2006

P9-CRE-294

Foundation
GRANTS TO
INDIVIDUALS

DISCARDED

FOUNDATION
CENTER
Knowledge to build on.

FIFTEENTH EDITION

FOUNDATION
GRANTS TO
INDIVIDUALS

Phyllis Edelson
Editor

CONTRIBUTING STAFF

Senior Vice President for Information Resources and Publishing_____Rick Schoff

Senior Director of Database Publishing _____Jeffrey A. Falkenstein

Information Control Coordinator_____Yinebon Iniya

Assistant Editor _____Claire Charles

Editorial Associates _____Anshu Dutt
Linda Calderon
Marisa Leong

Editorial Assistant_____Carrie Levinson

Publishing Database Administrator _____Kathye Giesler

Network Assistant _____Emmy So

Communications Project Manager_____Cheryl L. Loe

Production Manager _____Christine Innamorato

Reference Librarian _____Deborah B. McKinney

The editor gratefully acknowledges the many other Foundation Center staff who contributed support, encouragement, and information that was indispensable to the preparation of this volume. Special mention should also be made of the staff members of the New York, Washington, DC, Cleveland, San Francisco, and Atlanta libraries who assisted in tracking changes in foundation information. We would like to express our appreciation as well to the many foundations that cooperated fully in updating information prior to the compilation of the *Foundation Grants to Individuals*.

70862891

CONTENTS

INTRODUCTION

Foundation Grants to Individuals is the most comprehensive listing available of private grantmakers and public charities (also known as public foundations) in the United States that provide financial assistance to individuals. The 15th edition contains 6,211 entries from U.S. grantmakers that the Foundation Center has identified as conducting ongoing grantmaking programs for individuals. It describes giving for a variety of purposes, including scholarships, student loans, fellowships, travel internships, residencies, arts and cultural projects, research, and general welfare. It is intended to be both a grantseeker's guide and a reference tool for those interested in giving to individuals.

The 15th edition includes the most current information available for 6,060 entries listed in the previous edition (see the Appendix on p. 891 to review the list of ineligible entries) and 409 entries new to this edition. To prepare the 15th edition, Foundation Center staff researched a variety of public records, including 990-PFs and 990s (which all private foundations and public charities are required to file with the IRS), annual reports, newsletters, Web sites and other published information about grantmakers. Entries were then mailed to potential 15th edition grantmakers for review and correction, and were revised according to the information supplied.

It is important to note that this directory describes only those grantmaker programs to individuals. Most grantmakers also have funding programs for nonprofit organizations and institutions. Often these programs are much more substantial than those for individuals. Information about these programs can be found in *The Foundation 1000,* of the Foundation Center.

Many of the programs that grantmakers finance through nonprofit organizations are geared toward individual recipients (e.g., funds given by grantmakers to colleges and universities for setting up scholarship programs). Such programs are not included in this volume, as students must apply to their school rather than the grantmaker for assistance. However, information on these types of programs can be obtained through the appropriate financial aid offices. Keep in mind that many alternative sources of funding for individuals are available in the United States. Government grants, scholarships offered directly by colleges and universities, scholarships offered directly by corporations, research funds from nonprofit institutions, and other awards should be fully investigated as you search for financial assistance.

To help individual grantseekers of all kinds learn about alternative funding, a bibliography of reference guides to grants other than those made by grantmakers appears on page xxi. Relevant web addresses are also included here. For many grantseekers, the bibliography may be as useful as the grantmaker entries listed in this volume.

CRITERIA FOR INCLUS

In order to be included in [...] *n Grants to Individuals,* a grantmaker must meet fo [...] :

1. It must initially awa [...] to individuals totaling $10,000.

2. It must award gra [...] ividuals totaling at least $2,000 annually to maint [...] ility. (The latest financial information for t' [...] 2004 or 2005 were used. However, inform [...] n 2002 or 2003 was used in the absence of timely delivery of tax reporting forms from the IRS.) In addition, if a grantmaker gave less than $2,000 in grants to individuals in the latest year available, financial data from previous years was reviewed, and the grantmaker was included if a substantial giving pattern was found to exist.

3. Its grant recipients must be selected by its governing board or an independent selection committee.

4. It must accept applications from individuals directly or through an intermediary. The exception to this is funding by nomination only which includes information on award programs that require nominations from sources other than the individuals themselves (e.g., institutions or organizations affiliated with the grantmaker). These entries have been included for those interested in reviewing the full spectrum of grantmaker support for individuals. **Individuals should not apply directly to grantmakers described as only accepting nominations.**

ARRANGEMENT

The *Foundation Grants to Individuals,* now published annually is divided into four sections:

- **Educational Support:** In addition to general educational support, the section includes funding for company employees and/or their dependents, funding to individuals studying at specific schools or individuals who have attended specific schools, as well as entries relating to international applicants and by nomination only as appropriate.

- **General Welfare:** In addition to general funding for all types of support including grants, loans, and in-kind services on an emergency or long-term basis, the section includes funding for company employees and/or their dependents for general welfare assistance. Funding might be paid to the hospitals, doctors, or agencies that actually render the service rather than to the individuals. Some requests require a referral from a social service agency or a doctor; others accept direct applications from individuals.

- **Arts and Cultural Support:** Included here is all funding for the arts, which includes support for funding to artists for general welfare, awards/prizes and grants by nomination only that are only for artists. Artists seeking residencies when no monetary support is provided will also find lists of organizations here.

- **Research and Professional Support:** In addition to funding for those individuals working at the postgraduate level and above as well as those seeking support for projects within their professional careers, the section includes entries relating to international applicants and by nomination only as appropriate.

Entries within each section are arranged alphabetically by grantmaker name.

Many grantmakers have more than one type of grantmaking program. For example, a grantmaker might make scholarship awards and also give support to the needy elderly. Where breakdowns are available and both programs are of substantial size (usually over $2,000 in grant awards per program), separate entries are provided. When only one of the two programs makes grant awards totaling $2,000, there is only one entry.

Each entry includes, as available, the following:

1. The full legal **name of the foundation.**

2. The **former name** of the foundation.

3. The **street address, city and zip code** of the foundation's principal office.

4. The **telephone number** of the foundation.

5. The name and title of the **contact person** of the foundation.

6. The **application address** supplied by the foundation, if different from the grantmaker's principal address. Additional telephone or FAX numbers as well as e-mail and/or URL addresses may also be listed here.

7. **Foundation type:** community, company, independent, operating or public charity.

8. The **limitations** statement describing the restrictions (if any) on giving made by the grantmaker.

9. A list of **publications** of other materials made available by the foundation that describes its activities and giving programs. These can include annual or multi-year reports, newsletters, informational brochures, grants lists etc.

10. The **year-end date** for the foundation's accounting period for which financial data is supplied.

11. **Assets:** the total value of the foundation's investments at the end of the accounting period. In a few instances, foundations that act as 'pass-throughs" for individuals gifts report zero assets.

12. **Asset type:** generally, assets are reported at market value (M) or ledger value (L).

13. **Expenditures:** total disbursements of the foundation, including overhead expenses (salaries; investment, legal, and other professional fees; interest; rent; etc.) and federal excise taxes, as well as the total amount paid for grants, scholarships, and matching gifts.

14. The **total giving** amount and number of grants paid during the year, with the largest grant paid (high) and smallest grant paid (low). The Total Giving amount represents all the grants awarded by an organization during the fiscal year, and not necessarily funding to individuals.

15. The total amount and number of **grants made directly to or on behalf of individuals,** including scholarships, fellowships, awards, medical payments. When supplied by the foundation, high, low, and average range are also indicated. The grants to individuals amount represents the grants awarded by an organization with only one entry in the descriptive directory. When an organization has two or more entries in the publication the grants to individuals amount, unless otherwise noted, does not reflect the funding for each separate entry.

16. The number of **loans to individuals** and the total amount loaned. When supplied by the foundation, high, low and average are also indicated. The loans to individuals amount represents the loans awarded by an organization with only one entry in the descriptive directory. When an organization has two or more entries in the publication the loans to individuals amount, unless otherwise noted, does not reflect the funding for each separate entry.

17. The **fields of interest** reflected in the foundation's giving program relating to individuals. It is the subjects the grantmaker might support that are relevant to an individual's needs and does not include the giving interests the grantmaker provides to organization.

18. **Types of support** is generated to denote the types of support a grantmaker might provide to individuals and does not include the types of support the grantmaker provides to organizations.

19. **Application information,** including the preferred form of application, the number of copies of proposals requested, application deadlines, and the general amount of time the foundation requires notifying the applicant of the board's decision.

20. **Program description:** the name of the grant or award; its purpose, terms, and conditions; and grantee accountability to the grantmaker.

21. **EIN:** The Employer Identification Number assigned to the foundation by the Internal Revenue Service for tax purposes. This number can be useful when ordering or searching for copies of the foundation's annual information return, Form 990-PF or 990.

The absence of certain pieces of information in an entry indicates that such information is not pertinent or was not available for that grantmaker. Where full information is not provided and the available data seems to indicate that you might be eligible for assistance, it is advisable to write to the grantmaker. If a contact person isn't listed and no specific program is named or described, inquiries should simply be addressed to the grantmaker.

INDEXES

In order to facilitate your research and provide access to the many entries in this volume, seven indexes have been developed. The indexes are the best place to begin when using this directory.

The numbers listed in the indexes correspond to the sequence numbers of individual grantmaker entries in the Descriptive Directory section of the book. In the Grantmaker Name Index, the letter "A" refers to the Appendix, which lists 258 grantmakers from the 14th edition of *Foundation Grants to Individuals* that have not been included in the 15th edition. The grantmakers listed in the Appendix have either terminated their operations or no longer meet the criteria for inclusion in this volume. The indexes include the following:

1. **Geographic Focus Index.** This index provides access by state to all grantmaker entries in which a geographic preference or restriction is stated. Listings are further subdivided into categories of giving to provide more rapid access. Grantmakers in boldface type make grants on a national, regional or international basis; the others generally limit giving to the city, county, or state in which they are located.

2. **International Giving Index.** This index provides access to all grantmaker entries in which countries, continents, or regions have demonstrated giving interests. The index lists only those grantmakers whose giving goes directly overseas; to further access international interests of grantmakers, see the Subject Index for more information.

3. **Company Name Index.** This index provides access by company name to grantmaking programs that are open to a specific company's employees and/or former employees and their families.

4. **Specific School Index.** This index provides access to grantmakers that make grants to individuals who have attended or are attending specific schools.

5. **Type of Support Index.** This index provides access to grantmakers according to the particular kinds of grants they award, such as scholarships, medical expenses, or research grants. Entries are indexed under the applicable terms. Again, related types of support terms should be checked to make certain all potentially relevant entries are reviewed. Grantmakers in boldface type make grants on a national, regional or international basis; the others generally limit giving to the city, county, or state in which they are located. This index is generated to denote the types of support a grantmaker might provide to individuals and does not include the types of support the grantmaker provides to organizations.

6. **Subject Index.** This index provides access to grantmakers that make grants in specific subject areas. Entries are indexed under the applicable terms. Related subject terms should be checked to make certain all potentially relevant entries are reviewed. Grantmakers in boldface type make grants on a national, regional or international basis; the others generally limit giving to the city, county, or state in which they are located. This index is generated to denote the fields of interest a grantmaker might support that are relevant to an individual's needs and does not include the giving interests the grantmaker provides to organizations.

7. **Grantmaker Name Index.** This index provides access by grantmaker name to entries in the main section of the book, as well as to those listed in the Appendix (these entries are listed with an "A" next to them).

TO THE GRANTSEEKER: RESEARCHING GRANTMAKER GIVING

Used correctly, *Foundation Grants to Individuals* can be an important tool in the construction of a methodical research strategy designed to uncover those grantmakers that might be able to fulfill your funding needs. It is as much a guide to those programs to which you should not apply as it is a guide to those for which you may qualify. Many grantmakers making grants to individuals are small, have limited assets, and make a limited number of grants each year. Federal laws outline specific restrictions and requirements for grantmaker giving to individuals and have limited the extent and nature of such programs. (An excellent analysis of these laws follows this introduction.)

Remember, most of the grantmakers listed in this volume place specific limitations (i.e., by subject area, recipient type, and/or geographic focus) on their giving. Finding out about those limitations before you submit your application will save you time and increase your chances of obtaining assistance. Most grantmakers will automatically reject any applicant who does not qualify under their restrictions.

Do not waste time applying to inappropriate grantmakers. The law of averages does not apply when seeking grants. One hundred applications sent to one hundred grantmakers whose qualifications you do not meet will result in one hundred rejections, or in no responses at all. By demonstrating your knowledge of a grantmaker's programs, you have a better chance of getting your foot in the door. Grantmakers give only a limited amount of money and have a large number of applicants from which to choose. The grantmaker personnel who review your application will be looking for the candidate who best meets the standards and objectives of their programs.

Each entry in this book includes a statement of limitations outlining the specific constraints on that grantmaker's giving program for individuals. In addition, geographic limitations are indicated in the Subject Index, Type of Support Index, Geographic Focus Index and International Index.

REMEMBER: IF YOU DON'T QUALIFY, DON'T APPLY.

IDENTIFYING FUNDING POSSIBILITIES

As with all grantseeking, the key to obtaining grants is preparation. Preparation means identifying the grantmakers that make grants in your area and determining whether you qualify. It is important to pay close attention to grantmaker limitation statements, giving patterns, areas of interest, and average grant awards. Applying to a grantmaker that makes grants outside your field of study or to one that only makes grants of a few hundred dollars when you need thousands will prove futile. Instead, learn as much as you can about your funding prospects. Use all the available resources and do your homework.

Identify funding possibilities using the indexes provided in this book. These give you access to the grantmaker entries by subject, type of support, geographic focus, international giving focus, company-related grantmaking, and specific schools. Once you've identified the grantmakers likely to consider your request, try to find out more about their particular programs. Visit one of the Foundation Center's Cooperating Collections, which provide a core collection of Center publications as well as a variety of supplementary materials and services in areas useful to grantseekers.

If, upon further research, you believe a grantmaker may be receptive to your request, prepare your application or proposal according to the guidelines set up by the grantmaker. Be thorough. Provide all the information asked for, give references if required, and be sure to provide carefully planned budgets that show how the money will be spent.

Approach the application process as you would a job application. Explain why you are the best person for that grantmaker to support and emphasize your qualifications. Remember, there are more talented people around than there is money available. Take the time to make your case clearly and persuasively.

With all this in mind, you are now ready to begin the process that could lead to the funding you seek.

FEDERAL LAWS AND GRANTS TO INDIVIDUALS

LAWS REGARDING PRIVATE FOUNDATIONS

In general, careful foundations giving involves choices based on the capabilities of individuals, even though the foundation is *not* making a grant to an individual in the tax law sense. General support grants to colleges and universities, for example, may be based on perceptions of the capacities of the school's administrative leadership and faculty. Grantee selection for more specialized programs is all the more likely related to an applicant organization's leadership and staff. If, for example, a foundation wants to support an organization with programs that will provide housing and supporting services for homeless people, the foundation will take a good look at the background, experience, and track record of the individuals who determine the prospective grantee's policies, priorities, and directions. Foundations, it is frequently said, "bet on individuals," and this applies whether a grantmaker is making a grant to an individual or an organization.

SOME BACKGROUND INFORMATION

Provisions of the Internal Revenue Code establish some special requirements that certain foundation "grants to individuals" (GTIs) programs must meet. Individual grantees should be familiar with these rules, as they affect the grantee as well as the grantmaker grantor.

Charitable organizations in general, and foundations in particular, have traditionally enjoyed favorable treatment in the GTI area not enjoyed to the same extent by individual contributors. If you as an individual know a deserving and needy student, you can give that student the necessary funds for a college education, graduate degree, or research project (assuming you are financially able to do so)—but you won't get the benefit of a charitable contribution for doing so. However, charitable organizations, including foundations, whose funds are already exempt from income taxes and to which tax-deductible contributions can be made, have long been able to make individual grants without adversely affecting their tax status.

LEGISLATIVE HISTORY

This right came under close scrutiny in 1969, when the current elaborate private foundation rules and restrictions were first under consideration in Congress. The House Ways and Means Committee at one point tentatively decided that, with certain limited exceptions, private foundations should be denied the right to make grants directly to individuals for travel, study, or similar purposes. But the Committee changed its mind and reported a proposed bill allowing private foundations to award GTIs for travel, study, or similar purposes provided selection procedures for these grants were approved in advance by the Treasury Department on a one-time approval basis. This approach was enacted into law and remains in effect.

SOME GROUND RULES AND SOME QUESTIONS

Internal Revenue Code Section 4945 and the regulations to it provide the ground rules that private foundations must follow regarding GTIs. A grant to an individual for travel, study, or similar purposes is proscribed, unless the grant is awarded on an objective and nondiscriminatory basis under an approved procedure and the grant:

1. is a scholarship or fellowship as specially defined for study at an educational institution;

2. is a prize or award given for the achievement of exempt charitable purposes, where the recipient did not enter into a contest or other proceedings leading to the award and no substantial future services are required of the recipient as a condition to the prize or award; or

3. achieves a specific objective; produces a report or other similar product; or improves or enhances an artistic, scientific, or teaching capacity, skill, or talent of the grantee.

Though few foundations make such grants, the law also permits private foundations to provide direct support to needy individuals. Thus, the regulations to Section 4945 provide that a private foundation may make grants to indigent individuals enabling them to purchase furniture, without regard to whether the criteria cited above are met.

Let's take a closer look at the "objective and nondiscriminatory" and "approved procedure" requirements.

A question that has arisen with increasing frequency in other contexts is whether an educational program can be nondiscriminatory if it benefits particular groups (e.g., women, African Americans, the residents of a particular community or region). In the case of foundation GTIs, it still seems clear that prospective recipients can be limited to a group sufficiently broad to be recognized as a charitable class. The purpose of the individual grant rules was to ensure against arbitrary, whimsical, or personally motivated grants. If a foundation maintains a program of scholarship aids for residents of a particular county or state, or for a particular group that has been victimized by discrimination, the tax law rules do not require the foundation to change that focus so long as the program is administered in an objective and nondiscriminatory fashion within the group for whom benefits are available. The regulations also recognize that for grants to "achieve a specific objective," as noted in subparagraph three (3) above, selection from a group is not necessary where, taking the grant's purposes into account, one or more persons are selected because they are exceptionally qualified to accomplish these purposes.

Once a grant is made, a foundation and its individual grantees have additional responsibilities. The foundation must follow up to see to it the funds are being used by the individual grantee for the intended purposes. The foundation must obtain reports at least annually, though reporting and record keeping burdens can be lessened where the grants are paid to the educational institution for the benefit of the grantee rather than to the grantee directly.

A foundation also has a duty to investigate situations where there are indications that the grant is not being used for the purposes intended or is being diverted to improper purposes. A foundation would normally withhold any further funds under the grant until the situation is corrected and, where a diversion occurs, it is obliged to take all reasonable and appropriate steps to recover or to otherwise ensure the restoration of those funds.

Failure to comply with the requirements is sanctioned by a series of penalty excise taxes that can be imposed on the foundation and, in limited circumstances, on its managers. In flagrant cases, the foundation can lose its tax-exempt status.

SIGNIFICANT GUIDELINES FOR PUBLIC CHARITIES

Public charities, known alternately as public foundations (including a sub-class known as community foundations), sometimes administer programs of grants to individuals, but they do not have to meet the rules and regulations that apply to private foundation individual grant programs. Regulators do not provide as much oversight for these programs, so that more responsibility for the conduct of the programs is shifted to the charities. The upshot is that these charities must have in-depth legal knowledge and pay close attention to administrative detail.

Community foundations function along the same lines as private foundations. Many public charities also operate this way. While the tax rules and regulations are not binding, the charities often use the legal criteria set out in section 4945 to insure that they are within a safe zone when they file tax returns.

One requirement of grantmaking to individuals is that programs must be "objective and non- discriminatory"; public charities and private foundations use the same criteria. As a result of the wider interpretation of the phrase "objective and nondiscriminatory grants" public charities must investigate additional facets of the proposed granting to be sure it meets the legal criteria. Another important point to note is that public charities, in contrast to private foundations, are allowed to do some lobbying and are permitted to provide a limited amount of funding for lobbying purposes.

With regard to the approval procedure, contrary to the private foundation requirements, a public charity is not required to seek advance approval from the IRS, with the exception of company-related GTI programs where funds donated by a corporate foundation for company employee scholarships are to be administered by a community foundation. In addition, the IRS must be notified about amendments to the organization document when the charity undertakes a *new* GTI program not included in the original articles contained in that document.

Programs for public charity loans to individuals function along the same lines as GTI programs.

INCOME TAX CONSIDERATIONS

There is a substantial amount of law on the subject of whether scholarships and similar payments are taxable or tax-exempt income—a subject that is beyond the scope of this section. Only a few general observations will be made here.

Under prior law, private foundation scholarship and fellowship grants were generally income tax free to the recipient. However, this rule was substantially curtailed by the Tax Reform Act of 1986. The income-tax exemption is now generally limited to scholarships for degree candidates at educational institutions (also specially defined), and then only for amounts spent for tuition, fees, books, and supplies. Amounts spent for room, board, and other "personal expenses" are subject to tax. Similarly, prizes and awards are excluded from the recipient's income only if turned over to another charity or government.

Individuals lucky enough to receive a private foundation grant should surely not assume that their grant is nontaxable. They should be on notice that tax-exempt treatment is limited to a narrow area.

OTHER PROGRAMS

Bear in mind that many grantmakers provide substantial scholarship dollars but make these funds available to schools and other public charities, thus entrusting the responsibility to the institutions for selecting grant recipients. Students will often find that the source of the money for the scholarship awarded by the school or college of their choice is a grantmaker grant. The grantmaker community is a major source of support for organizations such as the Eisenhower Exchange Fellowships, the National Merit Scholarship Program, and others. However, such grant programs are generally treated as grants to organizations, and the detailed requirements for GTIs described here do not apply.

CONCLUSION

A relatively small number of grantmakers make grants to individuals as defined by federal law. However, for these grantmakers, the general consensus is that the rules are reasonable and provide assurance that grants to individuals made by grantmakers will be rational rather than whimsical, fair rather than arbitrary, and very much in the public interest.

SCHOLARSHIPS AND GRANTS TO INDIVIDUALS: WHERE TO FIND THEM

How can you get a grant to help pay for your education, write a book, make a film, or do research?

There are no easy answers but there are resources that can help you. *Foundation Grants to Individuals* is an excellent starting point. The purpose of this section, however, is to suggest additional resources on scholarships and grants.

FINANCIAL AID FOR EDUCATION

If you are a student and need financial support to further your education, your first stop should be the financial aid office of the school you plan to attend. Financial aid officers often have information about special scholarships or awards given by government agencies, local corporations, or foundations. Their advice can get you started in the right direction. You might also research the various financial aid directories available to you. A representative list of resources can be found in the bibliography that appears on page xxi. The best approach is to consider your own attributes and the connections you have to associations, corporations, or other organizations. Many scholarships are not based solely on academic merit or financial need. For example, there are scholarships for students from a particular county, for art history majors, for people with disabilities or for women. Consider your background and the type of support you need, and apply to those programs for which you qualify. Some of the more useful directories include *Peterson's Scholarships Grants and Prizes* 2006, 10th ed. (Lawrenceville, NJ: Peterson's Guides, 2006). The Scholarship Book 12th ed.: *The Complete Guide to Private-Sector Scholarships, Grants and Loans for the Undergraduate* (Paramus, NJ: Prentice-Hall, 2006), and *The College Student's Guide to Merit and Other No-Need Funding,* 2005–2007 (El Dorado Hills, CA: Reference Services Press, 2005). These books are well indexed and may suggest additional funding possibilities to you. For answers to frequently-asked questions about individual grant seeking (including information for those seeking financial aid) and links to other Web sites with scholarship information visit the Foundation Center's Web site: foundationcenter.org.

GENERAL RESOURCES FOR GRANTSEEKERS

In addition to the directories of financial aid for education, there are directories covering funding for non-educational purposes. *The Annual Register of Grant Support* 2005 (Medford, NJ: Information Today, Inc., published annually) covers grants for academic and scientific research, project development, travel and exchange programs, publication support, equipment and construction, in-service training, and competitive awards and prizes in a variety of fields. *The Grants Register* (New York: Palgrave Macmillan LTD, published annually) is intended for grantseekers at or above the graduate level and for all who require professional or advanced vocational training. It is international in scope and is useful to students from other countries seeking exchange opportunities or international scholarships. Volume 1 of *Awards, Honors, and Prizes* (Farmington Hills, MI: The Gale Group, published annually) contains details about more than 22,500 prizes and awards for all types of service and special achievement in the United States and Canada. Volume 2 covers awards from countries other than the U.S. and Canada. *The Directory of Research Grants* (Phoenix: Oryx Press, published annually) is a useful source for scholars, grant administrators, faculty members, and others seeking support for research projects. More than 5,100 programs are listed, including programs supported by private foundations, corporations, professional organizations, and a few state and foreign governments. Also of interest to the researcher is the *Research Centers Directory* (Farmington Hills, MI: The Gale Group, published annually), which lists university-related and other nonprofit research organizations in the U.S. and Canada.

SPECIALIZED RESOURCES FOR GRANTSEEKERS

In addition to the general directories, there are specialized resources compiled for specific population groups (e.g., women, minorities, etc.) or for specific disciplines and professions (e.g., grants in the arts, medicine, or sciences). Among these specialized resources are the *Directory of Financial Aids for Women* 2005–2007 (El Dorado Hills, CA: Reference Service Press, 2005), and *Financial Aid for African Americans* 2005–2007 (El Dorado Hills, CA: Reference Service Press, 2005), *Grants and Awards Available to American Writers* (New York: PEN American Center, 2005), the *Directory of Biomedical and Health Care Grants* (Phoenix: Oryx Press, published annually). For information on federal funding, the primary resource is the *Catalog of Federal Domestic Assistance* (Washington, DC: General Services Administration, free online at www.cfda.gov, or for purchase in print by calling toll free at 866-512-1800). Use this annual catalog as a starting point since much of the information may be outdated by the time it is published. Follow up by contacting the local or regional office of the appropriate agency. Another useful resource for finding Federal grantmaking agencies is the web site Grants.gov (www.grants.gov).

PROPOSAL WRITING FOR GRANTSEEKERS

Many grantmakers that give grants directly to individuals provide their own application forms and detailed guidelines. If you are applying to one of these grantmakers, be certain to follow their instructions to the letter. However, some funders provide very general application guidelines. The following information will be useful in constructing a proposal for these funders.

Each proposal is a unique document written with a specific funder in mind. The purpose of your proposal is to present you and your ideas in a positive and compelling way and to establish a link between you and the funder. Your proposal should suggest that you are a potential partner in accomplishing their mission, not just a person asking for money.

There are certain characteristics common to most successful proposals:

- They deliver an important idea and address a significant issue.

- They indicate that the applicant has chosen an innovative approach to that issue and has a reasonable plan for implementation.

- They assure the funder that the applicant is capable of success.

- They show how the grant will advance the funder's goals.

- They set forth anticipated results.

The standard elements of a proposal are:

- A **Cover Letter** addressed specifically to the appropriate contact person at the grantmaker.

- A brief **Abstract** (sometimes called an executive summary) that describes very concisely the information that will follow.

- An **Introduction** that helps to establish your credibility as a grant applicant.

- A **Statement of Need** that describes a problem and explains why you require a grant to address the issue.

- **Objectives** that refine your idea and tell exactly what you expect to accomplish in response to the need.

- **Procedures** that describe the methods you will use to accomplish your objectives within a stated time frame.

- An **Evaluation** method for determining how you and the funder will measure your results and effectiveness. This should closely correspond to the objectives you set forth.

- If the project is ongoing, a section about its **Future Funding,** with specific plans for feasible, continuing support.

- A separate **Budget** depicting in dollars precisely how much money will be required and how and when it will be spent in order to accomplish your objectives. Typical components of a budget for an individual's grant project include: wages for personnel (usually your own salary is "donated"), space and equipment costs, travel expenses, telephone, printing, postage, and other direct costs.

In general, proposals from individuals do not exceed five pages in addition to the budget. Begin by writing an outline to help you compose your thoughts will enable you to achieve clarity and conciseness. Good grammar and accurate spelling are important. The text should be divided into short paragraphs, with headings and sub-headings used for clarification. It's always good advice to ask someone else to read and critique your proposal before you submit it.

Funders' deadlines are very strict, so allow yourself enough time to do your research and to produce your most polished effort. Creating a checklist will help to ensure that your submission includes all the requested items in the proper order. If you are applying to more than one funder (which is common), you should mention this fact in your cover letter.

Remember one important rule of thumb: "If you don't qualify, don't apply." The ultimate success of your effort, like that of nonprofit grantseekers, will rest on the quality of your research aimed at uncovering the best prospective funder. Take your time in using *Foundation Grants to Individuals*— available in both online (gtionline.foundationcenter.org) and print formats—to ensure that you approach only grantmakers that have demonstrated an interest in your field and that give grants in your geographic area.

The Virtual Classroom on the Center's web site (foundationcenter.org/learn/classroom/index.jhtml) offers two courses that may be useful: "Finding Foundation Support for Your Education" and "Grantseeking Basics for Individuals."

AFFILIATION WITH A TAX-EXEMPT ORGANIZATION

If you are seeking support other than for your own education, you should be aware that few private foundations or corporations make grants directly to individuals. Most, in fact, make grants only to nonprofit tax-exempt organizations (e.g., universities, hospitals, museums, and other organizations with educational, scientific, religious, and/or charitable purposes) to which contributions are tax deductible. Some individual grantseekers become affiliated with tax-exempt organizations that serve as their sponsors in order to obtain the federal tax-exempt status that funders require. For a list of organizations to which contributions are tax-deductible, see the *Cumulative List of Organizations described in Section 170(c) of the Internal Revenue Code of 1986* (Washington, DC: Government Printing Office, published annually) or visit the Web site Taxbase (taxbase.tax.org). Newsletters, annual reports, and membership lists from state and local arts and humanities councils, Chambers of Commerce, and local United Ways may also help you to identify potential sponsors for your work or project. For a good discussion of the pros and cons of affiliation with a tax-exempt organization and of grantseeking in general, see *The Individual's Guide to Grants* (New York: Kluwer Academic/Plenum Press, 1983) by Judith Margolin. The author suggests a number of affiliation possibilities, including forming a consortium with other individuals interested in the same subject; finding a temporary, in name only, tax-exempt sponsor or umbrella group to serve as a fiscal agent for your project; making use of your current affiliations with professional societies, trade associations, clubs, alumni groups, etc.; or becoming an employee of a nonprofit institution. There are a number of creative strategies, including teaching in a college or university continuing education program on a part-time basis and developing a "scholar-in-residence" role for yourself.

Some organizations may fund your project directly or serve as fiscal agents for you. A fiscal agent is an organization that will accept funds on your behalf. It makes formal application for the grant and retains financial responsibility for the project. If you choose to work with a fiscal agent, be sure it has federal tax-exempt status and be aware that there may be strings attached. For example, the organization may insist on retaining administrative controls on your work; it may impose a service fee; it may want to share in subsidiary rights as a co-author; and so on. No two fiscal agency relationships are exactly alike. A detailed discussion of alternative arrangements may be found in *Fiscal Sponsorship: 6 Ways to Do It Right* (San Francisco: Study Center Press, 1993) by Gregory L. Colvin.

FORMING YOUR OWN NONPROFIT ORGANIZATION

Still another option to consider is forming your own nonprofit, tax-exempt organization. This will require careful thought and a good deal of administrative work on your part. It also entails legal and financial responsibilities that are likely to require the services of a lawyer. Don't try it alone. To learn more about what's involved in incorporating as a nonprofit or in forming an unincorporated association, there are a number of useful sources, including *Starting and Managing a Nonprofit Organization: A Legal Guide* (New York: John Wiley & Sons,

2005), and *How to Form a Nonprofit Corporation* (Berkeley, CA: Nolo Press, 2005) by Anthony Mancuso. Books covering incorporation for your particular state can be even more useful. In this category, see How to Form a Nonprofit Corporation in California (Berkeley, CA: Nolo Press, 2004) and *Getting Organized* (New York: Lawyers Alliance for New York, 1999).

Keep in mind that forming a nonprofit organization and obtaining tax-exempt status are two separate processes. Nonprofit incorporation is a procedure handled on the state level; tax-exempt status is a federal matter. For information on applying for tax-exempt status, see IRS publication 557, *Tax Exempt Status for Your Organization.* You can obtain copies by contacting the Internal Revenue Service at (800) 829-3676 or through their Web site: www.irs.gov/publications/index.html. Forming a nonprofit organization is not for everyone. In fact, many nonprofit organizations fail in their first few years because the people who established them did not understand what taking such a step would entail. By reviewing the resources mentioned above and discussing your options with a lawyer, you should be better able to decide if this approach is right for you.

Resources for Individual Grantseekers: A Bibliography on page xxi is a list of select resources that may prove valuable as you pursue your research. Scan the general directories first, and then check to see whether there are specific resources related to your status or interests.

Publishers' addresses frequently change, as do edition numbers and the price of publications. Before you order a particular title, check with the publisher to verify that it contains the most current information available. Copies of many of the works mentioned above are also available for reference use at the Foundation Center's New York, Washington, D.C., Cleveland, San Francisco, and Atlanta libraries as well as in many of its more than 260 Cooperating Collections. For the location of the Cooperating Collection nearest you, call the Foundation Center at (212) 620-4230 or check our web site: foundationcenter.org.

GLOSSARY

The following list, arranged alphabetically, includes common terms used by grantmakers and grantseekers.

Accredited institutions: Entities that meet specific standards for educational programs as determined by regional or national associations.

ACT: A test created by the American College Testing Program, which some colleges require students to take.

Annual report: A voluntary report issued by a grantmaker that provides financial data and descriptions of grantmaking activities. Annual reports vary in format from simple typewritten documents listing the year's grants to detailed publications that provide substantial information about the grantmaking program. Many organizations post the Annual Report of their Web site.

Award: A gift given in recognition of past achievements usually by nomination only.

Campership: A grant given to enable a child to attend summer camp.

Class rank: In secondary education, student rank based on GPA or grades relative to the other students in their class.

Community foundation: A 501(c)(3) organization that makes grants for charitable purposes in a specific community or region. Most community foundations are classified as public charities, which are eligible for maximum income tax-deductibility of contributions.

Company-sponsored foundation: (also referred to as Corporate Foundation) A private foundation whose grant funds are derived primarily from the contributions of a profit-making business organization.

Conferences/seminars: Grants that may cover registration, lodging or transportation for an individual to attend a conference, seminar, or workshop. Often, these grants are awarded in conjunction with a fellowship, internship or scholarship.

Curriculum vitae: In academe, a lengthy document providing a summary of an individual's accomplishments, including employment, education, research, published work, awards, professional memberships, and other biographical information.

Doctoral support: Grants to aid dissertation or thesis research.

Donee: The recipient of a grant or scholarship (Also known as the grantee or beneficiary).

Emergency funds: Grants to individuals and families to assist in paying for emergency needs resulting from disaster, natural or otherwise, including expenses for medical and dental care, shelter, repairs, utilities, transportation and clothing.

Employee-related scholarships/student loans: Scholarships and student loans to current or former company employees and/or their families.

Employee-related welfare: General welfare grants/loans to current or former employees and their families.

Exchange program: A program that sends students to study in other countries and allows students from those countries to exchange places with its participants.

Fellowships: Programs that award stipends to individuals for tuition, travel, books and other costs of research and study.

Financial Aid Form (FAF): Many private universities require this form, which is more detailed and requires a processing fee, in addition to the FAFSA, (see also Free Application for Student Aid).

Foreign applicants: Applicants from countries other than the U.S. are eligible to apply for certain programs administered by U.S. grantmakers.

Form 990: The annual information return that all public charities must submit to the IRS each year and which is also filed with appropriate state officials. The form requires information on the charity's assets, income, operating expenses, contributions and grants, paid staff and salaries, program funding areas, grantmaking guidelines.

Form 990-PF: The annual information return that all private foundations must submit to the IRS each year and which is also filed with appropriate state officials. The form requires information on the foundation's assets, income, operating expenses, contributions and grants, paid staff and salaries, program funding areas, grantmaking guidelines and restrictions, and grant application procedures.

Free Application for Student Aid (FAFSA): This is a form commonly used to apply for U.S. Government financial aid. Colleges and many non-institutional programs will use the data on this form to determine entitlement for financial aid (see also Financial Aid Form).

501(c)(3): The section of the Internal Revenue Code that defines nonprofit, charitable, tax-exempt organizations; 501(c)(3) organizations are further defined as public charities, private operating foundations, and private non-operating foundations (See also Operating foundation; Private foundation; Public Charity).

Graduate support: Funds awarded to individuals for graduate work through programs administered by the grantmaker.

Grants by nomination only: Scholarships, fellowships, research grants and other awards or grants which individuals must be nominated by the grantmaker, an allied institution or a third party in order to be considered.

Grants for special needs: Funds given directly to individuals or on their behalf, including grants and/or loans to cover medical expenses and other basic needs for economically disadvantaged individuals.

Independent foundation: A grantmaking organization classified by the IRS as a private foundation. Independent foundations may also be known as family foundations, general purpose foundations, special purpose foundations, or private non-operating foundations. The Foundation Center classifies independent foundations and company-sponsored foundations separately; however, federal law normally classifies them both as private, non-operating foundations, and both are subject to the same rules and requirements (see also Private foundation).

Internships: Programs that support individuals in gaining practical experience in their careers. Some internships are paid, and must be undertaken for college credit.

Letter of recommendation: A letter written by a teacher, school administrator, or professional in a relevant field that indicates the quality of an applicant's abilities or character.

Loans: Funds which usually must be repaid to the lending grantmaker, often with a pre-determined interest percentage added to the loaned amount.

Medical expenses: Funding which covers medical, dental, or eye care for needy individuals.

Operating foundation: A 501(c)(3) organization classified by the IRS as a private foundation whose primary purpose is to conduct research, social welfare, or other programs determined by its governing body or establishment charter. Some grants may be made, but the sum is generally small relative to the funds used for the foundation's own programs (see also 501(c)(3)).

Pell Grant: Federally-funded educational grants awarded almost exclusively to individuals who have not yet earned a bachelor's degree. Awards are based upon financial need, and the maximum award rarely exceeds $4,000.

Permanent resident: Non-U.S. citizens who have gained this status from the U.S. immigration and Naturalization Service.

Postdoctoral study: Funds for the pursuit of advanced research or study after receiving a doctorate degree.

Postgraduate study: Funds for the pursuit of advanced research or study after receiving a graduate degree.

Precollege scholarships/student loans: Scholarships and loans given for expenses related to elementary or secondary education, such as private school tuition.

Preliminary Student Aptitude Test (PSAT): A standardized test, often taken during the junior year of high school, which prepares the student for the Student Aptitude Test (SAT) (see also Student Apptitude Test).

Private foundation: A nongovernmental, nonprofit organization with funds and programs managed by its own trustees or directors, established to maintain or aid social, educational, religious, or other charitable activities serving the common welfare, primarily through making grants. A private foundation is tax exempt under code section 501(c)(3).

Prizes: Gifts to winners of competitions sponsored by nonprofits or an affiliated organization.

Professorships: Awards to individuals who will serve on the faculty of an institution of higher learning.

Program development: Grants to support specific projects or programs as opposed to general purpose grants.

Project support: Support given to individuals working at the postgraduate level or beyond and/or those seeking support for projects within their professional career.

Publication: Grants to fund reports or other publications issued by a nonprofit resulting from research or projects of interest to the grantmaker.

Public charity: In general, an organization that is tax exempt under code section 501(c)(3) and is classified by the IRS as "not a private foundation." Public charities derive their funding or support from the general public in carrying out social, educational, religious or other charitable activities serving the common welfare. Gifts to public charities are eligible for the maximum income tax-deductibility and are not subject to the same rules and restrictions as private foundations. Some are referred to as public foundations (See also 501(c)(3)).

Renewable: A scholarship or grant that may be renewed by the recipient, either automatically or through a reapplication process.

Request for Proposal (RFP): When the government issues a new contract or grant program, it sends out RFPs to agencies that might be qualified to participate. The RFP lists project specifications and application procedures. A few grantmakers occasionally use RFPs in specific fields that are initiated by applicants.

Research: Funds to cover the costs of investigations and clinical trials, including demonstration and pilot projects (research grants for individuals are usually referred to as fellowships).

Residencies: A nonmonetary award usually of short duration usually only for artists of all disciplines to further their creative talents. Meals, living quarters, equipment and studio space may be provided.

Resident: Usually, an individual qualifies for legal residency in a state by living there for a certain length of time. Criteria vary by state.

Resume: A one- to two-page document providing a summary of an individual's accomplishments, including employment, education, research positions, and other biographical information.

Sabbatical: A leave of absence, often with pay, usually granted every seventh year.

Scholarships—general: Funds awarded to individuals through programs administered by the grantmaker that are not specifically categorized elsewhere.

Seed money: Grants to start, establish, or initiate new projects or organizations; may cover salaries and other operating expenses of a new project. Also called "startup funds."

Seminary: An institution of higher education that offers religious training, usually to prepare the individual for ministry, priesthood or rabbinate.

Student Aid Report (SAR): The SAR is generated when students submit the FAFSA to College Scholarship Services. This report calculates the amount of money the study and/or the student's family should be able to contribute toward educational expenses. Both the student and his/her designated college will receive a copy of this report.

Student Aptitude Test (SAT): Students are often required to take this test for admission to many colleges. It is also administered by the College Board (see also Preliminary Student Apptitude Test).

Student loans—general: Loans distributed directly to individuals through programs administered by the grantmaker.

Loans for educational expenses which usually must be repaid to the lending grantmaker, often with a pre-paid interest percentage added to the loan amount.

Support for graduates or students of specific schools: Applicants are restricted to those who attend or have attended a specific school. Some programs may also specify institutions to be attended after graduation. In many cases, application must be made through the high school or college instead of the grantmaker.

Technical/Vocational school: Postsecondary institution that offers certificates in education directly related to preparation for specific careers, and which require no more than two years of study.

Transcript: An official record of a student's academic achievement available from the student's school. When a request is made to provide this document, an official copy must be submitted.

Travel grants: Awards that cover transportation and out-of-town living expenses. Enrollment in a college or university is not usually required.

Undergraduate support: Funds awarded to individuals for undergraduate work through programs administered by the grantmaker.

Welfare assistance: Grants or loans to cover basic needs for economically disadvantaged individuals.

Work study grants: Grants for educational expenses given to students who engage in a part-time work arrangement. A work commitment of 10-15 hours per week is usually required.

ABBREVIATIONS

The following lists contain standard abbreviations frequently used by the Foundation Center's editorial staff. These abbreviations are used most frequently in the addresses of grantmakers and the titles of corporate and grantmaker officers.

STREET ABBREVIATIONS

1st	First*	N.E.	Northeast
2nd	Second*	N.W.	Northwest
3rd	Third*	No.	Number
Apt.	Apartment	Pkwy.	Parkway
Ave.	Avenue	Pl.	Place
Bldg.	Building	Plz.	Plaza
Blvd.	Boulevard	R.R.	Rural Route
Cir.	Circle	Rd.	Road
Ct.	Court	Rm.	Room
Ctr.	Center	Rte.	Route
Dept.	Department	S.	South
Dr.	Drive	S.E.	Southeast
E.	East	S.W.	Southwest
Expwy.	Expressway	Sq.	Square
Fl.	Floor	St.	Saint
Ft.	Fort	St.	Street
Hwy.	Highway	Sta.	Station
Ln.	Lane	Ste.	Suite
M.C.	Mail Code	Terr.	Terrace
M.S.	Mail Stop	Tpke.	Turnpike
Mt.	Mount	Univ.	University
N.	North	W.	West

*Numerics used always

TWO LETTER STATE AND TERRITORY ABBREVIATIONS

AK	Alaska	NC	North Carolina
AL	Alabama	ND	North Dakota
AR	Arkansas	NE	Nebraska
AZ	Arizona	NH	New Hampshire
CA	California	NJ	New Jersey
CO	Colorado	NM	New Mexico
CT	Connecticut	NV	Nevada
DC	District of Columbia	NY	New York
DE	Delaware	OH	Ohio
FL	Florida	OK	Oklahoma
GA	Georgia	OR	Oregon
HI	Hawaii	PA	Pennsylvania
IA	Iowa	PR	Puerto Rico
ID	Idaho	RI	Rhode Island
IL	Illinois	SC	South Carolina
IN	Indiana	SD	South Dakota
KS	Kansas	TN	Tennessee
KY	Kentucky	TX	Texas
LA	Louisiana	UT	Utah
MA	Massachusetts	VA	Virginia
MD	Maryland	VI	Virgin Islands
ME	Maine	VT	Vermont
MI	Michigan	WA	Washington
MN	Minnesota	WI	Wisconsin
MO	Missouri	WV	West Virginia
MS	Mississippi	WY	Wyoming
MT	Montana		

ABBREVIATIONS USED FOR OFFICER TITLES

Acctg.	Accounting	Govt.	Government
ADM.	Admiral	Hon.	Judge
Admin.	Administration	Inf.	Information
Admin.	Administrative	Int.	Internal
Admin.	Administrator	Intl.	International
Adv.	Advertising	Jr.	Junior
Amb.	Ambassador	Lt.	Lieutenant
Assn.	Association	Ltd.	Limited
Assoc(s).	Associate(s)	Maj.	Major
Asst.	Assistant	Mfg.	Manufacturing
Bro.	Brother	Mgmt.	Management
C.A.O.	Chief Accounting Officer	Mgr.	Manager
C.A.O.	Chief Administration Officer	Mktg.	Marketing
		Msgr.	Monsignor
C.E.O.	Chief Executive Officer	Mt.	Mount
C.F.O.	Chief Financial Officer	Natl.	National
C.I.O.	Chief Information Officer	Off.	Officer
		Opers.	Operations
C.I.O.	Chief Investment Officer	Org.	Organization
		Plan.	Planning
C.O.O.	Chief Operating Officer	Pres.	President
Capt.	Captain	Prog(s).	Program(s)
Chair.	Chairperson	RADM.	Rear Admiral
Col.	Colonel	Rels.	Relations
Comm.	Committee	Rep.	Representative
Comms.	Communications	Rev.	Reverend
Commo.	Commodore	Rt. Rev.	Right Reverend
Compt.	Comptroller	Secy.	Secretary
Cont.	Controller	Secy.-Treas.	Secretary-Treasurer
Contrib(s).	Contribution(s)		
Coord.	Coordinator	Sen.	Senator
Corp.	Corporate, Corporation	Soc.	Society
Co(s).	Company(s)	Sr.	Senior
Dep.	Deputy	Sr.	Sister
Devel.	Development	Supvr.	Supervisor
Dir.	Director	Svc(s).	Service(s)
Distrib(s).	Distribution(s)	Tech.	Technology
Div.	Division	Tr.	Trustee
Exec.	Executive	Treas.	Treasurer
Ext.	External	Univ.	University
Fdn.	Foundation	V.P.	Vice President
Fr.	Father	VADM.	Vice Admiral
Genl.	General	Vice-Chair.	Vice Chairperson
Gov.	Governor		

ADDITIONAL ABBREVIATIONS

E-mail	Electronic mail
FAX	Facsimile
SASE	Self-Addressed Stamped Envelope
TDD, TTY	Telecommunication Device for the Deaf
Tel.	Telephone
URL	Uniform Resource Locator (web site)

Jan.	January
Feb.	February
Mar.	March
Apr.	April
Aug.	August
Sept.	September
Oct.	October
Nov.	November
Dec.	December

RESOURCES FOR INDIVIDUAL GRANTSEEKERS: A BIBLIOGRAPHY

The following is a selective bibliography of publications and electronic resources relevant to the individual grantseeker. These items were selected from a variety of sources. Entries with a descriptive abstract were taken from the Foundation Center's bibliographic database, Literature of the Nonprofit Sector Online (lnps.foundationcenter.org/) or the publisher's Web site. The bibliography is divided into these sections:

- General
- Arts and Humanities
- International Travel and Study
- Media and Communications
- Medicine and Health
- Minorities and Special Populations
- Research
- Scholarships, Fellowships, and Loans
- Writing

GENERAL

Annual Register of Grant Support: A Directory of Funding Sources. 39th ed. Medford, NJ: Information Today, Inc. 2005.
Includes details of the grant support programs of government agencies, public and private foundations, corporations, community trusts, unions, educational and professional associations, and special-interest organizations. Each complete program description contains details of the type, purpose, and duration of the grant; amount of funding available for each award and for the entire program; eligibility requirements; geographic restrictions; number of applicants and recipients; and other pertinent information and special stipulations. Published annually. URL: www.infotoday.com

Catalog of Federal Domestic Assistance. Executive Office of the President. Office of Management and Budget, and General Services Administration. Washington, DC: U.S. Government Printing Office, 2005.
Official directory of federal programs that provide assistance to American organizations, institutions, and individuals. Includes programs open to individual applicants or for individual beneficiaries in the areas of agriculture, commerce, community development, consumer protection, arts and culture, education, employment, energy, environmental quality, nutrition, health, housing, social services, information sciences, law, natural resources, regional development, science and technology, and transportation. Arranged by administering agency, with indexes by applicant eligibility, subject, and authorizing legislation. Published annually, with a semi-annual update. To purchase in print call 866-512-1800, toll free. Available free online. URL: www.cfda.gov

The Grants Register, 2006. 24th ed. New York, NY: Palgrave Publishers LTD. 2005.
Lists scholarships, fellowships, and awards at all levels of graduate study, from regional, national, and international sources; arranged alphabetically by name of organization. Entries provide contact information, subject, eligibility, purpose, type, number of awards offered, frequency, amount of award, length of study, country of study, and application procedure. Includes subject and eligibility guide to awards. Published annually. URL: www.palgrave.com

Margolin, Judith B. *The Individual's Guide to Grants.* New York: Kluwer Academic/Plenum Publishers, 1983.
An excellent starting guide to grantseeking for individuals. Discusses finding a sponsor or umbrella group, identifying and researching potential funders, writing and submitting proposals, and following up successful and rejected grant applications. Chapter two is particularly useful in explaining the role of institutional affiliation or project sponsorship. URL: www.wkap.nl

Webster, Valerie J., ed. *Awards, Honors, and Prizes.* Volume 1: United States and Canada. 25th ed. Farmington Hills, MI: Gale Group, Inc., 2006.
Directory of approximately 22,500 awards recognizing achievement in a wide variety of fields, including arts, business, communications, science, and public affairs. Sponsors are foundations, corporations, universities, nonprofit organizations, and governments. Indexed by sponsoring organization, award, and subject area. URL: www.gale.com

Webster, Valerie J., ed. *Awards, Honors, and Prizes.* Volume 2: International and Foreign. 25th ed. Farmington Hills, MI: Gale Group, Inc., 2006.
Contains descriptions of awards offered by organizations in countries outside the U.S. and Canada. Arranged by country, with indexes by organization, award name, and subject area. URL: www.gale.com

ARTS AND HUMANITIES

Alliance of Artists Communities. Artists Communities: A Directory of Residencies in the United States That Offer Time and Space for Creativity. 3rd ed. New York: Allworth Press, 2005.
Lists nonprofit residencies for performing and visual artists, composers, and writers, with basic information about programs, facilities, participants, and application procedures. URL: www.allworth.com

American Art Directory 2005–2006. 60th ed. New Providence, NJ: National Register Publishing Co., 2004.

> Includes a section on scholarships and fellowships awarded by colleges and universities, art schools, and arts organizations. URL: www.nationalregisterpub.com

Bessler, Ian, ed. 2006 *Songwriter's Market.* Cincinnati, OH: Writer's Digest Books, 2005

> Over 1000 totally updated listings for record companies, booking agents and music producers. URL: www.writersdigest.com

Breen, Nancy, ed. 2006 *Poet's Market.* Cincinnati, OH: Writer's Digest Books. 2005.

> Entries include contact information and submission instructions for periodicals, book publishers, and other outlets for poetry. URL: www.writersdigest.com

Christensen, Warren and Debbie McAfee, eds. *National Directory of Arts Internships.* 10th ed. Los Angeles: National Network for Artist Placement, 2005.

> Profiles 3,000 internship opportunities offered by 800 host organizations. Presents a broad range of disciplines, including arts management, dance, theater, music, literature, film and video, photography, performing arts, and design. Entries give brief program description and eligibility requirements. URL: www.artistplacement.com

Cox, Mary, ed. 2006 *Artist's and Graphic Designer's Market.* Cincinnati, OH: Writer's Digest Books. 2005.

> Covers magazines, books, posters, galleries, cartoons, clip art, record labels, greeting cards, and other related markets. Entries include contact information, how to query the publisher, typical fees paid, and other specifications for aspiring and professional graphic designers. URL: www.writersdigest.com

Crawford, Tad. *Legal Guide for the Visual Artist.* 4th ed. New York: Allworth Press, 1999.

> Provides information for artists on copyright law, sales and commissions contracts, publishing and reproduction rights, and taxation. Includes a short section on researching grants and contact information for artists' organizations and state arts councils. URL: www.allworth.com

Directory of Grants in the Humanities: 2005/2006. 19th ed. Westport, CT: Oryx Press, 2004.

> Directory contains more than 3,650 programs by 2,106 foundations, federal and state government agencies, corporations, and professional organizations and associations. Indexed by subject, sponsoring organization, program type, and geographic area. Published annually. E-mail: Greenwood.enquiries@ harcourteducation.co.uk; URL: www.greenwood.com

Grant, Daniel. *The Business of Being an Artist.* 3rd ed. New York: Allworth Press, 2000.

> Emerging artists are taught how to market and sell artwork on their own and through dealers. It shows how to create and market on a website, examines censorship, copyright, and more. URL: www.allworth.com

Michels, Caroll. *How to Survive and Prosper as an Artist: Selling Yourself Without Selling Your Soul.* 5th ed. New York: Henry Holt & Co., 2001.

> Includes a chapter on grantseeking, and an appendix of useful resources, including art colonies and residencies, publications with internships and apprenticeships, competitions, arts organizations, and an annotated bibliography on grants and funding. E-mail: publicity@hholt.com; URL: www.hholt.com

Middleton, Robyn, et. al. *Artists and Writers Colonies: Retreats, Residencies, and Respites for the Creative Mind.* 2nd ed. Portland, OR: Blue Heron Publishing, Inc., 2000.

> Includes more than 260 programs for the U.S. and overseas. Indexed by geographic area, with information on places for photographers, poets, playwrights, screenwriters, fiction and nonfiction writers, visual artists, performing artists, scientists, journalists, and scholars.

Moran-Lever, Terry, ed. *Musical America: International Directory of the Performing Arts. East Windsor, NJ:* Commonwealth Business Media, Inc., 2006.

> Includes a "Contests, Foundations, and Awards" section with information on scholarships, fellowships, prizes, and competitions in music and dance. Published annually. URL: www.musicalamerica.com

Poehner, Donna, ed. 2006 *Photographer's Market.* Cincinnati, OH: Writer's Digest Books. 2005.

> Covers numerous markets for photography professionals, including addresses, contacts and terms, specifications, and fees paid. URL: www.writersdigest.com

Schlachter, Gail Ann, and R. David Weber. *Money for Graduate Students in the Arts & Humanities 2005–2007 (Money for Graduate Students in the Humanities).* El Dorado Hills, CA: Reference Service Press, 2005.

> Graduate students working on a master's, professional, or doctoral degree can find out about the 1,000 biggest and best fellowships grants in a myriad of fields in the arts and humanities. URL: www.rspfunding.com

Vitali, Julius. *The Fine Artist's Guide to Marketing and Self-Promotion.* Rev. ed. New York, NY: Allworth Press, 2003.

> Explains how artists can be successful small-business entrepreneurs by marketing and promoting their work. Chapter 7 addresses corporate support for the arts, while Chapter 8 deals specifically with grants for individuals. URL: www.allworth.com

Wilder, Judith Luther. *Breaking Through the Clutter: Business Solutions for Women, Artists, and Entrepreneurs.* Los Angeles: National Network for Artist Placement, 1999.

> A guide for artists who want to create business plans, market their work, reach an audience, and seek outside funding. URL: www.artistplacement.com

Internet Sources

American Music Center (www.amc.net)

> A listing of ongoing American and foreign competitions, grants, commissioning programs, workshops, calls for scores, and artist's colonies. Includes opportunities for performers, both individuals and ensembles, in jazz and contemporary concert music, with subject index. This source is only available online by paid subscription.

Americans for the Arts (www.artsusa.org)
Information clearinghouse that provides material on funding for individuals in all areas of the arts.

American Society of Composers, Authors, and Publishers Awards Programs (www.ascap.com/about/support.html)
Lists prizes and awards to composers in various areas of music.

Arts Deadlines List (artdeadlineslist.com)
Monthly Internet publication with funding opportunities in the visual arts.

BMI Foundation (www.bmifoundation.org)
Describes programs established to encourage young composers and support the work of accomplished concert-music composers in such areas as classical music, jazz, and musical theater.

Creative Capital's Artist Toolbox (toolbox.creative-capital.org)
A listing of career-resource sites for individual artists.

Grammy Foundation (www.grammy.com/GRAMMY_Foundation/)
Provides information on grants that support the archiving and preserving of the music and recorded sound heritage of the Americas.

Musical Online (www.musicalonline.com/foundation_grants.htm)
A compilation of funding resources including foundations and associations, grants, scholarships, and organizations.

National Endowment for the Arts (arts.endow.gov)
Provides information on fellowships in the areas of poetry, prose, music, and the arts.

New York Foundation for the Arts (NYFA) (www.nyfa.org)
The "For Artists" section provides information on fellowships and fiscal sponsorship for artists. NYFA also has a listing of organizations that operate fiscal sponsorship programs for visual artists and a fact sheet for artists with disabilities, both available in PDF format.

INTERNATIONAL TRAVEL AND STUDY

Fulbright U.S. Student Program; Grants for Graduate Study, Research or Teaching Assistantships Abroad, 2006–2007. New York: Institute of International Education, 2005.
Describes fellowships available to U.S. graduate students, young professionals, and artists for study or research in over 100 foreign countries. Includes general program description and eligibility requirements. E-mail: info@iie.org; URL: www.iie.org

International Exchange Locator: A Resource Directory for Educational and Cultural Exchange. Washington, DC: Alliance for International Educational and Cultural Exchange, 2005.
Lists organizations involved in international exchanges, industry-specific exchanges, research/support organizations, foreign affairs agencies and exchange programs, other federal government exchanges, and key congressional committees and members of congress. Entries contain name and address of the organization, statement of purpose, types of exchange programs, availability of financial assistance, geographic focus, and a list of selected publications. URL: www.alliance-exchange.org

IIE Passport Academic Year Abroad, 2006 35th Edition. New York: Institute of International Education, 2006.
Includes information on more than 3,000 semester and academic-year study abroad programs, most sponsored by U.S. colleges and universities. Arranged geographically, with indexes by level and field of study, sponsor, and tuition range. E-mail: info@iiepassport.org; URL: www.iie.org

IIE Passport: Academic Year Abroad: The Most Complete Guide to Planning Academic Year Study Abroad. New York: Institute of International Education, 2006.
Includes information on more than 3,000 semester and academic-year study abroad programs, most sponsored by U.S. colleges and universities. Arranged geographically, with indexes by level and field of study, sponsor, and tuition range. E-mail: info@iie.org; URL: www.iie.org

IIE Passport: Short-Term Study Abroad: The Most Complete Guide to Summer and Short-Term Study Abroad 2006. New York: Institute of International Education, 2006.
Includes a listing of more than 3,000 short-term study abroad programs sponsored by U.S. colleges and universities as well as foreign universities, language schools and other organizations. E-mail: info@iie.org; URL: www.iie.org

Peterson's Study Abroad 2006. 13th ed. Lawrenceville, NJ: Peterson's Guides, 2005.
A complete A–Z guide to more than 1,900 overseas programs. URL: www.petersons.com

Schlachter, Gail Ann, and R. David Weber. *Financial Aid for Research and Creative Activities Abroad 2006-2008.* El Dorado Hills, CA: Reference Service Press, 2006.
Lists over 1,100 scholarships, fellowships, loans, grants, awards, and internships available for research, artistic, and professional pursuits abroad. Indexed by program title, sponsoring organization, geographic area, subject, and filing deadline. URL: www.rspfunding.com

Schlachter, Gail Ann, and R. David Weber. *Financial Aid for Study and Training Abroad 2006-2008.* El Dorado Hills, CA: Reference Service Press, 2006.
Describes nearly 1,000 financial aid programs sponsored by government agencies, professional organizations, foundations, educational associations, and other public and private agencies. Includes an annotated bibliography of financial aid directories. Indexed by program title, sponsoring organization, geographic area, subject, and filing deadline. URL: www.rspfunding.com

United Nations Educational, Scientific and Cultural Organization. *Study Abroad: Etudes a L'Etranger, Estudios en el Extranjero, 2006-2007.* 33rd ed. Paris, France: United Nations Educational, Scientific and Cultural Organization, 2006.
Profiles more than 2,700 international study programs in all academic and professional fields. Includes information about financial assistance offered by international organizations, governments, foundations, universities and other institutions in more than 120 countries. Indexed by organization and subject of study. URL: www.unesco.org

Internet Sources

EduPASS! The SmartStudent Guide to Studying in the USA
(www.edupass.org)

Institute of International Education Online (www.iie.org)
Includes information about international education and training programs, including Fulbright scholarships.

International Documentary Association
(www.documentary.org/resources/index.php)
Provides links to production resources such as fiscal sponsorship, grants, and documentary educational materials.

NAFSA: Association of International Educators (www.nafsa.org)
Information on financial aid for foreign nationals studying in the United States: bibliographies and links to other information sites.

Social Science Research Council (www.ssrc.org)
Supports international fellowships and grant programs in the social sciences.

Study in the USA (www.studyusa.com)
Provides international students with information about hundreds of colleges, universities and English-language programs in the United States.

StudyAbroad.com
(www.studyabroad.com/forum/financial_aid.html)
Lists sources and tips on obtaining financial aid including minority scholarships, studying in countries such as Germany, England, Commonwealth Universities, France, and Turkey.

MEDIA AND COMMUNICATIONS

The Journalist's Road to Success: A Career and Scholarship Guide. Princeton, NJ: Dow Jones Newspaper Fund, 2005.
Annual guide to aid offered through schools and departments of journalism at U.S. and Canadian colleges and universities, by newspapers, professional societies, and miscellaneous sources. There is a section on grants specifically designed for minority students. E-mail: newsfund@wsj.dowjones.com; URL: www.dowjones.com

Schlachter, Gail Ann and R. David Weber. *How to Pay for Your Degree in Journalism & Related Fields 2004–2006.* El Dorado Hills, CA: Reference Service Press, 2005. URL: www.rspfunding.com

Wiese, Michael. *The Independent Film and Videomaker's Guide.* 2nd ed. Studio City, CA: Michael Wiese Productions, 1998.
Chapters cover developing, distributing, financing, and marketing of independent film and television works. Extensive bibliography includes Web sites of interest. URL: www.mwp.com

Internet Sources

Association of Independent Video and Filmmakers
(www.aivf.org)
Supports a variety of programs and services for the independent media community.

Independent Television Service
(www.itvs.org/producers/funding.html)
Funds proposals by independent producers and provides production, promotion, marketing and distribution support.

The Journalist's Road to Success
(djnewspaperfund.dowjones.com/fund/pubcareerguide.asp)
This is an online version of the book with the same title, created by The Dow Jones Newspaper Fund.

Morrie Warshawski (www.warshawski.com)
Provides an extensive bibliography on fundraising for independent film and video projects.

National Endowment for the Humanities (www.neh.fed.us)
Supports learning in all areas of the humanities and funds research and education.

Newswise (www.newswise.com)
Includes descriptions, deadlines, and contact information for more than 90 awards, grants, and fellowships in journalism.

MEDICINE AND HEALTH

Directory of Biomedical and Health Care Grants 2006. 20th ed. Phoenix, AZ: Oryx Press, 2005.
Contains descriptions of more than 2,750 health-related funding programs. Areas covered include clinical and programmatic studies in gerontology and mental health; clinical studies of the cause, detection, and elimination of cancer; health care delivery and maintenance; and studies of infectious and immunologic diseases, including programs researching all areas related to AIDS. Provides each program's requirements (including eligibility statements), restrictions, contact information, deadlines, and funding amounts. Contains a subject index, a sponsoring organization index, and an index by program type. Published annually. E-mail: info@oryxpress.com; URL: www.oryxpress.com

Medical School Admission Requirements 2007-2008, United States and Canada. Washington, DC: Association of American Medical Colleges, 2006.
Provides an overview of the complete medical school application process, with application procedures and deadlines, tuition and student fees, and statistics on acceptance rates from every accredited medical school in the United States and Canada. Published annually. URL: www.aamc.org

Schlachter, Gail Ann and R. David Weber. *Money for Graduate Students in the Biological and Health Sciences 2005–2007.* El Dorado Hills, CA: Reference Service Press, 2005.
Describes the biggest and best fellowships, grants, and awards available to support graduate study, training, research, or creative activities in the biological and health sciences. URL: www.rspfunding.com

Schlachter, Gail Ann and R. David Weber. *RSP Funding for Nursing Students and Nurses 2004–2006.* El Dorado Hills, CA: Reference Service Press, 2004.
A list of scholarships, fellowships, grants, awards, loans, traineeships, and other funding programs in support of study, training, research, and creative activities for nursing students and nurses. URL: www.rspfunding.com

MINORITIES AND SPECIAL POPULATIONS

Getting Money for College: Scholarships for African American Students. Lawrenceville, NJ: Petersons, 2003.
Describes scholarships, grants, prizes, forgivable loans, and fellowships for African Americans. URL: www.petersons.com/

Getting Money for College: Scholarships for Asian American Students. Lawrenceville, NJ: Petersons, 2003.
Supplies profiles of scholarships, grants, prizes, forgivable loans, and fellowships for Asian American students. URL: www.petersons.com/

Getting Money for College: Scholarships for Hispanic American Students. Lawrenceville, NJ: Petersons, 2003.
Offers detailed descriptions of scholarships, grants, prizes, forgivable loans, and fellowships for Hispanic students. URL: www.petersons.com/

Schlachter, Gail Ann and R. David Weber. *Financial Aid for African Americans, 2005–2007.* El Dorado Hills, CA: Reference Service Press, 2005.
Provides nearly 1,500 descriptions of scholarships, fellowships, loans, grants, awards, and internships available to African Americans from high school through professional and postdoctoral levels. URL: www.rspfunding.com

Schlachter, Gail Ann and R. David Weber. *Financial Aid for Asian Americans, 2005–2007.* El Dorado Hills, CA: Reference Service Press, 2005.

Describes 1,100 scholarships, fellowships, loans, grants, awards, or internship opportunities for Americans of Asian/Pacific Islander origins. URL: www.rspfunding.com

Schlachter, Gail Ann and R. David Weber. *Financial Aid for the Disabled and Their Families, 2004–2006.* El Dorado Hills, CA: Reference Service Press, 2004.
Lists hundreds of scholarships, loans, grants-in-aid, and awards from federal, state, and private sources, arranged by disability type, with subject, geographic, sponsor, and filing date indexes. URL: www.rspfunding.com

Schlachter, Gail Ann and R. David Weber. *Financial Aid for Hispanic Americans, 2005–2007.* El Dorado Hills, CA: Reference Service Press, 2005.
Provides detailed entries of 1,300 scholarships, loans, fellowships, grants, awards, and internships available to Hispanic Americans. URL: www.rspfunding.com

Schlachter, Gail Ann and R. David Weber. *Financial Aid for Native Americans, 2005–2007.* El Dorado Hills, CA: Reference Service Press, 2005.
Contains more than 1,500 grants, scholarships, fellowships, internships, and awards open to American Indians, Native Alaskans, and Native Hawaiians. The funding opportunities cover major subject areas; are sponsored by more than 800 private and public agencies and organizations. URL: www.rspfunding.com

Schlachter, Gail Ann, and R. David Weber. *Financial Aid for Veterans, Military Personnel and Their Dependents, 2004–2006.* El Dorado Hills, CA: Reference Service Press, 2004.
Lists more than 1,200 scholarships, grants-in-aid, loans and other benefit programs for Americans affiliated with the military, from federal, state, and private sources. Indexed by subject, sponsor, geographic area, and filing deadline. URL: www.rspfunding.com

Schlachter, Gail Ann and R. David Weber. *Funding for Persons with Visual Impairments.* Large print ed. El Dorado Hills, CA: Reference Service Press, 2006.
A large-print listing of the scholarships, fellowships, loans, grants-in-aid, awards, and internships that are designated for persons with visual impairments (from high school seniors through professionals and others). Almost 270 funding opportunities are described. URL: www.rspfunding.com

Schlachter, Gail Ann. *Directory of Financial Aids for Women 2005–2007.* El Dorado Hills, CA: Reference Service Press, 2005.
Describes close to 1,500 scholarships, fellowships, loans, grants, awards, internships, and state sources of educational benefits for women. Entries include program title, sponsoring organization, availability, purpose, eligibility, financial data, duration, limitations, number of awards, and application deadline. Includes annotated bibliography of general financial aid directories. Indexed by program title, sponsoring organization, geographic area, subject focus, and calendar deadlines. URL: www.rspfunding.com

The 2005 Hispanic Scholarship Directory: Over 1,000 Ways to Finance Your Education. Carlsbad, CA: WPR Publishing and National Hispanic Press Foundation, 2005.
Contains scholarships available to Hispanic students and international students from Latin America. Information includes specifics on: Private and public scholarships, loan programs, national grant programs sponsored by the federal government, and resources provided by a number of state programs. URLs: www.westernpublicationresearch.com/ and www.nahp.org/nahpf/8.html
Winds of Change Magazine's Annual College Guide for American Indians. Boulder, CO: Winds of Change, 2005. E-mail: woc@indra.com; URL: www.wocmag.org

Internet Sources

Federal Benefits for Veterans and Dependents. Washington, DC: United States Department of Veterans Affairs, 2006. (bookstore.gpo.gov/) and (www1.va.gov/opa/vadocs/current_benefits.htm)
This resource may be downloaded from the link above or a print version may be ordered through the Government Printing Office.

Financial Aid for Lesbian, Gay and Bisexual Students (www.finaid.org/otheraid/gay.phtml)
This site gives a relatively comprehensive listing of many different scholarship funds, dividing them into general, regional, and campus specific.

Financial Aid and Scholarship Resources for Lesbian, Gay, Bisexual, and Transgender Students (www.american.edu/ocl/glbta/resources/info_scholarships.html)
This site is maintained by American University and lists various regional, national, and international grant and scholarship sources for LGBT students or researchers working on LGBT issues.

Scholarships for Hispanics (www.scholarshipsforhispanics.org/)
This free online directory, sponsored by the National Education
Association, is a joint project of WPR Publishing and the National
Hispanic Press Foundation. The searchable directory identifies
scholarships and fellowships for Hispanics/Latinos.

RESEARCH

*Directory of Research Grants 2007. Phoenix, AZ: Oryx Press,
2006.*
Describes more than 5,100 grant programs that support research
projects in medicine, the physical and social sciences, humanities
and the arts, and education. Annotations describe program
requirements with eligibility statements, program restrictions and
exclusions, contacts, deadlines, and funding amounts. Indexed by
subject, sponsoring organization, and program type (i.e.,
fellowships, travel grants). Published annually. E-mail:
info@oryxpress.com; URL: www.oryxpress.com

Grants, Fellowships, and Prizes of Interest to Historians 2005.
Washington, DC: American Historical Association Publications,
2005.
Describes more than 450 organizations that grant fellowships,
awards, and prizes to historians. Includes bibliography. Available
online, only to members of AHA. URL: www.theaha.org

Hellebust, Lynn, ed. *Think Tank Directory: A Guide to Nonprofit
Public Policy Research Organizations.* 2nd Rev.ed. Topeka, KS:
Government Research Service, 2003.
Over 1,200 academic and independent research organizations are
profiled, with information on their purposes, policy areas, research
priorities, budgets and funding sources, publications, staff, and
governance. Includes geographic and policy area indexes. E-mail:
grs@cjnetworks.com

International Research Centers Directory. 20th ed. Farmington
Hills, MI: Thomson Gale, 2006.
More than 10,000 government, university, independent, nonprofit,
and commercial research and development organizations in nearly
150 countries worldwide, indexed by name, subject, and country.
URL: www.gale.com

Schlachter, Gail Ann and R. David Weber. *Money for Graduate
Students in the Physical and Earth Sciences 2005–2007.* El
Dorado Hills, CA: Reference Service Press, 2005.
Describes 800 of the biggest and best fellowships, grants, and
awards available to support graduate study, training, research, or
creative activities in the physical and earth sciences. URL:
www.rspfunding.com

Schlachter, Gail Ann and R. David Weber. *Money for Graduate
Students in the Social and Behavioral Sciences 2005–2007.* El
Dorado Hills, CA: Reference Service Press, 2005.
Describes over 1,100 of the biggest and best fellowships, grants,
and awards available to support graduate study, training, research,
or creative activities in the social sciences.
URL: www.rspfunding.com

Schlachter, Gail Ann and R. David Weber. *How to Pay for Your
Degree in Engineering, 2004–2006.* (formerly issued as RSP
Funding for Engineering Students). El Dorado Hills, CA:
Reference Service Press, 2004.
A list of 800 scholarships, fellowships, loans, awards, prizes, and
internships available to undergraduate and graduate students
majoring in engineering. URL: www.rspfunding.com

Wood, Donna, ed. *Research Centers Directory.* 34th ed.
Farmington Hills, MI: Thomson Gale, 2006.
Guide to over 13,800 university-related and other nonprofit
research organizations in a broad range of subject areas, providing
information on programs, staffing, publications, and educational
efforts. Includes subject, geographic, personal name, and master
indexes. Published annually. URL: www.gale.com

Internet Sources

GrantsNet (www.grantsnet.org)
A "one-stop" resource for funds related to training in the sciences
and undergraduate science education.

International Education Financial Aid (www.iefa.org/)
This online directory lists college scholarship and grant
information for international students wishing to study abroad.

National Endowment for the Humanities (www.neh.fed.us)
Supports learning in all areas of the humanities and funds
research and education.

National Institutes of Health (www.nih.gov)
Funds research and education in science and engineering through
grants, contracts, and cooperative agreements.

National Science Foundation (www.nsf.gov)
Funds research and education in science and engineering through
grants, contracts and cooperative agreements.

Social Science Research Council (www.ssrc.org)
The SSRC provides fellowship and grant programs mostly targeting
the social sciences; although many are also open to applicants
from the humanities, natural sciences, and relevant professional
and practitioner communities.

SCHOLARSHIPS, FELLOWSHIPS, AND LOANS

Cassidy, Daniel J. *The Scholarship Book: The Complete Guide to
Private-Sector Scholarships, Grants, and Loans for
Undergraduates.* 12th ed. New York, NY: Prentice-Hall. 2006.
Describes scholarships awarded by foundations, associations,
corporations, unions, and fraternal organizations. Includes indexes
by major fields of study and scholarship name, and a Quick Find
index for state of residence, ethnic background, physical
handicaps, and state of intended study. Book also includes
CD-ROM.

Chronicle Financial Aid Guide 2005-2006: Scholarships and Loans for High School Students, College Undergraduates, Graduates, and Adult Learners. Moravia, NY: Chronicle Guidance Publications, Inc., 2005.

Information on scholarship programs in all fields of study, from undergraduate to postdoctoral levels. Sources include public and private organizations. Indexed by sponsoring organization and subject area. Published annually. URL: www.chronicleguidance.com

College Blue Book. 33rd ed. New York: Macmillan Reference USA, 2005.

Lists over 10,000 entries of financial aid awards, arranged by area of study and type of recipient, and indexed by title, subject, sponsor, and academic level.

College Board Scholarship Handbook 2006. New York, NY: College Board Publications, 2005.

Descriptions of private and government scholarship and internship programs for undergraduates. URL: www.collegeboard.com

Getting Money for Graduate School. Lawrenceville, NJ: Peterson's Guides, 2002.

Specifically targeted for the graduate and post-graduate student, this one-of-a-kind resource identifies more than 1,000 scholarships, grants, prizes, forgivable loans and fellowships available to help pay for these advanced studies.

Guernsey, Lisa. *College.edu: On-line Resources for the Cyber-Savvy Student.* Version 9.0. Alexandria, VA: Octameron Associates, 2005.

Recommended Web sites, with descriptions of how they are helpful to students in assessing colleges and in their search for scholarship funds. E-mail: info@octameron.com; URL: www.octameron.com

Leider, Anna. *The A's and B's of Academic Scholarships.* 25th ed. Alexandria, VA: Octameron Associates, 2005.

Describes in tabular form academic merit-based scholarships at over 1,200 colleges and universities. E-mail: info@octameron.com; URL: www.octameron.com

Leider, Anna. *Loans and Grants from Uncle Sam: Am I Eligible and for How Much?* 13th ed. Alexandria, VA: Octameron Associates, 2005.

This book contains simple explanations and useful worksheets to help readers understand loans and grants offered by the U.S. government.

Leider, Robert, and Anna Leider. *Don't Miss Out: The Ambitious Student's Guide to Financial Aid.* 30th ed. Alexandria, VA: Octameron Associates, 2005.

Planning guide that discusses procedures and strategies for students seeking financial aid, with tips about public and private funding sources. Special sections on academic and athletic scholarships, funding for women and minorities. E-mail: info@octameron.com; URL: www.octameron.com

Meeting College Costs: What You Need to Know Before Your Child and Your Money Leave Home. New York, NY: College Board Publications, 2005.

This book provides insight into the application process and how aid eligibility is determined. Many worksheets are included to calculate expected eligibility for aid or financing.

Need a Lift? to Educational Opportunities, Careers, Loans, Scholarships & Employment. 54th ed. Indianapolis, IN: American Legion, 2005.

Emphasis on scholarship opportunities for veterans and their dependents, or children of deceased or disabled veterans. Includes information on federal, state, and private sources of funding, American Legion benefit programs, and annotated bibliography. E-mail: emblem@legion.org; URL: www.legion.org

Peterson's College Money Handbook 2006. 23rd ed. Lawrenceville, NJ: Peterson's Guides, 2005.

Details on financial aid programs offered by over 2,000 American colleges and universities, along with general information about federal and state loan programs. URL: www.petersons.com

Peterson's Scholarships, Grants and Prizes 2006. 10th ed. Lawrenceville, NJ: Peterson's Guides, 2005.

Lists more than 2,800 private sources of financial aid, as well as state-controlled grant programs. URL: www.petersons.com

Schlachter, Gail Ann, and R. David Weber. *The College Student's Guide to Merit and Other No-Need Funding, 2005–2007.* El Dorado Hills, CA: Reference Service Press, 2005.

More than 1,200 non-need-based funding programs for currently enrolled or returning students, with subject, geographic, and calendar date indexes. URL: www.rspfunding.com

Schlachter, Gail Ann and R. David Weber. *High School Senior's Guide to Merit and Other No-*

Need Funding 2005–2007. El Dorado Hills, CA: Reference Service Press, 2005. URL: www.rspfunding.com

Schlachter, Gail Ann. *How to Find out about Financial Aid and Funding: A Guide to Print, Electronic, and Internet Resources Listing Scholarships, Fellowships, Loans, Grants, Awards, and Internships.* El Dorado Hills, CA: Reference Service Press, 2003.

An annotated bibliographic guide to the resources available for both undergraduate and graduate levels. Covers scholarships, grants to organizations, grants to individuals, awards or prizes, and internship opportunities. Entries indicate format of the item (Internet, electronic, or print), publisher, scope, and ordering information. A separate section describes federal government Web sites. Indexed by title of work, author's name, publisher, geographic area, and subject. URL: www.rspfunding.com

Schlachter, Gail Ann and R. David Weber. *How to Pay for Your Degree in Business & Related Fields 2004–2006.* El Dorado Hills, CA: Reference Service Press, 2004. URL: www.rspfunding.com

Schlachter, Gail Ann and R. David Weber. *How to Pay for Your Degree in Education & Related Fields 2004–2006.* El Dorado Hills, CA: Reference Service Press, 2004. URL: www.rspfunding.com

Scholarship Almanac 2005. 8th ed. Lawrenceville, NJ: Peterson's Guides, 2004. URL: www.petersons.com

Scholarships, Fellowships and Loans: A Guide to Education-Related Financial Aid Programs for Students and Professionals. 22nd ed. Farmington Hills, MI: Gale Group, Inc., 2005.

Lists a wide range of scholarships, fellowships, loans, grants, and awards not controlled by a college or university. URL: www.gale.com

The Student Guide 2005–2006/Guía para Estudiantes 2005–2006. Washington, DC: United States Department of Education, 2005.

> Published annually, available in English or Spanish, this is the federal government's official guide to its financial aid programs, including Pell Grants, Stafford and Perkins Loans, PLUS Loans, and Work-Study. Includes general information on applications, eligibility, determination of need, and college tuition financing. The entire guide may be downloaded via the URL: http://studentaid.ed.gov or request a copy by calling 1-800-4-FED-AID (1-800-433-3243).

Vuturo, Christopher. *The Scholarship Advisor: Hundreds of Thousands of Scholarships Worth More Than $1 Billion.* New York, NY: Princeton Review, 2002.

> Obtain a list of scholarships worth more than $1 billion. Learn to research and find scholarships; write quality inquiry letters, personal statements and essays; techniques for interviews with scholarship committees, and how to complete an application.

Weber, R. David, Douglas Bucher, and Gail Ann Schlachter. *Kaplan Scholarships 2006.* New York, NY: Simon & Schuster, 2005.

> Information on programs that offer significant and unrestricted scholarships combined with tips and advice on how to get them.

Internet Sources

AFL-CIO (66.109.241.150/unionplus/scholarship.html)
> Connects to the AFL-CIO's Union Plus Scholarship Database that offers information on union-sponsored scholarships and aid.

Broke Scholar (www.scholarships.brokescholar.com)
> Provides a free scholarship search engine of undergraduate, graduate, and professional awards. After completing a profile, it will deliver scholarship notifications via e-mail and tools to assist with tracking scholarship applications.

College Board's Scholarship Search (www.collegeboard.com)
> Users can create a personal profile of educational level, talents, and background to search among 2,300 undergraduate scholarships, loans, internships, and other financial aid programs from non-college sources.

College Answer (www.collegeanswer.com/index.jsp)
> Formerly Wired Scholar, this site offers guidance on college preparation, evaluation, selection, application, and financing. Free registration is required in order to use the database.

Fastweb.com (www.fastweb.com)
> A scholarship search engine that prompts users to enter information about themselves, including area of study, and responds with an appropriate list of available scholarships.

Federal Student Aid (studentaid.ed.gov)
> The U.S. Department of Education's Federal Student Aid (FSA) programs, described on this Web site, are the largest source of student aid in America. The information provided is designed to assist college planning. It provides access to and information about the products and services that needed throughout the financial aid process.

FinAid: The Financial Aid Information Page (www.finaid.org)
> Links to funding sources such as scholarships, fellowships, and grants, some of which are focused towards those with particular needs or interests: disabled, minorities and international students.
> The Foundation Center's Youth in Philanthropy-Scholarship Information (http://youth.foundationcenter.org/youth_scholarships.html) Here you will find an alphabetical listing of Web-based scholarship resources detailing a wide range of ways to find financial aid.

Info.Gradschools.com (www.gradschools.com/info/financial.html)

Petersons.com: Financial Aid (iiswinprd03.petersons.com/finaid)
> Provides help, guidance, and answers to frequently-asked questions on financial aid, as well as information on organizations that offer private and federal loans. Petersons' Scholarship Search provides information on over 1.7 million scholarships, grants, and prizes worth nearly $7.6 billion. (Free registration is required in order to use the database).

Scholarship Resource Network Express (www.srnexpress.com)

WRITING

Breen, Nancy, ed. 2006 *Poet's Market.* 2006 ed. Cincinnati, OH: Writer's Digest Books. 2005.

> Entries include contact information and submission instructions for periodicals, book publishers, and other outlets for poetry. URL: www.writersdigest.com

Brogan, Kathryn Struckel and Robert Brewer, eds. *2006 Writer's Market.* Cincinnati, OH: Writer's Digest Books, 2005.

> Contains a "Contests and Awards" section listing fellowships and prizes for fiction, nonfiction, poetry, playwriting, screenwriting, journalism, children's literature, and translation. Includes information on programs sponsored by state arts councils. Published annually. URL: www.writersdigest.com

Literary Market Place 2006: The Directory of the American Book Publishing Industry with Industry Yellow Pages. Medford, NJ: Information Today Inc., 2005.

> Includes a section listing literary prizes, contests, residencies, fellowships, and grants. Published annually. E-mail: info@bowker.com; URL: www.bowker.com

Grants and Awards Available to American Writers. New York: PEN American Center, 2005.

> Comprehensive list of awards available to American and Canadian writers for use in the U.S. or abroad. Includes appendix of state arts councils. Only available in electronic format via the website. URL: www.pen.org

Poets & Writers Magazine. New York, NY: Poets & Writers, Inc. URL: www.pw.org

Sova, Kathy, and Samantha Rachel Healy, eds. *Dramatists Sourcebook 24th ed.* New York: Theatre Communications Group, 2006.
Contains a "Fellowship and Grants" section listing foundations and organizations that offer funding to playwrights, composers, translators, librettists, and lyricists. Notes guidelines, application procedures, deadlines, remuneration, and frequency of these funding sources. Includes a list of sources of emergency funds for writers in severe temporary financial difficulties, the addresses and phone numbers of state arts agencies, and artists' colonies and residencies. Published annually. E-mail: tcg@tcg.org; URL: www.tcg.org

Wright, Michael, and Christi Pyland. *The Student's Guide to Playwriting Opportunities.* 3rd ed. Dorset, VT: American Theatre Works, 2002.
Includes developmental programs that may have internships, fellowships, summer employment, and other opportunities of interest to student playwrights. URL: www.theatredirectories.com

Internet Sources

Americans for the Arts (www.artsusa.org)
Information clearinghouse that provides material on funding for individuals in all areas of the arts.

National Endowment for the Arts (www.arts.endow.gov/)
Provides information on fellowships in the areas of poetry, prose, music, and the arts.

Newswise (www.newswise.com/resources/j_grants/)
Includes descriptions, deadlines, and contact information for awards, grants, and fellowships in journalism.

Poets & Writers Online (www.pw.org/mag/grantsawards.htm)
Contains an extensive list of upcoming deadlines for state and national poetry, fiction, and creative nonfiction prizes.

RESOURCES OF THE FOUNDATION CENTER

The Foundation Center is a national service organization founded and supported by foundations to provide a single authoritative source of information on foundation and corporate giving. The Center's programs are designed to help grantseekers select those funders that may be most interested in their projects from more than 80,000 active U.S. grantmakers. Among its primary activities toward this end are offering searchable databases online and on CD-ROM as well as publishing print directories covering foundation and corporate philanthropy; disseminating information on grantmaking, grantseeking, and related subjects through its site on the Internet; offering educational courses and workshops; and maintaining a nationwide network of library/learning centers and Cooperating Collections.

Databases and publications of the Foundation Center are the primary working tools of every serious grantseeker. They are also used by grantmakers, scholars, journalists, and legislators—in short, by anyone seeking any type of factual information on philanthropy. All private foundations and a significant number of corporate grantmakers and public charities actively engaged in grantmaking, regardless of size or geographic location, are included in one or more of the Center's databases or publications.

For those who wish to access information on grantmakers and their grants electronically, *The Foundation Directory Online* offers five plans to meet the needs of grantseekers—from *Basic*, featuring profiles of the 10,000 largest U.S. foundations to *Professional*, our most comprehensive option with more than 80,000 funders, half a million grants, and 250,000+ IRS 990s. The Center also issues *FC Search: The Foundation Center's Database on CD-ROM* containing the full universe of more than 80,000 foundations, grantmaking public charities, corporate givers and more than 334,000 associated grants.

Foundation Center print publications include directories that describe specific funders, characterizing their program interests and providing fiscal and personnel data; grants indexes that list and classify by subject recent foundation and corporate awards; fundraising and nonprofit management guides; and research reports on the field.

In addition, the Center's award-winning web site features a wide array of free information about the philanthropic community. The Foundation Center's electronic and print products may be ordered from the Foundation Center, 79 Fifth Avenue, New York, NY 10003-3076, or online at our web site. For more information about any aspect of the Center's products or services or for the name of the Center's library collection nearest you, call (800) 424-9836, or visit us on the web at foundationcenter.org.

ONLINE DATABASES

THE FOUNDATION DIRECTORY ONLINE SUBSCRIPTION PLANS

The Foundation Directory Online Basic
Search for foundation funding prospects from among the nation's largest 10,000 foundations and search the index of over 68,000 names of trustees, officers, and donors. Perform searches using up to twelve search fields.
MONTHLY SUBSCRIPTIONS START AT $19.95 PER MONTH
ANNUAL SUBSCRIPTIONS START AT $195 PER YEAR

The Foundation Directory Online Plus
Plus service allows users to search the 10,000 largest foundations in the U.S. and the index of over 68,000 names of trustees, officers, and donors—plus half a million grants awarded by major foundations.
MONTHLY SUBSCRIPTIONS START AT $29.95 PER MONTH
ANNUAL SUBSCRIPTIONS START AT $295 PER YEAR

The Foundation Directory Online Premium
In addition to featuring 20,000 of the nation's large and mid-sized foundations and an index of more than 117,000 names of trustees, officers, and donors—*Premium* service includes a searchable database of half a million grants awarded by major U.S. foundations.
MONTHLY SUBSCRIPTIONS START AT $59.95 PER MONTH
ANNUAL SUBSCRIPTIONS START AT $595 PER YEAR

The Foundation Directory Online Platinum
Search our entire universe of U.S. foundations, corporate giving programs, and grantmaking public charities—more than 80,000 funders in all. In addition to more funders, you'll get access to more in-depth data and an index of more than 364,000 names of trustees, officers, and donors. *The Foundation Directory Online Platinum* offers extensive program details and detailed application guidelines for more than 7,000 foundations; and sponsoring company information for corporate givers. This service also includes a searchable file of half a million grants awarded by the largest U.S. foundations.
MONTHLY SUBSCRIPTIONS START AT $149.95 PER MONTH
ANNUAL SUBSCRIPTIONS START AT $995 PER YEAR

The Foundation Directory Online Professional
The Foundation Directory Online Professional provides top-tier intelligence on grantmakers and their grants. Professional features our most comprehensive database, updated weekly: 80,000 funders, half a million grants, and 364,000 trustee, officer, and donor names—fully-indexed—plus a fully text-searchable database of 250,000+ 990s for grantmaking organizations, and unique funder portfolios including foundation news, RFPs, key staff affiliations, and full-color grant distribution charts.
MONTHLY SUBSCRIPTIONS START AT $179.95 PER MONTH
ANNUAL SUBSCRIPTIONS START AT $1,295 PER YEAR
Foundation and grants data are updated weekly for the above databases. Monthly, annual, and multi-user plans are available. Two-year subscription and Institution-wide Access plans are available for Platinum and Professional options. Please visit fconline.fdncenter.org to subscribe.

Foundation Grants to Individuals Online

Foundation Grants to Individuals Online features more than 6,200 foundation funding sources for individual grantseekers in education, research, arts and culture, or for special needs. Updated quarterly, users may choose from up to nine different search fields to discover prospective funders. Foundation records include current, authoritative data on the funder, including the name, address, and contact information; fields of interest; types of support; application information; and descriptions of funding opportunities for individual grantseekers.

ONE-MONTH SUBSCRIPTION: $9.95
THREE-MONTH SUBSCRIPTION: $26.95
ANNUAL SUBSCRIPTION: $99.95
Please visit gtionline.foundationcenter.org to subscribe.

CD-ROMs

FC SEARCH: The Foundation Center's Database on CD-ROM, Version 10.0

The Foundation Center's comprehensive database of grantmakers and their associated grants can be accessed in this fully searchable CD-ROM format. *FC Search* contains more than 80,000 grantmaker records, including all known active foundations and corporate giving programs in the United States. It also includes more than 334,000 newly reported grants from the largest foundations and the names of more than 364,000 trustees, officers, and donors which can be quickly linked to their foundation affiliations. Users can also link from *FC Search* to the Web sites of 6,100+ grantmakers and 2,600 corporations.

Grantseekers and other researchers may select multiple criteria and create customized prospect lists that can be printed or saved. Basic or Advanced search modes and special search options enable users to make searches as broad or as specific as required. Up to 21 different criteria may be selected:

- grantmaker name
- grantmaker type
- grantmaker city
- grantmaker state
- geographic focus
- fields of interest
- types of support
- total assets
- total giving
- trustees, officers, and donors
- establishment date
- corporate name
- corporate location
- recipient name
- recipient city
- recipient state
- recipient type
- subjects
- grant amount
- year grant authorized
- text search field

FC Search is a user friendly, yet sophisticated fundraising research tool. It has been developed with both the novice and experienced researcher in mind. Assistance is available through Online Help, a *User Manual* that accompanies *FC Search,* as well as through a free User Hotline.

APRIL 2006 / STANDALONE (SINGLE USER) VERSION: $1,195
LOCAL AREA NETWORK (2–8 USERS IN ONE BUILDING) VERSION: $1,895*
ADDITIONAL COPIES OF USER MANUAL: $19.95
Prices include fall 2006 Update disk plus one User Manual.
New editions of *FC Search* are released each spring.
*Larger local area network versions, site licenses, and wide area network versions are also available. For more information, call the Electronic Product Support Line (Mon.–Fri., 9am–5pm EST) (800) 478-4661.

THE FOUNDATION DIRECTORY 1 & 2 ON CD-ROM, Version 6.0

We've combined the authoritative data found in our two print classics, *The Foundation Directory* and *The Foundation Directory Part 2,* to bring you 20,000 of the nation's largest and mid-sized foundations in this searchable CD-ROM. Search for funding prospects by choosing from 12 search fields:

- grantmaker name
- grantmaker state
- grantmaker city
- fields of interest
- types of support
- trustees, officers, and donors
- geographic focus
- grantmaker type
- total giving
- total assets
- establishment date
- text search

The CD-ROM includes links to more than 2,000 foundation Web sites, more than 93,000 sample grants, and a searchable index of more than 117,000 trustees, officers, and donors.

MARCH 2006 / STANDALONE (SINGLE-USER) VERSION: $495
LOCAL AREA NETWORK VERSION (2-8 USERS IN ONE BUILDING): $795
Prices include fall 2006 Update disk

THE FOUNDATION GRANTS INDEX ON CD-ROM, Version 6.0

This CD-ROM enables grantseekers to search our database of 125,000 recently awarded grants by the largest 1,150 funders. Featuring 12 search fields:

- Recipient Name
- Recipient State
- Recipient City
- Recipient Type
- Grantmaker Name
- Grantmaker State
- Geographic Focus
- Subject
- Types of Support
- Grant Amount
- Year Authorized
- Text Search

DECEMBER 2005/ SINGLE USER / ISBN 1-59542-063-0 / $195
Call (800) 424-9836 for network versions.

GUIDE TO GREATER WASHINGTON D.C. GRANTMAKERS ON CD-ROM, Version 4.0

Compiled with the assistance of Washington Grantmakers, this CD-ROM covers more than 2,500 grantmakers located in the D.C. region or that have an interest in DC-area nonprofits. Users can generate prospect lists using 12 search fields. Grantmaker portraits feature crucial information: address, phone number, contact name, financial data, giving limitations, and names of key officials. For the first time, this CD-ROM features a separate searchable Grants database including summaries of thousands of grants awarded to nonprofits in the Washington, DC area, or from funders in the region.

JUNE 2006 / SINGLE USER / ISBN 1-59542-084-3 / $75

GUIDE TO OHIO GRANTMAKERS ON CD-ROM, Version 3.0

This CD-ROM features a searchable Foundation database, including profiles of more than 4,000 foundations with over 400 funders outside the state that award grants in Ohio. A separate searchable Grants database includes more than 30,000 summaries of grants awarded in Ohio nonprofits or from Ohio funders. Produced in collaboration with the Ohio Grantmakers Forum and the Ohio Association of Nonprofit Organizations.

MAY 2006 / ISBN 1-59542-085-1 / $125

SYSTEM CONFIGURATIONS FOR CD-ROM PRODUCTS

- Windows-based PC
- Microsoft 95 or above
- Pentium microprocessor
- 64mb memory

Internet access required to access grantmaker web sites and Foundation Center web site.

GENERAL RESEARCH DIRECTORIES

THE FOUNDATION DIRECTORY, 2006 Edition

The Foundation Directory has been widely known and respected in the field for more than 40 years. It includes the latest information on the 10,000 largest U.S. foundations based on total giving. The 2006 Edition includes more than 1,200 foundations that are new to this edition. *Directory* foundations hold more than $443 billion in assets and award over $28 billion in grants annually.

Each *Directory* entry contains information on application procedures, giving limitations, types of support awarded, the publications of each foundation, and foundation staff. In addition, each entry features such vital data as the grantmaker's giving interests, financial data, grant amounts, address, and telephone number. This edition includes more than 50,000 selected grants. The Foundation Center works closely with foundations to ensure the accuracy and timeliness of the information provided.

The *Directory* includes indexes by foundation name; subject areas of interest; names of donors, officers, and trustees; geographic location; international interests; types of support awarded; and grantmakers new to the volume. Also included are analyses of the foundation community by geography, asset and grant size, and the different foundation types.
MARCH 2006 / ISBN 1-59542-079-7 / $215 / PUBLISHED ANNUALLY

THE FOUNDATION DIRECTORY PART 2, 2006 Edition

The Foundation Directory Part 2 brings you the same thorough coverage for the next largest set of 10,000 foundations. It includes *Directory*-level information on mid-sized foundations, an important group of grantmakers responsible for millions of dollars in funding annually. Essential data on foundations is included along with more than 43,000 recently awarded foundation grants, providing an excellent overview of the foundations' giving interests. Quick access to foundation entries is facilitated by seven indexes, including foundation name; subject areas of interest; names of donors, officers, and trustees; geographic location; international interests; types of support awarded; and grantmakers new to the volume.
MARCH 2006 / ISBN 1-59542-081-9 / $185 / PUBLISHED ANNUALLY

THE FOUNDATION DIRECTORY SUPPLEMENT, 2006 Edition

The Foundation Directory Supplement provides new information on *Foundation Directory* and *Foundation Directory Part 2* grantmakers six months after those volumes are published. The *Supplement* ensures that users of the *Directory* and *Directory Part 2* always have the latest addresses, contact names, policy statements, application guidelines, and financial data for the foundations they're approaching for funding.
SEPTEMBER 2006 / ISBN 1-59542-086-X / $125 / PUBLISHED ANNUALLY

GUIDE TO U.S. FOUNDATIONS, THEIR TRUSTEES, OFFICERS, AND DONORS, 2006 Edition

This fundraising reference tool provides fundraisers with current, accurate information on more than 70,000 private and community foundations in the U.S. The three-volume set also includes a master list of the names of the people who establish, oversee, and manage those institutions so that fundraisers can discover the philanthropic connections of current donors, board members, volunteers, and prominent families in their geographic area. Each entry includes asset and giving amounts as well as geographic limitations, allowing fundraisers to quickly determine whether or not to pursue a particular grant source.

The *Guide to U.S. Foundations* is the only source of published data on thousands of local foundations. (It includes nearly 50,000 grantmakers not covered in other print publications.) Each entry also tells you whether you can find more extensive information on the grantmaker in another Foundation Center reference work.
APRIL 2006/ 1-59542-082-7 / $395 / PUBLISHED ANNUALLY

THE FOUNDATION 1000, 2005/2006 Edition

The Foundation 1000 provides access to extensive and accurate information on 1,000 of the largest foundations in the country. *Foundation 1000* grantmakers hold nearly $301 billion in assets and awarded over 190,000 grants worth over $17 billion to nonprofit organizations nationwide in the most current year of record. *The Foundation 1000* provides thorough analyses of 1,000 of the largest foundations and their grant programs, including all the data fundraisers need when applying for grants from these top-level foundations. Each multi-page foundation profile features a full foundation portrait, a detailed breakdown of the foundation's grant programs, and extensive lists of recently awarded foundation grants. Five indexes target potential funders in a variety of ways: by subject field, type of support, geographic location, international giving, and the names of foundation officers, donors, and trustees.
OCTOBER 2005 / ISBN 1-59542-056-8 / $295 / PUBLISHED ANNUALLY

NATIONAL DIRECTORY OF CORPORATE GIVING, 11th Edition

The *National Directory of Corporate Giving* offers authoritative information on nearly 4,100 company-sponsored foundations and direct corporate giving programs. It features detailed portraits of nearly 2,900 company-sponsored foundations plus more than 1,200 direct corporate giving programs.

Fundraisers will find essential information on these corporate grantmakers, including application information, key personnel, types of support generally awarded, giving limitations, financial data, and purpose and activities statements. Also included in the 11th Edition are more than 7,800 selected grants, providing the best indication of a grantmaker's funding priorities by identifying nonprofits it has already funded. The volume also provides data on the companies that sponsor foundations and direct-giving programs. Each entry gives the company's name and address, a listing of its types of business, its financial data (complete with *Forbes* and *Fortune* ratings), a listing of its subsidiaries, divisions, plants, and offices, and a charitable-giving statement. The *National Directory of Corporate Giving* features an extensive bibliography to guide you to further research on corporate funding. Seven essential indexes target funding prospects by geographic region; international giving; types of support; subject area; officers, donors, and trustees; types of business; and the names of the corporation, its foundation, and its direct-giving program.
AUGUST 2005/ ISBN 1-59542-051-7 / $195 / PUBLISHED ANNUALLY

DIRECTORY OF MISSOURI GRANTMAKERS, 6th Edition

The *Directory of Missouri Grantmakers* provides a comprehensive guide to grantmakers in the state or that have an interest in Missouri nonprofits—more than 1,800 foundations, corporate giving programs, and public charities—from the largest grantmakers to local family foundations. The volume will facilitate your grantseeking with entries that list giving amounts, fields of interest, purpose statements, selected grants, and more. Indexes help you target the most appropriate funders by subject interest, types of support, and names of key personnel.
JUNE 2005 / ISBN 1-59542-043-6 / $75 / PUBLISHED BIENNIALLY

FOUNDATION GRANTS TO INDIVIDUALS, 15th Edition

The only publication devoted entirely to foundation grant opportunities for qualified individual applicants, the 15th Edition of this volume features more than 6,200 entries, all of which profile grantmaker giving to individuals. Entries include grantmaker addresses and telephone numbers, financial data, giving limitations, and application guidelines.

This volume will save individual grantseekers countless hours of research. Indexes include:

- Geographic Focus
- International Focus
- Company Name
- Specific Schools
- Types of Support
- Subject
- Grantmaker Name

JULY 2006 / ISBN 1-59542-089-4 / $65 / PUBLISHED ANNUALLY

SUBJECT DIRECTORIES

The Foundation Center's *National Guide to Funding in . . .* series is designed to facilitate grantseeking within specific fields of nonprofit activity. Each of the directories described below identifies a set of grantmakers that have already stated or demonstrated an interest in a particular field. Entries provide access to foundation addresses, financial data, giving priorities, application procedures, contact names, and key officials. Many entries also feature recently awarded grants, the best indication of a grantmaker's funding priorities. A variety of indexes help fundraisers target potential grant sources by subject area, geographic preferences, types of support, and the names of donors, officers, and trustees.

GUIDE TO FUNDING FOR INTERNATIONAL AND FOREIGN PROGRAMS, 8th Edition

The *Guide to Funding for International and Foreign Programs* covers more than 1,400 grantmakers interested in funding projects with an international focus, both within the U.S. and abroad. Program areas covered include international relief, disaster assistance, human rights, civil liberties, community development, education, and more. The volume also includes descriptions of more than 9,300 recently awarded grants.
MAY 2006 / ISBN 1-59542-088-6 / $125

NATIONAL GUIDE TO FUNDING IN AIDS, 4th Edition

This volume covers nearly 600 foundations, corporate giving programs, and public charities that support AIDS- and HIV-related nonprofit organizations involved in direct relief, medical research, legal aid, preventative education, and other programs for persons with AIDS and AIDS-related diseases. More than 750 recently awarded grants show the types of projects funded by grantmakers.
APRIL 2005/ ISBN 1-59542-040-1 / $125

NATIONAL GUIDE TO FUNDING IN ARTS AND CULTURE, 8th Edition

This volume covers more than 9,600 grantmakers with an interest in funding dance companies, museums, theaters, and other types of arts and culture projects and institutions. The volume also includes more than 18,700 descriptions of recently awarded grants.
MAY 2004 / ISBN 1-931923-94-9 / $155

NATIONAL GUIDE TO FUNDING FOR THE ENVIRONMENT AND ANIMAL WELFARE, 7th Edition

This guide covers over 3,500 grantmakers that fund nonprofits involved in international conservation, ecological research, waste reduction, animal welfare, and more. The volume includes descriptions of over 9,500 recently awarded grants.
JUNE 2004 / ISBN 1-931923-93-0 / $125

NATIONAL GUIDE TO FUNDING IN HEALTH, 9th Edition

The *National Guide to Funding in Health* contains essential facts on over 11,500 grantmakers interested in funding hospitals, universities, research institutes, community- based agencies, national health associations, and a broad range of other health-related programs and

services. The volume also includes descriptions of more than 21,000 recently awarded grants.
APRIL 2005 / ISBN 1-59542-038-X / $175

NATIONAL GUIDE TO FUNDING FOR LIBRARIES AND INFORMATION SERVICES, 8th Edition

This volume provides data on more than 1,500 grantmakers that support a wide range of organizations and initiatives, from the smallest public libraries to major research institutions, academic/research libraries, art, law, and medical libraries, and other specialized information centers. The volume also includes descriptions of more than 1,100 recently awarded grants.
MAY 2005 / ISBN 1-59542-039-8 / $125

NATIONAL GUIDE TO FUNDING IN RELIGION, 8th Edition

With this volume, fundraisers who work for nonprofits affiliated with religious organizations have access to information on nearly 9,000 grantmakers that have a demonstrated or stated interest in funding churches, missionary societies, religious welfare and education programs, and many other types of projects and institutions. The volume also includes descriptions of more than 14,000 recently awarded grants.
MAY 2005/ ISBN 1-59542-037-1 / $175

GRANT DIRECTORIES

GRANT GUIDES

Designed for fundraisers who work within defined fields of nonprofit development, this series of guides lists actual foundation grants of $10,000 or more in 12 key areas of grantmaking.

Each title in the series affords immediate access to the names, addresses, and giving limitations of the foundations listed. The grant descriptions provide fundraisers with the grant recipient's name and location; the amount of the grant; the date the grant was authorized; and a description of the grant's intended use.

In addition, each *Grant Guide* includes three indexes: by the type of organization generally funded by the grantmaker, the subject focus of the foundation's grants, and the geographic area in which the foundation has already funded projects.

Each *Grant Guide* also includes a concise overview of the foundation spending patterns within the specified field. The introduction uses a series of statistical tables to document such important findings as 1) the 25 top funders in the given area of interest (by total dollar amount of grants); 2) the 15 largest grants reported; 3) the total dollar amount and number of grants awarded for specific types of support, recipient organization type, and population group; and 4) the total grant dollars received in each U.S. state and many foreign countries.
2005-2006 EDITIONS / $75 EACH / SERIES PUBLISHED ANNUALLY IN DECEMBER

FUNDRAISING GUIDES

FOUNDATION FUNDAMENTALS, 7th Edition

Foundation Fundamentals, often used as a basic primer in academic programs on the nonprofit sector, has been thoroughly updated to introduce beginners to the world of foundations. While prior editions of this guide focused on effective use of print resources, this edition places particular emphasis on harnessing electronic databases and the Web to uncover information on grantmakers and their grants. Research strategies are explored that utilize subject, geographic and types of support approaches to finding funders. In addition, the guide features chapters on planning a funding research strategy, corporate giving, and

presenting ideas to funders. A variety of worksheets and illustrations are provided throughout the text. The expanded and updated bibliography includes the latest publications as well as descriptions of the most relevant Web sites.
SEPTEMBER 2004 / ISBN 1-59542-006-1 / $24.95

THE FOUNDATION CENTER'S GRANTS CLASSIFICATION SYSTEM INDEXING MANUAL WITH THESAURUS, Revised Edition

A complete "how-to" guide, the *Grants Classification Manual* is an excellent resource for any organization that wants to classify foundation grants or their recipients. The *Manual* includes a complete set of classification codes to facilitate precise tracking of grants and recipients by subject, recipient type, and population categories. It also features a revised thesaurus to help identify the "official" terms and codes that represent thousands of subject areas and recipient types in the Center's system of grants classification.
MAY 1995 / ISBN 0-87954-644-1 / $95

THE FOUNDATION CENTER'S GUIDE TO GRANTSEEKING ON THE WEB, Revised Edition

Packed with a wealth of information, the *Guide to Grantseeking on the Web* provides both novice and experienced Web users with a gateway to the numerous online resources available to grantseekers. Foundation Center staff experts have team-authored this guide, contributing their extensive knowledge of Web content as well as their tips and strategies on how to evaluate and use Web-based funding materials. Presented in a concise, "how-to" style, the *Guide* will introduce you to the Web and structure your funding research with a toolkit of resources. These resources include foundation and corporate Web sites, searchable databases for grantseeking, government funding sources, online journals, and interactive services on the Web for grantseekers.
SEPTEMBER 2003 / BOOK / ISBN 1-931923-67-1 / $29.95
CD-ROM / ISBN 1-931923-73-6 / $29.95
BOOK AND CD-ROM / $49.95

THE FOUNDATION CENTER'S GUIDE TO PROPOSAL WRITING, 4th Edition

The *Guide* is a comprehensive manual on the strategic thinking and mechanics of proposal writing. It covers each step of the process, from pre-proposal planning to the writing itself to the essential post-grant follow-up. The book features many extracts from actual grant proposals and also includes candid advice from grantmakers on the "do's and don'ts" of proposal writing. Written by a professional fundraiser who has been creating successful proposals for more than 25 years, *The Foundation Center's Guide to Proposal Writing* offers the kind of valuable tips and in-depth, practical instruction that no other source provides.
MARCH 2004 / ISBN 1-931923-92-2 / $34.95

THE FOUNDATION CENTER'S GUIDE TO WINNING PROPOSALS

The *Guide to Winning Proposals* features 20 grant proposals reprinted in their entirety that have been funded by some of today's most influential grantmakers.

To represent the diversity of nonprofits throughout the country, proposals have been selected from large and small, local and national organizations, and for many different support purposes, including basic budgetary support, special projects, construction, staff positions, and more. The *Guide to Winning Proposals* also includes actual letters of inquiry, budgets, cover letters, and supplementary documents needed to develop a complete proposal.
OCTOBER 2003 / ISBN 1-931923-47-7/ $34.95

THE FOUNDATION CENTER'S GUIDE TO WINNING PROPOSALS II

A companion to *Guide to Winning Proposals*, volume II features 31 compelling grant proposals from some of the nation's most influential funders. Each proposal, reprinted in its entirety, includes a critique by the decision-maker who approved the grant. The accompanying commentary points to the strengths and weaknesses of each proposal and provides insight into what makes some proposals more successful than others. In addition to cover letters and budgets, volume II includes winning proposals for general operating support, special projects, and more.
OCTOBER 2005 / ISBN 1-59542-054-1/ $34.95

GUÍA PARA ESCRIBIR PROPUESTAS

The Spanish language edition of the 3rd edition of the *Guide to Proposal Writing* includes a special appendix listing consultants and technical assistance providers who can help Spanish speakers craft proposals in English, or give advice on fundraising.
MARCH 2003 / ISBN 1-931923-16-7 / $34.95

SECURING YOUR ORGANIZATION'S FUTURE: A Complete Guide to Fundraising Strategies, Revised Edition
by Michael Seltzer

In this completely updated edition, Michael Seltzer acts as your personal fundraising consultant. Beginners get bottom-line facts and easy-to-follow worksheets; veteran fundraisers receive a complete review of the basics plus new money-making ideas. Seltzer supplements his text with an extensive bibliography of selected readings and resource organizations. Highly recommended for use as a text in nonprofit management programs at colleges and universities.
FEBRUARY 2001 / ISBN 0-87954-900-9 / $34.95

RAISE MORE MONEY FOR YOUR NONPROFIT ORGANIZATION: A Guide to Evaluating and Improving Your Fundraising
by Anne L. New

In *Raise More Money*, Anne New sets guidelines for a fundraising program that will benefit the incipient as well as the established nonprofit organization. The author divides her text into three sections: "The Basics," which delineates the necessary steps a nonprofit must take before launching a development campaign; "Fundraising Methods," which encourages organizational self-analysis and points the way to an effective program involving many sources of funding; and "Fundraising Resources," a 20-page bibliography that highlights useful research and funding directories.
JANUARY 1991 / ISBN 0-87954-388-4 / $14.95

NONPROFIT MANAGEMENT GUIDES

THE 21ST CENTURY NONPROFIT
by Paul B. Firstenberg

In *The 21st Century Nonprofit*, Paul B. Firstenberg provides nonprofit managers with the know-how to make their organizations effective agents of change. *The 21st Century Nonprofit* encourages managers to adopt strategies developed by the for-profit sector in recent years. These strategies will help them to expand their revenue base by diversifying grant sources, exploit the possibilities of for-profit enterprises, and develop human resources by learning how to attract and retain talented people. The book also explores the nature of leadership through short profiles of three nonprofit CEOs.
JULY 1996 / ISBN 0-87954-672-7 / $34.95

AMERICA'S NONPROFIT SECTOR: A Primer, 2nd Edition
by Lester M. Salamon

In this revised edition of his classic book, Lester M. Salamon clarifies the basic structure and role of the nonprofit sector in the U.S. He places the nonprofit sector into context in relation to the government and business sectors. He also shows how the position of the nonprofit sector has changed over time, both generally and in the major fields in which the sector is active. Illustrated with numerous charts and tables,

Salamon's book is an easy-to-understand primer for government officials, journalists, and students—in short, for anyone who wants to comprehend the makeup of America's nonprofit sector.
FEBRUARY 1999 / ISBN 0-87954-801-0 / $14.95

BEST PRACTICES OF EFFECTIVE NONPROFIT ORGANIZATIONS: A Practitioner's Guide
by Philip Bernstein
This volume provides guidance for any nonprofit professional eager to advance their organization's goals. Philip Bernstein has drawn on his own extensive experience as a nonprofit executive, consultant, and volunteer to produce this review of "best practices" adopted by successful nonprofit organizations. Topics include defining purposes and goals, creating comprehensive financing plans, evaluating services, and effective communication.
FEBRUARY 1997 / ISBN 0-87954-755-3 / $29.95

THE BOARD MEMBER'S BOOK: Making a Difference in Voluntary Organizations, 3rd Edition
by Brian O'Connell
The revised and expanded edition of this popular title by former Independent Sector President, Brian O'Connell, is a guide to the issues, challenges, and possibilities that emerge from the interchange between a nonprofit organization and its board. O'Connell offers practical advice on how to be a more effective board member as well as on how board members can help their organizations make a difference.
MARCH 2003 / ISBN 1-931923-17-5 / $29.95

CAREERS FOR DREAMERS AND DOERS: A Guide to Management Careers in the Nonprofit Sector
by Lilly Cohen and Dennis R.Young
A timeless guide to management positions in the nonprofit world, Careers for Dreamers and Doers offers practical advice for starting a job search and suggests strategies used by successful managers throughout the voluntary sector.
NOVEMBER 1989 / ISBN 0-87954-294-2 / $29.95

ECONOMICS FOR NONPROFIT MANAGERS
by Dennis R. Young and Richard Steinberg
In Economics for Nonprofit Managers, Young and Steinberg treat micro-economic analysis as an indispensable skill for nonprofit managers. They introduce and explain concepts such as opportunity cost, analysis at the margin, market equilibrium, market failure, and cost-benefit analysis. This volume also focuses on issues of particular concern to nonprofits, such as the economics of fundraising and volunteer recruiting, the regulatory environment, the impact of competition on nonprofit performance, interactions among sources of revenue, and more.
JULY 1995 / ISBN 0-87954-610-7 / $34.95

EFFECTIVE ECONOMIC DECISION-MAKING BY NONPROFIT ORGANIZATIONS
by Dennis R. Young
Editor Dennis R. Young offers useful, practical guidelines to support today's nonprofit managers in their efforts to maximize the effectiveness with which their organizations employ their valuable resources. A group of expert authors explores core operating decisions that face all organizations and provides solutions that are unique to nonprofits of any size. Chapters cover such decision-making areas as pricing of services, compensation of staff, outsourcing, fundraising expenditures, and investment and disbursement of funds. Published by the National Center on Nonprofit Enterprise and the Foundation Center.
DECEMBER 2003 / ISBN 1-931923-69-8 / $34.95

WISE ECONOMIC DECISION-MAKING FOR NONPROFITS IN UNCERTAIN TIMES
by Dennis R. Young
Available May 2006. For details and to order, visit foundationcenter.org/marketplace.

INVESTING IN CAPACITY BUILDING: A Guide To High-impact Approaches
by Barbara Blumenthal
This publication by Barbara Blumenthal offers guidance to grantmakers and consultants in designing better approaches to helping nonprofits, while showing nonprofit managers how to obtain more effective assistance. Based on interviews with more than 100 grantmakers, intermediaries, and consultants; 30 evaluations of capacity building programs; and a review of research on capacity building; Investing in Capacity Building: A Guide to High-Impact Approaches identifies the most successful strategies for helping nonprofits improve organizational performance.
SEPTEMBER 2003 / ISBN 1-931923-65-5 / $34.95

THE NONPROFIT ENTREPRENEUR: Creating Ventures to Earn Income
Edited by Edward Skloot
In a well-organized topic-by-topic approach to nonprofit venturing, nonprofit consultant and entrepreneur Edward Skloot demonstrates how nonprofits can launch successful earned-income enterprises without compromising their missions. Skloot has compiled a collection of writings by the nation's top practitioners and advisors in nonprofit enterprise. Topics covered include legal issues, marketing techniques, business planning, avoiding the pitfalls of venturing for smaller nonprofits, and a special section on museums and their retail operations.
SEPTEMBER 1988 / ISBN 0-87954-239-X / $19.95

A NONPROFIT ORGANIZATION OPERATING MANUAL: Planning for Survival and Growth
by Arnold J. Olenick and Philip R. Olenick
This straightforward, all-inclusive desk manual for nonprofit executives covers all aspects of starting and managing a nonprofit. The authors discuss legal problems, obtaining tax exemption, organizational planning and development, and board relations; operational, proposal, cash, and capital budgeting; marketing, grant proposals, fundraising, and for-profit ventures; computerization; and tax planning and compliance.
JULY 1991 / ISBN 0-87954-293-4 / $29.95

PEOPLE POWER: Service, Advocacy, Empowerment
by Brian O'Connell
People Power, a selection of O'Connell's most powerful writings, provides thought-provoking commentary on the nonprofit world. The 25+ essays included in this volume range from keen analyses of the role of voluntarism in American life, to sound advice for nonprofit managers, to suggestions for developing and strengthening the nonprofit sector of the future.
OCTOBER 1994 / ISBN 0-87954-563-1 / $24.95

PHILANTHROPY'S CHALLENGE
Building Nonprofit Capacity Through Venture Grantmaking
by Paul B. Firstenberg
In this book, Paul Firstenberg challenges grantors to proactively assist grantee management as the way to maximize the social impact of nonprofit programs, while showing grantseekers how the growing grantor emphasis on organizational capacity building will impact their efforts to win support. The author draws on his years of experience working in both nonprofit and for-profit organizations to explore the

roles of grantor and grantee within various models of venture grantmaking. A full chapter is devoted to governance issues and responsibilities.
JANUARY 2003 / SOFTBOUND: ISBN 1-931923-15-9 / $29.95
HARDBOUND: ISBN 1-931923-53-1 / $39.95

PROMOTING ISSUES AND IDEAS: A Guide to Public Relations for Nonprofit Organizations, Third Edition
by M Booth & Associates
Available September 2006. For details and to order, visit: foundationcenter.org/marketplace.

SUCCEEDING WITH CONSULTANTS:
Self-Assessment for the Changing Nonprofit
by Barbara Kibbe and Fred Setterberg
This inspirational book, written by Barbara Kibbe and Fred Setterberg and supported by the David and Lucile Packard Foundation, guides nonprofits through the process of selecting and utilizing consultants to strengthen their organizations' operations. The book emphasizes self assessment tools and covers six different areas in which a nonprofit organization might benefit from a consultant's advice: governance, planning, fund development, financial management, public relations and marketing, and quality assurance.
APRIL 1992 / ISBN 0-87954-450-3 / $19.95

RESEARCH REPORTS

ARTS FUNDING IV: An Update on Foundation Trends
Prepared in cooperation with Grantmakers in the Arts, this report provides a framework for understanding trends in foundation funding for arts and culture through 2001. Based on a sample of 800+ foundations, it compares growth in arts funding with other sources of public and private support, examines changes in giving for specific arts disciplines, analyzes giving patterns by region, and explores shifts in the types of support funders award.
JULY 2003 / ISBN 1-931923-48-5 / $19.95

FAMILY FOUNDATIONS: A Profile of Funders and Trends
Prepared in cooperation with the National Center for Family Philanthropy, *Family Foundations* is an essential resource for anyone interested in understanding the fastest growing segment of foundation philanthropy. The report provides a comprehensive measurement of the size and scope of the U.S. family foundation community. Through the use of objective and subjective criteria, the report identifies the number of family foundations and their distribution by region and state, size, geographic focus, and decade of establishment; and includes analyses of staffing and public reporting by these funders. *Family Foundations* also examines trends in giving by a sample of larger family foundations between 1993 and 1998 and compares these patterns with independent foundations overall.
AUGUST 2000 / ISBN 0-87954-917-3 / $19.95

FOUNDATIONS TODAY SERIES, 2006 Edition
The *Foundations Today Series* provides the latest information on foundation growth and trends in foundation giving.
THREE BOOK SET / ISBN 1-59542-087-B / $95

Foundation Giving Trends: Update on Funding Priorities—Examines 2004 grantmaking patterns of a sample of more than 1,000 larger U.S. foundations and compares current giving priorities with trends since 1980.
FEBRUARY 2006 / ISBN 1-59542-087-8 / $45

Foundation Growth and Giving Estimates: 2005 Preview—Provides a first look at estimates of foundation giving for 2005 and final

statistics on actual giving and assets for 2004. Presents new top 100 foundation lists.
APRIL 2006 / ISBN 1-59542-092-4 / $20

Foundation Yearbook: Facts and Figures on Private and Community Foundations—Documents the growth in number, giving, and assets of all active U.S. foundations from 1975 through 2004.
JUNE 2006 / ISBN 1-59542-101-7 / $45

INTERNATIONAL GRANTMAKING III:
An Update on U.S. Foundation Trends
Prepared in cooperation with the Council on Foundations as an update to the 2000 *International Grantmaking II* study, this report examines perspectives on the post-9/11 funding climate and the current outlook for the field based on a 2004 survey of more than 65 leading U.S. international grantmakers. It also documents actual trends in international giving based on the grants of over 600 larger U.S. foundations. In particular, the study analyzes shifts in giving priorities, countries/regions targeted for support, and the impact of large new funders.
NOVEMBER 2004 / ISBN 1-59542-008-8 / $40

THE PRI DIRECTORY: Charitable Loans and Other Program-Related Investments by Foundations, 2nd Edition
Certain foundations have developed an alternative financing approach—known as program-related investing—for supplying capital to the nonprofit sector. PRIs have been used to support community revitalization, low-income housing, microenterprise development, historic preservation, human services, and more. This directory lists leading PRI providers and includes tips on how to seek out and manage PRIs. Foundation listings include funder name and state; recipient name, city, and state (or country); and a description of the project funded. There are several helpful indexes by foundation/recipient location, subject/type of support, and recipient name, as well as an index to donors, officers, and trustees.
SEPTEMBER 2003 / ISBN 1-931923-49-3 / $75

SOCIAL JUSTICE GRANTMAKING
Independent Sector and the Foundation Center have partnered in developing this groundbreaking research, resulting in a quantitative study of social justice funding by 1,000 of the largest private and community foundations in the U.S.

Social Justice Grantmaking is the first study to benchmark foundation funding for nonprofit organizations working to make structural changes that increase opportunities for those who are least well off economically, socially, or politically. Presented here for the first time: a definition of the social justice grantmaking field developed by grantmakers and practitioners; profiles of the top social justice funders; principle grantmaking priorities and funding trends; geographic distribution of funding within and outside of the U.S. Through interviews with key funders, the report also lends perspective on the motivations and challenges faced by social justice funders. From economic development to healthcare to civil and human rights, this report will enhance both the practice and understanding of social justice philanthropy.
AUGUST 2005 / ISBN 1-59542-052-5/ $24.95

NEW YORK METROPOLITAN AREA FOUNDATIONS:
A Profile of the Grantmaking Community
Prepared in cooperation with the New York Regional Association of Grantmakers, this study examines the size, scope, and giving patterns of foundations based in the eight-county New York metropolitan area. It documents the New York area's share of all U.S. foundations; details the growth of area foundations through 2000; profiles area foundations by type, size, and geographic focus; compares broad giving trends of

New York area and all U.S. foundations between 1992 and 2000; and examines giving by non-New York area grantmakers to recipients in the New York area.
DECEMBER 2002 / ISBN 1-931923-52-3/ $24.95

SOUTHEASTERN FOUNDATIONS II: A Profile of the Region's Grantmaking Community, 2nd Edition

Produced in cooperation with the Southeastern Council of Foundations, *Southeastern Foundations II* provides a detailed examination of foundation philanthropy in the 12-state Southeast region. The report includes an overview of the Southeast's share of all U.S. foundations, measures the growth of Southeastern foundations since 1992, profiles Southeastern funders by type, size, and geographic focus, compares broad giving trends of Southeastern and all U.S. foundations in 1992 and 1997, and details giving by non-Southeastern grantmakers to recipients in the region.
NOVEMBER 1999 / ISBN 0-87954-775-8 / $19.95
MEMBERSHIP PROGRAM

ASSOCIATES PROGRAM

Essential facts and figures are at your fingertips through this e-mail and toll-free telephone reference service, helping you to:

◆ Identify potential sources of foundation and corporate funding for your organization; and
◆ Gather important information to use in targeting and presenting your proposals effectively.

An annual $995 membership in the Associates Program gives you vital information on a timely basis, saving you hundreds of hours of research time. As a member, you may place an unlimited number of requests for assistance. Our staff will refer to any print or online resource available to us in any of our five library/learning centers.

Members also receive a special monthly e-newsletter and have access to an exclusive extranet site, which provides news that includes information about the newest foundations, changes at more established foundations, special discounts and invitations to members-only briefings, and more.

Since the mid-1970s, thousands of professional fundraisers have discovered the Associates Program to be a highly reliable and extremely cost-effective service. In times when budgets are tight, nonprofit staffers wearing many hats at once find it especially useful. For more information, call (800) 634-2953 or visit us online to learn how we can serve your specific needs.

FOUNDATION CENTER'S WEB SITE

foundationcenter.org

The premier online source for fundraising information you can trust and tools you can use, our site is updated and expanded daily, providing grantseekers, grantmakers, researchers, journalists, and the general public with easy access to valuable resources. Registered visitors receive news, announcements, and job alerts based on their region and subject interests.

GET STARTED

◆ Find answers to questions about seeking funds, nonprofit management, and how to start a nonprofit organization. Search comprehensive FAQs, ask our Online Librarian a question by e-mail, or find a reference guide to meet your needs.
◆ Learn about foundations and fundraising, proposal writing, nonprofit management, and how to use our tools and resources. You'll also find books, free orientations, training courses, and online tutorials to help your nonprofit.

◆ See the full curriculum of training courses—at locations nationwide and online—to get you started or develop your expertise in grantseeking and nonprofit management. Visit often for dates and locations of classroom courses.
◆ Visit our library/learning center homepages to find out what's happening at Foundation Center locations in Atlanta, Cleveland, New York, San Francisco, and Washington, DC. Find a library near you among our network of more than 230 cooperating collections throughout the U.S.

FINDING FUNDERS

◆ Look up nonprofit organizations with our free Foundation Finder tool that will help you find addresses, web sites and fiscal data. Or use our 990 Finder to access IRS returns for foundations and nonprofits.
◆ Check statistics . . . national, state, and metropolitan area data on U.S. foundations and their grants is at your fingertips. You'll learn about the assets and giving of the nation's grantmaking foundations, how they distribute their grant dollars, and the top recipients of their gifts.
◆ Identify funding sources with monthly or annual subscriptions to *The Foundation Directory Online,* the leading grantseeking database on the web. Search up to 80,000 comprehensive foundation and corporate giver profiles and half a million grant descriptions.

GAIN KNOWLEDGE

◆ Find information on grantmakers using our online, print, and CD-ROM directories. Learn the skills you need to write a winning proposal or ensure the future of your nonprofit through Foundation Center books and training courses.
◆ Access Research Studies to discover the latest data available on U.S. foundation philanthropy. Our research staff analyzes and interprets the data we collect on foundations. Learn about national and regional trends, and get the latest statistics on foundation giving.
◆ Search the *Catalog of Nonprofit Literature,* a bibliographic database of nearly 25,000 entries on the field of philanthropy—more than 16,700 include abstracts. Or look up a foundation-sponsored report on a topic of interest in PubHub.
◆ Get the news you need from *Philanthropy News Digest* (PND), a daily digest of philanthropy-related articles. Read interviews with leaders, look for RFPs, learn from the experts, and share ideas with others in the field.

LEARN AT YOUR OWN PACE WITH ONLINE TRAINING.

The Foundation Center's online training courses include:

◆ Grantseeking Basics for Nonprofit Organizations—Designed for anyone in the nonprofit sector who wants to learn more about identifying and researching foundations as potential sources of funding.
◆ Proposal Writing: The Statement of Need—Designed for beginners as well as experienced grantseekers, this course will help you construct a compelling statement of need.
◆ Proposal Writing: The Project Description—Designed for grantseekers at any level of experience, this course explores every aspect of drafting a compelling project description—from stating objectives to outlining key components.
◆ Proposal Writing: The Budget—Designed for beginning fundraisers who want to master the art of preparing project budgets for proposals to private foundations and corporations.

The Foundation Center provides a host of free and affordable services and information resources—all focused on strengthening the sector's ability to serve its constituents. For more information visit foundationcenter.org

FOUNDATION CENTER
Knowledge to build on.

COOPERATING COLLECTIONS

Free Funding Information Centers

The Foundation Center's mission is to strengthen the nonprofit sector by advancing knowledge about U.S. philanthropy. An authoritative source of information on grantmaker and corporate giving, we ensure free public access to a wide variety of services and comprehensive resources on grantmakers and grants through our five library/learning centers and a national network of Cooperating Collections. Cooperating Collections are libraries, community foundations, and other nonprofit agencies that make accessible a collection of Foundation Center print and electronic resources, as well as a variety of supplementary materials and educational programs in areas useful to grantseekers. The collection includes:

- Foundation Directory Online Professional or FC Search: The Foundation Center's Database on CD-ROM
- The Foundation Directory, Part 2, and Supplement
- Foundation Fundamentals
- The Foundation 1000

- Foundations Today Series
- Foundation Grants to Individuals
- Foundation Grants to Individuals Online
- The Foundation Center's Guide to Proposal Writing

- The Foundation Center's Guide to Winning Proposals
- Guide To U.S. Foundations, Their Trustees, Officers, and Donors
- National Directory of Corporate Giving
- Guide to Funding for International & Foreign Programs

All five Foundation Center libraries provide free access to both *The Foundation Directory Online* and *FC Search: The Foundation Center's Database on CD-ROM*. All Cooperating Collections provide access to either the online service or the CD-ROM, and all provide Internet access. Those seeking information on fundraising and nonprofit management can also refer to our web site (foundationcenter.org) for a wealth of data and advice on grantseeking, including links to grantmaker IRS information returns (990s and 990-PFs). Because the Cooperating Collections vary in their hours, it is recommended that you call a collection in advance of a visit. To check on new locations or current holdings, call toll-free (800) 424-9836 or visit foundationcenter.org/collections/.

FOUNDATION CENTER LIBRARY/LEARNING CENTERS

THE FOUNDATION CENTER
79 Fifth Ave., 2nd Floor
New York, NY 10003
(212) 620-4230

THE FOUNDATION CENTER
312 Sutter St., Suite 606
San Francisco, CA 94108
(415) 397-0902

THE FOUNDATION CENTER
1627 K St., NW, 3rd floor
Washington, DC 20006
(202) 331-1400

THE FOUNDATION CENTER
Kent H. Smith Library
1422 Euclid Ave., Suite 1600
Cleveland, OH 44115
(216) 861-1934

THE FOUNDATION CENTER
Hurt Bldg., 50 Hurt Plaza
Suite 150, Grand Lobby
Atlanta, GA 30303
(404) 880-0094

COOPERATING COLLECTIONS

ALABAMA

BIRMINGHAM PUBLIC LIBRARY
2100 Park Place
Birmingham 35203
(205) 226-3620

HUNTSVILLE PUBLIC LIBRARY
915 Monroe St.
Huntsville 35801
(256) 532-5940

MOBILE PUBLIC LIBRARY
West Regional Library
5555 Grelot Rd.
Mobile 36609
(251) 340-8555

AUBURN UNIVERSITY AT
MONTGOMERY LIBRARY
74-40 E. Dr.
Montgomery 36117-3596
(334) 244-3200

ALASKA

CONSORTIUM LIBRARY
3211 Providence Dr.
Anchorage 99508
(907) 786-1848

JUNEAU PUBLIC LIBRARY
292 Marine Way
Juneau 99801
(907) 586-5267

ARIZONA

FLAGSTAFF CITY-COCONINO COUNTY
PUBLIC LIBRARY
300 W. Aspen Ave.
Flagstaff 86001
(928) 779-7670

PHOENIX PUBLIC LIBRARY
1221 N. Central Ave.
Phoenix 85004
(602) 262-4636

TUCSON PIMA PUBLIC LIBRARY
101 N. Stone Ave.
Tucson 87501
(520) 791-4393

ARKANSAS

UNIVERSITY OF ARKANSAS—FORT SMITH
Boreham Library
5210 Grand Ave.
Fort Smith 72913
(479) 788-7204

CENTRAL ARKANSAS LIBRARY SYSTEM
100 Rock St.
Little Rock 72201
(501) 918-3000

CALIFORNIA

KERN COUNTY LIBRARY
Beale Memorial Library
701 Truxtun Ave.
Bakersfield 93301
(661) 868-0701

HUMBOLDT AREA FOUNDATION
Rooney Resource Center
373 Indianola
Bayside 95524
(707) 442-2993

VENTURA COUNTY COMMUNITY FOUNDATION
Resource Center for Nonprofit
  Management
1317 Del Norte Rd., Suite 150
Camarillo 93010
(805) 988-0196

FRESNO Nonprofit Advancement council
1752 L St.
Fresno 93721
(559) 264-1513

CENTER FOR NONPROFIT MANAGEMENT
Nonprofit Resource Library
Center for Healthy Communities
1000 N. Alameda St.
Los Angeles 90012
(213) 687-9511

LOS ANGELES PUBLIC LIBRARY
Mid-Valley Regional Branch Library
16244 Nordhoff St.
North Hills 91343
(818) 895-3654

FLINTRIDGE FOUNDATION
Philanthropy Resource Center
1040 Lincoln Ave., Suite 100
Pasadena 91103
(626) 449-0839

SHASTA REGIONAL COMMUNITY FOUNDATION
Center for Nonprofit Resources
2280 Benton Dr.
Bldg. C, Suite A
Redding 96003
(530) 244-1219

RICHMOND PUBLIC LIBRARY
352 Civic Center Plaza
Richmond 94804
(510) 620-6561

RIVERSIDE CITY PUBLIC LIBRARY
3581 Mission Inn Ave.
Riverside 92501
(909) 826-5201

NONPROFIT RESOURCE CENTER
828 I St., 2nd Floor
Sacramento 95814
(916) 264-2772

SAN DIEGO FOUNDATION
Funding Information Center
1420 Kettner Blvd., Suite 500
San Diego 92101
(619) 235-2300

COMPASSPOINT NONPROFIT SERVICES
Nonprofit Development Library
1922 The Alameda, Suite 212
San Jose 95126
(408) 248-9505

LOS ANGELES PUBLIC LIBRARY
San Pedro Regional Branch
931 S. Gaffey St.
San Pedro 90731
(310) 548-7779

VOLUNTEER CENTER ORANGE COUNTY
Nonprofit Resource Center
1901 E. 4th St., Suite 100
Santa Ana 92705
(714) 953-5757

SANTA BARBARA PUBLIC LIBRARY
40 E. Anapamu St.
Santa Barbara 93101-1019
(805) 962-7653

SANTA MONICA PUBLIC LIBRARY
601 Santa Monica Blvd
Santa Monica 90401
(310) 458-8600

SONOMA COUNTY LIBRARY
3rd & E. Sts.
Santa Rosa 95404
(707) 545-0831

SEASIDE BRANCH LIBRARY
550 Harcourt Ave.
Seaside 93955
(831) 899-2055

SIERRA NONPROFIT SUPPORT CENTER
39 N. Washington St. #F
Sonora 95370-0905
(209) 533-1093

COLORADO

EL POMAR NONPROFIT RESOURCE CENTER
Penrose Library
20 N. Cascade Ave.
Colorado Springs 80903
(719) 531-6333

DENVER PUBLIC LIBRARY
10 W. 14th Ave. Pkwy.
Denver 80204
(720) 865-1111

DURANGO PUBLIC LIBRARY
1188 E. 2nd Ave.
Durango 81301
(970) 375-3380

PUEBLO CITY-COUNTY LIBRARY DISTRICT
100 E. Abriendo Ave.
Pueblo 81004-4232
(719) 562-5600

FOUNDATION CENTER COOPERATING COLLECTIONS

CONNECTICUT

GREENWICH LIBRARY
101 W. Putnam Ave.
Greenwich 06830
(203) 622-7900

HARTFORD PUBLIC LIBRARY
500 Main St.
Hartford 06103
(860) 695-6300

NEW HAVEN FREE PUBLIC LIBRARY
133 Elm St.
New Haven 06510-2057
(203) 946-7431

DELAWARE

UNIVERSITY OF DELAWARE
Hugh Morris Library
181 S. College Ave.
Newark 19717-5267
(302) 831-2432

FLORIDA

BARTOW PUBLIC LIBRARY
2151 S. Broadway Ave.
Bartow 33830
(863) 534-0931

VOLUSIA COUNTY LIBRARY CENTER
City Island
105 E. Magnolia Ave.
Daytona Beach 32114-4484
(386) 257-6036

NOVA SOUTHEASTERN UNIVERSITY
Alvin Sherman Library, Research, and
Information Technology Center
3100 Ray Ferrero Jr. Blvd.
Fort Lauderdale 33314
(954) 262-4613

INDIAN RIVER COMMUNITY COLLEGE
Learning Resources Center
3209 Virginia Ave.
Fort Pierce 34981-5596
(772) 462-4757

JACKSONVILLE PUBLIC LIBRARY
Nonprofit Resources
303 N. Laura St.
Jacksonville 32202
(904) 630-2665

MIAMI-DADE PUBLIC LIBRARY
101 W. Flagler St.
Miami 33130
(305) 375-5575

ORANGE COUNTY LIBRARY SYSTEM
101 E. Central Blvd.
Orlando 32801
(407) 835-7323

SELBY PUBLIC LIBRARY
1331 1st St.
Sarasota 34236
(941) 861-1100

STATE LIBRARY OF FLORIDA
R.A. Gray Bldg.
500 S. Bronough St.
Tallahassee 32399-0250
(850) 245-6600

HILLSBOROUGH COUNTY PUBLIC LIBRARY
COOPERATIVE
John F. Germany Public Library
900 N. Ashley Dr.
Tampa 33602
(813) 273-3652

COMMUNITY FOUNDATION OF PALM BEACH &
MARTIN COUNTIES
700 S. Dixie Hwy., Suite 200
West Palm Beach 33401
(561) 659-6800

GEORGIA

HALL COUNTY LIBRARY SYSTEM
127 Main St. NW
Gainesville 30501
(770) 532-3311

METHODIST HOME FOR CHILDREN AND YOUTH
Rumford Center
304 Pierce Ave., 1st floor
Macon 31203
(478) 751-2800

THOMAS COUNTY PUBLIC LIBRARY
201 N. Madison St.
Thomasville 31792
(229) 225-5252

HAWAII

UNIVERSITY OF HAWAII AT MĀNOA
Hamilton Library
2550 The Mall
Honolulu 96822
(808) 956-7214

IDAHO

BOISE PUBLIC LIBRARY
Funding Information Center
715 S. Capitol Blvd.
Boise 83702
(208) 384-4024

CALDWELL PUBLIC LIBRARY
1010 Dearborn St.
Caldwell 83605
(208) 459-3242

MARSHALL PUBLIC LIBRARY
113 S. Garfield
Pocatello 83204
(208) 232-1263

ILLINOIS

CARBONDALE PUBLIC LIBRARY
405 W. Main St.
Carbondale 62901
(618) 457-0354

DONORS FORUM OF CHICAGO LIBRARY
208 S. LaSalle, Suite 740
Chicago 60604
(312) 578-0175

EVANSTON PUBLIC LIBRARY
1703 Orrington Ave.
Evanston 60201
(847) 866-0300

ROCK ISLAND PUBLIC LIBRARY
401 19th St.
Rock Island 61201-8143
(309) 732-7323

CENTRAL ILLINOIS NONPROFIT
RESOURCE CENTER
Brookens Library
University of Illinois at Springfield
One University Plaza, MS Lib 140
Springfield 62703-5407
(217) 206-6633

INDIANA

EVANSVILLE-VANDERBURGH PUBLIC LIBRARY
200 SE Martin Luther King Jr. Blvd.
Evansville 47708
(812) 428-8200

ALLEN COUNTY PUBLIC LIBRARY
200 East Berry St.
Fort Wayne 46802
(260) 421-1238

INDIANAPOLIS–MARION COUNTY PUBLIC
LIBRARY
202 N. Alabama St.
Indianapolis 46206
(317) 269-1700

VIGO COUNTY PUBLIC LIBRARY
One Library Square
Terre Haute 47807
(812) 232-1113

VALPARAISO UNIVERSITY
Christopher Center Library Services
1410 Chapel Dr.
Valparaiso 46383
(219) 464-5364

IOWA

CEDAR RAPIDS PUBLIC LIBRARY
500 1st St., SE
Cedar Rapids 52401
(319) 398-5123

SOUTHWESTERN COMMUNITY COLLEGE
Learning Resource Center
1501 W. Townline Rd.
Creston 50801
(641) 782-7081

KANSAS

DES MOINES PUBLIC LIBRARY
1000 Grand Ave.
Des Moines 50309-3027
(515) 283-4152

SIOUX CITY PUBLIC LIBRARY
Siouxland Funding Research Center
529 Pierce St.
Sioux City 51101-1203
(712) 255-2933

PIONEER MEMORIAL LIBRARY
375 West 4th St.
Colby 67701
(785) 460-4470

DODGE CITY PUBLIC LIBRARY
1001 2nd Ave.
Dodge City 67801
(620) 225-0248

KEARNY COUNTY LIBRARY
101 E. Prairie
Lakin 67860
(620) 355-6674

SALINA PUBLIC LIBRARY
301 W. Elm
Salina 67401
(785) 825-4624

TOPEKA AND SHAWNEE COUNTY
PUBLIC LIBRARY
1515 SW 10th Ave.
Topeka 66604
(785) 580-4400

WICHITA PUBLIC LIBRARY
223 S. Main St.
Wichita 67202
(316) 261-8500

KENTUCKY

WESTERN KENTUCKY UNIVERSITY
Helm-Cravens Library
110 Helm Library
Bowling Green 42101-3576
(270) 745-6163

LEXINGTON PUBLIC LIBRARY
140 E. Main St.
Lexington 40507-1376
(859) 231-5520

LOUISVILLE FREE PUBLIC LIBRARY
301 York St.
Louisville 40203
(502) 574-1617

LOUISIANA

COMMUNITY DEVELOPMENT WORKS LEARNING
LAB
The Rapides Foundation Building
1101 4th St., Suite 101B
Alexandria 71301
(318) 443-7880

EAST BATON ROUGE PARISH LIBRARY
River Center Branch
120 St. Louis St.
Baton Rouge 70802
(225) 389-4967

BEAUREGARD PARISH LIBRARY
205 S. Washington Ave.
DeRidder 70634
(337) 463-6217

OUACHITA PARISH PUBLIC LIBRARY
1800 Stubbs Ave.
Monroe 71201
(318) 327-1490

NEW ORLEANS PUBLIC LIBRARY
219 Loyola Ave.
New Orleans 70112
(504) 596-2580

SHREVE MEMORIAL LIBRARY
424 Texas St.
Shreveport 71120-1523
(318) 226-5894

MAINE

MAINE PHILANTHROPY CENTER
University of Southern Maine
Glickman Family Library
314 Forest Ave.
Portland 04104-9301
(207) 780-5039

MARYLAND

ENOCH PRATT FREE LIBRARY
400 Cathedral St.
Baltimore 21201
(410) 396-5320

MASSACHUSETTS

ASSOCIATED GRANT MAKERS
55 Court St.
Suite 520
Boston 02108
(617) 426-2606

BOSTON PUBLIC LIBRARY
700 Boylston St.
Boston 02116
(617) 536-5400

BERKSHIRE ATHENAEUM
1 Wendell Ave.
Pittsfield 01201-6385
(413) 499-9480

WESTERN MASSACHUSETTS FUNDING
RESOURCE CENTER
65 Elliot St.
Springfield 01101-1730
(413) 452-0697

WORCESTER PUBLIC LIBRARY
Grants Resource Center
3 Salem Square
Worcester 01608
(508) 799-1655

MICHIGAN

ALPENA COUNTY LIBRARY
211 N. 1st St.
Alpena 49707
(989) 356-6188

UNIVERSITY OF MICHIGAN
Graduate Library
209 Hatcher N.
Ann Arbor 48109-1205
(734) 763-1539

WILLARD PUBLIC LIBRARY
Nonprofit & Funding Resource
Collection
7 W. Van Buren St.
Battle Creek 49017
(269) 969-2100

WAYNE STATE UNIVERSITY
Purdy/Kresge Library
5265 Cass Ave.
Detroit 48202
(313) 577-6424

MICHIGAN STATE UNIVERSITY LIBRARIES
Main Library
Funding Center
100 Library
East Lansing 48824-1048
(517) 432-6123

FARMINGTON COMMUNITY LIBRARY
32737 W. 12 Mile Rd.
Farmington Hills 48334
(248) 553-0300

FLINT PUBLIC LIBRARY
1026 E. Kearsley St.
Flint 48502-1994
(810) 232-7111

GRAND RAPIDS PUBLIC LIBRARY
111 Library St. NE
Grand Rapids 49503-3268
(616) 988-5400

MICHIGAN TECHNOLOGICAL UNIVERSITY
Corporate Services
ATDC Bldg, Suite 200
1402 E. Sharon Ave.
Houghton 49931-1295
(906) 487-2228

WEST SHORE COMMUNITY COLLEGE LIBRARY
3000 N. Stiles Rd.
Scottville 49454-0277
(231) 845-6211

TRAVERSE AREA DISTRICT LIBRARY
610 Woodmere Ave.
Traverse City 49686
(231) 932-8500

MINNESOTA

BRAINERD PUBLIC LIBRARY
416 S. 5th St.
Brainerd 56401
(218) 829-5574

DULUTH PUBLIC LIBRARY
520 W. Superior St.
Duluth 55802
(218) 723-3802

SOUTHWEST STATE UNIVERSITY
University Library
N. Hwy. 23
Marshall 56253
(507) 537-6108

MINNEAPOLIS PUBLIC LIBRARY
Hosmer Library
347 E. 36th St.
Minneapolis 55408

ROCHESTER PUBLIC LIBRARY
101 2nd St. SE
Rochester 55904-3777
(507) 285-8002

SAINT PAUL PUBLIC LIBRARY
90 W. 4th St.
Saint Paul 55102
(651) 266-7000

MISSISSIPPI

LIBRARY OF HATTIESBURG, PETAL
AND FORREST COUNTY
329 Hardy St.
Hattiesburg 39401-3824
(601) 582-4461

JACKSON/HINDS LIBRARY SYSTEM
300 N. State St.
Jackson 39201
(601) 968-5803

MISSOURI

COUNCIL ON PHILANTHROPY
University of Missouri—Kansas City
4747 Troost, Rm. 207
Kansas City 64110
(816) 235-6259

KANSAS CITY PUBLIC LIBRARY
14 W. 10th St.
Kansas City 64105-1702
(816) 701-3400

ST. LOUIS PUBLIC LIBRARY
1301 Olive St.
St. Louis 63103
(314) 241-2288

SPRINGFIELD-GREENE COUNTY LIBRARY
The Library Center
4653 S. Campbell
Springfield 65810
(417) 874-8110

MONTANA

FALLON COUNTY LIBRARY
6 W. Fallon Ave.
Baker 59313-1037
(406) 778-7160

MONTANA STATE UNIVERSITY—BILLINGS
1500 N. 30th St.
Billings 59101
(406) 657-2262

BOZEMAN PUBLIC LIBRARY
220 E. Lamme
Bozeman 59715
(406) 582-2402

LINCOLN COUNTY PUBLIC LIBRARIES
Libby Public Library
220 W. 6th St.
Libby 59923
(406) 293-2778

MANSFIELD LIBRARY
University of Montana
32 Campus Dr.
Missoula 59812-9936
(406) 243-6800

NEBRASKA

BUTLER MEMORIAL LIBRARY
621 Penn St.
Cambridge 69022
(308) 697-3836

UNIVERSITY OF NEBRASKA—LINCOLN
University Libraries
14th & R Sts.
Lincoln 68588-2848
(402) 472-2848

OMAHA PUBLIC LIBRARY
W. Dale Clark Library
215 S. 15th St.
Omaha 68102
(402) 444-4826

NEVADA

GREAT BASIN COLLEGE LIBRARY
1500 College Pkwy.
Elko 89801
(775) 753-2222

CLARK COUNTY LIBRARY
1401 E. Flamingo
Las Vegas 89119
(702) 507-3400

WASHOE COUNTY LIBRARY
301 S. Center St.
Reno 89501
(775) 327-8300

NEW HAMPSHIRE

CONCORD PUBLIC LIBRARY
45 Green St.
Concord 03301
(603) 225-8670

PLYMOUTH STATE UNIVERSITY
Herbert H. Lamson Library
Plymouth 03264
(603) 535-2258

NEW JERSEY

FREE PUBLIC LIBRARY OF ELIZABETH
11 S. Broad St.
Elizabeth 07202
(908) 354-6060

COUNTY COLLEGE OF MORRIS
Learning Resource Center
214 Center Grove Rd.
Randolph 07869
(973) 328-5296

NEW JERSEY STATE LIBRARY
185 W. State St.
Trenton 08625-0520
(609) 292-6220

NEW MEXICO

ALBUQUERQUE/BERNALILLO COUNTY
LIBRARY SYSTEM
501 Copper Ave. NW
Albuquerque 87102
(505) 768-5141

NEW MEXICO STATE LIBRARY
1209 Camino Carlos Rey
Santa Fe 87507
(505) 476-9702

NEW YORK

NEW YORK STATE LIBRARY
Cultural Education Center, 6th Floor
Empire State Plaza
Albany 12230
(518) 474-5355

BROOKLYN PUBLIC LIBRARY
Grand Army Plaza
Brooklyn 11238
(718) 230-2122

BUFFALO & ERIE COUNTY PUBLIC LIBRARY
1 Lafayette Square
Buffalo 14203-1887
(716) 858-7097

SOUTHEAST STEUBEN COUNTY LIBRARY
300 Nasser Civic Center Plaza
Corning 14830
(607) 936-3713

HUNTINGTON PUBLIC LIBRARY
338 Main St.
Huntington 11743
(631) 427-5165

QUEENS BOROUGH PUBLIC LIBRARY
89-11 Merrick Blvd.
Jamaica 11432
(718) 990-0700

LEVITTOWN PUBLIC LIBRARY
1 Bluegrass Ln.
Levittown 11756
(516) 731-5728

ADRIANCE MEMORIAL LIBRARY
93 Market St.
Poughkeepsie 12601
(845) 485-3445

RIVERHEAD FREE LIBRARY
330 Court St.
Riverhead 11901
(631) 727-3228

ROCHESTER PUBLIC LIBRARY
115 S. Ave.
Rochester 14604
(585) 428-8130

ONONDAGA COUNTY PUBLIC LIBRARY
447 S. Salina St.
Syracuse 13202-2494
(315) 435-1900

UTICA PUBLIC LIBRARY
303 Genesee St.
Utica 13501
(315) 735-2279

WHITE PLAINS PUBLIC LIBRARY
100 Martine Ave.
White Plains 10601
(914) 422-1480

YONKERS PUBLIC LIBRARY
Riverfront Library
One Larkin Center
Yonkers 10701
(914) 337-1500

NORTH CAROLINA

COMMUNITY FOUNDATION OF WESTERN
NORTH CAROLINA
Pack Memorial Library
67 Haywood St.
Asheville 28802
(828) 254-4960

THE DUKE ENDOWMENT
100 N. Tryon St., Suite 3500
Charlotte 28202-4012
(704) 376-0291

DURHAM COUNTY PUBLIC LIBRARY
300 N. Roxboro St.
Durham 27702
(919) 560-0100

CAMERON VILLAGE REGIONAL LIBRARY
1930 Clark Ave.
Raleigh 27605
(919) 856-6710

NEW HANOVER COUNTY PUBLIC LIBRARY
201 Chestnut St.
Wilmington 28401-3942
(910) 798-6301

FORSYTH COUNTY PUBLIC LIBRARY
660 W. 5th St.
Winston-Salem 27101
(336) 727-2264

NORTH DAKOTA

BISMARCK PUBLIC LIBRARY
515 N. 5th St.
Bismarck 58501-4081
(701) 222-6410

FARGO PUBLIC LIBRARY
102 N. 3rd St.
Fargo 58102
(701) 241-1491

MINOT PUBLIC LIBRARY
516 2nd Ave. SW
Minot 58701-3792
(701) 852-1045

OHIO

STARK COUNTY DISTRICT LIBRARY
715 Market Ave. N.
Canton 44702
(330) 452-0665

PUBLIC LIBRARY OF CINCINNATI & HAMILTON
COUNTY
800 Vine St.
Cincinnati 45202-2071
(513) 369-6000

COLUMBUS METROPOLITAN LIBRARY
96 S. Grant Ave.
Columbus 43215
(614) 645-2590

DAYTON METRO LIBRARY
215 E. 3rd St.
Dayton 45402
(937) 227-9500

MANSFIELD/RICHLAND COUNTY PUBLIC
LIBRARY
43 W. 3rd St.
Mansfield 44902
(419) 521-3110

PORTSMOUTH PUBLIC LIBRARY
1220 Gallia St.
Portsmouth 45662
(740) 354-5688

TOLEDO–LUCAS COUNTY PUBLIC LIBRARY
325 N. Michigan St.
Toledo 43624
(419) 259-5207

PUBLIC LIBRARY OF YOUNGSTOWN &
MAHONING COUNTY
305 Wick Ave.
Youngstown 44503
(330) 744-8636

OKLAHOMA

OKLAHOMA CITY UNIVERSITY
Dulaney Browne Library
2501 N. Blackwelder
Oklahoma City 73106
(405) 521-5822

TULSA CITY–COUNTY LIBRARY
400 Civic Center
Tulsa 74103
(918) 596-7977

OREGON

OREGON INSTITUTE OF TECHNOLOGY
3201 Campus Dr.
Klamath Falls 97601-8801
(541) 885-1772

JACKSON COUNTY LIBRARY SERVICES
205 S. Central Ave.
Medford 97501
(541) 774-8689

MULTNOMAH COUNTY LIBRARY
801 SW 10th Ave.
Portland 97205
(503) 988-5123

OREGON STATE LIBRARY
250 Winter St. NE
Salem 97301-3950
(503) 378-4243

PENNSYLVANIA

NORTHAMPTON COMMUNITY COLLEGE
Paul and Harriett Mack Library
3835 Green Pond Rd.
Bethlehem 18020
(610) 861-5359

ERIE COUNTY LIBRARY SYSTEM
160 E. Front St.
Erie 16507
(814) 451-6927

DAUPHIN COUNTY LIBRARY SYSTEM
East Shore Area Library
4501 Ethel St.
Harrisburg 17109
(717) 652-9380

HAZLETON AREA PUBLIC LIBRARY
55 N. Church St.
Hazleton 18201
(570) 454-2961

LANCASTER PUBLIC LIBRARY
125 N. Duke St.
Lancaster 17602
(717) 394-2651

FREE LIBRARY OF PHILADELPHIA
1901 Vine St., 2nd Fl.
Philadelphia 19103-1189
(215) 686-5423

FOUNDATION CENTER COOPERATING COLLECTIONS

CARNEGIE LIBRARY OF PITTSBURGH
612 Smithfield St.
Pittsburgh 15222
(412) 281-7143

NONPROFIT & COMMUNITY
RESOURCE CENTER
1151 Oak St.
Pittston 18640
(570) 655-5581

READING PUBLIC LIBRARY
100 S. 5th St.
Reading 19602
(610) 655-6355

JAMES V. BROWN LIBRARY
19 E. 4th St.
Williamsport 17701
(570) 326-0536

MARTIN LIBRARY
159 E. Market St.
York 17401
(717) 846-5300

RHODE ISLAND

PROVIDENCE PUBLIC
LIBRARY
150 Empire St.
Providence 02903
(401) 455-8088

SOUTH CAROLINA

ANDERSON COUNTY LIBRARY
300 N. McDuffie St.
Anderson 29622
(864) 260-4500

CHARLESTON COUNTY LIBRARY
68 Calhoun St.
Charleston 29401
(843) 805-6930

SOUTH CAROLINA STATE LIBRARY
1500 Senate St.
Columbia 29211
(803) 734-8026

GREENVILLE COUNTY LIBRARY SYSTEM
25 Heritage Green Place
Greenville 29601-2034
(864) 242-5000

SOUTH DAKOTA

DAKOTA STATE UNIVERSITY
Nonprofit Management Institute
820 N. Washington
Madison 57042
(605) 367-5382

SOUTH DAKOTA STATE LIBRARY
800 Governors Dr.
Pierre 57501-2294
(605) 773-3131
(800) 423-6665 (SD residents)

E.Y. BERRY LIBRARY-LEARNING CENTER
Black Hills State University
1200 University St. Unit 9676
Spearfish 57799-9676
(605) 642-6834

TENNESSEE

UNITED WAY OF GREATER CHATTANOOGA
Center for Nonprofits
630 Market St.
Chattanooga 37402
(423) 752-0300

KNOX COUNTY PUBLIC LIBRARY
500 W. Church Ave.
Knoxville 37902
(865) 215-8751

MEMPHIS & SHELBY COUNTY PUBLIC LIBRARY
3030 Poplar Ave.
Memphis 38111
(901) 415-2734

NASHVILLE PUBLIC LIBRARY
615 Church St.
Nashville 37219
(615) 862-5800

TEXAS

AMARILLO AREA FOUNDATION NONPROFIT
SERVICE CENTER
801 S. Filmore, Suite 700
Amarillo 79101
(806) 376-4521

HOGG FOUNDATION FOR MENTAL HEALTH
Regional Foundation Library
3001 Lake Austin Blvd., Suite 400
Austin 78703
(512) 471-5041

BEAUMONT PUBLIC LIBRARY
801 Pearl St.
Beaumont 77704-3827
(409) 838-6606

CORPUS CHRISTI PUBLIC LIBRARY
805 Comanche St.
Corpus Christi 78401
(361) 880-7000

DALLAS PUBLIC LIBRARY
1515 Young St.
Dallas 75201
(214) 670-1487

SOUTHWEST BORDER NONPROFIT
RESOURCE CENTER
1201 W. University Dr.
Edinburg 78539-2999
(956) 384-5920

UNIVERSITY OF TEXAS AT EL PASO
500 W. University, Benedict Hall, Rm. 103
El Paso 79968-0547
(915) 747-5643

FUNDING INFORMATION CENTER OF
FORT WORTH
329 S. Henderson St.
Fort Worth 76104
(817) 334-0228

HOUSTON PUBLIC LIBRARY
500 McKinney Ave.
Houston 77002
(832) 393-1313

LAREDO PUBLIC LIBRARY
Nonprofit Management and
Volunteer Center
1120 E. Calton Rd.
Laredo 78041
(956) 795-2400

LONGVIEW PUBLIC LIBRARY
222 W. Cotton St.
Longview 75601
(903) 237-1350

LUBBOCK AREA FOUNDATION, INC.
1655 Main St., Suite 209
Lubbock 79408
(806) 762-8061

NONPROFIT RESOURCE CENTER OF TEXAS
Davidson Bldg.
7404 US Hwy. 90 W., Suite 120
San Antonio 78212-8270
(210) 227-4333

WACO-MCLENNAN COUNTY LIBRARY
1717 Austin Ave.
Waco 76701
(254) 750-5941

NONPROFIT MANAGEMENT CENTER OF
WICHITA FALLS
2301 Kell Blvd., Suite 218
Wichita Falls 76308
(940) 322-4961

UTAH

GRAND COUNTY PUBLIC LIBRARY
25 South 100 E.
Moab 84532
(435) 259-5421

SALT LAKE CITY PUBLIC LIBRARY
210 E. 400 S.
Salt Lake City 84111
(801) 524-8200

VERMONT

ILSLEY PUBLIC LIBRARY
75 Main St.
Middlebury 05753
(802) 388-4095

VERMONT DEPT. OF LIBRARIES
109 State St.
Montpelier 05609
(802) 828-3261

VIRGINIA

WASHINGTON COUNTY PUBLIC LIBRARY
205 Oak Hill St.
Abingdon 24210
(276) 676-6222

HAMPTON PUBLIC LIBRARY
4207 Victoria Blvd.
Hampton 23669
(757) 727-1314

RICHMOND PUBLIC LIBRARY
325 Civic Center Plaza
Richmond 94804
(804) 620-6561

ROANOKE PUBLIC LIBRARY SYSTEM
Main Library
706 S. Jefferson St.
Roanoke 24016
(540) 853-2473

WASHINGTON

MID-COLUMBIA LIBRARY
1620 S. Union St.
Kennewick 99338
(509) 783-7878

REDMOND REGIONAL LIBRARY
Nonprofit and Philanthropy Resource
Center
15990 NE 85th
Redmond 98052
(425) 885-1861

SEATTLE PUBLIC LIBRARY
1000 4th Ave.
Seattle 98104
(206) 386-4636

SPOKANE PUBLIC LIBRARY
906 W. Main Ave.
Spokane 99201
(509) 444-5300

UNIVERSITY OF WASHINGTON TACOMA
LIBRARY
1902 Commerce St.
Tacoma 98402
(253) 692-4440

WEST VIRGINIA

KANAWHA COUNTY PUBLIC LIBRARY
123 Capitol St.
Charleston 25301
(304) 343-4646

WEST VIRGINIA UNIVERSITY AT
PARKERSBURG LIBRARY
300 Campus Dr.
Parkersburg 26101
(304) 424-8260

SHEPHERD UNIVERSITY
Scarborough Library
King St.
Shepherdstown 25443-3210
(304) 876-5420

WISCONSIN

UNIVERSITY OF WISCONSIN—MADISON
Memorial Library
728 State St.
Madison 53706
(608) 262-3242

MARQUETTE UNIVERSITY
Raynor Memorial Libraries
1355 W. Wisconsin Ave.
Milwaukee 53201-3141
(414) 288-1515

UNIVERSITY OF WISCONSIN—
STEVENS POINT
University Library
900 Reserve St.
Stevens Point 54481-3897
(715) 346-2540

WYOMING

LARAMIE COUNTY COMMUNITY COLLEGE
Instructional Resources Center
1400 E. College Dr.
Cheyenne 82007
(307) 778-1206

CAMPBELL COUNTY PUBLIC LIBRARY
2101 4-J Rd.
Gillette 82718
(307) 687-0115

TETON COUNTY LIBRARY
125 Virginian Ln.
Jackson 83001
(307) 733-2164

SHERIDAN COUNTY FULMER PUBLIC LIBRARY
335 W. Alger St.
Sheridan 82801
(307) 674-8585

PUERTO RICO

UNIVERSIDAD DEL SAGRADO CORAZON
M.M.T. Guevara Library
Santurce 00914
(787) 728-1515

Participants in the Foundation Center's Cooperating Collections network are libraries or nonprofit information centers that provide fundraising information and other funding-related technical assistance in their communities. Cooperating Collections agree to provide free public access to a basic collection of Foundation Center resources during a regular schedule of hours, along with free funding research guidance to all visitors. Many also provide a variety of services for local nonprofit organizations, using staff or volunteers to prepare special materials, organize workshops, or conduct orientations.

A key initiative of the Foundation Center is to reach under-resourced and underserved populations throughout the United States who are in need of useful information and training to become successful grantseekers. One of the ways we accomplish this goal is by designating new Cooperating Collection libraries in regions that have the ability to serve the nonprofit communities most in need of Foundation Center resources. We are seeking proposals from qualified institutions (e.g., public, academic, or special libraries, community foundations, nonprofit resource centers, and other technical assistance providers) that can help us carry out this important initiative.

If you are interested in establishing a funding information library in your area, or would like to learn more about the program, please contact:
Coordinator of Cooperating Collections, The Foundation Center, 79 Fifth Avenue, New York, NY 10003 (E-mail: ccmail@foundationcenter.org).

DESCRIPTIVE DIRECTORY

EDUCATIONAL SUPPORT

This section of the directory lists sources of educational support for secondary, undergraduate, and graduate study.

Major types of educational assistance available include the following:

- **Scholarships**—grants awarded directly to students, or to schools for the benefit of students, to help meet tuition costs, at the undergraduate and graduate level. Also included are company employee-related scholarships/loans

- **Fellowships**—grants awarded to graduate students in colleges, universities, and other institutions

- **Loans**—funds for educational expenses which usually must be repaid to the lending grantmaker

- **Internships**—grants to support undergraduate or graduate students in gaining practical experience

Not listed in this section are company-sponsored foundations whose scholarship programs for children of employees are administered by outside organizations, since the selection and grant payment process is carried on independently of the foundation.

Entries are arranged alphabetically by grantmaker name. Access to grants by the above types of support, as well as specific subject areas and geographic focus, is provided in the "Subject," "Types of Support," "Geographic Focus," and "International Giving" indexes in the back of the book.

Limitations on grantmaking are indicated in the entry when available. *The limitations statement should be checked carefully as a grantmaker will reject any application that does not fall within its stated geographic area, recipient type, or area of interest.*

This section also lists grantmakers giving educational support only to the graduates of specific high schools or school districts, or students of specific institutions of higher education. Some grantmakers provide support to the graduates of more than one school. Some may also specify institutions to be attended after graduation or areas of study. In many cases, application must be made through the high school or college instead of the grantmaker.

REMEMBER: IF YOU DON'T QUALIFY, DON'T APPLY.

1
100 Black Men of America, Inc.
141 Auburn Ave.
Atlanta, GA 30303 (404) 688-5100
Contact: Anthony B. O'Neill Sr. Esq., Secy.
FAX: (404) 688-1028; Additional tel.: (800) 598-3411; URL: http://www.100blackmen.org

Foundation type: Public charity
Limitations: Scholarships to deserving matriculating students who will be full-time students at accredited, post-secondary institutions based on the foundation's eligibility criteria.
Financial data: Year ended 12/31/2004. Assets, $2,129,692 (M); Expenditures, $2,712,333; Total giving, $236,200.
Type of support: Undergraduate support.
Application information: Applications accepted. Application form required. Application form available on the grantmaker's Web site.
  Initial approach: Telephone or letter.
  Deadline(s): Feb. 28
  Applicants should submit the following:
    1) Essay
    2) Transcripts
    3) Letter(s) of recommendation
    4) GPA
  Additional information: See Web site for complete program guidelines.
Program description:
  100 Black Men of America Scholarship: Eligibility criteria includes:
  · Minimum GPA of 2.5
  · Completed 50 hours of active community service within past 12 months with certified documentation
  · leadership involvement
EIN: 581974429

2
100 Black Men of Greater Charlotte, Inc.
500 E. Morehead St., Ste. 318
Charlotte, NC 28202 (704) 375-7300
Contact: Jacqueline Peters
FAX: (704) 375-5151;
E-mail: charlottethe100@aol.com

Foundation type: Public charity
Limitations: Scholarships to African American students residing in the Charlotte, NC, area, for undergraduate education.
Publications: Annual report; Financial statement; Informational brochure.
Financial data: Year ended 12/31/2003. Assets, $44,957 (M); Expenditures, $198,055; Total giving, $28,566; Grants to individuals, totaling $28,566.
Fields of interest: Youth development, community service clubs; African Americans/Blacks.
Type of support: Precollege support; Undergraduate support.
Application information: Contact foundation for current application deadline/guidelines.
Program descriptions:
  Movement of Youth Scholarships: Awards $10,000 to African American students with GPAs of at least 3.0 and $3,000 to African American students with GPAs of between 2.0 and 2.9.
  Malcolm Robinson Memorial Community Service Scholarship: Awards $500 to a local high school student who exhibits solid scholarship and a commitment to community service.
EIN: 561795371

3
The 13th Regional Heritage Foundation
c/o Scholarship Comm.
1156 Industry Dr., Bldg. 40, Unit A
Seattle, WA 98188 (206) 575-6229
FAX: (206) 575-6283; URL: http://www.the13thregion.com/Scholarships/

Foundation type: Company-sponsored foundation
Limitations: Scholarships to Alaska Natives (Eskimos, Indians, and Aleuts) enrolled under Section 5 of the Alaska Native Claims Settlement Act (ANCSA) to the 13th Regional Corporation and direct descendants of those original enrollees currently accepted to, or enrolled in, nationally or regionally accredited institutions of higher education or vocational schools.
Publications: Application guidelines.
Financial data: Year ended 12/31/2004. Assets, $87,516 (M); Expenditures, $18,042; Total giving, $18,000; Grants to individuals, 35 grants totaling $18,000 (high: $1,000, low: $500).
Fields of interest: Native Americans/American Indians.
Type of support: Technical education support; Undergraduate support.
Application information: Applications accepted. Application form required. Application form available on the grantmaker's Web site.
  Initial approach: Letter.
  Deadline(s): Mar. 1 and June 30
  Additional information: See Web site for complete program guidelines.
EIN: 912002448

4
3-H Farms Charitable Foundation
c/o U.S. Bank, N.A., Trust Tax Svcs.
P.O. Box 64713
St. Paul, MN 55164-0713
Application address: c/o Guidance Off., Litchfield High School, 901 Gilman Ave. N., Litchfield, MN 55355

Foundation type: Independent foundation
Limitations: Scholarships to students from Litchfield, MN, for study in the fields of health or agriculture.
Financial data: Year ended 06/30/2005. Assets, $143,674 (M); Expenditures, $7,407; Total giving, $6,000; Grants to individuals, 2 grants totaling $6,000 (high: $3,000, low: $3,000).
Fields of interest: Health sciences school/education; Agriculture/food, formal/general education.
Type of support: Scholarships—to individuals.
Application information: Application form required.
  Deadline(s): Apr. 1
EIN: 416466247

5
A-Peeling Charitable Foundation, Inc.
46 Gunpowder Ridge
Fort Thomas, KY 41075-1001

Foundation type: Independent foundation
Limitations: Scholarships for higher education to students in Cincinnati, OH.
Financial data: Year ended 12/31/2004. Assets, $12,449 (M); Expenditures, $72,735; Total giving, $72,650; Grants to individuals, totaling $67,150.
Type of support: Scholarships—to individuals.
Application information: Contact foundation for current application deadline/guidelines.
EIN: 611350974

6
AAA Scholarship Fund of AAA East Penn
(formerly AAA Scholarship Fund of the Lehigh Valley Motor Club)
1020 Hamilton St.
Allentown, PA 18101-1085 (610) 434-5141
Contact: John H. Kern, Treas.

Foundation type: Independent foundation
Limitations: Scholarships by nomination only to former members of the AAA safety patrol and to graduates of high schools located within the AAA Lehigh Valley, PA, territory.
Financial data: Year ended 12/31/2004. Assets, $165,356 (M); Expenditures, $12,000; Total giving, $12,000; Grants to individuals, 12 grants totaling $12,000.
Fields of interest: Vocational education.
Type of support: Awards/grants by nomination only; Undergraduate support.
Application information:
  Deadline(s): Jan. 30
  Applicants should submit the following:
    1) Transcripts
    2) SAT
  Additional information: Completion of formal application required, including two letters of reference, class rank, and a copy of the first page of PHEA application; Applications must be made through high school guidance offices.
Program description:
  Scholarship Program: Each participating school selects one nominee for a college scholarship, and one nominee for a vocational school scholarship. These nominees are then forwarded to the foundation by Mar. 15.
EIN: 232325177

7
AAAA Foundation, Inc.
c/o AAAA, Inc.
405 Lexington Ave.
New York, NY 10174-1801
Contact: O. Burtch Drake, Pres.
URL: http://www.aaaa.org

Foundation type: Public charity
Limitations: Scholarships to people of color and to women for undergraduate and graduate education leading towards media, art, and advertising careers.
Financial data: Year ended 12/31/2003. Assets, $1,052,290 (M); Expenditures, $216,945; Total giving, $185,000; Grants to individuals, 25 grants totaling $185,000 (high: $10,000, low: $2,000).
Fields of interest: Media/communications; Minorities; Asians/Pacific Islanders; African Americans/Blacks; Hispanics/Latinos; Native Americans/American Indians; Women.
Type of support: Graduate support; Undergraduate support.
Application information: Application form required.
  Additional information: See Web site for further application and program information.
Program descriptions:
  Bill Bernbach Minority Scholarship: Scholarships to African Americans, Asian Americans, Latinos and Native Americans who are studying to become art directors or copywriters. Applicants must demonstrate financial need, be full-time students in the last year of portfolio school, and be U.S. citizens or permanent residents.
  John Mack Carter Scholarship: Awards a scholarship to a woman pursuing a Master's degree in a media or planning program. Applicants must be

registered full-time in the Ad Center's media sequence, demonstrate leadership skills, financial need, career commitment, and strategic thinking, and be U.S. citizens or permanent residents.

Operation Jump Start: Provides up to five years of financial assistance to individuals of color who aspire to be copywriters and art directors.

The Ornelas Advertising Scholarship Fund: Scholarships to individuals with at least one Latino grandparent for undergraduate studies. Applicant must be AAAA MAIP interns in good standing, have a GPA of at least 3.0 an a 4.0 scale, and be U.S. citizens attending an accredited U.S. college or university.
EIN: 133949950

8

Mary M. Aaron Memorial Trust Scholarship Fund
1190 Civic Center Blvd.
Yuba City, CA 95993-3004

Foundation type: Independent foundation
Limitations: Scholarships to residents of Sutter and Yuba counties, CA, who are high school and junior college students of the Yuba City, CA, area, to attend CA institutions of higher learning.
Financial data: Year ended 06/30/2005. Assets, $2,320,256 (M); Expenditures, $134,674; Total giving, $93,500; Grants to individuals, 51 grants totaling $93,500.
Type of support: Support to graduates or students of specific schools; Undergraduate support.
Application information: Application form required.
Initial approach: Letter.
Additional information: Mar. 15.
Program description:
Scholarship Program: The fund provides charitable relief for worthy and deserving students attending Marysville Union High School, Yuba City Union High School and Yuba City Junior College who are residents of California and who need financial assistance to complete their high school or junior college education. Financial assistance is also given to worthy and deserving graduates of said high schools and junior college in order to complete their college or professional education within the state of California. Applications for grants (including renewals) are not reviewed by the trustees until an official transcript of the current school year is received. The amount of the grant, therefore, may vary from year to year. The average grant is $400 for students attending a community college and $750 for those attending four-year colleges. Grants are awarded on the basis of financial need rather than scholastic grades or courses of study. The fund does not award scholarship grants for graduate studies.
EIN: 941561354

9

AAST Scholarship Foundation
(formerly American Association of State Troopers Scholarship Foundation, Inc.)
1949 Raymond Diehl Rd.
Tallahassee, FL 32308-3841 (850) 385-7904
Contact: Beverly Harris Elliott
Email: beverly@statetroopers.org; URL: http://statetroopers.org/scholarship_found.asp

Foundation type: Operating foundation
Limitations: Scholarships to children of members of the American Association of State Troopers, Inc., for higher education.
Financial data: Year ended 12/31/2004. Assets, $349,395 (M); Expenditures,

$1,532,734; Total giving, $102,500; Grants to individuals, 162 grants totaling $102,500 (high: $1,000, low: $500).
Fields of interest: Crime/law enforcement, police agencies.
Type of support: Scholarships—to individuals.
Application information: Application form required.
Copies of proposal: 1
Deadline(s): June 1
Additional information: Completion of formal application required, including an official transcript indicating a minimum 2.5 GPA, a 500-word essay entitled "How Will My Education Advance My Career Plans," and a 2"x2" photograph.
EIN: 593054670

10

The Clara Abbott Foundation
1505 White Oak Dr.
Waukegan, IL 60085 (800) 972-3859
Contact: Glenn S. Warner, V.P. and Exec. Dir.
URL: http://clara.abbott.com

Foundation type: Independent foundation
Limitations: Scholarships to dependents of employees and retirees of Abbott Laboratories.
Publications: Annual report (including application guidelines); Financial statement; Informational brochure.
Financial data: Year ended 12/31/2004. Assets, $274,447,766 (M); Expenditures, $22,380,946; Total giving, $13,613,681; Grants to individuals, totaling $13,613,681; Loans to individuals, totaling $417,000.
Type of support: Employee-related scholarships.
Application information: Application form required.
Deadline(s): Dec. 15 for domestic applicants and Aug. 15 for international applicants
Applicants should submit the following:
1) Transcripts
2) Financial information
Program description:
Scholarship Program: Applicants must be dependents of Abbott employees or retirees who have continuously worked for three or more years at Abbott Laboratories. Applicants must also be between the ages of 17 and 29, with plans to attend an accredited undergraduate, trade, or vocational school on a full-time basis. In addition, they must demonstrate financial need.
EIN: 366069632

11

Frances H. Abbott Memorial Foundation
c/o Fifth Third Bank
P.O. Box 3636
Grand Rapids, MI 49501-3636
Application address: c/o Gwendolyn Harris, Riverside-Brookfield High School, 1st Ave. and Ridgewood Rd., Riverside, IL 60546

Foundation type: Independent foundation
Limitations: Scholarships for graduating seniors from Riverside-Brookfield High School, IL.
Financial data: Year ended 12/31/2004. Assets, $54,998 (M); Expenditures, $9,415; Total giving, $5,300; Grants to individuals, totaling $5,300.
Type of support: Support to graduates or students of specific schools; Undergraduate support.
Application information: Applications accepted.
Initial approach: Application by letter.
Deadline(s): First Tues. in May
EIN: 366672535

12

James N. Abbott, Jr. Trust
c/o Frederik C. Hoffman
P.O. Box 330
Gloucester, MA 01930
Application address: c/o Maria Bagaco, Trust Off., Cape Ann Savings Bank, 109 Main St., Gloucester, MA 01930

Foundation type: Independent foundation
Limitations: Scholarships to residents of Gloucester, Essex, and Rockport, MA, who have graduated from Gloucester High School, MA, or Rockport High School, MA, and plan to return to the area to practice their professions after college. Applicants must have consistent strong academic records, and possess high moral standards.
Financial data: Year ended 12/31/2004. Assets, $769,987 (M); Expenditures, $41,403; Total giving, $36,000; Grants to individuals, 10 grants totaling $36,000.
Type of support: Support to graduates or students of specific schools; Undergraduate support.
Application information: Applications accepted. Application form required.
Initial approach: Letter.
Deadline(s): Contact trust for current application deadline.
Applicants should submit the following:
1) Essay
2) Transcripts
Additional information: Completion of formal application required, including letter indicating qualifications, and proof of acceptance to an accredited school of higher education.
EIN: 046707573

13

Edward and Marie Abele Memorial Fund
c/o Citizens Bank Wealth Mgmt., N.A.
328 S. Saginaw St., M/C 00272
Flint, MI 48502
Application address: c/o Abele Loan Comm., 5800 Weiss St., Saginaw, MI 48603, tel.: (989) 799-7910

Foundation type: Independent foundation
Limitations: Graduate and undergraduate student loans to practicing Catholics residing in Saginaw County, MI, with preference given to those entering seminaries for priesthood.
Financial data: Year ended 07/31/2004. Assets, $371,210 (M); Expenditures, $7,683; Total giving, $0; Loans to individuals, 4 loans totaling $6,600.
Fields of interest: Theological school/education; Roman Catholic agencies & churches.
Type of support: Graduate support; Undergraduate support.
Application information: Application form required.
Deadline(s): May 5
EIN: 386356628

14

Jennie G. and Pearl Abell Education Trust
717 Main St.
P.O. Box 487
Ashland, KS 67831 (620) 635-2228

Foundation type: Independent foundation
Limitations: Scholarships to financially needy graduates of Clark County, KS, high schools and current Clark County, KS, residents.
Publications: Program policy statement.

Financial data: Year ended 05/31/2005. Assets, $1,901,855 (M); Expenditures, $117,693; Total giving, $75,875; Grants to individuals, 52 grants totaling $75,875 (high: $3,000, low: $500).
Type of support: Support to graduates or students of specific schools; Undergraduate support.
Application information: Deadline June 15; Completion of formal application required, including college transcripts; Interviews granted upon request.
Program description:
Scholarship Program: The student must enroll full-time and maintain a minimum GPA of 2.0. If the student fails to meet the minimum academic standard, the college is instructed not to disburse the next semester's grant. Summer school grants are available and require a separate application.
EIN: 237454791

15
Abernathy Black Community Development & Educational Fund
(formerly ABCDE Fund)
P.O. Box 177
Washington, PA   15301   (724) 228-1245

Foundation type: Operating foundation
Limitations: Scholarships to African American students from Washington, PA, to attend colleges and technical schools.
Financial data: Year ended 12/31/2003. Assets, $36,981 (M); Expenditures, $9,665; Total giving, $7,500; Grants to individuals, totaling $7,500.
Fields of interest: Vocational education; African Americans/Blacks.
Type of support: Technical education support; Undergraduate support.
Application information:
Initial approach: Letter.
Deadline(s): Contact fund for current application deadline
Additional information: Completion of formal application required, including biographical and educational information; Interviews required.
EIN: 237336423

16
George Abrahamian Foundation
P.O. Box 41726
Providence, RI   02904-1726   (401) 433-5832

Foundation type: Operating foundation
Limitations: Scholarships to students of Armenian ancestry who are U.S. citizens and residents of the greater Providence, RI, area.
Financial data: Year ended 12/31/2003. Assets, $122,009 (M); Expenditures, $5,883; Total giving, $4,000.
Type of support: Undergraduate support.
Application information: Applications accepted. Application form required.
Deadline(s): Sept. 30
Additional information: Interviews required. Most recipients attend colleges and universities in RI.
Program description:
Scholarship Program: Scholarship candidates are recommended by Armenian churches in the area. Selections are based upon good character, scholastic ability, and financial need. Periodic follow-ups are made after a scholarship is awarded.
EIN: 237039366

17
Samuel L. Abrams Foundation
P.O. Box 3053
Harrisburg, PA   17105-3053   (717) 233-7927
Contact: Richard E. Abrams, Pres.
E-mail: support@slabramsfoundation.org;
URL: http://www.slabramsfoundation.org

Foundation type: Independent foundation
Limitations: Scholarships and interest-free loans to graduates of specific high schools in the greater Harrisburg, PA, area.
Publications: Application guidelines.
Financial data: Year ended 12/31/2004. Assets, $2,692,264 (M); Expenditures, $108,740; Total giving, $97,500; Loans to individuals, 47 loans totaling $97,500.
Fields of interest: Vocational education; Business school/education; Nursing school/education.
Type of support: Support to graduates or students of specific schools; Undergraduate support.
Application information: Applications accepted. Application form required.
Deadline(s): May 30
Applicants should submit the following:
1) Transcripts
2) Financial information
Additional information: Interviews required.
Program description:
Loan Program: The foundation makes grants or loans to graduates of area schools who want to continue their education at an approved institution of higher learning including, but not limited to, accredited colleges, universities, junior colleges, community colleges, business schools, technical schools, and schools of nursing. Graduates of the following PA schools are eligible: all public or parochial high schools within the City of Harrisburg, Camp Hill High School, Cedar Cliff High School, Central Dauphin East High School, Central Dauphin High School, Red Land High School, Steelton-Highspire High School, Susquehanna Township High School, The Harrisburg Academy, and Trinity High School. Applicants must demonstrate strong initiative, a desire to improve themselves, and a need for financial assistance. They must also have been accepted by an approved institution of learning. Applications may be submitted at any time during a student's undergraduate or graduate career. Prior-year recipients must submit new applications each year. Repayment of loan is to be made in equal installments within a period of five years after completion or termination of study. The co-signature of a parent or guardian is required.
EIN: 236408237

18
The Frederick B. Abramson Memorial Foundation
734 15th St., N.W., Ste. 502
Washington, DC   20005   (202) 463-6585
Contact: Lori Jackson, Exec. Dir.
FAX: (202) 828-6490;
E-mail: info@abramsonfoundation.org;
URL: http://www.abramsonfoundation.org

Foundation type: Public charity
Limitations: Scholarships to DC public high school seniors for higher education at a four-year college.
Publications: Application guidelines; Informational brochure; Newsletter.
Financial data: Year ended 06/30/2003. Assets, $165,737 (M); Expenditures, $210,163; Total giving, $70,750; Grants to individuals, 32 grants totaling $70,750 (high: $5,000, low: $100).

Application information: Applications accepted. Application form required.
Deadline(s): Mar. 31
Applicants should submit the following:
1) Transcripts
2) Financial information
3) Letter(s) of recommendation
Additional information: Consult foundation's Web site for full application requirements and forms.
EIN: 521800184

19
Louis & Mary J. Abstine College Scholarship Fund
c/o National City Bank
P.O. Box 94651
Cleveland, OH   44101-4651
Application address: c/o Denise Andorfer, National City Bank of Indiana, P.O. Box 110, Fort Wayne, IN 46801, tel.: (260)461-6218

Foundation type: Independent foundation
Limitations: Scholarships to residents of Shelby County, IN.
Financial data: Year ended 02/29/2004. Assets, $1,267,451 (M); Expenditures, $75,268; Total giving, $61,250; Grants to individuals, 38 grants totaling $61,250.
Type of support: Scholarships—to individuals.
Application information: Application form required.
Deadline(s): Mar. 15
EIN: 351787469

20
Accel Foundation
c/o James M. Strathmeyer
9012 Carrington Ridge Dr.
Raleigh, NC   27615

Foundation type: Independent foundation
Limitations: Scholarships for higher education, primarily to residents of Lancaster County, PA.
Financial data: Year ended 08/31/2004. Assets, $1,383,294 (M); Expenditures, $89,419; Total giving, $86,545; Grants to individuals, 18 grants totaling $44,000 (high: $4,000, low: $1,000).
Type of support: Undergraduate support.
Application information: Unsolicited requests for funds not considered or acknowledged.
EIN: 561900007

21
Access Foundation
181 Bonetti Dr.
San Luis Obispo, CA   93401   (805) 549-0161
Contact: Felicia Cashin, Pres.

Foundation type: Independent foundation
Limitations: Scholarships to students for higher education who are residents of CA.
Financial data: Year ended 11/30/2004. Assets, $57,407 (M); Expenditures, $6,353; Total giving, $5,700; Grants to individuals, totaling $3,000.
Type of support: Scholarships—to individuals.
Application information: Applications accepted. Application form required.
Deadline(s): None
Additional information: Application should include a letter describing the person's background, two letters of reference, and a

reason why attendance at a particular school is needed.
EIN: 954457341

22

Mary Margaret Ackers Charitable Trust
3040 West Point Rd.
Lancaster, OH 43130 (740) 653-0461
Contact: William J. Sitterley, Tr.

Foundation type: Independent foundation
Limitations: Scholarships to graduates of Berne Union High School, Fairfield County, OH.
Financial data: Year ended 05/31/2005. Assets, $329,818 (M); Expenditures, $18,459; Total giving, $14,500; Grants to individuals, 5 grants totaling $14,500 (high: $6,000, low: $1,000).
Type of support: Support to graduates or students of specific schools; Technical education support; Undergraduate support.
Application information: Application form required.
Deadline(s): 2nd Mon. in May
Applicants should submit the following:
1) Class rank
2) Transcripts
3) GPA
4) ACT
Additional information: This trust shares an application process with the Alice Kindler Scholarship Fund, the J. Colin Campbell Scholarship Fund, and the Mildred L. Herzberger Charitable Trust.
Program description:
Mary Ackers Scholarship: Recipients must be residents of Berne Township, OH, for a minimum of three years, and must have attended Berne Union High School for the last three years of their secondary education, including graduation. Recipients must maintain a good scholastic record, attend accredited state-supported colleges or universities or technical or vocational schools in OH, be full-time students with a minimum of 15 hours per term and maintain a 2.0 GPA. Applicants need not be recent high school graduates.
EIN: 311327096

23

ADA Foundation
(formerly American Dental Association Health Foundation)
211 E. Chicago Ave.
Chicago, IL 60611-2678 (312) 440-2547
Contact: Arthur A. Dugoni D.D.S., Pres.
FAX: (312) 440-3526; E-mail: adaf@ada.org; URL: http://www.ada.org/ada/prod/adaf/index.asp

Foundation type: Public charity
Limitations: Scholarships to dental students.
Publications: Application guidelines; Annual report; Informational brochure; Newsletter.
Financial data: Year ended 12/31/2004. Assets, $22,713,944 (M); Expenditures, $6,374,074; Total giving, $645,778.
Fields of interest: Dental school/education; Minorities.
Type of support: Graduate support; Undergraduate support.
Application information: Applications accepted. Application form required.
Initial approach: E-mail.
Deadline(s): Vary
Applicants should submit the following:
1) Essay
2) Letter(s) of recommendation

3) Financial information
Additional information: Application forms for all ADA Foundation scholarships are available at dental schools and allied dental health programs.
Program descriptions:
Dental Student Scholarship: The maximum annual award for the Dental Student Scholarship is $2,500. Applicants must be entering second year students at the time of application and currently attending or enrolled at a dental school accredited by the Commission on Dental Accreditation. Applicants must demonstrate a minimum financial need of $2,500, and must have an accumulative grade point average of 3.0 based on a 4.0 scale.
Minority Dental Student Scholarship: The maximum annual award for the Dental Student Scholarship is $2,500. Certain minority groups have been identified as being underrepresented in dental school enrollment. At this time, African American, Hispanic and Native American students are eligible to apply for this scholarship. Applicants must be entering second year students at the time of application and currently attending or enrolled at a dental school accredited by the Commission on Dental Accreditation. Applicants must demonstrate a minimum financial need of $2,500, and must have an accumulative grade point average of 3.0 based on a 4.0 scale.
Allied Dental Health Scholarships: The maximum annual award for Allied Dental Health Scholarships is $1,000.
EIN: 366132046

24

Ada Scholarship Foundation, Inc.
318 E. Main St.
Ada, MN 56510-1340
Application address: c/o Betty Johnson, 700 E. 1st Ave., Ada, MN 56510, tel.: (218) 784-7157

Foundation type: Independent foundation
Limitations: Scholarships to high school students in the City of Ada, MN, and Norman County, MN.
Financial data: Year ended 05/31/2005. Assets, $2,171,795 (M); Expenditures, $102,532; Total giving, $90,600; Grants to individuals, 64 grants totaling $90,600 (high: $2,800, low: $500).
Type of support: Scholarships—to individuals.
Application information: Applications accepted throughout the year; Completion of formal application required, including recommendations from principal and church official, employment history, class rank, transcripts, and parents' and student's financial information.
EIN: 411566681

25

Wesley G. Adair Scholarship Trust
c/o Synovus Trust Co.
P.O. Box 1747
Athens, GA 30603-1747 (706) 357-7115
Contact: Cynthia H. Lester, Trust Off., Synovus Trust Co.

Foundation type: Operating foundation
Limitations: Scholarships to individuals for undergraduate and vocational education. Applicants must be residents of Baurow County, GA, or lineal descendents of Wesley G. Adair.
Financial data: Year ended 12/31/2004. Assets, $573,992 (M); Expenditures, $43,724; Total giving, $31,500; Grants to individuals, 15 grants totaling $31,500.

Fields of interest: Vocational education, post-secondary.
Type of support: Undergraduate support.
Application information: Application form required.
Deadline(s): May 15
Applicants should submit the following:
1) Essay
2) Financial information
3) Letter(s) of recommendation
4) Transcripts
EIN: 586376451

26

Adams County Community Foundation
102 N. 2nd St.
Decatur, IN 46733-1660 (260) 724-3939
Contact: Coni Mayer, Exec. Dir.
FAX: (260) 724-2299;
E-mail: accfoundation@earthlink.com

Foundation type: Community foundation
Limitations: Scholarships to residents of Adams County, IN, for undergraduate education.
Publications: Annual report.
Financial data: Year ended 12/31/2004. Assets, $7,663,766 (M); Expenditures, $563,693; Total giving, $343,764; Grants to individuals, 37 grants totaling $10,819.
Type of support: Undergraduate support.
Application information: Application form required.
Deadline(s): 1st Thurs. of Feb. and June
Additional information: Application form available at the foundation's office or each of the Adams County Public Libraries.
EIN: 351834664

27

Adams Educational Fund, Inc.
P.O. Box 1012
Willmar, MN 56201 (320) 235-5720
Contact: Wayne S. Nelson, Pres.
Additional contacts: William Gulbrandsen, tel.: (320) 235-0499; Brett N. Aarmot, tel.: (320) 235-3311

Foundation type: Independent foundation
Limitations: Loans to graduates of the Willmar School System, MN, and surrounding areas. Maximum loan is $1,000 per year for four years.
Financial data: Year ended 12/31/2004. Assets, $1 (M); Expenditures, $4,520; Total giving, $0; Loans to individuals, 15 loans totaling $12,250.
Type of support: Student loans—to individuals; Support to graduates or students of specific schools; Undergraduate support.
Application information: Applications accepted. Application form required.
Deadline(s): None
EIN: 416038636

28

The William L. and Victorine Q. Adams Foundation, Inc.
1040 Park Ave., Ste. 300
Baltimore, MD 21201
Application address: c/o Adams Future Business Leader Scholarship Fund, Associated Black Charities, 1114 Cathedral St., 2nd Fl., Baltimore, MD 21201, tel.: (410) 659-0000

Foundation type: Operating foundation
Limitations: Undergraduate scholarships to financially needy African American residents of the

City of Baltimore, MD, who are U.S. citizens, for the study of business.

Financial data: Year ended 09/30/2003. Assets, $1,775,965 (M); Expenditures, $165,244; Total giving, $73,750; Grants to individuals, 13 grants totaling $43,400 (high: $13,000, low: $250).

Fields of interest: Business school/education; Business/industry; Economics; African Americans/Blacks.

Type of support: Undergraduate support.

Application information:

Deadline(s): May 1

Additional information: Applications available Nov. 1 to Apr. 1; Completion of formal application required, including GPA, transcripts, financial statement, recommendation from high school official, two-page letter outlining applicant's career goals, letter of acceptance from college or university, and notification of eligibility for federal and MD state student aid; Interviews required; Recipients notified by July 30.

Program description:

Scholarship Program: Applicants must have at least a 3.0 GPA and must intend to pursue the study of accounting, economics, business, or finance at the undergraduate level. Recipients are required to volunteer for community service while receiving a scholarship from the foundation. Scholarships are renewable for up to four years.

EIN: 521369556

29

James K. Adams & Arlene L. Adams Foundation

20 Erford Rd., Ste. 200
Lemoyne, PA 17043
Contact: David H. Radcliff, Tr.

Foundation type: Independent foundation

Limitations: Student loans to students graduating from high schools in eastern Cumberland County, PA.

Financial data: Year ended 12/31/2004. Assets, $356,374 (M); Expenditures, $64,861; Total giving, $62,300; Loans to individuals, 14 loans totaling $32,300.

Type of support: Student loans—to individuals; Support to graduates or students of specific schools; Undergraduate support.

Application information:

Initial approach: Letter.

Deadline(s): Dec. 31

EIN: 251665127

30

Adams Rotary Memorial Fund B

(formerly Charles & Lovie Adams Rotary Memorial Fund B Trust)
c/o KeyBank N.A., Trust Div.
202 S. Michigan St.
South Bend, IN 46601
Application address: c/o KeyBank N.A., Attn.: Maria Meredith, P.O. Box 89464, OH-01-27-1614, Cleveland, OH 44101-1717

Foundation type: Independent foundation

Limitations: Scholarships to high school graduates of Howard County, IN, to study medicine or nursing at any accredited college, university, or nursing school in the U.S.

Financial data: Year ended 12/31/2004. Assets, $377,149 (M); Expenditures, $26,141; Total giving, $22,000; Grants to individuals, 13

grants totaling $22,000 (high: $2,500, low: $1,000).

Fields of interest: Medical school/education; Nursing school/education.

Type of support: Scholarships—to individuals; Support to graduates or students of specific schools.

Application information: Application form required.

Additional information: Contact fund for current application deadline.

EIN: 356388193

31

John & Olive Adams Scholarship Foundation, Inc.

c/o John Murdock
690 John Adams Pkwy.
Idaho Falls, ID 83401
Application address: c/o Ann Howell, 2784 Science Ctr. Dr., Idaho Falls, ID 83402

Foundation type: Independent foundation

Limitations: Scholarships to students in eastern ID.

Financial data: Year ended 06/30/2005. Assets, $75,534 (M); Expenditures, $19,468; Total giving, $18,750; Grants to individuals, 32 grants totaling $18,750 (high: $1,500, low: $250).

Type of support: Scholarships—to individuals.

Application information: Applications accepted throughout the year; Completion of formal application required.

EIN: 943168497

32

Sally Adams Scholarship Fund

c/o JPMorgan Chase Bank, N.A.
P.O. Box 1308
Milwaukee, WI 53201
Application address: c/o JPMorgan Chase Bank, N.A., West Virginia, Wheeling, N.A., Attn.: Ed Johnson, 1114 Market St., Wheeling, WV 26003, tel.: (304) 234-4130

Foundation type: Independent foundation

Limitations: Scholarships to legal residents of Ohio County, WV, who are financially needy, aged 17 to 25, and graduates of public high schools in Wheeling, WV.

Financial data: Year ended 12/31/2004. Assets, $347,177 (M); Expenditures, $21,259; Total giving, $16,000; Grants to individuals, 6 grants totaling $16,000 (high: $4,000, low: $1,250).

Type of support: Support to graduates or students of specific schools; Undergraduate support.

Application information: Applications accepted. Application form required.

Deadline(s): Spring

Program description:

Scholarship Program: Applicants will be considered on the basis of personality, extracurricular activities, deportment, spirit of cooperation with school authorities, good citizenship, and grades. In general the scholarship is for one year only. No scholarship will be awarded for more than four years.

EIN: 556085702

33

Dr. E. W. Adamson Scholarship Fund

c/o JPMorgan Chase Bank, N.A.
P.O. Box 1308
Milwaukee, WI 53201
Application address: c/o Principal, Douglas High School, 1500 15th St., Douglas, AZ 85607, tel.: (520) 364-3462

Foundation type: Independent foundation

Limitations: Scholarships to male graduates of Douglas High School, AZ.

Financial data: Year ended 03/31/2005. Assets, $406,757 (M); Expenditures, $56,460; Total giving, $52,000; Grants to individuals, totaling $52,000.

Fields of interest: Men.

Type of support: Support to graduates or students of specific schools; Undergraduate support.

Application information: Application form required.

Deadline(s): Apr. 1

Program description:

Scholarship Program: Applicants must have a good scholastic and moral record. Scholarships are renewable, provided the recipient maintains at least a "B" GPA.

EIN: 866042761

34

Lena A. & Paul F. Addison Trust

c/o Fifth Third Bank
P.O. Box 630858
Cincinnati, OH 45263
Application address: c/o Guidance Counselor, Mount Vernon Senior High School, 700 Harriett St., Mount Vernon, IN 47620

Foundation type: Independent foundation

Limitations: Scholarships to graduating students of Mount Vernon Senior High School, IN, for higher education.

Financial data: Year ended 12/31/2004. Assets, $609,471 (M); Expenditures, $41,488; Total giving, $30,000; Grants to individuals, 3 grants totaling $30,000.

Type of support: Support to graduates or students of specific schools; Undergraduate support.

Application information: Application form required.

Deadline(s): Apr. 1

Applicants should submit the following:

1) Transcripts
2) Essay
3) Letter(s) of recommendation
4) FAFSA

Program description:

Lena A. and Paul F. Addison Scholarship: Two scholarships are awarded to graduating members of the Mount Vernon Senior High School class. Selection is based on academic achievement, leadership achievement, or future potential in either of these areas. Financial need will also be considered.

EIN: 356639866

35

Additon Scholarship Fund

c/o Citizens Bank of NH
870 Westminster St., 2nd Fl.
Providence, RI 02903-4089
Application address: c/o Bill Sirak, 875 Elm St., Manchester, NH 03105, tel.: (603) 634-7752

Foundation type: Independent foundation

Limitations: Scholarships limited to former employees, or issue of same of Numerica Financial

Corp., Manchester, NH, or Citizens Bank New Hampshire, Manchester, NH.
Financial data: Year ended 09/30/2005. Assets, $464,004 (M); Expenditures, $26,684; Total giving, $17,000; Grants to individuals, 12 grants totaling $17,000.
Type of support: Employee-related scholarships.
Application information: Application form required.
> *Deadline(s):* May 15
> *Additional information:* Application attainable from the trustee.
EIN: 237435466

36
Adelphic Educational Fund, Inc.
c/o George McKelvey Co.
529 Washington Blvd.
P.O. Box 375
Sea Girt, NJ 08750
Application address: c/o Erhard F. Konerding, 10 Yellow Cir., Middletown, CT 06459, tel.: (860) 685-3882

Foundation type: Independent foundation
Limitations: Scholarships and student loans to financially needy undergraduate students at Wesleyan University, CT. Recipients are chosen on the basis of financial need and scholastic aptitude.
Financial data: Year ended 04/30/2005. Assets, $1,123,645 (M); Expenditures, $48,145; Total giving, $30,584.
Type of support: Student loans—to individuals; Support to graduates or students of specific schools.
Application information: Applications accepted. Application form required.
> *Initial approach:* Letter.
> *Deadline(s):* Oct. 1
> *Additional information:* Interviews required.
EIN: 066023615

37
Leo Adler Community Trust
(formerly Leo Adler Trust)
c/o U.S. Bank, N.A.
P.O. Box 3168
Portland, OR 97208-3168
Contact: Marlyn Norquist, Trust Off., U.S. Bank, N.A.

Foundation type: Independent foundation
Limitations: Scholarships to graduates of high schools in Baker County, OR.
Publications: Informational brochure.
Financial data: Year ended 06/30/2005. Assets, $25,748,773 (M); Expenditures, $1,448,273; Total giving, $1,112,739; Grants to individuals, 148 grants totaling $1,112,739 (high: $109,741, low: $30).
Type of support: Support to graduates or students of specific schools; Undergraduate support.
Application information: Applications accepted.
> *Deadline(s):* Mar. 1 and Apr. 1
> *Additional information:* Contact foundation for current application guidelines.
EIN: 936289087

38
AEI Scholarship Fund
c/o KeyBank N.A.
800 Superior Ave., 4th Fl.
Cleveland, OH 44114
Application address: c/o Donna O'Malley, P.O. Box 89464, Cleveland, OH 44101

Foundation type: Independent foundation
Limitations: Scholarships to financially needy female students accepted to, or attending, accredited medical schools in the U.S.
Financial data: Year ended 06/30/2005. Assets, $273,942 (M); Expenditures, $17,052; Total giving, $12,653; Grants to individuals, 2 grants totaling $12,653.
Fields of interest: Medical school/education; Women.
Type of support: Graduate support.
Application information:
> *Deadline(s):* May 31
> *Additional information:* Completion of formal application required, including transcripts, reference letter, and verified financial information; Interviews granted upon request.
Program description:
> *Scholarship Program:* The applicants must maintain at least a "C+" average. If this average has not been maintained or the school does not evaluate by grades, applicants are then judged on the basis of faculty recommendations, MCAT scores, work experience, scholarly publications, and research experience. In addition, applicants must have net income of less than $15,000 per year with assets of no more than $10,000. Scholarships are intended to cover "necessary expenditures" such as tuition, books, food, clothing, housing, transportation, medical and dental expenses, insurance, and child care.
EIN: 382088329

39
Affordable Housing Management Training Foundation
c/o Maloney Properties, Inc.
200 Reservoir St., Ste. 200
Needham, MA 02494-2146 (781) 237-4893
Application address: 27 Mica Ln., Wellesley, MA 02481-1707
FAX: (781) 237-3200; E-mail: info@ahmtf.org; URL: http://www.ahmtf.org

Foundation type: Independent foundation
Limitations: Scholarships to individuals who work in the affordable housing management industry for training in housing management and maintenance.
Financial data: Year ended 09/30/2004. Assets, $192,848 (M); Expenditures, $27,021; Total giving, $15,200; Grants to individuals, totaling $15,200.
Fields of interest: Housing/shelter, management/technical aid; Housing/shelter, repairs.
Type of support: Scholarships—to individuals; Graduate support; Technical education support; Precollege support; Undergraduate support.
Application information: Applications accepted. Application form required. Application form available on the grantmaker's Web site.
> *Initial approach:* Letter or Web site.
EIN: 043528460

40
African Methodist Episcopal Church
Lindell Professional Bldg.
4144 Lindell Blvd., Ste. 216
St. Louis, MO 63108-2932 (314) 534-3064
Contact: Harold L. Whitfield, Exec. Dir.

Foundation type: Public charity
Limitations: Scholarships to students residing in the 5th District of St. Louis, MO.
Financial data: Year ended 12/31/2003. Assets, $4,010,491 (M); Expenditures,

$280,885; Total giving, $81,735; Grants to individuals, 59 grants totaling $59,000 (high: $1,000, low: $1,000).
Type of support: Scholarships—to individuals.
Application information: Contact foundation for current application deadline/guidelines.
EIN: 431127614

41
AFTRA Heller Memorial Foundation, Inc.
260 Madison Ave., 7th Fl.
New York, NY 10016 (212) 532-0800
Contact: Martha Greenhouse, Pres.
E-mail: info@aftra.com; URL: http://www.aftra.org/benefits/scholarship.htm

Foundation type: Public charity
Limitations: Scholarships and death benefits to AFTRA members and their dependents.
Financial data: Year ended 04/30/2004. Assets, $270,156 (M); Expenditures, $42,629; Total giving, $36,000; Grants to individuals, totaling $36,000.
Fields of interest: Television; Radio.
Type of support: Graduate support; Undergraduate support.
Application information: Application form required. Application form available on the grantmaker's Web site.
> *Deadline(s):* May 1
> *Applicants should submit the following:*
> 1) Essay
> 2) Transcripts
> 3) Letter(s) of recommendation
> 4) Financial information
> 5) SASE
Program description:
> *Scholarships:* Twelve to fifteen scholarships of no more than $2,500 each are awarded to AFTRA member or dependent child in good standing for at least five years, or the dependent child of a deceased member who, at the time of death, was an AFTRA member in good standing for at least five years. Scholarships are not renewable.
EIN: 237052868

42
AGC of Washington Education Foundation
1200 Westlake Ave. N., Ste. 301
Seattle, WA 98109 (206) 284-4500
Contact: Leanne Liddicoat, Exec. Dir.
FAX: (206) 284-4595;
E-mail: lliddicoat@agcwa.com; URL: http://www.constructionfoundation.org

Foundation type: Public charity
Limitations: Scholarships to high school and college students who are pursuing a career in the construction industry.
Financial data: Year ended 06/30/2004. Assets, $1,838,173 (M); Expenditures, $711,728; Total giving, $56,222; Grants to individuals, 14 grants totaling $29,030 (high: $4,030, low: $1,000).
Fields of interest: Vocational education.
Type of support: Employee-related scholarships; Scholarships—to individuals.
Application information: Applications accepted. Application form required. Application form available on the grantmaker's Web site.
> *Deadline(s):* Mar. 1
> *Applicants should submit the following:*
> 1) Transcripts
> 2) Letter(s) of recommendation
> *Additional information:* See Web site for complete scholarship guidelines.

Program description:
Scholarships: Several scholarships will be awarded ranging from $500 to $5,000 per student per year . Scholarship recipients may be designated to receive one of the following awards:
· Camilla Bishop Scholarship
· Chester H. & Elizabeth N. Johnson Memorial Scholarship
· Employees of GLY Construction Scholarship
· Mr. Robert W. Austin Memorial Scholarship
· Mr. & Mrs. Donald Bocek Scholarship
· Mr. A.E. DeAtley Memorial Scholarship
· Mr. and Mrs. Robert L. Landau Scholarship
· Mr. Howard S. Lease Memorial Scholarship
· Mr. Robert B. McEachern Memorial Scholarship
· Mr. & Mrs. Allan F. Osberg Scholarship
· Mr. and Mrs. William N. Scott Scholarship
· Mr. Hugh S. Ferguson Scholarship
· MulvannyG2 Scholarship in Memory of Patricia Chikamoto Lee
· Prime Construction Scholarship
EIN: 911157971

43

Harry Agganis Memorial Foundation
c/o Eastern Bank & Trust Co.
265 Franklin St.
Boston, MA   02110-3120
Contact: Nicholas P. Kostan, Tr.
Application address: 83 Grant Rd., Lynn, MA 01904, tel.: (781) 595-7420

Foundation type: Independent foundation
Limitations: Scholarships to residents of Lynn, MA.
Financial data: Year ended 12/31/2004.
Assets, $418,977 (M); Expenditures, $94,845; Total giving, $60,900; Grants to individuals, 61 grants totaling $60,900 (high: $1,000, low: $900).
Type of support: Scholarships—to individuals.
Application information: Applications accepted throughout the year; Initial approach by letter or telephone requesting application forms; Completion of formal application required.
EIN: 046032027

44

Agilent Technologies Employee Scholarship Foundation
c/o Agilent Technologies, Inc.
395 Page Mill Rd., M.S. A3-10
Palo Alto, CA   94303-0870
Contact: Gene Edicott, Pres.

Foundation type: Public charity
Limitations: Scholarships to children of employees of Agilent Technologies, Inc., who reside in CA.
Financial data: Year ended 12/31/2003.
Assets, $57,146 (M); Expenditures, $120,090; Total giving, $120,000; Grants to individuals, 60 grants totaling $120,000 (high: $20,000, low: $20,000).
Type of support: Employee-related scholarships.
Application information: Deadline Feb. 21; Completion of formal application required.
EIN: 776176364

45

Agnew Foundation
P.O. Box 820
Cambridge, OH   43725   (740) 432-3688
Contact: H. William Davis, Pres.

Foundation type: Independent foundation
Limitations: Scholarships to high school seniors in Guernsey County, OH.
Financial data: Year ended 12/31/2004.
Assets, $548,704 (M); Expenditures, $40,616; Total giving, $40,000; Grants to individuals, 40 grants totaling $40,000.
Type of support: Support to graduates or students of specific schools; Undergraduate support.
Application information: Application form required.
Deadline(s): May 1
EIN: 316077699

46

Agsource DHI Foundation, Inc.
P.O. Box 930230
Verona, WI   53593-0230

Foundation type: Independent foundation
Limitations: Scholarships primarily to residents of WI for higher education.
Financial data: Year ended 12/31/2004.
Assets, $581,726 (M); Expenditures, $35,427; Total giving, $29,818; Grants to individuals, 39 grants totaling $20,650 (high: $325).
Type of support: Scholarships—to individuals.
Application information: Contact foundation for current application deadline; Completion of formal application required.
EIN: 391909207

47

Aiea General Hospital Association Scholarship Fund
c/o Bank of Hawaii
P.O. Box 3170
Honolulu, HI   96802-3170
Application address: c/o Grants Admin., The Hawaii Community Foundation, 900 Fort St. Mall, Ste. 1300, Honolulu, HI 96813, tel.: (808) 566-5570

Foundation type: Independent foundation
Limitations: Scholarships to financially needy individuals who major in a health-related field and live within one of the following Leeward Oahu, HI, zip codes: 96701, 96706, 96707, 96782, 96792, or 96797.
Publications: Informational brochure (including application guidelines).
Financial data: Year ended 03/31/2004.
Assets, $451,859 (M); Expenditures, $30,154; Total giving, $19,500; Grants to individuals, 20 grants totaling $19,500 (high: $1,000, low: $500).
Fields of interest: Health sciences school/ education.
Type of support: Scholarships—to individuals.
Application information:
Initial approach: Letter or telephone.
Deadline(s): Mar. 1
Applicants should submit the following:
1) Transcripts
2) SAR
Additional information: Completion of formal application required, including a personal statement, and two letters of recommendation.
Program description:
Scholarship Program: Applicants are notified of the fund's decision within three months of the application deadline. Applicants to this foundation may automatically be considered for other scholarship programs administered by the Hawaii Community Foundation. Employees and direct

relatives of employees of Bancorp Hawaii and the Hawaii Community Foundation are ineligible.
EIN: 990241566

48

Air Force Association
(formerly Aerospace Education Foundation, Inc.)
1501 Lee Hwy.
Arlington, VA   22209-1198   (703) 247-5800
Contact: Donald L. Peterson, Exec. Dir.
FAX: (703) 247-5853; E-mail: afastaff@afa.org; URL: http://www.afa.org

Foundation type: Public charity
Limitations: Undergraduate and graduate scholarships to Air Force personnel, their spouses, and AFROTC graduates.
Financial data: Year ended 12/31/2004.
Assets, $4,428,849 (M); Expenditures, $1,651,536; Total giving, $350,706.
Fields of interest: Science; Space/aviation; Mathematics; Engineering/technology; Military/ veterans' organizations.
Type of support: Graduate support; Undergraduate support.
Application information: Application form required.
Deadline(s): Contact foundation for current application deadlines
Additional information: See Web site for a complete listing of scholarships and awards guidelines and programs.
Program description:
Award Programs:
· AEF Scholarship for Air Force Spouses: $1,000 stipend for educational support is available to spouses of Air Force personnel for undergraduate and graduate study
· Spatz Award: $1,000 stipend to an ACSC graduate who writes the best paper on advocacy of Air Force aerospace power
· Captain Jodi Callahan Memorial Scholarship: $1,000 scholarships are given to Air Force active duty, full-time guards and reserve members who are also Air Force Association members pursuing graduate degrees in nontechnical fields
· Pitsenbarger Award: $500 scholarships are given to the Air Force's top enlisted graduates from the Community College of the Air Force to pursue bachelor's degrees.
EIN: 526043929

49

Air Force Officers Wives Club of Washington DC Welfare Fund
50 Theisen St.
Bolling AFB
Washington, DC   20032-5411   (202) 574-8377

Foundation type: Public charity
Limitations: Scholarships to high school graduates and spouses of Air Force members in the Air Force. Scholarships are awarded to individuals in three categories: college-bound high school seniors; spouses of USAF members; and learning-disabled high school seniors.
Financial data: Year ended 05/31/2004.
Assets, $81,264 (M); Expenditures, $315,033; Total giving, $288,807; Grants to individuals, totaling $13,700.
Fields of interest: Military/veterans' organizations.
Type of support: Scholarships—to individuals.

Application information:
Deadline(s): Contact foundation for current application deadline/guidelines.
EIN: 526057758

50

Airport High School Educational Foundation, Inc.
P.O. Box 2044
West Columbia, SC 29171 (803) 794-3712
Contact: Donald H. Burkett, Dir.

Foundation type: Public charity
Limitations: Scholarships to graduating seniors of Airport High School in SC for higher education.
Financial data: Year ended 06/30/2004. Assets, $47,747 (M); Expenditures, $27,283; Total giving, $21,068; Grants to individuals, 35 grants totaling $21,068 (high: $1,750, low: $31). Subtotal for scholarships—to individuals: grants totaling (high: $1,250, low: $500).
Fields of interest: Higher education.
Type of support: Support to graduates or students of specific schools.
Application information:
Initial approach: Letter.
EIN: 562194610

51

Alabama Forestry Foundation
555 Alabama St.
Montgomery, AL 36104-4309 (334) 265-8733
Contact: Robert P. Sharp, Pres.

Foundation type: Public charity
Limitations: Scholarships to forestry students based on economic achievement and involvement in extra-curricular activities and leadership positions.
Financial data: Year ended 12/31/2003. Assets, $1,418,959 (M); Expenditures, $580,088; Total giving, $12,500; Grants to individuals, totaling $12,500.
Fields of interest: Environment, forests.
Type of support: Scholarships—to individuals.
Application information: Contact foundation for current application deadline/guidelines.
EIN: 630756161

52

Alabama Law Foundation, Inc.
415 Dexter Ave.
Montgomery, AL 36104-3742 (334) 269-1515
Contact: Tracy Daniel, Exec. Dir.
E-mail: tdaniel@alfinc.org; URL: http://www.alfinc.org

Foundation type: Public charity
Limitations: Scholarships to AL residents.
Publications: Application guidelines; Grants list; Informational brochure; Newsletter.
Financial data: Year ended 03/31/2005. Assets, $2,031,454 (M); Expenditures, $419,035; Total giving, $177,700.
Fields of interest: Law school/education; Human services.
Type of support: Graduate support; Technical education support; Precollege support; Undergraduate support.
Application information: Application form required. Application form available on the grantmaker's Web site.

Copies of proposal: 1
Deadline(s): June 19 for Cabaniss, Johnston, and May 1 for Kids' Chance
Applicants should submit the following:
1) Transcripts
2) GPA
3) Financial information
4) FAFSA
5) Budget Information
Additional information: Applications should be sent by mail or submitted online; Time for response to an application is one month.
Program descriptions:
Cabaniss, Johnston Scholarship Fund: This $5,000 scholarship is available for the second year of law school to an extremely bright Alabama resident attending an ABA-accredited law school. A runner-up scholarship of $1,000 may be awarded at the committee's discretion.
Kids' Chance Scholarship Fund: Provides high school, technical school, and college scholarships for young people who have had a parent killed or permanently totally disabled in an on-the-job accident.
EIN: 630951482

53

Alabama Power Foundation, Inc.
600 N. 18th St.
P.O. Box 2641
Birmingham, AL 35291-0011 (205) 257-2508
FAX: (205) 257-1860; URL: http://www.southerncompany.com/alpower/foundation

Foundation type: Company-sponsored foundation
Limitations: Scholarships to children of Alabama Power employees.
Publications: Application guidelines; Annual report (including application guidelines); Grants list; Informational brochure (including application guidelines).
Financial data: Year ended 12/31/2004. Assets, $142,620,531 (M); Expenditures, $9,200,813; Total giving, $7,906,013; Grants to individuals, 252 grants totaling $126,334 (high: $1,000, low: $334).
Type of support: Employee-related scholarships.
Application information: Contact foundation after Jan. 15 for current application deadline/guidelines. Scholarship application address: c/o Dr. Nyles C. Ayres, Pres., Scholarship Prog. Administers, Inc., 3314 West End Ave., Ste. 604, Nashville, TN 37203-1022.
EIN: 570901832

54

Robert J. Alander Scholarship Fund
2938 Wheelock Rd.
Charlotte, NC 28211

Foundation type: Independent foundation
Limitations: Scholarships to graduating high school seniors enrolled in the Marketing and Distributive Education Program of the City of Charlotte/Mecklenburg County, NC, school system.
Financial data: Year ended 06/30/2004. Assets, $28,153 (M); Expenditures, $4,452; Total giving, $4,000; Grants to individuals, totaling $4,000.
Fields of interest: Business/industry.
Type of support: Support to graduates or students of specific schools; Undergraduate support.
Application information:
Deadline(s): Mar. 1
Additional information: Completion of formal application required, including GPA,

transcripts, personal references, and personal statement.
EIN: 566235792

55

The Alaska Community Foundation
701 W. 8th Ave., Ste. 230
Anchorage, AK 99501 (907) 265-6044
Contact: Marcia Hastings, Dir.
FAX: (907) 263-3801;
E-mail: mhastings@alaskacf.org; URL: http://www.alaskacf.org

Foundation type: Community foundation
Limitations: Scholarships to residents of AK who are attending the University of Alaska.
Publications: Annual report; Grants list; Informational brochure.
Financial data: Year ended 12/31/2004. Assets, $9,974,724 (M); Expenditures, $280,299; Total giving, $107,749.
Fields of interest: Music; Business school/education; Engineering school/education; Athletics/sports, baseball.
Type of support: Support to graduates or students of specific schools; Technical education support; Precollege support; Undergraduate support.
Application information: Applications accepted. Application form required.
Initial approach: E-mail.
Additional information: Contact foundation for current application deadline; Application by letter outlining financial need and/or request application from foundation.
Program descriptions:
Alaska Youth Development Fund Scholarship: Provides scholarships to Alaskan youths to attend the Prudential Leadership Institute.
McKinley Capital Management Inc. Scholarship Fund: Awards ten $5,000 scholarships to students interested in pursuing course-work in a money-management-related field.
Sven E. and Lorraine Ericksson Scholarship Fund: Scholarships awarded to students attending the University of Alaska, who intend to study engineering or music.
Harry H. Hirshik Scholarship Fund: Scholarships to students of auto mechanics.
Scott Fibranz Memorial Baseball Scholarship Fund: Awards scholarships to baseball players to further their college education.
The Jim Snead Memorial Scholarship: Established by Anchorage Air Cargo to support Alaska students studying transportation.
Ray and Maxine Stephens Memorial Scholarship Fund: The fund seeks to further the education of qualified students from rural Alaska.
EIN: 920155067

56

Alaska Pulp Scholarship Foundation
1301 5th Ave., Ste. 3008
Seattle, WA 98101 (206) 682-6400
Contact: Franklin Roppel, Pres.

Foundation type: Public charity
Limitations: Scholarships to high school seniors in the Sitka and Wrangell, AK, areas to pursue a higher education.
Financial data: Year ended 12/31/2003. Assets, $1,447,364 (M); Expenditures, $52,500; Total giving, $52,500; Grants to individuals, 21 grants totaling $52,500 (high: $2,500, low: $2,500).
Fields of interest: Higher education.
Type of support: Undergraduate support.

Application information: Applications accepted.
   Initial approach: Letter.
EIN: 911481897

57

Ralph Buchanan Albaugh Trust

c/o Bank of America, N.A.
P.O. Box 831041
Dallas, TX   75283-1041
Application address: c/o Lindy Dehn, Methodist
Home, Waco, TX 76702, tel.: (254) 753-0181

Foundation type: Independent foundation
Limitations: Scholarships to residents of Methodist
Home, Waco, TX, to attend postsecondary
educational institutions.
Financial data: Year ended 12/31/2004.
Assets, $1,503,642 (M); Expenditures, $77,339;
Total giving, $63,000; Grants to individuals,
totaling $63,000.
Fields of interest: Protestant agencies & churches.
Type of support: Scholarships—to individuals.
Application information: Applications accepted.
   Deadline(s): None
   Additional information: Completion of formal
      application required, including financial and
      educational data.
EIN: 746041694

58

Albemarle Scholarship Foundation

c/o Mark S. Myrtue
451 Florida St.
Baton Rouge, LA   70801

Foundation type: Company-sponsored foundation
Limitations: Scholarships only to employees of the
Albemarle Corp. in AR, LA, SC, TX, and VA.
Financial data: Year ended 12/31/2004.
Assets, $3,359 (M); Expenditures, $28,772; Total
giving, $25,000; Grants to individuals, 10 grants
totaling $25,000 (high: $2,500, low: $2,500).
Type of support: Employee-related scholarships;
Undergraduate support.
Application information: Applications not
accepted.
   Additional information: Applications only to
      preselected individuals.
EIN: 311473843

59

Teya Albertani Foundation for Involvement, Inc.

1281 Tallevast Rd.
Sarasota, FL   34234
Contact: Judith Dewalt, Dir.

Foundation type: Independent foundation
Limitations: Scholarships to two graduating seniors
who have shown outstanding leadership qualities
and have excelled in their involvement in school and
community activities.
Publications: Application guidelines.
Financial data: Year ended 01/31/2004.
Assets, $72,885 (M); Expenditures, $8,764; Total
giving, $5,000; Grants to individuals, totaling
$5,000.
Type of support: Undergraduate support.
Application information: Applications accepted.
Application form required.
   Initial approach: Letter requesting application.
   Deadline(s): Mar. 15
   Applicants should submit the following:
      1) Transcripts

2) Essay
   Additional information: Application should also
      include three letters of recommendations;
      Financial need is not a criteria for selection.
      Two scholarships of $2,500 are awarded.
EIN: 592981976

60

Max H. Alberts Scholarship Trust

c/o Marshall & Ilsley Bank
P.O. Box 2980
Milwaukee, WI   53201-2980
Application address: c/o Johnson Creek High
School, 111 South St., Johnson Creek, WI 53038

Foundation type: Independent foundation
Limitations: Scholarships for undergraduate study
to graduates of Johnson Creek High School, WI.
Financial data: Year ended 04/30/2005.
Assets, $757,977 (M); Expenditures, $67,568;
Total giving, $55,970.
Type of support: Support to graduates or students
of specific schools; Undergraduate support.
Application information: Contact John Creek High
School for current application deadline/guidelines;
Initial approach by letter.
EIN: 396498404

61

Albion High School Alumni Foundation, Inc.

c/o Albion High School
P.O. Box 345
Albion, NY   14411-0345

Foundation type: Operating foundation
Limitations: Scholarships to students or alumni of
Albion High School, NY.
Financial data: Year ended 12/31/2003.
Assets, $230,992 (M); Expenditures, $13,001;
Total giving, $12,000; Grants to individuals, 10
grants totaling $12,000 (high: $1,500, low: $500).
Type of support: Support to graduates or students
of specific schools; Precollege support;
Undergraduate support.
Application information: Deadline mid-Apr.; Initial
approach by letter; Completion of formal application
required, including transcript, statement of goals,
and list of school and community activities.
EIN: 222925068

62

Albuquerque Community Foundation

3301 Menaul Blvd. N.E., Ste. 2
P.O. Box 36960
Albuquerque, NM   87176-6960
(505) 883-6240
Contact: For grants: Nancy Johnson, Prog. Dir.
FAX: (505) 883-3629;
E-mail: acf@albuquerquefoundation.org; Additional
E-mail: njohnson@albuquerquefoundation.org;
URL: http://www.albuquerquefoundation.org

Foundation type: Community foundation
Limitations: Scholarships and financial aid awards
to residents of the state of NM. Recipients may be
graduating high school seniors or continuing
education adults.
Publications: Annual report (including application
guidelines); Newsletter.
Financial data: Year ended 06/30/2005.
Assets, $39,283,237 (M); Expenditures,
$2,338,653; Total giving, $1,849,658; Grants to
individuals, 130 grants totaling $100,400.

Fields of interest: Continuing education;
Community development, volunteer services;
Science; Mathematics.
Type of support: Support to graduates or students
of specific schools; Undergraduate support.
Application information: See Web site for current
programs and application guidelines.
EIN: 850295444

63

Alcoa Foundation

Alcoa Corporate Ctr.
201 Isabella St.
Pittsburgh, PA   15212-5858   (412) 553-2348
E-mail: alcoafoundation@alcoa.com; URL: http://
www.alcoa.com/global/en/community/
foundation.asp

Foundation type: Company-sponsored foundation
Limitations: Scholarships only to children of current
or retired employees of Aluminum Company of
America.
Publications: Application guidelines; Annual report
(including application guidelines); Corporate giving
report; Informational brochure (including
application guidelines).
Financial data: Year ended 12/31/2004.
Assets, $512,821,331 (M); Expenditures,
$20,937,970; Total giving, $16,999,076; Grants
to individuals, totaling $428,500.
Type of support: Employee-related scholarships.
Application information: Application form required.
   Initial approach: Letter.
   Deadline(s): Oct. 31 of year prior to actual
      scholarship award year
Program description:
   Alcoa Sons and Daughters Scholarship:
Scholarships are $7,500 each and are not
renewable. Applicants must be high school seniors
with at least a "C+" grade average, or be in the
upper 50 percent of their classes.
EIN: 251128857

64

The Aleut Foundation

4000 Old Seward Hwy., Ste. 300
Anchorage, AK   99503   (907) 561-4300
Contact: Sharon Lind, Pres.
FAX: (907) 563-4328; E-mail: slind@aleutcorp.com

Foundation type: Company-sponsored foundation
Limitations: Scholarships to original enrollees of
the Aleut Corporation, AK, and their descendants;
and to Aleut WWII evacuees and their descendants.
Publications: Annual report.
Financial data: Year ended 03/31/2002.
Assets, $264,293 (M); Expenditures, $189,142;
Total giving, $118,952; Grants to individuals, 103
grants totaling $118,952 (high: $5,000, low:
$400).
Type of support: Scholarships—to individuals.
Application information: Application form required.
   Deadline(s): July 1
   Additional information: Completion of formal
      application required, including letter of
      acceptance, letter of recommendation, letter
      of intent, official transcripts, and class
      schedule for the upcoming fall semester/
      quarter.
EIN: 920124517

65
John Alexander Memorial Scholarship Fund
c/o Trustco Bank, N.A.
P.O. Box 380
Schenectady, NY 12305-0380
Application address: c/o C. Koury, 525 State St., Schenectady, NY 12305, tel.: (518) 374-1200

Foundation type: Independent foundation
Limitations: Scholarships to residents of Schenectady, NY, attending a law school in NY.
Financial data: Year ended 12/31/2004. Assets, $561,793 (M); Expenditures, $24,682; Total giving, $21,569; Grants to individuals, 25 grants totaling $21,569 (high: $1,171, low: $500).
Fields of interest: Law school/education.
Type of support: Graduate support.
Application information:
Deadline(s): Contact school
Additional information: Application by letter including home and legal address, and outlining financial need and professional objectives.
EIN: 146111436

66
Thomas L., Myrtle R., Arch, and Eva Alexander Scholarship Fund
c/o Trust Tax Dept.
P.O. Box 630858
Cincinnati, OH 45263
Application address: c/o Posey County School Districts, Posey County, IN 47620-0543, tel.: (812) 838-4333

Foundation type: Independent foundation
Limitations: Scholarships to students of Posey County, IN, high schools.
Financial data: Year ended 02/28/2005. Assets, $1,140,804 (M); Expenditures, $61,569; Total giving, $42,275; Grants to individuals, 10 grants totaling $42,275 (high: $2,000, low: $825).
Type of support: Scholarships—to individuals; Support to graduates or students of specific schools.
Application information:
Deadline(s): May 1
Additional information: Contact schools for current application guidelines.
EIN: 356333739

67
Olga V. Alexandria Trust
c/o U.S. Bank, N.A.
P.O. Box 3168
Portland, OR 97208
Contact: Carl Buck, Financial Aid Off., University of Utah
Application address: c/o University of Utah, Financial Aid & Scholarships, University & 200 S., Salt Lake City, UT 84112

Foundation type: Independent foundation
Limitations: Scholarships to young women studying business, law, medicine, or theater at the University of Utah.
Financial data: Year ended 05/31/2005. Assets, $647,655 (M); Expenditures, $40,104; Total giving, $32,037; Grants to individuals, totaling $32,037.
Fields of interest: Theater; Performing arts, education; Business school/education; Law school/education; Medical school/education; Women.

Type of support: Support to graduates or students of specific schools; Undergraduate support.
Application information: Applications accepted. Application form required.
Deadline(s): Mar. 1
Additional information: Apply at the University of Utah.
Program description:
Olga V. Alexandria Trust Scholarship Fund: The fund seeks to further the education of young women who have completed their high school education, or equivalent and who desire to study business, law, theater, ballet or medicine and who are orphans or whose parents are unable to provide the means for their education.
EIN: 942936907

68
Horatio Alger Association of Distinguished Americans, Inc.
99 Canal Ctr. Plz., Ste. 320
Alexandria, VA 22314 (703) 684-9444
Contact: Terrence Giroax, Exec. Dir.
FAX: (703) 684-9445; URL: http://www.horatioalger.org

Foundation type: Public charity
Limitations: Scholarships to high school seniors for higher education.
Financial data: Year ended 12/31/2003. Assets, $42,437,560 (M); Expenditures, $4,385,557; Total giving, $9,000; Grants to individuals, totaling $9,000.
Type of support: Undergraduate support.
Application information: Application form required.
Deadline(s): Oct. 15
Additional information: See Web site for current application guidelines.
Program descriptions:
National Scholarship Program: Annually awards scholarships of $10,000 to eligible students in all 50 states, DC and Puerto Rico. Recipients must be enrolled full-time as a high school senior progressing normally toward graduation, have plans to enter college no later than the fall after graduation, possess a strong commitment toward pursuing a bachelor's degree at an accredited institution (students may start their studies at a two-year institution and then transfer to a four-year institution), display critical financial need, have involvement in co-curricular and community activities, have a GPA of a minimum of 2.0, and be U.S. citizens (or be in the process of obtaining U.S. citizenship).
National Scholarships Finalist Program: Awards annual scholarships of $1,000 to 200 eligible students in states where the Association does not offer a state scholarship program.
State Scholarship Program: Annually awards scholarships of $2,500, $3,000 or $7,500 to worthy students in each of the following states: CA, DE, FL (Broward, Martin and St. Lucie counties), IA, LA, MN (Anoka, Carver, Dakota, Hennepin, Ramsey, Scott, and Washington counties), MO, NE and PA.
EIN: 131669975

69
All Saints' Scholarship Fund
1968 Woodside Ln.
Virginia Beach, VA 23454

Foundation type: Independent foundation
Limitations: Scholarships to students at Virginia Beach high schools, Cape Henry Academy, Norfolk

Academy and to children of All Saint's Episcopal Church, VA.
Financial data: Year ended 03/31/2005. Assets, $1,176,944 (M); Expenditures, $58,708; Total giving, $53,790; Grants to individuals, 41 grants totaling $51,790.
Fields of interest: Protestant agencies & churches.
Type of support: Support to graduates or students of specific schools; Graduate support; Undergraduate support; Postgraduate support; Doctoral support.
Application information: Application form required.
Initial approach: Letter outlining financial need.
Additional information: Contact foundation for current application deadline.
EIN: 541643750

70
All Stars Project, Inc.
543 W. 42nd St.
New York, NY 10036 (212) 941-9400
Contact: Gabrielle Kurlander, Pres.
Additional tel.: (800) 435-7453; URL: http://www.allstars.org

Foundation type: Public charity
Limitations: Scholarships to individuals residing in New York, NY, for undergraduate education.
Publications: Newsletter.
Financial data: Year ended 12/31/2004. Assets, $14,643,456 (M); Expenditures, $5,393,731; Total giving, $86,363; Grants to individuals, 13 grants totaling $45,780 (high: $5,446, low: $1,408).
Type of support: Undergraduate support.
Application information: Contact foundation for current application deadline/guidelines.
EIN: 133148295

71
Allegany County Area Foundation, Inc.
P.O. Box 494
Wellsville, NY 14895 (716) 593-5644

Foundation type: Community foundation
Limitations: Scholarships to residents of Allegany County, NY.
Publications: Annual report; Informational brochure.
Financial data: Year ended 12/31/2004. Assets, $4,461,767 (M); Expenditures, $383,103; Total giving, $270,382; Grants to individuals, totaling $249,697.
Type of support: Undergraduate support.
Application information: Applications accepted. Application form required.
Deadline(s): Contact foundation for current application deadline
EIN: 222506596

72
R. E. & Joan S. Allen Foundation, Inc.
c/o Wachovia Bank, N.A.
815 Colorado Ave.
Stuart, FL 34994
Application address: c/o Karen Allen, 2400 S. Federal Hwy., Ste. 200, Stuart, FL 34994

Foundation type: Independent foundation
Limitations: Scholarships to residents of Hardin County, OH, and employees of Imperial Bondware of Kenton, OH, and their children.
Financial data: Year ended 12/31/2004. Assets, $1,137,807 (M); Expenditures,

$150,176; Total giving, $136,800; Grants to individuals, 129 grants totaling $136,800 (high: $2,500, low: $500).

Type of support: Employee-related scholarships; Scholarships—to individuals.

Application information: Applications accepted throughout the year; Completion of formal application required, including biographical statement, academic and professional report, statement of educational plans, and letters of reference.

EIN: 650225533

73
Iona M. Allen Music Scholarship Fund
c/o Wachovia Bank, N.A.
P.O. Box 3099, NC6732
Charlotte, NC 28288-5709
Application address: Chris Spaugh, c/o Wachovia Charitable Svcs., P.O. Box 3099, Winston-Salem, NC 27150-6732, tel.: (336) 732-5991

Foundation type: Independent foundation
Limitations: Scholarships to high school seniors who demonstrate musical aptitude and are residents of the following western NC counties: Cherokee, Clay, Graham, Macon, Swain, Haywood, Transylvania, Henderson, Polk, Jackson, Buncombe, and Madison.
Financial data: Year ended 12/31/2004. Assets, $1,084,534 (M); Expenditures, $82,818; Total giving, $4,494; Grants to individuals, totaling $4,494.
Fields of interest: Performing arts, education.
Type of support: Undergraduate support.
Application information: Application form required.
  Initial approach: Letter.
  Deadline(s): Contact fund for current application deadline
  Additional information: Interview required.
EIN: 586189987

74
Walter H. Allen Scholarship Fund Trust
c/o National City Bank
P.O. Box 94651
Cleveland, OH 44101-4651
Application address: S. Patrick Cassady, Principal, c/o Dunlap High School, 5220 W. Legion Hall Rd., Dunlap, IL 61525, tel.: (309) 243-7751

Foundation type: Independent foundation
Limitations: Scholarships to graduates of Dunlap High School, IL.
Financial data: Year ended 04/30/2005. Assets, $6,851 (M); Expenditures, $9,126; Total giving, $8,000; Grants to individuals, 4 grants totaling $8,000.
Type of support: Support to graduates or students of specific schools; Undergraduate support.
Application information:
  Initial approach: Letter or telephone.
  Deadline(s): May 1
  Additional information: Contact high school for current application guidelines.
EIN: 376224404

75
William M. and Louise O. Allen Scholarship Fund
c/o National City Bank of Indiana
P.O. Box 94651
Cleveland, OH 44101-4651
Contact: Joseph Gaafar, Trust Off., National City Bank of Indiana
Application address: P.O. Box 5031, Indianapolis, IN 46201, tel.: (317) 267-7085

Foundation type: Independent foundation
Limitations: Scholarships to high school graduates in Montgomery County, IN, who plan to attend IN colleges and universities.
Financial data: Year ended 12/31/2003. Assets, $145,538 (M); Expenditures, $11,665; Total giving, $9,000; Grants to individuals, totaling $9,000.
Type of support: Undergraduate support.
Application information: Application form required.
  Deadline(s): May 31
  Additional information: Completion of formal application required, including a letter outlining financial need and future plans.
EIN: 356033947

76
Alliance Francaise of Tucson
3801 Calle Cortez
Tucson, AZ 85716 (520) 327-3279
Contact: Antoinette Wagner, Pres.

Foundation type: Independent foundation
Limitations: Scholarships, book awards, and medals to university and high school students in the Tucson, AZ, area who are enrolled in French classes.
Financial data: Year ended 12/31/2004. Assets, $10,564 (M); Expenditures, $7,164; Total giving, $2,585; Grants to individuals, 2 grants totaling $2,300.
Fields of interest: Language (foreign); France.
Type of support: Precollege support; Undergraduate support.
Application information: Application form required.
  Initial approach: Letter.
  Deadline(s): Mar. 10
  Additional information: Contact French teacher for application information; Interviews required.
EIN: 237295606

77
Allied Educational Foundation
467 Sylvan Ave.
Englewood Cliffs, NJ 07632 (201) 569-8180
Contact: Admin.

Foundation type: Independent foundation
Limitations: Scholarships to members of Union Local 815 and the Allied Trades Council in NY and NJ, to attend school full-time and maintain at least a "B+" average.
Financial data: Year ended 12/31/2004. Assets, $8,004,677 (M); Expenditures, $661,322; Total giving, $146,754; Grants to individuals, 51 grants totaling $145,754 (high: $7,500, low: $1,500).
Type of support: Scholarships—to individuals.
Application information:
  Initial approach: Letter in the form of an autobiography.
  Deadline(s): Apr. 15
  Additional information: Letter should also include include a 3" x 4" photograph of self,

transcripts, FFS, and letters of recommendation from faculty advisors, professors, or teachers.
EIN: 136202432

78
Allied Exeter Scholarship Foundation, Inc.
1601 E. Olympic Blvd., No. 105
Los Angeles, CA 90021-1936
Application address: c/o Jeanne Wilkinson, P.O. Box 217, Exeter, CA 93221

Foundation type: Independent foundation
Limitations: Scholarships to graduates of Exeter Union High School, CA.
Financial data: Year ended 07/31/2004. Assets, $80 (M); Expenditures, $15,091; Total giving, $14,969; Grants to individuals, 9 grants totaling $14,969 (high: $4,000, low: $113).
Type of support: Support to graduates or students of specific schools; Undergraduate support.
Application information: Deadline May 1; Completion of formal application required.
EIN: 942863726

79
Allman Medical Scholarship Foundation
2 Ocean Way, Ste. 1000
Atlantic City, NJ 08401 (609) 345-7571
FAX: (609) 345-6079; Application address: c/o Sharon J. Becker, Miss America Organization, P.O. Box 119, Atlantic City, NJ 08404; URL: http://www.missamerica.org/scholarships/allmanmedical.asp

Foundation type: Operating foundation
Limitations: Scholarships to women pursuing careers in medicine who have competed in a Miss America competition at the local, state, or national level.
Publications: Application guidelines.
Financial data: Year ended 07/31/2004. Assets, $151,250 (M); Expenditures, $7,265; Total giving, $7,200; Grants to individuals, totaling $7,000.
Fields of interest: Medical school/education; Women.
Type of support: Scholarships—to individuals.
Application information: Applications accepted. Application form required.
  Initial approach: Letter.
  Deadline(s): June 30
  Additional information: Application should include MCAT scores, GPA, transcripts, letter of medical school acceptance, 500-word essay, and financial aid information.
Program description:
  Scholarship Program: The scholarship is administered by the Miss America Pageant. Selections are based upon the applicant's GPA, class rank, MCAT scores, extracurricular activities, and financial need.
EIN: 237414385

80
Ebba Alm Educational Fund
c/o SunTrust Bank
825 Broadway
Dunedin, FL 34698-5708 (727) 823-4181
Contact: Jack McLean, Sr. Trust Off., SunTrust Bank

Foundation type: Independent foundation
Limitations: Scholarships to financially needy, worthy male students who are residents of Pinellas

County, FL, to attend Eckerd College and St. Petersburg Junior College, both in FL.
Financial data: Year ended 05/31/2005. Assets, $262,769 (M); Expenditures, $17,610; Total giving, $12,750; Grants to individuals, totaling $12,750.
Fields of interest: Men.
Type of support: Support to graduates or students of specific schools; Undergraduate support.
Application information: Applications accepted.
  Deadline(s): None
  Additional information: Applications by letter, including brief resume of academic qualifications; Recipients must be in good standing in their communities.
EIN: 510225186

81
Almanor Scholarship Fund
c/o Collins Pine Co.
P.O. Box 796
Chester, CA 96020
Contact: Terry S. Collins, Tr.

Foundation type: Independent foundation
Limitations: Scholarships only to graduates of Chester High School, CA.
Financial data: Year ended 12/31/2004. Assets, $1,680,116 (M); Expenditures, $129,343; Total giving, $110,500; Grants to individuals, 74 grants totaling $110,500 (high: $2,700, low: $600).
Type of support: Support to graduates or students of specific schools; Undergraduate support.
Application information: Application form required.
  Deadline(s): Aug. 1
Program description:
  Scholarship Program: Scholarships are awarded for undergraduate and graduate study to individuals who will be full-time students and single at the time of registration, and have maintained at least a 3.25 GPA in high school and at least a 3.0 GPA in college. Recipients must have exhibited leadership potential in school, engaged in community activities, and have employment experience.
EIN: 946066722

82
Alpha Chi Omega Foundation, Inc.
5939 Castle Creek Pkwy. N. Dr.
Indianapolis, IN 46250-4343 (317) 579-5050
Contact: Suzette E. Bewley Mathis, Exec. Dir.
URL: http://www.alphachiomega.org

Foundation type: Public charity
Limitations: Scholarships and grants to collegiate and alumnae members of Alpha Chi Omega.
Publications: Application guidelines; Annual report; Informational brochure; Newsletter.
Financial data: Year ended 07/31/2004. Assets, $7,971,302 (M); Expenditures, $1,207,598; Total giving, $488,350; Grants to individuals, 88 grants totaling $80,940 (high: $2,000, low: $295).
Fields of interest: Students, sororities/fraternities.
Type of support: Fellowships; Scholarships—to individuals; Student loans—to individuals.
Application information: Application form required.
  Deadline(s): Mar. 15
EIN: 310949882

83
Alpha Delta Kappa Foundation
1615 W. 92nd St.
Kansas City, MO 64114 (816) 363-5525
Contact: Janice M. Estell, Exec. Admin.
FAX: (816) 363-4010;
E-mail: headquarters@alphadeltakappa.org;
Additional tel.: (800) 363-5525; URL: http://www.alphadeltakappa.org

Foundation type: Public charity
Limitations: Scholarships to female education students, who are non-US citizens living outside of the U.S., for study at American colleges and universities.
Financial data: Year ended 05/31/2003. Assets, $1,520,429 (M); Expenditures, $228,293; Total giving, $167,361; Grants to individuals, totaling $72,000 (high: $10,000).
Fields of interest: Teacher school/education; Leadership development; Women.
Type of support: Foreign applicants; Undergraduate support.
Application information: Application form required.
  Initial approach: Letter, telephone, fax or E-mail.
  Deadline(s): Jan. 1
  Additional information: See Web site for additional information.
Program description:
  International Teacher Education Program: Scholarships of $10,000 each to foreign education students to study at an American institution of higher learning. Scholarships are renewable for an additional year. Recipients must have completed at least one year of college, carry sufficient credit hours to qualify as a full-time student and plan to enter the teaching profession or be engaged in the same. In addition recipients must:
  · be single women with no dependents and must maintain such status throughout the scholarship period
  · be at least 20 years of age and no more than 35 at the time of the application deadline of year study is to begin
  · be a non-U.S. citizen living outside of the U.S. and retain such status throughout the duration of the scholarship
  · rank in the top 25 percent of their class
  · have well-rounded personalities and display strong leadership qualities
  · have a genuine interest in the promotion of a better world understanding through education
  · have the ability and willingness to adapt readily to new situations
EIN: 431280111

84
Alpha Delta Pi Foundation, Inc.
1386 Ponce De Leon Ave., N.E.
Atlanta, GA 30306-4604 (404) 378-3164
Contact: Lisa Owen Newham, Exec. Dir.
FAX: (404) 378-5935;
E-mail: inewham@alphadeltapi.com; URL: http://www.alphadeltapi.org

Foundation type: Public charity
Limitations: Scholarships to members and alumni of the Alpha Delta Pi Sorority.
Publications: Application guidelines; Annual report; Financial statement; Newsletter.
Financial data: Year ended 07/31/2004. Assets, $2,727,081 (L); Expenditures, $570,002; Total giving, $263,350; Grants to individuals, totaling $69,400.
Fields of interest: Students, sororities/fraternities; Women.

Type of support: Scholarships—to individuals.
Application information: Application form required.
  Initial approach: Telephone, FAX or e-mail.
  Deadline(s): Apr. 1
  Applicants should submit the following:
    1) Letter(s) of recommendation
    2) Transcripts
EIN: 581507941

85
Alpha Epsilon Pi Foundation, Inc.
8815 Wesleyan Rd.
Indianapolis, IN 46268-1171 (317) 876-1913
Contact: Andy Barans, Exec. Dir.
FAX: (317) 876-1057; E-mail: office@aepi.org;
URL: http://www.aepi.org/foundation/

Foundation type: Public charity
Limitations: Educational grants and loans to members of Alpha Epsilon Pi and their families in the U.S. and Canada.
Publications: Informational brochure.
Financial data: Year ended 05/31/2004. Assets, $2,606,333 (M); Expenditures, $386,985; Total giving, $64,621; Grants to individuals, 36 grants totaling $15,458 (high: $1,000, low: $26).
Fields of interest: Students, sororities/fraternities.
Type of support: Fellowships; Internship funds; Scholarships—to individuals; Student loans—to individuals.
Application information: Contact foundation for current application deadline/guidelines.
EIN: 136141078

86
Alpha Omicron Pi Foundation
(formerly Alpha Omicron Pi Philanthropic Foundation)
P.O. Box 395
Brentwood, TN 37024-0395 (615) 370-0920
Contact: Bobby Stanton, Exec. Dir.
E-mail: foundation@alphaomicronpi.org;
URL: http://www.aoiifoundation.org

Foundation type: Public charity
Limitations: Scholarships to collegiate and alumnae members of Alpha Omicron Pi.
Publications: Biennial report; Grants list; Informational brochure.
Financial data: Year ended 06/30/2005. Assets, $3,267,819 (M); Expenditures, $628,847; Total giving, $344,725; Grants to individuals, 40 grants totaling $77,500.
Fields of interest: Students, sororities/fraternities.
Type of support: Scholarships—to individuals.
Application information: Application form required.
  Deadline(s): Mar. 1
  Additional information: Contact foundation for current application guidelines.
Program description:
  Diamond Jubilee Scholarships: Scholarships are awarded to collegiate and alumnae members who exhibit academic excellence as well as dedication to serving the community and Alpha Omicron Pi. Yearly awards are given in installments based on recipient's school semester schedules.
EIN: 581343315

87

Alpha Tau Omega Foundation, Inc.

32 E. Washington St., Ste. 1350
Indianapolis, IN   46204   (317) 472-0935
Contact: Cheri Dillon
FAX: (317) 472-0945;
E-mail: foundation@atofoundation.org;
URL: http://www.ato.org/foundation.shtml

Foundation type: Public charity
Limitations: Graduate and undergraduate
scholarships to members of Alpha Tau Omega
Fraternity.
Publications: Annual report; Grants list;
Informational brochure; Newsletter; Occasional
report.
Financial data: Year ended 12/31/2003.
Assets, $8,420,732 (M); Expenditures,
$908,984; Total giving, $422,986; Grants to
individuals, 150 grants totaling $358,598.
Fields of interest: Journalism/publishing; Law
school/education; Students, sororities/
fraternities; Public affairs.
Type of support: Fellowships; Internship funds;
Support to graduates or students of specific
schools; Graduate support; Undergraduate
support.
Application information: Application form available
on the grantmaker's Web site.
  Deadline(s): Contact foundation for current
    application deadline
  Applicants should submit the following:
    1) Transcripts
  Additional information: Completion of formal
    application required, including three letters of
    recommendation; Applicant must be an
    initiated member of Alpha Tau Omega in good
    standing, and have a GPA of 3.5 on a 4.0
    scale; See Web site for further application
    information.
Program descriptions:
National Scholarships:
· Graduate Scholarship
· Lawrence A. Long Memorial Law
  Scholarship
· J. Milton Richardson Theological Fellowship
· J.D. Sinnock Memorial Scholarship
· Undergraduate Scholarship
· William D. Krahling Excellence in
  Journalism
· Richard A. Portis Public Affairs Internship
· LeaderShape Scholarship.
Regional Scholarships:
· Lee G. Barthold Memorial Scholarship
· Epsilon Nu
· Frederick C. Philbrick Memorial Scholarship
· Robert J. Simmonds (2nd Century Fund)
· Patrick Doherty Memorial Scholarship
· Brian Keech Memorial Scholarship
· Kenneth P. Murrah Educational Endowment
· William Lloyd Muir II and John Thomas Muir
  Memorial Award
· L. Allyn Laybourn Scholastic Excellence
  Award
· Kenneth P. Murrah Scholarship
· Giles, Jones & Woods
· G.A. Ross Scholarship Award.
EIN: 237154214

88

Alpha Zeta Delta of Chi Psi Educational Foundation

1010 Revere Ct.
Naperville, IL   60540
Application address: c/o: Stan Thoren, 723
Sheridan Rd., Wilmette, IL 60091, tel.: (847)
256-3984

Foundation type: Independent foundation
Limitations: Undergraduate scholarships and
graduate fellowships to University of Illinois
students.
Financial data: Year ended 12/31/2004.
Assets, $718,615 (M); Expenditures, $58,445;
Total giving, $44,956; Grants to individuals,
totaling $32,931.
Fields of interest: Students, sororities/fraternities.
Type of support: Support to graduates or students
of specific schools; Graduate support;
Undergraduate support.
Application information: Application form required.
  Initial approach: Letter or telephone.
  Deadline(s): May 1 and Oct. 1
EIN: 363947662

89

W. R. Alsobrook Scholarship Trust

c/o Regions Bank
P.O. Box 1471
Little Rock, AR   72203-1471
Application address: c/o Regions Bank, Attn.: Trust
Off., 400 W. Capitol, Little Rock, AR 72201,
tel.: (501) 371-6723

Foundation type: Independent foundation
Limitations: Scholarships to graduating high school
seniors residing in Saline County, AR.
Financial data: Year ended 12/31/2004.
Assets, $141,261 (M); Expenditures, $9,686;
Total giving, $7,000; Grants to individuals, totaling
$7,000.
Type of support: Scholarships—to individuals;
Support to graduates or students of specific
schools.
Application information: Application form required.
  Deadline(s): Contact trust for current application
    deadline
EIN: 710517178

90

Miriam E. Alsobrooks Educational Fund

c/o Wachovia Bank, N.A.
100 N. Main St., 13th Fl.
Winston-Salem, NC   27150
Application address: c/o Dir. of Guidance, Marlboro
County High School, 951 Fayetteville Ave. EXT.,
Bennettsville, SC 29512

Foundation type: Independent foundation
Limitations: Scholarships to graduates of Marlboro
County high schools, SC.
Financial data: Year ended 12/31/2004.
Assets, $199,149 (M); Expenditures, $11,739;
Total giving, $7,750.
Type of support: Support to graduates or students
of specific schools; Undergraduate support.
Application information: Application form required.
  Deadline(s): Mar. 25
EIN: 576037000

91

Alumnae Association of the College of St. Teresa Scholarship Fund

(also known as Teresan Scholarship Fund)
357 Gould St.
Winona, MN   55987   (507) 454-2930
Contact: Colleen Kocer Peplinski, Exec. Dir.

Foundation type: Public charity
Limitations: Scholarships to residents of Winona,
MN, who are Catholic school undergraduates in the
upper 25% of their class.
Financial data: Year ended 12/31/2003.
Assets, $941,928 (M); Expenditures, $26,105;
Total giving, $13,800; Grants to individuals, 28
grants totaling $13,800 (high: $1,000, low: $300).
Type of support: Undergraduate support.
Application information:
  Initial approach: Letter.
  Additional information: Contact foundation for
    current application deadlines.
EIN: 411688308

92

Alumni Foundation Fund of the Illinois Chapter of Alpha Delta Phi

723 Forest Ave.
Glen Ellyn, IL   60137
Contact: Thomas Vogelsinger, Tr.

Foundation type: Independent foundation
Limitations: Awards restricted to undergraduate
students attending the University of Illinois at
Urbana-Champaign, IL, who are needy and
deserving.
Financial data: Year ended 06/30/2004.
Assets, $211,381 (M); Expenditures, $2,689;
Total giving, $2,600; Grants to individuals, totaling
$2,000; Loans to individuals, totaling $345.
Fields of interest: Men.
Type of support: Support to graduates or students
of specific schools; Awards/prizes; Undergraduate
support.
Application information: Applications accepted.
  Deadline(s): None
  Additional information: Applications by letter,
    including approval of the Dean of Men,
    University of Illinois at Urbana-Champaign.
EIN: 366047021

93

Marshall H. and Nellie Alworth Memorial Fund

402 Alworth Bldg.
306 W. Superior St., Ste. 402
Duluth, MN   55802   (218) 722-9366
Contact: Richard H. Carlson, Exec. Dir.
FAX: (218) 720-6996

Foundation type: Independent foundation
Limitations: Scholarships only to financially needy
graduates of high schools located in 15
northeastern MN counties who are majoring in one
of the basic sciences or medicine at accredited
colleges and universities. See program description
for further limitations.
Publications: Application guidelines; Program
policy statement.
Financial data: Year ended 12/31/2004.
Assets, $8,002,164 (M); Expenditures,
$2,474,615; Total giving, $2,159,500; Grants to
individuals, 639 grants totaling $2,159,500 (high:
$4,300, low: $2,150).
Fields of interest: Architecture; Medical school/
education; Nursing school/education;

Neuroscience; Agriculture; Physical/earth sciences; Space/aviation; Chemistry; Mathematics; Computer science; Biological sciences.
Type of support: Graduate support; Undergraduate support.
Application information: Application form required.
  Initial approach: Letter.
  Deadline(s): Mar. 1
  Additional information: Application forms available from high school counselors in northern MN.
Program description:
  Scholarship Program: Scholarships to persons who have graduated from a high school in one of the northeastern MN counties of Aitken, Beltrami, Carlton, Cass, Clearwater, Cook, Crow Wing, Hubbard, Itasca, Kanabec, Koochiching, Lake, Lake of the Woods, Pine, and St. Louis. Applicants must have a desire to specialize as a full-time student in one of the following fields of study: aeronautics, agriculture, animal science, architecture, biochemistry, biology (most phases), botany, chemistry (most phases), clinical laboratory science, computer science, dentistry, dietetics, engineering (most phases), environmental science, genetics, geology, mathematics, medicine, meteorology, neuroscience, nursing (bachelors degree programs only), occupational therapy, pharmacy, physical therapy, physics (most phases), pre-dentistry, pre-engineering, pre-medicine, pre-occupational therapy, pre-pharmacy, pre-physical therapy, pre-veterinary medicine, soil science, statistics, teaching basic sciences, teaching classical mathematics, veterinary medicine, wildlife management, and zoology. All pre-fields require a science major. Specifically excluded fields of study are accounting, actuarial science, business math, chiropractic, horticulture, information systems management, kinesiology, management science, podiatry, and sports medicine. Applicants must have an exemplary scholastic record, demonstrate high personal qualities, and show evidence of financial need. Scholarships are renewable up to five years for undergraduate and up to eight years for graduate and medical students, provided recipient maintains full-time status and a GPA of at least 2.6 for first-year college students, or at least 2.85 for all other students.
EIN: 410797340

94
Edmond Amateis Irrevocable Trust Foundation
(formerly Edmond Amateis Foundation)
c/o SunTrust Bank
P.O. Box 1908
Orlando, FL   32802-1908
Application address: c/o Jeffery Bay, 900 N. 14th St., Leesburg, FL, 34748

Foundation type: Independent foundation
Limitations: Scholarships to graduates of Lake County high schools and students currently attending Lake/Sumter Community College, FL.
Financial data: Year ended 03/31/2005. Assets, $779,131 (M); Expenditures, $52,355; Total giving, $50,281; Grants to individuals, 28 grants totaling $12,021 (high: $750, low: $750).
Type of support: Support to graduates or students of specific schools; Undergraduate support.
Application information: Application form required.
  Deadline(s): June 30

Program description:
  Scholarship Program: Recipients must maintain a 2.5 GPA and demonstrate financial need.
EIN: 596974154

95
Elizabeth Raymond Ambler Trust
P.O. Box 7266
Wilton, CT   06897-7266

Foundation type: Independent foundation
Limitations: Scholarships of $2,500 to $4,000 to students who are residents of the town of Wilton, CT, and surrounding areas.
Financial data: Year ended 12/31/2004. Assets, $9,555,570 (M); Expenditures, $369,417; Total giving, $260,450; Grants to individuals, 49 grants totaling $134,450 (high: $6,000, low: $1,000).
Type of support: Undergraduate support.
Application information: Application form required.
  Deadline(s): None
  Additional information: .
EIN: 066473263

96
Clifford L. & Daisie B. Amburn Memorial Scholarship Fund
c/o Merchants Trust Co.
200 E. Jackson St.
Muncie, IN   47305
Contact: Laura Moorman, Trust Off.

Foundation type: Independent foundation
Limitations: Scholarships to graduating high school seniors who are residents of Delaware County, IN. Preference is given to elementary education majors.
Financial data: Year ended 12/31/2004. Assets, $490,414 (M); Expenditures, $34,130; Total giving, $29,000; Grants to individuals, 12 grants totaling $29,000 (high: $2,500, low: $1,500).
Fields of interest: Elementary school/education; Teacher school/education.
Type of support: Scholarships—to individuals; Undergraduate support.
Application information: Application form required.
  Deadline(s): Mar. 31
  Additional information: Applicants should submit forms to their respective schools; Applications are then forwarded to Terri Robertson.
EIN: 356051256

97
Alan Ameche Memorial Foundation
P.O. Box 978
Narberth, PA   19072   (610) 664-8477

Foundation type: Public charity
Limitations: Grants to motivated, economically disadvantaged youth in fifth through twelfth grade to help them achieve their educational goals at private, vocational and parochial schools. Giving primarily in Delaware Valley, PA.
Publications: Program policy statement.
Financial data: Year ended 12/31/2004. Assets, $75,013 (M); Expenditures, $41,922; Total giving, $28,000; Grants to individuals, 19 grants totaling $28,000 (high: $1,250, low: $500).
Fields of interest: Youth development; Economically disadvantaged.
Type of support: Technical education support; Precollege support.

Application information: Application form required.
  Initial approach: Telephone.
  Deadline(s): Contact foundation for current application deadline
EIN: 232550681

98
American Academy of Nurse Practitioners Foundation
P.O. Box 10729
Glendale, AZ   85318-0729   (623) 376-9467
Contact: Judith Dempster, Exec. Dir.
FAX: (623) 376-0369;
E-mail: foundation@aanp.org; URL: http://www.aanpfoundation.org

Foundation type: Public charity
Limitations: Scholarships for individuals who are interested in pursuing a career as a nurse practitioner.
Financial data: Year ended 12/31/2003. Assets, $212,359 (M); Expenditures, $152,844; Total giving, $48,900; Grants to individuals, 29 grants totaling $45,950 (high: $6,000, low: $1,000).
Fields of interest: Nursing school/education.
Type of support: Scholarships—to individuals.
Application information: Applications accepted. Application form required.
  Initial approach: Telephone, E-mail, or Fax.
  Deadline(s): Apr. for 1st funding cycle; Oct. for 2nd funding cycle
  Additional information: Contact foundation to request application material; a $10 non refundable application/administration fee is due with each scholarship applied for.
Program description:
  Scholarships: Awards the following 16 scholarships:
  · NP Doctoral Education Scholarship
  · Post-MS NP Student Scholarship
  · Daiichi Pharmaceutical Corporation NP Student Scholarship
  · dela Cruz-Millman Filipino-American NP Student Scholarship
  · Fitzgerald Health Education Association NP Student Scholarship
  · Julia Smith Memorial NP Student Scholarship
  · Novo Nordisk Pharmaceuticals NP Student Scholarship
  · O'Hara-Johnson International Student Scholarship
  · Organon Pharmaceutical NP Student Scholarship
  · sanofi-aventis Group NP Student Scholarship
EIN: 742861018

99
American Arabic Educational Foundation
5742 Wish Ave.
Encino, CA   91316

Foundation type: Independent foundation
Limitations: Scholarships for higher education to CA residents of Arab American heritage with ancestors from Jordan, Libya, Palestine, or Syria.
Financial data: Year ended 12/31/2004. Assets, $550,719 (M); Expenditures, $38,423; Total giving, $31,500; Grants to individuals, totaling $31,500.
Fields of interest: Libya; Israel; Jordan; Syria; West Bank/Gaza.
Type of support: Scholarships—to individuals.

Application information: Applications not accepted.
EIN: 237423734

100
The American Architectural Foundation, Inc.
1799 New York Ave., N.W.
Washington, DC 20006-5209 (202) 626-7318
Contact: LaShawn Nichols, Admin. Asst.
FAX: (202) 626-7420;
E-mail: info@archfoundation.org; URL: http://www.archfoundation.org

Foundation type: Public charity
Limitations: Scholarships by nomination only to high school seniors and college freshmen who plan to study architecture in a program accredited by the National Architectural Accrediting Board (NAAB).
Publications: Application guidelines; Informational brochure (including application guidelines); Newsletter.
Financial data: Year ended 12/31/2004. Assets, $7,807,125 (M); Expenditures, $2,221,871; Total giving, $279,754; Grants to individuals, totaling $83,000.
Fields of interest: Architecture.
Type of support: Awards/grants by nomination only; Undergraduate support.
Application information: Application form required.
  Initial approach: Telephone.
  Deadline(s): Early Dec. for nomination form, mid-Jan. for supporting materials
  Applicants should submit the following:
   1) Letter(s) of recommendation
   2) Essay
  Additional information: Applicant should also include a statement of disadvantaged circumstances, and drawing; See Web site for further information.
Program description:
  AIA/AAF Minority/Disadvantaged Scholarship: Twenty awards per year are made and may be renewed for two additional years. Scholarship amounts range from $500 to $2,600, and are determined by evaluation of financial need information provided by the student and school.
EIN: 520847434

101
American Association of Airport Executives Foundation
601 Madison St., Ste. 400
Alexandria, VA 22314 (703) 824-0500
FAX: (703) 820-1395; URL: http://www.aaae.org/members/275_AAAE_Foundation

Foundation type: Public charity
Limitations: Scholarships to full-time undergraduate or graduate students attending accredited colleges or universities.
Financial data: Year ended 12/31/2004. Assets, $1,329,790 (M); Expenditures, $151,776; Total giving, $138,420; Grants to individuals, 120 grants totaling $138,420 (high: $2,000, low: $900).
Fields of interest: Adult/continuing education; Space/aviation.
Type of support: Graduate support; Undergraduate support.
Application information: Application form required.
  Deadline(s): May 15 for AAAE Foundation Scholarship

Program descriptions:
  AAAE Foundation Scholarship: Grants $1,000 each year to a number of students with a junior class standing or higher, who are enrolled in an aviation program and have a GPA of 3.0 or higher. Eligibility is unrelated to membership in AAAE. Only one student from each school may participate. Criteria used are academic records, financial need, participation in school and community activities, work experience, and a personal statement. Applicants should contact their scholarship or financial aid office for an application.
  AAE Scholarship: Offered exclusively to accredited airport executive (AAE) members of AAAE, their spouses and/or children. Accredited members are sent information on the program annually in the early spring and awards are made in July.
EIN: 516018128

102
American Association of Law Libraries
53 W. Jackson Blvd., Ste. 940
Chicago, IL 60604 (312) 939-4764
Contact: Susan E. Fox, Exec. Dir.
E-mail for scholarships: scholarships@aall.org
FAX: (312) 431-1097; E-mail: sfox@aall.org;
URL: http://www.aallnet.org

Foundation type: Public charity
Limitations: Scholarships to students majoring in library science.
Publications: Application guidelines; Occasional report.
Financial data: Year ended 09/30/2004. Assets, $4,067,451 (M); Expenditures, $2,945,803; Total giving, $31,300; Grants to individuals, 28 grants totaling $31,300 (high: $3,500, low: $195).
Fields of interest: Law school/education; Minorities.
Type of support: Scholarships—to individuals; Graduate support.
Application information: Applications accepted. Application form required.
  Initial approach: Telephone or letter.
  Deadline(s): Apr. 1
  Applicants should submit the following:
   1) Resume
   2) SASE
   3) Letter(s) of recommendation
  Additional information: Application must also include a stamped, self-addressed postcard, and evidence of financial need.
Program descriptions:
  AALL & Thomson West - George A. Strait Minority Scholarship: A $3,000 scholarship is awarded to college graduates with law library experience who are members of a minority group as defined by current U.S. Government guidelines and are degree candidates in accredited library or law schools and who intend to have a career in law librarianship.
  James F. Connolly LexisNexis Academic & Library Solutions Scholarship: Awards a $3,000 scholarship to a library school graduate with meaningful law library experience, who is pursuing a degree in an accredited law school with the intention of having a career in law librarianship and has no more than 36 semester credit hours remaining before qualifying for the degree.
  Institute for Court Management Scholarship: This award of $1,700 covers tuition and expenses for attendance at an ICM seminar or conference. Recipients must be a current member of AALL and also a current member of the State, Court and County Law Libraries Special Interest Section. Two Scholarships are awarded annually.

  AALL Educational Scholarships: Educational scholarships are available to assist individuals studying to become law librarians with their educational expenses.
EIN: 362536424

103
American Association of University Women Honolulu Branch Educational Fund
1802 Keeaumoku St.
Honolulu, HI 96822

Foundation type: Operating foundation
Limitations: Fellowships to females who have been residents of HI for at least three years. Awards also provided to Asian and Pacific women professionals for specific two- to six-month projects or graduate study in HI, on topics related to Pacific Rim countries (not the U.S.) or the Pacific Islands.
Financial data: Year ended 06/30/2003. Assets, $821,958 (M); Expenditures, $34,697; Total giving, $24,000; Grants to individuals, 12 grants totaling $24,000 (high: $4,000, low: $1,000).
Fields of interest: International exchange, students; Asians/Pacific Islanders; Women.
Type of support: Support to graduates or students of specific schools; Foreign applicants; Undergraduate support; Travel grants.
Application information: Applications accepted. Application form required.
  Initial approach: letter, received from Oct. 1 to Jan. 15, requesting application.
  Deadline(s): Mar. 1
Program descriptions:
  Ruth E. Black Scholarship Fund: Scholarships to HI residents for undergraduate study at an accredited institution in HI.
  The Pacific Fellowship Fund: Scholarships for graduate study to Asian and Pacific women, for use only at the University of Hawaii at Manoa. After study is completed, grantees must return "to help their own countries".
  Pacific Fellowships: Grants to non-American women from Asia and the Pacific who are already engaged in a profession, so that they may enrich their learning with a three- to four-month sabbatical in HI. Applicants must be employed at an institution that contributed to the development of the country; be able to present a proposal for special study; and contribute, if possible, to travel expenses. Selection will be based on:
   · academic record after completion of undergraduate college/university study
   · proof of acceptance at the graduate level
   · career plans
   · personal involvement in school and community activities
   · financial need
   · residence in HI for at least three years.
EIN: 990117668

104
American Bar Association Fund for Justice & Education
321 N. Clark St.
Chicago, IL 60611 (312) 988-5404
Contact: Robert A. Stein, Exec. Dir.
FAX: (312) 988-6392; E-mail: fje@staff.abanet.org;
URL: http://www.abanet.org/fje

Foundation type: Public charity
Limitations: Scholarships to minority students for attendance at law school.

Financial data: Year ended 08/31/2003. Assets, $18,553,254 (M); Expenditures, $50,750,855; Total giving, $5,606,545; Grants to individuals, 547 grants totaling $688,042 (high: $10,000, low: $32).
Fields of interest: Law school/education; Minorities.
Type of support: Graduate support.
Application information: Application form required.
Deadline(s): Feb. 28
Additional information: Completion of formal application required, including personal statement; See Web site for further information.
Program description:
Legal Opportunity Scholarship Fund: Scholarships of $5,000 annually awarded to students of racial and ethnic minority to attend an ABA-accredited law school. Awards made to entering first-year students may be renewable for two additional years for a total of $15,000 in financial assistance during student's time in law school. Recipients are chosen based on: whether they are a member of a racial and/or ethnic minority that has been underrepresented in the legal profession; financial need; personal, family and educational background; and participation in community service activities. To be eligible, applicant must: be an entering first-year law student; have a minimum 2.5 GPA (on a 4.0 scale) at his/her undergraduate institution; and be a citizen or permanent resident of the U.S.
EIN: 366110299

105
American Council of the Blind, Inc.
1155 15th St., N.W., Ste. 1004
Washington, DC 20005 (202) 467-5081
Contact: Melanie Brunson, Acting Exec. Dir.
FAX: (202) 467-5085; E-mail: info@acb.org;
Additional tel.: (800) 424-8666; URL: http://www.acb.org

Foundation type: Public charity
Limitations: Undergraduate and graduate scholarships to provide financial assistance to outstanding blind and visually impaired students.
Publications: Annual report; Financial statement; Informational brochure; Newsletter.
Financial data: Year ended 12/31/2003. Assets, $1,363,567 (M); Expenditures, $1,754,782; Total giving, $39,100; Grants to individuals, 22 grants totaling $39,100 (high: $2,500, low: $500).
Fields of interest: Eye diseases; Disabilities, people with.
Type of support: Graduate support; Undergraduate support.
Application information: Application form required.
Initial approach: Letter, telephone, or e-mail.
Deadline(s): Mar.
EIN: 580914436

106
American Dental Education Association
1400 K St., NW, Ste. 1100
Washington, DC 20005 (202) 289-7201
Contact: Richard Valachovic D.M.D., M.P.H., Exec. Dir.
FAX: (202) 289-7204;
E-mail: ValachovicR@adea.org; URL: http://www.adea.org
Foundation type: Public charity

Limitations: Scholarships to dental hygiene students who are individual members of the American Dental Association (ADEA).
Financial data: Year ended 06/30/2004. Assets, $7,887,996 (M); Expenditures, $10,798,192; Total giving, $1,735,838; Grants to individuals, 25 grants totaling $61,630 (high: $12,730, low: $250).
Fields of interest: Dental school/education; Dental care.
Type of support: Undergraduate support.
Application information:
Deadline(s): Jan. 27 for Secretary's Award and Dec. 15 for Oral-B Scholarship
Additional information: Completion of formal application, including project description, narrative, and budget for Secretary's Award and transcript, professional license, statement of purpose, and three letters of recommendation for Oral-B Scholarship; See Web site for further application information.
Program descriptions:
ADEA/Oral-B Scholarship for Dental Hygiene Students Pursuing Academic Careers: Awards two $2,500 scholarships to dental hygiene students pursuing education beyond an Associate's degree and considering an academic career. Candidates must:
· have graduated from an accredited dental hygiene program with an associate's degree or certificate to practice dental hygiene
· be enrolled in a degree completion program for a Bachelor's degree or graduate degree at an ADEA member institution or program
· show a commitment to pursuing an academic career in dental hygiene
· be an individual member of the American Dental Education Association.
Secretary's Award for Innovations in Health Promotion and Disease Prevention: Awards three single Discipline Awards of $1,500, $2,500, and $3,500 each, and three Interdisciplinary Awards of $3,000, $5,000 and $7,500 each to dental hygiene students for innovative projects that address health promotion or disease prevention. Applicants must be attending institutions that are affiliated with the Federation of Associations of Schools of the Health Professional. After submitting an application to the institution, each member institution submits one application to ADEA.
EIN: 911993281

107
American Dental Hygienist Association Institute for Oral Health
444 N. Michigan Ave., Ste. 3400
Chicago, IL 60611 (312) 440-8900
Contact: Ann Battrell RDH, MSDH(c), Exec. Dir.
E-mail: institute@adha.net; Additional tel: (800) 243-2432; URL: http://www.adha.org/institute

Foundation type: Public charity
Limitations: Scholarships to undergraduate and graduate dental hygiene students who have completed at least one year in a dental hygiene program.
Financial data: Year ended 06/30/2004. Assets, $879,516 (M); Expenditures, $242,490; Total giving, $94,631; Grants to individuals, 73 grants totaling $94,631.
Fields of interest: Dental care.
Type of support: Graduate support; Undergraduate support.
Application information: Application form required.
Deadline(s): May 1

Additional information: Application should include financial information; See Web site for further application information and for application forms.
Program description:
Scholarship Program: Applicants must be members of the Student American Dental Hygienists' Association or the American Dental Hygienists' Association and have a minimum GPA of 3.0 on a 4.0 scale. See Web site for the complete list of scholarships.
EIN: 363468143

108
American Dietetic Association Foundation
120 S. Riverside Plz.; Ste. 2000
Chicago, IL 60606 (800) 877-1600
Contact: Mary Beth Whalen, V.P. and Exec. Dir.
E-mail: foundation@eatright.org; URL: http://www.adaf.org

Foundation type: Public charity
Limitations: Scholarships for the study of dietetics to members of the American Dietetic Association.
Financial data: Year ended 05/31/2003. Assets, $8,277,676 (M); Expenditures, $1,865,669; Total giving, $427,175; Grants to individuals, 240 grants totaling $361,175 (high: $5,000, low: $100).
Fields of interest: Health sciences school/education; Nutrition.
Type of support: Graduate support; Undergraduate support.
Application information: Application form required.
Initial approach: Telephone or e-mail.
Deadline(s): Feb. 15
Program descriptions:
Baccalaureate or Coordinated Program Scholarships: Applicants must have completed the academic requirements in a CADE-accredited/approved college or university program for minimum standing as a junior. Applicants must demonstrate or show promise of being a valuable, contributing member of the profession, and be a U.S. citizen or permanent resident.
Dietetic Technician Program Scholarships: Applicants must be in their first year of study in a CADE-approved or accredited dietetic technician program. If selected, the student may use the scholarship for study during the second year. Applicants must show evidence of leadership and academic ability, and be a U.S. citizen or permanent resident.
Graduate Scholarship: Applicants must plan to or currently be enrolled in an advanced degree program in a U.S.-regionally accredited college/university. Students who are currently completing a dietetic internship (DI) or pre-professional practice program (AP4) that is combined with a graduate program and will be completing the graduate degree requirements should apply for a graduate scholarship. Applicants must intend to practice in the field of dietetics, and be a U.S. citizen or permanent resident.
EIN: 366150906

109
The American Electric Power System Educational Trust Fund
c/o American Electric Power Co., Inc., Tax Dept.
P.O. Box 16428
Columbus, OH 43216-0428

Foundation type: Company-sponsored foundation

Limitations: Undergraduate scholarships to children of employees of American Electric Power Co., Inc. who reside in IN, OH and MA.
Publications: Program policy statement.
Financial data: Year ended 02/28/2005. Assets, $2,915,690 (M); Expenditures, $206,097; Total giving, $198,500; Grants to individuals, 99 grants totaling $198,500 (high: $2,500, low: $1,500).
Type of support: Employee-related scholarships.
Application information: Application form required.
   Deadline(s): Oct.
   Additional information: Scholarship application address: c/o American Electric Power Co., Inc., Personnel Svcs. and EEO, 1 Riverside Plz., Columbus, OH 43215.
EIN: 237418083

110
American Express Foundation

World Financial Ctr.
200 Vesey St., 48th Fl.
New York, NY   10285-4804   (212) 640-5661
Contact: For organizations located outside the U.S.: Cornelia W. Higginson, V.P., Intl. Prog., and Secy.
URL: http://home3.americanexpress.com/corp/giving_back.asp

Foundation type: Company-sponsored foundation
Limitations: Scholarships only to children of employees of American Express Co. and its subsidiaries.
Publications: Grants list.
Financial data: Year ended 12/31/2004. Assets, $10,565,668 (M); Expenditures, $20,610,016; Total giving, $20,046,545; Grants to individuals, totaling $338,500.
Type of support: Employee-related scholarships.
Application information: Contact foundation for current application deadline/guidelines.
Program description:
   Employee Scholarships: Scholarship awards range from $1,000 to $3,000 per year, for a maximum of four consecutive years based on a combination of merit and financial need. Potential recipients who demonstrate no financial need are considered for a one-time honorarium of $500.
EIN: 136123529

111
American Finnish Workers Society Memorial Educational Trust

c/o U.S. Bank, N.A.
P.O. Box 64713
St. Paul, MN   55164-0713
Application address: c/o Superintendent of Schools, Hibbing, MN 55746

Foundation type: Independent foundation
Limitations: Scholarships and interest-free loans to students of Hibbing, MN, high schools.
Financial data: Year ended 12/31/2004. Assets, $127,244 (M); Expenditures, $6,090; Total giving, $2,001; Grants to individuals, 3 grants totaling $2,001 (high: $667, low: $667); Loans to individuals, totaling $20,000.
Type of support: Support to graduates or students of specific schools; Undergraduate support.
Application information: Application form required.
   Deadline(s): Contact schools for current application deadline
EIN: 416018271

112
American Floral Endowment

P.O. Box 945
Edwardsville, IL   62025   (618) 692-0045
Contact: Sten Crissey, Secy.-Treas.
FAX: (618) 692-4045; E-mail: afe@endowment.org;
URL: http://www.endowment.org

Foundation type: Public charity
Limitations: Scholarships and internships for students studying floriculture and horticulture.
Publications: Application guidelines; Annual report; Informational brochure; Newsletter.
Financial data: Year ended 06/30/2004. Assets, $10,850,210 (M); Expenditures, $1,048,324; Total giving, $677,828; Grants to individuals, 19 grants totaling $428,828 (high: $314,432, low: $400).
Fields of interest: Horticulture/garden clubs.
Type of support: Internship funds; Undergraduate support.
Application information: Application form required.
   Deadline(s): Mar. 1 and Nov. 1
Program descriptions:
   Vic and Margaret Ball Internship Program: Provides paid internship experiences to full-time students enrolled in either two- or four-year schools/universities interested in a career in commercial production (grower). Ten awards are available annually, and each includes paid training for three- or six-month periods and cash awards of up to $6,000 upon completion.
   Mosmiller Scholarship Program: Provides retail, wholesale, or allied trade paid internship experience to floriculture or business students enrolled at two- or four-year schools/universities. Seven awards are available annually, and each includes paid training for 10 to 16 weeks and a $2,000 cash award upon completion.
EIN: 236268380

113
American Foundation for Pharmaceutical Education

1 Church St., Ste. 202
Rockville, MD   20850   (301) 738-2160
Contact: Robert Bachman, Pres. and Secy.
FAX: (301) 738-2161; E-mail: info@afpenet.org;
URL: http://www.afpenet.org

Foundation type: Public charity
Limitations: Scholarships and fellowships to undergraduate and graduate students for pharmaceutical studies.
Financial data: Year ended 12/31/2003. Assets, $9,180,644 (M); Expenditures, $1,204,218; Total giving, $748,451; Grants to individuals, 89 grants totaling $545,451 (high: $7,500, low: $3,000).
Fields of interest: Health sciences school/education; Pharmacy/prescriptions.
Type of support: Graduate support; Undergraduate support; Doctoral support.
Application information: Application form required.
   Initial approach: Letter or telephone.
   Deadline(s): Contact foundation for current application deadline
Program descriptions:
   Gateway Research Scholarship Program: Provides awards of up to $5,000 to undergraduate and graduate students.
   First Year Graduate Scholarship Program: Provides scholarships of $5,000 to $7,500 to graduate pharmacy students.

Predoctoral Fellowship Program: Provides fellowships of $6,000 to $10,000 to doctoral pharmacy students. Deadline Mar. 1.
EIN: 530214882

114
American Foundation for the Blind

(also known as AFB)
11 Penn Plz., Ste. 300
New York, NY   10001   (212) 502-7600
Contact: Carl R. Augusto, Pres.
FAX: (212) 502-7777; E-mail: afbinfo@afb.net;
URL: http://www.afb.org

Foundation type: Public charity
Limitations: Undergraduate and graduate scholarships to legally blind and visually impaired individuals.
Publications: Annual report; Informational brochure; Newsletter.
Financial data: Year ended 06/30/2003. Assets, $40,700,682 (M); Expenditures, $21,708,382; Total giving, $87,090; Grants to individuals, 9 grants totaling $14,500 (high: $2,500, low: $500).
Fields of interest: Eye diseases; Disabilities, people with.
Type of support: Graduate support; Undergraduate support.
Application information:
   Deadline(s): Contact foundation for current application deadline
   Applicants should submit the following:
   1) Transcripts
   Additional information: Application by typewritten statement, proof of acceptance into college or program, three letters of recommendation, official and evidence of legal blindness; All applicants must be U.S. citizens.
Program description:
   Scholarship Funds:
   · Gladys C. Anderson Memorial Scholarship: Provides one $1,000 scholarship to a woman who is legally blind, and is studying religion or classical music at the college level
   · Karen D. Carsel Memorial Scholarship: Provides one $500 scholarship to a full-time graduate student who is legally blind and who presents evidence of economic need
   · Rudolph Dillman Memorial Scholarship: Provides four $2,500 scholarships to undergraduate and graduate students who are legally blind and studying in the field of rehabilitation and/or education of persons who are visually impaired or blind
   · Frederick A. Downes Scholarship: Provides two $1,500 scholarships to persons who are 22 years of age or younger, legally blind and enrolled in a course of study leading to credentials in a profession or vocation
   · R.L. Gillette Scholarship: Provides two $1,000 scholarships to women who are legally blind and enrolled in a four-year undergraduate degree program in literature or music
   · Paul W. Ruckes Scholarship: Provides one $1,000 scholarship to an undergraduate or graduate student who is blind or visually-impaired pursuing a degree in engineering, computer, physical or life sciences.
EIN: 135562161

115
American Friends of Even Yisroel Charitable Foundation

c/o Lisker
25 Dakota St.
Passaic, NJ 07055
Contact: Solomon Sobel, Tr.

Foundation type: Independent foundation
Limitations: Scholarships to members for religious study.
Financial data: Year ended 12/31/2004.
Assets, $14,923 (M); Expenditures, $373,763; Total giving, $333,574; Grants to individuals, 38 grants totaling $333,574 (high: $8,500).
Fields of interest: Theological school/education.
Type of support: Scholarships—to individuals.
Application information: Applications accepted.
Deadline(s): None
EIN: 137173269

116
The American Friends of Needy Israeli Sephardic Children

c/o Play Knits, Inc.
240 W. 40th St., 3rd Fl.
New York, NY 10018 (212) 391-0170
Contact: Ralph Tawil, Pres.

Foundation type: Public charity
Limitations: Grants to Sephardic Israeli children who come from economically disadvantaged families. Recipients must be residents of Israel, of Sephardic extraction, and come from a family that earns no more than $300 per week.
Financial data: Year ended 12/31/2003.
Assets, $60,910 (M); Expenditures, $88,719; Total giving, $88,646; Grants to individuals, totaling $38,646.
Fields of interest: Economically disadvantaged.
Type of support: Foreign applicants; Grants for special needs.
Application information: Application form available on the grantmaker's Web site.
Additional information: Contact foundation for current application deadline/guidelines.
EIN: 133180929

117
American General Finance Foundation, Inc.

(formerly American General Finance, Inc.—Richard E. Meier Foundation, Inc.)
601 N.W. 2nd St.
P.O. Box 59
Evansville, IN 47701-0059 (812) 468-5413
Contact: Michelle Dixon, Mgr., Mktg. Prog.

Foundation type: Company-sponsored foundation
Limitations: Scholarships to children of current, disabled, retired, or deceased employees of American General Finance, Inc. and its subsidiaries, primarily in IN. Applicants must rank in the top third of their high school class.
Publications: Application guidelines.
Financial data: Year ended 12/31/2004.
Assets, $97,776 (M); Expenditures, $426,802; Total giving, $426,595; Grants to individuals, 11 grants totaling $22,000 (high: $2,000, low: $2,000).
Type of support: Employee-related scholarships.
Application information: Application form required.
Initial approach: Letter.
Deadline(s): Mar. 1
Applicants should submit the following:

1) Transcripts
2) Class rank
Additional information: Application should also include standardized test scores; Recipients notified by Apr.
Program description:
Scholarship Program: Employees must have at least two years of full-time, consecutive employment with the corporation. Retired, disabled, and deceased employees must have had at least two years of consecutive service with the corporation prior to leaving. Scholarships are awarded for four years of study, provided an average of at least "B" is maintained. Recipients are chosen by a panel from the University of Southern Indiana on the basis of academic and standardized testing performance.
EIN: 356042566

118
American Hotel and Lodging Educational Foundation

(formerly American Hotel and Lodging Foundation)
1201 New York Ave., N.W., Ste. 600
Washington, DC 20005-3931 (202) 289-3100
Contact: Michelle Poinelei, Dir., Progs.
FAX: (202) 289-3199; E-mail: ahlef@ahlef.org;
URL: http://www.ahlef.org

Foundation type: Public charity
Limitations: Scholarships to college students pursuing an undergraduate degree in hospitality management.
Publications: Application guidelines; Annual report.
Financial data: Year ended 12/31/2003.
Assets, $18,910,241 (M); Expenditures, $1,342,270; Total giving, $941,993; Grants to individuals, 323 grants totaling $457,777.
Fields of interest: Business/industry.
Type of support: Undergraduate support.
Application information: Application form required.
Deadline(s): See Web site for current application deadline
EIN: 136095316

119
American Hungarian Foundation

300 Somerset St.
P.O. Box 1084
New Brunswick, NJ 08903-1004
(732) 846-5777
Contact: August J. Molnar, Pres.
FAX: (732) 249-7033;
E-mail: info@ahfoundation.org; URL: http://www.ahfoundation.org

Foundation type: Public charity
Limitations: Scholarships to students of Hungarian descent, for higher education.
Financial data: Year ended 06/30/2004.
Assets, $2,706,129 (M); Expenditures, $455,145; Total giving, $5,574.
Fields of interest: Hungary.
Type of support: Undergraduate support.
Application information: Contact foundation for current application deadline; Application by letter, including interest in Hungarian studies, program to be pursued, biography, sources to which applied for assistance and three references.
EIN: 366085165

120
American Indian Heritage Foundation

(also known as AIHF)
P.O. Box 6301
Falls Church, VA 22040 (703) 819-0979
Contact: Princess Pale Moon, Chair. and Pres.
URL: http://www.indians.org

Foundation type: Public charity
Limitations: Grants, scholarships and awards to Native Americans.
Financial data: Year ended 12/31/2002.
Assets, $228,370 (M); Expenditures, $1,496,486; Total giving, $1,223,338; Grants to individuals, totaling $1,223,338.
Fields of interest: Native Americans/American Indians.
Type of support: Grants to individuals; Scholarships—to individuals; Awards/prizes.
Application information: Contact foundation for current application deadline/guidelines.
EIN: 541222903

121
American Institute of Architects Scholarship Fund

(also known as AIA St. Louis Scholarship Fund)
911 Washington Ave., Ste. 225
St. Louis, MO 63101 (314) 621-3484
Contact: Michelle C. Swatek, Exec. Dir.
E-mail: chapter@aia-stlouis.org; URL: http://www.aia-stlouis.org

Foundation type: Public charity
Limitations: Scholarships to St. Louis, MO, area students for study at the Washington University School of Architecture, MO.
Financial data: Year ended 12/31/2003.
Assets, $2,414,232 (M); Expenditures, $83,665; Total giving, $69,750; Grants to individuals, 28 grants totaling $61,750 (high: $6,000, low: $1,000).
Fields of interest: Architecture.
Type of support: Support to graduates or students of specific schools; Graduate support; Undergraduate support.
Application information:
Initial approach: Letter or telephone.
Deadline(s): Feb. 15 and Dec. 15 for Ranft, June 1 for St. Louis Chapter.
Additional information: Interviews required.
Program descriptions:
Ranft Scholarship: Provides scholarships to students in their fifth year of study at graduate school. Scholarships are between $6,000 and $12,000.
St. Louis Chapter Scholarship: Offered during the third, fourth, and fifth year of undergraduate study at an accredited architectural school.
George E. Kassabaum Scholarship: Provides scholarships to graduate students at the Washington University School of Architecture. The maximum annual award is $1,000.
EIN: 436060703

122
American Legion Charles F. Moran Trust

(also known as American Legion Charles F. Moran Post No. 475, Scholarship Trust and Baseball Trust)
c/o First Financial Bank
100 E. Lancaster Ave.
Downingtown, PA 19335
Application address: Downingtown Area Senior High Schools, Downingtown, PA 19335

Foundation type: Independent foundation
Limitations: Scholarships to residents of the Downingtown, PA, area, for higher education.
Financial data: Year ended 12/31/2004.
Assets, $137,358 (M); Expenditures, $7,057; Total giving, $5,000; Grants to individuals, totaling $5,000.
Type of support: Undergraduate support.
Application information: Contact foundation for current application deadlines/guidelines.
EIN: 237718697

123

American Legion Memorial Scholarship Funds, Inc.

c/o Wachovia Bank, N.A.
255 S. County Rd.
Palm Beach, FL 33480
Application address: 3201 S. Dixie Hwy., West Palm Beach, FL 33405, tel.: (561)655-4305

Foundation type: Independent foundation
Limitations: Scholarships and student loans to financially needy residents of Palm Beach County, FL, who are U.S. citizens. Recipients may study at any accredited U.S. college or university.
Financial data: Year ended 12/31/2003.
Assets, $632,642 (M); Expenditures, $54,254; Total giving, $2,700; Grants to individuals, totaling $2,700.
Type of support: Graduate support; Undergraduate support.
Application information: Application form required.
   Deadline(s): May 15
   Applicants should submit the following:
      1) Transcripts
      2) FAFSA
      3) Photograph
   Additional information: Application should also include three letters of recommendation; Interviews required.
Program descriptions:
   Anson A. Bigelow Grant: Scholarships are available to graduate students. Preference is given to applicants whose parent(s) or close relative served in the Naval Forces of the U.S. (i.e., U.S. Navy, U.S. Marine Corp., U.S. Coast Guard).
   Helen Hoover West Grant: Both graduate and undergraduate students are eligible for this scholarship; however, freshman are generally not recipients.
EIN: 596151027

124

American Library Association

50 E. Huron St.
Chicago, IL 60611-2795 (800) 545-2433
Contact: Michael Gorman, Pres.
FAX: (312) 944-9374; E-mail: ala@ala.org; TDD: (888) 814-7692; URL: http://www.ala.org

Foundation type: Public charity
Limitations: Graduate scholarships for study in ALA-accredited master's degree programs.
Financial data: Year ended 08/31/2004.
Assets, $50,503,470 (M); Expenditures, $42,296,023; Total giving, $623,561; Grants to individuals, 73 grants totaling $256,069 (high: $5,000; low: $2,000).
Fields of interest: Libraries/library science.
Type of support: Graduate support.
Application information: Applications accepted.
   Deadline(s): Nov. 4 for Women's National Book Association/Ann Heidbreder Eastman Grant, Mar. 1 for all others.

Additional information: Application by a one-page, typewritten statement of no more than 300 words; See Web site for further program information.
Program description:
   Scholarship Funds: The following scholarships (except for the NMRT/EBSCO) all award $3,000, require recipient to enter an ALA-accredited master's degree program, allow full- or part-time students to apply, require applicant to be a citizen or permanent resident of the U.S. or Canada, and award one scholarship per year.
   · David H. Clift Scholarship
   · Marshall Cavendish Scholarship
   · Tom and Roberta Drewes Scholarship: For library support staff currently working in a library
   · Mary V. Gaver Scholarship: For individuals who plan to specialize in the field of library youth services
   · Miriam L. Hornback Scholarship: For library support staff currently working in a library
   · Hoy/ERT Scholarship
   · Tony B. Leisner Scholarship: For library support staff currently working in a library
   · New Members Round Table (NMRT)/ EBSCO Scholarship: An award of $1,000 to a member of ALA and NMRT who has been a member of ALA for 10 years
   · Women's National Book Association/Ann Heidbreder Eastman Grant: Awards $500-$750 annually to a librarian to take a course or participate in an intensive institute devoted to aspects of publishing as a profession, or to provide reimbursement for such study completed within the past year (this would not include courses, institutes, seminars or workshops devoted to desktop publishing for purposes of setting up a newsletter or an individual home office). Librarians holding the MLS or its equivalent master's level credential and having at least two years of post-master's work experience in a library are eligible to apply.
EIN: 362166947

125

American Meteorological Society

45 Beacon St.
Boston, MA 02108-3693 (617) 227-2425
Contact: Keith L. Seitter, Exec. Dir.
FAX: (617) 742-8718;
E-mail: amsinfo@ametsoc.org; Additional address: 1120 G. St., N.W., Ste. 800, Washington, DC 20005, tel.: (202) 737-9006, FAX: (202) 737-9050; URL: http://www.ametsoc.org/ams

Foundation type: Public charity
Limitations: Scholarships and fellowships for the study of meteorology and other related sciences.
Publications: Application guidelines; Annual report; Financial statement; Grants list; Informational brochure; Newsletter; Program policy statement.
Financial data: Year ended 12/31/2004.
Assets, $14,675,733 (M); Expenditures, $13,806,696.
Fields of interest: Science; Physical/earth sciences; Mathematics; Engineering/technology; Minorities.
Type of support: Fellowships; Awards/prizes; Graduate support; Undergraduate support.
Application information:
   Initial approach: Telephone or e-mail.
   Deadline(s): Varies
   Additional information: Candidates must be U.S. citizens or hold permanent resident status,

and should specify the program about which they are inquiring and the year of academic study they will be entering in the fall, when requesting an application.
Program descriptions:
   AMS Graduate Fellowships in the History of Science: Awards a $15,000 stipend for one year of research to a student to complete a dissertation on the history of the atmospheric, or related oceanic or hydrologic sciences. A close working relation is fostered between historians and scientists. An effort will be made to place the fellow into a mentoring relationship with an AMS member at an appropriate institution. Deadline Mar. 16.
   AMS/Industry/Government Graduate Fellowships: Awards $15,000 fellowships for nine months to promising young scientists who are preparing for careers in the meteorological, oceanic, and hydrologic fields. Students entering their first year of graduate study in the fall who wish to pursue advanced degrees in the atmospheric and related oceanic and hydrologic sciences, chemistry, computer sciences, mathematics, engineering, environmental sciences, and physics are eligible to apply. Awards are based on the applicant's performance as an undergraduate student and his or her qualifications to pursue a career in the atmospheric and related oceanic and hydrologic sciences. Deadline Feb. 16.
   AMS/Industry Minority Scholarships: Awards two-year scholarships of $3,000 per year to minority students who have been traditionally underrepresented in the sciences. Minority students entering their freshman year of college in the fall are eligible to apply. Students must plan to pursue careers in the atmospheric or related oceanic and hydrologic sciences. Second-year funding depends on successful completion of the first academic year.
   AMS/Industry Undergraduate Scholarships: Awards scholarships to outstanding undergraduate students planning to pursue careers in the atmospheric and related oceanic and related oceanic and hydrologic sciences. Applicants studying atmospheric sciences, oceanography, hydrology, chemistry, computer sciences, mathematics, engineering, and physics are encouraged to apply. The scholarship award is $2,000 for the junior year and a subsequent $2,000 for the senior year. Second-year funding is based on the recipient's performance and the recommendation of a faculty advisor. Deadline Feb. 23.
   AMS Undergraduate Scholarships: The following are all single-year scholarships:
   · Howard T. Orville Scholarship in Meteorology- $2,000
   · Howard H. Hanks, Jr. Scholarship in Meteorology- $700
   · Dr. Pedro Grau Undergraduate Scholarship- $2,500
   · AMS 75th Anniversary Scholarship- $2,000
   · Mark J. Schroeder Scholarship in Meteorology- $5,000
   · Richard and Helen Hagemeyer Scholarship- $3,000
   · Ethan and Allen Murphy Scholarship- $2,000; Applicants must be majoring in atmospheric or related oceanic and hydrologic science and must show clear intent to make the atmospheric or related sciences their careers.
Applicants must be enrolled full-time in an accredited U.S. institution and must have a cumulative GPA of at least 3.0 on a scale of 4.0 at the time of application.
   Father James B. Macelwane Annual Awards in Meteorology: Awards $300 to a college student for

an original student paper about an aspect of the atmospheric sciences. The student must be enrolled as an undergraduate at the time the paper is written, and no more than two students from any one institution may enter papers in any one contest. Deadline June 12.
EIN: 042103657

126
American Occupational Therapy Foundation

4720 Montgomery Ln.
P.O. Box 31220
Bethesda, MD 20824-1220 (301) 652-6611
Contact: Martha Kirkland, Exec. Dir.; Scholarships: Jane Huntington
FAX: (301) 656-3620; E-mail: aotf@aotf.org;
URL: http://www.AOTF.org

Foundation type: Public charity
Limitations: Scholarships to members of the American Occupational Therapy Association who are studying at the associate's, bachelor's, graduate, and professional levels.
Publications: Annual report; Financial statement; Informational brochure; Newsletter.
Financial data: Year ended 09/30/2004. Assets, $9,947,508 (M); Expenditures, $894,563; Total giving, $39,600; Grants to individuals, 34 grants totaling $39,600 (high: $5,000, low: $300).
Fields of interest: Physical therapy.
Type of support: Graduate support; Undergraduate support; Postgraduate support.
Application information: Applications accepted. Application form required. Application form available on the grantmaker's Web site.
Deadline(s): Oct. 1 to Jan. 15.
Additional information: Completion of formal application required, including two personal references, Curriculum Directors Statement, and official transcripts.
Program description:
AOTF Scholarship Program: Each year the American Occupational Therapy Foundation (AOTF) offers scholarships from the AOTF Scholarship Fund, the Association of Student Delegates, Kappa Delta Phi and State Associations funds administered by the Foundation. The scholarships, ranging from $250 to $5,000, are offered to occupational therapy students studying undergraduate and graduate levels. Applicants should have a record of outstanding scholastic ability and demonstrate a need for financial assistance. Awards are made by May 1. Funds are to be used solely for qualified tuition and educational expenses.
EIN: 136189382

127
American Optical Foundation

c/o American Optical Corp.
14 Mechanic St.
Southbridge, MA 01550 (508) 765-7085
Contact: Gary Bridgeman, Tr.

Foundation type: Company-sponsored foundation
Limitations: Scholarships and student loans to children of employees of American Optical Corporation who reside in MA.
Financial data: Year ended 12/31/2003. Assets, $1,422,557 (M); Expenditures, $102,737; Total giving, $89,926; Grants to individuals, 62 grants totaling $36,650 (high: $1,500, low: $25).

Type of support: Employee-related scholarships.
Application information: Application form required.
Deadline(s): Apr. 25
Applicants should submit the following:
1) SAT
2) Essay
3) Transcripts
4) Letter(s) of recommendation
EIN: 046028058

128
American Osteopathic Foundation

(formerly National Osteopathic Foundation)
142 E. Ontario, Ste. 502
Chicago, IL 60611 (312) 202-8234
Contact: Vicki L. Heck, Prog. Mgr.
FAX: (312) 202-8216;
E-mail: info@aof-foundation.org; Additional tels.: (800) 621-1773, ext. 8230, 8232, 8233, 8234;
URL: http://www.aof-foundation.org

Foundation type: Public charity
Limitations: Scholarships to students specializing in osteopathic medicine, and some support for doctors practicing osteopathic medicine.
Financial data: Year ended 05/31/2005. Assets, $9,913,849 (M); Expenditures, $932,337; Total giving, $277,656; Grants to individuals, 67 grants totaling $143,865 (high: $10,000, low: $313).
Fields of interest: Education.
Type of support: Awards/prizes; Graduate support.
Application information: Application form required.
Deadline(s): Vary
Additional information: See Web site for further application and program information.
Program description:
Scholarship Funds: The foundation administers the following funds:
· William G. Anderson, D.O., Scholarship for Minority Students
· Russell C. McCaughan Education Fund Scholarship
· Paul S. McCord, D.O., Memorial Scholarship Fund
· Donna Jones Moritsugu Award
· Pfizer Outstanding Resident Award
· Wyeth Emerging Leader Award.
EIN: 366056120

129
American Paint Horse Association Youth Development Foundation

P.O. Box 961023
Fort Worth, TX 76161-0023 (817) 834-2742
Contact: Mary Parrott, Pres.
FAX: (817) 834-3152; URL: http://www.apha.com/ydf/

Foundation type: Public charity
Limitations: Scholarships to hard-working young horsemen and horsewomen who are members of the AJPHA.
Financial data: Year ended 12/31/2002. Assets, $554,488 (M); Expenditures, $41,538; Total giving, $34,000; Grants to individuals, 38 grants totaling $34,000 (high: $1,000, low: $500).
Fields of interest: Athletics/sports, training; Athletics/sports, equestrianism.
Type of support: Undergraduate support.
Application information: Application form required.
Deadline(s): Mar. 1
Applicants should submit the following:
1) Letter(s) of recommendation
2) Essay

Additional information: See Web site for application forms.
EIN: 751729447

130
American Psychological Foundation

750 1st St. N.E.
Washington, DC 20002-4242 (202) 336-5843
Contact: Elizabeth H. Merck, Asst. Dir.
FAX: (202) 336-5812; E-mail: foundation@apa.org;
URL: http://www.apa.org/apf/

Foundation type: Public charity
Limitations: Scholarships for the study of psychology.
Publications: Annual report; Financial statement; Informational brochure (including application guidelines); Newsletter.
Financial data: Year ended 12/31/2004. Assets, $13,187,658 (M); Expenditures, $1,077,771; Total giving, $561,091; Grants to individuals, 82 grants totaling $546,091 (high: $30,000, low: $250).
Fields of interest: Psychology/behavioral science.
Type of support: Awards/prizes; Precollege support.
Application information: Application form required.
Initial approach: Letter or telephone.
Deadline(s): Contact foundation for current application deadlines
Program descriptions:
APF/TOPSS Excellence in High School Student Research Awards: Provides four scholarships to high school students of psychology. Awards are $1,500 for first place, $1,000 for second place, $500 for third place, and $250 for fourth place.
APF/TOPSS Scholar (Student Essay) Competition: Three $1,000 awards are given to the winners of the TOPSS Student Essay Contest.
Paul E. Henkin School Psychology Travel Award: Provides awards to defer the costs of registration, lodging, and travel for the student members of APA Division 16 to attend the APA annual convention.
EIN: 526051733

131
American Road & Transportation Builders Association Foundation

1219 28th St., NW
Washington, DC 20007-3389 (202) 289-4434
Contact: Brad Sant, Exec. Dir.
E-mail for scholarships: rbritton@artba.org
FAX: (202) 289-4435; URL: http://www.artba.org

Foundation type: Public charity
Limitations: Scholarships to children of highway workers who died or were permanently disabled at work. Awards also to undergraduate and graduate students for papers on transportation issues.
Financial data: Year ended 12/31/2004. Assets, $1,003,778 (M); Expenditures, $507,357; Total giving, $96,358; Grants to individuals, 10 grants totaling $18,500 (high: $2,000, low: $1,000).
Fields of interest: Transportation.
Type of support: Graduate support; Undergraduate support.
Application information: Applications accepted. Application form required.
Deadline(s): Mar. 31 for Highway Worker Memorial Scholarship and Apr. 14 for Student Paper Competition
Applicants should submit the following:
1) Photograph
2) Transcripts

3) Letter(s) of recommendation
4) FAFSA
5) Essay
Additional information: Application must also include documentation of parent's death or disability, and college acceptance letter for scholarships; See Web site for further information.
Program descriptions:
Highway Worker Memorial Scholarship: Awards scholarships of around $2,000 to children and adopted children of highway workers killed or disabled in the line if duty. Applicants must maintain a "C" average.
Student Paper Competition: Awards $500 to an undergraduate and graduate student for papers on transportation themes. Any junior, senior or graduate student enrolled at a college or university with an ARTBA-member faculty member is eligible to enter. The paper and abstract must be submitted, via the faculty member of ARTBA.
EIN: 526283894

132

American Savings Foundation
(formerly American Savings Charitable Foundation, Inc.)
185 Main St.
New Britain, CT 06051 (860) 827-2556
Contact: David Davison, Pres.
E-mail: info@asfdn.org; URL: http://www.asfdn.org

Foundation type: Independent foundation
Limitations: Scholarships to undergraduate CT students at a two- or four-year college, university or technical/vocational school who are full-time residents of one of the towns served by the foundation.
Publications: Application guidelines; Annual report; Financial statement; Grants list; Informational brochure; Informational brochure (including application guidelines); Occasional report.
Financial data: Year ended 12/31/2004. Assets, $83,463,632 (M); Expenditures, $4,147,239; Total giving, $3,086,264; Grants to individuals, 652 grants totaling $461,888 (high: $2,500, low: $250, average grant: $500-$1,500).
Type of support: Technical education support; Undergraduate support.
Application information: Application form required. Application form available on the grantmaker's Web site.
  Deadline(s): Mar. 31
  Applicants should submit the following:
    1) Transcripts
    2) Letter(s) of recommendation
    3) GPA
    4) Financial information
    5) FAFSA
    6) Essay
  Additional information: Applications should be submitted online.
EIN: 061563163

133

American Society for Industrial Security Foundation
(also known as ASIS Foundation)
1625 Prince St.
Alexandria, VA 22314-2818 (703) 519-6200
Contact: Robert Rowe, Dir., Devel.
FAX: (703) 519-6299;
E-mail: foundation@asisonline.org; URL: http://www.asisonline.org/foundation/index.xml

Foundation type: Public charity
Limitations: Scholarships to those who are interested in the security profession and who have demonstrated potential to make a contribution to the field of business security.
Publications: Application guidelines; Informational brochure; Newsletter.
Financial data: Year ended 12/31/2004. Assets, $784,746 (M); Expenditures, $318,926; Total giving, $128,167; Grants to individuals, 114 grants totaling $97,902 (high: $20,000, low: $128).
Fields of interest: Crime/law enforcement, association.
Type of support: Graduate support; Undergraduate support.
Application information: Applications accepted. Application form required.
  Initial approach: E-mail.
  Deadline(s): Contact foundation for current application deadline/guidelines
  Applicants should submit the following:
    1) Transcripts
    2) Letter(s) of recommendation
  Additional information: See Web site for additional information.
Program description:
Matching Chapter Scholarship: This program supports ASIS chapters that provide scholarships to students within the chapter area. The foundation matches the dollar amount a chapter will be giving up to $500. If the awardee is a chapter member, the foundation doubles the match up to $1,000. The foundation provides between 40-50 of these matching scholarships a year.
EIN: 520848090

134

American Society for Military Comptrollers
415 N. Alfred St.
Alexandria, VA 22314 (703) 549-0360
FAX: (703) 549-3181;
E-mail: asmchg@asmconline.org; Toll-free tel.: (800) 462-5637; Additional tel. for scholarships: (301) 227-6143; URL: http://www.asmconline.org

Foundation type: Public charity
Limitations: Scholarships to outstanding graduating high school seniors for academic achievement.
Financial data: Year ended 06/30/2005. Assets, $3,978,783 (M); Expenditures, $2,553,519; Total giving, $15,000; Grants to individuals, 10 grants totaling $15,000 (high: $2,000, low: $1,000).
Fields of interest: Business school/education; Computer science; Economics; Leadership development.
Type of support: Scholarships—to individuals.
Application information: Application form required. Application form available on the grantmaker's Web site.
  Initial approach: Telephone.
  Deadline(s): Mar. 31
  Applicants should submit the following:
    1) SAT
    2) ACT
    3) Financial information
    4) Letter(s) of recommendation
  Additional information: Application should also include copy of college acceptance letter, scholastic achievement, leadership ability, career and academic goals.
Program description:
Scholarships: One $3,000 scholarship is awarded to a high school senior who demonstrates

exemplary leadership abilities, an interest in the financial management career field, and academic promise. The individual will also have his/her name engraved on a perpetual plaque at National Headquarters. Five $2,000 scholarships and five $1,000 scholarships will also be awarded.
EIN: 541025128

135

American Society of Interior Designers Foundation
608 Massachusetts Ave., N.E.
Washington, DC 20002-6006 (202) 546-3480
Contact: Catherine Fraser, Dir., Devel.
FAX: (202) 546-3420;
E-mail: foundation@asid.org; URL: http://www.asidfoundation.org

Foundation type: Public charity
Limitations: Scholarships to individuals who are entering the field of interior design.
Publications: Application guidelines; Grants list.
Financial data: Year ended 09/30/2004. Assets, $2,114,813 (M); Expenditures, $22,197; Total giving, $8,750; Grants to individuals, 5 grants totaling $5,750 (high: $2,000, low: $750).
Fields of interest: Design; Historic preservation/historical societies.
Type of support: Awards/prizes; Graduate support; Undergraduate support.
Application information: Application form required.
  Initial approach: Telephone.
  Deadline(s): Mar. 15
Program descriptions:
Mabelle Wilhelmina Boldt Scholarship: Awards one $2,000 scholarship to a graduate-level student of interior design. Recipient must have been a practicing designer for at least five years previous to graduate school.
Dora Brahms Award: Award of $3,000 to a student of historic preservation and/or restoration services.
Joel Polsky Academic Achievement Award: Award of $1,000 to an undergraduate or graduate for interior design research or thesis project. Research papers or doctoral and master's theses should address such interior design topics as educational research, behavioral science, business practice, design process, theory or other technical subjects.
Joel Polsky Prize: Award of $1,000 to recognize outstanding academic contributions to the discipline of interior design through literature or visual communication. Entries should address the needs of the public, designers, and students on such topics as educational research, behavioral science, business practice, design process, theory or other technical subjects.
Yale R. Burge Competition: Awards $750 to students in their final year of undergraduate study who are enrolled in at least a three-year program of interior design. The competition is designed to encourage students to seriously plan their portfolios.
Irene Winifred Eno Grant: Award of $1,000 to individuals or groups engaged in the creation of an education program or an interior design research project dedicated to health, safety and welfare.
EIN: 132852954

136
American Speech-Language-Hearing Association Foundation
10801 Rockville Pike
Rockville, MD 20852-3226 (301) 897-5700
Contact: Nancy J. Minghetti, Exec. Dir.
FAX: (301) 571-0457;
E-mail: foundation@asha.org; URL: http://www.ashfoundation.org

Foundation type: Public charity
Limitations: Scholarships and research grants to graduate and postgraduate students in the areas of communication sciences and disorders.
Financial data: Year ended 12/31/2004. Assets, $4,389,743 (M); Expenditures, $458,443; Total giving, $148,000; Grants to individuals, 36 grants totaling $107,500 (high: $10,000, low: $500).
Fields of interest: Language/linguistics; Speech/hearing centers; Ear & throat research; Psychology/behavioral science; Disabilities, people with; Minorities.
Type of support: Research; Graduate support; Postgraduate support.
Application information: Application form required.
  Initial approach: Letter or FAX.
Program descriptions:
  Graduate Student Scholarship: $4,000 scholarships to full-time graduate students in communication sciences and disorders programs demonstrating outstanding academic achievement.
  Graduate Scholarship for Minority Student: A $4,000 scholarship is awarded to a racial/ethnic minority student who is a U.S. citizen and is accepted for graduate study in speech-language pathology or audiology. Other scholarships available through the International/Minority Student Graduate Scholarship program. See Web site for award information.
  Graduate Scholarship for Student with Disability: Full-time graduate students with a disability who are enrolled in a communication sciences and disorders program and demonstrating outstanding academic achievement are eligible to compete for a $2,000 scholarship.
  Student Research Grant in Audiology: Graduate and postgraduate students in communication sciences and disorders may apply for a $2,000 research grant in audiology. Only one applicant will be selected each year.
  Student Research Grant in Early Childhood Language Development: Graduate and postgraduate students may apply for a $2,000 research grant in the area of early childhood language development. One recipient is selected each year.
EIN: 526055761

137
Everett L. Amis Foundation
1911 Kenwood Pkwy.
Minneapolis, MN 55405 (612) 381-0886
Contact: Robert W. Amis, Jr., Pres.

Foundation type: Independent foundation
Limitations: Scholarships to students beginning study at Daystar University in Kenya or at Rhodes College in TN. Scholarships also to employees of Dyersberg, Inc., TN.
Financial data: Year ended 12/31/2004. Assets, $892,942 (M); Expenditures, $28,444; Total giving, $26,000; Grants to individuals, 7 grants totaling $26,000.
Application information:
  Initial approach: Letter or telephone.

Additional information: Contact foundation for current application deadlines; Completion of formal application required, including recommendation letters.
EIN: 411431074

138
L. A. Amundson Scholarships, Inc.
c/o Barbara J. Hegelund
P.O. Box 469
Sleepy Eye, MN 56085-0469
Scholarship application address: c/o A.R. Mixner, P.O. Box 1270, Sioux Falls, SD 57101

Foundation type: Independent foundation
Limitations: Scholarships to MN, MT, and ND high school graduates pursuing careers in health care, business, commerce, or technical training who reside in Benson, Byron, Canby, Detroit Lakes, Henning, Lake Benton, Sanborn or Sleepy Eye, MN; Beulah or Robinson, ND; or Fairview, MT.
Publications: Application guidelines.
Financial data: Year ended 12/31/2004. Assets, $4,585,759 (M); Expenditures, $242,905; Total giving, $228,000.
Fields of interest: Business school/education; Health care.
Type of support: Undergraduate support.
Application information: Application form required.
  Deadline(s): Mar. 15
  Additional information: Application should include a letter of acceptance from accredited college or vocational school, official transcript, two letters of recommendation, an essay under 500 words describing applicant's goals, and copy of parents' 1040 form to be considered for financial need.
EIN: 411692528

139
J. Wilfred Anctil Foundation
c/o Citizens Bank
870 Westminster St.
Providence, RI 02903
Application address: c/o Wayne Nelson, P.O. Box 96, Nashua, NH 03061-0096

Foundation type: Independent foundation
Limitations: Scholarships for higher education to needy residents of the greater Nashua, NH, area.
Financial data: Year ended 12/31/2004. Assets, $1,228,842 (M); Expenditures, $90,633; Total giving, $74,300; Grants to individuals, totaling $74,300.
Type of support: Scholarships—to individuals.
Application information:
  Deadline(s): May 1
  Additional information: Application by letter, including high school or college transcripts and a statement of need.
EIN: 026007760

140
Dick Anderson Chapter 75 (1896) United Daughters of the Confederacy Trust
c/o National Bank of South Carolina
P.O. Box 1798
Sumter, SC 29151-1798

Foundation type: Independent foundation
Limitations: Scholarships to students in Sumter and contiguous counties, SC, and to students in SC schools.

Financial data: Year ended 12/31/2004. Assets, $319,187 (M); Expenditures, $12,671; Total giving, $7,205; Grants to individuals, 4 grants totaling $7,000 (high: $2,000, low: $1,000).
Type of support: Scholarships—to individuals.
Application information: Application form required.
  Deadline(s): Mar.
EIN: 576108972

141
Harold C. Anderson Educational Trust
P.O. Box 98
Comfrey, MN 56019 (507) 877-2511
Contact: Ronald Winch, Chair.

Foundation type: Operating foundation
Limitations: Scholarships to graduates of Comfrey High School, MN, for higher education.
Financial data: Year ended 12/31/2004. Assets, $190,672 (M); Expenditures, $5,430; Total giving, $4,140; Grants to individuals, totaling $4,140.
Type of support: Support to graduates or students of specific schools; Undergraduate support.
Application information: Applications accepted. Application form required.
  Initial approach: Letter.
  Deadline(s): None
EIN: 416325121

142
Sophie L. Anderson Educational Trust
c/o Bank of America, N.A.
P.O. Box 34345
Seattle, WA 98124-1345

Foundation type: Independent foundation
Limitations: Scholarships to WA residents attending small colleges in WA, such as Whitman College, Whitworth College, Puget Sound Christian College, and Seattle Pacific College. Scholarships are awarded in the following order of preference: history majors, liberal arts majors, premedical majors, nursing majors, and teaching majors.
Financial data: Year ended 03/31/2005. Assets, $237,593 (M); Expenditures, $10,115; Total giving, $6,825; Grants to individuals, totaling $6,825.
Fields of interest: History/archaeology; Medical school/education; Nursing school/education; Teacher school/education.
Type of support: Support to graduates or students of specific schools; Undergraduate support.
Application information: Contact trust or listed colleges for application deadline/guidelines.
EIN: 916076066

143
Anderson Family Scholarship Trust u/w of Barbara Olson
c/o Dewit Bank & Trust Co.
815 6th Ave.
Dewitt, IA 52742
Contact: Rojer J. Hill, Sr. V.P. & Trust Off.
Application address: c/o DeWitt Bank & Trust Co., P.O. Box 260, Dewitt, IA 52742, tel.: (563) 659-3211

Foundation type: Independent foundation
Limitations: Scholarships to graduating seniors of Clinton County, IA, high schools.
Financial data: Year ended 12/31/2004. Assets, $619,554 (M); Expenditures, $30,295;

Total giving, $15,750; Grants to individuals, totaling $15,750.
Type of support: Undergraduate support.
Application information: Application form required.
  Deadline(s): Apr. 1
  Additional information: Applications available at area high schools.
EIN: 426615782

144
Kay M. Anderson Foundation
P.O. Box 307
Shenandoah, IA 51601
Contact: Terry Miller, Pres.

Foundation type: Independent foundation
Limitations: Scholarships to students of Shenandoah High School, IA, for higher education.
Publications: Annual report.
Financial data: Year ended 12/31/2004.
Assets, $1,425,226 (M); Expenditures, $61,121; Total giving, $43,466; Grants to individuals, 24 grants totaling $24,700 (high: $1,000, low: $500).
Type of support: Scholarships—to individuals; Support to graduates or students of specific schools.
Application information: Application form required.
  Deadline(s): Mar. 1
EIN: 421363292

145
Anderson Memorial Educational Trust
P.O. Box 519
Dubois, WY 82513-0519
Application address: c/o Scholarship Comm., P.O. Box 1270, Dubois, WY 82513

Foundation type: Independent foundation
Limitations: Scholarships only to graduates of Dubois High School, WY.
Financial data: Year ended 04/30/2004.
Assets, $616,164 (M); Expenditures, $32,206; Total giving, $31,800; Grants to individuals, 19 grants totaling $31,800 (high: $600, low: $300).
Type of support: Support to graduates or students of specific schools; Undergraduate support.
Application information:
  Initial approach: Letter.
  Deadline(s): Apr. 15
EIN: 836025176

146
E. & E. Anderson Scholarship Foundation
c/o KeyBank N.A.
800 Superior Ave., 4th Fl.
Cleveland, OH 44114

Foundation type: Independent foundation
Limitations: Scholarships to students, primarily in ME, for higher education.
Financial data: Year ended 12/31/2004.
Assets, $586,713 (M); Expenditures, $60,277; Total giving, $47,400; Grants to individuals, totaling $47,400.
Type of support: Undergraduate support.
Application information: Applications not accepted.
EIN: 527115055

147
Eugene and Daniela Anderson Scholarship Foundation
309 W. Foster Ave.
Pampa, TX 79065-6401 (806) 669-3397
Contact: Robert L. Finney, Secy.

Foundation type: Operating foundation
Limitations: Scholarships only to graduates of Pampa High School, TX.
Financial data: Year ended 09/30/2003.
Assets, $872,682 (M); Expenditures, $66,929; Total giving, $62,500; Grants to individuals, 15 grants totaling $62,500 (high: $6,000, low: $1,500).
Type of support: Support to graduates or students of specific schools; Undergraduate support.
Application information: Application form required.
  Deadline(s): Dec. 1
  Additional information: Applications available at Pampa High School.
EIN: 752848433

148
The Anderson Scholarship Fund
(formerly Carrie and Frances Anderson Memorial Scholarship Fund)
41 S. High St., 32nd Fl.
Columbus, OH 43215-6101
Contact: Jon M. Anderson, Tr.
Application address: c/o Principal, Carrollton High School, 252 3rd St. N.E., Carrollton, OH 44615

Foundation type: Independent foundation
Limitations: Scholarships to graduates of Carrollton High School, OH, for higher education.
Financial data: Year ended 12/31/2004.
Assets, $134,239 (M); Expenditures, $8,264; Total giving, $8,000; Grants to individuals, totaling $8,000.
Type of support: Support to graduates or students of specific schools; Undergraduate support.
Application information: Application form required.
  Deadline(s): Mar. 31
  Additional information: Applications available at Carrollton High School.
EIN: 311130710

149
Elizabeth M. Anderson Scholarship Trust
c/o MetroBank, Trust Dept.
1523 8th St.
East Moline, IL 61244

Foundation type: Independent foundation
Limitations: Scholarships to graduates of United Township High School, East Moline, IL. Preference is shown to students accepted to Augustana College; Iowa State University of Science and Technology; University of Michigan; and Washington University, MO.
Financial data: Year ended 02/28/2005.
Assets, $811,614 (M); Expenditures, $37,759; Total giving, $28,000; Grants to individuals, 31 grants totaling $28,000 (high: $1,050, low: $1,000).
Type of support: Support to graduates or students of specific schools; Undergraduate support.
Application information: Application form required.
  Deadline(s): End of Apr.
  Applicants should submit the following:
    1) Class rank
    2) GPA
    3) SAT
    4) Transcripts
    5) ACT

Additional information: Application should include a personal statement.
Program description:
  Scholarship Program: Recipients are chosen on the basis of their academic record, involvement in school and community activities, and educational and occupational goals. Applicants must have a cumulative GPA of at least 2.5 during the first seven semesters of high school. Scholarships are renewable provided the recipient maintains full-time status and a cumulative grade average of at least a "C.".
EIN: 366768317

150
Olson L. Anderson and Catherine Bastow Anderson Scholarship Trust
c/o National City Bank
2322 Tittabawassee Rd.
Saginaw, MI 48604-9476
Application address: c/o Central Michigan Univ., Financial Aid Office, 204 Warriner Hall, Mount Pleasant, MI 48858, tel.: (989) 775-3674

Foundation type: Independent foundation
Limitations: Scholarships to full-time, on-campus undergraduates with demonstrated financial need who are attending Central Michigan University, and who have graduated from high schools in Bay County, MI.
Financial data: Year ended 12/31/2004.
Assets, $1,233,080 (M); Expenditures, $67,257; Total giving, $53,560; Grants to individuals, totaling $53,560.
Type of support: Support to graduates or students of specific schools; Undergraduate support.
Application information: Application form required.
  Initial approach: Letter or telephone to C.M.U.'s financial aid office.
  Deadline(s): May 15
  Applicants should submit the following:
    1) Essay
    2) FAFSA
    3) Letter(s) of recommendation
Program description:
  Scholarship Program: Freshmen and transfer students must have at least a 3.0 cumulative GPA from their previous schools. Scholarships are renewable for up to three additional years provided at least a 2.75 cumulative GPA is maintained.
EIN: 386345071

151
Ralph W. Anderson Veterans Trust
27 Mayridge Dr.
Shenandoah, IA 51601-2233
Contact: Janice J. Billings, Secy.-Treas.

Foundation type: Independent foundation
Limitations: Scholarships to needy veterans of the U.S. military who reside in the Northboro, Shenandoah, or Farragut, IA, areas, and to their spouses, children, and grandchildren.
Financial data: Year ended 06/30/2005.
Assets, $91,920 (M); Expenditures, $21,719; Total giving, $20,662; Grants to individuals, totaling $20,662.
Fields of interest: Vocational education; Military/veterans' organizations.
Type of support: Scholarships—to individuals.
Application information: Applications accepted.
  Deadline(s): Jan. 30
  Additional information: Completion of formal application required, including copy of veteran's active military service release,

DD-214 or other similar release from active military service, list of three personal references, and personal statement. Scholarships are renewable for up to four years.
EIN: 426523038

152
Andona Society

P.O. Box 256
Andover, MA   01810-0005   (978) 475-6268
Contact: Sheila Graham, Pres.
E-mail: info@andonasociety.org; URL: http://www.andonasociety.org

Foundation type: Public charity
Limitations: Awards five scholarships of $2,000 each to permanent residents of Andover, MA, graduating from Andover High School, Greater Lawrence Technical School, or an area private school.
Financial data: Year ended 07/31/2003. Assets, $106,640 (M); Expenditures, $53,279; Total giving, $42,748; Grants to individuals, 5 grants totaling $10,000 (high: $2,000, low: $2,000).
Type of support: Support to graduates or students of specific schools; Undergraduate support.
Application information: Application form required.
   Deadline(s): Apr. 13
EIN: 046192700

153
The Andrew Family Foundation

14628 John Humphrey Dr.
Orland Park, IL   60462
Contact: Kim Llumiquinga

Foundation type: Independent foundation
Limitations: Scholarships to graduates of Carl H. Sandburg High School.
Financial data: Year ended 10/31/2004. Assets, $12,492,549 (M); Expenditures, $673,080; Total giving, $609,316; Grants to individuals, 10 grants totaling $39,666.
Type of support: Support to graduates or students of specific schools; Undergraduate support.
Application information: Applications accepted. Application form required.
   Initial approach: Letter.
   Deadline(s): Contact foundation for current application deadline
EIN: 363926511

154
Aileen S. Andrew Foundation

10701 Winterset Dr.
Orland Park, IL   60467-1106   (708) 349-4445
Contact: Robert E. Hord, Jr., Pres.

Foundation type: Independent foundation
Limitations: Scholarships to children of Andrew Corporation employees and to graduates of a local high school in Orland Park, IL.
Financial data: Year ended 11/30/2004. Assets, $54,431,869 (M); Expenditures, $2,380,722; Total giving, $2,018,824; Grants to individuals, 28 grants totaling $338,132 (high: $16,605, low: $576, average grant: $2,000-$6,000).
Type of support: Employee-related scholarships; Undergraduate support.
Application information: Application form required.
   Deadline(s): Apr. 1

Applicants should submit the following:
   1) Letter(s) of recommendation
   2) Essay
   3) ACT
   4) SAT
   5) Transcripts
Program description:
   Scholarship Program: Recipients may attend college, technical school, or training programs. Scholarships are renewable.
EIN: 366049910

155
The Lillian P. Andrews Foundation

P.O. Box 835
Jackson, AL   36545-0835

Foundation type: Independent foundation
Limitations: Scholarships to seniors of Clarke county high schools, AL, for higher education.
Financial data: Year ended 12/31/2003. Assets, $2,289,196 (M); Expenditures, $176,996; Total giving, $110,400; Grants to individuals, 22 grants totaling $110,000.
Type of support: Support to graduates or students of specific schools; Undergraduate support.
Application information: Applications not accepted.
EIN: 721396945

156
The Emily B. Andrews Memorial Foundation

626 Windwood Ln.
Boone, NC   28607   (828) 262-1731
Contact: James T. Mackorell, Jr., Chair.

Foundation type: Independent foundation
Limitations: Scholarships primarily to students of NC.
Financial data: Year ended 12/31/2004. Assets, $1,156,545 (M); Expenditures, $218,823; Total giving, $191,000; Grants to individuals, 16 grants totaling $16,000 (high: $1,000, low: $1,000).
Type of support: Undergraduate support.
Application information:
   Deadline(s): None
   Additional information: Applications by letter.
EIN: 561667607

157
Leah Andrews Scholarship Trust

c/o Fort Madison Bank & Trust Co.
7th & Ave. G
Fort Madison, IA   52627
Contact: Doyle Ruble, Tr.

Foundation type: Independent foundation
Limitations: Scholarships to graduates of high schools in Fort Madison, IA.
Financial data: Year ended 12/31/2004. Assets, $206,762 (M); Expenditures, $15,381; Total giving, $11,500; Grants to individuals, 8 grants totaling $11,500.
Type of support: Scholarships—to individuals; Support to graduates or students of specific schools.
Application information: Application form required.
   Additional information: Applications are available at Fort Madison Bank and at area high schools.
EIN: 426529065

158
Marie B. Andrews Trust

c/o U.S. Trust Co., N.A.
P.O Box 55122
Boston, MA   02101
Application address: c/o Robert A. Pederson, Principal, Spaulding High School, Wakefield St., Rochester, NH 03867, tel.: (603) 332-0757

Foundation type: Independent foundation
Limitations: Scholarships for higher education to graduates of Spaulding High School, Rochester, NH, with preference given to applicants receiving their education within the commercial department of the school.
Financial data: Year ended 02/29/2004. Assets, $1,579,001 (M); Expenditures, $84,943; Total giving, $68,715; Grants to individuals, totaling $18,000.
Fields of interest: Business school/education.
Type of support: Support to graduates or students of specific schools; Undergraduate support.
Application information:
   Initial approach: Letter or telephone.
   Additional information: Contact trust for current application deadline/guidelines.
EIN: 026061834

159
Alice A. Andrus Foundation

c/o National City Bank, Northeast
P.O. Box 94651
Cleveland, OH   44101-4651
Application address: c/o Principal of Wellington High School, 629 Main St., Wellington, OH 44090, tel.: (440) 647-3734

Foundation type: Independent foundation
Limitations: Scholarships only to graduates of Wellington High School, OH.
Financial data: Year ended 03/31/2004. Assets, $423,840 (M); Expenditures, $11,310; Total giving, $9,000; Grants to individuals, 16 grants totaling $9,000 (high: $1,000, low: $500).
Fields of interest: Vocational education.
Type of support: Support to graduates or students of specific schools; Undergraduate support.
Application information:
   Deadline(s): Apr. 1
   Additional information: Application by letter outlining financial need and purpose.
EIN: 346653271

160
The Angelo Brothers Company Founders Scholarship Foundation

c/o Barton Pasternak
12401 McNulty Rd.
Philadelphia, PA   19154-3297   (215) 671-2000

Foundation type: Independent foundation
Limitations: Scholarships to children of full-time PA employees of Angelo Brothers Company or an affiliate.
Financial data: Year ended 12/31/2004. Assets, $362,424 (M); Expenditures, $27,750; Total giving, $27,750; Grants to individuals, totaling $27,750.
Type of support: Employee-related scholarships.
Application information: Application form required.
   Deadline(s): May 1
   Additional information: Completion of formal application required, including transcript and recommendations from academic and community advisors and officials.

Program description:
Scholarship Program: Children of Angelo Brothers Company employees are eligible to apply provided the combined family income of the applicant and his or her parents does not exceed $40,000 per year. Criteria for selection includes academic achievement, financial need, extracurricular activities and achievements, community involvement, economic self-help (e.g., part-time and summer employment of the applicant), and recommendations. Scholarships are renewable up to four years provided the recipient continues to be a matriculated degree candidate, maintains a 3.0 GPA, and has not been the subject of disciplinary punishment for misconduct, or convicted of a criminal charge other than routine traffic violations.
EIN: 232825756

161

Animal Welfare Trust

141 Halstead Ave., Ste. 301
Mamaroneck, NY 10543 (914) 381-6177
Contact: Brad Goldberg, Pres.
*E-mail for internships:*ali@animalwelfaretrust.org
FAX: (914) 381-6176;
E-mail: email@animalwelfaretrust.org; Mailing and application address: P.O. Box 737, Mamaroneck, NY 10543; URL: http://foundationcenter.org/grantmaker/awt/

Foundation type: Operating foundation
Limitations: Grants to students to fund independent animal-related research projects, and grants to fund otherwise unpaid internship positions within established animal-related organizations.
Publications: Application guidelines; Grants list.
Financial data: Year ended 12/31/2005.
Assets, $5,054,241 (M); Expenditures, $345,214; Total giving, $144,250; Grants to individuals, 2 grants totaling $5,000 (high: $2,500, low: $2,500).
Fields of interest: Animal welfare.
Type of support: Internship funds.
Application information: Applications accepted.
Initial approach: E-mail.
Deadline(s): Apr. 30
Applicants should submit the following:
1) Essay
2) Transcripts
3) Resume
4) Letter(s) of recommendation
Additional information: Application by letter. See Web site for further program guidelines.
Program description:
Student Internship Grant: The foundation seeks to make a meaningful contribution to animal welfare by encouraging students to work on projects that facilitate positive reform for animals. The program was created to fund independent student research projects or provide funding to otherwise unpaid internship positions within established animal-related organizations. The foundation's primary areas of focus are factory farming and farm animal welfare issues, pro-vegetarian campaigns and humane education. Applicant requirements:
· must be a student or individual at the time of the application
· must have a demonstrated interest in animal welfare
· internship funding must be for an independent project approved by and under the supervision of a university professor or for an unpaid position within an established organization
· internships can be for a summer, semester or year-long duration

Priority will be given to post-undergraduate students and individuals. In addition, applications submitted for PhD dissertations will be considered only if there is a practical scope for the project beyond the completion of a final paper. The award is approximately $5,000, depending on a variety of factors, including type of project proposed, length of internship and whether alternate sources of funding are also available.
EIN: 134131408

162

Ann Arbor Area Community Foundation

(formerly Ann Arbor Area Foundation)
201 S. Main St., Ste. 501
Ann Arbor, MI 48104-2113 (734) 663-0401
Contact: Cheryl Elliott, C.E.O. and Pres.; For grants: Martha Bloom, V.P., Prog.
FAX: (734) 663-3514; E-mail: info@aaacf.org; Additional tel.: (734) 663-2173; Additional E-mail: mbloom@aaacf.org; URL: http://www.aaacf.org

Foundation type: Community foundation
Limitations: Scholarships to residents of the Ann Arbor, MI, area.
Publications: Application guidelines; Annual report (including application guidelines); Informational brochure (including application guidelines); Newsletter; Program policy statement.
Financial data: Year ended 12/31/2004.
Assets, $35,318,035 (M); Expenditures, $2,210,148; Total giving, $1,439,370.
Fields of interest: Music; Athletics/sports, training; Women.
Type of support: Employee-related scholarships; Undergraduate support; Camperships.
Application information: Applications accepted. Application form required.
Deadline(s): Varies by fund
Additional information: Interview required; See Web site for program descriptions and further guidelines.
Program description:
Scholarship Funds: The following scholarship funds are administered by the foundation:
· Josee L. Alvarez Memorial Fund
· Ann Arbor Ad Club Scholarship Fund
· Morse B. Barker Scholarship Fund: Awards approximately fifty $1,000 scholarships to students of the Ann Arbor Public Schools, Washtenaw Community College, and Cleary College
· Jack and Mary Ann Brown Scholarship Fund: Generally awards two scholarships per year to children of employees of Control Gaging
· Lucile B. Conger Alumni Group Agency Fund
· Andrea Greiner Memorial Scholarship Fund
· Marge Gallagher Scholarship Fund: Provides camperships for attendance at the Ann Arbor YMCA
· Andrew J. Lum Young Artist Scholarship Fund: Provides a $500 scholarship through the Ann Arbor Concert Band's Young Soloist Competition
· Beth Moffat Memorial Scholarship Fund: Provides a four-year scholarship to a female senior athlete of Hartland High School
· Midwest Financial Credit Union Scholarship Fund: Provides scholarships for credit union members.
EIN: 386087967

163

AnnMarie Foundation

c/o Phillips Plastics Technology Ctr.
N4660 1165th St.
P.O. Box 185
Prescott, WI 54021-7644 (715) 262-8000
Contact: Lori Feiten
FAX: (715) 262-8080; URL: http://www.phillipsplastics.com/corporateoverview/community/annmarie.html

Foundation type: Company-sponsored foundation
Limitations: Scholarships to graduates of Phillips High School, WI.
Financial data: Year ended 04/30/2005.
Assets, $4,302,432 (M); Expenditures, $433,214; Total giving, $410,522; Grants to individuals, 79 grants totaling $69,077 (high: $2,078, low: $500).
Type of support: Support to graduates or students of specific schools.
Application information: Applications not accepted.
EIN: 237301323

164

The Barbara Cox Anthony Foundation

1132 Bishop St., Ste. 1200
Honolulu, HI 96813-2870
Contact: Garner Anthony, V.P.
Application address: P.O. Box 4316, Honolulu, HI 96812, tel.: (808) 536-1877

Foundation type: Independent foundation
Limitations: Scholarships to residents of the Honolulu, HI, area.
Financial data: Year ended 12/31/2004.
Assets, $250,544 (M); Expenditures, $378,034; Total giving, $378,029.
Type of support: Undergraduate support.
Application information: Applications accepted. Application form required.
Initial approach: Letter.
Additional information: Contact foundation for further application guidelines.
EIN: 996005049

165

Aorn Foundation

2170 S. Parker Rd., Ste. 300
Denver, CO 80231-5711 (303) 755-6300
Contact: Sheri J. Voss RN,MS,CNOR, Pres.
FAX: (303) 755-4219; E-mail: tbarlow@aorn.org; Additional tel.: (800) 755-2676, ext. 8229; URL: http://www.aorn.org

Foundation type: Public charity
Limitations: Scholarships to AORN members pursuing bachelor's, master's, and doctoral degrees.
Publications: Annual report; Newsletter.
Financial data: Year ended 12/31/2003.
Assets, $1,456,484 (M); Expenditures, $447,384; Total giving, $322,195.
Fields of interest: Medical school/education; Nursing care.
Type of support: Fellowships; Graduate support; Undergraduate support; Doctoral support.
Application information: Applications accepted. Application form required.
Initial approach: Letter.
Deadline(s): Contact foundation for current application deadline.
EIN: 841193583

166
The Bryan and Helen Applefield Charitable Trust
2330 Montgomery Hwy.
Dothan, AL   36303

Foundation type: Independent foundation
Limitations: Scholarships to individuals residing in AL for elementary and secondary education.
Financial data: Year ended 06/30/2005.
Assets, $1,305 (M); Expenditures, $3,258; Total giving, $3,252; Grants to individuals, 2 grants totaling $3,152 (high: $2,652, low: $500).
Fields of interest: Elementary school/education; Secondary school/education.
Type of support: Precollege support.
Application information: Applications not accepted.
EIN: 636180210

167
Grace G. Appleton Student Loan Fund
c/o KeyBank N.A.
800 Superior Ave., 4th Fl.
Cleveland, OH   44114
Application address: c/o Dir. of Financial Aid, State University of New York at Plattsburgh, 101 Broad St., Plattsburgh, NY 12901

Foundation type: Independent foundation
Limitations: Interest-free student loans to junior or senior students attending SUNY-Plattsburgh, NY.
Financial data: Year ended 12/31/2004.
Assets, $95,584 (M); Expenditures, $12,792; Total giving, $12,000; Loans to individuals, totaling $12,000.
Type of support: Student loans—to individuals; Support to graduates or students of specific schools.
Application information: Applications accepted.
   Deadline(s): None
EIN: 237416731

168
Aquinas Foundation
2115 Summit Ave.
St. Paul, MN   55105-1048

Foundation type: Independent foundation
Limitations: Incentive grants by nomination only to students at the University of St. Thomas, MN.
Financial data: Year ended 06/30/2004.
Assets, $2,498,649 (M); Expenditures, $224,317; Total giving, $165,149.
Type of support: Awards/grants by nomination only; Undergraduate support.
Application information: Applications not accepted.
EIN: 411694561

169
Arab American Institute Foundation
1600 K St., N.W., Ste. 601
Washington, DC   20006   (202) 429-9210
Contact: Helen Samhan, Exec. Dir.; Internship: Dianne Davidson
FAX: (202) 429-9214; URL: http://www.aaiusa.org

Foundation type: Public charity
Limitations: Internship funds, scholarships and research grants to students of Arab descent as well as to individuals working on behalf of the Arab-American community.

Financial data: Year ended 12/31/2004.
Assets, $332,327 (M); Expenditures, $1,036,001; Total giving, $88,893; Grants to individuals, 22 grants totaling $58,038 (high: $14,127, low: $230).
Fields of interest: Community development; Immigrants/refugees.
Type of support: Internship funds; Awards/prizes; Graduate support; Undergraduate support.
Application information: Applications accepted. Application form required. Application form available on the grantmaker's Web site.
   Deadline(s): Mar. 15 for Helen Abott Community Service Awards and Raymond Jallow Awards for Public Service; Apr. 9, and Dec. 6 for Internships; and Apr. 15 for Youth Leadership Awards
   Applicants should submit the following:
   1) Resume
   Additional information: See Web site for complete application guidelines.
Program descriptions:
The Helen Abott Community Service Awards: Honors students and student organizations whose devotion to community service, selfless acts of care, and interest in improving the quality of life for others reflect the life of the Awards' namesake. Three awards are presented annually: one $1,000 prize to a student and two $500 grants to student organizations with impressive community service records.
Internships: The Institute offers paid internship positions to part-time students, graduate students and recent college graduates.
The Raymond Jallow Awards for Public Service: Awards are presented to two deserving candidates whose commitment to public service reflects the life of the Awards' namesake. Two $500 grants are given annually to students and adults who are actively involved in or plan to participate in public service.
Youth Leadership Awards: Awards cash awards to Arab Americans who are 30 years-old or younger to recognize public and community service.
EIN: 521959306

170
Arab Student Aid International Corp.
P.O. Box 3546
Dublin, OH   43016   (614) 889-9420
FAX: (614) 889-9430; E-mail: info@asai2000.org; URL: http://www.asai2000.org

Foundation type: Operating foundation
Limitations: Interest-free student loans to people of Arab descent.
Publications: Application guidelines; Newsletter.
Financial data: Year ended 06/30/2005.
Assets, $5,087,512 (M); Expenditures, $637,364; Total giving, $351,233; Loans to individuals, 42 loans totaling $117,500.
Fields of interest: Minorities.
Type of support: Student loans—to individuals.
Application information:
   Initial approach: Letter.
   Deadline(s): May 1
   Additional information: Contact foundation for current application guidelines.
Program description:
Student Loan Program: Students must maintain a "B" average and demonstrate financial need.
EIN: 223519297

171
Arby's Foundation, Inc.
1000 Corporate Dr.
Fort Lauderdale, FL   33334   (800) 487-2729
Contact: Candace Hawkins
URL: http://www.arby.com/arb07.html

Foundation type: Public charity
Limitations: Undergraduate scholarships by nomination only to participants in the Big Brothers Big Sisters program.
Financial data: Year ended 12/31/2003.
Assets, $5,323,721 (M); Expenditures, $3,809,166; Total giving, $2,658,548; Grants to individuals, 12 grants totaling $50,000 (high: $20,000, low: $1,000).
Type of support: Awards/grants by nomination only; Undergraduate support.
Application information: Applications not accepted.
Program description:
   Scholarship Program: Provides two four-year $20,000 scholarships and ten one-year $1,000 scholarships annually.
EIN: 581692997

172
The Arcadian Foundation
c/o Gordon E. Devens
2760 N.E. 55th St.
Fort Lauderdale, FL   33308-3448

Foundation type: Independent foundation
Limitations: Scholarships to Newark Senior High School students in Newark, NY for higher education.
Financial data: Year ended 12/31/2004.
Assets, $22,592 (M); Expenditures, $16,020; Total giving, $16,000; Grants to individuals, totaling $16,000.
Type of support: Support to graduates or students of specific schools; Undergraduate support.
Application information: Applications not accepted.
Program description:
   Scholarship Program: Four-year undergraduate scholarships to selected members of the Junior class of Newark Senior High School in Newark, NY.
EIN: 364014560

173
Virginia A. Archer Scholarship Trust Fund
520 N.W. Torrey View Ln.
Portland, OR   97229-6540   (503) 229-2733
Contact: Laura H. Shepherd, Tr.

Foundation type: Operating foundation
Limitations: Scholarships to graduating seniors of high schools in Multnomah County, OR, to attend OR colleges and universities.
Financial data: Year ended 06/30/2004.
Assets, $200,951 (M); Expenditures, $17,933; Total giving, $9,750; Grants to individuals, 11 grants totaling $9,750 (high: $900, low: $750).
Type of support: Support to graduates or students of specific schools; Undergraduate support.
Application information: Application form required.
   Initial approach: Letter requesting application.
   Deadline(s): Apr. 15
EIN: 936107007

174
Arctic Education Foundation
3900 C St., Ste. 801
Anchorage, AK 99503 (907) 852-8633
Contact: Leona Okakok
FAX: (907) 852-2774; E-mail: lokakok@asrc.com;
Application address: P.O. Box 129, Barrow, AK
99723; Additional tel.: (800) 770-2772; Additional
E-mail: dcook@asrc.com; URL: http://
www.asrc.com/aef/aef.html

Foundation type: Company-sponsored foundation
Limitations: Scholarships to worthy and financially
needy Native Alaskan students residing in the Arctic
and descendents of persons residing in the Arctic
for postsecondary education.
Publications: Annual report.
Financial data: Year ended 12/31/2003.
Assets, $581,823 (M); Expenditures, $417,598;
Total giving, $408,073; Grants to individuals, 236
grants totaling $408,073 (high: $5,025, low: $50).
Fields of interest: Science; Native Americans/
American Indians.
Type of support: Undergraduate support.
Application information: Applications accepted.
Application form required.
Initial approach: Letter.
Deadline(s): None
EIN: 920068447

175
The Area Fund of Dutchess County
(formerly The Area Fund)
80 Washington St., Ste. 201
Poughkeepsie, NY 12601 (845) 452-3077
Contact: Andrea L. Reynolds, C.E.O.
FAX: (845) 452-3083;
E-mail: cfdc@communityfoundationdc.org;
Additional E-mail:
areynolds@communityfoundationdc.org;
URL: http://www.communityfoundationdc.org

Foundation type: Community foundation
Limitations: Scholarships to Dutchess County, NY,
residents.
Publications: Application guidelines; Annual report;
Newsletter.
Financial data: Year ended 06/30/2004.
Assets, $19,924,579 (M); Expenditures,
$2,861,454; Total giving, $1,185,480; Grants to
individuals, 271 grants totaling $249,565 (high:
$6,000, low: $20).
Type of support: Scholarships—to individuals.
Application information: Applications accepted.
Initial approach: Letter or telephone.
Additional information: Contact fund for current
application deadline/guidelines.
Program description:
Scholarship Funds: The foundation administers
numerous scholarship funds, each with specific
guidelines and requirements. See the foundation's
Web site for information on specific funds.
EIN: 237026859

176
Ariens Foundation, Ltd.
655 W. Ryan St.
Brillion, WI 54110-1072
Contact: Mary M. Ariens, Pres.

Foundation type: Company-sponsored foundation
Limitations: Grants to residents of Brillion, WI, and
the surrounding area, primarily for educational
purposes.
Financial data: Year ended 06/30/2005.
Assets, $368,150 (M); Expenditures, $123,139;

Total giving, $122,375; Grants to individuals,
totaling $8,575.
Type of support: Scholarships—to individuals.
Application information: Applications accepted.
Deadline(s): None
Additional information: Individuals should submit
brief resume of qualifications.
EIN: 396102058

177
The Arise Charitable Trust
P.O. Box 1014
Freeland, WA 98249-1014
Contact: Charles W. Edwards, Mgr.

Foundation type: Independent foundation
Limitations: Scholarships to women of South
Whidbey Island, WA.
Publications: Informational brochure.
Financial data: Year ended 09/30/2005.
Assets, $3,279,378 (M); Expenditures,
$161,963; Total giving, $122,975; Grants to
individuals, 85 grants totaling $62,975 (high:
$1,750, low: $96).
Fields of interest: Women.
Type of support: Scholarships—to individuals.
Application information: Application form required.
Initial approach: Letter requesting application.
Deadline(s): Apr. 1 and Oct. 1
Additional information: Completion of formal
application required, including IRS Form
1040, FAF, and two letters of
recommendation.
EIN: 911350780

178
Arizona Community Foundation
2201 E. Camelback Rd., Ste. 202
Phoenix, AZ 85016 (602) 381-1400
Contact: Sharon Landis, Sr. V.P., Finance and
Admin.
FAX: (602) 381-1575;
E-mail: slandis@azfoundation.org; Additional tel.:
(800) 222-8221; Grant application E-mail:
grants@azfoundation.org; URL: http://
www.azfoundation.org

Foundation type: Community foundation
Limitations: Scholarships to residents of AZ to
attend Arizona State University, Northern Arizona
University, and University of Arizona.
Publications: Application guidelines; Annual report;
Financial statement; Informational brochure;
Newsletter; Program policy statement.
Financial data: Year ended 12/31/2005.
Assets, $430,919,000 (M); Expenditures,
$25,886,000; Total giving, $18,148,000.
Type of support: Support to graduates or students
of specific schools; Undergraduate support.
Application information: Applications accepted.
Application form required. Application form
available on the grantmaker's Web site.
Initial approach: Letter.
Deadline(s): Apr. 1 and Oct. 1
EIN: 860348306

179
The Arizona Cowpuncher's Scholarship Organization, Inc.
35550 9 Irons Ranch Rd.
Wickenburg, AZ 85390 (928) 684-2109
Contact: Bill Owens, Pres.
FAX: (928) 684-2125;
E-mail: info@allaboutacso.com; URL: http://
www.allaboutacso.com

Foundation type: Public charity
Limitations: Scholarships to students residing in
Arizona who are employed, or whose parents are
employed in ranching.
Financial data: Year ended 12/31/2003.
Assets, $149,325 (M); Expenditures, $44,814;
Total giving, $35,140; Grants to individuals, 24
grants totaling $35,140 (high: $3,140, low: $500).
Type of support: Undergraduate support.
Application information: Application form required.
Deadline(s): Feb. 1
Additional information: Completion of formal
application required, including birth
certificate, two letters of recommendation,
and letter of intent; See Web site for further
application information.
EIN: 860825426

180
Arizona Foundation for Legal Services and Education
4201 N. 24th St., Ste. 210
Phoenix, AZ 85016-6288 (602) 252-4804
Contact: Kevin Ruegg, Exec. Dir.; for Loans: Lara
Slifko
FAX: (602) 271-4930

Foundation type: Public charity
Limitations: Loans to law school graduates to
assist them in paying their law school loans.
Financial data: Year ended 12/31/2003.
Assets, $2,624,341 (M); Expenditures,
$3,560,270; Total giving, $2,149,688; Loans to
individuals, 16 loans totaling $24,221.
Fields of interest: Law school/education.
Type of support: Loans—to individuals.
Application information: Applications accepted.
Application form required. Application form
available on the grantmaker's Web site.
Deadline(s): Jan. 12
Additional information: See Web site for
complete application information.
Program description:
Loan Repayment Assistance Program: Assists
attorneys employed in non-profit organizations
dedicated to serving the legal needs of low-income
individuals and families in Arizona. The program
assists attorneys who have incurred significant
debt to finance their law school educations by giving
them forgivable loans to pay their education loans,
allowing attorneys to work in legal aid programs for
the poor. Applicants must be members of the State
Bar of Arizona with the possibility of waiver of this
requirement; or be licensed by another state and
employed by an approved non-profit legal
organization.
EIN: 953351710

181
Arizona Kidney Foundation
4203 E. Indian School Rd., Ste. 140
Phoenix, AZ 85018 (602) 840-1644
Contact: Glenna Jones Shapiro, C.E.O.
FAX: (602) 840-2360; E-mail: info@azkidney.org;
URL: http://www.azkidney.org

Foundation type: Public charity
Limitations: Scholarships to kidney patients residing in AZ.
Financial data: Year ended 06/30/2003. Assets, $2,617,920 (M); Expenditures, $1,821,400; Total giving, $24,751; Grants to individuals, totaling $24,751.
Fields of interest: Kidney diseases.
Type of support: Undergraduate support.
Application information: Application form required. Application form available on the grantmaker's Web site.
  Deadline(s): Contact foundation for current application deadline
Program description:
  Scholarship Program: Applications must be submitted by the patient's renal social worker.
EIN: 866052343

182
Arizona Scholarship Fund
P.O. Box 2576
Mesa, AZ   85214-2576   (480) 497-4564
Contact: ChamBria Henderson, Pres. and Exec. Dir.
FAX: (480) 497-4737;
E-mail: chambria@azscholarships.org; URL: http://www.azscholarships.org

Foundation type: Public charity
Limitations: Scholarships to families residing in AZ to send their children to private schools, from K-12th grade.
Publications: Informational brochure; Program policy statement; Program policy statement (including application guidelines).
Financial data: Year ended 06/30/2003. Assets, $462,925 (M); Expenditures, $1,128,898; Total giving, $1,038,250; Grants to individuals, totaling $1,038,250.
Fields of interest: Elementary/secondary education.
Type of support: Scholarships—to individuals; Precollege support.
Application information: Applications accepted. Application form required.
  Copies of proposal: 1
  Deadline(s): None
  Applicants should submit the following:
    1) Letter(s) of recommendation
    2) Financial information
    3) FAF
    4) Essay
  Additional information: See Web site for further application information.
Program description:
  Scholarship Program: Scholarships of up to $1,000 per child are awarded on a first-come, first-served basis. Scholarships are renewable. Students must be Arizona residents, enrolled in grades K-12.
EIN: 860938314

183
Arizona School Choice Trust, Inc.
1951 W. Camelback Rd., Ste. 445
Phoenix, AZ   85015   (602) 454-1360
Contact: Keith P. DeGreen, Pres.
FAX: (602) 995-1449; E-mail: info@asct.org;
URL: http://www.asct.org/

Foundation type: Public charity
Limitations: Scholarships to low-income families residing in AZ for tuition at K-12 schools.
Financial data: Year ended 07/31/2004.
Assets, $1,623,445 (M); Expenditures,

$1,064,087; Total giving, $1,064,087; Grants to individuals, 855 grants totaling $936,087.
Fields of interest: Elementary/secondary education; Economically disadvantaged.
Type of support: Precollege support.
Application information: Applications accepted. Application form required.
  Deadline(s): None
  Additional information: See Web site for further application information.
Program description:
  McVaugh Educational Opportunity Scholarship: The scholarship awards up to $3,000 per child per school year. Awards are first-come, first-served. Preference is given to students transferring from public school or into private school from home school or pre-K programs. Scholarships are renewable annually until graduation from grade 12.
EIN: 860712553

184
Arkansas Eastman Scholarship Trust
c/o Citizens Bank
P.O. Box 2156
Batesville, AR   72503
Application address: c/o Scholarship Comm., P.O. Box 2357, Batesville, AR 72503, tel.: (807) 698-5524

Foundation type: Operating foundation
Limitations: Scholarships to full-time students from North Central AR with an interest in math and/or science or other related studies for higher education.
Financial data: Year ended 12/31/2003. Assets, $162,976 (M); Expenditures, $7,722; Total giving, $5,200; Grants to individuals, totaling $5,200.
Fields of interest: Science; Mathematics.
Type of support: Undergraduate support.
Application information: Applications accepted.
  Deadline(s): None
  Additional information: Contact foundation for current application guidelines.
EIN: 582024178

185
Arkansas Farm Bureau Scholarship Foundation
(formerly Farm Bureau-Arkansas Scholarship Foundation, Inc.)
10720 Kanis Rd.
Little Rock, AR   72211
Application address: c/o Tim King, Attn.: Scholarship Form, P.O. Box 31, Little Rock, AR 72203, tel.: (501) 228-1270

Foundation type: Independent foundation
Limitations: Scholarships to residents of AR planning a career in or related to the agricultural industry. Applicants must be must be children of Farm Bureau members.
Financial data: Year ended 10/31/2004. Assets, $330,809 (M); Expenditures, $8,476; Total giving, $8,000; Grants to individuals, 14 grants totaling $8,000 (high: $1,000, low: $500).
Fields of interest: Agriculture.
Type of support: Undergraduate support.
Application information: Application form required.
  Initial approach: Letter.
  Applicants should submit the following:
    1) Financial information
    2) Essay

Additional information: Contact foundation for further application guidelines.
EIN: 710888051

186
Arkema Inc. Foundation
(formerly Atofina Chemicals, Inc. Foundation)
2000 Market St.
Philadelphia, PA   19103-3222   (215) 419-7000
Contact: Diane Milici, Exec. Asst.

Foundation type: Company-sponsored foundation
Limitations: Scholarships to high school seniors who are children of active or deceased employees of Arkema, Inc.
Financial data: Year ended 12/31/2004. Assets, $130,699 (M); Expenditures, $573,854; Total giving, $571,067.
Type of support: Employee-related scholarships.
Application information: Application form not required.
  Initial approach: Letter.
  Deadline(s): None.
Program description:
  Scholarship Program: Each year, 10 scholarships of $3,000 per year for four years of study are awarded to children of employees. Scholarships are paid in increments of $1,500 each semester. Eight scholarships are given in the U.S., one is given in Canada, and one is given in Mexico.
EIN: 236256818

187
Arlington Catholic High School Scholarship Fund
c/o Bank of America, N.A.
P.O. Box 6768
Providence, RI   02940-6768
Application address: c/o Carol Gray, Bank of America, N.A., 100 Federal St., Boston, MA 02110

Foundation type: Independent foundation
Limitations: Scholarships to graduating students of Arlington Catholic High School, MA.
Financial data: Year ended 12/31/2004. Assets, $274,382 (M); Expenditures, $12,736; Total giving, $9,000; Grants to individuals, totaling $9,000.
Fields of interest: Roman Catholic agencies & churches.
Type of support: Support to graduates or students of specific schools; Undergraduate support.
Application information:
  Initial approach: Letter.
  Deadline(s): Sept. 15 and Jan. 15
EIN: 046116950

188
Armstrong Family Foundation
P.O. Box 451248
Los Angeles, CA   90045-1248

Foundation type: Independent foundation
Limitations: Scholarships to graduates of Garfield High School, Los Angeles, CA, for higher education.
Financial data: Year ended 12/31/2004. Assets, $30,903 (M); Expenditures, $53,593; Total giving, $39,200; Grants to individuals, totaling $39,200.
Type of support: Support to graduates or students of specific schools; Undergraduate support.
Application information: Applications not accepted.
EIN: 954251068

189
Cecil Armstrong Foundation
c/o Lake City Bank
P.O. Box 1387
Warsaw, IN 46581-1387   (574) 267-9110

Foundation type: Independent foundation
Limitations: Scholarships to Kosciusko County, IN, students to improve skills or advance education by attending any properly accredited or certified educational program in IN.
Financial data: Year ended 12/31/2004.
Assets, $225,154 (M); Expenditures, $8,920; Total giving, $6,750; Grants to individuals, 16 grants totaling $6,750 (high: $450, low: $250).
Fields of interest: Vocational education; Health sciences school/education.
Type of support: Technical education support; Undergraduate support.
Application information: Application form required.
> *Deadline(s):* Apr. 1
> *Additional information:* Completion of formal application required, including transcript, activities, attendance, and three letters of recommendation; Applications available from local schools and Lake City Bank.

Program description:
> *Scholarship Program:* Grants for tuition, housing, and school expenses are awarded to students attending colleges, universities, vocational schools, rehabilitation training, or any properly accredited course in IN. For college-bound applicants, SAT, ACT, PSAT, or equivalent test scores will be required. No specific rank in class is required. For vocational, rehabilitation, or any other type of training, sufficient evidence of skills and ability to pursue such a course of study is required. Applicants applying for assistance to continue a course in which they are already enrolled must submit a transcript of grades and present status from the institution or program they are attending. Recipients are chosen by a five-member awards committee, composed of people from the community. Scholarships are renewable.

EIN: 237128298

190
Ethel Louise Armstrong Foundation, Inc.
c/o Penny Huff
130 La Vereda Rd.
Santa Barbara, CA 93108   (626) 398-8840
Contact: For Scholarships: Deborah Lewis
Scholarship application address: 2460 North Lake Ave., PMB No. 128, Altadena, CA 91001
FAX: (626) 398-8843; E-mail: info@ela.org;
URL: http://www.ela.org

Foundation type: Independent foundation
Limitations: Scholarships to female graduate students with physical disabilities.
Publications: Grants list; Informational brochure (including application guidelines).
Financial data: Year ended 12/31/2004.
Assets, $1,880,907 (M); Expenditures, $176,184; Total giving, $20,039; Grants to individuals, totaling $6,000.
Fields of interest: Disabilities, people with; Women.
Type of support: Graduate support.
Application information: Applications accepted. Application form required.
> *Deadline(s):* June 1
> *Additional information:* Formal application should include ELA verification of Disability form from Vocational Rehabilitation counselor or physician, two typed letters of recommendation from teachers, faculty

members or employers (on letterhead), copy of transcript, and typewritten 1,000-word essay explaining "How I Will Change the Face of Disability on the Planet"; See Web site for further information.

Program description:
> *Scholarship Program:* Scholarships range up to a maximum of $1,000 to $2,000 per year. Recipients must be currently enrolled or actively applying to a graduate program in an accredited college or university in the U.S., must be active in a local, state or national disability organization (either in person or electronically), which is providing services and/or advocacy for people with disabilities. Students must be willing, as ELA scholars, to network with the ELA Board of Directors and current alumni scholarship recipients on foundation's listserv. This will enhance the ELA scholar's support base in professional and political arenas. Students must also be willing to update ELA with an annual letter on their progress in academic and working careers.

EIN: 582147887

191
Benjamin A. Armstrong Trust
c/o Bank of America, N.A., P.C. Group
P.O. Box 2864
Hartford, CT 06101-9928
Application address: c/o: Bank of America, 777 Main St., CT2-102-22-02, Hartford, CT 06115

Foundation type: Independent foundation
Limitations: Scholarships to male graduates of New London High School, CT, and female graduates of the Williams School, for higher education.
Financial data: Year ended 12/31/2003.
Assets, $708,535 (M); Expenditures, $43,062; Total giving, $32,000; Grants to individuals, 8 grants totaling $16,000 (high: $5,000, low: $1,000).
Type of support: Support to graduates or students of specific schools; Undergraduate support.
Application information: Applications accepted. Application form required.
> *Deadline(s):* June 1
> *Additional information:* Application should include letters of recommendation, transcripts, a copy of parent's and applicant's income tax returns.

EIN: 066026283

192
George S. Arnold Educational Trust
c/o Wachovia Bank, N.A.
100 N. Main St., 13th Fl.
Winston-Salem, NC 27150
Application address: c/o Romney Rotary Club, Romney, WV 26757

Foundation type: Independent foundation
Limitations: Scholarships to students in Hampshire County, WV, for higher education.
Financial data: Year ended 12/31/2004.
Assets, $239,129 (M); Expenditures, $15,432; Total giving, $11,552.
Type of support: Undergraduate support.
Application information: Applications by letter accepted throughout the year.
EIN: 546191759

193
Arnold Foundation
c/o Paciotti, C.P.A.
Plaza 315, 1994 Rte. 315
Wilkes Barre, PA 18702-6943   (570) 823-8855
Contact: Arnold K. Biscontini, Pres.

Foundation type: Independent foundation
Limitations: Scholarships to residents of NC and Luzerne County, PA.
Financial data: Year ended 03/31/2005.
Assets, $147,094 (M); Expenditures, $80,513; Total giving, $69,083; Grants to individuals, 6 grants totaling $49,033 (high: $30,975, low: $500).
Type of support: Scholarships—to individuals.
Application information: Applications accepted throughout the year; Application by letter including brief resume of academic qualifications.
EIN: 236417708

194
Maude E. Arnold Memorial Fund
(formerly Maude E. Arnold Trust for Memorial Fund)
c/o Bank of America, N.A., P.C. Group
P.O. Box 6768
Providence, RI 02940-6768
Application address: c/o Scholarship Comm. Chair., First Baptist Church, P.O. Box 121, 2-4 North St., Plymouth, CT 06782, tel.: (860) 283-6181

Foundation type: Independent foundation
Limitations: Scholarships to students who have been residents of Waterbury, CT, for the previous five years; preference given to girls.
Financial data: Year ended 12/31/2003.
Assets, $209,142 (M); Expenditures, $13,339; Total giving, $12,100; Grants to individuals, 3 grants totaling $12,100 (high: $8,500, low: $1,800).
Fields of interest: Women.
Type of support: Undergraduate support.
Application information:
> *Deadline(s):* Apr. 30
> *Additional information:* Application requires transcript sent directly from college to church, including family financial status, activities and grades.

EIN: 066140957

195
Heather Lynn Arnold Memorial Scholarship
159 Emmer Rd. S.W.
Gridley, KS 66852-9244   (620) 836-4787
Contact: Doris E. Arnold, Tr.

Foundation type: Independent foundation
Limitations: Scholarships to graduating seniors at Gridley High School, KS, for higher education.
Financial data: Year ended 12/31/2004.
Assets, $172,151 (M); Expenditures, $9,752; Total giving, $9,200; Grants to individuals, totaling $9,200.
Type of support: Support to graduates or students of specific schools; Undergraduate support.
Application information: Application form required.
> *Deadline(s):* Contact foundation for current application deadline

Program description:
> *Scholarship Program:* Recipients must carry a GPA of at least 2.5 and have attended their entire senior year of high school at Gridley High School.

EIN: 481170140

196
Arnsberg Scholarship Trust
711 S. Clark Ave.
P.O. Box 386
Republic, WA 99166
Contact: Gary Anderson, Tr.

Foundation type: Operating foundation
Limitations: Scholarships to students of Republic, WA high schools for higher education at an WA institution.
Financial data: Year ended 12/31/2004.
Assets, $184,705 (M); Expenditures, $8,603; Total giving, $8,000; Grants to individuals, 5 grants totaling $8,000 (high: $3,000, low: $1,000).
Type of support: Support to graduates or students of specific schools; Undergraduate support.
Application information:
Initial approach: Letter.
Deadline(s): First Fri. after spring break
EIN: 916443732

197
Jack Arpajian Armenian Educational Foundation, Inc.
P.O. Box 1090
Exton, PA 19341
Contact: Marguerite Parkinson, Pres.

Foundation type: Independent foundation
Limitations: Scholarships to students of Armenian heritage for higher education.
Financial data: Year ended 12/31/2004.
Assets, $941,642 (M); Expenditures, $85,450; Total giving, $50,000; Grants to individuals, totaling $50,000.
Type of support: Undergraduate support.
Application information: Application form required.
Initial approach: Letter.
Deadline(s): Aug. 1 and Dec. 1
Program description:
Scholarship Program: Scholarships are awarded based on GPA, financial need, extracurricular activities and Armenian heritage.
EIN: 232761002

198
Ernest G. Arps Memorial Fund
c/o BB&T, Trust Dept.
P.O. Box 2907
Wilson, NC 27894-2907
Application address: c/o Samuel J. Styons, P.O. Box 127, Plymouth, NC 27962

Foundation type: Independent foundation
Limitations: Scholarships to residents of Washington County, NC, to attend four-year colleges in NC.
Financial data: Year ended 09/30/2004.
Assets, $839,716 (M); Expenditures, $51,893; Total giving, $41,500; Grants to individuals, totaling $41,500.
Type of support: Undergraduate support.
Application information: Applications accepted. Application form required.
Deadline(s): None
Applicants should submit the following:
1) Photograph
EIN: 566228126

199
Arques Charitable Education Trust
30 Liberty Ship Way, Ste. 3380
Sausalito, CA 94965
Contact: William Ziegler, Tr.

Foundation type: Independent foundation
Limitations: Scholarships to students majoring in veterinary fields, classical voice, and mechanical arts.
Financial data: Year ended 12/31/2004.
Assets, $2,933,196 (M); Expenditures, $271,411; Total giving, $187,545; Grants to individuals, 8 grants totaling $72,365 (high: $17,900, low: $3,500).
Fields of interest: Music; Opera; Veterinary medicine.
Type of support: Scholarships—to individuals; Student loans—to individuals; Graduate support.
Application information: Applications accepted. Application form required.
Initial approach: Letter.
Copies of proposal: 1
Deadline(s): Mar. 31
Applicants should submit the following:
1) Resume
2) Proposal
3) Letter(s) of recommendation
4) Budget Information
5) Financial information
Additional information: Time for response to an application is 30 days.
EIN: 686044627

200
Arrow International, Inc. Scholarship Fund
600 Penn St., PA 6497
P.O. Box 1102
Reading, PA 19603-1102

Foundation type: Independent foundation
Limitations: Scholarships to employees of Arrow International, and their children.
Financial data: Year ended 11/30/2004.
Assets, $2,376,343 (M); Expenditures, $118,740; Total giving, $94,917; Grants to individuals, 10 grants totaling $94,917 (high: $17,321, low: $2,543).
Type of support: Employee-related scholarships.
Application information: Applications not accepted.
Additional information: Unsolicited requests for funds not considered or acknowledged.
EIN: 232801942

201
Art League of Marco Island, Inc.
1010 Winterberry Dr.
Marco Island, FL 34145 (239) 394-4221
Contact: Dolores Lindberg, Pres.
E-mail: mail@marcoislandart.com; URL: http://www.marcoislandart.com

Foundation type: Public charity
Limitations: Scholarships to students from Collier County, FL high schools for higher education in the arts.
Financial data: Year ended 04/30/2004.
Assets, $2,197,136 (M); Expenditures, $465,920; Total giving, $15,000; Grants to individuals, totaling $15,000.
Fields of interest: Arts education.
Type of support: Support to graduates or students of specific schools; Undergraduate support.

Application information: Contact foundation for current application deadline/guidelines.
EIN: 591754367

202
Arthur's Enterprises, Inc. Scholarship Foundation
P.O. Box 5654
Huntington, WV 25703-0654
Contact: Joan Weisberg, Secy.

Foundation type: Company-sponsored foundation
Limitations: Scholarships to children of employees of Arthur's Enterprises, Inc., WV.
Financial data: Year ended 06/30/2005.
Assets, $1,048 (M); Expenditures, $14,250; Total giving, $14,250; Grants to individuals, 13 grants totaling $14,250 (high: $1,000, low: $250).
Type of support: Employee-related scholarships.
Application information: Application form required.
Deadline(s): Mar. 1
Applicants should submit the following:
1) SAT
2) GPA
3) ACT
Program description:
Scholarship Program: Applicants must have at least one parent who has been a full-time employee of Arthur's Enterprises, Inc. or its subsidiaries for the previous three years; be a high school senior, graduate, or student currently enrolled in college; have a minimum GPA of 2.5, ACT score of 18, and SAT score of 750; and be a full-time undergraduate degree candidate. Scholarships are renewable.
EIN: 550709058

203
Royale B. and Eleanor M. Arvig Memorial Scholarship Fund
(formerly Royale B. Arvig Memorial Scholarship Fund)
160 2nd Ave. S.W.
Perham, MN 56573

Foundation type: Independent foundation
Limitations: Scholarships to graduating high school seniors from specific MN school districts for further education at a college, university, vocational-technical school, or other postsecondary educational organization.
Financial data: Year ended 12/31/2004.
Assets, $179,464 (M); Expenditures, $33,052; Total giving, $33,000; Grants to individuals, totaling $33,000.
Fields of interest: Vocational education.
Type of support: Undergraduate support.
Application information:
Initial approach: Letter.
Additional information: Contact fund for current application deadline/guidelines.
EIN: 411574208

204
Asbestos Workers Local 14 Scholarship Fund
6513 Bustleton Ave.
Philadelphia, PA 19149-2906 (215) 289-4303
Contact: David Andrew, Co-Chair.
FAX: (215) 289-8655; E-mail: info@local-14.org; URL: http://www.local-14.org

Foundation type: Public charity
Limitations: Scholarships to members of Asbestos Workers Local 14 who are employed by participating

employers, or their children, for undergraduate education.

Financial data: Year ended 06/30/2003. Assets, $5,212 (M); Expenditures, $29,608; Total giving, $29,000; Grants to individuals, 28 grants totaling $29,000 (high: $2,000, low: $1,000).

Fields of interest: Labor unions/organizations.

Type of support: Employee-related scholarships; Undergraduate support.

Application information:
Deadline(s): Contact organization for current application deadlines/guidelines
Additional information: Recipients selected according to leadership, academics, and inability to afford college.

EIN: 311729117

205

Stanley and Blanche Ash Foundation

P.O. Box 310
Greenville, MI   48838-0310
Contact: Blanche E. Ash, Pres.

Foundation type: Independent foundation

Limitations: Scholarships to students residing in the Montcalm County, MI area, who show financial need and have satisfactory grades.

Financial data: Year ended 12/31/2004. Assets, $6,309,565 (M); Expenditures, $253,825; Total giving, $235,468; Grants to individuals, 119 grants totaling $99,773.

Type of support: Research; Graduate support; Technical education support; Undergraduate support.

Application information:
Deadline(s): None
Additional information: Application by standard scholarship form used by school of applicant's choice.

EIN: 382966745

206

Ashcraft Foundation, Inc.

2437 Eastridge Dr.
Billings, MT   59102   (406) 482-4272
Contact: Jimmie L. Ashcraft, Tr.

Foundation type: Independent foundation

Limitations: Scholarships to individuals for undergraduate support, primarily in MT.

Financial data: Year ended 09/30/2004. Assets, $73,349 (M); Expenditures, $28,000; Total giving, $28,000; Grants to individuals, 28 grants totaling $28,000 (high: $1,000, low: $1,000).

Type of support: Undergraduate support.

Application information: Applications accepted.
Initial approach: Letter.
Deadline(s): None
Additional information: Contact foundation for current application guidelines.

EIN: 810472889

207

Ashland County Community Foundation

300 College Ave.
Ashland, OH   44805   (419) 281-4733
Contact: Lucille G. Ford, Pres.
FAX: (419) 289-5540; E-mail: accf@hmcltd.net;
URL: http://
www.ashlandcountycommunityfoundation.org

Foundation type: Community foundation

Limitations: Educational loans to residents or students of Ashland County high schools who plan matriculation into college prior to the age of 23. Residents must be age 23 and over and be U.S. citizens.

Publications: Application guidelines; Annual report; Informational brochure; Newsletter.

Financial data: Year ended 06/30/2005. Assets, $7,870,462 (M); Expenditures, $423,223; Total giving, $275,503; Loans to individuals, totaling $34,200.

Type of support: Student loans—to individuals; Support to graduates or students of specific schools.

Application information: Applications accepted. Application form required.
Initial approach: Letter or e-mail.
Copies of proposal: 1
Deadline(s): Apr. 15, June 15 and Nov. 15 for Loans
Additional information: See foundation Web site for further information.

EIN: 341812908

208

The Ashtabula Foundation, Inc.

4510 Collins Blvd., Ste. 6
Ashtabula, OH   44004   (440) 992-6818
Contact: Roberta Martin, Admin.
FAX: (440) 992-0724;
E-mail: grants@ashtabulafoundation.org;
URL: http://www.ashtabulafoundation.org

Foundation type: Independent foundation

Limitations: Scholarships to residents of Ashtabula, OH, who are graduates of Ashtabula high schools. One scholarship is also awarded each year to an Ashtabula County high school senior who is a football letter winner with at least a 2.5 GPA.

Publications: Application guidelines; Informational brochure.

Financial data: Year ended 12/31/2004. Assets, $17,106,550 (M); Expenditures, $991,968; Total giving, $851,238.

Type of support: Support to graduates or students of specific schools; Undergraduate support.

Application information: Applications accepted. Application form required.
Deadline(s): May 1 for Edward J. Harvey scholarship
Applicants should submit the following:
1) Pell Grant
2) Transcripts
Additional information: A copy of SET may be submitted in place of the Pell Grant application.

Program description:
Edward J. Harvey Scholarship: Open to legal residents of Ashtabula, OH, who graduated from a high school in Ashtabula. These $1,000 per year scholarships must be used at accredited institutions by full-time students.

EIN: 346538130

209

Asian Pacific Fund

225 Bush St., Ste. 590
San Francisco, CA   94104-4224
(415) 433-6859
Contact: Gail Kong, Pres. and Exec. Dir.
FAX: (415) 433-2425;
E-mail: info@asianpacificfund.org; URL: http://
www.asianpacificfund.org

Foundation type: Public charity

Limitations: Scholarships and awards to Asian Americans, primarily in the Bay Area, CA, region.

Financial data: Year ended 06/30/2003. Assets, $1,149,904 (M); Expenditures, $884,483; Total giving, $351,329; Grants to individuals, 26 grants totaling $24,100 (high: $2,730, low: $500).

Fields of interest: Asians/Pacific Islanders.

Type of support: Support to graduates or students of specific schools; Awards/prizes; Undergraduate support.

Application information:
Initial approach: E-mail.
Additional information: See Web site for additional application information.

Program descriptions:
Banata Filipino American College Scholarship: Awards five scholarships of $5,000 to qualified high school seniors who will be enrolled at 4-year colleges or universities. Applicants must be of Filipino heritage with a GPA of at least "B", and plan to attend a four-year college or university. Award is based on financial need.

Growing Up Asian in America: An essay and art competition for students grades K through 12. Winning students are honored in May sharing $27,000 in savings bond awards and merchandise prizes. Their entries are featured in community exhibits that are displayed by Bay Area public libraries.

Banata Filipino American College Prep Scholarship: Awards 24 scholarships of $1,500 to qualified high school juniors for SAT preparation and college admissions counseling. Applicant must be of Filipino heritage with a high school 2.7 GPA, plan to attend a four-year college or university with interest and skills in engineering, math or science.

Maria Elena Yuchengco Memorial Journalism Scholarship: Awards two to three scholarships of $5,000 each year to full-time undergraduate students at San Francisco State University, who are journalism majors, of Filipino heritage and have a cumulative GPA of 3.0. Award is based on merit and financial need, and applicants must be a U.S. citizen or permanent resident.

Soledad Fernandez Scholarship Fund: Awards one to three scholarships totaling $5,000 each year to public high school seniors of Filipino heritage with a maximum cumulative GPA of 3.0, and plan to attend a four-year college or university. Award is based on merit and financial need.

EIN: 943201522

210

George W. Askren Memorial Scholarship Trust

(formerly Caroline L. Askren Trust)
c/o JPMorgan Chase Bank, N.A.
P.O. Box 1308
Milwaukee, WI   53201
Application address: c/o Principal, Warren Central High School, 9500 E. 16th St., Indianapolis, IN 46229, tel.: (317) 898-6133

Foundation type: Independent foundation

Limitations: Scholarships to graduates of Warren Township Schools, Indianapolis, IN, who are in the upper half of their class.

Financial data: Year ended 10/31/2004. Assets, $333,828 (M); Expenditures, $20,587; Total giving, $17,000; Grants to individuals, totaling $17,000.

Type of support: Support to graduates or students of specific schools; Undergraduate support.

Application information: Application form required.
Deadline(s): Early Spring

EIN: 356231596

211
Hazel Aslakson Scholarship Trust
c/o Associated Banc-Corp.
P.O. Box 408
Neenah, WI   54957-0408
Application address: c/o First Lutheran Church, 521
N. 8th St., Manitowoc, WI 54220

Foundation type: Independent foundation
Limitations: Scholarships to residents of
Manitowoc, WI, who are members of the First
Lutheran Church and attend an Evangelical
Lutheran Church of an American college, university,
or seminary.
Financial data: Year ended 12/31/2004.
Assets, $117,687 (M); Expenditures, $12,289;
Total giving, $9,950; Grants to individuals, 4 grants
totaling $9,950 (high: $4,500, low: $475).
Fields of interest: Theological school/education.
Type of support: Graduate support; Undergraduate
support.
Application information: Applications accepted.
   Deadline(s): Contact foundation for current
      application guidelines
   Additional information: Applicant must include
      good character references and have good
      grades.
EIN: 396638318

212
Asparagus Club
c/o National Grocers Assn.
1005 N. Glebe Rd., Ste. 250
Arlington, VA   22201   (703) 516-0700
Contact: Michael Needler, Pres.; Scholarships:
Rachel R. Sayes
Scholarship Selection and Review Committee: c/o
Baton Rouge Area Foundation, 402 N. Fourth St,
Baton Rouge, LA 70802; URL: http://
www.braf.org/images/asparagus1.pdf
URL: http://www.braf.org/images/asparagus1.pdf

Foundation type: Public charity
Limitations: Scholarships from $1,500 a year, for
up to two years, for sophomores and juniors who
demonstrate financial need and a desire to pursue
a career in the grocery industry.
Financial data: Year ended 05/31/2004.
Assets, $75,850 (M); Expenditures, $62,511;
Total giving, $18,000; Grants to individuals, 12
grants totaling $18,000 (high: $1,500, low:
$1,500).
Fields of interest: Higher education.
Type of support: Scholarships—to individuals.
Application information: Applications accepted.
Application form required. Application form
available on the grantmaker's Web site.
   Deadline(s): May 15
   Applicants should submit the following:
      1) ACT
      2) Essay
      3) Financial information
      4) Letter(s) of recommendation
      5) SAT
      6) Transcripts
EIN: 133208336

213
The Aspen Institute
1 Dupont Cir., N.W., Ste. 700
Washington, DC   20036   (202) 736-5814
Contact: Winnifred Levy, Comms. Mgr.
FAX: (202) 293-0525; E-mail: info@aspeninst.org;
E-mail (for Winnifred Levy):

winnifred.levy@aspeninstitute.org; URL: http://
www.nonprofitresearch.org
http://www.aspeninstitute.org

Foundation type: Public charity
Limitations: Assistance in the form of tuition,
travel, lodging and meals to young leaders in the
private, public, and not-for-profit sectors, to attend
the foundation's Socrates Society seminars.
Publications: Application guidelines; Annual report;
Grants list; Informational brochure; Newsletter.
Financial data: Year ended 12/31/2003.
Assets, $75,312,572 (M); Expenditures,
$35,673,968; Total giving, $1,047,725; Grants to
individuals, totaling $119,463.
Fields of interest: Education.
Type of support: Scholarships—to individuals;
Travel grants.
Application information: Applications accepted.
Application form required. Application form
available on the grantmaker's Web site.
   Initial approach: E-mail.
   Applicants should submit the following:
      1) Essay
      2) Curriculum vitae
   Additional information: Contact foundation for
      further application guidelines.
Program description:
   Socrates Society Seminar Scholarship: This
program invites young leaders from a broad
spectrum of organizations in the private, public, and
not-for-profit sectors. By bringing together
individuals with very different backgrounds, the
program ensures a level of diversity that enriches
the experience for all participants. The foundation
offers both full and partial scholarship assistance
in the form of tuition, travel, lodging and meals.
Applicants who are seriously considered will be
individuals whose wisdom and professional
experience will add a significant dimension to the
dialogue. To be eligible for financial assistance,
professional and personal attributes will be taken
into account: ethnic and/or geographic diversity;
leadership in fields such as academia, medicine,
journalism, non-profit management, government
office, and social service organizations; financial
need. Financial need will also dictate the level of
scholarship funds for which candidate is eligible.
For scholarship information, please contact
katie.bartel@aspeninstitute.org.
EIN: 840399006

214
The Aspire Foundation
1 Oxford Ctr., Ste. 3300
Pittsburgh, PA   15219
Contact: David Borroni, Treas.
Application address : c/o Scholarship Comm., 200
Allegheny Ctr., Pittsburgh, PA 15212

Foundation type: Company-sponsored foundation
Limitations: Scholarships and grants to western PA
area high school juniors and seniors for higher
education.
Financial data: Year ended 12/31/2004.
Assets, $59,123 (M); Expenditures, $56,691;
Total giving, $33,750; Grants to individuals, 31
grants totaling $33,750 (high: $2,500, low:
$1,250).
Type of support: Undergraduate support.
Application information: Application form required.
   Deadline(s): Mar. 17
   Applicants should submit the following:
      1) Letter(s) of recommendation
   Additional information: Application should
      include three letters of recommendation.

Program description:
   Scholarship Program: The foundation offers an
outreach mentorship program for western PA area
high school juniors and seniors to familiarize them
with working and help clarify goals of higher
learning. Participants in the mentorship program
are eligible for $5,000 scholarships which are
renewable, as long as sufficient progress is shown,
for up to five years.
EIN: 251759917

215
Assistance League of Houston
1902 Commonwealth St.
Houston, TX   77006   (713) 526-7983

Foundation type: Public charity
Limitations: Scholarships to grade school children
with learning disabilities in Houston, TX.
Financial data: Year ended 05/31/2005.
Assets, $1,722,029 (M); Expenditures,
$366,512; Total giving, $83,762; Grants to
individuals, totaling $69,144.
Fields of interest: Learning disorders.
Type of support: Precollege support.
Application information: Contact foundation for
current application deadline/guidelines.
EIN: 746081914

216
Associated Banc-Corp Founders
Scholarship, Inc.
c/o Associated Bank Green Bay, N.A.
P.O. Box 408
Neenah, WI   54957-0408
Contact: Jonathan Drayna, Secy.

Foundation type: Company-sponsored foundation
Limitations: Scholarships to children of employees
of Associated Banc-Corp and its affiliates, primarily
in WI.
Financial data: Year ended 12/31/2004.
Assets, $510,569 (M); Expenditures, $80,720;
Total giving, $72,750; Grants to individuals,
totaling $72,750.
Type of support: Employee-related scholarships.
Application information: Application form required.
   Deadline(s): Mar. 15
   Applicants should submit the following:
      1) Essay
   Additional information: Formal application should
      also include three teacher references;
      Application address: 112 N. Adams St., P.O.
      Box 13307, Green Bay, WI 54307-3307.
Program description:
   Scholarship Program: To be eligible, the applicant
must have maintained at least a "B" average
throughout high school, and plan to attend an
accredited, degree-granting U.S. undergraduate or
graduate program on a full-time basis. Scholarships
are renewable for up to four years provided the
recipient maintains at least a "B" average in
college, and his/her parent remains a current
employee of Associated Banc-Corp or its affiliates,
with the exceptions of death or disability.
EIN: 391482448

217

Associated General Contractors of Maine, Inc. Education Foundation
c/o John Butts
P.O. Box 5519
Augusta, ME 04332-5519
Application address: P.O. Box N, Augusta, ME 04332

Foundation type: Independent foundation
Limitations: Scholarships to ME students interested in a career in the construction industry.
Financial data: Year ended 12/31/2004. Assets, $480,272 (M); Expenditures, $19,500; Total giving, $19,500; Grants to individuals, 11 grants totaling $19,500 (high: $4,000, low: $1,000).
Fields of interest: Business/industry.
Type of support: Scholarships—to individuals.
Application information: Applications accepted.
  Deadline(s): None
  Additional information: Completion of formal application required, including written goals summary.
EIN: 010445998

218

Association of Former State Troopers Educational Fund
(formerly Association of Former New Jersey States Troopers Educational Fund)
P.O. Box 285
Richwood, NJ 08074-0285   (856) 627-3912
Contact: Frederick J. Weidman

Foundation type: Independent foundation
Limitations: Student loans to children and spouses of deceased NJ state troopers for full-time attendance at approved schools.
Financial data: Year ended 06/30/2005. Assets, $416,624 (M); Expenditures, $653; Total giving, $0; Loan to an individual, 1 loan totaling $6,000.
Fields of interest: Crime/law enforcement, police agencies.
Type of support: Employee-related scholarships.
Application information: Applications accepted. Application form required.
  Deadline(s): None
EIN: 226065219

219

Association of Moving Image Archivists
1313 N. Vine St.
Los Angeles, CA 90028   (323) 463-1500
FAX: (323) 463-1506; E-mail: amia@amianet.org;
URL: http://www.amianet.org

Foundation type: Public charity
Limitations: Scholarships and fellowships to students who wish to pursue careers in moving image archive management.
Publications: Newsletter.
Financial data: Year ended 12/31/2004. Assets, $505,929 (M); Expenditures, $531,953; Total giving, $25,000; Grants to individuals, 7 grants totaling $25,000 (high: $4,000, low: $1,000).
Fields of interest: Arts education; Film/video.
Type of support: Fellowships; Graduate support.
Application information: Applications accepted. Application form required. Application form available on the grantmaker's Web site.

  Initial approach: Telephone, Fax or E-mail.
  Deadline(s): May 1 for fellowships and May 15 for scholarships
  Applicants should submit the following:
    1) Transcripts
    2) Resume
    3) Letter(s) of recommendation
    4) Essay
    5) Curriculum vitae
Program descriptions:
  AMIA Scholarship Program: The program awards five annual scholarships: the Mary Pickford Scholarship; the Sony Pictures Scholarship; the CFI Sid Solow Scholarship; Universal Studios Preservaton Scholarship; and the Rick Chace Scholarship. Financial assistance in the amount of $4,000 is given to students of merit who intend to pursue careers in moving-image archiving.
  Kodak Fellowship: Provides students with financial assistance in the amount of a $4,000 scholarship for their formal education, practical experience through an intensive six-week summer internship at Kodak, and an introduction to the film archive community through participation in the AMIA conference.
EIN: 954386715

220

Assurant Foundation
(formerly Fortis Foundation)
1 Chase Manhattan Plz., 41st Fl.
New York, NY 10005
Contact: Kristy Hall
E-mail: kristy.hall@assurant.com; URL: http://www.assurant.com/inc/assurant/community/new-york.html

Foundation type: Company-sponsored foundation
Limitations: Scholarships to the natural or adopted children of employees of at least two years of Fortis, Inc. or its subsidiaries.
Financial data: Year ended 12/31/2003. Assets, $347,376 (M); Expenditures, $305,752; Total giving, $299,716; Grants to individuals, 103 grants totaling $153,750 (high: $1,500, low: $750).
Type of support: Employee-related scholarships.
Application information: Application form required.
  Initial approach: Letter requesting application information.
  Applicants should submit the following:
    1) Transcripts
  Additional information: Application should also include standardized test scores, and at least two recommendations from instructors; Interviews required.
Program description:
  Scholarship Program: Most of the scholarships are given for undergraduate study, but scholarships for graduate and pre-college study may also be awarded. No member of the selection committee is an employee of the foundation or the company. Recipients are selected based on academic performance, standardized test scores, teachers' recommendations, and personal interviews. Scholarships are at least $1,500 per year, and are renewable. In circumstances of financial need, scholarship amount will exceed $1,500 per year.
EIN: 133156497

221

Nina Heard Astin Charitable Trust
c/o Wells Fargo Bank, N.A., Trust Dept.
3000 Briarcrest Dr., MAC T5177-020
Bryan, TX 77802   (979) 776-5402
Scholarship application addresses: c/o Bryan High School Counselors, 3401 E. 29th St., Bryan, TX 77802, tel.: (979) 774-3273; c/o A&M Consolidated High School, 701 W. Loop S., College Station, TX 77840, tel.: (979) 696-0544

Foundation type: Independent foundation
Limitations: Scholarships only to graduates of Bryan High School, TX, and A&M Consolidated High School, TX.
Financial data: Year ended 03/31/2005. Assets, $6,319,613 (M); Expenditures, $394,978; Total giving, $330,584; Grants to individuals, totaling $99,917.
Type of support: Support to graduates or students of specific schools; Undergraduate support.
Application information: Applications accepted. Application form required.
  Deadline(s): May 1
EIN: 741721901

222

Edward Thatcher Astle Memorial Scholarship Foundation
24 West St.
P.O. Box 182
Annandale, NJ 08801   (908) 735-5339

Foundation type: Independent foundation
Limitations: Scholarships to high school seniors from central NJ who are U.S. citizens, have at least a "B" average, and require financial assistance to attend college or trade school.
Financial data: Year ended 04/30/2005. Assets, $811,180 (M); Expenditures, $56,686; Total giving, $53,135; Grants to individuals, 13 grants totaling $24,900 (high: $4,000, low: $600).
Fields of interest: Vocational education.
Type of support: Technical education support; Undergraduate support.
Application information: Application form required.
  Deadline(s): Mar. 19
  Additional information: Completion of formal application required, including tax return and written recommendation from the guidance dept. or a teacher; Applications available from foundation; Interviews required where goals, ideals, and attitudes will be discussed.
Program description:
  Scholarship Program: Awards $6,000 annually to graduating seniors. There are no restrictions on areas of study that applicants must pursue. However, recipients will be selected based on the importance of the area of study to our society. Applicants over 18 must be registered to vote in NJ. Candidates must have shown that they are willing to help pay for their education by working during the summer or after school hours. If a student leaves college or trade school during the school year, any unused scholarship funds must be donated to the college or trade school's general scholarship fund. Individuals who have known drug involvement or involvement in unlawful activities are discouraged from applying.
EIN: 222817002

223
AT&T Foundation
(formerly SBC Foundation)
130 E. Travis, Ste. 350
San Antonio, TX 78205   (210) 351-2218
Contact: Laura Sanford, Pres.
FAX: (210) 351-2599;
E-mail: sbcfdn@txmail.sbc.com; Additional tel.:
(800) 591-9663; URL: http://att.sbc.com/gen/
corporate-citizenship?pid=7736

Foundation type: Company-sponsored foundation
Limitations: Scholarships to children of Southwest
Bell employees.
Publications: Application guidelines.
Financial data: Year ended 12/31/2004.
Assets, $233,864,354 (M); Expenditures,
$48,438,028; Total giving, $48,159,537.
Type of support: Employee-related scholarships;
Undergraduate support.
Application information: Contact foundation for
current application deadlines/guidelines.
EIN: 431353948

224
Athanasiades Cultural Foundation, Inc.
30-96 42nd St.
Astoria, NY 11103-3031   (718) 278-3014

Foundation type: Operating foundation
Limitations: Scholarships to individuals in NY for
higher education.
Financial data: Year ended 12/31/2003.
Assets, $2,029,429 (M); Expenditures, $66,958;
Total giving, $13,567; Grants to individuals, 21
grants totaling $11,100.
Type of support: Scholarships—to individuals.
Application information:
Initial approach: Telephone.
Deadline(s): Oct. 31
Additional information: Application by letter.
EIN: 133614414

225
Atherton Family Foundation
c/o Hawaii Community Foundation
1164 Bishop St., Ste. 800
Honolulu, HI 96813   (808) 566-5524
Contact: Lissa Schiff, Private Fdn. Svcs. Off.
FAX: (808) 521-6286;
E-mail: Foundations@hcf-hawaii.org; Additional tel.:
(888) 731-3863 (Hawaii and neighbor islands only);
URL: http://www.Athertonfamilyfoundation.org

Foundation type: Independent foundation
Limitations: Scholarships to HI residents who are
children of Protestant ministers, graduate
theological students at a Protestant seminary, or
ministers seeking further education.
Publications: Annual report; Financial statement;
Grants list.
Financial data: Year ended 12/31/2004.
Assets, $96,076,217 (M); Expenditures,
$6,055,475; Total giving, $4,777,009; Grants to
individuals, 75 grants totaling $124,350 (high:
$5,000, low: $400).
Fields of interest: Theological school/education;
Christian agencies & churches; Protestant
agencies & churches.
Type of support: Graduate support; Postgraduate
support.
Application information: Application form required.
Initial approach: Letter or telephone.
Deadline(s): Mar. 1
Applicants should submit the following:
1) SAR
2) Letter(s) of recommendation
3) Transcripts
4) Essay
Additional information: See program description
for further information.
Program description:
Juliette M. Atherton Scholarship: Scholarships to
eligible applicants who are HI residents, and have
demonstrated financial need and promise of
achievement. Scholarship requests are accepted
from individuals in the following categories only:
· dependent sons and daughters of ordained
and active Protestant ministers of HI to
attend accredited postsecondary
educational institutions
· individuals desiring to attend accredited
graduate schools of theology with the goal
of becoming an ordained Protestant
minister
· ordained Protestant ministers of HI seeking
an advanced degree related to the ministry
at an accredited institution
· ordained Protestant ministers of HI
planning to pursue education in a field
related to ministry through course work,
workshops, or seminars.
Ministers and sons and daughters of ministers
must also include in their personal statements the
minister's current position, church or parish name,
denomination, place and date of ordination, and the
name of seminary attended. Ordained Protestant
ministers intending to further their education with
course work, workshops, or seminars are not
required to submit the SAR or transcript. Applicants
in this category must submit a special financial form
available from the Hawaii Community Foundation.
Applicants are notified of the fund's decision within
three months of the application deadline. Some
applicants to this foundation may automatically be
considered for other scholarship programs
administered by the Hawaii Community Foundation.
Employees or direct relatives of employees of the
Hawaii Community Foundation are ineligible.
EIN: 510175971

226
Grace Atkins Charities
c/o Bank of America, N.A., Fdn. and Philanthropic
Svcs.
P.O. Box 1802
Providence, RI 02901-1802
Application address: c/o Bank of America, N.A., Fdn.
and Philanthropic Svcs., 777 Main St.,
CT2-102-22-02, Hartford, CT 06115

Foundation type: Independent foundation
Limitations: Scholarships and educational grants
to residents of Bristol, CT, attending four-year
colleges.
Financial data: Year ended 12/31/2003.
Assets, $1,407,808 (M); Expenditures, $83,952;
Total giving, $66,486; Grants to individuals, 25
grants totaling $22,000 (high: $1,400, low: $400).
Type of support: Scholarships—to individuals.
Application information: Application form required.
Deadline(s): Mar. 15
Additional information: Application forms are
available from public libraries and high school
guidance departments.
EIN: 066138990

227
Atlantic County Medical Society
Scholarship Fund
599 Shore Rd., No. 99
Somers Point, NJ 08244
Contact: Carol Simpson

Foundation type: Independent foundation
Limitations: Scholarships to medical students who
are residents of Atlantic County, NJ.
Financial data: Year ended 04/30/2004.
Assets, $287,103 (M); Expenditures, $20,948;
Total giving, $16,583; Grants to individuals, 6
grants totaling $16,583 (high: $3,750, low:
$2,375).
Fields of interest: Medical school/education.
Type of support: Graduate support.
Application information: Application form required.
Deadline(s): Mid-June
Additional information: Completion of formal
application required, including tax return,
MCAT scores, college and medical school
grades, letter of acceptance and statement of
marital status. Recipients must be U.S.
citizens.
EIN: 237024987

228
ATO Foundation of Berkeley, Inc.
c/o Frederic A. Sawyer
2656 Ptarmigan Dr., No. 1
Walnut Creek, CA 94595-3116
Contact: Chris Johnson, V.P.
Application address: 5378 Lockfley Ave., Oakland,
CA 94618, tel.: (510) 597-0929

Foundation type: Independent foundation
Limitations: Undergraduate leadership
scholarships to members of Greek organizations
who are leaders, have excelled academically, and
have made notable contributions to the Greek
system, the campus, and/or the community at the
University of California, Berkeley.
Financial data: Year ended 12/31/2004.
Assets, $474,035 (M); Expenditures, $26,254;
Total giving, $16,100; Grants to individuals, 15
grants totaling $13,100 (high: $1,500, low: $300).
Fields of interest: Students, sororities/fraternities;
Leadership development.
Type of support: Support to graduates or students
of specific schools; Undergraduate support.
Application information: Application form required.
Initial approach: Letter or telephone.
Deadline(s): Contact foundation for current
application deadline
Additional information: Completion of formal
application required, including GPA,
extracurricular activities, transcripts, and two
letters of recommendation, one from chapter
and one from a member of the college,
community, or place of employment;
Interviews required for finalists.
EIN: 942880554

229
Atsinger Family Foundation
855 Aviation Dr.
Camarillo, CA 93010
Contact: Brian J. Counsil

Foundation type: Independent foundation
Limitations: Scholarships to students attending
Christian colleges and universities, primarily in CA.
Financial data: Year ended 12/31/2004.
Assets, $10,533 (M); Expenditures, $18,836;

Total giving, $18,076; Grants to individuals, totaling $18,076.
Fields of interest: Christian agencies & churches.
Type of support: Scholarships—to individuals.
Application information: Contact foundation for current application deadline/guidelines.
EIN: 770460697

230
Eugene Atwood Fund
68 Federal St.
New London, CT 06320-0270 (860) 443-4357
Contact: James C. McGuire, Tr.
Application address: P.O. Box 270, New London, CT 06320

Foundation type: Independent foundation
Limitations: Scholarships and student loans to New London County, CT, residents enrolled at the undergraduate level only.
Publications: Annual report.
Financial data: Year ended 04/30/2005.
Assets, $1,735,315 (M); Expenditures, $145,081; Total giving, $115,500; Grants to individuals, totaling $19,000; Loans to individuals, totaling $96,500.
Type of support: Undergraduate support.
Application information: Application form required.
  Initial approach: Letter or telephone.
  Deadline(s): May 1
  Applicants should submit the following:
    1) Transcripts
    2) Letter(s) of recommendation
    3) GPA
    4) Financial information
    5) FAFSA
  Additional information: Recipients notified in July.
EIN: 066044477

231
Florence D. Atwood Trust for Brooks Scholarship Fund
c/o KeyBank N.A.
800 Superior Ave., 4th Fl.
Cleveland, OH 44114
Application address: c/o Charles O'Conner, Superintendent of Schools, Chazy, NY 12921

Foundation type: Independent foundation
Limitations: Scholarships to financially needy residents of Chazy Central School District, NY, who have attended Chazy Central Rural High School and will attend college full-time.
Financial data: Year ended 06/30/2004.
Assets, $62,983 (M); Expenditures, $3,974; Total giving, $3,150; Grants to individuals, totaling $3,150.
Type of support: Support to graduates or students of specific schools; Undergraduate support.
Application information:
  Initial approach: Letter.
  Deadline(s): Apr. 1
EIN: 222753510

232
Auburn Foundry Foundation
c/o Tower Bank
116 E. Berry St.
Fort Wayne, IN 46802
Contact: Sharon Peters

Foundation type: Company-sponsored foundation
Limitations: Scholarships to graduates of DeKalb Central High School, IN.

Financial data: Year ended 02/28/2005.
Assets, $1,150,158 (M); Expenditures, $60,066; Total giving, $51,200; Grants to individuals, totaling $26,300.
Fields of interest: Engineering/technology; Biological sciences.
Type of support: Support to graduates or students of specific schools; Undergraduate support.
Application information: Applications accepted. Application form required.
  Initial approach: Letter.
  Deadline(s): None
Program description:
  Applied Science Scholarship: Provides scholarships to promote interest in physical sciences and encourage careers in such fields as engineering, technology and life sciences. Scholarships are worth $3,000 per year and are renewable for up to four years. Applicants must rank in the top 25 percent of their graduating class.
EIN: 356019220

233
Audio Engineering Society Educational Foundation, Inc.
(also known as AES Educational Foundation, Inc.)
60 E. 42nd St., No. 2520
New York, NY 10165
Contact: Emil Torick, Pres.
E-mail: HQ@aes.org; URL: http://www.aes.org/education/edu_foundation.html

Foundation type: Independent foundation
Limitations: Graduate scholarships to talented students in the U.S. and abroad, who are preparing to enter the audio engineering profession and related fields.
Publications: Application guidelines.
Financial data: Year ended 12/31/2004.
Assets, $204,958 (M); Expenditures, $48,112; Total giving, $44,400.
Fields of interest: Engineering.
Type of support: Graduate support.
Application information: Application form required. Application form available on the grantmaker's Web site.
  Initial approach: Letter.
  Deadline(s): Applications accepted only from Mar. 15 through May 15
  Applicants should submit the following:
    1) Letter(s) of recommendation
  Additional information: Awards are made in Aug.
Program description:
  Scholarship Program: Scholarship awards are granted on an international basis to students who have completed an undergraduate degree, have demonstrated their commitment to audio engineering or a related field, and have been accepted or are awaiting acceptance to a graduate degree program leading to a master's or higher degree, or an internationally recognized equivalent. Awards are typically in the amount of $4,000 for one year of study. They may be renewed once upon successful completion of at least one year of graduate study.
EIN: 112664807

234
Red Auerbach Youth Foundation, Inc.
101 Arch St., 9th Fl.
Boston, MA 02110 (617) 345-8998
Contact: Stewart F. Grossman Esq., Pres.
E-mail: rayf@redauerbach.org; URL: http://www.redauerbach.org

Foundation type: Public charity
Limitations: Scholarships to youths exhibiting outstanding athletic and academic achievement.
Financial data: Year ended 06/30/2004.
Assets, $305,514 (M); Expenditures, $144,639; Total giving, $23,000.
Fields of interest: Education.
Type of support: Scholarships—to individuals.
Application information: Applications accepted.
  Initial approach: Letter.
EIN: 043254418

235
Fannie August Charitable Trust
c/o Bank of America, N.A., P.C. Group
P.O. Box 6768
Providence, RI 02940-6768
Application address: c/o Bank of America, N.A., Attn.: Carol Gray, Trust Off., 100 Federal St., Boston, MA 02110

Foundation type: Independent foundation
Limitations: Scholarships to needy, worthy students in the metropolitan Boston, MA, area for medical school.
Financial data: Year ended 12/31/2003.
Assets, $313,134 (M); Expenditures, $22,681; Total giving, $20,000; Grants to individuals, 5 grants totaling $20,000 (high: $5,000, low: $3,750).
Fields of interest: Medical school/education.
Type of support: Graduate support.
Application information: Applications accepted.
  Initial approach: Letter.
  Deadline(s): None
EIN: 046027010

236
Augusta Kiwanis Scholarship Foundation
P.O. Box 966
Augusta, ME 04332-0966

Foundation type: Independent foundation
Limitations: Scholarships by nomination only to high school students in ME.
Financial data: Year ended 12/31/2004.
Assets, $302,155 (M); Expenditures, $13,747; Total giving, $13,200; Grants to individuals, totaling $13,200.
Type of support: Awards/grants by nomination only; Precollege support.
Application information: Applications not accepted.
EIN: 237089761

237
Aurora Foundation
c/o Jeffrey Bronfman
520 Cypress Creek Ln.
Wimberley, TX 78676

Foundation type: Operating foundation
Limitations: Scholarships and travel grants primarily to residents of Santa Fe, NM.
Financial data: Year ended 09/30/2003.
Assets, $100,879 (M); Expenditures, $287,211; Total giving, $269,761.
Type of support: Scholarships—to individuals; Travel grants.
Application information: Application accepted throughout the year; Contact foundation for current application guidelines.
EIN: 742660772

238
The Aurora Foundation
111 W. Downer Pl., Ste. 312
Aurora, IL 60506-5136 (630) 896-7800
Contact: Sharon Stredde, C.E.O.
FAX: (630) 896-7811; E-mail: info@aurorafdn.org;
Additional E-mails: sstredde@aurorafdn.org and
grant@aurorafdn.org; URL: http://
www.aurorafdn.org

Foundation type: Community foundation
Limitations: Scholarships and loans to full-time
students who reside in the Aurora, IL, area,
including Kendall and Southern Kane counties.
Scholarships are available to graduating high
school seniors, undergraduates, and graduate
students. See program description for further
limitations.
Publications: Application guidelines; Annual report;
Newsletter.
Financial data: Year ended 12/31/2005.
Assets, $35,692,953 (M); Expenditures,
$1,813,535; Total giving, $1,385,124; Grants to
individuals, totaling $447,850.
Type of support: Graduate support; Undergraduate
support.
Application information: Application form required.
Application form available on the grantmaker's Web
site.
Initial approach: Letter or telephone.
Applicants should submit the following:
1) Transcripts
2) SAT
3) Letter(s) of recommendation
4) GPA
5) Financial information
6) FAFSA
7) Essay
8) ACT
Additional information: Interviews required.
Program description:
Scholarship Funds: The foundation administers
approximately 60 scholarship funds. Some funds
are for graduates of specific IL schools, including:
Aurora Christian School, East Aurora High School,
West Aurora High School, City of Aurora high
schools, Marmion Academy, Rosary High School,
Yorkville High School, Kaneland High School, and
Hinckley-Big Rock High School.
EIN: 366086742

239
William Harold Francis Austin Trust
c/o Eastern Bank & Trust Co.
605 Broadway, LF4
Saugus, MA 01906 (781) 581-4274
Contact: Robert M. Wallask, V.P., Eastern Bank &
Trust Co.

Foundation type: Independent foundation
Limitations: Non-interest bearing student loans for
postsecondary education to residents of MA with
deceased fathers.
Financial data: Year ended 07/31/2005.
Assets, $827,229 (M); Expenditures, $42,642;
Total giving, $29,500; Loans to individuals, 8 loans
totaling $29,500.
Fields of interest: Residential/custodial care.
Type of support: Student loans—to individuals.
Application information: Applications accepted.
Application form required.
Deadline(s): June 1
Additional information: Application should
include transcripts and copy of father's death
certificate.

Program description:
Student Loan Program: The trust generally
awards five-ten loans of $1,000 to $5,000 each,
annually.
EIN: 042714929

240
Jean B. Authier Trust
c/o Paul Walter, Jr.
P.O. Box 718
New Lebanon, NY 12125-0718
Application addresses: c/o Delaware Valley High
School, 252 Rte. 6 & 209, Milford, PA
18337-9454, c/o Dieruff High School, 815 N. Irving
St., Allentown, PA 18109-1832

Foundation type: Independent foundation
Limitations: Scholarships to residents of Delaware
Valley, Wilford, Dieruff, and Allentown, PA, for
attendance at Johnson and Wales University.
Financial data: Year ended 12/31/2004.
Assets, $1,224,925 (M); Expenditures, $45,272;
Total giving, $38,118; Grants to individuals, 2
grants totaling $38,118 (high: $20,931, low:
$17,187).
Type of support: Support to graduates or students
of specific schools.
Application information:
Initial approach: Letter.
Additional information: Contact trust for
additional application guidelines.
EIN: 256820083

241
Avery Scholarship Foundation
P.O. Box 772
Livingston Manor, NY 12758
Application address: c/o Livingston Manor Central
School, Guidance Dept., Livingston Manor, NY
12758

Foundation type: Independent foundation
Limitations: Scholarships to graduating seniors of
Livingston Manor High School, NY, for
undergraduate education at a four-year college.
Financial data: Year ended 12/31/2004.
Assets, $461,098 (M); Expenditures, $10,831;
Total giving, $10,000; Grants to individuals,
totaling $10,000.
Type of support: Support to graduates or students
of specific schools; Undergraduate support.
Application information: Applications accepted.
Application form required.
Initial approach: Requesting form from Guidance
Dept.
Deadline(s): May 1
EIN: 141798357

242
The Avoda Club of Atlantic County
P.O. Box 3120
Margate City, NJ 08402-3120

Foundation type: Public charity
Limitations: Scholarships to graduates of Atlantic
County, NJ, high schools for undergraduate
education.
Financial data: Year ended 11/30/2004.
Assets, $576,411 (M); Expenditures, $78,028;
Total giving, $49,498; Grants to individuals,
totaling $49,498.
Type of support: Support to graduates or students
of specific schools; Undergraduate support.

Application information: Application form required.
Deadline(s): Apr.
Additional information: Applications available at
Atlantic County, NJ, high school guidance
counselors' offices.
EIN: 226085397

243
AWS Foundation
550 N.W. Lejeune Rd.
Miami, FL 33126 (305) 443-9353
Contact: Frank G. Delaurier, Exec. Dir.
Additional tel.: (800) 443-9353, ext. 293;
FAX: (305) 443-7559; E-mail: found@aws.org;
URL: http://www.aws.org/awards

Foundation type: Public charity
Limitations: Scholarships, fellowships and student
loans to individuals who wish to enter the field of
welding.
Financial data: Year ended 05/31/2004.
Assets, $4,239,298 (M); Expenditures,
$498,910; Total giving, $276,796; Grants to
individuals, totaling $276,796.
Fields of interest: Engineering/technology.
Type of support: Fellowships; Research; Student
loans—to individuals; Foreign applicants;
Postdoctoral support; Graduate support; Technical
education support; Doctoral support.
Application information: Application form required.
Deadline(s): Varies
Additional information: See Web site for further
guidelines and forms.
Program descriptions:
District Scholarship Program: Awards
scholarships to students for the expenses of
tuition, books, supplies and related institutional
costs. Scholarship is renewable. Deadline Mar. 1.
National Scholarship Program: Offers numerous
scholarships to students pursuing degrees in
welding or related fields.
International Scholarship Program: Awards
scholarships to international students wishing to
pursue their education in welding and related
joining technologies who are not assigned to an
AWS section. Recipients must be full-time students
pursuing a bachelor's degree and must be in the
top 20 percent of the institution's grading system.
Proof of country citizenship is required. Deadline
Apr. 1.
Student Loan Program: Awards student loans to
AWS members wishing to continue their studies in
welding and related fields of education. Recipients
must be at least 18 years of age, have a high school
diploma or G.E.D. equivalent, and a minimum GPA
of 2.0. All recipients must be members in good
standing with the American Welding Society.
Non-members will be charged a $15 application fee
and will receive a one-year membership in the AWS.
Research Fellowships: Awards up to $25,000 per
year to graduate students seeking a master's or
Ph.D. degree in welding or related fields.
Fellowships are renewable. Deadline Jan. 4.
EIN: 650148545

244
The Axelrod Family Foundation, Inc.
c/o Muchnick, Golieb & Golieb
200 Park Ave. S., Ste. 1700
New York, NY 10003-1503
Contact: Mrs. Mott
Application address for scholarships: 45 W. 139th
St., New York, NY 10037, tel.: (212)236-8810

Foundation type: Independent foundation

Limitations: Scholarships to secondary school students who reside in Delano Village, NY.
Financial data: Year ended 12/31/2004. Assets, $2,396 (M); Expenditures, $31,824; Total giving, $30,085; Grants to individuals, 12 grants totaling $28,788.
Type of support: Scholarships—to individuals.
Application information: Application form required.
Additional information: Applications accepted throughout the year; Contact foundation for current application guidelines.
EIN: 133775791

245
Waldo & Alice Ayer Trust
c/o Citizens Bank of NH
870 Westminster St.
Providence, RI 02903
Contact: Bill Sirak
Application address: c/o Citizens Bank New Hampshire, 875 Elm St., Manchester, NH 03101, tel.: (603) 634-7752

Foundation type: Independent foundation
Limitations: Scholarships to music students primarily in the state of NH, who are studying to become professional musicians or music teachers.
Financial data: Year ended 09/30/2005. Assets, $836,035 (M); Expenditures, $46,121; Total giving, $33,000; Grants to individuals, 16 grants totaling $21,000 (high: $2,500, low: $1,000).
Fields of interest: Music; Performing arts, education; Teacher school/education.
Type of support: Scholarships—to individuals.
Application information:
Initial approach: Letter.
Additional information: Applications accepted throughout the year.
EIN: 026059690

246
Aylesworth Foundation for Advancement of Marine Sciences, Inc.
1295 28th St., S.
St. Petersburg, FL 33712-1909
(727) 327-8608
Contact: Robert Aylesworth, Pres.
URL: http://www.flseagrant.org/students/scholarships/2005ayles_appli.htm

Foundation type: Public charity
Limitations: Scholarships to students in all Florida universities who are enrolled in the study of marine science.
Financial data: Year ended 12/31/2003. Assets, $993,077 (M); Expenditures, $49,680; Total giving, $16,500; Grants to individuals, 8 grants totaling $16,500 (high: $4,000, low: $500).
Fields of interest: Higher education; Marine science.
Application information: Applications accepted. Application form required.
Deadline(s): Nov.
EIN: 592623744

247
The Lucy C. Ayres Foundation, Inc.
(formerly The Lucy C. Ayres Home for Nurses, Inc.)
300 Centerville Rd., Ste. 300S
Warwick, RI 02886 (401) 246-1326
Contact: Helen Raynor, Pres.

Foundation type: Operating foundation

Limitations: Scholarships to nursing students, primarily in RI.
Financial data: Year ended 03/31/2004. Assets, $690,267 (M); Expenditures, $39,792; Total giving, $22,000; Grants to individuals, 21 grants totaling $22,000 (high: $3,000, low: $750).
Fields of interest: Nursing school/education.
Type of support: Scholarships—to individuals.
Application information: Application form required.
Deadline(s): Contact foundation for current application deadline
EIN: 050264853

248
Mabel Brickey Ayres Memorial Foundation, Inc.
709 N. Ermen Ln.
Osceola, AR 72370 (870) 563-2990
Contact: Ann Moore, Dir.

Foundation type: Independent foundation
Limitations: Scholarships to residents of Mississippi County, AR.
Financial data: Year ended 12/31/2004. Assets, $176,163 (M); Expenditures, $29,845; Total giving, $27,000; Grants to individuals, totaling $27,000.
Type of support: Scholarships—to individuals.
Application information: Contact foundation for current application deadline/guidelines; Initial approach by letter or telephone; Completion of formal application required.
EIN: 237408205

249
Dr. Samuel & Mildred L. Ayres Student Fund
(formerly Mildred L. Ayres Trust)
c/o Bank of America, N.A.
P.O. Box 831041
Dallas, TX 75283-1041
Contact: James J. Mueth, Trust Off., Bank of America, N.A.
Application address: P.O. Box 419119, Kansas City, MO 64141-6119, tel.: (816) 979-7481

Foundation type: Independent foundation
Limitations: Student loans and scholarships to residents of MO attending Midwestern Baptist Seminary, MO, William Jewell College, MO, or the University of Missouri—Columbia to assist with theological and medical training and living expenses. Preference is given to residents of metropolitan Kansas City.
Financial data: Year ended 12/31/2004. Assets, $307,606 (M); Expenditures, $12,019; Total giving, $8,500; Grants to individuals, 5 grants totaling $8,500.
Application information: Applications accepted. Application form required.
Initial approach: Letter.
Deadline(s): None
Additional information: Applications available from applicant's high school financial aid office or trust office, and must include financial statement, personal statement, photograph, transcripts, and four letters of reference, two personal and two from instructors or advisor.
EIN: 446008191

250
AZHHA Education Foundation
2901 N. Central Ave., Ste. 900
Phoenix, AZ 85012-2729 (602) 445-4300
Contact: John Rivers, Pres. and C.E.O.

Foundation type: Public charity
Limitations: Scholarships to residents of AZ who are enrolled in accredited healthcare programs, with a focus on nursing.
Financial data: Year ended 12/31/2003. Assets, $1,259,525 (M); Expenditures, $1,167,432; Total giving, $271,382; Grants to individuals, 52 grants totaling $99,375 (high: $7,000, low: $500).
Fields of interest: Nursing school/education.
Type of support: Graduate support.
Application information:
Initial approach: Letter.
Additional information: Contact foundation for further program information.
EIN: 942851811

251
John C. Babcock Fund
(formerly Betsey E. Babcock Trust)
c/o Bank of America, N.A.
P.O. Box 6768
Providence, RI 02940-6768
Application address: c/o Lillian B. Collyer, 29 Buchanan Cir., Lynn, MA 01902

Foundation type: Independent foundation
Limitations: Scholarships to residents of the greater Lynn area, including Swampscott, Nahant, and Saugus, MA.
Financial data: Year ended 12/31/2004. Assets, $230,347 (M); Expenditures, $11,092; Total giving, $8,800; Grants to individuals, totaling $8,800.
Type of support: Scholarships—to individuals.
Application information: Application form required.
Deadline(s): June 15
EIN: 046043639

252
Quintus C. Babcock Memorial Fund
5620 Highland Dr.
Salt Lake City, UT 84121-1303
Application address: c/o Dir. of Student Financial Planning, Upper Iowa Univ., Fayette, IA 52142, tel.: (319) 425-5200

Foundation type: Independent foundation
Limitations: Scholarships to IA residents, with preference given to those from Fayette, IA.
Financial data: Year ended 12/31/2003. Assets, $114,265 (M); Expenditures, $5,136; Total giving, $4,000; Grants to individuals, 3 grants totaling $4,000 (high: $1,500, low: $1,000).
Type of support: Scholarships—to individuals.
Application information: Application form required.
Deadline(s): June 1
EIN: 426075871

253
Weisell Baber Foundation, Inc.
132 E. Main St.
P.O. Box 162
Peru, IN 46970-0162 (765) 473-7526
Contact: Eric R. Baber, Mgr.

Foundation type: Independent foundation
Limitations: Student loans to graduates of Miami County High School, IN.

Financial data: Year ended 12/31/2004. Assets, $5,556,171 (M); Expenditures, $488,296; Total giving, $113,250; Loans to individuals, 35 loans totaling $103,250.
Type of support: Student loans—to individuals; Support to graduates or students of specific schools; Undergraduate support.
Application information: Applications accepted.
  Initial approach: Apply in person.
  Deadline(s): None
  Additional information: Interviews required.
EIN: 356024561

254
Babson's Midwest Memorial Foundation, Inc.
408 E. 3rd St.
Eureka, KS   67045-2031   (620) 583-7525
Contact: Irlene Huntington, Pres.
Application address: Route 3, Box 74, Eureka, KS 67045

Foundation type: Independent foundation
Limitations: Scholarships to graduates of high schools in Greenwood County, KS.
Publications: Newsletter.
Financial data: Year ended 12/31/2004. Assets, $763,451 (M); Expenditures, $48,569; Total giving, $32,000; Grants to individuals, 36 grants totaling $31,300 (high: $1,500, low: $500).
Type of support: Support to graduates or students of specific schools; Undergraduate support.
Application information: Application form required.
  Deadline(s): Apr. 15
  Applicants should submit the following:
    1) Essay
    2) Financial information
    3) Transcripts
EIN: 237086922

255
Daisy S. Bacon Scholarship Fund
14 Vanderventer Ave.
Port Washington, NY   11050-3737
Contact: Harry J. Mulry, Jr., Tr.

Foundation type: Independent foundation
Limitations: Scholarships to residents of Port Washington, NY, who have demonstrated high academic standards, character, and financial need, and who are seeking a college degree.
Publications: Application guidelines; Annual report; Grants list.
Financial data: Year ended 12/31/2004. Assets, $613,889 (M); Expenditures, $50,280; Total giving, $35,000; Grants to individuals, 34 grants totaling $35,000.
Type of support: Scholarships—to individuals.
Application information: Application form required.
  Initial approach: Letter outlining financial need.
  Deadline(s): Apr. 1
  Applicants should submit the following:
    1) Letter(s) of recommendation
  Additional information: Interviews required.
EIN: 116386052

256
Badger Mining Scholarship Trust
c/o Markesan State Bank
P.O. Box 270
Markesan, WI   53946

Foundation type: Company-sponsored foundation

Limitations: Scholarships to high school graduates from Taylor, Berlin, or Markesan, WI, for degrees in mining engineering, engineering curriculum, or environmental science.
Financial data: Year ended 12/31/2004. Assets, $1,181 (M); Expenditures, $12,802; Total giving, $12,500; Grants to individuals, 10 grants totaling $12,500 (high: $2,000, low: $500).
Fields of interest: Engineering school/education; Natural resources; Environment; Business/industry.
Type of support: Undergraduate support.
Application information: Application form required.
  Deadline(s): Contact trust for current application deadline
  Additional information: Application forms available from the high schools.
Program description:
  Scholarship Program: Children of officers of Badger Mining Corporation are ineligible. Recipients must be full-time students and maintain at least a 2.0 GPA.
EIN: 396433973

257
The Bagby Foundation for the Musical Arts, Inc.
501 5th Ave., Ste. 801
New York, NY   10017   (212) 986-6094
Contact: J. Andrew Lark, Exec. Dir.

Foundation type: Independent foundation
Limitations: Musical study grants based on talent and need to residents of NY.
Financial data: Year ended 12/31/2004. Assets, $2,118,090 (M); Expenditures, $141,316; Total giving, $70,705; Grants to individuals, totaling $55,706.
Fields of interest: Music; Performing arts, education.
Type of support: Scholarships—to individuals.
Application information: Applications by letter, outlining financial need, accepted throughout the year.
EIN: 131873289

258
The Bailey Family Foundation, Inc.
P.O. Box 803
Newington, VA   22122-0803   (703) 971-6203
FAX: (703) 971-6205;
E-mail: bailey@bailey-family.org; Additional address: 550 Reo St., Tampa, FL 33609-1065, tel.: (813) 261-2741; FAX: (813) 261-5194;
URL: http://www.bailey-family.org/

Foundation type: Operating foundation
Limitations: Scholarships to students attending specific schools in northern VA and FL for higher education. See Web site for full listing of schools.
Financial data: Year ended 12/31/2004. Assets, $57,363,604 (M); Expenditures, $3,004,130; Total giving, $2,085,463; Grants to individuals, 454 grants totaling $1,272,278 (high: $15,000, low: $191).
Type of support: Support to graduates or students of specific schools; Undergraduate support.
Application information: Application form required.
  Initial approach: Letter or e-mail.
  Deadline(s): Apr. 15
EIN: 541850780

259
Bailey Family Memorial Trust
c/o Bank of Oklahoma, N.A.
P.O. Box 880
Tulsa, OK   74101-0880
Contact: Cynthia L. Sutton, Trust Off., Bank of Oklahoma, N.A.
Application address: c/o William A. Ivy, Dir., Ctr. for Global Studies, College of Arts & Science, Oklahoma State Univ., Stillwater, OK 74078, tel.: (405) 744-5650, ext. 054

Foundation type: Independent foundation
Limitations: Grants and fellowships to students at Oklahoma State University studying liberal arts.
Publications: Application guidelines.
Financial data: Year ended 08/31/2005. Assets, $2,216,702 (M); Expenditures, $128,971; Total giving, $107,229; Grants to individuals, 17 grants totaling $107,229.
Fields of interest: Humanities.
Type of support: Fellowships; Support to graduates or students of specific schools; Undergraduate support.
Application information: Applications not accepted.
  Additional information: Candidates are recommended by Oklahoma State University faculty members.
Program description:
  Scholarship Program: Students must be recommended by a faculty member. Financial need of a proposed recipient will be considered, but is not of overriding importance. Recipients must submit a report of courses taken and grades received each semester. For noncourse study, recipients must submit a progress report at least annually. Recipients are chosen by a committee made up of the Dean of the School of Arts and Sciences of Oklahoma State University, the Sr. Trust Officer of the Bank of Oklahoma, N.A.
EIN: 736210018

260
Bailey Foundation
c/o U.S. Trust Co.
P.O. Box 55122
Boston, MA   02205-8670
Application address: c/o Edwin Bailey, 414 Main St., Amesbury, MA 01913

Foundation type: Independent foundation
Limitations: Undergraduate scholarships to residents of Amesbury, MA, who are U.S. citizens and students or graduates of Amesbury High School.
Financial data: Year ended 06/30/2005. Assets, $308,511 (M); Expenditures, $19,964; Total giving, $16,604; Grants to individuals, totaling $16,604.
Type of support: Support to graduates or students of specific schools; Undergraduate support.
Application information: Application form required.
  Deadline(s): Apr. 15
  Additional information: Completion of formal application required, including references, hobbies, and activities; Applications from outside the specified geographic area will not be considered.
Program description:
  Scholarship Program: The scholarship is awarded to one new individual each year who is a graduate of Amesbury High School or a resident of Amesbury, MA. The scholarship is to be used for tuition, books and supplies, and laboratory expenses for a student pursuing a B.S. or B.A. degree, and is usually renewable for a four-year period. Selection

is based on a combination of financial need and scholastic record.
EIN: 046095808

261
The Bailey Foundation
P.O. Box 494
Clinton, SC   29325   (864) 938-2628
Contact: Garth Silvey, Admin.
FAX: (864) 938-2669

Foundation type: Company-sponsored foundation
Limitations: Scholarship to one financially needy graduating senior of Laurens District 55 high schools and Clinton High School in Laurens County, SC, for study at accredited four-year colleges and universities.
Publications: Annual report; Informational brochure (including application guidelines).
Financial data: Year ended 08/31/2005. Assets, $4,916,689 (M); Expenditures, $300,610; Total giving, $272,740; Grants to individuals, 9 grants totaling $30,690 (high: $7,500, low: $1,690).
Type of support: Support to graduates or students of specific schools; Undergraduate support.
Application information: Application form required.
  Initial approach: Letter.
  Deadline(s): Apr. 15 of senior year in high school
  Additional information: Application forms available from high school guidance counselors; Interviews preferred, but not required; Scholarships are given to financially needy graduates ranking in the top quarter of their graduating classes.
EIN: 576018387

262
Bainbridge Arts & Crafts, Inc.
151 Winslow Way E.
Bainbridge Island, WA   98110-2425
(206) 842-3132
Contact: Susan Jackson, Exec. Dir.
FAX: (206) 780-8149;
E-mail: info@bainbridgeartscrafts.org; URL: http://www.bainbridgeartscrafts.org

Foundation type: Public charity
Limitations: Scholarships to graduates of Bainbridge High School, WA, who intend to pursue full-time art studies.
Financial data: Year ended 06/30/2004. Assets, $113,911 (M); Expenditures, $316,090; Total giving, $7,179; Grants to individuals, totaling $7,179.
Fields of interest: Arts education.
Type of support: Support to graduates or students of specific schools.
Application information: Applications accepted. Application form required.
  Initial approach: E-mail or letter.
  Applicants should submit the following:
    1) Letter(s) of recommendation
  Additional information: Contact foundation for further application information.
EIN: 910714664

263
Bainbridge-Ometepe Sister Islands Association
P.O. Box 4484
Rollingbay, WA   98061-0484   (206) 842-8148
Contact: Lee Robinson, Treas.
FAX: (206) 842-6907; E-mail: info@bosia.org;
URL: http://www.bosia.org

Foundation type: Public charity
Limitations: Scholarships to students from Ometepe Island, on Lake Nicaragua, to attend universities in Nicaragua; and grants to residents of Bainbridge Island, WA, and Ometepe Island to visit one another's islands.
Publications: Annual report; Newsletter.
Financial data: Year ended 12/31/2004. Assets, $201,680 (M); Expenditures, $164,878; Total giving, $81,524; Grants to individuals, totaling $43,052.
Type of support: Exchange programs; Foreign applicants; Undergraduate support.
Application information: Contact foundation for current application deadline/guidelines.
Program description:
  Scholarship Program: Scholarships of $60 per month are given to Ometepe college students. Students are selected by three committees of teachers from three different towns on Ometepe. Students must all be from low-income families.
EIN: 911433369

264
Charles M. Bair Memorial Trust
c/o U.S. Bank, N.A.
P.O. Box 30678
Billings, MT   59115   (406) 657-8134

Foundation type: Independent foundation
Limitations: Scholarships to graduating seniors and former graduates of Harlowton and White Sulphur Springs high schools, MT, and to graduates of high schools located in Meagher and Wheatland counties, MT.
Financial data: Year ended 01/31/2005. Assets, $50,498,124 (M); Expenditures, $1,959,871; Total giving, $1,881,814; Grants to individuals, totaling $366,814.
Fields of interest: Vocational education.
Type of support: Support to graduates or students of specific schools; Undergraduate support.
Application information: Application form required.
  Deadline(s): Apr.
  Additional information: Completion of formal application required, including Financial Assistance Questionnaire signed by parent or guardian.
Program description:
  Scholarship Program: Selection is based on achievement in high school, good citizenship, moral character, financial need, and apparent ability to benefit by a college education or vocational training. Scholarships are for a period of four years.
EIN: 810370774

265
Jessie H. Baker Educational Fund
c/o Alliance Bank, N.A.
241 Main St., Ste. 200
Buffalo, NY   14203

Foundation type: Independent foundation
Limitations: Student loans to Broome County, NY, high school students.
Financial data: Year ended 08/31/2004. Assets, $2,642,566 (M); Expenditures,

$151,902; Total giving, $122,000; Grants to individuals, 86 grants totaling $122,000 (high: $4,000, low: $500).
Type of support: Support to graduates or students of specific schools; Undergraduate support.
Application information: Applications not accepted.
EIN: 222478098

266
Thomas E. and Linda O. Baker Family Foundation
17 Glennon Farm Ln.
Lebanon, NJ   08833   (908) 832-2505
Contact: Cecile McKenzie, Prog. Dir.
FAX: (908) 832-2772;
E-mail: info@bakerfamilyfoundation.org; Additional tel. in Florida: (239) 481-5821; URL: http://www.bakerfamilyfoundation.org

Foundation type: Independent foundation
Limitations: Scholarships for continuing education to disadvantaged individuals residing in NJ and NY who may not have considered attending a four-year college program given their personal situation.
Financial data: Year ended 12/31/2004. Assets, $5,147,562 (M); Expenditures, $727,729; Total giving, $600,768.
Fields of interest: Scholarships/financial aid.
Type of support: Scholarships—to individuals.
Application information: Applications accepted. Application form available on the grantmaker's Web site.
  Initial approach: Letter.
  Deadline(s): None
Program description:
  Opportunity for Higher Education Program: Grants and stipends may be awarded for college tuition, room and board, book expenses, transportation, college prep classes, private secondary schooling, computer training, day care expenses, or family assistance. Candidates should have demonstrated a level of academic achievement sufficient to be considered college material; generally, candidates have at least a 3.0 GPA. Each candidate is required to have a sponsor, e.g., an established educator, guidance counselor, or mentor, to help in the application process.
EIN: 256611063

267
Clark and Ruby Baker Foundation
c/o Bank of America, N.A.
101 S. Tryon St., NC1-002-11-18
Charlotte, NC   28255-0001
Contact: Amber Gratwick
Application address: c/o Bank of America, N.A., 600 Peachtree St., Ste. 1100, Atlanta, GA 30308

Foundation type: Independent foundation
Limitations: Scholarships primarily to residents of GA who are attending Methodist-affiliated colleges or universities. Also provides assistance for retired Methodist ministers.
Financial data: Year ended 12/31/2004. Assets, $3,109,686 (M); Expenditures, $119,058; Total giving, $102,500.
Fields of interest: Health care; Protestant agencies & churches.
Type of support: Undergraduate support; Grants for special needs.
Application information: Applications accepted.
  Initial approach: Letter.
  Deadline(s): None
EIN: 581429097

268
Carl & Grace Baker Memorial Scholarship Loan Fund Trust
c/o Bank of Stockton, Trust Dept.
P.O. Box 1110
Stockton, CA 95201 (209) 941-1500
Contact: Robert W. Friedberger, Chair.

Foundation type: Independent foundation
Limitations: Educational loans to students in the public school system within the territorial jurisdiction of Stockton, CA, Scottish Rite Bodies.
Publications: Informational brochure.
Financial data: Year ended 10/31/2004.
Assets, $1,579,265 (M); Expenditures, $20,672; Total giving, $0; Loans to individuals, totaling $96,000.
Type of support: Student loans—to individuals.
Application information: Applications accepted. Application form required.
Deadline(s): May 15 for fall semester, Oct. 15 for spring semester
Additional information: Application should include transcripts and three references.
EIN: 946618012

269
Charles Milton Baker Memorial Trust
c/o Trustmark National Bank
P.O. Box 777
Greenville, MS 38701
Application address: c/o W.E. Bradley, Advisory Comm., P.O. Box 932, Greenville, MS 38702-0932, tel.: (662) 378-2286

Foundation type: Independent foundation
Limitations: Scholarships to students in the Washington County, MS, area, for higher education.
Financial data: Year ended 12/31/2004.
Assets, $127,738 (M); Expenditures, $6,661; Total giving, $6,000; Grants to individuals, totaling $6,000.
Type of support: Undergraduate support.
Application information: Contact trust for current application deadline/guidelines.
EIN: 646172203

270
J. H. Baker Trust
c/o Thomas V. Dechant
P.O. Box 280
La Crosse, KS 67548-0280 (785) 222-2537

Foundation type: Independent foundation
Limitations: Low-interest undergraduate student loans to graduates of high schools in Rush, Barton, Ellis, Ness, and Pawnee counties, KS, who are under 25 years of age.
Financial data: Year ended 12/31/2004.
Assets, $1,147,158 (M); Expenditures, $78,706; Total giving, $45,000; Loans to individuals, totaling $13,900.
Fields of interest: Vocational education; College; University.
Type of support: Student loans—to individuals; Support to graduates or students of specific schools; Undergraduate support.
Application information: Applications accepted. Application form required.
Deadline(s): Jan. 1 for spring, July 1 for fall
Applicants should submit the following:
1) GPA
2) Class rank
3) Transcripts
Additional information: Application should also include letter of recommendation from a

former teacher, guidance counselor, or principal; Recipients notified by Aug. 15.
Program description:
Student Loan Program: Applicants must be full-time undergraduates at colleges, universities, or vocational/technical schools, and maintain a cumulative GPA of 2.0 or greater.
EIN: 510210925

271
Lillian M. Baker Trust
c/o Bank of America, N.A., P.C. Group
P.O. Box 1802
Providence, RI 02901-1802
Contact: Sharon M. Driscoll, Trust Off., Bank of America, N.A.
Application address for individuals: 100 Federal St., Boston, MA 02110, tel.: (617) 434-5669

Foundation type: Independent foundation
Limitations: Scholarships to financially needy graduates of Rockland District High School, ME, and for the education of young doctors, particularly at Colby College and Bowdoin College.
Financial data: Year ended 12/31/2004.
Assets, $771,596 (M); Expenditures, $34,531; Total giving, $29,500.
Fields of interest: Medical school/education.
Type of support: Support to graduates or students of specific schools; Graduate support; Undergraduate support.
Application information: Deadline Apr. 15 for new applications, Apr. 20 for renewals; Completion of formal application required; Scholarships awarded in mid-July.
Program description:
Scholarship Program: Application forms are available from the Rockland Regional High School Guidance Office, and from the trustees. Recipients are selected based on financial need, academic excellence, and extracurricular activities. Scholarships are renewable.
EIN: 046010588

272
Baker-Adams Scholarship Fund
c/o Bank of America, N.A., P.C. Group
P.O. Box 1802
Providence, RI 02940-1802
Application address: c/o Georgetown School Dept., Office of the Superintendent, 51 North St., Georgetown, MA 01833

Foundation type: Independent foundation
Limitations: Scholarships to individuals graduating from Georgetown High School, MA, for undergraduate education at American universities.
Financial data: Year ended 12/31/2004.
Assets, $657,994 (M); Expenditures, $38,113; Total giving, $33,500; Grants to individuals, totaling $33,500.
Type of support: Support to graduates or students of specific schools; Undergraduate support.
Application information: Applications accepted. Application form required.
Deadline(s): May 10
Applicants should submit the following:
1) Financial information
EIN: 316636824

273
Baker/Geary Memorial Fund, Inc.
2000 Waterfront Plz.
325 W. Main St.
Louisville, KY 40202
Contact: Michael Conliffe, Dir.

Foundation type: Independent foundation
Limitations: Scholarships to financially needy individuals with passing grades who are active in extracurricular activities and have an interest in golf.
Financial data: Year ended 12/31/2004.
Assets, $800,025 (M); Expenditures, $165,282; Total giving, $149,863; Grants to individuals, 37 grants totaling $83,523 (high: $5,000, low: $500).
Fields of interest: Athletics/sports, golf; Recreation.
Type of support: Scholarships—to individuals.
Application information: Application form required.
Initial approach: Letter or telephone.
Deadline(s): Dec. 1
EIN: 611234349

274
John E. Bakes Scholarship Trust Fund
c/o National City Bank
P.O. Box 94651
Cleveland, OH 44101-4651

Foundation type: Independent foundation
Limitations: Scholarships to graduating seniors of Switzerland County and Rising Sun high schools, IN.
Financial data: Year ended 12/31/2004.
Assets, $333,523 (M); Expenditures, $19,587; Total giving, $16,000; Grants to individuals, totaling $16,000.
Type of support: Support to graduates or students of specific schools; Undergraduate support.
Application information:
Deadline(s): Mar. 1
Additional information: Application by brief resume of academic qualifications.
EIN: 356406002

275
Nellie L. Ball Trust
P.O. Box 106
Wellston, OH 45692 (740) 384-3827
Contact: Peggy Murdock, Secy.
Application address: 1020 S. Wisconsin Ave., Wellston, OH 45692
Additional tel.: (740) 384-3659

Foundation type: Independent foundation
Limitations: Scholarships to graduates of Wellston High School, OH for attendance at U.S. colleges or universities.
Financial data: Year ended 12/31/2003.
Assets, $252,676 (M); Expenditures, $16,096; Total giving, $15,300; Grants to individuals, 15 grants totaling $15,300 (high: $2,000, low: $500).
Type of support: Support to graduates or students of specific schools.
Application information: Applications accepted. Application form required.
Applicants should submit the following:
1) GPA
2) Financial information
3) Essay
Additional information: Applicants must maintain a 3.0 G.P.A.
EIN: 316543187

276
John & Ann Ballard Foundation
2001 E. 70th St.
Shreveport, LA 71105-5360 (318) 797-0206
Contact: Hon. John R. Ballard, Tr.

Foundation type: Independent foundation
Limitations: Scholarships to seniors attending
North Caddo High School, LA.
Financial data: Year ended 11/30/2004.
Assets, $125,300 (M); Expenditures, $4,746;
Total giving, $4,375; Grants to individuals, totaling
$4,375.
Type of support: Support to graduates or students
of specific schools; Undergraduate support.
Application information: Applications accepted.
Application form required.
Deadline(s): None
EIN: 726100666

277
**Edward L. Ballard Memorial Scholarship
Fund**
c/o Wachovia Bank, N.A.
100 N. Main St., 13th Fl.
Winston-Salem, NC 27150-6732
Application address: c/o Guidance Dept., Ridgefield
High School, N. Salem Rd., Ridgefield, CT 06877

Foundation type: Independent foundation
Limitations: Scholarships only to graduates of
Ridgefield High School, CT.
Financial data: Year ended 09/30/2004.
Assets, $501,255 (M); Expenditures, $38,435;
Total giving, $32,500; Grants to individuals,
totaling $32,500.
Type of support: Support to graduates or students
of specific schools; Undergraduate support.
Application information: Application form required.
Deadline(s): Apr. 15
Additional information: Forms available at high
school guidance office and family aid room.
EIN: 066042949

278
The Balso Foundation
c/o Frank Loehman, Jr.
130 Nob Hill Rd.
Cheshire, CT 06410
Application address: c/o Guidance Dept., Cheshire
High School, 525 S. Main St., Cheshire, CT
06410-3167, tel.: (203) 272-5361

Foundation type: Company-sponsored foundation
Limitations: Scholarships to high school seniors
and college undergraduates in Cheshire, CT, and
surrounding towns. Scholarships are only available
for undergraduate study and are renewable.
Financial data: Year ended 12/31/2004.
Assets, $424,371 (M); Expenditures, $29,595;
Total giving, $17,000; Grants to individuals, 17
grants totaling $17,000 (high: $1,000, low:
$1,000).
Type of support: Undergraduate support.
Application information: Application form required.
Deadline(s): Apr. 1
EIN: 237159876

279
**The Baltimore School for the Arts
Foundation, Inc.**
712 Cathedral St.
Baltimore, MD 21201-5210
FAX: (410) 539-1430; URL: http://www.bsfa.org/
foundation.html

Foundation type: Public charity
Limitations: Scholarships to students attending
Baltimore School for the Arts, MD.
Financial data: Year ended 06/30/2004.
Assets, $7,628,158; Expenditures, $1,454,981;
Total giving, $553,413.
Fields of interest: Arts.
Type of support: Support to graduates or students
of specific schools; Undergraduate support.
Application information: Applications not
accepted.
EIN: 521174284

280
**Ruth Eleanor Bamberger and John Ernest
Bamberger Memorial Foundation**
136 S. Main St., Ste. 418
Salt Lake City, UT 84101-1690
(801) 364-2045
Contact: Eleanor Roser, Member
E-mail: bambergermemfdn@qwest.net;
URL: http://
www.ruthandjohnbambergermemorialfdn.org

Foundation type: Independent foundation
Limitations: Undergraduate scholarships to UT
residents, with preference given to nursing
students. Occasional loans awarded for medical
education.
Financial data: Year ended 12/31/2004.
Assets, $25,598,877 (M); Expenditures,
$924,902; Total giving, $716,622; Grants to
individuals, 57 grants totaling $133,490 (high:
$9,040, low: $752).
Fields of interest: Medical school/education;
Nursing school/education.
Type of support: Support to graduates or students
of specific schools; Undergraduate support.
Application information: Applications accepted.
Initial approach: Letter.
Deadline(s): None
Additional information: Interviews sometimes
required; Students are usually referred by
colleges or universities in UT.
EIN: 876116540

281
The Bamford-Lahey Children's Foundation
2995 Woodside Rd., Ste. 400
Woodside, CA 94062
E-mail: info@bamford-lahey.org; URL: http://
www.bamford-lahey.org

Foundation type: Operating foundation
Limitations: Scholarships to doctoral students who
intend to pursue study and research language
disorders in children.
Financial data: Year ended 12/31/2003.
Assets, $327,129 (M); Expenditures, $140,970;
Total giving, $70,865; Grants to individuals, 9
grants totaling $31,665 (high: $5,000, low:
$1,500).
Fields of interest: Learning disorders research.
Type of support: Doctoral support.
Application information:
Initial approach: E-mail.
Deadline(s): Apr. 1

Additional information: Completion of formal
application required, including budget.
Funding limit is $10,000 per year.
EIN: 943368601

282
BancTrust Opportunity Foundation
101 S. Central Ave.
P.O. Box 880
Paris, IL 61944 (217) 465-6381
Contact: Terry Howard

Foundation type: Company-sponsored foundation
Limitations: College scholarships to high school
students in Edgar and Clark counties, IL.
Financial data: Year ended 12/31/2004.
Assets, $19,914 (M); Expenditures, $25,890;
Total giving, $24,800; Grants to individuals, 26
grants totaling $24,800 (high: $2,000, low: $100).
Fields of interest: Higher education.
Type of support: Scholarships—to individuals.
Application information: Applications accepted.
Application form required.
Initial approach: Letter.
EIN: 300109336

283
Earl Bane Foundation
P.O. Box 201
Salina, KS 67402-0201
Application address: c/o Sandra Buster, Pres., 315
N. 9th St., Salina, KS 67401, tel.: (785) 827-1492

Foundation type: Independent foundation
Limitations: Scholarships to individuals from Salina
County schools, KS, for attendance at KS
universities and colleges.
Financial data: Year ended 04/30/2005.
Assets, $11,055,264 (M); Expenditures,
$689,756; Total giving, $588,225; Grants to
individuals, 37 grants totaling $175,000 (high:
$5,000, low: $2,500).
Type of support: Undergraduate support.
Application information: Contact foundation for
current application deadline/guidelines.
EIN: 481152429

284
Bank of Hawaii Charitable Foundation
(formerly Bancorp Hawaii Charitable Foundation)
c/o Foundation Admin. #758
P.O. Box 3170
Honolulu, HI 96802-3170 (808) 538-4944
Contact: Elaine Moniz, Trust Specialist
FAX: (808) 538-4006; E-mail: emoniz@boh.com;
Additional tel.: (808) 538-4945; Additional E-mail:
pboyce@boh.com; URL: https://www.boh.com/
about/community/471_504.asp

Foundation type: Company-sponsored foundation
Limitations: Scholarships to residents of HI for
higher education.
Publications: Application guidelines; Grants list.
Financial data: Year ended 12/31/2004.
Assets, $8,486,984 (M); Expenditures,
$2,796,411; Total giving, $2,650,692; Grants to
individuals, 80 grants totaling $755,392 (high:
$15,000, low: $1,098).
Type of support: Undergraduate support.
Application information: Applications not
accepted.
EIN: 990210467

285
Bank of Stockton Educational Foundation, Inc.
P.O. Box 1110
Stockton, CA 95201 (209) 929-1244
Contact: Ray Robinson, Secy.

Foundation type: Company-sponsored foundation
Limitations: Scholarships to children of full-time employees of the Bank of Stockton, for full-time undergraduate degree programs.
Financial data: Year ended 06/30/2002.
Assets, $302,633 (M); Expenditures, $106,500; Total giving, $106,500; Grants to individuals, 8 grants totaling $106,500 (high: $20,000, low: $6,500).
Type of support: Employee-related scholarships.
Application information: Application form required.
  Deadline(s): Apr. 15
EIN: 311801280

286
Baptist Health Care Foundation, Inc.
P.O. Box 17500
Pensacola, FL 32522
Contact: Jerry L. Maygarden, Sr. V.P.

Foundation type: Public charity
Limitations: Scholarships to Baptist Hospital, Inc., employees and to Pensacola, FL, area students for health care education.
Financial data: Year ended 09/30/2004.
Assets, $4,795,422 (M); Expenditures, $1,782,427; Total giving, $1,645,989; Grants to individuals, 36 grants totaling $35,500 (high: $1,000, low: $500).
Fields of interest: Health sciences school/education.
Type of support: Employee-related scholarships; Undergraduate support.
Application information: Contact foundation for current application deadline/guidelines.
EIN: 590192265

287
C. Glenn Barber Foundation
c/o National City Bank
P.O. Box 94651
Cleveland, OH 44101-4651

Foundation type: Independent foundation
Limitations: Scholarships to students who reside in OH for undergraduate education.
Financial data: Year ended 12/31/2004.
Assets, $3,167,136 (M); Expenditures, $146,069; Total giving, $131,116; Grants to individuals, 2 grants totaling $51,116 (high: $25,558, low: $25,558).
Type of support: Undergraduate support.
Application information: Applications not accepted.
EIN: 346765153

288
George and Hazel Barber Scholarship Trust
c/o Farmers & Merchants Bank & Trust
P.O. Box 938
Hannibal, MO 63401
Application address: Superintendent of Schools, George and Hazel Barber Scholarship, 4650 McMasters Ave., Hannibal, MO 63401

Foundation type: Independent foundation
Limitations: Scholarships only to graduating seniors in Marion County, MO, and Pike County, IL.
Financial data: Year ended 12/31/2004.
Assets, $396,560 (M); Expenditures, $20,846; Total giving, $17,639; Grants to individuals, totaling $17,639.
Type of support: Support to graduates or students of specific schools; Undergraduate support.
Application information: Application form required.
  Deadline(s): Apr. 1
  Additional information: Application must be notarized; Completed application should be returned to local school official who will forward it to the trust; Interviews required.
EIN: 237214882

289
The Barden Foundation, Inc.
34 Hawley Road Ext.
Danbury, CT 06811-4907 (203) 792-9369
Contact: Thomas F. Loughman, Secy.-Treas.
FAX: (203) 790-6760;
E-mail: loughman@comcast.net

Foundation type: Independent foundation
Limitations: Scholarships to children of employees of The Barden Corp. who reside in CT.
Publications: Informational brochure.
Financial data: Year ended 10/31/2004.
Assets, $5,739,818 (M); Expenditures, $348,027; Total giving, $294,500; Grants to individuals, 42 grants totaling $63,000 (high: $3,000, low: $500).
Type of support: Employee-related scholarships.
Application information: Application form required.
  Copies of proposal: 1
  Additional information: Application should also include a High School Certification completed by the candidate's high school principal and College Board Entrance Exam score.
Program description:
  Scholarship Program: Recipients must meet briefly with an officer of the corporation or a trustee of the foundation at least once each academic year while receiving the scholarship. Recipients must also send an official transcript of their academic and attendance records to the scholarship committee at the end of each academic year. Scholarships are renewable. Recipients are notified the first week of May.
EIN: 066054855

290
Barking Foundation, Inc.
P.O. Box 855
Bangor, ME 04401 (207) 990-2910
Contact: Stephanie Leonard, Admin.
FAX: (207) 990-2975;
E-mail: info@barkingfoundation.org; URL: http://www.barkingfoundation.org

Foundation type: Independent foundation
Limitations: Scholarships to residents of ME for post-secondary education.
Publications: Application guidelines; Informational brochure.
Financial data: Year ended 12/31/2004.
Assets, $1,774,913 (M); Expenditures, $177,176; Total giving, $163,478; Grants to individuals, 55 grants totaling $163,478 (high: $3,000, low: $1,478).
Type of support: Scholarships—to individuals.
Application information: Application form required. Application form available on the grantmaker's Web site.
  Initial approach: Letter or E-mail.
  Deadline(s): Mar. 1
  Applicants should submit the following:
    1) Essay
    2) SAT
    3) Letter(s) of recommendation
    4) Financial information
  Additional information: Application by fax or e-mail not accepted.
Program description:
  Scholarship Program: Applicants must have been residents of ME for four consecutive years immediately prior to application. Grants are made for one academic year, and recipients may reapply for a second year only.
EIN: 010511020

291
William A. Barlocker Foundation
841 S. 54th Cir.
Mesa, AZ 85206
Application address: 723 W. 6th Ave., Mesa, AZ 85210

Foundation type: Independent foundation
Limitations: Scholarships to students in AZ and UT for higher education.
Financial data: Year ended 12/31/2003.
Assets, $0 (M); Expenditures, $11,683; Total giving, $8,265.
Type of support: Undergraduate support.
Application information:
  Initial approach: Letter.
  Deadline(s): Contact foundation for current application deadline
EIN: 742395114

292
Barnard Scholarship
c/o Marshall & Ilsley Bank
P.O. Box 2980
Milwaukee, WI 53201

Foundation type: Independent foundation
Limitations: Scholarships to graduates of River Valley High School, WI, for attendance at WI institutions.
Financial data: Year ended 08/31/2005.
Assets, $307,007 (M); Expenditures, $27,171; Total giving, $22,600; Grants to individuals, totaling $22,600.
Type of support: Support to graduates or students of specific schools; Undergraduate support.
Application information: Applications not accepted.
EIN: 396719890

293
Raeburn E. Barnes Estate Trust
P.O. Box 499
Sidney, OH 45365-0499
Contact: Eugene P. Elsass, Tr.
Application address: P.O. Box 652, Sidney, OH 45365

Foundation type: Independent foundation
Limitations: Educational loans to citizens of Shelby County, OH.
Financial data: Year ended 12/31/2003.
Assets, $6,557,543 (M); Expenditures, $127,593; Total giving, $1,000; Loans to individuals, totaling $775,594.
Type of support: Student loans—to individuals.

Application information: Applications accepted. Application form required.

Initial approach: Letter requesting application.

Deadline(s): July 1

EIN: 346639060

294

Fay T. Barnes Scholarship Trust

c/o JPMorgan Chase Bank
P.O. Box 550
Austin, TX 78789-0001 (512) 479-2647
Contact: Sonia Garza, Trust Admin.
E-mail: sonia.Garza@chase.com

Foundation type: Independent foundation
Limitations: Scholarships to graduating seniors of high schools in Williamson and Travis counties, TX, to attend TX universities and colleges.
Publications: Informational brochure (including application guidelines).
Financial data: Year ended 12/31/2003. Assets, $2,821,298 (M); Expenditures, $210,972; Total giving, $181,086; Grants to individuals, 53 grants totaling $181,086 (high: $5,250, low: $1,750).
Type of support: Support to graduates or students of specific schools; Undergraduate support.
Application information: Application form required.

Deadline(s): Jan. 15

Applicants should submit the following:

1) Letter(s) of recommendation

2) Essay

Additional information: Contact high school counselor only for specific application guidelines.

Program description:

Scholarship Program: Students are required to submit applications to their high school principal or counselor. A committee of three to five faculty administrators in each school selects eligible candidates. Each high school may submit to the trust one application for every 200 students, or part thereof, in its graduating senior class. The trustee administers the fund and selects approximately nine to ten recipients from the eligible candidates submitted by each high school. Recipients are chosen on the basis of the following criteria:

· Scholarship—minimum overall "B" (85) average at graduation
· Citizenship Character—activities, accomplishments, and recommendations
· Financial need may also be considered

Scholarships are $12,000 for four years, paid out at $3,000 per year. Recipients must maintain a 2.5 GPA and full-time status in college to remain eligible.

EIN: 742256469

295

Barnitz Fund

c/o JPMorgan Chase Bank, N.A.
P.O. Box 1308
Milwaukee, WI 53201
Application address: c/o JPMorgan Chase Bank, N.A., 2 S. Main St., Middletown, OH 45042

Foundation type: Independent foundation
Limitations: Scholarships to graduates of high schools in Middletown, OH, who plan to go into Christian work.
Financial data: Year ended 12/31/2004. Assets, $2,353,412 (M); Expenditures, $108,803; Total giving, $91,086.
Fields of interest: Christian agencies & churches.
Type of support: Support to graduates or students of specific schools; Undergraduate support.

Application information: Applications accepted. Application form required.

Additional information: Application should also include proof of church membership, letters of recommendation, transcript, financial information, list of school activities, and name of college to attend.

EIN: 316020687

296

Tom C. Barnsley Foundation

c/o Bank of America, N.A.
P.O. Box 831041
Dallas, TX 75283-1041

Foundation type: Independent foundation
Limitations: Scholarships to graduates of Crane High School, TX, studying animal sciences, agriculture, or associated studies.
Financial data: Year ended 12/31/2004. Assets, $739,998 (M); Expenditures, $59,210; Total giving, $38,000.
Fields of interest: Agriculture.
Type of support: Support to graduates or students of specific schools; Undergraduate support.
Application information: Applications accepted.

Deadline(s): None

EIN: 756248739

297

The Robert M. Barr and Roberta Armstrong Barr Foundation

c/o Rod Humble
P.O. Box 1779
Durango, CO 81302 (970) 247-1579

Foundation type: Independent foundation
Limitations: Scholarships to residents of CO aspiring to get a degree in education.
Financial data: Year ended 06/30/2005. Assets, $39,809 (M); Expenditures, $13,523; Total giving, $13,000; Grants to individuals, totaling $13,000.
Fields of interest: Teacher school/education.
Type of support: Undergraduate support.
Application information: Contact foundation for current application deadline/guidelines.

EIN: 880493403

298

Shelley & Terry Barr Foundation

29600 Northwestern Hwy., Ste. 102
Southfield, MI 48034

Foundation type: Independent foundation
Limitations: Scholarships only to graduates of Grand Rapids Central High School, MI.
Financial data: Year ended 12/31/2004. Assets, $69,374 (M); Expenditures, $8,000; Total giving, $8,000; Grants to individuals, totaling $8,000.
Type of support: Support to graduates or students of specific schools; Undergraduate support.
Application information: Applications accepted throughout the year; Contact foundation for current application guidelines.

EIN: 382258156

299

Barrand & Bradford Scholarship Foundation

c/o National City Bank
P.O. Box 94651
Cleveland, OH 44101-4651
Application address for individuals: c/o Taylor University, Dir. of Financial Aid, 1025 W. Rudisill Blvd., Fort Wayne, IN 46807, tel.: (219) 456-2111

Foundation type: Independent foundation
Limitations: Scholarships to incoming freshman applying to attend Taylor University, IN, full-time.
Financial data: Year ended 07/31/2004. Assets, $629,973 (M); Expenditures, $102,679; Total giving, $99,458; Grants to individuals, 5 grants totaling $99,458 (high: $25,634, low: $16,822).
Type of support: Support to graduates or students of specific schools; Undergraduate support.
Application information: Application form required.

Deadline(s): None

Additional information: Application should include financial information, 150-word essay, and two letters of recommendation.

EIN: 356615379

300

Barrick Mercur Gold Mine Foundation, Inc.

60 Benchview Dr.
Tooele, UT 84074
Contact: A. Bruce Cummings, Tr.

Foundation type: Operating foundation
Limitations: Scholarships to graduates of Grantsville High School and Tooele High School, both in UT, for higher education.
Financial data: Year ended 12/31/2004. Assets, $193,407 (M); Expenditures, $11,147; Total giving, $8,000; Grants to individuals, totaling $8,000.
Type of support: Support to graduates or students of specific schools; Undergraduate support.
Application information: Applications accepted.

Deadline(s): None

Additional information: Applications by letter.

EIN: 742546494

301

Leslie Bartell Scholarship Foundation, Inc.

c/o Leonard J. Krieger, Jr., C.P.A.
49 Roberts Rd.
Clark, NJ 07066

Foundation type: Independent foundation
Limitations: Scholarships to graduating seniors of Johnson High School, NJ, for higher education.
Financial data: Year ended 08/31/2004. Assets, $543,759 (M); Expenditures, $33,000; Total giving, $33,000; Grants to individuals, 3 grants totaling $33,000 (high: $11,000, low: $11,000).
Type of support: Support to graduates or students of specific schools; Undergraduate support.
Application information:

Deadline(s): May

Additional information: Application by letter, including transcript and activity participation.

Program description:

Scholarship Program: Recipients must be Clark, NJ, residents attending a four-year college.

EIN: 223504274

302
Bartholomew Family Scholarship & Loan Fund
c/o Bank of America, N.A.
P.O. Box 34345
Seattle, WA 98124-1345
Application address: Bartholomew Family Scholarship Comm., c/o First Congregational Church, 700 Marion St., N.E., Salem, OR 97301, tel.: (503) 363-3660

Foundation type: Independent foundation
Limitations: Scholarships to members of First Congregational Church, Salem, OR, for college, university, technical school, or ministry study.
Financial data: Year ended 04/30/2005. Assets, $503,349 (M); Expenditures, $30,115; Total giving, $25,000; Grants to individuals, 6 grants totaling $25,000 (high: $8,500; low: $1,000).
Fields of interest: Vocational education; Theological school/education; Protestant agencies & churches.
Type of support: Technical education support; Undergraduate support.
Application information: Applications accepted. Application form required.
  Deadline(s): Apr. 30
EIN: 936091422

303
The Frank H. Bartholomew Foundation
c/o William M. Godward
1 Maritime Plz., Ste. 2000
San Francisco, CA 94111
Application address: c/o Jan V. Haraszthy, P.O. Box 311, Sonoma, CA 95176-0311

Foundation type: Operating foundation
Limitations: Scholarships to graduating seniors of Sonoma Valley High School, CA, for study at the University of California, Davis, with emphasis on viticulture program.
Financial data: Year ended 12/31/2004. Assets, $16,894,016 (M); Expenditures, $766,337; Total giving, $5,200; Grant to an individual, 1 grant totaling $5,000.
Type of support: Support to graduates or students of specific schools; Undergraduate support.
Application information: Applications by letter accepted throughout the year.
EIN: 943129676

304
Lyle P. Bartholomew Scholarship & Loan Fund
c/o Bank of America, N.A.
P.O. Box 34345
Seattle, WA 98124-1345
Application address: c/o University of Oregon, School of Architecture, Lawrence Hall, Rm. 212, Eugene, OR 97403, tel.: (503) 686-3656

Foundation type: Independent foundation
Limitations: Scholarships to graduate and undergraduate students of architecture at the University of Oregon.
Financial data: Year ended 04/30/2005. Assets, $543,124 (M); Expenditures, $30,248; Total giving, $25,000; Grants to individuals, totaling $25,000.
Fields of interest: Architecture.
Type of support: Support to graduates or students of specific schools; Graduate support; Undergraduate support.

Application information: Applications accepted. Application form required.
  Deadline(s): May 10
  Additional information: Application should also include applicant's statement, financial statement and one letter of recommendation from a faculty member.
EIN: 936091423

305
W. P. Bartlett Trust Fund
27349 Ave. 138
Porterville, CA 93257
Contact: John C. Richardson, Secy.-Treas.

Foundation type: Independent foundation
Limitations: Scholarships to students of Porterville and Monache high schools and Porterville College, all in CA, to attend CA colleges and universities.
Publications: Informational brochure.
Financial data: Year ended 12/31/2004. Assets, $1,399,083 (M); Expenditures, $69,491; Total giving, $64,000; Grants to individuals, totaling $64,000.
Type of support: Support to graduates or students of specific schools; Undergraduate support.
Application information:
  Deadline(s): Feb.
  Additional information: Application by letter stating residence, schools attended, present school status, and name of prospective school; Interviews required; Recipients notified in May.
Program description:
  Scholarship Program: Scholarship recipients are recommended by scholarship committees of Porterville College, Porterville High School, and Monache High School. The aim of the fund is to assist financially needy, qualified students in meeting school expenses for each quarter for two years of schooling. Recipients of the scholarships must have been attending their high school or college for at least two years prior to application. Applicants are judged on prior academic performance, performance on college aptitude tests, recommendations from instructors, financial need, and an interview with the selection committee.
EIN: 946102005

306
Russell T. & Olive V. Bartlett Trust
c/o Citizens Bank of NH
870 Westminster St., 2nd Fl.
Providence, RI 02903
Application address: c/o Guidance Counselor, Woodsville High School, Woodsville, NH 03785, tel.: (603) 747-2451

Foundation type: Independent foundation
Limitations: Scholarships to residents of Bath and Haverhill, NH, to attend Dartmouth College, NH. Applicants must have been residents for at least five years prior to application.
Financial data: Year ended 09/30/2005. Assets, $830,670 (M); Expenditures, $57,799; Total giving, $42,000; Grants to individuals, totaling $42,000.
Type of support: Support to graduates or students of specific schools; Undergraduate support.
Application information: Applications accepted throughout the year; Applications made in person at the guidance office of Woodsville High School.
EIN: 026003957

307
Harold & Martha Barto Scholarship Trust
c/o Bank of America, N.A.
P.O. Box 34345
Seattle, WA 98124-1345
Contact: Jen Gray, Dir. of Fdn. and Comm. Relations
Application address for scholarships: c/o Central WA University Foundation, 400 E. 8th Ave., Ellensburg, WA 98926-7508, tel.: (509) 963-2111
Application address: Jen Gray, Dir., Fdn. & Community Rels., CWU Foundation, 400 E. 8th Ave., Ellensburg, WA 98926-7508

Foundation type: Independent foundation
Limitations: Scholarships restricted to full-time students actively pursuing a degree from Central Washington University, WA.
Financial data: Year ended 04/30/2005. Assets, $371,398 (M); Expenditures, $41,692; Total giving, $37,653; Grants to individuals, totaling $37,653.
Type of support: Support to graduates or students of specific schools; Undergraduate support.
Application information: Application form required.
  Deadline(s): Prior to fall semester
  Applicants should submit the following:
    1) Letter(s) of recommendation
EIN: 916267640

308
Bashinsky Foundation, Inc.
3432 E. Briarcliff Rd.
Birmingham, AL 35223

Foundation type: Company-sponsored foundation
Limitations: Scholarships to children of employees of Golden Flake Snack Foods, Inc.
Financial data: Year ended 12/31/2003. Assets, $11,244,905 (M); Expenditures, $472,590; Total giving, $437,884; Grants to individuals, 15 grants totaling $37,500 (high: $2,500, low: $2,500).
Type of support: Employee-related scholarships; Graduate support; Technical education support; Undergraduate support.
Application information: Application form required.
  Deadline(s): Mar. 1 for application request, Mar. 30 for application.
  Applicants should submit the following:
    1) Transcripts
  Additional information: Recipients must be dependent, unmarried and under the age of 25, and high school seniors or graduates, college undergraduates or graduate students who are enrolled or are planning to enroll in a full-time course of study at an accredited two- or four-year college, university, vocational-technical school or graduate school; Scholarship application address: c/o Golden Enterprises, Inc. Scholarship Prog., Scholarship Management Svcs., Scholarship America, Inc., P.O. Box 297, St. Peter, MN 56082, tel.: (507) 931-0407.
EIN: 630968201

309
G. Basila Scholarship Fund
P.O. Box 1383
Scranton, PA 18501-1383 (570) 342-2676
Contact: Joseph A. Karam, Tr.

Foundation type: Operating foundation
Limitations: Scholarships to students with financial need who attend St. Ann's Maronite Church, Scranton, PA, or St. Joseph's Melkite Church, Scranton, PA.

Financial data: Year ended 12/31/2003. Assets, $566,071 (M); Expenditures, $42,883; Total giving, $40,567; Grants to individuals, 13 grants totaling $40,567 (high: $14,500, low: $954).

Type of support: Scholarships—to individuals.

Application information: Applications accepted anytime prior to start of semester; Application by letter outlining financial need and including copy of financial aid forms.

EIN: 232614309

310
Basilica of St. Adalbert Foundation
701 4th St., N.W.
Grand Rapids, MI   49504-5104

Foundation type: Public charity

Limitations: Scholarships to student parishioners of St. Adalbert's Basilica, Grand Rapids, MI, for attendance at Catholic elementary schools or Catholic high schools.

Financial data: Year ended 06/30/2004. Assets, $411,675; Expenditures, $25,151; Total giving, $25,096; Grants to individuals, totaling $11,405.

Fields of interest: Roman Catholic agencies & churches.

Type of support: Precollege support.

Application information:
Initial approach: Letter.
Additional information: Contact foundation for further application guidelines.

EIN: 382685451

311
Graham Sefton Baskin & Anna Mae Sweeney Baskin Foundation
131 Cambridge St.
Indiana, PA   15701
Contact: Edward E. Mackey, Tr.

Foundation type: Independent foundation

Limitations: Scholarships to students who are attending or have attended a high school in Indiana County, PA, to pursue a degree in nursing or physical education.

Financial data: Year ended 12/31/2004. Assets, $1,163,802 (M); Expenditures, $69,336; Total giving, $49,500; Grants to individuals, totaling $49,500.

Fields of interest: Medical school/education; Nursing care; Recreation.

Type of support: Support to graduates or students of specific schools; Undergraduate support.

Application information: Application form required.
Deadline(s): Mar. 1

EIN: 251777790

312
R. Aumon & Mary Scott Bass Endowment Fund, Inc.
c/o First Virginia Bank, Trust Dept.
700 E. Main St.
Richmond, VA   23219
Contact: Race Drake, Pres.
Application address: c/o VSDB-Staunton, P.O. Box 2069, Staunton, VA 24401

Foundation type: Independent foundation

Limitations: Scholarships to graduates of Virginia School for the Deaf and the Blind in Staunton, VA, to attend colleges, universities, and technical and vocational schools.

Financial data: Year ended 09/30/2004. Assets, $147,752 (M); Expenditures, $7,199; Total giving, $4,255; Grants to individuals, totaling $4,255.

Fields of interest: Vocational education; Disabilities, people with.

Type of support: Support to graduates or students of specific schools; Technical education support; Undergraduate support.

Application information: Applications accepted throughout the year; Completion of formal application required.

Program description:
Scholarship Funds: Scholarship funds may be used for tuition, books, room, board, and other official college fees.

EIN: 541296056

313
Lillian M. Bassett Foundation
c/o Eastern Bank & Trust Co.
605 Broadway, Ste. LF41
Saugus, MA   01906   (781) 581-4290
Contact: Shawn McCarthy

Foundation type: Independent foundation

Limitations: Scholarships to seniors of Swampscott High School, MA.

Financial data: Year ended 12/31/2004. Assets, $250,897 (M); Expenditures, $17,596; Total giving, $14,000; Grants to individuals, totaling $14,000.

Type of support: Support to graduates or students of specific schools; Undergraduate support.

Application information: Applications accepted. Application form required.
Deadline(s): None

EIN: 046606391

314
Will Paul Bateman Scholarship Fund Trust
c/o Wachovia Bank, N.A.
100 N. Main St., 13th Fl.
Winston-Salem, NC   27150

Foundation type: Independent foundation

Limitations: Scholarships to financially needy male students for study at colleges and universities in FL.

Financial data: Year ended 04/30/2005. Assets, $739,987 (M); Expenditures, $48,390; Total giving, $35,709.

Fields of interest: Men.

Type of support: Scholarships—to individuals.

Application information: Applications accepted.
Deadline(s): None
Additional information: Contact school for current application guidelines.

EIN: 596149634

315
Oswald and Sophia Bathalter Scholarship Trust
c/o DeWitt Bank & Trust Co.
P.O. Box 260
DeWitt, IA   52742-0260
Contact: Roger J. Hill

Foundation type: Independent foundation

Limitations: Scholarships to graduating seniors of Central Community School District in Clinton County, IA. Graduating seniors of other schools in Clinton County, IA, are given second priority.

Financial data: Year ended 03/31/2005. Assets, $367,483 (M); Expenditures, $29,955;

Total giving, $24,000; Grants to individuals, totaling $24,000.

Fields of interest: Roman Catholic agencies & churches.

Type of support: Support to graduates or students of specific schools; Undergraduate support.

Application information: Applications accepted. Application form required.
Deadline(s): None
Applicants should submit the following:
1) Transcripts
Additional information: Application should also include a personal statement, and references.

Program description:
Scholarship Program: Special consideration is given to Roman Catholics. Recipients must maintain at least a 2.0 GPA, and provide transcripts from each term to the trust.

EIN: 421368307

316
Baton Rouge Area Foundation
402 N. 4th St.
Baton Rouge, LA   70802   (225) 387-6126
Contact: John G. Davies, C.E.O.
FAX: (225) 387-6153; E-mail: jdavies@braf.org; Additional tel.: (877) 387-6126; Grant information E-mail: grantmaking@braf.org; URL: http://www.braf.org

Foundation type: Community foundation

Limitations: Scholarships to residents of the Baton Rouge, LA, area.

Publications: Application guidelines; Annual report (including application guidelines); Informational brochure; Newsletter.

Financial data: Year ended 12/31/2004. Assets, $363,767,711 (M); Expenditures, $20,083,252; Total giving, $13,301,520; Grants to individuals, totaling $95,250.

Type of support: Undergraduate support.

Application information: Applications accepted. Application form required. Application form available on the grantmaker's Web site.
Initial approach: E-mail.
Additional information: See Web site for a complete listing of programs.

EIN: 726030391

317
Lloyd Batre Scholarship Trust Fund
c/o Regions Bank
P.O. Box 2527
Mobile, AL   36622
Application address: c/o Betty H. Harlan, Dir., Financial Aid Office, Spring Hill College, 40000 Dauphin St., Mobile, AL 36608

Foundation type: Independent foundation

Limitations: Scholarships to financially needy students attending Spring Hill College, AL.

Financial data: Year ended 01/31/2005. Assets, $152,522 (M); Expenditures, $9,780; Total giving, $7,525; Grants to individuals, totaling $7,525.

Type of support: Support to graduates or students of specific schools; Undergraduate support.

Application information: Applications by letter accepted throughout the year.

EIN: 636020978

318
Ruth M. Batson Educational Foundation
250 Cambridge St., Ste. 701
Boston, MA   02114-3135   (617) 742-1070
Contact: Ruth M. Batson, Treas.

Foundation type: Independent foundation
Limitations: Scholarships to minorities and disadvantaged individuals for tuition and related expenses residing primarily in the Boston, MA, area.
Financial data: Year ended 12/31/2004. Assets, $287,418 (M); Expenditures, $45,521; Total giving, $22,063; Grants to individuals, 10 grants totaling $14,763.
Fields of interest: Minorities.
Type of support: Scholarships—to individuals.
Application information: Applications by letter, outlining financial need, accepted throughout the year.
EIN: 237083481

319
Fred (B. A.) Batterton Fund Trust
c/o Kentucky Bank
P.O. Box 157
Paris, KY   40362-0157   (859) 987-3640

Foundation type: Independent foundation
Limitations: Scholarships to residents of Bourbon County, KY, for medical education.
Financial data: Year ended 10/31/2004. Assets, $981,253 (M); Expenditures, $47,312; Total giving, $40,310; Grants to individuals, 18 grants totaling $40,310 (high: $5,850; low: $1,000).
Fields of interest: Medical school/education.
Type of support: Graduate support.
Application information: Applications by letter accepted throughout the year.
EIN: 616128598

320
Battle Creek Community Foundation
(formerly Greater Battle Creek Foundation)
1 Riverwalk Ctr.
34 W. Jackson St.
Battle Creek, MI   49017-3505   (269) 962-2181
Contact: Brenda L. Hunt, C.E.O.; For grants: Kelly Boles Chapman, V.P., Progs.
FAX: (269) 962-2182;
E-mail: bccf@bccfoundation.org; Grant inquiry E-mail: kelly@bccfoundation.org; URL: http://www.bccfoundation.org

Foundation type: Community foundation
Limitations: Scholarships to residents of the greater Battle Creek, MI, area, for attendance at colleges and universities in the U.S.
Publications: Application guidelines; Annual report; Biennial report (including application guidelines); Financial statement; Grants list; Informational brochure; Newsletter; Program policy statement.
Financial data: Year ended 03/31/2005. Assets, $82,360,581 (M); Expenditures, $5,203,743; Total giving, $2,700,511; Grants to individuals, totaling $202,052.
Type of support: Scholarships—to individuals.
Application information: Applications accepted. Application form required.
   Initial approach: Contacting high school guidance counselors.
   Deadline(s): Late Feb.
   Additional information: Interviews required.
EIN: 382045459

321
Bauer Foundation
c/o Shipman & Goodwin
P.O. Box 1784, Porter St.
Lakeville, CT   06039   (860) 435-9282
Contact: Joan Wilkinson

Foundation type: Independent foundation
Limitations: Scholarships to residents of Regional School District No. 1 in Lakeville, CT.
Financial data: Year ended 12/31/2004. Assets, $1,255,989 (M); Expenditures, $58,818; Total giving, $53,000; Grants to individuals, totaling $53,000.
Type of support: Scholarships—to individuals.
Application information: Application form required.
   Deadline(s): May 2
EIN: 066032985

322
Frederick R. Bauer Fund
c/o Stuyvesant K. Bearns
P.O. Box 1784, Porter St.
Lakeville, CT   06039   (860) 435-9282

Foundation type: Independent foundation
Limitations: Scholarships to students residing in Salisbury, CT.
Financial data: Year ended 12/31/2004. Assets, $627,846 (M); Expenditures, $30,123; Total giving, $26,500; Grants to individuals, 5 grants totaling $26,500.
Type of support: Scholarships—to individuals; Support to graduates or students of specific schools.
Application information: Application form required.
   Deadline(s): July 15
EIN: 066032984

323
Baumberger Endowment
P.O. Box 6067
San Antonio, TX   78209-0067

Foundation type: Independent foundation
Limitations: Scholarships only to graduating seniors of high schools in Bexar County, TX.
Publications: Application guidelines; Program policy statement.
Financial data: Year ended 12/31/2004. Assets, $28,370,527 (M); Expenditures, $1,065,194; Total giving, $756,294.
Type of support: Support to graduates or students of specific schools; Undergraduate support.
Application information: Application form required.
   Deadline(s): Feb. 15
   Applicants should submit the following:
      1) ACT
      2) SAT
      3) GPA
      4) Transcripts
      5) Financial information
   Additional information: Applications available from high school counselors.
Program description:
   Baumberger Endowment: Applicants must have resided in TX for at least ten years, graduate in the top half of their class, have test scores of at least 1000 on the SAT, or 22 on the ACT, demonstrate financial need, plan to attend a state-supported or nondenominational school in TX, and be of good character. Scholarships are renewable. Funds are disbursed directly to the recipient's school.
EIN: 237225925

324
K. & F. Baxter Family Foundation, Inc.
P.O. Box 13053
Berkeley, CA   94712-4053   (510) 524-8145
Contact: Stacey K. Bell, Exec. Dir.
FAX: (510) 524-4101;
E-mail: kfbaxterfound@aol.com; URL: http://www.kfbaxterfoundation.com

Foundation type: Independent foundation
Limitations: Scholarships to multiracial children from Alameda, Contra Costa, San Francisco and Los Angeles county schools, CA.
Publications: Application guidelines; Grants list; Occasional report.
Financial data: Year ended 12/31/2004. Assets, $2,061,739 (M); Expenditures, $623,170; Total giving, $573,274.
Type of support: Precollege support; Undergraduate support.
Application information: Applications accepted.
   Initial approach: Letter, telephone, or E-mail.
   Copies of proposal: 4
   Deadline(s): Feb. 1 and Aug. 1 for the Foundation's Of Many Colors Scholarship
   Additional information: Application by proposal.
EIN: 954633505

325
Bay Area Community Foundation
703 Washington Ave.
Bay City, MI   48708-5732   (989) 893-4438
Contact: Roger Merrifield, C.E.O. and Pres.
FAX: (989) 893-4448;
E-mail: bacfnd@bayfoundation.org; Additional tel.: (800) 926-3217; URL: http://www.bayfoundation.org

Foundation type: Community foundation
Limitations: Scholarships to Bay County, MI, area residents and graduates of Bay County high schools.
Publications: Annual report; Financial statement; Grants list; Informational brochure.
Financial data: Year ended 12/31/2003. Assets, $22,216,122 (M); Expenditures, $1,171,964; Total giving, $1,027,738.
Fields of interest: Arts education; Journalism/publishing; Dance; Performing arts, education; History/archaeology; Education, research; Vocational education; Business school/education; Medical school/education; Nursing school/education; Students, sororities/fraternities; Physical therapy; Home economics; Athletics/sports, training; Athletics/sports, baseball; Athletics/sports, golf; Race/intergroup relations; Science; Economics; Native Americans/American Indians; Men.
Type of support: Employee-related scholarships; Graduate support; Technical education support; Undergraduate support.
Application information: Applications accepted. Application form available on the grantmaker's Web site.
   Additional information: See Web site for program descriptions and deadlines.
EIN: 382418086

326
Bernard H. Beal Scholarship Foundation
c/o National City Bank
2322 Tittabawassee Rd.
Saginaw, MI 48604
Application address: c/o Millington High School, 8780 Dean Dr., Millington, MI 48746, tel.: (989) 871-5220

Foundation type: Independent foundation
Limitations: Scholarships to graduates of Millington High School, MI.
Financial data: Year ended 12/31/2004. Assets, $577,888 (M); Expenditures, $26,065; Total giving, $22,550; Grants to individuals, totaling $22,550.
Type of support: Support to graduates or students of specific schools; Undergraduate support.
Application information: Application form required.
Deadline(s): Mar. 31
Applicants should submit the following:
1) Essay
Additional information: Application should also include two letters of recommendation, and a FAFSA or SAR.
EIN: 383381079

327
Anna Beal Trust
c/o U.S. Bank, N.A.
P.O. Box 2043
Milwaukee, WI 53201-9116
Contact: LuAnn Ray, Trust Off., U.S. Bank, N.A.
Scholarship application address: c/o: U.S. Bank, N.A., 425 Cedar St., Waterloo, IA 50701, tel.: (319) 235-2301

Foundation type: Independent foundation
Limitations: Scholarships to financially needy residents of IA, studying in agriculture and biology-related fields, who attend colleges and universities previously selected by the trustee.
Publications: Application guidelines; Financial statement; Grants list; Informational brochure; Newsletter.
Financial data: Year ended 12/31/2004. Assets, $649,449 (M); Expenditures, $35,238; Total giving, $28,125; Grants to individuals, 9 grants totaling $28,125.
Fields of interest: Agriculture; Biological sciences.
Type of support: Scholarships—to individuals.
Application information: Applications accepted. Application form required.
Deadline(s): None
Additional information: Applications must be submitted in writing from the college or university through the Nature Conservancy in Des Moines, IA.
EIN: 426193621

328
Jon C. Beal, Jr. Memorial Trust
1611 Country Rd. 2
Lubbock, TX 79423
Contact: Arlen W. Hastings, Tr.

Foundation type: Independent foundation
Limitations: Scholarships only to graduates of Fredonia High School, KS.
Financial data: Year ended 12/31/2004. Assets, $127,473 (M); Expenditures, $5,576; Total giving, $5,500; Grants to individuals, 5 grants totaling $5,500.
Type of support: Support to graduates or students of specific schools; Undergraduate support.

Application information: Applications accepted.
Deadline(s): None
Additional information: Applications by letter; Applicant must include social security number, parents' names, school activities, college plans, and a 200-word essay on why he/she wishes to attend college.
EIN: 480959834

329
The Robert and Aldona Beall Family Foundation, Inc.
(formerly The Beall Family Foundation)
1806 38th Ave. E.
Bradenton, FL 34208
Application address: c/o Palmetto Youth Center, Attn.: Scholarship Committee Chair., P.O. Box 608, Palmetto, FL 34220

Foundation type: Operating foundation
Limitations: Scholarships to members of the Palmetto Youth Center, FL.
Financial data: Year ended 10/30/2004. Assets, $903,958 (M); Expenditures, $44,782; Total giving, $42,000; Grants to individuals, 7 grants totaling $42,000 (high: $6,000, low: $6,000).
Fields of interest: Neighborhood centers; Children/youth, services.
Type of support: Scholarships—to individuals.
Application information: Applications accepted. Application form required.
Deadline(s): None
EIN: 650545213

330
R. M. Beall, Sr. Charitable Foundation
1806 38th Ave. E.
Bradenton, FL 34208
Contact: Patricia Johnson, Admin.

Foundation type: Company-sponsored foundation
Limitations: Scholarships to graduating seniors at Southeast High School, Brandenton, FL, for study at Manatee Community College, FL. Scholarships also to children and minor dependents of full-time Beall's, Inc. employees in AZ, FL and GA.
Financial data: Year ended 12/31/2002. Assets, $1,780,693 (M); Expenditures, $404,854; Total giving, $385,826; Grants to individuals, 80 grants totaling $333,336 (high: $6,636, low: $1,250).
Type of support: Employee-related scholarships; Support to graduates or students of specific schools; Undergraduate support.
Application information: Application form required.
Deadline(s): Apr. 1
Applicants should submit the following:
1) Letter(s) of recommendation
2) Transcripts
Additional information: Tel.: (941) 747-2355, ext. 309.
Program description:
Southeast Scholarship: Graduating seniors at Southeast High School, Brandenton, FL, and dependents of individuals who have been employed full-time at Beall's, Inc. for at least one year may apply for these renewable scholarships. In the first two years, recipients receive up to $1,600 per year. In the second two years, recipients receive up to $2,600 per year. Applicants must have a 2.5 minimum GPA and be formally accepted to Manatee Community College, FL. Recipients are chosen on the basis of:
· academic achievement

· involvement in extracurricular activities
· financial need
· sincerity of interest as demonstrated by thorough completion of the scholarship application and accompanying information
Scholarships are renewable each year for up to four years provided that the student maintains at least a 2.5 GPA, and that they are not suspended, expelled, or convicted of a crime in a court of law. To apply for a renewal, the student must submit a letter of intent to continue study, including intended course work, school attending or transferring to, other financial and eligibility information, and change of address or phone number if applicable, in June of each year.
EIN: 592851924

331
L. Carl Bean Scholarship Fund
c/o KeyBank N.A.
800 Superior Ave., 4th Fl.
Cleveland, OH 44114

Foundation type: Independent foundation
Limitations: Scholarships to attend colleges and universities in ME.
Financial data: Year ended 04/30/2005. Assets, $243,153 (M); Expenditures, $19,320; Total giving, $15,000; Grants to individuals, 20 grants totaling $15,000 (high: $1,000, low: $500).
Type of support: Scholarships—to individuals.
Application information: Applications not accepted.
EIN: 016068112

332
Beane Family Foundation
502 Holgate Ave.
Defiance, OH 43512
Contact: Evan J. Beane, Dir.

Foundation type: Independent foundation
Limitations: Scholarships to residents of IA, primarily in Marshalltown, for higher education.
Financial data: Year ended 12/31/2004. Assets, $745,030 (M); Expenditures, $41,487; Total giving, $40,578; Grants to individuals, 4 grants totaling $31,500 (high: $24,000, low: $2,500).
Type of support: Undergraduate support.
Application information: Contact foundation for current application deadline; Application by letter.
EIN: 341662821

333
Bearden Lumber Company Scholarship Foundation, Inc.
c/o Bearden Lumber Co., Inc.
P.O. Box 137
Bearden, AR 71720 (870) 687-2246

Foundation type: Company-sponsored foundation
Limitations: Scholarships to graduates of Bearden High School, AR, for higher education.
Financial data: Year ended 12/31/2004. Assets, $0 (M); Expenditures, $21,250; Total giving, $21,250; Grants to individuals, 10 grants totaling $21,250 (high: $2,500, low: $1,250).
Type of support: Support to graduates or students of specific schools; Undergraduate support.
Application information: Application form required.
Deadline(s): Mar. 15
EIN: 710510772

334
John J. and Mildred M. Beattie Scholarship Fund
c/o Wachovia Bank, N.A.
100 N. Main St., 13th Fl.
Winston-Salem, NC 27150
Contact: Scholarships: Elizabeth Bradshaw

Foundation type: Independent foundation
Limitations: Scholarships to graduates of Lebanon School District, PA, for higher education.
Financial data: Year ended 12/31/2004.
Assets, $327,583 (M); Expenditures, $15,608; Total giving, $12,000.
Type of support: Undergraduate support.
Application information: Applications not accepted.
Additional information: Contact school guidance office for application information.
EIN: 236851059

335
Harold W. & Emily K. Beattie Scholarship Trust Fund
P.O. Box 1119
St. Joseph, MO 64502-1119

Foundation type: Independent foundation
Limitations: Scholarships to graduates of Savannah, MO, high schools who are in the top ten percent of their classes.
Financial data: Year ended 12/31/2004.
Assets, $1,167,298 (M); Expenditures, $72,161; Total giving, $60,292; Grants to individuals, 10 grants totaling $60,292.
Type of support: Scholarships—to individuals.
Application information: Contact trust for current application deadline/guidelines.
EIN: 436355648

336
The E. Perry & Grace Beatty Memorial Foundation
c/o National City Bank, Northeast
P.O. Box 94651
Cleveland, OH 44101
Application address: c/o Myra Vitto, National City Bank, Northeast, P.O. Box 450, Youngstown, OH 45501, tel.: (330) 742-4289

Foundation type: Independent foundation
Limitations: Scholarships to residents of OH for higher education.
Financial data: Year ended 12/31/2004.
Assets, $999,469 (M); Expenditures, $54,288; Total giving, $43,220; Grants to individuals, 18 grants totaling $43,220 (high: $2,500, low: $720).
Fields of interest: Vocational education.
Type of support: Scholarships—to individuals.
Application information: Applications accepted throughout the year; Contact foundation for current application guidelines.
EIN: 346515791

337
Cordelia Lunceford Beatty Trust
Security Bank Bldg., 2nd Fl.
P.O. Box 514
Blackwell, OK 74631 (580) 363-3684
Contact: James R. Rodgers, Tr.
Application address: 105 N. Main St., Blackwell, OK 74631

Foundation type: Independent foundation

Limitations: Postsecondary scholarships and preschool tuition to financially needy residents of Blackwell, OK, who are under the age of 19.
Financial data: Year ended 12/31/2004.
Assets, $2,886,354 (M); Expenditures, $174,465; Total giving, $130,286; Grants to individuals, 89 grants totaling $84,527 (high: $2,000, low: $33).
Fields of interest: Early childhood education.
Type of support: Precollege support; Undergraduate support.
Application information: Applications accepted. Application form required.
Initial approach: Letter requesting application.
Deadline(s): Prior to start of school year.
Additional information: Application should include photograph, GPA, and copy of first two pages of parents' most recent tax return.
EIN: 736094952

338
Beaver Dam Scholarship Foundation, Inc.
P.O. Box 98
Beaver Dam, WI 53916 (920) 887-0532
Contact: Ayaz M. Samadani, Pres.

Foundation type: Public charity
Limitations: Scholarships to residents of the Beaver Dam Unified School District, WI, for attendance at college and technical schools. Scholarships also to children of Conley's Publishing, and Apache Stainless Steel, WI.
Publications: Application guidelines; Annual report; Financial statement.
Financial data: Year ended 12/31/2003.
Assets, $2,533,624 (L); Expenditures, $121,458; Total giving, $100,375; Grants to individuals, 78 grants totaling $100,375.
Type of support: Employee-related scholarships; Technical education support; Undergraduate support.
Application information: Application form required.
Deadline(s): Contact foundation for exact application deadline
EIN: 411700851

339
The Dennis and Anne Beaver Foundation
1311 L St.
Bakersfield, CA 93301

Foundation type: Independent foundation
Limitations: Scholarships and travel grants to pre-selected, gifted students at Bakersfield Universities and high schools to study abroad in Sweden or France.
Financial data: Year ended 12/31/2004.
Assets, $158,312 (M); Expenditures, $33,644; Total giving, $31,129; Grants to individuals, 7 grants totaling $31,129.
Type of support: Undergraduate support; Travel grants.
Application information: Applications not accepted.
EIN: 770557208

340
Patrick Beaver Scholarship Foundation, Inc.
2421 N. Center St., Ste. 227
Hickory, NC 28601
Contact: Angela B. Simmons, Secy.

Foundation type: Independent foundation

Limitations: Scholarships to high school, college, university or graduate students of Catawba and surrounding counties, NC, to attend school in NC.
Financial data: Year ended 08/31/2004.
Assets, $762,686 (M); Expenditures, $55,138; Total giving, $50,025; Grants to individuals, 24 grants totaling $50,000 (high: $2,500, low: $1,250).
Type of support: Exchange programs; Graduate support; Technical education support; Undergraduate support.
Application information: Application form required.
Initial approach: Letter.
Deadline(s): Contact foundation for current application deadline
Additional information: Interviews required.
Program description:
Beaver Scholarship Program: Recipients must demonstrate the following characteristics:
· Possess an average of "A" or "B" or demonstrate to the committee the ability to do the same
· Extraordinary character (i.e., ability to get along with classmates, teachers, professors and administrators; leadership qualities are a plus, and recommendations are required)
· Be focused on an enriching school experience and on expected educational goals (based on two-page essay)
· Active in extracurricular activities (on and off campus)
· Have established career goals and express the same in a short essay.
Special consideration will be given to students diagnosed with learning disabilities, disadvantaged home environments, and/or financial difficulties (guidance counselor or other official testimony to these considerations are necessary). Financial need will be a consideration but not a determining factor. Scholarships are renewable. Summer studies and internships may be funded at scholarship-awarded student's request (must be in writing with program description)
EIN: 562048446

341
Paul Bechtner Education Foundation
(formerly American Colloid Company Foundation)
c/o AMCOL International Corp.
1500 W. Shure Dr., Ste. 500
Arlington Heights, IL 60004

Foundation type: Company-sponsored foundation
Limitations: Scholarships for higher education limited to children of employees of AMCOL International Corp.
Financial data: Year ended 12/31/2004.
Assets, $6,356 (M); Expenditures, $25,500; Total giving, $25,500; Grants to individuals, 17 grants totaling $25,500 (high: $1,500, low: $1,500).
Type of support: Employee-related scholarships; Undergraduate support.
EIN: 363892273

342
BECU Foundation
(also known as Boeing Employees Credit Union Foundation)
c/o Bradford Canfield
12770 Gateway Dr., Ste. 1011-1
Tukwila, WA 98168-3309 (206) 439-5907
Contact: Deborah Wege, Secy.

Foundation type: Independent foundation

Limitations: Scholarships to BECU members and their families.
Financial data: Year ended 12/31/2004. Assets, $1,220,334 (M); Expenditures, $124,036; Total giving, $98,000; Grants to individuals, 49 grants totaling $98,000 (high: $2,000, low: $2,000).
Type of support: Undergraduate support.
Application information: Application form required.
Deadline(s): Mar. 31
EIN: 911703337

343

Bedford Community Health Foundation
P.O. Box 1104
Bedford, VA   24523   (540) 586-5292
Contact: Donna M. Proctor, Exec. Dir.
FAX: (540) 587-5819; E-mail: bchf@bchf.org;
URL: http://www.bchf.org

Foundation type: Public charity
Limitations: Scholarships to Bedford residents, who are students or graduates of Bedford City and Bedford County, VA, schools to prepare for careers in nursing and other non-physician allied health professions, and tuition assistance to professional nurses for continuing education at VA colleges.
Publications: Application guidelines; Annual report; Grants list; Informational brochure; Newsletter.
Financial data: Year ended 12/31/2004. Assets, $4,401,058 (M); Expenditures, $369,107; Total giving, $221,682.
Fields of interest: Nursing school/education; Health sciences school/education.
Type of support: Support to graduates or students of specific schools; Graduate support; Technical education support; Undergraduate support.
Application information: Applications accepted.
Initial approach: Letter or telephone.
Deadline(s): Contact foundation for current application guidelines
Additional information: Interviews required.
Program description:
Scholarship Funds: The following funds are administered by the foundation:
· Emma Allie Scholarship Fund: Provides scholarship assistance to an outstanding first-year student in the Bedford Science and Technology Center/Bedford Memorial Hospital's L.P.N. school
· Allied Scholarship: Provides scholarships to individuals studying in the Allied Health field and a resident of Bedford City or County
· Maxwell Dudley Davidson Scholarship Fund: Provides tuition assistance to a nursing student who has committed to work at Carilion Bedford Memorial Hospital upon graduation
· Janet Bowyer Wood Scholarship Fund: Provides tuition assistance to nurses who are employed in Bedford City or Bedford County to continue their education
· Bedford Memorial Hospital Employment Scholarship: Provides tuition assistance to nursing students who have committed to work at Bedford Memorial Hospital upon graduation
· Connie Bohon Parker Scholarship: Provides scholarship assistance to the outstanding second-year student in the Bedford Science & Technology Center/Bedford Memorial Hospital's CNA program.
EIN: 541088024

344

The J. L. Bedsole Foundation
P.O. Box 1137
Mobile, AL   36633   (251) 432-3369
Contact: Mabel B. Ward, Exec. Dir.
FAX: (251) 432-1134;
E-mail: info@jlbedsolefoundation.org; URL: http://www.jlbedsolefoundation.org

Foundation type: Independent foundation
Limitations: Scholarships to entering college freshmen from southwest AL to attend AL colleges and universities.
Publications: Application guidelines.
Financial data: Year ended 12/31/2004. Assets, $80,444,473 (M); Expenditures, $5,304,402; Total giving, $3,877,919; Grants to individuals, 166 grants totaling $767,250 (high: $9,000, low: $500, average grant: $1,000-$6,000).
Type of support: Undergraduate support.
Application information: Applications by letter accepted throughout the year.
Program description:
J.L. Bedsole Scholars Program: Recipients are selected on the basis of leadership ability, academic competency, and financial need. Scholarships are renewable.
EIN: 237225708

345

Charles A. Beebe Scholarship Fund
c/o Soy Capital Bank & Trust Co.
455 N. Main St.
Decatur, IL   62523-1103
Application address: c/o William Heinhorst, Pres., Peoples State Bank, 105 S. Adams St., Manito, IL 61546, tel.: (309) 968-6689

Foundation type: Independent foundation
Limitations: Scholarships to graduates of Forman Community High School, Manito, IL.
Financial data: Year ended 12/31/2004. Assets, $908,145 (M); Expenditures, $62,554; Total giving, $32,620; Grants to individuals, 115 grants totaling $32,620.
Type of support: Support to graduates or students of specific schools; Undergraduate support.
Application information: Application form required.
Deadline(s): May 15
Additional information: Applications available from People's State Bank.
EIN: 376164013

346

John & Nesbeth Bees School Foundation
c/o Citizens Bank Wealth Mgmt., N.A.
328 S. Saginaw St., M/C 002072
Flint, MI   48502
Application address: c/o Helen James, Citizens Bank Wealth Mgmt., N.A., 101 N. Washington Ave., Saginaw, MI 48607, tel.: (989) 776-7368

Foundation type: Independent foundation
Limitations: Scholarships to residents of Saginaw County, MI.
Financial data: Year ended 12/31/2004. Assets, $652,719 (M); Expenditures, $38,613; Total giving, $25,740; Grants to individuals, 36 grants totaling $25,740 (high: $715, low: $715).
Type of support: Scholarships—to individuals.
Application information: Application form required.
Deadline(s): May 1
EIN: 386601371

347

E. R. Behrend Trust Fund
c/o Erie Community Foundation
127 W. 6th St.
Erie, PA   16501   (814) 870-5854
Contact: Thomas C. Guelcher, Chair.

Foundation type: Independent foundation
Limitations: Scholarships to children of International Paper, Erie, PA, employees who are also residents of Erie, PA.
Financial data: Year ended 12/31/2004. Assets, $0 (M); Expenditures, $419,928; Total giving, $366,322; Grants to individuals, totaling $363,331.
Type of support: Employee-related scholarships.
Application information: Contact fund for current application deadline/guidelines.
Program description:
Scholarship Program: International Paper of Erie, PA, recommends qualified applicants, and the fund selects final recipients. Scholarships are awarded in May.
EIN: 256037040

348

George C. Beinke Scholarship Fund
c/o KeyBank N.A.
P.O. Box 10099
Toledo, OH   43699-0099   (419) 259-8218
Contact: Marilyn Brown, Trust Off.

Foundation type: Independent foundation
Limitations: Scholarships to financially needy graduates of Lucas County, OH, high schools to attend the University of Toledo.
Financial data: Year ended 08/31/2004. Assets, $553,026 (M); Expenditures, $35,386; Total giving, $24,000; Grants to individuals, totaling $24,000.
Type of support: Support to graduates or students of specific schools; Undergraduate support.
Application information: Application form required.
Initial approach: Letter.
Deadline(s): Mar. 1
EIN: 346542089

349

Joseph C. Belden Foundation
396 Feather Ct.
Carol Stream, IL   60188
Contact: David A. Vanden Brook, Dir.

Foundation type: Independent foundation
Limitations: Undergraduate scholarships to children of employees of Belden, Inc., and its wholly-owned subsidiaries in Canada and the U.S.
Financial data: Year ended 06/30/2005. Assets, $1,692,838 (M); Expenditures, $185,766; Total giving, $114,548; Grants to individuals, totaling $114,548.
Type of support: Employee-related scholarships.
Application information: Application form required.
Deadline(s): Applications accepted Sept. 1 to Dec. 31; Deadline for biographical and secondary reports Feb. 1
EIN: 363781852

350
Belgian American Educational Foundation, Inc.
195 Church St.
New Haven, CT 06510 (203) 777-5765
Contact: Emile L. Boulpaep M.D., Pres.
FAX: (203) 785-4951;
E-mail: emile.boulpaep@yale.edu; URL: http://www.baef.be

Foundation type: Public charity
Limitations: Fellowships by nomination only to Belgian graduate students and to American graduate students who are proficient in Dutch, French, or German.
Publications: Application guidelines; Financial statement; Newsletter.
Financial data: Year ended 08/31/2004.
Assets, $60,315,869 (M); Expenditures, $2,639,241; Total giving, $2,414,417; Grants to individuals, 70 grants totaling $2,134,264 (high: $48,784, low: $6,075).
Fields of interest: Graduate/professional education; International exchange, students.
Type of support: Fellowships; Exchange programs; Awards/grants by nomination only; Graduate support.
Application information:
  Initial approach: Letter.
  Deadline(s): Jan. 31; Submit proposal preferably in Dec.
  Additional information: Candidates must be nominated by the deans of their graduate schools.
Program description:
  Graduate Fellowships for Study or Research in Belgium: The fellowships were established to promote the exchange of intellectual ideas between the two countries. Predoctoral Fellowships are awarded to American graduate students to enable them to pursue study and research in Belgium on projects for which Belgium provides special advantages. The $13,000 awards are made for ten-month periods. Through the nominating dean, candidates must submit:
  · a statement of the dissertation or research project and its current status
  · a proposed program of study to be undertaken during the period of the grant
  · a curriculum vitae and a short personal biography
  · official transcripts of both undergraduate and graduate courses
  · evidence of language proficiency in French, German, and/or Dutch
  · reasons for choice of university or other institutions including the scholars with whom he or she plans to study
Applicants can expect to receive notification of final action on their proposals before Mar. 31.
EIN: 131606002

351
Stephen P. Bell and Tricia Flynn Caley Memorial Scholarship Fund
(formerly Stephen P. Bell Memorial Scholarship Fund)
c/o Citizens Bank of NH
154 Water St.
Exeter, NH 03833-2433
Application address: c/o Principal, Exeter High School, 30 Linden St., Exeter, NH 03833, tel.: (603) 775-8402

Foundation type: Independent foundation
Limitations: Scholarships to graduates of Exeter Area High School, NH, who have been active in student affairs.
Financial data: Year ended 12/31/2004.
Assets, $230,103 (M); Expenditures, $13,623; Total giving, $10,000; Grants to individuals, 3 grants totaling $10,000.
Type of support: Support to graduates or students of specific schools; Undergraduate support.
Application information: Application form required.
  Initial approach: Letter.
  Deadline(s): Apr. 1
EIN: 020364166

352
Louis E. Bell Charitable Trust
P.O. Box 308
St. Joseph, MO 64502-0308
Application address: c/o Advisory Committee, Atchison County School District, 500 Main St., Fairfax, MO 64446-9121

Foundation type: Independent foundation
Limitations: Scholarships to graduates of Atchinson County, MO, public high schools.
Financial data: Year ended 12/31/2004.
Assets, $139,135 (M); Expenditures, $12,630; Total giving, $9,700; Grants to individuals, totaling $9,700.
Type of support: Support to graduates or students of specific schools.
Application information: Applications accepted. Application form required.
  Deadline(s): None
  Applicants should submit the following:
  1) Photograph
  2) Transcripts
  3) SAT
  4) GPA
  5) ACT
  Additional information: Applications should also include extracurricular activities, employment, financial and family information, students and parents' tax return, three references.
EIN: 436406133

353
Dr. Richard C. and Esther Bellamy Educational Trust
c/o First Liberty National Bank
P.O. Box 10109
Liberty, TX 77575
Application address: c/o Charles W. Fisher, Jr., Trust Off., First Liberty National Bank, 1900 Sam Houston St., Liberty, TX 77575, tel.: (936) 336-6471

Foundation type: Independent foundation
Limitations: Scholarships to financially needy graduates of Liberty County, TX, Independent School Districts, primarily those who rank in the top ten percent of their class. Recipients must attend colleges, universities, or vocational schools in TX.
Financial data: Year ended 12/31/2002.
Assets, $840,409 (M); Expenditures, $81,359; Total giving, $71,000; Grants to individuals, 19 grants totaling $71,000.
Fields of interest: Vocational education.
Type of support: Support to graduates or students of specific schools; Technical education support; Undergraduate support.
Application information: Application form required.
  Initial approach: Letter or through school counselor.
  Deadline(s): Mar. 15
  Applicants should submit the following:

1) Transcripts
2) Photograph
Additional information: Applications should also include three references, SAT or ACT scores, and a handwritten personal statement of about 150 words.
Program description:
  Scholarship Program: Scholarships are awarded on the basis of character, attitude, initiative, stability, leadership, and potential for achievement. Applicants who do not rank in the top ten percent of their graduating classes will be considered if they have a documented extraordinary or outstanding talent. Recipients must attend school full-time at a two-year vocational or technical training program or a four-year college or university in TX. Scholarships are renewable.
EIN: 766002566

354
Don & Iva Bellinger Scholarship Fund
c/o Citizens Bank Wealth Mgmt., N.A.
328 S. Saginaw St., M/C 002072
Flint, MI 48502 (989) 776-7368
Application address: c/o Helen M. James, Citizens Bank Wealth Mgmt., N.A., 101 N. Washington Ave., Saginaw, MI 48607, tel.: (989) 776-7368

Foundation type: Independent foundation
Limitations: Scholarships to students attending the nursing program at Saginaw Valley State University, MI.
Financial data: Year ended 12/31/2004.
Assets, $1,050,407 (M); Expenditures, $50,069; Total giving, $35,650.
Fields of interest: Nursing school/education.
Type of support: Scholarships—to individuals; Support to graduates or students of specific schools.
Application information: Application form required.
  Deadline(s): Jan. 31
EIN: 386615679

355
Samuel L. Bemis Scholarship Fund
c/o Fifth Third Bank
P.O. Box 3636
Grand Rapids, MI 49501-3636

Foundation type: Independent foundation
Limitations: Scholarships to female graduating seniors at Brattleboro Union High School, VT.
Financial data: Year ended 12/31/2004.
Assets, $1,399,439 (M); Expenditures, $65,340; Total giving, $49,378; Grants to individuals, 7 grants totaling $26,554.
Fields of interest: Women.
Type of support: Support to graduates or students of specific schools; Undergraduate support.
Application information:
  Initial approach: Letter or telephone.
  Deadline(s): May 10
  Additional information: Contact fund for current application guidelines.
EIN: 367112890

356
Otto Bender Scholarship Trust
c/o First National Bank
P.O. Box 280
Carlyle, IL   62231
Contact: Deborah Keilbach, Trust Off., First National
Bank
Application address: 891 Fairfax St., Carlyle, IL
62231, tel.: (618) 594-2491

Foundation type: Independent foundation
Limitations: Scholarships to graduates or potential
graduates of Community Unit District No. 1 High
School, Carlyle, IL, who plan to attend four years of
college.
Financial data: Year ended 05/31/2005.
Assets, $330,736 (M); Expenditures, $13,669;
Total giving, $11,180; Grants to individuals, 4
grants totaling $11,180.
Type of support: Support to graduates or students
of specific schools; Undergraduate support.
Application information: Application form required.
   Deadline(s): Apr. 1
EIN: 376341841

357
Phyllis A. Beneke Scholarship Fund
c/o JPMorgan Chase Bank, N.A.
P.O. Box 1308
Milwaukee, WI   53201   (414) 977-1210
Application address: c/o George S. Krelis, Comm.
Member, R.D. No. 4, Box 1976, Wheeling, WV
26003, tel.: (304) 243-0400

Foundation type: Public charity
Limitations: Scholarships to graduates of Ohio
County, WV, high schools.
Publications: Informational brochure (including
application guidelines).
Financial data: Year ended 02/29/2004.
Assets, $2,821,406 (M); Expenditures,
$146,734; Total giving, $118,750; Grants to
individuals, 61 grants totaling $118,750 (high:
$5,000, low: $500).
Type of support: Scholarships—to individuals;
Support to graduates or students of specific
schools.
Application information: Application form required.
   Deadline(s): Third week of May
   Applicants should submit the following:
      1) Transcripts
   Additional information: Application should also
      include two teachers' recommendations,
      personal statement of 200 words or less,
      copy of financial aid form, recent ACT or SAT
      scores, student information sheet, and
      transcripts.
EIN: 556106147

358
George H. Benford Charities
c/o PNC Advisors
620 Liberty Ave., P2-PTPP-10-2
Pittsburgh, PA   15222-2719   (412) 762-6633

Foundation type: Independent foundation
Limitations: Student loans only to graduates of the
Meyersdale Joint High School, PA.
Financial data: Year ended 09/30/2004.
Assets, $2,046,308 (M); Expenditures, $81,709;
Total giving, $55,736; Loans to individuals, 35
loans totaling $23,650.
Type of support: Student loans—to individuals;
Support to graduates or students of specific
schools; Undergraduate support.

Application information: Application form required.
   Deadline(s): None
   Applicants should submit the following:
      1) Financial information
      2) Essay
   Additional information: Loan decisions are based
      on the character and scholastic record of the
      candidates, their serious determination to
      succeed in some worthwhile vocation, and
      their need for financial assistance.
Program description:
   Student Loan Program: The maximum loan is
$1,550. Repayments in ten installments must start
three years after graduation. The interest rate is five
percent.
EIN: 256038490

359
Benjamin Trust Fund
c/o State Bank of Illinois
600 E. Washington St.
P.O. Box 250
West Chicago, IL   60186-0250
Application address: c/o Superintendent of
Schools, 326 Joliet St., West Chicago, IL 60185

Foundation type: Independent foundation
Limitations: Scholarships to graduates of West
Chicago Community High School District No. 94, IL.
Financial data: Year ended 02/28/2005.
Assets, $307,088 (M); Expenditures, $21,029;
Total giving, $15,564; Grants to individuals,
totaling $15,564.
Type of support: Support to graduates or students
of specific schools; Undergraduate support.
Application information: Application form required.
   Deadline(s): Apr. 15
   Additional information: Applications available
      from Superintendent of schools.
EIN: 366552295

360
The James Gordon Bennett Memorial Corporation
c/o John Campbell
100 Bertwell Rd.
Lexington, MA   02420-3313

Foundation type: Independent foundation
Limitations: Scholarships to children of journalists
who have worked in New York, NY, on a daily
newspaper for 10 years or more.
Financial data: Year ended 12/31/2004.
Assets, $5,450,612 (M); Expenditures,
$261,842; Total giving, $211,950; Grants to
individuals, 97 grants totaling $211,950 (high:
$12,000, low: $250).
Fields of interest: Journalism/publishing.
Type of support: Employee-related scholarships.
Application information: Applications accepted.
Application form required.
   Initial approach: Letter requesting application.
   Deadline(s): Mar. 1
Program description:
   Scholarship Program: Amounts available for
scholarships vary each year because the
foundation's priority is to supply aid to needy
journalists who have worked in New York, NY, for 10
or more years. After aiding these journalists, the
foundation dispenses surplus funds among "the
issue of members of the immediate families of
persons employed for 10 years or more on any daily
newspaper published in New York or to such
persons themselves".
EIN: 136150414

361
Joe and Mary Helen Bennett Scholarship Fund
369 Walnut Dr.
Danville, IN   46122
Application address: c/o Danville Comm. High
School, Principal's Office-Bennett Scholarship, 100
Westview Dr., Danville, IN 46122, tel.: (317)
745-2212

Foundation type: Operating foundation
Limitations: Scholarships to graduates of Danville
Community High School to further their education in
any educational institution.
Financial data: Year ended 12/31/2003.
Assets, $88,229 (M); Expenditures, $16,952;
Total giving, $14,000; Grants to individuals, 28
grants totaling $14,000 (high: $500, low: $500).
Type of support: Support to graduates or students
of specific schools; Undergraduate support.
Application information: Application form required.
   Deadline(s): Apr. 15
   Applicants should submit the following:
      1) Transcripts
EIN: 356605585

362
M. A. & L. J. Bennett Scholarship Fund
c/o JPMorgan Chase Bank
345 Park Ave.
New York, NY   10154
Application address: c/o John Fitzgerald, Chair.,
NYPD Emerald Society, 2121 New York Ave.,
Brooklyn, NY 11210, tel.: (718) 258-4273

Foundation type: Independent foundation
Limitations: Scholarships to children of police
officers of the NYPD, who are either active, retired,
or killed in the line of duty.
Financial data: Year ended 05/31/2005.
Assets, $2,992,791 (M); Expenditures,
$163,041; Total giving, $129,500.
Fields of interest: Crime/law enforcement, police
agencies.
Type of support: Employee-related scholarships.
Application information: Applications accepted
throughout the year; Contact fund for current
application guidelines.
EIN: 133544931

363
Simon Benson Fund, Inc.
6441 S.W. Canyon Ct., Ste. 10
Portland, OR   97221-1458

Foundation type: Independent foundation
Limitations: Scholarships to graduates of Benson
High School, OR, for higher education.
Financial data: Year ended 12/31/2004.
Assets, $294,133 (M); Expenditures, $16,211;
Total giving, $15,000; Grants to individuals, 3
grants totaling $15,000.
Type of support: Support to graduates or students
of specific schools; Undergraduate support.
Application information: Recipients are chosen by
High School Scholarship Committee.
EIN: 936041516

364
Anne Benson Scholarship Trust Fund
c/o U.S. Bank, N.A., Trust Tax Dept.
P.O. Box 3168
Portland, OR 97208
Application address: c/o U.S. Bank, N.A., P.O. Box 30678, Billings, MT 59115

Foundation type: Independent foundation
Limitations: Scholarships to graduates of Judith Gap High School, MT, for higher education.
Financial data: Year ended 04/30/2004. Assets, $304,794 (M); Expenditures, $10,569; Total giving, $6,000; Grants to individuals, totaling $6,000.
Type of support: Support to graduates or students of specific schools; Undergraduate support.
Application information: Application form required.
  Deadline(s): Mar. 31
  Applicants should submit the following:
    1) Transcripts
  Additional information: Application should also include FFS and at least two letters of recommendation.
Program description:
  Scholarship Program: Recipients must be pursuing a degree in education, however, if no qualified applicants are majoring in education, those seeking a college education who have graduated from Judith Gap High School may be considered. Scholarships are for payment costs of tuition, books, expenses, room and board. Relatives of trustee or scholarship committee are ineligible for scholarship.
EIN: 816087202

365
Frank F. Bentley Trust
c/o KeyBank N.A.
800 Superior Ave., OH-01-02-0420
Cleveland, OH 44114
Application address: c/o Joyce A. May, Turner & May, 800 2nd National Bank Bldg., 108 Main Ave. S.W., Ste. 800, Warren, OH 44481, tel.: (330) 399-8801

Foundation type: Independent foundation
Limitations: Scholarships to residents of Trumbull County, OH. Preference is given first to orphans, then to persons from foster homes, and then to those from "broken" homes.
Financial data: Year ended 09/30/2004. Assets, $352,937 (M); Expenditures, $28,306; Total giving, $19,857; Grants to individuals, 45 grants totaling $19,857 (high: $750, low: $250).
Fields of interest: Residential/custodial care.
Type of support: Scholarships—to individuals.
Application information: Application form required.
  Initial approach: Letter requesting application.
  Deadline(s): June 30
EIN: 346508762

366
Benton Community Foundation
P.O. Box 351
Fowler, IN 47944 (765) 884-8022
Contact: Kathy Jane Chambery, Exec. Dir.
FAX: (765) 884-8023; E-mail: info@bentoncf.org;
Additional E-mail: director@bentoncf.org;
URL: http://www.bentoncf.org

Foundation type: Community foundation
Limitations: Scholarships by nomination only, to residents of Benton County, IN.
Publications: Application guidelines; Annual report; Grants list.

Financial data: Year ended 12/31/2004. Assets, $3,595,067 (M); Expenditures, $74,887; Total giving, $12,000.
Type of support: Awards/grants by nomination only; Undergraduate support.
Application information: Applications not accepted.
  Additional information: Unsolicited requests for funds not considered or acknowledged.
EIN: 260074023

367
Benton County Foundation
P.O. Box 911
Corvallis, OR 97339 (541) 753-1603
Contact: Richard Thompson, Pres.
E-mail: bcf@peak.org; URL: http://bentoncountyfoundation.org

Foundation type: Community foundation
Limitations: Scholarships to students in Benton County, OR.
Publications: Application guidelines; Informational brochure; Newsletter.
Financial data: Year ended 12/31/2004. Assets, $7,631,190 (M); Expenditures, $230,246; Total giving, $201,920; Grants to individuals, 15 grants totaling $41,490.
Type of support: Undergraduate support.
Application information: Application form required.
  Initial approach: Letter.
  Deadline(s): Spring
EIN: 936022916

368
William L. & Margaret L. Benz Foundation
c/o Mellon Bank, N.A.
1 Mellon Ctr., 500 Grant St., Ste. 3825
Pittsburgh, PA 15258-0001 (412) 234-0023
Contact: Laurie A. Moritz, V.P., Mellon Financial Corp.

Foundation type: Independent foundation
Limitations: Scholarships to students of Blairsville High School, PA.
Financial data: Year ended 05/31/2005. Assets, $3,744,011 (M); Expenditures, $172,434; Total giving, $160,421; Grants to individuals, 210 grants totaling $160,421 (high: $16,400, low: $150).
Type of support: Scholarships—to individuals; Support to graduates or students of specific schools.
Application information: Application form required.
  Deadline(s): Apr. 30
  Additional information: Contact Blairsville High School to request application.
EIN: 256276186

369
The Berek Scholarship Foundation, Inc.
9 Old Army Post Rd.
Morristown, NJ 07960
Application address: c/o Guidance Dept., Morristown High School, 50 Early St., Morristown, NJ 07960, tel.: (973) 292-2000

Foundation type: Independent foundation
Limitations: Scholarships to graduating seniors attending Morristown High School, NJ.
Financial data: Year ended 12/31/2004. Assets, $83,989 (M); Expenditures, $9,493; Total giving, $8,000; Grants to individuals, 4 grants totaling $8,000.

Type of support: Support to graduates or students of specific schools; Undergraduate support.
Application information: Contact foundation for current application deadline/guidelines.
EIN: 223286509

370
Lois & Max Beren Foundation
100 N. Main St., Ste. 700
Wichita, KS 67202-1384
Contact: Carla Beren Garrity, Tr.
Application address: 3360 S. Columbine Cir., Englewood, CO 80113

Foundation type: Independent foundation
Limitations: Scholarships to individuals for higher education. Preference is given to students at specific high schools.
Financial data: Year ended 12/31/2004. Assets, $1,637,146 (M); Expenditures, $76,263; Total giving, $62,000; Grants to individuals, 16 grants totaling $62,000 (high: $4,000, low: $2,500).
Type of support: Scholarships—to individuals.
Application information: Applications not accepted.
EIN: 486107224

371
Stefan Bergman Trust
c/o Wells Fargo Bank, N.A., Trust Dept.
P.O. Box 63954
San Francisco, CA 94163

Foundation type: Independent foundation
Limitations: Scholarships for the study of mathematics.
Financial data: Year ended 12/31/2004. Assets, $611,207 (M); Expenditures, $36,439; Total giving, $27,477; Grants to individuals, 3 grants totaling $27,477.
Fields of interest: Mathematics.
Type of support: Scholarships—to individuals.
Application information: Applications not accepted.
EIN: 946483652

372
Bergman-Davison-Webster Charitable Trust
2301 Israel Rd.
Livingston, TX 77351-2531 (936) 327-8642
Contact: Carolyn Davison Nixon, Tr.

Foundation type: Independent foundation
Limitations: Scholarships to individuals residing in Livingston and Corrigan, TX, as well as Polk County, TX, for undergraduate education.
Financial data: Year ended 06/30/2005. Assets, $8,623,320 (M); Expenditures, $603,214; Total giving, $477,334; Grants to individuals, 28 grants totaling $47,854 (high: $3,000, low: $780).
Type of support: Undergraduate support.
Application information: Applications accepted.
  Deadline(s): None
  Additional information: Application by letter.
EIN: 760521612

373
Bering Straits Foundation
P.O. Box 1008
Nome, AK 99762-1008 (907) 443-5252
Contact: Carolyn Crowder, Pres.
FAX: (907) 443-2985; Toll-free tel.: (800)
478-5079; URL: http://www.beringstraits.com/
bsf/bsfhome.htm

Foundation type: Public charity
Limitations: Scholarships to individuals primarily in
AK, who are members of Bering Straits Corporation
or the children of members, for undergraduate
education.
Publications: Application guidelines.
Financial data: Year ended 12/31/2004.
Assets, $403,384 (M); Expenditures, $130,212;
Total giving, $51,519; Grants to individuals, 93
grants totaling $51,519 (high: $1,000, low: $250).
Fields of interest: Native Americans/American
Indians.
Type of support: Technical education support;
Undergraduate support.
Application information:
Deadline(s): June 30 and Dec. 30 for Higher
Education and Vocational Training
Scholarship, June 30 for Martin Olson
Memorial Scholarship
Additional information: Completion of formal
application required, including transcript, two
letters of recommendation, personal
statement and copy of birth certificate; See
Web site for further application information
and application form.
Program descriptions:
*Higher Education and Vocational Training
Scholarship:* Applicants must have a high school
GPA of at least 3.0, or 2.5 if entering vocational
school. Once applicant is in college, university, or
vocational school, s/he must maintain a minimum
GPA of 2.0 for the first semester and 2.5 thereafter.
Applicants must maintain full-time status.
Scholarships may be renewable.
Martin Olson Memorial Scholarship: Applicants
must be at least 25 percent Alaskan Native (Aleut,
Eskimo, or Native American and maintain a 2.0 GPA
as a full-time college, university, or vocational
school student. Scholarships may be renewable.
EIN: 920138528

374
Berkeley Community Fund
800 Jones St.
Berkeley, CA 94710 (510) 525-5272
Contact: Eugenia Bowman, Exec. Dir.
FAX: (510) 525-5599; E-mail: info@berkfund.org;
URL: http://www.berkfund.org

Foundation type: Public charity
Limitations: Scholarships to seniors at Berkeley
High School, CA. and to continuing and transfer
students of Vista Community College.
Publications: Application guidelines; Annual report;
Grants list; Newsletter; Program policy statement.
Financial data: Year ended 06/30/2005.
Assets, $793,619 (M); Expenditures, $395,493;
Total giving, $126,000; Grants to individuals, 21
grants totaling $39,500 (high: $4,000, low: $500).
Type of support: Support to graduates or students
of specific schools; Undergraduate support.
Application information: Applications accepted.
Application form required. Application form
available on the grantmaker's Web site.
Initial approach: Application.
Copies of proposal: 1
Deadline(s): Mar. 7
Applicants should submit the following:

1) SASE
2) GPA
3) Budget Information
4) Essay
5) Financial information
6) Transcripts
7) SAR
8) FAFSA
9) ACT
10) SAT
11) Letter(s) of recommendation
Additional information: A minimum of 2.5 GPA is
required. Scholarships range from $500 to
$3,000; Response to application given by
May 20; Applications should be sent by mail.
EIN: 943264327

375
Berks County Community Foundation
501 Washington St., Ste. 801
P.O. Box 212
Reading, PA 19603-0212 (610) 685-2223
Contact: Kevin K. Murphy, Pres.; For grants: Richard
C. Mappin, V.P., Grantmaking
FAX: (610) 685-2240; E-mail: info@bccf.org; Grant
program E-mail: richardm@bccf.org; URL: http://
www.bccf.org

Foundation type: Community foundation
Limitations: Scholarships to individuals in Berks
County, PA, for higher education.
Publications: Application guidelines; Annual report;
Financial statement; Grants list; Newsletter.
Financial data: Year ended 06/30/2005.
Assets, $38,489,236 (M); Expenditures,
$4,302,847; Total giving, $3,261,693; Grants to
individuals, 213 grants totaling $402,625.
Type of support: Support to graduates or students
of specific schools; Undergraduate support.
Application information: Applications accepted.
Application form required.
Initial approach: Telephone.
Deadline(s): None
Program description:
Scholarship Program: The foundation offers
numerous scholarships and awards to individuals
in the Berks County, PA, area. See the foundation's
Web site for further information.
EIN: 232769892

376
**John & Ina Berkshire Educational
Operating Foundation, Inc.**
c/o Michael L. Hatcher
6901 Sherwood Dr.
Knoxville, TN 37919
Contact: Jerry L. Wear, Secy.-Treas.
Application address: 3428 Rena St., Pigeon Forge,
TN 37863, tel.: (865) 453-2401

Foundation type: Operating foundation
Limitations: Scholarships to seniors graduating
from Sevier County, TN, high schools.
Financial data: Year ended 12/31/2003.
Assets, $611,854 (M); Expenditures, $40,395;
Total giving, $30,000; Grants to individuals, 20
grants totaling $30,000 (high: $1,500, low:
$1,500).
Type of support: Support to graduates or students
of specific schools; Undergraduate support.
Application information: Application form required.
Deadline(s): May 30
EIN: 582004367

377
Berlin Family Educational Foundation
1325 Carnegie Ave., 3rd Fl.
Cleveland, OH 44115
Contact: Thomas Berlin, Pres.
Application address: 37500 Eagle Rd., Willoughby,
OH 44094, tel.: (216) 951-2655

Foundation type: Independent foundation
Limitations: Scholarships for higher education only
to residents of Willoughby Hills, OH, attending
South High School and greater Cleveland private
and parochial high schools. The foundation also
awards Teacher Excellence Awards to teachers in
the Willoughby-East Lake Community School
District, OH.
Financial data: Year ended 12/31/2004.
Assets, $694,803 (M); Expenditures, $24,348;
Total giving, $17,000; Grants to individuals, 7
grants totaling $17,000.
Fields of interest: Education.
Type of support: Support to graduates or students
of specific schools; Awards/prizes; Undergraduate
support.
Application information: Contact foundation for
current application deadline/guidelines.
EIN: 341817284

378
Mary Anne Berliner Foundation Trust
c/o First National Bank
P.O. Box AA
Artesia, NM 88211-7526 (505) 748-8005
Contact: Susan Holmes, Trust Off., First National
Bank
URL: http://www.1stnbnm.com/
trustberlinerfoundationscholarship.htm

Foundation type: Independent foundation
Limitations: Scholarships to students residing in
southeast NM for undergraduate and graduate
education.
Financial data: Year ended 12/31/2004.
Assets, $957,861 (M); Expenditures, $61,712;
Total giving, $48,000; Grants to individuals, 26
grants totaling $48,000 (high: $3,750, low:
$1,000).
Type of support: Graduate support; Undergraduate
support.
Application information: Application form available
on the grantmaker's Web site.
Deadline(s): Mar. 15
Additional information: Completion of formal
application required, including financial
information, three letters of recommendation
and essay; See Web site for further
information.
Program description:
Berliner Scholarships: Applicant must:
· be a resident of southeastern NM for at
least one year prior to application
· have been accepted for enrollment in an
institution of higher learning
· if applicant is a high school senior, have a
3.5 GPA on a scale of 4.0, and scores on
the SAT or ACT of 1170 and 26,
respectively
· if applicant is a current college student,
have a 2.75 GPA on a scale of 4.0, and be
a full-time student for the upcoming
semester
· maintain a GPA of 2.75 on a scale of 4.0,
and must maintain status as a full-time
student
· be a well-rounded individual with
outstanding personal character.
EIN: 856122581

379
Viola W. Bernard Foundation, Inc.
(formerly Tappanz Foundation, Inc.)
c/o Cary A. Koplin
605 3rd Ave., 21st Fl.
New York, NY 10158
Application address: c/o Perry Ottenberg, M.D., 210 W. Washington Sq., Ste. 750, Philadelphia, PA 19106; URL: http://www.violawbernardfoundation.org

Foundation type: Independent foundation
Limitations: Grants to individuals for the research of the social conditions and psychological health of children and families, primarily in NY.
Financial data: Year ended 12/31/2004. Assets, $4,637,458 (M); Expenditures, $281,420; Total giving, $226,712.
Application information: Applications accepted. Application form available on the grantmaker's Web site.
Initial approach: Letter.
Deadline(s): None
EIN: 132621140

380
Bernards Area Scholarship Assistance, Inc.
49 Old Chester Rd.
Gladstone, NJ 07934-2031
Contact: Nina Vitale, Chair.

Foundation type: Independent foundation
Limitations: Scholarships to residents of the Bernardsville/Basking Ridge, NJ, area who demonstrate academic ability and financial need.
Financial data: Year ended 06/30/2004. Assets, $13,958 (M); Expenditures, $69,626; Total giving, $68,500; Grants to individuals, 26 grants totaling $68,500.
Type of support: Scholarships—to individuals.
Application information: Application form required.
Deadline(s): Feb. 15
Applicants should submit the following:
1) Transcripts
EIN: 222590097

381
The Berner Charitable and Scholarship Foundation
221 N. LaSalle St., Ste. 2900
Chicago, IL 60601-1504 (312) 782-5885
Contact: Ruben R. Vernof, Tr.

Foundation type: Independent foundation
Limitations: Scholarships and student loans to GA residents, primarily for the study of veterinary medicine, at any AL or GA institution.
Financial data: Year ended 12/31/2003. Assets, $11,073,422 (M); Expenditures, $657,425; Total giving, $548,000; Grants to individuals, 5 grants totaling $65,000 (high: $20,000, low: $5,000).
Fields of interest: Veterinary medicine.
Type of support: Scholarships—to individuals; Student loans—to individuals; Graduate support; Postgraduate support.
Application information:
Initial approach: Letter.
Deadline(s): Mar.
Program description:
Scholarship Program: Half of the scholarship is given as an interest-free student loan, to be repaid six months after graduation. Recipients generally have five to six years to complete repayment. All

applicants must have a "C" average, and be full-time students. Scholarships can be used for undergraduate, Master's, or postgraduate degrees.
EIN: 363923844

382
Bernhard-Wentz Scholarship Fund
c/o The Huntington National Bank
P.O. Box 1558, EA4E86
Columbus, OH 43216-1558
Application address: c/o Advisory Comm., Dover High School Administrative Bldg., 219 W. 6th St., Dover, OH 44622, tel.: (216) 343-7746

Foundation type: Independent foundation
Limitations: Scholarships to graduates of Dover High School, OH.
Financial data: Year ended 12/31/2004. Assets, $1,709,751 (M); Expenditures, $76,409; Total giving, $60,020; Grants to individuals, totaling $60,020.
Type of support: Scholarships—to individuals; Support to graduates or students of specific schools; Undergraduate support.
Application information:
Deadline(s): June 1
Additional information: Contact fund for current application guidelines.
EIN: 316334477

383
Bernowski Scholarship Trust Fund
c/o National City Bank
P.O. Box 94651
Cleveland, OH 44101-4651
Contact: Joanna Mayo, Trust Off., National City Bank
Application address: 20 Stanwix St., LOC 09-066, Pittsburgh, PA 15222, tel.: (412) 644-8002

Foundation type: Independent foundation
Limitations: Scholarships to graduating seniors of Belle Vernon, Charleroi, and Ringgold, PA, high schools who are under 22, to attend local colleges.
Financial data: Year ended 12/31/2004. Assets, $305,717 (M); Expenditures, $15,218; Total giving, $10,567; Grants to individuals, 9 grants totaling $10,567 (high: $2,000, low: $500).
Type of support: Support to graduates or students of specific schools; Undergraduate support.
Application information: Contact fund for current application deadline/guidelines; Completion of formal application required.
EIN: 256534799

384
Nathan Bernstein Scholarship Fund
c/o AmSouth Bank
333 Texas St., SH 2069
Shreveport, LA 71101
Application address: c/o Aid Office, LSU Medical Center, P.O. Box 33932, Shreveport, LA 71130-3932

Foundation type: Independent foundation
Limitations: Scholarships to students at Louisiana State University School of Medicine. Entering students must have a GPA of 3.0 or better and a high score on the Medical College Aptitude Test. Continuing students must have a GPA of 3.0 or better and the recommendation of a faculty member.
Financial data: Year ended 09/30/2004. Assets, $2,467,616 (M); Expenditures, $113,285; Total giving, $90,000; Grants to

individuals, 30 grants totaling $90,000 (high: $3,000, low: $3,000).
Fields of interest: Medical school/education.
Type of support: Support to graduates or students of specific schools; Graduate support.
Application information: Application form required.
Deadline(s): June 15
Applicants should submit the following:
1) FAFSA
Additional information: Application should also include two letters of recommendation discussing the applicant's citizenship, motivation, and character.
EIN: 726103061

385
The Sadie Bernstine and Henrietta Harris Scholarship Fund
c/o Whachovia Bank, N.A.
1525 W. WT Harris Blvd.
Charlotte, NC 28288-5709
Application address: c/o Principal, Atlantic City High School, 1400 N. Albany Ave., Atlantic City, NJ 08401-1208

Foundation type: Independent foundation
Limitations: Scholarships to Jewish graduating seniors from Atlantic City High School, NJ.
Financial data: Year ended 09/30/2004. Assets, $1,417,559 (M); Expenditures, $102,481; Total giving, $88,500.
Fields of interest: Jewish agencies & temples.
Type of support: Support to graduates or students of specific schools; Undergraduate support.
Application information: Applications accepted. Application form required.
Deadline(s): Mar. 31.
Additional information: Applications may be received from and returned to principal of Atlantic City High School.
EIN: 226347842

386
Janice T. Berry Trust
c/o Citizens Bank of NH
870 Westminster St.
Providence, RI 02903
Application address: c/o Citizen's Bank of NH, Attn.: Renee Hall, 1 Capital Plz., Concord, NH 03301, tel.: (603) 229-3573

Foundation type: Independent foundation
Limitations: Scholarships to nursing students, with preference given to students in Manchester, NH.
Financial data: Year ended 12/31/2004. Assets, $439,651 (M); Expenditures, $29,652; Total giving, $21,000; Grants to individuals, 12 grants totaling $21,000.
Fields of interest: Nursing school/education.
Type of support: Undergraduate support.
Application information:
Initial approach: Letter or telephone.
Deadline(s): May 31
Additional information: Contact trust for current application guidelines.
EIN: 026067436

387
Bertelsmann Foundation U.S., Inc.
1540 Broadway
New York, NY 10036-4094 (888) 369-3434

Foundation type: Company-sponsored foundation

Limitations: Scholarships to graduating seniors of New York City public high schools and some Company-related scholarships and student loans.
Financial data: Year ended 12/31/2002.
Assets, $585,632 (M); Expenditures, $1,443,926; Total giving, $232,500; Grants to individuals, 82 grants totaling $132,500 (high: $10,000, low: $200).
Fields of interest: Music; Literature.
Type of support: Student loans—to individuals; Precollege support; Undergraduate support.
Application information: Application form required.
   Deadline(s): Feb. 1
   Additional information: Contact foundation for current application guidelines.
EIN: 133777740

388

Celia Berwin Memorial Foundation

1880 CR 3615
Bigfoot, TX   78005
Contact: Janie Mann, Treas.

Foundation type: Independent foundation
Limitations: Scholarships to students in TX for higher education.
Financial data: Year ended 12/31/2004.
Assets, $711,800 (M); Expenditures, $43,830; Total giving, $36,000; Grants to individuals, 5 grants totaling $36,000.
Type of support: Undergraduate support.
Application information: Applications accepted.
   Deadline(s): None
   Applicants should submit the following:
      1) Transcripts
      2) Resume
   Additional information: Contact foundation for current application guidelines; Applicant must include professional, educational and character references.
EIN: 746074127

389

Charles G. Berwind Foundation

3000 Ctr. Sq. W.
1500 Market St.
Philadelphia, PA   19102
Contact: Jessica M. Berwind

Foundation type: Independent foundation
Limitations: Scholarships to children of active, retired, or deceased Berwind Corp. employees who served the company for at least one year. Occasional scholarships to residents of areas of company operations who are not related to a Berwind employee.
Financial data: Year ended 09/30/2004.
Assets, $2,177,428 (M); Expenditures, $168,219; Total giving, $142,155; Grants to individuals, 30 grants totaling $142,155 (high: $10,500, low: $250).
Type of support: Employee-related scholarships.
Application information: Application form required.
   Deadline(s): Contact foundation for current application deadline
   Additional information: Completion of formal application required, including biographical questionnaire and parents' confidential statement.
EIN: 237382896

390

Best Buy Children's Foundation

7601 Penn Ave. S.
Richfield, MN   55423-3645
FAX: (612) 292-4001; Application address: P.O. Box 9448, Minneapolis, MN 55440-9448;
URL: http://www.bestbuy.com/communityrelations

Foundation type: Company-sponsored foundation
Limitations: Award scholarships to three graduating high school seniors in each U.S. Congressional District and the District of Columbia. Scholarships are for $1,000 to $2,000. Scholarships recipients are selected based on community service and academic achievement and must be entering an accredited U.S. university, college or technical school in the fall immediately after graduation.
Publications: Application guidelines.
Financial data: Year ended 03/01/2005.
Assets, $6,817,549 (M); Expenditures, $15,419,954; Total giving, $13,984,888.
Type of support: Undergraduate support.
Application information: Contact foundation for current application deadline/guidelines.
Program description:
   Scholarship Program: Scholarships are for $1,000 to $2,000. Scholarships recipients are selected based on community service and academic achievement and must be entering an accredited U.S. university, college or technical school in the fall immediately after graduation.
EIN: 411784382

391

Best Friends Foundation

5335 Wisconsin Ave., NW, Ste., 440
Washington, DC   20015   (202) 478-9677
Contact: Elayne G. Bennett, Pres.
FAX: (202) 478-9678;
E-mail: ebennett@bestfriendsfoundation.org;
URL: http://www.bestfriendsfoundation.org

Foundation type: Public charity
Limitations: Scholarships to girls who have been members of the foundation's Diamond Girls Program for at least two years of elementary or middle school.
Financial data: Year ended 07/31/2004.
Assets, $996,702 (M); Expenditures, $1,873,946; Total giving, $24,500; Grants to individuals, 43 grants totaling $24,500 (high: $1,000, low: $500).
Fields of interest: Youth development, ethics; Girls.
Type of support: Precollege support; Undergraduate support.
Application information:
   Deadline(s): Varies
   Additional information: Applicants should abstain from pre-marital sex, alcohol, and drugs. Funds must be used for undergraduate education. Contact local affiliate for complete application information.
EIN: 521844471

392

Beta Lambda Alumnae Scholarship Foundation of Gamma Phi Beta Sorority

8052 Hudson Dr.
San Diego, CA   92119
Contact: Laurie Larrabee-Baker, Pres.
Application address: 5311 E. Palisades Rd., San Diego, CA 92116

Foundation type: Independent foundation

Limitations: Scholarships to active members of the Beta Lambda Chapter at San Diego State University, CA, who are in good standing and have no outstanding financial obligations to the Chapter or the House Corp.
Financial data: Year ended 03/31/2004.
Assets, $373,218 (M); Expenditures, $17,426; Total giving, $14,129; Grants to individuals, 9 grants totaling $14,129 (high: $2,000, low: $229).
Fields of interest: Students, sororities/fraternities.
Type of support: Support to graduates or students of specific schools; Undergraduate support.
Application information: Application form required.
   Deadline(s): Apr. 29
   Applicants should submit the following:
      1) Transcripts
Program description:
   Scholarship Program: Scholarships are awarded on the basis of financial need (50 percent), GPA as verified by college transcripts (25 percent), and chapter, school, and community activities (25 percent).
EIN: 330041323

393

Beta Pi Sigma Sorority, Inc.

539 Crocker Ave.
Daly City, CA   94014
Contact: Dolores E. Giles, Chair.

Foundation type: Public charity
Limitations: Scholarships to residents of CA for higher education.
Financial data: Year ended 06/30/2004.
Assets, $114,255 (M); Expenditures, $213,783; Total giving, $46,311; Grants to individuals, totaling $38,057. Subtotal for scholarships—to individuals: grants totaling $38,057.
Fields of interest: Students, sororities/fraternities.
Type of support: Scholarships—to individuals.
Application information: Contact foundation for current application deadline/guidelines.
EIN: 954199699

394

Better Minerals & Aggregates Company Education Foundation

(formerly U.S. Silica Company Education Foundation)
c/o John A. Ulizio
106 Sand Mine Rd.
Berkeley Springs, WV   25411

Foundation type: Company-sponsored foundation
Limitations: Renewable scholarships to individuals.
Financial data: Year ended 12/31/2004.
Assets, $24,002 (M); Expenditures, $16,000; Total giving, $16,000; Grants to individuals, 4,000 grants totaling $16,000 (high: $4,000, low: $4,000).
Type of support: Undergraduate support.
Application information: Applications not accepted.
EIN: 550760222

395

Betts Foundation

c/o Byrleen K. Terry
730 Fonville Dr.
Marlin, TX   76661-2203

Foundation type: Independent foundation

Limitations: Scholarships to graduates of Marlin, TX, area high schools, primarily for undergraduate education at TX institutions.
Financial data: Year ended 12/31/2004. Assets, $119,492 (M); Expenditures, $12,622; Total giving, $11,250; Grants to individuals, 14 grants totaling $11,250.
Type of support: Undergraduate support.
Application information: Applications accepted. Application form not required.
  Deadline(s): Applications by letter accepted throughout the year.
  Additional information: Contact foundation for further application information.
EIN: 751014070

396
BF Foundation
c/o David Chase
607 Cerrillos Rd., Ste. D-2
Santa Fe, NM 87501

Foundation type: Independent foundation
Limitations: Undergraduate scholarships primarily to AZ residents who are U.S. citizens and enrolled full-time at Northern Arizona University. Continuing education students at Arizona State University who are AZ residents and U.S. citizens may also be eligible.
Financial data: Year ended 06/30/2005. Assets, $4,477,438 (M); Expenditures, $349,403; Total giving, $218,150.
Fields of interest: Adult/continuing education.
Type of support: Support to graduates or students of specific schools; Undergraduate support.
Application information: Applications accepted. Application form required.
Program description:
  Scholarship Program: Recipients are required to correspond with the foundation periodically and to maintain at least a 2.5 GPA. Final selection is made by the foundation. The foundation no longer gives loans to individuals.
EIN: 366141070

397
Bernard Bianco Foundation
1518 Mississippi St.
Trinidad, CO 81082
Contact: Mark Argo, Tr.
Application address: 805 Park St., Trinidad, CO 81082

Foundation type: Independent foundation
Limitations: Scholarships to graduating seniors in Las Animas County, CO.
Financial data: Year ended 12/31/2004. Assets, $0 (M); Expenditures, $26,150; Total giving, $26,000; Grants to individuals, 40 grants totaling $26,000.
Type of support: Support to graduates or students of specific schools; Undergraduate support.
Application information: Application form required.
  Deadline(s): May 31
EIN: 841418124

398
William Bicket Memorial Scholarship Fund
5 Wren Ln.
Hamilton, NJ 08690

Foundation type: Independent foundation

Limitations: Scholarships to graduates of the Trenton, NJ, public school system to attend accredited four-year colleges in the following year.
Financial data: Year ended 04/30/2005. Assets, $0 (M); Expenditures, $6,349; Total giving, $5,100; Grants to individuals, 3 grants totaling $5,100.
Type of support: Support to graduates or students of specific schools; Undergraduate support.
Application information: Contact foundation for current application deadline/guidelines.
EIN: 226049584

399
D. A. Biglane Foundation
P.O. Box 966
Natchez, MS 39121-0966
Application address: 75 Melrose-Monterello Pkwy., Natchez, MS 39120

Foundation type: Independent foundation
Limitations: Scholarships only to residents of the Natchez, MS, area.
Financial data: Year ended 12/31/2004. Assets, $2,059,697 (M); Expenditures, $91,580; Total giving, $89,200; Grants to individuals, 12 grants totaling $51,700 (high: $5,000, low: $2,200).
Type of support: Scholarships—to individuals.
Application information: Applications accepted.
  Deadline(s): None
  Additional information: Completion of formal application required, including transcripts and financial information.
EIN: 646028044

400
The Biomet Foundation, Inc.
P.O. Box 587
Warsaw, IN 46581-0587
Contact: Darlene K. Whaley, Secy.

Foundation type: Company-sponsored foundation
Limitations: Scholarships to financially needy children of full-time Team Members of Biomet, Inc. and its subsidiaries, primarily in IN.
Publications: Informational brochure.
Financial data: Year ended 12/31/2005. Assets, $7,059,548 (M); Expenditures, $375,270; Total giving, $373,871; Grants to individuals, 44 grants totaling $87,000 (high: $2,000, low: $1,000).
Type of support: Employee-related scholarships.
Application information: Application form required.
  Deadline(s): Feb. 15
  Applicants should submit the following:
    1) Transcripts
    2) SAT
    3) Letter(s) of recommendation
    4) GPA
    5) Financial information
    6) ACT
  Additional information: Application should also include parents' financial statement; High school students must have their guidance counselor forward the application to the foundation, along with transcripts and letter of recommendation from a teacher; College students must send application directly to the foundation, along with certified college transcripts and the recommendations of two professors.
Program description:
  Scholarship Program: The children of officers and directors of Biomet, subsidiaries, and members of

the foundation are ineligible. Scholarships are renewable.
EIN: 351806314

401
Lester R. Birbeck Charitable Trust
c/o Gold Trust Co.
P.O. Box 846
St. Joseph, MO 64502
Application address: c/o Gold Trust Co., 4305 Frederick Blvd., Ste. 102, St. Joseph, MO 64506

Foundation type: Independent foundation
Limitations: Scholarships to high school students from King City or Stanberry, MO, schools for higher education.
Financial data: Year ended 12/31/2004. Assets, $2,065,918 (M); Expenditures, $121,218; Total giving, $111,500; Grants to individuals, totaling $111,500.
Type of support: Support to graduates or students of specific schools; Undergraduate support.
Application information: Application form required.
  Deadline(s): Apr. 1
  Applicants should submit the following:
    1) Photograph
    2) Transcripts
EIN: 431725748

402
Birtwistle Family Foundation
(formerly Donald B. Birtwistle Foundation)
300 S. Rath Ave., Apt. 25
Ludington, MI 49431   (616) 843-2501
Contact: Donald B. Birtwistle, Pres.

Foundation type: Independent foundation
Limitations: Scholarships to graduates of the Ludington Area School District, MI, for college and graduate school.
Financial data: Year ended 12/31/2004. Assets, $1,769,533 (M); Expenditures, $90,208; Total giving, $86,550; Grants to individuals, 4 grants totaling $16,000.
Type of support: Support to graduates or students of specific schools; Graduate support; Undergraduate support.
Application information: Application form required.
  Deadline(s): Apr. 1 of senior year of high school or college
EIN: 382787567

403
Bishop Educational Trust
c/o First National Bank
300 E. 2nd St.
Muscatine, IA 52761
Application address: c/o Scott Snow, 200 E. 2nd St., Muscatine, IA 52761, tel.: (563) 263-4221

Foundation type: Independent foundation
Limitations: Scholarships to deserving students to attend IA colleges, with preference given to students attending Muscatine Community College.
Financial data: Year ended 12/31/2004. Assets, $3,155,913 (M); Expenditures, $229,776; Total giving, $207,522; Grants to individuals, 86 grants totaling $207,522 (high: $8,250, low: $500).
Type of support: Scholarships—to individuals; Support to graduates or students of specific schools.
Application information: Application form required.

Initial approach: Letter or telephone.
Deadline(s): June 1
Additional information: Contact trust for current application guidelines.
EIN: 426531722

404

Edward and Lillian Bishop Foundation

(formerly E. K. and Lillian F. Bishop Foundation)
c/o Bank of America, N.A.
701 5th Ave., 22nd Fl.
Seattle, WA 98104
Application address: c/o Bank of America, N.A., Aberdeen Branch, Attn.: Thomas J. Nevers, Grant Mgr., Bishop Scholarship Comm., P.O. Box 128, Aberdeen, WA 98520
FAX: (520) 749-2990

Foundation type: Independent foundation
Limitations: Scholarships only to financially needy students who are residents of Grays Harbor County, WA, and entering their third year of college or beyond.
Publications: Application guidelines; Informational brochure (including application guidelines); Program policy statement.
Financial data: Year ended 04/30/2005. Assets, $11,926,659 (M); Expenditures, $4,829,101; Total giving, $4,711,949.
Type of support: Graduate support; Undergraduate support.
Application information: Applications accepted. Application form required.
Initial approach: Letter.
Deadline(s): June 1
Program description:
Scholarship Program: Scholarships are provided to students enrolled in either their third or fourth year of approved four-year colleges and universities, or their first two years at approved graduate schools. Applicants must have maintained a GPA of at least 3.0 or the equivalent. Only students who are residents of Grays Harbor County, WA, are eligible.
EIN: 916116724

405

Warren H. Bishop Memorial Scholarship Fund

(also known as Priscilla Hill-Warren Bishop Scholarship Fund)
c/o U.S. Bank, N.A., Trust Tax Svcs.
P.O. Box 3168
Portland, OR 97208
Application address: c/o Scholarship Fund Comm., 70 Jackson County Medical Society, Rogue Valley Medical Arts Bldg., 691 Murphy Rd., Ste. 216, Medford, OR 97501

Foundation type: Independent foundation
Limitations: Scholarships to residents of Jackson, Josephine, and Klamath counties, OR, who are members of the sophomore, junior, or senior class at an accredited medical school.
Financial data: Year ended 06/30/2005. Assets, $62,073 (M); Expenditures, $8,016; Total giving, $5,000; Grants to individuals, 2 grants totaling $5,000.
Fields of interest: Medical school/education.
Type of support: Graduate support.
Application information: Applications accepted.
Deadline(s): Contact fund for current application deadline/guidelines.

Program description:
Bishop Memorial Scholarship: Scholarships may also be granted to graduates of accredited medical schools who are residents of these counties, who intend to practice in the counties, and who are resident student interns at accredited medical schools or hospitals specializing in internal medicine. Selection is based on need, medical aptitude and ability.
EIN: 936153739

406

Rex & Christine Bishop Perpetual Scholarship Fund for Iowa Valley Community School District

P.O. Box 267
Marengo, IA 52301-0267 (319) 642-5521
Contact: Julie A. Read, Tr.

Foundation type: Independent foundation
Limitations: Scholarships to graduates of the Iowa Valley Community School District, Marengo, IA, for higher education, including college, trade, and technical education within the state of IA.
Financial data: Year ended 12/31/2004. Assets, $807,932 (M); Expenditures, $56,979; Total giving, $54,244; Grants to individuals, 24 grants totaling $54,244.
Fields of interest: Vocational education.
Type of support: Support to graduates or students of specific schools; Technical education support; Undergraduate support.
Application information: Application form required.
Deadline(s): May 2
EIN: 421187973

407

Black Hawk College Foundation

6600 34th Ave.
Moline, IL 61265

Foundation type: Public charity
Limitations: Scholarships and grants to residents of Community College District No. 503, IL.
Publications: Application guidelines; Annual report; Informational brochure; Newsletter.
Financial data: Year ended 06/30/2005. Assets, $1,478,054 (M); Expenditures, $96,606; Total giving, $41,353; Grants to individuals, totaling $39,853.
Type of support: Undergraduate support.
Application information: Applications accepted.
Deadline(s): Contact foundation for current application deadline/guidelines.
EIN: 363240562

408

Abner & Eliza Black Memorial Fund

c/o Farmers & Merchants State Bank
P.O. Box 230
Winterset, IA 50273-0230 (515) 462-3731
Contact: Lewis H. Jordan, Tr.

Foundation type: Independent foundation
Limitations: Scholarships to residents of Madison County, IA, who are physically disabled and under the age of 21 at the time of application.
Financial data: Year ended 12/31/2004. Assets, $326,399 (M); Expenditures, $12,755; Total giving, $10,500; Grants to individuals, 7 grants totaling $10,500.
Fields of interest: Children/youth, services; Disabilities, people with.
Type of support: Scholarships—to individuals.

Application information: Applications accepted throughout the year; Completion of formal application required, including two personal references.
EIN: 426062134

409

Jim Black Memorial Scholarship Trust

P.O. Box 2020
Tyler, TX 75710
Application address: c/o Robert E. Lee High School, 411 E. Southeast Loop 323, Tyler, TX 75701, tel.: (903) 561-3911

Foundation type: Independent foundation
Limitations: Scholarships to graduates of Robert E. Lee High School, TX.
Financial data: Year ended 12/31/2004. Assets, $61,281 (M); Expenditures, $5,200; Total giving, $3,500; Grants to individuals, 5 grants totaling $3,500.
Type of support: Support to graduates or students of specific schools; Undergraduate support.
Application information: Deadline Feb.; Completion of formal application required, including personal references, financial information, and work experience.
Program description:
Scholarship Program: Scholarships are renewable for up to four years provided the recipient maintains at least a 2.0 GPA.
EIN: 756265235

410

The Black Student Fund

3636 16th St., N.W., 4th Fl.
Washington, DC 20010-1146 (202) 387-1414
Contact: Barbara Patterson, Pres.
E-mail: mail@blackstudentfund.org; Additional tel.: (703) 506-3553; URL: http://www.blackstudentfund.org

Foundation type: Public charity
Limitations: Scholarships to African American pre-K-12th grade students residing in the Washington, DC, metropolitan area.
Publications: Annual report; Informational brochure; Newsletter.
Financial data: Year ended 06/30/2004. Assets, $1,670,864 (M); Expenditures, $1,324,338; Total giving, $277,151; Grants to individuals, 275 grants totaling $277,151.
Fields of interest: Elementary/secondary education; Early childhood education; African Americans/Blacks.
Type of support: Precollege support.
Application information: Contact fund for current application deadline/guidelines.
EIN: 526053597

411

Evelyn H. Black Trust

(also known as Art B. and Evelyn H. Black Scholarship Fund)
c/o Bank of America, N.A.
100 Federal St., MADE 10020B
Boston, MA 02110
Contact: Beth Thut, Program Asst.

Foundation type: Independent foundation
Limitations: Scholarships to students who are attending or have attended Concord, MA, public schools.
Publications: Application guidelines.

Financial data: Year ended 12/31/2003. Assets, $1,290,207 (M); Expenditures, $71,784; Total giving, $60,500; Grants to individuals, 32 grants totaling $60,500 (high: $13,000, low: $750).

Fields of interest: Arts education; Vocational education.

Type of support: Support to graduates or students of specific schools; Undergraduate support.

Application information: Applications accepted. Application form required.

Deadline(s): Apr. 20

Applicants should submit the following:
1) GPA
2) Transcripts

Additional information: Application should include copy of parents' tax return.

Program description:

Scholarship Program: The fund was established to provide scholarships to financially needy, worthy, and able high school students. To qualify, applicants must have maintained a scholastic standing above their class average during the preceding year. Applicants must also wish to pursue studies or develop a talent in areas where no instruction or additional instruction is available free of charge in the Concord public schools. Scholarships are provided for college or university study, and advanced training in any one of the fine arts, practical arts, or vocations.

EIN: 046141425

412

Blade Foundation

c/o Gary J. Blair
541 N. Superior St.
Toledo, OH   43660-1000   (419) 245-6210
Contact: William Block, Jr., Pres.

Foundation type: Company-sponsored foundation

Limitations: Scholarships to children or legal dependents of full-time Toledo Blade employees with at three years' tenure.

Financial data: Year ended 12/31/2004. Assets, $9,486 (M); Expenditures, $149,175; Total giving, $149,075; Grants to individuals, 7 grants totaling $10,500 (high: $1,500, low: $1,500).

Type of support: Employee-related scholarships.

Application information: Application form required.

Deadline(s): Mar. 1

Applicants should submit the following:
1) SAT

Additional information: Allowance for SAT scores arriving after deadline.

EIN: 346559843

413

F. Kelsay Blair Scholarship Trust

c/o Fairmount State Bank
P.O. Box 8
Fairmount, IN   46928   (765) 948-4330
Contact: David Crouse, V.P. and Asst. Trust Off., Fairmount State Bank

Foundation type: Independent foundation

Limitations: Scholarships to high school students in Fairmount Township, Grant County, IN, for higher education.

Financial data: Year ended 12/31/2004. Assets, $531,327 (M); Expenditures, $26,745; Total giving, $25,196; Grants to individuals, 18 grants totaling $25,196.

Type of support: Undergraduate support.

Application information: Applications accepted.

Deadline(s): None

Additional information: Contact trust for current application guidelines.

EIN: 356532077

414

Lula Mae Blair Scholarship Trust

c/o Fairmount State Bank
P.O. Box 8
Fairmount, IN   46928   (765) 948-4330
Contact: David Crouse, V.P. and Asst. Trust Off., Fairmount State Bank

Foundation type: Independent foundation

Limitations: Scholarships to high school students residing in Fairmount Township, Grant County, IN, for higher education.

Financial data: Year ended 12/31/2004. Assets, $355,033 (M); Expenditures, $18,249; Total giving, $16,863; Grants to individuals, 7 grants totaling $16,863.

Type of support: Undergraduate support.

Application information: Applications accepted.

Deadline(s): None

Additional information: Contact trust for current application guidelines.

EIN: 356532078

415

James Hubert Blake Scholarship Fund

(also known as Eubie Blake Scholarship Fund)
c/o Beldock, Levine & Hoffman
99 Park Ave., Ste. 1600
New York, NY   10016-1503   (212) 490-0400
Contact: Elliot L. Hoffman, Tr.

Foundation type: Independent foundation

Limitations: Scholarships to instrumental music students, particularly those who intend to be musical performers (i.e. "working musicians").

Financial data: Year ended 03/31/2003. Assets, $469,892 (M); Expenditures, $27,949; Total giving, $18,000; Grants to individuals, 9 grants totaling $18,000 (high: $3,000, low: $1,500).

Fields of interest: Music; Performing arts, education.

Type of support: Undergraduate support.

Application information: Application form required.

Deadline(s): Apr. 30 for fall term, Nov. 30 for spring term

Additional information: Application must include at least two references preferably from music teachers, proof of admission or enrollment at an educational institution, financial need statement, official transcripts, and a recorded cassette tape or CD (maximum of 30 minutes) of recent musical performances.

Program description:

Eubie Blake Scholarship Fund: Only participants in studies of instrumental music who are preparing for careers as instrumental performing artists are considered. Preference may be shown to applicants who are interested in traditional American ragtime piano studies. Selection criteria include demonstrated musical talent and ability, motivation, and financial need. Scholarships are renewable. Eubie Blake Scholarships are administered as two separate foundations established under two separate wills, those of James Hubert Blake and of Marion Tyler Blake. While the specific fiscal figures differ, the programs, nomination procedures, contact person, and address are identical. Each foundation gives grants of either $1,500 or $3,000 per student per year.

EIN: 136836085

416

Marion Tyler Blake Trust

c/o Beldock, Levine & Hoffman
99 Park Ave., Ste. 1600
New York, NY   10016-1503   (212) 490-0400
Contact: Elliot L. Hoffman, Tr.

Foundation type: Independent foundation

Limitations: Scholarships by nomination only to instrumental music students, particularly those who intend to be musical performers (i.e. "working musicians").

Financial data: Year ended 03/31/2005. Assets, $189,325 (M); Expenditures, $14,771; Total giving, $12,000; Grants to individuals, 5 grants totaling $12,000.

Fields of interest: Music; Performing arts, education.

Type of support: Awards/grants by nomination only; Undergraduate support.

Application information: Application form required.

Deadline(s): Apr. 30 for Fall term, Nov. 30 for Spring term

Additional information: Applications must include at least two nominations preferably from music teachers, financial infromation, proof of admission or enrollment at an educational institution, financial need statement, official transcripts, a personal statement, and a recorded cassette tape (maximum 30 minutes) of recent musical performances.

Program description:

Eubie Blake Scholarship Fund: All candidates are nominated by pre-selected professors of music. Only participants in studies of instrumental music who are preparing for careers as instrumental performing artists are considered. Preference may be shown to applicants who are interested in traditional American ragtime piano studies. Selection criteria include demonstrated musical talent and ability, motivation, and financial need. Scholarships are renewable. Eubie Blake Scholarships are administered as two separate foundations established under two separate wills, those of James Hubert Blake and of Marion Tyler Blake. While the specific fiscal figures differ, the programs, nomination procedures, contact person, and address are identical. Each foundation gives grants of either $1,500 or $3,000 per student per year.

EIN: 136836084

417

Henry L. & Nellie E. Blakeslee Trust for Scholarships

c/o Bank of America, N.A.
P.O. Box 1802
Providence, RI   02901-1802
Application Address: c/o Susan Kaniewski, Probate Court, 158 Main St., Thomaston, CT 06787

Foundation type: Independent foundation

Limitations: Scholarship grants to residents of Thomaston, CT.

Financial data: Year ended 12/31/2004. Assets, $2,215,847 (M); Expenditures, $145,389; Total giving, $121,851; Grants to individuals, totaling $121,851.

Type of support: Scholarships—to individuals.

Application information: Contact foundation for current application deadline; Completion of formal application required, including general and financial information.

EIN: 066025519

418
Arthur F. Blanchard Trust
c/o Adelisa L. Gonzales, A.V.P., Mellon Financial Group
1 Boston Pl., Rm. 024-0024
Boston, MA 02108-4408
Application address: c/o Sandra Brown-Mullen, Mellon Financial Corp., 1 Boston Pl., Rm. 024-0092, Boston, MA 02108, tel.: (617) 722-7341

Foundation type: Independent foundation
Limitations: Scholarships to residents of Boxborough, MA who attended Blanchard Memorial School, MA.
Publications: Application guidelines; Program policy statement.
Financial data: Year ended 08/31/2004. Assets, $18,122,188 (M); Expenditures, $727,690; Total giving, $648,000; Grants to individuals, 60 grants totaling $68,000 (high: $5,000, low: $250).
Type of support: Support to graduates or students of specific schools; Undergraduate support.
Application information: Applications accepted.
   Initial approach: Letter.
   Additional information: Contact trust for current application deadline/guidelines.
EIN: 046093374

419
Grace T. Blanchard Trust
c/o Eastern Bank & Trust Co.
605 Broadway, LF41
Saugus, MA 01906
Contact: Shawn McCarthy

Foundation type: Independent foundation
Limitations: Scholarships to MA residents attending Harvard University or Radcliffe College.
Financial data: Year ended 12/31/2004. Assets, $233,088 (M); Expenditures, $14,691; Total giving, $11,250; Grants to individuals, 3 grants totaling $11,250.
Type of support: Support to graduates or students of specific schools; Undergraduate support.
Application information: Application form required.
   Additional information: Applications accepted throughout the year.
EIN: 046015965

420
Lenora Ford Bland and W. Jennings Bland Scholarship Trust
402 Main St.
Coshocton, OH 43812-1511   (740) 622-0130
Contact: Van Blanchard II, Tr.

Foundation type: Independent foundation
Limitations: Scholarships to students of Riverview High School, Ridgewood High School, and Coshocton High School, OH, for undergraduate education.
Financial data: Year ended 12/31/2004. Assets, $429,412 (M); Expenditures, $24,477; Total giving, $7,417; Grants to individuals, 9 grants totaling $7,417.
Type of support: Support to graduates or students of specific schools; Undergraduate support.
Application information:
   Initial approach: Letter or telephone.
   Additional information: Contact trust for current application deadline/guidelines.
EIN: 316430828

421
The Blandin Foundation
(formerly Charles K. Blandin Foundation)
100 N. Pokegama Ave.
Grand Rapids, MN 55744   (218) 326-0523
Contact: James Hoolihan, Pres.
FAX: (218) 327-1949;
E-mail: bfinfo@blandinfoundation.org; Additional tel.: (877) 882-2257; URL: http://www.blandinfoundation.org

Foundation type: Independent foundation
Limitations: Scholarships for undergraduate and vocational study to recent graduates of Itasca County, Hill City, and Remer high schools, all in MN. Candidates must be under the age of 25 as of Sept. 1 of the effective school year.
Publications: Financial statement; Informational brochure (including application guidelines).
Financial data: Year ended 12/31/2004. Assets, $413,253,276 (M); Expenditures, $36,559,072; Total giving, $30,006,595; Grants to individuals, 631 grants totaling $589,916 (high: $2,184, low: $250, average grant: $500-$1,500).
Fields of interest: Vocational education.
Type of support: Support to graduates or students of specific schools; Technical education support; Undergraduate support.
Application information: Application form required.
   Initial approach: Telephone, requesting brochure and application.
   Deadline(s): May 15
   Applicants should submit the following:
      1) SAR
      2) FAFSA
   Additional information: Application should also include a copy of parents' or independent students' 1040 income tax form; Interviews available to students with unusual circumstances; See program description for further application information.
Program description:
   Blandin Educational Awards Program: Students planning to attend Itasca Community College should not apply directly to the foundation. They should apply directly to the financial aid office at Itasca Community College. Students must be working toward their first baccalaureate degree or other undergraduate certificate or diploma.
EIN: 416038619

422
Blarney Fund Education Trust
c/o Bell & Co.
350 5th Ave., Ste. 7412
New York, NY 10118
Contact: M. Bell, C.P.A.
Application address: P.O. Box 214, Swanton, VT 05488, tel.: (802) 868-2755

Foundation type: Independent foundation
Limitations: Scholarships to graduating seniors of Bellows Free Academy and Missisquoi Valley Union High School, Franklin County, VT, who are entering or pursuing a two-year or four-year college degree program.
Financial data: Year ended 05/31/2004. Assets, $343,158 (M); Expenditures, $21,515; Total giving, $21,000; Grants to individuals, totaling $21,000.
Type of support: Support to graduates or students of specific schools; Undergraduate support.
Application information:
   Deadline(s): May
   Additional information: Contact trust for current application guidelines.

Program description:
   Scholarship Program: Recipients will be chosen by the Guidance Dept. and/or scholarship committee in each of the two schools.
EIN: 036051035

423
Blaske-Hill Foundation
25001 Battle Creek Hwy.
Bellevue, MI 49021-9603
Contact: E. Robert Blaske, Secy.-Treas.

Foundation type: Independent foundation
Limitations: Scholarships to graduates of Battle Creek Central, Battle Creek St. Philip, and Niles high schools, MI.
Financial data: Year ended 02/28/2005. Assets, $395,733 (M); Expenditures, $27,307; Total giving, $26,000; Grants to individuals, 13 grants totaling $26,000.
Type of support: Support to graduates or students of specific schools; Undergraduate support.
Application information: Application form required.
   Initial approach: Letter.
   Deadline(s): Mar. 15
EIN: 382525817

424
Joseph Blazek Foundation
8 S. Michigan Ave., No. 801
Chicago, IL 60603-3350   (312) 236-3882

Foundation type: Independent foundation
Limitations: Scholarships to high school seniors in public or private secondary schools in Cook County, IL, planning to major in engineering, mathematics, chemistry, physics, or related scientific fields.
Publications: Application guidelines.
Financial data: Year ended 06/30/2005. Assets, $128,327 (M); Expenditures, $86,034; Total giving, $17,034; Grants to individuals, 23 grants totaling $17,034.
Fields of interest: Engineering school/education; Science; Chemistry; Mathematics; Physics.
Type of support: Support to graduates or students of specific schools; Undergraduate support.
Application information: Application form required.
   Deadline(s): Mar. 15
Program description:
   Scholarship Program: All grants are automatically renewed for each succeeding undergraduate year for a maximum of four years, dependent upon the grantee's continued enrollment. Grants are made directly to the school.
EIN: 237015800

425
John M. & Elizabeth Beeman Bleuer Scholarship Fund
P.O. Box 289
Biloxi, MS 39533-0289
Contact: Mildred B. Page, Tr.; For Scholarships: Lyle M. Page
Application address for scholarships: P.O. Box 4779, Biloxi, MS 39535, tel.: (228) 374-2100

Foundation type: Operating foundation
Limitations: Scholarships to qualified high school seniors residing in Biloxi, MS.
Publications: Informational brochure (including application guidelines).
Financial data: Year ended 12/31/2003. Assets, $1,691,650 (M); Expenditures, $63,321;

Total giving, $55,000; Grants to individuals, 58 grants totaling $55,000 (high: $1,000, low: $500).
Type of support: Scholarships—to individuals.
Application information:
  Deadline(s): Mar. 30
  Additional information: Contact fund for current application guidelines.
EIN: 646197850

426
Jim Blevins Foundation
P.O. Box 150056
Nashville, TN 37215 (615) 298-5000
Contact: James V. Blevins, Tr.

Foundation type: Independent foundation
Limitations: Scholarships primarily to residents of TN and GA.
Financial data: Year ended 10/31/2004.
Assets, $2,521,036 (M); Expenditures, $145,704; Total giving, $141,401; Grants to individuals, 17 grants totaling $72,401 (high: $7,500, low: $2,000).
Type of support: Scholarships—to individuals.
Application information: Applications accepted.
  Deadline(s): None
EIN: 626043234

427
Bloch-Selinger Educational Trust Fund
c/o Wachovia Bank, N.A.
100 N. Main St., 13th Fl.
Winston-Salem, NC 27150
Application address: c/o Superintendent of Danville Schools, P.O. Box 139, Danville, PA 17821

Foundation type: Independent foundation
Limitations: Scholarships to honor students graduating from Danville Senior High School, PA.
Financial data: Year ended 12/31/2004.
Assets, $435,965 (M); Expenditures, $25,851; Total giving, $22,800; Grants to individuals, 10 grants totaling $22,800 (high: $3,600, low: $1,100).
Type of support: Support to graduates or students of specific schools; Undergraduate support.
Application information: Applications accepted. Application form required.
  Initial approach: Letter.
EIN: 236558579

428
James J. Bloomer Charitable Trust
c/o Chemung Canal Trust Co.
P.O. Box 1522
Elmira, NY 14902-1522
Application address: c/o St. Patrick's Roman Catholic Church Society, Elmira, NY 1490, tel.: (607) 733-6661

Foundation type: Independent foundation
Limitations: Scholarships to residents of Elmira, NY, who are members of St. Anthony and St. Patrick parishes, for attendance at Catholic colleges and universities in the U.S.
Financial data: Year ended 12/31/2004.
Assets, $238,564 (M); Expenditures, $13,938; Total giving, $13,241; Grants to individuals, 19 grants totaling $13,241.
Fields of interest: Roman Catholic agencies & churches.
Type of support: Undergraduate support.
Application information: Applications accepted.
  Deadline(s): None

Additional information: Interviews required.
EIN: 166022129

429
Charles H. and Isabell Blosser Foundation
3001 Blosser Cir.
Concordia, KS 66901
Contact: Beldon Blosser, Tr.

Foundation type: Independent foundation
Limitations: Scholarships primarily to residents of Cloud County, KS.
Financial data: Year ended 12/31/2004.
Assets, $1,123,093 (M); Expenditures, $42,289; Total giving, $38,424.
Type of support: Scholarships—to individuals.
Application information: Contact foundation for current application deadline/guidelines.
EIN: 481153247

430
Peter J. Blosser Student Loan Fund
(also known as Peter J. Blosser Scholarship Trust)
P.O. Box 6160
Chillicothe, OH 45601-6160 (740) 773-0043
Contact: Marie Rosebrook
E-mail: Blossertrust@horizonview.net

Foundation type: Independent foundation
Limitations: Student loans and scholarships to residents of Ross County, OH.
Publications: Application guidelines; Annual report; Informational brochure.
Financial data: Year ended 12/31/2004.
Assets, $2,284,646 (M); Expenditures, $65,370; Total giving, $16,000; Grants to individuals, 8 grants totaling $16,000 (high: $2,000, low: $2,000); Loans to individuals, 16 loans totaling $68,000.
Type of support: Scholarships—to individuals; Student loans—to individuals.
Application information: Applications accepted. Application form required.
  Initial approach: Letter, telephone, or email.
  Copies of proposal: 1
  Deadline(s): None
  Applicants should submit the following:
    1) Letter(s) of recommendation
    2) Transcripts
    3) GPA
    4) Financial information
  Additional information: Interviews required.
EIN: 310629687

431
Marlin E. Blosser Trust
c/o M&T Bank
1 M&T Plz., 8th Fl.
Buffalo, NY 14203
Application address for scholarships: c/o Carlisle High School, Counseling Center, 623 W. Penn St., Carlisle, PA 17013

Foundation type: Independent foundation
Limitations: Scholarships to graduates of Carlisle High School, PA, for higher education.
Financial data: Year ended 12/31/2003.
Assets, $266,342 (M); Expenditures, $11,903; Total giving, $9,540; Grants to individuals, totaling $9,540.
Fields of interest: Vocational education, post-secondary.
Type of support: Support to graduates or students of specific schools; Technical education support.

Application information: Application form required.
  Deadline(s): Contact foundation for current application deadline
  Additional information: Application should also include family information, employment history, higher education preferences, and essay.
EIN: 256579913

432
The Mildred W. Blount Educational & Charitable Foundation
(formerly Mildred Weedon Blount Educational & Charitable Foundation, Inc.)
P.O. Box 780607
Tallassee, AL 36078
Contact: Arnold B. Dopson, Chair.

Foundation type: Independent foundation
Limitations: Scholarships to students in Elmore County, AL.
Financial data: Year ended 06/30/2005.
Assets, $3,582,279 (M); Expenditures, $136,815; Total giving, $106,500.
Type of support: Scholarships—to individuals.
Application information: Application form required.
  Deadline(s): Early May
EIN: 630817472

433
David Strouse Blount Educational Foundation
c/o SunTrust Bank
P.O. Box 1908
Orlando, FL 32802-1908
Application address: c/o Carolyn McCoy, SunTrust Bank, 510 S. Jefferson St., Roanoke, VA 24038, tel.: (540) 982-3014

Foundation type: Independent foundation
Limitations: Scholarships to VA residents with scholastic ability and financial need attending colleges and universities in VA.
Financial data: Year ended 03/31/2005.
Assets, $3,232,875 (M); Expenditures, $90,054; Total giving, $54,000; Grants to individuals, totaling $54,000.
Type of support: Scholarships—to individuals.
Application information: Application form required.
  Deadline(s): None
  Additional information: Apply through financial aid office of a VA college or university.
EIN: 546111717

434
Hilda Blowers Scholarship Foundation
750 E. Green St., Ste. 209
Pasadena, CA 91101
E-mail: brian@hbfoundation.org; Application address: c/o Brian Molohan, 3140 Neil Armstrong Blvd., Ste. 311, Eagan, MN 55121, tel.: (651) 209-3067

Foundation type: Independent foundation
Limitations: Post-secondary college scholarships to residents of Minneapolis, MN, who have achieved a certain level of chess playing success based upon their United States Chess Federation rating.
Financial data: Year ended 12/31/2003.
Assets, $1,735,703 (M); Expenditures, $146,474; Total giving, $15,424; Grants to individuals, 4 grants totaling $11,250 (high: $5,626, low: $375).

Type of support: Undergraduate support.
Application information: Applications accepted.
Initial approach: E-mail or telephone.
Additional information: Contact foundation for additional application information.
Program description:
HB Foundation Scholarships: The applicant must be a graduate from a high school in Minnesota, as well as having a USCF rating of at least 1800.
EIN: 411876372

435
Blue Coats of Louisville, Inc.
c/o National City Bank, Kentucky
P.O. Box 94651
Cleveland, OH 44101-4651
Contact: Arthur C. Peters
Application address: c/o Hilliard Lyons, P.O. Box 32760, Louisville, KY 40232, tel.: (502) 895-8858

Foundation type: Independent foundation
Limitations: Scholarships and awards to outstanding police and fire department officers in Louisville and Jefferson counties, KY.
Financial data: Year ended 12/31/2004.
Assets, $649,736 (M); Expenditures, $30,686; Total giving, $24,862; Grants to individuals, 3 grants totaling $15,062.
Fields of interest: Crime/law enforcement, police agencies; Disasters, fire prevention/control.
Type of support: Scholarships—to individuals; Awards/prizes.
Application information: Contact foundation for current application deadline/guidelines.
EIN: 616022331

436
Blue Grass Community Foundation, Inc.
(formerly Blue Grass Foundation, Inc.)
250 W. Main St., Ste. 1220
Lexington, KY 40507-1714 (859) 225-3343
Contact: For grant applications: Barbara A. Fischer, Grants Off.
FAX: (859) 243-0770; E-mail: info@bgcf.org; Grant information E-mail: bfischer@bgcf.org; URL: http://www.bgcf.org

Foundation type: Community foundation
Limitations: Scholarships to central Kentucky area students for higher education.
Publications: Application guidelines; Annual report; Financial statement; Informational brochure (including application guidelines).
Financial data: Year ended 12/31/2005.
Assets, $26,221,968 (M); Expenditures, $2,141,972; Total giving, $1,531,743; Grants to individuals, 161 grants totaling $248,046 (high: $4,000, low: $140).
Type of support: Employee-related scholarships; Graduate support; Undergraduate support.
Application information: Applications not accepted.
Additional information: High schools recommend recipients.
EIN: 616053466

437
Blue Mountain Community Foundation
(formerly Blue Mountain Area Foundation)
8 S. 2nd, Ste. 618
P.O. Box 603
Walla Walla, WA 99362-0015 (509) 529-4371
Contact: Lawson F. Knight, Exec. Dir.
FAX: (509) 529-5284;
E-mail: bmcf@bluemountainfoundation.org;
URL: http://www.bluemountainfoundation.org

Foundation type: Community foundation
Limitations: Scholarships only to graduates of high schools in the Blue Mountain area of WA and OR.
Publications: Application guidelines; Annual report; Grants list; Informational brochure; Newsletter.
Financial data: Year ended 06/30/2005.
Assets, $21,632,098 (M); Expenditures, $1,201,187; Total giving, $891,178; Grants to individuals, 159 grants totaling $241,618 (high: $7,717, low: $80).
Type of support: Support to graduates or students of specific schools; Graduate support; Undergraduate support.
Application information: Applications accepted. Application form required. Application form available on the grantmaker's Web site.
Initial approach: Letter.
Deadline(s): May 1
EIN: 911250104

438
The Blue River Foundation, Inc.
54 W. Broadway, Ste. 1
P.O. Box 808
Shelbyville, IN 46176 (317) 392-7955
Contact: Elaine Haehl, Exec. Dir.; For grant applications: Lynne Ensminger, Prog. Admin.
FAX: (317) 392-4545;
E-mail: brf@blueriverfoundation.com; Additional E-mail: ehaehl@blueriverfoundation.com; Grant application E-mail: lensminger@blueriverfoundation.com; URL: http://www.blueriverfoundation.com

Foundation type: Community foundation
Limitations: Scholarships to financially needy residents of Shelby County, IN.
Publications: Application guidelines; Annual report; Financial statement; Informational brochure.
Financial data: Year ended 12/31/2004.
Assets, $11,917,222 (M); Expenditures, $709,925; Total giving, $329,738; Grants to individuals, 72 grants totaling $55,967 (high: $3,000, low: $54).
Type of support: Scholarships—to individuals; Graduate support; Undergraduate support.
Application information: Application form required.
Additional information: Contact foundation for current application deadline; Interviews required for some scholarships.
EIN: 351756331

439
BMI Foundation, Inc.
320 W. 57th St.
New York, NY 10019-3705
Contact: Ralph N. Jackson, Pres.
E-mail: info@bmifoundation.org; TN tel.: (615) 401-2411; URL: http://www.bmifoundation.org

Foundation type: Public charity
Limitations: Awards and scholarships to young songwriters and composers.
Financial data: Year ended 12/31/2003.
Assets, $1,476,769 (M); Expenditures, $138,248; Total giving, $135,450; Grants to individuals, 29 grants totaling $57,450 (high: $7,500, low: $100).
Fields of interest: Music; Music composition; Women.
Type of support: Support to graduates or students of specific schools; Awards/grants by nomination only; Awards/prizes; Undergraduate support.
Application information:
Initial approach: E-mail.
Deadline(s): Jan. 13 for peermusic Latin Scholarship
Additional information: See Web site for further application information.
Program descriptions:
The peermusic Latin Scholarship: The annual competition offers a $5,000 scholarship, which is awarded for the best song or instrumental work in any Latin genre. The competition is open to songwriters and composers who are current students at colleges and universities located in California, Florida, Illinois, Massachusetts, New York, Puerto Rico, or Texas. Applicants must be between the ages of 16 and 24. All words and music must be original.
The John Lennon Scholarship Program: The program recognizes young songwriters working in any genre between the ages of 15 and 25 and has awarded over $100,000 in scholarships over the past seven years. Entries are solicited from a select group of schools, which are listed on the Web site. Questions may be addressed to LennonScholarship@bmifoundation.org.
The BMI Student Composer Awards: The BMI Student Composer Awards is a competition for young composers of classical music. The awards are made on an annual basis for compositions submitted by students actively engaged in the study of music and all works are judged under pseudonyms. Applicants must be citizens of countries in the Western Hemisphere and must be either enrolled in accredited public, private or parochial secondary schools, in accredited colleges or conservatories of music, or engaged in private study of music with recognized and established teachers. Applicants must be under the age of 26. The postmark deadline is usually in early February and applications are available as of the preceding November. Questions may be addressed to classical@bmi.com.
The Jean Pratt Scholarship: The scholarship is given annually to a music student at Coffeyville Community College in Coffeyville, Kansas. This scholarship is by nomination only, no applications accepted.
The Joseph A. Carriere Scholarship: This scholarship is given to a worthy student each year chosen by the University of Tennessee Knoxville.
The Milton Adolphus Award: This award is given on an annual basis to a student at the LaGuardia High School of Music and Art in New York City for excellence in jazz improvisation. The award is by nomination only, no applications accepted.
The Harriette Schiff Roth Scholarship: The scholarship consists of an award to a female student at or graduate of Jackson Memorial High School, NJ, for the purpose of assisting in paying for voice lessons either under private tutelage or at a college, university or music school. The scholarship is by invitation only, no applications accepted.
EIN: 133249311

440
Board Family Foundation
7444 E. Florence Ave., Ste. C
Downey, CA 90240

Foundation type: Independent foundation
Limitations: Scholarships to students and awards to teachers of Downey High School, CA.
Financial data: Year ended 12/31/2004.
Assets, $1,093,065 (M); Expenditures, $58,060; Total giving, $54,400.
Fields of interest: Education.
Type of support: Scholarships—to individuals; Support to graduates or students of specific schools; Awards/prizes.
Application information: Contact foundation for current application deadline; Application by letter outlining financial need, evidence of good character, and reference.
EIN: 954262373

441
A. W. Bodine—Sunkist Memorial Foundation
c/o Sunkist Growers, Inc.
P.O. Box 7888
Van Nuys, CA 91409-7888
Contact: Claire H. Smith, Dir.
FAX: (703) 321-9319; URL: http://www.sunkist.com/about/bodine_scholarship.asp

Foundation type: Company-sponsored foundation
Limitations: Undergraduate scholarships to financially needy students who have a background in CA or AZ agriculture and at least a 3.0 GPA.
Publications: Annual report.
Financial data: Year ended 12/31/2003.
Assets, $456,712 (M); Expenditures, $30,073; Total giving, $30,000; Grants to individuals, 15 grants totaling $30,000 (high: $2,000, low: $2,000).
Fields of interest: Agriculture.
Type of support: Undergraduate support.
Application information:
Initial approach: Letter or telephone.
Deadline(s): Applications accepted Jan. 1 to Apr. 30
Additional information: Completion of formal application required, including most recent tax return, essay describing personal and agricultural background, transcripts, college board test scores, and two letters of reference.
Program description:
Scholarship Program: The applicant or someone in the applicant's immediate family must have derived the majority of his or her income from agriculture in CA or AZ. Scholarships are for undergraduate study only. They may be up to $2,000 per year, and are renewable for a total of four years. Recipients must take at least 12 credits per term and maintain at least a 2.7 GPA.
EIN: 953958439

442
Arthur C. Boehmer and Florence Schubert Boehmer Scholarship Fund
(also known as The Boehmer Scholarship Fund)
125 N. Pleasant Ave.
Lodi, CA 95240

Foundation type: Independent foundation
Limitations: Scholarships only to students who have graduated from high schools in the Lodi Unified School District, CA, and who plan to attend a CA college or university to prepare for a medical career. Participating schools are Lodi High School, Tokay High School, Liberty High School, Plaza Robles High School, Bear Creek High School, and Lodi Academy.

Financial data: Year ended 06/30/2004.
Assets, $726,176 (M); Expenditures, $32,630; Total giving, $17,925; Grants to individuals, 22 grants totaling $17,925 (high: $975, low: $475).
Type of support: Emergency funds; Support to graduates or students of specific schools.
Application information: Application form required.
Initial approach: Letter.
Deadline(s): June 15
Additional information: Recipients notified by early Aug. Scholarships are renewable.
EIN: 942683571

443
The Beau Bogan Foundation
c/o U.S. Trust
P.O. Box 15178
Washington, DC 20003

Foundation type: Independent foundation
Limitations: Scholarships to individuals from the Palm Beach, FL, and New York, NY, areas.
Financial data: Year ended 12/31/2004.
Assets, $94,619 (M); Expenditures, $13,257; Total giving, $12,000; Grants to individuals, totaling $12,000.
Type of support: Scholarships—to individuals.
Application information: Applications not accepted.
EIN: 650126326

444
Katherine Bogardus Trust
c/o John Warner Bank
301 S. Side Sq.
Clinton, IL 61727-0679
Contact: Katherine McNees, Trust Off., John Warner Bank

Foundation type: Independent foundation
Limitations: Educational loans to graduates of high schools in DeWitt County, IL, and to descendants of the first cousins of the creator of this trust.
Financial data: Year ended 12/31/2004.
Assets, $1,475,880 (M); Expenditures, $133,171; Total giving, $123,231; Loans to individuals, 36 loans totaling $123,231.
Type of support: Student loans—to individuals.
Application information: Application form required.
Deadline(s): Contact trust for current application deadline
Additional information: Application should also include high school transcript and proposed budget of expenses; Interviews required.
Program description:
Student Loan Program: Renewals of grants and loans are available provided recipients present evidence that they have a reasonable chance of success in pursuing their academic course and goals. In this respect, grant recipients are required to provide evidence, by transcript, that they have successfully completed their academic training for the preceding term or academic period. Grants or loans are made for one term or academic period only.
EIN: 376062479

445
Paul O. & Mary Boghossian Foundation
(formerly Paul O. & Mary Boghossian Memorial Trust)
c/o Bank of America, N.A.
P.O. Box 1802
Providence, RI 02901-1802
Application address: c/o Charitable Trust Svcs., Attn: Emma Greene, 100 Federal St., Boston, MA 02110, tel.: (617) 434-0329

Foundation type: Independent foundation
Limitations: Scholarships to RI residents. See program description for further limitations.
Financial data: Year ended 04/30/2005.
Assets, $1,798,566 (M); Expenditures, $117,540; Total giving, $98,750; Grants to individuals, 21 grants totaling $40,000 (high: $6,000, low: $750).
Fields of interest: Boys & girls clubs; YM/YWCAs & YM/YWHAs; Christian agencies & churches.
Type of support: Scholarships—to individuals.
Application information: Applications accepted. Application form required.
Deadline(s): None
Program description:
Scholarship Program: Scholarships are awarded to residents of Kent County, RI; members and former members of the Kent County branch of the YMCA or the Pawtucket Boys Club; members or descendants of members of Park Place Congregation Church in Pawtucket; and individuals who are Armenian by national origin or descent.
EIN: 056051815

446
E. Dante Bogni Trust
c/o TD Banknorth, N.A., Investment Mgmt. Group
P.O. Box 595
Williston, VT 05495
Application addresses: c/o Guidance Counselor, Spaulding High School, Barre, VT 05641, c/o Guidance Counselor, Montpelier High School, Montpelier, VT 05602

Foundation type: Independent foundation
Limitations: Scholarships to graduating seniors of Montpelier and Spaulding high schools, VT, for higher education.
Financial data: Year ended 12/31/2004.
Assets, $996,761 (M); Expenditures, $61,812; Total giving, $50,909; Grants to individuals, 4 grants totaling $50,909 (high: $21,572, low: $13,265).
Type of support: Support to graduates or students of specific schools; Undergraduate support.
Application information: Applications accepted.
Deadline(s): None
Additional information: Contact trust for current application guidelines.
EIN: 036044565

447
Violet R. and Nada V. Bohnett Memorial Foundation
(formerly Violet R. Bohnett Memorial Foundation)
7981 168th Ave. N.E., Ste. 220
Redmond, WA 98052 (425) 883-0208
Contact: James N. Bohnett, Dir.
FAX: (425) 883-2729; E-mail: jnbohnett@aol.com; URL: http://www.bohnettmemorial.org/

Foundation type: Independent foundation
Limitations: Scholarships to financially needy individuals, primarily in western WA, CA, AZ, CO,

and HI for the study of Christian ministry. Priority is given to students from western WA.
Publications: Informational brochure (including application guidelines); Newsletter.
Financial data: Year ended 12/31/2004. Assets, $0 (M); Expenditures, $210,953; Total giving, $80,141.
Fields of interest: Theological school/education; Christian agencies & churches.
Type of support: Scholarships—to individuals.
Application information: Applications accepted.
  Deadline(s): None.
  Additional information: Applications by letter of no more than one page.
EIN: 956225968

448
The Mary Bonham Educational Trust
P.O. Box 1007
Sulphur Springs, TX   75483-1007
(903) 885-1044
Contact: Carl D. Bryan, Tr.

Foundation type: Independent foundation
Limitations: Scholarships to undergraduate students in TX.
Financial data: Year ended 12/31/2004. Assets, $318,060 (M); Expenditures, $12,820; Total giving, $12,488; Grants to individuals, 4 grants totaling $12,488 (high: $6,666, low: $1,739).
Type of support: Undergraduate support.
Application information:
  Initial approach: Letter.
  Deadline(s): May 1
EIN: 756454600

449
The Corella & Bertram F. Bonner Foundation, Inc.
10 Mercer St.
Princeton, NJ   08540   (609) 924-6663
Contact: Wayne Meisel, Pres.
FAX: (609) 683-4626; E-mail: info@bonner.org;
URL: http://www.bonner.org

Foundation type: Independent foundation
Limitations: Community service scholarships to college students with high financial need and a commitment to service.
Publications: Informational brochure.
Financial data: Year ended 06/30/2005. Assets, $107,479,136 (M); Expenditures, $5,476,903; Total giving, $3,692,887; Grants to individuals, 4 grants totaling $12,000 (high: $3,000, low: $3,000).
Fields of interest: Community development, volunteer services; Voluntarism promotion; Economically disadvantaged.
Type of support: Scholarships—to individuals; Support to graduates or students of specific schools.
Application information: Applications accepted.
  Initial approach: Telephone.
  Deadline(s): Vary
  Additional information: Contact financial aid office for current application deadline/ guidelines.
Program description:
  Bonner Scholars Program: Offers financial support to academically qualified students from low-income backgrounds who want to attend college. In return, the scholars are expected to participate in community service activities. The

foundation works closely with 25 selected colleges and universities to identify deserving students.
EIN: 222316452

450
Bonner-Price Student Loan Fund Trust
c/o Wells Fargo Bank Texas, N.A., Trust Dept.
P.O. Box 10517
Lubbock, TX   79408

Foundation type: Independent foundation
Limitations: Loans to students of McMurry University, TX.
Financial data: Year ended 12/31/2004. Assets, $993,617 (M); Expenditures, $36,046; Total giving, $0; Loans to individuals, 14 loans totaling $35,900.
Type of support: Student loans—to individuals; Support to graduates or students of specific schools.
Application information: Applications accepted. Application form required.
  Deadline(s): Contact trust for current application deadline
  Applicants should submit the following:
    1) Transcripts
    2) Financial information
Program description:
  Student Loan Program: Loans may be given for up to $3,000 per year, but no more than $12,000 per student's school career. Upon graduation or termination from McMurry University, the recipient repays the principal and interest on the loan on a monthly installment basis. The interest rate shall be established by the Trust Investment Committee.
EIN: 726084752

451
Blancheola Bontrager Medical Scholarship Trust
c/o Wayne County National Bank
P.O. Box 94651
Cleveland, OH   44101-4651   (330) 264-7111
Contact: Stephen Kitchen, Sr. Trust Off., Wayne County National Bank

Foundation type: Independent foundation
Limitations: Scholarships to medical students who are residents of Wayne or Holmes counties, OH.
Financial data: Year ended 12/31/2004. Assets, $172,191 (M); Expenditures, $6,493; Total giving, $4,300; Grants to individuals, totaling $4,300.
Fields of interest: Medical school/education.
Type of support: Graduate support.
Application information:
  Deadline(s): May 1
  Additional information: Contact foundation for current application guidelines; Application by letter, outlining financial need, including three character references.
EIN: 347034110

452
Boogies Diner Foundation
(formerly The Weinglass Foundation, Inc.)
P.O. Box 11509
Aspen, CO   81612

Foundation type: Independent foundation
Limitations: Scholarships to individuals, primarily for athletics, in Aspen, CO and MD.
Financial data: Year ended 12/31/2004. Assets, $2,568,180 (M); Expenditures,

$568,622; Total giving, $528,163; Grants to individuals, totaling $168,330. Subtotal for scholarships—to individuals: 19 grants totaling $61,996 (high: $10,000, low: $500).
Fields of interest: Athletics/sports, training.
Type of support: Scholarships—to individuals.
Application information: Applications not accepted.
  Additional information: Contributes only to preselected individuals.
EIN: 521307628

453
James S. Boonshot Memorial Scholarship Trust
c/o GAFA
P.O. Box 810
Jasper, IN   47547-0810   (812) 482-1314
Contact: Bonnie Hochgesang

Foundation type: Independent foundation
Limitations: Scholarships for graduates of Pike Central High School, IN, for undergraduate and graduate education.
Financial data: Year ended 12/31/2003. Assets, $1,130,546 (M); Expenditures, $73,648; Total giving, $51,968; Grants to individuals, 75 grants totaling $51,968 (high: $1,555, low: $450).
Type of support: Support to graduates or students of specific schools; Graduate support; Undergraduate support.
Application information: Application form required.
  Deadline(s): Apr. 15
  Applicants should submit the following:
    1) SAT
    2) Photograph
    3) Class rank
  Additional information: Application should also include a brief letter to Pres. of Citizen's State Bank and three letters of character reference.
EIN: 356075332

454
Alex and Roxanna Booth Foundation, Inc.
2001 Sailfish Point Blvd., Apt. 316
Stuart, FL   34996
Application address for individuals: c/o Christa Weiss, 940 NW Fresco Way, Apt. 202, Jensen Beach, FL 34957
E-mail: seasideweiss@cs.com

Foundation type: Independent foundation
Limitations: Financial assistance to residents of the Port Saint Lucie, FL, area, who are studying nursing and other medically-related courses.
Financial data: Year ended 12/31/2004. Assets, $21,178 (M); Expenditures, $502,141; Total giving, $476,846; Grants to individuals, 36 grants totaling $74,831 (high: $8,506, low: $300).
Type of support: Grants to individuals.
Application information:
  Initial approach: Letter or e-mail.
  Deadline(s): Contact foundation for further application guidelines
  Additional information: Funds go towards books, supplies, exam fees, living expenses, and child care.
EIN: 134230772

455
The Bootstrap Foundation
700 Front St., Ste. 1904
San Diego, CA   92101
Contact: Andrew R. Cohen, Pres.

Foundation type: Independent foundation
Limitations: Scholarships to individuals residing in the San Diego, CA area.
Financial data: Year ended 12/31/2004. Assets, $4,955,662 (M); Expenditures, $106,129; Total giving, $97,305; Grants to individuals, 2 grants totaling $33,939.
Type of support: Undergraduate support.
Application information: Applications by letter accepted throughout the year.
EIN: 330492207

456

The Bootstraps Foundation of the Kiwanis Club of Nashville, Inc.
(formerly Bootstrap Awards, Inc.)
P.O. Box 290305
Nashville, TN 37229-0305 (615) 391-0123

Foundation type: Public charity
Limitations: Scholarships by nomination only to high school seniors in Davidson, Robertson, Rutherford, Cheatham, Sumner, Wilson and Williamson counties, TN, who have coped with difficulties, problems, or obstacles and are still successful students.
Financial data: Year ended 12/31/2004. Assets, $267,092 (M); Expenditures, $70,354; Total giving, $60,966; Grants to individuals, 17 grants totaling $60,966 (high: $4,830; low: $150).
Type of support: Awards/grants by nomination only; Undergraduate support.
Application information: Applications not accepted.
EIN: 621336039

457

The Borax Education Foundation
26877 Tourney Rd.
Valencia, CA 91355-1847

Foundation type: Company-sponsored foundation
Limitations: Scholarships to dependents of U.S. Borax, Inc. employees.
Financial data: Year ended 12/31/2004. Assets, $2,599 (M); Expenditures, $36,065; Total giving, $36,000; Grants to individuals, 9 grants totaling $36,000 (high: $4,000, low: $4,000).
Type of support: Employee-related scholarships.
Application information:
Initial approach: Letter or telephone.
Additional information: Contact foundation for current application deadline/guidelines.
EIN: 954497752

458

Walter & Cecile Borchert Scholarship Fund
c/o M&T Bank
1 M&T Plz., 8th Fl.
Buffalo, NY 14203 (716) 842-5506
Application addresses: c/o Fayetteville-Manlius High School, Attn.: Dir. of Career Ctr., 8201 E. Seneca Tpke., Manlius NY 13104; c/o Skaneateles High School, Attn.: Dir. of Career Ctr., 49 E. Elizabeth St., Skaneateles, NY 13152

Foundation type: Independent foundation
Limitations: Scholarships to graduating seniors of Fayetteville-Manlius and Skaneateles high schools, NY, for undergraduate education.
Financial data: Year ended 02/28/2005. Assets, $798,923 (M); Expenditures, $44,300;

Total giving, $35,000; Grants to individuals, totaling $35,000.
Type of support: Support to graduates or students of specific schools; Undergraduate support.
Application information: Application form required.
Deadline(s): Mar. 2
Applicants should submit the following:
1) Resume
2) FAFSA
3) Essay
Additional information: Application should also include financial aid information (as soon as this becomes available; students apply through high school Career Centers).
EIN: 166384392

459

Frank & Sallie Borden Foundation Trust
c/o Wachovia Bank, N.A.
100 N. Main St., 13th Fl.
Winston-Salem, NC 27150
Application address: c/o Wachovia Bank, N.A., Attn.: James A. Gallaher, P.O. Box 3099, Winston-Salem, NC 27150, tel.: (336) 732-6478

Foundation type: Independent foundation
Limitations: Scholarships and loans to residents of Goldsboro, NC, who are graduating seniors of Goldsboro High School, NC.
Financial data: Year ended 12/31/2004. Assets, $797,960 (M); Expenditures, $43,870; Total giving, $34,700.
Type of support: Support to graduates or students of specific schools; Undergraduate support.
Application information: Applications accepted. Application form required.
Deadline(s): None
Additional information: Applications available from principal of Goldsboro High School.
EIN: 566035962

460

Borders Group Foundation
100 Phoenix Dr.
Ann Arbor, MI 48108 (734) 477-1100
E-mail: bgf@bordersgroupinc.com; URL: http://www.bordersgroupinc.com/community/foundation.htm

Foundation type: Public charity
Limitations: Scholarships to employees and children of employees of Borders Group, Inc., for higher education.
Financial data: Year ended 12/31/2004. Assets, $2,878,749; Expenditures, $422,495; Total giving, $396,717; Grants to individuals, totaling $396,717. Subtotal for employee-related scholarships: 35 grants totaling $54,500 (high: $3,000, low: $1,000).
Type of support: Employee-related scholarships; Support to graduates or students of specific schools.
Application information: Application form required.
Deadline(s): Contact foundation for current application deadline
Program descriptions:
David H. Carpenter Scholarship Fund: This award aids Borders Group employees or their dependent children who are enrolled at or have been accepted to Michigan State University. Preference is given to those who demonstrate financial need. Each year, one student receives this $1,000 award.
Borders Group Foundation Scholarship Fund: Awards scholarships to regular full-time or part-time Borders Group employees with a minimum of two consecutive years of employment with the

company. Applicants must already be enrolled in an undergraduate or graduate course of study at an accredited school and have achieved a cumulative GPA of 3.0 or higher. Winners receive a $1,000 award. Up to 25 scholarships are awarded each year.
EIN: 383279018

461

Borton-Ryder Memorial Trust
c/o Bank of America, N.A.
P.O. Box 831041
Dallas, TX 75283-1041
Application address: Attn.: Jonathan Lantz, P.O. Box 830259, Dallas, TX, 75283-0259, tel.: 1-800-257-0332

Foundation type: Independent foundation
Limitations: Scholarships to students attending the Newman Memorial School of Nursing, Emporia, KS. A small number of grants for medical expenses are also given.
Financial data: Year ended 06/30/2004. Assets, $456,956 (M); Expenditures, $37,562; Total giving, $33,312; Grants to individuals, 12 grants totaling $33,312 (high: $2,776, low: $2,776).
Fields of interest: Nursing school/education; Health care.
Type of support: Support to graduates or students of specific schools; Graduate support; Undergraduate support.
Application information: Applications accepted.
Deadline(s): None
Additional information: Applications by letter.
EIN: 486110157

462

Willard & Lillian Bosaw Memorial Scholarship Fund
c/o First Financial Bank
300 High St.
Hamilton, OH 45011

Foundation type: Independent foundation
Limitations: Scholarships to high school graduates of Switzerland County, IN.
Financial data: Year ended 12/31/2004. Assets, $829,020 (M); Expenditures, $43,175; Total giving, $34,251; Grants to individuals, totaling $34,251.
Type of support: Scholarships—to individuals.
Application information: Applications accepted.
Deadline(s): None
Additional information: Applications by letter.
EIN: 351967183

463

Boscov-Berk-Tek, Inc., Scholarship Fund
c/o Kevin St. Cyr, Nexans, Inc.
132 White Oak Rd.
New Holland, PA 17557-9722 (717) 354-6200

Foundation type: Company-sponsored foundation
Limitations: Scholarships to children and spouses of employees and qualifying former employees of Berk-Tek, Inc., PA.
Financial data: Year ended 12/31/2004. Assets, $325,928 (M); Expenditures, $17,600; Total giving, $17,000; Grants to individuals, 3 grants totaling $17,000 (high: $6,000, low: $5,000).
Type of support: Employee-related scholarships.
Application information: Application form required.

Additional information: Contact fund for current application deadline.
EIN: 237763668

464
Boston Adult Literacy Fund

1 Milk St., 3rd Fl.
Boston, MA   02109   (617) 482-3336
Contact: Joanne Appleton Arnaud, Exec. Dir.
FAX: (617) 482-2554; E-mail: balf@balf.net;
URL: http://www.balf.net

Foundation type: Public charity
Limitations: Scholarships to individuals residing in the Boston, MA, area who have completed Adult Basic Education or English for Speakers of Other Languages. Some support also to individuals who mentor such students.
Publications: Application guidelines; Annual report; Grants list; Newsletter.
Financial data: Year ended 06/30/2003. Assets, $1,530,850 (M); Expenditures, $526,787; Total giving, $225,100; Grants to individuals, totaling $31,100.
Fields of interest: Adult education—literacy, basic skills & GED; Education, ESL programs.
Type of support: Technical education support; Undergraduate support.
Application information: Applications accepted. Application form required.
   Deadline(s): May 30
   Additional information: Completion of formal application required, including personal statement and two letters of recommendation.
Program description:
   Scholarships: Awards scholarships of up to $1,000 to students who have completed their basic education of English for Speakers of Other Languages (ESOL) studies in a Belmont, Boston, Brookline, Cambridge, Somerville, or Waterville program. Scholarships can be used for undergraduate or vocational education.
EIN: 042997446

465
Boston Post Office Employees Credit Union Charitable Foundation

175 McClellan Hwy., Ste. 10
East Boston, MA   02128

Foundation type: Independent foundation
Limitations: Scholarships to residents of MA for higher education.
Financial data: Year ended 12/31/2004. Assets, $5,761 (M); Expenditures, $22,325; Total giving, $13,087; Grants to individuals, 10 grants totaling $10,000 (high: $1,000, low: $1,000).
Type of support: Scholarships—to individuals.
Application information: Deadline varies; Application by letter.
EIN: 043553922

466
Boule Foundation

50 Hurt Plz.
Atlanta, GA   30303   (773) 779-8277
Contact: Robert V. Franklin, Chair.
Application address: 9 Alta Vista Dr., Yonkers, NY 10710, tel.: (914) 253-3011

Foundation type: Public charity
Limitations: Scholarships to individuals for undergraduate education.

Financial data: Year ended 12/31/2004. Assets, $8,187,614; Expenditures, $733,602; Total giving, $116,640.
Type of support: Undergraduate support.
Application information: Applications accepted.
   Initial approach: Proposal.
   Additional information: Contact foundation for current application guidelines.
EIN: 341304336

467
Chris and Katherine Boulos Foundation

c/o National Bank & Trust Co.
230 W. State St., MSC M-300
Sycamore, IL   60178   (815) 845-2125
Contact: Diane Florschuetz, V.P. and Secy., National Bank & Trust Co.

Foundation type: Independent foundation
Limitations: Scholarships to graduates of DeKalb High School, IL, and Sycamore High School, IL, for study at Kishwaukee College, in Malta, IL.
Financial data: Year ended 12/31/2004. Assets, $1,803,525 (M); Expenditures, $131,035; Total giving, $110,176.
Type of support: Support to graduates or students of specific schools; Undergraduate support.
Application information: Applications accepted. Application form required.
   Initial approach: Letter or telephone.
   Deadline(s): May 1
EIN: 363727751

468
Bound To Stay Bound Books Foundation

73 Central Park Plz. E.
Jacksonville, IL   62650-2070

Foundation type: Company-sponsored foundation
Limitations: Scholarships to students graduating with library degrees.
Financial data: Year ended 12/31/2002. Assets, $3,714,618 (M); Expenditures, $192,465; Total giving, $161,750; Grants to individuals, 4 grants totaling $24,000 (high: $6,000, low: $6,000).
Fields of interest: Libraries/library science.
Type of support: Undergraduate support.
Application information:
   Initial approach: Letter or telephone.
   Additional information: Contact foundation for current application deadline/guidelines.
EIN: 376227827

469
Bour Memorial Scholarship Fund

c/o Bank of America, N.A.
P.O. Box 831041
Dallas, TX   75283-1041
Contact: David P. Ross, Sr. V.P., Bank of America, N.A.
Application address: P.O. Box 419119, Kansas City, MO 64141-6119, tel.: (816) 979-7481

Foundation type: Independent foundation
Limitations: Scholarships to financially needy high school graduates residing in Lafayette County, MO, to attend any accredited MO college.
Financial data: Year ended 12/31/2004. Assets, $664,703 (M); Expenditures, $38,920; Total giving, $32,500; Grants to individuals, totaling $32,500.
Type of support: Undergraduate support.

Application information: Applications accepted. Application form required.
   Deadline(s): Apr. 1
   Additional information: Application forms available early each year from Bank of America, N.A., or school guidance counselors.
EIN: 436225461

470
Harriet Bouslog Labor Scholarship Fund

1149 Bethel St., Ste. 207
Honolulu, HI   96813
Contact: Stephen Sawyer, Pres.
Application address: 63 Merchant St., Honolulu, HI 96813

Foundation type: Independent foundation
Limitations: Scholarships to residents of HI. Preference is given to applicants whose parents are members of labor organizations.
Financial data: Year ended 11/30/2004. Assets, $521,320 (M); Expenditures, $21,000; Total giving, $21,000; Grants to individuals, 21 grants totaling $21,000 (high: $1,000, low: $1,000).
Fields of interest: Labor unions/organizations.
Type of support: Scholarships—to individuals.
Application information: Applications accepted.
   Deadline(s): None
   Additional information: Applications must include a brief resume of academic qualifications.
EIN: 990268061

471
The Mervin Bovaird Foundation

401 S. Boston Ave., Ste. 3300
Tulsa, OK   74103-4070   (918) 592-3300
Contact: R. Casey Cooper, Pres.

Foundation type: Independent foundation
Limitations: Scholarships to graduates of Tulsa public high schools and Tulsa Community College for attendance at The University of Tulsa.
Publications: Program policy statement.
Financial data: Year ended 12/31/2004. Assets, $46,552,502 (M); Expenditures, $2,459,778; Total giving, $2,036,020; Grants to individuals, 69 grants totaling $335,420.
Type of support: Support to graduates or students of specific schools; Undergraduate support.
Application information:
   Deadline(s): Aug. 1
   Additional information: Contact foundation for current application guidelines.
Program description:
   Scholarship Program: Students must maintain proper academic standing and demonstrate financial need.
EIN: 736102163

472
Ethel N. Bowen Foundation

c/o First Century Bank, N.A.
500 Federal St.
Bluefield, WV   24701   (304) 325-8181

Foundation type: Independent foundation
Limitations: Scholarships to students from the coal mining areas of southern WV and southwestern VA.
Financial data: Year ended 12/31/2004. Assets, $10,948,563 (M); Expenditures, $544,691; Total giving, $486,221; Grants to individuals, 477 grants totaling $276,808 (high: $3,595, low: $184).

Type of support: Scholarships—to individuals.
Application information:
   Deadline(s): Jan. 1 through Apr. 30
   Applicants should submit the following:
   1) Resume
   2) Transcripts
   Additional information: Applications by letter should also include a biographical outline; Interviews required.
EIN: 237010740

473

Bowen Foundation, Inc.
c/o Robert L. Bowen
8182 Dean Rd.
Indianapolis, IN 46240-2918

Foundation type: Independent foundation
Limitations: Scholarships to individuals who reside in Marion county, IN, and attend vocational/technical schools.
Financial data: Year ended 12/31/2004. Assets, $1,073,570 (M); Expenditures, $103,451; Total giving, $96,273.
Type of support: Scholarships—to individuals.
Application information: Applications not accepted.
EIN: 351906672

474

Virginia A. Bowmaker Scholarship Trust
(formerly V. A. Bowmaker Scholarship Trust)
c/o Bank of America, N.A.
P.O. Box 1802
Providence, RI 02940-1802
Application address: c/o Bank of America, N.A., 268 Genessee St., Utica, NY 13502

Foundation type: Independent foundation
Limitations: Scholarships to graduates of Utica, NY, public and parochial schools.
Financial data: Year ended 12/31/2004. Assets, $1,463,063 (M); Expenditures, $122,239; Total giving, $107,000; Grants to individuals, 34 grants totaling $107,000 (high: $18,500, low: $1,000).
Type of support: Support to graduates or students of specific schools; Undergraduate support.
Application information: Applications accepted. Application form required.
EIN: 161381376

475

Robert T. & Beatrice V. Bowman Scholarship Fund
c/o M&T Bank
21 E. Market St., M/C 402-130
York, PA 17401-1205
Application address: c/o Guidance Office, South Western High School, 200 Bowman Rd., Hanover, PA 17331

Foundation type: Independent foundation
Limitations: Scholarships to graduates of South Western High School, PA, who are residents of Penn, Manheim, or West Manheim townships, PA.
Financial data: Year ended 12/31/2004. Assets, $665,872 (M); Expenditures, $34,987; Total giving, $32,000; Grants to individuals, totaling $32,000.
Type of support: Support to graduates or students of specific schools; Undergraduate support.
Application information:
   Deadline(s): Apr. 1

Additional information: Contact fund for current application guidelines.
EIN: 237684863

476

Nelson P. Bowsher Foundation
c/o Wells Fargo Bank Nevada, N.A.
4707 S. 96th St.
Omaha, NE 68127
Application address: c/o Wells Fargo Bank Iowa, N.A., 112 Jefferson Blvd., South Bend, IN 46601

Foundation type: Independent foundation
Limitations: Scholarships to financially needy male graduates of Saint Joseph County, IN, high schools to attend colleges and universities.
Financial data: Year ended 12/31/2003. Assets, $608,229 (M); Expenditures, $37,825; Total giving, $30,000; Grants to individuals, totaling $30,000.
Fields of interest: Men; Young adults, male.
Type of support: Support to graduates or students of specific schools; Undergraduate support.
Application information: Applications accepted.
   Deadline(s): Mar. 31
   Additional information: Application by letter to local principal that describes the applicant's creativity, imagination, and originality in any field, including three letters of character reference, IQ rating, class rank, transcripts, GPA, attendance record, and school activity record; Applicants must file a FAF (Scholarship Program Code 0346) prior to Mar. 1.
Program description:
   Scholarship Program: Applicants must be U.S. citizens. Scholarships are renewable for a total of four years.
EIN: 356012966

477

The Box Project, Inc.
100 Business Center Dr., Ste. 26
Ormond Beach, FL 32174 (386) 677-8094
Contact: Cindy Shearer, Pres.
FAX: (386) 677-8617; E-mail: info@boxproject.org; Toll-free tel.: (800) 268-9928; URL: http://www.boxproject.org

Foundation type: Public charity
Limitations: Scholarships to individuals living in rural poverty for higher education, MS.
Publications: Application guidelines; Annual report; Financial statement; Newsletter (including application guidelines).
Financial data: Year ended 12/31/2004. Assets, $207,598 (M); Expenditures, $153,697.
Type of support: Graduate support; Technical education support; Undergraduate support.
Application information: Contact foundation for current application deadline/guidelines.
EIN: 060854618

478

Polly Boyd Scholarship Fund
c/o The Honors Course, Inc.
P.O. Box 23176
Chattanooga, TN 37422-3176
Contact: Joel W. Richardson, Jr., Tr.
Application address: 820 Broad St. Market Ctr., Ste. 400, Chattanooga, TN 37402-2524

Foundation type: Independent foundation

Limitations: Scholarships to employees, including caddies at The Honors Course, Inc., in TN.
Financial data: Year ended 12/31/2004. Assets, $655,839 (M); Expenditures, $55,586; Total giving, $54,966; Grants to individuals, totaling $54,966.
Fields of interest: Athletics/sports, golf.
Type of support: Employee-related scholarships.
Application information: Application form required.
   Additional information: Applications accepted throughout the year; Interviews required.
EIN: 626184352

479

Boye Scholarship Trust
c/o Wells Fargo Bank, N.A., Trust Tax Dept.
P.O. Box 63954
San Francisco, CA 94163

Foundation type: Independent foundation
Limitations: Scholarships to residents of Sacramento County, CA, with preference given to those pursuing agricultural studies.
Financial data: Year ended 06/30/2005. Assets, $798,073 (M); Expenditures, $72,541; Total giving, $59,470; Grant to an individual, 1 grant totaling $21,700.
Fields of interest: Agriculture.
Type of support: Graduate support; Undergraduate support.
Application information: Applications not accepted.
   Additional information: Candidates are identified by teachers and interviews are held to approve funding.
Program description:
   Scholarship Program: Recipients are guaranteed funding for four years, subject to maintenance of acceptable grades. Further funding may be approved for work above the undergraduate level.
EIN: 946067623

480

The Marvin Boyer Memorial Scholarship Fund
3737 Camino del Rio S., Ste. 109
San Diego, CA 92108
Contact: John C. Mowry, Tr.
Application address: P.O. Box 412, Patosi, MO 63664

Foundation type: Company-sponsored foundation
Limitations: Scholarships to attend the University of Missouri at Rolla or Columbia.
Financial data: Year ended 12/31/2004. Assets, $0 (M); Expenditures, $5,000; Total giving, $5,000; Grant to an individual, 1 grant totaling $5,000.
Type of support: Support to graduates or students of specific schools; Undergraduate support.
Application information:
   Deadline(s): Dec. 15 of applicant's senior year of high school
   Additional information: Application by letter.
EIN: 330245562

481

Bernard F. Boyle Memorial Scholarship Fund
c/o Mellon Bank, N.A.
P.O. Box 185
Pittsburgh, PA 15230-9877

Foundation type: Independent foundation

Limitations: Scholarships to students majoring in accounting. First priority is given to residents of Nesquehoning, PA. Second priority is given to residents of Wilkes-Barre, PA.
Financial data: Year ended 12/31/2004.
Assets, $1,087,350 (M); Expenditures, $46,219; Total giving, $38,568; Grants to individuals, totaling $38,568.
Fields of interest: Business school/education.
Type of support: Scholarships—to individuals.
Application information: Applications not accepted.
EIN: 236790683

482
Hazel Marie Boyle Scholarship Fund
c/o Citizens First National Bank
606 S. Main St.
Princeton, IL   61356
Application address: c/o Clifford Jones, Superintendent, Putnam County Schools, Granville, IL 61326, tel.: (815) 339-2238

Foundation type: Independent foundation
Limitations: Scholarships to graduates of Putnam County High School, IL.
Financial data: Year ended 12/31/2004.
Assets, $214,724 (M); Expenditures, $13,909; Total giving, $11,500; Grants to individuals, totaling $11,500.
Type of support: Support to graduates or students of specific schools; Undergraduate support.
Application information:
  Deadline(s): Feb. 1
  Additional information: Contact fund for current application guidelines.
EIN: 364091370

483
Margaret Hess Boyle Trust
1903 N. St.
P.O. Box 541
Belleville, KS   66935
Contact: Rodney R. Peake, Tr.

Foundation type: Independent foundation
Limitations: Scholarships to students who are residents of KS.
Financial data: Year ended 06/30/2004.
Assets, $913,467 (M); Expenditures, $44,555; Total giving, $23,800; Grants to individuals, 18 grants totaling $23,800 (high: $3,000, low: $500).
Type of support: Scholarships—to individuals.
Application information: Application form required.
  Deadline(s): Apr. 1
  Applicants should submit the following:
    1) Transcripts
    2) Letter(s) of recommendation
    3) Financial information
    4) Essay
EIN: 481216273

484
Boynton Gillespie Memorial Fund
P.O. Box 245
165 W. Broadway
Sparta, IL   62286   (618) 443-2148
Contact: John F. Clendenin, Tr.

Foundation type: Independent foundation
Limitations: Scholarships to students residing within a 30-mile radius of Sparta, IL.
Financial data: Year ended 12/31/2004.
Assets, $2,463,895 (M); Expenditures,

$145,937; Total giving, $118,000; Grants to individuals, 88 grants totaling $66,000 (high: $750, low: $750).
Fields of interest: Medical school/education.
Type of support: Scholarships—to individuals.
Application information: Application form required.
  Initial approach: Letter to request application.
  Deadline(s): May 1
EIN: 376028930

485
Boys & Girls Clubs of America
1230 W. Peachtree St. N.W.
Atlanta, GA   30309-3494   (404) 487-5700
Contact: Roxanne Spillett, Pres.
E-mail: info@bgca.org; *URL:* http://www.bgca.org

Foundation type: Public charity
Limitations: Scholarships to active Boys & Girls Club members who exhibit service to the Club and community, academic performance, and spiritual and family dedication.
Financial data: Year ended 12/31/2004.
Assets, $244,017,176 (M); Expenditures, $135,801,746; Total giving, $82,330,203.
Fields of interest: Boys & girls clubs.
Type of support: Undergraduate support.
Application information: Contact local Boys & Girls Club for current application deadline/guidelines.
Program description:
  Youth of the Year: Clubs select a Youth of the Year who receives a certificate and medallion then enters state competition. State winners receive a plaque and enter the regional competition. Regional winners receive a $5,000 scholarship and enter a national competition held in Washington, DC. The National Youth of the Year receives an additional $10,000 scholarship and is installed by the President of the United States.
EIN: 135562976

486
The Brackett Foundation
P.O. Box 8
Hamilton, NY   13346
Contact: Thomas E. Brackett, Pres.
FAX: (315) 824-4910; *E-mail:* tomb@twcny.rr.com; *URL:* http://brackett.colgate.edu/

Foundation type: Public charity
Limitations: Educational support to refugees, hill tribe people and displaced persons in Thailand and Mizoram State of India.
Publications: Annual report; Financial statement; Newsletter.
Financial data: Year ended 12/31/2003.
Assets, $165,000 (M); Expenditures, $93,741; Total giving, $78,216; Grants to individuals, 103 grants totaling $43,068.
Fields of interest: Elementary school/education; Secondary school/education; International relief; Immigrants/refugees.
Type of support: Foreign applicants; Undergraduate support; Grants for special needs.
Application information:
  Initial approach: Letter.
  Deadline(s): Mar. 1
  Additional information: Interviews required; Application forms distributed in Thailand and India in Jan.
Program description:
  Special Needs Grant: Support of projects directed by target population to provide elementary schools (where there are no schools) and boarding houses (to bring children from remote villages to areas

providing schools) and to supplement teacher's salaries.
EIN: 161523586

487
Bradford-Nye Trust
P.O. Box 359
Tyler, TX   75710-0359   (903) 597-8311
Application address: c/o First Baptist Church, Attn.: Dorothy Land, Scholarship Comm., 300 W. Ferguson St., P.O. Box 277, Tyler, TX 75710, tel.: (903) 597-4436

Foundation type: Independent foundation
Limitations: Scholarships to residents of Smith County, TX, for study at an educational institution sponsored and supported by the Baptist General Convention of TX, or the Southern Baptist Convention within the state of TX.
Financial data: Year ended 12/31/2004.
Assets, $171,650 (M); Expenditures, $7,931; Total giving, $7,000; Grants to individuals, totaling $7,000.
Fields of interest: Christian agencies & churches.
Type of support: Scholarships—to individuals.
Application information: Application form required.
  Deadline(s): Apr. 10.
  Applicants should submit the following:
    1) SAT
    2) ACT
    3) Transcripts
  Additional information: Application should include two letters of recommendation, one from a high school official and one from applicant's pastor, and a handwritten letter summarizing accomplishments, goals, and financial need.
Program description:
  Scholarship Program: Scholarships are awarded on the basis of scholastic merit and potential, citizenship, financial need, and proven Christian leadership.
EIN: 756329248

488
Bradish Memorial Scholarship Fund
(formerly Norman C. Bradish Trust)
P.O. Box 40200, MC FL9-100-10-19
Jacksonville, FL   32203-0200
Application Address: c/o Bank of America, N.A., 390 N. Orange Ave., Orlando, Fl 32801

Foundation type: Independent foundation
Limitations: Scholarships to male graduates of Decorah High School, IA.
Financial data: Year ended 06/30/2005.
Assets, $1,740,930 (M); Expenditures, $128,121; Total giving, $108,565; Grants to Individuals, 6 grants totaling $107,865 (high: $35,305, low: $200).
Fields of interest: Men.
Type of support: Support to graduates or students of specific schools.
Application information: Applications accepted. Application form required.
  Initial approach: Letter.
  Deadline(s): None
  Additional information: Contact foundation for current application deadline.
EIN: 596161559

489
The Bradley Foundation
1672 Main St., Ste. E-364
Ramona, CA 92065 (760) 789-2235
Contact: Barbara Teets

Foundation type: Independent foundation
Limitations: Scholarships to individuals residing in San Diego, CA.
Financial data: Year ended 12/31/2004. Assets, $6,536,659 (M); Expenditures, $545,641; Total giving, $458,735; Grants to individuals, 7 grants totaling $92,235 (high: $39,743, low: $913).
Type of support: Scholarships—to individuals.
Application information: Contact foundation for current application deadline; Application by letter.
EIN: 330771070

490
Don L. Bradley Scholarship Trust Fund
301 N. Burlington Blvd.
Burlington, WA 98233
Contact: Jim Clem, Tr.

Foundation type: Independent foundation
Limitations: Scholarships to graduates of Burlington-Edison High School, WA, who have participated in high school sports.
Financial data: Year ended 12/31/2004. Assets, $262,182 (M); Expenditures, $25,255; Total giving, $24,200; Grants to individuals, totaling $24,200.
Fields of interest: Athletics/sports, school programs.
Type of support: Support to graduates or students of specific schools; Undergraduate support.
Application information: Application form required.
Initial approach: Letter.
Deadline(s): Apr. 1
EIN: 916291543

491
Lorraine M. & Eugene P. Brady Memorial Scholarship Trust
P.O. Box 456
Lockport, NY 14095-0456
Contact: Paul Foster, Chair.
Application address: c/o Lockport High School, Lockport, NY 14094, tel.: (716) 439-6422

Foundation type: Operating foundation
Limitations: Scholarships to graduates of Lockport School District, NY, who do not qualify for financial aid but would otherwise be unable to attend the college of their choice.
Financial data: Year ended 12/31/2003. Assets, $452,738 (M); Expenditures, $60,390; Total giving, $42,208; Grants to individuals, 29 grants totaling $42,208 (high: $5,000, low: $250).
Type of support: Support to graduates or students of specific schools; Undergraduate support.
Application information: Applications accepted. Application form required.
Deadline(s): Nov. 30
Additional information: Contact foundation to request application.
EIN: 166411714

492
Herbert E. & Marion K. Bragg Foundation
c/o SunTrust Bank
P.O. Box 1908
Orlando, FL 32802-1908
Application address: c/o Carolyn McCoy, Trust Off., SunTrust Bank, 510 S. Jefferson St., Roanoke, VA 24011

Foundation type: Independent foundation
Limitations: Scholarships to students at colleges and universities in ME and VA. Preference is shown to those from ME.
Financial data: Year ended 10/31/2004. Assets, $1,482,753 (M); Expenditures, $73,241; Total giving, $45,000; Grants to individuals, totaling $45,000.
Type of support: Scholarships—to individuals.
Application information:
Deadline(s): June 15
Additional information: Applications are received only from colleges and universities through their financial aid departments.
EIN: 546313244

493
Bran, Inc.
10730 Pacific St., Ste. 218
Omaha, NE 68114 (402) 397-9785
Contact: Ray Weinberg, Pres.

Foundation type: Operating foundation
Limitations: Scholarships to undergraduate students attending universities or colleges in NE.
Financial data: Year ended 06/30/2004. Assets, $272,488 (M); Expenditures, $63,425; Total giving, $24,750; Grants to individuals, 24 grants totaling $24,750 (high: $1,500, low: $500).
Type of support: Undergraduate support.
Application information: Applications accepted.
Deadline(s): None
Additional information: Apply through the school's scholarship office.
EIN: 363449742

494
Branch County Community Foundation
2 W. Chicago St., Ste. E-1
Coldwater, MI 49036-1602 (517) 278-4517
Contact: Colleen Knight, Exec. Dir.
FAX: (517) 279-2319;
E-mail: info@brcofoundation.org; Additional E-mail: colleen@brcofoundation.org; URL: http://www.brcofoundation.org

Foundation type: Community foundation
Limitations: Scholarships to individuals residing in the Coldwater, MI, area for undergraduate education at colleges and universities in the U.S.
Publications: Application guidelines; Annual report; Financial statement; Informational brochure; Newsletter; Occasional report.
Financial data: Year ended 09/30/2004. Assets, $4,138,566 (M); Expenditures, $583,168; Total giving, $449,622.
Type of support: Undergraduate support.
Application information: Applications accepted. Application form required.
Deadline(s): Mar. 31
Applicants should submit the following:
1) Transcripts
2) Resume
3) GPA
4) Financial information
5) ACT

Additional information: Contact foundation for application form.
EIN: 383021071

495
John Brandt Memorial Foundation
831 66th Ave. N.E.
Minneapolis, MN 55432-4502 (800) 366-2477
Contact: Terry Anderson, Pres.

Foundation type: Independent foundation
Limitations: Scholarships to graduate students of dairy and animal science at upper Midwest institutions.
Financial data: Year ended 04/30/2005. Assets, $844,790 (M); Expenditures, $68,495; Total giving, $52,000; Grants to individuals, totaling $52,000.
Fields of interest: Agriculture.
Type of support: Graduate support.
Application information: Application form required.
Initial approach: Letter containing plan of study.
Deadline(s): Apr.
Additional information: Application should include transcripts and a personal history.
EIN: 416027683

496
Brandt Scholarship Fund
c/o Wells Fargo Bank, N.A.
P.O. Box 63954
San Francisco, CA 94163

Foundation type: Independent foundation
Limitations: Four-year scholarships to graduating seniors of high schools in the southern San Joaquin Valley, CA, area.
Financial data: Year ended 07/31/2005. Assets, $213,877 (M); Expenditures, $17,751; Total giving, $16,000; Grants to individuals, totaling $16,000.
Type of support: Undergraduate support.
Application information: Applications accepted. Application form required.
Deadline(s): Apr. 15
Additional information: Applications available from the area high school scholastic committees.
EIN: 956053020

497
Braswell Fund
P.O. Box 857
Madison, GA 30650
Contact: Hon. Michael F. Bracewell, Tr.
Application address: c/o Morgan County Courthouse, Madison, GA 30650

Foundation type: Independent foundation
Limitations: Scholarships to financially needy, deserving orphans who are residents of Morgan County, GA.
Financial data: Year ended 06/30/2005. Assets, $363,531 (M); Expenditures, $27,372; Total giving, $13,034; Grants to individuals, totaling $13,034.
Fields of interest: Residential/custodial care.
Type of support: Scholarships—to individuals.
Application information: Application form required.
Initial approach: Letter or telephone.
Deadline(s): Contact fund for current application deadline
Applicants should submit the following:
1) Financial information

2) Essay
Additional information: Application should also include a notarized signature.
Program description:
Scholarship Program: Applicants must have resided in Morgan County, GA, for at least one year prior to application, be deprived of one or both parents due to death, and plan to enroll in an accredited postsecondary institution on a full-time basis for three consecutive quarters or two consecutive semesters within the 13-month period starting June 1st. In addition, applicants must be high school graduates under the age of 26.
EIN: 586033308

498
Joel Braverman Foundation, Inc.
1609 Ave. J
Brooklyn, NY   11230-3711
Contact: Joel B. Wolowelsky M.D., Mgr.

Foundation type: Operating foundation
Limitations: Scholarships to graduates of the Yeshiva of Flatbush Joel Braverman High School in Brooklyn, NY, for one year of study at universities or yeshivas in Israel.
Financial data: Year ended 07/31/2004.
Assets, $330,424 (M); Expenditures, $10,325; Total giving, $8,658; Grants to individuals, totaling $8,658.
Fields of interest: Theological school/education; Jewish agencies & temples.
Type of support: Support to graduates or students of specific schools; Undergraduate support.
Application information: Applications accepted.
Deadline(s): None
Additional information: Application by letter demonstrating ability and need; Interviews required.
EIN: 116036594

499
Bread and Roses Community Fund
(formerly The People's Fund)
1500 Walnut St., Ste. 1305
Philadelphia, PA   19102   (215) 731-1107
Contact: Christie Balka, Exec. Dir.
FAX: (215) 731-0453;
E-mail: info@breadrosesfund.org; URL: http://www.breadrosesfund.org/

Foundation type: Public charity
Limitations: Scholarships awarded to gay men attending accredited colleges, graduate or professional schools anywhere or to men attending such schools within the Philadelphia region.
Publications: Application guidelines; Grants list; Informational brochure; Newsletter.
Financial data: Year ended 06/30/2004.
Assets, $1,713,130 (M); Expenditures, $841,212; Total giving, $276,534; Grants to individuals, 8 grants totaling $55,000 (high: $20,000, low: $5,000).
Fields of interest: LGBTQ.
Application information: Application form required. Application form available on the grantmaker's Web site.
Initial approach: Letter or telephone.
Deadline(s): Jan. 16
Program description:
LAX Scholarship Fund for Gay Men: Scholarship are awarded either in the sum of $20,000 (at least one per year) or several $5,000 scholarships are distributed annually to encourage gay men to obtain additional education, aspire to positions in which they contribute to society, be open about their sexual preference, and act as role models for other gay men with similar potential.
EIN: 232047297

500
Elizabeth Breckinridge Scholarship Fund
c/o JPMorgan Chase Bank, N.A.
P.O. Box 1308
Milwaukee, WI   53201

Foundation type: Independent foundation
Limitations: Scholarships to public high school seniors in Jefferson County, KY, who are interested in teaching.
Financial data: Year ended 05/31/2005.
Assets, $309,767 (M); Expenditures, $6,066; Total giving, $3,600.
Fields of interest: Teacher school/education.
Type of support: Support to graduates or students of specific schools; Undergraduate support.
Application information: Contact fund for current application deadline/guidelines.
Program description:
Scholarship Program: Recipients are chosen by each high school's Scholastic Awards Committee. Only one student per high school is chosen each year.
EIN: 616019485

501
Jonathan D. Brege Memorial Foundation
c/o JPMorgan Chase Bank, N.A.
P.O. Box 1308
Milwaukee, WI   53201-1308
Application address: c/o Donald R. Brege, 5224 Byron Rd., Corunna, MI 48817

Foundation type: Independent foundation
Limitations: Scholarships primarily to graduating students from Onaway High School and New Lothrop High School, MI.
Financial data: Year ended 09/30/2004.
Assets, $454,010 (M); Expenditures, $38,902; Total giving, $33,500.
Type of support: Support to graduates or students of specific schools; Undergraduate support.
Application information: Applications accepted.
Deadline(s): None
Additional information: Applications by letter.
EIN: 386477703

502
The J. P. Brenneman & M. H. Brenneman Fund
c/o Mellon Bank, N.A.
P.O. Box 185
Pittsburgh, PA   15230-9897
Contact: Robert O. Beers
Application address: c/o Blakey, Yost, Bupp & Schauman, 17 E. Market St., York, PA 17401

Foundation type: Independent foundation
Limitations: Scholarships to residents of York County, PA, for higher education at a university, college, or four-year technical school.
Financial data: Year ended 12/31/2004.
Assets, $1,464,302 (M); Expenditures, $62,236; Total giving, $60,375; Grants to individuals, totaling $60,375.
Fields of interest: Vocational education.
Type of support: Technical education support; Undergraduate support.
Application information: Application form required.
Deadline(s): May 1

Additional information: Contact the fund in Feb.
EIN: 237850463

503
The Hilda E. Bretzlaff Foundation, Inc.
1550 N. Milford Rd., Ste. 101
Milford, MI   48381-1058
Contact: Janelle M. Radtke, V.P.
E-mail: klindbeck@hebf.org; URL: http://www.hebf.org

Foundation type: Independent foundation
Limitations: Scholarships to U.S. citizens who are financially needy, moral, and conservative.
Financial data: Year ended 12/31/2004.
Assets, $25,381,022 (M); Expenditures, $1,439,104; Total giving, $974,937.
Fields of interest: Elementary/secondary education; College; University; Graduate/professional education.
Type of support: Precollege support; Undergraduate support.
Application information: Application form required.
Initial approach: Through high school, college, or university office.
Deadline(s): May 15
Applicants should submit the following:
1) Letter(s) of recommendation
2) Essay
3) ACT
4) SAT
5) Transcripts
Additional information: Application should also include copy of parents' and personal tax returns.
Program description:
Scholarship Program: Candidates must have at least a 2.0 cumulative GPA and maintain it during college. Scholarships are awarded to individuals who demonstrate a financial need; are creative, moral, ambitious and conservative; and will be a credit to America. The scholarships will help these individuals attend educational institutions that promote high educational, moral and conservative ideas. Interested students should apply through the university at which they are enrolled.
EIN: 382619845

504
Brevard Heart Foundation, Inc.
1901 S. Harbor City Blvd., Ste. 806
Melbourne, FL   32901   (321) 725-2292
Contact: Robert H. Rosequist, Pres.

Foundation type: Independent foundation
Limitations: Scholarships and loans for residents of Brevard County, FL, for nursing and medical education. See program description for specific requirements.
Financial data: Year ended 12/31/2003.
Assets, $465,864 (M); Expenditures, $29,470; Total giving, $16,900; Grants to individuals, 11 grants totaling $16,900 (high: $3,500, low: $750).
Fields of interest: Medical school/education; Nursing school/education.
Type of support: Graduate support; Undergraduate support.
Application information: Application form required.
Initial approach: By letter in person.
Deadline(s): May 15
Additional information: Interviews required for first-time applicants, recommended for reapplicants; photo required for file identification.

Program description:
Brevard Heart Scholarships: Nursing Scholarship Applicant Requirements:
- a certificate from the dean's office verifying that the applicant is regularly enrolled in a nursing program, with some indication of relative academic standing. In making the awards, the foundation will consider the level of students in the following order: (a) year four of a four-year degree program; (b) year three of a four-year degree program; (c) year two of a two-year degree program; or (d) advanced nursing degree. Awards are based on academic and professional qualifications
- a recent photograph of first-time applicants
- a short essay concerning needs, aspirations, and whether applicant intends to repay this achievement award.

Medical Scholarship Applicant Requirements:
- a certificate from the dean's office verifying that the applicant is regularly in a college of medicine, with some indication of relative academic standing. In making awards, the foundation will consider students in the following order: (a) rising medical school sophomore; (b) rising medical school junior; (c) rising medical school senior; or (d) rising medical school first-year student. Awards will be based primarily on academic and professional qualifications
- if applicant received an achievement award in a previous year, a short letter telling how the money was spent is required. Priority will be given to students who have received a previous scholarship. Financial need will play a secondary role
- a recent photograph for first-time applicants
- a short essay concerning needs, aspirations, and whether the applicant intends to repay this achievement award
- first-time applicants must arrange an interview. Those reapplying for an award are recommended to do so as well. The monetary amount and number of awards vary, depending on available funds.

EIN: 596150538

505

Robert N. Brewer Family Foundation

115 W. Jefferson St., Ste. 200
Bloomington, IL 61702-3217
Application address: 2 N. Park Ave., Herrin, IL 62948, tel.: (618) 942-8000

Foundation type: Independent foundation
Limitations: Scholarships to graduates of Marion and Herrin high schools, IL.
Financial data: Year ended 12/31/2003. Assets, $12,129,732 (M); Expenditures, $326,610; Total giving, $225,725; Grants to individuals, 84 grants totaling $225,375 (high: $4,250, low: $1,250).
Type of support: Support to graduates or students of specific schools; Undergraduate support.
Application information: Application form required.
  Deadline(s): Contact foundation for current application deadline.
Program description:
  Scholarship Program: Recipients must have a cumulative GPA of C or better. Preference is given to students with financial need.
EIN: 364129119

506

Brewer Foundation, Inc.

P.O. Box 7906
Rocky Mount, NC   27804
Contact: Joseph B. Brewer, Jr., Pres.

Foundation type: Company-sponsored foundation
Limitations: Scholarships for higher education to residents of NC.
Financial data: Year ended 08/31/2002. Assets, $949,309 (M); Expenditures, $151,343; Total giving, $120,927; Grants to individuals, 10 grants totaling $12,627 (high: $5,300, low: $85).
Type of support: Undergraduate support.
Application information: Contact foundation for current application deadline/guidelines.
EIN: 560941242

507

Brewster Education Foundation, Inc.

P.O. Box 320
Brewster, NY   10509-0320   (845) 279-5051
Contact: Nicholas Simonelli, Pres.
URL: http://www.bef.org

Foundation type: Public charity
Limitations: Scholarships to graduating students attending high school in the Brewster Central School District, NY.
Publications: Application guidelines; Financial statement; Informational brochure.
Financial data: Year ended 06/30/2005. Assets, $460,897 (M); Expenditures, $72,296; Total giving, $65,686; Grants to individuals, 44 grants totaling $39,756 (high: $2,500, low: $500).
Type of support: Support to graduates or students of specific schools; Undergraduate support.
Application information: Application form required.
  Initial approach: Letter.
  Deadline(s): Contact foundation for current application deadline
EIN: 222553348

508

Claude Brey and Ina L. Brey Memorial Endowment Fund

c/o U.S. Bank, N.A.
P.O. Box 387
St. Louis, MO   63166-0387
Application address: c/o Pat West, R.R. 2, Box 23, Mound City, KS 66056

Foundation type: Independent foundation
Limitations: Scholarships to fourth-degree Kansas Grange members to attend colleges and accredited trade schools.
Financial data: Year ended 04/30/2005. Assets, $142,895 (M); Expenditures, $8,826; Total giving, $2,000; Grants to individuals, totaling $2,000.
Fields of interest: Vocational education; Agriculture, farm bureaus/granges.
Type of support: Technical education support; Undergraduate support.
Application information: Application form required.
  Deadline(s): Apr. 15
  Additional information: Contact local Grange chapter for application forms; Interviews required.
EIN: 486187137

509

Helen Brice Scholarship Fund

c/o Mellon Bank, N.A.
P.O. Box 185
Pittsburgh, PA   15230-0185
Contact: Laurie Moritz, Trust Off., Mellon Financial Corp.
Application address: c/o 1 Mellon Bank Ctr., Ste. 3825, 500 Grant St., Pittsburgh, PA 15258

Foundation type: Independent foundation
Limitations: Undergraduate scholarships by nomination only to students of Uniontown High School, PA.
Financial data: Year ended 12/31/2004. Assets, $246,294 (M); Expenditures, $10,311; Total giving, $8,000; Grants to individuals, totaling $8,000.
Type of support: Awards/grants by nomination only; Undergraduate support.
Application information: Contact high school guidance counselor for current nomination deadline/guidelines.
EIN: 256119807

510

Bridgebuilder Scholarship Fund

c/o Stonewall Jackson High School
150 Stonewall Ln.
Quicksburg, VA   22847-1429   (540) 477-2732
Contact: William L. Pirtle, Chair.

Foundation type: Operating foundation
Limitations: Scholarships only to graduating seniors at Stonewall Jackson High School, Mt. Jackson, VA.
Financial data: Year ended 11/30/2003. Assets, $138,267 (M); Expenditures, $4,965; Total giving, $4,375; Grants to individuals, 4 grants totaling $4,375 (high: $1,250, low: $625).
Type of support: Support to graduates or students of specific schools; Undergraduate support.
Application information: Application form required.
  Deadline(s): Nov. 1
  Applicants should submit the following:
    1) SAT
    2) Class rank
    3) GPA
    4) Financial information
  Additional information: Application should also include work history, and personal statement.
Program description:
  Scholarship Program: Scholarships are awarded on the basis of academic ability, leadership and good citizenship, desire for higher education, financial need, and likelihood applicant will live in the area upon graduation.
EIN: 521262074

511

The Greater Bridgeport Area Foundation, Inc.

211 State St., 3rd Fl.
Bridgeport, CT   06604   (203) 334-7511
Contact: Cindy Kissin, C.E.O. and Pres.
FAX: (203) 333-4652;
E-mail: info@gbafoundation.org; URL: http://www.gbafoundation.org

Foundation type: Community foundation
Limitations: Scholarships to students of the greater Bridgeport area, which includes Easton, Fairfield, Milford, Monroe, Shelton, Stratford, Trumbull and Westport, CT, for higher education.
Publications: Application guidelines; Annual report; Financial statement.

Financial data: Year ended 12/31/2004. Assets, $38,693,418 (M); Expenditures, $2,091,653; Total giving, $1,287,477; Grants to individuals, 133 grants totaling $104,114 (high: $7,500, low: $195, average grant: $1,234).
Type of support: Awards/prizes; Graduate support; Technical education support; Precollege support; Undergraduate support.
Application information: Application form required.
  Deadline(s): Varies
  Additional information: Contact foundation for current application deadline.
Program description:
  The Greater Bridgeport Area Foundation Scholarship Program: Scholarships to students and grants to area agencies in five program areas including the arts, community and economic development, education, the environment, and health/human services.
EIN: 066103832

512
Alton Bridges Memorial Scholarship
c/o Carroll Tedder Bass
324 Boswell Rd.
Kenly, NC   27542   (919) 284-4397

Foundation type: Independent foundation
Limitations: Scholarships to high school graduates in Wilson County, NC, for higher education.
Financial data: Year ended 12/31/2004. Assets, $281,855 (M); Expenditures, $10,951; Total giving, $10,000; Grants to individuals, totaling $10,000.
Type of support: Undergraduate support.
Application information: Applications accepted.
  Deadline(s): None
  Additional information: Applications by letter.
EIN: 566486563

513
Briggs & Stratton Corporation Foundation, Inc.
12301 W. Wirth St.
Wauwatosa, WI   53222   (414) 259-5496
Contact: Robert F. Heath, Secy.-Treas.
Application address: P.O. Box 702, Milwaukee, WI 5320; Additional tel.: (414) 259-5333

Foundation type: Company-sponsored foundation
Limitations: Scholarships only to children of employees of the Briggs & Stratton Corporation, who have been employed full-time by the company for at least two years as of the Sept. 1 preceding the deadline.
Financial data: Year ended 11/30/2004. Assets, $25,002,808 (M); Expenditures, $2,026,172; Total giving, $2,016,400; Grants to individuals, 33 grants totaling $33,500.
Type of support: Employee-related scholarships.
Application information:
  Deadline(s): Jan. 31
  Additional information: Interviews required.
EIN: 396040377

514
Bright Star Foundation, Inc.
c/o Shale D. Stiller
6225 Smith Ave.
Baltimore, MD   21209-3600
Contact: Kenneth L. Greif, Pres.
Application address: 3707 Greenway, Baltimore, MD 21218, tel.: (410) 235-2287

Foundation type: Independent foundation
Limitations: Scholarships to residents of Baltimore, MD, for secondary and postsecondary education.
Financial data: Year ended 12/31/2004. Assets, $7,005 (M); Expenditures, $6,940; Total giving, $6,940; Grants to individuals, totaling $6,940.
Type of support: Precollege support; Undergraduate support.
Application information: Unsolicited applications not considered or acknowledged.
EIN: 237083731

515
Brighten Your Future
188 W. Main St.
Logan, OH   43138
Contact: Larry Kienzle, Tr.
Application address: 30436 Hideaway Hills Rd., Logan, OH 43138, tel.: (740) 385-8561

Foundation type: Independent foundation
Limitations: Scholarships to students of Logan High School, OH, who qualify under the FAF form.
Financial data: Year ended 06/30/2004. Assets, $1,242,307 (M); Expenditures, $81,268; Total giving, $53,657; Grants to individuals, totaling $53,657.
Type of support: Support to graduates or students of specific schools; Undergraduate support.
Application information:
  Deadline(s): June 15
  Additional information: Application should include FAF..
EIN: 311255015

516
Lou and Lucienne Brightman Scholarship Foundation
c/o Eastern Bank & Trust Co.
605 Broadway, Ste. LF42
Saugus, MA   01906   (781) 581-4274
Contact: Robert M. Wallask, V.P., Eastern Bank & Trust Co.

Foundation type: Independent foundation
Limitations: Scholarships to graduating high school seniors who are residents of MA and will attend an accredited college or university.
Financial data: Year ended 07/31/2005. Assets, $435,111 (M); Expenditures, $20,874; Total giving, $15,000; Grants to individuals, totaling $15,000.
Type of support: Undergraduate support.
Application information: Application form required.
  Deadline(s): June 1
  Additional information: Application should include transcripts; Scholarships are renewable.
EIN: 046500798

517
A. T. Brightwell School, Inc.
254 Oakland Ave.
Athens, GA   30606-4340   (706) 543-6450
Contact: Harold Darden, Exec. Secy.

Foundation type: Independent foundation
Limitations: Scholarships to unmarried or divorced (proof of divorce necessary) students under 25 years of age who have lived within the strictly defined Maxeys, GA, area for at least two years prior to effective date of scholarship. Parents of student

must live and remain in Maxeys area for the duration of the scholarship.
Publications: Annual report; Informational brochure.
Financial data: Year ended 06/30/2004. Assets, $57,542 (M); Expenditures, $66,547; Total giving, $52,375; Grants to individuals, 7 grants totaling $52,375 (high: $9,804, low: $1,776).
Fields of interest: Vocational education; Business school/education.
Type of support: Technical education support; Undergraduate support.
Application information: Applications accepted. Application form required.
  Initial approach: Letter.
  Deadline(s): None
  Additional information: Interviews required.
Program description:
  Scholarship Program: Scholarships may be used to attend any college, university, vocational, technical, or business school. Recipients must enter college within 18 months after graduation from high school or receipt of G.E.D.
EIN: 586066256

518
Marion Brill Scholarship Foundation, Inc.
P.O. Box 480
Ilion, NY   13357-0480   (315) 895-7771
Application address: c/o Guidance Office, Ilion Central School District High School, P.O. Box 480, Ilion, NY 13357

Foundation type: Operating foundation
Limitations: Scholarships to residents of Ilion, NY, who are also graduates of Ilion High School, NY.
Financial data: Year ended 06/30/2004. Assets, $345,485 (M); Expenditures, $37,324; Total giving, $30,000; Grants to individuals, 25 grants totaling $30,000 (high: $2,000, low: $500).
Type of support: Support to graduates or students of specific schools.
Application information: Application form required.
  Deadline(s): Apr. 15
  Additional information: Application should include financial aid forms, transcripts, and a college letter of acceptance for high school seniors.
EIN: 222373170

519
E. Brink Trust Scholarship Fund
c/o Alliance Bank, N.A.
241 Main St., Ste. 200
Buffalo, NY   14203

Foundation type: Independent foundation
Limitations: Scholarships to male graduates of Union-Endicott High School, NY, for higher education.
Financial data: Year ended 12/31/2004. Assets, $923,882 (M); Expenditures, $47,374; Total giving, $39,900; Grants to individuals, 29 grants totaling $39,900 (high: $1,500, low: $400).
Fields of interest: Men.
Type of support: Support to graduates or students of specific schools; Undergraduate support.
Application information: Applications not accepted.
EIN: 166076060

520
Dorothea Brinker Scholarship Fund
c/o Wells Fargo Bank Nevada, N.A.
P.O. Box 95021
Henderson, NV 89009
Application address: c/o Student Financial Svcs., University of Nevada, Las Vegas, 4505 S. Maryland Pkwy., Las Vegas, NV 89154, tel.: (702) 739-3424

Foundation type: Independent foundation
Limitations: Scholarships to residents of Clark County, GA, to attend the University of Las Vegas.
Financial data: Year ended 12/31/2004.
Assets, $294,325 (M); Expenditures, $15,087; Total giving, $11,430; Grants to individuals, totaling $11,430.
Type of support: Support to graduates or students of specific schools; Undergraduate support.
Application information: Applications accepted. Application form required.
Deadline(s): Mar. 15
Additional information: Application should include transcripts.
EIN: 886005302

521
Brisley Scholarship Loan Fund
(formerly Ella Frances Brisley & Noma Brisley Phillips Scholarship Loan Fund)
c/o Bank of America, N.A.
P.O. Box 831041
Dallas, TX 75283-1041
Application address: c/o Bank of America, N.A., Attn.: James J. Mueth, P.O. Box 419119, Kansas City, MO 64141-6119, tel.: (816) 979-7405

Foundation type: Independent foundation
Limitations: Scholarships to financially needy, deserving medical and nursing students attending accredited schools, and to financially needy students attending Methodist colleges. Preference is shown to American-born residents of KS and MO.
Financial data: Year ended 02/28/2005.
Assets, $3,111,767 (M); Expenditures, $168,174; Total giving, $132,650; Grants to individuals, 3 grants totaling $7,500 (high: $2,500, low: $2,500).
Fields of interest: Medical school/education; Nursing school/education; Protestant agencies & churches.
Type of support: Awards/grants by nomination only; Graduate support.
Application information: Application form required.
Additional information: Applications available from school.
Program description:
Scholarship Program: Application forms must be filed with the financial aid office or committee at each school. The financial aid office or committee will be responsible for providing a list of recommended applicants to the trustee of the fund with whom the final decision of selection rests.
EIN: 431343600

522
Bristol Bay Native Corp. Education Foundation
800 Cordova St., Ste. 200
Anchorage, AK 99501-6299 (907) 278-3602
Contact: Andria Agli

Foundation type: Company-sponsored foundation
Limitations: Scholarships to shareholders of Bristol Bay Native Corporation, located in AK.
Financial data: Year ended 12/31/2004.
Assets, $1,823,469 (M); Expenditures, $95,086; Total giving, $81,818; Grants to individuals, 129 grants totaling $81,818 (high: $2,975, low: $75).
Type of support: Scholarships—to individuals.
Application information: Application form required.
Deadline(s): June 1 and Sept. 1
EIN: 920141709

523
Bristol Yale Scholarship Fund, Inc.
96 Bradley St.
Bristol, CT 06010-5105 (860) 589-4845
Contact: K. David Graham, Treas.

Foundation type: Independent foundation
Limitations: Scholarships to graduates of Bristol and Terryville, CT, area high schools to attend Yale University.
Financial data: Year ended 12/31/2004.
Assets, $617,420 (M); Expenditures, $34,488; Total giving, $33,500; Grants to individuals, totaling $33,500.
Type of support: Support to graduates or students of specific schools; Undergraduate support.
Application information:
Deadline(s): May 20
Additional information: Contact fund for current application guidelines.
Program description:
Scholarship Program: Scholarships are renewable. Generally, one or two new recipients are chosen each year.
EIN: 066023679

524
Mervin Britton Memorial Scholarship Fund
c/o Security National Bank
40 S. Limestone St.
Springfield, OH 45502
Application address: c/o Clark County Board of Education, 1115 N. Limestone St., Springfield, OH 45503, tel.: (937) 325-7671

Foundation type: Independent foundation
Limitations: Scholarships for students from Clark County, OH, high schools, excluding city high schools, who are attending or will attend a college or university for the purpose of receiving formal training in the field of education.
Financial data: Year ended 12/31/2004.
Assets, $1,179,432 (M); Expenditures, $55,923; Total giving, $43,550; Grants to individuals, totaling $43,550. Subtotal for scholarships—to individuals: 21 grants totaling $50,000.
Fields of interest: Teacher school/education.
Type of support: Support to graduates or students of specific schools.
Application information: Contact Office of Education for application deadline; Completion of formal application required, including essay discussing why applicant desires to be an educator, photograph and two letters of recommendation from secondary school teachers.
EIN: 316511170

525
The Broadbent Family Foundation
(formerly The Broadbent Foundation)
c/o John H. Broadbent, Jr.
1 Chestnut Hill Dr.
Mohnton, PA 19540

Foundation type: Independent foundation

Limitations: Scholarships to students at Governor Mifflin High School, Shillington, PA, for higher education.
Financial data: Year ended 06/30/2005.
Assets, $1,163,712 (M); Expenditures, $48,525; Total giving, $45,783; Grants to individuals, 9 grants totaling $45,783 (high: $6,250, low: $158).
Type of support: Support to graduates or students of specific schools; Undergraduate support.
Application information:
Initial approach: Letter.
Deadline(s): Contact foundation for current application deadline/guidelines
Additional information: Completion of formal application required by high school principal, guidance counselor, or faculty advisor, and verification from school that applicant is currently in good standing; Interviews required.
EIN: 232703271

526
Broadcast Education Association
1771 N St., N.W.
Washington, DC 20036-2891 (202) 429-3935
Contact: For Scholarships: Peter B. Orlick Ph.D.
Application address for individuals: 344 Moore Hall, Central Michigan University, Mt. Pleasant, MI, 48859; tel.: (989) 774-7279 on Mon., Wed., Fri.; Additional tel.: (888) 380-7222; Additional URL: http://www.nab.org
E-mail: LNielsen@nab.org; URL: http://www.nab.org
http://www.beaweb.org

Foundation type: Public charity
Limitations: Scholarships to students planning careers in broadcasting.
Publications: Application guidelines.
Financial data: Year ended 12/31/2003.
Assets, $999,800; Expenditures, $505,628; Total giving, $50,750; Grants to individuals, 19 grants totaling $50,750 (high: $5,000, low: $1,000).
Fields of interest: Media/communications; Television; Radio.
Type of support: Graduate support; Undergraduate support.
Application information: Application form required. Application form available on the grantmaker's Web site.
Deadline(s): Sept. 15
Additional information: Application should include four typed copies of application, waiver sheet, three letters of reference, college transcripts, and NAB station or employment internship affidavit; Applications by fax or e-mail not accepted.
Program description:
Broadcast Scholarships: The foundation administers the following scholarships:
· Helen J. Sioussat/Fay Wells: Awards two scholarships of $1,250 each for study in any area of broadcasting
· Andrew H. Economos: Awards one $3,500 scholarship for study in radio
· Philo T. Farnsworth: Awards one $1,500 scholarship to a graduate or undergraduate student
· Harold E. Fellows: Awards four scholarships of $1,250 each for study in any area of broadcasting
· Joseph and Marcia Silbergleid: Awards one $1,500 scholarship for graduate study in digital television
· Walter S. Patterson: Awards two $1,250 scholarships for a career in radio

- Alexander M. Tanger: Awards one $5,000 scholarship for study in any area of broadcasting
- Two Year/Community College BEA Award: Awards two $1,500 scholarships for study at a BEA two-year/community college
- Abe Voron Award: One $5,000 scholarship for study toward a career in radio
- Vincent T. Wasilewski Award: $2,500 for graduate study in any area of broadcasting.

EIN: 526057288

527
Mary E. Brock Trust
c/o Citizens Bank of NH
870 Westminster St.
Providence, RI 02903

Foundation type: Independent foundation
Limitations: Scholarships to individuals, primarily in N.H.
Financial data: Year ended 12/31/2004. Assets, $588,287 (M); Expenditures, $38,627; Total giving, $30,152; Grants to individuals, totaling $30,152.
Type of support: Undergraduate support.
Application information: Unsolicited requests for funds not considered or acknowledged.
EIN: 026030934

528
Leo J. Brockman Trust
c/o Bank of America, N.A.
P.O. Box 34345, CSC-9
Seattle, WA 98124-1345
Application address: c/o Financial Aid Advisor, Gonzaga Univ., Spokane, WA 99207

Foundation type: Independent foundation
Limitations: Loans to financially needy students of Gonzaga University, WA.
Financial data: Year ended 12/31/2003. Assets, $422,854 (M); Expenditures, $27,496; Total giving, $26,000; Loans to individuals, 26 loans totaling $26,000.
Type of support: Student loans—to individuals; Support to graduates or students of specific schools.
Application information: Applications accepted. Application form required.
Deadline(s): None
EIN: 916024372

529
Brockton Rotary Charitable & Educational Fund, Inc.
195 Westgate Dr.
P.O. Box 537
Brockton, MA 02303
Contact: Stanley T. Belastock, Pres.

Foundation type: Public charity
Limitations: Scholarships to needy individuals in the Brockton, MA, area.
Financial data: Year ended 06/30/2003. Assets, $276,256 (M); Expenditures, $10,050; Total giving, $10,000; Grants to individuals, totaling $10,000.
Type of support: Scholarships—to individuals.
Application information:
Deadline(s): Apr. 1
Additional information: Contact foundation for current application guidelines.
EIN: 046071645

530
Dan Broida/Sigma-Aldrich Scholarship Fund, Inc.
3050 Spruce St.
St. Louis, MO 63103-2530

Foundation type: Operating foundation
Limitations: Scholarships for the study of science to children of employees of Sigma-Aldrich Corp. or its subsidiaries in MO.
Financial data: Year ended 03/31/2005. Assets, $817,203 (M); Expenditures, $75,265; Total giving, $70,000; Grants to individuals, 14 grants totaling $70,000 (high: $5,000, low: $5,000).
Fields of interest: Science.
Type of support: Employee-related scholarships.
Application information: Application form required.
Deadline(s): Apr. 10
Additional information: Children of officers and directors of Sigma-Aldrich Corp. are ineligible.
EIN: 431253095

531
Bromley Trust and Educational Fund
c/o Wells Fargo Bank Indiana, N.A.
841 N. Cass St.
Wabash, IN 46992 (260) 563-6378
Contact: William C. Coleman, Trust Off., Wells Fargo Bank Indiana, N.A.

Foundation type: Independent foundation
Limitations: Scholarships to graduates of Wabash, IN, high schools for further education in a science or postsecondary school.
Financial data: Year ended 08/31/2002. Assets, $208,535 (M); Expenditures, $13,073; Total giving, $7,798; Grants to individuals, 35 grants totaling $7,798 (high: $250, low: $123).
Fields of interest: Science.
Type of support: Support to graduates or students of specific schools; Undergraduate support.
Application information:
Deadline(s): Mar. 15
Additional information: Completion of formal application required, including high school transcript, proof of enrollment in post-secondary school, financial statements, and references.
EIN: 316236153

532
R. Carlyle Bronson Scholarship Foundation, Inc.
2375 Sue Dr.
Kissimmee, FL 34741 (407) 847-4169
Contact: Betty Gilbert, Dir.

Foundation type: Independent foundation
Limitations: Scholarships to residents of Osceola County, FL.
Financial data: Year ended 12/31/2004. Assets, $443,947 (M); Expenditures, $23,017; Total giving, $22,000; Grants to individuals, totaling $22,000.
Type of support: Scholarships—to individuals.
Application information: Application form required.
Deadline(s): Prior to beginning of school year
EIN: 593392431

533
Sunshine Brooks Foundation
4649 Morena Blvd.
San Diego, CA 92117 (858) 812-1392
Contact: Michael Kearney, Dir.
E-mail: mkearney@costco.com; URL: http://www.sunshinebrooks.com

Foundation type: Independent foundation
Limitations: Scholarships to CA employees and children of employees of Price Costco, or any of its direct or indirect wholly-owned subsidiaries. Scholarships are renewable.
Financial data: Year ended 06/30/2004. Assets, $1,826,454 (M); Expenditures, $162,559; Total giving, $154,000; Grants to individuals, 40 grants totaling $154,000 (high: $15,000, low: $500).
Type of support: Employee-related scholarships.
Application information:
Deadline(s): May 1
Additional information: Completion of formal application required.
EIN: 330190411

534
Verl I. Brooks Scholarship Foundation
P.O. Box 9
New Windsor, IL 61465-0009
Contact: Arnold R. Bonnett, Tr.

Foundation type: Independent foundation
Limitations: Scholarships to high school graduates who were residents of Rivoli Township, Mercer County, IL, for at least two years prior to graduation.
Financial data: Year ended 12/31/2004. Assets, $2,186,310 (M); Expenditures, $70,707; Total giving, $45,875; Grants to individuals, 29 grants totaling $45,875 (high: $4,550, low: $700).
Type of support: Scholarships—to individuals.
Application information:
Deadline(s): May 1
Additional information: Unsolicited requests for funds outside of Tivoli township not considered or acknowledged.
EIN: 363967580

535
Brookville Foundation
919 Main St.
Brookville, IN 47012
Contact: Donald M. Jobe, Pres.

Foundation type: Independent foundation
Limitations: Scholarships to residents of Franklin County, IN, attending Franklin County High School, Batesville High School, Union County High School, or Oldenburg High School, IN.
Financial data: Year ended 10/31/2004. Assets, $943,824 (M); Expenditures, $55,312; Total giving, $50,455; Grants to individuals, totaling $3,715.
Type of support: Support to graduates or students of specific schools; Precollege support.
Application information: Applications accepted. Application form required.
Initial approach: Letter or by contacting local school.
Deadline(s): Apr. 9
Program description:
Brookville Scholarship Awards:
- Humig-Wiebe Scholarship
- John Lane Scholarship
- Hannah Popper Scholarship
- James Runyon Scholarship
- Donald L. Wolber Scholarship

- Jennifer Brown Scholarship
- Richard and Helen Maley Scholarship
- James R. Kaffenberger Scholarship.

EIN: 237130825

536

The Brossman Family Charitable Trust for Scholarships

c/o The Ephrata National Bank
P.O. Box 457
Ephrata, PA 17522-0457
Contact: Carl L. Brubaker, V.P. and Trust Off., The Ephrata National Bank

Foundation type: Independent foundation
Limitations: Scholarships to graduates of Ephrata Senior High School, Ephrata, PA, or high school residents in an area served by Denver & Ephrata Telephone & Telegraph Co.
Financial data: Year ended 10/31/2004.
Assets, $3,821 (M); Expenditures, $369,126; Total giving, $355,500.
Type of support: Support to graduates or students of specific schools; Undergraduate support.
Application information: Application form required.
Deadline(s): June 15
Additional information: Application available from selection committee.
EIN: 232860047

537

The Brown Brothers Harriman & Co. Undergraduate Fund

140 Broadway
New York, NY 10005

Foundation type: Company-sponsored foundation
Limitations: Scholarships to children of employees of The Brown Brothers Harriman & Co., based on scholastic ability and financial need.
Financial data: Year ended 07/31/2004.
Assets, $812,279 (M); Expenditures, $67,720; Total giving, $63,500.
Type of support: Employee-related scholarships; Undergraduate support.
Application information: Application form required.
Deadline(s): May 1
Applicants should submit the following:
1) SAT
Additional information: Applications distributed to employees only; Scholarships are renewable.
EIN: 136169140

538

Brown County Community Foundation, Inc.

P.O. Box 191
Nashville, IN 47448 (812) 988-4882
Contact: For grants: Spring Smith, Prog. Off.; For scholarships: Lisa Terry
FAX: (812) 988-0299;
E-mail: info@browncountycommunityfoundation.org
; Grant application E-mail:
spring@BrownCountyCommunityFoundation.org;
URL: http://
www.browncountycommunityfoundation.org

Foundation type: Community foundation
Limitations: Scholarships to individuals in the Brown County area, IN.
Publications: Application guidelines; Annual report; Informational brochure (including application guidelines); Newsletter.

Financial data: Year ended 12/31/2005.
Assets, $7,652,245 (M); Expenditures, $619,237; Total giving, $324,336.
Type of support: Scholarships—to individuals.
Application information: Applications accepted. Application form required. Application form available on the grantmaker's Web site.
Initial approach: Letter or telephone.
Copies of proposal: 6
Deadline(s): Jan. 31
Applicants should submit the following:
1) Transcripts
2) SAT
3) Letter(s) of recommendation
4) GPA
5) Financial information
6) Essay
7) ACT
Additional information: .
EIN: 351960379

539

Selma McKrill Brown Educational Trust

c/o Lake City Bank
P.O. Box 1387
Warsaw, IN 46581-1387 (574) 267-9110
Contact: Peggy Michel, Trust Dept.

Foundation type: Independent foundation
Limitations: Scholarships to U.S. citizen residents of Kosciusko County, IN, who are active church members.
Publications: Annual report (including application guidelines).
Financial data: Year ended 12/31/2004.
Assets, $63,787 (M); Expenditures, $25,475; Total giving, $17,600; Grants to individuals, totaling $17,600.
Fields of interest: Religion.
Type of support: Scholarships—to individuals.
Application information: Applications accepted. Application form required.
Initial approach: Applications available at area high schools, as well as the trust department of Lake City Bank, Warsaw, IN.
Deadline(s): Apr. 1
Applicants should submit the following:
1) Photograph
2) Transcripts
Additional information: Application should also include a letter from high school principal and pastor of church.
EIN: 356455007

540

Lucille R. Brown Foundation, Inc.

4949 Bear Paw Dr.
Castle Rock, CO 80104
Contact: Cecilia A. Wells, Secy.

Foundation type: Independent foundation
Limitations: Scholarships only to Colorado residents doing undergraduate work at Colorado schools.
Financial data: Year ended 12/31/2004.
Assets, $518,691 (M); Expenditures, $25,625; Total giving, $22,500; Grants to individuals, totaling $22,500.
Type of support: Scholarships—to individuals.
Application information: Applications accepted.
Deadline(s): None
Additional information: Apply by letter, giving name, address, telephone number, and brief description of purpose for which grant will be used.
EIN: 846025298

541

The Sunny Brown Foundation

1760 N. Palm Ave.
Upland, CA 91784
Contact: Sherran Velto, C.F.O.

Foundation type: Independent foundation
Limitations: Scholarships to graduating seniors at De Ridder High School, LA, and to U.S. citizens, allowing them to study and train in their artistic fields.
Financial data: Year ended 12/31/2002.
Assets, $1,173,437 (M); Expenditures, $188,991; Total giving, $122,500; Grants to individuals, 27 grants totaling $122,500 (high: $7,000, low: $3,500).
Fields of interest: Arts.
Type of support: Support to graduates or students of specific schools; Undergraduate support.
Application information: Deadline Mar. 31; Completion of formal application required, including transcripts and essays.
Program descriptions:
Sunny Brown Memorial Scholarships for De Ridder High School: One scholarship per year is awarded to an outstanding senior at De Ridder High School on the basis of merit. Applicants must have an overall GPA of 3.5 and a minimum of 20 on the ACT test, demonstrate outstanding academic talent and exceptional school and/or community service, and plan to attend a four-year college or university. Recipients receive a $12,000 award.
Sunny Brown Memorial Scholarships for the Arts: Scholarships are awarded to talented graduating high school seniors who are U.S. citizens to pursue study in the creative arts at colleges, universities, and other accredited professional companies or private institutions allowing them to study and train in their artistic fields. Recipients are selected on the basis of talent and achievement in the arts.
EIN: 954190924

542

Brown Memorial Foundation

409 N.W. 3rd St., Ste. G
P.O. Box 187
Abilene, KS 67410-0187
Application address: c/o Abilene High School, 1101 N. Mulberry St., Abilene, KS 67410-2044, tel.: (785) 263-1260

Foundation type: Operating foundation
Limitations: Scholarships to graduating seniors of Abilene High School, KS, to attend accredited colleges, universities, and technical schools in KS. Scholarships are awarded on the basis of financial need, grades, class rank, test scores, moral character, citizenship, and motivation.
Financial data: Year ended 12/31/2004.
Assets, $17,423,110 (M); Expenditures, $741,205; Total giving, $16,850; Grants to individuals, totaling $14,250.
Application information: Application form required.
Deadline(s): Apr. 25
Additional information: Applications available from Abilene High School. Unsolicited applications not accepted or acknowledged.
EIN: 480573809

543

Fern Brown Memorial Fund

c/o JPMorgan Chase Bank, N.A.
P.O. Box 1308
Milwaukee, WI 53201
Contact: Mike Bartel, Trust Off., JPMorgan Chase Bank, N.A.
Application address: P.O. Box 1, Tulsa, OK 74193

Foundation type: Independent foundation
Limitations: Scholarships to residents of OK.
Financial data: Year ended 06/30/2005.
Assets, $207,314 (M); Expenditures, $11,969;
Total giving, $8,769.
Type of support: Scholarships—to individuals.
Application information: Applications accepted.
   Deadline(s): None
   Additional information: Applications by letter.
EIN: 736162573

544

The Lorene Brown Scholarship Foundation

c/o National Bank & Trust Co.
230 W. State St.
Sycamore, IL 60178
Contact: Diane Florschuetz, Asst. V.P. and Trust Off., National Bank & Trust Co.

Foundation type: Independent foundation
Limitations: Scholarships to graduates of Genoa-Kingston High School who are attending the University of Illinois or Northern Illinois University.
Financial data: Year ended 12/31/2004.
Assets, $283,155 (M); Expenditures, $19,742;
Total giving, $15,000; Grants to individuals, totaling $15,000.
Type of support: Support to graduates or students of specific schools; Undergraduate support.
Application information: Application form required.
   Deadline(s): Apr. 15
EIN: 366939275

545

Marion D. Brown Scholarship Trust

c/o Integra Bank, N.A.
P.O. Box 868
Evansville, IN 47705-0868 (812) 464-9661

Foundation type: Independent foundation
Limitations: Scholarships to students of high schools in Vanderburgh County, IN.
Financial data: Year ended 12/31/2004.
Assets, $595,967 (M); Expenditures, $38,593;
Total giving, $31,500; Grants to individuals, totaling $31,500.
Type of support: Support to graduates or students of specific schools; Undergraduate support.
Application information: Applications accepted.
   Initial approach: Students apply for aid at their respective school's financial aid office during the school year, and are then recommended by the institution for the award.
   Additional information: Unsolicited applications not accepted; Selection is based on high school record, desire for a college education and financial need.
EIN: 356050689

546

Marguerite V. Brown Testamentary Trust

(also known as Le Roy C. Brown Memorial Scholarships)
c/o U.S. Bank, N.A.
P.O. Box 2043
Milwaukee, WI 53201-9116

Foundation type: Independent foundation
Limitations: Scholarships for attendance at colleges and trade schools to financially needy graduates of Abraham Lincoln High School, Thomas Jefferson High School, Lewis Central Senior High School, and the high school at the Iowa School for the Deaf, all in Council Bluffs, IA.
Financial data: Year ended 12/31/2004.
Assets, $758,350 (M); Expenditures, $20,749;
Total giving, $13,695; Grants to individuals, totaling $13,695.
Fields of interest: Vocational education; Disabilities, people with.
Type of support: Support to graduates or students of specific schools; Technical education support; Undergraduate support.
Application information: Applications accepted. Application form required.
   Deadline(s): 2nd Mon. in Mar.
   Applicants should submit the following:
      1) GPA
      2) Financial information
   Additional information: Application should also include school and community activities, self-evaluation and applications should be submitted to individual high schools.
Program description:
   Scholarship Program: Applicants must have a GPA of at least "C" to apply for vocational or technical scholarships, and at least a "B" to apply for four-year college scholarships. Scholarships may be used for tuition, books, and supplies. A scholarship committee at each school selects the scholarship recipients for that school.
EIN: 426353639

547

R. D. Brown Trust B

c/o JPMorgan Chase Bank
1211 6th Ave., 34th Fl.
New York, NY 10036

Foundation type: Independent foundation
Limitations: Loans and grants primarily to financially needy employees of The Chase Manhattan Bank who live in NY.
Financial data: Year ended 12/31/2003.
Assets, $1,925,105 (M); Expenditures, $108,348; Total giving, $80,189; Loans to individuals, 81 loans totaling $73,789.
Type of support: Employee-related scholarships.
Application information: Applications not accepted.
EIN: 136030429

548

Gabriel J. Brown Trust Loan Fund

112 W. Ave. E
Bismarck, ND 58501 (701) 223-5916
Contact: Student Loans: Susan Lundberg
Additional tel.: (701) 223-5119

Foundation type: Independent foundation
Limitations: Student loans to financially needy residents of ND.
Financial data: Year ended 03/31/2005.
Assets, $1,392,204 (M); Expenditures, $12,468;

Total giving, $85,500; Loans to individuals, 10 loans totaling $85,500.
Type of support: Student loans—to individuals; Undergraduate support.
Application information: Applications accepted. Application form required.
   Initial approach: Letter or telephone.
   Applicants should submit the following:
      1) GPA
      2) Financial information
Program description:
   Educational Loans: Applicants must meet the following qualifications:
   · be residents of ND and in attendance at a college or university for four semesters or six quarters, or have acquired 48 credits or its equivalent in quarter hours. Students at Bismarck State College, Medcenter One College of Nursing, or the University of Mary need to have attended only two semesters or three quarters, or have acquired 24 credits or its quarter-hour equivalent
   · have maintained a GPA of at least a 2.5 based upon a 4.0 grading system in their college or university work
   · be in need of financial assistance to continue their education. Interest is charged at the rate of six percent per year.
EIN: 237086880

549

Raena Brown Trust No. 363

c/o AMCORE Bank, N.A.
501 7th St.
Rockford, IL 61104
Application address: c/o AMCORE Investment Group, N.A., 801 Washington St., Mendota, IL 61342, tel.: (815) 539-9346

Foundation type: Independent foundation
Limitations: Scholarships to medical students from the Mendota, IL, area.
Financial data: Year ended 12/31/2004.
Assets, $342,583 (M); Expenditures, $13,053;
Total giving, $10,400; Grants to individuals, totaling $10,400.
Fields of interest: Medical school/education.
Type of support: Graduate support.
Application information: Applications accepted. Application form required.
   Initial approach: Letter or telephone.
   Deadline(s): None
EIN: 366692001

550

Florence H. Brown Trust

(also known as H. Fletcher Brown Trust)
c/o PNC Advisors
1600 Market St.
Philadelphia, PA 19103-7240
Contact: Donald Davis, Trust Off., PNC Advisors

Foundation type: Independent foundation
Limitations: Scholarships to financially needy DE residents, who were born in DE, and are studying chemistry, engineering, law, medicine, or dentistry.
Financial data: Year ended 12/31/2004.
Assets, $404,080 (M); Expenditures, $27,642;
Total giving, $20,750; Grants to individuals, totaling $20,750.
Fields of interest: Dental school/education; Law school/education; Medical school/education; Chemistry; Engineering.
Type of support: Scholarships—to individuals.
Application information: Application form required.
   Deadline(s): Mar. 22

Applicants should submit the following:
1) Financial information
2) SAT
3) Transcripts
Additional information: Applications should also include birth certificate, last two tax returns, letter of recommendation from principal, college advisor, or dean, personal reference from a friend or relative, and a personal statement; Interviews required.
Program description:
Scholarship Program: To be eligible, recipients must have SAT scores of 1000 or higher, rank in the upper 20 percent of their class, and have a family income of less than $75,000, unless extenuating circumstances are demonstrated. Scholarships are renewable until the completion of the course of study, provided the recipient maintains at least a 2.5 GPA.
EIN: 516010596

551
T. Wistar Brown Trust
(also known as T. Wistar Brown Teacher's Fund)
c/o PNC Advisors
620 Liberty Ave., P2 PTPP-10-2
Pittsburgh, PA 15222-2705

Foundation type: Independent foundation
Limitations: Grants to financially needy members of Philadelphia Yearly Meeting who are 21 years of age or older preparing themselves to teach at the elementary or secondary school level, or to take advanced courses to enrich their teaching talents.
Financial data: Year ended 09/30/2002.
Assets, $1,561,475 (M); Expenditures, $37,143; Total giving, $27,769; Grants to individuals, totaling $27,769.
Fields of interest: Teacher school/education; Education.
Type of support: Scholarships—to individuals.
Application information:
Deadline(s): Apr. 15 for summer study, July 1 for fall or winter study, Dec. 15 for spring study
Additional information: Completion of formal application required, including essay, letter of support from the clerk of applicant's monthly meeting or its overseers, recommendation letter from principal of the school or from educator who is familiar with the applicant's circumstances.
EIN: 236200741

552
Dr. & Mrs. C. R. Brownell, Jr. Charitable Fund
1030 2nd St.
Morgan City, LA 70380
Contact: Michael W. Vanover, Secy.
Application address: 580 Fairview Dr., Berwick, LA 70342, tel.: (504) 384-3191

Foundation type: Independent foundation
Limitations: Scholarships to full-time students who maintain a 3.0 GPA, and attend a LA university or college.
Financial data: Year ended 12/31/2004.
Assets, $206,158 (M); Expenditures, $13,384; Total giving, $12,000; Grants to individuals, totaling $12,000.
Type of support: Scholarships—to individuals.
Application information: Applications accepted throughout the year; Completion of formal application required, including thesis, high school transcript, and ACT score.
EIN: 721228886

553
Blanche A. Bruce Trust
95 Market St.
Manchester, NH 03101 (603) 669-4140
Contact: Theodore Wadleigh, Tr.

Foundation type: Independent foundation
Limitations: Scholarships to NH residents.
Financial data: Year ended 06/30/2005.
Assets, $2,777,960 (M); Expenditures, $112,230; Total giving, $80,455; Grants to individuals, 4 grants totaling $10,455 (high: $4,000, low: $15).
Type of support: Scholarships—to individuals.
Application information: Applications accepted.
Deadline(s): None
Additional information: Contact foundation for current application guidelines.
EIN: 026014968

554
Michael A. Bruder Foundation
600 Reed Rd.
P.O. Box 600
Broomall, PA 19008-0600

Foundation type: Company-sponsored foundation
Limitations: Scholarships to children of employees of M.A. Bruder and Sons, Inc.
Financial data: Year ended 12/31/2004.
Assets, $261,821 (M); Expenditures, $42,027; Total giving, $36,500; Grants to individuals, 13 grants totaling $32,750 (high: $10,000, low: $1,000).
Type of support: Employee-related scholarships.
Application information: Unsolicited requests for funds not considered or acknowledged.
EIN: 236298481

555
The Brummer-Stiles-Duncan Scholarship Fund
c/o Cherokee State Bank
212 W. Willow St.
Cherokee, IA 51012-1857
Contact: Leon Klotz, V.P.

Foundation type: Independent foundation
Limitations: Scholarships to graduates of high schools in Cherokee County, IA.
Financial data: Year ended 09/30/2005.
Assets, $177,296 (M); Expenditures, $11,865; Total giving, $10,000; Grants to individuals, 10 grants totaling $10,000.
Type of support: Support to graduates or students of specific schools; Undergraduate support.
Application information: Application form required.
EIN: 426371803

556
W. J. Brundred Charitable Fund
c/o Mellon Bank, N.A.
P.O. Box 185
Pittsburgh, PA 15230-9897
Application address: c/o Marilyn King, MPWM, 100 State St., Ste. 200, Erie, PA 16507, tel.: (814) 874-5209

Foundation type: Independent foundation
Limitations: Scholarships to residents of Venango County, PA, primarily for attendance at Yale University or Massachusetts Institute of Technology.

Financial data: Year ended 12/31/2002.
Assets, $1,020,780 (M); Expenditures, $72,822; Total giving, $65,000; Grants to individuals, 17 grants totaling $65,000 (high: $32,000, low: $2,000).
Type of support: Scholarships—to individuals; Support to graduates or students of specific schools.
Application information:
Deadline(s): Apr. 1
Additional information: Completion of formal application required, including parental confidential statement.
EIN: 256031974

557
Joseph & Angela Bruneo Foundation
3505 30th Ave.
Kenosha, WI 53144 (262) 652-5050
Contact: Bruno M. Rizzo, Dir.

Foundation type: Independent foundation
Limitations: Scholarships to students in WI pursuing a two- or four-year degree in a medical field, with an emphasis on nursing.
Financial data: Year ended 12/31/2004.
Assets, $61,940 (M); Expenditures, $11,555; Total giving, $10,000; Grants to individuals, 5 grants totaling $10,000 (high: $2,000, low: $2,000).
Fields of interest: Medical school/education; Nursing school/education.
Type of support: Scholarships—to individuals.
Application information: Contact foundation for current application deadline/guidelines.
EIN: 391917743

558
Paul W. Bruning Testamentary Trust f/b/ o Bruning Scholarship Fund
c/o Citizens State Bank & Trust Co.
610 Oregon St.
Hiawatha, KS 66434-2101
Contact: Lori Nigus, Trust Off., Citizens State Bank & Trust Co.

Foundation type: Independent foundation
Limitations: Scholarships to graduates of Brown County, KS, high schools.
Financial data: Year ended 05/31/2005.
Assets, $51,466 (M); Expenditures, $35,802; Total giving, $34,200; Grants to individuals, totaling $34,200.
Type of support: Support to graduates or students of specific schools; Undergraduate support.
Application information: Application form required.
Deadline(s): Contact trust for current application deadline
Additional information: Applications available at Citizens State Bank and Hiawatha High School.
EIN: 486234280

559
The Brunswick Foundation, Inc.
1 N. Field Ct.
Lake Forest, IL 60045-4811 (847) 735-4467
Contact: Carol Stame, Pres.

Foundation type: Company-sponsored foundation
Limitations: Scholarships only to children of full-time Brunswick Corporation employees who have at least one year of service prior to application due date.

Publications: Application guidelines.
Financial data: Year ended 12/31/2003.
Assets, $5,844,890 (M); Expenditures,
$2,159,028; Total giving, $503,896; Grants to
individuals, 225 grants totaling $411,500 (high:
$2,000, low: $500).
Type of support: Employee-related scholarships.
Application information: Application form required.
  Initial approach: Letter.
  Deadline(s): Contact foundation for current
    application deadline
  Additional information: Application should
    include transcripts.
Program description:
  Scholarship Program: Recipients may receive
  either a one-year scholarship ($1,000 to $2,000)
  or a multi-year scholarship ($2,000 to $8,000).
EIN: 366033576

560
Benjamin F. & Ernestine Bruton Foundation
P.O. Box 201328
Chicago, IL   60620
Application address: c/o Alice S. Walker, Secy.,
4212 Cedarwood, Matteson, IL 60443, tel.: (708)
747-4945

Foundation type: Independent foundation
Limitations: Scholarships to individuals in IL
pursuing a career in veterinary medicine.
Financial data: Year ended 12/31/2002.
Assets, $817,250 (M); Expenditures, $55,506;
Total giving, $46,825; Grants to individuals, 27
grants totaling $28,400 (high: $2,000, low:
$1,000).
Fields of interest: Veterinary medicine.
Type of support: Scholarships—to individuals.
Application information: Applications accepted.
  Deadline(s): None
  Additional information: Contact foundation for
    current application guidelines.
EIN: 363385677

561
Bryan Area Foundation, Inc.
102 N. Main St.
P.O. Box 651
Bryan, OH   43506   (419) 633-1156
Contact: Mitchell S. Owens, Exec. Dir.
E-mail: foundation@cityofbryan.net; URL: http://
www.bryanareafoundation.org

Foundation type: Community foundation
Limitations: Scholarships to residents of the Bryan,
OH area.
Publications: Application guidelines; Occasional
report.
Financial data: Year ended 06/30/2005.
Assets, $14,852,676 (M); Expenditures,
$1,111,249; Total giving, $720,231; Grants to
individuals, totaling $102,855.
Type of support: Undergraduate support.
Application information: Applications accepted.
Application form required.
  Initial approach: E-mail.
  Additional information: Contact foundation for
    further application guidelines.
EIN: 237041310

562
Fred A. Bryan Collegiate Students Fund
c/o Wells Fargo Bank, N.A.
P.O. Box 53456, MAC S4035-014
Phoenix, AZ   85072
Application address: c/o: Wells Fargo Bank of
Indiana, N.A., P.O. Box 960, Fort Wayne, IN 46801

Foundation type: Independent foundation
Limitations: Scholarships to male graduates of
high schools in South Bend, IN, with preference
given to those who have been Boy Scouts in good
standing for a period of two years at some time prior
to application.
Financial data: Year ended 12/31/2004.
Assets, $287,394 (M); Expenditures, $10,313;
Total giving, $6,000; Grants to individuals, totaling
$6,000.
Fields of interest: Boy scouts; Men; Young adults,
male.
Type of support: Support to graduates or students
of specific schools; Undergraduate support.
Application information: Application form required.
  Initial approach: Letter to high school principal
    stating general information about the
    applicant and his qualifications.
  Deadline(s): Mar. 31
  Additional information: Nomination application
    should also include three letters of character
    reference, IQ rating, class rank, attendance
    record, GPA, transcripts, and school activity
    record; Applicant must also file a FAF prior to
    Mar. 1 and, if a Boy Scout, include a copy of
    Scout Record.
Program description:
  Scholarship Program: Scholarship awards are
  determined by a committee made up of the
  principals of the South Bend, IN, high schools, the
  superintendent of the school district, and a
  representative of the fund's trustees. Generally,
  awards are renewable for a maximum of four years.
EIN: 356012911

563
Dodd and Dorothy L. Bryan Foundation
2 N. Main St., No. 401
Sheridan, WY   82801   (307) 672-3535
Application address: c/o Rose Marie Madia, P.O.
Box 6287, Sheridan, WY 82601

Foundation type: Independent foundation
Limitations: Loans to students from Sheridan,
Campbell, and Johnson counties, WY, and from
Powder River, Rosebud, and Big Horn counties, MT,
who have lived in the county for at least two years
prior to application.
Publications: Application guidelines.
Financial data: Year ended 12/31/2004.
Assets, $6,365,993 (M); Expenditures,
$101,426; Total giving, $15,012; Loans to
individuals, 92 loans totaling $349,407.
Fields of interest: Vocational education.
Type of support: Student loans—to individuals;
Loans—to individuals.
Application information: Application form required.
  Initial approach: Letter or in person.
  Deadline(s): June 15
  Applicants should submit the following:
    1) Transcripts
    2) Financial information
  Additional information: Application should also
    include parents' financial statement;
    Interviews required.
Program description:
  Student Loan Program: Loans are made for
  higher or vocational education for recipients
  selected on the basis of financial need and

academic achievement. Applicants must be under
the age of 25 to be eligible for academic loans.
There is no age limit for vocational loans.
Recipients must have at least a 2.5 GPA and
maintain full-time status. Both of the recipient's
parents must co-sign the loan note. Recipients
must also carry life insurance with a collateral
assignment to the foundation in an amount at least
equal to the loan. Repayments are approximately
$25 per month per $1,000. Loans are
automatically renewed provided the recipient
maintains eligibility.
EIN: 836006533

564
Bryant Chucking Grinder Company Charitable Foundation
53 Cutler Dr.
Springfield, VT   05156   (802) 885-5812
Contact: Richard H. Dexter, II, Pres.

Foundation type: Independent foundation
Limitations: Scholarships to students who reside in
New England.
Financial data: Year ended 12/31/2004.
Assets, $1,081,192 (M); Expenditures, $22,119;
Total giving, $16,000; Grants to individuals,
totaling $16,000.
Type of support: Scholarships—to individuals.
Application information: Applications accepted.
  Initial approach: Letter.
  Deadline(s): None
  Additional information: Applications by letter;
    Contact foundation for current application
    guidelines.
EIN: 036009332

565
The Samuel & Esther Buchalter Foundation, Inc.
c/o Gilbert Buchalter, Tr.
c/o Pharmaceutical Innovations, Inc.
897 Frelinghuysen Ave.
Newark, NJ   07114-2122   (973) 242-2900

Foundation type: Company-sponsored foundation
Limitations: Scholarships to employees or
dependents of employees of Pharmaceutical
Innovations.
Financial data: Year ended 12/31/2004.
Assets, $382,505 (M); Expenditures, $14,035;
Total giving, $14,000; Grants to individuals, 10
grants totaling $14,000 (high: $2,000, low: $500).
Type of support: Employee-related scholarships.
Application information:
  Initial approach: Letter.
  Additional information: Contact foundation for
    application guidelines.
EIN: 223269458

566
C. A. Buck Educational Foundation
c/o Wells Fargo Bank, N.A.
P.O. Box 63954
San Francisco, CA   94163-0001
Application address: c/o Victor Mangini,
Educational Secy., 1100 Industrial Rd., Ste. 17,
San Carlos CA 94070

Foundation type: Independent foundation
Limitations: Scholarships by nomination only for
higher education to financially needy students of
San Mateo County, CA, schools.

Financial data: Year ended 11/30/2004. Assets, $536,099 (M); Expenditures, $27,054; Total giving, $2,000; Grants to individuals, totaling $2,000.
Type of support: Awards/grants by nomination only; Undergraduate support.
Application information: Applications not accepted.
  Additional information: Selected schools recommend students.
EIN: 946100778

567
The Frank H. and Eva B. Buck Foundation
P.O. Box 5610
Vacaville, CA 95696-5610 (707) 446-7700
Contact: Robert Walker, Exec. Dir.
FAX: (707) 446-7766;
E-mail: rwalker@buckfoundation.org; URL: http://www.buckfoundation.org

Foundation type: Independent foundation
Limitations: Scholarships only to residents, or people enrolled in school in Solano, Napa, Yolo, Sacramento, San Joaquin, and Contra Costa counties.
Publications: Application guidelines; Informational brochure; Newsletter.
Financial data: Year ended 03/31/2005. Assets, $57,259,594 (M); Expenditures, $4,961,273; Total giving, $3,964,601; Grants to individuals, 119 grants totaling $3,543,632 (high: $63,664, low: $125, average grant: $10,000-$50,000).
Type of support: Scholarships—to individuals; Graduate support; Technical education support; Undergraduate support; Postgraduate support; Doctoral support.
Application information: Applications accepted. Application form required. Application form available on the grantmaker's Web site.
  Initial approach: Letter, telephone or e-mail.
  Copies of proposal: 3
  Deadline(s): 1st Sat. in Dec.
  Applicants should submit the following:
    1) Transcripts
    2) SAT
    3) Resume
    4) Letter(s) of recommendation
    5) GPA
    6) Financial information
    7) Essay
    8) Curriculum vitae
    9) ACT
  Additional information: Application should include teacher's assessment and parental authorization for release of school records; Interviews required.
EIN: 770233870

568
Helen Ann Buckley Foundation
P.O. Box 2229
Sonoma, CA 95476
Contact: James Kemp, Tr.
Application address: 428 1st St., East Sonoma, CA 95476

Foundation type: Operating foundation
Limitations: Scholarships to students who have been residents of Sonoma Valley, CA, for at least one year, for undergraduate and vocational education.
Financial data: Year ended 12/31/2003. Assets, $991,328 (M); Expenditures, $70,134;

Total giving, $49,750; Grants to individuals, 71 grants totaling $49,750 (high: $1,500, low: $250).
Type of support: Technical education support; Undergraduate support.
Application information: Applications accepted. Application form required.
  Deadline(s): Apr. 15
EIN: 686183386

569
Margaret G. Buckner Scholarship Trust
P.O. Box 721
Marshall, MO 65340-0721
Application address: c/o William G. Bucker, P.O. Box 625, Marshall, MO 65340, tel.: (660) 886-3408

Foundation type: Operating foundation
Limitations: Scholarships to students in Saline County, MO, for higher education.
Financial data: Year ended 12/31/2003. Assets, $1,092,339 (M); Expenditures, $62,730; Total giving, $57,253; Grants to individuals, 15 grants totaling $57,253 (high: $6,888, low: $1,125).
Type of support: Undergraduate support.
Application information: Applications accepted. Application form required.
  Deadline(s): None
EIN: 431735027

570
Bobby Buerger Scholarship Fund
c/o MainSource Bank
P.O. Box 87
Greensburg, IN 47240
Application address: c/o Superintendent, Greensburg Community Schools, Greensburg, IN 47240

Foundation type: Independent foundation
Limitations: Scholarships to graduating seniors of Greensburg Community High School, IN.
Financial data: Year ended 12/31/2004. Assets, $712,585 (M); Expenditures, $35,932; Total giving, $29,500.
Type of support: Support to graduates or students of specific schools; Undergraduate support.
Application information: Application form required.
  Deadline(s): May 1
  Applicants should submit the following:
    1) GPA
    2) Class rank
  Additional information: Application should also include personal statement, financial statement, and copy of page one of FAF.
EIN: 356415393

571
Buffalo Urban League, Inc.
15 E. Genesee St.
Buffalo, NY 14203 (716) 854-7625
Contact: Brenda McDuffie, Pres. and C.E.O.
FAX: (716) 854-8960; URL: http://www.buffalourbanleague.org

Foundation type: Public charity
Limitations: Scholarships to students of color residing in the Buffalo, NY, area for undergraduate and graduate education.
Financial data: Year ended 03/31/2005. Assets, $1,457,136 (M); Expenditures, $3,531,963.
Fields of interest: Minorities.

Type of support: Graduate support; Undergraduate support.
Application information: Application form required.
  Deadline(s): Apr. 16
  Applicants should submit the following:
    1) Letter(s) of recommendation
    2) Transcripts
    3) SAR
    4) Financial information
    5) Essay
  Additional information: Application should also include college acceptance letter. See Web site for further application information.
EIN: 160743940

572
The Susan Thompson Buffett Foundation
(formerly The Buffett Foundation)
222 Kiewit Plz.
Omaha, NE 68131
Contact: Allen Greenberg, Pres.
Scholarship application address: c/o Devon Buffett, P.O. Box 4508, Decatur, IL 62525, tel.: (402) 451-6011
E-mail: scholarships@stbfoundation.org; Tel. for scholarship information: (402) 943-1383

Foundation type: Independent foundation
Limitations: Scholarships to residents of NE to attend NE state colleges and universities. Scholarships are for tuition and fees at NE state colleges and universities only.
Financial data: Year ended 12/31/2004. Assets, $5,052,931 (M); Expenditures, $36,704,755; Total giving, $35,644,506; Grants to individuals, 15 grants totaling $150,000 (high: $10,000, low: $10,000).
Application information: Applications accepted. Application form required.
  Deadline(s): Apr. 15 and Oct. 5
EIN: 476032365

573
Build-A-Bear Workshop Foundation, Inc.
1954 Innerbelt Business Center Dr.
St. Louis, MO 63114-5760 (314) 423-8000
Contact: Maxine Clark, Pres.
E-mail: giving@buildabear.com; URL: http://www.buildabear.com/aboutus/community/BabwFoundation.aspx

Foundation type: Public charity
Limitations: Prizes to winners of the Huggable Heroes competition, for kids who demonstrate extraordinary service to their local communities.
Financial data: Year ended 12/31/2004. Assets, $387,065 (M); Expenditures, $245,937; Total giving, $242,757.
Fields of interest: Community development, volunteer services.
Type of support: Awards/prizes.
Application information: Application form required. Application form available on the grantmaker's Web site.
  Initial approach: Letter or telephone.
  Deadline(s): Feb. 14
  Applicants should submit the following:
    1) Essay
  Additional information: See Web site for further information.
Program description:
  Huggable Heros: This program seeks to reward kids who demonstrate extraordinary service to their local communities. Nominations will be accepted of young people who are 18 years of age or younger and are legal residents of the United States, District

of Columbia, Puerto Rico, and Canada. Twelve young people will be selected and recognized as Huggable Heroes. Each of the twelve honorees will be rewarded with a $2,500 donation to help further their cause along with a trip to Los Angeles, where they will be recognized for their achievements. Nominees may perform their community service as an individual working within a group or on an individual basis. Self-nominations will be accepted.
EIN: 331007188

574

Builders Exchange of Santa Clara County Scholarship Fund

400 Reed St.
Santa Clara, CA 95052
URL: http://www.bxscco.com/benefits.html

Foundation type: Independent foundation
Limitations: Scholarships to children and grandchildren of general members of the Builders Exchange of Santa Clara County and children and grandchildren of employees of member firms that have worked four hundred hours or more for a general member within the previous or current calendar year, who are pursuing a career in the construction and business industry at a college, university or trade school.
Financial data: Year ended 12/31/2004. Assets, $0 (M); Expenditures, $28,033; Total giving, $26,000; Grants to individuals, 9 grants totaling $26,000 (high: $5,000, low: $250).
Fields of interest: Vocational education; Business school/education; Business/industry.
Type of support: Technical education support; Undergraduate support.
Application information:
    Deadline(s): Early Mar.
    Additional information: Contact foundation for current application guidelines.
EIN: 770304794

575

Elizabeth Roosa Buisch Memorial Scholarship Fund

c/o Steuban Trust Co.
1 Steuban Sq.
Hornell, NY 14843-1699

Foundation type: Independent foundation
Limitations: Scholarships by nomination only to graduating seniors of Hornell High School, NY.
Financial data: Year ended 12/31/2004. Assets, $275,598 (M); Expenditures, $17,597; Total giving, $13,500; Grants to individuals, totaling $13,500.
Type of support: Support to graduates or students of specific schools; Awards/grants by nomination only; Undergraduate support.
Application information: Unsolicited requests for funds not accepted.
Program description:
    Scholarship Program: Recipient must maintain a passing average of at least "C" or a 2.5 GPA in college.
EIN: 161501166

576

Trustees of the Bulkeley School

14 Crocker St.
New London, CT 06320
Contact: William J. Smith, Treas.

Foundation type: Independent foundation

Limitations: Scholarships only to residents of New London, CT.
Financial data: Year ended 04/30/2005. Assets, $1,378,168 (M); Expenditures, $81,445; Total giving, $68,800; Grants to individuals, totaling $68,800.
Type of support: Scholarships—to individuals.
Application information: Application form required.
    Initial approach: Mar. 15.
    Deadline(s): Apr. 1
    Additional information: Application should include a copy of financial aid statement; Interviews required.
EIN: 066040926

577

The Everett S. Bulkley, Jr. Trust

(formerly The Bulkley Foundation Trust)
c/o JPMorgan Chase Bank
P.O. Box 31412
Rochester, NY 14603-1412
Contact: Pamela Detoro, V.P., JPMorgan Chase Bank
Application address: 122 Main St., New Canaan, CT 06840, tel.: (203) 972-2205

Foundation type: Independent foundation
Limitations: Scholarships to graduating seniors at Norwalk High School, CT.
Financial data: Year ended 12/31/2004. Assets, $3,997,699 (M); Expenditures, $268,620; Total giving, $228,198.
Type of support: Support to graduates or students of specific schools; Undergraduate support.
Application information: Contact trust for current application deadline/guidelines.
EIN: 066332021

578

Jesse David & Katie B. Bundy Scholarship Trust

c/o Bank of America, N.A.
101 S. Tryon St., NC1-002-11-18
Charlotte, NC 28255-0001
Contact: Lula Cook, Trust Off., Bank of America, N.A.
Application address: 380 Knollwood St., Winston-Salem, NC 27103

Foundation type: Independent foundation
Limitations: Scholarship to residents of Wilkes County, NC, who are enrolled in educational programs leading to medical careers in technical and supporting fields.
Financial data: Year ended 08/31/2004. Assets, $159,171 (M); Expenditures, $12,440; Total giving, $10,500.
Type of support: Undergraduate support.
Application information: Applications accepted. Application form required.
    Initial approach: Letter.
    Deadline(s): Apr. 15
    Applicants should submit the following:
        1) Class rank
        2) SAT
        3) GPA
        4) Essay
        5) Letter(s) of recommendation
        6) SAR
        7) Financial information
        8) Transcripts
    Additional information: Contact trust for additional application guidelines.
EIN: 566501861

579

Henry Bunn Memorial Fund

c/o JPMorgan Chase Bank, N.A.
P.O. Box 1308
Milwaukee, WI 53201
Contact: JoAnn Ley, Trust Off., JPMorgan Chase Bank, N.A.
Application address: 1 E. Old State Capitol Plz., Springfield, IL 62701

Foundation type: Independent foundation
Limitations: Scholarships to high school seniors who are residents of Sangamon County, IL.
Financial data: Year ended 12/31/2004. Assets, $1,136,823 (M); Expenditures, $66,092; Total giving, $54,000; Grants to individuals, 94 grants totaling $54,000 (high: $1,000, low: $500).
Type of support: Undergraduate support.
Application information: Application form required.
    Deadline(s): Mar. 1
    Additional information: Application should include transcript and standardized test scores; Applications accepted through local high school counselors.
Program description:
    Scholarship Program: Scholarship recipients must exhibit high moral character, industry, and good study habits. Their high school record and qualifications must be superior, indicating the potential for successful college work. They also must demonstrate a need for financial assistance beyond reasonable levels of parent and self-help. The scholarship may be renewed annually for a maximum of three years, provided the student remains in financial need and good academic standing.
EIN: 376041599

580

Burch-Setton Student Loan Fund

c/o Wells Fargo Bank Texas, N.A.
P.O. Box 10517
Lubbock, TX 79408-3517 (806) 293-1311
Contact: Sherrie Gibson
Application address: c/o Board of Stewards, First United Methodist Church, 1001 W. 7th St., Plainview, TX 79072, tel.: (806) 293-3658

Foundation type: Independent foundation
Limitations: Student loans to graduates of high schools in Briscoe, Castro, Floyd, Hale, Lamb, and Swisher counties, TX, who have at least an "80" average.
Financial data: Year ended 12/31/2004. Assets, $1,349,621 (M); Expenditures, $69,046; Total giving, $0; Loans to individuals, totaling $115,204.
Type of support: Student loans—to individuals; Support to graduates or students of specific schools; Undergraduate support.
Application information: Applications accepted. Application form required.
    Deadline(s): June 1
    Applicants should submit the following:
        1) Transcripts
        2) GPA
        3) Financial information
Program description:
    Student Loan Program: Maximum amount to be loaned to a student is $10,000 for undergraduate degrees and $15,000 for graduate degrees. The maximum time to complete a degree is six years for an undergraduate and nine years for a graduate degree. Parents must sign all guarantees. Repayment begins six months after termination of school. The loan repayment schedule is five years for a loan of up to $4,000, seven years for a loan

of $4,100 to $7,500, and ten years for a loan of $7,600 to $10,000. Interest does not accrue until after the recipient graduates or terminates attendance in college. Minimum monthly payment is $50. The current interest rate is eight percent. Recipients must be enrolled for at least nine semester hours and maintain at least a 2.0 GPA.
EIN: 756056226

581
Daisy L. Burchfield Trust
205 E. Main St.
P.O. Box 477
Panora, IA 50216-0477

Foundation type: Independent foundation
Limitations: Educational loans to graduates of Panorama Community School District of Panora, IA, for postsecondary educational expenses.
Financial data: Year ended 12/31/2004.
Assets, $774,236 (M); Expenditures, $9,090; Total giving, $28,619; Loans to individuals, 7 loans totaling $28,619.
Type of support: Student loans—to individuals; Support to graduates or students of specific schools; Undergraduate support.
Application information: Applications not accepted.
EIN: 426359761

582
The William, Agnes & Elizabeth Burgess Memorial Scholarship Fund
c/o First Mid-Illinois Bank & Trust
P.O. Box 499
Mattoon, IL 61938 (217) 234-7454
Contact: Gary Kuhns, Trust Off., First Mid-Illinois Bank & Trust

Foundation type: Independent foundation
Limitations: Scholarships to financially needy graduating seniors of Mattoon High School, IL.
Financial data: Year ended 03/31/2005.
Assets, $2,027,294 (M); Expenditures, $194,656; Total giving, $125,000; Grants to individuals, 125 grants totaling $125,000.
Type of support: Support to graduates or students of specific schools; Undergraduate support.
Application information:
Deadline(s): Mar. 15
Additional information: Application forms available at Mattoon High School.
EIN: 376024599

583
John P. Burke Memorial Fund
1 Button Hole Dr., Ste. 2
Providence, RI 02909-5750 (401) 272-1350
Contact: Maury C. Davitt, Exec. Dir.
FAX: (401) 331-3627;
E-mail: burkefund@rigalinks.org; URL: http://www.burkefund.org

Foundation type: Public charity
Limitations: Scholarships to individuals who have worked as golf caddies to pursue higher education.
Financial data: Year ended 12/31/2004.
Assets, $405,712 (M); Expenditures, $134,122; Total giving, $86,975; Grants to individuals, totaling $86,975.
Fields of interest: Higher education.
Type of support: Scholarships—to individuals.

Application information: Applications accepted.
Initial approach: Letter.
EIN: 056008795

584
Burke-Weber Memorial Fund
c/o Wells Fargo Bank, N.A.
P.O. Box 63954, MAC A0330-011
San Francisco, CA 94163-0001
Application address: c/o Superintendent of Schools, Monterey County, Monterey, CA 93901

Foundation type: Independent foundation
Limitations: Scholarships to students from Salinas Valley, CA, high schools to study pharmacy.
Financial data: Year ended 11/30/2005.
Assets, $261,993 (M); Expenditures, $14,501; Total giving, $10,000; Grants to individuals, 3 grants totaling $5,250.
Fields of interest: Pharmacy/prescriptions.
Type of support: Scholarships—to individuals; Support to graduates or students of specific schools.
Application information: Applications accepted.
Deadline(s): None
Additional information: Contact fund for current application guidelines.
EIN: 946449131

585
The Burkhalter Educational Fund
P.O. Box 367
Louisiana, MO 63353
Contact: Leone Cadwallader

Foundation type: Independent foundation
Limitations: Scholarships to students living in the area serviced by First Baptist Church, Louisiana, MO.
Financial data: Year ended 12/31/2004.
Assets, $1 (M); Expenditures, $9,260; Total giving, $6,600; Grants to individuals, totaling $6,600.
Type of support: Scholarships—to individuals.
Application information: Application form required.
Deadline(s): June 15
Additional information: Application should include parents' tax return; Completed applications must be returned to the Louisiana R-II High School guidance counselor; Interviews required.
EIN: 431228710

586
Belle C. Burnett Foundation
P.O. Box 573
Salem, NY 12865-0573
Application address: c/o Guidance Office, Salem Central School, E. Broadway, Salem, NY 12865, tel.: (518) 854-7855

Foundation type: Independent foundation
Limitations: Scholarships to graduating seniors from Salem Central High School, NY, who have been accepted at four-year accredited colleges and universities.
Financial data: Year ended 12/31/2004.
Assets, $89,434 (M); Expenditures, $6,135; Total giving, $5,500; Grants to individuals, totaling $5,500.
Type of support: Support to graduates or students of specific schools; Undergraduate support.
Application information: Application form required.
Deadline(s): Jan. 1 through June 1
EIN: 146018940

587
John & Ellen Burnham Educational Trust
c/o KeyBank N.A.
800 Superior Ave., 4th Fl.
Cleveland, OH 44114

Foundation type: Independent foundation
Limitations: Scholarships to individuals, primarily in ME, for higher education.
Financial data: Year ended 12/31/2004.
Assets, $145,757 (M); Expenditures, $11,633; Total giving, $8,500; Grants to individuals, totaling $8,500.
Type of support: Scholarships—to individuals.
Application information: Unsolicited requests for funds not accepted.
EIN: 016131036

588
John A. Burns Foundation
P.O. Box 861149
Wahiawa, HI 96786
Contact: Robert C. Oshiro, Pres.

Foundation type: Independent foundation
Limitations: Scholarships only to Hawaiian students from HI.
Financial data: Year ended 02/28/2005.
Assets, $2,861,505 (M); Expenditures, $227,298; Total giving, $210,000; Grants to individuals, 9 grants totaling $18,000.
Type of support: Scholarships—to individuals.
Application information: Applications accepted.
Deadline(s): None
Additional information: Applications by letter, including any supporting materials; Only Hawaiian applicants welcomed; Other applicants not considered or acknowledged.
EIN: 237391086

589
The Warren and Betty Burnside Foundation, Inc.
300 W. Pike St.
Clarksburg, WV 26301 (304) 623-3668
Contact: James C. West, Jr., Pres.
Application address: 360 Washington Ave., Clarksburg, WV 26301, tel.: (304) 624-5501

Foundation type: Independent foundation
Limitations: Scholarships restricted to residents of Harrison County, WV, who have attended a Harrison County high school for four years for attendance at colleges, universities, and technical schools.
Financial data: Year ended 01/31/2003.
Assets, $2,689,519 (M); Expenditures, $147,635; Total giving, $93,625; Grants to individuals, totaling $93,625.
Fields of interest: Vocational education.
Type of support: Support to graduates or students of specific schools; Undergraduate support.
Application information: Application form required.
Deadline(s): Mar. 20
Additional information: Completion of formal application required, including SAT or ACT scores, two letters of recommendation, a recent photograph, a list of financial aid received, a personal statement of 200 words or less, and if applicable, college transcripts.
Program description:
Scholarship Program: Applicants must have demonstrated a high scholastic achievement and shown leadership, good character, and initiative. Scholarships cover tuition and fees only, and are renewable.
EIN: 550709158

590
N. R. Burroughs Educational Fund
c/o BB&T, Trust Dept.
P.O. Box 2907
Wilson, NC   27894-2907   (276) 666-3198
Application address: c/o Lynanne Newman, P.O. Box 5228, Martinsville, VA 24115; tel.: (212) 666-3105

Foundation type: Independent foundation
Limitations: Student loans to qualified, deserving, and credit-worthy residents residing within a 200-mile radius of Martinsville, VA.
Financial data: Year ended 06/30/2005. Assets, $5,684,325 (M); Expenditures, $758,643; Total giving, $700,500; Grants to individuals, 244 grants totaling $697,933 (high: $3,000, low: $1,350).
Type of support: Student loans—to individuals.
Application information: Applications accepted. Application form required.
  Deadline(s): None
EIN: 521303602

591
Burrows Memorial Trust
306 E. Summit St.
Wilton, IA   52778
Contact: Jerry Grings, Secy.

Foundation type: Independent foundation
Limitations: Scholarships to high school seniors and graduates of Wilton Community School District, IA, who live within the boundaries of the school district. Scholarships are awarded on the basis of financial need, academic achievement, individual desire, and aptitude.
Financial data: Year ended 03/31/2005. Assets, $172,029 (M); Expenditures, $7,877; Total giving, $7,700; Grants to individuals, totaling $7,700.
Type of support: Support to graduates or students of specific schools; Undergraduate support.
Application information: Application form required.
  Deadline(s): Apr. 15.
  Additional information: Application should include trancripts.
EIN: 426097247

592
Fran & Jean Burst Educational Foundation, Inc.
105 S. Broadway
Greensburg, IN   47240   (812) 663-8478
Contact: G. Daryl Smith, Pres.

Foundation type: Independent foundation
Limitations: Scholarships to Batesville, IN, residents who attend Batesville High School or Oldenbug Academy.
Financial data: Year ended 06/30/2005. Assets, $264,128 (M); Expenditures, $18,437; Total giving, $13,000; Grants to individuals, 6 grants totaling $13,000.
Type of support: Support to graduates or students of specific schools; Undergraduate support.
Application information: Application form required.
  Initial approach: Letter requesting application.
  Deadline(s): July 1
EIN: 352000893

593
Abraham Burtman Charity Trust
c/o Christine R. Marshall
P.O. Box 608
Dover, NH   03820-4103

Foundation type: Independent foundation
Limitations: Undergraduate scholarships to financially needy NH residents.
Financial data: Year ended 12/31/2004. Assets, $1,625,353 (M); Expenditures, $110,048; Total giving, $82,000.
Type of support: Undergraduate support.
Application information: Application form required.
  Initial approach: Letter.
  Deadline(s): May 10
  Additional information: Application should include financial information.
EIN: 026004364

594
The William T. and Ethel Lewis Burton Foundation
641 W. Prien Lake Rd.
Lake Charles, LA   70601
Contact: William B. Lawton, Chair.

Foundation type: Independent foundation
Limitations: Scholarships for southwest LA high school seniors and the McNeese State University, LA, football team.
Financial data: Year ended 05/31/2004. Assets, $4,935,119 (M); Expenditures, $164,812; Total giving, $153,011; Grants to individuals, 27 grants totaling $26,000 (high: $1,500, low: $500).
Fields of interest: Athletics/sports, school programs; Athletics/sports, football.
Type of support: Support to graduates or students of specific schools; Undergraduate support.
Application information: Applications accepted. Application form required.
  Initial approach: Letter.
  Deadline(s): None
  Additional information: Recipients are selected by their institutions.
Program description:
  Scholarship Program: A scholarship committee of three education administrators and three members of the business community receives the applications and makes the final selection of the recipients. After notification by the committee, the foundation makes the scholarship payments directly to the college or university in the name of the individual recipient. The foundation makes payments of up to $500 per semester toward the cost of tuition, instructional materials, room and board, and all required and usual fees. Students must maintain a 2.5 GPA.
EIN: 726027957

595
Lila Draper Burton Trust
c/o JPMorgan Chase Bank, N.A
P.O. Box 1308
Milwaukee, WI   53201
Application address: c/o Carol Ruekert, Coord., School District of Waukesha, 222 Maple Ave., Waukesha, WI 53186, tel: (414) 521-5809

Foundation type: Independent foundation
Limitations: Undergraduate scholarships are awarded to residents of Waukesha County, WI, who have graduated from a Waukesha County, WI, high school and who have demonstrated academic achievement, personality and character qualities, school citizenship, high ACT and SAT scores, and financial need.
Financial data: Year ended 12/31/2004. Assets, $1,993,651 (M); Expenditures, $107,954; Total giving, $87,100; Grants to individuals, 313 grants totaling $87,100.
Type of support: Support to graduates or students of specific schools; Undergraduate support.
Application information: Contact guidance office of any Waukesha County high school for application forms and deadlines.
EIN: 396146782

596
Busch Family Foundation
148 S. Industrial Dr.
Saline, MI   48176
Application address: c/o Clinton High School, Attn.: Tim Wilson, Principal, 341 E. Michigan Ave., Clinton, MI 49236

Foundation type: Independent foundation
Limitations: Scholarships to graduates of Clinton High School, MI.
Financial data: Year ended 12/31/2004. Assets, $93,756 (M); Expenditures, $32,307; Total giving, $28,000; Grants to individuals, 14 grants totaling $25,000 (high: $3,750, low: $500).
Fields of interest: Vocational education.
Type of support: Support to graduates or students of specific schools; Undergraduate support.
Application information:
  Initial approach: Letter or telephone.
  Deadline(s): Mar. 27
  Additional information: Contact high school guidance office for current application guidelines; Completion of formal application required, including short biographical sketch, essays, high school transcripts, SAT and ACT scores, and three personal references.
EIN: 382671217

597
Busey-Mills Community Foundation
c/o Douglas C. Mills
201 W. Main St.
Urbana, IL   61801-2621

Foundation type: Independent foundation
Limitations: Scholarships to residents of IL, primarily in Champaign, for higher education.
Financial data: Year ended 12/31/2004. Assets, $835,849 (M); Expenditures, $23,485; Total giving, $19,208; Grants to individuals, totaling $14,208.
Type of support: Undergraduate support.
Application information: Unsolicited requests for funds not accepted.
EIN: 371267247

598
William E. and Margaret N. Bush Memorial Scholarship Fund
P.O. Box 247
Apollo, PA   15613

Foundation type: Independent foundation
Limitations: Scholarships to residents of Pittsburgh, PA.
Financial data: Year ended 12/31/2004. Assets, $592,282 (M); Expenditures, $25,908; Total giving, $19,000; Grants to individuals, 3 grants totaling $19,000.
Type of support: Scholarships—to individuals.

Application information: Applications not accepted.
EIN: 251814240

599
Elizabeth B. Bush Memorial Scholarship Trust
c/o KeyBank N.A.
800 Superior Ave., 4th Fl.
Cleveland, OH 44114

Foundation type: Independent foundation
Limitations: Scholarships to high school graduates who are residents of Lewis, NY. Recipients must seek at least a two-year program of higher study after graduation.
Financial data: Year ended 12/31/2003. Assets, $205,424 (M); Expenditures, $11,479; Total giving, $9,068; Grants to individuals, totaling $9,068.
Type of support: Undergraduate support.
Application information: Applications not accepted.
Additional information: Unsolicited requests for funds not accepted.
EIN: 146123826

600
Florence Evans Bushee Foundation, Inc.
c/o Palmer & Dodge, LLP
111 Huntington Ave. at Prudential Ctr.
Boston, MA 02199-7613 (617) 239-0556
Contact: Brenda Taylor, Fdn. Admin.

Foundation type: Independent foundation
Limitations: Undergraduate scholarships to residents of the Newbury, MA, area. Applicants must be graduates of Triton, Pentucket, Newburyport, Governor, or Dummer high schools.
Publications: Application guidelines; Informational brochure.
Financial data: Year ended 12/31/2004. Assets, $5,300,293 (M); Expenditures, $264,208; Total giving, $187,979; Grants to individuals, 136 grants totaling $183,979 (high: $3,800, low: $500).
Type of support: Support to graduates or students of specific schools; Undergraduate support.
Application information:
Initial approach: Letter.
Deadline(s): May 1
Additional information: Completion of formal application required, including transcripts; Interviews required.
EIN: 046035327

601
The Business and Professional Women's Foundation
(formerly BPW Foundation)
1900 M St., N.W., Ste. 310
Washington, DC 20036 (202) 293-1200
FAX: (202) 861-0298; URL: http://www.bpwusa.org/i4a/pages/index.cfm?pageid=4212

Foundation type: Public charity
Limitations: Scholarships and loans to financially needy female students over the age of 25 to pursue further education in order to enter, re-enter, or advance in the work force.
Publications: Annual report; Informational brochure.

Financial data: Year ended 09/30/2003. Assets, $7,036,874 (M); Expenditures, $1,264,399; Total giving, $65,000; Grants to individuals, 50 grants totaling $65,000 (high: $5,000, low: $500).
Fields of interest: Vocational education; Women.
Type of support: Scholarships—to individuals; Student loans—to individuals.
Application information: Application form required.
Deadline(s): Apr. 15
Program description:
Scholarships and Loans: All applicants must be female, at least 25 years of age, and a U.S. citizen. In addition, the individual must be within 12 to 24 months of graduating; be officially accepted into an accredited program or course of study at an institution in the U.S. or its territories; have a definite plan to use the desired training to upgrade skills for career advancement, to train for a new career field, or to enter or re-enter the job market; and demonstrate critical financial need.
EIN: 530237067

602
Alice Butler Foundation
(formerly J. D. and Alice Butler Memorial Scholarship Foundation)
c/o Wachovia Bank, N.A.
100 N. Main St., 13th Fl.
Winston-Salem, NC 27150
Application address: c/o Principal, Deerfield Beach Senior High School, 910 S.W. 15th St., Deerfield Beach, FL 33461

Foundation type: Independent foundation
Limitations: Scholarships to graduates of Deerfield Beach Senior High School, FL.
Financial data: Year ended 08/31/2005. Assets, $9,810,146 (M); Expenditures, $559,881; Total giving, $467,677; Grants to individuals, 820 grants totaling $467,677 (high: $34,357, low: $49).
Type of support: Support to graduates or students of specific schools; Undergraduate support.
Application information: Application form required.
Initial approach: Letter.
Deadline(s): Contact foundation for current application deadline
EIN: 596878169

603
The Butler Foundation
(formerly Neslab Charitable Foundation)
c/o Charter Trust Co.
P.O. Box 2530
Concord, NH 03302-2530

Foundation type: Independent foundation
Limitations: Scholarships to individuals studying environmental conservation.
Financial data: Year ended 12/31/2002. Assets, $6,321,804 (M); Expenditures, $299,883; Total giving, $288,226; Grants to individuals, 6 grants totaling $12,886 (high: $5,000, low: $500).
Fields of interest: Natural resources.
Type of support: Scholarships—to individuals.
Application information: Unsolicited requests for funds not accepted.
EIN: 222701588

604
Butler Manufacturing Company Foundation
P.O. Box 419917
Kansas City, MO 64141-0917 (816) 968-3208
Contact: Pamela Bird Yeater, Dir.
FAX: (816) 627-8946;
E-mail: psbirdyeater@butlermfg.com; URL: http://www.butlermfg.com/faq/Foundationguidelines.pdf

Foundation type: Company-sponsored foundation
Limitations: Scholarships only to children of full-time employees of Butler Manufacturing Company, and its wholly-owned subsidiaries.
Publications: Application guidelines; Informational brochure (including application guidelines).
Financial data: Year ended 12/31/2004. Assets, $6,166,062 (M); Expenditures, $295,049; Total giving, $275,201; Grants to individuals, 3 grants totaling $4,000 (high: $2,000, low: $1,000).
Type of support: Employee-related scholarships.
Application information: Application form required.
Initial approach: Telephone.
Deadline(s): Feb.
Additional information: Applications available at human resources offices at all company locations; Scholarships are paid directly to the student's academic institution.
Program description:
Scholarship Program: An independent committee of educators and professionals recommends eight new $2,500 scholarship winners to the foundation each year. Recipients are selected on the basis of academic achievement, financial need, character, and future promise. Scholarships are continued over a four-year period of study leading to a baccalaureate degree at an accredited college or university, providing the student performs in the upper half of the class academically, maintains conduct acceptable to the school and to the foundation, and carries a normal academic load.
EIN: 440663648

605
Butte Creek Foundation
901 Bruce Rd., Ste. 270
Chico, CA 95928 (530) 895-1512
Contact: John L. Burghardt, Dir.

Foundation type: Independent foundation
Limitations: Scholarships to residents of Butte County, CA.
Financial data: Year ended 12/31/2004. Assets, $1,761,574 (M); Expenditures, $94,260; Total giving, $92,295; Grants to individuals, totaling $8,100.
Type of support: Scholarships—to individuals.
Application information: Applications accepted.
Deadline(s): None
Additional information: Applications by letter.
EIN: 680111634

606
M. Verna Butterer Educational Trust
P.O. Box 273
Fountainville, PA 18923 (215) 249-0503
Contact: Elissa J. Kirkegard, Fdn. Admin.
URL: http://butterer.org/

Foundation type: Independent foundation
Limitations: Scholarships to graduates of Bucks County, PA, high schools for higher education.
Financial data: Year ended 01/31/2005. Assets, $4,657,639 (M); Expenditures, $258,818; Total giving, $214,352; Grants to

individuals, 39 grants totaling $214,352 (high: $16,500, low: $418).

Type of support: Support to graduates or students of specific schools; Undergraduate support.

Application information: Application form required.

Deadline(s): Contact foundation for current application deadline

Additional information: Applications available at public high school guidance departments in Bucks County, PA.

EIN: 237751390

607
Jane Buttrey Memorial Trust

c/o U.S. Bank, N.A.
P.O. Box 3168
Portland, OR   97208-3168

Foundation type: Independent foundation

Limitations: Scholarships to graduating high school seniors or undergraduate college students pursuing a course of study in the humanities or social sciences at specific MT and TX colleges and universities. See program description for further limitations.

Financial data: Year ended 06/30/2005. Assets, $1,435,975 (M); Expenditures, $102,275; Total giving, $90,000; Grants to individuals, totaling $90,000.

Fields of interest: Humanities; Social sciences.

Type of support: Support to graduates or students of specific schools; Undergraduate support.

Application information: Applications not accepted.

Program description:

Scholarship Program: Applicants must have at least a "B" average. No more than two years of awards are granted to each individual. The trust grants scholarships only to students of the following institutions: Montana State University, Bozeman; University of Montana, Missoula; Montana State University, Billings; Western Montana College of the University of Montana; Rocky Mountain College; Montana Tech of the University of Montana; Carroll College; Montana State University, Northern; St. Edward's University; Episcopal Theological Seminary of the Southwest, TX; St. Stephen's Episcopal School, Austin, TX.

EIN: 816014941

608
Gertrude Butts Memorial Home Association

31 Mulberry St.
Newark, NJ   07102   (973) 622-4306
Contact: Rt. Rev Jack M. McKelvey, Exec. Secy.

Foundation type: Independent foundation

Limitations: Scholarships to individuals in NJ for higher education.

Financial data: Year ended 12/31/2004. Assets, $2,274,445 (M); Expenditures, $70,754; Total giving, $61,000; Grants to individuals, totaling $60,000.

Type of support: Undergraduate support.

Application information: Applications accepted. Application form required.

Deadline(s): None

Additional information: Scholarships are renewable; Contact foundation for current application guidelines.

EIN: 226043630

609
Art & Clara Butts Scholarship Foundation

P.O. Box 577
Burwell, NE   68823-0577
Contact: Jo Ann Vodehnal

Foundation type: Independent foundation

Limitations: Scholarships to residents of Garfield County, NE, and the surrounding areas.

Financial data: Year ended 06/30/2004. Assets, $185,277 (M); Expenditures, $12,015; Total giving, $11,250; Grants to individuals, 13 grants totaling $11,250 (high: $1,000, low: $250).

Type of support: Scholarships—to individuals.

Application information: Application form required.

Deadline(s): June 1

Additional information: Application should include academic transcripts, college application letter, and two letters of recommendation.

EIN: 362899308

610
James F. Byrnes Foundation

P.O. Box 6781
Columbia, SC   29260   (803) 254-9325
Contact: Genny White, Exec. Secy.
FAX: (803) 254-9354;
E-mail: info@byrnesscholars.org; URL: http://www.byrnesscholars.org

Foundation type: Operating foundation

Limitations: Undergraduate scholarships to young residents of SC who are high school seniors or college freshmen to attend a 4-year college or university, and whose parent or parents are deceased.

Publications: Application guidelines; Informational brochure; Newsletter.

Financial data: Year ended 06/30/2004. Assets, $1,973,689 (M); Expenditures, $234,352; Total giving, $133,003; Grants to individuals, totaling $133,003.

Fields of interest: Residential/custodial care.

Type of support: Undergraduate support.

Application information: Applications accepted. Application form required.

Initial approach: Letter or telephone.

Deadline(s): Feb. 15

Applicants should submit the following:

1) Photograph
2) Class rank
3) Transcripts
4) ACT
5) SAT
6) Financial information

Additional information: Application should also include a brief autobiography; Interviews required.

Program description:

Byrnes Scholarship: College scholarships are awarded to high school seniors and college freshmen planning to pursue B.A. or B.S. degrees. Scholarships are not available for technical education or associate degrees. Recipients may attend four-year colleges or universities within or outside of SC. Applicants must demonstrate financial need, a satisfactory scholastic record, at least a 2.5 GPA if in college, and qualities of character, ability, and enterprise that indicate a worthwhile contribution to society. The scholarships are in the amount of approximately $2,750 each year and are renewable for a maximum of four years, contingent upon maintenance of adequate academic standing, personal involvement in the Byrnes Scholarship Program, and continuing need. The foundation recognizes that students with a

deceased parent or parents have more than a financial need. As such, the foundation's executive secretary is available to scholarship recipients as a counselor. Directors of the foundation and graduate Byrnes scholars also volunteer time and counsel recipients. The foundation hosts a number of events where scholars and graduates can meet, including fall dinners near college campuses, a weekend retreat in Mar. and an awards luncheon in June.

EIN: 576024756

611
C & E Foundation

c/o Norman A. Peil, Jr., Treas.
P.O. Box 20467
Lehigh Valley, PA   18002-0467

Foundation type: Independent foundation

Limitations: Scholarships to graduating students of two Warren county, NJ and one Carbon county, PA high schools.

Financial data: Year ended 12/31/2004. Assets, $4,959,529 (M); Expenditures, $335,281; Total giving, $294,507; Grants to individuals, totaling $194,507.

Type of support: Undergraduate support.

Application information: Applications by letter accepted throughout the year.

EIN: 232929096

612
Cabot Scholarship Foundation

200 W. Main St.
Cabot, AR   72023   (501) 843-6515
Contact: Calvin Aldridge, Treas.
URL: http://cabot.k12.ar.us/schools/chs/scholar/csf.htm

Foundation type: Public charity

Limitations: Scholarships to graduates of Cabot High School, AR.

Financial data: Year ended 07/31/2004. Assets, $344,865 (M); Expenditures, $19,000; Total giving, $19,000; Grants to individuals, 17 grants totaling $19,000 (high: $1,500, low: $500).

Type of support: Support to graduates or students of specific schools.

Application information: Application form required.

Additional information: Contact guidance counselor for current application deadline/guidelines.

EIN: 710713554

613
Cabot Scholarship Fund

c/o JPMorgan Chase Bank
P.O. Box 31412
Rochester, NY   14603-1412
Application address: c/o Anthony Teravainen, Scholarship America, Inc., Shepaug Valley Regional High School, South St., Washington, CT 06793

Foundation type: Independent foundation

Limitations: Scholarships to graduates of Shepaug Valley High School, CT, who are residents of Washington, CT.

Financial data: Year ended 02/28/2005. Assets, $260,369 (M); Expenditures, $15,770; Total giving, $12,000; Grants to individuals, 7 grants totaling $12,000 (high: $1,800, low: $1,600).

Type of support: Support to graduates or students of specific schools; Undergraduate support.

Application information: Application form required.
Deadline(s): Feb. 20 for FAFSA, Apr. 5 for
application including SAR.
EIN: 066113079

614
Robert and Mary Cade Foundation, Inc.
1106 N.W. 57th St.
Gainesville, FL 32605-4494   (352) 332-3093
Contact: Arnold Zimmerman, Secy.-Treas.

Foundation type: Operating foundation
Limitations: Scholarships to individuals residing in
FL and NC for undergraduate education.
Financial data: Year ended 12/31/2004.
Assets, $67,419 (M); Expenditures, $258,679;
Total giving, $195,736; Grants to individuals, 16
grants totaling $88,170 (high: $12,000, low:
$1,500).
Type of support: Undergraduate support.
Application information: Applications accepted.
Deadline(s): None
Additional information: Applications by letter
outlining financial need accepted.
EIN: 592938184

615
George A. Cady Educational Trust
c/o Wells Fargo Bank Nevada, N.A.
P.O. Box 95021
Henderson, NV 89009-5021
Application address: c/o Counselor, Valley High
School, Menlo, WA 98561, tel.: (206) 942-5855

Foundation type: Independent foundation
Limitations: Scholarships to graduating seniors
from Valley High School, Menlo, WA.
Financial data: Year ended 12/31/2004.
Assets, $110,956 (M); Expenditures, $6,187;
Total giving, $3,225; Grants to individuals, 3 grants
totaling $3,225.
Type of support: Support to graduates or students
of specific schools; Undergraduate support.
Application information: Applications accepted.
Application form required.
Deadline(s): First Fri. in May
Additional information: Application should also
include GPA, name of college or university to
attend, and future plans; Application
information available from Valley High School
guidance counselor.
EIN: 916088092

616
The William M. & A. Cafaro Family Foundation
c/o The Cataro Co.
2445 Belmont Ave.
P.O. Box 2186
Youngstown, OH 44504-0186
Contact: Joseph S. Nohra, Tr.

Foundation type: Independent foundation
Limitations: Scholarships to qualifying residents of
the greater Youngstown, OH area.
Financial data: Year ended 03/31/2005.
Assets, $14,675,306 (M); Expenditures,
$604,069; Total giving, $544,887; Grants to
individuals, 8 grants totaling $20,000 (high:
$5,000, low: $2,000).
Type of support: Undergraduate support.

Application information: Applications accepted.
Application form required.
Deadline(s): May 1
EIN: 311550874

617
Cahp Foundation
2030 V St.
Sacramento, CA 95818-1730   (916) 452-6751
Contact: William Admire, Tr.

Foundation type: Public charity
Limitations: Scholarships to dependents of
uniformed California Highway Patrol Officers for
undergraduate education.
Financial data: Year ended 12/31/2004.
Assets, $464,964 (M); Expenditures, $29,822;
Total giving, $24,750; Grants to individuals, 29
grants totaling $24,750 (high: $2,000, low: $750).
Type of support: Employee-related scholarships;
Undergraduate support.
Application information: Contact foundation for
current application deadline/guidelines.
EIN: 942716339

618
The Cain Family Foundation
121 E. Kern Ave. H.
Tulare, CA 93274   (559) 686-3832

Foundation type: Independent foundation
Limitations: Scholarships to graduates of Tulare,
CA, high schools.
Financial data: Year ended 06/30/2005.
Assets, $1,234 (M); Expenditures, $56,426; Total
giving, $55,226; Grants to individuals, totaling
$55,226.
Type of support: Support to graduates or students
of specific schools.
Application information: Applications accepted.
Initial approach: Letter.
Deadline(s): None
Additional information: Contact foundation for
current application guidelines.
EIN: 770455208

619
Calcot-Seitz Foundation
c/o Scholarship Comm.
P.O. Box 259
Bakersfield, CA 93302-0259

Foundation type: Independent foundation
Limitations: Scholarships to students from
cotton-producing areas in CA and AZ to pursue
four-year degrees in agriculture.
Financial data: Year ended 08/31/2005.
Assets, $685,803 (M); Expenditures, $41,035;
Total giving, $38,950; Grants to individuals,
totaling $38,950.
Fields of interest: Agriculture.
Type of support: Scholarships—to individuals.
Application information: Application form required.
Deadline(s): Mar. 31
Applicants should submit the following:
1) Letter(s) of recommendation
2) Essay
3) Transcripts
4) GPA
Program description:
Scholarship Program: Applicants must be
full-time students and have at least a 3.0 GPA in
high school and college. Recipients are chosen on
the basis of scholastic aptitude, leadership

potential, and financial need. Scholarships are not
renewable. The Joe and Joyce Sheely Memorial
Scholarship is a $3,000 award granted to the top
applicant from AZ.
EIN: 953434180

620
The Caleb Foundation, Inc.
c/o Randy Alan Weiss
P.O. Box 988
Arlington, VA 22216
E-mail: hbrauner@thecalebfoundation.org;
Additional address: 491 Humphrey St.,
Swampscott, MA 01907, tel.: (781) 595-4665,
FAX: (781) 592-0770; URL: http://
www.thecalebfoundation.org

Foundation type: Operating foundation
Limitations: Scholarships primarily to residents of
Gainsville, VA.
Financial data: Year ended 11/30/2003.
Assets, $485,104 (M); Expenditures, $49,972;
Total giving, $22,232.
Type of support: Scholarships—to individuals.
Application information: Applications not
accepted.
EIN: 541527522

621
California Alpha Delta Phi Memorial Foundation
c/o Dale Sartor
930 Paramount Rd.
Oakland, CA 94610

Foundation type: Independent foundation
Limitations: Scholarships to members of the
University of California, Berkeley, chapter of Alpha
Delta Phi Fraternity, CA.
Financial data: Year ended 12/31/2004.
Assets, $1,213,933 (M); Expenditures, $52,586;
Total giving, $49,900; Grants to individuals,
totaling $49,900.
Fields of interest: Students, sororities/fraternities.
Type of support: Support to graduates or students
of specific schools; Undergraduate support.
Application information: Application form required.
Deadline(s): Apr. and Oct
Additional information: Interviews required.
Program description:
Scholarship Program: Scholarships are awarded
twice per year on the basis of financial need,
service to the fraternity and the community, and
academic achievement. Prospective applicants are
encouraged to consider fraternities as a housing
option.
EIN: 946065541

622
California Association of Realtors Scholarship Foundation
525 S. Virgil Ave.
Los Angeles, CA 90020   (213) 739-8200
FAX: (213) 480-7724; E-mail: scholarship@car.org;
URL: http://www.car.org/index.php?id=ODU=

Foundation type: Public charity
Limitations: Scholarships to students enrolled at a
CA college or university for careers related to real
estate. Awards are for $3,000 to students of
four-year colleges/universities and $1,000 to
students of two-year colleges/universities.
Financial data: Year ended 12/31/2004.
Assets, $1,095,550 (M); Expenditures, $44,586;

Total giving, $38,750; Grants to individuals, 37 grants totaling $38,750 (high: $2,000, low: $500).
Fields of interest: Housing/shelter, formal/general education.
Type of support: Undergraduate support.
Application information: Applications accepted. Application form required. Application form available on the grantmaker's Web site.
  Deadline(s): Sept. 18
  Applicants should submit the following:
    1) Letter(s) of recommendation
    2) GPA
    3) Financial information
    4) Essay
  Additional information: Applicants must have completed at least 12 college credits and have at least a 2.6 GPA.
EIN: 237230340

623
California Japanese-American Alumni Association

c/o Emiko Yamada
1060 Tahoe Dr.
Belmont, CA 94002-3011
Contact: Katherine Yoshii, Tr.
Application address: P.O. Box 15235, San Francisco, CA 94115-9991, tel.: (510) 622-7804

Foundation type: Independent foundation
Limitations: Scholarships to Japanese-American students enrolled at one of the nine University of California campuses for undergraduate or graduate education.
Financial data: Year ended 06/30/2005.
Assets, $300,758 (M); Expenditures, $12,016; Total giving, $6,600; Grants to individuals, 5 grants totaling $6,500.
Fields of interest: Asians/Pacific Islanders; Japan.
Type of support: Support to graduates or students of specific schools; Graduate support; Undergraduate support.
Application information: Application form required.
  Initial approach: Letter.
  Applicants should submit the following:
    1) Letter(s) of recommendation
    2) Essay
    3) Transcripts
  Additional information: Contact association for current application deadline; Application must also include career objectives.

Program description:
  Scholarship Program: Each year the association focuses its scholarships on specific fields of study. Scholarships are awarded on the basis of academic excellence and commitment to community and social concerns. Previous recipients of awards of $1,000 or more are ineligible. Recipients who are awarded more than $5,000 from other scholarships and grants in the same academic year will have the excess amount over $5,000 deducted from the amount of their CJAAA awards.
EIN: 941179725

624
California Job's Daughters Foundation

303 W. Lincoln Ave., Ste. 210
Anaheim, CA 92805 (714) 491-4994
Contact: Jo-Ann Anderson, Pres.
Scholarship address: Betty Klotz, Schol. Chair., 1228 Moss Rock Ct., Santa Rosa, CA 95404
E-mail: caiojdfund@hotmail.com

Foundation type: Public charity

Limitations: Scholarships to California Job's Daughters based on academic merit.
Financial data: Year ended 12/31/2004.
Assets, $359,663 (M); Expenditures, $22,752; Total giving, $17,660; Grants to individuals, 13 grants totaling $8,200 (high: $1,200, low: $500).
Fields of interest: Higher education.
Type of support: Scholarships—to individuals.
Application information: Applications accepted. Application form required.
  Initial approach: Letter or E-mail.
  Deadline(s): Apr. 1
  Applicants should submit the following:
    1) Transcripts
    2) Letter(s) of recommendation
EIN: 330692562

625
California Masonic Foundation

1111 California St.
San Francisco, CA 94108
Contact: Angel Alvarez-Mapp, Coord.
E-mail: foundation@Freemason.org; URL: http://www.freemason.org

Foundation type: Independent foundation
Limitations: Undergraduate scholarships to financially needy U.S. citizens, who are high school seniors and have been residents of CA for at least one year, for study at accredited two- and four-year schools.
Publications: Application guidelines.
Financial data: Year ended 06/30/2004.
Assets, $12,687,783 (M); Expenditures, $816,362; Total giving, $484,250; Grants to individuals, 195 grants totaling $6,000 (high: $2,500, low: $625).
Fields of interest: Fraternal societies.
Type of support: Undergraduate support.
Application information: Application form required.
  Initial approach: Web site, requesting application form between Sept. 1 and Feb. 15.
  Deadline(s): Feb. 15
  Applicants should submit the following:
    1) Letter(s) of recommendation
    2) Essay
    3) SAT
    4) Transcripts
  Additional information: Application should also include name of college where accepted, parents' and students' latest tax returns; Interviews required for some programs.

Program description:
  California Masonic Foundation Scholarships: In addition to its general scholarship fund, the foundation manages other scholarship programs that grant awards to CA residents. These programs include:
  · Robinson Scholarships: Provides scholarships of $2,500
  · Lister Scholarships: Provides scholarships of $2,500
  · MacKechnie Scholarships: Provides scholarships of $2,500
  · Coalinga Scholarships: Provides scholarships of $2,500
  · Cazneaux Scholarships: Provides scholarships of $2,500
  · Brotherhood Scholarships: Provides scholarships of $2,500
  · Blomseth Scholarships: Provides scholarships of $2,500
  · Starr King Scholarships: Provides scholarships of $2,500
  · Arnold Wilmott Scholarships: Provides scholarships of $2,500

  · Wade/Amaranth Scholarships: Provides scholarships of $2,500
  · McElwain Scholarships: Provides scholarships of $2,500
  · Soquel-Pajaro Scholarships: Provides scholarships of $2,500
  · C.E. Towne Scholarship: Provides scholarships of $10,000
  · Chowchilla Scholarships: Provides scholarships of $500
  · The Amaranth Scholarships: Provides scholarships of $2,500 to female high school seniors
All applications will be evaluated on academic standing, financial need, and student's essay. All scholarships are renewable annually. Applicants should submit only one application for consideration in all scholarship funds. While not required, some preference is given to applicants with Masonic relationships and/or Masonic youth group membership.
EIN: 237013074

626
Calista Scholarship Fund

(formerly David K. Nicolai Memorial Scholarship Fund)
301 Calista Ct., Ste. A
Anchorage, AK 99518-3028 (907) 279-5516
Contact: Bob Charles, Pres.
FAX: (907) 272-5060;
E-mail: calista@calistacorp.com; Additional tel.: (800) 277-5516; URL: http://www.calistacorp.com/share2.html

Foundation type: Public charity
Limitations: Scholarships to AK Natives for continuing educational activities, for the benefit of the region and its people.
Financial data: Year ended 12/31/2004.
Assets, $283,594 (M); Expenditures, $109,656; Total giving, $102,736; Grants to individuals, 77 grants totaling $102,736 (high: $2,000, low: $236).
Fields of interest: Native Americans/American Indians.
Type of support: Scholarships—to individuals.
Application information: Application form required.
  Initial approach: Letter or telephone.
  Deadline(s): June 30
  Additional information: Application should include transcripts of career and educational goals.

Program description:
  Scholarship Program: Recipients must be accepted to an accredited institution of higher education, an Alaskan Native shareholder, or lineal descendant of an Alaskan Native shareholder with ties to the Calista, AK, region. Recipients must have at least a 2.0 GPA.
EIN: 920088631

627
Ina Calkins Foundation

c/o Bank of America, N.A.
P.O. Box 419119
Kansas City, MO 64141-6119
Contact: David P. Ross, Sr. V.P.
Application address: c/o Bank of America, Attn.: Spence Heddens, 1200 Main St., 14th Fl., P.O. Box 419119, Kansas City, MO 64141-6119; URL: http://www.calkinsboard.org

Foundation type: Independent foundation
Limitations: Scholarships to residents of Kansas City, MO.

Financial data: Year ended 12/31/2003. Assets, $6,048,927 (M); Expenditures, $252,444; Total giving, $245,448; Grants to individuals, 9 grants totaling $24,200 (high: $3,300, low: $1,800).
Type of support: Scholarships—to individuals.
Application information:
Deadline(s): Jan. 1, Apr. 1, July 1 and Oct. 11
Additional information: Application by letter of no more than three pages, including appropriate attachments.
EIN: 526994869

628
Fuller E. Callaway Foundation
P.O. Box 790
LaGrange, GA 30241 (706) 884-7348
Contact: H. Speer Burdette III, Genl. Mgr.
FAX: (706) 884-0201; E-mail: hsburdette@callaway-foundation.org

Foundation type: Independent foundation
Limitations: Scholarships to individuals who have been residents of Troup County or La Grange, GA, for at least two years. See program description for further limitations.
Publications: Informational brochure.
Financial data: Year ended 12/31/2004. Assets, $50,574,972 (M); Expenditures, $6,979,463; Total giving, $1,193,103; Grants to individuals, 97 grants totaling $321,570 (low: $500 average grant: $500-$10,000).
Fields of interest: Graduate/professional education.
Type of support: Employee-related scholarships; Scholarships—to individuals; Graduate support; Undergraduate support.
Application information: Application form required.
Initial approach: Letter for Hatton Lovejoy Graduate Studies Fund.
Deadline(s): Feb. 15 for undergraduate scholarships and June 30 for graduate scholarships
Additional information: Applications available through high school guidance counselor; Interviews required.
Program description:
Hatton Lovejoy Scholarship Plan: Applicants must have been residents of Troup County, GA, for at least two years before submitting applications. Additionally, applicants must be graduates of, or within six months of graduation from, an accredited high school with a scholastic standing in the upper 25 percent of their classes. While in college, recipients must maintain a cumulative scholastic standing in the upper 50 percent of their college classes. The maximum scholarship award is $1,200 per quarter or $1,800 per semester of college attendance for 12 quarters or 8 semesters for a total maximum of $14,400. Hatton Lovejoy Graduate Studies Fund: Scholarships are awarded to those seeking a graduate degree. First preference is given to sons of former employees of Callaway Mills Company, and second to those residing within 50 miles of LaGrange who are graduates of LaGrange public schools. Award amounts vary depending on specific circumstances.
EIN: 580566148

629
Callejo-Botello Foundation
(formerly Callejo-Botello Foundation Charitable Trust)
4314 N. Central Expwy.
Dallas, TX 75206-6536 (214) 741-6710
Contact: William F. Callejo, Tr.

Foundation type: Independent foundation
Limitations: Scholarships primarily to students planning to attend educational institutions in TX.
Financial data: Year ended 12/31/2004. Assets, $177,455 (M); Expenditures, $53,622; Total giving, $46,585; Grants to individuals, totaling $46,585.
Type of support: Scholarships—to individuals.
Application information: Applications accepted. Application form required.
Initial approach: Letter requesting application.
Deadline(s): Apr. 23
EIN: 751678195

630
Stephen G. Calvert Memorial Merit Scholarship Foundation
c/o 5 Tower Bridge
300 Barr Harbor Dr., Ste. 600
West Conshohocken, PA 19428-2998
Contact: Geraldine Livingston

Foundation type: Company-sponsored foundation
Limitations: Scholarships to dependents of Keystone Foods Corp. employees.
Financial data: Year ended 10/31/2002. Assets, $0 (M); Expenditures, $142,120; Total giving, $123,691; Grants to individuals, 24 grants totaling $123,691 (high: $6,750, low: $1,000).
Type of support: Employee-related scholarships.
Application information: Application form required.
Initial approach: Letter.
Deadline(s): None
EIN: 232816413

631
Francis L. Calvi Memorial Foundation
14 S. California Ave.
Atlantic City, NJ 08401-6413 (609) 345-0151

Foundation type: Company-sponsored foundation
Limitations: Scholarships only to employees and children of employees of Calvi Electric Company, residing in the NJ jurisdiction of Local No. 211.
Financial data: Year ended 12/31/2004. Assets, $161,168 (M); Expenditures, $16,113; Total giving, $16,000; Grants to individuals, 9 grants totaling $16,000 (high: $2,000, low: $1,000).
Type of support: Employee-related scholarships.
Application information: Application form required.
Additional information: Application should include transcripts.
EIN: 222769316

632
Camden County Hero Scholarship 200 Club, Inc.
191 White Horse Pike
Berlin, NJ 08009 (856) 546-0607
Contact: Muriel Mansmann, Secy.

Foundation type: Independent foundation
Limitations: Scholarships to spouses and children of Camden County, NJ, firefighters and law enforcement officers who lost their lives or became disabled in the line of duty. Scholarships are for attendance at colleges, junior colleges, or postsecondary vocational schools. Some work-related continuing education grants for firefighters and officers are also available. Selection is based on need, scholarship, character, and extracurricular activities.
Financial data: Year ended 09/30/2004. Assets, $0 (M); Expenditures, $145,536; Total giving, $36,768; Grants to individuals, 10 grants totaling $36,768 (high: $8,271, low: $967).
Fields of interest: Vocational education; Adult/continuing education; Crime/law enforcement, police agencies; Disasters, fire prevention/control.
Type of support: Technical education support; Undergraduate support.
Application information: Applications accepted.
Deadline(s): None
Additional information: Application by letter.
EIN: 226105887

633
The Dave Cameron Educational Foundation
P.O. Box 181
York, SC 29745-0181 (803) 684-4968

Foundation type: Independent foundation
Limitations: Educational grants to undergraduate students within the York, SC, area who maintain a minimum GPA of 2.0. Preference given to those studying agriculture.
Financial data: Year ended 03/31/2005. Assets, $292,487 (M); Expenditures, $12,522; Total giving, $11,000; Grants to individuals, totaling $11,000.
Fields of interest: Agriculture.
Type of support: Undergraduate support.
Application information: Applications accepted. Application form required.
Deadline(s): None
EIN: 237080657

634
Camp Foundation
P.O. Box 813
Franklin, VA 23851
Contact: Bobby B. Worrell, Exec. Dir.

Foundation type: Independent foundation
Limitations: Scholarships to graduating high school seniors who are residents of the city of Franklin and the counties of Southampton and Isle of Wight, VA.
Publications: Application guidelines.
Financial data: Year ended 12/31/2004. Assets, $19,580,051 (M); Expenditures, $1,040,494; Total giving, $905,418; Grants to individuals, 28 grants totaling $90,000 (high: $4,500, low: $3,000).
Type of support: Undergraduate support.
Application information: Application form required.
Initial approach: Applicants file with their high school principals who then file with the foundation.
Deadline(s): Feb. 20 for new applicants, Mar. 1 for renewals
Applicants should submit the following:
1) Photograph
2) Transcripts
Additional information: Applications should also include three letters of recommendation, family financial statement, and evaluation of applicant by principal; Recipients announced on or after June 5.

Program description:
Scholarship Program: Recipients are selected on the basis of character, leadership, community service, academic achievement, and value to the community after graduation.
- Camp Foundation Colgate W. Darden Scholarship: Each year one new scholarship of $4,500 is awarded. The recipient is chosen solely on the basis of academic achievement, without regard for financial need.
- Camp Foundation Scholarships: Each year six new scholarships of $3,000 are awarded. Recipients are chosen with regard for financial need.

Both scholarship programs are renewable for up to three additional years.
EIN: 546052488

635
Camp Mohawk Scholarship Trust
P.O. Box 232
Alvin, TX   77512-0232
Application address: 802 S. Johnson, Alvin, TX 77511; tel.: (281) 585-6224

Foundation type: Independent foundation
Limitations: Scholarships to graduating seniors of Alvin High School, TX.
Financial data: Year ended 07/31/2005. Assets, $488,198 (M); Expenditures, $32,195; Total giving, $24,000; Grants to individuals, 4 grants totaling $24,000.
Type of support: Support to graduates or students of specific schools; Undergraduate support.
Application information: Applications accepted. Application form required.
Deadline(s): Apr.15
Applicants should submit the following:
1) Financial information
2) Transcripts
3) Essay
Additional information: Application should also include SAT or ACT scores, proof of financial need and three letters of recommendation.
EIN: 376387595

636
Lucille Camp Trust
c/o JPMorgan Chase Bank, N.A.
P.O. Box 1308
Milwaukee, WI   53201
Contact: Steve Eikenberry
Application address: c/o Wabash High School, 580 N. Miami St., Wabash, IN 46992

Foundation type: Independent foundation
Limitations: Scholarships to graduating seniors of Wabash High School, IN or graduates not more than three years prior to applying for award.
Financial data: Year ended 02/28/2005. Assets, $477,575 (M); Expenditures, $11,019; Total giving, $6,550; Grants to individuals, 10 grants totaling $6,550 (high: $655, low: $655).
Type of support: Support to graduates or students of specific schools; Undergraduate support.
Application information: Application form required.
Deadline(s): 1st Fri. in Mar.
EIN: 356648622

637
Alfred Campanelli Charitable Foundation
P.O. Box 850985
Braintree, MA   02185-0985
Contact: Robert DeMarco, Tr.
Application address: 1 Campanelli Dr., Braintree, MA 02184-5215

Foundation type: Independent foundation
Limitations: Scholarships to local MA high school students for higher education.
Financial data: Year ended 12/31/2004. Assets, $449,088 (M); Expenditures, $94,075; Total giving, $93,950; Grants to individuals, totaling $10,000.
Type of support: Undergraduate support.
Application information:
Initial approach: Letter or telephone.
Additional information: Contact foundation for current application deadline/guidelines.
EIN: 042991588

638
Ruth Camp Campbell Charitable Trust
(formerly Ruth Camp McDougall Charitable Trust)
c/o Brown Brothers Harriman Trust Co.
140 Broadway, 4th Fl.
New York, NY   10005
Application address: c/o Victoria Peaper, Brown Brothers Harriman Trust Co., 240 Royal Palm Way, Palm Beach, FL 33480

Foundation type: Independent foundation
Limitations: Scholarships to residents of VA, with preference to Southampton, Sussex, Surrey, Isle of Wight, Nansemond and Greenville counties.
Financial data: Year ended 12/31/2004. Assets, $10,886,640 (M); Expenditures, $463,456; Total giving, $395,000.
Type of support: Undergraduate support.
Application information: Applications accepted.
Initial approach: Letter.
Deadline(s): None
Additional information: Contact foundation for current application guidelines; Application by letter.
EIN: 546162697

639
Ernest and Lillian E. Campbell Foundation
P.O. Box 51
Julesburg, CO   80737
Contact: Anna R. Scott, Exec. Dir.

Foundation type: Independent foundation
Limitations: Scholarships to graduating seniors of high schools in Sedgwick County, CO only.
Financial data: Year ended 12/31/2004. Assets, $2,441,424 (M); Expenditures, $148,740; Total giving, $74,900; Grants to individuals, 25 grants totaling $14,500 (high: $2,250, low: $250).
Type of support: Support to graduates or students of specific schools; Undergraduate support.
Application information: Applications not accepted.
Program description:
Scholarship Program: Recipients must maintain a GPA of at least 3.0 to remain eligible for scholarship in future years.
EIN: 841271390

640
W. C. & Pearl Campbell Scholarship Fund for Linfield College Students
c/o U.S. Bank, N.A.
P.O. Box 3168
Portland, OR   97208-3168

Foundation type: Independent foundation
Limitations: Scholarships to undergraduate and graduate students studying full-time at Linfield College, OR.
Financial data: Year ended 06/30/2005. Assets, $188,153 (M); Expenditures, $18,060; Total giving, $14,500; Grants to individuals, totaling $14,500.
Type of support: Support to graduates or students of specific schools; Graduate support; Undergraduate support.
Application information:
Deadline(s): May 1
Additional information: Contact fund for current application guidelines.
Program description:
Scholarship Program: High school applicants must have at least a 2.5 GPA, college student applicants must have at least a 2.0 GPA. Preference is shown to students with financial need and whose GPAs exceed the minimum requirement.
EIN: 936021036

641
The J. Colin Campbell Scholarship Fund
3040 West Point Rd.
Lancaster, OH   43130
Contact: William J. Sitterley, Tr.

Foundation type: Independent foundation
Limitations: Scholarships to graduates of Fairfield County, OH, high schools.
Financial data: Year ended 05/31/2005. Assets, $1,705,227 (M); Expenditures, $85,084; Total giving, $71,300; Grants to individuals, 20 grants totaling $71,300 (high: $5,800, low: $1,500).
Type of support: Support to graduates or students of specific schools; Technical education support; Undergraduate support.
Application information: Application form required.
Deadline(s): 2nd Mon. in Mar.
Applicants should submit the following:
1) Class rank
2) Transcripts
3) GPA
4) ACT
Additional information: This fund shares an application process with the Mildred J. Herzberger Charitable Trust, the Mary Margaret Ackers Charitable Trust, and the Alice Kindler Scholarship Fund.
Program description:
J. Colin Campbell Scholarship: Recipients must be residents of Fairfield County for a minimum of three years, and have attended a high school in Fairfield County the last three years of their secondary education, including graduation. Recipients must maintain a good scholastic record, attend accredited state-supported colleges or universities or technical or vocational schools in OH, and must be full-time students with a minimum of 15 hours per term and maintain a 2.0 GPA. Applicants need not be recent high school graduates.
EIN: 316204632

642
Canaan Exchange Club Charitable Trust
c/o Trust Co. of the Berkshires
99 North St.
Pittsfield, MA 01201-5106
Contact: Eugene Cornell, Trust Off., Trust Co. of the Berkshires
Application address: 100 Main St., Canaan, CT 06018

Foundation type: Independent foundation
Limitations: Scholarships to local area Canaan, CT, high school students for higher education.
Financial data: Year ended 12/31/2004. Assets, $35,700 (M); Expenditures, $12,102; Total giving, $11,000; Grants to individuals, totaling $11,000.
Type of support: Undergraduate support.
Application information: Application form required.
Deadline(s): 30 days prior to award date
Additional information: Application should include transcripts and parents' financial information.
EIN: 061030724

643
Jesse W. Cannon Scholarship Foundation
c/o Bank of America, N.A.
P.O. Box 831041
Dallas, TX 75283-1041
Contact: Lewis D. Jones, Dir.
Application address: P.O. Box 1284, Fayetteville, AR 72702-1284, tel.: (501) 443-4313

Foundation type: Independent foundation
Limitations: Low-interest educational loans to students attending the University of Arkansas, Fayetteville.
Financial data: Year ended 04/30/2005. Assets, $2,371,490 (M); Expenditures, $28,461; Total giving, $0; Loans to individuals, totaling $21,000.
Type of support: Student loans—to individuals; Support to graduates or students of specific schools; Undergraduate support.
Application information: Applications accepted. Application form required.
Initial approach: Letter requesting application.
Deadline(s): None
Additional information: Applications should also include grades and explanation of extenuating circumstances.
EIN: 716099820

644
Canton Community Foundation
50430 School House Rd., Ste. 200
Canton, MI 48187 (734) 495-1200
Contact: Joan Noricks, Pres.
FAX: (734) 495-1212;
E-mail: info@cantonfoundation.org; Additional E-mail: jnoricks@cantonfoundation.org;
URL: http://www.cantonfoundation.org

Foundation type: Community foundation
Limitations: Scholarships to residents of Canton or Plymouth, MI.
Publications: Annual report; Grants list; Informational brochure (including application guidelines).
Financial data: Year ended 06/30/2005. Assets, $1,760,767 (M); Expenditures, $318,480; Total giving, $87,878; Grants to individuals, 30 grants totaling $35,591.
Type of support: Scholarships—to individuals.
Application information: Application form required.

Initial approach: Letter or telephone.
Deadline(s): None
Program description:
Scholarship Program: Recipient must maintain a GPA of at least 2.5.
EIN: 382898615

645
Jasmine L. Cantor Foundation, Inc.
P.O. Box 1279
Jamestown, NY 14702

Foundation type: Independent foundation
Limitations: Scholarships to the top ten graduates of Jamestown High School, NY, to attend four-year colleges.
Financial data: Year ended 12/31/2004. Assets, $278,963 (M); Expenditures, $19,152; Total giving, $15,000; Grants to individuals, 10 grants totaling $15,000.
Type of support: Support to graduates or students of specific schools; Undergraduate support.
Application information:
Initial approach: Letter.
Deadline(s): Contact foundation for current application deadline/guidelines.
EIN: 161287432

646
CAP Charitable Foundation USA
1160 Pepsi Pl., Ste. 206
Charlottesville, VA 22901-0807
(434) 964-1588
Contact: Fran Hardey, Exec. Asst.
FAX: (434) 964-1589; E-mail: franh@ronbrown.org

Foundation type: Independent foundation
Limitations: Scholarships to academically talented, highly motivated African American students for undergraduate education.
Publications: Application guidelines; Informational brochure; Newsletter.
Financial data: Year ended 12/31/2004. Assets, $37,797 (M); Expenditures, $809,998; Total giving, $270,689; Grants to individuals, 50 grants totaling $270,689.
Fields of interest: African Americans/Blacks.
Type of support: Undergraduate support.
Application information: Application form required.
Initial approach: Applications by Fax or E-mail not accepted.
Deadline(s): Jan. 9
Applicants should submit the following:
  1) Transcripts
  2) Financial information
Additional information: Application should also include SAT or ACT scores, two essays, and two letters of recommendation; See Web site for further application information.
Program description:
Scholarship Program: Awards at least ten scholarships of $10,000 annually for four years, for a total of $40,000. Recipients may attend any four-year college or university, and are required to participate in at least one pre-professional internship.
EIN: 541832314

647
The Cape Cod Foundation
(formerly The Community Foundation of Cape Cod)
259 Willow St.
P.O. Box 406
Yarmouthport, MA 02675 (508) 790-3040
Contact: Elizabeth Gawron, Pres.
FAX: (508) 790-4069;
E-mail: info@capecodfoundation.org; Additional tel.: (800) 947-2322; Additional E-mail: egawron@capecodfoundation.org; URL: http://www.capecodfoundation.org

Foundation type: Community foundation
Limitations: Scholarships to residents of Barnstable, Duke and Nantucket counties, MA, for undergraduate education.
Publications: Application guidelines; Informational brochure; Newsletter.
Financial data: Year ended 12/31/2004. Assets, $24,067,970 (M); Expenditures, $4,979,767; Total giving, $4,101,568.
Fields of interest: Music; Medical school/education.
Type of support: Undergraduate support.
Application information: Application form required.
Initial approach: Telephone.
Deadline(s): Apr. 1
Additional information: See Web site for program listings, further application information and guidelines.
EIN: 510140462

648
The Capricorn Foundation
2 Lower Waverly Rd.
Pawleys Island, SC 29585
Contact: L.E. Jones, Pres.

Foundation type: Independent foundation
Limitations: Scholarships to individuals of the southeastern U.S. who have been residents for at least six months.
Financial data: Year ended 12/31/2002. Assets, $119,941 (M); Expenditures, $67,883; Total giving, $65,817; Grants to individuals, 6 grants totaling $40,817 (high: $23,151, low: $518).
Type of support: Scholarships—to individuals.
Application information: Applications accepted. Application form required.
Deadline(s): None
Additional information: Application should include a request for personal information, educational institutions which have been applied to, and a written summary of the basis for the request to the foundation to receive a scholarship grant.
EIN: 571011351

649
Robert C. Carco 31 Charitable Foundation
7 Wainwright Rd., Ste. 109
Winchester, MA 01890-2394 (781) 729-4424
Contact: Mario P. Carco, Tr.

Foundation type: Independent foundation
Limitations: Scholarships to graduates of Belmont High School, MA, and students of Roman Catholic elementary and high schools.
Financial data: Year ended 12/31/2004. Assets, $192,580 (M); Expenditures, $13,880; Total giving, $13,000; Grants to individuals, totaling $13,000.
Fields of interest: Roman Catholic agencies & churches.

Type of support: Support to graduates or students of specific schools; Precollege support; Undergraduate support.
Application information: Application form required.
  Deadline(s): Contact high school for current application deadline
  Additional information: Applications should include transcripts, recommendations from faculty and/or community leaders, financial statements, and proposed course of study.
Program description:
  Scholarship Program: Scholarships are awarded on the basis of financial need, community and civic involvement, industry, and scholastic ability as measured by grades, performance, and recommendations.
EIN: 043060962

650

Florence Lewis Carkeek Trust

c/o Union Bank of California, N.A.
P.O. Box 84495
Seattle, WA 98124-5795

Foundation type: Independent foundation
Limitations: Scholarships to graduating seniors of the ten public high schools in Seattle School District No. 1 WA, to attend state-supported institutions.
Financial data: Year ended 03/31/2005.
Assets, $3,095,467 (M); Expenditures, $136,680; Total giving, $103,967; Grants to individuals, 553 grants totaling $88,970 (high: $1,333, low: $56).
Type of support: Support to graduates or students of specific schools; Undergraduate support.
Application information:
  Deadline(s): Mar. 15
  Additional information: Applications made through the principals of schools in Seattle School District No. 1.
EIN: 916022715

651

Board of Trustees of Carleton College

P.O. Box 78
Syracuse, OH 45779
Contact: John Lisle

Foundation type: Independent foundation
Limitations: Scholarships to residents of Syracuse, OH, for attendance at Carleton College.
Financial data: Year ended 12/31/2004.
Assets, $48,653 (M); Expenditures, $3,670; Total giving, $3,500; Grants to individuals, totaling $3,500.
Type of support: Support to graduates or students of specific schools; Undergraduate support.
Application information: Application form required.
  Deadline(s): Sept. 1
EIN: 311000137

652

Carlsbad Foundation, Inc.

116 S. Canyon St.
Carlsbad, NM 88220   (505) 887-1131
Contact: Jim Harrison, Exec. Dir.

Foundation type: Community foundation
Limitations: Scholarships and loans to students and residents in the South Eddy County and Carlsbad, NM, area.
Publications: Annual report (including application guidelines); Newsletter.

Financial data: Year ended 06/30/2005.
Assets, $19,668,552 (M); Expenditures, $760,828; Total giving, $480,704; Grants to individuals, totaling $112,449.
Type of support: Employee-related scholarships; Student loans—to individuals; Support to graduates or students of specific schools; Undergraduate support.
Application information: Applications accepted. Application form required.
  Deadline(s): None
Program descriptions:
  New Mexico State University/Carlsbad Memorial Scholarship Trust: The trust provides tuition, fees, and textbook scholarships to students of New Mexico State University, in Carlsbad, maintaining a GPA of 2.5 or better who are not recipients of other scholarships.
  JoAnna Wills Light Loving High School Scholarship Fund: Provides a scholarship to a graduate of Loving High School, NM.
  Carlsbad Rotary Charity Fund: Administers a scholarship to a resident of South Eddy County and Carlsbad, NM.
  New Directions College Loan Program: Provides loans to residents of South Eddy County and Carlsbad, NM, who make mid-life career changes by obtaining baccalaureate degrees. Candidates must have completed high school at least 10 years prior to applying and must not already be college graduates. Loans are for $625 a semester for up to four years. Program participants may have their loans forgiven if they obtain their degrees and such licensure or certification as might be appropriate.
  Don and Sarrah Kidd NMSU Scholarship Fund: Assists gifted students as they move from New Mexico State University, in Carlsbad, to the main campus of New Mexico State University in Las Cruces.
  Kiwanis Scholarship and Community Service Fund: Provides scholarships to residents of South Eddy County and Carlsbad, NM.
  Jim Skinner Memorial Fund: Provides a scholarship to a graduate of Carlsbad High School, NM.
  Carlsbad Rotary Memorial Scholarship Fund: Funds multiple scholarships to graduating seniors of local high schools. Demonstrated academic excellence is the major criteria for selection. The scholarships are awarded for the first year of college.
  Dowling Family Scholarship Fund: Provides scholarships to the three students graduating from Carlsbad High School, NM, with the highest GPAs.
  R.E. Willis Memorial Scholarship Fund: Provides scholarships to students who have completed a minimum of 30 credit hours at New Mexico State University, in Carlsbad, and plan to transfer to a four-year institution.
  Donna Umstead Markle Nursing Scholarship Fund: Scholarships given to Carlsbad High School graduates or others wishing to obtain an Associate Degree in Nursing at New Mexico State University, in Carlsbad or other regional schools. Financial need as well as demonstrated academic excellence are the key selection criteria.
EIN: 850206472

653

Nellie Martin Carman Scholarship Trust

c/o Sheri Ashleman
P.O. Box 60052
Seattle, WA 98160-0052

Foundation type: Independent foundation
Limitations: Scholarships by nomination only to public high school seniors in King, Snohomish, and

Pierce counties, WA, to attend colleges and universities in WA. Candidates must be U.S. citizens.
Publications: Application guidelines.
Financial data: Year ended 05/31/2005.
Assets, $2,660,369 (M); Expenditures, $176,660; Total giving, $125,300; Grants to individuals, 205 grants totaling $124,200 (high: $1,000, low: $500).
Type of support: Scholarships—to individuals; Awards/grants by nomination only; Undergraduate support.
Application information:
  Deadline(s): Mar. 1 for new applicants, and Apr. 1 for renewals
  Additional information: Candidates must be nominated by their high schools; Completion of formal nomination required; Nomination forms only available from high school principals and counselors; Interviews required.
Program description:
  Nellie Martin Carman Scholarship: Scholarships of up to $2,000 awarded for one academic year at any university or college in WA. Scholarships are renewable, providing a GPA of at least 3.0 is maintained. First-time applicants must be nominated by their high schools. Renewals must apply directly to the trust. Students majoring in music, sculpture, drawing, interior decorating, or domestic science are ineligible.
EIN: 916023774

654

Helen K. Carney Scholarship Fund

c/o National City Bank, Kentucky
P.O. Box 94651
Cleveland, OH 44101-4651
Application address: c/o Principal, Russell High School, 709 Red Devil Ln., Russell, KY 41169, tel.: (606) 836-9658

Foundation type: Operating foundation
Limitations: Scholarships to financially needy graduates of Russell High School, KY, for higher education.
Financial data: Year ended 12/31/2003.
Assets, $313,308 (M); Expenditures, $15,377; Total giving, $13,500; Grants to individuals, totaling $13,500.
Type of support: Scholarships—to individuals; Support to graduates or students of specific schools.
Application information: Deadline Mar. 15; Completion of formal application required, including KY FAF.
EIN: 611163331

655

Carpe Diem Foundation of Illinois

208 S. LaSalle St., Ste. 1400
Chicago, IL 60604
Contact: Gordon V. Levine, Exec. Dir.
Application address: c/o Gordon V. Levine, Exec. Dir., P.O. Box 3194, Chicago, IL 60690-3194
E-mail: glevine@carpediemfoundation.org;
URL: http://www.carpediemfoundation.org

Foundation type: Operating foundation
Limitations: Scholarships to exceptional students for undergraduate education.
Financial data: Year ended 12/31/2003.
Assets, $693,582 (M); Expenditures, $79,968; Total giving, $42,500; Grants to individuals, 15 grants totaling $42,500 (high: $2,500, low: $1,250).

Fields of interest: Architecture; Music; Arts; Health sciences school/education; Education; Chemistry; Engineering/technology; Biological sciences; Political science.

Type of support: Undergraduate support.

Application information:

Deadline(s): May 7

Applicants should submit the following:

1) Transcripts
2) Essay
3) SAT

Additional information: Completion of formal application required, including $14 payment by check or money order, teacher recommendation and community service recommendation; See Web site for further application information.

Program description:

Carpe Diem Scholarships: These scholarships of $2,500-$5,000 are used for tuition, room and board, books and related expenses. Scholarships are awarded in the following six categories:

· Political Science
· Pre-Med, Biomedical Engineering, Biology or Chemistry
· Science and Technology
· Education
· Art and Architecture
· Music Performance or Composition.

EIN: 731625173

656

Milton Carpenter Foundation, Inc.

P.O. Box 226
Jefferson Valley, NY   10535-0226
(845) 621-2819
Contact: Arlene Stoffel, Secy.
FAX: (845) 621-2819; E-mail: mcfarlane@rcn.com

Foundation type: Independent foundation

Limitations: Scholarships to financially needy residents of northern Westchester and Putnam counties, NY, who have alcohol impairment in their immediate families.

Publications: Informational brochure (including application guidelines).

Financial data: Year ended 12/31/2004. Assets, $1,137,934 (M); Expenditures, $84,208; Total giving, $68,320; Grants to individuals, totaling $68,320.

Fields of interest: Substance abuse, treatment; Alcoholism.

Type of support: Undergraduate support.

Application information:

Deadline(s): Feb. 1

Applicants should submit the following:

1) Financial information
2) Letter(s) of recommendation
3) FAF
4) Transcripts
5) SAT
6) ACT

Additional information: Application by nomination letter from a principal, teacher, counselor, member of the clergy, or other adult; Students must also submit a handwriting sample on any subject (not exceeding 500 words), list of colleges applied to, and verification of alcoholism in the family; Interviews required.

Program description:

Scholarship Program: Recipients must attend accredited colleges that are considered competitive, be in the upper quarter of their high school class, and have a combined SAT score of at least 1100 or a comparable ACT score. Financial need must be indicated by the institution attended, at the discretion of the directors. The foundation

may advance application fees for not more than three colleges for students they find qualified. The advancing of such fees does not assure the granting of a scholarship, but is to encourage students to reach for excellence. Applicants must advise the foundation of the colleges they have been accepted to no later than Apr. 20. Awards will be continued for four years of college, providing satisfactory progress toward a degree is maintained. Maximum award is $24,000, or $6,000 per year. Recipients are notified by May 15.

EIN: 061102502

657

John S. Carpenter Trust

c/o Wachovia Bank, N.A.
100 N. Main St., 13th Fl.
Winston-Salem, NC   27150-6732
(800) 576-5135
Contact: Michael Boyles
FAX: (336) 732-6537;
E-mail: michael.boyles@wachovia.com

Foundation type: Independent foundation

Limitations: Scholarships to students of Salem High School, NJ or Salem Meeting in a school affiliated with the Religious Society of Friends for higher education.

Financial data: Year ended 12/31/2004. Assets, $1,109,193 (M); Expenditures, $31,003; Total giving, $26,250; Grants to individuals, 7 grants totaling $26,250.

Fields of interest: Religion, formal/general education.

Type of support: Undergraduate support.

Application information: Applications accepted.

Initial approach: Letter.

Additional information: Contact foundation for current application deadline/guidelines.

EIN: 226501059

658

Carpenter-Dent Trust Fund

c/o BB&T, Trust Dept.
P.O. Box 7340
Paducah, KY   42002-7348   (866) 820-4179
Contact: Townsend Quinn, Trust Off.

Foundation type: Independent foundation

Limitations: Scholarships to students of Allen, Simpson, and Warren counties, KY for pharmacy education.

Financial data: Year ended 12/31/2003. Assets, $315,678 (M); Expenditures, $16,937; Total giving, $14,300; Grants to individuals, 10 grants totaling $14,300 (high: $3,000, low: $300).

Fields of interest: Pharmacy/prescriptions.

Type of support: Undergraduate support.

Application information:

Deadline(s): June 15

Additional information: Contact foundation for current application guidelines.

EIN: 616019528

659

Clinton J. Carr Foundation, Inc.

P.O. Box 1547
Lebanon, MO   65536-0158

Foundation type: Independent foundation

Limitations: Scholarships to high school graduates who reside in MO.

Financial data: Year ended 07/31/2004. Assets, $1,373,677 (M); Expenditures, $75,518;

Total giving, $63,144; Grants to individuals, 61 grants totaling $58,144 (high: $2,344, low: $600).

Type of support: Undergraduate support.

Application information: Application form required.

Deadline(s): Contact high school for current application deadline

Additional information: Application should include a one- two-page essay, GPA, and SAT/ACT scores; Applications are submitted to the foundation through participating high schools.

EIN: 431534880

660

Reynaldo J. Carreon, M.D. Foundation

P.O. Box 1420
Indio, CA   92202-1420
Contact: Martin Martinez, Exec. Dir.
FAX: (760) 347-2733

Foundation type: Independent foundation

Limitations: Scholarships to residents of Coachella Valley, Riverside County, CA, of Mexican descent for undergraduate study.

Financial data: Year ended 12/31/2004. Assets, $1,777,738 (M); Expenditures, $139,668; Total giving, $89,250; Grants to individuals, 72 grants totaling $89,250 (high: $2,000, low: $750).

Fields of interest: Mexico.

Type of support: Undergraduate support.

Application information: Application form required.

Additional information: Contact foundation for current application deadline.

EIN: 330426210

661

Carrier & Bryant Distributors' Educational Foundation

(formerly William A. Blees Educational Foundation)
c/o Peggy Hotaling
P.O. Box 4808, Carrier Pkwy.
Syracuse, NY   13221   (315) 433-4512
Application address: c/o Matt Richardson, P.O. Box 770728, Lakewood, OH 44107
FAX: (315) 433-4213

Foundation type: Independent foundation

Limitations: Scholarships to employees and children of employees of HVAC dealers and contractors for attendance at four-year colleges and universities.

Financial data: Year ended 07/31/2005. Assets, $409,991 (M); Expenditures, $40,648; Total giving, $37,500; Grants to individuals, totaling $37,500.

Type of support: Employee-related scholarships; Undergraduate support.

Application information: Application form required.

Deadline(s): May 30

Applicants should submit the following:

1) Class rank
2) Transcripts

Additional information: Application should also include SAT/ACT scores; Applications available from Carrier dealers.

EIN: 161153992

662

Glen Carrier Charitable Trust

P.O. Box 1453
Beaver, OK   73932   (580) 625-3710
Contact: V. Pauline Hodges, Tr.
FAX: (580) 625-3275; E-mail: vphodges@ptsi.net

Foundation type: Independent foundation
Limitations: Renewable scholarships to students residing in Beaver County, OK, for undergraduate or vocational education.
Publications: Annual report.
Financial data: Year ended 12/31/2004. Assets, $1,727,796 (M); Expenditures, $103,368; Total giving, $85,000; Grants to individuals, totaling $85,000.
Fields of interest: Vocational education, post-secondary.
Type of support: Undergraduate support.
Application information: Application form required.
   Deadline(s): Mar. 31
   Applicants should submit the following:
      1) Transcripts
      2) Financial information
   Additional information: Application should also include three letters of recommendation.
EIN: 731531180

663
Robert M. and Lenore W. Carrier Foundation
c/o Union Planters Bank, Trust Dept.
P.O. Box 387
Memphis, TN 38147   (901) 383-6196
Contact: Steve Spencer, Trust Off., Union Planters Bank

Foundation type: Independent foundation
Limitations: Scholarships primarily to MS residents attending the University of Mississippi.
Financial data: Year ended 10/31/2004. Assets, $2,037,178 (M); Expenditures, $155,609; Total giving, $132,661; Grants to individuals, totaling $132,661.
Type of support: Support to graduates or students of specific schools; Undergraduate support.
Application information: Application form required.
   Deadline(s): Prior to high school graduation
   Additional information: Application should include transcripts and brief academic resume.
EIN: 626035575

664
The Anne Carroll Foundation, Inc.
361 Main St.
Winchester, MA 01890
Contact: John J. Carroll, Jr., Pres.

Foundation type: Independent foundation
Limitations: Grants to graduating seniors from Eastern MA high schools for undergraduate education.
Financial data: Year ended 11/30/2004. Assets, $119,043 (M); Expenditures, $12,324; Total giving, $10,025; Grants to individuals, 3 grants totaling $10,025.
Type of support: Undergraduate support.
Application information:
   Deadline(s): Applications accepted throughout the year
   Additional information: Contact foundation for current application guidelines.
EIN: 043493735

665
Kit Carson Electric Education Foundation, Inc.
P.O. Box 587
Taos, NM 87571   (505) 758-2258
Contact: Rudy Martinez, Pres.

Foundation type: Company-sponsored foundation
Limitations: Scholarships to NM students residing in households that have received electric service from Kit Carson Electric for a minimum of six months.
Financial data: Year ended 12/31/2004. Assets, $204,330 (M); Expenditures, $44,881; Total giving, $42,440; Grants to individuals, 70 grants totaling $40,640 (high: $1,000, low: $40).
Type of support: Undergraduate support.
Application information:
   Deadline(s): Apr. 12
   Additional information: Contact foundation for current application guidelines; Applicant must include letters of recommendation from teachers, principals, or counselors from school they are currently attending.
EIN: 311578049

666
Carson Scholars Fund, Inc.
305 W. Chesapeake Ave., Ste. L-020
Towson, MD 21204   (410) 828-1005
Contact: Ixchel B. Tate, Exec. Dir.
E-mail: ibtate@carsonscholars.org; *URL:* http://www.carsonscholars.org

Foundation type: Public charity
Limitations: Scholarships by nomination only to grades 4-12 students attending targeted schools in MD, DE, DC, Lancaster, PA, Battle Creek, MI, Atlanta, GA, and Santa Ana, CA.
Publications: Annual report; Informational brochure; Newsletter.
Financial data: Year ended 06/30/2003. Assets, $1,376,137 (M); Expenditures, $770,173; Total giving, $430,206; Grants to individuals, totaling $430,206.
Fields of interest: Education, gifted students.
Type of support: Awards/grants by nomination only; Precollege support.
Application information: Applications are sent to qualifying students; See Web site for further information.
Program description:
   Carson Scholars: Nominees must have a minimum 3.75 GPA. Each winner receives a $1,000 award to be invested for college.
EIN: 521851346

667
Eula Carter & Graham Smith Memorial Scholarship Fund
201 N. Kaufman St.
P.O. Box 985
Mount Vernon, TX 75457

Foundation type: Independent foundation
Limitations: Scholarships to the top five graduates of Mount Vernon High School, TX.
Financial data: Year ended 12/31/2004. Assets, $409,463 (M); Expenditures, $23,699; Total giving, $20,856; Grants to individuals, 8 grants totaling $20,856.
Type of support: Support to graduates or students of specific schools; Undergraduate support.

Application information: Applications not accepted.
EIN: 756364952

668
Carter Family Foundation
c/o United Bank
129 Main St.
Beckley, WV 25801
Application address: c/o Dianna Hunt, United Bank Trust Dept., P.O. Box 1269, Beckley, WV 25802-1269

Foundation type: Operating foundation
Limitations: Grants to specific WV colleges and universities for scholarships. Priority is shown to WV students, with an emphasis on Raleigh county, WV students.
Financial data: Year ended 06/30/2005. Assets, $16,373,959 (M); Expenditures, $835,992; Total giving, $762,287.
Fields of interest: Education.
Type of support: Support to graduates or students of specific schools.
Application information: Applications accepted.
   Additional information: Applications through financial aid offices at specific schools.
EIN: 550606479

669
Amon G. Carter Star-Telegram Employees Fund
P.O. Box 17480
Fort Worth, TX 76102   (817) 332-3535
Contact: Nenetta Carter Tatum, Pres.

Foundation type: Company-sponsored foundation
Limitations: Scholarships to children of employees of the Fort Worth Star-Telegram, KXAS-TV, and WBAP-Radio, all in TX.
Financial data: Year ended 04/30/2005. Assets, $25,929,797 (M); Expenditures, $1,202,457; Total giving, $1,065,072; Grants to individuals, 227 grants totaling $416,092 (high: $7,352, low: $70).
Type of support: Employee-related scholarships.
Application information:
   Initial approach: Letter.
   Deadline(s): None
EIN: 756014850

670
Marie L. & John L. Carter Trust Fund
c/o Legacy Bank
215 Center Ave. S.
Mitchellville, IA 50169
Application address: c/o District Superintendent, 8379 N.E. University Ave., Runnells, IA 50237

Foundation type: Independent foundation
Limitations: Scholarships to Southeast Polk High School, Runnells, IA, graduates who will attend four-year IA colleges and universities, who will not become trained in social work, and who have excelled in American History, Government, and Citizenship.
Financial data: Year ended 03/31/2005. Assets, $321,582 (M); Expenditures, $13,760; Total giving, $9,700; Grants to individuals, totaling $9,700.
Type of support: Emergency funds; Support to graduates or students of specific schools; Undergraduate support.

Application information: Applications accepted. Application form required.
Deadline(s): None
Additional information: Scholarships are for one year, and renewable for a maximum of four years.
EIN: 421179937

671
Evelyn C. Carter Trust
c/o JPMorgan Chase Bank, N.A.
P.O. Box 1308
Milwaukee, WI 53201
Application address: c/o Guidance Counselor, Bridgeport Senior High School, Bridgeport, WV 26330, tel.: (304) 842-3693

Foundation type: Independent foundation
Limitations: Scholarships to graduates of Bridgeport High School, WV, who are attending West Virginia University in Morgantown, WV, and who indicate financial need.
Financial data: Year ended 12/31/2004. Assets, $1,774,705 (M); Expenditures, $88,898; Total giving, $75,564; Grants to individuals, 26 grants totaling $18,891.
Type of support: Support to graduates or students of specific schools; Undergraduate support.
Application information:
Initial approach: Letter.
Deadline(s): Apr. 30
EIN: 556129783

672
Carver Scholarship Fund, Inc.
75 W. 125th St.
New York, NY 10027 (212) 876-4747
Contact: Richard T. Greene, Chair.

Foundation type: Company-sponsored foundation
Limitations: Scholarships to residents of the New York, NY, area.
Publications: Informational brochure.
Financial data: Year ended 12/31/2004. Assets, $575,618 (M); Expenditures, $103,735; Total giving, $53,200; Grants to individuals, 48 grants totaling $53,200 (high: $2,000, low: $1,000).
Type of support: Scholarships—to individuals.
Application information: Contact fund for current application deadline/guidelines.
EIN: 133277661

673
Isaac Harris Cary Educational Fund
c/o David Wells
41 Woodland Rd.
Lexington, MA 02420-5321 (781) 861-0650
Contact: Steven T. Balthaser

Foundation type: Independent foundation
Limitations: Scholarships to male graduates of Lexington High School, MA, who are of New England parentage.
Financial data: Year ended 04/30/2005. Assets, $1,367,238 (M); Expenditures, $83,154; Total giving, $55,625; Grants to individuals, totaling $55,625.
Fields of interest: Men.
Type of support: Support to graduates or students of specific schools; Undergraduate support.
Application information: Application form required.
Deadline(s): Apr. 15

Additional information: Application forms available at Lexington High School.
EIN: 046023807

674
William J. & Gertrude R. Casper Foundation
c/o U.S. Bank, N.A.
P.O. Box 2043
Milwaukee, WI 53201-9116 (715) 723-6618
Contact: M. Berry
Application address: c/o The Edward Rutledge Charity, Betty Manning, 404 N. Bridge St., Chippewa Falls, WI 54729

Foundation type: Independent foundation
Limitations: Scholarships to residents of the Chippewa Falls, WI, area for study at technical schools, colleges, and universities.
Financial data: Year ended 05/31/2004. Assets, $17,186,591 (M); Expenditures, $820,734; Total giving, $743,327; Grants to individuals, 109 grants totaling $95,800 (high: $800, low: $300).
Fields of interest: Vocational education.
Type of support: Technical education support; Undergraduate support.
Application information: Applications accepted. Application form required.
Initial approach: Letter.
Program description:
Scholarship Program: Selection is based on financial need, past academic achievement, and character.
EIN: 396484669

675
The Cassner Foundation
835 S. High St.
Hillsboro, OH 45133-9602 (937) 393-3426
Scholarship application address: c/o Frederick Slater, Superintendent, Hillsboro City School, 358 W. Main St., Hillsboro, OH 45133, tel.: (937) 393-3475

Foundation type: Independent foundation
Limitations: Four-year scholarships to high school seniors in the Highland County school system, OH, for tuition or room and board at a university or college within a 500-mile radius of Highland County.
Financial data: Year ended 03/31/2004. Assets, $3,253,536 (M); Expenditures, $136,031; Total giving, $135,020; Grants to individuals, 17 grants totaling $42,500 (high: $2,500, low: $2,500).
Type of support: Support to graduates or students of specific schools; Undergraduate support.
Application information: Application form required.
Deadline(s): Mar. 1
EIN: 386090665

676
Dr. and Mrs. Theodore J. Castele Foundation
c/o The Catholic Diocese of Cleveland Fdn.
1404 E. 9th St., 8th Fl.
Cleveland, OH 44114-1722 (216) 696-6525
Contact: Valerie Raines

Foundation type: Public charity
Limitations: Scholarships based on academic merit and financial need to residents of the Cleveland, OH area.
Type of support: Undergraduate support.

Application information:
Initial approach: Letter.
Additional information: Contact foundation for further information.
EIN: 341528050

677
Castelli Charitable Trust
c/o PNC Advisors, P2-PTPP-25-1
620 Liberty Ave., 10th Fl.
Pittsburgh, PA 15222-2719
For scholarship application address: Gregory T. Nichols, Exec. Dir., Deno Castelli Charitable School Fund, 35 W. Pittsburgh St., Greensburg, PA 15601, tel.: (724) 834-3405

Foundation type: Independent foundation
Limitations: Scholarships to financially needy high school seniors and residents of Westmoreland County, PA.
Financial data: Year ended 05/30/2005. Assets, $1,643,423 (M); Expenditures, $138,624; Total giving, $102,000; Grants to individuals, 102 grants totaling $102,000.
Type of support: Undergraduate support.
Application information: Application form required.
Deadline(s): May 1
Additional information: Form available from high school guidance counselors.
EIN: 256242226

678
Casten Family Foundation, Inc.
8 E. 3rd St.
Hinsdale, IL 60521
Contact: Judith A. Casten, Pres.

Foundation type: Independent foundation
Limitations: Undergraduate and graduate scholarships to individuals studying international or multicultural subjects.
Financial data: Year ended 12/31/2003. Assets, $3,232,697 (M); Expenditures, $150,001; Total giving, $140,940; Grants to individuals, 2 grants totaling $35,892 (high: $29,780, low: $6,112).
Fields of interest: International affairs, formal/general education.
Type of support: Graduate support; Undergraduate support.
Application information: Applications accepted. Application form required.
Deadline(s): None
Additional information: Contact foundation for current application guidelines.
EIN: 134074089

679
Castle Pines Scholarship Foundation
1000 Hummingbird Dr.
Castle Rock, CO 80104 (303) 688-6000

Foundation type: Public charity
Limitations: Scholarships to caddies or employees of the Castle Pines Golf Club who are pursuing higher education.
Financial data: Year ended 12/31/2003. Assets, $1,120,436 (M); Expenditures, $82,292; Total giving, $76,200; Grants to individuals, 65 grants totaling $76,200 (high: $8,400, low: $800).
Fields of interest: Higher education.
Type of support: Employee-related scholarships.
Application information: Applications accepted.
EIN: 742270452

680
The Dante Castrodale Scholarship Foundation

c/o First Community Bank, Inc.
P.O. Box 950
Bluefield, WV 24701
Contact: Dante Enrico Castrodale, Selection Comm. Member
Application address: c/o Vecellio & Grogan, Drawer V, Beckley, WV 25801

Foundation type: Independent foundation
Limitations: Scholarships to residents of McDowell County, WV.
Financial data: Year ended 12/31/2004.
Assets, $539,766 (M); Expenditures, $19,708; Total giving, $15,000; Grants to individuals, 6 grants totaling $15,000 (high: $2,500, low: $2,500).
Type of support: Scholarships—to individuals.
Application information: Application form required.
Deadline(s): Jan. to May
Applicants should submit the following:
1) Class rank
2) GPA
Additional information: Application should also include a personal statement; Recipients notified in June.
EIN: 626198751

681
Catawissa Lumber & Specialty Co., Inc. College Educational Fund

c/o First Columbia Bank & Trust Co.
11 W. Main St.
Bloomsburg, PA 17815
Contact: Janice Dreese, Trust Off., First Columbia Bank & Trust Co.

Foundation type: Company-sponsored foundation
Limitations: Scholarships to graduates of Shamokin Area Senior High School, Mt. Carmel Area High School, Southern Columbia Area High School, Bloomsburg Area High School, Central Columbia High School, and Danville Senior High School, all in PA. No more than one recipient is selected from each school per year.
Financial data: Year ended 12/31/2004.
Assets, $117,839 (M); Expenditures, $13,791; Total giving, $12,500; Grants to individuals, 7 grants totaling $12,500 (high: $2,000, low: $1,250).
Type of support: Support to graduates or students of specific schools; Undergraduate support.
Application information: Application form required.
Deadline(s): May 15
EIN: 237676581

682
Catholic Education Foundation Diocese of Evansville

4200 N. Kentucky Ave.
P.O. Box 4169
Evansville, IN 47724-0169 (812) 424-5536
Contact: Linda Montejano; Scholarships: Margaret Angermeier

Foundation type: Public charity
Limitations: Scholarships to Evansville Deanery students in need so they may attend a Catholic high school within the Evansville diocese, IN.
Publications: Application guidelines; Informational brochure.
Financial data: Year ended 12/31/2003.
Assets, $595,027 (M); Expenditures, $186,715;

Total giving, $160,600; Grants to individuals, 102 grants totaling $149,400 (high: $2,500, low: $500).
Fields of interest: Religion, formal/general education; Roman Catholic agencies & churches.
Type of support: Support to graduates or students of specific schools; Precollege support.
Application information: Applications accepted. Application form required.
Deadline(s): Mar. 1 for first consideration, July 1 for appeals.
Additional information: Contact foundation for current application deadline/guidelines. Completion of formal application required, including W-2 forms and tax returns.
EIN: 356078141

683
Catholic Teachers Association of the Diocese of Brooklyn, Inc.

191 Joralemon St.
Brooklyn, NY 11201-4353
Contact: Frank Steele, Pres.

Foundation type: Public charity
Limitations: Scholarships and study grants to NY members based on merit and need.
Financial data: Year ended 06/30/2003.
Assets, $72,860 (M); Expenditures, $43,767; Total giving, $20,946; Grants to individuals, totaling $20,946.
Fields of interest: Education, association; Religion, formal/general education; Roman Catholic agencies & churches.
Type of support: Scholarships—to individuals.
Application information: Contact foundation for current application deadline/guidelines.
EIN: 111687465

684
Frank & Edith Catt Educational Fund

c/o Jersey State Bank, Trust Dep't.
1000 S. State St.
Jerseyville, IL 62052

Foundation type: Operating foundation
Limitations: Educational loans to graduates of Jersey Community High School, IL, for higher education.
Financial data: Year ended 12/31/2004.
Assets, $5,973,772 (M); Expenditures, $308,844; Total giving, $252,236; Grants to individuals, totaling $252,236.
Type of support: Student loans—to individuals; Support to graduates or students of specific schools; Undergraduate support.
Application information: Application form required.
Deadline(s): Contact fund for current application deadline
Additional information: Application should include two references with different addresses, one of which from a parent or legal guardian, the other from a person unrelated to applicant.
Program description:
Student Loan Program: Loans are for $500 per college semester and $4,000 total and are interest-free. Recipients must be enrolled in an institution of higher learning on a full-time basis and provide a copy of their transcript for each semester within 10 days of receipt. Recipient must also acknowledge that in the event their GPA falls below a "C" average, they will receive loans for one more semester, and that if GPA does not improve (to at least a "C"), they will be ineligible for further loans.
EIN: 376352751

685
Caves Valley Scholars Foundation, Inc.

2910 Blendon Rd.
Owings Mills, MD 21117-2360

Foundation type: Independent foundation
Limitations: Scholarships to students who caddie at golf courses in the greater Baltimore, MD, area, for higher education.
Financial data: Year ended 09/30/2004.
Assets, $434,405 (M); Expenditures, $23,388; Total giving, $19,000; Grants to individuals, 8 grants totaling $19,000.
Type of support: Undergraduate support.
Application information: Applications not accepted.
EIN: 521900251

686
The Cawasa Grange Memorial Scholarship Fund, Inc.

23 Thayer Ave.
Collinsville, CT 06019
Application address: c/o Guidance Dept., Canton High School, Canton, CT 06019, tel.: (860) 693-7707

Foundation type: Independent foundation
Limitations: Scholarships to graduates of Canton High School who are residents of Canton, CT. for undergraduate study.
Financial data: Year ended 06/30/2005.
Assets, $792,581 (M); Expenditures, $22,535; Total giving, $15,000; Grants to individuals, 3 grants totaling $15,000.
Type of support: Undergraduate support.
Application information: Applications accepted. Application form required.
Deadline(s): Last business day in Apr.
Applicants should submit the following:
1) FAFSA
2) FAF
Additional information: Application should also include most recent report card, and most recent tax return.
Program description:
Scholarship Program: Scholarships are paid in two $2,500 installments to recipient's college or university. Selection is based on academic performance with at least a "B" average, community service, and financial need.
EIN: 061552895

687
CCSU Foundation, Inc.

P.O. Box 612
New Britain, CT 06050-0612 (860) 832-2278
Contact: William J. McCue, Secy.
FAX: (860) 832-1768; URL: http://www.ccsu.edu/Instiadv/foundationinc.html

Foundation type: Public charity
Limitations: Scholarships to students attending Central Connecticut State University, CT.
Financial data: Year ended 06/30/2005.
Assets, $18,582,053 (M); Expenditures, $1,070,264; Total giving, $126,838.
Type of support: Support to graduates or students of specific schools.
Application information: Application form required.
Initial approach: Letter.
Deadline(s): Feb. 1
Additional information: Contact foundation for current application guidelines; See Web site for complete list of scholarship programs.
EIN: 237354328

688

Cecil County Bar Foundation, Inc.

c/o Charles L. Scott
157 E. Main St.
Elkton, MD   21921-5917   (410) 398-1918
Contact: Robert Jones, Dir.

Foundation type: Independent foundation
Limitations: Scholarships to students who reside in the Elkton, MD, area.
Financial data: Year ended 02/28/2005.
Assets, $50,403 (M); Expenditures, $10,374; Total giving, $7,800; Grants to individuals, 26 grants totaling $7,800.
Type of support: Scholarships—to individuals.
Application information: Applications by letter, including transcripts, accepted throughout the year.
EIN: 522058962

689

Center for Alternative Media and Culture

c/o CRM Mgmt.
P.O. Box 778
New York, NY   10013

Foundation type: Operating foundation
Limitations: Scholarships to Flint, MI, area students.
Financial data: Year ended 12/31/2003.
Assets, $439,855 (M); Expenditures, $43,651; Total giving, $36,000.
Type of support: Scholarships—to individuals.
Application information: Contact foundation for current application deadline/guidelines.
EIN: 382415253

690

Central Alabama Community Foundation, Inc.

(formerly Montgomery Area Community Foundation, Inc.)
P.O. Box 427
Montgomery, AL   36101-0427   (334) 264-6223
FAX: (334) 263-6225; E-mail: cacf@bellsouth.net;
URL: http://www.cacfinfo.org

Foundation type: Community foundation
Limitations: Scholarships to residents of Montgomery, Elmore and Lowndes counties, AL.
Publications: Application guidelines; Annual report; Newsletter.
Financial data: Year ended 12/31/2004.
Assets, $27,809,922 (M); Expenditures, $2,784,041; Total giving, $1,880,041.
Type of support: Undergraduate support.
Application information: Applications accepted. Application form required. Application form available on the grantmaker's Web site.
  Initial approach: E-mail.
  Deadline(s): Apr. 1
  Applicants should submit the following:
    1) Financial information
    2) Letter(s) of recommendation
    3) Transcripts
EIN: 630842355

691

Central Carolina Community Foundation

P.O. Box 11222
Columbia, SC   29211-1222   (803) 254-5601
Contact: Marjorie L. Gilbert, C.E.O.; For grant application: Joan Fail Hoffman, Dir., Grantmaking and Progs.
FAX: (803) 799-6663;
E-mail: info@yourfoundation.org; Grant application E-mail: joan@yourfoundation.org; URL: http://www.yourfoundation.org

Foundation type: Community foundation
Limitations: Scholarships to residents of Calhoun, Clarendon, Fairfield, Kershaw, Lee, Lexington, Newberry, Orangeburg, Richland, Saluda and Sumter counties, SC.
Publications: Annual report; Informational brochure; Newsletter.
Financial data: Year ended 06/30/2004.
Assets, $55,053,962 (M); Expenditures, $4,639,057; Total giving, $3,942,739; Grants to individuals, 40 grants totaling $80,221 (high: $3,280, low: $250).
Type of support: Scholarships—to individuals.
Application information: Application form required.
  Initial approach: Letter of intent or telephone.
  Deadline(s): Feb. 15 and Aug. 15 for letter of intent, Apr. 15 and Oct. 15 for proposal
  Applicants should submit the following:
    1) Proposal
  Additional information: See Web site for further information.
EIN: 570793960

692

Central Minnesota Community Foundation

101 S. 7th Ave., Ste. 100
St. Cloud, MN   56301   (320) 253-4380
Contact: Steven R. Joul, Pres.; Greta Stark-Kraker, Office Mgr.
FAX: (320) 240-9215;
E-mail: gstark@communitygiving.org; Additional Tel.: (877) 253-4380; E-mail for Susan Lorenz: slorenz@communitygiving.org; URL: http://www.communitygiving.org

Foundation type: Community foundation
Limitations: Scholarships primarily to individuals residing in the St. Cloud, MN, area for undergraduate education at U.S. colleges and universities.
Publications: Application guidelines; Annual report; Informational brochure; Newsletter.
Financial data: Year ended 06/30/2004.
Assets, $42,451,244 (M); Expenditures, $3,716,096; Total giving, $3,057,291.
Type of support: Undergraduate support.
Application information: Applications accepted. Application form required. Application form available on the grantmaker's Web site.
  Additional information: Application eligibility and guidelines vary with each scholarship; please contact foundation for current guidelines.
EIN: 363412544

693

Central Montana Foundation

224 W. Main, Ste. 300
Lewistown, MT   59457   (406) 538-2352
Contact: Vern Peterson, Pres.

Foundation type: Public charity
Limitations: Scholarships to residents of central MT for higher education.

Financial data: Year ended 12/31/2004.
Assets, $7,901,203 (M); Expenditures, $667,906; Total giving, $616,005; Grants to individuals, totaling $59,560.
Type of support: Scholarships—to individuals.
Application information: Application form required.
  Additional information: Contact foundation for current application deadline.
EIN: 810425314

694

The Central National-Gottesman Foundation

3 Manhattanville Rd.
Purchase, NY   10577-2110

Foundation type: Company-sponsored foundation
Limitations: Scholarships to children of full-time employees of Central National Gottesman Division for full-time study leading to a B.A. degree, or the equivalent.
Financial data: Year ended 12/31/2004.
Assets, $23,021,293 (M); Expenditures, $1,186,253; Total giving, $763,783; Grants to individuals, 21 grants totaling $138,733 (high: $13,705, low: $934).
Type of support: Employee-related scholarships; Undergraduate support.
Application information: Application form required.
  Additional information: Contact foundation for current application deadline.
EIN: 133047546

695

Central Susquehanna Community Foundation

(formerly Berwick Health and Wellness Foundation)
309 Vine St.
Berwick, PA   18603   (570) 752-3930
Contact: Eric DeWald, Exec. Dir.; For grants: Rita Boyle, Dir., Progs.
FAX: (570) 752-7435;
E-mail: edewald@csgiving.org; Additional E-mail: rboyle@csgiving.org; URL: http://www.csgiving.org

Foundation type: Community foundation
Limitations: Scholarships to individuals residing Columbia and lower Luzerne counties, PA, for the study of health and wellness.
Publications: Application guidelines; Annual report; Grants list; Newsletter.
Financial data: Year ended 12/31/2004.
Assets, $30,670,398 (M); Expenditures, $1,785,358; Total giving, $1,306,158; Grants to individuals, totaling $20,500.
Fields of interest: Health sciences school/education.
Type of support: Seed money; Awards/prizes; Undergraduate support.
Application information: Applications accepted. Application form required.
  Additional information: Contact foundation for current application deadline/guidelines.
EIN: 232982141

696

Central Valley Electric Education Foundation

c/o Scholarship Comm.
P.O. Box 230
Artesia, NM   88211-0230   (505) 746-3571
Contact: Mike Anderson

Foundation type: Company-sponsored foundation

Limitations: Scholarships to members, or children of members, of the Central Valley Electric Cooperative, Inc. to attend NM colleges and universities.
Financial data: Year ended 12/31/2004. Assets, $732,224 (M); Expenditures, $56,417; Total giving, $56,000; Grants to individuals, 38 grants totaling $56,000 (high: $2,000, low: $1,000).
Type of support: Scholarships—to individuals.
Application information:
Deadline(s): Apr. 15
Additional information: Contact foundation for current application guidelines.
EIN: 850323120

697
Central Valley High School Scholarship Fund
P.O. Box 494312
Redding, CA   96049-4312   (530) 221-0199
Contact: Kate Baker, Tr.

Foundation type: Independent foundation
Limitations: Scholarships to graduates of Central Valley High School, Redding, CA.
Financial data: Year ended 07/31/2004. Assets, $891 (M); Expenditures, $15,082; Total giving, $9,668; Grants to individuals, 12 grants totaling $9,668 (high: $1,600, low: $100).
Type of support: Scholarships—to individuals; Support to graduates or students of specific schools.
Application information: Deadline before end of school year; Completion of formal application required, including justification for need and college attendance.
EIN: 946293818

698
Centralia Foundation
115 E. 2nd St.
Centralia, IL   62801
Application address: c/o William Sprehe, P.O. Box 709, Centralia, IL 62801-9111

Foundation type: Operating foundation
Limitations: Scholarships primarily to students of Centralia, Sandoval, and Odin high schools who are residents of the Centralia, IL, area for graduate or undergraduate study.
Financial data: Year ended 09/30/2004. Assets, $23,114,964 (M); Expenditures, $1,463,609; Total giving, $115,820; Grants to individuals, 67 grants totaling $71,774 (high: $3,500, low: $225).
Type of support: Support to graduates or students of specific schools; Graduate support; Undergraduate support.
Application information: Application form required.
Additional information: Contact foundation for current application deadline.
EIN: 376029269

699
Cessna Foundation, Inc.
P.O. Box 7706
Wichita, KS   67277   (316) 517-7810
Contact: Marilyn Richwine, Secy.-Treas.

Foundation type: Company-sponsored foundation
Limitations: Scholarships to children or grandchildren of employees or retirees of The Cessna Aircraft Co., KS.

Publications: Application guidelines.
Financial data: Year ended 12/31/2002. Assets, $14,034,013 (M); Expenditures, $1,608,834; Total giving, $1,501,709; Grants to individuals, 42 grants totaling $12,066 (high: $518, low: $98).
Type of support: Employee-related scholarships.
Application information:
Deadline(s): May 15
Additional information: Application should be sent by letter.
EIN: 486108801

700
The Ralph M. Cestone Foundation, Inc.
2 PNC Plz., 30th Fl.
620 Liberty Ave.
Pittsburgh, PA   15222
Contact: Bruce Bickel
FAX: (412) 762-4160;
E-mail: bruce.bickel@pncadvisors.com

Foundation type: Independent foundation
Limitations: Scholarships to individuals for undergraduate education, primarily in NJ, OH and PA.
Financial data: Year ended 12/31/2004. Assets, $7,699,153 (M); Expenditures, $443,298; Total giving, $377,498.
Type of support: Undergraduate support.
Application information: Application form required.
Initial approach: Letter.
Copies of proposal: 1
Deadline(s): Nov. 1
Applicants should submit the following:
1) Transcripts
2) GPA
3) Financial information
Additional information: Contact foundation for current application guidelines.
EIN: 226703196

701
Chadwick Foundation
P.O. Box 486
Soda Springs, ID   83276-0486   (208) 547-2166
Contact: Frank Chadwick, Pres.

Foundation type: Independent foundation
Limitations: Scholarships to individuals with preference to applicants from the immediate southeastern ID area.
Financial data: Year ended 12/31/2004. Assets, $1,034,925 (M); Expenditures, $45,576; Total giving, $24,959; Grants to individuals, 24 grants totaling $18,340.
Type of support: Scholarships—to individuals.
Application information: Applications accepted. Application form required.
Initial approach: Letter or telephone.
EIN: 820456503

702
Joyce A. Chaffer Scholarship Trust
c/o Wells Fargo Bank Northwest, N.A.
P.O. Box 21927
Seattle, WA   98111
Contact: Matthew Hillman
Application address: c/o Gay H. Pool, Scholarship Chair., Idaho Federated Music Clubs, Boise Tuesday Musicale, 1517 Shenandoah Dr., Boise, ID 83712; E-mail: gpiano83712@earthlink.net

Foundation type: Independent foundation

Limitations: Scholarships for music education to residents of ID and students at ID schools.
Financial data: Year ended 09/30/2004. Assets, $930,638 (M); Expenditures, $58,716; Total giving, $45,000; Grants to individuals, totaling $45,000.
Fields of interest: Music; Performing arts, education.
Type of support: Scholarships—to individuals.
Application information:
Deadline(s): Apr. 1
EIN: 826079845

703
Chairman's Award Foundation
P.O. Box 4567
Houston, TX   77210-4567   (713) 207-3000
Contact: Preston Johnson, Tr.

Foundation type: Company-sponsored foundation
Limitations: Scholarships to children of employees of Reliant Energy Ventures, Inc. in recognition of volunteer and community service activities.
Financial data: Year ended 12/31/2004. Assets, $975,228 (M); Expenditures, $48,739; Total giving, $46,000; Grants to individuals, 23 grants totaling $46,000 (high: $2,000, low: $2,000).
Fields of interest: Community development, volunteer services.
Type of support: Employee-related scholarships.
Application information: Contributes only to pre-selected individuals.
EIN: 760321771

704
Frank A. & Gladys F. Chamberlin Scholarship Fund
c/o Bank of America, N.A.
P.O. Box 831041
Dallas, TX   75283-1041
Contact: Dennis McCabe
Application address: c/o Office of Financial Aid, Tarleton State Univ., Box T-0001, Administration Bldg. 228, Stephenville, TX 76401

Foundation type: Independent foundation
Limitations: Seven undergraduate and seven graduate scholarships awarded annually to high school graduates of Earth County, TX, and residents of Earth County, TX, who are attending Tarleton State University, TX.
Financial data: Year ended 07/31/2003. Assets, $824,539 (M); Expenditures, $43,756; Total giving, $36,301; Grants to individuals, 14 grants totaling $36,301 (high: $2,214, low: $1,107).
Type of support: Support to graduates or students of specific schools; Graduate support; Undergraduate support.
Application information:
Deadline(s): Apr. 15
Additional information: Application by FAF available from College Entrance Examination Board.
EIN: 756234715

705
The Mary Cecile Chambers Charitable Trust
(formerly The Mary Cecile Chambers Scholarship Fund)
c/o Moody National Bank
P.O. Box 1139
Galveston, TX 77553 (409) 765-5561
Contact: G. Luann Bland, Asst. V.P. and Trust Off., Moody National Bank
E-mail: lbland@moodytrust.com

Foundation type: Independent foundation
Limitations: Scholarships to financially needy male residents of Chambers, Galveston and Brazoria counties, TX, for full-time study at colleges, universities, and trade schools.
Publications: Application guidelines.
Financial data: Year ended 03/31/2005.
Assets, $5,202,612 (M); Expenditures, $187,594; Total giving, $126,749; Grants to individuals, totaling $125,749.
Fields of interest: Vocational education; Men; Young adults, male.
Type of support: Scholarships—to individuals; Support to graduates or students of specific schools; Undergraduate support.
Application information: Application form required.
  Initial approach: Letter or telephone.
  Deadline(s): Apr. 15
  Applicants should submit the following:
    1) Class rank
    2) Transcripts
    3) SAT
    4) Letter(s) of recommendation
    5) GPA
    6) Financial information
    7) Essay
    8) ACT
  Additional information: Applications should also include parents' and applicant's financial statements; Application forms available from the trustee or any high school in Chambers, Galveston or Brazoria counties.
Program description:
  Scholarship Program: First-year students are given priority. Automatic renewal of scholarship if required criteria is met. Recipients are notified by June 30.
EIN: 766071425

706
Esther Chandler Trust
c/o Bank of America, N.A., P.C. Group
P.O. Box 6767
Providence, RI 02940-6767
Application address for individuals: c/o Bank of America, N.A., Attn.: Deborah Dillon Pearce, Trust Admin., 100 Federal St., Boston, MA 02110

Foundation type: Independent foundation
Limitations: Scholarships to students who are residents of Kingston, MA, for higher education.
Financial data: Year ended 10/31/2004.
Assets, $282,123 (M); Expenditures, $24,856; Total giving, $20,300; Grants to individuals, totaling $20,300.
Type of support: Undergraduate support.
Application information:
  Deadline(s): Apr. 11
  Additional information: Application by letter.
EIN: 046589692

707
Hazel M. Chaney Scholarship Trust
c/o KeyBank N.A.
800 Superior Ave., 4th Fl.
Cleveland, OH 44114
Contact: Christina Cook, Trust Off., KeyBank N.A.
Application address: c/o KeyBank N.A., Augusta, ME 04330

Foundation type: Independent foundation
Limitations: Scholarships to high school graduates from Wilton, ME, and Franklin County, ME.
Financial data: Year ended 08/31/2005.
Assets, $153,939 (M); Expenditures, $7,693; Total giving, $4,500; Grants to individuals, totaling $4,500.
Type of support: Support to graduates or students of specific schools; Undergraduate support.
Application information: Applications not accepted.
EIN: 016007065

708
William H. Chapman Foundation
P.O. Box 1321
New London, CT 06320
Contact: Caroline K. Driscoll, Admin.

Foundation type: Independent foundation
Limitations: Undergraduate scholarships to residents of New London County, CT, whose family income is less than $100,000 per year (income amount varies) for full-time study at an accredited institution.
Financial data: Year ended 03/31/2003.
Assets, $2,268,909 (M); Expenditures, $157,413; Total giving, $121,250; Grants to individuals, 107 grants totaling $121,250 (high: $1,500, low: $900, average grant: $1,200).
Type of support: Technical education support; Undergraduate support.
Application information: Application form required.
  Initial approach: Letter before Mar. 20.
  Deadline(s): Apr. 1
  Additional information: Formal application required, including three letters of recommendation sent directly to the foundation from the writer, copies of high school and, if appropriate, college transcripts. Interviews required.
Program description:
  Scholarship Program: Recipients are selected on the basis of academic achievement and financial need. No awards are made for graduate study or for families with incomes exceeding $100,000, although extenuating circumstances are considered.
EIN: 066034290

709
Chapman Fund
(formerly The Chapman Foundation)
c/o W.A. Chapman
P.O. Box 1278
Sun City, AZ 85372-1278
Application address: 10484 W. Thunderbird Blvd., Sun City, AZ 85351, tel.: (623) 876-5352

Foundation type: Independent foundation
Limitations: Scholarships to individuals residing in the Sun City, AZ, area, for undergraduate education.
Financial data: Year ended 12/31/2004.
Assets, $292,163 (M); Expenditures, $4,385; Total giving, $4,000; Grants to individuals, 4 grants totaling $4,000.
Type of support: Undergraduate support.

Application information: Application form required.
  Deadline(s): Feb. 28
  Applicants should submit the following:
    1) Transcripts
    2) Financial information
  Additional information: Application should also include two letters of recommendation.
EIN: 860731311

710
Chapman Trust Fund
P.O. Box 2918
Clearwater, FL 33757-2918
Application address: c/o AmSouth Bank, Trust Dept., P.O. Box 23100, Jackson, MS 39225-3100

Foundation type: Independent foundation
Limitations: Loans to males residing in Lawrence County, MS.
Financial data: Year ended 12/31/2004.
Assets, $254,534 (M); Expenditures, $18,759; Total giving, $12,000; Grants to individuals, totaling $12,000.
Fields of interest: Men.
Type of support: Student loans—to individuals.
Application information: Applications accepted.
  Initial approach: Letter or telephone.
  Deadline(s): Contact foundation for current application deadline
  Additional information: Applications by letter including resume, financial information, and references.
EIN: 646023166

711
Corabelle Chappell Memorial Fund
c/o Wachovia Bank, N.A.
100 N. Main St, 13th Fl.
Winston-Salem, NC 27150
Application address: 130 Wyoming Ave., Scranton, PA 18503

Foundation type: Independent foundation
Limitations: Scholarships to financially needy students of Keystone Junior College, PA.
Financial data: Year ended 12/31/2004.
Assets, $1,390,393 (M); Expenditures, $56,042; Total giving, $43,250.
Type of support: Support to graduates or students of specific schools; Undergraduate support.
Application information: Applications accepted.
  Deadline(s): None
  Additional information: Applications by letter, outlining financial need.
EIN: 237710777

712
Charleston Scientific & Cultural Educational Fund
P.O. Box 340
Charleston, SC 29402-0340 (843) 722-3366
Contact: Charlton deSaussure, Jr., Secy.

Foundation type: Independent foundation
Limitations: Grants to SC natives for scientific, cultural, or educational pursuits in Charleston, SC.
Financial data: Year ended 12/31/2004.
Assets, $338,364 (M); Expenditures, $23,339; Total giving, $19,799; Grants to individuals, totaling $19,799.
Fields of interest: Arts education; Arts; Science.
Type of support: Scholarships—to individuals.

Application information: Application form required.
Deadline(s): June 1
EIN: 576019987

713
Charlevoix County Community Foundation
507 Water St.
P.O. Box 718
East Jordan, MI   49727   (231) 536-2440
Contact: Robert G. Tambellini, C.E.O.
FAX: (231) 536-2640; E-mail: bob@3cf.org;
URL: http://www.c3f.org

Foundation type: Community foundation
Limitations: Scholarships to financially needy
residents of Charlevoix County, MI. See program
description for further limitations.
Publications: Application guidelines; Annual report;
Informational brochure.
Financial data: Year ended 09/30/2005.
Assets, $16,735,100 (M); Expenditures,
$792,900; Total giving, $524,800.
Application information: Application form required.
Application form available on the grantmaker's Web
site.
Initial approach: Telephone.
Deadline(s): Apr. 30 and Oct. 31
Additional information: See Web site or contact
foundation for current list of programs and
Scholarship manual.
EIN: 383033739

714
Charlotte Hall School Board of Trustees,
Inc.
24665 Hollywood Rd.
Charlotte Hall, MD   20622

Foundation type: Independent foundation
Limitations: Scholarships only to high school
students of Charles and St. Mary's counties, MD,
for higher education.
Financial data: Year ended 12/31/2004.
Assets, $724,338 (M); Expenditures, $42,945;
Total giving, $31,500; Grants to individuals,
totaling $31,500.
Type of support: Scholarships—to individuals.
Application information: Applications not
accepted.
EIN: 521609924

715
The Charter Fund
370 17th St., Ste. 5300
Denver, CO   80202-5653   (303) 572-1727
Contact: Jeanette Montoya, Secy.

Foundation type: Independent foundation
Limitations: Scholarships to CO high school
seniors to attend an accredited college or university
in the U.S.
Financial data: Year ended 09/30/2004.
Assets, $71,534 (M); Expenditures, $190,812;
Total giving, $174,250; Grants to individuals, 87
grants totaling $126,750 (high: $2,500; low:
$250).
Type of support: Scholarships—to individuals.
Application information: Application form required.
Initial approach: Letter or telephone after Feb. 1
to request application.
Deadline(s): May 15
Additional information: Interviews required for
finalists.
EIN: 841049083

716
The Bishop Joseph Chartrand Memorial
Scholarship Trust Fund
P.O. Box 1743
Carmel, IN   46032
Application address: P.O. Box 1763, Carmel, IN
46082

Foundation type: Independent foundation
Limitations: Scholarships to individuals studying or
planning to study for Catholic ministry as a priest,
permanent deacon, or a religious man or woman,
primarily in IN.
Financial data: Year ended 12/31/2004.
Assets, $191,248 (M); Expenditures, $10,255;
Total giving, $7,000; Grants to individuals, totaling
$7,000.
Fields of interest: Theological school/education;
Roman Catholic agencies & churches.
Type of support: Scholarships—to individuals.
Application information: Applications accepted.
Application form required.
Deadline(s): None
Program description:
Scholarship Program: Recipient must have a
need for financial assistance.
EIN: 351940230

717
Hal S. Chase Family Scholarship Fund
c/o Farmers & Merchants State Bank
P.O. Box 230
Winterset, IA   50273-0230
Contact: James W. Mease, Tr.
Application address: c/o James W. Mease, Tr.,
Farmers & Merchants State Bank, Farmers &
Merchants State Bank Bldg., Winterset, IA 50273

Foundation type: Independent foundation
Limitations: Scholarships to students graduating
from Winterset High School, IA, Interstate 35 High
School, IA, and Orient-Macksburg High School, IA.
Financial data: Year ended 12/31/2004.
Assets, $788 (M); Expenditures, $5,500; Total
giving, $5,500; Grants to individuals, totaling
$5,500.
Type of support: Support to graduates or students
of specific schools; Undergraduate support.
Application information: Application form required.
Deadline(s): Mar. 1
EIN: 421240720

718
Chatham Kiwanis Scholarship Fund
c/o Stockholm
P.O. Box 422
Chatham, NJ   07928-0422
Application address: c/o Chair., Guidance Dept.,
Chatham High School, Lafayette Ave., Chatham, NJ
07928, tel.: (973) 635-2814

Foundation type: Independent foundation
Limitations: Scholarships to graduates of Chatham
High School, NJ, for higher education.
Financial data: Year ended 09/30/2004.
Assets, $196,576 (M); Expenditures, $13,220;
Total giving, $13,000; Grants to individuals,
totaling $13,000.
Fields of interest: Business school/education;
Teacher school/education; Natural resources;
Youth development; Community development,
volunteer services; Voluntarism promotion;
Leadership development.
Type of support: Support to graduates or students
of specific schools; Undergraduate support.

Application information: Application form required.
Deadline(s): Mar.
Additional information: Applications available at
Chatham High School; Scholarships are
renewable for a maximum of three additional
years.
EIN: 237438319

719
Chautauqua Region Community
Foundation, Inc.
418 Spring St.
Jamestown, NY   14701   (716) 661-3390
Contact: Randall J. Sweeney, Exec. Dir.; For grant
inquiries: June Diethrick, Grants Coord.; For
scholarship inquiries: Lisa W. Lynde, Scholarship
Coord.
FAX: (716) 488-0387; E-mail: crcf@crcfonline.org;
Grant inquiries tel.: (716) 661-3392 and E-mail:
jdiethrick@crcfonline.org; Scholarship inquiries
E-mail: llynde@crcfonline.org; Kids First Mini-Grants
E-mail: ccy@crcfonline.org; URL: http://
www.crcfonline.org

Foundation type: Community foundation
Limitations: Scholarships to graduates of 18
school districts in the Chautauqua County, NY,
area, as well as Allegheny and Cattaraugus
counties, NY.
Publications: Application guidelines; Annual report
(including application guidelines); Informational
brochure; Newsletter.
Financial data: Year ended 12/31/2004.
Assets, $44,172,553 (M); Expenditures,
$2,141,353; Total giving, $1,472,363; Grants to
individuals, 149 grants totaling $516,437.
Fields of interest: Arts education; Journalism/
publishing; Performing arts, education; Education,
research; Business school/education; Medical
school/education; Nursing school/education;
Education; Engineering/technology; Economics.
Type of support: Program development;
Conferences/seminars; Scholarships—to
individuals; Awards/prizes; Graduate support;
Undergraduate support.
Application information: Applications accepted.
Application form required.
Initial approach: Telephone.
Deadline(s): June 1.
Additional information: Applications available
from the foundation, high school guidance
counselors, and Jamestown banks.
Program description:
Scholarship Funds: The foundation administers
over 140 separate scholarship funds, many of
which are for students interested in specific
subjects, such as music, art, nursing, education,
business, and engineering. Almost all awards are
for undergraduate college study, although a few
awards are made to graduate students, primarily for
medical education. Some awards are given to
graduates of specific schools. Contact foundation
for specific limitations.
EIN: 161116837

720
The Chazen Foundation
c/o Nathan Berkman & Co., Inc.
29 Broadway, Ste. 2900
New York, NY   10006
Application address: 767 5th Ave., 26th Fl., New
York, NY 10153

Foundation type: Independent foundation

Limitations: Scholarships to residents of Rockland County, NY.
Publications: Application guidelines; Informational brochure.
Financial data: Year ended 12/31/2004. Assets, $37,576,834 (M); Expenditures, $2,308,522; Total giving, $1,916,436; Grants to individuals, 49 grants totaling $137,000 (high: $5,000, low: $500).
Type of support: Scholarships—to individuals.
Application information: Applications by letter accepted throughout the year.
Program description:
Chazen Scholarship Project: For high achieving, financially needy students (including middle class families.) Scholarship grants range from $1,000 to $5,000 per year with a guarantee of 4 years, provided the student maintains a 3.0 average.
EIN: 133229474

721

T. Franklin Cheek, Jr. Scholarship Fund
227 Anthony St.
Ripley, TN 38063
Application address: c/o Bobby Baker, Principal, Ripley High School, 254 Jefferson, Ripley, TN 38063, tel.: (731) 635-2642

Foundation type: Independent foundation
Limitations: Scholarships to graduating seniors of Ripley High School, TN, for higher education.
Financial data: Year ended 06/30/2004. Assets, $851,024 (M); Expenditures, $27,029; Total giving, $22,500; Grants to individuals, 15 grants totaling $22,500 (high: $1,500, low: $1,500).
Type of support: Support to graduates or students of specific schools; Undergraduate support.
Application information: Deadline Apr. 1 of graduating year; Completion of formal application required.
EIN: 621849685

722

CHEMCENTRAL Charitable Trust
P.O. Box 730
Bedford Park, IL 60499-0730 (708) 594-7000

Foundation type: Company-sponsored foundation
Limitations: Scholarships to children of employees of CHEMCENTRAL Corporation.
Financial data: Year ended 12/31/2004. Assets, $105,911 (M); Expenditures, $41,848; Total giving, $38,000; Grants to individuals, 19 grants totaling $38,000 (high: $2,000, low: $2,000).
Type of support: Employee-related scholarships.
Application information:
Initial approach: Letter or telephone.
Additional information: Contact foundation for current application deadline/guidelines.
EIN: 363803848

723

Chenango County Medical Society & Otsego County Medical Society, Trustees for the Van Wagner Scholarship
c/o NBT Bank, N.A.
52 S. Broad St.
Norwich, NY 13815-1646
Application address: c/o Kathleen E. Dyman, 4311 Middle Settlement Rd., New Hartford, NY 13413

Foundation type: Independent foundation
Limitations: Scholarships to residents of Chenango or Otsego counties, NY, who are attending medical or osteopathic school.
Financial data: Year ended 04/30/2005. Assets, $325,123 (M); Expenditures, $19,208; Total giving, $14,000; Grants to individuals, totaling $14,000.
Fields of interest: Medical school/education; Health organizations.
Type of support: Scholarships—to individuals.
Application information: Application form required.
Deadline(s): June 1
EIN: 237325443

724

Chenega Future, Inc.
4000 Old Seward Hwy., Ste. 101
Anchorage, AK 99503 (907) 561-0500
Contact: Patricia Totemoff Andrews, Dir.

Foundation type: Operating foundation
Limitations: Scholarships to shareholders of record and descendants of the Chenega Corporation, AK.
Financial data: Year ended 12/31/2004. Assets, $0 (M); Expenditures, $89,347; Total giving, $72,599; Grants to individuals, 24 grants totaling $72,599 (high: $17,852, low: $75).
Type of support: Employee-related scholarships.
Application information: Application form required.
Deadline(s): Apr., Aug. and Dec.
EIN: 943111730

725

Elizabeth Chenoweth Foundation, Inc.
117 E. Washington St.
P.O. Box 1373
Paris, TN 38242-1373 (901) 642-1322
Contact: John Etheridge, Secy.-Treas.

Foundation type: Independent foundation
Limitations: Scholarships to students who attended Henry County High School, IN, for four years.
Financial data: Year ended 12/31/2004. Assets, $332,080 (M); Expenditures, $15,544; Total giving, $15,000; Grants to individuals, totaling $15,000.
Type of support: Support to graduates or students of specific schools; Undergraduate support.
Application information: Deadline Apr. 30; Completion of formal application required.
EIN: 237044756

726

Chesapeake Corporation Foundation
1021 E. Cary St., 22nd Fl.
Richmond, VA 23219 (804) 697-1000
Contact: Shannon E. Rivera, Secy.
FAX: (804) 697-1192; Application address: P.O. Box 2350, Richmond, VA 23218

Foundation type: Company-sponsored foundation
Limitations: Scholarships to children of employees of the Chesapeake Corporation, VA for higher education. Awards are for $3,500 year for up to four years, or until Bachelor's Degree is completed.
Publications: Application guidelines.
Financial data: Year ended 12/31/2004. Assets, $1,444,027 (M); Expenditures, $126,276; Total giving, $124,258; Grants to individuals, totaling $26,656.
Type of support: Employee-related scholarships.

Application information: Application form required.
Deadline(s): Nov. 14
EIN: 540605823

727

B. H. Chesley Foundation
370 Quail Rd.
Dellwood, MN 55110

Foundation type: Operating foundation
Limitations: Scholarships to individuals who live within 100 miles of Mankato, MN, and plan to attend a technical college or a state university within 200 miles of Mankato, MN.
Financial data: Year ended 12/31/2003. Assets, $237,460 (M); Expenditures, $3,995; Total giving, $2,000; Grants to individuals, totaling $2,000.
Fields of interest: Vocational education.
Type of support: Technical education support; Undergraduate support.
Application information:
Initial approach: Letter.
Deadline(s): Apr. 15
Additional information: Contact foundation for current application guidelines.
EIN: 411674753

728

William A. Chessall Memorial Scholarship Fund
P.O. Box 419
Ukiah, CA 95482-0419

Foundation type: Independent foundation
Limitations: Scholarships to financially needy graduates of Ukiah High School, CA, to study full-time at two- and four-year colleges and universities.
Financial data: Year ended 03/31/2005. Assets, $738,765 (M); Expenditures, $37,314; Total giving, $34,416; Grants to individuals, totaling $34,416.
Type of support: Support to graduates or students of specific schools; Undergraduate support.
Application information: Application form required.
Deadline(s): May1
Applicants should submit the following:
1) Class rank
2) Transcripts
3) GPA
Additional information: Completion of formal application in triplicate required, including personal statement, SAT or ACT test results, and activity sheet to be completed by applicant, and attendance record to be completed by counselor.
Program description:
Scholarship Program: Scholarships are for $10,000 to be paid over four years. Recipients need only to maintain full-time status and make satisfactory progress toward a degree. Two or three new recipients are chosen each year. The fund selects recipients who fall into one or more of the following categories:
· demonstrate financial need, especially in the case of students who cannot afford full-time study but whose family income is above that of most financial aid criteria
· are academic "late bloomers" in high school and whose cumulative GPA may not accurately reflect their capabilities
· have foregone many school activities because of the need to work or have family duties after school and on weekends

- have definable and achievable career goals
- desire to attend a community college, such as Mendocino Community College, before transferring to a four-year institution
- have completed advanced placement classes while in high school.

EIN: 946515834

729
Trustees of Chester Academy
c/o TD Banknorth, N.A., Investment Mgmt. Group
P.O. Box 595
Williston, VT 05495

Foundation type: Independent foundation
Limitations: Scholarships to high school graduates residing in Chester, VT. Scholarships are renewable.
Financial data: Year ended 03/31/2005.
Assets, $588,382 (M); Expenditures, $33,144; Total giving, $26,200; Grants to individuals, 24 grants totaling $26,200.
Type of support: Undergraduate support.
Application information: Applications not accepted.
  Additional information: Scholarship recipients are selected by the Board of Trustees.
EIN: 036007034

730
Chester County Community Foundation
The Lincoln Bldg.
28 W. Market St.
West Chester, PA 19382 (610) 696-8211
Contact: Karen A. Simmons, C.E.O.; For grant applications: Beth Harper Briglia, V.P., Donors Svcs. and Grantmaking
FAX: (610) 696-8213; E-mail: info@chescocf.org;
Additional E-mail: Karen@chescocf.org; Grant application E-mail: Beth@chescocf.org;
URL: http://www.chescocf.org

Foundation type: Community foundation
Limitations: Scholarships to residents of Chester County, PA, for the study of a trade, art or craft which requires working with their hands to build, restore or finish a home.
Publications: Application guidelines; Annual report; Financial statement; Informational brochure; Newsletter.
Financial data: Year ended 06/30/2005.
Assets, $21,504,040 (L); Expenditures, $2,196,127; Total giving, $1,109,746; Grants to individuals, 67 grants totaling $117,798.
Type of support: Scholarships—to individuals; Undergraduate support.
Application information: Applications accepted. Application form required.
  Initial approach: Letter.
Program description:
  Natalie A.W. Leaf Fund: Scholarships range from $300 to $5,000 and may be used for tuition, books, incidental fees, commuting expenses, room and board and family maintenance.
EIN: 232773822

731
Chester High School Alumni Association
Skyline Trail
Middlefield, MA 01243 (413) 623-5519
Contact: Maurice H. Pease, Treas. of Scholarship Program

Foundation type: Operating foundation

Limitations: Scholarships to financially needy residents of Chester, MA, for study at graduate and undergraduate colleges and universities, and technical schools. Scholarships are renewable.
Financial data: Year ended 06/30/2004.
Assets, $0 (M); Expenditures, $19,882; Total giving, $5,875; Grants to individuals, 18 grants totaling $5,872 (high: $500, low: $125).
Type of support: Technical education support; Undergraduate support.
Application information: Application form required.
  Deadline(s): Applications accepted throughout the year.
EIN: 046058373

732
Chesterfield Charitable Foundation
P.O. Box 177
Chesterfield, NH 03443 (603) 256-8045
Contact: Caren B. Foisie, Dir.
FAX: (860) 388-3077;
E-mail: info@chesterfieldfoundation.com;
URL: http://www.chesterfieldfoundation.com

Foundation type: Independent foundation
Limitations: Scholarships to students, primarily to residents of CT, NH, PA and VT for higher education.
Financial data: Year ended 12/31/2004.
Assets, $467,080 (M); Expenditures, $519,995; Total giving, $518,842; Grants to individuals, 100 grants totaling $518,842 (high: $10,000, low: $1,000).
Type of support: Undergraduate support.
Application information: Contact foundation for current application deadline/guidelines.
EIN: 020533669

733
Judge C. C. Chevelle Foundation
P.O. Box 4742
Rollingbay, WA 98061-0742 (206) 842-6272
Contact: Karen C. Keefe, Tr.

Foundation type: Independent foundation
Limitations: Scholarships to individuals born in the state of WA, for higher education.
Financial data: Year ended 06/30/2005.
Assets, $569,429 (M); Expenditures, $26,823; Total giving, $12,986; Grants to individuals, totaling $12,986.
Type of support: Undergraduate support.
Application information: Applications accepted. Application form required. Application form available on the grantmaker's Web site.
  Initial approach: Letter.
  Deadline(s): Aug. 1
  Additional information: Application should include a personal statement of 300 words or less, employment history, the addresses and telephone numbers of three references, college entrance exam scores, and cumulative GPA; Applicants must provide birth certificates.
EIN: 911123055

734
Chicago Engineers' Foundation of the Union League Club
(formerly Chicago Engineers' Club Foundation)
65 W. Jackson Blvd., Ste. 901
Chicago, IL 60604-3598 (312) 427-7800
Contact: John L. Donnelly, Treas.

Foundation type: Independent foundation

Limitations: Scholarships to Chicago, IL, public high school students who plan to pursue engineering degrees.
Financial data: Year ended 05/31/2003.
Assets, $81,873 (M); Expenditures, $79,083; Total giving, $58,500; Grants to individuals, 89 grants totaling $57,000 (high: $700, low: $600).
Fields of interest: Engineering school/education.
Type of support: Support to graduates or students of specific schools; Undergraduate support.
Application information: Deadline Mar. 31; Application by letter including class rank and counselor's recommendation.
EIN: 366109433

735
Chicago Symphony Orchestra
220 S. Michigan Ave.
Chicago, IL 60604 (312) 294-3333
Contact: Deborah Card, Pres.
FAX: (312) 294-3329; Additional tel.: (800) 223-7114; URL: http://www.cso.org

Foundation type: Public charity
Limitations: Scholarships to music students who are members of the Civic Orchestra of Chicago, IL.
Financial data: Year ended 06/30/2003.
Assets, $414,362,918 (M); Expenditures, $60,152,262; Total giving, $442,106; Grants to individuals, 110 grants totaling $442,106 (high: $7,669, low: $50).
Fields of interest: Music; Performing arts, education.
Type of support: Scholarships—to individuals.
Application information: Contact foundation for current application deadline/guidelines.
Program description:
  Scholarship Program: All Regular members of the Civic Orchestra of Chicago receive a $2,800 scholarship intended to further the Civic members' musical education. Associate members receive scholarship funds if asked to perform in a concert as a sub or an extra player. Approximately twenty-five graduate string players, all of whom are Regular members, receive a $3,500 fellowship annually towards the institution they are attending.
EIN: 362167823

736
Chicago White Metal Charitable Foundation
Rte. 83 & Fairway Dr.
Bensenville, IL 60106 (630) 595-4424

Foundation type: Company-sponsored foundation
Limitations: Scholarships to children of employees of Chicago White Metal Casting, Inc., who have been employed by the corporation for at least three years, and who are not officers or directors of the corporation.
Financial data: Year ended 10/31/2003.
Assets, $96,521 (M); Expenditures, $110,081; Total giving, $109,884; Grants to individuals, 17 grants totaling $67,502 (high: $3,000, low: $559).
Fields of interest: Education.
Type of support: Employee-related scholarships; Graduate support; Undergraduate support.
Application information: Application form required.
EIN: 366069669

737
Child Development Center of the Houston-Galveston Psychoanalytic

900 Lovett Blvd.
Houston, TX 77006 (713) 526-2046
Contact: T. Kevin Dillon, Pres.
FAX: (713) 526-9126; URL: http://www.hgpsai.org

Foundation type: Public charity
Limitations: Scholarships for enrollment in the center's therapeutic pre-school program, located in TX.
Financial data: Year ended 09/30/2003. Assets, $1,975,775 (M); Expenditures, $1,000,367; Total giving, $78,608; Grants to individuals, 16 grants totaling $78,608 (high: $14,695, low: $400).
Fields of interest: Early childhood education.
Type of support: Precollege support.
Application information:
Deadline(s): Contact foundation for current application deadline/guidelines.
EIN: 760287971

738
Child Nutrition Foundation

(formerly School Food Service Foundation)
700 S. Washington St., Ste. 300
Alexandria, VA 22314 (703) 739-3900
Contact: Barbara Belmont CAE, Exec. Dir.
FAX: (703) 739-3915; E-mail: cnf@asfsa.org;
URL: http://www.schoolnutrition.org/CNF.aspx?id=36

Foundation type: Public charity
Limitations: Scholarships to American School Food Service Association (ASFSA) members for undergraduate and graduate education related to food services.
Publications: Application guidelines; Annual report; Informational brochure; Newsletter.
Financial data: Year ended 07/31/2003. Assets, $3,513,630 (M); Expenditures, $1,172,396; Total giving, $155,114; Grants to individuals, totaling $155,114.
Fields of interest: Food services; Nutrition.
Type of support: Graduate support; Technical education support; Undergraduate support.
Application information: Applications accepted. Application form required.
Initial approach: Telephone.
Deadline(s): Apr. 15
Applicants should submit the following:
1) Letter(s) of recommendation
2) Transcripts
3) Essay
Additional information: Five copies of the application package are required.
Program descriptions:
Tony's/Schwan's Food Service Scholarship: Fifty scholarships ranging from $200 to $1,500 are awarded to eligible active ASFSA members with a history of employment in school food service and/or their dependents, who are attending a college or vocational/technical institution and pursuing a program designed to improve school food service. Applicants or applicants' parents (for dependent applicants) must be ASFSA members for at least one year prior to application. In addition, they must have satisfactory academic records, express a desire to make school service a career; be enrolled or enrolling in real-time interactive classroom instruction coursework; and be pursuing associate's, bachelor's, or in some cases, a master's degree.
Professional Growth Scholarship: Six to ten scholarships ranging from $200 to $1,500 are

awarded to eligible, active ASFSA members with a history of employment in school food service who are enrolled in and pursuing graduate studies in graduate programs at accredited institutions in the field of food service management or nutrition. To be eligible, the individual must provide proof of acceptance to a graduate program in food service and nutrition or food service management at an accredited institution, have a minimum GPA of 2.7, and provide a transcript showing completion of at least one course of the planned program.
Heinz Scholarship: Seven $2,500 scholarships are awarded to ASFSA members, school food service professionals, and their dependants who have been accepted to, or are currently registered at an accredited college, university, or vocational/technical institution. Scholarships are not limited to those pursuing a food service-related field of study and are primarily merit-based.
EIN: 846039412

739
Children at the Crossroads Foundation

711 W. Monroe St.
Chicago, IL 60661-3512

Foundation type: Public charity
Limitations: Scholarships to students at Frances Xavier Warde School, IL.
Type of support: Support to graduates or students of specific schools; Undergraduate support.
Application information: Applications not accepted.
EIN: 363654481

740
Children's Aid Association of Amsterdam, NY

P.O. Box 327
Amsterdam, NY 12010-0327
Application address: c/o Jacque Bresonis, 321 Guy Park Ave., Amsterdam, NY 12010

Foundation type: Operating foundation
Limitations: Scholarships to financially needy, single high school seniors or graduates of Montgomery County, NY, to attend accredited colleges.
Financial data: Year ended 05/31/2003. Assets, $1,252,985 (M); Expenditures, $70,915; Total giving, $67,064; Grants to individuals, totaling $17,000.
Type of support: Scholarships—to individuals; Undergraduate support; Camperships.
Application information: Applications accepted. Application form required.
Deadline(s): May 30
Additional information: Application should include financial information.
Program description:
Scholarship Program: To be eligible, an applicant must be:
· a high school senior or graduate of good record and a resident of Montgomery County
· accepted to an accredited college or in an otherwise approved institution of learning
· in need of financial assistance
· able to maintain at least a "C" average
· reliable, dependable, determined, interested in school and community affairs, in accordance with past school and community records
· single

In general, students renewing grants from the previous year are given preference over new applicants provided they have maintained at least a "C" average during the prior year.
EIN: 141340035

741
Children's Aid Society

105 E. 22nd St.
New York, NY 10010-5493 (212) 949-4800
Contact: C. Warren Moses, C.E.O.
URL: http://www.childrensaidsociety.org

Foundation type: Public charity
Limitations: Scholarships to individuals for higher education.
Publications: Annual report; Financial statement; Newsletter.
Financial data: Year ended 06/30/2004. Assets, $281,973,051 (M); Expenditures, $78,137,871; Total giving, $9,700,320; Grants to individuals, totaling $9,700,320.
Type of support: Undergraduate support.
Application information: Contact foundation for current application deadline/guidelines.
Program description:
CAS Scholarship Program: Awards scholarships to students to provide financial aid and emotional support to help them make the transition from high school to college. To qualify for financial assistance, applicant must be a member of a CAS center or school and have participated in a Youth Development Services program. Students need proof of high school or GED completion, a referral from a Youth Development Services staff person and proof of acceptance and registration in a community or four-year college as a full-time student. In addition, as part of the scholarship requirement, each applicant must complete 30 hours of community service with The Children's Aid Society or in another community-based, non-profit organization.
EIN: 135562191

742
Children's Educational Opportunity Foundation

60 Bowling Dr.
Oakland, CA 94618
Scholarship address: c/o Admin., P.O. Box 21456, Oakland, CA 94620, tel.: (510) 483-7971

Foundation type: Operating foundation
Limitations: Scholarships to students from low-income Oakland, CA, families to attend the private school of their choice.
Financial data: Year ended 06/30/2005. Assets, $575 (M); Expenditures, $350,514; Total giving, $345,780; Grants to individuals, 229 grants totaling $345,780.
Type of support: Scholarships—to individuals.
Application information:
Deadline(s): Apr. 1 to May 1
Additional information: Completion of formal application required, including copies of current-year income tax returns. Recipient's family must qualify for the federal school lunch program.
EIN: 943201181

743

Children's Foundation for the Arts, Inc.

(formerly Ira B. Brown Foundation, Inc.)
500 Rte. 17 S.
Hasbrouck Heights, NJ   07604   (201) 288-5301
Contact: Maria Beerman, Mgr. Dir.
FAX: (201) 288-5305; E-mail: cfa.nj@verizon.net

Foundation type: Operating foundation
Limitations: Grants to children under the age of 17 who are skilled in the performing arts and who have been emotionally deprived due to a lack of a relationship with a grandparent, and who reside in the New York, NY metropolitan area or Houston, TX.
Publications: Annual report; Informational brochure; Newsletter.
Financial data: Year ended 08/31/2004. Assets, $1,660,254 (M); Expenditures, $236,804; Total giving, $88,611; Grants to individuals, 133 grants totaling $88,611 (high: $1,500; low: $250).
Fields of interest: Music; Arts.
Type of support: Grants to individuals.
Application information: Application form required.
   Deadline(s): Dec. 31
   Additional information: Interviews required.
Program description:
   Grant Program: Grants are given in amounts up to $2,000 for eligible children to award achievement in the arts. Candidates must receive no emotional or financial support from grandparents (i.e., grandparents are all deceased).
EIN: 223329717

744

The Children's Museum of Indianapolis, Inc.

3000 N. Meridian St.
Indianapolis, IN   46208-4716   (317) 334-3206
Contact: Donna Lolla, Dir., Public and Media Relations
FAX: (317) 921-4019;
E-mail: communic@childrensmuseum.org;
URL: http://www.childrensmuseum.org

Foundation type: Public charity
Limitations: Scholarships to residents of Marion County who possess artistic or musical talent and have high grades and participation in neighborhood activities.
Financial data: Year ended 12/31/2003. Assets, $346,503,387 (M); Expenditures, $28,294,447; Total giving, $34,500; Grants to individuals, 33 grants totaling $34,500 (high: $2,500; low: $167).
Fields of interest: Museums (children's).
Type of support: Support to graduates or students of specific schools; Undergraduate support.
Application information: Contact foundation for current application/guidelines.
EIN: 350867985

745

Children's Scholarship Fund

8 W. 38th St., 9th Fl.
New York, NY   10018   (212) 515-7100
FAX: (212) 515-7111;
E-mail: info@scholarshipfund.org; URL: http://www.scholarshipfund.org

Foundation type: Public charity
Limitations: Tuition assistance to economically disadvantaged children for attendance at private elementary and parochial schools.
Publications: Financial statement; Informational brochure.

Financial data: Year ended 08/31/2004. Assets, $12,121,530 (M); Expenditures, $9,416,145; Total giving, $7,840,883; Grants to individuals, 4,500 grants totaling $7,840,883.
Fields of interest: Elementary/secondary education; Economically disadvantaged.
Type of support: Precollege support.
Application information: Unsolicited requests for funds not considered or acknowledged.
EIN: 134002189

746

China Times Cultural Foundation

1499 Bayshore Hwy., No. 212
Burlingame, CA   94010   (718) 460-4900
Contact: Sophia Hsieh
E-mail: ctcfmail@yahoo.com

Foundation type: Independent foundation
Limitations: Undergraduate scholarships to individuals of Chinese ancestry. Scholarships for Chinese language school students.
Financial data: Year ended 12/31/2004. Assets, $2,246,653 (M); Expenditures, $123,638; Total giving, $27,500; Grants to individuals, 10 grants totaling $27,500 (high: $2,750; low: $2,750).
Fields of interest: International studies.
Type of support: Undergraduate support.
Application information:
   Deadline(s): June 30
   Additional information: Completion of formal application required, including report cards for previous four semesters, recent photographs, and parents' income.
Program description:
   Scholarship Program: Preference is given to individuals with the purpose of promoting Chinese culture or improving Chinese communities throughout the world; also for Sino-American cultural exchanges, Chinese language education, and scholarly discourses relating to Chinese studies.
EIN: 222711422

747

Chinese American Citizens Alliance Foundation

763 Yale St.
Los Angeles, CA   90012
Contact: James B. Wong, Pres.
Application address: 2460 Venus Dr., Los Angeles, CA 90046

Foundation type: Independent foundation
Limitations: Scholarships to students of Chinese ancestry who are entering their junior year at colleges and universities in the southern CA area.
Financial data: Year ended 12/31/2004. Assets, $140,725 (M); Expenditures, $7,533; Total giving, $6,000; Grants to individuals, 6 grants totaling $6,000.
Fields of interest: Asians/Pacific Islanders.
Type of support: Undergraduate support.
Application information: Application form required.
   Initial approach: Letter.
   Deadline(s): July 31
   Applicants should submit the following:
   1) Transcripts
   2) SASE
Program description:
   Scholarship Program: Scholarships are awarded primarily on the basis of academic achievement,

but consideration is also given to community and extracurricular activities.
EIN: 237106480

748

Hung Wo & Elizabeth Lau Ching Foundation

841 Bishop St., Ste. 940
Honolulu, HI   96813-3910   (808) 521-4961
Contact: Han Hsin Ching, V.P.; Han Ping Ching, V.P.

Foundation type: Independent foundation
Limitations: Academic achievement awards to students attending Farrington High School and Molokai High School, HI.
Financial data: Year ended 01/31/2005. Assets, $8,398,727 (M); Expenditures, $369,763; Total giving, $328,210; Grants to individuals, 4 grants totaling $10,000 (high: $2,500; low: $2,500).
Type of support: Support to graduates or students of specific schools; Awards/prizes; Precollege support.
Application information: Applications by letter accepted throughout the year.
EIN: 996008990

749

Melanie V. Chmielewski Educational Foundation

2448 S. 102nd St., Ste. 170
West Allis, WI   53227
Contact: Alfred A. Drosen, Jr., Tr.

Foundation type: Independent foundation
Limitations: Scholarships for higher education to individuals who have expressed an interest in teaching academic subjects. Individuals interested in teaching subjects such as physical education and home economics are ineligible.
Financial data: Year ended 12/31/2004. Assets, $56,871 (M); Expenditures, $19,827; Total giving, $14,750; Grants to individuals, totaling $14,750.
Fields of interest: Teacher school/education.
Type of support: Undergraduate support.
Application information: Applications accepted. Application form required.
   Initial approach: Letter or telephone.
   Deadline(s): None
   Additional information: Interviews are required.
Program description:
   Scholarship Program: Preference is shown to qualified graduating high school seniors entering their freshman year at any university or college. A GPA of at least a "B" is required.
EIN: 396531505

750

The Thomas Cholnoky Foundation, Inc.

100 Old Church Rd.
Greenwich, CT   06830
Contact: Thomas Cholnoky, Pres.

Foundation type: Independent foundation
Limitations: Scholarships, research grants, and travel expenses to students and graduates of certain Hungarian universities for study in the U.S.
Financial data: Year ended 12/31/2004. Assets, $328,923 (M); Expenditures, $54,295; Total giving, $51,831; Grants to individuals, totaling $31,494.
Type of support: Research; Foreign applicants; Undergraduate support; Travel grants.

Application information: Applications accepted throughout the year; Completion of formal application required, including academic standing, financial need, personal history, cost of program, and purpose.
EIN: 222610435

751
Stanley & Marvel Chong Foundation
c/o Herman J. Ratelle
7760 France Ave. S., Ste. 340
Bloomington, MN 55435

Foundation type: Independent foundation
Limitations: Scholarships to individuals for higher education in MN and OR.
Financial data: Year ended 12/31/2004. Assets, $498,883 (M); Expenditures, $24,986; Total giving, $17,484; Grants to individuals, 2 grants totaling $8,484 (high: $4,961, low: $3,523).
Type of support: Scholarships—to individuals.
Application information: Applications not accepted.
Additional information: Unsolicited requests for funds not considered or acknowledged.
EIN: 363411371

752
Albert A. Christ Scholarship Fund
c/o JPMorgan Chase Bank, N.A.
P.O. Box 1308
Milwaukee, WI 53201
Application address: c/o JPMorgan Chase Bank, N.A., Attn.: Edward Johnson, 1114 Market St., Wheeling, WV 26003

Foundation type: Independent foundation
Limitations: Scholarships to deserving young people who reside in the Wheeling, WV, area to attend a college or university or to pursue graduate studies.
Financial data: Year ended 06/30/2005. Assets, $5,672,348 (M); Expenditures, $397,405; Total giving, $268,848; Grants to individuals, 297 grants totaling $268,848 (high: $4,000, low: $98).
Type of support: Graduate support; Undergraduate support.
Application information: Applications accepted.
Initial approach: Letter.
Deadline(s): None
Additional information: Contact foundation for current application guidelines.
EIN: 556129775

753
Elmer S. and Frances R. Christ Scholarship Fund
c/o Union Bank & Trust Co.
121 N. Progress Ave.
Pottsville, PA 17901 (570) 622-9528
Contact: Bert R. Cramer, Trust Off., V.P., Union Bank & Trust Co.

Foundation type: Operating foundation
Limitations: Scholarships restricted to applicants who have lived within the Pottsville area school district or who have graduated from either Pottsville, PA, area or Nativity BVM high schools.
Financial data: Year ended 12/31/2003. Assets, $1,106,170 (M); Expenditures, $45,306; Total giving, $37,500; Grants to individuals, 19 grants totaling $37,500 (high: $3,750, low: $1,250).
Type of support: Support to graduates or students of specific schools; Undergraduate support.
Application information: Contact fund for current application deadline; Completion of formal application required, including financial information, 3 character references and 3 academic references.
EIN: 232534508

754
Christamore House Guild, Inc.
(formerly Christamore Aid Society, Inc.)
40 E. 43rd. St.
Indianapolis, IN 46205
Contact: Suzy Dilts, Treas.

Foundation type: Public charity
Limitations: Scholarships to high school graduates in IN, and Christamore House Staff.
Financial data: Year ended 05/31/2004. Assets, $222,253 (M); Expenditures, $320,359; Total giving, $62,606; Grants to individuals, totaling $62,606.
Type of support: Employee-related scholarships.
Application information: Unsolicited requests for funds not considered or acknowledged.
EIN: 311019216

755
Christian Fellowship Foundation of the Peace United Church of Christ, Inc.
P.O. Box 9003
Rochester, MN 55903

Foundation type: Independent foundation
Limitations: Scholarships to students enrolling in an accredited academic or vocational program for work in the fields of religion or nursing who attend high school in Rochester, MN, and its surrounding areas.
Financial data: Year ended 12/31/2004. Assets, $435,804 (M); Expenditures, $23,951; Total giving, $18,825; Grants to individuals, totaling $17,500.
Fields of interest: Nursing school/education; Religion.
Type of support: Support to graduates or students of specific schools; Technical education support; Undergraduate support.
Application information:
Deadline(s): Apr. 1
Applicants should submit the following:
1) Transcripts
2) Financial information
Additional information: Contact foundation for current application guidelines; Application should also include grade statement of educational plans, colleges to be attended, and financial data on college costs.
EIN: 410694748

756
Christian Foundation of Indiana, Inc.
8445 Keystone Crossing, Ste. 200
Indianapolis, IN 46240-4318

Foundation type: Independent foundation
Limitations: Grants to individuals at the Heritage Christian School, IN.
Financial data: Year ended 12/31/2004. Assets, $51,868 (M); Expenditures, $186,057;

Total giving, $185,613; Grants to individuals, totaling $147,366.
Type of support: Support to graduates or students of specific schools; Undergraduate support.
Application information: Applications accepted. Application form required.
Deadline(s): None
EIN: 356048268

757
Christian Legal Society
8001 Braddock Rd., Ste. 300
Springfield, VA 22151 (703) 642-1070
Contact: Samuel B. Casey, Exec. Dir. and C.E.O.
FAX: (703) 642-1075; E-mail: clshq@clsnet.org;
URL: http://www.clsnet.org

Foundation type: Public charity
Limitations: Scholarships to law students throughout the country to aid in becoming Christian law practitioners.
Financial data: Year ended 12/31/2004. Assets, $546,427 (M); Expenditures, $2,202,359; Total giving, $61,042; Grants to individuals, 190 grants totaling $61,042 (high: $7,552, low: $50).
Fields of interest: Law school/education.
Type of support: Scholarships—to individuals.
Application information:
Initial approach: Letter.
EIN: 366101090

758
Christian Scholarship Fund of Arizona
P.O. Box 31101
Tucson, AZ 85751-1101 (520) 322-0966
Contact: Thomas R. Lavoie, Pres.

Foundation type: Public charity
Limitations: Scholarships to AZ students to attend private schools.
Financial data: Year ended 06/30/2004. Assets, $414,382 (M); Expenditures, $402,642; Total giving, $383,166; Grants to individuals, totaling $383,166.
Fields of interest: Elementary/secondary education; Religion.
Type of support: Precollege support.
Application information: Application form available on the grantmaker's Web site.
Initial approach: Application through a school.
Copies of proposal: 1
Deadline(s): None
Additional information: Contact foundation for current application deadline/guidelines; Completion of formal application required, including guidelines.
EIN: 860940166

759
Van and Joanna Christy Scholarship Fund
c/o Citizens Bank of NH
870 Westminster St.
Providence, RI 02903
Contact: Bill Sirak, Trust Off., Citizens Bank of NH
Application address: 875 Elm St., Manchester, NH 03101, tel.: (603) 634-7752

Foundation type: Independent foundation
Limitations: Scholarships only to students of Greek descent in the Manchester, NH, area, for higher education.
Financial data: Year ended 08/31/2005. Assets, $1,325,316 (M); Expenditures, $65,642;

Total giving, $51,000; Grants to individuals, totaling $51,000.
Fields of interest: Greece.
Type of support: Scholarships—to individuals.
Application information: Application form required.
Deadline(s): May 31
EIN: 020484968

760

The Chubb Foundation

15 Mountain View Rd.
Warren, NJ 07059 (908) 903-3580
Contact: Roger Lehecka
Scholarship address: c/o R & R Consultants, P.O. Box 250861, Columbia University Station, New York, NY 10025

Foundation type: Independent foundation
Limitations: Scholarships only to qualified relatives of employees of the Chubb Group Insurance Co., including Chubb and Son, Inc., the Colonial Life Insurance Company of America, and the Chubb Corp.
Financial data: Year ended 12/31/2002. Assets, $15,376,957 (M); Expenditures, $1,028,514; Total giving, $978,750; Grants to individuals, totaling $978,750.
Type of support: Employee-related scholarships.
Application information:
Deadline(s): Dec. 31 for application, Feb. 24 for Student Financial Statement, Mar. 1 for Secondary School Report from applicant's principal or guidance counselor.
Additional information: Application requests should include: name, home address, and zip code; whether student is presently attending high school or college and in what class; and employee information—name and relationship to student, employer branch, and date of employment.
EIN: 226058567

761

Chung Kun Ai Foundation

c/o City Mill Co., Ltd.
P.O. Box 1559
Honolulu, HI 96806

Foundation type: Independent foundation
Limitations: Scholarships to financially needy HI residents who have at least a 2.8 GPA.
Financial data: Year ended 12/31/2004. Assets, $2,033,442 (M); Expenditures, $123,925; Total giving, $78,300; Grants to individuals, 7 grants totaling $17,500 (high: $2,500, low: $2,500).
Type of support: Scholarships—to individuals.
Application information: Applications accepted. Application form required.
Deadline(s): None
Applicants should submit the following:
1) Photograph
2) Transcripts
Additional information: Application should also include three letters of recommendation, and a personal letter stating reasons for desiring a scholarship, academic interests and vocational plans, family financial situation, applicant's financial situation, and participation in student activities or community services; Interviews required.
EIN: 996003289

762

Bradford & Dorothy Church Memorial Fund

c/o State Street Bank and Trust Co.
P.O. Box 55122
Boston, MA 02205

Foundation type: Independent foundation
Limitations: Scholarships to students of Martha's Vineyard Regional High School, MA.
Financial data: Year ended 12/31/2004. Assets, $4,274,993 (M); Expenditures, $247,819; Total giving, $211,649; Grants to individuals, 83 grants totaling $77,500 (high: $2,000, low: $500).
Type of support: Support to graduates or students of specific schools; Undergraduate support.
Application information: Applications not accepted.
Additional information: Unsolicited requests for funds not considered or acknowledged.
EIN: 046135552

763

Churches Homes Foundation, Inc.

c/o Bank of America, N.A.
Bank of America Plz., NC1-002-11-18
Charlotte, NC 28255
Application address: c/o V. Faye White, Atlanta Financial Ctr., S. Twr., Ste. 500, 3353 Peachtree Rd. N.E., Atlanta, GA 30326

Foundation type: Independent foundation
Limitations: Scholarships to residents of metropolitan Atlanta, GA where there exists evidence of financial need and a satisfactory prior academic performance.
Financial data: Year ended 03/31/2005. Assets, $5,373,868 (M); Expenditures, $355,935; Total giving, $312,843; Grants to individuals, 54 grants totaling $235,843.
Type of support: Scholarships—to individuals.
Application information: Applications accepted.
Initial approach: Letter.
Additional information: Application should include a resume. Interviews required.
EIN: 580568689

764

CIACO, Inc.

4563 W. 200 N.
Anderson, IN 46011-8788 (317) 637-2050
Contact: Nancy M. Arellano, Dir.

Foundation type: Independent foundation
Limitations: Undergraduate scholarships to residents of the Chicago, IL, metropolitan area.
Financial data: Year ended 12/31/2004. Assets, $742 (M); Expenditures, $33,104; Total giving, $32,090; Grants to individuals, 15 grants totaling $29,712 (high: $6,371, low: $250). Subtotal for scholarships—to individuals: 16 grants totaling $28,184 (high: $6,371, low: $250).
Type of support: Undergraduate support.
Application information: Application form required.
Deadline(s): Contact foundation for current application deadline/guidelines.
Additional information: In addition, the foundation awards some grants to economically disadvantaged individuals for medical expenses, food, shelter and clothing.
EIN: 351756007

765

Joseph D. Ciatti Memorial Foundation

1101 5th Ave., No. 170
San Rafael, CA 94901

Foundation type: Independent foundation
Limitations: Scholarships to graduates of San Rafael High School, CA.
Financial data: Year ended 10/31/2004. Assets, $215,960 (M); Expenditures, $9,455; Total giving, $8,000; Grants to individuals, 2 grants totaling $6,000 (high: $3,000, low: $3,000).
Type of support: Support to graduates or students of specific schools; Undergraduate support.
Application information: Applications accepted.
Additional information: Contact foundation for current application deadline/guidelines.
EIN: 680113940

766

Cibrowski Family Foundation

6059 S. Quebec St., No. 202
Englewood, CO 80111 (303) 740-9497
Contact: Deon E. Fitch, Chair.
FAX: (303) 740-9593

Foundation type: Independent foundation
Limitations: Scholarships in engineering and chemistry to full-time students at University of Denver and Colorado School of Mines, who are U.S. citizens.
Financial data: Year ended 12/31/2004. Assets, $112,253 (M); Expenditures, $17,250; Total giving, $9,900; Grants to individuals, totaling $9,900.
Fields of interest: Engineering school/education; Chemistry.
Type of support: Support to graduates or students of specific schools; Undergraduate support.
Application information:
Initial approach: Letter or through High School Counselor.
Deadline(s): Apr. 1
Additional information: Completion of formal application required, including GPA, standardized test scores, reference letters, list of academic and community achievements, and an essay; Interviews required.
Program description:
Scholarship Program: Scholarships are awarded on the basis of academic achievement, community involvement, and work ethic. Scholarships are $2,500 annually for students at University of Denver and $600 annually for students at Colorado School of Mines.
EIN: 841255065

767

Elwin L. Cilley Trust

c/o Citizens Bank
870 Westminster St.
Providence, RI 02903
Application address: c/o Bill Sirak, 875 Elm St., Manchester, NH 03101, tel.: (603) 634-7752

Foundation type: Independent foundation
Limitations: Scholarships to individuals who have resided in Nottingham, NH, for the past five years.
Financial data: Year ended 06/30/2005. Assets, $460,258 (M); Expenditures, $29,070; Total giving, $19,800; Grants to individuals, 6 grants totaling $19,800.
Type of support: Undergraduate support.

Application information:
Initial approach: Letter.
Deadline(s): Mar. 31
Additional information: Application should include an essay. Contact trust for further application guidelines.
EIN: 026044555

768
Circuit City Foundation
9950 Mayland Dr.
Richmond, VA 23233-1464 (804) 527-4000
Contact: Jane Gurganus

Foundation type: Operating foundation
Limitations: Scholarships to children and spouses of employees of Circuit City Stores, Inc.
Financial data: Year ended 02/28/2005.
Assets, $2,295,796 (M); Expenditures, $1,892,146; Total giving, $1,828,778; Grants to individuals, 150 grants totaling $192,950.
Type of support: Employee-related scholarships.
Application information: Application form not required.
Deadline(s): June 15.
Additional information: Application by letter.
EIN: 546048660

769
The CIRI Foundation
(also known as The Cook Inlet Region, Inc. Foundation)
2600 Cordova St., Ste. 206
Anchorage, AK 99503 (907) 263-5582
Contact: Paneen Petersen, Prog. Off.
Toll-free tel.: (800) 764-3382; FAX: (907) 263-5588; E-mail: tcf@ciri.com; URL: http://www.thecirifoundation.org

Foundation type: Company-sponsored foundation
Limitations: Scholarships, internships, and fellowships to AK Natives enrolled to the Cook Inlet Region under the Alaska Native Settlement Claims Act of 1971. Recipients are original enrollees, their descendants, or are their legally adopted descendants.
Publications: Application guidelines; Informational brochure (including application guidelines); Program policy statement.
Financial data: Year ended 12/31/2002.
Assets, $38,030,217 (M); Expenditures, $2,512,826; Total giving, $1,131,583; Grants to individuals, totaling $1,050,930.
Fields of interest: Education; Native Americans/American Indians.
Type of support: Fellowships; Internship funds; Research; Graduate support; Technical education support; Undergraduate support.
Application information: Application form required.
Deadline(s): Mar. 31, June 1 and Dec. 1
Applicants should submit the following:
1) Letter(s) of recommendation
2) Transcripts
Additional information: Application should also include proof of eligibility, and statement of purpose.
EIN: 920087914

770
Citizens Union Bank Foundation, Ltd.
P.O. Box 89
Greensboro, GA 30642
Contact: Bobby L. Voyles, Chair.
Scholarship application address: 200 N. East St., Greensboro, GA 30642, tel.: (706) 453-2236
Application address: 200 N. East St., Greensboro, GA 30642, tel.: (706) 453-2236

Foundation type: Company-sponsored foundation
Limitations: Scholarships by nomination only to residents of Greene County, GA.
Financial data: Year ended 12/31/2004.
Assets, $485,536 (M); Expenditures, $13,479; Total giving, $11,100; Grants to individuals, 4 grants totaling $4,000 (high: $1,000, low: $1,000).
Type of support: Awards/grants by nomination only.
Application information: Applications not accepted.
Additional information: Recipients are nominated by schools.
EIN: 581541701

771
The City College 21st Century Foundation, Inc.
138th St. and Convent Ave.
New York, NY 10031 (212) 650-6781
Contact: Zeev Dagan, Secy.

Foundation type: Public charity
Limitations: Scholarships to students of City College, NY.
Financial data: Year ended 12/31/2004.
Assets, $24,371,712 (M); Expenditures, $2,855,234; Total giving, $774,077; Grants to individuals, 33 grants totaling $774,077 (high: $5,500, low: $500).
Type of support: Support to graduates or students of specific schools.
Application information: Applications accepted. Application form required.
Initial approach: Letter.
Deadline(s): Varies
Applicants should submit the following:
1) Essay
2) SAR
3) Transcripts
4) Letter(s) of recommendation
Additional information: Contact foundation for additional application guidelines.
Program descriptions:
Alumni Association Economics Department Scholarships: Awards funds, prizes and internships to qualified students in the economics department.
Howard Wexler Scholarship: Awards $5,000 to graduate students demonstrating financial need.
Mellon Mays Undergraduate Fellowships: Awards a stipend of $1,000 per semester and support of $3,000 for summer research following sophomore and junior years and repayment of up to $10,000 in undergraduate or graduate loans to minority students who desire to matriculate in a Ph.D. program and to pursue a career in research and teaching at the college or university level.
Rudin Research Fellowships: Awards $2,500 stipends to biomedical students to undertake at least 250 hours of research that must be mentored by a faculty member of the Sophie Davis program.
Zitrin Foundation Scholarships: Awards $5,000 to juniors or seniors in the Student Support Services Program (SSSP) to tutor and mentor other SSSP students and help with SSSP activities.
EIN: 133850823

772
Civitan International Foundation
P.O. Box 130744
Birmingham, AL 35213-0744 (205) 591-8910
FAX: (205) 592-6307; E-mail: civitan@civitan.org; URL: http://www.civitan.org

Foundation type: Public charity
Limitations: Undergraduate and graduate scholarships, based on grades, leadership, and community service, to members of Civitan, spouses or children of members, or junior Civitan members.
Publications: Application guidelines.
Financial data: Year ended 09/30/2004.
Assets, $1,689,615 (M); Expenditures, $1,591,110; Total giving, $947,406; Grants to individuals, 29 grants totaling $27,575 (high: $2,000, low: $603).
Fields of interest: Voluntarism promotion.
Type of support: Graduate support; Undergraduate support.
Application information:
Deadline(s): Contact foundation for current application deadline/guidelines.
EIN: 636052990

773
The Clan MacBean Foundation
c/o Raymond L. Heckethorn
441 Wadsworth Blvd., Ste. 213
Lakewood, CO 80226-1546

Foundation type: Operating foundation
Limitations: Scholarships to undergraduate and graduate students primarily for studies and projects related to Scottish culture.
Financial data: Year ended 12/31/2002.
Assets, $142,069 (M); Expenditures, $19,780; Total giving, $12,000; Grants to individuals, 4 grants totaling $12,000 (high: $3,000, low: $3,000).
Fields of interest: Scotland.
Type of support: Graduate support; Undergraduate support.
Application information: Application form required.
Initial approach: Letter or telephone.
Deadline(s): May. 1
Additional information: Application should include transcripts.
EIN: 411445203

774
Helen Miller Clancy Scholarship Foundation
P.O. Box 4
Vashon, WA 98070 (206) 463-3608
URL: http://www.hmcsf.org

Foundation type: Independent foundation
Limitations: Scholarships to graduating high school seniors who are residents of Vashon Island, WA, based on academics, financial need, leadership, and other personal achievements.
Financial data: Year ended 12/31/2004.
Assets, $475,291 (M); Expenditures, $38,472; Total giving, $30,500; Grants to individuals, totaling $30,500.
Type of support: Undergraduate support.
Application information: Applications accepted. Application form required.
Deadline(s): Apr. 25.
Applicants should submit the following:
1) Letter(s) of recommendation
2) Transcripts
3) Essay
EIN: 911658180

775
The Clareth Fund: The Philadelphia Association of Zeta Psi Fraternity
c/o Duanne Morris, LLP
30 S. 17th St.
Philadelphia, PA 19103-4196
Contact: Frank G. Cooper, Esq.
Application address: c/o David L. Sims, Designtex, 2400 Market St., Philadelphia, PA 19103

Foundation type: Independent foundation
Limitations: Scholarships to students attending the University of Pennsylvania Wharton School, Dental School, or Medical School, or who are in the Sigma chapter of Zeta Psi Fraternity.
Financial data: Year ended 12/31/2004. Assets, $5,614,256 (M); Expenditures, $295,736; Total giving, $233,410; Grants to individuals, 51 grants totaling $188,410 (high: $7,000, low: $250).
Fields of interest: Dental school/education; Medical school/education; Students, sororities/fraternities.
Type of support: Support to graduates or students of specific schools.
Application information:
  Deadline(s): None
  Additional information: Contact fund for current application guidelines.
EIN: 232092500

776
Clark Community College District 14 Foundation
1800 E McLoughlin Blvd
Vancouver, WA 98663 (360) 992-2301
Contact: Lisa Gilbert, Pres.
E-mail: foundation@clark.edu; URL: http://www.clarkcollegefoundation.org

Foundation type: Public charity
Limitations: Scholarships to students attending Clark Community College, WA.
Publications: Annual report; Newsletter.
Financial data: Year ended 06/30/2004. Assets, $59,367,014 (M); Expenditures, $3,964,648; Total giving, $288,721; Grants to individuals, totaling $288,721.
Type of support: Support to graduates or students of specific schools.
Application information: Applications accepted. Application form required.
  Initial approach: E-mail.
  Applicants should submit the following:
    1) Transcripts
    2) Letter(s) of recommendation
  Additional information: Contact foundation for further application guidelines.
EIN: 237315006

777
B. M. Clark Foundation
P.O. Box 185
Union, ME 04862 (207) 735-4411
Contact: Randall N. Clark, Treas.

Foundation type: Independent foundation
Limitations: Scholarships to residents of Union, ME.
Financial data: Year ended 12/31/2004. Assets, $0 (M); Expenditures, $3,217; Total giving, $2,700; Grants to individuals, totaling $2,700.
Type of support: Scholarships—to individuals.

Application information: Applications by letter accepted throughout the year.
EIN: 010282855

778
James T. Clark Foundation
c/o American National Bank
3033 E. 1st Ave.
Denver, CO 80206 (303) 394-5129
Contact: Mary Rolsch, Trust Off., American National Bank
FAX: (303) 394-5320

Foundation type: Independent foundation
Limitations: Scholarships to graduates of Fort Morgan High School, CO, to attend Colorado College, Colorado School of Mines, Colorado State University, University of Colorado, or University of Denver.
Financial data: Year ended 09/30/2005. Assets, $1,241,010 (M); Expenditures, $61,938; Total giving, $50,000; Grants to individuals, totaling $50,000.
Type of support: Support to graduates or students of specific schools; Undergraduate support.
Application information: Application form required.
  Deadline(s): Mar. 15
  Additional information: Application should include letter of acceptance from college, transcripts, ACT/SAT scores, two letters of recommendation, and a personal statement outlining future plans and goals; Interviews required for finalists.
Program description:
  Scholarship Program: Completed applications should be delivered to the Fort Morgan High School counselor's office. Applications are then forwarded to the foundation. Recipients are notified by May 1.
EIN: 841070259

779
The Clark Foundation
1 Rockefeller Plz., 31st Fl.
New York, NY 10020-2102
Contact: Charles H. Hamilton, Exec. Dir.

Foundation type: Independent foundation
Limitations: Fellowships by nomination only to high school graduates of Cooperstown, NY and surrounding areas, who are students at the college junior level or above, and who are interested in nonprofit or community-based work. Also, undergraduate scholarships to students residing in the Cooperstown, NY, area. A limited number of grants given to residents of New York, NY.
Publications: Application guidelines; Program policy statement.
Financial data: Year ended 06/30/2005. Assets, $544,631,091 (M); Expenditures, $28,821,942; Total giving, $21,603,356; Grants to individuals, 4 grants totaling $37,462 (high: $18,600, low: $262).
Fields of interest: Community development, volunteer services; Leadership development.
Type of support: Fellowships; Scholarships—to individuals; Awards/grants by nomination only; Graduate support; Undergraduate support.
Application information: Direct applications from students not accepted for fellowships; ineligible requests for funds not considered or acknowledged. Most scholarship applicants are referred to the program by their high schools during their senior year. Interviews required.
Program description:
  Clark Fellowship Program: Nominations are accepted annually from New York City colleges and

universities only for students who are graduates of Cooperstown, NY and the immediate surrounding area high schools. Up to six students per year will be selected to enter the three-year fellowship program offering financial support for graduate study and the first years of work in the nonprofit sector.
EIN: 135616528

780
Mary Clark League Trust
(also known as Clark-AFF League Memorial Fund)
c/o Mellon Financial Corp.
P.O. Box 185
Pittsburgh, PA 15230-9897

Foundation type: Independent foundation
Limitations: Scholarships to students attending medical schools in Philadelphia, PA, including the School of Podiatric Medicine.
Financial data: Year ended 06/30/2005. Assets, $510,915 (M); Expenditures, $29,291; Total giving, $29,000; Grants to individuals, totaling $29,000.
Fields of interest: Medical school/education; Podiatry.
Type of support: Support to graduates or students of specific schools; Graduate support.
Application information: Application form required.
  Additional information: Contact local medical school financial aid office for current application deadline.
EIN: 236225542

781
Henry H. Clark Medical Education Foundation
c/o Mellon Financial Corp.
P.O. Box 185
Pittsburgh, PA 15230-9897

Foundation type: Independent foundation
Limitations: Scholarships and fellowships to residents of Allegheny County, PA, who are attending the University of Pittsburgh School of Medicine.
Financial data: Year ended 12/31/2002. Assets, $1,095,251 (M); Expenditures, $61,952; Total giving, $57,000.
Fields of interest: Medical school/education.
Type of support: Fellowships; Support to graduates or students of specific schools; Graduate support.
Application information: Applications not accepted.
  Additional information: Contact financial aid office at the University of Pittsburgh School of Medicine for information.
EIN: 256018886

782
Welsford Starr and Mildred M. Clark Medical Memorial Fund
(formerly W. S. Clark & M. M. Clark Memorial Trust Fund)
c/o Bank of America, N.A.
777 Main St., CT2-102-22-03
Hartford, CT 06115 (860) 952-7407
Application address: c/o Waterbury Medical Assn., P.O. Box 30, Bloomfield, CT 06002

Foundation type: Independent foundation
Limitations: Scholarships to medical students who have been CT residents for at least five years.

Financial data: Year ended 12/31/2004. Assets, $3,205,157 (M); Expenditures, $230,951; Total giving, $180,000; Grants to individuals, 20 grants totaling $180,000 (high: $9,000, low: $9,000).
Fields of interest: Medical school/education.
Type of support: Undergraduate support.
Application information: Application form required.
 Deadline(s): Jan. 1 of applicant's third year of medical school
 Additional information: Application should include transcript, test results of Part I of the National Boards, 2 letters of recommendation, financial statement, and statement of medical school expenses; Interviews required.
EIN: 066326364

783
Alvin T. Clark Memorial Fund
(formerly Alvin T. Clark Family Memorial Fund)
c/o George Schafer
P.O. Box 400
Buffalo, WY   82834-0400

Foundation type: Independent foundation
Limitations: Student loans to graduating seniors of Buffalo, WY, for postsecondary education in nursing, forestry, and medicine at accredited schools.
Financial data: Year ended 12/31/2004. Assets, $245,380 (M); Expenditures, $2,220; Total giving, $0; Loans to individuals, totaling $57,800.
Fields of interest: Nursing school/education; Environment, forests.
Type of support: Student loans—to individuals; Support to graduates or students of specific schools.
Application information: Applications accepted. Application form required.
 Deadline(s): None
 Additional information: .
EIN: 836025848

784
Claude Clark Memorial Scholarship Fund
788 Santa Ray Ave.
Oakland, CA   94610
Contact: Claude L. Clark, Pres.
Scholarship address: P.O. Box 8172, Emeryville, CA 94622

Foundation type: Independent foundation
Limitations: Scholarships to high school graduates residing in Oakland, CA, for undergraduate education.
Financial data: Year ended 12/31/2004. Assets, $25,233 (M); Expenditures, $11,539; Total giving, $9,880; Grants to individuals, totaling $9,880.
Type of support: Undergraduate support.
Application information: Applications accepted. Application form required.
 Deadline(s): May 31
 Additional information: Contact organization for current application deadlines/guidelines.
EIN: 912152552

785
The Royce W. Clark Memorial Trust
c/o The National Bank of Delaware County
P.O. Box 389
Walton, NY   13856-0389   (607) 865-4126

Foundation type: Independent foundation
Limitations: Scholarships to graduates of Walton Central School District #1, NY, for undergraduate education.
Financial data: Year ended 12/31/2004. Assets, $159,715 (M); Expenditures, $8,170; Total giving, $7,500; Grants to individuals, totaling $7,500.
Type of support: Support to graduates or students of specific schools; Undergraduate support.
Application information:
 Deadline(s): May 31
 Additional information: Completion of written application required.
EIN: 166333418

786
Clark Scholarship Fund
c/o Centennial Bank of the West
P.O. Box 1
Longmont, CO   80502
Application address: c/o Duke Aschenmenner, Principal, Longmont High School, 1040 Sunset, Longmont, CO 80501

Foundation type: Independent foundation
Limitations: Scholarships to financially needy graduates of Longmont High School, CO, attending two- or four-year colleges and universities. Scholarships are awarded on the basis of financial need, and academic and leadership abilities.
Financial data: Year ended 09/30/2005. Assets, $2,262,780 (M); Expenditures, $145,315; Total giving, $125,000; Grants to individuals, 25 grants totaling $125,000 (high: $5,000, low: $5,000).
Fields of interest: Leadership development.
Type of support: Support to graduates or students of specific schools.
Application information: Application form required.
 Deadline(s): Apr. 1
 Applicants should submit the following:
 1) SAT
 2) Financial information
 3) GPA
 4) Class rank
 5) ACT
 Additional information: Application must also include PSAT score, and counselor recommendation; Applications available at Longmont High School, CO.
EIN: 846270490

787
Clark Scholarship Trust
(also known as Grace W. Clark, Thomas R. & Elsie T. Clark Scholarship Trust)
c/o Bank of America, N.A.
10 Light St., MD4-302-17-06
Baltimore, MD   21202
Application address: Bruce Love, V.P., c/o Bank of America, N.A., 302 S. Jefferson St., Roanoke, VA 24011, tel.: (540) 265-3169

Foundation type: Independent foundation
Limitations: Scholarships primarily to residents of Halifax County, VA.
Financial data: Year ended 12/31/2004. Assets, $1,359,801 (M); Expenditures, $84,912; Total giving, $69,300; Grants to individuals, totaling $69,300.
Type of support: Scholarships—to individuals.
Application information: Application form required.
 Initial approach: Letter or telephone.
 Deadline(s): May 1
 Applicants should submit the following:

 1) GPA
 2) Financial information
EIN: 540907369

788
Donald Clark Scholarship Trust
P.O. Box A
Alliance, NE   69301
Application address: Dan Kadden, Principal c/o Bridgeport Public Schools, P.O. Box 430, Bridgeport, NE 69336, tel.: (308) 262-0346

Foundation type: Independent foundation
Limitations: Scholarships to graduates of Bridgeport High School, NE, who are attending or are planning to attend, the University of Nebraska.
Financial data: Year ended 12/31/2004. Assets, $689,788 (M); Expenditures, $52,961; Total giving, $34,748; Grants to individuals, totaling $34,748.
Type of support: Support to graduates or students of specific schools; Undergraduate support.
Application information: Applications accepted. Application form required.
 Deadline(s): Apr. 1
 Additional information: Completion of formal application required, including a letter of no more than 200 words demonstrating need from self (if not a minor) or parent or guardian, tax returns and certified transcript.
EIN: 476213232

789
Rachel Fiero Clarke Trust
c/o KeyBank N.A.
800 Superior Ave., 4th Fl.
Cleveland, OH   44114-1306
Application address: c/o Catskill Board of Education, Catskill, NY 12414

Foundation type: Independent foundation
Limitations: Scholarships to graduates of Catskill High School, NY.
Financial data: Year ended 06/30/2005. Assets, $1,809,736 (M); Expenditures, $85,240; Total giving, $66,596; Grants to individuals, totaling $66,596.
Type of support: Support to graduates or students of specific schools; Undergraduate support.
Application information: Application form required.
 Deadline(s): Apr. 15
EIN: 237122166

790
George M. and Florence M. Clarkson Scholarship Foundation
c/o First Interstate Bank
P.O. Box 1299
Polson, MT   59860

Foundation type: Independent foundation
Limitations: Scholarships to seniors and graduates of Polson High School, MT, for study at any accredited college, university, or technical or vocational training school.
Financial data: Year ended 12/31/2004. Assets, $211,101 (M); Expenditures, $12,311; Total giving, $10,000; Grants to individuals, totaling $10,000.
Fields of interest: Vocational education.
Type of support: Support to graduates or students of specific schools; Technical education support; Undergraduate support.

Application information: Applications accepted. Application form required.
> *Deadline(s):* Apr. 1
> *Applicants should submit the following:*
> 1) Transcripts
> 2) Letter(s) of recommendation
> 3) FAF
> *Additional information:* Application should include three references.

EIN: 363802270

791
Class of 1968 Scholarship, Inc.
119 Putnam Park
Greenwich, CT 06830-6735 (203) 661-2161
Contact: Robert S.V. Platten, Pres.

Foundation type: Operating foundation
Limitations: Scholarships to children of members of the Hobart College and William Smith College classes of 1968.
Financial data: Year ended 05/31/2005. Assets, $1,364 (M); Expenditures, $8,149; Total giving, $8,000; Grants to individuals, totaling $8,000.
Type of support: Support to graduates or students of specific schools; Undergraduate support.
Application information: Application form required.
> *Initial approach:* Letter outlining financial need.
> *Deadline(s):* May 31

EIN: 222573776

792
The Claudia Foundation
(formerly The Claudia Bloodworth Company)
c/o Gelfand Rennert & Feldman
1880 Century Park E., Ste. 1600
Los Angeles, CA 90067
Application address: c/o Stacey M. Kalich, 626 Cynthia St., Poplar Bluff, MO 53901, tel.: (573) 686-3040

Foundation type: Independent foundation
Limitations: Scholarships to female students at Three Rivers Community College, MO, who attended Poplar Bluff School District or Sacred Heart School of Poplar Bluff. Awards up to six full scholarships, which are need-based and challenge women to assume leadership roles and professional positions in a variety of careers.
Financial data: Year ended 12/31/2004. Assets, $4,174,305 (M); Expenditures, $66,049; Total giving, $12,000.
Fields of interest: Women.
Type of support: Support to graduates or students of specific schools; Undergraduate support.
Application information:
> *Initial approach:* Letter.
> *Deadline(s):* Mar. 1
> *Additional information:* Contact foundation for current application guidelines.

EIN: 431574170

793
William L. Clay Scholarship & Research Fund
6023 Waterman, Ste. 1W
St. Louis, MO 63112
Contact: Hazel Mallory, Dir.
Application address: P.O. Box 4693, Field Station, St. Louis, MO 63108

Foundation type: Independent foundation

Limitations: Scholarships to financially needy full-time students who are residents of the First Congressional District of MO.
Financial data: Year ended 12/31/2004. Assets, $29,195 (M); Expenditures, $107,749; Total giving, $75,182; Grants to individuals, totaling $75,182.
Type of support: Undergraduate support.
Application information: Contact fund for current application deadline; Completion of formal application required, including personal statement, transcripts, three recommendations, and copy of parents' most recent tax return; Interviews required.
Program description:
> *Scholarship Program:* Scholarships are awarded on the basis of academic achievement, potential, and financial need. Applicants must be first-time freshmen, currently enrolled undergraduates, or transfer students from an accredited college with at least two years remaining before the completion of a degree. Applicants must be at least 18 years old and registered voters. Scholarships are renewable.

EIN: 431288222

794
Clayman Family Foundation, Inc.
P.O. Box 200
Canfield, OH 44406

Foundation type: Independent foundation
Limitations: Scholarships primarily to residents of Niles, OH.
Financial data: Year ended 06/30/2005. Assets, $856,154 (M); Expenditures, $63,694; Total giving, $62,375; Grants to individuals, totaling $62,375.
Type of support: Scholarships—to individuals.
Application information: Applications not accepted.
EIN: 341685923

795
Bernard and Anna Clayton Scholarship Trust
c/o HNB Bank, N.A.
100 N. Main St.
Hannibal, MO 63401

Foundation type: Independent foundation
Limitations: Scholarships to residents of the A.D. Stowell School attendance area of Hannibal, MO, School District No. 60, for study at colleges and technical schools.
Financial data: Year ended 12/31/2004. Assets, $475,262 (M); Expenditures, $25,765; Total giving, $21,525; Grants to individuals, totaling $21,525.
Fields of interest: Vocational education.
Type of support: Support to graduates or students of specific schools; Technical education support; Undergraduate support.
Application information: Unsolicited requests for application not accepted.
EIN: 431652040

796
The Clemens Foundation
c/o Kelly Howard, Exec. Dir.
P.O. Box 427
Philomath, OR 97370

Foundation type: Independent foundation

Limitations: Scholarships to graduates of high schools in the Alsea, Crane, Eddyville, and Philomath, OR, school districts.
Financial data: Year ended 12/31/2004. Assets, $31,728,279 (M); Expenditures, $1,990,134; Total giving, $1,787,894.
Fields of interest: Vocational education; Athletics/sports, water sports.
Type of support: Support to graduates or students of specific schools; Undergraduate support.
Application information: Applications not accepted.
Program description:
> *Scholarship Program:* Scholarships are awarded for college-level education, to students attending recognized institutions or accredited vocational schools on a full-time basis. Tuition grants will not exceed the amount of tuition charged by Oregon State University to resident students. In addition, two grants of slightly higher amounts are awarded to the first- and second-place swimmers at Philomath High School, OR, provided they plan to attend college.

EIN: 936023941

797
H. Loren Clements Scholarship Fund
c/o Wachovia Bank, N.A.
100 N. Main St., 13th Fl.
Winston-Salem, NC 27150

Foundation type: Independent foundation
Limitations: Scholarships to graduates of North Pocono High School in Moscow, PA.
Financial data: Year ended 12/31/2004. Assets, $373,873 (M); Expenditures, $17,138; Total giving, $14,000; Grants to individuals, 14 grants totaling $14,000 (high: $1,000, low: $1,000).
Type of support: Support to graduates or students of specific schools; Undergraduate support.
Application information: Applications accepted.
> *Deadline(s):* Mar. 19
> *Additional information:* Contact fund for current application guidelines.

EIN: 236523865

798
Cleveland Alumnae Panhellenic Endowment Fund, Inc.
1335 W. 49th St.
Cleveland, OH 44102
Contact: Rea Wedekamm, Scholarship Chair.
Application address: 7654 Sherman Rd., Chesterland, OH 44026, tel.: (440) 729-9001, E-mail: DawneeDee@aol.com

Foundation type: Independent foundation
Limitations: Scholarships to residents of the metropolitan Cleveland, OH, area who are members of the National Panhellenic Conference and are full-time students in graduate, senior, junior, or sophomore years.
Financial data: Year ended 05/31/2005. Assets, $226,116 (M); Expenditures, $11,076; Total giving, $10,000; Grants to individuals, 10 grants totaling $10,000 (high: $1,000, low: $1,000).
Fields of interest: Students, sororities/fraternities.
Type of support: Graduate support; Undergraduate support.
Application information: Deadline Mar. 1; Completion of formal application required, including two letters of recommendation.
EIN: 341476473

799

Cleveland National Air Show Charitable Foundation, Inc.

c/o Burke Lakefront Airport
1501 N. Marginal Rd.
Cleveland, OH 44114 (216) 241-5587
Contact: Miria Batig

Foundation type: Independent foundation
Limitations: Scholarships to aviation students.
Financial data: Year ended 10/31/2003.
Assets, $302,854 (M); Expenditures, $406,942;
Total giving, $16,000; Grants to individuals, 3
grants totaling $15,000 (high: $5,000, low:
$5,000).
Fields of interest: Space/aviation.
Type of support: Scholarships—to individuals.
Application information: Applications accepted
throughout the year; Completion of formal
application required.
EIN: 341741796

800

Cleveland Scholarship Programs, Inc.

(also known as CSP)
BP Tower
200 Public Sq., Ste. 3820
Cleveland, OH 44114-3304 (216) 241-5587
Contact: Maria Boss, Pres. and C.E.O.
E-mail: csp@cspohio.org; URL: http://
www.cspohio.org

Foundation type: Public charity
Limitations: Scholarships to residents of the
following OH counties: Ashtabula, Cuyahoga,
Geauga, Lake, Lorain, Mahoning, Medina, Portage,
Stark, Summit, and Trumbull.
Publications: Application guidelines; Annual report;
Financial statement; Newsletter.
Financial data: Year ended 07/31/2004.
Assets, $11,590,142 (M); Expenditures,
$6,688,896; Total giving, $3,054,903; Grants to
individuals, totaling $3,054,903.
Fields of interest: Teacher school/education;
Adult/continuing education.
Type of support: Graduate support; Precollege
support; Undergraduate support.
Application information: Application form required.
Deadline(s): Vary
Applicants should submit the following:
1) Transcripts
2) Letter(s) of recommendation
3) Essay
4) Financial information
Additional information: See Web site for
complete guidelines and application forms.
Program descriptions:
*Adult Learning Scholarships for Ages 25 and
Above:* Scholarships to adult students pursuing an
associate's or bachelor's degree. Applicants must
be age 25 or older by Sept. 1 of the next academic
year; have at least a 2.5 cumulative GPA if currently
enrolled in college or if college work has been
completed within the past five years; and be able to
demonstrate financial need. Individuals who
already hold a bachelor's degree are not eligible.
Some Adult Learner students may also be eligible
for an additive scholarship that rewards a high GPA
in conjunction with a high number of credit hours
per semester. Deadlines Apr. 15 (1st priority -
$1,000) and Oct. 15 (2nd priority - $500). CSP also
provides scholarships to a select number of adults,
ages 19 to 24, currently employed and pursuing an
associate's degree in a one- to two-year
occupational career program. All other criteria are
the same as for the 25 and over scholarship.

*Adult Learner Scholarship for Non-Degree
Certificates:* This $500 to $1,000 award is meant
for individuals planning to pursue training in a
Pell-eligible certificate program not associated with
an associate or bachelor's degree and which lasts
from several months to two years in length.
Applicants must be at least 19 years old, a high
school graduate or GED holder, and have financial
need. Applications must be submitted at least two
months before the beginning of the program.

*CSP/Cuyahoga Community College Transfer
Scholarships:* This program provides a scholarship
fund for Cleveland Public School students assisted
by CSP who attend Tri-C and then transfer to any
four-year college or university to pursue a
bachelor's degree. The award is $2,000 each year
for two years. Twelve area colleges have agreed to
match this $2,000 scholarship with one of their
own: The University of Akron, Baldwin-Wallace
College, Case Western Reserve University,
Cleveland Institute of Music, Cleveland State
University, David N. Myers College, Hiram College,
John Carroll University, Lake Erie College, Notre
Dame College of Ohio, Oberlin College, Ursuline
College.

CSP Finalist Scholarships for High School Seniors:
Applicants must attend a high school serviced by a
CSP Advisor. Winners are selected based on
recommendations by the CSP Advisor, and students
must also meet CSP criteria for academic
performance (grades and SAT/ACT scores) and
financial need. Awards start at $500 per year.

*Jennings Post-Baccalaureate Teacher
Certification Scholarship:* This $2,500 scholarship
is open to students who already have a bachelor's
degree and are returning to school to obtain a
teacher certification/licensure by itself or in
conjunction with a Master's degree in education.
Applicants must have had a GPA of at least 2.5 at
time of undergraduate graduation, and a 3.0 in
post-bachelor or graduate courses, if applicable.
Financial need is a requirement. Deadline June 1.

CSP Administered Scholarships: CSP manages
scholarship programs for a number of outside
organizations and corporations. See Web site for a
list of these scholarships.
EIN: 346580096

801

Clifford Foundation, Inc.

P.O. Box 1001
Corsicana, TX 75151 (903) 874-4725
Contact: C.L. Brown III, Pres.

Foundation type: Independent foundation
Limitations: Scholarships to financially needy
residents of TX, with preference given to residents
of Navarro County.
Financial data: Year ended 06/30/2005.
Assets, $1,993,410 (M); Expenditures,
$107,735; Total giving, $104,508; Grants to
individuals, 13 grants totaling $104,508 (high:
$16,623, low: $966).
Type of support: Scholarships—to individuals.
Application information: Application form required.
Initial approach: Letter.
Deadline(s): Apr. 1
Applicants should submit the following:
1) Financial information
2) Essay
3) SAT
4) ACT
Additional information: Application should also
include a copy of parents' previous year's tax
return, Interviews required.
EIN: 752506394

802

Ted & Elinor Clifford Scholarship

c/o Northeast Investment Management
150 Federal St., Ste. 1000
Boston, MA 02110-1745
Contact: Elinor C. Huntley, Tr.
Application address: R.D. 1, Box 27, Bethel, VT
05032, tel.: (800) 233-0111

Foundation type: Independent foundation
Limitations: Scholarships to graduates of
Whitcomb Senior High School, Bethel, VT, pursuing
undergraduate or graduate degrees.
Financial data: Year ended 12/31/2004.
Assets, $435,446 (M); Expenditures, $20,042;
Total giving, $18,000; Grants to individuals,
totaling $18,000.
Type of support: Support to graduates or students
of specific schools; Graduate support;
Undergraduate support.
Application information: Applications not
accepted.
Additional information: Recipients are chosen by
a scholarship committee at Whitcomb High
School.
EIN: 036051878

803

Clifton Trust

664 Commanche Dr.
Macon, GA 31210
Contact: Horace L. McSwain III

Foundation type: Independent foundation
Limitations: Scholarships to graduates of public
and private high schools in the middle of GA.
Financial data: Year ended 07/31/2002.
Assets, $271,351 (M); Expenditures, $33,262;
Total giving, $23,400; Grants to individuals, 26
grants totaling $23,400 (high: $900, low: $900).
Type of support: Undergraduate support.
Application information: Applications accepted.
Application form required.
Initial approach: Letter.
Deadline(s): Varies
EIN: 586396554

804

Charles O. & Hazel E. Cline Memorial Scholarship Fund

c/o KeyBank N.A.
1211 S.W. 5th Ave., Ste. 560
Portland, OR 97204

Foundation type: Independent foundation
Limitations: Scholarships to graduates of high
schools in Linn and Crook counties, OR, to attend
postsecondary educational institutions in OR.
Financial data: Year ended 03/31/2005.
Assets, $1,190,099 (M); Expenditures,
$126,785; Total giving, $104,700; Grants to
individuals, 127 grants totaling $104,700 (high:
$1,500, low: $600).
Type of support: Support to graduates or students
of specific schools; Undergraduate support.
Application information: Application form required.
Initial approach: Letter.
Deadline(s): Mar. 15
Program description:
Scholarship Program: Students graduating from
the following high schools in Linn and Crook
counties, OR, are eligible: Crook County High
School, West Albany High School, Harrisburg High
School, Sweet Home High School, Central Linn High
School, South Albany High School, Lebanon High
School, Scio High School, Santiam High School,

and East Linn Christian Academy. Scholarships are renewable.
EIN: 930931552

805
The Clint Foundation
1015 Atlantic Blvd., PMB 252
Atlantic Beach, FL 32233

Foundation type: Independent foundation
Limitations: Scholarships by nomination only to students who will work during the school year to help pay a portion of their own education costs.
Financial data: Year ended 03/31/2004.
Assets, $307,971 (M); Expenditures, $103,536; Total giving, $97,714; Grants to individuals, 8 grants totaling $97,714.
Type of support: Awards/grants by nomination only; Undergraduate support.
Application information: Unsolicited requests for funding not considered or acknowledged.
Program description:
Scholarship Program: Students will be required to participate in a "service" component during the year. Awards are $2,000 each. Students must maintain a 2.5 GPA, participate in volunteer service, and make a moral commitment at some time in the future to help others with their education.
EIN: 593226849

806
The Club Foundation
1733 King St.
Alexandria, VA 22314 (703) 739-9500
Contact: Rhonda Schaver, Mgr., Admin. & Schol.
FAX: (703) 739-0124;
E-mail: rhonda.schaver@clubfoundation.org;
URL: http://www.clubfoundation.org/

Foundation type: Public charity
Limitations: Scholarships to those pursuing a career in private club management.
Financial data: Year ended 10/31/2004.
Assets, $3,294,711 (M); Expenditures, $1,117,917; Total giving, $391,149; Grants to individuals, 12 grants totaling $26,022 (high: $2,500, low: $117).
Fields of interest: Business school/education.
Type of support: Scholarships—to individuals; Undergraduate support.
Application information:
Deadline(s): mid-Apr.
Additional information: Contact foundation for current application guidelines.
Program description:
Student Scholarship: Awards two $2,500 scholarships annually to students currently attending an accredited, four-year college or university and pursuing careers in private club management. The candidate must have achieved and continue to maintain a GPA of at least 2.5 on a 4.0 scale, or a 4.5 on a 6.0 scale.
EIN: 521642692

807
CMCD Scholarship Foundation
1415 L St., Ste. 700
Sacramento, CA 95814 (916) 441-2599
Contact: Bruce Sedlezky

Foundation type: Independent foundation
Limitations: Scholarships to high school graduates who have been accepted to any of the three

Norwood University campuses, in Midland, MI, Cedar Hill, TX, or West Palm Beach, FL.
Financial data: Year ended 12/31/2004.
Assets, $258,394 (M); Expenditures, $14,855; Total giving, $13,500; Grants to individuals, 4 grants totaling $13,500.
Type of support: Support to graduates or students of specific schools; Undergraduate support.
Application information: Applications accepted. Application form required.
Initial approach: Letter.
Deadline(s): Aug. 1
Additional information: Application must include a letter of recommendation and a letter of admission acceptance.
Program description:
Scholarship Program: Recipients must maintain at least a 2.5 GPA in high school and be able to demonstrate a sincere interest in the franchised new motor vehicle business.
EIN: 954454279

808
Coast Guard Foundation, Inc.
394 Taugwonk Rd.
Stonington, CT 06378-1807 (860) 535-0786
Contact: James C. Link, Pres.
FAX: (860) 535-0944; E-mail: info@cgfdn.org;
URL: http://www.cgfdn.org

Foundation type: Public charity
Limitations: Scholarships to Coast Guard enlisted personnel and their dependents.
Financial data: Year ended 12/31/2003.
Assets, $5,392,760 (M); Expenditures, $2,924,021; Total giving, $412,510; Grants to individuals, totaling $412,510.
Fields of interest: Military/veterans' organizations.
Type of support: Support to graduates or students of specific schools; Undergraduate support.
Application information: Applications accepted. Application form required.
Initial approach: E-mail.
Deadline(s): Varies
Applicants should submit the following:
1) Essay
2) Transcripts
3) SAT
4) ACT
5) Letter(s) of recommendation
Additional information: See Web site for further program descriptions.
Program descriptions:
Enlisted Education Grant: This grant program is open to active duty enlisted personnel in pay grades E-3 to E-9 with two or more years of Coast Guard Service. This grant may be used in conjunction with the Coast Guard Tuition Assistance Program (i.e. to pay the member's 25% of the course cost), or other non-funded relevant education items. Maximum payable is $350 per member per year. For more information, please contact: The Coast Guard Institute at (405) 954-7240 or www.uscg.mil/hq/cgi on the web.
Keiser College Coast Guard Scholarship: The candidate for this scholarship must meet Keiser College admission criteria and Coast Guard eligibility requirements as follows: Verification of high school graduation or GED completion and an entrance exam (SAT or ACT, for example). Coast Guard requirements include: a minimum of four years in the Coast Guard, 2nd tour of duty, demonstrated leadership skill, an essay and a recommendation from his or her Commanding Officer. On-going requirements must also be met to remain in good standing. Keiser College will award two full-tuition scholarships, valued at $50,000

each. The Award Recipients will be responsible for the costs associated with education fees, books and supplies, when applicable. However, the one time application and registration fees will be waived. For more information, please contact: Dr. Ronnie Ellen Kramer via email at rkramer@keisercollege.edu with "Coast Guard Scholarship" in the subject line or by phone at 866-534-7371 or visit the Keiser College website at www.keisercollege.edu.
USAA Family Reserve Enlisted Scholarship: Applicants must be a US Coast Guard Enlisted Reservist or a Dependent (defined as a spouse or child) of a Coast Guard Drilling Enlisted Reservist Listed Registered in Deers. The scholarship can be applied to tuition, fees, books and school supplies. Four $750 scholarships are awarded each year. The applicant must meet the following requirements:
· Enrolled in (or have been accepted to) an accredited institution in a degree (associates, bachelors masters, doctoral) program or a two or four year course of study at an accredited technical or vocational training school
· Maintain minimum GPA established by their institution to remain in degree status
· Pursuing his/her first associates, bachelors, masters or doctoral degree or technical/vocational certificate
For more information, please contact:
· LCDR Rob Hanley, Chief, Reserve Communications, US Coast Guard Headquarters: (202) 267-6443 rhanley@comdt.uscg.mil
· LT Scott Toves, US Coast Guard Headquarters: (202) 267-0622 stoves@comdt.uscg.mil
· LTJG Jae-Won Kwon, US Coast Guard Headquarters: (202) 267-0192 jkwon@comdt.uscg.mil
Arnold Sobel Scholarship/Coast Guard Foundation Scholarship: This scholarship is awarded to dependent children of enlisted men and women of the US Coast Guard on active duty, retired or deceased, and dependent children of enlisted personnel in the Coast Guard Reserve currently on extended active duty 180 days or more. Students applying to and currently attending college are eligible to apply. Awards range up to $5,000 per year, renewable for up to 4 consecutive years as long as the student, in the opinion of the selection committee, continues to qualify. The Arnold Sobel Scholarship fund offers four scholarships per year. The Coast Guard Foundation Scholarship awards vary year to year. Questions and requests for applications may to directed to Mrs. Yvette Wright at 202-267-6728 or email ywright@comdt.uscg.mil.
Captain Ernest Fox Perpetual Scholarship: This scholarship is available to employees of ARSC (active duty, federal civil service and their dependents.) One $500 scholarship is awarded each year. Members of the ARSC interested in applying for this grant should contact MCPO Don Staubin of the ARSC at 252-335-6034.
EIN: 042899862

809
The Coastal Banc Foundation
c/o Coastal Banc Savings Assn.
5718 Westheimer Rd., Ste. 600
Houston, TX 77057-5733

Foundation type: Operating foundation
Limitations: Scholarships to financially needy graduating seniors from TX high schools located within the Coastal Banc market area. Recipients

must attend two- and four-year state-supported colleges and universities in TX.
Financial data: Year ended 05/31/2004. Assets, $0 (M); Expenditures, $17,323; Total giving, $17,312; Grants to individuals, 9 grants totaling $17,312 (high: $5,000, low: $1,000).
Type of support: Undergraduate support.
Application information: Deadline Mar. 11; Completion of formal application required, including personal statement, high school transcripts, GPA, SAT or ACT scores, and a copy of parents' last two tax returns; Interviews required.
Program description:
  Scholarship Program: To be eligible, applicants must have at least a 3.0 GPA and SAT score of at least 1000, or ACT score of at least 20. Recipients must attend college on a full-time basis and must maintain at least a 2.75 GPA. Scholarships are available for full-time summer study and are also renewable. Students living with, or related to Coastal Banc employees are ineligible.
EIN: 760390265

810
Coastal Bend Community Foundation
The Six Hundred Bldg.
600 Leopard St., Ste. 1716
Corpus Christi, TX 78473   (361) 882-9745
FAX: (361) 882-2865;
E-mail: eh@cbcfoundation.org; URL: http://www.cbcfoundation.org

Foundation type: Community foundation
Limitations: Scholarships to residents of Aransas, Bee, Jim Wells, Kleberg, Nueces, Refugio, and San Patricio counties, TX.
Publications: Application guidelines; Annual report; Grants list; Informational brochure.
Financial data: Year ended 12/31/2004. Assets, $35,978,712 (M); Expenditures, $4,040,424; Total giving, $3,105,217; Grants to individuals, totaling $243,791.
Type of support: Undergraduate support.
Application information:
  Initial approach: Letter requesting guidelines.
  Deadline(s): Mar. 15.
EIN: 742190039

811
Coastal Community Foundation of South Carolina
(formerly The Community Foundation Serving Coastal South Carolina)
90 Mary St.
Charleston, SC 29403-6230   (843) 723-3635
Contact: Madeleine McGee, C.E.O.
FAX: (843) 577-3671;
E-mail: mmcgee@ccfgives.org; Alternate E-mail: info@ccfgives.org; URL: http://www.ccfgives.org

Foundation type: Community foundation
Limitations: Scholarships primarily to residents of Berkeley, Charleston, and Dorchester counties, SC.
Publications: Application guidelines; Biennial report; Financial statement; Grants list; Informational brochure (including application guidelines); Newsletter; Occasional report.
Financial data: Year ended 06/30/2005. Assets, $115,416,742 (M); Expenditures, $7,662,173; Total giving, $5,489,958.
Fields of interest: Athletics/sports, golf; Business/industry; Roman Catholic agencies & churches; Minorities; African Americans/Blacks.
Type of support: Graduate support; Undergraduate support.

Application information: Applications accepted. Application form required. Application form available on the grantmaker's Web site.
  Copies of proposal: 1
  Deadline(s): Mar. 24.
  Applicants should submit the following:
    1) Letter(s) of recommendation
    2) SASE
    3) ACT
    4) Essay
    5) Financial information
    6) GPA
    7) SAT
    8) Transcripts
  Additional information: Application must also include personal statement and photocopy of financial requirements page from catalogs of first- and second-choice colleges; Faxed applications not accepted.
Program descriptions:
  Banks-Williams-Banks Scholarship: Provides a scholarship to a high school senior at Summerville High School. One award of $1,200, renewable throughout college if certain standards are met.
  Seymour I. Barkowitz Scholarship: Provides scholarships to students in Charleston, Berkeley, and Dorchester Counties intending to pursue a four-year degree at the College of Charleston. One award of $500.
  Thaddeus J. Bell, II Memorial Scholarship: Provides scholarships to students who are pursuing or who intend to pursue a bachelor's degree at Morehouse College, in Atlanta. Applicants' permanent residence must be in SC. One award of $500, renewable with conditions during four years of college.
  William Melvin Brown, Jr. Scholarship: Provides scholarships to African-Americans in Charleston County who are about to begin studies at a four-year college; preference is given to applicants who are members of the Roman Catholic Church. Two awards of $1,000 or one award of $2,000, renewable with conditions through college.
  Catfish Row Co./P&B Music Scholarship: Provides scholarships to African-American students who have lived in Charleston, Berkeley or Dorchester Counties for five years or more, and who are pursuing a four-year college major related to music or music education. Applicants must be musically talented (voice or instrumental)
  Charles E. Eiserhart, Sr. Scholarships: Provides a college scholarship each year to a senior at BEHS.
  Eve K. Evans Scholarship: Provides financial assistance to selected youth (to age 21, with a preference for African-American males) to experience a positive difference in a direction of their lives and development by improving their education. Assistance may be given for public or private educational experiences, to a maximum of $5,000.
  Morris Finkelstein Scholarship: Provides a scholarship which is renewable for up to four years to help a deserving athlete receive a degree from the College of Charleston. One award of $500.
  Future Military Officers Scholarship: Provides an annual scholarship to a college-bound (or in-college) student living in the 294** zip code area. The student must be in a ROTC program and intend to become a military officer. One award of $1,000.
  Donna and Michael Griffith Fund: Awards renewable college scholarships to students from St. John's High School.
  The Gadsden Fund: Provides scholarships to help high school seniors in Berkeley or Dorchester counties to attend either Winthrop or Clemson. One award of $500.
  Philip O'Neill Hanvey Memorial Scholarship: To Charleston County students who attend either

undergraduate or graduate school. Awards total $1,000.
  Frene Nichole Haynes Scholarship: College scholarship awards to Ashley Hall students who possess passion for the fine arts and music.
  Randall G. Heffron Scholarship: Provides scholarship to a Charleston County high school senior nominated by either Bishop England High School or Porter-Gaud School, based on tennis ability, sportsmanship, scholarship, character and service. One award of $1,000 to $1,500.
  J.C. and Alberta Long Scholarship: Provides scholarships to high school seniors who have lived in Charleston, Berkeley, or Dorchester counties for at least the past four years; college students who have received a J.C. and Alberta Long Award in the past may also apply; three to five awards are made, totaling $4,500.
  Mount Pleasant Rotary Scholarship: When this "endowment-in-progress" is fully capitalized, it will accept applications from high school seniors who live east of Cooper. Awards are renewable, in increasing amounts ($1,000, $1,500, $2,000, $2,500) through college.
  Jack C. Muller Scholarship Fund: Provides a scholarship annually to a high school senior about to enter a four-year college. Applicants must be residents of properties owned by and/or managed by the Housing Authority of the City of Charleston. One award of $350, renewable throughout college.
  National Golf Course Owners' Association Scholarship: Provides a scholarship to a student pursuing a degree in sports management. One award of $1,000.
  Porter-Gaud Minority Scholarship: Provides scholarships for minority students.
  Ester Lorraine Bailey Rivers Scholarship: Provides scholarship assistance for minority students.
  Felix Turner Scholarship Fund: Provides scholarships for low-income youth.
  Wofford College Scholarship: This fund accepts applications from Charleston, Berkeley, and Dorchester county students intending to pursue a four-year degree at Wofford College. One award of $500.
EIN: 237390313

812
Coats North American Educational Foundation
(formerly American Thread Educational Foundation, Inc.)
c/o Coats American Inc.
3430 Toringdon Way, Ste. 301
Charlotte, NC 28277
Contact: Alan Demillo, Treas.

Foundation type: Company-sponsored foundation
Limitations: Scholarships to children of employees of Coats American, Inc., and Coats & Clark, who earn below a certain salary level, primarily in GA, NC, and SC.
Financial data: Year ended 12/31/2004. Assets, $1,071,395 (M); Expenditures, $58,076; Total giving, $57,214; Grants to individuals, 18 grants totaling $57,214 (high: $5,625, low: $964).
Type of support: Employee-related scholarships.
Application information: Application form required.
  Deadline(s): Feb. 28
  Additional information: Interviews required.
EIN: 566093510

813
Ty Cobb Educational Fund
P.O. Box 937
Sharpsburg, GA 30277
Contact: Cathy Scott, Secy.
E-mail: tycobb@mindspring.com; URL: http://
www.tycobbfoundation.com

Foundation type: Independent foundation
Limitations: Scholarships to needy and deserving residents of GA who have completed one year in an accredited institution of higher learning. Graduate school scholarships available to medical or dental students only.
Publications: Application guidelines; Informational brochure.
Financial data: Year ended 12/31/2004.
Assets, $12,277,046 (M); Expenditures, $574,441; Total giving, $455,502.
Fields of interest: Dental school/education; Law school/education; Medical school/education.
Type of support: Graduate support; Undergraduate support.
Application information: Application form required.
Initial approach: Letter or e-mail.
Deadline(s): June 15.
Applicants should submit the following:
1) Transcripts
2) Letter(s) of recommendation
Program description:
Scholarship Program: Scholarships are awarded to students who have demonstrated financial need and completed at least one academic year of "B" quality or higher work. Ordinarily, scholarships are awarded for undergraduate study, but awards may also be made for professional study in law, medicine, and dentistry. Scholarships are paid directly to the institution for a full academic year of nine months and are renewable.
EIN: 586026003

814
Frank and Ellen Cobb Memorial Scholars
c/o Bank of America, N.A.
P.O. Box 6767
Providence, RI 02940-6767
Application address: c/o Hingham High School, Guidance Department, 17 Union St., Hingham, MA 02043

Foundation type: Independent foundation
Limitations: Scholarships to graduates of Hingham High School, MA, for higher education.
Financial data: Year ended 08/31/2002.
Assets, $1,738,294 (M); Expenditures, $37,185; Total giving, $25,500; Grants to individuals, 10 grants totaling $25,500 (high: $4,500, low: $1,000).
Type of support: Support to graduates or students of specific schools; Undergraduate support.
Application information: Applications accepted. Application form required.
Deadline(s): Mar. 15
EIN: 036088605

815
E. B. Coburn Scholarship Trust
c/o Brownsville Bank, Trust Dept.
P.O. Box 879
Brownsville, TN 38012-0879
Application address: c/o Gordon Perry, Haywood County High School, Brownsville, TN 38012

Foundation type: Independent foundation
Limitations: Scholarships only to students at Haywood County High School, TN.

Financial data: Year ended 12/31/2004.
Assets, $0 (M); Expenditures, $8,530; Total giving, $6,500; Grants to individuals, 7 grants totaling $6,500 (high: $1,000, low: $500).
Type of support: Support to graduates or students of specific schools; Undergraduate support.
Application information: Application form required.
Initial approach: Letter.
Deadline(s): May 1
EIN: 626199961

816
Coca-Cola Scholars Foundation, Inc.
P.O. Box 442
Atlanta, GA 30301-0442 (404) 733-5420
Contact: Patricia A. Cohen, V.P.
FAX: (404) 733-5439;
E-mail: scholars@na.ko.com; Application address: P.O. Box 1615, Atlanta, GA 30301-1615; Additional tel.: (800) 306-2653; URL: http://
www.coca-colascholars.org

Foundation type: Public charity
Limitations: Scholarships to well-rounded, college-bound high school students with highly developed ethics and goals for higher education at accredited two- or four-year institutions in the U.S.
Publications: Application guidelines; Annual report; Informational brochure (including application guidelines); Newsletter.
Financial data: Year ended 12/31/2003.
Assets, $41,762,987 (M); Expenditures, $4,873,147; Total giving, $2,687,145; Grants to individuals, totaling $2,687,145.
Type of support: Scholarships—to individuals.
Application information: Applications accepted. Application form required.
Deadline(s): Deadline Oct. 31, initial application and Jan. 31, semi-finalist's candidacy material;
Additional information: Applications available through high school guidance office.
Program description:
Scholarship Program: Selection is based on a number of factors, with emphasis on each individual's character, personal merit, and background. Merit is demonstrated in a variety of ways, including leadership in school, civic, and other extracurricular activities; academic achievement; and motivation to serve and succeed in all endeavors.
EIN: 581686023

817
Gifford A. Cochran Trust
c/o Mellon Financial Corp.
P.O. Box 185
Pittsburgh, PA 15230-0185
Telephone for Sandra Brown Mc-Mullen, Boston, MA: (617) 722-3891

Foundation type: Independent foundation
Limitations: Scholarships to graduates of high schools in Hancock County, ME, with preference to students from Ellsworth High School, ME.
Financial data: Year ended 08/31/2004.
Assets, $250,301 (M); Expenditures, $11,060; Total giving, $7,250; Grants to individuals, 14 grants totaling $7,250 (high: $1,000, low: $250).
Type of support: Support to graduates or students of specific schools; Undergraduate support.
Application information:
Initial approach: Telephone.
Additional information: Contact trust for current application deadline/guidelines.
EIN: 046078603

818
Code Scholarship Fund
c/o Bankers Trust Co.
665 Locust St.
Des Moines, IA 50309

Foundation type: Independent foundation
Limitations: Scholarships to individuals in IA for higher education.
Financial data: Year ended 12/31/2004.
Assets, $597,583 (M); Expenditures, $49,934; Total giving, $43,750; Grants to individuals, totaling $43,750.
Type of support: Scholarships—to individuals.
Application information:
Initial approach: Letter or telephone.
Deadline(s): Contact fund for current application deadline/guidelines
EIN: 426472809

819
Cody Medical Foundation
721 Sheridan Ave.
Cody, WY 82414 (307) 587-9030
Contact: Marty Coe, Exec. Dir.

Foundation type: Independent foundation
Limitations: Scholarships to financially needy residents of the West Park Hospital District, WY, including the towns of Cody and Meeteetse, for study in a medical-related field.
Financial data: Year ended 06/30/2005.
Assets, $1,480,023 (M); Expenditures, $118,994; Total giving, $73,000; Grants to individuals, totaling $73,000.
Fields of interest: Medical school/education; Nursing school/education.
Type of support: Graduate support; Undergraduate support.
Application information: Applications accepted.
Deadline(s): None
EIN: 836006491

820
William H. Coe Medical & Surgical Fund for Education
c/o Bank of America, N.A.
P.O. Box 6767
Providence, RI 02940-6767
Application address: c/o Auburn Board of Education, Thornton Ave., Auburn, NY 13021

Foundation type: Independent foundation
Limitations: Scholarships to financially needy residents of Cayuga County, NY, who are graduates of high schools within the Auburn School District in NY, primarily those pursuing study in the areas of medicine and/or surgery.
Financial data: Year ended 12/31/2004.
Assets, $356,423 (M); Expenditures, $18,960; Total giving, $13,900; Grants to individuals, totaling $13,900.
Fields of interest: Medical school/education.
Type of support: Support to graduates or students of specific schools; Undergraduate support.
Application information: Application form required.
Deadline(s): Mar. 15
Additional information: Application should include financial information.
EIN: 156018065

821
Helen R. Coe Trust
c/o Bank of America, N.A.
P.O. Box 1802
Providence, RI 02901-1802
Loan application address: c/o Coe Governing
Committee, P.O. Box 185, Center Lovell, ME 04016

Foundation type: Independent foundation
Limitations: Student loans to residents of Lovell,
ME.
Financial data: Year ended 03/31/2005.
Assets, $2,089,389 (M); Expenditures,
$107,850; Total giving, $86,650; Grants to
individuals, totaling $59,000.
Type of support: Student loans—to individuals.
Application information: Applications, including
letter showing proof of residency in Lovell, ME, a
statement of prior academic performance,
achievement test scores, a teacher
recommendation, and proof of financial need,
accepted throughout the applicant's senior year of
high school.
EIN: 010351827

822
Regina Coeli Foundation, Inc.
739 N. Lake St.
Mundelein, IL 60060
Contact: Rev. John R. Hoffman, Pres.

Foundation type: Independent foundation
Limitations: Scholarships to financially needy
students primarily in the Chicago, IL, area.
Financial data: Year ended 05/31/2005.
Assets, $13,338 (M); Expenditures, $13,174;
Total giving, $13,120; Grants to individuals,
totaling $7,420.
Type of support: Scholarships—to individuals.
Application information: Applications accepted
throughout the year; Application by letter outlining
financial need.
EIN: 366126117

823
The Coffey Foundation, Inc.
P.O. Box 1170
Lenoir, NC 28645
Contact: Harriet Hailey
Application address: 406 Norwood St. S.W., Lenoir,
NC 28645

Foundation type: Independent foundation
Limitations: Scholarships and student loans
limited to residents of Caldwell County, NC.
Financial data: Year ended 11/30/2004.
Assets, $9,029,646 (M); Expenditures,
$548,981; Total giving, $378,600; Grants to
individuals, 37 grants totaling $244,500 (high:
$7,000, low: $3,500).
Type of support: Scholarships—to individuals;
Student loans—to individuals.
Application information: Application form required.
Deadline(s): Apr. 15
Applicants should submit the following:
1) Transcripts
2) Photograph
Additional information: Application forms
available at high schools in Caldwell County,
NC; Application should also include essay
explaining chosen course of study and future
work, letter of recommendation (from
principal, guidance counselor, pastor, or
community leader), and results of any
supplemental tests (SAT, ACT, etc.).
EIN: 566047501

824
John F. Coffman Scholarship Trust
c/o Wells Fargo Bank Northwest, N.A.
P.O. Box 21927
Seattle, WA 98111
Application address: c/o Student Counselor, W.F.
West High School, Chehalis, WA 98532

Foundation type: Independent foundation
Limitations: Scholarships to graduates of Chehalis,
WA, high schools, who are U.S. citizens and
demonstrate financial need.
Financial data: Year ended 12/31/2004.
Assets, $725,591 (M); Expenditures, $41,271;
Total giving, $28,000; Grants to individuals,
totaling $28,000.
Type of support: Support to graduates or students
of specific schools; Undergraduate support.
Application information: Deadline within one year
after graduation; Completion of formal application
required; Application forms available from W.F.
West High School.
EIN: 916274936

825
George T. Cogan Trust
c/o Portsmouth Hight School, Scholarship Coord.
50 Andrew Jarvis Dr.
Portsmouth, NH 03801
Contact: Michael G. Modern, Tr.

Foundation type: Independent foundation
Limitations: Scholarships to male students who
have resided in Portsmouth, NH, for at least four
years prior to graduation from either Portsmouth
High School or St. Thomas Aquinas High School.
Financial data: Year ended 12/31/2004.
Assets, $590,759 (M); Expenditures, $44,066;
Total giving, $30,500; Grants to individuals,
totaling $30,500.
Fields of interest: Men.
Type of support: Support to graduates or students
of specific schools; Undergraduate support.
Application information: Application form required.
Deadline(s): Apr. 15
Applicants should submit the following:
1) SAR
2) FAF
3) Transcripts
4) Letter(s) of recommendation
EIN: 026019789

826
Cogar Foundation, Inc.
1001 Broad St.
Utica, NY 13501
Application address for individuals: c/o Phillip
Hubbard, Dir. of Financial Aid, Herkimer Community
College, Reservoir Rd., Herkimer, NY 11350,
tel.: (315) 866-0300

Foundation type: Independent foundation
Limitations: Scholarships to Herkimer County High
School, NY, students and to Herkimer County
Community College graduates.
Financial data: Year ended 12/31/2004.
Assets, $787,920 (M); Expenditures, $46,291;
Total giving, $37,400; Grants to individuals,
totaling $37,400.
Type of support: Support to graduates or students
of specific schools; Undergraduate support.
Application information: Application form required.
Deadline(s): 1st quarter of the year; Contact
foundation for current application deadline
Applicants should submit the following:
1) Transcripts

2) Financial information
EIN: 237035415

827
Martin D. Cohen Family Foundation
(formerly J & J Charitable Foundation)
P.O. Box 1127
Easton, PA 18044-1127
Contact: Martin D. Cohen, Pres.

Foundation type: Independent foundation
Limitations: Scholarships only to high school
seniors in Lehigh Valley PA, for higher education.
Financial data: Year ended 12/31/2004.
Assets, $1,370,374 (M); Expenditures,
$155,385; Total giving, $134,310; Grants to
individuals, 84 grants totaling $27,000 (high:
$3,000, low: $250).
Type of support: Scholarships—to individuals.
Application information: Applications not
accepted.
EIN: 232294358

828
The David J. and Rosetta Adler Cohen Foundation
3255 Wilshire Blvd., Ste. 1034
Los Angeles, CA 90010-1414 (213) 386-1773
Contact: Jerry Michaels, Pres.

Foundation type: Independent foundation
Limitations: Scholarships for higher education.
Financial data: Year ended 12/31/2004.
Assets, $795,652 (M); Expenditures, $213,513;
Total giving, $88,439; Grants to individuals,
totaling $88,439.
Type of support: Scholarships—to individuals.
Application information: Applications accepted.
Initial approach: Letter.
Deadline(s): None
EIN: 954420751

829
Sarah Cohen Scholarship Fund
c/o Bank of America, N.A.
10 Light St.
Baltimore, MD 21202
Application address: c/o Rabbi, Ohef Sholom
Temple, Stockley Gardens, Raleigh Ave., Norfolk,
VA 23507, tel.: (804) 625-4595

Foundation type: Independent foundation
Limitations: Scholarships to residents of Norfolk,
VA.
Financial data: Year ended 12/31/2004.
Assets, $323,422 (M); Expenditures, $14,584;
Total giving, $11,574; Grants to individuals,
totaling $11,574.
Type of support: Scholarships—to individuals.
Application information: Application form not
required.
Deadline(s): Aug. 1.
Additional information: Application by letter.
EIN: 546033744

830
Rueben J. and Dorothy S. Cohen Scholarship Trust Fund
c/o Bank of America, N.A., P.C. Group
P.O. Box 441, NJ6-219-02-03
Ridgefield Park, NJ 07660-9984
Application address: c/o Bank of America, N.A., Attn.: Cindy Leip, V.P., Charitable Asset Div., 1125 Route 22 W., Bridgewater, NJ 08807-2965

Foundation type: Independent foundation
Limitations: Scholarships to financially needy Jewish students admitted to fully accredited medical schools located in Philadelphia, PA.
Financial data: Year ended 12/31/2004. Assets, $478,187 (M); Expenditures, $30,069; Total giving, $24,000; Grants to individuals, 4 grants totaling $20,000 (high: $8,000; low: $4,000).
Fields of interest: Medical school/education; Jewish agencies & temples.
Type of support: Support to graduates or students of specific schools; Graduate support.
Application information: Application form required.
Deadline(s): None.
EIN: 226618260

831
Deo B. Colburn Education Foundation
P.O. Box 824
Lake Placid, NY 12946-0824
Contact: Margaret E. Doran, Treas.

Foundation type: Independent foundation
Limitations: Scholarships to residents of school districts of northeast portions of the Adirondack Park in northern NY for attendance at colleges, universities, and technical schools.
Financial data: Year ended 06/30/2005. Assets, $6,058,055 (M); Expenditures, $331,678; Total giving, $284,500; Grants to individuals, 436 grants totaling $284,500 (high: $1,000, low: $500).
Fields of interest: Vocational education.
Type of support: Technical education support; Undergraduate support.
Application information: Deadline Apr. 15; Application forms available after Feb. 1; Completion of formal application required, including transcripts, class rank, GPA, copy of financial aid award letter, resume, and a handwritten statement of future plans.
Program description:
Scholarship Program: If a recipient maintains at least a 2.5 GPA, he or she may apply for a scholarship for the next year. There is no guarantee that a scholarship will be awarded or that it will be awarded for the same amount as the prior year.
EIN: 222777121

832
William Cullen Colburn Memorial Fund
c/o Wachovia Bank, N.A.
100 N. Main St., 13th Fl.
Winston-Salem, NC 27150 (800) 576-5135
Contact: Scholarships: Elizabeth Bradshaw
Application address: c/o CSA, P.O. Box 1465, Taylors, SC 29687-0031

Foundation type: Independent foundation
Limitations: Scholarships to residents of Buncombe County, NC, for higher education.
Financial data: Year ended 12/31/2004. Assets, $448,516 (M); Expenditures, $15,155; Total giving, $13,000; Grants to individuals, 10 grants totaling $13,000 (high: $2,000, low: $500).

Type of support: Scholarships—to individuals.
Application information: Applications accepted. Application form required.
Initial approach: Letter or telephone.
Deadline(s): Apr. 1
Additional information: Application must also include financial information, honors and awards, and extracurricular, civic, and community activities. Interviews required.
EIN: 566049108

833
The Cold Heading Foundation
(formerly DeSeranno Educational Foundation, Inc.)
c/o Edward Miller
21777 Hoover Rd.
Warren, MI 48089

Foundation type: Independent foundation
Limitations: Scholarships primarily to students attending Madonna University.
Financial data: Year ended 12/31/2004. Assets, $29,486,456 (M); Expenditures, $1,535,345; Total giving, $1,095,113.
Type of support: Support to graduates or students of specific schools; Undergraduate support.
Application information: Applications not accepted.
EIN: 237005737

834
Olive B. Cole Foundation, Inc.
6207 Constitution Dr.
Fort Wayne, IN 46804
Contact: Maclyn T. Parker, Pres.

Foundation type: Independent foundation
Limitations: Scholarships to graduates of secondary schools in Noble County, IN, and to residents of Noble County, IN.
Publications: Application guidelines; Program policy statement.
Financial data: Year ended 03/31/2005. Assets, $31,194,046 (M); Expenditures, $1,550,895; Total giving, $1,094,607; Grants to individuals, 233 grants totaling $216,816.
Type of support: Undergraduate support.
Application information: Applications accepted throughout the year; Initial approach by letter; Completion of formal application required; Interviews granted upon request; Application forms available from the foundation or any office in the Noble County, IN, secondary school system.
EIN: 356040491

835
Harold M. Cole Scholarship Trust
c/o Branch Banking and Trust Co.
P.O. Drawer 1149
Pinehurst, NC 28370-1149 (910) 215-2620

Foundation type: Independent foundation
Limitations: Scholarships to financially needy residents of Moore County, NC, who are attending NC institutions and pursuing undergraduate and graduate accounting degrees.
Financial data: Year ended 03/31/2005. Assets, $1,499,879 (M); Expenditures, $122,699; Total giving, $92,745; Grants to individuals, 18 grants totaling $92,745 (high: $7,500, low: $2,000).
Fields of interest: Business school/education.
Type of support: Graduate support; Undergraduate support.

Application information: Applications accepted throughout the year; Initial approach by letter or telephone; Completion of formal application required, including transcripts, letter of recommendation, a handwritten essay of two pages or less, a copy of birth certificate, a copy of parents' most recent tax return, and a copy of acceptance letter from the college or university.
EIN: 586212292

836
Lillian R. Coleman Scholarship Trust
(formerly William S. and Lillian R. Coleman Scholarship Trust)
c/o JPMorgan Chase Bank, N.A.
P.O. Box 1308
Milwaukee, WI 53201
Contact: Jacqueline Weitz, V.P. and Trust Off., JPMorgan Chase Bank, N.A.
Application address: 111 Monument Cir., Ste. 1701, Indianapolis, IN 46277-0117, tel.: (317) 321-7544

Foundation type: Independent foundation
Limitations: Scholarships for postsecondary education to graduates of high schools in Rush County, IN.
Financial data: Year ended 06/30/2005. Assets, $2,817,593 (M); Expenditures, $95,476; Total giving, $79,288; Grants to individuals, totaling $79,288.
Type of support: Support to graduates or students of specific schools; Undergraduate support.
Application information: Deadline Apr. 1 or 60 days prior to beginning of school term; Completion of formal application required, including parents' financial statement.
EIN: 356279390

837
Coleman Student Fund, Inc.
P.O. Box 284
Trumansburg, NY 14886

Foundation type: Independent foundation
Limitations: Interest-free student loans to graduates of Charles O. Dickerson High School, Trumansburg, NY, for study at the undergraduate level.
Financial data: Year ended 07/31/2004. Assets, $194,815 (M); Expenditures, $165; Total giving, $0; Loans to individuals, totaling $18,740.
Type of support: Student loans—to individuals; Support to graduates or students of specific schools; Undergraduate support.
Application information: Application form required.
Deadline(s): May 31
Additional information: Application must include a letter outlining need, GPA, and co-signatures of parent(s) or guardian(s).
Program description:
Loans: Selection is based on academic performance, type of academic program, repayment status of other members of the household who have already borrowed from the fund, and the number of years the applicant attended schools in the Trumansburg District. For first-time applicants, the initial loan will not be disbursed until the fund receives a semester grade report from the college attended indicating the applicant has achieved at least a 2.0 GPA. All applicants must maintain at least a 2.0 GPA in order to be eligible to receive any further loans from the fund. Loans are renewable for up to four years. Loan repayment is scheduled

at $50 per month beginning six months after program termination.
EIN: 222387137

838
Mary D. Coles Foundation
c/o Bank of America, N.A.
P.O. Box 441
Ridgefield Park, NJ 07660-9984

Foundation type: Independent foundation
Limitations: Scholarships to graduates of Martha's Vineyard Regional High School who intend to pursue the study of art, music, architecture, painting, sculpture, theater or other fine arts at the higher education level.
Financial data: Year ended 12/31/2004. Assets, $1,019,387 (M); Expenditures, $47,626; Total giving, $40,000; Grants to individuals, totaling $40,000.
Fields of interest: Arts education; Visual arts; Architecture; Sculpture; Painting; Theater; Music.
Type of support: Support to graduates or students of specific schools; Undergraduate support.
Application information: Applications accepted.
Deadline(s): None
Additional information: Applications should be sent by letter.
EIN: 527054900

839
Colf Family Foundation
c/o Bank of America, N.A.
P.O. Box 34345
Seattle, WA 98124-1345

Foundation type: Independent foundation
Limitations: Scholarships to residents of WA for higher education.
Financial data: Year ended 12/31/2004. Assets, $613,051 (M); Expenditures, $92,567; Total giving, $88,109; Grants to individuals, 8 grants totaling $39,230.
Type of support: Scholarships—to individuals.
Application information: Applications not accepted.
EIN: 911815575

840
College Art Association
(formerly College Art Association of America, Inc.)
275 7th Ave., 18th Fl.
New York, NY 10001-6708 (212) 691-1051
Contact: Susan Ball, Exec. Dir.
FAX: (212) 627-2381;
E-mail: nyoffice@collegeart.org; Additional E-mail: fellowship@collegeart.org; URL: http://www.collegeart.org

Foundation type: Public charity
Limitations: Fellowships limited to M.F.A., M.A., and Ph.D. students studying art and art history. Applicants must be U.S. citizens or permanent residents and be part of a community that has been traditionally marginalized.
Publications: Application guidelines; Biennial report; Financial statement; Grants list; Informational brochure; Newsletter.
Financial data: Year ended 06/30/2004. Assets, $9,839,525 (M); Expenditures, $4,131,768; Total giving, $57,000; Grants to individuals, 10 grants totaling $57,000 (high: $7,500, low: $1,500).
Fields of interest: Visual arts; Art history.

Type of support: Fellowships; Graduate support; Doctoral support.
Application information: Application form required.
Initial approach: Letter, telephone, or e-mail.
Deadline(s): Jan. 31
Program description:
Professional Development Fellowships: $5,000 fellowships are provided to help M.F.A., M.A., and Ph.D. students in their second-to-last year of a visual arts or art history degree bridge the gap between graduate work and professional careers. The foundation hopes to encourage future students from underrepresented communities to study art and art history and to pursue careers in the visual arts. Recipients are notified by May 30th.
EIN: 131671148

841
College Careers Fund of Westchester, Inc.
P.O. Box 1530
White Plains, NY 10602 (914) 428-3435
Contact: Blanche Walker, Exec. Dir.
FAX: (914) 428-3328

Foundation type: Public charity
Limitations: Scholarships to economically disadvantaged young people for higher education with unique counseling services.
Financial data: Year ended 12/31/2004. Assets, $827,704 (M); Expenditures, $381,540.
Fields of interest: Economically disadvantaged.
Type of support: Undergraduate support.
Application information: Contact fund for current application deadline/guidelines.
EIN: 132628725

842
The College Club of Cleveland Foundation
c/o Scholarship Committee
2348 E. Overlook Rd.
Cleveland Heights, OH 44106

Foundation type: Independent foundation
Limitations: Scholarships only to female residents of the Cleveland, OH, area.
Financial data: Year ended 12/31/2004. Assets, $484,717 (M); Expenditures, $25,425; Total giving, $24,130; Grants to individuals, totaling $24,130.
Fields of interest: Women.
Type of support: Scholarships—to individuals.
Application information: Deadline prior to start of school year; Completion of formal application required.
EIN: 341569601

843
College Club of St. Louis
439 Conway Meadows Dr.
Chesterfield, MO 63017
Contact: Mildred Winter
Application address: 26 Lake Pembroke Dr., St. Louis, MO 63135

Foundation type: Independent foundation
Limitations: Scholarships to female graduates of high schools in St. Louis County, MO, for tuition and fees for their first year of college. Recipients must have taken the ACT or SAT and rank in the upper 25 percent of their class.
Financial data: Year ended 05/31/2005. Assets, $1,327,269 (M); Expenditures, $48,294;

Total giving, $13,556; Grants to individuals, totaling $13,056.
Type of support: Undergraduate support.
Application information: Application form required.
Deadline(s): Jan. 31
Additional information: Application should include an essay.
EIN: 436031163

844
College First Foundation
P.O. Box 2176
Hurst, TX 76053 (817) 656-3811
Contact: Vantisa Hudson, Admin.

Foundation type: Independent foundation
Limitations: Scholarships to children, agents, and members of participating companies and associations.
Financial data: Year ended 12/31/2003. Assets, $282,906 (M); Expenditures, $558,830; Total giving, $504,000; Grants to individuals, 182 grants totaling $504,000 (high: $12,000, low: $500).
Type of support: Employee-related scholarships.
Application information: Contact foundation for current application deadline/guidelines; Initial approach by letter or telephone.
EIN: 752638941

845
Coller Foundation
35 S. Elk St.
Sandusky, MI 48471
Contact: John Paterson, Pres.
Application address: P.O. Box 311, Sandusky, MI 48471, tel.: (810) 648-2414

Foundation type: Independent foundation
Limitations: Scholarships to financially needy graduates of high schools in Tuscola and Sanilac counties, MI.
Financial data: Year ended 12/31/2004. Assets, $1,795,904 (M); Expenditures, $49,306; Total giving, $43,000; Grants to individuals, totaling $43,000.
Type of support: Support to graduates or students of specific schools; Undergraduate support.
Application information: Deadline Mar. 1; Completion of formal application required.
EIN: 382832816

846
Joseph Collins Foundation
c/o Willkie Farr & Gallagher
787 7th Ave., Rm. 3950
New York, NY 10019-6099
Contact: Augusta L. Packer, Secy.-Treas.

Foundation type: Independent foundation
Limitations: Scholarships to medical students in their second, third, or fourth year who are in the top half of their class and intend to specialize in neurology or psychiatry, or to become a general practitioner. Students must attend an accredited medical school in states east of or contiguous to the Mississippi River.
Publications: Application guidelines; Annual report; Program policy statement.
Financial data: Year ended 06/30/2005. Assets, $25,781,264 (M); Expenditures, $1,487,651; Total giving, $1,160,000.

Fields of interest: Medical school/education; Mental health, treatment; Neuroscience; Psychology/behavioral science.

Type of support: Undergraduate support.

Application information: Deadline Jan. 15 for application requests, Mar. 1 for filing; Initial approach by proposal; Application forms are required and are available only through the medical school financial aid office, to whom completed forms should also be returned for forwarding to the foundation with a supporting letter from the dean of the medical school.

Program description:

Scholarship Program: Applicants must also demonstrate interest in arts and letters or other cultural pursuits outside the field of medicine. Additional factors considered are: evidence of good moral character of the applicant; age (applicants commencing their medical education before attaining the age of 30 are preferred); marital status; geographical proximity (applicants residing within 200 miles of the medical school are preferred); and financial need. Maximum grant per student is $10,000. Awards are not made for the benefit of premedical or postgraduate medical students.

EIN: 136404527

847

Collins McDonald Trust Fund

1618 S.W. 1st Ave., Ste. 500
Portland, OR 97201-5706
Contact: James C. Lynch
Application address: 620 N. 1st St., Lakeview, OR 97630, tel.: (541) 947-2196

Foundation type: Independent foundation

Limitations: Scholarships to graduates of Lake County, OR, high schools. Applicants must have attended a Lake County, OR, high school for four years, or received a GED after attending a Lake County school, and have resided with their parents or guardian in Lake County for those four years. Scholarships also to children of Fremont Sawmill employees, OR.

Financial data: Year ended 12/31/2004. Assets, $10,367,967 (M); Expenditures, $574,995; Total giving, $567,397; Grants to individuals, 21 grants totaling $538,500 (high: $99,000, low: $15,000).

Type of support: Employee-related scholarships; Support to graduates or students of specific schools; Undergraduate support.

Application information: Applications accepted. Application form required.

Deadline(s): May 1

Applicants should submit the following:
1) GPA
2) SAT

Additional information: Interviews required; Recipients notified by Aug. 1.

Program description:

Scholarship Program: Recipients are required to have at least a 2.2 GPA if they are entering their sophomore year, a 2.35 if they are entering their junior year, and a 2.5 if they are entering their senior year. In addition, recipients must complete at least 15 credit hours per semester and be enrolled as full-time students. Scholarships are renewable for a total of eight semesters of study.

EIN: 936021894

848

Paul and Mary Collins Trust No. 2

c/o U.S. Bank, N.A.
P.O. Box 2043
Milwaukee, WI 53201-9668 (712) 472-2581
Application address: c/o U.S. Bank, 203 S. 2nd Ave., Rock Rapids, IA 51246-1509

Foundation type: Independent foundation

Limitations: Scholarships to students attending a college or university in Northwestern IA who have the surname of Beardsley, Boldholdt, Collins, Eppright, Rohloff, or any name listed in the 1968 telephone directory for Manhattan Borough of the City of New York, NY. Name may be acquired by birth, marriage, or adoption. Relatives of Paul & Mary Collins are ineligible.

Financial data: Year ended 05/31/2005. Assets, $756,306 (M); Expenditures, $63,511; Total giving, $34,226; Grants to individuals, 56 grants totaling $34,226 (high: $675, low: $338).

Type of support: Scholarships—to individuals.

Application information: Application form required.

Deadline(s): June 1

Additional information: Application must also include financial statement.

EIN: 426120024

849

Roberta Collister Scholarship Trust

205 W. Alvarado St.
Fallbrook, CA 92028-2002 (760) 728-1154
Contact: Robert H. James, Tr.

Foundation type: Independent foundation

Limitations: Scholarships to disabled students at Fallbrook High School, CA.

Financial data: Year ended 12/31/2004. Assets, $312,542 (M); Expenditures, $11,315; Total giving, $5,500; Grants to individuals, totaling $5,500.

Fields of interest: Disabilities, people with.

Type of support: Support to graduates or students of specific schools; Undergraduate support.

Application information: Application form required.

Initial approach: Letter.

Deadline(s): Contact foundation for current application deadline

Additional information: Applications available from high school.

EIN: 336208197

850

The Colom Foundation

P.O. Box 101
Columbus, MS 39703
Application Address: c/o Deborah Schumaker, 200 6th St. N., Ste. 102, Columbus, MS 39701

Foundation type: Independent foundation

Limitations: Scholarships to individuals residing in FL and TX.

Financial data: Year ended 12/31/2004. Assets, $344,027 (M); Expenditures, $170,652; Total giving, $157,173; Grants to individuals, 6 grants totaling $12,205 (high: $7,061, low: $144).

Type of support: Undergraduate support.

Application information: Applications accepted throughout the year; Contact foundation for current application guidelines; Completion of formal application required.

EIN: 640932723

851

Colorado League in Defense of Teens, Inc.

c/o Frank Morriss
3505 Owens St.
Wheat Ridge, CO 80033-5571

Foundation type: Independent foundation

Limitations: Scholarships to CO students attending or accepted to Franciscan University, OH, Christendom College, VA, St. Thomas Aquinas College, CA, or Colorado Catholic Academy, CO.

Financial data: Year ended 12/31/2003. Assets, $52,257 (M); Expenditures, $30,444; Total giving, $30,400; Grants to individuals, 31 grants totaling $30,400 (high: $17,000, low: $1,000).

Type of support: Support to graduates or students of specific schools; Undergraduate support.

Application information: Contact league for current application deadline; Initial approach by letter stating financial need.

EIN: 841195369

852

Colorado Masons Benevolent Fund Association

c/o Scottish Rite Masonic Center
1370 Grant St., Ste. 212
Denver, CO 80203-2347
Contact: Robert L. Bartholic, Exec. Secy.

Foundation type: Operating foundation

Limitations: Scholarships only to graduating seniors of public high schools in CO planning to attend institutions of higher learning in CO.

Financial data: Year ended 10/30/2004. Assets, $11,216,093 (M); Expenditures, $762,103; Total giving, $642,621; Grants to individuals, totaling $591,501.

Fields of interest: Fraternal societies.

Type of support: Undergraduate support.

Application information: Applications not accepted.

EIN: 840406813

853

Columbia Basin Foundation

234 1st Ave. N.W. , Ste. B
Ephrata, WA 98823 (509) 754-4596
Contact: Stephanie Hawkins, Fdn. Mgr.
FAX: (509) 754-4194;
E-mail: info@columbiabasinfoundation.org;
URL: http://www.columbiabasinfoundation.org

Foundation type: Community foundation

Limitations: Scholarships to individuals in Grant and Adams counties, WA.

Publications: Annual report; Informational brochure; Newsletter.

Financial data: Year ended 12/31/2004. Assets, $2,008,522 (M); Expenditures, $326,321; Total giving, $275,742; Grants to individuals, 32 grants totaling $99,534.

Type of support: Scholarships—to individuals.

Application information:

Initial approach: Letter.

Deadline(s): None

Additional information: Contact foundation for current application guidelines.

EIN: 911733104

854

The Columbus Phipps Foundation

10 Light St., MD4-302-17-06
Baltimore, MD 21202
Application address: c/o Paul D. Buchanan, P.O.
Box 1145, Clintwood, VA 24228, tel.: (540)
926-8152

Foundation type: Independent foundation
Limitations: Scholarships to high school graduates of Dickenson County, VA. Scholarships are renewable.
Financial data: Year ended 03/31/2004.
Assets, $10,290,852 (M); Expenditures, $394,495; Total giving, $298,787; Grants to individuals, 133 grants totaling $298,787.
Type of support: Support to graduates or students of specific schools; Undergraduate support.
Application information:
Initial approach: letter.
Deadline(s): May 15 for new applications, June 15 for renewal applications
Applicants should submit the following:
1) Financial information
2) Essay
3) GPA
4) ACT
5) SAT
Additional information: Application should include references and copy of returned Pell Grant Index form.
EIN: 546338751

855

Thomas S. Colvin Scholarship Trust

c/o South Valley Bank & Trust
P.O. Box 5210
Klamath Falls, OR 97601
Application address: c/o Ruthann Brown, Clatskanie High School, P.O. Box 68, Clatskanie, OR 97016

Foundation type: Independent foundation
Limitations: Scholarships to graduates of Clatskanie High School, OR, for the pursuit of a vocational education at a university, college or trade school.
Financial data: Year ended 12/31/2004.
Assets, $535,479 (M); Expenditures, $29,914; Total giving, $22,536; Grants to individuals, totaling $22,536.
Fields of interest: Vocational education, post-secondary.
Type of support: Support to graduates or students of specific schools; Technical education support; Undergraduate support.
Application information: Deadline Mar. 1; Application by letter outlining financial need, including high school GPA, SAT scores, school and community activities, future plans, and honors received.
EIN: 936267268

856

Commercial Bank Foundation

c/o Commercial Bank of Grayson
208 E. Main St.
Grayson, KY 41143 (606) 474-7811
Contact: Jack W. Strother, Jr., Tr.
Additional contact: Mark Strother, Tr.

Foundation type: Company-sponsored foundation
Limitations: Scholarships to students graduating from Carter County high schools, KY.
Financial data: Year ended 12/31/2004.
Assets, $568,103 (M); Expenditures, $32,419;

Total giving, $32,000; Grants to individuals, totaling $13,000 (high: $1,000, low: $1,000).
Type of support: Support to graduates or students of specific schools; Undergraduate support.
Application information: Deadline Apr. 15; Completion of formal application required.
EIN: 611087988

857

Common Grace Ministries, Inc.

3800 Commerce St., Ste. 217
Dallas, TX 75226 (214) 370-5750
Contact: Martin Hironaga, Exec. Dir.

Foundation type: Operating foundation
Limitations: Scholarships to East Dallas, TX residents who attend Dallas Theological Seminary and who plan to serve the community, as well as scholarships to East Dallas, TX students who plan to serve the community.
Financial data: Year ended 12/31/2004.
Assets, $161,621 (M); Expenditures, $435,359; Total giving, $127,952.
Fields of interest: Religion, formal/general education; Christian agencies & churches.
Type of support: Support to graduates or students of specific schools; Undergraduate support.
Application information: Application form required.
Deadline(s): Aug. 1.
Program descriptions:
Community Servant Leadership Scholarship: Awards scholarships to financially needy students to attend institutions of higher education. Students must agree with the core principles of Common Grace Ministries, Inc. and must be able and willing to attend weekly seminars and have the desire to serve in East Dallas in any capacity. Students must be residents or be somehow connected to East Dallas.
Community Connection Scholarship Program: Awards scholarships to students at Dallas Theological Seminary who have financial needs, who agree with the core principles of Common Grace Ministries, Inc., are able and willing to attend weekly seminars, and who desire to serve in East Dallas, TX, in any capacity.
EIN: 752727006

858

Communications Workers of America Disaster Relief Fund

501 3rd St., N.W.
Washington, DC 20001-2797 (202) 797-8700
Contact: Morton Bahr, Pres.
URL: http://www.cwa-union.org

Foundation type: Public charity
Limitations: Thirty partial college scholarships of $3,000 each, to CWA members and their spouses, children and grandchildren, including those of retired or deceased members.
Financial data: Year ended 12/31/2003.
Assets, $197,288 (M); Expenditures, $42,033; Total giving, $41,328; Grants to individuals, totaling $41,328.
Fields of interest: Labor unions/organizations.
Type of support: Undergraduate support.
Application information: Applications accepted. Application form required. Application form available on the grantmaker's Web site.
Initial approach: Letter or telephone.
Deadline(s): Mar. 31
Applicants should submit the following:
1) Essay

Program description:
CWA Joe Beirne Foundation Scholarship: Thirty (30) two-year scholarships, to be paid at the rate of $3,000 annually, are awarded each year to applicants from the U.S.A. and Canada. A second-year award is contingent on academic accomplishment of the first year. Winners are chosen by lottery drawing and only winners will be notified. CWA members, their spouses, children and grandchildren (including dependents of laid-off, retired or deceased CWA members) may apply. Applicants must be high school graduates or at least high school students who will graduate during the year in which they apply. Undergraduate and graduate students returning to schooling may also apply. Prior winners may not reapply.
EIN: 522128973

859

Communities Foundation of Oklahoma

(formerly Oklahoma Communities Foundation, Inc.)
2932 N.W. 122nd St., Ste. D
Oklahoma City, OK 73120-1955
(405) 488-1450
Contact: Susan R. Graves, Exec. Dir.
FAX: (405) 755-0938; E-mail: sgraves@cfok.org; Additional tel.: (877) 689-7726; URL: http://www.cfok.org

Foundation type: Community foundation
Limitations: Scholarships to students in OK.
Publications: Financial statement; Grants list; Informational brochure.
Financial data: Year ended 06/30/2004.
Assets, $8,096,355 (M); Expenditures, $1,465,103; Total giving, $1,203,557; Grants to individuals, 69 grants totaling $171,800.
Type of support: Undergraduate support.
Application information: Contact foundation for current application deadline/guidelines.
EIN: 731396320

860

Community Foundation Alliance, Inc.

123 N.W. 4th Ave., Ste. 322
Evansville, IN 47708-1712 (812) 429-1191
Contact: Marilyn J. Klenck, C.E.O.; Carol M. Pace, Mgr., Comms. and Donor Svcs.
FAX: (812) 429-0840; E-mail: info@alliance9.org; Additional Tel.: (877) 429-1191; Additional E-mail: mklenck@alliance9.org; URL: http://www.alliance9.org

Foundation type: Community foundation
Limitations: Scholarships to individuals living in Daviess, Gibson, Knox, Perry, Pike, Posey, Spencer, Vanderburgh, and Warrick counties, IN.
Publications: Application guidelines; Annual report; Financial statement; Grants list; Informational brochure; Newsletter.
Financial data: Year ended 06/30/2004.
Assets, $50,019,227 (M); Expenditures, $3,177,275; Total giving, $2,147,928.
Fields of interest: History/archaeology; Arts; Business school/education; Agriculture.
Type of support: Technical education support; Undergraduate support.
Application information: Application form required.
Initial approach: Telephone.
Deadline(s): Contact foundation for current application deadline.
Additional information: Please see Web site for complete program listing.
Program description:
Daviess County Scholarships:

· Friends of Daviess County Fund: Provides support to the selected alternates of the Lilly Endowment Community Scholarship for Daviess County
· Lilly Endowment Community Scholarship Fund: One full-tuition scholarship is available to a student admitted into a baccalaureate program at an accredited IN college or university. Applicants must be residents of Daviess County, IN, or be students of high schools in Daviess County, or graduates of accredited Daviess County or IN high schools or academies by June of the application year, and be available for an interview with the scholarship committee if selected as a finalist
· McKinley Vance Agri-Business Scholarship Fund: Available to a graduating senior of Washington High School, IN, who ranks in the upper one-third of his/her class. Participation for a minimum of four years in 4-H and enrollment in a bachelor degree program at a college or university in a field of study in agriculture such as farming, agri-sales, agri-research, veterinary science, etc., is required. Grade requirements; active participation in school, church, community, and work; and financial need will be considered
· National Service Scholarships Fund: For a graduating senior from each Daviess County high school. Three scholarships are awarded annually
· Dwight Risley Scholarship Fund: Is available to a graduating senior at any Daviess County high school to be used for tuition, books, and required fees for post-high school education. Applicants must demonstrate financial need and good scholastic standing.

EIN: 351830262

861
Community Foundation for Delta County, Michigan, Inc.

2500 7th Ave. S., Ste. 103, Box 5
Escanaba, MI   49829   (906) 786-6654
Contact: Gary LaPlant, Exec. Dir.
FAX: (906) 786-9124; E-mail: cffdc@chartermi.net

Foundation type: Community foundation
Limitations: Scholarships to individuals residing in the Delta County, MI, area for undergraduate education.
Publications: Application guidelines; Annual report; Informational brochure.
Application information: Applications accepted. Application form required.
  Initial approach: Letter or telephone.
  Additional information: Contact foundation for current application deadline/guidelines.
EIN: 382907795

862
Community Foundation for Greater Atlanta, Inc.

(formerly Metropolitan Atlanta Community Foundation, Inc.)
50 Hurt Plz., Ste. 449
Atlanta, GA   30303   (404) 688-5525
Contact: For Scholarships: David Gibbs
Additional E-mail: vweekes@atlcf.org (for scholarship opportunities).
FAX: (404) 688-3060; E-mail: info@atlcf.org; Additional E-mail: grants@atlcf.org (for grant guidelines and grant orientation session registration); URL: http://www.atlcf.org

Foundation type: Community foundation
Limitations: Scholarships to students in Atlanta, GA, who are pursuing higher education.
Publications: Application guidelines; Annual report; Informational brochure; Newsletter; Program policy statement.
Financial data: Year ended 06/30/2005. Assets, $560,410,937 (M); Expenditures, $56,810,022; Total giving, $49,998,065; Grants to individuals, totaling $343,919.
Fields of interest: Vocational education; Higher education; Medical school/education; Teacher school/education; Social work school/education; Health sciences school/education; Journalism school/education; Adult/continuing education; Women.
Type of support: Employee-related scholarships; Scholarships—to individuals; Support to graduates or students of specific schools; Undergraduate support.
Application information: Applications accepted. Application form required. Application form available on the grantmaker's Web site.
  Initial approach: Letter of inquiry.
  Deadline(s): Varies
  Additional information: Applications sent by fax or e-mail will not be accepted; see Web site for complete application and guideline information.

Program descriptions:
Ron Autry Scholarship: Awards up to $2,000 to a student with demonstrated financial need enrolled in undergraduate studies in journalism. Eligible candidate must be:
  · A legal resident of Georgia
  · Enrolled in college and pursuing studies in journalism (news, advertising, circulation, or human resources)
  · A junior or senior level undergraduate college student
  · Have a minimum GPA of 2.0 for the previous academic year
Atlanta Insurance Women's Club Scholarship: Awards up to $2,000 to women pursuing careers in the insurance field. Eligible candidates must:
  · Be a female student enrolled at Georgia State University
  · A minimum GPA of 3.0 required to apply
  · Commitment to pursue a career in insurance
  · Demonstrate financial need
Helen and Vernon Crawford Scholarship: Awards up to $500 to adults who have completed a literacy program and wish to pursue post-secondary education. Eligibility requirements:
  · Persons who have completed a literacy program and obtained a high school diploma or GED
  · Legal resident of Georgia
  · Accepted for enrollment or enrolled in a post-secondary institution
  · Recommended by either Literacy Action or the Certified Literate Community Program

Steve Dearduff Scholarship: Awards up to $2,500 for undergraduate and graduate students pursuing degrees in medicine and social work. Eligibility:
  · Legal resident of Georgia
  · Enrollment in or acceptance to an accredited institution of higher learning
  · Demonstrated history of outstanding community service
  · Potential for success in chosen field
  · Minimum "C" average (2.0 GPA)
Preference given to candidates entering the field of medicine (research or clinical practice) or social work.
Dreams2 Scholarship Fund: Awards up to $2,000 to deserving students who want to pursue their education. Eligibilty:
  · GPA between 2.0 and 3.0
  · Enrollment in or acceptance to an accredited 2- or 4-year college, university, or technical school to pursue an undergraduate degree
  · Demonstrated financial need
  · Full-time enrollment
William Lucas Foundation Scholarship: Awards up to $1,250 to deserving students interested in pursuing an undergraduate degree in Social Work, Education, or an Allied Health field. Eligibilty:
  · A graduating high school senior beginning college
  · Resident of the city of Atlanta or the city of Gainesville, Georgia
  · Minimum 2.5 GPA
  · Acceptance to an accredited institution of higher learning
  · Demonstrated history of commitment to community service
Nancy Penn Lyons Scholarship Fund: Awards up to $5,000 to students with financial need who have been accepted for enrollment at prestigious or out-of-state universities. Eligibility:
  · Legal resident of Georgia for at least one year prior to application
  · A graduating high school senior
  · A combined SAT score of 1000 or higher/ ACT composite of 22 or higher
  · Demonstrated financial need
  · Preference will be given to students attending selective private or out-of-state institutions
  · Cumulative 3.0 GPA
Patrick Family Scholarship Fund: Awards up to $5,000 to a senior graduating from Decatur High School who demonstrates financial need. Eligibility:
  · Acceptance or enrollment at an accredited college or university
  · High potential for attaining academic or career goal
  · Strong grades in topics related to that field
  · History of activities in that field
  · Demonstrated financial need
Patillo Scholarship Fund: Awards up to $3,500 to students pursuing an undergraduate degree with preference shown to employees of Pattillo Construction Corporation and their dependents. Eligibility:
  · Grade 'C' or better average(2.0 GPA) through the two previous quarters or the previous semester
  · Eligible applicants include, but are not limited to, employees of Pattillo Construction Corporation, its affiliates, and their dependents
  · Employees must be full-time employees of Pattillo Construction Corporation or its affiliates for a minimum of three (3) years
  · Students who have completed at least one semester or two quarters of college study must have a minimum cumulative 2.0 GPA

Russell Scholarship Fund: Awards up to $5,000 to support dependents of Russell Corporation employees in their pursuit of an undergraduate degree. Eligibility:
- Enrollment at an accredited college or university
- Minimum cumulative 3.0 GPA through the two previous quarters or the previous semester
- Parents of applicants must be full-time employees of Russell Corporation for a minimum of two (2) years

Jean Simmons After-Divorce Scholarship: Awards up to $1,000 a year to individuals for post-divorce assistance through education which will help recipients improve upon existing job skills and provide the opportunity to acquire new ones. Eligibility:
- Have a high school diploma or GED with a minimum of 2.5 GPA
- Hold U.S. citizenship
- Legal resident of Bartow, Cherokee, Cobb, Fulton, Paulding, or Pickens County for at least one year
- Divorce must be final within the past five years
- Accepted for enrollment or enrolled at an accredited college, university, or vocational school

James M. & Virginia M. Smyth Scholarship Fund: Awards up to $2,500 to provide financial support to students enrolled at an accredited college pursuing an undergraduate degree in the arts and sciences, human services, music or ministry field. Eligibility:
- Cumulative 3.0 GPA
- Accepted for enrollment or enrolled at an accredited college, university, or technical school
- Demonstrated financial need
- Commitment to community service through school, community, or religious organizations
- Preference will be given to applicants from Missouri, Mississippi, Georgia, Illinois, Oklahoma, Texas, and Tennessee
- Adults returning to school in order to increase employability are eligible

George W. and Pearl D. Strickland Scholarship: Awards up to $1,500 to students with financial need pursuing a degree at the University Center colleges. Eligibility:
- Legal resident of Georgia
- Enrolled or accepted for enrollment at Clark Atlanta University, Morehouse College, Morehouse School of Medicine, Morris Brown College or Spelman College
- Demonstrated financial need
- Potential for success in chosen field
- Evidence of extra-curricular involvement in community activities
- Grade C or better average (2.0 GPA) through the 2 previous quarters or the previous semester

Morgan Thomas Scholarship: Awards up to $1,000 For Cobb County high school seniors seeking an undergraduate degree. Eligibility:
- U.S. citizenship
- Legal resident of Cobb County for at least six (6) months prior to application
- Certified by her/his high school as a current candidate for graduation
- Accepted to a post-secondary institution in the United States to pursue an Associate or Bachelor's degree
- 2.5 GPA for high school course work in Grades 10, 11 and 12 for first-time applicants

- Preference shown for students achieving 3.0-3.5 GPA

Women's Chamber of Commerce Scholarship: Awards up to $3,000 to students enrolled in undergraduate studies at an accredited four-year college. Eligibility:
- A graduating senior at any metropolitan Atlanta high school
- Cumulative high school GPA of 3.0 (B) or higher
- SAT scores of at least 422 Verbal and 472 Math or ACT composite of 22 or higher
- Acceptance to a college or university to pursue an undergraduate degree

EIN: 581344646

863
Community Foundation for Greater Buffalo

(formerly The Buffalo Foundation)
712 Main St.
Buffalo, NY 14202-1720 (716) 852-2857
Contact: Myra S. Lawrence, V.P., Finance and Admin.
FAX: (716) 852-2861; E-mail: mail@cfgb.org;
URL: http://www.cfgb.org

Foundation type: Community foundation
Limitations: Scholarships from designated scholarship funds for purposes designated by the donors to financially needy residents of Buffalo and Erie County, NY, who have been accepted for admission to colleges. First consideration is given to full-time undergraduate students.
Publications: Application guidelines; Annual report (including application guidelines); Informational brochure; Newsletter; Program policy statement.
Financial data: Year ended 12/31/2004.
Assets, $90,204,606 (M); Expenditures, $5,108,123; Total giving, $3,541,193.
Fields of interest: Medical school/education; International human rights; Civil rights, advocacy; Engineering.
Type of support: Graduate support; Undergraduate support.
Application information: Application form required. Application form available on the grantmaker's Web site.
Initial approach: Letter.
Deadline(s): June 1
Additional information: Application must include SASE sent between Mar. 1 and May 1.
Program description:
Scholarship Program: The foundation administers 160 designated funds that give grants to individuals. Please see Web site for the current list of programs.
EIN: 160743935

864
Community Foundation for Muskegon County

(formerly Muskegon County Community Foundation, Inc.)
425 W. Western Ave., Ste. 200
Muskegon, MI 49440 (231) 722-4538
Contact: Chris Ann McGuigan, Pres.; For grants: Arnold "Arn" Boezaart, V.P., Grant Progs.
FAX: (231) 722-4616; E-mail: info@cffmc.org;
Grant application E-mail: aboezaart@cffmc.org;
URL: http://www.cffmc.org

Foundation type: Community foundation
Limitations: Scholarships to residents of Muskegon County, MI.

Publications: Application guidelines; Annual report (including application guidelines); Financial statement; Grants list; Informational brochure (including application guidelines); Newsletter; Program policy statement.
Financial data: Year ended 12/31/2004.
Assets, $88,320,829 (M); Expenditures, $4,879,031; Total giving, $2,726,558.
Type of support: Scholarships—to individuals; Undergraduate support.
Application information: Application form required.
Initial approach: Telephone.
Deadline(s): Mar. 1.
Additional information: Interviews required; Application must also include $5 application fee; See Web site for complete listing of programs and guidelines.
Program description:
Scholarship Funds: The foundation administers three types of scholarships including 198 different scholarship funds. See Web site to download an application.
EIN: 386114135

865
Community Foundation for Palm Beach and Martin Counties, Inc.

(formerly Palm Beach County Community Foundation)
700 S. Dixie Hwy., Ste. 200
West Palm Beach, FL 33401 (561) 659-6800
Contact: For grants: Linda Raybin, V.P., Progs.; For scholarships: Carolyn Jenco
FAX: (561) 832-6542; E-mail: info@cfpbmc.org;
Temporary address: 319 Clematis St., Ste. 900, West Palm Beach, FL 33401; Additional tel.: (888) 853-4438; Grant application E-mail: lraybin@cfpbmc.org; URL: http://www.yourcommunityfoundation.org
Additional URL: http://www.cfpbmc.org

Foundation type: Community foundation
Limitations: Scholarships to residents of Palm Beach County and Martin County, FL.
Publications: Application guidelines; Annual report (including application guidelines); Grants list; Informational brochure; Newsletter.
Financial data: Year ended 06/30/2005.
Assets, $111,772,572 (M); Expenditures, $8,111,292; Total giving, $5,226,021.
Fields of interest: Media/communications; Journalism/publishing; Performing arts, education; Language (foreign); Arts; Vocational education; Business school/education; Law school/education; Teacher school/education; Athletics/sports, training; Leadership development; Religion; Disabilities, people with; Minorities; African Americans/Blacks.
Type of support: Employee-related scholarships; Technical education support; Undergraduate support.
Application information: Applications accepted. Application form required.
Initial approach: Letter.
Deadline(s): Mar. 1
Additional information: Application should include ACT scores; Some scholarships are not awarded on an annual basis; new scholarships are added annually. See Web site for program listings and guidelines. Interviews required.
EIN: 237181875

866

Community Foundation for Southeastern Michigan

333 W. Fort St., Ste. 2010
Detroit, MI 48226 (313) 961-6675
Contact: Mariam C. Noland, Pres.
FAX: (313) 961-2886; E-mail: cfsem@cfsem.org;
URL: http://www.cfsem.org

Foundation type: Community foundation
Limitations: Scholarships to individuals in southeastern MI for postsecondary education. Scholarships also to employees of American Tape Co. and English Gardens Co., MI, and their children.
Publications: Application guidelines; Annual report (including application guidelines); Informational brochure (including application guidelines); Newsletter.
Financial data: Year ended 12/31/2004. Assets, $410,447,703 (M); Expenditures, $31,945,335; Total giving, $28,178,465.
Type of support: Employee-related scholarships; Undergraduate support.
Application information: Contact foundation for current application guidelines.
Program description:
Scholarships:
· Renaissance of Values Scholarship Fund: The fund helps assist students to attain a college education and higher values.
· Economic Club of Detroit Education Endowment Fund: Provides scholarships to students in Wayne, Oakland, and Macomb counties.
· Robert Holmes Scholarship Fund: Provides scholarships to children of MI members of the International Brotherhood of Teamsters.
· Southern Wayne County Chamber of Commerce Fund: Provides educational scholarships to individuals residing in the Chamber's service area.
· Otis M. Smith Scholarship Fund: Provides scholarships to selected single mothers residing in Wayne, Oakland, or Macomb counties, MI, for postsecondary education.
· Cris M. Kurzweil Scholarship Fund
· Enrico and Marie Vespa Scholarship Fund.
EIN: 382530980

867

Community Foundation for Southern Arizona

2250 E. Broadway Blvd.
Tucson, AZ 85719-6014 (520) 770-0800
Contact: Steve Alley, C.E.O.
FAX: (520) 770-1500;
E-mail: philanthropy@cfsoaz.org; Additional
E-mails: bbrown@cfsoaz.org and salley@cfsoaz.org;
URL: http://www.cfsoaz.org

Foundation type: Community foundation
Limitations: Scholarships by nomination only to students graduating from or attending AZ educational institutions; arts awards by nomination and application.
Publications: Application guidelines; Annual report; Financial statement; Informational brochure.
Financial data: Year ended 06/30/2004. Assets, $69,691,516 (M); Expenditures, $12,628,122; Total giving, $8,399,361.
Fields of interest: Arts education; Visual arts; Performing arts; Music; Opera; Literature.
Type of support: Awards/grants by nomination only; Undergraduate support.
Application information: Application form required.

Additional information: Contact foundation for current nomination deadline/guidelines; See Web site for complete program listing.
EIN: 942681765

868

The Community Foundation for the Capital Region, Inc.

6 Tower Place
Albany, NY 12203 (518) 446-9638
Contact: Judith Lyons, Exec. Dir.
FAX: (518) 446-9708; E-mail: info@cfcr.org;
URL: http://www.cfcr.org

Foundation type: Community foundation
Limitations: Scholarships to students at high schools in the NY Capital Region.
Publications: Application guidelines; Annual report; Financial statement; Informational brochure; Newsletter.
Financial data: Year ended 12/31/2004. Assets, $32,137,809 (M); Expenditures, $4,488,410; Total giving, $3,883,522.
Fields of interest: Media/communications; Vocational education; Business school/education; Medical school/education; Teacher school/education; Athletics/sports, training; Science, formal/general education; Women.
Type of support: Employee-related scholarships; Support to graduates or students of specific schools; Awards/grants by nomination only; Undergraduate support.
Application information:
Initial approach: Letter or telephone.
Additional information: See Web site for current application deadline/guidelines.
Program description:
Scholarship Program: The complete listing of programs is available on the foundation Web site.
EIN: 141505623

869

The Community Foundation for the National Capital Region

(formerly The Foundation for the National Capital Region)
1201 15th St. N.W., Ste. 420
Washington, DC 20005 (202) 955-5890
Contact: Terri Lee Freeman, Pres.; For grant applications: Alicia Reid, Grants Coord.
FAX: (202) 955-8084; E-mail: tfreeman@cfncr.org;
Tel. for grant applications: (202) 955-5890, ext. 119; E-mail for grant applications: areid@cfncr.org;
URL: http://www.cfncr.org

Foundation type: Community foundation
Limitations: Scholarships to residents of the metropolitan Washington, DC, area, and to students from China.
Publications: Application guidelines; Annual report; Financial statement; Program policy statement.
Financial data: Year ended 03/31/2005. Assets, $329,576,002 (M); Expenditures, $86,599,528; Total giving, $83,251,153.
Fields of interest: Engineering school/education.
Type of support: Scholarships—to individuals.
Application information: Contact foundation for current application deadline/guidelines.
Program descriptions:
101 Scholarship Fund: Provides scholarships to the children of U.S. Forest Service personnel.
China Education Fund: Provides graduate scholarships to students from the People's Republic of China for study in the U.S.

Dunbar Scholarship Fund: Provides scholarships to students in the field of civil engineering.
Edward Mahoney Scholarship: Provides scholarships to seniors of Pompton Lakes High School in north central NJ who are in the second ten percent of their class, demonstrate some artistic ability, and who cannot qualify for government-funded financial aid.
Mayor's Scholarship Fund: Provides scholarships to graduates of Washington, DC, public schools.
Margaret McNamara Memorial Fund: Provides scholarships to women from developing countries studying in the U.S.
Scholarship Fund of Alexandria: Provides scholarships to students from Alexandria, VA.
Roy Smith Memorial Scholarship: Provides scholarships to graduating seniors of Eastern High School, DC.
Presidential Internship Fund: Provides awards to outstanding students who have been accepted into the White House Internship Program in order to assist with their travel and living expenses, with preference given to minority applicants.
James Brady Presidential Fund: Provides for the care, rehabilitation, and support of Federal employees, their dependents, and other innocent bystanders who are victims of assassination attempts on the President, Vice-President, or other senior U.S. officials.
EIN: 237343119

870

The Community Foundation for the Ohio Valley, Inc.

3 Heiskell Ave.
P.O. Box 3048
Wheeling, WV 26003 (304) 242-3144
Contact: C.J. Kaiser, Jr., Pres.
FAX: (304) 242-3278; E-mail: director@cfov.org;
Additional E-mail: mfisher@cfov.org; URL: http://www.cfov.org

Foundation type: Community foundation
Limitations: Scholarships to qualified students in OH and WV.
Publications: Application guidelines; Annual report (including application guidelines); Grants list; Informational brochure; Newsletter.
Financial data: Year ended 05/31/2004. Assets, $18,273,284 (M); Expenditures, $921,549; Total giving, $829,316.
Type of support: Scholarships—to individuals.
Application information: Applications accepted. Application form required.
Initial approach: Letter or telephone.
Additional information: Contact foundation for current application deadline/guidelines.
EIN: 310908698

871

Community Foundation of Bloomington and Monroe County, Inc.

(formerly Bloomington Community Foundation, Inc.)
101 W. Kirkwood, Ste. 321
Bloomington, IN 47404
Contact: Kathleen Wissing, Exec. Dir.
E-mail: cf@bloomington.in.us

Foundation type: Community foundation
Limitations: Scholarships and grants to residents of Bloomington and Monroe counties, IN.
Publications: Application guidelines; Annual report; Informational brochure; Newsletter.
Financial data: Year ended 06/30/2004. Assets, $19,201,787 (M); Expenditures,

$1,376,383; Total giving, $331,989; Grants to individuals, 11 grants totaling $14,746 (high: $5,161, low: $127).
Type of support: Grants to individuals; Scholarships—to individuals.
Application information: Application form required.
  Initial approach: Letter.
  Deadline(s): Mar., June, Sept. and Dec
EIN: 351811149

872

Community Foundation of Boone County, Inc.

60 E. Cedar St.
P.O. Box 92
Zionsville, IN 46077 (317) 873-0210
Contact: Lisa Latz John, Exec. Dir.
FAX: (317) 873-0219; E-mail: cfbc@in-motion.net;
Additional tel.: (765) 482-0024; URL: http://www.bccn.boone.in.us/cf

Foundation type: Community foundation
Limitations: Scholarships to residents of Boone County, IN.
Publications: Application guidelines; Annual report; Informational brochure; Newsletter.
Financial data: Year ended 12/31/2004.
Assets, $13,945,414 (M); Expenditures, $799,043; Total giving, $481,266; Grants to individuals, 13 grants totaling $9,740 (high: $1,200, low: $100).
Fields of interest: Journalism/publishing; Medical school/education; Athletics/sports, training.
Type of support: Technical education support; Precollege support; Undergraduate support.
Application information: Applications accepted. Application form required.
  Deadline(s): Most scholarships Mar. 1, other deadlines vary
  Additional information: See Web site for complete list of programs.
EIN: 351829585

873

The Community Foundation of Brazoria County, Texas

P.O. Box 2392
Angleton, TX 77516-2392 (979) 848-2628
Contact: Vicki Kirby, Exec. Dir.
FAX: (979) 848-0031;
E-mail: cfbrzco@brazosport.edu; URL: http://www.cfbr.org

Foundation type: Community foundation
Limitations: Scholarships through Dow Chemical to residents of Brazoria County, TX.
Publications: Informational brochure; Newsletter.
Financial data: Year ended 06/30/2004.
Assets, $818,190 (M); Expenditures, $177,641; Total giving, $140,834; Grants to individuals, 38 grants totaling $34,500.
Type of support: Employee-related scholarships.
Application information: Contact foundation for current application deadline/guidelines.
EIN: 760427068

874

Community Foundation of Central Illinois

(formerly Peoria Area Community Foundation)
331 Fulton St., Ste. 310
Peoria, IL 61602 (309) 674-8730
Contact: Shanna Miller, Exec. Dir.
FAX: (309) 674-8754;
E-mail: jim@communityfoundationci.org;
URL: http://www.communityfoundationci.org

Foundation type: Community foundation
Limitations: Scholarships to residents in the Peoria, IL, area.
Publications: Application guidelines; Annual report (including application guidelines); Financial statement; Informational brochure; Newsletter.
Financial data: Year ended 06/30/2004.
Assets, $11,130,226 (M); Expenditures, $709,803; Total giving, $437,128; Grants to individuals, 31 grants totaling $71,500 (high: $6,000, low: $500).
Fields of interest: Nursing school/education; Epilepsy; Military/veterans.
Type of support: Technical education support; Undergraduate support.
Application information: Applications accepted. Application form required.
  Deadline(s): Apr. 15 and June 1
  Additional information: See Web site for application guidelines.
Program descriptions:
  Dr. Valentine Jobst III Educational Fund: This $1,500 award is given to a student attending high school in Peoria, IL, who wishes to attend a vocational technical school, or a junior or community college.
  Vietnam Veteran's Moving Wall Scholarship: This $250 award is given to a student attending a high school within a 50-mile radius of Peoria, IL. The student must be a child of a Vietnam veteran. The award will be given during the student's senior year to further education at a junior college or a four-year university/college.
  Jean M. Brown Nursing Scholarship: This $250 award is given to an individual who resides within a 50-mile radius of Peoria, IL, who is pursuing an education in the field of nursing, with special preference given to those interested in studying Occupational Nursing.
  Epilepsy Foundation Scholarship Fund: This $500 award is given to an individual who resides within a 50-mile radius of Peoria, IL, and is diagnosed with epilepsy. Recommendation by one teacher and a physician are required supplemental application information.
EIN: 371185713

875

The Community Foundation of Davie County, Inc.

194 Wilkesboro St.
P.O. Box 546
Mocksville, NC 27028 (336) 753-6903
Contact: Jane Simpson, C.E.O.
FAX: (336) 753-6904;
E-mail: info@daviefoundation.org; URL: http://www.daviefoundation.org

Foundation type: Community foundation
Limitations: Scholarships to residents of Davie County, NC, for attendance at a 2-year or 4-year accredited college/university in NC on a full-time basis.
Publications: Application guidelines; Annual report; Financial statement; Grants list; Informational brochure; Newsletter.

Financial data: Year ended 12/31/2004.
Assets, $3,267,993 (M); Expenditures, $200,248; Total giving, $82,056; Grants to individuals, totaling $4,875.
Type of support: Undergraduate support.
Application information:
  Initial approach: E-mail.
  Deadline(s): Mar. 24
  Additional information: Various scholarships may have specific requirements for applicants.
EIN: 581850531

876

The Community Foundation of Frederick County, MD, Inc.

312 E. Church St.
Frederick, MD 21701 (301) 695-7660
Contact: Elizabeth Y. Day, Pres.
FAX: (301) 695-7775; E-mail: info@cffredco.org;
Additional E-mail: donor.services@cffredco.org;
URL: http://www.cffredco.org

Foundation type: Community foundation
Limitations: Scholarships to residents of Frederick County, MD, for higher education.
Publications: Application guidelines; Annual report; Grants list; Newsletter.
Financial data: Year ended 06/30/2004.
Assets, $26,979,473 (M); Expenditures, $2,202,263; Total giving, $1,656,180; Grants to individuals, 232 grants totaling $212,551 (high: $4,855, low: $75).
Type of support: Scholarships—to individuals.
Application information: Application form required.
  Deadline(s): Mar. 30
EIN: 521488711

877

Community Foundation of Gaston County, Inc.

P.O. Box 123
Gastonia, NC 28053 (704) 864-0927
Contact: John A. Edgerton, Exec. Dir.
FAX: (704) 869-0222; E-mail: info@cfgaston.org;
Additional E-mail: jedgerton@cfgaston.org;
URL: http://www.cfgaston.org

Foundation type: Community foundation
Limitations: Scholarships to residents of Gaston County, NC.
Publications: Annual report; Informational brochure; Newsletter.
Financial data: Year ended 12/31/2004.
Assets, $85,165,926 (M); Expenditures, $6,837,266; Total giving, $6,349,836.
Type of support: Undergraduate support.
Application information: Applications accepted. Application form required. Application form available on the grantmaker's Web site.
  Initial approach: E-mail.
  Deadline(s): Varies
  Additional information: Each program has its own specific criteria. See Web site for a complete listing of programs.
EIN: 581340834

878

Community Foundation of Grant County
505 W. 3rd St.
Marion, IN   46952   (765) 662-0065
Contact: Elizabeth Wright, Exec. Dir.
FAX: (765) 662-1438;
E-mail: foundationoffice@comfdn.org; URL: http://www.comfdn.org

Foundation type: Community foundation
Limitations: Student loans and scholarships to graduates of Grant County high schools, IN.
Publications: Application guidelines; Annual report; Newsletter.
Financial data: Year ended 03/31/2005. Assets, $15,976,001 (M); Expenditures, $1,416,625; Total giving, $1,066,540.
Type of support: Scholarships—to individuals; Support to graduates or students of specific schools; Graduate support; Undergraduate support.
Application information: Applications accepted. Application form required.
> *Deadline(s):* Apr. 1.
> *Applicants should submit the following:*
> 1) Transcripts
> 2) SAT
> 3) Resume
> 4) Letter(s) of recommendation
> 5) GPA
> 6) Financial information
> 7) FAFSA
> 8) Essay
> 9) ACT

EIN: 311117791

879

The Community Foundation of Greater Chattanooga, Inc.
1270 Market St.
Chattanooga, TN   37402   (423) 265-0586
Contact: Peter T. Cooper, Pres.; For scholarships: Rebecca Smith, Scholarship Off.; For grants: Pamela Bracher, Dir., Progs.
Scholarship E-mail: rsmith@cfgc.org
FAX: (423) 265-0587; E-mail: info2@cfgc.org; Additional E-mail: pcooper@cfgc.org; Grant E-mail: pbracher@cfgc.org; URL: http://www.cfgc.org

Foundation type: Community foundation
Limitations: Scholarships to residents of the Hamilton County, TN, area for undergraduate study.
Publications: Application guidelines; Annual report; Biennial report (including application guidelines); Informational brochure; Informational brochure (including application guidelines).
Financial data: Year ended 12/31/2004. Assets, $59,739,119 (M); Expenditures, $23,495,398; Total giving, $22,309,018; Grants to individuals, 145 grants totaling $168,503 (high: $20,000, low: $7).
Type of support: Undergraduate support.
Application information: Applications accepted. Application form required. Application form available on the grantmaker's Web site.
> *Deadline(s):* Mar.
> *Applicants should submit the following:*
> 1) Transcripts
> 2) GPA
> 3) FAFSA
> 4) ACT
> *Additional information:* Interviews required; See Web site for a complete listing of funds.

Program description:
> *Scholarship Funds:* The following scholarship funds are administered by the community foundation:

- Together We Can Scholarship Fund
- Mary Adams Memorial Scholarship Fund
- Harold Cheney Cash & Ellen Lewis Cash Scholarship Fund
- Japanese-American Understanding Scholarship Fund
- Coca-Cola Centennial Scholarship Fund

EIN: 626045999

880

Community Foundation of Greater Flint
502 Church St.
Flint, MI   48502-1206   (810) 767-8270
Contact: Kathi Horton, Pres.
FAX: (810) 767-0496; E-mail: cfgf@cfgf.org; Additional E-mail: Khorton@cfgf.org; URL: http://www.cfgf.org

Foundation type: Community foundation
Limitations: Scholarships to individuals from the Flint, MI, area for undergraduate education at American colleges and universities.
Publications: Application guidelines; Annual report; Financial statement; Grants list; Informational brochure (including application guidelines); Occasional report; Program policy statement.
Financial data: Year ended 12/31/2004. Assets, $122,605,447 (M); Expenditures, $8,269,565; Total giving, $5,542,758.
Fields of interest: Performing arts, education; Business school/education; Dental school/education; Nursing school/education; Teacher school/education; Engineering school/education; Medical care, community health systems; Health care; Athletics/sports, water sports; Athletics/sports, winter sports; Boy scouts; Engineering/technology; Economics; Ethnic studies; Women.
Type of support: Support to graduates or students of specific schools; Awards/prizes; Graduate support; Technical education support; Undergraduate support.
Application information: Applications accepted. Application form required. Application form available on the grantmaker's Web site.
> *Additional information:* Scholarship are based on academic achievement.

Program description:
> *Scholarships:* The foundation administers over 60 scholarship funds to Flint, MI, area students. Please see Web site for a complete listing.

EIN: 382190667

881

Community Foundation of Greater Fort Wayne, Inc.
(formerly Fort Wayne Community Foundation)
701 S. Clinton St., Ste. 210
Fort Wayne, IN   46802   (260) 426-4083
Contact: David J. Bennett, Exec. Dir.; For grant application: Christine Meek, Prog. Off.
FAX: (260) 424-0114; E-mail: info@cfgfw.org; Grant application tel.: (260) 426-4083, ext. 318 and E-mail: cmeek@cfgfw.org; URL: http://www.cfgfw.org

Foundation type: Community foundation
Limitations: Scholarships to financially needy graduates of high schools in Fort Wayne, and Allen county IN, and to employees of Grabill Bank, and Rae Magnet Wire.
Publications: Application guidelines; Annual report; Financial statement; Grants list; Informational brochure; Informational brochure (including application guidelines); Newsletter; Occasional report.

Financial data: Year ended 12/31/2004. Assets, $85,555,500 (M); Expenditures, $7,252,553; Total giving, $6,331,323; Grants to individuals, 260 grants totaling $1,300,000.
Type of support: Scholarships—to individuals; Exchange programs; Support to graduates or students of specific schools; Undergraduate support; Camperships.
Application information: Applications accepted. Application form required. Application form available on the grantmaker's Web site.
> *Copies of proposal:* 1
> *Deadline(s):* Varies
> *Applicants should submit the following:*
> 1) Financial information
> 2) Letter(s) of recommendation
> 3) SAT
> 4) Curriculum vitae
> 5) Essay
> 6) FAFSA
> 7) GPA
> 8) Transcripts
> *Additional information:* Application must also include a personal data sheet and a list of high school activities. See Web site for additional programs.

EIN: 351119450

882

Community Foundation of Greater Greensboro, Inc.
(formerly The Foundation of Greater Greensboro, Inc.)
Foundation Place
330 S. Greene St., Ste. 100
Greensboro, NC   27401   (336) 379-9100
Contact: H. Walker Sanders, Pres.; For grant applications: Tara Sandercock, V.P., Progs.; For scholarship applications: Michiko Stavert, Dir., Scholarships
Scholarship application E-mail: mstavert@cfgg.org
FAX: (336) 378-0725; E-mail: info@cfgg.org; Application address: P.O. Box 20444, Greensboro, NC 27420; Grant application E-mail: grants@cfgg.org; URL: http://www.cfgg.org

Foundation type: Community foundation
Limitations: Scholarships to students of the greater Greensboro, NC, area.
Publications: Application guidelines; Annual report; Financial statement; Grants list; Informational brochure; Newsletter; Program policy statement.
Financial data: Year ended 12/31/2004. Assets, $83,379,047 (M); Expenditures, $15,969,741; Total giving, $13,390,745.
Fields of interest: Education.
Type of support: Scholarships—to individuals.
Application information: Applications accepted. Application form required.
> *Initial approach:* Letter or telephone.
> *Additional information:* Contact foundation for current application deadline/guidelines, as well as for the complete program listing.

Program description:
> *Scholarship Program:* Scholarships range from $500 to $10,000 offering financial assistance to individuals pursuing education through various scholarship funds. Individuals are selected on a competitive basis, considering academic and non-academic factors and demonstrated financial need. The funds target students from areas of interest including performance in high school, high school attended, and academic or career focus. For additional information on the various scholarships contact mstavert@cfgg.org.

EIN: 561380249

883
Community Foundation of Greater Jackson

(formerly Greater Jackson Foundation)
c/o 640845750
525 E. Capitol St., Ste. 5B
Jackson, MS 39201 (601) 974-6044
Contact: Linda Montgomery, Pres.
FAX: (601) 974-6045;
E-mail: info@cfgreaterjackson.org; URL: http://www.cfgreaterjackson.org

Foundation type: Community foundation
Limitations: Scholarships to students in LA and MS. See programs for further information on each scholarship fund.
Publications: Application guidelines; Annual report; Informational brochure; Newsletter; Occasional report.
Financial data: Year ended 03/31/2005. Assets, $13,351,359 (M); Expenditures, $1,539,676; Total giving, $1,151,214; Grants to individuals, 18 grants totaling $23,877 (high: $2,000, low: $500, average grant: $500-$2,000).
Fields of interest: Media/communications; Journalism/publishing; Business school/education; Engineering school/education; Journalism school/education; Education; Public affairs, formal/general education; Young adults, female.
Type of support: Scholarships—to individuals; Support to graduates or students of specific schools; Awards/grants by nomination only; Awards/prizes; Undergraduate support.
Application information: Applications accepted. Application form required. Application form available on the grantmaker's Web site.
Initial approach: Letter.
Copies of proposal: 1
Deadline(s): Mid-Apr.
Applicants should submit the following:
1) SAT
2) GPA
3) Financial information
4) ACT
Program descriptions:
Ryan Kirkpatrick Memorial Scholarship Fund: Awards scholarships to graduating seniors of Madison Central High School. Applications available from Senior Counselor.
Outstanding Educators Award Fund: Provides cash awards to public school teachers selected as the year's Outstanding Educators by the local chapter of Parents for Public Schools. No application necessary.
Bill Minor Journalism Awards Fund: Provides cash awards to winners selected in certain categories of the Mississippi Press Association's Better Newspaper Contest. No applications necessary.
American Public Works Association Scholarship Fund: Scholarship to a full-time junior or senior at a public university in MS studying to enter the field of public works. Recipient must have attended high school in MS. The award is based on both merit and need.
John Robert Boswell: Scholarship to an outstanding senior majoring in chemical engineering at Ole Miss. Recipient must be a full-time student and cannot belong to a social sorority or fraternity. The award is based on both merit and need.
Thomas Scholarship Fund: Scholarships to students at Jackson State University who are studying mass communications and to students at Alcorn State University who are studying business. Awards are based on financial need.
Harrison Clark Scholarship Awards Fund: Awards scholarships of $500 to graduating seniors of

Madison Central High School. Awards are intended for good students who have been active in the school and plan to attend a two- or four-year college on a full-time basis. Students with GPAs of 2.75 or better and ACT scores of 19-25 are encouraged to apply. Awards are made strictly based on merit. Applications are only available at Madison Central High School counselor's office.
Anthony "Tony" Gobar Juvenile Justice Scholarship: Scholarship to a full-time junior or senior majoring in criminal justice, political science, or counseling at a public university in Mississippi or Southern University in Louisiana.
Robert E. Luckett Memorial Scholarship Fund: Awards scholarships to graduates of Richland High School, MS. Awards are based on a combination of merit, need and teacher recommendation. Applications are only available at Richland High School counselor's office.
Bill Hunsberger Scholarship Fund: Scholarship to a female upperslassman majoring in journalism at the University of Mississippi or University of Southern Mississippi, or political science at Mississippi State University.
EIN: 640845750

884
The Community Foundation of Greater Lorain County

1865 N. Ridge Rd. E., Ste. A
Lorain, OH 44055 (440) 277-0142
Contact: Brian R. Frederick, C.E.O.
FAX: (440) 277-6955;
E-mail: foundation@peoplewhocare.org; Additional tel.: (440) 323-4445; Additional E-mail: info@peoplewhocare.org; URL: http://www.peoplewhocare.org

Foundation type: Community foundation
Limitations: Scholarships to residents of Lorain County, OH.
Publications: Application guidelines; Annual report (including application guidelines); Financial statement; Informational brochure (including application guidelines); Newsletter; Program policy statement.
Financial data: Year ended 12/31/2004. Assets, $70,361,297 (M); Expenditures, $4,138,570; Total giving, $3,306,909; Grants to individuals, 229 grants totaling $245,237 (high: $3,400, low: $200).
Fields of interest: Journalism/publishing; Medical care, community health systems; Dental care; Nursing care; Health care; Substance abuse, services; Business/industry; Business/industry, trade boards; Engineering; Religion.
Type of support: Graduate support; Technical education support; Undergraduate support.
Application information: Application form required.
Initial approach: Letter or telephone.
Deadline(s): Feb. 10
Additional information: Contact foundation for current application deadline; Application forms may be obtained from any Lorain County high school counselor for Nord Scholarships, from the newspaper's offices in Elyria for Chronicle-Telegram Scholarships, and from the foundation for other scholarship programs; Interviews may be required; See Web site for complete program listing.
EIN: 341322781

885
Community Foundation of Greater Memphis

1900 Union Ave.
Memphis, TN 38104 (901) 728-4600
Contact: Gid H. Smith, C.E.O. and Pres.; For grants and scholarships: Melissa Wolowicz, Dir., Progs.
FAX: (901) 722-0010; E-mail: gsmith@cfgm.org; Tel. for scholarships: (901) 722-0054; E-mail for grants and scholarships: mwolowicz@cfgm.org; URL: http://www.cfgm.org

Foundation type: Community foundation
Limitations: Scholarships to students residing in the Memphis, TN, area for undergraduate education.
Publications: Application guidelines; Annual report; Newsletter.
Financial data: Year ended 04/30/2005. Assets, $254,302,778 (M); Expenditures, $38,260,973; Total giving, $35,715,659.
Fields of interest: Music; Business school/education.
Type of support: Support to graduates or students of specific schools; Undergraduate support.
Application information: Application form required.
Deadline(s): Apr. 1
Applicants should submit the following:
1) ACT
2) SAT
3) SAR
4) Transcripts
Additional information: Application should also include letter outlining career goals and two letters of recommendation; The foundation administers numerous scholarships; See Web site for further application and program information.
Program descriptions:
Indian Community of Memphis Scholarship Fund: Scholarships to graduates of Central, East, Treadwell, Booker T. Washington and Whitehaven high schools, TN. Applicants must:
· maintain a 3.0 GPA
· be accepted into an accredited four-year college or university.
Community Foundation of Greater Memphis Scholarship Fund: Awards scholarships of $1,250 to students in the metropolitan Memphis, TN area. Scholarships are renewable, provided that recipient maintains a "B" average and reapplies annually. Applicants must:
· be graduating high school seniors
· plan to attend an accredited college or university
· maintain a "B" average
· show economic need.
James A. Hyter Vocal Music Scholarship Fund: Awards scholarships of $1,000 to $2,000 each to students who possess vocal talent. Applicants must:
· have a 3.0 GPA
· attend or plan to attend a two- or four-year program at an accredited institution.
Qualified applicants are invited to audition.
Allen Jones/ Marjorie Barringer/ Barkays Scholarship Fund: Awards scholarships of $2,000 to $2,500 to Memphis, TN, seniors for attendance at LeMoyne-Owen College, TN. Applicants must:
· have a "C" average
· demonstrate financial need.
Stephen Lowe Memorial Scholarship Fund: Awards scholarships of $150 to $2,000 to graduating seniors of Bolton High School or Faith Baptist High School, TN. Applicants must have 3.0 GPAs and participate in extracurricular activities.
EIN: 581723645

886
Community Foundation of Greater Rochester

(formerly Greater Rochester Area Community Foundation)
P.O. Box 80431
Rochester, MI 48308-0431 (248) 608-2804
Contact: Peggy Hamilton, Exec. Dir.
Scholarship application address for hand delivery:
Community Fdn. Office, 127 W. University Dr.,
Rochester, MI 48307
FAX: (248) 608-2826; E-mail: cfound@cfound.org;
URL: http://www.cfound.org

Foundation type: Community foundation
Limitations: Scholarships to graduating high school students in the greater Rochester area, MI, including the following schools: Adams High School, Avondale High School, Clawson High School, and Rochester High School.
Publications: Annual report (including application guidelines); Financial statement; Informational brochure; Newsletter.
Financial data: Year ended 12/31/2004.
Assets, $0 (M); Expenditures, $845,111; Total giving, $660,469; Grants to individuals, 98 grants totaling $141,587 (high: $4,000, low: $63).
Type of support: Support to graduates or students of specific schools; Undergraduate support.
Application information: Contact foundation for current application deadline/guidelines; See Web site or contact foundation for information about specific scholarship programs.
EIN: 382476777

887
Community Foundation of Henderson County, Inc.

401 N. Main St., 3rd Fl.
P.O. Box 1108
Hendersonville, NC 28793 (828) 697-6224
Contact: McCray V. Benson, C.E.O.; For grants:
Kathryn McConnell, V.P., Community Philanthropy;
For scholarships: Amy Robinson
FAX: (828) 696-4026;
E-mail: info@cfhendersoncounty.org; Grant application E-mail:
kmcconnell@cfhendersoncounty.org; Scholarship application E-mail:
arobinson@cfhendersoncounty.org; URL: http://www.cfhendersoncounty.org

Foundation type: Community foundation
Limitations: Scholarships to scholastic achievers and financially needy residents of Henderson County, NC.
Publications: Application guidelines; Annual report; Informational brochure; Newsletter.
Financial data: Year ended 06/30/2005.
Assets, $55,532,411 (M); Expenditures, $3,136,131; Total giving, $2,256,872; Grants to individuals, 136 grants totaling $218,843 (high: $5,000, low: $500).
Type of support: Scholarships—to individuals.
Application information: Application form required.
Deadline(s): Mar. 1
Additional information: Applications available at high school guidance counselor's office.
EIN: 561330792

888
The Community Foundation of Howard County, Inc.

202 N. Main St.
Kokomo, IN 46901-4624 (765) 454-7298
Contact: Hilda Burns, V.P.
FAX: (765) 868-4123; E-mail: hilda@cfhoward.org;
Additional tel.: (800) 964-0508; URL: http://www.cfhoward.org

Foundation type: Community foundation
Limitations: Scholarships to students in the Howard County, IN, area, for higher education.
Publications: Application guidelines; Annual report (including application guidelines); Informational brochure; Newsletter.
Financial data: Year ended 12/31/2004.
Assets, $26,555,173 (M); Expenditures, $823,620; Total giving, $493,215; Grants to individuals, 81 grants totaling $98,524.
Type of support: Support to graduates or students of specific schools; Undergraduate support.
Application information: Applications accepted.
Application form required.
Initial approach: Letter.
Deadline(s): Vary
Additional information: Application should include FAFSA; See Web site for application guidelines.
Program description:
Scholarship Program: The complete listing of programs is available on the foundation Web site.
EIN: 351844891

889
The Community Foundation of Jackson County, Inc.

P.O. Box 1231
Seymour, IN 47274 (812) 523-4483
Contact: C.W. "Bud" Walther, C.E.O.
FAX: (812) 523-1433; E-mail: cfjc@htonline.net;
Additional E-mail: jccf@hsonline.net

Foundation type: Community foundation
Limitations: Scholarships to students at Jackson County high schools, IN.
Publications: Application guidelines; Annual report; Financial statement; Informational brochure (including application guidelines); Newsletter.
Financial data: Year ended 12/31/2004.
Assets, $7,061,837 (L); Expenditures, $287,924; Total giving, $115,826; Grants to individuals, 11 grants totaling $37,575 (high: $11,112).
Type of support: Seed money; Support to graduates or students of specific schools; Awards/grants by nomination only; Technical education support; Undergraduate support.
Application information: Application form required.
Deadline(s): Contact foundation for current application deadline
EIN: 311119856

890
The Community Foundation of Louisville, Inc.

(formerly Louisville Community Foundation, Inc.)
Waterfront Plz. Bldg.
325 W. Main St., Ste. 1110
Louisville, KY 40202-4251 (502) 585-4649
Contact: C. Dennis Riggs, C.E.O.; For grants:
Alexandra M. Spoelker, Dir., Grants
FAX: (502) 587-7484; E-mail: info@cflouisville.org;
Grant application E-mail: alexs@cflouisville.org;
URL: http://www.cflouisville.org

Foundation type: Community foundation
Limitations: Scholarships to individuals in the greater Louisville, KY, area.
Publications: Annual report; Informational brochure; Newsletter; Program policy statement.
Financial data: Year ended 06/30/2004.
Assets, $177,841,869 (M); Expenditures, $12,631,041; Total giving, $8,361,478.
Fields of interest: Vocational education; Business school/education; Nursing school/education; Adult/continuing education; Environmental education; Agriculture; Jewish agencies & temples; Women.
Type of support: Program development; Employee-related scholarships; Graduate support; Technical education support; Precollege support; Undergraduate support.
Application information: Applications accepted. Application form required. Application form available on the grantmaker's Web site.
Deadline(s): Mar. 1 for Darcy Blair Fund and Artist Bill Fischer Foundation for Working Artists and Feb. 1 for all other funds
Additional information: See Web site for complete program listing.
EIN: 310997017

891
Community Foundation of Madison and Jefferson County, Inc.

214 E. Main St.
P.O. Box 306
Madison, IN 47250-0306 (812) 265-3327
Contact: Louise Markel, C.E.O.
FAX: (812) 273-0181; E-mail: jeffcom@cfmjc.org;
URL: http://www.cfmjc.org

Foundation type: Community foundation
Limitations: Scholarships for post-high school education to qualified students of Madison Consolidated Schools, Madison, IN, and Southwestern Consolidated Schools, Hanover, IN.
Publications: Application guidelines; Annual report; Financial statement; Grants list; Informational brochure; Newsletter; Program policy statement.
Financial data: Year ended 12/31/2005.
Assets, $14,746,800 (M); Expenditures, $991,881; Total giving, $416,900; Grants to individuals, totaling $30,900.
Type of support: Scholarships—to individuals; Support to graduates or students of specific schools; Technical education support; Undergraduate support.
Application information: Application form required.
Initial approach: Telephone or e-mail.
Deadline(s): Mar. 15
Applicants should submit the following:
1) SAT
2) Transcripts
3) Resume
4) Letter(s) of recommendation
5) GPA
6) Financial information
7) FAFSA
8) Curriculum vitae
Additional information: Applications should be sent by mail; Recipients notified in six weeks.
EIN: 351847297

892
Community Foundation of Monroe County
P.O. Box 627
Monroe, MI 48161 (734) 242-1976
Contact: Kristyn Theisen, Exec. Dir.
FAX: (734) 242-1234; E-mail: info@cfmonroe.org;
URL: http://www.cfmonroe.org

Foundation type: Community foundation
Limitations: Scholarships to graduates of Monroe County, MI, who are pursuing careers in technical schools, pre-med, pre-law, journalism, engineering, computer tech education.
Publications: Application guidelines; Annual report; Financial statement; Grants list; Informational brochure; Newsletter.
Financial data: Year ended 03/31/2005.
Assets, $3,799,971 (M); Expenditures, $412,713; Total giving, $173,463; Grants to individuals, 68 grants totaling $52,025 (high: $4,245, low: $200).
Fields of interest: Journalism/publishing; Law school/education; Medical school/education; Engineering.
Type of support: Graduate support; Technical education support.
Application information: Applications accepted. Application form required.
   Copies of proposal: 15
   Deadline(s): Contact foundation for deadline.
   Applicants should submit the following:
      1) Transcripts
      2) SAT
      3) GPA
      4) Essay
      5) ACT
EIN: 382236628

893
Community Foundation of Mount Vernon & Knox County
(formerly The Mount Vernon/Knox County Community Trust)
c/o The First-Knox National Bank
1 S. Main St.
P.O. Box 1270
Mount Vernon, OH 43050 (740) 392-3270
Contact: Sam Barone, Exec. Dir.
FAX: (740) 399-5296;
E-mail: sbarone@mvkcfoundation.org; URL: http://www.mvkcfoundation.org

Foundation type: Community foundation
Limitations: Scholarships and student loans to residents of Knox County, OH.
Publications: Application guidelines; Annual report; Informational brochure; Occasional report.
Financial data: Year ended 12/31/2004.
Assets, $27,797,399 (M); Expenditures, $896,552; Total giving, $645,647; Grants to individuals, 154 grants totaling $195,289 (high: $10,000, low: $400).
Type of support: Scholarships—to individuals; Student loans—to individuals.
Application information: Application form required.
   Initial approach: Letter.
   Deadline(s): Feb. 21
EIN: 311768219

894
The Community Foundation of Muncie and Delaware County, Inc.
P.O. Box 807
Muncie, IN 47308-0807 (765) 747-7181
Contact: Roni Johnson, Pres.
FAX: (765) 289-7770;
E-mail: commfound@cfmdin.org; URL: http://www.cfmdin.org

Foundation type: Community foundation
Limitations: Scholarships to individuals from the Muncie, IN, area for undergraduate education at U.S. colleges and universities.
Publications: Application guidelines; Annual report; Financial statement; Grants list; Informational brochure; Newsletter; Occasional report.
Financial data: Year ended 12/31/2004.
Assets, $36,341,209 (M); Expenditures, $3,508,712; Total giving, $3,004,881; Grants to individuals, 92 grants totaling $265,251 (high: $14,756, low: $100).
Fields of interest: Business school/education; Health care, alliance; Athletics/sports, golf; Protestant agencies & churches; Physically disabled; Women; Economically disadvantaged.
Type of support: Employee-related scholarships; Support to graduates or students of specific schools; Technical education support; Undergraduate support.
Application information: Applications accepted. Application form required.
   Initial approach: Telephone.
   Deadline(s): Vary
   Additional information: Contact foundation for further application and program information.
Program descriptions:
   E.A. and E.E. Burgess Scholarship: Awarded to a graduate of Muncie Central High School or Connersville Senior High School who is enrolled in Ball State University College of Applied Science and Technology.
   Hurley C. and Fredine (Wynn) Goodall Scholarship: Awarded annually to economically disadvantaged students of color enrolled in the two-year associate program at Ivy Tech State College.
   "J" Scholarship: Awarded to a student from a county high school in Delaware County who is interested in obtaining a business degree from the Ball State University School of Business.
   Rozelle-Camplin Scholarship: Awarded to a graduate of Daleville High School. Selection is based on scholarship, community service, citizenship, and participation in student activities.
   Van Laningham Scholarship: Awarded to entrepreneurship students in the Small Business Management/Entrepreneurship Program at Ball State University.
   Sarah E. Adams Scholarship: Awarded to a member of a Delaware County High School girls' golf team who has displayed good citizenship and a positive attitude for life, this scholarship is for use while attending an accredited college or university in the State of Indiana.
   Michael Broadhead Scholarship: Awarded to a Delaware County High School college-bound senior who has overcome a physical disability while achieving a high level of academics and participating in other activities outside the classroom.
   Creviston Scholarship: Awarded to a graduate of Cowan High School who wishes to attend a post-high school institution.
   Ollie Mae Hammond Scholarship: Awarded to graduating students who are active members of the Youth Group of Antioch Baptist Church. Recipients must plan to attend college, university or business school.
   Lilly Endowment Community Scholarships: Awards six scholarships to exceptional area students.
   Grace Maring Scholarships: Awards scholarships to three graduates of Wapahani High School, IN.
   McDonald's Restaurants of Delaware and Madison Counties Scholarships: Awards five $1,000 scholarships to employees of the Terhune McDonald's restaurants in Delaware or Madison Counties.
   Yorktown Lions Club Scholarships: Awards scholarships to Yorktown High School graduates who maintain an 8.0/12.0 GPA and display good citizenship.
   Community Foundation Scholarships: Awards 15 scholarships to honor nominees of the Lilly Endowment Community Scholars Program.
EIN: 351640051

895
Community Foundation of North Central Washington
(formerly Greater Wenatchee Community Foundation)
P.O. Box 3332
Wenatchee, WA 98807-3332 (509) 663-7716
Contact: Beth A. Stipe, Exec. Dir.; For grants: Lila Edlund, Prog. and Office Mgr.
FAX: (509) 667-2208;
E-mail: foundaton@cfncw.org; Additional E-mails: beth@cfncw.org and judy@cfncw.org; Grant inquiry E-mail: lila@cfncw.org; URL: http://www.cfncw.org

Foundation type: Community foundation
Limitations: Scholarships to students who are residents of Chelan, Douglas, Grant, and Okanogan counties, WA, for higher education.
Publications: Application guidelines; Annual report; Grants list; Informational brochure; Informational brochure (including application guidelines); Newsletter; Occasional report.
Financial data: Year ended 06/30/2005.
Assets, $23,715,814 (M); Expenditures, $2,062,816; Total giving, $1,695,911.
Fields of interest: Higher education; Women.
Type of support: Scholarships—to individuals.
Application information: Application form required.
   Initial approach: Telephone.
   Deadline(s): Feb. 29
   Applicants should submit the following:
      1) Financial information
      2) Letter(s) of recommendation
      3) FAFSA
      4) Transcripts
Program descriptions:
   Altrusa Club of Wenatchee Scholarship: Provides a scholarship to a female high school graduate who will be attending a four-year college full-time. The award is given every other year and is renewable a second year.
   Brewster High School Rawson Scholarship: Provides scholarships to graduating seniors at Brewster High School who are enrolled in an accredited educational program.
   Chelan County Fire District No. 1 Volunteer Association Scholarship: Provides two scholarships to a member or retired member in good standing of the association for at least one year, or a spouse, child, or grandchild of a member.
   Rudolph and Carolyn Christianson Scholarship: Provides two scholarships to graduating seniors. Each year, the scholarship award will alternate between Eastmont High School and Wenatchee High School until there are sufficient funds to offer the scholarship to all NCW high schools.
   Cone Family Scholarship: Provides scholarships to graduating seniors at Chelan High School.

Donna A. Corbin Memorial Scholarship: Provides scholarships to graduating high school seniors who are affiliated with the First Presbyterian Church of Wenatchee.

Melvin P. "Mel" and Lyndell Crowder NCW Memorial Horticulture Scholarship: Provides scholarships to students enrolled in the Tree Fruit Production Program at Wenatchee Valley College or Tree Fruit Management in the Horticulture Program at Washington State University.

Doell Family Scholarship: Provides scholarships to graduating seniors of NCW high schools for accredited educational programs, with emphasis on journalism or music.

EIN: 911349486

896

The Community Foundation of Northwest Connecticut, Inc.

(formerly Torrington Area Foundation for Public Giving)
32 City Hall Ave.
P.O. Box 1144
Torrington, CT   06790   (860) 626-1245
Contact: Guy Rovezzi, Pres.
FAX: (860) 489-7517; E-mail: info@cfnwct.org;
Grant application E-mail: jobrien@cfnwct.org;
URL: http://www.cfnwct.org

Foundation type: Community foundation
Limitations: Scholarships to residents of the foundation's 20-town service area for higher education.
Publications: Application guidelines; Annual report; Financial statement; Informational brochure; Informational brochure (including application guidelines); Newsletter; Occasional report.
Financial data: Year ended 12/31/2004.
Assets, $10,329,916 (M); Expenditures, $932,196; Total giving, $599,553; Grants to individuals, 162 grants totaling $110,000 (high: $5,000, low: $100).
Type of support: Graduate support; Undergraduate support.
Application information: Application form required. Application form available on the grantmaker's Web site.
   Initial approach: Letter or telephone.
   Copies of proposal: 3
   Deadline(s): Apr. 1
   Applicants should submit the following:
      1) Transcripts
      2) SAT
      3) SAR
      4) Letter(s) of recommendation
      5) GPA
      6) Essay
   Additional information: Applications should be sent by mail.
EIN: 066114199

897

Community Foundation of Randolph County, Inc.

213 S. Main St.
Winchester, IN   47394   (765) 584-9077
Contact: Suzan Dillion Myers, Pres.

Foundation type: Community foundation
Limitations: Scholarships to graduates of Randolph County, IN, high schools for attendance at any accredited IN college or university.
Financial data: Year ended 02/28/2004.
Assets, $4,092,011 (L); Expenditures, $287,322; Total giving, $184,364; Grants to individuals, 33

grants totaling $123,307 (high: $14,756, low: $93).
Type of support: Support to graduates or students of specific schools.
Application information: Contact foundation for current application deadline; Completion of formal application required; Applications available at Randolph County high school guidance offices.
Program description:
   Scholarship Program: Scholarships include full tuition and a $700 annual stipend for books. Applicants must be graduating seniors with a GPA of at least 3.0.
EIN: 351903148

898

The Community Foundation of Santa Cruz County

(formerly Greater Santa Cruz County Community Foundation)
2425 Porter St., Ste. 17
Soquel, CA   95073-2453   (831) 477-0800
Contact: Lance Linares, Exec. Dir.; For grants: Christina Cuevas, Prog. Dir.
FAX: (831) 477-0991; E-mail: info@cfscc.org;
Additional E-mails: lance@cfscc.org and christina@cfscc.org; URL: http://www.cfscc.org

Foundation type: Community foundation
Limitations: Scholarships to high school graduates from Santa Cruz County, CA. See program description for further limitations.
Publications: Application guidelines; Annual report; Financial statement; Grants list.
Financial data: Year ended 12/31/2004.
Assets, $31,767,568 (M); Expenditures, $4,177,776; Total giving, $3,004,904.
Fields of interest: Agriculture; Athletics/sports, training; Recreation.
Type of support: Support to graduates or students of specific schools; Undergraduate support.
Application information: Application form required.
   Initial approach: Letter, telephone, or e-mail.
   Deadline(s): Apr. 31
   Applicants should submit the following:
      1) Transcripts
Program descriptions:
   Emmett and Elsie Geiser Scholarships: This fund provides scholarships to students of Watsonville and Aptos high schools in the Pajaro Valley Unified School District. Applicants must have earned a varsity letter in an athletic program and have maintained at least a 3.0 GPA. Financial need is a factor in selection, but not a requirement. Awards must be used at four-year universities and state colleges (not community colleges) in the U.S. Applications must include a letter from the school verifying that the student received a varsity letter in at least one sport. Applications must be made to the high school scholarship committee who will forward their suggestions to the foundation's board of directors. Each scholarship is $625 per year for four years. Annual renewal is dependent on proof of enrollment and maintenance of at least a 2.0 GPA.
   The John L. Turner Scholarship: One $1,000 scholarship to a student who is a graduating senior of Watsonville High School at the time of the application. Applicants must be worthy individuals with the sincere desire to further their education and who would not be able to do so otherwise.
   R.H. Beel Memorial Scholarships: This fund provides scholarships to graduating seniors of Santa Cruz High School who demonstrate academic achievement, socially responsible activities, and financial need. Priority is given to students who will attend fully accredited two- or four-year colleges or universities or vocational institutions in CA, in

particular, Santa Cruz County. Applicants must be U.S. citizens. Priority is given to students who do not receive other scholarships. Applicants should show plans for partial self-support for educational costs. Renewal of scholarships is contingent on verification of self-support. The maximum award is $1,000.

   Ernest V. Cowell Scholarship: This fund provides $1,000 scholarships to financially needy graduates of public high schools in the Santa Cruz High School District and to graduating seniors from high schools in Santa Cruz County, CA, to attend a University of California campus. Recipients must show proof of enrollment at a University of California campus before the award is disbursed. This scholarship is non-renewable.

   The Dan Wood Scholarship: Two $500 scholarships are awarded to individuals who are graduating from a high school in the Santa Cruz City School District and who have demonstrated significant interest in their community via involvement and volunteer work.

   Mary Ellen and Louis Schultz Scholarship: This fund provides scholarships to graduates of Santa Cruz County high schools for attendance at colleges, community colleges, and vocational schools.
EIN: 942808039

899

The Community Foundation of Sarasota County, Inc.

(formerly The Sarasota County Community Foundation, Inc.)
P.O. Box 49587
Sarasota, FL   34230-6587   (941) 955-3000
Contact: Stewart W. Stearns, C.E.O.; For grant applications: Wendy Hopkins, V.P., Grant & Prog. Svcs.
FAX: (941) 952-1951;
E-mail: info@sarasota-foundation.org; Office address: 2635 Fruitville Rd., Sarasota, FL 34237; Grant application tel.: (941) 556-7152; Grant inquiry E-mail: wendy@sarasota-foundation.org; URL: http://www.sarasota-foundation.org

Foundation type: Community foundation
Limitations: Scholarships, awards and professional support to financially needy residents of Charlotte, Manatee, and Sarasota counties, FL, who are graduates of the specific schools named in the program descriptions.
Publications: Application guidelines; Annual report; Grants list; Informational brochure; Newsletter; Occasional report (including application guidelines); Program policy statement.
Financial data: Year ended 05/31/2004.
Assets, $109,600,000 (M); Expenditures, $6,368,675; Total giving, $5,200,000.
Fields of interest: Vocational education; Health care.
Type of support: Support to graduates or students of specific schools; Awards/prizes; Undergraduate support.
Application information: Application form required. Application form available on the grantmaker's Web site.
   Copies of proposal: 1
   Deadline(s): Vary
   Additional information: See Web site for complete program listing.
EIN: 591956886

900

The Community Foundation of Shelby County

(formerly The Community Foundation of Sidney and Shelby County)
100 S. Main Ave., Ste. 202
Sidney, OH 45365-2771 (937) 497-7800
Contact: Marian Spicer, Exec. Dir.
FAX: (937) 497-7799;
E-mail: info@commfoun.com; Additional E-mail: mspicer@commfoun.com; URL: http://www.commfoun.com

Foundation type: Community foundation
Limitations: Scholarships to graduates of Shelby County, OH, high schools, and loans to graduates of Botkins, OH, local schools.
Publications: Informational brochure; Newsletter.
Financial data: Year ended 12/31/2004.
Assets, $8,067,533 (M); Expenditures, $2,594,464; Total giving, $2,416,722; Grants to individuals, totaling $87,738.
Type of support: Support to graduates or students of specific schools; Undergraduate support.
Application information: Contact foundation for current application deadline/guidelines; Application by letter outlining financial need.
EIN: 346565194

901

Community Foundation of South Lake County, Inc.

(formerly South Lake County Community Foundation, Inc.)
P.O. Box 121543
Clermont, FL 34712-1543 (352) 394-3818
Contact: Bruce Greer, Exec. Dir.; For grants: Cheryl Fishel, Prog. Mgr.
FAX: (352) 394-7739; E-mail: info@cfslc.org;
Additional E-mail: bruce@cfslc.org; Grant inquiry E-mail: slcfishel@earthlink.net; URL: http://www.cfslc.org

Foundation type: Community foundation
Limitations: Scholarships to college bound seniors from South Lake County high schools, FL.
Publications: Application guidelines; Annual report; Financial statement; Grants list; Informational brochure; Newsletter.
Financial data: Year ended 09/30/2005.
Assets, $9,381,091 (M); Expenditures, $571,144; Total giving, $334,505; Grants to individuals, totaling $45,200.
Type of support: Support to graduates or students of specific schools.
Application information:
Initial approach: Letter or telephone.
Additional information: Contact foundation for current application deadline/guidelines.
EIN: 593343026

902

The Community Foundation of Southeastern Connecticut

(formerly The Pequot Community Foundation, Inc.)
147 State St.
P.O. Box 769
New London, CT 06320 (860) 442-3572
Contact: Alice F. Fitzpatrick, Pres.
FAX: (860) 442-0584; E-mail: jennob@cfsect.org;
URL: http://www.cfsect.org

Foundation type: Community foundation

Limitations: Scholarships by nomination only to graduating high school students at particular schools in southeastern CT.
Publications: Application guidelines; Annual report (including application guidelines); Financial statement; Grants list; Informational brochure; Newsletter.
Financial data: Year ended 12/31/2003.
Assets, $22,777,129 (L); Expenditures, $1,551,600; Total giving, $1,063,348; Grants to individuals, totaling $141,094.
Type of support: Awards/grants by nomination only; Undergraduate support.
Application information: Application form required.
Deadline(s): Apr. 1
Program description:
Scholarships: The foundation administers scholarship programs with varying eligibility requirements. Applicants must be graduating from one of the following CT schools: East Lyme High School, Fitch High School, Ledyard High School, Lyme High School, Montville High School, New London High School, St. Bernard High School, Stonington High School, Waterford High School, Wheeler High School, or Williams School.
EIN: 061080097

903

Community Foundation of Southern Wisconsin, Inc.

(formerly United Community Foundation, Inc.)
111 N. Main St.
Janesville, WI 53545 (608) 758-0883
Contact: Sue S. Conley, Exec. Dir.
FAX: (608) 758-8551; E-mail: info@cfsw.org;
Additional Tel.: (800) 995-CFSW; Additional E-mail: sconley.cfsw@sbcglobal.net; URL: http://www.cfsw.org

Foundation type: Community foundation
Limitations: Scholarships only to residents of Monroe, WI, and northern Rock, Iowa, Lafayette, Grant, Green, Jefferson, and Walworth counties, WI.
Publications: Application guidelines; Annual report; Informational brochure (including application guidelines); Newsletter.
Financial data: Year ended 06/30/2005.
Assets, $20,017,240 (M); Expenditures, $2,360,959; Total giving, $1,684,002; Grants to individuals, 89 grants totaling $590,400 (high: $96,950, low: $200).
Fields of interest: Language (foreign); Arts; Business school/education; Nursing school/education; Teacher school/education; Government/public administration; Public affairs, citizen participation.
Type of support: Employee-related scholarships; Support to graduates or students of specific schools; Undergraduate support.
Application information: Application form required.
Initial approach: Letter directly through school.
Deadline(s): May1
Program description:
Scholarship Funds: The foundation administers numerous scholarship funds. See Web site for a complete listing of these scholarship programs.
EIN: 391711388

904

Community Foundation of Southwest Georgia, Inc.

135 N. Broad St., Ste. 202
P.O. Box 2654
Thomasville, GA 31799-2654 (229) 228-5088
Contact: Wade Miller, Pres.
FAX: (229) 228-0848; Additional tel.: (888) 544-2317; URL: http://www.cfsga.org

Foundation type: Community foundation
Limitations: Scholarships to individuals in southwestern GA.
Financial data: Year ended 12/31/2004.
Assets, $18,837,621 (M); Expenditures, $1,931,485; Total giving, $1,453,030; Grants to individuals, 56 grants totaling $32,747 (high: $5,500, low: $44).
Type of support: Scholarships—to individuals.
Application information: Unsolicited requests for funds not accepted.
EIN: 582210876

905

Community Foundation of St. Clair County

516 McMorran Blvd.
Port Huron, MI 48060 (810) 984-4761
Contact: Randy D. Maiers, C.E.O.
FAX: (810) 984-3394;
E-mail: info@stclairfoundation.org; Grant application E-mail: grants@stclairfoundation.org; Additional E-mail: randy@stclairfoundation.org (for Randy Maiers); URL: http://www.stclairfoundation.org

Foundation type: Community foundation
Limitations: Scholarships only to students in St. Clair County, MI.
Publications: Application guidelines; Annual report; Financial statement; Grants list; Informational brochure.
Financial data: Year ended 12/31/2004.
Assets, $27,914,951 (M); Expenditures, $1,617,994; Total giving, $1,095,716.
Type of support: Scholarships—to individuals.
Application information:
Deadline(s): Mar. 15
Additional information: See Web site for application guidelines.
EIN: 381872132

906

Community Foundation of St. Joseph County

205 W. Jefferson Blvd.
P.O. Box 837
South Bend, IN 46624-0837 (574) 232-0041
Contact: Angela Butiste, Prog. Off.
FAX: (574) 233-1906; E-mail: info@cfsjc.org;
Additional E-mail: angela@cfsjc.org; URL: http://www.cfsjc.org

Foundation type: Community foundation
Limitations: Scholarships to individuals residing in the St. Joseph County, IN, area for undergraduate education.
Publications: Application guidelines; Financial statement; Grants list; Newsletter.
Financial data: Year ended 06/30/2005.
Assets, $74,461,662 (M); Expenditures, $3,702,665; Total giving, $2,916,160; Grants to individuals, 54 grants totaling $215,144 (high: $14,373, low: $250).
Fields of interest: Historic preservation/historical societies; Teacher school/education; Engineering

906—Community—EDUCATIONAL SUPPORT

school/education; Crime/law enforcement, formal/general education; Athletics/sports, school programs.
Type of support: Employee-related scholarships; Scholarships—to individuals; Support to graduates or students of specific schools; Graduate support; Undergraduate support.
Application information: Applications accepted. Application form required. Application form available on the grantmaker's Web site.
  Deadline(s): Varies
  Applicants should submit the following:
    1) Transcripts
    2) SAT
    3) Letter(s) of recommendation
    4) GPA
    5) Financial information
    6) Essay
  Additional information: See Web site for complete program and application information.
Program descriptions:
  Champions of Early Childhood Education Scholarship: Awards up to 15 scholarships for to full tuition plus a stipend for books and supplies to individuals committed to raising the quality of early childhood education (0-5) through pursuit of a Master of Science in Education Degree with a Concentration in Early Childhood at Indiana University South Bend. Deadline June 1.
  The Charles W. Cole Scholarship Program: Awards up to $1,000 toward tuition and fees to graduating seniors of John Adams High School, IN. Deadline Mar. 1.
  Donald C. and Marion E. Currier Scholarship: Scholarships of up to full tuition, required fees, and allowance for books, and a living allowance of up to 150% of the typical room and board amount charged by Purdue University. St Joseph County students who have been accepted into the School of Mechanical Engineering at Purdue University with a minimum 3.0 GPA are eligible. Deadline June 15.
  Officer Paul R. Deguch Memorial Scholarship: One award of up to $1,000 to St. Joseph County, IN, residents who have minimum GPA's of 2.5 and plan to pursue criminal justice degrees at Indiana University South Bend. Deadline Feb. 1.
  1st Source Scholarship Fund for Indiana University: Awards up to 50 percent tuition and book expenses to natural or legally adopted children of current 1st Source employees with thee years consecutive employment. Applicants must have a minimum 2.5 GPA. Deadline Mar. 1.
  International Brotherhood of Electrical Workers Local #153 Scholarship: Awards one scholarship of 20 percent of the per credit hour tuition cost of attendance at Indiana University South Bend to children and stepchildren of active union members. Deadline Mar. 1.
  Lilly Endowment Community Scholarships: Awards nine four-year, full-tuition scholarships to outstanding St. Joseph County, IN, high school seniors attending college in IN. Minimum 3.8 GPA or 1300 SAT score. Deadline Jan. 15.
  Katie McCloskey Memorial Scholarship: Awards one $1,000 award renewable for up to 7 semesters to a John Adams High School senior with athletic involvement for undergraduate education. Minimum GPA 2.5. Deadline Mar. 1.
  Southhold Historic Preservation Scholarship: One award of up to $1,000 to full-time graduate students or undergraduate students in their Junior or Senior year who are pursuing studies at the University of Notre Dame, University of Evansville, or Ball State University leading toward a degree in or related to historic preservation. Applicants must

be permanent residents of the state of Indiana, with preference given to St. Joseph County residents.
EIN: 237365930

907
Community Foundation of Switzerland County, Inc.
317 Ferry St.
P.O. Box 46
Vevay, IN 47043   (812) 427-9160
Contact: Pam Acton, Exec. Dir.
FAX: (812) 427-9173; E-mail: cfsci@cfsci.org;
URL: http://www.cfsci.org

Foundation type: Community foundation
Limitations: Scholarships to individuals residing in the Switzerland County, IN, area for undergraduate education.
Publications: Application guidelines; Annual report; Grants list; Informational brochure; Program policy statement; Program policy statement (including application guidelines).
Financial data: Year ended 12/31/2004. Assets, $6,785,124 (M); Expenditures, $281,161; Total giving, $106,548.
Type of support: Scholarships—to individuals; Support to graduates or students of specific schools; Undergraduate support.
Application information: Applications accepted. Application form required. Application form available on the grantmaker's Web site.
  Applicants should submit the following:
    1) SAT
    2) GPA
    3) Letter(s) of recommendation
    4) Transcripts
    5) Essay
  Additional information: See foundation Web site for complete listing of scholarship programs.
EIN: 352087649

908
The Community Foundation of the Elmira-Corning Area
(formerly The Community Foundation of the Chemung County Area and Corning Community Foundation)
307B E. Water St.
Elmira, NY 14901-3402   (607) 734-6412
Contact: Suzanne Lee, Pres.; For grant applications: Randi Hewitt, Prog. Off.
FAX: (607) 734-7335;
E-mail: shl@communityfund.org; E-mail for grant applications: rlh@communityfund.org; URL: http://www.communityfund.org

Foundation type: Community foundation
Limitations: Scholarships to NY area students.
Publications: Application guidelines; Annual report (including application guidelines); Financial statement; Newsletter.
Financial data: Year ended 06/30/2005. Assets, $15,720,450 (M); Expenditures, $1,253,662; Total giving, $897,729; Grants to individuals, 47 grants totaling $90,150 (high: $14,000, low: $150).
Fields of interest: Education, research; Nursing school/education; Athletics/sports, training; Human services; Business/industry; Science; Engineering.
Type of support: Employee-related scholarships; Scholarships—to individuals; Support to graduates or students of specific schools; Awards/grants by nomination only; Awards/prizes; Graduate support;

Technical education support; Undergraduate support; Camperships.
Application information: Application form required. Application form available on the grantmaker's Web site.
  Initial approach: Letter or e-mail.
  Copies of proposal: 1
  Deadline(s): Feb. 23
  Applicants should submit the following:
    1) Transcripts
    2) SAT
    3) Resume
    4) Letter(s) of recommendation
    5) GPA
    6) Financial information
    7) Essay
    8) ACT
  Additional information: Contact foundation for current application deadline/guidelines.
Program descriptions:
  Daniel Dobson Memorial Scholarship: Scholarships to employees of Cameron Fabricating Corporation and their family members who possess the desire, dedication, and interest in furthering their education either at the university level or at a technical school in the fields of engineering and the sciences.
  Chemung Canal Trust Company Scholarship: Four-year $6,000 scholarships to financially needy graduates of secondary schools in Chemung County or in any of the following school districts: Bath, Haverling, Corning East and West High Schools, Odessa-Montour, Spencer-VanEtten, Watkins Glen, Owego, and Waverly, all in NY.
  Carolyn Matthews Memorial Scholarship: $500 scholarships to high school seniors who have demonstrated a positive attitude, and made a significant contribution to the betterment of their school and community.
  West Elmira Volunteer Fire Department Scholarship: One-year $500 scholarships to residents of Fire District Number One in the Town of Elmira (includes most of West Elmira), seeking either an associate's or bachelor's degree. Recipients are selected on the basis of grades and scholarship, financial need, citizenship, community and school activities, and active membership in the West Elmira Fire Department.
  The Kurt and Ellen Wohl Scholarship: One-year scholarships to financially needy individuals who have lived in Chemung County, NY, for more than two years, are 25 or older, and have been accepted for a minimum of six credits per semester at a college, university, technical school, or nursing school within 55 miles of Elmira, NY. To be eligible, individuals must meet very specific household income requirements.
  Joyce P. Conroy Scholarship: $1,000 scholarships to matriculated, graduating seniors at Corning East/Corning West High schools, who intend on pursuing advanced education, including vocational training.
  William M. Cooper Scholarship: Four-year $6,000 scholarships to well-rounded Chemung County, NY, residents who are graduates from accredited Chemung County high schools, demonstrate maturity, leadership, and outstanding citizenship, and who have benefited from extracurricular activities.
  David P. Courtney Memorial Scholarship: Two-year $500 scholarships to financially needy graduates of Elmira Free Academy with average grades and a willingness to work hard, for tuition at Corning Community College. Preference may be shown toward students pursuing degrees in business administration, nursing, social work, or criminal justice.

Creighton-Buckley Scholarship: $500 scholarships to worthwhile and deserving students to attend Notre Dame High School.

Ernie Davis Scholarship: $12,000 scholarships to financially needy residents of Chemung County, NY, who have graduated from an accredited high school in Chemung County or from a public high school in Corning, NY. Candidates should have participated as a member of the varsity sports team in their high schools, exhibit excellent character, and plan to attend a four-year college, or a two-year college with the intent on transferring to a four-year college. In addition, applicants must be nominated by their high school principals and have demonstrated good citizenship in their high schools and in their communities.

Ann Baldwin Dedrick Scholarship: $500 scholarships to financially needy Horseheads High School graduates who are in the top fifth of their graduating classes. Preference is given to students majoring in education.

George Douglas/LPGA Corning Classic Scholarship: Four-year $4,000 scholarships to students of and graduating seniors at schools in the following counties: Chemung, Steuben, Schuyler, Allegany, and Tompkins, all in NY, or Bradford or Tioga counties, PA.

Evans Service Company Scholarship: One-year $1,000 scholarships to students with good scholastic records, evidence of good citizenship, a strong work ethic, and evidence of a firm desire for further education. Priority will be given to employees of Evans Service Company, Inc. and its subsidiaries, and their children.

Rodney H. Faught Memorial Scholarship: One-year $200 scholarships to physically disabled graduates from Chemung County, NY, high schools who have demonstrated qualities of excellence and determination in pursuit of their academic and career goals, for attendance at two- and four-year colleges and universities.

Harvey O. Hutchinson Memorial Scholarship: $4,000 scholarship to residents of Chemung County, NY, who have graduated from an accredited high school in the county.

The Stuart Komer Family Student Aid Fund Award: Graduate and undergraduate scholarships to Chemung County, NY, residents who are graduates of Chemung County, NY, high schools, and will attend two- or four-year accredited colleges and universities taking at least six credits per semester. Scholarships are renewable.

Mikkelsen Memorial Scholarship: Four-year $6,000 scholarships to Chemung County, NY, residents who have graduated from accredited high schools in that county. Preference is given to qualified children of employees, retirees, or deceased employees of Zeiser-Wilber Vault.

Josh Palmer Scholarship: One-year $250 scholarships to graduates of accredited high schools in Chemung, Steuben, and Schuyler, NY, and Tioga County, PA, who have participated in at least one year of a varsity sport.

Thomas J. Rosettie Memorial Scholarship: $1,000 scholarships to graduating seniors from Corning East High School, who have earned a varsity baseball letter during their senior year and have contributed the most to the varsity team based upon sportsmanship, integrity, the balancing of academic achievement, and athletic pursuit. Recipients are selected by the varsity baseball coach.

Rotary Ann's Scholarship: One-year $1,000 scholarships for attendance at two- or four-year accredited colleges and universities to Chemung County, NY, residents who have graduated from Chemung County, NY, high schools, and who embody the Rotary's motto of "service above self.".

Amy Snow Memorial Scholarship: Scholarships to graduating seniors at Corning Painted Post East High School who show a zest for life and learning, a strong commitment to schools and community, and the demonstrated belief in the good in all people.

Twin Tiers Youth For Christ Scholarship: $4,000 scholarships to Christian residents of Chemung County, NY, or an adjacent county, who have been residents for at least six months, and who are recommended by a pastor of a Christian church. Candidates must be enrolled in an accredited four-year college or university.

Harriet I. Wixon Memorial Scholarship: Four-year $4,000 scholarships to financially needy residents of Chemung County, NY, who are graduates of an accredited high school within that county.
EIN: 161100837

909
Community Foundation of the Great River Bend

(formerly Davenport Area Foundation)
111 E. 3rd St., Ste. 710
Davenport, IA 52801 (563) 326-2840
Contact: Susan S. Skora, C.E.O.
FAX: (563) 326-2870; E-mail: info@cfgrb.org;
Additional E-mail: susankora@cfgrb.org;
URL: http://www.cfgrb.org

Foundation type: Community foundation
Limitations: Scholarships, grants, and loans to individuals in the 12-county area of eastern IA and western IL who attend school in those areas.
Publications: Application guidelines; Annual report; Grants list; Informational brochure.
Financial data: Year ended 12/31/2004. Assets, $30,703,898 (M); Expenditures, $1,408,145; Total giving, $922,420; Grants to individuals, 57 grants totaling $169,911 (high: $22,000, low: $500).
Type of support: Program development; Conferences/seminars; Seed money; Technical education support; Precollege support; Undergraduate support; Travel grants.
Application information: Deadline Sept. 1 for Grants, Jan. 5 for Scholarships; Initial approach by letter; Completion of formal application required.
Program description:
Scholarship Program: The foundation offers several scholarship programs. See Web site for further information.
EIN: 426122716

910
The Community Foundation of the Holland/Zeeland Area

(formerly Holland Community Foundation, Inc.)
70 W. 8th St., Ste. 100
Holland, MI 49423 (616) 396-6590
Contact: Janet DeYoung, Exec. Dir.
FAX: (616) 396-3573; E-mail: info@cfhz.org;
Additional E-mail: janet@cfhz.org; URL: http://www.cfhz.org

Foundation type: Community foundation
Limitations: Scholarships to graduates of the Holland-Zeeland School District, MI.
Publications: Application guidelines; Annual report; Informational brochure; Informational brochure (including application guidelines); Newsletter.
Financial data: Year ended 12/31/2004. Assets, $22,308,089 (M); Expenditures, $2,916,521; Total giving, $2,579,111.

Type of support: Employee-related scholarships; Support to graduates or students of specific schools; Undergraduate support.
Application information: Application form required.
Deadline(s): Apr. 14
Applicants should submit the following:
1) Financial information
2) FAFSA
Additional information: Application available only at high school counseling offices.
EIN: 386095283

911
Community Foundation of the Ozarks

(formerly Community Foundation, Inc.)
425 E. Trafficway
Springfield, MO 65806 (417) 864-6199
Contact: Gary Funk, C.E.O.; Concept letter: Randy Russell, Sr. Prog. Off.; Concept letter: Gay Lynn Russell, Scholarship Coord.
FAX: (417) 864-8344; E-mail: gfunk@cfozarks.org; Additional tel.: (888) 266-6815; Concept letter E-mails: rrussell@cfozarks.org or grussell@cfozarks.org; URL: http://www.cfozarks.org

Foundation type: Community foundation
Limitations: Scholarships, grants, and awards to residents of Greene County, MO. See program description for further limitations.
Publications: Application guidelines; Annual report (including application guidelines); Informational brochure; Newsletter.
Financial data: Year ended 06/30/2005. Assets, $87,846,197 (M); Expenditures, $6,190,741; Total giving, $4,614,480.
Fields of interest: Vocational education; Teacher school/education; Students, sororities/fraternities; Athletics/sports, training; Chemistry; Mathematics; Physics; Government/public administration; Military/veterans' organizations.
Type of support: Seed money; Internship funds; Scholarships—to individuals; Support to graduates or students of specific schools; Awards/prizes; Technical education support; Undergraduate support; Grants for special needs.
Application information: Applications accepted. Application form required.
Initial approach: Letter.
Deadline(s): None
Additional information: See Web site for complete program and application information.
EIN: 237290968

912
Community Foundation of the Rappahannock River Region, Inc.

P.O. Box 208
Fredericksburg, VA 22404 (540) 373-9292
Contact: Teri McNally, Exec. Dir.
FAX: (540) 373-3050;
E-mail: cfrrr@midatlanticbb.com; Additional E-mail: TeriMcNally@cfrrr.org; URL: http://cfrrr.org

Foundation type: Community foundation
Limitations: Scholarships to residents of the Rappannock River region, VA.
Publications: Grants list; Informational brochure; Occasional report; Program policy statement.
Financial data: Year ended 06/30/2004. Assets, $2,469,598 (M); Expenditures, $263,233; Total giving, $169,305; Grants to individuals, totaling $9,300.
Type of support: Undergraduate support.

Application information: Application form required.
Initial approach: E-mail.
Applicants should submit the following:
   1) Essay
Additional information: Contact foundation for
   further application guidelines.
EIN: 541843987

913
Community Foundation of the Upper Peninsula

(formerly Upper Peninsula Community Foundation Alliance)
2500 7th Ave. S., Ste. 103
Escanaba, MI 49829-1176 (906) 789-5972
Contact: Gary LaPlant, Exec. Dir.
FAX: (906) 786-9124; E-mail: cfup@chartermi.net;
URL: http://cfup.org/about_CFUP.htm

Foundation type: Community foundation
Limitations: Scholarships to residents of the Upper Peninsula area of MI.
Publications: Application guidelines; Annual report; Financial statement; Informational brochure; Informational brochure (including application guidelines).
Financial data: Year ended 12/31/2004.
Assets, $8,356,884 (M); Expenditures, $1,192,119; Total giving, $886,119; Grants to individuals, 29 grants totaling $40,100 (high: $9,250, low: $200).
Type of support: Technical education support; Undergraduate support.
Application information: Applications accepted. Application form required.
Initial approach: Letter.
Additional information: Contact foundation for
   current application deadline.
EIN: 383227080

914
Community Foundation of Warren County

(formerly The Warren Foundation)
P.O. Box 691
Warren, PA 16365-0691 (814) 726-9553
Contact: Charles E. MacKenzie, Dir.
FAX: (814) 726-7099; E-mail: cfwc@westpa.net;
Additional E-mail: info@communityfoundationofwarrencounty.org;
URL: http://www.communityfoundationofwarrencounty.org
Alternate URL: http://www.warrenfoundationpa.org

Foundation type: Community foundation
Limitations: Scholarships only to residents of Warren County, PA, for nursing education, medical education, and general undergraduate education; also employee family scholarships for employees of Blair Corporation.
Publications: Annual report.
Financial data: Year ended 12/31/2004.
Assets, $36,431,527 (M); Expenditures, $1,440,493; Total giving, $1,266,752; Grants to individuals, 755 grants totaling $497,731 (high: $5,000, low: $250). Subtotal for scholarships—to individuals, 755 grants totaling $497,731 (high: $5,000, low: $250).
Fields of interest: Medical school/education; Nursing school/education.
Type of support: Employee-related scholarships; Graduate support; Technical education support; Undergraduate support.
Application information: Applications accepted. Application form required. Application form available on the grantmaker's Web site.

Initial approach: Application.
Copies of proposal: 1
Deadline(s): May 7
Applicants should submit the following:
   1) Transcripts
   2) SAT
   3) Letter(s) of recommendation
   4) GPA
   5) Financial information
EIN: 251380549

915
The Community Foundation of Western North Carolina, Inc.

The BB&T Bldg., Ste. 1600
1 W. Pack Sq., P.O. Box 1888
Asheville, NC 28802 (828) 254-4960
Contact: Pat Smith, Pres.; For scholarships: Maria Juarez, Scholarship Off.; Virginia Dollar, Prog. Admin.
FAX: (828) 251-2258; E-mail: dollar@cfwnc.org;
Additional E-mail: sandlin@cfwnc.org; Scholarship E-mail: juarez@cfwnc.org; URL: http://www.cfwnc.org

Foundation type: Community foundation
Limitations: Scholarships and research support, primarily to western NC students for higher education. Scholarships also to children of Shadowline, Inc. employees, NC.
Publications: Application guidelines; Annual report; Informational brochure (including application guidelines); Newsletter.
Financial data: Year ended 06/30/2005.
Assets, $125,267,848 (M); Expenditures, $8,007,919; Total giving, $6,496,545; Grants to individuals, totaling $408,136 (high: $10,000, low: $250).
Fields of interest: Music; Higher education; College (community/junior); Education.
Type of support: Employee-related scholarships; Scholarships—to individuals.
Application information: Application form required.
Initial approach: Letter or e-mail.
Copies of proposal: 1
Deadline(s): Varies
Applicants should submit the following:
   1) Transcripts
   2) SAT
   3) Letter(s) of recommendation
   4) GPA
   5) Financial information
   6) FAFSA
   7) Essay
   8) ACT
Additional information: See Web site for additional programs and current application guidelines; Applications available at local high schools guidance offices. Interviews may be required.
Program descriptions:
Richard (Yogi) Crowe Memorial Scholarship: Offers enrolled members of the Eastern Band of Cherokee Indians who are pursuing graduate or postgraduate education.
Little Mountaineer Scholarships: Provides scholarships for Western Carolina residents who are (in order of preference) dairy youths/students pursuing education related to the dairy industry, agriculture youths/students pursuing education related to the agriculture industry, or rural youths/students pursuing education that will lead to employment in a rural setting.
Ernest S. DeWick Memorial Scholarship: Provides scholarships for residents or former residents of the Swannanoa Valley (C.D. Owen High School district)

Carolina High Country Section 1103: American Society of Quality Scholarships: Provides scholarships for students in a field related to quality control and enrolled at Asheville-Buncombe Technical Community College, Blue Ridge Community College, Mayland Community College, McDowell Technical Community College, or the University of North Carolina at Asheville.
Cheri Roth Nate Scholarship: Provides scholarships for cello students in the Brevard Music Center summer program.
Rebekah Parker Memorial Scholarship: Scholarships for members of the Crossroads Assembly of God who are pursuing higher education or mission activities.
EIN: 561223384

916
Community Foundation Serving Greeley and Weld County

711 8th Ave.
Greeley, CO 80631-3955 (970) 304-9970
Contact: Judy Knapp, Pres.
FAX: (970) 352-1271;
E-mail: information1@greeleyweldcomfound.org;
Additional E-mails: info@greeleyweldcomfound.org and judy@greeleyweldcomfound.org; URL: http://www.greeleyweldcomfound.org

Foundation type: Community foundation
Limitations: Scholarships to individuals residing in Greeley and Weld counties, CO.
Publications: Application guidelines; Annual report; Financial statement; Informational brochure; Newsletter.
Financial data: Year ended 12/31/2004.
Assets, $10,447,103 (M); Expenditures, $1,247,283; Total giving, $1,101,593; Grants to individuals, totaling $288,676.
Fields of interest: Arts education; Arts; Vocational education; Nursing school/education; Hispanics/Latinos.
Type of support: Student loans—to individuals; Support to graduates or students of specific schools; Graduate support; Technical education support; Undergraduate support.
Application information: Applications accepted. Application form required.
Deadline(s): Varies
Additional information: See Web site for complete program and application information.
Program description:
Arts Alive Scholarship: Awards two scholarships of $1,000 each for attendance at Aims Community College or University of Northern Colorado. The foundation administers numerous other programs. See Web site for complete listing.
EIN: 841315296

917
The Community Foundation Serving Richmond & Central Virginia

(formerly Greater Richmond Community Foundation)
7325 Beaufant Springs Dr., Ste. 210
Richmond, VA 23225-5546 (804) 330-7400
Contact: Darcy S. Oman, C.E.O. and Pres.; For grants: Jill A. McCormick, Sr. Prog. Off.
FAX: (804) 330-5992;
E-mail: info@tcfrichmond.org; Additional E-mail: doman@tcfrichmond.org; Grant application E-mail: jmccormick@tcfrichmond.org; URL: http://www.tcfrichmond.org

Foundation type: Community foundation
Limitations: The foundation administers approximately 19 scholarship funds benefiting high school seniors from schools throughout central VA. Scholarships are paid directly to undergraduate colleges and universities.
Publications: Application guidelines; Annual report; Biennial report.
Financial data: Year ended 12/31/2004. Assets, $161,627,393 (M); Expenditures, $13,927,079; Total giving, $11,935,299.
Type of support: Support to graduates or students of specific schools; Undergraduate support.
Application information: Application form required.
  Deadline(s): Mar. 8
  Applicants should submit the following:
    1) Financial information
  Additional information: Interviews required.
EIN: 237009135

918

Community Foundation Sonoma County

(formerly The Sonoma County Community Foundation)
250 D St., Ste. 205
Santa Rosa, CA 95404-4773 (707) 579-4073
Contact: Kay M. Marquet, C.E.O.; For grants: Robert Judd, Dir., Progs.
FAX: (707) 579-4801;
E-mail: jharrison@sonomacf.org; Additional E-mail: Kmarquet@sonomacf.org; Grant inquiry E-mail: rjudd@sonomacf.org; URL: http://www.sonomacf.org

Foundation type: Community foundation
Limitations: Scholarships to individuals who are Sonoma County, CA, residents.
Publications: Application guidelines; Annual report; Financial statement; Informational brochure; Newsletter.
Financial data: Year ended 12/31/2004. Assets, $99,400,199 (M); Expenditures, $8,286,827; Total giving, $5,116,404.
Fields of interest: Arts, artist's services.
Type of support: Program development; Scholarships—to individuals.
Application information: Applications accepted. Application form required.
  Deadline(s): Mid-Mar., contact foundation for exact deadline.
  Additional information: Interviews required.
EIN: 680003212

919

The Community Hospital Auxiliary Scholarship Trust

(also known as Munster Medical Foundation, Inc.)
901 MacArthur Blvd.
Munster, IN 46321-2901

Foundation type: Independent foundation
Limitations: Scholarships to eligible dependents of qualified employees of Munster Medical Research Foundation, Inc.
Financial data: Year ended 01/31/2005. Assets, $552,596 (M); Expenditures, $26,004; Total giving, $21,000; Grants to individuals, totaling $21,000.
Type of support: Employee-related scholarships.
Application information: Contact trust for current application deadline/guidelines; Initial approach by letter or telephone.
EIN: 356595973

920

Community Nursing Services in Greensburg, Inc.

P.O. Box 98
Greensburg, PA 15601 (724) 837-6827

Foundation type: Independent foundation
Limitations: Scholarships to individuals studying in a health care field, who reside in South Greensburg, Southwest Greensburg, Youngwood, West Newton, Hempfield, North Huntingdon, Salem, Sewicky or Unity, PA.
Financial data: Year ended 04/30/2005. Assets, $1,411,114 (M); Expenditures, $71,993; Total giving, $57,000; Grants to individuals, totaling $57,000.
Fields of interest: Health sciences school/education.
Type of support: Graduate support; Undergraduate support.
Application information: Deadline Mar. 20; Initial approach by letter; Completion of formal application required; Interviews required.
EIN: 250967471

921

Community Projects, Inc.

715 Franklin St.
Napa, CA 94559-2920 (707) 226-7585
Contact: Gaylon Castner, Pres.; Scholarships: J. Miller

Foundation type: Public charity
Limitations: Four-year scholarships to graduating students attending one of the following Napa Valley, CA, schools: Callistoga High School, St. Helena High School, Justin-Siaena High School, Vintage High School, Napa High School, New Technology High School, Napa Valley College.
Financial data: Year ended 12/31/2003. Assets, $1,669,131 (M); Expenditures, $393,443; Total giving, $231,951.
Type of support: Support to graduates or students of specific schools; Undergraduate support.
Application information: Application by letter outlining financial need; Applications available through guidance counselors at the specified schools.
EIN: 941229581

922

Community Welfare Association of Colquitt County, GA

P.O. Box 38
Moultrie, GA 31776-0038 (229) 890-6142
Contact: Fay T. Smith, Guidance Coord.
Application address: c/o Colquitt County High School, 1800 Park Ave., Moultrie, GA 31768

Foundation type: Independent foundation
Limitations: Scholarships to residents of Colquitt County, GA, and to graduates of Colquitt County High School, GA.
Financial data: Year ended 12/31/2004. Assets, $4,711,170 (M); Expenditures, $265,252; Total giving, $210,720; Grants to individuals, 6 grants totaling $6,000 (high: $1,500, low: $750).
Type of support: Support to graduates or students of specific schools; Undergraduate support.
Application information: Applications accepted throughout the year; Completion of formal application required; For Colquitt County High School program one student per year is selected to receive this scholarship.
EIN: 586032259

923

Noel Compass Foundation, Inc.

1145 Clark St.
Stevens Point, WI 54481
Contact: Carol Torline, Secy.

Foundation type: Operating foundation
Limitations: Scholarships to financially needy students from at-risk environments attending the University of Wisconsin, Stevens Point, who have shown academic or leadership qualities in their high school careers.
Financial data: Year ended 12/31/2004. Assets, $229,697 (M); Expenditures, $125,298; Total giving, $81,319; Grants to individuals, 13 grants totaling $80,919.
Type of support: Undergraduate support.
Application information: Deadline Jan. 31; Completion of formal application required.
EIN: 391837771

924

The Compass Fund, Inc.

(formerly Navarro Family Foundation, Inc.)
95 Glastonbury Blvd., Box 22
Glastonbury, CT 06033 (860) 659-0050
Contact: Michele Hull
URL: http://www.thecompassfund.org

Foundation type: Independent foundation
Limitations: Scholarships to children of low and moderate-income families residing in New London, CT.
Financial data: Year ended 12/31/2004. Assets, $1,076,080 (M); Expenditures, $153,529; Total giving, $131,012; Grants to individuals, 64 grants totaling $121,191 (high: $2,500, low: $1,288).
Fields of interest: Economically disadvantaged.
Type of support: Precollege support.
Application information: Unsolicited requests for funds not considered or acknowledged.
Program description:
  The Compass Scholarship Program: Families awarded the scholarship will be able to enroll their children in the school of their choice. The fund will pay eighty percent of the tuition, up to $2,500 for any public or private school.
EIN: 061602643

925

Compton Courts Scholarship Fund

1228 Dimondale Dr.
Carson, CA 90746-3159
Contact: Thomas N. Townsend, Chair.
Application address: P.O. Box 4383, Carson, CA 90749-4383, tel.: (310) 604-8311

Foundation type: Independent foundation
Limitations: Scholarships to residents of Compton, Carson, Lynwood, Paramount, Athens, and Willowbrook, CA.
Financial data: Year ended 12/31/2004. Assets, $9,911 (M); Expenditures, $9,389; Total giving, $8,900; Grants to individuals, totaling $8,900.
Type of support: Scholarships—to individuals; Undergraduate support.
Application information: Applications accepted.
  Deadline(s): Apr. 3
  Additional information: Application by letter outlining financial need, including name, address, and telephone number, transcripts, letter of recommendation signed by at least one teacher, a list of other scholarships

received or applied for, and all other relevant information.

Program description:

Scholarship Program: Scholarship recipients are required to commit to help their community through church activities, school activities, and community service programs. In addition, all applicants must participate in an interview at the courthouse and attend a luncheon in their honor. Residents of Long Beach, Wilmington, and South Gate, CA, are not within the jurisdictional boundaries of the scholarship program. Applicants must live in Compton Judicial District and recipients must maintain a "B" average and provide documented services to the community.

EIN: 953752951

926

Comstock Memorial Scholarship Trust

(formerly James A. Comstock Memorial Scholarship Trust)
c/o Bank of America, N.A.
10 Light St., MD4-302-17-06
Baltimore, MD   21202
Application address: c/o Bank of America, N.A., 10 Fountain Plz., Buffalo, NY 14202

Foundation type: Independent foundation
Limitations: Scholarships to children of employees of Acme Electric Corp.
Financial data: Year ended 05/31/2005.
Assets, $2,384,456 (M); Expenditures, $129,182; Total giving, $108,100.
Type of support: Employee-related scholarships.
Application information:
  Deadline(s): Jan. 31
  Additional information: Completion of formal application required, including a personal essay, teacher recommendation, transcript, and SAT or ACT scores.
EIN: 222327403

927

Moses Cone-Wesley Long Community Health Foundation

(formerly Wesley Long Community Health Foundation, Inc.)
721 Green Valley Rd., Ste. 102
P.O. Box 4426
Greensboro, NC   27404-4426   (336) 832-9555
Contact: Antonia Reaves, V.P. and Chief Prog. Off.
FAX: (336) 832-9559;
E-mail: foundation@mosescone.com; URL: http://www.mcwlhealthfoundation.org

Foundation type: Public charity
Limitations: Scholarships to Greensboro, NC, students who are pursuing a degree in nursing.
Publications: Application guidelines; Annual report; Informational brochure; Newsletter.
Financial data: Year ended 09/30/2004.
Assets, $110,213,975 (M); Expenditures, $6,594,251; Total giving, $5,233,620.
Fields of interest: Nursing school/education.
Type of support: Graduate support.
Application information: Applications not accepted.
  Additional information: Unsolicited requests for funds not considered or acknowledged.
EIN: 562001399

928

Confort Foundation Trust

c/o Martin L. Riker
660 White Plains Rd., Ste. 450
Tarrytown, NY   10591
Application address: c/o Scholarship Coordinator, 47-47 Austell Pl., Long Island City, NY 11101

Foundation type: Independent foundation
Limitations: Scholarships to high school seniors and eighth-grade students who are dependent children of Confort & Co., Inc. employees in good standing with at least two years of service. Scholarships also to qualified students who are unrelated to employees, but are recommended by them. Recipients may attend accredited colleges, universities, or private high schools.
Financial data: Year ended 12/31/2004.
Assets, $426,329 (M); Expenditures, $143,709; Total giving, $141,225; Grants to individuals, 54 grants totaling $123,500 (high: $37,500, low: $989).
Fields of interest: Secondary school/education; Higher education.
Type of support: Employee-related scholarships; Undergraduate support.
Application information:
  Deadline(s): Mar. 15
  Additional information: For college scholarships, completion of formal application required, including SAT scores, GPA, letters of recommendation from guidance counselor and at least one teacher, parents' or student's tax return, and FAFSA form or SAR; For high school scholarships, completion of formal application required, including seventh grade report and co-op scores (if taken).
Program description:
  Scholarship Program: Scholarships are awarded on the basis of scholastic aptitude and achievement, personal integrity and responsibility, and financial need. Scholarships are renewable provided recipient maintains full-time status and a 2.0 GPA.
EIN: 137053704

929

Congressional Hispanic Caucus Institute

911 2nd St., N.E.
Washington, DC   20002   (202) 543-1771
Contact: Ingrid Duran, Pres. and C.E.O.
FAX: (202) 546-2143; Additional tel.: (800) EXCEL-DC; URL: http://www.chci.org/

Foundation type: Public charity
Limitations: Internships, including transportation reimbursement, housing, and stipends, to promising Latino undergraduate students. The Caucus also provides scholarships to undergraduate and graduate Latinos as well as fellowships to allow promising Latinos to participate in public service.
Financial data: Year ended 12/31/2003.
Assets, $5,191,713 (M); Expenditures, $2,128,640; Total giving, $256,000; Grants to individuals, 54 grants totaling $256,000 (high: $5,000, low: $1,500).
Fields of interest: Leadership development; Public affairs; Hispanics/Latinos.
Type of support: Fellowships; Internship funds; Graduate support; Undergraduate support; Travel grants; Stipends.
Application information: Applications accepted. Application form required. Application form available on the grantmaker's Web site.
  Deadline(s): Jan. 31 for internships; Feb. 28 for fellowship; Apr. 15 for scholarships

Applicants should submit the following:
  1) Transcripts
  2) Letter(s) of recommendation
  3) SAR
  4) Resume
  5) Financial information
  6) Essay
Program descriptions:
  Fellowship Program: Available to 21 promising Latinos from across the country, providing the opportunity to gain hands-on experience at the national level in the public policy area of their choice. Participants are provided round-trip transportation to Washington, DC, health insurance and a monthly stipend of $2,061. Fellows with a graduate degree receive a monthly stipend of $2,500.
  Scholarships: Awards scholarships to Latino students who have a history of performing public service-oriented activities in their communities and who plan to continue contributing in the future. Scholarships of $2,500 are given to recipients to attend a four-year or graduate-level academic institution or $1,000 to attend a two-year community college.
  Summer Internship Program: Available to 30 promising Latino undergraduate students and recent college graduates to explore their interests in the public policy arena while living in Washington, D.C. Participants are provided with a $2,000 stipend, round-trip transportation, and summer housing.
EIN: 521114225

930

Conn Appliances Charitable Foundation, Inc.

3295 College St.
Beaumont, TX   77701
Additional address: P.O. Box 2358, Beaumont, TX 77704, tel.: (409) 835-3496

Foundation type: Company-sponsored foundation
Limitations: Scholarships to children of employees of Conn Appliances, Inc.
Financial data: Year ended 11/30/2004.
Assets, $3,488 (M); Expenditures, $27,300; Total giving, $26,700.
Type of support: Employee-related scholarships.
Application information:
  Deadline(s): None
  Additional information: Applications should be sent by letter.
EIN: 741884559

931

Conn Memorial Foundation, Inc.

2910 W. Bay to Bay Blvd., Ste. 200
Tampa, FL   33629   (813) 282-4922
Contact: Maggie Osborn, Dir., Grants

Foundation type: Independent foundation
Limitations: Scholarships to residents of Hillsborough and Pinellas counties, FL.
Publications: Informational brochure (including application guidelines).
Financial data: Year ended 07/31/2005.
Assets, $22,550,138 (M); Expenditures, $1,282,598; Total giving, $889,905.
Type of support: Scholarships—to individuals.
Application information: Applications accepted. Application form required.
  Initial approach: Letter.
  Deadline(s): May 15 and Nov. 15
EIN: 590978713

932
The Connecticut Community Foundation
(formerly The Waterbury Foundation)
43 Field St.
Waterbury, CT 06702 (203) 753-1315
FAX: (203) 756-3054; E-mail: info@conncf.org;
URL: http://conncf.org

Foundation type: Community foundation
Limitations: Undergraduate scholarships to students residing in the foundation's 21-town service area. Priority is given to students with a "B" average, attending schools in CT.
Publications: Application guidelines; Annual report; Newsletter.
Financial data: Year ended 12/31/2004. Assets, $45,044,484 (M); Expenditures, $2,555,025; Total giving, $1,667,423; Grants to individuals, 217 grants totaling $283,824 (high: $5,200, low: $75).
Fields of interest: Arts education; Media/communications; Journalism/publishing; Humanities; Literature; Education, research; Secondary school/education; Education, special; Nursing school/education; Reading; Education; Mathematics; Disabilities, people with; African Americans/Blacks; Women.
Type of support: Scholarships—to individuals; Undergraduate support.
Application information: Application form required. Application form available on the grantmaker's Web site.
   Initial approach: Telephone, e-mail, or
      application.
   Copies of proposal: 4
   Deadline(s): Mar. 1
   Applicants should submit the following:
      1) Essay
      2) Financial information
      3) GPA
      4) Letter(s) of recommendation
   Additional information: Applications should be
      mailed; Responses to applications given 8
      weeks after submission.
Program description:
   Scholarship Program: The foundation administers approximately 40 scholarship funds. Most recipients must live in the foundation's service area. Preference is shown to students attending local colleges. Criteria for specific funds may vary.
EIN: 066038074

933
John F. Connelly Scholarship Fund
1 Crown Way, Tax Dept.
Philadelphia, PA 19154-4599
Contact: Gary Burgess

Foundation type: Independent foundation
Limitations: Scholarships only to children of employees of Crown Cork & Seal Co., Inc. to pursue undergraduate study at accredited colleges, universities, and technical/vocational schools in the U.S. and worldwide.
Financial data: Year ended 12/31/2004. Assets, $3,247,995 (M); Expenditures, $193,167; Total giving, $192,000; Grants to individuals, 96 grants totaling $192,000 (high: $2,000, low: $2,000).
Fields of interest: Vocational education.
Type of support: Employee-related scholarships; Technical education support.
Application information: Applications accepted throughout the year; Contact fund for current application guidelines.

Program description:
   Scholarship Program: Scholarships of up to $2,500 are for one year and are not renewable. One hundred recipients are chosen through a random drawing of qualified applicants on the 4th Thursday of Apr. each year.
EIN: 232667541

934
Edward & Elizabeth Conner Foundation
c/o Larussi, Gelhaus & Hauskens
3189 Danville Blvd., Ste. 160
Alamo, CA 94507-1982
E-mail: connerfound@aol.com; Application address: c/o Kathleen Conner, 1164 Van Buren Ave., Venice, CA 90291

Foundation type: Operating foundation
Limitations: Scholarships to graduates of Liberty High School, Brentwood, CA, and Greene Central High School, NY, for postsecondary education in 2-year institution.
Financial data: Year ended 12/31/2004. Assets, $2,105,017 (M); Expenditures, $136,513; Total giving, $114,550; Grants to individuals, 48 grants totaling $92,050 (high: $4,000, low: $150).
Type of support: Support to graduates or students of specific schools; Undergraduate support.
Application information: Deadline 45 days before scholarship is required; Applications must be made through Liberty High School or Greene Central High School guidance departments.
EIN: 946131053

935
James C. & Elizabeth R. Conner Foundation
204 S. Wellington St., Ste. A
Marshall, TX 75670-4056 (903) 938-0331
Contact: Robert L. Duvall, Chair.; R. Michael Hallum, Secy.
FAX: (903) 938-0334; E-mail:
bd-kdh&co@internetgcs.net

Foundation type: Independent foundation
Limitations: Graduate and doctoral scholarships to deserving students in the fields of business, engineering, medical science, or physical science, who graduated in the top ten percent of their undergraduate class.
Publications: Annual report; Annual report (including application guidelines).
Financial data: Year ended 12/31/2004. Assets, $3,751,495 (M); Expenditures, $244,822; Total giving, $220,094; Grants to individuals, 15 grants totaling $220,094 (high: $37,434, low: $768).
Fields of interest: Business school/education; Medical school/education; Engineering school/education; Science; Physical/earth sciences.
Type of support: Fellowships; Graduate support; Doctoral support.
Application information: Applications accepted. Application form required.
   Initial approach: Letter or telephone.
   Deadline(s): May 31 for Fall
   Applicants should submit the following:
      1) Transcripts
      2) Photograph
   Additional information: Interviews required for
      finalists.
EIN: 752302882

936
The Jim Conner Foundation
1030 State St.
Erie, PA 16501 (814) 456-9322
Contact: William B. Conner, Pres.

Foundation type: Independent foundation
Limitations: Scholarships to graduates of McDowell High School, Erie, PA, for higher education.
Financial data: Year ended 06/30/2005. Assets, $245,077 (M); Expenditures, $30,485; Total giving, $29,750; Grants to individuals, 18 grants totaling $27,750 (high: $2,000, low: $750).
Type of support: Support to graduates or students of specific schools; Undergraduate support.
Application information: Deadline one month prior to graduation; Application by letter, including transcript and evidence of need.
EIN: 251320114

937
Alice Conner Trust
c/o Iowa State Bank & Trust Co.
612 Locust St.
Des Moines, IA 50309-3701
Application address: c/o Scholarship Selection Comm., P.O. Box 16268, Des Moines, IA 50316

Foundation type: Independent foundation
Limitations: Scholarships to residents of IA to attend IA colleges and universities.
Financial data: Year ended 12/31/2004. Assets, $353,292 (M); Expenditures, $22,186; Total giving, $18,000; Grants to individuals, totaling $18,000.
Type of support: Scholarships—to individuals.
Application information: Application form required.
   Initial approach: Letter.
   Deadline(s): Mar. 1
   Applicants should submit the following:
      1) Transcripts
      2) Letter(s) of recommendation
Program description:
   Scholarship Program: Applicants must have at least a 2.5 GPA.
EIN: 426430160

938
ConocoPhillips Dependent Scholarship Program Trust
(formerly Educational Fund for Children of Phillips Petroleum Company Employees)
1650 PB
Bartlesville, OK 74004
Contact: Ron Stanley, Dir., Educational Funds

Foundation type: Company-sponsored foundation
Limitations: Scholarships to high school seniors who are children, adopted children, stepchildren, or fully-dependent wards of present, former, or deceased full-time employees of ConocoPhillips or its domestic subsidiaries.
Financial data: Year ended 08/31/2002. Assets, $0 (M); Expenditures, $372,155; Total giving, $369,000; Grants to individuals, 180 grants totaling $369,000 (high: $6,000, low: $1,000).
Fields of interest: Higher education.
Type of support: Employee-related scholarships.
Application information: Application form required.
   Deadline(s): Mar. 1
   Applicants should submit the following:
      1) Photograph
   Additional information: Application should also
      include family financial statement,
      standardized test scores, and a report from

student's school principal; Scholarship application address: 1646 Phillips Bldg., Bartlesville, OK 74004, tel.: (918) 661-6248.

Program description:

Scholarship Program: Recipients are chosen by an independent selection committee based on financial need, academic achievement, and future promise. Scholarship awards are $8,000 each, payable over four years at $2,000 per year. Yearly extensions of the award must be consecutive unless the recipient is in active military service. Recipients must maintain full-time status and must submit a formal progress report at the end of each semester. Recipients may attend accredited junior colleges if they work towards bachelor's degree requirements. Students who are not children of employees but are full, live-in dependents of an employee-relative may be judged eligible by the selection committee. In order for an employee's dependent to be eligible, the employee must have been working full-time for at least two years. Children of permanently disabled or deceased employees who worked full-time for at least three years are also eligible. Children of the principal officers of ConnocoPhillips are ineligible.

EIN: 736095141

939
R. J. Conrad Charitable Foundation

P.O. Box 144
Oakmont, PA 15139
Contact: Jeffrey M. Thompson, Tr.

Foundation type: Independent foundation
Limitations: Scholarships to students in PA for higher education.
Financial data: Year ended 12/31/2004. Assets, $261,415 (M); Expenditures, $17,871; Total giving, $15,000; Grants to individuals, totaling $15,000.
Type of support: Undergraduate support.
Application information: Contact foundation for current application deadline/guidelines.
EIN: 237863991

940
Construction Careers Foundation

P.O. Box 965
Cheyenne, WY 82003
Contact: Charles Ware, Exec. V.P.

Foundation type: Public charity
Limitations: Scholarships to individuals for education and training in the construction industry.
Publications: Informational brochure; Occasional report.
Financial data: Year ended 12/31/2004. Assets, $2,737,252 (M); Expenditures, $101,544; Total giving, $48,664.
Fields of interest: Vocational education.
Type of support: Technical education support; Undergraduate support.
Application information: Contact foundation for current application deadlines/guidelines.
EIN: 830319926

941
Rosalie Conte Foundation

c/o First Tennessee Bank, N.A.
P.O. Box 84
Memphis, TN 38101
Application address: c/o Andrea Conte, Dir., 1724 Chickering Rd., Nashville, TN 37215

Foundation type: Independent foundation
Limitations: Scholarships for higher education to at least one student who resides within the public school district serving the Great Barrington, MA, area.
Financial data: Year ended 12/31/2004. Assets, $298,150 (M); Expenditures, $17,217; Total giving, $13,500; Grants to individuals, totaling $13,500.
Type of support: Undergraduate support.
Application information: Applications accepted throughout the year.
EIN: 581849183

942
Sally Conti Scholarship

13035 Willow Way
Golden, CO 80401-6307 (303) 237-6685
Contact: Richard F. Conti, Pres.

Foundation type: Independent foundation
Limitations: Scholarships to seniors at Arvada West High School who attended Fremont Elementary School, CO, for higher education.
Financial data: Year ended 12/31/2004. Assets, $4,922 (M); Expenditures, $4,040; Total giving, $4,000; Grants to individuals, totaling $4,000.
Type of support: Support to graduates or students of specific schools; Technical education support; Undergraduate support.
Application information: Deadline May 10; Completion of formal application required, including transcript, essay of no more than one page, and two letters of recommendation (one from a teacher or counselor and one from someone who is not a relative).

Program description:

Scholarship Program: Scholarships are meant to cover tuition and fees at the university, college or trade school of recipient's choice. Scholarships are renewable annually for a total of four years. Recipients must maintain a minimum GPA of "C.".
EIN: 841331801

943
Continental Divide Electric Education Foundation

P.O. Box 1087
Grants, NM 87020 (505) 285-6656
Contact: Lynn Head, Pres.

Foundation type: Company-sponsored foundation
Limitations: Undergraduate scholarships to active members, or the immediate family of active members, of Continental Divide Electric Cooperative, Inc. to attend accredited colleges and universities in AZ and NM.
Financial data: Year ended 12/31/2004. Assets, $1,669,393 (M); Expenditures, $81,187; Total giving, $66,750; Grants to individuals, totaling $66,750.
Type of support: Undergraduate support.
Application information: Application form required.
   Deadline(s): May 1
   Applicants should submit the following:
      1) Transcripts
      2) Essay
   Additional information: Application should also include basic information on applicant's background and academic achievements, and three letters of recommendation from guidance counselors, principals, superintendent, or teachers; Applicants notified by May 31.

Program description:

Scholarship Program: Recipients are awarded $1,500 per year for up to four years, provided a GPA of at least 2.5 is maintained. Recipients must use the scholarship to attend a school in their state of residence, either AZ or NM. Recipients are chosen on the basis of academic accomplishment and character. For the purposes of this scholarship, an "active member" of Continental Divide Electric Cooperative is defined as any consumer who has paid the $5 cooperative membership and receives power from the cooperative.
EIN: 850365720

944
Marvin H. & Gretchen V. Cook Educational Trust

c/o The Fountain Trust Co.
P. O. Box 8
Covington, IN 47932-0008 (765) 793-2237

Foundation type: Independent foundation
Limitations: Scholarships to residents of Troy, Wabash, Fulton, Van Buren, and Milcreek townships in Fountain County, IN.
Financial data: Year ended 12/31/2004. Assets, $434,751 (M); Expenditures, $11,316; Total giving, $10,600; Grants to individuals, totaling $10,600.
Type of support: Undergraduate support.
Application information: Deadline June 1; Completion of formal application required, including financial information, personal statement, high school transcripts, class rank, and SAT scores.
EIN: 356040497

945
Loring Cook Foundation

P.O. Box 1060
McAllen, TX 78505
Scholarship application address: c/o Counselor, McAllen Memorial High School, McAllen, TX 78501, tel.: (956) 686-5491

Foundation type: Independent foundation
Limitations: Scholarships to graduating seniors of McAllen Memorial High School, TX.
Financial data: Year ended 12/31/2004. Assets, $3,319,912 (M); Expenditures, $176,273; Total giving, $170,900.
Type of support: Support to graduates or students of specific schools; Undergraduate support.
Application information: Application form required.
   Deadline(s): Mar. 1.
   Additional information: Interviews required.
EIN: 746050063

946
Kelly Gene Cook, Sr. Charitable Foundation, Inc.

278 Waterford Way
Montgomery, TX 77356-8334
Contact: Peggy Cook Pool, Pres.
Application address: c/o Carolyn Bost, 1675 Lakeland Dr., Ste. 507; Jackson, MS 39216, tel.: (601) 981-1116; FAX: (601) 981-1146; E-mail: Pegpool@aol.com, or kgccf@ayrix.net

Foundation type: Independent foundation
Limitations: Undergraduate and graduate scholarships to students attending specific schools in IL, LA, MS, NC, TN, and TX. See program description for school list.

Financial data: Year ended 12/31/2004. Assets, $31,572,062 (M); Expenditures, $1,602,062; Total giving, $1,315,124; Grants to individuals, 85 grants totaling $708,630.
Type of support: Support to graduates or students of specific schools; Graduate support; Undergraduate support.
Application information: Application form required.
  Deadline(s): Apr. 15
  Additional information: Applications should include financial information, and be sent to the financial aid office of the named institutions. Interviews required.
Program description:
  Scholarship Awards: To be eligible, students must attend school full-time (15 hours) and maintain a satisfactory GPA. Recipients cannot be physical education majors, married, or have children. Recipients who maintain a 3.0 GPA in their undergraduate studies are eligible to receive $6,000 for their first year of graduate study. Students at the following schools may be eligible: Blinn Community College, TX, Duke University, NC, Holmes Community College, MS, Millsaps College, MS, Mississippi College, MS, Mississippi State University, MS, Northeast Mississippi Community College, MS, Northwestern University, IL, Rhodes College, TN, Southwest Texas State University, TX, Tougaloo College, MS, Tulane University, LA, University of Memphis, TN, University of Mississippi, MS, University of North Carolina School of Law, NC, University of Tennessee Medical School, TN, Vanderbilt University, TN, Vanderbilt University School of Law, TN.
EIN: 760201807

947
Robert W. Cooke Educational Fund
c/o Wells Fargo Bank Northwest, N.A.
P.O. Box 21927, MAC P8540-144
Seattle, WA 98111
Application address: c/o J.F. and R.W. Cooke Educational Fund Comm., Attn.: Secy., Scholarship Comm., Condon, OR 97823

Foundation type: Independent foundation
Limitations: Scholarships to graduates of Gilliam County High School who are residents of Gilliam County, OR.
Financial data: Year ended 05/31/2004. Assets, $524,241 (M); Expenditures, $31,683; Total giving, $23,175; Grants to individuals, totaling $23,175.
Type of support: Support to graduates or students of specific schools; Undergraduate support.
Application information: Deadline June 30; Completion of formal application required.
Program description:
  Scholarship Program: For each year of assistance, recipients must maintain a GPA of 2.0 and complete a minimum of 45 quarter hours, or the equivalent.
EIN: 936017308

948
Jack Kent Cooke Foundation
44325 Woodridge Pkwy.
Lansdowne, VA 20176 (703) 723-8000
Contact: Matthew J. Quinn, Exec. Dir.
Application address: Jack Kent Cooke Foundation, ACT, P.O. Box 4030, Iowa City, IA 52243
FAX: (703) 723-8030;
E-mail: jkc@jackkentcookefoundation.org;
URL: http://www.jackkentcookefoundation.org

Foundation type: Independent foundation

Limitations: Scholarships by nomination only to students or recent alumni from community colleges or two-year institutions who plan to transfer to four-year institutions and to students or recent bachelor's degree recipients who plan to enter a full-time graduate or professional degree program. Scholarships also to students entering high school as well as to dependents of Sept. 11 victims.
Publications: Application guidelines; Financial statement; Grants list; Informational brochure.
Financial data: Year ended 05/31/2005. Assets, $592,886,751 (M); Expenditures, $17,792,770; Total giving, $10,475,884; Grants to individuals, 387 grants totaling $7,699,297 (high: $50,000, low: $302).
Fields of interest: College (community/junior); Disasters, 9/11/01.
Type of support: Awards/grants by nomination only; Graduate support; Precollege support; Undergraduate support.
Application information: Applications accepted. Application form required.
  Deadline(s): Varies
  Additional information: See Web site for further application and program information.
Program descriptions:
  Graduate Scholarship Program: Awards approximately 35 scholarships by nomination only for tuition, room and board, required fees, and books for up to six years of graduate or professional study. Criteria include academic ability, financial need, and will to succeed. Scholarship amounts vary for each recipient based on several factors, including costs at the institution he or she attends; awards cannot exceed $50,000 annually. Applicants must have a cumulative undergraduate GPA of at least 3.5 on a 4.0 scale. Candidates must be nominated by the Jack Kent Cooke Foundation faculty representative at their undergraduate institution. Deadline generally May 1.
  Young Scholars Program: Selects highly able youth (7th graders) and provides them throughout high school with individualized educational counseling and services to help them develop their talents and abilities. Criteria include academic ability, financial need, and will to succeed. Deadline May 1.
  Undergraduate Transfer Scholarship: Awards approximately 25 scholarships to students currently attending community colleges or two-year institutions and planning to transfer to four-year institutions in the fall. Scholarships awards provide funding for tuition, room and board, books, and other required fees for the remainder of the Jack Kent Cooke Scholar's bachelor's degree, generally two years. The amount and duration of awards will vary by student based on the cost of attendance and the length of the program as well as other scholarships or grants received. The maximum available per student is $30,000 per year. Candidates must have a minimum GPA of 3.5 on a 4.0 scale, demonstrate financial need, and the will to succeed. Candidates for this scholarship must be nominated by the Jack Kent Cooke Foundation Faculty Representative at their two-year institution. Deadline generally Feb. 1.
  Bridges to Tomorrow Grant Program: Provides undergraduate scholarships to any two-year, four-year, technical or trade school in the U.S. to spouses or dependents of people killed or permanently disabled in the attacks on the Pentagon and World Trade Center, the crash of United Airlines Flight 93 in PA, and the Sept. and Oct. 2001 anthrax attacks. Deadlines Jan. 15 and Sept. 15.
EIN: 541896244

949
J. S. Cooley Educational Trust Fund
c/o Marshall National Bank & Trust Co.
P.O. Box 38
Marshall, VA 20116-0038

Foundation type: Independent foundation
Limitations: Educational loans to residents of Clarke, Culpeper, Fauquier, Frederick, Loudoun, Rappahanock, and Warren counties, VA, for four-year college and university programs in VA.
Financial data: Year ended 08/31/2003. Assets, $102,598 (M); Expenditures, $179; Total giving, $0; Loans to individuals, totaling $20,067.
Type of support: Student loans—to individuals.
Application information: Applications accepted throughout the year; Initial approach by contacting trustee bank.
EIN: 521274701

950
Verne Cooper Foundation, Inc.
1400 W. Russell Ave.
Bonham, TX 75418-2341 (903) 583-5574
Contact: Steve Mohundro, Secy.

Foundation type: Independent foundation
Limitations: Scholarships to residents of Fanin County, TX.
Financial data: Year ended 12/31/2004. Assets, $2,328,430 (M); Expenditures, $94,247; Total giving, $85,367.
Type of support: Scholarships—to individuals.
Application information: Deadline May 1; Completion of formal application required.
EIN: 752547151

951
Charles Cooper Industrial School
c/o Laraine B. Smith, Chittenden Trust Co.
87 West St.
Rutland, VT 05701
Application address: c/o Dorothy Smith, 255 Union St., Bennington, VT 05201

Foundation type: Independent foundation
Limitations: Student loans for higher education to Bennington County, VT, residents.
Financial data: Year ended 12/31/2004. Assets, $1,282,452 (M); Expenditures, $23,870; Total giving, $0; Loans to individuals, totaling $69,000.
Type of support: Student loans—to individuals.
Application information: Completion of formal application required, including application fee and 3 reference letters.
EIN: 036010636

952
William F. Cooper Scholarship Trust
c/o Wachovia Bank, N.A.
100 N. Main St., 13th Fl.
Winston-Salem, NC 27150 (404) 332-4987
Contact: Randy Karesh, Trust Off.
Scholarship Web site: URL: http://www.wachoviascholars.com.copr_2006_ins.htm

Foundation type: Independent foundation
Limitations: Scholarships to financially needy, worthy females of "good family." Preference is given to those residing in Chatham County, GA. No support is given for the study of theology, law, or medicine.
Financial data: Year ended 12/31/2004. Assets, $1,923,163 (M); Expenditures, $83,841;

Total giving, $80,612; Grants to individuals, totaling $80,612.
Fields of interest: Women.
Type of support: Undergraduate support.
Application information: Application form required.
Deadline(s): May 15
Applicants should submit the following:
1) GPA
Additional information: Application should also include GPA and a copy of prior year's tax return or W-2.
Program description:
Scholarship Program: The scholarship is open to women only and based on financial need and GPA. The scholarship will cover any field of undergraduate study except law, theology, or medicine. The field of nursing is an approved area of study. The scholarship grant may be used for any expense related to enrollment such as tuition, books, meal plans, housing, etc. Once a scholarship has been granted, funds are distributed to the school in the student's name for her use each term.
EIN: 586029952

953
Cooper Student Aid Fund
(formerly John Lamar Cooper Scholarship Loan Fund)
c/o U.S. Bank, N.A., Trust Tax Svcs.
P.O. Box 3168
Portland, OR 97208-3168
Application address: c/o Oregon Student Assistance Commission "OSAC", 1500 Valley River Dr., No. 100, Eugene, OR 97401, tel.: (541) 687-7400- Eugene/ Springfield area, (800) 452-8807, FAX: (541) 687-7419

Foundation type: Independent foundation
Limitations: Student loans to graduates of high schools in Hood River County, OR, who enroll as full-time undergraduates in OR colleges and universities, or who pursue a vocational education.
Publications: Informational brochure (including application guidelines).
Financial data: Year ended 06/30/2005.
Assets, $880,492 (M); Expenditures, $68,936; Total giving, $49,000.
Fields of interest: Vocational education.
Type of support: Student loans—to individuals; Support to graduates or students of specific schools; Technical education support; Undergraduate support.
Application information: Application form required.
Deadline(s): Applications accepted from June 1 through June 15 and Aug. 1 through Aug. 15.
Additional information: Interviews required.
Program description:
Student Loan Program: Loans are typically five percent interest on principal, contingent upon satisfactory academic performance. High school students must have at least a 2.5 GPA for consideration. Continuing college students must maintain at least a 2.0 GPA to keep their loans in good standing.
EIN: 936155856

954
Copper Mountain Foundation
P.O. Box 650
Cordova, AK 99574 (907) 424-3777
Contact: Carroll Kompkoff, Treas.

Foundation type: Company-sponsored foundation
Limitations: Scholarships to Native Alaskans or Native Alaskan descendants with ancestral ties to

the native village of Tatitlek, AK, for postsecondary education.
Financial data: Year ended 12/31/2004.
Assets, $0 (M); Expenditures, $33,039; Total giving, $28,958; Grants to individuals, 18 grants totaling $19,420.
Fields of interest: Native Americans/American Indians.
Type of support: Scholarships—to individuals.
Application information: Application form required.
Additional information: Contact foundation for current application deadline.
EIN: 920137461

955
Corbett Student Loan Program
(formerly Laura R & William Corbett Trust)
c/o Bank of America, N.A.
101 S. Tryon St., NC1-002-08-12
Charlotte, NC 28255-0001

Foundation type: Public charity
Limitations: Low-interest loans to medical students attending the University of South Carolina School of Medicine.
Financial data: Year ended 12/31/2003.
Assets, $2,535,986 (M); Expenditures, $332,695; Total giving, $239,100.
Fields of interest: Medical school/education.
Type of support: Student loans—to individuals; Support to graduates or students of specific schools; Graduate support.
Application information: Application form required.
Initial approach: Letter.
Deadline(s): Contact foundation for current application deadline.
Additional information: Applications available at the Office of Student Affairs at the School of Medicine.
Program description:
Corbett Trust Loan Program: The primary program is for long-term loans to cover costs associated with medical education and provides for extended repayment. The secondary program is for short-term loans designed to meet emergency needs and to be repaid within one calendar year, or upon leaving school, whichever occurs first. The Office of Student Affairs at the School of Medicine forwards all completed applications to the Scholarship and Loan Committee for review, which submits the applications with recommendations to the Citizen and Southern Trust Company (South Carolina), N.A. A student borrower's indebtedness under the trust's long-term program will not exceed $3,500 per year with a cumulative indebtedness of $14,000 per individual. The repayment period may extend for up to ten years after graduation, dismissal, or withdrawal. There is no interest charged or accrued while the student is enrolled in good standing. A borrower may apply for a deferment of scheduled payments on the principal of a long-term loan for the lesser of five years or the period of postgraduate medical training. Under the short-term program, qualified students may borrow up to $1,000 for a period not to exceed one year. This program is to be used as an emergency fund and must be repaid within one year. There will be no interest charged on the portion of the loan repaid within 60 days; thereafter, interest will be charged from the date of the note on the balance. Applications for the long-term loan program will be considered for disbursement only at the beginning of either the fall or spring terms. Application processing for the short-term loan program takes approximately 30 days at any time during the year.
EIN: 570685862

956
John Byron Corbin Charitable Trust
P.O. Box 550
Nevada, MO 64772
Contact: Don Hutchison, Tr.

Foundation type: Independent foundation
Limitations: Scholarships to U.S. citizens who are graduating high school seniors within 50 miles of Nevada, MO.
Financial data: Year ended 12/31/2004.
Assets, $2,792,563 (M); Expenditures, $104,379; Total giving, $53,560; Grants to individuals, totaling $53,560.
Type of support: Undergraduate support.
Application information: Application form required.
Deadline(s): Apr. 15
Additional information: Application should include a resume.
EIN: 436250034

957
Hubert & Alice Corke Educational Trust
P.O. Box 1543
Mountain Home, AR 72654 (501) 425-3100
Contact: Sara Zimmerman, Tr.

Foundation type: Independent foundation
Limitations: Scholarships to residents of Baxter and Marion counties, AR, who are children of Century Telephone Enterprises or Yelcot Telephone Company, Inc. employees, or who reside in the service areas of those two companies. Preference is given to dependents of employees of Century and Yelcot.
Financial data: Year ended 07/31/2005.
Assets, $1,961,338 (M); Expenditures, $146,880; Total giving, $130,450; Grants to individuals, 13 grants totaling $130,450 (high: $11,593, low: $3,864).
Type of support: Employee-related scholarships.
Application information: Deadlines July 31 for fall semester and Dec. 31 for spring semester; Completion of formal application required.
EIN: 716142206

958
Corn Products Educational Foundation
c/o Corn Products International, Inc.
5 Westbrook Corp. Ctr.
Westchester, IL 60154

Foundation type: Company-sponsored foundation
Limitations: Scholarships to children of full-time employees of Corn Products International, Inc., and its affiliates, who have at least one year of service as of the date of the scholarship award.
Financial data: Year ended 12/31/2004.
Assets, $2,899,901 (M); Expenditures, $79,702; Total giving, $35,566; Grants to individuals, 20 grants totaling $35,566 (high: $17,200, low: $300).
Type of support: Employee-related scholarships.
Application information: For additional information, contact: Linda Salcito-Bozek, 137 Park Ave., Teaneck, NJ 07666.
EIN: 364477522

959
J. B. Cornelius Foundation
181 Rutledge Rd.
Greenwood, SC 29649 (864) 229-7151
Contact: John L. Sherrill, Secy.-Treas.

Foundation type: Independent foundation

Limitations: Scholarships to financially needy female students attending Bennett College, Brevard College, Duke University, Greensboro College, High Point University and Pfeiffer College, all supported by the Western North Carolina Conference of the United Methodist Church, NC.
Financial data: Year ended 04/30/2005. Assets, $1,881,753 (M); Expenditures, $101,102; Total giving, $82,550; Grants to individuals, 90 grants totaling $82,550 (high: $1,000, low: $1,000, average grant: $1,000-$1,000).
Fields of interest: Women.
Type of support: Support to graduates or students of specific schools.
Application information: Application form required.
Deadline(s): May 1
Additional information: Applications available through colleges.
EIN: 566060705

960
The Cornell Delta Phi Educational Fund
c/o Snow Becker Krauss
605 3rd Ave.
New York, NY 10158
Contact: P. Michael Puleo, Tr.

Foundation type: Independent foundation
Limitations: Scholarships to full-time students who are selected according to prior academic performance, financial need, extracurricular activities, and character at Cornell University, Ithaca, NY, for undergraduate or graduate study.
Financial data: Year ended 03/31/2003. Assets, $347,817 (M); Expenditures, $35,273; Total giving, $7,655; Grants to individuals, 25 grants totaling $7,655.
Type of support: Support to graduates or students of specific schools; Graduate support; Undergraduate support.
Application information: Application form required.
Initial approach: Letter.
Deadline(s): Mar. 1 and Nov. 30
Additional information: Application must include resume indicating academic qualifications and financial need, and most recent Cornell transcript.
EIN: 136123284

961
Flora Corpening Trust
c/o JPMorgan Chase Bank, N.A.
P.O. Box 1308
Milwaukee, WI 53201
Application address: Principal, Bridgeport High School, 515 Johnson Ave., Bridgeport, WV 26330-1311

Foundation type: Independent foundation
Limitations: Scholarships to graduating seniors at Bridgeport High School, WV.
Financial data: Year ended 12/31/2004. Assets, $178,823 (M); Expenditures, $14,170; Total giving, $8,200; Grants to individuals, 37 grants totaling $8,200 (high: $250, low: $200).
Type of support: Support to graduates or students of specific schools; Undergraduate support.
Application information: Deadline Apr. 1; Completion of formal application required, including personal letter.
EIN: 556035695

962
Corson Foundation
P.O. Box 710
Plymouth Meeting, PA 19462
Contact: John E.F. Corson, Tr.

Foundation type: Independent foundation
Limitations: Scholarships to high school graduates primarily from schools located in the Plymouth-Whitemarsh, PA, area for attendance at colleges or universities.
Financial data: Year ended 12/31/2004. Assets, $2,611,841 (M); Expenditures, $136,199; Total giving, $114,500.
Type of support: Undergraduate support.
Application information: Applications accepted throughout the year; Application by letter, including proof of acceptance by an accredited college or university, and two recommendations from high school teachers or from the high school principal.
EIN: 236390878

963
Corti Family Agricultural Fund
c/o Wells Fargo Bank, N.A.
P.O. Box 63954
San Francisco, CA 94163
Contact: Lynn James
Application addresses: c/o Kern County Superintendent of Schools, Attn.: Theresa Corti, Scholarship Comm., 5801 Sundale Ave., Bakersfield, CA 93309, tel.: (805) 398-3600; c/o Wells Fargo Bank, N.A., Attn.: Lynn James, 111 W. Ocean Blvd., Long Beach, CA 90802, tel.: (800) 352-3705

Foundation type: Independent foundation
Limitations: Scholarships to graduates of Kern County, CA, high schools who are pursuing an agricultural education at a college or university.
Financial data: Year ended 03/31/2005. Assets, $1,201,229 (M); Expenditures, $74,562; Total giving, $53,700; Grants to individuals, totaling $53,700.
Fields of interest: Agriculture.
Type of support: Support to graduates or students of specific schools; Undergraduate support.
Application information: Deadline Feb. 28; Completion of formal application required, including two reference letters (one from an academic source, one from a personal source), transcript of grades, and a letter stating goals and plans; Interviews granted upon request; Application forms may be obtained from either of the two application contacts.
EIN: 956053041

964
William Henry Cosby, Jr. and Camille Olivia Cosby Foundation, Inc.
c/o John P. Schmitt
1133 Ave. of the Americas, Ste. 2200
New York, NY 10036-6710

Foundation type: Independent foundation
Limitations: Scholarships by nomination only to financially needy students enrolled in selected colleges and universities in the U.S., primarily in NY and PA, on the basis of academic achievement.
Financial data: Year ended 06/30/2004. Assets, $8,834 (M); Expenditures, $8,947; Total giving, $5,000; Grants to individuals, totaling $5,000.
Type of support: Awards/grants by nomination only; Undergraduate support.

Application information: Applications not accepted.
Additional information: Recipients are nominated by selected educational institutions that the foundation has invited to participate in the program.
EIN: 133408842

965
Arthur & David Cosgrove Memorial Fund
228 S. Main St.
Le Sueur, MN 56058
Contact: Peter Schoeppner, Tr.

Foundation type: Independent foundation
Limitations: Student loans to residents of the Le Sueur, MN, area.
Financial data: Year ended 12/31/2004. Assets, $1,321,308 (M); Expenditures, $60,335; Total giving, $55,794; Loans to individuals, totaling $55,794.
Type of support: Student loans—to individuals.
Application information: Applications by letter, outlining financial need, and including attendance report and year of graduation, accepted throughout the year.
EIN: 416022638

966
Coshocton Foundation
220 S. 4th St.
P.O. Box 55
Coshocton, OH 43812 (740) 622-0010
Contact: James Gauerke, Treas.
FAX: (740) 622-1660;
E-mail: jamesg@coshoctonfoundation.org;
URL: http://www.coshoctonfoundation.org

Foundation type: Community foundation
Limitations: Scholarships to graduates of high schools in Coshocton County, OH.
Publications: Application guidelines; Annual report; Financial statement; Informational brochure (including application guidelines); Newsletter; Occasional report.
Financial data: Year ended 09/30/2004. Assets, $18,084,742 (M); Expenditures, $1,114,076; Total giving, $827,120; Grants to individuals, 48 grants totaling $343,700.
Fields of interest: Nursing school/education.
Type of support: Conferences/seminars; Scholarships—to individuals; Undergraduate support.
Application information: Applications accepted. Application form required.
Initial approach: Letter.
Additional information: Contact foundation for current application deadline; Interviews required.
Program description:
Educational Program:
· Adolph Golden Scholarships: One $5,000 scholarship is given each year to a graduating senior from each of the three Coshocton County high schools. The awards are based on academic achievement and personal interviews with the foundation's Distribution Committee.
· Baughman Scholarship: Two $1,850 scholarships are given to graduating seniors of Coshocton High School. Scholarships are renewable for up to four years.
· Blue River Scholarship: Two $5,000 one-year scholarships are given to graduating seniors of Coshocton High

School, OH, Blue River Valley High School, IN, and Hobart High School, IN, to attend four-year, degree-granting colleges and universities.

- Coshocton High School Class of 1944 Scholarship: One $700 scholarship is given to a graduating senior of Coshocton High School.
- R.R. and Mary M. Jones Memorial Scholarship: One $600 scholarship is given to a graduating senior of Coshocton County Joint Vocational School.
- Coshocton Lions Memorial Scholarship: One $500 scholarship is given to a graduating senior of Coshocton High School to attend a four-year, degree-granting institution.
- Brownfield Scholarships: Upon application and recommendation of the high school principal, one $600 Brownfield scholarship is given to a graduating senior from each of the three county high schools. Scholarships are renewable for four years.
- Custer Scholarships: Two $600 Custer scholarships are awarded to Coshocton High School graduates upon recommendation of high school principal. Scholarships are renewable for two years.
- Pomerene Scholarship: One $700 Pomerene Scholarship is awarded to a student graduating through the Coshocton JVS.
- Alice L. Clift Scholarship: One $2,000 scholarship to a graduating senior of Coshocton High School to attend a degree-granting college of nursing. The scholarship is renewable for four years.
- Joe Johnston Memorial Scholarships: Two $4,500 scholarships, payable over one year, to students graduating from Coshocton High School.
- James A. Lee Scholarship: One $500 scholarship to a student graduating from Coshocton High School.

EIN: 316064567

967
The Jennie & Samuel J. Costa Educational Trust
c/o Kirkpatrick & Lockhart, LLP
75 State St.
Boston, MA 02109-1808
Contact: Sarita W. Beebe

Foundation type: Independent foundation
Limitations: Scholarships to current seniors or recent graduates of Waltham High School, MA, who are of Italian descent.
Financial data: Year ended 12/31/2004.
Assets, $333,695 (M); Expenditures, $14,770; Total giving, $5,000; Grants to individuals, totaling $5,000.
Fields of interest: Italy.
Type of support: Support to graduates or students of specific schools; Undergraduate support.
Application information: Applications accepted throughout the year; Completion of formal application required; Applications available at Waltham High School.
EIN: 043031308

968
Mary P. Costa Scholarship Fund Trust
(formerly John D. Costa Scholarship Fund Trust)
c/o Bank of America, N.A., P.C. Group
P.O. Box 6767
Providence, RI 02940-6767
Contact: Deborah Dillon Pearce, Trust Admin., Bank of America, N.A.

Foundation type: Independent foundation
Limitations: Scholarships by nomination only to the highest ranking graduate of Plymouth-Carver High School, MA.
Financial data: Year ended 07/31/2005.
Assets, $214,315 (M); Expenditures, $18,487; Total giving, $13,746; Grants to individuals, 3 grants totaling $13,746 (high: $5,000, low: $4,373).
Type of support: Support to graduates or students of specific schools; Awards/grants by nomination only; Undergraduate support.
Application information: Applications not accepted.
  Additional information: Recipients selected by Plymouth-Carver High School staff.
EIN: 046144750

969
Theresa Costa Scholarship Fund
c/o Alliance Bank, N.A.
241 Main St., Ste. 200
Buffalo, NY 14203

Foundation type: Independent foundation
Limitations: Scholarships for higher education, primarily in Schuyler County, NY.
Financial data: Year ended 02/28/2005.
Assets, $305,527 (M); Expenditures, $11,942; Total giving, $9,000.
Type of support: Scholarships—to individuals.
Application information:
  Initial approach: Letter.
  Additional information: Contact trust for current application deadline/guidelines.
EIN: 166417356

970
The Costello Family Foundation, Inc.
P.O. Box 2724
La Jolla, CA 92038-2724
Contact: Joseph D. Costello, Pres.

Foundation type: Independent foundation
Limitations: Support for K-12 education for the disadvantaged.
Financial data: Year ended 10/31/2005.
Assets, $1,062,853 (M); Expenditures, $54,695; Total giving, $50,000; Grants to individuals, 2 grants totaling $2,000.
Fields of interest: Education.
Type of support: Precollege support.
Application information: Applications accepted.
  Deadline(s): None
  Additional information: Applications by letter.
EIN: 820464641

971
O. W. Costilow Scholarship Trust
c/o Bank of America, N.A.
231 S. LaSalle St.
Chicago, IL 60697
Application address: 9120 Bristol Ave., St. Louis, MO 63114, tel.: (314) 429-3500

Foundation type: Independent foundation

Limitations: Scholarships to graduates of Ritenour Senior High School, MO.
Financial data: Year ended 09/30/2005.
Assets, $262,870 (M); Expenditures, $14,704; Total giving, $11,596; Grants to individuals, totaling $11,596.
Type of support: Support to graduates or students of specific schools; Undergraduate support.
Application information: Contact trust for current application deadline/guidelines.
EIN: 436253991

972
Cottington Trust for Gifted Children
c/o Bank of Hawaii
P.O. Box 3170
Honolulu, HI 96802-3170
Scholarship address: c/o Hawaii Community Fdn., 1164 Bishop St., Ste. 800, Honolulu, HI 96813

Foundation type: Independent foundation
Limitations: Scholarships to intellectually gifted children of HI who demonstrate intellectual giftedness by scoring at or above the 98th percentile on a standard IQ test.
Publications: Application guidelines.
Financial data: Year ended 12/31/2004.
Assets, $945,249 (M); Expenditures, $50,341; Total giving, $37,250; Grants to individuals, totaling $37,250.
Fields of interest: Education, gifted students.
Type of support: Precollege support; Undergraduate support.
Application information: Deadline Apr. 1; Contact foundation for current application guidelines; Initial approach by letter; Completion of formal application required, including IQ test scores, report card, references, narrative essay, and statement from the educational institution for which the applicant is being considered or has been accepted.
Program description:
  Scholarship Program: The Trust defines gifted children as those between the ages of 2 and 18-scholarships can be used for educational expenses such as tuition, fees, and books.
EIN: 996044219

973
County North Foundation
P.O. Box 791
Bryan, OH 43506
Contact: Patricia A. Pool, C.P.A.
Application address: 05691 St., Ste. 15, Bryan, OH 43506

Foundation type: Operating foundation
Limitations: Scholarships to students for higher education.
Financial data: Year ended 12/31/2003.
Assets, $821,365 (M); Expenditures, $51,070; Total giving, $46,837; Grants to individuals, 15 grants totaling $46,837 (high: $4,000, low: $500).
Type of support: Undergraduate support.
Application information: Contact foundation for current application deadline; Application by letter, including high school, graduation date, class rank and transcript.
EIN: 311596311

974

Covington Memorial Scholarship Trust

106 W. Stoddard St.
Dexter, MO 63841
Contact: Bryce Matthews, Tr.
Application addresses: c/o Dexter High School,
Dexter, MO 63841, tel.: (573) 614-1000; c/o
Marilyn Jackson, U.S. Bank, N.A., Bloomfield, MO
63825, tel.: (573) 568-4553

Foundation type: Independent foundation
Limitations: Scholarships to graduates of Dexter
and Bloomfield, MO, high schools.
Financial data: Year ended 12/31/2004.
Assets, $103,031 (M); Expenditures, $3,500;
Total giving, $3,250; Grants to individuals, totaling
$3,250.
Type of support: Scholarships—to individuals;
Support to graduates or students of specific
schools.
Application information:
Deadline(s): None
Additional information: Applications by letter.
Scholarships are renewable provided student
maintains satisfactory grades.
EIN: 431201123

975

Edith May Cox Charitable Trust

7655 2075 Rd.
Delta, CO 81416-9364 (970) 874-4438
Contact: Mike McMillan, Tr.

Foundation type: Independent foundation
Limitations: Scholarships to graduating seniors of
high schools in Delta County, CO, to study music at
accredited colleges and universities.
Financial data: Year ended 12/31/2004.
Assets, $39,149 (M); Expenditures, $3,167; Total
giving, $3,000.
Fields of interest: Music; Performing arts,
education.
Type of support: Support to graduates or students
of specific schools; Undergraduate support.
Application information:
Deadline(s): Apr.21
Applicants should submit the following:
1) Financial information
2) Letter(s) of recommendation
3) Essay
Additional information: Scholarships by
nomination. Contact high school or
superintendent's office for nomination forms;
Completion of formal nomination required.
Nomination form is submitted to the music
teachers of each school; Each school sends
one nomination form to the trust; Interviews
required; Recipients notified at graduation.
Program description:
Scholarship Program: Scholarships are awarded
on the basis of musical talent, financial need, and
academic and leadership abilities. Recipients must
maintain at least a 2.5 GPA.
EIN: 846190844

976

Opal G. Cox Charitable Trust

c/o Bank of America, N.A.
P.O. Box 831041
Dallas, TX 75283-1041
Scholarship application addresses: c/o William J.
Dube III, Office of Baylor Academic Scholarships
and Financial Aid, Baylor Univ., Box 7028, Waco, TX
76798-7028, tel.: (817) 755-2611; or c/o David G.
McQuitty, Dir. of Student Aid, Southwestern Baptist

Theological Seminary, P.O. Box 22000, Fort Worth,
TX 76122, tel.: (817) 923-1921

Foundation type: Independent foundation
Limitations: Scholarships to students attending
Southwestern Baptist Theological Seminary and
Baylor University, TX, with preference given to
students in the top 25 percent of the class,
studying as missionaries, or foreign students. Any
student studying to become a medical missionary
will be eligible for continued support during the term
he or she attends medical school.
Financial data: Year ended 08/31/2005.
Assets, $3,627,478 (M); Expenditures,
$327,096; Total giving, $270,000.
Fields of interest: Medical school/education;
Theological school/education; International
exchange, students; Christian agencies &
churches.
Type of support: Support to graduates or students
of specific schools; Foreign applicants; Graduate
support.
Application information: Application form required.
Deadline(s): Mar. 21 for Baylor University and
Apr. 1 for Southwestern Baptist Theological
Seminary.
Additional information: Application should
include transcripts.
Program description:
Scholarship Program: Applicants must have a
GPA of 3.2 or above and, if selected, enroll in a
minimum of 12 semester hours of undergraduate
studies per semester. The final selection is based
on merit and need as revealed in the application
provided by the trustees. Faculty recommendations
should be forwarded directly to the financial aid
office by the faculty.
EIN: 746307500

977

The Marshall G. Cox Family Foundation

2642 Vista Dr.
Newport Beach, CA 92663
Contact: Donna Cox, Pres.

Foundation type: Operating foundation
Limitations: Four-year scholarships to Asian
students from single parent families of Santa Clara
County for higher education, who have at least a "B"
average in high school and have participated in
extracurricular activities. One scholarship is given
each year.
Financial data: Year ended 12/31/2004.
Assets, $1,169,108 (M); Expenditures, $97,579;
Total giving, $76,930.
Fields of interest: Asians/Pacific Islanders.
Type of support: Undergraduate support.
Application information: Application form required.
Deadline(s): Contact foundation for current
application deadline.
EIN: 770456887

978

Cox Foundation

c/o Cox Wood Preserving Co.
P.O. Box 1124
Orangeburg, SC 29116 (803) 534-7467
Contact: Cathy C. Yeadon, Dir.

Foundation type: Company-sponsored foundation
Limitations: Scholarships are granted to family
members of full-time SC employees of Cox Wood
Preserving or related companies.
Financial data: Year ended 04/30/2005.
Assets, $805,007 (M); Expenditures, $31,557;

Total giving, $29,662; Grants to individuals, 17
grants totaling $29,662 (high: $3,160, low: $755).
Type of support: Employee-related scholarships.
Application information: Application form required.
Deadline(s): Jan. 31
EIN: 570823753

979

The William J. and Dorothy H. Cox Foundation, Inc.

2084 Hydesville Rd.
Newark, NY 14513-9729
Contact: William Tatro, Tr.

Foundation type: Independent foundation
Limitations: Scholarships by nomination only to
students at secondary schools in the western NY
Section V athletic zone. Applicants must be
nominated by his/her high school principal.
Financial data: Year ended 12/31/2004.
Assets, $183,400 (M); Expenditures, $9,576;
Total giving, $9,200; Grants to individuals, totaling
$9,200.
Type of support: Awards/grants by nomination only;
Undergraduate support.
Application information:
Initial approach: Letter or telephone.
Additional information: Contact foundation for
current nomination deadline/guidelines;
Nomination by letter from nominee's high
school principal, including recommendation
letters from student's athletic coach and
community leader who can attest to
nominee's character and Christian values.
EIN: 161353302

980

James M. Cox Foundation

1500 Woodmen Twr.
Omaha, NE 68102 (402) 344-0500
Contact: Ronald C. Jensen, Secy.

Foundation type: Independent foundation
Limitations: Scholarships by nomination only to
residents of the eastern-most third of NE.
Publications: Application guidelines.
Financial data: Year ended 12/31/2004.
Assets, $2,652,660 (M); Expenditures,
$198,311; Total giving, $158,500; Grants to
individuals, 95 grants totaling $94,500 (high:
$1,000, low: $500).
Type of support: Awards/grants by nomination only;
Undergraduate support.
Application information: Application form not
required.
Initial approach: Letter.
Deadline(s): None
Additional information: Contact foundation for
current application guidelines.
EIN: 470719195

981

Cozad Public Schools Foundation

P.O. Box 540
Cozad, NE 69130 (308) 784-2212

Foundation type: Operating foundation
Limitations: Scholarships to residents of Cozad,
NE.
Financial data: Year ended 08/31/2004.
Assets, $413,072 (M); Expenditures, $81,776;
Total giving, $80,772; Grants to individuals, 4
grants totaling $20,000 (high: $5,000, low:
$5,000).

Type of support: Scholarships—to individuals.
Application information: Applications by letter accepted throughout the year.
EIN: 470688549

982
William & Ruth Cozard Educational Scholarship Trust

c/o Wells Fargo Bank South Dakota, N.A., Trust Dept.
425 S. Main St.
Winner, SD   57580   (605) 842-8217
Contact: Lynnette Kucera, Trust Off., Wells Fargo Bank South Dakota, N.A.

Foundation type: Independent foundation
Limitations: Student loans to graduates of Chamberlain High School, SD, for undergraduate study.
Financial data: Year ended 12/31/2004. Assets, $138,897 (M); Expenditures, $26,635; Total giving, $22,000; Grants to individuals, totaling $22,000.
Type of support: Student loans—to individuals; Support to graduates or students of specific schools; Undergraduate support.
Application information: Deadline June 1; Initial approach by letter; Completion of formal application required, including financial statement, transcripts, and copy of applicant's, spouse's, or parents' most recent tax return.
Program description:
Student Loan Program: Normally, repayment of the loan is made over a four-year period. Recipients must pay at least $600 a year toward the loan unless otherwise authorized by the bank. Often, annual payments of over $600 are required. The exact repayment schedule is determined by the size of the debt and the recipient's ability to repay.
EIN: 466039141

983
CPCU- Loman Education Foundation

(also known as CPCU- Harry J. Loman Foundation)
P.O. Box 3009
Malvern, PA   19355-0709   (610) 251-2744
Contact: Roger W. Joyce, Chair.
E-mail: loman@cpcusociety.org; URL: http://www.cpculoman.cpcusociety.org

Foundation type: Public charity
Limitations: Scholarships and awards to individuals by CPCU society chapters.
Financial data: Year ended 12/31/2004. Assets, $1,102,751 (M); Expenditures, $203,487; Total giving, $99,570; Grants to individuals, 106 grants totaling $99,570 (high: $5,000, low: $250).
Fields of interest: Insurance, providers.
Type of support: Awards/prizes; Undergraduate support.
Application information: Contact foundation for current application deadline/guidelines.
Program description:
Scholarship Program: Scholarship recipients must be enrolled full- or part-time in an insurance or insurance-related field of study. Scholarships are usually in amounts of $1,500 each. CPCU- Loman Education Foundation matches scholarship funds given by individual CPCU chapters.
EIN: 232031260

984
Jennifer Craig Memorial Fund for the Arts, Inc.

13300-56 S. Cleveland Ave., PMB No. 214
Fort Myers, FL   33907-4203   (239) 275-0057
Contact: Ruth Kostush Christman, Exec. Dir.
E-mail: jennyfund@aol.com; URL: http://www.music-foundation.org

Foundation type: Public charity
Limitations: Scholarships to southwest FL high school seniors for study as music majors at the University of Central Florida.
Publications: Newsletter.
Financial data: Year ended 12/31/2003. Assets, $76,865; Expenditures, $60,135; Total giving, $2,570; Grants to individuals, totaling $2,570.
Fields of interest: Music; Performing arts, education.
Type of support: Support to graduates or students of specific schools; Undergraduate support.
Application information:
Deadline(s): Contact foundation for current application deadline/guidelines.
EIN: 650264107

985
J. P. Crain Family Scholarship Fund

c/o KeyBank N.A.
P.O. Box 10099
Toledo, OH   43699-0099   (419) 259-8218
Contact: Diane Ohns, Tr.

Foundation type: Independent foundation
Limitations: Scholarships to financially needy graduates of Paulding County High School, OH, who are U.S. citizens and are pursuing careers as teachers, doctors of medicine, lawyers, dentists, ministers, engineers, business administrators, farmers, or veterinarians.
Financial data: Year ended 03/31/2005. Assets, $1,072,157 (M); Expenditures, $71,769; Total giving, $59,912; Grants to individuals, totaling $59,912.
Fields of interest: Business school/education; Dental school/education; Law school/education; Medical school/education; Teacher school/education; Engineering school/education; Theological school/education; Veterinary medicine; Agriculture.
Type of support: Support to graduates or students of specific schools; Undergraduate support.
Application information: Applications accepted throughout the year; Application by letter outlining financial need, grades, reasons for request, and a statement of motivation; Completion of formal application required.
EIN: 346985380

986
Zenas Crane Fund for Student Aid

c/o TD Banknorth, N.A., Investment Mgmt. Group
P.O. Box 174
New Britain, CT   06050   (413) 445-8249
Application address: c/o Wahconah Regional High School, 150 Windsor Rd., Dalton, MA 01226,

Foundation type: Independent foundation
Limitations: Scholarships to graduates of Wahconah Regional High School, Dalton, MA.
Financial data: Year ended 04/30/2005. Assets, $1,674,307 (M); Expenditures, $102,073; Total giving, $85,355; Grants to individuals, 180 grants totaling $85,355.

Type of support: Support to graduates or students of specific schools; Undergraduate support.
Application information: Deadline May 1; Completion of formal application required; Applications available at Wahconah Regional High School.
EIN: 046048993

987
The Cranston Foundation

c/o The Cranston Fdn. Trustees
1381 Cranston St.
Cranston, RI   02920-6739   (401) 943-4800

Foundation type: Company-sponsored foundation
Limitations: Scholarships for two years only to children of employees, excluding directors and officers, of the Cranston Print Works Company, its divisions, and subsidiaries.
Financial data: Year ended 06/30/2005. Assets, $2,557 (M); Expenditures, $212,661; Total giving, $212,522; Grants to individuals, 43 grants totaling $84,087 (high: $4,000, low: $27).
Type of support: Employee-related scholarships.
Application information:
Initial approach: Letter.
Deadline(s): May 1
EIN: 056015348

988
Cranston High School Athletic Scholarship Fund

c/o Leslie Kenney
1000 Jefferson Blvd.
Warwick, RI   02886-2201
Contact: Edward L. Rondeau, Secy.
Application address: 1052 Park Ave., Cranston, RI 02910, tel.: (401) 461-5056

Foundation type: Independent foundation
Limitations: Scholarships to athletes who are graduating seniors of Cranston High School East and Cranston High School West, RI.
Financial data: Year ended 12/31/2004. Assets, $100,848 (M); Expenditures, $6,374; Total giving, $3,200; Grants to individuals, totaling $3,200.
Fields of interest: Athletics/sports, training; Athletics/sports, school programs.
Type of support: Support to graduates or students of specific schools; Undergraduate support.
Application information: Deadline Apr. 30; Completion of formal application required.
EIN: 222982274

989
Bruce L. Crary Foundation, Inc.

c/o Hand House, River St.
P.O. Box 396
Elizabethtown, NY   12932   (518) 873-6496
Contact: Hanna Kissam, Exec. Dir.

Foundation type: Independent foundation
Limitations: Scholarships based on financial need to residents of Clinton, Essex, Franklin, Hamilton, and Warren counties, NY.
Financial data: Year ended 06/30/2005. Assets, $8,536,502 (M); Expenditures, $493,675; Total giving, $334,680; Grants to individuals, 473 grants totaling $329,430 (high: $5,000, low: $125).
Type of support: Undergraduate support.
Application information: Application form required.
Deadline(s): Apr. 15

Additional information: Applications available from guidance offices at local high schools; Scholarships awarded in early July.

Program description:

Crary Education Fund: There are approximately 125 new awards available each year. There are no scholastic requirements other than the ability to complete the educational requirements of the attending institution. Although there is no obligation to repay the award, recipients are encouraged to do so. Scholarships are renewable.

EIN: 237366844

990

G. Kenneth Crawford and Margaret B. Crawford Memorial Scholarship Fund

c/o U.S. Bancorp Trust Co.
P.O. Box 520
Johnstown, PA 15907-0520
Application address: c/o Deborah Madden, Thomas Jefferson High School, P.O. Box 18019, Pleasant Hills, PA 15236-0019

Foundation type: Independent foundation
Limitations: Scholarships to graduating seniors and alumni of Thomas Jefferson High School, in Jefferson Hills, Clairton, PA.
Financial data: Year ended 12/31/2004. Assets, $319,812 (M); Expenditures, $18,455; Total giving, $15,000; Grants to individuals, totaling $15,000.
Type of support: Support to graduates or students of specific schools; Undergraduate support.
Application information: Contact fund for current application deadline/guidelines; Initial approach by letter.
EIN: 251738804

991

Ethel W. Crawley Memorial Educational Fund

c/o BB&T
P.O. Box 2907
Wilson, NC 27894-2907
Application address: c/o Heather Stall, 434 Fayetteville St., Raleigh, NC 27601, tel.: (919) 716-6259

Foundation type: Independent foundation
Limitations: Scholarships to individuals who have resided in Halifax County, NC, for at least two years, for higher education.
Financial data: Year ended 12/31/2004. Assets, $4,531,440 (M); Expenditures, $299,311; Total giving, $207,964; Grants to individuals, 28 grants totaling $207,964 (high: $15,769, low: $385).
Type of support: Undergraduate support.
Application information: Deadline Mar. 15; Completion of formal application required, including copies of parents' W2 forms; Applications available at local high schools or academy office in Halifax County, NC.
EIN: 566534286

992

J. Fletcher Creamer & Son Scholarship Foundation

101 E. Broadway
Hackensack, NJ 07601-6832 (201) 488-9800
Contact: Estelle R. Marafino, Tr.

Foundation type: Company-sponsored foundation

Limitations: Scholarships to children and grandchildren of current employees of J. Fletcher Creamer & Son, Inc., Creamer Bros., Inc., and Signs of Safety, exclusive of these companies' owners.
Financial data: Year ended 11/30/2004. Assets, $17,473 (M); Expenditures, $10,108; Total giving, $10,000; Grants to individuals, 4 grants totaling $10,000 (high: $2,500, low: $2,500).
Type of support: Employee-related scholarships.
Application information: Application form required.
Deadline(s): Mar. 1
EIN: 222870454

993

CREATE Foundation

(formerly Create Christian Research Education Action Technical Enterprise, Inc.)
P.O. Box 1053
Tupelo, MS 38802-1053 (662) 844-8989
Contact: Michael K. Clayborne, Pres.
FAX: (662) 844-8149;
E-mail: info@createfoundation.com; URL: http://www.createfoundation.com

Foundation type: Public charity
Limitations: Scholarships to graduating students attending Tupelo High School, MS, and Baldwin High School in Lee County, MS.
Publications: Application guidelines; Annual report; Informational brochure; Newsletter.
Financial data: Year ended 12/31/2004. Assets, $33,590,272 (M); Expenditures, $3,234,223; Total giving, $2,437,766; Grants to individuals, totaling $77,523.
Type of support: Support to graduates or students of specific schools; Undergraduate support.
Application information: Contact specified schools for current application deadline/guidelines.
EIN: 237248582

994

Credit Bureau of Fort Dodge Trust

312 11th Ave. N.
P.O. Box 722
Fort Dodge, IA 50501-0722
Application addresses: c/o Jack Grandgeorge, 244 11th Ave. N., Fort Dodge, IA 50501; c/o Bruck McCullough, 2749 21st Ave. N, Fort Dodge, IA 50501; c/o Tom Chalstrom, 825 Central Ave., Fort Dodge, IA 50501

Foundation type: Operating foundation
Limitations: Scholarships to residents of Fort Dodge, IA.
Financial data: Year ended 12/31/2003. Assets, $109,874 (M); Expenditures, $8,802; Total giving, $8,200; Grants to individuals, 11 grants totaling $8,200 (high: $1,000, low: $300).
Type of support: Scholarships—to individuals.
Application information: Contact trust for current application deadline; Completion of formal application required.
EIN: 421319169

995

The Crescent Moon Foundation, Inc.

P.O. Box 22388
Houston, TX 77227-2388 (713) 541-2093
Contact: Harold Warren Moon, Jr., Chair.

Foundation type: Public charity
Limitations: Scholarships for higher education to residents of the Greater Houston, TX, area.

Financial data: Year ended 12/31/2003. Assets, $29,823 (M); Expenditures, $1,022.
Fields of interest: Higher education.
Type of support: Scholarships—to individuals.
Application information: Applications accepted. Application form required.
Initial approach: Letter.
Applicants should submit the following:
1) Essay
2) Financial information
3) Letter(s) of recommendation
4) GPA
Additional information: Interview required.
EIN: 760279428

996

Crescent Scholarship Foundation

777 Main St., Ste. 2100
Fort Worth, TX 76102 (817) 321-1000
Contact: Kathy Rosenthal, Secy.

Foundation type: Company-sponsored foundation
Limitations: Scholarships to children of employees of Crescent Real Estate Equities, Ltd.
Financial data: Year ended 12/31/2004. Assets, $398,362 (M); Expenditures, $15,832; Total giving, $11,000; Grants to individuals, 12 grants totaling $11,000 (high: $1,500, low: $500).
Type of support: Employee-related scholarships.
Application information:
Initial approach: Letter.
Applicants should submit the following:
1) Resume
2) Financial information
3) Letter(s) of recommendation
4) Photograph
5) Essay
6) ACT
7) Transcripts
8) GPA
EIN: 752993151

997

Criswell Scholarship Fund

c/o U.S. Bank, N.A.
P.O. Box 3168
Portland, OR 97208-3168
Application address: Clare Winkle c/o St. Luke's Episcopal Church, 224 N.W., D St., Grants Pass, OR 97526

Foundation type: Independent foundation
Limitations: Scholarships to financially needy seniors of Grants Pass High School, OR, to attend any college. Preference is given to those who choose to attend Oregon State University.
Financial data: Year ended 06/30/2005. Assets, $237,717 (M); Expenditures, $14,246; Total giving, $10,002; Grants to individuals, totaling $10,002.
Type of support: Support to graduates or students of specific schools; Undergraduate support.
Application information: Contact Fr. Shulda of St. Luke's Episcopal Church, Grants Pass, OR 97526, for current application deadline/guidelines.
Program description:
Scholarship Program: The award may be received for up to four years. Preference is given to previous recipients.
EIN: 936020612

998
Croatian Fraternal Union Scholarship Foundation, Inc.
100 Delaney Dr.
Pittsburgh, PA 15235-5416 (412) 351-3909
Contact: Bernard M. Luketich, Pres.

Foundation type: Public charity
Limitations: Scholarships to individuals of Croatian descent residing in Pittsburgh, PA. Applicants should be members of the Croation Fraternal Union, for higher education.
Financial data: Year ended 12/31/2003.
Assets, $2,457,426; Expenditures, $124,857; Total giving, $118,000; Grants to individuals, totaling $118,000.
Fields of interest: Croatia.
Type of support: Undergraduate support.
Application information: Contact foundation for current application deadline/guidelines.
EIN: 256066985

999
Alton & Mildred Cross Scholarship Fund
3330 Peach St., Ste. 101
Erie, PA 16508
Contact: Eugene Cross, Tr.

Foundation type: Independent foundation
Limitations: Scholarships to graduates of Fort Leboeuf High School in Waterford, PA.
Financial data: Year ended 12/31/2004.
Assets, $0 (M); Expenditures, $97,776; Total giving, $84,500; Grants to individuals, 83 grants totaling $84,500 (high: $2,000, low: $400).
Type of support: Support to graduates or students of specific schools; Undergraduate support.
Application information:
  Initial approach: Letter or telephone.
  Additional information: Contact fund for current application deadline/guidelines.
EIN: 251709602

1000
R. Elaine Croston Scholarship Fund
c/o Bank of America, N.A., P.C. Group
P.O. Box 6767
Providence, RI 02940-6767
Application address: c/o Karen K. Baker, Principal, Haverhill High School, 137 Monument St., Haverhill, MA 01832-2697, tel.: (508) 374-5712

Foundation type: Independent foundation
Limitations: Scholarships for higher education to graduates of Haverhill High School, MA.
Financial data: Year ended 12/31/2003.
Assets, $508,145 (M); Expenditures, $25,298; Total giving, $20,225; Grants to individuals, 30 grants totaling $17,500 (high: $1,000, low: $500).
Type of support: Support to graduates or students of specific schools; Undergraduate support.
Application information: Applications not accepted.
EIN: 046079522

1001
Mary G. Croston Trust
c/o Citizens Bank of NH
870 Westminster St.
Providence, RI 02903
Application address: c/o Fr. Frederick B. McGowan, St. James Parish, 6 Cottage St., Haver Hill, MA 01830, tel.: (508) 327-8537

Foundation type: Independent foundation
Limitations: Scholarships to high school graduates who are members of Saint James Parish in Haverhill, MA.
Financial data: Year ended 08/31/2005.
Assets, $259,319 (M); Expenditures, $17,544; Total giving, $13,000; Grants to individuals, totaling $13,000.
Fields of interest: Christian agencies & churches.
Type of support: Scholarships—to individuals.
Application information: Contact trust for current application deadline/guidelines; Initial approach by letter or telephone.
EIN: 026027098

1002
Croul Family Foundation
1901 Bayadere Terr.
Corona del Mar, CA 92625
Contact: Spencer Behr Croul, Secy.
FAX: (949) 548-1026;
E-mail: Foundation@croul.com

Foundation type: Independent foundation
Limitations: Scholarships to children of employees of Behr Process Corp., Santa Ana, CA.
Publications: Application guidelines; Program policy statement.
Financial data: Year ended 12/31/2004.
Assets, $17,212,660 (M); Expenditures, $1,535,645; Total giving, $1,359,800; Grants to individuals, 6 grants totaling $30,652 (high: $7,404, low: $3,650).
Type of support: Employee-related scholarships.
Application information: Contact foundation for current application deadline/guidelines.
EIN: 330749543

1003
Robert Lloyd Crozier and Myrtle Madge Crozier Educational Trust
P.O. Box 268
Knoxville, IA 50138-0268
Application address: c/o Ned Job, Trust Off., Iowa Savings Bank, 222 E. Robinson St., Knoxville, IA 50138, tel.: (641) 828-8000

Foundation type: Independent foundation
Limitations: Scholarships to financially needy Knoxville High School, IA, graduates for higher education at recognized colleges and universities.
Financial data: Year ended 12/31/2004.
Assets, $521,447 (M); Expenditures, $20,654; Total giving, $15,500; Grants to individuals, totaling $15,500.
Type of support: Support to graduates or students of specific schools; Undergraduate support.
Application information: Applications accepted. Application form required.
  Additional information: Applications accepted throughout the year; Completion of formal application required, including financial data, class rank, name of the accredited state or private school applicant will attend.
EIN: 426469990

1004
George M. Cruise Charitable Foundation
c/o First Community Bank, Inc.
P.O. Box 950
Bluefield, WV 24701
Contact: Selection Comm.

Foundation type: Independent foundation

Limitations: Scholarships to residents of Mercer County, WV, and Tazewell County, VA, to attend U.S. colleges.
Financial data: Year ended 12/31/2004.
Assets, $3,222,481 (M); Expenditures, $171,749; Total giving, $141,900; Grants to individuals, 124 grants totaling $64,957.
Type of support: Scholarships—to individuals.
Application information: Applications accepted. Application form required.
  Deadline(s): May of each year for fall semester scholarships
EIN: 626214545

1005
Roy L. Crume Trust
c/o First National Bank, Trust Dept.
P.O. Box 9012
Kokomo, IN 46904-9012

Foundation type: Independent foundation
Limitations: Scholarships to graduating seniors of Carroll, Cass, Clinton, Grant, Howard, Miami, and Tipton counties, IN, who will attend a trade school, college or university.
Financial data: Year ended 12/31/2004.
Assets, $489,554 (M); Expenditures, $72,668; Total giving, $68,500; Grants to individuals, totaling $68,500.
Fields of interest: Vocational education, post-secondary.
Type of support: Technical education support; Undergraduate support.
Application information: Applications accepted. Application form required.
  Deadline(s): Mar. 31
EIN: 356630304

1006
Joe and Jessie Crump Fund
c/o JPMorgan Chase Bank, N.A
P.O. Box 1308
Milwaukee, WI 53201-1308

Foundation type: Independent foundation
Limitations: Student loans for study at an Episcopal theological seminary in TX.
Financial data: Year ended 09/30/2004.
Assets, $18,763,213 (M); Expenditures, $1,058,065; Total giving, $715,396.
Fields of interest: Theological school/education; Protestant agencies & churches.
Type of support: Student loans—to individuals.
Application information: Applications not accepted.
EIN: 756045044

1007
CTS Foundation
c/o CTS Corp.
905 N. West Blvd.
Elkhart, IN 46514 (574) 293-7511

Foundation type: Company-sponsored foundation
Limitations: Interest-free student loans for undergraduate education to employees and children of employees of the CTS Corp. and its subsidiaries.
Financial data: Year ended 06/30/2005.
Assets, $2,273,787 (M); Expenditures, $128,459; Total giving, $98,500; Loans to individuals, totaling $83,675.
Type of support: Employee-related scholarships; Loans—to individuals.

Application information: Application form required.
Deadline(s): Deadline prior to beginning of school term
Program description:
Student Loan Program: When the student's first promissory note matures, usually soon after graduation, the student shall arrange to pay back the full amount within one year with no interest. After one year, interest at the rate of 10 percent per year is accrued.
EIN: 356014484

1008
CTW Foundation, Inc.
(formerly Beneficial Foundation, Inc.)
c/o Finn M.W. Casperson, V.P.
P.O. Box 911
Wilmington, DE   19899-0911   (302) 429-9425
Contact: Robert A. Tucker, Pres.
Application address: P.O. Box 2205, Wilmington, DE 19899; NJ tel.: (908) 781-3010

Foundation type: Company-sponsored foundation
Limitations: Scholarships to children of employees of Beneficial Corporation and its affiliated corporations, primarily in DE, NJ and PA.
Financial data: Year ended 12/31/2004.
Assets, $13,526,721 (M); Expenditures, $1,021,884; Total giving, $817,525; Grants to individuals, 3 grants totaling $14,000 (high: $7,000, low: $3,000).
Type of support: Employee-related scholarships.
Application information: Applications accepted. Application form required.
Deadline(s): None
Additional information: Application should include financial information, biographical and scholastic information.
EIN: 516011637

1009
Cuan Foundation, Inc.
c/o Morrison & Assocs.
P.O. Box 1926
La Crosse, WI   54602-1926
Contact: Jane Ann Quinlisk, Dir.
Application address: 521 S. 23rd St., La Crosse, WI 54601, tel.: (608) 785-0005

Foundation type: Operating foundation
Limitations: Scholarships to residents of the greater La Crosse, WI, area.
Financial data: Year ended 12/31/2003.
Assets, $743,445 (M); Expenditures, $42,732; Total giving, $19,505; Grants to individuals, 9 grants totaling $19,505 (high: $6,823, low: $100).
Type of support: Scholarships—to individuals.
Application information: Applications by letter accepted throughout the year; Contact foundation for current application guidelines; Initial approach by letter.
EIN: 391714380

1010
Culver's V.I.P. Foundation, Inc.
540 Water St.
Prairie du Sac, WI   53578

Foundation type: Company-sponsored foundation
Limitations: Scholarships to students for higher education, primarily in WI.
Financial data: Year ended 10/31/2004.
Assets, $511,071 (M); Expenditures, $225,018; Total giving, $205,633; Grants to individuals, 140 grants totaling $136,000 (high: $1,500, low: $500).
Type of support: Undergraduate support.
Application information: Applications not accepted.
Additional information: Unsolicited requests for funds not accepted.
EIN: 392042139

1011
Cameron Cunningham Foundation
P.O. Box 1786
Danville, IL   61834-1786
Contact: Leesa A. Cunningham Hubbard, Exec. Dir.

Foundation type: Operating foundation
Limitations: Scholarships primarily to students residing in the Vermilion County, IL, area. Some support also to seriously ill children.
Financial data: Year ended 12/31/2002.
Assets, $109,470 (M); Expenditures, $28,289; Total giving, $19,500; Grants to individuals, 17 grants totaling $19,500 (high: $2,500, low: $500).
Type of support: Emergency funds; Scholarships—to individuals.
Application information: Application form required.
Deadline(s): Mar. 31
Applicants should submit the following:
1) Transcripts
2) Financial information
3) ACT
Additional information: Scholarship applications available at area high schools; Applications by letter for medical assistance.
EIN: 371346422

1012
The Louis Cunningham Scholarship Foundation
21411 Civic Center Dr., Ste. 206
Southfield, MI   48076   (248) 263-7630
Contact: Louis E. Cunningham, Treas.

Foundation type: Independent foundation
Limitations: Scholarships to individuals for study at institutions of higher learning.
Financial data: Year ended 12/31/2004.
Assets, $144,489 (M); Expenditures, $11,577; Total giving, $11,500; Grants to individuals, totaling $11,500.
Type of support: Scholarships—to individuals.
Application information: Application form required.
Deadline(s): Spring
Additional information: Application should include transcript.
Program description:
Scholarship Program: Awards are restricted to expenses for tuition, books, room and board. GPA requirements must be maintained.
EIN: 383197360

1013
Cuno Foundation
c/o Bank of America, N.A.
P.O. Box 6767
Providence, RI   02940-6767
Application address: c/o Trudy Magnolia, Secy., Bank of America, N.A., 18 Devon Ct., Meriden, CT 06450

Foundation type: Independent foundation
Limitations: Scholarships to residents of Meriden, CT.

Financial data: Year ended 12/31/2004.
Assets, $9,888,363 (M); Expenditures, $528,525; Total giving, $450,525.
Type of support: Scholarships—to individuals.
Application information: Contact foundation for current application deadline/guidelines; Initial approach by letter.
EIN: 066033040

1014
The Curley Foundation
4961 Campanile Dr.
San Diego, CA   92115-2332
Contact: Carmen J. Berry, V.P.
Application address: 8405 Zeta St., La Mesa, CA 91942, tel.: (619) 589-8151

Foundation type: Independent foundation
Limitations: Scholarships to individuals for higher education, with preference given to those who received their primary and secondary education in San Diego County, CA.
Financial data: Year ended 12/31/2004.
Assets, $328,166 (M); Expenditures, $98,154; Total giving, $66,250; Grants to individuals, totaling $66,250.
Type of support: Support to graduates or students of specific schools; Undergraduate support.
Application information: Applications accepted throughout the year; Completion of formal application required, including essay, transcripts, and recommendation letters from instructors, employers/supervisors, or others who have known the applicant for a significant amount of time; Application forms are available from high school guidance counselor.
EIN: 330640939

1015
Curran Music Scholarship Fund
(also known as Gertrude D. Curran Trust f/b/o Curran Music School)
c/o Alliance Bank, N.A.
241 Main St.
Buffalo, NY   14203

Foundation type: Independent foundation
Limitations: Music scholarships to residents of Utica, NY who are or were students of Proctor High School or other schools of the Utica, NY public school system.
Financial data: Year ended 12/31/2004.
Assets, $187,654 (M); Expenditures, $12,021; Total giving, $7,500; Grants to individuals, totaling $7,500.
Fields of interest: Music.
Type of support: Support to graduates or students of specific schools; Undergraduate support.
Application information: Contact trust for current application deadline/guidelines.
EIN: 156015514

1016
T. Manning Curtis Athletic Scholarship Fund
c/o PNC Advisors
P.O. Box 937, P2-PTPP-10-3
Pittsburgh, PA   15222
Application address: c/o Superintendent, Stroudsburg Area School District, 123 Linden St., Stroudsburg, PA 18360, tel.: (717) 421-1990

Foundation type: Independent foundation

Limitations: Scholarships to graduates of Stroudsburg High School, PA, who have participated in a school athletic program and demonstrate financial need.
Financial data: Year ended 12/31/2004. Assets, $247,657 (M); Expenditures, $18,206; Total giving, $16,000; Grants to individuals, totaling $16,000.
Fields of interest: Athletics/sports, training.
Type of support: Support to graduates or students of specific schools; Undergraduate support.
Application information: Applications and deadline available from high school guidance office; Completion of formal application required.
EIN: 236979929

1017
Charles Curtis & Patricia Morse Curtis Foundation

1 Penrose Ln.
Colorado Springs, CO   80906   (719) 635-9470
Contact: Charles Curtis, Pres.

Foundation type: Independent foundation
Limitations: Scholarships to individuals in CO.
Financial data: Year ended 08/31/2004. Assets, $1,596,404 (M); Expenditures, $100,046; Total giving, $32,592; Grants to individuals, 7 grants totaling $12,416 (high: $3,000, low: $666).
Type of support: Scholarships—to individuals.
Application information: Applications accepted throughout the year; Contact foundation for current application guidelines; Initial approach by letter.
EIN: 841473110

1018
The Frances Blayney Curtis Foundation

P.O. Box 451
Ranchester, WY   82839
Contact: Don Steadman, Secy.-Treas.
tel.: (307) 655-2595

Foundation type: Independent foundation
Limitations: Loans to residents of the Sheridan, WY, area to attend colleges, universities, trade schools, and vocational schools in the Rocky Mountain area.
Financial data: Year ended 12/31/2004. Assets, $495,196 (M); Expenditures, $4,753; Total giving, $0; Loans to individuals, totaling $29,000.
Fields of interest: Vocational education.
Type of support: Student loans—to individuals; Technical education support; Undergraduate support.
Application information: Application form required.
   Deadline(s): 2 months prior to need for funds
   Applicants should submit the following:
      1) Photograph
Program description:
   Student Loan Program: Loans are to be repaid within ten years after education is completed. Payments begin six months after graduation. For loans $5,000 or less, monthly payment is $70. For loans over $5,000, monthly payment is $14 per $1,000. Recipients, their spouses, and both parents are required to sign a loan agreement. Students must show proof every semester of passing at least 12 credit hours and maintaining at least a 2.0 GPA.
EIN: 830300312

1019
Charles B. & Margaret E. Cushwa Foundation

c/o KeyBank N.A.
800 Superior Ave., 4th Fl.
Cleveland, OH   44114
Contact: Kim Mayle, Trust Off., KeyBank N.A.
Application address: 126 Central Plz. N., Canton, OH 44702, tel.: (330) 489-5434

Foundation type: Independent foundation
Limitations: Scholarships to individuals in OH for higher education.
Financial data: Year ended 12/31/2004. Assets, $1,764,414 (M); Expenditures, $94,681; Total giving, $85,000; Grants to individuals, totaling $78,500.
Type of support: Scholarships—to individuals.
Application information: Applications by letter accepted throughout the year.
EIN: 341787513

1020
Cut Bank Elks Lodge Charitable Corp.

38B S. Central Ave.
Cut Bank, MT   59427
Contact: Robert Smith, Secy.
Application address: P.O. Box 2117, Cut Bank, MT 59427

Foundation type: Independent foundation
Limitations: Scholarships to MT students in their second, third or fourth year of postsecondary education who are members of the Cut Bank Elks Lodge, No. 1632, or whose spouse, parent, or grandparent is a member thereof for the past three years.
Financial data: Year ended 12/31/2004. Assets, $248,871 (M); Expenditures, $12,868; Total giving, $12,400; Grants to individuals, totaling $12,400.
Fields of interest: Fraternal societies.
Type of support: Undergraduate support.
Application information: Application form required.
   Deadline(s): June 30
EIN: 810495546

1021
William H. & Sadie R. Cutter Trust Fund, Inc.

P.O. Drawer 310
Summit, NJ   07902-0310
Contact: Donald Geddis, Tr.
Application address: c/o Summit High School, Kent Place Blvd., Summit, NJ 07901

Foundation type: Independent foundation
Limitations: Scholarships to students of Summit and Woodbridge high schools, NJ.
Financial data: Year ended 12/31/2004. Assets, $531,911 (M); Expenditures, $31,429; Total giving, $18,100; Grants to individuals, totaling $6,000.
Type of support: Support to graduates or students of specific schools; Undergraduate support.
Application information: Deadline Mar. 31; Initial approach by letter; Completion of formal application required, including high school transcript and resume of non-academic activities.
EIN: 237096467

1022
CVS/pharmacy Charitable Trust, Inc.

(formerly CVS Charitable Trust, Inc.)
1 CVS Dr.
Woonsocket, RI   02895
URL: http://www.cvs.com/corpInfo/community/charitable_mission.html

Foundation type: Company-sponsored foundation
Limitations: Scholarships to children of full-time employees of CVS Corporation and its subsidiaries.
Publications: Grants list.
Financial data: Year ended 09/30/2005. Assets, $81,287,564 (M); Expenditures, $3,621,902; Total giving, $3,438,565; Grants to individuals, 94 grants totaling $280,590 (high: $5,000, low: $1,000).
Type of support: Employee-related scholarships.
Application information: Application form required.
   Deadline(s): Spring
EIN: 223206973

1023
Cypress-Fairbanks Educational Foundation

(also known as CFEF)
P.O. Box 690445
Houston, TX   77269-0445   (832) 615-5730
Contact: Marie Homes, Exec. Dir.
Scholarship application address: P.O. Box 690445, Houston, TX 77269-0445
FAX: (281) 582-6231; *URL:* http://www.thecfef.org

Foundation type: Public charity
Limitations: Scholarships to individuals in the Cypress Fairbanks Independent School District who are pursuing higher education.
Financial data: Year ended 06/30/2004. Assets, $2,655,631 (M); Expenditures, $245,090; Total giving, $210,148; Grants to individuals, 32 grants totaling $132,500 (high: $20,000, low: $500).
Fields of interest: Higher education.
Type of support: Scholarships—to individuals.
Application information: Applications accepted. Application form available on the grantmaker's Web site.
   Deadline(s): Feb. 2
   Applicants should submit the following:
      1) Financial information
      2) Transcripts
Program description:
   Scholarships: Awards the following ten scholarships:
   · The Cypress Fairbanks Educational Foundation Assistance Scholarship
   · The Cecil Hall Scholarship
   · The Sterling Bank Scholarship
   · The Adam Jackson Skinner Memorial Scholarship
   · The Dynegy Scholarship
   · The Watson Family Foundation Scholarship
   · The Tenet Healthcare Foundation/CY-Fair Medical Center Scholarship
   · The Kevin Borgfeldt Memorial Scholarship
   · Houston Super Bowl XXXVIII Host Committee Scholarship
EIN: 237079589

1024
The Paul H. D'Amour Fellowship Foundation

c/o Scholarship Comm.
2145 Roosevelt Ave.
Springfield, MA   01104   (413) 504-4203

Foundation type: Company-sponsored foundation
Limitations: Scholarships only to students in the Big Y marketing areas of CT and central and western MA.
Financial data: Year ended 07/03/2005.
Assets, $116,370 (M); Expenditures, $10,460; Total giving, $10,000; Grants to individuals, 5 grants totaling $10,000 (high: $2,000, low: $2,000).
Type of support: Scholarships—to individuals.
Application information:
Deadline(s): Feb. 1
Additional information: Application should include transcripts, college board scores and three letters of recommendation; Applications should be sent by letter.
EIN: 222626366

1025

The Gerald and Paul D'Amour Founders Scholarship for Academic Excellence

P.O. Box 7840
2145 Roosevelt Ave.
Springfield, MA 01102-7840 (413) 784-0600

Foundation type: Company-sponsored foundation
Limitations: Scholarships to students residing in the Big Y Foods, Inc. marketing area (central and western MA and parts of CT).
Financial data: Year ended 07/03/2005.
Assets, $1,065,942 (M); Expenditures, $170,155; Total giving, $169,500; Grants to individuals, 250 grants totaling $169,500 (high: $1,000, low: $500).
Type of support: Scholarships—to individuals.
Application information:
Deadline(s): Feb. 1
Additional information: Application should include college board scores, transcripts, and three letters of recommendation; Applications should be sent by letter.
EIN: 223305742

1026

Dade Community Foundation, Inc.

(formerly Dade Foundation)
200 S. Biscayne Blvd., Ste. 505
Miami, FL 33131-2343 (305) 371-2711
Contact: Ruth Shack, Pres.; For grant applications: Charisse Grant, Dir., Progs.; For grant applications: Betty Alonso, Prog. Off.; For scholarships: Joe Pena
FAX: (305) 371-5342;
E-mail: ruth.shack@dadecommunityfoundation.org;
Additional E-mails:
Charisse.grant@dadecommunityfoundation.org,
Betty.alonso@dadecommunityfoundation.org, and
Todd.weeks@dadecommunityfoundation.org;
URL: http://www.dadecommunityfoundation.org

Foundation type: Community foundation
Limitations: Scholarships to high school students and residents of Dade County, FL.
Publications: Application guidelines; Annual report; Newsletter; Occasional report.
Financial data: Year ended 12/31/2004.
Assets, $117,643,735 (M); Expenditures, $9,304,384; Total giving, $6,663,021.
Fields of interest: Arts education; Journalism/publishing; Performing arts, education; Hispanics/Latinos.
Type of support: Scholarships—to individuals; Support to graduates or students of specific schools; Undergraduate support.
Application information: Application form available on the grantmaker's Web site.

Initial approach: Application by letter.
Deadline(s): Vary
Additional information: See Web site for current list of programs and deadlines.
EIN: 650350357

1027

Frank C. Dailey College Scholarship Fund

c/o Than Richburg
R.R. 1, Box 98
Grapeland, TX 75844-9705
Application address: c/o Karen Bridges, 116 W. Myrtle St., Grapeland, TX, 75844, tel.: (936) 687-4661

Foundation type: Independent foundation
Limitations: Scholarships to graduating seniors of Grapeland Independent School District, TX, for undergraduate education.
Financial data: Year ended 12/31/2004.
Assets, $217,631 (M); Expenditures, $5,559; Total giving, $5,500; Grants to individuals, totaling $5,500.
Type of support: Support to graduates or students of specific schools.
Application information: Deadline May 15; Completion of formal application required, including transcript.
EIN: 752383547

1028

Daiwa Securities America Foundation

c/o Gary Mass
32 Old Slip
New York, NY 10005-3504

Foundation type: Company-sponsored foundation
Limitations: Scholarships to children of employees of Daiwa Securities America, Inc. and its U.S. affiliates. Awards are renewable and limited to $2,500 per semester, or $5,000 per year.
Financial data: Year ended 02/28/2005.
Assets, $594,256 (M); Expenditures, $28,576; Total giving, $28,576; Grants to individuals, 4 grants totaling $17,500 (high: $5,000, low: $2,500).
Type of support: Employee-related scholarships.
Application information: Application form required.
Deadline(s): Nov. 30
EIN: 133637516

1029

Jim & Doris Daley Scholarship Foundation

P.O. Box 343
Somers, MT 59932
Contact: Ashley Mason
Application address: c/o Career Center, Ashley Mason, Flathead High School, Kalispell, MT 59901

Foundation type: Operating foundation
Limitations: Scholarships to graduates of Flathead High School, MT.
Financial data: Year ended 12/31/2003.
Assets, $26,407 (M); Expenditures, $15,561; Total giving, $15,000; Grants to individuals, 3 grants totaling $15,000 (high: $5,000, low: $5,000).
Type of support: Support to graduates or students of specific schools; Undergraduate support.
Application information: Deadline May 1; Completion of formal application required.
EIN: 810533021

1030

Margaret E. Dallas Scholarships

400 E. 6th St.
Tipton, IA 52772

Foundation type: Independent foundation
Limitations: Scholarships to residents of Cedar County, IA, for study at accredited colleges, universities, nursing schools, technical schools, or area schools.
Publications: Application guidelines.
Financial data: Year ended 02/28/2005.
Assets, $202,042 (M); Expenditures, $10,840; Total giving, $9,000.
Fields of interest: Vocational education; Nursing school/education.
Type of support: Technical education support; Undergraduate support.
Application information: Contact foundation for current application deadline; Initial approach by letter; Completion of formal application required, including two letters of recommendation, transcripts, and personal biography.
Program description:
Scholarship Program: Scholarships are renewable. At least one $1,500 scholarship per year will be available to a qualified applicant who has demonstrated a commitment to becoming a kindergarten or early childhood teacher.
EIN: 421238258

1031

Bernard Daly Educational Fund

P.O. Box 351
Lakeview, OR 97630 (541) 947-2196
Contact: James C. Lynch, Secy.-Treas.

Foundation type: Independent foundation
Limitations: Scholarships only to students in Lake County, OR, for study at OR state-supported universities, colleges, and technical schools.
Publications: Application guidelines.
Financial data: Year ended 05/31/2005.
Assets, $4,625,710 (M); Expenditures, $249,065; Total giving, $204,000; Grants to individuals, 39 grants totaling $204,000 (high: $7,250, low: $250).
Fields of interest: Vocational education.
Type of support: Scholarships—to individuals; Technical education support.
Application information: Deadline May 1; Application by letter; Scholarships are renewable.
EIN: 936025466

1032

Elizabeth B. Damato Scholarship Trust

c/o Lawson Products, HR Dept.
1666 E. Touhy Ave.
Des Plaines, IL 60018 (847) 827-9666
Contact: Sidney L. Port, Tr.

Foundation type: Independent foundation
Limitations: Undergraduate scholarships to children of internal employees of Lawson Products who have been working at any Lawson distribution center for at least three years prior to scholarship period, primarily in GA and IL.
Financial data: Year ended 12/31/2004.
Assets, $204,524 (M); Expenditures, $15,131; Total giving, $15,000; Grants to individuals, totaling $15,000.
Type of support: Employee-related scholarships; Undergraduate support.
Application information: Contact trust for current application deadline; Initial approach by letter or

telephone; Completion of formal application required, including class rank, GPA, and transcripts.
Program description:
Betty Damato Scholarship Award: Only graduating high school seniors may apply for this $2,500 scholarship. Applicants must also be dependents of Lawson Products employees of at least three years. Funds may not be used for any college requiring less than two years of study in order to graduate. No grants will be made for graduate school.
EIN: 367034538

1033
Dana Corporation Foundation
P.O. Box 1000
Toledo, OH   43697   (419) 535-4500
Contact: Ed McNeal

Foundation type: Company-sponsored foundation
Limitations: Scholarships only to children of employees of the Driveshaft division of the Dana Corporation.
Publications: Informational brochure (including application guidelines).
Financial data: Year ended 03/31/2004. Assets, $4,762,609 (L); Expenditures, $2,554,895; Total giving, $2,513,662; Grants to individuals, 7 grants totaling $14,000 (high: $2,000, low: $2,000).
Type of support: Employee-related scholarships.
Application information:
Deadline(s): None
Additional information: Contact foundation for current application guidelines.
EIN: 346544909

1034
Opal Dancey Memorial Foundation
c/o Plante Moran Trust
27400 Northwestern Hwy.
Southfield, MI   48037
Contact: Sandra K. Campbell
Application address: c/o Betty D. Godard, Chair., 2637 Revere Rd., Akron, OH 44313;
E-mail: bethinbath@juno.com

Foundation type: Independent foundation
Limitations: Scholarships to students pursuing theological education in the Great Lakes region.
Financial data: Year ended 10/31/2004. Assets, $2,160,150 (M); Expenditures, $112,389; Total giving, $96,000; Grants to individuals, 32 grants totaling $96,000.
Fields of interest: Theological school/education.
Type of support: Scholarships—to individuals.
Application information: Deadline June 15; Completion of formal application required.
EIN: 386361282

1035
David Kendall Danciger Charitable Foundation
12221 Merit Dr., Ste. 1700
Dallas, TX   75251
Contact: Cameron Dee Sewell, V.P.
Application address: 1919 Park Central, Dallas, TX 75271, tel.: (972) 739-1919

Foundation type: Operating foundation
Limitations: Scholarships to individuals in Denver, CO, and Dallas, TX.
Financial data: Year ended 12/31/2003. Assets, $68 (M); Expenditures, $29,997; Total

giving, $29,840; Grants to individuals, 6 grants totaling $29,840 (high: $10,460, low: $428).
Type of support: Scholarships—to individuals.
Application information: Applications accepted.
Initial approach: Letter outlining educational pursuits.
Additional information: Applications should include transcripts.
EIN: 752510985

1036
Danicas Foundation, Inc.
3250 S.W. Doschdale Dr.
Portland, OR   97239-1158   (503) 246-2886
Contact: Daniel E. Casey M.D., Dir.

Foundation type: Independent foundation
Limitations: Scholarships to individuals studying the arts and sciences at an institution of higher learning.
Financial data: Year ended 12/31/2004. Assets, $476,316 (M); Expenditures, $28,859; Total giving, $16,500; Grants to individuals, totaling $16,500.
Fields of interest: Arts; Science.
Type of support: Undergraduate support.
Application information: Applications by letter accepted throughout the year.
EIN: 930875917

1037
Daniels Fund
(formerly Daniels Foundation)
101 Monroe St.
Denver, CO   80206   (303) 393-7220
Contact: Peter Droege, V.P. and Dir., Comms.
FAX: (303) 393-7339;
E-mail: Contact@danielsfund.org; URL: http://www.danielsfund.org

Foundation type: Independent foundation
Limitations: Scholarships to individuals in CO, NM, UT, and WY for higher education.
Publications: Annual report; Financial statement; Grants list.
Financial data: Year ended 12/31/2004. Assets, $1,040,647,749 (M); Expenditures, $43,527,644; Total giving, $34,204,475; Grants to individuals, totaling $7,658,569.
Type of support: Scholarships—to individuals.
Application information: Applications not accepted.
EIN: 841393308

1038
Dante Foundation of Nassau County, Inc.
99 Quentin Roosevelt Blvd.
Garden City, NY   11530   (516) 794-1300
Contact: Hon. Joseph M. Margiotta, Pres.

Foundation type: Public charity
Limitations: Scholarships to deserving students of Italian decent to further their education.
Financial data: Year ended 12/31/2003. Assets, $80,086 (M); Expenditures, $92,792; Total giving, $79,900; Grants to individuals, 17 grants totaling $57,000 (high: $5,000, low: $1,000).
Fields of interest: Higher education; Italy.
Type of support: Scholarships—to individuals.
Application information: Applications accepted.
Initial approach: Letter.
EIN: 112843055

1039
Thomas R. Dargan Minority Scholarship Fund
(formerly KATU Thomas R. Dargan Minority Scholarship Fund)
c/o KATU, Human Resources
P.O. Box 2
Portland, OR   97207-0002   (503) 231-4222
Contact: Rhonda Shelby, Tr.
URL: http://www.katu.com/insidekatu/scholarship.asp

Foundation type: Company-sponsored foundation
Limitations: Scholarships to students of color from OR or WA who are pursuing careers in broadcasting or communications at out-of-state institutions.
Publications: Informational brochure (including application guidelines).
Financial data: Year ended 03/31/2005. Assets, $197,057 (M); Expenditures, $4,119; Total giving, $4,000; Grant to an individual, 1 grant totaling $4,000.
Fields of interest: Media/communications; Minorities.
Type of support: Scholarships—to individuals; Undergraduate support.
Application information:
Deadline(s): Apr. 30
Additional information: Application by letter including letters of recommendation, grades, GPA and essay; Interviews required; Recipients notified by July 1.
Program description:
Scholarship Program: Applicants must be Native American, African American, Latino or Asian. Applicant must have a minimum 3.0 GPA. Scholarship award is $4,000, and is renewable. Winners are eligible for a paid internship in selected departments at Fisher Broadcasting/KATU.
EIN: 943101223

1040
Meredyth Anne Dasburg Foundation
2650 Marshland Rd.
Woodland, MN   55391

Foundation type: Independent foundation
Limitations: Scholarships for elementary and secondary school education, primarily in FL, MN and WA.
Financial data: Year ended 12/31/2004. Assets, $488,170 (M); Expenditures, $467,453; Total giving, $463,676.
Fields of interest: Elementary school/education; Secondary school/education.
Type of support: Precollege support.
Application information: Unsolicited proposals or applications not considered or acknowledged.
EIN: 521608565

1041
Datatel Scholars Foundation
4375 Fair Lakes Ct.
Fairfax, VA   22033   (703) 968-9000
FAX: (703) 968-4625;
E-mail: scholars@datatel.com; Additional tel.: (800) 486-4332; URL: http://www.datatel.com/global/scholarships/

Foundation type: Company-sponsored foundation
Limitations: Scholarships to undergraduate and graduate students attending institutions of higher learning that use Datatel's software.
Publications: Application guidelines.
Financial data: Year ended 12/31/2003. Assets, $143,435 (M); Expenditures, $478,333;

Total giving, $478,100; Grants to individuals, 361 grants totaling $478,100 (high: $2,500, low: $700).
Type of support: Graduate support; Undergraduate support.
Application information:
Deadline(s): Feb. 15
Additional information: Contact college financial aid office or the foundation for current application guidelines; If foundation is contacted, the name of college or university must be indicated to determine eligibility; Applications submitted directly to the foundation are not considered; Applications are returned to college financial aid office which may forward up to two applications to the foundation for consideration.
EIN: 541604129

1042
Daughters of the Cincinnati
c/o Scholarship Admin.
122 E. 58th St
New York, NY   10022   (212) 319-6915
URL: http://foundationcenter.org/grantmaker/cincinnati/

Foundation type: Independent foundation
Limitations: Scholarships to high school seniors who are daughters of regular commissioned officers (on active duty, retired, or deceased) in the Army, Navy, Air Force, Coast Guard, or Marines.
Publications: Annual report.
Financial data: Year ended 12/31/2004.
Assets, $2,355,437 (M); Expenditures, $198,148; Total giving, $74,825; Grants to individuals, 28 grants totaling $73,075 (high: $5,500, low: $500).
Fields of interest: Military/veterans' organizations; Women.
Type of support: Undergraduate support.
Application information: Applications accepted. Application form required.
Deadline(s): Mar. 15
Additional information: Initial approach by letter requesting application forms, including parent's name, rank, branch of service, and applicant's current year in high school.
Program description:
Scholarship Program: Undergraduate scholarships, awarded to high school seniors, are available in amounts up to $1,500 annually for four years, subject to a review each year of the candidate's academic record. The foundation requires copies of the applicant's SAT or ACT scores in addition to completion of the Biographical Questionnaire and a letter of recommendation from a member of the community other than family or school. Applicant's school must complete the Secondary School Questionnaire and submit an official transcript. The applicant's parents must file a FAF with The College Scholarship Service, Princeton, NJ. On the FAF the applicant should indicate that a copy is to be sent to the foundation, code number 0174. The applicant must include $5 for postage and handling to the foundation.
EIN: 136096069

1043
Henry & Sidney T. Davenport Educational Family Foundation
(formerly Henry & Sidney T. Davenport Educational Fund)
c/o Centura Bank
P.O. Box 1220
Rocky Mount, NC   27803   (252) 454-4017
Contact: Sharon M. Stephens, Trust Off., Centura Bank

Foundation type: Independent foundation
Limitations: Student loans to financially needy residents of Nash and Edgecombe counties, NC, who are U.S. citizens.
Financial data: Year ended 06/30/2005.
Assets, $786,207 (M); Expenditures, $2,410; Total giving, $2,200; Loans to individuals, totaling $2,200.
Type of support: Student loans—to individuals.
Application information: Applications accepted. Application form required.
Deadline(s): June 1
Applicants should submit the following:
1) SAT
2) ACT
3) Financial information
4) Transcripts
Program description:
Loans: Recipients are selected on the basis of financial need, qualities of leadership, good citizenship, force of character and community spirit, and scholarship. Preference is given to graduates of schools in Nash and Edgecombe counties, NC. Loans are renewable for subsequent academic years provided that the student maintains satisfactory academic standing. Recipients must repay their loans within five years of graduation. No interest is paid while the student is still in school.
EIN: 237422939

1044
John K. and Thirza F. Davenport Foundation
c/o TD Banknorth, N.A.
P.O. Box 1180
South Yarmouth, MA   02664
Application address: c/o Dewitt P. Davenport, 20 N. Main St., South Yarmouth, MA 02664

Foundation type: Independent foundation
Limitations: Scholarships to students of the arts who are residents of Barnstable County, MA.
Financial data: Year ended 06/30/2005.
Assets, $633,684 (M); Expenditures, $35,899; Total giving, $31,025; Grants to individuals, totaling $16,625.
Fields of interest: Arts education.
Type of support: Scholarships—to individuals.
Application information: Applications accepted throughout the year; Completion of formal application required.
EIN: 222647795

1045
Davey Scholarship Foundation
c/o JPMorgan Chase Bank, N.A
P.O. Box 1308
Milwaukee, WI   53201-1308
Contact: JoAnn Ley, Trust Off., JPMorgan Chase Bank, N.A.
Application address: 1 E. Old State Capitol Plz., Springfield, IL 62701-1320, tel.: (217) 525-9747

Foundation type: Independent foundation

Limitations: Loans awarded to high school graduates of Sangamon, Morgan, and Christian counties, IL. Applicants must be between 16 and 25 years of age.
Financial data: Year ended 06/30/2005.
Assets, $2,519,140 (M); Expenditures, $45,219; Total giving, $0; Loans to individuals, totaling $100,726.
Type of support: Student loans—to individuals.
Application information: Application form required.
Deadline(s): June 15
EIN: 376057502

1046
The Paul & Carol David Foundation
(formerly The David Family Foundation)
6283 Frank Ave. N.W.
North Canton, OH   44720   (330) 490-2600
Contact: Jeffrey David, Pres.
FAX: (330) 497-4499

Foundation type: Independent foundation
Limitations: Scholarships to qualified high school students in Stark County, OH.
Financial data: Year ended 12/31/2004.
Assets, $52,733,259 (M); Expenditures, $2,264,931; Total giving, $1,826,226; Grants to individuals, 109 grants totaling $330,201.
Type of support: Scholarships—to individuals.
Application information: Applications accepted throughout the year; Completion of formal application required.
EIN: 341319236

1047
The Davidson Krueger Foundation
5002 2nd Ave.
Brooklyn, NY   11232

Foundation type: Independent foundation
Limitations: Scholarships to children of FL and NY employees of Davidson Pipe Supply Co., Inc., for higher education.
Financial data: Year ended 11/30/2004.
Assets, $1,550,420 (M); Expenditures, $186,827; Total giving, $183,960; Grant to an individual, 1 grant totaling $11,100.
Type of support: Employee-related scholarships.
Application information: Deadline Mar. 15; Application by letter including transcripts.
EIN: 116005674

1048
Daisy Davies Educational Fund
(formerly Daisy Davies Educational Foundation of Friendship Class of Peachtree Road Methodist Church)
4534 Tall Pines Dr.
Atlanta, GA   30327
Contact: William F. Lozier, Secy.

Foundation type: Independent foundation
Limitations: Scholarships to individuals in GA, including for theological study.
Financial data: Year ended 05/31/2005.
Assets, $263,135 (M); Expenditures, $10,107; Total giving, $10,000; Grants to individuals, totaling $10,000.
Fields of interest: Theological school/education.
Type of support: Scholarships—to individuals.
Application information: Deadline Sept. 1; Application by letter, explaining goals and

objectives supported by a budget proposal of income and expenses.
EIN: 586030091

1049
John and Shirley Davies Foundation
(formerly Bishopric Foundation)
8044 Montgomery Rd., Ste. 163
Cincinnati, OH 45236-2923 (513) 791-6699
Contact: S. John Davies, Jr., Pres.

Foundation type: Independent foundation
Limitations: Scholarships to students who graduated from Goshen School District, OH, who are members of One Earth One People (OEOP), Cincinnati, OH.
Financial data: Year ended 12/31/2004. Assets, $507,149 (M); Expenditures, $577,701; Total giving, $550,546; Grants to individuals, 2 grants totaling $2,400 (high: $1,200, low: $1,200).
Type of support: Support to graduates or students of specific schools; Undergraduate support.
Application information: Applications accepted.
  Deadline(s): None
Program description:
  Scholarship Program: Recipients must maintain an overall GPA of 3.0. Applicants must demonstrate financial need.
EIN: 311335126

1050
Walter L. J. Davies Memorial Scholarship
c/o U.S. Bank, N.A.
P.O. Box 3168
Portland, OR 97208-3168
Application address: c/o State Scholarship Commission, 1445 Williamette St., Eugene, OR 97401, URL: http://www.getcollegefunds.org

Foundation type: Independent foundation
Limitations: Scholarships for full-time undergraduate or vocational study to financially needy employees or children of employees of U.S. Bancorp who have graduated from a high school in OR.
Financial data: Year ended 06/30/2005. Assets, $1,079,705 (M); Expenditures, $68,527; Total giving, $49,700; Grants to individuals, totaling $49,700.
Fields of interest: Vocational education.
Type of support: Employee-related scholarships; Technical education support.
Application information: Deadline Apr. 1; Completion of Private Award application required, including transcripts, GPA, SAT or ACT scores, and a federally-approved need analysis form; Application form available from the State Scholarship Commission.
Program description:
  Scholarship Program: Applicants are ranked by the State Scholarship Committee according to GPA, aptitude test scores, and financial need. Recipients are notified by July 1. Scholarships are renewable.
EIN: 936163624

1051
Joe Davies Scholarship Foundation
4600 East West Hwy., Ste. 900
Bethesda, MD 20814
Contact: Lawrence R. Beebe, V.P. and Treas.

Foundation type: Independent foundation

Limitations: Scholarships to financially needy graduating high school seniors who are residents of Dodge, Jefferson, and Dane counties, WI, for attendance at the University of Wisconsin.
Financial data: Year ended 12/31/2004. Assets, $774,873 (M); Expenditures, $44,731; Total giving, $40,370; Grants to individuals, 7 grants totaling $40,370.
Type of support: Support to graduates or students of specific schools; Undergraduate support.
Application information: Application form required.
  Deadline(s): Contact foundation for current application deadline.
  Additional information: Application form available from the Board of Education in each community.
EIN: 530218110

1052
William G. Davis Charitable Trust
c/o PNC Advisors
620 Liberty Ave., 10th Fl.
Pittsburgh, PA 15222-2705
Application address: c/o David L. Wylie, Doric Lodge No. 630, 409 Chestnut Rd., Sewickley, PA 15143

Foundation type: Independent foundation
Limitations: Undergraduate scholarships to children of Master Members of Doric Lodge No. 630.
Financial data: Year ended 12/31/2003. Assets, $642,084 (M); Expenditures, $36,241; Total giving, $30,450; Grants to individuals, 12 grants totaling $29,950 (high: $5,529, low: $524).
Fields of interest: Fraternal societies; Greece.
Type of support: Undergraduate support.
Application information: Deadline Dec. 1; Completion of formal application required.
EIN: 251289600

1053
Edward Davis Education Foundation
585 E. Larned St., Ste. 100
Detroit, MI 48226 (877) 847-9060
URL: http://www.onwheelsinc.com/EDEFoundation/

Foundation type: Public charity
Limitations: Scholarships to minorities pursuing careers in the auto industry.
Financial data: Year ended 12/31/2003. Assets, $149,007; Expenditures, $256,100; Total giving, $28,500; Grants to individuals, 17 grants totaling $28,500 (high: $2,000, low: $1,500).
Fields of interest: Safety, automotive safety; Minorities.
Type of support: Undergraduate support.
Application information: Applications accepted. Application form required.
  Deadline(s): Sept. 30
  Applicants should submit the following:
    1) Transcripts
    2) Essay
  Additional information: Application must also include photo and two letters of recommendation.
EIN: 383431880

1054
Grace Davis Education Trust
c/o S&T Trust Co.
43 S. 9th St.
Indiana, PA 15701

Foundation type: Independent foundation
Limitations: Scholarships to individuals enrolled at a college or university in PA.
Financial data: Year ended 12/31/2004. Assets, $594,458 (M); Expenditures, $27,305; Total giving, $20,000; Grants to individuals, 10 grants totaling $20,000.
Type of support: Scholarships—to individuals.
Application information: Applications not accepted.
  Additional information: Unsolicited requests for funds not considered or acknowledged.
EIN: 256494236

1055
Charles E. Davis Educational Foundation
c/o Wells Fargo Bank Northwest, N.A.
P.O. Box 21927, MAC P6540-144
Seattle, WA 98111
Application address: c/o Sherman County Scholarship Assoc., P.O. Box 0444, Moro, OR 97039-0444

Foundation type: Independent foundation
Limitations: Scholarships to graduates of Sherman County, OR, high schools.
Financial data: Year ended 07/31/2004. Assets, $359,234 (M); Expenditures, $57,153; Total giving, $44,642; Grants to individuals, totaling $44,642.
Type of support: Support to graduates or students of specific schools; Undergraduate support.
Application information: Deadline May 30; Completion of formal application required.
EIN: 936170500

1056
James A. and Juliet L. Davis Foundation, Inc.
1 Compound Dr.
Hutchinson, KS 67502-4349 (620) 662-8331
Contact: Merl F. Sellers, Pres.

Foundation type: Independent foundation
Limitations: Scholarships strictly limited to students graduating from Hutchinson High School, KS. The foundation also gives Educator of the Year Awards.
Financial data: Year ended 12/31/2004. Assets, $4,711,502 (M); Expenditures, $223,682; Total giving, $196,567.
Fields of interest: Education; Global programs.
Type of support: Support to graduates or students of specific schools; Awards/prizes; Undergraduate support.
Application information: Deadline Mar. 15; Recipients are chosen by a review committee.
EIN: 486105748

1057
Jones S. Davis Foundation
c/o JPMorgan Chase Bank, N.A.
P.O. Box 1308
Milwaukee, WI 53201
Application address: c/o JPMorgan Chase Bank, N.A., P.O. Box 91210, Baton Rouge, FL 70821

Foundation type: Independent foundation
Limitations: Scholarships to individuals in LA for higher education.
Financial data: Year ended 08/31/2004. Assets, $1,177,974 (M); Expenditures, $79,940; Total giving, $68,000.
Type of support: Undergraduate support.

Application information: Applications by letter, including transcripts, ACT scores, major, and college choice, accepted throughout the year.
EIN: 726023237

1058
Lewis J. & Nelle A. Davis Foundation
c/o National City Bank
P.O. Box 94651
Cleveland, OH 44101-4651
Application address: c/o Superintendent, Galion School District, Galion, OH 44833

Foundation type: Independent foundation
Limitations: Scholarships to students who rank in the upper half of the senior class of Galion High School, OH.
Financial data: Year ended 11/30/2004.
Assets, $2,409,108 (M); Expenditures, $116,232; Total giving, $111,000; Grants to individuals, 37 grants totaling $111,000 (high: $4,000, low: $2,000).
Type of support: Support to graduates or students of specific schools; Undergraduate support.
Application information: Applications by letter accepted throughout the year.
EIN: 346942736

1059
William E. & Rose Marie Davis Foundation
2391 Davis Mountain Ln.
Omaha, NE 68112-5159 (402) 250-3599
Contact: Heather Abbott, Secy.

Foundation type: Independent foundation
Limitations: Scholarships to high school graduates or GED recipients, primarily in NE, for higher education.
Financial data: Year ended 12/31/2004.
Assets, $860,489 (M); Expenditures, $68,550; Total giving, $47,863; Grants to individuals, 10 grants totaling $17,363 (high: $5,000, low: $500).
Type of support: Scholarships—to individuals.
Application information: Application form required.
Initial approach: Telephone.
Copies of proposal: 1
Deadline(s): July 1 and Jan. 1
Applicants should submit the following:
  1) Transcripts
  2) SAT
  3) Letter(s) of recommendation
  4) ACT
Additional information: Application should also include essay of no more than 300 words about experiences and/or potential as a leader.
Program description:
Scholarship Program: Recipients must maintain at least a 2.2 cumulative GPA. Scholarships are renewable.
EIN: 911787066

1060
Fred W. Davis Memorial Foundation
c/o Wachovia Bank, N.A.
100 N. Main St., 13th Fl.
Winston-Salem, NC 27150

Foundation type: Independent foundation
Limitations: Scholarships only to Episcopal seminary students in FL for their second year of study.
Financial data: Year ended 08/31/2004.
Assets, $745,006 (M); Expenditures, $43,243;

Total giving, $34,500; Grants to individuals, totaling $34,435.
Fields of interest: Theological school/education; Protestant agencies & churches.
Type of support: Scholarships—to individuals.
Application information: Deadline 30 days prior to semester; Application by letter, including financial need and scholastic achievements; Applicants must be recommended by Dean of their Episcopalian seminary.
EIN: 596717509

1061
Dorothy Davis Scholarship Fund
c/o PNC Advisors
1600 Market St., Tax Dept., 4th Fl.
Philadelphia, PA 19103-7240 (215) 585-3977
Application address: c/o Trust Dept., PNC Bank, N.A., 150 Broad St., 2nd Fl., Red Bank, NJ 07701

Foundation type: Independent foundation
Limitations: Merit-based scholarships to residents of Rumson, NJ, who have been nominated by their high school principals.
Financial data: Year ended 12/31/2004.
Assets, $838,086 (M); Expenditures, $62,797; Total giving, $54,000; Grants to individuals, totaling $54,000.
Type of support: Awards/grants by nomination only; Undergraduate support.
Application information:
Deadline(s): None
Additional information: Application by letter, including personal statement and letters of recommendation.
Program description:
George Walter Davis Scholarship: Each year, two scholarships are awarded, one to a male applicant and one to a female applicant. Applicants must have distinguished academic accomplishments over their last three years. In addition, they must have demonstrated significant accomplishment in a non-academic area (e.g., art, music, sports, community services, leadership). Recipients receive a $3,000 scholarship award for the first year of study. Scholarships are renewable for up to four years provided the student remains in good standing. Award amounts may be increased after the first year.
EIN: 226631276

1062
Helen S. Davis Scholarship Trust No. 3
(also known as Davis Medical School Scholarships)
c/o Wells Fargo Bank Northwest, N.A.
P.O. Box 21927, MAC P6540-144
Seattle, WA 98111
Application address: c/o Wells Fargo Bank Montana, N.A., P.O. Box 597, Helena, MT 59624

Foundation type: Independent foundation
Limitations: Scholarships only to residents of MT attending accredited medical schools.
Financial data: Year ended 08/31/2004.
Assets, $1,777,209 (M); Expenditures, $102,464; Total giving, $82,000; Grants to individuals, 25 grants totaling $82,000 (high: $7,000, low: $1,000).
Fields of interest: Medical school/education.
Type of support: Graduate support.
Application information: Deadline May 30; Completion of formal application required, including undergraduate transcripts, three reference letters, federal income tax forms, and letter of acceptance from, or proof of enrollment at, an accredited

medical school; Applications can be obtained at Wells Fargo Bank, N.A., PCS.
EIN: 816056734

1063
Margaret L. Davis Trust Fund
c/o JPMorgan Chase Bank, N.A.
P.O. Box 1308
Milwaukee, WI 53201-1308
Application addresses: c/o Principal, Perry Meridian High School, 410 W. Meridian School Rd., Indianapolis, IN 46217 or c/o Southport High School, 971 E. Banta Rd., Indianapolis, IN 46227

Foundation type: Independent foundation
Limitations: Scholarships to current graduates of Perry Meridian High School, Indianapolis, IN, and Southport High School, IN. Scholarships are renewable for up to four years of study provided that the student maintains at least a "B" average.
Financial data: Year ended 10/31/2004.
Assets, $523,114 (M); Expenditures, $32,766; Total giving, $27,000; Grants to individuals, 12 grants totaling $27,000 (high: $2,500, low: $2,000).
Type of support: Support to graduates or students of specific schools; Undergraduate support.
Application information: Applications accepted. Application form required.
Initial approach: Letter or telephone.
Deadline(s): Apr. 12
Additional information: Application must include an essay and a list of extracurricular activities.
EIN: 351973505

1064
Jean M. Davis Trust
c/o Elmira Sundell
3390 Hazelton Ave.
Rochester Hills, MI 48307-4922

Foundation type: Independent foundation
Limitations: Scholarships to students studying veterinary medicine at Michigan State University, Ohio State University, and Perdue University, IN.
Financial data: Year ended 12/31/2004.
Assets, $90,228 (M); Expenditures, $24,470; Total giving, $21,000; Grants to individuals, totaling $21,000.
Fields of interest: Veterinary medicine.
Type of support: Support to graduates or students of specific schools; Undergraduate support.
Application information: Applications not accepted.
EIN: 596828711

1065
Davis-Roberts Scholarship Fund, Inc.
P. O. Box 20645
Cheyenne, WY 82003 (307) 632-0491
Contact: Gary D. Skillern, Secy.- Treas.
Application address: 342 Bocage Dr., Cheyenne, WY 82009-3524

Foundation type: Independent foundation
Limitations: Scholarships to members or former members of the Order of DeMolay or Job's Daughters in WY, for full-time study at any college or university.
Financial data: Year ended 12/31/2004.
Assets, $84,727 (M); Expenditures, $3,219; Total giving, $3,000; Grants to individuals, totaling $3,000.
Type of support: Scholarships—to individuals.

Application information: Deadline June 15; Initial approach by letter or telephone; Completion of formal application required, including transcripts, letter from applicant's Chapter Dad or Bethel Guardian, letter of endorsement from an individual unrelated to the applicant, and photograph of applicant.
Program description:
Scholarship Program: Scholarships are awarded on the basis of financial need and character. Awards are renewable.
EIN: 836011403

1066
DaVita Children's Foundation
c/o DaVita Inc., Tax Dept.
1423 Pacific Ave.
Tacoma, WA 98402

Foundation type: Company-sponsored foundation
Limitations: Scholarships to children and grandchildren of WA employees of DaVita, Inc.
Financial data: Year ended 12/31/2005.
Assets, $434,055 (M); Expenditures, $29,230; Total giving, $28,888; Grants to individuals, totaling $28,888.
Type of support: Employee-related scholarships.
Application information: Unsolicited requests for funds not accepted.
EIN: 330932587

1067
Blanche L. Dawson Nursing Scholarship Fund
c/o Belvidere National Bank & Trust Co.
600 S. State St.
Belvidere, IL 61008-4322 (815) 547-5200
Contact: Mark Stearns, Tr.

Foundation type: Independent foundation
Limitations: Scholarships to young women residing in Boone County, IL, who are nursing students.
Financial data: Year ended 05/31/2005.
Assets, $296,338 (M); Expenditures, $9,991; Total giving, $6,250.
Fields of interest: Nursing school/education; Women.
Type of support: Undergraduate support.
Application information: Deadline Apr. 30; Completion of formal application required.
EIN: 366877151

1068
Muriel R. Dawson Scholarship Trust
c/o The Citizens National Bank of Paris
P.O. Box 790
Paris, IL 61944 (217) 465-7641
Contact: Chris Jurcin, Trust Off., The Citizens National Bank of Paris

Foundation type: Independent foundation
Limitations: Scholarships to residents of the Shiloh Unit Two School District in Edgar County, IL, for study at a public university or college in IL.
Financial data: Year ended 12/31/2004.
Assets, $237,145 (M); Expenditures, $13,408; Total giving, $9,497; Grants to individuals, totaling $9,497.
Type of support: Scholarships—to individuals.
Application information: Deadline May 15; Completion of formal application required.
EIN: 376134534

1069
The Carl and Virginia Day Trust
125 E. Jefferson St.
Yazoo City, MS 39194-4552 (662) 746-4901
Contact: Carolyn Johnson

Foundation type: Independent foundation
Limitations: Interest-free student loans to residents of MS who are under 25 years old, have a 2.0 GPA, and attend MS schools.
Publications: Annual report; Financial statement.
Financial data: Year ended 12/31/2003.
Assets, $3,271,954 (M); Expenditures, $360,558; Total giving, $320,750; Loans to individuals, 187 loans totaling $320,750.
Type of support: Student loans—to individuals; Undergraduate support.
Application information:
Deadline(s): July 4 for fall loans and Nov. 4 for spring loans
Additional information: Application by letter, including statement of school planning to attend, transcripts, state of residence, parents' financial statements and four references.
Program description:
Student Loan Program: Approximately 100 students are assisted annually. Loans are repaid at the rate of $100 per month.
EIN: 640386095

1070
The Dayton Foundation
2300 Kettering Twr.
Dayton, OH 45423-1395 (937) 222-0410
Contact: Michael M. Parks, Pres.; For discretionary grants: Marilyn Shannon, Sr. Prog. Off.
FAX: (937) 222-0636;
E-mail: info@daytonfoundation.org; Additional tel.: (877) 222-0410; Additional E-mails: Dtimmons@daytonfoundation.org and Mshannon@daytonfoundation.org; URL: http://www.daytonfoundation.org

Foundation type: Community foundation
Limitations: Scholarships to students from the greater Dayton, OH, area for postsecondary education.
Publications: Application guidelines; Financial statement; Newsletter; Program policy statement.
Financial data: Year ended 06/30/2005.
Assets, $260,578,404 (M); Expenditures, $40,716,582; Total giving, $30,381,725; Grants to individuals, 1,063 grants totaling $1,532,936.
Fields of interest: Media/communications; Journalism/publishing; Visual arts; Photography; Dance; Arts; Vocational education; Business school/education; Teacher school/education; Engineering school/education; Crime/law enforcement, police agencies; Community development, volunteer services; African Americans/Blacks.
Type of support: Employee-related scholarships; Support to graduates or students of specific schools; Awards/prizes; Undergraduate support.
Application information: Contact foundation for current application deadline.
Program descriptions:
Scholarship: Scholarships are available for students who are graduating from one of the 30 area high schools. Scholarships are also available for students already enrolled in school pursuing degrees in photojournalism, mathematics, turfgrass management and music. These, however, are limited to certain colleges/universities. The foundation also administers scholarships for children of employees of certain corporations

including, but not limited to Dayton Superior, Unibilt Industries, and GM/Frigidaire/Delphi.
Friendship Award: Awards to Dayton-area students who are making a difference in the fight against bigotry, bias and hate.
EIN: 316027287

1071
Dayton Masonic Foundation
P.O. Box 932
Dayton, OH 45401-0932
Contact: Marvin Olinsky, Exec. Dir.
URL: http://www.daytonmasoniccenter.org

Foundation type: Public charity
Limitations: Scholarships to students from the fourteen-county Dayton, OH, area for higher education.
Financial data: Year ended 07/31/2004.
Assets, $565,971 (M); Expenditures, $215,083; Total giving, $31,349; Grants to individuals, 16 grants totaling $29,600 (high: $2,000, low: $800).
Type of support: Undergraduate support.
Application information:
Initial approach: Letter.
Additional information: Contact foundation for further application information.
EIN: 311385609

1072
Faye H. Deane Scholarship Fund
c/o Thomas A. Maddigan
P.O. Box 714
Middleboro, MA 02346
Application address: c/o Principal, Middleboro High School, 71 E. Grove St., Middleboro, MA 02346, tel.: (508) 946-2010

Foundation type: Independent foundation
Limitations: Scholarships to financially needy students who have graduated or are graduating from Middleborough High School, MA, for higher education.
Financial data: Year ended 12/31/2004.
Assets, $495,602 (M); Expenditures, $35,241; Total giving, $28,450; Grants to individuals, totaling $28,450.
Type of support: Scholarships—to individuals; Support to graduates or students of specific schools.
Application information: Application form required.
Deadline(s): Apr. 30
Additional information: Application should include needs and grades; Application form available from the high school principal.
EIN: 042900642

1073
Dearborn Community Foundation
(formerly Dearborn County Community Foundation)
204 Short St.
Lawrenceburg, IN 47025 (812) 539-4115
Contact: Fred McCarter, Exec. Dir.; For grants: Alyson K. Glaze, Dir., Progs.
FAX: (812) 539-4119; E-mail: info@dearborncf.org; Grant information E-mail: dcf@suscom.net; URL: http://www.dearborncf.org

Foundation type: Community foundation
Limitations: Grants and scholarships for residents of Dearborn County, IN.
Publications: Annual report; Newsletter.
Financial data: Year ended 12/31/2004.
Assets, $10,307,228 (M); Expenditures,

$3,503,505; Total giving, $3,184,661; Grants to individuals, totaling $681,437.

Fields of interest: Engineering school/education.

Type of support: Support to graduates or students of specific schools; Technical education support; Undergraduate support.

Application information: Application form required.

Deadline(s): Jan. 14

Additional information: Interviews required.

Program description:

Dearborn Community Scholarships: The foundation administers the following funds:

- Dearborn Community Foundation Scholarships: This program awards up to nine $1,000 scholarships to finalists in the Lilly Endowment Community Scholarship Program
- Ray Peterson Memorial Scholarship Fund: This program provides assistance for higher education to individuals seeking degrees in engineering
- Ronald Selmeyer Memorial Scholarship: This program is for graduates of Lawrenceville High School who are pursuing a bachelor's or master's degree
- Michael Cleary Memorial Scholarship: Awards scholarships to graduates of East Central High School who are planning to attend an accredited vocational school
- Lawrenceburg Kiwanis Club Scholarship: Awards to students pursuing a two- or four-year degree
- Lilly Endowment Community Scholarship: Awards for four-year's tuition and stipends to students attending an accredited college or university in IN
- Perpetual Rotary Scholarship: Awards to graduates of South Dearborn High School.

EIN: 352036110

1074

W. G. Dearing Educational Trust Fund

c/o Marshall National Bank & Trust Co.

P.O. Box 38

Marshall, VA 20116-0038

Foundation type: Independent foundation

Limitations: Educational loans to residents of Marshall, VA.

Financial data: Year ended 12/31/2004. Assets, $336,365 (M); Expenditures, $164; Total giving, $0; Loans to individuals, totaling $10,000.

Type of support: Student loans—to individuals.

Application information: Contact fund for current application deadline/guidelines.

EIN: 546039319

1075

The Edward J. DeBartolo Memorial Scholarship Foundation

7620 Market St.

Youngstown, OH 44512   (330) 965-2000

Contact: Cindy Miller

Foundation type: Independent foundation

Limitations: Scholarships to individuals in Youngstown, OH, for higher education.

Financial data: Year ended 12/31/2004. Assets, $575,774 (M); Expenditures, $126,588; Total giving, $30,000; Grants to individuals, totaling $30,000.

Type of support: Scholarships—to individuals.

Application information: Deadline within 15 days of receiving application; Completion of formal application required.

EIN: 311527910

1076

Debenham-Alaska Scholarships, Inc.

2932 C St., Ste. C

Anchorage, AK 99503   (907) 562-9330

Foundation type: Independent foundation

Limitations: Scholarships to residents of AK, UT, WA, for full-time study at an approved educational institution.

Financial data: Year ended 06/30/2005. Assets, $500 (M); Expenditures, $15,145; Total giving, $15,000; Grants to individuals, totaling $15,000.

Type of support: Scholarships—to individuals.

Application information: Deadline May 31; Completion of formal application required, including transcripts, two black and white photographs, and two-page personal essay.

Program description:

Scholarship Program: Scholarships are renewable, provided that the recipient maintains at least a 2.7 GPA.

EIN: 920076887

1077

Decatur County Community Foundation, Inc.

101 E. Main St., Ste. 1

P.O. Box 72

Greensburg, IN 47240   (812) 662-6364

Contact: Sharon Hollowell, Exec. Dir.

FAX: (812) 662-8704;

E-mail: contact@dccfound.org; URL: http://www.dccfound.org

Foundation type: Community foundation

Limitations: Scholarships to residents of Decatur County, IN, for undergraduate education at American colleges and universities.

Publications: Application guidelines; Annual report (including application guidelines); Financial statement; Informational brochure; Informational brochure (including application guidelines); Newsletter; Occasional report.

Financial data: Year ended 12/31/2004. Assets, $14,590,332 (M); Expenditures, $790,709; Total giving, $628,442.

Fields of interest: Arts education; Music; Nursing school/education; Teacher school/education; Engineering school/education; Health sciences school/education; Agriculture/food, formal/general education; Athletics/sports, school programs; Science, formal/general education.

Type of support: Support to graduates or students of specific schools; Technical education support; Undergraduate support.

Application information: Applications accepted. Application form required.

Deadline(s): Vary

Additional information: Scholarship applications are available at Foundation Office or at guidance counselor's office.

Program description:

Scholarships: The foundation administers approximately 30 scholarships for local students. Please see Web site for a complete listing of programs.

EIN: 351870979

1078

C. H. Deem Scholarship Fund

c/o JPMorgan Chase Bank, N.A.

P.O. Box 1308

Milwaukee, WI 53201

Application address: c/o Tom Honderich, JPMorgan Chase Bank, N.A., 111 Monument Cir., IN1-0169, Indianapolis, IN 46277-0115, tel.: (317) 321-1355

Foundation type: Independent foundation

Limitations: Scholarships to graduates who are residents of the State of Victoria, Australia, who are studying food technology in the U.S., primarily to attend Purdue University.

Financial data: Year ended 02/28/2005. Assets, $358,604 (M); Expenditures, $48,225; Total giving, $41,519.

Fields of interest: Nutrition; Business/industry.

Type of support: Foreign applicants; Graduate support.

Application information: Applications by letter accepted throughout the year.

Program description:

Scholarship Program: Scholarships are awarded on the basis of attendance, progress, physical fitness, conduct, personality, general intelligence, character, initiative, integrity, and a general grounding in basic subjects, such as mathematics, physics, biology, and chemistry. Preference is shown to applicants who are not married and who are working toward a graduate degree at Purdue University in the field of food technology. Applicants are expected to provide:

- evidence of an interest in food technology and its problems, including the applicant's experience in the field
- evidence of the applicant's potential for development in the science or art of food technology
- evidence of an ability to set up an improved quality control program and make necessary laboratory determinations

The fund pays recipients a monthly stipend based on the student's requirements, the available income of the trust, and a pre-established budget. After a recipient has received a stipend for three years, the fund will request that he or she seek other support. The fund also provides housing and one roundtrip airfare from Australia. Recipients are expected to progress at a reasonable rate of success toward a degree. Students must maintain a superior GPA and send copies of grade reports to the fund.

EIN: 356381311

1079

Deering Foundation, Inc.

4 Kona Rd.

Darien, CT 06820

Application address: c/o Thomas Copadis, Peter Hill Rd., Deering, NH 03244, tel.: (603) 529-2441

Foundation type: Independent foundation

Limitations: Scholarships to Deering, Hillsboro, and Weare, NH, area students. Preference is given to those majoring in medicine, social service, and related fields.

Financial data: Year ended 05/31/2005. Assets, $0 (M); Expenditures, $22,854; Total giving, $21,500; Grants to individuals, 16 grants totaling $20,000 (high: $2,000, low: $1,000).

Fields of interest: Medical school/education; Social sciences.

Type of support: Scholarships—to individuals.

Application information: Deadline May 1; Initial approach by letter, including present and proposed school, field of interest, financial support available

from family, and personal income; Completion of formal application required; Scholarships are renewable.
EIN: 026012645

1080

Mark Deering Foundation

c/o John F. Sheehy, Jr.
510 N. Valley Hills Dr., Ste. 500
Waco, TX 76710
Contact: Msgr. Msgr. Mark Deering, Dir.
Application address: 4700 Westchester Dr., Waco, TX 76710, tel.: (254) 772-5263

Foundation type: Independent foundation
Limitations: Scholarships to individuals who attend Roman Catholic schools in the greater Waco, TX, area.
Financial data: Year ended 12/31/2004. Assets, $302,250 (M); Expenditures, $25,792; Total giving, $24,505; Grants to individuals, totaling $24,505.
Fields of interest: Roman Catholic agencies & churches.
Type of support: Scholarships—to individuals.
Application information: Applications by letter, outlining financial needs and student qualifications, accepted throughout the year; Recipients usually notified within one month.
EIN: 742726640

1081

DeKalb County Community Foundation

The Atrium Office Ctr.
2600 DeKalb Ave., Ste. J
Sycamore, IL 60178 (815) 748-5383
Contact: Jerome A. Smith, Secy.
FAX: (815) 748-5873;
E-mail: jerry@dekalbcountyfoundation.org;
URL: http://www.dekalbcountyfoundation.org

Foundation type: Community foundation
Limitations: Scholarships to students who are residents of DeKalb County, IL, for higher education.
Publications: Application guidelines; Annual report; Informational brochure; Newsletter; Occasional report.
Financial data: Year ended 12/31/2004. Assets, $17,944,763 (M); Expenditures, $1,034,472; Total giving, $816,347; Grants to individuals, 49 grants totaling $67,454 (high: $11,150).
Type of support: Graduate support; Undergraduate support.
Application information: Deadlines Feb. 23 and Sept. 1; Contact foundation for current application guidelines; Initial approach by proposal.
Program description:
Scholarship Program: The foundation offers numerous scholarships in the DeKalb County, IL, area. See Web site for complete listing of scholarship funds.
EIN: 363788167

1082

DeKalb County Producers' Supply and Farm Bureau Scholarship Trust Fund

c/o DeKalb County Farm Bureau
1350 W. Prairie Dr.
Sycamore, IL 60178-3166 (815) 756-6361

Foundation type: Independent foundation

Limitations: Scholarships to IL residents obtaining a medical education (including veterinary medicine, nursing, and pharmacology) whose parents have been members of the DeKalb County Farm Bureau in good standing for at least two years.
Financial data: Year ended 09/30/2002. Assets, $99,867 (M); Expenditures, $5,150; Total giving, $2,525; Grants to individuals, totaling $2,525.
Fields of interest: Medical school/education; Nursing school/education; Veterinary medicine.
Type of support: Graduate support.
Application information: Contact foundation for current application deadline; Completion of formal application required.
EIN: 237136011

1083

Delaware Community Foundation

P.O. Box 1636
Wilmington, DE 19899 (302) 571-8004
Contact: Elizabeth Bouchelle, Dir., Grants Admin.;
For administered scholarships: Richard Gentsch
FAX: (302) 571-1553; E-mail: info@delcf.org; Tel. for grant application inquiries: (302) 504-5239; E-mail for grant application inquiries: bbouchelle@delcf.org; Tel. for administered scholarships: (302) 504-5222, E-mail for administered scholarships: rgentsch@delcf.org; URL: http://www.delcf.org

Foundation type: Community foundation
Limitations: Scholarships to students and professionals residing in DE for attendance at U.S. colleges and universities.
Publications: Application guidelines; Annual report; Informational brochure; Newsletter.
Financial data: Year ended 06/30/2004. Assets, $163,306,665 (M); Expenditures, $13,870,528; Total giving, $10,645,468.
Fields of interest: Arts, formal/general education; Ballet; Theater; Vocational education; Vocational school, secondary; Law school/education; Medical school/education; Nursing school/education; Engineering school/education; Nonprofit management.
Type of support: Program development; Support to graduates or students of specific schools; Awards/prizes; Graduate support; Technical education support; Undergraduate support.
Application information: Application form required. Application form available on the grantmaker's Web site.
Deadline(s): Vary
Additional information: See Web site and program descriptions for complete application and program information.
Program descriptions:
Roxanna C. Arscht Fellowship: Awarded to law students, recent law school graduates and attorneys admitted to the Bar of the Supreme Court of Delaware who plan to work in the public or nonprofit sector in Delaware. Deadline May 1.
Cape Thespian Scholarship: Awarded to a Henlopen High School senior who is pursuing studies in the field of theatre arts.
Richard S. Cordrey Scholarship: Awards a one-time payment of $1,000 to seniors who attend a public high school in the Cape Henlopen, Indian River or Sussex Vocational-Technical school districts and have been accepted at a Delaware college or university. A preference will be given to students who will be attending Goldey-Beacom College or Delaware Technical & Community College. Deadline Mar. 31.
Peter A. DeCoursey Memorial Award: Awards $1,000 to a high school senior enrolled in a Junior

Achievement program, completed application, advisor recommendation, and interview. Exceptional leadership ability and enthusiasm to motivate others. Deadline Apr. 26.
Donald W. & Nancy S. Edwards Scholarship: Scholarships to students identified through the Upward Bound program at the University of Delaware with demonstrated academic ability and financial need who plan to pursue a four-year college degree.
Helen L. & Douglas Eliason Scholarship: Scholarships are awarded to help deserving students lead productive lives and return something to their community. Priority is given to working adults who want to improve their employment potential through continuing education. Low- and moderate-income high school students will also be considered (call in Spring for application for the Fall semester). Scholarships may be used at Delaware-based programs. Aid is available for credit, or non-credit courses in special circumstances. Deadline Jan. 1 for summer semester, May 1 for fall semester, July 15 for winter semester, and Nov. 1 for spring semester.
Endsley P. Fairman Fellowship: Fellowships to senior executives of nonprofit organizations in Delaware and the Brandywine Valley with budgets of $1 million and above. The fund offers nonprofit executives the opportunity to acquire concrete business skills and a broad, strategic view of general management in the nonprofit sector. Fellowship provides tuition, room, board and travel expenses for "Strategic Perspectives in Nonprofit Management" at the Harvard Business School Executive Education Program in Cambridge, Massachusetts. Fairman Fellows will be expected to share what they learn in an effort to strengthen other Delaware nonprofits. Deadline Apr. 15.
Bill Frank Prize for Excellence in Communications: Scholarships to three Delaware high school seniors active in journalism and/or communication activities, including participation in activities such as school newspapers and magazines and/or television and radio programs. Each high school may nominate one student. Each recipient receives $1,000. Deadline Feb. 19.
James Jamieson Memorial Scholarship: Scholarships by nomination only to dance students who reside in or study dance in the state of Delaware. Consideration will be given to all facets of the student's education that would point to a successful professional ballet career. Race, religion or sex will not be a factor in the selection of candidates. Each applicant will be required to submit a short essay on why he or she desires to undertake a career in ballet. Finalists will be required to attend a personal interview and audition.
Caesar Rodney Rotary Scholarship: Two renewable awards to seniors who attend Howard High School of Technology and Cab Calloway School of the Arts in Wilmington. Preferences will be given to students who show potential for achievement, are involved in activities outside the classroom and demonstrate financial need. Deadline Apr. 23.
John J. Ryan Scholarship: Awards $500 to seniors at Caesar Rodney High School who have been accepted in any college or university. Students should be planning to have a career in education or teaching. It is expected that all scholarship recipients will seek to improve the quality of life in our society through teaching ideals.This is a one-time scholarship to be paid in January after the successful completion of the student's first semester in college. Deadline Apr. 15.
John B. & Marion A. Smitheman Scholarship: Awards $8,000 to be paid in four equal installments of $2,000 over four years to seniors at any Kent County public high school who have been accepted

to a Delaware college or university. Applicants must aspire to a career in engineering and submit a short statement to that effect. Deadline May 31.

Margaret A. Stafford Nursing Scholarship Fund: Awards approximately $1,000 to a Delaware resident who has been accepted into an accredited college or university nursing program within or outside Delaware, with the intention of pursuing a career in nursing and ensuring that patients' needs are a priority. A preference will be given to those students most in need of financial support. Deadline Mar. 31.

Youth Opportunity Scholarship: Scholarships to students or former students of Delaware schools who have experienced a chronic illness, lasting six months or longer, that has impaired the individual's ability to pursue his or her education. Priority will be given to students of the First State School. Scholarship awards will be based on financial need, demonstrated academic promise and potential for success.

Henry H. Stroud, MD. Memorial Scholarship: Scholarships to Delaware residents who have been accepted at an accredited school of medicine. Scholarship awards shall be based on the applicant's demonstrated commitment to pursuing the highest standards of excellence, ethics, and compassion in the medical profession, as well as his or her academic promise and financial need. Special consideration will be given to applicants demonstrating an entrepreneurial and innovative approach to medicine. While there is no guarantee of continuing support, recipients are eligible to re-apply in successive years, for a maximum of four (4) annual awards. The same criteria will be used in determining renewal awards.
EIN: 222804785

1084
Greater Delaware County Community Foundation
217 N. Franklin St.
Manchester, IA   52057-1538

Foundation type: Community foundation
Limitations: Scholarships to graduating seniors of the Edgewood-Colesburg and West Delaware community school districts, IA.
Financial data: Year ended 10/31/2004.
Assets, $1,602,823 (M); Expenditures, $386,626; Total giving, $341,903; Grants to individuals, 23 grants totaling $40,914 (high: $14,886, low: $170).
Type of support: Support to graduates or students of specific schools; Undergraduate support.
Application information: Contact foundation for current application deadline/guidelines.
EIN: 421045184

1085
Delaware State Golf Association Scholarship Fund, Inc.
(also known as DSGA Junior Golf Scholarship Fund, Inc.)
240 West Side Dr.
Rehoboth Beach, DE   19971-0101
(302) 227-3616

Foundation type: Operating foundation
Limitations: Scholarships to DE high school seniors and graduates who are involved in golf.
Financial data: Year ended 12/31/2002.
Assets, $176,204 (M); Expenditures, $43,031; Total giving, $42,799; Grants to individuals, 23 grants totaling $42,799 (high: $4,000, low: $500).

Fields of interest: Athletics/sports, training; Athletics/sports, golf.
Type of support: Scholarships—to individuals.
Application information: Deadline Apr. 1; Completion of formal application required, including letter from member club and two other letters of reference, a brief essay, transcripts, a list of other scholarships applied for or received, and a statement outlining financial need, if any.
EIN: 510297378

1086
Delaware Valley Senior Citizens Scholarship Trust
115 Connard Dr.
Easton, PA   18042
Contact: Louis DiLullo, Tr.
Application address: c/o Delaware Valley Regional High School, 19 Senator Stout Rd., Frenchtown, NJ 08825-3721

Foundation type: Independent foundation
Limitations: Scholarships to graduates of Delaware Valley Regional High School, Frenchtown, NJ.
Financial data: Year ended 12/31/2004.
Assets, $427,484 (M); Expenditures, $21,780; Total giving, $20,500; Grants to individuals, totaling $20,500.
Type of support: Support to graduates or students of specific schools; Undergraduate support.
Application information: Applications accepted throughout the year; Contact foundation for current application guidelines; Initial approach by letter.
EIN: 226555205

1087
Ray Dellinger Scholarship Fund, Inc.
P.O. Box 460
Cartersville, GA   30120-0387
Contact: Dot Hall
Application address: c/o Dot Hall, Chair., Selection Comm., 70 Cassville Rd., Cartersville, GA 30120

Foundation type: Independent foundation
Limitations: Scholarships to individuals primarily in the Bartow County, GA, area.
Financial data: Year ended 02/28/2005.
Assets, $898,561 (M); Expenditures, $39,421; Total giving, $39,000; Grants to individuals, totaling $39,000.
Type of support: Scholarships—to individuals.
Application information: Application form required.
Deadline(s): Apr. 15
Additional information: Application should include transcripts.
EIN: 586041060

1088
James E. DeLong Foundation, Inc.
1101 W. St. Paul Ave.
Waukesha, WI   53188

Foundation type: Company-sponsored foundation
Limitations: Scholarships only to children of WI employees of the Waukesha Engine Division.
Financial data: Year ended 09/30/2004.
Assets, $126,507 (M); Expenditures, $9,901; Total giving, $9,750; Grants to individuals, 8 grants totaling $9,750 (high: $1,500, low: $750).
Type of support: Employee-related scholarships.
Application information:
Deadline(s): First Mon. in Apr.
Additional information: Application forms available from Waukesha Engine Division;

Application address: c/o Pres., Carrol College, 100 N. East Ave., Waukesha, WI 53186.
EIN: 396050331

1089
Delta Delta Delta Foundation
2331 Brookhollow Plz. Dr.
Arlington, TX   76005   (817) 633-8001
Contact: Anne Leary

Foundation type: Public charity
Limitations: Scholarships to members of Delta Delta Delta fraternity.
Financial data: Year ended 07/31/2003.
Assets, $3,967,605 (M); Expenditures, $820,785; Total giving, $311,158; Grants to individuals, totaling $311,158.
Fields of interest: Students, sororities/fraternities.
Type of support: Undergraduate support.
Application information: Applications accepted. Application form required.
Initial approach: Letter.
Additional information: Contact foundation for current application deadlines.
EIN: 752184529

1090
Delta Phi Epsilon Educational Foundation
16A Worthington Dr.
Maryland Heights, MO   63043   (314) 275-2626
Contact: Harriette Hirsch, Pres.
E-mail: info@dphie.org; URL: http://www.dphie.org/home.shtml

Foundation type: Public charity
Limitations: Scholarships to members of Delta Phi Epsilon and their children.
Publications: Annual report.
Financial data: Year ended 12/31/2004.
Assets, $71,237 (M); Expenditures, $24,578; Total giving, $5,515; Grants to individuals, totaling $5,515.
Fields of interest: Students, sororities/fraternities.
Type of support: Scholarships—to individuals.
Application information: Application form required.
Deadline(s): Mar. 15
Additional information: Application should include official transcripts and three supporting letters of recommendation; Interviews required.
EIN: 431661725

1091
Delta Sigma Delta Educational Foundation
301 Ebbtide Dr., Ste. F
North Palm Beach, FL   33408
Contact: Harold R. Lyboldt, Admin.

Foundation type: Operating foundation
Limitations: Educational loans to students attending dental schools with an undergraduate chapter of Delta Sigma Delta.
Financial data: Year ended 06/30/2005.
Assets, $615,752 (M); Expenditures, $69,865; Total giving, $25,000.
Fields of interest: Dental school/education; Students, sororities/fraternities.
Type of support: Student loans—to individuals.
Application information: Applications accepted.
Deadline(s): None
Additional information: Applications available from a Deputy at Delta Sigma Delta.

Program description:
Student Loan Program: Loan limit per student is $2,000. Students must have a co-signer for the promissory note.
EIN: 386089377

1092
Elizabeth B. Demarest Trust
c/o Mellon Financial Corp.
P.O. Box 185
Pittsburgh, PA   15230-0185
Contact: Laurie Moritz, Trust Off., Mellon Financial Corp.
Application address: c/o 1 Mellon Center, 500 Grant St., Ste. 3825, Pittsburgh, PA 15258, tel.: (412) 234-0023

Foundation type: Independent foundation
Limitations: Grants by nomination only to exceptionally gifted individuals in archaeology or the arts.
Financial data: Year ended 12/31/2004. Assets, $349,585 (M); Expenditures, $16,124; Total giving, $15,000; Grants to individuals, totaling $15,000.
Fields of interest: Visual arts; Performing arts; Music; History/archaeology; Literature; Arts.
Type of support: Awards/grants by nomination only.
Application information:
Deadline(s): June 1
Additional information: Nominations accepted from institutions on behalf of individual candidates; Completion of formal nomination required; Individual applications without nominations not accepted.
Program description:
Grant Program: Initial contact is by an organization or a member of the Demarest Council recommending a candidate for a grant. Grants are awarded to exceptionally gifted individuals in literature, music, visual or performing arts, or in archaeology. One award is given each year.
EIN: 256108821

1093
Demolay Foundation, Inc.
10200 N. Executive Hills Blvd.
Kansas City, MO   64153   (816) 891-8333
Contact: Tony R. Krall, Pres.
URL: http://www.demolay.org

Foundation type: Public charity
Limitations: Scholarships to Demolay members for undergraduate and postgraduate education.
Financial data: Year ended 12/31/2003. Assets, $4,168,667 (M); Expenditures, $242,211; Total giving, $17,150; Grants to individuals, 18 grants totaling $17,150 (high: $1,500, low: $800).
Fields of interest: Dental school/education; Medical school/education.
Type of support: Graduate support; Undergraduate support.
Application information: Deadline Apr. 1; Initial approach by e-mail; Completion of formal application required, including two letters of recommendation and two reference letters.
Program descriptions:
Grotto Scholarship: Awards four $1,500 pre-medical/dental scholarships to "active" members of DeMolay or a "Senior DeMolay," a member who is at least 21 years old.
Frank S. Land Scholarship: Applicant must be an active member of DeMolay to be eligible for one of the several scholarships awarded each year. Applicants must be under 21 years old.

York Rite Grand Chapter Royal Arch Masons Scholarship: Awards five $1,000 scholarships to "active" or Senior Demolay members for post-undergraduate education.
EIN: 430893446

1094
Greater Denfeld Foundation, Inc.
c/o Trust Tax Svcs.
P.O. Box 64713
St. Paul, MN   55164-0713

Foundation type: Public charity
Limitations: Scholarships to graduates of Denfeld High School, MN, for higher education.
Financial data: Year ended 04/30/2004. Assets, $2,761,233 (M); Expenditures, $107,947; Total giving, $94,075; Grants to individuals, 10 grants totaling $6,075 (high: $1,250, low: $25).
Type of support: Support to graduates or students of specific schools; Undergraduate support.
Application information: Deadline Jan. 6; Completion of formal application required; Application forms available through high school counselors.
EIN: 237182610

1095
Robert E. & Olive L. Denton Scholarship Trust
c/o Corydon State Bank
P.O. Box 228
Corydon, IA   50060-0228
Application address: c/o William H. Miles, 107 W. Jackson St., Corydon, IA 50060, tel.: (641) 872-2343

Foundation type: Independent foundation
Limitations: Scholarships to graduating seniors at Wayne Community Junior Senior High School in Corydon, IA, who are in the upper fifth of their graduating classes.
Financial data: Year ended 12/31/2004. Assets, $351,962 (M); Expenditures, $19,845; Total giving, $19,000; Grants to individuals, totaling $19,000.
Type of support: Support to graduates or students of specific schools; Undergraduate support.
Application information: Applications by letter accepted throughout the year; Initial approach by telephone.
EIN: 426424290

1096
Des Moines Golf and Country Club Educational Foundation
1600 Jordan Creek Pkwy.
West Des Moines, IA   50266

Foundation type: Independent foundation
Limitations: Scholarships only to employees of the Des Moines Golf and Country Club in IA for undergraduate study.
Financial data: Year ended 12/31/2004. Assets, $63,794 (M); Expenditures, $59,148; Total giving, $51,000; Grants to individuals, totaling $51,000.
Type of support: Employee-related scholarships.
Application information: Contact foundation for current application deadline/guidelines only if you are an employee of the Des Moines Golf and Country Club.
EIN: 421402068

1097
Descendants of the Signers of the Declaration of Independence
8507 Henrico Ave.
Richmond, VA   23229
URL: http://www.dsdi1776.com

Foundation type: Public charity
Limitations: Scholarships to descendents and members of Descendents of the Signers of the Declaration of Independence.
Financial data: Year ended 12/31/2004. Assets, $542,400 (M); Expenditures, $51,573; Total giving, $9,300; Grants to individuals, totaling $9,300.
Fields of interest: Historic preservation/historical societies.
Type of support: Undergraduate support.
Application information: Unsolicited requests for funds not considered or acknowledged.
EIN: 236397427

1098
Anthony W. DeSio & Delores J. DeSio Foundation
5880 Chambery Cir.
Reno, NV   89511-5024
Contact: Darcy L. Lessard, Exec. Dir.
Application address: 27475 Ynez Rd., Box 431, Temecula, CA 92591, tel.: (909) 695-5491, Fax.: (909) 694-3358, darcylew@aol.com

Foundation type: Independent foundation
Limitations: Undergraduate scholarships based on academic record, participation in school and community activities, honors, work experience, a statement of education and career goals, and an outside appraisal, to residents of Washoe County, Nevada attending the University of Nevada, Reno.
Publications: Occasional report (including application guidelines).
Financial data: Year ended 09/30/2004. Assets, $1,801,531 (M); Expenditures, $101,295; Total giving, $37,376.
Type of support: Scholarships—to individuals; Support to graduates or students of specific schools.
Application information: Applications accepted. Application form required.
Initial approach: Letter.
Deadline(s): May 15.
Applicants should submit the following:
1) GPA
2) Financial information
3) Essay
4) Transcripts
EIN: 330727889

1099
deStwolinski Family Foundation
17330 W. Center Rd., Ste. 110
Omaha, NE   68130
Contact: T. Geoffrey Lieben
Additional address: 100 Scoular Bldg., 2027 Dodge St., Omaha, NE 68102, tel.: (402) 344-4000

Foundation type: Independent foundation
Limitations: Scholarships to residents of AZ, IA, NE and NM for higher education. Awards for teachers in Sioux City, IA are also given.
Financial data: Year ended 05/31/2005. Assets, $2,384,636 (M); Expenditures, $157,948; Total giving, $151,669; Grant to an individual, 1 grant totaling $10,000.
Fields of interest: Education.

Type of support: Awards/prizes; Undergraduate support.
Application information: Unsolicited requests for funds not accepted.
EIN: 470812539

1100

Detroit Diesel Scholarship Foundation, Inc.

c/o Detroit Diesel Corp.
13400 Outer Dr. W.
Detroit, MI 48239-4001
Contact: Ken Holman

Foundation type: Company-sponsored foundation
Limitations: Scholarships to qualified dependents of employees of Detroit Diesel Corporation, MI.
Financial data: Year ended 12/31/2004. Assets, $1,575 (M); Expenditures, $5,027; Total giving, $5,000; Grants to individuals, 5 grants totaling $5,000 (high: $1,000, low: $1,000).
Type of support: Employee-related scholarships.
Application information: Application form required.
  Additional information: Application should include GPA.
EIN: 382964503

1101

Leroy E. Dettman Foundation, Inc.

4401 N. Federal Hwy., Ste. 100
Boca Raton, FL 33431 (561) 367-9811

Foundation type: Independent foundation
Limitations: Undergraduate and graduate scholarships to temporary employees of Personnel Pool of America and their children.
Publications: Application guidelines.
Financial data: Year ended 10/31/2004. Assets, $1,143,939 (M); Expenditures, $134,211; Total giving, $29,515; Grants to individuals, totaling $29,515.
Type of support: Employee-related scholarships.
Application information: Deadline Mar. 15; Initial approach by letter; Completion of formal application required, including transcripts, ACT and SAT scores, and FAF.
EIN: 591784551

1102

Daniel B. Deupree Foundation

P.O. Box 345
Bonham, TX 75418

Foundation type: Independent foundation
Limitations: Scholarships to those residing in Fannin County.
Financial data: Year ended 12/31/2004. Assets, $1,509,252 (M); Expenditures, $85,139; Total giving, $77,900; Grants to individuals, totaling $77,900.
Type of support: Scholarships—to individuals.
Application information: Applications accepted throughout the year; Completion of formal application required.
EIN: 759033769

1103

Dick DeVoe Buick Cadillac Scholarship Trust

2601 Airport Rd. S.
Naples, FL 34112-4855 (239) 261-3538
Application address: c/o Guidance Dept., Naples High School, 1110 Golden Eagle Cir., Naples, FL 33940

Foundation type: Company-sponsored foundation
Limitations: Scholarships to graduates of Naples High School, or Collier County or Estero high schools, FL, for higher education.
Financial data: Year ended 12/31/2004. Assets, $103,558 (M); Expenditures, $119,516; Total giving, $110,960; Grants to individuals, 11 grants totaling $110,960 (high: $11,756, low: $9,921).
Type of support: Scholarships—to individuals; Support to graduates or students of specific schools.
Application information:
  Deadline(s): Contact trust for current application deadline; High school advisory board determines deadlines.
  Additional information: Application by letter stating name, address, extracurricular activities, honors/awards, state test scores, GPA, class rank, and demonstration of need.
Program description:
  Scholarship Program: Students must be graduates of Naples High School. Recipients of Florida prepaid tuition scholarships must be students of Collier County or Estero high schools.
EIN: 237296264

1104

Dewuhs-Keckritz Educational Trust

706 Hillcrest Dr.
La Grande, OR 97850
Contact: Wilbur Smith

Foundation type: Independent foundation
Limitations: Scholarships of up to $5,000 each to the top male and female students in Union and Wallowa counties, OR.
Financial data: Year ended 12/31/2004. Assets, $695,680 (M); Expenditures, $49,366; Total giving, $38,500; Grants to individuals, totaling $38,500.
Type of support: Undergraduate support.
Application information: Applications accepted. Application form required.
  Deadline(s): Apr. 10
EIN: 936092788

1105

Murray DeYoung Educational Foundation, Inc.

135 Stratford Ct.
Haines City, FL 33844-8475 (863) 419-8286
Contact: Thomas Matthews, Pres.

Foundation type: Independent foundation
Limitations: Scholarships to individuals based on financial need and recommendations from teachers, counselors, and welfare agencies.
Financial data: Year ended 06/30/2005. Assets, $4,479,537 (M); Expenditures, $235,756; Total giving, $144,516; Grants to individuals, 12 grants totaling $61,462 (high: $8,000, low: $500).
Type of support: Scholarships—to individuals.

Application information: Applications by letter outlining financial need accepted throughout the year.
EIN: 592758439

1106

Albert Dial Educational Trust

104 Creek Dr.
Laurens, SC 29360
Application address: c/o Palmetto Bank, Attn.: David Martin, Trust Off., P.O. Box 49, Laurens, SC 29360, tel.: (864) 984-4551

Foundation type: Independent foundation
Limitations: Scholarships to residents of Laurens County, SC, and to graduates of public high schools in Laurens, SC.
Financial data: Year ended 10/31/2005. Assets, $426,446 (M); Expenditures, $24,728; Total giving, $19,505; Grants to individuals, 8 grants totaling $19,505 (high: $3,400, low: $1,000).
Type of support: Scholarships—to individuals.
Application information: Applications by letter outlining financial need accepted throughout the year.
EIN: 237203948

1107

Dialysis Research Foundation

5575 S. 500 E.
Ogden, UT 84405 (801) 479-0351
FAX: (801) 476-1766

Foundation type: Independent foundation
Limitations: Educational assistance and textbook stipends to individuals who have undergone dialysis.
Financial data: Year ended 12/31/2004. Assets, $4,617,452 (M); Expenditures, $747,786; Total giving, $453,165; Grants to individuals, 23 grants totaling $62,051 (high: $9,355, low: $240).
Fields of interest: Kidney diseases.
Type of support: Undergraduate support.
Application information: Applications accepted.
  Deadline(s): None
  Additional information: Contact foundation for current application guidelines.
EIN: 942819009

1108

The Dickens Family Foundation

c/o Robert E. Dickens, Jr.
31 Clarendon Ave.
Avondale Estates, GA 30002-1402

Foundation type: Independent foundation
Limitations: Scholarships to students graduating from Gaffney High School, SC, for undergraduate education at a SC institution.
Financial data: Year ended 12/31/2004. Assets, $3,056,988 (M); Expenditures, $169,526; Total giving, $115,791; Grants to individuals, totaling $115,791.
Type of support: Support to graduates or students of specific schools.
Application information: Application form required.
  Deadline(s): End of each semester
  Additional information: Applicantion should include transcripts.Contact Gaffney High School Career Services Counseling Center for current application guidelines.
EIN: 582581077

1109
Dickinson Area Community Foundation

(formerly Dickinson County Area Community Foundation)
427 S. Stephenson, Ste. 207
Iron Mountain, MI 49801-0648
(906) 774-3131
Contact: Debra J. Flannery, Exec. Dir.
FAX: (906) 774-7640; E-mail: dcacf@uplogon.com;
URL: http://www.dcacf.org

Foundation type: Community foundation
Limitations: Scholarships to college students in Dickinson County, MI, and surrounding MI and WI communities.
Publications: Application guidelines; Annual report; Financial statement; Grants list.
Financial data: Year ended 04/30/2005. Assets, $4,755,081 (M); Expenditures, $201,528; Total giving, $107,142; Grants to individuals, 106 grants totaling $88,891 (high: $1,500, low: $45).
Type of support: Undergraduate support.
Application information: Contact foundation for current application deadline; Completion of formal application required.
EIN: 383218990

1110
John T. and Ada Diederich Educational Trust Fund

c/o National City Bank, Kentucky
P.O. Box 94651
Cleveland, OH 44101-4651
Application address: c/o Jenny Tempeton, Exec. Dir., P.O. Box 1919, Ashland, KY 41105-1919, tel.: (606) 836-8186

Foundation type: Independent foundation
Limitations: Scholarships to students in Boyd, Greenup, Martin, Lawrence, and Carter counties, KY.
Financial data: Year ended 12/31/2004. Assets, $4,869,689 (M); Expenditures, $237,963; Total giving, $188,704; Grants to individuals, 44 grants totaling $188,704 (high: $10,000, low: $227).
Type of support: Scholarships—to individuals.
Application information: Deadline May 30; Completion of formal application required; Applications and information available in high school guidance offices.
EIN: 316271680

1111
Harlan O. Diehl Trust

7452 N. 95th Ave. W.
Baxter, IA 50028
Application address: c/o Guidance Office, Baxter Community High School, Baxter, IA 50028

Foundation type: Independent foundation
Limitations: Scholarships to seniors of Baxter Community High School, IA, for higher education.
Financial data: Year ended 05/31/2005. Assets, $173,570 (M); Expenditures, $19,072; Total giving, $18,750; Grants to individuals, totaling $18,750.
Type of support: Support to graduates or students of specific schools; Undergraduate support.
Application information: Deadline Apr. 15; Completion of formal application required.
EIN: 426338687

1112
Emma Fanny Dietrich Trust

c/o B.B. Massagee III
240 3rd Ave. W.
Hendersonville, NC 28739
Contact: Charles Byrd, Tr.
Application address: 1970 Cambridge Dr., Hendersonville, NC 28792, tel.: (828) 692-6642

Foundation type: Operating foundation
Limitations: Scholarships to male students for post high school education who are graduates of Henderson County, NC high school and are residents of Henderson County, NC.
Financial data: Year ended 12/31/2003. Assets, $1,281,669 (M); Expenditures, $73,399; Total giving, $68,700; Grants to individuals, 38 grants totaling $68,700 (high: $26,000, low: $1,000).
Fields of interest: Men.
Type of support: Scholarships—to individuals; Support to graduates or students of specific schools.
Application information: Applications accepted. Application form required.
   Deadline(s): None
   Additional information: Application should include vital statistics, financial need, and explanation of desire for further education.
EIN: 566152201

1113
H. J. Diffenbaugh Trust for Baker University

c/o Bank of America, N.A.
P.O. Box 831041
Dallas, TX 75283-1041
Application address: c/o David P. Ross, Sr. V.P. and Trust Off., c/o Bank of America, N.A., P.O. Box 419119, Kansas City, MO 64141-6119, tel.: (816) 979-7481

Foundation type: Independent foundation
Limitations: Scholarships to MO residents attending Baker University in Baldwin, KS.
Financial data: Year ended 12/31/2004. Assets, $237,481 (M); Expenditures, $15,978; Total giving, $10,000; Grants to individuals, totaling $10,000.
Type of support: Support to graduates or students of specific schools; Undergraduate support.
Application information: Applications by letter of no more than three pages accepted throughout the year.
EIN: 446008351

1114
H. J. Diffenbaugh Trust for Kansas University

c/o Bank of America, N.A.
P.O. Box 831041
Dallas, TX 75283-1041
Application address: c/o David P. Ross, Sr. V.P. and Trust Off., c/o Bank of America, N.A., P.O. Box 419119, Kansas City, MO 64141-6119, tel.: (816) 979-6119

Foundation type: Independent foundation
Limitations: Scholarships and student loans to financially needy MO residents who wish to attend the University of Kansas.
Financial data: Year ended 12/31/2004. Assets, $264,444 (M); Expenditures, $13,944; Total giving, $8,000.

Type of support: Scholarships—to individuals; Student loans—to individuals; Support to graduates or students of specific schools.
Application information: Contact foundation for current application deadline; Application by letter outlining financial need.
EIN: 446008349

1115
H. J. Diffenbaugh Trust for University of Illinois

c/o Bank of America, N.A.
P.O. Box 831041
Dallas, TX 75283-1041
Application address: c/o David P. Ross, Sr. V.P. and Trust Off., c/o Bank of America, N.A., P.O. Box 419119, 14 W. 10th St., Kansas City, MO 64141-6119, tel.: (816) 979-7481

Foundation type: Independent foundation
Limitations: Student loans to MO residents attending the University of Illinois at Urbana-Champaign.
Financial data: Year ended 12/31/2004. Assets, $518,401 (M); Expenditures, $34,505; Total giving, $30,120; Grants to individuals, totaling $30,120.
Fields of interest: Education.
Type of support: Student loans—to individuals; Support to graduates or students of specific schools; Undergraduate support.
Application information: Applications accepted.
   Initial approach: Letter or telephone.
EIN: 446008350

1116
Harry J. and Mollie S. Dilcher Student Loan Fund

c/o Wachovia Bank, N.A.
100 N. Main St., 13th Fl.
Winston-Salem, NC 27150

Foundation type: Independent foundation
Limitations: Scholarships to members of The Ashbury Methodist Church in Allentown, PA.
Financial data: Year ended 12/31/2004. Assets, $304,256 (M); Expenditures, $14,525; Total giving, $9,750; Grants to individuals, totaling $9,750.
Fields of interest: Protestant agencies & churches.
Type of support: Scholarships—to individuals.
Application information: Applications not accepted.
EIN: 236955204

1117
Max E. & Maude M. Dinger Scholarship Fund

c/o National City Bank of Pennsylvania
P.O. Box 94651
Cleveland, OH 44101
Application address: c/o Punxsutawney Area High School, Guidance Dept., Punxsutawney, PA 15767

Foundation type: Independent foundation
Limitations: Scholarships to graduates of Punxsutawney Area High School, PA, who intend to pursue a degree in nursing.
Financial data: Year ended 12/31/2003. Assets, $217,248 (M); Expenditures, $9,269; Total giving, $8,265; Grants to individuals, totaling $8,265.
Fields of interest: Nursing school/education.

Type of support: Support to graduates or students of specific schools; Undergraduate support.
Application information: Application form required.
Initial approach: Letter.
Deadline(s): Apr. 14
EIN: 256291080

1118

William Orr Dingwall Foundation, Inc.

1200 New Hampshire Ave. N.W., No. 440
Washington, DC 20036-6802
Contact: John D. Ward, Dir.
E-mail: woding@aol.com

Foundation type: Independent foundation
Limitations: Scholarships to individuals of Korean ancestry for higher education at accredited institutions and to graduate students of any national origin to study the neural basis of language.
Financial data: Year ended 12/31/2004. Assets, $82,238 (M); Expenditures, $104,371; Total giving, $90,425; Grants to individuals, 5 grants totaling $90,425 (high: $27,000, low: $9,000).
Fields of interest: Language/linguistics; Neuroscience; Asians/Pacific Islanders.
Type of support: Graduate support; Undergraduate support.
Application information:
Deadline(s): Feb. 1
Additional information: Completion of formal application required, including academic record, evidence of financial need, purpose of application and recommendations; Application may be submitted through Web site.
Program description:
Scholarship Program: This program distributes one or more grants of up to $18,000 per year to students who meet its goals. The amount of the stipend will depend on the grantee's justified need. The normal duration of the grant is three years, but may be extended for one additional year. Grantees must be able to maintain at least a 3.0 GPA out of 4.0, and must submit transcripts of their grades each semester as well as annual progress reports.
EIN: 521877552

1119

Nancy Dinwiddle Scholarship Trust

(formerly Dinwiddle Scholarship Trust)
c/o Wells Fargo Bank, N.A.
P.O. Box 63954
San Francisco, CA 94163-0001

Foundation type: Independent foundation
Limitations: Scholarships to residents of Falbrook, CA.
Financial data: Year ended 10/31/2004. Assets, $473,581 (M); Expenditures, $23,794; Total giving, $17,000; Grants to individuals, totaling $17,000.
Type of support: Scholarships—to individuals.
Application information: Contact trust for current application deadline/guidelines; Initial approach by letter.
EIN: 946646383

1120

The Walt Disney Company Foundation

(formerly Disney Foundation)
500 S. Buena Vista St.
Burbank, CA 91521-3603
Contact: Tillie J. Baptie, Exec. Dir.
URL: http://disney.go.com/disneyhand/contributions/wdcfoundation.html

Foundation type: Company-sponsored foundation
Limitations: Undergraduate scholarships to children of full-time, regular employees of The Walt Disney Company and its subsidiaries or affiliated companies. Recipients must be residents of CA, FL or NY, graduating high school seniors who rank in the upper third of their classes and who plan to attend accredited four-year colleges and universities.
Publications: Financial statement.
Financial data: Year ended 09/30/2004. Assets, $1,469,839 (M); Expenditures, $3,220,402; Total giving, $3,198,257; Grants to individuals, totaling $1,246,550.
Type of support: Employee-related scholarships.
Application information: Application form required.
Deadline(s): Dec. 30
Applicants should submit the following:
1) SAT
Additional information: Application should also include biographical questionnaire, college choice form, and a secondary school report completed by applicant's counselor.
Program description:
Scholarship Program: The parents of applicants must be U.S. citizens or residents who are full-time, regular employees of the company with a record of at least one year of continuous service as of Oct. 1 of the year of application. Scholarships are awarded on the basis of SAT scores, academic achievement, citizenship, leadership, and college and career potential. Depending on the type awarded, scholarships provide either full tuition or half tuition. The minimum full-tuition scholarship amount is $1,000 per year. The minimum half-tuition amount is $500 per year. The stipend may be used for tuition, room and board, or books. In addition, recipients of full- and half-tuition scholarships receive $200 annually to cover costs other than tuition. Scholarships are renewable for up to eight semesters or twelve quarters of full-time study.
EIN: 956037079

1121

Distilled Spirits Wholesalers of Florida Education Foundation, Inc.

215 South Monroe St., Ste. 800A
Tallahassee, FL 32301

Foundation type: Public charity
Limitations: Scholarships to residents of FL enrolled in a College of Business at any of the nine universities in the Florida University system.
Financial data: Year ended 06/30/2003. Assets, $304,206 (M); Expenditures, $20,084; Total giving, $19,039; Grants to individuals, 9 grants totaling $19,039 (high: $2,691, low: $400).
Type of support: Support to graduates or students of specific schools.
Application information: Applications accepted. Application form required.
Initial approach: Letter.
Deadline(s): Mar. 31
Applicants should submit the following:
1) Transcripts
2) Financial information

Additional information: Application must also include recent photograph.
EIN: 237002435

1122

District of Columbia Library Association

P.O. Box 14177
Benjamin Franklin Sta.
Washington, DC 20044-4177 (202) 872-1112
Additional telephone for student loans: (202) 707-6785
URL: http://www.dcla.org

Foundation type: Public charity
Limitations: Awards and interest-free student loans to residents of the District of Columbia.
Publications: Newsletter.
Financial data: Year ended 06/30/2005. Assets, $215,397 (M); Expenditures, $29,018; Total giving, $10,000; Grants to individuals, 2 grants totaling $10,000 (high: $5,000, low: $5,000).
Fields of interest: Law school/education; Libraries/library science; Libraries (public).
Type of support: Student loans—to individuals; Awards/prizes.
Application information: Applications accepted. Application form required.
Initial approach: Telephone.
Deadline(s): Apr. 14 for Student Loans
Applicants should submit the following:
1) Letter(s) of recommendation
Additional information: See Web site for additional information for loans.
Program descriptions:
Ainsworth Rand Spofford President's Award: This award recognizes contributions to the development or improvement of library and information services as evidence by outstanding achievement.
Distinguished Service Award: This award recognizes outstanding contributions by an active, current member of DCLA.
Community Service Award: Individuals must have volunteered their library expertise to develop or improve a library service, program, or facility unrelated to their employment. The nomination must demonstrate a significant, long-term level of service and commitment that directly benefited the community in the greater Washington area. Preference will be given to current DCLA members.
Ruth Fine Memorial Student Loans: Awards two $5,000 each for the financial assistance of library school students. The loans are awarded based on commitment, academic background, previous work experience, and financial need. Preference will be given to District of Columbia residents or someone employed in the District of Columbia.
EIN: 237225161

1123

District One Foundation for Quality Education

702 5th St.
Carrollton, IL 62016-1404
Contact: Michael Barry, Superintendent

Foundation type: Independent foundation
Limitations: Scholarships to graduates of Carrolton High School, IL, for higher education at a university, college or trade school.
Financial data: Year ended 06/30/2004. Assets, $93,049 (M); Expenditures, $28,724; Total giving, $26,350; Grants to individuals, 37 grants totaling $26,350 (high: $2,500, low: $150).

Type of support: Support to graduates or students of specific schools; Technical education support; Undergraduate support.
Application information: Deadline Apr. 30; Completion of formal application required.
EIN: 371314937

1124

Dixie Foundation, Inc.
c/o Lexington Furniture Industries
P.O. Box 1008
Lexington, NC   27292

Foundation type: Company-sponsored foundation
Limitations: Undergraduate scholarships to children of Lexington Furniture Industries employees.
Financial data: Year ended 09/30/2004. Assets, $520 (M); Expenditures, $49,454; Total giving, $49,454; Grants to individuals, 13 grants totaling $49,454 (high: $7,000, low: $1,000).
Type of support: Employee-related scholarships.
Application information: Application form required.
   Additional information: Contact foundation for current application deadline.
EIN: 566042530

1125

The Dixie Group Foundation, Inc.
(formerly Dixie Yarns Foundation, Inc.)
c/o The Dixie Group, Inc.
P.O. Box 25107
Chattanooga, TN   37422-5107
Contact: Starr T. Klein, Secy.-Treas.

Foundation type: Company-sponsored foundation
Limitations: Scholarships to children of employees of The Dixie Group, Inc., Chattanooga, TN.
Financial data: Year ended 12/31/2004. Assets, $834,190 (M); Expenditures, $119,810; Total giving, $119,331; Grants to individuals, 48 grants totaling $39,031.
Type of support: Employee-related scholarships.
Application information: Applications not accepted.
   Additional information: Contributes only to preselected individuals.
EIN: 620645090

1126

George & Addie Dixon Educational Foundation
c/o Wells Fargo Bank, N.A.
P.O. Box 63954, E2076-021
San Francisco, CA   94163

Foundation type: Independent foundation
Limitations: Scholarships to graduating seniors of Folsom High School, CA.
Financial data: Year ended 12/31/2004. Assets, $84,693 (M); Expenditures, $72,107; Total giving, $65,000; Grants to individuals, 16 grants totaling $65,000 (high: $5,000, low: $4,000).
Type of support: Support to graduates or students of specific schools; Undergraduate support.
Application information: Applications not accepted.
EIN: 946587263

1127

W. J. and Amy C. Dodd Educational Trust
c/o The Citizens National Bank of Paris
P.O. Box 790
Paris, IL   61944-0790   (217) 465-7641
Contact: Chris Hollowell, Trust Off., The Citizens National Bank of Paris

Foundation type: Independent foundation
Limitations: Scholarships to graduates of Shiloh C.U.S.D. No. 1 and enrolled in institutions of higher learning.
Financial data: Year ended 09/30/2003. Assets, $292,656 (M); Expenditures, $11,892; Total giving, $7,500; Grants to individuals, totaling $7,500.
Type of support: Scholarships—to individuals; Support to graduates or students of specific schools.
Application information: Deadline Apr. 15; Completion of formal application required; Applications available at Citizens National Bank of Paris.
EIN: 376331158

1128

Dodd Foundation
c/o Judy C. West
P.O. Box 8247
St. Joseph, MO   64508

Foundation type: Independent foundation
Limitations: Scholarships primarily to residents of the St. Joseph, MO, area.
Financial data: Year ended 06/30/2005. Assets, $279,148 (M); Expenditures, $15,534; Total giving, $12,800; Grants to individuals, totaling $12,800.
Type of support: Scholarships—to individuals.
Application information:
   Deadline(s): May 15
   Additional information: Unsolicited applications not considered or acknowledged.
EIN: 436048719

1129

Norris E. Dodd Foundation
c/o Wells Fargo Bank Nevada, N.A.
P.O. Box 95021
Henderson, NV   89009

Foundation type: Independent foundation
Limitations: Scholarships to students in OR for higher education.
Financial data: Year ended 12/31/2004. Assets, $235,533 (M); Expenditures, $13,102; Total giving, $9,600; Grants to individuals, totaling $9,600.
Type of support: Scholarships—to individuals.
Application information: Applications not accepted.
EIN: 916449509

1130

Verna Lilly Dodd Scholarship Trust
c/o JPMorgan Chase Bank, N.A
P.O. Box 1308
Milwaukee, WI   53201
Application address: c/o Mer Rouge Methodist Church, Attn: W.T. Blackwell, P.O. Box 400, Mer Rouge, LA 71261

Foundation type: Independent foundation
Limitations: Scholarships to financially needy residents of the Mer Rouge, LA, area who rank in the top half of their class and have at least an 18 on the ACT and a cumulative GPA of 2.75 or greater.
Financial data: Year ended 05/31/2005. Assets, $266,496 (M); Expenditures, $15,284; Total giving, $10,500; Grants to individuals, 3 grants totaling $10,500.
Type of support: Undergraduate support.
Application information: Deadline June 10; Completion of formal application required.
Program description:
   Scholarship Program: If there are no qualified applicants from the Mer Rouge, LA, area, awards will be made to residents of Morehouse Parish, LA, who are not residents of Mer Rouge. Scholarship recipients must obtain the consent of the trust before accepting another financial award.
EIN: 726118421

1131

Dodge City Business & Professional Women's Club-Elma Schmidt Fund
P.O. Box 1803
Dodge City, KS   67801   (620) 225-6100
Contact: Velda Thomas, Tr.

Foundation type: Independent foundation
Limitations: Scholarships to financially needy women from southwestern KS who are U.S. citizens, have a high school degree or GED, and are enrolled in six or more credits per semester or in a qualified vocational program.
Financial data: Year ended 03/31/2005. Assets, $184,610 (M); Expenditures, $9,196; Total giving, $7,195; Grants to individuals, totaling $7,195.
Fields of interest: Vocational education; Women.
Type of support: Technical education support; Undergraduate support.
Application information: Deadlines Apr. 1 for fall semester and Nov. 1 for spring semester; Completion of formal application required, including high school transcripts or GED certificate, a photograph, and a personal statement of 300 words or less.
EIN: 237430868

1132

Dodge Scholarship Trust for Girls
(formerly Adelaide Dodge Scholarship Trust)
95 Market St.
Manchester, NH   03101-1933
Application address: c/o Guidance Office, Manchester Central High School, 270 Lowell St., Manchester, NH 03101

Foundation type: Independent foundation
Limitations: Scholarships to female graduates of Manchester High School Central NH for higher education.
Financial data: Year ended 12/31/2004. Assets, $451,787 (M); Expenditures, $13,344; Total giving, $8,000; Grants to individuals, totaling $8,000.
Fields of interest: Women.
Type of support: Scholarships—to individuals; Support to graduates or students of specific schools.
Application information: Deadline May 15; Contact foundation for current application guidelines.
EIN: 020439653

1133
Hans & Margaret Doe Charitable Trust
600 W. Broadway, 8th Fl.
San Diego, CA 92101   (619) 239-3444
Contact: Anton Dimitroff
FAX: (619) 232-6828

Foundation type: Independent foundation
Limitations: Scholarships to students who are children of employees of Vista Irrigation District.
Financial data: Year ended 12/31/2003. Assets, $2,768,842 (M); Expenditures, $160,054; Total giving, $92,000; Grants to individuals, 5 grants totaling $45,000 (high: $15,000, low: $2,000).
Type of support: Employee-related scholarships.
Application information: Applications by letter accepted throughout the year; Initial approach by letter or telephone.
EIN: 336080541

1134
Ray and Rosetta Doerhoff Scholarship Trust
P.O. Box 6
St. Elizabeth, MO 65075
Contact: Bert Doerhoff, Tr.
Application address: 1301 Southwest Blvd., Jefferson City, MO 65109

Foundation type: Independent foundation
Limitations: Scholarships to graduating seniors at St. Elizabeth Public School, MO.
Financial data: Year ended 03/31/2005. Assets, $40,719 (M); Expenditures, $2,250; Total giving, $2,250; Grants to individuals, 4 grants totaling $2,250 (high: $1,000, low: $250).
Type of support: Support to graduates or students of specific schools; Undergraduate support.
Application information:
  Initial approach: Letter.
  Deadline(s): Apr.
  Additional information: Contact foundation for current application guidelines.
EIN: 431565655

1135
Dog Writers Educational Trust
P.O. Box 22322
St. Petersburg, FL 33742-2322
Contact: Allene McKewen, Secy.-Treas.
Tel.: (727) 507-9233

Foundation type: Operating foundation
Limitations: Undergraduate and graduate scholarships to students with a strong background in the ownership and care of dogs, as well as a special award to journalism majors.
Financial data: Year ended 12/31/2002. Assets, $92,117 (M); Expenditures, $9,036; Total giving, $5,000; Grants to individuals, totaling $5,000.
Fields of interest: Journalism/publishing; Animals/wildlife, training; Animals/wildlife, exhibition.
Type of support: Graduate support; Undergraduate support.
Application information: Deadline Dec. 31; Initial approach by letter including SASE; Completion of formal application required, including transcripts, personal essay, and up to three optional recommendations.
Program description:
  Scholarship Program: Grants are limited to college students who have participated in organized

activities with dogs (dog shows, obedience or field trials, raising guide dogs, etc.).
EIN: 046088171

1136
James E. Doherty Scholarship Fund
c/o U.S. Bank, N.A.
P.O. Box 7900
St. Paul, MN 55164-0713

Foundation type: Independent foundation
Limitations: Scholarships to Cretin-Derham High School, MN, students.
Financial data: Year ended 07/31/2005. Assets, $980,191 (M); Expenditures, $82,525; Total giving, $80,000; Grants to individuals, totaling $80,000.
Fields of interest: Education.
Type of support: Scholarships—to individuals; Support to graduates or students of specific schools.
Application information: Applications not accepted.
EIN: 416257985

1137
Sabina Dolan & Gladys Saulsbury Foundation, Inc.
400 Orange St.
New Haven, CT 06511-6405   (203) 787-3513
Contact: Edward J. Dolan, Pres.

Foundation type: Independent foundation
Limitations: Scholarships to students participating in interscholastic athletics at public high schools in New Haven, CT.
Financial data: Year ended 01/31/2005. Assets, $1,299 (M); Expenditures, $18,696; Total giving, $18,495; Grants to individuals, totaling $18,495.
Fields of interest: Athletics/sports, training.
Type of support: Scholarships—to individuals; Support to graduates or students of specific schools; Precollege support.
Application information: Applications accepted. Application form required.
  Deadline(s): None
EIN: 061088838

1138
Stephen Dexter and Emily Jane Tipton Dole Scholarship Trust
(also known as Emily Oblinger Trust f/b/o Stephen Dexter and Emily Jane Tipton Dole Scholarship)
c/o First National Bank
507 Lake Land Blvd.
P.O. Box 685
Mattoon, IL 61938   (217) 234-6430
Contact: Tabby Bell

Foundation type: Independent foundation
Limitations: Scholarships to high school students in Mattoon, Charleston, Neogad Arcola, IL, who will attend the University of Illinois.
Financial data: Year ended 12/31/2004. Assets, $2,008,669 (M); Expenditures, $138,237; Total giving, $70,150; Grants to individuals, 30 grants totaling $70,150 (high: $3,450, low: $2,300).
Type of support: Support to graduates or students of specific schools; Undergraduate support.
Application information: Deadline Apr. 15; Completion of formal application required;

Applications available at The First National Bank and at area high schools.
EIN: 376023196

1139
The Christine A. Dolechek Medical Scholarship Trust Fund
c/o Citizens State Bank
P.O. Box 128
Ellsworth, KS 67439-0128
Contact: Heather Y. Barta, V.P. and Trust Off., Citizens State Bank & Trust Co.
Application address: 203 N. Douglas, Ellsworth, KS 67439, tel.: (785) 472-3141

Foundation type: Independent foundation
Limitations: Medical scholarships to residents of Ellsworth County, KS.
Financial data: Year ended 01/31/2005. Assets, $267,076 (M); Expenditures, $14,119; Total giving, $10,885; Grants to individuals, totaling $10,885.
Fields of interest: Medical school/education.
Type of support: Graduate support.
Application information: Deadline Apr. 1; Contact fund for current application guidelines.
EIN: 481042904

1140
The Dollywood Foundation
1020 Dollywood Ln.
Pigeon Forge, TN 37863-4113   (865) 428-9606
Contact: David C. Dotson, Exec. Dir.
FAX: (865) 428-9612;
E-mail: dollywoodfoundation@aol.com

Foundation type: Public charity
Limitations: Scholarships to graduating high school seniors from Gatlinburg-Pitman High School, Sevier County High School, and Seymour High School, TN, who excel in music, academics, or environmental studies.
Publications: Annual report.
Financial data: Year ended 12/31/2004. Assets, $7,384,838 (M); Expenditures, $922,828; Total giving, $368,348; Grants to individuals, 4 grants totaling $37,500.
Fields of interest: Music; Natural resources.
Type of support: Scholarships—to individuals; Support to graduates or students of specific schools.
Application information:
  Deadline(s): Contact foundation for current application deadlines and guidelines.
Program description:
  Dollywood Foundation Scholarships: Nine college scholarships are provided annually to graduating high school seniors from Gatlinburg, Sevier County, and Seymour high schools, in the following areas: Music ($1,500), Academics ($1,200), and Environment ($1,000). Three students from each school are selected by a faculty committee at each high school.
EIN: 621348105

1141
Henry & Elizabeth Donaghey Foundation
c/o Regina D. Pruitt, Bank of Texas Trust Co.
P.O. Box 1088
Sherman, TX 75091-1088
Contact: Regina D. Pruitt

Foundation type: Independent foundation

Limitations: Scholarships to graduating students attending Trenton High School, TX, for up to two continuous years of undergraduate study.
Financial data: Year ended 12/31/2004.
Assets, $514,412 (M); Expenditures, $30,070; Total giving, $22,200; Grants to individuals, totaling $16,000.
Type of support: Support to graduates or students of specific schools; Undergraduate support.
Application information: Application form not required.
  Deadline(s): None
  Additional information: Contact foundation for current application guidelines.
Program description:
  Scholarship Program: Applicants will be judged on citizenship, leadership, and intent to continue education beyond high school. Applicants should rank in the upper 25 percent of their senior class. Recipients must maintain a "C" average in college courses.
EIN: 751937116

1142
Kenneth S. Donnell Trust
c/o Craig Hunter
P.O. Box 354
Nantucket, MA 02554
Application address: c/o E. Foley Vaughan, P.O. Box 659, Nantucket, MA 02554

Foundation type: Independent foundation
Limitations: Scholarships and camperships to people under age 17 who are residents of Nantucket, MA.
Financial data: Year ended 12/31/2004.
Assets, $552,204 (M); Expenditures, $41,419; Total giving, $35,697; Grants to individuals, totaling $35,697.
Type of support: Scholarships—to individuals; Precollege support; Camperships.
Application information: Application form required.
  Additional information: Contact trust for current application deadline.
EIN: 046635207

1143
Herbert A. "Mike" Donovan Scholarship Fund
c/o Bank of America, N.A.
10 Light St.
Baltimore, MD 21202
Application address: c/o Rector, Christ Episcopal Church, 120 W. High St., Charlottesville, VA 22901

Foundation type: Independent foundation
Limitations: Scholarships primarily to residents of Charlottesville, VA, and to Episcopalians in the diocese of VA to study in preparation for ordination and parish ministry. Priority is given to members of Christ Episcopal Church, VA.
Financial data: Year ended 12/31/2004.
Assets, $211,907 (M); Expenditures, $7,849; Total giving, $4,355; Grants to individuals, totaling $4,355.
Fields of interest: Theological school/education; Christian agencies & churches; Protestant agencies & churches.
Type of support: Scholarships—to individuals.
Application information:
  Initial approach: Letter.
EIN: 546063123

1144
The Donald J. Doody Foundation
15 Salt Creek Ln., Ste. 312
Hinsdale, IL 60521
Contact: Sandra McGovern, Dir.
Application address: 413 Sagebrush Rd., Naperville, IL 69565-4133, tel.: (630) 983-9381

Foundation type: Independent foundation
Limitations: Scholarships to students at St. Laurence High School, Marist High School, and Regis High School, IL.
Financial data: Year ended 12/31/2004.
Assets, $6,951 (M); Expenditures, $41,611; Total giving, $38,850; Grants to individuals, totaling $38,850.
Fields of interest: Education.
Type of support: Support to graduates or students of specific schools; Undergraduate support.
Application information: Applications accepted. Application form required.
EIN: 364092822

1145
Clifford Doolin Foundation, Inc.
c/o Larry Sargent
P.O. Box 157
Meadville, MO 64659

Foundation type: Independent foundation
Limitations: Scholarships to residents of MO for higher education.
Financial data: Year ended 12/31/2004.
Assets, $582,750 (M); Expenditures, $26,385; Total giving, $25,528; Grants to individuals, totaling $13,000.
Type of support: Scholarships—to individuals.
Application information: Applications not accepted.
EIN: 431573474

1146
Blanche Doolittle Private Foundation
c/o Wells Fargo Bank Minnesota, N.A.
230 W. Superior St.
Duluth, MN 55802
Application address: c/o Wells Fargo Bank Minnesota, N.A., Attn.: Robin Aden, 101 N. Phillips Ave., Sioux Falls, SD 57104-6714

Foundation type: Independent foundation
Limitations: Scholarships to graduates of Sioux Falls high schools, SD, for higher education.
Financial data: Year ended 12/31/2004.
Assets, $363,018 (M); Expenditures, $28,833; Total giving, $25,000; Grants to individuals, 10 grants totaling $25,000 (high: $4,000; low: $1,000).
Type of support: Support to graduates or students of specific schools; Undergraduate support.
Application information: Applications not accepted.
EIN: 466056120

1147
The James and Shirley Dora Foundation
2501 S. High School Rd.
Indianapolis, IN 46241

Foundation type: Independent foundation
Limitations: Scholarships to residents of IN, primarily from Indianapolis and surrounding communities.
Financial data: Year ended 12/31/2004.
Assets, $845 (M); Expenditures, $43,164; Total giving, $38,250; Grants to individuals, totaling $38,250.
Type of support: Scholarships—to individuals.
Application information: Applications not accepted.
EIN: 351807219

1148
The Marie A. Dornhecker Foundation
308 Cedar Lakes Dr., 2nd Fl.
Chesapeake, VA 23322-8343 (757) 312-0924
Contact: Steven L. Baldwin, Secy.-Treas.
E-mail: admin@dornheckerfoundation.org;
URL: http://www.dornheckerfoundation.org

Foundation type: Operating foundation
Limitations: Scholarships to students who reside in the Hampton Roads, VA, area for undergraduate or graduate study of French language and culture.
Financial data: Year ended 12/31/2003.
Assets, $7,729 (M); Expenditures, $48,629; Total giving, $25,500; Grants to individuals, totaling $25,500.
Fields of interest: Language (foreign); France.
Type of support: Graduate support; Undergraduate support.
Application information: Application form required.
  Deadline(s): Aug. 15
  Applicants should submit the following:
    1) GPA
    2) Financial information
    3) Essay
EIN: 541945504

1149
Dorot Foundation
439 Benefit St.
Providence, RI 02903 (401) 351-8866
Contact: Michael Hill, Exec. V.P.
FAX: (401) 351-4975; *E-mail:* info@dorot.org;
URL: http://www.dorot.org

Foundation type: Independent foundation
Limitations: Fellowships to American and Canadian Jews in their 20s or 30s for study in Israel.
Publications: Application guidelines; Financial statement; Grants list.
Financial data: Year ended 03/31/2004.
Assets, $57,829,735 (M); Expenditures, $4,697,996; Total giving, $3,314,140.
Fields of interest: International exchange, students; Canada.
Type of support: Fellowships; Foreign applicants.
Application information: Applications not accepted.
EIN: 136116927

1150
John Dotson, M.D. Fund
c/o PNC Advisors
620 Liberty Ave., 10th Fl.
Pittsburgh, PA 15222-2705
Contact: Judy Rice, Trust Off., PNC Advisors
Application address: James Hohn, c/o PNC Bank, N.A., 2 Tower Ctr., East Brunswick, NJ 08816-1100, tel.: (908) 220-3153

Foundation type: Independent foundation
Limitations: Scholarships to financially needy young women from Closter, NJ.
Financial data: Year ended 12/31/2003.
Assets, $223,261 (M); Expenditures, $11,324; Total giving, $8,750; Grants to individuals, totaling $8,750.

Fields of interest: Women.
Type of support: Scholarships—to individuals.
Application information: Deadline Apr. 30; Completion of formal application required.
EIN: 226040599

1151
Dougherty Foundation, Inc.
3507 N. Central, Ste. 404
Phoenix, AZ   85012-2020   (602) 264-7478
Contact: Linda M. Czarnecki, Secy.-Treas.

Foundation type: Independent foundation
Limitations: Undergraduate and graduate student loans and undergraduate scholarships to financially needy AZ residents who are U.S. citizens and enrolled in degree programs at accredited colleges in AZ.
Publications: Financial statement; Informational brochure.
Financial data: Year ended 12/31/2004. Assets, $6,771,970 (M); Expenditures, $523,059; Total giving, $374,268; Grants to individuals, totaling $276,768; Loans to individuals, totaling $97,500.
Type of support: Graduate support; Undergraduate support.
Application information: Application form required.
  Additional information: Application forms available at financial aid offices of AZ universities; Interviews required.
EIN: 866051637

1152
J. & R. Doverspike Charitable Foundation
c/o S&T Bank, Trust Dept.
P.O. Box 220
Indiana, PA   15701
Application address: c/o Selection Committee, P.O. Box 1034, Punxsutawney, PA 15767

Foundation type: Independent foundation
Limitations: Scholarships to graduates of Punxsutawney School District, PA.
Financial data: Year ended 12/31/2004. Assets, $1,944,882 (M); Expenditures, $82,787; Total giving, $77,305; Grants to individuals, totaling $25,500.
Type of support: Scholarships—to individuals; Support to graduates or students of specific schools.
Application information:
  Initial approach: Letter.
  Deadline(s): Sept. 30
  Additional information: Contact foundation for current application guidelines.
EIN: 256571881

1153
Dow Jones Newspaper Fund, Inc.
P.O. Box 300
Princeton, NJ   08543-0300   (609) 452-2820
Contact: Richard S. Holden, Exec. Dir.
FAX: (609) 520-5804;
E-mail: newsfund@wsj.dowjones.com; Street address: 4300 Rte. 1 N., South Brunswick, NJ 08852; URL: http://djnewspaperfund.dowjones.com

Foundation type: Independent foundation
Limitations: Monetary awards by nomination only to high school journalism students. Scholarships by nomination only to minority high school seniors who attend the High School Journalism Workshop for Minorities or students of teachers selected through the High School Journalism Teacher of the Year Program.
Publications: Application guidelines; Annual report; Grants list.
Financial data: Year ended 12/31/2003. Assets, $492,975 (M); Expenditures, $551,507; Total giving, $475,414; Grants to individuals, 13 grants totaling $243,214 (high: $38,245, low: $167).
Fields of interest: Journalism/publishing; Education; Minorities.
Type of support: Awards/grants by nomination only; Awards/prizes; Undergraduate support.
Application information:
  Initial approach: Letter.
  Deadline(s): July 31 for Special Awards Program and Sept. 1 for Summer Workshops Writing Competition
  Additional information: Completion of formal nomination required; Individual applications not accepted; Grants awarded to recipient's school.
Program description:
  Scholarships By Nomination: The Newspaper Fund awards two categories of grants by nomination.
  • Special Awards Program: Open to high school seniors intending to major in journalism in college and who are nominated by teachers who have received distinction as National Journalism Teacher of the Year or Distinguished Advisers (runners-up). Teachers may be nominated by newspapers, press associations, or high school principals for their outstanding abilities as journalism teachers by July 1 of each year. Winning teachers subsequently nominate students from their respective high schools to enter a writing competition. Prizes are awarded to winning students in honor of their teachers: $1,000 scholarships for the student of the teacher selected as Journalism Teacher of the Year, and $500 for each of the four students of the Distinguished Advisors.
  • The Summer Workshops Writing Competition: Gives grants to minority high school students who write news and/or feature articles under the direction of professional newspaper reporters, editors, and journalism teachers in High School Journalism Workshops for Minorities operated by the Dow Jones Newspaper Fund in the summer. Candidates who are high school seniors or first-year college students the fall semester following the workshops, are nominated by workshop directors, and if successful, receive $1,000 college scholarships renewable for up to one year based on need, continued interest in journalism career, and grades.
EIN: 136021439

1154
Adrian & Marie Downing Educational Trust
c/o BancTrust Co.
P.O. Box 469
Brewton, AL   36427   (251) 809-2238
Contact: Elaine Cato, V.P., South Alabama Trust Co.

Foundation type: Independent foundation
Limitations: Scholarships to residents of Escambia County, AL, who have at least a 3.0 GPA.
Financial data: Year ended 12/31/2004. Assets, $527,651 (M); Expenditures, $30,653; Total giving, $24,622; Grants to individuals, totaling $24,622.
Type of support: Scholarships—to individuals.
Application information: Deadline Mar. 1; Completion of formal application required.
EIN: 586320669

1155
The Frank M. Doyle Foundation, Inc.
3732 Lakeside Dr., Ste. 202A
Reno, NV   89509   (775) 329-1972
FAX: (775) 329-8917;
E-mail: FMDFoundation@aol.com; URL: http://www.frankmdoyle.org

Foundation type: Operating foundation
Limitations: Scholarships to high school graduates of the Huntington Beach Union High School District and students or graduates of Golden West Community College and Huntington Beach Adult High School.
Financial data: Year ended 08/31/2004. Assets, $5,027,045 (M); Expenditures, $749,213; Total giving, $267,377.
Type of support: Scholarships—to individuals; Exchange programs; Graduate support; Technical education support; Undergraduate support; Postgraduate support; Doctoral support.
Application information: Application form required.
  Deadline(s): Mar. 1
EIN: 880372802

1156
Mary Doyle Memorial Fund
(formerly Dr. Edgar Clay Doyle and Mary Cherry Doyle Memorial Fund)
c/o Wachovia Bank, N.A.
100 N. Main St., 13th Fl.
Winston-Salem, NC   27150
Application address: c/o SC Fdn. of Independent Colleges, P.O. Box 1465, Taylors, SC 29687-1465, tel.: (864) 268-4002 or (864) 268-3363

Foundation type: Independent foundation
Limitations: Scholarships to seniors and graduates of Oconee County High School, SC, for undergraduate study at SC colleges and universities.
Publications: Annual report.
Financial data: Year ended 01/31/2005. Assets, $1,293,278 (M); Expenditures, $69,746; Total giving, $46,000; Grants to individuals, totaling $46,000.
Fields of interest: Education.
Type of support: Support to graduates or students of specific schools; Undergraduate support.
Application information: Applications accepted. Application form required.
  Deadline(s): Mar. 1.
  Additional information: Application must include curriculum vitae, transcripts, SAT and ACT scores, letters of recommendation, GPA, and first two pages of most recent 1040 form.
Program description:
  Scholarship Program: One-year partial scholarships are renewable if grade requirements are met. Approximately 30 new awards are available annually. Doyle family relatives are ineligible. Recipients may attend an institution outside of SC if their course of study is not available within the state.
EIN: 576019447

1157
The Doyon Foundation
1 Doyon Pl., Ste. 300
Fairbanks, AK 99701 (888) 478-4755
FAX: (905) 459-2065;
E-mail: foundation@doyon.com; Additional tel.:
(907) 459-2050; URL: http://
www.doyonfoundation.com/

Foundation type: Company-sponsored foundation
Limitations: Scholarships to shareholders of Doyon
Ltd., and their spouses and lineal descendants
attending an accredited college, university,
vocational or technical school program that is at
least six weeks long.
Publications: Application guidelines; Annual report;
Newsletter.
Financial data: Year ended 06/30/2005.
Assets, $8,334,048 (M); Expenditures,
$1,705,020; Total giving, $338,822; Grants to
individuals, 511 grants totaling $329,524 (high:
$3,910, low: $141).
Fields of interest: Vocational education.
Type of support: Employee-related scholarships;
Technical education support; Undergraduate
support.
Application information: Application form required.
Deadline(s): None
EIN: 943089624

1158
Dreams Scholarship Foundation
3103 N. Cardinal Rd.
Azle, TX 76020
Contact: Trisha McAda, Chair.
Application address: P.O. Box 667, Azle, TX 76098,
tel.: (817) 444-2252

Foundation type: Operating foundation
Limitations: Scholarships to graduating seniors of
Azle and Springtown high schools, TX.
Financial data: Year ended 02/29/2004.
Assets, $209,569 (M); Expenditures, $20,392;
Total giving, $20,000; Grants to individuals, 8
grants totaling $20,000 (high: $2,500, low:
$2,500).
Type of support: Support to graduates or students
of specific schools; Undergraduate support.
Application information: Deadline Apr. 15;
Completion of formal application required, including
transcript.
Program description:
Scholarship Program: Recipients must be
planning to attend any TX university except the
University of Texas at Austin.
EIN: 752738823

1159
Grace D. Dreher Memorial Scholarship Fund
c/o Wachovia Bank, N.A.
100 N. Main St., 13th Fl.
Winston-Salem, NC 27150-6732
Contact: Michael Boyles, Scholarship Prog.

Foundation type: Independent foundation
Limitations: Scholarships to graduates of
Stroudsburg High School, PA, for undergraduate
education.
Financial data: Year ended 04/30/2003.
Assets, $675,595 (M); Expenditures, $43,551;
Total giving, $39,000; Grants to individuals, 53
grants totaling $39,000 (high: $1,500, low: $250).
Type of support: Support to graduates or students
of specific schools; Undergraduate support.

Application information: Applications accepted.
Application form required.
Deadline(s): Contact foundation for current
application deadlines.
Additional information: Application available at
Stroudsburg High School.
EIN: 236478635

1160
The Dreman Foundation, Inc.
(formerly David Dreman Foundation)
c/o Contrarian Services Corp.
10 Exchange Pl., Ste. 2150
Jersey City, NJ 07302

Foundation type: Independent foundation
Limitations: Fellowships to individuals primarily in
CO, NJ and NY for academic research,
investigation, analysis, or writing, as well as
internship opportunities.
Financial data: Year ended 11/30/2004.
Assets, $10,006,062 (M); Expenditures,
$437,643; Total giving, $195,055.
Type of support: Fellowships; Internship funds;
Research.
Application information: Applications not
accepted.
EIN: 222764782

1161
The Dressage Foundation, Inc.
Wells Fargo Ctr., Ste. 732
1248 "O" St.
Lincoln, NE 68508 (402) 434-8585
Contact: John F. Boomer, Pres. and C.E.O.
FAX: (402) 436-3053;
E-mail: john@dressagefoundation.org; URL: http://
www.dressagefoundation.org

Foundation type: Public charity
Limitations: Scholarships and grants to individuals
to study abroad to improve his or her teaching and
training of Dressage.
Financial data: Year ended 12/31/2003.
Assets, $1,213,995 (M); Expenditures,
$176,801; Total giving, $62,771; Grants to
individuals, totaling $62,771.
Fields of interest: Athletics/sports, equestrianism.
Type of support: Scholarships—to individuals.
Application information: Applications accepted.
Application form required.
Initial approach: Telephone.
Program description:
Major Anders Lindgren Scholarship: Awards
$6,000 to an individual to study abroad to improve
his/her teaching and training of Dressage.
Applicants are requested, but not limited to, study
at the following: Deurne in Holland; Samur in
France; Flyinge in Sweden; and Aerhus in Denmark.
The funds must be used within two years of the date
of the award. 80 percent of the scholarship will be
paid to the recipient prior to his/her departure for
the overseas training trip; 20 percent will be paid
after the recipient returns home and has submitted
his/her written report.
EIN: 363670953

1162
John Lynn Driscoll, Jr. Scholarship Trust
c/o Wells Fargo Bank, N.A.
P.O. Box 21927, MAC P6540-144
Seattle, WA 98111
Application address: c/o Boise State Univ.,
Attn.: Diane Morton, 1910 University Dr., Boise, ID
83725, tel.: (208) 426-1156

Foundation type: Independent foundation
Limitations: Scholarships to residents of Ada
County, ID, attending postsecondary schools in Ada
County.
Financial data: Year ended 12/31/2004.
Assets, $115,006 (M); Expenditures, $6,708;
Total giving, $4,715; Grants to individuals, totaling
$4,715.
Type of support: Scholarships—to individuals.
Application information: Application form required.
Deadline(s): Mar. 1
EIN: 237275638

1163
Bruce V. Drowns Educational Foundation
c/o UMB Bank, N.A.
P.O. Box 419692, M/S 1020305
Kansas City, MO 64141-6692
Application address: c/o Benton High School, 5655
S. 4th St., St. Joseph, MO 64505

Foundation type: Independent foundation
Limitations: Scholarships to disadvantaged,
financially needy students and graduates of Benton
High School, St. Joseph, MO.
Financial data: Year ended 06/30/2004.
Assets, $1,153,314 (M); Expenditures, $93,367;
Total giving, $79,500; Grants to individuals,
totaling $79,500.
Type of support: Scholarships—to individuals;
Support to graduates or students of specific
schools; Graduate support; Technical education
support; Undergraduate support.
Application information: Application form required.
Deadline(s): Apr. 1
EIN: 436371635

1164
Druckenmiller Foundation
c/o Duquesne Capital Mgmt.
40 W. 57th St., 25th Fl.
New York, NY 10019

Foundation type: Independent foundation
Limitations: Undergraduate scholarships to
students who have caddied for at least two seasons
at Oakmont Country Club in PA.
Financial data: Year ended 11/30/2004.
Assets, $4,945,554 (M); Expenditures,
$204,495; Total giving, $195,250; Grants to
individuals, 29 grants totaling $195,250 (high:
$14,750, low: $2,500).
Fields of interest: Athletics/sports, golf.
Type of support: Undergraduate support.
Application information: Application form required.
Initial approach: Letter or telephone.
Deadline(s): Contact foundation for current
application deadline
Applicants should submit the following:
1) Transcripts
2) SAT
3) ACT
Additional information: The Druckenmiller
Foundation administers the Oakmont
Scholarship Program. Application should
include letter of recommendation from caddie
master at Oakmont Country Club, student's

and parents' income tax returns, and two reference letters (at least one from a teacher).
EIN: 133735187

1165
Alfred A. & Tia Juana Drummond Foundation
c/o JPMorgan Chase Bank
111 E. Wisconsin Ave., Ste. 940
Milwaukee, WI 53220

Foundation type: Independent foundation
Limitations: Scholarships to graduating seniors of public high schools in Marshall County, OK.
Financial data: Year ended 10/31/2004. Assets, $349,980 (M); Expenditures, $32,829; Total giving, $28,000; Grants to individuals, 16 grants totaling $28,000 (high: $3,000, low: $1,000).
Type of support: Support to graduates or students of specific schools; Undergraduate support.
Application information: Recipients are selected by scholarship selection committees at participating Marshall County, OK, high schools.
EIN: 731157648

1166
Cora Du Bois Charitable Trust
c/o Palmer & Dodge
111 Huntington Ave.
Boston, MA 02199
Contact: Eric F. Menoyo, Tr.

Foundation type: Independent foundation
Limitations: Scholarships to graduate students in anthropology and other fields.
Financial data: Year ended 12/31/2004. Assets, $1,327,616 (M); Expenditures, $74,717; Total giving, $60,000; Grants to individuals, totaling $60,000.
Fields of interest: Anthropology/sociology.
Type of support: Graduate support.
Application information: Deadline Feb. 15; Completion of formal application required, including two letters of recommendation and transcript.
EIN: 046689812

1167
The Dudley Foundation
c/o Cowles Liipfert
1080 Old Greensboro Rd.
Kernersville, NC 27284 (336) 993-8800
Contact: Eunice M. Dudley, Secy.-Treas.

Foundation type: Independent foundation
Limitations: Scholarships primarily to high school students of Greensboro, NC for higher education.
Financial data: Year ended 12/31/2002. Assets, $0 (M); Expenditures, $22,479; Total giving, $21,253; Grants to individuals, totaling $6,942.
Type of support: Scholarships—to individuals.
Application information: Contact foundation for current application deadline; Completion of formal application required; Applications available from high school guidance office.
EIN: 562026106

1168
Grace Norton Dudley Fund
c/o JPMorgan Chase Bank
P.O. Box 31412
Rochester, NY 14603

Foundation type: Independent foundation
Limitations: Scholarships to students graduating from Bridgeport, CT, high schools for studies at an accredited music school.
Financial data: Year ended 12/31/2004. Assets, $1,368,024 (M); Expenditures, $238,563; Total giving, $220,843; Grants to individuals, 14 grants totaling $220,843 (high: $30,374, low: $1,468).
Type of support: Support to graduates or students of specific schools; Undergraduate support.
Application information: Applications by letter accepted throughout the year, including letter of acceptance into an accredited music school, transcripts, character reference from high school and standard FAF.
EIN: 066079557

1169
Dudley-Vehmeyer-Brown Memorial Foundation, Inc.
385 Solana Dr.
Los Altos, CA 94022
Contact: Chet Frankenfield, Treas.

Foundation type: Operating foundation
Limitations: Scholarships to graduating seniors of Palo Alto High School and Gunn High School, both in Palo Alto, CA; Lowell High School, San Francisco, CA; and Roseville High School, CA.
Financial data: Year ended 12/31/2003. Assets, $1,534,896 (M); Expenditures, $89,387; Total giving, $60,500; Grants to individuals, 24 grants totaling $28,000 (high: $2,000, low: $1,000).
Type of support: Support to graduates or students of specific schools; Undergraduate support.
Application information: Recommendations are made to the foundation by the participating high schools; Contact the high school for current application deadline/guidelines.
EIN: 237355824

1170
D. C. Duer Foundation
P.O. Box 10
Norton, KS 67654
Contact: Karen C. Griffith

Foundation type: Independent foundation
Limitations: Scholarships to residents of Smith County, KS.
Financial data: Year ended 09/30/2004. Assets, $174,222 (M); Expenditures, $8,420; Total giving, $7,764; Grants to individuals, totaling $7,764.
Type of support: Scholarships—to individuals.
Application information: Applications accepted.
Additional information: Contact foundation for current application deadline/guidelines.
EIN: 480947751

1171
George Duffy Foundation
1 Claire Pass
Saratoga Springs, NY 12866-7505
Contact: Richard J. Cordovano
Application address for individuals: P.O. Box 230, Fort Plain, NY 13339

Foundation type: Independent foundation
Limitations: Scholarships to graduates of Canajoharie High School, Fort Plain High School, and St. Johnsville High School, Montgomery County, NY, for study in a medical or health-related field.
Publications: Informational brochure.
Financial data: Year ended 12/31/2004. Assets, $2,724,078 (M); Expenditures, $157,116; Total giving, $123,750; Grants to individuals, totaling $123,750.
Fields of interest: Medical school/education; Health sciences school/education.
Type of support: Support to graduates or students of specific schools; Undergraduate support.
Application information: Application form required.
Initial approach: Letter.
Deadline(s): July 15
Additional information: Applications available Mar. 1 from the foundation and guidance offices of the three schools; Application should include transcripts, two letters of recommendation, and a copy of the acceptance letter from, or application to, the college; Recipients are notified by mail by Aug. 1; Award checks are mailed to schools by Aug. 15.
EIN: 146016445

1172
Martin W. Dugan Foundation
(also known as Martin W. Dugan Trust)
c/o Eastern Bank & Trust Co.
605 Broadway, LF41
Saugus, MA 01906 (781) 581-4220
Contact: Shawn McCarthy, Trust Off., Eastern Bank & Trust Co.

Foundation type: Independent foundation
Limitations: Scholarships to financially needy residents of Newbury, Newburyport, or West Newbury, MA, for studies in science, technology, law, medicine, or the Roman Catholic priesthood.
Financial data: Year ended 12/31/2004. Assets, $551,673 (M); Expenditures, $40,051; Total giving, $30,500; Grants to individuals, totaling $30,500.
Fields of interest: Law school/education; Medical school/education; Theological school/education; Science; Engineering/technology; Roman Catholic agencies & churches.
Type of support: Scholarships—to individuals.
Application information: Contact foundation for current application deadline; Completion of formal application required.
EIN: 046193022

1173
Cornelius Duggan Scholarship Trust
c/o Security National Bank, Trust Dept.
P.O. Box 147
Sioux City, IA 51102-0147

Foundation type: Independent foundation
Limitations: Scholarships to individuals for higher education in IA.
Financial data: Year ended 12/31/2004. Assets, $4,164,465 (M); Expenditures,

$304,465; Total giving, $283,750; Grants to individuals, totaling $283,750.
Type of support: Undergraduate support.
Application information: Unsolicited requests for funds not accepted.
EIN: 426136907

1174
Margaret S. Duke Scholarship Fund, Inc.
5 Summerville Ln.
Augusta, GA 30909-1813 (706) 737-7850
Contact: Jon D. Simowitz, Pres.

Foundation type: Independent foundation
Limitations: Scholarships to students in Augusta, GA, for higher education.
Financial data: Year ended 12/31/2004.
Assets, $93,983 (M); Expenditures, $5,290; Total giving, $5,000; Grants to individuals, totaling $5,000.
Type of support: Undergraduate support.
Application information: Applications by letter accepted throughout the year.
EIN: 582270126

1175
John H. Dulany Memorial, Inc.
P.O. Box 2949
Salisbury, MD 21802-2949 (410) 546-2053

Foundation type: Independent foundation
Limitations: Scholarships to residents of Wicomico County, MD.
Financial data: Year ended 12/31/2004.
Assets, $321,554 (M); Expenditures, $17,689; Total giving, $15,950; Grants to individuals, totaling $14,100.
Fields of interest: Education.
Type of support: Technical education support; Undergraduate support.
Application information: Applications accepted. Application form required.
  Deadline(s): Apr. 15.
  Additional information: Applications available from Wicomico County, MD, high schools.
EIN: 526051399

1176
Duluth-Superior Area Community Foundation
Medical Arts Bldg.
324 W. Superior St., Ste. 212
Duluth, MN 55802-1707 (218) 726-0232
Contact: Holly C. Sampson, C.E.O.
FAX: (218) 726-0257;
E-mail: info@dsacommunityfoundation.com; Grant application E-mail: grantsinfo@dsacommunityfoundation.com;
URL: http://www.dsacommunityfoundation.com

Foundation type: Community foundation
Limitations: Scholarships to residents of Douglas and Bayfield counties, WI, and Koochiching, Itasca, St. Louis, Lake, Cook, Carlton, and Aitkin counties in northeastern MN. Recipients may attend college or technical school.
Publications: Application guidelines; Annual report; Grants list; Informational brochure (including application guidelines); Newsletter.
Financial data: Year ended 12/31/2004.
Assets, $37,984,757 (M); Expenditures, $2,550,334; Total giving, $1,942,542; Grants to individuals, 261 grants totaling $946,800 (high: $5,500, low: $195).

Fields of interest: Vocational education.
Type of support: Technical education support; Undergraduate support.
Application information: Deadline Jan. 15; Initial approach by letter or telephone; Completion of formal application required; Interviews required.
EIN: 411429402

1177
Evangeline L. Dumesnil Trust
c/o National City Bank of MI/IL
P.O. Box 94651
Cleveland, OH 44101-4651

Foundation type: Independent foundation
Limitations: Scholarships to undergraduate and graduate students enrolled in the musical arts program at the University of Michigan and Wayne State University, MI.
Financial data: Year ended 12/31/2004.
Assets, $4,986,718 (M); Expenditures, $196,561; Total giving, $158,676.
Fields of interest: Music; Performing arts, education.
Type of support: Support to graduates or students of specific schools; Graduate support; Undergraduate support.
Application information: Applications not accepted.
EIN: 386473007

1178
Howard W. Dunbar Scholarship Trust A
c/o SunTrust Bank
800 S. Federal Hwy.
Boca Raton, FL 33432 (561) 362-3530
Contact: Leslie A. McCullough, Trust Off., SunTrust Bank

Foundation type: Independent foundation
Limitations: Scholarships to children of employees or former employees of The Norton Company, Worcester, MA, to study engineering.
Financial data: Year ended 08/31/2004.
Assets, $641,463 (M); Expenditures, $29,703; Total giving, $22,500; Grants to individuals, 11 grants totaling $22,500 (high: $3,000, low: $1,500).
Fields of interest: Engineering school/education.
Type of support: Employee-related scholarships.
Application information: Applications accepted. Application form required.
  Initial approach: Letter.
  Copies of proposal: 1
  Deadline(s): May 31
  Applicants should submit the following:
    1) Transcripts
    2) GPA
    3) Financial information
  Additional information: Application should include two letters of recommendation, a recent photograph, and a copy of parents' and applicant's most recent tax returns.
Program description:
  Scholarship Program: Recipients are chosen on the basis of financial need and academic achievement. Applicants must rank in the upper third of their classes or have at least a 2.8 GPA. Recipients who maintain at least a 2.8 GPA receive priority consideration for renewals. The scholarship may cover the costs of tuition, board, lodging, books, fees, supplies, study materials, and other necessities.
EIN: 656000044

1179
Harry F. Duncan Foundation, Inc.
c/o Friedman & Friedman, LLP
409 Washington Ave., Ste. 900
Towson, MD 21204-4905

Foundation type: Independent foundation
Limitations: Scholarships to individuals in FL and MO for higher education.
Financial data: Year ended 12/31/2004.
Assets, $3,403,101 (M); Expenditures, $191,595; Total giving, $177,316; Grants to individuals, 12 grants totaling $31,316 (high: $5,000, low: $1,000).
Type of support: Undergraduate support.
Application information: Applications not accepted.
EIN: 526054187

1180
Dewey C. Duncan Trust
c/o Wachovia Bank, N.A.
100 N. Main St., 13th Fl.
Winston-Salem, NC 27150

Foundation type: Independent foundation
Limitations: Scholarships to members of the Buchanan First Presbyterian Church of Grundy, VA, and the First Christian Church of Pulaski, VA, who are also Buchanan, VA, residents.
Financial data: Year ended 12/31/2004.
Assets, $335,089 (M); Expenditures, $16,407; Total giving, $12,038; Grants to individuals, 8 grants totaling $12,038 (high: $5,516, low: $486).
Fields of interest: Christian agencies & churches; Protestant agencies & churches.
Type of support: Scholarships—to individuals.
Application information: Application form required.
  Deadline(s): Apr. 5
  Applicants should submit the following:
    1) Transcripts
    2) Essay
Program description:
  Anne Bevins Duncan Scholarship: Provides scholarships to financially needy residents of Buchanan County, VA, who are members of Buchanan First Presbyterian Church. Scholarships are awarded on the basis of financial need, academic achievement, and character. Scholarships are renewable for up to four years. Application forms are available at the above address from Rev. Woody Alexander.
EIN: 546066637

1181
Arlenn and Arthur H. Dunham Educational Trust
247 Oyster Pond Dr.
Woods Hole, MA 02543-1529 (508) 823-4567
Application address: c/o Principal, Middleboro High School, 71 E. Grove St., Middleboro, MA 02346

Foundation type: Independent foundation
Limitations: Scholarships to students who have graduated from Middleborough High School, MA, with sufficient grades and financial need for higher education.
Financial data: Year ended 12/31/2004.
Assets, $206,029 (M); Expenditures, $7,473; Total giving, $4,282; Grants to individuals, totaling $4,282.
Type of support: Scholarships—to individuals; Support to graduates or students of specific schools.
Application information: Deadline for Apr. 30; Completion of formal application required, including

letter of need and grades; Applications available at Middleborough High School.
EIN: 046252943

1182
Dunkin' Donuts Charitable Trust
c/o Dunkin' Donuts, Inc., Total Rewards Off.
P.O. Box 317, 14 Pacella Park Dr.
Randolph, MA   02368-0317   (781) 961-4000

Foundation type: Company-sponsored foundation
Limitations: Scholarships to dependent children of employees or franchise owners of Dunkin' Donuts, Baskin-Robbins, or Togo's eateries.
Publications: Application guidelines; Biennial report; Newsletter.
Financial data: Year ended 12/31/2004.
Assets, $183,813 (M); Expenditures, $9,122; Total giving, $7,000; Grants to individuals, 7 grants totaling $7,000 (high: $1,000, low: $1,000).
Type of support: Employee-related scholarships.
Application information: Application form required.
Deadline(s): Mar. 31
Additional information: Application should include FAF.
EIN: 042733961

1183
Frank R. "Bo" Dunlap Foundation, Inc.
4701 Hickory Bend Rd.
Circleville, OH   43113
Scholarship application address: 26541 Immel Rd., Circleville, OH 43113

Foundation type: Independent foundation
Limitations: Scholarships to undergraduates who are residents of Wayne or Union Township, OH, for college expenses such as tuition, books, fees and on-campus room and board.
Financial data: Year ended 12/31/2004.
Assets, $922,916 (M); Expenditures, $64,755; Total giving, $45,200; Grants to individuals, totaling $35,500.
Type of support: Undergraduate support.
Application information: Applications accepted. Application form required.
Deadline(s): May 15
EIN: 311496488

1184
David R. Dunlap, Jr. Memorial Trust
c/o Regions Bank
P.O. Box 2527
Mobile, AL   36622   (251) 690-1419
Contact: David R. Dunlap, Jr.

Foundation type: Independent foundation
Limitations: Student loans to residents of Mobile and Baldwin counties, AL, and to employees of Regions Bank and Atlantic Marine, Inc.
Financial data: Year ended 12/31/2004.
Assets, $2,194,297 (M); Expenditures, $295,678; Total giving, $248,868; Loans to individuals, 73 loans totaling $248,868.
Type of support: Employee-related scholarships; Student loans—to individuals.
Application information:
Deadline(s): July
Additional information: Completion of formal application required, including transcripts and educational expenses.
EIN: 636020944

1185
Mary Frances Dunlop Scholarship Trust
c/o HNB Bank, N.A.
100 N. Main St.
Hannibal, MO   63401-3537
Application address: c/o Superintendent, Mark Twain High School, Ralls County, MO 63401

Foundation type: Independent foundation
Limitations: Scholarships to needy high school graduates residing in Ralls County, MO.
Financial data: Year ended 12/31/2004.
Assets, $108,864 (M); Expenditures, $6,884; Total giving, $5,300; Grants to individuals, totaling $5,300.
Type of support: Undergraduate support.
Application information: Applications accepted.
Program description:
Scholarship Program: The foundation's purpose is to assist students in obtaining a college or university education. Application forms, supplied by the awards committee, may be obtained from the superintendent of Mark Twain High School.
EIN: 436116557

1186
Dr. Ferrell W. Dunn Memorial Fund Trust
200 E. Jackson St.
Muncie, IN   47305
Contact: Torey Cook, Trust Off., First Merchants Bank, N.A.

Foundation type: Independent foundation
Limitations: Scholarships to students from Delaware County, IN, schools who have demonstrated an aptitude and desire to study and practice medicine.
Financial data: Year ended 05/31/2005.
Assets, $632,737 (M); Expenditures, $22,339; Total giving, $15,500; Grants to individuals, totaling $15,500.
Fields of interest: Medical school/education.
Type of support: Support to graduates or students of specific schools; Undergraduate support.
Application information: Deadline Apr. 1; Initial approach by letter; Completion of formal application required; Scholarships are renewable.
EIN: 356398629

1187
Margaret Dunn Scholarship Fund
c/o Bank of America, N.A.
P.O. Box 34345
Seattle, WA   98124-1345

Foundation type: Independent foundation
Limitations: Scholarships to graduates of Yakima School District 7, WA, for attendance at accredited institutions in WA.
Financial data: Year ended 08/31/2004.
Assets, $273,305 (M); Expenditures, $12,690; Total giving, $10,092; Grants to individuals, 27 grants totaling $10,092 (high: $1,200, low: $40).
Type of support: Support to graduates or students of specific schools; Undergraduate support.
Application information: Application form required.
Deadline(s): Apr. 15
Additional information: See high school counselor for application.
EIN: 916365396

1188
Caroline F. Dunton Scholarship Fund
c/o KeyBank N.A.
800 Superior Ave., 4th Fl.
Cleveland, OH   44114

Foundation type: Independent foundation
Limitations: Scholarships to graduates of Belfast High School, ME, for postsecondary education.
Financial data: Year ended 08/31/2004.
Assets, $103,986 (M); Expenditures, $10,520; Total giving, $7,375; Grants to individuals, totaling $7,375.
Fields of interest: Vocational education.
Type of support: Support to graduates or students of specific schools; Undergraduate support.
Application information: Applications not accepted.
EIN: 016026835

1189
Mabel E. Dupee Foundation, Inc.
c/o Union National Bank & Trust Co.
124 W. Oak St.
Sparta, WI   54656-1713   (608) 269-6737

Foundation type: Independent foundation
Limitations: Scholarships to graduates of Sparta Senior High School, WI, for undergraduate education. Students beyond their 4th year of post-high school education are ineligible.
Financial data: Year ended 12/31/2004.
Assets, $275,299 (M); Expenditures, $15,634; Total giving, $14,800; Grants to individuals, totaling $14,800.
Type of support: Support to graduates or students of specific schools; Undergraduate support.
Application information: Deadline Mar. 31; Completion of formal application required.
EIN: 391383645

1190
The Naasson K. & Florrie S. Dupre Permanent Educational Scholarship Fund Trust
c/o American State Bank
P.O. Box 1401
Lubbock, TX   79408-1401   (806) 767-7000
Application address: c/o Dean of Agriculture, Texas Tech University, Lubbock, TX 79409, tel.: (806) 742-2808

Foundation type: Independent foundation
Limitations: Scholarships to juniors, seniors, and graduate students enrolled in the College of Agricultural Sciences at Texas Tech University, who are residents of TX and have maintained at least a "B" average in the semester preceding application.
Financial data: Year ended 12/31/2004.
Assets, $174,849 (M); Expenditures, $11,820; Total giving, $9,100; Grants to individuals, totaling $9,100.
Fields of interest: Natural resources; Agriculture.
Type of support: Support to graduates or students of specific schools; Graduate support; Undergraduate support.
Application information: Contact school for application deadline; Completion of formal application required; Interviews required; Scholarships are renewable.
EIN: 756103694

1191
Duran Foundation
1035 Carleton St.
Berkeley, CA 94710

Foundation type: Independent foundation
Limitations: Scholarships to individuals for higher education.
Financial data: Year ended 12/31/2004.
Assets, $425,007 (M); Expenditures, $25,184; Total giving, $4,000; Grants to individuals, totaling $4,000.
Type of support: Undergraduate support.
Application information: Applications by letter accepted throughout the year.
EIN: 943316076

1192
Hildegard Durfee Scholarship Fund
c/o Charles R. Cummings
P.O. Box 677
Brattleboro, VT 05302-0677

Foundation type: Independent foundation
Limitations: Undergraduate and graduate scholarships to residents of Windham County, VT. Relatives of the fund's trustees or selection committee are ineligible.
Financial data: Year ended 12/31/2004.
Assets, $605,974 (M); Expenditures, $37,141; Total giving, $25,000; Grants to individuals, totaling $25,000.
Type of support: Graduate support; Undergraduate support.
Application information: Application form required.
Deadline(s): Deadline Apr. 15.
Applicants should submit the following:
1) Transcripts
2) FAF
EIN: 226546128

1193
The Dan Dutko Memorial Foundation
412 First St., S.E.
Washington, DC 20003 (202) 484-4884
Contact: G. Stephen Perry, Pres.; Fellowships: Mindy Nierenberg
Address for fellowships: c/o Tufts University College of Citizenship and Public Service, Lincoln Filene Hall, Tufts University, Medford, MA 02155

Foundation type: Public charity
Limitations: Fellowships to individuals graduating from Tufts University College of Citizenship and Public Service.
Financial data: Year ended 12/31/2003.
Assets, $147,620 (M); Expenditures, $42,451; Total giving, $40,000; Grants to individuals, 4 grants totaling $40,000 (high: $12,000, low: $8,000).
Fields of interest: Higher education.
Type of support: Fellowships; Support to graduates or students of specific schools.
Application information: Applications accepted.
Deadline(s): Feb. 25
Applicants should submit the following:
1) Transcripts
2) Resume
3) Letter(s) of recommendation
4) Essay
EIN: 522248030

1194
Duvall Family Foundation
3002 Taralane Dr.
Birmingham, AL 35216-4110 (205) 979-0276

Foundation type: Independent foundation
Limitations: Scholarships to individuals residing in AL.
Financial data: Year ended 12/31/2002.
Assets, $100,707 (M); Expenditures, $10,485; Total giving, $10,485; Grants to individuals, 4 grants totaling $10,085 (high: $4,421, low: $418).
Type of support: Scholarships—to individuals.
Application information: Applications not accepted.
EIN: 631239622

1195
Fred H. DuVall Scholarship Fund
c/o Wachovia Bank, N.A.
100 N. Main St., 13th Fl.
Winston-Salem, NC 27150

Foundation type: Independent foundation
Limitations: Scholarships by nomination only to financially needy students residing in Swain City, NC.
Financial data: Year ended 08/31/2005.
Assets, $387,417 (M); Expenditures, $25,978; Total giving, $22,000; Grants to individuals, totaling $22,000.
Type of support: Scholarships—to individuals; Awards/grants by nomination only.
Application information: Nominations accepted throughout the year; Completion of formal application required.
EIN: 566415001

1196
Duxbury Yacht Club Charitable Foundation
c/o U.S. Trust Company, N.A.
P.O. Box 55122, 3rd Fl.
Boston, MA 02205
Application address: c/o Powell Robinson, Jr., 19 Depot St., P.O. Box 2801, Duxbury, MA 02331

Foundation type: Independent foundation
Limitations: Scholarships to Duxbury, MA, high school graduates.
Financial data: Year ended 12/31/2004.
Assets, $265,157 (M); Expenditures, $20,488; Total giving, $18,935; Grants to individuals, totaling $13,000.
Type of support: Support to graduates or students of specific schools; Undergraduate support.
Application information:
Initial approach: Letter requesting financial aid.
Deadline(s): May 1
EIN: 046115247

1197
James W. & Betty Dye Foundation, Inc.
900 Ridge Rd., Ste. M
Munster, IN 46321 (219) 836-1100
Contact: Scholarship Comm.

Foundation type: Independent foundation
Limitations: Scholarships to graduates of Griffith High School and Hammond High School, IN, who hold a GPA of 2.75 or are in the top third of their graduating classes and who will be attending Bloomington Campus of Indiana University or West Layfayette Campus of Purdue University on a full-time basis.
Financial data: Year ended 12/31/2004.
Assets, $4,029,987; Expenditures, $201,169; Total giving, $177,579; Grants to individuals, 45 grants totaling $176,079 (high: $5,872, low: $962).
Type of support: Support to graduates or students of specific schools.
Application information: Deadline Apr. 1; Completion of formal application required, including copy of letter of admission to the university, two letters of recommendation, and a short personal essay; Applications available in high school guidance offices.
Program description:
Scholarship Program: Recipients receive support for eight consecutive undergraduate semesters of full-time study. Each academic year, recipients must forward a copy of their transcripts to the foundation prior to July 1, in order to renew their award.
EIN: 351884798

1198
J. Franklin Dyer Trust
109 Main St.
Gloucester, MA 01930
Contact: J. Michael Faherty, Tr.
Application address: 111 Main St., Gloucester, MA 01930

Foundation type: Independent foundation
Limitations: Scholarships to graduating students attending Gloucester High School, MA.
Financial data: Year ended 03/31/2004.
Assets, $130,566 (M); Expenditures, $6,474; Total giving, $5,000; Grants to individuals, totaling $5,000.
Type of support: Support to graduates or students of specific schools; Undergraduate support.
Application information: Contact foundation for current application deadline/guidelines.
EIN: 046545848

1199
Herbert T. Dyett Foundation, Inc.
218 N. Washington St.
Rome, NY 13440 (315) 336-1441
Contact: James P. Kehoe, Jr., Secy.
Scholarship application addresses: c/o Principal, Rome Free Academy, Rome, NY 13440, tel.: (315) 338-2222, or c/o Principal, Rome Catholic High School, Rome, NY 13440, tel.: (315) 336-6190

Foundation type: Independent foundation
Limitations: Scholarships for the first two years of college only to financially needy graduating seniors at Rome Free Academy and Rome Catholic High School, both in Rome, NY. Applicants must have attended the schools for two years prior to graduation and rank in the top third of their classes.
Financial data: Year ended 12/31/2004.
Assets, $1,661,596 (M); Expenditures, $97,569; Total giving, $91,250; Grants to individuals, totaling $91,250.
Type of support: Support to graduates or students of specific schools; Undergraduate support.
Application information: Applications accepted throughout the year; Completion of formal application required; Interviews required.
Program description:
Scholarship Program: Scholarships are awarded on the basis of financial need, personality, character, leadership, citizenship, and health.
EIN: 166041857

1200
EAA Aviation Foundation, Inc.
P.O. Box 3086
Oshkosh, WI   54903-3086   (920) 426-6884
Contact: Thomas P. Poberezny, Pres.
FAX: (920) 426-6865; E-mail: hsanchez@eaa.org;
URL: http://www.eaa.org/education/
scholarships/

Foundation type: Public charity
Limitations: Scholarships to individuals studying the technologies and skills needed in the field of aviation.
Financial data: Year ended 02/28/2003.
Assets, $27,538,694 (M); Expenditures, $9,226,583; Total giving, $112,008; Grants to individuals, totaling $60,200.
Fields of interest: Engineering school/education; Space/aviation.
Type of support: Support to graduates or students of specific schools; Technical education support; Undergraduate support.
Application information: Deadline Mar. 30; Completion of formal application required; See Web site for additional information.
Program descriptions:
EAA Aviation Achievement Scholarship: Awards of $500 each to deserving students who are active in recreational aviation endeavors. Scholarships are to further training or education.
Teledyne Continental Aviation Excellence Scholarship: Awards $500 to an individual displaying the potential to become a professional in any field of aviation.
Herbert L. Cox Memorial Scholarship: Awards $500 to an individual accepted at or attending a four-year accredited college or university in pursuit of a degree leading to an aviation profession. Recipient must show need for financial support.
Richard Lee Vernon Aviation Scholarship: Awards $500 to a student pursuing training leading to a professional aviation occupation. Scholarship is awarded to a person accepted to a course of study in a recognized professional aviation training program in either an institution of higher learning or aviation technical school. Recipient must show need for financial support.
Hansen Scholarship: Awards a renewable scholarship of $1,000 to a student in good academic standing who is enrolled in an accredited college, university or technical school and is pursuing a degree in Aerospace Engineering or Aeronautical Engineering. Financial need is a consideration.
Payzer Scholarship: Awards $5,000 to an individual accepted at or enrolled in an accredited college, university or postsecondary school with an emphasis on technical information. Recipient must be intent on pursuing a professional career in engineering, mathematics, or the physical or biological sciences.
Friendship One Flight Training Scholarships: Awards two $5,000 scholarships to individuals for commercial flight training and two $2,500 scholarships for private pilot training. Recipients must have attended the resident youth EAA Air Academy in Oshkosh, WI.
Clay Lacy Professional Pilot Scholarship: Awards $25,000 per year to highly qualified flight students from the University of North Dakota, John D. Odegard School of Aerospace to earn a degree as a professional pilot and earn commercial, instrument, multi-engine and all-fixed wing flight instructor ratings. Recipients must meet FAA criteria and licensure and must have their private pilot's license to be eligible for scholarship. Recipients must also show financial need.

David Alan Quick Scholarship: Awards $1,000 to a junior or senior, in good standing, enrolled in an accredited college or university. Recipient must be pursuing a degree in Aerospace or Aeronautical Engineering. Scholarship is renewable.
H.P. "Bud" Milligan Aviation Scholarship: Awards $1,000 to students enrolled in an accredited aviation program at a college, technical school or aviation academy. Financial need is not a requirement.
EIN: 391033301

1201
The Eagle Foundation, Inc.
2 Walsh Ln.
Greenwich, CT   06830-7039   (203) 661-4011
Contact: Brenda Landsman, Tr.
E-mail: eagle06830@aol.com

Foundation type: Independent foundation
Limitations: Undergraduate scholarships to high school seniors, who are residents of CT, NJ, and NY. Ten four-year undergraduate scholarships of up to $10,000 are awarded per student per year with scholarship amount dependent on family need.
Financial data: Year ended 12/31/2003.
Assets, $340,898 (M); Expenditures, $198,027; Total giving, $113,850; Grants to individuals, 31 grants totaling $113,850 (high: $9,200, low: $500).
Type of support: Undergraduate support.
Application information: Applications accepted. Application form required.
Deadline(s): Deadline Apr.15.
Additional information: Contact local high school for application.
EIN: 061442187

1202
Edna & Harvey Eagle Scholarship Trust
c/o U.S. Bank, N.A.
P.O. Box 1118, ML CN-OH-W10X
Cincinnati, OH   45201
Application address: c/o Jan Wagner, 175 S. Third St., 4th Fl., ML CN-OH-9281, Columbus, OH 43215

Foundation type: Independent foundation
Limitations: Scholarships to students of Newark High School, OH, and Leipsic High School, OH, through the recommendation of employees at these schools.
Financial data: Year ended 09/30/2005.
Assets, $190,326 (M); Expenditures, $16,106; Total giving, $13,500; Grants to individuals, totaling $13,500.
Fields of interest: Education.
Type of support: Support to graduates or students of specific schools; Awards/grants by nomination only; Undergraduate support.
Application information: Contact foundation for current application deadline/guidelines.
EIN: 316546256

1203
Eagles Memorial Foundation, Inc.
4710 14th St. W.
Bradenton, FL   34207   (941) 755-1976
Contact: Thomas J. McGriff, Exec. Secy.
Additional tel.: (941) 758-4042; Application address for individuals: c/o Richard J. Steinberg, Golden Eagle Fund, P.O. Box 25916, Milwaukee, WI 53225-0916
E-mail: memorial@foe.com; URL: http://www.foe.com/memorial/index.html

Foundation type: Public charity
Limitations: Scholarships to the children of deceased Eagle servicemen and women, law officers, or firefighters, and to graduates of Home on the Range for Boys in Sentinel Butte, ND, High Sky Girls Ranch in Midland, TX, and Bob Hope High School in Port Arthur, TX.
Publications: Financial statement; Informational brochure.
Financial data: Year ended 05/31/2004.
Assets, $12,582,388 (M); Expenditures, $1,745,005; Total giving, $670,150.
Fields of interest: Vocational education; Business school/education; Nursing school/education; Disasters, fire prevention/control; Military/veterans' organizations.
Type of support: Support to graduates or students of specific schools; Technical education support; Undergraduate support.
Application information: Applications accepted. Application form required.
Additional information: Application should include transcripts. Contact foundation for current application deadline.
Program description:
Scholarship Program: To be eligible for scholarship assistance, individuals must be graduates of the aforementioned institutions, or the children of members of the Fraternal Order of Eagles and the Ladies Auxiliary who died from injuries or diseases incurred or aggravated while serving:
  · in the armed forces
  · as a law enforcement officer
  · as a full-time or volunteer firefighter or EMS officer
Educational assistance is available to eligible individuals up to the age of 25, unless married or self-supporting before that time. The re-marriage of either parent does not change an individual's eligibility. Educational grants shall not exceed $4,000 per school year, or a total of $20,000 for all years per recipient. Grants may be used to help defray the cost of college education or vocational school training after high school. The term "vocational school" includes any continuous trade training schools, such as business, beauty, nursing, or other technical schools. Scholarships are renewable annually provided the recipient maintains at least a cumulative "C" average.
EIN: 396126176

1204
Eagleton War Memorial Scholarship Fund, Inc.
P.O. Box 980
Bridgehampton, NY   11932-0980
Application address: c/o Superintendent of Schools, Bridgehampton High School, Bridgehampton, NY 11932

Foundation type: Independent foundation
Limitations: Scholarships to graduating seniors of Bridgehampton High School, NY.
Financial data: Year ended 12/31/2004.
Assets, $251,655 (M); Expenditures, $9,594; Total giving, $9,000; Grants to individuals, totaling $9,000.
Type of support: Support to graduates or students of specific schools; Undergraduate support.
Application information: Deadline June 1; Application by letter outlining financial need.
EIN: 237149864

1205
Harrison Earl & Frances Smith Scholarship Fund
c/o Chemung Canal Trust Co.
P.O. Box 1522
Elmira, NY 14902
Application address: c/o Board of Education, Elmira Heights Central School District, Elmira Heights, NY 14903, tel.: (607) 734-7114

Foundation type: Independent foundation
Limitations: Scholarships to graduates of Thomas A. Edison High School, Elmira, NY.
Financial data: Year ended 12/31/2002. Assets, $71,599 (M); Expenditures, $4,367; Total giving, $4,106; Grants to individuals, totaling $4,006.
Type of support: Support to graduates or students of specific schools; Undergraduate support.
Application information: Contact fund for current application deadline/guidelines.
EIN: 166038545

1206
East Lake Foundation, Inc.
(formerly East Lake Community Foundation, Inc.)
2606 Alston Dr.
Atlanta, GA 30317   (404) 373-4351
Contact: Rhonda Davidson, Dir., Devel.
FAX: (404) 373-4354;
E-mail: rdavidson@eastlakecommunityfdn.org;
URL: http://www.eastlakefoundation.org

Foundation type: Public charity
Limitations: Scholarships to high school and college students employed by the Charlie Yates Golf Course in Atlanta, GA.
Publications: Annual report; Informational brochure; Newsletter.
Financial data: Year ended 12/31/2003. Assets, $38,585,661 (M); Expenditures, $4,469,593; Total giving, $282,530; Grants to individuals, 9 grants totaling $16,500 (high: $2,500, low: $1,000).
Type of support: Employee-related scholarships; Undergraduate support.
Application information:
Initial approach: E-mail.
Additional information: Contact foundation for current application guidelines.
EIN: 582204306

1207
East Longmeadow Rotary Memorial Scholarship Foundation
c/o Rotary Scholarship Comm.
537 Prospect St.
East Longmeadow, MA 01028
Application address: c/o Scholarship Comm., P.O. Box 571, East Longmeadow, MA 01028

Foundation type: Independent foundation
Limitations: Scholarships to graduating seniors of East Longmeadow High School and residents of East Longmeadow, MA.
Publications: Application guidelines.
Financial data: Year ended 06/30/2004. Assets, $241,904 (M); Expenditures, $16,496; Total giving, $12,000.
Type of support: Support to graduates or students of specific schools; Undergraduate support.
Application information: Application form required.
Initial approach: Letter or telephone.
Deadline(s): Mar. 1

Additional information: Applications should include 3 references.
Program description:
Scholarship Program: One scholarship to a culinary or vocational school student. Other scholarships awarded on merit. Additional scholarships available from East Longmeadow Rotary Club.
EIN: 042961763

1208
Eastcliff Foundation
P.O. Box 1455
Capitola, CA 95010-1455   (831) 465-8399
Contact: Jeannine Baker, Secy.
E-mail: info@eastcliff.org; URL: http://www.eastcliff.org

Foundation type: Independent foundation
Limitations: Scholarships to graduates of Santa Cruz County, CA, public high schools for undergraduate education.
Financial data: Year ended 09/30/2004. Assets, $344,080 (M); Expenditures, $115,817; Total giving, $112,000; Grants to individuals, 56 grants totaling $112,000 (high: $2,000, low: $2,000).
Type of support: Support to graduates or students of specific schools; Undergraduate support.
Application information: Application form required.
Initial approach: Telephone.
Applicants should submit the following:
1) Transcripts
2) Financial information
3) Essay
Additional information: Contact foundation for current application deadline.
Program description:
Scholarship Program: Awards scholarships of $2,000, renewable for four years provided that the recipient maintains good standing with his or her university. Recipients must have a minimum GPA of 3.0 and demonstrate financial need.
EIN: 912150715

1209
Eastern Choral Society
(also known as Washington Youth Choir)
P.O. Box 50361
Washington, DC 20091
Contact: Heather Infantry, Exec. Dir.
FAX: (202) 293-7509;
E-mail: heather@washingtonyouthchoir.org;
URL: http://www.washingtonyouthchoir.org/

Foundation type: Public charity
Limitations: Scholarships to members of the Washington Youth Choir, DC, for higher education.
Publications: Annual report; Financial statement.
Financial data: Year ended 06/30/2004. Assets, $72,877 (M); Expenditures, $169,228; Total giving, $25,500; Grants to individuals, 9 grants totaling $25,500 (high: $3,500, low: $2,000).
Fields of interest: Higher education.
Type of support: Scholarships—to individuals.
Application information: Contact foundation for current application deadline/guidelines.
Program description:
Scholarship Fund: Scholarships of $500 to $4,000 awarded to choir members towards their first year of college.
EIN: 521833176

1210
Eastern Star Charity Foundation of New Jersey
111 Finderne Ave.
Bridgewater, NJ 08807-3100
Contact: Lynn Billingham, Pres.

Foundation type: Public charity
Limitations: Scholarships and student loans to members of the Eastern Star of NJ.
Financial data: Year ended 05/31/2003. Assets, $1,694,604 (M); Expenditures, $178,405; Total giving, $165,734; Grants to individuals, totaling $64,416.
Type of support: Scholarships—to individuals; Student loans—to individuals.
Application information: Applications accepted. Application form required.
Applicants should submit the following:
1) SAT
2) ACT
3) Letter(s) of recommendation
Additional information: Contact foundation for current application deadline.
EIN: 221613650

1211
Arthur G. Eastman Memorial Scholarship Fund
c/o Chittenden Bank
P.O. Box 820
Burlington, VT 05402
Application address: c/o Katherine James, Guidance Dir., Whitingham High School, Jacksonville, VT 05342, tel.: (802) 368-2929

Foundation type: Independent foundation
Limitations: Scholarships to graduates of Whitingham High School, Jacksonville, VT, who have completed their last two high school years at Whitingham.
Financial data: Year ended 12/31/2004. Assets, $145,922 (M); Expenditures, $13,068; Total giving, $10,047; Grants to individuals, totaling $10,047.
Type of support: Scholarships—to individuals; Support to graduates or students of specific schools.
Application information: Contact fund for current application deadline; Completion of formal application required, including transcripts and student's or parents' financial statement.
Program description:
Scholarship Program: Students must be accepted to the school of their choice before applying, and must go directly to college when the next scholastic year begins. Recipients must continue as full-time students without interruption until graduation.
EIN: 030279845

1212
Eaton & Reed Scholarship Fund Trust
c/o Bank of America, N.A., P.C. Group
P.O. Box 1802
Providence, RI 02940-1802
Application address: c/o Guidance Office, Manchester High School, 134 Middle Tpke., East Manchester, CT 06040

Foundation type: Independent foundation
Limitations: Scholarships to seniors and graduates of Manchester High School, CT.
Financial data: Year ended 09/30/2005. Assets, $672,586 (M); Expenditures, $35,334;

Total giving, $28,467; Grants to individuals, totaling $28,467.
Type of support: Support to graduates or students of specific schools; Undergraduate support.
Application information:
Deadline(s): May 24
Additional information: Completion of formal application required, including page one of parents' 1040 form, and the financial aid award package from institution applicant plans to attend or the Needs Analysis Form.
EIN: 237146710

1213
Ebell of Los Angeles Scholarship Endowment Fund
743 S. Lucerne Blvd.
Los Angeles, CA 90005 (323) 931-1277
Contact: Kay Lachter, Scholarship Chair.
FAX: (323) 937-0272;
E-mail: scholarship@ebellla.com; URL: http://www.ebellla.com

Foundation type: Independent foundation
Limitations: Undergraduate scholarships to full-time students who are U.S. citizens, registered voters, residents of Los Angeles County, CA, and attending colleges and universities in Los Angeles County. Applicants must be sophomores or above in financial need, and have at least a 3.25 GPA.
Publications: Application guidelines.
Financial data: Year ended 06/30/2004.
Assets, $4,225,731 (M); Expenditures, $266,409; Total giving, $181,625; Grants to individuals, 89 grants totaling $181,625 (high: $3,500, low: $125).
Type of support: Undergraduate support.
Application information: Applications accepted. Application form required.
Deadline(s): Mar. 1
Applicants should submit the following:
1) Photograph
2) Letter(s) of recommendation
3) Essay
4) Financial information
5) Transcripts
6) GPA
Additional information: Applications available from the fund or the financial aid office of student's college or university.
Program description:
Scholarship Program: Scholarships are awarded on the basis of grades, character, financial need, and leadership. Generally, scholarship payments are made in monthly installments from Sept. to June. Scholarships are renewable through the completion of undergraduate study. This scholarship program is administered as two separate funds: The Ebell of Los Angeles Scholarship Endowment Fund and the Mr. and Mrs. Charles N. Flint Scholarship Endowment Fund. While the specific fiscal figures for each fund differ, the programs, application procedures, contact person, and address are identical.
EIN: 237049580

1214
Elsie C. Eberhardt Trust
200 W. Harrison St.
Sullivan, IL 61951-1954 (217) 728-7369
Contact: Steven K. Wood, Tr.

Foundation type: Independent foundation
Limitations: Scholarships to high school graduates of Arthur Community School District schools in IL.

Financial data: Year ended 12/31/2004.
Assets, $1,279,571 (M); Expenditures, $63,333; Total giving, $56,200; Grants to individuals, totaling $14,050.
Type of support: Support to graduates or students of specific schools; Undergraduate support.
Application information: Deadline June 10; Completion of formal application required, including transcripts, letter of college acceptance, letters of recommendation from principal, counselor, or department head and from someone else other than a teacher or relative, personal statement, and for dependent students, parents' financial statement.
EIN: 376311757

1215
Hazel C. Ebert Memorial Fund
c/o Commerce Bank, N.A.
P.O. Box 419248
Kansas City, MO 64141-6248
Contact: Kenneth Niemeyer, Dean, School of Veterinary Medicine
Application address: c/o University of Missouri-Columbia, Columbia, MO 65211

Foundation type: Independent foundation
Limitations: Scholarships to third- and fourth-year veterinary medicine students at the University of Missouri—Columbia who have financial need and academic potential.
Financial data: Year ended 12/31/2004.
Assets, $744,185 (M); Expenditures, $35,868; Total giving, $32,448; Grants to individuals, totaling $32,448.
Fields of interest: Veterinary medicine.
Type of support: Scholarships—to individuals; Support to graduates or students of specific schools.
Application information: Applications accepted throughout the year; Initial approach by letter; Completion of formal application required; Interviews required.
EIN: 431260509

1216
Dr. Robert R. Eckert Memorial Fund
c/o The National Bank of Delaware County
P.O. Box 389
Walton, NY 13856 (607) 865-4126

Foundation type: Independent foundation
Limitations: Scholarships to students of Roscoe Central and Downsville school districts, NY.
Financial data: Year ended 12/31/2003.
Assets, $793,689 (M); Expenditures, $45,733; Total giving, $40,985; Grants to individuals, 25 grants totaling $40,985 (high: $4,000, low: $27).
Type of support: Scholarships—to individuals; Support to graduates or students of specific schools.
Application information: Applications by letter accepted throughout the year.
EIN: 166280587

1217
C. K. Eddy Family Memorial Fund
c/o Citizens Bank Wealth Mgmt., N.A.
328 S. Saginaw St., M/C 002072
Flint, MI 48502
Application address: Helen James, Trust Off., c/o Citizens Bank Wealth Mgmt., N.A., 101 N. Washington Ave., Saginaw, MI 48007, tel.: (989) 776-7368

Foundation type: Independent foundation
Limitations: Student loans to financially needy individuals between the ages of 15 and 30, who have been residents of Saginaw County, MI, for at least one year prior to application deadline, and are or will be attending colleges in MI.
Publications: Application guidelines.
Financial data: Year ended 06/30/2005.
Assets, $16,004,061 (M); Expenditures, $918,201; Total giving, $703,191; Loans to individuals, 64 loans totaling $225,200.
Type of support: Student loans—to individuals.
Application information: Application form required.
Deadline(s): May 1
Applicants should submit the following:
1) Transcripts
2) ACT
3) SAT
4) GPA
5) Financial information
6) Essay
Program description:
C.K. Eddy Student Loan Fund: The need for economic assistance in the form of a student loan must be proven. If the applicant has not attained his or her 23rd birthday as of the application deadline, the financial need will be based upon the financial status of the parents. If the applicant reaches his or her 23rd birthday prior to the deadline, financial need will be based upon the applicant's financial status. GPA requirement for the loan is at least 2.0 cumulative during high school and college. A loan recipient may attend any institution in MI. However, funds available for out-of-state schools are limited. The interest rate of the loan will be three percent while attending school as a full-time student. Interest will begin to accrue upon receipt of the loan. It will be to the recipient's advantage to request the actual payment no sooner than the funds are needed. As long as the recipient is a full-time student, annual payment of only the interest is required. Monthly payments of the principal and interest will begin no later than nine months after completion of education. The terms of the loan will be up to ten years with payments of no less than $30 and no more than $125 per month, at five percent per annum. Deferment on loan payment may be requested if the student pursues graduate studies.
EIN: 386040506

1218
Eddy Foundation
(formerly Eddy Foundation Charitable Trust)
c/o Wells Fargo Bank Minnesota, N.A.
230 W. Superior St., Ste. 400
Duluth, MN 55802
Application addresses: For University of Minnesota-Duluth students: Dept. of Communication Sciences and Disorders, University of Minnesota, 221 Bohannon Hall, 10 University Dr., Duluth, MN 55812-2496; For non-University students and special situations: Edwin H. Eddy Foundation Scholarship, Northwest Bank Minnesota North, N.A., Trust Dept., P.O. Box 488, Duluth, MN 55801-0488

Foundation type: Independent foundation
Limitations: Scholarships to Duluth, MN, area residents who are full-time college seniors or graduate students studying communication disorders at accredited colleges and universities. Grants also to nonresidents attending the University of Minnesota, Duluth.
Publications: Application guidelines; Informational brochure (including application guidelines); Program policy statement.

Financial data: Year ended 06/30/2005. Assets, $4,361,584 (M); Expenditures, $335,273; Total giving, $282,152; Grants to individuals, 39 grants totaling $84,350 (high: $3,000, low: $750).
Fields of interest: Learning disorders research; Disabilities, people with.
Type of support: Scholarships—to individuals; Graduate support; Undergraduate support.
Application information: Applications accepted. Application form required.
  Initial approach: Letter.
  Deadline(s): Mar. 31
  Additional information: Application should include transcripts; Interviews required; Recipients notified by June 1.
Program description:
  Scholarship Program: Applicants must have a minimum 3.0 GPA to qualify. The maximum scholarship amount is $1,200 for undergraduate study and $3,000 for two years of graduate study, or $467 per quarter for up to six quarters. Priorities for granting scholarships are as follows:
  · Duluth area residents attending the University of Minnesota, Duluth
  · Duluth area residents attending other accredited institutions
  · Non-area residents attending the University of Minnesota, Duluth
Interviews must be arranged by the applicant at the Office of Communicative Disorders Department at the University of Minnesota, Duluth.
EIN: 416242226

1219
The Sidney and Arthur Eder Foundation, Inc.
11 Eder Rd.
West Haven, CT   06516

Foundation type: Independent foundation
Limitations: Undergraduate scholarships to children of present or former employees of Eder Brothers, Inc.
Financial data: Year ended 12/31/2004. Assets, $5,577,229 (M); Expenditures, $349,089; Total giving, $330,650.
Type of support: Employee-related scholarships.
Application information: Applications not accepted.
EIN: 066035306

1220
William Edgar Charitable Foundation
c/o U.S. Bank, N.A., Private Client Group
P.O. Box 387
St. Louis, MO   63166
Contact: R. David Bray

Foundation type: Independent foundation
Limitations: Scholarships to graduates of Ironton High School, MO.
Publications: Application guidelines.
Financial data: Year ended 06/30/2005. Assets, $4,513,241 (M); Expenditures, $301,463; Total giving, $250,140.
Type of support: Scholarships—to individuals; Support to graduates or students of specific schools; Awards/grants by nomination only; Technical education support; Undergraduate support.
Application information: Application form required.
  Copies of proposal: 5
  Deadline(s): Feb. 15
  Applicants should submit the following:

1) Class rank
2) GPA
3) SAT
4) ACT
  Additional information: Application should also include the most relevant standardized test that is applicable to an applicant's chosen avenue of further education (if not the SAT or ACT), and verification of graduation or impending graduation from Ironton High School, MO.
Program description:
  Scholarship Program: Scholarships are renewable if recipient maintains a cumulative GPA of at least 3.0 on a 4.0 scale, or the equivalent.
EIN: 436829350

1221
Edgar County Bank & Trust Foundation
c/o The Edgar County Bank & Trust Co.
P.O. Box 400
Paris, IL   61944-0400   (217) 465-4154
Contact: John D. Carrington, Secy.-Treas.

Foundation type: Company-sponsored foundation
Limitations: Scholarships to students at secondary schools located in Edgar County and contiguous counties of IL and IN, for study at the postsecondary level.
Financial data: Year ended 07/31/2005. Assets, $7,275 (M); Expenditures, $39,585; Total giving, $38,835; Grants to individuals, 35 grants totaling $16,300 (high: $1,500, low: $200).
Type of support: Scholarships—to individuals.
Application information: Application form required.
  Deadline(s): None
EIN: 371286227

1222
Edgerton Area Foundation
P.O. Box 399
Edgerton, OH   43517-0399
Contact: Roger D. Strup, Pres.

Foundation type: Community foundation
Limitations: Scholarships to students in the Edgerton, OH, area, for higher education.
Financial data: Year ended 06/30/2005. Assets, $1,005,631 (M); Expenditures, $59,811; Total giving, $26,184; Grants to individuals, 28 grants totaling $22,300 (high: $1,500, low: $250).
Type of support: Undergraduate support.
Application information: Contact foundation for current application deadline/guidelines.
EIN: 341593384

1223
George Walter & Violet C. Edmonds Scholarship Trust
c/o Wachovia Bank, N.A.
100 N. Main St., 13th Fl.
Winston-Salem, NC   27150
Application address: c/o Herb Tschappat, Principal, Palmetto High School, 1200 17th St., Palmetto, FL 34221, tel.: (941) 722-4848

Foundation type: Independent foundation
Limitations: Scholarships only to graduates of Palmetto High School, FL, who are enrolled in Palmetto, FL, area junior colleges or four-year colleges or universities.
Financial data: Year ended 09/30/2004. Assets, $250,622 (M); Expenditures, $16,676;

Total giving, $13,500; Grants to individuals, totaling $13,470.
Type of support: Support to graduates or students of specific schools; Undergraduate support.
Application information: Applications by letter, outlining financial need, GPA, college entrance exam scores, and community service, accepted throughout the year.
EIN: 596804593

1224
V. Faith Edmunds Scholarship Trust
c/o TD Banknorth, N.A., Investment Mgmt. Group
P.O. Box 595
Williston, VT   05495
Application address: c/o Principal of People's Academy, Rd. No. 3, Box 40, Morrisville, VT 05661

Foundation type: Independent foundation
Limitations: Scholarships to students at People's Academy in Morrisville, VT, for higher education. Scholarships range up to $1,000 per year for a maximum of four years of study.
Financial data: Year ended 12/31/2004. Assets, $115,180 (M); Expenditures, $7,375; Total giving, $5,500; Grants to individuals, totaling $5,500.
Type of support: Support to graduates or students of specific schools; Undergraduate support.
Application information:
  Initial approach: Letter.
  Deadline(s): Contact the Academy for current application deadline/guidelines.
EIN: 946443878

1225
T. Murrell Edmunds Testamentary Trust
c/o JPMorgan Chase Bank, N.A.
P.O. Box 1308
Milwaukee, WI   53201
Application address: c/o John LaFargue, 201 St. Charles Ave., 29th Fl., New Orleans, LA 70170

Foundation type: Independent foundation
Limitations: Scholarships to high school graduates from Lynchburg, VA.
Financial data: Year ended 12/31/2004. Assets, $292,889 (M); Expenditures, $11,575; Total giving, $7,000.
Type of support: Undergraduate support.
Application information: Contact trust for current application deadline/guidelines.
EIN: 756533776

1226
Educare Scholarship Fund
P.O. Box 8393
Scottsdale, AZ   85252-8393   (602) 980-2680
Contact: Hon. Carl J. Kunasek, Pres.
E-mail: educaresecretary@yahoo.com; URL: http://www.educarescholarshipfund.com

Foundation type: Public charity
Limitations: Scholarships to attend school in AZ.
Financial data: Year ended 12/31/2003. Assets, $158,797 (M); Expenditures, $70,525; Total giving, $66,094; Grants to individuals, 66 grants totaling $66,094.
Type of support: Undergraduate support.
Application information: Applications accepted. Application form required.
  Initial approach: E-mail or letter.

Additional information: Application should include transcripts; Contact foundation for further program information.
EIN: 860967764

1227
Educational Advancement Foundation

c/o Grant Committee
2303 Rio Grande St.
Austin, TX 78705
E-mail: info@educationaladvancementfoundation.org; *URL:* http://www.educationaladvancementfoundation.org

Foundation type: Independent foundation
Limitations: Scholarships primarily to individuals residing in the Austin, TX, area for undergraduate education. Scholarships are generally by nomination only.
Publications: Application guidelines; Informational brochure.
Financial data: Year ended 12/31/2004. Assets, $897,924 (M); Expenditures, $1,353,592; Total giving, $977,693; Grants to individuals, 2 grants totaling $76,000 (high: $40,000, low: $36,000).
Type of support: Awards/grants by nomination only; Undergraduate support.
Application information: Applications not accepted.
Additional information: Unsolicited requests for funds not considered or acknowledged.
EIN: 237001761

1228
Educational Communications Scholarship Foundation

(also known as ECI Scholarship Foundation)
7211 Circle S Rd.
Austin, TX 78745
Contact: Jeffrey J. Fix, Genl. Mgr.
Application address: c/o Scholarship Coord., 7211 Circle S Rd., P.O. Box 149319, Austin, TX 78714-9319
URL: http://www.ecisf.org

Foundation type: Company-sponsored foundation
Limitations: Scholarships to high school students who have demonstrated ability and effort.
Publications: Application guidelines.
Financial data: Year ended 06/11/2003. Assets, $262,489 (M); Expenditures, $16,600; Total giving, $11,450; Grants to individuals, 6 grants totaling $5,250.
Type of support: Graduate support; Undergraduate support.
Application information: Application form required.
Deadline(s): May 15
Additional information: Applications available from high school guidance offices; Finalists must provide financial information and respond to essay questions; Winners notified by Aug. 5.
Program description:
Scholarship Program: High school students with a GPA of "B" or better who are legal residents of the U.S. may apply. The foundation awards 200 scholarships annually of $1,000 each. Ability and performance are the major criteria for selection, with some consideration given to financial need. Semi-finalists are selected on the basis of aptitude test scores, GPA, leadership qualifications, student interests, and work experience.
EIN: 237032032

1229
Educational Foundation of Alpha Gamma Rho

10101 N. Ambassador Dr.
Kansas City, MO 64153-1395   (816) 891-9200
Contact: Philip Josephson, Secy. and Exec. Dir.
FAX: (816) 891-9401; *URL:* http://www.agrs.org

Foundation type: Public charity
Limitations: Scholarships to undergraduate members of Alpha Gamma Rho.
Financial data: Year ended 06/30/2004. Assets, $1,990,473 (M); Expenditures, $1,189,862; Total giving, $826,030.
Fields of interest: Students, sororities/fraternities.
Type of support: Undergraduate support.
Application information: Applications accepted. Application form required.
Initial approach: Letter or telephone.
Deadline(s): Apr. 30
Applicants should submit the following:
1) GPA
2) Essay
3) Transcripts
Additional information: Contact foundation for a complete program listing.
EIN: 366158409

1230
Educational Foundation of the Missouri Society of Certified Public Accountants, Inc.

275 N. Lindbergh Blvd., Ste. 10
St. Louis, MO 63141   (314) 997-7966
Contact: Stephen C. Smith C.P.A., Secy.
Additional Web site for scholarship application: www.mocpa.org/leap/application.html; e-mail address: scholarships@mocpa.org
FAX: (314) 997-2592;
E-mail: member@mocpa.org; Additional tel.: (800) 264-7966; *URL:* http://www.mocpa.org/cpe.html

Foundation type: Public charity
Limitations: Scholarships of $1,000 to residents of MO, or children of MSCPA members, who are enrolled in a MO college studying accounting.
Financial data: Year ended 06/30/2004. Assets, $392,483 (M); Expenditures, $1,714,732; Total giving, $76,500; Grants to individuals, 57 grants totaling $76,500 (high: $3,000, low: $500).
Fields of interest: Business school/education.
Type of support: Undergraduate support.
Application information: Applications accepted. Application form required. Application form available on the grantmaker's Web site.
Initial approach: E-mail.
Deadline(s): Jan. 15
Applicants should submit the following:
1) ACT
2) SAT
3) Transcripts
4) Essay
Additional information: Applicants must provide proof of enrollment.
EIN: 237028488

1231
The Educational Foundation, Inc. at Ozaukee Bank

(formerly Ozaukee Bank Educational Foundation, Inc.)
P.O. Box 3
Cedarburg, WI 53012   (262) 377-9000
Contact: Terri A. Haas, Mgr.
E-mail: haas@ozaukeebank.com

Foundation type: Company-sponsored foundation
Limitations: Scholarships to graduating high school seniors who live in or attend high school in Ozaukee County, WI.
Financial data: Year ended 12/31/2004. Assets, $1,532,597 (M); Expenditures, $144,186; Total giving, $142,562; Grants to individuals, totaling $20,500.
Type of support: Scholarships—to individuals.
Application information: Application form required.
Initial approach: Letter or telephone.
Deadline(s): None
Additional information: Ineligible applications will not be considered or acknowledged.
EIN: 391745307

1232
Educational Fund of the Rochester New York Branch of the American Association of University Women

494 East Ave.
Rochester, NY 14607-1911   (716) 244-8890
Contact: Louise Spivack, Treas.

Foundation type: Independent foundation
Limitations: Student loans only for undergraduate or graduate study to women who reside in Monroe County, NY, or who attend an accredited college or university in Monroe County, and who have completed two years of college study.
Financial data: Year ended 06/30/2004. Assets, $147,057 (M); Expenditures, $4,545; Total giving, $4,136; Loans to individuals, totaling $4,136.
Fields of interest: Women.
Type of support: Support to graduates or students of specific schools; Graduate support; Undergraduate support.
Application information: Applications accepted. Application form required.
Deadline(s): None
Additional information: Application must include three letters of reference, two professional and one character; Interviews required; Applications from individuals outside of the specified geographic area not considered or acknowledged.
Program description:
Student Loan Program: Loans are usually given in amounts of $1,000 to $1,500. Repayment must begin within six months after graduation or termination of the course of study for which the loan was made. No interest will be charged for one-and-one-half calendar years after graduation or termination of the course of study. In any event, the entire loan repayment is expected two years after graduation or termination of the course of study for which the loan was made. A guarantor for the loan is required.
EIN: 510204285

1233
Educational Loan Foundation of Spokane, Inc.
1420 U.S. Bank Bldg.
Spokane, WA   99201   (509) 747-2158
Contact: Joan Bergdorf

Foundation type: Independent foundation
Limitations: Student loans to residents of Spokane, WA.
Financial data: Year ended 05/31/2005.
Assets, $78,902 (M); Expenditures, $9,219; Total giving, $8,100; Loans to individuals, totaling $8,100.
Type of support: Student loans—to individuals.
Application information: Applications accepted. Application form required.
   Deadline(s): None
EIN: 916031887

1234
Educational Theatre Association
2343 Auburn Ave.
Cincinnati, OH   45219-2815   (513) 421-3900
Contact: Michael J. Peitz, Exec. Dir.
FAX: (513) 421-7077; URL: http://www.edta.org

Foundation type: Public charity
Limitations: Scholarships to high school theatre students to attend the International Thespian Festival.
Publications: Annual report; Informational brochure.
Financial data: Year ended 07/31/2004.
Assets, $4,774,193 (M); Expenditures, $2,877,043; Total giving, $24,250; Grants to individuals, 69 grants totaling $24,250 (high: $2,500; low: $100).
Fields of interest: Theater.
Type of support: Scholarships—to individuals; Travel grants.
Application information: Applications accepted. Application form required. Application form available on the grantmaker's Web site.
   Applicants should submit the following:
   1) Letter(s) of recommendation
   2) Essay
   3) Resume
   Additional information: See Web site for current application guidelines.
Program description:
   Doug Finney Festival Grant: Each student will receive round-trip airfare. Festival registration fees will be waived. Recipients are chosen based on theatre contributions to school, to the community, and on financial need.
EIN: 310743605

1235
EducationQuest Foundation
(formerly Foundation for Educational Funding, Inc.)
P.O. Box 82552
Lincoln, NE   68501-2552   (402) 479-6735
Contact: Liz Fieselman, Pres. and C.E.O.
FAX: (402) 479-6658;
E-mail: info@educationquest.org; Additional address: 1300 O St., Lincoln, NE 68508, tel.: (800) 303-3745; URL: http://www.educationquest.org/about.asp

Foundation type: Public charity
Limitations: Scholarships by nomination only to low-income NE residents for undergraduate education. Some scholarships also to high school guidance counselors.

Financial data: Year ended 09/30/2004.
Assets, $20,326,467 (M); Expenditures, $1,077,919; Total giving, $851,000; Grants to individuals, 771 grants totaling $851,000.
Fields of interest: Economically disadvantaged.
Type of support: Awards/grants by nomination only; Undergraduate support.
Application information: Application form required.
   Additional information: Contact foundation for current application deadline/guidelines; See Web site for further program and application information.
Program description:
   Scholarship Program: The foundation administers the following programs:
   · Guidance Counselor Enrichment Scholarship
   · Reaching Your Potential: Applicants are referred by community agencies.
EIN: 470606382

1236
Glade M. Edwards Foundation, Inc.
c/o Karen Sinclair
636 W. Sunnyside Ln.
Thermopolis, WY   82443
Application address: c/o R.C. Johnson, 1001 Araphoe, Thermopolis, WY 82443, tel.: (307) 864-5164

Foundation type: Independent foundation
Limitations: Scholarships to graduating high school seniors of Hot Springs, WY, for tuition and books for higher education.
Financial data: Year ended 06/30/2005.
Assets, $604,693 (M); Expenditures, $19,192; Total giving, $17,750.
Type of support: Scholarships—to individuals.
Application information: Applications by letter accepted throughout the year; Contact foundation for current application guidelines; Initial approach by letter or telephone.
EIN: 830271524

1237
The Winifred, Ruth, Frances & Dorothy Edwards Foundation, Inc.
6443 Glenwood Rd.
Omaha, NE   68132-1844   (402) 556-4769
Contact: Gerald L. Adcock, V.P.

Foundation type: Independent foundation
Limitations: Scholarships to individuals in IA and NE for higher education, with preference given to students of the behavioral sciences.
Financial data: Year ended 12/31/2004.
Assets, $947,425 (M); Expenditures, $52,427; Total giving, $40,800; Grants to individuals, 39 grants totaling $40,800 (high: $1,600; low: $800).
Fields of interest: Psychology/behavioral science.
Type of support: Scholarships—to individuals.
Application information: Deadlines Jan. 10 and June 10; Completion of formal application required, including transcript and references.
EIN: 470623166

1238
Edwards Scholarship Fund
200 Clarendon St., 27th Fl.
Boston, MA   02116   (617) 654-8628
Contact: Brenda McCarthy, Exec. Secy.

Foundation type: Independent foundation

Limitations: Educational loans to financially needy students under the age of 25 whose families have resided in Boston, MA, since the start of the student's junior year in high school.
Publications: Application guidelines.
Financial data: Year ended 07/31/2004.
Assets, $8,383,654 (M); Expenditures, $387,168; Total giving, $284,750; Grants to individuals, 133 grants totaling $284,750.
Type of support: Graduate support; Undergraduate support.
Application information: Application form required. Application form available on the grantmaker's Web site.
   Initial approach: Letter, telephone or e-mail.
   Deadline(s): Mar. 1
   Applicants should submit the following:
   1) Transcripts
   2) SAT
   3) SAR
   4) Financial information
   Additional information: Application should also include two letters of recommendation and copies of parents' W-2 forms; Interviews required.
Program description:
   Scholarship Program: The purpose of the fund is to further the development of good citizenship through education. The fund offers scholarships to men and women of good character and ability who are in need of financial aid for higher education. Students must have their family home in Boston and be enrolled in a program that leads to an associate's, bachelor's, or higher degree. Undergraduates receive preference. Applicants must be under 25 years of age, and may receive scholarship aid for six years. Recipients have a moral obligation to repay any amount granted when they are able to do so.
EIN: 046002496

1239
Marguerite R. Edwards Scholarship Trust
c/o Union Planters Bank
P.O. Box 232
Alvin, TX   77512-0232
Application address: c/o Principal, Alvin High School, 802 S. Johnson, Alvin, TX 77511, tel.: (281) 585-6224

Foundation type: Independent foundation
Limitations: Scholarships to graduating seniors of Alvin High School, TX, who are in the top 15 percent of their class.
Financial data: Year ended 07/31/2004.
Assets, $566,935 (M); Expenditures, $37,034; Total giving, $26,100; Grants to individuals, 27 grants totaling $26,100 (high: $3,000, low: $400).
Type of support: Support to graduates or students of specific schools; Undergraduate support.
Application information: Application form required.
   Deadline(s): Apr. 15
   Applicants should submit the following:
   1) Transcripts
   2) Class rank
   Additional information: Application should also include personal statement and standardized test scores.
Program description:
   Scholarship Program: Recipients are selected on the basis of academic standing; standardized test scores; leadership, recognition, honors, and activities; and goals and plans. Scholarships are not renewable.
EIN: 746216234

1240
Eggleston Educational Trust
P.O. Box 188
Medicine Lodge, KS   67104
Contact: Nola Fowler, Tr.

Foundation type: Independent foundation
Limitations: Scholarships to financially needy graduates of high schools in Barber County, KS.
Financial data: Year ended 08/31/2004. Assets, $309,065 (M); Expenditures, $14,573; Total giving, $12,000; Grants to individuals, totaling $12,000.
Type of support: Support to graduates or students of specific schools; Undergraduate support.
Application information: Deadline Apr.1; Completion of formal application required.
EIN: 486320356

1241
V. M. Ehlers Foundation
(formerly V. M. Ehlers Memorial Fund, Inc.)
1106 Clayton Ln., Ste. 101 E.
Austin, TX   78723-1093
Contact: Ronald H. Bearden, Tr.
Application address: 1504 Lime Rock Dr., Round Rock, TX 78681-6303, tel.: (512) 255-3846
E-mail: twua@twua.org; URL: http://www.twua.org/vmehlers.htm

Foundation type: Independent foundation
Limitations: Scholarships to TX residents studying in environmental health fields.
Financial data: Year ended 06/30/2004. Assets, $440,040 (M); Expenditures, $53,310; Total giving, $52,655; Grants to individuals, totaling $52,655.
Fields of interest: Health sciences school/education; Environmental education.
Type of support: Scholarships—to individuals.
Application information: Deadline July 1; Completion of formal application required, including transcripts.
Program description:
  Scholarship Program: The fund was established to further the water utility-related educations of members and the children of members of the Texas Water Utilities Association, the Texas Water Pollution Control Association, and the Texas Section of the American Water Works Association. Presently, the fund awards scholarships to members and non-members alike.
EIN: 746062790

1242
Eisenhauer Scholarship Fund
(formerly John Henry & Clarissa A. Eisenhauer, et al. Scholarship Fund)
403 E. Maple St.
Annville, PA   17003-1519
Contact: Jane L. Kaylor, Tr.
Application address: 225 Bainbridge, Elizabethtown, PA 17022

Foundation type: Operating foundation
Limitations: Scholarships to financially needy high school seniors of Lebanon County, PA, to attend college.
Financial data: Year ended 06/30/2004. Assets, $196,266 (M); Expenditures, $14,986; Total giving, $14,470; Grants to individuals, 23 grants totaling $14,470 (high: $925, low: $350).
Type of support: Support to graduates or students of specific schools; Undergraduate support.
Application information: Applications accepted.
  Deadline(s): None

Additional information: Initial approach by letter, including recommendations from high school principal.
EIN: 232020120

1243
Marie and Margaret Ekstrand Educational Trust
c/o Sherry C. Powers
P.O. Box 153
Elmwood, IL   61529
Application address: c/o Thomas Kahn, Superintendent, Elmwood Community High School, 301 W. Butternut, Elmwood, IL 61529, tel.: (309) 742-8464

Foundation type: Independent foundation
Limitations: Scholarships to individuals who graduated from Elmwood Junior Senior High School, IL, in School District No. 322, after 1982.
Financial data: Year ended 12/31/2004. Assets, $827,262 (M); Expenditures, $39,901; Total giving, $33,656; Grants to individuals, totaling $33,656.
Type of support: Scholarships—to individuals; Support to graduates or students of specific schools.
Application information: Deadline May; Contact trust for current application guidelines; Initial approach by letter or telephone; Completion of formal application required.
EIN: 366773809

1244
El Paso Community Foundation
310 N. Mesa, 10th Fl.
P.O. Box 272
El Paso, TX   79943   (915) 533-4020
Contact: Janice W. Windle, Pres.
FAX: (915) 532-0716; E-mail: info@epcf.org; URL: http://www.epcf.org

Foundation type: Community foundation
Limitations: Scholarships to individuals residing in the El Paso, TX, area for undergraduate education.
Publications: Application guidelines; Annual report; Informational brochure; Newsletter.
Financial data: Year ended 12/31/2004. Assets, $93,108,757 (M); Expenditures, $17,282,353; Total giving, $13,005,101.
Fields of interest: Disabilities, people with.
Type of support: Scholarships—to individuals; Undergraduate support.
Application information: Application form required.
  Initial approach: Letter or telephone.
  Copies of proposal: 1
  Deadline(s): Jan. 31
  Applicants should submit the following:
    1) Transcripts
    2) Letter(s) of recommendation
    3) Financial information
    4) Essay
  Additional information: See Web site for complete listing of programs.
EIN: 741839536

1245
El Paso County Salute to Education
4445 N. Mesa St., Ste. 121
El Paso, TX   79902-1107   (915) 532-1930
Scholarship application address: Ford Salute to Education, Attn: Public Relations Mgr., P.O. Box 961178, El Paso, TX 79996, tel.: (915) 532-1930

Foundation type: Company-sponsored foundation
Limitations: Scholarships to graduating seniors of Hudspeth and El Paso counties, TX, for higher education.
Financial data: Year ended 12/31/2004. Assets, $168,517 (M); Expenditures, $162,030; Total giving, $120,106; Grants to individuals, 107 grants totaling $120,106 (high: $14,606, low: $500).
Type of support: Undergraduate support.
Application information: Application form required.
  Initial approach: Letter requesting application.
  Deadline(s): First quarter of the calendar year
EIN: 742871171

1246
E. O. Elam Scholarship Trust Fund
P.O. Box 111
Hamilton, TX   76531
Contact: Robert W. Witzsche, Tr.
Application address: P.O. Box 311, Hamilton, TX 76531, tel.: (254) 386-8937

Foundation type: Independent foundation
Limitations: Scholarships to students residing in and attending public school in Hamilton County, TX.
Financial data: Year ended 12/31/2004. Assets, $57,973 (M); Expenditures, $16,348; Total giving, $16,000; Grants to individuals, totaling $16,000.
Type of support: Support to graduates or students of specific schools; Undergraduate support.
Application information: Deadline May 1; Initial approach by letter, including address, parent's name and income range, school activities, awards, references, and a statement explaining goals.
EIN: 746306225

1247
Louis J. Elbert Trust
c/o The Citizens State Bank
200 N. Main St.
Pocahontas, IA   50574
Application address: c/o Kate Schiek, Guidance Counselor, Pocahontas Area Community School, Pocahontas, IA 50574, tel.: (712) 335-4848

Foundation type: Independent foundation
Limitations: Scholarships to graduates of Pocahontas Area Community School, IA, with a minimum 2.0 GPA.
Financial data: Year ended 12/31/2004. Assets, $360,199 (M); Expenditures, $16,076; Total giving, $12,875; Grants to individuals, totaling $12,875.
Type of support: Support to graduates or students of specific schools; Undergraduate support.
Application information: Deadline Feb. 15; Completion of formal application required, including three references and transcripts.
EIN: 421301198

1248
Elburn Scholarship Fund
611 Plamondon Ct.
Wheaton, IL   60187-6305   (630) 665-2776
Contact: Donald G. Westlake, Pres.

Foundation type: Independent foundation
Limitations: Scholarships to graduating seniors of Kaneland High School, Maple Park, IL, for attendance at community colleges or universities in IL.

Financial data: Year ended 12/31/2004. Assets, $1,144,148 (M); Expenditures, $33,698; Total giving, $33,000; Grants to individuals, totaling $33,000.
Type of support: Support to graduates or students of specific schools; Undergraduate support.
Application information: Deadline Mar. 1; Completion of formal application required; Application forms are available at Kaneland High School, Maple Park, IL.
EIN: 363366640

1249
Charles and Anna Elenberg Foundation, Inc.
c/o Jack Scharf
630 3rd Ave., 18th Fl.
New York, NY 10017

Foundation type: Independent foundation
Limitations: Scholarships to financially needy students of Hebrew faith, who are attending high school or college, with preference given to orphans. No grants to married students.
Financial data: Year ended 06/30/2004. Assets, $776,748 (M); Expenditures, $38,518; Total giving, $22,500; Grants to individuals, 50 grants totaling $22,500 (high: $500; low: $300).
Fields of interest: Residential/custodial care; Jewish agencies & temples.
Type of support: Precollege support; Undergraduate support.
Application information: Individual applications no longer accepted; Application forms are distributed to preselected educational institutions on a rotating basis.
EIN: 116042334

1250
Jessie Elfers Scholarship Trust No. 2
c/o U.S. Bank, N.A.
P.O. Box 2043, LC4NE
Milwaukee, WI 53201-9116

Foundation type: Independent foundation
Limitations: Scholarships to graduating seniors of Marshalltown High School, Marshalltown, IA.
Financial data: Year ended 01/31/2005. Assets, $237,458 (M); Expenditures, $13,623; Total giving, $10,956; Grants to individuals, totaling $10,956.
Type of support: Support to graduates or students of specific schools; Undergraduate support.
Application information: Unsolicited requests for funds not accepted.
EIN: 426546523

1251
Elizabeth City Foundation
P.O. Box 574
Elizabeth City, NC 27907-0574
Contact: Ray S. Jones, Jr., Exec. Dir.

Foundation type: Independent foundation
Limitations: Scholarships only to residents of Camden County, NC.
Publications: Application guidelines; Financial statement; Informational brochure.
Financial data: Year ended 07/31/2005. Assets, $3,179,868 (M); Expenditures, $144,945; Total giving, $113,250; Grants to individuals, totaling $35,450.

Type of support: Scholarships—to individuals; Support to graduates or students of specific schools.
Application information: Application form required.
Initial approach: Letter.
Deadline(s): Mar. 5
Additional information: Application forms available at Wachovia Bank and Trust Company and Camden High School.
EIN: 237076018

1252
Maria Elizondo Scholarship Trust
c/o Board of Trustees
P.O. Box 327
Montrose, CO 81402-0327

Foundation type: Independent foundation
Limitations: Scholarships to individuals in the top 10 percent of the graduating classes of Mesa and Montrose County high schools, CO.
Financial data: Year ended 06/30/2005. Assets, $1,346,853 (M); Expenditures, $82,913; Total giving, $69,233; Grants to individuals, totaling $69,233.
Type of support: Support to graduates or students of specific schools; Undergraduate support.
Application information: Deadline Mar. 21; Completion of formal application required, including copy of transcript and SAT or ACT scores.
EIN: 846328479

1253
Elk County Community Foundation
111 Erie Ave.
St. Marys, PA 15857 (814) 834-2125
Contact: Martha A. Engel, Secy.
FAX: (814) 834-2126;
E-mail: info@elkcountyfoundation.com; Additional E-mail: eccf@penn.com; URL: http://www.elkcountyfoundation.com

Foundation type: Community foundation
Limitations: Scholarships to individuals residing in Elk County, PA.
Publications: Application guidelines; Annual report; Informational brochure; Informational brochure (including application guidelines); Newsletter.
Financial data: Year ended 12/31/2004. Assets, $2,461,304 (M); Expenditures, $149,628; Total giving, $64,451; Grants to individuals, 43 grants totaling $47,291 (high: $4,236, low: $350).
Fields of interest: Nursing school/education.
Type of support: Undergraduate support.
Application information: Application form required.
Deadline(s): Vary
Additional information: See Web site for further application and program information.
EIN: 251859637

1254
Elk Grove Community Foundation
P.O. Box 2021
Elk Grove, CA 95759 (916) 685-7118
FAX: (916) 689-7875; E-mail: egcf@pjcpa.org

Foundation type: Community foundation
Limitations: Scholarships to individuals in the Elk Grove, CA, area.
Publications: Application guidelines; Financial statement; Informational brochure; Program policy statement.

Financial data: Year ended 12/31/2004. Assets, $1,172,740 (M); Expenditures, $96,465; Total giving, $81,935; Grants to individuals, 40 grants totaling $81,935 (high: $24,000, low: $500).
Type of support: Scholarships—to individuals.
Application information: Contact foundation for current application deadline/guidelines.
EIN: 946097642

1255
Elkhart County Community Foundation, Inc.
KeyBank Bldg.
101 S. Main St., P.O. Box 2932
Elkhart, IN 46515-2932 (574) 295-8761
Contact: W. Earl Taylor, Pres.
FAX: (574) 389-7497; E-mail: elk.ccf@verizon.net; Additional E-mail: weteccf@aol.com; URL: http://www.elkhartccf.org

Foundation type: Community foundation
Limitations: Scholarships to residents of Elkhart County for higher education.
Publications: Application guidelines; Annual report (including application guidelines); Grants list; Informational brochure; Newsletter; Occasional report.
Financial data: Year ended 06/30/2004. Assets, $34,205,947 (M); Expenditures, $2,007,517; Total giving, $1,526,227; Grants to individuals, 75 grants totaling $300,320.
Fields of interest: Higher education; College.
Type of support: Scholarships—to individuals.
Application information: Application form available on the grantmaker's Web site.
Initial approach: Contact Elkhart County area high schools.
Deadline(s): Feb. 1 for Lilly Endowment Community Scholarship; June 1 for all other scholarships
Applicants should submit the following:
1) Transcripts
2) SAT
3) Letter(s) of recommendation
4) Essay
5) Curriculum vitae
6) ACT
Additional information: See Web site for additional program listings.
Program descriptions:
IUSB Elkhart County Scholarship: Scholarships to residents of Elkhart County of at leats one year and who are enrolled as a student at IUSB in good standing pursuing a degree. Students can be traditional or non-traditional.
Claude S. and Hanna M. Kegerreis Scholarship: Annual scholarships to worthy and needy students of an Elkhart County high school who plan to attend an accredited college or university.
Henry and Alice Pederson Education Scholarship: Scholarships to young residents of Elkhart County for higher education.
Walter O. Wells Scholarship: Provides scholarships for post-secondary education for students residing in Elkhart County.
Lilly Endowment Community Scholarship: Awards four year, full tuition scholarships to four Elkhart County seniors. Students may attend any accredited Indiana college.
EIN: 311255886

1256
Elks National Foundation
2750 N. Lakeview Ave.
Chicago, IL 60614-1889 (773) 755-4728
FAX: (773) 755-4729; E-mail: enf@elks.org;
URL: http://www.elks.org/enf/

Foundation type: Public charity
Limitations: Scholarships and awards to
individuals for higher education and for specific
achievements.
Publications: Annual report; Financial statement;
Informational brochure; Newsletter.
Financial data: Year ended 03/31/2004.
Assets, $402,725,075 (M); Expenditures,
$15,221,347; Total giving, $12,840,623; Grants
to individuals, totaling $30,000.
Fields of interest: Girls clubs; Mutual aid societies.
Type of support: Scholarships—to individuals;
Precollege support; Undergraduate support.
Application information: Deadlines vary; See Web
site for guidelines for each program.
Program descriptions:

Most Valuable Student Scholarships: Provides
awards of $1,000 to $15,000 per year to students
pursuing a four-year degree, on a full-time basis, at
a U.S. college or university. Male and female
students compete separately. Awards go to 500 of
the highest-rated boys and girls, who are high
school seniors and citizens of the U.S. Recipients
need not be related to a member of the Elks.
Applicants are judged based on financial need,
leadership and scholarship. Deadline mid-Jan.

Eagle Scout Awards: Awards four $8,000
scholarships ($2,000 per year for four years) and
four $4,000 scholarships ($1,000 per year for four
years) to registered Scouts who have achieved the
rank of Eagle, have an SAT score of at least 1090
and/or equivalent ACT score of 26, and will
graduate from high school during the year they are
applying. Applicant must demonstrate financial
need. Application forms are available at the Scout
Council Service Center or online at http://
www.scouting.org/nesa/scholar. For additional
information, contact: National Office, Boy Scouts of
America, P.O. Box 152079, Irving, TX 75015-2079,
tel.: (972) 580-2000.

Gold Awards Scholarships: Scholarships of
$6,000 ($1,500 per year for four years) awarded to
one girl from each Girl Scout Service area.
Recipients are selected based on academics,
activities, community involvement, leadership and
pursuit of individual interests. Applicants must be
Gold Award winners and graduating high school
seniors. Recipients should contact their Girl Scout
Council, or see the Web site http://
jfg.girlscouts.org/whatsup/whatsup.htm
poundsign ContestsandOpportunities for further
information.

Legacy Awards: Awards up to 500 scholarships
of $1,000 for one year to children or grandchildren,
step-children or step-grandchildren or legal wards of
an Elk who has been a member in good standing for
at least two years. Elks must be active members or
a charter member of a Lodge that was instituted
since same date in order for individuals to be
eligible. Elks must have paid up membership dues
through Mar. 31. Great-grandchildren are ineligible.
Recipients must be high school seniors and take
the SAT or ACT. See Web site for additional
information. Deadline mid-Jan.

Emergency Educational Fund Grants: Grants to
children or step-children of deceased or completely
disabled Elks members. Deceased members must
have been in good standing at the time of his/her
death. Disabled members also must have been in
good standing before he/she became so and must
continue to be an Elk in good standing at time of

application. Recipients must be unmarried, under
the age of 23 on the date application is signed and
attend a U.S. college or university. They must be
enrolled full-time (12 hours minimum per semester)
and be undergraduate students. Assistance will not
extend beyond four years. Deadline for new
applicants between July 1 and Dec. 31. Deadline
for renewing applicants between July 1 and Oct. 31.
EIN: 046038176

1257
Ella Mount Burr Trust
c/o Wachovia Bank, N.A.
1525 W. WT Harris Blvd.
Charlotte, NC 28262-8522

Foundation type: Independent foundation
Limitations: Scholarships to individuals for higher
education.
Financial data: Year ended 07/31/2005.
Assets, $578,641 (M); Expenditures, $27,448;
Total giving, $19,000.
Type of support: Undergraduate support.
Application information: Unsolicited requests for
funds not accepted.
EIN: 223527315

1258
Mabel M. Elliott Educational Foundation
P.O. Box 1930
San Marcos, CA 92079-1930 (760) 744-9101
Contact: James L. Richmond, Pres.
Application address: 427 Washington Dr., San
Marcos, CA 92078-5033

Foundation type: Operating foundation
Limitations: Scholarships to financially needy
individuals residing in CA who attend college prep
programs in high school, and are willing to work
part-time while attending postsecondary school.
Financial data: Year ended 12/31/2003.
Assets, $246,916 (M); Expenditures, $23,188;
Total giving, $12,250; Grants to individuals, 12
grants totaling $12,250 (high: $2,000, low: $500).
Type of support: Graduate support; Undergraduate
support.
Application information: Applications accepted.
Application form required.
Deadline(s): Apr. 15.
Applicants should submit the following:
1) Letter(s) of recommendation
2) Transcripts
EIN: 330617739

1259
Elliott-Hemingford Scholarship Foundation
(formerly Hemingford Scholarship Foundation)
324 Hillcrest Dr.
Alliance, NE 69301
Application address: c/o Ramona Hocke or Lannie
Shelmadine, P.O. Box 217, Hemingford, NE 69348,
tel.: (308) 487-3327

Foundation type: Independent foundation
Limitations: Scholarships to graduates of
Hemingford High School, NE, in their second, third,
or fourth year of college.
Financial data: Year ended 07/31/2004.
Assets, $695,418 (M); Expenditures, $43,527;
Total giving, $42,428; Grants to individuals, 44
grants totaling $42,428 (high: $1,482, low: $390).
Type of support: Support to graduates or students
of specific schools; Undergraduate support.

Application information: Deadline June 15; Initial
approach by letter; Completion of formal application
required, including recommendations, scholastic
standing, and financial need.
EIN: 363504495

1260
Danny and Willa Ellis Foundation
P.O. Box 54
Fort Scott, KS 66701 (620) 223-2232
Contact: Danny Ellis, Pres.; Willa Ellis, Secy.-Treas.
FAX: (620) 223-2236;
E-mail: dan@theellisfoundation.org; Additional
E-mail:chris@theellisfoundation.org;
julie@theellisfoundation.org; URL: http://
www.theellisfoundation.org

Foundation type: Independent foundation
Limitations: Scholarships to residents of KS for
higher education.
Financial data: Year ended 12/31/2004.
Assets, $3,996,771 (M); Expenditures,
$300,080; Total giving, $231,213; Grants to
individuals, 303 grants totaling $215,213 (high:
$1,000, low: $223).
Type of support: Undergraduate support.
Application information: Applications by letter
accepted throughout the year.
EIN: 481093604

1261
Charles E. Ellis Grant and Scholarship Fund
c/o PNC Advisors
1600 Market St., Tax Dept., 4th Fl.
Philadelphia, PA 19103-7240
Application address: c/o White-Williams Scholars,
215 S. Broad St., 5th Fl., Philadelphia, PA 19102

Foundation type: Independent foundation
Limitations: Scholarships to functionally orphaned
female students who reside in Philadelphia County,
PA, for high school-level education. Scholarships
not available for college-level education.
Publications: Application guidelines; Informational
brochure; Program policy statement.
Financial data: Year ended 06/30/2004.
Assets, $34,412,495 (M); Expenditures,
$1,592,739; Total giving, $1,383,746.
Fields of interest: Secondary school/education;
Women.
Type of support: Precollege support.
Application information: Applications accepted.
Additional information: Applications by letter
accepted throughout the year.
Program description:
Scholarship Program: The scholarship grants are
awarded to individually named recipients. However,
all funds are paid directly to the educational
institution the individual attends. The fund's use of
the term "functionally orphaned" includes girls from
single-parent families.
EIN: 236725618

1262
John G. Ellis Scholarship Fund
c/o Commerce Bank
P.O. Box 637
Wichita, KS 67201 (316) 261-4891
Contact: Yvonne Lee, Trust Off., Commerce Bank

Foundation type: Independent foundation
Limitations: Scholarships to graduates of Butler
County, KS, high schools to attend Kansas State

University, California Maritime Academy, or the University of Southern California. First priority is given to engineering students, who are graduates of El Dorado, KS, high schools.
Financial data: Year ended 12/31/2004. Assets, $449,150 (M); Expenditures, $25,727; Total giving, $23,000; Grants to individuals, totaling $23,000.
Fields of interest: Engineering.
Type of support: Support to graduates or students of specific schools; Undergraduate support.
Application information: Applications accepted throughout the year; Contact fund for current application guidelines; Initial approach by letter.
EIN: 486250894

1263
Jeffrey Wallace Ellis Trust
c/o McDermott & Miller, PC
P.O. Box 1317
Hastings, NE 68902-1317
Contact: Lloyd H. Ellis, Jr., Pres.
Application address: c/o Lloyd H. Ellis, Jr., 32250 Woodsdale Ln., Solon, OH 44139, tel.: (216) 498-3914

Foundation type: Independent foundation
Limitations: Graduate and advanced study scholarships in professional arts, sciences, or equivalent fields to NE residents. Applicants must rank in the upper ten percent of their undergraduate classes to qualify.
Financial data: Year ended 12/31/2004. Assets, $1,637,187 (M); Expenditures, $90,669; Total giving, $70,000; Grant to an individual, 1 grant totaling $20,000.
Fields of interest: Arts; Science.
Type of support: Graduate support; Postgraduate support.
Application information: Applications accepted.
Initial approach: Letter or telephone.
Deadline(s): None
Additional information: Application by letter including undergraduate transcripts, GMAT or equivalent scores, recommendations from college professors, and description of extracurricular activities.
EIN: 363494704

1264
Harold Ellison Scholarship Fund
c/o Merchants Trust Co.
200 E. Jackson St.
Muncie, IN 47305 (317) 916-7444
Contact: Laura Moorman, Trust. Off.

Foundation type: Independent foundation
Limitations: Scholarships to graduates of Delaware County high schools, IN, attending Ball State University, IN, with special skills in fine and performing arts, writing, or athletics.
Financial data: Year ended 10/31/2005. Assets, $1,266,368 (M); Expenditures, $139,498; Total giving, $128,113; Grant to an individual, 1 grant totaling $128,113.
Fields of interest: Performing arts; Literature; Arts; Athletics/sports, training.
Type of support: Support to graduates or students of specific schools; Undergraduate support.
Application information: Applications accepted. Application form required.
Deadline(s): Nov. 2 through Feb. 28.
Additional information: A complete listing of school and community activities, awards or honors achieved, musical or theatrical

performances, items written for publication, athletic activities, and a self description.
EIN: 356375836

1265
Henry E. Ellsworth Scholarship Fund
c/o Bank of America, N.A.
P.O. Box 1802
Providence, RI 02901-1802
Application address: c/o Scholarship Comm., 34 Farms Village Rd., Simsbury High School, Simsbury, CT 06070

Foundation type: Independent foundation
Limitations: Scholarships to students in the senior class of Simsbury High School, CT.
Financial data: Year ended 12/31/2004. Assets, $98,975 (M); Expenditures, $6,830; Total giving, $5,000; Grants to individuals, totaling $5,000.
Type of support: Support to graduates or students of specific schools; Undergraduate support.
Application information: Contact guidance office for current application deadline; Completion of formal application required.
EIN: 066032904

1266
Henry Elm Trust
c/o Stockman Bank
101 S. Central Ave.
Sidney, MT 59270
Contact: Robert Goss, Tr.; Robert Williamson, Tr.

Foundation type: Independent foundation
Limitations: Scholarships to graduating seniors of Richland County, MT.
Financial data: Year ended 12/31/2004. Assets, $253,519 (M); Expenditures, $20,927; Total giving, $15,041; Grants to individuals, totaling $15,041.
Type of support: Support to graduates or students of specific schools; Undergraduate support.
Application information: Deadline Apr. 7; Completion of formal application required.
EIN: 237418092

1267
Catherine Marie Elvins and Naomi Libby Elvins Scholarship Trust
c/o Jill Richardson
16702 N.E. 103rd Pl.
Redmond, WA 98052
Application address: c/o Washington State Society Daughters of the American Rev., Attn.: Barbara Carlson, State Regent, 3406 Shyleen St., Gig Harbor, 98335-1246, tel.: (253) 851-2617

Foundation type: Independent foundation
Limitations: Scholarships to female medical students from WA who are attending or plan to attend the University of Washington Medical School.
Financial data: Year ended 12/31/2004. Assets, $3,334,886 (M); Expenditures, $119,767; Total giving, $100,000; Grants to individuals, 12 grants totaling $100,000 (high: $12,000, low: $2,000).
Fields of interest: Medical school/education; Women.
Type of support: Support to graduates or students of specific schools.
Application information: Deadline May 1; Completion of formal application required, including

letter stating importance of obtaining scholarship, future goals, biographical sketch and activities, two letters of recommendation, and transcripts.
EIN: 916470080

1268
Ely-Winton Hospital Association Scholarship Fund Trust
c/o U.S. Bank, N.A.
P.O. Box 64713
St. Paul, MN 55164-0713
Application address: c/o Terrence Merfeld, Superintendent of Schools, ISD No. 694, 601 Harvey St., Ely, MN 55731

Foundation type: Independent foundation
Limitations: Scholarships to graduates of Ely High School, MN, pursuing medical-related fields of study.
Financial data: Year ended 07/31/2005. Assets, $462,527 (M); Expenditures, $29,138; Total giving, $23,500; Grants to individuals, 7 grants totaling $23,500 (high: $4,500, low: $2,500).
Fields of interest: Medical school/education; Public health school/education; Health sciences school/education.
Type of support: Support to graduates or students of specific schools; Undergraduate support.
Application information: Deadline Oct. 31; Completion of formal application required.
EIN: 416045814

1269
The Emergency Aid of Pennsylvania Foundation, Inc.
221 Conestoga Rd., Ste. 300
Wayne, PA 19087 (610) 225-0944
Contact: Joanne Platt, Office Mgr.
FAX: (610) 225-0945; E-mail: eapa@erols.com;
URL: http://www.eafoundation.org/

Foundation type: Independent foundation
Limitations: Scholarships to young women who receive the foundation's Founders Award in their ninth grade of school, and who live in the five counties of the Philadelphia, PA, area.
Publications: Annual report; Informational brochure; Newsletter.
Financial data: Year ended 06/30/2004. Assets, $2,654,668 (M); Expenditures, $159,189; Total giving, $77,200; Grants to individuals, 35 grants totaling $23,950 (high: $1,000, low: $500).
Fields of interest: Women.
Type of support: Scholarships—to individuals; Precollege support.
Application information: Contact foundation for current application deadline; Application by letter.
EIN: 232321913

1270
Emerson Charitable Trust
8000 W. Florissant Ave.
P.O. Box 4100
St. Louis, MO 63136 (314) 553-2000
Contact: Robert M. Cox, Jr.
FAX: (314) 553-1605

Foundation type: Company-sponsored foundation
Limitations: Scholarships only to children of employees of Emerson Electric Company, St. Louis, MO.

Financial data: Year ended 09/30/2004. Assets, $18,543,347 (M); Expenditures, $16,424,684; Total giving, $15,907,672; Grants to individuals, 129 grants totaling $96,120 (high: $750, low: $30).
Type of support: Employee-related scholarships.
Application information: Employees are notified directly when and how to apply.
EIN: 526200123

1271
Harland and Genevieve Emerson Foundation
c/o Wells Fargo Bank Nevada, N.A.
1248 O St., 4th Fl., MAC N8032-042
Lincoln, NE   68508-0837
Application address: c/o James E. Van Werden, P.O. Box 99, 1009 Main St., Adel, IA 50003, tel.: (515) 993-4545

Foundation type: Independent foundation
Limitations: Scholarships to graduates of Adel-Minburn-Desoto High School, IA, to attend college, university, trade or business school.
Financial data: Year ended 09/30/2004. Assets, $827,324 (M); Expenditures, $78,632; Total giving, $66,375; Grants to individuals, 50 grants totaling $66,375 (high: $5,000, low: $250).
Fields of interest: Vocational education.
Type of support: Support to graduates or students of specific schools; Technical education support; Undergraduate support.
Application information: Deadlines July 1 and Dec. 1; Completion of formal application required, including an essay, high school and college transcripts, and tax returns of parent and student for 3 years.
EIN: 426543700

1272
Emmons County Sports Alumni, Inc.
c/o Terry Gimbel
420 N. Broadway
Linton, ND   58552

Foundation type: Independent foundation
Limitations: Scholarships to residents of Emmons County, ND.
Financial data: Year ended 12/31/2004. Assets, $11,082 (M); Expenditures, $8,277; Total giving, $2,500; Grants to individuals, totaling $2,500.
Type of support: Scholarships—to individuals.
Application information: Applications accepted. Application form required.
Deadline(s): Apr. 15
EIN: 363442049

1273
Endowment of the U.S. Institute of Peace
1200 17th St., N.W., Ste. 200
Washington, DC   20036-3011   (202) 457-1700
Contact: Richard H. Solomon, Pres.
FAX: (202) 429-6063;
E-mail: grant_program@usip.org; URL: http://www.usip.org

Foundation type: Public charity
Limitations: Fellowships for the research and writing of doctoral dissertations concerning international conflict and resolution. Scholarships are also awarded.
Publications: Application guidelines; Annual report; Newsletter; Occasional report.

Financial data: Year ended 09/30/2004. Assets, $6,034,134 (M); Expenditures, $9,415,453; Total giving, $6,576,209; Grants to individuals, totaling $6,576,209.
Fields of interest: International peace/security; International conflict resolution; International affairs.
Type of support: Fellowships; Doctoral support.
Application information: Application form required.
Initial approach: Letter or e-mail.
Deadline(s): Nov. 1
Program description:
Jennings Randolph Program - Peace Scholar Dissertation Fellowships: These fellowships support the research and writing of doctoral dissertations addressing the sources and nature of international conflict and strategies to prevent or end conflict and to sustain peace. Peace Scholars work at their universities or appropriate field research sites. Dissertation projects from a broad range of disciplines are welcome. Priority will be given to projects that contribute knowledge relevant to the formulation of policy on international peace and conflict issues. Doctoral students applying for support must be enrolled in universities in the U.S., but citizens of all countries are eligible. Awards support 12 months of dissertation research or writing, beginning in Sept. Stipends for Peace Scholars are currently set at $17,000 per year and are paid directly to the individual.
EIN: 521503251

1274
Mildred Engel Nurse Scholarship Fund
125 Churchill Hubbard Rd.
Youngstown, OH   44505
Contact: J. Newman Levy, Tr.
Application address: c/o Nurse Scholarship Comm., 517 Gypsy Ln., Youngstown, OH 44501, tel.: (330) 746-1076

Foundation type: Independent foundation
Limitations: Scholarships for nursing education.
Financial data: Year ended 12/31/2004. Assets, $500,235 (M); Expenditures, $33,990; Total giving, $28,419; Grants to individuals, totaling $5,419.
Fields of interest: Nursing school/education.
Type of support: Scholarships—to individuals.
Application information: Deadline June 1; Application by letter outlining financial need and personal goals.
EIN: 346987176

1275
The Engine Rebuilders Educational Foundation
330 Lexington Dr.
Buffalo Grove, IL   60089-6933   (847) 541-4555
Contact: Ellen Mechlin

Foundation type: Public charity
Limitations: Scholarships for higher education to individuals interested in a career in engine rebuilding.
Financial data: Year ended 06/30/2004. Assets, $184,209 (M); Expenditures, $30,343; Total giving, $21,000; Grants to individuals, 20 grants totaling $21,000 (high: $2,000, low: $1,000).
Fields of interest: Vocational education.
Type of support: Scholarships—to individuals.
Application information: Applications accepted.
Initial approach: Letter.

Additional information: Application should include letters of recommendation.
EIN: 364163715

1276
Frank F. England Scholarship Fund
c/o Community National Bank
P.O. Box 120
Newport, VT   05855-0120
Application addresses: c/o Guidance Off., Northfield High School, Northfield, VT 05663, tel.: (802) 485-8644, or c/o Lucinda Buck Conti, 5 Burnside Ave., Barre, VT 05641

Foundation type: Independent foundation
Limitations: Scholarships to graduates of Northfield Elementary and Middle-High School, VT. Recipients must be the first generation of college-bound individuals in their family.
Financial data: Year ended 12/31/2004. Assets, $103,288 (M); Expenditures, $10,637; Total giving, $3,750; Grants to individuals, totaling $3,750.
Type of support: Support to graduates or students of specific schools; Undergraduate support.
Application information:
Deadline(s): Deadline 1st Mon. in June.
Additional information: Application by letter, including two references pertaining to extracurricular and community service involvement and character, and essay.
EIN: 036054992

1277
Elizabeth R. England Trust
c/o Mellon Financial Corp.
P.O. Box 185
Pittsburgh, PA   15230-9897

Foundation type: Independent foundation
Limitations: Scholarships to female performing arts majors at Philadelphia, PA, high schools.
Financial data: Year ended 06/30/2004. Assets, $18,833,973 (M); Expenditures, $892,779; Total giving, $884,956; Grants to individuals, totaling $884,956.
Fields of interest: Performing arts, education; Women.
Type of support: Support to graduates or students of specific schools; Undergraduate support.
Application information:
Deadline(s): None.
Additional information: Contact trust for current application guidelines.
EIN: 236606334

1278
Englewood BPO Elks Scholarship Trust
c/o Englewood Elks Lodge No. 2378, Schol. Comm.
401 N. Indiana Ave.
Englewood, FL   34223

Foundation type: Independent foundation
Limitations: Scholarships to students of Lemon Bay High School, FL, or to members of the Englewood Elks Lodge, for higher education.
Financial data: Year ended 03/31/2005. Assets, $335,186 (M); Expenditures, $17,138; Total giving, $14,000; Grants to individuals, 8 grants totaling $14,000.
Type of support: Support to graduates or students of specific schools; Undergraduate support.
Application information: Contact foundation for current application deadline; Initial approach by

letter or telephone; Completion of formal application required.
EIN: 596687568

1279
Englewood Youth Foundation, Inc.
P.O. Box 176
Englewood, FL 34295-0176 (941) 473-1392
Contact: Leslie Gift, Pres.

Foundation type: Public charity
Limitations: Scholarships to individuals in Englewood, FL, for higher education.
Financial data: Year ended 06/30/2003.
Assets, $1,024,989 (M); Expenditures, $52,582; Total giving, $45,782; Grants to individuals, totaling $32,000.
Type of support: Scholarships—to individuals.
Application information: Contact foundation for current application deadline/guidelines; Initial approach by letter.
EIN: 596208459

1280
Fenton E. English Charitable Trust
c/o JPMorgan Chase Bank, N.A
P.O. Box 1308
Milwaukee, WI 53201

Foundation type: Independent foundation
Limitations: Scholarships to students at Paris High School, IL, and McLean County High School, Calhoun, KY.
Financial data: Year ended 12/31/2004.
Assets, $3,039,639 (M); Expenditures, $129,039; Total giving, $100,619; Grants to individuals, 87 grants totaling $81,169 (high: $2,500; low: $26).
Fields of interest: Education.
Type of support: Support to graduates or students of specific schools; Undergraduate support.
Application information: Applications not accepted.
EIN: 376121328

1281
The English Foundation
(formerly The English Foundation-Trust)
c/o English's Inc.
1522 Main St.
Altavista, VA 24517 (434) 369-4771
Contact: E.R. English, Jr., Tr.

Foundation type: Independent foundation
Limitations: Scholarships to students of Altavista High School, VA.
Publications: Annual report.
Financial data: Year ended 12/31/2004.
Assets, $3,113,244 (M); Expenditures, $221,995; Total giving, $163,600.
Type of support: Support to graduates or students of specific schools; Undergraduate support.
Application information: Application form required.
 Initial approach: letter requesting application form.
 Deadline(s): Contact foundation for current application deadline
EIN: 546036409

1282
The W. C. English Scholarship Foundation
P.O. Box P7000
Lynchburg, VA 24505-7000

Foundation type: Independent foundation
Limitations: Scholarships to students of Lynchburg, VA, attending four-year accredited institutions.
Financial data: Year ended 12/31/2004.
Assets, $419,775 (M); Expenditures, $32,184; Total giving, $31,950; Grants to individuals, totaling $31,950.
Type of support: Scholarships—to individuals.
Application information: Deadline Apr. 1; Initial approach by letter; Completion of formal application required.
EIN: 541658362

1283
ENMR Education Foundation
(formerly ENMR Telephone Education Foundation)
c/o ENMR-Plateau, Scholarship Comm.
P.O. Box 1947
Clovis, NM 88102-1947
Contact: Jay Gurley
Additional tel.: (800) 432-2389

Foundation type: Company-sponsored foundation
Limitations: Scholarships to active members receiving service from ENMR Telephone Cooperative and their immediate families and dependents, who wish to attend an institution of higher learning.
Publications: Application guidelines; Annual report; Grants list; Informational brochure (including application guidelines); Newsletter; Program policy statement.
Financial data: Year ended 12/31/2004.
Assets, $1,308,092 (M); Expenditures, $34,883; Total giving, $19,500; Grants to individuals, 42 grants totaling $19,500 (high: $1,600, low: $250).
Type of support: Employee-related scholarships; Technical education support.
Application information: Application form required.
 Deadline(s): Feb. 1
 Additional information: Application should include transcripts; scholarships are renewable.
Program description:
 Scholarship Program: Recipients must maintain a GPA of at least 2.5, must be of good character, and must demonstrate a coherent degree and willingness to pursue a course of higher learning and vocational training. Scholarships shall not exceed $300 per semester and may be made on a semester, term, or one-year basis.
EIN: 850385194

1284
Envirosafe Services of Idaho, Inc. Charitable Trust
(also known as Envirosafe Charitable Trust)
c/o Farmers & Merchants Bank & Trust
P.O. Box 328
Meridian, ID 83680
Contact: Rosalie J. Hadlow, Asst. V.P. and Sr. Trust Off., Farmers & Merchants Bank & Trust
FAX: (208) 383-3870

Foundation type: Company-sponsored foundation
Limitations: Scholarships to students residing in Mountain Home and Owyhee County, ID.
Publications: Application guidelines; Occasional report.
Financial data: Year ended 02/28/2005.
Assets, $13,923 (M); Expenditures, $21,832; Total giving, $20,332.
Type of support: Scholarships—to individuals.
Application information: Application form required.

Initial approach: Letter.
Deadline(s): None
Additional information: Request application from selection committee.
EIN: 826067761

1285
EOG Scholarship Fund
333 Clay St., Ste. 4200
Houston, TX 77002

Foundation type: Company-sponsored foundation
Limitations: Scholarships to the unmarried children, adopted children, stepchildren and foster children of employees or retirees of EOG Resources, Inc., or its subsidiary.
Financial data: Year ended 12/31/2004.
Assets, $865,561 (M); Expenditures, $52,882; Total giving, $51,250; Grants to individuals, 28 grants totaling $51,250 (high: $2,000, low: $1,500).
Type of support: Employee-related scholarships.
Application information: Application form required.
 Deadline(s): Feb. 1 through Mar. 31
 Additional information: Application should include transcripts.
Program description:
 Scholarship Program: Scholarships may be used for attending an accredited college or university, excluding military academies. Scholarships are based on financial need, scholastic achievement, writing skills, demonstrated leadership and community service.
EIN: 760479501

1286
Mabel S. Epler Scholarship Fund
c/o First Merchants Bank, N.A.
200 E. Jackson St.
Muncie, IN 47305
Application address: c/o Yorktown High School, 1100 S. Tiger Dr., Yorktown, IN 47396

Foundation type: Independent foundation
Limitations: Scholarships to graduates of Yorktown High School, IN.
Financial data: Year ended 12/31/2004.
Assets, $126,644 (M); Expenditures, $8,692; Total giving, $6,600.
Type of support: Support to graduates or students of specific schools; Undergraduate support.
Application information: Deadline Mar. 31; Completion of formal application required.
EIN: 356326717

1287
The Samuel Epstein Foundation Trust
c/o National City Bank
20 Stanwix St., Ste. 25 162
Pittsburgh, PA 15222-4801

Foundation type: Independent foundation
Limitations: Scholarships to residents of PA, primarily from the towns of Sheffield and Clarendon.
Financial data: Year ended 12/31/2004.
Assets, $5,503,765 (M); Expenditures, $370,622; Total giving, $332,566; Grants to individuals, 26 grants totaling $121,975 (high: $14,279, low: $750).
Type of support: Scholarships—to individuals.
Application information: Applications not accepted.
EIN: 256311365

1288
ERI Educational Foundation

c/o Equitable Resources, Inc.
225 North Shore Dr.
Pittsburgh, PA 15212   (412) 553-5700
Contact: Christine Bodzenski

Foundation type: Company-sponsored foundation
Limitations: Scholarships to children of full-time employees of Equitable Resources, Inc., and its affiliates for higher education.
Financial data: Year ended 12/31/2004.
Assets, $36 (M); Expenditures, $14,711; Total giving, $12,500; Grants to individuals, 5 grants totaling $12,500 (high: $2,500, low: $2,500).
Fields of interest: Higher education.
Type of support: Employee-related scholarships.
Application information: Application form required.
   Deadline(s): Apr. 30
   Applicants should submit the following:
      1) GPA
      2) Transcripts
   Additional information: Transcript should indicate class rank and board scores (for high school seniors, and course(s) of study for current college students); application available through the human resources department.
Program description:
   ERI Scholarship Program: Student candidates must currently be high school seniors or attending an accredited two-year institution or four-year college or university at the undergraduate level. It is not a prerequisite that a high school senior be accepted to an institution for consideration under this program; however, proof of acceptance will be required prior to payment of a scholarship award. Applicants must have at least a 2.5 GPA to apply. Graduate school programs are not eligible. Scholarships must be used for tuition, books, and supplies. Students who received awards in past years are not eligible to apply again.The selection process will be conducted by a committee of faculty and staff from Duquesne University in Pittsburgh. The selection criteria will be based on academic achievement, leadership and participation in related extracurricular activities. The program awards five $2,500 scholarships.
EIN: 251789716

1289
Arnold & Mildred Erickson Charitable Foundation, Inc.

c/o National Bank & Trust Co. of Sycamore
230 W. State St.
Sycamore, IL 60178   (815) 895-2125
Contact: Diane Florschuetz, Asst. V.P. and Trust Off., National Bank & Trust Co. of Sycamore

Foundation type: Independent foundation
Limitations: Scholarships to graduates of Kaneland and Central Community School District No.1, IL, who are attending a four-year college or university, and to residents who are attending Waubonsee Community College and studying the manual or cultural arts.
Financial data: Year ended 12/31/2004.
Assets, $1,601,996 (M); Expenditures, $96,378; Total giving, $78,400; Grants to individuals, totaling $58,900.
Fields of interest: Arts education; Arts.
Type of support: Support to graduates or students of specific schools.
Application information: Application form required.
   Deadline(s): Mar. 1
EIN: 366998667

1290
Carl J. Erickson Scholarship Educational Fund

c/o Bank of America, N.A.
P.O. Box 34345
Seattle, WA 98124-1345
Application address: c/o Merilyn Baker, Superintendent, Educational Service District 123, 124 S. 4th Ave., Pasco, WA 99301

Foundation type: Independent foundation
Limitations: Scholarships to financially needy graduating seniors of high schools in Benton County, WA, to study horticulture or agriculture at Washington State University. See program description for more limitations.
Financial data: Year ended 12/31/2004.
Assets, $91,684 (M); Expenditures, $7,998; Total giving, $4,200; Grants to individuals, totaling $4,200.
Fields of interest: Horticulture/garden clubs; Agriculture.
Type of support: Support to graduates or students of specific schools; Undergraduate support.
Application information: Deadline Apr. 27; Completion of formal application required, including transcripts, photograph, essay, description of achievements, and letters of recommendation.
Program description:
   Scholarship Program: Applicants must have ranked in the upper third of their class and completed three years of 4-H or FFA work and must be regularly enrolled during the year of their application. Preference is given to high school seniors who reside on farms in Benton County, WA, and whose family has received its principal income from farming during the preceding two-year period.
EIN: 916025631

1291
Leroy Erickson Scholarship Fund

c/o National City Bank
P. O. Box 94651
Cleveland, OH 44101
Application address: Chris Junker, c/o Pennbank, Leroy G. Erickson Scholarship Comm., Trust Dept., 71 Main St., Bradford, PA 16701

Foundation type: Independent foundation
Limitations: Scholarships to students who have been residents of the city of Bradford, the borough of Lewis Run, or the townships of Bradford, Corydon, Foster, or Lafayette, PA, for at least the past two school years and who are graduates of Bradford, PA, area high schools.
Financial data: Year ended 10/31/2004.
Assets, $866,318 (M); Expenditures, $39,361; Total giving, $30,000; Grants to individuals, totaling $30,000.
Type of support: Scholarships—to individuals; Support to graduates or students of specific schools.
Application information: Deadline Apr. 1; Completion of formal application required.
EIN: 256358243

1292
The Erie Community Foundation

127 W. 6th St.
Erie, PA 16501-1001   (814) 454-0843
Contact: Michael L. Batchelor, Pres.; For grants: Donna Douglass, Prog. and Scholarship Off.
FAX: (814) 456-4965;
E-mail: mbatchelor@cferie.org; Additional E-mail: ddouglass@cferie.org; URL: http://www.cferie.org

Foundation type: Community foundation
Limitations: Scholarships to individuals residing in the Erie, PA, area for undergraduate education.
Publications: Annual report; Informational brochure (including application guidelines); Newsletter.
Financial data: Year ended 12/31/2004.
Assets, $114,627,596 (M); Expenditures, $7,214,530; Total giving, $5,330,819; Grants to individuals, 36 grants totaling $307,126 (high: $128,870, low: $300).
Type of support: Undergraduate support.
Application information: Deadlines vary; Completion of formal application required; Applications available at local high schools.
EIN: 256032032

1293
Alfred Erk Charitable Education Trust

c/o JPMorgan Chase Bank
P.O. Box 31412, Ste. S-5
Rochester, NY 14603
Application address: c/o Cheryl Kleiman, JPMorgan Chase Bank, 20 S. Clinton Ave., Ste. S-4, Rochester, NY 14606, tel.: (800) 850-7222

Foundation type: Independent foundation
Limitations: Scholarships to residents of Middlebury, CT.
Financial data: Year ended 09/30/2004.
Assets, $199,762 (M); Expenditures, $9,193; Total giving, $5,250; Grants to individuals, totaling $5,250.
Type of support: Scholarships—to individuals.
Application information: Applications accepted Jan. 1 through Apr. 30; Completion of formal application required.
EIN: 066287322

1294
Helen R. Ernst Charitable Trust

c/o Ramsey National Bank & Trust Co.
P.O. Box 160
Devils Lake, ND 58301-0160
Contact: Joanne Crosswhite, Comm. Member
Application address: c/o Higher Educ. Office, Spirit Lake Nation, P.O. Box 359, Fort Totten, ND 58375

Foundation type: Independent foundation
Limitations: Scholarships to Native Americans in ND who are members of the Fort Trotten Spirit Lake Nation enrolled or enrolling in an accredited postsecondary institution on a full time basis.
Financial data: Year ended 06/30/2005.
Assets, $158,748 (M); Expenditures, $12,104; Total giving, $8,794; Grants to individuals, totaling $8,794.
Fields of interest: Native Americans/American Indians.
Type of support: Scholarships—to individuals.
Application information: Deadline July 30; Completion of formal application required, including BIA and Pell grants applied for; Applicants must take a full course load and have a 2.0 GPA.
EIN: 456050423

1295
Catherine Ernst Memorial Educational Trust Fund

21116 County Rd. 30
Corcoran, MN 55340   (763) 420-2985
Contact: Anne Eisenzimmer, Tr.

Foundation type: Independent foundation

Limitations: Scholarships only to descendants of Catherine Ernst.
Financial data: Year ended 06/30/2004. Assets, $265,326 (M); Expenditures, $22,441; Total giving, $21,747; Grants to individuals, 13 grants totaling $21,747 (high: $2,000, low: $747).
Type of support: Scholarships—to individuals.
Application information: Deadline Aug. 31; Initial approach by letter or telephone; Completion of formal application required.
EIN: 416307139

1296
Dacy Espy Foundation, Inc.
c/o James Boulware & Co.
2221 Peachtree Rd. N.E., Ste. D-330
Atlanta, GA   30309
Application address: c/o Ann Petty, Treas., 6267 Hwy. 43, Jackson, AL 36545; tel.: (251) 246-2492

Foundation type: Independent foundation
Limitations: Scholarships primarily to individuals residing in the South, with a focus on GA, for undergraduate education.
Financial data: Year ended 12/31/2004. Assets, $32,792 (M); Expenditures, $54,978; Total giving, $19,248; Grants to individuals, totaling $19,248.
Type of support: Undergraduate support.
Application information: Applications accepted. Application form required.
   Deadline(s): Prior to beginning of school year
EIN: 582657354

1297
Essex Classical Institute
62 Learned Dr.
Westford, VT   05494

Foundation type: Independent foundation
Limitations: Scholarships to graduates of Essex High School who are residents of Essex, VT.
Financial data: Year ended 12/31/2004. Assets, $0 (M); Expenditures, $3,666; Total giving, $3,000; Grant to an individual, 1 grant totaling $3,000.
Type of support: Support to graduates or students of specific schools; Undergraduate support.
Application information: Applications accepted.
   Additional information: Applicants chosen and submitted by Essex High School.
EIN: 036006448

1298
Essex County Bar Foundation
354 Eisenhower Pkwy., Plz. 11
Livingston, NJ   07039   (973) 622-6207
Contact: Brian G. Steller, Pres.
FAX: (973) 622-4341

Foundation type: Public charity
Limitations: Scholarships to financially needy second- or third-year law students with ties to Essex County, NJ. Preference is given to students attending Rutgers University School of Law, NJ, or Seton Hall University School of Law, NJ. Law scholarships without geographic restriction to those who have a permanent physical disability or mental impairment.
Publications: Application guidelines; Newsletter.
Financial data: Year ended 05/31/2003. Assets, $371,876 (L); Expenditures, $142,113; Total giving, $13,500; Grants to individuals, totaling $13,500.

Fields of interest: Law school/education; Disabilities, people with.
Type of support: Graduate support.
Application information: Application form required.
   Initial approach: Letter or telephone.
   Deadline(s): Apr. 25
   Additional information: Interviews required.
Program description:
   Biunno Scholarship Fund: This fund is specifically for law students with physical or mental disabilities. The following additional guidelines apply:
   · the scholarship must be awarded to a person with a disability. Some objective demonstration of a present and permanent disability must be submitted
   · the recipient must be attending law school or be accepted to and commencing studies in law school. Preference is given to persons attending Rutgers Law or Seton Hall Law, and to those seeking to pursue a career in the field of advocacy for persons with disabilities. Applicants seeking to secure the benefit of such a preference need to demonstrate their intent, either by having completed a course in law school relating to advocacy, having worked in an advocacy-type clinic or, potentially, having had prior job experience—either at the undergraduate or law school level—in an advocacy field or with a public interest organization
   · the recipient must have attained at least a 3.0 or equivalent GPA
An appropriate use of scholarship money would be for personal expenses during the time when the individual is not studying or pursuing his or her education, but is, in effect, pursuing education in the broader sense by securing employment experience. It is for this purpose that even a third-year law student might be an appropriate recipient of a scholarship grant. A student who has already graduated from law school, but who is encountering difficulty in securing employment and is in need of supplemental funding to enter a public interest or advocacy field, or who is in need of supplemental funding to secure ordinary employment, will also be considered as eligible for a scholarship grant. The only limitation is that funds should not, under any circumstances, be permitted to be used, in effect, to "retrofit" an employer's place of business, or a law school itself for that matter, in order to make it accessible. Since accessibility will, in any event, be a requirement of ADA, it is one to which these funds should not be addressed.
EIN: 221661299

1299
Essex Veterans of World War II
c/o First National Bank of Ipswich
31 Market St.
Ipswich, MA   01938
Application address: c/o Essex Scholarship Comm., Attn.: Armand LaSalva, Superintendent of Schools, 12 Story St., Essex, MA 01929

Foundation type: Independent foundation
Limitations: Scholarships to graduating seniors of Essex, MA, public schools, and to veterans of the U.S.
Financial data: Year ended 12/31/2004. Assets, $203,988 (M); Expenditures, $12,023; Total giving, $10,000; Grants to individuals, totaling $10,000.
Fields of interest: Military/veterans' organizations.
Type of support: Scholarships—to individuals.

Application information: Applications by essay accepted throughout the year.
EIN: 046697373

1300
Estonian-Revelia Academic Fund, Inc.
c/o Juri Taht
12901 Clearfield Dr.
Bowie, MD   20715-1106

Foundation type: Operating foundation
Limitations: Scholarships to students residing in Estonia for higher education.
Financial data: Year ended 12/31/2002. Assets, $862,694 (M); Expenditures, $67,032; Total giving, $52,560; Grants to individuals, 63 grants totaling $52,500 (high: $1,000, low: $500).
Type of support: Foreign applicants; Undergraduate support.
Application information:
   Deadline(s): Mid-Oct.
   Additional information: Contact foundation for current application guidelines; Application should include transcripts, biographical resume and certificate of enrollment.
EIN: 521901554

1301
The Ethridge Scholarship Foundation
P.O. Box 2087
Centennial, CO   80161-2087

Foundation type: Operating foundation
Limitations: Scholarships to Denver, CO, female high school seniors for teacher education programs.
Financial data: Year ended 06/30/2004. Assets, $481,277 (M); Expenditures, $33,000; Total giving, $34,724; Grants to individuals, 14 grants totaling $33,000 (high: $3,000, low: $1,500).
Fields of interest: Teacher school/education; Women.
Type of support: Support to graduates or students of specific schools.
Application information: Deadline Mar. 1; Applications by letter including three letters of reference, (one from a high school counselor and another reference from a non-related person in the community), transcripts, GPA, ACT and/or SAT scores, class rank, extracurricular activities, community activities, record of employment, essay stating educational goals, and income tax returns for parents/students; Interviews required.
EIN: 841270799

1302
Oliver Etnier Charitable Trust
c/o Wilmington Trust Co.
1100 N. Market St.
Wilmington, DE   19890-0001
Contact: Elizabeth Fallon, Trust Off.

Foundation type: Independent foundation
Limitations: Scholarships to PA residents with preference for Huntington County, majoring in engineering, physics, applied mathematics, or computer science at one of six qualifying universities.
Financial data: Year ended 04/30/2004. Assets, $16,186,149 (M); Expenditures, $867,930; Total giving, $641,478; Grants to individuals, totaling $641,478.
Type of support: Undergraduate support.

Application information: Application form required.
Deadline(s): Jan. 1.
Additional information: Application should include SAT scores, transcripts, and a copy of application to one of the qualifying universities.
EIN: 516170516

1303
Zelia Stephans Evans Educational Trust
c/o Glenda Freeman
P.O. Box 431
Montgomery, AL   36101-0431

Foundation type: Independent foundation
Limitations: Scholarships to full-time students from AL who maintain a B average and a continuous course of study.
Financial data: Year ended 12/31/2004.
Assets, $441,586 (M); Expenditures, $14,004; Total giving, $6,000; Grants to individuals, 6 grants totaling $6,000.
Type of support: Scholarships—to individuals.
Application information: Applications accepted.
Deadline(s): None
Additional information: Application by essay describing previous experiences, plan of action and desired outcome, and outside sources of income.
EIN: 636202940

1304
Clyde R. Evans Scholarship Award Trust
c/o JPMorgan Chase Bank, N.A
P.O. Box 1308
Milwaukee, WI   53201

Foundation type: Independent foundation
Limitations: Scholarships to residents of OK for higher education.
Financial data: Year ended 06/30/2005.
Assets, $245,549 (M); Expenditures, $12,590; Total giving, $10,000; Grants to individuals, 2 grants totaling $10,000.
Type of support: Scholarships—to individuals.
Application information: Applications not accepted.
EIN: 736296081

1305
LaVerna Evans Teacher's Scholarship Trust
4387 N. Illinois St.
Swansea, IL   62226-1836
Application address: c/o O'Fallon Township High School, 600 S. Smiley St., O'Fallon, IL 62269

Foundation type: Independent foundation
Limitations: Scholarships to graduates of O'Fallon Township High School, IL, who intend to become elementary or secondary education teachers.
Financial data: Year ended 12/31/2004.
Assets, $291,162 (M); Expenditures, $13,722; Total giving, $9,616; Grants to individuals, totaling $9,616.
Fields of interest: Education, research; Elementary school/education; Secondary school/education.
Type of support: Support to graduates or students of specific schools.
Application information: Application form required.
Additional information: Contact local high school superintendent for current application deadline.
EIN: 371179974

1306
Evans-Moss Fund
c/o Wells Fargo Bank Nevada, N.A.
4707 S. 96th St., MAC N9311-140
Omaha, NE   68127   (260) 461-6470
Application address: c/o Wells Fargo Bank Indiana, N.A., P.O. Box 960, Fort Wayne, IN 46801, tel.: (260) 461-6470

Foundation type: Independent foundation
Limitations: Scholarships to financially needy children living in Fort Wayne, IN, or attending Fort Wayne community schools.
Financial data: Year ended 11/30/2004.
Assets, $487,928 (M); Expenditures, $21,455; Total giving, $13,700; Grants to individuals, 9 grants totaling $13,700 (high: $3,850, low: $700).
Fields of interest: Economically disadvantaged.
Type of support: Support to graduates or students of specific schools; Undergraduate support.
Application information: Application form required.
Initial approach: Letter.
Deadline(s): Apr. 1
EIN: 356332797

1307
Evereg-Fenesse Mesrobian-Roupinian Educational Society, Inc.
4140 Tanglewood Ct.
Bloomfield Hills, MI   48301-1218

Foundation type: Independent foundation
Limitations: Scholarships to students attending Armenian day schools, and to full-time undergraduate or graduate students of Armenian descent attending colleges and universities in CA, MI, NJ, or NY.
Financial data: Year ended 07/31/2003.
Assets, $8,706 (M); Expenditures, $11,805; Total giving, $11,400; Grants to individuals, 43 grants totaling $11,400.
Fields of interest: Armenia.
Type of support: Graduate support; Precollege support; Undergraduate support.
Application information: Application form required.
Deadline(s): Dec. 15
Additional information: Standard application forms available from, and submitted to, designated local chapter representatives.
EIN: 136154468

1308
Everett McKinley Dirksen Endowment Fund
2815 Broadway
Pekin, IL   61554   (309) 347-7113
Contact: Frank Mackaman, Exec. Dir.
FAX: (309) 347-6432;
E-mail: info@dirksencenter.org; Additional e-mail: fmackaman@dirksencenter.org; URL: http://dirksencenter.org

Foundation type: Public charity
Limitations: Scholarships to study American government at one of the specified IL universities, and also to a student at Bradley University, IL, who is majoring in the arts, music, art education, or music education.
Financial data: Year ended 09/30/2004.
Assets, $8,698,802 (M); Expenditures, $450,487; Total giving, $55,964; Grants to individuals, totaling $55,964.
Fields of interest: Government/public administration.

Type of support: Support to graduates or students of specific schools; Undergraduate support.
Application information: Applications accepted. Application form required. Application form available on the grantmaker's Web site.
Initial approach: Letter, telephone or e-mail.
Deadline(s): June 1 for Ray LaHood Scholarships
Applicants should submit the following:
1) Letter(s) of recommendation
2) Transcripts
Additional information: See Web site for complete program information.
Program descriptions:
Ray LaHood Scholarships: Provides financial support for tuition, fees, and books to college and university juniors who are majoring in a discipline related to The Dirksen Center's purpose and interest or in a subject related to the study of the federal government. The Center will award up to five $1,000 scholarships. In order to be considered for a LaHood Scholarship, students must meet the following requirements:
· They are a junior in good standing who will enter their senior year of study in a field related to the study of the U.S. government (e.g., political science, public administration, American studies, U.S. history)
· They attend one of the following: Bradley University, Eureka College, Illinois University, Knox College, Lincoln Christian College, MacMurray College, Millikin University, Quincy University, or Springfield College in Illinois
· Their permanent residence lies within the 18th congressional district or a county touched by the district
· They have a GPA (on a four-point scale) of at least 3.0 overall and 3.75 in their major
Corrine W. Michel Scholarship: The Center will award $1,500 annually to a student at Bradley University, IL, who is majoring in the arts, music, art education, or music education.
EIN: 366132816

1309
Andree T. & Gladys E. Everhart Scholarship Fund Trust
c/o KeyBank N.A., Trust Div.
800 Superior Ave., 4th Fl.
Cleveland, OH   44114
Application address: c/o KeyBank N.A., 1211 S.W. 5th Ave., Ste. 560, Portland, OR 97204

Foundation type: Independent foundation
Limitations: Scholarships to Oregon City high school graduates majoring in a social science at OR public schools of higher education.
Financial data: Year ended 12/31/2004.
Assets, $777,396 (M); Expenditures, $52,440; Total giving, $42,000; Grants to individuals, totaling $42,000.
Fields of interest: Social sciences.
Type of support: Support to graduates or students of specific schools; Undergraduate support.
Application information: Deadline Apr. 1; Application by letter outlining financial need, grades, and character.
EIN: 936212186

1310

Everly Scholarship Fund, Inc.
4300 Haddonfield Rd.
Fairway Corp. Ctr., Ste. 311
Pennsauken, NJ 08109
Contact: John R. Lolio, Jr., Pres.
FAX: (856) 662-0165; E-mail: jlolio@sskrplaw.com

Foundation type: Operating foundation
Limitations: Undergraduate scholarships to graduating high school students of the Camden, Burlington, and Gloucester counties, NJ school districts.
Publications: Application guidelines.
Financial data: Year ended 03/31/2005. Assets, $2,415,674 (M); Expenditures, $71,267; Total giving, $47,500; Grants to individuals, 19 grants totaling $47,500 (high: $2,500, low: $1,250).
Type of support: Support to graduates or students of specific schools; Undergraduate support.
Application information: Application form required.
Initial approach: Letter or telephone.
Deadline(s): May 15
Applicants should submit the following:
1) SAT
2) GPA
EIN: 223161410

1311

Paul B. Evers Trust
133 E. Market St.
Xenia, OH 45385-3158
Contact: David L. Pendry, Tr.
Application address: c/o Vicki Huff, Xenia High School, 303 Kinsey Rd., Xenia, OH 45385, tel.: (937) 372-6983

Foundation type: Independent foundation
Limitations: Student loans to graduates of Xenia High School, OH.
Financial data: Year ended 12/31/2003. Assets, $243,502 (M); Expenditures, $5,555; Total giving, $0; Loans to individuals, 5 loans totaling $13,965.
Type of support: Support to graduates or students of specific schools; Undergraduate support.
Application information: Deadline Mar. 15; Contact trust for current application guidelines; Initial approach by letter.
Program description:
Student Loan Program: Interest-free loans, for tuition only, are given to graduates of Xenia High School who live within the city limits of Xenia, OH. Loans are interest-free as long as they are repaid in full within ten years from the date of the student's college graduation. If loans are not repaid by the due date, interest accrues at ten percent per annum. Each student must be enrolled for at least 12 hours per quarter or semester. If the student drops out of school or fails to maintain passing grades, loans become due in full immediately.
EIN: 316120701

1312

Evrytanian Association of America
121 Greenwich Rd.
Charlotte, NC 28211-2313 (704) 366-6571

Foundation type: Public charity
Limitations: Scholarships to children of Evrytanian origin, based on academic excellence and financial need.
Financial data: Year ended 05/31/2005. Assets, $756,619 (M); Expenditures, $87,483;

Total giving, $32,300; Grants to individuals, totaling $6,500.
Fields of interest: Greece.
Type of support: Scholarships—to individuals.
Application information: Contact foundation for current application deadline/guidelines.
EIN: 566061036

1313

H. T. Ewald Foundation
15450 E. Jefferson Ave., Ste. 180
Grosse Pointe, MI 48230 (313) 821-1278
Contact: Shelagh K. Czuprenski, Secy.
FAX: (313) 821-3299;
E-mail: ewaldfndtn@aol.com; URL: http://www.ewaldfoundation.org

Foundation type: Independent foundation
Limitations: Undergraduate scholarships to high school seniors who are residents of the metropolitan Detroit, MI, area.
Publications: Informational brochure (including application guidelines).
Financial data: Year ended 12/31/2004. Assets, $2,826,168 (M); Expenditures, $149,501; Total giving, $81,450; Grants to individuals, 40 grants totaling $80,800 (high: $5,500, low: $500).
Fields of interest: Higher education.
Type of support: Undergraduate support.
Application information: Application form required.
Initial approach: Letter or telephone.
Deadline(s): Mar. 1
Additional information: Application should include three letters of recommendation, photograph, biography, high school transcripts, and SAT and ACT scores; Interviews required for finalists only.
Program description:
Scholarships: Financial need is one of the most important considerations. Scholastic record, extracurricular activities, honors or awards, and character are also used as criteria for selection. The amount of the scholarship varies with the financial need of the applicant. The awards are renewable for up to four years during pursuit of a B.A. degree, contingent upon maintenance of a satisfactory GPA. Approximately 10-15 new awards are available each year.
EIN: 386007837

1314

Exacto Foundation, Inc.
P.O. Box 24
Grafton, WI 53024-0024

Foundation type: Operating foundation
Limitations: Scholarships for undergraduate study to residents of Grafton, WI.
Financial data: Year ended 07/31/2003. Assets, $1,550,363 (M); Expenditures, $32,431; Total giving, $32,370; Grants to individuals, 27 grants totaling $20,750 (high: $7,500, low: $250).
Fields of interest: Education; Health care.
Type of support: Undergraduate support.
Application information: Applications not accepted.
EIN: 237076890

1315

Excelsior Scottish Rite Bodies Charity Fund, Inc.
c/o Secy's Office, Scottish Rite Temple
315 White Horse Pike
West Collingswood, NJ 08107

Foundation type: Independent foundation
Limitations: Scholarships to the sons and daughters of any living or deceased Master Freemason who resides in Atlantic, Burlington, Camden, Cape May, Cumberland, Gloucester, Ocean, or Salem counties, NJ. This scholarship is $2,000 per year, for up to four years, and may be used for undergraduate education.
Publications: Application guidelines.
Financial data: Year ended 07/31/2004. Assets, $1,957,342 (M); Expenditures, $136,151; Total giving, $96,564; Grants to individuals, totaling $29,000.
Fields of interest: Fraternal societies.
Type of support: Undergraduate support.
Application information:
Deadline(s): Apr. 1
Additional information: Completion of formal application required, including information on scholastic honors, extracurricular and community activities, hobbies, work experience, transcripts, family background, and anticipated course of study.
EIN: 222917990

1316

The Exchange Club of Vero Beach Scholarship Foundation Trust
P.O. Box 1982
Vero Beach, FL 32961-1982 (772) 567-9217
Contact: George Foote, Chair.

Foundation type: Independent foundation
Limitations: Scholarships to graduates of Indian River County, FL, public high schools.
Financial data: Year ended 08/31/2004. Assets, $195,854 (M); Expenditures, $11,293; Total giving, $11,000; Grants to individuals, 7 grants totaling $11,000 (high: $2,000, low: $1,000).
Type of support: Support to graduates or students of specific schools; Undergraduate support.
Application information: Application form required.
Deadline(s): Apr. 1
Additional information: Completion of formal application required, including transcript, SAT and ACT scores, and letter of recommendation from counselor.
EIN: 592967807

1317

Fabri-Kal Foundation
c/o Fabri-Kal Corp.
Plastics Pl.
Kalamazoo, MI 49001 (269) 385-5050
Contact: Robert P. Kittredge, Pres.

Foundation type: Company-sponsored foundation
Limitations: Scholarships for higher education to children of employees of Fabri-Kal Corporation, primarily in MI, PA and SC.
Financial data: Year ended 12/31/2003. Assets, $113 (M); Expenditures, $503,649; Total giving, $503,639; Grants to individuals, 72 grants totaling $357,462 (high: $17,374, low: $259).
Type of support: Employee-related scholarships.
Application information:
Deadline(s): None

Additional information: Applications should be sent by letter, and should outline financial need.

EIN: 237003366

1318

The Fadel Educational Foundation, Inc.

1348 Walton Way, No. 5500
Augusta, GA 30901
Contact: Hossam E. Fadel, Pres.
E-mail: fef_grants@hotmail.com

Foundation type: Operating foundation
Limitations: Scholarships to American students of Islamic faith for college or post graduate study.
Financial data: Year ended 06/30/2004. Assets, $454,123 (M); Expenditures, $73,984; Total giving, $62,732; Grants to individuals, 79 grants totaling $62,732 (high: $3,325, low: $200).
Fields of interest: Islam.
Type of support: Graduate support; Technical education support; Undergraduate support.
Application information: Deadline Mar. 15; Initial approach by letter; Completion of formal application required.
EIN: 582330050

1319

Charles E. Fahrney Education Foundation

(also known as Fahrney Education Foundation)
c/o U.S. Bank, N.A., Trust Dept.
123 E. 3rd St.
Ottumwa, IA 52501
Contact: Scholarship Comm.

Foundation type: Independent foundation
Limitations: Undergraduate scholarships to residents of Wapello County, IA, to attend colleges and universities in IA.
Publications: Application guidelines.
Financial data: Year ended 02/28/2005. Assets, $5,368,148 (M); Expenditures, $248,674; Total giving, $205,000; Grants to individuals, 49 grants totaling $205,000 (high: $2,500, low: $1,250).
Fields of interest: Higher education.
Type of support: Undergraduate support.
Application information: Applications accepted. Application form required.
Deadline(s): Feb. 15
Additional information: Application should include transcripts and one-page letter expressing educational and occupational interests and goals, along with description of other personal interests and any extraordinary factors which should be considered by the scholarship committee.
Program description:
Scholarships: Scholarships of $2,250 are awarded on the basis of academic performance and citizenship. Should the recipient fail, drop out, or drop below full-time status, the scholarship will immediately terminate and funds will be returned to the foundation. Applications may be obtained after Dec. 1 each year from Firstar Bank, Ottumwa, at IA colleges and universities, and Wapello County High School. Applicants must reapply annually. Scholarships are granted on a yearly basis. No applicant will be eligible to receive more than four scholarship awards. Applicants must be enrolled in a full-time course of study in one of the following:
  • a four-year accredited IA college or university program leading toward a bachelor degree

  • a two-year IA college associate arts or science program leading to a four-year course of study and bachelor degree.
EIN: 426295370

1320

Fairbanks-Horix Charitable Trust

c/o National City Bank of PA
P.O. Box 94651
Cleveland, OH 44101-4651
Application address: c/o Stephen L. Guin, Ph.D., Consultants, PSP The Union Trust Bldg., Ste. 470, Pittsburgh, PA 15219

Foundation type: Company-sponsored foundation
Limitations: Scholarships to children of full-time or deceased employees of Horix Manufacturing Company, PA.
Financial data: Year ended 12/31/2004. Assets, $711,534 (M); Expenditures, $26,017; Total giving, $22,000; Grants to individuals, 3 grants totaling $4,500 (high: $2,250, low: $750).
Type of support: Employee-related scholarships.
Application information:
Deadline(s): May 1
Additional information: Application should include transcripts, a copy of parents' confidential statement, college aptitude test scores, and proof of financial need; Applications should be sent by letter.
Program description:
Scholarship Program: Applicants must be graduating high school seniors, or have graduated within the past two years, or be enrolled in four-year colleges as full-time undergraduate students. Employees must have at least two years of service as of May 1. Children of officers may not apply.
EIN: 256084211

1321

Kittie M. Fairey Educational Fund

c/o Wachovia Bank, N.A.
100 N. Main St., 13th Fl.
Winston-Salem, NC 27150
Application address: c/o The Foundation Scholarship Program, Attn.: Sandra Lee, P.O. Box 1465, Taylors, SC 29687-1465. Scholarship Program URL: http://www.wachoviascholars.com/kmfr/kmfr_2006_ins.htm

Foundation type: Independent foundation
Limitations: Undergraduate scholarships to residents of SC attending a four-year college or university within the state.
Financial data: Year ended 09/30/2005. Assets, $3,321,233 (M); Expenditures, $163,111; Total giving, $128,357; Grants to individuals, totaling $128,357.
Type of support: Undergraduate support.
Application information: Application form required.
Initial approach: Letter.
Deadline(s): Mar. 15.
EIN: 576037140

1322

Freeman E. Fairfield - Meeker Charitable Trust

c/o Wells Fargo Bank West, N.A.
1740 Broadway, No. C7300-483
Denver, CO 80274
Contact: Peggy Toal, Sr. Trust Admin., Wells Fargo Bank West, N.A.
Application address: Judy Dowling, c/o Wells Fargo Bank, 633 17th St., Denver, CO 80270

Foundation type: Independent foundation
Limitations: Scholarships to graduates of Meeker High School, CO.
Financial data: Year ended 11/30/2004. Assets, $4,529,751 (M); Expenditures, $308,400; Total giving, $282,245.
Type of support: Support to graduates or students of specific schools; Undergraduate support.
Application information: Application form not required.
Additional information: Applications by letter accepted throughout the year.
EIN: 846068906

1323

Fairfield County Foundation

162 E. Main St.
P.O. Box 159
Lancaster, OH 43130 (740) 654-8451
Contact: Amy Eyman, Exec. Dir.
FAX: (740) 654-3971;
E-mail: info@fairfieldcountyfoundation.org;
Additional E-mail:
aeyman@fairfieldcountyfoundation.org;
URL: http://www.fairfieldcountyfoundation.org

Foundation type: Community foundation
Limitations: Grants and scholarships to individuals in the Fairfield County, OH, area.
Publications: Application guidelines; Annual report; Financial statement; Grants list; Informational brochure (including application guidelines); Newsletter.
Financial data: Year ended 12/31/2003. Assets, $18,474,336 (M); Expenditures, $974,923; Total giving, $591,302; Grants to individuals, 345 grants totaling $224,172 (high: $3,500, low: $12).
Type of support: Grants to individuals; Scholarships—to individuals.
Application information: Application form required.
Deadline(s): Mid-Mar. and mid-Oct.
Additional information: Contact foundation for application form.
EIN: 341623983

1324

Fairmount Tire Charitable Foundation, Inc.

11766 Wilshire Blvd., Ste. 900
Los Angeles, CA 90025
Contact: Alvie Kracek
Application address: 56816 Aspen Dr., Springville, CA 93265, tel.: (559) 542-2639

Foundation type: Company-sponsored foundation
Limitations: Scholarships to economically disadvantaged students residing in South Central Los Angeles, CA, to study nursing.
Financial data: Year ended 12/31/2002. Assets, $100,234 (M); Expenditures, $129,774; Total giving, $124,622; Grants to individuals, 4 grants totaling $40,189 (high: $36,342, low: $1,800).
Fields of interest: Nursing school/education.
Type of support: Undergraduate support.
Application information: Deadline Fall; Contact foundation for current application deadline/guidelines; Completion of formal application required.
EIN: 954424035

1325
Herbert Fales Educational Trust
c/o Bank of America, N.A., P.C. Group
P.O. Box 1802
Providence, RI 02901-1802
Application address: c/o Bank of America, N.A.,100
Federal St., Boston, MA 02109

Foundation type: Independent foundation
Limitations: Scholarships to individuals who reside
within ten miles of Framingham, MA, and have a
GPA of at least 2.5.
Financial data: Year ended 12/31/2004.
Assets, $865,947 (M); Expenditures, $42,845;
Total giving, $31,738; Grants to individuals, 22
grants totaling $11,138 (high: $600, low: $463).
Type of support: Scholarships—to individuals.
Application information: Deadline June 30;
Completion of formal application required.
EIN: 046044998

1326
Fallon Foundation
100 Front St., 14th Fl.
Worcester, MA 01608 (508) 368-5498
Contact: Johanna Lolax, Mgr., Fundraising & Devel.
Scholarship application address: Attn. Karen
Rodrigues, c/o Fallon Clinic, Human Resources
Dept., 630 Plantation St., Worcester, MA 01605
E-mail: johanna.lolax@fallon-clinic.com;
URL: http://www.fallonfoundation.org

Foundation type: Public charity
Limitations: Scholarships to employees and
dependants of employees of Fallon Clinic and Fallon
Community Health Plan, MA.
Publications: Application guidelines; Financial
statement; Grants list; Informational brochure.
Financial data: Year ended 12/31/2004.
Assets, $4,090,180 (M); Expenditures,
$730,877; Total giving, $248,132; Grants to
individuals, 11 grants totaling $29,225 (high:
$5,650, low: $1,000).
Type of support: Employee-related scholarships.
Application information: Applications accepted.
Application form required. Application form
available on the grantmaker's Web site.
  Initial approach: Letter or telephone.
  Deadline(s): June 24
  Applicants should submit the following:
    1) GPA
    2) Financial information
    3) SAT
    4) Transcripts
  Additional information: See Web site for full
    listing of programs.
EIN: 222912515

1327
Charlotte Fanning Foundation, Inc.
(formerly Fanning Orphan School)
101 Hill Heaven Dr.
Waverly, TN 37185 (931) 296-1144
Contact: Norma Morefield

Foundation type: Independent foundation
Limitations: Scholarships to students to attend a
Christian college or university who have at least one
deceased parent and work at least 40 hours per
week on campus.
Financial data: Year ended 05/31/2005.
Assets, $515,005 (M); Expenditures, $37,354;
Total giving, $25,000; Grants to individuals,
totaling $25,000.
Fields of interest: Christian agencies & churches.
Type of support: Scholarships—to individuals.

Application information: Deadline June 1;
Application by letter, outlining applicant's history
and orphan status.
EIN: 620541810

1328
The Kate Fansler Foundation, Inc.
c/o Susan Heath
845 West End Ave., Ste. 9A
New York, NY 10025

Foundation type: Independent foundation
Limitations: Provides financial and other
assistance to individuals, with special attention to
women in need of such assistance, in order to
improve their lives through study, work, or support
in their creative efforts.
Financial data: Year ended 05/31/2004.
Assets, $43,694 (M); Expenditures, $37,740;
Total giving, $37,022; Grants to individuals, 17
grants totaling $37,022 (high: $5,471, low: $500).
Fields of interest: Women.
Type of support: Scholarships—to individuals;
Awards/grants by nomination only.
Application information: Applications not
accepted.
  Additional information: Unsolicited applications
    not considered or acknowledged.
EIN: 133979080

1329
Fansteel Scholarship Foundation
c/o The Northern Trust Co.
P.O. Box 803878
Chicago, IL 60680

Foundation type: Company-sponsored foundation
Limitations: Scholarships to children or, in limited
cases, grandchildren of Fansteel employees,
retirees, or deceased employees. Maximum
scholarship awarded is $3,000.
Financial data: Year ended 12/31/2004.
Assets, $86,501 (M); Expenditures, $34,784;
Total giving, $33,500; Grants to individuals, 30
grants totaling $33,500 (high: $3,000, low: $250).
Type of support: Employee-related scholarships.
Application information: Application form required.
  Deadline(s): Apr. 3
  Applicants should submit the following:
    1) SAT
    2) ACT
    3) Transcripts
  Additional information: Application should also
    include parents' confidential statement and
    high school counselor's report.
EIN: 362614698

1330
Charles C. Faranna Scholarship Trust
4008 S. Elm Pl., Ste. F
Broken Arrow, OK 74011
Contact: Mark Harper, Tr.

Foundation type: Independent foundation
Limitations: Scholarships to residents of OK.
Financial data: Year ended 06/30/2005.
Assets, $4,427,807 (M); Expenditures,
$172,854; Total giving, $94,387; Grants to
individuals, totaling $94,387.
Type of support: Undergraduate support.
Application information: Contact trust for current
application deadline/guidelines.
EIN: 736251335

1331
Farber Foundation, Inc.
1845 Walnut St., Ste. 800
Philadelphia, PA 19103-4711
Contact: Jacqueline A. Tully, Coord., Scholarship
Prog.

Foundation type: Company-sponsored foundation
Limitations: Scholarships to financially needy,
full-time juniors studying in the College of Allied
Health Sciences at Thomas Jefferson University
who have at least a 3.3 GPA. Scholarships also to
children of employees of CSS Industries, Inc., or its
subsidiaries, whose parents have been employees
for at least two years.
Financial data: Year ended 12/31/2002.
Assets, $2,759,235 (M); Expenditures,
$419,642; Total giving, $415,177; Grants to
individuals, 29 grants totaling $176,779 (high:
$75,000, low: $1,000).
Fields of interest: Medical school/education;
Health sciences school/education; Physical
therapy.
Type of support: Employee-related scholarships;
Undergraduate support.
Application information: Application form required.
  Deadline(s): June 15 for Thomas Jefferson
    University scholarships and Apr. for CSS
    Industries, Inc. scholarships
  Applicants should submit the following:
    1) Letter(s) of recommendation
    2) Essay
    3) Financial information
  Additional information: Contact foundation for
    further application information; Address for
    Health Professions Scholars Prog.: c/o Univ.
    Office of Financial Aid, College of Health
    Professions, Thomas Jefferson Univ., 1025
    Walnut St., Philadelphia, PA 19107, tel.:
    (215) 955-2867.
Program descriptions:
  *Farber Foundation Health Professions Scholars
  Program:* Scholarships cover full tuition for a
  maximum of two years to three outstanding
  students who are planning to enter a health-related
  profession. Farber Scholars must work with a
  mentor to create and implement an honors project.
  An additional $1,000 award will help the recipient
  carry out this project. Projects directed at some
  facet of community service are encouraged.
  Students in the Physical Therapy program are not
  eligible until their senior year whereupon funding
  will be provided for the senior year and for the first
  year of graduate study. Recipients are chosen by a
  committee made up of university faculty and staff.
  Employee-related Scholarships: Scholarships are
  awarded on the basis of academic performance,
  standardized test scores, recommendations,
  personal motivation, financial need, and
  participation in community and extracurricular
  activities. Recipients are selected by the Thomas
  Jefferson University Selection Committee of
  Philadelphia, PA. Scholarships are renewable.
EIN: 236254221

1332
Elizabeth Farmen Trust/ St. Marks Church
c/o Alliance Bank, N.A.
241 Main St.
Buffalo, NY 14203

Foundation type: Independent foundation
Limitations: Scholarships to members of St.
Mark's Episcopal Church, NY, for undergraduate
education at U.S. universities.

Financial data: Year ended 11/30/2004. Assets, $1,210,292 (M); Expenditures, $73,032; Total giving, $56,000.
Fields of interest: Protestant agencies & churches.
Type of support: Undergraduate support.
Application information: Contact trust for current application deadlines/guidelines.
EIN: 527044240

1333
Farmers' Electric Education Foundation
P.O. Box 550
Clovis, NM 88102-0550 (505) 762-4466
Contact: Lance R. Adkins, Genl. Mgr.
URL: http://www.farmerselectric.org/scholarships.htm

Foundation type: Company-sponsored foundation
Limitations: Scholarships to members of Farmers' Electric Cooperative, Inc. of NM, and their immediate families. Scholarships for "Government in Action" youth tour program to eleventh-grade students who are dependents of members of Farmers' Electric Cooperative, Inc. of NM.
Financial data: Year ended 12/31/2004. Assets, $692,054 (M); Expenditures, $23,924; Total giving, $23,250; Grants to individuals, 31 grants totaling $23,250 (high: $750, low: $750).
Fields of interest: Vocational education; Business/industry; Government/public administration.
Type of support: Conferences/seminars; Technical education support; Precollege support; Undergraduate support.
Application information: Application form required.
Initial approach: Letter.
Deadline(s): Feb. 1
Additional information: Applications should include two letters of recommendation and essays.
Program descriptions:
Farmers' Electric Education Foundation Scholarship Fund: Scholarships are granted to attend accredited colleges, universities, vocational schools, or technical schools. Applicants must have at least a 2.5 GPA and be enrolled full-time. First preference is given to graduating seniors from high schools in the service area of the cooperative. Economic need is a secondary consideration. Recipients are announced by Apr. 1. Scholarships are renewable.
Government in Action Youth Tour Program: This program is endorsed by the National Rural Electric Cooperative Association in Washington, DC. Farmers' Electric sponsors 11th grade students who are dependents of active members of the cooperative to participate in the program, which takes place in June. Farmers' Electric provides transportation, lodging, meals, and tour expenses. Parents of selected recipients must sign a Parents' Consent and Release Form and complete a Personal Data Sheet. Further information on this program is available by contacting Lance Adkins or Phyllis Lewis at (800) 445-8541.
EIN: 850348498

1334
Juli Ann Farrell Charitable Trust
c/o Wanda Jane Farrell
104 Walnut St.
Hudson, IA 50643

Foundation type: Independent foundation
Limitations: Scholarships to individuals for higher education.
Financial data: Year ended 12/31/2004. Assets, $302,069 (M); Expenditures, $24,637;

Total giving, $21,000; Grants to individuals, totaling $19,500.
Type of support: Undergraduate support.
Application information: Applications not accepted.
EIN: 426591048

1335
Eleanor E. Farrington Trust
c/o Bank of America, N.A.
100 Federal St., MC-MADE10020B
Boston, MA 02110
Application address: c/o Alenia Miles Guidance Dir., Kennett High School, 176 Main St., Conway, NH 03818

Foundation type: Independent foundation
Limitations: Scholarships to high school seniors from the North Conway, NH school district, who have demonstrated financial need.
Financial data: Year ended 12/31/2003. Assets, $2,586,538 (M); Expenditures, $110,553; Total giving, $87,000; Grants to individuals, 39 grants totaling $87,000 (high: $4,000, low: $1,000).
Type of support: Support to graduates or students of specific schools; Undergraduate support.
Application information: Application form required.
Deadline(s): May 29
Additional information: Application should include copy of financial aid award letter and copy of first page of SAR.
EIN: 046433574

1336
Ruth T. Farrow Trust
c/o Wachovia Bank, N.A.
401 S. Tryon St., 4th Fl.
Charlotte, NC 28288-1159
Contact: Andrew Davis, Trust Off., Wachovia Bank, N.A.
Application address: 765 Broad St., Newark, NJ 07101

Foundation type: Independent foundation
Limitations: Scholarships to high school graduates of Delaware Valley Regional High School, Hunterdon Central Regional High School, North Hunterdon High School, South Hunterdon Regional High School, and Voorhees High School, all in Hunterdon County, NJ.
Financial data: Year ended 12/31/2003. Assets, $15,180 (M); Expenditures, $14,708; Total giving, $13,900; Grants to individuals, 4 grants totaling $13,900 (high: $3,475, low: $3,475).
Type of support: Support to graduates or students of specific schools.
Application information: Applications not accepted.
Additional information: Candidates are nominated by preselected high schools, and recipients are then chosen by the foundation.
EIN: 226298532

1337
Fary Memorial Scholarship Fund
P.O. Box 485
Tappahannock, VA 22560 (804) 443-3373
Contact: William L. Lewis, Tr.
FAX: (804) 443-9303

Foundation type: Independent foundation
Limitations: Scholarships to residents of VA.

Financial data: Year ended 12/31/2003. Assets, $3,065,750 (M); Expenditures, $202,283; Total giving, $136,556; Grants to individuals, 39 grants totaling $125,556 (high: $9,000, low: $176).
Type of support: Scholarships—to individuals.
Application information: Contact foundation for current application deadline/guidelines.
EIN: 541827276

1338
The Fasken Foundation
P.O. Box 162786
Austin, TX 78716-2786 (512) 708-1003
Contact: Andrew C. Elliot, Jr., Dir.

Foundation type: Independent foundation
Limitations: Scholarships to graduates of Midland County public high schools and Midland Community College for attendance at TX institutions.
Publications: Application guidelines.
Financial data: Year ended 12/31/2004. Assets, $23,038,870 (M); Expenditures, $1,771,461; Total giving, $1,151,091; Grants to individuals, 43 grants totaling $92,841 (high: $4,971, low: $1,500).
Type of support: Support to graduates or students of specific schools; Undergraduate support.
Application information: Applications accepted throughout the year; Initial approach by letter; Completion of formal application required.
EIN: 756023680

1339
The Fassino Foundation, Inc.
42 Eliot Hill Rd.
Natick, MA 01760
Contact: Edward G. Fassino, Pres.
E-mail: efassino@mediaone.net

Foundation type: Independent foundation
Limitations: Scholarships to individuals for higher education.
Financial data: Year ended 09/30/2005. Assets, $3,431,388 (M); Expenditures, $327,700; Total giving, $322,450; Grants to individuals, 10 grants totaling $46,000 (high: $5,000, low: $4,000).
Type of support: Scholarships—to individuals.
Application information: Applications not accepted.
EIN: 043177633

1340
Ethel & Emery Fast Scholarship Foundation, Inc.
12620 Rolling Rd.
Potomac, MD 20854 (301) 762-1102
Contact: Carol A. Minami, Secy.-Treas.
FAX: (301) 279-0201

Foundation type: Operating foundation
Limitations: Graduate and undergraduate scholarships to financially needy Native Americans who have successfully completed one year of postsecondary studies and are full-time students.
Financial data: Year ended 12/31/2003. Assets, $2,067,021 (M); Expenditures, $139,929; Total giving, $57,700; Grants to individuals, 59 grants totaling $57,700 (high: $3,000, low: $500).
Fields of interest: Native Americans/American Indians.

Type of support: Graduate support; Undergraduate support.
Application information: Deadlines Dec. 15 for spring semester and Aug. 15 for fall semester; Initial approach by letter or telephone; Completion of formal application required.
EIN: 521817707

1341
Father Daily Scholarship Foundation
c/o Boerner & Goldsmith Law Firm, P.C.
500 2nd St.
Ida Grove, IA 51445
Contact: For scholarships: Fr. Gerald Fisch
Application address: Sacred Heart Rectory, Ida Grove, IA 51445, tel.: (712) 364-2718

Foundation type: Operating foundation
Limitations: Scholarships to high school seniors who are parishioners of Sacred Heart Parish, IA, to attend college or technical school.
Financial data: Year ended 12/31/2003. Assets, $185,126 (M); Expenditures, $25,614; Total giving, $23,600; Grants to individuals, totaling $23,600.
Fields of interest: Vocational education, post-secondary.
Type of support: Technical education support; Undergraduate support.
Application information: Contact foundation for current application deadline/guidelines.
EIN: 421372214

1342
Harriet M. Faunce Trust
c/o TD Banknorth, N.A.
P.O. Box 10
Orleans, MA 02653-0010
Contact: Gladys M. Burgess, Tr.
Application address: P.O. Box 3067, Bourne, MA 02532-0767

Foundation type: Independent foundation
Limitations: Scholarships to eligible students from the towns of Bourne and Sandwich, MA.
Financial data: Year ended 12/31/2004. Assets, $657,196 (M); Expenditures, $37,719; Total giving, $29,000; Grants to individuals, totaling $28,000.
Type of support: Scholarships—to individuals.
Application information: Applications accepted. Application form required.
Deadline(s): None
Additional information: Forms are obtained from the guidance department of eligible schools.
EIN: 046035572

1343
Fava Scholarship Foundation
(formerly Philip V. Fava and Nancy Owen D. Fava Scholarship Foundation)
c/o Wachovia Bank, N.A.
100 N. Main St., 13th Fl.
Winston-Salem, NC 27150

Foundation type: Independent foundation
Limitations: Scholarships to students attending Blackburn College, IL, Caldwell College, NJ, and Tufts University School of Medicine, MA.
Financial data: Year ended 12/31/2004. Assets, $1,940,713 (M); Expenditures, $112,346; Total giving, $95,955; Grants to individuals, totaling $95,955.

Type of support: Support to graduates or students of specific schools.
Application information:
Deadline(s): Oct.
Additional information: Applications are made through institutions.
EIN: 237149743

1344
Fayette County Foundation
P.O. Box 844
Connersville, IN 47331 (765) 827-9966
Contact: Anna Dungan, Secy. and Exec. Dir.
FAX: (765) 827-5836;
E-mail: info@fayettefoundation.com; URL: http://www.fayettefoundation.com

Foundation type: Community foundation
Limitations: Scholarships to individuals residing in Fayette County, IN, for undergraduate education.
Publications: Annual report; Grants list; Informational brochure; Newsletter.
Financial data: Year ended 12/31/2003. Assets, $4,987,519 (M); Expenditures, $350,454; Total giving, $174,180; Grants to individuals, 15 grants totaling $83,252.
Fields of interest: Nursing school/education.
Type of support: Undergraduate support.
Application information: Applications accepted. Application form required.
Initial approach: Telephone or e-mail.
Additional information: Contact foundation for current application deadline/guidelines; See Web site for complete program listing.
EIN: 311185980

1345
Federal Employees Scholarship Foundation, Inc.
(formerly Fed-Mart Foundation)
1022 Laguna Seca Loop
Chula Vista, CA 91915
E-mail: civilwar49@aol.com

Foundation type: Independent foundation
Limitations: Scholarships to graduating seniors of high schools in San Diego County, CA, who have at least a 3.5 GPA. Some grants are also given to community college students pursuing a certificate program.
Financial data: Year ended 12/31/2004. Assets, $614,182 (M); Expenditures, $30,652; Total giving, $21,000; Grants to individuals, totaling $21,000.
Type of support: Support to graduates or students of specific schools; Undergraduate support.
Application information: Deadline Apr. 15; Completion of formal application required, including high school transcripts with the first semester of senior year; Applications available in Jan. from San Diego County high schools.
Program description:
Scholarship Program: Academic achievement is the primary criterion for selection, and individuals should have a minimum GPA of 3.5 to apply. Applicants must show active participation in school and community activities.
EIN: 330727818

1346
The Federated Church of Columbus Foundation, Inc.
2704 15th St.
Columbus, NE 68601
Application address: c/o Scholarship Committee, P.O. Box 564, Columbus, NE 68602-0564

Foundation type: Independent foundation
Limitations: Scholarships to residents of Columbus, NE, for higher education.
Financial data: Year ended 12/31/2004. Assets, $819,268 (M); Expenditures, $48,884; Total giving, $44,100; Grants to individuals, totaling $44,100.
Type of support: Undergraduate support.
Application information: Application form required.
Deadline(s): June 15
Additional information: Application should include most recent transcripts; scholarships are renewable.
Program description:
Scholarship Program: Scholarships are renewable.
EIN: 470818736

1347
Federman Scholarship Fund
c/o M&T Bank
1 M&T Plz., 8th Fl.
Buffalo, NY 14203 (716) 842-5526
Application address: c/o Peter Fleisch, 787 Delaware Ave., Buffalo, NY 14209, tel.: (716) 882-1166

Foundation type: Independent foundation
Limitations: Scholarships to residents of Erie County, NY, who are members of the Jewish faith.
Financial data: Year ended 12/31/2004. Assets, $298,889 (M); Expenditures, $16,536; Total giving, $10,000; Grants to individuals, totaling $10,000.
Fields of interest: Jewish agencies & temples.
Type of support: Scholarships—to individuals.
Application information: Applications accepted throughout the year; Contact trust for current application guidelines.
EIN: 166223968

1348
Feiga-Olch Trust
44 Front St., Ste. 210
Worcester, MA 01608 (508) 792-1972
Contact: Carl Emmett Baylis, Tr.

Foundation type: Independent foundation
Limitations: Scholarships to individuals who have resided in Worcester, MA, for at least two years. Priority is given to individuals whose families belong to a local temple or synagogue.
Financial data: Year ended 06/30/2004. Assets, $344,535 (M); Expenditures, $39,285; Total giving, $18,750; Grants to individuals, totaling $18,750.
Fields of interest: Jewish agencies & temples.
Type of support: Scholarships—to individuals.
Application information: Applications by letter accepted throughout the year.
EIN: 046791032

1349
Feild Co-Operative Association, Inc.
4270 I-55 N., Ste. 107
Jackson, MS   39296-5054   (601) 713-2312
Contact: Virginia G. Chill, Secy. and Dir. of Student Loans
FAX: (601) 713-2314; URL: http://www.feildstudentloans.org

Foundation type: Independent foundation
Limitations: Student loans to MS residents who are undergraduate juniors or seniors, or graduate students at accredited colleges and universities.
Publications: Application guidelines; Informational brochure.
Financial data: Year ended 12/31/2003. Assets, $16,390,931 (M); Expenditures, $853,489; Total giving, $571,126; Loans to individuals, totaling $412,126.
Fields of interest: Higher education.
Type of support: Graduate support; Undergraduate support.
Application information: Application form required.
  Initial approach: Letter.
  Deadline(s): Six to eight weeks before each semester begins
  Additional information: Applications should include student's employment history, photograph, transcripts, financial information, three personal references, three academic references, and three business references for applicant and/or parents; Interviews required.
Program description:
  Loan Program: Loans are made to supplement other funds available to students, but never to cover all expenses. The maximum loan amount is $3,000 per calendar year, for a total of no more than $9,000 over a three-year period. Students of good character who have satisfactorily completed two years of college work, graduate students, and students in special fields may apply for loans. Students must show evidence of financial need, and promise of social and financial responsibility. Application should be made for only one year at a time. Loans are made at six percent interest. First payment on account is due no later than three months from date of graduation or withdrawal from college for any reason, military or otherwise. Loan repayment schedule is not less than $50 per month if loan is less than $2,500.
EIN: 640155700

1350
Bruce M. Fellman Charitable Foundation Trust
809 N. 96th St.
Omaha, NE   68114-2538
Contact: Howard M. Kooper, Tr.
Application address: c/o Broadmoor Dev. Co., 801 N. 96th St., Omaha, NE 68114

Foundation type: Independent foundation
Limitations: Scholarships to financially needy individuals pursuing an undergraduate degree from Omaha, NE and surrounding areas.
Financial data: Year ended 12/31/2004. Assets, $352,519 (M); Expenditures, $23,864; Total giving, $23,836; Grants to individuals, 23 grants totaling $23,836 (high: $1,886, low: $500).
Type of support: Undergraduate support.
Application information: Deadline Apr. 1; Contact trust for current application guidelines; Initial approach by letter; Completion of formal application required.
EIN: 476146480

1351
J. Hugh and Earle W. Fellows Memorial Fund
P.O. Box 12950
Pensacola, FL   32576
Contact: Charles A. Atwell, Pres.
Application address: c/o Pensacola Junior College, 1000 College Blvd., Pensacola, FL 32504

Foundation type: Independent foundation
Limitations: Low-interest loans to students of nursing, medicine, medical technology, and the ministry who reside in Escambia, Santa Rosa, Okaloosa, and Bay counties, FL.
Publications: Informational brochure (including application guidelines).
Financial data: Year ended 04/30/2005. Assets, $5,589,298 (M); Expenditures, $83,733; Total giving, $0; Loans to individuals, totaling $161,943.
Fields of interest: Medical school/education; Nursing school/education; Theological school/education.
Type of support: Graduate support; Undergraduate support.
Application information: Applications accepted throughout the year; Initial approach by letter; Completion of formal application required, including financial statement, transcripts, and outline of financial need; Interviews occasionally required.
Program description:
  Student Loan Program: Applicants must be of good moral character, have qualified scholastically and intellectually for the education desired, and been accepted by, or enrolled in, accredited schools in the appropriate fields. Loans to ministerial students are limited to those whose religious beliefs are not in substantial conflict with Episcopal doctrines. Ordinarily, interest is not charged until one year after graduation. Approximately ten new applicants are awarded loans each year.
EIN: 596132238

1352
Gertrude A. Fenner Educational Trust
c/o Associated Banc-Corp.
P.O. Box 408
Neenah, WI   54957-0408
Application address: c/o Lincoln High School, Attn.: Carla Von Haden, 143 S. 8th St., Manitowoc, WI 54220

Foundation type: Independent foundation
Limitations: Scholarships to graduates of Lincoln High School, WI, for undergraduate education.
Financial data: Year ended 12/31/2004. Assets, $234,796 (M); Expenditures, $18,041; Total giving, $14,000; Grants to individuals, totaling $14,000.
Type of support: Support to graduates or students of specific schools.
Application information: Deadline Mar. 17; Completion of formal application required.
EIN: 396741325

1353
Charles H. Feoppel Educational Loan Trust
c/o The Huntington National Bank
P.O. Box 633, WE3013
Charleston, WV   25322-0633   (304) 348-5093
Contact: Carla D. Parsons, Trust Off.
FAX: (304) 348-4552

Foundation type: Independent foundation
Limitations: Student loans to financially needy, unmarried high school graduates who are residents of Harrison County, WV, to pursue higher education at WV institutions. Loans may be used for undergraduate, graduate, or technical education.
Publications: Informational brochure (including application guidelines).
Financial data: Year ended 12/31/2004. Assets, $3,143,216 (M); Expenditures, $41,310; Total giving, $0; Loans to individuals, totaling $97,500.
Fields of interest: Vocational education.
Type of support: Graduate support; Technical education support; Undergraduate support.
Application information: Deadline May 31; Completion of formal application required.
Program description:
  Student Loan Program: Financial need is the prime determinant in granting loans. Loans are given for one year and recipients must reapply each year. Repayment of loans begins six months after the recipient ceases full-time study at a postsecondary institution. The interest rate fluctuates, but always remains well below the federal Guaranteed Student Loan rate.
EIN: 556107185

1354
William Pablo Feraldo Memorial Fund
c/o U.S. Bank, N.A.
P.O. Box 387
St. Louis, MO   63166
Contact: Angela Pearson

Foundation type: Independent foundation
Limitations: Renewable scholarships to male high school graduates residing in the St. Louis, MO, area, for undergraduate education.
Financial data: Year ended 12/31/2004. Assets, $15,380,072 (M); Expenditures, $654,703; Total giving, $534,640; Grants to individuals, 44 grants totaling $104,400 (high: $4,600, low: $2,000).
Fields of interest: Men.
Type of support: Undergraduate support.
Application information: Deadline Feb. 1; Completion of formal application required, including transcript, recommendation, financial information, and copy of student's or parent's tax return.
EIN: 436019398

1355
Percy B. Ferebee Endowment
c/o Wachovia Bank, N.A.
100 N. Main St., 13th Fl.
Winston-Salem, NC   27150   (800) 576-5135
Contact: Shane Thomas
Scholarship Fund URL: http://www.wachoviascholars.com/ferb/csaw_ferebee_deadline.php

Foundation type: Independent foundation
Limitations: Scholarships to residents of the NC counties of Cherokee, Clay, Graham, Jackson, Macon, and Swain, and the Cherokee Indian Reservation, for study only at NC colleges and universities.
Publications: Informational brochure (including application guidelines).
Financial data: Year ended 12/31/2003. Assets, $3,523,526 (M); Expenditures, $174,586; Total giving, $146,500; Grants to individuals, 65 grants totaling $108,000 (high: $4,000, low: $1,000).

Fields of interest: Native Americans/American Indians.
Type of support: Scholarships—to individuals.
Application information: Applications accepted. Application form required.
  Initial approach: Letter.
  Deadline(s): Feb. 15 for scholarships and Oct. 1 for grants
  Additional information: Interviews required; Applications made to high school principals and guidance counselors in the eligible counties.
Program description:
  Scholarship Program: Scholarships are granted annually to worthy young men and women and will not exceed the cost of tuition, books, fees, and reasonable living and travel expenses. Applications from candidates recommended by the high schools are forwarded to the trustee. The committee takes into consideration the respective abilities, educational goals, career ambitions, and financial needs of the applicants. The amount of each scholarship and the manner in which it will be paid is determined by the awards committee. A scholarship may be renewed annually if the student is making satisfactory academic progress.
EIN: 566118992

1356
Enrico Fermi Educational Fund of Yonkers, Inc.
c/o Anthony Maddalena
13 Ann Marie Pl.
Yonkers, NY 10703
Application address: c/o Rosalind Mariani, Scholarship Comm., 67 Garfield St., Yonkers, NY 10701

Foundation type: Independent foundation
Limitations: Scholarships and awards to Italian-American high school students in Yonkers, NY.
Financial data: Year ended 06/30/2005. Assets, $243,287 (M); Expenditures, $37,159; Total giving, $26,500; Grants to individuals, totaling $26,500.
Fields of interest: Arts education; Science.
Type of support: Undergraduate support.
Application information: Deadline Feb. 1; Initial approach by letter requesting application, including a brief resume and academic qualifications; Completion of formal application required.
Program description:
  Scholarship Program: In addition to scholarships to Italian-Americans from Yonkers, the fund grants two science awards of $1,000 each to a resident of NJ and a resident of Westchester County, NY. One fine arts award of $1,000 is given annually on the basis of audition material.
EIN: 136159001

1357
Robert W. & Caroline A. Fernstrum Scholarship Foundation Trust
P.O. Box 137
Marinette, WI 54143
Application address: c/o Superintendent of Schools, 1230 13th St., Menominee, MI 49858, tel.: (906) 863-9951

Foundation type: Independent foundation
Limitations: Scholarships to graduating seniors of Menominee High School, MI, for higher education.
Financial data: Year ended 12/31/2004. Assets, $627,058 (M); Expenditures, $32,931;

Total giving, $27,000; Grants to individuals, totaling $27,000.
Type of support: Support to graduates or students of specific schools; Undergraduate support.
Application information: Application form required.
  Deadline(s): Apr. 17
  Additional information: Application should include class rank, GPA, SAT and ACT scores.
EIN: 396625465

1358
The Ferraro Foundation for Science and the Disabled, Inc.
77 Povershon Rd.
Nutley, NJ 07110
FAX: (201) 664-6693; URL: http://www.theferrarofoundation.org

Foundation type: Independent foundation
Limitations: Scholarships to disabled individuals primarily in DC and NJ, for the study of biology, chemistry, physics, engineering, biotechnology, allied health sciences and medicine.
Financial data: Year ended 12/31/2004. Assets, $0 (M); Expenditures, $32,204; Total giving, $16,024; Grants to individuals, totaling $7,250.
Fields of interest: Medical school/education; Engineering school/education; Public health school/education; Health sciences school/education; Science; Disabilities, people with.
Type of support: Undergraduate support.
Application information: Contact foundation for current application deadline/guidelines.
EIN: 223537772

1359
The Luis A. Ferre Foundation, Inc.
P.O. Box 9066590
San Juan, PR 00906-6590 (787) 848-0505
Contact: Hiromi Shiba, Exec. Dir.

Foundation type: Public charity
Limitations: Scholarships to residents of PR.
Publications: Financial statement.
Financial data: Year ended 12/31/2003. Assets, $54,639,906 (M); Expenditures, $4,274,464; Total giving, $45,071.
Type of support: Scholarships—to individuals.
Application information: Applications not accepted.
EIN: 660235625

1360
Ferree Educational & Welfare Fund
P.O. Box 2207
Asheboro, NC 27204-2207 (336) 629-2040
Contact: Linda R. Cranford, Exec. Dir.
E-mail: sprouse@asheboro.com

Foundation type: Independent foundation
Limitations: Student loans, up to $1,000, and scholarships, up to $2,000, to residents of Randolph County, NC, who have a minimum GPA of 2.0.
Financial data: Year ended 12/31/2004. Assets, $2,558,246 (M); Expenditures, $80,297; Total giving, $37,500; Grants to individuals, totaling $37,500; Loans to individuals, totaling $108,500. Subtotal for student loans—to individuals: loans totaling $108,500. Subtotal for scholarships—to individuals: 19 grants totaling $37,500 (high: $2,000, low: $1,500).

Type of support: Scholarships—to individuals; Student loans—to individuals.
Application information: Applications accepted. Application form required.
  Deadline(s): May 15
  Additional information: Application must include financial information, letter of acceptance from school to be attended, and personal statement. Interviews required; All applicants notified in June.
Program description:
  Student Loan Program: Consideration for student loans is based on requirements similar to those of federal government loans. Loans are granted at rates between one percent and six percent, only to students attending institutions of higher learning, and are limited to $1,000 per student per academic year. No interest is charged while students are enrolled full-time. Loans are for one year only, so students must reapply each year. Each applicant is responsible for making an appointment for an interview which must be completed before May 10. Students who are reapplying may wish to have an interview during spring break.
EIN: 566062560

1361
The Clifford G. and Grace A. Ferris Foundation
c/o Marshall & Ilsley Bank
1000 N. Water St.
Milwaukee, WI 53202
Application address: c/o David Guillion, Marshall & Ilsley Bank, 500 3rd St., P.O. Box 209, Wausau, WI 54402

Foundation type: Independent foundation
Limitations: Scholarships to graduating seniors of Wausau, WI, high schools.
Financial data: Year ended 05/31/2005. Assets, $239,407 (M); Expenditures, $11,858; Total giving, $8,000; Grants to individuals, totaling $8,000.
Type of support: Support to graduates or students of specific schools; Undergraduate support.
Application information: Applications by letter accepted throughout the year.
EIN: 396716441

1362
Fieldcrest Cannon Foundation
(formerly Fieldcrest Foundation)
c/o Dir.
1 Lake Circle Dr.
Kannapolis, NC 28081-3435 (704) 939-2775
Contact: Karen Cobb

Foundation type: Company-sponsored foundation
Limitations: Scholarships limited to children of employees of Fieldcrest Cannon, Inc., in NC and SC.
Financial data: Year ended 12/31/2003. Assets, $798,423 (M); Expenditures, $402,050; Total giving, $401,800; Grants to individuals, totaling $401,800.
Type of support: Employee-related scholarships.
Application information:
  Deadline(s): Mar. 1
EIN: 566046659

1363
Laura Fields Trust
P.O. Box 2394
Lawton, OK 73502-2394
Contact: Jay Dee Fountain, Mgr.

Foundation type: Independent foundation
Limitations: Scholarships to the top two students in each of the Comanche County, OK, high schools only to attend Cameron University, OK. Student loans to residents of southwest OK.
Publications: Annual report.
Financial data: Year ended 06/30/2005. Assets, $2,077,508 (M); Expenditures, $121,060; Total giving, $79,896; Loans to individuals, totaling $54,100.
Fields of interest: Vocational education.
Type of support: Support to graduates or students of specific schools; Undergraduate support.
Application information: Application form required.
　Initial approach: Letter.
　Additional information: Applications accepted throughout the year.
Program description:
　Scholarships and Loans:
　· Student Loan Program: Provides loans to residents of southwest OK to attend accredited U.S. colleges and universities
　· Cameron University Valedictorian/ Salutatorian Scholarship Program: Provides first-year scholarships only to the top two students in each of the Comanche County, OK, high schools to attend Cameron University
　· Speech Scholarships: Given to deserving debate students at Cameron University
Applicants who do not meet the residency requirements will not be considered for scholarships or loans.
EIN: 736095854

1364
Files Foundation
P.O. Box 429
Anahuac, TX　77514-0429　(409) 267-3171
Contact: Douglas M. Cameron, Pres.

Foundation type: Independent foundation
Limitations: Scholarships to graduating seniors of Chambers County, TX, high schools.
Publications: Application guidelines; Financial statement; Program policy statement.
Financial data: Year ended 12/31/2002. Assets, $196,394 (M); Expenditures, $38,362; Total giving, $30,453; Grants to individuals, 19 grants totaling $19,453 (high: $2,000, low: $500).
Type of support: Support to graduates or students of specific schools; Undergraduate support.
Application information: Deadline Mar. 1; Completion of formal application required, including transcript, financial statement, and three references; Interviews required.
EIN: 741921896

1365
Findlay Hancock County Community Foundation
101 W. Sandusky St., Ste. 207
Findlay, OH　45840　(419) 425-1100
Contact: Barbara Deerhake, Exec. Dir.; Julie Alford, Financial Off.; for scholarships: Marie Swaisgood
For scholarships:
mswaisgood@community-foundation.com
FAX: (419) 425-9339;
E-mail: commfdn@bright.net; URL: http:// www.community-foundation.com

Foundation type: Community foundation
Limitations: Scholarships to residents of Hancock County, OH.

Publications: Application guidelines; Annual report; Financial statement; Informational brochure; Informational brochure (including application guidelines).
Financial data: Year ended 12/31/2004. Assets, $29,798,247 (M); Expenditures, $2,323,566; Total giving, $1,808,629; Grants to individuals, 213 grants totaling $218,387 (high: $2,500, low: $100).
Type of support: Undergraduate support.
Application information: Applications accepted. Application form required. Application form available on the grantmaker's Web site.
　Initial approach: E-mail.
　Copies of proposal: 2
　Deadline(s): Apr. 1
　Applicants should submit the following:
　　1) Transcripts
　　2) SAT
　　3) SAR
　　4) Letter(s) of recommendation
　　5) GPA
　　6) FAFSA
　　7) Essay
　　8) Curriculum vitae
　　9) Budget Information
　　10) ACT
　Additional information: See Web site for complete listing of scholarship programs.
EIN: 341713261

1366
The Findlay-Conso Education Foundation
c/o Conso Products, Inc.
244 Shopping Ave., Ste. 175
Sarasota, FL　34237
Contact: J. Cary Findlay, Pres.
Application address: 513 N. Duncan Bypass, Union, SC 29379, tel.: (864) 427-9004

Foundation type: Independent foundation
Limitations: Scholarships to children and grandchildren of employees of the Conso Products Co. in SC for higher education.
Financial data: Year ended 12/31/2004. Assets, $41,546 (M); Expenditures, $72,642; Total giving, $64,848; Grants to individuals, totaling $64,848.
Type of support: Employee-related scholarships.
Application information: Applications accepted Feb. 1 through June 15; Completion of formal application required.
EIN: 582315882

1367
Morris Fingersh Scholarship Fund
(formerly Morris Fingersh Charitable Trust Fund)
c/o UMB Bank, N.A.
P.O. Box 419692
Kansas City, MO　64141-6692
Application address: c/o Hyman-Brand Hebrew Academy, 5901 College Blvd., Overland Park, KS 66211

Foundation type: Independent foundation
Limitations: Scholarships to students attending the Hyman Brand Hebrew Academy in Overland Park, KS.
Financial data: Year ended 03/31/2005. Assets, $291,808 (M); Expenditures, $15,588; Total giving, $12,099; Grants to individuals, totaling $12,099.
Fields of interest: Elementary school/education; Secondary school/education; Jewish agencies & temples.

Type of support: Scholarships—to individuals; Support to graduates or students of specific schools.
Application information: Application form not required.
　Deadline(s): June 1.
　Additional information: Application by letter.
Program description:
　Fingersh Scholarship Fund: The Morris Fingersh Scholarships are administered as two separate funds through different banks. While the specific fiscal figures differ, the programs, application address, and contact person are the same. Both funds are expressly for the purpose of providing scholarships to students in grades K-12 to attend the Hyman Brand Hebrew Academy in Overland Park, KS.
EIN: 510214040

1368
Finis Heidel Trust
P.O. Box 165
Hobbs, NM　88241-0165　(505) 392-0503
Contact: Vikki Arnwine, Exec. Dir.

Foundation type: Independent foundation
Limitations: Scholarships to graduates of Lea County high schools, NM, for higher education. Recipient may pursue a two-year associate degree, a four-year academic degree, or a vocational certificate at an accredited NM school.
Financial data: Year ended 12/31/2004. Assets, $1,652,780 (M); Expenditures, $97,675; Total giving, $71,000; Grants to individuals, totaling $71,000.
Type of support: Technical education support; Undergraduate support.
Application information: Deadline Feb. 21; Completion of formal application required.
EIN: 856117343

1369
Henry J. & Helen Finkbeiner Memorial Fund for Benton High School Graduates
422 N. Main St.
Benton, AR　72015
Contact: Fred E. Briner, Tr.

Foundation type: Independent foundation
Limitations: Scholarships to Benton High School, AR, seniors for higher education.
Financial data: Year ended 12/31/2004. Assets, $236,765 (M); Expenditures, $13,678; Total giving, $13,000; Grants to individuals, totaling $13,000.
Type of support: Support to graduates or students of specific schools; Undergraduate support.
Application information: Contact fund for current application deadline; Completion of formal application required, including transcripts.
EIN: 710557061

1370
Curtis Finlay Foundation, Inc.
P.O. Box 298
Brewton, AL　36427　(251) 867-7706
Contact: Richard D. Finlay, Dir.

Foundation type: Independent foundation
Limitations: Scholarships to residents of Escambia County, AL, and students attending Jefferson Davis Community College, Brewton, AL.
Financial data: Year ended 12/31/2004. Assets, $10,575,451 (M); Expenditures,

$605,336; Total giving, $440,500; Grants to individuals, 11 grants totaling $43,000 (high: $4,000, low: $3,000).
Type of support: Support to graduates or students of specific schools; Undergraduate support.
Application information: Applications accepted throughout the year; Contact foundation for current application guidelines.
EIN: 631080992

1371
The Rose McFarland Finley Foundation
c/o Wachovia Wealth Mgmt.
255 S. County Rd. FL 6091
Palm Beach, FL 33480
Scholarship application address: 1053 Palmetto Ave., Sebastian, FL 32958, tel.: (772) 589-4502

Foundation type: Operating foundation
Limitations: Scholarships to graduates of schools in Indian River County, FL.
Financial data: Year ended 04/30/2004. Assets, $1,363,164 (M); Expenditures, $115,992; Total giving, $86,250.
Type of support: Support to graduates or students of specific schools; Undergraduate support.
Application information: Deadline Mar. 15; Completion of formal application required, including transcripts, FAFSA report, and parents' tax returns.
EIN: 237414902

1372
The Dred and Lula Finnell Trust
c/o Norman Bentley
P.O. Box 204
Keytesville, MO 65261   (660) 288-3233

Foundation type: Independent foundation
Limitations: Scholarships to graduates of the Keytesville Township School District, MO.
Financial data: Year ended 12/31/2004. Assets, $2,312,034 (M); Expenditures, $108,204; Total giving, $82,796; Grants to individuals, totaling $82,796.
Type of support: Support to graduates or students of specific schools; Undergraduate support.
Application information: Deadline last Fri. in June for fall semester and last Fri. in Nov. for spring semester; Contact trust for current application guidelines.
EIN: 431589370

1373
J. B. Firestone Charitable Trust
c/o FirstMerit Bank, N.A.
106 S. Main St., Ste. 1600
Akron, OH 44308
Contact: Corinne F. Neff, Trust Off., FirstMerit Bank, N.A.
Application address: 105 Court St., ELY20, Elyria, OH 44035

Foundation type: Independent foundation
Limitations: Student loans to students and alumni of Black River High School, OH.
Financial data: Year ended 12/31/2004. Assets, $1,665,801 (M); Expenditures, $139,149; Total giving, $126,046.
Type of support: Student loans—to individuals; Support to graduates or students of specific schools.
Application information: Applications accepted throughout the year; Completion of formal

application required, including applicant's and parents' financial information.
EIN: 346577308

1374
First Command Educational Foundation
(formerly USPA & IRA Educational Foundation)
P.O. Box 901091
Fort Worth, TX 76101
Contact: Pam Elliott
E-mail: edufoundation@firstcommand.org;
URL: http://www.firstcommand.org

Foundation type: Independent foundation
Limitations: Undergraduate scholarships to children of active duty, retired, and deceased military personnel. The maximum scholarship amount is $3,000.
Financial data: Year ended 12/31/2003. Assets, $130,606 (L); Expenditures, $864,329; Total giving, $193,000.
Fields of interest: Military/veterans' organizations.
Type of support: Undergraduate support.
Application information: Application form required.
  Deadline(s): None
  Applicants should submit the following:
    1) Class rank
    2) SAT
    3) GPA
    4) ACT
  Additional information: Applications are solicited by the officers' wives clubs of local military officers.
EIN: 751973894

1375
First Data Western Union Foundation
6200 S. Quebec St., Ste. 370AU
Greenwood Village, CO 80111   (303) 967-6606
Contact: Luella Chavez D'Angelo, Pres.
FAX: (303) 967-6492;
E-mail: luella.dangelo@firstdata.com; Application address for organizations located outside the U.S.: Ellen Y. Brown, Sr. Prog. Dir., 6200 S. Quebec St., Ste. 370AU, Greenwood Village, CO 80111, tel.: (303) 967-6535; Additional tel.: (303) 967-6305; URL: http://www.firstdatawesternunion.org

Foundation type: Operating foundation
Limitations: Scholarships to non-traditional students for higher education.
Publications: Annual report.
Financial data: Year ended 12/31/2004. Assets, $2,783,846 (M); Expenditures, $9,220,047; Total giving, $8,393,382; Grants to individuals, 178 grants totaling $257,174 (high: $5,000, low: $500).
Type of support: Scholarships—to individuals; Technical education support; Undergraduate support.
Application information: Application form required.
  Copies of proposal: 1
  Deadline(s): June 1 and Dec. 1
  Applicants should submit the following:
    1) Transcripts
    2) SAT
    3) Letter(s) of recommendation
    4) GPA
    5) Financial information
    6) Essay
    7) ACT
  Additional information: Application available on Web site; Application should be submitted online; Application attachments may be sent by mail.

Program description:
  Scholarship Program: Recipients must have overcome personal challenges, exemplify initiative, exhibit a commitment to learning and working hard, and demonstrate financial need. The foundation looks beyond criteria such as GPA, SAT scores, class rank or career choice. Special consideration is given to applicants who show academic promise and a strong desire for advancing their educational and career goals. Scholarships are one-time and range from $500 to $3,000. Applicants can re-apply each year.
EIN: 311738614

1376
First Gaston Foundation, Inc.
(formerly Myers-Ti-Caro Foundation, Inc.)
P.O. Box 2696
Gastonia, NC 28053   (704) 864-9242
Contact: B. Frank Matthews II, Chair.

Foundation type: Independent foundation
Limitations: Scholarships to graduating seniors at Gaston County High School, NC.
Financial data: Year ended 09/30/2004. Assets, $9,406,082 (M); Expenditures, $333,374; Total giving, $299,093; Grants to individuals, 44 grants totaling $143,693 (high: $6,000, low: $331).
Type of support: Support to graduates or students of specific schools; Undergraduate support.
Application information: Applications accepted throughout the year; Completion of formal application required, including extracurricular and civic activities and employment history.
EIN: 560770083

1377
Karl Fischer Trust
c/o Mellon Financial Corp.
P.O. Box 185
Pittsburgh, PA 15230-0185
Contact: Sandra Brown-McMullen, V.P., Mellon Financial Corp.
Application address: 1 Boston Pl., Boston, MA 02106, tel.: (617) 722-3891

Foundation type: Independent foundation
Limitations: Scholarships primarily to residents of Marblehead, Salem, and Swampscott, MA.
Financial data: Year ended 08/31/2003. Assets, $586,394 (M); Expenditures, $33,870; Total giving, $26,000; Grants to individuals, 24 grants totaling $26,000 (high: $2,000, low: $1,000).
Type of support: Scholarships—to individuals.
Application information: Contact trust for current application deadline/guidelines; Initial approach by letter.
EIN: 046411644

1378
Velma Klamm & Ruth Fishburn Foundation
18 N. Adair St.
Pryor, OK 74361-2433
Contact: Julia L. Neftzger, V.P.
Application address: Court Pl. and N. Vann, Pryor, OK 74361, tel.: (918) 825-0332

Foundation type: Independent foundation
Limitations: College scholarships to high school students from Pryor and Adair, OK.
Financial data: Year ended 12/31/2004. Assets, $882,841 (M); Expenditures, $44,545;

Total giving, $32,000; Grants to individuals, 6 grants totaling $32,000 (high: $8,000, low: $8,000).
Type of support: Undergraduate support.
Application information: Applications accepted. Application form required.
Deadline(s): Apr. 30
Additional information: Application should include transcripts.
EIN: 731575833

1379
The Myron Fishel Scholarship Trust
c/o U.S. Bank, N.A.
P.O. Box 400
Cambridge, OH 43725-0400
Contact: Jeffrey C. East, Tr.
Application address: 819 Wheeling Ave., Cambridge, OH 43725; tel.: (740) 432-1334

Foundation type: Independent foundation
Limitations: Scholarships to financially needy high school seniors in Guernsey, OH, for undergraduate and graduate study at accredited colleges and universities. The trust considers candidates who are residents of other counties in OH if funds are available.
Financial data: Year ended 09/30/2004. Assets, $648,423 (M); Expenditures, $31,440; Total giving, $30,000; Grants to individuals, 15 grants totaling $30,000 (high: $7,500, low: $1,500).
Type of support: Graduate support; Undergraduate support.
Application information: Deadline Apr.; Completion of formal application required; Interviews may be required.
Program description:
Scholarship Program: Candidates are evaluated on the basis of academic achievement, financial need, tuition costs, and the ability of the applicant to hold a job during schooling. Scholarships are renewable.
EIN: 237407789

1380
Fisher Broadcasting Minority Scholarship Fund
(formerly KOMO Radio and Television Minority Scholarship Fund)
100 4th Ave. N., Ste. 513
Seattle, WA 98109 (206) 404-6766
Contact: Judy Endejan, Legal Counsel; Ann Marie Hitchcock, Human Resources Specialist
Application address: 100 4th Ave. N., Ste. 510, Seattle, WA 98121
FAX: (206) 404-6013; E-mail: jendejan@fsci.com; URL: http://www.fsci.com/x100.xml

Foundation type: Company-sponsored foundation
Limitations: Scholarships to minority broadcasting students attending WA, OR, ID, and MT schools.
Publications: Informational brochure.
Financial data: Year ended 12/31/2004. Assets, $278,052 (M); Expenditures, $14,000; Total giving, $14,000; Grants to individuals, 4 grants totaling $14,000 (high: $5,000, low: $1,000).
Fields of interest: Media/communications; Television; Radio; Minorities.
Type of support: Technical education support; Undergraduate support.
Application information: Application form required.
Deadline(s): Apr. 30
Applicants should submit the following:

1) Transcripts
2) Letter(s) of recommendation
3) Essay
Additional information: Interviews required.
Program description:
Minority Scholarship Fund: Applicants must be non-white sophomores enrolled in a broadcast, marketing or journalism curriculum at a four-year college or university; or a broadcast curriculum at a community college or vocational-technical school. Applicants must have a minimum 2.5 GPA in broadcast, marketing, or journalism courses, and must be U.S. citizens.
EIN: 911500276

1381
The Steven and Lynn Fisher Foundation
1310 W. Island Cir.
Chandler, AZ 85248-3700 (480) 899-2907
Contact: Steven D. Fisher, Pres.

Foundation type: Independent foundation
Limitations: Scholarships to individuals for higher education.
Financial data: Year ended 12/31/2004. Assets, $0 (M); Expenditures, $38,255; Total giving, $37,304; Grants to individuals, totaling $36,904.
Type of support: Scholarships—to individuals.
Application information: Applications by letter accepted throughout the year.
EIN: 860686929

1382
Fisher House Foundation, Inc.
1401 Rockville Pike, Ste. 600
Rockville, MD 20852 (301) 294-8560
Contact: David A. Coker, Exec. Dir.
FAX: (301) 294-8562;
E-mail: info@fisherhouse.org; Additional tel.: (888) 294-8560; URL: http://www.fisherhouse.org

Foundation type: Public charity
Limitations: Scholarships to children of active duty military personnel, reserve/guard members, and retired commissary customers.
Financial data: Year ended 12/31/2004. Assets, $9,701,721 (M); Expenditures, $5,022,659; Total giving, $3,981,723.
Fields of interest: Military/veterans' organizations.
Type of support: Undergraduate support.
Application information: Applications accepted. Application form required. Application form available on the grantmaker's Web site.
Deadline(s): Feb. 16
Applicants should submit the following:
1) Transcripts
2) Letter(s) of recommendation
3) Essay
Additional information: Applications by e-mail not accepted; See Web-site for further application or program information.
Program description:
Scholarship: One $1,500 scholarship will be awarded at every commissary location where qualified applications are received. The scholarship provides for payment of tuition, books, lab fees, and room and board. Applicant must have a cumulative 3.0 GPA or above on a 4.0 basis.
EIN: 113158401

1383
T. S. Fitch Memorial Scholarship Fund
c/o Mellon Financial Corp.
P.O. Box 185
Pittsburgh, PA 15230-0185 (412) 234-0023
Contact: Laurie Moritz, Trust Off., Mellon Financial Corp.
Application address: c/o 1 Mellon Bank Ctr., 500 Grant St., Ste. 3825, Pittsburgh, PA 15259

Foundation type: Independent foundation
Limitations: Scholarships to students for higher education.
Financial data: Year ended 12/31/2004. Assets, $256,059 (M); Expenditures, $12,205; Total giving, $11,000; Grants to individuals, 6 grants totaling $11,000 (high: $2,357, low: $1,310).
Fields of interest: Higher education.
Type of support: Undergraduate support.
Application information: Contact fund for current application deadline/guidelines.
EIN: 256123538

1384
Father James M. Fitzgerald Scholarship Trust
c/o National City Bank of the Midwest
P.O. Box 94651
Cleveland, OH 44101-4651
Application address: 301 S.W. Adams, Peoria, IL 61652, tel.: (309) 655-5322

Foundation type: Independent foundation
Limitations: Scholarships to priesthood students attending Catholic colleges and universities, and to the two highest-ranking male and female students at St. Mark's Catholic School, Peoria, IL, enrolling in any Roman Catholic high school.
Financial data: Year ended 12/31/2004. Assets, $2,927,432 (M); Expenditures, $116,327; Total giving, $107,977.
Fields of interest: Secondary school/education; Theological school/education; Roman Catholic agencies & churches.
Type of support: Scholarships—to individuals; Support to graduates or students of specific schools; Precollege support.
Application information:
Initial approach: Letter indicating desire to enroll and acceptance as a seminarian.
Deadline(s): None.
EIN: 376050189

1385
Rev. William J. Fitzpatrick Memorial Scholarship Fund
c/o M&T Bank
21 E. Market St.
York, PA 17401 (717) 852-3051
Application address: c/o York Catholic High School, Attn.: Principal, 601 Springettsbury Ave., York, PA 17403

Foundation type: Independent foundation
Limitations: Scholarships to graduates of York Catholic High School, PA, for higher education in the field of engineering or scientific studies related to engineering.
Financial data: Year ended 12/31/2004. Assets, $273,099 (M); Expenditures, $15,841; Total giving, $12,250; Grants to individuals, totaling $12,250.
Fields of interest: Engineering school/education.
Type of support: Support to graduates or students of specific schools; Undergraduate support.

Application information: Deadline Mar. 1; Completion of formal application required.
EIN: 236692323

1386

Alois A. and Nina M. Fix Scholarship Fund

c/o John W. Drew
308 Fox Cir.
Tomah, WI 54660
Application address: c/o Tomah Senior High School, Attn.: Ronald Geurkink, Counselor, Tomah, WI 54660, tel.: (608) 372-5986

Foundation type: Independent foundation
Limitations: Scholarships to graduates of Tomah Senior High School, WI.
Financial data: Year ended 07/31/2005. Assets, $243,718 (M); Expenditures, $41,987; Total giving, $35,750; Grants to individuals, totaling $35,750.
Type of support: Support to graduates or students of specific schools; Undergraduate support.
Application information: Deadline Mar. 23; Completion of formal application required.
EIN: 396257879

1387

Flathead Educational Foundation

P.O. Box 759
Kalispell, MT 59903 (406) 752-6644
Application address: P.O. Box 7130, Kalispell, MT 59901, tel.: (406) 752-5202

Foundation type: Independent foundation
Limitations: Scholarships by nomination only to graduating students attending high school in Flathead County, MT.
Financial data: Year ended 12/31/2003. Assets, $388,090 (M); Expenditures, $14,582; Total giving, $10,675; Grants to individuals, 42 grants totaling $10,675 (high: $750, low: $250).
Type of support: Support to graduates or students of specific schools; Awards/grants by nomination only; Undergraduate support.
Application information:
Deadline(s): Contact foundation for current application deadline
Program description:
Scholarship Program: Principals and heads of the guidance departments will submit the names of eligible applicants to the selection committee, which will then choose recipients based on worth and need. Eligible students will have minimum 2.5 GPAs, but the selection committee may select persons having a GPA of not less than 2.0 if the student has outstanding qualities of leadership, scientific or forensic ability, good citizenship and community participation, and a strong potential for improvement.
EIN: 816013249

1388

The Flatirons Foundation

950 Cemetary Ln.
Aspen, CO 81611 (970) 920-4653
Contact: Rob Gile, Tr.

Foundation type: Operating foundation
Limitations: Scholarships to graduates of Aspen High School, CO.
Financial data: Year ended 12/31/2004. Assets, $262,790 (M); Expenditures, $15,722; Total giving, $15,000; Grants to individuals, 4

grants totaling $13,000 (high: $6,000, low: $1,500).
Type of support: Support to graduates or students of specific schools; Undergraduate support.
Application information: Applications accepted. Application form required.
Initial approach: Letter from high school seniors.
Deadline(s): May 1
Additional information: Application should include financial information; Applications from outside the stated limitations will not be considered.
EIN: 840563062

1389

Clark Flegal Educational Trust

c/o County National Bank, Trust Dept.
P.O. Box 42
Clearfield, PA 16830-0042 (814) 765-1683

Foundation type: Independent foundation
Limitations: Educational loans to residents of Clearfield, PA.
Financial data: Year ended 10/31/2004. Assets, $366,569 (M); Expenditures, $6,648; Total giving, $0; Loans to individuals, totaling $7,000.
Type of support: Student loans—to individuals.
Application information: Applications accepted throughout the year; Contact trust for current application guidelines.
Program description:
Loan Program: Maximum total loan amount is $4,000 per person. No interest is charged if loan is repaid within two years of termination of schooling. Minimum monthly payment is $35. Interest is charged at the rate of six percent per annum throughout the two- to five-year period after termination of schooling. After the five-year period, interest is charged at the rate of ten percent per annum.
EIN: 256030462

1390

Foreman Fleisher Trust

(also known as Foreman Fleisher Trust No. 2)
c/o PNC Advisors
620 Liberty Ave., P2-PTPP-10-2
Pittsburgh, PA 15222-2705
Contact: Richard Nassau
Application address: c/o The Federation of Jewish Agencies of Greater Philadelphia, 2100 Arch St., Philadelphia, PA 19103-1300

Foundation type: Independent foundation
Limitations: Scholarships to Jewish women who seek professional education, primarily in PA.
Financial data: Year ended 09/30/2002. Assets, $392,642 (M); Expenditures, $27,448; Total giving, $25,400; Grants to individuals, 7 grants totaling $25,400 (high: $7,000, low: $1,000).
Fields of interest: Jewish agencies & temples; Women.
Type of support: Scholarships—to individuals.
Application information: Applications by letter accepted throughout the year.
EIN: 236201637

1391

Albert W. Fleming Insurance Trust

c/o Hale & Dorr, LLP
P.O. Box 9350
Boston, MA 02114 (617) 526-6054
Contact: Anne Marie Towle
E-mail: annemarie.towle@haledorr.com

Foundation type: Independent foundation
Limitations: Scholarships to individuals who are enrolled or have been accepted for enrollment at any college or university in the U.S. Preference is given to residents of Mills and Watertown, MA.
Publications: Application guidelines.
Financial data: Year ended 10/31/2004. Assets, $388,385 (M); Expenditures, $29,988; Total giving, $26,000; Grants to individuals, totaling $26,000.
Type of support: Undergraduate support.
Application information: Deadline Apr. 30; Initial approach by letter; Completion of formal application required, including personal statement, transcripts, and one recommendation.
EIN: 046646727

1392

Mary E. Fleming & John J. Fleming Scholarship Trust for Holy Cross College

29 Sohier St.
Cohasset, MA 02025
Contact: Owen O'Malley, Tr.

Foundation type: Independent foundation
Limitations: Scholarships to residents of Cohasset, MA, who have been admitted to or are enrolled at College of the Holy Cross.
Financial data: Year ended 12/31/2004. Assets, $264,501 (M); Expenditures, $15,601; Total giving, $14,000; Grants to individuals, totaling $14,000.
Type of support: Scholarships—to individuals; Support to graduates or students of specific schools.
Application information: Applications by letter describing qualifications accepted throughout the year.
EIN: 223115094

1393

Fleshman Memorial Scholarship Fund

c/o JPMorgan Chase Bank, N.A
P.O. Box 1308
Milwaukee, WI 53201
Application address: c/o Jeffersonville High School, Jeffersonville, IN 47130

Foundation type: Independent foundation
Limitations: Scholarships to graduating students attending Jeffersonville High School, IN, who are not studying physical education.
Financial data: Year ended 02/29/2004. Assets, $425,790 (M); Expenditures, $53,107; Total giving, $42,211; Grants to individuals, 7 grants totaling $42,211 (high: $7,727, low: $2,520).
Type of support: Support to graduates or students of specific schools; Undergraduate support.
Application information: Deadline Mar. 1; Completion of formal application required.
EIN: 356639411

1394
The Flinn Foundation

1802 N. Central Ave.
Phoenix, AZ 85004-1506 (602) 744-6800
Contact: John W. Murphy, C.E.O.
FAX: (602) 744-6815; E-mail: info@flinn.org; E-mail for scholarship information: fscholars@flinn.org;
URL: http://www.flinn.org

Foundation type: Independent foundation
Limitations: Undergraduate scholarships to AZ residents.
Publications: Annual report; Financial statement; Newsletter; Occasional report.
Financial data: Year ended 12/31/2004.
Assets, $178,440,413 (M); Expenditures, $11,871,476; Total giving, $7,801,343.
Fields of interest: University.
Type of support: Undergraduate support.
Application information: Application form required. Application form available on the grantmaker's Web site.
Deadline(s): Oct. 26
Applicants should submit the following:
   1) Transcripts
   2) GPA
   3) ACT
   4) SAT
Program description:
Flinn Scholars Program: Each year the foundation selects 20 outstanding AZ high school graduates and provides them with a four-year scholarship and personal enrichment opportunity at any AZ university. The scholars, who apply directly to the foundation, are selected solely on merit. Selections are made by a distinguished advisory committee. The goal of the program is to provide students with an undergraduate educational experience without equal and to enable AZ's universities to strengthen their educational programs for gifted students. Applicants must rank in the top 5 percent of their graduating class; have a 3.5 GPA in academic subjects; score a minimum of 1280 on the SAT I or 29 on the ACT; participate in a breadth of extracurricular activities and demonstrate leadership in them; and be a U.S. citizen and have lived in AZ the prior two years. Scholars receive the full cost of tuition and fees for four years at an AZ university; a three-week seminar in Budapest, Hungary, on democratization issues in central and eastern Europe, plus an additional summer or semester of study-related travel abroad; personal mentor assistance by a university faculty member; and opportunities to meet leaders in business, government, education, and the arts.
EIN: 860421476

1395
Mr. & Mrs. Charles N. Flint Scholarship Endowment Fund

(formerly The Ebell of Los Angeles/Charles N. Flint Scholarship Endowment Fund)
743 S. Lucerne Blvd.
Los Angeles, CA 90005-3707 (323) 931-1277
FAX: (323) 937-0272;
E-mail: scholarship@ebellla.com; URL: http://www.ebellla.com

Foundation type: Independent foundation
Limitations: Undergraduate scholarships to full-time students attending school in Los Angeles County, CA, who are U.S. citizens. Applicants must be sophomores or second-term freshmen, in financial need, and have at least a 3.25 GPA.
Financial data: Year ended 06/30/2004.
Assets, $2,176,559 (M); Expenditures,

$123,862; Total giving, $83,750; Grants to individuals, totaling $83,750.
Fields of interest: Higher education.
Type of support: Technical education support; Undergraduate support.
Application information: Application form required.
Initial approach: E-mail.
Deadline(s): Mar. 15
Applicants should submit the following:
   1) Letter(s) of recommendation
   2) Essay
   3) Financial information
   4) Transcripts
   5) GPA
Additional information: Interviews required; Applications available from the fund or the financial aid office of student's university or college.
Program description:
Scholarship Fund: Scholarships are awarded on the basis of grades, character, financial need, and leadership. Generally, scholarship payments are made in monthly installments from September to June. Scholarships are renewable through the completion of undergraduate study. This scholarship program is administered as two separate funds, The Ebell of Los Angeles Scholarship Endowment Fund and the Mr. and Mrs. Charles N. Flint Scholarship Endowment Fund. While the specific fiscal figures for each fund differ, the programs, application procedures, contact person, and address are identical.
EIN: 956100327

1396
Floriculture Industry Research and Scholarship Trust

(formerly Bedding Plants Foundation)
P.O. Box 280
East Lansing, MI 48826-0280 (517) 333-4617
Contact: William T. Willbrandt, Exec. Dir.
FAX: (517) 333-4944;
E-mail: first@firstinfloriculture.org; URL: http://www.firstinfloriculture.org/

Foundation type: Public charity
Limitations: Scholarships to individuals to encourage study in budding and container plant industry.
Financial data: Year ended 03/31/2004.
Assets, $1,754,688 (M); Expenditures, $250,599; Total giving, $76,010; Grants to individuals, 19 grants totaling $20,500 (high: $3,000, low: $500).
Fields of interest: Horticulture/garden clubs.
Type of support: Scholarships—to individuals.
Application information: Deadline Jan. 1 to May 1; Completion of formal application required; Applications available on Web site.
EIN: 591975717

1397
Florida Air Academy Scholarship Fund, Inc.

(formerly South Florida Air Academy, Inc.)
1950 S. Academy Dr.
Melbourne, FL 32901-0000 (321) 723-3211
Contact: James Dwight, Tr.

Foundation type: Independent foundation
Limitations: Scholarships primarily to residents of FL.
Financial data: Year ended 06/30/2004.
Assets, $0 (M); Expenditures, $23,727; Total

giving, $23,314; Grants to individuals, 17 grants totaling $23,314 (high: $7,602, low: $257).
Type of support: Scholarships—to individuals.
Application information: Applications accepted throughout the year; Completion of formal application required.
EIN: 591056104

1398
Florida Alliance for Arts Education, Inc.

402 Office Plz.
Tallahassee, FL 32301-2757 (850) 205-2010
Contact: Jayne Ellspermann, Pres.; Scholarships: Joe Monserrat
FAX: (850) 942-1793; E-mail: info@faae.org;
Toll-free tel.: (866) 919-3223; Additional tel. (for Scholarship Contact): (407) 882-2791;
URL: http://www.faae.org

Foundation type: Public charity
Limitations: Scholarship awards to high school students residing in FL who specialize in visual arts, music, dance, media and theatre.
Financial data: Year ended 06/30/2005.
Assets, $77,371 (M); Expenditures, $104,270.
Fields of interest: Arts education; Media/communications; Visual arts; Dance; Theater; Music; Arts.
Type of support: Undergraduate support.
Application information: Applications accepted. Application form required.
Initial approach: E-mail.
Additional information: Applications must include essay and portfolio of work. Contact foundation for current application deadline/guidelines.
Program description:
First Lady Awards: Students residing in FL are eligible for a $1,000 scholarship, which must be used for higher education in an art form. Students are required to submit a portfolio of their work and an essay on an established topic. The winners will be honored during a reception at the Governor's Mansion.
EIN: 592563990

1399
The Florida Bar Foundation

109 E. Church St., Ste. 405
P.O. Box 1553
Orlando, FL 32802-1553 (407) 843-0045
Contact: Jane Curran, Exec. Dir.
FAX: (407) 839-0287;
E-mail: flabarfndn@worldnet.att.net; Additional tel.: (800) 541-2195; URL: http://www.flabarfndn.org/

Foundation type: Public charity
Limitations: Loans and scholarships to law students.
Financial data: Year ended 06/30/2004.
Assets, $13,780,937 (M); Expenditures, $14,660,445; Total giving, $12,839,296.
Fields of interest: Law school/education.
Type of support: Student loans—to individuals.
Application information: Contact foundation for current application deadline/guidelines.
EIN: 591004604

1400
Florida Land Surveyors Scholarship Foundation, Inc.

1689A Mahan Center Blvd.
Tallahassee, FL 32308 (850) 942-1900
Contact: Marilyn Evers

Foundation type: Independent foundation
Limitations: Scholarships to University of Florida students.
Financial data: Year ended 10/31/2004. Assets, $7,829 (M); Expenditures, $26,960; Total giving, $26,200; Grants to individuals, totaling $26,200.
Type of support: Support to graduates or students of specific schools.
Application information: Applications accepted. Application form required.
Initial approach: Letter or telephone.
Deadline(s): Apr. 30
Additional information: Contact foundation for current application guidelines.
EIN: 596209248

1401

Flying Horse Foundation, Inc.
1061 Rahway Rd.
Plainfield, NJ 07060-3407

Foundation type: Independent foundation
Limitations: Scholarships to individuals who reside in Plainfield, NJ.
Financial data: Year ended 12/31/2004. Assets, $1,928,449 (M); Expenditures, $113,727; Total giving, $89,800; Grants to individuals, totaling $34,600.
Type of support: Scholarships—to individuals.
Application information: Applications not accepted.
EIN: 223337841

1402

Margaret and Thomas Flynn Scholarship Fund
c/o Hunziker, Jones, and Champion
155 U.S. Hwy. 46, Plz. II
Wayne, NJ 07470

Foundation type: Independent foundation
Limitations: Scholarships to individuals residing in NJ for higher education.
Financial data: Year ended 12/31/2004. Assets, $86,232 (M); Expenditures, $28,400; Total giving, $22,250; Grants to individuals, totaling $22,250.
Type of support: Scholarships—to individuals.
Application information: Applications not accepted.
EIN: 226690913

1403

Joseph G. & Clara T. Flynn Scholarship Trust
(formerly Joseph G. & Clara T. Flynn Scholarship Fund)
c/o TD Banknorth, N.A., Wealth Mgmt. Group
178 Main St.
P.O. Box 174
New Britain, CT 06050
Application address: c/o TD Banknorth, N.A., Wealth Mgmt. Group, Attn: Michelle Sullivan, 153 Merrimack St., Haverhill, MA 01830 tel.: (978) 556-1183

Foundation type: Independent foundation
Limitations: Scholarships to residents of Fitchburg, MA, who attend Fitchburg High School or St. Bernard's High School, Fitchburg, MA.
Financial data: Year ended 12/31/2004. Assets, $880,544 (M); Expenditures, $72,163;

Total giving, $60,000; Grants to individuals, 25 grants totaling $60,000.
Type of support: Scholarships—to individuals; Support to graduates or students of specific schools.
Application information: Deadline June 1; Completion of formal application required, including a letter from student's guidance counselor.
EIN: 046215821

1404

FMI Scholarship Foundation, Inc.
(formerly Franklin Mutual Insurance Scholarship Foundation, Inc.)
P.O. Box 400
Branchville, NJ 07826-0400

Foundation type: Company-sponsored foundation
Limitations: Scholarships to residents of Sussex, NJ, for undergraduate education.
Financial data: Year ended 12/31/2004. Assets, $80,876 (M); Expenditures, $29,395; Total giving, $27,750; Grants to individuals, 27 grants totaling $27,750 (high: $1,500, low: $500).
Type of support: Undergraduate support.
Application information: Unsolicited requests for funds not considered or acknowledged.
EIN: 223394738

1405

Harry Foley Scholarship Foundation
c/o Gerald F. Johansen
P.O. Box 418
Winnebago, MN 56098
Application address: c/o Kevin Grant, Admin., Winnebago Elem. School, 132 1st Ave. S.E., Winnebago, MN 56098, tel.: (507) 893-3176

Foundation type: Independent foundation
Limitations: Scholarships to resident students of the Winnebago School District, MN.
Financial data: Year ended 12/31/2004. Assets, $188,352 (M); Expenditures, $8,926; Total giving, $8,000; Grants to individuals, totaling $8,000.
Type of support: Support to graduates or students of specific schools; Undergraduate support.
Application information: Deadline Apr. 1; Completion of formal application required, including a letter from student's guidance counselor.
EIN: 411499816

1406

Follett Educational Foundation
c/o Follett Corp., Human Resources
2233 West St.
River Grove, IL 60171-1817 (708) 437-2402

Foundation type: Company-sponsored foundation
Limitations: Scholarships to children of Follett Corporation employees with at least two years of service.
Financial data: Year ended 12/31/2004. Assets, $1,836,412 (M); Expenditures, $249,671; Total giving, $223,031; Grants to individuals, 125 grants totaling $223,031 (high: $3,500, low: $250).
Type of support: Employee-related scholarships.
Application information: Applications accepted.
EIN: 366104348

1407

Maud Glover Folsom Foundation, Inc.
25 Patterson Ave.
Greenwich, CT 06830
Contact: Douglas M. Burdett, Pres.
E-mail: sarahdouglas.burdett@snet.net

Foundation type: Independent foundation
Limitations: Scholarships to male U.S. citizens of Anglo-Saxon or German descent between the ages of 14 and 19.
Publications: Informational brochure (including application guidelines).
Financial data: Year ended 07/31/2004. Assets, $7,218,109 (M); Expenditures, $504,362; Total giving, $364,250.
Fields of interest: Genealogy; Children/youth, services; Men.
Type of support: Graduate support; Precollege support; Undergraduate support.
Application information: Applications accepted. Application form required.
Initial approach: letter.
Deadline(s): None
Additional information: Interviews required in CT at applicant's expense.
Program description:
Scholarship Program: Grants are made for preparatory school, high school, college, professional and graduate school, or any advanced school the individual selects to advance his education. Ancestry for three complete generations (both sides) prior to the applicant must be English and/or German. Annual grants of $5,000 maximum may continue through graduate school provided that the grantee maintains at least a C+ or numerical 77 average.
EIN: 111965890

1408

Fond Rev. Edmond Gelinas, Inc.
39 Carpenter St.
Manchester, NH 03104-2206 (603) 623-6979
Contact: Donald N. Fournier, Pres.

Foundation type: Operating foundation
Limitations: Scholarships to NH students who are Catholic and of French Canadian ancestry.
Financial data: Year ended 12/31/2003. Assets, $223,584 (M); Expenditures, $10,691; Total giving, $9,125; Grants to individuals, totaling $9,125.
Fields of interest: Roman Catholic agencies & churches; Canada; France.
Type of support: Undergraduate support.
Application information: Deadline May 15; Completion of formal application required, including financial information, high school transcripts, photograph, and letter of recommendation; Grants are given based on ethnic background and financial need.
EIN: 020262914

1409

Stuart and Margaret L. Forbes Foundation, Inc.
c/o Office of William H. Miller, Esq.
84 Pacolet St.
Tryon, NC 28782 (828) 859-3137
Contact: Cindy Allen

Foundation type: Independent foundation
Limitations: Scholarships to students at high schools in the Polk County public school system, NC and the Landrum public school system, SC.

Financial data: Year ended 02/28/2005. Assets, $931,114 (M); Expenditures, $106,656; Total giving, $93,557; Grants to individuals, totaling $49,607.
Type of support: Support to graduates or students of specific schools; Undergraduate support.
Application information: Applications accepted throughout the year; Completion of formal application required.
EIN: 562079528

1410
Fannie Forbes Trust f/b/o Westborough High School

(formerly Fannie E. Forbes Trust)
c/o Bank of America, N.A.
P.O. Box 6768
Providence, RI   02940-6768
Application address: c/o Dr. John P. Dotherty Jr., Superintendent of Schools, Phillips St., Westborough, MA, tel.: (508) 366-8551

Foundation type: Independent foundation
Limitations: Student loans to graduates of Westborough High School, MA, who plan to attend college.
Financial data: Year ended 06/30/2005. Assets, $179,151 (M); Expenditures, $14,911; Total giving, $12,000; Grants to individuals, totaling $12,000.
Type of support: Student loans—to individuals; Support to graduates or students of specific schools; Undergraduate support.
Application information:
Initial approach: Contact Supt.'s office requesting application form.
Deadline(s): Aug. 15 and Dec. 15.
EIN: 046036977

1411
The Ford Family Foundation

1600 N.W. Stewart Pkwy.
Roseburg, OR   97470   (541) 957-5574
Contact: Norman J. Smith, Pres.
FAX: (541) 957-5720; E-mail: info@tfff.org;
URL: http://www.tfff.org

Foundation type: Independent foundation
Limitations: Scholarships to deserving high school and community college graduates throughout OR and Siskiyou County, CA, to be used toward a four-year, in-state baccalaureate degree.
Publications: Informational brochure (including application guidelines); Newsletter.
Financial data: Year ended 03/31/2005. Assets, $522,129,631 (M); Expenditures, $24,479,180; Total giving, $17,003,353; Grants to individuals, 850 grants totaling $7,457,296 (high: $45,860, low: $333, average grant: $1,000-$15,000).
Fields of interest: Adult/continuing education.
Type of support: Employee-related scholarships; Scholarships—to individuals; Technical education support; Undergraduate support.
Application information: Application form required. Application form available on the grantmaker's Web site.
Copies of proposal: 1
Deadline(s): Mar. 1
Applicants should submit the following:
1) Transcripts
2) SAT
3) Letter(s) of recommendation
4) Essay

Additional information: See Web site for application guidelines.
Program description:
Ford Scholarships: The foundation administers the following scholarships:
· Ford Scholars: for students graduating from high schools or community colleges pursuing an undergraduate degree
· Ford Opportunity Scholars: for single parents pursuing undergraduate degrees
· Ford ReStart Scholars: for nontraditional students pursuing college after an absence from education (high school or college) of at least five years
· Roseburg Forest Products Sons and Daughters Scholarship: Scholarships to children or stepchildren of Roseburg Forest Products employees.
EIN: 936026156

1412
The S. N. Ford and Ada Ford Fund

c/o KeyBank N.A
P.O. Box 10099
Toledo, OH   43699
Contact: Nick Gesouras, Trust Off., KeyBank N.A
Application address: c/o KeyBank N.A., 42 N. Main St., Mansfield, OH 44902, tel.: (419) 525-7665

Foundation type: Independent foundation
Limitations: Scholarships only to qualified residents of Richland County, OH.
Publications: Annual report.
Financial data: Year ended 12/31/2004. Assets, $11,811,909 (M); Expenditures, $578,966; Total giving, $541,500.
Fields of interest: Vocational education.
Type of support: Scholarships—to individuals.
Application information: Application form required.
Initial approach: Telephone.
Deadline(s): None
Program description:
Scholarship Program: The fund provides postsecondary scholarships for study that is preferably designed for the purpose of earning a living.
EIN: 340842282

1413
Formosa Plastics Corporation, Texas— Calhoun High School Scholarship Foundation, Inc.

c/o Superintendent, Calhoun County School District
525 N. Commerce St.
Port Lavaca, TX   77979-3034   (361) 552-9728

Foundation type: Company-sponsored foundation
Limitations: Scholarships to graduates of Calhoun High School, Port Lavaca, TX, for the first year of postsecondary education. Scholarships are renewable.
Financial data: Year ended 12/31/2004. Assets, $1,048,896 (M); Expenditures, $42,120; Total giving, $40,544; Grants to individuals, 21 grants totaling $40,544 (high: $2,000, low: $2,000).
Type of support: Support to graduates or students of specific schools; Undergraduate support.
Application information: Application form required.
Initial approach: Letter.
Deadline(s): Contact foundation for current application deadline.
EIN: 742634043

1414
Forsyth Educational Fund

(formerly Fred Forsyth Educational Trust Fund)
c/o Bank of America, N.A.
P.O. Box 6768
Providence, RI   02940-6768
Application address: c/o Bucksport High School Guidance Office, Bucksport, ME 04416

Foundation type: Independent foundation
Limitations: Scholarships to graduates of Bucksport High School, ME, attending college.
Financial data: Year ended 07/31/2004. Assets, $798,891 (M); Expenditures, $33,624; Total giving, $21,300; Grants to individuals, totaling $21,300.
Type of support: Support to graduates or students of specific schools; Undergraduate support.
Application information: Applications by letter, including financial, scholastic, and employment records, accepted throughout the year.
EIN: 016059631

1415
Fort Atkinson Community Foundation

c/o Premier Bank
244 N. Main St.
Fort Atkinson, WI   53538   (920) 563-3210
E-mail: facf@idcnet.com; URL: http:// www.fortfoundation.org

Foundation type: Community foundation
Limitations: Scholarships to individuals in the Fort Atkinson, WI, area.
Financial data: Year ended 06/30/2005. Assets, $15,770,300 (M); Expenditures, $533,053; Total giving, $437,162; Grants to individuals, 81 grants totaling $176,988 (high: $7,500, low: $500).
Type of support: Scholarships—to individuals.
Application information: Contact foundation for current application deadline/guidelines.
EIN: 396220899

1416
Ernest Fortin Memorial Foundation, Inc.

330 Market St.
Brighton, MA   02135
Contact: Rev. John Franck, Pres.

Foundation type: Independent foundation
Limitations: Scholarships to individuals residing in the Brighton, MA, area for graduate education.
Financial data: Year ended 12/31/2004. Assets, $406,626 (M); Expenditures, $37,105; Total giving, $32,930; Grants to individuals, totaling $32,930.
Type of support: Graduate support.
Application information: Contact foundation for current application deadlines/guidelines.
EIN: 043544279

1417
Forum Communications Foundation

(also known as Norman Black Foundation)
P.O. Box 2020
Fargo, ND   58107-2020
Contact: Lloyd G. Case, Secy.-Treas.

Foundation type: Independent foundation
Limitations: Grants primarily to residents of Moorhead, MN, and Fargo, ND.
Financial data: Year ended 07/31/2005. Assets, $1,739,530 (M); Expenditures, $78,424;

Total giving, $77,000; Grants to individuals, totaling $55,889.
Type of support: Scholarships—to individuals.
Application information: Applications accepted throughout the year.
EIN: 456012365

1418
Ralph H. Foss Memorial Trust
c/o U.S. Bank, N.A.
P.O. Box 3168
Portland, OR 97208
Contact: Lynn Caraveau, Trust Off., U.S. Bank, N.A.
Application address: P.O. Box 30678, Billings, MT 30678, tel.: (406) 657-8139

Foundation type: Independent foundation
Limitations: Scholarships to high school graduates in Richland and Dawson counties, MT.
Financial data: Year ended 12/31/2004.
Assets, $526,948 (M); Expenditures, $30,596; Total giving, $22,250.
Type of support: Undergraduate support.
Application information: Application form required.
  Deadline(s): Apr. 1
  Applicants should submit the following:
    1) Essay
    2) Financial information
    3) Class rank
    4) GPA
  Additional information: Application should also include employment history and two letters of recommendation, preferably from adults not affiliated with applicant's school.
Program description:
  Scholarship Program: Scholarships are awarded to one male and one female from each county for an initial period of two years each, and are limited to an annual minimum amount of $1,500. Scholarships are renewable annually for up to two further years of study.
EIN: 816048184

1419
Foster Foundation
(formerly Foster Welfare Foundation)
161 Ottawa Ave. N.W., Ste. 511
Grand Rapids, MI 49503-2712
Contact: Karley D. Johns, Exec. Dir.
Application address: 581 Alta Dale S.E., Grand Rapids, MI 49546, tel.: (616) 676-5958

Foundation type: Independent foundation
Limitations: Scholarships to financially needy students with demonstrated academic aptitude attending accredited colleges in Kent County, MI.
Financial data: Year ended 04/30/2005.
Assets, $56,257 (M); Expenditures, $34,868; Total giving, $24,500; Grants to individuals, totaling $24,500.
Type of support: Support to graduates or students of specific schools; Undergraduate support.
Application information: Deadline Feb. 1; Contact foundation for current application guidelines.
EIN: 380831533

1420
Sid & Mary Foulger Foundation, Inc.
9600 Blackwell Rd, Ste. 200
Rockville, MD 20850-3659

Foundation type: Independent foundation
Limitations: Scholarships to residents of AZ, FL, MD and UT for higher education.

Financial data: Year ended 12/31/2003.
Assets, $206,779 (M); Expenditures, $434,184; Total giving, $430,692; Grants to individuals, 31 grants totaling $353,967 (high: $30,285, low: $1,500).
Type of support: Undergraduate support.
Application information: Applications not accepted.
EIN: 522062781

1421
The Foundation Chapter of Theta Chi Fraternity, Inc.
3330 Founders Rd.
Indianapolis, IN 46268-1333 (317) 824-1881
Contact: James L. Hosterman, Jr., Secy.

Foundation type: Independent foundation
Limitations: Scholarships to members of Theta Chi Fraternity.
Financial data: Year ended 06/30/2004.
Assets, $2,868,804 (M); Expenditures, $399,463; Total giving, $99,278; Grants to individuals, totaling $99,278.
Fields of interest: Students, sororities/fraternities.
Type of support: Scholarships—to individuals.
Application information: Applications accepted throughout the year; Initial approach by letter requesting application; Completion of formal application required.
EIN: 214014559

1422
The Foundation for College Christian Leaders
(formerly Eckmann Foundation)
2658 Del Mar Heights Rd., Ste. 266
Del Mar, CA 92014 (858) 481-0848
Contact: Helen L. Eckmann, Dir.
E-mail: LMHays@aol.com; URL: http://www.collegechristianleader.com

Foundation type: Operating foundation
Limitations: Scholarships to financially needy Christian leaders, who are residents of southern CA or attending schools in southern CA, to obtain a four-year degree in higher education.
Financial data: Year ended 12/31/2003.
Assets, $1,333,390 (M); Expenditures, $82,132; Total giving, $56,000; Grants to individuals, 22 grants totaling $56,000 (high: $4,000, low: $1,200).
Fields of interest: Christian agencies & churches.
Type of support: Scholarships—to individuals.
Application information: Applications accepted. Application form required.
  Deadline(s): Apr. 22
EIN: 330323974

1423
Foundation for Educational Excellence
4908 Tower Rd., Ste. 108
Denver, CO 80249
Application address: c/o Angela Hutton-Howard, 1445 Market St., No. 350, Denver, CO 80202, tel.: (303) 820-5603

Foundation type: Independent foundation
Limitations: Scholarships to residents of the northeastern Denver, CO, area.
Financial data: Year ended 12/31/2004.
Assets, $915,236 (M); Expenditures, $205,719; Total giving, $100,728.

Type of support: Technical education support; Undergraduate support.
Application information:
  Deadline(s): Vary
  Additional information: Contact foundation for current application guidelines.
EIN: 841396597

1424
The Foundation for Enhancing Communities
(formerly The Greater Harrisburg Foundation)
200 N. 3rd St., 8th Fl.
P.O. Box 678
Harrisburg, PA 17108-0678 (717) 236-5040
Contact: Janice R. Black, C.E.O.; For grants: Mary Hall, Prog. Off.; For scholarships: Dawn Morns
Scholarships inquiry E-mail: Dawn@tfec.org
FAX: (717) 231-4463; Grant application E-mail: Mary@tfec.org;; URL: http://www.tfec.org

Foundation type: Community foundation
Limitations: Scholarships to individuals who are residents of Cumberland, Dauphin, Franklin, Lebanon and Perry counties, PA.
Publications: Application guidelines; Annual report (including application guidelines); Financial statement; Grants list; Informational brochure (including application guidelines); Program policy statement.
Financial data: Year ended 12/31/2005.
Assets, $41,207,227 (M); Expenditures, $6,295,728; Total giving, $2,255,492; Grants to individuals, 185 grants totaling $251,535 (high: $20,000, low: $13).
Type of support: Scholarships—to individuals; Undergraduate support.
Application information: Application form required.
  Initial approach: Letter or telephone.
  Deadline(s): Contact foundation for current application deadline/guidelines
  Applicants should submit the following:
    1) Transcripts
    2) SAT
    3) Letter(s) of recommendation
    4) GPA
    5) FAFSA
    6) Essay
    7) Financial information
Program description:
  Scholarship Program: The foundation offers numerous scholarships in Cumberland, Dauphin, Franklin, Lebanon and Perry counties in PA. See Web site for more information.
EIN: 010564355

1425
The Foundation for Geriatric Education
P.O. Box 1398
Murfreesboro, TN 37133-1398
(615) 890-2020
Contact: Robert G. Adams, Pres.

Foundation type: Public charity
Limitations: Grants to purchase textbooks for those who are studying the field of geriatrics.
Financial data: Year ended 12/31/2003.
Assets, $25,222,716 (M); Expenditures, $107,436; Total giving, $103,847; Grants to individuals, 66 grants totaling $13,929 (high: $594, low: $33).
Fields of interest: Geriatrics.
Type of support: Grants to individuals.
Application information:
  Initial approach: Letter.

Additional information: Contact foundation for further application information.
EIN: 621179417

1426
The Foundation for Hellenic Culture, Inc.
7 W. 57th St., Ste. 1
New York, NY 10019 (212) 308-6908
FAX: (212) 308-0919;
E-mail: iep.ny@ix.netcom.com; URL: http://www.foundationhellenicculture.com

Foundation type: Operating foundation
Limitations: Awards to students for the study and enhancement of Greek culture and language.
Financial data: Year ended 12/31/2003.
Assets, $212,729 (M); Expenditures, $488,090; Total giving, $99,055; Grant to an individual, 1 grant totaling $10,143.
Fields of interest: Language (foreign); Greece.
Type of support: Awards/prizes.
Application information: Applications accepted.
Deadline(s): None
Additional information: Contact foundation for current application guidelines.
EIN: 133802490

1427
Foundation for Rural Education & Development, Inc.
(formerly Fund for Rural Education & Development)
21 Dupont Cir., N.W., Ste. 700
Washington, DC 20036-1109 (202) 659-5990
Contact: Dan Hatzenbuehler, Pres.
FAX: (202) 659-4619; E-mail: mak@opastco.org;
URL: http://www.fred.org/

Foundation type: Public charity
Limitations: Scholarships to students living in or attending high school in an Organization for Promotion and Advancement of Small Telecommunications Companies (OPASTCO) member company's service area for undergraduate education.
Publications: Annual report; Grants list; Informational brochure (including application guidelines); Newsletter.
Financial data: Year ended 09/30/2004.
Assets, $1,314,612 (M); Expenditures, $455,363; Total giving, $63,500; Grants to individuals, 73 grants totaling $63,500 (high: $5,000, low: $500).
Fields of interest: Rural development; Telecommunications.
Type of support: Undergraduate support.
Application information:
Deadline(s): Feb. 13
Additional information: Completion of formal application required, including transcript, essay, financial information, letter of recommendation, OPASTCO member nomination letter, and recent photograph; Submit one original and two copies of all information; See Web site for further information.
Program description:
Scholarship Program: Scholarships range from $500 to $5,000.
EIN: 521676879

1428
Foundation for Seacoast Health
100 Campus Dr., Ste. 1
Portsmouth, NH 03801 (603) 422-8200
Contact: Susan Bunting, C.E.O.
FAX: (603) 422-8207;
E-mail: ffsh@communitycampus.org; URL: http://www.ffsh.org

Foundation type: Independent foundation
Limitations: Scholarships to students in health-related fields who have been residents of one of the following communities for at least two years: Greenland, New Castle, Newington, North Hampton, Portsmouth, and Rye, NH; Eliot, Kittery, and York, ME.
Publications: Application guidelines; Annual report (including application guidelines); Newsletter; Occasional report.
Financial data: Year ended 12/31/2004.
Assets, $69,871,210 (M); Expenditures, $4,133,470; Total giving, $1,220,572; Grants to individuals, 17 grants totaling $48,000 (high: $4,500, low: $1,000).
Fields of interest: Medical school/education; Health sciences school/education; Health care, formal/general education.
Type of support: Scholarships—to individuals; Graduate support; Undergraduate support.
Application information: Application form required. Application form available on the grantmaker's Web site.
Copies of proposal: 1
Deadline(s): Feb. 1
Applicants should submit the following:
  1) Resume
  2) Letter(s) of recommendation
  3) GPA
  4) Financial information
  5) Essay
  6) Transcripts
  7) SAT
  8) ACT
Additional information: Recipients notified in Mar.
Program description:
Seacoast Health Scholarships: Recipients are selected on a competitive basis with highest priority given to academic achievement and potential exemplified by such factors as class rank, GPA, course difficulty, and test scores. Other factors considered are financial need, school and community participation, work experience, personal recommendations, applicant's educational goals, written communication skills, and any unusual personal or family circumstances. Scholarships are renewable. The foundation also awards the Edwina Foye Scholarship Award to eligible graduate students in a health-related field and the Steven Cutter Award for eligible undergraduate students in a health-related field.
EIN: 020386319

1429
Foundation for the Carolinas
217 S. Tryon St.
Charlotte, NC 28202 (704) 973-4500
Contact: Donald K. Jonas Ph.D., Sr. V.P., Community Philanthropy
FAX: (704) 973-4599; E-mail: infor@fftc.org;
Additional tel.: (800) 973-7244; Additional E-mail: djonas@fftc.org; URL: http://www.fftc.org

Foundation type: Community foundation
Limitations: Scholarships to students residing in the greater Charlotte, NC, area. The foundation also provides undergraduate and vocational

scholarships to children of employees of National Welders Supply Company, Inc., National Realty Sales Corporation, and Wikoff Color Corporation, in NC and SC.
Publications: Application guidelines; Annual report (including application guidelines); Newsletter.
Financial data: Year ended 12/31/2004.
Assets, $349,127,277 (M); Expenditures, $92,191,230; Total giving, $82,821,824.
Fields of interest: Education, research; Nursing school/education; Community development, volunteer services; Engineering/technology.
Type of support: Employee-related scholarships; Graduate support; Technical education support; Undergraduate support.
Application information: Application form required.
Initial approach: Letter.
Deadline(s): Vary
Additional information: Interviews required.
Program description:
Scholarship Funds: The foundation administers 45 scholarship programs. Recipients for most funds are nominated by their school. The nine scholarship funds that accept applications are listed below:
- William Tasse Alexander Scholarship Fund: Provides merit scholarships to college juniors and seniors who are residents of Mecklenburg County, NC, for undergraduate study in the field of education. Deadline Mar. 1
- Carolinas/Virginias Retail Hardware Scholarship Fund: Provides scholarships to children of members of the National Retail Hardware Association in NC, SC, VA, and WV. Deadline Feb. 15
- Charlotte Housing Authority Scholarship Fund: Provides scholarships to residents of Charlotte public housing for college, technical, and vocational school. Deadlines May 1 and Dec. 1
- Crowder Scholarship Fund: Provides scholarships to children of employees of general contracting companies located in Mecklenburg County. Deadline Mar. 1
- Richard Goolsby Scholarship Fund: Provides scholarships to enrolled college students pursuing careers in the plastics industry. Deadline Feb. 1
- North Carolina League for Nursing Academic Scholarship Fund: Provides graduate scholarships in nursing and related fields. Deadline Aug. 1
- Henry DeWitt Plyler Scholarship Fund: Provides undergraduate scholarships to students from Lancaster County, SC, to attend Winthrop University. Deadline Feb. 1
- Rotary Scholarship Fund: Provides scholarships to graduates of Central Piedmont Community College pursuing a four-year degree from a senior college in Mecklenburg County. Scholarships are awarded on the basis of merit, financial need, and community service. Deadline Apr. 1.
EIN: 566047886

1430
Foundation for United Methodists, Inc.
204 N. Lexington Ave.
Wilmore, KY 40390-1199 (859) 858-2283
Contact: Dexter W. Porter, Treas.

Foundation type: Public charity
Limitations: Scholarships to attend Asbury Theological Seminary, KY.

Financial data: Year ended 04/30/2005.
Assets, $989,360 (M); Expenditures, $126,981;
Total giving, $124,080; Grants to individuals, 144
grants totaling $124,080.
Type of support: Support to graduates or students
of specific schools.
Application information: Applications accepted.
Initial approach: Letter or telephone.
Additional information: Contact foundation for
current application deadline/guidelines.
EIN: 237015220

1431

Foundation of the Pierre Fauchard Academy

c/o Windes & McClaughry
P.O. Box 87
Long Beach, CA   90801-0087

Foundation type: Independent foundation
Limitations: Scholarships to dental school
students to promote the study and research of
dentistry.
Financial data: Year ended 12/31/2004.
Assets, $6,998,677 (M); Expenditures,
$522,131; Total giving, $425,693; Grants to
individuals, totaling $136,000.
Fields of interest: Dental school/education.
Type of support: Scholarships—to individuals.
Application information: Contact foundation for
current application deadline/guidelines.
EIN: 770120371

1432

Foundation of the Wall & Ceiling Industry

(formerly Association of the Wall & Ceiling
Industry-Foundation Office)
803 W. Broad St., Ste. 600
Falls Church, VA   22042   (703) 534-8300
Contact: R. Gabe Reitter II, Pres.
FAX: (703) 534-8307; E-mail: info@awci.org;
URL: http://www.awci.org/thefoundation.shtml

Foundation type: Public charity
Limitations: Scholarships to members and
dependents of the Association of the Wall and
Ceiling Industries who are students pursuing a
post-high school education in the fields of
construction management, engineering, or
architecture at a technical school, community
college, four-year college, or graduate school.
Publications: Application guidelines; Program
policy statement.
Financial data: Year ended 06/30/2005.
Assets, $965,383 (M); Expenditures, $124,461;
Total giving, $12,500; Grants to individuals, 3
grants totaling $12,500 (high: $5,000, low:
$2,500).
Fields of interest: Architecture; Vocational
education; Engineering school/education;
Business/industry.
Type of support: Graduate support; Technical
education support; Undergraduate support.
Application information: Deadline Aug. 2; Initial
approach by telephone or e-mail; Completion of
formal application required.
Program description:
Scholarship Program: One scholarship of
$10,000 will be awarded each year. Applicants
must have had a cumulative 3.0 GPA for the last
two full-time semesters of study.
EIN: 521244895

1433

Founders Memorial Fund of the American Sterilizer Company

2424 W. 23rd St.
Erie, PA   16506

Foundation type: Company-sponsored foundation
Limitations: Scholarships to dependent children of
active and retired employees of the American
Sterilizer Co. to attend accredited colleges,
universities, vocational schools, or adult education
facilities.
Financial data: Year ended 12/31/2004.
Assets, $1,795,479 (M); Expenditures, $76,980;
Total giving, $62,880; Grants to individuals, 69
grants totaling $62,880 (high: $930, low: $500).
Fields of interest: Vocational education.
Type of support: Employee-related scholarships.
Application information: Application form required.
Deadline(s): Apr. 15
Applicants should submit the following:
1) Class rank
2) Financial information
3) Transcripts
Additional information: Application should also
include standardized test scores.
Program description:
Scholarship Program: Dependent children may
include natural children, stepchildren, adopted
children, or legal wards. Employee must have at
least one year of continuous service with AMSCO or
its subsidiaries. Dependents of retired or disabled
employees are also eligible. Grants are to be used
to cover tuition, room and board, books, and fees.
The number of scholarships awarded is limited to
25 percent of the total number of applicants.
Scholarships are renewable.
EIN: 256062068

1434

The Foundry Educational Foundation

(also known as FEF)
1695 N. Perry Ln.
Schaumburg, IL   60173   (847) 490-9200
Contact: William W. Sorensen, Exec. Dir.
FAX: (847) 890-6270; E-mail: info@fefoffice.org;
URL: http://www.fefoffice.org

Foundation type: Public charity
Limitations: Scholarships to individuals for
education related to careers in metal casting.
Publications: Annual report.
Financial data: Year ended 04/30/2005.
Assets, $5,534,041 (M); Expenditures,
$809,080; Total giving, $296,785; Grants to
individuals, 211 grants totaling $296,785.
Fields of interest: Engineering school/education.
Type of support: Support to graduates or students
of specific schools; Graduate support;
Undergraduate support.
Application information: Deadlines vary; Initial
approach by online registration form; Completion of
formal application required; See Web site for further
program and application information.
Program descriptions:
George J. Barker Memorial Scholarship:
Scholarships to individuals pursuing educational
programs related to cast metal. Applicants must
attend WI institutions. Deadline on or before Jan.
16.
David Laine Memorial Scholarship: Scholarships
to North American citizens pursuing education
related to die casting. Deadline on or before Oct.
15.
Keith Dwight Millis Scholarship: Scholarships to
undergraduate and graduate students who are

interested in ductile iron. International students are
eligible. Deadline on or before Nov. 5.
R. Conner Warren/Auburn University Scholarship:
Scholarships to students at Auburn University,
primarily those in the departments of engineering,
who are interested in the metal casting industry.
Applicants must be North American citizens.
Current students must have ACT scores of 25 and
3.5 GPA.
EIN: 340714666

1435

Four County Community Foundation

(formerly Four County Foundation)
231 E. Saint Clair St.
P.O. Box 539
Almont, MI   48003-0539   (810) 798-0909
Contact: Janet Bauer, Exec. Dir.
FAX: (810) 798-0908; E-mail: info@4ccf.org;
Additional E-mail: janet@4ccf.org; URL: http://
www.4ccf.org

Foundation type: Community foundation
Limitations: Scholarships to residents of southeast
Lapeer, northwest Macomb, northeast Oakland,
and southwest St. Clair counties, MI. See program
description for further limitations.
Publications: Application guidelines; Annual report;
Newsletter; Program policy statement.
Financial data: Year ended 12/31/2004.
Assets, $9,355,205 (M); Expenditures,
$604,553; Total giving, $440,052.
Fields of interest: Engineering school/education;
Computer science.
Type of support: Scholarships—to individuals;
Undergraduate support.
Application information: Applications accepted.
Application form required.
Initial approach: Letter or telephone.
Deadline(s): Apr. 1.
Program description:
*Russell Ligon Memorial Engineering Scholarship
Fund:* This fund awards scholarships to students
pursuing careers in engineering or computer
science. Awards are granted on the basis of
academic excellence, engineering promise, and
community involvement.
EIN: 382736601

1436

Sadie and Hobert Fouts Scholarship Fund

c/o High Point Bank & Trust Co.
P.O. Box 2278
High Point, NC   27261-2278
Contact: Ron Venable, C.F.O.
Application address for individuals: c/o Catawba
College, Attn.: Office of Financial Aid, 2300 W.
Innes St., Salisbury, NC 28144, tel.: (800)
CATAWBA

Foundation type: Independent foundation
Limitations: Scholarships to students from
Davidson County, NC, who will be attending
Catawba College.
Financial data: Year ended 12/31/2004.
Assets, $181,990 (M); Expenditures, $10,270;
Total giving, $8,100; Grants to individuals, totaling
$8,100.
Type of support: Support to graduates or students
of specific schools; Undergraduate support.
Application information: Contact fund for current
application deadline/guidelines.
EIN: 566481132

1437
Blanche N. Fowler Charitable Trust
c/o AmSouth Bank
P.O. Box 2028
Tuscaloosa, AL 35403 (205) 391-5729
Contact: Lynn Shaw, V.P.

Foundation type: Independent foundation
Limitations: Scholarships to students attending
four-year colleges in AL.
Financial data: Year ended 12/31/2004.
Assets, $339,944 (M); Expenditures, $21,345;
Total giving, $14,900; Grants to individuals,
totaling $14,900.
Type of support: Scholarships—to individuals.
Application information: Deadline Mar. 31;
Completion of formal application required.
EIN: 636158965

1438
Louis B. Fox & Julian Karger Scholarship Fund
(formerly Louis B. Fox & Julian Karger Trust)
c/o Bank of America, N.A.
P.O. Box 1802
Providence, RI 02940-1802
Application address: c/o Scholarship Comm.,
Revere High School, Revere, MA 02151

Foundation type: Independent foundation
Limitations: Scholarships to the highest-ranking
graduating seniors of Revere High School, MA, who
wish to attend institutions of higher education.
Financial data: Year ended 12/31/2004.
Assets, $107,302 (M); Expenditures, $3,842;
Total giving, $1,500.
Type of support: Support to graduates or students
of specific schools; Undergraduate support.
Application information: Applications by letter
accepted throughout the year.
EIN: 046334789

1439
Jacob L. & Lewis Fox Foundation
c/o Del Negro, Feldman, LLC
Goodwin Sq.
225 Asylum St.
Hartford, CT 06115-1516 (860) 633-1429
Contact: MaryLou Rosadini, Admin. Asst.

Foundation type: Independent foundation
Limitations: Scholarships to graduates of Hartford,
CT, public high schools.
Financial data: Year ended 12/31/2004.
Assets, $4,497,259 (M); Expenditures,
$307,702; Total giving, $212,521; Grants to
individuals, 75 grants totaling $212,521 (high:
$8,569, low: $194).
Type of support: Support to graduates or students
of specific schools; Undergraduate support.
Application information: Application form required.
  Deadline(s): Usually late Jan. or early Feb.
  Additional information: Application must be made
    through the public high schools; The trust
    does not accept applications directly.
EIN: 066067700

1440
Evelyn Fraites Foundation, Inc.
61 Broadway, 18th Fl.
New York, NY 10006-2794

Foundation type: Independent foundation

Limitations: Scholarships to graduates of Cranford
High School, NJ.
Financial data: Year ended 11/30/2004.
Assets, $241,217 (M); Expenditures, $20,000;
Total giving, $20,000; Grants to individuals, 5
grants totaling $20,000.
Type of support: Support to graduates or students
of specific schools; Undergraduate support.
Application information: Contact foundation for
current application deadline/guidelines; Initial
approach by letter.
EIN: 113241845

1441
Francies Scholarship Fund
c/o JPMorgan Chase Bank, N.A.
P.O. Box 1308
Milwaukee, WI 53201
Contact: Delores Dukes, Admin., JPMorgan Chase
Bank, N.A.
Application address: 50 S. Main St., Akron, OH
44308, tel.: (216) 972-1594

Foundation type: Independent foundation
Limitations: Scholarships to students in the fields
of political science, government, and social
studies, primarily in OH.
Financial data: Year ended 04/30/2005.
Assets, $231,364 (M); Expenditures, $18,219;
Total giving, $13,500; Grants to individuals, 5
grants totaling $13,500.
Fields of interest: Social sciences; Political
science; Government/public administration.
Type of support: Undergraduate support.
Application information: Contact fund for current
application deadline/guidelines.
EIN: 316415216

1442
Franciscan Foundation for the Holy Land
(formerly The Holy Land Foundation)
c/o The Franciscan Monastery
1400 Quincy St. N.E
Washington, DC 20017 (866) 905-3787
Contact: Rev. Peter F. Vasko O.F.M., Pres.
FAX: (866) 905-3788; E-mail: info@ffhl.org;
URL: http://www.ffhl.org

Foundation type: Public charity
Limitations: Scholarships to Christian Palestinian
students in Israel and the Occupied Territories.
Parents' economic income is a major criteria for
deciding whether student will receive a partial or full
scholarship.
Financial data: Year ended 12/31/2003.
Assets, $2,283,100 (M); Expenditures,
$517,526; Total giving, $129,000; Grants to
individuals, totaling $129,000.
Fields of interest: Christian agencies & churches.
Type of support: Scholarships—to individuals.
Application information: Contact foundation for
current application deadline/guidelines.
EIN: 330628775

1443
Elenore Francisco Educational Trust
c/o Old National Bank
P.O. Box 390
Morganfield, KY 42437
Contact: J. David Buckman, V.P., Old National Bank

Foundation type: Operating foundation

Limitations: Student loans to graduates of Union
County High School, KY. Maximum loan amount per
academic year per student is $2,500.
Financial data: Year ended 12/31/2004.
Assets, $422,787 (M); Expenditures, $9,021;
Total giving, $0; Loans to individuals, 6 loans
totaling $7,500.
Type of support: Support to graduates or students
of specific schools; Undergraduate support.
Application information: Applications accepted
throughout the year; Completion of formal
application required, including transcripts.
EIN: 616151610

1444
Frank Family Memorial Scholarship
(formerly Simon Frank Scholarship Fund)
c/o Wells Fargo Bank, N.A.
4707 S. 96th St.
Phoenix, AZ 85072
Application address: c/o Secy., Homestead High
School, 500 W. Mequon Rd., Mequon, WI 53092

Foundation type: Independent foundation
Limitations: Scholarships to Homestead High
School, Mequon, WI, graduates only.
Financial data: Year ended 12/31/2004.
Assets, $2,549,648 (M); Expenditures,
$188,829; Total giving, $164,000; Grants to
individuals, 188 grants totaling $164,000 (high:
$1,250, low: $500).
Type of support: Support to graduates or students
of specific schools; Undergraduate support.
Application information: Deadline Feb. 1;
Completion of formal application required.
EIN: 396270979

1445
Jacob, Lillian & Nathan M. Frank Scholarship Fund
c/o Integra Bank
P.O. Box 868
Evansville, IN 47705-0868 (812) 464-9661

Foundation type: Independent foundation
Limitations: Scholarships to financially needy high
school students and residents of Vanderburgh
County, IN, for higher educational purposes.
Recipients are selected on the basis of grades,
desire for high school or college education and
financial need.
Financial data: Year ended 12/31/2004.
Assets, $524,411 (M); Expenditures, $33,576;
Total giving, $24,000; Grants to individuals,
totaling $24,000.
Application information: Applications accepted
throughout the year; Completion of formal
application required.
EIN: 356338764

1446
Franklin County Community Foundation, Inc.
527 Main St.
Brookville, IN 47012 (765) 647-6810
Contact: Shelly Lunsford, Exec. Dir.
FAX: (765) 647-0238;
E-mail: fcfoundation@yahoo.com; URL: http://
www.franklincountyindiana.info

Foundation type: Community foundation
Limitations: Scholarships to students in IN for
books and tuition, primarily in Franklin County.

Publications: Annual report; Financial statement; Informational brochure; Newsletter.
Financial data: Year ended 08/31/2005.
Assets, $2,075,862 (M); Expenditures, $303,660; Total giving, $67,336; Grants to individuals, 35 grants totaling $67,336.
Type of support: Technical education support; Undergraduate support.
Application information: Application form required.
Initial approach: Letter.
Deadline(s): Varies
Additional information: Contact foundation for current application deadline/guidelines.
EIN: 352034336

1447
The Franklin Electric—Edward J. Schaefer and T. W. Kehoe Charitable and Educational Foundation, Inc.
c/o Franklin Electric Co., Inc.
400 E. Spring St.
Bluffton, IN 46714-3798 (260) 824-2900
Contact: William H. Lawson, Pres.

Foundation type: Company-sponsored foundation
Limitations: Scholarships to children of employees of Franklin Electric Co., Inc. or its wholly-owned subsidiaries to attend accredited institutions. Employees must have at least two years' experience with Franklin Electric or have retired under the company's retirement plan.
Financial data: Year ended 12/31/2003.
Assets, $514,179 (M); Expenditures, $396,685; Total giving, $396,565; Grants to individuals, 17 grants totaling $12,000 (high: $1,500, low: $750).
Type of support: Employee-related scholarships.
Application information: Application form required.
Applicants should submit the following:
1) Transcripts
2) Class rank
3) SAT
Additional information: Deadline during senior year of high school; Application should also include SAT or National Merit Scholarship Qualifying Test scores.
Program description:
Scholarship Program: Employees who are qualified but on official leave of absence for medical or military purposes are eligible. Applicants must graduate in the upper half of their high school class. Scholarships are awarded on the basis of scholastic achievement, standardized test scores, character, and citizenship. Scholarships are $1,500 for each full year of study, $750 for each half year, and are automatically renewed for up to four years of study.
EIN: 237399324

1448
Anna Collins Franklin Foundation
P.O. Box 144
Ardmore, OK 73401
Application address: c/o Glenn Hendrix, Tr., Rte. 3, Box 174, Ardmore, OK 73401

Foundation type: Independent foundation
Limitations: Scholarships to residents of Carter County, OK.
Financial data: Year ended 12/31/2004.
Assets, $2,089,306 (M); Expenditures, $134,065; Total giving, $90,000; Grants to individuals, totaling $90,000.
Type of support: Scholarships—to individuals.

Application information: Applications by letter accepted throughout the year.
EIN: 731361437

1449
Franklin Park Rotary Club Foundation
P.O. Box 154
Franklin Park, IL 60131
Contact: Donald Knapp, Pres.

Foundation type: Public charity
Limitations: Scholarships to individuals residing in the area of Franklin Park, IL, for the first year of college.
Financial data: Year ended 12/31/2004.
Assets, $165,823 (M); Expenditures, $34,452; Total giving, $27,600; Grants to individuals, totaling $14,900.
Type of support: Scholarships—to individuals.
Application information: Applications not accepted.
EIN: 363273843

1450
Franks Foundation
c/o Kermit V. Jones
P.O. Box 250
Booneville, MS 38829-0250
Contact: C.J. Roper, Dir.
Application address: 2075 1st St., Booneville, MS 38829, tel.: (662) 728-5342

Foundation type: Independent foundation
Limitations: Scholarships to individuals in the First Congressional District of MS, for higher education.
Financial data: Year ended 12/31/2004.
Assets, $3,414,111 (M); Expenditures, $76,642; Total giving, $65,000; Grants to individuals, 175 grants totaling $65,000 (high: $500, low: $250).
Type of support: Undergraduate support.
Application information: Deadline 30 days prior to start of semester; Completion of formal application required.
EIN: 640845922

1451
Franks Foundation Fund
c/o U.S. Bank, N.A.
P.O. Box 3168
Portland, OR 97208-3168
Contact: Marlyn J. Norquist, Loan Off., U.S. Bank, N.A.
Application address: c/o Oregon State Scholarship Commission, 1500 Valley River Dr., Ste. 100, Eugene, OR 97401-2148; URL: http://www.osac.state.or.us/

Foundation type: Independent foundation
Limitations: Student loans to high school students in OR.
Financial data: Year ended 06/30/2005.
Assets, $453,364 (M); Expenditures, $40,438; Total giving, $30,000; Grants to individuals, totaling $30,000.
Type of support: Undergraduate support.
Application information: Applications accepted. Application form required.
Deadline(s): June 1 to June 15.
Additional information: Interviews required.
EIN: 930666994

1452
Fraser Area Educational Foundation
33466 Garfield Rd.
Fraser, MI 48026-1892

Foundation type: Public charity
Limitations: Scholarships to graduates of Fraser High School, MI.
Financial data: Year ended 06/30/2004.
Assets, $229,785 (M); Expenditures, $18,446; Total giving, $17,744; Grants to individuals, totaling $17,744.
Type of support: Support to graduates or students of specific schools; Undergraduate support.
Application information: Applications accepted. Application form required.
Deadline(s): Mar. 4
Applicants should submit the following:
1) Essay
2) ACT
3) Letter(s) of recommendation
4) Transcripts
Additional information: Applications are available at the office of the guidance counselor.
EIN: 382785496

1453
William G. & Margaret B. Frasier Charitable Foundation
c/o Wachovia Bank, N.A.
P.O. Box 3099
Winston-Salem, NC 27150-1022
(336) 732-5991
Contact: Ed Loflin, Trust Off., Wachovia Bank, N.A.
Scholarship URL: http://www.wachoviascholars.com/frsr/frsr_2006_ins.htm

Foundation type: Independent foundation
Limitations: Scholarships to Baptist ministerial candidates at Southeastern Baptist Theological Seminary and Wake Forest University Divinity School, NC.
Financial data: Year ended 12/31/2004.
Assets, $1,767,843 (M); Expenditures, $98,265; Total giving, $76,600; Grants to individuals, totaling $76,600.
Fields of interest: Theological school/education; Protestant agencies & churches.
Type of support: Support to graduates or students of specific schools; Undergraduate support.
Application information: Applications not accepted.
EIN: 566144594

1454
John Cowles Frautschy Scholarship Trust Fund
501 7th St.
Rockford, IL 61104

Foundation type: Independent foundation
Limitations: Scholarships to male Protestant graduating seniors of Monroe High School, WI.
Financial data: Year ended 05/31/2005.
Assets, $305,453 (M); Expenditures, $20,929; Total giving, $18,650; Grants to individuals, totaling $18,650.
Fields of interest: Vocational education; Protestant agencies & churches; Men.
Type of support: Support to graduates or students of specific schools; Undergraduate support.
Application information: Applications available from guidance counselors at Monroe High School, WI; Completion of formal application required.

Program description:

Scholarship Fund: Selected guidance counselors submit application forms to the Scholarship Selection Group. If requested, the counselors will also present additional information about the applicants, including class rank, aptitude test scores, and an appraisal of financial need. Primary emphasis is given to financial need of the applicants and their record of scholastic accomplishment. Emphasis is also placed on attitude and aptitude. Grants are made for college scholarships or for other training and are awarded to adults as well as to high school seniors.
EIN: 930799642

1455
Harry S. Fredenburgh Scholarship Fund
c/o JPMorgan Chase Bank
P.O. Box 31412
Rochester, NY   14603
Application address: c/o Janis Mosher, V.P., JPMorgan Chase Bank, 31 Main St., Canandaigua, NY 14424, tel.: (716) 394-7675

Foundation type: Independent foundation
Limitations: Scholarships to graduates of Mynders Academy, Seneca Falls, NY.
Financial data: Year ended 12/31/2004. Assets, $1,490,228 (M); Expenditures, $95,663; Total giving, $80,875; Grants to individuals, totaling $80,875.
Type of support: Support to graduates or students of specific schools; Undergraduate support.
Application information: Applications accepted throughout the year; Contact school district office or school for information.
EIN: 166229781

1456
Freedom Alliance
22570 Markey Ct., Ste. 240
Dulles, VA   20166   (703) 444-7940
Contact: Thomas Kilgannon, Pres.
FAX: (703) 444-9893; Additional tel.: (800) 475-6620; URL: http://www.freedomalliance.org

Foundation type: Public charity
Limitations: Scholarships to dependents of an active duty service member who died or was permanently disabled in the line of duty, or who is currently certified as POW or MIA.
Financial data: Year ended 12/31/2003. Assets, $3,825,129 (M); Expenditures, $4,352,169; Total giving, $88,000.
Fields of interest: Military/veterans' organizations.
Type of support: Undergraduate support.
Application information: Applications accepted. Application form required. Application form available on the grantmaker's Web site.
Initial approach: Telephone or letter.
Deadline(s): June 30
Applicants should submit the following:
  1) Letter(s) of recommendation
  2) Transcripts
  3) Essay
  4) Financial information
Additional information: Applications must also include photo and certificate of service/dependency.
Program description:
Freedom Alliance Scholarship: One-year scholarships are awarded annually to high school seniors, high school graduates, or registered to undergraduate students to accredited colleges or post-high school vocational/technical institutions.

Applicants must maintain a GPA within a 2.00/4.00 scale.
EIN: 541411430

1457
Freedom Forge Corporation Foundation
(formerly American Welding & Manufacturing Company Foundation)
c/o Kish Bank Asset Mgmt.
1 Gateway Dr.
Reedsville, PA   17084
Application address: 500 N. Walnut St., Burnham, PA 17009, tel.: (717) 248-4911

Foundation type: Company-sponsored foundation
Limitations: Scholarships to individuals for higher education, primarily in PA.
Financial data: Year ended 12/31/2004. Assets, $1,308,687 (M); Expenditures, $56,889; Total giving, $49,172; Grants to individuals, 8 grants totaling $20,000 (high: $2,500, low: $2,500).
Type of support: Scholarships—to individuals.
Application information: Applications by letter accepted throughout the year.
EIN: 346516721

1458
The Freedom Forum, Inc.
1101 Wilson Blvd.
Arlington, VA   22209-2248   (703) 528-0800
Contact: Charles L. Overby, Chair.
FAX: (703) 284-3770;
E-mail: news@freedomforum.org; URL: http://www.freedomforum.org

Foundation type: Operating foundation
Limitations: Scholarships to attend the annual American Indian Journalism Institute, a training program for Native American journalism students.
Publications: Annual report; Occasional report.
Financial data: Year ended 12/31/2004. Assets, $924,229,500 (M); Expenditures, $57,848,576; Total giving $23,152,188; Grants to individuals, 133 grants totaling $100,249 (high: $10,000, low: $25).
Fields of interest: Journalism/publishing; Native Americans/American Indians.
Type of support: Stipends.
Application information: Applications accepted.
Initial approach: Letter or telephone.
Deadline(s): Mar. 31
Additional information: See Web site for complete program information.
Program description:
American Indian Journalism Institute: Any Native American college student with an interest in becoming a newspaper journalist may apply. Once accepted into the program, participants will be placed in one of four courses according to their interests and experience. Tuition, fees, books, room, and board are provided free to enrollees. To be eligible, Native students must have completed at least one year of college. Program graduates will earn four hours of college credit from the University of South Dakota that students may transfer to their current school. In addition, graduates will receive a $500 stipend/scholarship from the Freedom Forum, paid when the student resumes full-time classes in the fall.
EIN: 541604427

1459
J. C. Freels Scholarship Awards Trust
c/o Union Planters Bank, N.A.
P.O. Box 15993
Knoxville, TN   37901-5993

Foundation type: Independent foundation
Limitations: Scholarships to graduates of Morristown High School, TN.
Financial data: Year ended 12/31/2004. Assets, $154,778 (M); Expenditures, $5,921; Total giving, $3,440; Grants to individuals, totaling $3,440.
Type of support: Support to graduates or students of specific schools; Undergraduate support.
Application information: Recipients chosen by Hamblen County School Superintendent and committee.
EIN: 626049363

1460
Isabel Freer Memorial Scholarship Trust
146 E. Center St.
Marion, OH   43302
Contact: John C. Bartram, Tr.

Foundation type: Independent foundation
Limitations: Scholarships to graduates of Marion Harding High School, OH.
Financial data: Year ended 12/31/2004. Assets, $105,818 (M); Expenditures, $9,261; Total giving, $7,500; Grants to individuals, totaling $7,500.
Type of support: Support to graduates or students of specific schools; Undergraduate support.
Application information: Applications by letter providing details of purpose and use of grant accepted throughout the year.
EIN: 346866821

1461
Charles Frees Educational Fund
c/o U.S. Bank, N.A.
P.O. Box 387
St. Louis, MO   63166-0387   (314) 993-5982
Contact: Morris E. Blitz, Committee Chair.
Application address: 508 Coeur De Royale Dr., No. 202, St. Louis, MO 63141, tel.: (314) 516-5461, or (314) 993-5982

Foundation type: Independent foundation
Limitations: Scholarships to male high school seniors in St. Louis County, MO, for their first year of college.
Financial data: Year ended 09/30/2003. Assets, $869,956 (M); Expenditures, $67,195; Total giving, $46,800; Grants to individuals, 27 grants totaling $46,800 (high: $2,000, low: $1,000).
Fields of interest: Men.
Type of support: Support to graduates or students of specific schools; Undergraduate support.
Application information: Deadline Apr. 1; Initial approach through counselor at high school; Completion of formal application required.
EIN: 436059806

1462
Irene Frees Teaching Scholarship Trust
c/o First National Bank of Monterey
P.O. Box 8
Monterey, IN   46960
Contact: Claiborn Wamsley

Foundation type: Independent foundation

Limitations: Scholarships to graduating seniors at North Judson San Pierre High School, IN, to pursue teaching degrees.
Financial data: Year ended 12/31/2004. Assets, $173,796 (M); Expenditures, $7,110; Total giving, $6,200; Grants to individuals, totaling $6,200.
Fields of interest: Teacher school/education.
Type of support: Support to graduates or students of specific schools; Undergraduate support.
Application information: Application form required.
  Initial approach: letter or telephone.
  Deadline(s): Apr. 1
EIN: 356530824

1463
Fremont Area Community Foundation
(formerly The Fremont Area Foundation)
4424 W. 48th St.
P.O. Box B
Fremont, MI   49412   (231) 924-5350
Contact: Elizabeth Cherin, C.E.O.
FAX: (231) 924-5391; E-mail: info@tfacf.org;
Additional FAX: (231) 924-7637; Additional E-mails: echerin@tfacf.org and gzerlaut@tfacf.org;
URL: http://www.tfacf.org

Foundation type: Community foundation
Limitations: Scholarships to graduates of high schools in Newaygo County, MI.
Publications: Application guidelines; Annual report; Financial statement; Grants list; Informational brochure; Newsletter.
Financial data: Year ended 12/31/2005. Assets, $194,738,922 (M); Expenditures, $11,557,038; Total giving, $9,386,427.
Fields of interest: Design; Teacher school/education; Theological school/education; Health sciences school/education; Agriculture; Athletics/sports, school programs; Athletics/sports, basketball; Protestant agencies & churches.
Type of support: Support to graduates or students of specific schools; Awards/grants by nomination only; Awards/prizes; Undergraduate support.
Application information: Application form required.
  Initial approach: Telephone.
  Deadline(s): Mar. 1
  Additional information: Interviews required.
Program descriptions:
  John K. Rottier Fund: The fund offers a basketball clinic campership. Recipient selection is made by a private advisory committee.
  Bessie B. Slautterback Scholarship: The scholarship is awarded annually to one high school senior from each of the five high schools in Newaygo County, MI. These seniors are chosen by selection committees from each high school.
  Nellie McCarty Fund: Selection is limited to residents of Newaygo County, MI, for health and medically related scholarships. Final selection is made by an advisory committee at Gerber Memorial Hospital.
  Excellence in Education Scholarships: Awards are given to the top five percent of the graduating high school seniors in Newaygo County, MI.
  Fremont Public Schools Fund: Awards are given for college scholarships to top academic high school seniors as selected by a school advisory committee.
  Carl G. and Viola C. Smith Advised Fund: Annually awards college scholarships to three Hesperia High School seniors as selected by a school advisory committee.
  Harnden Scholarship Fund: Annually awards college scholarships to one male and one female senior from Fremont High School, excelling in both

academics and athletics as selected by school administrators.
  Dodge Scholarship Fund: Annually awards college scholarships to one high school senior from each of the five high schools in Newaygo County. These seniors are chosen by selection committees from each high school.
  Newaygo County Career-Tech Center Outstanding Student Awards: Awards are granted annually to one student selected by school administrators.
  Charleen J. Erber Scholarship Fund: The fund provides a renewable scholarship to a graduate of Fremont High School preparing for a career in education or the ministry.
  Janene Hogancamp Memorial Graphic Arts Scholarship Fund: One scholarship is awarded to a Newaygo County graduate pursuing a career in graphic arts.
  Kenneth & Pauline Bull Scholarship Fund: Scholarships to students from Grant High School.
  Agricultural Scholarship Fund: Assistance is provided to graduating Newaygo County seniors who are pursuing careers in agriculture.
  Kristy Auw Couch Memorial Scholarship: A scholarship is awarded to a graduating senior of White Cloud High School.
  Robert and Elsie Geeting Scholarship Fund: Scholarships are awarded to Newaygo County students.
  Head Family Scholarship Fund: Awards scholarships to Newaygo County graduates with preference given to members of St. John's Episcopal Church.
  William A. and Colleen Mee Fund: Scholarships to graduating seniors of Newaygo County.
  Brenda G. Price Scholarship Fund: A scholarship is provided to a Newaygo County high school graduate to attend Hope College or the University of Michigan.
  Vanderwier Scholarship Fund: Scholarships are provided to a deserving student from each Newaygo County high school.
EIN: 381443367

1464
Fremont Area Community Foundation
605 N. Broad St.
P.O. Box 182
Fremont, NE   68025   (402) 721-4252
Contact: Elizabeth Mulliken, Exec. Dir.
FAX: (402) 721-9359;
E-mail: inquire@facfoundation.org; URL: http://www.facfoundation.org

Foundation type: Community foundation
Limitations: Scholarships to residents of Fremont, NE, and surrounding communities.
Publications: Application guidelines; Annual report; Informational brochure (including application guidelines); Newsletter.
Financial data: Year ended 06/30/2005. Assets, $7,383,381 (M); Expenditures, $548,101; Total giving, $454,271; Grants to individuals, 37 grants totaling $21,250 (high: $2,500, low: $100, average grant: $1,000-$2,500).
Type of support: Technical education support; Undergraduate support.
Application information: Application form required. Application form available on the grantmaker's Web site.
  Copies of proposal: 1
  Deadline(s): Apr. 1
  Applicants should submit the following:
    1) ACT
    2) GPA
    3) Resume

    4) Transcripts
  Additional information: Applications submitted through area high school guidance counselors. See Web site for further information.
EIN: 470629642

1465
The French Benevolent Society of Philadelphia
c/o Clairmont Paciello & Co.
250 Tanglewood Ln.
King of Prussia, PA   19406-2365
Application address: c/o Directors or Scholarship Comm., 1301 Medical Arts Bldg., 1601 Walnut St., Philadelphia, PA 19102, tel.: (215) 563-3276

Foundation type: Independent foundation
Limitations: Scholarships for higher education, either in the U.S. or France, to financially needy French citizens or immigrants and their descendants, now living in the Philadelphia, PA, metropolitan area.
Publications: Informational brochure (including application guidelines).
Financial data: Year ended 10/31/2004. Assets, $1,187,792 (M); Expenditures, $76,953; Total giving, $38,410; Grants to individuals, 6 grants totaling $38,410 (high: $9,900, low: $939).
Fields of interest: France.
Type of support: Scholarships—to individuals.
Application information: Applications accepted.
  Deadline(s): None
  Additional information: Completion of formal application required, including an official transcript of high school and/or college work done in the U.S. or abroad, a financial disclosure form, and curriculum vitae.
EIN: 231401532

1466
Ed French Charitable Foundation, Inc.
517 Yale St.
Mexico, MO   65265   (573) 581-6010
Contact: Ruby Hamlett, Mgr.
Application address: P.O. Box 38, Laddonia, MO 63352-0038, tel.: (573) 373-5644

Foundation type: Independent foundation
Limitations: Undergraduate scholarships to individuals who are residents of Ranges 6 and 7 in Audrain County, MO.
Financial data: Year ended 06/30/2005. Assets, $2,273,811 (M); Expenditures, $108,335; Total giving, $89,300; Grants to individuals, totaling $82,000.
Type of support: Undergraduate support.
Application information: Unsolicited requests for applications not accepted.
EIN: 431393163

1467
R. E. French Family Educational Foundation
P.O. Box 203
Gridley, KS   66852   (620) 836-3285
Contact: R.E. French, Tr.

Foundation type: Independent foundation
Limitations: Scholarships to graduating high school students in KS based on high school grades, ACT scores, chosen vocation, financial need, motivation, and character.

Financial data: Year ended 06/30/2005. Assets, $6,088,504 (M); Expenditures, $163,341; Total giving, $98,651.
Type of support: Undergraduate support.
Application information: Applications accepted. Application form required.
Initial approach: Letter or telephone.
Deadline(s): Contact foundation for current application deadline
Additional information: Application must include essay, ACT scores, transcripts, letters of recommendation, recent photograph and attendance records.
EIN: 480926521

1468
Blanche E. French Scholarship Foundation
P.O. Box 768
Iola, KS 66749-0768 (913) 266-5736
Application address: c/o Charlotte Young, 605 S.W. Fairland Rd., Topeka, KS 66611

Foundation type: Independent foundation
Limitations: Scholarships by nomination only to graduating seniors of high schools in Coffey, Woodson, Greenwood, and Bourbon counties, KS.
Financial data: Year ended 09/30/2004. Assets, $249,372 (M); Expenditures, $4,221; Total giving, $4,200; Grants to individuals, totaling $4,200.
Type of support: Support to graduates or students of specific schools; Awards/grants by nomination only; Undergraduate support.
Application information: Recipients are recommended by high school principals; Completion of formal application required.
EIN: 480868018

1469
Henry W. French Trust f/b/o Susan E. French Scholarship
185 Lincoln St., Ste. 300
Hingham, MA 02043
Application address: c/o Oliver Ames High School, Attn.: Principal, Lothrop St., North Easton, MA 02356

Foundation type: Independent foundation
Limitations: One four-year scholarship awarded every four years to a graduating senior at Oliver Ames High School, North Easton, MA.
Financial data: Year ended 12/31/2004. Assets, $181,969 (M); Expenditures, $5,606; Total giving, $4,650; Grants to individuals, totaling $4,650.
Type of support: Support to graduates or students of specific schools; Undergraduate support.
Application information: Completion of formal application required.
EIN: 046026812

1470
Fresno Musical Club
2689 W. San Carlos Ave.
Fresno, CA 93711
Contact: Saskia Dyer, Treas.
Application address: 2672 E. Alluvial Ave., Clovis, CA 93611

Foundation type: Operating foundation
Limitations: Scholarships to young musicians and artists in the community of Clovis, CA, to assist in their music studies.

Financial data: Year ended 06/30/2004. Assets, $191,468 (M); Expenditures, $12,380; Total giving, $9,700; Grants to individuals, 13 grants totaling $9,700.
Fields of interest: Music; Performing arts, education.
Type of support: Undergraduate support.
Application information: Applications by letter, including resume of musical background and description of needs, accepted throughout the year.
EIN: 946075667

1471
Fresno Regional Foundation
3425 N. 1st St., Ste. 101
Fresno, CA 93726 (559) 226-5600
Contact: Daniel G. DeSantis, C.E.O.
FAX: (559) 230-2078;
E-mail: info@fresnofoundation.org; Additional E-mail: frfdan@pacbell.net; URL: http://www.fresnoregfoundation.org

Foundation type: Community foundation
Limitations: Scholarships to individuals residing in the San Joaquin Valley, CA, area, for undergraduate education.
Financial data: Year ended 12/31/2004. Assets, $19,723,196 (M); Expenditures, $3,951,202; Total giving, $2,936,012; Grants to individuals, 42 grants totaling $18,540 (high: $1,300, low: $10).
Type of support: Undergraduate support.
Application information: Contact foundation for current application deadline/guidelines. See Web site for complete program listing.
EIN: 770478025

1472
Frets Educational Trust
P.O. Box 1108
Mount Vernon, WA 98273-1108
Contact: David A. Welts, Tr.

Foundation type: Independent foundation
Limitations: Scholarships to high school and college students of Skagit County, WA.
Financial data: Year ended 12/31/2004. Assets, $144,304 (M); Expenditures, $10,930; Total giving, $4,312; Grants to individuals, totaling $4,312.
Type of support: Undergraduate support.
Application information: Contact trust for current application deadline; Initial approach by letter or telephone; Application by letter, including resume, transcripts, budget, and letters of recommendation.
EIN: 916341455

1473
William and Lena Fricke Foundation
c/o Hentzen Law Offices
127 Canterbury Rd.
Eau Claire, WI 54701-7105
Application address: c/o Robert E. Fricke, 2434 Remington Dr., Napersville, IL, tel.: (630) 305-3201

Foundation type: Independent foundation
Limitations: Scholarships to students between the ages of 10 and 20, primarily in the Midwest.
Financial data: Year ended 12/31/2004. Assets, $324,695 (M); Expenditures, $7,440; Total giving, $5,000; Grants to individuals, totaling $5,000.
Type of support: Undergraduate support.

Application information: Deadline Dec. 1; Application by letter.
Program description:
Scholarship Program: Scholarships are in maximum amounts of $500 each. Applications must include family background and reasons for willingness to participate in one-year program of total abstinence from alcohol and tobacco use.
EIN: 396677792

1474
Friedberger Educational Fund
c/o Bank of Stockton
P.O. Box 201014
Stockton, CA 95201-9014

Foundation type: Independent foundation
Limitations: Scholarships by nomination only to residents of San Joaquin County, CA, who graduate from preparatory schools and attend colleges and universities within CA.
Financial data: Year ended 12/31/2004. Assets, $1,325,133 (M); Expenditures, $80,934; Total giving, $59,477; Grants to individuals, totaling $59,477.
Type of support: Awards/grants by nomination only; Undergraduate support.
Application information: Each public and private high school may nominate two applicants; Students should notify guidance counselor if interested; Do not write to fund.
Program description:
Scholarship Program: Recipients are selected by an independent committee made up of the school superintendent of San Joaquin County, CA, the school superintendent of Stockton, CA, and a third member selected by the superintendents. Scholarships are renewable.
EIN: 946081078

1475
Friedman Scholarship Fund
(formerly Friedman Loan & Scholarship Fund)
c/o Wells Fargo Bank Northwest, N.A.
877 W. Main St., 3rd Fl., U1858-035
Boise, ID 83702
Contact: Chris Peters

Foundation type: Independent foundation
Limitations: Scholarships to graduates of Wood River High School, Hailey, ID.
Financial data: Year ended 04/30/2005. Assets, $589,972 (M); Expenditures, $29,660; Total giving, $20,500; Grants to individuals, 44 grants totaling $20,500 (high: $1,500, low: $250).
Type of support: Support to graduates or students of specific schools; Undergraduate support.
Application information: Application form required.
Initial approach: Letter.
Deadline(s): Mar. 15 and Oct. 1
EIN: 826066650

1476
Friend & B. Kerr Trust
c/o National City Bank
P.O. Box 94651
Cleveland, OH 44101-4651
Application address: c/o Ronald Joyce, Titusville Area High School, Guidance Ctr., 302 E. Walnut, Titusville, PA 16354, tel.: (814) 827-9687

Foundation type: Independent foundation
Limitations: Scholarships only to graduating seniors of Titusville, PA, area high schools.

Financial data: Year ended 12/31/2004.
Assets, $185,468 (M); Expenditures, $9,146;
Total giving, $6,500; Grants to individuals, totaling
$6,500.
Type of support: Support to graduates or students
of specific schools; Undergraduate support.
Application information: Deadline Mar. 31;
Completion of formal application required.
EIN: 256086650

1477
Kennedy T. Friend Education Fund

c/o PNC Advisors
620 Liberty Ave.
Pittsburgh, PA   15222-2719

Foundation type: Independent foundation
Limitations: Scholarships to the children of lawyers
of Allegheny County, PA, to attend Yale University or
University of Paris, Sorbonne, France.
Financial data: Year ended 12/31/2002.
Assets, $5,509,527 (M); Expenditures,
$103,030; Total giving, $88,458; Grants to
individuals, totaling $88,458.
Type of support: Support to graduates or students
of specific schools; Undergraduate support.
Application information: Applications accepted.
Application form required.
Initial approach: Letter.
Deadline(s): May 1
EIN: 256026198

1478
Friendship Fund, Inc.

c/o Mellon Financial Corp.
P.O. Box 185
Pittsburgh, PA   15230-0185
Application address: Eleanor Millan, c/o Mellon
Trust of New England, 1 Boston Pl., Boston, MA
02108

Foundation type: Independent foundation
Limitations: Grants for the advancement of the
humanities, the sciences, and the welfare of
humanity with emphasis on environmental
protection, social services, and international
affairs.
Financial data: Year ended 06/30/2004.
Assets, $4,900,390 (M); Expenditures,
$298,277; Total giving, $270,000.
Fields of interest: Humanities; Natural resources;
Human services; International affairs.
Type of support: Undergraduate support.
Application information: Unsolicited applications
no longer accepted; All funds for scholarship grants
are committed in advance by the trustees.
Program description:
Scholarship Program: A very small number of
scholarship grants are awarded each year to
institutions on behalf of individuals whose needs
are known to the trustees. Grants are not normally
made to graduate students.
EIN: 136089220

1479
Walter and Mabel Fromm Scholarship
Trust

c/o U.S. Bank, N.A.
P.O. Box 3194, Ste. MK-WI-TWPT
Milwaukee, WI   53201-3194
Contact: Gil Lindemann
E-mail: Gil.Lindemann@USbank.com

Foundation type: Independent foundation

Limitations: Scholarships to graduates of Maple
Grove (elementary) School in Hamburg, WI, and
Merrill Senior Public High School in Merrill, WI.
Publications: Application guidelines.
Financial data: Year ended 02/28/2005.
Assets, $3,458,346 (M); Expenditures,
$179,049; Total giving, $156,775; Grants to
individuals, 36 grants totaling $156,775 (high:
$4,725, low: $750).
Fields of interest: Vocational education; Nursing
school/education.
Type of support: Support to graduates or students
of specific schools; Undergraduate support.
Application information: Contact trust for current
application deadline/guidelines.
Program description:
Scholarship Fund: Applicants are divided into four
classes of qualification. Preference is shown to
applicants in Class I. Consideration is then given to
Classes II, III, and IV, respectively. Class I: Students
who are already enrolled in a four-year degree
program or three-year nursing school program and
have:
· attended grades 1-6 and graduated from
  Maple Grove School, Hamburg, WI
· attended grades 7-12 in the City of Merrill,
  WI Public School System and graduated
  from Merrill Senior Public High School
· maintained at least a 2.5 GPA in grades
  9-12
Class II: Students who are intending to enroll in a
four-year degree program or three-year nursing
school program, have attended grade six at and
graduated from Maple Grove School, Hamburg, WI,
and have met the last two requirements stated
above for Class I. Class III: Students who are
intending to enroll in a four-year degree program or
three-year nursing school program and have met
requirements 2 and 3 for Class I. Class IV: Students
intending to enroll in a two-year degree or associate
program at North Central Technical College, WI, who
otherwise meet all Class I or II requirements. The
total number of Class IV students selected to
receive scholarships in any one year must not
exceed the total number of Class III students
selected in that year.
EIN: 396250027

1480
Frontiers of Science Foundation of
Oklahoma

P.O. Box 26967
Oklahoma City, OK   73126   (405) 290-5600

Foundation type: Independent foundation
Limitations: Scholarships to students at OK high
schools that have participated in The Frontiers of
Science Symposium in the current year, for study at
OK colleges and universities.
Financial data: Year ended 06/30/2004.
Assets, $903,970 (M); Expenditures, $38,300;
Total giving, $37,250; Grants to individuals,
totaling $6,000.
Fields of interest: Science.
Type of support: Undergraduate support.
Application information: Deadline Apr. 1; Initial
approach by letter or telephone; Completion of
formal application required.
EIN: 730642039

1481
Ruth Perrin Fues Memorial Scholarship
Fund

c/o St. Clair County State Bank
P.O. Box 539
Osceola, MO   64776-0539
Contact: Robin Smith, Trust Off., St. Clair City State
Bank

Foundation type: Independent foundation
Limitations: Scholarships to graduates of Osceola
public schools and any public school in St. Clair
County, MO, to attend a college or university.
Financial data: Year ended 12/31/2003.
Assets, $234,211 (M); Expenditures, $10,864;
Total giving, $9,132; Grants to individuals, totaling
$9,132.
Type of support: Support to graduates or students
of specific schools; Undergraduate support.
Application information: Application form required.
Deadline(s): May 15
Additional information: Application must include
short statement, extracurricular and work
experience, and two references.
EIN: 431788109

1482
Fukunaga Scholarship Foundation

P.O. Box 2788
Honolulu, HI   96803   (808) 564-1386
Contact: Sandy Wong, Scholarship Admin.
FAX: (808) 523-3937;
E-mail: sandyw@servco.com; For applications
include: c/o Scholarship Selection Committee.;
URL: http://www.servco.com/scholarship

Foundation type: Independent foundation
Limitations: Scholarships to residents of HI for a
minimum of one year to study business
administration at the University of Hawaii or other
accredited universities.
Publications: Application guidelines.
Financial data: Year ended 12/31/2004.
Assets, $4,010,341 (M); Expenditures,
$163,573; Total giving, $132,917; Grants to
individuals, 56 grants totaling $132,917 (high:
$2,500, low: $833).
Fields of interest: Business school/education.
Type of support: Undergraduate support.
Application information: Deadline Feb. 15; Initial
approach by telephone; Completion of formal
application, including transcripts, SAT scores, and
at least two letters of reference (one from high
school principal, teacher, or counselor, one from
business or professional person in the community)
required; Interviews required for semi-finalists.
Program description:
*Annual Four-Year Scholarships in Business
Administration:* Applicants must demonstrate
academic ability, leadership qualities, interest in
business in the Pacific Basin area, and financial
need. Applicants must have a high school
cumulative 3.0 GPA. Applicants must plan to return
to HI or the Pacific Island region to work and live.
EIN: 990600370

1483
W. C. Fuller Educational Trust

c/o Bank of America, N.A.
P.O. Box 831041
Dallas, TX   75283-1041
Application addresses: c/o Southern Methodist
University, Office of Financial Aid, P.O. Box 196,
SMU, Dallas, TX 75275, tel.: (214) 692-3417, c/o
Paul Quinn College, Dir., Financial Aid or Chair. of

Admissions and Financial Aid Comm., Dallas, TX 75241

Foundation type: Independent foundation
Limitations: Scholarships to students accepted to or currently enrolled at Southern Methodist University or Bishop College, TX.
Financial data: Year ended 10/31/2004. Assets, $670,256 (M); Expenditures, $36,484; Total giving, $30,000; Grants to individuals, totaling $30,000.
Type of support: Support to graduates or students of specific schools; Undergraduate support.
Application information: Applications accepted. Application form required.
  Deadline(s): For SMU: Feb. 1 for freshmen and transfer students and Jan. 1 for continuing students, For Bishop College: Aug. 1
  Additional information: Applicants should apply by completing the standard application and financial aid forms required by their respective schools.
EIN: 756234718

1484
C. G. Fuller Foundation

c/o Bank of America, N.A.
P.O. Box 448, SC3-240-04-17
Columbia, SC   29201
Contact: Pamela S. Carroll

Foundation type: Independent foundation
Limitations: Scholarships to incoming first-year students who are residents of SC to attend SC colleges and universities.
Financial data: Year ended 12/31/2004. Assets, $3,845,579 (M); Expenditures, $205,775; Total giving, $170,000.
Type of support: Undergraduate support.
Application information: Application form required.
  Initial approach: Contact university financial aid office.
  Deadline(s): Mar. 31
  Additional information: Interviews required.
EIN: 576050492

1485
Frank R. Fuller Trust

c/o Bank of America, N.A.
777 Main St., CT2-102-22-02
Hartford, CT   06115   (860) 952-7387
Application address: c/o Fuller Scholarship Committee, 300 Summit St., Hartford, CT 06106, tel.: (203) 527-3157, ext. 365

Foundation type: Independent foundation
Limitations: Scholarships and student loans to seniors of the Protestant faith, attending Hartford County, CT, high schools who are members of the Congregational Church and who plan to attend an accredited degree program at a four-year college or university.
Financial data: Year ended 12/31/2003. Assets, $4,623,459 (M); Expenditures, $129,831; Total giving, $88,150; Grants to individuals, 78 grants totaling $88,150 (high: $2,500, low: $80).
Fields of interest: Christian agencies & churches.
Type of support: Scholarships—to individuals; Support to graduates or students of specific schools; Undergraduate support.
Application information: Deadline Apr. 15 for application, Mar. 1 for letter requesting application form; Completion of formal application required, including recommendations, transcripts, and financial aid form.

Program description:
  Frank Roswell Fuller Scholarship Fund: The grant portion of the award is applied to the recipient's total expenses for room, board, travel to and from college, and personal expenses. If there is remaining need, the loan portion of the award is applied against the recipient's total expenses for tuition, books, and supplies. The loans are interest-free and payable within ten years of the termination of study at a mutually agreed upon installment rate. Awards are for one semester and are renewable. Six new awards are made per year.
EIN: 066028136

1486
Fulton Bank Scholarship Foundation

c/o Fulton Financial Advisors, N.A.
P.O. Box 3215
Lancaster, PA   17604-3215

Foundation type: Company-sponsored foundation
Limitations: Scholarships to financially needy dependents of employees of Fulton Financial Corporation.
Financial data: Year ended 12/31/2004. Assets, $90 (M); Expenditures, $36,000; Total giving, $36,000; Grants to individuals, 24 grants totaling $36,000 (high: $1,500, low: $1,500).
Type of support: Employee-related scholarships.
Application information: Application form required.
  Deadline(s): Contact foundation for current application deadline
  Additional information: Application should include transcripts.
EIN: 236769593

1487
The Fund for American Studies

1706 New Hampshire Ave., N.W.
Washington, DC   20009   (202) 986-0384
Contact: Roger Ream, Pres.
FAX: (202) 986-0390; E-mail: info@tfas.org;
Additional tel.: (800) 741-6964; URL: http://www.tfas.org

Foundation type: Public charity
Limitations: Scholarships to undergraduate students for attendance at specific summer programs involving coursework at Georgetown University, Charles University in Prague, Czech Republic, Greece, and the University of Hong Kong.
Publications: Annual report; Financial statement; Informational brochure; Newsletter.
Financial data: Year ended 09/30/2004. Assets, $20,747,114 (M); Expenditures, $5,901,260; Total giving, $1,161,002.
Fields of interest: Journalism/publishing; International affairs, public policy; International exchange, students; International affairs; Economics; Political science.
Type of support: Internship funds; Support to graduates or students of specific schools; Undergraduate support.
Application information: Contact fund for current application deadline/guidelines; See Web site for further information.

Program description:
  Scholarship Fund: These programs, for students with demonstrated leadership skills, instill in young people an understanding of the concepts that sustain America's commitment to freedom-limited government, the rule of law, personal responsibility, and a market economy. Scholarships are given based on financial need, but only to students accepted into one of the specified seven institutes. Institutes are held at Georgetown University,

Washington DC, Indiana University, Indianapolis, IN, Charles University, Prague, Greece, and the University of Hong Kong.
EIN: 136223604

1488
Fund for the Advancement of the State System of Higher Education, Inc.

2986 N. 2nd St.
Harrisburg, PA   17110   (717) 720-4051
Contact: Charles R. Agnew, Pres.

Foundation type: Public charity
Limitations: Scholarships to residents of PA for higher education.
Financial data: Year ended 06/30/2003. Assets, $2,883,848 (M); Expenditures, $696,319; Total giving, $117,551; Grants to individuals, 133 grants totaling $117,551.
Type of support: Undergraduate support.
Application information: Contact fund for current application deadline/guidelines.
EIN: 222686249

1489
Fundacao Beneficente Faialense, Inc.

P.O. Box 14291
East Providence, RI   02914
Contact: Conselho Supremo

Foundation type: Independent foundation
Limitations: Scholarships primarily to students residing in Portugal, in the Azores, and in the U.S.
Financial data: Year ended 06/30/2005. Assets, $244,399 (M); Expenditures, $24,381; Total giving, $13,000; Grants to individuals, totaling $13,000.
Fields of interest: International exchange, students; Portugal.
Type of support: Technical education support; Undergraduate support.
Application information: Application form required.
  Initial approach: Letter.
  Deadline(s): Feb. 22
EIN: 042722163

1490
The Mark R. Fusco Foundation

555 Long Wharf Dr.
New Haven, CT   06535   (203) 777-7451
Application address: c/o Nancy Meyerjack, Fusco Corp., P.O. Box 9618, New Haven, CT 06535

Foundation type: Independent foundation
Limitations: Scholarships primarily to residents of CT.
Financial data: Year ended 06/30/2002. Assets, $192,983 (M); Expenditures, $93,935; Total giving, $51,540; Grant to an individual, 1 grant totaling $2,000.
Type of support: Scholarships—to individuals.
Application information: Applications by letter accepted throughout the year.
Program description:
  Scholarship Program: Selection is based upon academic record, performance on SAT/ACT examinations, financial need, and recommendations from instructors.
EIN: 222566615

1491
Susan C. Fusco Memorial Scholarship Fund
8813 Hawthorne Ln., Ste. T4
Laurel, MD   20708
Contact: Edward C. Diggs, V.P.

Foundation type: Operating foundation
Limitations: Scholarships for college or trade school education limited to high school graduates who attended Beacon Heights Elementary School, MD.
Financial data: Year ended 06/30/2003. Assets, $157,951 (M); Expenditures, $18,944; Total giving, $16,000; Grants to individuals, 7 grants totaling $16,000 (high: $4,000, low: $1,000).
Fields of interest: Vocational education.
Type of support: Support to graduates or students of specific schools; Technical education support; Undergraduate support.
Application information: Deadline July 1; Completion of formal application required, including high school transcripts and proof of attendance at Beacon Heights Elementary School, MD.
EIN: 521739989

1492
Future Foundation
753 St. Francis Pl., Ste. 4003A
Mobile, AL   36602
Contact: Chris W. Cole, Pres.

Foundation type: Independent foundation
Limitations: Scholarships to individuals in Mobile, AL, for higher education.
Financial data: Year ended 12/31/2003. Assets, $1,900 (M); Expenditures, $18,726; Total giving, $18,036; Grants to individuals, 5 grants totaling $18,036 (high: $6,836, low: $400).
Type of support: Scholarships—to individuals.
Application information: Applications accepted throughout the year; Contact foundation for current application guidelines; Initial approach by proposal.
EIN: 631249602

1493
Arthur Gabler Scholarship Fund
(formerly Arthur Gabler Scholarship Trust)
c/o JPMorgan Chase Bank
P.O. Box 31412
Rochester, NY   14603-1412
Application address: c/o Trumbull High School, Guidance Dept., 72 Strobel Rd., Trumbull, CT 06611

Foundation type: Independent foundation
Limitations: Scholarships to students living in Trumbull, CT, who are attending Trumbull High School.
Financial data: Year ended 06/30/2005. Assets, $397,371 (M); Expenditures, $56,360; Total giving, $47,420; Grants to individuals, totaling $47,420.
Type of support: Scholarships—to individuals; Support to graduates or students of specific schools.
Application information: Deadline Mar. 1; Completion of formal application required, including parents' and student's tax returns and a financial aid form.
Program description:
  Scholarship Program: In the past, the trust has paid $2,500 each year for four years of undergraduate studies for each of the students

selected. Usually one student is selected each year.
EIN: 066244605

1494
Robert Gaffney Trust
c/o Marshall & Illsley Trust Co.
P.O. Box 2980
Milwaukee, WI   53201
Application address: c/o Thomas P. Gaffney, 503 Russell Ave., Long Beach, MS, 39560-6013, tel.: (228) 363-0387

Foundation type: Independent foundation
Limitations: Scholarships to graduates of Northern Pines High School, and Rhinelander High School, WI, for undergraduate education, with a focus upon those studying education.
Financial data: Year ended 01/31/2005. Assets, $775,335 (M); Expenditures, $38,864; Total giving, $31,500; Grants to individuals, totaling $31,500.
Fields of interest: Teacher school/education.
Type of support: Support to graduates or students of specific schools; Undergraduate support.
Application information: Application form required.
  Deadline(s): Contact foundation for current application deadline/guidelines
  Additional information: Application should include GPA.
EIN: 816106700

1495
Carmela Gagliardi Foundation
789 Upper Scotsborough Way
Bloomfield Hills, MI   48304-3827

Foundation type: Independent foundation
Limitations: Scholarships primarily to students of Italian descent who have been accepted to a recognized medical school.
Financial data: Year ended 12/31/2004. Assets, $75,005 (M); Expenditures, $26,763; Total giving, $25,000; Grants to individuals, totaling $25,000.
Fields of interest: Medical school/education; Italy.
Type of support: Graduate support.
Application information: Unsolicited requests for funds not considered or acknowledged.
EIN: 382895105

1496
Gala Foundation
10621 Calle Lee, No. 141
Los Alamitos, CA   90720
Contact: Dineshchandra Gala, Pres.

Foundation type: Operating foundation
Limitations: Scholarships to individuals of Indian descent for higher education.
Financial data: Year ended 09/30/2004. Assets, $364,915 (M); Expenditures, $106,744; Total giving, $106,450; Grants to individuals, 12 grants totaling $36,000 (high: $5,000, low: $2,500).
Fields of interest: India.
Type of support: Scholarships—to individuals.
Application information: Deadline Sept. 1; Contact foundation for current application guidelines; Initial approach by letter.
EIN: 330777331

1497
Galena Park ISD Education Foundation, Inc.
14705 Woodforest Blvd.
Houston, TX   77015   (832) 386-1000
Contact: Dr. Mark Henry, Superintendent
URL: http://www.galenaparkisd.com/foundati.htm

Foundation type: Public charity
Limitations: Scholarships to students of Galena Park Independent School District, TX.
Financial data: Year ended 12/31/2003. Assets, $224,005 (M); Expenditures, $170,069; Total giving, $117,418; Grants to individuals, totaling $117,418.
Type of support: Support to graduates or students of specific schools.
Application information: Applications accepted. Application form required. Application form available on the grantmaker's Web site.
  Initial approach: Letter or telephone.
  Additional information: Contact foundation for current application deadline/guidelines.
EIN: 760563596

1498
Galesburg-Augusta Education Foundation
(formerly Galesburg-Augusta Community Foundation)
1076 N. 37th St.
Galesburg, MI   49053   (269) 484-2000

Foundation type: Operating foundation
Limitations: Scholarships to students who graduate from Galesburg-Augusta Community Schools, MI, including one award to a student studying forestry at Michigan State University.
Publications: Informational brochure.
Financial data: Year ended 06/30/2002. Assets, $0 (M); Expenditures, $47,243; Total giving, $46,915; Grants to individuals, totaling $46,915.
Fields of interest: Environment, forests.
Type of support: Support to graduates or students of specific schools; Undergraduate support.
Application information:
  Initial approach: Letter to high school counselor.
  Deadline(s): Feb.
  Additional information: Contact foundation for current application guidelines.
EIN: 383082334

1499
Galion Community Foundation
135 Harding Way W.
Galion, OH   44833   (419) 468-9047
Contact: Steven J. Erlsten, Chair.
Application address for scholarships: c/o Galion Community Foundation Board, 380 Tidd Dr., Galion, OH 44833

Foundation type: Independent foundation
Limitations: Scholarships to residents of Galion, OH.
Financial data: Year ended 06/30/2003. Assets, $1,423,889 (M); Expenditures, $88,306; Total giving, $68,138; Grants to individuals, 10 grants totaling $16,350 (high: $5,500, low: $500).
Type of support: Scholarships—to individuals.
Application information:
  Deadline(s): Nov. 15.
  Additional information: Contact foundation for current application guidelines.
EIN: 316023104

1500
Catherine M. Gallagher Scholarship Fund
c/o Kathryn A. Heily
24 Burning Tree Dr.
Novato, CA 94949-6111

Foundation type: Independent foundation
Limitations: Scholarships to Novato, CA, residents for higher education.
Financial data: Year ended 12/31/2004.
Assets, $26,095 (M); Expenditures, $21,673; Total giving, $20,000; Grants to individuals, 2 grants totaling $20,000.
Type of support: Scholarships—to individuals.
Application information: Applications not accepted.
EIN: 943187129

1501
Laura Schriber Gallik Memorial Scholarship Fund
c/o The National Bank of Delaware County
P.O. Box 389
Walton, NY 13856 (607) 865-4126

Foundation type: Independent foundation
Limitations: Scholarships to graduates of Walton Central High School, NY.
Financial data: Year ended 12/31/2004.
Assets, $209,659 (M); Expenditures, $8,331; Total giving, $7,500; Grants to individuals, totaling $7,500.
Type of support: Support to graduates or students of specific schools; Undergraduate support.
Application information: Deadline Apr.; Initial approach by letter or telephone; Completion of formal application required.
EIN: 161406866

1502
Romaine Gallmeier Seminarian Scholarship Fund
c/o Associated Banc-Corp
P.O. Box 408
Neenah, WI 54957-0408
Application address: c/o East Central Synod of Wisconsin, 33003 B N. Richmond St., Appleton, WI 54911, tel.: (920) 734-5381

Foundation type: Independent foundation
Limitations: Scholarships only to theological students of the American Lutheran Synod.
Financial data: Year ended 12/31/2004.
Assets, $2,890,445 (M); Expenditures, $10,551; Total giving, $7,393; Grants to individuals, totaling $7,393.
Fields of interest: Theological school/education.
Type of support: Graduate support.
Application information:
  Initial approach: Letter.
  Deadline(s): Applications accepted throughout the year.
  Additional information: Contact foundation for current application guidelines.
EIN: 396550978

1503
Ira M. Gambill Medical Education Trust
c/o AmSouth Bank
P.O. Box 1981
Kingsport, TN 37662 (423) 229-0291
Contact: Terry L. Moretz, V.P.

Foundation type: Independent foundation

Limitations: Scholarships to Johnson County, TN students attending East Tennessee State University Medical School with preference to medical students.
Financial data: Year ended 06/30/2005.
Assets, $587,854 (M); Expenditures, $39,521; Total giving, $32,290; Grants to individuals, totaling $32,290.
Fields of interest: Medical school/education.
Type of support: Support to graduates or students of specific schools; Graduate support.
Application information:
  Initial approach: Letter.
  Deadline(s): Contact trust for current application deadline
  Additional information: The principal of Mountain City High School and the superintendent of Johnson County schools will screen applicants and recommend eligible applicants to the trust.
Program description:
  Scholarship Program: Scholarships for up to four years may be provided to students with a "C" or better grade average. If sufficient applications are not received from medical students, additional scholarship applications will be accepted with preference in the following order:
  · Nursing Education
  · Physical Therapy
  · Scientific Education
  · Medical Technicians.
EIN: 626186726

1504
Dr. R. A. Gandy, Jr./Mercy Hospital Medical Staff, Inc. Scholarship Fund
2148 Evergreen Rd.
Toledo, OH 43606 (419) 536-8224
Contact: Yvonne M. Gandy, Pres.

Foundation type: Independent foundation
Limitations: Scholarships to students for postgraduate study in a science field at the University of Toledo or the Medical College of Ohio, OH.
Financial data: Year ended 12/31/2004.
Assets, $117,825 (M); Expenditures, $9,065; Total giving, $9,000; Grants to individuals, 2 grants totaling $9,000 (high: $5,000, low: $4,000).
Fields of interest: Medical school/education; Science, formal/general education.
Type of support: Support to graduates or students of specific schools; Postgraduate support.
Application information:
  Deadline(s): July 20.
  Additional information: Contact fund for current application guidelines.
EIN: 311491102

1505
Wanda K. Ganyard Scholarship Trust
(formerly The Lyle B. & Wanda K. Ganyard Scholarship Trust)
c/o FirstMerit Bank, N.A.
121 S. Main St., Ste. 200
Akron, OH 44308 (330) 384-7302
Application addresses: c/o Copley High School, 3807 Ridgewood Rd., Copley, OH 44321-1697, tel.: (330) 668-3227, or c/o Revere High School, 3420 Everett Rd., Richfield, OH 44286, tel.: (330) 659-6111

Foundation type: Independent foundation
Limitations: Scholarships to graduates of Copley High School and Revere High School, both in OH,

who have family residing in one of these schools districts.
Financial data: Year ended 09/30/2004.
Assets, $660,668 (M); Expenditures, $61,845; Total giving, $51,489; Grants to individuals, totaling $49,489.
Type of support: Support to graduates or students of specific schools; Undergraduate support.
Application information:
  Initial approach: Letter or telephone.
  Additional information: Contact high school for current application deadline/guidelines.
EIN: 346820819

1506
Allan C. & Leila J. Garden Foundation
c/o Bank of America, N.A.
P.O. Box 4007
Macon, GA 31213 (478) 744-6455
Scholarship application address: P.O. Box 308, Fitzgerald, GA 31750

Foundation type: Independent foundation
Limitations: Scholarships and student loans to residents of Fitzgerald, GA, and Ben Hill, Irwin, and Wilcox counties, GA.
Financial data: Year ended 05/31/2005.
Assets, $4,864,653 (M); Expenditures, $285,633; Total giving, $240,000.
Type of support: Scholarships—to individuals; Student loans—to individuals.
Application information: Applications accepted. Application form required.
  Deadline(s): None
EIN: 586103546

1507
George Gardner & Fanny Whiting Blanchard Scholarship Fund
c/o Bank of America, N.A.
P.O. Box 1802
Providence, RI 02901-1802
Application address: c/o Bank of America, N.A., P.O. Box 3730, Nashua, NH 03061

Foundation type: Independent foundation
Limitations: Scholarships to graduates of Wilton High School, NH.
Financial data: Year ended 03/31/2005.
Assets, $433,550 (M); Expenditures, $18,516; Total giving, $16,400; Grants to individuals, 18 grants totaling $16,400 (high: $2,300, low: $500).
Type of support: Scholarships—to individuals; Support to graduates or students of specific schools.
Application information: Applications accepted throughout the year; Completion of formal application required, including transcripts.
Program description:
  Scholarship Program: Scholarships are awarded based on financial need, academic standing, and character. Preference is shown to residents of the town of Wilton and to those who completed their entire course of study at Wilton High School. Scholarships are renewable.
EIN: 026004699

1508
Annie Gardner Foundation
620 S. 6th St.
Mayfield, KY 42066-2316
Contact: Nancy H. Sparks, Dir., Education

Foundation type: Operating foundation

Limitations: Student loans to residents of Graves County, KY, who are graduates of Graves County High School or Mayfield High School.
Financial data: Year ended 05/31/2005. Assets, $9,979,771 (M); Expenditures, $543,029; Total giving, $278,529; Grants to individuals, totaling $278,529; Loans to individuals, totaling $297,250.
Type of support: Support to graduates or students of specific schools; Undergraduate support.
Application information: Application form required.
  Deadline(s): July 1
Program description:
  Student Loan Program: Maximum loan amounts are $2,000 and $3,000 per year for undergraduate and graduate students respectively. If student attends summer school, he or she may receive an additional $500.
EIN: 610564889

1509
The Gardner Foundation
304 S. Highview Rd.
Middletown, OH   45044
Contact: Martha Sorrell, Business Mgr.

Foundation type: Independent foundation
Limitations: Scholarships to graduating seniors of high schools in Edgewood, Franklin, Hamilton County, Madison, and Middletown, OH.
Publications: Application guidelines; Program policy statement.
Financial data: Year ended 05/31/2005. Assets, $4,712,860 (M); Expenditures, $320,803; Total giving, $298,000.
Type of support: Support to graduates or students of specific schools; Undergraduate support.
Application information: Applications accepted. Application form required.
  Deadline(s): None
  Additional information: Applications available through high school guidance counselors in the specified school districts.
Program description:
  Scholarship Program: Scholarships are for students who will immediately enroll in a four-year baccalaureate program. Only graduating seniors in the following school districts are eligible: Edgewood, Franklin, Hamilton County, Madison, and Middletown. Scholarship amount is based on need and is payable to the qualified educational institution.
EIN: 316050604

1510
Mary K. Garr Scholarship Foundation Trust
c/o First Merchants Bank, N.A.
200 E. Jackson St.
Muncie, IN   47305   (765) 747-1521
Contact: Stacy Terhune; Laura Moorman

Foundation type: Independent foundation
Limitations: Scholarships to worthy high school graduates who are U.S. citizens and residents of Delaware County, IN. Preference is given to those studying medicine or nursing.
Financial data: Year ended 12/31/2004. Assets, $1,913,378 (M); Expenditures, $112,528; Total giving, $97,800; Grants to individuals, 17 grants totaling $97,800 (high: $8,350, low: $2,750).
Fields of interest: Medical school/education; Nursing school/education.
Type of support: Scholarships—to individuals.

Application information: Application form required.
  Deadline(s): Mar. 22
EIN: 351938040

1511
Frederick S. & Emma Gartner Charitable Trust
P.O. Box 1151
Bellingham, WA   98227   (360) 671-1500
Contact: Mark B. Packer, Tr.
FAX: (360) 676-5123; E-mail: packer@nas.com

Foundation type: Independent foundation
Limitations: Scholarships to residents of WA, primarily in Whatcom County, of either Jewish faith or who have a declared interest in Jewish studies and/or Jewish community activities.
Financial data: Year ended 07/31/2005. Assets, $0 (M); Expenditures, $8,970; Total giving, $8,625; Grants to individuals, 3 grants totaling $8,625 (high: $4,500, low: $1,875).
Fields of interest: Jewish agencies & temples.
Type of support: Scholarships—to individuals.
Application information: Deadline June 30; Completion of formal application required.
EIN: 911733246

1512
Garwin Family Foundation
1102 W. Chautauqua St.
Carbondale, IL   62901-2453
Contact: Leo Garwin, Pres.
Application address: 35 Hillcrest Dr., Carbondale, IL 62901-2444, tel.: (618)529-2005

Foundation type: Operating foundation
Limitations: Scholarships to law and medical students at Southern Illinois University.
Financial data: Year ended 12/31/2002. Assets, $516,575 (M); Expenditures, $78,274; Total giving, $44,300; Grants to individuals, 4 grants totaling $18,100 (high: $10,000, low: $100).
Fields of interest: Law school/education; Medical school/education.
Type of support: Support to graduates or students of specific schools; Graduate support.
Application information: Applications accepted throughout the year; Contact foundation for current application guidelines.
EIN: 731440816

1513
Cora Belle Gates Education Trust Fund
P.O. Box 640
Vinton, IA   52349
Application address: c/o Donna Meyocks, 3033 55th St., Vinton, IA 52349, tel.: (319) 443-2120

Foundation type: Independent foundation
Limitations: Scholarships to students graduating from high schools within a 50-mile radius of the Gates's farm, Northern Benton County, IA.
Financial data: Year ended 12/31/2004. Assets, $58,854 (M); Expenditures, $12,710; Total giving, $12,000; Grants to individuals, totaling $12,000.
Type of support: Undergraduate support.
Application information: Deadline May 1; Completion of formal application required, including college major and institution, and list of high school activities.
EIN: 426445183

1514
John B. Gates Memorial Scholarship Fund
P.O. Box 846
Clearfield, PA   16830

Foundation type: Independent foundation
Limitations: Scholarships to graduating seniors at Curwensville High School, PA.
Financial data: Year ended 06/30/2005. Assets, $293,340 (M); Expenditures, $22,964; Total giving, $22,000; Grants to individuals, totaling $22,000.
Type of support: Support to graduates or students of specific schools; Undergraduate support.
Application information: Applications not accepted.
EIN: 251721073

1515
Hilliard Gates Scholarship Foundation
c/o National City Bank
P.O. Box 94651
Cleveland, OH   44101-4651   (216) 575-2934
Application address: c/o Michelle Herald, National City Bank of Indiana, P.O. Box 110, Fort Wayne, IN 46802, tel.: (219) 461-7115

Foundation type: Independent foundation
Limitations: Scholarships to high school graduates living within a 75-mile radius of Allen County, IN, who are incoming freshman athletes attending the University of St. Francis, IU-PU, Ft. Wayne, or the Indiana Institute of Technology.
Financial data: Year ended 07/31/2004. Assets, $17,196 (M); Expenditures, $7,652; Total giving, $7,000; Grants to individuals, totaling $7,000.
Fields of interest: Athletics/sports, training.
Type of support: Support to graduates or students of specific schools; Undergraduate support.
Application information: Contact foundation for current application deadline/guidelines.
EIN: 311180053

1516
Mildred E. Gates Trust
c/o Bank of America, N.A., P.C. Group
P.O. Box 6768
Providence, RI   02940-6768
Application address: c/o Guidance Counselor, Gardner High School, 200 Catherine St., Gardner, MA 01440

Foundation type: Independent foundation
Limitations: Scholarships for higher education to residents living within a 20 mile radius of Gardner City Hall in Gardner, MA.
Financial data: Year ended 12/31/2004. Assets, $840,019 (M); Expenditures, $43,968; Total giving, $33,000.
Type of support: Scholarships—to individuals.
Application information: Application form required.
  Initial approach: Letter.
  Deadline(s): Mar. 15
EIN: 046643614

1517
Katharine and Calvin Gatlin Scholarship Fund
c/o The Trust Co. of Oklahoma
P.O. Box 3627
Tulsa, OK   74101

Foundation type: Independent foundation

Limitations: Scholarships to high school seniors in Vinita, OK.
Financial data: Year ended 12/31/2004.
Assets, $1,255,813 (M); Expenditures, $58,991; Total giving, $46,176; Grants to individuals, totaling $46,176.
Type of support: Undergraduate support.
Application information: Applications not accepted.
EIN: 736266862

1518
Charles L. and Anna N. Gault Memorial Scholarship Fund
c/o Unizan Bank, N.A.
514 Market St.
Parkersburg, WV 26101-5144 (304) 424-8832
Contact: Tracy Wharton, Trust Off., Unizan Bank, N.A.

Foundation type: Independent foundation
Limitations: Scholarships by nomination only to financially needy senior students attending high schools in Wood and Wirt counties, WV, who are members of the Methodist church.
Financial data: Year ended 12/31/2004.
Assets, $894,176 (M); Expenditures, $41,275; Total giving, $32,000; Grants to individuals, totaling $32,000.
Fields of interest: Protestant agencies & churches.
Type of support: Support to graduates or students of specific schools; Awards/grants by nomination only; Undergraduate support.
Application information:
Deadline(s): Three months prior to graduation date.
Additional information: Individual applications not accepted; Principals and guidance counselors nominate one applicant from each school.
EIN: 556096793

1519
Arthur J. Gavrin Foundation, Inc.
1865 Palmer Ave., Ste. 108
Larchmont, NY 10538-3037
Application address: c/o New Rochelle High School, Attn.: Guidance Dept., 265 Clove Rd., New Rochelle, NY 10801, tel.: (914) 576-4542

Foundation type: Independent foundation
Limitations: Scholarships to graduating students from New Rochelle High School, NY, for higher education.
Financial data: Year ended 12/31/2004.
Assets, $396,492 (M); Expenditures, $19,570; Total giving, $19,500; Grants to individuals, totaling $19,500.
Type of support: Support to graduates or students of specific schools; Undergraduate support.
Application information: Deadline Apr. 15; Application by letter, including transcripts, test results, statement of need and personal and family history.
EIN: 136265245

1520
The Norbert Gazin Educational Foundation
c/o KeyBank N.A.
800 Superior Ave., 4th Fl.
Cleveland, OH 44114

Foundation type: Independent foundation

Limitations: Scholarships to individuals for higher education.
Financial data: Year ended 12/31/2004.
Assets, $2,129,248 (M); Expenditures, $147,309; Total giving, $126,575; Grants to individuals, 196 grants totaling $126,575 (high: $1,400, low: $500).
Type of support: Undergraduate support.
Application information: Applications not accepted.
EIN: 527124691

1521
GBU Foundation
4254 Clairton Blvd.
Pittsburgh, PA 15227-3394 (412) 884-5100
Contact: James R. Stoker, Secy.-Treas.
FAX: (412) 884-9815; *E-mail:* info@gbu.org;
URL: http://www.gbu.org

Foundation type: Public charity
Limitations: Scholarships to GBU members or annuitants for secondary or postsecondary education.
Financial data: Year ended 12/31/2003.
Assets, $1,104,066 (M); Expenditures, $47,768; Total giving, $43,250; Grants to individuals, 74 grants totaling $43,250 (high: $1,000, low: $500).
Fields of interest: Secondary school/education; Higher education.
Type of support: Scholarships—to individuals.
Application information: Applications accepted. Application form required. Application form available on the grantmaker's Web site.
Deadline(s): May 31 for high school freshman grants; Feb.1 for all other grants
Applicants should submit the following:
1) Transcripts
2) SAT
3) Letter(s) of recommendation
4) Essay
5) ACT
EIN: 256076646

1522
Gehl Foundation, Inc.
143 Water St.
West Bend, WI 53095 (262) 334-9461
Contact: Thomas M. Rettler, Treas.

Foundation type: Company-sponsored foundation
Limitations: Postsecondary scholarships to individuals in communities where Gehl Company has facilities.
Financial data: Year ended 12/31/2004.
Assets, $715,445 (M); Expenditures, $23,823; Total giving, $23,500; Grants to individuals, 19 grants totaling $23,500 (high: $1,500, low: $250).
Type of support: Scholarships—to individuals.
Application information:
Deadline(s): None
Additional information: Contact foundation for current application guidelines.
EIN: 391039217

1523
GEICO Philanthropic Foundation
c/o GEICO Corp.
5260 Western Ave.
Chevy Chase, MD 20815 (301) 986-3802
Contact: David L. Schindler, Chair.

Foundation type: Company-sponsored foundation

Limitations: Scholarships to military personnel, and both active and retired federal employees, and their natural, or legally adopted children or step children.
Financial data: Year ended 12/31/2004.
Assets, $32,042,376 (M); Expenditures, $3,524,193; Total giving, $3,508,835; Grants to individuals, 6 grants totaling $15,000 (high: $2,500, low: $2,500).
Type of support: Employee-related scholarships.
Application information: Contact foundation for current application deadline/guidelines.
Program description:
Geico Family Scholarship Programs/Snyder and Byrne Scholarships: Scholarship applicants must meet these requirements:
· Full-time associates must have worked for the companies for at least one continuous year by the application deadline, Mar. 1.
· Part-time associates must have been employed by GEICO for three years and worked for a minimum of 1,000 hours in the previous year.
· Dependent children must be unmarried and primarily supported by the associate. They may be natural or legally adopted children or stepchildren.
· High school seniors, high school graduates, college undergraduates, or graduate students who are enrolled or planning to enroll in a full-time course of study at an accredited two or four year college, university or vocational-technical school.
Children of officers of the companies above grade 8 are not eligible for these scholarships.
EIN: 521202740

1524
Victoria S. & Bradley L. Geist Foundation
c/o Hawaii Community Foundation
1164 Bishop St., Ste. 800
Honolulu, HI 96813 (808) 566-5524
Contact: Robin Johnson, Prog. Off., Private Foundations
E-mail: foundations@hcf-hawaii.org; *Tel. for Robin Johnson:* (808) 537-6333; *URL:* http://www.hawaiicommunityfoundation.org/grants/pfGrants.php

Foundation type: Independent foundation
Limitations: Scholarships to individuals in HI for higher education who are or have been in foster care.
Publications: Application guidelines.
Financial data: Year ended 12/31/2004.
Assets, $42,292,428 (M); Expenditures, $2,143,001; Total giving, $1,820,411; Grants to individuals, 120 grants totaling $283,000 (high: $4,000, low: $500).
Type of support: Scholarships—to individuals.
Application information:
Initial approach: Letter or telephone.
Additional information: Contact foundation for current application deadline/guidelines.
EIN: 990163400

1525
Robert Gemmill Foundation
c/o Union Planters Bank
P.O. Box 449
Marion, IN 46952-0449
Application address: c/o Timothy L. Faust, V.P. & Trust Off., 402 S. Washington, St., Marion, IN, tel.: (765) 668-5851

Foundation type: Independent foundation
Limitations: Scholarships to residents of Grant County, IN.
Financial data: Year ended 12/31/2004.
Assets, $720,294 (M); Expenditures, $38,370; Total giving, $29,375; Grants to individuals, totaling $29,375.
Fields of interest: Higher education; Law school/education.
Type of support: Undergraduate support.
Application information: Application form required.
  Deadline(s): May 15
  Additional information: Application should include transcripts, a personal essay, recent photograph, and three letters of recommendation.
Program descriptions:
  Willard B. Gemmill Law Scholarship: Awards funds to Grant County residents to attend law school full-time.
  Florence J. Gemmill Scholarship: Awards funds to female residents of Grant County for full-time study. Applicants must include their class rank, GPA, and SAT or ACT scores.
  Willard B. Gemmill Scholarship: Awards funds to male residents of Grant County for full-time study. Applicants must include their class rank, GPA, and SAT or ACT scores.
EIN: 356494321

1526
General Charitable Society of Newburyport

P.O. Box 365
Newburyport, MA 01950
Contact: Sara-Anne Eames, Pres.

Foundation type: Independent foundation
Limitations: Scholarships to residents of Newburyport, MA.
Financial data: Year ended 10/31/2004.
Assets, $1,216,544 (M); Expenditures, $79,357; Total giving, $53,961.
Type of support: Scholarships—to individuals.
Application information: Application form required.
  Deadline(s): May 1.
EIN: 042589680

1527
General Education Fund, Inc.

c/o Merchants Trust Co.
P.O. Box 8490
Burlington, VT 05402
Application address: Attn: General Education Fund (GEF), Inc., Scholarship-NEW, VSAC Scholarship Program, P.O. Box 2000, Champlain Mill, Winooski, VT, 05404-2601

Foundation type: Independent foundation
Limitations: Scholarships by nomination only to financially needy VT residents for study in the U.S. Students may not apply directly.
Financial data: Year ended 07/31/2005.
Assets, $31,346,556 (M); Expenditures, $1,490,306; Total giving, $1,308,467; Grants to individuals, 901 grants totaling $1,308,467.
Type of support: Scholarships—to individuals; Awards/grants by nomination only.
Application information: Applicants must be nominated; Unsolicited applications not accepted or acknowledged; Eligible individuals will be contacted by the fund by mail.
EIN: 036009912

1528
Geneseo Foundation

c/o Central Bank Illinois, Trust Dept.
P.O. Box 89
Geneseo, IL 61254
Contact: John DuBois, Trust Off., Central Bank Illinois
Application address: c/o Central Bank Illinois, 101 N. State St., Geneseo, IL 61254

Foundation type: Independent foundation
Limitations: Scholarships only to graduates of Geneseo High School, IL.
Financial data: Year ended 03/31/2005.
Assets, $6,714,800 (M); Expenditures, $346,277; Total giving, $316,205; Grants to individuals, totaling $19,575.
Type of support: Scholarships—to individuals; Support to graduates or students of specific schools.
Application information: Deadline first week of each month; Completion of formal application required.
EIN: 366079604

1529
Genesis Foundation, Inc.

3323 N. 45th St.
Omaha, NE 68104 (402) 451-7545
Application address: c/o Robert K. Gjere, P.O. Box 540456, Omaha, NE 68154, tel.: (402) 289-4984

Foundation type: Independent foundation
Limitations: Scholarships to young Christians residing in urban Omaha, NE, who are pursuing theological education. Major emphasis for determining eligibility will be given to their living environments, financial need, other available resources, and commitment to the ministry.
Financial data: Year ended 12/31/2004.
Assets, $5,929,699; Expenditures, $497,633; Total giving, $300,680.
Fields of interest: Theological school/education.
Type of support: Undergraduate support.
Application information: Applications accepted. Application form required.
  Deadline(s): Contact foundation for current application deadlines
  Applicants should submit the following:
    1) Financial information
    2) Essay
  Additional information: Interviews required.
EIN: 470799762

1530
Genesis Health Services Foundation

1227 E. Rusholme St.
Davenport, IA 52803 (563) 421-6865
Contact: Missy Gowey, Exec. Dir.
FAX: (563) 421-6869;
E-mail: goweym@genesishealth.com; URL: http://www.genesishealth.com/media/charitable_contributions.aspx

Foundation type: Public charity
Limitations: Forgivable student loans to nursing students residing in IA. Scholarships also to Genesis Medical Center staff for professional development.
Publications: Application guidelines; Informational brochure.
Financial data: Year ended 06/30/2003.
Assets, $14,048,471 (M); Expenditures, $1,532,924; Total giving, $1,223,020; Grants to individuals, 12 grants totaling $69,650.
Fields of interest: Nursing school/education.
Type of support: Employee-related scholarships; Undergraduate support.
Application information:
  Deadline(s): Mar. 5 for Gala Nursing Scholarship
  Additional information: Completion of formal application required, including transcript, copy of college/university acceptance letter, essay, and three letters of recommendation. Applicants must have a minimum high school GPA of 3.0 or college GPA of 2.5. Half of the loan will be forgiven if the student works as a nurse for Genesis Health Services full-time for one year. The entire loan will be forgiven if the student does so for two years.
Program descriptions:
  Carlen Brinser Award: Awarded annually to one or more members of Genesis Medical Center nursing staff for continuing professional education.
  Gala Nursing Scholarship: Awards $5,000 as a forgivable loan to current high school seniors or past high school graduates planning to enter nursing at area colleges/universities offering a Bachelor's degree.
  Virginia I. Pilcher, R.N. Scholarship: Scholarship awarded to an R.N. employed by Genesis Medical Center for higher education toward a Bachelor's or advanced degree in nursing.
EIN: 421421670

1531
Mabelle M. George Educational Trust

c/o Melvin McMillan
43 Kayla Dr.
Montesano, WA 98563-9654
Application address: c/o Brookings-Harbor Scholarship Foundation, Inc., P.O. Box 7673, Brookings, OR 97415

Foundation type: Operating foundation
Limitations: Scholarships to graduates of Brookings-Harbor High School, OR, attending a four-year college or university.
Financial data: Year ended 12/31/2004.
Assets, $300,082 (M); Expenditures, $30,107; Total giving, $23,667; Grants to individuals, 8 grants totaling $23,667 (high: $7,500, low: $2,000).
Type of support: Support to graduates or students of specific schools; Undergraduate support.
Application information: Applications accepted throughout the year; Initial approach by letter; Completion of formal application required.
EIN: 916358636

1532
Georgia Dental Education Foundation, Inc.

5100 Lavista Rd.
P.O. Box 49
Tucker, GA 30085-0049 (770) 931-9246
Contact: Randall J. Phillips, D.D.S., Pres.
URL: http://www.gadental.org/GDEF.htm

Foundation type: Public charity
Limitations: Scholarships of $1,000 each to dental students attending The Medical College of Georgia.
Financial data: Year ended 08/31/2004.
Assets, $806,839 (M); Expenditures, $55,729; Total giving, $39,000; Grants to individuals, totaling $39,000.
Fields of interest: Dental school/education.
Type of support: Support to graduates or students of specific schools.

Application information: Contact foundation for current application deadline/guidelines.
EIN: 581623147

1533
Georgia Engineering Foundation
100 Peachtree St., Ste. 2150
Atlanta, GA   30303   (404) 521-2324
Contact: Jeff Dingle, Pres.; Schol. Chair.: Roger Austin
FAX: (404) 521-0283; E-mail: info@GEFinc.org;
URL: http://www.gefinc.org

Foundation type: Public charity
Limitations: Scholarships to residents of GA who are pursuing a career in engineering or engineering technology.
Publications: Application guidelines; Annual report.
Financial data: Year ended 09/30/2005.
Assets, $539,618 (M); Expenditures, $80,767;
Total giving, $58,660; Grants to individuals, totaling $58,660.
Fields of interest: Engineering school/education.
Type of support: Scholarships—to individuals.
Application information: Applications accepted. Application form required. Application form available on the grantmaker's Web site.
Deadline(s): Aug. 31
Applicants should submit the following:
1) Transcripts
2) SAT
3) Letter(s) of recommendation
4) GPA
Additional information: Applications should be submitted online.
EIN: 237193629

1534
Georgia-Pacific Foundation, Inc.
133 Peachtree St. N.E.
Atlanta, GA   30303   (404) 652-4182
Contact: Curley M. Dossman, Jr., Pres.
FAX: (404) 749-2754; URL: http://www.gp.com/center/community/index.html

Foundation type: Company-sponsored foundation
Limitations: Scholarships only to high school juniors whose parents are employees of Georgia-Pacific Corporation in areas where there are major plants/offices.
Publications: Application guidelines; Biennial report; Corporate giving report.
Financial data: Year ended 12/31/2004.
Assets, $163,637 (M); Expenditures, $4,029,638; Total giving, $4,029,080; Grants to individuals, 119 grants totaling $122,000 (high: $2,000, low: $2,000).
Type of support: Employee-related scholarships; Precollege support.
Application information: Application form required.
Deadline(s): Feb. 1
Additional information: Applications by letter accepted Sept. through Feb. 1; Applicants must take PSAT and apply during junior year of high school.
EIN: 936023726

1535
The Gerber Foundation
(formerly The Gerber Companies Foundation)
4747 W. 48th St., Ste. 153
Fremont, MI   49412-8119   (231) 924-3175
Contact: Catherine A. Obits, Prog. Mgr.
FAX: (231) 924-7906; E-mail: tgf@ncresa.org;
Additional E-mail (for Catherine A. Obits): cobits@ncresa.org; URL: http://www.gerberfoundation.org

Foundation type: Independent foundation
Limitations: Scholarships to residents of Newaygo and Muskegon Counties, MI.
Publications: Application guidelines; Annual report (including application guidelines); Program policy statement.
Financial data: Year ended 12/31/2005.
Assets, $82,646,107 (M); Expenditures, $5,141,405; Total giving, $4,277,576.
Type of support: Scholarships—to individuals; Undergraduate support.
Application information: Application form required. Application form available on the grantmaker's Web site.
Initial approach: E-mail.
Deadline(s): Feb. 28
Applicants should submit the following:
1) Transcripts
2) Letter(s) of recommendation
3) GPA
4) Essay
5) Budget Information
6) ACT
Additional information: Application available from the high school guidance counselor's office or the foundation office.
Program descriptions:
Gerber Foundation Merit Scholarship: Students from Newaygo and Muskegon Counties, MI, must have a GPA of 3.7 or lower. The scholarship provides a one-time payment of $1,700 to be applied to tuition, fees and books for a course of study at a post-secondary institution.
Dan Gerber, Sr. Medallion Scholarship: Students from Newaygo County, MI, must have a GPA of 3.71 or higher. The scholarship provides $6,800 to be applied to tuition, fees and books.
EIN: 386068090

1536
Sgt. Philip German Memorial Foundation
c/o M&T Bank
21 E. Market St.
York, PA   17401-1500
Contact: Joe Macri, Trust Off., M&T Bank
Application address: P.O. Box 2961, Harrisburg, PA 17105

Foundation type: Independent foundation
Limitations: Scholarships to children of veterans living in Cumberland and Dauphin counties, PA.
Financial data: Year ended 12/31/2004.
Assets, $1,537,478 (M); Expenditures, $82,059; Total giving, $74,400; Grants to individuals, totaling $74,400.
Fields of interest: Military/veterans' organizations.
Type of support: Undergraduate support.
Application information: Deadline June 10; Completion of formal application required.
EIN: 236745697

1537
The German Society of Maryland, Inc.
8058 Old Montgomery Rd.
Ellicott City, MD   21043
Application address: P.O. Box 22585, Baltimore, MD 21203

Foundation type: Independent foundation
Limitations: Scholarships to individuals of German descent attending colleges in MD.
Financial data: Year ended 12/31/2004.
Assets, $568,158 (M); Expenditures, $55,336; Total giving, $6,300; Grants to individuals, totaling $6,300.
Fields of interest: Germany.
Type of support: Undergraduate support.
Application information: Deadline Apr. 15; Application by letter, including FAF and transcript.
EIN: 520326115

1538
Gerondelis Foundation, Inc.
56 Central Ave., Ste. 201
Lynn, MA   01901   (781) 595-3311
Contact: Gregory C. Demakis, Pres.

Foundation type: Independent foundation
Limitations: Scholarships to Essex County, MA, high school graduates who are of at least one half Greek descent and rank in the top 15 percent of their classes.
Financial data: Year ended 12/31/2004.
Assets, $4,928,493 (L); Expenditures, $453,087; Total giving, $363,000; Grants to individuals, 28 grants totaling $81,000 (high: $3,000, low: $3,000).
Fields of interest: Greece.
Type of support: Undergraduate support.
Application information: Applications accepted throughout the year; Contact foundation for current application deadline; Initial approach by letter outlining financial need; Completion of formal application required.
EIN: 046130871

1539
John & Dorothy Geyer Scholarship Fund
c/o JPMorgan Chase Bank, N.A
P.O. Box 1308
Milwaukee, WI   53201
Application address: c/o Beverly Rodgers-Nemeth, 121 W. Franklin St., Elkhart, IN 46516, tel.: (219) 524-3521

Foundation type: Independent foundation
Limitations: Scholarships to individuals for higher education.
Financial data: Year ended 12/31/2004.
Assets, $2,533,119 (M); Expenditures, $115,260; Total giving, $99,500.
Type of support: Undergraduate support.
Application information: Contact fund for current application deadline/guidelines.
EIN: 352113954

1540
William & Marian Ghidotti Foundation
c/o Wells Fargo Bank, N.A.
P.O. Box 63954, 17th Fl.
San Francisco, CA   94163
Application address: c/o William Toms, Tr., 3961 DeSabla Rd., Cameron Park, CA 95682, tel.: (530) 677-3994

Foundation type: Independent foundation

Limitations: Scholarships to residents of Nevada County, CA.
Financial data: Year ended 12/31/2004. Assets, $11,896,732 (M); Expenditures, $656,348; Total giving, $590,454; Grants to individuals, 145 grants totaling $480,333 (high: $7,000, low: $750).
Type of support: Scholarships—to individuals.
Application information: Deadlines Feb. for new scholarships, Aug. for renewals; Completion of formal application required, including transcripts, student and family income statement, and personal resume.
EIN: 946181833

1541
Giant Eagle Foundation
c/o Giant Eagle, Inc.
101 Kappa Dr.
Pittsburgh, PA 15238 (412) 963-6200

Foundation type: Company-sponsored foundation
Limitations: Scholarships to PA Giant Eagle employees and their children.
Financial data: Year ended 08/31/2005. Assets, $32,172,579 (M); Expenditures, $1,601,623; Total giving, $1,460,522; Grants to individuals, 75 grants totaling $75,000 (high: $1,000, low: $1,000).
Type of support: Employee-related scholarships.
Application information: Application form required.
  Deadline(s): Nov. 1
  Applicants should submit the following:
   1) Transcripts
   2) SAT
   3) ACT
  Additional information: Application should also include two letters of recommendation and supporting information.
Program description:
  Scholarship Program: Fifteen scholarships will be awarded to employees and twelve will be awarded to the children of employees. All winners will receive $1,000 per year for up to four years. To qualify for renewal, the recipient must remain a full-time student in good academic standing with evidence of progression toward a degree. Family income cannot exceed $45,000 per year.
EIN: 256033905

1542
Giants Community Fund
c/o SBC Park
24 Willie Mays Plz.
San Francisco, CA 94107
Contact: Sue Petersen, Exec. Dir.
URL: http://www.giants.mlb.com/NASApp/mlb/sf/community/sf_community_communityfund.jsp

Foundation type: Public charity
Limitations: Scholarships to Junior Giants students for higher education.
Publications: Application guidelines; Newsletter.
Financial data: Year ended 12/31/2003. Assets, $528,892 (M); Expenditures, $1,252,202; Total giving, $1,100,863.
Fields of interest: Higher education.
Type of support: Scholarships—to individuals.
Application information: Applications accepted. Application form required.
  Additional information: Applications can be obtained from your local Junior Giants commissioner or coach.
EIN: 943200061

1543
Esther A. and Bruce S. Gibbs Charitable Trust
c/o Citizens Bank & Trust
101 N. Main St.
P.O. Box 70
Rock Port, MO 64482-0070
Contact: Jerry Moore, Trust Off.; Karen Tiemeyer, Asst. Trust. Off.

Foundation type: Independent foundation
Limitations: Scholarships for Atchison County, MO, students.
Financial data: Year ended 12/31/2004. Assets, $856,992 (M); Expenditures, $64,188; Total giving, $38,750; Grants to individuals, totaling $38,750.
Type of support: Scholarships—to individuals.
Application information: Applications accepted.
  Deadline(s): None
  Additional information: Contact trust for current application guidelines.
EIN: 436370943

1544
Ruby L. Gibbs Charitable Trust
c/o Citizens Bank Wealth Mgmt., N.A.
328 S. Saginaw St., M/C 002072
Flint, MI 48502
Application addresses: c/o Ovid-Elsie High School, 8989 E. Colony Rd., Elsie, MI 48831, or c/o Arthur Hill High School, 3115 Mackinaw St., Saginaw, MI 49602-3221

Foundation type: Independent foundation
Limitations: Scholarships to students of Arthur Hill High School who will be attending an accredited college in MI and students of Ovid-Elsie High School attending a college in central MI.
Financial data: Year ended 12/31/2004. Assets, $1,138,276 (M); Expenditures, $71,428; Total giving, $58,735; Grants to individuals, 12 grants totaling $37,115 (high: $5,850, low: $1,105).
Type of support: Support to graduates or students of specific schools; Undergraduate support.
Application information: Applications accepted. Application form required.
  Deadline(s): May 1
EIN: 386658848

1545
Addison H. Gibson Foundation
1 PPG Pl., Ste. 2230
Pittsburgh, PA 15222-5401 (412) 261-1611
Contact: Rebecca Wallace, Exec. Dir.
FAX: (412) 261-5733;
E-mail: rwallace@gibson-fnd.org; *URL:* http://www.gibson-fnd.org

Foundation type: Independent foundation
Limitations: Student loans to financially needy residents of Allegheny, Armstrong, Beaver, Butler, Clarion, Crawford, Erie, Fayette, Forest, Greene, Lawrence, Mercer, Venango, Warren, Washington, and Westmoreland counties, PA and the westernmost portions of Cambria, Elk, Indiana, Jefferson, and Somerset counties, PA, who have completed at least one year in an undergraduate or graduate degree program.
Financial data: Year ended 12/31/2004. Assets, $27,584,622 (M); Expenditures, $1,451,079; Total giving, $1,009,665; Grants to individuals, 104 grants totaling $1,009,665 (high: $30,000, low: $1,000); Loans to individuals, 138 loans totaling $791,415.

Fields of interest: Higher education.
Type of support: Student loans—to individuals; Graduate support; Undergraduate support.
Application information: Applications accepted. Application form required.
  Initial approach: Letter, telephone or e-mail.
  Deadline(s): None
  Additional information: Interviews required.
Program description:
  Gibson Educational Loan Program: Applicants must have successfully completed at least one year of undergraduate school and remain full-time students at accredited colleges and universities. First-year undergraduate students are ineligible. Full-time graduate students may be eligible after completing one or more years of graduate studies. Transferring students must complete at least one year of full-time study at the new school. Those wishing to verify their eligibility may telephone or e-mail the foundation office for more information. The application process begins with an interview in the foundation's offices. Loans are awarded on the basis of character, reputation, academic record, and sense of responsibility. Interest at the rate of two percent per annum will be charged on loans from date of issue. The interest rate will increase to five percent per annum one year after graduation, or one month after education is otherwise terminated. At that time, the recipient is also required to begin repayment of the principal. Students are required to submit transcripts to the foundation at regular intervals.
EIN: 250965379

1546
E. L. Gibson Foundation
5626 Ash Grove St.
Montgomery, AL 36116 (334) 353-1490
Contact: Tim Alford, Exec. Dir.
FAX: (334) 393-4553;
E-mail: gateway135@aol.com

Foundation type: Independent foundation
Limitations: Scholarships for health-related study to residents of Coffee County, AL, and bordering counties attending approved universities in AL.
Financial data: Year ended 12/31/2003. Assets, $3,590,705 (M); Expenditures, $214,274; Total giving, $167,154; Grants to individuals, 34 grants totaling $16,252 (high: $1,228, low: $45).
Fields of interest: Health sciences school/education.
Type of support: Scholarships—to individuals.
Application information: Applications accepted throughout the year; Initial approach by letter to Enterprise State Junior College; Completion of formal application required.
EIN: 630383929

1547
Gibson Foundation, Inc.
c/o Karen Noll
P.O. Box 146
Plymouth, IN 46563-0146

Foundation type: Independent foundation
Limitations: Scholarships primarily to graduates of Marshall County, IN, schools for higher education; some scholarships also to graduates of St. Joseph County Schools, both in IN.
Financial data: Year ended 12/31/2004. Assets, $1,697,008 (M); Expenditures, $100,120; Total giving, $96,100.
Type of support: Support to graduates or students of specific schools; Undergraduate support.

Application information: Application form required.
Initial approach: Letter.
Deadline(s): Apr. 1.
EIN: 351422779

1548
Goldie Gibson Scholarship Fund
302 S. Osage Ave.
Bartlesville, OK   74003-3522   (918) 336-0008
Contact: Ruth Andrews, Secy.-Treas.

Foundation type: Independent foundation
Limitations: Student loans primarily to residents of OK. Loans are renewable.
Financial data: Year ended 02/28/2005.
Assets, $620,404 (M); Expenditures, $4,891; Total giving, $0; Loans to individuals, totaling $3,712.
Type of support: Student loans—to individuals.
Application information: Applications accepted. Application form required.
Deadline(s): None
EIN: 736183311

1549
Giddings & Lewis Foundation, Inc.
142 Doty St.
Fond du Lac, WI   54935   (920) 921-9400
Contact: Terri Groth

Foundation type: Company-sponsored foundation
Limitations: Scholarships to children of Giddings and Lewis employees with excellent academic standing.
Financial data: Year ended 12/31/2004.
Assets, $1,834,309 (M); Expenditures, $186,888; Total giving, $177,060; Grants to individuals, 30 grants totaling $34,250 (high: $2,000, low: $250).
Type of support: Employee-related scholarships; Undergraduate support.
Application information: Contact foundation for application deadlines and guidelines.
EIN: 396061306

1550
Alice & Murray Giddings Foundation
c/o Dr. Joseph Lalka
P.O. Box 182
Chatham, NY   12037

Foundation type: Independent foundation
Limitations: Scholarships to residents of Columbia County, NY for higher education.
Financial data: Year ended 12/31/2004.
Assets, $871,054 (M); Expenditures, $61,455; Total giving, $47,627; Grants to individuals, 14 grants totaling $47,627 (high: $5,000, low: $986).
Type of support: Undergraduate support.
Application information: Contact foundation for current application deadline/guidelines.
EIN: 141781248

1551
Mary Louise Gidley Scholarship Fund
P.O. Box 54
Shenandoah, IA   51601
Contact: Richard Profit, Superintendant
Application address: 304 W. Nishna Rd., Shenandoah, IA 51601, tel.: (712) 246-1581

Foundation type: Independent foundation

Limitations: Student loans only to graduates of Shenandoah High School, IA.
Financial data: Year ended 12/31/2004.
Assets, $452,955 (M); Expenditures, $32,109; Total giving, $30,000; Grants to individuals, totaling $30,000.
Type of support: Support to graduates or students of specific schools; Undergraduate support.
Application information: Deadline May 15; Completion of formal application required; Interviews required.
EIN: 421091743

1552
Elvine and Leroy Gienger Foundation, Inc.
P.O. Box 337
Chiloquin, OR   97624-0337

Foundation type: Operating foundation
Limitations: Scholarships to residents of the Chiloquin, OR, area.
Financial data: Year ended 11/30/2002.
Assets, $604,651 (M); Expenditures, $26,075; Total giving, $23,208; Grants to individuals, 23 grants totaling $23,208 (high: $2,500, low: $250).
Type of support: Scholarships—to individuals.
Application information: Application form required.
Deadline(s): Two weeks before graduation
Additional information: Scholarships are renewable. Generally, the foundation chooses two or three new recipients per year.
EIN: 930981050

1553
The Gifford Foundation, Inc.
165 Farm Rd.
Woodside, CA   94062

Foundation type: Independent foundation
Limitations: Scholarships to individuals residing in CA and HI for undergraduate education.
Financial data: Year ended 05/31/2004.
Assets, $18,354,600 (M); Expenditures, $1,054,892; Total giving, $918,759; Grants to individuals, 3 grants totaling $55,000 (high: $20,000, low: $15,000).
Type of support: Undergraduate support.
Application information: Contact foundation for current application deadlines/guidelines.
EIN: 943303273

1554
Hazel Chase Gifford Fund
c/o TD Banknorth, N.A
P.O. Box 1180
South Yarmouth, MA   02664
Application address: c/o Guidance Counselor, Dennis-Yarmouth Regional High School, Yarmouth, MA 02675

Foundation type: Independent foundation
Limitations: Scholarships to residents of Yarmouth, MA, who are students of Dennis-Yarmouth Regional High School.
Financial data: Year ended 10/31/2004.
Assets, $318,429 (M); Expenditures, $20,701; Total giving, $15,800; Grants to individuals, 14 grants totaling $15,800 (high: $1,200, low: $1,000).
Type of support: Support to graduates or students of specific schools; Undergraduate support.
Application information: Deadline Apr. 15; Completion of formal application required;

Application forms may be obtained from Dennis-Yarmouth Regional High School.
EIN: 046208360

1555
Harold C. Gift Scholarship Trust
c/o Wachovia Bank, N.A.
100 N. Main St., 13th Fl.
Winston-Salem, NC   27150-6732
(800) 576-5135
Contact: Scholarship Prog.: Michael Boyles

Foundation type: Independent foundation
Limitations: Scholarship to a graduate of Reading High School, PA, to attend the University of Pennsylvania. One scholarships to a graduate of Muhlenburg High School, PA, to attend Albright College, PA. One scholarship also to a graduate of Reading High School, PA, for attendance at Philadelphia University, PA.
Financial data: Year ended 12/31/2004.
Assets, $1,846,396 (M); Expenditures, $65,467; Total giving, $52,139.
Type of support: Support to graduates or students of specific schools; Undergraduate support.
Application information: Applications accepted. Application form required.
Additional information: Applications available at Reading and Muhlenberg High Schools.
EIN: 236524243

1556
Muriel Gilbert Memorial Scholarship Fund
c/o KeyBank N.A.
800 Superior Ave., 4th Fl.
Cleveland, OH   44114
Application addresses: c/o James Hause, Prof., Eastern Michigan Univ., Music Dept., 1215 Huron River Dr., Ypsilanti, MI 48197, or c/o Superintendent of Schools, Milan Area Schools, 920 North St., Milan, MI 48160

Foundation type: Independent foundation
Limitations: Scholarships to Eastern Michigan University full-time music majors concentrating on voice with a 3.0 GPA or higher. One-year scholarships also to Milan, MI, area high school seniors who intend to major in music.
Financial data: Year ended 09/30/2005.
Assets, $526,151 (M); Expenditures, $5,064; Total giving, $0.
Fields of interest: Music; Music (choral); Performing arts, education.
Type of support: Support to graduates or students of specific schools; Undergraduate support.
Application information: Applications accepted. Application form required.
Additional information: Contact Eastern Michigan University or Milan area schools for current application deadline.
Program description:
Scholarship Program: Milan, MI high school senior recipients are selected by a panel of music dept. staff from Milan area schools.
EIN: 386525706

1557
Edwin Gilbert Trust - Georgetown School Fund
c/o Wachovia Bank, N.A.
100 N. Main St., 13th Fl.
Winston-Salem, NC   27150
Application address: c/o James C. Driscoll III, P.O. Box 248, Bethel, CT 06801, tel.: (203) 744-5000

Foundation type: Independent foundation
Limitations: Scholarships to individuals living in the area that is formerly known as the Tenth School District of Georgetown, CT.
Financial data: Year ended 12/31/2004.
Assets, $519,627 (M); Expenditures, $32,054; Total giving, $25,000.
Type of support: Support to graduates or students of specific schools.
Application information: Deadline May 1; Initial approach by letter requesting application; Completion of formal application required.
EIN: 066044834

1558
The Lucille P. and Edward C. Giles Foundation
(formerly The Edward C. Giles Foundation)
P.O. Box 830
Mooresville, NC   28115
Contact: Bernard R. Fitzgerald, Pres.

Foundation type: Independent foundation
Limitations: Scholarships only to children of employees of Carauster Industries, Inc. and its subsidiaries.
Financial data: Year ended 12/31/2004.
Assets, $14,999,891 (L); Expenditures, $613,334; Total giving, $524,658; Grants to individuals, 43 grants totaling $250,658 (high: $6,000, low: $2,600).
Type of support: Employee-related scholarships; Scholarships—to individuals.
Application information: Application form required.
   Deadline(s): Mar. 1
   Applicants should submit the following:
      1) Financial information
   Additional information: Application should also include biographical, scholastic, extracurricular and civic information.
EIN: 581450874

1559
Emily Gill Trust
c/o Bank of America, N.A., P.C. Group
P.O. Box 1802
Providence, RI   02940-1802
Application addresses: c/o Chicopee High School, 650 Front St., Chicopee, MA 01013, c/o Chicopee Comprehensive High School, 617 Montgomery St., Chicopee, MA 01020

Foundation type: Independent foundation
Limitations: Scholarships to graduates of Chicopee High School and Chicopee Comprehensive High School, MA.
Financial data: Year ended 12/31/2004.
Assets, $309,914 (M); Expenditures, $16,393; Total giving, $12,000.
Type of support: Support to graduates or students of specific schools; Undergraduate support.
Application information: Applications by letter accepted throughout the year.
EIN: 046021060

1560
Conrad H. and Anna Belle Gillen Scholarship Fund
(formerly Conrad H. and Anna Belle Gillen Trust Fund)
52 S. Broad St.
Norwich, NY   13815-1646

Foundation type: Independent foundation

Limitations: Scholarships to current-year high school graduates residing in Fulton County, NY, and attending Gloversville High School, Northville Central School, Johnstown High School, Mayfield Central School, Broadalbin-Perth, and Perth Christian Bible Academy, NY, with preference shown to those entering the ministry or pursuing Christian work. Scholarships are $500 per year for up to four years.
Publications: Application guidelines.
Financial data: Year ended 12/31/2004.
Assets, $306,680 (M); Expenditures, $13,386; Total giving, $12,000; Grants to individuals, 24 grants totaling $12,000 (high: $500, low: $500).
Type of support: Scholarships—to individuals; Support to graduates or students of specific schools.
Application information: Application form required.
   Deadline(s): May 15
   Applicants should submit the following:
      1) Transcripts
      2) Letter(s) of recommendation
      3) GPA
      4) Financial information
   Additional information: Applications must be submitted to guidance director of eligible high schools.
EIN: 146016128

1561
Herbert & Florence Gilles Scholarship Trust
c/o Citizens Bank, N.A., Wealth Mgmt.
328 S. Saginaw St., M/C 002072
Flint, MI   48502
Application address: c/o Ann Siminowski, Nouvel Catholic Central High School, 2555 Wieneke Rd., Saginaw, MI 48602, tel.: (989) 797-6605

Foundation type: Independent foundation
Limitations: Scholarships only to students at Nouvel Catholic Central High School, MI.
Financial data: Year ended 12/31/2004.
Assets, $191,869 (M); Expenditures, $9,897; Total giving, $7,400; Grants to individuals, 3 grants totaling $7,400.
Type of support: Support to graduates or students of specific schools; Undergraduate support.
Application information: Applications accepted. Application form required.
   Deadline(s): 2nd Mon. in May
EIN: 386738557

1562
Gillespie Family Charity Trust
P.O. Box 3010
Russellville, AR   72811-3010   (479) 967-6763
Contact: Jim Lanier, Trust Off., Simmons First National Bank

Foundation type: Independent foundation
Limitations: Scholarships to graduates of Pope County high schools, AR.
Financial data: Year ended 12/31/2004.
Assets, $454,796 (M); Expenditures, $15,251; Total giving, $12,034; Grants to individuals, totaling $9,625.
Type of support: Support to graduates or students of specific schools; Undergraduate support.
Application information: Contact foundation for current application deadline/guidelines; Initial approach by letter, including academic ability, financial need, disability status and three letters of character reference.
EIN: 716145471

1563
Henry William Gillet Memorial, Inc.
c/o Ken E. Malm Financial Services Center
P.O. Box 730
Pine Bluffs, WY   82082-0730   (307) 245-3222
Contact: J. William Parsons, V.P.

Foundation type: Independent foundation
Limitations: Student loans to graduates of Laramie County School District No. 2, WY.
Financial data: Year ended 06/30/2005.
Assets, $91,059 (M); Expenditures, $12,558; Total giving, $10,500; Loans to individuals, 2 loans totaling $10,500.
Type of support: Support to graduates or students of specific schools; Undergraduate support.
Application information: Applications by letter, outlining financial need and intentions of education, accepted throughout the year.
Program description:
   Student Loan Program: A maximum of four individuals are selected each semester.
EIN: 237135637

1564
James P. & Ruth C. Gillroy Foundation, Inc.
480 Mamaroneck Ave.
Harrison, NY   10528
Contact: Edmund C. Grainger, Jr., Pres.
Application address: 480 Harrison Ave., Harrison, NY 10528, tel.: (914) 282-6306

Foundation type: Independent foundation
Limitations: Undergraduate scholarships primarily to residents of the five boroughs of the City of New York.
Publications: Application guidelines.
Financial data: Year ended 05/31/2005.
Assets, $1,290,867 (M); Expenditures, $45,086; Total giving, $28,750; Grants to individuals, totaling $28,750.
Type of support: Undergraduate support.
Application information: Deadline is at least two months prior to the date payment is due the college; Application by letter, including a secondary school transcript and college transcript (if applicable), a statement of extracurricular activities and educational goals, the name and address of the college to be attended, the courses to be undertaken, the anticipated total annual expenses, and how these expenses are to be met.
Program description:
   Scholarship Program: Generally, 50 percent of the foundation's total giving to individuals goes to residents of New York City. Maximum award for each student is $1,250 per semester, or $2,500 per year.
EIN: 237129473

1565
Marian Leota Gilmore Scholarship Trust for Sullivan High School Students
80 E. Jefferson St.
Franklin, IN   46131
Contact: Robert D. Heuchan, Tr.

Foundation type: Independent foundation
Limitations: Scholarships to graduates of Sullivan High School, IN, for higher education.
Financial data: Year ended 12/31/2004.
Assets, $581,320 (M); Expenditures, $28,965; Total giving, $19,000; Grants to individuals, 13 grants totaling $19,000 (high: $5,200, low: $600).

Type of support: Support to graduates or students of specific schools; Undergraduate support.
Application information: Applications accepted. Application form required.
 Additional information: Contact trust for current application deadline.
EIN: 356700224

1566
The Clyde O. Ginder Memorial Foundation
c/o Wells Fargo Bank Nebraska, N.A.
1919 Douglas St.
Omaha, NE 68102-1310   (260) 461-6470
Application address: c/o Mount Pleasant United Methodist Church, 7380 State Rd. 8, Butler, IN 46721

Foundation type: Independent foundation
Limitations: Scholarships to high school graduates who are U.S. citizens and members of the Mount Pleasant United Methodist Church in Butler, IN.
Financial data: Year ended 06/30/2005. Assets, $887,098 (M); Expenditures, $19,825; Total giving, $8,002; Grants to individuals, totaling $5,602.
Fields of interest: Protestant agencies & churches.
Type of support: Scholarships—to individuals.
Application information: Applications accepted. Application form required.
 Deadline(s): Applications accepted throughout the year.
 Applicants should submit the following:
  1) Transcripts
  2) Financial information
EIN: 356484641

1567
Giovanini Foundation
P.O. Box 160
Jackson, WY 83001
Application address: P.O. Box 607, Teton Village, WY 83205, tel.: (307) 739-1426

Foundation type: Independent foundation
Limitations: Scholarships to students graduating from DuBois High School or Jackson High School, WY.
Financial data: Year ended 12/31/2004. Assets, $1,628,636 (M); Expenditures, $93,053; Total giving, $69,750; Grants to individuals, totaling $40,000.
Type of support: Support to graduates or students of specific schools; Undergraduate support.
Application information: Deadline Mar. 15; Contact schools for current application guidelines.
EIN: 830308568

1568
Glades Electric Educational Foundation, Inc.
P.O. Box 519
Moore Haven, FL 33471   (863) 946-0061
Contact: Jeffrey R. Brewington, Secy.-Treas.

Foundation type: Company-sponsored foundation
Limitations: Scholarships to graduating seniors whose permanent, legal residence is served directly or indirectly by Glades Electric Cooperative, Inc.
Financial data: Year ended 12/31/2004. Assets, $197,339 (M); Expenditures, $42,193; Total giving, $14,000; Grants to individuals, 14 grants totaling $14,000 (high: $1,000; low: $1,000).
Type of support: Undergraduate support.

Application information:
 Initial approach: Letter.
 Applicants should submit the following:
  1) ACT
  2) SAT
  3) GPA
  4) Class rank
  5) Transcripts
  6) Financial information
 Additional information: Contact foundation for further program information.
EIN: 651083705

1569
Sheldon Glaser Trust
c/o Fifth Third Bank
101 W. Stephenson St.
Freeport, IL 61032   (815) 233-6003
Contact: Troy Lessman, Tr.

Foundation type: Independent foundation
Limitations: Scholarships to students enrolled at a qualifying educational institution that qualifies as a public charity, primarily in Lena, IL.
Financial data: Year ended 12/31/2004. Assets, $309,780 (M); Expenditures, $20,105; Total giving, $15,600; Grants to individuals, totaling $15,600.
Type of support: Scholarships—to individuals.
Application information: Deadline Mar.; Contact foundation for current application deadline/ guidelines; Completion of formal application required.
EIN: 367074441

1570
Howard Glasgow Charity Foundation
6743 E. Camino Principal
Tucson, AZ 85715
Contact: Howard L. Glasgow, Pres.
Application address: P.O. Box 1779, Oracle, AZ 85623-1779

Foundation type: Independent foundation
Limitations: Scholarships to individuals to cover the costs of tuition and books for higher education, primarily in OR.
Financial data: Year ended 12/31/2004. Assets, $8,829 (M); Expenditures, $72,482; Total giving, $71,982; Grants to individuals, totaling $71,982.
Type of support: Scholarships—to individuals.
Application information: Contact foundation for current application deadline; Application by letter, including cost of tuition and books.
EIN: 860762974

1571
Louis and Florence Glasgow Foundation
c/o NBT Bank, N.A.
52 S. Broad St.
Norwich, NY 13815
Application address: Norwich High School, Attn.: Guidance Dept., Midland Dr., Norwich, New York 13815

Foundation type: Operating foundation
Limitations: Scholarships to graduating seniors of Norwich High School, NY, for higher education.
Financial data: Year ended 12/31/2003. Assets, $339,098 (M); Expenditures, $33,247; Total giving, $17,250; Grants to individuals, 10 grants totaling $17,250 (high: $1,725; low: $1,725).

Type of support: Support to graduates or students of specific schools; Undergraduate support.
Application information: Deadline 60 days prior to graduation; Completion of formal application required.
EIN: 237304980

1572
Charles G. Glazer Scholarship Fund
c/o M&T Bank
21 E. Market St., M/C 402-130
York, PA 17401-1500
Application address: c/o James Buchanan High School, Gudiance Officer, 4773 Fort Loudon Rd., Mercersburg, PA 17236, tel.: (717) 328-2146

Foundation type: Independent foundation
Limitations: Scholarships to graduates of James Buchanan High School, PA.
Financial data: Year ended 12/31/2004. Assets, $55,274 (M); Expenditures, $63,219; Total giving, $62,204; Grants to individuals, totaling $62,204.
Type of support: Support to graduates or students of specific schools; Undergraduate support.
Application information: Deadline Apr. 1; Completion of formal application required.
EIN: 236485096

1573
Gleaner Life Insurance Society Scholarship Foundation
5200 W. U.S. Hwy. 223
P.O. Box 1894
Adrian, MI 49221   (800) 992-1894
FAX: (517) 265-7745;
E-mail: gleaner@gleanerlife.com; URL: http:// www.gleanerlife.com/memben.htm

Foundation type: Operating foundation
Limitations: Scholarships only to members of the society.
Financial data: Year ended 06/30/2004. Assets, $100,528 (M); Expenditures, $115,641; Total giving, $113,400; Grants to individuals, 117 grants totaling $113,400 (high: $1,000, low: $400).
Fields of interest: Fraternal societies (501(c)(8)).
Type of support: Scholarships—to individuals.
Application information: Applications not accepted.
EIN: 383006741

1574
Glen Rock High School Unified Scholarship Council, Inc.
c/o Guidance Counselor, Glen Rock High School
400 Hamilton Ave.
Glen Rock, NJ 07452-2399   (201) 445-7700

Foundation type: Operating foundation
Limitations: Scholarships to seniors at Glen Rock High School, NJ, for attendance at accredited colleges, universities, and training programs.
Financial data: Year ended 06/30/2004. Assets, $100,393 (M); Expenditures, $23,479; Total giving, $22,000; Grants to individuals, 9 grants totaling $22,000 (high: $3,000, low: $1,800).
Fields of interest: Vocational education.
Type of support: Support to graduates or students of specific schools; Undergraduate support.

Application information:
Initial approach: Letter.
Deadline(s): Deadline June 1.
EIN: 226053789

1575
Glendale Community Foundation
327 Arden Ave., Ste. 201
P.O. Box 313
Glendale, CA 91203-0313 (818) 241-8040
Contact: Thomas R. Miller, Exec. Dir.
FAX: (818) 241-8045;
E-mail: Tom@glendalecommunityfoundation.org;
Application E-mail:
info@glendalecommunityfoundation.org;
URL: http://
www.glendalecommunityfoundation.org

Foundation type: Community foundation
Limitations: Scholarships to individuals from La Crescenta, La Canada Flintridge, Glendale, Montrose and Verdugo City, CA, for undergraduate education.
Publications: Application guidelines; Annual report; Financial statement; Grants list; Informational brochure; Newsletter; Program policy statement (including application guidelines).
Financial data: Year ended 12/31/2004. Assets, $7,078,905 (M); Expenditures, $736,717; Total giving, $440,284; Grants to individuals, 30 grants totaling $20,050 (high: $2,000, low: $100).
Fields of interest: Education, special; Vocational education, post-secondary; Medical school/education; Teacher school/education; Journalism school/education.
Type of support: Exchange programs; Student loans—to individuals; Support to graduates or students of specific schools; Technical education support; Undergraduate support.
Application information: Applications accepted. Application form required. Application form available on the grantmaker's Web site.
Initial approach: Letter, telephone or e-mail.
Copies of proposal: 1
Deadline(s): Mar. 12.
Applicants should submit the following:
1) Letter(s) of recommendation
2) ACT
3) SAT
4) Transcripts
5) Essay
Additional information: Interviews required.
Program descriptions:
Chuck Benedict Student Loan: Interest-free $1,000 loans to students from southern California (generally southern Santa Barbara) who are studying for a career in sports journalism and are enrolled in classes at recognized universities. Secondary considerations include academic achievement, financial need and potential ability to repay the loan. The loans are to be repaid after the student's graduation. A committee of current or past professional journalists will screen the application and/or perform the interviews. The loan may be renewable for one additional year, but is not automatic. It is not available for graduate students.
Phyllis Campbell Student Loan: Provides an interest-free $1,000 loan each year to one local student who is studying to become an educator of the handicapped. The student is evaluated on the basis of his or her interest to teach the handicapped, financial need, community involvement, academic success, and potential ability to repay the loan.
Dr. John and Mae Benjamin Scholarship: Scholarship to a local student who is studying for a medical career. The award may be renewable, but is not automatic.
Christopher A. Burrows Memorial Scholarship: At least two scholarships for a minimum of $1,500 each will be awarded to college-bound seniors from the Crescenta-Canada Valley. Scholarship recipients must reside in La Canada Flintridge, La Crescenta, Montrose or Verdugo City and attend high school in La Canada or La Crescenta.
Katherine Bush Memorial Scholarship: Awards $750 to a Crescenta Valley High School senior whose career goal is in teaching or a related field of working with youth. The award may be renewable, but is not automatic.
Phil Ellis Scholarship: Awards up to $500 to students involved in We Care For Youth, who have a 2.5 GPA or better who are pursuing higher education in college or vocational or technical institutions, and who are residents of Glendale, Montrose, Verdugo City or La Crescenta.
Pearl A. Gray Student Loan: Interest-free, $1,000 loans to local students for their studies at college or a vocational or technical institution. The loans are to be repaid after the student's graduation. Students are evaluated on the basis of financial need, community involvement, academic success, and potential ability to repay the loan. There is no specific GPA required.
Frank and Ann Leone Scholarship: A $1,000 scholarship which rotates among the Glendale public high schools. Criteria for the scholarships include a GPA of 3.5 better, good citizenship, plans for college or vocational or technical institution, and community involvement.
Tuesday Afternoon Club Scholarship: Provides a scholarship to one graduating student each from Glendale high, Hoover High, Crescenta Valley High, and Allan Daily Continuation for continuing education to a college or vocational or technical institute; and one to a full-time student at Glendale Community College.
EIN: 956068137

1576
The Glens Falls Foundation
16 Maple St.
Glens Falls, NY 12801 (518) 761-7350
Contact: John G. Zeis, Admin.
FAX: (518) 798-8620

Foundation type: Community foundation
Limitations: Scholarships to residents of Warren, Washington, and Saratoga counties, NY, to attend Dartmouth College, Harvard University, or any accredited medical school.
Publications: Application guidelines; Annual report; Informational brochure.
Financial data: Year ended 12/31/2004. Assets, $9,934,981 (M); Expenditures, $378,997; Total giving, $332,199; Grants to individuals, 129 grants totaling $165,085 (high: $12,000, low: $50).
Fields of interest: Medical school/education.
Type of support: Graduate support; Undergraduate support.
Application information: Application form required.
Deadline(s): Contact foundation for current application deadline.
Additional information: Only medical school students may apply.
EIN: 146036390

1577
GMAA Grover Loening Scholarship Fund
c/o James Montie
P.O. Box 0184
Miami Springs, FL 33266-0184
(305) 215-4622

Foundation type: Operating foundation
Limitations: Scholarships to south FL college students majoring in aviation, who have completed at least 30 credits of college work, 15 of which must be in aviation, and have a GPA no less than 3.0.
Financial data: Year ended 12/31/2002. Assets, $682,469 (M); Expenditures, $70,831; Total giving, $36,000; Grants to individuals, 14 grants totaling $36,000 (high: $3,600, low: $1,000).
Fields of interest: Space/aviation.
Type of support: Support to graduates or students of specific schools; Undergraduate support.
Application information: Deadline Apr. 28; Completion of formal application required, including official transcripts, a statement describing leadership qualities, goals, and reasons for applying, and a letter of recommendation from an employer or instructor; Interviews required.
EIN: 650270346

1578
Richard E. Gnade Charitable Trust
c/o Frost National Bank
P.O. Box 2950
San Antonio, TX 78299-2950 (210) 220-4997
Contact: Susan T. Palmer, V.P., and Trust Off., Frost National Bank
FAX: (210) 220-5011;
E-mail: spalmer@frostbank.com

Foundation type: Independent foundation
Limitations: Scholarships to financially needy young men in Bandera County, TX.
Financial data: Year ended 10/31/2004. Assets, $597,057 (M); Expenditures, $39,827; Total giving, $30,116; Grants to individuals, totaling $30,116.
Fields of interest: Men.
Type of support: Scholarships—to individuals.
Application information:
Deadline(s): Contact trust for current application deadline
Additional information: Application by letter including a biographical sketch and financial information.
EIN: 746032311

1579
William Jesse Godwin Foundation
P.O. Box 739
Whitesboro, TX 76273
Contact: Gene Bryan, Pres.

Foundation type: Independent foundation
Limitations: Scholarships to residents of Grayson County, TX.
Financial data: Year ended 12/31/2004. Assets, $0 (M); Expenditures, $28,509; Total giving, $18,200; Grants to individuals, totaling $4,000.
Type of support: Scholarships—to individuals.
Application information: Applications by letter, outlining tuition cost, room and board fees, major field of study, and student's future plans, accepted throughout the year.
EIN: 756036128

1580
Reynold A. Gogarn Scholarship Fund
c/o Comerica Bank
P.O. Box 75000, M/C 3302
Detroit, MI 48275-3302
Application address: c/o Robert J. Hermann, Grant
Comm., 201 McDonald, Midland, MI 48640-0993

Foundation type: Independent foundation
Limitations: Scholarships to students of West
Branch and Rose City school districts, MI.
Financial data: Year ended 12/31/2002.
Assets, $481,524 (M); Expenditures, $43,411;
Total giving, $27,000; Grants to individuals,
totaling $27,000.
Type of support: Support to graduates or students
of specific schools; Undergraduate support.
Application information: Applications by letter,
outlining financial need and school to attend,
accepted throughout the year.
EIN: 386461123

1581
Rita & Herbert Z. Gold Charitable Trust
P.O. Box 319
Rockville Centre, NY 11570

Foundation type: Independent foundation
Limitations: Scholarships to students of South
Side High School, Rockville Centre, NY, who started
school in the Head Start program.
Financial data: Year ended 12/31/2004.
Assets, $313,881 (M); Expenditures, $25,467;
Total giving, $24,525; Grants to individuals,
totaling $24,525.
Type of support: Scholarships—to individuals;
Support to graduates or students of specific
schools.
Application information: Applications not
accepted.
EIN: 116465852

1582
Raymond and Marie Goldbach Foundation, Inc.
(formerly Goldbach Charitable Foundation, Inc.)
304 East St.
Marathon, WI 54448
Contact: John L. Skoug, Pres.

Foundation type: Independent foundation
Limitations: Scholarships to residents of WI for
higher education.
Financial data: Year ended 12/31/2004.
Assets, $7,102,869 (M); Expenditures,
$324,981; Total giving, $300,924.
Type of support: Undergraduate support.
Application information: Applications not
accepted.
EIN: 391877824

1583
Golden Gate Family Foundation
c/o Boyd C. Smith
3201 Ash St.
Palo Alto, CA 94306-2240

Foundation type: Independent foundation
Limitations: Scholarships for higher education.
Financial data: Year ended 12/31/2004.
Assets, $211,740 (M); Expenditures, $71,795;
Total giving, $62,540; Grants to individuals,
totaling $43,477.
Type of support: Scholarships—to individuals.

Application information: Applications not
accepted.
EIN: 770259505

1584
Golden Gate Restaurant Association Scholarship Foundation
(formerly David Rubenstein Memorial Scholarship
Foundation)
c/o Michael Rubenstein
120 Montgomery St., Ste. 1280
San Francisco, CA 94104 (415) 781-5348
Contact: Donnalyn Murphy
URL: http://www.ggra.org

Foundation type: Independent foundation
Limitations: Scholarships to CA residents planning
to attend a CA college on a full-time basis in the
field of food services.
Financial data: Year ended 12/31/2004.
Assets, $225,515 (M); Expenditures, $24,452;
Total giving, $9,500; Grants to individuals, 10
grants totaling $9,500 (high: $2,300, low: $200).
Fields of interest: Business/industry.
Type of support: Graduate support; Undergraduate
support.
Application information: Application form required.
Initial approach: Letter or telephone.
Deadline(s): Mar. 31
Additional information: Interviews required.
Program description:
Scholarship Fund: Recipients are selected on the
basis of a commitment to pursuing a career in the
hospitality industry, personal merit, and evidence of
ability to benefit from additional training. In the case
of applicants with equal qualifications, preference
may be given to students who are immediate family
or employees of GGRA members and students
attending San Francisco Bay Area foodservice
programs.
EIN: 237012819

1585
William Goldman Foundation
42 S. 15th St., Ste. 1116
Philadelphia, PA 19102 (215) 568-0411
Contact: William R. Goldman, Vice-Chair.

Foundation type: Independent foundation
Limitations: Scholarships to residents of the
metropolitan Philadelphia, PA, area for full-time
graduate or medical study at specific Philadelphia
institutions.
Publications: Application guidelines.
Financial data: Year ended 12/31/2004.
Assets, $3,840,723 (M); Expenditures,
$206,015; Total giving, $155,205.
Fields of interest: Medical school/education.
Type of support: Support to graduates or students
of specific schools; Graduate support.
Application information: Application form required.
Initial approach: Letter.
Deadline(s): Mar. 15.
Additional information: Interviews required.
Program description:
Scholarship Fund: Scholarships are for the
benefit of students attending the following nine
graduate and medical schools: Bryn Mawr College,
Drexel University, Hahnemann University, Medical
College of Pennsylvania, Philadelphia College of
Osteopathic Medicine, Temple University, Thomas
Jefferson University, Jefferson Medical College,
University of Pennsylvania, and Villanova University.
Grants only cover tuition and are renewable.
First-year students must be accepted to one of the

above schools in order to apply. Applicants must
rank in top third of their class.
EIN: 236266261

1586
Goldman Sachs Charitable Fund
c/o Goldman, Sachs & Co.
10 Hanover Sq., 22nd Fl.
New York, NY 10005
Application addresses: H.R. Young Graduate
Scholarship Prog. and Walter F. Blain Scholarship
Prog.: c/o Scholarship America, Inc., 1505
Riverview Rd., P.O. Box 297, St. Peter, MN 56082,
tel.: (507) 931-1682, George E. Doty Master's
Degree Fellowship Prog.: c/o Gregg Bloom, Human
Resources Dept., 180 Maiden Ln., 21st Fl., New
York, NY 10038-4958

Foundation type: Company-sponsored foundation
Limitations: Scholarships to children of employees
of Goldman Sachs & Co. for graduate and
undergraduate school education.
Financial data: Year ended 06/30/2003.
Assets, $21,581 (L); Expenditures, $340,250;
Total giving, $340,250; Grants to individuals, 74
grants totaling $340,250 (high: $7,500, low:
$2,500).
Type of support: Employee-related scholarships;
Graduate support; Undergraduate support.
Application information: Application form required.
Deadline(s): Varies
Additional information: Applicants should submit
transcripts.
Program descriptions:
H.R. Young Graduate Scholarship: Awards as
many as ten $7,500 scholarships to graduate
students for the attainment of an initial graduate
degree. Scholarships are awarded for a maximum
of three years and recipients may attend any
accredited university and select any course of study
leading to a graduate degree. Recipients must be a
child or spouse of a Goldman Sachs employee who
has been employed for at least one year by Jan. 1
of application year and will be an employee at the
time scholarship is awarded. Recipient must be
pursuing his/her first graduate degree, in his/her
last year of college and due to graduate during the
current academic year and enter graduate school no
later than Sept. and a student in good standing.
Recipient may also be a bachelor's degree holder
applying to a graduate school. Deadline Jan. 15.
Walter E. Blaine Scholarship: Awards as many as
15 scholarships of $2,500 to $4,000 to
undergraduate students for a maximum of four
years. Recipients must be children of employees of
Goldman Sachs who have been employed for at
least one year by Jan. 1 of application year and will
be an employee by the time scholarship is awarded.
Recipients may attend any accredited college or
university and select any course leading to a
bachelor's degree. Recipients must be in his/her
last year of high school and due to graduate during
the current academic year and enter an institution
of higher learning as a full-time student no later
than Sept. Deadline Jan. 15.
George E. Doty Master's Degree Fellowship:
Awards graduate scholarships to eligible Goldman
Sachs employees. This program recognizes
outstanding achievement and encourages the
continuing development of professional full-time
employees by providing qualified individuals with
the opportunity to attend an Executive MBA or other
Executive Master's Degree program. Recipients
may complete their degree in two years. Program
pays all program-related expenses during the two

years, provided recipient remains a full-time employee with the firm. Deadline Dec. 14.
EIN: 311678646

1587
Goldring Family Foundation
809 Jefferson Hwy.
Jefferson, LA 70121
Contact: Trudi Briede, Dir.
FAX: (504) 849-6515; Application address: P.O. Box 53333, New Orleans, LA 70153

Foundation type: Independent foundation
Limitations: Scholarships to children of employees of Goldring Affiliates and Magnolia Marketing, for higher education at accredited colleges and universities.
Publications: Informational brochure (including application guidelines).
Financial data: Year ended 11/30/2004. Assets, $82,289,380 (M); Expenditures, $4,669,047; Total giving, $3,789,983; Grants to individuals, 140 grants totaling $224,500 (high: $3,000, low: $1,500).
Type of support: Employee-related scholarships.
Application information: Application form required.
  Deadline(s): Jan. 1 and July 1
EIN: 726022666

1588
Goldstein Family Foundation
6 Vincent Rd.
Spring Valley, NY 10977 (212) 239-7500

Foundation type: Independent foundation
Limitations: Scholarships to Jewish residents of NY, primarily in Brooklyn.
Financial data: Year ended 12/31/2004. Assets, $586,539 (M); Expenditures, $65,450; Total giving, $65,450; Grants to individuals, totaling $55,350.
Type of support: Undergraduate support.
Application information:
  Initial approach: Letter.
  Additional information: Contact foundation for further information.
EIN: 020581239

1589
Sarah and Tena Goldstein Memorial Scholarship
c/o Jewish Family and Children's Svcs.
5743 Bartlett St.
Pittsburgh, PA 15217 (412) 422-7200

Foundation type: Independent foundation
Limitations: Undergraduate and graduate scholarships to Jewish students residing in the following western PA counties: Allegheny, Beaver, Butler, Clarion, Crawford, Erie, Lawrence, Mercer, Venango, Washington, and Westmoreland. Preference is shown to residents of Titusville, PA.
Financial data: Year ended 12/31/2003. Assets, $2,868,004 (M); Expenditures, $155,530; Total giving, $132,749; Grants to individuals, 18 grants totaling $132,749 (high: $25,000, low: $5,335).
Fields of interest: Jewish agencies & temples.
Type of support: Graduate support; Undergraduate support.
Application information: Applications accepted Dec. to Feb. 16; Initial approach by telephone; Completion of formal application required, including essay, personal financial statement, tax forms,

SAR, and three references; Interviews required for new applicants.
Program description:
  Scholarship Program: Scholarships are awarded on a highly competitive basis. Recipients are selected on the basis of financial need, grades, and community service.
EIN: 251229795

1590
Noble Symond Golub and Leila J. Golub Educational Trust
99 Fordham Rd.
P.O. Box 1008
Wilmington, MA 01887-0578
Contact: Harvey J. Waugh, Tr.

Foundation type: Independent foundation
Limitations: Scholarships to students for higher education, with emphasis on residents of MA.
Financial data: Year ended 12/31/2004. Assets, $239,854 (M); Expenditures, $12,126; Total giving, $11,000; Grants to individuals, totaling $11,000.
Type of support: Undergraduate support.
Application information:
  Deadline(s): May 1
  Additional information: Completion of formal application required, including transcript and personal letter.
EIN: 046796825

1591
Mary Gonter & Sara O'Brien Scholarship Foundation
c/o The Huntington National Bank
P.O. Box 1558, EA4E86
Columbus, OH 43216
Application address: Larry Markworth, V.P., c/o The Huntington National Bank, P.O. Box 232, Dover, OH 44622, tel.: (330) 364-7421

Foundation type: Independent foundation
Limitations: Scholarships to young OH residents studying to become ordained Protestant Christian ministers.
Financial data: Year ended 06/30/2004. Assets, $380,145 (M); Expenditures, $16,056; Total giving, $11,000; Grants to individuals, 5 grants totaling $11,000 (high: $2,200, low: $2,200).
Fields of interest: Theological school/education; Protestant agencies & churches.
Type of support: Undergraduate support.
Application information:
  Deadline(s): Applications by letter accepted throughout the year.
EIN: 316317421

1592
Good Samaritan Hospital Foundation
4503 N. 2nd Ave., Ste 209
P.O. Box 1810
Kearney, NE 68848-1810 (308) 865-7900
Contact: Randall DeFreece, Pres.
FAX: (308) 865-2933; Additional tel.: (308) 865-2703; URL: http://www.gshs.org

Foundation type: Public charity
Limitations: Scholarships to individuals for health-related education at institutions located in the Kearney, NE, area.
Publications: Annual report; Informational brochure; Newsletter.

Financial data: Year ended 06/30/2003. Assets, $6,270,772 (M); Expenditures, $3,424,433; Total giving, $2,910,457; Grants to individuals, totaling $16,043.
Fields of interest: Health care.
Type of support: Undergraduate support.
Application information: Applications accepted. Application form required. Application form available on the grantmaker's Web site.
  Deadline(s): June 1
  Additional information: Application should include two letters of recommendation, transcript, verification of enrollment, and essay outlining future goals.
EIN: 470659443

1593
Edwin C. Goodenough Scholarship Trust
(formerly Edwin C. Goodenough Scholarship Fund)
c/o Pioneer Trust Bank, N.A.
P.O. Box 2305
Salem, OR 97308-2305
Application address: c/o Pioneer Trust Bank, N.A., 109 Commercial St. N.E., Salem, OR 97308, tel.: (503) 363-3136

Foundation type: Independent foundation
Limitations: Scholarships to residents of Salem, OR, who are graduating seniors from schools located in the area comprising School District No. 24J in Salem, OR.
Financial data: Year ended 06/30/2005. Assets, $136,216 (M); Expenditures, $9,705; Total giving, $6,939; Grants to individuals, totaling $6,939.
Type of support: Support to graduates or students of specific schools; Undergraduate support.
Application information: Contact trust for current application deadline; Initial approach by letter, including SASE; Completion of formal application required; Interviews required.
EIN: 936119287

1594
George L. Gooding Trust
c/o State Street Bank and Trust Co.
P.O. Box 551122
Boston, MA 02205
Application address: c/o Chairperson, Plymouth Carver High School, 41 Obrey St., Plymouth, MA 02360

Foundation type: Independent foundation
Limitations: Scholarships to financially needy residents of Plymouth, MA, who demonstrate good character and potential.
Financial data: Year ended 12/31/2003. Assets, $666,725 (M); Expenditures, $33,386; Total giving, $25,000; Grants to individuals, 14 grants totaling $25,000 (high: $2,600, low: $1,260).
Type of support: Scholarships—to individuals.
Application information: Deadline May 1; Contact trust for current application guidelines.
EIN: 046095797

1595
Goodlark Educational Foundation, Inc.
404 E. College St., Ste. D
Dickson, TN 37055 (615) 446-9156
Contact: Vanessa Smith

Foundation type: Operating foundation

Limitations: Scholarships for undergraduate studies to financially needy residents of Dickson, Hickman, and Humphreys counties, TN.
Publications: Application guidelines.
Financial data: Year ended 12/31/2002. Assets, $2,491,514 (M); Expenditures, $101,699; Total giving, $75,608; Grants to individuals, totaling $75,608.
Fields of interest: Vocational education.
Type of support: Undergraduate support.
Application information:
Deadline(s): Feb.
Additional information: Completion of formal application required, including GPA, transcripts, and most recent W-2 and income tax forms.
Program description:
Scholarship Program: Scholarships of up to $1,000 are provided for college or technical school education. Scholarships are renewable provided the recipient maintains at least a 2.0 GPA.
EIN: 581764987

1596
David Goodrich College Education Fund

c/o Fifth Third Bank
P.O. Box 3636
Grand Rapids, MI 49501-3636
Application address: c/o Wayne Petroelje, Elsie Area Superintendent of Schools, 8989 E. Colony Rd., Elsie, MI 48831

Foundation type: Independent foundation
Limitations: Scholarships to financially needy students living within a four-mile radius of Ovid, MI, who have high scholastic averages.
Financial data: Year ended 12/31/2004. Assets, $779,872 (M); Expenditures, $51,443; Total giving, $45,246; Grants to individuals, totaling $45,246.
Type of support: Scholarships—to individuals.
Application information: Deadline May 1; Contact foundation for current application guidelines.
EIN: 386658237

1597
Howard D. and Rose E. Goodwin
Scholarship Trust

c/o Wachovia Bank, N.A.
100 N. Main St., 13th Fl.
Winston-Salem, NC 27150

Foundation type: Independent foundation
Limitations: Scholarships to financially needy residents of the Antietam School District, Berks County, PA, who have graduated from Antietam Junior/Senior High School, PA.
Financial data: Year ended 12/31/2004. Assets, $119,195 (M); Expenditures, $6,036; Total giving, $5,500; Grants to individuals, totaling $5,500.
Type of support: Support to graduates or students of specific schools; Undergraduate support.
Application information: Applications not accepted.
EIN: 236476039

1598
Goolsby Educational Fund

111 N. Church St.
Marion, VA 24354-2705 (540) 783-8102
Contact: Donald G. Hammer, Tr.

Foundation type: Operating foundation

Limitations: Scholarships and student loans to financially needy high school graduates in Smyth County, VA.
Financial data: Year ended 12/31/2002. Assets, $692,083 (M); Expenditures, $48,151; Total giving, $33,850; Loans to individuals, 64 loans totaling $33,850.
Type of support: Undergraduate support.
Application information: Applications accepted. Application form required.
Initial approach: Letter or telephone.
Deadline(s): June 30
Applicants should submit the following:
1) FAF
2) Letter(s) of recommendation
3) Essay
4) Transcripts
Program description:
Scholarship and Loan Program: Recipients are granted both a scholarship and a loan, generally in the same amount. Repayment of loans begins within five years after graduation or termination of study, with deferments granted to students immediately attending graduate school. Loans will bear a ten percent interest rate per annum, thereafter.
EIN: 546067955

1599
George E. Gordy Family Educational Trust
Fund

c/o Wilmington Trust Co.
1100 N. Market St., Ste. 310780
Wilmington, DE 19801-1243 (302) 855-2814
Contact: Deanne Welsh

Foundation type: Independent foundation
Limitations: Scholarships to financially needy graduates of Sussex County, DE, high schools for higher education.
Financial data: Year ended 06/30/2005. Assets, $2,692,188 (M); Expenditures, $299,562; Total giving, $272,856; Grants to individuals, 216 grants totaling $272,856 (high: $3,000, low: $281).
Fields of interest: Vocational education.
Type of support: Support to graduates or students of specific schools; Undergraduate support.
Application information: Application form required.
Deadline(s): Feb. 15
Additional information: Recipients notified by May 15.
Program description:
Scholarship Fund: Applicants must be Sussex County high school graduates and must have evidence of acceptance to accredited institutions of postsecondary education. Screening is done by the Scholarship Advisory Committee and a list of qualified applicants is provided to the Selection Committee to determine award recipients. The application must contain a budget including additional expenses which might occur (uniforms, equipment, etc.) to be reviewed by the Selection Committee. Also required is a handwritten paragraph that answers the following questions:
· Why do I qualify for this scholarship?
· Why do I want to attend college?
· What are my career goals?
A letter of acceptance from the institution an applicant wishes to attend must be submitted to the bank prior to any disbursement of funds. The scholarship must be applied to tuition, room, board, books, transportation, lab fees and student activities. The funds will be sent directly to the college of the student's choice for ultimate disbursement. It is the responsibility of the student to authorize the appropriate official of the school to

forward a copy of their transcript for each academic year to the bank. No disbursement will be made prior to the transcript being received by the bank. To remain eligible, the student must maintain a minimum cumulative GPA of 2.5. The maximum amount of each award is $3,000. In general, participation is limited to four years and to those enrolled in baccalaureate and associate degrees or toward completion of the vocational or other educational program in which student is enrolled.
EIN: 222561832

1600
Gore Family Memorial Foundation

c/o SunTrust Bank
P.O. Box 14728
Fort Lauderdale, FL 33302
Application address: 4747 N. Ocean Dr., Ste. 204, Fort Lauderdale, FL 33308

Foundation type: Independent foundation
Limitations: Scholarships only to Broward County, FL, residents, except for severely physically disabled individuals who may apply from other parts of the U.S.
Financial data: Year ended 01/31/2005. Assets, $20,528,309 (M); Expenditures, $1,343,113; Total giving, $761,302.
Fields of interest: Disabilities, people with; Physically disabled.
Type of support: Scholarships—to individuals; Undergraduate support.
Application information:
Initial approach: Letter.
Deadline(s): Applications accepted throughout the year.
Program description:
Scholarship Program: Scholarships are granted to FL residents and to the physically disabled. Most scholarships are for college education, but there are some for secondary education. No scholarships are awarded for graduate studies, except to physically disabled individuals.
EIN: 596497544

1601
Gorman Foundation

7777 Bonhomme Ave., Ste. 2300
Clayton, MO 63105
Application addresses: University of Missouri-Riolla: Undergraduate: c/o Student Financial Aid Off., 106 Parker Hall, Rolla, MO 65401-0249, tel.: (314)341-4282; Graduate: c/o Office of the Dean, 210 Parker Hall, Rolla, MO 65401-0249, tel.: (314) 341-4142; MIT: Undergraduate: c/o Student Financial Aid Off., 77 Massachusetts Ave., Rm. 5-119, Cambridge, MA 02139; Graduate: c/o Dean of Graduate School, 77 Massachusetts Ave., Bldg. 3, Room 132, Cambridge, MA 02139, tel.: (617) 253-1957

Foundation type: Operating foundation
Limitations: Scholarships to residents of St. Louis, MO, who graduated from high schools located in the city of St. Louis, and who will pursue an undergraduate and/or graduate education in engineering at the Massachusetts Institute of Technology or the University of Missouri—Rolla. Awards are based on financial need as well as excellence in scholastic performance.
Publications: Application guidelines; Annual report; Informational brochure.
Financial data: Year ended 06/30/2004. Assets, $573,411 (M); Expenditures, $45,992; Total giving, $35,000; Grants to individuals, 28

grants totaling $35,000 (high: $1,250, low: $1,250).

Fields of interest: Engineering school/education.
Type of support: Support to graduates or students of specific schools; Graduate support; Undergraduate support.
Application information: Application form required.
  Deadline(s): Oct. 1 for fall semester, Dec. 15 for winter semester
  Additional information: Upon selection of qualified applicants, the foundation trustees shall authorize scholarship awards and direct payment to each school. For further information contact the specific school relating to your application.
EIN: 431377593

1602
Alva O., Adie E. & Mary J. Goslee Student Loan Fund

c/o Wells Fargo Bank Nebraska, N.A.
4707 S. 96th St.
Omaha, NE 68127-2019
Application address: Attn.: Joyce Fulford, Twin Lakes School Corp., Monticello, IN 47960

Foundation type: Independent foundation
Limitations: Scholarships and loans to students of Jefferson & Adams High School and Twin Lakes High School, IN.
Financial data: Year ended 12/31/2004.
Assets, $961,537 (M); Expenditures, $44,045; Total giving, $19,300; Grants to individuals, totaling $19,300.
Fields of interest: Vocational education.
Type of support: Support to graduates or students of specific schools.
Application information: Deadline Mar. 31; Completion of formal application required, including transcripts and letter of recommendation.
Program description:
  Scholarship and Loan Program: Loans are repaid at four percent interest. Payment begins six months after completion or termination of study.
EIN: 356369633

1603
Beatrice I. Goss Educational Testamentary Trust

c/o Fifth Third Bank
P.O. Box 3636
Grand Rapids, MI 49501
Application address: c/o Fifth Third Bank, 56 S. Washington, Valparaiso, IN 46383, tel.: (219) 465-6706

Foundation type: Independent foundation
Limitations: Scholarships to residents of Marshall County, IN, for higher education.
Financial data: Year ended 09/30/2004.
Assets, $171,651 (M); Expenditures, $10,837; Total giving, $9,134; Grants to individuals, totaling $9,134.
Type of support: Undergraduate support.
Application information: Application form required.
  Deadline(s): Mar. 15
EIN: 356361029

1604
Earl J. Gossett Foundation

c/o William Dempsey
8200 N. Austin Ave.
Morton Grove, IL 60053   (847) 966-3700
Contact: Jan Blackburn
Additional tel.: (847) 966-3700, ext. 3349

Foundation type: Company-sponsored foundation
Limitations: Student loans to employees of ITT Bell & Gossett and their dependents. All student loans issued are charged two percent per year simple interest.
Financial data: Year ended 04/30/2005.
Assets, $228,314 (M); Expenditures, $43,528; Total giving, $43,400; Loans to individuals, 14 loans totaling $43,400.
Type of support: Student loans—to individuals.
Application information: Application form required.
  Deadline(s): Apr. 30
EIN: 366084312

1605
Gould Inc. Foundation

c/o Scholarship Dir.
34929 Curtis Blvd.
Eastlake, OH 44095   (440) 953-5000

Foundation type: Company-sponsored foundation
Limitations: Scholarships based on leadership and merit to graduating high school seniors who are children of employees of Gould, Inc. and its U.S. subsidiaries.
Publications: Application guidelines.
Financial data: Year ended 12/31/2003.
Assets, $2,278,607 (M); Expenditures, $134,902; Total giving, $134,626.
Type of support: Employee-related scholarships; Undergraduate support.
Application information: Application form required.
  Deadline(s): Jan. 31
  Applicants should submit the following:
    1) ACT
    2) SAT
  Additional information: Application should also include biographical information; Applicants notified in Apr.; Scholarship application address: c/o Dir., Gould Inc. Fdn. Scholarship Prog., 35129 Curtis Blvd., Eastlake, OH 44095.
Program description:
  Scholarship Awards: Scholarships cover up to four years of full-time study at regionally-accredited four-year colleges, or two-year U.S. colleges leading to a four-year bachelor's degree. Students who enroll in junior colleges will only be eligible if they are pursuing a program of study that is specifically aimed at subsequent matriculation to full four-year colleges. Recipients must rank in the upper 25 percent of their graduating classes. Special consideration is given to awards and prizes won by the applicant, and involvement in school programs, athletics, clubs, and groups. Equally important are demonstrations of self-reliance, such as earnings for college, scientific inventions, outdoorsmanship (such as Outward Bound), political involvement, and significant accomplishment in arts and crafts. Some scholarships are set aside for children of employees whose Gould salary is less than $35,000 a year.
EIN: 346525555

1606
Gould Scholarship Fund

(formerly Norman J. and Anna B. Gould Scholarship Fund)
c/o Bank of America, N.A.
1 East Ave., 3rd Fl., NY7-144-03-04
Rochester, NY 14604

Foundation type: Company-sponsored foundation
Limitations: Scholarships for Goulds Pumps employees who are residents of Seneca Falls, NY.
Financial data: Year ended 12/31/2004.
Assets, $183,488 (M); Expenditures, $16,325; Total giving, $14,000; Grants to individuals, 15 grants totaling $14,000 (high: $2,000, low: $500).
Type of support: Employee-related scholarships.
Application information:
  Initial approach: Letter.
  Deadline(s): None
  Additional information: Application address: c/o M.J. Catoe, Gould Pumps, Inc., 240 Fall St., Seneca Falls, NY 13148.
EIN: 166051306

1607
Norman J. and Anna B. Gould Scholarship Fund

c/o Bank of America, N.A., P.C. Group
P.O. Box 6767
Providence, RI 02940-6767
Application address: c/o Dick Landers, Goulds Pumps, Inc., 291 Fall St., Seneca Falls, NY 13148

Foundation type: Independent foundation
Limitations: Scholarships to children of Goulds Pumps, NY, employees and scholarships to children of Seneca Falls, NY residents.
Financial data: Year ended 09/30/2004.
Assets, $1,123,279 (M); Expenditures, $46,119; Total giving, $35,600; Grants to individuals, totaling $35,600.
Type of support: Employee-related scholarships; Scholarships—to individuals.
Application information: Applications accepted throughout the year; Contact fund for current application guidelines.
EIN: 166318641

1608
The Mary I. Gourley Scholarship Foundation

(formerly M.I.G. Scholarship Foundation)
P.O. Box 161235
Fort Worth, TX 76161-1235
Contact: Robert C. Albritton, Jr., Pres.
FAX: (817) 834-5093

Foundation type: Public charity
Limitations: Scholarships to students of six specified colleges in the Fort Worth, TX, area. Preference is given to mature individuals, including heads of households. See program description for a list of participating colleges.
Financial data: Year ended 06/30/2004.
Assets, $12,646,658 (M); Expenditures, $608,364; Total giving, $369,505; Grants to individuals, 122 grants totaling $369,505 (high: $5,850, low: $100).
Fields of interest: Theological school/education; Christian agencies & churches.
Type of support: Support to graduates or students of specific schools.
Application information: Contact foundation for current application deadline; Completion of formal application required; Applications must be

submitted through the office of the Director of Financial Aid of the college, university, or seminary.

Program description:

Scholarship Program: Grants are meant to be combined with any financial aid students can qualify for through their educational institution. Scholarships are awarded to students attending the following schools: Southwestern Baptist Theological Seminary, Tarrant County College, Texas Christian University, Texas Wesleyan University, Texas Woman's University, and University of Texas at Arlington.

EIN: 752052592

1609
John N. Graber Irrevocable Scholarship Trust

c/o Marshall & Ilsley Bank
P.O. Box 2980
Milwaukee, WI   53201
Application address: c/o Mineral Point Unified School District, Attn.: Gary Galle, 705 Ross St., Mineral Point, WI 53565

Foundation type: Independent foundation
Limitations: Scholarships to graduates of the Mineral Point Unified School District, WI, for higher education.
Financial data: Year ended 10/31/2004. Assets, $675,104 (M); Expenditures, $47,181; Total giving, $40,000; Grants to individuals, totaling $40,000.
Type of support: Support to graduates or students of specific schools; Undergraduate support.
Application information: Deadline Apr. 1; Completion of formal application required.
EIN: 396603480

1610
Grace Foundation

P.O. Box 924
Menlo Park, CA   94026-0924
Contact: Hari Adisasmito, Chair., Awards Comm.

Foundation type: Operating foundation
Limitations: Scholarships to economically deprived students of China and Southeast Asia only, to work towards improving the welfare of persons in their native countries and promoting the Christian faith.
Publications: Application guidelines; Informational brochure.
Financial data: Year ended 06/30/2005. Assets, $962,723 (M); Expenditures, $33,985; Total giving, $30,750; Grants to individuals, 16 grants totaling $30,750 (high: $3,500, low: $500).
Fields of interest: Christian agencies & churches.
Type of support: Grants to individuals; Scholarships—to individuals; Foreign applicants.
Application information: Application form required.
Initial approach: Letter in Sept. or Oct. to request application, including applicant's name and address, intended course of study, statement of financial need, brief background, Christian testimony, and name and address of applicant's college or university.
Copies of proposal: 1
Deadline(s): Feb. 1
Additional information: Recipients notified by May 15.
Program description:
Grace Foundation Program: Recipients must meet the following criteria:
 · have satisfactorily completed one or more years at an accredited four-year college or university in or near their native country, or

in a developed country where specialized training is offered; special permission may be granted for Bible Schools that offer in-depth postsecondary school training
 · have excellent character with a strong Christian witness
 · have strong academic achievement with a minimum GPA of 3.0 or equivalent; for students studying in the U.S., a minimum TOEFL score of 500 is required
 · be following a course of study in Christian ministry, teaching, health care, or other fields that can be used to assist needy persons in their native country
 · have financial need. A student must be unable to pursue studies without some form of financial assistance
 · have the ability to express himself/herself clearly and to personally complete the Grace Foundation Application Form in English

Preference is shown to students who express a strong commitment to return to their native country upon completion of their studies to provide service in Christian ministry, teaching, health care, or welfare assistance to the poor and uneducated. Scholarships are in amounts of up to $3,500 and cover the costs of tuition only. Scholarships are renewable for up to four years of full-time study provided recipient maintains at least a 3.0 GPA. The foundation does not:
 · accept second party referrals
 · sponsor students for their entire educational cost
 · provide aid for more than four years, or for additional degrees
 · provide transportation or living expenses for students and their families.

EIN: 237294779

1611
Graff Educational Foundation, Inc.

1405 E. Main St.
Grand Prairie, TX   75050   (972) 264-0700
Contact: Jean Van Schaick

Foundation type: Company-sponsored foundation
Limitations: Scholarships to residents of the Grand Prairie, TX, area.
Financial data: Year ended 11/30/2004. Assets, $421,154 (M); Expenditures, $70,294; Total giving, $55,775; Grants to individuals, 33 grants totaling $29,775 (high: $6,000, low: $125).
Type of support: Undergraduate support.
Application information:
Initial approach: Letter.
Deadline(s): None
Additional information: Contact foundation for current application guidelines.
EIN: 752913161

1612
Florence B. Graham & Clemma B. Fancher Scholarship Fund

149 Josephine St., Ste. A
Santa Cruz, CA   95060-2798
Contact: Robert H. Darrow, Tr.

Foundation type: Independent foundation
Limitations: Scholarships to graduating seniors from high schools in northern Santa Cruz County, CA.
Financial data: Year ended 04/30/2005. Assets, $83,231 (M); Expenditures, $4,288; Total giving, $3,400; Grants to individuals, totaling $3,400.

Type of support: Support to graduates or students of specific schools; Undergraduate support.
Application information: Deadline May 31; Completion of formal application required; Application forms available through eligible high schools.
Program description:
Scholarship Program: Scholarships are awarded primarily on the basis of need, but academic standing and high school achievements are also considered.
EIN: 946233118

1613
The Graham Foundation, Inc.

79 Main St.
Unionville, CT   06085-1117

Foundation type: Independent foundation
Limitations: Scholarships to graduates of Farmington High School, CT, who are or were residents of Farmington at the time of graduation.
Financial data: Year ended 12/31/2004. Assets, $0 (L); Expenditures, $20,411; Total giving, $14,000; Grants to individuals, 13 grants totaling $14,000 (high: $2,000, low: $1,000).
Type of support: Support to graduates or students of specific schools; Undergraduate support.
Application information: Contact foundation for current application deadline/guidelines.
EIN: 061337821

1614
Dorothy D. Graham Scholarship Fund

c/o Wells Fargo Bank South Dakota, N.A.
101 N. Phillips Ave.
Sioux Falls, SD   57117-5953   (605) 575-7400
Contact: Robin Aden, Trust Off.

Foundation type: Independent foundation
Limitations: Scholarships to individuals, primarily in SD, for higher education.
Financial data: Year ended 12/31/2002. Assets, $309,075 (M); Expenditures, $22,861; Total giving, $18,500; Grants to individuals, totaling $9,250.
Type of support: Scholarships—to individuals.
Application information: Applications accepted throughout the year; Initial approach by letter or telephone; Completion of formal application required.
EIN: 466034811

1615
Gramberg-Millner Scholarship Fund

c/o Wells Fargo Bank South Dakota, N.A.
P.O. Box 1040
Rapid City, SD   57709-1040

Foundation type: Independent foundation
Limitations: Scholarships to residents of rural Pennington County in the area west of the Cheyenne River or rural Custer County, SD, who plan to attend a college, university, or nursing school in SD.
Financial data: Year ended 11/30/2004. Assets, $209,598 (M); Expenditures, $12,845; Total giving, $9,200; Grants to individuals, totaling $9,200.
Fields of interest: Nursing school/education.
Type of support: Undergraduate support.
Application information: Contact fund for current application deadline; Completion of formal application required.
EIN: 466018116

1616
The GRAMMY Foundation
(also known as The NARAS Foundation)
3402 Pico Blvd.
Santa Monica, CA   90405-2118
(310) 392-3777
Contact: Kristen Murphy, Grants Prog. Coord.
FAX: (310) 392-2188;
E-mail: grants@grammy.com; URL: http://
www.grammy.com/foundation

Foundation type: Public charity
Limitations: Scholarships to law students for the research, analyzation, and submission of essays regarding important issues facing the entertainment industry.
Publications: Application guidelines; Financial statement; Grants list.
Financial data: Year ended 07/31/2004. Assets, $3,957,462 (M); Expenditures, $2,990,938; Total giving, $151,000; Grants to individuals, 5 grants totaling $11,000 (high: $5,000, low: $1,500).
Type of support: Scholarships—to individuals.
Application information:
   Initial approach: Letter or e-mail.
   Additional information: Contact foundation for further program guidelines.
Program description:
   Entertainment Law Initiative: One of the premier educational initiatives of the foundation is the national legal writing contest and scholarship program, which awards $11,000 in scholarships. Law students nationwide are invited to research, analyze and submit essays regarding important legal issues facing the entertainment industry. Consisting of two components, a writing competition and a luncheon, the foundation invites entertainment law students to write a 3,000-word essay on a legal topic facing today's music industry. At the luncheon, a cash scholarship of $5,000 is awarded to the author of the winning paper, and $1,500 is awarded to each of four runners-up.
EIN: 953199223

1617
Grand Haven Area Community Foundation, Inc.
1 S. Harbor Dr.
Grand Haven, MI   49417
Contact: Ann Irish Tabor, Pres.; For grants: Carol Bedient, Prog. Admin.
FAX: (616) 842-9518; E-mail: info@ghacf.org;
Grant application E-mail: cbedient@ghacf.org;
URL: http://www.ghacf.org

Foundation type: Community foundation
Limitations: Scholarships to residents of northwest Ottawa County, MI, including the City of Grand Haven, Grand Haven Township, the Village of Spring Lake, Spring Lake Township, the City of Ferrysburg, and Robinson Township.
Publications: Application guidelines; Annual report (including application guidelines); Financial statement; Informational brochure (including application guidelines); Newsletter; Program policy statement.
Financial data: Year ended 03/31/2004. Assets, $37,641,101 (M); Expenditures, $2,763,806; Total giving, $2,385,118.
Type of support: Undergraduate support.
Application information: Applications accepted. Application form required.
   Initial approach: Letter.
   Deadline(s): Apr. 1

Additional information: Application must include SAR, academic achievements, desire to pursue higher education, and career goals.
Program description:
   Scholarship Funds: The foundation administers several scholarship funds. The funds require that recipients be students of one of the following MI schools: Grand Haven High School; Spring Lake High School; Holland Christian High School; Catholic Central High School, Muskegon; West Michigan Christian High School, Muskegon; West Ottawa High School; and Fruitport High School. Students must reside in the foundation's service area of northwest Ottawa County, MI.
EIN: 237108776

1618
Grand Island Community Foundation, Inc.
410 W. 2nd St., Ste. 2
P.O. Box 430
Grand Island, NE   68801   (308) 381-7767
Contact: Lisa Katzberg, Exec. Dir.
FAX: (308) 381-6567; E-mail: info@gicf.org;
URL: http://www.gicf.org

Foundation type: Community foundation
Limitations: Scholarships to individuals residing in the greater Hall County, NE, area for undergraduate education.
Publications: Application guidelines; Annual report; Annual report (including application guidelines); Financial statement; Grants list; Informational brochure; Informational brochure (including application guidelines); Newsletter; Occasional report.
Financial data: Year ended 12/31/2005. Assets, $3,813,753 (L); Expenditures, $272,218; Total giving, $116,517; Grants to individuals, 35 grants totaling $32,400.
Type of support: Undergraduate support.
Application information: Application form required. Application form available on the grantmaker's Web site.
   Copies of proposal: 2
   Deadline(s): Mar. 1
   Applicants should submit the following:
      1) GPA
      2) ACT
      3) Transcripts
      4) Essay
   Additional information: See Web site for further application information and complete program listing.
EIN: 476032570

1619
The Grand Marnier Foundation
717 5th Ave., 22nd Fl.
New York, NY   10022
Contact: Michel Roux, Pres.
Fellowship application address: c/o Grand Marnier Film Fellowships, 165 W. 65th St., 4th Fl., New York, NY 10023

Foundation type: Company-sponsored foundation
Limitations: Fellowships to graduate-level film students.
Financial data: Year ended 12/31/2004. Assets, $5,848,209 (L); Expenditures, $221,179; Total giving, $59,000.
Fields of interest: Film/video.
Type of support: Fellowships; Graduate support.
Application information: Applications accepted. Application form required. Application form available on the grantmaker's Web site.
   Deadline(s): July 18

Program description:
   Grand Marnier Film Fellowships: Awards three fellowships of $5,000 each to graduate-level film students in three categories: 1) shows originality and excellence in the craft of filmmaking; 2) shows originality and excellence using the medium of video; and 3) aspiring film historian or critic writing on the subject of film or video. Recipients must be students residing in states other than CA or TX and be at least 21 years of age. U.S. citizenship is not required. Fellowships are open to students who have graduated in May of the current year. Submissions are limited to one film, one essay and one video per applicant.
EIN: 133258414

1620
Grand Rapids Area Community Foundation
201 N.W. 4th St., Central Sq. Mall
Grand Rapids, MN   55744   (218) 327-8855
Contact: Wendy Roy, Exec. Dir.
FAX: (218) 327-8865; E-mail: info@gracf.org; Grant application E-mail: wroy@gracf.org; URL: http://www.gracf.org

Foundation type: Community foundation
Limitations: Scholarships to high school graduates of Grand Rapids and Itasca, MN, for higher education.
Publications: Application guidelines; Annual report; Informational brochure; Newsletter.
Financial data: Year ended 12/31/2004. Assets, $6,670,295 (L); Expenditures, $1,992,371; Total giving, $1,772,645; Grants to individuals, 300 grants totaling $90,000 (high: $5,000, low: $50). Subtotal for scholarships—to individuals: 50 grants totaling $50,000 (high: $5,000, low: $2,000).
Type of support: Support to graduates or students of specific schools; Undergraduate support.
Application information: Applications accepted. Application form required. Application form available on the grantmaker's Web site.
   Copies of proposal: 1
   Deadline(s): Mar. 15.
   Applicants should submit the following:
      1) ACT
      2) GPA
      3) Letter(s) of recommendation
EIN: 411761590

1621
Grand Rapids Community Foundation
(formerly The Grand Rapids Foundation)
161 Ottawa Ave. N.W., Ste. 209-C
Grand Rapids, MI   49503-2757   (616) 454-1751
Contact: Diana R. Sieger, Pres.; For grant inquiries: Ann Puckett, Admin. Asst.
FAX: (616) 454-6455;
E-mail: grfound@grfoundation.org; Grant inquiry tel.: (616) 454-1751, ext. 123, and E-mail: apuckett@grfoundation.org; URL: http://www.grfoundation.org

Foundation type: Community foundation
Limitations: Scholarships to residents of Kent and Ottawa counties (Greater Grand Rapids), MI.
Publications: Application guidelines; Annual report; Informational brochure; Newsletter.
Financial data: Year ended 06/30/2005. Assets, $194,189,277 (M); Expenditures, $10,696,786; Total giving, $7,691,957.
Fields of interest: Arts education; Theater; Performing arts, education; Business school/

education; Health sciences school/education; Nutrition; Race/intergroup relations; African Americans/Blacks.
Type of support: Support to graduates or students of specific schools; Undergraduate support; Postgraduate support.
Application information: Applications accepted. Application form required. Application form available on the grantmaker's Web site.
  Initial approach: Letter, telephone, or by contacting school's financial aid office.
  Deadline(s): Apr. 1
  Applicants should submit the following:
    1) SAT
    2) GPA
    3) Essay
    4) Financial information
  Additional information: See Web site for further application and program information.
EIN: 382877959

1622
Grannis-Martin Memorial Foundation, Inc.
c/o Merton Hubbard
315 Waite Ave. S.
St. Cloud, MN 56301
Application address: c/o Scholarship Comm., Chair., First United Methodist Church, 302 S. 5th Ave., St. Cloud, MN 56301, tel.: (320) 251-0804

Foundation type: Independent foundation
Limitations: Scholarships to prospective clergy in the United Methodist Church.
Financial data: Year ended 12/31/2004. Assets, $210,409 (M); Expenditures, $11,716; Total giving, $11,000; Grants to individuals, totaling $11,000.
Fields of interest: Theological school/education; Protestant agencies & churches.
Type of support: Scholarships—to individuals; Undergraduate support.
Application information: Applications are accepted throughout the year; Completion of formal application required, including pastoral recommendations, financial needs and type of service summary.
EIN: 411378657

1623
Leon L. Granoff Foundation
P.O. Box 2148
Gardena, CA 90247

Foundation type: Independent foundation
Limitations: Undergraduate scholarships for CA residents to attend CA colleges and universities.
Financial data: Year ended 08/31/2005. Assets, $0 (M); Expenditures, $709,270; Total giving, $700,460.
Type of support: Undergraduate support.
Application information: Contact foundation for current application deadline/guidelines.
Program description:
  Scholarship Program: Scholarships are renewable providing recipients maintain at least a 3.25 GPA.
EIN: 953184779

1624
Tom Grant Foundation
c/o Lab One, Inc.
10101 Renner Rd.
Lenexa, KS 66219

Foundation type: Operating foundation
Limitations: Scholarships to individuals participating in the foundation's sports programs in KS and MO.
Financial data: Year ended 12/31/2002. Assets, $13,411 (M); Expenditures, $115,679; Total giving, $8,227; Grants to individuals, totaling $8,227.
Fields of interest: Athletics/sports, training.
Type of support: Scholarships—to individuals.
Application information: Contact foundation for current application deadline/guidelines; Initial approach by letter or telephone.
EIN: 431623254

1625
William T. & Frances D. Grant Foundation
c/o UMB Bank, N.A.
P.O. Box 419692
Kansas City, MO 64141-6692

Foundation type: Independent foundation
Limitations: Scholarships to individuals, primarily in the Kansas City, MO, area for undergraduate education.
Financial data: Year ended 12/31/2003. Assets, $2,328,942 (M); Expenditures, $143,052; Total giving, $123,393; Grants to individuals, 3 grants totaling $10,831.
Type of support: Undergraduate support.
Application information: Contact foundation for current application deadlines/guidelines.
EIN: 446010325

1626
The Arthur E. Grasso Memorial Scholarship Foundation
7155 E. Ridgeview Pl.
Carefree, AZ 85377
Contact: Arthur D. Grasso, Pres.

Foundation type: Independent foundation
Limitations: Scholarships to graduating high school seniors from Hammonton, NJ.
Financial data: Year ended 12/31/2004. Assets, $73,238 (M); Expenditures, $5,520; Total giving, $5,500; Grants to individuals, totaling $5,500.
Type of support: Support to graduates or students of specific schools; Undergraduate support.
Application information: Applications not accepted.
EIN: 226555120

1627
Grays Harbor Community Foundation
707 J St.
P.O. Box 615
Hoquiam, WA 98550   (360) 532-1600
Contact: Stan Pinnick, Pres.
FAX: (360) 532-8111; E-mail: info@gh-cf.org; URL: http://www.gh-cf.org

Foundation type: Community foundation
Limitations: Scholarships to graduates of any high school in Grays Harbor County, WA.
Publications: Application guidelines; Annual report; Financial statement; Grants list; Informational brochure.
Financial data: Year ended 12/31/2004. Assets, $10,030,857 (M); Expenditures, $402,536; Total giving, $336,919.
Fields of interest: Human services, emergency aid.

Type of support: Graduate support; Undergraduate support.
Application information: Deadline Apr. 1; Completion of formal application required; See Web site for detailed application information.
EIN: 911607005

1628
Great Lakes Castings Corporation Foundation
800 N. Washington Ave.
Ludington, MI 49431   (231) 843-2501
Contact: Carol Henke

Foundation type: Company-sponsored foundation
Limitations: Scholarships to high school graduates from Ludington, MI, area school districts.
Financial data: Year ended 12/31/2004. Assets, $743,435 (M); Expenditures, $21,383; Total giving, $15,000; Grants to individuals, 4 grants totaling $5,000 (high: $1,250, low: $1,250).
Type of support: Undergraduate support.
Application information:
  Initial approach: Letter or telephone.
  Deadline(s): Apr. 1
  Additional information: Application by letter outlining personal, academic, and professional data.
EIN: 382250546

1629
Grede Foundation, Inc.
P.O. Box 26499
Milwaukee, WI 53226-0499   (414) 257-3600
Contact: Burleigh E. Jacobs, Pres.
Additional contact: Loretta Tesch

Foundation type: Company-sponsored foundation
Limitations: Scholarships to graduating high school seniors whose parent is an employee of Grede Foundries, Inc., or its subsidiaries, and has been employed for two years prior to application. Applicants must be accepted for full-time enrollment the following year in a four- or five-year undergraduate program leading to a bachelor's degree.
Financial data: Year ended 12/31/2004. Assets, $98,309 (M); Expenditures, $51,494; Total giving, $51,050; Grants to individuals, 14 grants totaling $14,000 (high: $1,000, low: $1,000).
Type of support: Employee-related scholarships; Undergraduate support.
Application information: Application form required.
  Deadline(s): Dec. 31
  Additional information: Application address: 9898 W. Bluemound Rd., Milwaukee, WI 53226-0499.
EIN: 396042977

1630
Greater Green Bay Community Foundation, Inc.
310 W. Walnut St., Ste. 350
Green Bay, WI 54303   (920) 432-0800
Contact: Steve Schmeisser, Finance Off.; For grants: Martha Ahrendt Ph.D., Prog. Off.
FAX: (920) 432-5577; E-mail: steve@ggbcf.org; Grant application E-mail: martha@ggbcf.org; URL: http://www.ggbcf.org

Foundation type: Community foundation

Limitations: Scholarships to graduates of Brown County high schools, WI.
Publications: Application guidelines; Annual report; Financial statement; Informational brochure.
Financial data: Year ended 06/30/2004.
Assets, $38,902,169 (M); Expenditures, $2,505,636; Total giving, $2,004,116; Grants to individuals, 55 grants totaling $254,350 (high: $40,000, low: $350, average grant: $350-$40,000).
Fields of interest: Performing arts, education; Vocational education; Nursing school/education; Agriculture; Women.
Type of support: Support to graduates or students of specific schools; Graduate support; Technical education support; Precollege support; Undergraduate support.
Application information: Applications accepted. Application form required.
> *Initial approach:* See high school counselor.
> *Deadline(s):* Mar. 1
> *Additional information:* Applications accepted only through schools; See Web site for further application information.
EIN: 391699966

1631
Walter & Frances Green Charitable Trust
c/o Wells Fargo Bank South Dakota, N.A.
P.O. Box 1040
Rapid City, SD 57709
Application address: c/o Green Scholarship Comm., 320 S. Main, Lead, SD 57754

Foundation type: Independent foundation
Limitations: Scholarships to high school seniors at Lead High School, SD, for study at colleges or vocational/technical schools.
Financial data: Year ended 12/31/2004.
Assets, $1,472,704 (M); Expenditures, $83,881; Total giving, $72,864; Grants to individuals, totaling $49,500.
Fields of interest: Vocational education.
Type of support: Support to graduates or students of specific schools; Technical education support; Undergraduate support.
Application information: Applications accepted throughout the year; Completion of formal application required, including list of extracurricular activities, special awards, transcripts, essay, and for vocational/technical students, work history and recommendation letter from past or current employer.
EIN: 466096446

1632
Allen P. & Josephine B. Green Foundation
222 S. Jefferson, Rm. 108
P.O. Box 523
Mexico, MO 65265 (573) 581-5568
Contact: Walter G. Staley, Jr., Secy.-Treas.
FAX: (573) 581-1714;
E-mail: wstaley@greenfdn.org; Additional E-mail: nrcox@greenfdn.org; URL: http://www.greenfdn.org

Foundation type: Independent foundation
Limitations: Awards scholarships of $5,000 to graduates of Mexico High School, MO.
Publications: Application guidelines; Annual report (including application guidelines); Grants list.
Financial data: Year ended 12/31/2004.
Assets, $12,384,166 (M); Expenditures, $736,335; Total giving, $615,435; Grants to individuals, 4 grants totaling $20,000 (high: $5,000, low: $5,000).

Type of support: Support to graduates or students of specific schools; Undergraduate support.
Application information: Applications accepted. Application form required.
> *Initial approach:* Application.
> *Copies of proposal:* 1
> *Deadline(s):* Jan. 15
> *Applicants should submit the following:*
> 1) Financial information
> 2) Essay
> 3) Curriculum vitae
> *Additional information:* Applications available at Mexico High School; application and attachments should be submitted to the high school counselor.
EIN: 436030135

1633
Green Scholarship Fund
c/o Bank of America, N.A., P.C. Group
P.O. Box 441
Ridgefield Park, NJ 07660-9984

Foundation type: Independent foundation
Limitations: Scholarships to students of Central Regional High School, NJ, for higher education.
Financial data: Year ended 12/31/2004.
Assets, $108,014 (M); Expenditures, $11,292; Total giving, $10,000.
Fields of interest: Science.
Type of support: Support to graduates or students of specific schools; Undergraduate support.
Application information: Applications accepted. Application form required.
Program description:
> *Scholarship Program:* Recipients are chosen by school board members. Award is given annually to one male and one female student who have excelled in science.
EIN: 527140821

1634
Anna C. & R. J. Green Scholarship Fund
c/o Bank of America, N.A.
10 Light St., MD4-302-17-06
Baltimore, MD 21202
Application addresses: c/o Superintendent of Schools, Greensville, VA 24440, or c/o Principal, Greensville County School, 403 Harding St., Emporia, VA 23847

Foundation type: Independent foundation
Limitations: Scholarships to graduates of Greenville County High School, VA, for higher education.
Financial data: Year ended 12/31/2004.
Assets, $54,695 (M); Expenditures, $14,956; Total giving, $11,000; Grants to individuals, totaling $11,000.
Type of support: Support to graduates or students of specific schools; Undergraduate support.
Application information: Applications accepted.
> *Additional information:* Applications by letter accepted throughout the year.
EIN: 546053477

1635
George B. Green Scholarship Trust
c/o Simone Masse
180 Locust St.
Dover, NH 03820 (603) 742-1300
Contact: William Tanguay, Tr.

Foundation type: Independent foundation

Limitations: Scholarships to financially needy students residing in Barrington, NH, to pursue undergraduate degrees in nursing, forestry, or medicine at colleges and universities.
Financial data: Year ended 12/31/2004.
Assets, $1,022,368 (M); Expenditures, $54,162; Total giving, $47,000; Grants to individuals, totaling $47,000.
Fields of interest: Medical school/education; Nursing school/education; Environment, forests.
Type of support: Undergraduate support.
Application information: Deadline Apr.; Completion of formal application required, including transcripts and two letters of recommendation, at least one from a teacher; Applicants must also complete the FAFSA and submit the resulting report to the foundation.
EIN: 223208678

1636
Marcella Green Scholarship Trust
c/o PNC Advisors
620 Liberty Ave., 10th Fl.
Pittsburgh, PA 15222-2705

Foundation type: Independent foundation
Limitations: Scholarships to individuals for higher education.
Financial data: Year ended 12/31/2003.
Assets, $314,891 (M); Expenditures, $17,220; Total giving, $14,112; Grants to individuals, 8 grants totaling $14,112 (high: $1,764, low: $1,764).
Type of support: Scholarships—to individuals.
Application information: Applications not accepted.
EIN: 226475773

1637
Vera Grace Greenlaw Trust
c/o Bank of America, N.A., P.C. Group
P.O. Box 6768
Providence, RI 02940-6768
Application addresses: c/o Principal, East Belfast High School, Belfast, 04915, c/o Principal, Searsport District High School, 20 Church St., Searsport, ME 04974, c/o Principal, Mountain View High School, Franklyn, ME 04607

Foundation type: Independent foundation
Limitations: Scholarships for higher education to residents of Waldo County, ME, and graduates of Waldo County secondary schools.
Financial data: Year ended 04/30/2005.
Assets, $582,164 (M); Expenditures, $33,128; Total giving, $24,095; Grants to individuals, 25 grants totaling $24,095 (high: $2,520, low: $225).
Type of support: Support to graduates or students of specific schools; Undergraduate support.
Application information: Deadline Apr. 30; Application by letter including all relevant personal data, such as employment history, transcripts, and references.
EIN: 016080221

1638
E. E. & Maud Greenwell Scholarship Trust
c/o First State Bank
P.O. Box 309
Brazil, IN 47834

Foundation type: Independent foundation
Limitations: Scholarships to Clay County High School, IN, students for higher education.

Financial data: Year ended 12/31/2004. Assets, $2,082,462 (M); Expenditures, $148,618; Total giving, $138,987; Grants to individuals, 18 grants totaling $138,987 (high: $32,817, low: $667).
Type of support: Support to graduates or students of specific schools; Undergraduate support.
Application information: Deadline Mar. 1; Application by letter.
EIN: 356613402

1639
Gregg-Graniteville Foundation, Inc.
P.O. Box 418
Graniteville, SC   29829
Contact: Patricia H. Knight, Admin.

Foundation type: Independent foundation
Limitations: Scholarships only for children of Graniteville Company employees and residents of Graniteville, Vaucluse, and Warrenville, SC.
Publications: Annual report.
Financial data: Year ended 12/31/2004. Assets, $18,571,854 (M); Expenditures, $1,008,314; Total giving, $280,916; Grants to individuals, 26 grants totaling $82,600 (high: $6,000, low: $2,000).
Type of support: Employee-related scholarships.
Application information: Application form required.
  Initial approach: Letter or proposal.
  Deadline(s): None
EIN: 570314400

1640
Abbie M. Griffin Educational Fund
c/o Winer & Bennett
378 Main St.
Nashua, NH   03060
Contact: William M. Prizer III, Tr.
Application address: William Prizer, c/o The William Mann Co., 155 Main Dunstable Rd., Ste. 105, Nashua, NH 03060, tel.: (603) 881-5633

Foundation type: Independent foundation
Limitations: Scholarships to graduating high school seniors who are residents of Merrimack, NH.
Financial data: Year ended 06/30/2005. Assets, $347,643 (M); Expenditures, $18,067; Total giving, $10,000; Grants to individuals, totaling $10,000.
Type of support: Undergraduate support.
Application information: Applications by letter accepted throughout the year.
EIN: 026021466

1641
Griffin Family Foundation, Inc.
1722 Huntingfield Dr.
Mexico, MO   65265   (573) 581-4583
Contact: Anna Margaret Griffin, Dir.

Foundation type: Independent foundation
Limitations: Scholarships to residents of MO, with emphasis on Mexico, Moberly and Springfield counties.
Financial data: Year ended 12/31/2004. Assets, $586,121 (M); Expenditures, $34,538; Total giving, $24,500; Grants to individuals, totaling $19,500.
Type of support: Undergraduate support.
Application information: Contact foundation for current application deadline/guidelines.
EIN: 431822804

1642
The Griffin Foundation, Inc.
303 W. Prospect Rd.
Fort Collins, CO   80526   (970) 482-3030
Contact: David L. Wood, Dir.

Foundation type: Independent foundation
Limitations: Scholarships to students attending an accredited university or junior college in CO and WY.
Financial data: Year ended 12/31/2004. Assets, $6,933,301 (M); Expenditures, $1,571,386; Total giving, $1,243,925; Grants to individuals, 25 grants totaling $126,842 (high: $5,830, low: $5,000).
Type of support: Undergraduate support.
Application information: Applications by letter accepted throughout the year.
EIN: 841171483

1643
The Neil and Elaine Griffin Foundation
P.O. Box 291910
Kerrville, TX   78029-1910   (830) 896-6667
Contact: Richard D. Griffin, Managing Tr.
Scholarship application address: 301 Junction Hwy., Ste. 320, Kerrville, TX 78028
E-mail: rgriffin@ktc.com

Foundation type: Independent foundation
Limitations: Scholarships to graduates of Kerr County High School, TX, for higher education.
Financial data: Year ended 09/30/2004. Assets, $6,502,948 (M); Expenditures, $1,084,121; Total giving, $526,198; Grants to individuals, 53 grants totaling $509,348 (high: $18,000, low: $5,245).
Type of support: Support to graduates or students of specific schools; Undergraduate support.
Application information: Applications accepted. Application form required.
  Additional information: Applications by letter accepted throughout the year.
EIN: 742729281

1644
The Lewis, Philip and Andrew Griffith Foundation
620 Main St.
P.O. Box 313
Neodesha, KS   66757-0313   (620) 325-2626
Contact: Dennis D. Depew, Secy.-Treas.
FAX: (620) 325-2636;
E-mail: Dennis@depewlaw.biz

Foundation type: Independent foundation
Limitations: Scholarships to graduates of Neodesha High School, KS, who reside in USD No. 461.
Publications: Application guidelines.
Financial data: Year ended 12/31/2004. Assets, $14,302 (M); Expenditures, $75,963; Total giving, $68,175; Grants to individuals, totaling $61,051.
Type of support: Support to graduates or students of specific schools; Undergraduate support.
Application information: Deadline Apr. 1; Completion of formal application required, including transcripts.
EIN: 481076347

1645
Paul and Mary Griffith Scholarship Fund
c/o Farmers and Merchants Bank
P.O. Box 29
Winterset, IA   50273-0029
Application address: c/o Winterset High School, Winterset, IA 50273

Foundation type: Independent foundation
Limitations: Scholarships to graduates of Winterset High School, IA. Scholarship must not exceed $1,000 per year, and may be renewed up to $4,000.
Financial data: Year ended 12/31/2004. Assets, $151,017 (M); Expenditures, $7,422; Total giving, $7,000; Grants to individuals, totaling $7,000.
Application information: Applications accepted. Application form required.
  Deadline(s): None
  Additional information: Interviews required; Further application information available through Winterset High School.
EIN: 421172652

1646
Clifford D. and Virginia S. Grim Educational Fund
(formerly Clifford D. Grim and Virginia S. Grim Educational Fund)
c/o Wachovia Bank, N.A.
100 N. Main St., 13th Fl.
Winston-Salem, NC   27150-6732
Contact: Caroline Beck, Trust Off., Wachovia Bank, N.A.
Scholarship URL: http://www.wachoviascholars.com/grim/grim_2006_ins.htm

Foundation type: Independent foundation
Limitations: Educational loans to students in the Winchester, VA, area only.
Financial data: Year ended 07/31/2005. Assets, $1,469,959 (M); Expenditures, $12,106; Total giving, $0; Loans to individuals, totaling $23,500.
Type of support: Student loans—to individuals.
Application information: Application form required.
  Deadline(s): May 1
  Additional information: Application must also include three references, statement form filled out by school, and personal financial statement; Interviews required; Applications are not mailed.
EIN: 546046865

1647
Grimley Scholarship Trust
c/o Wachovia Bank, N.A.
401 S. Tryon St., 4th Fl.
Charlotte, NC   28288-5709
Contact: For Scholarships: Michael Boyles

Foundation type: Independent foundation
Limitations: Scholarships to members of the top half graduating class of Kutztown Area High School, PA.
Financial data: Year ended 12/31/2003. Assets, $556,579 (M); Expenditures, $27,296; Total giving, $26,000; Grants to individuals, 18 grants totaling $26,000 (high: $1,500, low: $1,000).
Type of support: Support to graduates or students of specific schools; Undergraduate support.

Application information: Applications not accepted.
EIN: 236408183

1648
Jessie E. Griswold Trust
520 N. Main
White Hall, IL   62092   (217) 374-2306
Contact: Howard Piper, Tr.

Foundation type: Independent foundation
Limitations: Student loans to students from Green County, IL, for higher education. Renewal of loans will depend on a satisfactory scholastic record.
Financial data: Year ended 12/31/2004. Assets, $8,471,793 (M); Expenditures, $241,078; Total giving, $174,500; Loans to individuals, 136 loans totaling $174,500.
Type of support: Student loans—to individuals.
Application information: Applications accepted. Application form required.
Deadline(s): Contact trust for current application deadline.
Additional information: Application should include transcripts.
EIN: 376105072

1649
Mike & Bev Groeniger College Scholarship Fund
P.O. Box 3629
Hayward, CA   94540   (510) 786-3333
Contact: Richard Groeniger, Tr.
Application address: 27750 Industrial Blvd., Hayward, CA 94540

Foundation type: Company-sponsored foundation
Limitations: Scholarships only to children of employees of Groeniger & Company who are high school seniors with a GPA of 2.5 or higher.
Financial data: Year ended 12/31/2004. Assets, $470,775 (M); Expenditures, $21,522; Total giving, $21,500; Grants to individuals, 5 grants totaling $21,500 (high: $5,000, low: $1,500).
Type of support: Employee-related scholarships.
Application information:
Initial approach: Letter.
Applicants should submit the following:
1) GPA
2) Curriculum vitae
Additional information: Application address: c/o Richard Groeniger, 27750 Industrial Blvd., Hayward, CA 94540.
EIN: 946757910

1650
Frank and Louise Groff Foundation
c/o Susan Rechel
15 Floyd Wycoff Rd.
Morganville, NJ   07751   (732) 842-8000

Foundation type: Independent foundation
Limitations: Scholarships to graduates of public schools in Monmouth County, NJ, who are preparing to become registered nurses or medical doctors. Awards are granted first to graduates of Monmouth County public high schools, NJ, and then to graduates of any public school in NJ.
Publications: Application guidelines.
Financial data: Year ended 06/30/2004. Assets, $453,193 (M); Expenditures, $31,380; Total giving, $17,000; Grants to individuals, totaling $17,000.

Fields of interest: Medical school/education; Nursing school/education.
Type of support: Support to graduates or students of specific schools; Undergraduate support.
Application information: Application form required.
Deadline(s): Apr. 1
Additional information: Interviews required; Applications available at Monmouth County, NJ, public high school guidance offices and the foundation office.
Program description:
Scholarship Program: Recipients are chosen on the basis of demonstrated financial need, high school records, recommendations, sincere interest in a course leading to certification as a registered nurse or medical doctor, and admission to and maintenance of satisfactory progress in a nursing or medical school. Students preparing to be physical therapists, X-ray technicians, or licensed practical nurses are ineligible.
EIN: 237082026

1651
Mary S. Groff Scholarship Trust
c/o Wachovia Bank, N.A.
100 N. Main St., 13th Fl.
Winston-Salem, NC   27150

Foundation type: Independent foundation
Limitations: Scholarships to graduates of Columbia High School, PA.
Financial data: Year ended 12/31/2004. Assets, $217,993 (M); Expenditures, $9,406; Total giving, $9,000; Grants to individuals, totaling $9,000.
Type of support: Support to graduates or students of specific schools; Undergraduate support.
Application information: Applications not accepted.
EIN: 236479982

1652
The Beverly W. Grogan & Mabel Tudor Grogan Educational Fund, Inc.
c/o BB&T
P.O. Box 5228
Martinsville, VA   24115-5228
Application address: c/o Priscilla Diggs, Patrick County High School, 215 Cougar Ln., Stuart, VA 24171

Foundation type: Independent foundation
Limitations: Scholarships and educational loans to students at Patrick County High School, VA.
Financial data: Year ended 10/31/2004. Assets, $807,712 (M); Expenditures, $13,756; Total giving, $4,500; Grants to individuals, totaling $4,500.
Type of support: Support to graduates or students of specific schools; Undergraduate support.
Application information: Deadline Mar. 1; Completion of formal application required.
EIN: 541511938

1653
Gromack Scholarship Fund
c/o Bank of America, N.A., P.C. Group
P.O. Box 1802
Providence, RI   02940-1802

Foundation type: Independent foundation
Limitations: Scholarships to students of New Britain High School, CT, who plan on pursuing a Bachelor's degree in the Arts or Sciences, and must

have a good academic standing and show financial need.
Financial data: Year ended 04/30/2005. Assets, $417,833 (M); Expenditures, $28,869; Total giving, $22,400; Grants to individuals, 14 grants totaling $22,400 (high: $1,500, low: $1,500).
Type of support: Support to graduates or students of specific schools; Undergraduate support.
Application information: Application form required.
Deadline(s): Apr. 13
Additional information: Application must include transcripts, class rank and mid-year grades.
EIN: 061514838

1654
The Janice & Ben Gromet Fund for Disadvantaged Children
(formerly J & B Fund for Disadvantaged Children)
1188 Bishop St., Ste. 2701
Honolulu, HI   96813-3311
Contact: Charles Rolles, Pres. and Treas.
E-mail: info@gromet.org

Foundation type: Independent foundation
Limitations: Scholarships to financially needy residents of HI, who have graduated from HI high schools.
Financial data: Year ended 12/31/2004. Assets, $8,455,357 (M); Expenditures, $706,373; Total giving, $203,623; Grants to individuals, 55 grants totaling $203,623 (high: $5,000, low: $750).
Type of support: Scholarships—to individuals.
Application information: Application form required.
Deadline(s): Contact Hawaii Community Foundation for current application deadline
Applicants should submit the following:
1) Letter(s) of recommendation
2) SAT
3) GPA
4) Financial information
Additional information: Interviews required.
Program description:
Scholarship Program: Scholarships are awarded on the basis of academic achievement, financial need, special talents, and results of a personal interview. Scholarships are renewable.
EIN: 990281966

1655
Mary Sullivan Gross Scholarship Fund
17404 Spring Tree Ln.
Boca Raton, FL   33487

Foundation type: Operating foundation
Limitations: Scholarship awards to Florida residents for postsecondary study.
Financial data: Year ended 12/31/2003. Assets, $31,180 (M); Expenditures, $12,300; Total giving, $11,800; Grants to individuals, 13 grants totaling $11,800 (high: $2,200, low: $600).
Fields of interest: Higher education.
Type of support: Scholarships—to individuals.
Application information: Applications accepted.
Initial approach: Letter.
EIN: 756654263

1656
Alexander J. Grossman Scholarship Foundation

c/o AmSouth Bank
P.O. Box 2918
Clearwater, FL 33757-2918

Foundation type: Independent foundation
Limitations: Undergraduate scholarships in science and engineering to graduates of Dunedin Comprehensive High School, FL, who were in the top ten percent of their class and have been accepted to accredited U.S. colleges and universities.
Financial data: Year ended 03/31/2005. Assets, $2,096,480 (M); Expenditures, $122,955; Total giving, $100,000; Grants to individuals, 19 grants totaling $100,000 (high: $11,000, low: $2,500).
Fields of interest: Engineering school/education; Science.
Type of support: Support to graduates or students of specific schools; Undergraduate support.
Application information: Applications not accepted.
>   *Additional information:* Candidates are sought by the awards committee. Unsolicited requests for funds not considered or acknowledged.

EIN: 596782085

1657
George Grotefend Scholarship Fund

c/o Wells Fargo Bank, N.A., Tax Dept.
P.O. Box 63954
San Francisco, CA 94168
Application address: c/o Scholarship Board, 1644 Magnolia Ave., Redding, CA 96001

Foundation type: Independent foundation
Limitations: Graduate and undergraduate scholarships to financially needy students who have received their entire high school education in Shasta County, CA.
Financial data: Year ended 04/30/2005. Assets, $1,259,815 (M); Expenditures, $90,729; Total giving, $63,220; Grants to individuals, totaling $63,220.
Type of support: Support to graduates or students of specific schools; Graduate support; Undergraduate support.
Application information: Deadline May 1; Completion of formal application required; Initial approach through high school.
EIN: 946069688

1658
Thomas O. Grove Scholarship Fund

c/o KeyBank N.A., Trust Div.
P.O. Box 10099
Toledo, OH 43699-0099   (419) 259-8655
Contact: Diane Ohns, Trust Admin., KeyBank N.A.

Foundation type: Independent foundation
Limitations: Scholarships to graduating students of any high school in Sylvania, OH.
Financial data: Year ended 12/31/2004. Assets, $252,939 (M); Expenditures, $20,555; Total giving, $16,000; Grants to individuals, totaling $16,000.
Type of support: Support to graduates or students of specific schools; Undergraduate support.
Application information: Contact fund for current application deadline/guidelines.
EIN: 346942668

1659
Freeman and Emma Grow Memorial Scholarship Fund

P.O. Box 134
Goldendale, WA 98620   (509) 773-4646
Contact: Daryl G. Erdman, Secy.

Foundation type: Independent foundation
Limitations: Scholarships only to graduating seniors of Goldendale High School, WA, to attend institutions of higher learning in WA.
Financial data: Year ended 12/31/2004. Assets, $0 (M); Expenditures, $3,228; Total giving, $3,000; Grants to individuals, totaling $3,000.
Type of support: Support to graduates or students of specific schools; Undergraduate support.
Application information: Applications accepted throughout the year; Completion of formal application required; Scholarships are not renewable.
EIN: 237123616

1660
Augusta Schultz Grubbs Charitable Trust

P.O. Drawer 635
Clifton Forge, VA 24422-0635
Application address: c/o Alleghany High School, Attn.: Scholarship Comm., 1 Mountaineer Dr., Covington, VA 24426

Foundation type: Independent foundation
Limitations: Scholarships to Alleghany High School seniors, VA, who have a GPA in the top ten percent of their graduating class.
Financial data: Year ended 05/31/2005. Assets, $1,284,158 (M); Expenditures, $43,751; Total giving, $28,680; Grants to individuals, totaling $28,680.
Type of support: Support to graduates or students of specific schools; Undergraduate support.
Application information:
>   *Deadline(s):* Deadline Mar. 1.
>   *Additional information:* Application by letter explaining plans for college education or career in 200 words or less, grade reports and other academic progress, and transcript.

EIN: 541902317

1661
The Gruenberg Foundation, Inc.

50 N. Franklin Tpke., Ste. 206
Ho-Ho-Kus, NJ 07423

Foundation type: Independent foundation
Limitations: Scholarships to high school seniors who attend Tri-State University, IN, as undergraduates, are U.S. citizens, and have been residents of Ridgewood, NJ, for four years.
Financial data: Year ended 09/30/2004. Assets, $5,950,860 (M); Expenditures, $344,975; Total giving, $187,023; Grants to individuals, 33 grants totaling $187,023 (high: $13,000, low: $2,500).
Type of support: Support to graduates or students of specific schools; Undergraduate support.
Application information: Contact foundation for current application deadline; Initial approach by letter or telephone.
EIN: 223381175

1662
William F. Grupe Foundation, Inc.

c/o TD Banknorth, N.A, Wealth Mgmt. Group
55 Madison Ave.
Morristown, NJ 07960   (973) 889-3771
Contact: David Paterson, Secy.-Treas.

Foundation type: Independent foundation
Limitations: Medical, nursing, and paramedical scholarships only to residents of Bergen, Essex, and Hudson counties, NJ, planning to practice within the state.
Publications: Application guidelines.
Financial data: Year ended 12/31/2004. Assets, $1,234,935 (M); Expenditures, $92,526; Total giving, $72,000; Grants to individuals, totaling $72,000.
Fields of interest: Medical school/education; Nursing school/education.
Type of support: Graduate support; Undergraduate support.
Application information: Applications by letter accepted throughout the year.
EIN: 226094704

1663
Guardian Industries Educational Foundation

2300 Harmon Rd.
Auburn Hills, MI 48326-1714
Contact: Kenneth J. Battjes, V.P.

Foundation type: Company-sponsored foundation
Limitations: Scholarships to children of full-time employees of Guardian Industries and its U.S. subsidiaries for attendance at accredited two- and four-year colleges, vocational and technical schools, and hospital schools of nursing in the U.S.
Financial data: Year ended 12/31/2003. Assets, $57,159 (M); Expenditures, $823,512; Total giving, $782,816; Grants to individuals, 206 grants totaling $782,816 (high: $9,250, low: $900).
Fields of interest: Vocational education; Nursing school/education.
Type of support: Employee-related scholarships; Technical education support; Undergraduate support.
Application information: Application form required.
>   *Deadline(s):* Nov. 30
>   *Additional information:* Application should include SAT; Scholarship application address: c/o Guardian Scholarship Prog., Educational Testing Svc., Scholarship and Recognition Progs., Rosedale Rd., M.S. 02-L, Princeton, NJ 08541, tel.: (609) 683-2325.

EIN: 382707035

1664
Paul Gubitosi Charitable Fund, Inc.

5 Joshua Dr.
Hillsborough, NJ 08844

Foundation type: Independent foundation
Limitations: Scholarships to individuals.
Financial data: Year ended 12/31/2004. Assets, $7,075 (M); Expenditures, $56,418; Total giving, $34,000; Grants to individuals, 7 grants totaling $10,000 (high: $2,500, low: $1,000).
Type of support: Scholarships—to individuals.
Application information: Contact foundation for current application deadline/guidelines.
EIN: 810547982

1665
The Guenther Scholarship Fund
c/o Steuben Trust Co.
1 Steuben Sq.
Hornell, NY 14843-1699

Foundation type: Independent foundation
Limitations: Scholarships awarded to graduates of Hornell High School District, NY.
Financial data: Year ended 12/31/2004. Assets, $712,215 (M); Expenditures, $32,562; Total giving, $30,000; Grants to individuals, totaling $30,000.
Type of support: Support to graduates or students of specific schools; Undergraduate support.
Application information: Applications not accepted.
Program description:
  Scholarship Program: The student must prove outstanding citizenship to the committee and must demonstrate leadership, capability, and perceptiveness. These traits may be evaluated in part by the nature of extracurricular activities and the extent of success in them. Scholarships are to be used at accredited four-year colleges for courses in subjects which are usually considered to be valuable in producing desirable citizens. Very specialized courses should be considered carefully. They must be part of the college's prescribed degree program.
EIN: 222314303

1666
Ernest Guertin Trust
c/o Bank of America, N.A., P.C. Group
P.O. Box 1802
Providence, RI 02940-1802
Application address: c/o Endowment, 650 Elm St., Manchester, NH 03110

Foundation type: Independent foundation
Limitations: Scholarships to students of Lebanon High School, NH, for higher education.
Financial data: Year ended 12/31/2004. Assets, $378,952 (M); Expenditures, $29,206; Total giving, $23,841.
Application information: Application form required.
  Deadline(s): First week in May
  Additional information: The Ernest Guertin Trust administers the Evelyn "Burgess" Guertin Scholarship Program. Application should include essay, copies of letter of acceptance and financial aid award letter from the college that will be attended, and FAF acknowledgement form.
EIN: 026075479

1667
W. H. Guest & E. M. Guest Educational Trust
(formerly William H. Guest & Edith M. Guest Educational Trust)
P.O. Box 250
Cherokee, IA 51012-0250   (712) 225-3120
Contact: Violet L. Guest, Mgr.

Foundation type: Independent foundation
Limitations: Scholarships to residents of Cherokee, IA, for study at a two-year trade or vocational school.
Financial data: Year ended 12/31/2004. Assets, $469,806 (M); Expenditures, $8,550; Total giving, $5,400; Grants to individuals, totaling $5,400.
Fields of interest: Vocational education.
Type of support: Technical education support.

Application information: Application form required.
  Deadline(s): May 1
EIN: 426278426

1668
Simon Guggenheim Scholarship Fund
c/o Wachovia Bank, N.A.
100 N. Main St., 13th Fl.
Winston-Salem, NC 27150
Application address: c/o Pres., Central High School, Ogontz Ave., Philadelphia, PA 19122

Foundation type: Independent foundation
Limitations: Scholarships to seniors of Central High School in Philadelphia, PA.
Financial data: Year ended 12/31/2004. Assets, $1,084,324 (M); Expenditures, $131,877; Total giving, $126,073; Grants to individuals, totaling $126,073.
Type of support: Support to graduates or students of specific schools; Undergraduate support.
Application information: Applications accepted throughout the year; Completion of formal application required.
EIN: 236219173

1669
Albert Guiliani Scholarship Foundation
c/o First National Bank
P.O. Box 1010
Danville, IL 61834-1010

Foundation type: Independent foundation
Limitations: Scholarships to students at Danville Area Community College, IL.
Financial data: Year ended 12/31/2004. Assets, $157,795 (M); Expenditures, $10,484; Total giving, $8,000; Grants to individuals, totaling $8,000.
Type of support: Support to graduates or students of specific schools; Undergraduate support.
Application information: Unsolicited requests for funds not accepted.
EIN: 376134954

1670
A. B. Guslander Masonic Lodge Scholarship Fund
P.O. Box 67
Willits, CA 95490

Foundation type: Independent foundation
Limitations: Scholarships to graduates of Willits High School, CA, in their junior or senior year of college, or in graduate school.
Financial data: Year ended 12/31/2004. Assets, $0 (M); Expenditures, $10,689; Total giving, $10,110; Grants to individuals, totaling $10,110.
Type of support: Support to graduates or students of specific schools; Graduate support; Undergraduate support.
Application information: Deadline Aug. 31; Application by letter, including transcript of high school grades and student statement.
EIN: 237323314

1671
Dwight R. & Julia Guthrie Scholarship Fund
c/o National City Bank
P.O. Box 94651
Cleveland, OH 44101-4651

Foundation type: Independent foundation
Limitations: Scholarships to students in PA, for higher education.
Financial data: Year ended 01/31/2005. Assets, $314,501 (M); Expenditures, $15,120; Total giving, $11,250; Grants to individuals, 2 grants totaling $11,250 (high: $7,500, low: $3,750).
Type of support: Undergraduate support.
Application information: Unsolicited requests for funds not accepted.
EIN: 256638149

1672
Gygi and von Wyss Foundation
(formerly Hans Gygi Foundation)
P.O. Box 122
Dundee, MI 48131
Contact: Karen Dierks, Asst. Secy.
E-mail: karen.dierks@holcim.com; Application address: 6211 N. Ann Arbor Rd., Dundee, MI 48131-0122; URL: http://www.holcim.com/USA/EN/b/null/oid/57272/module/gnm50/jsp/templates/editorial/editorial.html

Foundation type: Company-sponsored foundation
Limitations: Scholarships to high school seniors who are children or stepchildren of employees of Holcim (U.S.), Inc. and its wholly-owned subsidiaries.
Financial data: Year ended 12/31/2004. Assets, $59,421 (M); Expenditures, $104,838; Total giving, $75,064; Grants to individuals, 24 grants totaling $75,064 (high: $4,000, low: $1,455).
Type of support: Employee-related scholarships; Undergraduate support.
Application information: Application form required.
  Deadline(s): Jan. 11
  Applicants should submit the following:
    1) Transcripts
    2) SAT
    3) Letter(s) of recommendation
    4) Essay
    5) ACT
  Additional information: Application address: 6211 N. Ann Arbor Rd., Dundee, MI 48131-0122.
Program description:
  Scholarship Award: Employees must have been employed full-time for at least 12 consecutive months and have accrued 1,000 hours of service. In addition, they must be actively employed on the date of the scholarship award or have retired from active employment between Sept. 1 and the date of the scholarship award. Applicants must have at least a 2.5 cumulative GPA to be considered for this scholarship.
EIN: 382472472

1673
H.E.R.O. Scholarship Fund
2074 Lake Tahoe Blvd., Ste. 6
South Lake Tahoe, CA 96150   (530) 544-2121
Contact: Douglas Rosner, Pres.

Foundation type: Public charity
Limitations: Scholarships to high school graduates of schools in the Lake Tahoe, CA, area.

Financial data: Year ended 03/31/2004.
Assets, $37,895 (M); Expenditures, $14,387;
Total giving, $14,375; Grants to individuals, 14
grants totaling $14,375 (high: $1,250, low: $625).
Fields of interest: Vocational education,
post-secondary.
Type of support: Scholarships—to individuals.
Application information: Applications accepted.
Initial approach: Letter.
Program description:
Scholarships: Recipients must be high school
graduates pursuing post secondary higher
education. Eligible students must have overcome
some obstacle to their continuing education . The
recipients are required to provide proof of
enrollment in 9 or more units of higher education
before they receive the first half of their award. The
second half is given after verification of enrollment
of 9 or more units in the next academic period.
Initial eligibility requires the recipient to be
nominated for the award by a high school
administrator, counselor or teacher.
EIN: 680473751

1674
H.O.P.E. Foundation of Darke County
c/o Rodney Oda
300 W. Main St.
Greenville, OH 45331
Application address: c/o Office of Education,
Courthouse, Greenville, OH 45331

Foundation type: Independent foundation
Limitations: Applicants must be residents of Drake
County, OH. The foundation does not generally
grant scholarships for first-year studies.
Financial data: Year ended 06/30/2004.
Assets, $1,364,323 (M); Expenditures, $89,281;
Total giving, $75,479.
Type of support: Undergraduate support.
Application information: Application form required.
Deadline(s): June 15
Applicants should submit the following:
1) Transcripts
Additional information: Application should
include transcripts; Contact foundation for the
areas in which they are making grants;
Interviews required.
Program description:
Scholarship Program: Scholarships are
renewable for up to three years. Applicants must
have a 3.0 GPA to be considered.
EIN: 311177601

1675
Paul and Mary Haas Foundation
P.O. Box 2928
Corpus Christi, TX 78403-2928
(361) 887-6955
Contact: Karen L. Wesson, Admin. Dir.
FAX: (361) 883-5992; E-mail: haasfdn@aol.com

Foundation type: Independent foundation
Limitations: Scholarships to graduates of Corpus
Christi High School, TX, who were previously named
as Haas scholars in the 8th grade, while attending
Paul R. Haas Middle School, TX.
Publications: Application guidelines; Financial
statement; Grants list; Informational brochure
(including application guidelines).
Financial data: Year ended 12/31/2004.
Assets, $2,454,442 (M); Expenditures,
$369,320; Total giving, $299,353; Grants to
individuals, 45 grants totaling $111,000 (high:
$3,000, low: $1,000).

Type of support: Support to graduates or students
of specific schools; Undergraduate support.
Application information: Applications not
accepted.
Additional information: Unsolicited requests for
funds not considered or acknowledged.
EIN: 746031614

1676
Hach Scientific Foundation
2114 N. Lincoln Ave., Ste. 104
Loveland, CO 80538

Foundation type: Independent foundation
Limitations: Scholarships to high school graduates
in IA, CO, and WY, who are pursuing B.S. degrees
in chemistry or chemical engineering, and are in the
top ten percent of their classes.
Financial data: Year ended 09/30/2004.
Assets, $38,358,316 (M); Expenditures,
$1,480,414; Total giving, $1,174,286.
Fields of interest: Science; Chemistry; Engineering.
Type of support: Undergraduate support.
Application information: Applications not
accepted.
EIN: 840900668

1677
D. D. Hachar Charitable Trust Fund
c/o The Laredo National Bank
P.O. Box 59
Laredo, TX 78042-0059   (956) 723-1151
FAX: (956) 764-1592

Foundation type: Independent foundation
Limitations: Scholarships to financially needy
residents of Laredo, Webb County, and surrounding
counties, TX.
Publications: Application guidelines; Annual report;
Informational brochure; Program policy statement.
Financial data: Year ended 04/30/2005.
Assets, $27,512,904 (M); Expenditures,
$1,283,899; Total giving, $905,959; Grants to
individuals, 271 grants totaling $348,825 (high:
$4,000, low: $250).
Type of support: Scholarships—to individuals.
Application information:
Deadline(s): Last Friday in Apr. for fall and spring
semester grants, last Friday in Oct. for spring
semester only
Applicants should submit the following:
1) Letter(s) of recommendation
2) Transcripts
Additional information: Completion of formal
application required, including photograph,
copy of parents' and/or applicant's tax
returns with notarized affidavit, letter
awarding or denying financial aid from college,
and acceptance letter from college; Interviews
required and must be scheduled before last
Friday in Oct.
Program description:
Scholarship Program: Freshmen and sophomore
applicants must have at least a 2.0 GPA; juniors
and seniors must have at least a 2.5 GPA.
Applicants with family incomes over $50,000 are
ineligible. Part-time students are ineligible. No
scholarships are granted for summer school.
EIN: 742093680

1678
Starr Hacker Memorial Scholarship Fund
350 Daniel St.
Lindenhurst, NY 11757-3547
Contact: Daniel Giordano, Tr.
Application address: 300 Charles St., Lindenhurst,
NY 11757, tel.: (631) 226-7567

Foundation type: Independent foundation
Limitations: Scholarships to graduates of
Lindenhurst High School, NY, who show distinction
in English and/or Drama. Applicants must have an
average of at least 85 percent in English.
Financial data: Year ended 11/30/2004.
Assets, $230,308 (M); Expenditures, $9,706;
Total giving, $9,000; Grants to individuals, totaling
$9,000.
Fields of interest: Theater; Literature.
Type of support: Employee-related scholarships;
Support to graduates or students of specific
schools; Undergraduate support.
Application information: Deadline Nov. 19;
Completion of formal application required, including
teacher recommendations and essay; Interviews
required; Finalists announced Dec. 3; Finalists
submit a poem, short story, critical review, or
dramatic performance by Jan. 7; Recipients
announced Feb. 4.
EIN: 112487557

1679
Edna Haddad Welfare Trust Fund
7215 Creveling Dr.
St. Louis, MO 63130-4124
Contact: Evelyn B. Goldberg, Dir.

Foundation type: Independent foundation
Limitations: Scholarships to residents of MO for
higher education.
Financial data: Year ended 03/31/2005.
Assets, $302,335 (M); Expenditures, $19,966;
Total giving, $19,089; Grants to individuals,
totaling $19,089.
Type of support: Scholarships—to individuals.
Application information: Contact fund for current
application deadline/guidelines.
EIN: 431434151

1680
Mary Catherine Hagedorn Trust
P.O. Box 305
Lake View, IA 51450-0305
Contact: William Vonnahme, Tr.

Foundation type: Operating foundation
Limitations: Scholarships to students for higher
education, primarily in IA.
Financial data: Year ended 10/31/2002.
Assets, $441,901 (M); Expenditures, $17,032;
Total giving, $12,375; Grants to individuals, 24
grants totaling $12,375 (high: $750, low: $375).
Type of support: Undergraduate support.
Application information: Applications by letter
accepted throughout the year.
EIN: 426291418

1681
Hager Hanger Club Foundation
2511 Santa Clara Ave.
Alameda, CA 94501   (510) 337-9025
Contact: James Hager, Pres.

Foundation type: Operating foundation
Limitations: Scholarships for flight training to
underprivileged students in CA and Mexico.

Financial data: Year ended 12/31/2002. Assets, $509,886 (M); Expenditures, $29,693; Total giving, $23,985; Grants to individuals, totaling $23,985.
Fields of interest: Space/aviation; Economically disadvantaged; Mexico.
Type of support: Scholarships—to individuals.
Application information: Applications by letter accepted throughout the year.
EIN: 943245672

1682
Roy Haggerty Memorial Scholarship Fund
c/o Indiana Lawrence Bank
P.O. Box 502
North Manchester, IN 46962-0502
Application address: c/o Indiana Lawrence Bank, 729 Main St., Rochester, IN 46975, tel.: (219) 223-3105

Foundation type: Independent foundation
Limitations: Scholarships to residents of Fulton County, IN, for attendance at Indiana University, IN.
Financial data: Year ended 06/30/2005. Assets, $508,677 (M); Expenditures, $28,447; Total giving, $25,500; Grants to individuals, totaling $25,500.
Type of support: Support to graduates or students of specific schools; Undergraduate support.
Application information: Applications accepted. Application form required.
Applicants should submit the following:
1) Financial information
2) Essay
Additional information: Application should also include personal, family, educational, and extracurricular information.
EIN: 352050033

1683
Robert L. Hahn Foundation, Inc.
2800 Casey Key Rd.
Nokomis, FL 34275-3323

Foundation type: Independent foundation
Limitations: Scholarships to individuals for higher education, primarily in FL.
Financial data: Year ended 12/31/2004. Assets, $3,235 (M); Expenditures, $14,150; Total giving, $13,500; Grants to individuals, totaling $13,500.
Type of support: Undergraduate support.
Application information: Applications not accepted.
EIN: 593100586

1684
William Haines Memorial Scholarship Trust
5 Brookwood Dr.
Voorhees, NJ 08043
Contact: John Morelli, Tr.

Foundation type: Independent foundation
Limitations: Scholarships to residents of the Voorhees or Gibbsboro, NJ areas, for four-year programs.
Financial data: Year ended 12/31/2004. Assets, $86,325 (M); Expenditures, $39,666; Total giving, $39,000; Grants to individuals, 15 grants totaling $39,000 (high: $4,000, low: $2,000).
Fields of interest: Scholarships/financial aid.
Type of support: Scholarships—to individuals.

Application information: Applications accepted.
Deadline(s): None
Additional information: Contact foundation for current application guidelines.
EIN: 226853625

1685
The Jeanette Hajjar Foundation
2422 Manoa Ln. N.
Toledo, OH 43615-2432
Contact: Sami Sayegh, Tr.

Foundation type: Independent foundation
Limitations: Scholarships to women of Lebanese descent from Beirut, Lebanon.
Financial data: Year ended 12/31/2004. Assets, $203,356 (M); Expenditures, $90,936; Total giving, $56,532; Grants to individuals, totaling $30,555.
Fields of interest: Women; Lebanon.
Type of support: Scholarships—to individuals.
Application information: Applications accepted. Application form required.
Additional information: Contact foundation for current application deadline.
EIN: 341893921

1686
The Jen Hale Memorial Foundation, Inc.
P.O. Box 1400
Voorhees, NJ 08043-1400 (856) 768-1300
Contact: Barry J. Hale, Tr.

Foundation type: Independent foundation
Limitations: Scholarships and student loans to graduating seniors from local high schools for undergraduate education.
Financial data: Year ended 12/31/2004. Assets, $175,157 (M); Expenditures, $23,253; Total giving, $22,000; Grants to individuals, totaling $22,000.
Type of support: Student loans—to individuals; Undergraduate support.
Application information: Deadline May 8; Completion of formal application required, including essay and SAT scores.
EIN: 311703194

1687
Benton & Louise Hale Memorial Scholarship Fund
c/o Marshall & Ilsley Bank Trust Co., N.A.
P.O. Box 2980
Milwaukee, WI 53201-2980
Application address: c/o Marshall & Ilsley Trust Co., N.A., 5935 7th Ave., Kenosha, WI 53140, tel.: (252) 658-5580

Foundation type: Independent foundation
Limitations: Scholarships for higher education to Burlington High School, WI, graduates.
Financial data: Year ended 12/31/2004. Assets, $417,152 (M); Expenditures, $14,520; Total giving, $10,892; Grants to individuals, totaling $10,892.
Type of support: Support to graduates or students of specific schools; Undergraduate support.
Application information: Application form required.
Deadline(s): Apr.
EIN: 396257040

1688
Martha K. Hall Educational Trust
c/o U.S. Bank, N.A.
P.O. Box 3168
Portland, OR 97208-3168
Application address: c/o U.S. Bank, N.A., P.O. Box 3588 (WSA 680), Spokane, WA 9920

Foundation type: Independent foundation
Limitations: Scholarships to graduates of Lincoln County high schools, WA.
Financial data: Year ended 09/30/2002. Assets, $720,028 (M); Expenditures, $61,071; Total giving, $45,666; Grants to individuals, 18 grants totaling $45,666 (high: $12,299, low: $300).
Type of support: Support to graduates or students of specific schools; Undergraduate support.
Application information: Application form required.
Initial approach: Letter.
Deadline(s): Apr. 15
Applicants should submit the following:
1) Transcripts
2) Financial information
EIN: 916173039

1689
Hall Family Foundation
P.O. Box 419580, Dept. 323
Kansas City, MO 64141-6580
Contact: Tracy McFerrin Foster, V.P.; Jeanne Bates, V.P.; Sally Groves, Prog. Off.
FAX: (816) 274-8547; URL: http://www.hallfamilyfoundation.org

Foundation type: Independent foundation
Limitations: Scholarships only to children of employees of Hallmark Cards, Inc.
Publications: Annual report; Grants list; Informational brochure (including application guidelines).
Financial data: Year ended 12/31/2004. Assets, $785,079,156 (M); Expenditures, $41,330,373; Total giving, $35,588,948; Grants to individuals, 325 grants totaling $243,000 (high: $750, low: $750).
Type of support: Undergraduate support.
Application information: Applications through dedicated URL accepted from Hallmark employees only.
EIN: 446006291

1690
John T. Hall Trust
c/o SunTrust Bank
P.O. Box 1908
Orlando, FL 32802-1908 (404) 813-9105
Contact: Allen Mast
Application address: c/o SunTrust Bank, P.O. Box 4655, MC-221, Atlanta, GA 30302

Foundation type: Independent foundation
Limitations: Student loans to residents of GA, for undergraduate and graduate education at GA colleges.
Financial data: Year ended 12/31/2004. Assets, $2,305,224 (M); Expenditures, $13,509; Total giving, $2,757; Loans to individuals, totaling $2,757.
Type of support: Graduate support; Undergraduate support.
Application information: Applications by letter, including resume, accepted throughout the year.
EIN: 586026022

1691
Albert Haller Foundation
P.O. Box 2739
Sequim, WA   98382
Contact: Alan Millet, Atty.
Additional address: c/o Clallam County United Way,
P.O. Box 937, Port Angeles, WA 98362

Foundation type: Independent foundation
Limitations: Scholarships to residents of Clallam
County, WA.
Publications: Informational brochure (including
application guidelines).
Financial data: Year ended 12/31/2004.
Assets, $6,655,428 (M); Expenditures,
$599,421; Total giving, $493,699; Grants to
individuals, 32 grants totaling $113,583 (high:
$4,250, low: $1,250).
Type of support: Scholarships—to individuals.
Application information: Applications not
accepted.
> *Additional information:* Applications should be
> sent by letter; Applications made through
> office of the superintendent of applicant's
> school district.

EIN: 911556810

1692
James & Lena Halsey Educational Trust
100 W. Elm St.
Canton, IL   61520
Application address: c/o Canton Senior High
School, Attn.: Principal, 1001 N. Main St., Canton,
IL 61520-1199

Foundation type: Independent foundation
Limitations: Scholarships to graduates of Canton
High School, IL, for higher education.
Financial data: Year ended 12/31/2004.
Assets, $647,143 (M); Expenditures, $44,850;
Total giving, $40,000; Grants to individuals,
totaling $40,000.
Type of support: Support to graduates or students
of specific schools; Undergraduate support.
Application information: Applications accepted
throughout the year; Completion of formal
application required.
EIN: 367139856

1693
Halton Foundation
P.O. Box 3377
Portland, OR   97208
Contact: Susan Halton Findlay, Mgr.

Foundation type: Company-sponsored foundation
Limitations: Scholarships only to children of
employees of The Halton Company or related
companies. Employees must have worked for at
least one year. Applicants must be full-time
students and under 28 years of age. Scholarships
are not available to the general public.
Financial data: Year ended 08/31/2004.
Assets, $1,225,876 (M); Expenditures, $62,714;
Total giving, $62,370; Grants to individuals, 13
grants totaling $51,270 (high: $6,849, low: $822).
Fields of interest: Higher education.
Type of support: Graduate support; Technical
education support; Undergraduate support.
Application information: Application form required.
> *Deadline(s):* Jan. 31
> *Applicants should submit the following:*
> 1) Transcripts
> 2) Essay
> *Additional information:* Interviews required.

Program description:
> *Scholarship Awards:* Scholarship recipients,
> known as Halton Scholars, must be high school
> graduates and may attend graduate school,
> undergraduate school, junior college, or nursing
> school, but may not study through correspondence
> courses or at night school. Scholarships may be
> used to pay for tuition and books. Each award is for
> one year only, but is renewable. Only children of
> Halton Company employees and related companies
> are eligible to apply. Applicants are evaluated on
> the basis of financial need, academic achievement,
> and participation in extracurricular activities, which
> include athletics, a part-time job, volunteer work,
> etc. The applicant's ability to demonstrate
> long-term planning for achievement of his or her
> educational goal is also considered. Recipients who
> do not fit eligibility requirements should not apply.

EIN: 936036295

1694
John Alvin Halverson Scholarship
c/o Marshall & Ilsley Bank
P.O. Box 2980
Milwaukee, WI   53201
Contact: Sharon Blank, Trust Off.
Application address: c/o Marshall & Ilsley Bank,
401 N. Segoe Rd., Ste. 2N, Madison, WI 53708,
tel.: (608) 232-2056

Foundation type: Independent foundation
Limitations: Scholarships to individuals residing in
IA for higher education.
Financial data: Year ended 12/31/2003.
Assets, $0 (M); Expenditures, $2,450; Total giving,
$2,000; Grants to individuals, totaling $2,000.
Type of support: Scholarships—to individuals.
Application information: Unsolicited requests for
applications not accepted.
EIN: 391749711

1695
Hamilton Community Foundation, Inc.
1216 L St.
P.O. Box 283
Aurora, NE   68818   (402) 694-3200
Contact: Sidney L. Widga, Exec. Secy.-Treas.
FAX: (402) 694-6160

Foundation type: Community foundation
Limitations: Scholarships to residents of Hamilton
County, NE.
Publications: Annual report.
Financial data: Year ended 12/31/2003.
Assets, $3,184,239 (M); Expenditures,
$305,765; Total giving, $281,199; Grants to
individuals, 88 grants totaling $119,957 (high:
$16,430, low: $400).
Type of support: Scholarships—to individuals.
Application information: Contact foundation for
current application deadline; Initial approach by
letter; Completion of formal application required.
EIN: 476038289

1696
Robert W. Hamilton Foundation
P.O. Box 898
Alamogordo, NM   88311   (505) 437-5573
Contact: Marion Ledford, V.P.

Foundation type: Independent foundation
Limitations: Scholarships to graduates of Otero
County, NM, high schools who are residents of NM.

Financial data: Year ended 12/31/2003.
Assets, $276,430 (M); Expenditures, $36,668;
Total giving, $34,500; Grants to individuals, 27
grants totaling $34,500 (high: $2,000, low: $500).
Type of support: Support to graduates or students
of specific schools; Undergraduate support.
Application information: Deadline Apr. 1;
Completion of formal application required.
Program description:
> *Scholarship Program:* Recipients must be U.S.
> citizens and maintain a GPA of at least 2.5.

EIN: 311679675

1697
Esther Hamilton Fund
(also known as Santa Claus Club Scholarship Fund)
c/o National City Bank
P.O. Box 94651
Cleveland, OH   44101
Application address: c/o Myra Vitto, National City
Bank, P.O. Box 450, Youngstown, OH 44503,
tel.: (330) 742-4289

Foundation type: Independent foundation
Limitations: Scholarships to financially needy
graduating seniors who are in the top 25 percent of
their classes at city, county, and parochial high
schools in Mahoning County, OH. Recipients must
attend Youngstown State University.
Financial data: Year ended 12/31/2004.
Assets, $208,096 (M); Expenditures, $10,926;
Total giving, $9,930; Grants to individuals, totaling
$9,930.
Type of support: Support to graduates or students
of specific schools; Undergraduate support.
Application information: Deadline May; Completion
of formal application required; Applications
available from high school principals.
EIN: 346575611

1698
Joann Hamilton Memorial Fund
c/o U.S. Bank, N.A.
P.O. Box 3168
Portland, OR   97208-3168

Foundation type: Independent foundation
Limitations: Scholarships to graduates of Newport
Senior High School, OR, or any other Lincoln
County, OR, high school who have demonstrated
academic excellence in any field of study including,
but not limited to, speech, drama, and vocational
skills.
Financial data: Year ended 06/30/2005.
Assets, $1,540,849 (M); Expenditures, $97,870;
Total giving, $72,350; Grants to individuals,
totaling $72,350.
Fields of interest: Theater; Vocational education.
Type of support: Support to graduates or students
of specific schools; Undergraduate support.
Application information: Deadline Mar. 1;
Completion of formal application required, including
transcripts, two letters of recommendation, a
one-page personal statement, SAT scores (for
academic applicants only), and a copy of the first
page of parents' latest 1040 federal tax form.
Program description:
> *Scholarship Program:* Aforementioned vocational
> skills include, but are not restricted to, carpentry,
> cabinet making, metal working, welding,
> mechanics, electronics, and mechanical drawing.

EIN: 936249490

1699
Marie H. Hamilton Scholarship Fund
c/o Bank of America, N.A.
P.O. Box 34345, CSC-10
Seattle, WA   98124-1345
Contact: Lisa Nelson, Principal
Application address: c/o Nancey Olson, Ocean
Beach School District, P.O. Box I, No. 100, Iwalco,
WA 98624

Foundation type: Independent foundation
Limitations: Scholarships to graduating seniors of
Ilwaco High School, WA, for attendance at colleges,
universities, junior colleges, trade and technical
schools, and business colleges.
Financial data: Year ended 03/31/2005.
Assets, $860,093 (M); Expenditures, $43,555;
Total giving, $35,938; Grants to individuals,
totaling $35,938.
Fields of interest: Vocational education; Business
school/education.
Type of support: Support to graduates or students
of specific schools; Technical education support;
Undergraduate support.
Application information: Deadline Apr. 26;
Completion of formal application required, including
recommendations from two teachers, a nonfamily
member, and the school principal.
Program description:
 Scholarship Program: Applications will be
reviewed by a selection committee consisting of the
Ocean Beach Board of School Directors and the
Superintendent of the Ocean Beach School District.
Scholarships will be awarded on the basis of
academic performance, extracurricular activities,
financial need, and "general worthiness.".
EIN: 916068558

1700
Helen and June Hamilton Teachers Scholarship Fund
c/o U.S. Bank, N.A.
P.O. Box 387
St. Louis, MO   63166
Application address: c/o Mary Jo Janssen, U.S.
Bank, N.A., P.O. Box 19264, Springfield, IL
62794-9264, tel.: (217) 753-7358

Foundation type: Independent foundation
Limitations: Loans and scholarships to graduates
of Sangamon County High School, IL, between the
ages of 16 and 25, who are residents of Sangamon
County, IL, to study education at a college, graduate
or professional school, with the intent of becoming
a school teacher.
Financial data: Year ended 08/31/2003.
Assets, $188,404 (M); Expenditures, $2,969;
Total giving, $11,250; Loans to individuals, 13
loans totaling $11,250.
Type of support: Student loans—to individuals;
Support to graduates or students of specific
schools; Undergraduate support.
Application information: Applications accepted.
Application form required.
 Deadline(s): Apr. 1
 Additional information: Application should
  include acceptance letter from university,
  transcript, and information concerning merit,
  promise and need.
Program description:
 Scholarship and Loan Program: The awards are
given as loans. If the student completes an
education degree and teaches as a full-time
elementary or secondary school teacher for two
consecutive years after graduation, the loan is
forgiven. The maximum amount of any loan is

two-thirds of the cost of one year in college,
graduate, or professional school.
EIN: 376325303

1701
Harry O. Hamm Foundation
P.O. Box 469
Van Buren, AR   72957
Application address: c/o Senior Class Counselor,
Van Buren High School, 1221 Pointer Trail, Van
Buren, AR 72956, tel.: (501) 474-2621

Foundation type: Operating foundation
Limitations: Scholarships to graduates of Van
Buren High School, AR, for higher education.
Financial data: Year ended 12/31/2004.
Assets, $4,100,190 (M); Expenditures,
$216,433; Total giving, $189,972.
Fields of interest: Higher education.
Type of support: Support to graduates or students
of specific schools; Undergraduate support.
Application information: Applications accepted.
Application form required.
 Deadline(s): Apr. 1
EIN: 710800702

1702
George and Mary Josephine Hamman Foundation
3336 Richmond, Ste. 310
Houston, TX   77098-3022   (713) 522-9891
Contact: E. Alan Fritsche, Exec. Dir.
FAX: (713) 522-9693;
E-mail: HammanFdn@aol.com; *URL:* http://
www.hammanfoundation.org

Foundation type: Independent foundation
Limitations: Undergraduate scholarships to
graduating high school seniors residing in the
Bragoria, Fort Bend, Galveston, Harris, Liberty,
Montgomery, or Waller counties, TX. Students must
be U.S. citizens.
Publications: Application guidelines; Financial
statement; Grants list.
Financial data: Year ended 12/31/2004.
Assets, $69,091,755 (M); Expenditures,
$3,977,354; Total giving, $3,042,000; Grants to
individuals, 206 grants totaling $604,500 (high:
$3,000, low: $1,500, average grant:
$1,500-$3,000).
Type of support: Scholarships—to individuals;
Undergraduate support.
Application information: Application form required.
Application form available on the grantmaker's Web
site.
 Initial approach: Letter or Web site.
 Copies of proposal: 1
 Deadline(s): Feb. 28
 Applicants should submit the following:
  1) Transcripts
  2) SAT
  3) GPA
  4) ACT
  5) Financial information
 Additional information: Interviews required for
  finalists.
Program description:
 Scholarship Program: Scholarship recipients
receive $12,000 over four years ($3,000 per year).
Scholarships are paid in semester increments.
EIN: 746061447

1703
Hammel-Delangis Scholarship Trust
c/o Northern Michigan Bank & Trust Co.
1502 W. Washington St.
Marquette, MI   49855-3195
Application address: c/o Scholarship Selection
Comm., City of Iron Mountain School Dist., Iron
Mountain, MI 49801

Foundation type: Independent foundation
Limitations: Scholarships to graduates of Iron
Mountain High School, MI, for study in optometry,
medicine, or other health-related fields leading to a
bachelor's degree.
Financial data: Year ended 09/30/2004.
Assets, $88,306 (M); Expenditures, $9,294; Total
giving, $6,100; Grants to individuals, totaling
$6,100.
Fields of interest: Medical school/education;
Health sciences school/education; Health
organizations.
Type of support: Support to graduates or students
of specific schools; Undergraduate support.
Application information: Deadline Apr. 25;
Completion of formal application required, including
ACT scores, transcripts, and one letter of
recommendation.
EIN: 386513191

1704
C. Arthur and Elizabeth Hammers Charitable Trust
c/o Wachovia Bank, N.A.
401 S. Tryon St., 4th FL
Charlotte, NC   28288-5709
Contact: Scholarships: Michael Boyles

Foundation type: Public charity
Limitations: Scholarships only to graduates of
Lehighton Area High School, PA.
Fields of interest: Education.
Type of support: Support to graduates or students
of specific schools; Undergraduate support.
Application information: Applications accepted.
 Additional information: Contact high school
  guidance office for current application
  deadline/guidelines.
EIN: 237840919

1705
W. R. Hammond Foundation
c/o Wells Fargo Bank Texas, N.A.
P.O. Box 9129
Wichita Falls, TX   76308

Foundation type: Independent foundation
Limitations: Scholarships to individuals studying
medicine, primarily in TX and UT.
Financial data: Year ended 12/31/2004.
Assets, $420,554 (M); Expenditures, $25,129;
Total giving, $19,432; Grants to individuals,
totaling $19,432.
Fields of interest: Medical school/education.
Type of support: Graduate support.
Application information: Applications not
accepted.
EIN: 756524028

1706
Mike Hampton Pitching In Foundation
P.O. Box 1168
Lecanto, FL   34460   (352) 527-3297
Contact: Brent Hall, Exec. Dir.

Foundation type: Public charity
Limitations: Scholarships to residents of Citrus County, FL.
Publications: Financial statement; Informational brochure.
Financial data: Year ended 06/30/2003.
Assets, $180,341 (M); Expenditures, $614,895; Total giving, $314,917; Grants to individuals, totaling $7,500.
Type of support: Undergraduate support.
Application information: Applications accepted only from Citrus County residents; all other requests for funding not considered or acknowledged.
Program description:
 Scholarship: The foundation intends to fund an annual, four-year scholarship to a high school senior in Citrus County, Fl, based upon academic performance, leadership potential, athletic ability, and financial need. The student will receive $2,500 per year, providing that the student remains a full-time student and maintains a 2.0 grade point average.
EIN: 760660225

1707
Hana Maui Trust
P.O. Box 463
Kula, HI 96790

Foundation type: Community foundation
Limitations: One scholarship each year is provided to a graduating student of Hana High School, HI and some assistance to those individuals in the community with special needs.
Financial data: Year ended 12/31/2004.
Assets, $1,169,174 (M); Expenditures, $25,730; Total giving, $9,250. Subtotal for grants for special needs: grants totaling $3,000.
Type of support: Support to graduates or students of specific schools; Grants for special needs.
Application information:
 Initial approach: Letter.
 Additional information: Contact trust for additional application deadline/guidelines.
EIN: 996011303

1708
Sumner O. Hancock Scholarship Fund
P.O. Box 299
Casco, ME 04015
Contact: Elizabeth W. Hancock, Pres.
Application address: P.O. Box 116, Casco, ME 04015, tel.: (207) 627-4354

Foundation type: Independent foundation
Limitations: Scholarships to residents of the Casco, ME, area, including graduates of Lake Region High School, Naples, ME.
Financial data: Year ended 12/31/2004.
Assets, $97,139 (M); Expenditures, $7,079; Total giving, $6,000; Grants to individuals, totaling $6,000.
Type of support: Support to graduates or students of specific schools; Undergraduate support.
Application information: Deadline May 15; Completion of formal application required.
EIN: 016028898

1709
The Hand Foundation, Inc.
1499 Forest Hill Blvd., Ste. 116
West Palm Beach, FL 33406
Contact: Ruben Ledesma, Jr., Dir.

Foundation type: Independent foundation
Limitations: Scholarships to residents of FL for higher education.
Financial data: Year ended 12/31/2003.
Assets, $11,874 (M); Expenditures, $130,063; Total giving, $130,000; Grants to individuals, 31 grants totaling $130,000 (high: $33,767, low: $382).
Type of support: Undergraduate support.
Application information: Applications by letter, including information about personal history, education, economic situation and goals, accepted throughout the year.
EIN: 650118848

1710
Cecelia Hand Nelson and Morgan Hand II Memorial Scholarship Fund
c/o Wachovia Bank, N.A.
100 N. Main St., 13th Fl.
Winston-Salem, NC 27150
Contact: Martha Johnson, Trust Off., Wachovia Bank, N.A.

Foundation type: Independent foundation
Limitations: Scholarships to graduates of Ocean City High School, NJ.
Financial data: Year ended 07/31/2005.
Assets, $1,885,452 (M); Expenditures, $112,697; Total giving, $84,000; Grants to individuals, totaling $84,000.
Type of support: Support to graduates or students of specific schools; Undergraduate support.
Application information: Applications accepted. Application form required.
 Initial approach: Letter.
 Deadline(s): June
EIN: 237790152

1711
The George T. Handyside Memorial Scholarship Foundation
c/o The Selection Committee
1019 Rte. 519, Bldg. 6
Eighty Four, PA 15330-2813 (724) 228-8820
Contact: Daniel Wallach

Foundation type: Independent foundation
Limitations: Scholarships to sons, daughters, and spouses of active 84 Lumber Company employees.
Financial data: Year ended 12/31/2004.
Assets, $1,582,398 (M); Expenditures, $81,247; Total giving, $74,000; Grants to individuals, totaling $74,000.
Type of support: Employee-related scholarships.
Application information: Contact a company office for current application deadline/guidelines; Initial approach by letter or telephone.
EIN: 251667394

1712
Albert G. and Bernice F. Hansen Charitable Foundation
12165 W. Center Rd., Ste. 56
Omaha, NE 68144-3974 (402) 758-6631
Contact: Robert Roh, Tr.

Foundation type: Independent foundation
Limitations: Scholarships to students graduating from high schools in Chase, Dundy, Frontier, Hayes, Hitchcock and Red Willow counties, NE, for postsecondary education.
Financial data: Year ended 12/31/2004.
Assets, $5,951,762 (M); Expenditures,

$388,268; Total giving, $291,231; Grants to individuals, totaling $72,000.
Type of support: Support to graduates or students of specific schools; Undergraduate support.
Application information: Applications accepted throughout the year; Application by letter outlining financial need and qualifications.
EIN: 363847506

1713
Dane G. Hansen Foundation
P.O. Box 187
Logan, KS 67646 (785) 689-4832
Contact: Don Stahr, Tr.
URL: http://www.hansenfoundationscholarships.com

Foundation type: Independent foundation
Limitations: Scholarships to graduating seniors of high schools in northwest KS to attend KS colleges and universities. See program description for eligible counties.
Financial data: Year ended 09/30/2004.
Assets, $61,443,397 (M); Expenditures, $2,953,540; Total giving, $2,167,126; Grants to individuals, totaling $603,628.
Fields of interest: Vocational education.
Type of support: Awards/prizes; Technical education support; Undergraduate support.
Application information:
 Deadline(s): Oct. 9 for Vocational Education Scholarships
 Additional information: Completion of formal application required for Vocational Education Scholarships, including personal statement, transcripts, GPA, photograph, and three references; Reference questionnaires are due Oct. 26; See program description for further information. Interviews required.
Program descriptions:
 Scholarship Awards: Students residing in the following counties of northwest KS are eligible: Cheyenne, Cloud, Decatur, Ellis, Ellsworth, Gove, Graham, Jewell, Lincoln, Logan, Mitchell, Norton, Osborne, Ottawa, Phillips, Rawlins, Republic, Rooks, Russell, Saline, Sheridan, Sherman, Smith, Thomas, Trego, and Wallace. Students interested in the Hansen Leaders of Tomorrow, the Hansen Student, or the Hansen Merit Scholarships must register with their school counselor or principal and take the qualifying test. No formal application is required. Prior to Sept. 25, the principal or counselor must provide the Hansen Foundation with a list of students who plan to take the qualifying tests. Reference questionnaires are sent only to the candidates selected for interviews after taking the test.
 Hansen Leaders of Tomorrow Scholarships: Scholarships of $5,000 each are awarded annually to students planning to attend four-year KS colleges and universities of their choice. Recipients must be graduating high school seniors with at least a 3.5 high school GPA and a record of service and extracurricular activities. Scholarships are awarded on the basis of their "moral and leadership qualities as shown through past participation in community, church, scout, school, and other youth activities, with special emphasis on diligence towards chosen tasks, the recognition accorded them by their peers and a final evaluation by the screening board." Recipients must be proficient in written and verbal skills. Scholarships are renewable for up to three additional years contingent upon recipient maintaining a 3.0 GPA in college.
 Hansen Student Scholarships: The same general conditions as set forth in the Leaders of Tomorrow Scholarships are observed in the Hansen Student

Scholarships. Up to 60 scholarships of $2,000 each are awarded annually. Recipients may attend any two- or four-year college or university in KS. These scholarships are not renewable.

Vocational Education Scholarships: Up to 80 Vocational Education Scholarships of $1,500 each are awarded annually. Recipients must be of good character and intend to enroll in any vocational course in KS not leading to a four-year degree. Students interested in these scholarships must complete an application form and submit it to the foundation by Oct. 1. A transcript with GPA circled must accompany the application. Applications are available in the office of the school counselor.

Hansen Merit Scholar Awards: The same general conditions as set forth in the Leaders of Tomorrow scholarships are observed in the Merit Scholar competition. Up to thirty Hansen Merit Scholar Awards are offered annually. They have a stipend of $3,000 and are renewable for one additional year.
EIN: 486121156

1714
Carl M. Hansen Foundation, Inc.
2714 E. Foxwood Dr.
Spokane, WA   99223-3419

Foundation type: Independent foundation
Limitations: Scholarships to residents of the Pacific Northwest for the study of engineering.
Financial data: Year ended 12/31/2004. Assets, $3,806,613 (M); Expenditures, $283,054; Total giving, $243,500; Grants to individuals, 6 grants totaling $21,000 (high: $3,500, low: $3,500).
Fields of interest: Engineering school/education.
Type of support: Scholarships—to individuals.
Application information: Applications not accepted.
EIN: 916063191

1715
Hansen-Furnas Foundation, Inc.
(formerly Furnas Foundation, Inc.)
28 S. Water St., Ste. 310
Batavia, IL   60510

Foundation type: Independent foundation
Limitations: Undergraduate and graduate scholarships to students who are U.S. citizens and reside within 12 miles of the Batavia Government Center, Batavia, IL, or in Clarke County, IA.
Publications: Application guidelines; Informational brochure; Program policy statement.
Financial data: Year ended 12/31/2004. Assets, $964,223 (M); Expenditures, $536,955; Total giving, $482,328; Grants to individuals, 52 grants totaling $265,376.
Fields of interest: African Americans/Blacks; Women.
Type of support: Graduate support; Undergraduate support.
Application information: Application form required.
Initial approach: Letter requesting application.
Deadline(s): Mar. 1
Applicants should submit the following:
1) Financial information
2) Class rank
3) Transcripts
Additional information: Application should also include three character references; Interviews required; Recipients notified by Apr. 15.
Program description:
Hansen-Furnas Scholarships: The foundation administers the following scholarship programs:

· William Carlyle Furnas Scholarship: Provides a full tuition undergraduate scholarship to a student for study at Purdue University
· Robert Buckner Scholarship for African Americans: Awarded to African Americans for full-time undergraduate study at accredited colleges and universities
· Leto M. Furnas Graduate Scholarship for Women: Awarded to female students who have already earned their bachelor's degrees, for graduate study at accredited colleges and universities
· Furnas Foundation Scholarships: Awarded to full-time undergraduate students at accredited colleges and universities.
EIN: 366049894

1716
E. L. & Maudean Hanson Foundation
P.O. Box 131
Beulah, CO   81023   (719) 485-3172
Contact: David A. Bleichrodt, V.P.

Foundation type: Independent foundation
Limitations: Scholarships to graduates of Pueblo County high school, Pueblo County, CO.
Financial data: Year ended 02/28/2005. Assets, $252,461 (M); Expenditures, $11,597; Total giving, $11,000; Grants to individuals, totaling $11,000.
Type of support: Support to graduates or students of specific schools; Undergraduate support.
Application information: Deadline varies; Application by letter.
EIN: 841150453

1717
Hapke Educational Fund
c/o Wells Fargo Bank Nebraska, N.A.
1248 O St., 4th Fl.
Lincoln, NE   68508
Application address: c/o Delta Kappa Gamma Society, Davenport, IA 52801

Foundation type: Independent foundation
Limitations: Scholarships to graduates of Davenport high schools, IA for study at accredited four-year colleges in the U.S.
Financial data: Year ended 05/31/2005. Assets, $444,542 (M); Expenditures, $21,145; Total giving, $16,625; Grants to individuals, totaling $16,625.
Type of support: Support to graduates or students of specific schools.
Application information:
Deadline(s): Mid-Apr.
Additional information: Application by letter.
EIN: 426344503

1718
The Haraldson Foundation
25025 I-45 N., Ste. 410
The Woodlands, TX   77380   (281) 362-9909
Contact: Dale A. Dossey, Dir.
FAX: (281) 298-6001; E-mail: ndossey@yahoo.com
E-mail: ndossey@haraldsonfoundation.org;
URL: http://www.haraldsonfoundation.org

Foundation type: Operating foundation
Limitations: Scholarships to full-time students attending the University of Texas, and to high school seniors planning to attend.

Publications: Application guidelines; Annual report; Grants list; Informational brochure (including application guidelines); Newsletter.
Financial data: Year ended 09/30/2004. Assets, $4,961,202 (M); Expenditures, $304,026; Total giving, $155,000.
Type of support: Support to graduates or students of specific schools; Undergraduate support.
Application information: Applications accepted. Application form required.
Initial approach: Letter or e-mail.
Applicants should submit the following:
1) Essay
2) Letter(s) of recommendation
Additional information: Scholarships are renewable if recipients continue to demonstrate financial need and maintain at least a 3.0 GPA; Interviews required.
EIN: 760420758

1719
Anna M. Harber Educational Trust Foundation
c/o 1st Source Bank, Trust Dept.
100 N. Michigan St.
South Bend, IN   46601   (574) 235-2790
Contact: Lee Morton, Trust Off., 1st Source Bank

Foundation type: Independent foundation
Limitations: Scholarships to graduates of Roman Catholic high schools in St. Joseph County, IN.
Financial data: Year ended 12/31/2004. Assets, $384,643 (M); Expenditures, $25,063; Total giving, $20,000; Grants to individuals, totaling $20,000.
Fields of interest: Roman Catholic agencies & churches.
Type of support: Support to graduates or students of specific schools; Undergraduate support.
Application information: Applications accepted throughout the year; Completion of formal application required, including three letters of recommendation, high school transcripts, class rank, IQ, SAT scores, GPA, attendance record, health records, record of school activities, and financial statement; Interviews required.
EIN: 356034473

1720
Harbison Scholarship Trust
P.O. Box 3262
San Bernardino, CA   92413-3262
Contact: Doreen Thornes, Tr.
FAX: (909) 335-6024

Foundation type: Operating foundation
Limitations: Scholarships to students of San Bernardino County, CA, high schools.
Financial data: Year ended 10/31/2004. Assets, $6,292,915 (M); Expenditures, $471,325; Total giving, $388,904.
Type of support: Support to graduates or students of specific schools.
Application information: Deadline Feb. 5; Contact high school for current application guidelines.
Program description:
Scholarship Program: Scholarships are awarded on the basis of scholarship, character, motivation, interests and skills, extracurricular activities, and financial need. Scholarships are for four years of study.
EIN: 330621341

1721
Ralph Dean & Evelyn Peake Harby Scholarship Fund

c/o The National Bank of Delaware County
P.O. Box 389
Walton, NY 13856 (607) 865-4126

Foundation type: Independent foundation
Limitations: Scholarships to students of Walton Central High School, NY.
Financial data: Year ended 12/31/2004.
Assets, $268,452 (M); Expenditures, $5,029;
Total giving, $4,000; Grants to individuals, totaling $4,000.
Type of support: Support to graduates or students of specific schools; Precollege support.
Application information: Deadline July 31; Initial approach by letter; Completion of formal application required.
EIN: 166210926

1722
Harden Foundation, Inc.

8550 Mill Pond Way
McConnellsville, NY 13401 (315) 245-1000
Contact: David Harden, Dir.

Foundation type: Independent foundation
Limitations: Scholarships for children of employees of Harden Furniture Company, primarily in NY.
Financial data: Year ended 12/31/2004.
Assets, $869,608 (M); Expenditures, $42,132;
Total giving, $35,464; Grants to individuals, totaling $27,500.
Type of support: Employee-related scholarships.
Application information: Applications by letter, detailing need, accepted throughout the year.
EIN: 156017586

1723
Hardin Memorial Scholarship Foundation

c/o Bank of America, N.A.
231 S. LaSalle St., IL1-231-14-19
Chicago, IL 60697
Application address: c/o Karen Ladd, Trust Off., Bank of America, N.A., 100 N. Broadway, St. Louis, MO 63102, tel.: (314) 466-3477

Foundation type: Independent foundation
Limitations: Scholarships to graduates of high schools in the city of Louisiana, Pike County, MO for study at colleges, universities, and technical schools.
Financial data: Year ended 06/30/2005.
Assets, $1,812,693 (M); Expenditures, $135,151; Total giving, $112,574; Grants to individuals, 21 grants totaling $112,574 (high: $18,418, low: $1,941).
Fields of interest: Vocational education.
Type of support: Support to graduates or students of specific schools; Technical education support; Undergraduate support.
Application information: Applications accepted. Application form required.
Deadline(s): May 1.
Applicants should submit the following:
1) Transcripts
2) GPA
3) ACT
4) Letter(s) of recommendation
5) Essay
EIN: 436395032

1724
The Harding Foundation

Harding Fdn. Bldg.
P.O. Box 130, 5th and Hidalgo
Raymondville, TX 78580 (956) 689-2706
Contact: Glenn Harding, Pres.
FAX: (956) 698-5740

Foundation type: Independent foundation
Limitations: Graduate scholarships to seminary students pursuing master's degrees in theology, leading to ordination in a mainline Protestant church, with special consideration given to those willing to serve in the South Texas Conference.
Financial data: Year ended 12/31/2004.
Assets, $1,189,078 (M); Expenditures, $224,866; Total giving, $52,650; Grants to individuals, totaling $42,500.
Fields of interest: Theological school/education; Protestant agencies & churches.
Type of support: Graduate support.
Application information: Deadline Jan. 15; Initial approach by letter or telephone; Completion of formal application required, including transcripts, two letters of recommendation, one from a teacher and one from a minister, and personal statement of no more than 500 words.
Program description:
Scholarship Program: Special consideration is given to bilingual theology students committed to work in the South Texas Conference, McAllen District, or Rio Grande Valley Conference of the Methodist Church. Applicants must be enrolled in a master's program on a full-time basis. Individuals involved in practice preaching or those working on theses but not enrolled in school are ineligible. The maximum scholarship awarded is $3,000 a year for up to three years of study.
EIN: 746025883

1725
The George Harding Scholarship Fund

18270 Manor Ln.
Livonia, MI 48152
Contact: Gerald A. Johnson, Tr.
Application address: 611 Woodward Ave., No. MI1-8077, Detroit, MI 48226

Foundation type: Independent foundation
Limitations: Scholarships to MI residents who are full-time students, enrolled in a four-year out-of-state or MI college or university, and pursuing finance-related degrees. Scholarships are available for the junior and senior year of college, or first year of graduate school. Students must maintain Michigan residency and an overall GPA of 3.0 or higher.
Financial data: Year ended 12/31/2004.
Assets, $53,009 (M); Expenditures, $35,200;
Total giving, $19,000; Grants to individuals, totaling $19,000.
Fields of interest: Business school/education; Economics.
Type of support: Graduate support; Undergraduate support.
Application information: Application form required.
Additional information: Applications accepted throughout the year.
EIN: 382527040

1726
Hariri Foundation

7501 Wisconsin Ave., Ste. 715
Bethesda, MD 20814 (301) 656-1666
FAX: (301) 656-1613; Application address: Hariri Bldg., Jnah, Opposite Summerland Hotel, Beirut, Lebanon

Foundation type: Independent foundation
Limitations: Student loans to deserving Lebanese high school students for study at Lebanese institutions of higher learning in order to build up the human resources of Lebanon through educational programs.
Publications: Informational brochure; Multi-year report; Newsletter.
Financial data: Year ended 12/31/2004.
Assets, $1,664,287 (M); Expenditures, $518,432; Total giving, $53,500; Loans to individuals, totaling $53,500.
Type of support: Student loans—to individuals; Undergraduate support.
Application information: Application form required.
Additional information: Contact foundation for current application deadline; Initial application must be made in Beirut, Lebanon; Interviews required.
EIN: 521386338

1727
Sylvia M. Harley Nursing Scholarship Fund

c/o Sovereign Bank
P.O. Box 1100
Pottsville, PA 17901-7100
Application address: c/o Sovereign Bank, 120 S. Centre St., Pottsville, PA 17901, tel.: (570) 628-6640

Foundation type: Independent foundation
Limitations: Scholarships to financially needy residents of the Pottsville Area School District, PA, who are pursuing a career in nursing in either a two- or four-year degree program. Vocational/technical school programs do not qualify.
Financial data: Year ended 12/31/2003.
Assets, $756,232 (M); Expenditures, $47,238;
Total giving, $38,000; Grants to individuals, 10 grants totaling $38,000 (high: $3,800, low: $3,800).
Fields of interest: Nursing school/education.
Type of support: Support to graduates or students of specific schools; Undergraduate support.
Application information: Application form required.
Deadline(s): May
Additional information: Interviews may be required.
Program description:
Scholarship Program: Residents of the following PA towns are eligible: City of Pottsville, Palo Alto, Mechanicsville, Mount Carbon, Norwegian Township, and Port Carbon. Preference is given to residents of the City of Pottsville. Eligibility also extends to any localities of any other school districts that become part of the Pottsville School District.
EIN: 232402538

1728
Carlyle and Delta Harmon Scholarship Foundation

(formerly Harmon Women's Scholarship Fund)
2481 W. 1425 S.
Syracuse, UT 84075
Contact: Richard McDermott, Tr.

Foundation type: Independent foundation

Limitations: Scholarships to students in UT for higher education.
Financial data: Year ended 12/31/2004. Assets, $1,290,319 (M); Expenditures, $141,370; Total giving, $71,307; Grants to individuals, totaling $3,550.
Type of support: Undergraduate support.
Application information: Applications accepted throughout the year; Initial approach by letter; Completion of formal application required, including transcripts.
EIN: 870508363

1729
Harness Horsemen International Foundation, Inc.
64 Rte. 33
Manalapan, NJ 07726-8301   (609) 259-3717
Contact: Michael Izzo, Exec. Dir.

Foundation type: Independent foundation
Limitations: Scholarships to a child of a full-time groom or a member of a Harness Horsemen International member association.
Financial data: Year ended 12/31/2004. Assets, $0 (M); Expenditures, $13,976; Total giving, $10,000; Grants to individuals, totaling $10,000.
Type of support: Undergraduate support.
Application information: Applications accepted.
  Initial approach: Letter.
  Deadline(s): June 1
  Applicants should submit the following:
    1) Photograph
    2) SAT
    3) ACT
    4) Essay
    5) Transcripts
    6) Letter(s) of recommendation
Program description:
  Jerome L. Hauck Scholarship: Must be used at a four-year college or university for any field of study. $1,000 per school year renewable four times. Applicant must be a full-time student. High school students not considered.
EIN: 061182260

1730
Laura Brooks Harney/P. J. Harney Scholarship Trust
c/o Bank of America, N.A., P.C. Group
P.O. Box 1802
Providence, RI 02940-1802   (401) 276-7316
Application address: c/o David Clark, Chair., Town of Webb Schools, Crosby Blvd., Old Forge, NY 13420

Foundation type: Independent foundation
Limitations: Scholarships to students graduating from Town of Webb High School, NY, who will attend school at one of six specific institutions of higher education.
Financial data: Year ended 12/31/2004. Assets, $228,699 (M); Expenditures, $13,059; Total giving, $10,000.
Type of support: Support to graduates or students of specific schools; Undergraduate support.
Application information: Application form required.
  Initial approach: Letter.
  Deadline(s): June 20
  Additional information: Application should include transcripts.
EIN: 166283916

1731
Harper Brush Works Foundation, Inc.
P.O. Box 608
Fairfield, IA 52556-0608
Contact: Wendall King, Dir.
Application address: 701 E. Madison Ave., Fairfield, IA 52556

Foundation type: Company-sponsored foundation
Limitations: Scholarships to individuals for higher education and a teacher of the year award, primarily in IA and TX.
Financial data: Year ended 08/31/2004. Assets, $67,368 (M); Expenditures, $53,095; Total giving, $52,963; Grants to individuals, 22 grants totaling $16,750 (high: $3,000; low: $250).
Fields of interest: Education.
Type of support: Scholarships—to individuals; Awards/prizes.
Application information: Contact foundation for current application deadline/guidelines.
EIN: 421145331

1732
Carrie M. Harper Trust
c/o JPMorgan Chase Bank, N.A.
P.O. Box 1308
Milwaukee, WI 53201
Application address: c/o Pres. of Board of Ed., Supt., or Principal of East Liverpool High School, East Liverpool, OH 43920

Foundation type: Independent foundation
Limitations: Scholarships to graduates of East Liverpool High School, OH.
Financial data: Year ended 12/31/2003. Assets, $1,226,058 (M); Expenditures, $64,076; Total giving, $52,103; Grants to individuals, 93 grants totaling $52,103 (high: $600; low: $400).
Type of support: Support to graduates or students of specific schools; Undergraduate support.
Application information: Applications accepted throughout the year; Contact trust for current application guidelines.
EIN: 346582259

1733
Clyde W. Harrell Educational Fund
c/o AmSouth Bank
315 Deaderick St., 4th Fl.
Nashville, TN 37237-0401

Foundation type: Independent foundation
Limitations: Scholarships to graduates of public high schools in the upper end of Hawkins County, TN, to attend colleges and universities in TN.
Financial data: Year ended 02/28/2005. Assets, $166,891 (M); Expenditures, $64,525; Total giving, $62,500; Grants to individuals, totaling $62,500.
Type of support: Support to graduates or students of specific schools; Undergraduate support.
Application information: Deadline Apr. 30; Scholarship recipients are chosen by their high school principal with final approval by the First American Trust Comm.
EIN: 626085008

1734
Dwight H. Harrelson Memorial Scholarship Trust
c/o Bank of America, N.A.
101 S. Tryon St., NC1-002-11-18
Charlotte, NC 28255-0001

Foundation type: Independent foundation
Limitations: Scholarships to graduating seniors of Cherryville High School, NC.
Financial data: Year ended 12/31/2004. Assets, $283,521 (M); Expenditures, $21,854; Total giving, $17,150.
Type of support: Support to graduates or students of specific schools; Undergraduate support.
Application information: Applications by letter accepted throughout the year.
EIN: 237159114

1735
Adolph & Edith Harries & Eleanor Tippens Scholarship Trust
(also known as Tippens Charitable Trust)
c/o WesBanco Bank, Inc.
415 Market St.
Parkersburg, WV 26101
Contact: Michelle Sandy, Trust Off.

Foundation type: Independent foundation
Limitations: Scholarships to financially needy high school students of Wood County, WV, for study at a college, university, or trade school in WV.
Financial data: Year ended 12/31/2004. Assets, $3,094,209 (M); Expenditures, $264,702; Total giving, $250,432; Grants to individuals, 35 grants totaling $250,432 (high: $22,193, low: $515).
Fields of interest: Vocational education.
Type of support: Support to graduates or students of specific schools; Technical education support; Undergraduate support.
Application information: Applications not accepted.
  Additional information: Candidates are nominated by the principal and guidance counselor of each high school in Wood County; Generally, only two recipients are chosen each year.
EIN: 556118733

1736
The Harrington Foundation
4248 Park Glen Rd.
Minneapolis, MN 55416
Contact: Edward A. Harrington, Pres.

Foundation type: Operating foundation
Limitations: Scholarships to individuals in MN for higher education.
Financial data: Year ended 12/31/2003. Assets, $86,307 (M); Expenditures, $55,451; Total giving, $45,010; Grants to individuals, 43 grants totaling $44,000 (high: $2,000, low: $1,000).
Type of support: Scholarships—to individuals.
Application information: Applications accepted throughout the year; Contact foundation for current application guidelines; Initial approach by letter.
EIN: 411894989

1737
Charles M. & Julia C. Harrington Scholarship Fund
c/o KeyBank N.A., Trust Div.
800 Superior Ave., 4th Fl.
Cleveland, OH 44114
Application address: c/o KeyBank N.A., Attn.: Harrington Scholarship Committee, 35 State St., Albany, NY 12207

Foundation type: Independent foundation

Limitations: Scholarships to graduates of Plattsburg High School, NY, who plan to attend one of several specified colleges.
Financial data: Year ended 12/31/2004.
Assets, $117,032 (M); Expenditures, $19,198; Total giving, $17,500; Grants to individuals, totaling $17,500.
Type of support: Support to graduates or students of specific schools; Undergraduate support.
Application information: Deadline Apr. 1; Application by letter.
EIN: 146014863

1738
Phil Harris & Alice Faye Scholarship Foundation, Inc.

P.O. Box 236
Lyons, IN   47443
Contact: Barbara Rollison, Tr.
Application address: c/o Phil Harris Scholarship Comm., 489 N. Main St., Linton, IN 47441, tel.: (812) 847-9263

Foundation type: Independent foundation
Limitations: Scholarships to graduating seniors of Linton-Stockton high schools, IN, who are attending Vincennes University, IN.
Financial data: Year ended 12/31/2002.
Assets, $373,913 (M); Expenditures, $38,952; Total giving, $17,000; Grants to individuals, 5 grants totaling $17,000 (high: $3,750, low: $2,000).
Type of support: Support to graduates or students of specific schools; Undergraduate support.
Application information: Deadline Apr. 28; Completion of formal application required.
EIN: 310992482

1739
George M. Harris & Faye Tabor Harris Charitable Foundation

c/o Wells Fargo Bank Northwest, N.A.
P.O. Box 21927, MAC P6540-144
Seattle, WA   98111
Application addresses: For general scholarships: c/o John A. Mercer, 301 1st. E., Polson, MT 59860, tel.: (406) 883-5367, or for PEO scholarships: c/o Ann Tribbey, MT Cottey Chair., 703 S. Cale, Miles City, MT 59301, or for Ohio Northern Univ. Scholarships: c/o Henry H. Hixon III, V.P., Development Office, Ada, OH 45810, tel.: (419) 772-2035

Foundation type: Independent foundation
Limitations: Scholarships to female residents of MT to attend Cottey College in Nevada, MO, a two-year college for women. Scholarships also to MT high school graduates, with preference to Lake County graduates, for attendance at accredited colleges and universities.
Financial data: Year ended 01/31/2005.
Assets, $1,061,662 (M); Expenditures, $56,249; Total giving, $39,819.
Fields of interest: Women.
Type of support: Support to graduates or students of specific schools; Undergraduate support.
Application information:
  Deadline(s): Mar. 15 for Cottey College program, May 1 for Lake County graduates
  Additional information: Application by letter outlining financial need and educational goals, and including transcripts, recent photograph, and three letters of reference, one from the high school principal.

Program description:
  Tabor Harris Education Program: The Cottey College program is administered under the name PEO Scholarships.
EIN: 816010110

1740
Ray M. Harris Educational Fund

c/o Bank of America, N.A.
10 Light St.
Baltimore, MD   21202
Application address: c/o Bank of America, N.A., Attn.: Bruce Love, Trust Off., 302 Jefferson St., Roanoke, VA 24011-2010, tel.: (804) 528-2483

Foundation type: Independent foundation
Limitations: Student loans primarily to graduates of high schools in Pittsylvania County, VA, for undergraduate, graduate, and vocational studies.
Financial data: Year ended 12/31/2004.
Assets, $1,222,752 (M); Expenditures, $106,800; Total giving, $86,680; Loans to individuals, totaling $3,500.
Fields of interest: Vocational education.
Type of support: Support to graduates or students of specific schools; Graduate support; Technical education support; Undergraduate support.
Application information: Deadline Apr. 15; Completion of formal application required, including transcripts, letter of recommendation, financial information, and copies of all financial aid notices.
Program description:
  Student Loan Program: Loans are granted on the basis of financial need and academic ability. Repayments begin after graduation or termination of study and are generally made in monthly payments of $40 to $100.
EIN: 546065353

1741
Raymond J. Harris Educational Trust

c/o Mellon Financial Corp.
P.O. Box 185
Pittsburgh, PA   15230-9897

Foundation type: Independent foundation
Limitations: Scholarships to Christian men for professional education in medicine, law, engineering, dentistry, or agriculture at nine Philadelphia, PA, area colleges.
Financial data: Year ended 09/30/2004.
Assets, $1,046,310 (M); Expenditures, $34,003; Total giving, $34,000; Grants to individuals, totaling $34,000.
Fields of interest: Dental school/education; Law school/education; Medical school/education; Engineering school/education; Agriculture; Christian agencies & churches; Men.
Type of support: Support to graduates or students of specific schools; Graduate support; Undergraduate support.
Application information: Deadline Feb. 1; Completion of formal application required, including high school transcripts, copies of financial statements, and letters of recommendation from teachers; Applications may be obtained from the nine area colleges.
EIN: 236224306

1742
H. H. Harris Foundation

30 S. Wacker Dr., Ste. 2300
Chicago, IL   60606   (312) 346-7900
Contact: John W. Hough, Tr.
FAX: (312) 346-0904; E-mail: JohnHH@aol.com;
URL: http://www.afsinc.org/Harris/Harris.html

Foundation type: Independent foundation
Limitations: Scholarships and other forms of educational aid to students and professionals who are U.S. citizens studying in the metallurgical and metal casting fields.
Financial data: Year ended 06/30/2005.
Assets, $3,650,753 (M); Expenditures, $235,657; Total giving, $151,625; Grants to individuals, 65 grants totaling $103,400 (high: $2,500, low: $1,000).
Fields of interest: Vocational education; Science; Chemistry.
Type of support: Scholarships—to individuals.
Application information: Applications accepted. Application form required.
  Deadline(s): June 15
  Applicants should submit the following:
    1) Letter(s) of recommendation
    2) Financial information
    3) GPA
  Additional information: Application should also include two letters of reference.
EIN: 362615318

1743
Harris Scholarship Fund

c/o PNC Bank, N.A.
1600 Market St., 4th Fl.
Philadelphia, PA   19103-7240

Foundation type: Independent foundation
Limitations: Scholarships to academically qualified and financially needy graduates of Salem High School, NJ.
Financial data: Year ended 12/31/2004.
Assets, $640,463 (M); Expenditures, $35,102; Total giving, $28,500; Grants to individuals, totaling $28,500.
Type of support: Support to graduates or students of specific schools; Undergraduate support.
Application information:
  Initial approach: Letter.
  Additional information: Applications accepted throughout the year.
EIN: 226485592

1744
Paul Hyland Harris Trust

c/o National City Bank
248 Seneca St.
Oil City, PA   16301
Contact: Christopher A. Junker, V.P., National City Bank
FAX: (814) 678-3552;
E-mail: christopher.junker@nationalcity.com

Foundation type: Independent foundation
Limitations: Scholarships to students graduating from Crawford, Venango, and Warren county high schools, PA, who plan to attend Allegheny College or Harvard University, MA.
Financial data: Year ended 12/31/2004.
Assets, $3,525,812 (M); Expenditures, $168,136; Total giving, $155,645.
Type of support: Support to graduates or students of specific schools; Undergraduate support.

Application information: Applications accepted. Application form required.

Deadline(s): Apr. 1

Applicants should submit the following:
1) Transcripts
2) SAT
3) GPA
4) Financial information
5) FAFSA
6) Essay
7) ACT
8) Resume

Additional information: Applications available at high school guidance offices.

EIN: 256013264

1745

Harrison County Community Foundation, Inc.

405 N. Capitol, Ste. 104
P.O. Box 279
Corydon, IN 47112 (812) 738-6668
Contact: Steve A. Gilliland, Exec. Dir.
FAX: (812) 738-6864;
E-mail: steveg@hccfindiana.org; Additional E-mail: staff@hccfindiana.org; URL: http://www.hccfindiana.org

Foundation type: Community foundation
Limitations: Scholarships to residents of the Harrison County, IN, area.
Publications: Application guidelines; Annual report; Financial statement; Grants list; Multi-year report.
Financial data: Year ended 12/31/2004. Assets, $47,087,608 (M); Expenditures, $5,438,746; Total giving, $5,052,243; Grants to individuals, 130 grants totaling $300,000 (high: $12,000, low: $200).
Type of support: Undergraduate support.
Application information: Contact foundation for current application deadline; Completion of formal application required.
EIN: 351986569

1746

Fred G. Harrison Foundation

101 S. Park Ave.
Herrin, IL 62948-3609
Application address: c/o The Bank of Herrin, P.O. Box B, Herrin, IL 62948, tel.: (618) 942-6666

Foundation type: Independent foundation
Limitations: Scholarships primarily to seniors of Herrin High School, IL.
Financial data: Year ended 12/31/2003. Assets, $13,313,811 (M); Expenditures, $181,498; Total giving, $106,562; Grants to individuals, 4 grants totaling $4,000 (high: $1,000, low: $1,000).
Type of support: Support to graduates or students of specific schools; Undergraduate support.
Application information: Applications accepted throughout the year; Initial approach by letter or telephone.
EIN: 376085205

1747

The Reese & Sis Hart Foundation

1309 Highmarket St.
Georgetown, SC 29440
Contact: J.S. Bourne, Dir.
Application address: P.O. Box 423, Georgetown, SC 29442

Foundation type: Operating foundation
Limitations: Scholarships to individuals, primarily in SC, for higher education.
Financial data: Year ended 12/31/2002. Assets, $536,326 (M); Expenditures, $123,816; Total giving, $99,437; Grants to individuals, 20 grants totaling $99,437 (high: $10,500, low: $1,437).
Type of support: Conferences/seminars; Postdoctoral support; Graduate support; Technical education support; Undergraduate support; Travel grants; Doctoral support.
Application information: Application form required.

Deadline(s): None

Applicants should submit the following:
1) Transcripts
2) Letter(s) of recommendation

Additional information: Interviews required.

Program description:

Scholarship Program: Once scholarship is accepted, student must sign a statement agreeing to maintain a C average and remain felon- and drug-free during the time they are receiving assistance. If infractions occur, scholarship is automatically terminated.

EIN: 582435805

1748

Marjorie Hart Trust

23 E. Broadway
P.O. Box 284
Wellston, OH 45692

Foundation type: Independent foundation
Limitations: Scholarships to residents of Wellston, OH.
Financial data: Year ended 12/31/2004. Assets, $378,143 (M); Expenditures, $24,439; Total giving, $14,225; Grants to individuals, totaling $14,225.
Type of support: Scholarships—to individuals.
Application information: Contact foundation for current application deadline/guidelines.
EIN: 311428420

1749

The Selma J. Hartke Community Foundation

c/o U.S. Bank, N.A.
P.O. Box 19264
Springfield, IL 62794
Application address: c/o Edwin E. Hardt, 13105 E. 1st Rd., Litchfield, IL 62056

Foundation type: Independent foundation
Limitations: Scholarships primarily to individuals residing in IL for undergraduate education.
Financial data: Year ended 03/31/2005. Assets, $10,167,083 (M); Expenditures, $604,245; Total giving, $468,635; Grants to individuals, 103 grants totaling $322,135 (high: $6,000, low: $75).
Type of support: Undergraduate support.
Application information: Applications by letter accepted throughout the year.
EIN: 371406237

1750

Betty Wycoff Hartley and Randall D. Hartley Memorial Scholarship Fund

c/o Wayne County National Bank
1776 Beall Ave.
Wooster, OH 44691 (330) 264-7111
Contact: Stephen Kitchen, Tr.

Foundation type: Independent foundation
Limitations: Scholarships to students attending Ohio State University, Ohio University, University of Pittsburgh or Berea College, who are residents of Guernsey County, OH and are pursuing an education in the teaching profession.
Financial data: Year ended 12/31/2004. Assets, $222,468 (M); Expenditures, $9,610; Total giving, $7,000; Grants to individuals, totaling $7,000.
Fields of interest: Teacher school/education.
Type of support: Support to graduates or students of specific schools; Undergraduate support.
Application information: Applications by letter, clearly outlining financial need, accepted throughout the year.
EIN: 341907881

1751

The Chester and Sylvia Hartley Scholarship Trust

10751 N.W. 50 St.
Penalosa, KS 67035-8204

Foundation type: Independent foundation
Limitations: Scholarships for children and grandchildren of members of Penalosa United Methodist Church and area KS students who are not members.
Financial data: Year ended 12/31/2004. Assets, $264,485 (M); Expenditures, $13,792; Total giving, $13,190; Grants to individuals, totaling $13,190.
Fields of interest: Protestant agencies & churches.
Type of support: Undergraduate support.
Application information: Contact trust for current application deadline/guidelines.
Program description:

Scholarship Program: Recipients not related to members of the church must meet financial requirements and attend a college or university in the U.S.

EIN: 486353578

1752

Dan Hartman Foundation for Music

6439 Deep Dell Pl.
Los Angeles, CA 90068 (323) 465-9565
Contact: Charles Kaufman, Tr.

Foundation type: Independent foundation
Limitations: Scholarships to students who are receiving education in the arts, CA and MI.
Financial data: Year ended 12/31/2004. Assets, $862,298 (M); Expenditures, $99,719; Total giving, $50,000; Grants to individuals, totaling $50,000.
Fields of interest: Music; Performing arts, education.
Type of support: Scholarships—to individuals.
Application information: Applications accepted.

Initial approach: Letter.

Deadline(s): None

Additional information: Grants are generally limited to $5,000 per applicant to further education of individuals in the arts.

EIN: 954520564

1753
Russell L. Hartman Trust
c/o Mellon Financial Corp.
P.O. Box 185
Pittsburgh, PA   15230-0185
Application address: c/o William Becker, Mellon
Bank, N.A., P.O. Box 7899, Philadelphia, PA 19103

Foundation type: Independent foundation
Limitations: Scholarships to financially needy
residents of Boyertown, PA, and its surrounding
areas.
Financial data: Year ended 09/30/2004.
Assets, $970,682 (M); Expenditures, $58,964;
Total giving, $50,600; Grants to individuals, 46
grants totaling $50,600 (high: $2,325, low: $200).
Type of support: Scholarships—to individuals.
Application information: Deadline May 1;
Completion of formal application required, including
information on academic performance and financial
need.
EIN: 236810792

1754
Hartselle Scholarship Foundation
P.O. Box 267
Huntsville, AL   35804   (256) 551-4126
Contact: Dean Johnson

Foundation type: Independent foundation
Limitations: Scholarships to graduates of Hartselle
High School, AL, for higher education.
Financial data: Year ended 12/31/2004.
Assets, $1,589,608 (M); Expenditures, $88,629;
Total giving, $77,789; Grants to individuals, 186
grants totaling $77,789.
Fields of interest: Vocational education.
Type of support: Support to graduates or students
of specific schools; Undergraduate support.
Application information: Applications accepted.
Application form required.
Deadline(s): Apr. 1.
EIN: 631045867

1755
Hartzell-Norris Charitable Trust
c/o Fifth Third Bank
P.O. Box 630858
Cincinnati, OH   45263
URL: http://www.hartzellindustries.com/
community.htm

Foundation type: Company-sponsored foundation
Limitations: Scholarships to students, primarily in
OH, for higher education.
Financial data: Year ended 12/31/2003.
Assets, $5,409,967 (M); Expenditures,
$347,206; Total giving, $279,853; Grants to
individuals, 17 grants totaling $40,000 (high:
$2,500, low: $1,250).
Type of support: Undergraduate support.
Application information: Unsolicited requests for
funds not accepted.
EIN: 316024521

1756
Harvard Club of Minnesota Foundation
c/o Christopher R. Morris
P.O. Box 2421
Minneapolis, MN   55402
Application address: c/o Harvard University,
Attn.: Financial Aid Office, 8 Garden St., 312 Byerly
Hall, Cambridge, MA 02138, tel.: (617) 495-1581

Foundation type: Independent foundation
Limitations: Scholarships to MN students to attend
Harvard University.
Financial data: Year ended 06/30/2004.
Assets, $446,804 (M); Expenditures, $28,061;
Total giving, $18,802; Grants to individuals,
totaling $18,802.
Type of support: Support to graduates or students
of specific schools.
Application information: Applications accepted.
Additional information: Contact school's financial
aid office for current application deadline/
guidelines.
EIN: 416083667

1757
O. J. & Mary Christine Harvey Educational Foundation
(formerly The Foundation for Educational
Advancement)
435 S. 68th St.
Boulder, CO   80303

Foundation type: Independent foundation
Limitations: Scholarships to students in CO or OK,
for higher education.
Financial data: Year ended 12/31/2003.
Assets, $278,570 (M); Expenditures, $14,126;
Total giving, $13,000; Grants to individuals, 6
grants totaling $13,000 (high: $3,000, low:
$1,000).
Type of support: Undergraduate support.
Application information: Applications not
accepted.
EIN: 841441530

1758
Harvey Foundation, Inc.
1st Federal Bldg.
1519 Ponce de Leon Ave., Ste. 507
San Juan, PR   00909
Contact: Charles M. Hitt, Pres.

Foundation type: Independent foundation
Limitations: Scholarships to residents of PR.
Publications: Annual report.
Financial data: Year ended 12/31/2004.
Assets, $2,145,715 (M); Expenditures,
$106,573; Total giving, $92,200; Grants to
individuals, totaling $27,700.
Type of support: Undergraduate support.
Application information: Unsolicited applications
not accepted.
EIN: 660271454

1759
Takehiko Hasegawa Scholarship Fund
P.O. Box 1047
Lihue, HI   96766
Application address: c/o Scholarship Board, P.O.
Box 3290, Lihue, HI 96766

Foundation type: Independent foundation
Limitations: Scholarships to residents of Kauai, HI,
for higher education.
Financial data: Year ended 07/31/2005.
Assets, $153,521 (M); Expenditures, $11,370;
Total giving, $9,000; Grants to individuals, totaling
$9,000.
Type of support: Undergraduate support.
Application information: Contact fund for current
application deadline; Completion of formal
application required.
EIN: 990250582

1760
The Hassel Foundation
United Plz.
30 S. 17th St., Rm. 1800
Philadelphia, PA   19103   (215) 893-8740
Contact: Michael H. Krekstein, Tr.

Foundation type: Independent foundation
Limitations: Scholarships to graduating seniors of
Reading Senior High School and Exeter Township
Senior High School, both in PA.
Financial data: Year ended 12/31/2004.
Assets, $8,767,020 (M); Expenditures,
$483,603; Total giving, $391,500.
Type of support: Support to graduates or students
of specific schools; Undergraduate support.
Application information: Applications accepted
throughout the year; Applications are available
through high school principal's office.
EIN: 236251862

1761
Hasselhofer-Wolf Scholarship Fund
c/o U.S. Bank, N.A.
P.O. Box 7900
Madison, WI   53707-7900
Application address: c/o St. Peter Claver Parish,
1444 S. 11 St., Sheboygan, WI 53081

Foundation type: Independent foundation
Limitations: Scholarships to graduates or high
school seniors of St. Peter Claver School in
Sheboygan, WI, to attend college or technical
school.
Financial data: Year ended 05/31/2005.
Assets, $262,487 (M); Expenditures, $13,268;
Total giving, $10,000; Grants to individuals,
totaling $10,000.
Type of support: Support to graduates or students
of specific schools; Undergraduate support.
Application information:
Initial approach: Initial approach by letter.
Deadline(s): Deadline May 13. Applicants will be
notified by June 1 as to acceptance or
rejection.
Additional information: Contact fund for current
application guidelines.
EIN: 396514224

1762
The Hassell Charitable Foundation
P.O. Box 183
Clifton, TN   38425   (931) 676-3371
Contact: Autry Gobbell, Tr.; Martha Gobbell, Tr.
Additional tel.: (931) 676-3371

Foundation type: Operating foundation
Limitations: Scholarships to residents within a
125-mile radius of Clifton, TN.
Financial data: Year ended 12/31/2004.
Assets, $11,807,353 (M); Expenditures,
$1,585,249; Total giving, $18,200.
Type of support: Scholarships—to individuals.
Application information: Applications accepted
throughout the year; Initial approach by letter;
Completion of formal application required.
EIN: 581485616

1763
Dorothy S. Hastings Student Aid Fund
(also known as Hastings Student Aid Fund)
c/o TD Banknorth, N.A., Investment Mgmt. Group
P.O. Box 595
Williston, VT   05495-0595
Application address: 89 Merchants Row, Rutland, VT 05701

Foundation type: Independent foundation
Limitations: Scholarships to graduates of Lake Region Union High School, VT, and Weeks Scholarship recipients.
Publications: Application guidelines; Financial statement; Grants list; Informational brochure; Program policy statement.
Financial data: Year ended 03/31/2005. Assets, $429,122 (M); Expenditures, $27,193; Total giving, $18,983; Grants to individuals, totaling $18,983.
Type of support: Support to graduates or students of specific schools; Undergraduate support.
Application information: Deadline July 15; Initial approach by letter; Completion of formal application required, including high school transcripts.
EIN: 036048694

1764
The Harold D. and Hazel H. Hathcoat Educational Trust
P.O. Box 286
Nowata, OK   74048

Foundation type: Independent foundation
Limitations: Loans to individuals for higher education.
Financial data: Year ended 12/31/2004. Assets, $561,631 (M); Expenditures, $6,120; Total giving, $0; Loans to individuals, totaling $6,120.
Type of support: Student loans—to individuals.
Application information: Applications not accepted.
EIN: 736300011

1765
The Hatterscheidt Foundation, Inc.
c/o Wells Fargo Bank, N.A.
P.O. Box 849
Aberdeen, SD   57402-0849
Contact: Lisa Grote, Trust Officer, Wells Fargo Bank, N.A.

Foundation type: Independent foundation
Limitations: Scholarships to SD high school seniors, and to students planning to attend colleges and universities in SD, or Jamestown College, North Dakota State School of Science, or Trinity Bible College, all in ND.
Financial data: Year ended 12/31/2004. Assets, $5,182,523 (M); Expenditures, $291,767; Total giving, $242,550; Grants to individuals, 45 grants totaling $200,200.
Fields of interest: Education.
Type of support: Support to graduates or students of specific schools; Undergraduate support.
Application information: Applications accepted. Application form required.
 Deadline(s): None
 Additional information: Students should apply directly through selected colleges.
Program description:
 Scholarship Program: Scholarship amount is $1,400 for the freshman year of college and cannot be renewed. Scholarships are generally made only to SD residents, except for scholarships to

Jamestown College, Trinity Bible College, and North Dakota School of Science. Applicants must be high school seniors with at least a 3.0 GPA.
EIN: 466012543

1766
Haugse-Cossey Foundation
P.O. Box 196870
Boise, ID   83709
Contact: William A. Hon, Tr.
Application address for Boise residents only: P.O. Box 828, Boise, ID 83701

Foundation type: Independent foundation
Limitations: Scholarships to graduates from Ada County high schools, ID.
Financial data: Year ended 06/30/2005. Assets, $1,618,505 (M); Expenditures, $100,239; Total giving, $82,500; Grants to individuals, totaling $82,500.
Type of support: Support to graduates or students of specific schools; Undergraduate support.
Application information: Applications not accepted. Unsolicited requests for funds not considered or acknowledged.
EIN: 826055666

1767
Ruth Haulenbeek St. John - Helena L. Cable Scholarship Fund
c/o Francis Cucciarre
25 Maple St.
Walton, NY   13856

Foundation type: Independent foundation
Limitations: Educational loans to students of Walton Central School, NY, for higher education.
Financial data: Year ended 12/31/2004. Assets, $295,521 (M); Expenditures, $1,079; Total giving, $895; Loans to individuals, totaling $33,000.
Type of support: Support to graduates or students of specific schools; Undergraduate support.
Application information: Application form required.
 Deadline(s): July 3
EIN: 161372173

1768
The Hauss-Helms Foundation, Inc.
P.O. Box 25
Wapakoneta, OH   45895   (419) 738-4911
E-mail: information@hauss-helmsfoundation.org;
URL: http://www.hauss-helmsfoundation.org

Foundation type: Independent foundation
Limitations: Scholarships to financially needy graduating high school students who are residents of Auglaize and Allen counties, OH, and who wish to continue their education at colleges, universities, and technical schools.
Financial data: Year ended 12/31/2004. Assets, $11,845,645 (M); Expenditures, $337,184; Total giving, $268,408; Grants to individuals, 118 grants totaling $268,408 (high: $6,827, low: $334).
Fields of interest: Vocational education.
Type of support: Technical education support; Undergraduate support.
Application information: Application form required.
 Initial approach: Letter or telephone.
 Deadline(s): Apr. 15
 Applicants should submit the following:
  1) Letter(s) of recommendation
  2) Financial information

Additional information: Interviews required.
Program description:
 Educational Grants: Applicants must be of good moral character, rank in the top half of their graduating classes, be unable to fund college on their own, and be recommended for the grant by the principal, guidance counselor, or faculty member in their high school. If already in college, they must be recommended by a faculty advisor at that college. Scholarships are for one year of full-time study, and are renewable providing the student has maintained a GPA of at least 2.0 or its equivalent. In addition, grant recipients will have their grant revoked if they become a member of, or associate with, the Communist Party or any other group advocating the violent overthrow of our government.
EIN: 340975903

1769
Nina Haven Charitable Foundation
555 Colorado Ave.
Stuart, FL   34994-3013
Scholarship application address: c/o Guidance Office, Martin County High School, 2801 S. Kanner Hwy., Stuart, FL 34994, tel.: (561) 287-0710

Foundation type: Independent foundation
Limitations: Scholarships to graduates of Martin County, FL, high schools and local community colleges.
Financial data: Year ended 12/31/2004. Assets, $4,354,477 (M); Expenditures, $145,817; Total giving, $131,477.
Type of support: Support to graduates or students of specific schools; Undergraduate support.
Application information: Contact school guidance counselor for current application deadline; Completion of formal application required.
EIN: 136099012

1770
Havens Foundation, Inc.
25132 Oakhurst Dr., Ste. 220
Spring, TX   77386
Contact: Joe D. Havens, Pres.

Foundation type: Independent foundation
Limitations: Undergraduate scholarships primarily to residents of TX.
Financial data: Year ended 12/31/2004. Assets, $1,621,735 (M); Expenditures, $128,284; Total giving, $121,490.
Type of support: Undergraduate support.
Application information: Applications accepted throughout the year; Completion of formal application required.
EIN: 760317434

1771
Harry A. Haverlah Foundation
c/o East Texas National Bank
P.O. Box 770
Palestine, TX   75802   (903) 729-6091
Contact: Jerry L. Nowlin, V.P. & Trust Off.

Foundation type: Independent foundation
Limitations: Student loans to financially needy graduates of high schools in Anderson County, TX, who have at least a "B" average. Recipients must attend four-year colleges or universities in TX.
Financial data: Year ended 12/31/2004. Assets, $359,457 (M); Expenditures, $23,866; Total giving, $10,838; Loans to individuals, totaling $10,838.

Type of support: Support to graduates or students of specific schools; Undergraduate support.
Application information: Application form required.
Deadline(s): July 25
Applicants should submit the following:
1) Financial information
2) ACT
3) Transcripts
4) SAT
Additional information: Application must also include attendance records, physician's authorization letter, college or university letter, and latest income tax return.
Program description:
Student Loan Program: Repayment of loans are amortized over a period of twice the number of months the recipient attends college or university. Payment begins six months after completion or termination of study.
EIN: 751242215

1772
Hawaii Community Foundation
(formerly The Hawaiian Foundation)
1164 Bishop St., Ste. 800
Honolulu, HI 96813 (808) 537-6333
Contact: Kelvin H. Taketa, C.E.O. and Pres.
FAX: (808) 521-6286; E-mail: info@hcf-hawaii.org;
Additional tel.: (888) 731-3863; Scholarship inquiry E-mail: scholarships@hcf-hawaii.org; URL: http://www.hawaiicommunityfoundation.org

Foundation type: Community foundation
Limitations: Scholarships to residents of the state of HI.
Publications: Application guidelines; Annual report; Informational brochure; Newsletter; Program policy statement.
Financial data: Year ended 12/31/2004.
Assets, $263,717,137 (M); Expenditures, $23,951,706; Total giving, $18,130,056; Grants to individuals, totaling $2,627,817.
Fields of interest: Folk arts; Arts education; Media/communications; Journalism/publishing; Arts; Vocational education; Business school/education; Dental school/education; Medical school/education; Nursing school/education; Teacher school/education; Engineering school/education; Health sciences school/education; Agriculture; Athletics/sports, training; Youth development; International peace/security; International affairs; Science; Physical/earth sciences; Engineering; Protestant agencies & churches; Women.
Type of support: Employee-related scholarships; Graduate support; Undergraduate support.
Application information: Application form required.
Deadline(s): Mar. 1 unless otherwise stated for scholarships using the foundation's common application form
Applicants should submit the following:
1) SAR
2) Transcripts
Additional information: Application must also include personal statement, and two letters of recommendation; Applications may be obtained through high school guidance counselors and college financial aid offices or by contacting the foundation; Applicants notified Apr. to June; See program description for specific information and guidelines for other scholarships.
EIN: 990261283

1773
Hawaii Foundation for Dietetics
P.O. Box 235751
Honolulu, HI 96823-3512   (808) 547-4255
Contact: Joy Kunimitsu

Foundation type: Independent foundation
Limitations: Scholarships and awards to high school students residing in HI.
Financial data: Year ended 05/31/2004.
Assets, $45,384 (M); Expenditures, $14,957; Total giving, $14,057; Grants to individuals, 23 grants totaling $14,057 (high: $1,000, low: $100).
Fields of interest: Nutrition.
Type of support: Awards/prizes; Undergraduate support.
Application information: Application form required.
Deadline(s): Apr. 1
EIN: 990274646

1774
Robert and Cecilia Hawk Citizenship Foundation
c/o PMB
519 Interstate 30, Ste. 704
Rockwall, TX 75087-5408   (972) 722-9218
Contact: Robert Hawk, Pres.

Foundation type: Independent foundation
Limitations: Scholarships by teacher nomination only to graduating seniors of Rockwall Independent School District, TX, for higher education or trade schools.
Financial data: Year ended 12/31/2004.
Assets, $1,490,658 (M); Expenditures, $39,777; Total giving, $35,000; Grants to individuals, totaling $35,000.
Type of support: Support to graduates or students of specific schools; Awards/grants by nomination only; Technical education support; Undergraduate support.
Application information: Nominations accepted throughout the year; Completion of formal nomination required.
Program description:
Scholarship Program: Scholarships to recipients who are members of high income household shall be reduced as follows:
· Twenty percent for income between $100,000 and $125,000
· Forty percent for income between $125,000 and $150,000
· Sixty percent for income between $150,000 and $175,000
· Eighty percent for income in excess of $175,000
Recipients must be nominated by a high school teacher to be eligible for scholarship.
EIN: 752617169

1775
Hawkes Scholarship Fund
c/o KeyBank N.A.
800 Superior Ave., 4th Fl.
Cleveland, OH 44114-1306

Foundation type: Independent foundation
Limitations: Scholarships to graduating seniors of Tobique Valley High School in New Brunswick, Canada and Governor Baxter School for the Deaf in Portland, ME. Scholarships also to graduating seniors who are residents of Opportunity Farm for Boys or Sweetser-Children's Home, both in ME, and to members of the Boys and Girls Club of Portland, ME only for the first year of study at a U.S. college, university or technical school.

Financial data: Year ended 07/31/2005.
Assets, $1,366,209 (M); Expenditures, $55,665; Total giving, $41,643; Grants to individuals, totaling $41,643.
Fields of interest: Vocational education; Boys & girls clubs; Disabilities, people with.
Type of support: Support to graduates or students of specific schools; Undergraduate support.
Application information: Applications not accepted.
EIN: 010441158

1776
E. Maurine Hawkins Memorial Scholarship Fund
c/o Trust Co. of Knoxville
P.O. Box 789
Knoxville, TN 37901-0789
Contact: Whitney Walling, Chair.
Application address: c/o Tennessee High School, 1112 Edgemont Ave., Bristol, TN 37620, tel.: (423) 652-9317

Foundation type: Independent foundation
Limitations: Scholarships to graduates of Tennessee High School, Bristol, TN; and full-time students at University of Tennessee, Knoxville, and Carson Newman College, TN, and Union College, KY.
Financial data: Year ended 12/31/2004.
Assets, $291,691 (M); Expenditures, $18,371; Total giving, $16,000; Grants to individuals, totaling $16,000.
Type of support: Support to graduates or students of specific schools; Undergraduate support.
Application information: Deadline May 1; Contact fund for current application guidelines.
EIN: 621338535

1777
Hawkins Scholarship Foundation
c/o Davidson Trust Co.
P.O. Box 152
Kalispell, MT 59903-0152

Foundation type: Independent foundation
Limitations: Scholarships to graduating students attending high schools in Flathead County, MT.
Financial data: Year ended 12/31/2004.
Assets, $4,192,512 (M); Expenditures, $273,263; Total giving, $241,000; Grants to individuals, 165 grants totaling $241,000 (high: $2,000, low: $1,000).
Type of support: Support to graduates or students of specific schools; Undergraduate support.
Application information: Contact foundation for current application deadline/guidelines.
EIN: 816018444

1778
The Hawks Foundation
1044 N. 115th St., Ste. 400
Omaha, NE 68154 (402) 691-9500
Contact: Howard L. Hawks, Tr.

Foundation type: Independent foundation
Limitations: Scholarships primarily to Omaha, NE, area residents.
Financial data: Year ended 12/31/2003.
Assets, $12,608,988 (M); Expenditures, $773,001; Total giving, $722,959; Grants to individuals, 22 grants totaling $34,138 (high: $13,238, low: $200).
Type of support: Scholarships—to individuals.

Application information: Applications accepted throughout the year; Completion of formal application required, including transcripts and ACT scores.

Program description:

Scholarship Program: Scholarship applicants must be high school graduates enrolled or in the process of being enrolled full-time in an accredited institution of higher learning. In addition, they must have maintained at least a 2.8 cumulative GPA.

EIN: 476194021

1779

Esther H. Hawks Trust

c/o Nutter, McClennen & Fish
P.O. Box 51400
Boston, MA 02205-8982
Contact: John B. Newhall, Tr.
Scholarship application address for first-time applicants: c/o Charles L. Newhall, P.O. Box 2056, Salem, MA 01970, tel.: (978) 744-1626

Foundation type: Independent foundation
Limitations: Scholarships limited to graduating high school students of Lynn, MA, for full-time study at U.S. colleges. Preference is shown to renewal applicants.
Publications: Application guidelines.
Financial data: Year ended 12/31/2002. Assets, $1,722,195 (M); Expenditures, $124,505; Total giving, $102,500; Grants to individuals, 41 grants totaling $102,500 (high: $2,500, low: $2,500).
Type of support: Undergraduate support.
Application information: Deadlines May 1 for first-time applicants, May 15 for renewal applicants; Completion of formal application required, including transcripts, two references, GPA, SAT, or ACT scores, financial information, and SAR; Recipients notified in early June; Applications available from guidance counselors at Lynn high schools and, for renewal applicants only, from trustees.

Program description:

Scholarship Program: Scholarships are awarded on the basis of financial need and achievement. Awards range from $2,000 to $4,000 per year, but do not exceed the amount of tuition and fees. High school seniors receive preference for first-time awards, although college students and high school graduates not currently in school also qualify.

EIN: 046035212

1780

Hawley Foundation for Children

P.O. Box 1017
Saratoga Springs, NY 12866

Foundation type: Independent foundation
Limitations: Scholarships to graduates of high schools in Saratoga Springs, NY, for undergraduate or vocational study.
Financial data: Year ended 10/31/2004. Assets, $2,558,898 (M); Expenditures, $141,743; Total giving, $107,036; Grants to individuals, 28 grants totaling $41,319 (high: $3,000, low: $500).
Fields of interest: Vocational education.
Type of support: Support to graduates or students of specific schools; Technical education support; Undergraduate support.
Application information: Deadline May; Completion of formal application required, including FAF or FSS form and parents' or guardians' income tax form;

Applications are available from the guidance office of each high school after Feb. 1.
EIN: 141340069

1781

Josiah Willard Hayden Recreation Centre, Inc.

c/o Donald K. Mahoney
24 Lincoln St.
Lexington, MA 02421 (781) 862-8480

Foundation type: Operating foundation
Limitations: Four-year scholarships to students pursuing postsecondary education and who are residents of Lexington, MA.
Financial data: Year ended 08/31/2004. Assets, $19,566,000 (M); Expenditures, $2,343,026; Total giving, $36,600; Grants to individuals, 69 grants totaling $36,600 (high: $1,100, low: $300).
Type of support: Undergraduate support.
Application information: Deadline Apr. 15; Completion of formal application required, including tuition cost and family financial information.
EIN: 042203700

1782

Dale Irwin Hayes Scholarship Fund

c/o U.S. Bank, N.A.
P.O. Box 387
St. Louis, MO 63166
Application address: c/o University of Missouri-Rolla, Office of Admissions and Financial Aid, 106 Parker Hall, 1870 Miner Cir., Rolla, MO 65409-1060

Foundation type: Independent foundation
Limitations: Scholarships of at least $2,000 to students enrolled at the University of Missouri-Rolla, with priority given to students at the undergraduate level to study engineering or a related subject. Students should demonstrate financial need.
Financial data: Year ended 09/30/2004. Assets, $1,219,577 (M); Expenditures, $70,394; Total giving, $46,000; Grants to individuals, 19 grants totaling $46,000 (high: $2,000, low: $2,000).
Fields of interest: Engineering school/education.
Type of support: Support to graduates or students of specific schools; Undergraduate support.
Application information: Application form required.
Deadline(s): Contact fund for current application deadline/guidelines.
EIN: 436619759

1783

Mildred & Milo Hayes Scholarship Trust

(formerly Mildred & Milo Hayes Educational Foundation)
c/o Bank of America, N.A.
231 S. LaSalle St., ILI-231-14-19
Chicago, IL 60697
Application address for individuals: c/o Howard D. Hamilton, 205 Snell Bldg., Fort Dodge, IA 50501

Foundation type: Independent foundation
Limitations: Scholarships to graduates of Webster County High School, IA, who graduated in the upper 50 percent of the class, for study at IA colleges and universities.
Financial data: Year ended 03/31/2004. Assets, $629,510 (M); Expenditures, $30,227;

Total giving, $25,300; Grants to individuals, totaling $25,300.
Type of support: Support to graduates or students of specific schools; Undergraduate support.
Application information: Application form required.
Deadline(s): Apr. 1
Applicants should submit the following:
1) ACT
2) GPA
Additional information: Provide a list of your extracurricular activities.
EIN: 426344913

1784

Walter Hayes, Sr., Beulah Buffum Hayes & Walter H. Hayes, Jr. Foundation

(also known as The Hayes Foundation)
P.O. Box 129
Wallingford, VT 05773 (802) 446-2877
E-mail: abchayes@sover.net

Foundation type: Independent foundation
Limitations: Grants for educational assistance to intellectually gifted children from preschool to grade 12, who reside in Rutland County, VT. Priority is given to younger children and children of needy families.
Financial data: Year ended 12/31/2002. Assets, $478,867 (M); Expenditures, $64,816; Total giving, $10,855; Grants to individuals, 25 grants totaling $10,855.
Fields of interest: Elementary school/education; Secondary school/education; Children/youth, services.
Type of support: Precollege support.
Application information: Applications accepted. Application form required.
Initial approach: Letter or through guidance counselor or teacher.
Additional information: Application should include essay.
Program description:
Grant Program: The foundation sponsors a summer enrichment program for gifted children, with financial assistance as needed for individual students.
EIN: 030284264

1785

Haymarket Lodge Charitable Foundation, Inc.

P.O. Box 313
Haymarket, VA 20168-0313

Foundation type: Independent foundation
Limitations: Scholarships to individuals in VA.
Financial data: Year ended 12/31/2004. Assets, $1,125,132 (M); Expenditures, $63,321; Total giving, $10,002; Grants to individuals, totaling $9,002.
Type of support: Scholarships—to individuals.
Application information: Applications not accepted.
EIN: 541679008

1786

The Charles O. and Elsie Haynes Trust

5375 State Hwy. 7, Ste. 4
Oneonta, NY 13820
Contact: Thomas J. Trelease, Mgr.

Foundation type: Operating foundation
Limitations: Scholarships to residents of Charlotte Valley Central School District, Davenport, NY.

Financial data: Year ended 12/31/2003. Assets, $331,561 (M); Expenditures, $16,333; Total giving, $14,000; Grants to individuals, 5 grants totaling $14,000 (high: $6,000, low: $2,000).
Type of support: Scholarships—to individuals.
Application information: Application form required.
Initial approach: Letter.
Deadline(s): First Mon. in June
Applicants should submit the following:
1) Transcripts
2) GPA
3) Financial information
4) Essay
EIN: 222429332

1787
Mary F. & Annie M. Hazard Memorial Foundation
1526 Hickory Ln.
Columbus, MS 39705   (662) 328-3088
Contact: Eulalie H. Davis, Tr.

Foundation type: Independent foundation
Limitations: Scholarships to individuals attending Mississippi University for Women, Belhaven College, MS, or The McCallie School in Chattanooga, TN.
Financial data: Year ended 12/31/2004. Assets, $169,823 (M); Expenditures, $12,651; Total giving, $8,000; Grants to individuals, totaling $8,000.
Fields of interest: Women.
Type of support: Support to graduates or students of specific schools; Undergraduate support.
Application information: Deadline prior to the beginning of the semester; Completion of formal application required; Forms are available from eligible schools.
EIN: 646024825

1788
Della Lucille Hazelton Charitable Trust
c/o Wells Fargo Bank Nevada, N.A.
P.O. Box 95021, MAC 4753-028
Henderson, NV 89009

Foundation type: Independent foundation
Limitations: Scholarships by nomination only to Native Americans in AZ and MT.
Financial data: Year ended 12/31/2004. Assets, $347,906 (M); Expenditures, $13,622; Total giving, $8,289; Grants to individuals, totaling $8,289.
Fields of interest: Native Americans/American Indians.
Type of support: Scholarships—to individuals; Awards/grants by nomination only.
Application information: Applications not accepted.
Additional information: Two Native American tribes within each state are contacted on a rotating basis to select needy applicants.
EIN: 746366878

1789
Vivien B. Head Testamentary Trust
c/o Wells Fargo Bank New Mexico, N.A.
P.O. Box 2169
Las Cruces, NM 88004   (505) 521-6883

Foundation type: Public charity
Limitations: Scholarships to students majoring in the fine arts and electrical engineering at New Mexico State University, NM and New York University, NY.
Fields of interest: Arts education; Arts; Engineering.
Type of support: Support to graduates or students of specific schools; Undergraduate support.
Application information: Applications not accepted.
EIN: 850319081

1790
Headliners Foundation of Texas
221 W. 6th St., Ste. 2100
Austin, TX 78701
Contact: Cindy Bradshaw
Application address: c/o Mike Quinn, Dept. of Journalism, University of TX, Austin TX 78712

Foundation type: Public charity
Limitations: Undergraduate scholarships to residents of TX in the field of communications at specified schools in TX.
Financial data: Year ended 07/31/2005. Assets, $1,798,635 (M); Expenditures, $129,964; Total giving, $43,730; Grants to individuals, 17 grants totaling $43,730 (high: $3,000).
Fields of interest: Media/communications; Journalism/publishing.
Type of support: Support to graduates or students of specific schools; Undergraduate support.
Application information: Applications accepted. Application form required.
Initial approach: Letter.
Deadline(s): Feb. 1
Program description:
Scholarship Program: The foundation awards scholarships at the University of Texas at Austin, and at each of the following: St. Edward's University, Texas A&M University, Baylor University, and Southwestern University.
EIN: 742281076

1791
William H. Heald Scholarship Fund
c/o PNC Bank, N.A.
1600 Market St., Tax Dept.
Philadelphia, PA 19103-7240
Contact: Richard Sutton
Application address: P.O. Box 1347, Wilmington, DE 19899

Foundation type: Independent foundation
Limitations: Scholarships to male residents of New Castle County, DE, to attend the University of Delaware.
Financial data: Year ended 12/31/2004. Assets, $874,572 (M); Expenditures, $56,129; Total giving, $48,000.
Fields of interest: Men.
Type of support: Support to graduates or students of specific schools; Undergraduate support.
Application information: Deadline May 1; Application by letter.
EIN: 516010547

1792
B. L. & W. H. Heald Scholarship Trust
c/o Bank of America, N.A., P.C. Group
P.O. Box 6767
Providence, RI 02940-6767

Foundation type: Independent foundation

Limitations: Scholarships to graduates of Stafford Springs High School, CT, with an "A" average.
Financial data: Year ended 09/30/2004. Assets, $329,497 (M); Expenditures, $20,015; Total giving, $14,500.
Type of support: Support to graduates or students of specific schools; Undergraduate support.
Application information: Applications not accepted.
EIN: 066087125

1793
Health Professions Education Foundation
(formerly Minority Health Professions Education Foundation)
818 K. St., Ste. 210
Sacramento, CA 95814   (916) 324-6500
Contact: Robyn D. Boyer, Exec. Dir.
FAX: (916) 324-6585; Additional tel.: (800) 773-1669; URL: http:// www.healthprofessions.ca.gov/application.htm

Foundation type: Public charity
Limitations: Scholarships to young residents of CA for the pursuit of a degree in a health care profession.
Publications: Application guidelines; Annual report; Informational brochure; Newsletter.
Financial data: Year ended 06/30/2004. Assets, $6,092,754 (M); Expenditures, $2,502,710; Total giving, $1,980,225; Grants to individuals, totaling $1,980,225.
Fields of interest: Reproductive health, sexuality education; Health care.
Type of support: Technical education support; Undergraduate support.
Application information: Deadline Nov. 15; Initial approach by telephone; See Web site for application guidelines and forms.
Program description:
Youth for Adolescent Pregnancy Prevention (YAPP): Awards to recognize CA youth ages 16-24 who have made outstanding contributions in their local communities within the last five years by actively promoting healthy adolescent sexuality and lifestyle choices for other youth. Recipients receive an educational scholarship of up to $5,000 per year for up to five years. Award money may be used to pursue a health professional degree at an accredited CA vocational school, college or university.
EIN: 680178150

1794
Healthcare and Nursing Education Foundation
(formerly Visiting Nurse Association of Houston Foundation)
3815 Montrose Blvd., Ste. 200
Houston, TX 77006-4665   (713) 802-7865
FAX: (713) 868-2619; E-mail: info@hnef.org; Leslie Winesett tel.: (713) 802-7870; URL: http:// www.hnef.org

Foundation type: Independent foundation
Limitations: Scholarships to individuals with financial need who are pursuing a professional nursing career.
Publications: Application guidelines; Grants list.
Financial data: Year ended 06/30/2005. Assets, $7,955,757 (M); Expenditures, $503,269; Total giving, $369,762; Grants to individuals, 7 grants totaling $32,000 (high: $6,000, low: $4,000).
Fields of interest: Nursing school/education.

Type of support: Scholarships—to individuals.
Application information: Applications accepted.
Deadline(s): Mar. 25
Program description:
Nursing Scholarships: Scholarships are awarded based on academics, leadership ability, community involvement, financial need, and commitment to pursuing a nursing career. Scholarship recipients receive up to $3,000 per year for their freshman and sophomore year and $4,000 per year for their junior and senior year to be used for tuition, books, and fees at Houston area colleges and universities providing programs leading to a nursing degree. Scholarships are awarded to students:
  - who have graduated from high school and will be attending an accepted undergraduate program in preparation for entry into an accredited college program leading to a bachelor's degree in nursing
  - who have been accepted into an accredited bachelor's-level nursing program, or
  - who have been accepted into an accredited graduate-level nursing program leading to a master's degree in nursing or a Nurse Practitioner degree
EIN: 760454511

1795
Hearn Educational Fund Trust
c/o PNC Advisors, Delaware, Trust Dept.
222 Delaware Ave., 16th Fl.
Wilmington, DE   19899   (302) 429-1186
Contact: Amy Davis, V.P., PNC Advisors

Foundation type: Independent foundation
Limitations: Scholarships to students who reside in the Milford, DE, school district.
Publications: Application guidelines; Program policy statement.
Financial data: Year ended 12/31/2003.
Assets, $1,724,607 (M); Expenditures, $100,100; Total giving, $82,000; Grants to individuals, 45 grants totaling $82,000 (high: $3,000, low: $800).
Type of support: Scholarships—to individuals; Support to graduates or students of specific schools.
Application information: Applications accepted. Application form required.
Deadline(s): May 24
Program description:
Scholarship Program: Selection criteria include merit and financial need. Scholarships are renewable for up to four years and are for associate and baccalaureate degrees only.
EIN: 516015401

1796
Heart of Variety Fund
1520 Locust St., 9th Fl.
Philadelphia, PA   19103   (215) 735-0803
Contact: Andrew M. Pack, Exec. Dir.

Foundation type: Public charity
Limitations: Scholarships to handicapped children.
Financial data: Year ended 09/30/2004.
Assets, $704,086 (M); Expenditures, $1,933,347; Total giving, $855,959; Grants to individuals, totaling $35,959.
Fields of interest: Children; Disabilities, people with.
Type of support: Scholarships—to individuals.
Application information:
Initial approach: Letter.

Additional information: Contact fund for application guidelines.
EIN: 236392728

1797
The Heath Educational Fund
c/o Bank of America, N.A.
P.O. Box 40200, MC FL9-100-10-19
Jacksonville, FL   32203-0200
Application address: c/o: Bank of America, N.A., P.O. Box 15507, St. Petersburg, FL 33733

Foundation type: Independent foundation
Limitations: Scholarships only to male high school graduates from the southeastern U.S. who wish to study for the ministry, missionary activities, or social work, primarily in the Methodist or Episcopalian denominations.
Financial data: Year ended 09/30/2005.
Assets, $95,299 (M); Expenditures, $9,349; Total giving, $4,928; Grants to individuals, totaling $4,928.
Fields of interest: Theological school/education; Social work school/education; Christian agencies & churches; Men.
Type of support: Graduate support; Undergraduate support.
Application information:
Deadline(s): June 30
Applicants should submit the following:
  1) Transcripts
  2) Letter(s) of recommendation
Additional information: Application by letter, including brief background of applicant, copy of high school diploma, and birth certificate.
Program description:
Scholarship Program: Students must be under the age of 35 and pursuing an undergraduate or graduate degree in order to serve in the ministry, as a missionary or as a social worker. Scholarship awards range from $300 to $800.
EIN: 596218458

1798
Steve Heath Memorial ROTC Scholarship
12618 Sandpiper
Live Oak, TX   78233-7236   (210) 655-5317
Contact: Donald Heath, Tr.

Foundation type: Independent foundation
Limitations: Scholarships to individuals who have completed at least one year with the University of Texas at San Antonio AFROTC, Detachment 842.
Financial data: Year ended 12/31/2004.
Assets, $479 (M); Expenditures, $15,408; Total giving, $15,345; Grants to individuals, totaling $13,250.
Fields of interest: Military/veterans' organizations.
Type of support: Support to graduates or students of specific schools; Undergraduate support.
Application information: Applications accepted throughout the year; Completion of formal application required, including transcripts and a 200-300 word handwritten personal history.
EIN: 742591005

1799
Donald & Gladys Heath Scholarship Memorial Fund
c/o Bank of America, N.A.
P.O. Box 6768
Providence, RI   02940-6768

Foundation type: Independent foundation

Limitations: Scholarships to the valedictorians and salutatorians of Livonia High School, NY, Mount Morris High School, NY, and York High School, Retsof, NY.
Financial data: Year ended 02/29/2004.
Assets, $590,084 (M); Expenditures, $23,781; Total giving, $17,185; Grants to individuals, 6 grants totaling $17,185 (high: $2,865, low: $2,864).
Type of support: Support to graduates or students of specific schools; Undergraduate support.
Application information: Applications not accepted.
Additional information: Awards are determined by each school's records.
EIN: 166355023

1800
The Gary & Diane Heavin Community Fund Inc.
(formerly The Curves Community Fund, Inc.)
400 Schroeder Dr.
Waco, TX   76710

Foundation type: Company-sponsored foundation
Limitations: Scholarships to current employees of Curves, and their dependents, who plan on studying a subject relating to health.
Financial data: Year ended 04/30/2002.
Assets, $2,171,437 (M); Expenditures, $1,256,494; Total giving, $1,256,494; Grants to individuals, 19 grants totaling $44,109 (high: $16,967, low: $380).
Type of support: Employee-related scholarships.
Application information:
Initial approach: Letter.
Additional information: Contact the Corporate Office for further application information.
EIN: 743003293

1801
Maurice and Virginia Hecht Scholarship Fund
c/o Citizens Bank Wealth Mgmt., N.A.
328 S. Saginaw St., M/C 002072
Flint, MI   48502   (866) 308-7878
Contact: Donna Sumbera, Trust Off., Citizens Bank, N.A.

Foundation type: Independent foundation
Limitations: Scholarships to graduates of Burr Oak High School, MI.
Financial data: Year ended 03/31/2005.
Assets, $181,540 (M); Expenditures, $9,501; Total giving, $5,500; Grants to individuals, totaling $5,500.
Type of support: Support to graduates or students of specific schools; Undergraduate support.
Application information: Applications accepted.
Deadline(s): None
Additional information: Applications by letter, including a list of academic and nonacademic achievements and goals, a statement of financial need, and recommendations from the superintendent and principal of Burr Oak High School.
Program description:
Scholarship Program: Scholarships are renewable for up to four years. There are a maximum of ten new scholarships per year.
EIN: 382923150

1802
The George and Lucile Heeringa Foundation
P.O. Box 9016
Holland, MI   49422-9016

Foundation type: Operating foundation
Limitations: Scholarships to western MI area high school students for higher education.
Financial data: Year ended 12/31/2002. Assets, $553,962 (M); Expenditures, $37,581; Total giving, $35,500; Grants to individuals, 22 grants totaling $19,000 (high: $1,000, low: $500).
Type of support: Undergraduate support.
Application information: Contact foundation for current application deadline/guidelines.
EIN: 383024217

1803
Hefflefinger Scholarship Fund
c/o Bank of America, N.A.
P.O. Box 513189
Los Angeles, CA   90051-1189
Application address: c/o Tulare Union High School, Attn.: Gregory DeMuth, 755 E. Tulare Ave., Tulare, CA 93274, tel.: (209) 686-4761

Foundation type: Independent foundation
Limitations: Scholarships only to students of the Tulare High School District, CA.
Financial data: Year ended 10/31/2004. Assets, $210,705 (M); Expenditures, $7,429; Total giving, $4,700; Grants to individuals, totaling $4,700.
Type of support: Support to graduates or students of specific schools; Undergraduate support.
Application information: Deadline Apr. 1; Initial approach by letter; Completion of formal application required.
EIN: 953820054

1804
Frances Sawyer Hefti Trust
c/o JPMorgan Chase Bank, N.A.
P.O. Box 1308
Milwaukee, WI   53201
Application address: c/o JPMorgan Chase Bank, N.A., 200 W. College Ave., Appleton, WI 54911, tel.: (920) 735-1383

Foundation type: Independent foundation
Limitations: Scholarships to high school seniors at Neenah or Menasha Joint School Districts, WI.
Financial data: Year ended 03/31/2005. Assets, $943,763 (M); Expenditures, $44,840; Total giving, $36,000.
Type of support: Support to graduates or students of specific schools; Undergraduate support.
Application information: Deadline Feb. 15; Completion of formal application required; Forms available from guidance counselors.
EIN: 396474920

1805
Hein Family Foundation Corporation
1944 Levine Ln.
Clearwater, FL   33760

Foundation type: Independent foundation
Limitations: Scholarships to students for higher education.
Financial data: Year ended 12/31/2004. Assets, $63,984 (M); Expenditures, $37,907;

Total giving, $35,194; Grants to individuals, totaling $35,194.
Type of support: Undergraduate support.
Application information: Deadline two months prior to post-high school education; Completion of formal application required, including goals, transcript and letter of recommendation.
Program description:
Scholarship Program: Scholarships are limited to tuition, fees, books and room and board at accredited institutions of higher education. Recipients must maintain at least a 2.7 GPA at their chosen institution and must submit transcripts at the conclusion of each term.
EIN: 593708543

1806
Geraldine Heiserman Trust f/b/o Cottey College
(formerly Geraldine Cottey College Trust)
c/o U.S. Bank, N.A., Trust Tax Svcs.
P.O. Box 3168
Portland, OR   97208-3168
Contact: Scholarship: Katherine K. West
Application address: c/o Cottey College, 1000 W. Austin Blvd., Nevada, MO 64772-2763, tel.: (888) 526-8839

Foundation type: Independent foundation
Limitations: Scholarships to residents of CO to attend Cottey College in Nevada, MO.
Financial data: Year ended 12/31/2003. Assets, $399,608 (M); Expenditures, $17,615; Total giving, $12,736; Grants to individuals, totaling $12,736.
Type of support: Support to graduates or students of specific schools.
Application information: Applications accepted.
Additional information: Contact college for current application deadline/guidelines.
EIN: 846049131

1807
The Heisey Foundation
c/o U.S. Bank, N.A.
P.O. Box 5000
Great Falls, MT   59403

Foundation type: Independent foundation
Limitations: Awards by nomination only to students attending specific public and parochial schools in the Great Falls, MT, trade area.
Financial data: Year ended 12/31/2004. Assets, $6,185,661 (M); Expenditures, $289,094; Total giving, $251,975; Grants to individuals, 15 grants totaling $15,000 (high: $1,000, low: $1,000).
Type of support: Support to graduates or students of specific schools; Awards/grants by nomination only; Awards/prizes.
Application information: Applications are accepted by nomination only.
Program description:
Scholarship Awards: Awards by nomination only are given to those students making the most improvement in citizenship, effort, and scholarship to the best of his/her ability. The selection committees will give the greatest weight to improvement in citizenship (50 percent). The balance will be divided equally between effort and scholarship. An award of $50 may be given to one student for every 20. There are separate selection committees for Great Falls public high school students, Great Falls parochial high school students, and for students attending schools in the

approximately 22 other locations in the Great Falls trade area.
EIN: 816009624

1808
The Helaman Foundation
11 Quietwood Ln.
Sandy, UT   84092

Foundation type: Independent foundation
Limitations: Scholarships to residents of AZ, CO, ID and UT, for higher education.
Financial data: Year ended 12/31/2004. Assets, $10,158 (M); Expenditures, $195,380; Total giving, $195,380; Grants to individuals, 52 grants totaling $195,380 (high: $57,000, low: $750).
Type of support: Undergraduate support.
Application information: Applications not accepted.
EIN: 311234291

1809
A. M. Helbing Trust for Nursing Education
c/o Mauch Chunk Trust Co.
P.O. Box 289
Jim Thorpe, PA   18229

Foundation type: Independent foundation
Limitations: Scholarships to residents of Carbon County, PA, pursuing nursing education.
Financial data: Year ended 12/31/2004. Assets, $323,042 (M); Expenditures, $20,889; Total giving, $17,600; Grants to individuals, totaling $17,600.
Fields of interest: Nursing school/education.
Type of support: Graduate support.
Application information: Applications accepted. Application form required.
Deadline(s): Apr. 30
EIN: 237681690

1810
The Hellenic Foundation
12051 Rosemount Dr.
Fort Myers, FL   33912
Contact: John F. Grove, Jr., Tr.

Foundation type: Company-sponsored foundation
Limitations: Scholarships to financially needy residents of PA, for attendance at colleges and universities. Scholarships cover tuition, books and living expenses.
Financial data: Year ended 06/30/2005. Assets, $394,599 (M); Expenditures, $32,228; Total giving, $28,750; Grants to individuals, 2 grants totaling $7,000 (high: $5,000, low: $2,000).
Type of support: Scholarships—to individuals.
Application information: Applications by letter including academic records, recommendations, and statement of financial need accepted throughout the year.
EIN: 222536161

1811
Pauline and Edna Hellstern Foundation
c/o U.S. Bank, N.A.
P.O. Box 3168
Portland, OR   97208
Application address: c/o Pueblo Centennial High School, 2525 Montview Dr., Pueblo, CO 81008

Foundation type: Independent foundation
Limitations: Scholarships to graduates of Pueblo County, CO, schools.
Financial data: Year ended 02/28/2005.
Assets, $294,802 (M); Expenditures, $16,285; Total giving, $12,000; Grants to individuals, 9 grants totaling $12,000 (high: $5,000, low: $500).
Type of support: Support to graduates or students of specific schools; Undergraduate support.
Application information: Applications accepted. Application form required.
   Additional information: Applications available from School District No. 60, Pueblo, CO.
EIN: 742536168

1812

John Y. Helm & Willie Mae Helm Scholarship Fund

c/o First National Bank of Santa Fe
P.O. Box 609
Santa Fe, NM   87504
Contact: Fredrica E. Smith M.D., Secy.-Treas.
Application address: c/o Los Alamos Medical Center, 3917 West Rd., Ste. D, Los Alamos, NM 87544, tel.: (505) 662-9400

Foundation type: Independent foundation
Limitations: Scholarships to medical students who are or have been residents of Los Alamos County, NM.
Financial data: Year ended 01/31/2005.
Assets, $305,344 (M); Expenditures, $19,343; Total giving, $14,020; Grants to individuals, totaling $14,020.
Fields of interest: Medical school/education.
Type of support: Graduate support.
Application information: Deadline July 31; Initial approach by letter or telephone; Applications by letter outlining background, extracurricular activities, career goals, and transcripts.
EIN: 856108694

1813

Help Our Students Succeed Foundation

3131 N. Hwy. 161
Irving, TX   75062   (972) 257-1244
FAX: (972) 594-0622

Foundation type: Independent foundation
Limitations: Scholarships to individuals for higher education.
Financial data: Year ended 12/31/2004.
Assets, $2,074 (M); Expenditures, $17,668; Total giving, $17,500; Grants to individuals, totaling $17,500.
Type of support: Scholarships—to individuals.
Application information: Application form required.
   Additional information: Contact foundation for current application deadline.
EIN: 752622539

1814

R. L. and Elsa Helvering Trust

1114 Broadway
P.O. Box 468
Marysville, KS   66508   (785) 562-2375
Contact: Edward F. Wiegers, Tr.

Foundation type: Independent foundation
Limitations: Scholarships by nomination only to financially needy graduating seniors of Marshall County, KS, high schools to attend a college or university in KS.

Financial data: Year ended 03/31/2005.
Assets, $1,617,887 (M); Expenditures, $83,152; Total giving, $74,838.
Type of support: Support to graduates or students of specific schools; Awards/grants by nomination only; Undergraduate support.
Application information: Applications accepted. Application form required.
   Deadline(s): May 1.
   Additional information: Interviews required.
Program description:
   Scholarship Program: Two four-year scholarships are awarded annually for attendance at a KS college or university. Selection criteria used by the trustee include:
   · The recipient must have been recommended by his or her high school principal
   · The recipient must have a high scholastic average during his or her high school career
   · The recipient must be deserving and show financial need
   · The recipient's parents must have a financial condition, such that they are not reasonably able to pay for their child's college education without a scholarship.
EIN: 480924200

1815

Charles R. Hemenway Scholarship Trust

c/o Bank of Hawaii
P.O. Box 3170
Honolulu, HI   96802
Application address: c/o Univ. of Hawaii, Financial Aid Office, 2442 Campus Rd., Honolulu, HI 96822, tel.: (808) 956-7251

Foundation type: Public charity
Limitations: Undergraduate scholarships to residents of HI attending the University of Hawaii, or Hawaii community colleges, who are committed to HI and its people.
Financial data: Year ended 06/30/2004.
Assets, $4,535,124 (M); Expenditures, $297,704; Total giving, $285,060.
Type of support: Support to graduates or students of specific schools; Undergraduate support.
Application information: Application form required.
   Deadline(s): Apr. 1
   Additional information: Applications available from the financial aid offices of the Manoa and Hilo campuses of the University of Hawaii; Interviews required.
Program description:
   Scholarship Program: Selection of recipients, scholarship amounts, and manner of paying the scholarships are determined jointly by the trust scholarship committee and the University of Hawaii. Eligible applicants are selected upon the following criteria:
   · financial need as determined by FAF
   · academic promise or performance at the University of Hawaii
   · evidence of good character and citizenship
Grants are made through the financial aid offices of the University of Hawaii. Do not contact trustee regarding grant applications.
EIN: 996003089

1816

Susan Hay Hemminger Scholarship Foundation

P.O. Box 9242
Michigan City, IN   46361-9242

Foundation type: Independent foundation
Limitations: Scholarships to graduates of LaPorte County, IN, high schools residing in LaPorte County, who are accepted to or enrolled at two- or four-year colleges and universities.
Financial data: Year ended 08/31/2005.
Assets, $792,468 (M); Expenditures, $50,934; Total giving, $42,000; Grants to individuals, totaling $42,000.
Type of support: Support to graduates or students of specific schools; Undergraduate support.
Application information: Application form required.
   Deadline(s): Apr. 15
   Applicants should submit the following:
      1) Transcripts
      2) GPA
      3) Financial information
   Additional information: Application must also include references, 500-word essay, and proof of acceptance to or enrollment at an accredited institution; Interviews required.
Program description:
   Scholarship Program: Scholarships are awarded on the basis of financial need, academic achievement, service and leadership, and ability and commitment. Students must attend on a full-time basis. The foundation awards up to $5,000 or the amount of full-time tuition at the recipient's school, whichever is less. Scholarships are renewable annually.
EIN: 351900696

1817

Helen L. Henderson Scholarship Fund

c/o Fowler State Bank
P.O. Box 511
Fowler, IN   47944-0511
Contact: Anne Molter, Tr.
Application address: 300 E. 5th St., Fowler, IN 47944, tel.: (765) 884-1200

Foundation type: Independent foundation
Limitations: Loans to residents of Benton County and/or students of Benton Central Junior/Senior High School, IN.
Financial data: Year ended 12/31/2004.
Assets, $323,384 (M); Expenditures, $6,861; Total giving, $0; Loans to individuals, 24 loans totaling $36,329.
Type of support: Support to graduates or students of specific schools; Undergraduate support.
Application information: Applications accepted. Application form required.
   Deadline(s): None
EIN: 356479328

1818

Herbert & Gertrude Henderson Scholarship Fund

P.O. Box 650
Iola, KS   66749-0650

Foundation type: Independent foundation
Limitations: Scholarships to full-time students at Allen County Community College, KS.
Financial data: Year ended 12/31/2004.
Assets, $324,676 (M); Expenditures, $10,387; Total giving, $7,493; Grants to individuals, totaling $7,493.
Type of support: Support to graduates or students of specific schools; Undergraduate support.
Application information: Contact fund for current application deadline/guidelines; Initial approach by letter or telephone.

Program description:

Scholarship Program: Scholarships are renewable provided that the recipient maintains at least a 3.0 GPA each semester. There is no support for summer semesters. Recipients must either live in the school's residence hall or commute from home.
EIN: 486322955

1819

Hendricks County Community Foundation

(formerly The White Lick Heritage Community Foundation, Inc.)
5055 E. Main St., Ste. A
Avon, IN   46123   (317) 718-1200
Contact: Delynn A. Daniel, Exec. Dir.
E-mail: deedee@hendrickscountycf.org;
URL: http://www.whitelick.org

Foundation type: Community foundation
Limitations: Scholarships to students in Hendricks County, IN, for higher education.
Publications: Annual report; Financial statement; Informational brochure; Newsletter.
Financial data: Year ended 12/31/2004. Assets, $4,837,987 (M); Expenditures, $481,178; Total giving, $244,232.
Type of support: Undergraduate support.
Application information: Application form required.
Deadline(s): Vary
Additional information: Contact the local Guidance Counselor, or see Web site, for complete application and program information.
Program description:
Lilly Endowment Community Scholarship: Full four-year undergraduate scholarships to all Hendricks County, IN, high school seniors who are ranked in the top 15 percent of their class. Students must be involved in the school's extracurricular program and community service activities. Students must choose to attend any IN college or university. A $700 stipend is provided for books and supplies.
EIN: 351878973

1820

Father Leo Henkel Scholarship Trust

c/o Citizens First National Bank
606 S. Main St.
Princeton, IL   61356
Application address: c/o William Novotney, LaSalle City Regional Superintendent of Schools, Ottawa, IL 61350, tel.: (815) 434-0780

Foundation type: Independent foundation
Limitations: Scholarships to residents of LaSalle, IL, who have graduated from local, state-accredited high schools for undergraduate study at accredited colleges or universities.
Financial data: Year ended 12/31/2004. Assets, $149,242 (M); Expenditures, $12,261; Total giving, $10,033; Grants to individuals, totaling $10,033.
Type of support: Support to graduates or students of specific schools; Undergraduate support.
Application information: Deadline Apr. 1; Completion of formal application required, including class rank, GPA, and ACT scores.
Program description:
Scholarship Program: Scholarships are renewable for up to four years of study, provided that the student maintains a minimum GPA of 3.51 on a 5.0 scale.
EIN: 363711096

1821

Keith Henney Trust

c/o Bank of America, N.A.
P.O. Box 1802
Providence, RI   02940-6768
Application address: c/o Leona Hurley, P.O. Box 2, Eaton Center, NH 03832

Foundation type: Independent foundation
Limitations: Scholarships to students of Kennett High School, NH, who have lived in Eaton, NH, for at least two years.
Financial data: Year ended 12/31/2004. Assets, $614,470 (M); Expenditures, $35,137; Total giving, $27,301; Grants to individuals, totaling $4,500.
Type of support: Support to graduates or students of specific schools; Undergraduate support.
Application information: Deadline Apr. 10; Initial approach by letter; Completion of formal application required.
EIN: 026065480

1822

Henrico Education Foundation

3820 Nine Mile Rd.
P.O. Box 23120
Richmond, VA   23223-0420   (804) 652-3869
Contact: Susan Stanley, Exec. Dir.
FAX: (804) 652-3856;
E-mail: sfstanle@henrico.k12.va.us; URL: http://www.cvco.org/education/henedf/about.htm

Foundation type: Public charity
Limitations: Scholarships to graduates of Henrico County public schools, VA.
Financial data: Year ended 06/30/2004. Assets, $472,623 (M); Expenditures, $139,949; Total giving, $71,999; Grants to individuals, 28 grants totaling $56,750 (high: $5,000, low: $1,000).
Type of support: Support to graduates or students of specific schools.
Application information:
Initial approach: E-mail or letter.
Additional information: Contact foundation for further application information.
EIN: 541893274

1823

Chester Henrizi Scholarship Fund

P.O. Box 100
Sussex, WI   53089-0100
Contact: Paul E. Schmidt, Tr.

Foundation type: Independent foundation
Limitations: Undergraduate scholarships to male graduates of Menomonee Falls High School, WI, who attend any campus or branch of the University of Wisconsin. Scholarships are renewable for up to four years of undergraduate study.
Financial data: Year ended 11/30/2004. Assets, $257,382 (M); Expenditures, $27,891; Total giving, $23,153; Grants to individuals, totaling $23,153.
Fields of interest: Men.
Type of support: Support to graduates or students of specific schools; Undergraduate support.
Application information: Application form required.
Initial approach: Letter or telephone.
Deadline(s): Apr. 27
EIN: 391501364

1824

The John Henry Company—Lou Brand Scholarship Foundation

5800 W. Grand River Ave.
Lansing, MI   48906-9111   (517) 886-2460
Contact: Shahriar Ghoddousi, Vice-Chair.

Foundation type: Company-sponsored foundation
Limitations: Scholarships to children of employees of the John Henry Company.
Financial data: Year ended 06/30/2002. Assets, $422,340 (M); Expenditures, $22,301; Total giving, $22,050; Grants to individuals, 37 grants totaling $22,050 (high: $1,500, low: $100).
Type of support: Employee-related scholarships.
Application information: Application form required.
Deadline(s): 3rd Monday in May
Additional information: Application should include transcripts and letter of recommendation from counselor.
EIN: 383243055

1825

Henry County Community Foundation, Inc.

P.O. Box 6006
New Castle, IN   47362   (765) 529-2235
Contact: Jerry Schaeffer, Exec. Dir.
FAX: (765) 529-2284;
E-mail: jerry@henrycountycf.org; URL: http://www.henrycountycf.org

Foundation type: Community foundation
Limitations: Scholarships to Henry County, IN, residents.
Publications: Application guidelines; Annual report; Grants list; Informational brochure (including application guidelines); Newsletter.
Financial data: Year ended 12/31/2004. Assets, $20,980,570 (M); Expenditures, $1,068,590; Total giving, $528,321.
Type of support: Scholarships—to individuals.
Application information: Applications accepted. Application form required. Application form available on the grantmaker's Web site.
Initial approach: Letter, telephone, or in person.
Copies of proposal: 1
Deadline(s): Mar. 20
Applicants should submit the following:
1) Transcripts
2) SAT
3) Letter(s) of recommendation
4) GPA
5) Financial information
6) Curriculum vitae
Additional information: Interviews required.
EIN: 311170412

1826

Henry County Health Center Foundation

Saunders Park
Mount Pleasant, IA   52641

Foundation type: Independent foundation
Limitations: Student loans and grants to attract and retain physicians who will provide medical care to citizens of Henry County, IA. Generally, the grants are given to cover the cost of interest on previously given loans.
Financial data: Year ended 06/30/2004. Assets, $628,911 (M); Expenditures, $48,878; Total giving, $38,199; Grants to individuals, totaling $28,199.
Fields of interest: Health care.
Type of support: Student loans—to individuals.

Application information: Applications not accepted.
EIN: 421354383

1827
Patrick Henry High School Foundation
4320 Newton Ave. N.
Minneapolis, MN 55412
Contact: Ann Kaan, Pres.

Foundation type: Independent foundation
Limitations: Scholarships to students from Patrick Henry High School, MN.
Financial data: Year ended 12/31/2004. Assets, $29,405 (M); Expenditures, $34,416; Total giving, $25,500; Grants to individuals, totaling $25,500.
Type of support: Support to graduates or students of specific schools; Undergraduate support.
Application information: Application form required.
   Additional information: Contact foundation for current application deadline.
EIN: 411970958

1828
Iva W. and Roy Henry Scholarship Trust
c/o The Citizens National Bank of Paris, Trust Dept.
P.O. Box 790
Paris, IL 61944-0790   (217) 465-7641
Contact: Chris Jurcin, Trust Off., The Citizens National Bank of Paris

Foundation type: Independent foundation
Limitations: Scholarships only to residents of Edgar County, IL.
Financial data: Year ended 12/31/2004. Assets, $240,770 (M); Expenditures, $9,692; Total giving, $6,000; Grants to individuals, totaling $6,000.
Type of support: Scholarships—to individuals.
Application information:
   Deadline(s): Apr. 15
   Additional information: Application forms are available at the bank.
EIN: 376115083

1829
May Thompson Henry Trust
(formerly Thompson Henry Trust)
c/o Central National Bank & Trust Co. of Enid
P.O. Box 3448
Enid, OK 73702-3448
Contact: Karen Holland, Trust Off., Central National Bank & Trust Co. of Enid
URL: http://onecentralsource.us/PDF_files/MayTHenryOnlineApp02.pdf

Foundation type: Independent foundation
Limitations: Scholarships to high school graduates for attendance at OK state-supported colleges, universities, and technical schools.
Financial data: Year ended 12/31/2004. Assets, $354,609 (M); Expenditures, $14,632; Total giving, $9,000; Grants to individuals, totaling $9,000.
Type of support: Scholarships—to individuals; Graduate support; Technical education support; Undergraduate support.
Application information: Application form required.
   Deadline(s): None
   Applicants should submit the following:
      1) Transcripts
      2) GPA
      3) Essay

Additional information: Application should include three letters of recommendation.
EIN: 731308178

1830
Charles D. "Bud" Hering, Jr. Foundation
634 W. Market St.
Tiffin, OH 44883-2516
Application address: c/o William C. Felton, 189 Gross St., Tiffin, OH 44883

Foundation type: Independent foundation
Limitations: Scholarships to students residing in the Tiffin, OH, area, for higher education.
Financial data: Year ended 12/31/2004. Assets, $271,529 (M); Expenditures, $15,474; Total giving, $13,375; Grants to individuals, totaling $13,375.
Type of support: Undergraduate support.
Application information: Applications by letter accepted throughout the year.
EIN: 341702565

1831
Heritage Club-A Christian Molokan Association
P.O. Box H
Downey, CA 90241-1556   (562) 861-2148
Contact: Morrie Adnoff, Pres.

Foundation type: Public charity
Limitations: Scholarships to university students who are residents of CA.
Financial data: Year ended 12/31/2003. Assets, $243,644 (M); Expenditures, $77,484; Total giving, $24,000; Grants to individuals, 25 grants totaling $24,000 (high: $2,000, low: $500).
Type of support: Undergraduate support.
Application information: Contact foundation for current application deadline/guidelines.
EIN: 953622329

1832
Heritage Fund - The Community Foundation of Bartholomew County
(formerly Heritage Fund of Bartholomew County, Inc.)
538 Franklin St.
P.O. Box 1547
Columbus, IN 47202-1547   (812) 376-7772
Contact: Sharon Risk Stark, C.E.O. and Pres.; For grants: Lyn Morgan, Prog. Off.
FAX: (812) 376-0051;
E-mail: hfgrants@sbcglobal.net; Additional E-mail: hfceo@sbcglobal.net; URL: http://www.heritagefundbc.com

Foundation type: Community foundation
Limitations: Scholarships primarily to residents of Bartholomew County, IN.
Publications: Application guidelines; Annual report; Informational brochure; Newsletter; Program policy statement.
Financial data: Year ended 12/31/2004. Assets, $41,418,537 (M); Expenditures, $3,715,478; Total giving, $2,508,868; Grants to individuals, 79 grants totaling $105,806 (high: $8,500, low: $250).
Type of support: Support to graduates or students of specific schools; Undergraduate support.
Application information: Applications accepted. Application form required.
   Initial approach: Letter.

Additional information: See Web site for current application deadline/guidelines and program listings.
EIN: 351343903

1833
Irvin E. Herr Foundation
c/o M&T Bank
21 E. Market St.
York, PA 17401-1500
Contact: Joe A. Macri, Trust Admin.
Application address: P.O. Box 2961, Harrisburg, PA 17105-2961

Foundation type: Independent foundation
Limitations: Scholarships to graduating high school seniors in Cumberland, Dauphin, Northumberland, and Perry counties, PA.
Financial data: Year ended 12/31/2004. Assets, $483,146 (M); Expenditures, $27,730; Total giving, $25,000; Grants to individuals, totaling $25,000.
Type of support: Support to graduates or students of specific schools; Undergraduate support.
Application information: Deadline Apr. 1; Contact foundation for current application guidelines.
EIN: 222550087

1834
Edith Fitton Herrin Trust
c/o Mellon Financial Corp.
P.O. Box 185
Pittsburgh, PA 15230-9897

Foundation type: Independent foundation
Limitations: Scholarships to medical students entering or attending any accredited medical school in Philadelphia, PA.
Financial data: Year ended 06/30/2005. Assets, $551,716 (M); Expenditures, $39,479; Total giving, $32,500; Grants to individuals, totaling $32,500.
Fields of interest: Medical school/education.
Type of support: Graduate support.
Application information: Contact financial aid offices for current application deadlines; Completion of formal application required; Applications available at medical schools' financial aid offices.
EIN: 236500294

1835
Fannie and John Hertz Foundation
2456 Research Dr.
Livermore, CA 94550-3850   (925) 373-1642
Contact: Linda Kubiak, Fellowship Admin.
FAX: (925) 373-6329; E-mail: askhertz@aol.com; URL: http://www.hertzfoundation.org

Foundation type: Independent foundation
Limitations: Graduate fellowships to students in physical applied sciences at specified nationwide institutions whose education may be of value to the defense of the U.S.
Publications: Informational brochure (including application guidelines).
Financial data: Year ended 06/30/2004. Assets, $27,418,680 (M); Expenditures, $4,529,982; Total giving, $3,265,851; Grants to individuals, 95 grants totaling $3,065,851 (high: $43,000, low: $400, average grant: $1,000-$40,000).
Fields of interest: Engineering school/education; Science, research; Science; Physical/earth

sciences; Astronomy; Chemistry; Mathematics; Physics; Computer science; Biological sciences.
Type of support: Fellowships; Support to graduates or students of specific schools; Graduate support.
Application information: Application form required.
Deadline(s): Nov. 2
Additional information: Applications should include 2 copies of transcripts, GPA, references, and personal statement; Technical interviews covering topics in physics, chemistry, mathematics, and engineering may be required; Application may be completed online.
Program description:
Graduate Fellowships in Applied Physical Sciences: These fellowships are awarded to worthy students of engineering and other applied physical sciences whose education may be of value to the defense of the U.S. Awards are made to outstanding students who seem likely to have an impact on scientific and technological advancement or to become exemplars of teaching skills in the applied sciences. Awards are made to enable such candidates to complete advanced degrees at the following selected universities: California Institute of Technology; all campuses of The University of California; Carnegie Mellon University; University of Chicago; University of Colorado at Boulder; Cornell University; Georgia Institute of Technology; Harvard University; Johns Hopkins University; University of Illinois at Urbana-Champaign; Massachusetts Institute of Technology; University of Michigan; University of Minnesota, Twin Cities Campus; New York University; Northwestern University; Polytechnic University; Princeton University; Purdue University; Rensselaer Polytechnic Institute; Rice University; University of Rochester; Stanford University; Texas A&M University; University of Texas at Austin; Vanderbilt University; University of Washington; University of Wisconsin—Madison; and Yale University. No professional degree programs (M.D., L.L.B., M.B.A., etc.), joint Ph.D./professional degree programs, or biological science studies are supported. Approximately 25 fellowships are awarded each year and are renewable for up to five years. The fellowship consists of a cost-of-education allowance and a living stipend of $25,000 per year based on a nine-month study year.
EIN: 362411723

1836
Mildred L. Herzberger Charitable Trust
3040 West Point Rd.
Lancaster, OH   43130   (740) 653-9730

Foundation type: Independent foundation
Limitations: Scholarships to graduates of Fairfield County, OH, high schools.
Financial data: Year ended 05/31/2005.
Assets, $456,286 (M); Expenditures, $24,263; Total giving, $19,400; Grants to individuals, 4 grants totaling $19,400 (high: $5,800, low: $3,900).
Type of support: Support to graduates or students of specific schools; Undergraduate support.
Application information: Application form required.
Deadline(s): 2nd Mon. in Mar.
Applicants should submit the following:
1) Transcripts
2) GPA
3) ACT
Additional information: This trust shares an application process with the J. Colin Campbell Scholarship Fund, the Alice Kindler Scholarship Fund, and the Mary Margaret Ackers Scholarship Trust.

Program description:
Harzberger Scholarship: Recipients must be residents of Fairfield County for a minimum of three years, and must have attended a high school in Fairfield County the last three years of their secondary education, including graduation. Recipients must maintain a good scholastic record, attend accredited state-supported colleges or universities or technical or vocational schools in the state of OH, and be full-time students with a minimum of fifteen hours per term and maintain a 2.0 GPA. Applicants need not be recent high school graduates.
EIN: 311435269

1837
George Hess Educational Fund
(also known as Hazel Porter Hess and George R. Hess Educational Trust)
c/o Wachovia Bank, N.A.
100 N. Main St., 13th Fl.
Winston-Salem, NC   27150

Foundation type: Independent foundation
Limitations: Scholarships to graduates of Loudoun County and Loudoun Valley high schools, PA, for higher education.
Financial data: Year ended 12/31/2004.
Assets, $563,563 (M); Expenditures, $41,606; Total giving, $35,000; Grants to individuals, 27 grants totaling $35,000 (high: $1,250, low: $1,250).
Type of support: Support to graduates or students of specific schools; Undergraduate support.
Application information: Applications and deadline/guidelines are available at Loudoun County and Loudoun Valley high schools.
EIN: 546200977

1838
Elmer E. Hester Foundation
503 6th Ave.
Benkelman, NE   69021
Contact: Edith Roundtree, Treas.

Foundation type: Independent foundation
Limitations: Scholarships to high school graduates of Dundy County, NE, for higher education.
Financial data: Year ended 12/31/2004.
Assets, $1,134,255 (M); Expenditures, $99,417; Total giving, $62,790; Grants to individuals, totaling $37,575.
Fields of interest: Education.
Type of support: Support to graduates or students of specific schools.
Application information: Applications accepted. Application form required.
Initial approach: Letter.
Deadline(s): July 15
Additional information: The Elmer E. Hester Foundation administers the Homesteader Awards Program.
EIN: 476026486

1839
Leonard W. & Helen L. Hester Trust
c/o B.G. Wolfe, Jr., C.P.A.
1626 Hedges Plz.
Nevada, MO   64772   (417) 667-3057
Application address: c/o David Swearingen, P.O. Box 388, Nevada, MO 64772

Foundation type: Independent foundation

Limitations: Scholarships for higher education to members of farm families in Vernon and Cedar counties, MO, seeking degrees in medicine, dentistry, veterinary medicine, teaching, or missionary studies.
Financial data: Year ended 12/31/2004.
Assets, $1,606,286 (M); Expenditures, $89,434; Total giving, $72,550; Grants to individuals, totaling $72,550.
Fields of interest: Dental school/education; Medical school/education; Nursing school/education; Teacher school/education; Theological school/education; Veterinary medicine; Christian agencies & churches.
Type of support: Scholarships—to individuals.
Application information: Application form required.
Deadline(s): Jan. 5 and June 15
Applicants should submit the following:
1) Transcripts
2) SAT
3) Letter(s) of recommendation
4) GPA
5) ACT
Additional information: Application must also include extracurricular activities list, and tax returns.
Program description:
Scholarship Program: Applicants must be in the upper one-fourth of their high school graduating classes. Recipients must attend school full-time.
EIN: 436478437

1840
Hewlett-Packard Company Foundation
3000 Hanover St., M.S. 20AH
Palo Alto, CA   94304-1112
Contact: Bess Stephens, Exec. Dir.
FAX: (650) 857-2982;
E-mail: philanthropy_ed@hp.com; Application address: P.O. Box 10301, Palo Alto, CA 94303; URL: http://www.hp.com/go/grants

Foundation type: Company-sponsored foundation
Limitations: Scholarships to individuals of African American, Latino or Native American descent for study in computer engineering and sciences.
Financial data: Year ended 10/31/2004.
Assets, $5,794,048 (M); Expenditures, $1,159,413; Total giving, $1,160,000.
Fields of interest: Engineering/technology; Computer science; Engineering; African Americans/Blacks; Hispanics/Latinos; Native Americans/American Indians.
Type of support: Scholarships—to individuals; Undergraduate support.
Application information: Applications accepted. Application form required.
Initial approach: Proposal.
Deadline(s): Nov. 22.
Additional information: Application available on Web site.
Program description:
Community College Pre-Engineering/Computer Science Grant Initiative: Grants to African American, Latino and Native American students engaged in pre-engineering courses so that they can successfully transfer into computer engineering and computer science majors at four-year universities. Deadline for proposals, Feb. 12.
EIN: 942618409

1841
Patricia Hickey Scholarship Fund
22563 Gill Rd.
Farmington Hills, MI 48335-4037
(248) 471-3048
Contact: Mary O. Hickey, Secy.

Foundation type: Operating foundation
Limitations: Scholarships to students of St. Agatha High School, MI, whose parents belong to the parish.
Financial data: Year ended 06/30/2003. Assets, $17,383 (M); Expenditures, $10,608; Total giving, $10,500; Grants to individuals, 3 grants totaling $10,500 (high: $3,500, low: $3,500).
Fields of interest: Roman Catholic agencies & churches.
Type of support: Support to graduates or students of specific schools; Undergraduate support.
Application information: Deadline Apr.; Completion of formal application required.
Program description:
   Scholarship Program: Recipients must be sophomores or above, carry a GPA of 2.8 or better and have a need for financial aid.
EIN: 382927699

1842
Ethel Brickey Hicks Charitable Corporation
P.O. Box 1990
Knoxville, TN 37901
Contact: James S. Tipton, Jr., Pres.

Foundation type: Independent foundation
Limitations: Scholarships to medical students who will practice in rural AR.
Financial data: Year ended 12/31/2004. Assets, $560,790 (M); Expenditures, $114,891; Total giving, $101,000; Grants to individuals, 7 grants totaling $101,000 (high: $25,000, low: $9,500).
Fields of interest: Medical school/education.
Type of support: Graduate support.
Application information: Applications accepted throughout the year; Completion of formal application required.
EIN: 710698966

1843
Hidalgo Independent School District Scholarship Foundation
P.O. Drawer D
Hidalgo, TX 78557 (956) 843-3124

Foundation type: Public charity
Limitations: Scholarships to graduates of Hidalgo Independent School District, TX, for undergraduate education.
Financial data: Year ended 08/31/2004. Assets, $902,577 (M); Expenditures, $60,279; Total giving, $57,279; Grants to individuals, totaling $57,279 (average grant: $300-$1,500).
Type of support: Support to graduates or students of specific schools; Undergraduate support.
Application information: Contact foundation for current application deadline/guidelines; Recipients are selected on the basis of academic merit, school and community involvement, and financial need.
EIN: 742895923

1844
Thomas and Jennie Hiebler Memorial Scholarship Fund Trust
c/o Union Bank of California, N.A.
400 California St.
San Francisco, CA 94104

Foundation type: Independent foundation
Limitations: Scholarships to deserving and financially needy students from Montrose High School and Mancos High School, both in CO, who will be attending a university in CO.
Financial data: Year ended 06/30/2005. Assets, $354,303 (M); Expenditures, $22,056; Total giving, $15,000.
Fields of interest: Education.
Type of support: Scholarships—to individuals; Support to graduates or students of specific schools; Undergraduate support; Grants for special needs.
Application information: Applications accepted.
   Deadline(s): Application by letter before graduation.
Program description:
   Scholarship Program: The scholarship committees of the school districts have been provided with the qualifications set forth in the Hieblers' will. Each year, based on these qualifications, the committees recommend graduating seniors. A trust committee then acts upon their recommendations.
EIN: 956111386

1845
David Downs Higbee Trust
c/o PNC Advisors
1600 Market St., 4th Fl.
Philadelphia, PA 19103-7240

Foundation type: Independent foundation
Limitations: Scholarships to graduates of Audubon High School, NJ.
Financial data: Year ended 12/31/2004. Assets, $422,146 (M); Expenditures, $29,330; Total giving, $23,561; Grants to individuals, totaling $23,561.
Type of support: Support to graduates or students of specific schools; Undergraduate support.
Application information: Applications not accepted.
EIN: 226375372

1846
Mary E. Higgins Educational Fund
c/o KeyBank N.A.
800 Superior Ave., 4th Fl.
Cleveland, OH 44114
Application address: c/o Guidance Dept., Gray-Gloucester High School, Lobby Hill Rd., Gray, ME 04034

Foundation type: Independent foundation
Limitations: Scholarships to residents of Gray, ME, who have graduated from Sadis, are made payable to the student and the school upon certification of completion of the first semester.
Financial data: Year ended 06/30/2003. Assets, $570 (M); Expenditures, $7,400; Total giving, $5,000; Grants to individuals, totaling $5,000.
Fields of interest: Vocational education.
Type of support: Support to graduates or students of specific schools; Undergraduate support.

Application information: Applications accepted throughout the year; Completion of formal application required.
EIN: 016067064

1847
Charles F. High Foundation
1232 St. Rt. 4 S.
Bucyrus, OH 44820 (419) 562-2074
Contact: John R. Clime, Admin.

Foundation type: Independent foundation
Limitations: Scholarships to male residents of OH to attend Ohio State University.
Financial data: Year ended 12/31/2004. Assets, $4,595,152 (M); Expenditures, $239,649; Total giving, $221,293; Grants to individuals, 104 grants totaling $221,293 (high: $3,542, low: $177).
Fields of interest: Men.
Type of support: Scholarships—to individuals; Support to graduates or students of specific schools.
Application information: Deadline June 1; Application by letter.
EIN: 346527860

1848
The High Foundation
P.O. Box 10008
Lancaster, PA 17605-0008
Contact: Sadie H. High, Chair.

Foundation type: Independent foundation
Limitations: Scholarships to children of employees of High Industries, Inc., and its affiliates and divisions, for undergraduate education at universities and colleges in the U.S.
Publications: Application guidelines; Program policy statement.
Financial data: Year ended 08/31/2005. Assets, $4,729,290 (M); Expenditures, $272,480; Total giving, $249,560; Grants to individuals, 8 grants totaling $26,400 (high: $3,000, low: $3,000).
Type of support: Employee-related scholarships.
Application information: Applications accepted. Application form required.
   Deadline(s): Dec. 15
   Additional information: Applications available from human resources departments.
EIN: 232149972

1849
Paul Hill and Julia Mercer Hill Charitable Foundation
c/o The Bank of Herrin
P.O. Box B
Herrin, IL 62948-3609 (618) 942-6666

Foundation type: Independent foundation
Limitations: Scholarships to Carterville High School, IL, graduates that are planning on attending John A. Logan College in Carterville, IL, only.
Financial data: Year ended 12/31/2004. Assets, $1,377,315 (M); Expenditures, $72,886; Total giving, $64,604; Grants to individuals, totaling $60,350.
Type of support: Scholarships—to individuals.
Application information: Applications by letter accepted throughout the year.
EIN: 371394605

1850
Hill Country Community Foundation
P.O. Box 10
Burnet, TX   78611

Foundation type: Community foundation
Limitations: Scholarships to graduating seniors of Hill County high schools, TX, for higher education.
Financial data: Year ended 12/31/2004.
Assets, $3,870,245 (M); Expenditures, $117,041; Total giving, $106,658; Grants to individuals, 100 grants totaling $83,592.
Type of support: Support to graduates or students of specific schools; Undergraduate support.
Application information:
    Initial approach: Letter.
    Additional information: Contact foundation for current application deadline/guidelines.
EIN: 742452519

1851
Hill Country Student Help
P.O. Box 1092
Fredericksburg, TX   78624-1092
Contact: Helen V. Birck, Secy.-Treas.

Foundation type: Independent foundation
Limitations: Student loans to graduates of Gillespie County high schools, TX, who have lived in Gillespie County for at least two years and are currently residents. Recipients may attend graduate schools, universities, colleges, or trade, business, or professional schools.
Financial data: Year ended 12/31/2004.
Assets, $771,776 (M); Expenditures, $8,503; Total giving, $0; Loans to individuals, 26 loans totaling $37,500.
Fields of interest: Higher education.
Type of support: Graduate support; Undergraduate support.
Application information: Application form required.
    Deadline(s): June 30 for fall semester, Nov. 30 for spring semester, Apr. 30 for summer semester
    Additional information: Applications must include a recent photograph and a brief letter outlining educational plans and goals.
Program description:
    Educational Loans: Loan amount is limited to $1,500 a year for four years of college or university education, or $2,000 a year for two years of trade, business, or professional education. Repayment of the loan begins six months after the recipient ceases to be a full-time student. Interest accrues at the rate of five percent per annum beginning with the first day of the loan disbursement. The recipient, spouse, and parents must sign a promissory note prior to fund disbursement.
EIN: 741473060

1852
Harold Newlin Hill Foundation
c/o Mellon Financial Corp.
P.O. Box 185
Pittsburgh, PA   15230-9897

Foundation type: Independent foundation
Limitations: Scholarships to children of employees of Asten Group, Inc.
Financial data: Year ended 06/30/2005.
Assets, $380,326 (M); Expenditures, $27,000; Total giving, $22,000; Grants to individuals, totaling $22,000.
Type of support: Employee-related scholarships.

Application information: Applications not accepted.
EIN: 236228294

1853
Elizabeth Hill Trust
212 W. Broadway
Eagle Grove, IA   50533-1710
Application address: c/o Opal Gibson, 1405 S.W. 2nd St., Eagle Grove, IA 50533-1924

Foundation type: Independent foundation
Limitations: Loans for higher education to needy and deserving residents of Eagle Grove, IA. No interest will be charged until six months after completion or termination of training.
Financial data: Year ended 12/31/2004.
Assets, $0 (M); Expenditures, $89,148; Total giving, $77,200; Loans to individuals, totaling $77,200.
Type of support: Student loans—to individuals.
Application information: Applications accepted. Application form required.
    Deadline(s): None
EIN: 426375488

1854
Ruth A. Hill Trust
c/o Mellon Financial Corp.
P.O. Box 185
Pittsburgh, PA   15230
Application address: c/o Marilyn King, 100 State St., Erie, PA 16507, tel.: (814) 874-5209

Foundation type: Independent foundation
Limitations: Scholarships to financially needy students who reside in Oil City, PA, and to African American students who reside in Venango County, City of Titusville, or areas served by Forest County Area Vocational School.
Financial data: Year ended 12/31/2004.
Assets, $7,212,137 (M); Expenditures, $332,372; Total giving, $328,805; Grants to individuals, 17 grants totaling $111,906 (high: $18,621, low: $265).
Fields of interest: Minorities.
Type of support: Support to graduates or students of specific schools; Undergraduate support.
Application information: Applications accepted. Application form required.
    Deadline(s): Deadline Mar. 15.
EIN: 256031644

1855
Hillsdale County Community Foundation
52 E. Bacon St.
P.O. Box 276
Hillsdale, MI   49242-0276   (517) 439-5101
Contact: Sharon E. Bisher, Exec. Dir.
FAX: (517) 439-5109; E-mail: info@abouthccf.org; URL: http://www.abouthccf.org

Foundation type: Community foundation
Limitations: Scholarships to Hillsdale County, MI, residents.
Publications: Application guidelines; Annual report; Financial statement; Informational brochure (including application guidelines); Newsletter.
Financial data: Year ended 09/30/2004.
Assets, $8,103,365 (M); Expenditures, $463,436; Total giving, $217,080.
Fields of interest: Education.
Type of support: Scholarships—to individuals.
Application information: Applications accepted.

Initial approach: Telephone or in person.
Deadline(s): Apr. 1 and Aug. 1.
Additional information: Contact foundation for current application guidelines.
EIN: 383001297

1856
William & Alice Hinckley Fund
2000 Broadway
Redwood City, CA   94063
Scholarship application address: c/o The Unitarian Church, 1187 Franklin St., San Francisco, CA 94109

Foundation type: Independent foundation
Limitations: Graduate scholarships limited to northern CA residents, studying in the Bay Area, in the humanitarian professions, including nurses, physicians, counselors, and ministers.
Financial data: Year ended 12/31/2004.
Assets, $2,298,486 (M); Expenditures, $123,690; Total giving, $120,410; Grants to individuals, 18 grants totaling $45,000 (high: $3,000, low: $2,000).
Fields of interest: Medical school/education; Nursing school/education; Theological school/education; Health care; Mental health, treatment; Leadership development.
Type of support: Graduate support.
Application information: Applications not accepted.
EIN: 946080975

1857
E. A. Hinderman Scholarship Memorial, Inc.
P.O. Box 236
Whitefish, MT   59937
Application address: c/o Guidance Counselor, Whitefish High School, 600 E. 2nd St., Whitefish, MT 59937

Foundation type: Operating foundation
Limitations: Scholarships to financially needy graduating seniors who attend Whitefish High School, MT.
Financial data: Year ended 12/31/2003.
Assets, $8,805 (M); Expenditures, $29,359; Total giving, $27,500; Grants to individuals, 6 grants totaling $27,500 (high: $5,000, low: $2,500).
Type of support: Support to graduates or students of specific schools; Undergraduate support.
Application information: Deadline Apr. 30; Application by letter, including high school transcript and college application.
EIN: 810392053

1858
Jud W. Hines Honorary Scholarship Trust
c/o Neil Detrich
P.O. Box 589
Chapman, KS   67431-0589
Application address: 437 N. Marshall, Chapman, KS 67431, tel.: (785) 922-6225

Foundation type: Independent foundation
Limitations: Scholarships to graduates of Chapman High School, KS.
Financial data: Year ended 12/31/2004.
Assets, $233,852 (M); Expenditures, $7,787; Total giving, $7,250; Grants to individuals, totaling $7,250.
Type of support: Support to graduates or students of specific schools; Undergraduate support.

Application information: Deadline Apr. 1; Application by letter.
EIN: 480930179

1859
Grove W. & Agnes M. Hinman Charitable Foundation

P.O. Box 209
Hamilton, NY 13346-0209
Contact: Susan Schapiro, Tr.

Foundation type: Independent foundation
Limitations: Scholarships to students in the Morrisville-Eaton, Hamilton, and Madison, NY, school districts.
Financial data: Year ended 04/30/2005. Assets, $827,717 (M); Expenditures, $63,508; Total giving, $50,100; Grants to individuals, totaling $41,500.
Type of support: Support to graduates or students of specific schools; Undergraduate support.
Application information: Applications accepted after May 1; Completion of formal application required.
EIN: 237194828

1860
Hinton Area Foundation

P.O. Box 217
Hinton, WV 25951-0217 (304) 466-5232
Contact: William "Skip" Mills, Pres.
E-mail: skipmills@stargate.net; Application address: c/o Richard Lawrence, 110 James St., Hinton, WV 25951; URL: http://givetowestvirginia.org/localcom/index.htm

Foundation type: Community foundation
Limitations: Scholarships to graduates of Summers County, WV, public schools, for higher education.
Financial data: Year ended 12/31/2004. Assets, $1,598,840 (M); Expenditures, $49,758; Total giving, $41,285; Grants to individuals, 11 grants totaling $19,180 (high: $1,680, low: $250).
Fields of interest: Medical school/education.
Type of support: Support to graduates or students of specific schools; Undergraduate support.
Application information: Deadline May 18; Completion of formal application required.
Program descriptions:
Campaign 2000 Scholarship Fund: Scholarships to graduates of Summers County public schools or to residents of Summers County who have maintained at least a 3.0 GPA for the four years of high school.
CHPR Gwinn Family Scholarship Fund: Scholarships to graduates of Summers County public schools or to residents of Summers County for undergraduate study at Concord College.
Claude Johnson Memorial Scholarship Fund: Scholarships of $500 each to graduates of Summers County public schools who have maintained at least a 2.75 GPA for the four years of high school.
First National Bank of Hinton Scholarship Trust: Scholarships to graduates of Summers County public schools or to residents of Summers County. Each recipient will be chosen based on evaluation of his or her application information rather than by academic records.
First Presbyterian Church Scholarship Fund: Scholarships to graduates of Summers County High School, for undergraduate study at an accredited college or university. Scholarships may be renewed for up to four years annually.
Joyce Jarrell Memorial Scholarship Fund: Scholarships to graduates of Summers County public schools or to residents of Summers County, who have maintained a GPA or at least 3.0 for the four years of high school and have an ACT score of at least 20.
Dr. Matthew Ellison Memorial Scholarship Fund: Scholarships to graduates of Summers County public schools for undergraduate study at colleges and universities, with priority given to students entering the field of medicine. Recipients must have maintained a GPA of 3.0 during the four years of high school.
National Bank of Summers Scholarship Fund: Scholarships to graduates of Summers County public schools or to residents of Summers County, for undergraduate study at colleges and universities.
Paul Hess Memorial Scholarship Fund: Scholarships to graduates of Summers County public schools for undergraduate study at colleges and universities.
EIN: 550716276

1861
Florence Hirsch Educational Endowment Fund

c/o Commerce Bank of St. Joseph, N.A.
P.O. Box 1119
St. Joseph, MO 64502-9983
Application address: c/o St. Joseph School District, 10th & Felix Sts., St. Joseph, MO 64501

Foundation type: Independent foundation
Limitations: Scholarships for St. Joseph, MO, residents attending four-year colleges.
Financial data: Year ended 12/31/2004. Assets, $1,351,472 (M); Expenditures, $72,758; Total giving, $57,750; Grants to individuals, totaling $57,750.
Type of support: Undergraduate support.
Application information: Applications accepted throughout the year; Completion of formal application required.
EIN: 436068192

1862
Eric G. Hirsch Memorial Trust

5297 Sycamore Valley Ln.
Navasota, TX 77868-6019
Application address: c/o Joyce Finch, Klein Forest High School, 11400 Misty Valley, Houston, TX 77066

Foundation type: Independent foundation
Limitations: Scholarships to graduating seniors of Klein Forest High School, Houston, TX.
Financial data: Year ended 12/31/2004. Assets, $96,634 (M); Expenditures, $8,812; Total giving, $8,750; Grants to individuals, totaling $8,750.
Type of support: Support to graduates or students of specific schools; Undergraduate support.
Application information: Deadline Apr. 20; Completion of formal application required; Applications available at high school.
EIN: 760148604

1863
Harold Hirsch Scholarship Fund

c/o Stack & Rogers
1 Buckhead Plz., Ste. 920
3060 Peachtree Rd. N.W.
Atlanta, GA 30305 (404) 231-1313
Contact: Ronald W. Rogers, Tr.

Foundation type: Independent foundation
Limitations: Scholarships to financially needy Atlanta, GA, residents for secondary and college education.
Financial data: Year ended 06/30/2005. Assets, $2,497,104 (M); Expenditures, $123,802; Total giving, $100,000.
Fields of interest: Secondary school/education.
Type of support: Precollege support; Undergraduate support.
Application information: Applications accepted.
Initial approach: Letter.
Deadline(s): At least six months to the date when assistance is needed.
Applicants should submit the following:
1) Transcripts
2) Financial information
EIN: 586036125

1864
L. Hirsch Scholarship Fund

(also known as The Hirsch Foundation)
c/o Wilmington Trust Co.
Rodney Sq. N.
1100 N. Market St., Ste. 505610
Wilmington, DE 19890-0900

Foundation type: Independent foundation
Limitations: Undergraduate scholarships to students of Milford High School, DE.
Financial data: Year ended 12/31/2004. Assets, $211,704 (M); Expenditures, $9,373; Total giving, $6,000; Grants to individuals, totaling $6,000.
Type of support: Support to graduates or students of specific schools; Undergraduate support.
Application information: Applications accepted throughout the year; Completion of formal application required; Applications available from Milford High School guidance office.
EIN: 516013661

1865
Hirth Family Foundation, Inc.

c/o Steven H. Hirth
36 W. 44th St., Ste. 1412
New York, NY 10036-8105
FAX: (646) 416-6290; E-mail: shhirt@aol.com

Foundation type: Independent foundation
Limitations: Scholarships to residents of CT to attend any college or university in CT.
Financial data: Year ended 12/31/2004. Assets, $18,348 (M); Expenditures, $57,426; Total giving, $55,000; Grants to individuals, totaling $50,000.
Type of support: Undergraduate support.
Application information: Applications not accepted.
Additional information: Unsolicited requests for funds not considered or acknowledged.
EIN: 651179388

1866
Orris C. Hirtzel and Beatrice Dewey Hirtzel Memorial Foundation

(formerly Elec Material Hirtzel Memorial Foundation)
c/o Mellon Financial Corp.
P.O. Box 185
Pittsburgh, PA 15230 (412) 234-0023
Contact: Laurie Moritz

Foundation type: Independent foundation
Limitations: Scholarships to students completing secondary school with close geographical proximity to the North East, PA, and Erie County, PA.
Financial data: Year ended 12/31/2004. Assets, $22,738,299 (M); Expenditures, $1,053,461; Total giving, $943,900.
Type of support: Undergraduate support.
Application information: Application form required.
Initial approach: Letter.
EIN: 256018933

1867
His Storehouse Foundation
699 W. Line St., Ste. E
Bishop, CA 93514-3334
Contact: Leslie L. Chapman, C.F.O.

Foundation type: Independent foundation
Limitations: Scholarships to students residing in Mammoth Lakes, CA, for higher education.
Financial data: Year ended 12/31/2004. Assets, $27,621 (M); Expenditures, $36,355; Total giving, $26,000; Grants to individuals, totaling $26,000.
Type of support: Undergraduate support.
Application information: Contact foundation for current application deadline/guidelines; Completion of formal application required.
EIN: 770457212

1868
Hispanic Association of Colleges and Universities
8415 Datapoint Dr., Ste. 400
San Antonio, TX 78229 (210) 692-3805
Contact: Antonio Flores Ph.D., Pres.
FAX: (210) 692-0823; E-mail: hacu@hacu.net;
URL: http://www.hacu.net

Foundation type: Public charity
Limitations: Scholarships to Hispanic students who wish to study engineering and science at a HACU member institution.
Financial data: Year ended 12/31/2003. Assets, $3,153,372 (M); Expenditures, $9,278,180; Total giving, $275,408; Grants to individuals, 15 grants totaling $29,408.
Fields of interest: Hispanics/Latinos.
Type of support: Undergraduate support.
Application information:
Initial approach: E-mail.
Applicants should submit the following:
1) Letter(s) of recommendation
Additional information: Contact foundation for further application information.
EIN: 742466103

1869
Hispanic Heritage Foundation
(formerly Hispanic Heritage Awards)
2600 Virginia Ave., N.W., Ste. 406
Washington, DC 20037 (202) 861-9797
Contact: Jose Antonio Tijerino, Pres. and C.E.O.; For scholarships: Clarissa Sandoval
FAX: (202) 861-9799;
E-mail: contact@hispanicheritage.org; URL: http://www.hispanicheritage.org

Foundation type: Public charity
Limitations: Scholarships to graduating high school seniors of Hispanic descent, based on academic achievement and community service.
Financial data: Year ended 12/31/2003. Assets, $340,946 (M); Expenditures, $2,594,179; Total giving, $2,300,000.
Fields of interest: Hispanics/Latinos.
Type of support: Undergraduate support.
Application information: Applications accepted. Application form required. Application form available on the grantmaker's Web site.
Initial approach: E-mail.
Copies of proposal: 3
Deadline(s): Feb. 3
Applicants should submit the following:
1) Transcripts
2) Work samples
3) Letter(s) of recommendation
4) GPA
5) Essay
Additional information: See Web site for further program information.
EIN: 521818255

1870
Hispanic Scholarship Fund
(formerly National Hispanic Scholarship Fund, Inc.)
55 2nd St., Ste. 1500
San Francisco, CA 94105 (415) 808-2300
Contact: Selection Comm.
FAX: (415) 808-2302; E-mail: info@hsf.net;
URL: http://www.hsf.net

Foundation type: Public charity
Limitations: Scholarships to outstanding Latino students throughout the U.S. and Puerto Rico, for higher education.
Publications: Annual report; Informational brochure (including application guidelines); Newsletter.
Financial data: Year ended 03/31/2005. Assets, $41,473,414 (M); Expenditures, $32,515,861; Total giving, $25,342,091; Grants to individuals, 7,148 grants totaling $25,342,091 (high: $23,000, low: $166).
Fields of interest: African Americans/Blacks; Hispanics/Latinos.
Type of support: Undergraduate support; Grants for special needs.
Application information: Application form required.
Initial approach: Letter with SASE.
Deadline(s): Applications accepted throughout the year
Additional information: See Web site for further application information.
Program descriptions:
College Scholarship: This program assists U.S. citizens and permanent residents of Latino background earning their degrees at four-year institutions. Basic program requirements are that the students have completed 12 credits of college work, have a minimum 2.7 GPA, and are enrolled full-time at accredited colleges in the U.S. and Puerto Rico. Scholarships ranging from $1,000 to $3,000 are available based on donor restrictions which may include fields of study, specific

geographical areas, etc. The program is open to undergraduate and graduate students.
Community College Transfer Program: This program was recently developed to assist Latinos in making the transition from community college to four-year institutions. Scholarships are available for full-time community college students who are transferring to a four-year institution.
High School Program: This program is designed to assist Latinos making the transition from high school to a four-year institution. Funded mainly through public school district workplace giving campaigns, this program focuses on helping graduating high school seniors from participating areas. Seniors are eligible for scholarships if they have a minimum GPA of 3.0 and have been accepted to attend college in the fall. In addition, there are a small number of other targeted regional programs.
New Horizons Scholarships Program: The New Horizon Scholars Program is offered in partnership with the Hispanic Scholarship Fund and the Thurgood Marshall Scholarship Fund. The scholarship supports Hispanic and African American students who are infected with Hepatitis C or who are dependents of someone with Hepatitis C. Deadline Feb. 20.
EIN: 521051044

1871
Hispanic Scholarship Fund Institute
1001 Connecticut Ave., N.W., Ste. 632
Washington, DC 20036 (202) 296-0009
Contact: Sara Martinez Tucker, Pres. and C.E.O.
FAX: (202) 296-3633; E-mail: info@hsfi.org;
URL: http://www.hsfi.org

Foundation type: Public charity
Limitations: Scholarships to needy Hispanic American students for higher education.
Financial data: Year ended 03/31/2004. Assets, $99,100 (M); Expenditures, $834,920; Total giving, $294,000; Grants to individuals, 104 grants totaling $294,000 (high: $3,000, low: $200).
Fields of interest: Higher education; Hispanics/Latinos.
Type of support: Scholarships—to individuals.
Application information: Applications accepted. Application form required.
Initial approach: Letter.
EIN: 542014609

1872
The Hitachi Foundation
1509 22nd St., N.W.
Washington, DC 20037-1073 (202) 457-0588
Contact: Barbara Dyer, C.E.O. and Pres.; Mark Popovich, Sr. Prog. Off.
URL: http://www.hitachifoundation.org

Foundation type: Independent foundation
Limitations: Awards by nomination only to high school seniors who make significant contributions in community service.
Publications: Application guidelines; Annual report; Financial statement; Grants list; Informational brochure; Occasional report.
Financial data: Year ended 12/31/2004. Assets, $22,731,308 (M); Expenditures, $2,579,322; Total giving, $1,015,615.
Fields of interest: Education; Children/youth, services; Community development, volunteer services.
Type of support: Awards/grants by nomination only; Awards/prizes; Undergraduate support.

Application information:
Deadline(s): Apr. 1
Additional information: Nomination should include letters of recommendation; Students may not nominate themselves.
Program description:
Yoshiyama Award for Exemplary Community Service: Each award is $5,000, dispensed over two years, and is to be used at the discretion of the recipient. The award recognizes exemplary service rather than academic achievement. It is not a scholarship. Recipients are selected by a national panel of outstanding leaders representing various professions but all committed to the development of leadership and civic responsibility. Selection of recipients is based on service rather than on academic achievement or extracurricular activities. GPA, SAT scores, and school club memberships are not considered in the selection process. Recipients are invited, but not required, to participate in a special award ceremony in Washington, DC, and a retreat. These activities allow recipients to exchange ideas and strategies, develop a network, and increase their knowledge and skills in leadership and effective social change.
EIN: 521429292

1873
Trustees of Hitchcock Free Academy
P.O. Box 155
Brimfield, MA   01010
Application address: c/o Guidance Office, Tantasqua Regional H.S., 319 Brookfield Rd., Sturbridge, MA 01566

Foundation type: Operating foundation
Limitations: Scholarships to high school seniors of Brimfield, Holland, Sturbridge, and Wales, MA, and carry at least a 2.5 GPA.
Financial data: Year ended 12/31/2004. Assets, $2,468,136 (M); Expenditures, $165,934; Total giving, $6,850; Grants to individuals, 21 grants totaling $6,850.
Type of support: Undergraduate support.
Application information: Application form required.
Deadline(s): Mar.
Additional information: Interview required.
Program description:
Scholarship Program: Scholarships are awarded on the basis of accomplishments, scholarship, and merit. These are assessed by evaluating grades, class rank, extracurricular activities, effort, work record, and standardized test scores. Financial need is not a primary consideration. Payment of scholarships is made directly to the student upon proof of enrollment in a college level program.
EIN: 042277210

1874
Jimmy V. & Lucile A. Hoar Memorial Scholarship Fund
P.O. Box 103
Lewis, KS   67552-0103
Contact: Bill Updegrove, Treas.
Application address: P.O. Box 86, Lewis, KS 67522, tel.: (620) 324-5434

Foundation type: Independent foundation
Limitations: Scholarships to graduates of Lewis High School, KS.
Financial data: Year ended 12/31/2004. Assets, $882,012 (M); Expenditures, $57,722; Total giving, $54,000.
Type of support: Support to graduates or students of specific schools.

Application information: Application form required.
Deadline(s): May 25
EIN: 431917366

1875
Bertram & Alta Heartt Hochmark Scholarship Foundation
(also known as B. A. Hochmark Scholarship Trust)
c/o Well Fargo Bank Northwest, N.A.
P.O. Box 21927
Seattle, WA   98111

Foundation type: Independent foundation
Limitations: Scholarships to graduates of Polson High School, MT.
Financial data: Year ended 10/31/2004. Assets, $276,715 (M); Expenditures, $16,066; Total giving, $12,000; Grants to individuals, totaling $12,000.
Type of support: Support to graduates or students of specific schools; Undergraduate support.
Application information: Contact foundation for current application deadline; Initial approach by letter or telephone.
EIN: 816064383

1876
Charles Hockenberry Foundation
c/o City National Bank
116 S. Blossom St.
Shenandoah, IA   51601-1732   (712) 246-2205
Contact: George Perry, Pres.

Foundation type: Independent foundation
Limitations: Scholarships to disadvantaged youths residing in Page County, IA.
Financial data: Year ended 12/31/2004. Assets, $1,472,664 (M); Expenditures, $86,814; Total giving, $67,052; Grants to individuals, totaling $66,352.
Fields of interest: Music; Education.
Type of support: Scholarships—to individuals.
Application information: Applications accepted throughout the year; Completion of formal application required, including a copy of parents' most recent tax return.
EIN: 421382905

1877
Al Hodes Charitable Trust
c/o Marshall & Ilsley Bank
P.O. Box 2980
Milwaukee, WI   53201

Foundation type: Independent foundation
Limitations: Scholarships to nursing students attending North Central Technical College in Wausau, WI.
Financial data: Year ended 06/30/2005. Assets, $352,302 (M); Expenditures, $26,502; Total giving, $23,000; Grants to individuals, totaling $23,000.
Fields of interest: Nursing school/education.
Type of support: Support to graduates or students of specific schools; Technical education support; Undergraduate support.
Application information: Applications not accepted.
EIN: 396480058

1878
The Helen Hodges Educational Charitable Foundation
c/o American State Bank, Trust Dept.
P.O. Box 1401
Lubbock, TX   79408   (806) 767-7000
Contact: Marion Bryant, Trust Off., American State Bank

Foundation type: Independent foundation
Limitations: Scholarships to junior and senior high school students in Lubbock, TX.
Financial data: Year ended 12/31/2004. Assets, $411,247 (M); Expenditures, $23,703; Total giving, $18,250; Grants to individuals, 15 grants totaling $18,250.
Type of support: Support to graduates or students of specific schools; Undergraduate support.
Application information: Deadline July 15; Completion of formal application required, including transcripts, college letter of acceptance, and handwritten statement of 250 words or less describing personal goals and career plans.
EIN: 510183778

1879
J. M. Hodges Educational Fund Trust
c/o Community Bank, N.A.
201 N. Union St.
Olean, NY   14760-2738

Foundation type: Independent foundation
Limitations: Student loans to high school students within a ten-mile radius of Olean, NY.
Financial data: Year ended 12/31/2004. Assets, $281,145 (M); Expenditures, $17,211; Total giving, $13,425; Loans to individuals, totaling $13,425.
Fields of interest: Education.
Type of support: Student loans—to individuals.
Application information:
Deadline(s): May 15
Additional information: Application by letter.
EIN: 166136464

1880
Mary E. Hodges Fund
c/o Masonic Grand Lodge Charities
222 Taunton Ave.
East Providence, RI   02914   (401) 435-4650
Contact: John M. Faulhaber, Secy.

Foundation type: Independent foundation
Limitations: Student aid to individuals who have a RI masonic affiliation or who have been residents of RI for at least five years.
Financial data: Year ended 10/31/2004. Assets, $3,938,647 (M); Expenditures, $442,543; Total giving, $388,050; Grants to individuals, totaling $146,250.
Fields of interest: Fraternal societies.
Type of support: Scholarships—to individuals.
Application information: Deadline Apr. 18; Initial approach by letter; Completion of formal application required.
EIN: 056049444

1881
Hodnefield Family Foundation, Inc.
P.O. Box 549
Railroad Flat, CA   95248
Contact: Gerald E. Hodnefield, Secy.

Foundation type: Independent foundation

Limitations: Scholarships to residents of CA for higher education.
Financial data: Year ended 12/31/2004. Assets, $146,512 (M); Expenditures, $13,937; Total giving, $12,727; Grants to individuals, totaling $12,727.
Type of support: Undergraduate support.
Application information: Unsolicited requests for funds not accepted.
EIN: 943302456

1882
John F. Hoeting Scholarship Fund

c/o Bank of America, N.A.
P.O. Box 40200
Jacksonville, FL   32203-0200
Application address: c/o Bank of America, N.A., Attn.: Sally Herny, 600 Cleveland St., 3rd Fl., Clearwater, FL 33755-4151

Foundation type: Independent foundation
Limitations: Scholarships to graduating seniors of Hudson High School, FL, for higher education.
Financial data: Year ended 06/30/2005. Assets, $461,035 (M); Expenditures, $25,278; Total giving, $17,916; Grants to individuals, 7 grants totaling $17,916 (high: $3,333, low: $2,500).
Type of support: Support to graduates or students of specific schools; Undergraduate support.
Application information: Applications by letter accepted throughout the year.
EIN: 597102513

1883
James R. Hoffa Memorial Scholarship Fund, Inc.

25 Louisiana Ave. N.W.
Washington, DC   20001-2130   (202) 624-7471
Contact: Cheryl L. Johnson, Pres.
E-mail: scholarship@teamster.org; URL: http://www.teamster.org/resources/students/scholarship/scholarship.htm

Foundation type: Public charity
Limitations: Scholarships to children, grandchildren, and financial dependents of Teamster members for undergraduate education.
Financial data: Year ended 12/31/2004. Assets, $4,290,517 (M); Expenditures, $452,990; Total giving, $404,000; Grants to individuals, 125 grants totaling $404,000 (high: $10,000, low: $1,000).
Fields of interest: Labor unions/organizations.
Type of support: Undergraduate support.
Application information: Deadline Mar. 31. Completion of formal application required, including two letters of recommendation for American applicants and three letters of recommendation for Canadian applicants, SAT or ACT scores, and transcript.
EIN: 522206826

1884
Valeria E. Hoffert Scholarship Trust

c/o M&T Bank
21 E. Market St., MC 402130
York, PA   17401-1500

Foundation type: Independent foundation
Limitations: Scholarships to graduates of Reading Senior High School, PA.
Financial data: Year ended 12/31/2004. Assets, $1,148,202 (M); Expenditures, $63,506; Total giving, $58,000; Grants to individuals, totaling $58,000.
Type of support: Support to graduates or students of specific schools; Undergraduate support.
Application information: Deadline Apr. 1; Initial approach by letter or telephone; Completion of formal application required; Interviews required.
EIN: 237763256

1885
Augustus L. & Jennie D. Hoffman Foundation

c/o JPMorgan Chase Bank
P.O. Box 31412
Rochester, NY   14603-1412
Application address: Marjorie Perez for Scholarships or James Brady for grants, c/o Wayne County Historical Society, 22 Butternut St., Lyon, NY 14489, tel.: (315) 946-6191

Foundation type: Operating foundation
Limitations: Scholarships to Wayne County, NY, high school seniors for two or four years. Also, one-time payment awards to winners of the Original Historical Research Essay Contest, open only to Wayne County, NY, high school seniors.
Publications: Application guidelines.
Financial data: Year ended 12/31/2003. Assets, $981,371 (M); Expenditures, $26,715; Total giving, $5,325; Grants to individuals, totaling $5,325.
Fields of interest: History/archaeology.
Type of support: Support to graduates or students of specific schools; Awards/prizes; Undergraduate support.
Application information: Deadline on or before Apr. 30; Initial approach by letter.
Program description:
   Hoffman Foundation's Original Historical Research Essay Contest: For Wayne County High School seniors, enrolled since Oct. 1 of the current school year. The research paper must be at least 2,000 words. The topic of the paper must be concerned with some phase of Wayne County historic or civic affairs. The paper must include original research, accurately documented. It is recommended that applicants register their topic at the County Historian's office to prevent papers with the same topic. Papers will be evaluated by the following guidelines: form, creativity, historical content, accuracy, documentation, and miscellaneous (e.g. pictures, illustrations, diagrams).
EIN: 166014973

1886
James M. Hoffman Scholarship Trust

c/o Wachovia Bank, N.A
P.O. Box 1000
Anniston, AL   36202-1000

Foundation type: Independent foundation
Limitations: Scholarships to seniors at Calhoun County, AL, schools.
Publications: Application guidelines.
Financial data: Year ended 09/30/2004. Assets, $175,446 (M); Expenditures, $9,684; Total giving, $7,150; Grants to individuals, 10 grants totaling $6,500.
Type of support: Support to graduates or students of specific schools; Undergraduate support.
Application information: Applications accepted. Application form required.
   Initial approach: Letter.
   Deadline(s): Mar.

Additional information: Application must include a copy of applicant's W-2 form; Applications not accepted from individuals residing outside of stated geographic restriction.
EIN: 636077959

1887
Robert E. Hogsett Foundation, Inc

P.O. Box 995
Fort Morgan, CO   80701-0995   (970) 867-2447
Contact: Eric C. Jorgenson, Pres.

Foundation type: Independent foundation
Limitations: Scholarships to graduates of Brush and Fort Morgan high schools, CO.
Financial data: Year ended 06/30/2005. Assets, $1,418,866 (M); Expenditures, $86,750; Total giving, $81,250; Grants to individuals, totaling $8,000.
Type of support: Support to graduates or students of specific schools; Undergraduate support.
Application information: Applications accepted.
   Initial approach: Letter.
EIN: 742272978

1888
Joseph J. Hohner Scholarship Fund

c/o Harris Trust and Savings Bank
P.O. Box 755
Chicago, IL   60690   (312) 461-6735
Contact: Cheryl Fair, V.P., Harris Trust & Savings Bank

Foundation type: Independent foundation
Limitations: Scholarships to worthy students at all educational levels who are residents of LaSalle County, IL.
Financial data: Year ended 05/31/2004. Assets, $1,264,029 (M); Expenditures, $64,908; Total giving, $50,400; Grants to individuals, totaling $50,400.
Fields of interest: Education.
Type of support: Scholarships—to individuals.
Application information: Applications accepted.
   Additional information: Application should include a proposal.
Program description:
   Scholarship Program: Students should show promise of intellectual or moral ability and be deserving of financial support.
EIN: 366644741

1889
Holce Logging Company Scholarship Fund, Inc.

P.O. Box 127
Vernonia, OR   97064-0127

Foundation type: Company-sponsored foundation
Limitations: Scholarships to recent graduates (within five years) of Vernonia High School, OR.
Publications: Application guidelines.
Financial data: Year ended 04/30/2005. Assets, $247,319 (M); Expenditures, $12,284; Total giving, $12,200; Grants to individuals, 12 grants totaling $12,200 (high: $2,000, low: $300).
Type of support: Support to graduates or students of specific schools; Undergraduate support.
Application information:
   Applicants should submit the following:
   1) Transcripts
   2) SAT
   3) Resume
   4) Letter(s) of recommendation

5) GPA
6) Essay
7) ACT
Additional information: Contact high school counselor for current application deadline/ guidelines. Application address: c/o Guidance Counselor, Vernonia High School, 399 Bridge St., Vernonia, OR 97064.
EIN: 930845692

1890
Holland Family Scholarship Foundation
(formerly C.V. Holland, Maybelle Holland, & John Holland Scholarship Fund)
c/o AmSouth Bank
315 Deaderick St., 4th Fl.
Nashville, TN 37237-0401
Contact: Harry Brittain
Application address: P.O. Box 520, Tullahoma, TN 37388

Foundation type: Independent foundation
Limitations: Scholarships to seniors at Tullahoma High School, TN.
Financial data: Year ended 05/31/2005. Assets, $476,734 (M); Expenditures, $27,098; Total giving, $22,900; Grants to individuals, 62 grants totaling $22,900.
Type of support: Support to graduates or students of specific schools; Undergraduate support.
Application information: Deadline Apr. 1; Initial approach by letter; Completion of formal application required.
EIN: 626141452

1891
Dewitt and Parke Holland Foundation, Inc.
79 W. Monroe St., Ste. 1119
Chicago, IL 60603-4993

Foundation type: Independent foundation
Limitations: Scholarships to students of agriculture at Joliet Junior College.
Financial data: Year ended 10/31/2004. Assets, $792,472 (M); Expenditures, $81,654; Total giving, $81,649; Grants to individuals, totaling $81,649.
Fields of interest: Agriculture.
Type of support: Support to graduates or students of specific schools; Undergraduate support.
Application information: Applications not accepted.
EIN: 363397703

1892
Audrey Holliday Scholarship Fund
c/o Patricia J. Brenner
3116 Wilderness Dr. S.E.
Olympia, WA 98501-4963
Application address: c/o Scholarship Comm., Gresham Union High School, Gresham, OR 97030

Foundation type: Operating foundation
Limitations: Scholarships to students at Gresham High School, OR, intending to major in the physical or sciences, or liberal arts.
Financial data: Year ended 12/31/2002. Assets, $405,887 (M); Expenditures, $15,556; Total giving, $14,000; Grants to individuals, 3 grants totaling $14,000 (high: $6,750, low: $3,625).
Fields of interest: Humanities; Science; Social sciences.

Type of support: Support to graduates or students of specific schools; Undergraduate support.
Application information: Applications accepted throughout the year; Contact fund for current application guidelines.
Program description:
Scholarship Program: Recipients must maintain at least a 3.5 GPA in college.
EIN: 916340777

1893
Hazel Holm Scholarship Fund
c/o Arthur P. Folden
2508 Buckingham Dr. S.E.
Olympia, WA 98501 (360) 352-1845

Foundation type: Operating foundation
Limitations: Scholarships to graduates of Raymond, South Bend and Willapa Valley high schools, WA.
Financial data: Year ended 12/31/2002. Assets, $65,417 (M); Expenditures, $24,238; Total giving, $24,000; Grants to individuals, 22 grants totaling $24,000 (high: $2,000, low: $500).
Type of support: Support to graduates or students of specific schools; Undergraduate support.
Application information: Deadline Mar. 31; Application by letter, including grades, plans for future education, activities, abilities and family information.
EIN: 911868960

1894
The Jeffrey S. Holman Foundation
c/o Archer & Greiner, PC
1 Centennial Sq.
Haddonfield, NJ 08033
Contact: Frank R. Demmerly, Jr., Tr.

Foundation type: Independent foundation
Limitations: Loans to graduating seniors of Haddonfield Memorial High School, NJ, for higher education.
Financial data: Year ended 12/31/2004. Assets, $2,991,153 (M); Expenditures, $130,559; Total giving, $114,644.
Type of support: Student loans—to individuals; Support to graduates or students of specific schools.
Application information: Deadline Apr. 15; Completion of formal application required, including statement outlining financial need, grades, SAT scores, essay and standard Haddonfield Memorial High School loan application.
EIN: 223351283

1895
Holmes County Education Foundation
(also known as HCEF)
28 W. Jackson St., Lower Level
P.O. Box 226
Millersburg, OH 44654 (330) 674-7303
Contact: Darla DiFabio, Exec. Dir.
FAX: (330) 674-7313; E-mail: hcef@valkyrie.net;
URL: http://www.HCEF.net

Foundation type: Public charity
Limitations: Scholarships to residents of Holmes County, OH, who demonstrate financial need.
Publications: Application guidelines; Annual report; Grants list; Informational brochure; Newsletter.
Financial data: Year ended 12/31/2004. Assets, $7,537,179 (M); Expenditures, $548,309; Total giving, $358,657; Grants to

individuals, 268 grants totaling $330,285 (high: $11,317, low: $500).
Type of support: Graduate support; Technical education support; Undergraduate support.
Application information: Deadline Apr. 30; Completion of formal application required.
EIN: 341631041

1896
Bonnie L. Holmes Scholarship Fund
9708 Lawrence 2130
Mount Vernon, MO 65712-8314
(417) 466-3454

Foundation type: Independent foundation
Limitations: Scholarships to financially needy students who have demonstrated academic ability for success in higher education.
Financial data: Year ended 12/31/2004. Assets, $165,727 (M); Expenditures, $8,610; Total giving, $8,000; Grants to individuals, totaling $8,000.
Type of support: Scholarships—to individuals.
Application information: Applications not accepted.
EIN: 431603665

1897
Ruth H. Holmes Trust
(formerly Ruth H. Holmes Trust f/b/o Elizabeth V. Cushman Scholarship Fund)
c/o Rockland Trust Co.
2036 Washington St.
Hanover, MA 02339 (781) 982-6766

Foundation type: Independent foundation
Limitations: Scholarships to graduates of high schools in Middleboro, Lakeville, and Carver, MA.
Financial data: Year ended 12/31/2004. Assets, $639,222 (M); Expenditures, $32,190; Total giving, $24,750; Grants to individuals, totaling $24,750.
Type of support: Support to graduates or students of specific schools; Undergraduate support.
Application information: Application form required.
Deadline(s): May 1
Additional information: Applications available from guidance counselors at high schools in Middleboro, Lakeville, and Carver, MA.
EIN: 046044854

1898
The George Holopigian Memorial Fund
c/o Bank of America, N.A., P.C. Group
P.O. Box 1802
Providence, RI 02940-1802
Application addresses: c/o Armenian Students' Assn. of America, Inc., P.O. Box 6947, Providence, RI 02904, or c/o Armenian General Benevolent Union, 585 Saddle River Rd., Saddlebrook, NJ 07662

Foundation type: Independent foundation
Limitations: Scholarships for postsecondary schooling to students of Armenian descent residing in RI.
Financial data: Year ended 06/30/2005. Assets, $458,184 (M); Expenditures, $24,932; Total giving, $17,667; Grants to individuals, totaling $17,667.
Fields of interest: Armenia.
Type of support: Undergraduate support.
Application information: Application form required.
Deadline(s): None

Additional information: Applications are available from the Armenian Students Assn. and Armenian General Benevolent Union.
EIN: 056044531

1899
Holt Family Scholarship Foundation
c/o Marshall & Ilsley Bank
P.O. Box 2980
Milwaukee, WI   53211-2980   (414) 287-7181

Foundation type: Independent foundation
Limitations: Scholarships to graduates of Wautoma or Wild Rose High Schools, WI.
Financial data: Year ended 07/31/2005. Assets, $1,084,023 (M); Expenditures, $61,052; Total giving, $52,400; Grants to individuals, totaling $52,400.
Type of support: Support to graduates or students of specific schools; Undergraduate support.
Application information: Applications accepted throughout the year; Contact foundation for current application guidelines.
EIN: 391734323

1900
Lois Holt Foundation of Central Florida, Inc.
530 E. Central Ave., Ste. 1201
Orlando, FL   32801-4345   (407) 841-6938
Contact: John P. Stilwell II, Admin.

Foundation type: Independent foundation
Limitations: Scholarships to FL residents for higher education.
Financial data: Year ended 06/30/2005. Assets, $1,347,676 (M); Expenditures, $107,040; Total giving, $56,750; Grants to individuals, totaling $45,050.
Type of support: Scholarships—to individuals.
Application information: Applications accepted throughout the year; Initial approach by telephone; Completion of formal application required.
EIN: 593143622

1901
R. B. Holt Foundation
(formerly R. B. Holt Corporate Foundation)
P.O. Box 370434
Denver, CO   80237
Contact: David Fowler, Secy.-Treas.

Foundation type: Independent foundation
Limitations: Scholarships to graduating seniors of public high schools in Baca County, CO.
Financial data: Year ended 12/31/2004. Assets, $211,575 (M); Expenditures, $8,318; Total giving, $7,500; Grants to individuals, 3 grants totaling $7,500.
Type of support: Support to graduates or students of specific schools; Undergraduate support.
Application information: Application form not required.
Initial approach: Letter.
Copies of proposal: 1
Deadline(s): Apr. 1
Applicants should submit the following:
   1) Transcripts
   2) SAT
   3) GPA
   4) ACT
Additional information: Application should also include work history and community services.
EIN: 846036673

1902
Hiram W. & Cecil J. Holtsford Scholarship Fund
P.O. Box 692
Lawrenceburg, TN   38464   (931) 762-6620
Contact: Charles Doerflinger, Tr.

Foundation type: Independent foundation
Limitations: Scholarships to single students from Lawrence County, TN, high schools to attend four-year accredited colleges.
Financial data: Year ended 06/30/2005. Assets, $555,450 (M); Expenditures, $28,403; Total giving, $27,504; Grants to individuals, totaling $27,504.
Type of support: Support to graduates or students of specific schools; Undergraduate support.
Application information: Deadline Feb. 15; Completion of formal application required.
EIN: 626169638

1903
Holy Family High School Foundation
7100 W. 44th Ave., Ste. 101
Wheat Ridge, CO   80033
Application address: c/o Gloria Olson, Holy Family High School, 5195 W. 144th Ave., Bloomfield, CO 80020

Foundation type: Independent foundation
Limitations: Scholarships by nomination only to students at Holy Family High School, CO.
Financial data: Year ended 12/31/2002. Assets, $22,181 (M); Expenditures, $16,799; Total giving, $16,200; Grants to individuals, 3 grants totaling $16,200 (high: $5,900; low: $4,400).
Type of support: Support to graduates or students of specific schools; Awards/grants by nomination only; Undergraduate support.
Application information: Application form required.
   Deadline(s): Feb. 7
EIN: 841251938

1904
Mark B. Holzman Graduate Education Foundation
c/o Wilmington Trust Co.
1100 N. Market St., Trust Tax
Wilmington, DE   19890-0900   (302) 856-2816
Application address: c/o D. Lunblad, Trust Off., Wilmington Trust Co., Georgetown, DE 19947

Foundation type: Independent foundation
Limitations: Scholarships to residents of DE for graduate study in the fields of dentistry, law, medicine, and the ministry.
Financial data: Year ended 09/30/2004. Assets, $274,793 (M); Expenditures, $12,026; Total giving, $8,000; Grants to individuals, totaling $8,000.
Fields of interest: Dental school/education; Law school/education; Medical school/education; Theological school/education; Christian agencies & churches.
Type of support: Graduate support.
Application information: Application form required.
   Deadline(s): June 15
EIN: 516012582

1905
Home & Building Association Foundation
(formerly Greater Grand Rapids Home Builders Association Foundation, also known as HBA Foundation)
c/o Housing Center of West Michigan
1633 E. Beltline Ave., N.E.
Grand Rapids, MI   49525-4509   (616) 447-7262
Contact: Bobbie Talsma, Exec. Dir.
FAX: (616) 281-4500; *URL:* http://hbaggr.com/CommunityInvolvement/HBAFoundation/tabid/92/Default.aspx

Foundation type: Independent foundation
Limitations: Scholarships to students pursuing a career related to the building industry.
Publications: Annual report; Newsletter.
Financial data: Year ended 12/31/2004. Assets, $245,984 (M); Expenditures, $62,397; Total giving, $35,250; Grants to individuals, totaling $12,000.
Fields of interest: Housing/shelter, development.
Type of support: Scholarships—to individuals.
Application information: Deadlines Mar. 31 and Oct. 31; Initial approach by telephone or e-mail; Completion of formal application required; Application available on Web site; Foundation Grants and Community Projects Committee reviews all requests.
EIN: 382836920

1906
Home Builders Foundation of Western Massachusetts, Inc.
c/o Bradford Campbell
240 Cadwell Dr.
Springfield, MA   01104   (413) 733-3126

Foundation type: Independent foundation
Limitations: Scholarships to students who attend a secondary educational vocational institution, an accredited college or university on a full-time basis or a graduate program of or relating to the construction industry.
Financial data: Year ended 12/31/2004. Assets, $30,828 (M); Expenditures, $18,830; Total giving, $14,000; Grants to individuals, totaling $14,000.
Fields of interest: Vocational school, secondary; Business/industry.
Type of support: Graduate support; Technical education support; Precollege support; Undergraduate support.
Application information: Contact foundation for current application deadline; Completion of one page questionnaire at the close of the first semester, detailing credits received, present course of study and future plans.
EIN: 043212851

1907
Homer Incentive Trust, Inc.
1060 E. End Rd.
Homer, AK   99603-3249

Foundation type: Independent foundation
Limitations: Financial support to high school students residing in AK who are at risk or under financial or environmental limitations that jeopardize the completion of their high school degree programs.
Financial data: Year ended 12/31/2004. Assets, $67 (M); Expenditures, $5,687; Total giving, $5,086; Grants to individuals, totaling $5,086.

Type of support: Grants to individuals; Precollege support.
Application information: Applications accepted.
Additional information: Contact trust for current application deadline/guidelines.
EIN: 920141200

1908
HomeStar Education Foundation, Inc.
3 Diversatech Dr.
Manteno, IL 60950 (815) 468-2357
Contact: Deborah S. Maw, Treas.
Scholarship application addresses: For HomeStar Customer Scholarships Program: HomeStar Bank, Mktg. Dept., 435 E. North St., Bradley, IL 60915; For HomeStar-NAACP Scholarship Program: NAACP Education Comm., P.O. Box 1986, Kankakee, IL 60901
E-mail: starmail@homestarbank.com; URL: http://www.homestarbank.com/Scholarship.htm

Foundation type: Company-sponsored foundation
Limitations: Scholarships of $2,000, to high school seniors residing in IL whose parent or grandparent is a customer of HomeStar Bank, HomeStar Insurance Services, HomeStar Investment Services or HomeStar Trust Services. Scholarships are renewable for up to four years provided applicant maintains a "C" average.
Financial data: Year ended 12/31/2004.
Assets, $0 (M); Expenditures, $42,000; Total giving, $42,000; Grants to individuals, 21 grants totaling $42,000 (high: $2,000, low: $2,000).
Type of support: Undergraduate support.
Application information: Applications accepted. Application form required.
Deadline(s): Feb. 10
Applicants should submit the following:
1) Letter(s) of recommendation
2) Transcripts
3) Essay
Additional information: See Web site for further application information.
EIN: 364452037

1909
A. E. Hood Foundation
P.O. Box 367
Amite, LA 70422-0367
Contact: Gloria V. Hood, Pres.
Application address: P.O. Box 917, Amite, LA 70422, tel.: (985) 748-4471

Foundation type: Independent foundation
Limitations: Scholarships to residents of Amite, LA, for higher education.
Financial data: Year ended 12/31/2004.
Assets, $53,684 (M); Expenditures, $17,519; Total giving, $14,700; Grants to individuals, totaling $14,700.
Type of support: Scholarships—to individuals.
Application information: Contact foundation for current application deadline/guidelines.
EIN: 726032071

1910
Charles H. Hood Fund
c/o Ropes & Gray
1 International Pl.
Boston, MA 02110-2624
Scholarship application address: c/o Exec. Dir., 90 Everett Ave., Chelsea, MA 02150-2301, tel.: (617) 887-8475

Foundation type: Independent foundation
Limitations: Scholarships to children of employees of H.P. Hood, Inc. and Agri-Mark, Inc. only, for higher education.
Publications: Application guidelines.
Financial data: Year ended 12/31/2004.
Assets, $3,136,479 (M); Expenditures, $132,143; Total giving, $112,000; Grants to individuals, 30 grants totaling $112,000 (high: $4,000, low: $2,000).
Type of support: Employee-related scholarships.
Application information: Deadline Feb. 15; Completion of formal application required.
Program description:
Scholarship Program: Generally, scholarships are up to $5,000 per year per student. Three to four high school seniors and three to four upperclassmen are selected each year.
EIN: 046036788

1911
Esther Gowen Hood Music Fund
c/o Mellon Financial Corp.
P.O. Box 185
Pittsburgh, PA 15230-9897
Contact: Wanda Caviness
Application address: 1735 Market St., Philadelphia, PA 19101

Foundation type: Independent foundation
Limitations: Scholarships to local PA students attending music schools.
Financial data: Year ended 09/30/2003.
Assets, $239,573 (M); Expenditures, $14,082; Total giving, $10,000.
Fields of interest: Music; Performing arts, education.
Type of support: Scholarships—to individuals.
Application information: Applications accepted.
Initial approach: Letter.
Deadline(s): Apr. 15.
Applicants should submit the following:
1) Transcripts
2) Financial information
EIN: 236223620

1912
Hooker Educational Foundation
c/o Branch Banking and Trust
P.O. Box 5228
Martinsville, VA 24115

Foundation type: Company-sponsored foundation
Limitations: Scholarships to children and spouses of full-time VA employees of Hooker Furniture Corp.
Financial data: Year ended 12/31/2004.
Assets, $1,530,033 (M); Expenditures, $97,918; Total giving, $88,028; Grants to individuals, 39 grants totaling $88,028 (high: $3,000, low: $500).
Type of support: Employee-related scholarships.
Application information: Application form required.
Deadline(s): Apr. 1
Applicants should submit the following:
1) Transcripts
2) Letter(s) of recommendation
Additional information: Applications should also include college board scores; Application address: c/o Dir., Personnel, Hooker Furniture Corp., P.O. Box 4708, Martinsville VA 24115.
EIN: 541583948

1913
Hoop Dreams Scholarship Fund
(formerly Hoop Dreams Tournament Corporation)
800 K St., N.W., Ste. 1100 S.
Washington, DC 20001 (202) 414-4774
Contact: Susie Kay, Pres.
FAX: (202) 408-5111;
E-mail: info@hoopdreams.org; URL: http://hoopdreams.org/

Foundation type: Public charity
Limitations: Scholarships to inner-city Washington, DC, public high school students.
Financial data: Year ended 08/31/2004.
Assets, $612,536 (M); Expenditures, $1,231,909; Total giving, $205,915; Grants to individuals, totaling $205,915.
Type of support: Undergraduate support.
Application information: Apr. 21 for Scholarship Fund, Apr. 30 for Scholarship Fund for Continuing Students; Initial approach by e-mail; Completion of formal application required, including acceptance letter, standardized test scores, letters of recommendation, resume, essay, personal statement, FAFSA, SAR, SAT or ACT scores, and financial aid letter; See Web site for further application information.
Program description:
Scholarship Program: Scholarships are for one year. Students must maintain a GPA of 2.0. Continuing students must submit an official transcript from all institutions attended. See Web site for additional guidelines.
EIN: 522079470

1914
The J. Edgar Hoover Foundation
P.O. Box 5914
Hilton Head Island, SC 29938-5914
(843) 671-5020
Contact: Cartha D. DeLoach, Chair.
Application address: 50 Gull Point Rd., Hilton Head Island, SC 29928

Foundation type: Independent foundation
Limitations: Scholarships for the study of government and the promotion of good citizenship.
Financial data: Year ended 12/31/2003.
Assets, $648,453 (M); Expenditures, $227,306; Total giving, $128,250; Grants to individuals, 65 grants totaling $78,250 (high: $25,000, low: $500).
Fields of interest: Government/public administration; Public affairs, citizen participation.
Type of support: Scholarships—to individuals.
Application information: Applications accepted throughout the year; Contact foundation for current application guidelines.
Program description:
Scholarship Program: The foundation strives to safeguard the heritage and freedom of the U.S., to promote good citizenship through an appreciation of the American form of government, and to perpetuate the ideals and purposes to which the Hon. J. Edgar Hoover dedicated his life, including combating communism or any other ideology or doctrine which is opposed to the principles set forth in the Constitution of the U.S.
EIN: 526060988

1915
O. Robert Hoover Scholarship Foundation
c/o National Bank & Trust Co.
230 W. State St.
Sycamore, IL 60178-1419
Contact: Diane Florschuetz, V.P. and Trust Off.

Foundation type: Independent foundation
Limitations: Scholarships to graduates of
Genoa-Kingston High School, IL, for undergraduate
education.
Financial data: Year ended 12/31/2004.
Assets, $297,482 (M); Expenditures, $18,534;
Total giving, $13,500; Grants to individuals,
totaling $13,500.
Type of support: Support to graduates or students
of specific schools.
Application information: Applications accepted.
Application form required.
Initial approach: Letter.
Deadline(s): Mar. 15
Additional information: Contact foundation for
current application guidelines.
EIN: 363986816

1916
Daniel R. Hoover Trust Fund
c/o Wachovia Bank, N.A.
100 N. Main St., 13th Fl.
Winston-Salem, NC 27150-6732
Application address: c/o Wachovia Bank, N.A., P.O.
Box 467, Concord, NC 28026-0467; Scholarship
URL: http://www.wachoviascholars.com/hovr/
csaw_hoover_deadline.php

Foundation type: Independent foundation
Limitations: Scholarships to ministerial students
from Cabarrus County, NC, who plan to study at a
southern theological or divinity school or a
seminary.
Financial data: Year ended 12/31/2004.
Assets, $1,027,690 (M); Expenditures, $13,324;
Total giving, $10,720; Grants to individuals,
totaling $10,720.
Fields of interest: Theological school/education;
Religion.
Type of support: Scholarships—to individuals.
Application information: Applications accepted
throughout the year; Completion of formal
application required.
EIN: 566034863

1917
Hoover-Koken Foundation, Inc.
811 N. Washington St.
Junction City, KS 66441-2446

Foundation type: Independent foundation
Limitations: Scholarships to residents of Geary
County, KS, Jasper County, MO, and Fort Riley, KS.
Financial data: Year ended 12/31/2004.
Assets, $157,528 (M); Expenditures, $56,159;
Total giving, $54,840; Grants to individuals,
totaling $54,840.
Type of support: Scholarships—to individuals.
Application information: Applications not
accepted.
EIN: 481026087

1918
Blanche and Thomas Hope Memorial Fund
c/o National City Bank
P.O. Box 94651
Cleveland, OH 44101-4651
Application address: c/o Donna J. Wimbec, National
City Bank, 101 S. 5th St., Louisville, KY 40233,
tel.: (502) 581-5107

Foundation type: Independent foundation
Limitations: Scholarships limited to students
graduating from high schools in Boyd and Greenup
counties, KY, and Lawrence County, OH.
Scholarships are based on need, although
character, grades, and inclination are important.
Financial data: Year ended 12/31/2004.
Assets, $3,461,158 (M); Expenditures,
$194,539; Total giving, $179,345; Grants to
individuals, totaling $179,345.
Type of support: Support to graduates or students
of specific schools.
Application information: Application form required.
Deadline(s): Mar. 1
Applicants should submit the following:
1) Transcripts
2) FAF
Additional information: Interviews required.
EIN: 616067105

1919
The Hopedale Foundation
43 Hope St.
P.O. Box 123
Hopedale, MA 01747-0123
Contact: Vincent J. Arone

Foundation type: Independent foundation
Limitations: Student loans to graduates of
Hopedale High School, MA.
Financial data: Year ended 10/31/2004.
Assets, $8,344,679 (M); Expenditures,
$487,226; Total giving, $439,978.
Fields of interest: Education.
Type of support: Student loans—to individuals;
Support to graduates or students of specific
schools; Undergraduate support.
Application information: Applications accepted.
Additional information: Contact foundation for
application deadline; Application by letter.
EIN: 046044779

1920
Charles & Alda Horgan Charitable Trust
c/o Citizens Bank Wealth Mgmt., N.A.
328 S. Saginaw St., N/C 002027
Flint, MI 48502
Application address: c/o Helen James, Trust Off.,
Citizens Bank Wealth Mgmt., N.A.,101 N.
Washington St., Saginaw, MI 48607, tel.: (989)
776-7368

Foundation type: Operating foundation
Limitations: Scholarships to residents of Saginaw
Township, MI.
Financial data: Year ended 09/30/2004.
Assets, $1,089,939 (M); Expenditures, $67,037;
Total giving, $50,196; Grants to individuals, 27
grants totaling $18,468 (high: $684, low: $684).
Type of support: Scholarships—to individuals.
Application information: Application form required.
Initial approach: Letter.
Deadline(s): July 1
Additional information: Recipients must maintain
a GPA of at least 2.5 and display ambition and
leadership skills.
EIN: 386661683

1921
The Horizon Foundation, Inc.
999 Ponce de Leon Blvd., No. 625
Coral Gables, FL 33133

Foundation type: Operating foundation
Limitations: Grants to Jamaicans for freediving and
for undergraduate education in Jamaica and in the
U.S.
Financial data: Year ended 12/31/2003.
Assets, $3,435,934 (M); Expenditures,
$345,074; Total giving, $199,577; Grants to
individuals, 6 grants totaling $20,186 (high:
$10,000, low: $1,008).
Fields of interest: Athletics/sports, water sports;
Jamaica.
Type of support: Foreign applicants; Undergraduate
support.
Application information:
Initial approach: Letter.
Additional information: Contact foundation for
current application deadline/guidelines.
EIN: 651121440

1922
Horizons Foundation
870 Market St., Ste. 728
San Francisco, CA 94102 (415) 398-2333
FAX: (415) 398-4733;
E-mail: info@horizonsfoundation.org; URL: http://
www.horizonsfoundation.org

Foundation type: Public charity
Limitations: Scholarships to children with at least
one gay or lesbian parent residing in the San
Francisco Bay area, CA.
Publications: Application guidelines; Annual report;
Financial statement; Grants list; Informational
brochure; Newsletter.
Financial data: Year ended 12/31/2004.
Assets, $3,332,444 (M); Expenditures,
$1,798,648; Total giving, $911,754.
Fields of interest: Vocational education; LGBTQ.
Type of support: Scholarships—to individuals;
Technical education support; Undergraduate
support.
Application information: Applications accepted.
Application form required.
Initial approach: Letter.
Deadline(s): June 15.
Additional information: Scholarships to LGBT
students are made through specific
scholarship funds established at the
foundation. Each scholarship fund has a
competitive application process open to all
qualifying students. See Web site for
additional information.
Program description:
Scholarship Program: These scholarships are
provided through the Joseph Towner Fund. Each
scholarship is $500 and is to be used for
postsecondary education.
EIN: 942686530

1923
Horn Educational Trust
(formerly Lee A. & Mabel H. Horn Educational Trust)
c/o Wells Fargo Bank Nebraska, N.A.
1248 O St., 4th Fl., MAC N8032-042
Lincoln, NE 68508
Application address: 666 Walnut St., Des Monies,
IA 50304-0837

Foundation type: Independent foundation

Limitations: Scholarships to single students who graduated from Ida Grove High School, IA, in the upper third of their class.
Financial data: Year ended 12/31/2004.
Assets, $165,729 (M); Expenditures, $15,610; Total giving, $12,000; Grants to individuals, 5 grants totaling $12,000 (high: $3,000, low: $1,500).
Type of support: Support to graduates or students of specific schools; Undergraduate support.
Application information: Applications accepted.
  Initial approach: Letter.
  Deadline(s): None
EIN: 426051539

1924
Evelyn Horn Scholarship Trust
c/o Westamerica Bank
2893 Sunrise Blvd., Ste. 106
Rancho Cordova, CA   95742   (916) 852-5096
Contact: Christa Nordstrom, Sr. Trust Off., Westamerica Bank
FAX: (916) 853-2085

Foundation type: Independent foundation
Limitations: Scholarships to graduates and students who have completed at least two years at Folsom Lake College- Placerville Campus, graduates of El Dorado Union High School, Placerville; and graduates of Black Oak Mine School District High School, all in CA.
Financial data: Year ended 09/30/2005.
Assets, $347,102 (M); Expenditures, $21,753; Total giving, $16,487; Grants to individuals, totaling $16,487.
Type of support: Support to graduates or students of specific schools; Undergraduate support.
Application information: Deadline Jan. 15; Completion of formal application required.
Program description:
  Scholarship Program: Scholarships to graduates of Folsom Lake College, Placerville Campus, CA, are limited to two years. Scholarships to graduates of El Dorado Union High School and Black Oak Mine School District High School are limited to four years. Scholarships will be terminated if student obtains less than a "C" average or fails to carry an average, full-time course load. Financial need is not a consideration. Decisions are made by March 30.
EIN: 686060391

1925
Ednah Horner Charitable Foundation
c/o Eastern Bank & Trust Co.
605 Broadway, LF41
Saugus, MA   01906

Foundation type: Independent foundation
Limitations: Scholarships to individuals in the Peabody, MA, area.
Financial data: Year ended 12/31/2003.
Assets, $763,927 (M); Expenditures, $47,777; Total giving, $39,500; Grants to individuals, totaling $27,500.
Type of support: Scholarships—to individuals.
Application information: Contact foundation for current application deadline/guidelines.
EIN: 043468419

1926
The Fredrick H. & Kathleen M. Hornlein Educational Trust
c/o First National Bank
P.O. Box Drawer 1928
Mountain Home, AR   72654-1928
(870) 425-1863

Foundation type: Independent foundation
Limitations: Scholarships based on financial need, character, and scholastic ability, to graduates of Mountain Home Arkansas High School, AR, who are enrolled in institutions within the continental U.S. for vocational, undergraduate, and graduate degrees.
Publications: Annual report (including application guidelines); Informational brochure.
Financial data: Year ended 12/31/2004.
Assets, $1,912,020 (M); Expenditures, $67,648; Total giving, $44,600; Grants to individuals, totaling $44,600.
Type of support: Support to graduates or students of specific schools; Graduate support; Technical education support; Undergraduate support.
Application information: Applications accepted. Application form required.
  Deadline(s): Dec. 31.
  Applicants should submit the following:
    1) Letter(s) of recommendation
    2) SAT
    3) ACT
    4) Transcripts
    5) Financial information
EIN: 716157456

1927
Ivy B. Horr Charitable Revocable Trust
c/o Shasta College
P.O. Box 496006
Redding, CA   96049-6006
Contact: Margaret L. Dominici, V.P., College and Community Relations

Foundation type: Independent foundation
Limitations: Student loans for medical education, primarily to residents of CA.
Financial data: Year ended 12/31/2004.
Assets, $1,596,229 (M); Expenditures, $11,348; Total giving, $0; Loans to individuals, totaling $79,500.
Fields of interest: Medical school/education.
Type of support: Graduate support.
Application information: Application form required.
  Additional information: Contact trust for current application deadline.
EIN: 680068577

1928
Horsey Educational Fund
c/o Wells Fargo Bank Iowa, N.A.
203 W. 3rd St.
Davenport, IA   52801
Application addresses: c/o Scholarship Comm., Trinity Episcopal Cathedral, 121 W. 12th St., Davenport, IA 52803, c/o Scholarship Comm., Embury Methodist Church, R.R. No. 2, 411 Dowey, Donnellson, IA 52625

Foundation type: Independent foundation
Limitations: Scholarships to members of Trinity Episcopal Cathedral and Embury Methodist Church, IA.
Financial data: Year ended 12/31/2002.
Assets, $559,806 (M); Expenditures, $23,684; Total giving, $17,275; Grants to individuals, 21 grants totaling $12,100 (high: $750, low: $300).

Fields of interest: Christian agencies & churches; Protestant agencies & churches.
Type of support: Scholarships—to individuals.
Application information: Deadline Mar. 1; Completion of formal application required.
EIN: 426468681

1929
Horsman Foundation
c/o Davidson Trust Co.
P.O. Box 152
Kalispell, MT   59903-0152
Application address: c/o Guidance Counselor, Flathead High School, 644 4th Ave. W., Kalispell, MT 59901, tel.: (406) 751-3504

Foundation type: Independent foundation
Limitations: Scholarships to graduates of Flathead High School, MT, who are planning to attend an accredited four-year program of higher education.
Financial data: Year ended 09/30/2004.
Assets, $1,155,107 (M); Expenditures, $100,251; Total giving, $80,672; Grants to individuals, totaling $80,672.
Type of support: Support to graduates or students of specific schools; Undergraduate support.
Application information: Application form required.
  Deadline(s): Apr. 13
  Additional information: Application information packet available at guidance counselor's office.
EIN: 810520094

1930
Jessie R. Horton Trust
c/o KeyBank N.A., Trust Div.
800 Superior Ave., 4th Fl.
Cleveland, OH   44114
Application address: c/o Greg Maynard, KeyBank N.A., 1 Canal Plz., Portland, ME 04107

Foundation type: Independent foundation
Limitations: Scholarships to residents of Harrison, ME, who are under the age of 25.
Financial data: Year ended 12/31/2003.
Assets, $82,603 (M); Expenditures, $6,971; Total giving, $4,100; Grants to individuals, totaling $4,100.
Type of support: Scholarships—to individuals.
Application information: Deadline May 31; Application by letter.
EIN: 016021432

1931
Dr. Arthur J. & Helen M. Horvat Foundation
c/o Wachovia Bank, N.A.
100 N. Main St., 13th Fl.
Winston-Salem, NC   27150
Application address: c/o David Glickman, Wachovia Bank, N.A., 123 S. Broad St., Philadelphia, PA 19109

Foundation type: Independent foundation
Limitations: Scholarships for the study of science to residents of the Duryea, PA, area whose family income is below $30,000.
Publications: Informational brochure (including application guidelines).
Financial data: Year ended 12/31/2004.
Assets, $5,649,725 (M); Expenditures, $409,931; Total giving, $331,387; Grants to individuals, totaling $331,387.
Fields of interest: Science.

Type of support: Scholarships—to individuals.
Application information: Deadline May 15; Contact foundation for current application guidelines.
EIN: 236846849

1932
Lois U. Horvitz Foundation
(formerly HRH Family Foundation)
c/o Parkland Mgmt. Co.
1001 Lakeside Ave., Ste. 900
Cleveland, OH   44114-1151   (216) 479-2200
Contact: Thomas H. Oden, Treas.
Scholarship application address: c/o Dr. Nyles C. Ayers, Scholarship Prog. Admin., 3314 W. End Ave., Nashville, TN 37203-1022, tel.: (615) 292-4379
FAX: (216) 479-2222

Foundation type: Independent foundation
Limitations: Scholarships to descendants of an employee of The Mainfield Journal, The Lake County News Herald, The Dover-New Philadelphia Times Reporter, The Troy Times Record, The Multi-Channel TV Co., and The Lorain Journal. Scholarships also to high school seniors of Lake, Lorain, Richland, Tuscarawas counties, OH, or Rensselaer County, NY.
Financial data: Year ended 12/31/2004.
Assets, $3,657,897 (M); Expenditures, $1,234,413; Total giving, $1,210,908; Grants to individuals, totaling $63,638.
Type of support: Employee-related scholarships; Support to graduates or students of specific schools; Technical education support; Undergraduate support.
Application information: Application form required.
Deadline(s): Apr. 1
Program description:
Scholarship Program: Academic merit is not the most important factor. Awards must be used at an accredited college, university, or nonprofit trade school. Awards are automatically renewable. Payments of the scholarships will be made directly to the schools.
EIN: 341594655

1933
Dr. R. S. Hosler Memorial Educational Fund
P.O. Box 5
Ashville, OH   43103-0005
Application address: c/o Leo J. Hall, 50 Bortz St., Ashville, OH 43103, tel.: (740) 983-2557

Foundation type: Independent foundation
Limitations: Scholarships to high school graduates of Teays Valley and Amanda Clearcreek, OH, school systems.
Financial data: Year ended 12/31/2004.
Assets, $4,773,706 (M); Expenditures, $196,079; Total giving, $101,750; Grants to individuals, 6 grants totaling $101,750 (high: $22,500, low: $5,250).
Type of support: Support to graduates or students of specific schools; Undergraduate support.
Application information: Deadline Mar. 1; Completion of formal application required.
EIN: 311073939

1934
Hospitalers Committee of Detroit Commandery No. 1 Knights Templar
500 Temple Ave.
Detroit, MI   48201   (313) 831-7072
Contact: Don J. Williams, Treas.

Foundation type: Independent foundation
Limitations: Scholarships to individuals.
Financial data: Year ended 12/31/2004.
Assets, $1,595,626 (M); Expenditures, $136,293; Total giving, $57,600; Grants to individuals, 3 grants totaling $12,600 (high: $6,000, low: $2,400).
Type of support: Scholarships—to individuals.
Application information: Application form required.
Initial approach: Letter.
Additional information: Applications accepted throughout the year.
EIN: 383476671

1935
Everett R. & Frieda G. Houghton Memorial Trust
c/o First National Bank of Monterey
P.O. Box 8
Monterey, IN   46960-0008   (574) 542-2121
Contact: Claiborn Wamsley, Pres. and Trust Off., First National Bank of Monterey

Foundation type: Independent foundation
Limitations: Scholarships to graduating seniors of Culver Community School, IN and Eastern Pulaski Community School, IN, for higher education.
Financial data: Year ended 12/31/2004.
Assets, $511,864 (M); Expenditures, $8,115; Total giving, $7,400; Grants to individuals, totaling $7,400.
Type of support: Scholarships—to individuals; Support to graduates or students of specific schools.
Application information: Deadline spring; Contact trust for current application deadline; Application by letter including statement of whether applicant intends to attend college or other postsecondary educational institution in the fall following graduation.
EIN: 351899190

1936
Susan Cook House Educational Trust
c/o JPMorgan Chase Bank, N.A.
P.O. Box 1308
Milwaukee, WI   53201-1308
Application address: c/o Lin Jones, JPMorgan Chase Bank, N.A., 1 E. Old Capitol Plz., Springfield, IL 62701, tel.: (217) 525-9737

Foundation type: Independent foundation
Limitations: Scholarships only to residents of Sangamon County, IL.
Financial data: Year ended 11/30/2004.
Assets, $2,932,391 (M); Expenditures, $128,786; Total giving, $88,035.
Type of support: Scholarships—to individuals.
Application information: Applications by letter accepted throughout the year.
EIN: 376087675

1937
Houston Osteopathic Foundation
1603 N. Main St.
Pearland, TX   77581
Contact: Joe Martin
Application address: c/o Grant Comm., P.O. Box 746, Pearland, TX 77588, tel: (281) 485-1612

Foundation type: Independent foundation
Limitations: Scholarships to students at Texas College of Osteopathic Medicine, TX.
Financial data: Year ended 12/31/2004.
Assets, $1,176,957 (M); Expenditures, $51,775; Total giving, $19,325; Grants to individuals, totaling $19,325.
Fields of interest: Medical school/education; Health organizations.
Type of support: Support to graduates or students of specific schools; Graduate support; Undergraduate support.
Application information: Initial approach by letter; Completion of formal application required, including evidence of enrollment in Texas College of Osteopathic Medicine, as well as biographical, educational, and financial information.
EIN: 742426837

1938
Trustees of the Howard Funds in West Bridgewater
c/o State Street Bank & Trust Co.
P.O. Box 351, MAO-10
Boston, MA   02101
Application address: c/o Howard High School Schol. Comm., 155 West Center, West Bridgewater, MA 02379, tel.: (508) 583-7506

Foundation type: Independent foundation
Limitations: Scholarships to residents of West Bridgewater, MA. Scholarships are renewable.
Financial data: Year ended 06/30/2005.
Assets, $1,062,020 (M); Expenditures, $65,314; Total giving, $44,000; Grants to individuals, totaling $44,000.
Type of support: Scholarships—to individuals.
Application information:
Deadline(s): Apr. 11
Additional information: Completion of formal application required.
EIN: 042105774

1939
Howard Memorial Fund
120 Wall St., 8th Fl.
New York, NY   10005   (212) 558-5420
Contact: DeLoris W. Greene, Chair.

Foundation type: Independent foundation
Limitations: Scholarships for undergraduate study and technical school to young high school graduates of the City of New York and Nassau and Suffolk counties, NY.
Financial data: Year ended 06/30/2004.
Assets, $923,803 (M); Expenditures, $50,070; Total giving, $41,850; Grants to individuals, 58 grants totaling $41,850 (high: $750, low: $600).
Fields of interest: Vocational education.
Type of support: Technical education support; Undergraduate support.
Application information:
Initial approach: Letter.
Deadline(s): Apr. 30
Additional information: Completion of formal application required, including references of two people not family members, high school transcript or official record of GED test scores,

verification of U.S. citizenship, verification of family income, and one-page essay.

Program description:

Scholarship Awards: Scholarships are awarded to disadvantaged students whose academic averages may not qualify them for other scholarships, but who have the potential to pursue a bona fide course of study, either academic or vocational, at a college or professional institution. Applicants must be accepted by a school of their choice and demonstrate financial need. The grants may be used for tuition, books or living expenses. Maximum award per individual per school year is $1,000. Scholarships are renewable. One-half of the grant is paid in Sept., the other half is paid in Jan.

EIN: 136161770

1940

Howard Memorial Fund

P.O. Box 114
Aberdeen, SD   57402-0114
Contact: Carlyle Richards, Secy.-Treas.
Application address: 222 Midwest Capitol Bldg., Aberdeen, SD 57401, tel.: (605) 225-1200

Foundation type: Independent foundation
Limitations: Scholarships to students attending Presentation College or Northern State University, SD.
Financial data: Year ended 12/31/2004. Assets, $890,581 (M); Expenditures, $48,006; Total giving, $42,000; Grants to individuals, totaling $28,500.
Fields of interest: Education.
Type of support: Technical education support; Undergraduate support.
Application information: Deadline Apr. 1; Contact fund for current application guidelines.
EIN: 466014133

1941

M. P. Howard Trust

c/o Bank of America, N.A.
P.O. Box 1802
Providence, RI   02901-1802
Application address: c/o Drury High School, Attn.: Mortimer P. Howard Scholarship Comm., 1130 S. Church St., North Adams, MA 02144, tel.: (413) 662-3245

Foundation type: Independent foundation
Limitations: Scholarships to graduates of Drury High School, RI, who are about to enter their junior or senior year of a four-year college.
Financial data: Year ended 12/31/2004. Assets, $201,365 (M); Expenditures, $14,075; Total giving, $10,700; Grants to individuals, 25 grants totaling $10,700 (high: $500, low: $300).
Type of support: Support to graduates or students of specific schools.
Application information: Application form required.
   Initial approach: Letter.
   Deadline(s): June 1
   Applicants should submit the following:
   1) Transcripts
   2) Essay
   Additional information: Contact the school's Guidance Office for further application guidelines.
EIN: 046385719

1942

Marjorie W. Howe & Howard C. Howe Scholarship Trust

c/o 789
1701 Golf Rd.
Rolling Meadows, IL   60008   (847) 354-7248
Contact: Kristina Modrow, Tr.

Foundation type: Independent foundation
Limitations: Scholarships to students at Waukegan High School, IL.
Financial data: Year ended 12/31/2004. Assets, $845,569 (M); Expenditures, $71,009; Total giving, $51,250; Grants to individuals, totaling $51,250.
Type of support: Scholarships—to individuals; Support to graduates or students of specific schools.
Application information: Contact trust for current application deadline; Completion of formal application required, including class rank, GPA, ACT and SAT scores, recommendation letter from a teacher, and transcripts; Interviews required.
EIN: 364005689

1943

Samuel C. Howes Trust

c/o Nutter, McClennen & Fish, LLP
World Trade Ctr. West, 155 Seaport Blvd.
Boston, MA   02210-2604   (617) 439-2000
Contact: Thomas P. Jalkut, Tr.

Foundation type: Independent foundation
Limitations: Scholarships to financially needy and deserving college students attending the following schools: Calvary Bible College, Columbia International University, Gordon-Conwell Theological Seminary, Gordon College, Houghton College, Moody Bible Institute, and Wheaton College, IL.
Financial data: Year ended 09/30/2004. Assets, $2,331,576 (M); Expenditures, $125,934; Total giving, $98,150; Grants to individuals, totaling $98,150.
Type of support: Scholarships—to individuals; Support to graduates or students of specific schools.
Application information: Applications not accepted.
EIN: 046077889

1944

George Hoy Family Scholarship Fund

201 South Mill
P.O. Box 607
Beloit, KS   67420-0607
Application addresses: c/o Beloit High School, Office of Principal, 1711 N. Walnut, Beloit, KS 67420, tel.: (785) 738-3593; c/o St. John's High School, Office of Principal, 209 Cherry, Beloit, KS 67420, tel.: (738) 738-2942

Foundation type: Independent foundation
Limitations: Scholarships to graduating seniors at Beloit and St. John's high schools, Beloit, KS.
Financial data: Year ended 12/31/2004. Assets, $62,475 (M); Expenditures, $4,644; Total giving, $4,000; Grants to individuals, totaling $4,000.
Type of support: Support to graduates or students of specific schools; Undergraduate support.
Application information: Deadlines one month before each school term ends; Application by letter stating college and career objectives, and why financial aid is necessary.

Program description:

Scholarship Program: Scholarships are awarded for the first year of college, and are renewable for three consecutive years thereafter. The fund awards one new scholarship to a student from Beloit High School and one to a student from St. John's High School each year.
EIN: 486203636

1945

Hubbard Family Foundation

c/o Bank of America, N.A.
P.O. Box 34345
Seattle, WA   98124-1345
Contact: Ruth Graven
Application address: Bank of America, N.A., P.O. Box 24565, Seattle, WA 98124, tel.: (206) 358-3367

Foundation type: Independent foundation
Limitations: Scholarships to residents of Edmonds and South Snomish counties, WA, for higher education.
Financial data: Year ended 07/31/2005. Assets, $2,341,961 (M); Expenditures, $117,452; Total giving, $95,075; Grants to individuals, totaling $86,075.
Type of support: Undergraduate support.
Application information: Applications accepted throughout the year; Contact foundation for current application guidelines.
EIN: 916253897

1946

Hubbard Farms Charitable Foundation

P.O. Box 505
Walpole, NH   03608-0505   (603) 756-3311
Contact: Jane F. Kelly, Clerk

Foundation type: Company-sponsored foundation
Limitations: Scholarships to financially needy students in the fields of poultry science, genetics, and other life sciences.
Publications: Application guidelines.
Financial data: Year ended 12/31/2004. Assets, $1,369,152 (M); Expenditures, $56,223; Total giving, $52,950.
Fields of interest: Genetics/birth defects; Agriculture, livestock issues; Science.
Type of support: Scholarships—to individuals.
Application information:
   Deadline(s): Apr. 1 and Oct. 1
   Additional information: Contact foundation for current application guidelines.

Program description:

Scholarship Program: The foundation is sponsored by Hubbard Farms, Inc. and "wishes to encourage continued progress in technology and efficiency of production of poultry products." Scholarships are for study at universities that the foundation trustees consider to be leaders in these fields of interest.
EIN: 026015114

1947

Leonard D. Hubbard Onodaga Nation School Trust

c/o Bank of America, N.A., Private Clients Group
P.O. Box 6767
Providence, RI   02940-6767
Application address: c/o Principal, Lafayette Central School, Lafayette, NY 12401

Foundation type: Independent foundation

Limitations: Scholarships to graduates of Lafayette Central School who are certified members of Onondaga Nation and enrolled in an accredited college, NY.
Financial data: Year ended 05/31/2004.
Assets, $273,035 (M); Expenditures, $17,127; Total giving, $13,000; Grants to individuals, totaling $13,000.
Type of support: Support to graduates or students of specific schools; Undergraduate support.
Application information: Contact school for current application deadline; Completion of formal application required.
EIN: 226500878

1948
Leo Huber Foundation
c/o U.S. Bank, N.A.
P.O. Box 64713
St. Paul, MN 55164-0713
Application address: c/o David J. Scarpino, Educational Dir., Nekoosa Public Schools, 600 S. Section St., Nekoosa, WI 54455, tel.: (715) 886-8000

Foundation type: Independent foundation
Limitations: Scholarships to high school seniors at Nekoosa High School, WI.
Financial data: Year ended 08/31/2002.
Assets, $170,832 (M); Expenditures, $19,913; Total giving, $13,300; Grants to individuals, 19 grants totaling $13,300 (high: $700, low: $700).
Type of support: Support to graduates or students of specific schools; Undergraduate support.
Application information: Deadline prior to graduation; Completion of formal application required, including financial need information.
EIN: 237168868

1949
Henry P. Huber Scholarship Trust
c/o The Huntington National Bank
P.O. Box 1558
Columbus, OH 43216
Application address: c/o Scholarship Comm., 101 N. Elizabeth, Lima, OH 45801

Foundation type: Independent foundation
Limitations: Scholarships to students of the Bluffton School District, OH, and contiguous districts for the study of agriculture and related fields.
Financial data: Year ended 06/30/2005.
Assets, $160,598 (M); Expenditures, $19,325; Total giving, $16,250; Grants to individuals, totaling $16,250.
Fields of interest: Agriculture.
Type of support: Support to graduates or students of specific schools; Undergraduate support.
Application information:
Initial approach: Letter.
EIN: 346766601

1950
The Huether/McClelland Foundation, Inc.
(formerly The Huether Foundation, Inc.)
P.O. Box 370
1300 Brass Mill Rd.
Belcamp, MD 21017
Contact: H. Douglas Huether, Chair.

Foundation type: Independent foundation

Limitations: Scholarships to seniors at Harford County, MD, high schools to pursue postsecondary education in engineering.
Financial data: Year ended 12/31/2004.
Assets, $3,651,604 (M); Expenditures, $174,320; Total giving, $174,320; Grants to individuals, 4 grants totaling $23,500 (high: $11,000, low: $2,500).
Fields of interest: Engineering school/education.
Type of support: Support to graduates or students of specific schools; Undergraduate support.
Application information: Contact foundation for current application deadline/guidelines.
EIN: 521435090

1951
Carrie & Luther Huffines Educational Fund
c/o RBC Centura Bank
P.O. Box 1220
Rocky Mount, NC 27802

Foundation type: Independent foundation
Limitations: Loans to students residing in Nash and Edgecombe counties, NC.
Financial data: Year ended 06/30/2005.
Assets, $119,532 (M); Expenditures, $12,382; Total giving, $11,500; Loans to individuals, totaling $11,500.
Type of support: Student loans—to individuals.
Application information: Applications accepted. Application form required.
Deadline(s): June 1.
EIN: 566046187

1952
Huffman-Cornwell Foundation
c/o Wachovia Bank of North Carolina, N.A.
100 N. Main St., 13th Fl.
Winston-Salem, NC 27150   (864) 467-2836
Contact: Mary Louise McCombs, Dir.
Application address: P.O. Box 1113, Morganton, NC 28680-1113, tel.:(828) 437-5872

Foundation type: Independent foundation
Limitations: Scholarships only to students of Freedom High School in Morganton, NC.
Financial data: Year ended 12/31/2004.
Assets, $2,901,215 (M); Expenditures, $142,558; Total giving, $107,500; Grants to individuals, 7 grants totaling $13,500 (high: $3,500, low: $1,000).
Type of support: Support to graduates or students of specific schools; Undergraduate support.
Application information: Applications accepted. Application form required.
Initial approach: Letter.
Deadline(s): None
Additional information: Applications available through guidance counselors.
EIN: 566065286

1953
Leola W. and Charles H. Hugg Trust
c/o JPMorgan Chase Bank
P.O. Box 31412
Rochester, NY 14603

Foundation type: Independent foundation
Limitations: Scholarships for students from Williamson County, TX, to attend colleges and universities.
Financial data: Year ended 12/31/2004.
Assets, $4,406,074 (M); Expenditures, $202,408; Total giving, $150,500; Grants to

individuals, 190 grants totaling $150,500 (high: $1,000, low: $250).
Type of support: Undergraduate support.
Application information: Application form required.
Initial approach: Letter.
Deadline(s): May 1.
Additional information: Application forms and guidelines are available upon request from participating high schools, or from the director of the Texas Baptist Children's Home in Round Rock, TX, or the Office of Student Financial Aid at Southwestern University in Georgetown, TX.
Program description:
Scholarship Program: Awards are given based on satisfaction of residence requirements and demonstrated financial need. Successful applicants must reapply annually with documentation of being in the top quarter of class and continued financial need.
EIN: 741907673

1954
Grace Graves Huggins Foundation
P.O. Box 127
Chestertown, MD 21620   (410) 348-5408

Foundation type: Independent foundation
Limitations: Scholarships to graduates of Corcoran school in Washington, DC.
Financial data: Year ended 05/31/2004.
Assets, $203,042 (M); Expenditures, $22,458; Total giving, $18,500; Grants to individuals, 11 grants totaling $16,500 (high: $2,000, low: $1,500).
Type of support: Scholarships—to individuals; Support to graduates or students of specific schools; Undergraduate support.
Application information: Application form required.
Deadline(s): after Feb. 1
Additional information: Application should include copy of letter of acceptance from school, resume listing school and community activities, 2- to 3-page essay, transcripts, two letters of reference (one from faculty member and one from employer), and copy of FAFSA and SAR.
EIN: 526854449

1955
Walter M. Hughes Educational Trust
c/o JPMorgan Chase Bank, N.A
P.O. Box 1308
Milwaukee, WI 53201
Application address: c/o JPMorgan Chase Bank, N.A, 100 E. Broad St., 9th Fl., Columbus, OH 43215-0192, tel.: (614) 248-5911

Foundation type: Independent foundation
Limitations: Scholarships to worthy young people of Muskingum County, OH.
Financial data: Year ended 12/31/2004.
Assets, $1,236,552 (M); Expenditures, $58,081; Total giving, $55,000; Grants to individuals, 26 grants totaling $55,000 (high: $3,500, low: $1,000).
Type of support: Scholarships—to individuals.
Application information: Deadline Mar. 15; Initial approach by letter; Completion of formal application required.
EIN: 316024847

1956
Charles J. Hughes Foundation
P.O. Box 1498
Pagosa Springs, CO 81147 (970) 264-2228
Contact: Terrence P. Alley, Pres.

Foundation type: Independent foundation
Limitations: Scholarships to students with learning disabilities, primarily those who live in CO.
Financial data: Year ended 08/31/2004.
Assets, $867,307 (M); Expenditures, $73,813; Total giving, $32,190.
Fields of interest: Learning disorders.
Type of support: Scholarships—to individuals.
Application information: Applications by letter outlining financial need accepted throughout the year.
EIN: 841148636

1957
James E. Hughes Scholarship Fund
c/o JPMorgan Chase Bank, N.A.
P.O. Box 1308
Milwaukee, WI 53201

Foundation type: Independent foundation
Limitations: Scholarships to financially needy residents of Marion County, IN, attending Butler University, University of Indianapolis, or Marian College in Indianapolis, IN.
Financial data: Year ended 05/31/2005.
Assets, $728,895 (M); Expenditures, $21,376; Total giving, $18,000.
Type of support: Support to graduates or students of specific schools; Undergraduate support.
Application information: Applications accepted.
Deadline(s): None
Additional information: Applicant must be in the upper one-third of his or her class.
EIN: 356009013

1958
Cedric L. Hughes Scholarship Trust
c/o Wells Fargo Bank Minnesota, N.A., P.C. Svcs.
230 W. Superior St., Ste. 400
Duluth, MN 55802
Application address: c/o Earl W. Bedard, 200 5th St., P.O. Box 417, Ironton, MN 56455, tel.: (218) 546-6449

Foundation type: Independent foundation
Limitations: Scholarships to graduates of Crosby-Ironton High School, MN, who demonstrate both an ability to excel and a need for financial assistance.
Financial data: Year ended 03/31/2005.
Assets, $499,104 (M); Expenditures, $45,290; Total giving, $38,000; Grants to individuals, 19 grants totaling $38,000 (high: $2,000, low: $2,000).
Type of support: Scholarships—to individuals; Support to graduates or students of specific schools.
Application information: Contact foundation for current application deadline; Completion of formal application required, including transcript indicating GPA and essay on school participation, achievements, and activities, and why this scholarship is important.
EIN: 416415622

1959
Ruth M. Hughes Scholarship Trust
c/o Unizan Financial Svcs. Group, N.A.
P.O. Box 2307
Zanesville, OH 43702-2307 (740) 455-7060

Foundation type: Independent foundation
Limitations: Scholarships to graduates of high schools in Muskingum County, OH.
Publications: Annual report.
Financial data: Year ended 12/31/2004.
Assets, $5,920,622 (M); Expenditures, $265,773; Total giving, $228,250; Grants to individuals, 53 grants totaling $228,250 (high: $5,000, low: $250).
Type of support: Support to graduates or students of specific schools; Undergraduate support.
Application information:
Deadline(s): May 1
Additional information: Contact foundation for current application guidelines.
EIN: 316442501

1960
Raymond Hughes Scholarship
(formerly Raymond Hughes Business Scholarship)
2023 J Saunders Rd.
Dothan, AL 36305-9215

Foundation type: Independent foundation
Limitations: Scholarships to students of Enterprise High School, and Slocomb High School, AL, for business education.
Financial data: Year ended 12/31/2004.
Assets, $43,382 (M); Expenditures, $2,537; Total giving, $2,500; Grants to individuals, totaling $2,500.
Fields of interest: Business school/education.
Type of support: Support to graduates or students of specific schools; Undergraduate support.
Application information: Application form required.
Deadline(s): Contact schools for application deadline
Additional information: Application should include transcripts.
EIN: 582085356

1961
Teresa F. Hughes Trust
P.O. Box 3170
Honolulu, HI 96802-3170
Application address: c/o Grants Admin., Hawaii Community Foundation, 1164 Bishop St., Ste. 800, Honolulu, HI 96813, tel.: (808) 537-6333

Foundation type: Independent foundation
Limitations: Scholarships to financially needy HI residents who are orphans, half-orphans, social orphans (neglected or abused), and children born out-of-wedlock, for preschool, summer programs, private school, and college.
Financial data: Year ended 03/31/2004.
Assets, $9,373,224 (M); Expenditures, $426,842; Total giving, $367,400.
Fields of interest: Elementary school/education; Secondary school/education; Education; Children, services; Residential/custodial care.
Type of support: Precollege support; Undergraduate support.
Application information: Applications accepted. Application form required.
Deadline(s): None
EIN: 990042494

1962
W. Marshall Hughes, Jr. Scholarship Foundation
c/o W. Marshall Hughes, Jr., National Penn Investors Trust
2201 Ridgewood Rd., Ste. 180
Wyomissing, PA 19610 (800) 826-5534

Foundation type: Independent foundation
Limitations: Scholarships to graduates of Berks County, PA, secondary schools to study architecture, literature, music, or theater. Scholarships are awarded on the basis of merit and are renewable for up to seven years (five undergraduate years and two graduate years).
Financial data: Year ended 12/31/2004.
Assets, $2,915,186 (M); Expenditures, $165,490; Total giving, $137,391; Grants to individuals, 31 grants totaling $137,391 (high: $17,382, low: $720).
Fields of interest: Architecture; Theater; Music; Performing arts, education; Literature.
Type of support: Support to graduates or students of specific schools; Undergraduate support.
Application information: Application form required.
Deadline(s): None
Applicants should submit the following:
1) Letter(s) of recommendation
2) Transcripts
Additional information: Application should also include a letter of recommendation from the applicant's high school principal, guidance counselor, or faculty advisor, description of extracurricular and community activities, statement of career objectives, certificate of acceptance to institution, and supporting artistic materials, if applicable; Interviews required; Auditions may be required.
EIN: 236934996

1963
Herbert J. and Geneva S. Hull Scholarship Fund, Inc.
c/o Rev. Elbridge Holland
85 Laurel Ln.
Greentown, PA 18426
Contact: John Frank, Treas.
Application address: c/o John Frank, 28 Hillside Ave., NJ 07860

Foundation type: Independent foundation
Limitations: Scholarships to residents of Sussex County, NJ, who are preparing for a career in conservation or environmental science through full-time postsecondary education.
Financial data: Year ended 12/31/2004.
Assets, $421,712 (M); Expenditures, $14,328; Total giving, $11,250; Grants to individuals, totaling $11,250.
Fields of interest: Natural resources; Animals/wildlife, preservation/protection.
Type of support: Undergraduate support.
Application information: Application form required.
Deadline(s): May 1
Applicants should submit the following:
1) Transcripts
2) Letter(s) of recommendation
Additional information: Application must also include letter of reference, citizenship, scholarship, and career potential in conservation; Interviews required; Applications may be requested from and returned to John Frank.
Program description:
Scholarship Program: Applicants must be full-time residents of Sussex County, NJ, for at least five years prior to application and exhibit good

citizenship and sound moral character. Applicant must plan to pursue postsecondary education on a full-time basis to prepare him/her for a career in conservation, including areas of environmental science, ecology, wildlife management and preservation, and enhancement of our environment and natural resources.
EIN: 223173661

1964
J. Brannon Hull Scholarship Fund, Inc.
c/o Superintendent's Office
4065 School Dr.
Crooksville, OH 43731 (740) 982-7040

Foundation type: Independent foundation
Limitations: Scholarships to graduates of Crooksville High School, OH, or children of employees of Hull Pottery Company, OH. First-time applicants must be under 23 years of age and have a high school GPA of 2.5 or greater.
Financial data: Year ended 12/31/2004. Assets, $720,017 (M); Expenditures, $54,125; Total giving, $45,332; Grants to individuals, totaling $45,332.
Fields of interest: Higher education.
Type of support: Employee-related scholarships; Support to graduates or students of specific schools.
Application information: Application form required.
Deadline(s): Jan. 15 to Mar. 15
Applicants should submit the following:
1) Transcripts
2) SAT
3) Letter(s) of recommendation
Program description:
Scholarship Fund: Priority shall be given to applicants who show a probability of success in higher education. Once an initial award is made, the fund will consider the recipient's application continuous as long as said recipient remains a student in good standing. Scholarships are awarded for education purposes, not to afford a person an opportunity to develop his or her manual skills or to obtain proficiency in a trade or business. Scholarship support will be provided only for attendance at institutions requiring at least two full years for the completion of course work and leading to an associate's degree or higher. Maximum benefits available in a given academic year will not exceed $1,000. No recipient will receive more than a total of $4,000.
EIN: 311090015

1965
Phyllis Perry Hulton Educational Trust
P.O. Box 1635
Marshalltown, IA 50158-7635 (641) 753-9337
Contact: Robert H. Bowman, Tr.
Application address: 24 E. Main St., Marshalltown, IA 50158, tel.: (641) 753-9337

Foundation type: Independent foundation
Limitations: Scholarships to graduates of any Marshall County, IA, high school.
Financial data: Year ended 11/30/2004. Assets, $1,352,982 (M); Expenditures, $41,037; Total giving, $40,000; Grants to individuals, totaling $40,000.
Type of support: Support to graduates or students of specific schools; Undergraduate support.
Application information: Deadline Apr. 20; Completion of formal application required, including academic qualifications, any physical disabilities,

and a proposed educational budget; Applications available in Jan.
EIN: 426526655

1966
Humane Society of Macomb Foundation, Inc.
11350 22 Mile Rd.
Utica, MI 48317 (586) 739-6870
Contact: George Fox, Pres.

Foundation type: Independent foundation
Limitations: Scholarships, primarily to MI residents, to study veterinary medicine.
Financial data: Year ended 12/31/2004. Assets, $1,461,060 (M); Expenditures, $66,325; Total giving, $64,800; Grants to individuals, totaling $12,300.
Fields of interest: Veterinary medicine.
Type of support: Scholarships—to individuals.
Application information: Contact foundation for current application deadline/guidelines.
EIN: 383183238

1967
Paul A. Humbert Scholarship Trust
c/o Fifth Third Bank
P.O. Box 3636
Grand Rapids, MI 49501-3636
Application address: c/o Culver Community High School, Guidance Off., N. School St., Culver, IN 46511, tel.: (219) 842-3391

Foundation type: Independent foundation
Limitations: Scholarships to students or graduates of Culver Community School Corporation, IN.
Financial data: Year ended 06/30/2005. Assets, $641,730 (M); Expenditures, $37,626; Total giving, $34,015; Grants to individuals, totaling $34,015.
Type of support: Support to graduates or students of specific schools; Undergraduate support.
Application information: Deadline Apr. 15; Completion of formal application required.
EIN: 356505726

1968
The Humboldt Area Foundation
373 Indianola Rd.
Bayside, CA 95524 (707) 442-2993
Contact: Peter H. Pennekamp, Exec. Dir.
FAX: (707) 442-3811;
E-mail: irener@hafoundation.org; Additional E-mails: peter@hafoundation.org and laurao@hafoundation.org; URL: http://www.hafoundation.org

Foundation type: Community foundation
Limitations: Scholarships to students who reside in the Bayside, CA, area for undergraduate education.
Publications: Application guidelines; Annual report; Financial statement; Grants list.
Financial data: Year ended 06/30/2004. Assets, $54,655,373 (M); Expenditures, $3,592,180; Total giving, $3,094,737; Grants to individuals, 1,141 grants totaling $575,883.
Fields of interest: Architecture; Vocational education, post-secondary; Nursing school/education.
Type of support: Support to graduates or students of specific schools; Foreign applicants; Undergraduate support.

Application information: Applications accepted. Application form required. Application form available on the grantmaker's Web site.
Initial approach: Application.
Deadline(s): Apr. 1
Additional information: See Web site for complete program listing.
EIN: 237310660

1969
Esther Hume Educational Endowment Fund, Inc.
613 1st St.
Glasgow, MO 65254 (660) 338-2144
Contact: William J. Daily, Pres.

Foundation type: Independent foundation
Limitations: Scholarships to graduates of high schools in Howard County, MO.
Financial data: Year ended 12/31/2003. Assets, $156,178 (M); Expenditures, $6,919; Total giving, $6,600; Grants to individuals, totaling $6,600.
Type of support: Support to graduates or students of specific schools; Undergraduate support.
Application information: Applications accepted throughout the year; Contact foundation for current application guidelines.
EIN: 431284451

1970
Grace H. Humphrey Residuary Trust
c/o Bank of America, N.A., P.C. Group
P.O. Box 1802
Providence, RI 02901-1802

Foundation type: Independent foundation
Limitations: Scholarships to students and graduates of Simsbury High School, CT.
Financial data: Year ended 12/31/2004. Assets, $317,480 (M); Expenditures, $14,196; Total giving, $10,600; Grants to individuals, totaling $10,600.
Type of support: Support to graduates or students of specific schools; Undergraduate support.
Application information: Applications not accepted.
EIN: 066055126

1971
Huna Heritage Foundation
9301 Glacier Hwy., Ste. A-103
Juneau, AK 99801 (907) 790-4937
FAX: (907) 789-1896;
E-mail: info@hunaheritage.org; Additional tel.: (800) 428-8298; URL: http://www.hunaheritage.org

Foundation type: Company-sponsored foundation
Limitations: Scholarships to AK Huna Totem Shareholders and Descendants for full-time graduate, undergraduate, cultural education, or vocational study.
Publications: Application guidelines.
Financial data: Year ended 12/31/2004. Assets, $177,672 (M); Expenditures, $198,701; Total giving, $78,424; Grants to individuals, 49 grants totaling $55,977 (high: $6,300, low: $40).
Fields of interest: Vocational education; Native Americans/American Indians.
Type of support: Graduate support; Technical education support; Undergraduate support; Workstudy grants.

Application information: Application form required. Application form available on the grantmaker's Web site.

Copies of proposal: 1

Deadline(s): Oct. 15 for fall term, Jan. 30 for spring term

Applicants should submit the following:
1) Letter(s) of recommendation
2) Financial information
3) Budget Information

Additional information: Application should also include transcripts or GED certificate, letter of recommendation from school administrator, and letter of acceptance from college, university, vocational school, or administrators of the Apprenticeship Program or Intern Program of On-The-Job-Training (OJT); Applications available on Web site.

Program description:

Huna Heritage Program: The term 'Descendant' is defined in accordance with the Alaska Native Claims Settlement Act Amendments of 1987 as follows: A person who is descended from a Native, or adopted by a Native, or adopted by a descendant of a Native. The foundation also provides a career counseling program to assist Huna Totem Shareholders and Descendants in selecting a postsecondary school and applying for financial assistance. These services continue once the student is in college via the identification of support services both on and off campus, and continued exploration for sources of funding.

EIN: 943113818

1972

Robert Hungerford Chapel Trust

P.O. Box 2822
Winter Park, FL 32790
Contact: Leroy Brown, Jr., Chair.

Foundation type: Independent foundation
Limitations: Scholarships to economically disadvantaged individuals of color attending FL high schools and colleges.
Financial data: Year ended 12/31/2003. Assets, $480,110 (M); Expenditures, $18,134; Total giving, $6,250; Grants to individuals, 7 grants totaling $6,250 (high: $1,000, low: $700).
Fields of interest: Minorities.
Type of support: Scholarships—to individuals.
Application information: Applications accepted throughout the year; Completion of formal application required, including SAT or ACT results, transcripts and financial information.
EIN: 592350325

1973

H. Jack Hunkele Foundation

c/o The Northern Trust Co.
50 S. LaSalle St., Ste. L-5
Chicago, IL 60675

Foundation type: Independent foundation
Limitations: Scholarships to residents of FL for higher education.
Financial data: Year ended 12/31/2004. Assets, $638,030 (M); Expenditures, $17,503; Total giving, $10,000.
Type of support: Undergraduate support.
Application information: Unsolicited requests for funds not accepted.
EIN: 656101273

1974

Minnie H. Hunt Educational Fund

c/o National City Bank
P.O. Box 94651
Cleveland, OH 44101-4651
Contact: Joseph Gaafar, Trust Off., National City Bank
Application address: P.O. Box 5031, Indianapolis, IN 46255, tel.: (317) 267-7280

Foundation type: Independent foundation
Limitations: Student loans to residents of Madison County, IN, who are under 25 years of age and are attending an accredited institution of higher education.
Financial data: Year ended 06/30/2005. Assets, $220,240 (M); Expenditures, $6,262; Total giving, $0; Loans to individuals, totaling $2,000.
Type of support: Undergraduate support.
Application information: Application form required.
Deadline(s): mid-Apr.
Additional information: Application forms available from the principals of local high schools.

Program description:

Student Loan Program: An official from the student's secondary school must complete a formal evaluation form, including the student's class rank, GPA, transcript, standardized test scores, and recommendations. This form also requires the signature of the school principal.
EIN: 356337245

1975

William C. and Mabel D. Hunt Memorial Scholarship

c/o Bank of America, N.A.
P.O. Box 441
Ridgefield Park, NJ 07660-9984

Foundation type: Independent foundation
Limitations: Scholarships to residents of Cape May County, NJ.
Financial data: Year ended 12/31/2004. Assets, $668,289 (M); Expenditures, $75,258; Total giving, $67,500; Grants to individuals, totaling $67,500.
Type of support: Scholarships—to individuals.
Application information: Application form required.
Deadline(s): May 1
EIN: 222690724

1976

Helena W. Hunt Trust

c/o Rockland Trust Co.
2036 Washington St.
Hanover, MA 02339
Application address: c/o Rockland High School, Attn.: Principal, 34 MacKinlay, Rockland, MA 02370

Foundation type: Independent foundation
Limitations: Scholarships to graduates of Rockland High School, MA.
Financial data: Year ended 06/30/2005. Assets, $384,895 (M); Expenditures, $21,648; Total giving, $16,000; Grants to individuals, totaling $16,000.
Type of support: Support to graduates or students of specific schools; Undergraduate support.
Application information: Applications accepted throughout the year; Completion of formal application required; Application forms available at Rockland High School.
EIN: 046384141

1977

Hunter Douglas Foundation, Inc.

c/o Kathy O'Keefe
2 Park Way & Rt. 17 S.
Upper Saddle River, NJ 07458 (201) 327-8200

Foundation type: Operating foundation
Limitations: Scholarships to children of employees of Hunter Douglas, Inc. and its subsidiaries, primarily in NJ.
Financial data: Year ended 12/31/2004. Assets, $128,148 (M); Expenditures, $246,415; Total giving, $242,925; Grants to individuals, 126 grants totaling $242,925 (high: $6,000, low: $250).
Type of support: Employee-related scholarships.
Application information: Application form required.
Deadline(s): Mid-Sept.
EIN: 223694713

1978

Eileen M. Hunter Scholarship Fund

c/o Wells Fargo Bank Northwest, N.A.
P.O. Box 21927
Seattle, WA 98111
Application address: c/o Teton County School Dist. No. 1, Attn.: Matt Rodosky, P.O. Box 568, Jackson, WY 83001, tel.: (307) 733-2767

Foundation type: Independent foundation
Limitations: Scholarships to high school graduates of the Teton County School District No. 1, WY.
Financial data: Year ended 12/31/2004. Assets, $603,893 (M); Expenditures, $30,447; Total giving, $25,338; Grants to individuals, totaling $25,338.
Type of support: Support to graduates or students of specific schools; Undergraduate support.
Application information: Contact fund for current application deadline/guidelines.
EIN: 836034396

1979

Larry and Gladys Hunter Scholarship Fund, Inc.

412 Pine St.
Minden, LA 71055-3120 (318) 377-6846
Contact: Ben Hunter, Pres.

Foundation type: Independent foundation
Limitations: Scholarships to graduates of the Minden Public School System, LA, for undergraduate education. Scholarships are renewable, for a maximum of $6,000 over four years.
Financial data: Year ended 12/31/2002. Assets, $126,108 (M); Expenditures, $14,534; Total giving, $14,412; Grants to individuals, 11 grants totaling $14,412 (high: $2,500, low: $625).
Type of support: Support to graduates or students of specific schools; Undergraduate support.
Application information: Applications accepted. Application form required.
Deadline(s): Mar. 10
Additional information: Application should include essay.
EIN: 720942291

1980

Ralph and Lucile Hunter Scholarship Trust

c/o Emprise Bank, N.A.
1200 Main St.
Hays, KS   67601
Application address: c/o Fort Hays State Univ.,
Office of Student Financial Assistance, Hays, KS
67601, tel.: (785) 628-4408

Foundation type: Independent foundation
Limitations: Scholarships to female students from
western KS, who are attending Fort Hays State
University.
Financial data: Year ended 12/31/2004.
Assets, $1,554,454 (M); Expenditures,
$110,176; Total giving, $93,000; Grants to
individuals, totaling $93,000.
Fields of interest: Women.
Type of support: Support to graduates or students
of specific schools; Undergraduate support.
Application information: Deadline Mar. 15;
Completion of formal application required.
Program description:
  Scholarship Program: Students must have
graduated from a KS high school, be a full-time
student, maintain a 3.0 GPA, and display
outstanding citizenship.
EIN: 486297085

1981

Jane E. Hunter Testamentary Trust

c/o KeyBank N.A. Tax Dept.
800 Superior Ave., 4th Fl.
Cleveland, OH   44114

Foundation type: Independent foundation
Limitations: Scholarships to young women from
Ohio and South Carolina for higher education.
Financial data: Year ended 12/31/2004.
Assets, $2,154,002 (M); Expenditures,
$103,062; Total giving, $87,283; Grants to
individuals, totaling $87,283.
Type of support: Undergraduate support.
Application information: Deadline May 1; Initial
approach by letter; Completion of formal application
required.
EIN: 346699212

1982

Huntingburg Foundation, Inc.

309 N. Geiger St.
P.O. Box 255
Huntingburg, IN   47542-0255   (812) 683-5799
Contact: Christine L. Prior, Exec. Dir.
FAX: (812) 683-3524;
E-mail: chambered@huntingburg.org; Additional
E-mail: huntingburg@psci.net; URL: http://
www.huntingburg.org/foundation.htm

Foundation type: Community foundation
Limitations: Scholarships to individuals residing in
the Huntingburg, IN, area for undergraduate
education.
Publications: Annual report; Grants list;
Informational brochure.
Financial data: Year ended 12/31/2004.
Assets, $4,301,153 (M); Expenditures,
$312,685; Total giving, $167,304.
Type of support: Undergraduate support.
Application information: Applications accepted.
Application form required. Application form
available on the grantmaker's Web site.
  Copies of proposal: 7
  Deadline(s): Mar. 1
  Applicants should submit the following:
    1) Essay

    2) ACT
    3) GPA
    4) SAT
    5) Transcripts
    6) Letter(s) of recommendation
  Additional information: Applicants must submit
    letter of acceptance to college/university for
    funds to be dispersed.
Program descriptions:
  Larry Dugle Scholarship: Awarded annually to a
graduate of Southridge High School interested in
pursuing a college education.
  Jason Feldmeyer Scholarship: One scholarship to
a senior at Southridge while the second scholarship
shall be open to a graduating senior of any of the
four Dubois County high schools: Jasper, Northeast
Dubois, Forest Park, and Southridge, who is a
member of that school's golf team.
  Sarah Gobert Scholarship: Awarded to students
graduating from any of the four school districts of
Dubois County who wish to pursue further
education in a career in the medical profession.
  Huntingburg Foundation Scholarship: Awarded
annually to a graduate of Southridge High School
interested in pursuing a college education.
  Frosty and Muriel Jones Scholarship: Awarded
annually to a graduate of Southridge High School
interested in pursuing a college degree in aviation
or a related field of study.
  Irene Mendel Scholarship: For three years, a
$1,000 scholarship shall be given to either the
Valedictorian or Solitarian of the graduating class of
Southridge High School. For four years the Musical
Department of Southridge shall choose a student
who has participated in vocal or band to receive a
$1,000 scholarship.
  *Jeanette Rauscher/Southwest Dubois County
Scholarship Fund:* Awarded annually to a graduate
of Southridge High School interested in pursuing a
college education.
  Marian Klausmeier Roettger Scholarship:
Awarded annually to a graduating senior of
Southridge High School interested in pursuing a
college degree in business or accounting. The
amount and number of scholarships to be awarded
shall be at the discretion of the selection
committee, but shall not be less than $1,000.
  Owen Roettger Scholarship: Awarded annually to
a graduating senior of Southridge interested in
pursuing a college degree in music with a
preference of voice over a musical instrument. The
amount and number of scholarships to be awarded
shall be at the discretion of the selection
committee, but shall not be less than $1,000.
  Marcia Scanlon Scholarship: Awarded annually to
a graduate of Southridge High School interested in
pursuing a college degree in education.
  Arnold Schwartz Scholarship: Awarded annually
to a graduate of Southridge High School interested
in pursuing a college degree in math, science, or
engineering.
  Ruby and Dick Smith Scholarship: Awarded
annually to a graduating senior of Southridge High
School who plans on attending a college or
technical school.
  Uebelhor Family Scholarship: Awarded annually
to a graduate of Southridge High School interested
in pursuing a college degree in elementary
education.
EIN: 351410928

1983

Huntington County Help, Inc. for Disabled Citizens

c/o Thomas R. Edington
P.O. Box 1032
Huntington, IN   46750-1032

Foundation type: Independent foundation
Limitations: Scholarships to residents of
Huntington, IN, who are disabled.
Financial data: Year ended 08/31/2004.
Assets, $1,292,544 (M); Expenditures, $92,783;
Total giving, $58,000; Grants to individuals, 14
grants totaling $18,000 (high: $1,500, low:
$1,500).
Fields of interest: Physically disabled.
Type of support: Undergraduate support.
Application information: Applications not
accepted.
  Additional information: Unsolicited requests for
    funds not considered or acknowledged.
EIN: 351903337

1984

The Samuel Huntington Fund, Inc.

25 Research Dr.
Westborough, MA   01582   (508) 389-3390
Contact: Don F. Goodwin, V.P.
E-mail: amy.stacy@us.ngrid.com; URL: http://
www.nationalgridus.com/education

Foundation type: Independent foundation
Limitations: Awards to graduating college seniors
to perform a one-year public service project
anywhere in the world immediately following
graduation. Generally awards two grants of
$10,000 each annually.
Financial data: Year ended 06/30/2005.
Assets, $132,738 (M); Expenditures, $21,191;
Total giving, $20,000; Grants to individuals, 2
grants totaling $20,000.
Application information: Application form required.
Application form available on the grantmaker's Web
site.
  Copies of proposal: 1
  Deadline(s): Feb. 15
  Applicants should submit the following:
    1) Resume
    2) Proposal
    3) Transcripts
    4) Budget Information
  Additional information: Application should also
    include three letters of recommendation;
    Interviews required of semi-finalists.
EIN: 043021374

1985

Horace C. Hurlbutt Memorial Fund

90 Post Rd. E., 3rd Fl.
Westport, CT   06880

Foundation type: Independent foundation
Limitations: Undergraduate scholarships only to
residents of Westport, CT. Maximum scholarship
per individual is $2,000.
Financial data: Year ended 12/31/2004.
Assets, $681,642 (M); Expenditures, $24,414;
Total giving, $14,508; Grants to individuals, 39
grants totaling $8,500.
Type of support: Undergraduate support.
Application information: Applications not
accepted.
EIN: 066035912

1986
Ed and Gladys Hurley Trust Foundation
c/o Bank of America, N.A.
P.O. Box 831041
Dallas, TX 75283-1041 (214) 209-6486
Application address: c/o Bonnie L. Rainey, 5500
Preston Rd., Dallas, TX 75205-6303, tel.: (214)
559-6303

Foundation type: Independent foundation
Limitations: Scholarships to residents of the U.S.
who are studying at schools or colleges in AR, LA
and TX to become ministers, or those in other
phases of religious education of the Protestant
faith.
Publications: Informational brochure (including
application guidelines).
Financial data: Year ended 08/31/2005.
Assets, $2,545,061 (M); Expenditures,
$193,309; Total giving, $146,500; Grants to
individuals, 11 grants totaling $146,500 (high:
$30,000, low: $3,000).
Fields of interest: Theological school/education;
Protestant agencies & churches.
Type of support: Graduate support.
Application information: Application form required.
  Deadline(s): Apr. 30.
  Additional information: Applications are available
     at schools.
EIN: 756006961

1987
Huron County Community Foundation
1160 S. Van Dyke Rd.
Bad Axe, MI 48413-9615 (989) 269-2850
FAX: (989) 269-8209

Foundation type: Community foundation
Limitations: Scholarships to individuals in MI for
higher education.
Financial data: Year ended 12/31/2004.
Assets, $1,146,580 (M); Expenditures,
$136,032; Total giving, $47,568; Grants to
individuals, 24 grants totaling $14,672 (high:
$1,222, low: $250).
Type of support: Scholarships—to individuals.
Application information: Applications accepted
throughout the year; Contact foundation for current
application guidelines; Initial approach by letter or
telephone.
EIN: 383160009

1988
Lonnie Bob Hurst Scholarship Trust
11465 75th Dr.
Live Oak, FL 32060-7118 (386) 364-5210
Contact: Donna C. Long, Tr.

Foundation type: Operating foundation
Limitations: Scholarships to adults wishing to enter
the LPN program at Suwannee-Hamilton Area
Voc-Tech; to Suwannee High School seniors wishing
to enroll in Suwannee-Hamilton Area Voc-Tech after
graduation; and to Suwannee High School seniors
wishing to enroll in a community or four-year college
after graduation, all in FL.
Financial data: Year ended 06/30/2004.
Assets, $96,343 (M); Expenditures, $2,657; Total
giving, $2,000; Grants to individuals, totaling
$2,000.
Fields of interest: Vocational education,
post-secondary.
Type of support: Support to graduates or students
of specific schools; Technical education support;
Undergraduate support.

Application information: Deadline May 1 for high
school seniors and Aug. 1 for LPN students;
Application by letter outlining financial need,
including transcript, one character reference letter,
one reference from teacher or employer, and 2.0
GPA; Interviews required.
EIN: 597011644

1989
Hurst-Sorenson Memorial Fund
P.O. Box 428
Stanford, MT 59479-0428 (406) 566-2238
Contact: Mike Zacher, Tr.; Peggy Petersen, Tr.
Additional tel.: (406) 566-2645

Foundation type: Independent foundation
Limitations: Scholarships to graduates of Stanford
High School, MT, who attend Protestant universities
or vocational or technical schools.
Financial data: Year ended 06/30/2005.
Assets, $534,414 (M); Expenditures, $31,880;
Total giving, $27,795; Grants to individuals,
totaling $27,795.
Fields of interest: Vocational education; Vocational
education, post-secondary; Protestant agencies &
churches.
Type of support: Support to graduates or students
of specific schools; Undergraduate support.
Application information: Deadline July 1;
Application by letter.
EIN: 810372356

1990
Helen Huss Charitable Trust
P.O. Box 189
Salisbury, MO 65281 (660) 388-6608
Contact: Ray Widmer, Tr.

Foundation type: Independent foundation
Limitations: Scholarships to graduates of Salisbury
High School, MO, for higher education.
Financial data: Year ended 12/31/2004.
Assets, $14,051 (M); Expenditures, $21,318;
Total giving, $21,000; Grants to individuals,
totaling $21,000.
Type of support: Support to graduates or students
of specific schools.
Application information: Applications accepted.
Application form required.
  Deadline(s): None
  Additional information: Application forms
     available from the high school's guidance
     counselor.
EIN: 436766144

1991
Theodore Huss, Sr. and Elsie Endert Huss Memorial Fund
c/o Citizens Bank Wealth Mgmt., N.A.
328 S. Saginaw St., M/C 002072
Flint, MI 48502
Application address: c/o Helen James, Citizens
Bank, N.A., Wealth Mgmt., 101 N. Washington Ave.,
Saginaw, MI 48607, tel.: (989) 776-7368

Foundation type: Independent foundation
Limitations: Scholarships to full-time
undergraduate students of Saginaw County, MI.
Financial data: Year ended 12/31/2004.
Assets, $390,679 (M); Expenditures, $23,837;
Total giving, $15,640; Grants to individuals, 23
grants totaling $15,640 (high: $680, low: $380).
Type of support: Undergraduate support.

Application information: Deadline June 1;
Completion of formal application required.
EIN: 386476850

1992
Harold J. Hutchins Foundation Fund
c/o U.S. Bank, N.A.
P.O. Box 387
St. Louis, MO 63166
Contact: Tom Feig
Application address: c/o U.S.Bank, N.A., 235 N.
Elm, P.O. Box, Centralia, IL 62801, tel.: (618)
545-1217

Foundation type: Independent foundation
Limitations: Scholarship loans to graduates of
Mount Vernon High School, IL, for undergraduate
study.
Financial data: Year ended 09/30/2004.
Assets, $209,951 (M); Expenditures, $13,942;
Total giving, $10,525; Loans to individuals, totaling
$10,525.
Type of support: Student loans—to individuals;
Support to graduates or students of specific
schools.
Application information: Application form required.
  Initial approach: Interview.
EIN: 376235717

1993
Hutchinson Community Foundation
1 N. Main St., Ste. 501
P.O. Box 298
Hutchinson, KS 67504-0298 (620) 663-5293
Contact: Lynette S. Lacy, Pres. and Exec. Dir.
FAX: (620) 663-9277; E-mail: info@hutchcf.org;
Grant application E-mail: aubrey@hutchcf.org;
URL: http://www.hutchcf.org

Foundation type: Community foundation
Limitations: Scholarships for postsecondary
education to individuals in Hutchison and Reno
County, KS.
Publications: Annual report; Financial statement;
Grants list; Informational brochure; Newsletter;
Occasional report; Program policy statement.
Financial data: Year ended 12/31/2004.
Assets, $26,036,767 (M); Expenditures,
$4,971,250; Total giving, $4,797,237; Grants to
individuals, 19 grants totaling $63,088.
Type of support: Undergraduate support.
Application information: Applications accepted.
Application form required.
  Initial approach: Letter.
  Copies of proposal: 15
  Deadline(s): June 1
  Additional information: Applications should
     include financial information and be sent to
     the foundation from the schools; Recipients
     notified within 90 days.
EIN: 481076910

1994
Otto A. Huth Scholarship Fund
c/o Wells Fargo Bank, N.A.
P.O. Box 40908
Reno, NV 89504-4908 (775) 823-4810
Contact: David Hess, Dir., Wells Fargo Bank, N.A.

Foundation type: Independent foundation
Limitations: Scholarships to financially needy high
school seniors who are orphans, and who are
primarily residents of NV.

Financial data: Year ended 12/31/2004. Assets, $1,218,903 (M); Expenditures, $65,273; Total giving, $42,712; Grants to individuals, totaling $42,712.
Fields of interest: Children, services; Residential/custodial care.
Type of support: Scholarships—to individuals.
Application information: Deadline prior to college semester; Completion of formal application required, including verification of high school senior status, estimated cost of education, and a list of other aid for which student has applied.
EIN: 886059683

1995
Edward L. Hutton Foundation
2600 Chemed Ctr.
255 E. 5th St.
Cincinnati, OH   45202-4726
Contact: Sandra E. Laney, V.P.

Foundation type: Independent foundation
Limitations: Scholarships to students from I.U. Bedford N. Lawrence high school, and to residents of Centi, Hamilton City, OH.
Publications: Annual report.
Financial data: Year ended 12/31/2004. Assets, $5,373,972 (M); Expenditures, $351,299; Total giving, $299,692; Grants to individuals, 19 grants totaling $27,546 (high: $5,000, low: $500).
Type of support: Grants to individuals; Awards/grants by nomination only; Undergraduate support; Postgraduate support.
Application information: Applications not accepted.
EIN: 311334189

1996
Hy-Vee Foundation, Inc.
5820 Westown Pkwy.
West Des Moines, IA   50266-8223
Contact: Rose Kleyweg Mitchell, Pres.

Foundation type: Company-sponsored foundation
Limitations: Scholarships to a predetermined number of current Hy-Vee, Inc. employees and their children in ten regions of company operations, principally IA, IL, KS, MN, MO, NE, and SD.
Financial data: Year ended 09/27/2004. Assets, $139 (M); Expenditures, $73,036; Total giving, $67,000; Grants to individuals, 67 grants totaling $67,000 (high: $1,000, low: $1,000).
Type of support: Employee-related scholarships.
Application information: Application form required.
Initial approach: Letter.
Deadline(s): Jan. 10
Additional information: Recipients notified in May.
EIN: 420942086

1997
Hyde Family Foundations
17 W. Pontotoc Ave., Ste. 200
Memphis, TN   38103   (901) 685-3400
Contact: Teresa Sloyan, Exec. Dir.
FAX: (901) 683-3147;
E-mail: info@hydefamilyfoundations.org;
URL: http://www.hydefamilyfoundations.org

Foundation type: Independent foundation
Limitations: Scholarships and loans only to children of current TN employees of The Autozone Inc. Co., who are entering their freshman year of

college. Scholarship is paid directly to the institution.
Publications: Application guidelines.
Financial data: Year ended 12/31/2004. Assets, $128,830,819 (M); Expenditures, $8,721,048; Total giving, $6,560,150.
Type of support: Employee-related scholarships.
Application information: Applications accepted. Application form required.
Deadline(s): Mar. 31.
Additional information: Application process coordinated through AutoZone Community Relations; Recipients notified in Apr.

1998
Hypertronics Corporation Charitable Foundation
c/o Hypertronics Corp.
16 Brent Dr.
Hudson, MA   01749   (978) 568-0451
Contact: Margaret S. McDonald, Tr.

Foundation type: Company-sponsored foundation
Limitations: Scholarships to graduating seniors at public schools in Hudson, Maynard, and Marlboro, MA, who are majoring in physical sciences, engineering, or math.
Financial data: Year ended 12/31/2004. Assets, $35,650 (M); Expenditures, $10,035; Total giving, $10,000; Grants to individuals, 10 grants totaling $10,000 (high: $1,000, low: $1,000).
Fields of interest: Mathematics; Engineering.
Type of support: Support to graduates or students of specific schools; Undergraduate support.
Application information:
Initial approach: Letter or telephone.
Deadline(s): Contact foundation for current application deadline.
EIN: 043062594

1999
I Have a Dream Foundation
P.O. Box 4567
Carmel, IN   46082-4567

Foundation type: Operating foundation
Limitations: Scholarships to students attending the University of Indiana, IN.
Financial data: Year ended 12/31/2003. Assets, $2,204 (M); Expenditures, $34,965; Total giving, $34,950; Grants to individuals, 5 grants totaling $34,950 (high: $22,950, low: $1,000).
Type of support: Support to graduates or students of specific schools; Undergraduate support.
Application information: Applications not accepted.
EIN: 351769495

2000
I Have a Dream Foundation - Oregon
4317 N.E. Emerson St.
Portland, OR   97218
E-mail: info@ihad.org; URL: http://www.ihad.org

Foundation type: Operating foundation
Limitations: Scholarships to individuals for higher education, primarily to residents of OR.
Financial data: Year ended 08/31/2003. Assets, $106,402 (M); Expenditures, $964,568; Total giving, $93,177; Grants to individuals, totaling $93,177.
Type of support: Undergraduate support.

Application information: Unsolicited requests for funds not accepted.
EIN: 931037323

2001
I Have a Dream Foundation - Port Huron
5538 Lakeshore Rd.
Fort Gratiot, MI   48059
Contact: Chris M. Kurzweil, Pres.

Foundation type: Independent foundation
Limitations: Scholarships to economically disadvantaged graduating students attending high schools in the Port Huron, MI, area.
Financial data: Year ended 06/30/2005. Assets, $73,529 (M); Expenditures, $136,666; Total giving, $119,267; Grants to individuals, 32 grants totaling $119,267 (high: $9,309, low: $278).
Type of support: Support to graduates or students of specific schools; Undergraduate support.
Application information: Contact foundation for current application deadline/guidelines.
EIN: 383193498

2002
I Have a Dream Foundation of Delaware
1907 N. Van Buren St.
Wilmington, DE   19802

Foundation type: Operating foundation
Limitations: Scholarships to pre-selected individuals residing in DE.
Financial data: Year ended 06/30/2003. Assets, $10,637 (M); Expenditures, $4,590; Total giving, $3,133; Grants to individuals, 3 grants totaling $3,133 (high: $2,700, low: $109).
Type of support: Scholarships—to individuals.
Application information: Applications not accepted.
EIN: 510313759

2003
I.O.O.F. Grand Lodge Educational Fund, Inc.
c/o Paul L. Hevner
1465 Tremont Ave.
Morgantown, WV   26505-5335
Contact: Carl C. Williams, Secy.
Application address: Rte. 6, P.O. Box 295, Clarksburg, WV 26301

Foundation type: Independent foundation
Limitations: Scholarships to members of The Independent Order of Odd Fellows of WV and their children. Applicants must be high school graduates who are members or the children of WV Odd Fellows members, who are in good standing or are deceased.
Financial data: Year ended 12/31/2004. Assets, $405,956 (M); Expenditures, $33,759; Total giving, $32,400; Grants to individuals, totaling $32,400.
Type of support: Scholarships—to individuals.
Application information: Applications accepted throughout the year; Completion of formal application required, including transcripts, personal statement, and a letter from the Lodge of I.O.O.F., under seal of Lodge, stating that applicant is eligible.
EIN: 237003391

2004
IATAN Foundation

(also known as IATAN-Ronald A. Santana Memorial Foundation)
300 Garden City Plz.
Garden City, NY 11530-3302 (516) 663-6000
Contact: Christopher Gilbey, Chair.
PR tel.: (514) 868-8800; Additional tel.: (800) 294-2826 ext. 4; FAX: (516) 747-4462;
URL: http://www.iatan.org/

Foundation type: Public charity
Limitations: Scholarships to individuals who plan to pursue or enhance their careers in travel.
Financial data: Year ended 12/31/2003. Assets, $194,334 (M); Expenditures, $8,410; Total giving, $6,000; Grants to individuals, totaling $6,000.
Fields of interest: Visitors/convention bureau/tourism promotion.
Type of support: Scholarships—to individuals.
Application information: Application form available on the grantmaker's Web site.
> *Deadline(s):* Apr. 1
> *Applicants should submit the following:*
> 1) Resume
> 2) Transcripts
> *Additional information:* Completion of formal application required, including letter of recommendation from study supervisor, letter from employer if applicable, photocopies of recent awards related to the travel industry, and a 750-1,000 word essay.

Program description:
> *Scholarship Program:* Awards scholarships to students who meet the following criteria:
> · be at least 17 years of age
> · reside in the U.S. or its commonwealth or territories
> · have already begun study or plan to shortly
> · have courses in Travel and Tourism, Hospitality, and/or related fields of study

EIN: 113361043

2005
ICRDA/SDA Scholarship Foundation

(formerly Systems Dealers Association Scholarship Foundation)
4115 Taggart Creek Rd.
Charlotte, NC 28208

Foundation type: Independent foundation
Limitations: Scholarships to children of employees, members or dealers of ICRDA/SDA.
Financial data: Year ended 04/30/2005. Assets, $9,545 (M); Expenditures, $36,000; Total giving, $36,000; Grants to individuals, totaling $36,000.
Type of support: Employee-related scholarships.
Application information: Deadline June 15; Completion of formal application required, including current FAF, essay, list of school activities, leadership positions, work experience and awards, and transcript.
EIN: 364130326

2006
Idaho Community Foundation

c/o Cathy Silak
210 W. State St.
Boise, ID 83702 (208) 342-3535
Contact: Holly Motes, Cont.; For grants: Kay Harper, Grant Specialist
FAX: (208) 342-3577; E-mail: info@idcomfdn.org; Mailing address: P.O. Box 8143, Boise, ID 83707;

Additional tel.: (800) 657-5357; Additional E-mail: hmotes@idcomfdn.org; Grant inquiry E-mail: grants@idcomfdn.org; URL: http://www.idcomfdn.org

Foundation type: Community foundation
Limitations: Scholarships to residents of ID.
Publications: Application guidelines; Annual report; Financial statement; Informational brochure (including application guidelines); Newsletter; Program policy statement.
Financial data: Year ended 12/31/2004. Assets, $60,309,541 (M); Expenditures, $4,762,040; Total giving, $3,382,730; Grants to individuals, 79 grants totaling $250,626 (high: $5,000, low: $500).
Type of support: Undergraduate support.
Application information: Applications accepted. Application form required. Application form available on the grantmaker's Web site.
> *Initial approach:* E-mail.
> *Deadline(s):* Vary
> *Additional information:* Each scholarship has its own application process and deadline. See Web site for a complete listing of all scholarships.

EIN: 820425063

2007
May H. Ilgenfritz Testamentary Trust

c/o Bank of America, N.A.
P.O. Box 831041
Dallas, TX 75283-1041
Application address: c/o Virginia Swearingen, 717 W. 6th St., Sedalia, MO 65302, tel.: (816) 979-7405

Foundation type: Independent foundation
Limitations: Scholarships to financially needy high school students in the Sedalia, MO, area, who rank in the upper third of their classes.
Financial data: Year ended 12/31/2004. Assets, $4,207,869 (M); Expenditures, $206,304; Total giving, $153,700; Grants to individuals, 83 grants totaling $152,500 (high: $4,000, low: $400).
Type of support: Undergraduate support.
Application information: Deadlines July and Dec.; Application by letter of no more than three pages, accompanied by two letters of recommendation, one related to character and the other to academic potential.

Program description:
> *Scholarship Program:* Students must rank in the upper third of their high school graduating classes (but this requirement may be waived in special cases) and have demonstrable financial need. If student is attending a junior college and plans to transfer to a four-year college, he or she must rank in the upper one-third of his or her class and/or have at least a "C+" average.

EIN: 440663403

2008
Illinois Broadcasters Association Minority Intern Program, Inc.

300 N. Pershing B.
Energy, IL 62933

Foundation type: Operating foundation
Limitations: Educational support to students of color studying in colleges of communication at IL institutes of higher education.
Financial data: Year ended 12/31/2003. Assets, $33,245 (M); Expenditures, $17,837; Total giving, $14,000; Grants to individuals, 10

grants totaling $14,000 (high: $1,800, low: $1,200).
Fields of interest: Media/communications; Minorities.
Type of support: Scholarships—to individuals.
Application information:
> *Initial approach:* Letter or telephone.
> *Additional information:* Contact college dean for current application deadline/guidelines.

EIN: 371231448

2009
Illinois High School Activities Foundation

2715 McGraw Dr.
Bloomington, IL 61704-2715

Foundation type: Independent foundation
Limitations: Scholarships only to IL high school students on the Illinois High School Association's All-State Academic Team.
Financial data: Year ended 12/31/2004. Assets, $50,577 (M); Expenditures, $45,113; Total giving, $26,000; Grants to individuals, totaling $26,000.
Type of support: Precollege support; Undergraduate support.
Application information: Contact foundation for current application deadline; Initial approach by letter or telephone; Completion of formal application required, including scholastic standing, participation in high school athletics, community service, and two letters of recommendation.
EIN: 371322645

2010
Illinois Historic Preservation Agency Trust

Old State Capitol Plz.
Springfield, IL 62701

Foundation type: Public charity
Limitations: Scholarships to Ph.D. candidates studying historic or library science, primarily in IL.
Fields of interest: Historic preservation/historical societies; Libraries/library science.
Type of support: Doctoral support.
Application information: Applications not accepted.
EIN: 376332661

2011
Illinois Scholarship Foundation

9N978 N. Leland Ct.
Elgin, IL 60123

Foundation type: Independent foundation
Limitations: Scholarships and grants by nomination only to residents of IL.
Financial data: Year ended 12/31/2004. Assets, $21,835 (M); Expenditures, $60,076; Total giving, $40,118; Grants to individuals, totaling $40,118.
Type of support: Awards/grants by nomination only.
Application information: Applications not accepted.
> *Additional information:* Unsolicited requests for funds not considered or acknowledged.

EIN: 364291185

2012
Illinois Tool Works Foundation
3600 W. Lake Ave.
Glenview, IL   60025-5811   (847) 724-7500
Contact: Mary Ann Mallahan, Secy.
FAX: (847) 657-4505;
E-mail: mmallahan@itw.com; URL: http://
www.itw.com/itw_foundation.html

Foundation type: Company-sponsored foundation
Limitations: Employee-related scholarships to
children of Illinois Tool Works employees.
Publications: Newsletter.
Financial data: Year ended 02/28/2005.
Assets, $21,916,937 (M); Expenditures,
$8,683,130; Total giving, $8,695,554.
Type of support: Employee-related scholarships.
Application information:
  Deadline(s): None
  Additional information: Applications should be
    sent by brief letter and should outline financial
    need.
EIN: 366087160

2013
Illinois Valley Educational Foundation, Inc.
79 W. Monroe St., Ste. 1119
Chicago, IL   60603-4950

Foundation type: Independent foundation
Limitations: Scholarships to financially needy
students attending La Salle Catholic Schools in La
Salle, IL, for payment of tuition.
Financial data: Year ended 10/31/2004.
Assets, $12,452 (M); Expenditures, $28,222;
Total giving, $28,100; Grants to individuals,
totaling $28,100.
Type of support: Scholarships—to individuals;
Support to graduates or students of specific
schools.
Application information: Contact foundation for
current application deadline; Completion of formal
application required; Applications are distributed
through the school.
EIN: 364120388

2014
IMM-MIN-ED Foundation
212-75 Whitehall Terr.
Queens Village, NY   11427
Contact: Eleanor Bollag, V.P.

Foundation type: Independent foundation
Limitations: Scholarships to students, primarily in
NY, for higher education.
Financial data: Year ended 05/31/2005.
Assets, $5,625 (M); Expenditures, $3,775; Total
giving, $3,400; Grants to individuals, totaling
$3,400.
Type of support: Undergraduate support.
Application information: Applications by letter
accepted throughout the year.
EIN: 112556291

2015
Immagia Foundation, Inc.
306 N.W. 32nd St.
Corvallis, OR   97330-5023
Contact: Paul Ahrens, Pres.

Foundation type: Independent foundation
Limitations: Scholarships to graduates of Corvallis
high schools, OR.

Financial data: Year ended 12/31/2004.
Assets, $1,103 (M); Expenditures, $70,518; Total
giving, $54,000; Grants to individuals, totaling
$54,000.
Type of support: Support to graduates or students
of specific schools; Undergraduate support.
Application information: Applications accepted
throughout the year; Contact foundation for current
application guidelines.
EIN: 931188930

2016
Immokalee Foundation, Inc.
4100 Corporate Sq., Ste. 156
Naples, FL   34104   (239) 430-9122
Contact: Ed Laudise
E-mail: Immfound@earthlink.net

Foundation type: Public charity
Limitations: Scholarships to graduates of
Immokalee High School, FL.
Publications: Application guidelines; Annual report;
Grants list; Informational brochure; Newsletter.
Financial data: Year ended 03/31/2005.
Assets, $3,900,388 (M); Expenditures,
$567,657; Total giving, $445,693; Grants to
individuals, totaling $204,305.
Type of support: Support to graduates or students
of specific schools; Undergraduate support.
Application information: Application form required.
  Initial approach: Letter.
  Copies of proposal: 7
  Deadline(s): Jan.15
  Applicants should submit the following:
    1) Proposal
    2) Financial information
    3) Budget Information
  Additional information: Applications should be
    mailed.
EIN: 650315664

2017
Immune Deficiency Foundation, Inc.
40 W. Chesapeake Ave., Ste. 308
Towson, MD   21204   (800) 296-4433
Contact: Donald Weinapple, C.F.O.
FAX: (410) 321-9165;
E-mail: idf@primaryimmune.org; URL: http://
www.primaryimmune.org/

Foundation type: Public charity
Limitations: Scholarships of $500 to $1,000 for
one or two years for undergraduate or technical
training to students with primary immune
deficiencies requiring financial assistance for
undergraduate studies.
Publications: Application guidelines; Newsletter.
Financial data: Year ended 12/31/2003.
Assets, $2,763,350 (M); Expenditures,
$4,555,503; Total giving, $26,500; Grants to
individuals, 34 grants totaling $26,500 (high:
$1,000, low: $750).
Fields of interest: Vocational education.
Type of support: Undergraduate support.
Application information: Application form required.
  Initial approach: Initial approach by letter or
    telephone.
  Deadline(s): Deadline Mar. 31.
  Additional information: Application must include
    diagnosis of a primary immune deficiency
    disease.
EIN: 521214782

2018
Indiana Elks Charities, Inc.
908 Maple Dr.
Rockville, IN   47872   (765) 643-4786
Contact: Joe Erp, Pres.

Foundation type: Public charity
Limitations: Scholarships to local students for
college and vocational education. Some
scholarships also to the finalists and winner of the
Miss Indiana Pageant.
Financial data: Year ended 03/31/2005.
Assets, $395,924 (M); Expenditures, $361,470;
Total giving, $331,743; Grants to individuals, 88
grants totaling $81,600 (high: $1,000, low: $300).
Fields of interest: Vocational education,
post-secondary.
Type of support: Undergraduate support.
Application information: Contact foundation for
current application deadline/guidelines.
EIN: 237289798

2019
Indonesian Cultural Foundation, Inc.
605 3rd Ave., Ste. 1501
New York, NY   10158
Contact: Carl J. Morelli, Secy.-Treas.

Foundation type: Independent foundation
Limitations: University scholarships to citizens of
Indonesia with genuine financial need and a
superior academic record for graduate study in the
U.S.
Publications: Annual report.
Financial data: Year ended 12/31/2004.
Assets, $1,769,821 (M); Expenditures,
$125,583; Total giving, $69,191; Grants to
individuals, 27 grants totaling $67,333 (high:
$4,000, low: $1,332).
Fields of interest: International exchange,
students.
Type of support: Foreign applicants; Graduate
support.
Application information: Applications accepted.
Application form required.
  Initial approach: Letter.
  Deadline(s): May 15 for fall semester and Nov.
    15 for spring semester
  Applicants should submit the following:
    1) Transcripts
    2) Letter(s) of recommendation
EIN: 237055841

2020
Joe Ingram Trust
c/o Bank of America, N.A.
211 South Broadway
Salisbury, MO   65281

Foundation type: Independent foundation
Limitations: Student loans to residents of Chariton
County, MO, and awards to valedictorians and
salutatorians of graduating classes of Chariton
County high schools for undergraduate and
vocational education.
Financial data: Year ended 12/31/2004.
Assets, $14,270,352 (M); Expenditures,
$902,559; Total giving, $744,090; Grants to
individuals, 61 grants totaling $32,759 (high:
$1,000, low: $500); Loans to individuals, 398
loans totaling $690,320.
Type of support: Student loans—to individuals;
Support to graduates or students of specific
schools.
Application information: Application form required.

Initial approach: Letter.
Deadline(s): None
Applicants should submit the following:
 1) GPA
 2) Financial information
Additional information: Application should also include recommendation form filled out by counselor, first two pages of federal tax returns, biographical sketch, and, for college students, current transcripts.

Program descriptions:

Student Loans: High school students must have a cumulative GPA of at least 3.0 on a 4.0 scale or the equivalent, or an 8.5 on the 11.0 scale. To continue loans in college, students must have at least a 2.0 GPA and be enrolled on a full-time basis. High school students who do not have the required average may be eligible after their first semester of college if they obtain at least a 2.0 GPA as a full-time student. Loans for trade schools are not determined by high school GPA. College loans are to be repaid over a maximum of ten years, and trade school loans over five years, in monthly, quarterly, semi-annual, or annual installments. The four percent interest rate becomes active twelve months following graduation or when the student leaves school. However, there is no such grace period for the loan itself, with payments beginning immediately upon graduation. Students are expected to seek other sources of financial aid as well.

Valedictorian and Salutatorian Awards: These grants are given to graduating high school seniors attending schools within Chariton County, MO.
EIN: 446006475

2021

Initiative Foundation

(formerly Central Minnesota Initiative Fund)
405 1st St., S.E.
Little Falls, MN 56345 (320) 632-9255
Contact: Kathy Gaalswyk, Pres.
FAX: (320) 632-9258; E-mail: info@ifound.org;
Additional tel: (877) 632-9255; Additional E-mail: Kgaalswyk@ifound.org; URL: http://www.ifound.org

Foundation type: Community foundation
Limitations: Scholarships to high school seniors who reside in the 14-county area of Benton, Cass, Chisago, Crow Wing, Isanti, Kanabec, Mille Lacs, Morrison, Pine, Sherburne, Stearns, Todd, Wadena, and Wright, MN.
Publications: Application guidelines; Annual report; Grants list; Informational brochure; Newsletter; Program policy statement.
Financial data: Year ended 06/30/2004. Assets, $36,309,311 (L); Expenditures, $3,118,067; Total giving, $769,858; Grants to individuals, 57 grants totaling $44,455 (high: $2,000, low: $500).
Type of support: Undergraduate support.
Application information: Applications accepted. Application form required.
 Initial approach: Telephone.
EIN: 363451562

2022

Inman-Riverdale Foundation

P.O. Box 207
Inman, SC 29349 (864) 472-2121

Foundation type: Company-sponsored foundation
Limitations: Scholarships only to dependents of Inman Mills employees, SC.

Financial data: Year ended 11/30/2004. Assets, $6,236,139 (M); Expenditures, $551,508; Total giving, $456,436; Grants to individuals, 12 grants totaling $47,648 (high: $8,867, low: $400).
Type of support: Employee-related scholarships.
EIN: 576019736

2023

The INNW Fund

250 Oak Grove Ave., Ste. A
Menlo Park, CA 94025-3218 (650) 327-0248
Contact: Susan K. Lang, Pres.

Foundation type: Public charity
Limitations: Awards and scholarships to individuals for undergraduate education.
Financial data: Year ended 10/31/2004. Assets, $160,276 (M); Expenditures, $376,896; Total giving, $203,800.
Type of support: Support to graduates or students of specific schools; Undergraduate support.
Application information: Contact foundation for current application deadline/guidelines; Completion of formal application required, including transcript, essay, and financial information.
EIN: 770293402

2024

Institute for Better Education

5151 E. Broadway, Ste. 1600
Tucson, AZ 85711 (520) 512-5438
Contact: Louise Gilbert, Prog. Coord.
FAX: (520) 512-5401;
E-mail: info@ibescholarships.org; URL: http://www.ibescholarships.org

Foundation type: Public charity
Limitations: Scholarships primarily to individuals residing in the Tucson, AZ, area for attendance at parochial and private schools.
Publications: Informational brochure; Newsletter.
Financial data: Year ended 08/31/2004. Assets, $334,237 (M); Expenditures, $1,025,243; Total giving, $947,988; Grants to individuals, 1,300 grants totaling $947,988.
Type of support: Precollege support.
Application information: Applications accepted. Application form required. Application form available on the grantmaker's Web site.
 Deadline(s): Rolling
 Applicants should submit the following:
  1) Financial information
 Additional information: Application should include a letter of circumstances, if needed.
EIN: 237102832

2025

Institute for Humane Studies

c/o George Mason University
3301 N. Fairfax Dr., Ste. 440
Arlington, VA 22201-4432 (703) 993-4880
Contact: Marty Zupan, Pres.
FAX: (703) 993-4890; E-mail: ins@gmu.edu;
Additional tel.: (800) 697-8799; URL: http://www.theihs.org/

Foundation type: Public charity
Limitations: Fellowships and internships to humanities and arts students.
Financial data: Year ended 08/31/2004. Assets, $5,232,154 (M); Expenditures, $3,787,842; Total giving, $421,134; Grants to

individuals, 190 grants totaling $403,027 (high: $12,500, low: $100).
Fields of interest: Media/communications; Film/video; Theater (playwriting); Humanities; Literature; Journalism school/education; Public policy, research.
Type of support: Fellowships; Internship funds; Graduate support; Undergraduate support; Postgraduate support; Travel grants.
Application information: Application form required.
 Deadline(s): Vary
 Additional information: See Web site for deadlines and further information.
Program descriptions:

Charles G. Koch Summer Fellow Program: Awards a $1,500 stipend to individuals for the Washington, DC Public Policy Internship. Includes airfare, housing, and career development workshops. Deadline Feb. 15.

IHS Journalism Internships: Internships to journalism students at Freedom Communications Newspaper, including a $1,500 stipend, housing allowance, travel, and seminar and career workshops. Deadline Jan. 15.

Young Communicators Fellowships: Up to $5,000 awarded to advanced students and recent graduates pursuing specified non-academic careers. Fellowships are awarded to appropriate candidates to help them take advantage of strategic short-term opportunities that can enhance their abilities and credentials to pursue careers that involve the communication of ideas. Each fellowship consists of a stipend of up to $2,500 for a 12-week period, and housing and travel assistance of up to $2,500 if required. Fellowships are not for tuition or living expenses associated with pursuing a degree. To qualify for consideration, recipient must: be a college junior or senior, a graduate student or a recent graduate; have a clearly demonstrated interest in the "classical liberal" tradition of individual rights and market economies; be intent on pursuing a career in journalism, film, writing (fiction or nonfiction), publishing or market-oriented public policy; and have arranged or applied for an internship, training program or other short-term opportunity related to their intended career. Recipient must submit a proposal of 500-1,000 words explaining: what specific opportunity/opportunities he/she has arranged or applied for; and what financial assistance is needed. Recipient must include a cover letter, current resume, a writing sample, and the names, addresses and telephone numbers of two academic and/or professional references. Deadline Mar. 15.

Humane Studies Fellowship: Awards of up to $12,000 to individuals for graduate or undergraduate study in the U.S. or abroad. Recipients must have an interest in the classical liberal tradition. Deadline Dec. 31.

Film & Fiction Scholarships: Awards of up to $10,000 for tuition, plus stipend to students who are pursuing a Master of Fine Arts (M.F.A.) degree in filmmaking, fiction writing or playwriting. Recipients must have a demonstrated interest in classical liberal ideas and application in contemporary society, and must possess the desire, motivation and creative ability to succeed in their chosen profession.

Summer Graduate Research Fellowships: Awards a $3,000 stipend and travel expenses to Fellows to spend the summer completing their own writing projects. Recipients interact with a community of scholars. Deadline Feb. 15.
EIN: 941623852

2026
Institute for the Study of Human Resources

1017 S. Arlington Ave.
Los Angeles, CA 90019-3513

Foundation type: Operating foundation
Limitations: Scholarships to individuals residing in CA to study human resources.
Financial data: Year ended 12/31/2003. Assets, $0 (M); Expenditures, $34,933; Total giving, $28,850; Grant to an individual, 1 grant totaling $25,850.
Fields of interest: Business school/education.
Type of support: Scholarships—to individuals.
Application information: Applications not accepted.
EIN: 952369815

2027
InterBel Telephone Cooperative Education Foundation

c/o Gerald L. Hanson
P.O. Box 1398
Whitefish, MT 59937-1398

Foundation type: Company-sponsored foundation
Limitations: Scholarships to students with a parent or guardian who is, or has been, a member of InterBel Telephone Cooperative, MT, for two of the past five years.
Financial data: Year ended 12/31/2004. Assets, $146,633 (M); Expenditures, $5,388; Total giving, $3,500; Grants to individuals, 9 grants totaling $3,500 (high: $750, low: $250).
Type of support: Employee-related scholarships.
Application information: Application form required.
Deadline(s): None
Additional information: Application address: c/o InterBel Telephone Cooperative Inc., P.O. Box 128, Eureka, MT 59917, tel.: (406) 889-3311.
EIN: 363684131

2028
Intermountain Electrical Association Education Fund Scholarship Program

(also known as IEA Educational Scholarship Program)
2125 W. 2300 S.
West Valley City, UT 84119-2017
Contact: Klaas DeBoer

Foundation type: Independent foundation
Limitations: Scholarships to individuals for higher education, primarily in UT.
Financial data: Year ended 12/31/2004. Assets, $695,287 (M); Expenditures, $64,725; Total giving, $62,000; Grants to individuals, totaling $62,000.
Type of support: Scholarships—to individuals.
Application information: Applications not accepted.
EIN: 742520009

2029
Internal Medicine Associates Scholarship Fund, Inc.

121 N. 20th St.
Opelika, AL 36801 (334) 749-3385
Contact: W. Park McGehee, Chair.

Foundation type: Independent foundation

Limitations: Scholarships to an AL graduating senior planning to enter a health career of any type.
Financial data: Year ended 12/31/2004. Assets, $173,468 (M); Expenditures, $11,860; Total giving, $11,460; Grants to individuals, totaling $11,460.
Type of support: Undergraduate support.
Application information:
Initial approach: Letter.
Deadline(s): Apr. 1
Applicants should submit the following:
  1) ACT
Additional information: Contact foundation for current application guidelines.
EIN: 570884128

2030
The International Association of Culinary Professionals Foundation

(formerly Cooking Advancement Research and Education Foundation)
304 W. Liberty St., Ste. 201
Louisville, KY 40202-3068 (502) 583-3783
Contact: Christopher Papagni, Secy.
FAX: (502) 589-3602;
E-mail: emcknight@hqtrs.com; URL: http://www.iacpfoundation.com/

Foundation type: Public charity
Limitations: Awards and scholarships for training at both the primary and continuing education level to students interested in culinary careers.
Publications: Application guidelines; Annual report; Financial statement; Newsletter.
Financial data: Year ended 06/30/2004. Assets, $244,734 (M); Expenditures, $255,052; Total giving, $26,000; Grants to individuals, 6 grants totaling $26,000 (high: $5,000, low: $1,000).
Fields of interest: Adult/continuing education; Business/industry.
Type of support: Awards/prizes; Undergraduate support.
Application information:
Initial approach: Letter.
Deadline(s): Dec. 1
Additional information: Contact foundation for current application guidelines.
Program description:
Culinary Scholarships: Scholarships ranging from $500 to $10,000 are given for basic, continuing and specialty education courses in the U.S. and abroad. Awards are tuition credit and cash. Awards cover partial tuition costs; however, they may be occasionally used to cover course-related expenses such as research, room and board, or travel.
EIN: 521333505

2031
International Council of Airshows Foundation, Inc.

751 Miller Dr., SE, F-4
Leesburg, VA 20175
Contact: Caroline Trinkwalder, Chair.
E-mail: scholarship@icasfoundation.org;
URL: http://icasfoundation.org

Foundation type: Public charity
Limitations: Scholarships to aspiring pilots, air performers and flight instructors.
Publications: Application guidelines; Financial statement; Program policy statement.
Financial data: Year ended 06/30/2005. Assets, $120,669 (M); Expenditures, $21,021; Total giving, $16,000; Grants to individuals, 9

grants totaling $16,000 (high: $5,000, low: $1,000).
Fields of interest: Scholarships/financial aid; Space/aviation.
Type of support: Grants to individuals; Scholarships—to individuals.
Application information: Application form required. Application form available on the grantmaker's Web site.
Copies of proposal: 1
Deadline(s): Sept. 1
Applicants should submit the following:
  1) Essay
Additional information: Application should include a short biography.
Program descriptions:
Charlie Hillard Memorial Scholarship: Awards $1,000 each to two U.S. citizens 16 years or older. The scholarship monies must be used towards instruction in tailwheel aircraft operations or acrobatic flight.
Family Fund: Provides financial aid to individuals in the air show profession and their families who have suffered a catastrophic event.
French Connection Memorial Scholarship: Awards $1,000 each to a male and female certified flight instructor (CFI), and the scholarship monies must be used for aerobatic flight training.
Jan Jones Memorial Scholarship: Awards $1,000 to a female holding a private pilot certificate. The grant is for aerobatic flight training.
Leo Loudenslager Memorial Scholarship: Awards of $2,000 is given in rotation to an enlisted member of the US Navy Blue Angels, the US Air Force Thunderbirds, and the Canadian Forces Snowbirds. Recipient must use the scholarship monies for flight training.
Red Barons Memorial Scholarship: Awards $1,000 to a U.S. citizen 16 years or older. The scholarship money must be used towards instruction in tailwheel aircraft operations or acrobatic flight.
Sean DeRosier Memorial Scholarship: Applicants must have a private pilot's license, be between the ages of 18 and 31, and must be a resident of the western U.S., defined as the states of CA, OR, WA, NV or ID. The scholarship monies must be applied towards aerobatic flight training or schooling towards obtaining his or her A & P license.
EIN: 382885409

2032
International Council of Shopping Centers Educational Foundation, Inc.

1221 Ave. of the Americas, 41st Fl.
New York, NY 10020-1099 (646) 728-3800
Contact: Sarah Ritchie, Educational Fdn. Mgr.
FAX: (212) 589-5555; E-mail: icsc@icsc.org;
Additional tel.: (646) 728-3490; Additional E-mail: sritchie@icsc.org; URL: http://www.icsc.org/srch/education/education_univlinks.php

Foundation type: Independent foundation
Limitations: Scholarships to individuals employed by ICSC member companies for professional education in the shopping center industry or real estate at the John T. Riordan School for Professional Development.
Financial data: Year ended 12/31/2003. Assets, $599,058 (M); Expenditures, $377,564; Total giving, $150,873; Grant to an individual, 1 grant totaling $8,500.
Fields of interest: Business school/education.
Type of support: Scholarships—to individuals; Foreign applicants; Travel grants.
Application information:
Deadline(s): Mar. 15

Additional information: Completion of formal application required, including resume or C.V., letters or recommendation, essay, and future plans; See Web site for further application and for application form.
Program description:
Scholarship Program: At least one scholarship will be awarded to an international professional to attend a member school outside the U.S.
EIN: 133525440

2033
International Palace of Sports, Inc.
P.O. Box 332
North Webster, IN   46555-0332
(574) 834-7556
Contact: Marilyn Cassell, Secy.-Treas.

Foundation type: Independent foundation
Limitations: Scholarships and student loans to graduates of Wawasee, Warsaw, and Whitko school districts, all in IN.
Financial data: Year ended 03/31/2005.
Assets, $4,181,866 (M); Expenditures, $256,752; Total giving, $223,080; Grants to individuals, 59 grants totaling $136,330 (high: $13,000, low: $250).
Type of support: Support to graduates or students of specific schools; Undergraduate support.
Application information: Application form required.
  Deadline(s): Apri. 1
  Applicants should submit the following:
    1) Class rank
    2) Financial information
EIN: 351331032

2034
The Intuit Scholarship Foundation
1015 Middlefield Rd.
Palo Alto, CA   94301
Contact: Bryn Roe Ostby, Secy.

Foundation type: Company-sponsored foundation
Limitations: Scholarships to individuals to attend colleges or secondary schools.
Financial data: Year ended 07/31/2005.
Assets, $20,121 (M); Expenditures, $66,480; Total giving, $57,350; Grants to individuals, 20 grants totaling $57,350 (high: $5,000, low: $500).
Type of support: Scholarships—to individuals.
Application information: Contact foundation for current application deadline/guidelines.
EIN: 770417277

2035
Iowa Foundation for Agricultural Advancement
6770 Rising Sun Dr.
Des Moines, IA   50327
Contact: Harold Hodson, V.P.
Application address: c/o Swine Genetics, Cambridge, IA 50046, tel.: (515) 383-4386

Foundation type: Independent foundation
Limitations: Scholarships to individuals studying any area related to the animal industry at two-year and four-year colleges in IA.
Financial data: Year ended 12/31/2004.
Assets, $157,845 (M); Expenditures, $113,620; Total giving, $84,500; Grants to individuals, totaling $84,500.
Fields of interest: Agriculture.
Type of support: Scholarships—to individuals.

Application information: Deadline June 1; Initial approach by letter or telephone; Completion of formal application required.
EIN: 421183067

2036
Iowa Pharmacy Foundation
8515 Douglas Ave., Ste. 16
Urbandale, IA   50322-2900
Contact: Thomas R. Temple, Secy.-Treas.

Foundation type: Operating foundation
Limitations: Scholarships and research grants in pharmacology to residents of IA.
Financial data: Year ended 12/31/2003.
Assets, $1,276,070 (M); Expenditures, $257,336; Total giving, $17,000; Grants to individuals, 2 grants totaling $2,000.
Fields of interest: Pharmacy/prescriptions.
Type of support: Research; Scholarships—to individuals.
Application information: Applications by letter accepted throughout the year.
EIN: 426075767

2037
Iowa West Foundation
25 Main Pl., Ste. 550
Council Bluffs, IA   51503   (712) 309-3003
FAX: (712) 322-2267;
E-mail: grantinfo@iowawestfoundation.org;
URL: http://www.iowawestfoundation.org

Foundation type: Independent foundation
Limitations: Scholarships to students in IA and NE, for higher education.
Publications: Application guidelines; Annual report; Quarterly report.
Financial data: Year ended 12/31/2004.
Assets, $307,889,409 (M); Expenditures, $19,109,764; Total giving, $16,424,419; Grants to individuals, 25 grants totaling $500,000.
Type of support: Scholarships—to individuals.
Application information: Application form required.
  Deadline(s): Apr.
  Additional information: Application must also include transcript.
Program description:
Scholarship Program: Twenty-five scholarships of $20,000 are given to students annually from accredited high schools in Audubon, Cass, Fremont, Harrison, Mills, Montgomery, Page, Pottawattamie and Shelby counties, IA, and in Douglas, Sarpy and Washington counties in NE. Recipients must be current high school graduates, have an ACT score of at least 25 and enroll as a full-time student in a four-year program leading to a bachelor's degree. Recipients must maintain a GPA or at least 2.5 on a 4.0 scale.
EIN: 421391990

2038
A. G. & Rosalee W. Ireland Scholarship Trust
c/o Wells Fargo Bank Nebraska, N.A.
1248 O St., 4th Fl.
Lincoln, NE   68508

Foundation type: Independent foundation
Limitations: Scholarships for high school seniors from Woodbury County, IA, or South Sioux City, NE.
Financial data: Year ended 10/31/2004.
Assets, $225,457 (M); Expenditures, $16,492;

Total giving, $14,000; Grants to individuals, totaling $14,000.
Type of support: Undergraduate support.
Application information: Applications not accepted.
EIN: 426346940

2039
Ironwood Area Scholarship Foundation
650 E. Ayer St.
Ironwood, MI   49938
Contact: Tim Kolesar, Pres.

Foundation type: Public charity
Limitations: Scholarships to graduates of Ironwood Area School District, MI.
Financial data: Year ended 06/30/2004.
Assets, $541,537 (M); Expenditures, $24,026; Total giving, $20,250; Grants to individuals, totaling $20,250.
Type of support: Support to graduates or students of specific schools.
Application information:
  Initial approach: Letter.
  Additional information: Contact foundation for current application information.
EIN: 382822183

2040
Mary Ann Irvin Scholarship Foundation
c/o S&T Bank, Trust Dept.
P.O. Box 220
Indiana, PA   15701-0220
Application address: c/o Punxsutawney High School, Attn.: Emily Cassidy, 465 Beyer Ave., Punxsutawney, PA 15767, tel.: (724) 456-1443

Foundation type: Independent foundation
Limitations: Scholarships to financially needy graduates of Punxsutawney Area High School, PA, entering college or trade school.
Financial data: Year ended 12/31/2004.
Assets, $467,440 (M); Expenditures, $25,285; Total giving, $19,620; Grants to individuals, totaling $19,620.
Fields of interest: Vocational education.
Type of support: Support to graduates or students of specific schools; Graduate support; Technical education support; Undergraduate support.
Application information: Deadline Apr. 15; Completion of formal application required; Applications available from guidance counselors at Punxsutawney Area High School.
EIN: 256079669

2041
Irwindale Educational Foundation
(formerly Irwindale Educational & Scholarship Foundation)
16102 Arrow Hwy.
P.O. Box 2307
Irwindale, CA   91706   (626) 960-6606

Foundation type: Operating foundation
Limitations: Scholarships to individuals who have been residents of Irwindale, CA, for at least three years. A limited number of grants are available to Irwindale Chamber of Commerce members and their children.
Publications: Informational brochure (including application guidelines).
Financial data: Year ended 12/31/2003.
Assets, $70,213 (M); Expenditures, $35,862;

Total giving, $22,000; Grants to individuals, 13 grants totaling $22,000 (high: $2,000, low: $500).
Type of support: Scholarships—to individuals; Grants for special needs.
Application information: Application form required.
Initial approach: Letter or telephone.
Deadline(s): Contact foundation for deadline
Applicants should submit the following:
1) Transcripts
Additional information: Application must also include proof of college acceptance, and demonstration of financial need.
EIN: 954274826

2042
Betty & Kan Isaac Scholarship Foundation, Inc.
3234 Weidner Rd.
Newton, NC 28658   (828) 464-0920
Contact: Betty D. Isaac, Secy.-Treas.

Foundation type: Independent foundation
Limitations: Scholarships to financially needy residents of Catawba County, NC, who demonstrate an interest in golf to attend a North Carolina college.
Financial data: Year ended 12/31/2004.
Assets, $477,134 (M); Expenditures, $21,901; Total giving, $20,000; Grants to individuals, totaling $20,000.
Fields of interest: Athletics/sports, golf.
Type of support: Scholarships—to individuals.
Application information: Application form required.
Deadline(s): Jan. 31
Applicants should submit the following:
1) Letter(s) of recommendation
2) Transcripts
3) SAT
Additional information: Application forms may be obtained from the foundation.
Program description:
Scholarship Program: The award is $20,000 for a four-year scholarship. Applicants must maintain a 2.5 GPA.
EIN: 561875423

2043
Harry Z. Isaacs Scholarship Fund, Inc.
901 S. Bond St.
Baltimore, MD 21231
Application addresses: c/o D. Chennault, Carthage Co., 511 E. Franklin, Carthage, MS 39051, c/o T. Bradley, Newton Co., 300 N. Newton Ave., Newton, MS 39345, c/o W.G. Butler, Raleigh Co., Hwy. 18 W., P.O. Box 278, Raleigh, MS 39153; c/o A.J. Adkisson, Sussex Co., S.E. 4th & Columbia, Milford, DE 19963, c/o D. Derencz, I.C. Isaacs Co., 3840 Bank St., Baltimore, MD 21224

Foundation type: Independent foundation
Limitations: Scholarships to children of employees of I.C. Isaacs Co. L.P., who reside in DE, MD and MS.
Financial data: Year ended 12/31/2002.
Assets, $283,273 (M); Expenditures, $15,068; Total giving, $11,400; Grant to an individual, 1 grant totaling $11,400.
Fields of interest: Higher education.
Type of support: Employee-related scholarships.
Application information: Deadline Apr. 30; Completion of formal application required, including transcripts and a letter of recommendation; Application forms available from the application address or the Personnel Dir. of each facility of I.C. Isaacs Co. L.P.

Program description:
Scholarship Fund: Scholarships are renewable provided recipient has maintained at least a 3.0 GPA. I.C. Isaacs Co. L.P. owns and operates facilities in Carthage, Newtown, and Raleigh, MS, and Milford, DE. The headquarters of the I.C. Isaacs Co. L.P. are in Baltimore, MD.
EIN: 521713003

2044
Abdol H. Islami, M.D. Foundation, Inc.
(formerly Comprehensive Medical Review Course, Inc.)
14 Forest Ave.
Caldwell, NJ 07006
Contact: Joan Islami, Pres.

Foundation type: Independent foundation
Limitations: Scholarships to NJ residents for the study of medicine and related fields.
Financial data: Year ended 12/31/2004.
Assets, $2,689,854 (M); Expenditures, $155,043; Total giving, $126,000; Grants to individuals, 18 grants totaling $126,000 (high: $12,500, low: $500).
Fields of interest: Medical school/education.
Type of support: Scholarships—to individuals.
Application information: Deadline Mar. 15; Contact foundation for current application guidelines.
EIN: 222111419

2045
Italian American Cultural Foundation
3659 Green Rd., Ste. 124
Beachwood, OH 44122

Foundation type: Independent foundation
Limitations: Grants to educate, implement and strengthen the knowledge of Italian American heritage among OH residents.
Financial data: Year ended 03/31/2005.
Assets, $59,741 (M); Expenditures, $33,339; Total giving, $16,850; Grants to individuals, totaling $16,850.
Type of support: Support to graduates or students of specific schools.
Application information:
Deadline(s): Mar. 15 for essays
Additional information: Contact foundation for current application guidelines.
Program description:
Essay Competition: The IACF Essay Competition is open to high school students of Italian descent at participating schools, and all students at participating colleges. Students read a text from the foundation's Literary Collection, which has been donated to each school's library. Students prepare an essay discussing how the test influenced their perspective on Italian American heritage. Essays are judged by a Committee of Academics for content, insight, knowledge, style, grammar and punctuation.
EIN: 341213061

2046
Caroline Lawson Ivey Memorial Foundation, Inc.
c/o William L. Stephens, C.P.A.
2210 Gateway Dr., Ste. C
Opelika, AL 36801
Contact: Callie Brooks, Prog. Dir.
Additional address: P.O. Box 2028, Auburn, AL 36831-2028; E-mail: climf@mindspring.com

Foundation type: Independent foundation
Limitations: Scholarships to AL junior and senior college students who plan to be social studies teachers and have been accepted into a teacher certification program.
Publications: Application guidelines.
Financial data: Year ended 12/31/2004.
Assets, $1,137,933 (M); Expenditures, $39,950; Total giving, $8,500; Grants to individuals, totaling $4,500.
Fields of interest: Secondary school/education.
Type of support: Undergraduate support.
Application information: Contact foundation for current application deadline; Initial approach by letter or e-mail; Completion of formal application required, including an essay stating why applicant wants to be a social studies teacher and a letter of intent to teach social studies in a public school.
Program description:
Scholarship Program: Applicants must have an outstanding academic record and maintain a 3.0 GPA.
EIN: 630940413

2047
Ivy Foundation of Suffolk/Nassau Counties
167 Moore Ave.
Freeport, NY 11520-1441   (516) 868-6554
Contact: C. Yvette Long, Pres.

Foundation type: Public charity
Limitations: Scholarships to residents of Long Island, NY, with a GPA of 85.
Financial data: Year ended 03/31/2005.
Assets, $32,594 (M); Expenditures, $105,619; Total giving, $89,504; Grants to individuals, totaling $89,504.
Type of support: Undergraduate support.
Application information:
Initial approach: Letter.
Applicants should submit the following:
1) Essay
2) Letter(s) of recommendation
Additional information: Contact foundation for further application guidelines. Application must also include proof of enrollment in an undergraduate program. Interviews required.
EIN: 113551213

2048
Amelia G. Jachym Scholarship Fund
600 Hotel Jamestown Office Bldg.
Jamestown, NY 14702-3236

Foundation type: Independent foundation
Limitations: Scholarships to graduates of Pine Valley Central School, South Dayton, NY.
Financial data: Year ended 08/31/2005.
Assets, $293,813 (M); Expenditures, $21,591; Total giving, $20,000; Grants to individuals, totaling $20,000.
Type of support: Scholarships—to individuals; Support to graduates or students of specific schools; Undergraduate support.
Application information: Applications accepted throughout the year; Applicants must contact the guidance counselor of Pine Valley Central School.
Program description:
Scholarship Program: Scholarship recipients are selected on the basis of character, citizenship, and leadership. Winners are selected from the top 20 percent of the graduating class. One new student is

selected each year. Generally, each scholarship is $2,500 per year for four years.
EIN: 112599257

2049
Jack and Jill of America Foundation
1930 17th St., N.W.
Washington, DC 20009 (202) 232-5290
Contact: Grace E. Speights Esq., Pres.
FAX: (202) 232-1747;
E-mail: adminstration@jackandjillfoundation.org;
URL: http://www.jackandjillfoundation.org

Foundation type: Public charity
Limitations: Scholarships to African American high school seniors.
Financial data: Year ended 03/31/2004.
Assets, $279,485 (M); Expenditures, $530,753; Total giving, $146,720.
Fields of interest: African Americans/Blacks.
Type of support: Undergraduate support.
Application information: Applications accepted. Application form required. Application form available on the grantmaker's Web site.
Initial approach: E-mail or letter.
Deadline(s): Mar. 14
Applicants should submit the following:
1) Resume
2) GPA
3) Letter(s) of recommendation
4) Transcripts
5) Essay
Additional information: Applicants must have performed 60 hours of community service prior to the application deadline.
Program description:
National College Scholarship: Applicants must be African American high school seniors with a minimum GPA of 3.0 who will be pursuing a Bachelor's degree at any accredited post-secondary institution in the United States. Maximum awards are $1,500 to $2,500 for a single year, which can be applied to tuition, room and board.
EIN: 510224656

2050
The Jackson County Community Foundation
(formerly The Jackson Community Foundation)
1 Jackson Sq., Ste. 110A
Jackson, MI 49201-1406 (517) 787-1321
Contact: Shelly Saines, C.E.O.; For grants: Jan Maino, V.P., Progs.
FAX: (517) 787-4333; E-mail: info@jacksoncf.org;
Additional E-mail: ssaines@jacksoncf.org;
URL: http://www.jacksoncf.org

Foundation type: Community foundation
Limitations: Scholarships and student loans primarily to students in Jackson County, MI.
Publications: Application guidelines; Annual report (including application guidelines); Newsletter.
Financial data: Year ended 12/31/2004.
Assets, $17,832,222 (M); Expenditures, $1,206,688; Total giving, $688,343.
Fields of interest: Medical school/education; Engineering school/education; Theological school/education; Science; Christian agencies & churches.
Type of support: Employee-related scholarships; Student loans—to individuals; Support to graduates or students of specific schools; Undergraduate support.
Application information: Applications accepted. Application form required.
Deadline(s): April 15

Applicants should submit the following:
1) Essay
2) Budget Information
3) ACT
Additional information: See Web site for complete program and application information.
Program description:
Scholarship and Loan Program: The complete listing of programs is available on the foundation Web site.
EIN: 386070739

2051
C. Daniel Jackson Foundation
P.O. Box 510
Opelika, AL 36803
Contact: Durward W. Jackson II, Pres.

Foundation type: Independent foundation
Limitations: Scholarships to residents of AL.
Financial data: Year ended 12/31/2002.
Assets, $213,274 (M); Expenditures, $8,038; Total giving, $4,500; Grants to individuals, totaling $4,500.
Type of support: Scholarships—to individuals.
Application information: Applications by letter accepted throughout the year.
EIN: 631186158

2052
Corwill and Margie Jackson Foundation
c/o Comerica Bank
P.O. Box 75000, M/C 3302
Detroit, MI 48275-3302
Application address: c/o David J. Hall, 6954 W. Jackson Rd., Ludington, MI 49431-9428

Foundation type: Independent foundation
Limitations: Scholarships to high school seniors in Mason County, MI, for the first year of college. Four four-year awards are also given annually.
Financial data: Year ended 12/31/2004.
Assets, $2,578,564 (M); Expenditures, $159,942; Total giving, $131,500; Grants to individuals, 82 grants totaling $131,500.
Type of support: Support to graduates or students of specific schools; Undergraduate support.
Application information: Application form required.
Deadline(s): May 1
EIN: 386064502

2053
Dr. J. M. Jackson Memorial Trust Fund
c/o Al Werner
P.O. Box 15
Lawrenceburg, IN 47025 (812) 537 0349

Foundation type: Independent foundation
Limitations: Scholarships to residents of Dearborn, OH, and Ripley and Switzerland counties, IN, to pursue nursing careers.
Financial data: Year ended 08/31/2004.
Assets, $0 (M); Expenditures, $6,000; Total giving, $6,000; Grants to individuals, 10 grants totaling $6,000 (high: $1,000, low: $500).
Fields of interest: Nursing school/education.
Type of support: Undergraduate support.
Application information:
Deadline(s): Contact foundation or high school for current application deadline

Additional information: Completion of formal application required, including copy of grades and financial need information.
EIN: 356051394

2054
George Jackson Scholarship Foundation
(formerly George Jackson Trust)
c/o Peapack Gladstone Bank
190 Main St.
Gladstone, NJ 07934

Foundation type: Independent foundation
Limitations: Scholarships to students of Sussex County high schools, NJ, who are also residents of Sussex County.
Financial data: Year ended 12/31/2004.
Assets, $1,889,535 (M); Expenditures, $132,065; Total giving, $119,500; Grants to individuals, totaling $119,500.
Type of support: Support to graduates or students of specific schools; Undergraduate support.
Application information: Contact trust for current application deadline; Completion of formal application required.
EIN: 226474357

2055
Colonel William J. & Helen Jackson Scholarship Fund
c/o William C. Krantz
1470 N. Main St.
Lakeport, CA 95453-3847 (707) 263-0242
Contact: Phil N. Crawford, Mgr.

Foundation type: Operating foundation
Limitations: Scholarships to graduating seniors from Lake County, CA, high schools.
Financial data: Year ended 12/31/2002.
Assets, $44,510 (M); Expenditures, $5,373; Total giving, $4,500; Grants to individuals, totaling $4,500.
Fields of interest: Vocational education.
Type of support: Support to graduates or students of specific schools; Undergraduate support.
Application information: Application form required.
Deadline(s): Mid-May
Additional information: Interviews required.
Program description:
Scholarship Program: Selection is based upon the following four criteria: financial need, scholastic record, citizenship (including school and community services), and the purpose and need for education. Applicants must be residents of Lake County, CA, for at least one full year prior to application, and must be accepted for enrollment in an accredited university, college, or recognized trade or vocational school.
EIN: 946287540

2056
Beatrice Jackson Scholarship
c/o Ballard County Board of Education
3465 Paducah Rd.
Barlow, KY 42024

Foundation type: Independent foundation
Limitations: Scholarships by nomination only to students and graduates of Ballard Memorial High School, KY, who are of African descent, for higher education, including vocational training. Scholarships are renewable.
Financial data: Year ended 08/31/2004.
Assets, $159,742 (M); Expenditures, $13,476;

Total giving, $12,824; Grants to individuals, totaling $12,824.
Fields of interest: Minorities.
Type of support: Awards/grants by nomination only; Technical education support; Undergraduate support.
Application information: Candidates are nominated by Ballard Memorial High School counselors and administration.
EIN: 611225206

2057

James A. Jackson Trust
(formerly James A. Jackson and Beatrice D. Jackson Scholarship Trust)
c/o KeyBank N.A.
800 Superior Ave., 4th Fl.
Cleveland, OH 44114
Contact: Superintendent of the Oxford County School District

Foundation type: Independent foundation
Limitations: Scholarships to graduating high school seniors who are residents of West Paris, ME, to be used in pursuing Bachelor of Arts degrees. One female and one male resident are selected to receive these scholarships.
Financial data: Year ended 06/30/2005.
Assets, $0 (M); Expenditures, $185,710; Total giving, $162,059; Grants to individuals, totaling $162,059.
Type of support: Undergraduate support.
Application information: Applications accepted.
Additional information: Applications by letter accepted throughout the year.
EIN: 016128257

2058

Wilhelmina W. Jackson Trust
c/o Bank of America, N.A.
100 Federal St., MADE10020B
Boston, MA 02110
Scholarship application address: c/o Marcia Hostetter (for art scholarships), P.O. Box 47, Marblehead, MA 01945; c/o Rev. Dean Pederson (for medical scholarships), 40 Monument Ave., Swampscott, MA 01907

Foundation type: Independent foundation
Limitations: Scholarships to residents of Swampscott and Marblehead, MA, for the study of any form of the creative arts at a college, university, or art school, or for the study of medicine.
Financial data: Year ended 12/31/2004.
Assets, $8,538,904 (M); Expenditures, $403,020; Total giving, $300,420; Grants to individuals, totaling $300,420.
Fields of interest: Arts education; Visual arts; Photography; Sculpture; Design; Painting; Ceramic arts; Art history; Medical school/education.
Type of support: Undergraduate support; Doctoral support.
Application information: Deadlines Feb. 15 for art scholarships, June 1 for medical scholarships; Completion of formal application required, including recent photograph, transcripts, and three letters of recommendation; Interviews required.
Program descriptions:
Roland Jackson Medical Scholarships: Scholarships are given for the study of medicine.
Wilhemina Denning Jackson Art Scholarships: Selection is based on financial need, artistic ability, character and work habits, and GPA. The scholarship is awarded for up to four years. Forms of the creative arts included are painting, sculpture,

graphics, printmaking, industrial design, illustration, photography, ceramics, and art history.
EIN: 046024405

2059

Maria C. Jackson-Gen. George A. White Student Aid for Children of War Veterans Foundation
c/o U.S. Bank, N.A., Trust Tax Svcs.
P.O. Box 3168
Portland, OR 97208-3168 (503) 275-4456
Application address: c/o U.S. Bank, N.A. of Oregon, Trust Student Aid, Portland, OR 97208-3168

Foundation type: Independent foundation
Limitations: Scholarships and student loans to U.S. Armed Forces veterans or children of veterans who are high school graduates or long-time residents of OR and are studying at institutions of higher learning in OR.
Financial data: Year ended 06/30/2005.
Assets, $712,946 (M); Expenditures, $47,492; Total giving, $33,800; Grants to individuals, totaling $33,800.
Fields of interest: Military/veterans' organizations.
Type of support: Undergraduate support.
Application information: Application form required.
Initial approach: Letter.
Deadline(s): Scholarship applications accepted Jan. 1 to Apr. 1, loan applications accepted June 1 to June 15
Additional information: Interviews required.
Program description:
Student Aid for Children of War Veterans Program: Loans and scholarships must be approved by a committee of three persons who are residents of OR and appointed by the foundation's trustees. Both scholastic ability and the financial need of the applicant will be taken into consideration. To qualify for scholarships, applicants who are graduating high school seniors must have a cumulative GPA of at least 3.5, college students must have at least a 3.0 GPA. Scholarship applicants who are unsuccessful may apply for loans. Generally, $750 is the maximum loan amount awarded to any one applicant for each school year, although successive loans up to this amount may be made available during a full college course. Payments to graduating seniors will be scheduled to begin three months following graduation. The interest rate on student loans is nine percent and begins to accrue the day the promissory note is drawn. Applicants are notified of their status by June 30.
EIN: 936020316

2060

Charles D. Jacobus Family Foundation
11815 W. Bradley Rd.
Milwaukee, WI 53224 (414) 577-0252
Contact: Missy MacLeod, Pres.
FAX: (414) 359-1357;
E-mail: quickinfo@jacobusenergy.com; Mailing address: P.O. Box 13009, Milwaukee, WI 53213-0009; Additional tel.: 1 (800) JACOBUS ext. 252; URL: http://www.cdjff.org

Foundation type: Independent foundation
Limitations: Scholarships to children of employees of Jacobus Energy in the Milwaukee County, WI, area.
Financial data: Year ended 12/31/2003.
Assets, $4,937,281 (M); Expenditures, $326,155; Total giving, $243,740; Grants to individuals, 3 grants totaling $5,000 (high: $2,000, low: $1,000).

Type of support: Employee-related scholarships.
Application information: See Web site for application deadline/guidelines.
EIN: 391559892

2061

William E. and Janet Burrows James Foundation
160 Federal St., 18th Fl.
Boston, MA 02110

Foundation type: Independent foundation
Limitations: Scholarships to individuals for higher education, primarily in MA.
Financial data: Year ended 12/31/2004.
Assets, $684,878 (M); Expenditures, $307,572; Total giving, $298,800.
Type of support: Undergraduate support.
Application information: Application form required.
Initial approach: Letter.
Deadline(s): June 1
EIN: 046835740

2062

William & Glenna James Scholarship Fund
c/o TD Banknorth, N.A., Investment Mgmt. Group
P.O. Box 595
Williston, VT 05495-0595
Application address: c/o TD Banknorth, N.A., Investment Mgmt. Group, 89 Merchants Row, Rutland, VT 05701

Foundation type: Independent foundation
Limitations: Scholarships to residents of Proctor, VT, to attend the University of Vermont.
Financial data: Year ended 12/31/2004.
Assets, $482,509 (M); Expenditures, $35,006; Total giving, $29,600; Grants to individuals, totaling $29,600.
Type of support: Support to graduates or students of specific schools; Graduate support; Undergraduate support.
Application information: Applications accepted throughout the year; Initial approach by letter; Completion of formal application required.
EIN: 036064491

2063

Janesville Foundation, Inc.
121 N. Parker Dr.
P.O. Box 8123
Janesville, WI 53547-8123 (608) 752-1032
Contact: Bonnie Lynne Robinson, Pres. and Exec. Dir.
FAX: (608) 752-1952

Foundation type: Independent foundation
Limitations: Scholarships to graduating seniors of public high schools in Janesville, WI, for attendance at colleges, universities, and vocational schools.
Publications: Informational brochure (including application guidelines).
Financial data: Year ended 12/31/2004.
Assets, $7,769,295 (M); Expenditures, $579,263; Total giving, $400,000; Grants to individuals, totaling $54,374. Subtotal for scholarships—to individuals: 25 grants totaling $54,374 (high: $3,500, low: $1,000).
Fields of interest: Vocational education.
Type of support: Support to graduates or students of specific schools; Technical education support; Undergraduate support.
Application information: Deadlines Mar. 1; Completion of formal application required;

Applications available only from principals of Janesville public high schools.

Program description:

Scholarship Program: Selection is based on scholastic rank in the graduating class and recommendation by the principal. Written application is made through the principal of each high school. Some scholarships are $1,625 per year over four years. Other scholarships are $1,000 for one year. All payments are made upon presentation of evidence of a "B" average or better at an accredited higher education institution.
EIN: 396034645

2064
Janson Foundation
c/o Bank of America, N.A.
P.O. Box 34345
Seattle, WA 98124-1345
Application address for individuals: c/o Janson Scholarship Fund Comm., Attn.: Robert Suttles, Emmanuel Baptist Church, 1515 East College Way, Mount Vernon, WA 98273
Application address for organizations: c/o Heidi Gordon, Bank of America, N.A., P.O. Box 24565, Seattle, WA 98124

Foundation type: Independent foundation
Limitations: Scholarships are awarded on the basis of character, mental and physical abilities, and financial need to residents of Skagit County, WA, who have at least a 2.5 GPA.
Publications: Application guidelines.
Financial data: Year ended 11/30/2005. Assets, $2,329,166 (M); Expenditures, $136,169; Total giving, $109,285; Grants to individuals, 53 grants totaling $59,557 (high: $1,150, low: $575).
Type of support: Undergraduate support.
Application information: Application form required.
   Deadline(s): Apr. 15.
   Applicants should submit the following:
      1) Financial information
      2) Transcripts
EIN: 916251624

2065
Donald Janssen, Sr. Memorial Foundation
16 Evesboro Rd.
Medford, NJ 08055

Foundation type: Company-sponsored foundation
Limitations: Scholarships to high school students for undergraduate education.
Financial data: Year ended 12/31/2002. Assets, $215,004 (M); Expenditures, $11,373; Total giving, $11,000; Grants to individuals, totaling $11,000.
Type of support: Undergraduate support.
Application information: Contact foundation for current application deadline/guidelines.
EIN: 232744775

2066
Gregory B. Jarvis Memorial Scholarship Foundation
c/o The DIRECTV Group, Inc.
2250 E. Imperial Hwy.
El Segundo, CA 90245-0956   (310) 662-9824
Contact: Robin Preston

Foundation type: Company-sponsored foundation

Limitations: Scholarships to dependents of employees of Hughes Electronics Corporation or its subsidiaries and affiliates.
Financial data: Year ended 12/31/2004. Assets, $103,637 (M); Expenditures, $12,000; Total giving, $12,000; Grants to individuals, 2 grants totaling $12,000 (high: $7,200, low: $4,800).
Type of support: Employee-related scholarships.
Application information:
   Initial approach: Letter.
   Deadline(s): Jan. 9
   Additional information: This $6,000 scholarship is granted on a one-time basis. To apply, contact: Nissen Davis (310) 964-0719 or Robin Preston (310) 964-0846.
EIN: 954089695

2067
Jasper Foundation, Inc.
P.O. Box 295
Rensselaer, IN 47978   (219) 866-5899
Contact: Linda Reiners, Exec. Dir.
FAX: (219) 866-0555;
E-mail: jasper@liljasper.com; URL: http://www.jasperfdn.org

Foundation type: Community foundation
Limitations: Scholarships to individuals residing in Jasper and Newton counties, IN.
Financial data: Year ended 12/31/2004. Assets, $6,866,547 (M); Expenditures, $568,499; Total giving, $378,302; Grants to individuals, totaling $199,563.
Fields of interest: Health sciences school/education.
Type of support: Undergraduate support.
Application information: Application form required.
   Deadline(s): Apr. 9 for Dr. Cecil and Gladys Johnson Memorial Scholarship
   Applicants should submit the following:
      1) Financial information
      2) GPA
      3) Transcripts
   Additional information: See Web site for further application information.
Program description:
   Dr. Cecil and Gladys Johnson Memorial Scholarship: Awards scholarships of up to $5,000 to individuals planning medical or medical-related careers.
EIN: 351842404

2068
The Jacob K. Javits Foundation, Inc.
c/o Marion B. Javits
322 E. 57th St., 12th Fl.
New York, NY 10022
Application addresses: c/o Duke University, Division of Student Affairs, 102 Flowers Bldg., P.O. Box 90937, Durham NC 27708; tel.: (919) 684-3737, or c/o Columbia University, Division of Student Affairs, 405 Alfred Lerner Hall, 2920 Broadway, New York, NY 10027, tel.: (212) 854-2446

Foundation type: Independent foundation
Limitations: Scholarships to graduate students at Columbia University, NY, and Duke University, NC.
Financial data: Year ended 12/31/2004. Assets, $2,906,070 (M); Expenditures, $81,755; Total giving, $43,434.
Fields of interest: Government/public administration.
Type of support: Support to graduates or students of specific schools; Graduate support.

Application information: Deadline Jan. 31; Completion of formal application required, including essay of approximately 600 words on one of Javits' legislative commitments; Applications available at Students Affairs Office.
Program description:
   Scholarship Program: Applicants must have at least a 3.5 GPA and commit to working for the U.S. Senate or for a Senate Committee for at least a year after graduation.
EIN: 133226735

2069
George S. & Grace A. Jay Memorial Trust
612 1/2 W. Sheridan Ave.
P.O. Box 57
Shenandoah, IA 51601   (712) 246-3399
Contact: Eileen Dinville

Foundation type: Independent foundation
Limitations: Student loans only to graduates of high schools in Shenandoah, Essex, and Farragut, IA, for use at accredited colleges, universities, and trade schools.
Financial data: Year ended 03/31/2005. Assets, $2,157,285 (M); Expenditures, $66,307; Total giving, $0; Loans to individuals, 115 loans totaling $155,800.
Fields of interest: Vocational education.
Type of support: Support to graduates or students of specific schools; Technical education support; Undergraduate support.
Application information: Application form required.
   Initial approach: Telephone inquiries only accepted on Tuesdays.
   Deadline(s): May 31
   Additional information: Recipients notified by June 30.
Program description:
   Student Loan Program: Loans do not exceed the amount of $500 per student, per semester, or $350 per student, per summer session. Loans are repayable bearing an interest rate of three percent.
EIN: 426061515

2070
JBL Scholarship Trust
10 Montchanin Rd.
P.O. Box 4248
Wilmington, DE 19807-0248   (302) 654-3444
Contact: Catherine S. Malone, Prog. Admin.

Foundation type: Independent foundation
Limitations: Undergraduate scholarships to financially needy students under the age of 30, who are graduating from DE high schools, attending DE colleges, or residing in an adjoining state (NJ, MD, PA) within 20 miles of the DE border.
Financial data: Year ended 12/31/2003. Assets, $1,753,911 (M); Expenditures, $108,273; Total giving, $101,000; Grants to individuals, 212 grants totaling $101,000 (high: $3,000, low: $700).
Type of support: Undergraduate support.
Application information: Deadline Mar. 15; Completion of formal application required, including three personal references, GPA, financial statement, recommendation from an official of the college applicant is attending, transcripts, class rank, SAT scores, photograph, and a personal essay; Recipients notified after June 20.
Program description:
   Scholarship Program: To be eligible, undergraduate applicants must have at least a 2.75 GPA, and high school seniors must have at least a 3.0 GPA or a score of at least 1100 on the

SAT. Scholarships are limited to $6,000 over a period of four years of study. Scholarships are renewable annually, provided the recipient maintains at least a 2.75 GPA.
EIN: 516016533

2071
Boyd & Stephen Jefferies Educational Grant Program
11100 Santa Monica Blvd.
Los Angeles, CA 90025 (310) 914-1025
Contact: Regina de Wetter, Coord.
FAX: (201) 221-7520; E-mail: rdewette@jefco.com;
URL: http://www.jefferiesgrant.org

Foundation type: Public charity
Limitations: Financial assistance to students who are children of employees of Jefferies Group, Inc.
Financial data: Year ended 06/30/2004.
Assets, $6,097,233 (M); Expenditures, $711,480; Total giving, $336,026; Grants to individuals, 46 grants totaling $336,026 (high: $8,000, low: $685).
Fields of interest: Higher education.
Type of support: Undergraduate support.
Application information: Applications accepted. Application form required. Application form available on the grantmaker's Web site.
  Deadline(s): Apr. 15
  Applicants should submit the following:
    1) Transcripts
EIN: 953594410

2072
Michael Jeffers Memorial Education Fund
c/o Citizens Bank Wealth Mgmt., N.A.
328 S. Saginaw St., M/C 002072
Flint, MI 48502
Application address: c/o Helen James, Citizens Bank, N.A., Wealth Mgmt., 101 N. Washington Ave., Saginaw, MI 48607, tel.: (989) 776-7368

Foundation type: Independent foundation
Limitations: Educational loans to residents of Saginaw, MI, who are ages 16 to 19 and have an economic need.
Financial data: Year ended 12/31/2004.
Assets, $6,231,589 (M); Expenditures, $93,940; Total giving, $0; Loans to individuals, 71 loans totaling $248,000.
Type of support: Student loans—to individuals.
Application information: Applications accepted. Application form required.
  Deadline(s): June 1 for renewals and June 15 for new loans
EIN: 383431990

2073
Greater Jefferson County Community Foundation
P.O. Box 1325
Fairfield, IA 52556-1325

Foundation type: Community foundation
Limitations: Scholarships to students in Jefferson County, IA, for higher education.
Financial data: Year ended 03/31/2005.
Assets, $1,928,349 (M); Expenditures, $162,744; Total giving, $148,988; Grants to individuals, 45 grants totaling $95,181.
Type of support: Undergraduate support.
Application information: Contact foundation for current application deadline/guidelines.
EIN: 510172078

2074
Jefferson County Tuberculosis Association, Inc.
P.O. Box 610
Charles Town, WV 25414
Contact: Lacie Mumaw, Treas.
Application address: 112 Court St., Charles Town, WV 25414, tel.: (304) 725-9616

Foundation type: Independent foundation
Limitations: Support for education about, prevention of, and rehabilitation of those afflicted with, cardio-pulmonary diseases.
Financial data: Year ended 12/31/2004.
Assets, $145,173 (M); Expenditures, $30,476; Total giving, $28,437; Grants to individuals, totaling $13,856.
Fields of interest: Health sciences school/education; Heart & circulatory diseases; Heart & circulatory research.
Type of support: Scholarships—to individuals; Grants for special needs.
Application information: Applications accepted.
  Deadline(s): None
  Additional information: Verbal and written requests stating intent of request, cost, and other information. Camperships are also provided.
EIN: 550713040

2075
Ethel Jefferson Scholarship Fund
c/o First National Bank & Trust Co. of Newtown
34 S. State St.
Newtown, PA 18940 (215) 968-4872

Foundation type: Independent foundation
Limitations: Scholarships primarily to residents of Bucks County, PA.
Financial data: Year ended 12/31/2004.
Assets, $1,276,875 (M); Expenditures, $60,237; Total giving, $48,000; Grants to individuals, totaling $48,000.
Type of support: Scholarships—to individuals.
Application information: Deadline Apr. 15; Completion of formal application required.
EIN: 237749232

2076
Jellison Benevolent Society, Inc.
P.O. Box 145
Junction City, KS 66441-0145 (785) 762-5566
Contact: Susan E. Williams, Secy.
FAX: (785) 762-4242;
E-mail: s_williams1948@yahoo.com

Foundation type: Independent foundation
Limitations: Scholarships to residents of KS, with preference shown toward residents of Geary County, KS, to attend undergraduate colleges and technical schools.
Publications: Application guidelines.
Financial data: Year ended 12/31/2004.
Assets, $3,552,979 (M); Expenditures, $225,031; Total giving, $195,215.
Fields of interest: Vocational education.
Type of support: Undergraduate support.
Application information: Application form required.
  Initial approach: Letter or telephone.
  Deadline(s): June 20 for fall semester and Nov. 20 for spring semester.
  Applicants should submit the following:
    1) GPA
    2) Budget Information
    3) Letter(s) of recommendation
    4) Resume

5) Transcripts
6) Financial information
  Additional information: Application should also include ACT scores, if applicant has them; Applications should be sent by mail or fax.
EIN: 486106092

2077
Wyatt F. & Mattie M. Jeltz Scholarship Foundation
3017 Martin Luther King
P.O. Box 36575
Oklahoma City, OK 73136-6575

Foundation type: Independent foundation
Limitations: Scholarships to minority students who have completed one year of studies at an accredited college or university in OK.
Publications: Informational brochure (including application guidelines).
Financial data: Year ended 12/31/2004.
Assets, $274,632 (M); Expenditures, $32,380; Total giving, $25,500; Grants to individuals, totaling $25,500.
Fields of interest: Minorities.
Type of support: Scholarships—to individuals.
Application information: Deadlines Aug. and Dec.; Contact foundation for current application guidelines.
EIN: 730994084

2078
Melvin H. & Thelma N. Jenkins Scholarship Fund
c/o M&T Bank
21 E. Market St.
York, PA 17401-1205
Application address: Ann L. Rich, Trust Off., c/o M&T Trust Co., One South Center St., Pottsville, PA 17901, tel.: (570) 628-9270

Foundation type: Independent foundation
Limitations: Scholarships to graduates of Minersville Area High School, PA.
Financial data: Year ended 12/31/2004.
Assets, $886,699 (M); Expenditures, $54,632; Total giving, $42,750; Grants to individuals, totaling $42,750.
Type of support: Employee-related scholarships; Undergraduate support.
Application information: Applications accepted Dec. 1 to Feb. 15; Completion of formal application required, including transcripts and verification of school activities.
EIN: 256373763

2079
Jenkins Student Aid Fund
c/o U.S. Bank, N.A.
P.O. Box 3168
Portland, OR 97208-3168 (503) 275-4456
Application address: 1500 Valley River Dr., Ste. 100, Eugene, OR 97401, tel.: (800) 452-8807

Foundation type: Independent foundation
Limitations: Undergraduate and graduate student loans first to OR residents studying in the U.S., and then to WA and ID residents attending school in OR.
Publications: Application guidelines; Program policy statement.
Financial data: Year ended 06/30/2005.
Assets, $1,079,689 (M); Expenditures, $79,754; Total giving, $52,750; Grants to individuals, totaling $52,750.

Type of support: Graduate support; Undergraduate support.
Application information: Application form required. Application form available on the grantmaker's Web site.
Initial approach: Letter.
Deadline(s): Jan. 2
Applicants should submit the following:
1) Letter(s) of recommendation
2) Transcripts
Additional information: Recipients notified by July 15.
Program description:
Student Loan Program: To be eligible, applicants must have at least a 2.5 GPA and must be graduates of accredited high schools planning to enroll full-time in undergraduate and graduate programs at accredited U.S. colleges and universities. Loans are awarded on the basis of financial need and maintenance of satisfactory academic progress. Loans of up to $2,500 are repayable at eight percent interest. Recipients may reapply in subsequent years.
EIN: 936020672

2080

Carolyn Jenkins Trust
245 Main St.
Oneonta, NY 13820-2502 (607) 432-1700
Application address: c/o Donald Moore, State University College, Education Bldg., Rm. 123, Oneonta, NY 13820-2502, tel.: (607) 432-2532

Foundation type: Independent foundation
Limitations: Scholarships by nomination only to students of State University of New York College at Oneonta.
Financial data: Year ended 06/30/2005. Assets, $427,516 (M); Expenditures, $24,640; Total giving, $22,100; Grants to individuals, totaling $22,100.
Fields of interest: Minorities.
Type of support: Exchange programs; Support to graduates or students of specific schools; Awards/grants by nomination only; Foreign applicants; Undergraduate support.
Application information: Scholarships granted by nomination only.
Program descriptions:
Scott-Jenkins Work Grants: These grants are open to any full-time matriculated student. Grants of $750 are paid to financially needy students who work a minimum of 11 hours per week on average for 30 weeks. Interested students must be recommended to the selection committee by Aug. 1. Recipients are chosen by Aug. 15.
Scott-Jenkins Foreign Student Scholarships: These scholarships are open to any foreign student who is matriculated. Grants pay for room, board, and/or maintenance costs for students living on campus. Applicants must be recommended by the Dir. of International Education by Aug. 1. Recipients are chosen by Aug. 15.
Scott-Jenkins Memorial Scholarships: These scholarships are open to minority students of State University of New York College at Oneonta. Recipients must be in good academic standing and in financial need. Candidates are identified by the Office of Special Programs and the Financial Aid Office, and recommended to the selection committee by May 1. Recipients are chosen by June 1. Scholarships are renewable.
Scott-Jenkins Foreign Study Scholarships: These scholarships are open to any financially needy full-time matriculated State University of New York College at Oneonta student in a foreign study program sponsored by the State University or

Hartwick College. Scholarships cover program costs over and above those which are not covered by financial aid, but not to exceed $500 per student. Candidates are identified by the Dir. of International Education and the Financial Aid Office, and recommended to the selection committee by Apr. 1 for summer, May 1 for fall, and Dec. 1 for spring. Recipients are chosen by May 1 for summer, June 1 for fall, and Jan. 3 for spring.
EIN: 166183805

2081

Vernon & Leoma Jenniges Education Trust
c/o Farmers & Merchants State Bank
P.O. Box 126
Springfield, MN 56087 (507) 723-4234

Foundation type: Operating foundation
Limitations: Scholarships to students from the Springfield School District, MN, for postsecondary education.
Financial data: Year ended 12/31/2003. Assets, $436,322 (M); Expenditures, $15,723; Total giving, $15,000; Grants to individuals, 34 grants totaling $15,000 (high: $900, low: $250).
Type of support: Support to graduates or students of specific schools; Undergraduate support.
Application information: Applications accepted. Application form required.
Deadline(s): None
EIN: 416325986

2082

The John J. & Nora Jennings Foundation, Inc.
46 Gaston St.
Medford, MA 02155 (781) 391-5016
Contact: David C. Johnson, Treas.

Foundation type: Independent foundation
Limitations: Scholarships to residents of MA for undergraduate education.
Financial data: Year ended 12/31/2004. Assets, $110,353 (M); Expenditures, $22,210; Total giving, $20,000; Grants to individuals, totaling $20,000.
Type of support: Undergraduate support.
Application information: Contact foundation for current application deadline/guidelines.
EIN: 550797079

2083

The Robert H. Jentes Scholarship Fund
c/o FirstMerit Bank, N.A.
106 S. Main St., Ste. 1600
Akron, OH 44308 (330) 479-4378
Contact: Amanda Miller, Admin. Asst.

Foundation type: Independent foundation
Limitations: Scholarships to students attending Wittenberg College in Springfield, OH, and Malone College in Canton, OH. Scholarships also to children of former employees of Fleming Foods, Co., OH.
Financial data: Year ended 12/31/2004. Assets, $1,041,822 (M); Expenditures, $61,826; Total giving, $46,100; Grants to individuals, totaling $46,100.
Type of support: Employee-related scholarships; Support to graduates or students of specific schools; Undergraduate support.
Application information: Applications accepted. Application form required.
Initial approach: Letter.

Copies of proposal: 1
Deadline(s): Apr. 1
Applicants should submit the following:
1) Transcripts
2) FAFSA
EIN: 346779406

2084

The Jerusalem Fund for Education and Community Development
(formerly The Jerusalem Fund)
2425 Virginia Ave., N.W.
Washington, DC 20037 (202) 338-1958
Contact: Samar Assad, Exec. Dir.
FAX: (202) 333-7742;
E-mail: info@palestinecenter.org; URL: http://www.palestinecenter.org

Foundation type: Public charity
Limitations: Scholarships to Palestinians in the West Bank and the Gaza Strip.
Publications: Annual report; Financial statement; Grants list; Newsletter.
Financial data: Year ended 12/31/2004. Assets, $6,584,904 (M); Expenditures, $920,470; Total giving, $49,354; Grants to individuals, totaling $49,354.
Fields of interest: West Bank/Gaza.
Type of support: Foreign applicants; Graduate support; Technical education support; Undergraduate support.
Application information:
Initial approach: Letter, including biographical record with supporting material, report on academic and/or professional careers and statement of training plans.
Deadline(s): Aug. 31 and Dec. 15
Additional information: Contact foundation for current application guidelines.
EIN: 521238142

2085

The Daniel Ashley and Irene Houston Jewell Memorial Foundation
c/o George M. McMillan, Jr.
2221 Fox Run Dr.
Signal Mountain, TN 37377
Application address: c/o D. Ashley Jewell V, 115 Old Homestead Dr., Chickamauga, GA 30707, tel.: (404) 624-7636

Foundation type: Independent foundation
Limitations: Undergraduate scholarships to graduates of Gordon Lee High School, Chickamauga, GA, and graduate scholarships to individuals without restriction, to attend accredited colleges in GA, AL, and TN. Recipients are recommended to the trustees by a scholarship committee.
Financial data: Year ended 06/30/2005. Assets, $4,971,712 (M); Expenditures, $260,890; Total giving, $224,000; Grants to individuals, 9 grants totaling $35,000 (high: $4,000, low: $3,000).
Application information: Applications by letter accepted throughout the year.
EIN: 586034213

2086
Jewish Children's Home of Rochester, New York, Inc., Fund

c/o Harter, Secrest & Emery, LLP
1600 Bausch & Lomb Pl.
Rochester, NY   14604-2711   (585) 231-1134
Contact: Nathan J. Robfogel, Pres.

Foundation type: Operating foundation
Limitations: Scholarships to undergraduate college students. All grants are paid to Jewish Family Services of New York which distributes the awards.
Financial data: Year ended 12/31/2003. Assets, $50,361 (M); Expenditures, $4,900; Total giving, $4,500; Grants to individuals, totaling $4,500.
Fields of interest: Jewish agencies & temples.
Type of support: Undergraduate support.
Application information: Applications accepted throughout the year; Contact fund for current application guidelines; Initial approach by letter.
EIN: 166040408

2087
Jewish Endowment Foundation

234 Loyola Bldg., Ste. 611
New Orleans, LA   70112-2015   (504) 524-4559
Contact: Sandra K. Levy, Exec. Dir.
FAX: (504) 524-4259; E-mail: skljef@aol.com;
URL: http://www.jefno.org

Foundation type: Public charity
Limitations: Scholarships to graduate students residing in AL, AR, FL, LA, MS, OK, TN, or TX who are enrolled in or will be enrolled in a professional career in Jewish service.
Financial data: Year ended 12/31/2003. Assets, $16,347,217 (M); Expenditures, $2,202,062; Total giving, $1,754,446.
Fields of interest: Jewish agencies & temples.
Type of support: Graduate support.
Application information: Contact foundation for current application deadline; Completion of formal application required, including essay, transcript, three letters of recommendation, GRE scores, tax return, and photograph; See Web site for further application information.
Program description:
Willy and Erna Wolff Memorial Scholarship: Awards up to $7,500 to individuals who have demonstrated a strong personal commitment to Jewish life, exemplary personal qualities and interpersonal skills, and excellence in academic achievement. Scholarships may be renewed for one successive year but renewal is not guaranteed.
EIN: 720638456

2088
Jewish Family and Children's Services of San Francisco, the Peninsula, Marin and Sonoma Counties

(formerly JFCS)
2150 Post St.
San Francisco, CA   94115   (415) 449-1226
Contact: Anita Friedman Ph.D., Exec. Dir.
FAX: (415) 922-5938; E-mail: EricS@jfcs.org; TDD: (415) 567-1044; URL: http://www.jfcs.org

Foundation type: Public charity
Limitations: Scholarships and grants to Jewish permanent residents of San Francisco, the Peninsula, Marin, and Sonoma counties, CA. Student loans are also available to permanent residents of the East Bay, CA.

Publications: Application guidelines; Annual report; Informational brochure.
Financial data: Year ended 06/30/2005. Assets, $44,314,334 (M); Expenditures, $24,303,721; Total giving, $1,216,050; Grants to individuals, totaling $838,656.
Fields of interest: Humanities; Education, special; Vocational education; Reading; Children/youth, services; Business/industry; Jewish agencies & temples.
Type of support: Student loans—to individuals; Technical education support; Undergraduate support.
Application information: Applications accepted. Application form required.
Initial approach: Telephone.
Deadline(s): None
Additional information: Interviews required; See program description for further application information.
Program descriptions:
Fogel Loan Fund: This fund provides loans to assist individuals of all ages for college, university, or vocation study, and for personal, business, or professional purposes. Applicants must have an appropriate and sound plan for the type of loan requested. Interest of 80 percent of the current prime rate may be waived under special circumstances. No collateral security is required, but guarantors or co-makers may be required. Contact JCFS for application guidelines.
Scholarship Program: Applicants must be Jewish, accepted to a vocational school, college, or university, have financial need, and demonstrate academic achievement (usually indicated by at least a 3.0 GPA). Other qualifications are specified in individual scholarship fund descriptions. In addition to the following programs, aid is available for children and youth with special needs for remedial education. Loans are also available for participation in a valuable social or educational experience, and for adults to begin a new business or attend a professional or vocational training program.
Anna and Charles Stockwitz Children and Youth Fund: This fund provides loans and grants of up to $5,000 to assist Jewish children and teens with a variable educational, social, or psychological experience, or to assist them in attending undergraduate school. The term of loan repayment is flexible. Interest at 80 percent of the prime rate may be waived under special circumstances. No collateral security is required, but guarantors or co-makers may be required. Applicants must be under the age of 26 and must have a plan for use of the funds. If applying for a loan applicant must demonstrate ability to repay. If applying for a grant applicant must demonstrate financial need. Contact JFCS for current application guidelines.
College Loan Fund: This fund provides student loans of up to $5,000 to worthy college students with financial need but demonstrated ability to repay. The term of loan repayment is flexible. Interest at 80 percent of the current prime rate may be waived under special circumstances. No collateral security is required, but co-signers may be required. Contact JFCS for current application guidelines.
Vivienne S. Camp Scholarship Fund: This fund provides $8,000 to one Jewish man and one Jewish woman on the basis of demonstrated academic achievement, promise, and financial need. Students must be accepted in a college, university, or vocational school in CA. Deadline Mar. 1. Completion of formal application required.
Jacob Rassen Memorial Scholarship Fund: This fund provides a scholarship of up to $2,000 to a Jewish youth under age 22 who demonstrates a

desire to enhance Jewish identity and increase his or her knowledge of, and connection to, Israel by studying in Israel. Contact JFCS for current application guidelines.
Stanley Olson Youth Scholarship: This fund provides a scholarship of up to $2,500 to a Jewish youth for graduate or undergraduate study at a college or university, with preference to those pursuing studies in the humanities or liberal arts. Scholarships are awarded on the basis of academic achievement and financial need. Contact JFCS for current application guidelines.
EIN: 941156528

2089
Jewish Foundation for Education of Women

135 E. 64 St.
New York, NY   10021   (212) 288-3931
Contact: Marge Goldwater, Exec. Dir.
FAX: (212) 288-5798;
E-mail: FdnScholar@aol.com; URL: http://www.jfew.org

Foundation type: Independent foundation
Limitations: Scholarships and loans to financially needy female residents of New York City for study in the area of the arts, health care, teaching, and social work.
Publications: Application guidelines; Informational brochure.
Financial data: Year ended 06/30/2004. Assets, $52,602,845 (M); Expenditures, $2,692,601; Total giving, $2,326,549; Grants to individuals, 505 grants totaling $2,326,549.
Fields of interest: Medical school/education; Nursing school/education; Health sciences school/education; Health care; Jewish agencies & temples; Women; Immigrants/refugees.
Type of support: Graduate support; Undergraduate support.
Application information: Contact foundation for current application deadline; Initial approach by letter or e-mail; Completion of formal application required; Interviews required for some programs.
Program descriptions:
Scholarships for Emigres in the Health Professions: Awards are $5,000 each for undergraduate and graduate study at a designated school in New York, NY. Approximately 48 awards are granted. Applicants must demonstrate financial need.
Scholarships for Emigres Training for Careers in Jewish Education: Awards range from $10,000-$20,000 for graduate study at medicine, dental, pharmacy, nursing, dental hygiene, occupational and physical therapy, and physician assistant programs in New York. Approximately 60 awards are granted to female emigres studying Rabbinical, Cantorial, Jewish education or Jewish studies. Scholarships are awarded for one year and are renewable subject to academic performance and continuing financial need. Application deadline is Feb. 15.
EIN: 131860415

2090
Jewish Home for Children, Inc.

129 Church St., Ste. 806
New Haven, CT   06510-2005
Contact: Hinda Massey, Secy.
Application address: 99 Carroll Rd., Hamden, CT 06517, tel.: (203) 288-2618

Foundation type: Independent foundation

Limitations: Scholarships to residents of the greater New Haven, CT, area.
Financial data: Year ended 12/31/2004. Assets, $1,046,685 (M); Expenditures, $47,109; Total giving, $33,950; Grants to individuals, totaling $33,350.
Type of support: Scholarships—to individuals.
Application information: Applications accepted throughout the year; Completion of formal application required.
EIN: 237059701

2091
Jewish Social Service Agency
6123 Montrose Rd.
Rockville, MD 20852 (301) 881-3700
Contact: Jonathan Weinberg, Pres.; For scholarships: Donna Becker
FAX: (301) 770-0901; E-mail: info@jssa.org;
URL: http://www.jssa.org

Foundation type: Public charity
Limitations: Scholarships to Jewish residents of the Washington DC metropolitan area.
Financial data: Year ended 06/30/2004. Assets, $35,279,393 (M); Expenditures, $8,772,609; Total giving, $616,959; Grants to individuals, totaling $616,959.
Fields of interest: Jewish agencies & temples.
Type of support: Undergraduate support.
Application information: Applications accepted. Application form required. Application form available on the grantmaker's Web site.
   Initial approach: E-mail.
   Deadline(s): Mar. 10
   Applicants should submit the following:
      1) Essay
      2) Letter(s) of recommendation
      3) Transcripts
      4) FAFSA
   Additional information: Applications must also include financial aid award letter and letter of admission. See Web site for complete listing of scholarship programs.
EIN: 530196598

2092
Ruth T. Jinks Foundation
P.O. Box 375
Colquitt, GA 39837
Contact: G.C. Jinks, Jr., Pres.

Foundation type: Independent foundation
Limitations: Student loans to individuals, primarily in GA.
Financial data: Year ended 11/30/2005. Assets, $30,147,229 (M); Expenditures, $1,654,027; Total giving, $1,588,221.
Type of support: Student loans—to individuals.
Application information: Unsolicited requests not considered or acknowledged.
EIN: 586043856

2093
JMEC Foundation
(also known as Jemez Mountains Electric Foundation)
P.O. Box 128
Espanola, NM 87532-0128 (505) 753-2105
Contact: Olivar A. Barela

Foundation type: Company-sponsored foundation

Limitations: Scholarships to high school students residing within the Jemez Mountains Electrical Coop.'s service area, primarily in NM.
Financial data: Year ended 12/31/2004. Assets, $609,652 (M); Expenditures, $23,518; Total giving, $19,200; Grants to individuals, 37 grants totaling $18,500 (high: $500; low: $500).
Type of support: Scholarships—to individuals.
Application information:
   Initial approach: Letter or telephone.
   Deadline(s): Mar. 22
   Additional information: Completion of formal application required, including transcripts, GPA, ACT scores, brief personal statement, two letters of recommendation from teachers, and copy of FAFSA.
EIN: 237022094

2094
Jo Daviess County Extension & 4-H Foundation
P.O. Box 600
Elizabeth, IL 61028-0600 (815) 858-2221
Contact: Dennis Guenzler, Treas.
Application address: c/o Joe Daviess, 204 Vine St., Elizabeth, IL 61028, tel.: (815) 858-2221

Foundation type: Independent foundation
Limitations: Scholarships to residents of Jo Daviess County, IL, who are studying agriculture or agricultural-related issues.
Financial data: Year ended 12/31/2004. Assets, $124,894 (M); Expenditures, $14,363; Total giving, $14,300; Grants to individuals, totaling $14,300.
Fields of interest: Agriculture/food, formal/general education.
Type of support: Undergraduate support.
Application information: Deadline Mar. 26; Completion of formal application required; Applications must be typewritten.
Program descriptions:
   Floyd & Alice Bale Scholarship: Awards scholarships of $500 each to students studying agriculture at an accredited institution of higher learning. Recipients must be Jo Daviess County, IL, residents, enrolled in a two- or four-year program of study, and be full-time students taking a minimum of 12 hours of school per semester.
   Ralph & Katherine Norris Scholarship: Awards scholarships of $1,000 each to students studying agriculture at an accredited institution of higher learning. Recipients must be Jo Daviess County, IL, residents, enrolled in a two- or four-year program of study, and be full-time students, taking a minimum of 12 hours of school per semester.
EIN: 363731543

2095
Johns Manville Fund, Inc.
(formerly Schuller Fund, Inc.)
P.O. Box 17086
Denver, CO 80217 (303) 978-3863
FAX: (303) 978-2108; Application address: c/o Fund Admin., P.O. Box 5108, Denver, CO 80217-5108; URL: http://www.jm.com/corporate/1116.htm

Foundation type: Company-sponsored foundation
Limitations: Scholarships to children of employees of Johns Manville.
Publications: Informational brochure (including application guidelines).

Financial data: Year ended 12/31/2004. Assets, $224,022 (M); Expenditures, $75,503; Total giving, $72,743.
Type of support: Employee-related scholarships.
Application information: Application form required.
   Initial approach: Application.
   Deadline(s): Feb. 1
EIN: 136034039

2096
Marvin A. and Lillie Mae Johns Scholarships
c/o SunTrust Bank
P.O. Box 1314
Rome, GA 30162-1314

Foundation type: Independent foundation
Limitations: Scholarships to students who are residents of Chattooga County, GA.
Financial data: Year ended 12/31/2004. Assets, $290,401 (M); Expenditures, $21,382; Total giving, $19,000; Grants to individuals, totaling $19,000.
Fields of interest: Education.
Type of support: Scholarships—to individuals.
Application information: Contact the foundation for current application deadline/guidelines.
EIN: 581846123

2097
Donald K. Johnson Charitable Trust
c/o Wells Fargo Bank Minnesota, N.A.
1248 O St., 4th Fl.
Lincoln, NE 68508

Foundation type: Independent foundation
Limitations: Scholarships to Webster County, IA, youth who have attended the local St. Paul's Lutheran Elementary School.
Financial data: Year ended 12/31/2004. Assets, $305,088 (M); Expenditures, $7,621; Total giving, $5,250; Grants to individuals, totaling $5,250.
Type of support: Support to graduates or students of specific schools; Precollege support.
Application information: Applications accepted.
   Initial approach: Letter or telephone.
   Additional information: Contact trust for current application deadline/guidelines.
EIN: 426401180

2098
The Ralph and Marguerita Johnson Charitable Trust
P.O. Box 1434
Arroyo Grande, CA 93421-1434
Contact: Arlene Pilkington, Tr.

Foundation type: Independent foundation
Limitations: Scholarships to high school graduates of San Luis Obispo County, CA, who are U.S. citizens.
Financial data: Year ended 12/31/2004. Assets, $1,028,870 (M); Expenditures, $25,396; Total giving, $19,000; Grants to individuals, totaling $19,000.
Type of support: Undergraduate support.
Application information: Contact foundation for current application deadline/guidelines; Completion of formal application required, including statement of financial need.
EIN: 776180529

2099
Johnson Controls Foundation
5757 N. Green Bay Ave.
P.O. Box 591
Milwaukee, WI 53201 (414) 524-2296
Contact: Valerie Adisek, Coord.
URL: http://www.johnsoncontrols.com/
corpvalues/foundation.htm

Foundation type: Company-sponsored foundation
Limitations: Scholarships to children and
dependents of employees of Johnson Controls, Inc.
Publications: Application guidelines.
Financial data: Year ended 12/31/2004.
Assets, $47,747,034 (M); Expenditures,
$6,267,905; Total giving, $6,125,188.
Type of support: Employee-related scholarships.
Application information:
  Deadline(s): None
  Additional information: Applications by letter,
  outlining financial need.
Program description:
  Scholarship Program: Each year, up to 16
four-year scholarships are awarded. Recipients are
selected by a distinguished three-person
committee. Each scholarship is in the amount of
$2,000 per year.
EIN: 396036639

2100
Johnson County Community Foundation, Inc.
(formerly Greater Johnson County Community
Foundation)
398 S. Main St.
P.O. Box 217
Franklin, IN 46131-2311 (317) 738-2213
Contact: Sandy Daniels, C.E.O. and Pres.
FAX: (317) 738-9113; E-mail: sandyd@jccf.org;
URL: http://www.jccf.org

Foundation type: Community foundation
Limitations: Scholarships to high school seniors,
students already enrolled in college, and
non-traditional students from Johnson County, IN.
Publications: Application guidelines; Annual report
(including application guidelines); Informational
brochure (including application guidelines);
Newsletter.
Financial data: Year ended 12/31/2004.
Assets, $11,612,133 (M); Expenditures,
$771,842; Total giving, $440,677; Grants to
individuals, 143 grants totaling $108,607 (high:
$12,000, low: $100).
Fields of interest: Nursing school/education;
Nutrition; Voluntarism promotion; Engineering/
technology; Disabilities, people with.
Type of support: Support to graduates or students
of specific schools; Awards/prizes; Technical
education support; Undergraduate support.
Application information: Application form required.
Application form available on the grantmaker's Web
site.
  Initial approach: Letter or telephone.
  Copies of proposal: 1
  Deadline(s): Mar. 1
  Applicants should submit the following:
    1) ACT
    2) Essay
    3) Financial information
    4) GPA
    5) Letter(s) of recommendation
    6) SAT
    7) Transcripts

Additional information: See Web site for
  complete application and program
  information.
EIN: 351797437

2101
Johnson County High School Scholarship Fund Charitable Trust
P.O. Box 400
Buffalo, WY 82834 (307) 684-2211
Contact: Raymond Holt, Tr.

Foundation type: Independent foundation
Limitations: Scholarships to graduates of Johnson
County, WY, secondary schools for bachelor's
degrees and other postsecondary education.
Scholarships are renewable for up to four years.
Financial data: Year ended 12/31/2004.
Assets, $979,429 (M); Expenditures, $48,980;
Total giving, $47,567; Grants to individuals,
totaling $47,567.
Type of support: Support to graduates or students
of specific schools; Undergraduate support.
Application information:
  Deadline(s): Deadline Apr. 1.
  Additional information: Application by letter
  indicating references, plans for higher
  education, name of school planning to attend,
  courses of study, and dates of attendance;
  Applicants must be recommended by school
  administration.
EIN: 836003627

2102
Dexter G. Johnson Educational and Benevolent Trust
P.O. Box 1620
Tulsa, OK 74101-1620
Contact: Betty Crews
Application address: P.O. Box 850250, Oklahoma
City, OK 73085

Foundation type: Independent foundation
Limitations: Educational loans limited to financially
needy residents of OK for study at OK high schools
and vocational schools, and Oklahoma State
University, Oklahoma City University, and the
University of Oklahoma. Preference is given to
physically disabled students, and students who, by
misfortune or calamity, cannot otherwise complete
their education.
Financial data: Year ended 12/31/2003.
Assets, $3,864,936 (M); Expenditures,
$239,817; Total giving, $145,385; Grants to
individuals, totaling $145,385.
Type of support: Student loans—to individuals.
Application information: Application form required.
  Deadline(s): None
  Additional information: Applications must also
  include financial information, family history,
  physical condition, age, education goals, and
  other data necessary to show need.
EIN: 237389204

2103
Ethan Allen Johnson and Caroline H. Johnson Educational Trust
c/o Soy Capital Bank & Trust Co.
455 N. Main St.
Decatur, IL 62523-1103 (217) 429-8714
Contact: Andy Mihm

Foundation type: Independent foundation

Limitations: Scholarships to residents of Kankakee
County, IL, who are under the age of 22.
Financial data: Year ended 12/31/2004.
Assets, $564,901 (M); Expenditures, $36,136;
Total giving, $16,000; Grants to individuals,
totaling $16,000.
Type of support: Scholarships—to individuals.
Application information: Application form required.
  Deadline(s): Contact trust for current application
  deadline.
  Applicants should submit the following:
    1) SAT
    2) ACT
EIN: 363467018

2104
Johnson Family Foundation
P.O. Box 483
Junction, TX 76849
Contact: Dennis Heap, Secy.

Foundation type: Independent foundation
Limitations: Scholarships to residents of Kimble,
Kerr or Gillespie counties, TX, for higher education.
Financial data: Year ended 12/31/2004.
Assets, $245,357 (M); Expenditures, $28,598;
Total giving, $26,200; Grants to individuals,
totaling $17,000.
Type of support: Undergraduate support.
Application information: Deadline Mar. 31;
Completion of formal application required.
EIN: 752568312

2105
Magic Johnson Foundation, Inc.
9100 Wilshire Blvd., E. Twr., Ste. 700
Beverly Hills, CA 90212 (310) 246-4400
FAX: (310) 246-1106;
E-mail: mjscholarship@aol.com; Additional tel.:
(888) 624-4205; URL: http://
www.magicjohnson.org

Foundation type: Public charity
Limitations: Undergraduate scholarships to
inner-city high school students who are residents of
Atlanta, GA; Cleveland, OH; Houston, TX; Los
Angeles, CA; or New York, NY.
Publications: Application guidelines; Informational
brochure; Newsletter.
Financial data: Year ended 06/30/2003.
Assets, $378,432 (M); Expenditures,
$1,202,773; Total giving, $518,351; Grants to
individuals, 97 grants totaling $270,651 (high:
$23,154, low: $250).
Fields of interest: Economically disadvantaged.
Type of support: Undergraduate support.
Application information: Application form required.
  Initial approach: Letter.
  Deadline(s): Feb. 3.
  Applicants should submit the following:
    1) Letter(s) of recommendation
    2) Transcripts
    3) Financial information
    4) Essay
  Additional information: See Web site for further
  information and application form.
Program description:
  Taylor Michaels Scholarship Fund: Applicants
must exemplify a strong potential for academic
achievement, but face socio-economic conditions
that hinder them from reaching their full potential.
Applicants must be planning to attend a four-year
college or university in the fall; have at least a 2.5
GPA; and attend an awards ceremony and
seminars.
EIN: 954349860

2106
The Johnson Foundation, Inc.
5112 W. Cove St.
Boise, ID 83703
Contact: Jerald D. Johnson Sr., Pres.

Foundation type: Independent foundation
Limitations: Scholarships to students for the purchase of textbooks.
Financial data: Year ended 12/31/2004.
Assets, $19,822 (M); Expenditures, $28,651;
Total giving, $28,000; Grants to individuals, totaling $28,000.
Type of support: Scholarships—to individuals; Foreign applicants.
Application information: Application form required.
Deadline(s): Aug.
EIN: 943144095

2107
The Paul and Louise Johnson Foundation
525 S. Main St., Ste. 700
Tulsa, OK 74103-4508 (918) 585-9211
Contact: Jerry Zimmerman, Pres.

Foundation type: Operating foundation
Limitations: Scholarships and grants for educational endeavors in the field of dentistry.
Financial data: Year ended 08/31/2003.
Assets, $482,722 (M); Expenditures, $88,491;
Total giving, $65,761; Grants to individuals, 6 grants totaling $65,761 (high: $27,651, low: $2,500).
Fields of interest: Dental school/education.
Type of support: Scholarships—to individuals.
Application information: Applications accepted throughout the year; Initial approach by letter or telephone; Completion of formal application required.
EIN: 731506406

2108
The Paul T. and Frances B. Johnson Foundation
787 Michigan Ave.
P.O. Box 203
Benzonia, MI 49616-0203 (231) 882-4681
Contact: Jon M. Haugen, Chair.

Foundation type: Independent foundation
Limitations: Scholarships and honoraria to graduating students attending high schools in Grand Traverse, Leelanau, and Benzie counties, MI.
Financial data: Year ended 06/30/2005.
Assets, $3,653,256 (M); Expenditures, $203,217; Total giving, $193,900; Grants to individuals, 111 grants totaling $183,900 (high: $8,000, low: $600).
Type of support: Support to graduates or students of specific schools; Undergraduate support.
Application information: Application form required.
Deadline(s): May 1
Applicants should submit the following:
1) Transcripts
2) FAFSA
Additional information: Interviews required.
EIN: 383382755

2109
The Samuel S. Johnson Foundation
P.O. Box 356
Redmond, OR 97756-0079 (541) 548-8104
Contact: Elizabeth Hill Johnson, Pres.
FAX: (541) 548-2014; E-mail: mary@tssjf.org

Foundation type: Independent foundation
Limitations: Scholarships and student loans to residents of the state of OR who are studying traditional, mainstream health care and allied arts fields, and who have attained at least a sophomore status.
Publications: Application guidelines.
Financial data: Year ended 05/31/2005.
Assets, $9,252,180 (M); Expenditures, $461,200; Total giving, $398,653; Grants to individuals, 4 grants totaling $8,100.
Fields of interest: Health care.
Type of support: Graduate support; Undergraduate support.
Application information: Applications accepted. Application form required.
Initial approach: Letter.
Deadline(s): None
Additional information: Recipients must be currently enrolled in their sophomore, junior, senior, or graduate years of college at an accredited institution.
EIN: 946062478

2110
Johnson Matthey Electronics Employee's of Spokane Scholarship Foundation
E. 15128 Euclid Ave.
Spokane, WA 99216

Foundation type: Company-sponsored foundation
Limitations: Scholarship awards to employees of Johnson Matthey Electronics and their children.
Financial data: Year ended 12/31/2003.
Assets, $25,662 (M); Expenditures, $29,915;
Total giving, $29,574; Grants to individuals, totaling $29,574.
Fields of interest: Higher education.
Type of support: Employee-related scholarships.
Application information: Application form required.
Initial approach: Letter.
EIN: 911769103

2111
Alfred N. Johnson Memorial Fund Trust
c/o Bank of America, N.A.
P.O. Box 6768
Providence, RI 02940-6768
Application address: c/o Guidance Secy., Gloversvile High School, 199 Lincoln St., Gloversville, NY 12078-1999, tel.: (518) 725-0671

Foundation type: Independent foundation
Limitations: Scholarships to graduates of Gloversville High School, NY.
Financial data: Year ended 01/31/2005.
Assets, $631,773 (M); Expenditures, $39,189;
Total giving, $30,000; Grants to individuals, totaling $30,000.
Type of support: Support to graduates or students of specific schools; Undergraduate support.
Application information: Deadline May 15; Completion of formal application required, including three letters of reference (one from teacher, one from fellow student, one from neighbor), letter of acceptance from college, and detailed financial information.
EIN: 146099201

2112
Ray & Vesta Johnson Memorial Scholarship Fund
c/o Bank of America, N.A.
701 5th Ave
P.O. Box 34345
Seattle, WA 98124-1345
Application address: c/o Pastor, Almira Community Church, P.O. Box 55, Almira, WA 99103

Foundation type: Independent foundation
Limitations: Scholarships to graduating, needy female students attending Almira High School, WA, who plan to attend a public college or university in WA.
Financial data: Year ended 03/31/2005.
Assets, $280,323 (M); Expenditures, $18,266;
Total giving, $14,844; Grants to individuals, 3 grants totaling $14,844.
Fields of interest: Women.
Type of support: Support to graduates or students of specific schools; Undergraduate support.
Application information: Deadline 2nd Thurs. in Apr.; Completion of formal application required, including transcripts, a letter from the mayor certifying residence, and a letter of recommendation from the minister of a local church; Scholarships are renewable.
EIN: 237375893

2113
Johnson Scholarship Foundation, Inc.
1002 Rolling Meadow Dr.
Mount Juliet, TN 37122 (615) 758-3617
Contact: Dan York, Treas.

Foundation type: Independent foundation
Limitations: Scholarships to students at David Lipscomb University, TN.
Financial data: Year ended 12/31/2002.
Assets, $113,596 (M); Expenditures, $11,994;
Total giving, $11,040; Grants to individuals, 11 grants totaling $11,040 (high: $1,426, low: $696).
Type of support: Scholarships—to individuals; Support to graduates or students of specific schools.
Application information: Deadline Dec. 31; Application by letter.
EIN: 626047142

2114
Ervin W. Johnson Scholarship Fund
434 N. Main St.
P.O. Box 209
Darlington, WI 53530-1428

Foundation type: Independent foundation
Limitations: Scholarships to financially needy high school graduates currently residing in Lafayette County, WI, for study at any recognized institution of higher learning.
Financial data: Year ended 12/31/2004.
Assets, $802,517 (M); Expenditures, $31,482;
Total giving, $30,900; Grants to individuals, totaling $30,900.
Type of support: Undergraduate support.
Application information: Applications accepted. Application form required.
Deadline(s): May 1
EIN: 391297197

2115
The Sandra and Bill Johnson Scholarship Fund, Inc.

c/o John T. Bobo
P.O. Box 169
Shelbyville, TN 37162 (931) 684-4611
Contact: Kathy Anderson

Foundation type: Independent foundation
Limitations: Scholarships to students who are members of the Walking Horse Training Association, or are otherwise connected with the walking horse industry to pursue postsecondary education.
Financial data: Year ended 12/31/2004.
Assets, $1,787 (M); Expenditures, $79,319; Total giving, $68,293; Grants to individuals, totaling $68,293.
Fields of interest: Athletics/sports, training; Athletics/sports, equestrianism.
Type of support: Scholarships—to individuals.
Application information: Applications are accepted up to the beginning of the current academic year; Completion of formal application required.
EIN: 621622697

2116
Ray & Nell Johnson Scholarship Fund

c/o Wells Fargo Bank West, N.A.
P.O. Box 21927
Seattle, WA 98111
Application address: c/o Harlowton High School, Attn.: Superintendent, 304 Division St., Harlowton, MT 59036, tel.: (496) 632-4324

Foundation type: Independent foundation
Limitations: Scholarships to graduates of Harlowton High School, MT.
Financial data: Year ended 05/31/2005.
Assets, $151,667 (M); Expenditures, $14,891; Total giving, $12,850; Grants to individuals, totaling $12,850.
Type of support: Support to graduates or students of specific schools; Undergraduate support.
Application information: Deadline 1st Mon. in May; Application by letter, including current scholarship status, extracurricular activities, educational goals, financial status, need for scholarship, transcript, and moral character references.
EIN: 816013476

2117
Magda M. Johnson Scholarship Trust Fund

c/o Legacy Portfolio Mgmt.
99 North St.
Pittsfield, MA 01202

Foundation type: Independent foundation
Limitations: Undergraduate and graduate scholarships to students residing in North Canaan and Canaan, CT.
Financial data: Year ended 11/30/2002.
Assets, $253,876 (M); Expenditures, $13,757; Total giving, $8,430; Grants to individuals, totaling $8,430.
Type of support: Graduate support; Undergraduate support.
Application information: Deadline July 1; Completion of formal application required.
EIN: 066082582

2118
Gladys L. Johnson Scholarship Trust

c/o Wells Fargo Bank Minnesota, N.A.
625 Marquette Ave., N9311-142
Minneapolis, MN 55402
Application address: P.O. Box 175, Center City, MN 55012

Foundation type: Independent foundation
Limitations: Scholarships to residents of east central MN, WI, SD, ND, MI, and IA.
Financial data: Year ended 01/31/2005.
Assets, $154,956 (M); Expenditures, $7,293; Total giving, $4,619; Grants to individuals, totaling $4,619.
Type of support: Scholarships—to individuals.
Application information: Deadline May 1; Initial approach by letter requesting application; Completion of formal application required; Interviews required.
EIN: 416225081

2119
Johnson Student Scholarship & Loan Foundation

P.O. Box 248
Ord, NE 68862-0248
Application address: c/o Lu Lansman, Chair., Selection Comm., Ord Public Schools, Ord, NE 68862

Foundation type: Independent foundation
Limitations: Scholarships for higher education to graduating seniors of Ord public high schools, NE.
Financial data: Year ended 11/30/2004.
Assets, $217,644 (M); Expenditures, $2,240; Total giving, $0; Loans to individuals, 7 loans totaling $9,500.
Type of support: Support to graduates or students of specific schools; Undergraduate support.
Application information: Application form required.
  Deadline(s): May 1
EIN: 470606386

2120
Addie Kate M. Johnson Trust

(also known as Morton Johnson Scholarship)
P.O. Box 250
Gray, GA 31032
Contact: Patricia J. Childs, Tr.
Application address: P.O. Box 257, Gray, GA 31032, tel.: (478) 986-3410

Foundation type: Independent foundation
Limitations: Scholarships to residents of Jones County, GA.
Financial data: Year ended 12/31/2003.
Assets, $167,784 (M); Expenditures, $10,335; Total giving, $9,000; Grants to individuals, 9 grants totaling $9,000 (high: $1,000, low: $1,000).
Type of support: Scholarships—to individuals.
Application information: Deadline May 1; Application by letter detailing school accomplishments, activities, contributions to school and community, grades, and future plans.
EIN: 586157940

2121
F. W. Johnston Scholarship Fund

(formerly F. W. Johnston Foundation)
c/o SunTrust Bank, Trust Tax Svcs.
P.O. Box 1908
Orlando, FL 32802-1908
Application address: c/o SunTrust Bank, P.O. Box 85024, Richmond, VA 23285-5024

Foundation type: Independent foundation
Limitations: Scholarships to students from the Roanoke Valley and Gile County areas, VA.
Financial data: Year ended 12/31/2004.
Assets, $1,778,719 (M); Expenditures, $53,698; Total giving, $25,133; Grants to individuals, totaling $18,000.
Type of support: Support to graduates or students of specific schools; Undergraduate support.
Application information: Applications accepted throughout the year; Contact fund for current application guidelines.
EIN: 546456401

2122
Joint Council No. 73 Scholarship Fund

(also known as Josephine Provenzano Scholarship Fund)
2414 Morris Ave.
Union, NJ 07083

Foundation type: Independent foundation
Limitations: Scholarships of up to $750 per semester to children of Joint Council No. 73 members in NJ to attend four-year colleges.
Financial data: Year ended 12/31/2004.
Assets, $374,895 (M); Expenditures, $25,034; Total giving, $24,000; Grants to individuals, totaling $24,000.
Fields of interest: Labor unions/organizations.
Type of support: Undergraduate support.
Application information: Application form required.
  Deadline(s): Apr. 1
  Applicants should submit the following:
    1) Letter(s) of recommendation
    2) Transcripts
    3) SAT
EIN: 226017773

2123
Thomas B. Jones & Grace Stevenson Jones Charitable Foundation

c/o National Bank & Trust Co.
230 W. State St.
Sycamore, IL 60178 (815) 895-2125
Contact: Marilyn Knetsch, V.P., National Bank and Trust Co.

Foundation type: Independent foundation
Limitations: Scholarships to residents of Grant, Iowa, and Lafayette counties in WI, who are attending four-year colleges or universities.
Financial data: Year ended 12/31/2004.
Assets, $1,452,760 (M); Expenditures, $91,791; Total giving, $72,075; Grants to individuals, totaling $72,075.
Type of support: Scholarships—to individuals.
Application information: Deadline Mar. 1; Completion of formal application required.
EIN: 363470630

2124

The Harvey and Bernice Jones Charitable Trust No. 2
P.O. Box 2035
Springdale, AR 72765

Foundation type: Independent foundation
Limitations: Scholarships to individuals.
Financial data: Year ended 11/30/2004.
Assets, $347,365 (M); Expenditures, $50,678;
Total giving, $44,583; Grants to individuals,
totaling $44,583.
Type of support: Scholarships—to individuals.
Application information: Applications not
accepted.
EIN: 716143264

2125

Emmett & Beulah Jones Educational Fund
c/o Gold Trust Co.
P.O. Box 846
St. Joseph, MO 64502
Application addresses: c/o Office of Student
Financial Planning, William Jewell College, 500
College Hill, Liberty, MO 54068-1896, c/o Financial
Aid Office, College of the Ozarks, Point Lookout, MO
65726

Foundation type: Independent foundation
Limitations: Scholarships to residents of Point
Lookout and Liberty, MO, primarily for those who are
pursuing a Christian ministry or service.
Financial data: Year ended 02/28/2005.
Assets, $374,229 (M); Expenditures, $33,794;
Total giving, $30,258; Grants to individuals, 15
grants totaling $30,258.
Fields of interest: Theological school/education.
Type of support: Scholarships—to individuals.
Application information: Applications accepted
throughout the year; Completion of formal
application required.
EIN: 436765443

2126

Walter S. and Evan C. Jones Foundation
(also known as Jones Foundation, Inc.)
527 Commercial St., Rm. 501
Emporia, KS 66801-4081
Contact: Sharon L. Tidwell, Exec. Dir.
URL: http://www.jonesfdn.org

Foundation type: Independent foundation
Limitations: Scholarships to financially needy
individuals who have been continuous residents of
Lyon, Coffey, or Osage counties, KS, for a minimum
of one year.
Publications: Informational brochure; Program
policy statement.
Financial data: Year ended 06/30/2005.
Assets, $171,427 (M); Expenditures, $915,050;
Total giving, $793,218; Grants to individuals, 770
grants totaling $793,218 (high: $19,600, low:
$375).
Fields of interest: Vocational education.
Type of support: Technical education support;
Undergraduate support.
Application information: Applications accepted.
Application form required. Application form
available on the grantmaker's Web site.
Initial approach: Telephone or in person.
Deadline(s): July 20 and Dec. 20
Applicants should submit the following:
 1) FAFSA
 2) Transcripts
 3) SAR
 4) GPA

5) Financial information
Program description:
 Scholarship Program: Recipients may attend
four-year colleges and universities, two-year
colleges, or technical schools. Grants are given for
tuition and books. Some recipients receive multiple
grants.
EIN: 237384087

2127

Claude R. and Sadie B. Jones Loan Fund
c/o Wells Fargo Bank Northwest, N.A.
P.O. Box 21927
Seattle, WA 98111
Application address: c/o James Armstrong, Branch
Mgr., Wells Fargo Bank Northwest, N.A., P.O. Box
365, Oakridge, OR 97463

Foundation type: Independent foundation
Limitations: Student loans to graduates of
Oakridge High School, OR.
Financial data: Year ended 09/30/2002.
Assets, $626,979 (M); Expenditures, $51,502;
Total giving, $36,810; Grants to individuals, 50
grants totaling $36,810 (high: $1,500, low: $334).
Type of support: Support to graduates or students
of specific schools; Undergraduate support.
Application information: Deadline Aug. 15;
Completion of formal application required, including
transcript and proof of enrollment.
EIN: 936055774

2128

Clinton O. & Lura Curtis Jones Memorial Trust
66 West St., 3rd Fl.
Pittsfield, MA 01201 (413) 443-4771
Contact: Frederick M. Myers, Tr.

Foundation type: Independent foundation
Limitations: Scholarships to Berkshire County, MA,
residents.
Financial data: Year ended 12/31/2004.
Assets, $1,186,989 (M); Expenditures, $38,176;
Total giving, $29,000; Grants to individuals,
totaling $29,000.
Type of support: Scholarships—to individuals.
Application information: Deadline Apr. 15; Initial
approach by letter; Completion of formal application
required, including financial information,
transcripts, parents' federal income tax return, and
brief personal essay.
EIN: 046173271

2129

Adora S. Jones Ministerial Trust
c/o Wells Fargo Bank Iowa, N.A.
101 3rd Ave. S.W.
Cedar Rapids, IA 52406-1967

Foundation type: Operating foundation
Limitations: Scholarships to Presbyterian, Baptist
or Congregational ministerial students in IA.
Financial data: Year ended 12/31/2002.
Assets, $321,017 (M); Expenditures, $24,692;
Total giving, $17,500; Grants to individuals,
totaling $17,500.
Fields of interest: Theological school/education.
Type of support: Scholarships—to individuals.
Application information: Applications accepted
throughout the year; Contact trust for current
application guidelines; Initial approach by letter.
EIN: 426506484

2130

Joseph Jones Scholarship Fund
c/o National City Bank
P.O. Box 94651
Cleveland, OH 44101-4651
Contact: C.A. Kelsey, Trust Off., National City Bank
Application address: 20 Stanwix St., Pittsburgh, PA
15222

Foundation type: Independent foundation
Limitations: Scholarships to individuals residing in
PA for medical education.
Financial data: Year ended 12/31/2003.
Assets, $44,224 (M); Expenditures, $6,145; Total
giving, $4,800; Grants to individuals, 3 grants
totaling $4,800 (high: $2,400, low: $1,200).
Fields of interest: Health sciences school/
education.
Type of support: Scholarships—to individuals.
Application information: Applications accepted.
Application form required.
Deadline(s): Nov. 1
Additional information: Contact foundation for
 application form.
EIN: 256021372

2131

Grace B. Jones Trust
c/o TD Banknorth, N.A, Wealth Mgmt. Group
P.O. Box 1180
South Yarmouth, MA 02664-0180
Application address: c/o Guidance Dir.,
Attn: Andrew Kalinick, Nauset Regional High
School, 100 Cable Rd., North Eastham, MA 02651

Foundation type: Independent foundation
Limitations: Scholarships to graduates of Nauset
Regional High School, North Eastham, MA.
Financial data: Year ended 12/31/2004.
Assets, $478,799 (M); Expenditures, $30,382;
Total giving, $23,383.
Type of support: Support to graduates or students
of specific schools; Undergraduate support.
Application information: Applications accepted by
letter throughout the year stating background and
qualifications; Initial approach by letter.
EIN: 046466327

2132

Jordaan Foundation, Inc.
111 E. 8th St.
P.O. Box 360
Larned, KS 67550-0360
Contact: Donald L. Burnett, Dr.

Foundation type: Independent foundation
Limitations: Scholarships to graduates of Pawnee
County, KS, high schools to attend KS colleges and
universities.
Publications: Application guidelines.
Financial data: Year ended 12/31/2004.
Assets, $1,132,772 (M); Expenditures, $79,140;
Total giving, $57,000; Grants to individuals,
totaling $37,000.
Type of support: Support to graduates or students
of specific schools; Undergraduate support.
Application information: Application form required.
Initial approach: In person.
Deadline(s): Apr. 5
Additional information: Applications available
 from Pawnee County high school principals,
 foundation, or trustee bank; Applications not
 accepted by mail.
EIN: 480950585

2133
Roderick J. & Gertrude B. Jordan Charitable Trust
P.O Box 448
Murfreesboro, NC 27855-0448
(252) 398-4171
Contact: J. Guy Revelle, Jr., Tr.

Foundation type: Independent foundation
Limitations: Scholarships to high school students who are residents of Northampton County, NC.
Financial data: Year ended 03/31/2005. Assets, $917,808 (M); Expenditures, $87,925; Total giving, $67,838; Grants to individuals, totaling $67,838.
Type of support: Support to graduates or students of specific schools.
Application information: Deadline June 1; Completion of formal application required; Applications available from high schools.
EIN: 566302665

2134
Jordan Education Foundation
9361 S. 300 E.
Sandy, UT 84070-2998 (801) 567-8125
Contact: Martin A. Nielsen, Pres.
FAX: (801) 567-8092;
E-mail: martin.nielsen@jordan.k12.ut.us;
URL: http://www.jordandistrict.org/foundation

Foundation type: Public charity
Limitations: Scholarships to Jordan School District, UT, students, for financial need and academic achievement.
Financial data: Year ended 06/30/2004. Assets, $677,891 (M); Expenditures, $584,144; Total giving, $584,144; Grants to individuals, 38 grants totaling $41,850 (high: $3,000, low: $400).
Type of support: Support to graduates or students of specific schools.
Application information: Contact foundation for current application deadline/guidelines; Completion of formal application required.
EIN: 746356280

2135
Leon M. Jordan Scholarship & Monument Fund, Inc.
5540 Wayne Ave.
Kansas City, MO 64110
Contact: Alexander Ellison, Treas.
Application address: c/o Advisory Comm., P.O. Box 15544, Kansas City, MO 64106

Foundation type: Independent foundation
Limitations: Scholarships to residents of MO.
Financial data: Year ended 06/30/2004. Assets, $74,189 (M); Expenditures, $12,229; Total giving, $10,000; Grants to individuals, 10 grants totaling $10,000 (high: $1,000, low: $1,000).
Type of support: Scholarships—to individuals.
Application information: Applications accepted. Application form required.
Deadline(s): Sept.
Additional information: Application authorizing release of financial information must be submitted to college Financial Aid Officer.
EIN: 431248204

2136
The B. N. & W. L. Jordan Scholarship Fund
c/o Wachovia Bank, N.A.
100 N. Main St., 13th Fl.
Winston-Salem, NC 27150
Application address: c/o Ed Loflin, P.O. Box 3099, Winston-Salem, NC 27150-6732, tel.: (336) 732-6488

Foundation type: Independent foundation
Limitations: Scholarships to graduates of Henderson County public high schools, NC, for higher education.
Financial data: Year ended 12/31/2004. Assets, $1,377,690 (M); Expenditures, $73,279; Total giving, $59,000; Grants to individuals, totaling $59,000.
Type of support: Support to graduates or students of specific schools.
Application information: Deadline Apr. 1; Completion of formal application required, including transcripts, SAT score, GPA, essay, and financial statement.
EIN: 566487341

2137
The Jostens Foundation, Inc.
5501 American Blvd. W.
Minneapolis, MN 55437 (952) 830-3235
Contact: Mary Klimek, Dir. and Admin.
E-mail: foundation@jostens.com; URL: http://www.jostens.com/company/community/index.asp

Foundation type: Company-sponsored foundation
Limitations: Scholarships to high school seniors who are full-time dependents of a Jostens employee or sales representative for higher education.
Publications: Application guidelines; Informational brochure (including application guidelines).
Financial data: Year ended 12/31/2004. Assets, $72,651 (M); Expenditures, $462,302; Total giving, $479,427.
Type of support: Employee-related scholarships.
Application information:
Initial approach: Proposal.
Additional information: Contact foundation for current application deadline/guidelines.
Program description:
Jostens Scholars Awards: One-time scholarships of $1,000 to high school seniors for tuition and academic fees for the first year of full-time study at any postsecondary school. Recipient must be a dependent of a full-time Jostens employee or sales representative. All applicants are automatically eligible for the Jack M. Holt Memorial Scholarship award. The Holt scholarship is a $1,500 award and is renewable for up to three additional years for a maximum of $6,000.
EIN: 411280587

2138
Journalism Foundation of Metropolitan St. Louis
c/o Bank of America, N.A.
231 S. LaSalle St., IL1-231-14-19
Chicago, IL 60697
Contact: Pat Rice, Pres.
Application address: c/o St. Louis Post Dispatch, 900 N. 12th St., St. Louis, MO 63101

Foundation type: Independent foundation
Limitations: Scholarships to students of journalism at recognized schools and departments of journalism.
Financial data: Year ended 12/31/2004. Assets, $60,321 (M); Expenditures, $23,864; Total giving, $19,400; Grants to individuals, totaling $19,400.
Fields of interest: Journalism/publishing.
Type of support: Scholarships—to individuals.
Application information: Applications by letter accepted throughout the year.
EIN: 436121179

2139
The Joyard Foundation
2056 Lyans Dr.
La Canada Flintridge, CA 91011-1537

Foundation type: Independent foundation
Limitations: Scholarships to individuals for higher education.
Financial data: Year ended 12/31/2003. Assets, $1,188,195 (M); Expenditures, $411,391; Total giving, $405,048; Grants to individuals, 10 grants totaling $305,048 (high: $55,508).
Type of support: Undergraduate support.
Application information: Contact foundation for current application deadline/guidelines.
EIN: 954636168

2140
Melvin S. Jozwiak Scholarship Trust
825 N. Jefferson St., Ste. 300
Milwaukee, WI 53202-3737 (414) 271-2718
Contact: Janet F. Resnick, Tr.

Foundation type: Independent foundation
Limitations: Scholarships to children of Vilter Manufacturing Corporation employees.
Financial data: Year ended 12/31/2004. Assets, $49,752 (M); Expenditures, $13,050; Total giving, $10,000; Grants to individuals, totaling $10,000.
Type of support: Employee-related scholarships.
Application information: Deadline Spring; Contact foundation for current application deadline; Completion of formal application required.
EIN: 396696457

2141
JSA Foundation
306 Gay St., Ste. 400
Nashville, TN 37201 (615) 254-2291
Contact: Margaret L. Behm, Dir.

Foundation type: Operating foundation
Limitations: Scholarships to female residents of TN, 23 years of age or older, who are attending college.
Financial data: Year ended 08/31/2003. Assets, $302,245 (M); Expenditures, $19,881; Total giving, $13,740; Grants to individuals, 5 grants totaling $13,740 (high: $3,000, low: $1,740).
Fields of interest: Women.
Type of support: Scholarships—to individuals.
Application information: Application form required.
Deadline(s): One month prior to registration
Additional information: Application should include transcript.
EIN: 581488121

2142
JSJ Family Foundation
c/o UMB Bank, N.A.
P.O. Box 419692
Kansas City, MO 64141-6692

Foundation type: Operating foundation
Limitations: Scholarships to individuals for higher education.
Financial data: Year ended 01/31/2005.
Assets, $3,350,048 (M); Expenditures, $180,110; Total giving, $136,264.
Type of support: Undergraduate support.
Application information: Applications not accepted.
EIN: 436797334

2143

Bryan W. & Minnie Judge Foundation

c/o Judge Fdn. Scholarship Comm.
P.O. Box 6973
Vero Beach, FL   32961-6973   (772) 778-6903

Foundation type: Operating foundation
Limitations: Scholarships to students for higher education.
Financial data: Year ended 12/31/2003.
Assets, $599,943 (M); Expenditures, $40,995; Total giving, $31,250; Grants to individuals, 67 grants totaling $31,250 (high: $500, low: $250).
Type of support: Scholarships—to individuals.
Application information: Applications accepted. Application form required.
Deadline(s): Feb. 28
Additional information: Completion of formal application required, including transcripts, three recommendations and personal letter.
Program description:
Scholarship Program: Scholarships are awarded based on financial need, academic performance and church and community activities. Most awards are limited to $1,000 per year.
EIN: 592691650

2144

Judges Athletic Association

P.O. Box 2213
Winchester, VA   22604-1413
Contact: Damon DeArment, Pres.

Foundation type: Public charity
Limitations: Scholarships to Handley High School, VA students who are in an athletic program.
Financial data: Year ended 07/31/2004.
Assets, $425,349 (M); Expenditures, $104,832; Total giving, $99,129; Grants to individuals, 600 grants totaling $84,500.
Type of support: Support to graduates or students of specific schools.
Application information: Application form required.
Initial approach: Letter.
Deadline(s): Contact foundation for application guidelines
EIN: 546060341

2145

George W. & Sadie Marie Juhl Scholarship Fund

c/o Southern Michigan Bank & Trust
51 W. Pearl St.
Coldwater, MI   49036-1933
Contact: Mary Guthrie

Foundation type: Independent foundation
Limitations: Scholarships to students residing in Branch County, MI, to attend schools of higher education in MI.
Financial data: Year ended 03/31/2005.
Assets, $2,807,331 (M); Expenditures, $145,516; Total giving, $127,000; Grants to individuals, 64 grants totaling $127,000 (high: $2,000, low: $1,000).
Fields of interest: Vocational education.
Type of support: Scholarships—to individuals.
Application information: Applications accepted throughout the year; Completion of formal application required; Forms are available at each high school in Branch County.
Program description:
Scholarship Program: The maximum scholarship is $2,000 per year. Scholarships will not exceed 50 percent of one year's costs. There is no age limit or limit on how many times an individual may apply.
EIN: 386372257

2146

Just Foundation

(also known as F. Ward Just Scholarship Foundation)
2508 Walnut St.
Waukegan, IL   60087-3123   (847) 623-0411
Contact: Frederic J. Woldt, V.P.

Foundation type: Independent foundation
Limitations: Scholarships to Lake County, IL, high school graduates intending to establish an undergraduate major in journalism or media communications.
Financial data: Year ended 08/31/2005.
Assets, $354,552 (M); Expenditures, $29,253; Total giving, $17,500; Grants to individuals, totaling $17,500.
Fields of interest: Media/communications; Journalism/publishing.
Type of support: Support to graduates or students of specific schools; Undergraduate support.
Application information: Deadline Apr. 15; Completion of formal application required, including college entrance exam scores, transcripts, letter of reference from school and parent/guardian, and confidential financial statement.
Program description:
Scholarship Program: Grants do not exceed $4,000 per year. Candidates must rank in the upper half of their classes, establish clear financial need, and be outstanding in character and promise.
EIN: 366162896

2147

Justice Lodge No. 285 F. & A.M., Educational Trust

420 N. Douglass Ave.
Margate City, NJ   08402-1929   (609) 822-0520
Application address: c/o Michael D. Karsevar, 24 West Dr., Margate, NJ 08402

Foundation type: Operating foundation
Limitations: Scholarships to relatives of members of NJ 23rd Masonic District Encompassing Atlantic County.
Financial data: Year ended 12/31/2002.
Assets, $536,210 (M); Expenditures, $65,793; Total giving, $31,438; Grants to individuals, 11 grants totaling $31,438 (high: $4,125, low: $875).
Fields of interest: Fraternal societies.
Type of support: Scholarships—to individuals.
Application information: Deadline May 1; Completion of formal application required, including transcripts.
EIN: 222857778

2148

JWF Quanza Foundation, Inc.

5101 N. Classen Blvd., Ste. 404
Oklahoma City, OK   73118   (405) 843-8444
Contact: Jerry Crabb, Pres.

Foundation type: Independent foundation
Limitations: Scholarships to OK residents for attendance at OK universities and grants for hearing aids for underprivileged children.
Financial data: Year ended 12/31/2004.
Assets, $3,555,295 (M); Expenditures, $235,793; Total giving, $148,860; Grants to individuals, 67 grants totaling $148,860 (high: $7,300, low: $228).
Fields of interest: Ear & throat diseases; Economically disadvantaged.
Type of support: Undergraduate support; Grants for special needs.
Application information: Applications accepted. Application form required.
Additional information: Applications available at OK universities' financial aid offices and OK audiologists' offices.
EIN: 731467915

2149

The Henry J. Kaiser Family Foundation

2400 Sand Hill Rd.
Menlo Park, CA   94025   (650) 854-9400
Contact: Renee Wells, Grants and Contracts Mgr.
Additional E-mail: pduckham@kff.org; Washington, DC Office: 1330 G St., N.W., Washington, DC 20005, tel.: (202) 347-5270; FAX: (202) 347-5274
FAX: (650) 854-4800; E-mail: rwells@kff.org; URL: http://www.kff.org

Foundation type: Operating foundation
Limitations: Scholarships to students of color for health policy research at Howard University, DC.
Publications: Annual report; Informational brochure (including application guidelines).
Financial data: Year ended 12/31/2004.
Assets, $547,983,207 (M); Expenditures, $66,214,838; Total giving, $839,393.
Fields of interest: Public health school/education; Minorities.
Type of support: Support to graduates or students of specific schools; Undergraduate support.
Application information: Applications accepted. Application form required.
Deadline(s): Jan. 7
Program description:
Barbara Jordan Health Policy Scholars: The program brings talented Latino, African American, Asian/Pacific Islander, and American Indian/Alaska Native college seniors and recent graduates to Washington, D.C., where they work in congressional offices and learn about health policy. Through the nine-week program (May 24-July 29), scholars gain knowledge about federal legislative procedure and health policy issues, while further developing their critical thinking and leadership skills. In addition to an internship in a congressional office, scholars participate in seminars and site visits to augment their knowledge of healthcare issues and write and present a health policy research memo. Eligible candidates must be U.S. citizens who are members of a racial/ethnic minority group and will be seniors or recent graduates of an accredited U.S. college or university in the fall. Scholars receive approximately $5,000 in support, which includes a stipend of $1,500 upon completion of the program; a daily expense allowance for meals and local transportation; transportation/airfare to and from

Washington, D.C.; and lodging at Howard University.
EIN: 946064808

2150
Kaiser Foundation, Inc.
c/o Lawrence L. Lang
1660 Lincoln St., No. 2350
Denver, CO 80264
Contact: Edward W. Hunter, Exec. Dir.
Application address: 1025 Aspen Dr., Cody, WY 82414

Foundation type: Independent foundation
Limitations: Scholarships to WY high school students.
Financial data: Year ended 12/31/2004. Assets, $1,638,325 (M); Expenditures, $14,134; Total giving, $10,000; Grants to individuals, totaling $10,000.
Type of support: Support to graduates or students of specific schools; Undergraduate support.
Application information: Applications accepted. Application form required.
  Deadline(s): Deadline May 1
EIN: 840278210

2151
Kaiulani Home for Girls Trust
c/o Bank of Hawaii
P.O. Box 3170
Honolulu, HI 96802
Scholarship address: c/o Hawaii Community Fdn., 1164 Bishop St., Ste. 800, Honolulu, HI 96813, tel.: (808) 537-6333

Foundation type: Independent foundation
Limitations: Undergraduate and graduate scholarships to financially needy females who are legal residents of HI, with preference given to those of Hawaiian or part Hawaiian ancestry, to attend colleges and universities in the U.S.
Publications: Informational brochure (including application guidelines).
Financial data: Year ended 03/31/2005. Assets, $2,972,246 (M); Expenditures, $181,293; Total giving, $141,600; Grants to individuals, 286 grants totaling $141,600 (high: $950, low: $150).
Fields of interest: Women.
Type of support: Graduate support; Undergraduate support.
Application information: Deadline Mar. 1; Initial approach by letter or telephone; Completion of formal application required, including transcripts, personal statement, two letters of recommendation, and Student Aid Report (SAR).
Program description:
  Scholarship Program: Scholarships are renewable. Applicants to this foundation may automatically be considered for other scholarship programs administered by the Hawaii Community Foundation. Employees and relatives of employees of Bancorp Hawaii and the Hawaii Community Foundation are ineligible.
EIN: 996003331

2152
Kalamazoo Community Foundation
(formerly Kalamazoo Foundation)
151 S. Rose St., Ste. 332
Kalamazoo, MI 49007-4775 (269) 381-4416
Contact: David D. Gardiner, V.P., Comm. Invest.
FAX: (269) 381-3146; E-mail: info@kalfound.org; Additional E-mails: dgardiner@kalfound.org and sspringgate@kalfound.org; URL: http://www.kalfound.org

Foundation type: Community foundation
Limitations: Scholarships to students from Kalamazoo County high schools, Kalamazoo, MI.
Publications: Application guidelines; Annual report; Financial statement; Informational brochure; Informational brochure (including application guidelines); Newsletter; Quarterly report.
Financial data: Year ended 12/31/2004. Assets, $262,256,195 (M); Expenditures, $18,844,111; Total giving, $15,158,481.
Type of support: Research; Support to graduates or students of specific schools; Graduate support; Technical education support; Undergraduate support.
Application information: Contact foundation for current application deadline; Initial approach by telephone; Completion of formal application required.
Program description:
  Scholarship Program: The foundation offers numerous scholarship programs, primarily in the Kalamazoo, MI, area. See Web site for further information.
EIN: 383333202

2153
Kalamazoo Public Education Foundation
714 S. Westnedge Ave., Ste. 214
Kalamazoo, MI 49007-5094 (269) 337-0498
Contact: Pamela Kingery, Exec. Dir.
FAX: (269) 337-0496; E-mail: kpefcec@aol.com; URL: http://www.geocities.com/kpef_2000/

Foundation type: Public charity
Limitations: Scholarships to residents of the Kalamazoo, MI, area, primarily to minorities, for teaching education.
Publications: Application guidelines; Grants list.
Financial data: Year ended 12/31/2005. Assets, $2,693,959 (M); Expenditures, $2,091,893; Total giving, $59,631.
Fields of interest: Teacher school/education; Minorities.
Type of support: Undergraduate support.
Application information:
  Deadline(s): Apr. 16
  Additional information: Completion of formal application required, including statement of personal goals, two letters of recommendation and transcripts; See Web site for a complete listing of scholarships.
Program description:
  Home Growth Scholarship: The applicant must be African American, Latino, Native American, or Asian American, and must have experience working with youth in a leadership role. The applicant must be pursuing a course of study leading to a degree in teaching. If selected as a scholarship recipient, the applicant must be willing to teach at least three years in the Kalamazoo Public Schools if offered a position upon completion of his/her teaching certificate.
EIN: 382873188

2154
Stephanie Kamenski Trust
c/o Bank of America, N.A., P.C. Group
P.O. Box 6767
Providence, RI 02940-6767
Application address: c/o Thomas Gavin, Principal, Berlin High School, 139 Patterson St., Berlin, CT 06037

Foundation type: Independent foundation
Limitations: Scholarships to graduates of Berlin and New Britain high schools, CT.
Financial data: Year ended 07/31/2004. Assets, $406,305 (M); Expenditures, $21,880; Total giving, $14,100; Grants to individuals, 5 grants totaling $14,100 (high: $4,000, low: $2,000).
Type of support: Support to graduates or students of specific schools; Undergraduate support.
Application information: Applications by letter accepted throughout the year, including copy of parents' 1040 form and transcripts.
EIN: 066288857

2155
Sylvester and Tessie Kaminski Foundation
c/o Wells Fargo Bank, N.A.
P.O. Box 53456
Phoenix, AZ 85072

Foundation type: Independent foundation
Limitations: Scholarships primarily to residents of South Bend, IN.
Financial data: Year ended 12/31/2004. Assets, $1,097,564 (M); Expenditures, $88,249; Total giving, $70,222; Grants to individuals, totaling $55,763.
Type of support: Scholarships—to individuals.
Application information: Applications by letter accepted throughout the year.
EIN: 237355916

2156
The Greater Kanawha Valley Foundation
1600 Huntington Sq.
900 Lee St. E.
Charleston, WV 25301 (304) 346-3620
Contact: Rebecca Ceperley, C.E.O.; For grants: Christina Williams, Receptionist; For grants: Kim Barbara Tiemon, Sr. Prog. Off.
FAX: (304) 346-3640; E-mail: tgkvf@tgkvf.org; Additional address: P.O. Box 3041, Charleston, WV 25331; Additional tel.: (800) 467-5909; Grant application E-mails: ktieman@tgkvf.org and cwilliams@tgkvf.org; URL: http://www.tgkvf.org

Foundation type: Community foundation
Limitations: Scholarships to residents of WV for undergraduate, graduate, vocational, and technical education.
Publications: Application guidelines; Annual report (including application guidelines); Financial statement; Grants list; Informational brochure; Occasional report.
Financial data: Year ended 12/31/2004. Assets, $128,779,492 (M); Expenditures, $4,920,762; Total giving, $3,770,838; Grants to individuals, totaling $731,540.
Fields of interest: Vocational education.
Type of support: Graduate support; Technical education support; Undergraduate support.
Application information: Application form required.
  Deadline(s): Feb. 14

Program description:

Scholarship Funds: The foundation administers 70 separate scholarship funds, each with its own criteria. Some of these funds benefit students of the following schools: Dunbar High School, WV, Nicholas County High School, WV, Washington and Lee University, West Virginia Wesleyan College, and The Conservatory of Music and Fine Arts at the University of Charleston.
EIN: 556024430

2157
Stephen D. Kander Scholarship Fund
c/o JPMorgan Chase Bank, N.A.
P.O. Box 1308
Milwaukee, WI 53201-1308
Application addresses: c/o Luxemburg-Casco High School, Attn.: Fred Yagodinsky, Counselor, 512 Center St., Luxemburg, WI 54217, tel.: (920) 845-2336; c/o Green Bay East High School, Attn.: Gerry Erickson, Counselor, 1415 E. Walnut St., Green Bay, WI 54301, tel.: (920) 448-2092

Foundation type: Independent foundation
Limitations: Scholarships to graduates of Luxembourg-Casco High School and Green Bay East High School, WI, who are math, science, or education majors and show academic promise and/or financial need.
Financial data: Year ended 07/31/2004.
Assets, $299,675 (M); Expenditures, $16,796; Total giving, $12,000; Grants to individuals, 9 grants totaling $12,000 (high: $3,000, low: $857).
Fields of interest: Teacher school/education; Education; Science; Mathematics.
Type of support: Support to graduates or students of specific schools; Undergraduate support.
Application information: Application form required.
   Deadline(s): Mar. 31
EIN: 396631861

2158
Kane Paper Scholarship Fund, Inc.
12 Marjorie Dr.
Suffern, NY 10901
Contact: James G. Kane, Treas.
Application address: 2365 Milburn Ave., Baldwin, NY 11510-3384, tel.: (516) 223-8120

Foundation type: Company-sponsored foundation
Limitations: Scholarships to NY students for higher education.
Financial data: Year ended 12/31/2004.
Assets, $1,404 (M); Expenditures, $4,475; Total giving, $3,700.
Type of support: Scholarships—to individuals.
Application information: Applications accepted throughout the year; Contact fund for current application guidelines; Initial approach by letter or telephone.
EIN: 116082733

2159
S. Y. Kang Scholarship Trust
c/o Tom Chun
2600 Michelson Dr., No. 1120
Irvine, CA 92612 (949) 752-1211
Application address for scholarships: Scott Martin, Anderson University, 1100 E. 5th St., Anderson, IN 46012, tel.: (765) 641-1849, fax (765) 641-4091

Foundation type: Independent foundation
Limitations: Scholarships for attendance at Anderson University, IN.

Financial data: Year ended 12/31/2004.
Assets, $200,230 (M); Expenditures, $109,620; Total giving, $107,410; Grants to individuals, 5 grants totaling $107,410 (high: $23,810, low: $17,990).
Type of support: Support to graduates or students of specific schools; Undergraduate support.
Application information: Contact trust for current application deadline/guidelines.
EIN: 336183568

2160
L. Kanhofer Trust
(also known as Lee McKinney Scholarship Trust)
c/o National City Bank
P.O. Box 94651
Cleveland, OH 44101-4651
Application address: c/o Ronald Joyce, Guidance Dir., Titusville Area High School, Guidance Ctr., 302 E. Walnut St., Titusville, PA 16354, tel.: (814) 827-9687

Foundation type: Independent foundation
Limitations: Scholarships to graduates of Titusville, PA, area high schools for undergraduate education at U.S. universities and colleges.
Financial data: Year ended 12/31/2003.
Assets, $324,726 (M); Expenditures, $28,206; Total giving, $25,000; Grants to individuals, 9 grants totaling $25,000 (high: $5,000, low: $2,000).
Type of support: Support to graduates or students of specific schools; Undergraduate support.
Application information: Applications accepted. Application form required.
   Deadline(s): Mar. 1
   Additional information: Contact guidance office for application forms.
EIN: 256227057

2161
Greater Kansas City Community Foundation
(formerly The Greater Kansas City Community Foundation and Affiliated Trusts)
1055 Broadway, Ste. 130
Kansas City, MO 64105-1595 (816) 842-0944
Contact: Janice C. Kreamer, C.E.O.
FAX: (816) 842-8079; E-mail: info@gkccf.org; Tel. for Donor Svcs. Ctr.: (816) 842-7444; URL: http://www.gkccf.org

Foundation type: Community foundation
Limitations: Scholarships to students in the greater Kansas City, MO, area.
Publications: Annual report; Informational brochure; Newsletter.
Financial data: Year ended 12/31/2004.
Assets, $895,377,250 (M); Expenditures, $70,760,164; Total giving, $63,388,075.
Fields of interest: Education, research; Elementary school/education; Secondary school/education; Education, special; Reading; Athletics/sports, training.
Type of support: Undergraduate support.
Application information:
   Initial approach: Letter.
   Deadline(s): Varies by fund
   Additional information: Contact foundation for current application deadline/guidelines; See Web site for complete program listing.
EIN: 431152398

2162
Kansas State Alpha Tau Omega Students' Aid Endowment Fund
14402 Briarwood Ln.
Urbandale, IA 50323-2038
Contact: William L. Muir, Pres.
Application address: c/o Kansas State University, 2040 Shirley Ln., Manhattan, KS 66502, tel.: (785) 539-5050

Foundation type: Independent foundation
Limitations: Scholarships to members of Alpha Tau Omega Fraternity at Kansas State University who are living in the fraternity chapter house or in an approved annex.
Financial data: Year ended 06/30/2005.
Assets, $102,003 (M); Expenditures, $28,276; Total giving, $25,683; Grants to individuals, totaling $25,683.
Fields of interest: Students, sororities/fraternities.
Type of support: Conferences/seminars; Support to graduates or students of specific schools; Undergraduate support.
Application information: Deadline Oct. 1; Completion of formal application required, including transcripts, GPA, and highly-detailed financial statement.
Program description:

Muir Memorial Grant-in-Aid Awards: Applicants must have maintained at least a 2.0 GPA during the previous spring semester and cumulatively. In making its decision, the foundation considers each applicant's financial situation (including outstanding debt and annual expenses), GPA, and extracurricular activities. Muir Awards are made jointly to the recipient and to his chapter of Delta Theta of Alpha Tau Omega. Funds must be used to cover housing bills or annex fees. The maximum award for members living in the chapter house is $1,700 per year or one-half of the annual basic house bill. The maximum award for a member living in an approved annex is $160 per year or one half of the annex fees plus national fees.
EIN: 486111125

2163
Lazare and Charlotte Kaplan Foundation, Inc.
c/o Rouis & Co., LLP
P.O. Box 209
Wurtsboro, NY 12790
Contact: Leon Siegel, Pres.
Application address: P.O. Box 456, Livingston Manor, NY 12758

Foundation type: Independent foundation
Limitations: Scholarships to students from Livingston Manor, Roscoe, Liberty, and Jeffersonville, all in Sullivan County, NY. Preference is shown to Livingston Manor High School graduates.
Financial data: Year ended 12/31/2004.
Assets, $1,685,181 (M); Expenditures, $100,702; Total giving, $79,100; Grants to individuals, totaling $65,250.
Type of support: Undergraduate support.
Application information: Deadline May 1; Initial approach by school guidance counselor; Completion of formal application required, including FAF; Interviews required.
Program description:

Scholarship Program: Scholarships are awarded on the basis of prior academic performance, college aptitude test scores, recommendations from instructors, financial need, and personal interviews. Officers, directors, trustees, and

employees of the foundation and their relatives are ineligible.
EIN: 136193153

2164
The Seymour L. Kaplan Scholarship Foundation
c/o Natalie J. Roberts
P.O. Box 7
White Plains, NY 10602

Foundation type: Independent foundation
Limitations: Scholarships to students of the Columbia Presbyterian Medical Center and the Mount Sinai School of Medicine.
Financial data: Year ended 12/31/2004. Assets, $407,941 (M); Expenditures, $22,060; Total giving, $20,000; Grants to individuals, 4 grants totaling $20,000.
Fields of interest: Medical school/education.
Type of support: Support to graduates or students of specific schools; Graduate support.
Application information: Application form required.
 Deadline(s): Nov. 12
EIN: 137004964

2165
Kappa Alpha Theta Foundation
8740 Founders Rd.
Indianapolis, IN 46268
URL: http://www.kappaalphatheta.org

Foundation type: Public charity
Limitations: Scholarships and grants to collegiate and alumna members of the Kappa Alpha Theta fraternity.
Financial data: Year ended 06/30/2003. Assets, $15,066,636 (M); Expenditures, $1,628,810; Total giving, $1,052,785.
Fields of interest: Leadership development; Fraternal societies.
Type of support: Graduate support; Undergraduate support.
Application information: Application form required.
 Deadline(s): Feb. 1 for scholarships
 Additional information: Application should include letters of recommentdation.
Program descriptions:
 Scholarships: Scholarships are merit-based, and are for undergraduate or graduate study. Applications are available by calling (888) 526-1870, ext. 336.
 Grants: Awards include graduate scholarships; grants to pursue leadership training or educational programs related to professional or personal development; and alumni grants for attending workshops, seminars and classes. Contact Gary Hand at ghand@kappaalphatheta.org for more information.
EIN: 366066531

2166
The Karnes Memorial Fund
c/o Thomas Brucker
606 W. Oak St.
P.O. Box 288
Fairbury, IL 61739-0288
Application address: c/o Board of Governors, P.O. Box 302, Fairbury, IL 61739

Foundation type: Independent foundation
Limitations: Scholarships to graduates of Prairie Central Community Unit District 8, who are residents of Fairbury, Forrest, and Chatsworth, IL.

Financial data: Year ended 12/31/2004. Assets, $1,423,390 (M); Expenditures, $93,490; Total giving, $43,150; Grants to individuals, totaling $43,150.
Type of support: Support to graduates or students of specific schools; Undergraduate support.
Application information: Deadline Mar. 1; Completion of formal application required; Applicants must submit parental financial analysis, general background information, and school and community activities.
EIN: 376243213

2167
Karyae Benevolent Foundation
P.O. Box 37169
Charlotte, NC 28237-7169
Scholarship address: c/o Selection Committee, P.O. Box 37169, Charlotte, NC 28236

Foundation type: Independent foundation
Limitations: Loans, scholarships, and general welfare grants to residents and descendents of residents of Karyae, Greece. Scholarships are to be used for education at universities, colleges, and trade schools. Loans are generally $500 per year.
Financial data: Year ended 12/31/2004. Assets, $397,404 (M); Expenditures, $10,597; Total giving, $8,200; Grants to individuals, totaling $7,200.
Fields of interest: Vocational education.
Type of support: Scholarships—to individuals; Student loans—to individuals.
Application information: Contact foundation for current application deadline; Completion of formal application required, including letters of recommendation.
EIN: 566058576

2168
Kasser Family Foundation
26 Park St.
Montclair, NJ 07042 (973) 744-4470
Contact: Mary V. Mochary, Mgr.

Foundation type: Independent foundation
Limitations: Scholarships to students at Israeli public school K.B. Beit Haemek for the Aryanl Prize.
Financial data: Year ended 05/31/2004. Assets, $2,566,600 (M); Expenditures, $35,970; Total giving, $13,100; Grants to individuals, totaling $2,500.
Fields of interest: Jewish agencies & temples.
Type of support: Support to graduates or students of specific schools; Foreign applicants.
Application information: Applications accepted.
 Initial approach: Letter or telephone.
 Deadline(s): None
 Additional information: Formal application must be filed through the applicant's school.
EIN: 237043288

2169
Irfan Kathwari Foundation, Inc.
1875 Palmer Ave.
Larchmont, NY 10538
Contact: Irfan Kathwari

Foundation type: Independent foundation
Limitations: Scholarships to children of Ethan Allen employees and other economically disadvantaged individuals for undergraduate education.
Financial data: Year ended 06/30/2004. Assets, $6,553,797 (M); Expenditures,

$424,719; Total giving, $391,808; Grants to individuals, 61 grants totaling $30,250 (high: $500, low: $250).
Type of support: Employee-related scholarships; Undergraduate support.
Application information: Application form required.
 Initial approach: Letter.
 Additional information: Contact foundation for current application guidelines.
EIN: 133681135

2170
Kerri Ann Kattar Memorial Fund, Inc.
11 Dupont Cir. N.W., No. 775
Washington, DC 20036
Contact: Candace Kattar, Pres.

Foundation type: Independent foundation
Limitations: Scholarships to students pursuing careers in academic, athletic or sports-related fields, and in the arts.
Financial data: Year ended 12/31/2004. Assets, $61,484 (M); Expenditures, $21,774; Total giving, $13,400; Grants to individuals, totaling $10,300.
Fields of interest: Arts; Recreation.
Type of support: Undergraduate support.
Application information: Application form required.
 Initial approach: Letter.
 Applicants should submit the following:
  1) Letter(s) of recommendation
  2) Financial information
  3) Essay
 Additional information: Application must also include federal or state tax return.
EIN: 042725274

2171
Gene Kauffman Scholarship Foundation, Inc.
P.O. Box 113
Princeton, MO 64673-0113
Application addresses: c/o George Scurlock, V.P., 1008 E. Coleman St., Princeton, MO 64673-1210, tel.: (660) 748-3490, or c/o Alan Hamilton, Pres., P.O. Box 648, Mercer, MO 64661-0648, tel.: (660) 382-4214

Foundation type: Independent foundation
Limitations: Scholarships to unmarried female non-smokers who have graduated from a Mercer County, MO, high school for attendance at a MO college.
Financial data: Year ended 06/30/2005. Assets, $1,861 (M); Expenditures, $204,089; Total giving, $200,271; Grants to individuals, 52 grants totaling $200,271 (high: $4,725, low: $927).
Fields of interest: Women.
Type of support: Support to graduates or students of specific schools; Undergraduate support.
Application information: Application form required.
 Initial approach: Letter.
 Deadline(s): June 10 and Dec. 2
 Applicants should submit the following:
  1) GPA
  2) FAFSA
EIN: 431825689

2172
Kaufman & Coffman Scholarship Fund
c/o JPMorgan Chase Bank, N.A
P.O. Box 1308
Milwaukee, WI 53201
Application address: c/o Debra Kennedy, 416 W.
Jefferson St., Louisville, KY 40202

Foundation type: Independent foundation
Limitations: Scholarships to residents of Louisville,
KY, who attained the age of 30 before beginning the
first year of higher education.
Financial data: Year ended 12/31/2004.
Assets, $836,554 (M); Expenditures, $24,929;
Total giving, $20,194.
Type of support: Undergraduate support.
Application information: Contact fund for current
application deadline/guidelines.
EIN: 616252774

2173
Charles and Pauline Kautz Foundation
c/o Rouis and Co., LLP
P.O. Box 209
Wurtsboro, NY 12790
Application address: c/o Robert Curtis, Bank of
America, N.A., Bridge St., Callicoon, NY 12723

Foundation type: Independent foundation
Limitations: Scholarships to graduates of Delaware
Valley Central High School, Callicoon, NY.
Financial data: Year ended 12/31/2004.
Assets, $5,170,264 (M); Expenditures,
$280,672; Total giving, $219,850; Grants to
individuals, totaling $219,850.
Type of support: Support to graduates or students
of specific schools; Undergraduate support.
Application information: Deadline May 1;
Applications available through the Guidance Dept.
of Delaware Valley High School.
EIN: 141579429

2174
H. G. and A. G. Keasbey Memorial Fund
c/o Wachovia Bank, N.A.
100 N. Main St., 13th Fl.
Winston-Salem, NC 27150
Application address: c/o Angus Russell, Esq., Lewis
& Backus, 1 Logan Sq., Ste. 2000, Philadelphia, PA
19103-6993

Foundation type: Independent foundation
Limitations: Scholarships to individuals primarily
for study in the United Kingdom.
Financial data: Year ended 12/31/2004.
Assets, $7,408,934 (M); Expenditures,
$534,131; Total giving, $475,177; Grants to
individuals, 66 grants totaling $475,177.
Fields of interest: United Kingdom.
Type of support: Scholarships—to individuals.
Application information: Application form required.
Deadline(s): Contact foundation for current
application deadline.
EIN: 236447014

2175
The Keel Foundation
P.O. Box 1778
Morristown, TN 37816

Foundation type: Independent foundation
Limitations: Scholarships to individuals.
Financial data: Year ended 12/31/2004.
Assets, $1,687,918 (M); Expenditures,
$117,963; Total giving, $89,000; Grants to

individuals, 8 grants totaling $13,500 (high:
$2,500, low: $1,500).
Type of support: Scholarships—to individuals.
Application information: Applications not
accepted.
Additional information: Unsolicited requests for
funds not considered or acknowledged.
EIN: 621722004

2176
The Harold and Berta Keen Family Scholarship Foundation
1951 Harrisburg Pike
Carlisle, PA 17013 (717) 243-6622
Contact: William R. Keen, Pres.

Foundation type: Company-sponsored foundation
Limitations: Scholarships to Keen Transport Co.
employees and their children, as well as residents
of central PA.
Financial data: Year ended 12/31/2004.
Assets, $3,699 (M); Expenditures, $10,000; Total
giving, $10,000; Grants to individuals, 12 grants
totaling $10,000 (high: $1,000, low: $800).
Type of support: Employee-related scholarships.
Application information: Application form required.
Deadline(s): Prior to school term
EIN: 251843433

2177
Lorene Lobner Keena Trust
c/o Wells Fargo Bank, N.A., Trust Tax Dept.
P.O. Box 63954
San Francisco, CA 94163-0001
Application address: c/o Lorene Lobner Keena,
Scholarship Comm., 24995 Ben Taylor Rd., Colfax,
CA 95713, tel.: (530) 816-2284

Foundation type: Independent foundation
Limitations: Scholarships to students of the Placer
Joint High School District, CA.
Financial data: Year ended 08/31/2004.
Assets, $640,692 (M); Expenditures, $84,906;
Total giving, $76,300; Grants to individuals,
totaling $76,300.
Type of support: Support to graduates or students
of specific schools; Undergraduate support.
Application information: Deadline Apr.; Initial
approach by letter; Completion of formal application
required, including transcripts and three letters of
recommendation, two from school personnel and
one from a friend, neighbor, employer, or other
non-school person.
EIN: 946429682

2178
Robert W. Keener and Barbara J. Keener Foundation
P.O. Box 9360
Salt Lake City, UT 84109

Foundation type: Independent foundation
Limitations: Scholarships to students of Benton
High School and Bishop LeBlond High School, UT,
planning to attend Kansas University and Missouri
Western State College, and to students enrolled in
these institutions.
Financial data: Year ended 05/31/2005.
Assets, $1,202,366 (M); Expenditures, $99,480;
Total giving, $57,350; Grants to individuals,
totaling $29,850.
Type of support: Support to graduates or students
of specific schools; Undergraduate support.

Application information:
Initial approach: Letter.
Deadline(s): Contact foundation for deadline.
EIN: 876232895

2179
E. R. Keig and Alice Keig Scholarship Trust
P.O. Box 1567
Mason City, IA 50402-1567

Foundation type: Independent foundation
Limitations: Scholarships to graduates of North
Fayette Senior High School, West Union, IA.
Scholarships are generally renewable in amounts of
$5,000 per year to each recipient, for up to four
years.
Financial data: Year ended 12/31/2004.
Assets, $836,354 (M); Expenditures, $45,784;
Total giving, $42,000; Grants to individuals,
totaling $42,000.
Type of support: Support to graduates or students
of specific schools; Undergraduate support.
Application information: Applications not
accepted.
EIN: 596952608

2180
Ruth Keith Scholarship Fund
c/o The First National Bank & Trust Co. of Newtown,
Trust Dept.
34 S. State St.
Newtown, PA 18940 (215) 968-4872

Foundation type: Independent foundation
Limitations: Scholarships primarily to students
from Bucks County, PA. Scholarships are
renewable.
Financial data: Year ended 12/31/2004.
Assets, $604,120 (M); Expenditures, $27,296;
Total giving, $21,200; Grants to individuals,
totaling $20,000.
Type of support: Undergraduate support.
Application information: Application form required.
Deadline(s): Apr. 15
Additional information: Scholarships are
renewable.
Program description:
Scholarship Program: Scholarships are
renewable.
EIN: 236503403

2181
Charles B. & Lenore M. Keitzer Memorial Trust C
c/o First National Bank of Monterey
655 Main St.
Monterey, IN 46960 (574) 542-2121
Contact: Claiborn Wamsley

Foundation type: Independent foundation
Limitations: Scholarships to individuals who have
resided within a radius of five miles from the central
point in the town of Monterey, IN, for at least one
year while a high school student, or be a member
of the parish of St. Ann's Catholic Church,
Monterey, IN. Awards are limited to study for
religious or educational purposes.
Financial data: Year ended 09/30/2004.
Assets, $858,042 (M); Expenditures, $30,795;
Total giving, $24,000; Grants to individuals,
totaling $24,000.
Fields of interest: Theological school/education.
Type of support: Scholarships—to individuals.

Application information: Applications accepted throughout the year; Completion of formal application required.
EIN: 356354152

2182
Kelben Foundation, Inc.
225 E. Mason St., Ste. 800
Milwaukee, WI 53202 (262) 242-4794
Contact: Mary Kellner, Pres.
Additional tels.: Judy Shane (262) 241-4563; Janet Larscheid (262) 241-4086; Patty Schuyler (262) 354-7968; FAX: (262) 242-4760;
E-mail: kellner@ameritech.net

Foundation type: Independent foundation
Limitations: Scholarships to financially needy graduating seniors in the Milwaukee, WI, public school system who have ranked in the top 50 percent of their class from ninth to twelfth grades. See program description for a list of eligible schools.
Financial data: Year ended 11/30/2003.
Assets, $19,623,941 (M); Expenditures, $374,760; Total giving, $317,450; Grants to individuals, totaling $30,750 (high: $1,000, low: $500).
Type of support: Support to graduates or students of specific schools; Undergraduate support.
Application information: Deadline Apr. 1; Completion of formal application required, including transcripts, SAT/ACT scores, and two letters of recommendation; Applications available from school guidance offices.
Program description:
   Scholarship Program: Scholarships are for one year and are not renewable. Students from the following high schools are eligible: Custer High School, Hamilton High School, Juneau Business High School, Rufus King High School, Madison University High School, Marshall High School, Milwaukee High School of the Arts, Milwaukee Trade Technical High School, North Division High School, Riverside University High School, South Division High School, Vincent High School, Washington High School, Greenfield High School, and Homestead High School.
EIN: 391494625

2183
Lucille L. Keller Foundation
c/o Irwin Union Bank & Trust Co.
P.O. Box 929
Columbus, IN 47202 (812) 376-1795
Contact: For Student Loans: Melissa Fleetwood
Application address for individuals: 500 Washington St., Columbus, IN 47201

Foundation type: Independent foundation
Limitations: Interest-free student loans for higher education to Bartholomew County, IN, residents, as well awards for a special honors program and awards to Ivy Tech Nursing Students.
Financial data: Year ended 12/31/2004.
Assets, $278,112 (M); Expenditures, $16,637; Total giving, $12,315; Grants to individuals, totaling $3,050; Loans to individuals, totaling $3,265.
Type of support: Student loans—to individuals; Awards/prizes; Undergraduate support.
Application information: Application form required.
   Initial approach: Letter or telephone.
   Deadline(s): May 31.
   Applicants should submit the following:
      1) Transcripts
      2) Financial information

Additional information: Applicant for interest-free student loan must have at least a 2.0 GPA. Loans are eligible for renewable for four consecutive years, but re-apply each year.
EIN: 356016638

2184
Melvin G. & Mary F. Keller Scholarship Fund
c/o National City Bank
P.O. Box 94651
Cleveland, OH 44101-4651
Contact: Chris Junker, Trust Off., National City Bank of Pennsylvania
Application address: 315 2nd Ave., Warren, PA 16365, tel.: (814) 871-1279

Foundation type: Independent foundation
Limitations: Scholarships to graduates of the Warren County School District, PA, who have resided in Warren County and are pursuing careers in public school teaching.
Financial data: Year ended 12/31/2004.
Assets, $1,078,305 (M); Expenditures, $80,019; Total giving, $68,389; Grants to individuals, totaling $65,889.
Fields of interest: Teacher school/education.
Type of support: Support to graduates or students of specific schools; Undergraduate support.
Application information: Deadline Apr. 30; Completion of formal application required.
EIN: 256344325

2185
Clarence Keller Scholarship Trust
c/o U.S. Bank, N.A.
P.O. Box 663
Sheboygan, WI 53082-0663
Contact: Paul Callan
Application address: P.O. Box 0663, Sheboygan, WI 53081

Foundation type: Independent foundation
Limitations: Giving limited to members of the Foundation Park Methodist Church or participants in the Big Brothers/Big Sisters Program, WI.
Financial data: Year ended 07/31/2005.
Assets, $528,310 (M); Expenditures, $15,965; Total giving, $12,275; Grants to individuals, totaling $12,275.
Fields of interest: Big Brothers/Big Sisters; Protestant agencies & churches.
Type of support: Scholarships—to individuals.
Application information: Applications not accepted.
EIN: 396500681

2186
Edward Bangs Kelley and Elza Kelley Foundation, Inc.
243 South St.
P.O. Drawer M
Hyannis, MA 02601 (508) 775-3117
Contact: Henry L. Murphy, Jr., Pres.
E-mail: contact@kelleyfoundation.org; URL: http://www.kelleyfoundation.org

Foundation type: Independent foundation
Limitations: Scholarships to residents of Barnstable County, MA, and to individuals who intend to reside in Barnstable County subsequent to completion of their education. Preference is given to students in health-related fields.

Publications: Annual report (including application guidelines).
Financial data: Year ended 12/31/2004.
Assets, $5,164,307 (M); Expenditures, $247,145; Total giving $163,936; Grants to individuals, 25 grants totaling $19,000 (high: $2,000, low: $250).
Fields of interest: Health sciences school/ education.
Type of support: Scholarships—to individuals.
Application information: Application form required.
   Initial approach: Letter or telephone.
   Deadline(s): Apr. 30
   Additional information: Interviews required for new applicants.
EIN: 046039660

2187
The Kellner Foundation
c/o Kellner, Dileo, & Co.
900 3rd. Ave., 10th Fl.
New York, NY 10022
URL: http://www.kellner.hu/main.html

Foundation type: Independent foundation
Limitations: Scholarships to Hungarian students from the Eotvos Lorand University in Budapest to study in the US for two semesters at Trinity College, CT, or at Bard College, NY.
Financial data: Year ended 12/31/2004.
Assets, $3,513,489 (M); Expenditures, $586,663; Total giving, $559,951.
Fields of interest: Hungary.
Type of support: Foreign applicants.
Application information: Application form required.
   Deadline(s): Mar. 1
   Additional information: Contact foundation for current application deadline/guidelines; See Web site for additional requirements.
EIN: 137084979

2188
C. L. Kelly Charitable Trust
c/o Comerce Bank, Agent
P.O. Box 75000
Detroit, MI 48275-3302
Contact: Claudia Moore, Trust Rep., RBC Centura Bank

Foundation type: Independent foundation
Limitations: Student loans to U.S. citizens who are residents of Halifax County, NC.
Financial data: Year ended 01/31/2005.
Assets, $1,501,578 (M); Expenditures, $89,984; Total giving, $70,070; Loans to individuals, totaling $17,500.
Type of support: Student loans—to individuals.
Application information: Applications accepted. Application form required.
   Initial approach: Letter.
   Deadline(s): June 15
EIN: 566218777

2189
Kelly Family Charitable Foundation
c/o The Northern Trust Co.
50 S. LaSalle St.
Chicago, IL 60675

Foundation type: Independent foundation
Limitations: Scholarships to eighth grade graduates of Holy Rosary Catholic School in Warrenton, MO, who will attend St. Francis Borgia Regional High School or St. Dominic High School.

Financial data: Year ended 08/31/2004.
Assets, $290,192 (M); Expenditures, $61,998;
Total giving, $57,500; Grants to individuals,
totaling $57,500.
Type of support: Support to graduates or students
of specific schools; Precollege support.
Application information: Application form required.
   Deadline(s): Contact foundation for current
      application deadline.
   Additional information: Applications should be
      submitted to the Holy Rosary Catholic Grade
      School office.
Program description:
   Scholarship Program: Ten $2,500 scholarships
are awarded. Scholarships may be renewed for
each of three consecutive years as long as the
recipient is a full-time student at the high school
named and maintains a cumulative GPA of at least
3.0 on a 4.0 scale.
EIN: 436685888

2190
Kelly Family Foundation
(formerly Stephen P. and Sandra Lu Kelly
Foundation)
9 Stonebrook Ct.
Brownwood, TX   76801-6036   (325) 643-3561
Contact: Sandra Kelly, Pres.

Foundation type: Independent foundation
Limitations: Scholarships to high school seniors
who are residents of Brown County, TX.
Financial data: Year ended 08/31/2004.
Assets, $245,754 (M); Expenditures, $24,150;
Total giving, $23,550; Grants to individuals,
totaling $11,000.
Type of support: Undergraduate support.
Application information: Applications accepted
throughout the year; Applications by letter, including
a brief resume of academic qualifications.
EIN: 752298202

2191
Kelly Foundation of Washington
(formerly KCPQ-TV/Kelly Foundation of Washington)
4212 Soundview Dr. W.
University Place, WA   98466   (253) 706-8486
Contact: Mary Low, Exec. Dir.
Application address: c/o Ewing C. Kelly Scholarship,
P.O. Box 19208, Seattle, WA 98109

Foundation type: Independent foundation
Limitations: Scholarships to graduates of high
schools in the Cascade Region, WA.
Financial data: Year ended 12/31/2004.
Assets, $3,538,668 (M); Expenditures,
$159,528; Total giving, $117,500; Grants to
individuals, 35 grants totaling $87,500 (high:
$2,500, low: $2,500).
Type of support: Support to graduates or students
of specific schools; Undergraduate support.
Application information: Application form required.
   Deadline(s): Feb. 14.
   Applicants should submit the following:
      1) Letter(s) of recommendation
      2) ACT
      3) SAT
      4) Transcripts
      5) Financial information
   Additional information: Applications by FAX not
      accepted; Applications available through high
      school counselors.
Program description:
   Ewing C. Kelly Scholarship: The scholarships
reward students who demonstrate good citizenship
while striving to attain their academic goals.

Applicants must have earned a composite score of
20 on the ACT or of 840 on the SAT. Finalists will
be contacted by the scholarship committee by Mar.
31. Recipients will be informed by Apr. 15, and will
be presented with the scholarship at a banquet in
Seattle in May.
EIN: 911620836

2192
Kelly Foundation, Inc.
801 E. Sugarland Hwy.
Clewiston, FL   33440-2621   (941) 983-8177
Contact: Alden M. Wyse, Secy.-Treas.

Foundation type: Company-sponsored foundation
Limitations: Scholarships to children of Kelly
Tractor Company employees and residents of FL.
Financial data: Year ended 12/31/2004.
Assets, $10,724,511 (M); Expenditures,
$444,662; Total giving, $430,465; Grants to
individuals, 99 grants totaling $177,300 (high:
$5,250, low: $500).
Type of support: Employee-related scholarships.
Application information: Application form required.
   Initial approach: Letter.
   Deadline(s): None
EIN: 596153269

2193
Mary A. Kelly Scholarship Fund
P.O. Box 464
Newburyport, MA   01950-7364

Foundation type: Independent foundation
Limitations: Scholarships to students pursuing
studies in science at a four-year college or
university, whose parents are members of the
Congregation of Immaculate Conception Roman
Catholic Church, Newburyport, MA.
Financial data: Year ended 12/31/2004.
Assets, $656,532 (M); Expenditures, $26,431;
Total giving, $13,000; Grants to individuals,
totaling $13,000.
Fields of interest: Science; Roman Catholic
agencies & churches.
Type of support: Undergraduate support.
Application information: Application form required.
   Initial approach: Letter.
   Deadline(s): Apr. 15
EIN: 046042274

2194
The Forest C. & Ruth V. Kelsey Foundation
P.O. Box 404
Montesano, WA   98563
Contact: Charles Caldwell, Pres.

Foundation type: Independent foundation
Limitations: Scholarships to residents of Grays
Harbor County, WA.
Financial data: Year ended 12/31/2004.
Assets, $11,865,957 (M); Expenditures,
$561,235; Total giving, $464,126; Grants to
individuals, totaling $233,293.
Type of support: Scholarships—to individuals.
Application information: Application form required.
   Additional information: Application should
      include transcripts, four references, and
      anticipated expenditures.
EIN: 912013369

2195
Harris and Eliza Kempner Fund, Inc.
2201 Market St., Ste. 601
Galveston, TX   77550-1529   (409) 762-1603
Contact: Barbara K. Crews, Exec. Dir.
FAX: (409) 762-5435;
E-mail: information@kempnerfund.org;
URL: http://www.kempnerfund.org

Foundation type: Independent foundation
Limitations: Interest-free, need-based loans
primarily to full-time students in Galveston, TX.
Publications: Annual report (including application
guidelines).
Financial data: Year ended 12/31/2003.
Assets, $40,024,619 (M); Expenditures,
$1,925,174; Total giving, $1,439,131.
Fields of interest: Higher education.
Type of support: Student loans—to individuals.
Application information: Application form required.
   Deadline(s): Mar. 31.
   Additional information: Application forms
      available from selected colleges.
Program description:
   Loan Fund: Loans are limited to $1,250 per
regular semester, with a maximum loan per student
of $10,000. Two co-signers are required. Forms will
be mailed to co-signers immediately upon receipt of
the student's letter accepting the terms of the loan.
These co-signer forms must be mailed back no later
than May 1. A minimum of $20 monthly repayment
must begin in Sept. and continue until termination
of schooling. Once schooling has terminated,
schedule will be adjusted to complete repayment
within five years. Repayment is interest-free,
provided required payments are current. The fund's
loan program is limited in scope and dependent on
the rate of repayments received from prior
recipients.
EIN: 760680130

2196
Edward R. Kengla Foundation, Inc.
c/o Alexandria American Legion Post 24
P.O. Box 402
Alexandria, VA   22313

Foundation type: Independent foundation
Limitations: Scholarships to residents of the
Alexandria, VA area for college education.
Financial data: Year ended 12/31/2002.
Assets, $533,053 (M); Expenditures, $28,257;
Total giving, $26,500; Grants to individuals, 4
grants totaling $10,000 (high: $4,000, low:
$2,000).
Type of support: Undergraduate support.
Application information: Contact foundation for
current application deadline/guidelines;
Completion of formal application required.
EIN: 541826229

2197
Keniston and Dane Educational Fund
P.O. Box 22
Sheffield, VT   05866
Application address for individuals: c/o Town Clerk,
Town of Wheelock, VT 05851

Foundation type: Operating foundation
Limitations: Scholarships to residents of Wheelock
and Sheffield, VT.
Financial data: Year ended 12/31/2003.
Assets, $1,468,271 (M); Expenditures, $56,137;
Total giving, $42,968; Grants to individuals, 55
grants totaling $38,382 (high: $825, low: $688).
Type of support: Scholarships—to individuals.

Application information: Application form required.
Deadline(s): Prior to school year
EIN: 030341752

2198
Kennard Educational Fund, Inc.
c/o Planters Bank & Trust Co. of VA, Trust Dept.
P.O. Box 1268
Staunton, VA 24402-1268 (540) 885-1232

Foundation type: Independent foundation
Limitations: Educational loans to residents of the cities of Staunton or Waynesboro, or the county of Augusta, VA.
Financial data: Year ended 09/30/2004.
Assets, $719,110 (M); Expenditures, $10,096; Total giving, $0; Loans to individuals, 4 loans totaling $9,500.
Type of support: Student loans—to individuals.
Application information:
Deadline(s): July 1.
Applicants should submit the following:
1) Financial information
2) Transcripts
Additional information: Application by letter stating purpose, and employment history.
EIN: 541157065

2199
Kennedy Foundation
6901 S. Pierce St., Ste. 100
Littleton, CO 80128
Application address: P.O. Box 27296, Denver, CO 80227

Foundation type: Independent foundation
Limitations: Scholarships to high school students who are residents of CO.
Financial data: Year ended 06/30/2004.
Assets, $531,122 (M); Expenditures, $37,607; Total giving, $28,000; Grants to individuals, totaling $28,000.
Type of support: Undergraduate support.
Application information: Applications accepted. Application form required.
Initial approach: Letter.
Deadline(s): None
Additional information: Application should include SASE.
EIN: 840748729

2200
Francis Nathaniel and Katheryn Padgett Kennedy Foundation
933 Sunset Dr.
Greenwood, SC 29646
Contact: Don Johnson, Admin. Asst.

Foundation type: Independent foundation
Limitations: Student grants only to individuals preparing for full-time Christian service at the college or seminary level. Grants shall be made only to students who are from the South Carolina counties of Abbeville, Anderson, Cherokee, Greenville, Greenwood, Laurens, McCormick, Oconee, Pickens, Spartanburg, Union and York counties. Students from Laurens County shall be given first preference.
Publications: Informational brochure (including application guidelines).
Financial data: Year ended 06/30/2005.
Assets, $1,377,303 (M); Expenditures, $79,381; Total giving, $58,250; Grants to individuals, 16 grants totaling $44,250 (high: $3,000, low: $750).

Fields of interest: Theological school/education; Christian agencies & churches.
Type of support: Graduate support; Undergraduate support.
Application information: Application form required.
Initial approach: Letter or telephone.
Copies of proposal: 1
Deadline(s): May 1
Applicants should submit the following:
1) Transcripts
2) Letter(s) of recommendation
3) Financial information
4) Budget Information
EIN: 237347655

2201
Kennedy Health System, Inc.
(formerly Kennedy Health Care Foundation, Inc.)
500 Marlboro Ave.
Cherry Hill, NJ 08034 (856) 661-5188
URL: http://www.kennedyhealth.org

Foundation type: Public charity
Limitations: Scholarships to students residing in Southern NJ for education toward health care careers.
Financial data: Year ended 12/31/2003.
Assets, $8,542,937 (M); Expenditures, $330,915; Total giving, $12,750; Grants to individuals, 10 grants totaling $12,750 (high: $2,250, low: $750).
Fields of interest: Health sciences school/education.
Type of support: Undergraduate support.
Application information: Contact foundation for current application deadline/guidelines.
EIN: 222442036

2202
Margaret Kennedy Scholarship Trust
c/o Bank of America, N.A.
P.O. Box 6768
Providence, RI 02901-1802
Application address: c/o Guidance Counselor, Bucksport High School, Bucksport, ME 04416, tel.: (207) 469-7300

Foundation type: Independent foundation
Limitations: Scholarships only to students at Bucksport High School, ME.
Financial data: Year ended 04/30/2005.
Assets, $340,537 (M); Expenditures, $17,998; Total giving, $12,925; Grants to individuals, 39 grants totaling $12,925 (high: $495, low: $220).
Type of support: Support to graduates or students of specific schools; Undergraduate support.
Application information: Deadline Apr. 30; Completion of formal application required.
EIN: 016027394

2203
Arthur Kennett Educational Fund
c/o U.S. Bank, N.A.
P.O. Box 387
St. Louis, MO 63166
Contact: James B. Gerdes
Application address: c/o Fund Scholarship Board, Attn.: James B. Gerdes, 6501 Clayton Rd., St. Louis, MO 63117, tel.: (314) 721-1200

Foundation type: Independent foundation
Limitations: Scholarships to financially needy high school seniors and graduates of secondary schools in St. Louis County, MO, who are U.S. citizens with

demonstrated ability to succeed in postsecondary work. Scholarships are for one academic year only.
Financial data: Year ended 06/30/2005.
Assets, $683,108 (M); Expenditures, $44,200; Total giving, $24,000; Grants to individuals, totaling $24,000.
Type of support. Support to graduates or students of specific schools; Undergraduate support.
Application information: Applications accepted. Application form required.
Deadline(s): Mar. 18.
Additional information: Application should include transcripts and a 250-word essay and two letters of recommendation.
EIN: 436517200

2204
Walter J. Kenney Scholarship Fund
c/o Bank of America, N.A.
777 Maint. St., CT2-102 2202
Hartford, CT 06115
Application address: Gary J.C. Woodfield, 41 Lexington St., New Britain, CT 06052

Foundation type: Independent foundation
Limitations: Scholarships to specifically designated residents of New Britain, CT, who have been accepted to an engineering college or a seminary.
Financial data: Year ended 12/31/2004.
Assets, $3,451,723 (M); Expenditures, $252,349; Total giving, $219,078; Grants to individuals, 13 grants totaling $219,078 (high: $42,569, low: $392).
Fields of interest: Engineering school/education; Theological school/education.
Type of support: Scholarships—to individuals.
Application information: Application form required.
Deadline(s): Apr. 15
EIN: 066111411

2205
Monsignor Simon E. Kenny Education Fund
c/o Thomas A. Burke
3859 Prospect Rd.
Street, MD 21154-1517

Foundation type: Independent foundation
Limitations: Scholarships to students from St. Mary's Parish, Pylesville, MD.
Financial data: Year ended 12/31/2002.
Assets, $66,091 (M); Expenditures, $4,066; Total giving, $4,000; Grants to individuals, totaling $4,000.
Type of support: Scholarships—to individuals.
Application information: Applications not accepted.
EIN: 521084609

2206
Kenosha Scholarship Foundation, Inc.
5800 7th Ave.
Kenosha, WI 53140 (262) 657-1000
Contact: Arleen Wermeling

Foundation type: Independent foundation
Limitations: Scholarships to employees and children of employees of Kenosha News, WI, who are full-time students, for study at accredited institutions.
Publications: Application guidelines.
Financial data: Year ended 12/31/2004.
Assets, $64,424 (M); Expenditures, $7,422; Total

giving, $6,600; Grants to individuals, totaling
$6,600.
Type of support: Employee-related scholarships;
Technical education support.
Application information: Application form required.
Initial approach: Letter or employee notice.
Deadline(s): May
Additional information: Scholarships are
renewable for up to four years of full-time
study.
EIN: 391501320

2207
Senah C. and C. A. Kent Foundation
c/o Wachovia Bank, N.A.
P.O. Box 3099
Winston-Salem, NC   27199-2217
(336) 732-5991
Contact: Christopher Spaugh CTFA, V.P.
Application addresses: c/o Wayne E. Johnson, Asst.
Dir., Student Financial Aid, Wake Forest University,
P.O. Box 7305, Winston-Salem, NC 27109,
tel.: (336) 761-5265; c/o Pamela Butts, Assoc.
Dir. of Financial Aid, Salem College, P.O. Box
10548, Winston-Salem, NC 27108-0548,
tel.: (336) 721-2808; or c/o Ginger Klock, Student
Dir., NC School of the Arts, P.O. Box 12189,
Winston-Salem, NC 27117-2189, tel.: (336)
770-3297; Scholarship URL: http://
www.wachoviascholars.com/kent/
kent_2006_ins.htm

Foundation type: Independent foundation
Limitations: Scholarships to students attending
Wake Forest University, North Carolina School of
the Arts, and Salem College, NC.
Financial data: Year ended 12/31/2004.
Assets, $2,375,015 (M); Expenditures,
$134,193; Total giving, $107,526; Grants to
individuals, totaling $107,526.
Type of support: Support to graduates or students
of specific schools; Undergraduate support.
Application information: Applications accepted.
Application form required.
Deadline(s): July 1.
Additional information: Contact individual
schools for current application guidelines;
See program description for further
information.
Program description:
Scholarship Program: Scholarship
recommendations are made to the foundation by
the specified educational institutions. Submit
applications to:
- G. William Joyner, Jr., V.P., Devel., Wake
Forest University, 7227 Reynolda Sta.,
Winston-Salem, NC 27109; Tel.: (919)
761-5265
- William Cox, Dir., Financial Aid, North
Carolina School of the Arts, Box 12189,
Winston-Salem, NC 27107; Tel.: (919)
784-7170
- Mrs. Neville C. Watkins, Dir., Financial Aid,
Salem College, Winston-Salem, NC 27108.
EIN: 566037248

2208
The Kentucky Safety & Health Network Foundation, Inc.
P.O. Box 4087
Frankfort, KY   40604-4087
Contact: Benny Adair, Pres.

Foundation type: Independent foundation

Limitations: Scholarships to undergraduate and
graduate students from or studying in KY, who are
studying occupational safety and health, industrial
hygiene, or public health.
Financial data: Year ended 12/31/2002.
Assets, $99,695 (M); Expenditures, $15,464;
Total giving, $12,000; Grants to individuals, 10
grants totaling $12,000 (high: $2,000, low:
$1,000).
Fields of interest: Public health; Public health,
occupational health.
Type of support: Graduate support; Undergraduate
support.
Application information:
Deadline(s): Mar. 1
Additional information: Completion of formal
application required, including resume, essay,
transcript, two letters of recommendation,
and proof of enrollment; See Web site for
further application information.
Program description:
*Scholastic Achievement for Education "SAFE"
Awards:* Undergraduate students must be classified
as Juniors in the academic year for which the
scholarship is awarded.
EIN: 611269280

2209
Ralph A. Kerber Memorial Foundation
32 Castellina Dr.
Newport Coast, CA   92657   (949) 715-3474
Contact: Janet C. Kerber, Tr.

Foundation type: Independent foundation
Limitations: Scholarships to college students
residing in southern CA enrolled in a business or
other technical program.
Publications: Application guidelines; Newsletter;
Newsletter (including application guidelines).
Financial data: Year ended 12/31/2004.
Assets, $780,604 (M); Expenditures, $48,599;
Total giving, $38,000; Grants to individuals, 18
grants totaling $38,000 (high: $5,000, low: $500).
Fields of interest: Vocational education,
post-secondary; Business school/education.
Type of support: Scholarships—to individuals;
Undergraduate support.
Application information: Application form required.
Initial approach: Letter or telephone.
Deadline(s): Apr. 1 to request application; Feb.
10 to submit application
Applicants should submit the following:
1) Financial information
2) Essay
Additional information: Application should
include two letters of recommendation.
Program description:
Scholarship Program: Applicants must have a
GPA of "B" or above, and provide one letter of
recommendation from a school counselor and one
from a participant in the pool and spa industry.
EIN: 336289007

2210
Keren Tifereth Yisroel Foundation
45 White St.
New York, NY   10013   (212) 219-3944
Contact: Yehuda Lieb Braun, Tr.

Foundation type: Independent foundation
Limitations: Scholarships to graduates of Sinai
Academy, NY, to study the Torah in Israel.
Financial data: Year ended 06/30/2004.
Assets, $25,500 (M); Expenditures, $76,587;
Total giving, $75,909; Grants to individuals, 33
grants totaling $51,269 (high: $6,000, low: $60).

Fields of interest: Jewish agencies & temples;
Israel.
Type of support: Support to graduates or students
of specific schools.
Application information: Applications by proposal
accepted throughout the year.
EIN: 134073684

2211
Kershaw County Vocational Education Foundation, Inc.
P.O. Box 10
Lugoff, SC   29078-0010
Contact: Larry B. Kilgore, Dir.
Application address: c/o Selection Comm., 1095
Pepper Ridge Dr., Lugoff, SC 29078, tel.: (803)
438-3708

Foundation type: Operating foundation
Limitations: Scholarships to residents of Kershaw
County, SC, for vocational study.
Financial data: Year ended 12/31/2003.
Assets, $724,780 (M); Expenditures, $15,910;
Total giving, $13,700; Grants to individuals,
totaling $7,500.
Fields of interest: Vocational education.
Type of support: Technical education support.
Application information: Contact foundation for
current application deadline; Completion of formal
application required, including financial and
educational information.
EIN: 570805522

2212
Edgar E. Kessel Scholarship Fund
(formerly Edgar E. Kessel Trust)
c/o KeyBank N.A.
800 Superior Ave., 4th Fl.
Cleveland, OH   44114-1306
Application address: c/o Kate Blaszak, Trust Off.,
KeyBank N.A., 127 Public Sq., 18th Fl., Cleveland,
OH 44114-1306

Foundation type: Independent foundation
Limitations: Scholarships to current graduates of
Euclid public schools, OH.
Financial data: Year ended 09/30/2005.
Assets, $7,767 (M); Expenditures, $29,350; Total
giving, $22,000; Grants to individuals, totaling
$22,000.
Type of support: Scholarships—to individuals;
Support to graduates or students of specific
schools; Undergraduate support.
Application information: Contact superintendent of
Euclid public schools for application; Completion of
formal application required.
Program description:
Scholarship Program: Recipients are chosen by
the superintendent or chief administrative officer of
the City of Euclid, OH public schools, the principal
or chief administrative officer of Euclid Senior High
School, OH, and the trust officer assigned to the
administration of the trust by Key Trust Co. of Ohio,
N.A. Applicants from the Euclid, OH, public school
district will be given priority.
EIN: 346505938

2213
Key Charitable Trust
P.O. Box 389
Fort Scott, KS   66701   (620) 223-2000
Contact: William K. Pollock, Tr.

Foundation type: Independent foundation

Limitations: Scholarships to individuals in KS for higher education.
Financial data: Year ended 12/31/2004. Assets, $3,401,639 (M); Expenditures, $133,336; Total giving, $131,981; Grants to individuals, 22 grants totaling $47,337 (high: $8,000, low: $337).
Type of support: Undergraduate support.
Application information: Applications by proposal accepted throughout the year.
EIN: 486107304

2214
Key West Rotary Foundation, Inc.

c/o John G. Parks, Jr.
815 Peacock Plz.
Key West, FL 33040

Foundation type: Independent foundation
Limitations: Scholarships to graduating high school seniors from Key West High School, FL.
Financial data: Year ended 12/31/2003. Assets, $204,928 (M); Expenditures, $26,660; Total giving, $25,825; Grants to individuals, totaling $18,825.
Type of support: Support to graduates or students of specific schools; Undergraduate support.
Application information: Contact foundation for current application deadline/guidelines.
EIN: 592826669

2215
Bernice A. B. Keyes Trust

c/o Keybank, N.A.
800 Superior Ave.
Cleveland, OH 44114
Contact: Michael Steadman, V.P.

Foundation type: Independent foundation
Limitations: Scholarships to high school students in the Tacoma, WA, area, selected by Tacoma area high schools.
Financial data: Year ended 12/31/2004. Assets, $2,067,867 (M); Expenditures, $117,876; Total giving, $93,380; Grants to individuals, 35 grants totaling $93,380.
Type of support: Support to graduates or students of specific schools; Awards/grants by nomination only; Undergraduate support.
Application information: Applications not accepted.
EIN: 916111944

2216
Kia Ora Foundation

5980 Norton St., Ste. 390
Emeryville, CA 94608
URL: http://www.kiaora.org

Foundation type: Independent foundation
Limitations: Scholarships to music students residing in New Zealand to continue their studies at a renowned international music school or conservatorium.
Financial data: Year ended 12/31/2004. Assets, $1,829,899 (M); Expenditures, $69,104; Total giving, $56,400; Grants to individuals, 4 grants totaling $36,400.
Type of support: Foreign applicants.
Application information: Unsolicited requests for funds not accepted.
EIN: 133947823

2217
Kibble Foundation

P.O. Box 723
Pomeroy, OH 45769

Foundation type: Independent foundation
Limitations: Scholarships only to graduates of Meigs County, OH, high schools pursuing four-year degrees or technical degrees on a full-time basis.
Financial data: Year ended 12/31/2004. Assets, $0 (M); Expenditures, $178,573; Total giving, $163,450.
Fields of interest: Vocational education.
Type of support: Support to graduates or students of specific schools; Technical education support; Undergraduate support.
Application information: Unsolicited applications not considered or acknowledged.
EIN: 316175971

2218
Kids' Chance, Inc.

P.O. Box 623
Valdosta, GA 31603 (229) 244-0153
Contact: Cheryl G. Oliver, Exec. Dir.
FAX: (229) 245-0413;
E-mail: Kids300@Bellsouth.net; URL: http://www.kidschance.org/georgia.htm

Foundation type: Public charity
Limitations: Scholarships to the children of Georgia workers who have been seriously, catastrophically or fatally injured in work-related accidents.
Financial data: Year ended 12/31/2004. Assets, $830,062 (M); Expenditures, $248,560; Total giving, $176,286; Grants to individuals, 67 grants totaling $176,286 (high: $5,372, low: $15).
Fields of interest: Disabilities, people with.
Type of support: Undergraduate support.
Application information: Contact foundation for current application deadline/guidelines; Initial approach by e-mail; Completion of formal application required.
EIN: 581827365

2219
Helen U. Kiely Trust

c/o Bank of America, N.A.
P.O. Box 1802
Providence, RI 02940-1802
Application address: c/o Bank of America, N.A., 100 Federal St., Boston, MA 02110

Foundation type: Independent foundation
Limitations: Prizes to chemistry students and one-year scholarships to graduating seniors of Northampton, MA, high schools. Some scholarships are limited to those attending Catholic schools.
Financial data: Year ended 12/31/2004. Assets, $1,273,027 (M); Expenditures, $59,618; Total giving, $46,100; Grants to individuals, 10 grants totaling $46,100.
Fields of interest: Chemistry; Roman Catholic agencies & churches.
Type of support: Support to graduates or students of specific schools; Awards/prizes; Undergraduate support.
Application information: Deadline July 1; Initial approach by letter requesting application between May 15 and June 20; Completion of formal application required, including transcripts, parents' financial information, and tax return.
EIN: 046278297

2220
Robert W. Kiersted Memorial Scholarship Fund

c/o Russell F. Rowen
P.O. Box 755
Fairfax, CA 94978-0755
Application address: c/o Principal, Saratoga High School, 20300 Herriman Ave., Saratoga, CA 95070, tel.: (408) 867-3411

Foundation type: Independent foundation
Limitations: Scholarships to residents of Saratoga, CA.
Financial data: Year ended 12/31/2004. Assets, $161,192 (M); Expenditures, $22,621; Total giving, $19,510; Grants to individuals, 6 grants totaling $19,510 (high: $8,000, low: $1,500).
Type of support: Scholarships—to individuals; Support to graduates or students of specific schools.
Application information: Contact fund for current application deadline/guidelines.
EIN: 943064364

2221
Kieve-Wavus Education, Inc.

(formerly Kieve Affective Education)
P.O. Box 169
Nobleboro, ME 04555 (207) 563-5172
Contact: Henry R. Kennedy, Exec. Dir.
FAX: (207) 563-5215; URL: http://www.kieve.org

Foundation type: Public charity
Limitations: Grants to individuals to attend Kieve Affective Education, Inc., for the summer.
Financial data: Year ended 12/31/2004. Assets, $15,402,578 (M); Expenditures, $4,528,132; Total giving, $809,046.
Fields of interest: Elementary/secondary education; Camps.
Type of support: Precollege support.
Application information: Contact organization for current application deadlines/guidelines.
EIN: 237352599

2222
Peter Kiewit Foundation

8805 Indian Hills Dr., Ste. 225
Omaha, NE 68114 (402) 344-7890
Contact: Lyn Wallin Ziegenbein, Secy.
FAX: (402) 344-8099

Foundation type: Independent foundation
Limitations: Undergraduate scholarships only to high school students in the Omaha, NE—Council Bluffs, IA, area, specifically Douglas and Sarpy counties, NE, and Pottawattamie County, IA. Grants also to NE teachers for excellence in classroom teaching.
Publications: Application guidelines; Annual report; Informational brochure (including application guidelines).
Financial data: Year ended 06/30/2005. Assets, $380,416,544 (M); Expenditures, $20,101,243; Total giving, $16,840,372; Grants to individuals, totaling $3,244,323.
Fields of interest: Education.
Type of support: Undergraduate support.
Application information: Contact foundation for current application deadline; Initial approach by letter or telephone requesting application; Completion of formal application required.
Program description:
Scholarship Program: Scholarships are awarded annually based primarily on financial need.

Scholarships are for four years of study, given satisfactory achievement.
EIN: 476098282

2223

Kil Chung-Hee Fellowship Fund, Inc.

7818 Oak Lane Rd.
Cheltenham, PA 19012-1015
Contact: Sangduk Kim, Dir.

Foundation type: Independent foundation
Limitations: Research grants to students and alumni of Korea University Medical College. Upon completion of project, recipient must return to Korea University Medical College within three years to teach or do additional research for a period of no less than three years.
Financial data: Year ended 12/31/2004. Assets, $131,285 (M); Expenditures, $4,467; Total giving, $3,000; Grant to an individual, 1 grant totaling $3,000.
Fields of interest: Medical school/education; Korea.
Type of support: Research; Support to graduates or students of specific schools; Postgraduate support.
Application information:
Deadline(s): Applications accepted throughout the year.
Additional information: Application by proposal.
EIN: 232199550

2224

Kilgore-Ramsey Scholarship Trust

P.O. Box 249
Chapman, KS 67431-0411
Contact: Richard Hall, Tr.
Application address: c/o Chapman High School, Chapman, KS 67431

Foundation type: Operating foundation
Limitations: Scholarships to students of Chapman High School, KS, for higher education.
Financial data: Year ended 12/31/2003. Assets, $118,637 (M); Expenditures, $11,576; Total giving, $11,250; Grants to individuals, 8 grants totaling $11,250 (high: $1,500, low: $750). Subtotal for support to graduates or students of specific schools: 8 grants totaling $11,250 (high: $1,500, low: $750).
Type of support: Support to graduates or students of specific schools; Undergraduate support.
Application information: Contact trust for current application deadline; Application by letter, including financial need, personal reference and academic record.
EIN: 486343752

2225

J. A. & Ophelia Killgore Scholarship Trust Fund

c/o Regions Bank, Trust Dept.
P.O. Box 2527
Mobile, AL 36622-0001

Foundation type: Independent foundation
Limitations: Scholarships to graduates of schools in Lee County, AL. Recipients are selected by the three local Boards of Education.
Financial data: Year ended 09/30/2004. Assets, $3,115,018 (M); Expenditures, $210,249; Total giving, $197,750; Grants to individuals, totaling $197,750.
Type of support: Support to graduates or students of specific schools; Undergraduate support.

Application information:
Initial approach: Letter.
Deadline(s): Contact fund for current application deadline.
EIN: 636055718

2226

The Kilts Foundation

P.O. Box 339
Somonauk, IL 60552 (815) 498-3429
Application address: c/o Jules S. Gershon, 111 W. Washington St., Ste. 815, Chicago, IL 60602, tel.: (312) 269-8570

Foundation type: Independent foundation
Limitations: Scholarships primarily to residents of Kendall County, IL.
Financial data: Year ended 12/31/2004. Assets, $460,398 (M); Expenditures, $35,108; Total giving, $25,250; Grants to individuals, 46 grants totaling $25,250 (high: $1,000, low: $250).
Type of support: Scholarships—to individuals.
Application information: Contact foundation for current application deadline; Completion of formal application required.
EIN: 363815138

2227

The Kimball International—Habig Foundation, Inc.

(formerly The Habig Foundation)
1600 Royal St.
Jasper, IN 47549 (812) 482-1600

Foundation type: Company-sponsored foundation
Limitations: Scholarships to children of full-time employees of Kimball International, Inc. and its subsidiaries, for attendance at two- and four-year institutions.
Financial data: Year ended 06/30/2005. Assets, $1,636,101 (M); Expenditures, $437,621; Total giving, $436,095; Grants to individuals, 87 grants totaling $128,700 (high: $1,500, low: $600).
Type of support: Employee-related scholarships; Undergraduate support.
Application information: Application form required.
Initial approach: Letter.
Deadline(s): Apr. 1
Additional information: Additional application tel.: (812) 482-8513, E-mail: kathy.herndon@kimball.com.
Program description:
Scholarship Program: Four-year scholarships are available toward bachelor's degrees at accredited four-year colleges. Two-year scholarships are available toward associate's degrees at accredited learning institutions. There are no restrictions on the field of study chosen. Applicants must be graduating in the upper 30 percent of their classes. No more than 25 percent of the applicants may be awarded scholarships, and at least 50 percent of those awarded scholarships must be children of hourly-paid employees.
EIN: 356022535

2228

The Kimbo Foundation

430 Shotwell St.
San Francisco, CA 94110 (415) 285-4100
Contact: Jennifer Chung
Scholarship application addresses: Northern CA: SF Korea Daily, 2811 Adeline St., Oakland, CA 94608, Attn.: June Park, tel.: (510) 272-4605, FAX: (510)

272-4606, E-mail: junep@joongangusa.com; Southern CA and other states: LA Korean Central Daily, 690 Wilshire Pl., Los Angeles, CA 90005, Attn.: Jung-Hoon Lee,
E-mail: info@joongangusa.com
FAX: (415) 285-4103;
E-mail: info@kimbofoundation.org; URL: http://www.kimbofoundation.org

Foundation type: Company-sponsored foundation
Limitations: Scholarships to financially needy students of Korean descent residing in CA for attendance at four-year colleges and universities. High school seniors and current undergraduates may apply.
Financial data: Year ended 06/30/2004. Assets, $1,954,403 (M); Expenditures, $109,032; Total giving, $102,500; Grants to individuals, totaling $102,500 (high: $1,500, low: $1,500).
Type of support: Undergraduate support.
Application information:
Deadline(s): June 30
Additional information: Completion of formal application required, including transcripts, parents' or student's tax return, and essay in English or Korean; Letter of recommendation suggested, but not required.
Program description:
Scholarship Program: The scholarship program is announced in the Korea Central Daily paper in Mar. or Apr. every year.
EIN: 943047547

2229

Eugene E. Kimmel Scholarship Trust

4707 S. 96th St.
Omaha, NE 68127
Application address: c/o Wells Fargo Bank Indiana, N.A, Attn.: Jennifer King, Trust Off., P.O. Box 960, Fort Wayne, IN 46801-6632

Foundation type: Independent foundation
Limitations: Scholarships to graduates of Catholic high schools in Fort Wayne, IN.
Financial data: Year ended 11/30/2004. Assets, $745,285 (M); Expenditures, $31,317; Total giving, $21,925; Grants to individuals, 23 grants totaling $21,925 (high: $3,000, low: $300).
Fields of interest: Roman Catholic agencies & churches.
Type of support: Support to graduates or students of specific schools; Undergraduate support.
Application information: Application form required.
Initial approach: Letter.
Deadline(s): Apr. 1
Applicants should submit the following:
1) Financial information
2) Essay
EIN: 311019032

2230

Kincaid Foundation, Inc.

c/o Central Bank & Trust Co.
P.O. Box 1360
Lexington, KY 40590-1360
Application address: c/o Marcia Wade, V.P., Central Bank & Trust Co., 510 Kincaid Twrs., Lexington, KY 40507, tel.: (859) 253-6251

Foundation type: Independent foundation
Limitations: Scholarships to financially needy graduates of Fayette County, KY, high schools who are enrolling in four-year college degree programs.
Financial data: Year ended 12/31/2004. Assets, $314,231 (M); Expenditures, $28,759;

Total giving, $24,000; Grants to individuals, 14 grants totaling $24,000 (high: $2,000, low: $1,000).

Type of support: Support to graduates or students of specific schools; Undergraduate support.

Application information: Deadline Apr. 1; Completion of formal application required, including GPA, statement of need, and parents' financial information.

Program description:

Scholarship Program: Scholarships are renewable provided that the recipient maintains passing grades, as verified by each semester's transcripts. Scholarships are awarded first on the basis of financial need, and then on the basis of academic achievement.

EIN: 616033698

2231
Kent Rogers Kincaid Foundation

(also known as Kent Rogers Kincaid Charitable Foundation)
809 Mt. View Dr.
Lafayette, CA 94549
Contact: Wayne Lawson, Pres.

Foundation type: Independent foundation

Limitations: Scholarships to financially needy students at Tamalpais High School, Mill Valley, CA, for higher education.

Financial data: Year ended 12/31/2004. Assets, $1,943,799 (M); Expenditures, $55,705; Total giving, $46,500; Grants to individuals, 20 grants totaling $46,500 (high: $4,000, low: $2,000).

Type of support: Support to graduates or students of specific schools; Undergraduate support.

Application information: Deadline prior to Tamalpais High School graduation date; Contact foundation for current application guidelines.

EIN: 680179679

2232
The Kincaid Foundation

1125 S. Ball St., Ste. 104
Grapevine, TX 76051 (972) 501-0007
Contact: Thomas R. Kincaid, Tr.; Richard Jones, Tr.

Foundation type: Independent foundation

Limitations: Scholarships to special education school students in TX.

Financial data: Year ended 12/31/2004. Assets, $1,036,914 (M); Expenditures, $518,308; Total giving, $496,306; Grants to individuals, 23 grants totaling $298,377 (high: $25,000, low: $1,913, average grant: $9,500-$15,100).

Fields of interest: Education, special; Disabilities, people with.

Type of support: Undergraduate support.

Application information: Deadline Mar. 31; Application by letter.

EIN: 752687930

2233
Alice Kindler Charitable Fund

3040 West Point Rd.
Lancaster, OH 43130
Contact: William J. Sitterley, Tr.
Application address: 4307 Bauman Hill Rd., Lancaster, OH 43130

Foundation type: Independent foundation

Limitations: Scholarships to graduates of Fairfield County, OH, high schools.

Financial data: Year ended 05/31/2005. Assets, $1,218,359 (M); Expenditures, $63,560; Total giving, $53,591; Grants to individuals, 14 grants totaling $53,591 (high: $6,400, low: $1,400).

Type of support: Support to graduates or students of specific schools; Technical education support; Undergraduate support.

Application information: Deadline 2nd Mon. in Mar.; Completion of formal application required, including high school transcript, ACT scores, class rank, and GPA; This fund shares an application process with the Mary Margaret Ackers Charitable Trust, the J. Colin Campbell Scholarship Fund, and the Mildred J. Herzberger Charitable Trust.

Program description:

Alice Kindler Scholarship: Recipients must be residents of Fairfield County for a minimum of three years, and must have attended a high school in Fairfield County the last three years of their secondary education, including graduation. Recipients must maintain a good scholastic record, attend accredited state-sponsored colleges or universities or technical or vocational schools in OH, be full-time students with a minimum of 15 hours per term, and maintain a 2.0 GPA. Applicants need not be recent high school graduates.

EIN: 311337515

2234
Jane R. King Charity Fund

P.O. Box 453
Jewell, IA 50130-0453
Contact: Keith Peterson, Treas.
Application address: 1510 Linden Dr., Ames, IA 50010, tel.: (515) 232-5240

Foundation type: Independent foundation

Limitations: Student loans only to graduates of South Hamilton School District, IA.

Financial data: Year ended 12/31/2004. Assets, $357,177 (M); Expenditures, $4,671; Total giving, $1,000; Loans to individuals, 3 loans totaling $3,000.

Type of support: Student loans—to individuals.

Application information: Applications accepted. Application form required.

Deadline(s): None

EIN: 426081131

2235
Maurice & Evelyn King Education Trust

c/o Springs Valley Bank & Trust
P.O. Box 830
Jasper, IN 47547-0830 (800) 843-4947

Foundation type: Independent foundation

Limitations: Scholarships to Springs Valley high school graduates for undergraduate education.

Financial data: Year ended 12/31/2004. Assets, $247,025 (M); Expenditures, $13,926; Total giving, $12,000; Grants to individuals, 10 grants totaling $12,000 (high: $2,000, low: $1,000).

Type of support: Support to graduates or students of specific schools.

Application information: Applications by letter accepted throughout the year.

EIN: 356678200

2236
William Toben King Educational Trust

c/o James Counts
320 Robidoux Ctr.
St. Joseph, MO 64501
Scholarship address: Julie Walker, c/o Commerce Bank, St. Joseph, P.O. Box 1119, St. Joseph, MO 64502, tel.: (816) 364-3131

Foundation type: Independent foundation

Limitations: Scholarships only to high school graduates of Andrew and Buchanon counties, MO, for higher education based on financial need and academic merit.

Financial data: Year ended 09/30/2005. Assets, $7,202,803 (M); Expenditures, $430,936; Total giving, $366,837; Grants to individuals, totaling $366,837.

Type of support: Scholarships—to individuals.

Application information: Deadline June 1; Completion of formal application required, including student's and parents' tax returns, extracurricular activities, work experience, detailed financial information, GPA, ACT or P-ACT scores, transcripts, guidance counselor's recommendation and signature, and one additional reference letter.

EIN: 431582893

2237
Charles & Lucille King Family Foundation, Inc.

366 Madison Ave., 10th Fl.
New York, NY 10017 (212) 682-2913
Contact: Michael Donovan, Educational Dir.; Karen E. Kennedy, Asst. Educational Dir.
E-mail: info@kingfoundation.org; URL: http://www.kingfoundation.org

Foundation type: Independent foundation

Limitations: Tuition scholarships to television and film undergraduate students who are juniors or seniors and demonstrate academic excellence, financial need, and professional potential.

Publications: Application guidelines; Informational brochure (including application guidelines).

Financial data: Year ended 12/31/2004. Assets, $3,466,639 (M); Expenditures, $647,591; Total giving, $530,940.

Fields of interest: Film/video.

Type of support: Undergraduate support.

Application information: Applications accepted. Application form required.

Initial approach: Letter.
Deadline(s): Apr. 15.
Applicants should submit the following:
1) Letter(s) of recommendation
2) Transcripts
3) Financial information

Program description:

Scholarship Program: Recipients must attend schools in the U.S. Scholarships are awarded for a maximum of two years. Recipients must maintain at least a "B" semester grade average.

EIN: 133489257

2238
Carl B. and Florence E. King Foundation

2929 Carlisle St., Ste. 222
Dallas, TX 75204 (214) 750-1884
Contact: Michelle D. Monse, Pres.
FAX: (214) 750-1651;
E-mail: michellemonse@kingfoundation.com;
URL: http://www.kingfoundation.com

Foundation type: Independent foundation

Limitations: Scholarships to TX high school and college students for the study of math, science, or English. Preference is shown to residents of the Dallas area.
Publications: Informational brochure (including application guidelines).
Financial data: Year ended 12/31/2005. Assets, $51,487,899 (M); Expenditures, $3,187,621; Total giving, $1,894,110.
Fields of interest: Literature; Science; Mathematics.
Type of support: Undergraduate support.
Application information:
Initial approach: Letter.
Deadline(s): Contact Texas Interscholastic League or the Dallas YMCA for current application deadline
Additional information: Completion of formal application required, including high school transcripts.
EIN: 756052203

2239
Basil L. King Scholarship Foundation, Inc.
(formerly Fort Pierce Memorial Hospital Scholarship Foundation, Inc.)
403 S. 6th St.
Fort Pierce, FL 34950-8318
Application address: c/o Indian River Community College Foundation, 3209 Virginia Ave., Ft. Pierce, FL 34981; tel.: (772) 462-7247

Foundation type: Independent foundation
Limitations: Scholarships to residents of St. Lucie County, FL, who are following a graduate or undergraduate course of study leading to a career in the health field. Undergraduate students must be unmarried.
Financial data: Year ended 09/30/2005. Assets, $5,916,011 (M); Expenditures, $360,133; Total giving, $305,441; Grants to individuals, totaling $3,700.
Fields of interest: Dental school/education; Medical school/education; Health sciences school/education.
Type of support: Graduate support; Undergraduate support.
Application information: Deadline Apr. 15; Completion of formal application required, including transcripts and declaration of domicile and citizenship completed by Clerk of the Circuit Court.
Program description:
Scholarship Program: Applicants must already have been accepted to an accredited medical or dental school at the time of application. Recipients are selected by the foundation's scholarship committee.
EIN: 590651084

2240
King Scholarship Fund
(also known as Cora E. King Scholarship Fund)
c/o Bank of America, N.A.
P.O. Box 1802
Providence, RI 02901-1802
Application address: c/o First Presbyterian Church, 112 South St., Auburn, NY 13021

Foundation type: Independent foundation
Limitations: Scholarships for residents (of at least one year) of Cayuga County, NY, for higher education.
Financial data: Year ended 12/31/2004. Assets, $634,575 (M); Expenditures, $33,246; Total giving, $24,500; Grants to individuals, 30 grants totaling $24,500 (high: $1,500, low: $500).

Type of support: Scholarships—to individuals.
Application information: Applications accepted. Application form required.
Deadline(s): June 6
Applicants should submit the following:
1) Transcripts
2) Letter(s) of recommendation
3) Financial information
Additional information: Application must also include autobiography of no more than 300 words, and copy of financial aid form.
EIN: 222589716

2241
George Leech King-St. Ferdinand College Scholarship Foundation
(formerly Ray Tyo-St. Ferdinand College Scholarship Foundation)
c/o M&T Bank
21 E. Market St., M/C 402-130
York, PA 17401-1205
Application address: c/o Msgr. Edward Quinlan, P.O. Box 3553, Harrisburg, PA 17105-3553, tel.: (717) 657-4804

Foundation type: Independent foundation
Limitations: Scholarships to financially needy graduates of Harrisburg Diocesan high schools in PA who will be attending Catholic colleges and universities for undergraduate study.
Financial data: Year ended 12/31/2004. Assets, $1,992,156 (M); Expenditures, $94,544; Total giving, $90,200; Grants to individuals, 45 grants totaling $90,200 (high: $2,100, low: $1,000).
Fields of interest: Roman Catholic agencies & churches.
Type of support: Undergraduate support.
Application information: Contact high school for current application deadline; Completion of formal application required, including transcripts, financial statement, and personal essay; Scholarships are paid each semester.
EIN: 236508132

2242
Kingsbury Fund
c/o Kingsbury Corp.
80 Laurel St.
Keene, NH 03431 (603) 352-5212
Contact: William G. Cogger, Exec. Tr.

Foundation type: Company-sponsored foundation
Limitations: Scholarships to high school seniors who are children of employees of the Kingsbury Corp. and to company-related undergraduate students, for attendance at technical institutes, colleges, or other accredited schools.
Financial data: Year ended 12/31/2004. Assets, $3,426,106 (M); Expenditures, $155,199; Total giving, $129,803; Grants to individuals, 11 grants totaling $11,000 (high: $1,000, low: $1,000).
Fields of interest: Vocational education.
Type of support: Employee-related scholarships.
Application information: Application form required.
Deadline(s): Mar. 25
Applicants should submit the following:
1) Transcripts
2) Essay
Program description:
Scholarship Program: All applicants must be in financial need, be students of good standing or meet college admission requirements, be active in school affairs or have a part-time job, demonstrate

qualities of leadership, and show evidence of good citizenship. The winners of scholarships are those who have the best combination of high need and good grades, and the best overall level of activity for the other factors. A written statement from each applicant is also used as an additional selection factor.
EIN: 026004465

2243
Mr. & Mrs. Henry B. Kingsbury Scholarship Fund
c/o H.F. Magnuson & Co.
P.O. Box 469
Wallace, ID 83873
Contact: Dennis O'Brien, Secy.

Foundation type: Independent foundation
Limitations: Scholarships to high school graduates of Shoshone County, ID.
Financial data: Year ended 12/31/2004. Assets, $84,558 (M); Expenditures, $9,992; Total giving, $6,000; Grants to individuals, 20 grants totaling $6,000 (high: $300, low: $300).
Type of support: Undergraduate support.
Application information: Application form required.
Initial approach: Letter.
Deadline(s): Apr. 15
EIN: 826005448

2244
Clair H. Kinney Scholarship Fund
(formerly Clair H. Kinney Scholarship and Library Science Reference Fund)
c/o First Columbia Bank & Trust Co.
11 W. Main St.
Bloomsburg, PA 17815-1702 (570) 387-4609
Contact: John Thompson, V.P. and Trust Off., First Columbia Bank & Trust Co.

Foundation type: Independent foundation
Limitations: Scholarships to graduates of public high schools in Columbia and Montour counties, PA.
Financial data: Year ended 12/31/2004. Assets, $190,242 (M); Expenditures, $30,088; Total giving, $27,879; Grants to individuals, 3 grants totaling $9,000 (high: $3,000, low: $3,000).
Type of support: Support to graduates or students of specific schools; Undergraduate support.
Application information: Deadline May 1; Completion of formal application required, including transcript, SAT scores, class rank, financial information, copy of parents' federal income tax return, and two references.
EIN: 236664657

2245
James Edward Kinsley Trust
(formerly James Edward Kinsley Educational Foundation)
c/o Bank of America, N.A.
P.O. Box 1802
Providence, RI 02901-1802
Application address: c/o Acton Boxbourough Regional High School, Attn.: James Kesler, Superintendent, 96 Hayward Rd., Acton, MA 01720

Foundation type: Independent foundation
Limitations: Scholarships by nomination only to young, unwed mothers who are students of the Acton, MA public school system.

Financial data: Year ended 05/31/2005.
Assets, $300,135 (M); Expenditures, $20,850;
Total giving, $15,900; Grants to individuals, 12
grants totaling $15,900 (high: $2,000, low:
$1,000).
Fields of interest: Women.
Type of support: Support to graduates or students
of specific schools; Awards/grants by nomination
only; Undergraduate support.
Application information: Recipients are selected by
school committee.
EIN: 046342377

2246

The Kirchner Family Foundation, Inc.
P.O. Box 404
Queenstown, MD   21658
Contact: Suzanne Kirchner, Pres.

Foundation type: Operating foundation
Limitations: Scholarship awards to residents of
Queenstown, MD.
Financial data: Year ended 12/31/2003.
Assets, $8,102 (M); Expenditures, $23,539; Total
giving, $20,079; Grants to individuals, 5 grants
totaling $20,079 (high: $10,340, low: $1,033).
Fields of interest: Higher education.
Application information: Applications accepted.
Application form required.
  Initial approach: Letter.
  Deadline(s): Apr. 1 for Summer and Fall
    semesters; Oct. 1 for Spring semester
  Applicants should submit the following:
    1) Letter(s) of recommendation
    2) SAT
    3) GPA
EIN: 134222352

2247

John E. Kirschner Educational Trust
c/o Commerce Bank of St. Joseph, N.A.
P.O. Box 1119
St. Joseph, MO   64502   (816) 364-3131
Contact: Julie Walker, Advisory Comm.

Foundation type: Independent foundation
Limitations: Scholarships in the fields of religion,
religious services, social work, education, and
ministry to members of the Zion United Church of
Christ in St. Joseph, MO, students graduating from
the St. Joseph Public School System, MO, and
students attending Missouri Western State College.
Financial data: Year ended 09/30/2002.
Assets, $1,346,488 (M); Expenditures,
$112,180; Total giving, $101,287; Grants to
individuals, 54 grants totaling $88,287 (high:
$24,250, low: $389).
Fields of interest: Education, research; Human
services; Christian agencies & churches; Religion.
Type of support: Scholarships—to individuals;
Support to graduates or students of specific
schools; Undergraduate support.
Application information: Applications accepted.
Application form required.
  Deadline(s): June 1
Program description:
  Scholarship Program: Preference is shown to
members of the Zion United Church of Christ. If
funds allow, the trust will ask the St. Joseph Public
School System and Missouri Western State College
to submit candidates for scholarships.
EIN: 436385089

2248

Clara Louise Kiser Memorial Fund
c/o National City Bank
P.O. Box 94651
Cleveland, OH   44101-4651
Application address: c/o Stephen P. Kosak, P.O.
Box 374, Oil City, PA 16301, tel.: (814) 677-5085

Foundation type: Independent foundation
Limitations: Scholarships to graduating seniors of
Clarion High School, PA. Children of parents
employed by National City Bank are not eligible to
apply.
Financial data: Year ended 12/31/2004.
Assets, $664,472 (M); Expenditures, $38,908;
Total giving, $30,405; Grants to individuals, 12
grants totaling $15,000.
Type of support: Support to graduates or students
of specific schools; Undergraduate support.
Application information: Contact fund for current
application deadline; Completion of formal
application required, including letter outlining
financial need and college CSS profile.
EIN: 256191759

2249

Kiwanis of Little Havana Foundation
701 S.W. 27th Ave., Ste. 900
Miami, FL   33135-3026

Foundation type: Independent foundation
Limitations: Scholarships to Hispanic students
with financial difficulties, residing in Miami, FL.
Financial data: Year ended 09/30/2002.
Assets, $394,924 (M); Expenditures, $207,106;
Total giving, $144,933; Grants to individuals, 43
grants totaling $69,410 (high: $4,220, low: $264).
Type of support: Undergraduate support.
Application information: Applications not
accepted.
  Additional information: Unsolicited requests for
    funds not accepted.
EIN: 650093807

2250

**Ray & Mary Klapmeyer Grandview High
School Foundation**
c/o UMB Bank, N.A.
P.O. Box 419692
Kansas City, MO   64141-6692
Application address: c/o Grandview High School,
Attn.: Sara Barrows, Counseling Office, 2300 High
Grove Rd., Grandview, MO 64030, tel.: (816)
761-3388

Foundation type: Independent foundation
Limitations: Scholarships to students graduating
from Grandview High School, MO.
Financial data: Year ended 02/28/2005.
Assets, $105,816 (M); Expenditures, $7,507;
Total giving, $3,653; Grants to individuals, 4 grants
totaling $3,500 (high: $1,500, low: $500).
Type of support: Support to graduates or students
of specific schools; Undergraduate support.
Application information: Application form required.
  Deadline(s): Mar. 31
  Applicants should submit the following:
    1) Photograph
EIN: 237382733

2251

A. M. Kleeman, Jr. Scholarship Fund
c/o Orange County Trust Co.
212 Dolson Ave.
Middletown, NY   10940
Contact: Joseph Natale, Superintendent
Application address: c/o Warwick Valley Central
School District, Warwick, NY 10990

Foundation type: Independent foundation
Limitations: Scholarships to students who
graduated from Central School District No. 1 in
Warwick and Chester, Orange County, NY.
Financial data: Year ended 05/31/2005.
Assets, $219,876 (M); Expenditures, $10,244;
Total giving, $7,000; Grants to individuals, totaling
$7,000.
Type of support: Support to graduates or students
of specific schools; Undergraduate support.
Application information: Applications accepted
throughout the year; Completion of formal
application required.
EIN: 133586537

2252

Cecil H. Kleppe Scholarship Fund
117 S. 6th St.
P.O. Box 240
Hiawatha, KS   66434-2306   (785) 742-2181
Contact: Michael K. Schmitt, Tr.
Application address: 117 S. 6th St., Hiawatha, KS
66434, tel.: (785) 742-2181

Foundation type: Independent foundation
Limitations: Scholarships only to graduating
resident students of high schools in Brown County,
KS, who are enrolled in a college, university or
vocational school.
Financial data: Year ended 06/30/2005.
Assets, $1,269,504 (M); Expenditures,
$105,646; Total giving, $53,500; Grants to
individuals, 53 grants totaling $53,500 (high:
$1,000, low: $500).
Fields of interest: Vocational education.
Type of support: Support to graduates or students
of specific schools; Technical education support;
Undergraduate support.
Application information: Applications accepted.
Application form required.
  Deadline(s): Mar. 15
EIN: 486364390

2253

Jessie Klicka Foundation
c/o Wells Fargo Bank, N.A.
85 Cleveland Rd., 1st Fl.
Pleasant Hill, CA   94523-3478

Foundation type: Independent foundation
Limitations: Scholarships to graduates of high
schools in San Diego City and County, CA.
Financial data: Year ended 12/31/2003.
Assets, $2,010,029 (M); Expenditures, $94,699;
Total giving, $47,000.
Type of support: Support to graduates or students
of specific schools; Undergraduate support.
Application information: Application form required.
  Deadline(s): Apr. 20
Program description:
  Scholarship Program: The foundation prefers to
award scholarships in special situations where the
need is not adequately met by other sources. There
has to be proven financial need and students must
have the necessary scholastic requirements to be

admitted to the school of their choice. The award is renewable for four years of undergraduate study.
EIN: 956093455

2254
Verne O. & Dorothy M. Kling Scholarship Fund
c/o Comerica Bank
P.O. Box 7500, M/C 8280
Detroit, MI 48275
Application address: c/o Comerica Bank, 101 N Main St., Ste. 100, Ann Arbor, MI 48104, tel.: (734) 930-2413

Foundation type: Independent foundation
Limitations: Scholarships to members of the Protestant Church, preferably those who reside in Shelby County, IN. Secondary consideration is given in order of preference to Protestants residing anywhere within IN, then within MI, and lastly in other states of the U.S.
Financial data: Year ended 06/30/2005. Assets, $59,249 (M); Expenditures, $15,875; Total giving, $11,500; Grants to individuals, 18 grants totaling $11,500.
Fields of interest: Protestant agencies & churches.
Type of support: Scholarships—to individuals.
Application information: Applications accepted.
   Initial approach: Letter.
   Deadline(s): Apr. 1
   Applicants should submit the following:
      1) Transcripts
      2) Letter(s) of recommendation
      3) Financial information
   Additional information: Application must also include a list of extracurricular activities.
EIN: 386302950

2255
Louise Kling Trust
1392 Collinswood Ln.
Marion, OH 43302
Contact: Vickie Davidson, Tr.

Foundation type: Independent foundation
Limitations: Scholarships to seniors of Warren G. Harding High School, OH, for the study of music or medicine.
Financial data: Year ended 12/31/2004. Assets, $2,070,695 (M); Expenditures, $280,001; Total giving, $254,965; Grants to individuals, 6 grants totaling $154,525 (high: $26,119, low: $11,126).
Fields of interest: Music; Performing arts, education; Medical school/education.
Type of support: Support to graduates or students of specific schools; Undergraduate support.
Application information: Applications by letter throughout the year.
Program description:
   Scholarship Program: Scholarships are renewable. No more than two new recipients are chosen each year.
EIN: 346841720

2256
Edward M. and Henrietta M. Knabusch Scholarship Foundation
c/o Monroe Bank & Trust
102 E. Front St.
Monroe, MI 48161

Foundation type: Independent foundation

Limitations: Undergraduate scholarships to children of La-Z-Boy, Inc. employees who are graduating high school seniors.
Financial data: Year ended 12/31/2004. Assets, $2,512,423 (M); Expenditures, $146,977; Total giving, $127,661; Grants to individuals, 70 grants totaling $127,661 (high: $2,000, low: $1,000).
Type of support: Employee-related scholarships.
Application information: Application form required.
   Deadline(s): Contact foundation for deadline
   Applicants should submit the following:
      1) Letter(s) of recommendation
      2) SAT
      3) ACT
Program description:
   Scholarship Program: Applicants are chosen based on scholastic achievement, extracurricular activities, community activities, citizenship and moral character, educational goals, job history, and financial need. Students who receive these scholarships may reapply for awards in their second, third, and fourth years of undergraduate study if they maintain a minimum 3.0 GPA as a full-time student.
EIN: 383450698

2257
Russell and Edna Knapp Foundation Trust
(also known as Knapp Foundation)
c/o Wells Fargo Bank Nevada, N.A.
P.O. Box 95021, MAC S4753-028
Henderson, NV 89009-5021

Foundation type: Independent foundation
Limitations: Scholarships to graduates from any high school in the Elko County School District, NV, and to residents of Elko County, NV, who out of necessity and not choice attend a high school outside the county. Recipients may attend colleges, universities, and technical schools.
Financial data: Year ended 01/31/2005. Assets, $1,198,389 (M); Expenditures, $48,827; Total giving, $35,167; Grants to individuals, totaling $35,167.
Fields of interest: Vocational education.
Type of support: Technical education support; Undergraduate support.
Application information: Applications accepted. Application form required.
   Deadline(s): None
Program description:
   Scholarship Program: Scholarships are limited to $1,000 per year, per student, and $4,000 per baccalaureate degree. Students enrolled in a program less than four years in duration would be limited to $1,000 per year, if selected. Recipients must be enrolled full-time and maintain at least a 2.5 GPA. Criteria for selection include character, scholarship, and economic need.
EIN: 942938337

2258
Beulah Knecht Trust
c/o Shelby County State Bank
130 S. Morgan St.
Shelbyville, IL 62565 (217) 774-3911

Foundation type: Independent foundation
Limitations: Scholarships to graduates of Shelbyville High School, IL, who have been accepted to four-year colleges.
Financial data: Year ended 02/28/2005. Assets, $210,687 (M); Expenditures, $8,928; Total giving, $7,000; Grants to individuals, 7 grants totaling $7,000 (high: $1,000, low: $1,000).

Type of support: Support to graduates or students of specific schools; Undergraduate support.
Application information: Applications accepted. Application form required.
   Deadline(s): Apr. 15
Program description:
   Scholarship Program: Students applying for renewals must have maintained at least a 2.75 GPA. Scholarships are renewable for up to four years of college.
EIN: 376291914

2259
Louise Knight Scholarship Trust
P.O. Box 925
Madisonville, TX 77864-0924
Contact: Roger Knight, Jr., Tr.

Foundation type: Independent foundation
Limitations: Scholarships to graduates of Madisonville High School, TX, for undergraduate education.
Financial data: Year ended 12/31/2004. Assets, $1 (M); Expenditures, $8,000; Total giving, $8,000; Grants to individuals, 8 grants totaling $8,000 (high: $1,000, low: $1,000).
Type of support: Support to graduates or students of specific schools; Undergraduate support.
Application information: Applications accepted. Application form required.
   Deadline(s): Feb. 1
   Applicants should submit the following:
      1) Photograph
      2) Letter(s) of recommendation
      3) Essay
   Additional information: Application must include proof of undergraduate enrollment.
EIN: 746387730

2260
Knights of Columbus Charities, Inc.
1 Columbus Plz.
New Haven, CT 06510-3326 (203) 752-4000
Contact: Carl A. Anderson, Pres.
FAX: (203) 752-4118; URL: http://www.kofc.org

Foundation type: Public charity
Limitations: Scholarships to graduating high school students for higher education.
Financial data: Year ended 12/31/2003. Assets, $49,953,652 (M); Expenditures, $4,716,199; Total giving, $2,351,525; Grants to individuals, totaling $1,280,701.
Type of support: Undergraduate support.
Application information: Application form required.
   Deadline(s): Vary
   Additional information: See Web site for further application and program information.
Program description:
   Scholarship Program: The foundation administers the following scholarships:
      · Fourth-Degree Pro Deo and Pro Patria Scholarships
      · John W. McDevitt (Fourth Degree) Scholarships
      · Francis P. Matthews and John E. Swift Educational Trust Scholarships
      · Bishop Charles P. Greco Graduate Fellowships
      · Fourth Degree Pro Deo and Pro Patria (Canada) Scholarships
Scholarships are awarded annually to students for education at universities for four-year programs and at colleges for two- or three-year programs immediately following graduation from high school. Scholarships are renewable for one additional year,

subject to evidence of continued enrollment and good standing at the university or college of student's choice.
EIN: 237227608

2261
Knoche-Guett Scholarship Fund
c/o Wells Fargo Bank, N.A., Trust Tax Dept.
P.O. Box 63954
San Francisco, CA 94163

Foundation type: Independent foundation
Limitations: Scholarships to graduates of Carlsbad High School, CA, for study at two- and four-year colleges and universities. Scholarships are limited to $5,000 per year, per recipient.
Financial data: Year ended 06/30/2005. Assets, $4,591 (M); Expenditures, $81,087; Total giving, $72,250; Grants to individuals, 24 grants totaling $72,250 (high: $40,000, low: $150).
Fields of interest: Vocational education.
Type of support: Support to graduates or students of specific schools; Undergraduate support.
Application information: Applications not accepted.
EIN: 330215414

2262
The Knoll Charitable Foundation
P.O. Box 157
East Greenville, PA 18041

Foundation type: Company-sponsored foundation
Limitations: Scholarships to children, between the ages of 17 and 25, of full-time Knoll, Inc. employees, primarily in MI and PA. Recipients must plan to pursue full-time study at the accredited college, university, or vocational school of their choice.
Financial data: Year ended 12/31/2004. Assets, $4,818,223 (M); Expenditures, $218,397; Total giving, $195,000; Grants to individuals, 31 grants totaling $195,000 (high: $8,000, low: $3,000).
Type of support: Employee-related scholarships.
Application information: Application form required.
  Deadline(s): Mar. 15
  Additional information: Scholarship application address: c/o Knoll Educational Scholarship Prog., Scholarship America, Inc., P.O. Box 297, St. Peter, MN 56082, tel.: (507) 931-1682.
EIN: 232939762

2263
Knoop Scholarship Fund
c/o U.S. Bank, N.A.
P.O. Box 387
St. Louis, MO 63166
Application address: c/o Margaret Garrison, 13853 Country Club Dr., Versailles, MO 65084

Foundation type: Independent foundation
Limitations: Scholarships to graduates of Morgan County High School, MO.
Financial data: Year ended 07/31/2004. Assets, $198,355 (M); Expenditures, $10,593; Total giving, $7,250; Grants to individuals, totaling $7,250.
Type of support: Support to graduates or students of specific schools; Undergraduate support.
Application information: Contact fund for current application deadline/guidelines.
EIN: 431717989

2264
Leonora H. Knowles Trust B
c/o KeyBank N.A., Trust Div.
800 Superior Ave., 4th Fl.
Cleveland, OH 44114-2601

Foundation type: Independent foundation
Limitations: Scholarships to financially needy residents of Hancock and Oxford counties, ME, for postsecondary education, including nursing.
Financial data: Year ended 12/31/2004. Assets, $6,465,592 (M); Expenditures, $508,991; Total giving, $434,969; Grants to individuals, 84 grants totaling $95,000 (high: $3,750, low: $500).
Fields of interest: Nursing school/education.
Type of support: Undergraduate support.
Application information: Contact trust for current application deadline/guidelines.
EIN: 222789214

2265
Ellen Beck Knox-MKB Foundation
(also known as MKB Foundation)
c/o Bank of America, N.A.
P.O. Box 831041
Dallas, TX 75283-1041
Application address: c/o Bank of America, N.A., Attn.: Susan Bullard, Trust Off., P.O. Box 830259, Dallas, TX 75283-0259, tel.: (214) 508-6674

Foundation type: Independent foundation
Limitations: Scholarships to residents of Coleman County, TX, for vocational or technical school.
Financial data: Year ended 05/31/2004. Assets, $369,627 (M); Expenditures, $99,263; Total giving, $94,000; Grants to individuals, 83 grants totaling $94,000 (high: $15,000, low: $500).
Fields of interest: Vocational education.
Type of support: Technical education support.
Application information: Applications by letter accepted throughout the year.
EIN: 756233396

2266
Robert & Margaret Koch Bomarko Founders Scholarship Fund
c/o Fifth Third Bank
P.O. Box 3636
Grand Rapids, MI 49501-3636

Foundation type: Independent foundation
Limitations: Scholarships for attendance at Ancilla College to graduates of the Argos, Bremen, Culverd, Laville, Plymouth or Triton school corporations, IN, and to employees of BoMarko, Plymouth, IN.
Financial data: Year ended 09/30/2004. Assets, $112,455 (M); Expenditures, $6,021; Total giving, $4,900; Grants to individuals, totaling $4,900.
Type of support: Employee-related scholarships; Support to graduates or students of specific schools; Undergraduate support.
Application information: Applications accepted. Application form required.
  Deadline(s): Apr. 15
  Applicants should submit the following:
    1) Transcripts
    2) SAT
    3) Financial information
EIN: 351781577

2267
The Fred C. and Mary R. Koch Foundation, Inc.
(formerly The Fred C. Koch Foundation)
P.O. Box 2256
Wichita, KS 67201-2256 (316) 828-2646
Contact: Roger Ramseyer, V.P.
E-mail: ramseyer@kochind.com

Foundation type: Independent foundation
Limitations: Scholarships only to dependents of employees of Koch Industries, Inc., and its subsidiaries.
Financial data: Year ended 12/31/2003. Assets, $24,908,437 (M); Expenditures, $1,230,075; Total giving, $1,099,803; Grants to individuals, 109 grants totaling $109,000 (high: $1,000, low: $1,000).
Type of support: Employee-related scholarships.
Application information:
  Deadline(s): Mar. 1
  Applicants should submit the following:
    1) Resume
    2) Transcripts
  Additional information: Application must also include two reference letters from high school officials; Recipients notified between May 2 and Aug. 1.
Program description:
  Koch Scholarship Awards: Scholarships are given to eligible applicants who are under the age of 25, for full-time study at an institution of higher education. In order to be eligible, applicants must be children of employees of Koch Industries, Inc., and its subsidiaries with at least one year of service as of the application deadline. Scholarships are automatically renewed, provided that the recipient maintains a 3.5 GPA.
EIN: 486113560

2268
John G. Koehler Fund
c/o Herr & Herr
103 N. Main St.
Pontiac, IL 61764-1978 (815) 844-7128
Contact: James Herr

Foundation type: Independent foundation
Limitations: Scholarships to local IL area students for full-time study.
Financial data: Year ended 12/31/2004. Assets, $1,225,074 (M); Expenditures, $54,795; Total giving, $45,600; Grants to individuals, 29 grants totaling $45,600 (high: $1,800, low: $700).
Type of support: Scholarships—to individuals.
Application information: Applications accepted.
  Initial approach: Letter.
  Deadline(s): June 1
  Applicants should submit the following:
    1) Financial information
  Additional information: Application must also include last three years' tax returns and student's general background.
EIN: 376141953

2269
Herb Kohl Educational Foundation
825 N. Jefferson St.
Milwaukee, WI 53202
Scholarship address: c/o Greg Doyle, Wisconsin Dept. of Public Instruction, P.O. Box 7841, Madison, WI 53707-7841, tel.: (608) 266-1098,
E-mail: greg.doyle@dpi.state.wi.us
URL: http://www.kohleducation.org

Foundation type: Independent foundation

Limitations: Scholarships to students who are WI residents.
Financial data: Year ended 12/31/2004. Assets, $2,776,677 (M); Expenditures, $409,427; Total giving, $388,157; Grants to individuals, 285 grants totaling $284,657 (high: $1,000, low: $657).
Fields of interest: Vocational education.
Type of support: Undergraduate support.
Application information:
Deadline(s): Feb. 1
Additional information: Completion of formal application required, including several essays, transcripts, and four letters of recommendation, one each from a teacher, counselor or principal, community member, and family friend.
Program description:
Kohl Student Scholarship Program: WI residents who are graduating high school students may apply for $1,000 scholarships to be used for tuition and fees related to their first year of postsecondary education. Recipients are selected through a competitive process on the basis of their leadership, citizenship, school and community involvement, and academic achievement. Students are also evaluated on their ability to articulate educational, personal, community, and career goals in the application essay. Applications are reviewed by school district officials for public school students and by similar entities for non-public school students, who select a limited number of applicants to nominate for the scholarship.
EIN: 391661743

2270
Leila Kohl Scholarship Trust
c/o Marshall & Ilsley Bank
P.O. Box 2980
Milwaukee, WI 53201-2980
Application address: c/o School District of Tomahawk, Dist. Admin. Off., 18 E. Washington Ave., Tomahawk, WI 54487, tel.: (715) 453-5551

Foundation type: Independent foundation
Limitations: Scholarships to graduates of the Tomahawk School District, WI.
Financial data: Year ended 03/31/2005. Assets, $1,105,601 (M); Expenditures, $68,090; Total giving, $56,000; Grants to individuals, 51 grants totaling $56,000 (high: $2,500, low: $500).
Type of support: Support to graduates or students of specific schools; Undergraduate support.
Application information: Applications accepted. Application form required.
EIN: 396611696

2271
Kohler Foundation, Inc.
725 Woodlake Rd., Ste. X
Kohler, WI 53044 (920) 458-1972
Contact: Terri Yoho, Exec. Dir.
FAX: (920) 458-4280; E-mail: terri.yoho@kohlerco.com; URL: http://www.kohlerfoundation.org

Foundation type: Independent foundation
Limitations: Scholarships only to Sheboygan County, WI, graduating high school seniors recommended by their schools.
Financial data: Year ended 12/31/2003. Assets, $155,175,261 (M); Expenditures, $7,105,155; Total giving, $5,746,578; Grants to individuals, 94 grants totaling $214,042 (high: $10,000, low: $250).

Fields of interest: Humanities; Science; Mathematics.
Type of support: Undergraduate support.
Application information: Application form required.
Initial approach: Letter.
Deadline(s): May 1
Additional information: Candidates must be recommended by their schools; Interviews may be required.
Program description:
Scholarship Program: The foundation's program includes scholarship awards, awards in the humanities, and awards in mathematics and science. Scholarships may be used to attend any accredited college or university in the U.S.
EIN: 390810536

2272
Cynthia McKinley Kolasinski Scholarship Trust
P.O. Box 218
Fort Atkinson, WI 53538-0218
Application address: c/o Greg Banaszynski, 611 Sherman Ave., Fort Atkinson, WI 53538

Foundation type: Operating foundation
Limitations: Scholarships to residents of Fort Atkinson and Watertown, WI, for study in medical fields.
Financial data: Year ended 12/31/2003. Assets, $234,328 (M); Expenditures, $18,735; Total giving, $17,000; Grants to individuals, 14 grants totaling $17,000 (high: $3,000, low: $500).
Fields of interest: Medical school/education.
Type of support: Graduate support; Undergraduate support.
Application information:
Initial approach: Letter.
EIN: 396290565

2273
The Kolob Foundation
c/o Randy J. Green
423 Wakara Way, Ste. 212
Salt Lake City, UT 84108-1242
(801) 583-8811

Foundation type: Independent foundation
Limitations: Scholarships to economically disadvantaged individuals in the Salt Lake City, UT, area.
Financial data: Year ended 12/31/2004. Assets, $137,645 (M); Expenditures, $29,525; Total giving, $29,236; Grants to individuals, 8 grants totaling $29,236 (high: $7,230, low: $333).
Fields of interest: Economically disadvantaged.
Type of support: Scholarships—to individuals.
Application information: Applications accepted. Application form required.
Initial approach: Letter.
EIN: 876231892

2274
Susan G. Komen Breast Cancer Foundation
Occidental Twr.
5005 Lyndon B. Johnson Freeway, Ste. 250
Dallas, TX 75244 (972) 855-1600
Contact: Patrice Tosi, C.O.O.
FAX: (972) 855-1605; E-mail: grants@komen.org; Additional tel.: (800) 462-9273; URL: http://www.komen.org

Foundation type: Public charity

Limitations: Five scholarships of up to $10,000 are awarded annually to recipients who have lost a parent to breast cancer.
Publications: Annual report; Grants list; Informational brochure; Newsletter.
Financial data: Year ended 03/31/2005. Assets, $116,598,410 (M); Expenditures, $95,390,752; Total giving, $53,323,199; Grants to individuals, 61 grants totaling $650,158 (high: $37,333, low: $1,530).
Fields of interest: Cancer.
Type of support: Undergraduate support.
Application information: Application form required.
Initial approach: Letter, telephone, or e-mail.
Deadline(s): Nov. 8.
EIN: 751835298

2275
Louis and Ella I. Kondur Memorial Foundation, Inc.
2945 Orchard Pl.
Orchard Lake, MI 48324

Foundation type: Independent foundation
Limitations: Scholarships to the top ten graduating seniors from each of West Bloomfield High School and St. Mary's High School, MI.
Financial data: Year ended 12/31/2004. Assets, $441,348 (M); Expenditures, $53,120; Total giving, $52,500; Grants to individuals, 21 grants totaling $52,500 (high: $2,500, low: $2,500).
Type of support: Undergraduate support.
Application information: Contact foundation for current application deadline/guidelines.
EIN: 383314192

2276
Koniag Education Foundation
6927 Old Seward Hwy., Ste. 103
Anchorage, AK 99518 (888) 562-9093
Contact: Tyan Selby, Exec. Dir.
FAX: (907) 562-9023; E-mail: kef@alaska.com; URL: http://www.koniageducation.org

Foundation type: Company-sponsored foundation
Limitations: Scholarships to Native Alaskan students for undergraduate, graduate, vocational, or other educational endeavors.
Publications: Application guidelines; Financial statement; Grants list; Informational brochure; Newsletter.
Financial data: Year ended 03/31/2005. Assets, $5,104,121 (M); Expenditures, $367,655; Total giving, $187,758; Grants to individuals, 132 grants totaling $187,758 (high: $6,800, low: $98).
Fields of interest: Native Americans/American Indians.
Type of support: Graduate support; Technical education support; Undergraduate support.
Application information: Applications accepted. Application form required. Application form available on the grantmaker's Web site.
Initial approach: Letter.
Deadline(s): Mar. 15 and June 1
Applicants should submit the following:
1) Resume
2) Letter(s) of recommendation
3) GPA
4) Essay
5) Transcripts
Additional information: Application must also include two letters of assessment, applicants

letter, achievements, activities and responsibilities.
EIN: 920145017

2277
The Elmer J. Kooi, Beatrice A. Kooi and Robert J. Kooi Education Fund
c/o Harris Bank, N.A.
P.O. Box 755, Tax Div.
Chicago, IL 60690
Application address: c/o Marengo Community High School, Marengo, IL 60152

Foundation type: Independent foundation
Limitations: Loans to students who have graduated from Marengo Community High School, IL, for undergraduate and vocational education.
Financial data: Year ended 12/31/2004. Assets, $2,307,403 (M); Expenditures, $160,131; Total giving, $129,500; Loans to individuals, 19 loans totaling $129,500.
Type of support: Student loans—to individuals; Support to graduates or students of specific schools; Undergraduate support.
Application information: Applications accepted. Application form required.
  Initial approach: Letter.
  Deadline(s): None
Program description:
  Student Loan Program: Students who have graduated from Marengo Community High School may apply for an annual $6,000 loan. Each year, two students, one male and one female, will be selected by the high school principal or by a committee appointed by him. Loans are renewable for up to four years of study, over an eight-year period.
EIN: 363899844

2278
Koomruian Armenian Education Fund
(formerly Koomruian Education Fund)
c/o Bank of America, N.A.
P.O. Box 513189, GMF
Los Angeles, CA 90051-1189
Application address: c/o Robert Britton, 555 S. Flower St., 11th Fl., Los Angeles, CA 90071, tel.: (213) 346-0485

Foundation type: Independent foundation
Limitations: Scholarships to students of Armenian descent residing in CA.
Financial data: Year ended 12/31/2004. Assets, $475,581 (M); Expenditures, $26,486; Total giving, $18,000; Grants to individuals, 12 grants totaling $18,000 (high: $1,500, low: $1,500).
Fields of interest: Armenia.
Type of support: Graduate support; Undergraduate support.
Application information: Application form required.
  Initial approach: Letter requesting information and application form.
  Deadline(s): None
  Additional information: Applicants must be attending college, are in need of financial assistance and whose academic performance is above average or excellent.
EIN: 956837992

2279
Alice W. C. Koon Scholastic Fund
c/o Alliance Bank, N.A.
241 Main St.
Buffalo, NY 14203
Application address: c/o Cayuga Central School, Superintendent of schools

Foundation type: Independent foundation
Limitations: Scholarships to Cayuga County, NY, residents who graduated from the Southern Cayuga Central School District.
Financial data: Year ended 12/31/2003. Assets, $1,602,939 (M); Expenditures, $99,727; Total giving $80,889; Grants to individuals, 18 grants totaling $80,889 (high: $7,500, low: $539).
Type of support: Scholarships—to individuals; Support to graduates or students of specific schools.
Application information: Applications not accepted.
EIN: 166071002

2280
Ida C. Koran Trust
c/o U.S. Bank, N.A.
P.O. Box 64713
St. Paul, MN 55164-0704

Foundation type: Independent foundation
Limitations: Scholarships and student loans to dependents of Ecolab employees, MN.
Financial data: Year ended 12/31/2004. Assets, $39,764,035 (M); Expenditures, $1,983,499; Total giving, $1,667,266; Grants to individuals, totaling $1,635,266; Loans to individuals, totaling $339,654.
Type of support: Employee-related scholarships.
Application information: Applications not accepted.
EIN: 416124022

2281
Ellen Korpy Foundation, Inc.
1104 9th Ave. S.
Virginia, MN 55792
Application address: c/o Virginia Secondary School Independent School District No. 706, Sr. High Counselor, 411 5th Ave., Virginia, MN 55792, tel.: (218) 742-3909

Foundation type: Operating foundation
Limitations: Scholarships to students in the Virginia Secondary Independent School District No. 706, MN, for higher education.
Financial data: Year ended 12/31/2003. Assets, $107,747 (M); Expenditures, $35,553; Total giving, $34,140; Grants to individuals, 6 grants totaling $34,140 (high: $6,500, low: $1,500).
Type of support: Support to graduates or students of specific schools; Undergraduate support.
Application information: Applications accepted. Application form required.
  Deadline(s): Apr. 15
EIN: 411908484

2282
Kosciusko County Community Foundation, Inc.
102 E. Market St.
Warsaw, IN 46580 (574) 267-1901
Contact: Suzanne M. Light, Exec. Dir.
FAX: (574) 268-9780;
E-mail: kcf@kcfoundation.org; URL: http://www.kcfoundation.org

Foundation type: Community foundation
Limitations: Scholarships to residents of Kosciusko County, IN for attendance at a college, university or trade school.
Publications: Application guidelines; Annual report (including application guidelines); Newsletter.
Financial data: Year ended 06/30/2005. Assets, $26,026,404 (M); Expenditures, $1,475,462; Total giving, $1,009,917; Grants to individuals, 708 grants totaling $130,582.
Fields of interest: Arts education; Performing arts, education; Medical school/education; Nursing school/education; Pharmacy/prescriptions; Athletics/sports, training; Women.
Type of support: Support to graduates or students of specific schools; Technical education support; Undergraduate support.
Application information: Applications accepted. Application form required. Application form available on the grantmaker's Web site.
  Deadline(s): Apr. 1 and July 15
  Additional information: See Web site for complete guidelines and to download application; new scholarships are added annually.
EIN: 356086777

2283
Kosciuszko Foundation, Inc.
15 E. 65th St.
New York, NY 10021-6595 (212) 734-2130
Contact: Maryla Janiak, Dir., Educ. Progs.
Address in Poland: ul. Nowy Swiat 4, Rm. 118, 03-921 Warszawa, tel.: (48) (22) 21-7067
FAX: (212) 628-4552; E-mail: thekf@aol.com;
URL: http://www.kosciuszkofoundation.org

Foundation type: Public charity
Limitations: Scholarships for Americans of Polish descent and study/research programs for Americans in Poland.
Publications: Annual report; Informational brochure (including application guidelines); Newsletter.
Financial data: Year ended 06/30/2003. Assets, $24,885,967 (M); Expenditures, $3,086,666; Total giving, $1,414,593; Grants to individuals, totaling $1,414,593.
Fields of interest: Music.
Type of support: Graduate support; Undergraduate support; Postgraduate support; Residencies; Travel grants.
Application information: Application form required.
  Initial approach: Letter.
  Deadline(s): Contact foundation for application deadlines.
Program descriptions:
  Music Scholarships: The Kosciuszko Foundation Chopin Piano Competition/Scholarship was designed to encourage highly talented American students of piano to study and play works of Chopin. The competition is held annually at the Foundation house on three consecutive days, during the middle of May, before a team of distinguished jurors. The competition is open to citizens and permanent residents of the U.S. and to international full-time students with valid student visas. Applicants must be between the ages of 16

and 22, as of the opening date of the competition. The Foundation awards $5,000 in cash prizes to the competition's top three winners, i.e. $2,500 as first prize, $1,500 as second prize, and $1,000 as third prize.

Study/Research Programs for Americans in Poland: The Foundation annually sponsors American students to pursue an undergraduate course of Polish language, literature, history, and culture at the Jagrellonian University in Poland. Students who will be entering their junior or senior year in college are eligible. Although it is an undergraduate program students enrolled in an M.A. or Ph.D. program with the exception of those at their dissertation level, can also apply. Selection criteria include overall academic performance and motivation for pursuing studies in Poland. Students receive tuition, housing, and a monthly stipend for living expenses. Transportation to and from Poland is at the expense of the participant. There is a $50 non-refundable application fee.

Graduate and Postgraduate Study in Poland: Each year the Foundation assists a number of Americans in continuing their graduate and postgraduate studies at institutions of higher learning in Poland. Grantees receive tuition and housing plus an allowance per month in Polish currency for living expenses. No provisions are made for dependents. Grantees wishing to have members of their family accompany them may do so at their own expense. Transportation to and from Poland is at the expense of the participant. The Foundation requires a non-refundable application fee of $50. Students must possess a working knowledge of the Polish language. Selection is based on overall academic performance, motivation for pursuing graduate studies in Poland, and a well-reasoned research proposal.

Graduate Scholarships: Scholarships are for full-time graduate study in the U.S. Eligible applicants are U.S. citizens of Polish descent, Poles who are permanent residents of the U.S. and Americans of non-Polish descent who are pursuing a course of study or research relating to Polish subjects. All applicants must furnish evidence of identification with the Polish community. The deadline for submitting applications is Jan. 15. Applications, together with all required supporting materials, must be at the Foundation by the deadline. Applications not received by Jan. 15 will not be given consideration. Applications should be accompanied by a $25 non-refundable processing fee. Only one family member may receive scholarship aid in any given academic year. Scholarships are granted for one academic year. All recipients and previous candidates may re-apply.

Summer Sessions in Poland: Each year the Foundation sponsors summer session programs in Poland. The sessions take place at Polish universities, academies and cultural institutions. The programs are geared toward students of Polish language, culture and history, as well as Polish Americans interested in learning about their Polish heritage and those with special interests in Polish contemporary life. Admission is open to American and Canadian citizens of all ethnic backgrounds. Minimum requirement is high school graduation prior to the commencement of the program. Four and six week courses are offered in Polish language, history, culture, art and folk art, economics and foreign trade. All programs include some travel within Poland. Program fees are inclusive of complete tuition, room, board and travel expenses connected with the program in Poland. Free health service is provided in Poland to all participants. Airfare to Poland is not included. For more information write: Summer Sessions.
EIN: 131628179

2284
Eugene R. Kotur Foundation
c/o PNC Advisors
1600 Market St., 4th Fl.
Philadelphia, PA   19103-7240
Application address: c/o Ukrainian Fraternal Association, 440 Wyoming Ave., Scranton, PA 18503-1290, tel.: (717) 342-0937

Foundation type: Independent foundation
Limitations: Scholarships to individuals of Ukrainian descent for higher education.
Financial data: Year ended 12/31/2004. Assets, $355,064 (M); Expenditures, $17,045; Total giving, $12,000; Grants to individuals, 6 grants totaling $12,000 (high: $2,500, low: $1,500).
Fields of interest: Ukraine.
Type of support: Undergraduate support.
Application information: Applications accepted. Application form required.
Deadline(s): June 15
EIN: 256394138

2285
The Trustees of Ivan V. Koulaieff Educational Fund
c/o Stadler, Rosenblum & Saris
451 Montgomery St., 3rd Fl.
San Francisco, CA   94104-1199

Foundation type: Independent foundation
Limitations: Grants and scholarships to Russians who were political immigrants between 1918 and 1945 throughout the world, and their descendants.
Financial data: Year ended 12/31/2004. Assets, $8,449,543 (M); Expenditures, $466,380; Total giving, $396,100; Grants to individuals, 11 grants totaling $155,100 (high: $43,800, low: $3,000).
Fields of interest: Immigrants/refugees; Russia.
Type of support: Scholarships—to individuals; Foreign applicants.
Application information: Applications accepted. Application form required.
Initial approach: Letter.
EIN: 946088762

2286
Judith Kirsch Kovach Memorial Trust
501 New County Rd.
Secaucus, NJ   07096

Foundation type: Independent foundation
Limitations: Scholarships to Edison High School, NJ, seniors based on the display of courage and perseverance in the face of adversity.
Financial data: Year ended 12/31/2004. Assets, $28,930 (M); Expenditures, $10,010; Total giving, $10,000; Grants to individuals, 2 grants totaling $10,000 (high: $5,000, low: $5,000).
Type of support: Support to graduates or students of specific schools; Undergraduate support.
Application information: Applications not accepted.
Additional information: Recipients are chosen by Edison High School Administration.
EIN: 226503902

2287
George Krambles Transit Scholarship Fund
1351 W. Whitmore Ct.
Lake Forest, IL   60045-1566
Contact: Joseph D. DiJohn, Dir.
Application address: c/o University of Illinois at Chicago, 421 S. Peoria St., Ste. 340, Chicago, IL 60607, tel.: (312) 996-1458

Foundation type: Independent foundation
Limitations: Scholarships by nomination only to full-time graduate students studying for a career in the transit industry, in fields relating to mass transit, such as business administration, economics, engineering, planning, and geography.
Financial data: Year ended 12/31/2004. Assets, $50,426 (M); Expenditures, $16,520; Total giving, $15,000; Grants to individuals, 6 grants totaling $15,000 (high: $2,500, low: $2,500).
Fields of interest: Business school/education; Engineering school/education; Business/industry; Economics; Transportation.
Type of support: Awards/grants by nomination only; Graduate support.
Application information: Application form required.
Initial approach: Letter.
Deadline(s): Mar. 1
Additional information: Students cannot apply directly, they must be nominated by a faculty member.
Program description:
Scholarship Program: Student must be nominated by a faculty member or a faculty member and a transit manager in conjunction with one another. There must be evidence submitted that the nominating school has a program that will aid those seeking careers in transit management. Nomination must include student's transcript, a letter of interest by the student indicating career aim, and a paper on a mass transit subject. The latter may be submitted from a course already taken.
EIN: 363124494

2288
Louie & Frank Kramer Educational Fund
c/o Wells Fargo Bank South Dakota, N.A.
425 S. Main St.
Winner, SD   57580
Application address: c/o Wells Fargo Bank SD, N.A., Trust Dept., Attn.: Lynnette Kucera, Winner, SD 57325, tel.: (605) 842-8217

Foundation type: Independent foundation
Limitations: Student loans to residents of Chamberlain, SD.
Financial data: Year ended 12/31/2004. Assets, $75,472 (M); Expenditures, $20,892; Total giving, $17,225; Grants to individuals, 13 grants totaling $17,225 (high: $1,675, low: $1,025).
Type of support: Student loans—to individuals.
Application information: Applications accepted. Application form required.
Applicants should submit the following:
1) Transcripts
Additional information: Application must also include tax returns.
EIN: 510190074

2289
Cmdr. and Mrs. Robert Krause Foundation
132 State St.
Harbor Beach, MI 48441
Contact: Marilyn S. Townley, Tr.

Foundation type: Independent foundation
Limitations: Scholarships to graduates of Harbor Beach Community School, MI, to attend a postsecondary institution.
Financial data: Year ended 12/31/2004.
Assets, $792,367 (M); Expenditures, $57,049; Total giving, $35,600; Grants to individuals, 26 grants totaling $35,600 (high: $2,000, low: $500).
Fields of interest: Higher education.
Type of support: Scholarships—to individuals.
Application information: Applications accepted. Application form required.
  Deadline(s): End of Apr.
  Applicants should submit the following:
    1) GPA
EIN: 527317516

2290
Essie W. Krausman Scholarship Trust
(also known as August P. & Essie W. Krausman Scholarships)
c/o Bank of America, N.A.
P.O. Box 40200, MC FL9-100-10-19
Jacksonville, FL 32203-0200
Application address: P.O. Box 11388, St. Petersburg, FL 33733

Foundation type: Independent foundation
Limitations: Scholarships to residents of Pinellas County, FL, for undergraduate education based on academic standing, financial need, and lack of other resources.
Financial data: Year ended 08/31/2004.
Assets, $706,691 (M); Expenditures, $51,361; Total giving, $37,650; Grants to individuals, 39 grants totaling $37,650 (high: $1,000, low: $500).
Application information: Application form required.
  Initial approach: Letter of telephone.
  Deadline(s): June 1
  Additional information: Application must include personal statement; Interview required.
EIN: 596161774

2291
Walter J. & Ada B. Kreager Memorial Scholarship Fund
c/o Hibernia National Bank
P.O. Box 3928
Beaumont, TX 77704
Application address: c/o Lana Walsh, Port Neches High School, 1401 Merriman St., Port Neches, TX 77651

Foundation type: Independent foundation
Limitations: Scholarships to individuals in the Port Neches and Groves, TX, areas.
Financial data: Year ended 05/31/2003.
Assets, $215,582 (M); Expenditures, $12,950; Total giving, $9,000; Grants to individuals, 9 grants totaling $9,000.
Type of support: Scholarships—to individuals.
Application information: Contact foundation for current application deadline/guidelines.
EIN: 760504933

2292
Helen and Rudy Krejci Trust
1905 Hollister Ave.
Tomah, WI 54660
Contact: Robert Steele, Tr.

Foundation type: Independent foundation
Limitations: Scholarships to graduates of Tomah High School, WI, for higher education.
Financial data: Year ended 12/31/2004.
Assets, $560,444 (M); Expenditures, $16,183; Total giving, $16,150; Grants to individuals, 26 grants totaling $12,650 (high: $700, low: $300).
Type of support: Support to graduates or students of specific schools; Undergraduate support.
Application information: Contact trust for current application guidelines.
EIN: 396643512

2293
The Scott S. Krueger Memorial Foundation, Inc.
11 Ranch Trail Ct.
Orchard Park, NY 14127
Application address: c/o Orchard Park High School, Guidance Dept., 4040 Baker Rd., Orchard Park, NY 14127

Foundation type: Independent foundation
Limitations: Scholarships to seniors at Orchard Park High School, NY, for higher education.
Financial data: Year ended 12/31/2004.
Assets, $1,153,181 (M); Expenditures, $86,459; Total giving, $70,000; Grants to individuals, 7 grants totaling $70,000 (high: $10,000, low: $10,000).
Type of support: Support to graduates or students of specific schools; Undergraduate support.
Application information:
  Deadline(s): Feb.
  Additional information: Contact foundation for current application guidelines.
EIN: 161599236

2294
The KT Family Foundation
21250 Hawthorne Blvd., Ste. 800
Torrance, CA 90503 (815) 675-2405
Contact: Kay Kargul, Secy.
Application address: 9802 Fox Bluff Ln., Spring Grove, IL 60081, tel.: (800) 310-4872, ext. 3736, fax: (815) 675-6923, E-mail: kkargul@davita.com

Foundation type: Independent foundation
Limitations: Scholarships to children of DaVita, Inc., employees for private education.
Financial data: Year ended 12/31/2002.
Assets, $84,472 (M); Expenditures, $16,010; Total giving, $16,000; Grants to individuals, 8 grants totaling $16,000 (high: $3,000, low: $1,000).
Fields of interest: Elementary/secondary education.
Type of support: Precollege support; Undergraduate support.
Application information: Application form required.
  Deadline(s): Feb. 24
  Applicants should submit the following:
    1) SAT
    2) Letter(s) of recommendation
    3) GPA
    4) ACT
    5) Essay
Program description:
  Scholarship Program: Awards $1,000-$3,000 to children of DaVita, Inc. for private junior high school, private high school, or undergraduate tuition. Applicants must currently be attending grades 5-11 and be the natural child, stepchild or adopted child of a full-time DaVita employee or a part-time benefit eligible DaVita employee.
EIN: 912151390

2295
Kuhner Scholarship Foundation
c/o First Merchants Bank, N.A.
200 E. Jackson St.
Muncie, IN 47305
Contact: Laura Moorman, Trust Off., First Merchants Bank, N.A.

Foundation type: Independent foundation
Limitations: Scholarships to students from Delaware County, IN, who are studying engineering.
Financial data: Year ended 12/31/2004.
Assets, $258,700 (M); Expenditures, $17,663; Total giving, $14,500; Grants to individuals, 15 grants totaling $14,500 (high: $1,000, low: $500).
Fields of interest: Theology; Engineering school/education; Science.
Type of support: Scholarships—to individuals; Support to graduates or students of specific schools; Undergraduate support.
Application information: Applications accepted. Application form required.
  Deadline(s): Mar. 31
  Additional information: Applications available from schools in Delaware County, IN.
EIN: 356017351

2296
Kurzweil Foundation, Inc.
15 Walnut St.
Wellesley Hills, MA 02481

Foundation type: Independent foundation
Limitations: Scholarships to visually impaired students.
Financial data: Year ended 04/30/2005.
Assets, $695 (M); Expenditures, $78,942; Total giving, $45,000; Grants to individuals, 31 grants totaling $45,000 (high: $15,000, low: $1,000).
Fields of interest: Eye diseases; Disabilities, people with.
Type of support: Undergraduate support.
Application information: Applications not accepted.
Program description:
  Scholarship Program: Scholarship recipients also receive scanners for computer usage.
EIN: 042921512

2297
Kuskokwim Educational Foundation, Inc.
4300 B St., Ste. 207
Anchorage, AK 99503 (907) 243-2944
Scholarship application address: P.O. Box 227, Aniak, AK 99557, Tel./FAX: (907) 675-4276

Foundation type: Company-sponsored foundation
Limitations: Scholarships to Native Americans and their descendants who are living in the region serviced by Kuskokwim Corporation, AK, for study at colleges, universities, and vocational schools.
Financial data: Year ended 05/31/2004.
Assets, $9,724 (M); Expenditures, $28,760; Total giving, $25,500; Grants to individuals, 26 grants totaling $25,500 (high: $1,500, low: $500).
Fields of interest: Vocational education; Native Americans/American Indians.

Type of support: Technical education support; Undergraduate support.
Application information: Applications accepted. Application form required.
Initial approach: Letter.
Deadline(s): June 15 for fall semester, Nov. 15 for spring semester
Applicants should submit the following:
1) Transcripts
Additional information: Application must also include letter from applicant, and budget form.
Program description:
Scholarship Awards: Applicants must be Alaskan Native or American Indian. Awards are generally for a one-year period. Scholarships are paid in two installments. The second installment will not be sent to the school until the foundation receives a transcript and letter of intent from the recipient. Recipients are announced on May 3.
EIN: 920081529

2298
L & L Educational Foundation
P.O. Box 308
Romeo, MI 48065
Application address: c/o Patti Lange, 160 McLean Dr., Romeo, MI 48065; tel.: (586) 336-3501; E-mail: patti_lange@llproducts.com

Foundation type: Operating foundation
Limitations: Scholarships to employees, former employees and children of employees of L & L Products, Inc.
Financial data: Year ended 12/31/2004. Assets, $5,309,668 (M); Expenditures, $197,654; Total giving, $166,823; Grants to individuals, 88 grants totaling $166,823 (high: $4,576, low: $28).
Type of support: Employee-related scholarships.
Application information: Applications accepted. Application form required.
Deadline(s): Apr. 1
Applicants should submit the following:
1) Transcripts
Program description:
Scholarship Program: Eligible employees must have at least one year of employment seniority by the application deadline. Former employees must have left the company due to death, disability, or retirement. Scholarships are renewable for up to four years.
EIN: 382785121

2299
La Crosse Community Foundation
(formerly La Crosse Foundation)
300 2nd St. N., Ste. 320
La Crosse, WI 54601
Contact: Sheila Garrity, Exec. Dir.
E-mail: lacrosscommfound@centurytel.net;
URL: http://www.laxcommfoundation.com

Foundation type: Community foundation
Limitations: Scholarships limited to residents of La Crosse County, WI, for higher education.
Publications: Annual report (including application guidelines).
Financial data: Year ended 12/31/2005. Assets, $23,827,733 (M); Expenditures, $1,216,456; Total giving, $859,555.
Fields of interest: Journalism/publishing; Music; Performing arts, education; Theological school/education; Environmental education; Chemistry; Mathematics.

Type of support: Support to graduates or students of specific schools; Undergraduate support.
Application information: Application form required.
Deadline(s): Feb. 15
Additional information: Applications available through the high school guidance office.
Program descriptions:
The Ella F. Ambrosius Fund: Provides music awards and scholarships.
The Mary Jane Bice Fund: Provides the Mary Lousia and Frederick T. Whitbeck Scholarship and the Alfred W. Rice Scholarship to area public high school students to study journalism or environmental studies.
The Nellie L. Case Fund: Provides scholarships for the education of needy students who desire to study chemistry at higher than the high school level. The awards are made directly to the educational institutions.
The Josephine Hintgen Fund: Provides scholarships to La Crosse Public High School students.
The Louis I. Rehfuss Fund: Provides scholarships to La Crosse area students, particularly advanced math students.
The Burton C. Smith Fund: Provides scholarships to La Crosse Logan High School students who attend the University of Wisconsin—Stout, in Menomonie.
The Jason David Koppelman Scholarship Fund: Provides scholarships to students interested in writing and film studies.
The Father Chris Pratt Memorial Fund: Provides financial aid to students interested in the ministry. Representatives from the La Crosse Catholic Diocese and Christ Episcopal Church recommend recipients.
The Harold E. Lemke Fund: Provides financial aid to students of Onalaska High School.
The Ernest and Olive Gershon Fund: Provides scholarships to nontraditional students.
EIN: 396037996

2300
Ladies Charitable Society of Keene
P.O. Box 271
Keene, NH 03431
Contact: Ruth Joslin, Treas.

Foundation type: Independent foundation
Limitations: Scholarships to students of Keene public schools and residents of Keene, NH, to attend institutions within the NH University system, or NH vocational-technical colleges.
Financial data: Year ended 12/31/2004. Assets, $731,455 (M); Expenditures, $26,691; Total giving, $26,502; Grants to individuals, 9 grants totaling $21,975 (high: $2,000, low: $1,000).
Fields of interest: Vocational education.
Type of support: Technical education support; Undergraduate support.
Application information: Application form required.
Initial approach: Letter.
Deadline(s): May 1
EIN: 026007047

2301
Ladies Education Society
c/o Millicent R. Deal
1146 W. College Ave.
Jacksonville, IL 62650-2213
Contact: Helen P. Hinde, Secy.
Application address: 13 Pitner Pl., Jacksonville, IL 62650

Foundation type: Independent foundation
Limitations: Scholarships to financially needy female students for higher education.
Financial data: Year ended 12/31/2004. Assets, $483,748 (M); Expenditures, $27,590; Total giving, $22,600; Grants to individuals, 19 grants totaling $22,600 (high: $1,800, low: $500).
Fields of interest: Women.
Type of support: Scholarships—to individuals.
Application information: Applications accepted. Application form required.
Deadline(s): Apr. 15
Applicants should submit the following:
1) Financial information
2) Letter(s) of recommendation
3) GPA
Additional information: Application must also include evidence of need; contact organization for application guidelines.
EIN: 376027579

2302
Greater Lafayette Community Foundation
1114 State St.
P.O. Box 225
Lafayette, IN 47902-0225 (765) 742-9078
Contact: Cheryl Ubelhor, Prog. Dir.; James E. Klusman, C.E.O.
FAX: (765) 742-2428; E-mail: info@glcfonline.org; Additional E-mails: cheryl@glcfonline.org, jklusman@glcfonline.org, and angela@glcfonline.org; URL: http://www.glcfonline.org

Foundation type: Community foundation
Limitations: Scholarships to high school seniors at Tippecanoe County high schools for higher education at IN colleges and universities.
Publications: Application guidelines; Annual report; Informational brochure; Newsletter.
Financial data: Year ended 12/31/2004. Assets, $21,881,259 (M); Expenditures, $1,290,742; Total giving, $515,691; Grants to individuals, 20 grants totaling $72,300 (high: $2,500, low: $500).
Type of support: Undergraduate support.
Application information: Application form required.
Initial approach: Telephone.
Deadline(s): Contact foundation for current application deadline
Additional information: Interviews required.
Program description:
Scholarship Awards: The foundation offers two scholarship programs:
· Tippecanoe County Lilly Endowment Scholarship Awards
· White County Lilly Endowment Community Scholarship Awards
Recipients must maintain a GPA of at least 2.75 and have a combined SAT score of 800 or better. Scholarships are for full tuition and fees for four years at a public or private IN college or university, and include a $800 annual stipend for required books and equipment.
EIN: 237147996

2303
William T. Laflin Scholarship Fund, Inc.
c/o Trustees
3226 Arthur Rd.
Remus, MI 49340-9541

Foundation type: Independent foundation
Limitations: Scholarships to graduates of Chippewa Hills School District, MI.

Financial data: Year ended 12/31/2004. Assets, $88,797 (M); Expenditures, $4,541; Total giving, $4,050; Grants to individuals, 8 grants totaling $4,050 (high: $500; low: $500).
Type of support: Scholarships—to individuals.
Application information: Applications accepted. Application form required.
Additional information: Application must also include proof of college acceptance.
EIN: 381579001

2304

H. Carl & William Lage Loan & Scholarship Trust Fund

2309B Chatburn Ave.
Harlan, IA 51537
Application address: c/o Robert J. Broomfield, Superintendent, Harlan Community Schools, 2102 Durant St., Harlan, IA 51537, tel.: (712) 755-2152

Foundation type: Operating foundation
Limitations: Student loans to financially needy graduates of Harlan Community High School, IA, who are in the top half of their classes and will be full-time students at four-year colleges and universities.
Financial data: Year ended 10/31/2002. Assets, $857,066 (M); Expenditures, $39,915; Total giving, $32,553; Loans to individuals, 43 loans totaling $32,553.
Type of support: Support to graduates or students of specific schools; Undergraduate support.
Application information: Applicants must contact the student counselor to document a request for application; Financial need must be verified by filing FAF and FFS forms with the corresponding services.
Program description:
Student Loan Program: Recipients are required to provide copies of their grades at the end of the first and second semesters of freshman year. Recipients must show substantial progress towards completion of their degrees.
EIN: 420369519

2305

LaGrange County Community Foundation, Inc.

109 E. Central Ave., Ste. 3
LaGrange, IN 46761 (260) 463-4363
Contact: Laura Lemings, Exec. Dir.
FAX: (260) 463-4856; E-mail: lccf@lccf.net; Additional E-mail: llemings@lccf.net; URL: http://www.lccf.net

Foundation type: Community foundation
Limitations: Scholarships to individuals from the Lagrange County, IN, area for undergraduate education at American colleges and universities.
Publications: Application guidelines; Annual report; Financial statement; Grants list; Informational brochure (including application guidelines); Newsletter; Occasional report.
Financial data: Year ended 12/31/2004. Assets, $9,381,024 (M); Expenditures, $594,722; Total giving, $222,419.
Fields of interest: Nursing school/education; Teacher school/education; Health sciences school/education; Journalism school/education; Agriculture/food, formal/general education; Athletics/sports, basketball.
Type of support: Scholarships—to individuals; Support to graduates or students of specific schools; Technical education support; Precollege support; Undergraduate support.

Application information: Applications accepted. Application form required.
Initial approach: Visit to school's guidance department.
Copies of proposal: 2
Deadline(s): Varies
Applicants should submit the following:
1) Transcripts
2) SAT
3) Letter(s) of recommendation
4) GPA
5) Financial information
6) FAFSA
7) Essay
8) ACT
Additional information: Contact foundation for current application guidelines. See Web site for complete program listing.
EIN: 351834679

2306

The Helen Laidlaw Foundation

314 Newman St.
East Tawas, MI 48730 (989) 362-5911
Contact: Nancy E. Huck, Pres.
FAX: (989) 362-7675

Foundation type: Independent foundation
Limitations: Scholarships to MI residents for the study of health care. Preference is shown to residents of northeastern MI.
Financial data: Year ended 12/31/2004. Assets, $558,793 (M); Expenditures, $35,974; Total giving, $28,500; Grants to individuals, 31 grants totaling $28,500 (high: $1,000; low: $500).
Fields of interest: Health care.
Type of support: Scholarships—to individuals.
Application information: Applications accepted. Application form required.
Deadline(s): Mar. 1
Applicants should submit the following:
1) FAF
2) Transcripts
3) Resume
4) GPA
5) Financial information
EIN: 382901107

2307

H. F. and B. M. Laird Memorial Education Foundation

(formerly Herbert Frank and Bertha Maude Laird Oakland Scottish Rite Memorial Educational Foundation)
1547 Lakeside Dr.
Oakland, CA 94612

Foundation type: Independent foundation
Limitations: Scholarships by nomination only to public high school students in northern and central CA. Preference is given to electrical engineering majors.
Financial data: Year ended 12/31/2004. Assets, $1,508,615 (M); Expenditures, $65,880; Total giving, $60,000; Grants to individuals, 16 grants totaling $60,000 (high: $5,000; low: $2,500).
Application information:
Deadline(s): Jan.
Additional information: Individual applications not accepted; Selection is based on responses of area public school superintendents to the foundation's questionnaire; Interviews required.
EIN: 237047350

2308

Lake Erie Marine Trades Association Educational Foundation, Inc.

1269 Bassett Rd.
Westlake, OH 44145-1116 (440) 899-5009

Foundation type: Independent foundation
Limitations: Grants to residents of OH for educational purposes in the field of recreational boating.
Financial data: Year ended 04/30/2005. Assets, $8,263 (M); Expenditures, $9,000; Total giving, $9,000; Grants to individuals, 15 grants totaling $9,000 (high: $1,000; low: $300).
Fields of interest: Education; Recreation.
Type of support: Grants to individuals.
Application information: Application form required.
Initial approach: Letter.
Additional information: Contact foundation for current application deadline.
EIN: 341835791

2309

Lake Travis Education Foundation

P.O. Box 340759
Austin, TX 78734 (512) 533-6095
Contact: Paula Baczewski, Admin. Dir.
FAX: (512) 261-5819;
E-mail: email@laketraviseducationfoundation.org;
URL: http://www.laketraviseducationfoundation.org

Foundation type: Public charity
Limitations: Scholarships to graduating seniors of Lake Travis Independent School District high schools. Some support also to K-12 students for medical assistance.
Publications: Grants list.
Financial data: Year ended 05/31/2004. Assets, $635,190 (M); Expenditures, $314,119; Total giving, $263,843; Grants to individuals, totaling $34,015.
Type of support: Support to graduates or students of specific schools; Precollege support; Grants for special needs.
Application information: Applications accepted. Application form required.
Initial approach: Telephone or e-mail.
Applicants should submit the following:
1) Letter(s) of recommendation
Additional information: Contact foundation for current application deadline; Application must also include proof of enrollment or acceptance at college or vocational school; Interviews required.
EIN: 742406134

2310

Lake-Matthews Educational Fund, Inc.

P.O. Box 307
Shenandoah, IA 51601
Contact: John Davis, V.P.
Application address: c/o Shenandoah Community School District, 1000 Mustang Dr., Shenandoah, IA 51601

Foundation type: Independent foundation
Limitations: Scholarships to students of the Shenandoah Community School District, IA, for higher education.
Financial data: Year ended 12/31/2004. Assets, $381,777 (M); Expenditures, $19,505; Total giving, $18,500; Grants to individuals, 18 grants totaling $18,500 (high: $1,500; low: $1,000).

Type of support: Support to graduates or students of specific schools; Undergraduate support.
Application information: Applications accepted. Application form required.
Deadline(s): Jan. 31
EIN: 421491841

2311

The Lakeland Group Foundation, Inc.
5735 Lindsay St.
Minneapolis, MN 55422

Foundation type: Company-sponsored foundation
Limitations: Scholarships to employees of Lakeland Engineering Equipment Co., Inc., primarily in MN.
Financial data: Year ended 01/31/2005. Assets, $229,097 (M); Expenditures, $14,502; Total giving, $14,000; Grants to individuals, 9 grants totaling $9,000 (high: $1,000, low: $1,000).
Fields of interest: Engineering school/education.
Type of support: Employee-related scholarships.
Application information: Contact foundation for current application deadline/guidelines.
EIN: 411738234

2312

Lakeland Health Foundation, Niles
(formerly Pawating Health Foundation)
31 N. St. Joseph Ave.
Niles, MI 49120-9910
Contact: Chickie Landgraf, Chair.

Foundation type: Public charity
Limitations: Scholarships to employees of Lakeland Niles Associates, MI, for education and skills training.
Financial data: Year ended 09/30/2004. Assets, $1,366,700 (M); Expenditures, $212,951; Total giving, $201,968; Grants to individuals, totaling $18,660.
Fields of interest: Health sciences school/education.
Type of support: Employee-related scholarships.
Application information: Contact foundation for current application deadline/guidelines.
EIN: 383130558

2313

Lakeland High School Scholarship Fund, Inc.
c/o Lakeland High School Scholarship Committee
P.O. Box 1129
Minocqua, WI 54548-1129
Contact: R.J. O'Leary

Foundation type: Operating foundation
Limitations: Scholarships to Lakeland High School, WI, graduates.
Publications: Application guidelines.
Financial data: Year ended 12/31/2004. Assets, $2,400,875 (M); Expenditures, $159,217; Total giving, $122,875; Grants to individuals, 25 grants totaling $115,125 (high: $5,875, low: $250).
Type of support: Support to graduates or students of specific schools; Undergraduate support.
Application information: Application form required.
Copies of proposal: 1
Deadline(s): Feb. 21
EIN: 391259200

2314

Lakewood Medical Center Foundation
(formerly Doctors Hospital of Lakewood Foundation)
c/o Lakewood Regional Medical Ctr.
3700 E. South St.
Lakewood, CA 90712
Contact: Larry A. Pasquali M.D., C.E.O.
Application address: Attn. Scholarship Coord., P.O. Box 6070, Lakewood, CA 90712, tel.: (562) 633-1150

Foundation type: Independent foundation
Limitations: Scholarships to students currently enrolled in accredited schools of medicine, nursing, and pharmacy who have a permanent address within a five-mile radius of Lakewood Regional Medical Center, in Lakewood, CA.
Financial data: Year ended 09/30/2004. Assets, $0 (M); Expenditures, $25,965; Total giving, $22,500; Grants to individuals, 7 grants totaling $22,500 (high: $6,000, low: $1,500).
Fields of interest: Medical school/education; Nursing school/education; Pharmacy/prescriptions.
Type of support: Graduate support; Undergraduate support.
Application information: Application form required.
Initial approach: Telephone.
Deadline(s): Apr. 15
Program description:
Scholarship Program: Scholarships are limited to residents of record of the following CA cities: Artesia, Bellflower, Cerritos, Compton, Cypress, Downey, Hawaiian Gardens, Lakewood, Long Beach, Norwalk, Paramount, and Signal Hill. Scholarships awarded based on academic achievement, financial circumstances, extracurricular activities and general merit.
EIN: 510154413

2315

The Lallinger Family Charitable Foundation
2121 Kirby Dr., Ste. 52
Houston, TX 77019-6065 (713) 961-2637

Foundation type: Independent foundation
Limitations: Scholarships to Catholic elementary school students, primarily in TX.
Financial data: Year ended 12/31/2003. Assets, $2,448,551 (M); Expenditures, $303,458; Total giving, $278,100.
Type of support: Precollege support.
Application information: Applications not accepted.
EIN: 760574234

2316

Lambda Chi Alpha Educational Foundation, Inc.
8741 Founders Rd.
Indianapolis, IN 46268 (317) 872-8000
Contact: Ronald A. Neville, Pres.
FAX: (317) 875-3828;
E-mail: cmolloy@lambdachi.org; FAX: (317) 875-3828; E-mail: cmolloy@lambdachi.org; URL: http://www.lambdachi.org/foundation

Foundation type: Public charity
Limitations: Educational scholarships to members of the fraternity.
Financial data: Year ended 06/30/2003. Assets, $3,538,646 (M); Expenditures, $1,491,255; Total giving, $640,350; Grants to individuals, totaling $139,000.

Fields of interest: Fraternal societies.
Type of support: Graduate support; Undergraduate support.
Application information: Applications accepted. Application form required.
Initial approach: Telephone or e-mail.
Deadline(s): Apr. 2
Program descriptions:
Graduate Fellowships: Awards $50,000 to twenty brothers who are in need of funds for graduate studies. Eligible applicants must have a 3.4 cumulative GPA, demonstrate chapter and/or campus participation, community service, and financial need.
Undergraduate Scholarships: Awards $50,000 to eighteen brothers who are in need of funds for undergraduate studies. Eligible applicants must have a 3.0 cumulative GPA, demonstrate chapter participation, community service, and financial need.
EIN: 136266432

2317

Lampstand Foundation
(formerly Agnes Klingensmith Charitable Foundation)
18160 Cottonwood Rd., No. 244
Sunriver, OR 97707
Contact: David "Tim" Winn, Tr.
E-mail: dtimwinn@xc.org

Foundation type: Independent foundation
Limitations: Scholarships and internships to individuals.
Publications: Application guidelines.
Financial data: Year ended 12/31/2004. Assets, $3,831,993 (M); Expenditures, $149,685; Total giving, $80,121.
Type of support: Internship funds; Scholarships—to individuals.
Application information: Applications by letter accepted throughout the year.
EIN: 911503479

2318

The Lancaster County Community Foundation
(formerly The Lancaster County Foundation)
P.O. Box 1745
Lancaster, PA 17608-1745 (717) 397-1629
Contact: Deborah B. Schattgen, C.E.O.; For grants: Doug Levering, Dir., Progs. and Initiatives
Scholarship e-mail:
scholarships@lancastercountyfoundation.org
FAX: (717) 397-6877;
E-mail: info@lancastercountyfoundation.org;
Additional E-mail:
debbie@lancastercountyfoundation.org; Grant application E-mail:
doug@lancastercountyfoundation.org; URL: http://www.lancastercountyfoundation.org

Foundation type: Community foundation
Limitations: Limited number of scholarships for residents of Lancaster County, PA, for the pursuit of a college education or for technical training beyond high school.
Publications: Application guidelines; Annual report; Newsletter.
Financial data: Year ended 04/30/2004. Assets, $47,099,405 (M); Expenditures, $1,293,750; Total giving, $993,801; Grants to individuals, totaling $25,000.
Type of support: Scholarships—to individuals.

Application information: Application form not required. Application form available on the grantmaker's Web site.
Initial approach: E-mail.
Copies of proposal: 2
Deadline(s): Jan.
Applicants should submit the following:
1) Budget Information
2) Transcripts
3) SAT
4) FAFSA
5) Financial information
EIN: 200874857

2319
Lela M. Lancaster Trust
c/o Normandin, Cheney & O'Neil
P.O. Box 575
Laconia, NH   03247
Application address: c/o Lakes Region Scholarship Foundation, Homebank, P.O. Box 100, Laconia, NH 03247

Foundation type: Independent foundation
Limitations: Scholarships to students from Laconia, Gilford, Gilmanton, and Sanbornton, NH.
Financial data: Year ended 05/31/2005.
Assets, $181,473 (M); Expenditures, $8,583; Total giving, $6,800.
Type of support: Scholarships—to individuals; Undergraduate support.
Application information: Applications accepted.
Deadline(s): None
Program description:
Scholarship Program: Some preference is shown to applicants from Gilford, NH, the town where Lela M. Lancaster resided.
EIN: 026036769

2320
Landscape Architecture Foundation
636 Eye St., N.W.
Washington, DC   20001-3736   (202) 898-2444
Contact: Melinda Sippel, Exec. Asst.
FAX: (202) 898-1185; E-mail: rfiguera@alsa.org;
URL: http://www.asla.org

Foundation type: Public charity
Limitations: Scholarships to students interested in landscape architecture-related fields, and to undergraduate and graduate students enrolled in landscape architecture programs at Arizona State University and several southern CA schools.
Financial data: Year ended 09/30/2003.
Assets, $3,167,123 (M); Expenditures, $451,187; Total giving, $32,000; Grant to an individual, 1 grant totaling $2,000.
Fields of interest: Architecture; Landscaping; Minorities.
Type of support: Support to graduates or students of specific schools; Graduate support; Undergraduate support.
Application information: Applications accepted.
Initial approach: Telephone or e-mail.
Deadline(s): Mar. 31
Additional information: Application by letter, including name of award applying for, contact information, academic summary of two pages or less, detailed financial information, copy of FAF, information on extracurricular activities, community involvement, and professional experiences; Consult Web site for more specific application guidelines.
Program descriptions:
Rain Bird Scholarship: Awarded to an outstanding student in need of financial assistance.

Hawaii Chapter/David T. Woolsey Scholarship: Awarded to an undergraduate or graduate student who is a permanent resident of Hawaii.
Edith H. Henderson Scholarship: Awarded to a landscape architecture student committed to the goal of developing practical communication skills in his/her role as a landscape architect.
William J. Locklin Scholarship: Awarded to a student with particular interest in lighting design.
Raymond E. Page Scholarship: Awarded to a student in need of financial aid.
Edward D.Stone Jr. and Associates Minority Scholarship: Awarded to African American, Latino, and minority students of other cultural and ethnic backgrounds entering their final two years of undergraduate study.
Harriett Barnhart Wimmer Scholarship: Awarded to a woman with exemplary design skills.
LAF/CLASS Fund Scholarships and Internships: Awarded to students enrolled in landscape architecture or ornamental horticulture programs at several southern California schools (University of California - Davis, Berkeley, and Los Angeles, and California Polytechnic State University - San Luis Obispo and Pomona)
Thomas P. Papandrew Scholarship: Awarded to meritorious minority students interested in pursuing a career in landscape architecture at Arizona State University.
EIN: 526065505

2321
Winthrop and Frances Lane Foundation
c/o U.S. Bank, N.A.
P.O. Box 64713
St. Paul, MN   55164-0713
Application address: U.S. Bank, N.A., 17th and Farnham Sts., Omaha, NE 68102, tel: (402) 963-2156

Foundation type: Independent foundation
Limitations: Scholarships to students at Creighton University School of Law, NE, and University of Nebraska College of Law.
Financial data: Year ended 12/31/2004.
Assets, $3,645,057 (M); Expenditures, $198,224; Total giving, $160,000; Grants to individuals, 17 grants totaling $120,000 (high: $18,000, low: $3,600).
Fields of interest: Law school/education.
Type of support: Support to graduates or students of specific schools; Graduate support.
Application information: Applications accepted throughout the year by the offices of the deans of the two law schools; Completion of formal application required, including class rank, GPA, LSAT scores, and financial information.
EIN: 470581778

2322
Ruth E. Patterson Lang Benevolent Trust
c/o La Salle Bank, N.A.
105 Marquette St.
P.O. Box 461
La Salle, IL   61301-2412
Application address: c/o Guidance Dir., Princeton High School, Princeton, IL 61356, tel.: (815) 875-3308

Foundation type: Independent foundation
Limitations: Scholarships to students who reside in Princeton and Berlin Townships of Bureau County, IL.
Financial data: Year ended 05/31/2005.
Assets, $654,362 (M); Expenditures, $22,256;

Total giving, $15,200; Grants to individuals, 19 grants totaling $15,200 (high: $1,100, low: $250).
Type of support: Scholarships—to individuals.
Application information: Application form required.
Deadline(s): June 9
EIN: 366818806

2323
The Fritz Lang Foundation
c/o Hibernia National Bank
1807 Lake St.
Lake Charles, LA   70601-5771   (337) 436-1600
Contact: Wanda N. Borel

Foundation type: Independent foundation
Limitations: Scholarships to graduating students from Vermilion and Jefferson Davis parishes, LA, who are pursuing undergraduate and graduate degrees in agriculture and related fields.
Publications: Application guidelines.
Financial data: Year ended 06/30/2004.
Assets, $1,935,150 (M); Expenditures, $274,042; Total giving, $244,800; Grants to individuals, 113 grants totaling $244,800 (high: $3,600, low: $1,200).
Fields of interest: Agriculture.
Type of support: Support to graduates or students of specific schools; Graduate support; Undergraduate support.
Application information: Application form required.
Deadline(s): Aug. 31 and Apr. 1
Applicants should submit the following:
1) Transcripts
2) Letter(s) of recommendation
Additional information: Application must also include a copy of parents' or personal tax return.
Program description:
Scholarship Program: Late applications may be considered and placed on a waiting list for unclaimed funds. Selection will be based on academic achievement and financial need. Students must have and maintain a 2.5 GPA or better.
EIN: 581854369

2324
Edith A. Langdale Scholarship Fund
c/o National City Bank
P.O. Box 94651
Cleveland, OH   44101-4651
Application address: c/o Guidance Office, Warren Area High School, 345 E. 5th Ave., Warren, PA 16365, tel.: (814) 723-5300

Foundation type: Independent foundation
Limitations: Scholarships only to graduates of Warren, PA, area high schools.
Financial data: Year ended 08/31/2003.
Assets, $228,440 (M); Expenditures, $11,215; Total giving, $8,400; Grants to individuals, totaling $8,400.
Type of support: Support to graduates or students of specific schools; Undergraduate support.
Application information: Applications accepted. Application form required.
Deadline(s): June 1
EIN: 256164317

2325
Bonnie Langston Memorial Scholarship Trust

P.O. Box 327
Montrose, CO 81402-0327 (970) 249-4531
Contact: Victor T. Roushar, Tr.

Foundation type: Operating foundation
Limitations: Scholarships to graduates of Montrose High School, CO, who are in the top twenty-five percent of their graduating class.
Financial data: Year ended 12/31/2003. Assets, $322,473 (M); Expenditures, $27,934; Total giving, $12,000; Grants to individuals, 2 grants totaling $12,000 (high: $6,000, low: $6,000).
Type of support: Support to graduates or students of specific schools; Undergraduate support.
Application information: Deadline prior to end of school year; Completion of formal application required.
EIN: 846268159

2326
Lanham Foundation

c/o Bank of America, N.A.
P.O. Box 34345, FAB-22
Seattle, WA 98124-1345
Application address: c/o Jay A. Johnson, 617 Washington St., P.O. Box 2136, Wenatchee, WA 98807

Foundation type: Independent foundation
Limitations: Scholarships to financially needy residents of Chelan County, WA, for study at junior colleges, community colleges, technical schools, and universities.
Financial data: Year ended 12/31/2004. Assets, $735,375 (M); Expenditures, $137,695; Total giving, $119,794; Grants to individuals, 63 grants totaling $119,794 (high: $2,500, low: $334).
Fields of interest: Vocational education.
Type of support: Technical education support; Undergraduate support.
Application information: Applications accepted. Application form required.
Deadline(s): Apr. 15
Applicants should submit the following:
1) Transcripts
2) Financial information
Additional information: Application must also include a statement on academic performance and progress towards graduation.
Program description:
Scholarship Program: Recipients must be full-time students and maintain at least a 2.5 GPA.
EIN: 916020593

2327
Lansing Art Gallery

113 S. Washington Sq.
Lansing, MI 48933 (517) 374-6400
Contact: Catherine A. Babcock, Exec. Dir.
E-mail: lansingartgallery@yahoo.com; URL: http://www.lansingartgallery.org

Foundation type: Public charity
Limitations: Scholarships to Lansing, MI, students in grades 9-12 who win the juried art competition.
Financial data: Year ended 06/30/2005. Assets, $73,984 (M); Expenditures, $223,281.
Fields of interest: Visual arts.
Type of support: Awards/prizes; Undergraduate support.

Application information: Contact foundation for current application deadline/guidelines.
Program description:
Sara Jane Venable Scholarship Award: To qualify for this $1,000 award the student must demonstrate an exceptional record of achievement and involvement in the visual arts and prove a commitment to advanced study, write an essay for review, and present a portfolio of artwork including slides. A special panel of jurors selects one senior each year to receive this prestigious award.
EIN: 381889973

2328
Lapan Sunshine Foundation, Inc.

(formerly Lapan Educational Loan Foundation, Inc.)
2121 Plaza de la Candela
Las Vegas, NV 89102-4041
Contact: Joseph Lapan, Board Member

Foundation type: Independent foundation
Limitations: Scholarships and loans to financially needy individuals residing in CA for higher education.
Financial data: Year ended 12/31/2004. Assets, $962,941 (M); Expenditures, $136,502; Total giving, $131,420; Grants to individuals, 19 grants totaling $77,800 (high: $25,900, low: $750).
Type of support: Scholarships—to individuals; Student loans—to individuals.
Application information:
Initial approach: Letter.
Deadline(s): May 1.
Applicants should submit the following:
1) Financial information
2) Transcripts
3) Resume
EIN: 880192311

2329
Hypoliet Lapeer Testamentary Trust

c/o National City Bank
1900 E. 9th St.
Cleveland, OH 44114 (800) 628-8151
Contact: Joseph Brettnacher, Mgr.
Application address: c/o Marian High School, 1311 S. Logan St, Mishawaka, IN 46544

Foundation type: Independent foundation
Limitations: Scholarships to Roman Catholic graduates of Marian High School, Mishawaka, IN, and St. Joseph High School, South Bend, IN, who have either Belgian or French ancestry and who plan to study engineering at Notre Dame University or Purdue University.
Financial data: Year ended 12/31/2004. Assets, $412,632 (M); Expenditures, $25,070; Total giving, $18,750; Grants to individuals, 3 grants totaling $18,750 (high: $7,500, low: $3,730).
Fields of interest: Engineering school/education; Roman Catholic agencies & churches; Belgium; France.
Type of support: Support to graduates or students of specific schools; Undergraduate support.
Application information: Application form required.
Initial approach: Letter.
Deadline(s): May 1
Additional information: Forms available from principal at application address.
EIN: 356508488

2330
Ted Larew Scholarship Fund of the New Jersey Steel Association, Inc.

c/o New Jersey Steel Assn., Inc.
11 Cleveland Pl.
Springfield, NJ 07081-1594 (973) 467-1625
Contact: Advisory Comm.
FAX: (201) 467-5562

Foundation type: Independent foundation
Limitations: Scholarships to employees or children of employees of member companies of the New Jersey Steel Association, Inc. Preference is given to those who are pursuing any degree or certificate that will lead directly to a vocation associated with the construction industry, such as architecture or engineering.
Financial data: Year ended 12/31/2002. Assets, $15,500 (M); Expenditures, $33,575; Total giving, $33,552; Grants to individuals, 19 grants totaling $33,552 (high: $2,000, low: $925).
Fields of interest: Architecture; Vocational education; Labor unions/organizations; Business/industry; Engineering.
Type of support: Employee-related scholarships.
Application information:
Initial approach: Letter.
Deadline(s): June 30
Additional information: Completion of formal application required, including name of union local (if any), list of institutions with tuition fees to which applicant has applied, including indication if accepted, indication of which institution applicant expects to attend, statement of any other scholarships which applicant may expect to receive, high school transcripts, results of college board examinations, and statement of intended field of study.
Program description:
Scholarship: The following individuals are eligible for scholarships:
· Children of members of Shopmen's Local 545 whose parent is employed by a firm operating under a labor agreement with Local 545.
· Children of ironworkers referred to work by the District Council of Ironworkers of Northern NJ (Local Unions 11, 45, 373, 480, and 483) as employees of a firm signatory to a labor agreement with these Locals and the Association.
· Children of operating engineers (Local Union 825) referred to work as employees of a firm signatory to a labor agreement with this Local and the Association.
· Children of members of Teamsters Local 408 whose parent is employed by a member firm of the New Jersey Steel Association, Inc., or is a contributor to the steel industry Advancement Fund.
· Any ironworker, operating engineer, or Teamster of the above-mentioned unions who are employed or have been employed by a member firm of the New Jersey Steel Association, Inc., or are contributors to the steel industry Advancement Fund.
· Employees as well as children of all other employees of member firms of the New Jersey Steel Association, Inc., except executives and directors of member firms and their children.
Scholarships awarded amount to 25 percent of the first year's tuition charges, not to exceed $2,000. Scholarships are renewable up to the completion of the course of study providing the recipient remains

in good academic standing. Applications for renewal are due June 30 with grades attached.
EIN: 226090565

2331
Gay R. Larsen Charitable Education Trust
P.O. Box 107
Wheeling, WV   26003
Contact: Douglas McKay, Tr.

Foundation type: Independent foundation
Limitations: Scholarships to high school graduates residing in the northern Panhandle counties of WV and OH.
Financial data: Year ended 12/31/2004. Assets, $1,668,435 (M); Expenditures, $86,523; Total giving, $69,550; Grants to individuals, 44 grants totaling $69,550 (high: $3,400, low: $1,000).
Type of support: Technical education support; Undergraduate support.
Application information: Applications accepted. Application form required.
  Initial approach: Telephone.
  Deadline(s): Feb. 1 for new applicants, and June 1 for renewals
  Applicants should submit the following:
    1) Essay
    2) SAT
    3) ACT
  Additional information: Application must also include extracurricular activities.
Program description:
  Scholarship Program: Scholarship funds are provided during the full term of normal progression toward graduation in an institution of higher learning. Scholarships are renewable if the recipient is enrolled in an accredited postsecondary nonprofit college or vocational or technical school, and is enrolled full-time.
EIN: 556128918

2332
Michael Lascaris Scholarship Trust
c/o McDermott, Will & Emery
227 W. Monroe St.
Chicago, IL   60606-5096

Foundation type: Independent foundation
Limitations: Scholarships to students in Greece.
Financial data: Year ended 12/31/2004. Assets, $7,148,338 (M); Expenditures, $541,191; Total giving, $255,000; Grants to individuals, 236 grants totaling $255,000 (high: $1,500, low: $750).
Type of support: Foreign applicants; Undergraduate support.
Application information: Applications not accepted.
EIN: 367144785

2333
Bill Latimer Family Foundation Trust
201 W. Main St., Ste. E
Union City, TN   38281
Contact: William H. Latimer III, Pres.

Foundation type: Independent foundation
Limitations: Student loans to individuals for undergraduate education.
Financial data: Year ended 12/31/2004. Assets, $18,913,514 (M); Expenditures, $323,048; Total giving, $310,030; Loans to individuals, 7 loans totaling $23,500.

Type of support: Student loans—to individuals.
Application information: Contact foundation for current application deadline/guidelines.
EIN: 621680941

2334
Lucile Latta Charitable Trust
c/o Security National Bank Trust Dept.
P.O. Box 147
Sioux City, IA   51102-0147

Foundation type: Independent foundation
Limitations: Scholarships to high school graduates who are residents of Harrison County, IA.
Financial data: Year ended 12/31/2004. Assets, $3,521,397 (M); Expenditures, $210,661; Total giving, $183,150.
Type of support: Scholarships—to individuals.
Application information: Applications not accepted.
EIN: 426554228

2335
Laub Foundation
2810 W. Charleston Blvd., Ste. 53
Las Vegas, NV   89102-1905

Foundation type: Independent foundation
Limitations: Scholarships to children of employees of Southwest Gas Corporation to attend an accredited college, university, or trade school. Applicants must be no older than 23 as of July 1, with exception to those who have served in the U.S. military, Peace Corps, or other such activity. Employees must have worked full-time for the company for at least one year.
Financial data: Year ended 12/31/2004. Assets, $653,305 (M); Expenditures, $33,245; Total giving, $30,200; Grants to individuals, 20 grants totaling $30,000 (high: $1,500, low: $1,500).
Fields of interest: Vocational education.
Type of support: Employee-related scholarships.
Application information: Applications accepted. Application form required.
  Deadline(s): July 1
  Additional information: Application forms are available in all district offices of Southwest Gas Corporation from human resources representatives. Interviews may be required.
Program description:
  Harold G. Laub Scholarships: Children of officers are ineligible. Selection criteria are academic performance, extracurricular activities, community service, performance on aptitude tests, recommendations, and the applicant's written personal statement. Scholarships are renewable for up to three years. Freshman recipients must maintain a GPA of at least 2.5, all others must maintain at least a 3.0 GPA.
EIN: 886006974

2336
Stephanie E. Laucius Educational and Charitable Foundation
521 Chilton St.
Elizabeth, NJ   07208-1609   (908) 353-6959
Contact: Stephanie E. Laucius, Tr.

Foundation type: Independent foundation
Limitations: Scholarships to graduating high school seniors for undergraduate education. Scholarships are renewable.

Financial data: Year ended 12/31/2004. Assets, $842,110 (M); Expenditures, $32,973; Total giving, $28,750; Grants to individuals, 21 grants totaling $24,750 (high: $2,000, low: $250).
Type of support: Undergraduate support.
Application information: Application form required.
  Initial approach: Letter.
  Deadline(s): July 1.
  Applicants should submit the following:
    1) Transcripts
EIN: 521947741

2337
Harry A. Laudermilch Scholarship Fund
c/o Fulton Financial Advisors, N.A.
P.O. Box 3215
Lancaster, PA   17604-3215
Application address: c/o Lebanon School District, Guidance Dept., 100 S. 8th St., Lebanon, PA 17042

Foundation type: Independent foundation
Limitations: Scholarships to graduates of Lebanon High School, PA.
Financial data: Year ended 09/30/2005. Assets, $484,547 (M); Expenditures, $29,064; Total giving, $24,000; Grants to individuals, 4 grants totaling $24,000 (high: $6,000, low: $6,000).
Type of support: Support to graduates or students of specific schools; Undergraduate support.
Application information: Applications accepted. Application form required.
  Additional information: Applications may be obtained from high school guidance office.
Program description:
  Scholarship Program: Two graduating seniors, one male and one female, are chosen annually to receive a scholarship. Selection criteria (in order of priority) are: academic achievement; civic responsibility; extracurricular involvement; personal attitude; and career goals.
EIN: 231989571

2338
Lauffer Scholarship Fund
(formerly Charles A. Lauffer Trust)
c/o Bank of America, N.A.
P.O. Box 40200, MC FL9-100-10-19
Jacksonville, FL   32203-0200
Application address: c/o Bank of America, N.A., 2 Central Ave., Ste. 300, St. Petersburg, FL 337

Foundation type: Independent foundation
Limitations: Student loans to third- and fourth-year medical students living in the St. Petersburg, FL, area and in the state of PA.
Financial data: Year ended 08/31/2005. Assets, $3,991,606 (M); Expenditures, $191,991; Total giving, $140,068; Loans to individuals, 6 loans totaling $39,000.
Fields of interest: Medical school/education.
Type of support: Graduate support.
Application information: Application form required.
  Initial approach: Letter.
  Deadline(s): June 15
  Applicants should submit the following:
    1) Financial information
    2) Class rank
    3) Letter(s) of recommendation
  Additional information: Application must also include documentation of school attendance and major course of study.
EIN: 596121126

2339
Lauterbach Scholarship Fund Trust
c/o U.S. Bank, N.A.
P.O. Box 2043
Milwaukee, WI 53201-9116
Application address: c/o Cedar Falls High School,
Attn.: Dean H. Dreyer, Principal, 10th & Division
Sts., Cedar Falls, IA 50613, tel.: (319) 277-3100

Foundation type: Independent foundation
Limitations: Scholarships to female graduates of
Cedar Falls High School, IA, for undergraduate
education at an IA four-year institution.
Financial data: Year ended 12/31/2004.
Assets, $272,561 (M); Expenditures, $21,774;
Total giving, $18,750; Grants to individuals,
totaling $18,750.
Fields of interest: Women.
Type of support: Support to graduates or students
of specific schools; Undergraduate support.
Application information: Applications accepted.
Application form required.
Deadline(s): Mar. 31 for applications and Apr. 10
for recommendations
Applicants should submit the following:
1) Letter(s) of recommendation
2) Financial information
3) GPA
4) Essay
EIN: 426470008

2340
Madalynne F. Laux Memorial Trust
c/o JPMorgan Chase Bank, N.A.
P.O. Box 1308
Milwaukee, WI 53201
Application addresses: c/o Glen LaFrombois,
Counselor, Appleton West H.S., 610 N. Badger
Ave., Appleton, WI 54911, tel.: (920) 832-6219;
Appleton East H.S., c/o Gary Ludwig or Maureen
Killian, Counselors, 2121 E. Emmers Dr., Appleton,
WI 54915, tel.: (920) 832-6203

Foundation type: Independent foundation
Limitations: Scholarships to graduating seniors of
Appleton High School East and Appleton High
School West, both in WI, who rank in the top 15
percent of their classes and whose permanent
residence is Appleton, WI.
Financial data: Year ended 05/31/2005.
Assets, $1,385,021 (M); Expenditures, $58,911;
Total giving, $46,000; Grants to individuals, 25
grants totaling $46,000.
Type of support: Support to graduates or students
of specific schools; Undergraduate support.
Application information: Application form required.
Deadline(s): Feb. 15.
Applicants should submit the following:
1) Essay
EIN: 396551972

2341
Paul Lauzier Scholarship Foundation
P.O. Box 1230
Ephrata, WA 98823-1230
Contact: Michael Rex Tabler, Tr.

Foundation type: Independent foundation
Limitations: Scholarships to individuals for higher
education who have attended Grant County, WA,
high schools.
Financial data: Year ended 12/31/2004.
Assets, $2,287,142 (M); Expenditures,
$719,560; Total giving, $401,000; Grants to
individuals, 189 grants totaling $401,000 (high:
$5,000, low: $1,000).

Type of support: Support to graduates or students
of specific schools; Undergraduate support.
Application information: Applications accepted.
Application form required.
Deadline(s): Mar. 1
Additional information: Applications are available
through the Grant County high school the
applicant attends or has graduated from.
EIN: 911701545

2342
**Daisy Harder LaVictoire Memorial
Scholarship**
c/o John Schaefer
7254 Michigan Ave.
Pigeon, MI 48755 (989) 453-2097
Contact: Robert Drury, Tr.

Foundation type: Independent foundation
Limitations: Scholarships to graduating students
attending high school in Elkton, Pigeon, or Bay Port,
MI.
Financial data: Year ended 03/31/2005.
Assets, $234,912 (M); Expenditures, $7,427;
Total giving, $5,069; Grants to individuals, 5 grants
totaling $5,069 (high: $1,267, low: $634).
Type of support: Support to graduates or students
of specific schools; Undergraduate support.
Application information: Applications accepted.
Application form required.
Deadline(s): Mar. 31
EIN: 386629469

2343
Lawler Foundation
P.O. Box 2558
Humble, TX 77347
Contact: Carol M. Lawler, Mgr.

Foundation type: Independent foundation
Limitations: Scholarships by nomination only to
graduating students attending high school in the
Houston, TX, area who will attend a four-year college
in TX and graduate within four years.
Financial data: Year ended 11/30/2004.
Assets, $123,434 (M); Expenditures, $32,153;
Total giving, $27,335; Grants to individuals, 5
grants totaling $22,335 (high: $5,000, low:
$2,500).
Type of support: Awards/grants by nomination only;
Undergraduate support.
Application information: Applications not
accepted.
Program description:
Scholarship Program: High school counselors
from the Houston area select and submit a list of
candidates that have the academic capabilities to
complete college within four years, and financial
hardship that would not make college possible
without assistance from the foundation.
EIN: 760386450

2344
Edna A. Layton Scholarship Fund
c/o First MainStreet Bank, N.A.
P.O. Box 1159
Longmont, CO 80502-1159 (303) 776-5800

Foundation type: Independent foundation
Limitations: Scholarships to graduates of Saint
Vrain district high schools, CO, to pursue a teaching
career.
Financial data: Year ended 03/31/2005.
Assets, $700,611 (M); Expenditures, $40,396;

Total giving, $31,800; Grants to individuals, 16
grants totaling $31,800 (high: $2,200, low: $500).
Fields of interest: Teacher school/education.
Type of support: Support to graduates or students
of specific schools; Undergraduate support.
Application information: Application form required.
Initial approach: Letter requesting application.
Deadline(s): Mar.
Applicants should submit the following:
1) Essay
EIN: 841494001

2345
Le Rosey Foundation
c/o N.B. Zoullas Mgmt.
909 Third Ave., 29th Fl.
New York, NY 10022 (212) 350-5315

Foundation type: Independent foundation
Limitations: Scholarships to individuals by
nomination only.
Financial data: Year ended 12/31/2004.
Assets, $591,149 (M); Expenditures, $59,270;
Total giving, $47,000; Grants to individuals, 3
grants totaling $47,000.
Type of support: Scholarships—to individuals;
Awards/grants by nomination only.
Application information: Unsolicited requests for
funds not considered or acknowledged.
EIN: 311502618

2346
Lea County Electric Education Foundation
P.O. Drawer 1447
Lovington, NM 88260

Foundation type: Company-sponsored foundation
Limitations: Scholarships to members receiving
electric service from Lea County Electric
Cooperative, Inc. and their dependents, who attend
recognized NM and TX institutions.
Publications: Application guidelines.
Financial data: Year ended 12/31/2004.
Assets, $810,768 (M); Expenditures, $57,138;
Total giving, $49,000; Grants to individuals, 61
grants totaling $49,000 (high: $1,750, low: $375).
Type of support: Undergraduate support.
Application information: Applications accepted.
Application form required.
Deadline(s): Feb. 16
Applicants should submit the following:
1) Letter(s) of recommendation
2) Essay
Additional information: Recipients notified within
90 days of deadline.
Program description:
Scholarship Program: Scholarships are $250
each per semester. Recipients may renew their
scholarships for eight semesters, providing they
maintain full-time status and at least a 2.5
cumulative GPA. Recipients must provide a copy of
their grades at the end of each semester to Lea
County Electric, in order to receive the following
semester's scholarship money.
EIN: 850351147

2347
Leach Nursing Scholarship Trust
c/o First Midwest Bank
2801 W. Jefferson St.
Joliet, IL 60435
Application address: c/o University of St. Francis,
St. Joseph College of Nursing, Attn.: Financial Aid

Office, 500 Wilcox St., Joliet, IL 60435, tel.: (815) 740-3360

Foundation type: Independent foundation
Limitations: Scholarships to individuals attending St. Joseph College of Nursing, IL.
Financial data: Year ended 12/31/2004. Assets, $571,415 (M); Expenditures, $40,230; Total giving, $35,365; Grants to individuals, 38 grants totaling $35,365 (high: $2,066, low: $83).
Fields of interest: Vocational education; Nursing school/education.
Type of support: Support to graduates or students of specific schools.
Application information:
 Initial approach: Letter.
 Additional information: Contact trust for current application deadline/guidelines.
EIN: 366980712

2348

League of United Latin American Citizens California Educational Foundation
7731 Laurelton Ave.
Garden Grove, CA 92841
Contact: Angelina Guirindola, V.P.; Scholarships: Vera Marcus

Foundation type: Public charity
Limitations: Scholarships of $500 for undergraduate education to students who reside in CA for attendance at U.S. colleges and universities.
Financial data: Year ended 03/31/2005. Assets, $7,550; Expenditures, $14,230; Total giving, $8,500; Grants to individuals, 17 grants totaling $8,500.
Type of support: Graduate support; Undergraduate support.
Application information: Applications accepted. Application form required.
 Initial approach: Letter.
 Deadline(s): June 16
 Applicants should submit the following:
  1) GPA
  2) Letter(s) of recommendation
  3) Financial information
 Additional information: Scholarships are matched by national organization; Financial need is a determining factor in selection; Application should include extracurricular activities.
EIN: 330297651

2349

Thomas H. and Mary H. C. Leath Foundation
c/o BB&T, Trust Dept
P.O. Box 2907
Wilson, NC 27894-2907
Contact: Patrice Cain
Application address: P.O. Drawer 1149, Pinehurst, NC 28370, tel.: (910) 215-2627

Foundation type: Independent foundation
Limitations: Scholarships to residents of Richmond County, NC, who will attend the University of North Carolina at Chapel Hill, Duke University, NC, or Salem College, NC. Scholarships are renewable.
Financial data: Year ended 07/31/2005. Assets, $2,436,023 (M); Expenditures, $140,386; Total giving, $100,900; Grants to individuals, 23 grants totaling $41,400 (high: $1,800, low: $1,800).
Type of support: Support to graduates or students of specific schools; Undergraduate support.

Application information: Applications accepted. Application form required.
 Applicants should submit the following:
  1) Essay
  2) Letter(s) of recommendation
  3) Transcripts
 Additional information: Application must also include copy of the acceptance letter from college or university, and estimate of total costs.
EIN: 566294400

2350

Elisha Leavenworth Foundation, Inc.
c/o Charles Heaven & Co.
207-231 Bank St., 5th Fl.
Waterbury, CT 06702

Foundation type: Independent foundation
Limitations: Scholarships to high school senior women who are residents of the greater Waterbury, CT, area.
Financial data: Year ended 12/31/2004. Assets, $2,786,968 (M); Expenditures, $172,515; Total giving, $150,325; Grants to individuals, 3 grants totaling $6,000 (high: $2,000, low: $2,000).
Fields of interest: Women.
Type of support: Undergraduate support.
Application information:
 Initial approach: Letter.
 Deadline(s): May 1
 Applicants should submit the following:
  1) Transcripts
 Additional information: Contact foundation for current application guidelines; Application must also include personal information, and explanation of financial needs; Interviews required.
Program description:
 Scholarship Program: Scholarships do not exceed $1,000 per student, per year. They are renewable for three years upon reapplication and submission by student of year-end transcript indicating completion of acceptable work and continuing financial need.
EIN: 066035206

2351

Thomas & Dorothy Leavey Foundation
10100 Santa Monica Blvd., Ste. 610
Los Angeles, CA 90067 (310) 551-9936
Contact: Kathleen L. McCarthy, Chair.

Foundation type: Independent foundation
Limitations: Scholarships based on merit and need only to children of employees or agents of Farmers Insurance Group, Inc.
Financial data: Year ended 12/31/2004. Assets, $243,072,931 (M); Expenditures, $14,006,143; Total giving, $11,270,218; Grants to individuals, totaling $294,478.
Type of support: Employee-related scholarships.
Application information: Applications by letter accepted throughout the year.
EIN: 956060162

2352

Carol J. Ledward Memorial Foundation
(formerly J. Dehaven Ledward Memorial Foundation)
c/o Wachovia Bank, N.A.
401 S. Tryon St., 4th Fl.
Charlotte, NC 28288-5709
Application address: c/o Dean of Admissions, Univ. of PA, 34th & Market Sts., Philadelphia, PA 19104

Foundation type: Independent foundation
Limitations: Scholarships to graduating seniors in the Lincoln County School System, NC, who have been in attendance for four years immediately prior to graduation. The recipient may attend any accredited college, university, vocational, or trade school.
Financial data: Year ended 06/30/2004. Assets, $294,050 (M); Expenditures, $17,609; Total giving, $14,925; Grants to individuals, totaling $14,925.
Fields of interest: Vocational education; Business school/education.
Type of support: Support to graduates or students of specific schools; Undergraduate support.
Application information: Applications accepted. Application form required.
 Applicants should submit the following:
  1) Transcripts
  2) SAT
  3) Letter(s) of recommendation
 Additional information: Submit application to high school guidance counselor.
Program description:
 Scholarship Program: Any graduate of the Lincoln County School System is eligible for scholarship consideration and may apply in the year following graduation. Scholarships will be awarded on the basis of ability demonstrated through scholastic records; character; citizenship and leadership in community, church, and school organizations; achievement; persistence, cooperation, and responsibility; and financial need.
EIN: 232112337

2353

Lee Endowment Foundation
c/o First Citizens Trust Co., N.A.
2601 4th St., S.W., P.O. Box 1708
Mason City, IA 50402-1708
Application address: c/o Howard Query, Chair., Charitable Fund Screening Comm., Globe-Gazette, Mason City, IA 50401, tel.: (641) 421-0507 (for Elizabeth Muse Norris Char. Fund and Lorraine & Ray Rorick Fund)

Foundation type: Independent foundation
Limitations: Scholarships primarily to residents of Mason City and Cerro Gordo County, IA.
Financial data: Year ended 12/31/2004. Assets, $32,044,794 (M); Expenditures, $1,339,438; Total giving, $1,297,038; Grants to individuals, 178 grants totaling $222,767 (high: $1,300, low: $650).
Fields of interest: Vocational education.
Type of support: Graduate support; Technical education support; Undergraduate support; Postgraduate support.
Application information: Applications accepted. Application form required.
 Deadline(s): Feb. 1
 Applicants should submit the following:
  1) Transcripts
  2) Financial information
Program description:
 Will F. Muse Scholarship Fund: Selection is made on the basis of scholarship, financial need, and good moral character. Scholarships may be used

for any course of study or education beyond the high school level. This includes, but is not limited to, trade schools, craft schools, college courses leading to degrees, and college postgraduate courses of every kind and nature. Scholarships are renewable. Scholarship application should be addressed: Muse Scholarship Program, 500 College Dr., Mason City, IA 50401, tel.: (515) 421-4200.
EIN: 421074052

2354
Lee Industries Educational Foundation, Inc.
c/o Scholarship Comm.
402 W. 25th St.
Newton, NC 28658

Foundation type: Company-sponsored foundation
Limitations: Scholarships to graduating students attending high school in Catawba County, NC, or adjacent counties, who demonstrate financial need. Scholarships also to dependents of Lee employees, Sipe's Orchard Home and the Salvation Army.
Financial data: Year ended 12/31/2004. Assets, $24,041 (M); Expenditures, $20,131; Total giving, $20,000; Grants to individuals, 14 grants totaling $20,000 (high: $2,000, low: $1,000).
Type of support: Support to graduates or students of specific schools; Undergraduate support.
Application information: Application form required.
　Deadline(s): Apr. 1
　Applicants should submit the following:
　　1) Transcripts
　　2) SAT
　　3) Financial information
　　4) Essay
　　5) Letter(s) of recommendation
EIN: 562046037

2355
Arthur K. and Sylvia S. Lee Scholarship Foundation
P.O. Box 681943
Franklin, TN 37068-1943
Contact: James B. Ford, Secy.-Treas.
Application address for scholarships: 810 Crescent Centre Dr., Ste. 600, Franklin, TN 37067

Foundation type: Independent foundation
Limitations: Scholarships primarily to children and dependents of employees of United Cities Gas Co.
Financial data: Year ended 12/31/2004. Assets, $1,325,618 (M); Expenditures, $125,516; Total giving, $93,658; Grants to individuals, 90 grants totaling $93,658 (high: $1,200, low: $467).
Type of support: Employee-related scholarships.
Application information: Application form required.
　Deadline(s): June 1
EIN: 366069067

2356
The Marvin L. Lee Scholarship Foundation
11 Embarcadero W., Ste. 140
Oakland, CA 94607-4543
Contact: Mary Catherine Bliss, Mgr.
Application address: 700 College Ave., Henderson, NV 89015, tel.: (702) 564-7484

Foundation type: Independent foundation

Limitations: Scholarships to students who are residents of NV for undergraduate study.
Financial data: Year ended 12/31/2004. Assets, $25,730 (M); Expenditures, $3,582; Total giving, $2,787; Grant to an individual, 1 grant totaling $2,787.
Type of support: Undergraduate support.
Application information: Applications accepted.
　Initial approach: Letter or telephone.
　Deadline(s): None
　Additional information: Contact foundation for current application guidelines.
EIN: 943251822

2357
Whilma B. Lee Scholarship Trust Fund
P.O. Box 247
Marcellus, MI 49067-0247
Contact: Donald R. France, Tr.

Foundation type: Independent foundation
Limitations: Scholarships to graduates of public and private schools in Van Buren, Cass, Kalamazoo, and St. Joseph counties, MI.
Financial data: Year ended 12/31/2004. Assets, $128,198 (M); Expenditures, $13,043; Total giving, $9,225; Grants to individuals, 25 grants totaling $9,225 (high: $500, low: $100).
Fields of interest: Nursing school/education; Teacher school/education; Theological school/education; Protestant agencies & churches.
Type of support: Support to graduates or students of specific schools; Undergraduate support.
Application information: Application form required.
　Initial approach: Letter.
　Deadline(s): Apr. 15
　Applicants should submit the following:
　　1) Transcripts
　Additional information: Interviews may be required.
Program description:
　Scholarship Program: Scholarships are awarded to applicants who are either training in the ministry of the Bible with the Missionary Church, North Central District; pursuing a teaching certificate with the promise of teaching full-time at any Protestant Church-approved school in MI for a minimum of three years after graduation; or who are training to be nurses at Southwestern Michigan College. At least one scholarship each year is awarded to a student at each of the following schools: Bethel College or Fort Wayne College, IN; Glen Oaks Community College, MI; Kalamazoo Valley Community College, MI; and Southwestern Michigan College.
EIN: 386547465

2358
Lee-Jackson Educational Foundation
(formerly The Lee-Jackson Foundation)
P.O. Box 8121
Charlottesville, VA 22906 (434) 977-1861
Contact: Thomas McLernon, Pres.
FAX: (434) 974-6083; URL: http://www.lee-jackson.org

Foundation type: Public charity
Limitations: Undergraduate scholarships to junior or senior students of public, private or home school who are VA residents.
Financial data: Year ended 03/31/2004. Assets, $3,651,093 (M); Expenditures, $285,823; Total giving, $160,392; Grants to individuals, 27 grants totaling $40,392 (high: $5,058, low: $1,000).
Type of support: Undergraduate support.

Application information: Contact foundation for current application deadline; Completion of formal application required.
Program description:
　Scholarship Program: Scholarships are given through an annual essay competition. Essays should demonstrate an appreciation of the exemplary character and soldierly virtues of Generals Lee and Jackson, and are judged on historical accuracy, quality of research, and clarity of written expression. Eight scholarships will be awarded, varying in amount from $1,000 to $8,000. Financial need is not a requirement.
EIN: 540581000

2359
R. W. Leet Electric Foundation
5411 McPherson Rd., Box 84-312
Laredo, TX 78041-6010
Contact: Richard Leet, Pres.

Foundation type: Company-sponsored foundation
Limitations: Scholarships to children of employees of, or who have a guardian who is an employee of, R. W. Leet Electric.
Financial data: Year ended 12/31/2004. Assets, $414,370 (M); Expenditures, $105,747; Total giving, $100,550.
Type of support: Employee-related scholarships.
Application information: Application form required.
　Deadline(s): Jan. 1 to Mar. 31
Program description:
　Scholarship Program: Recipients must be under the age of 25 and maintain a minimum GPA of 2.5 in high school. Parents/guardians employed by the company must work full-time (40 hours per week) for applicant to be eligible.
EIN: 383325851

2360
Legacy Foundation, Inc.
1000 E. 80th Pl., S. Tower, Ste. 302
Merrillville, IN 46410-5644 (219) 736-1880
Contact: Nancy K. Johnson, Pres.
FAX: (219) 736-1940;
E-mail: info@legacyfoundationlakeco.org;
URL: http://www.legacyfoundationlakeco.org

Foundation type: Community foundation
Limitations: Scholarships to residents of Lake County, IN.
Publications: Application guidelines; Annual report; Informational brochure; Newsletter.
Financial data: Year ended 06/30/2004. Assets, $18,073,333 (M); Expenditures, $1,871,299; Total giving, $1,563,293; Grants to individuals, 38 grants totaling $25,941 (high: $700, low: $421).
Fields of interest: Athletics/sports, training; Athletics/sports, academies; Recreation, social clubs.
Type of support: Technical education support; Undergraduate support.
Application information: Application form required.
　Deadline(s): Varies
EIN: 351872803

2361
Legal Foundation of Washington
1325 Fourth Ave., Ste. 1335
Seattle, WA 98101-2509 (206) 624-2536
Contact: Barbara C. Clark, Exec. Dir.
FAX: (206) 382-3396;
E-mail: dtheories@legalfoundation.org;
URL: http://www.legalfoundation.org

Foundation type: Public charity
Limitations: Summer internships to second-year law students and recent graduates from law schools across the country for internships with Washington state nonprofits that provide civil legal services to the poor.
Publications: Annual report.
Financial data: Year ended 12/31/2003.
Assets, $10,700,193 (L); Expenditures, $7,363,110; Total giving, $6,724,896; Grants to individuals, totaling $8,000.
Fields of interest: Law school/education; Legal services, public interest law.
Type of support: Internship funds; Awards/prizes.
Application information: Application form required.
Initial approach: Letter, outlining interest in working on behalf of low income people.
Deadline(s): 2nd Fri. in Oct
Additional information: Interviews required; Unofficial transcript reflecting current law school enrollment, and resume with letter required; See Web site for further information.
Program description:
Goldmark Internships: Internships are advertised with more than 50 schools nationwide. Three to five finalists are invited for interviews.
EIN: 911263533

2362
The Legion Foundation
1750 S. Telegraph Rd., Ste. 301
Bloomfield Hills, MI 48302
Contact: James E. Mulvoy, Tr.

Foundation type: Independent foundation
Limitations: Scholarships and grants for personal, physical and spiritual development, in order to facilitate and encourage the study and maintenance of Christian faith in the secular world.
Financial data: Year ended 12/31/2004.
Assets, $887,103 (M); Expenditures, $450,670; Total giving, $357,563; Grants to individuals, 47 grants totaling $350,263 (high: $29,677, low: $300).
Fields of interest: Christian agencies & churches; Religion.
Type of support: Scholarships—to individuals.
Application information: Application form required.
Deadline(s): June 30 for scholarships, none for grants;
Additional information: Financial need is not a factor in evaluating applicants.
EIN: 383330588

2363
Legislative Black Caucus of the Georgia General Assembly, Inc.
P.O. Box 38028
Atlanta, GA 30334 (404) 651-5569

Foundation type: Public charity
Limitations: Scholarships to minority students residing in GA for undergraduate education.
Financial data: Year ended 12/31/2003.
Assets, $110,508 (L); Expenditures, $163,468; Total giving, $8,700; Grants to individuals, 20 grants totaling $8,700.

Fields of interest: Minorities.
Type of support: Undergraduate support.
Application information: Contact foundation for current application deadline/guidelines.
EIN: 581500919

2364
Ivan F. LeGore Scholarship Fund
c/o Bank of America, N.A.
P.O. Box 40200, MC FL9-100-10-19
Jacksonville, FL 32203-0200
Application address: c/o Vickie Brandenburg, Guidance Counselor, Saratoga High School Board, 1960 Landings Blvd., Sarasota, FL 34231

Foundation type: Independent foundation
Limitations: Scholarships to graduates of Sarasota County, FL, high schools who have participated in one or more Sailor Circus performances.
Financial data: Year ended 03/31/2005.
Assets, $456,650 (M); Expenditures, $23,643; Total giving, $18,660; Grants to individuals, 9 grants totaling $18,660 (high: $2,170, low: $1,300).
Type of support: Support to graduates or students of specific schools; Undergraduate support.
Application information: Applications accepted.
Deadline(s): Apr. 15
Additional information: Contact fund for current application guidelines.
Program description:
Scholarship Program: Applicants are judged by all or some of the following criteria:
· prior academic performance
· performance on tests designed to measure ability and aptitude
· recommendations from instructors
· financial need
· conclusions drawn from a personal interview as to the applicant's motivation, character, ability, potential as a contributing member of society, deportment, and any other factors the trustees may deem appropriate
· participation in Sailor Circus.
EIN: 656008408

2365
Vernon S. Lehr Scholarship Fund
c/o Sterling Financial Trust
101 N. Pointe Blvd.
Lancaster, PA 17601-4133
FAX: (717) 633-4439

Foundation type: Independent foundation
Limitations: Scholarships to graduates of Bermudian Springs High School, Delone Catholic High School, Hanover High School, and New Oxford High School, all in PA.
Financial data: Year ended 12/31/2004.
Assets, $2,212,210 (M); Expenditures, $95,697; Total giving, $82,500; Grants to individuals, 16 grants totaling $82,500 (high: $10,000, low: $5,000).
Type of support: Support to graduates or students of specific schools; Undergraduate support.
Application information: Contact fund for current application deadline/guidelines.
EIN: 251872650

2366
Nellie E. Leighow Scholarship Fund
c/o Northumberland National Bank
245 Front St.
Northumberland, PA 17857

Foundation type: Independent foundation
Limitations: Scholarships to graduating seniors from Shikellamy High School, Sunbury, PA, to study nursing.
Financial data: Year ended 12/31/2004.
Assets, $117,180 (M); Expenditures, $6,963; Total giving, $6,000; Grants to individuals, 3 grants totaling $6,000 (high: $3,000, low: $1,500).
Fields of interest: Nursing school/education.
Type of support: Scholarships—to individuals; Support to graduates or students of specific schools.
Application information: Applications accepted. Application form required.
Initial approach: Telephone.
Deadline(s): Contact fund for deadline
Additional information: Applications are available through the guidance counselor at the high school.
EIN: 237692684

2367
Lemmer-Blazer Scholarship Fund
124 W. Market St.
Havana, IL 62644-1191 (309) 543-2291
Contact: Don P. Boggs, Tr.

Foundation type: Independent foundation
Limitations: Scholarships to graduates of Havana High School, IL.
Financial data: Year ended 12/31/2004.
Assets, $614,159 (M); Expenditures, $24,592; Total giving, $20,550; Grants to individuals, 32 grants totaling $20,550 (high: $1,000, low: $250).
Type of support: Support to graduates or students of specific schools; Undergraduate support.
Application information: Application form required.
Deadline(s): July 1
EIN: 376233127

2368
Lenawee Community Foundation
(formerly Tecumseh Community Fund Foundation)
P.O. Box 142
Tecumseh, MI 49286 (517) 423-1729
Contact: Suann Hammersmith, Exec. Dir.
FAX: (517) 424-6579;
E-mail: info@lenaweecf.com; Grant request E-mail: shammersmith@ubat.com; URL: http://www.lenaweecf.com

Foundation type: Community foundation
Limitations: Scholarships to residents in the Lenawee MI, area.
Publications: Application guidelines; Annual report (including application guidelines); Grants list; Informational brochure.
Financial data: Year ended 09/30/2005.
Assets, $5,557,456 (M); Expenditures, $628,358; Total giving, $458,989; Grants to individuals, 89 grants totaling $88,876 (high: $2,000, low: $250, average grant: $250-$2,000).
Type of support: Undergraduate support.
Application information: Applications not accepted.
Additional information: Unsolicited requests for funds not considered or acknowledged.
EIN: 386095474

2369
The Lenfest Foundation, Inc.
5 Tower Bridge
300 Barr Harbor Dr., Ste. 450
West Conshohocken, PA   19428
(610) 828-4510
Contact: Bruce Melgary, Exec. Dir.
FAX: (610) 828-0390;
E-mail: lenfestfoundation@lenfestfoundation.org;
URL: http://www.lenfestfoundation.org

Foundation type: Independent foundation
Limitations: Scholarships to students residing in
Franklin County, PA, for undergraduate education
and for attendance at college preparatory boarding
schools.
Publications: Application guidelines; Informational
brochure (including application guidelines).
Financial data: Year ended 06/30/2004.
Assets, $156,902,899 (M); Expenditures,
$10,140,729; Total giving, $8,710,484; Grants to
individuals, 106 grants totaling $1,032,968 (high:
$26,763, low: $1,000, average grant:
$7,500-$20,230).
Fields of interest: Education.
Type of support: Support to graduates or students
of specific schools; Precollege support;
Undergraduate support.
Application information:
  Deadline(s): Feb. 15 for Lenfest College
    Scholarship and Dec. 1 for Lenfest
    Scholarship
  Additional information: Completion of formal
    application required, including essay; See
    Web site for further application information.
Program descriptions:
  Lenfest Scholarship: Awards 12 to 16
  scholarships for tuition, room and board to Franklin
  County, PA, students to attend Mercersburg
  Academy, PA, Perkiomen School, PA, Westtown
  School, PA, and Wyoming Seminary, PA.
  Lenfest College Scholarship: Awards up to
  $15,000 per year for up to four years to students
  at Chambersburg Area Senior High School, PA,
  Fannett Metal High School, PA, James Buchanan
  High School, PA, Greencastle Antrim High School,
  PA, and Waynesboro Area Senior High School, PA.
  Applicants apply during their Junior year of high
  school.
EIN: 233031350

2370
Dorsey S. and Eugenie C. Lenz Foundation
c/o Wells Fargo Bank Northwest, N.A.
P.O. Box 21927
Seattle, WA 98111
Application address: c/o Norwest Investment
Management & Trust, P.O. Box 3298, Missoula, MT
59806

Foundation type: Independent foundation
Limitations: Scholarships to graduating students
attending Big Fork High School, MT.
Financial data: Year ended 12/31/2004.
Assets, $301,035 (M); Expenditures, $14,777;
Total giving, $10,666; Grants to individuals, 6
grants totaling $10,666 (high: $2,000, low: $666).
Type of support: Scholarships—to individuals;
Support to graduates or students of specific
schools.
Application information: Application form required.
  Deadline(s): Apr. 1
EIN: 816073154

2371
Margaret and Irwin Lesher Foundation
c/o National City Bank
P.O. Box 94651
Cleveland, OH 44101-4651
Contact: Stephen P. Kosak, Consultant
Application address: P.O. Box 374, Oil City, PA
16301, tel.: (814) 677-5085

Foundation type: Independent foundation
Limitations: Scholarships to financially needy
graduates of Union Joint School District of Clarion
County, PA. Children of employees of National City
Bank are not eligible to apply.
Publications: Application guidelines.
Financial data: Year ended 12/31/2003.
Assets, $2,942,485 (M); Expenditures,
$113,114; Total giving, $81,545; Grants to
individuals, 74 grants totaling $81,545.
Fields of interest: Vocational education.
Type of support: Support to graduates or students
of specific schools; Undergraduate support.
Application information: Application form required.
  Initial approach: Letter requesting application.
  Deadline(s): Apr. 30
Program description:
  Scholarship Program: Scholarships are granted
  on the basis of financial need. Students may attend
  the college, trade school, business school, or
  technical school of their choice. Applications may
  be obtained from the foundation or from Union High
  School in Rimersburg, PA.
EIN: 256067843

2372
Leslie Scholarship Fund
c/o Wells Fargo Bank Indiana, N.A.
P.O. Box 960, 3rd. Fl. MAC N8622-031
Fort Wayne, IN 46801
Application address: c/o Van Wert City Schools,
Attn.: Superintendent, 205 W. Crawford St., Van
Wert, OH 45891

Foundation type: Independent foundation
Limitations: Scholarships to individuals for
attendance at OH universities.
Financial data: Year ended 07/31/2005.
Assets, $237,170 (M); Expenditures, $12,784;
Total giving, $8,000; Grants to individuals, 4 grants
totaling $8,000 (high: $4,260, low: $2,130).
Type of support: Undergraduate support.
Application information: Application form required.
  Deadline(s): May 15
  Additional information: Contact foundation for
    application guidelines.
EIN: 346566216

2373
J. R. Lester Educational Fund
c/o SunTrust Bank
P.O. Box 1908
Orlando, FL 32802-1908
Application address for individuals: c/o Frances
Blankenship, Asst. V.P. and Trust Off., SunTrust
Bank, P.O. Box 491, Martinsville, VA 24115,
tel.: (540) 666-8316

Foundation type: Independent foundation
Limitations: Student loans to residents of Henry
and Franklin counties and Martinsville, VA, for
attendance at colleges, universities, and technical
schools.
Financial data: Year ended 12/31/2004.
Assets, $631,080 (M); Expenditures, $7,965;
Total giving, $27,200; Loans to individuals, totaling
$27,200.

Fields of interest: Vocational education.
Type of support: Technical education support;
Undergraduate support.
Application information: Applications accepted.
Application form required.
  Initial approach: Letter.
  Deadline(s): May 1
  Applicants should submit the following:
    1) Transcripts
    2) Financial information
  Additional information: Application must also
    include college entrance exam scores;
    Recipients notified in June; Interviews
    required.
Program description:
  Student Loan Program: Primary considerations
  for choosing recipients are total family income,
  number of family dependents, number of college
  students in family, total cost of recipient's
  education, and progress in studies. Additional
  loans are available for continuous years of full-time
  study. Loans are repayable over a ten-year period,
  beginning six months after completion of studies,
  at a rate of five percent per annum. Loans are
  interest-free until payments begin.
EIN: 546031460

2374
Raymond & Lorraine Letourneau Educational Foundation
P.O. Box 276
Burlington, VT 05402-0276   (802) 863-4549
Contact: Raymond Letourneau

Foundation type: Operating foundation
Limitations: Scholarships to Burlington, VT,
residents.
Financial data: Year ended 12/31/2003.
Assets, $262,163 (M); Expenditures, $19,162;
Total giving, $15,100; Grants to individuals, 5
grants totaling $15,100 (high: $8,698, low:
$1,000).
Type of support: Scholarships—to individuals.
Application information: Applications by letter
accepted throughout the year, including brief
resume of academic qualifications and financial
information; Notification before end of school year.
EIN: 030277007

2375
Mr. & Mrs. Walter F. Leverenz Scholarship Trust
c/o Wells Fargo Private Banking Group
P.O. Box 63954
San Francisco, CA 94163-0001
Contact: Linda Benton, Trust Admin., Wells Fargo
Bank, N.A.
Application address: c/o Wells Fargo Private
Banking group, P.O. Box 20160, Long Beach, CA
90801

Foundation type: Operating foundation
Limitations: Scholarships to financially needy
students graduating from Atascadero High School,
CA, to study math, science, or music.
Financial data: Year ended 09/30/2003.
Assets, $258,519 (M); Expenditures, $20,029;
Total giving, $14,900; Grants to individuals, 31
grants totaling $14,900 (high: $1,000, low: $100).
Fields of interest: Music; Performing arts,
education; Science; Mathematics.
Type of support: Support to graduates or students
of specific schools; Undergraduate support.

Application information: Applications accepted. Application form required.
> Deadline(s): Apr. 30
> Applicants should submit the following:
>   1) Transcripts
>   2) SAT
>   3) Letter(s) of recommendation
>   4) ACT
EIN: 956721631

2376
Harvey R. Lewis Foundation, Inc.
31 S. Bayles Ave.
Port Washington, NY   11050

Foundation type: Operating foundation
Limitations: Undergraduate and graduate scholarships to residents of Port Washington, NY.
Financial data: Year ended 06/30/2004. Assets, $2,816,934 (M); Expenditures, $182,853; Total giving, $141,205; Grants to individuals, 57 grants totaling $138,455.
Type of support: Graduate support; Undergraduate support.
Application information: Applications by letter accepted throughout the year, including academic records, and describing extracurricular activities and financial need.
EIN: 112630467

2377
T. W. Lewis Foundation
850 W. Elliot Rd., Ste. 101
Tempe, AZ   85284-1202   (480) 820-0807
FAX: (480) 820-1445;
E-mail: twlfoundation@twlewis.com; Additional E-mail: info@twlewis.com; URL: http://www.twlewisfoundation.org/

Foundation type: Independent foundation
Limitations: Scholarships to graduates of Maricopa County, AZ, high schools for undergraduate education.
Publications: Grants list.
Financial data: Year ended 12/31/2003. Assets, $4,152,529 (M); Expenditures, $265,382; Total giving, $245,227; Grants to individuals, 20 grants totaling $98,334 (high: $5,000, low: $3,334).
Type of support: Support to graduates or students of specific schools; Undergraduate support.
Application information: Applications accepted. Application form required.
> Deadline(s): Contact foundation for current application deadlines.
Program description:
> *Program:* Awards up to $5,000 per year for four years. Applicants must be Maricopa County high school students, be enrolled full-time (15 semester hours or more) in a course of study leading to a baccalaureate degree at an accredited college or university located within the United States, have a minimum SAT score of 1200, have a minimum high school cumulative GPA of 3.5 and rank in the top five percent of their graduating class academically.
EIN: 860989236

2378
Roberta Bachmann Lewis Scholarship Fund
2640 Grey Oaks Dr. N.
Naples, FL   34105   (312) 641-5765
Contact: Irving Lewis, Pres.

Foundation type: Public charity
Limitations: Scholarships to individuals in financial need for higher education.
Financial data: Year ended 12/31/2004. Assets, $411,604 (M); Expenditures, $31,701; Total giving, $23,500; Grants to individuals, totaling $23,500.
Fields of interest: Higher education.
Type of support: Scholarships—to individuals.
Application information: Applications accepted. Application form required.
> *Additional information:* Applicants must be recommended by a faculty member; Interviews are required.
EIN: 311705330

2379
Lewis-Gale Foundation
c/o Scholarship Committee
3807 Brandon Ave., Ste. 1000
Roanoke, VA   24018   (540) 774-4022
Contact: Judith Hagadorn, Pres.
E-mail: channah@healthfocuswva.org; URL: http://www.lewisgalefdn.org

Foundation type: Public charity
Limitations: Scholarships to residents of the southeastern U.S. who have been accepted into a pre-medical program at an accredited college or university.
Publications: Application guidelines.
Financial data: Year ended 12/31/2004. Assets, $940,666 (M); Expenditures, $401,718; Total giving, $110,725; Grants to individuals, totaling $110,725.
Fields of interest: Medical school/education.
Type of support: Undergraduate support.
Application information: Application form required.
> *Initial approach:* Letter or telephone.
> *Deadline(s):* May 15 and Dec. 1
EIN: 546051298

2380
Lexington Community Foundation
607 N. Washington St.
P.O. Box 422
Lexington, NE   68850   (308) 324-6704
Contact: Jacqueline Berke, Exec. Dir.
E-mail: lexfoundation@alltel.net; URL: http://www.lexfoundation.org

Foundation type: Community foundation
Limitations: Scholarships to graduating high school seniors at Lexington High School for higher education.
Publications: Application guidelines; Annual report; Grants list; Newsletter; Program policy statement.
Financial data: Year ended 12/31/2004. Assets, $2,950,209 (M); Expenditures, $521,334; Total giving, $369,502; Grants to individuals, 65 grants totaling $57,550 (high: $3,000, low: $500).
Fields of interest: Higher education; Engineering school/education; Computer science.
Type of support: Scholarships—to individuals; Undergraduate support.
Application information: Applications accepted. Application form required. Application form available on the grantmaker's Web site.
> *Copies of proposal:* 1
> *Deadline(s):* Varies
> Applicants should submit the following:
>   1) Transcripts
>   2) Resume
>   3) Letter(s) of recommendation
>   4) GPA

>   5) Financial information
>   6) Essay
>   7) ACT
Program descriptions:
> *Alumni Scholarship:* Awards two annual scholarships in the amount of $750 to high school seniors at Lexington High School. The scholarship will be given to a high school senior who has plans to attend any university, state college, community college or technical school within the state of Nebraska.
> *Edsel Newman Scholarship:* Awards a $1,500 scholarship to a graduating Lexington High School senior enrolled as a full-time student in an accredited curriculum leading to a B.S. degree in engineering and/or computer science.
EIN: 470794760

2381
Henry T. Leyendecker Fund
501 W. Broadway, Ste. 900
San Diego, CA   92101-3577   (619) 233-1155
Contact: John G. Davies, Tr.

Foundation type: Operating foundation
Limitations: Scholarships by nomination only to worthy and needy students residing in San Diego County, CA, to attend nonprofit secondary schools, colleges, and universities in CA.
Financial data: Year ended 12/31/2002. Assets, $64,867 (M); Expenditures, $28,199; Total giving, $23,050; Grants to individuals, 5 grants totaling $23,050 (high: $7,050, low: $2,500).
Type of support: Awards/grants by nomination only; Graduate support; Precollege support; Undergraduate support.
Application information: The trustee contacts educational institutions who in turn refer candidates to him; Completion of formal application required; Interviews required.
EIN: 330102774

2382
The Li Foundation, Inc.
57 Glen St.
Glen Cove, NY   11542   (516) 676-1315
Contact: Taie Li, Pres.
FAX: (516) 676-2538;
E-mail: thelifoundation@usa.net

Foundation type: Independent foundation
Limitations: Scholarships and fellowships by nomination only to graduate students from China (including Taiwan) for one to two years of master's degree study in the U.S.
Financial data: Year ended 12/31/2004. Assets, $9,017,453 (M); Expenditures, $686,497; Total giving, $544,297; Grants to individuals, 9 grants totaling $104,875 (high: $21,000, low: $6,000).
Fields of interest: International exchange, students; International affairs.
Type of support: Fellowships; Awards/grants by nomination only; Awards/prizes; Graduate support.
Application information:
> *Deadline(s):* Before the end of Dec. for the Heritage Prize and Jan. 31 for others
> *Additional information:* Nominations and application proposals must be from Chinese or U.S. institutions.
Program descriptions:
> *Heritage Prize:* The prize is awarded to returnees to China/Taiwan for excellent achievements done during their stay in the U.S. A $35,000 prize is awarded for two years ($17,500 each year)

Student Scholar Grants: The foundation assists needy promising students, sponsored by institutions in China (including Taiwan), to study in the U.S. for one to two years. Grants are not made directly to individuals, but only to scholars nominated by an approved Chinese educational or U.S. educational or research institution. The foundation invites academic institutions in the U.S. and China establishing a sister or joint-research relationship to jointly sponsor a student/scholar for support. The grant provides the student with $17,500 annually for living expenses, or the scholar with $20,000, transportation costs, health insurance, book allowance and an academic trip within the U.S. The institution in the U.S. is expected to waive tuition fees for the student or provide the necessary working conditions for the researcher and encourage them to return to China. Institutions selected on this program can expect to receive support for five years and can negotiate for renewal of the agreement after the fourth year. The institutions need to submit progress and financial reports every year.
EIN: 136098783

2383
Licking County Foundation

P.O. Box 4212
Newark, OH   43058-4212   (740) 349-3863
Contact: Michael Wolfe, Exec. Dir.
FAX: (740) 322-6260; E-mail: lcf@msmisp.com;
URL: http://www.thelcfoundation.org

Foundation type: Community foundation
Limitations: Scholarships to residents of Licking County, OH.
Publications: Annual report (including application guidelines); Informational brochure; Newsletter.
Financial data: Year ended 10/31/2004.
Assets, $33,068,120 (M); Expenditures, $2,240,533; Total giving, $1,882,754.
Fields of interest: Performing arts, education; Literature; Elementary school/education; Secondary school/education; Vocational education; Medical school/education; Nursing school/education; Teacher school/education; Natural resources; Environment, forests; Animals/wildlife, preservation/protection; Agriculture; Mathematics.
Type of support: Graduate support; Technical education support; Undergraduate support.
Application information: Application form required.
  Deadline(s): Apr. 1
  Additional information: Contact foundation for current application guidelines.
Program description:
  Scholarship Funds: The foundation administers several scholarship funds. Recipients must be residents of Licking County, OH. Scholarships are awarded primarily on the basis of financial need and scholastic achievement. Recipients may attend undergraduate, graduate, or technical/vocational schools. Scholarships may be specific as to high school or college attendance and/or course of study.
EIN: 316018618

2384
The Liebling Foundation for Worthy Students

(also known as The Liebling Foundation)
c/o U.S. Bank, N.A.
P.O. Box 308
St. Joseph, MO   64502

Foundation type: Independent foundation

Limitations: Scholarships to students of the St. Joseph, MO, school district for higher education.
Financial data: Year ended 12/31/2004.
Assets, $988,265 (M); Expenditures, $42,361; Total giving, $27,787; Grants to individuals, 34 grants totaling $27,787.
Type of support: Scholarships—to individuals; Support to graduates or students of specific schools.
Application information: Application form required.
  Deadline(s): Contact foundation for deadline
  Applicants should submit the following:
    1) Photograph
    2) Essay
    3) Letter(s) of recommendation
  Additional information: Application must also include federal tax returns.
EIN: 431722158

2385
The Dolores Zohrab Liebmann Fund

c/o JPMorgan Chase Bank, Global Foundations Group
345 Park Ave., 4th Fl.
New York, NY   10154   (212) 789-5682
Contact: Edward L. Jones, V.P.
E-mail: jones_ed_l@jpmorgan.com; Additional tel.: (212) 464-2470; URL: http://foundationcenter.org/grantmaker/liebmann/

Foundation type: Independent foundation
Limitations: Fellowships to graduate students for study in the humanities, social sciences, or natural sciences, including law, medicine, engineering, architecture, or other formal professional training.
Publications: Application guidelines; Grants list; Informational brochure.
Financial data: Year ended 12/31/2004.
Assets, $25,909,424 (M); Expenditures, $1,037,526; Total giving, $836,471; Grants to individuals, 4 grants totaling $36,200 (high: $14,500, low: $2,500).
Fields of interest: Architecture; Humanities; Law school/education; Medical school/education; Science; Engineering; Social sciences.
Type of support: Fellowships; Graduate support.
Application information: Application form required.
  Deadline(s): Jan. 31
  Additional information: Contact university fellowship office for application form.
EIN: 137060094

2386
The Lifeboat Foundation

515 N. State St., Rm. 2650
Chicago, IL   60610
Contact: Admin.

Foundation type: Independent foundation
Limitations: Scholarships to individuals for higher education.
Financial data: Year ended 12/31/2004.
Assets, $4,402,536 (M); Expenditures, $323,282; Total giving, $161,175.
Type of support: Scholarships—to individuals.
Application information: Applications by letter accepted throughout the year.
EIN: 364158875

2387
LifeCare Foundation, Inc.

4242 Rte. 1
Monmouth Junction, NJ   08852

Foundation type: Independent foundation
Limitations: Scholarships to individuals residing in NJ for undergraduate education.
Financial data: Year ended 12/31/2002.
Assets, $8,431,559 (M); Expenditures, $43,396; Total giving, $12,000; Grants to individuals, 2 grants totaling $12,000 (high: $8,000, low: $4,000).
Type of support: Undergraduate support.
Application information: Contact foundation for current application deadlines/guidelines.
EIN: 223625345

2388
Light Ranch at Old Snowmass Charitable Trust, Inc.

c/o Raymond E. Monahan
818 Colorado Ave.
P.O. Box 790
Glenwood Springs, CO   81602
Application address: c/o Basalt High School, Attn.: Scholarship Comm., 600 Southside Dr., Basalt, CO 81602

Foundation type: Independent foundation
Limitations: Scholarships to graduating seniors of Basalt High School, CO.
Financial data: Year ended 12/31/2004.
Assets, $18,454 (M); Expenditures, $10,005; Total giving, $10,000; Grants to individuals, 4 grants totaling $10,000 (high: $2,500, low: $2,500).
Type of support: Support to graduates or students of specific schools; Undergraduate support.
Application information: Application form required.
  Deadline(s): Contact trust for deadline
  Applicants should submit the following:
    1) Transcripts
    2) Letter(s) of recommendation
    3) Essay
Program description:
  Scholarship Program: Recipient must have attended Basalt High School for at least two semesters prior to submitting application, must maintain a minimum GPA of 3.0 during first semester, pursue course of study at an accredited school and be gainfully employed during summer breaks.
EIN: 841420992

2389
The E. L. & B. G. Lightfoot Foundation

c/o U.S. Bank, N.A.
P.O. Box 3168
Portland, OR   97208-3168
Contact: Michael W. Sullivan
Application address: P.O. Box 886 Meridian, ID 83642

Foundation type: Independent foundation
Limitations: Scholarships to residents of eastern OR and southern ID.
Financial data: Year ended 02/28/2005.
Assets, $21,004,739 (M); Expenditures, $982,095; Total giving, $773,392; Grants to individuals, 52 grants totaling $59,593 (high: $6,000, low: $93).
Type of support: Scholarships—to individuals.
Application information: Application form required.
  Initial approach: Letter.
  Deadline(s): None
EIN: 820454166

2390
Lighthouse International
111 E. 59th St.
New York, NY 10022-1202 (212) 821-9200
Contact: Tara A. Cortes R.N., Ph.D., Pres. and
C.E.O.; Scholarships: Kelly Boyle
E-mail for scholarships: kboyle@lighthouse.org
FAX: (212) 821-9707; Additional tel.: (800)
829-0500; URL: http://www.lighthouse.org

Foundation type: Public charity
Limitations: Scholarships to partially-sighted or
blind students.
Financial data: Year ended 06/30/2004.
Assets, $121,299,961 (M); Expenditures,
$48,056,891; Total giving, $50,000; Grants to
individuals, 5 grants totaling $50,000 (high:
$30,000, low: $5,000).
Fields of interest: Eye diseases; Disabilities,
people with.
Type of support: Graduate support; Undergraduate
support.
Application information:
Initial approach: E-mail or telephone.
Additional information: Contact foundation for
further application information.
Program description:
Lighthouse Scholarship: Lighthouse's
Scholarship Awards are designed to reward
excellence, recognize accomplishments and help
students who are blind or partially sighted achieve
their career goals. There are four categories:
College-bound Award, Undergraduate Award I,
Undergraduate Award II and Graduate Award, and
each carries a $5,000 prize.
· College-bound Award: College-bound high
school seniors or recent high school
graduates now planning to begin college
may apply
· Undergraduate Award I: College students
may apply at any time during their
undergraduate studies
· Undergraduate Award II: College students
pursuing an undergraduate degree after an
absence of ten years or more from high
school or an accredited program may apply
at any time immediately prior to, or during,
their course of study
· Graduate Award: College graduates or
college seniors planning to pursue a
graduate-level program may apply at any
time immediately prior to, or during, their
course of study
EIN: 131096620

2391
Oletha C. Likins & Loren E. Likins Memorial Trust
P.O. Box 53
Torrington, WY 82240 (307) 532-7109
Contact: Donna Beth Downer

Foundation type: Independent foundation
Limitations: Scholarships only to members of Job's
Daughters who are residents and graduates of an
accredited high school in Goshen County, WY, with
preference given to members of Bethel No. 20,
International Order of Job's Daughters, Torrington,
WY, for higher education at accredited schools.
Financial data: Year ended 12/31/2004.
Assets, $1,082,264 (M); Expenditures, $33,392;
Total giving, $31,700; Grants to individuals, 5
grants totaling $31,700 (high: $15,000, low:
$2,000).
Type of support: Scholarships—to individuals;
Support to graduates or students of specific
schools.

Application information: Application form required.
Deadline(s): Mar. 15
Applicants should submit the following:
1) Transcripts
2) Essay
Additional information: Application must include,
a written statement of occupational and life
goals, two letters of reference, one from a
current or past Bethel guardian or past Bethel
Council member; Preference will be given to
applicants for undergraduate programs.
Program description:
Scholarship Program: Scholarships may vary in
number and amount from year to year. Scholarships
are renewable so long as satisfactory progress is
demonstrated. Recipient must reapply each year,
and will be required to make an oral report to
Torrington Chapter No. 22 at the conclusion of each
year scholarship funding is provided.
EIN: 836039257

2392
Likins-Masonic Memorial Trust
121 E. 20th Ave.
Torrington, WY 82240-2811
Contact: Gerald Connolly, Tr.

Foundation type: Independent foundation
Limitations: Scholarships only to members of Max
Burk Chapter, Order of DeMolay, that graduate from
a Goshen County high school, WY.
Financial data: Year ended 12/31/2004.
Assets, $951,492 (M); Expenditures, $45,842;
Total giving, $44,584; Grants to individuals, 2
grants totaling $44,584 (high: $39,584, low:
$5,000).
Type of support: Scholarships—to individuals.
Application information: Applications not
accepted.
EIN: 836041098

2393
The William Limmer Scholarship Foundation
155 Rte. 46 W.
Wayne, NJ 07470-6831 (973) 256-0456
Contact: Rev. Ulrich M. Keemss, Tr.
Application address: c/o St. John Lutheran Church,
140 Lexington Ave., Passaic, NJ 07055, tel.: (973)
779-1166

Foundation type: Independent foundation
Limitations: Scholarships to residents of the
Passaic, NJ, area. Preference is given to graduates
of Passaic and Wallington high schools.
Financial data: Year ended 12/31/2004.
Assets, $809,967 (M); Expenditures, $71,306;
Total giving, $50,300; Grants to individuals, 35
grants totaling $30,700 (high: $1,500, low: $400).
Type of support: Undergraduate support.
Application information: Applications accepted.
Application form required.
Initial approach: Letter.
EIN: 222779308

2394
The James F. Lincoln Arc Welding Foundation
22801 St. Clair Ave.
Cleveland, OH 44117-1199 (216) 481-4300
Contact: Roy Morrow, Pres.
URL: http://www.jflf.org

Foundation type: Operating foundation

Limitations: Awards to high school, undergraduate,
and graduate students, for projects or papers
dealing with arc welding.
Publications: Informational brochure (including
application guidelines).
Financial data: Year ended 12/31/2003.
Assets, $310,462 (M); Expenditures, $161,252;
Total giving, $60,594; Grants to individuals,
totaling $60,594.
Fields of interest: Business/industry; Engineering.
Type of support: Awards/prizes; Graduate support;
Precollege support; Undergraduate support.
Application information: Applications accepted.
Application form required.
Deadline(s): June 1 for Student Awards, June 15
for Preprofessional Awards
Applicants should submit the following:
1) Work samples
Additional information: See Web site for
complete application guidelines.
Program description:
Arc Welding Awards: The purpose of the
foundation is to stimulate and encourage
educational development in the field of arc welding.
The awards that are made on a competitive basis
to students at various educational levels are for
projects or papers dealing with problems relating to
design or uses of arc welding. In addition to the
student awards, each school receives a small
amount for each award its students receive. Factors
considered in selection, particularly for awards at
the postsecondary level, are originality and
ingenuity, feasibility, practicality, results achieved
or expected, engineering competence, and clarity of
presentation. For all competitions, students may
enter as individuals or in groups of no more than
five. Individual awards range from $75 to $1,000.
· Arc Welding Awards for Students: Awards to
students in three separate noncompeting
divisions: Division I includes students 18
years of age or younger in any type of
school or training program; Division II
includes students over 18 years of age in
any type of school or training program;
Division III includes students involved in
the VICA program
· The Pre-professional Design Competition:
For undergraduates and graduates enrolled
in engineering and technology programs.
Students may submit papers representing
their work on design, engineering, or
fabrication problems related to structures,
machines, or mechanical apparatus or
their component parts. They may represent
work on problems related to the
conservation of materials, labor, and
energy, or appearance and performance
improvement in any type of building, bridge,
or other generally stationary structure; any
type of machine, product, or device; or
apparatus for research and development,
needed to solve the problems. The
structure, machine, device, etc. does not
have to be actually constructed. Individual
awards range from $250 to $2,000.
EIN: 346553433

2395
Lincoln Center for the Performing Arts, Inc.
70 Lincoln Center Plz.
New York, NY 10023-6583 (212) 875-5000
Contact: Reynold Levy, Pres.
URL: http://www.lincolncenter.org

Foundation type: Public charity

Limitations: Scholarships to attend Julliard School, NY, as well as career grants.
Financial data: Year ended 06/30/2004. Assets, $320,984,079 (M); Expenditures, $88,788,208; Total giving, $130,000; Grants to individuals, 7 grants totaling $120,000 (high: $50,000, low: $5,000).
Type of support: Support to graduates or students of specific schools; Undergraduate support.
Application information:
   Initial approach: Letter.
   Additional information: Contact foundation for further information.
EIN: 131847137

2396
The Lincoln-Lane Foundation
207 Granby St., Ste. 302
Norfolk, VA   23510   (757) 622-2557
Contact: Edith G. Grandy, Secy.-Treas.
FAX: (757) 623-2698;
E-mail: lincolnlane@earthlink.net

Foundation type: Independent foundation
Limitations: Scholarships to college students who are residents of the Tidewater, VA, area.
Publications: Application guidelines; Program policy statement.
Financial data: Year ended 07/31/2005. Assets, $8,726,031 (M); Expenditures, $581,241; Total giving, $379,500; Grants to individuals, 173 grants totaling $379,500 (high: $4,000, low: $500).
Type of support: Graduate support; Undergraduate support.
Application information: Application form required.
   Initial approach: Letter.
   Deadline(s): Sept. 1 to Oct. 15
   Additional information: Interviews required.
Program description:
   Scholarship Program: About 30 new scholarships are awarded annually to college students for full-time study at accredited postsecondary schools, colleges, and universities in the U.S. Applicants are selected on the basis of academic achievement, financial need, community service, and extracurricular activities. Recipients are required to submit periodic progress reports or transcripts to the foundation.
EIN: 540601700

2397
Arthur F. Lind Scholarship Fund
P.O. Box 215
Ganado, TX   77962-0215   (361) 771-3482
Application address: c/o Ganado Independent School District, Ganado, TX 77962, tel.: (361) 771-3482

Foundation type: Independent foundation
Limitations: Scholarships to graduating seniors of Ganado Independent School District, TX.
Financial data: Year ended 03/31/2005. Assets, $46,506 (M); Expenditures, $13,684; Total giving, $9,550; Grants to individuals, totaling $9,550.
Type of support: Support to graduates or students of specific schools; Undergraduate support.
Application information: Deadline May 15; Completion of formal application required; Application forms available from schools.
EIN: 742618872

2398
John and Mary Linda Foundation
714 Main St.
Boonton, NJ   07005   (973) 334-1900
Contact: John H. Dorsey, Tr.

Foundation type: Independent foundation
Limitations: Scholarships to graduates of Montville High School, NJ, who reside in Montville, NJ.
Financial data: Year ended 12/31/2004. Assets, $630,202 (M); Expenditures, $18,913; Total giving, $7,000; Grant to an individual, 1 grant totaling $7,000.
Type of support: Support to graduates or students of specific schools; Undergraduate support.
Application information: Applications accepted. Application form required.
   Deadline(s): May 1
   Applicants should submit the following:
      1) Letter(s) of recommendation
   Additional information: Application must also include a brief statement explaining why applicant is deserving of a scholarship.
EIN: 521566835

2399
Lindhart Educational Trust
c/o Humboldt Rotary Club
901 11th St. S.W.
Humboldt, IA   50548   (515) 332-2990
Contact: Delmar J. Cram, Secy.-Treas.

Foundation type: Independent foundation
Limitations: Student loans to graduates of high schools in Humboldt County, IA.
Publications: Application guidelines.
Financial data: Year ended 12/31/2004. Assets, $93,895 (M); Expenditures, $550; Total giving, $9,550; Loans to individuals, 4 loans totaling $9,500.
Fields of interest: Education.
Type of support: Student loans—to individuals.
Application information:
   Deadline(s): July 1
EIN: 426051376

2400
Franklin Lindsay Student Aid Fund
c/o JP Morgan Chase Bank, N.A.
P.O. Box 1308
Milwaukee, WI   53201   (866) 300-6222
Contact: JoAnn Parks, Admin. Off.
Additional tel.: (512) 479-5502; FAX: (512) 479-2656; E-mail: info@FranklinLindsay.org; URL: http://www.franklinlindsay.org

Foundation type: Independent foundation
Limitations: Undergraduate and graduate loans to U.S. citizens who have completed at least one year of college attending TX colleges or universities.
Publications: Application guidelines; Informational brochure; Program policy statement.
Financial data: Year ended 12/31/2004. Assets, $18,139,760 (M); Expenditures, $246,537; Total giving, $0; Loans to individuals, totaling $1,267,100.
Type of support: Graduate support; Undergraduate support.
Application information: Application form required.
   Deadline(s): Feb. 1 to Dec. 1
   Additional information: Application must also include loan co-signer; Applications available from any one of 16 loan committee members whose names and addresses are listed in a brochure available from the fund; Interviews required for first-time applicants.

Program description:
   Student Loan Program: Maximum loan amount is $5,000 per student, per year. Recipients may reapply in subsequent years up to a $20,000 total loan per student, providing the recipient maintains at least a "C" average.
EIN: 746031753

2401
Alma Verne Line Scholarship Fund Trust II
(formerly Claude & Verne Line Scholarship Fund Trust II)
c/o Old National Bank
P.O. Box 207
Evansville, IN   47702   (812) 634-5239
Application address: c/o Jasper High School, Attn.: Robert Johnson, Principal, Saint Charles St., Jasper, IN 47546

Foundation type: Independent foundation
Limitations: Scholarships to graduates of high schools in Dubois County, IN, who attend church.
Financial data: Year ended 11/30/2004. Assets, $5,699 (M); Expenditures, $22,420; Total giving, $22,000; Grants to individuals, totaling $22,000.
Fields of interest: Medical school/education; Religion.
Type of support: Support to graduates or students of specific schools; Undergraduate support.
Application information: Application form required.
   Deadline(s): Apr. 15
   Applicants should submit the following:
      1) Essay
      2) Letter(s) of recommendation
      3) Transcripts
      4) SAR
      5) Financial information
   Additional information: Application must also include list of previous awards and honors.
Program description:
   Scholarship Program: Half of all scholarships granted are for the study of medicine. Not more than one recipient is selected from the same church affiliation per selected field of study. Applicants must provide verification by clergy member of church membership.
EIN: 356370018

2402
Claude & Verne Line Scholarship Fund Trust
c/o Old National Bank
P.O. Box 550
Jasper, IN   47547
Application address: c/o Jasper High School, Attn.: Robert Johnson, Principal, St. Charles St., Jasper, IN 47546

Foundation type: Independent foundation
Limitations: Scholarships to graduates of Dubois County high schools, IN.
Financial data: Year ended 11/30/2004. Assets, $4,842 (M); Expenditures, $9,885; Total giving, $9,725; Grants to individuals, totaling $9,725.
Type of support: Scholarships—to individuals; Support to graduates or students of specific schools.
Application information: Applications accepted. Application form required.
   Initial approach: Letter.
   Deadline(s): Apr. 15.
   Applicants should submit the following:
      1) Class rank

2) Transcripts
3) SAR
4) GPA
5) Essay
Additional information: Application must include reference letter from clergy indicating, list of honors and awards, and reference letters from all employers over the past two years.
EIN: 311038789

2403
The Linhart Foundation
12050 W. Broad St.
Richmond, VA 23233 (804) 364-4504
Contact: J. Theodore Linhart, Pres.

Foundation type: Independent foundation
Limitations: Scholarships to Henrico County, VA, secondary school students.
Financial data: Year ended 12/31/2004.
Assets, $1,239,097 (M); Expenditures, $71,582; Total giving, $55,300; Grants to individuals, 8 grants totaling $28,000 (high: $3,500, low: $3,500).
Type of support: Scholarships—to individuals; Support to graduates or students of specific schools.
Application information:
Initial approach: Letter.
Additional information: Contact foundation for current application deadline/guidelines.
EIN: 540846082

2404
Lintner Scholarship Trust
c/o PNC Advisors
620 Liberty Ave., P2-PTPP-10-2, 10th Fl.
Pittsburgh, PA 15222-2705
Application address for scholarships: Blairsville/ Saltsburg School District, 102 School Ln., Blairsville, PA 15717

Foundation type: Independent foundation
Limitations: Undergraduate scholarships to residents and children of residents of Blairsville, Burrell, or Black Lick, IN, to attend Pennsylvania State University.
Financial data: Year ended 03/31/2005.
Assets, $2,076,698 (M); Expenditures, $93,113; Total giving, $87,550; Grants to individuals, 41 grants totaling $87,550 (high: $3,450, low: $875).
Type of support: Support to graduates or students of specific schools; Undergraduate support.
Application information: Applications accepted.
Initial approach: Letter.
Applicants should submit the following:
1) Financial information
EIN: 256406800

2405
Robert L. Lippert Foundation
512 Westline Dr., Ste. 300
Alameda, CA 94501
Contact: James A. Stonehouse, Pres.

Foundation type: Independent foundation
Limitations: Scholarships to graduates of Alameda Unified School District, and St. Joseph Notre Dame High School, CA.
Financial data: Year ended 12/31/2004.
Assets, $1,030,257 (M); Expenditures, $49,699; Total giving, $39,000; Grants to individuals, 9 grants totaling $13,000 (high: $2,000, low: $1,000).

Type of support: Support to graduates or students of specific schools; Undergraduate support.
Application information: Applications accepted.
Additional information: Contact foundation for current application guidelines.
EIN: 943108580

2406
The Lissak Foundation, Inc.
175 South St.
Morristown, NJ 07960 (973) 898-9494
Contact: Kenneth Lissak, Mgr.

Foundation type: Independent foundation
Limitations: Scholarships primarily to residents of New York, NY, Brooklyn, NY, New Fairfield, CT, and Los Angeles, CA.
Financial data: Year ended 11/30/2004.
Assets, $0 (M); Expenditures, $1,248,775; Total giving, $1,247,801; Grants to individuals, 16 grants totaling $273,049 (high: $50,383, low: $1,000).
Type of support: Undergraduate support.
Application information:
Initial approach: Letter.
Additional information: Contact foundation for application guidelines.
EIN: 061468915

2407
Litchfield County University Club
c/o Howard L. Aller
95 Interlaken Rd.
Lakeville, CT 06039-0749
Scholarship contact: Jean B. Vitalis, tel.: (860) 672-6880

Foundation type: Independent foundation
Limitations: Scholarships to financially needy graduates of Litchfield County, CT, secondary schools for postsecondary education.
Financial data: Year ended 05/31/2004.
Assets, $1,605,910 (M); Expenditures, $90,216; Total giving, $59,500; Grants to individuals, 50 grants totaling $59,500.
Type of support: Support to graduates or students of specific schools; Undergraduate support.
Application information: Application form required.
Deadline(s): May 7
Applicants should submit the following:
1) Photograph
Additional information: Application must also include tax return. Forms are available from principal or headmaster. Interviews required.
Program description:
Scholarship Program: Selection criteria include academic performance, college aptitude test scores, and financial need. Scholarships are for one year only.
EIN: 066055891

2408
Lithuanian Foundation
14911 127th St.
Lemont, IL 60439-6466 (630) 257-1616
FAX: (630) 257-1647; E-mail: admin@lithfund.org;
URL: http://www.lithfund.org

Foundation type: Public charity
Limitations: Scholarships to students worldwide who are of Lithuanian descent.
Financial data: Year ended 12/31/2003.
Assets, $11,440,797; Expenditures, $1,050,812;

Total giving, $833,608; Grants to individuals, totaling $833,608.
Fields of interest: Lithuania.
Type of support: Undergraduate support.
Application information: Application form required.
Deadline(s): Apr. 15
Additional information: Applications must be written in Lithuanian and are available on Web site.
EIN: 366118312

2409
Helen I. Little Education Trust
c/o Bank of America, N.A.
P.O. Box 831041
Dallas, TX 75283-1041
Application address: c/o Christ Episcopal Church, 505 E. Commerce St., Mexia, TX 76667-2862, tel.: (254) 562-5918

Foundation type: Independent foundation
Limitations: Scholarships to members of Christ Episcopal Church, St. Paul's Church, TX, and any Episcopal church, parish or mission in TX.
Financial data: Year ended 12/31/2004.
Assets, $1,492,963 (M); Expenditures, $73,591; Total giving, $58,282; Grants to individuals, 8 grants totaling $58,282 (high: $20,800, low: $624).
Fields of interest: Protestant agencies & churches.
Type of support: Undergraduate support.
Application information: Application form required.
Deadline(s): Apr. 1.
EIN: 756500051

2410
Edward Little High School Alumni Association Trust
c/o Bank of America, N.A.
P.O. Box 6768
Providence, RI 02940-6768
Application address for scholarship: c/o Edward Little High School, Guidance Office, Auburn, ME 04401

Foundation type: Independent foundation
Limitations: Scholarships to graduates of Edward Little High School, Auburn, ME, to attend colleges and universities in ME.
Financial data: Year ended 07/31/2004.
Assets, $120,633 (M); Expenditures, $8,858; Total giving, $8,000; Grants to individuals, totaling $8,000.
Type of support: Support to graduates or students of specific schools; Undergraduate support.
Application information: Applications accepted. Application form required.
Additional information: Application must also include personal records, financial data, employment records, school records, and references.
EIN: 016029596

2411
Solon E. & Espie Watts Little Scholarship Loan Fund, Inc.
43 Union St. S.
Concord, NC 28025
Contact: Steve L. Medlin, V.P.

Foundation type: Independent foundation
Limitations: Interest-free student loans to graduates of Alexander Central High School,

Taylorsville, NC, who have been residents of Alexander County, NC, for at least one year.
Financial data: Year ended 12/31/2004. Assets, $3,162,012 (M); Expenditures, $322,482; Total giving, $212,300; Loans to individuals, 86 loans totaling $212,300.
Type of support: Support to graduates or students of specific schools; Undergraduate support.
Application information: Application form required.
  Initial approach: Letter or telephone.
  Deadline(s): Feb. 15
  Additional information: Contact fund for current application guidelines.
EIN: 581491453

2412
Live Oak Foundation
P.O. Box 1202
George West, TX 78022   (512) 449-2508
Contact: Alfred West Ward, Pres.

Foundation type: Independent foundation
Limitations: Vocational education scholarships to financially deprived high school students in southern TX.
Financial data: Year ended 12/31/2004. Assets, $537,472 (M); Expenditures, $44,738; Total giving, $38,548; Grants to individuals, 5 grants totaling $38,548.
Fields of interest: Vocational education.
Type of support: Technical education support.
Application information: Applications accepted.
  Applicants should submit the following:
    1) Resume
EIN: 742119731

2413
Living Memorial Scholarship Fund, Inc.
503 W. Main St.
West Lafayette, OH 43845   (740) 545-0227
Contact: D. Sharlynn Smith, Treas.
Application address for scholarship: 503 Main St., West Lafayette, OH 43845

Foundation type: Independent foundation
Limitations: Scholarships to students who are graduates of Ridgewood High School, OH, for attendance at college or technical school.
Financial data: Year ended 06/30/2005. Assets, $317,543 (M); Expenditures, $10,791; Total giving, $10,000; Grants to individuals, 9 grants totaling $10,000 (high: $2,000, low: $1,000).
Type of support: Support to graduates or students of specific schools; Technical education support; Undergraduate support.
Application information: Applications accepted. Application form required.
EIN: 341321980

2414
James S. & Peggy M. Livingston Educational Trust
c/o Wells Fargo Bank Iowa, N.A.
150 1st Ave. N.E.
Cedar Rapids, IA 52401

Foundation type: Independent foundation
Limitations: Scholarships to graduates of Cedar Rapids, IA, high schools who have been accepted to an accredited college, university, or junior college.

Financial data: Year ended 10/31/2004. Assets, $231,290 (M); Expenditures, $17,361; Total giving, $13,000; Grants to individuals, 26 grants totaling $13,000 (high: $500, low: $500).
Type of support: Support to graduates or students of specific schools; Undergraduate support.
Application information: Applications not accepted.
  Additional information: Students are recommended by the high school principals.
Program description:
  Scholarship Program: The number of scholarships for each high school of Cedar Rapids, IA, equals the ratio of the number of seniors at that school compared to the number of all seniors in the Cedar Rapids School District. Scholarships are awarded at a school-wide awards assembly.
EIN: 426351732

2415
P. A. & Marie B. Loar Student Loan Fund
c/o Wells Fargo Bank Northwest, N.A.
P.O. Box 21927
Seattle, WA 98111
Application address: c/o Greg Snyder, Silverton High School, 802 Schlador St., Silverton, OR 97381

Foundation type: Independent foundation
Limitations: Student loans to graduates of Silverton High School, OR.
Financial data: Year ended 09/30/2004. Assets, $495,363 (M); Expenditures, $30,329; Total giving, $20,314.
Type of support: Support to graduates or students of specific schools; Undergraduate support.
Application information: Application form required.
  Deadline(s): Applications accepted throughout the year.
EIN: 936041499

2416
Local 758 S & E Fund
c/o Board of Trustees
330 W. 42nd St., 15th Fl.
New York, NY 10036-6902

Foundation type: Independent foundation
Limitations: Scholarships to residents of NY who are in Local 758, Service Employee International Union.
Financial data: Year ended 06/30/2004. Assets, $106,549 (M); Expenditures, $32,715; Total giving, $12,500; Grants to individuals, 9 grants totaling $12,500 (high: $2,000, low: $500).
Type of support: Scholarships—to individuals.
Application information:
  Initial approach: Letter.
EIN: 134181778

2417
Lockheed Martin Corporation Foundation
(formerly Martin Marietta Corporation Foundation)
6801 Rockledge Dr.
Bethesda, MD 20817
Contact: David Phillips, Secy.

Foundation type: Company-sponsored foundation
Limitations: Scholarships only to high school graduates who are children of Lockheed Martin Corporation employees.
Publications: Application guidelines.
Financial data: Year ended 12/31/2004. Assets, $1,960,348 (M); Expenditures, $7,183,885; Total giving, $7,052,605.

Type of support: Employee-related scholarships.
Application information:
  Deadline(s): Feb. 1.
  Additional information: Application guidelines and forms available from company human resource offices.
Program description:
  Scholarship Program: Scholarships are generally in amounts of up to $3,000 per year, and are renewable annually for three years, providing the recipient maintains a satisfactory level of accomplishment.
EIN: 136161566

2418
The William Loeb Memorial Fund
P.O. Box 750
Reno, NV 89504
Application address: c/o William Loeb Education Grants, P.O. Box 9555, Manchester, NH 03108, tel.: (800) 562-8218 or (800) 668-4321

Foundation type: Independent foundation
Limitations: Scholarships to high school seniors who have been residents of NH for at least two years for attendance at colleges, universities, and trade or technical schools.
Financial data: Year ended 12/31/2004. Assets, $93,169 (M); Expenditures, $9,865; Total giving, $8,000; Grants to individuals, 6 grants totaling $8,000 (high: $1,000, low: $1,000).
Fields of interest: Vocational education.
Type of support: Technical education support; Undergraduate support.
Application information: Application form required.
  Deadline(s): Mar. 15
  Applicants should submit the following:
    1) Photograph
    2) Letter(s) of recommendation
  Additional information: Application must include a brief letter of recommendation from a teacher or counselor, typed, no more than one double-spaced page, stating why applicant deserves a scholarship, and how they intend to better themselves and NH through the use of that scholarship.
Program description:
  Scholarship Program: Prime consideration is given to applicants who demonstrate initiative, involvement, and a high degree of volunteerism in community and school activities. The award is not based on GPA or financial need.
EIN: 942864613

2419
Logan County Nurses Scholarship Association
P.O. Box 1306
Sterling, CO 80751-1306
Contact: Mary Sutter, Pres.
Application address: 831 Elwood St., Sterling, CO 80751, tel.: (970) 522-6210

Foundation type: Independent foundation
Limitations: Scholarships to residents of six northeastern CO counties for study in a nursing or paramedical program.
Financial data: Year ended 06/30/2005. Assets, $116,632 (M); Expenditures, $7,237; Total giving, $7,125; Grants to individuals, 11 grants totaling $7,125 (high: $875, low: $500).
Fields of interest: Nursing school/education; Health sciences school/education.
Type of support: Scholarships—to individuals.

Application information: Applications accepted. Application form required.

Deadline(s): Apr. 2
Applicants should submit the following:
1) Transcripts
2) Letter(s) of recommendation
3) Essay
Additional information: Application must also include three references (only one of which may be from a school authority).

Program description:
Scholarship Program: Applicants must be residents of Logan, Morgan, Phillips, Sedgwick, Washington, or Yuma counties, all in CO. Scholarships do not exceed $1,000 per year and they are renewable pending review of applicant's yearly transcripts.

EIN: 840736731

2420
George & Frances London Educational Foundation

P.O. Box 20389
Raleigh, NC 27619-0389 (919) 787-8880
Contact: Howard E. Manning, Sr., Tr.

Foundation type: Independent foundation
Limitations: Scholarships to students from specified counties in NC for study at a four-year college or university.
Financial data: Year ended 12/31/2004. Assets, $2,778,802 (M); Expenditures, $184,765; Total giving, $160,515; Grants to individuals, 35 grants totaling $160,515 (high: $7,500, low: $2,500).
Type of support: Undergraduate support.
Application information: Application form required.

Deadline(s): Mar. 1
Applicants should submit the following:
1) Transcripts

Program description:
London Foundation Scholars: The foundation awards scholarships to high school seniors who have demonstrated, through school and community activities, a high level of academic scholarship, a sincere interest in pursuing higher education, involvement in their local community, leadership ability/potential, and an expectation of returning to their home county following graduation to live and work for four to five years. Applicants must have been enrolled in the local high school full time during his or her junior or senior year, have an unweighted GPA of 3.5, and at least a 1200 on the SAT. Financial need of the applicant is considered in the selection process. High school seniors from selected schools may apply on their own initiative, and nominations will be solicited from guidance counselors.

EIN: 582233144

2421
Dr. Ralph F. Long and Pearl A. Long Trust

c/o Bank of America, N.A.
777 Main St., CT2-102-22-02
Hartford, CT 06115 (860) 952-7387

Foundation type: Independent foundation
Limitations: Scholarships to financially needy students for higher education. Preference is given to graduates of Terryville High School, CT.
Financial data: Year ended 12/31/2004. Assets, $3,550,877 (M); Expenditures, $231,610; Total giving, $193,500; Grants to individuals, 19 grants totaling $47,000 (high: $4,000, low: $1,000).

Type of support: Support to graduates or students of specific schools; Undergraduate support.
Application information: Applications accepted. Application form required.

Deadline(s): Mar. 15, and June 15 for renewal
Applicants should submit the following:
1) Letter(s) of recommendation
2) Transcripts
3) Essay
Additional information: Application should include a copy of financial aid package from institution for the next academic year for renewals, and a list of extracurricular activities; Interviews may be required.

EIN: 223010188

2422
L. A. Long Trust

c/o First National Bank
P.O. Box 540
Graham, TX 76450-0540
Application address: c/o School Board of Trustees, Graham Independent School District, Graham, TX 76450

Foundation type: Independent foundation
Limitations: Student loans to graduates of Graham Independent School District and graduates of other Young County School District schools, TX.
Financial data: Year ended 07/31/2004. Assets, $569,808 (M); Expenditures, $69,123; Total giving, $46,099; Loans to individuals, totaling $46,099.
Type of support: Support to graduates or students of specific schools; Undergraduate support.
Application information: Applications by letter accepted throughout the year.
EIN: 750399970

2423
Loofbourrow Educational Trust

c/o H. Douglas Pfalzgraf
522 N. Washington Ave.
Wellington, KS 67152-4061

Foundation type: Independent foundation
Limitations: Scholarships to graduates of accredited Sumner County, KS high schools, for higher education.
Financial data: Year ended 12/31/2004. Assets, $936,459 (M); Expenditures, $53,429; Total giving, $42,125; Grants to individuals, 8 grants totaling $16,000 (high: $2,000, low: $2,000).
Type of support: Support to graduates or students of specific schools; Undergraduate support.
Application information: Application form required.

Deadline(s): Feb. 1

Program description:
Scholarship Program: Recipients must demonstrate good citizenship, have scholastic ability to perform the requirements of a college or university education endeavor, and have the need for financial assistance to achieve their educational goals. Descendants of trustees of the Trust are ineligible.

EIN: 486329154

2424
Loogootee Community School Scholarship Trust

c/o Peoples National Bank
P.O. Box 560
Washington, IN 47501 (812) 254-4630

Foundation type: Public charity
Limitations: Scholarships to graduating seniors of the Loogootee Community School District, IN.
Financial data: Year ended 12/31/2003. Assets, $779,351 (M); Expenditures, $43,297; Total giving, $37,793; Grants to individuals, 41 grants totaling $37,793 (high: $1,300, low: $222).
Type of support: Support to graduates or students of specific schools; Undergraduate support.
Application information: Contact trust for current application deadline/guidelines.
EIN: 356399803

2425
The Lorain Foundation

c/o Lorain National Bank
457 Broadway
Lorain, OH 44052

Foundation type: Independent foundation
Limitations: Scholarships to graduates of high schools in Lorain, OH.
Financial data: Year ended 12/31/2004. Assets, $1,387,661 (M); Expenditures, $89,464; Total giving, $65,121; Grants to individuals, 33 grants totaling $31,005 (high: $2,000, low: $334).
Type of support: Support to graduates or students of specific schools; Undergraduate support.
Application information: Application form required.

Deadline(s): Prior to spring break
Additional information: Applications must be submitted to counselor of participating high school.

EIN: 341022034

2426
Lord Educational Fund

c/o U.S. Bank, N.A.
P.O. Box 350
Taylorville, IL 62568 (217) 824-4955
FAX: (217) 287-1835; Additional tel.: (217) 287-1820

Foundation type: Independent foundation
Limitations: Scholarships and student loans to graduates of Taylorville Senior High School, IL, and graduates from any other high school who reside at Kemmerer Village Specialized Foster Home in Assumption, IL. Recipients may attend college, vocational, or business schools.
Financial data: Year ended 09/30/2004. Assets, $2,531,003 (M); Expenditures, $190,937; Total giving, $148,500; Grants to individuals, 60 grants totaling $148,500 (high: $4,000, low: $1,000).
Fields of interest: Vocational education; Business school/education.
Type of support: Technical education support; Undergraduate support.
Application information: Application form required.

Deadline(s): Apr. 1
Applicants should submit the following:
1) Financial information
Additional information: Interviews required for finalists.

Program description:
Scholarship and Loan Program: Any resident of Taylorville, IL, or Kemmerer Village Specialized Foster Home in Assumption, IL, who has not graduated from high school, but is in need of financial assistance to attend a trade or vocational school, may apply. If funds are available, scholarships will be opened to students residing in Christian County, IL, so they may attend college, vocational, or trade school. All recipients are

chosen on the basis of character, intelligence, and financial need. Scholarships are renewable.
EIN: 510175613

2427
Henry C. Lord Scholarship Fund Trust
c/o Citizens Bank of NH
870 Westminster St.
Providence, RI 02903
Application address for scholarships: Citizens Bank New Hampshire, Attn: Renee Hall, 1 Capital Plz., Concord, NH 03301, tel.: (603) 229-3573

Foundation type: Independent foundation
Limitations: Scholarships to needy residents of Peterborough, NH, and contiguous towns, pursuing an undergraduate program.
Financial data: Year ended 06/30/2005.
Assets, $11,940,729 (M); Expenditures, $867,146; Total giving, $753,000; Grants to individuals, 204 grants totaling $753,000 (high: $6,000, low: $3,000).
Type of support: Undergraduate support.
Application information: Application form required.
   Deadline(s): Apr. 30 for first-time applicants, June 15 for reapplicants
EIN: 026051741

2428
Los Alamos Community Foundation
1200 Trinity Dr.
Los Alamos, NM 87544
Application address: c/o Los Alamos High School, Attn.: Edwina Lieb, 1300 Diamond Dr., Los Alamos, NM 87544

Foundation type: Operating foundation
Limitations: Scholarship awards to graduates of Los Alamos High School, NM, who plan to pursue a degree in the field of education.
Financial data: Year ended 12/31/2003.
Assets, $250,270 (M); Expenditures, $32,500; Total giving, $32,500; Grants to individuals, 33 grants totaling $32,500 (high: $1,000, low: $750).
Type of support: Support to graduates or students of specific schools.
Application information:
   Initial approach: Letter.
EIN: 850453999

2429
Los Altos Community Foundation
183 Hillview Ave.
Los Altos, CA 94022 (650) 949-5908
Contact: Roy Lave, Exec. Dir.
FAX: (650) 949-0807; E-mail: lacf@losaltoscf.org; Additional E-mail: staff@losaltoscf.org; URL: http://www.losaltoscf.org

Foundation type: Community foundation
Limitations: Scholarships to graduates of Mountain View Los Altos Union School District, CA.
Publications: Application guidelines; Annual report; Financial statement; Grants list; Informational brochure; Newsletter; Occasional report; Program policy statement.
Financial data: Year ended 06/30/2005.
Assets, $4,408,097 (M); Expenditures, $1,079,284; Total giving, $823,578; Grants to individuals, 46 grants totaling $47,989 (high: $4,038, low: $28).
Type of support: Support to graduates or students of specific schools.

Application information: Applications accepted. Application form required.
   Initial approach: Letter.
   Copies of proposal: 1
   Applicants should submit the following:
      1) Transcripts
      2) Letter(s) of recommendation
      3) GPA
      4) Financial information
      5) FAFSA
      6) Essay
      7) Budget Information
EIN: 770273721

2430
Los Padres Foundation
658 Live Oak Dr.
McLean, VA 22101 (703) 790-9870
Application address for scholarships: Ms. Margarita Pagan, 289 Grant Ave., Ste. 1A, Jersey City, NJ 07305, tel.: (201) 451-6229
FAX: (703) 790-9742;
E-mail: lpfadmin@lospadresfoundation.com;
URL: http://www.lospadresfoundation.org/

Foundation type: Operating foundation
Limitations: Scholarships for tuition assistance to financially needy first-generation college attendees who meet specific academic achievement levels, primarily in NY.
Financial data: Year ended 09/30/2004.
Assets, $3,111,207 (M); Expenditures, $359,101; Total giving, $52,464; Grants to individuals, 44 grants totaling $52,464 (high: $2,500, low: $130).
Type of support: Undergraduate support.
Application information: Application form required.
   Deadline(s): Jan. 15
   Applicants should submit the following:
      1) Letter(s) of recommendation
      2) Financial information
      3) Essay
   Additional information: Interviews required.
EIN: 541772081

2431
Alfred J. Loser Memorial Scholarship Fund
c/o Lorain National Bank
457 Broadway
Lorain, OH 44052

Foundation type: Independent foundation
Limitations: Scholarships and awards to financially needy graduates of Admiral King High School, Southview High School, and Lorain Catholic High School, OH, who are in the top third of their classes.
Financial data: Year ended 12/31/2004.
Assets, $0 (M); Expenditures, $54,158; Total giving, $24,000; Grants to individuals, 20 grants totaling $24,000 (high: $2,000, low: $1,000).
Type of support: Support to graduates or students of specific schools; Awards/prizes; Undergraduate support.
Application information: Application form required.
   Deadline(s): Mar. 26
   Applicants should submit the following:
      1) Photograph
      2) Financial information
   Additional information: Interviews may be required.
EIN: 346742325

2432
Louisiana Poultry Industries Educational Foundation, Inc.
P.O. Box 931
Natchitoches, LA 71458-0931
Contact: Theresia Laverge Ph.D., Secy.
Application address for scholarships: Poultry Science, 120 Ingram Hall, LSU, Baton Rouge, LA 70803

Foundation type: Operating foundation
Limitations: Scholarships to students in LA institutes of higher learning who have completed 15 college credits and demonstrate a sincere interest in poultry.
Financial data: Year ended 12/31/2002.
Assets, $120,184 (M); Expenditures, $5,100; Total giving, $5,100; Grants to individuals, totaling $5,100.
Fields of interest: Agriculture.
Type of support: Scholarships—to individuals.
Application information: Application form required.
   Deadline(s): May 29
   Applicants should submit the following:
      1) Transcripts
      2) Letter(s) of recommendation
Program description:
   Scholarship Program: Applicants must meet the following requirements for eligibility: demonstrate a sincere interest in poultry by evidence of a poultry major, poultry course enrollment, or poultry-related activities; possess a minimum 2.5 GPA, have completed 15 college credits, and be a student at a LA institute of higher education.
EIN: 721148406

2433
Louisville Male High School Foundation, Inc.
2907 Iris Way
Louisville, KY 40220
Contact: George E. Mercker, Pres.
Applicaiton address: 1500 KY Home Life Bldg., Louisville, KY 40202

Foundation type: Independent foundation
Limitations: Scholarships to seniors at Louisville Male Traditional High School, KY.
Financial data: Year ended 12/31/2004.
Assets, $328,426 (M); Expenditures, $12,801; Total giving, $12,500; Grants to individuals, 11 grants totaling $11,500 (high: $1,500, low: $500).
Fields of interest: Men.
Type of support: Support to graduates or students of specific schools; Undergraduate support.
Application information: Applications by letter accepted throughout the year.
EIN: 616033780

2434
The Lucyle S. Love Foundation
P.O. Box 10045
Greenville, SC 29603
Contact: Ben R. Lever, Jr., Tr.; Susan H. Hart, Tr.; Donald R. McAlister, Tr.

Foundation type: Independent foundation
Limitations: Scholarships to high school, college, and graduate students, with preference given to Greenville County, SC, residents.
Financial data: Year ended 12/31/2004.
Assets, $2,998,532 (M); Expenditures, $210,471; Total giving, $140,250; Grants to individuals, 19 grants totaling $50,000 (high: $6,000, low: $500).

Application information: Application form required.
Initial approach: Letter.
Deadline(s): Contact foundation for deadline
Applicants should submit the following:
1) Transcripts
2) Essay
3) Financial information
Additional information: Application must also include employment history and personal references from individuals who are not related to the applicant.
EIN: 570902382

2435
Mary Friese Lowe Memorial Educational Fund

c/o Latanzi Spaulding & Landreth
P.O. Box 2300
Orleans, MA 02653
Application addresses: c/o Richard J. Barber, Jr., 211 Purchase St., Rye, NY 10580, tel.: (914) 967-3040; or c/o Brooks B. Thamer, Jr., 8 Cardinal Ln., P.O. Box 2300, Orleans, MA 02653, tel.: (508) 235-2133

Foundation type: Independent foundation
Limitations: Scholarships to graduating high school seniors who are residents of Orleans, MA, and Rye, NY.
Financial data: Year ended 06/30/2005.
Assets, $2,650,507 (M); Expenditures, $124,523; Total giving, $102,000; Grants to individuals, 54 grants totaling $102,000 (high: $2,000, low: $1,000).
Type of support: Undergraduate support.
Application information: Application form required.
Deadline(s): Apr. 15
Applicants should submit the following:
1) Transcripts
2) SAT
3) Letter(s) of recommendation
Additional information: Application must also include parents' tax return; Interviews may be required.
Program description:
Scholarship Program: Awards are generally $2,000 per recipient. Scholarships are renewable.
EIN: 133040569

2436
Amy Lowell 10th Clause Trust

c/o Choate, Hall & Stewart, LLP
2 International Pl.
Boston, MA 02110 (617) 248-5000
Contact: F. Davis Dassori, Tr.
E-mail: amylowell@choate.com; URL: http://www.amylowell.org

Foundation type: Public charity
Limitations: Scholarships to individuals in MA for higher education.
Financial data: Year ended 11/30/2004.
Assets, $10,756,973; Expenditures, $474,084; Total giving, $352,098; Grants to individuals, 4 grants totaling $26,000 (high: $18,500, low: $2,500).
Type of support: Undergraduate support.
Application information: Unsolicited requests for funds not accepted.
EIN: 046016148

2437
Leon Lowengard Scholarship Fund

c/o Mellon Financial Corp.
2 N. 2nd St., 12th Fl.
Harrisburg, PA 17108
Application address: c/o Harrisburg Area Community College, Admissions Office, Cameron St., Harrisburg, PA 17108, tel.: (717) 780-2319

Foundation type: Independent foundation
Limitations: Undergraduate and graduate scholarships to Jewish graduates of greater Harrisburg, PA, area high schools.
Financial data: Year ended 09/30/2004.
Assets, $3,213,452 (M); Expenditures, $159,717; Total giving, $153,825; Grants to individuals, 45 grants totaling $153,825 (high: $9,832, low: $500).
Fields of interest: Jewish agencies & temples.
Type of support: Support to graduates or students of specific schools; Graduate support; Undergraduate support.
Application information: Application form required.
Deadline(s): Apr. 1
Applicants should submit the following:
1) Transcripts
2) Financial information
EIN: 236236909

2438
Ora T. & Dessie H. Lower Memorial Scholarship Fund

c/o JPMorgan Chase Bank, N.A.
P.O. Box 1308
Milwaukee, WI 53201
Application address: c/o Jacqueline A. Weitz, V.P. and Trust Off., JPMorgan Chase Bank, N.A., 111 Monument Cir., Indianapolis, IN 46277-0117, tel.: (317) 321-7544

Foundation type: Independent foundation
Limitations: Scholarships to graduates of high schools in Rush County, IN, for college or other postsecondary education.
Financial data: Year ended 06/30/2005.
Assets, $937,469 (M); Expenditures, $33,256; Total giving, $24,588; Grants to individuals, 55 grants totaling $24,588 (high: $600, low: $238).
Fields of interest: Vocational education.
Type of support: Support to graduates or students of specific schools; Undergraduate support.
Application information: Application form required.
Deadline(s): Apr. 1 or 60 days prior to start of the school term
EIN: 237311043

2439
Pearl Lowrie Student Loan Fund

c/o HNB Bank, N.A.
100 N. Main St.
Hannibal, MO 63401-3537
Application address: c/o Hannibal LaGrange College, Financial Aid Office, 2800 Palmyra Rd., Hannibal, MO 63401; c/o Central Methodist College, 411 Central Methodist Sq., Fayette, MO 65248

Foundation type: Independent foundation
Limitations: Student loans to financially needy local students attending Hannibal-LaGrange College, Culver-Stocton College and Central Methodist College, MO.
Financial data: Year ended 12/31/2004.
Assets, $542,812 (M); Expenditures, $59,427; Total giving, $54,850; Loans to individuals, 19 loans totaling $54,850.

Type of support: Student loans—to individuals; Support to graduates or students of specific schools.
Application information: Unsolicited requests for loan applications not accepted.
EIN: 436029573

2440
The Sam J. Lucas, Jr. Foundation

1929 Allen Pkwy., 9th Fl.
Houston, TX 77019
Application address: c/o Human Resources, P.O. Box 130548, Houston, TX 77219-0548

Foundation type: Operating foundation
Limitations: Undergraduate scholarships to employees of SCI, their spouses and their children.
Financial data: Year ended 12/31/2003.
Assets, $23,479 (M); Expenditures, $27,012; Total giving, $22,500; Grants to individuals, 50 grants totaling $22,500 (high: $750, low: $250). Subtotal for employee-related scholarships: 50 grants totaling $22,500 (high: $750, low: $250).
Type of support: Employee-related scholarships.
Application information: Application form required.
Deadline(s): Feb. 1
Applicants should submit the following:
1) Transcripts
2) SAT
3) GPA
4) ACT
5) Essay
Program description:
Scholarship Program: Scholarships are awarded for two years only, and recipients must reapply for the second year. Full-time or part-time employees must have been employed at SCI or any or its subsidiaries for a minimum of one year prior to the application deadline.
EIN: 760066431

2441
Clare Boothe Luce Policy Institute

112 Elden St., Ste. P
Herndon, VA 20170 (703) 318-0730
Contact: Scholarships: Lil Tuttle
FAX: (703) 318-8867; E-mail: info@cblpi.org; Toll-Free tel.: (888) 891-4288; URL: http://www.cblpi.org

Foundation type: Public charity
Limitations: Scholarships to individuals for Virginia K through 12 students.
Financial data: Year ended 12/31/2004.
Assets, $900,917 (M); Expenditures, $862,130; Total giving, $19,000; Grants to individuals, 18 grants totaling $19,000 (high: $2,000, low: $1,000).
Fields of interest: Higher education.
Type of support: Scholarships—to individuals.
Application information: Application form required. Application form available on the grantmaker's Web site.
Initial approach: Telephone.
Deadline(s): None
Additional information: Interviews required.
Program description:
CHOICES Scholarship Program: Scholarships of $1,000 each are awarded on a competitive basis to students of compulsory school age K through 12 residing in Virginia. For further information, contact ltuttle@cblpi.org, tel.: (804) 337-9706.
EIN: 541672138

2442
Charles and Nancy Oden Luce Trust

c/o Bank of America, N.A.
P.O. Box 34345, CSC-10
Seattle, WA 98124-1345
Application address: c/o Financial Aid Off., Umatilla Indian Reservation, Pendelton, OR 97801

Foundation type: Independent foundation
Limitations: Scholarships to worthy, financially needy members of the federated tribes of the Umatilla Indian Reservation, OR, who wish to obtain a liberal arts, professional, or vocational education.
Financial data: Year ended 12/31/2003. Assets, $296,734 (M); Expenditures, $16,814; Total giving, $14,273; Grants to individuals, 12 grants totaling $14,273 (high: $2,250, low: $525). Subtotal for technical education support: 12 grants totaling $14,273 (high: $2,250, low: $525).
Fields of interest: Native Americans/American Indians.
Type of support: Technical education support; Undergraduate support.
Application information: Applications accepted.
  Additional information: Contact financial aid officer at Umatilla Reservation, Pendleton, OR, for current application guidelines.
EIN: 916026999

2443
Lucent Technologies Foundation

600 Mountain Ave., Rm. 6F4
Murray Hill, NJ 07974 (908) 582-7906
Contact: Michele Donato, Mgr., Finance and Opers.
E-mail: foundation@lucent.com; Application address for Graduate Research Fellowships: Bell Labs Graduate Research Fellowship Prog., Scholarship Management Svcs., Scholarship America, 1 Scholarship Way, P.O. Box 297, St. Peter, MN 56082, E-mail: coopgraduate@lucent.com; Tel. for Conqueror of the Hill: (908) 582-7436; E-mail for Conqueror of the Hill: lucentcoh@lucent.com;; URL: http://www.lucent.com/social/foundation/home.html

Foundation type: Company-sponsored foundation
Limitations: Prizes to winners of the Conqueror of the Hill contest, which is an annual applied physics/engineering competition for high school students in NJ.
Publications: Application guidelines.
Financial data: Year ended 09/30/2005. Assets, $929,640 (M); Expenditures, $5,258,577; Total giving, $5,951,645.
Type of support: Awards/prizes.
Application information:
  Initial approach: E-mail or telephone.
  Deadline(s): Mar.
  Additional information: For further details, contact (908) 582-7436 or lucentcoh@lucent.com.
Program description:
  Conqueror of the Hill Student Competition: Each year the competition focuses on a project made from common household items designed to complete a specific task on the playing field of a plywood hill. Teams consist of 1-3 New Jersey high school students (grades 9-12). Teams representing schools are expected to be the top finishers in a local school competition. Each school may send a maximum of two teams to the tournament. Prizes will be awarded as follows:
  · First Place - $3,000.00 U.S. Savings Bonds per team member present
  · Second Place - $2,000 U.S. Savings Bonds per team member present

· Third Place - $1,000.00 U.S. Savings Bond per team member present
· Fourth Place - $500 U.S. Savings Bond per team member present
· Honorary Prizes - Prizes for teams not placing in the first 4 spots $100 U.S Savings Bond per team member present
EIN: 223480423

2444
Oatha & Una Lucky Scholarship Trust

P.O. Box 56
Lakeport, CA 95453
Contact: Lauretta Deweese, Tr.; Mary Hopper-Paiva, Tr.
Application address: c/o Clear Lake High School, 350 Lange St., Lakeport, CA 95453

Foundation type: Independent foundation
Limitations: Scholarships to financially needy graduating seniors at Clear Lake High School, Lakeport, CA, who have maintained at least a 2.7 GPA in their junior and senior years.
Financial data: Year ended 09/30/2004. Assets, $1,622,796 (M); Expenditures, $71,664; Total giving, $30,500; Grants to individuals, 27 grants totaling $30,500.
Fields of interest: Vocational education; Business school/education.
Type of support: Support to graduates or students of specific schools; Undergraduate support.
Application information: Application form required.
  Deadline(s): May 1
  Additional information: Application forms may be requested at Clear Lake High School.
Program description:
  Scholarship Program: Scholarships are for tuition and educational costs, including reasonable maintenance and support while attending school. Funds primarily support study at vocational, technical, or trade schools; business colleges; institutions; junior college; or universities.
EIN: 686121297

2445
Merwin C. Ludwig Educational Trust

P.O. Box 119
Wardensville, WV 26851-0552
Contact: Patti Combs, Pres.
Application address: Rte. 1, Box 44E, Baker, WV 26801, tel.: (304) 874-3531

Foundation type: Independent foundation
Limitations: Scholarships to high school graduates from Hardy and Hampshire counties, WV, for undergraduate education.
Financial data: Year ended 06/30/2002. Assets, $209,493 (M); Expenditures, $11,536; Total giving, $10,800; Grants to individuals, 13 grants totaling $10,800 (high: $900, low: $450).
Type of support: Undergraduate support.
Application information: Applications by letter accepted throughout the year.
EIN: 550699102

2446
Founces M. Luley Scholarship & Educational Fund

c/o JPMorgan Chase Bank, N.A
P.O. Box 1308
Milwaukee, WI 53201

Foundation type: Independent foundation

Limitations: Scholarships to residents of Trumbull County, OH, who graduate in the top one-third of their class, have been accepted by an accredited college, and plan to major in music.
Financial data: Year ended 12/31/2004. Assets, $935,775 (M); Expenditures, $49,951; Total giving, $38,250; Grants to individuals, totaling $38,250.
Fields of interest: Music; Performing arts, education.
Type of support: Undergraduate support.
Application information: Contact foundation for current application deadline/guidelines.
Program description:
  Luley Scholarship and Educational Progam: Recipients are selected first from among the graduates of Warren G. Harding and John F. Kennedy high schools in the City of Warren, OH. If funds remain, recipients are then selected from among the graduates of high schools in Trumbull County, OH. Scholarship awards are limited to $3,500 annually per recipient. While attending college and continuing to receive the scholarship, the recipient must maintain a GPA of at least 2.8 and must continue to major in music.
EIN: 346672173

2447
The Luling Foundation

523 S. Mulberry St.
Luling, TX 78648-2940
Contact: Archie Abrameit, Mgr.
Tel./FAX: (830) 875-2438

Foundation type: Operating foundation
Limitations: Scholarships and educational loans to graduating high school seniors who are residents of Caldwell, Gonzales, and Guadalupe counties, TX, and are working toward an agricultural degree.
Publications: Application guidelines; Informational brochure; Occasional report.
Financial data: Year ended 12/31/2003. Assets, $3,338,445 (M); Expenditures, $372,901; Total giving, $9,800; Grants to individuals, totaling $8,500.
Fields of interest: Agriculture.
Type of support: Undergraduate support.
Application information: Application form required.
  Initial approach: Letter.
  Deadline(s): May 15
Program description:
  Scholarship and Loan Program: Scholarships are limited to $1,000. Loans are limited to $500.
EIN: 741143102

2448
Walter E. Lundquist Scholarship Testamentary Trust

c/o Wells Fargo Bank Northwest, N.A.
P.O. Box 21927
Seattle, WA 98111
Application address: c/o Walter E. Lundquist Scholarship Comm., Kalama School District, No. 402, P.O. Box 1097, Kalama, WA 98625, tel.: (360) 673-5225

Foundation type: Independent foundation
Limitations: Scholarships to graduates of Kalama High School, WA, who have resided in WA for at least one year.
Financial data: Year ended 03/31/2005. Assets, $768,124 (M); Expenditures, $43,513; Total giving, $31,252; Grants to individuals, 75 grants totaling $31,252 (high: $975, low: $46).

Type of support: Support to graduates or students of specific schools; Undergraduate support.
Application information: Application form required.
Deadline(s): Apr. 1
Applicants should submit the following:
1) Transcripts
2) Letter(s) of recommendation
3) Essay
Additional information: Application must also include three references, and a history of employment/volunteer service.
EIN: 936145913

2449
The Turner and Louise Lundy Foundation
(formerly The B-G Foundation)
c/o Wachovia Bank, N.A.
100 N. Main St., 13th Fl.
Winston-Salem, NC 27150
Contact: Nicole B. Bryan
Scholarship URL: http://www.wachoviascholars.com/lndy/csaw_lundy_deadline.php

Foundation type: Independent foundation
Limitations: Scholarships to high school students of Brunswick and Greensville counties, VA.
Financial data: Year ended 12/31/2004.
Assets, $1,211,730 (M); Expenditures, $82,660; Total giving, $51,000; Grants to individuals, 25 grants totaling $36,900 (high: $2,000, low: $750).
Type of support: Support to graduates or students of specific schools; Undergraduate support.
Application information:
Deadline(s): Contact foundation for current application deadline/guidelines.
EIN: 541526783

2450
Georges Lurcy Charitable and Educational Trust
125 W. 55th St.
New York, NY 10019
Contact: Seth E. Frank, Tr.

Foundation type: Independent foundation
Limitations: Fellowships to graduate students at American colleges and universities to study in France and to graduate students of French colleges and universities to study in the U.S.
Financial data: Year ended 06/30/2004.
Assets, $32,095,539 (M); Expenditures, $1,445,510; Total giving, $1,106,624.
Fields of interest: International exchange, students.
Type of support: Fellowships; Exchange programs; Awards/grants by nomination only; Foreign applicants; Graduate support.
Application information: Direct applications by individuals not accepted; Fellowship applicants from America must be recommended by their universities; Applicants from France must apply to the Franco-American Commission for Educational Exchange using the commission's application.
Program description:
Lurcy Fellowship Grants: Fellowship grants are awarded for one year of research and graduate study in France to permanent residents of the U.S. and to outstanding students of French colleges for study in American colleges and universities.
EIN: 136372044

2451
Lyden Foundation, Inc.
P.O. Box 700
Winter Park, FL 32790

Foundation type: Operating foundation
Limitations: Scholarships to individuals in CT, DE and FL.
Financial data: Year ended 05/31/2004.
Assets, $325,162 (M); Expenditures, $16,195; Total giving, $16,000; Grants to individuals, 3 grants totaling $11,000 (high: $4,000, low: $3,000).
Type of support: Scholarships—to individuals.
Application information: Unsolicited requests for funds not accepted.
EIN: 593469366

2452
Lyman Fund, Inc.
c/o Claire Darrow
19 Eaton Ln.
Georgetown, ME 04548
Contact: Charlotte Fardelmann, Pres.
Application address: 385 Little Harbor Rd., Portsmouth, NH 03801-5527, tel.: (603) 436-7652; E-mail: cfardelmann@attbi.com

Foundation type: Independent foundation
Limitations: Grants primarily to Quakers (members of the Religious Society of Friends) in the U.S.
Publications: Informational brochure (including application guidelines).
Financial data: Year ended 06/30/2005.
Assets, $730,073 (M); Expenditures, $46,500; Total giving, $38,000; Grants to individuals, 15 grants totaling $38,000 (high: $3,000, low: $1,000).
Fields of interest: Religion.
Type of support: Conferences/seminars; Seed money; Scholarships—to individuals; Support to graduates or students of specific schools; Graduate support; Travel grants; Project support.
Application information: Application form required.
Initial approach: Telephone.
Copies of proposal: 7
Deadline(s): Apr. 1 and Oct. 1
Applicants should submit the following:
1) Financial information
2) Essay
3) Budget Information
Additional information: Application must also include brief statement of proposal, spiritual journey, personal statement, anticipated expenses and income, photograph, two or more letters of reference from church or spiritual support group.
Program description:
Lyman Fund: Grants range from $1,000 to $3,000. The fund typically gives one-time grants. Recipients may apply for second grants for the original project.
EIN: 020471515

2453
John B. Lynch Scholarship Foundation
10 Montchanin Rd.
P.O. Box 4248
Wilmington, DE 19807-0247 (302) 654-3444
Contact: Catherine S. Malone, Prog. Mgr.

Foundation type: Independent foundation
Limitations: Undergraduate scholarships to economically disadvantaged individuals who are residents of DE, attending colleges and high schools in DE, or who live within 20 miles of the DE border in PA, NJ, or MD.
Publications: Application guidelines.
Financial data: Year ended 12/31/2004.
Assets, $6,891,530 (M); Expenditures, $409,214; Total giving, $311,570; Grants to individuals, 238 grants totaling $311,570 (high: $3,000, low: $750).
Type of support: Undergraduate support.
Application information: Applications accepted. Application form required.
Deadline(s): Mar. 15 for new applicants and Mar. 1 for renewal applicants
Applicants should submit the following:
1) Photograph
2) Essay
3) GPA
4) Financial information
5) Transcripts
6) Letter(s) of recommendation
Additional information: For current undergraduate applicants, a separate personal essay is also required. Recipients notified after June 20.
Program description:
John B. Lynch Scholarship Program: Undergraduate scholarships are awarded to financially needy students who are no more than 30 years of age, and who have demonstrated academic achievement. Current undergraduate students must have at least a 2.75 GPA and graduating high school seniors must have at least a 3.0 GPA or a score of at least 1100 on the SAT. A grant is generally made outright and repayment is not required. However, it is the hope of the founder that persons who benefit from grants will recognize a moral commitment to reimburse the foundation if able to do so later in life. In this way, benefits received by present-day recipients will extend to economically disadvantaged and deserving students in the future. Grants are renewable for up to four years of study, (not necessarily consecutive), except in cases where the normal undergraduate academic period is five years, as in pharmacy. The maximum total amount an individual can receive is $10,000. Applicants pursuing a second undergraduate degree are only eligible if they have not previously received assistance from the foundation for their first undergraduate degree.
EIN: 516017041

2454
Cornelius T. & Elizabeth Lynch Scholarship Fund
(formerly Cornelius T. & Elizabeth Lynch Scholarship Trust)
c/o M&T Bank
1 M&T Plz., 8th Fl.
Buffalo, NY 14203
Application address: c/o M&T Bank, Personal Trust, 225 East Ave., Rochester, NY 14604-2625

Foundation type: Independent foundation
Limitations: Scholarships to graduates of Geneva High School, NY, and LaSalle High School, Niagara Falls, NY.
Financial data: Year ended 03/31/2005.
Assets, $221,553 (M); Expenditures, $18,008; Total giving, $13,946; Grants to individuals, 14 grants totaling $13,946 (high: $1,930, low: $500).
Type of support: Support to graduates or students of specific schools; Undergraduate support.
Application information: Applications accepted throughout the year; Contact fund for current application guidelines.
EIN: 166014594

2455
William A. Lynch Trust
c/o Eastern Bank & Trust Co.
605 Broadway, LF41
Saugus, MA 01906
Application address: c/o Principal, Beverly High School, 100 Sohier Rd., Beverly, MA 01915

Foundation type: Independent foundation
Limitations: Scholarships to deserving Catholic graduates of public high schools in Beverly, MA, and nearby Catholic schools.
Financial data: Year ended 12/31/2004.
Assets, $63,238 (M); Expenditures, $4,630; Total giving, $3,200; Grants to individuals, 4 grants totaling $3,200.
Fields of interest: Roman Catholic agencies & churches.
Type of support: Undergraduate support.
Application information: Application form required.
Initial approach: Letter.
Deadline(s): June 1
EIN: 046016042

2456
William A. Lynch Trust
c/o Mellon Financial Corp.
P.O. Box 185
Pittsburgh, PA 15230-0185
Application address: c/o John S. Feenan, 45 Abbott St., Beverly, MA 01915

Foundation type: Independent foundation
Limitations: Scholarships to Catholic graduates of Beverly, MA, area high schools and Catholic schools.
Financial data: Year ended 08/31/2005.
Assets, $241,289 (M); Expenditures, $15,555; Total giving, $12,000; Grants to individuals, 5 grants totaling $12,000 (high: $2,000, low: $2,000).
Fields of interest: Roman Catholic agencies & churches.
Type of support: Support to graduates or students of specific schools; Undergraduate support.
Application information:
Initial approach: Letter.
Deadline(s): Contact trust for deadline
Additional information: Applications are handled by the selection committee through St. Mary's Rectory, Beverly, MA.
EIN: 046093002

2457
Greater Lynchburg Community Trust
P.O. Box 714
Lynchburg, VA 24505-0714 (434) 845-6500
Contact: George H. Murphy, Pres.
FAX: (434) 845-6530; E-mail: challglct@ntelos.net;
URL: http://www.lynchburgtrust.org

Foundation type: Community foundation
Limitations: Scholarships, fellowships, research grants, and loans to individuals in VA.
Publications: Application guidelines; Annual report; Informational brochure; Newsletter; Program policy statement.
Financial data: Year ended 09/30/2004.
Assets, $20,984,945 (M); Expenditures, $1,082,818; Total giving, $930,121; Grants to individuals, totaling $12,750.
Type of support: Grants to individuals; Scholarships—to individuals; Student loans—to individuals.

Application information: Application form required.
Deadline(s): Contact trust for deadline
EIN: 546112680

2458
Berneice U. Lynn Foundation
1901 Camino Vida Roble, Ste. 110
Carlsbad, CA 92008-6560 (760) 930-9668
Contact: Michael G. Perdue, Mgr.
URL: http://www.Lynnfoundation.org

Foundation type: Operating foundation
Limitations: Scholarships to graduating high school seniors of the high desert area of southern CA, who are studying science, technology or art.
Financial data: Year ended 12/31/2003.
Assets, $1,757,613 (M); Expenditures, $145,471; Total giving, $16,774; Grants to individuals, totaling $16,774.
Type of support: Undergraduate support.
Application information: Applications accepted. Application form required.
Deadline(s): Apr. 15
EIN: 330555611

2459
Charles Lyons Memorial Foundation, Inc.
P.O. Box 236
Lexington, MO 64067-0236 (660) 259-6151

Foundation type: Independent foundation
Limitations: Scholarships to graduates of Lafayette County, MO, high schools who are residents of the county at the time of application.
Financial data: Year ended 12/31/2003.
Assets, $682,695 (M); Expenditures, $92,936; Total giving, $69,050; Grants to individuals, 63 grants totaling $67,000 (high: $2,000, low: $1,000).
Type of support: Support to graduates or students of specific schools; Undergraduate support.
Application information: Application form required.
Deadline(s): Apr. 1
Program description:
Scholarship Program: Scholarships are not available to parents, spouses, lineal descendents, or spouses thereof of individuals who are substantial contributors, foundation managers, or members of the selection committee at the time the scholarship is granted.
EIN: 436056850

2460
The Marguerite Gambill Lyons Scholarship Fund
c/o National City Bank of Kentucky
P.O. Box 94651
Cleveland, OH 44101-4651
Application address: c/o National City Bank, P.O. Box 1270, Ashland, KY 41105, tel.: (502) 581-5107

Foundation type: Independent foundation
Limitations: Scholarships only to students in Boyd, KY, and surrounding counties.
Financial data: Year ended 12/31/2004.
Assets, $365,947 (M); Expenditures, $20,581; Total giving, $14,057; Grant to an individual, 1 grant totaling $14,057.
Type of support: Scholarships—to individuals.
Application information: Application form required.
Deadline(s): Mar. 31
EIN: 611121801

2461
The Ray C., Maude E. & Genevieve Lyons Scholarship Fund
501 7th St.
Rockford, IL 61104

Foundation type: Independent foundation
Limitations: Scholarships to seniors from Brodhead High School, WI.
Financial data: Year ended 04/30/2005.
Assets, $643,468 (M); Expenditures, $39,112; Total giving, $30,750; Grants to individuals, 27 grants totaling $30,750 (high: $2,000, low: $500).
Type of support: Scholarships—to individuals; Support to graduates or students of specific schools.
Application information: Application form required.
Deadline(s): Contact fund for deadline
Additional information: Applications available at the guidance office of Brodhead High School, WI.
EIN: 391363244

2462
Lytle Scholarship Trust
(formerly Carl H. Lytle Scholarship Trust)
c/o U.S. Bank, N.A.
P.O. Box 3168
Portland, OR 97208-3168
Application address: c/o Scholarship Counselor, University of Denver, 2199 S. Univ. Blvd., Denver, CO 80208, tel.: (303) 871-2904

Foundation type: Independent foundation
Limitations: Scholarships to financially needy residents of CO to attend the University of Denver. Applicants must have graduated in the upper 25 percent of their high school classes and maintain at least a 3.2 GPA.
Financial data: Year ended 08/31/2004.
Assets, $294,295 (M); Expenditures, $18,948; Total giving, $14,500; Grants to individuals, totaling $14,500.
Type of support: Support to graduates or students of specific schools; Undergraduate support.
Application information: Application form required.
Additional information: Application must also include student information sheet, certification sheet, SFAA, and FFS.
EIN: 846195232

2463
M & M Area Community Foundation
1101 11th Ave., Ste. 2
P.O. Box 846
Menominee, MI 49858-0846 (906) 864-3599
Contact: Richard O'Farrell, Exec. Dir.
FAX: (906) 864-3657;
E-mail: mmfoundation@czwireless.net; Additional E-mail: ricko@menominee.net; URL: http://www.mmcommunityfoundation.org

Foundation type: Community foundation
Limitations: Scholarships to graduating seniors from Nenominee, MI, and Marinette county WI, high schools.
Publications: Annual report; Financial statement; Grants list; Informational brochure.
Financial data: Year ended 12/31/2004.
Assets, $4,085,254 (M); Expenditures, $267,278; Total giving, $85,783.
Fields of interest: Education.
Type of support: Scholarships—to individuals.

Application information:
Initial approach: Telephone.
Deadline(s): See Web site for additional information
EIN: 383264725

2464
The MacCurdy-Salisbury Foundation, Inc.
P.O. Box 474
Old Lyme, CT   06371   (860) 434-2646
Contact: Ward Bing, Secy.-Treas.

Foundation type: Public charity
Limitations: Scholarships only to residents of Lyme and Old Lyme, CT.
Financial data: Year ended 12/31/2003.
Assets, $4,173,230 (M); Expenditures, $185,374; Total giving, $155,935; Grants to individuals, 121 grants totaling $155,935 (high: $2,000, low: $250).
Type of support: Scholarships—to individuals.
Application information: Application form required.
Deadline(s): Apr. 30 for 1st semester, Nov. 15 for 2nd semester
EIN: 066044250

2465
Muriel L. MacGregor Charitable Trust
c/o Eric D. Adams
P.O. Box 4675
Estes Park, CO   80517   (970) 586-3749
E-mail: info@macgregorranch.org

Foundation type: Operating foundation
Limitations: Scholarships to graduating seniors of Estes Park High School, CO, who are also Estes Park residents.
Publications: Informational brochure.
Financial data: Year ended 08/31/2004.
Assets, $21,477,601 (M); Expenditures, $420,308; Total giving, $28,250; Grants to individuals, totaling $28,250.
Type of support: Support to graduates or students of specific schools; Undergraduate support.
Application information: Application form required.
Additional information: Contact trust for current application deadline; Interviews required; Scholarships are renewable.
EIN: 846154601

2466
Mack Industrial School
c/o Cabot Money Mgmt.
216 Essex St.
Salem, MA   01970
Application address: c/o Diane Costa, 14 Atlantic Ave., Beverly, MA 01915, tel.: (978) 927-1982

Foundation type: Independent foundation
Limitations: Scholarships to female residents of Salem, MA, who are graduating high school seniors and have been accepted to a vocational school or college for the fall semester following graduation. Recipients are chosen on academic record and need.
Financial data: Year ended 08/31/2004.
Assets, $419,544 (M); Expenditures, $27,882; Total giving, $24,900; Grants to individuals, 37 grants totaling $24,900 (high: $900, low: $500).
Application information: Application form required.
Deadline(s): May 1

Additional information: Application forms available only at the guidance offices of eligible area high schools.
EIN: 046032773

2467
Helen H. Mackey Educational Awards Foundation
c/o National City Bank of the Midwest
P.O. Box 94651
Cleveland, OH   44101-9957
Application address: c/o Senior Counselor, Bay City Central High School, 1624 Columbus Ave., Bay City, MI 48708, tel.: (989) 893-9541

Foundation type: Independent foundation
Limitations: Scholarships to financially needy graduates of high schools within the school districts of the city of Bay City, MI, and Bay and Saginaw counties, MI, who attended T.L. Handy High School or T.L. Handy Intermediate, Bay City, MI.
Financial data: Year ended 12/31/2004.
Assets, $120,189 (M); Expenditures, $4,140; Total giving, $2,500; Grants to individuals, 10 grants totaling $2,500 (high: $250, low: $250).
Type of support: Support to graduates or students of specific schools; Undergraduate support.
Application information: Application form required.
Deadline(s): May 18
Additional information: Application must also include proof of attendance at T.L. Handy High School or T.L. Handy Intermediate, Bay City, MI; Applications available at the Bay City Central Guidance Center and the office of the Western High School Guidance Center.
Program description:
Scholarship Program: Recipients must be accepted by the postsecondary institutions of their choice. Awards are granted for one term, with the award for the next term being granted contingent upon satisfactory academic performance.
EIN: 386058127

2468
Arthur Rhodes Mackley Memorial Scholarship Fund Trust
(also known as Dorothy M. Corson Testamentary Trust)
c/o National City Bank, Columbus
P.O. Box 94651
Cleveland, OH   44101-4651
Scholarship application address: c/o Principal, Jackson High School, 21 Tropic St., Jackson, OH 45640, tel.: (740) 286-7575

Foundation type: Independent foundation
Limitations: Scholarships to graduating seniors and graduates of Jackson High School, OH, to attend member colleges of the Ohio Foundation of Independent Colleges, Inc.
Financial data: Year ended 12/31/2004.
Assets, $1,559,973 (M); Expenditures, $57,761; Total giving, $49,450; Grants to individuals, 32 grants totaling $49,450 (high: $3,000, low: $1,200).
Type of support: Support to graduates or students of specific schools; Undergraduate support.
Application information: Application form required.
Deadline(s): May 1
Applicants should submit the following:
 1) GPA
 2) Financial information
EIN: 316177708

2469
William & Ellen E. Macristy Foundation
259 Wood Pond Rd.
Glastonbury, CT   06033

Foundation type: Independent foundation
Limitations: Scholarships to children of employees who have at least two years of continuous service with Connecticut Stamping & Bending, or Tube Bends.
Financial data: Year ended 08/31/2004.
Assets, $1,650,409 (M); Expenditures, $94,699; Total giving, $92,625; Grants to individuals, 22 grants totaling $63,125 (high: $3,000, low: $500).
Fields of interest: Engineering.
Type of support: Student loans—to individuals.
Application information: Applications not accepted.
Program description:
Scholarship Program: Scholarships are awarded on the basis of character, attitude, academic standing, and financial need. Recipients may study at accredited colleges, universities, and engineering schools located within the continental U.S. Scholarships are renewable contingent upon the recipient remaining in good standing and earning money during the summer vacation.
EIN: 066034030

2470
J. F Maddox Foundation
P.O. Box 2588
Hobbs, NM   88241-2588   (505) 393-6338
Contact: Robert J. Reid, Exec. Dir.
FAX: (505) 397-7266; E-mail (for Robert Reid): bobreid@leaco.net; URL: http://www.jfmaddox.org/

Foundation type: Independent foundation
Limitations: Scholarships to residents of Lea County, NM.
Publications: Biennial report.
Financial data: Year ended 12/31/2004.
Assets, $170,079,275 (M); Expenditures, $9,247,279; Total giving, $5,523,130; Grants to individuals, 66 grants totaling $188,407 (high: $19,904, low: $152, average grant: $152-$19,904).
Type of support: Scholarships—to individuals; Undergraduate support.
Application information: Application form required. Application form available on the grantmaker's Web site.
Initial approach: Application.
Copies of proposal: 1
Deadline(s): June 30
Applicants should submit the following:
 1) Transcripts
 2) SAT
 3) Letter(s) of recommendation
 4) GPA
 5) Essay
 6) ACT
Additional information: Application should also include senior class schedule and extracurricular activities; Interviews required.
Program description:
Student Loan Program: Student loan program discontinued and phasing out with current loan recipients. The program is no longer open to new applicants. Students currently participating in this program may reapply for funding.
EIN: 756023767

2471
Madison County Community Foundation
33 W. 10th St.
P.O. Box 1056
Anderson, IN 46015-1056 (765) 644-0002
Contact: Sally A. DeVoe, Exec. Dir.
FAX: (765) 644-3392;
E-mail: info@madisonccf.org; Additional E-mail:
sdevoe@madisonccf.org; URL: http://
www.madisonccf.org

Foundation type: Community foundation
Limitations: Scholarships to residents of Madison
County, IN, for higher education.
Publications: Annual report (including application
guidelines); Informational brochure; Newsletter.
Financial data: Year ended 12/31/2004.
Assets, $11,229,455 (M); Expenditures,
$903,911; Total giving, $632,071.
Type of support: Support to graduates or students
of specific schools; Technical education support;
Undergraduate support.
Application information: Application form required.
Additional information: Contact foundation for
current application deadline.
Program description:
Scholarship Program: The foundation
administers the following nine scholarships, which
are open to applications from individuals who have
been Madison County, IN, residents for at least 12
months prior:
- Alexander Character in Athletics
Scholarship: Given to graduating high
school senior athletes in recognition of
demonstrated strength of character in
sports, classroom, and life. Scholarships
may be used for four-year colleges, junior
colleges, and technical schools
- Ralph and Lora Garriott Scholarship: Given
to students with a minimum cumulative
GPA of 2.5 and at least a 900 SAT score,
who might otherwise be overlooked
- Lilly Endowment Community Scholarship:
Given to graduating seniors at accredited
IN high schools for full-time study in a
baccalaureate program at accredited
four-year colleges and universities located
in IN. This scholarship provides for full
tuition, required fees, and special
allocation of up to $700 per year for
required books and equipment
- Mike Maley Scholarship: Given to
graduating seniors at Alexandria Monroe
High School who demonstrate financial
need and plan to attend technical schools,
junior colleges, two-year associate's
degree programs, or business schools that
will provide them with marketable skills.
This scholarship is only renewable once
- Betty Price Scholarship Fund: Given to
graduating high school graduates who are
members of First Presbyterian Church in
Anderson, IN, for continuation of their
education.
- Eulala Roettger Scholarship for Future
Teachers: Given to high school graduates
accepted for study in the field of education
at accredited colleges and universities.
This scholarship is nonrenewable
- Brad Stansberry Scholarship Fund: Given to
individuals accepted into Purdue
University's Engineering School
- Soroptimist Scholarship Grant: Given to
students from Anderson, Highland, and
Daleville high schools
- Nina P. Van Dorn Scholarship.
EIN: 351859959

2472
Madison Rotary Foundation
22 N. Carroll St., Ste. 202
Madison, WI 53703-3377
E-mail: office@rotarymadison.org; URL: http://
rotarymadison.org/rotary_foundation/
foundation.htm

Foundation type: Public charity
Limitations: Scholarships and awards by
nomination only to high school students residing in
the Madison, WI, area.
Publications: Newsletter.
Financial data: Year ended 06/30/2005.
Assets, $7,874,046 (M); Expenditures,
$652,623; Total giving, $526,964; Grants to
individuals, 54 grants totaling $194,856 (high:
$20,000, low: $250).
Fields of interest: Youth development.
Type of support: Awards/grants by nomination only;
Precollege support; Undergraduate support.
Application information: Applications not
accepted.
Additional information: Unsolicited requests for
funds not considered or acknowledged.
Program descriptions:
Scholarships:
- Frederic (Heggie) S. Brandenburg
- Harry L. French
- Louis Hirsig
- Thomas Leonard.
Youth Awards:
- Hunter Youth Awards: Certificates and
money to area high school seniors.
- Faye J. Meade Community Service Awards:
Awards $500 to a Madison high school
senior who has demonstrated outstanding
leadership and community service.
EIN: 930757050

2473
Madison Scholarship Committee
c/o Shirley Clement
14 W. Oak Ct.
Madison, NJ 07940
Contact: Robert Newhouse, Pres.
Scholarship application address: 78 Lincoln Ave.,
Florham Park, NJ 07932

Foundation type: Independent foundation
Limitations: Scholarships only to graduates of
Madison High School, NJ.
Financial data: Year ended 06/30/2005.
Assets, $101,565 (M); Expenditures, $20,082;
Total giving, $18,700; Grants to individuals, 19
grants totaling $18,700 (high: $2,500, low: $500).
Type of support: Support to graduates or students
of specific schools; Undergraduate support.
Application information: Application form required.
Deadline(s): Feb. 15
Additional information: Interviews required.
EIN: 226100079

2474
Minnie L. Maffett Scholarship Trust
c/o Bank of America, N.A.
P.O. Box 831041
Dallas, TX 75283-1041
Application address: c/o Southern Methodist
University, Attn.: Jenny DeMasi, Division of
Enrollment Svcs., P.O. Box 750181, Dallas, TX
75275-018196, tel.: (214) 768-2058

Foundation type: Independent foundation
Limitations: Scholarships to TX students to pursue
pre-med or pre-nursing undergraduate degrees.

Recipients must attend accredited colleges and
universities, state medical college, or an
AMA-approved nursing school in TX. Preference is
given to residents of Limestone County, TX;
Preference that at least one recipient is African
American.
Financial data: Year ended 04/30/2005.
Assets, $1,269,115 (M); Expenditures, $50,432;
Total giving, $35,734; Grants to individuals, 51
grants totaling $35,734 (high: $2,500, low: $300).
Fields of interest: Medical school/education;
Nursing school/education; African Americans/
Blacks.
Type of support: Undergraduate support.
Application information: Application form required.
Deadline(s): Apr. 1
Applicants should submit the following:
1) Transcripts
EIN: 756037885

2475
Magic Action Team Community Fund, Inc.
(formerly Magic Action Community Fund, Inc.)
8701 Maitland Summit Blvd.
Orlando, FL 32810
Contact: Scott Bowman, Dir.

Foundation type: Operating foundation
Limitations: Scholarships to students in Orange,
Osceola, Brevard, and Seminole counties, FL, for
study at Florida colleges.
Financial data: Year ended 06/30/2003.
Assets, $25,000 (M); Expenditures, $19,069;
Total giving, $19,000; Grants to individuals, 7
grants totaling $19,000 (high: $5,000, low:
$1,000).
Fields of interest: African Americans/Blacks.
Type of support: Undergraduate support.
Application information: Application form required.
Deadline(s): Feb. 27
Applicants should submit the following:
1) Photograph
2) Transcripts
3) Letter(s) of recommendation
Additional information: Application must also
include income profile, parent or guardian's
tax return or W2.
Program descriptions:
Magic Achievers Scholarship: This scholarship
provides a total of $4,000 ($1,000 annually) to a
high school senior in the Orange, Osceola, or
Seminole County, FL, area, who demonstrates
financial need, has a minimum 1010 SAT or 21 ACT
score, and a weighted GPA of 3.0 or above. The
recipient must perform 30 hours of community
service per semester to be determined by the Magic
Action Team Community Fund. Funds must be used
for attendance at a four-year college or university in
FL.
Orlando Magic UCF Minority Scholarship: This
scholarship provides a total of $20,000 ($5,000
annually) to an African American high school senior
in the four-county area to attend the University of
Central Florida. The applicant must have a minimum
1010 SAT or 21 ACT score, a weighted cumulative
GPA of 3.0 or above, and perform 30 hours of
community service per semester to be determined
by the Magic Action Team Community Fund.
EIN: 593287579

2476
Marguerite Magraw Trust
c/o Bank of America, N.A.
P.O. Box 6767
Providence, RI 02940-6767
Scholarship application address: c/o Scholarship Comm., Bank of America, N.A., 777 Main St., CT2-102-22-02, Hartford, CT 06115

Foundation type: Independent foundation
Limitations: Scholarships to financially needy students of Waterbury, CT, and contiguous towns to attend accredited colleges and universities.
Financial data: Year ended 11/30/2004. Assets, $1,447,032 (M); Expenditures, $15,945; Total giving, $3,950; Grants to individuals, totaling $3,950.
Type of support: Scholarships—to individuals.
Application information: Application form required.
  Deadline(s): Mar. 31
  Applicants should submit the following:
    1) Transcripts
    2) Financial information
  Additional information: Interviews required; Recipients notified by mail on June 25 or later.
EIN: 066113177

2477
Agnes T. Maguire Trust
c/o JPMorgan Chase Bank, N.A.
P.O. Box 91210, LA 2-2441
Baton Rouge, LA 70821-9120

Foundation type: Independent foundation
Limitations: Student loans to young girls who are residents of LA, pursuing a profession after high school graduation.
Publications: Application guidelines.
Financial data: Year ended 12/31/2004. Assets, $2,538,370 (M); Expenditures, $38,297; Total giving, $0; Loans to individuals, 40 loans totaling $126,000.
Fields of interest: Women.
Type of support: Student loans—to individuals; Technical education support; Undergraduate support.
Application information: Application form required.
  Initial approach: Letter.
  Deadline(s): July 1
EIN: 726021532

2478
Varoon Mahajan Memorial Trust, Inc.
154 Huyler Landing Rd.
Cresskill, NJ 07626 (201) 871-3607
Contact: Manjit S. Bains, Pres.

Foundation type: Independent foundation
Limitations: Awards to individuals who have or will have medical training at accredited medical institutions in the U.S., and who demonstrate a strong interest in promoting the advancement of medical care in India and the U.S.
Financial data: Year ended 06/30/2005. Assets, $119,764 (M); Expenditures, $11,536; Total giving, $10,930; Grants to individuals, 2 grants totaling $10,930 (high: $8,272, low: $2,658).
Fields of interest: Medical school/education; India.
Type of support: Graduate support.
Application information: Applications accepted throughout the year; Contact trust for current application guidelines.
EIN: 133387669

2479
Mahana Congregational Church Scholarship Foundation
619 S. Harlan St.
Algona, IA 50511 (515) 295-3565
Contact: Marilyn Deal, Pres.
Additional application addresses: Algona High School, 600 S. Hale, Algona, IA 50511 or Bishop Garrigan High School, 1224 N. McCoy St., Algona, IA 50511

Foundation type: Independent foundation
Limitations: Scholarships to graduating Algona, IA, Community School District students for higher education to attend any college or university in the world.
Publications: Application guidelines; Annual report; Grants list; Occasional report.
Financial data: Year ended 12/31/2004. Assets, $1,438,489 (M); Expenditures, $88,264; Total giving, $75,000; Grants to individuals, 27 grants totaling $75,000 (high: $3,000, low: $1,500).
Type of support: Support to graduates or students of specific schools; Graduate support; Undergraduate support.
Application information: Application form required.
  Initial approach: Letter.
  Deadline(s): 3rd week in Apr.
EIN: 421391307

2480
Dora L. Mahanay Educational Trust
P.O. Box 27
Jefferson, IA 50129-0027 (515) 386-3932
Contact: Verna Ball, Tr.

Foundation type: Independent foundation
Limitations: Student loans to residents of IA and NE for study at accredited schools.
Financial data: Year ended 12/31/2004. Assets, $0 (M); Expenditures, $129,969; Total giving, $0; Loans to individuals, totaling $98,750.
Type of support: Student loans—to individuals.
Application information: Applications accepted throughout the year; Completion of formal application required.
EIN: 426091712

2481
B. William Mahoney Trust
c/o Alliance Bank, N.A.
241 Main St., Ste. 200
Buffalo, NY 14203

Foundation type: Independent foundation
Limitations: Scholarships to students in CT and NY, for higher education.
Financial data: Year ended 09/30/2004. Assets, $140,023 (M); Expenditures, $13,809; Total giving, $11,645; Grants to individuals, 3 grants totaling $9,145 (high: $4,921, low: $1,224).
Type of support: Undergraduate support.
Application information: Unsolicited requests for funds not accepted.
EIN: 146186780

2482
Charles Main 1917 Scholarship Fund
c/o Bank of America, N.A.
P.O. Box 6768
Providence, RI 02940-6768
Application address: c/o Virginia Keist, Secy. and Trust Off., Auburn Board of Education, Thorton Ave., Auburn, NY 13021

Foundation type: Independent foundation
Limitations: Scholarships to graduating seniors or graduates of a high school in the public school system of Auburn, NY.
Financial data: Year ended 12/31/2003. Assets, $221,538 (M); Expenditures, $14,609; Total giving, $11,554; Grants to individuals, 16 grants totaling $11,554 (high: $1,663, low: $400).
Type of support: Support to graduates or students of specific schools; Graduate support; Undergraduate support.
Application information: Application form required.
  Initial approach: Letter.
  Deadline(s): Jan 1. to Mar. 1
EIN: 226407279

2483
Main Street Community Foundation
200 Main St.
P.O. Box 2702
Bristol, CT 06011-2702 (860) 583-6363
Contact: Cheryl Dumont-Smith, C.E.O.; For grants: Jarre B. Betts, Prog. Dir.
FAX: (860) 589-1252;
E-mail: office@mainstreetfoundation.org;
Additional E-mail: cheryl@mainstreetfoundation.org; Grant questions E-mail: jarre@mainstreetfoundation.org;
URL: http://www.mainstreetfoundation.org

Foundation type: Community foundation
Limitations: Scholarships to high school students in Bristol, Burlington, Plainville, Plymouth, Southington and Wolcott, CT for higher education.
Publications: Application guidelines; Annual report; Financial statement; Informational brochure; Newsletter.
Financial data: Year ended 12/31/2004. Assets, $22,590,110 (M); Expenditures, $924,339; Total giving, $721,911; Grants to individuals, 50 grants totaling $55,250 (high: $5,000, low: $200).
Type of support: Undergraduate support.
Application information: Application form required. Application form available on the grantmaker's Web site.
  Initial approach: Telephone.
  Deadline(s): Varies
EIN: 061433299

2484
The Maine Community Foundation, Inc.
245 Main St.
Ellsworth, ME 04605 (207) 667-9735
Contact: For grants: Peter Taylor, Dir., Grantmaking; For scholarships: Jean Warren, Scholarship Coord.
FAX: (207) 667-0447; E-mail: info@mainecf.org;
Additional tel: (877) 700-6800; Portland mailing address: 1 Monument Way, Ste. 200, P.O. Box 7380, Portland, ME 04101, tel.: (207) 761-2440, Fax: (207) 773-8832; Grant information E-mail: ptaylor@mainecf.org; URL: http://www.mainecf.org

Foundation type: Community foundation
Limitations: Scholarships, camperships, and fellowships to ME residents only.

Publications: Application guidelines; Annual report; Grants list; Informational brochure; Newsletter.
Financial data: Year ended 12/31/2004. Assets, $142,314,671 (M); Expenditures, $11,240,198; Total giving, $8,807,162; Grants to individuals, 731 grants totaling $792,029 (high: $10,000, low: $75).
Fields of interest: Music; Literature; Theology; Arts, artist's services; Education, research; Elementary/secondary education; Vocational education; Nursing school/education; Environmental education; Veterinary medicine; Mental health/crisis services, formal/general education; Agriculture; Athletics/sports, school programs; Marine science; Political science; Government/public administration; Military/veterans' organizations; Women.
Type of support: Scholarships—to individuals; Camperships.
Application information: Application form required.
  Additional information: See Web site for current application deadline/guidelines.
Program description:
  Campership and Scholarship Funds: Camperships and scholarship funds are available for students attending secondary, post-secondary and graduate education programs. Several scholarships are available for individuals to attend inspirational or non-traditional programs. Scholarships also available for students attending Friends (Quaker) secondary schools. Please note that each scholarship has its own application requirements, review process, and application deadline and that many scholarships are limited to residents of specific counties or graduates of specific high schools. The complete listing is available on the foundation Web site. For further information contact: jwarren@mainecf.org.
EIN: 010391479

2485
Maine Veterinary Education Foundation
P.O. Box 152
Hallowell, ME   04347-0152   (207) 622-4443
Contact: William Bell

Foundation type: Independent foundation
Limitations: Scholarships to students enrolled in approved colleges of veterinary medicine or veterinary technicians from the state of ME.
Financial data: Year ended 12/31/2004. Assets, $522,200 (M); Expenditures, $9,955; Total giving, $8,750; Grants to individuals, 5 grants totaling $8,750.
Fields of interest: Veterinary medicine.
Type of support: Scholarships—to individuals.
Application information:
  Initial approach: Letter.
  Additional information: Contact foundation for further application guidelines.
EIN: 311599553

2486
Major Junior Hockey Education Fund of Oregon, Inc.
c/o Fred T. Hanna
P.O. Box 6405
Portland, OR   97228-6405
Contact: William Deeks, Pres.
Application address: P.O. Box 1419, Beaverton, OR 97075, tel.: (503) 645-3935

Foundation type: Operating foundation
Limitations: Scholarships to Major Junior Hockey players living in the Portland, OR, metropolitan

region who are high school graduates and who do not have a career in professional hockey.
Financial data: Year ended 04/30/2004. Assets, $338,671 (M); Expenditures, $79,718; Total giving, $57,563; Grants to individuals, 20 grants totaling $57,563 (high: $4,554, low: $498).
Fields of interest: Athletics/sports, training; Athletics/sports, winter sports.
Type of support: Scholarships—to individuals.
Application information: Application form required.
  Initial approach: Letter.
  Deadline(s): Contact fund for deadline
  Applicants should submit the following:
    1) Transcripts
  Additional information: Application must also include school admission letter, tuition/fee statement and class schedule.
EIN: 930869476

2487
Major League Baseball Equipment Managers Association
2901 Jolly Rd.
Plymouth Meeting, PA   19462   (610) 279-9100
Contact: Ted Walsh, Pres.

Foundation type: Public charity
Limitations: Scholarships to baseball equipment managers, prospective equipment managers, and their personnel.
Financial data: Year ended 12/31/2004. Assets, $121,220 (M); Expenditures, $29,771; Total giving, $16,293; Grants to individuals, totaling $16,293.
Fields of interest: Athletics/sports, baseball.
Type of support: Undergraduate support.
Application information: Application form required.
  Additional information: Contact foundation for current application deadline/guidelines.
EIN: 341763294

2488
Emma F. Makinson Trust
c/o Bank of America, N.A.
P.O. Box 1802
Providence, RI   02901-1802
Application address: c/o Patricia Lowe, Superintendent of Schools, North Attleboro, MA 02703

Foundation type: Independent foundation
Limitations: Scholarships to high school students from North Attleboro, MA.
Financial data: Year ended 12/31/2004. Assets, $620,789 (M); Expenditures, $45,371; Total giving, $37,500; Grants to individuals, 25 grants totaling $37,500 (high: $1,500, low: $1,500).
Type of support: Support to graduates or students of specific schools; Undergraduate support.
Application information: Applications accepted. Application form required.
EIN: 046224805

2489
William E. Maloney Foundation
275 Massachusetts Ave.
Lexington, MA   02420-4088
Contact: John W. Maloney, Tr.
Application address: P.O. Box 515, Lexington, MA 02173

Foundation type: Independent foundation

Limitations: Scholarships to individuals for undergraduate education, primarily in MA.
Financial data: Year ended 12/31/2004. Assets, $882,184 (M); Expenditures, $67,727; Total giving, $62,500; Grants to individuals, 7 grants totaling $8,000 (high: $2,000, low: $1,000).
Type of support: Undergraduate support.
Application information: Applications accepted.
EIN: 046131998

2490
Mammoth Lakes Foundation
100 College Pkwy.
P.O. Box 1815
Mammoth Lakes, CA   93546   (760) 934-3781
Contact: Evan Russell, Pres.; for Scholarships: Stuart Brown
FAX: (760) 934-6019;
E-mail: foundation@mammothlakesfoundation.org;
URL: http://www.mammothlakesfoundation.org

Foundation type: Public charity
Limitations: Scholarships to high school graduates and residents of Mono County, CA, for higher education.
Financial data: Year ended 06/30/2004. Assets, $3,022,674 (M); Expenditures, $853,494; Total giving, $10,064; Grants to individuals, 10 grants totaling $10,064.
Fields of interest: College (community/junior); Nursing school/education; Journalism school/education; Athletics/sports, winter sports.
Type of support: Scholarships—to individuals.
Application information: Applications accepted. Application form required.
  Initial approach: Telephone.
Program descriptions:
  Scholarship Fund: College scholarships for high school graduates and residents of the Mono County, CA, area who wish to further their education at the Mammoth Campus of Cerro Coso Community College. Any graduate of Mono County high schools and current residents who have lived in the county for at least the past two years are eligible to apply. The scholarship covers the cost of enrollment fees and books for each scholarship recipient for up to sixty units or two years.
  Robyn R. Noll Memorial Scholarship: Awards two scholarships for students who wish to pursue a career in nursing or journalism. The nursing scholarship is awarded to a student in good academic standing, who will begin their higher education at the Mammoth campus of the Eastern Sierra College Center and who show financial need for assistance. The scholarship in journalism is a one-time award of $1,000 for payment of books and fees. The recipient must be enrolled as a full-time student with 12 or more units at the Mammoth campus.
  Chuck Tallman Scholarship: Scholarship to any local resident in Mono County who is pursuing the sport of ski racing and their Associate degree at the Mammoth Campos of Cerro Coso Community College. Financial assistance covers tuition fees and books for a semester.
EIN: 770245395

2491
Ione Mancini Trust
c/o Wells Fargo Bank, N.A.
P.O. Box 63954
San Francisco, CA   94163

Foundation type: Independent foundation

Limitations: Scholarships to graduates of Beyer, Davis, Downey, and Modesto, CA, high schools who will major in instrumental music.
Financial data: Year ended 02/28/2005. Assets, $438,455 (M); Expenditures, $21,755; Total giving, $15,517.
Fields of interest: Music; Performing arts, education.
Type of support: Support to graduates or students of specific schools; Undergraduate support.
Application information: Applications by statement outlining plans for ensuing year, including a copy of transcript, accepted throughout the year.
EIN: 946122937

2492
Manley Music Scholarship Trust
c/o Wells Fargo Bank Indiana, N.A.
P.O. Box 960, 3rd Fl.
Fort Wayne, IN 46801
Application address: c/o Wells Fargo Bank Indiana, N.A., 841 Cass St., Wabash, IN 46992

Foundation type: Independent foundation
Limitations: Scholarships to students at Wabash High School, IN to pursue a career in music or music education.
Financial data: Year ended 12/31/2002. Assets, $395,620 (M); Expenditures, $20,824; Total giving, $15,000; Grants to individuals, 7 grants totaling $15,000 (high: $3,000, low: $1,500).
Fields of interest: Music.
Type of support: Support to graduates or students of specific schools; Undergraduate support.
Application information: Application form required.
  Deadline(s): Mar. 1
  Applicants should submit the following:
    1) Transcripts
    2) Letter(s) of recommendation
EIN: 352028289

2493
Joe L. Mann, Jr. Memorial Fund
629 W. Plaza Dr.
Marshall, MO 65340-2442   (660) 259-2447
Contact: Joe Aull, Tr.

Foundation type: Independent foundation
Limitations: Scholarships only to young male students who reside in Lafayette County, MO, who have been nominated by their high school principals, based on leadership.
Financial data: Year ended 12/31/2004. Assets, $818,021 (M); Expenditures, $111,765; Total giving, $82,000; Grants to individuals, 41 grants totaling $82,000 (high: $3,000, low: $500).
Fields of interest: Leadership development; Men.
Type of support: Awards/grants by nomination only; Undergraduate support.
Application information: Applications not accepted.
  Additional information: Contact fund for current nomination deadline/guidelines; Interviews required.
Program description:
  Scholarship Program: There is no formal application process as students must be nominated. Scholarships are usually $3,000 each, but amounts may vary. In certain years, recipients may apply to renew their scholarship.
EIN: 431204485

2494
Mary B. Mannweiler Trust for Emil Mannweiler Scholarship Fund
c/o Bank of America, N.A.
P.O. Box 1802
Providence, RI 02901-1802
Application address: c/o Principal, Naugatuck High School, Naugatuck, CT 06770, tel.: (203) 720-5400

Foundation type: Independent foundation
Limitations: Scholarships to graduates of Naugatuck High School, CT who have been admitted to college.
Financial data: Year ended 12/31/2004. Assets, $120,873 (M); Expenditures, $5,906; Total giving, $3,700; Grants to individuals, 3 grants totaling $3,700 (high: $2,000, low: $700).
Type of support: Support to graduates or students of specific schools; Undergraduate support.
Application information: Applications accepted.
  Initial approach: Letter.
  Additional information: Contact fund for current application guidelines.
EIN: 066024961

2495
Manpower Foundation, Inc.
5301 N. Ironwood Rd.
Milwaukee, WI 53201   (414) 961-1000

Foundation type: Company-sponsored foundation
Limitations: Scholarships to children of employees of Manpower, Inc., its subsidiaries, or affiliated franchise corporations.
Financial data: Year ended 12/31/2004. Assets, $481,746 (M); Expenditures, $338,230; Total giving, $337,650; Grants to individuals, 3 grants totaling $6,000 (high: $2,000, low: $2,000).
Type of support: Employee-related scholarships.
Application information: Application form required.
  Deadline(s): May 31
  Applicants should submit the following:
    1) Letter(s) of recommendation
    2) Essay
    3) Transcripts
    4) Financial information
  Additional information: Scholarship application address: c/o Scholarship Prog. Coord., P.O. Box 2053, Milwaukee, WI 53201.
Program description:
  Scholarship Program: Children of the following are ineligible: members of the Board of Directors, corporate officers, and members of Manpower Foundation, Inc., any person who has been a substantial contributor to Manpower Foundation, Inc., and members of the Board of Directors and corporate officers of Manpower, Inc., and each of its subsidiaries.
EIN: 396052810

2496
Mansfield Family Foundation
109 E. 3rd St.
Washington, KS 66968
Application address: P.O. Box 104, Washington, KS 66968, tel.: (785) 325-2149

Foundation type: Independent foundation
Limitations: Scholarships to graduates of school districts that lie at least in part within Washington County, KS, for undergraduate or graduate studies. Special consideration for those who would not otherwise be able to continue education; who are pursuing studies in the medical profession; or who

will return to Washington County, KS, to pursue their occupation or profession after completing their education.
Financial data: Year ended 12/31/2004. Assets, $694,703 (M); Expenditures, $44,514; Total giving, $35,932; Grants to individuals, 15 grants totaling $22,500 (high: $1,500, low: $1,500).
Fields of interest: Medical school/education.
Type of support: Support to graduates or students of specific schools; Graduate support; Undergraduate support.
Application information: Application form required.
  Deadline(s): June 15
  Applicants should submit the following:
    1) Essay
    2) Transcripts
    3) GPA
    4) ACT
  Additional information: Application must also include PIN number from the Pell Grant Form, and three references. Interviews may be required.
EIN: 486256918

2497
Viola G. Manuel Trust
c/o TD Banknorth, N.A.
P.O. Box 1180
South Yarmouth, MA 02664
Application address: c/o Nauset Regional High School, Attn: Guidance Dept., 100 Cable Rd, North Eastham, MA 02651, tel.: (508) 255-1505

Foundation type: Independent foundation
Limitations: Scholarships to graduating students of Nauset Regional High School, North Eastham, MA.
Financial data: Year ended 06/30/2005. Assets, $509,334 (M); Expenditures, $33,383; Total giving, $26,506; Grants to individuals, 16 grants totaling $26,506 (high: $2,506, low: $500).
Type of support: Support to graduates or students of specific schools; Undergraduate support.
Application information: Application form required.
  Deadline(s): May 1
  Additional information: Applications available from the high school guidance department.
EIN: 046555836

2498
Lloyd R. and Stella Gibboney Manwiller Trust
c/o Bank of America, N.A.
P.O. Box 441
Ridgefield Park, NJ 07660-9984

Foundation type: Independent foundation
Limitations: Scholarships to members of any United Church of Christ, primarily in Berks County, PA for seminary education. Applicants must plan to serve in the ministry for five years after graduation, or risk repaying scholarship funds.
Financial data: Year ended 12/31/2004. Assets, $2,318,568 (M); Expenditures, $37,417; Total giving, $25,813.
Fields of interest: Theological school/education; Protestant agencies & churches.
Type of support: Graduate support.
Application information: Applications accepted. Application form required.
  Deadline(s): July 31 and Nov. 30
  Applicants should submit the following:
    1) Transcripts
    2) Letter(s) of recommendation
    3) Financial information
EIN: 236714082

2499
Maple Point Foundation, Inc.
P.O. Box 287
Lafayette, IN 47902-0287
Contact: Judith K. Hamman, Dir.
Application address: 1519 Ticonderoga Rd., Ft. Collins, CO 80525

Foundation type: Independent foundation
Limitations: Scholarships to financially needy young people who will be enrolled in the civil engineering program at Purdue University.
Financial data: Year ended 05/31/2005. Assets, $6,339 (M); Expenditures, $10,317; Total giving, $9,000.
Fields of interest: Engineering school/education.
Type of support: Support to graduates or students of specific schools; Undergraduate support.
Application information: Applications accepted. Application form required.
   Deadline(s): Mar. 21
   Applicants should submit the following:
      1) Essay
      2) Transcripts
      3) Letter(s) of recommendation
EIN: 310999380

2500
Maquoketa Area Community Foundation
(formerly Maquoketa Area Foundation)
120 1/2 S. Main St.
Maquoketa, IA 52060 (563) 652-4179
Contact: Kate Carinder, Exec. Dir.
FAX: (563) 652-4203; E-mail: maf@cis.net;
URL: http://www.maqarea.org

Foundation type: Community foundation
Limitations: Scholarships to students in the Jackson County, IA area, for higher education.
Publications: Application guidelines; Annual report; Financial statement; Grants list; Informational brochure; Newsletter.
Financial data: Year ended 12/31/2004. Assets, $3,997,001 (M); Expenditures, $382,237; Total giving, $336,833; Grants to individuals, 51 grants totaling $45,200 (high: $2,500, low: $200).
Type of support: Graduate support; Undergraduate support.
Application information: Application form required. Application form available on the grantmaker's Web site.
   Initial approach: Application.
   Copies of proposal: 1
   Deadline(s): Apr.
   Applicants should submit the following:
      1) Transcripts
      2) GPA
      3) FAFSA
      4) Curriculum vitae
      5) ACT
   Additional information: Contact foundation for current application deadline/guidelines.
EIN: 421197911

2501
William A. March Education Fund
c/o PNC Advisors
1600 Market St., 4th Fl.
Philadelphia, PA 19103-7240

Foundation type: Independent foundation
Limitations: Student loans to individuals in PA for higher education.
Financial data: Year ended 12/31/2003. Assets, $784,352 (M); Expenditures, $9,470;

Total giving, $0; Loans to individuals, totaling $16,250.
Type of support: Student loans—to individuals.
Application information: Contact fund for current application deadline/guidelines.
EIN: 236295283

2502
Clara A. March Scholarship Fund
15 Knoerl Ave.
Buffalo, NY 14210-2329
Contact: Dennis A. Nadler, Assoc. Dean
Application address: c/o Dean of the Medical School, 40 Biomedical Bldg., SUNY, Buffalo, NY 14214

Foundation type: Independent foundation
Limitations: Scholarships to medical students attending the State University of New York at Buffalo.
Publications: Annual report.
Financial data: Year ended 12/31/2004. Assets, $1,658,236 (M); Expenditures, $99,116; Total giving, $80,000.
Fields of interest: Medical school/education.
Type of support: Support to graduates or students of specific schools; Graduate support.
Application information:
   Initial approach: Letter outlining financial need.
   Deadline(s): None
EIN: 166119078

2503
Arthur and Ann Marciano Scholarship Fund
(formerly Arthur & Ann Marciano Scholarship & Charitable Trust)
88 Barnes Rd.
Stamford, CT 06902
Contact: Arthur Marciano

Foundation type: Independent foundation
Limitations: Grants to middle-income ($35,000-$110,000) U.S. citizens residing in CT for undergraduate education at accredited American colleges, universities or trade schools. Special consideration given when two or more children are in college at the same time.
Financial data: Year ended 12/31/2002. Assets, $77,042 (M); Expenditures, $14,910; Total giving, $13,100; Grants to individuals, 15 grants totaling $13,100 (high: $1,250, low: $650).
Type of support: Undergraduate support.
Application information:
   Initial approach: Letter.
   Deadline(s): June
   Applicants should submit the following:
      1) SASE
      2) Photograph
      3) Transcripts
      4) Financial information
      5) Essay
   Additional information: Application must also include a $55 application fee.
EIN: 510201994

2504
Marco Island Women's Club Foundation
P.O. Box 40200
Jacksonville, FL 32203-0200
Contact: June McGannon, Co-Chair.
Application address: 1857 Honduras Ct., Marco Island, FL 34145, tel.: (941) 394-8683

Foundation type: Independent foundation
Limitations: Scholarships only to Marco Island, FL residents.
Financial data: Year ended 04/30/2005. Assets, $171,258 (M); Expenditures, $17,113; Total giving, $15,567; Grants to individuals, 24 grants totaling $15,567 (high: $1,000, low: $250).
Type of support: Scholarships—to individuals.
Application information: Application form required.
   Initial approach: Letter.
   Deadline(s): Mar. 15
   Applicants should submit the following:
      1) Resume
   Additional information: Interviews required.
EIN: 650144269

2505
Joseph L. Marcum Scholarship Fund, Inc.
9450 Seward Rd.
Fairfield, OH 45014-5456
Contact: Stacey Andrews, Admin. Asst.
Scholarship application address: c/o Hamilton Community Fdn., 319 N. 3rd. St., Hamilton, OH 45011, tel.: (513) 863-1389
FAX: (513) 881-1327;
E-mail: stacey.andrews@ocas.com

Foundation type: Company-sponsored foundation
Limitations: Scholarships to children of employees of Ohio Casualty Corporation who have been in the continuous full-time employment of the corporation for at least 24 months.
Financial data: Year ended 12/31/2004. Assets, $150,611 (M); Expenditures, $15,921; Total giving, $15,000; Grants to individuals, 16 grants totaling $15,000 (high: $2,000, low: $500).
Type of support: Employee-related scholarships.
Application information: Application form required.
   Deadline(s): Feb.
   Applicants should submit the following:
      1) Essay
      2) Transcripts
      3) SAT
      4) ACT
      5) Letter(s) of recommendation
EIN: 311425290

2506
The Adele Marcus Foundation, Inc.
c/o Leonard B. Pack
1500 Broadway, 21st Fl.
New York, NY 10036
Contact: Elizabeth Ross, Secy.
Application address: c/o Ernest D. Loewenwarter & Co., 10 E. 40th St., Ste. 2105, New York, NY 10016, tel.: (212) 532-2777

Foundation type: Operating foundation
Limitations: Scholarships to students for the study of classical piano music in CA, NY and VA.
Financial data: Year ended 10/31/2003. Assets, $192,398 (M); Expenditures, $20,285; Total giving, $8,600; Grants to individuals, totaling $8,600.
Fields of interest: Music; Education.
Type of support: Undergraduate support.
Application information: Applications by letter accepted throughout the year.
EIN: 841426290

2507
Susan H. & Wilbur H. Marcy Trust
P.O. Box 1328
Winter Park, FL 32790-1328
Contact: Kenneth F. Murrah, Tr.

Foundation type: Public charity
Limitations: Scholarships and fellowships to individuals in FL and GA.
Financial data: Year ended 01/31/2005. Assets, $8,574,013 (M); Expenditures, $253,714; Total giving, $166,646; Grants to individuals, totaling $37,112.
Type of support: Fellowships; Scholarships—to individuals.
Application information: Unsolicited requests for funds not accepted.
EIN: 591932547

2508
Marek Trust Fund
c/o Central State Bank
301 Iowa Ave.
Muscatine, IA 52761
Application addresses: c/o Scholarship Comm., Washington Community School District, 404 W. Main, Washington, IA 52353, tel.: (319) 653-6543; c/o Scholarship Comm., Mid-Prairie School District, Hwy. 22 E., Wellman, IA 52356, tel.: (319) 646-6093, or c/o Scholarship Comm., Iowa Mennonite School, R.R. 1, Kalona, IA 52247, tel.: (319) 646-2475

Foundation type: Independent foundation
Limitations: Scholarships to financially needy individuals from Washington, Wellman, and Kalona, IA, who are pursuing degrees in medically-related, agriculturally-related, and other socially-related fields that benefit humanity.
Financial data: Year ended 12/31/2004. Assets, $217,625 (M); Expenditures, $9,318; Total giving, $6,000; Grants to individuals, 3 grants totaling $6,000 (high: $2,000, low: $2,000).
Fields of interest: Medical school/education; Agriculture; Human services.
Type of support: Scholarships—to individuals; Support to graduates or students of specific schools.
Application information: Applications accepted.
Initial approach: Letter.
Deadline(s): May 1
Additional information: Application must also include past academic performance, college aptitude test scores, and including instructors' recommendations; Interviews required.
EIN: 426397123

2509
Marietta Community Foundation
121 Putman St.
P.O. Box 77
Marietta, OH 45750-0070 (740) 373-3286
Contact: Jack Moberg, C.E.O., Pres., and Exec. Dir.; For grant information: Carol Wharff, Prog. and Donor Svcs. Off.
FAX: (740) 373-3937;
E-mail: info@mariettacommunityfoundation.org; Additional E-mail: jack@mariettacommunityfoundation.org; URL: http:// www.mariettacommunityfoundation.org

Foundation type: Community foundation
Limitations: Scholarships to individuals in the Marietta, OH, area. Recipients are identified and recommended by various school administrators in the area.
Publications: Application guidelines; Annual report; Informational brochure (including application guidelines).
Financial data: Year ended 12/31/2004. Assets, $1,039,063 (M); Expenditures, $512,354; Total giving, $338,242.
Type of support: Scholarships—to individuals.
Application information:
Initial approach: Letter or telephone.
Additional information: Contact foundation for current application deadline/guidelines.
EIN: 743054287

2510
Maria Marino Scholarship Fund
c/o Avon Town Treas.
Avon Town Hall
Avon, MA 02322
Application address: Marilyn Malcomson, Guidance Counselor, c/o Avon High School, Avon, MA 02322, tel.: (508) 583-4822

Foundation type: Independent foundation
Limitations: Scholarships to students at Avon High School, MA, for college education.
Financial data: Year ended 12/31/2004. Assets, $115,699 (M); Expenditures, $7,273; Total giving, $6,500; Grants to individuals, 11 grants totaling $6,500 (high: $1,000, low: $250).
Type of support: Support to graduates or students of specific schools; Undergraduate support.
Application information: Application form required.
Deadline(s): Apr. 1
Applicants should submit the following:
1) Transcripts
2) Essay
3) FAFSA
EIN: 510181012

2511
Marion Memorial Health Foundation
c/o Harlean Miller
P.O. Box 1815
Marion, IL 62959 (618) 997-5341

Foundation type: Independent foundation
Limitations: Scholarships to graduating seniors from Benton, Carrier Mills, Carterville, Christopher, Crab Orchard, Eldorado, Goreville, Harrisburg, Herrin, Johnston City, Marion, Thompsonville, Vienna and West Frankfort high schools, IL, for higher education.
Financial data: Year ended 12/31/2004. Assets, $1,033,159 (M); Expenditures, $37,180; Total giving, $33,500; Grants to individuals, 6 grants totaling $6,500 (high: $2,000, low: $500).
Fields of interest: Medical school/education; Public health.
Type of support: Support to graduates or students of specific schools; Undergraduate support.
Application information: Application form required.
Additional information: Contact foundation for current application deadline.
Program description:
Scholarship Program: Scholarships are in the amount of $1,000 to three seniors at area schools (Benton, Carrier Mills, Carterville, Christopher, Crab Orchard, Eldorado, Goreville, Harrisburg, Herrin, Johnston City, Thompsonville, Vienna or West Frankfort) who are planning a career in human health care. Two scholarships of $1,000 are provided to Marion graduating seniors pursuing a career in the human health care field. A $2,000 "R.D. Morgan, M.D." medical scholarship will be awarded to a Marion High School graduating senior who is pursuing a career as a medical doctor. If no graduating senior meets the necessary qualifications, the scholarship will be open to the previously-listed schools.
EIN: 371316969

2512
Irena Maris Scholarship Foundation
c/o First National Bank-Danville
P.O. Box 1010
Danville, IL 61834-1010

Foundation type: Independent foundation
Limitations: Scholarships to individuals in Danville, IL.
Financial data: Year ended 12/31/2004. Assets, $214,946 (M); Expenditures, $18,760; Total giving, $14,684; Grants to individuals, 5 grants totaling $14,684 (high: $4,000, low: $684).
Type of support: Scholarships—to individuals.
Application information: Unsolicited requests for funds not accepted.
EIN: 376261922

2513
The Markos Foundation, Inc.
c/o Stephanie Mott
P.O. Box 5507
Madison, WI 53705

Foundation type: Independent foundation
Limitations: Scholarships to individuals in IL, IN and WI for attendance at colleges, universities and technical schools.
Financial data: Year ended 06/30/2005. Assets, $2,389,266 (M); Expenditures, $177,247; Total giving, $144,000; Grants to individuals, 20 grants totaling $38,000 (high: $2,000, low: $1,000).
Type of support: Technical education support; Undergraduate support.
Application information: Applications not accepted.
EIN: 391836400

2514
Marquette Area Public Schools Education Foundation
1201 W. Fair Ave.
Marquette, MI 49855 (906) 225-4328
Contact: Linda Winslow, Pres.

Foundation type: Public charity
Limitations: Scholarships to students in the Marquette, MI, Public Schools area.
Financial data: Year ended 06/30/2004. Assets, $586,021 (M); Expenditures, $38,879; Total giving, $30,908; Grants to individuals, 17 grants totaling $11,800 (high: $1,000, low: $200).
Fields of interest: Education.
Type of support: Scholarships—to individuals.
Application information: Applications accepted.
Initial approach: Letter.
EIN: 382972673

2515
Marquette Community Foundation
401 E. Fair Ave.
Marquette, MI   49855   (906) 226-7666
Contact: Cathy Nardi, Exec. Dir.
FAX: (906) 226-2104; E-mail: mcf@chartermi.net;
Mailing address: P.O. Box 37, Marquette, MI 49855

Foundation type: Community foundation
Limitations: Scholarships to individuals from the Marquette County, MI, area, for undergraduate education at U.S. colleges and universities.
Publications: Application guidelines; Annual report; Financial statement; Informational brochure; Newsletter; Program policy statement.
Financial data: Year ended 12/31/2004.
Assets, $7,055,237 (M); Expenditures, $369,682; Total giving, $206,806; Grants to individuals, 44 grants totaling $26,500 (high: $2,000, low: $500).
Fields of interest: Music (choral); Teacher school/education.
Type of support: Precollege support; Undergraduate support.
Application information: Contact foundation for current applications deadlines/guidelines.
Program descriptions:
Lee Andrews Choral Music Scholarships: Supports attendance at a summer music camp for middle school children.
Meggan Eiben Memorial Scholarship: Scholarships to individuals studying education.
EIN: 382826563

2516
Louis & Temple Marsch Charitable Trust
c/o U.S. Bank, N.A.
P.O. Box 387
St. Louis, MO   63166
Contact: Mary Jo Janssen, Trust Off., U.S. Bank, N.A.
Additional tel.: (217) 753-7358

Foundation type: Independent foundation
Limitations: Scholarships to high school graduates from specific geographical areas of southern IL, pursuing engineering or scientific fields of study on a full-time basis. See program description for a list of counties and townships from which recipients are chosen.
Financial data: Year ended 06/30/2005.
Assets, $1,040,907 (M); Expenditures, $96,560; Total giving, $78,800; Grants to individuals, 146 grants totaling $70,800 (high: $1,000, low: $500).
Fields of interest: Engineering school/education; Science.
Type of support: Scholarships—to individuals.
Application information: Applications accepted.
Application form required.
Initial approach: Letter or telephone.
Deadline(s): Dec. 31 to Apr. 1
Applicants should submit the following:
1) Transcripts
2) Letter(s) of recommendation
Additional information: Application should also include acceptance letter.
Program description:
Scholarship Fund: Recipients must be from one of the following locales in southern IL: Christian, Montgomery, or Macoupin counties; the townships of Auburn, Pawnee, Divernon, Rochester, and Mechanicsburg in Sangamon County; or the townships of Moweaqua, Flat Branch, or Shelbyville in Shelby County. Generally five to fifteen new recipients are chosen each year. Students must be enrolled on a full-time basis, pursue an education in engineering or a scientific field, and maintain at

least a "C" average. Verified transcripts of courses taken and grades received are required during scholarship funding. The Board must be notified of any change in circumstances.
EIN: 376129244

2517
Marshall & Ilsley Foundation, Inc.
(formerly Marshall & Ilsley Bank Foundation, Inc.)
770 N. Water St.
Milwaukee, WI   53202   (414) 765-7835
Contact: Meg Sullivan, Asst. Secy.

Foundation type: Company-sponsored foundation
Limitations: Scholarships only to children of permanent full-time employees of the Marshall & Ilsley Corporation.
Financial data: Year ended 12/31/2004.
Assets, $93,993 (M); Expenditures, $2,845,594; Total giving, $2,844,850.
Type of support: Employee-related scholarships.
Application information:
Deadline(s): None
EIN: 396043185

2518
W. Marshall & Margaret Hughes Scholarship Foundation
1631 Farr Rd.
Wyomissing, PA   19610
Scholarship application address: c/o Investors Trust Co., 2201 Ridgewood Rd., Ste. 180, Wyomissing, PA 19610, tel.: (610) 372-6414

Foundation type: Independent foundation
Limitations: Scholarships to graduates of Berks County, PA, high schools for undergraduate education in architecture, creative literature, music, or theatre.
Financial data: Year ended 12/31/2004.
Assets, $564,607 (M); Expenditures, $29,934; Total giving, $21,601; Grants to individuals, 13 grants totaling $21,601 (high: $3,780, low: $265).
Fields of interest: Architecture; Theater; Music; Literature.
Type of support: Support to graduates or students of specific schools.
Application information: Applications accepted.
Application form required.
Deadline(s): Mar. 1
Applicants should submit the following:
1) Transcripts
2) Letter(s) of recommendation
3) Essay
Additional information: Application should include proof of enrollment, and supporting materials.
EIN: 237813648

2519
Marshall Community Foundation
(formerly Marshall Civic Foundation)
126 W. Michigan Ave., Ste. 202
Marshall, MI   49068   (269) 781-2273
Contact: Sherry Anderson, Exec. Dir.
FAX: (269) 781-9747;
E-mail: marshallcomfdn@aol.com; URL: http://www.marshallcf.org

Foundation type: Community foundation
Limitations: Scholarships to residents of Calhoun County, MI, for higher education.
Publications: Annual report; Informational brochure.

Financial data: Year ended 09/30/2004.
Assets, $7,461,104 (M); Expenditures, $280,381; Total giving, $184,245; Grants to individuals, 59 grants totaling $52,356 (high: $5,000, low: $50).
Fields of interest: Higher education.
Type of support: Scholarships—to individuals.
Application information: Applications accepted.
Application form required.
Initial approach: Letter.
Deadline(s): Mar. 1
Additional information: Interviews required.
EIN: 237011281

2520
Marshall County Community Foundation, Inc.
2701 N. Michigan St.
P.O. Box 716
Plymouth, IN   46563   (574) 935-5159
Contact: R. Jeffrey Honzik, Exec. Dir.
FAX: (574) 936-8040;
E-mail: info@marshallcountycf.org; Additional E-mail: jeff@marshallcountycf.org; URL: http://www.marshallcountycf.org

Foundation type: Community foundation
Limitations: Scholarships to graduates of schools in Marshall County, IN.
Publications: Application guidelines; Annual report (including application guidelines); Financial statement; Grants list; Informational brochure (including application guidelines); Newsletter; Program policy statement.
Financial data: Year ended 06/30/2005.
Assets, $20,310,357 (M); Expenditures, $984,667; Total giving, $568,460.
Type of support: Precollege support; Undergraduate support.
Application information: Application form required.
Initial approach: Letter.
Additional information: Contact foundation for current application deadline; See Web site for complete program descriptions and guidelines.
EIN: 351826870

2521
The Marshall Educational Trust Fund
517 Locust St.
P.O. Box 98
Marshall, IL   62441-0098   (217) 826-8051
Contact: Joseph R. Schroeder, Pres.

Foundation type: Independent foundation
Limitations: Student loans to graduates of Marshall High School, IL.
Financial data: Year ended 07/31/2004.
Assets, $479,240 (M); Expenditures, $6,657; Total giving, $0; Loans to individuals, 14 loans totaling $25,545.
Type of support: Support to graduates or students of specific schools; Undergraduate support.
Application information: Application form required.
Deadline(s): June 1 and Dec. 1
Program description:
Student Loan Program: Applicants must have attended Marshall High School for two full years; must plan to attend a two- or four-year college or university; must have a GPA of at least 2.5 for a four-year school or 2.0 for a two-year school; and must demonstrate financial need.
EIN: 371318513

2522
The Judge Elliott D. Marshall Foundation
5763 Salisbury Ln.
San Luis Obispo, CA 93405-8253
Application address: P.O. Box 1618, Front Royal, VA
22630, tel.: (540) 635-9415

Foundation type: Operating foundation
Limitations: Scholarships to residents of the 26th
Judicial Circuit of VA to attend law school.
Financial data: Year ended 12/31/2002.
Assets, $1,486 (M); Expenditures, $10,971; Total
giving, $10,000; Grant to an individual, 1 grant
totaling $10,000.
Fields of interest: Law school/education.
Type of support: Graduate support.
Application information: Application form required.
 Deadline(s): May 15
EIN: 311670725

2523
Marshfield Area Community Foundation
P.O. Box 456
Marshfield, WI 54449
Contact: Dean Markwardt, Exec. Dir.
E-mail: macf@tznet.com; Tel./fax: (715) 384-9029

Foundation type: Community foundation
Limitations: Scholarships to residents of the
Marshfield, WI, Marquette, WI and Turkey Valley, IA
areas for higher education.
Publications: Application guidelines; Annual report;
Financial statement; Grants list; Informational
brochure; Informational brochure (including
application guidelines); Newsletter.
Financial data: Year ended 12/31/2004.
Assets, $2,417,601 (M); Expenditures,
$157,271; Total giving, $110,965; Grants to
individuals, 42 grants totaling $37,449 (high:
$3,349, low: $250).
Type of support: Scholarships—to individuals;
Technical education support; Precollege support;
Undergraduate support; Camperships.
Application information: Application form required.
 Initial approach: Letter of no more than two
 pages.
 Copies of proposal: 1
 Deadline(s): Contact foundation for current
 application deadline
 Applicants should submit the following:
 1) Letter(s) of recommendation
 2) Financial information
 3) Essay
 Additional information: Applications should be
 sent by mail or fax; Application should also
 include any other information required in the
 agreement.
EIN: 396578767

2524
C. F. Martell Memorial Foundation
c/o First International Bank & Trust
P.O. Box 1088
Williston, ND 58802-1088
Contact: Hon. William W. McLees, Jr.
Scholarship loan application address: P.O. Box 546,
Watford City, ND 58854

Foundation type: Independent foundation
Limitations: Student loans to residents of Williams
and McKenzie counties, ND, for study at trade,
technical, and professional schools and colleges in
the U.S.
Financial data: Year ended 07/31/2005.
Assets, $977,630 (M); Expenditures, $121,916;

Total giving, $111,000; Loans to individuals, 26
loans totaling $52,000.
Fields of interest: Vocational education.
Type of support: Technical education support.
Application information: Application form required.
 Deadline(s): July 1
 Applicants should submit the following:
 1) Transcripts
 2) Financial information
 Additional information: Applications available
 from District Judge of Williams County, County
 Judge of McKenzie County, and Pastor of St.
 Joseph's Church in Williston, ND.
EIN: 456010183

2525
Marth Foundation, Ltd.
c/o Scholarship Comm.
6752 State Hwy. 107N
Marathon, WI 54448-9444

Foundation type: Independent foundation
Limitations: Scholarships to residents of WI who
plan on attending a WI college or university.
Financial data: Year ended 05/31/2005.
Assets, $15,746 (M); Expenditures, $15,218;
Total giving, $14,749; Grants to individuals, 7
grants totaling $14,749 (high: $3,000, low:
$1,000).
Type of support: Undergraduate support.
Application information:
 Initial approach: Letter.
 Applicants should submit the following:
 1) Financial information
 2) Essay
 Additional information: Contact foundation for
 further application guidelines.
EIN: 391410550

2526
Marti Foundation
1501-D N. Main St.
Cleburne, TX 76033
Contact: Hoylene Harris, Mgr.

Foundation type: Independent foundation
Limitations: Undergraduate scholarships and
student loans, and graduate student loans to
residents of TX for study at approved institutions.
Preference is given to residents of Johnson County.
Recipients must submit an academic and financial
report to the foundation within one month of
completing each semester or trimester of study.
Financial data: Year ended 05/31/2004.
Assets, $9,545,712 (M); Expenditures,
$448,681; Total giving, $439,786; Grants to
individuals, 210 grants totaling $415,657.
Type of support: Student loans—to individuals;
Undergraduate support.
Application information: Application form required.
 Deadline(s): Applications accepted throughout
 the year.
EIN: 752265837

2527
G. Roxy & Elizabeth C. Martin Charitable Trust
P.O. Box 1908
Orlando, FL 32802-1908

Foundation type: Independent foundation
Limitations: Scholarships to individuals in FL for
higher education.
Publications: Application guidelines.

Financial data: Year ended 11/30/2004.
Assets, $3,865,001 (M); Expenditures,
$215,333; Total giving, $206,875; Grants to
individuals, 62 grants totaling $61,875 (high:
$3,000, low: $250).
Type of support: Undergraduate support.
Application information: Applications accepted.
 Initial approach: Letter.
 Deadline(s): None
 Additional information: Contact trust for current
 application guidelines.
EIN: 596920693

2528
Loy Crump Martin Charitable Trust
720 E. Broadway
Columbia, MO 65201-4444

Foundation type: Independent foundation
Limitations: Scholarships to students of Southern
Boone High School, Ashland, MO.
Financial data: Year ended 09/30/2005.
Assets, $1,381,400 (M); Expenditures, $76,321;
Total giving, $52,918; Grant to an individual, 1
grant totaling $46,918.
Type of support: Support to graduates or students
of specific schools.
Application information:
 Initial approach: Letter.
 Additional information: The Loy Crump Martin
 Charitable Trust administers the Loy Crump
 Martin Ashland High School Scholarship
 Program. Contact trust for current application
 deadline/guidelines.
EIN: 436589909

2529
Martin Education Trust
c/o JPMorgan Chase Bank, N.A.
P.O. Box 1308
Milwaukee, WI 53201
Application address: c/o JPMorgan Chase Bank,
N.A., 101 Central Plz. S., Canton, OH 44711,
tel.: (330) 438-8354

Foundation type: Independent foundation
Limitations: Scholarships to residents of the City of
Wooster and Wayne Township in Wayne County, OH.
Financial data: Year ended 04/30/2005.
Assets, $382,481 (M); Expenditures, $31,772;
Total giving, $27,000; Grants to individuals, 14
grants totaling $27,000 (high: $5,000, low: $500).
Type of support: Scholarships—to individuals.
Application information: Application form required.
 Deadline(s): Mar. 1
EIN: 346742103

2530
S. J. Martin Endowment Fund
c/o BB&T, Trust Dept.
1820 Scottsville Rd.
Bowling Green, KY 42104
Application address: c/o H.A. Thurman, 427-1/2
Park Row, Bowling Green, KY 42101

Foundation type: Independent foundation
Limitations: Scholarships to children of members
of The Independent Order of Odd Fellows, KY.
Financial data: Year ended 12/31/2003.
Assets, $253,061 (M); Expenditures, $12,870;
Total giving, $10,679; Grants to individuals, 5
grants totaling $10,679 (high: $6,979, low: $700).
Type of support: Undergraduate support.

Application information: Applications accepted. Application form required.

Initial approach: Letter requesting application form.

Additional information: Contact fund for current application deadline.

EIN: 616031132

2531

Albert and Jessie D. Martin Scholarship Trust Fund

8016 N. County Hwy. 601
Boonville, NC 27011
Application address: c/o Craig Smythers, Starmount High School, 2516 Longtown Rd., Boonville, NC 27011, tel.: (336) 468-2891

Foundation type: Independent foundation
Limitations: Scholarships by nomination only to graduates of Starmount High School, NC.
Financial data: Year ended 12/31/2004. Assets, $283,209 (M); Expenditures, $17,231; Total giving, $16,500; Grants to individuals, 11 grants totaling $16,500 (high: $2,000, low: $1,000).
Type of support: Support to graduates or students of specific schools; Awards/grants by nomination only; Undergraduate support.
Application information:

Deadline(s): Apr. 1st to 15th

Additional information: Application by nomination only.

Program description:

Scholarship Program: Recipients must meet the following criteria to be eligible for scholarship: carry a 3.0 GPA in high school; demonstrate interest in the welfare of others, as evidenced by community and school activities not restricted to student government and athletic organizations; demonstrate ability for divergent thinking and creativity, particularly in writing and other arts; reflect in his/her work an unusual interest and aptitude for a career in education; gained the respect of peers and teachers for personal integrity and effort to live by convictions; and graduated from Boonville Elementary School or the elementary school serving the Boonville community.

EIN: 586241009

2532

Mary R. Martin Trust No. 2

P.O. Box 1739
Wolfeboro, NH 03894-1739
Contact: G. Thomas Bickford, Tr.

Foundation type: Independent foundation
Limitations: Scholarships to economically disadvantaged residents of Wolfeboro, NH.
Financial data: Year ended 12/31/2004. Assets, $556,047 (M); Expenditures, $21,004; Total giving, $18,651; Grants to individuals, 40 grants totaling $18,651 (high: $500, low: $150).
Fields of interest: Economically disadvantaged.
Type of support: Graduate support; Undergraduate support.
Application information: Applications accepted. Application form required.

Copies of proposal: 1

Deadline(s): June 30

EIN: 026009374

2533

Karl & Georgia Martin, Sr., Anna Belle Flynn, Karl & June Martin, Jr. Foundation

P.O. Box 3627
Tulsa, OK 74101-3627
Contact: William E. Meyer, Tr.

Foundation type: Operating foundation
Limitations: Scholarships to students majoring in petroleum and related fields at Oklahoma State University, University of Oklahoma and University of Tulsa, OK.
Financial data: Year ended 12/31/2002. Assets, $207,474 (M); Expenditures, $32,467; Total giving, $30,000; Grants to individuals, 16 grants totaling $20,000 (high: $2,000, low: $1,000).
Fields of interest: Environmental education.
Type of support: Support to graduates or students of specific schools; Undergraduate support.
Application information: Application form required.

Initial approach: Letter.

Deadline(s): Apr. 30

EIN: 731504147

2534

Joseph W. Martino Trust

c/o U.S. Bank, N.A.
P.O. Box 387
St. Louis, MO 63166 (314) 241-8600
Application addresses: c/o Hal Dygert, Benevolent & Protective Order of Elks Lodge No. 9, 12481 Ladue Rd., St. Louis, MO 63141, c/o Charles Nash, Boys Club of St. Louis, 2524 S. 11th St., St. Louis, MO 63104

Foundation type: Independent foundation
Limitations: Scholarships to members and children of members of the Boys Club of St. Louis, MO, or the B.P.O.E. Lodge, No. 9.
Financial data: Year ended 11/30/2004. Assets, $817,296 (M); Expenditures, $49,525; Total giving, $34,950; Grants to individuals, 29 grants totaling $34,950 (high: $3,450, low: $625).
Fields of interest: Boys clubs; Men.
Type of support: Scholarships—to individuals.
Application information: Applications accepted. Application form required.
EIN: 436274479

2535

Mother Joseph Rogan Marymount Foundation

18 Fordyce Ln.
St. Louis, MO 63124 (314) 993-1290
Contact: Joseph F. Imbs II, Pres.

Foundation type: Independent foundation
Limitations: Scholarships to financially needy high school students and student loans to college and university students. Applicants must be U.S. citizens and residents of greater St. Louis, MO.
Financial data: Year ended 06/30/2004. Assets, $173,297 (M); Expenditures, $164,554; Total giving, $160,065; Grants to individuals, 62 grants totaling $106,465 (high: $10,000, low: $100).
Type of support: Undergraduate support.
Application information: Applications by letter outlining financial need accepted throughout the year.
EIN: 237418805

2536

Daisy Mason Scholarship Fund

(formerly Mason Scholarship Fund)
c/o First Mid-Illinois Bank & Trust
P.O. Box 499
Mattoon, IL 61938 (217) 234-7454
Contact: Gary Kuhns, Trust Off., First Mid-Illinois Bank & Trust

Foundation type: Independent foundation
Limitations: Scholarships to graduates of Community Unit District No. 2, Mattoon Senior High School, IL.
Financial data: Year ended 12/31/2004. Assets, $1,080,532 (M); Expenditures, $107,563; Total giving, $55,000; Grants to individuals, 49 grants totaling $54,500 (high: $1,200, low: $500).
Type of support: Support to graduates or students of specific schools; Undergraduate support.
Application information: Application form required.

Deadline(s): Apr.

Additional information: Applications available at First Mid-Illinois Bank & Trust and Mattoon Senior High School.

EIN: 376024616

2537

Masonic Educational Foundation, Inc.

P.O. Box 12357
Alexandria, LA 71315
Contact: Roy B. Delaney, Pres.
Application address: 9416 Evergreen Dr., Shreveport, LA 71118

Foundation type: Independent foundation
Limitations: Scholarships only to residents of the state of LA.
Financial data: Year ended 09/30/2004. Assets, $1 (M); Expenditures, $17,791; Total giving, $15,496; Grants to individuals, 18 grants totaling $15,496 (high: $1,000, low: $500).
Type of support: Undergraduate support.
Application information: Applications accepted. Application form required.

Applicants should submit the following:

1) Financial information

Additional information: Application must include proof of college attendance; Funds severely limited; Applications from individuals residing outside of stated geographic restriction not accepted.

EIN: 237423947

2538

Masonic Foundation of Michigan, Inc.

233 E. Fulton St., Ste. 20
Grand Rapids, MI 49503-3270 (616) 459-2451
Contact: Richard I. Williams, Pres.
FAX: (616) 459-3912;
E-mail: mmhcf@masonichome.com

Foundation type: Public charity
Limitations: Scholarships to individuals residing in MI for undergraduate education.
Financial data: Year ended 03/31/2003. Assets, $2,176,950 (M); Expenditures, $401,929; Total giving, $90,675; Grants to individuals, totaling $90,675.
Type of support: Undergraduate support.
Application information: Contact foundation for current application deadline/guidelines.
EIN: 382284259

2539
Masonic Foundation of Utah
650 E. South Temple St.
Salt Lake City, UT 84102 (801) 363-2936
Contact: Blaine Simons, Secy.-Treas.
FAX: (801) 363-2938

Foundation type: Public charity
Limitations: Scholarships to individuals for undergraduate education, primarily in UT.
Financial data: Year ended 12/31/2003. Assets, $3,693,533 (M); Expenditures, $277,897; Total giving, $242,250; Grants to individuals, 30 grants totaling $48,000 (high: $1,600, low: $1,600).
Type of support: Undergraduate support.
Application information: Contact foundation for current application deadline/guidelines.
EIN: 870261722

2540
Masonic Grand Lodge Charities of Rhode Island, Inc.
222 Taunton Ave.
East Providence, RI 02914 (401) 435-4650
Contact: John M. Faulhaber, Secy.

Foundation type: Independent foundation
Limitations: Scholarships to individuals who have resided in RI for at least five years and to individuals whose parents or grandparents are RI masons.
Financial data: Year ended 10/31/2004. Assets, $1,812,524 (M); Expenditures, $291,488; Total giving, $221,634; Grants to individuals, totaling $209,122.
Fields of interest: Fraternal societies.
Type of support: Scholarships—to individuals.
Application information: Application form required.
  Deadline(s): May 1
  Applicants should submit the following:
    1) Financial information
EIN: 056014340

2541
Massachusetts Automatic Merchandising Council Scholarship Fund
462 Boston St., Ste. 7
Topsfield, MA 01983 (978) 887-9633
Contact: Allan Z. Gilbert, Tr.

Foundation type: Public charity
Limitations: Scholarships, fellowships, prizes, and awards to employees and members of the Massachusetts Automatic Merchandise Council, and to their children and spouses.
Financial data: Year ended 12/31/2003. Assets, $259,043 (M); Expenditures, $23,018; Total giving, $22,000; Grants to individuals, totaling $22,000.
Type of support: Employee-related scholarships.
Application information: Contact fund for current application deadline/guidelines; Initial approach by letter.
EIN: 046798624

2542
Massachusetts Bar Foundation, Inc.
20 West St.
Boston, MA 02111-1204 (617) 338-0500
Contact: Elizabeth Lynch, Exec. Dir.
FAX: (617) 338-0550;
E-mail: foundation@massbar.org; URL: http://www.massbarfoundation.org

Foundation type: Public charity
Limitations: Four stipends of $6,000 each awarded to law students who intern during the summer at nonprofit organizations providing civil legal services to low-income individuals in MA.
Publications: Application guidelines; Annual report; Grants list; Newsletter.
Financial data: Year ended 12/31/2004. Assets, $9,410,031 (M); Expenditures, $3,378,404; Total giving, $3,157,657.
Fields of interest: Law school/education.
Type of support: Internship funds; Graduate support.
Application information: Application form required.
  Deadline(s): Mar. 14
  Applicants should submit the following:
    1) Transcripts
    2) Essay
    3) Resume
    4) Letter(s) of recommendation
EIN: 046130261

2543
Master Brewers Association of the Americas Scholarship Foundation, Inc.
3340 Pilot Knob Rd.
St. Paul, MN 55121-2097
Contact: Joseph Weiss, Comm. Member
Application address: 1106 S. 3rd St., La Crosse, WI 54601, tel.: (608) 785-4528
FAX: (651) 454-0766; E-mail: mbaa@mbaa.com; URL: http://www.mbaa.com/scholarship/scholarship.html

Foundation type: Independent foundation
Limitations: Scholarships to children of individuals employed at least five years in the brewing industry in the Americas for study in brewing, malting, and packaging courses at the Master Brewers Assn. of the Americas. General scholarships also to children of members of the Master Brewers Assn. of the Americas. Applicants must be interested in working in the brewing industry.
Financial data: Year ended 12/31/2004. Assets, $10,162 (M); Expenditures, $6,551; Total giving, $4,000; Grant to an individual, 1 grant totaling $4,000.
Fields of interest: Business/industry.
Type of support: Employee-related scholarships.
Application information: Applications accepted.
  Deadline(s): June 1 for Brewing and Malting Courses, Nov. 1 for Packaging Course
  Additional information: Contact foundation for current application guidelines.
EIN: 391456157

2544
Master Educational Assistance Foundation
747 S. Euclid Ave.
Oak Park, IL 60304-1243
Contact: James F. Zangrilli, Exec. Dir.

Foundation type: Independent foundation
Limitations: Scholarships to economically disadvantaged individuals in IL for higher education.

Financial data: Year ended 12/31/2004. Assets, $5,725,863 (M); Expenditures, $341,113; Total giving, $264,388; Grants to individuals, totaling $115,705.
Type of support: Scholarships—to individuals.
Application information: Applications accepted. Application form required.
  Deadline(s): None
  Applicants should submit the following:
    1) FAFSA
    2) Essay
EIN: 363542174

2545
Edith L. Masters Trust Fund
c/o National Bank of Petersburg
P.O. Box 470
Petersburg, IL 62675
Application address: c/o Porta Community Unit School District No. 202, Attn.: Matthew Bruce, Superintendent, P.O. Box 202, Petersburg, IL 62675, tel.: (217) 632-2513

Foundation type: Independent foundation
Limitations: Undergraduate scholarships to PORTA District high school graduates, IL.
Financial data: Year ended 12/31/2004. Assets, $325,311 (M); Expenditures, $21,619; Total giving, $9,000; Grants to individuals, 12 grants totaling $9,000 (high: $750, low: $750).
Type of support: Scholarships—to individuals; Support to graduates or students of specific schools.
Application information: Application form required.
  Deadline(s): 1st week in May
  Additional information: Application must include previous year's tax return.
EIN: 376141924

2546
MATHCOUNTS Foundation
1420 King St.
Alexandria, VA 22314-2794 (703) 684-2850
Contact: Peggy Parnell Drane, Exec. Dir.
E-mail: info@mathcounts.org; FAX: (703) 836-4875; URL: http://mathcounts.org

Foundation type: Public charity
Limitations: Awards to sixth, seventh, and eight graders, "Mathletes," who win Mathcounts competitions.
Publications: Annual report; Financial statement; Informational brochure; Newsletter.
Financial data: Year ended 07/31/2003. Assets, $1,868,262 (M); Expenditures, $2,000,943; Total giving, $30,000; Grants to individuals, 7 grants totaling $30,000 (high: $10,000, low: $2,000).
Fields of interest: Secondary school/education; Mathematics.
Type of support: Awards/prizes; Precollege support.
Application information: See Web site for current application deadline/guidelines.
Program description:
  Awards Program: Awards to the top eight finishers in the national Mathcounts competition held each May in Washington, D.C. The amount of the awards may very each year. Mathcounts competitors, "Mathletes," are sixth, seventh, and eighth graders.
EIN: 541295407

2547
Margaret & Donald Matheson Scholarship Fund

c/o Bank of America, N.A.
P.O. Box 6767
Providence, RI 02940-6767
Application address: c/o Winslow High School, Scholarship Comm., 14 Danielson St., Winslow, ME 04901-6895

Foundation type: Independent foundation
Limitations: Scholarships to graduating seniors of Winslow High School, ME, for higher education. Students who demonstrate academic focus and financial need will be given highest priority.
Financial data: Year ended 12/31/2003. Assets, $605,877 (M); Expenditures, $27,149; Total giving, $20,750; Grants to individuals, 23 grants totaling $20,750 (high: $1,500, low: $250).
Type of support: Support to graduates or students of specific schools; Undergraduate support.
Application information: Applications accepted throughout the year; Contact foundation for current application guidelines.
EIN: 010504173

2548
James Matheson & Marian Matheson Scholarship Trust Fund

c/o Lincoln Savings Bank
508 Main St.
Reinbeck, IA 50669 (319) 788-6441

Foundation type: Independent foundation
Limitations: Scholarships to economically disadvantaged graduates of Reinbeck, IA, public schools for study at accredited colleges and comparable technical or vocational schools.
Financial data: Year ended 12/31/2004. Assets, $55,564 (M); Expenditures, $3,612; Total giving, $2,800; Grants to individuals, 4 grants totaling $2,800 (high: $700, low: $700).
Fields of interest: Vocational education.
Type of support: Support to graduates or students of specific schools; Technical education support; Undergraduate support.
Application information: Application form required.
Deadline(s): May 1
Applicants should submit the following:
1) Transcripts
2) Financial information
Additional information: Application must also include standardized test scores, and references.
EIN: 421172985

2549
Carol Hay Mathiesen Charitable Trust

3800 E. Lincoln Dr., Ste. 16
Phoenix, AZ 85018-1011
Application address: c/o Snell & Wilmer, LLP, Hay Scholarship, 1 Arizona Ctr., Phoenix, AZ 85004-0001, tel.: (602) 382-6000

Foundation type: Independent foundation
Limitations: Four-year scholarships to Maricopa County, AZ, high school students to attend college or vocational school.
Financial data: Year ended 12/31/2004. Assets, $549 (M); Expenditures, $16,003; Total giving, $16,003; Grant to an individual, 1 grant totaling $16,003.
Type of support: Support to graduates or students of specific schools; Technical education support; Undergraduate support.

Application information: Application form required.
Deadline(s): Mar. 1
Applicants should submit the following:
1) SAR
2) FAFSA
3) GPA
4) Letter(s) of recommendation
5) Transcripts
6) Essay
Additional information: Application must also include latest copy of student and parent(s) income tax returns; Interviews may be required.
EIN: 866247075

2550
Charles B. Mathis Memorial Trust

c/o Wachovia Bank, N.A.
100 N. Main St., 13th Fl.
Winston-Salem, NC 27150
Application address: c/o Wachovia Bank, N.A., 765 Broad St., Newark, NJ 07101

Foundation type: Independent foundation
Limitations: Scholarships to seniors at high schools in Ocean County, NJ, for study at NJ colleges.
Publications: Application guidelines.
Financial data: Year ended 12/31/2004. Assets, $1,841,692 (M); Expenditures, $105,501; Total giving, $94,375.
Type of support: Support to graduates or students of specific schools; Undergraduate support.
Application information: Applications accepted throughout the year; Contact trust for current application guidelines.
EIN: 232733573

2551
Lorraine D. Matson Trust

c/o Comerica Bank
P.O. Box 75000
Detroit, MI 48275
Application addresses: c/o Principal, Avondale High School, 2800 Waukegan, Auburn Hills, MI 48326, or c/o Auburn Hills Presbyterian Church, 3456 Primary, Auburn Hills, MI 48236

Foundation type: Independent foundation
Limitations: Scholarships to graduates of Avondale High School and to members of the Auburn Hills Presbyterian Church, MI.
Financial data: Year ended 11/30/2004. Assets, $234,102 (M); Expenditures, $15,716; Total giving, $11,700; Grants to individuals, 17 grants totaling $9,900 (high: $1,000, low: $300).
Fields of interest: Protestant agencies & churches.
Type of support: Support to graduates or students of specific schools; Undergraduate support.
Application information: Application form required.
Deadline(s): Jan. 1 to Apr. 1
EIN: 386523330

2552
Ernestine Matthews Trust

8507 Victory Lane
Potomac, MD 20854

Foundation type: Independent foundation
Limitations: Undergraduate scholarships to financially needy residents of Washington, DC, MD, PA, VA, and WV, who rank in the upper third of their high school classes.

Financial data: Year ended 12/31/2004. Assets, $1,328,626 (M); Expenditures, $104,549; Total giving, $75,000; Grants to individuals, 50 grants totaling $75,000 (high: $1,500, low: $1,500).
Type of support: Undergraduate support.
Application information: Application form required.
Deadline(s): Mar. 15
Applicants should submit the following:
1) Letter(s) of recommendation
2) Financial information
3) Transcripts
4) SASE
Additional information: Application must also include verification of class standing, and personal statement.
Program description:
Scholarship Program: Applicants must be of high moral character and sign a statement that they will neither smoke nor use alcoholic beverages while receiving money from the trust. The scholarship award must be used to defray the cost of tuition and/or room and board. Recipients may apply for renewals of their awards on an annual basis by completing a renewal form and furnishing a transcript showing a GPA of at least "C".
EIN: 526059006

2553
Frances Maude Children's Fund

c/o Bank of America, N.A.
P.O. Box 1802
Providence, RI 02901-1802
Application address: c/o Mulhark Regional High School, Attn.: Lizz Davin, Shelburne Falls, MA 01370

Foundation type: Independent foundation
Limitations: Scholarships to graduates of Mulhark Trail Regional High School, MA, who are also residents of Shelburne Falls Fire District.
Financial data: Year ended 08/31/2005. Assets, $583,260 (M); Expenditures, $29,741; Total giving, $19,000; Grants to individuals, 27 grants totaling $19,000 (high: $975, low: $350).
Type of support: Support to graduates or students of specific schools; Undergraduate support.
Application information:
Initial approach: Letter.
Deadline(s): Apr. 5
Applicants should submit the following:
1) Transcripts
2) Letter(s) of recommendation
3) Financial information
Additional information: Application must also include list of references.
EIN: 046019146

2554
Mauger Insurance Fund

c/o National City Bank, Columbus
P.O. Box 94651
Cleveland, OH 44101
Application address: c/o Watkins High School, Mauger Scholarship Fund, Attn.: Guidance Office, 8808 Watkins Rd., Pataskala, OH 43062

Foundation type: Independent foundation
Limitations: Scholarships to high school graduates who have attended Southwest Licking School District, OH, for at least nine years. Scholarships may be used for a university, college, or technical school.
Financial data: Year ended 12/31/2004. Assets, $917,366 (M); Expenditures, $76,399;

Total giving, $66,200; Grants to individuals, 32 grants totaling $66,200 (high: $3,400, low: $725).
Fields of interest: Vocational education.
Type of support: Support to graduates or students of specific schools; Undergraduate support.
Application information: Application form required.
Deadline(s): May 1
Applicants should submit the following:
1) Letter(s) of recommendation
2) Financial information
3) Transcripts
4) Class rank
5) GPA
Additional information: Application must also include standardized test scores, and handwritten personal statement.
EIN: 316198377

2555
Dennis & Marion Mavrogenis Trust Fund
30 Main St.
Peabody, MA 01960
Contact: Arthur J. Frawley, Tr.
Application address: c/o Shawn McCarthy, Eastern Bank & Trust Co., Trust Dept., 217 Essex St., Salem, MA 09170, tel.: (978) 740-6323

Foundation type: Independent foundation
Limitations: Scholarships to financially needy residents of Salem, MA, studying medicine, nursing, or engineering. Scholarships are renewable.
Financial data: Year ended 12/31/2003.
Assets, $2,398,758 (M); Expenditures, $130,983; Total giving, $108,600; Grants to individuals, 32 grants totaling $108,600 (high: $5,000, low: $500).
Fields of interest: Medical school/education; Nursing school/education.
Type of support: Undergraduate support.
Application information:
Deadline(s): Apr. 15.
Additional information: Application by letter.
EIN: 043179137

2556
Edmund F. Maxwell Foundation
P.O. Box 22537
Seattle, WA 98122-0537
Contact: Jane Thomas, Admin.
E-mail: admin@maxwell.org; URL: http://www.maxwell.org

Foundation type: Independent foundation
Limitations: Scholarships to residents of western WA who are entering or attending accredited, private institutions of higher learning in the western WA state area.
Publications: Informational brochure (including application guidelines).
Financial data: Year ended 12/31/2004.
Assets, $9,169,976 (M); Expenditures, $431,163; Total giving, $319,887; Grants to individuals, 98 grants totaling $319,887 (high: $3,500, low: $2,350, average grant: $1,000-$3,500).
Type of support: Undergraduate support.
Application information: Applications accepted. Application form required.
Initial approach: Letter or download application from Web site.
Deadline(s): Apr. 30
Applicants should submit the following:
1) Transcripts
2) SAT
3) Financial information

4) ACT
Additional information: Application must also include employment history, and a personal statement.
Program description:
Scholarship Program: Assistance is usually given in the amount of $3,500 per student per year. Those applying for financial assistance as first-year students should have outstanding scholastic records at their secondary schools, and SAT scores of at least 1200. Recipients are not selected on the basis of scholarship alone, but on the basis of all factors considered relevant by the trustees of the foundation, without regard to race, sex, color, ethnic origin, religious belief, marital status, or physical disability. Scholarships are renewable.
EIN: 916181008

2557
Maya Educational Foundation
P.O. Box 38, Rte. 106
South Woodstock, VT 05071
Contact: Armando J. Alfonzo, Treas.
E-mail: mayaedfund@mayaedufound.org;
URL: http://www.mayaedufound.org/

Foundation type: Public charity
Limitations: Scholarships to individuals of Mayan descent in Central America and Mexico.
Publications: Annual report; Informational brochure; Newsletter.
Financial data: Year ended 12/31/2003.
Assets, $535,058 (M); Expenditures, $150,181; Total giving, $145,463; Grants to individuals, totaling $75,200.
Fields of interest: Native Americans/American Indians.
Type of support: Program development; Graduate support; Technical education support; Precollege support; Undergraduate support; Doctoral support.
Application information: Applications accepted.
Initial approach: Letter.
Deadline(s): None
Additional information: Contact foundation for additional information.
EIN: 030335159

2558
Imogene M. Maybury Trust
c/o Bank of America, N.A.
P.O. Box 6768
Providence, RI 02940-6768
Application address: c/o Guidance Counselor, Dexter Regional High School, Dexter, ME 04930

Foundation type: Independent foundation
Limitations: Scholarships to graduates of Dexter Regional High School, Dexter, ME, for study at colleges, universities, and vocational schools.
Financial data: Year ended 04/30/2005.
Assets, $3,129,738 (M); Expenditures, $154,289; Total giving, $117,253; Grants to individuals, 89 grants totaling $117,253 (high: $2,650, low: $663).
Fields of interest: Vocational education.
Type of support: Support to graduates or students of specific schools; Undergraduate support.
Application information: Applications accepted throughout the year; Contact guidance counselor at high school; Applicants should provide all relevant personal data including employment information, transcripts, and references.
EIN: 016023401

2559
The M. L. Mayfield and Jessie Star Mayfield Foundation
27407 E. Fairway Oaks Dr.
Huffman, TX 77336
Contact: Charles F. Presley

Foundation type: Independent foundation
Limitations: Scholarships, initially provided as interest bearing loans, to residents of TX or LA to attend colleges in TX or LA.
Financial data: Year ended 12/31/2004.
Assets, $502,276 (M); Expenditures, $24,867; Total giving, $19,372; Grants to individuals, 3 grants totaling $19,372 (high: $14,320, low: $2,452).
Type of support: Scholarships—to individuals; Student loans—to individuals.
Application information:
Deadline(s): May 15
Additional information: Contact foundation for current application guidelines; Applicants must demonstrate financial need by submitting a copy of parents' and personal tax returns for three years.
Program description:
Scholarship Program: Applicants must have a 2.5 GPA or better. The grant will initially be given as an interest bearing loan, which the applicant's parents must co-guarantee. Upon proof of a 2.5 GPA or better, the loan will be converted to a grant, at which time all interest will be waived. Failure to provide grades or failure to perform at or in excess of a 2.5 GPA will cause the loan to be due and payable in full with the accrued interest.
EIN: 760133546

2560
The Charles G. & Alice R. Mayson Scholarship Grant Fund
c/o First National Bank of Atmore, Trust Dept.
P.O. Box 27
Atmore, AL 36504

Foundation type: Operating foundation
Limitations: Scholarships by nomination only to students at three local area high schools in AL.
Financial data: Year ended 12/31/2004.
Assets, $734,296 (M); Expenditures, $43,238; Total giving, $33,134; Grants to individuals, 12 grants totaling $33,132 (high: $2,761, low: $2,761).
Type of support: Awards/grants by nomination only; Undergraduate support.
Application information: Nominations accepted throughout the year.
Program description:
Scholarship Program: Scholarship nominations are based on ACT scores, GPA, class rank, and letter of recommendation.
EIN: 636161467

2561
The MBNA Foundation
1100 N. King St.
Wilmington, DE 19884-0723
Application tel.: Delaware Scholars Program and HBCU Scholarship Program: (302) 432-4800, option 2, or (800) 205-8877, option 2; Maine Scholars Program: (800) 386-6262, ext. 65878; Cleveland Scholars Program: (216) 545-4178 or (800) 410-6262, ext. 54178
Delaware Excellence in Education Grants, tel.: (302) 432-5288 or (800) 205-8877, option 1; Maine Excellence in Education Grants, tel.: (800)

386-6262, ext. 65886,
E-mail: mainegrants@mbna.com; Cleveland
Excellence in Education Grants, tel.: (216)
545-8000 or (800) 410-6262, ext. 58000; Helen
F. Graham Grants, tel.: (302) 432-5288 or (800)
205-8877, option 1,
E-mail: grahamgrants@mbna.com; Community
Donations Program, tel.: (302) 432-5205 or (800)
205-8877, option 3; URL: http://
www.mbnafoundation.org

Foundation type: Company-sponsored foundation
Limitations: Scholarships to students and
graduates of Cab Calloway School of Performing
Arts, DE. Scholarships also to children of full-time
employees of MBNA, for undergraduate education.
Financial data: Year ended 12/31/2004.
Assets, $69,704,941 (M); Expenditures,
$39,517,770; Total giving, $38,914,413; Grants
to individuals, 1,372 grants totaling $6,050,865
(high: $11,250, low: $99).
Fields of interest: Performing arts, education.
Type of support: Employee-related scholarships;
Support to graduates or students of specific
schools; Undergraduate support.
Application information: Application form required.
Initial approach: Letter.
Deadline(s): June 1 for Cab Calloway
Scholarships, and Feb. 1 for employee-related
scholarships
Additional information: Contact foundation for
current application guidelines; Application
must include two letters of recommendation;
See Web site for application addresses.
Program descriptions:
Employee-related Scholarships: Up to 25 percent
of eligible applicant pool of students will be
awarded scholarships for up to $5,000 in tuition
and fees for each academic year for up to four
years. Children of Senior Operating Members and
families with household incomes of $125,000 or
more are not eligible. Recipients must maintain a
GPA of at least 3.0 and full-time academic
undergraduate status. If these requirements are
maintained, students will retain the scholarship,
even if their parent leaves the employ of the
company.
Cab Calloway Scholarships: Awards scholarships
of up to $2,000 for students to pursue their arts
education. Recipients may also study music and
may use awards for instruments or supplies.
EIN: 522191136

2562

Donald C. and Helene Marienthal McCabe Charitable Foundation

c/o National City Bank
171 Monroe Ave. N.W.
Grand Rapids, MI 49503
Contact: Scott E. Campbell

Foundation type: Independent foundation
Limitations: Undergraduate scholarships primarily
to economically disadvantaged and Jewish or
Presbyterian residents of Bay, Midland, and
Saginaw counties, MI, for tuition at Delta
Community College, MI, or Saginaw Valley State
University, MI.
Financial data: Year ended 12/31/2004.
Assets, $925,525 (M); Expenditures, $57,635;
Total giving, $51,284; Grants to individuals, 11
grants totaling $37,551 (high: $5,384, low:
$2,208).
Fields of interest: Protestant agencies & churches;
Jewish agencies & temples.
Type of support: Support to graduates or students
of specific schools; Undergraduate support.

Application information: Application form required.
Deadline(s): Apr. 30
Applicants should submit the following:
1) SAR
2) FAFSA
Program descriptions:
Jewish Scholarship Fund: Undergraduate
scholarships covering tuition up to 32 credits per
academic year at Delta Community College, MI, or
Saginaw Valley State University, MI, are available to
students in Bay, Midland, and Saginaw counties,
MI, who demonstrate financial need. First priority is
given to Jewish students from Bay County who live
below the federally-defined poverty level. Second
priority is given to Jewish students from Bay County,
MI, who demonstrate financial need, but who live
above the poverty level. Third priority is given to
Jewish students in Midland and Saginaw counties,
MI, with financial need. Fourth priority is given to
Presbyterian students in Bay County, followed by
such students in Midland and Saginaw counties,
MI. Last priority is given to financially needy Bay
County residents of other religions. All Jewish
applicants must be recommended by the Bay City
Jewish Community Association. Scholarships are
renewable.
Presbyterian Scholarship Fund: Undergraduate
scholarships covering tuition up to 32 credits per
academic year at Delta Community College, MI, or
Saginaw Valley State University, MI, are available to
students in Bay, Midland, and Saginaw counties,
MI, who demonstrate financial need. First priority is
given to Presbyterian students from Bay County, MI,
who live below the federally-defined poverty level,
followed by such students who live above the
poverty level but still demonstrate financial need.
Second priority is given to Presbyterian students
from Midland and Saginaw counties, MI, with
financial need. Third priority is given to Jewish
students from Bay County, MI, followed by such
students in Midland and Saginaw counties, MI. Last
priority will be given to financially needy Bay County,
MI, residents of other religions. All Presbyterian
applicants must be recommended by the Board of
Trustees of the First Presbyterian Church in Bay
City, MI. Scholarships are renewable.
EIN: 383184550

2563

E. R. Warner McCabe Testamentary Trust-Georgia

(formerly Society of Cincinnati, Georgia Trust)
c/o SunTrust Bank
P.O. Box 1908
Orlando, FL 32802-1908
Application address: c/o Col. Ford P. Fuller, Jr.,
Chair., McCabe Scholarship Comm., Society of
Cincinnati State of Georgia, Savannah, GA 31406

Foundation type: Independent foundation
Limitations: Scholarships to commendable
children of members of the Society of Cincinnati in
GA.
Financial data: Year ended 06/30/2005.
Assets, $1,308,673 (M); Expenditures, $86,815;
Total giving, $72,000; Grants to individuals, 18
grants totaling $72,000 (high: $4,000, low:
$4,000).
Type of support: Scholarships—to individuals.
Application information: Application form not
required.
Deadline(s): July 15.
Applicants should submit the following:
1) Transcripts
Additional information: Application by letter from
parent.
EIN: 546131247

2564

E. R. Warner McCabe Testamentary Trust-Virginia

(formerly Society of Cincinnati-Virginia Trust)
c/o SunTrust Bank
P.O. Box 1908
Orlando, FL 32802-1908
Contact: Andrew H. Christian, Chair.,
Application address: c/o McCabe Scholarship
Comm., Society of Cincinnati in the State of
Virginia, P.O. Box 1357, Richmond, VA 23211

Foundation type: Independent foundation
Limitations: Scholarships to VA high school
students who are children of members of the
Virginia Society of Cincinnati for undergraduate or
graduate study at U.S. institutions.
Financial data: Year ended 06/30/2004.
Assets, $1,314,535 (M); Expenditures, $61,334;
Total giving, $50,400; Grants to individuals, 14
grants totaling $50,400 (high: $3,600, low:
$3,600).
Type of support: Graduate support; Undergraduate
support.
Application information:
Initial approach: Letter.
Deadline(s): June 1
Applicants should submit the following:
1) Transcripts
EIN: 546131246

2565

The McCaddin-McQuirk Foundation, Inc.

P.O. Box 5001
New York, NY 10185-5001 (212) 366-5893
Contact: Frank J. Hardart III, V.P.

Foundation type: Independent foundation
Limitations: Scholarships to students who wish to
become priests, deacons, catechists or lay
teachers of the Roman Catholic Church in the U.S.
or elsewhere.
Financial data: Year ended 12/31/2004.
Assets, $5,249,374 (M); Expenditures,
$314,840; Total giving, $299,200; Grants to
individuals, totaling $299,200.
Fields of interest: Theological school/education;
Roman Catholic agencies & churches.
Type of support: Scholarships—to individuals.
Application information: Applications accepted.
Deadline(s): Dec. 1
Additional information: Application by letter.
EIN: 136134444

2566

Edwin L. and Louis B. McCallay Educational Trust Fund

c/o First Financial Bank
300 High St.
Hamilton, OH 45011
Application address: c/o Trust Off., First Financial
Bank, 815 Breiel Blvd., Middletown, OH 45042,
tel.: (513) 425-7548

Foundation type: Independent foundation
Limitations: Scholarships to graduates of high
schools in the Middletown, OH, city school district,
including Fenwick High School, to attend colleges,
universities or other institutions of higher learning.
Financial data: Year ended 02/28/2005.
Assets, $486,685 (M); Expenditures, $27,761;
Total giving, $22,000; Grants to individuals, 15
grants totaling $22,000 (high: $2,500, low: $500).
Type of support: Support to graduates or students
of specific schools; Technical education support;
Undergraduate support.

Application information: Application form required.
Applicants should submit the following:
1) Financial information
Additional information: Contact school for current application deadline; Applications available from high schools in the Middletown, OH, city school district.
Program description:
Scholarship Program: Students must show academic ability and financial need. Scholarships are paid to cover tuition, school fees, and related incidentals.
EIN: 316111939

2567
The McCarthey Dressman Education Foundation
610 E. South Temple, Ste. 110
Salt Lake City, UT 84102 (801) 578-1260
Application address: c/o Kristy Carson, 802 Boston Building, No. 9 Exchange Pl., Salt Lake City, UT 84111, tel.: (801) 320-0765
FAX: (801) 578-1261;
E-mail: info@mccartheydressman.org; URL: http://www.mccartheydressman.org

Foundation type: Operating foundation
Limitations: Scholarships to students enrolled in teacher education programs at New Mexico State University, NM, and University of Texas at Austin, TX.
Financial data: Year ended 12/31/2003.
Assets, $56,958 (M); Expenditures, $132,617; Total giving, $78,478; Grants to individuals, 13 grants totaling $78,478 (high: $10,000, low: $868).
Fields of interest: Teacher school/education.
Type of support: Support to graduates or students of specific schools; Graduate support; Undergraduate support.
Application information: Applications accepted. Application form required.
Deadline(s): Apr. 20
Applicants should submit the following:
1) Transcripts
2) Letter(s) of recommendation
3) Essay
Additional information: Interviews required; See Web site for additional application information.
Program description:
Scholarship/Mentoring: Awards four $5,000 scholarships to full-time students in their final year of a teacher education program, who are specializing in elementary or secondary education. Applicants may be undergraduate or graduate students, and must maintain a "B" average.
EIN: 870646265

2568
McCaulay Memorial Masonic Fund
3346 Meadow Oaks Dr.
Garland, TX 75043-6229

Foundation type: Independent foundation
Limitations: Scholarships to former students of the Masonic Home and School of Texas.
Financial data: Year ended 12/31/2004.
Assets, $466,838 (M); Expenditures, $35,896; Total giving, $33,000; Grants to individuals, 12 grants totaling $33,000 (high: $4,500, low: $1,500).
Type of support: Scholarships—to individuals.
Application information:
Initial approach: Letter.

Additional information: Contact foundation for further program information.
EIN: 752443043

2569
Pauline Linebarger & Riley McClain Scholarship Trust
c/o Citizens National Bank
P.O. Box 790
Paris, IL 61944-0790
Contact: Chris Hollowell, Trust Off., Citizens National Bank

Foundation type: Independent foundation
Limitations: Student loans to residents of Edgar and Vermilion counties, IL, who are studying agriculture, nursing, teaching, law, medicine, or dentistry.
Financial data: Year ended 12/31/2004.
Assets, $1,184,857 (M); Expenditures, $13,286; Total giving, $0; Loans to individuals, 12 loans totaling $39,000.
Fields of interest: Dental school/education; Law school/education; Medical school/education; Nursing school/education; Teacher school/education; Agriculture.
Type of support: Graduate support; Undergraduate support.
Application information: Application form required.
Deadline(s): Apr. 15
EIN: 376185245

2570
J. Allen McClain Trust
133 E. Market St.
Xenia, OH 45385-3110
Contact: David L. Pendry, Tr.

Foundation type: Independent foundation
Limitations: Loans to residents of Greene County, OH, for medical school.
Financial data: Year ended 12/31/2004.
Assets, $495,218 (M); Expenditures, $8,449; Total giving, $0; Loans to individuals, 4 loans totaling $10,000.
Fields of interest: Medical school/education.
Type of support: Graduate support.
Application information:
Deadline(s): May 31
Additional information: Contact foundation for current application guidelines.
EIN: 316060712

2571
Frank McCleary Medical Scholarship Fund of the Mary Ball Chapter for the Daughters of the American Revolution
8419 45th St. W.
University Place, WA 98466
Contact: Hilda L. Walker, Pres.

Foundation type: Independent foundation
Limitations: Scholarships to worthy students primarily in the Seattle, WA, area who are U.S. citizens and are enrolled in approved medical schools, colleges, or universities.
Financial data: Year ended 12/31/2004.
Assets, $501,147 (M); Expenditures, $22,585; Total giving, $17,800; Grants to individuals, totaling $17,800.
Fields of interest: Medical school/education.
Type of support: Graduate support; Undergraduate support.

Application information: Applications accepted. Application form required.
Deadline(s): Aug. 23.
EIN: 510158972

2572
Glenn R. McClendon, Sr. Memorial Scholarship Foundation
P.O. Box 641
Lafayette, AL 36862-0641
Contact: James W. McClendon, Tr.
FAX: (334) 864-8865

Foundation type: Independent foundation
Limitations: Scholarships to children of McClendon Trucking company employees for higher education.
Financial data: Year ended 12/31/2002.
Assets, $133 (M); Expenditures, $19,153; Total giving, $17,780; Grants to individuals, 6 grants totaling $17,780 (high: $7,141, low: $919).
Type of support: Employee-related scholarships.
Application information: Applications are provided directly to employees; Ineligible applications not accepted or acknowledged.
EIN: 631041773

2573
W. H. "Howie" McClennan Scholarship Fund
c/o The International Assn. of Fire Fighters
1750 New York Ave. N.W.
Washington, DC 20006-5395 (202) 737-8418
URL: http://www.iaff.org/academy/scholarships/mcclennan.html

Foundation type: Independent foundation
Limitations: Scholarships to sons, daughters, dependents, and legally adopted children of fire fighters who were members in good standing of the IAFF and were killed in the line of duty.
Financial data: Year ended 09/30/2004.
Assets, $725,862 (M); Expenditures, $57,996; Total giving, $58,750; Grants to individuals, 24 grants totaling $58,750.
Fields of interest: Vocational education; Disasters, fire prevention/control.
Type of support: Graduate support; Technical education support; Undergraduate support.
Application information: Applications accepted. Application form required.
Deadline(s): Apr. 30
Applicants should submit the following:
1) Transcripts
2) Letter(s) of recommendation
3) Financial information
4) Essay
Program description:
McClennan Scholarship Fund: The applicant's parent must have been a member in good standing of the International Association of Fire Fighters, AFL-CIO-CLC at the time of death. Scholarships are awarded on the basis of financial need, promise, and academic achievement, and are renewable for up to four years. To be eligible, applicants must have at least a 2.0 GPA. Recipients may attend any postsecondary institution requiring a high school diploma or GED, including vocational/technical schools, training institutions, two- and four-year public or private accredited colleges, universities, and graduate schools. Renewal applications are given preference over new applications.
EIN: 521121279

2574

Charles A. McCloskey Memorial Scholarship Fund

c/o Austin Area School District
138 Costello Ave.
Austin, PA 16720
Application address: c/o Austin United Methodist Church, Attn.: Rev. Charles E. Gummo, 30 Turner St., Austin, PA 16720

Foundation type: Independent foundation
Limitations: Scholarships to graduates of the Austin Area School District, PA.
Financial data: Year ended 06/30/2005. Assets, $103,421 (M); Expenditures, $3,365; Total giving, $2,700; Grants to individuals, 4 grants totaling $2,700 (high: $675, low: $675).
Type of support: Support to graduates or students of specific schools; Undergraduate support.
Application information: Application form required.
  Deadline(s): Nov. 1 and May 15
  Additional information: Application forms available from Austin Area School District, PA; Recipients notified by June 5.
EIN: 256355191

2575

James G. K. McClure Educational and Development Fund, Inc.

11 Sugar Hollow Rd.
Fairview, NC 28730 (828) 628-2114
Contact: John Curtis Ager, Exec. Dir.
E-mail: jager@aol.com

Foundation type: Independent foundation
Limitations: Scholarships limited to residents of western NC, including the following counties: Allegheny, Ashe, Avery, Buncombe, Burke, Caldwell, Cherokee, Clay, Graham, Haywood, Henderson, Jackson, Macon, Madison, McDowell, Mitchell, Polk, Rutherford, Swain, Transylvania, Watauga, and Yancey.
Publications: Application guidelines; Biennial report; Informational brochure.
Financial data: Year ended 06/30/2003. Assets, $3,303,213 (M); Expenditures, $172,340; Total giving, $96,432.
Fields of interest: Vocational education; Nursing school/education; Health sciences school/education; Christian agencies & churches; Minorities.
Type of support: Undergraduate support.
Application information: Initial approach by letter; Completion of formal application required.
Program description:
  Scholarship Program: Scholarship payments are made directly to specific colleges on behalf of the recipients, and all applications must be submitted to these colleges. They include Appalachian State University, NC, Asheville-Buncombe Technical Community College, Berea College, Blue Ridge Community College, Brevard College, Caldwell Community College and Technical Institute, NC, East Tennessee State University, Gardner-Webb College, Haywood Community College, Isothermal Community College, Lees-McRae College, Mars Hill College, Mayland Community College, McDowell Community College, Montreat College, North Carolina School of the Arts, North Carolina State University, Southwestern Community College, Tri-County Technical College, University of North Carolina at Asheville, University of North Carolina at Greensboro, Warren Wilson College, Western Carolina University, Western Piedmont Community College, Wilkes Community College, and Young Harris College. The colleges must in turn submit scholarship recommendations to the fund by Apr.

15. The following factors will be considered: high school record for both scholarship and leadership; evidence of Christian character; financial need; intellectual promise; demonstrated ambition. A special effort is made to offer scholarships to minority students from the region, and students entering into nursing and other health career related fields. Students facing a sudden and catastrophic financial problem may apply for a hardship grant to finish their course of study.
  · Dumont Clarke Scholarship Fund: Available for active ministers in the region who would like to attend a course of study to enhance some aspect of their work. Application forms are available from the fund office.
  · Edward deZulueta Greenebaum Fund: This is a special scholarship fund reserved for promising students from western NC.
EIN: 560690982

2576

Lucille McComb Memorial Scholarship Fund

105 W. Main St.
Napoleon, OH 43545-1781
Application address: c/o Napoleon High School, Attn.: Jeffrey Schlade, Principal, 701 Briarheath Ave., Napoleon, OH 43545-1251, tel.: (419) 599-1050

Foundation type: Independent foundation
Limitations: Educational grants to economically disadvantaged students from Henry County, OH, to attend colleges, trade, or vocational schools. First consideration is given to Napoleon High School students.
Financial data: Year ended 12/31/2004. Assets, $554,532 (M); Expenditures, $26,958; Total giving, $15,900; Grants to individuals, 16 grants totaling $15,900 (high: $1,000, low: $900).
Fields of interest: Vocational education.
Type of support: Support to graduates or students of specific schools; Technical education support; Undergraduate support.
Application information: Application form required.
  Deadline(s): Apr. 1
  Additional information: Application must also include a copy of parents' and applicant's federal income tax forms for the previous three years; Interviews may be required.
Program description:
  Scholarship Program: Recipients repay 50 percent of the grant without interest after degree is completed or prior to the termination of studies. Scholarships are renewable for up to four years. The maximum grant per year is $1,500.
EIN: 346875773

2577

Ann McConahay Educational Foundation

c/o Unizan Financial Services Group
P.O. Box 24190
Canton, OH 44701
Application address: c/o Guidance Counselor, Alliance High School, Alliance, OH 44601

Foundation type: Independent foundation
Limitations: Scholarships to graduates of Alliance High School, OH.
Financial data: Year ended 12/31/2004. Assets, $1,255,248 (M); Expenditures, $145,422; Total giving, $136,162; Grants to individuals, 90 grants totaling $136,162 (high: $6,000, low: $96).
Type of support: Support to graduates or students of specific schools; Undergraduate support.

Application information: Application form required.
  Deadline(s): June 30
  Applicants should submit the following:
    1) Letter(s) of recommendation
  Additional information: Applications are available from Alliance High School guidance counselor.
Program description:
  Scholarship Funds: Applicants must demonstrate financial need, maintain at least a 3.0 cumulative GPA and demonstrate good character and integrity. Scholarship funds may be used for tuition and books at accredited colleges and universities in the continental U.S. Payments are made directly to the college or university. Recipients may reapply for a total of four years. Applications for renewal must include an official college transcript.
EIN: 341550065

2578

The Lynn E. and Mattie G. McConnell Foundation and Scholarship Fund

c/o Bath National Bank
44 Liberty St.
Bath, NY 14810
Contact: B. Graham, Trust Off., Bath National Bank

Foundation type: Independent foundation
Limitations: Educational loans to students for college, primarily in NY.
Publications: Annual report.
Financial data: Year ended 12/31/2004. Assets, $267,563 (M); Expenditures, $3,753; Total giving, $9,310; Loans to individuals, 2 loans totaling $9,310.
Type of support: Student loans—to individuals.
Application information: Application form required.
  Deadline(s): May 15
  Applicants should submit the following:
    1) Financial information
EIN: 166237917

2579

The McConnell Foundation

P.O. Box 492050
Redding, CA 96049-2050 (530) 226-6200
Contact: Lee W. Salter, C.E.O. and Pres.
FAX: (530) 226-6210;
E-mail: info@mcconnellfoundation.org;
URL: http://www.mcconnellfoundation.org

Foundation type: Independent foundation
Limitations: Scholarships to residents of Modoc, Shasta, Siskiyou, and Trinity counties, CA, as well as students of Big Valley High School in Lassen County.
Publications: Annual report; Newsletter.
Financial data: Year ended 12/31/2004. Assets, $367,694,308 (M); Expenditures, $19,302,474; Total giving, $11,293,566.
Type of support: Support to graduates or students of specific schools; Undergraduate support.
Application information:
  Initial approach: E-mail.
  Additional information: Contact foundation for further application guidelines.
Program descriptions:
  Scholars Program: This program will serve students who are pursuing baccalaureate degrees at four year colleges and universities. It consists of a need-based financial award that is renewable for up to a total of four years.
  Vista Program: This program will serve 'at-risk' students who are pursuing two year degree or certificate programs at either Shasta College or

College of the Siskiyous. It consists of a financial award that is renewable for up to a total of two years.
EIN: 946102700

2580
Robert W. McCormick Scholarship Fund
c/o Bank of Charles Town
P.O. Drawer 40
Charles Town, WV   25414-0040
(304) 728-2435

Foundation type: Independent foundation
Limitations: Scholarships to students graduating from Jefferson County, WV, high schools with at least a "B" average. Recipients must attend WV public colleges or universities full-time.
Financial data: Year ended 04/30/2005. Assets, $4,212,953 (M); Expenditures, $255,467; Total giving, $209,062; Grants to individuals, 30 grants totaling $209,062 (high: $14,992, low: $475).
Type of support: Support to graduates or students of specific schools; Undergraduate support.
Application information: Application form required.
  Deadline(s): Feb. 15
  Applicants should submit the following:
    1) Transcripts
    2) Letter(s) of recommendation
    3) FAFSA
    4) Essay
Program description:
  Scholarship Program: Scholarships are awarded on the basis of financial need, academic records, and citizenship. Scholarships are renewable provided recipients maintain at least a "B" average and full-time status.
EIN: 550734149

2581
Flora S. McCourtney Trust
c/o Bank of America, N.A.
231 S. LaSalle St., IL1-231-14-19
Chicago, IL   60697
Contact: Christine Secorsky
Application address: c/o Bank of America, N.A., 100 N. Broadway, P.O. Box 14737, St. Louis, MO 63178. tel.: (314) 466-4417

Foundation type: Independent foundation
Limitations: Scholarships primarily to graduates of high schools in Sangamon County, IL, who are seeking a technical or scientific education.
Financial data: Year ended 09/30/2005. Assets, $7,917,179 (M); Expenditures, $387,201; Total giving, $351,000.
Fields of interest: Vocational education; Science.
Type of support: Support to graduates or students of specific schools; Technical education support; Undergraduate support.
Application information: Applications accepted. Application form required.
  Initial approach: Letter.
EIN: 436023586

2582
Clark & Laura McCoy Scholarship Trust
c/o Wayne County National Bank
1776 Beall Ave.
Wooster, OH   44691

Foundation type: Public charity
Limitations: Scholarships to graduates of Wooster High School, OH.

Type of support: Support to graduates or students of specific schools.
Application information:
  Initial approach: Letter.
  Additional information: Contact foundation for complete application guidelines.
EIN: 346950704

2583
Stephen F. McCready Scholarship Fund
P.O. Box 1525
Pennington, NJ   08534-1525
Application address: c/o First United Methodist Church, Attn.: Secy., 1126 E. Silver Springs Blvd., Ocala, FL 34470

Foundation type: Independent foundation
Limitations: Student loans for higher education with preference given to Marion County, FL, residents who are attending theological seminaries or who have otherwise indicated intentions of entering full-time Christian service.
Financial data: Year ended 12/31/2004. Assets, $561,062 (M); Expenditures, $32,088; Total giving, $21,798; Loan to an individual, 1 loan totaling $21,798.
Fields of interest: Theological school/education; Christian agencies & churches.
Type of support: Student loans—to individuals.
Application information: Applications accepted. Application form required.
  Deadline(s): June 1 and Dec 1.
EIN: 596577844

2584
Dorsey McCrory Trust for Gonzales County, TX
414 St. Joseph St., Ste. 200
Gonzales, TX   78629
Application address: c/o Waelder ISD Counselor, 105 Ave. C, Waelder, TX 78959, tel.: (830) 788-7151

Foundation type: Independent foundation
Limitations: Scholarships to financially needy students from the Gonzales County Commissioner's Precinct No. 2, which includes Waelder, TX, for higher education.
Financial data: Year ended 10/31/2004. Assets, $607,709 (M); Expenditures, $25,254; Total giving, $19,380; Grants to individuals, 16 grants totaling $19,380 (high: $1,520, low: $570).
Type of support: Scholarships—to individuals.
Application information: Applications accepted.
  Initial approach: Letter.
  Deadline(s): Contact foundation for deadline
  Applicants should submit the following:
    1) Financial information
  Additional information: Application must also include evidence of college enrollment, and residency in the Waelder area.
EIN: 746414650

2585
C. N. McCune Scholarship Foundation Trust
c/o SunTrust Bank
P.O. Box 14728
Fort Lauderdale, FL   33302-4728
(954) 765-7413
Contact: Michael Jacobs, Trust Off., SunTrust Bank

Foundation type: Independent foundation

Limitations: Scholarships to residents of Broward County, FL, and eligible relatives of C.N. McCune toward degrees from community colleges, universities, and graduate schools. Scholarships are renewable.
Financial data: Year ended 08/31/2005. Assets, $298,016 (M); Expenditures, $33,416; Total giving, $26,543; Grants to individuals, 43 grants totaling $26,543 (high: $750, low: $74).
Type of support: Graduate support; Undergraduate support.
Application information: Application form required.
  Deadline(s): Apr. 15
  Applicants should submit the following:
    1) Photograph
    2) Letter(s) of recommendation
    3) Transcripts
  Additional information: Application must also include student's and parents' most recent tax returns.
EIN: 596667689

2586
McCurdy Memorial Scholarship Foundation
c/o Comerica Bank
49 W. Michigan Ave.
Battle Creek, MI   49017-3603
Contact: Lori Hill, Treas.

Foundation type: Independent foundation
Limitations: Undergraduate scholarships to residents of Calhoun County, MI.
Financial data: Year ended 12/31/2004. Assets, $682,718 (M); Expenditures, $41,689; Total giving, $36,000; Grants to individuals, 25 grants totaling $36,000 (high: $1,500, low: $750).
Type of support: Scholarships—to individuals; Undergraduate support.
Application information: Application form required.
  Deadline(s): Mar. 31
  Additional information: Interviews required.
Program description:
  Scholarship Program: Awards are made on the basis of excellence in scholastic and other activities and are renewable contingent upon the continuance of above-average work in college. Approximately six to eight new awards are available each year.
EIN: 381687120

2587
Edna P. McCurdy Scholarship Foundation
c/o Ounalashka Corp.
P.O. Box 149
Unalaska, AK   99685
Contact: Chris Salts

Foundation type: Company-sponsored foundation
Limitations: Scholarships to shareholders of Ounalashka Corp. and their descendents for educational training.
Financial data: Year ended 12/31/2003. Assets, $557,158 (M); Expenditures, $146,314; Total giving, $135,846; Grants to individuals, 9 grants totaling $135,846 (high: $36,697, low: $2,500).
Type of support: Internship funds; Technical education support; Undergraduate support.
Application information: Application form required.
  Deadline(s): Contact foundation for current application guidelines
  Additional information: Scholarship applications are attached to the Ounalashka Corp. newsletter, the Eider Pointer.

Program description:

Scholarship Program: The foundation provides support to shareholders of The Ounalashka Corp. and their descendents via scholarships, grants, student aid, stipends, and other means of support in connection with educational training through apprenticeships, internships, and other educational programs. Scholarships are for tuition, room and board, and stipends. Scholarships are available, by application, to full-time students who have been accepted into institutions of higher learning, including trade schools. Students must meet certain criteria including a base GPA.
EIN: 920157058

2588

The McCurry Foundation, Inc.

11645 Beach Blvd., Ste. 200
Jacksonville, FL 32246
Contact: Edgar W. McCurry, Jr., Dir.

Foundation type: Independent foundation
Limitations: Scholarships to students for undergraduate education, primarily in FL.
Financial data: Year ended 05/31/2005.
Assets, $219,429 (M); Expenditures, $27,477; Total giving, $26,250; Grants to individuals, 36 grants totaling $26,250 (high: $1,000, low: $500).
Type of support: Undergraduate support.
Application information: Applications accepted.
   Additional information: Applicants by letter accepted throughout the year.
EIN: 593287752

2589

McDavid Dental Educational Trust

(formerly G. N. and Edna McDavid Dental Education Trust)
c/o U.S. Bank, N.A.
P.O. Box 387
St. Louis, MO 63166
Application address: c/o University of Missouri of Kansas City, 4825 Troost Ave., Kansas City, MO 64110, tel.: (816) 932-4422; c/o St. Louis University, 3556 Caroline Mall, St. Louis, MO 63104, tel.: (314) 577-8186

Foundation type: Independent foundation
Limitations: Student loans to residents of MO attending an accredited dental school in MO. Preference given to residents of Madison County, MO.
Financial data: Year ended 12/31/2004.
Assets, $2,072,151 (M); Expenditures, $553,209; Total giving, $455,605; Grants to individuals, 2 grants totaling $455,605 (high: $284,105, low: $171,500); Loans to individuals, 70 loans totaling $458,395.
Fields of interest: Dental school/education.
Type of support: Graduate support.
Application information: Applications accepted. Application form required.
   Additional information: Forms available from Student Financial Aid office of accredited MO dental schools; Interviews required.
EIN: 436192984

2590

Joan B. and Frank E. McDonald Charitable Trust Memorial Scholarship Fund for Weir High School

c/o Richard J. Federowicz
2 PPG Pl., Ste. 400
Pittsburgh, PA 15222
Application address: c/o Guidance Dept., Weir High School, 100 Red Rider Rd., Weirton, WV 26062

Foundation type: Operating foundation
Limitations: Scholarships to financially needy graduates of Weir Senior High School, WV to attend a post high school technical school, college (2-year or 4-year), community college, university or accredited trade, industrial, or technical institution.
Financial data: Year ended 09/30/2004.
Assets, $483,817 (M); Expenditures, $17,704; Total giving, $16,250; Grants to individuals, 13 grants totaling $16,250 (high: $2,250, low: $1,000).
Type of support: Support to graduates or students of specific schools; Technical education support; Undergraduate support.
Application information: Application form required.
   Deadline(s): Apr. 15
EIN: 546478360

2591

Joan Bieberson McDonald Charitable Trust Memorial Scholarship Fund for Wheeling Park High School

c/o Richard J. Federowicz
2 PPG Pl., Ste. 400
Pittsburgh, PA 15222
Application address: c/o Guidance Dept., Wheeling Park High School, 1976 Park View Rd., Wheeling, WV 26003

Foundation type: Operating foundation
Limitations: Scholarships to students at Wheeling Park High School, PA, to attend a college, university, or accredited trade, industrial, or technical institution.
Financial data: Year ended 09/30/2004.
Assets, $726,466 (M); Expenditures, $26,677; Total giving, $25,000; Grants to individuals, 13 grants totaling $25,000 (high: $1,500, low: $1,000).
Type of support: Support to graduates or students of specific schools; Technical education support; Undergraduate support.
Application information: Contact trust for current application deadline/guidelines.
EIN: 546478362

2592

McDonald Memorial Fund Trust

(also known as Angus C. McDonald Memorial Trust)
c/o National City Bank
P.O. Box 94651
Cleveland, OH 44101-4651
Application address: c/o Superintendent of the Warsaw Community Schools, 1 Administrative Dr., Warsaw, IN 46580

Foundation type: Independent foundation
Limitations: Student loans for college and professional education to Kosciusko County, IN, residents only.
Publications: Informational brochure.
Financial data: Year ended 12/31/2004.
Assets, $2,599,186 (M); Expenditures, $46,836; Total giving, $250; Loans to individuals, totaling $78,000.

Type of support: Student loans—to individuals.
Application information: Applications accepted. Application form required.
   Applicants should submit the following:
      1) Letter(s) of recommendation
   Additional information: Interviews required.
Program description:
   Student Loan Fund: Students applying for loans must be enrolled and in good standing or have been accepted for enrollment at an eligible school (most public and private institutions meet these requirements). Selection is based on prior academic performance, recommendations, and a personal interview. Maximum loan per student is $6,000. Loans are interest-free while the recipient is in school and four months thereafter. However, all loans are interest-bearing during the repayment period, which begins five months after the recipient completes his or her course of study or leaves school, and normally lasts five to ten years. Minimum monthly amount is $50. Parents or guardians of recipients are generally required to co-sign student loans.
EIN: 356018326

2593

Katrina Overall McDonald Memorial Scholarship Fund

P.O. Box 130
Bay St. Louis, MS 39520-0130

Foundation type: Independent foundation
Limitations: Scholarships by nomination only to graduates of Bay High School in Bay St. Louis, MS.
Financial data: Year ended 12/31/2003.
Assets, $277,589 (M); Expenditures, $7,192; Total giving, $5,250; Grants to individuals, totaling $5,250.
Type of support: Support to graduates or students of specific schools; Awards/grants by nomination only; Undergraduate support.
Application information: Applications not accepted.
   Additional information: Recipients are selected from a list of nominees submitted by the school faculty committee.
EIN: 640725975

2594

Sam & Carrie McDonald Scholarship Fund

c/o Regions Bank, Trust Dept.
P.O. Box 2527
Mobile, AL 36622
Application address: c/o Lydia Houck, Dir. of Financial Aid, Mobile College, P.O. Box 13220, Mobile, AL 36613, tel.: (251) 675-5990

Foundation type: Independent foundation
Limitations: Scholarships for students of Mobile College, AL.
Financial data: Year ended 12/31/2004.
Assets, $145,867 (M); Expenditures, $9,780; Total giving, $8,000; Grants to individuals, 3 grants totaling $8,000.
Type of support: Support to graduates or students of specific schools; Undergraduate support.
Application information: Application form required.
   Initial approach: Letter.
   Deadline(s): May 1
   Applicants should submit the following:
      1) Transcripts
   Additional information: Application must also include anticipated educational expenses.
EIN: 636077642

2595
The Trustees of McDonough Charity School
P.O. Box 607
La Plata, MD   20646

Foundation type: Independent foundation
Limitations: Scholarships to residents of the McDonough Charity School District in Charles County, MD. Student loans to those residents outside the McDonough School District.
Financial data: Year ended 01/31/2003. Assets, $1,004,978 (M); Expenditures, $63,929; Total giving, $51,570; Grants to individuals, 8 grants totaling $35,570 (high: $5,000, low: $3,000).
Type of support: Scholarships—to individuals; Student loans—to individuals.
Application information: Applications accepted. Application form required.
   Applicants should submit the following:
      1) Letter(s) of recommendation
   Additional information: Applications available from district schools.
EIN: 526048878

2596
Frances and Ina McDougall Medical Scholarship Foundation
c/o SunTrust Bank
P.O. Box 1908
Orlando, FL   32802-1908
Application address: c/o Terese Gaffney, P.O. Box 1498, Tampa, FL 33601, tel.: (813) 224-2460

Foundation type: Independent foundation
Limitations: Scholarships to medical students at the University of South Florida, FL.
Financial data: Year ended 12/31/2004. Assets, $656,004 (M); Expenditures, $43,037; Total giving, $29,000; Grants to individuals, 13 grants totaling $29,000 (high: $4,900, low: $900).
Fields of interest: Medical school/education.
Type of support: Support to graduates or students of specific schools; Graduate support.
Application information: Applications accepted.
   Initial approach: Letter.
EIN: 596981356

2597
Verne Catt McDowell Corporation
P.O. Box 1336
Albany, OR   97321-0440
Contact: Emily Killin, Mgr.

Foundation type: Independent foundation
Limitations: Scholarships for graduate theological studies to ministers ordained or studying to meet the requirements to be ordained as a minister in the Christian Church (Disciples of Christ). Preference is given to OR residents.
Publications: Application guidelines.
Financial data: Year ended 12/31/2004. Assets, $352,982 (M); Expenditures, $23,074; Total giving, $17,905; Grants to individuals, 8 grants totaling $15,975 (high: $3,150, low: $500).
Fields of interest: Theological school/education; Christian agencies & churches.
Type of support: Graduate support.
Application information: Applications accepted. Application form required.
   Initial approach: Letter.
   Copies of proposal: 1
   Deadline(s): May 1st
   Applicants should submit the following:
      1) Transcripts

      2) Letter(s) of recommendation
      3) GPA
      4) Financial information
   Additional information: Application should include educational plans and confirmation by regional minister; Interviews required.
Program description:
   Verne Catt McDowell Corporation Scholarship: Applicants must have baccalaureate degrees from accredited liberal arts colleges or universities, and be accepted into professional degree programs at graduate institutions of theological education which are accredited by the General Assembly of the Christian Church (Disciples of Christ). Support is given in the form of a monthly stipend.
EIN: 936022991

2598
Ephraim McDowell Foundation
P.O. Box 636
Belfry, KY   41514

Foundation type: Independent foundation
Limitations: Scholarships to residents of the Tug Valley area (Pike and Martin counties, KY, and Mingo County, WV), with priority given to financially needy individuals pursuing health-related studies. Scholarships are awarded on the basis of financial need and GPA.
Financial data: Year ended 06/30/2005. Assets, $647,241 (M); Expenditures, $36,453; Total giving, $23,900; Grants to individuals, 17 grants totaling $23,500 (high: $2,400, low: $700).
Fields of interest: Health sciences school/education.
Type of support: Undergraduate support.
Application information:
   Deadline(s): June 10 and Nov. 10.
   Additional information: Application by letter including proof of enrollment in a health-related field of study.
EIN: 610647946

2599
John McElaney Trust f/b/o Town of Avon
c/o Heald Hoffmeister & Co.
105 Chestnut St., No. 10
Needham, MA   02492
Application address: c/o Guidance Counselor, Avon High School, Avon, MA 02322

Foundation type: Independent foundation
Limitations: Scholarships to graduates of Avon High School, MA, who plan to pursue studies at higher education institutions.
Financial data: Year ended 12/31/2004. Assets, $349,887 (M); Expenditures, $41,687; Total giving, $26,500; Grants to individuals, 14 grants totaling $10,000 (high: $1,500, low: $250).
Type of support: Support to graduates or students of specific schools; Undergraduate support.
Application information: Application form required.
   Deadline(s): Apr. 10
EIN: 046060702

2600
William E. McElroy Charitable
c/o U.S. Bank, N.A.
P.O. Box 19264
Springfield, IL   62794-9264   (217) 753-7362
Contact: Mary Jo Janssen

Foundation type: Independent foundation

Limitations: Scholarships to boys graduating from high schools in Sangamon County, IL.
Financial data: Year ended 07/31/2005. Assets, $3,572,582 (M); Expenditures, $191,952; Total giving, $153,254; Grants to individuals, 24 grants totaling $82,750 (high: $17,000, low: $500).
Fields of interest: Men.
Type of support: Support to graduates or students of specific schools; Undergraduate support.
Application information: Application form required.
   Deadline(s): Apr. 1
   Applicants should submit the following:
      1) SAT
      2) Letter(s) of recommendation
      3) ACT
EIN: 376306920

2601
William Preston and Belvah McFadden Scholarship Fund
c/o TeamBank, N.A., Trust Dept.
119 E. Madison St.
P.O. Box 650
Iola, KS   66749-0650   (620) 365-3101
Contact: Hellen Welch, Sr. V.P. and Trust Off., TeamBank, N.A.
FAX: (316) 365-3105

Foundation type: Independent foundation
Limitations: Two-year scholarships to financially needy graduates of high schools in Allen County, KS, and to children of residents of Allen County, KS, for full-time study at a four-year Kansas State Board of Regents' college or university.
Publications: Application guidelines; Informational brochure.
Financial data: Year ended 06/30/2005. Assets, $1,075,735 (M); Expenditures, $26,836; Total giving, $21,000; Grants to individuals, 6 grants totaling $21,000 (high: $3,500, low: $3,500).
Type of support: Undergraduate support.
Application information: Application form required.
   Deadline(s): Nov. 1
   Applicants should submit the following:
      1) Photograph
      2) Financial information
      3) Transcripts
      4) ACT
   Additional information: Application should include attendance record. Forms may be obtained from high school guidance counselors and Team Bank, N.A Scholarships are for $3,500 per year for two years (four semesters) only. At least one male and one female student will be chosen each year. No scholarship shall be given to any applicant who has been a student at a community college that is supported by taxes levied upon the taxpayers of that county.
EIN: 481070866

2602
McFarland Charitable Foundation
c/o Havana National Bank, Trust Dept.
P.O. Box 200, 112 S. Orange St.
Havana, IL   62644-0200   (309) 543-3361
Contact: Larry Thomson, V.P. and Sr. Trust Off., Havana National Bank
FAX: (309) 543-3441;
E-mail: info@havanabank.com; Additional tel.: (800) 921-5538

Foundation type: Independent foundation

Limitations: Scholarships to nursing students residing in the Havana, IL area.
Publications: Application guidelines.
Financial data: Year ended 12/31/2004. Assets, $3,093,158 (M); Expenditures, $210,411; Total giving, $160,892; Grants to individuals, 7 grants totaling $59,392 (high: $15,208, low: $4,122).
Fields of interest: Nursing school/education.
Type of support: Scholarships—to individuals; Undergraduate support.
Application information: Applications accepted. Application form required.
> *Initial approach:* Letter.
> *Deadline(s):* None
> *Additional information:* Application should include a $5 application fee; Forms are mailed to applicants by the Director of Nursing Services of the Mason District Hospital; Interviews required.
Program description:
> *Grant Program:* Students may apply during their senior year of high school. Grants normally cover three years of study. Students are obliged to work in the Havana community after graduation for one year for every year of assistance from the foundation. Students must sign written contracts and two co-signers are required. Breach of contract results in repayment plus interest from dates of disbursement, plus recruitment and replacement costs.
EIN: 376022376

2603
McFarland Medical Trust
c/o Havana National Bank
112 S. Orange St.
Havana, IL   62644-0200   (309) 543-3361
Contact: Larry Thomson, V.P. and Trust Off., Havana National Bank
E-mail: info@havanabank.com; Additional tel.: (800) 921-5538; FAX: (309) 543-3441; URL: http://www.havanabank.com

Foundation type: Independent foundation
Limitations: Scholarships to IL students in any field of medicine, except nursing. Students must return to the Havana area to practice for a number of years after graduation.
Publications: Informational brochure.
Financial data: Year ended 12/31/2004. Assets, $667,994 (M); Expenditures, $40,971; Total giving, $27,031.
Fields of interest: Medical school/education.
Type of support: Graduate support.
Application information:
> *Initial approach:* Letter.
> *Applicants should submit the following:*
> 1) Resume
Program description:
> *Scholarship Program:* Execution of written contract with two co-signers and an employment commitment is required. If recipient does not fulfill his or her contract, the grant must be repaid in full, including interest from the date of each disbursement.
EIN: 376095841

2604
John & Agnes McFarlane Scholarship Fund
5450 Telegraph Ln., No. 101
Ventura, CA   93003

Foundation type: Independent foundation

Limitations: Student loans to Ventura County, CA, residents, with preference given to juniors, seniors, and graduate students.
Financial data: Year ended 10/31/2004. Assets, $1,548,501 (M); Expenditures, $89,359; Total giving, $63,500; Loans to individuals, 13 loans totaling $63,500.
Fields of interest: Vocational education.
Type of support: Graduate support; Undergraduate support.
Application information: Application form required.
> *Deadline(s):* Apr. 5
> *Applicants should submit the following:*
> 1) Photograph
> 2) Transcripts
> 3) GPA
> 4) Essay
> *Additional information:* Application must also include two references, letter stating understanding of loan agreement, and an estimated budget if applicant is a senior or graduate student.
Program description:
> *Student Loan Program:* Loans are awarded on the basis of applicant's letter, financial need, academic achievement, ability to repay the loan, and the accuracy of application. Recipients may apply for additional loans in subsequent years. Students attending two-year junior colleges are also eligible.
EIN: 956066876

2605
The McGeehin Educational Foundation, Inc.
6905 Rockledge Dr., Ste. 700
Bethesda, MD   20817-1818
Application address: c/o Col. Zadok A. Magruder High School, 5939 Muncaster Mill Rd., Rockville, MD 20855, tel.: (301) 840-4600

Foundation type: Independent foundation
Limitations: Scholarships to students of Magruder High School, MD, pursuing a degree in education.
Financial data: Year ended 04/30/2004. Assets, $28,606 (M); Expenditures, $15,015; Total giving, $15,000; Grants to individuals, 5 grants totaling $15,000 (high: $5,000, low: $2,500).
Fields of interest: Teacher school/education.
Type of support: Support to graduates or students of specific schools.
Application information: Application form required.
> *Deadline(s):* Contact foundation for deadline
EIN: 521977515

2606
The Donald Ray McGill, Jr. Agape Foundation
11800 Old Katy Rd.
Houston, TX   77079

Foundation type: Operating foundation
Limitations: Scholarships to economically disadvantaged students residing in the Houston, TX, area. Some preference given to students attending Protestant institutions.
Financial data: Year ended 12/31/2003. Assets, $0 (M); Expenditures, $15,914; Total giving, $13,346; Grants to individuals, 3 grants totaling $13,346 (high: $7,346, low: $2,000).
Fields of interest: Protestant agencies & churches; Economically disadvantaged.
Type of support: Undergraduate support.
Application information: Applications accepted. Application form required.

Initial approach: Letter or telephone.
Deadline(s): None
Additional information: Contact foundation for current application guidelines; Applicants may apply directly or by referral.
EIN: 760671332

2607
McGinty Family Foundation
(formerly Alice and Patrick McGinty Foundation, Inc.)
2 Commerce Park Sq., Ste. 325
23220 Chagrin Blvd.
Beachwood, OH   44122-5403   (216) 831-5000
Contact: T.P. McGinty, Exec. Dir.
FAX: (216) 464-9531;
E-mail: jmcginnis9@aol.com; URL: http://www.mcgintyfamilyfoundation.org

Foundation type: Independent foundation
Limitations: Educational support only to school teachers in northeastern OH and western MA.
Publications: Application guidelines; Annual report (including application guidelines); Informational brochure (including application guidelines); Newsletter; Occasional report.
Financial data: Year ended 10/31/2004. Assets, $3,223,459 (M); Expenditures, $241,948; Total giving, $105,111; Grants to individuals, 4 grants totaling $3,699.
Fields of interest: Elementary school/education; Secondary school/education; Education.
Type of support: Program development; Grants to individuals.
Application information: Application form required.
> *Initial approach:* Letter or telephone.
> *Deadline(s):* Apr. 1 and Aug. 15
Program descriptions:
> *Grants to Schools Programs:* Over $1,000 is awarded to schools and administrators. Awards cannot be used for salaries or travel/transportation.
> *Grants to Teachers Program:* Up to $1,000 is awarded to teachers and administrators. Funds cannot be used for salaries or travel/transportation.
EIN: 341643124

2608
Ellanora McGinty Scholarship Fund Trust
c/o Sanford A. Minkoff
15800 Acorn Cir.
Tavares, FL   32778
Application address: c/o Tavares High School, Attn.: Coranell Glass, 603 N. New Hampshire Ave., Tavares, FL 32778, tel.: (352) 343-3007

Foundation type: Independent foundation
Limitations: Scholarships based on financial need and achievement to graduates of Tavares High School, FL.
Financial data: Year ended 12/31/2004. Assets, $246,904 (M); Expenditures, $24,627; Total giving, $24,177; Grants to individuals, 14 grants totaling $24,177 (high: $3,000, low: $212).
Fields of interest: Vocational school, secondary; African Americans/Blacks.
Type of support: Support to graduates or students of specific schools; Undergraduate support.
Application information: Application form required.
> *Deadline(s):* Mar. or Apr.
> *Applicants should submit the following:*
> 1) Essay
> 2) SAT
> 3) GPA
> 4) ACT
> *Additional information:* Interviews required.

Program description:

Scholarship Program: Awards at least one scholarship to an African American and one scholarship to a White student, one of whom must be female and one of whom must be male. The maximum amount per scholarship is $2,000 for up to 4 years, for a total of $8,000. Applicants must be full-time students at Tavares High School with a minimum GPA of 2.0 who intend to attend a public or private vocational center, public or private community college, state university, or private college or university.

EIN: 596964815

2609
Arthur B. & Anna F. McGlothlan Trust
c/o U.S. Bank, N.A.
P.O. Box 308
St. Joseph, MO   64502-0308
Application address: c/o U.S. Bank, N.A., 1 Roubidoux Ctr., St. Joseph, MO 64501

Foundation type: Independent foundation
Limitations: Scholarships to graduates of St. Joseph, MO, area high schools who will attend a church-related or affiliated college.
Financial data: Year ended 06/30/2005. Assets, $274,875 (M); Expenditures, $9,061; Total giving, $5,850; Grants to individuals, 17 grants totaling $5,850.
Fields of interest: Theological school/education; Christian agencies & churches.
Type of support: Support to graduates or students of specific schools; Undergraduate support.
Application information: Application form required.
Deadline(s): Apr. 1
Applicants should submit the following:
1) Photograph
2) Transcripts
3) GPA
4) Financial information
Additional information: Application must also include three references.

Program description:
Scholarship Program: Recipients will lose their grant money in most cases if they decide to get married while still in college.
EIN: 446009610

2610
The McIninch Scholarship Fund
c/o TD Banknorth, N.A.
P.O. Box 477
Concord, NH   03302-0477
Application address: c/o Manchester High School, Attn.: Principal, 207 Lowell St., Manchester, NH 03104

Foundation type: Independent foundation
Limitations: Scholarships to graduates of Manchester High School, NH, for study at four-year colleges and universities.
Publications: Application guidelines.
Financial data: Year ended 12/31/2004. Assets, $1,791,612 (M); Expenditures, $89,956; Total giving, $70,000; Grants to individuals, 14 grants totaling $70,000.
Type of support: Support to graduates or students of specific schools; Undergraduate support.
Application information: Application form required.
Deadline(s): May 10
Additional information: Application forms available from Manchester High School principal.
EIN: 026076262

2611
Eva E. McInnes College Scholarship Fund
c/o First Midwest Bank
3510 W. Elm St.
McHenry, IL   60050-4448

Foundation type: Independent foundation
Limitations: Scholarships to graduating high school students primarily in McHenry, IL.
Financial data: Year ended 12/31/2004. Assets, $1,392,604 (M); Expenditures, $82,464; Total giving, $66,400; Grants to individuals, 39 grants totaling $66,400 (high: $4,800, low: $500).
Type of support: Scholarships—to individuals.
Application information: Applications not accepted.
EIN: 363756004

2612
John McIntire Educational Fund
c/o Unizan Fin. Svcs. Group
422 Main St.
P.O. Box 2307
Zanesville, OH   43702-2307   (740) 455-7060
Contact: Neana Butler, Admin. Asst.

Foundation type: Independent foundation
Limitations: Scholarships to residents of Zanesville, OH, who are under 21 years of age.
Publications: Annual report.
Financial data: Year ended 06/30/2005. Assets, $11,314,887 (M); Expenditures, $558,688; Total giving, $502,783; Grants to individuals, 139 grants totaling $501,783 (high: $8,000, low: $1,000).
Type of support: Scholarships—to individuals.
Application information: Application form required.
Deadline(s): May 1
Applicants should submit the following:
1) Transcripts
2) Letter(s) of recommendation
3) Financial information
EIN: 316021239

2613
Lalitta Nash McKaig Foundation
c/o PNC Advisors
620 Liberty Ave.
Pittsburgh, PA   15222-2705   (412) 762-7941
Contact: Robert Dunlap
Application address (Cumberland office): 21 Prospect Sq., Cumberland, MD, 21502, tel.: (301) 777-1515

Foundation type: Independent foundation
Limitations: Scholarships to residents of Bedford and Somerset counties, PA, Mineral and Hampshire counties, WV, and Allegany and Garrett counties, MD, for undergraduate, graduate, or professional education at any accredited college or university located in the U.S.
Publications: Application guidelines.
Financial data: Year ended 09/30/2004. Assets, $10,861,358 (M); Expenditures, $1,077,123; Total giving, $979,498; Grants to individuals, 516 grants totaling $979,498 (high: $4,000, low: $100).
Type of support: Graduate support; Undergraduate support.
Application information: Applications accepted. Application form required.
Deadline(s): May 30
Additional information: Interviews required; Application forms available from Cumberland, MD, area high school guidance offices, Frostburg State College and Allegany

Community College financial aid offices, the PNC Bank, N.A., or the foundation's Cumberland office.
Program description:
Scholarship Program: Scholarship recipients are selected primarily on the basis of their financial need as computed by the College Scholarship Service from information contained on the FAF and Supplement. The foundation will not normally base any selection of a recipient on his or her past academic performance. Persons applying for a renewal grant, however, will also be evaluated on their scholarship performance during all prior periods of college level education. All persons are eligible to apply for renewal grants provided they resubmit their application and FAF and Supplement for the applicable year and continue to meet the residency requirement. A renewal applicant is not automatically guaranteed a renewal grant.
EIN: 256071908

2614
Edward Nixon McKay Memorial Scholarship Fund
c/o Wachovia Bank, N.A.
100 N. Main St., 13 Fl.
Winston-Salem, NC   27150
Application address: c/o Wachovia Bank, N.A., 191 Peachtree St., Atlanta, GA 30303

Foundation type: Independent foundation
Limitations: Scholarships to students enrolled at Armuchee, Coosa, Darlington, Rome, Model, and Pepperell high schools, GA.
Financial data: Year ended 11/30/2004. Assets, $331,167 (M); Expenditures, $7,667; Total giving, $6,330; Grants to individuals, 5 grants totaling $6,000.
Type of support: Scholarships—to individuals; Support to graduates or students of specific schools.
Application information: Applications not accepted.
Additional information: Recipients are recommended by high school principals.
Program description:
Scholarship Program: Scholarships are to be used for tuition, books, and supplies only.
EIN: 586161795

2615
McKee Educational Foundation
214 Kennith Dr.
Nashville, TN   37207   (615) 444-2569
Contact: C. William McKee, Tr.

Foundation type: Independent foundation
Limitations: Scholarships to students for higher education, primarily in GA and TX.
Financial data: Year ended 12/31/2004. Assets, $155,569 (M); Expenditures, $6,545; Total giving, $6,000; Grants to individuals, 9 grants totaling $6,000 (high: $1,500, low: $500).
Type of support: Undergraduate support.
Application information: Application form required.
Deadline(s): Aug. 8
Applicants should submit the following:
1) Essay
Program description:
Scholarship Program: Recipients must be U.S. citizens and demonstrate financial need and academic promise. They must also maintain at least a 2.5 GPA to be eligible for scholarship and to

retain it. Recipients must register for and complete the equivalent of 12 semester credits per term.
EIN: 911845996

2616
John W. McKee Educational Trust
c/o U.S. Bank, N.A.
P.O. Box 3168, No. 50255290, Trust Tax
Portland, OR   97208-3168   (503) 275-4327
Application address: c/o O'Toole Law Firm,
Attn.: McKee, 209 N. Main St., Plentywood, MT
59254, tel.: (406) 765-1630

Foundation type: Independent foundation
Limitations: Scholarships to undergraduate students who are residents of Sheridan, Roosevelt, or Daniels counties, MT.
Financial data: Year ended 12/31/2004.
Assets, $485,464 (M); Expenditures, $37,162; Total giving, $27,300; Grants to individuals, 89 grants totaling $27,300 (high: $350, low: $250).
Type of support: Undergraduate support.
Application information:
    Deadline(s): July 15
    Additional information: Contact foundation for current application guidelines.
EIN: 237058723

2617
Ella G. McKee Foundation
c/o First National Bank of Vandalia
P.O. Box 40, Trust Dept.
Vandalia, IL   62471

Foundation type: Independent foundation
Limitations: Interest-free student loans to individuals who have been residents of Fayette County, IL, for at least four years.
Financial data: Year ended 12/31/2004.
Assets, $1,584,935 (M); Expenditures, $162,016; Total giving, $150,950; Loans to individuals, 118 loans totaling $150,950.
Type of support: Student loans—to individuals.
Application information: Application form required.
    Deadline(s): Contact foundation for deadline
EIN: 376099863

2618
Elmer McKenney Scholarship Trust
c/o JPMorgan Chase Bank
P.O. Box 701
Abilene, TX   79604
Application addresses: c/o Marilyn Cluck, Sr. Counselor, Abilene High School, 842 N. 6th, Abilene, TX 79603, tel.: (915) 677-1444; c/o Isabel Anderson, 3639 Sayles Blvd., Abilene, TX 79602, tel.: (915) 691-1000; or c/o Billie McKeever, 600 North Ave. E., Haskell, TX 79521, tel.: (940) 864-2848

Foundation type: Independent foundation
Limitations: Scholarships to financially needy graduating seniors from Abilene High School, Cooper High School, and Haskell High School, TX, for attendance at junior or senior colleges and universities.
Financial data: Year ended 07/31/2004.
Assets, $179,360 (M); Expenditures, $18,995; Total giving, $4,400; Grants to individuals, 5 grants totaling $4,400.
Type of support: Support to graduates or students of specific schools; Undergraduate support.
Application information: Application form required.
    Deadline(s): Aug. 29

Applicants should submit the following:
    1) Transcripts
    Additional information: Application must also include three reference forms.
Program description:
    Scholarship Program: Applicants must have a GPA of 85 or above during their senior year and exemplify good citizenship.
EIN: 756319992

2619
McKesson Foundation, Inc.
(formerly McKesson HBOC Foundation, Inc.)
1 Post St.
San Francisco, CA   94104   (415) 983-8673
Contact: Marcia M. Argyris, Pres.
E-mail: community.relations@mckesson.com;
URL: http://www.mckesson.com/foundation.html

Foundation type: Company-sponsored foundation
Limitations: Scholarships to graduates of Ida B. Wells High School in San Francisco, CA, or other youth who participate in the McKesson programs.
Publications: Application guidelines; Annual report; Grants list.
Financial data: Year ended 03/31/2005.
Assets, $17,528,012 (M); Expenditures, $4,630,297; Total giving, $4,310,297; Grants to individuals, totaling $64,975.
Type of support: Scholarships—to individuals; Support to graduates or students of specific schools; Graduate support; Undergraduate support.
Application information: Contact foundation for current application deadline/guidelines.
Program description:
    Thomas E. Drohan Scholarships: These scholarships are awarded to motivated and deserving graduates of Ida B. Wells High School in San Francisco, CA. Recipients must maintain frequent contact with McKesson as long as they continue to receive funding. Throughout the program, the coordinator counsels scholarship recipients and works with the schools to ensure that the necessary resources are available to the students. Recipients are recommended by outreach workers, youth centers and counselors.
EIN: 943140036

2620
Edgar & Nona McKinney Charitable Foundation
c/o SunTrust Bank Foundation Svcs.
P.O. Box 620005
Orlando, FL   32862-0005
Contact: Candace Marshall, Acctg. Admin.

Foundation type: Independent foundation
Limitations: Scholarships to residents of FL for higher education.
Financial data: Year ended 05/31/2005.
Assets, $1,612,126 (M); Expenditures, $144,643; Total giving, $136,000; Grants to individuals, 25 grants totaling $43,000 (high: $3,000, low: $1,000).
Type of support: Scholarships—to individuals.
Application information: Applications accepted. Application form required.
    Additional information: Contact foundation for current application guidelines.
EIN: 597001925

2621
Charles Cecil McKinney Foundation
1006 Harvey St.
Raleigh, NC   27608   (919) 834-1317

Foundation type: Independent foundation
Limitations: Scholarships by nomination only to graduates of Mitchell High School, NC, for undergraduate education.
Financial data: Year ended 12/31/2004.
Assets, $488,857 (M); Expenditures, $25,426; Total giving, $21,429; Grants to individuals, 2 grants totaling $14,000 (high: $7,000, low: $7,000).
Type of support: Support to graduates or students of specific schools; Awards/grants by nomination only; Undergraduate support.
Application information: Application form required.
    Additional information: Contact high school for further application information. Interviews required.
EIN: 562026410

2622
The Ira and Dena McKinnis Educational Trust
P.O. Box H
Pratt, KS   67124-1108   (620) 672-5533
Contact: Bill Hampton, Jr., Tr.

Foundation type: Independent foundation
Limitations: Student loans and scholarships to graduates of high schools in Pratt County, KS.
Financial data: Year ended 12/31/2004.
Assets, $435,177 (M); Expenditures, $7,616; Total giving, $0; Loans to individuals, 20 loans totaling $40,800.
Type of support: Scholarships—to individuals; Student loans—to individuals; Support to graduates or students of specific schools.
Application information: Applications accepted.
    Initial approach: Letter.
    Additional information: Application must also include personal and academic information.
EIN: 486247592

2623
Dorothea van Dyke McLane Association
c/o Dorothea's House
120 John St., Ste. 1
Princeton, NJ   08542-3121   (609) 924-9713

Foundation type: Independent foundation
Limitations: Scholarships to graduates of secondary schools in the Princeton, NJ, area, based on academic ability and financial need.
Financial data: Year ended 12/31/2004.
Assets, $3,567,161 (M); Expenditures, $175,376; Total giving, $91,150; Grants to individuals, 89 grants totaling $57,150 (high: $1,775, low: $250).
Type of support: Support to graduates or students of specific schools; Undergraduate support.
Application information: Applications accepted.
    Deadline(s): None
    Additional information: Applications by letter accepted throughout the year.
EIN: 216000849

2624
McLaughlin Foundation
118 Woodland Rd.
Milton, MA   02186   (617) 361-6530
Contact: James McGrath, Pres.

Foundation type: Independent foundation
Limitations: Scholarships to MT residents attending Harvard University, MA, and other colleges.
Financial data: Year ended 12/31/2004. Assets, $875,358 (M); Expenditures, $39,475; Total giving, $32,000; Grants to individuals, 3 grants totaling $30,000.
Type of support: Scholarships—to individuals; Support to graduates or students of specific schools.
Application information: Applications accepted.
Deadline(s): None
Additional information: Contact foundation for current application guidelines; Applicants should submit a brief resume of academic qualifications.
EIN: 237416882

2625
McLoraine Family Educational Trust
c/o Kenneth J. Rudnick
980 W. Blue Fox Rd.
Green Valley, AZ 85614-4747
Contact: Dennis Carroll, Tr.
Application address: 1507 E. Ironwood Dr., MT Prospect, IL 60056

Foundation type: Independent foundation
Limitations: Scholarships to financially needy, scholastically worthy graduating seniors attending secondary Catholic education facilities in northern IL.
Financial data: Year ended 06/30/2005. Assets, $807,600 (M); Expenditures, $36,000; Total giving, $36,000; Grants to individuals, 12 grants totaling $36,000 (high: $3,000; low: $3,000).
Fields of interest: Roman Catholic agencies & churches.
Type of support: Scholarships—to individuals; Precollege support.
Application information:
Deadline(s): Mar. 30
Applicants should submit the following:
1) Financial information
Additional information: Application must also include primary scholastic information.
EIN: 363196087

2626
William J. McMannis and A. Haskell McMannis Educational Trust Fund
c/o PNC Advisors
620 Liberty Ave., P2-PTPP-10-2
Pittsburgh, PA 15222-2708
Scholarship address: c/o PNC Advisors, P.O. Box 8480, Erie, PA 16553, tel.: (814) 871-9362

Foundation type: Independent foundation
Limitations: Scholarships to students who are U.S. citizens, for study at Gannon University, PA; Mercyhurst College, PA; Pennsylvania State University at Erie, The Behrend College; Dickinson College, PA; University of Pittsburgh, PA; Edinboro University, PA; and Florida State University, Fl.
Publications: Informational brochure (including application guidelines).
Financial data: Year ended 08/31/2004. Assets, $4,492,569 (M); Expenditures, $298,974; Total giving, $242,500; Grants to individuals, totaling $242,500.
Type of support: Support to graduates or students of specific schools; Undergraduate support.
Application information: Application form required.
Deadline(s): Apr. 1

Additional information: Applications not accepted from individuals, and must be submitted through qualified schools.
EIN: 256191302

2627
McMaster-Moulthrop Scholarship Fund
480 Wolcott St.
Bristol, CT 06010
Contact: Dennis Siegmann, Tr.
Application address: Bristol Central High School, 480 Wolcott St., Bristol, CT 06010-6498, tel.: (860) 584-7735

Foundation type: Independent foundation
Limitations: Scholarships to financially needy graduating seniors of Bristol Central High School, CT, who have demonstrated service to school and community and superior academic achievement.
Financial data: Year ended 12/31/2004. Assets, $0 (L); Expenditures, $99,755; Total giving, $94,500; Grants to individuals, 63 grants totaling $94,500 (high: $5,000, low: $100).
Fields of interest: Community development, volunteer services.
Type of support: Support to graduates or students of specific schools; Undergraduate support.
Application information: Application form required.
Initial approach: Letter or telephone.
Deadline(s): Mar. 1
EIN: 066373995

2628
Bruce McMillan, Jr. Foundation, Inc.
P.O. Box 9
Overton, TX 75684 (903) 834-3148
Contact: Ralph Ward, Jr., Pres.

Foundation type: Independent foundation
Limitations: Scholarships to qualified graduates of eight high schools in the immediate Overton, TX, area.
Publications: Application guidelines.
Financial data: Year ended 06/30/2005. Assets, $18,627,466 (M); Expenditures, $1,344,898; Total giving, $714,873; Grants to individuals, 9 grants totaling $33,500 (high: $12,000, low: $500).
Type of support: Support to graduates or students of specific schools; Undergraduate support.
Application information: Application form required.
Initial approach: Letter.
Deadline(s): Apr. 15
Additional information: Interviews required during spring break period of respective high schools.
Program description:
Scholarship Program: The foundation provides scholarship support to qualified high school seniors attending the following high schools within an approximate 15-mile radius of Overton, TX: West Rusk High School, Overton High School, Henderson High School, Leverett Chapel High School, Kilgore High School, Troup High School, Arp High School, and Carlisle High School.
EIN: 750945924

2629
Wendell W. McMillen Foundation
203 Center St.
Sheffield, PA 16347 (814) 968-3241
Contact: Joyce E. Olson, Dir.

Foundation type: Independent foundation

Limitations: Student loans to residents of the Sheffield, PA, area.
Financial data: Year ended 03/31/2004. Assets, $483,552 (M); Expenditures, $19,312; Total giving, $0; Loans to individuals, 15 loans totaling $23,450.
Type of support: Student loans—to individuals.
Application information: Application form required.
Initial approach: Letter or telephone.
Additional information: Applications accepted throughout the year.
EIN: 256060174

2630
Lucy J. McMurtrie Foundation
(also known as McMurtrie Scholarship Fund)
c/o Bank of America, N.A.
P.O. Box 441
Ridgefield Park, NJ 07660-9984
Application address: c/o Office of the Principal, Roxbury High School, Succasunna, NJ 07876, tel.: (201) 584-1200

Foundation type: Independent foundation
Limitations: Scholarships to financially needy, deserving students of Roxbury High School, Succassunna, NJ.
Financial data: Year ended 12/31/2003. Assets, $533,737 (M); Expenditures, $34,324; Total giving, $29,500; Grants to individuals, 58 grants totaling $29,500 (high: $1,500, low: $250).
Type of support: Support to graduates or students of specific schools; Precollege support.
Application information:
Deadline(s): May
Additional information: Application by letter stating educational pursuits and financial need.
EIN: 226426610

2631
John F. McNair Memorial Fund Trust
c/o Wachovia Bank, N.A.
100 N. Main St., 13th Fl.
Winston-Salem, NC 27150
Application address: c/o Scholarship Coordinator, Scotland High School, 1000 W. Church St., Laurinburg, NC 28352, tel.: (919) 276-7370

Foundation type: Independent foundation
Limitations: Scholarships to graduates of public high schools in Laurinburg, NC.
Financial data: Year ended 12/31/2004. Assets, $157,383 (M); Expenditures, $9,747; Total giving, $9,000; Grants to individuals, 6 grants totaling $9,000.
Type of support: Support to graduates or students of specific schools; Undergraduate support.
Application information: Application form required.
Initial approach: Letter.
Additional information: Applications accepted throughout the year.
EIN: 566035967

2632
Dr. Francis McNaught Scholarship Fund
(formerly Grace I. McNaught-Dr. Francis McNaught Scholarship Fund)
c/o Wells Fargo Bank Arizona, N.A.
P.O. Box 53456
Phoenix, AZ 85072
Application address: c/o Wells Fargo Bank West, N.A., Attn.: Margaret Toal, Trust Off., 633 17th St., Denver, CO 80270

Foundation type: Independent foundation
Limitations: Loans only to students at the University of Colorado Medical School, CO, who are acquiring an advanced degree in medicine.
Financial data: Year ended 08/31/2005. Assets, $793,007 (M); Expenditures, $48,637; Total giving, $34,000; Grant to an individual, 1 grant totaling $34,000.
Fields of interest: Medical school/education.
Type of support: Support to graduates or students of specific schools; Graduate support.
Application information: Applications accepted.
Additional information: Applications by letter accepted throughout the year; Contact university financial aid office for current application guidelines.
EIN: 846020606

2633
Harry & Winnie McNay Educational Trust
c/o Great Western Bank
P.O. Box 4070
Omaha, NE 68104-0070
Application address: c/o Great Western Bank, Attn.: Keith Cueno, 201 N. Main St., Chariton, IA 50049

Foundation type: Independent foundation
Limitations: Low-interest student loans to residents of Lucas County, IA.
Financial data: Year ended 06/30/2004. Assets, $658,197 (M); Expenditures, $18,515; Total giving, $4,513; Grants to individuals, totaling $4,513; Loans to individuals, 23 loans totaling $34,500.
Type of support: Student loans—to individuals.
Application information: Applications accepted. Application form required.
Applicants should submit the following:
1) Financial information
EIN: 426252638

2634
Roy and Yvonne McNeil Scholarship Fund
5426 12th St. S
Fargo, ND 58104

Foundation type: Operating foundation
Limitations: Scholarships to residents of Traill County, ND.
Financial data: Year ended 12/31/2003. Assets, $295,425 (M); Expenditures, $17,517; Total giving, $12,000; Grants to individuals, 5 grants totaling $12,000 (high: $2,400, low: $2,400).
Type of support: Undergraduate support.
Application information: Applications accepted. Application form required.
Initial approach: Letter.
EIN: 456101161

2635
Gertrude L. McRae Scholarship Fund
c/o Wells Fargo Bank Northwest, N.A.
P.O. Box 21927, MAC P6540-144
Seattle, WA 98111
Application address: c/o Scholarship Fund Committee, Grant County Court House, Canyon City, OR 97820

Foundation type: Independent foundation
Limitations: Scholarships to graduates of high schools in Grant County, OR, who have completed one or more years of college. Secondary preference to students from Wheeler, Morrow, and Wasco county high schools, OR.
Financial data: Year ended 06/30/2005. Assets, $239,451 (M); Expenditures, $25,507; Total giving, $19,900; Grants to individuals, 13 grants totaling $19,900 (high: $4,150, low: $450).
Type of support: Support to graduates or students of specific schools; Undergraduate support.
Application information: Application form required.
Deadline(s): July 1
EIN: 936097780

2636
McRoberts Memorial Law Scholarship Fund
c/o National City Bank
P.O. Box 94651
Cleveland, OH 44101-4651
Application address: c/o National City Bank, Jo Ann Harlan, V.P. and Trust Off., 301 S.W. Adams St., Peoria, IL 61652

Foundation type: Independent foundation
Limitations: Scholarships to financially needy students who have been residents of Peoria County, IL, for at least five years, and who are pursuing law degrees.
Publications: Informational brochure (including application guidelines).
Financial data: Year ended 06/30/2005. Assets, $781,545 (M); Expenditures, $36,916; Total giving, $34,000; Grants to individuals, 6 grants totaling $34,000 (high: $13,000, low: $1,000).
Fields of interest: Law school/education.
Type of support: Scholarships—to individuals.
Application information: Application form required.
Deadline(s): May 15
Applicants should submit the following:
1) Transcripts
2) Letter(s) of recommendation
3) Financial information
Additional information: Application must also include LSAT scores.
EIN: 376043864

2637
MDU Resources Foundation
P.O. Box 5650
Bismarck, ND 58506-5650
Contact: Robert E. Wood, Pres.
FAX: (701) 222-7607; URL: http://www.mdu.com/the_vision/vision_foundation.htm

Foundation type: Company-sponsored foundation
Limitations: Scholarships only to children and spouses of active full-time employees of MDU Resources Group, Inc. and its subsidiaries in MT.
Publications: Annual report.
Financial data: Year ended 12/31/2002. Assets, $2,038,980 (M); Expenditures, $738,136; Total giving, $732,557; Grants to individuals, 20 grants totaling $24,000 (high: $1,200, low: $1,200).
Type of support: Employee-related scholarships.
Application information: Application form required.
Initial approach: Letter.
Deadline(s): None
EIN: 450378937

2638
Beth Rowell Mead Educational Trust
c/o Regions Morgan Keegan Trust
P.O. Box 2020
Tyler, TX 75710-2020
Contact: Suzanne Benefield, Tr.
Application address: P.O. Box 486, Jefferson, TX 75657, tel.: (903) 665-7700

Foundation type: Independent foundation
Limitations: Scholarships to residents of Marion, Harrison, Cass, Morris, Gregg, and Upshur counties, TX.
Financial data: Year ended 09/30/2004. Assets, $648,592 (M); Expenditures, $34,966; Total giving, $26,650; Grants to individuals, 23 grants totaling $26,650 (high: $1,750, low: $400).
Type of support: Scholarships—to individuals.
Application information: Applications accepted. Application form required.
Applicants should submit the following:
1) Letter(s) of recommendation
2) Photograph
3) Transcripts
Additional information: Application must also include a handwritten letter, and an outline of financial need.
Program description:
Scholarship Program: Recipients must maintain at least a 2.0 GPA and enroll in a minimum of 12 credits per semester.
EIN: 756310255

2639
Edwin Budge Mead Scholarship Trust
c/o Bank of America, N.A.
P.O. Box 40200, MC FL9-100-10-19
Jacksonville, FL 32203-0200
Application address: c/o Eustis High School, Attn.: Principal, 1300 E. Washington Ave., Eustis, FL 32726

Foundation type: Independent foundation
Limitations: Scholarships to individuals graduating in the top quarter of the senior class of Eustis High School, FL.
Financial data: Year ended 12/31/2004. Assets, $371,455 (M); Expenditures, $19,533; Total giving, $15,800; Grants to individuals, 23 grants totaling $15,800 (high: $1,100, low: $500).
Type of support: Support to graduates or students of specific schools.
Application information: Contact principal for current application deadline/guidelines.
EIN: 596190681

2640
Joseph F. Meade Memorial Science Fund
c/o JPMorgan Chase Bank
P.O. Box 31412
Rochester, NY 14603

Foundation type: Independent foundation
Limitations: Scholarships and interest-free loans to selected graduates of the Hammondsport Central School District, NY, who are continuing their education in engineering or allied fields at accredited universities and colleges, or other education or training institutions.
Financial data: Year ended 12/31/2004. Assets, $262,799 (M); Expenditures, $18,083; Total giving, $15,000; Grants to individuals, 5 grants totaling $15,000 (high: $7,500, low: $500).
Fields of interest: Vocational education; Engineering school/education.

Type of support: Scholarships—to individuals; Student loans—to individuals; Support to graduates or students of specific schools.
Application information: Applications not accepted.
EIN: 166015269

2641
L. & M. Meador Scholarship Trust
c/o Bank of America, N.A.
P.O. Box 26606
Richmond, VA 23261-6606
Application address: c/o Bank of America, N.A., Attn.: Sarah Kay, 1111 E. Main St., Richmond, VA 23219-3500

Foundation type: Independent foundation
Limitations: Scholarships to residents of Norton and Wise counties, VA, for higher education.
Financial data: Year ended 05/31/2005. Assets, $1,013,027 (M); Expenditures, $50,808; Total giving, $35,000; Grants to individuals, 12 grants totaling $35,000 (high: $14,500, low: $500).
Type of support: Scholarships—to individuals.
Application information:
  Initial approach: Letter or telephone.
  Additional information: Contact trust for current application deadline/guidelines.
EIN: 546385104

2642
Edith Mears Trust
c/o Peoples Bank & Trust Co.
202-204 N. Main St.
Greensburg, KY 42743

Foundation type: Independent foundation
Limitations: Scholarships by nomination only to graduating seniors of Green County High School, KY. Top 20 graduating students are selected by school and scholarship recipients are nominated by trustees of the trust.
Financial data: Year ended 12/31/2002. Assets, $819,568 (M); Expenditures, $44,540; Total giving, $43,982; Grants to individuals, 5 grants totaling $33,825 (high: $6,765, low: $6,765).
Type of support: Support to graduates or students of specific schools; Awards/grants by nomination only; Undergraduate support.
Application information: Applications not accepted.
EIN: 626284015

2643
The Benjamin and Mary Siddons Measey Foundation
225 N. Olive St.
P.O. Box 258
Media, PA 19063
Contact: James C. Brennan, Mgr.

Foundation type: Independent foundation
Limitations: Scholarships to students wishing to attend medical school in Philadelphia, PA.
Publications: Informational brochure.
Financial data: Year ended 12/31/2004. Assets, $52,985,348 (M); Expenditures, $2,677,211; Total giving, $2,531,500.
Type of support: Graduate support.
Application information:
  Initial approach: Letter.

Copies of proposal: 5
Deadline(s): Mar. 1, June 1, Sept. 1, Dec. 1
Applicants should submit the following:
  1) Proposal
Additional information: Grants are made to the medical institution, who in turn distribute funds for the benefit of students through scholarships.
EIN: 236298781

2644
Mecklenburg Scholarship Association, Inc.
504 E. 2nd St.
Chase City, VA 23924-1716 (434) 372-5353
Contact: A. Duke Reid, Secy.-Treas.

Foundation type: Independent foundation
Limitations: Scholarships to financially needy residents of Chase City District, VA. Student loans to financially needy residents of Mecklenburg County, VA.
Financial data: Year ended 05/31/2004. Assets, $21,785 (M); Expenditures, $10,399; Total giving, $8,600.
Type of support: Scholarships—to individuals; Student loans—to individuals.
Application information: Applications accepted.
  Initial approach: Letter.
  Deadline(s): Contact foundation for deadline
  Additional information: Application must also include information on parents' and student's incomes.
EIN: 546040510

2645
Medallion Foods Competitive Edge Scholarship Trust
3636 Delta Ave.
Newport, AR 72112-9096
Application address: c/o Newport Campus Charitable Foundation, Box 189, Newport, AR 72112, tel.: (870) 523-3300

Foundation type: Operating foundation
Limitations: Scholarships to financially needy residents of Jackson County, AR and children of employees of businesses in Jackson County, AR for higher education. Preference is given to qualified applicants to further their higher education at institutions located in Jackson County.
Financial data: Year ended 12/31/2003. Assets, $72,994 (M); Expenditures, $86,728; Total giving, $86,418; Grants to individuals, totaling $86,418.
Type of support: Undergraduate support.
Application information: Application form required.
  Deadline(s): Apr. 15 for summer students and high school seniors, June 30 for continuing and non-traditional students.
EIN: 710773955

2646
The Medic Educational Foundation
c/o Wachovia Bank, N.A.
100 N. Main St., 13th Fl.
Winston-Salem, NC 27150 (336) 732-5252

Foundation type: Independent foundation
Limitations: Scholarships to students for attendance at medical school.
Financial data: Year ended 12/31/2004. Assets, $208,473 (M); Expenditures, $78,732; Total giving, $71,000; Grants to individuals, 26

grants totaling $60,000 (high: $2,500, low: $1,250).
Fields of interest: Medical school/education.
Type of support: Graduate support.
Application information: Unsolicited requests for funds not accepted.
EIN: 582391110

2647
Medical Association of Georgia Foundation, Inc.
(also known as MAG Foundation)
1330 W. Peachtree St. N.W., Ste. 500
Atlanta, GA 30309-3990 (404) 876-7535
Contact: Leigh Skinner

Foundation type: Independent foundation
Limitations: Student loans to GA residents attending a GA medical school.
Financial data: Year ended 12/31/2004. Assets, $620,007 (M); Expenditures, $182,272; Total giving, $15,000.
Fields of interest: Medical school/education.
Type of support: Graduate support.
Application information: Applications accepted. Application form required.
EIN: 586066431

2648
The Medical Education Scholarship Trust
c/o Idaho Medical Assn.
P.O. Box 2668
Boise, ID 83701-2668 (208) 344-7888
Contact: Robert K. Seehusen, Tr.

Foundation type: Independent foundation
Limitations: Scholarships to ID residents for higher education.
Financial data: Year ended 12/31/2004. Assets, $284,422 (M); Expenditures, $15,261; Total giving, $14,950; Grants to individuals, 21 grants totaling $14,950 (high: $1,000, low: $150).
Type of support: Scholarships—to individuals.
Application information: Application form required.
  Deadline(s): Contact trust for deadline
EIN: 943105797

2649
Medical Research Foundation, Inc.
P.O. Box 109
Minden, NE 68959-0109 (308) 832-1475
Contact: Jerry C. Stirtz, Dir.

Foundation type: Independent foundation
Limitations: Scholarships to women in NE who are seeking education in medicine or medicine related-fields.
Financial data: Year ended 12/31/2004. Assets, $461,260 (M); Expenditures, $12,639; Total giving, $12,000; Grants to individuals, 14 grants totaling $12,000 (high: $2,000, low: $1,000).
Fields of interest: Medical school/education; Women.
Type of support: Scholarships—to individuals.
Application information:
  Initial approach: Letter.
  Deadline(s): June 1
EIN: 476026243

2650
Meehan Family Foundation, Inc.
(formerly Daniel E. Meehan Foundation, Inc.)
1473 E. Goodrich Ln.
Fox Point, WI 53217-2950
Contact: Daniel E. Meehan, Chair.

Foundation type: Independent foundation
Limitations: Scholarships to employees and
children of employees of Meehan Seaway Service,
Ltd. and its subsidiaries.
Publications: Application guidelines.
Financial data: Year ended 12/31/2004.
Assets, $3,226,333 (M); Expenditures,
$1,280,834; Total giving, $1,215,694.
Fields of interest: Education.
Type of support: Employee-related scholarships.
Application information: Applications accepted.
Application form required.
   Initial approach: Letter or intercompany mail
      outlining financial need and academic
      eligibility.
   Deadline(s): May 15.
   Applicants should submit the following:
      1) SAT
      2) Transcripts
      3) Letter(s) of recommendation
Program description:
   Scholarship Program: Employees of the following
companies are eligible: Meehan Seaway Service,
Ltd., Meehan Seaway Service of Milwaukee, Ltd.,
Meehan Overseas Terminal, Ltd., Meehan
Overseas Terminal of Albany, Ship and Cargo
Agency of Morehead City, Meehan Overseas
Terminal of New London, 4400 Packaging, Inc., and
Seaway Cartage, Ltd. Scholarships are awarded on
the basis of scholastic achievement, standardized
test scores, recommendations, and financial need.
Scholarships may be used for full-time study at the
undergraduate or graduate level. Scholarships
cover the cost of annual tuition, up to $4,000 per
year for up to four years. Recipients must maintain
full-time status and at least a 3.0 GPA to be eligible
for renewals. Applicants are notified of the
scholarship committee's decision by mail.
EIN: 391445333

2651
The Amy E. Mehaffy Foundation, Inc.
c/o South of City
P.O. Box 437
Baxter Springs, KS 66713

Foundation type: Independent foundation
Limitations: Scholarships to graduating seniors
from Baxter Springs High School, KS.
Financial data: Year ended 06/30/2005.
Assets, $334,469 (M); Expenditures, $12,989;
Total giving, $12,000; Grants to individuals, 4
grants totaling $12,000 (high: $3,000, low:
$3,000).
Type of support: Support to graduates or students
of specific schools.
Application information: Contact foundation for
current application deadline/guidelines.
EIN: 486284765

2652
Lena Y. Meharg Scholarship Trust
c/o Regions Bank, Trust Dept.
P.O. Box 2128
Anniston, AL 36202-2128
Contact: Cheryl Reid, Trust Off., Regions Bank

Foundation type: Independent foundation

Limitations: Scholarships for higher education to
financially needy young women of the First
Presbyterian Church of Anniston, the Presbyterian
Home for Children at Talladega, or who are
residents of Calhoun County, AL.
Financial data: Year ended 08/31/2005.
Assets, $374,285 (M); Expenditures, $19,299;
Total giving, $14,800; Grants to individuals, 9
grants totaling $14,800 (high: $2,000, low: $750).
Fields of interest: Children/youth, services;
Christian agencies & churches; Women.
Type of support: Scholarships—to individuals.
Application information: Applications not
accepted.
Program description:
   Scholarship Program: Scholarships are made to
qualified girls or young women who are members of
the First Presbyterian Church of Anniston, AL or who
are in or from the Presbyterian Home for Children at
Talladega, AL or who are residents of Calhoun
County, AL with financial need and creditable school
record.
EIN: 636017711

2653
**Bhupat and Jyott Mehta Family
Foundation**
738 Hwy. 6 S., Ste. 850
Houston, TX 77079-4033
Application address: c/o Janet Bertolino, U.S.
National Bank, 2201 Market St.., Galveston, TX
77553, tel.: (409) 770-7165

Foundation type: Independent foundation
Limitations: Student loans to TX residents for
full-time study at an accredited college or university.
Financial data: Year ended 09/30/2004.
Assets, $14,425,513 (M); Expenditures,
$709,033; Total giving, $675,210.
Type of support: Undergraduate support.
Application information: Application form required.
   Initial approach: Letter or telephone.
   Deadline(s): Jan. 1 to Mar. 31
Program description:
   Student Loan Program: Applicants must be U.S.
citizens.
EIN: 760522455

2654
Lucy E. Meiller Educational Trust
c/o SunTrust Bank
P.O. Box 1908
Orlando, FL 32802-1908
Contact: Carolyn McCoy, Trust Off., SunTrust Bank
Application address: P.O. Box 13888, Roanoke, VA
24038

Foundation type: Independent foundation
Limitations: Scholarships to financially needy VA
residents with scholastic ability to attend VA
colleges and universities.
Financial data: Year ended 08/31/2004.
Assets, $510,018 (M); Expenditures, $26,047;
Total giving, $19,500; Grants to individuals, 6
grants totaling $19,500 (high: $6,000, low:
$1,500).
Type of support: Scholarships—to individuals.
Application information: Application form required.
   Applicants should submit the following:
      1) Transcripts
   Additional information: Application must also
      include a biographical sketch, financial need
      analysis report (FNAR), and financial aid form
      or parents' confidential statement (PCS);

Apply through financial aid office of the VA
college or university.
EIN: 546238746

2655
The J. Robert and Rose Marie Melish Trust
P.O. Box 87
Galion, OH 44833
Application address: c/o Charles Neal, 200 Union
St., Galion, OH 44833, tel.: (419) 468-6500

Foundation type: Operating foundation
Limitations: Scholarships to graduating seniors of
Galion High School, OH.
Financial data: Year ended 12/31/2003.
Assets, $178,440 (M); Expenditures, $46,287;
Total giving, $45,900; Grants to individuals, 9
grants totaling $45,900 (high: $7,500, low:
$1,333).
Type of support: Support to graduates or students
of specific schools; Undergraduate support.
Application information: Application form required.
   Deadline(s): Apr. 1
EIN: 347041107

2656
**Edward Arthur Mellinger Educational
Foundation, Inc.**
1025 E. Broadway
P.O. Box 770
Monmouth, IL 61462   (309) 734-2419
FAX: (309) 734-4435; E-mail: info@mellinger.org;
URL: http://www.mellinger.org/

Foundation type: Independent foundation
Limitations: Scholarships to undergraduate
students and loans to graduate students residing
in western IL and eastern IA.
Publications: Application guidelines; Program
policy statement.
Financial data: Year ended 12/31/2004.
Assets, $22,579,624 (M); Expenditures,
$1,077,524; Total giving, $776,141; Grants to
individuals, totaling $749,917; Loans to
individuals, totaling $60,000.
Type of support: Graduate support; Undergraduate
support.
Application information: Application form required.
   Initial approach: Letter.
   Deadline(s): Feb. to May
Program description:
   Scholarship Program: The foundation awards
scholarships to undergraduate students and loans
to graduate students who are scholastically
qualified and in need of financial assistance to
attend accredited institutions. Scholarships are
renewable for up to four years contingent upon
evidence of satisfactory academic performance.
Loans may be renewed annually up to four years,
also contingent upon evidence of satisfactory
academic performance.
EIN: 362428421

2657
Mellinger Scholarship Fund
(formerly Gertrude & Clarence Mellinger
Scholarship Fund)
c/o The Ephrata National Bank
47 E. Main St.
Ephrata, PA 17522   (717) 733-6576
Contact: Carl Brubaker, Trust Off., Ephrata National
Bank

Foundation type: Independent foundation

Limitations: Scholarships to financially needy graduating seniors from Ephrata Area High School who have been residents of the school district for at least three years prior to graduation.
Financial data: Year ended 12/31/2004. Assets, $1,007,638 (M); Expenditures, $80,398; Total giving, $72,500; Grants to individuals, 59 grants totaling $72,500 (high: $1,250, low: $1,250).
Fields of interest: Nursing school/education.
Type of support: Support to graduates or students of specific schools; Undergraduate support.
Application information: Application form required.
Deadline(s): Apr. 25
Applicants should submit the following:
1) Class rank
2) ACT
Additional information: Application must also include extracurricular activities and achievements.
Program description:
Scholarship Program: Applicants must be in the top ten percent of their graduating classes and must be attending an institution of higher learning in a four-year degree program or a three-year nursing degree program. Recipients are selected on the basis of financial need, extracurricular activities, and SAT scores. Each scholarship is a $5,000 award, payable in equal installments of $1,250 per year over a four-year period. Scholarships are renewable provided that the student maintains at least a 2.5 cumulative GPA.
EIN: 232833247

2658
Melmac Education Foundation
185 Whitten Rd.
Augusta, ME 04330

Foundation type: Independent foundation
Limitations: Scholarships to high school seniors in ME for higher education.
Financial data: Year ended 12/31/2002. Assets, $27,050,886 (M); Expenditures, $520,318; Total giving, $235,712; Grants to individuals, 147 grants totaling $147,000 (high: $1,000, low: $1,000).
Type of support: Undergraduate support.
Application information: Contact foundation for current application deadline/guidelines.
EIN: 010390854

2659
Jenny Melton Scholarship Foundation
P.O. Box 267
Flowery Branch, GA 30542-0005

Foundation type: Independent foundation
Limitations: Scholarships by nomination only to individuals residing in the Flowery Branch, GA, area for undergraduate education.
Financial data: Year ended 12/31/2002. Assets, $14,272 (M); Expenditures, $14,567; Total giving, $10,000; Grants to individuals, 4 grants totaling $10,000 (high: $2,500, low: $2,500).
Type of support: Awards/grants by nomination only; Undergraduate support.
Application information: Unsolicited requests for funds not considered or acknowledged.
EIN: 010687979

2660
Melville House, Inc.
330 Willis Ave.
Roslyn Heights, NY 11577 (516) 621-1500
Contact: Alexander Casella, Chair.

Foundation type: Independent foundation
Limitations: Scholarships and periodic awards to college students.
Financial data: Year ended 06/30/2004. Assets, $1,312,821 (M); Expenditures, $48,531; Total giving, $35,923; Grants to individuals, 6 grants totaling $35,923.
Type of support: Awards/prizes; Undergraduate support.
Application information: Contact foundation for current application deadline/guidelines.
EIN: 112289338

2661
Memorial Hospital of Bedford County Foundation
10455 Lincoln Hwy.
Everett, PA 15537 (814) 623-3545
Contact: Sherry Obert

Foundation type: Independent foundation
Limitations: Scholarships to Bedford County, PA, residents pursuing degrees in health care professions to be determined annually.
Financial data: Year ended 06/30/2005. Assets, $6,011,216 (M); Expenditures, $144,024; Total giving, $83,471; Grants to individuals, 15 grants totaling $83,471 (high: $7,560, low: $332).
Fields of interest: Health sciences school/education; Health care.
Type of support: Scholarships—to individuals.
Application information: Contact foundation for current application deadline; Completion of formal application required.
EIN: 232938090

2662
Memorial Scholarship Foundation of the Rotary Club of Westminster, Maryland in Memory of Colonel Sherman E. Flanagan, Jr.
91 Walz Dr.
Westminster, MD 21158
Contact: Michael K. Billingslea, Pres.

Foundation type: Independent foundation
Limitations: Scholarships to students graduating from Westminster High School, MD.
Financial data: Year ended 06/30/2005. Assets, $107,374 (M); Expenditures, $4,113; Total giving, $4,000; Grants to individuals, 4 grants totaling $4,000 (high: $1,000, low: $1,000).
Type of support: Support to graduates or students of specific schools; Undergraduate support.
Application information: Application form required.
Initial approach: Letter.
Deadline(s): Apr. 1
Additional information: Application must also include name, college of choice, and accomplishments warranting selection; Applications available from high school guidance office.
Program description:
Scholarship Program: Scholarships are given each year to two graduates of Westminster High School. Each scholarship is for $1,000 and is paid for two years.
EIN: 237037815

2663
The Becky Menard Memorial Scholarship Fund
1600 Scripps Ctr.
312 Walnut St.
Cincinnati, OH 45202 (513) 762-7676
Contact: Joseph Bick, Tr.

Foundation type: Public charity
Limitations: Scholarships to student athletes graduating from Western Brown High School.
Financial data: Year ended 12/31/2004. Assets, $63,137 (M); Expenditures, $10,000; Total giving, $10,000; Grants to individuals, 2 grants totaling $10,000 (high: $5,000, low: $5,000).
Fields of interest: Higher education.
Type of support: Scholarships—to individuals.
Application information:
Initial approach: Letter.
EIN: 311729852

2664
Menasha Corporation Foundation
P.O. Box 367
Neenah, WI 54957-0367 (920) 751-1000
Contact: Kevin Schuh, Treas.

Foundation type: Company-sponsored foundation
Limitations: Scholarships only to children of employees of Menasha Corporation.
Publications: Application guidelines.
Financial data: Year ended 12/31/2003. Assets, $690,060 (M); Expenditures, $416,491; Total giving, $406,460; Grants to individuals, 51 grants totaling $50,625 (high: $1,125, low: $500).
Type of support: Employee-related scholarships.
Application information: Application form required.
Initial approach: Proposal.
Deadline(s): Jan. 15, Apr. 15, Aug. 15 and Nov. 15
EIN: 396047384

2665
Mendenhall-Tyson Scholarship Foundation
c/o PNC Advisors
620 Liberty Ave., P2-PTPP-10-2
Pittsburgh, PA 15222-2705 (412) 768-5192

Foundation type: Public charity
Limitations: Scholarships to graduates of Upper Darby School District, PA.
Financial data: Year ended 12/31/2003. Assets, $1,382,772 (M); Expenditures, $56,982; Total giving, $50,000; Grants to individuals, 13 grants totaling $50,000 (high: $4,000, low: $2,000).
Type of support: Support to graduates or students of specific schools.
Application information: Applications not accepted.
Additional information: Unsolicited requests for funds not accepted.
EIN: 232983986

2666
Gregory Menn Foundation
c/o JPMorgan Chase Bank, N.A.
P.O. Box 1308
Milwaukee, WI 53201
Application address: c/o C. Radtke, Guidance Office, Appleton East High School, Appleton, WI 54911

Foundation type: Independent foundation
Limitations: Scholarships to students and graduates of Appleton High School East, WI, who show academic excellence and school participation.
Financial data: Year ended 06/30/2005. Assets, $846,016 (M); Expenditures, $55,147; Total giving, $47,000.
Application information:
   Deadline(s): May 1
   Additional information: Contact foundation for current application guidelines.
EIN: 396143254

2667

Greater Menomonie Area Community Foundation, Inc.

500 Main St., Ste. 322
P.O. Box 53
Menomonie, WI 54751 (715) 232-8019
Contact: Michael Glapa, Exec. Dir.
FAX: (715) 232-9636; E-mail: gmacf@gmacf.org; Additional tel.: (715) 232-8029; Additional E-mail: info@gmacf.org; URL: http://www.gmacf.org

Foundation type: Community foundation
Limitations: Scholarships to residents of Dunn County, WI.
Publications: Annual report; Informational brochure (including application guidelines); Newsletter.
Financial data: Year ended 12/31/2004. Assets, $991,615 (M); Expenditures, $87,220; Total giving, $26,326.
Type of support: Undergraduate support.
Application information: Applications not accepted.
   Additional information: Unsolicited requests for funds not considered or acknowledged.
EIN: 391819945

2668

Mentzer Memorial Foundation

(formerly Charles T. Mentzer Memorial Trust)
c/o KeyBank N.A., Trust Div.
800 Superior Ave., 4th Fl.
Cleveland, OH 44111
Application address: c/o KeyBank N.A., Trust Client Svcs., 127 Public Sq., Cleveland, OH 44114, tel.: (800) 999-9658

Foundation type: Independent foundation
Limitations: Scholarships to students studying for holy orders.
Financial data: Year ended 12/31/2004. Assets, $491,237 (M); Expenditures, $25,236; Total giving, $19,141; Grants to individuals, 6 grants totaling $19,141 (high: $3,528, low: $1,500).
Fields of interest: Theological school/education.
Type of support: Graduate support; Undergraduate support.
Application information: Contact foundation for current application deadline/guidelines.
EIN: 916273732

2669

John P. Mentzer Scholarship Trust

c/o U.S. Bank, N.A.
P.O. Box 2043
Milwaukee, WI 53201-9116
Application address: c/o Guidance Counselor, Marion High School, Marion, IA 52302, tel.: (319) 377-9894

Foundation type: Independent foundation
Limitations: Scholarships to financially needy graduates of Marion and Linn-Mar high schools, Marion, IA.
Financial data: Year ended 09/30/2004. Assets, $170,227 (M); Expenditures, $9,223; Total giving, $6,650; Grants to individuals, totaling $6,650.
Type of support: Support to graduates or students of specific schools; Undergraduate support.
Application information: Application form required.
   Applicants should submit the following:
      1) Essay
      2) Class rank
      3) Transcripts
      4) GPA
   Additional information: Applications accepted during the second semester. Application must also include three references.
EIN: 426054056

2670

The Suzy Mercado Scholarship Foundation

4400 Post Oak Pkwy., No. 1610
Houston, TX 77027
Application address: c/o Suzy Mercado, 2201 San Felipe St., Houston, TX 77019-5605

Foundation type: Independent foundation
Limitations: Scholarships to individuals in the Houston, TX area.
Financial data: Year ended 12/31/2004. Assets, $919,133 (M); Expenditures, $67,023; Total giving, $65,000; Grants to individuals, 9 grants totaling $65,000 (high: $10,000, low: $5,000).
Type of support: Scholarships—to individuals.
Application information: Contact foundation for current application deadline/guidelines.
EIN: 760543418

2671

The Mercer County Civic Foundation, Inc.

119 W. Fulton St.
P.O. Box 439
Celina, OH 45822 (419) 586-9950
Contact: Rita S. Bair, Exec. Dir.
E-mail: mccf@bright.net; URL: http://www.mercercountycivicfdn.org

Foundation type: Community foundation
Limitations: Educational loans and scholarships to students who graduate from Mercer County, OH, high schools.
Publications: Application guidelines; Annual report (including application guidelines); Informational brochure; Newsletter.
Financial data: Year ended 12/31/2004. Assets, $4,885,018 (M); Expenditures, $227,885; Total giving, $156,234; Grants to individuals, totaling $42,859.
Fields of interest: Arts; Environment; Human services; Community development.
Type of support: Scholarships—to individuals; Student loans—to individuals.
Application information: Application form required.
   Initial approach: Letter.
   Deadline(s): June 1
EIN: 346539139

2672

Vandal and Winifred Mercer Texas A & M Educational Foundation

c/o Frost National Bank, Trust Dept.
P.O. Box 8210
Galveston, TX 77553-8210 (409) 770-5665
Additional tel.: (409) 770-5666

Foundation type: Operating foundation
Limitations: Educational loans to graduates of TX high schools who are attending Texas A&M University.
Publications: Informational brochure (including application guidelines).
Financial data: Year ended 12/31/2002. Assets, $1,242,257 (M); Expenditures, $93,505; Total giving, $63,750; Loans to individuals, 27 loans totaling $63,750.
Type of support: Student loans—to individuals; Support to graduates or students of specific schools; Undergraduate support.
Application information: Application form required.
   Initial approach: Letter or telephone.
   Deadline(s): Jan. 1 to Mar. 31
   Applicants should submit the following:
      1) Letter(s) of recommendation
Program description:
   Scholarship Program: Priority is given to students who are residents of Galveston, TX. Loans are interest-free.
EIN: 760472391

2673

The Meriden Foundation

c/o Webster Trust Co., N.A.
The Michaels Bldg.
Webster Plz.
Waterbury, CT 06702 (203) 782-4531
Contact: Jeffrey Otis, Dir.

Foundation type: Independent foundation
Limitations: Scholarships primarily to residents of the greater Meriden, CT, area.
Financial data: Year ended 12/31/2003. Assets, $21,809,932 (M); Expenditures, $1,324,143; Total giving, $1,101,551; Grants to individuals, 87 grants totaling $200,350 (high: $10,000, low: $175).
Type of support: Scholarships—to individuals.
Application information: Applications accepted. Application form required.
   Additional information: Application must also include proof of qualifications for scholarships.
EIN: 066037849

2674

Meriden Record Journal Foundation

P.O. Box 1802
Providence, RI 02901-1802
Contact: Elliott White
Application address: 11 Crown St., Meriden, CT 06450

Foundation type: Company-sponsored foundation
Limitations: Scholarships to the children of employees of the Meriden Record Journal, to carriers, and to residents of the CT circulation area who are studying journalism or journalism-related subjects, such as advertising.
Financial data: Year ended 12/31/2004. Assets, $219,624 (M); Expenditures, $73,473; Total giving, $69,450; Grants to individuals, 27 grants totaling $20,450 (high: $2,000, low: $500).
Fields of interest: Media/communications; Journalism/publishing; Business/industry.

Type of support: Employee-related scholarships; Scholarships—to individuals.
Application information: Application form required.
Deadline(s): Contact foundation for deadline
EIN: 066074903

2675
Merrick Foundation, Inc.
1530 17th Ave.
Central City, NE 68826 (308) 946-3707
FAX: (308) 946-3049;
E-mail: merrickf@hamilton.net; URL: http://www.merrick-foundation.org

Foundation type: Community foundation
Limitations: Scholarships to graduating high school students in the Merrick county area, and to individuals whose permanent address is in Merrick county and graduated from a Merrick county high school within the last five years.
Financial data: Year ended 10/31/2004.
Assets, $9,528,126 (M); Expenditures, $449,150; Total giving, $365,048; Grants to individuals, totaling $56,543.
Fields of interest: Education.
Type of support: Scholarships—to individuals.
Application information: Applications accepted. Application form required. Application form available on the grantmaker's Web site.
Initial approach: Telephone or letter.
Deadline(s): Jan.
Applicants should submit the following:
1) Class rank
2) Transcripts
3) Letter(s) of recommendation
4) GPA
5) Financial information
6) Essay
EIN: 476024770

2676
Albert & Helen C. Meserve Memorial Fund
c/o Wachovia Bank, N.A.
100 N. Main St., 13th Fl.
Charlotte, NC 28288-5709

Foundation type: Independent foundation
Limitations: Scholarships to residents of Bethel, Bridgewater, Brookfield, Danbury, New Fairfield, New Milford, Newton, Reading, Ridgefield, and Sherman, CT.
Financial data: Year ended 08/31/2005.
Assets, $4,283,577 (M); Expenditures, $174,019; Total giving, $106,432.
Type of support: Scholarships—to individuals.
Application information:
Deadline(s): Oct. 15 and Apr. 15;
Additional information: Contact fund for current application guidelines.
EIN: 066254956

2677
Metta Enlightenment Foundation, Inc.
c/o Commodore Funding Corp.
1841 Broadway, Ste. 1004
New York, NY 10023

Foundation type: Independent foundation
Limitations: Scholarships to individuals.
Financial data: Year ended 11/30/2004.
Assets, $1,120,539 (M); Expenditures, $57,023; Total giving, $53,324; Grants to individuals, 11 grants totaling $48,322 (high: $9,087; low: $1,497).

Type of support: Undergraduate support.
Application information: Applications not accepted.
Additional information: Unsolicited requests for funds not considered or acknowledged.
EIN: 030496347

2678
Henry James and Christie M. Metz Foundation
5125 Happy Canyon Rd.
Santa Ynez, CA 93460

Foundation type: Independent foundation
Limitations: Scholarships to individuals for veterinary education, with a specialization in equine medicine.
Financial data: Year ended 12/31/2004.
Assets, $902,256 (M); Expenditures, $112,620; Total giving, $106,565; Grants to individuals, 3 grants totaling $25,800 (high: $10,000; low: $6,300).
Fields of interest: Veterinary medicine.
Type of support: Scholarships—to individuals.
Application information: Applications accepted. Application form required.
Initial approach: Letter.
Deadline(s): None
Additional information: Contact foundation for further information.
EIN: 421324791

2679
Rene Metz Scholarship Trust
(also known as Metz Scholarship Trust)
c/o J. Gerber & Co.
6404 Nancy Ridge Dr.
San Diego, CA 92121 (858) 587-0400
Contact: Shanna Decker

Foundation type: Independent foundation
Limitations: Scholarships for higher education to full-time, part-time, and retired employees of J. Gerber & Co., Inc., and their dependents.
Financial data: Year ended 12/31/2004.
Assets, $112,823 (M); Expenditures, $8,948; Total giving, $8,781; Grants to individuals, 3 grants totaling $8,781 (high: $3,000; low: $3,000).
Type of support: Employee-related scholarships.
Application information: Application form required.
Deadline(s): Six months before the beginning of the academic period
Program description:
Scholarship Program: Scholarships may be used for undergraduate, graduate, technical, and professional education. Applicants are evaluated on the basis of "scholastic worthiness, economic needs, educational undertaking, and the specific institution they plan to attend.".
EIN: 133271084

2680
The Stella E. Metzger Scholarship Fund
c/o M&T Trust Co.
21 E. Market St., M/C 402-130
York, PA 17401-1500
Application address: c/o Superintendent, Lebanon School District, Scholarship Fund Comm., 1000 S. 8th St., Lebanon, PA 17042, tel.: (717) 273-9391

Foundation type: Independent foundation
Limitations: Scholarships to financially needy graduates of Lebanon High School, PA, who have outstanding academic records.

Financial data: Year ended 01/31/2005.
Assets, $90,046 (M); Expenditures, $5,372; Total giving, $4,550; Grants to individuals, 4 grants totaling $4,550 (high: $1,820, low: $910).
Type of support: Support to graduates or students of specific schools; Undergraduate support.
Application information: Applications accepted.
Initial approach: Letter.
Additional information: Application must also include academic record, financial need, and desire for a college degree accepted throughout the year.
EIN: 236853062

2681
The Mexico Foundation
(also known as Camellia Foundation)
401 B St., Ste. 920
San Diego, CA 92101 (619) 814-1400
Contact: Tobias Gorodzinsky, Secy.

Foundation type: Independent foundation
Limitations: Scholarships to Mexican students pursuing higher education.
Financial data: Year ended 01/31/2005.
Assets, $663,414 (M); Expenditures, $43,067; Total giving, $35,000; Grants to individuals, 14 grants totaling $35,000.
Fields of interest: Hispanics/Latinos.
Type of support: Scholarships—to individuals; Foreign applicants.
Application information: Applications accepted.
Initial approach: Letter.
Deadline(s): None
Applicants should submit the following:
1) Transcripts
Additional information: Application must also include intended area of study and reason, and amount of scholarship desired.
EIN: 330099230

2682
The Roy E. and Merle Meyer Foundation
P.O. Box 385573
Minneapolis, MN 55438-5573
Application address: c/o Beth Kelly, Dean's Office, Red Wing Central High School, Red Wing, MN 55066, tel.: (651) 385-4603

Foundation type: Independent foundation
Limitations: Scholarships to Red Wing Central High School, MN, seniors who intend to pursue a career in engineering or the sciences. Selection is based on financial need and past scholastic achievements, including GPA and college entrance exam results.
Financial data: Year ended 12/31/2004.
Assets, $75,986 (M); Expenditures, $4,834; Total giving, $4,800; Grants to individuals, 4 grants totaling $4,800 (high: $1,200, low: $1,200).
Application information: Contact Red Wing Central High School for current application deadline/guidelines.
EIN: 416078887

2683
Paul & Regina Meyer Scholarship Trust
P.O. Box 18
Caruthersville, MO 63830
Contact: Richard Adams, Tr.
Application address: P.O. Box 1830, Sikeston, MO 63801, tel.: (573) 471-2424

Foundation type: Operating foundation

Limitations: Scholarships to graduates of Sikeston High School, MO, for higher education at a MO institution.
Financial data: Year ended 03/31/2004. Assets, $1,516,639 (M); Expenditures, $83,299; Total giving, $75,577; Grants to individuals, totaling $75,577.
Type of support: Support to graduates or students of specific schools; Undergraduate support.
Application information: Application form required.
Deadline(s): Apr. 1
EIN: 436721837

2684
Edward E. Meyer Trust
c/o Fifth Third Bank
38 Fountain Sq. Plz.
Cincinnati, OH 45263

Foundation type: Independent foundation
Limitations: Scholarships to students from Vanderburgh County, IN, to attend U.S. institutions other than Indiana University.
Financial data: Year ended 12/31/2004. Assets, $2,096,342 (M); Expenditures, $114,729; Total giving, $92,300; Grants to individuals, totaling $92,300.
Application information: Applications not accepted.
EIN: 356259567

2685
Meyerhoff Charitable Trust
914 Prairie Meadow Ct.
Waterloo, IA 50701-4834
Contact: Joe Nutting, Tr.
Application address: c/o Waterloo Schools, Admin. Bldg., 1516 Washington St., Waterloo, IA 50702-1698, tel.: (319) 291-4800; E-mail: nutt@coam.net

Foundation type: Independent foundation
Limitations: Scholarships primarily to high school seniors in the Waterloo, IA, area, for higher education.
Financial data: Year ended 12/31/2002. Assets, $866,583 (M); Expenditures, $76,730; Total giving, $56,250; Grants to individuals, 120 grants totaling $56,250 (high: $700, low: $400).
Type of support: Support to graduates or students of specific schools; Undergraduate support.
Application information: Application form required.
Deadline(s): Mar. 10
Applicants should submit the following:
1) Transcripts
EIN: 426554728

2686
Allen H. and Nydia Meyers Foundation
(formerly Allen H. Meyers Foundation)
P.O. Box 100
Tecumseh, MI 49286-0100 (517) 423-8086

Foundation type: Independent foundation
Limitations: Scholarships limited to Lenawee County, MI, graduating high school seniors from Lenawee County High School, to study engineering, aeronautics, computer science, mathematics, medicine, or other physical sciences.
Financial data: Year ended 04/30/2005. Assets, $548,862 (M); Expenditures, $26,002; Total giving, $21,000.
Fields of interest: Medical school/education; Engineering school/education; Science; Physical/

earth sciences; Space/aviation; Chemistry; Mathematics; Computer science.
Type of support: Scholarships—to individuals; Support to graduates or students of specific schools.
Application information: Application form required.
Deadline(s): Mar. 1
Additional information: Applications may obtain from Lenawee County high schools or from Lenawee County Intermediate School district office.
Program description:
Scholarship Program: The foundation was established to encourage, support, and stimulate scientific education, teaching, research, and related efforts such as engineering and aerospace study and design. High school graduates and college students planning studies in the sciences and allied fields (e.g., natural sciences, physical sciences, medicine, chemistry, engineering, computer science, mathematics, aeronautics, space science) may apply for scholarships. Selection is based on character, academic purpose, financial need, and leadership qualities. Awards are made only once to any individual and are only renewable under exceptional circumstances.
EIN: 386143278

2687
MFA Foundation
201 Ray Young Dr.
Columbia, MO 65201
Contact: Larna Lavelle, Secy.-Treas.
URL: http://www.mfaincorporated.com/cooperative/scholarships/index.asp

Foundation type: Company-sponsored foundation
Limitations: Scholarships to high school seniors residing in areas where MFA agencies operate, including MFA Agri Service Centers and MFA Oil Company Bulk Plants and Propane Plants.
Publications: Financial statement; Informational brochure.
Financial data: Year ended 06/30/2005. Assets, $11,891,249 (M); Expenditures, $451,719; Total giving, $400,110; Grants to individuals, 294 grants totaling $342,210 (high: $1,500, low: $100).
Type of support: Undergraduate support.
Application information: Application form required.
Deadline(s): Mar. 15
Additional information: Applications available in Feb. through high school counselors.
Program description:
Scholarship Program: The foundation awards nonrenewable scholarships in the amount of $1,200 each, to be applied toward the student's freshman year in college. Selection is made by local committees of three to five members and includes farmers, one businessman, and high school officials. Selection is based upon the following attributes of each applicant:
· interest in furthering his/her education in preparation for a vocation
· participation and leadership in school, church, and community activities
· reputation for good citizenship and good moral character
· financial ability, sources of income, and willingness to work
· satisfactory academic progress.
EIN: 436026877

2688
MGM Charitable/Scholarship Foundation
2116 Broadway
Paducah, KY 42001

Foundation type: Independent foundation
Limitations: Scholarships to students residing in McCracken County, KY, for undergraduate education, with preference to those planning to study outside of KY.
Financial data: Year ended 11/30/2004. Assets, $0 (M); Expenditures, $191,800; Total giving, $189,400; Grants to individuals, 25 grants totaling $39,400 (high: $6,400, low: $500).
Type of support: Undergraduate support.
Application information: Application form required.
Deadline(s): Apr. 1
Applicants should submit the following:
1) Transcripts
2) SAT
3) Essay
4) Financial information
EIN: 616264013

2689
Miami County Foundation
(formerly Piqua-Miami County Foundation)
317 N. Wayne St.
P.O. Box 1526
Piqua, OH 45356-1526 (937) 773-9012
Contact: Cheryl Stiefel-Francis, Exec. Dir.
FAX: (937) 773-9012;
E-mail: mcfoundation@peoplepc.com; Additional E-mail: director@miamicountyfoundation.org;
URL: http://www.miamicountyfoundation.org

Foundation type: Independent foundation
Limitations: Scholarships to students who reside in Newton Township or Miami County, OH.
Publications: Application guidelines; Informational brochure; Newsletter.
Financial data: Year ended 12/31/2004. Assets, $10,783,132 (M); Expenditures, $511,346; Total giving, $426,384; Grants to individuals, 23 grants totaling $65,850 (high: $25,000, low: $850).
Fields of interest: Higher education; Science, formal/general education.
Type of support: Support to graduates or students of specific schools; Undergraduate support.
Application information: Application form required.
Deadline(s): Nov. 1 for Thelma Ross Dalton Memorial Scholarship;
Program descriptions:
Thelma Ross Dalton Memorial Scholarship: Scholarships to Miami County, OH, students for post-high school education, including trade schools, vocational schools, nursing and health-related schools, as well as college programs.
Don Favorite Deeter Memorial Scholarship: Scholarships to graduates of Newton High School, OH, for undergraduate study in science.
EIN: 311142558

2690
The Michael Foundation, Inc.
518 Kimberton Rd., PMB 320
Phoenixville, PA 19460
Contact: Edward R. Hill, Pres.
FAX: (610) 917-0800

Foundation type: Independent foundation
Limitations: Scholarships to individuals intending to obtain an education under the Waldorf method.

Publications: Informational brochure (including application guidelines).
Financial data: Year ended 06/30/2004. Assets, $1,990,193 (M); Expenditures, $157,947; Total giving, $88,125; Grants to individuals, 4 grants totaling $10,100 (high: $5,000, low: $100).
Type of support: Program development; Conferences/seminars; Publication; Research; Graduate support; Postgraduate support.
Application information:
Initial approach: Letter.
Deadline(s): Feb. 1
Additional information: Contact foundation for current application guidelines; Application must include statement of how funds will be used and three references.
EIN: 581992204

2691
Frank J. Michaels Scholarship Fund
4320-G Wade Hampton Blvd.
Taylors, SC 29687 (866) 608-0001
Contact: Sally King, V.P.
Scholarship application address: c/o Wachovia Bank, N.A., 123 S. Broad St., Philadelphia, PA 19109
E-mail: sallyking@bellsouth.net; URL: http://www.wachoviascholars.com/mike/michaels_2006_ins.htm

Foundation type: Independent foundation
Limitations: Scholarships to residents of Oxford, PA, or to those within 25 miles of Oxford, if there are insufficient Oxford applicants.
Financial data: Year ended 01/31/2005. Assets, $2,200,623 (M); Expenditures, $136,963; Total giving, $112,850; Grants to individuals, 111 grants totaling $112,850 (high: $1,500, low: $374).
Type of support: Scholarships—to individuals.
Application information: Application form required.
Deadline(s): Apr. 15
EIN: 236680399

2692
The Michaud Charitable Trust
c/o KeyBank N.A., Trust Div.
800 Superior Ave., 4th Fl.
Cleveland, OH 44114
Application address: c/o KeyBank N.A., Trust Svcs., 286 Water St., Augusta, ME 04330

Foundation type: Independent foundation
Limitations: Scholarships to students attending college in ME.
Financial data: Year ended 10/31/2004. Assets, $0 (M); Expenditures, $74,168; Total giving, $49,191; Grants to individuals, 34 grants totaling $12,905 (high: $375, low: $250).
Type of support: Scholarships—to individuals.
Application information:
Initial approach: Letter.
Additional information: Applications by letter accepted throughout the year.
EIN: 046013647

2693
Michels Family Educational Trust
c/o First National Bank
300 E. 2nd St.
Muscatine, IA 52761 (563) 263-4221
Contact: Scott Snow, Trust Off., First National Bank

Foundation type: Independent foundation
Limitations: Scholarships to financially needy students who wish to attend Muscatine Community College, IA, or Drake University, IA, of Des Moines, with preference given to students from Muscatine and Louisa counties, IA.
Financial data: Year ended 12/31/2004. Assets, $268,897 (M); Expenditures, $19,358; Total giving, $16,500; Grants to individuals, totaling $16,500.
Type of support: Support to graduates or students of specific schools; Undergraduate support.
Application information:
Deadline(s): Contact foundation for current application deadline.
Additional information: Application by letter outlining financial need and a desire to attend Muscatine Community College or Drake University of Des Moines.
EIN: 426570941

2694
Jimmie Michels Scholarship Foundation
P.O. Box 895
Sunnyside, WA 98944

Foundation type: Independent foundation
Limitations: Scholarships to residents of Grandview, WA.
Financial data: Year ended 12/31/2003. Assets, $10,090 (M); Expenditures, $10,158; Total giving, $10,000; Grants to individuals, 2 grants totaling $10,000 (high: $5,000, low: $5,000).
Type of support: Undergraduate support.
Application information:
Initial approach: Letter.
Additional information: Contact foundation for further program information.
EIN: 043630286

2695
Michigan Accountancy Foundation
5480 Corporate Dr., Ste. 200
P.O. Box 5068
Troy, MI 48007-5068 (248) 267-3700
FAX: (248) 267-3737; URL: http://www.michcpa.org/maf/s_criteria.asp

Foundation type: Public charity
Limitations: Scholarships to current accounting majors enrolled in a MI college or university, to fund their fifth graduate year.
Financial data: Year ended 06/30/2004. Assets, $48,525; Expenditures, $77,334; Total giving, $56,000; Grants to individuals, totaling $56,000.
Fields of interest: Business school/education.
Type of support: Graduate support.
Application information: Applications accepted. Application form required. Application form available on the grantmaker's Web site.
Initial approach: Letter.
Deadline(s): Jan. 15
Applicants should submit the following:
1) Letter(s) of recommendation
2) Resume
3) Transcripts
EIN: 386090334

2696
Michigan Agri-Business Association Educational Trust Fund
(also known as Michigan Agri-Dealers Educational Trust)
1501 Northshore Dr., Ste. A
East Lansing, MI 48823-7622 (517) 336-0223
Contact: James E. Byrum, Pres.

Foundation type: Independent foundation
Limitations: Scholarships to students in MI studying agri-business or a related field, such as grain elevator management.
Financial data: Year ended 12/31/2004. Assets, $370,971 (M); Expenditures, $17,989; Total giving, $16,500; Grants to individuals, 21 grants totaling $16,500 (high: $1,150, low: $550).
Fields of interest: Agriculture.
Type of support: Undergraduate support.
Application information: Application form required.
Initial approach: Letter.
Deadline(s): June 1 and Oct. 1
Applicants should submit the following:
1) Financial information
2) Transcripts
Additional information: Application must also include references, student affair participation, personal qualities of leadership, personality, and citizenship.
Program description:
Scholarship Program: Applicants are selected on the basis of high school grades, acceptance at an accredited college or university in an agri-business related program, financial need, references, participation in student affairs, and personal character.
EIN: 382086180

2697
Michigan Elks Association Charitable Grant Fund
43904 Lee Ann Ln.
Canton, MI 48187-2822

Foundation type: Independent foundation
Limitations: Scholarships to physically disabled students who are residents of MI.
Financial data: Year ended 03/31/2005. Assets, $333,143 (M); Expenditures, $36,186; Total giving, $31,017; Grants to individuals, 16 grants totaling $31,017 (high: $3,000, low: $1,017).
Fields of interest: Disabilities, people with.
Type of support: Scholarships—to individuals.
Application information: Application form required.
Deadline(s): Jan. 31
Applicants should submit the following:
1) Financial information
Additional information: Application must also include academic information; Applications should be made to individual Elk Lodges.
EIN: 382599208

2698
Michigan Gateway Community Foundation
(formerly Buchanan Area Foundation)
111 Days Ave.
Buchanan, MI 49107-1609 (269) 695-3521
Contact: Robert N. Habicht, Pres. and C.E.O.
FAX: (269) 695-4250; E-mail: mgcf@mgcf.org;
URL: http://www.mgcf.org

Foundation type: Community foundation

Limitations: Student loans and scholarships to high school seniors of Buchanan, MI, area for degree or certificate programs in any field of study.
Publications: Application guidelines; Annual report; Financial statement; Informational brochure; Newsletter.
Financial data: Year ended 03/31/2005. Assets, $4,761,078 (M); Expenditures, $362,838; Total giving, $135,554.
Type of support: Undergraduate support.
Application information: Applications accepted. Application form required.
   Deadline(s): Contact foundation for current application deadline.
EIN: 382180730

2699
Joseph & Lottie Michner Educational Foundation
P.O. Box 1128
Jackson, MI   49204-1128
Contact: Charles C. McClafferty, Tr.

Foundation type: Independent foundation
Limitations: Scholarships to students to attend Lumen Christi High School, Jackson, MI.
Financial data: Year ended 12/31/2004. Assets, $390,494 (M); Expenditures, $24,510; Total giving, $24,510; Grants to individuals, 6 grants totaling $24,510 (high: $4,085, low: $4,085).
Fields of interest: Secondary school/education.
Type of support: Support to graduates or students of specific schools; Undergraduate support.
Application information: Application form required.
   Initial approach: Letter.
   Deadline(s): May 15
Program description:
   Scholarship Program: Applicants must have a minimum GPA of "C." Selection is based on academic performance, general aptitude test scores, academic and/or personal recommendations, and financial need.
EIN: 382346759

2700
Micron Technology Foundation, Inc.
8000 S. Federal Way
Boise, ID   83707-0006   (208) 363-3675
E-mail: mtf@micron.com; Application address: P.O. Box 6, M.S. 407, Boise, ID 83707-0006;
URL: http://www.micron.com/foundation

Foundation type: Company-sponsored foundation
Limitations: Scholarships by nomination only to individuals for higher education in the areas of science and technology.
Publications: Application guidelines; IRS Form 990-PF.
Financial data: Year ended 12/31/2004. Assets, $105,598,235 (M); Expenditures, $4,622,888; Total giving, $3,773,158; Grants to individuals, 64 grants totaling $276,542 (high: $27,500, low: $2,500, average grant: $4,125-$13,750).
Fields of interest: Engineering/technology; Science.
Type of support: Awards/grants by nomination only; Undergraduate support.
Application information: Applications not accepted.
EIN: 820516178

2701
Mid-Columbia Health Foundation
19th and Nevada Sts.
The Dalles, OR   97058   (541) 296-1111
Contact: Joyce Powell-Morin, Dir.

Foundation type: Public charity
Limitations: Scholarships to employees of Mid-Columbia Medical Center, OR. Recipients must have been employees of Mid-Columbia Medical Center for at least one year.
Financial data: Year ended 12/31/2003. Assets, $2,575,191; Expenditures, $299,210; Total giving, $299,210; Grants to individuals, totaling $4,000.
Type of support: Employee-related scholarships.
Application information: Application form required.
   Deadline(s): Apr. 30
EIN: 930854433

2702
Mid-Nebraska Community Foundation, Inc.
120 N. Dewey
P.O. Box 1321
North Platte, NE   69103   (308) 534-3315
Contact: Eric Seacrest, Exec. Dir.
FAX: (308) 534-6117; E-mail: mncf@hamilton.net;
URL: http://www.midnebraskafoundation.org

Foundation type: Community foundation
Limitations: Scholarships to individuals in Custer, Dawson, Frontier, Hayes, Keith, Lincoln, Logan, McPherson and Perkins counties, NE, for post-secondary education.
Publications: Annual report; Biennial report; Informational brochure; Occasional report.
Financial data: Year ended 05/31/2005. Assets, $13,856,112 (M); Expenditures, $596,971; Total giving, $447,069; Grants to individuals, totaling $94,060.
Type of support: Scholarships—to individuals.
Application information: Application form required.
   Deadline(s): Mar. 1
   Additional information: Applications generally are available through area school counselors, except for non-traditional students.
EIN: 470604965

2703
Mid-Shore Community Foundation, Inc.
c/o Bullitt House
102 E. Dover St.
Easton, MD   21601   (410) 820-8175
FAX: (410) 820-8729; E-mail: info@mscf.org;
Additional E-mail: robbin@mscf.org; URL: http://www.mscf.org

Foundation type: Community foundation
Limitations: Scholarships to dependents of employees of specific companies, primarily in MD.
Publications: Application guidelines; Annual report; Financial statement; Informational brochure; Newsletter.
Financial data: Year ended 06/30/2004. Assets, $26,339,132 (M); Expenditures, $1,265,061; Total giving, $805,787.
Type of support: Employee-related scholarships.
Application information:
   Initial approach: Letter or telephone.
   Additional information: Contact foundation for current application deadline/guidelines.
EIN: 521782373

2704
Middlesex County Medical Society Foundation, Inc.
575 Cranbury Rd., Ste. B-7
East Brunswick, NJ   08816-5404
(732) 257-6800
Contact: Brian Obser
Application fax for individuals: (732) 257-6775

Foundation type: Independent foundation
Limitations: Scholarships to individuals who have been residents of Middlesex County, NJ, for at least five years for the study of medicine, nursing, or pharmacology.
Financial data: Year ended 09/30/2004. Assets, $331,631 (M); Expenditures, $23,971; Total giving, $14,800; Grants to individuals, 17 grants totaling $14,800 (high: $1,250, low: $500).
Fields of interest: Medical school/education; Nursing school/education; Pharmacy/prescriptions.
Type of support: Graduate support.
Application information: Application form required.
   Initial approach: Telephone.
   Deadline(s): Feb. 1
   Applicants should submit the following:
      1) Letter(s) of recommendation
      2) Transcripts
      3) Financial information
      4) Curriculum vitae
   Additional information: Applications should be sent by mail or fax.
EIN: 221767843

2705
Middletown Community Foundation
36 Donham Plz.
Middletown, OH   45042   (513) 424-7369
Contact: Kay Wright, Exec. Dir.
FAX: (513) 424-7555;
E-mail: info@mcfoundation.org; URL: http://www.mcfoundation.org/

Foundation type: Community foundation
Limitations: Scholarships to residents of the Middletown, OH, area for higher education.
Publications: Application guidelines; Annual report; Financial statement; Informational brochure (including application guidelines); Newsletter.
Financial data: Year ended 12/31/2003. Assets, $20,862,088 (M); Expenditures, $1,926,024; Total giving, $1,625,027; Grants to individuals, 351 grants totaling $633,936 (high: $4,000, low: $40).
Type of support: Scholarships—to individuals.
Application information: Contact foundation for current application deadline/guidelines.
EIN: 310898380

2706
Midwest Foundaton for Higher Education
3800 S. 48th St.
Lincoln, NE   68506-4300   (402) 486-2600
Contact: Gary Bollinger, Secy.

Foundation type: Public charity
Limitations: Scholarships to residents of the midwestern part of the U.S.
Financial data: Year ended 12/31/2003. Assets, $6,658,348 (M); Expenditures, $250,694; Total giving, $250,694; Grants to individuals, totaling $250,694.
Type of support: Undergraduate support.
Application information:
   Initial approach: Letter.

Additional information: Contact foundation for application guidelines.
EIN: 470698086

2707
Christina M. Mihos Youth Foundation
c/o Christy's Realty, LP
130 Liberty St., Ste. 4
Brockton, MA 02301 (508) 427-6111
Contact: Linda Ann Mihos, Tr.

Foundation type: Independent foundation
Limitations: Scholarships to graduating seniors of Oliver Ames High School, and to students who have completed at least one year of full-time study at Stonehill College, MA.
Financial data: Year ended 06/30/2005.
Assets, $110,173 (M); Expenditures, $118,353; Total giving, $106,500; Grants to individuals, 10 grants totaling $11,500 (high: $1,500, low: $1,000).
Type of support: Support to graduates or students of specific schools; Undergraduate support.
Application information: Applications accepted.
Initial approach: Letter.
Applicants should submit the following:
1) Transcripts
Additional information: Application must also include course of study.
Program description:
Scholarship Program: Recipients must be accepted full-time in an institution of higher learning. Students whose immediate family members are members in good standing of the Greek Orthodox Church in Brockton, MA, and who have been accepted as full-time students at a recognized institution of higher learning are also eligible for scholarships.
EIN: 043164157

2708
Miles Educational Foundation
c/o U.S. Bank, N.A.
P.O. Box 387
St. Louis, MO 63166
Contact: William Orendorff, Trust Off., U.S. Bank, N.A.
Application address: P.O. Box 368, Doniphan, MO 63935-0368

Foundation type: Independent foundation
Limitations: Scholarships to graduates of Doniphan High School, MO.
Financial data: Year ended 12/31/2002.
Assets, $734,212 (M); Expenditures, $47,619; Total giving, $33,900; Grants to individuals, 57 grants totaling $33,900 (high: $750, low: $400).
Type of support: Support to graduates or students of specific schools; Undergraduate support.
Application information: Contact foundation for current application deadline/guidelines.
EIN: 436072185

2709
Alice W. Miles HSSF Trust
(formerly Alice W. Miles Trust High School Scholarship)
c/o Bank of America, N.A.
P.O. Box 6767
Providence, RI 02940-6767
Application address: c/o Principal, Worcester Public High School, Worcester, MA 01613

Foundation type: Independent foundation

Limitations: Scholarships to graduating seniors of Worcester Public High School, MA.
Financial data: Year ended 10/31/2004.
Assets, $317,815 (M); Expenditures, $19,011; Total giving, $15,000; Grants to individuals, 5 grants totaling $15,000 (high: $3,000, low: $3,000).
Type of support: Scholarships—to individuals; Support to graduates or students of specific schools; Undergraduate support.
Application information: Application form required.
Deadline(s): Feb. 15.
Applicants should submit the following:
1) Financial information
EIN: 046019793

2710
Milford Chamber of Commerce Trust Fund
5 N. Broad St.
Milford, CT 06460 (203) 878-0681
Contact: Kathleen Alagno, Exec. V.P.

Foundation type: Independent foundation
Limitations: Scholarships to residents of Milford, CT.
Financial data: Year ended 12/31/2004.
Assets, $0 (M); Expenditures, $75,041; Total giving, $25,217; Grants to individuals, 27 grants totaling $20,217 (high: $2,500, low: $250).
Type of support: Undergraduate support.
Application information:
Initial approach: Letter.
Deadline(s): Contact foundation for deadline
Applicants should submit the following:
1) Financial information
Additional information: Application must also include individual information, school grades, and citizenship behavior.
EIN: 061053993

2711
The Military Officers Association of America Scholarship Fund
(formerly The Retired Officers Association Scholarship Fund)
201 N. Washington St.
Alexandria, VA 22314-2539
Contact: Laurie Wavering, Admin.
E-mail: edassist@moaa.org; URL: http://www.moaa.org/education

Foundation type: Public charity
Limitations: Interest-free student loans and a limited number of scholarships to full-time undergraduates who are dependent children of active, retired, or deceased military officers or enlisted personnel or members of the Retired Officers Association. Applicants must be single, under the age of 24, and have never received a bachelor's degree.
Publications: Application guidelines; Financial statement; Informational brochure.
Financial data: Year ended 12/31/2003.
Assets, $28,405,019 (M); Expenditures, $373,579; Total giving, $390,500; Grants to individuals, 481 grants totaling $390,500 (high: $5,000, low: $500).
Fields of interest: Vocational education; Military/veterans' organizations.
Type of support: Undergraduate support.
Application information:
Initial approach: Letter or telephone.
Deadline(s): Mar. 1
Applicants should submit the following:
1) Financial information
2) Transcripts

3) ACT
4) SAT
5) Resume
Additional information: Applications available Nov. 1 through Feb. 15; Recipients notified in June.
Program description:
Educational Assistance Programs: The Retired Officers Association is a membership organization for active duty, reserve, retired, and National Guard officers, for surviving spouses of deceased officers. There are four educational assistance programs open to dependent children of members, and to children of active, retired, and deceased enlisted service personnel who have never been discharged. Applicants must have a GPA of at least 3.0. Selection is based on scholastic ability, potential, character, leadership, and financial need. Male applicants must affirm that they have registered for the Selective Service.
- TROA Educational Loan Program: This is the only program to which eligible individuals may actually apply. Applying for this program entitles applicants to be considered for the three grant programs if they meet the other requirements specified below in each program's description. Applicants may apply for student loans of up to $3,000 per year for full-time study at accredited colleges and technical institutions in the U.S. Repayment at an agreed rate begins three to four months after graduation or after leaving school.
- Designated Scholar Program: Provides an additional $500 to TROA Educational Loan recipients.
- Garlinger and Crozier Grants: Provides $3,000 grants to former loan recipients entering their final year of college. Eligible individuals will receive information automatically.
- General John Paul Ratay Educational Fund: Provides $3,000 grants to children of widows of retired commissioned officers who have applied for the TROA Educational Loan. No student will receive both a TROA Loan and a Ratay Grant, however, eligible students applying for the TROA Educational Loan will automatically be considered for this grant.
EIN: 541659039

2712
The Milken Family Foundation
1250 4th St., 3rd Fl.
Santa Monica, CA 90401 (310) 570-4800
Contact: Richard Sandler, Exec. V.P.
FAX: (310) 570-4801; E-mail: admin@mff.org;
URL: http://www.mff.org

Foundation type: Independent foundation
Limitations: Awards to educators, and scholarships and educational opportunities to high school seniors.
Publications: Annual report.
Financial data: Year ended 11/30/2004.
Assets, $238,573,671 (M); Expenditures, $21,053,297; Total giving, $17,784,836.
Fields of interest: Education.
Type of support: Scholarships—to individuals; Awards/grants by nomination only; Awards/prizes; Undergraduate support.
Application information: Nominations not accepted for National Educator Awards; Unsolicited nominations/applications not accepted for Milken Scholars Program; See program description for nomination procedures.

Program descriptions:

Milken Scholars Program: Scholars are selected from more than 350 high schools in Washington, DC, Los Angeles, and New York City, in order to provide support to outstanding young people who will make a difference as future leaders in communities throughout the world. Scholars receive career-related counseling and internships, opportunities for volunteerism, and a graduate fund, in addition to $2,000 for each of their four years of college. Scholars are nominated by the foundation with the help of college advisors at area high schools. Eligible students will have a 3.6 minimum GPA; minimum SAT score of 1250 or ACT score of 27; active participation in community service activities; a record of leadership; financial need; and U.S. citizenship or permanent residency.

National Educator Awards: Provides public recognition and financial rewards of $25,000 each to elementary and secondary school teachers, principals, and other education professionals who are furthering excellence in education. The program is active in 43 states (all except DE, ID, LA, NY, NJ, SD, and VT). The program does not include nomination or application procedures, because participating states' departments of education appoint blue ribbon committees that identify candidates for evaluation and recommendation to the foundation.
EIN: 954073646

2713
Millar Scholarship Fund
c/o Bank of America, N.A.
P.O. Box 34345
Seattle, WA 98124-1345
Application address: c/o Reynolds High School, Attn.: Pat English, Scholarship Coordinator, 1698 S.W. Cherry Park Rd., Troutdale, OR 97060-1481, tel.: (503) 667-3186

Foundation type: Independent foundation
Limitations: Scholarships to financially needy graduates of Reynolds High School and Columbia High School, both in Troutdale, OR, for study at OR postsecondary institutions.
Financial data: Year ended 06/30/2005.
Assets, $381,457 (M); Expenditures, $21,789; Total giving, $18,200.
Fields of interest: Vocational education; Business school/education; Nursing school/education.
Type of support: Support to graduates or students of specific schools; Undergraduate support.
Application information: Application form required.
   Deadline(s): Apr. 23
   Applicants should submit the following:
      1) Transcripts
      2) SAT
      3) Financial information
      4) GPA
   Additional information: Application forms available from the school counseling offices in Feb. Interviews required.
Program description:
   Scholarship Program: Recipients are chosen by a selection committee which includes counselors from Reynolds High School, Columbia High School, and members of the Smith Memorial Church in Fairview, OR. Scholarships are renewable after the first year to provide up to four years of postsecondary education. Recipients may attend any college, university, community college, nursing school, business college, or other institution leading to a degree or certificate in OR.
EIN: 936054074

2714
The Miller Assistance Fund
c/o Hibernia National Bank
P.O. Box 3928
Beaumont, TX 77704-3928
Application address: c/o The Rabbi of Temple Emanuel, P.O. Box 423, Beaumont, TX 77704-0423

Foundation type: Independent foundation
Limitations: Scholarships to young residents of the Beaumont, TX, area.
Financial data: Year ended 06/30/2005.
Assets, $67,881 (M); Expenditures, $6,133; Total giving, $4,800; Grants to individuals, 3 grants totaling $4,800 (high: $1,600, low: $1,600).
Type of support: Scholarships—to individuals.
Application information:
   Initial approach: Letter.
   Deadline(s): Contact fund for deadline
EIN: 746255231

2715
The Colin U. Miller & Mary May Miller Charitable Trust for the Advancement of Education
c/o Ameriserve Trust & Financial Services Co.
P.O. Box 520
Johnstown, PA 15907-0520 (814) 533-5278
Contact: Carol Stern, Trust Off., Ameriserv Trust & Financial Svcs. Co.

Foundation type: Independent foundation
Limitations: Scholarships to graduate and undergraduate students who demonstrate financial need, dedication to their community, and academic achievement.
Financial data: Year ended 12/31/2004.
Assets, $317,386 (M); Expenditures, $20,757; Total giving, $16,000; Grants to individuals, 8 grants totaling $16,000 (high: $2,000, low: $2,000).
Type of support: Graduate support; Undergraduate support.
Application information: Application form required.
   Deadline(s): June 30
EIN: 256303529

2716
Larry H. Miller Education Foundation
9350 S. 150 E., Ste. 1000
Sandy, UT 84070-2721

Foundation type: Operating foundation
Limitations: Scholarships to individuals for higher education.
Financial data: Year ended 12/31/2003.
Assets, $0 (M); Expenditures, $462,274; Total giving, $460,799; Grants to individuals, 192 grants totaling $460,799 (high: $5,991, low: $167).
Type of support: Scholarships—to individuals.
Application information: Applications not accepted.
EIN: 870560678

2717
Miller Family Foundation
(formerly Arnold M. & Sydell L. Miller Foundation)
30575 Bainbridge Rd., Ste. 130
Solon, OH 44139-2275
Contact: Diane Gregerson; Scholarships: Sydell L. Miller
Application address: c/o Matrix Essentials, Inc., 30601 Carter St., Solon, OH 44139

Foundation type: Independent foundation
Limitations: Graduate and undergraduate scholarships primarily to fully-dependent children of employees of Matrix Essentials, Inc. and Davida's Salon & Spa, both in OH.
Publications: Financial statement.
Financial data: Year ended 06/30/2004.
Assets, $7,665,023 (M); Expenditures, $303,516; Total giving, $291,291.
Type of support: Employee-related scholarships; Graduate support.
Application information: Application form required.
   Deadline(s): Apr. 15
   Applicants should submit the following:
      1) Transcripts
      2) SAT
      3) ACT
      4) Class rank
      5) Letter(s) of recommendation
      6) Photograph
   Additional information: Application must also include duplicate of application to attending college, personal statement, copy of first page of parents' income tax return, or GRE scores for graduate students; Recipients notified after May 30.
Program description:
   Scholarship Program: Scholarships are awarded on the basis of financial need, academic ability, character, and motivation. Recipients must be full-time students attending accredited colleges, junior colleges, vocational or business schools, graduate, postgraduate, and professional schools. Scholarships are renewable provided recipient has maintained full-time status, worked while attending school, continued to exhibit financial need, and maintained a GPA commensurate with the averages required for other scholarship holders by the school attended.
EIN: 341460324

2718
J. William Miller & Lorraine M. Miller Family Foundation
2814 Canterbury Dr.
Midland, MI 48642 (989) 832-3454
Contact: Lorraine M. Miller, Secy.-Treas.

Foundation type: Independent foundation
Limitations: Scholarships to graduates of Midland County high schools, MI.
Financial data: Year ended 12/31/2004.
Assets, $758,351 (M); Expenditures, $38,386; Total giving, $36,500; Grants to individuals, 8 grants totaling $36,500 (high: $9,500, low: $2,000).
Type of support: Support to graduates or students of specific schools; Undergraduate support.
Application information: Application form required.
   Deadline(s): Apr. 10
   Applicants should submit the following:
      1) Transcripts
EIN: 383009465

2719
Don W. Miller Foundation
c/o Wells Fargo Bank Indiana, N.A.
4707 S. 96th St.
Omaha, NE 68127
Application address: c/o Wells Fargo Bank, P.O. Box 960, Fort Wayne, IN 46801

Foundation type: Independent foundation
Limitations: Scholarships to children of employees of Miller Pipeline or Miller Cable and to students

attending Clyde Greensprings High School in Clyde, OH.
Financial data: Year ended 12/31/2004.
Assets, $1,153,631 (M); Expenditures, $66,590;
Total giving, $56,667; Grants to individuals, 34
grants totaling $54,667 (high: $5,000, low: $500).
Type of support: Employee-related scholarships;
Support to graduates or students of specific
schools.
Application information: Application form required.
Deadline(s): Apr. 15
Applicants should submit the following:
1) Transcripts
2) Letter(s) of recommendation
3) Essay
EIN: 352004527

2720
Howard Miller Foundation
860 E. Main Ave.
Zeeland, MI 49464-1365

Foundation type: Independent foundation
Limitations: Scholarships to children of Howard
Miller Clock Co. employees for undergraduate
education.
Financial data: Year ended 12/31/2004.
Assets, $13,246,042 (L); Expenditures,
$691,997; Total giving, $622,000; Grants to
individuals, 13 grants totaling $25,000 (high:
$2,000, low: $1,000).
Type of support: Employee-related scholarships.
Application information: Applications not
accepted.
Additional information: Unsolicited requests for
funds not considered or acknowledged.
EIN: 382137226

2721
Arthur M. Miller Fund
c/o Bank of America, N.A.
P.O. Box 831041
Dallas, TX 75283-1041 (214) 209-3364

Foundation type: Independent foundation
Limitations: Scholarships to residents of KS for the
study of medicine or related fields at accredited
institutions.
Financial data: Year ended 12/31/2004.
Assets, $422,337 (M); Expenditures, $28,061;
Total giving, $23,500; Grants to individuals, 8
grants totaling $23,500 (high: $5,000, low:
$1,500).
Fields of interest: Medical school/education.
Type of support: Graduate support.
Application information: Application form required.
Applicants should submit the following:
1) Transcripts
2) Letter(s) of recommendation
3) Financial information
Additional information: Application must also
include personal statement; Interviews may
be required.
EIN: 481077714

2722
John R. Miller Nursing Scholarship
c/o Sovereign Bank
1900 Route 70
Lakehurst, NJ 08733

Foundation type: Independent foundation
Limitations: Scholarships only to nursing students
in PA.

Financial data: Year ended 12/31/2004.
Assets, $300,062 (M); Expenditures, $21,719;
Total giving, $16,500; Grants to individuals, 14
grants totaling $16,500 (high: $2,000, low: $500).
Fields of interest: Nursing school/education.
Type of support: Graduate support; Undergraduate
support.
Application information: Contact foundation for
current application deadline/guidelines.
EIN: 237985997

2723
Jayne L. Miller Scholarship Foundation
c/o U.S. Bank, N.A.
808 E. Main St.
Richmond, IN 47374
Application addresses: c/o Hagerstown
Junior-Senior High School, 701 Baker Rd.,
Hagerstown, IN 47346 or c/o U.S. Bank-Trust
Dept., P.O. Box 818, Richmond, IN 47374

Foundation type: Independent foundation
Limitations: Scholarships to residents of IN for
higher education.
Financial data: Year ended 12/31/2004.
Assets, $1,513,330 (M); Expenditures, $75,941;
Total giving, $62,000; Grants to individuals, 31
grants totaling $62,000 (high: $3,000, low:
$1,000).
Type of support: Scholarships—to individuals.
Application information: Contact foundation for
current application deadline/guidelines.
EIN: 352081769

2724
Morey and Helen McCarthy Miller Scholarship Fund
c/o Bank of America, N.A.
P.O. Box 1802
Providence, RI 02940-6768
Scholarship application address: c/o Beverly
Cochran, 56 Valley View Ln., Vernon, CT 06066

Foundation type: Independent foundation
Limitations: Scholarships to graduating seniors at
Rockville High School, CT, who have been accepted
into a college or university.
Financial data: Year ended 02/28/2005.
Assets, $3,453,750 (M); Expenditures,
$226,781; Total giving, $187,906; Grants to
individuals, 3 grants totaling $7,906 (high:
$4,000, low: $1,500).
Type of support: Support to graduates or students
of specific schools; Undergraduate support.
Application information: Application form required.
Deadline(s): Contact fund for deadline
EIN: 043222995

2725
Miller Scholarship Trust
c/o JPMorgan Chase Bank, N.A
P.O. Box 1308
Milwaukee, WI 53201

Foundation type: Independent foundation
Limitations: Scholarships to financially needy
graduates of Canton, Astoria, and Lewistown high
schools, WI.
Financial data: Year ended 12/31/2004.
Assets, $627,109 (M); Expenditures, $34,313;
Total giving, $27,786.
Type of support: Support to graduates or students
of specific schools; Undergraduate support.

Application information: Application form required.
Deadline(s): Contact trust for deadline
Applicants should submit the following:
1) Class rank
2) ACT
3) Transcripts
4) Letter(s) of recommendation
Additional information: Application must also
include verification of admissibility for the next
academic year, three personal references,
personal letter explaining reason for applying,
Applications available from the local high
school principals.
Program description:
Scholarship Program: Recipients are selected on
the basis of financial need, perceived future
contributions to community and profession and
likelihood of success as undergraduate students.
Applicants must be eligible to attend accredited
colleges or universities as full-time students.
Awards are renewable for a four-year period with
proof of good standing from a college
representative.
EIN: 376280528

2726
Ed & Edith Miller Scholarship Trust
c/o Wells Fargo Bank Nevada, N.A.
P.O. Box 95021, MAC P6540-144
Henderson, NV 89009
Application addresses: c/o Counseling Office, White
River School Colling, 2160 Collins Rd., Buckley, WA
98312, or c/o Counseling Office, White River
School Dist. 416-White River, 240 N. C St., Buckley,
WA 98321

Foundation type: Independent foundation
Limitations: Scholarships to graduates of public
high schools in Buckley, WA, to pursue higher
education in the areas of engineering, forestry, and
mathematics.
Financial data: Year ended 01/31/2005.
Assets, $309,013 (M); Expenditures, $12,753;
Total giving, $7,650; Grant to an individual, 1 grant
totaling $7,650.
Fields of interest: Engineering school/education;
Environment, forests; Mathematics.
Type of support: Support to graduates or students
of specific schools; Undergraduate support.
Application information: Applications accepted.
Initial approach: Letter.
Additional information: Applicants should contact
their high school counseling office to apply.
EIN: 916340047

2727
Daniel R. Miller Trust Fund for Education
c/o Wachovia Bank, N.A.
100 N. Main St., 13th Fl.
Winston-Salem, NC 27150
Contact: Scholarships: Michael Boyles

Foundation type: Independent foundation
Limitations: Scholarships to residents of the
following areas in order of preference: Borough of
Pinegrove, PA, Township of Pinegrove, PA, and Clear
Spring, Washington County, MD.
Financial data: Year ended 12/31/2004.
Assets, $692,033 (M); Expenditures, $37,917;
Total giving, $27,005; Grants to individuals, 69
grants totaling $27,005 (high: $610, low: $350).
Type of support: Scholarships—to individuals;
Undergraduate support.
Application information: Applications accepted.
Application form required.

Initial approach: Contacting high school guidance counselor.
Deadline(s): June 1.
EIN: 236246260

2728
F. Roger Miller Trust
c/o Bank of America, N.A.
P.O. Box 6768
Providence, RI   02940-6768
Application address: c/o Scholarship Comm.,
Waldoboro High School, Waldoboro, ME 03908

Foundation type: Independent foundation
Limitations: Scholarships to deserving students who reside in Waldoboro, ME, and attend a college or university in the state of ME.
Financial data: Year ended 12/31/2004.
Assets, $723,876 (M); Expenditures, $29,099;
Total giving, $21,312.
Type of support: Scholarships—to individuals.
Application information: Application form required.
Deadline(s): Contact trust for deadline
EIN: 016048187

2729
George and Wilma F. Miller Trust
P.O. Box 266
Lewistown, IL   61542
Application address: c/o Lewistown High School,
Attn.: Guidance Counselor, 15205 N. State 100
Hwy., Lewistown, IL 61542, tel.: (309) 547-2288

Foundation type: Independent foundation
Limitations: Scholarships, which are renewable, to students of Lewistown School District No. 97, IL, for higher education.
Financial data: Year ended 12/31/2004.
Assets, $589,031 (M); Expenditures, $29,292;
Total giving, $13,050; Grants to individuals, 64 grants totaling $13,050 (high: $300, low: $125).
Type of support: Support to graduates or students of specific schools; Undergraduate support.
Application information: Applications accepted.
Application form required.
Deadline(s): Apr. 30.
Applicants should submit the following:
   1) ACT
   2) SAT
   3) Transcripts
   4) Essay
   5) Letter(s) of recommendation
EIN: 371147868

2730
Sadie H. Miller Trust
c/o First National Bank of Elmer
10 S. Main St.
P.O. Box 980
Elmer, NJ   08318
Application address: c/o Schalick High School,
Attn.: Guidance Office, 718A Centerton Rd.,
Pittsgrove, NJ 08318, tel.: (856) 358-2054

Foundation type: Independent foundation
Limitations: Scholarships to graduates of Schalick High School, Pittsgrove, NJ.
Financial data: Year ended 12/31/2004.
Assets, $217,373 (M); Expenditures, $11,707;
Total giving, $9,088; Grants to individuals, 5 grants totaling $9,088 (high: $2,272, low: $1,136).
Type of support: Support to graduates or students of specific schools; Undergraduate support.

Application information:
Deadline(s): Varies
Additional information: Contact trust for application guidelines.
EIN: 226625423

2731
Nettie Millhollon Educational Trust
c/o Trustees
P.O. Box 643
Stanton, TX   79782   (432) 756-2261
FAX: (432) 756-3956;
E-mail: millhollon@earthlink.net; URL: http://www.millhollon.com

Foundation type: Independent foundation
Limitations: Student loans to financially needy residents of TX, who are under the age of 25.
Financial data: Year ended 06/30/2005.
Assets, $3,680,494 (M); Expenditures, $77,953;
Total giving, $285; Loans to individuals, totaling $244,833.
Type of support: Student loans—to individuals.
Application information: Application form required.
Initial approach: Letter or telephone.
Deadline(s): July 1 for fall semester and Jan. 2 for spring semester
Additional information: Interviews required.
EIN: 756024639

2732
Clinton G. Mills Fund
c/o Bank of America, N.A.
P.O. Box 6768
Providence, RI   02940-6768
Contact: Kerry Sullivan, Trust Admin., Bank of America, N.A.
Application address: 75 State St., Boston, MA
02109, tel.: (617) 346-1245

Foundation type: Independent foundation
Limitations: Scholarships to graduates of public high schools in Lynn and Swampscott, MA.
Financial data: Year ended 12/31/2003.
Assets, $601,343 (M); Expenditures, $39,409;
Total giving, $32,638; Grants to individuals, 27 grants totaling $32,638 (high: $2,425, low: $106).
Type of support: Support to graduates or students of specific schools; Undergraduate support.
Application information:
Deadline(s): Apr.
Additional information: Contact fund for current application guidelines.
EIN: 046024752

2733
Casper Mills Scholarship Foundation
6264 Nita Ave.
Woodland Hills, CA   91367-1821
Contact: Bernard Axelrad, Secy.
Application address: 12340 Santa Monica Blvd.,
Rm. 212, Los Angeles, CA 90025; tel.: (310) 826-9395

Foundation type: Independent foundation
Limitations: Graduate and undergraduate scholarships to financially needy orphans and individuals from broken homes, who reside in CA.
Publications: Program policy statement.
Financial data: Year ended 07/31/2004.
Assets, $1,070,773 (M); Expenditures, $196,040; Total giving, $54,000; Grants to individuals, 15 grants totaling $54,000 (high: $5,000, low: $2,000).

Fields of interest: Children, services; Residential/custodial care.
Type of support: Graduate support; Undergraduate support.
Application information: Application form required.
Initial approach: Letter.
Deadline(s): Aug.31
Additional information: Interviews required.
EIN: 510174623

2734
Thomas and Lois Mills Scholarship Trust
c/o Alliance Bank, N.A.
241 Main St.
Buffalo, NY   14203

Foundation type: Independent foundation
Limitations: Scholarships to students at Gowanda Central School, Gowanda, NY.
Financial data: Year ended 06/30/2003.
Assets, $525,669 (M); Expenditures, $42,052;
Total giving, $36,000; Grants to individuals, 10 grants totaling $36,000 (high: $6,050, low: $2,000).
Type of support: Awards/grants by nomination only; Undergraduate support.
Application information: Applications not accepted.
EIN: 166136606

2735
William R. Mills Trust B
600 Wilshire Blvd., Ste. 1515
Los Angeles, CA   90017
Contact: Lawrence Stone, Tr.
Application address: 3452 E. Foothill Blvd., Ste.
1100, Pasadena, CA 91107, tel.: (626) 844-3300

Foundation type: Independent foundation
Limitations: Scholarships to financially needy undergraduate students at the University of Southern California and Syracuse University, NY.
Financial data: Year ended 12/31/2003.
Assets, $891,699 (M); Expenditures, $30,395;
Total giving, $16,275; Grants to individuals, totaling $16,275.
Type of support: Support to graduates or students of specific schools; Undergraduate support.
Application information: Application form required.
Deadline(s): Apr. 1
EIN: 956487535

2736
Clinton G. Mills Trust
c/o Bank of America, N.A.
P.O. Box 6768
Providence, RI   02940-6768
Application address: c/o Bank of America, N.A., 75
State St., Boston, MA 02109,

Foundation type: Independent foundation
Limitations: Scholarships for higher education to graduates of high schools in Lynn and Swampscott, MA. Student must have at least a "B" average in high school.
Financial data: Year ended 12/31/2003.
Assets, $485,858 (M); Expenditures, $29,503;
Total giving, $24,000; Grants to individuals, 12 grants totaling $24,000 (high: $2,300, low: $1,400).
Type of support: Scholarships—to individuals; Support to graduates or students of specific schools; Undergraduate support.

Application information:
Deadline(s): Apr.
Additional information: Contact trust for current application guidelines.
EIN: 046111074

2737
The Hilda and Raymond Milne Foundation
c/o Wells Fargo Bank Wyoming, N.A.
P.O. Box 3004
Gillette, WY 82717-3004 (307) 682-1313
Contact: Thomas E. Lubnau II, Dir.

Foundation type: Independent foundation
Limitations: Scholarships to students in the Campbell County, WY, area, for higher education.
Financial data: Year ended 12/31/2004.
Assets, $1,068,108 (M); Expenditures, $42,108; Total giving, $23,750; Grants to individuals, 27 grants totaling $23,750 (high: $5,000, low: $500).
Type of support: Undergraduate support.
Application information: Applications by letter accepted throughout the year.
EIN: 830305556

2738
Alfred G. & Elma M. Milotte Scholarship Fund
c/o Bank of America, N.A., Tax Svcs.
P.O. Box 34345, FAB-22
Seattle, WA 98124-1345 (800) 832-9071
Application address: c/o Bank of America, N.A., 715 Peachtree St., 8th Fl., Atlanta, GA 30308
E-mail: info@milotte.org; URL: http://www.milotte.org

Foundation type: Independent foundation
Limitations: Graduate and undergraduate scholarships to college students who have lived in WA for at least five years and who have at least a 3.0 GPA and an interest in wilderness areas.
Financial data: Year ended 03/31/2005.
Assets, $956,649 (M); Expenditures, $53,097; Total giving, $43,576; Grants to individuals, 10 grants totaling $43,576 (high: $5,400, low: $35).
Fields of interest: Photography; Arts; Natural resources; Environment, forests; Psychology/behavioral science.
Type of support: Graduate support; Undergraduate support.
Application information: Application form required.
Deadline(s): Contact fund for deadline
Applicants should submit the following:
1) Financial information
Additional information: Application must also include educational and career goals, and two reference letters.
Program description:
Scholarship Program: Applicants should have an interest in photography of natural history, the arts, environmental studies, ecology, or an animal behavior related field of study. Relatives of officers, directors, trustees, and selection committee members of the foundation are ineligible.
EIN: 916307731

2739
James Forsythe Milroy Foundation
c/o Citizens Federal Bldg.
110 N. Main St.
Bellefontaine, OH 43311
Contact: Charles Earick, Tr.

Foundation type: Independent foundation

Limitations: Interest-free loans to residents of Logan County, OH, studying agriculture or related fields at OH colleges.
Financial data: Year ended 12/31/2004.
Assets, $983,052 (M); Expenditures, $41,388; Total giving, $22,859; Loans to individuals, totaling $21,000.
Fields of interest: Agriculture.
Type of support: Student loans—to individuals.
Application information: Applications accepted. Application form required.
Deadline(s): None
Additional information: Interviews required.
EIN: 346516844

2740
Milton-Freewater Area Foundation
c/o Baker Boyer Trust & Investment Svcs.
P.O. Box 1796
Walla Walla, WA 99362 (509) 525-2000

Foundation type: Community foundation
Limitations: Scholarships to residents of Milton-Freewater, OR.
Financial data: Year ended 12/31/2004.
Assets, $1,502,086 (M); Expenditures, $70,175; Total giving, $52,865; Grants to individuals, 12 grants totaling $10,250 (high: $2,300, low: $300).
Type of support: Scholarships—to individuals.
Application information: Applications accepted.
Deadline(s): None
EIN: 936025936

2741
Minbanc Foundation, Inc.
1513 P St. N.W.
Washington, DC 20005 (202) 588-5432
Contact: Christine LaRocco, Tr.
URL: http://www.minbanc.org

Foundation type: Public charity
Limitations: Scholarships to management and officer-level employees of minority- and women-owned banks.
Financial data: Year ended 12/31/2004.
Assets, $1,763,012 (M); Expenditures, $59,290; Total giving, $28,710; Grants to individuals, totaling $28,710.
Fields of interest: Minorities.
Type of support: Scholarships—to individuals.
Application information: Application form required.
Deadline(s): None
EIN: 510386370

2742
Ruth M. Minear Educational Trust
c/o Wells Fargo Bank Nebraska, N.A.
4707 S. 96th St.
Omaha, NE 68127
Application address: c/o Wells Fargo Bank Indiana, N.A., 841 N. Cass St., Wabash, IN 46992, tel.: (260) 563-1116

Foundation type: Independent foundation
Limitations: Scholarships to graduates of Wabash High School, IN, for study at an accredited postsecondary school in IN.
Financial data: Year ended 02/28/2005.
Assets, $2,261,563 (M); Expenditures, $129,353; Total giving, $103,007; Grants to individuals, 146 grants totaling $103,007 (high: $2,000, low: $636).
Type of support: Support to graduates or students of specific schools; Undergraduate support.

Application information: Application form required.
Deadline(s): Feb. 14
Applicants should submit the following:
1) Transcripts
Additional information: Application must also include IN financial aid forms, copy of high school diploma, and certification of acceptance at accredited college; Scholarships are renewable.
EIN: 356335021

2743
Minerva Club Trust Fund, Inc.
127 W. Boone St.
Santa Maria, CA 93454

Foundation type: Independent foundation
Limitations: Scholarships to individuals, primarily in Santa Maria, CA.
Financial data: Year ended 12/31/2004.
Assets, $363,602 (M); Expenditures, $22,774; Total giving, $17,600.
Type of support: Scholarships—to individuals.
Application information: Applications not accepted.
EIN: 770562319

2744
Minnesota Masonic Foundation, Inc.
200 E. Plato Blvd.
St. Paul, MN 55107-1618 (651) 222-6051
Additional tel.: (800) 245-6050; URL: http://www.mnmasonicfoundation.org

Foundation type: Independent foundation
Limitations: Scholarships primarily to those in the midwestern U.S.
Financial data: Year ended 02/28/2005.
Assets, $1,223,014 (M); Expenditures, $163,399; Total giving, $147,975; Grants to individuals, 334 grants totaling $124,382 (high: $8,830, low: $100).
Type of support: Scholarships—to individuals.
Application information: Applications by letter accepted throughout the year.
EIN: 237227879

2745
Rives C. Minor & Asalie M. Preston Educational Fund, Inc.
c/o Brian P. Menard
P.O. Box 274
Charlottesville, VA 22902-0274
(434) 963-9961

Foundation type: Independent foundation
Limitations: Scholarships to residents of the city of Charlottesville, VA, Albemarle County, VA, and all contiguous counties, who are members of a racial minority group or are otherwise culturally disadvantaged, and who are public high school students in the Charlottesville-Alexandria, VA, community.
Financial data: Year ended 02/28/2005.
Assets, $1,776,239 (M); Expenditures, $212,014; Total giving, $140,549; Grants to individuals, 78 grants totaling $140,549 (high: $3,000, low: $500).
Application information: Application form required.
Deadline(s): July 1
Additional information: Forms available from high schools.
EIN: 521279007

2746
The Berkeley Minor and Susan F. Minor Foundation
P.O. Box 1793
Charleston, WV   25326
Application address: c/o John L. Ray, 109 Capitol St., Ste. 700, Charleston, WV 25301, tel.: (304) 342-1141

Foundation type: Independent foundation
Limitations: Scholarships to residents of WV attending West Virginia University, University of Charleston, University of Virginia, and the Protestant Episcopal Theological Seminary of Virginia.
Financial data: Year ended 12/31/2004. Assets, $2,765,559 (M); Expenditures, $118,603; Total giving, $101,500.
Fields of interest: Theological school/education.
Type of support: Support to graduates or students of specific schools; Undergraduate support.
Application information:
  Deadline(s): Aug. 1.
  Additional information: Application by letter, including names and addresses of parents and siblings, grades and courses in school and college, results of aptitude tests, and recommendations of teachers or others; Only students attending West Virginia University should apply directly to the foundation; Other applicants must be admitted to and recommended for financial aid by The University of Charleston, the University of Virginia, or the Protestant Episcopal Theological Seminary of Virginia.
EIN: 556014946

2747
Minot Rotary Scholarship Foundation
P.O. Box 1584
Minot, ND   58702   (701) 852-7006
Contact: Thomas Hinzpeter, Secy.
FAX: (303) 964-9795

Foundation type: Independent foundation
Limitations: Scholarships to graduating students within a 50 mile radius of Minot, ND.
Financial data: Year ended 12/31/2004. Assets, $186,991 (M); Expenditures, $37,152; Total giving, $37,000; Grants to individuals, 36 grants totaling $37,000 (high: $2,000, low: $1,000).
Type of support: Undergraduate support.
Application information:
  Deadline(s): Apr. 15
  Applicants should submit the following:
    1) SAT
  Additional information: Contact foundation for current application guidelines; Considerations for scholarship include demographics, awards won, school activities, scholastic achievements, and employment.
EIN: 363369060

2748
Helen Lancaster Minton Educational Trust
c/o Centura Bank, Trust Dept.
P.O. Box 1220
Rocky Mount, NC   27802-1220   (252) 454-4017
Contact: Sharon Stephens, Trust Off., Centura Bank

Foundation type: Independent foundation
Limitations: Scholarships to financially needy residents of Nash and Edgecombe counties, NC, to attend North Carolina Wesleyan College.

Financial data: Year ended 03/31/2003. Assets, $604,354 (M); Expenditures, $44,344; Total giving, $35,900; Grants to individuals, totaling $35,900.
Type of support: Support to graduates or students of specific schools; Undergraduate support.
Application information: Application form required.
  Deadline(s): June 1.
  Applicants should submit the following:
    1) SAT
    2) Transcripts
  Additional information: Application must also include handwritten personal statement, photograph, and outline of high school activities.
Program description:
  Scholarship Program: Recipients must be of excellent character, financially needy, and have a GPA of "C+" or better. Scholarships are renewable.
EIN: 566180453

2749
Jessie Mintz Scholarship Trust
c/o Wells Fargo Bank West, N.A.
90 S. Cascade Ave., No. 200
Colorado Springs, CO   80903
Contact: Doug Dixon

Foundation type: Independent foundation
Limitations: Scholarships to graduates of certain Colorado Springs, CO, high schools.
Financial data: Year ended 12/31/2004. Assets, $8,489,468 (M); Expenditures, $446,019; Total giving, $365,000.
Type of support: Undergraduate support.
Application information: Application by invitation only.
EIN: 846301763

2750
Minyard Founders Foundation
777 Freeport Pkwy.
Coppell, TX   75019   (972) 393-8700

Foundation type: Public charity
Limitations: Scholarships only to full and part-time employees and family for higher education.
Financial data: Year ended 12/31/2004. Assets, $489,477 (M); Expenditures, $232,598; Total giving, $232,575; Grants to individuals, 89 grants totaling $39,750 (high: $500, low: $250).
Type of support: Employee-related scholarships.
Application information: Contact foundation for current application deadline/guidelines.
EIN: 752368233

2751
Mirage Resorts Family Scholarship Fund
3260 S. Industrial Rd.
Las Vegas, NV   89109

Foundation type: Company-sponsored foundation
Limitations: Scholarships to dependent children of Mirage Resorts employees with a critical financial need not met by other grants, scholarships, or loans who have a cumulative high school GPA of "C+" or better, and who are planning to enroll in the University of Nevada, Las Vegas, the University of Nevada, Reno, or the Community College of Southern Nevada.
Financial data: Year ended 12/31/2003. Assets, $33,229 (M); Expenditures, $161,555; Total giving, $160,875; Grants to individuals, 269

grants totaling $160,875 (high: $1,250, low: $250).
Type of support: Employee-related scholarships; Support to graduates or students of specific schools.
Application information: Application form required.
  Deadline(s): Mar. 15
  Applicants should submit the following:
    1) Transcripts
    2) FAFSA
  Additional information: Application address: Dir., P.O. Box 7700, Las Vegas, NV 89177, tel.: (702) 693-7111.
EIN: 880863207

2752
Ruth Mishler Memorial Trust
P.O. Box 37
Sheridan, OR   97378-0037   (503) 843-3888
Contact: Naomi Kelley, Secy.

Foundation type: Independent foundation
Limitations: Scholarships to residents of Sheridan and Willamina, OR.
Financial data: Year ended 12/31/2004. Assets, $356,950 (M); Expenditures, $19,692; Total giving, $17,500; Grants to individuals, 19 grants totaling $17,500 (high: $2,000, low: $250).
Type of support: Scholarships—to individuals.
Application information: Application form required.
  Deadline(s): Apr. 30
  Applicants should submit the following:
    1) Transcripts
  Additional information: Application must also include references, and tax returns.
EIN: 943234766

2753
Aimee and Frank Mishou Scholarship Trust
c/o KeyBank N.A. Trust Div.
800 Superior Ave., 4th Fl.
Cleveland, OH   44114
Application address: c/o Principal, Sumner High School, Sumner, ME 04607

Foundation type: Independent foundation
Limitations: Scholarships restricted to graduates of Sumner High School, ME, and residents of Sullivan, Gouldsboro, and Winter Harbor, ME.
Financial data: Year ended 04/30/2005. Assets, $371,759 (M); Expenditures, $26,257; Total giving, $21,000; Grants to individuals, totaling $21,000.
Type of support: Support to graduates or students of specific schools; Undergraduate support.
Application information: Applications accepted. Application form required.
  Additional information: Applications available from school.
EIN: 016070062

2754
Miss Connecticut Scholarship Corporation
72 Cambridge Dr.
Southington, CT   06489

Foundation type: Independent foundation
Limitations: Scholarships to women of Miss Connecticut title selected through the Miss American Beauty Pageant.

Financial data: Year ended 12/31/2004. Assets, $50,879 (M); Expenditures, $88,858; Total giving, $25,296.
Type of support: Scholarships—to individuals.
Application information: Contact foundation for current application deadline/guidelines.
EIN: 222708060

2755
Miss Massachusetts Scholarship Foundation, Inc.
170 N. Washington St.
North Attleboro, MA 02760-1733
(508) 695-5831
Contact: Dolores Rabuffo, Exec. Dir.

Foundation type: Independent foundation
Limitations: Scholarships to young women in MA who are involved in the Miss America organization.
Financial data: Year ended 09/30/2005. Assets, $12,962 (M); Expenditures, $33,408; Total giving, $13,762; Grants to individuals, totaling $13,762.
Fields of interest: Women.
Type of support: Undergraduate support.
Application information: Contact foundation for current application deadline/guidelines.
EIN: 222586251

2756
Mississippi Society of Certified Public Accountants Foundation
P.O. Box 16630
Jackson, MS 39236-6630 (601) 366-3473

Foundation type: Independent foundation
Limitations: Grants to senior college students majoring in accounting or working toward a Masters degree in accounting who are residents of MS.
Financial data: Year ended 04/30/2005. Assets, $315,157 (M); Expenditures, $9,231; Total giving, $9,000; Grants to individuals, 9 grants totaling $9,000 (high: $1,000, low: $1,000).
Fields of interest: Business school/education; Business/industry.
Type of support: Graduate support; Undergraduate support.
Application information: Application form required.
Deadline(s): July 1
Additional information: Applications provided in MS colleges and universities.
EIN: 646038540

2757
Bruce Mitchell Foundation
12038 W. Mesquite Dr.
Boise, ID 83713
Application address: c/o Glenda Leigh, P.O. Box 443, Parma, ID 83660, tel.: (208) 722-5295

Foundation type: Independent foundation
Limitations: Scholarships primarily to graduates of Parma High School, ID.
Financial data: Year ended 06/30/2005. Assets, $4,632,285 (M); Expenditures, $229,935; Total giving, $197,836; Grants to individuals, 65 grants totaling $145,582 (high: $3,600, low: $1,125).
Type of support: Support to graduates or students of specific schools; Undergraduate support.
Application information:
Deadline(s): Apr. 15

Additional information: Contact trust for current application guidelines.
EIN: 943107820

2758
Oscar Mitchell, Jr. Trust Scholarship Fund
c/o Wells Fargo Bank Minnesota, N.A.
230 W. Superior St., Ste. 400
Duluth, MN 55802
Scholarship application address: c/o Scholarship Office, Medical Arts Bldg., 324 W. Superior St., Ste. 212, Duluth, MN 55802

Foundation type: Independent foundation
Limitations: Scholarships for full-time study to graduating seniors of public and private high schools in Duluth, MN, and Carlton, Cloquet, Esko, Hermantown, Proctor, Two Harbors, and Wrenshall high schools, MN. Applicant must be in the upper ten percent of his/her class.
Publications: Informational brochure.
Financial data: Year ended 06/30/2005. Assets, $3,377,511 (M); Expenditures, $237,829; Total giving, $194,750; Grants to individuals, 48 grants totaling $194,750 (high: $4,100, low: $2,050).
Fields of interest: Education.
Type of support: Support to graduates or students of specific schools; Undergraduate support.
Application information: Application form required.
Deadline(s): Contact trust for deadline
Applicants should submit the following:
1) Letter(s) of recommendation
Additional information: Application must also include a Family Financial Statement (FFS); Forms available from the guidance department of each participating high school; All forms must be submitted to the student's counselor by the announced date.
Program description:
Scholarship Program: Scholarships are awarded on the basis of academic ability, standardized test scores, extracurricular activities, recommendations, purpose, and financial need. Approximately one-half of the scholarships will be awarded to students attending the University of Minnesota (all campuses) and one-half to students attending any accredited private four-year college or university. Grants are in the amount of $2,500 and are renewable annually for four years of undergraduate study, provided satisfactory grades are maintained. This scholarship may be accepted in addition to other awards, provided that the combined amount does not exceed the full amount of tuition, books, fees, and room and board charges. Summer school attendance may also be funded.
EIN: 416148927

2759
Mitchell-Gantz Educational & Charitable Trust
c/o Community First National Bank
P.O Box A
Alliance, NE 69301 (308) 762-4400

Foundation type: Independent foundation
Limitations: Scholarships to residents of Arthur, Box Butte, Cherry, Dawes, Garden, Grant, Hooker, Morrill, Sheridan, and Sioux counties, NE.
Financial data: Year ended 09/30/2005. Assets, $350,872 (M); Expenditures, $17,551; Total giving, $10,500; Grants to individuals, 9 grants totaling $10,500 (high: $1,500, low: $750).
Fields of interest: Law school/education; Medical school/education.

Type of support: Graduate support.
Application information: Application form required.
Deadline(s): Mar. 31
Applicants should submit the following:
1) Transcripts
2) Photograph
3) SAT
4) ACT
5) Essay
Additional information: Application must also include parents' tax returns; Applications available through high school guidance counselors.
EIN: 476080709

2760
Mitrani Family Foundation, Inc.
149 Madison Ave., 10th Fl.
New York, NY 10016

Foundation type: Independent foundation
Limitations: Scholarships to children and grandchildren of employees of Milco Industries, Inc., PA, to cover the costs of tuition, books, and supplies.
Financial data: Year ended 12/31/2004. Assets, $2,810,013 (M); Expenditures, $303,552; Total giving, $253,276.
Type of support: Employee-related scholarships.
Application information: Applications accepted.
Additional information: Contact foundation for current application guidelines.
EIN: 246018102

2761
John Joseph Moakley Charitable Foundation
c/o Shaevel & Krems
141 Tremont St.
Boston, MA 02111 (617) 556-0244
Contact: Frederick W. Clark, Jr., Pres.

Foundation type: Public charity
Limitations: Scholarships to residents of MA for a post high school vocational education program or to an institution of higher education for undergraduate or graduate support.
Financial data: Year ended 12/31/2003. Assets, $1,584,816 (M); Expenditures, $206,414; Total giving, $175,000; Grants to individuals, 20 grants totaling $100,000 (high: $5,000, low: $5,000).
Fields of interest: Higher education.
Type of support: Scholarships—to individuals.
Application information: Applications accepted.
Initial approach: Letter.
EIN: 043551974

2762
F. H. & Clara G. Moberly Trust Scholarship Program
c/o INTRUST Bank, N.A.
P.O. Box 1, Trust Tax Dept.
Wichita, KS 67201-5001
Application address: c/o Bob Bartkoski, Supt., Unified School District No. 300, Coldwater, KS 67029

Foundation type: Independent foundation
Limitations: Scholarships to graduates of Comanche County, KS, high schools.
Financial data: Year ended 04/30/2005. Assets, $245,388 (M); Expenditures, $18,586;

Total giving, $10,500; Grants to individuals, totaling $10,500.
Type of support: Support to graduates or students of specific schools; Undergraduate support.
Application information: Application form required.
Deadline(s): June 10
Applicants should submit the following:
1) Transcripts
Additional information: Application must also include Family Financial Statement (FFS), Financial Aid Package, personal statement, and three references.
EIN: 481002542

2763
Mobile Medical Mission Hospital, Inc.
1919 First Tennessee Plz.
Knoxville, TN 37929
Contact: Samuel O. Massey, Jr., Pres.
Application address: 310 Regatta Dr., Niceville, FL 32578

Foundation type: Independent foundation
Limitations: Scholarships to financially needy individuals pursuing health care education. Recipients must volunteer ten percent of their time to low-income areas.
Financial data: Year ended 10/31/2004. Assets, $748,601 (M); Expenditures, $113,827; Total giving, $92,471; Grants to individuals, 7 grants totaling $71,201 (high: $17,695, low: $50).
Fields of interest: Medical school/education.
Type of support: Undergraduate support.
Application information:
Deadline(s): None
Additional information: Contact foundation for current application guidelines.
EIN: 581348941

2764
John & Mary Mock Perpetual Memorial Scholarship Fund
c/o Union Bank of California, N.A.
P.O. Box 2742
Portland, OR 97208-2742
Application address: c/o Roosevelt High School District, Principal, P.O. Box 3107, Portland, OR 97208, tel.: (503) 916-2000

Foundation type: Independent foundation
Limitations: Scholarships to male graduates of Roosevelt High School, Portland, OR.
Financial data: Year ended 12/31/2004. Assets, $1,055,259 (M); Expenditures, $89,318; Total giving, $79,131.
Fields of interest: Men.
Type of support: Support to graduates or students of specific schools; Undergraduate support.
Application information: Application form required.
Deadline(s): Apr. 22.
Applicants should submit the following:
1) Letter(s) of recommendation
2) Transcripts
EIN: 930727584

2765
The Modglin Family Foundation
3100 Airway, Ste. 124
Costa Mesa, CA 92626

Foundation type: Independent foundation
Limitations: Scholarships to students for attendance at southern CA theological seminaries.

Financial data: Year ended 06/30/2004. Assets, $5,465,758 (M); Expenditures, $488,131; Total giving, $446,372; Grants to individuals, 76 grants totaling $446,372 (high: $50,000, low: $200).
Fields of interest: Theological school/education; Christian agencies & churches.
Type of support: Graduate support.
Application information: Applications not accepted.
EIN: 330266405

2766
Cecile Moeschle Scholarship Fund
c/o Regions Bank
P.O. Box 2392
Longview, TX 75606-2392

Foundation type: Independent foundation
Limitations: Scholarships to graduates of Longview High School, and Pine Tree High School, both in TX, for attendance at any TX college, university, or community college.
Financial data: Year ended 12/31/2004. Assets, $0 (M); Expenditures, $9,276; Total giving, $6,500; Grants to individuals, 9 grants totaling $6,500 (high: $1,000, low: $500).
Type of support: Support to graduates or students of specific schools; Undergraduate support.
Application information: Application form required.
Deadline(s): Apr. 1
Additional information: Applications are available at participating high schools.
EIN: 756349280

2767
Victor Mohr Memorial Trust
c/o Fifth Third Bank
38 Fountain Sq. Plz.
Cincinnati, OH 45263
Application address: c/o Principal, South Spencer High School, 1142 N. Country Rd. 275 W., Rockport, IN 47635

Foundation type: Independent foundation
Limitations: Scholarships to graduates of South Spencer High School, IN, who have a high school average of "C" or better.
Financial data: Year ended 12/31/2004. Assets, $1,123,905 (M); Expenditures, $66,855; Total giving, $48,850; Grants to individuals, totaling $47,850.
Type of support: Support to graduates or students of specific schools; Undergraduate support.
Application information: Application form required.
Deadline(s): Apr. 15
Applicants should submit the following:
1) GPA
2) Financial information
EIN: 356225418

2768
Mary Molloy Scholarship Fund
c/o JPMorgan Chase Bank, N.A.
P.O. Box 1308
Milwaukee, WI 53201
Contact: Julie Birdwell, Trust Off., JPMorgan Chase Bank, N.A.
Application address: 1125 17th St., Denver, CO 80202, tel.: (303) 244-3175

Foundation type: Independent foundation

Limitations: Scholarships to graduates of Loveland and Thompson Valley high schools, CO, for higher education.
Financial data: Year ended 12/31/2004. Assets, $324,611 (M); Expenditures, $22,725; Total giving, $16,900.
Type of support: Support to graduates or students of specific schools; Undergraduate support.
Application information: Contact fund for current application deadline/guidelines; Initial approach by letter.
EIN: 846214213

2769
The Michael A. Molloy Scholarship Trust Fund
c/o James C. Glidden
10 Bonavista St.
Lynn, MA 01905-1304
Application address: c/o Bradley, Moore, Primason, Cuffe & Weber, 85 Exchange St., Lynn, MA 01901, tel.: (781) 595-2050

Foundation type: Independent foundation
Limitations: Scholarships to graduates of St. Mary's Regional Junior/Senior High School, Lynn, MA.
Financial data: Year ended 12/31/2004. Assets, $487,565 (M); Expenditures, $35,033; Total giving, $24,000; Grants to individuals, 10 grants totaling $24,000 (high: $2,400, low: $2,400).
Type of support: Support to graduates or students of specific schools; Undergraduate support.
Application information: Application form required.
Deadline(s): May 1
EIN: 043484055

2770
Carroll C. Mongan Trust
c/o Loughlin Law Firm
P.O. Box 398
Cherokee, IA 51012

Foundation type: Independent foundation
Limitations: Scholarships and student loans to residents of Cherokee County, IA.
Financial data: Year ended 12/31/2004. Assets, $418,408 (M); Expenditures, $18,373; Total giving, $13,000; Grants to individuals, totaling $13,000.
Type of support: Scholarships—to individuals; Student loans—to individuals.
Application information: Contact trust for current application deadline/guidelines.
EIN: 426550538

2771
Ivy A. Monk Scholarship Trust
c/o UMB Bank, N.A.
P.O. Box 560
Salina, KS 67402-0560

Foundation type: Independent foundation
Limitations: Scholarships and loans to post high school students in Dickinson, Ottawa, and Saline counties, KS.
Financial data: Year ended 02/28/2005. Assets, $1,022,584 (M); Expenditures, $76,981; Total giving, $58,500; Grants to individuals, totaling $58,500.
Type of support: Support to graduates or students of specific schools; Undergraduate support.

Application information: Application form required.
Deadline(s): Varies
Additional information: No direct applications through trust, awards are made through high school principals, counselors, and other officials.
EIN: 486186267

2772
Monroe Foundation, Inc.
215 Betty St.
P.O. Box 71620
Fairbanks, AK 99707-1620
Contact: Nancy Cook, Exec. Dir.

Foundation type: Public charity
Limitations: Scholarships to individuals for attendance at Catholic schools in Fairbanks, AK.
Financial data: Year ended 06/30/2004. Assets, $2,751,696 (M); Expenditures, $1,325,322; Total giving, $765,554; Grants to individuals, totaling $11,098.
Fields of interest: Education; Roman Catholic agencies & churches.
Type of support: Precollege support.
Application information:
Deadline(s): Contact foundation for current application deadline/guidelines
Additional information: Scholarships are based on financial need and performance.
EIN: 930747034

2773
Monroe Welfare Foundation
P.O. Box 393A, Rt. 8
Waycross, GA 31503 (912) 285-9136
Contact: Moi M. Monroe III, Tr.

Foundation type: Independent foundation
Limitations: Scholarships to individuals in Ware County, GA.
Financial data: Year ended 05/31/2004. Assets, $2,672,952 (M); Expenditures, $122,910; Total giving, $120,000.
Type of support: Scholarships—to individuals.
Application information: Applications accepted.
Initial approach: Letter.
Additional information: Contact foundation for current application guidelines.
EIN: 586033825

2774
Ethel Lynn Monroe, Ella Jay Strugell, Martha Towler Educational Trust
(also known as Monroe, Sturgell, Towler Educational Foundation)
c/o Peoples Bank of Ohio
138 Putnam St.
Marietta, OH 45750
Application address: c/o James W. Lyon, Jr., Lyon & Kendall, P.O. Box 675, Greenup, KY 41144, tel.: (606) 473-5002

Foundation type: Independent foundation
Limitations: Scholarships to graduates of high schools in the Ashland, Boyd County, Greenup County, Raceland-Worthington Independent or Russell Independent school systems, OH, for higher education. Recipients must have attended one of the designated high schools for at least three years preceding their graduation.
Financial data: Year ended 12/31/2004. Assets, $924,952 (M); Expenditures, $134,022; Total giving, $98,500; Grants to individuals, 13

grants totaling $82,000 (high: $16,750, low: $1,500).
Type of support: Support to graduates or students of specific schools; Undergraduate support.
Application information: Applications accepted.
Initial approach: Letter.
EIN: 611355728

2775
Montana Community Foundation
101 N. Last Chance Gulch, Ste. 211
Helena, MT 59601 (406) 443-8313
Contact: Linda E. Reed, Exec. Dir.
FAX: (406) 442-0482; E-mail: mtcf@mt.net; Additional E-mails: lindareed@mtcf.org and mgorsich@mtcf.org; URL: http://www.mtcf.org

Foundation type: Community foundation
Limitations: Scholarships to students in MT for higher education.
Publications: Annual report; Newsletter.
Financial data: Year ended 06/30/2005. Assets, $49,909,125 (M); Expenditures, $3,287,614; Total giving, $1,734,972.
Type of support: Undergraduate support.
Application information: Application form required.
Deadline(s): Feb. 15, May 15, Aug. 15 and Nov. 15
EIN: 810450150

2776
Monterey Peninsula Board of Realtors Scholarship Trust
P.O. Box 108
Monterey, CA 93942-0108 (831) 422-9604
Contact: Sandy Haney

Foundation type: Independent foundation
Limitations: Scholarships to students in CA, for higher education.
Financial data: Year ended 12/31/2004. Assets, $0 (M); Expenditures, $20,679; Total giving, $20,000; Grants to individuals, 14 grants totaling $20,000 (high: $1,500, low: $1,000).
Type of support: Undergraduate support.
Application information:
Initial approach: Letter.
Deadline(s): Contact trust for deadline
EIN: 237165412

2777
Montgomery County Community Foundation
118 E. Main St.
P.O. Box 334
Crawfordsville, IN 47933 (765) 362-1267
Contact: L. Ann Malott, Exec. Dir.
FAX: (765) 361-0562; E-mail: ann@mc-cf.org; URL: http://www.mc-cf.org

Foundation type: Community foundation
Limitations: Scholarships to individuals from Montgomery County, IN, for higher education.
Publications: Application guidelines; Annual report; Grants list; Informational brochure (including application guidelines); Newsletter.
Financial data: Year ended 12/31/2004. Assets, $27,797,940 (M); Expenditures, $867,431; Total giving, $545,515; Grants to individuals, 94 grants totaling $226,743 (high: $55,180, low: $30).
Type of support: Support to graduates or students of specific schools; Undergraduate support.
Application information: Application form required.

Initial approach: Letter or telephone.
Deadline(s): Varies
Additional information: See Web site for further information.
Program description:
Lilly Endowment Community Scholarship: Scholarships for full tuition and required fees, plus special allocations of up to $700 per year for required books and equipment for four years of undergraduate study on a full-time basis leading to a bachelor's degree at any accredited IN public or private college or university. Deadline Feb. 1.
EIN: 351836315

2778
Hazel Montgomery, M.D., Memorial Scholarship Trust
c/o Southside Bank
P.O. Box 8444
Tyler, TX 75711-8444
Application address: c/o West Independent School District, Attn.: Jack Crain, Supt., 801 N. Reagan St., West, TX 76691-1158, tel.: (817) 826-3728

Foundation type: Independent foundation
Limitations: Scholarships to students of the West Independent School District, TX.
Financial data: Year ended 05/31/2005. Assets, $1,426,228 (M); Expenditures, $61,750; Total giving, $43,194; Grants to individuals, 98 grants totaling $43,194 (high: $654, low: $209).
Type of support: Support to graduates or students of specific schools; Undergraduate support.
Application information:
Initial approach: Letter.
Deadline(s): May 1
Additional information: Contact trust for current application guidelines.
EIN: 756498847

2779
The Moody Foundation
2302 Post Office St., Ste. 704
Galveston, TX 77550 (409) 797-1500
Contact: Peter M. Moore, Dir., Grants
FAX: (409) 763-5564; URL: http://www.moodyf.org

Foundation type: Independent foundation
Limitations: Scholarships to financially needy graduates of high schools in Galveston County, TX, who have a "B+" average. Recipients must attend colleges and universities in TX. Applicants must also be residents of Galveston County, TX.
Publications: Application guidelines; Annual report; Grants list.
Financial data: Year ended 12/31/2004. Assets, $1,056,384,643 (M); Expenditures, $62,690,327; Total giving, $57,621,881.
Type of support: Support to graduates or students of specific schools; Undergraduate support.
Application information: Application form required.
Deadline(s): Oct
Additional information: Application must include family background, family finances, and scholastic achievement; Applications available only through high school counselors' office.
Program description:
Scholarship Program: Recipients are chosen on the basis of scholastic achievement, test scores, school and community involvement, and financial need. Scholarships are renewable for a total of four years of study.
EIN: 741403105

2780
James B. Moore Charitable Foundation
706 Waynetown Rd.
Crawfordsville, IN 47933
Contact: James B. Moore, Tr.

Foundation type: Independent foundation
Limitations: Scholarships to individuals for higher education.
Financial data: Year ended 12/31/2004. Assets, $84,424 (M); Expenditures, $8,187; Total giving, $7,612; Grants to individuals, totaling $7,112.
Type of support: Scholarships—to individuals.
Application information: Application form required.
Deadline(s): Contact foundation for deadline
EIN: 351966383

2781
Orlene Drobisch Moore Charitable Trust
c/o National City Bank
P.O. Box 94651
Cleveland, OH 44101-4651
Contact: Jo Ann Harlan, Trust Off., National City Bank
Application address: 301 S. W. Adams St., Peoria, IL 61652, tel.: (309) 655-5227

Foundation type: Independent foundation
Limitations: Scholarships to high school graduates of Williamsville, IL, School District No. 15.
Financial data: Year ended 06/30/2005. Assets, $254,576 (M); Expenditures, $9,985; Total giving, $8,250; Grants to individuals, 13 grants totaling $8,250 (high: $750, low: $500).
Type of support: Support to graduates or students of specific schools; Undergraduate support.
Application information: Applications accepted. Application form required.
Applicants should submit the following:
1) Letter(s) of recommendation
2) SAT
3) Financial information
4) GPA
5) ACT
EIN: 371316048

2782
Benjamin Moore Educational Foundation, Inc.
51 Chestnut Ridge Rd.
Montvale, NJ 07645

Foundation type: Company-sponsored foundation
Limitations: Undergraduate scholarships to children of employees of Benjamin Moore, Inc.
Financial data: Year ended 12/31/2004. Assets, $245,302 (M); Expenditures, $66,621; Total giving, $59,000; Grants to individuals, 19 grants totaling $59,000 (high: $4,000, low: $1,000).
Type of support: Employee-related scholarships; Undergraduate support.
Application information: Application form required.
Deadline(s): Nov. 15
Applicants should submit the following:
1) SAT
Additional information: Application address: c/o Sponsored Scholarship Progs., CN 670, Princeton, NJ 08541.
EIN: 222637513

2783
Alfred Moore Foundation
367 S. Pine St.
Spartanburg, SC 29302-2623 (864) 573-5298
Contact: C.L. Page, Jr., Chair.

Foundation type: Independent foundation
Limitations: Three four-year scholarships to graduating seniors of Chapman High School, SC, Byrnes High School, SC, and Crescent High School, SC.
Financial data: Year ended 12/31/2004. Assets, $2,988,975 (M); Expenditures, $304,236; Total giving, $243,266; Grants to individuals, totaling $110,266.
Type of support: Support to graduates or students of specific schools; Undergraduate support.
Application information: Application form required.
Deadline(s): Mar. 29.
Additional information: Application forms available from high schools.
EIN: 576018424

2784
Elsie B. Moore Scholarship Foundation
c/o PNC Bank, Delaware
1600 Market St., Tax Dept.
Philadelphia, PA 19103-7240
Application address: c/o PNC Bank, Delaware, 222 Delaware Ave., 16th Fl., Wilmington, DE 19899, tel.: (302) 429-1338

Foundation type: Independent foundation
Limitations: Scholarships to residents of DE accepted by an accredited school of medicine.
Financial data: Year ended 08/31/2004. Assets, $351,911 (M); Expenditures, $26,130; Total giving, $20,500; Grants to individuals, 10 grants totaling $20,500.
Fields of interest: Medical school/education.
Type of support: Graduate support.
Application information: Application form required.
Deadline(s): Apr. 12
Applicants should submit the following:
1) Financial information
2) Letter(s) of recommendation
3) Transcripts
Additional information: Application must also include MCAT scores, copy of letter of acceptance, and letter describing professional aspirations; Interviews required.
EIN: 516154834

2785
Arlene Goist Moore Scholarship Fund
c/o Second National Bank of Warren
105 High St. N.E.
Warren, OH 44481
Contact: Jeff Hatchner, Trust Off., Second National Bank of Warren

Foundation type: Independent foundation
Limitations: Scholarships to Southington High School, OH graduates who are Southington Township residents and have attended Southington Schools for at least four years.
Financial data: Year ended 04/30/2005. Assets, $54,451 (M); Expenditures, $3,922; Total giving, $2,500; Grants to individuals, 5 grants totaling $2,500 (high: $500, low: $500).
Type of support: Support to graduates or students of specific schools; Undergraduate support.
Application information: Application form required.
Initial approach: Letter.
Deadline(s): Mar. 31

Additional information: Application must also include academic achievements, nonathletic extracurricular activities, and personal statement on applicant's character and reputation in the community.
EIN: 346863075

2786
Doris Floyd Moore Scholarship Fund
(formerly J. W. and Doris Floyd Moore Scholarships)
c/o Wachovia Bank, N.A.
100 N. Main St., 13th Fl.
Winston-Salem, NC 27150

Foundation type: Independent foundation
Limitations: Scholarships to residents of Dillon County, SC, for undergraduate and graduate study.
Financial data: Year ended 12/31/2004. Assets, $553,421 (M); Expenditures, $27,117; Total giving, $17,500.
Type of support: Graduate support; Undergraduate support.
Application information: Applications not accepted.
EIN: 576094970

2787
Roy L. Moore & Aleata M. Moore Scholarship Fund
117 S. 6th St.
P.O. Box 240
Hiawatha, KS 66434 (785) 742-2181
Contact: Michael K. Schmitt, Tr.

Foundation type: Independent foundation
Limitations: Scholarships to graduating seniors of Hiawatha High School, KS, who will enroll in a university, college, community college, graduate school, or vocational or proprietary school.
Financial data: Year ended 05/31/2005. Assets, $2,122,507 (M); Expenditures, $150,814; Total giving, $124,925; Grants to individuals, totaling $124,925.
Type of support: Scholarships—to individuals; Support to graduates or students of specific schools.
Application information: Application form required.
Deadline(s): Mar. 15
Applicants should submit the following:
1) Financial information
Additional information: Application must also include three reference questionnaires.
Program description:
Scholarship Program: Recipients must be graduates of Hiawatha High School, demonstrate academic achievement, have a GPA of 2.6 or greater, demonstrate financial need and potential success in post high school training, and be enrolled as a full-time student at a college or university.
EIN: 486348470

2788
M. Eddie Moore Scholarship Trust
8700 Ashwood Dr.
Capitol Heights, MD 20743 (301) 333-2356
Contact: Joe Savia, Tr.

Foundation type: Independent foundation
Limitations: Scholarships only to unmarried natural or adopted children and financial dependents of a member of the Steamfitters Local Union 602 of the United Association of Journeymen and apprentice

of the plumbing and pipefitting industry of the U.S. and Canada.

Financial data: Year ended 12/31/2004. Assets, $104,093 (M); Expenditures, $10,601; Total giving, $10,000; Grants to individuals, 2 grants totaling $10,000 (high: $5,000, low: $5,000).

Type of support: Scholarships—to individuals.

Application information: Application form required.

Deadline(s): Contact foundation for deadlines

Applicants should submit the following:
1) Transcripts
2) Letter(s) of recommendation

Additional information: Application must also include evidence of enrollment/acceptance to an accredited university, and a written statement of achievement.

EIN: 526489401

2789

Mildred Jayne & H. J. "Ham" Moore Trust

c/o U.S. Bank, N.A.
123 E. 3rd St., Scholarship Comm.
Ottumwa, IA 52501   (641) 683-1641

Foundation type: Independent foundation

Limitations: Scholarships to graduates of Albia High School, IA, and Twin Cedars Junior Senior High School, IA, pursuing postsecondary education.

Financial data: Year ended 02/28/2005. Assets, $566,209 (M); Expenditures, $29,529; Total giving, $23,555; Grants to individuals, 16 grants totaling $23,555 (high: $5,986, low: $200).

Type of support: Support to graduates or students of specific schools; Undergraduate support.

Application information: Application form required.

Initial approach: Letter or telephone.

Deadline(s): Apr. 1.

EIN: 426512721

2790

Moorestown Education Foundation

803 N. Stanwick Rd.
Moorestown, NJ 08057-2147   (856) 778-6600
Contact: Laurel Taron

Foundation type: Operating foundation

Limitations: Scholarships to graduates of Moorestown High School, NJ.

Financial data: Year ended 12/31/2004. Assets, $630,436 (M); Expenditures, $72,679; Total giving, $38,500; Grants to individuals, 46 grants totaling $38,500 (high: $4,000, low: $150).

Type of support: Support to graduates or students of specific schools; Undergraduate support.

Application information: Applications accepted. Application form required.

Deadline(s): May

EIN: 222699954

2791

James Moorman Orphans Home

2909 W. 200 N.
Winchester, IN 47394
Contact: W. Austin Cox, Secy.-Treas.

Foundation type: Independent foundation

Limitations: Scholarships to graduating seniors of high schools in Randolph County, IN, who have been residents of Randolph County for at least two years.

Financial data: Year ended 09/30/2005. Assets, $161,584 (M); Expenditures, $11,633;

Total giving, $10,990; Grants to individuals, 13 grants totaling $10,990 (high: $1,000, low: $490).

Fields of interest: Vocational education.

Type of support: Support to graduates or students of specific schools; Undergraduate support.

Application information: Applications accepted. Application form required.

Deadline(s): Late Apr. or early May

Applicants should submit the following:
1) Photograph
2) Transcripts
3) Financial information

Additional information: Application must also include a personal statement. Application forms available through Randolph County, IN, high schools.

Program description:

James F. Moorman Scholarship: Applicants must meet the following criteria:

· have attended a Randolph County high school their junior and senior years

· be recommended by the school's principal or guidance director

· have applied to or been accepted at an accredited college, university, technical school, or trade or business school

· have received no other major scholarship award

Scholarship awards are considered in relation to the applicant's probability of succeeding in his/her chosen field. Each scholarship is a single grant awarded for a one-year period. Maximum award is $1,500. Special grants may be awarded at the discretion of the governing board. Two applications will be accepted, upon proper recommendation, from each Randolph County high school for each school year.

EIN: 350883508

2792

Edward & Suzan Moran Scholarship Trust

c/o First United Bank
P.O. Box 557
Oakland, MD 21550-4557
Application address: c/o Principal, Westmar High School, Lonaconing, MD 21539

Foundation type: Independent foundation

Limitations: Scholarships to graduates of Westmar High School, MD.

Financial data: Year ended 07/31/2004. Assets, $250,970 (M); Expenditures, $13,727; Total giving, $10,500; Grants to individuals, 7 grants totaling $10,500 (high: $1,500, low: $1,500).

Type of support: Support to graduates or students of specific schools; Undergraduate support.

Application information:

Deadline(s): Prior to graduation

Additional information: Contact trust for current application guidelines.

EIN: 556069479

2793

Julia Moran Trust

c/o Fulton Financial Advisors, N.A.
P.O. Box 3215
Lancaster, PA 17604-3215
Application address: c/o Temple University, Attn.: Edward Moore, 3223 N. Broad St., Philadelphia, PA 19140

Foundation type: Independent foundation

Limitations: Student loans to male students attending the Temple University School of Dentistry, PA.

Financial data: Year ended 12/31/2004. Assets, $552,945 (M); Expenditures, $11,986; Total giving, $6,000; Loans to individuals, 3 loans totaling $6,000.

Fields of interest: Dental school/education; Men.

Type of support: Student loans—to individuals; Support to graduates or students of specific schools.

Application information: Applications accepted throughout the year; Applications made through the Temple University Financial Aid Office.

EIN: 236642828

2794

The John Motley Morehead Foundation

P.O. Box 690
Chapel Hill, NC 27514-0690
Contact: Charles E. Lovelace, Jr., Exec. Dir.
FAX: (919) 962-1615; E-mail: morehead@unc.edu;
URL: http://www.moreheadfoundation.org

Foundation type: Independent foundation

Limitations: Undergraduate scholarships by nomination only to high school students in NC and Canada, public schools in Great Britain, and selected secondary schools in the rest of the U.S. to be used for attendance at the University of North Carolina at Chapel Hill only.

Publications: Annual report; Informational brochure.

Financial data: Year ended 06/30/2004. Assets, $110,159,678 (M); Expenditures, $6,413,281; Total giving, $4,606,384; Grants to individuals, 196 grants totaling $3,490,650 (high: $26,835, low: $6,587, average grant: $13,173-$25,021).

Fields of interest: Education.

Type of support: Support to graduates or students of specific schools; Awards/grants by nomination only; Undergraduate support.

Application information:

Deadline(s): Contact foundation for current nomination deadline

Applicants should submit the following:
1) Photograph
2) Transcripts
3) Letter(s) of recommendation

Additional information: Completion of formal nomination required, and two-page school form; Interviews required.

Program description:

Morehead Award Program: This program for undergraduates is the primary focus of the foundation's activities and receives the major commitment of the foundation's resources. The awards are based solely on merit with no consideration of financial need. No individuals may apply for an award. Awards are made to high school and preparatory school students in the U.S., Canada, and Great Britain who have been nominated by their respective schools to compete for the awards. Each participating out-of-state school may nominate only one student for the Morehead Award. Nominations are invited from all secondary schools in NC and Canada; from all public schools in Great Britain; and from 140 select secondary schools in the U.S. outside of NC (see the foundation's Web site for a list of eligible schools). The program, which is limited to sponsoring undergraduate study at the University of North Carolina at Chapel Hill, has three components. Morehead Scholars receive an annual stipend to cover expenses, including room, board, books, and fees. The Tuition Program pays tuition for NC residents and out-of-state residents directly to the University. These awards are renewable for four years of study. The Summer Enrichment

Program is a four-year optional program designed to balance the academic education of Morehead Scholars with real-world experience. Arranged and financed by the foundation, this program is open to all Morehead Award recipients and involves a summer internship prior to each academic year. Prior to the first year, students participate in an outdoor leadership program, such as Outward Bound. Second-year student internships are with public service agencies in major U.S. cities. Third-year students intern with major American companies. Rising seniors work either in federal or foreign governments or on self-devised special projects. A third option prior to the senior year is a travel/study abroad project also of the scholar's own design.
EIN: 560599225

2795
The Morey Foundation
P.O. Box 1000
Winn, MI 48896
Contact: Lon Morey, Pres.

Foundation type: Independent foundation
Limitations: Scholarships to students at Central Michigan University.
Financial data: Year ended 12/31/2004. Assets, $35,976,559 (M); Expenditures, $535,432; Total giving, $73,405.
Type of support: Scholarships—to individuals; Support to graduates or students of specific schools.
Application information: Applications accepted. Application form required.
Deadline(s): Mar. 15.
EIN: 382965346

2796
Father John H. Morgan Charitable Irrevocable Trust
c/o National City Bank of Kentucky
P.O. Box 94651
Cleveland, OH 44101-4651

Foundation type: Independent foundation
Limitations: Scholarships to individuals residing in the Louisville, KY, area for undergraduate education.
Financial data: Year ended 07/31/2004. Assets, $1,260,433 (M); Expenditures, $72,820; Total giving, $63,000; Grants to individuals, 9 grants totaling $63,000 (high: $7,000, low: $7,000).
Type of support: Undergraduate support.
Application information: Contact foundation for current application deadline/guidelines.
EIN: 527231472

2797
Hardy & Bess Morgan Citzenship Award Fund
P.O. Box 790
Lamesa, TX 79331

Foundation type: Operating foundation
Limitations: Citizenship awards by nomination only to graduating seniors from high schools in Dawson County, TX.
Financial data: Year ended 12/31/2003. Assets, $0 (M); Expenditures, $3,525; Total giving, $3,375; Grants to individuals, totaling $3,375.
Fields of interest: Public affairs, citizen participation.

Type of support: Support to graduates or students of specific schools; Awards/grants by nomination only; Awards/prizes; Undergraduate support.
Application information:
Deadline(s): Spring
Applicants should submit the following:
1) Transcripts
Additional information: Completion of formal nomination required; Application must also include record of nominee's classwork and achievements, and faculty testimonials and vote; Contact high school principals for nomination guidelines; Recipients selected in spring.
EIN: 759630846

2798
Morgan Family Foundation, Inc.
6671 Owens Dr.
Pleasanton, CA 94588

Foundation type: Independent foundation
Limitations: Scholarships to students residing in CA for higher education.
Financial data: Year ended 12/31/2003. Assets, $596,561 (M); Expenditures, $399,406; Total giving, $397,800; Grants to individuals, 11 grants totaling $35,000 (high: $25,000, low: $1,000).
Type of support: Undergraduate support.
Application information: Applications not accepted.
EIN: 912081052

2799
Thomas D. Morgan Irrevocable Inter Vivos Trust No. 1
120 S. State St.
Norton, KS 67654-2142
Contact: Warren A. White, Tr.
Application address: 302 N. West St., Norton, KS 67654, tel.: (785) 877-3985

Foundation type: Independent foundation
Limitations: Scholarships to graduates of Norton Community High School, KS.
Financial data: Year ended 06/30/2005. Assets, $373,439 (M); Expenditures, $30,745; Total giving, $17,500; Grants to individuals, 10 grants totaling $17,500 (high: $3,000, low: $750).
Type of support: Support to graduates or students of specific schools; Undergraduate support.
Application information: Application form required.
Deadline(s): May 15 for fall semester, and two and one half months prior to start of semester for spring and summer
Additional information: Application forms are distributed by the school.
EIN: 481038549

2800
Griffith D. Morgan Memorial Fund
c/o PNC Advisors
620 Liberty Ave.
Pittsburgh, PA 15222-2705
Application address: c/o Mary L. Ferrara, Guidance Counselor, Armstrong Central Senior High School, Orr Ave., Kittanning, PA 15602, tel.: (412) 543-1591

Foundation type: Independent foundation
Limitations: Scholarships to graduates of the East Brady Area School District, PA.

Financial data: Year ended 12/31/2002. Assets, $1,332,781 (M); Expenditures, $89,290; Total giving, $86,209; Grants to individuals, 60 grants totaling $86,209 (high: $1,724, low: $1,034).
Type of support: Support to graduates or students of specific schools; Undergraduate support.
Application information: Application form required.
Initial approach: Letter requesting application.
Deadline(s): May 1
EIN: 256066552

2801
A. D. & A. L. Morgan Memorial Scholarship Fund
c/o UBS Financial Services Inc
1 Columbus Ctr.
Virginia Beach, VA 23462
Application address: c/o Old Dominion Univ., Financial Aid Office, 121 Old Administration Bldg., Norfolk, VA 23529-0052

Foundation type: Independent foundation
Limitations: Scholarships for residents of Tidewater south of Hampton Roads, VA, to attend Old Dominion University in Norfolk, VA. Students must maintain at least a "C" average to remain eligible. Professorships to teachers at Old Dominion University are also granted.
Financial data: Year ended 12/31/2004. Assets, $840,317 (M); Expenditures, $62,407; Total giving, $50,500; Grants to individuals, 10 grants totaling $50,500 (high: $28,000, low: $2,500).
Fields of interest: Education.
Type of support: Professorships; Scholarships—to individuals; Support to graduates or students of specific schools.
Application information: Application form required.
Deadline(s): May
Additional information: Applicatin must also include school records, personal history, and financial status.
EIN: 540309320

2802
George and Loraine Morgan Memorial Trust
126 S. Sherrin Ave.
Louisville, KY 40207
Contact: Junius Beaver, Dir.

Foundation type: Independent foundation
Limitations: Scholarships to residents of Louisville, KY, for higher education.
Financial data: Year ended 12/31/2004. Assets, $1,100,425 (M); Expenditures, $115,793; Total giving, $64,987; Grants to individuals, 10 grants totaling $64,987 (high: $10,850, low: $1,250).
Type of support: Undergraduate support.
Application information: Applications accepted throughout the year; Contact trust for current application guidelines.
EIN: 311532819

2803
Greater Morgantown Community Trust, Inc.
344 High St.
P.O. Box 409
Morgantown, WV 26507-0409 (304) 296-3433
E-mail: info@gmctfoundation.org; URL: http://www.gmctfoundation.org/

Foundation type: Community foundation
Limitations: Two $1500 scholarships to graduates of Monongalia County high schools, WV.
Financial data: Year ended 12/31/2004. Assets, $3,083,073 (M); Expenditures, $224,729; Total giving, $81,715; Grants to individuals, 22 grants totaling $27,940 (high: $6,515, low: $50).
Type of support: Support to graduates or students of specific schools; Undergraduate support.
Application information: Applications accepted. Application form required. Application form available on the grantmaker's Web site.
   Initial approach: E-mail or letter.
   Additional information: See Web site for additional application information.
Program description:
   Hope Works Scholarship: Provides two, $1500 scholarships to Monongalia County, West Virginia high school graduates who are regularly enrolled as undergraduate students in a college or university. The recipients shall have demonstrated:
   · need for financial assistance due to loss of parental support from death, divorce, or loss of family income due to special circumstances
   · excellence, commitment, and leadership through involvement in school and community organizations
   · high academic promise
EIN: 550776715

2804
The Morrill Foundation
c/o National City Bank
P.O. Box 94651
Cleveland, OH 44101-4651

Foundation type: Company-sponsored foundation
Limitations: Student loans to graduates of Garrett Kyser Butler Community Schools, IN, who reside in the school district, and to employees of Electric Motors and Specialties, Inc., and their children and grandchildren.
Financial data: Year ended 12/31/2004. Assets, $124,088 (M); Expenditures, $1,672; Total giving, $1,000; Loans to individuals, totaling $10,000.
Type of support: Employee-related scholarships; Student loans—to individuals.
Application information: Applications accepted.
   Initial approach: Letter.
   Deadline(s): None
   Applicants should submit the following:
   1) Letter(s) of recommendation
   2) Transcripts
   3) Financial information
   Additional information: Application must also include personal data; Application address: P.O. Box 116, Garrett, IN 46738.
EIN: 356040178

2805
James K. Morrill Scholarship Fund
c/o Fifth Third Bank
P.O. Box 3636
Grand Rapids, MI 49501-3636
Application address: c/o Brattleboro Union High School District, Attn.: Guidance Counselor, 131 Fairground Rd., Brattleboro, VT 05301 or c/o Holyoke High School, Attn.: Guidance Counselor, 500 Beech St., Holyoke, MA 01040

Foundation type: Independent foundation
Limitations: Scholarships to graduating female seniors of Holyoke High School, MA.
Financial data: Year ended 12/31/2004. Assets, $1,379,723 (M); Expenditures, $74,066; Total giving, $57,992; Grants to individuals, 8 grants totaling $57,992 (high: $7,600, low: $6,196).
Fields of interest: Women.
Type of support: Support to graduates or students of specific schools; Undergraduate support.
Application information: Application form required.
   Deadline(s): May 10
   Additional information: Applications available in guidance office.
EIN: 367112892

2806
Muriel M. Morris Educational Foundation
c/o Dorothy Wallace
6880 Dixon Ave. E.
Dixon, CA 95620-9685
Application address: c/o Dixon High School, Attn.: Dorothy Wallace, 6880 Dixon Ave. E., Dixon, CA 95620

Foundation type: Independent foundation
Limitations: Scholarships to graduates of Dixon High School, CA, for higher education.
Financial data: Year ended 12/31/2004. Assets, $741,211 (M); Expenditures, $28,958; Total giving, $28,000; Grants to individuals, 4 grants totaling $28,000 (high: $7,000, low: $7,000).
Type of support: Support to graduates or students of specific schools; Undergraduate support.
Application information: Application form required.
   Deadline(s): Apr.
EIN: 680311581

2807
Morrison Education Foundation
c/o William Burch
409 N. Cherry St.
Morrison, IL 61270

Foundation type: Independent foundation
Limitations: Scholarships to individuals in Morrison, IL, for higher education.
Financial data: Year ended 12/31/2004. Assets, $862,034 (M); Expenditures, $47,204; Total giving, $34,551; Grants to individuals, 16 grants totaling $21,627 (high: $3,000, low: $300).
Type of support: Scholarships—to individuals.
Application information: Contact foundation for current application deadline/guidelines.
EIN: 363583712

2808
Glenn W. & Hazelle Paxson Morrison Foundation, Inc.
P.O. Box 7518
Lakeland, FL 33807-7518
Contact: R. Lynn Noris, Exec. Dir.

Foundation type: Independent foundation
Limitations: Scholarships and loans primarily to individuals pursuing higher education at Christian schools in Polk County, FL.
Financial data: Year ended 06/30/2005. Assets, $4,084,475 (M); Expenditures, $188,967; Total giving, $150,358; Grants to individuals, 35 grants totaling $89,000 (high: $5,000; low: $1,000).
Fields of interest: Christian agencies & churches.
Type of support: Scholarships—to individuals; Student loans—to individuals.
Application information: Applications accepted.
   Initial approach: Letter.
EIN: 592220612

2809
Ollege and Minnie Morrison Foundation
c/o JPMorgan Chase Bank
P.O. Box 31412
Rochester, NY 14603

Foundation type: Independent foundation
Limitations: Scholarships only to graduating seniors of the Livingston Intermediate School District, Livingston, TX, area.
Financial data: Year ended 12/31/2004. Assets, $1,701,042 (M); Expenditures, $140,495; Total giving, $111,000; Grants to individuals, 46 grants totaling $111,000 (high: $4,500, low: $1,500).
Type of support: Support to graduates or students of specific schools; Undergraduate support.
Application information: Applications not accepted.
EIN: 237073336

2810
Darthea Morrow Scholarship Trust
c/o Bank of America, N.A.
P.O. Box 1802
Providence, RI 02901-1802
Application address: c/o Nauset Regional High School, Scholarship Comm., 100 Cable Rd., North Eastham, MA 02651

Foundation type: Independent foundation
Limitations: Scholarships to graduates of Nauset Regional High School, MA.
Financial data: Year ended 12/31/2004. Assets, $1,078,039 (M); Expenditures, $48,926; Total giving, $36,520; Grants to individuals, 25 grants totaling $36,520 (high: $3,720, low: $200).
Type of support: Support to graduates or students of specific schools; Undergraduate support.
Application information: Applications accepted. Application form required.
   Initial approach: Letter.
   Additional information: Applications accepted throughout the year; Recipients are chosen during the third week of May.
EIN: 042866532

2811
Morrow-Stevens Foundation
P.O. Box 3026
Oakton, VA   22124-3026   (703) 319-1527
Contact: Geraldine M. Graham, Pres.

Foundation type: Independent foundation
Limitations: Scholarships to VA residents for attendance at accredited VA colleges and universities.
Financial data: Year ended 12/31/2004. Assets, $226,493 (M); Expenditures, $31,951; Total giving, $30,317; Grants to individuals, 4 grants totaling $30,317 (high: $14,471, low: $2,549).
Type of support: Undergraduate support.
Application information: Application form required.
  Deadline(s): May 15
  Applicants should submit the following:
    1) Letter(s) of recommendation
    2) Transcripts
    3) SAT
    4) Essay
    5) FAFSA
    6) ACT
  Additional information: Application must also include proof of VA residency.
EIN: 541949631

2812
D. W. Morse Family Scholarship Fund
c/o Bank of America, N.A.
P.O. Box 34345
Seattle, WA   98124-1345
Application address: c/o Patrick Kane, Port Angeles Senior High, 304 E. Park Ave., Port Angeles, WA 98362, tel.: (360) 452-7602

Foundation type: Independent foundation
Limitations: Scholarships to graduates of Port Angeles Senior High School, WA. If funds are available, scholarships may also be given to students residing on the Olympic Peninsula, WA.
Financial data: Year ended 10/31/2004. Assets, $598,870 (M); Expenditures, $31,777; Total giving, $26,800; Grants to individuals, 35 grants totaling $26,800 (high: $2,000, low: $500).
Type of support: Support to graduates or students of specific schools; Undergraduate support.
Application information:
  Deadline(s): Jan. 6
  Additional information: Applicants must prepare a scholarship notebook.
EIN: 916218517

2813
Hugh Morson Memorial Scholarship Fund
c/o Wachovia Bank, N.A.
100 N. Main St., 13th Fl.
Winston-Salem, NC   27150   (704) 732-4090
Contact: Chris Spaugh, Trust Off., Charitable Svcs., Wachovia Bank, N.A.
Scholarship application address: 4320-G, Wade Hampton Blvd., Taylors, SC 29687
URL: http://www.wachoviascholars.com/mrsn/mrsn_2006_ins.htm

Foundation type: Independent foundation
Limitations: Undergraduate scholarships to high school seniors of Raleigh, NC.
Financial data: Year ended 12/31/2004. Assets, $849,089 (M); Expenditures, $54,996; Total giving, $45,000; Grant to an individual, 1 grant totaling $45,000.
Type of support: Support to graduates or students of specific schools; Undergraduate support.

Application information: Application form required.
  Deadline(s): Apr. 30
  Additional information: Applications available through high school guidance offices.
EIN: 237418060

2814
Mortar Board Alumni/Tolo Foundation
P.O. Box 53162
Bellevue, WA   98015-3162
Application address: 8041 19th Ave., N.E., Seattle, WA 98115

Foundation type: Independent foundation
Limitations: Scholarships to undergraduate and graduate students at the University of Washington and its branch campuses.
Financial data: Year ended 05/31/2004. Assets, $626,438 (M); Expenditures, $23,627; Total giving, $16,000; Grants to individuals, 10 grants totaling $16,000 (high: $3,000, low: $750).
Type of support: Graduate support; Undergraduate support.
Application information: Applications accepted. Application form required.
  Deadline(s): Mar. 27
  Applicants should submit the following:
    1) Transcripts
    2) Letter(s) of recommendation
    3) Essay
  Additional information: Application must include extracurricular activities. Four copies of all material are required.
EIN: 916054386

2815
Alan Morton Foundation
93 Thompson Blvd.
Greenport, NY   11944

Foundation type: Operating foundation
Limitations: Scholarships to individuals in NY.
Financial data: Year ended 08/31/2004. Assets, $155,758 (M); Expenditures, $112,232; Total giving, $92,102; Grants to individuals, 8 grants totaling $18,680 (high: $5,000, low: $1,680).
Type of support: Scholarships—to individuals.
Application information: Contact foundation for current application deadline/guidelines.
EIN: 133295743

2816
Alice E. Morton Memorial Scholarship Fund
c/o TD Banknorth, N.A., Investment Mgmt. Group
P.O. Box 595
Williston, VT   05495   (802) 879-2285
Application address: c/o Bellows Free Academy, 71 S. Main St., St. Albans, VT 05478

Foundation type: Independent foundation
Limitations: College scholarships to financially needy graduates of Bellows Free Academy, St. Albans, VT.
Financial data: Year ended 12/31/2004. Assets, $138,459 (M); Expenditures, $6,004; Total giving, $4,000.
Type of support: Support to graduates or students of specific schools; Undergraduate support.
Application information: Application form required.
  Deadline(s): May 1
  Applicants should submit the following:

    1) Financial information
EIN: 036005300

2817
Harvey H. Moses & Catherine Allis Moses Educational Fund
c/o Bank of America, N.A.
P.O. Box 1802
Providence, RI   02901-1802
Application address: c/o Ticonderoga Senior High School, Attn.: Guidance Off., 5 Calkins Pl., Ticonderoga, NY 12883

Foundation type: Independent foundation
Limitations: Scholarships to students of Ticonderoga High School, NY, for higher education.
Financial data: Year ended 08/31/2005. Assets, $307,968 (M); Expenditures, $14,697; Total giving, $11,500; Grants to individuals, 10 grants totaling $11,500 (high: $1,150, low: $1,150).
Type of support: Support to graduates or students of specific schools; Undergraduate support.
Application information: Application form required.
  Deadline(s): Apr. 30
EIN: 046487087

2818
Joseph R. Moss Educational & Charitable Trust
P.O. Box 299
York, SC   29745   (803) 684-3559
Contact: Melvin B. McKeown, Tr.

Foundation type: Independent foundation
Limitations: Scholarships to individuals for higher education.
Financial data: Year ended 08/31/2004. Assets, $1,454,190 (M); Expenditures, $77,517; Total giving, $73,600; Grants to individuals, 46 grants totaling $73,600 (high: $2,600, low: $750).
Type of support: Undergraduate support.
Application information: Applications accepted. Application form required.
  Initial approach: Letter.
EIN: 576162069

2819
Helen W. Moulton Scholarship Fund
(formerly Harold E. Moulton Scholarship Fund)
c/o Bank of America, N.A.
P.O. Box 6768
Providence, RI   02940
Contact: William A. McKee, Trust Off., Bank of America, N.A.
Application address: 159 E. Main St., Rm. 3089, Rochester, NY 14638

Foundation type: Independent foundation
Limitations: Scholarships to residents of Clarksville, NY, who are attending or have graduated from Bolivar Central School, NY; Richburg Central School, NY; Cuba Rushford School, NY; or Portville Central School, NY. Preference is given to students pursuing dairy or agricultural courses at four-year schools in NY.
Financial data: Year ended 04/30/2005. Assets, $377,615 (M); Expenditures, $27,591; Total giving, $22,000.
Type of support: Support to graduates or students of specific schools; Undergraduate support.
Application information: Applications accepted. Application form required.

Initial approach: Letter.
Deadline(s): Apr. 15.
Applicants should submit the following:
1) Financial information
2) Essay
3) Transcripts
4) SAT
5) ACT
EIN: 510197187

2820
Mount Angel Community Foundation
P.O. Box 1054
Mount Angel, OR 97362-1054
Contact: Jim Hall, Secy.-Treas.
FAX: (503) 845-6190;
E-mail: jerry@oktoberfest.org

Foundation type: Community foundation
Limitations: Scholarships to students of JFK High School, OR, for undergraduate study.
Publications: Financial statement.
Financial data: Year ended 12/31/2004.
Assets, $635,027 (M); Expenditures, $26,416; Total giving, $25,166; Grants to individuals, totaling $25,166.
Type of support: Support to graduates or students of specific schools; Undergraduate support.
Application information: Contact foundation for current application deadline/guidelines.
EIN: 931205915

2821
Mount Dora Community Trust
c/o First National Bank of Mount Dora
P.O. Box 1406
Mount Dora, FL 32756   (352) 383-2140
Contact: Kevin Batliner, Exec. Dir.
E-mail: trust@fnbmd.com; URL: http://www.fnbmd.com/_docs/com_trust.htm

Foundation type: Community foundation
Limitations: Scholarships to students at Mount Dora area high schools, FL, for higher education.
Publications: Annual report; Informational brochure.
Financial data: Year ended 08/31/2005.
Assets, $5,434,743 (M); Expenditures, $218,774; Total giving, $150,972; Grants to individuals, 38 grants totaling $37,508.
Type of support: Support to graduates or students of specific schools; Undergraduate support.
Application information: Application form required.
Additional information: Contact trust for current application deadline/guidelines.
EIN: 237227875

2822
Mount Pleasant Area Community Foundation
(formerly Mount Pleasant Community Foundation)
113 W. Broadway
P.O. Box 1283
Mount Pleasant, MI 48804-1283
(989) 773-7322
FAX: (989) 773-1517; E-mail: info@mpacf.org;
Additional E-mail: srathbun@mpacf.org;
URL: http://www.mpacf.org

Foundation type: Community foundation
Limitations: Scholarships and student loans to Mount Pleasant, MI, area residents.

Publications: Application guidelines; Annual report; Financial statement; Grants list; Informational brochure; Newsletter.
Financial data: Year ended 12/31/2004.
Assets, $4,572,440 (M); Expenditures, $232,395; Total giving, $74,450.
Type of support: Scholarships—to individuals; Student loans—to individuals.
Application information: Contact foundation for current application deadline/guidelines.
EIN: 382951873

2823
Mountain Chalet Cornerstone Foundation
1286 Snowbunny Ln.
Aspen, CO 81611-1055
Contact: Craig Melville, Pres.

Foundation type: Independent foundation
Limitations: Scholarships to students attending college in Avon or Menno, SD, and Quincy or Whitman, MA.
Financial data: Year ended 12/31/2002.
Assets, $70,582 (M); Expenditures, $15,324; Total giving, $15,150; Grants to individuals, 17 grants totaling $15,150 (high: $2,000, low: $250).
Type of support: Graduate support; Undergraduate support.
Application information: Application form required.
Deadline(s): Apr. 7
EIN: 841440601

2824
Mountain Protective Association Scholarship Fund
P.O. Box 253
Evergreen, CO 80437-0253   (303) 674-4733

Foundation type: Independent foundation
Limitations: Scholarships are awarded for a two- to four-year period to graduates of Evergreen and Conifer senior high schools, CO.
Financial data: Year ended 06/30/2004.
Assets, $154,960 (M); Expenditures, $9,298; Total giving, $7,500; Grants to individuals, totaling $7,500.
Application information: Contact fund for current application deadline/guidelines.
EIN: 237457169

2825
The Mountain West Track & Field Club, Inc.
P.O. Box 8081
Missoula, MT 59807
Contact: Mark William Timmons, Pres.

Foundation type: Operating foundation
Limitations: Awards by nomination only to athletes residing in MT who have completed their NCAA eligibility, to provide competitive and educational opportunities.
Financial data: Year ended 09/30/2002.
Assets, $123,315 (M); Expenditures, $687,307; Total giving, $554,652; Grants to individuals, 5 grants totaling $62,055 (high: $19,221, low: $9,167).
Fields of interest: Athletics/sports, training.
Type of support: Awards/grants by nomination only; Awards/prizes.
Application information: Applications not accepted.

Additional information: Eligibility and acceptance is by invitation only.
EIN: 810459511

2826
The Mountaintop Foundation
1432 W. 1st St.
Pella, IA 50219-1050   (641) 628-8173
Contact: Elizabeth A. Wilson, Pres.

Foundation type: Independent foundation
Limitations: Scholarships to students residing in PA and WV for undergraduate education.
Financial data: Year ended 12/31/2004.
Assets, $300,292 (M); Expenditures, $15,626; Total giving, $15,000; Grants to individuals, 15 grants totaling $15,000 (high: $1,000, low: $1,000).
Type of support: Undergraduate support.
Application information: Application form required.
Initial approach: Letter or telephone.
Deadline(s): Jan. 31
EIN: 421481840

2827
Jerry Don Mouser Foundation
c/o Brimer, Hobbs & Perry
4025 Woodland Park Blvd., Ste. 200
Arlington, TX 76013
Contact: Shirlene Miller, Secy.
Application address: P.O. Box 40672, Everman, TX 76140

Foundation type: Operating foundation
Limitations: Scholarships to graduating high school seniors from Grossmont Union High School District in La Mesa, CA, Mansfield Independent School District in Mansfield, TX, and Randolph Township Board of Education in Randolph, NJ, with priority given to Mouser Electronics Companies employees' dependents, regardless of where they attend school.
Financial data: Year ended 12/31/2003.
Assets, $9,868 (M); Expenditures, $54,611; Total giving, $53,716; Grants to individuals, 12 grants totaling $20,443 (high: $5,900, low: $303).
Type of support: Employee-related scholarships; Undergraduate support.
Application information: Application form required.
Deadline(s): Apr. 20
Applicants should submit the following:
1) Transcripts
2) Essay
3) SAT
4) Letter(s) of recommendation
5) ACT
Additional information: Application must also include PSAT/NMSQT, and list of achievements and honors; Recipients notified first week in June.
Program description:
Scholarship Program: Applicants must have at least a 3.0 GPA in high school and be entering college or junior college as a full-time student.
EIN: 752548171

2828
Moyer Brothers Educational Trust
P.O. Box 413
Abilene, KS 67410-0413   (785) 263-1370
Contact: Robert H. Royer, Jr., Tr.

Foundation type: Independent foundation

Limitations: Scholarships to graduating seniors from Abilene and Chapman high schools, KS.
Financial data: Year ended 12/31/2004. Assets, $128,522; Expenditures, $11,438; Total giving, $11,000; Grants to individuals, 6 grants totaling $11,000 (high: $2,000, low: $1,000).
Type of support: Support to graduates or students of specific schools; Undergraduate support.
Application information: Application form required.
Deadline(s): Apr. 15
EIN: 481010595

2829
The William and Louise Moyer Trust
c/o Trust Board
6736 Cetronia Rd.
Allentown, PA 18106-9202   (610) 398-1711
Contact: John Helfrich, Secy.

Foundation type: Independent foundation
Limitations: Scholarships to students with 24 hours of credited study at the college level, at one of the eligible colleges as specified by the Trust and the Moyer Will.
Financial data: Year ended 06/30/2005. Assets, $519,221 (M); Expenditures, $20,380; Total giving, $18,332; Grants to individuals, 10 grants totaling $18,332 (high: $5,000, low: $500).
Type of support: Undergraduate support.
Application information:
Initial approach: Letter.
Deadline(s): June 1
EIN: 237739199

2830
A. Marlyn Moyer, Jr. Scholarship Foundation
409 Hood Blvd.
Fairless Hills, PA 19030   (215) 943-7400
Contact: Susan M. Harkins, Recording Secy.

Foundation type: Independent foundation
Limitations: Scholarships to residents of Lower Bucks County, PA, who are attending Lower Bucks County high schools and have never attended postsecondary schools.
Financial data: Year ended 12/31/2004. Assets, $673,801 (M); Expenditures, $26,536; Total giving, $19,000; Grants to individuals, 7 grants totaling $19,000 (high: $3,000, low: $1,000).
Type of support: Support to graduates or students of specific schools; Undergraduate support.
Application information: Application form required.
Deadline(s): Apr. 30
Additional information: Contact guidance counselors at local area schools or Bucks County Chamber of Commerce for application forms.
EIN: 232037282

2831
Moynihan, Mattaliano, Perry Trust
(formerly The Joseph F. Moynihan, Jr. Memorial Charitable Trust)
15 Front St.
Salem, MA 01970-3707   (978) 740-2880
Contact: Carol A. Perry, Tr.
Application address: c/o Arthur Moore, 29 Grove St., Hudson, MA 01749

Foundation type: Public charity

Limitations: Scholarships to employees of Massachusetts State Police and their children for postsecondary education.
Financial data: Year ended 12/31/2003. Assets, $476,389 (M); Expenditures, $64,104; Total giving, $60,125; Grants to individuals, 30 grants totaling $60,000 (high: $2,000, low: $2,000).
Fields of interest: Crime/law enforcement, police agencies.
Type of support: Employee-related scholarships.
Application information: Contact trust for current application deadline/guidelines.
EIN: 046660317

2832
The Louis K. Mulford Scholarship Foundation
3 Brassie Way
Littleton, CO 80123
Contact: Joyce Latham, Tr.

Foundation type: Independent foundation
Limitations: Scholarships primarily to residents of CO who attend Littleton High School in Littleton, CO.
Financial data: Year ended 12/31/2004. Assets, $506,918 (M); Expenditures, $33,130; Total giving, $19,294; Grants to individuals, 10 grants totaling $19,294 (high: $3,000, low: $1,394).
Type of support: Scholarships—to individuals; Support to graduates or students of specific schools; Undergraduate support.
Application information: Applications accepted. Application form required.
Deadline(s): Apr. 15
Applicants should submit the following:
1) Letter(s) of recommendation
Additional information: Application must also include letter explaining request and outlining qualifications; Interviews required.
Program description:
Scholarship Program: All recipients are required to maintain a 2.9 grade average and graduate in four years. A maximum of $1,300 per quarter for eight quarters is paid directly to the college or university for tuition and fees only.
EIN: 237398275

2833
Multnomah Athletic Foundation, Inc.
P.O. Box 1799
Portland, OR 97207-1799   (503) 223-6251
Contact: Lorraine Miller, Exec. Dir.

Foundation type: Public charity
Limitations: Scholarships to athletes residing in the Portland, OR, area for undergraduate education.
Financial data: Year ended 12/31/2003. Assets, $690,045 (M); Expenditures, $159,207; Total giving, $109,394; Grants to individuals, totaling $93,844.
Fields of interest: Recreation.
Type of support: Employee-related scholarships; Awards/grants by nomination only; Undergraduate support.
Application information: Contact foundation for current application deadline/guidelines.
Program descriptions:
Mel Fox Scholarship: Recipients are selected by their high schools.
Joe Loprinzi Scholarship: Awards one scholarship to a graduating senior who has been nominated to the Scholar Athlete Program.

Fay Sasser Scholarship: Awards up to two scholarships to Multnomah Athletic Club employees or their children.
EIN: 931014651

2834
Henry J. & Marie Munger Scholarship Fund
550 E. Main St., No. 32
Branford, CT 06405
Contact: David P. Zuber, Tr.
URL: http://www.munger.org

Foundation type: Independent foundation
Limitations: Scholarships to first- and second-year college students who have resided for at least four years prior to college (excluding military service) in Guilford, Madison, or Clinton, CT for higher education.
Financial data: Year ended 05/31/2005. Assets, $348,017 (M); Expenditures, $33,081; Total giving, $24,000; Grants to individuals, 6 grants totaling $24,000 (high: $4,000, low: $4,000).
Type of support: Undergraduate support.
Application information: Application form required.
Deadline(s): Contact fund for deadline
Applicants should submit the following:
1) Transcripts
EIN: 060968106

2835
Robert L. Munger, Jr. Foundation
1 Cedar Point Dr.
Sandusky, OH 44870-5259
Application addresses: c/o Valleyfair Park, Personnel Dept., 1 Valleyfair Dr., Shakopee, MN 55379, c/o Dorney Park, Personnel Dept., 3830 Dorney Park Rd., Allentown, PA 18104, or Cedar Point, Personnel Dept., 1 Cedar Point Dr., Sandusky, OH 44870-5259

Foundation type: Independent foundation
Limitations: Scholarships to graduating high school seniors who are seasonal and part-time employees of the following amusement parks: Cedar Point in Sandusky, OH, Valleyfair in Shakopee, MN, and Dorney Park in Allentown, PA.
Financial data: Year ended 12/31/2004. Assets, $419,215 (M); Expenditures, $29,120; Total giving, $26,000; Grants to individuals, 13 grants totaling $26,000 (high: $2,000, low: $2,000).
Fields of interest: Education.
Type of support: Employee-related scholarships; Undergraduate support.
Application information: Applications accepted. Application form required.
Deadline(s): July 1
Applicants should submit the following:
1) Essay
Additional information: Interviews required.
Program description:
Scholarship Program: Scholarships are $2,000 and are not renewable. Applicants must have at least a "C" average. Forty finalists are selected from a random drawing, and from these finalists the scholarship committee generally selects 13 recipients. Selection criteria include academic performance, extracurricular activities, and financial need. Job performance is not considered when selecting recipients. Children and relatives of the selection committee, officers of Cedar Fair Management Co., and the Munger family are ineligible.
EIN: 341599255

2836
The Grant Munro Scholarship Trust
c/o National City Bank
P.O. Box 94651
Cleveland, OH 44101-4651
Contact: Charles H. Hodson, Chair.
Application address: c/o Fairfield Foundation, 109 N. Broad St., Lancaster, OH 43130

Foundation type: Independent foundation
Limitations: Scholarships to graduates of Lancaster High School or any other high school in Fairfield County, OH, for degrees in medicine or the ministry.
Financial data: Year ended 05/31/2005. Assets, $5,634,149 (M); Expenditures, $301,338; Total giving, $255,655; Grants to individuals, totaling $243,325.
Fields of interest: Medical school/education; Theological school/education.
Type of support: Support to graduates or students of specific schools; Undergraduate support.
Application information: Application form required.
   Deadline(s): Apr. 15
EIN: 316517313

2837
W. B. Munson Foundation
c/o JPMorgan Chase Bank, N.A.
P.O. Box 1308
Milwaukee, WI 53201
Application address: c/o JPMorgan Chase Bank, N.A., 8111 Preston Rd., Dallas, TX 75225, tel.: (214) 360-4391

Foundation type: Independent foundation
Limitations: Scholarships to seniors at Denison High School, TX.
Financial data: Year ended 12/31/2004. Assets, $7,999,982 (M); Expenditures, $443,884; Total giving, $382,433; Grants to individuals, 17 grants totaling $13,500 (high: $1,000, low: $500).
Type of support: Support to graduates or students of specific schools; Undergraduate support.
Application information: Applications not accepted.
EIN: 756015068

2838
William J. Munson Fund
c/o Bank of America, N.A.
P.O. Box 6768
Providence, RI 02940-6768
Contact: Alfred Morency, Chair.
Application address: 71 Scott Rd., Watertown, CT 06795, tel.: (203) 274-4288

Foundation type: Independent foundation
Limitations: Scholarships to residents of Watertown, CT. Only one award per family is granted.
Financial data: Year ended 12/31/2003. Assets, $1,773,312 (M); Expenditures, $107,297; Total giving, $80,648; Grants to individuals, 87 grants totaling $80,648 (high: $3,261, low: $8).
Type of support: Undergraduate support.
Application information: Application form required.
   Deadline(s): May 15 to June 15
EIN: 066024564

2839
Julia Blake Munster & Adele Blake Scholarship Trust
c/o Port Washington State Bank
206 N. Franklin St.
Port Washington, WI 53074
Application address: c/o Port Washington High School, Scholarship Comm., 427 W. Jackson St., Port Washington, WI 53074, tel.: (262) 268-5500

Foundation type: Independent foundation
Limitations: Scholarships to graduating seniors of Port Washington High School, WI.
Financial data: Year ended 05/31/2005. Assets, $695,324 (M); Expenditures, $35,278; Total giving, $28,000; Grants to individuals, 15 grants totaling $28,000 (high: $3,000, low: $1,000).
Type of support: Support to graduates or students of specific schools; Undergraduate support.
Application information: Contact trust for current application deadline/guidelines.
EIN: 396178832

2840
Duane & Evelyn Munter Charitable Trust
c/o Citizens State Bank
P.O. Box 4
Strawberry Point, IA 52076-0004

Foundation type: Operating foundation
Limitations: Scholarships to individuals in IA for higher education.
Financial data: Year ended 07/31/2003. Assets, $269,689 (M); Expenditures, $11,673; Total giving, $10,470; Grants to individuals, 12 grants totaling $8,899 (high: $804, low: $697).
Type of support: Undergraduate support.
Application information: Unsolicited requests for funds not accepted.
EIN: 421286829

2841
Murphy Education Program, Inc.
200 Peach St.
P.O. Box 7000
El Dorado, AR 71731-7000

Foundation type: Company-sponsored foundation
Limitations: Awards to teachers and students of the El Dorado School District, AR.
Financial data: Year ended 12/31/2004. Assets, $103,099 (M); Expenditures, $97,748; Total giving, $94,525.
Fields of interest: Education.
Type of support: Awards/prizes.
Application information: Applications not accepted.
EIN: 710814094

2842
The Murphy Foundation
Union Bldg.
El Dorado, AR 71730-6133
Application address: c/o Brett Williamson, Secy.-Treas., 200 N. Jefferson, Ste. 400, El Dorado, AR 71730, tel.: (870) 862-4961

Foundation type: Independent foundation
Limitations: Scholarships to students from southern AR.
Financial data: Year ended 04/30/2005. Assets, $57,925,340 (M); Expenditures, $2,134,999; Total giving, $1,937,880; Grants to individuals, 62 grants totaling $176,400 (high: $6,000, low: $1,000).
Type of support: Scholarships—to individuals.
Application information: Applications accepted.
   Initial approach: Letter.
   Deadline(s): Aug. 1
   Additional information: Application must also include copy of applicant's scholastic record.
Program description:
   Scholarship Program: Scholarships are awarded primarily for college level study. In the past, recipients have largely been local residents and received aid for personal expenses related to their education as well as tuition.
EIN: 716049826

2843
M. Catherine Murphy Memorial Fund
c/o First Columbia Bank & Trust Co.
11 W. Main St.
Bloomsburg, PA 17815 (570) 387-4609
Contact: John Thompson, Sr. V.P. & Trust Off., First Columbia Bank & Trust Co.

Foundation type: Independent foundation
Limitations: Interest-free student loans to residents of Catawissa, PA, who are graduates of Southern Columbia Area High School and attend Bloomsburg University, PA.
Financial data: Year ended 12/31/2004. Assets, $431,865 (M); Expenditures, $22,544; Total giving, $17,467; Loans to individuals, 6 loans totaling $17,467.
Type of support: Support to graduates or students of specific schools; Undergraduate support.
Application information: Applications accepted. Application form required.
   Additional information: Application must also include copy of parents' federal income tax return(s).
EIN: 236648433

2844
T. R. Murphy Residuary Trust
c/o Kincaid, Taylor & Geyer
50 N. 4th St.
Zanesville, OH 43701-1030 (740) 454-2591
Contact: R. William Geyer, Tr.

Foundation type: Independent foundation
Limitations: Scholarships to graduates of high schools in Muskingum County, OH. Scholarships may be renewed.
Financial data: Year ended 06/30/2005. Assets, $3,708,431 (M); Expenditures, $220,572; Total giving, $185,813; Grants to individuals, totaling $129,949.
Type of support: Support to graduates or students of specific schools; Undergraduate support.
Application information: Application form required.
   Deadline(s): Deadline May 1.
   Applicants should submit the following:
      1) Letter(s) of recommendation
      2) Financial information
      3) SAT
      4) ACT
      5) Transcripts
EIN: 316285970

2845
The Major Jeremiah P. Murphy Scholarship Foundation

c/o Home Loan & Investment Bank
1 Home Loan Plz., Ste. 3
Warwick, RI 02886-1765 (401) 739-8800
Contact: For scholarships: Rodrick Mortier

Foundation type: Independent foundation
Limitations: Scholarships to children of current and former Providence, RI, police officers.
Financial data: Year ended 12/31/2002.
Assets, $148,475 (M); Expenditures, $15,552;
Total giving, $14,032; Grants to individuals, 3 grants totaling $14,032 (high: $5,000, low: $4,032).
Fields of interest: Crime/law enforcement, police agencies.
Type of support: Employee-related scholarships.
Application information: Contact foundation for current application deadline/guidelines.
EIN: 050483640

2846
Dennis L. & Hildreth M. Murphy Scholarship Trust

c/o Corydon State Bank
201 W. Jackson St.
Corydon, IA 50060-1418
Application address: c/o William H. Miles, 107 W. Jackson, Corydon, IA 50060, tel.: (641) 872-2343

Foundation type: Independent foundation
Limitations: Scholarships to graduating seniors at Wayne Community High School, IA.
Financial data: Year ended 12/31/2004.
Assets, $880,862 (M); Expenditures, $52,729;
Total giving, $51,300; Grants to individuals, 34 grants totaling $51,300 (high: $3,400, low: $500).
Type of support: Support to graduates or students of specific schools; Undergraduate support.
Application information: Applications accepted throughout the year; Contact foundation for current application guidelines.
EIN: 421486268

2847
The Albert K. Murray Fine Arts Educational Fund

9665 Young America Rd.
Adamsville, OH 43802 (740) 796-4797
Contact: Marion C. Gilliland, Tr.

Foundation type: Independent foundation
Limitations: Scholarships to fine arts students.
Financial data: Year ended 12/31/2004.
Assets, $1,491,441 (M); Expenditures, $107,277; Total giving, $64,805; Grants to individuals, 36 grants totaling $64,805 (high: $4,100, low: $450).
Fields of interest: Arts.
Type of support: Scholarships—to individuals.
Application information: Applications not accepted.
EIN: 311404573

2848
William H. Murray Memorial Scholarship Trust Fund

c/o Bank of America, N.A.
P.O. Box 40200, NC FL9-100-10-19
Jacksonville, FL 32203-0200
Application address: c/o Daytona Beach Community College, Attn.: Financial Aid Office, 1200 W. International Speedway Blvd., Daytona Beach, FL 32114, tel.: (904) 255-8131

Foundation type: Independent foundation
Limitations: Scholarships to financially needy students enrolled in the nursing degree program at Daytona Beach Community College, FL.
Financial data: Year ended 04/30/2005.
Assets, $571,552 (M); Expenditures, $30,296;
Total giving, $21,300; Grants to individuals, 11 grants totaling $21,300 (high: $3,600, low: $300).
Fields of interest: Nursing school/education.
Type of support: Support to graduates or students of specific schools; Undergraduate support.
Application information: Applications accepted. Application form required.
  Additional information: Application forms available from the Student Financial Aid Office.
Program description:
  Scholarship Program: Recipients are chosen by the college nursing faculty on the basis of need and academic ability.
EIN: 596722136

2849
F. Leo Murray & Irene D. Murray Scholarship Fund

P.O. Box 250
Winchendon, MA 01475
Contact: Robert LaFortune, Tr.
Application address: 1 Summer Dr., Winchendon, MA 01475, tel.: (978) 297-2042

Foundation type: Operating foundation
Limitations: Scholarships to young men and women of Winchendon, MA.
Financial data: Year ended 12/31/2002.
Assets, $377,625 (M); Expenditures, $23,341;
Total giving, $17,500; Grants to individuals, 25 grants totaling $17,500 (high: $1,000, low: $500).
Type of support: Scholarships—to individuals.
Application information: Application form required.
  Deadline(s): Contact fund for deadline
EIN: 046635075

2850
Murray Trust

110 N. Marshall St.
Rock Rapids, IA 51246-1516
Application address: c/o Terry Tauz, Tr., Central Lyon Community School, 1010 S. Greene St., Rock Rapids, IA 51246

Foundation type: Independent foundation
Limitations: Scholarships to graduates of Central Lyon High School in Rock Rapids, IA.
Financial data: Year ended 12/31/2004.
Assets, $1,136,942 (M); Expenditures, $91,787;
Total giving, $51,775; Grants to individuals, 103 grants totaling $51,775 (high: $710, low: $310).
Type of support: Scholarships—to individuals;
Support to graduates or students of specific schools.
Application information: Application form required.
  Deadline(s): Apr. 30
  Applicants should submit the following:

1) Transcripts
2) Financial information
Additional information: Application must also include an affidavit of nonsupport if applicant is self-supporting.
EIN: 237181382

2851
The Music for Youth Foundation, Inc.

(formerly The New York Music For Youth Foundation, Inc.)
9 Murray St., 4th Fl.
New York, NY 10007 (646) 723-2713
Contact: Jon Marcus, Exec. Dir.
FAX: (212) 608-7780;
E-mail: info@musicforyouth.com; URL: http://www.musicforyouth.org

Foundation type: Public charity
Limitations: Scholarships to individuals, up to 22 years of age, with exceptional musical talent, to pursue musical careers, primarily in NY.
Publications: Annual report; Grants list; Informational brochure.
Financial data: Year ended 06/30/2004.
Assets, $312,598 (M); Expenditures, $467,271;
Total giving, $350,000; Grants to individuals, 2 grants totaling $50,000 (high: $25,000, low: $25,000).
Fields of interest: Music; Orchestra (symphony); Music composition.
Type of support: Scholarships—to individuals.
Application information: Applications accepted. Application form required.
  Initial approach: Telephone or e-mail.
  Deadline(s): Sept. 30
  Additional information: See Web site for additional information.
EIN: 133888983

2852
Music Institute of Chicago

(formerly Music Center of the North Shore)
300 Green Bay Rd.
Winnetka, IL 60093
Contact: Sel Kardan, Pres.
FAX: (847) 446-3876; E-mail: info@musicinst.org;
URL: http://www.musicinst.org

Foundation type: Public charity
Limitations: Scholarships to individuals for music study.
Publications: Annual report; Informational brochure (including application guidelines); Newsletter.
Financial data: Year ended 08/31/2004.
Assets, $12,006,992 (M); Expenditures, $5,106,026; Total giving, $257,949.
Fields of interest: Performing arts; Music; Art & music therapy.
Type of support: Scholarships—to individuals; Undergraduate support.
Application information:
  Initial approach: Telephone.
  Additional information: Contact foundation for current application deadline/guidelines.
EIN: 362374224

2853
Musical Research Society Endowment Fund, Inc.

(formerly Musical Research Society Endowment Foundation, Inc.)
804 S. Castle Rd.
Bartlesville, OK   74006-9023
Application address: c/o Diana Farris, P.O. Box 2105, Bartlesville, OK 74005, tel.: (918) 333-6719

Foundation type: Independent foundation
Limitations: Scholarships to college graduates and high school seniors for the study of music and summer music camp scholarships to students in grades 7-11. All applicants must be U.S. citizens and regional residents. See program description for further limitations.
Financial data: Year ended 06/30/2004. Assets, $0 (M); Expenditures, $5,689; Total giving, $3,740; Grants to individuals, 25 grants totaling $3,740 (high: $1,000, low: $50).
Fields of interest: Music; Performing arts, education.
Type of support: Awards/prizes; Graduate support; Undergraduate support.
Application information: Application form required.
  Deadline(s): Contact fund for deadline
  Additional information: Auditions required for all grants except Music Camp Scholarships and the Ruth Brush Composition Awards.
Program descriptions:
  Vocal Scholarship: One scholarship ($1,000-$1,650) to Inspiration Point Fine Arts Colony for tuition is awarded to a man or woman between the ages of 18 and 30 at the time of the audition. Auditions are held in conjunction with the Oklahoma Federation of Music Clubs Student and Young Artists Audition. They usually take place in Feb. in Oklahoma City.
  Stewart Graduate Grants: The first place $4,000 Stewart Grant and the second place $2,000 Stewart Grant are awarded to master's or doctorate degree candidates in piano or voice at all schools in OK, plus the University of Arkansas, Arkansas State University, University of North Texas, the Kansas City Conservatory of Music, University of Kansas, Kansas State University, and Wichita State University. A written application, current transcript showing at least a 3.0 GPA, a recommendation by a major professor, resume, list of repertoire, and a publicity photo are required. A nonrefundable $25 application fee must be paid by check to Musical Research Society Endowment Fund. Initial auditions are 15 minutes. Final auditions are 20 minutes, with judges choosing pieces from applicant's repertoire after applicant has performed his or her first choice. Applicants should have 30 minutes of material prepared for finals. Applicants must provide their own accompanist and two original copies of music for judges. Contact the scholarship committee for audition dates and locations. Former first place winners are ineligible.
  High School Grants: The $1,000 Stewart Grant and the Musical Research Society first place $500 and second place $250 grants are awarded to high school seniors of Bartlesville and Dewey high schools for the continued study of music in college. Auditions of 10-15 minutes are required. All music must be memorized. Applicants must supply judges with original copies of music. Application must include a letter of recommendation, biography, photograph, list of school and extracurricular activities and awards, and copy of audition program. Scholarship money will be sent directly to the college of enrollment after official notification is received. If music study is dropped, the award will be rescinded.
  Ruth Brush Composition Award: This competition with first place award of $50, and second place award of $25, is open to students in grades 7-12. The amount varies annually. Call chairperson for application details.
  Music Camp Scholarships: The ten $100 Stewart Summer Music Camp Scholarship Awards are given to Dewey or Bartlesville High School band, orchestra, and choir students in grades 7-11 who will be playing in the orchestra, band, or choir during the following school year. No audition is required. However, a letter of recommendation from a teacher is required. Recipients are chosen based on ability, leadership potential, attitude, dedication, teacher recommendations, and need. The awards are sent to the music camp at which the student is enrolled. Students should contact the foundation to find out which music camps are approved for award participation. Certain master classes are eligible for scholarships, especially those offered during the Oklahoma Mozart Festival held annually in Bartlesville.
EIN: 731282613

2854
Mustard Seed Foundation, Inc.

3330 N. Washington Blvd., Ste. 100
Arlington, VA   22201   (703) 524-5620
Contact: Brian Bakke, Regional Dir., North America
FAX: (703) 524-5643; URL: http://www.msfdn.org

Foundation type: Independent foundation
Limitations: Scholarships and fellowships to undergraduate students of top five universities and of Christian faith.
Publications: Application guidelines; Annual report.
Financial data: Year ended 12/31/2004. Assets, $12,337,734 (M); Expenditures, $6,100,771; Total giving, $4,804,253; Grants to individuals, 81 grants totaling $602,500 (high: $14,000, low: $3,015).
Type of support: Fellowships; Scholarships—to individuals; Graduate support; Doctoral support.
Application information: Applications accepted. Application form required.
  Additional information: Contact foundation for current application deadline.
Program descriptions:
  Harvey Fellows Program: Fellowships to Christian graduate students who possess a unique vision to impact society through their fields and who are pursuing graduate studies at the top five institutions in their disciplines in the U.S. or abroad. Through the fellowship, the foundation hopes to encourage recipients to integrate their faith and vocation and pursue leadership positions in strategic fields where Christians tend to be underrepresented.
  Theological Education: Scholarships to individuals at non-U.S. institutions who are pursuing degrees in theological education to prepare them for preaching, teaching, missions and evangelism.
EIN: 570748914

2855
Mutual Service Foundation Trust

2222 N. Cunningham Rd.
Indianapolis, IN   46224

Foundation type: Independent foundation
Limitations: Scholarships and aid to financially needy, self-supporting women residing in Marion County, IN. A limited amount of funds are available for welfare assistance.
Financial data: Year ended 12/31/2004. Assets, $426,668 (M); Expenditures, $25,731; Total giving, $21,525; Grants to individuals, 14 grants totaling $21,525 (high: $1,525, low: $500).
Fields of interest: Women; Economically disadvantaged.
Type of support: Scholarships—to individuals; Grants for special needs.
Application information: Applications not accepted.
EIN: 356047127

2856
My Brother's Keeper Foundation

9090 S. Sandy Pkwy.
Sandy, UT   84070
Contact: Leslie P. Layton, Tr.
Application address: 9090 Despain Way, Sandy, UT 84093

Foundation type: Independent foundation
Limitations: Scholarships to residents of Sandy, UT.
Financial data: Year ended 12/31/2004. Assets, $3,422 (M); Expenditures, $11,941; Total giving, $10,441; Grants to individuals, 13 grants totaling $10,441 (high: $2,500, low: $350).
Type of support: Undergraduate support.
Application information: Application form required.
  Initial approach: Letter.
  Deadline(s): 30 days after receipt of form
  Additional information: Contact foundation for further application guidelines.
Program description:
  Educational Program: Recipients must be enrolled in or accepted for enrollment at an institution of higher learning.
EIN: 870579029

2857
Myers Charitable Trust

c/o Wells Fargo Bank Nebraska, N.A.
1248 O St., 4th Fl., MAC N8032-042
Lincoln, NE   68508
Application address: c/o Anne Walters, Wells Fargo Bank Iowa, N.A., 203 W. 3rd St., 4th Fl., Davenport, IA 52801, tel.: (563) 383-3200

Foundation type: Independent foundation
Limitations: Scholarships primarily to students from IL, who are seeking a degree in medicine, dentistry, nursing or law in Geneseo, IL School District No. 228.
Financial data: Year ended 12/31/2004. Assets, $1,320,542 (M); Expenditures, $79,833; Total giving, $62,002; Grants to individuals, 7 grants totaling $34,002 (high: $5,439, low: $1,368).
Fields of interest: Dental school/education; Law school/education; Medical school/education; Nursing school/education.
Type of support: Graduate support.
Application information: Application form required.
  Initial approach: Telephone.
  Additional information: Applications accepted throughout the year.
EIN: 367233377

2858

Myers Church Scholarship

c/o Fifth Third Bank
P.O. Box 3636
Grand Rapids, MI 49501-3636 (888) 218-7878
Application address: c/o Rev. William Collins, 6108
Barnhart Rd., Ludington, MI 49431, tel.: (616)
843-9275

Foundation type: Independent foundation
Limitations: Scholarships to graduates of Mason
County, MI, high schools and to individuals whose
parents reside in Mason County, MI.
Financial data: Year ended 12/31/2002.
Assets, $155,536 (M); Expenditures, $12,118;
Total giving, $9,600; Grants to individuals, totaling
$9,600.
Type of support: Support to graduates or students
of specific schools; Undergraduate support.
Application information: Application form required.
Deadline(s): Mar. 1
Additional information: Application must also
includie two references and personal
statement.
EIN: 383288570

2859

G. Myers Memorial Scholarship Trust

c/o National City Bank
P.O. Box 94651
Cleveland, OH 44101-4651
Application address: c/o Guidance Dept.,
Logansport High School, 1 Berry Ln., Logansport, IN
46947

Foundation type: Independent foundation
Limitations: Scholarships to students who have
attended Logansport High School, IN, for the last
two years of high school, for higher education.
Publications: IRS Form 990-PF.
Financial data: Year ended 12/31/2003.
Assets, $219,213 (M); Expenditures, $14,411;
Total giving, $12,000; Grants to individuals, 7
grants totaling $12,000 (high: $3,000, low: $750).
Type of support: Support to graduates or students
of specific schools; Undergraduate support.
Application information: Applications accepted.
Application form required.
Deadline(s): Mar. 22
Applicants should submit the following:
1) Letter(s) of recommendation
2) Financial information
3) Transcripts
Additional information: Application must also
include parents' and student's tax returns,
and list of school and community activities.
Program description:
Scholarship Program: Scholarships of up to
$3,000 are renewable for up to three years
provided the recipient is a full-time student,
maintains a cumulative G.P.A. of at least 2.8 on a
4.0 scale and submits a copy of last semester's
grades to National City Bank. Initial criteria for
selection include character, financial need,
scholastic achievement and participation in school
and community activities.
EIN: 356648858

2860

Malcolm W. & Anna G. Myers Scholarship Fund

c/o Wachovia Bank, N.A.
100 N. Main St., 13th Fl.
Winston-Salem, NC 27150
Application address: c/o Brenton Hake, V.P., 12 E.
Market St., York, PA 17401-1206

Foundation type: Independent foundation
Limitations: Scholarships to graduating seniors
from Hanover and Southwestern, PA.
Financial data: Year ended 12/31/2004.
Assets, $3,177,983 (M); Expenditures,
$173,751; Total giving, $152,000; Grants to
individuals, 76 grants totaling $152,000 (high:
$2,000, low: $2,000).
Type of support: Scholarships—to individuals.
Application information: Contact fund for current
application deadline/guidelines.
EIN: 237879656

2861

The N Foundation, Inc.

c/o Eisman, Zucker, et al., LLP
120 Bloomingdale Rd. Ste 402
White Plains, NY 10605

Foundation type: Independent foundation
Limitations: Scholarships to residents of
Larchmont, NY.
Financial data: Year ended 08/31/2004.
Assets, $1 (M); Expenditures, $7,600; Total giving,
$7,600; Grants to individuals, 10 grants totaling
$7,600 (high: $800, low: $800).
Type of support: Scholarships—to individuals.
Application information: Applications not
accepted.
EIN: 133361672

2862

NAACP Legal Defense and Education Fund, Inc.

99 Hudson St., Ste. 1600
New York, NY 10013-2815 (212) 965-2200
URL: http://www.naacpldf.org

Foundation type: Public charity
Limitations: Scholarships to undergraduate and
law students.
Publications: Annual report; Financial statement;
Informational brochure (including application
guidelines); Newsletter.
Financial data: Year ended 06/30/2004.
Assets, $37,937,085 (M); Expenditures,
$7,050,594; Total giving, $42,000; Grants to
individuals, 7 grants totaling $42,000.
Fields of interest: Law school/education; African
Americans/Blacks.
Type of support: Graduate support; Undergraduate
support.
Application information: Application form required.
Initial approach: Letter.
Deadline(s): Apr. 1
Program description:
Herber Lehman Educational Program: Provides
scholarships to undergraduate and law students.
Also, the fund offers a limited number of $3,000
scholarships to African American students who are
entering or are enrolled in ABA approved law
schools. Awards are limited to U.S. citizens.
Applicants who have a well-defined interest in law
and/or civil rights, in addition to meeting the highly
competitive academic criteria, are given preference.
EIN: 131655255

2863

NAC Scholarship Fund, Inc.

1 New Whale St.
Nantucket, MA 02554

Foundation type: Independent foundation
Limitations: Scholarships to individuals.
Financial data: Year ended 03/31/2005.
Assets, $1,503,455 (M); Expenditures, $22,432;
Total giving, $13,000; Grants to individuals, 13
grants totaling $13,000 (high: $1,000, low:
$1,000).
Fields of interest: Higher education.
Type of support: Scholarships—to individuals.
Application information: Applications not
accepted.
EIN: 043518227

2864

Stella M. Nelson Nadeau & Louise E. Nelson Scholarship Foundation

(formerly Stella M. Nelson Nadeau & Louise E.
Nelson Senft Scholarship Foundation)
c/o Davidson Trust Co.
P.O. Box 152
Kalispell, MT 59903-0152

Foundation type: Independent foundation
Limitations: Scholarships to graduates of Flathead
High School, MT.
Financial data: Year ended 12/31/2004.
Assets, $133,572 (M); Expenditures, $10,163;
Total giving, $7,500; Grants to individuals, 3 grants
totaling $7,500 (high: $2,500, low: $2,500).
Type of support: Support to graduates or students
of specific schools.
Application information: Application form required.
Deadline(s): Mid-Apr.
EIN: 816087287

2865

Robert T. Nahas Educational Scholarship Foundation

102 S. 17th St., Ste. 300
Boise, ID 83702
Application address: c/o Scholarship Comm.,
20630 Patio Dr., Castro Valley, CA 94546

Foundation type: Independent foundation
Limitations: Scholarships to one male and one
female graduating senior from the following high
schools in ID: Caldwell, Contennial, Greenleaf,
Homedale, Kuna, Marsing, Melba, Meridian,
Middleton, Mountain View, Nampa, Nampa
Christian, Rimrock, Skyview, and Vallivue.
Financial data: Year ended 11/30/2004.
Assets, $179,386 (M); Expenditures, $11,615;
Total giving, $3,500; Grants to individuals, 3 grants
totaling $3,500 (high: $1,250, low: $1,000).
Type of support: Support to graduates or students
of specific schools; Undergraduate support.
Application information: Application form required.
Initial approach: Letter.
Deadline(s): Mar. 11
Applicants should submit the following:
1) Transcripts
2) Letter(s) of recommendation
Additional information: Application must also
include record of community service, and a
biographical essay; Interviews required.
EIN: 820392827

2866
Nansemond Charitable Foundation, Inc.
453 W. Washington St.
Suffolk, VA   23434   (757) 539-3421
Contact: Jack W. Webb, Jr., V.P.

Foundation type: Company-sponsored foundation
Limitations: Scholarships to high school graduates of Nansemond High School, Lakeland High School and Nansemond Academy, VA.
Financial data: Year ended 08/31/2004.
Assets, $233,628 (M); Expenditures, $21,570; Total giving, $21,488; Grants to individuals, 11 grants totaling $10,540 (high: $1,000, low: $540).
Type of support: Scholarships—to individuals; Support to graduates or students of specific schools.
Application information: Applications accepted. Application form required.
  Deadline(s): May 15
  Additional information: Application must also include letter outlining financial need.
EIN: 541291449

2867
Naples Yacht Club Blue Gavel Scholarship Fund
700 14th Ave. S.
Naples, FL   34102   (239) 262-6648
Contact: Joseph Schoenforf, Pres.

Foundation type: Public charity
Limitations: Scholarships to students for higher education.
Financial data: Year ended 12/31/2003.
Assets, $374,573 (M); Expenditures, $81,218; Total giving, $77,600; Grants to individuals, 56 grants totaling $53,600 (high: $3,000, low: $500).
Fields of interest: Higher education.
Type of support: Scholarships—to individuals.
Application information: Applications accepted.
  Initial approach: Letter.
  Applicants should submit the following:
    1) Transcripts
EIN: 593467966

2868
Richard T. Naples, Sr. Educational Foundation, Inc.
c/o Richard T. Naples, Sr.
2665 N. Main St.
Hubbard, OH   44425-3247   (330) 534-5145

Foundation type: Independent foundation
Limitations: Scholarships to individuals in OH.
Financial data: Year ended 06/30/2005.
Assets, $18,427 (M); Expenditures, $11,304; Total giving, $10,000; Grants to individuals, 20 grants totaling $10,000 (high: $500, low: $500).
Type of support: Scholarships—to individuals.
Application information: Applications not accepted.
EIN: 341851988

2869
The Nara Bank Scholarship Foundation
3701 Wilshire Blvd., Ste. 220
Los Angeles, CA   90010   (213) 427-6327
Contact: Jenny Mun
URL: http://www.narabank.com/n_scholar.asp

Foundation type: Company-sponsored foundation
Limitations: Scholarships to individuals residing in communities served by Nara Bank, N.A. Some preference given to students of Korean descent.
Financial data: Year ended 12/31/2004.
Assets, $19,959 (M); Expenditures, $133,337; Total giving, $88,000; Grants to individuals, 88 grants totaling $88,000 (high: $1,000, low: $1,000).
Fields of interest: Asians/Pacific Islanders.
Type of support: Undergraduate support.
Application information: Applications accepted. Application form required.
  Deadline(s): Nov. 13
  Applicants should submit the following:
    1) Transcripts
    2) Letter(s) of recommendation
  Additional information: Application must also include tax return. Applicants notified by Dec. 20.
Program description:
  Scholarship Program: Applicants must be U.S. citizens or permanent residents, be enrolled in an accredited four-year college, and have a GPA of 3.5 or higher.
EIN: 912156704

2870
NASA College Scholarship Fund, Inc.
c/o NASA Johnson Space Ctr.
2101 NASA Rd. 1, Mail Code AH12
Houston, TX   77058-3696
Contact: Doug Ming

Foundation type: Independent foundation
Limitations: Undergraduate scholarships to dependents of current and former NASA employees to study engineering and science at U.S. colleges and universities. Scholarships are a maximum of $2,000 per year, or $8,000 over six years.
Financial data: Year ended 12/31/2004.
Assets, $513,566 (M); Expenditures, $42,782; Total giving, $40,000; Grants to individuals, 26 grants totaling $40,000 (high: $2,000, low: $1,000).
Fields of interest: Engineering school/education; Science.
Type of support: Employee-related scholarships.
Application information: Application form required.
  Initial approach: Letter or telephone.
  Deadline(s): Mar. 31
  Additional information: Application must also include academic records.
EIN: 760039071

2871
NASB Foundation, Inc.
(formerly North American Savings Bank Foundation, Inc.)
c/o Barbara Cornwell
12498 S. 71 Hwy.
Grandview, MO   64030-1733   (816) 765-2200

Foundation type: Company-sponsored foundation
Limitations: Scholarships to graduating seniors in communities where North American Savings Bank, F.S.B. conducts business, who intend to attend any public college, community college, or accredited trade school in MO.
Financial data: Year ended 09/30/2004.
Assets, $0 (M); Expenditures, $35,850; Total giving, $35,835; Grants to individuals, 11 grants totaling $35,835 (high: $9,000, low: $294).
Fields of interest: Vocational education.
Type of support: Technical education support; Undergraduate support.

Application information: Application form required.
  Deadline(s): Contact foundation for deadline
  Applicants should submit the following:
    1) Letter(s) of recommendation
    2) Transcripts
  Additional information: Applications available through high school administrators.
EIN: 431796549

2872
Clayton Nash Scholarship Fund
c/o Bank of America, N.A.
P.O. Box 6767
Providence, RI   02940-6767
Application address: Mary Kelly, Trust Off., c/o Bank of America, N.A., 100 Federal St., Boston, MA 02110

Foundation type: Independent foundation
Limitations: Scholarships to graduates of Weymouth North and Weymouth South high schools, MA, for higher education.
Financial data: Year ended 05/31/2004.
Assets, $240,459 (M); Expenditures, $14,364; Total giving, $10,500.
Type of support: Support to graduates or students of specific schools; Undergraduate support.
Application information: Applications by letter accepted throughout the year.
EIN: 222480259

2873
Nation Foundation (Corporation)
P.O. Box 180849
Dallas, TX   75218   (214) 388-5751
Contact: James H. Nation, Dir.

Foundation type: Independent foundation
Limitations: Scholarships to individuals for higher education.
Financial data: Year ended 01/31/2005.
Assets, $5,061,740 (M); Expenditures, $374,806; Total giving, $374,798; Grants to individuals, 63 grants totaling $264,628 (high: $25,679, low: $500).
Fields of interest: Higher education.
Type of support: Scholarships—to individuals.
Application information: Applications by letter outlining financial need accepted throughout the year.
EIN: 752791965

2874
National Action Council for Minorities in Engineering, Inc.
(also known as NACME)
440 Hamilton Ave., Ste. 302
White Plains, NY   10601-1813   (914) 539-4010
Contact: John C. Eppolito, V.P. and C.F.O.
FAX: (914) 539-4032;
E-mail: jeppolito@nacme.org; URL: http://www.nacme.org

Foundation type: Public charity
Limitations: Scholarships and fellowships to minority undergraduate engineering students. The council also provides awards and prizes to high school seniors who have demonstrated excellence in pre-college math and science.
Publications: Annual report; Newsletter.
Financial data: Year ended 08/31/2003.
Assets, $13,440,410 (M); Expenditures, $9,709,238; Total giving, $6,055,983; Grants to

individuals, 510 grants totaling $6,055,983 (high: $35,000, low: $3,500).
Fields of interest: Engineering school/education; Environment; Minorities; African Americans/ Blacks; Hispanics/Latinos; Native Americans/ American Indians.
Type of support: Fellowships; Research; Awards/ grants by nomination only; Awards/prizes; Undergraduate support.
Application information: Application form required.
 Deadline(s): Vary
 Additional information: Applicants must be U.S. citizens or permanent residents; Fellowship applications are mailed to selected institutions in Dec.; See Web site for further application and program information.
Program descriptions:
 TechForce Pre-Engineering Prize: High school seniors with outstanding records and participation in pre-college math and science programs are eligible to compete for one of the 10 prizes awarded annually. Students must be nominated by directors of university-based programs, or those recognized by the National Association of Pre-College Directors. The scholar receives a $1,000 award, a plaque, and a paid trip to the NACME Forum to receive the award and make a presentation to an audience. Those who maintain a GPA of 3.0 also receive a renewable award for books and supplies. Winners are also eligible for: William Randolph Hearst Scholarships, 3M Engineering Award, and the Corporate Scholars Program.
 Bechtel Undergraduate Fellowship Award: This award is a financial support program that encourages and recognizes high academic achievement of students interested in pursuing a corporate career in a construction-related engineering discipline. The award is accompanied by internship and mentoring opportunities. The scholarship provides up to $10,000 over two years to engineering students from underrepresented minority population groups majoring in a construction-related engineering field. Students may apply during their second semester in the sophomore year.
 Elizabeth and Stephen D. Bechtel, Jr. Foundation Fellows: Provides up to $10,000 over two years to engineering students from underrepresented minority population groups. The award must be supplemented by work-study or other student contributions. Students may apply during their second semester in the sophomore year.
 Corporate Scholars Program: Offers high-performing, first-year students financial assistance, corporate mentoring, paid summer internships and professional leadership development. Full-time students with a GPA of 2.75 or better after the first semester, attending selected institutions, may apply. Scholars receive annual awards of up to $5,000 a year, based on academic performance, and attend special NACME leadership development conferences. Applications are available in Nov. and due by Feb.12.
 W. Lincoln Hawkins Undergraduate Research Fellowship: Honors an extraordinary scientist and engineer for her/his remarkable life and career. The fellowship offers an exceptional opportunity to outstanding African American, Latino, and Native American chemical engineering students by providing early research experience, one-on-one faculty mentoring, and exposure to leading-edge technologies. The award provides up to $20,000 over two years: $10,000 to be applied to a research project and $10,000 to be applied toward educational costs. Students may apply during their second semester in the sophomore year and must have a minimum GPA of 3.5.

 Philip D. Reed Undergraduate Award in Environmental Engineering: This award is designed to increase access to careers in this area among African American, Latino, and American Indian students. The award provides $10,000 payable over two years. Undergraduate students may apply during the second semester of the sophomore year. Applicants must have a GPA of 3.0 and a demonstrated interest in environmental engineering.
 Sustaining Fellow Award: Provides up to $20,000 scholarships payable over four years. Undergraduate engineering students from underrepresented population groups may apply during their freshman year after completing one semester. Applicants must have a minimum GPA of 3.0.
EIN: 521190664

2875

National Association of Insurance Women (International) Education Foundation

(also known as NAIW (International))
6528 E. 101st St.
PMB 750
Tulsa, OK 74182 (800) 766-6249
Contact: Billie Sleet, Exec. Dir.
Application address: P.O. Box 4410, Tulsa, OK 74159
FAX: (918) 743-1968; E-mail: joinnaiw@naiw.org; URL: http://www.naiw.org

Foundation type: Independent foundation
Limitations: Scholarships to individuals majoring in insurance/risk management.
Financial data: Year ended 06/30/2004. Assets, $833,053 (M); Expenditures, $256,882; Total giving, $42,425; Grants to individuals, 41 grants totaling $42,425 (high: $2,450, low: $78).
Fields of interest: Business school/education.
Type of support: Scholarships—to individuals; Undergraduate support.
Application information: Applications accepted. Application form required. Application form available on the grantmaker's Web site.
 Initial approach: E-mail.
 Deadline(s): Apr. 10
 Applicants should submit the following:
  1) Letter(s) of recommendation
 Additional information: See Web site for full program descriptions.
Program description:
 Educational Program:
  · College Scholarship in the Fields of Insurance/Risk Management
  · Professional Scholarship in the Fields of Insurance/Risk Management
EIN: 731429257

2876

National Charity League, Inc.

23545 Crenshaw Blvd., Ste. 103
Torrance, CA 90505-5280 (310) 784-2336
Contact: Marty Hunt, Pres.
URL: http://www.nationalcharityleague.org/

Foundation type: Public charity
Limitations: Scholarships to high school students who reside in CA for higher education.
Financial data: Year ended 05/31/2004. Assets, $283,362 (M); Expenditures, $161,260; Total giving, $103,700; Grants to individuals, 34 grants totaling $54,500 (high: $3,000, low: $500).
Type of support: Undergraduate support.

Application information: Contact foundation for current application deadline/guidelines.
EIN: 952136037

2877

National Charity League-Newport Chapter

540 W. 19th St.
Costa Mesa, CA 92627-2748 (949) 487-3637
Contact: Trudi Kern, Pres.

Foundation type: Public charity
Limitations: Scholarships to residents of CA for higher education.
Financial data: Year ended 05/31/2003. Assets, $554,099 (M); Expenditures, $296,738; Total giving, $162,720; Grants to individuals, totaling $12,250.
Type of support: Undergraduate support.
Application information: Contact foundation for current application deadline/guidelines.
EIN: 966055016

2878

National Council of Teachers of Mathematics

(also known as NCTM's Mathematics Education Trust (MET))
1906 Association Dr.
Reston, VA 20191-1502 (703) 620-9840
Contact: James M. Rubillo, Exec. Dir.
FAX: (703) 476-2970; E-mail: exec@nctm.org; URL: http://www.nctm.org/about/met

Foundation type: Public charity
Limitations: Grants to pre-K to 12th grade mathematics teachers for program development.
Publications: Application guidelines; Annual report; Grants list; Informational brochure.
Financial data: Year ended 05/31/2003. Assets, $21,169,455 (M); Expenditures, $18,197,842; Total giving, $377,196; Grants to individuals, totaling $14,302.
Fields of interest: Elementary/secondary education; Elementary school/education; Teacher school/education; Education; Mathematics.
Type of support: Program development; Research; Awards/prizes; Stipends.
Application information: Applications accepted. Application form required. Application form available on the grantmaker's Web site.
 Deadline(s): Dec. 5 for NCTM MET Awards; Jan. 9 for Toyota Time.
 Applicants should submit the following:
  1) Budget Information
 Additional information: See Web site for complete application guidelines.
Program descriptions:
 Edward G. Begle Grant for Classroom-Based Research: Provides up to $8,000 to support collaborative classroom-based research in precollege mathematics education.
 Mary Dolciani Grants for Grades 7-12 Teachers: Grants of up to $2,000 are provided to persons currently working at the grades 7-12 level to improve their own professional competence as classroom teachers of mathematics.
 Ernest Duncan Grants for Grades Pre-K to 6 Teachers: Grants of up to $2,000 are provided to persons currently working at the grades Pre-K to 6 level to improve their own professional competence as classroom teachers of mathematics.
 E. Glenadine Gibb Grants for Implementing the NCTM Teachers: Grants of up to $2,000 are provided to grades Pre-K to 12 teachers to carry out

a plan that implements some aspect of the NCTM standards in their own classrooms.

Future Leaders Annual Meeting Support (FLAMeS) Project Awards: Up to $1,000 is provided for travel, subsistence expenses, and substitute teacher costs of full-time mathematics teachers in grades K to 12 who have never attended an NCTM annual meeting, are NCTM members, and have taught three to ten years.

NCTM Lifetime Achievement Awards for Distinguished Service to Mathematics Education: Awards are designed to honor members of NCTM who have exhibited a lifetime of achievement in mathematics education. The awards are presented annually following a nomination and selection process.

Theoni Pappas Incentive Grants for Grades 9 to 12 Teachers: Grants of up to $2,000 are provided to grades 9 to 12 teachers to develop mathematical enrichment materials or lessons detailing an innovative teaching unit they have implemented in their own classroom.

Isabelle P. Rucker Awards for Future Teachers: Provides up to $1,000 for travel and subsistence expenses to help support attendance at an NCTM annual or regional meeting by full-time students who are preparing to be precollege mathematics teachers.

Dale Seymour Scholarships for Grades Pre-K to 12 Teachers: Scholarships of up to $2,000 are provided to grades Pre-K to 12 teachers to improve their own professional competence as classroom teachers of mathematics.

Toyota's Investment in Mathematics Excellence (Toyota TIME) Grants for Grades K to 12 Teachers: Grants of up to $10,000 each will be awarded to up to thirty-five teachers within the U.S., District of Columbia, Puerto Rico, and/or U.S. territory with three years experience teaching grades K to 12.

John and Stacey Wahl Grants for Grades Pre-K to 8 Teachers: Grants of up to $2,000 are awarded to Pre-K to 8 teachers to develop a project that will enable students to better appreciate and understand some aspect of geometry that is consistent with the NCTM standards.

EIN: 526057004

2879
National Fish and Wildlife Foundation

1120 Connecticut Ave., N.W., Ste. 900
Washington, DC   20036   (202) 857-0166
Contact: Jeff Trandahl, Exec. Dir.
Additional tel.: (503) 417-8700, ext. 21
FAX: (202) 857-0162; URL: http://www.nfwf.org/

Foundation type: Public charity
Limitations: Scholarships to graduate and undergraduate students for education in environmental science, natural resource management, biology, public policy, geography, political science, or related fields.
Publications: Application guidelines; Annual report; Grants list; Informational brochure; Newsletter.
Financial data: Year ended 09/30/2004.
Assets, $197,940,906 (M); Expenditures, $44,090,921; Total giving, $35,634,847.
Fields of interest: Natural resources; Environmental education; Science, public policy; Biological sciences; Political science.
Type of support: Graduate support; Undergraduate support.
Application information: Applications accepted. Application form required.
Deadline(s): Jan. 14
Applicants should submit the following:
1) Letter(s) of recommendation
2) Essay

Additional information: See Web site for further application and program information.
Program description:
Student Scholarship Awards: Awards up to ten scholarships of up to $10,000 each to cover students' expenses for tuition, fees, books, room and board and other expenses directly related to their studies. Awards are based on merit and take into consideration the students' academic achievements and their ability and commitment to develop innovative solutions that are designed to address real and pressing issues affecting fish, wildlife and plant conservation efforts. To be eligible for consideration, a student must be a U.S. citizen at least 21 years of age and enrolled in an accredited institution of higher education in the U.S. while pursuing a graduate or undergraduate degree (sophomores and juniors in the current academic year only) in environmental science, natural resource management, biology, public policy, geography, political science, or related disciplines. For further information see Web site, www.nfwf.org/budscholarship/index.cfm.
EIN: 521384139

2880
National Foundation, Inc.

2925 Professional Pl., Ste. 201
Colorado Springs, CO   80904-8105
E-mail: nfi@thefoundations.org; URL: http://www.thefoundations.org

Foundation type: Public charity
Limitations: Scholarships to individuals.
Publications: Financial statement; Informational brochure; Newsletter; Program policy statement.
Financial data: Year ended 12/31/2003.
Assets, $14,919,378 (M); Expenditures, $918,083; Total giving, $693,081.
Type of support: Scholarships—to individuals.
Application information: Applications not accepted.
EIN: 541230512

2881
National Headache Foundation

820 N. Orleans St., Ste. 217
Chicago, IL   60610   (888) 643-5552
Contact: Carolyn Smith, Exec. Asst.
E-mail: info@headaches.org; URL: http://www.headaches.org

Foundation type: Public charity
Limitations: Scholarships by nomination only to a worthy candidate for study in a program related to headache research.
Publications: Grants list; Informational brochure; Newsletter.
Financial data: Year ended 07/31/2004.
Assets, $7,569,611 (M); Expenditures, $2,319,570; Total giving, $38,938; Grants to individuals, 4 grants totaling $38,938.
Fields of interest: Medical research.
Type of support: Awards/grants by nomination only.
Application information: Applications not accepted.
Additional information: Unsolicited requests for funds not considered or acknowledged.
EIN: 237073022

2882
National Healthcare Scholars Foundation

(formerly United American Healthcare Foundation)
300 River Pl., Rm. 4700
Detroit, MI   48207   (313) 393-4549
Contact: J.V. Combs, M.D., Pres.
Additional tel.: (313) 393-7944
FAX: (313) 393-3394; E-mail: info@nhsfonline.org; URL: http://www.nhsfonline.org/

Foundation type: Independent foundation
Limitations: Scholarships by nomination only to minority students in health-care fields at participating schools. Preference is given to financially needy students. See program description for a list of participating schools.
Publications: Biennial report (including application guidelines); Grants list; Informational brochure.
Financial data: Year ended 09/30/2004.
Assets, $1,528 (M); Expenditures, $159,261; Total giving, $92,000.
Fields of interest: Medical school/education; Nursing school/education; Health care; Minorities.
Type of support: Scholarships—to individuals; Support to graduates or students of specific schools; Awards/grants by nomination only.
Application information:
Deadline(s): Contact foundation for current nomination deadline/guidelines
Additional information: Recipients are nominated by the Dean and/or financial aid officer of participating schools.
Program description:
Scholarship Program: The following schools submit nominations: Charles R. Drew University of Medicine & Science, CA; Georgetown University, School of Medicine, DC; Howard University College of Medicine, DC; Meharry Medical College, TN; Morehouse School of Medicine, GA; North Carolina Central University, Dept. of Nursing; Oakland University School of Nursing, CA; Spelman College, GA; University of Detroit Mercy, McAuley School of Nursing, MI; University of Memphis, Loewenberg School of Nursing, TN; Wayne State University College of Nursing, MI; Wayne State University School of Medicine, MI. Medical students receive $7,500 per school year, graduate nursing students receive $2,500 per school year, and undergraduate nursing students receive $1,500 per school year. Scholarships are renewable providing the student maintains a good academic standing.
EIN: 382894517

2883
National Intercollegiate Rodeo Foundation, Inc.

2316 Eastgate St. N., Ste. 160
Walla Walla, WA   99362-1576
Contact: Timothy L. Corfield, Pres.

Foundation type: Independent foundation
Limitations: Scholarships to individuals attending a National Intercollegiate Rodeo Association member college who maintain a GPA of at least 3.0, and who meet state financial assistance qualifications.
Financial data: Year ended 06/30/2004.
Assets, $161,361 (M); Expenditures, $57,163; Total giving, $26,100; Grants to individuals, 19 grants totaling $26,100 (high: $3,000, low: $150).
Fields of interest: Athletics/sports, equestrianism.
Type of support: Support to graduates or students of specific schools; Undergraduate support.
Application information: Application form required.
Initial approach: Letter.
Deadline(s): May 1
EIN: 911659631

2884
National Italian American Foundation, Inc.
Peter Secchia Bldg.
1860 19th St., N.W.
Washington, DC 20009-5501 (202) 387-0600
Contact: John Salamone, Exec. Dir.
FAX: (202) 387-0800; E-mail: info@niaf.org;
URL: http://www.niaf.org/scholarships

Foundation type: Public charity
Limitations: Undergraduate, graduate, and doctoral scholarships to students of Italian-American descent in any field of study; or to students of any ethnic background majoring in Italian language, Italian studies, Italian-American studies or a related field.
Financial data: Year ended 12/31/2003.
Assets, $6,529,555 (M); Expenditures, $6,836,817; Total giving, $3,884,058; Grants to individuals, totaling $2,091,314.
Fields of interest: Language (foreign).
Type of support: Graduate support; Undergraduate support; Doctoral support.
Application information: Application form available on the grantmaker's Web site.
  Deadline(s): Apr. 30
  Additional information: Completion of online application required.
Program description:
  Scholarship Program: Awards range from $2,000 to $5,000. Criteria for selection include academic merit, financial need, and community service.
EIN: 521071723

2885
National Kidney Foundation of Connecticut
2139 Silas Deane Hwy., Ste. 208
Rocky Hill, CT 06067-2336 (860) 257-3770
Contact: Kimberly Hathaway, C.E.O.
FAX: (860) 257-3429; E-mail: info@kidneyct.org;
URL: http://www.kidneyct.org

Foundation type: Public charity
Limitations: Scholarships to dialysis and kidney transplant patients, their dependents, and individuals with Childhood Nephrotic Syndrome, who reside in CT.
Financial data: Year ended 06/30/2005.
Assets, $660,178 (M); Expenditures, $103,253; Total giving, $40,062; Grants to individuals, totaling $40,062.
Fields of interest: Kidney diseases.
Type of support: Undergraduate support.
Application information: Application form required.
  Deadline(s): June 6
EIN: 060792956

2886
National Kidney Foundation of Indiana, Inc.
911 E. 86th St., Ste. 100
Indianapolis, IN 46240-1840 (317) 722-5640
Contact: Margie Fort, Exec. Dir.
FAX: (317) 722-5650; E-mail: nkfi@myvine.com;
Additional tel.: (800) 382-9971; URL: http://www.kidneyindiana.org

Foundation type: Public charity
Limitations: Scholarships for higher education to dialysis and kidney transplant patients residing in IN.
Financial data: Year ended 06/30/2005.
Assets, $623,717 (M); Expenditures,

$1,215,100; Total giving, $425,506; Grants to individuals, totaling $425,506.
Fields of interest: Kidney diseases.
Type of support: Technical education support; Undergraduate support.
Application information: Application form required.
  Initial approach: E-mail.
  Deadline(s): Contact foundation for application deadline
Program description:
  Larry Smock Scholarship: Provides scholarships to IN undergraduates who are on dialysis or have received kidney transplants, and wish to pursue higher education in an academic or monitored occupational setting. Applicants must have a high school diploma or its equivalent.
EIN: 351180274

2887
National Kidney Foundation of Maine
630 Congress St.
P.O. Box 1134
Portland, ME 04104 (207) 772-7270
Contact: Tammy Atwood, Exec. Dir.
FAX: (207) 772-4202; E-mail: info@kidneyme.org;
Toll-free tel.: (800) 639-7220; URL: http://www.kidneyme.org

Foundation type: Public charity
Limitations: Scholarships to kidney patients as well as immediate family members of patients residing in ME.
Publications: Newsletter.
Financial data: Year ended 06/30/2005.
Assets, $124,854 (M); Expenditures, $495,376; Total giving, $62,813; Grants to individuals, totaling $62,813.
Fields of interest: Kidney diseases.
Type of support: Undergraduate support.
Application information: Applications accepted.
  Deadline(s): May 15
  Additional information: Contact foundation for guidelines.
Program description:
  Scholarship Program: Applications are available through Dialysis Unit Social Workers and the NKFM office. Applicants must either be currently attending accredited institutions of higher learning or have proof of acceptance.
EIN: 010318150

2888
National Kidney Foundation of Massachusetts, Rhode Island, New Hampshire and Vermont, Inc.
11 Vanderbilt Ave., Ste. 105
Norwood, MA 02062 (781) 278-0222
Contact: BJ Weiss, C.E.O.
FAX: (781) 278-0333;
E-mail: bjweiss@kidneyhealth.org; Additional tel.:
(800) 542-4001; URL: http://www.kidneyhealth.org

Foundation type: Public charity
Limitations: Scholarships to undergraduate and/or graduate students from MA, RI, NH, or VT who are afflicted by or are first degree relatives of someone afflicted by a kidney disease. Also offers summer research opportunities for graduating seniors with an interest in the medical field.
Publications: Annual report; Informational brochure; Newsletter.
Financial data: Year ended 06/30/2003.
Assets, $374,640 (M); Expenditures,

$1,214,253; Total giving, $40,000; Grant to an individual, 1 grant totaling $35,000.
Fields of interest: Medical school/education; Kidney diseases; Kidney research; Minorities.
Type of support: Research; Graduate support; Undergraduate support.
Application information: Application form required.
  Deadline(s): Mar. 12 for Academic Award
  Applicants should submit the following:
    1) Transcripts
    2) Letter(s) of recommendation
  Additional information: Application must also include renal patient information, and financial form.
Program descriptions:
  Academic Award: Awards 13 $700 scholarships annually to students from MA, RI, NH and VT who are pursuing a postsecondary education and are afflicted by or are first-degree relatives of someone afflicted by a kidney disease.
  Summer Science Research Opportunity: Summer research opportunities with stipends, awarded annually to five graduating seniors who show an interest in the medical field and live in MA, RI, NH, or VT. Priority given to minorities.
EIN: 042305643

2889
National Kidney Foundation of North Carolina
5950 Fairview Rd., Ste. 550
Charlotte, NC 28210-2102 (704) 552-1351
FAX: (704) 552-7870; E-mail: info@kidney.org;
Toll-free tel.: (800) 356-5362; URL: http://www.nkfnc.org

Foundation type: Public charity
Limitations: Scholarships to End Stage Renal Disease patients and transplant recipients residing in NC.
Publications: Application guidelines.
Financial data: Year ended 06/30/2005.
Assets, $1,249,627 (M); Expenditures, $1,895,688; Total giving, $272,270; Grants to individuals, totaling $252,125.
Fields of interest: Kidney diseases.
Type of support: Undergraduate support.
Application information: Contact foundation for current application deadline/guidelines.
Program description:
  Scholarship Program: Scholarships are available ranging from $100 to $3,000 based on need, past academic performance and potential to succeed in the chosen academic program.
EIN: 237055496

2890
National Kidney Foundation of Northern California
611 Mission St., 3rd Fl.
San Francisco, CA 94105 (415) 543-3303
Contact: Christopher Kelley, C.E.O.
E-mail: melanie@kidneynca.org; FAX: (415) 543-3331; E-mail: info@kidneyca.org; URL: http://www.kidneynca.org

Foundation type: Public charity
Limitations: Scholarships to kidney patients residing in northern CA.
Publications: Application guidelines; Annual report; Financial statement; Informational brochure (including application guidelines); Newsletter.
Financial data: Year ended 06/30/2003.
Assets, $663,559 (M); Expenditures,

$1,253,452; Total giving, $265,154; Grants to individuals, totaling $75,256.
Fields of interest: Kidney diseases.
Type of support: Undergraduate support.
Application information: Contact foundation for current application deadline/guidelines.
Program description:
Scholarship Program: Scholarships are to cover tuition, books, and other classroom materials for patients demonstrating financial need. Applications are available each May for the following school year.
EIN: 946130713

2891
National Kidney Foundation of Upstate New York, Inc.
15 Prince St.
Rochester, NY   14607   (585) 697-0874
Contact: Jan Miller M.S., Ed., Exec. Dir.
FAX: (585) 607-0895;
E-mail: kidneyinfo@kidneynyup.org; Additional tel.: (800) 724-9421; URL: http://www.kidneynyup.org

Foundation type: Public charity
Limitations: Scholarships to high school students residing in NY to work alongside kidney disease researchers during the summer.
Publications: Annual report; Informational brochure; Newsletter; Program policy statement.
Financial data: Year ended 06/30/2003.
Assets, $911,752 (M); Expenditures, $1,296,409; Total giving, $64,540; Grants to individuals, totaling $34,540.
Fields of interest: Kidney research.
Type of support: Awards/prizes; Undergraduate support.
Application information: Application form required. Application form available on the grantmaker's Web site.
Deadline(s): Contact foundation for current application deadline
Program description:
Scholarship Program: Two $1,000 science scholarships are awarded to high school juniors and seniors.
EIN: 161169134

2892
National Machinery Foundation, Inc.
161 Greenfield St.
P.O. Box 747
Tiffin, OH   44883
Contact: Larry F. Baker, Pres.

Foundation type: Company-sponsored foundation
Limitations: Scholarships to high school seniors and first-year graduates who are children of employees of National Machinery Company, OH. Also, awards for good citizenship to children in Seneca County, OH.
Financial data: Year ended 12/31/2003.
Assets, $12,794,671 (M); Expenditures, $330,420; Total giving, $248,005; Grants to individuals, 190 grants totaling $73,450 (high: $8,000, low: $55).
Type of support: Employee-related scholarships; Awards/prizes; Graduate support; Undergraduate support.
Application information: Application form required.
Initial approach: Letter.
EIN: 346520191

2893
National Medical Fellowships, Inc.
5 Hanover Sq., 15th Fl.
New York, NY   10004   (212) 483-8880
Contact: Jeanne A. Reynolds, Dir., Devel. and Comm.
FAX: (212) 483-8897; E-mail: info@nmfonline.org; URL: http://www.nmf-online.org

Foundation type: Public charity
Limitations: Scholarships to medical students at specific schools in New York, NY.
Financial data: Year ended 06/30/2003.
Assets, $4,496,240 (M); Expenditures, $3,494,661; Total giving, $1,293,233; Grants to individuals, totaling $1,243,233.
Fields of interest: Medical school/education; Medical research; African Americans/Blacks; Hispanics/Latinos; Native Americans/American Indians.
Type of support: Support to graduates or students of specific schools; Graduate support; Undergraduate support.
Application information: Application form required.
Deadline(s): Oct. 26
Applicants should submit the following:
1) Transcripts
2) Essay
3) Letter(s) of recommendation
Additional information: See Web site for complete application guidelines.
Program description:
New York City Community Service Scholarship Program: Offers six two-year service scholarships worth $15,000 each to Native American, African American, Puerto Rican and Mexican American students enrolled full-time at M.D. and D.O. degree-granting schools in New York City. Eligible students will be interested in careers in community-based primary care or in conducting biomedical or clinical research in areas of "critical need," which include, but are not limited to, HIV/AIDS, cardiovascular disease, hypertension, diabetes, substance abuse, asthma, women's health issues, and public health policy. Students must be attending one of the following medical schools: Columbia University College of Physicians and Surgeons, Albert Einstein College of Medicine, Mount Sinai School of Medicine, New York Medical College, New York University School of Medicine, SUNY Health Science Center at Brooklyn, or the Weill Medical College of Cornell University.
EIN: 362125449

2894
National Multiple Sclerosis Society
733 3rd Ave.
New York, NY   10017-3288   (212) 986-3240
Contact: Michael J. Dugan, Pres.
FAX: (212) 986-7981;
E-mail: patricia.olooney@nmss.org; Additional tel.: (800) 344-4867; URL: http://www.nationalmssociety.org

Foundation type: Public charity
Limitations: Scholarships to students who have multiple sclerosis, to students who have a parent or guardian with multiple sclerosis, or to adults with multiple sclerosis who have never enrolled in a postsecondary institution.
Publications: Annual report; Financial statement; Informational brochure; Newsletter; Program policy statement.
Financial data: Year ended 09/30/2003.
Assets, $56,700,970 (M); Expenditures, $79,141,538; Total giving, $29,446,615; Grants

to individuals, 67 grants totaling $94,500 (high: $3,000, low: $1,410).
Fields of interest: Multiple sclerosis.
Type of support: Undergraduate support.
Application information: Applications accepted. Application form required. Application form available on the grantmaker's Web site.
Additional information: Applications accepted throughout the year.
Program description:
National MS Society Scholarship Program: Awards range in amount from $1,000 to $3,000. Recipients are chosen based on financial need, an academic record that shows the applicant is able to succeed in his or her chosen area, and on personal essay discussing the impact of MS on the applicant's life.
EIN: 135661935

2895
National Multiple Sclerosis Society, Minnesota Chapter
200 12th Ave. S.
Minneapolis, MN   55415   (612) 335-7900
Contact: Maureen Reeder, Pres.
FAX: (612) 335-7997;
E-mail: info@mssociety.com; Additional tel.: (800) 582-5296; URL: http://www.nationalmssociety.org/MNM/home/

Foundation type: Public charity
Limitations: Scholarships to residents of MN with Multiple Sclerosis. Grants for medical equipment and emergency needs are also given.
Financial data: Year ended 09/30/2003.
Assets, $4,358,194; Expenditures, $5,897,738; Total giving, $506,258; Grants to individuals, totaling $506,258.
Fields of interest: Multiple sclerosis.
Type of support: Scholarships—to individuals; Grants for special needs.
Application information: Contact foundation for current application deadline/guidelines.
EIN: 410790658

2896
National Restaurant Association Educational Foundation
(formerly National Institute for the Food Service Industry)
175 W. Jackson Blvd., Ste. 1500
Chicago, IL   60604-2702   (800) 765-2122
Contact: Ellen Nash
FAX: (312) 715-0807; E-mail: info@nraef.org; Additional tel.: (312) 715-1010, ext. 733; URL: http://www.nraef.org

Foundation type: Public charity
Limitations: Scholarships for undergraduate and graduate studies in the restaurant/hospitality area, and industry assistance and workstudy grants to teachers and administrators.
Publications: Annual report; Newsletter.
Financial data: Year ended 12/31/2004.
Assets, $27,027,459 (M); Expenditures, $22,171,834; Total giving, $968,669; Grants to individuals, 351 grants totaling $844,050 (high: $10,000, low: $850).
Fields of interest: Education, administration/regulation; Vocational education; Education; Business/industry.
Type of support: Graduate support; Undergraduate support; Workstudy grants.
Application information: Application form required.

Initial approach: Letter, telephone, or e-mail.
Deadline(s): Mar. 1 for Undergraduate Scholarships, Feb. 15 for Work-Study Grants and Heinz Fellowships, and Nov. 1 and May for ProManagement Scholarships
Additional information: Scholarship applications available Dec. 1; Fellowship applications available Nov. 15.

Program descriptions:

Teacher Work-Study Grants: Awarded to full-time teachers and administrators of Restaurant-Hotel-Institutional Management, Culinary Arts, and Commercial Foods programs in secondary and postsecondary schools. Applicant must arrange employment in a restaurant and hospitality line or staff position, working a minimum of 200 hours full-time within a two-month period, and be paid by the employer at a rate commensurate with the position. A letter of recommendation on school letterhead from an immediate supervisor or program director and a letter from the prospective employer must be included with a completed application. It is the objective of these grants to provide opportunities for the recipient in hands-on work experience in the industry. Up to 25 grants worth $2,000 each will be awarded.

ProMgmt. Undergraduate Scholarships: $850 scholarships are available to students in certificate, associate, or bachelor's degree programs in culinary arts, restaurant, or hospitality at ProMgmt. partner schools on a full-time, part-time, or home-study basis. Up to five students at each school may be selected on the basis of a personal essay; completion of at least two ProMgmt. courses; enrollment after application for the award and industry-related work experience that reflects a commitment to a restaurant/hospitality career. For each student receiving a scholarship, their school also receives $150.

Undergraduate Scholarship for High School Seniors: $2,000 scholarships are available to high school students who have demonstrated a commitment to both postsecondary hospitality education and to a career in the industry. Applicants must be U.S. citizens or permanent residents or be studying at schools in the U.S. or its territories; have a minimum 2.75 GPA on a 4.0 scale; have taken a minimum of one food service-related course with a minimum B-/80 grade, and/or have performed a minimum of 250 hours of restaurant and hospitality work experience verified by pay stubs or letter(s) from employer(s); and have applied for or gained acceptance to a hospitality-related postsecondary program on either a full- or part-time basis.

Undergraduate Scholarship for College Students: $2,000 scholarships are awarded to college students who are pursuing certificate, associate degrees, or bachelor's degrees in restaurant or hospitality programs. Applicants must have demonstrated a commitment to both postsecondary hospitality education and to a career in the industry, have a minimum 2.75 GPA, be enrolled for a minimum of nine semester hours, have completed the first semester of a two- or four-year degree, have a minimum of 750 hours of work experience in the restaurant and hospitality industry verified by pay stubs or letter(s) from employer(s), and be U.S. citizens/permanent residents.

EIN: 366103388

2897
National Society of Accountants Scholarship Foundation

(formerly National Society of Public Accountants Scholarship Foundation)
1010 N. Fairfax St.
Alexandria, VA 22314-1574 (703) 549-6400
Contact: Susan E. Noell, Dir., Edu. Progs.
FAX: (703) 549-2984; E-mail: giving@nsacct.org; URL: http://www.nsacct.org

Foundation type: Public charity
Limitations: Scholarships to U.S. or Canadian citizens studying accounting at an accredited U.S. business school, college, or university.
Publications: Application guidelines; Informational brochure; Newsletter.
Financial data: Year ended 08/31/2003. Assets, $599,618 (M); Expenditures, $116,102; Total giving, $92,200; Grants to individuals, totaling $92,200.
Fields of interest: Business school/education; Canada.
Type of support: Undergraduate support.
Application information: Application form required.
Deadline(s): Mar. 10
Applicants should submit the following:
1) Financial information
2) Transcripts
Additional information: See Web site for further program information.

Program description:

Scholarship Program: Students must be accounting majors with a minimum GPA of "B". The foundation also administers the following scholarships:
· The Charles Earp Memorial Scholarship
· The Louis and Fannie Sager Memorial Scholarship
· The Stanley H. Stearman Award.

EIN: 237112372

2898
National Society of Professional Engineers Educational Foundation

(formerly National Society of Professional Engineers)
1420 King St.
Alexandria, VA 22314-2794 (703) 684-2800
Contact: Mary Maul
FAX: (703) 836-4875; E-mail: mmaul@nspe.org; URL: http://www.nspe.org

Foundation type: Public charity
Limitations: Scholarships and fellowships in the field of engineering.
Financial data: Year ended 06/30/2004. Assets, $1,069,174 (M); Expenditures, $84,211; Total giving, $59,541; Grants to individuals, 12 grants totaling $59,541.
Fields of interest: Business school/education; Engineering school/education; Public affairs; Women.
Type of support: Graduate support; Undergraduate support.
Application information: Application form required.
Deadline(s): Vary

Program descriptions:

Auxiliary Scholarship: An award of $1,000 a year for four years for a female high school senior to attend the college or university of her choice. The program must be accredited by the Engineering Accreditation Commission of the Accreditation Board for Engineering and Technology. The scholarship is awarded strictly on the basis of achievement, and must be applied for in the fall of senior year of high school. A scholarship renewal

report will be required for subsequent payment. Deadline Dec. 1. Send eight copies of the application Attn: NSPE Headquarters, Education Services.

Virginia D. Henry Memorial Scholarship: Awards $1,000 for the freshman year of college to a female high school senior to attend the college or university of her choice. The program must be accredited by the Engineering Accreditation Commission of the Accreditation Board for Engineering and Technology. The scholarship is awarded strictly on the basis of achievement, and must be applied for in the fall of senior year of high school. Deadline Dec. 1. Send eight copies of the application Attn: NSPE Headquarters, Education Services.

Professional Engineers in Government (PEG) Management Study Fellowship: This is a scholarship for graduate students who are pursuing an M.B.A., a master's degree in engineering management, or a master's degree in public administration. This fellowship in the amount of $2,500 is to be awarded to an engineer pursuing advanced studies in management. It is available to any engineer intern or licensed professional engineer from any discipline. Applicants who are not U.S. citizens may apply if they are current NSPE members. Mail five copies of the application Attn.: Erin Garcia, PEG Management Study Fellowship, or e-mail application to egarcia@nspe.org. Deadline Mar. 15.

Professional Engineers in Industry (PEI) Scholarship: An award of $2,500 for one year of study. Applicants must be sponsored by a NSPE/PEI member. Students who are children, dependents, or relatives of NSPE members are given preference. Students must have completed a minimum of two semesters or three quarters of undergraduate engineering studies (or be enrolled in graduate study) in a program accredited by the Accreditation Board for Engineering and Technology. Send application and attachments to: Neal Illenberg, P.E., 35 Garden Ln., Rochester, NY 14626. Deadline June 1.

Paul H. Robbins, P.E., Honorary Scholarship: An award of $1,000 a year for two years is provided for the recipient to attend the college or university of his or her choice, which must be accredited by the Engineering Accreditation Commission of the Accreditation Board for Engineering and Technology. The scholarship is awarded strictly on the basis of achievement, and must be applied for in the fall of senior year of high school. A scholarship renewal report will be required for second year payment. Deadline Dec. 1. Send eight copies of the application Attn.: NSPE Headquarters, Education Services.

Steinman Fellowship: An award of $10,000 for one year will be awarded to an NSPE student member to assist in the pursuit of a graduate degree in engineering. The award will be given annually and will rotate among the six NSPE regions. Eligible candidates must be a senior in an undergraduate engineering program that is accredited by the Engineering Accreditation Commission of the Accreditation Board for Engineering and Technology. The candidate must also have registered to take or have passed the Fundamentals of Engineering (FE) exam, and must have been accepted into a graduate engineering degree program. Send eight copies of application and materials to Attn.: NSPE Education Services, Steinman Fellowship. Deadline Mar. 1.

EIN: 526056276

2899
National Urban League, Inc.
120 Wall St.
New York, NY 10005 (212) 558-5300
FAX: (212) 344-5332; E-mail: info@nul.org;
URL: http://www.nul.org

Foundation type: Public charity
Limitations: Scholarships to African Americans and individuals of other ethnicities in the achievement of social and economic equality.
Publications: Annual report.
Financial data: Year ended 12/31/2004.
Assets, $41,100,548 (M); Expenditures, $28,399,870; Total giving, $6,595,643.
Fields of interest: African Americans/Blacks.
Type of support: Support to graduates or students of specific schools; Undergraduate support.
Application information: Contact foundation for current application deadline/guidelines.
Program descriptions:
Campaign for African American Achievement Scholarship Program: Scholarships of $10,000 for four years to African American students for study at an accredited college or university.
University of Rochester Urban League Scholarship: Scholarships of $24,000 over a four-year period, in increments of $6,000 per year, awarded to students, based on financial need, who will attend the University of Rochester. Deadline Jan. 31. Applicant must submit an admissions application no later than Jan. 15 to the university. Applications may be obtained from a local Urban League or directly from the University's admissions office. There is a $50 admissions application fee.
American Chemical Society Minority Scholars Program: Scholarships to high school seniors who will be entering college in the coming year, college students who are currently pursuing, or planning to pursue, full-time study in a chemically-related field, or community college graduates and transfer students who plan to get their bachelor's degree. Scholarships are awarded based on merit and financial need. Recipients must be minority students with outstanding academic records combined with a strong interest in chemistry.
Gillette/National Urban League Scholarship and Intern Program for Minority Students: Scholarships to undergraduate college or university students who are classified as juniors. Recipients must be within the top 25 percent of their class and major in engineering, marketing, manufacturing operations, finance, business administration or human resource management, or related fields. Recipients must also have work experience in said field(s), extracurricular activities, leadership skills and volunteer work. Recipients will receive $5,000 annually, to go towards tuition, room and board, and to purchase required education materials and books, along with paid summer internships with one of the Gillette companies between their junior and senior year. Deadline Jan. 15.
EIN: 131840489

2900
National Wildlife Federation
11100 Wildlife Center Dr.
Reston, VA 20190-5362 (800) 822-9919
Contact: Larry J. Schweiger, Pres. and C.E.O.
URL: http://www.nwf.org

Foundation type: Public charity
Limitations: Fellowships to students for ecological projects on college and university campuses.
Financial data: Year ended 08/31/2004.
Assets, $76,207,459; Expenditures, $104,080,463; Total giving, $1,484,964; Grants

to individuals, 3 grants totaling $3,600 (high: $1,375, low: $1,000).
Fields of interest: Natural resources; Environment.
Type of support: Seed money; Fellowships; Awards/prizes; Graduate support; Undergraduate support.
Application information: Application form required.
Deadline(s): See Web site for current deadline
Additional information: Application must also include 3-5 page project proposal and other supporting materials.
Program description:
Campus Ecology Fellowship Program: Offers a nationally recognized opportunity for undergraduate and graduate students to implement projects that green their campuses and communities. Fellows may receive a grant of up to $1,200 per project period which may be used for direct project expenses and/or as salary. Grant funds are intended to serve as seed money, not to cover the full cost of the project. Proposals must include plans for measurable improvement on the campus and in the community; engagement of an advisor; commitment of staff or administrators to institutionalize and maintain the project; and matching funds. For further information, contact campus@nwf.org or www.nwf.org/campusecology.
EIN: 530204616

2901
The NATSO Foundation
1199 N. Fairfax St., Ste. 801
Alexandria, VA 22314 (703) 549-2100
Contact: Kim Viani, Exec. Dir.; Scholarships: Sharon Corigliano
FAX: (703) 684-9667;
E-mail: scorigliano@natso.com; URL: http://www.natsofoundation.org

Foundation type: Public charity
Limitations: Scholarships to truck stop industry employees or their dependents who plan to enroll on a full-time basis in postsecondary studies at an accredited school.
Publications: Application guidelines; Informational brochure (including application guidelines); Newsletter.
Financial data: Year ended 12/31/2003.
Assets, $2,307,731 (M); Expenditures, $181,171; Total giving, $12,500; Grants to individuals, 5 grants totaling $12,500 (high: $2,500, low: $2,500).
Fields of interest: Transportation.
Type of support: Employee-related scholarships.
Application information: Applications accepted. Application form required. Application form available on the grantmaker's Web site.
Deadline(s): May 1
Applicants should submit the following:
1) Essay
2) GPA
3) Financial information
4) Transcripts
Additional information: See web site for complete application information.
Program description:
Bill Moon Scholarship: Provides $2,500 scholarships to truck stop industry employees and their dependents for full-time postsecondary studies at accredited educational institutions.
EIN: 541519317

2902
NCR Scholarship Foundation
1700 S. Patterson Blvd.
Dayton, OH 45479 (937) 445-6298
Contact: Susan York
FAX: (937) 445-1607;
E-mail: ncr.scholarship@ncr.com

Foundation type: Company-sponsored foundation
Limitations: Scholarships to children of NCR Corporation employees.
Financial data: Year ended 12/31/2004.
Assets, $374,891 (M); Expenditures, $24,537; Total giving, $20,000; Grants to individuals, 10 grants totaling $20,000 (high: $2,000, low: $2,000).
Type of support: Employee-related scholarships.
Application information: Application form required.
Deadline(s): Mar. 2
Applicants should submit the following:
1) Transcripts
2) Essay
EIN: 237431180

2903
Ed Neal Memorial Scholarship Fund
1260 Brook Forest Dr. NE
Atlanta, GA 30374-3808
Contact: Donald F. Hampton, Chair.
Application address: c/o Susan S. Nerius, 2615 Majestic Way, Lawrenceville, GA 30244

Foundation type: Independent foundation
Limitations: Scholarships to graduates of any north Fulton County high school, GA, or from Cumberland County High School, TN.
Financial data: Year ended 03/31/2005.
Assets, $30,767 (M); Expenditures, $24,150; Total giving, $24,500; Grants to individuals, 25 grants totaling $24,500 (high: $1,000, low: $500).
Type of support: Support to graduates or students of specific schools.
Application information:
Initial approach: Letter.
Deadline(s): May 6
Applicants should submit the following:
1) Financial information
2) Transcripts
3) Photograph
4) Essay
EIN: 582153268

2904
The Charles and Dana Nearburg Foundation
P.O. Box 823085
Dallas, TX 75382-3085 (214) 739-1779
Contact: Charles E. Nearburg, Pres.

Foundation type: Operating foundation
Limitations: Scholarships and loans to children of employees of Nearburg Producing Company or other deserving TX community members for enrollment in a private middle or secondary school or an accredited institution of postsecondary education.
Financial data: Year ended 12/31/2002.
Assets, $599,228 (M); Expenditures, $464,225; Total giving, $464,225; Grants to individuals, 5 grants totaling $36,725 (high: $11,100, low: $4,625).
Type of support: Employee-related scholarships.
Application information: Applications accepted. Application form required.
Deadline(s): Aug. 1
Applicants should submit the following:
1) Transcripts

2) Letter(s) of recommendation
3) Financial information
Additional information: Application must include school ranking, and the results of a drug test taken within the previous 10 days.
EIN: 752658947

2905
Nebraska Medical Foundation, Inc.
c/o U.S. Bank, N.A.
1512 U.S. Bank Bldg.
233 S. 13th St., Ste.1200
Lincoln, NE 68508-2091   (402) 474-4472
Contact: Joel Johnson M.D., Secy.
E-mail: nebmed@nebmed.org; URL: http://www.nebmed.org/nma_foundation

Foundation type: Public charity
Limitations: Scholarships of $500-$2,500 to students attending a NE university.
Financial data: Year ended 01/31/2005. Assets, $1,553,902 (M); Expenditures, $55,591; Total giving, $33,645; Grants to individuals, totaling $33,645.
Type of support: Undergraduate support.
Application information: Application form required.
  Initial approach: E-mail or letter.
  Deadline(s): Apr. 10
  Additional information: Contact university for application guidelines.
EIN: 476036827

2906
Needham September 11th Scholarship Fund
c/o Needham & Co., Inc.
445 Park Ave.
New York, NY 10022   (212) 705-0314
Contact: Joseph J. Turano, Dir.
E-mail: jturano@needhamco.com; URL: http://www.needhamco.com/911Fund.asp

Foundation type: Company-sponsored foundation
Limitations: Scholarships to dependents of victims of the World Trade Center attacks.
Financial data: Year ended 12/31/2004. Assets, $1,717,308 (M); Expenditures, $86,811; Total giving, $85,400; Grants to individuals, 7 grants totaling $85,400 (high: $20,000, low: $5,000).
Fields of interest: Disasters, 9/11/01.
Type of support: Undergraduate support.
Application information: Applications accepted. Application form required. Application form available on the grantmaker's Web site.
  Initial approach: E-mail.
  Applicants should submit the following:
    1) Essay
    2) Financial information
    3) GPA
  Additional information: Contact foundation for further program information.
EIN: 134196881

2907
Harold M. Neel and Katharine Klepinger Neel Scholarship Fund
P.O. Box 909
Lafayette, IN 47902-0909
Contact: Charles Max Layden, Tr.
Application address: 201 N. Main St., Ste. 712, Lafayette, IN 47901

Foundation type: Independent foundation

Limitations: Undergraduate scholarships to graduating students of Frontier High School, IN, who are in the top 25 percent of their classes for attendance at state supported colleges and universities in IN.
Financial data: Year ended 12/31/2004. Assets, $1,654,628 (M); Expenditures, $134,426; Total giving, $72,432; Grants to individuals, 8 grants totaling $72,432 (high: $17,582, low: $3,857).
Type of support: Support to graduates or students of specific schools; Undergraduate support.
Application information: Application form required.
  Deadline(s): Apr. 1
EIN: 356529645

2908
Adeline L. Neilson Foundation
P.O. Box 930
Jackson, WY 83001-0930
Contact: Jennifer L. Flanagan, Pres.
FAX: (307) 733-9159

Foundation type: Operating foundation
Limitations: Scholarships to individuals, primarily in WY.
Financial data: Year ended 11/30/2004. Assets, $1,003,286 (M); Expenditures, $79,273; Total giving, $71,500; Grants to individuals, 20 grants totaling $71,500 (high: $4,000, low: $3,000).
Type of support: Scholarships—to individuals.
Application information: Application form required.
  Deadline(s): Spring
EIN: 841423057

2909
Maurice A. Neinken Scholarship Grant & Loan Foundation
(formerly Maurice A. Neinken Scholarship Grant)
c/o Wachovia Bank, N.A.
P.O. Box 193
Telford, PA 18969
Contact: Charles W. Apple, Chair.
Additional address: 164 Sussex at Lion's Gate, Souderston, PA 18964

Foundation type: Independent foundation
Limitations: Grants and loans to financially needy individuals who are graduating from Quakertown School District, Pennridge School District, Christopher Dock School District, or Souderton-Telford School District, all in PA.
Financial data: Year ended 12/31/2004. Assets, $2,778,490 (M); Expenditures, $319,206; Total giving, $294,500; Grants to individuals, 239 grants totaling $294,500 (high: $2,000, low: $500).
Type of support: Support to graduates or students of specific schools; Undergraduate support.
Application information: Application by letter outlining financial need; Contact fund for current application deadline.
Program description:
  Grant and Loan Program: Recipients are selected primarily on the basis of financial need with consideration to academic achievement. Approximately 20 new students are chosen each year. Grants are generally $2,000 to $5,000 per student per year, with a maximum limit of $20,000 per student over four years. Fifty percent of the grant is considered a scholarship. The other 50 percent is a loan. Loans are interest-free if repaid within five years of graduation. If not repaid by then, they accrue five percent interest on the balance for

the first five years, and eight percent interest after that.
EIN: 237760341

2910
Walter E. Neiswanger Educational Foundation
(also known as Neiswanger Educational Trust)
c/o Wells Fargo Bank Iowa, N.A.
203 W. 3rd St., N8236-020
Davenport, IA 52801
Application address: c/o Walter Neiswanger, 222 W. 30th St., Davenport, IA 52803

Foundation type: Independent foundation
Limitations: Scholarships to graduating seniors of Davenport, IA, public high schools who plan to pursue degrees in the medical field at an accredited four-year college or university in the U.S.
Financial data: Year ended 11/30/2004. Assets, $165,102 (M); Expenditures, $23,486; Total giving, $22,202; Grants to individuals, 5 grants totaling $22,202 (high: $7,202, low: $828).
Fields of interest: Medical school/education.
Type of support: Support to graduates or students of specific schools; Undergraduate support.
Application information: Contact fund for current application deadline/guidelines.
Program description:
  Scholarship Program: Scholarships are terminated if the student ceases to be a pre-medical or medical student. Scholarships are renewable. No graduate student who was not a recipient of a Neiswanger scholarship as an undergraduate may apply. Scholarships are limited to $5,000 per year and $20,000 total per student.
EIN: 426079112

2911
Zola N. & Lawrence R. Nell Educational Trust
c/o Commerce Bank, N.A.
P.O. Box 637
Wichita, KS 67201-0637
Contact: Scholarships: Jennifer Stullz

Foundation type: Independent foundation
Limitations: Scholarships to graduates of Sedgwick County, KS, high schools who are pursuing graduate study in medicine or some other healthcare field and will return to KS to practice.
Publications: Application guidelines.
Financial data: Year ended 09/30/2004. Assets, $644,626 (M); Expenditures, $42,302; Total giving, $36,250; Grants to individuals, 22 grants totaling $36,250 (high: $3,000, low: $1,000).
Fields of interest: Medical school/education; Health care.
Type of support: Support to graduates or students of specific schools; Graduate support; Undergraduate support.
Application information: Applications accepted. Application form required.
  Deadline(s): Apr. 15
EIN: 486274160

2912
Nelson Foundation, Inc.
(formerly NMC Projects, Inc.)
P.O. Box 428
Stoughton, WI 53589

Foundation type: Company-sponsored foundation

Limitations: Scholarships to individuals for higher education.
Publications: Annual report.
Financial data: Year ended 07/31/2002.
Assets, $387,520 (M); Expenditures, $191,108; Total giving, $190,930; Grants to individuals, totaling $38,000.
Type of support: Scholarships—to individuals.
Application information:
   Initial approach: Letter.
   Additional information: Contact foundation for current application deadline/guidelines.
EIN: 396043256

2913
Victor and Mary D. Nelson Scholarship Fund
c/o Marshall & Ilsley Bank
P.O. Box 2980
Milwaukee, WI   53201-2980
Application address: c/o William Retinstrand, Superior Senior High School, 2600 Catlin Ave., Superior, WI 54880, tel.: (715) 384-0271

Foundation type: Independent foundation
Limitations: Scholarships to graduates of Superior High School, WI, for higher education.
Financial data: Year ended 06/30/2004.
Assets, $5,296,211 (M); Expenditures, $388,223; Total giving, $353,619; Grants to individuals, 211 grants totaling $353,619 (high: $2,000, low: $811).
Type of support: Support to graduates or students of specific schools; Undergraduate support.
Application information:
   Deadline(s): Apr. 15
   Additional information: Contact foundation for current application guidelines.
EIN: 396184729

2914
Hazel T. Nelson Scholarship Trust
c/o Citizens State Bank & Trust Co.
P.O. Box 360
Hiawatha, KS   66434   (785) 742-2101
Contact: James Bush, Trust Off., Citizens State Bank & Trust Co.

Foundation type: Independent foundation
Limitations: Scholarships to graduates of Brown County, KS, high schools.
Financial data: Year ended 04/30/2005.
Assets, $235,846 (M); Expenditures, $22,760; Total giving, $20,500; Grants to individuals, 25 grants totaling $20,500 (high: $1,000, low: $500).
Type of support: Support to graduates or students of specific schools; Undergraduate support.
Application information: Application form required.
   Deadline(s): Vary
   Additional information: Applications available from Citizens State Bank, KS.
EIN: 481046006

2915
Catherine Hayes Nelson Scholarships, Inc.
1265 S. Garner St.
State College, PA   16801
Contact: John Hayes, Pres.

Foundation type: Independent foundation
Limitations: Scholarships to graduates of Brockway Area High School, Dubois area high schools, St. Mary's high schools and students who have been

accepted at the Dubois Campus of Penn State University, PA.
Financial data: Year ended 12/31/2004.
Assets, $20,842 (M); Expenditures, $75,985; Total giving, $72,312; Grants to individuals, 2 grants totaling $4,000 (high: $2,000, low: $2,000).
Type of support: Support to graduates or students of specific schools; Undergraduate support.
Application information: Applications accepted.
   Initial approach: Letter.
   Applicants should submit the following:
      1) Letter(s) of recommendation
      2) FAFSA
EIN: 251867007

2916
Nepal Educational Fund, Inc.
700 Front St., No. 2003
San Diego, CA   92101-6012
Application address: c/o Kedar G.C., Sajha Pasal Deva Pascal 1, Sajha Bhandar, KTM, Nepal

Foundation type: Operating foundation
Limitations: Scholarships to financially needy students born in Nepal.
Financial data: Year ended 12/31/2003.
Assets, $0 (M); Expenditures, $27,717; Total giving, $27,177; Grants to individuals, 5 grants totaling $27,177 (high: $13,714, low: $1,905).
Fields of interest: Nepal.
Type of support: Fellowships; Scholarships—to individuals; Graduate support; Technical education support; Undergraduate support.
Application information: Applications accepted.
   Initial approach: Letter.
   Deadline(s): Contact foundation for deadline
EIN: 330490545

2917
Nesbitt Medical Student Foundation
c/o National Bank & Trust Co.
230 W. State St., MSC M-300
Sycamore, IL   60178
Contact: Diane Florschuetz, V.P. and Trust Off., National Bank & Trust Co.

Foundation type: Independent foundation
Limitations: Scholarships to students attending an approved medical school who are in need of financial assistance and residents of IL. Preference given to women who are, or have been, residents of DeKalb County, IL.
Financial data: Year ended 12/31/2004.
Assets, $986,627 (M); Expenditures, $66,363; Total giving, $52,700; Grants to individuals, 11 grants totaling $52,700 (high: $6,300, low: $1,700).
Fields of interest: Medical school/education; Women.
Type of support: Graduate support.
Application information: Application form required.
   Initial approach: Letter.
   Deadline(s): Apr. 1
   Applicants should submit the following:
      1) Letter(s) of recommendation
   Additional information: Applications are also available in the appropriate office of applicant's medical college; Previous recipients must submit renewal application for each succeeding year.
Program description:
   Scholarship Program: Individual awards will generally not exceed $2,000 for any single academic year. The need of each applicant will be determined on an individual basis as a matter of

judgment by the NMSF Scholarship Committee. The committee will base its judgment on the financial information submitted by the applicant and by such information as may be available. The financial information must clearly show the inability of the student to meet educational expenses without assistance. Academic qualifications, letters of recommendation, and personal interviews will also be considered in evaluating the scholarship applications.
EIN: 510171682

2918
Mary Margaret Nestor Foundation
Reiff & West Sts.
Lykens, PA   17048
Contact: Donald E. Nestor, Pres.
Application address: c/o Reiff & Nestor Co., P.O. Box 147, Lykens, PA 17048-0147, tel.: (717) 453-7113

Foundation type: Independent foundation
Limitations: Scholarships to residents of Lykens, PA, and surrounding areas, primarily for medical students, including those studying nursing and dental hygiene.
Financial data: Year ended 06/30/2005.
Assets, $10,669 (M); Expenditures, $16,628; Total giving, $12,250; Grants to individuals, 28 grants totaling $12,250 (high: $500, low: $250).
Fields of interest: Dental school/education; Medical school/education; Nursing school/education.
Type of support: Scholarships—to individuals; Graduate support.
Application information: Applications not accepted.
EIN: 236277570

2919
The Netherland-America Foundation, Inc.
82 Wall St., Ste. 1101
New York, NY   10005   (212) 825-1221
Contact: Joan Carolyn Kuyper, Exec. Dir.
FAX: (212) 825-9105; E-mail: info@TheNAF.org;
URL: http://www.thenaf.org/

Foundation type: Public charity
Limitations: Fellowships and educational loans to graduate and postgraduate students in the Netherlands and the U.S.
Publications: Application guidelines; Annual report; Financial statement; Grants list; Newsletter; Program policy statement.
Financial data: Year ended 12/31/2003.
Assets, $4,034,915 (M); Expenditures, $513,612; Total giving, $443,335; Grants to individuals, 19 grants totaling $293,335 (high: $5,000, low: $500).
Fields of interest: Netherlands.
Type of support: Fellowships; Graduate support; Postgraduate support.
Application information:
   Initial approach: Letter or e-mail.
   Deadline(s): Contact foundation for deadline
   Additional information: American students should contact their on-campus Fullbright representative and the foundation, Attn. David B. Roosevelt.
EIN: 132989216

2920
Nevada Women's Fund
770 Smithridge Dr., Ste. 300
Reno, NV   89502   (775) 786-2335
Contact: Fritsi H. Ericson, Pres. and C.E.O.
FAX: (775) 786-8152;
E-mail: info@nevadawomensfund.org; URL: http://
www.nevadawomensfund.org

Foundation type: Public charity
Limitations: Scholarships to women residing in NV,
with preference to Northern NV students, and those
at the University of Nevada and its community
college system.
Publications: Application guidelines; Grants list;
Informational brochure; Newsletter.
Financial data: Year ended 12/31/2004.
Assets, $2,341,380 (M); Expenditures,
$709,330; Total giving, $319,829.
Fields of interest: Women.
Type of support: Graduate support; Technical
education support; Undergraduate support;
Doctoral support.
Application information: Application form required.
Application form available on the grantmaker's Web
site.
  Initial approach: E-mail or telephone.
  Deadline(s): Last Fri. in Feb.
EIN: 942860375

2921
Ladies Branch of the New Bedford Port Society
c/o Education Grant Chair.
15 Johnny Cake Hill
New Bedford, MA   02740

Foundation type: Operating foundation
Limitations: Scholarships only to needy students
from the greater New Bedford, MA, area, families or
descendants of seamen planning to attend a
maritime academy or majoring in marine sciences.
Publications: Application guidelines.
Financial data: Year ended 12/31/2003.
Assets, $371,795 (M); Expenditures, $17,980;
Total giving, $12,500; Grants to individuals,
totaling $9,000.
Fields of interest: Military/veterans' organizations.
Type of support: Undergraduate support.
Application information: Application form required.
  Initial approach: Letter.
  Deadline(s): Apr. 15
  Applicants should submit the following:
    1) GPA
    2) Financial information
    3) Essay
    4) Curriculum vitae
    5) Budget Information
    6) ACT
    7) SASE
  Additional information: Applications from
  individuals residing outside of stated
  geographic restriction not accepted;
  Application mailed to all area high schools
  and to Massachusetts Maritime Academy.
EIN: 046079892

2922
New England Education Society
c/o Day Berry & Howard, LLP
260 Franklin St.
Boston, MA   02110   (617) 951-2100
Application address: c/o Rev. Earl Beane, Boston
Univ., School of Theology, 745 Commonwealth
Ave., Boston, MA 02115

Foundation type: Independent foundation
Limitations: Loans to graduate students for
theological education in Christian ministry at
seminaries located in New England.
Financial data: Year ended 04/30/2005.
Assets, $958,094 (M); Expenditures, $11,104;
Total giving, $5,000.
Fields of interest: Theological school/education.
Type of support: Student loans—to individuals.
Application information: Applications by letter
accepted throughout the year.
EIN: 046067431

2923
New England Society in the City of Brooklyn
c/o David Goodrich
155 Congress St.
Brooklyn, NY   11201-6103   (718) 625-1291
Application address: c/o Harrison M. Davis, III, 215
Adams St., Apt. 2-J, Brooklyn, NY 11201

Foundation type: Independent foundation
Limitations: Scholarships limited to residents of
Brooklyn, NY, who attend either a preparatory
school or college in New England.
Publications: Application guidelines; Program
policy statement.
Financial data: Year ended 12/31/2004.
Assets, $608,245 (M); Expenditures, $36,210;
Total giving, $28,500; Grants to individuals, 9
grants totaling $28,000 (high: $6,000, low:
$1,500).
Type of support: Scholarships—to individuals;
Awards/prizes; Undergraduate support.
Application information: Application form required.
  Initial approach: Letter or telephone.
  Deadline(s): Contact foundation for deadline
  Applicants should submit the following:
    1) Letter(s) of recommendation
  Additional information: Interviews required.
Program description:
  Scholarship Program: Scholarships are generally
  renewed for four years of college. Applicants are
  selected based on their academic ability, need, an
  interview, and a "good representative posture.".
EIN: 116036708

2924
The New Hampshire Charitable Foundation
37 Pleasant St.
Concord, NH   03301-4005   (603) 225-6641
Contact: Racheal Stuart, V.P., Progs.; For grant
inquiries: Lorraine Albanese, Prog. Asst.
FAX: (603) 225-1700; E-mail: info@nhcf.org; Grant
inquiry E-mail: la@nhcf.org; NHCF-Piscataqua
Region application address: 446 Market St.,
Portsmouth, NH 03801; NHCF-Upper Valley Region
application address: 16 Buck Rd., Hanover, NH
03755-2700; URL: http://www.nhcf.org

Foundation type: Community foundation
Limitations: Scholarships and student loans to NH
residents pursuing undergraduate or graduate
study at accredited colleges, universities, and
vocational schools. Two programs open to
out-of-state applicants in specific fields of study.
Publications: Application guidelines; Annual report;
Financial statement; Grants list; Informational
brochure; Informational brochure (including
application guidelines); Newsletter; Program policy
statement.

Financial data: Year ended 12/31/2005.
Assets, $344,269,144 (M); Expenditures,
$31,187,329; Total giving, $25,528,024.
Fields of interest: Vocational education; Natural
resources.
Type of support: Fellowships; Graduate support;
Technical education support; Undergraduate
support.
Application information: Application form required.
  Initial approach: Telephone, letter, or e-mail.
  Deadline(s): Apr. 23
Program description:
  Scholarship and Student Loan Program: The
  single largest effort of the foundation is an annual
  statewide competition that attracts over 2,000
  applicants from all areas of the state. Grants and
  loans ranging from $100 to $2,500 are awarded in
  this program. Other awards are made from advised
  or designated funds through local scholarship
  committees, high schools, and colleges. Those
  programs include:
   · Emergency Funding Program: Awards given
     to students who experience an unforeseen
     emergency that threatens continuation of
     their education program
   · Adult Learner Program: Funds adults
     returning to school to upgrade skills for
     employment or career advancement
   · Switzer Environmental Fellowship:
     Supports exceptional graduate students in
     environmental fields at schools in New
     England.
EIN: 026005625

2925
New Hampshire Food Industries Education Foundation
(formerly Food Industry Scholarship Fund of New
Hampshire)
110 Stark St.
Manchester, NH   03101   (603) 669-9333

Foundation type: Independent foundation
Limitations: Scholarships to employees or family
members of employees of food stores that are
members of NH Retail Grocers Assn.
Financial data: Year ended 12/31/2004.
Assets, $256,133 (M); Expenditures, $50,463;
Total giving, $12,605.
Fields of interest: Business/industry.
Type of support: Employee-related scholarships.
Application information: Application form required.
  Deadline(s): Contact foundation for application
  guidelines
EIN: 020433248

2926
New Jersey Nets and Devils Foundation
(formerly New Jersey Nets Foundation, Inc.)
50 Rte. 120 N.
East Rutherford, NJ   07073   (201) 635-3140
Contact: Shane Harris, Exec. Dir.
FAX: (201) 935-8140; URL: http://www.nba.com/
nets/foundation/index.html

Foundation type: Company-sponsored foundation
Limitations: Scholarships to NJ high school
graduates attending certain NJ colleges.
Financial data: Year ended 12/31/2002.
Assets, $331,814 (M); Expenditures, $775,537;
Total giving, $356,948; Grants to individuals, 3
grants totaling $10,000 (high: $5,000, low:
$2,500).
Type of support: Scholarships—to individuals.

Application information:
Initial approach: Letter or telephone.
Deadline(s): Contact foundation for current application deadline/guidelines
EIN: 521815967

2927
New Jersey Osteopathic Education Foundation
One Distribution Way, Ste. 201
Monmouth Junction, NJ   08852-3001
(732) 940-9000
Contact: Shirley Belkoff, Secy.
URL: http://www.njosteo.com/aboutnjaops/njoef.asp

Foundation type: Public charity
Limitations: Scholarships to NJ residents accepted into their first year at any approved college of osteopathic medicine.
Financial data: Year ended 12/31/2003.
Assets, $777,719 (M); Expenditures, $96,577; Total giving, $33,635; Grants to individuals, 5 grants totaling $33,635 (high: $8,000, low: $1,635).
Fields of interest: Nerve, muscle & bone research.
Type of support: Doctoral support.
Application information: Applications accepted. Application form required. Application form available on the grantmaker's Web site.
Applicants should submit the following:
1) Essay
2) Financial information
3) Transcripts
4) Letter(s) of recommendation
Additional information: Application should include four references, MCAT scores and last year's tax return; Interviews required; See Web site for further information.
EIN: 226088562

2928
New Jersey State Elks Crippled Children's Committee
P.O. Box 1596
Woodbridge, NJ   07095-1596   (732) 257-7107
Contact: George M. Helock, Tr.

Foundation type: Public charity
Limitations: Scholarships to handicapped college students residing in NJ.
Financial data: Year ended 03/31/2004.
Assets, $4,952,114 (M); Expenditures, $664,190; Total giving, $16,250; Grants to individuals, 7 grants totaling $16,250 (high: $2,500, low: $1,250).
Fields of interest: Disabilities, people with.
Type of support: Undergraduate support.
Application information:
Initial approach: Letter.
Additional information: Contact foundation for further application information.
EIN: 221522929

2929
New London Service Organization, Inc.
c/o Lake Sunapee Bank
9 Main St.
P.O. Box 29
Newport, NH   03773-0029
Contact: Helen Tucker, Pres.
Application address: P.O. Box 191, New London, NH 03257-0191, tel.: (603) 526-6567

Foundation type: Operating foundation
Limitations: Scholarships to individuals from New London, NH, to attend U.S. colleges and universities.
Financial data: Year ended 12/31/2003.
Assets, $535,881 (M); Expenditures, $29,540; Total giving, $24,500; Grants to individuals, 7 grants totaling $10,000 (high: $2,000, low: $1,000).
Fields of interest: Education.
Type of support: Scholarships—to individuals.
Application information: Applications accepted. Application form required.
Applicants should submit the following:
1) Resume
Additional information: Application must also include personal history, academic record, and future goals.
EIN: 026007487

2930
The New Mexico Community Foundation
343 E. Alameda St.
Santa Fe, NM   87501   (505) 820-6860
Contact: Robert H. Stark, Exec. Dir.
FAX: (505) 820-7860; E-mail: nmcf@nmcf.org;
Additional address: 303 Roma N.W., Ste. 400, Albuquerque, NM 87102, tel.: (505) 821-6735;
URL: http://www.nmcf.org

Foundation type: Community foundation
Limitations: Scholarships to students who reside in NM.
Publications: Annual report; Newsletter; Occasional report.
Financial data: Year ended 12/31/2004.
Assets, $18,549,931 (M); Expenditures, $4,791,313; Total giving, $2,962,063.
Type of support: Scholarships—to individuals.
Application information: Applications not accepted.
EIN: 850311210

2931
New Orphan Asylum Scholarship Foundation
2300 Montana Ave., Ste. 218
Cincinnati, OH   45211   (513) 389-9400
Contact: Melody Sparks
FAX: (513) 389-9401

Foundation type: Independent foundation
Limitations: Scholarships to residents of, or graduates of high schools in, the greater Cincinnati, OH, area.
Financial data: Year ended 12/31/2004.
Assets, $3,248,471 (M); Expenditures, $141,556; Total giving, $79,200.
Fields of interest: Vocational education.
Type of support: Technical education support; Undergraduate support.
Application information: Application form required.
Deadline(s): Three months prior to commencement of semester or quarter.
Additional information: Interviews required.
Program description:
Scholarship Program: Scholarships may be used for undergraduate and technical school education. Scholarships for postgraduate study are given in limited amounts through the Samuel Bulluck Scholarship.
EIN: 310536683

2932
New World Gospel Mission, Inc.
272 8th St.
Palisades Park, NJ   07650

Foundation type: Independent foundation
Limitations: Scholarships to individuals, primarily on the East Coast of the US and in to Toronto, Canada.
Financial data: Year ended 12/31/2004.
Assets, $649,850 (M); Expenditures, $29,311; Total giving, $12,117; Grants to individuals, 17 grants totaling $12,117 (high: $1,400, low: $401).
Fields of interest: Canada.
Type of support: Scholarships—to individuals.
Application information: Applications not accepted.
EIN: 113325506

2933
New York City "Bravest" Scholarship Fund
225 Broadway, Ste. 401
New York, NY   10007-3001   (212) 293-9300
Contact: Mary Travers
FAX: (212) 292-1560; URL: http://www.ufoa.org

Foundation type: Public charity
Limitations: Scholarships to children of fire officers and firefighters of the New York City Fire Department who have died while active.
Financial data: Year ended 12/31/2003.
Assets, $2,409,176 (M); Expenditures, $127,965; Total giving, $122,000; Grants to individuals, 44 grants totaling $122,000 (high: $4,000, low: $2,000).
Fields of interest: Disasters, fire prevention/control.
Type of support: Emergency funds; Employee-related scholarships.
Application information: Application form required.
Deadline(s): May 1
EIN: 134055458

2934
New York City Police Foundation, Inc.
345 Park Ave.
New York, NY   10154   (212) 751-8170
Contact: Pamela D. Delaney, Pres.
FAX: (212) 750-7616;
E-mail: info@nycpolicefoundation.org; URL: http://www.nycpolicefoundation.org

Foundation type: Public charity
Limitations: Scholarships to eligible police officers employed with the NYPD.
Publications: Annual report; Financial statement; Grants list; Informational brochure; Program policy statement.
Financial data: Year ended 06/30/2004.
Assets, $13,490,738 (M); Expenditures, $5,411,229; Total giving, $3,280,473; Grants to individuals, 37 grants totaling $96,284 (high: $15,000, low: $250).
Fields of interest: Crime/law enforcement, police agencies; Crime/law enforcement.
Type of support: Employee-related scholarships.
Application information: Contact NYPD for current application/deadline; Interviews required.
EIN: 132711338

2935
The New York Classical Club, Inc.
39 Forest Ave.
Hastings on Hudson, NY   10706

Foundation type: Independent foundation
Limitations: Scholarships to graduating students from New York, NY, for higher education at the American Academy in Rome, Italy and/or the American School of Classical Studies in Athens, Greece.
Financial data: Year ended 03/31/2005. Assets, $339,122 (M); Expenditures, $21,335; Total giving, $12,050; Grants to individuals, totaling $12,050.
Fields of interest: Education; Greece; Italy.
Type of support: Support to graduates or students of specific schools; Undergraduate support.
Application information: Applications accepted.
  Deadline(s): None
EIN: 133970766

2936
New York Foundation for Architecture, Inc.

536 LaGuardia Pl.
New York, NY 10012 (212) 683-0023
Contact: Rick Bell FAIA, Exec. Dir.
FAX: (212) 696-5022; E-mail: infor@aiany.org;
Additional tel.: (212) 358-6110, e-mail:
bell@aiany.org; URL: http://www.aiany.org

Foundation type: Public charity
Limitations: Scholarships to residents of NY enrolled in architecture programs at New York City colleges and universities.
Financial data: Year ended 12/31/2003. Assets, $1,281,841 (M); Expenditures, $391,693; Total giving, $17,000; Grants to individuals, totaling $17,000.
Fields of interest: Architecture.
Type of support: Scholarships—to individuals.
Application information: Application form required.
  Deadline(s): Contact foundation for current application deadline
EIN: 223047700

2937
New York Library Association

252 Hudson Ave.
Albany, NY 12210 (518) 432-6952
FAX: (518) 427-1697; E-mail: info@nyla.org;
Toll-free tel.: (800) 252-6952; URL: http://www.nyla.org

Foundation type: Public charity
Limitations: Scholarships of $1,500 to students who wish to pursue a Master's Degree in Library Science at an ALA-accredited library school in NY.
Financial data: Year ended 12/31/2003. Assets, $681,575 (M); Expenditures, $728,856; Total giving, $12,000; Grants to individuals, 2 grants totaling $12,000 (high: $6,000, low: $6,000).
Fields of interest: Libraries/library science.
Type of support: Graduate support.
Application information: Applications accepted. Application form required. Application form available on the grantmaker's Web site.
  Initial approach: E-mail.
  Deadline(s): Sept. 23
  Additional information: See Web site for additional program guidelines.
EIN: 141407060

2938
The New York Times Company Foundation, Inc.

229 W. 43rd St., 10 Fl.
New York, NY 10036-3959 (212) 556-1091
Contact: Jack Rosenthal, Pres.
Additional tel. for scholarships: (212) 556-1923
FAX: (212) 556-4450; URL: http://www.nytimes.com/scholarship
  http://www.nytco.com/foundation

Foundation type: Company-sponsored foundation
Limitations: Scholarships to New York City high school seniors who have overcome financial, racial, ethnic, language or other difficulties.
Publications: Annual report (including application guidelines).
Financial data: Year ended 12/31/2004. Assets, $2,280,375 (M); Expenditures, $6,763,315; Total giving, $5,174,682; Grants to individuals, totaling $240,000.
Type of support: Undergraduate support.
Application information: Applications accepted. Application form required. Application form available on the grantmaker's Web site.
  Deadline(s): Oct. 28
  Additional information: Applications are available from principals and college counselors or see Web site to download application and access additional information; Additional tel.: (212) 556-1923.
Program description:
  The New York Times College Scholarship Program: Awarded to New York City high school seniors who demonstrate outstanding academic achievement, a commitment to community service and perseverance in the face of significant obstacles, whether financial, physical or family related. Priority is given to students whose parents are not college graduates. The foundation funds five scholarships annually at $12,000 a year for each of four years. Up to fifteen additional $6,000 a year scholarships are funded by public contributions.
EIN: 136066955

2939
Newaygo Public Schools Educational Advancement Foundation

c/o Selection Comm.
360 S. Mill St.
Newaygo, MI 49337

Foundation type: Independent foundation
Limitations: Scholarships to residents of Newaygo, MI, for higher education.
Financial data: Year ended 06/30/2005. Assets, $319,300 (M); Expenditures, $28,587; Total giving, $17,526; Grants to individuals, 16 grants totaling $17,526 (high: $4,500, low: $26).
Type of support: Undergraduate support.
Application information: Application form required.
  Deadline(s): Apr. 1
  Applicants should submit the following:
    1) GPA
    2) Financial information
  Additional information: Application must also include character information, and career choice.
EIN: 382989275

2940
Darold A. Newblom Foundation

1208 Laramie Ave.
Alliance, NE 69301-2538 (308) 762-4693
Contact: Wally A. Seiler, Treas.

Foundation type: Independent foundation
Limitations: Scholarships to residents of Box Butte and Dawes counties, NE.
Financial data: Year ended 12/31/2004. Assets, $294,998 (M); Expenditures, $15,361; Total giving, $10,250; Grants to individuals, 9 grants totaling $2,250 (high: $250, low: $250).
Type of support: Scholarships—to individuals.
Application information: Application form required.
  Deadline(s): Mar. 1
  Applicants should submit the following:
    1) Transcripts
    2) Letter(s) of recommendation
    3) Essay
EIN: 363696589

2941
Newell Scholarship Trust

(formerly Daniel James and Lavonne Newell Scholarship Trust Fund)
c/o Wells Fargo Bank Indiana, N.A.
P.O. Box 370
Peru, IN 46970 (765) 473-6661
Application address: c/o Wells Fargo Bank Indiana, N.A., 841 N. Cass St., Wabash, IN 46992, tel.: (260) 563-5598

Foundation type: Independent foundation
Limitations: Scholarships to graduates of Miami County, IN, high schools who are members of the St. Charles Catholic Church or Peru United Methodist Church.
Financial data: Year ended 04/30/2003. Assets, $363,883 (M); Expenditures, $21,795; Total giving, $17,900; Grants to individuals, 23 grants totaling $17,900 (high: $800, low: $550).
Fields of interest: Protestant agencies & churches; Roman Catholic agencies & churches.
Type of support: Support to graduates or students of specific schools; Undergraduate support.
Application information: Application form required.
  Deadline(s): Apr. 15
  Applicants should submit the following:
    1) Transcripts
    2) GPA
  Additional information: Scholarships are renewable.
EIN: 351144081

2942
Newhouse Scholarship Trust Fund

c/o Virginia Commonwealth Trust Co.
P.O. Box 1717
Culpeper, VA 22701

Foundation type: Independent foundation
Limitations: Scholarships primarily to individuals from the Culpeper, VA, area for attendance at colleges and universities in the U.S.
Financial data: Year ended 12/31/2004. Assets, $227,505 (M); Expenditures, $13,011; Total giving, $9,600; Grants to individuals, 4 grants totaling $9,600 (high: $2,400, low: $2,400).
Fields of interest: College; University.
Type of support: Scholarships—to individuals.
Application information: Contact foundation for current application deadlines/guidelines.
EIN: 546260176

2943
Robert "Aqqaluk" Newlin, Sr. Memorial Trust

c/o NANA Regional Corp.
1001 E. Benson Blvd.
Anchorage, AK   99508   (866) 442-1607
Contact: Toni Raye Bergan, Education Dir.
URL: http://aqqaluktrust.com

Foundation type: Public charity
Limitations: Scholarships to Native Alaskans of the Anchorage region for educational and vocational achievement.
Publications: Informational brochure (including application guidelines).
Financial data: Year ended 12/31/2003. Assets, $1,953,088 (M); Expenditures, $741,569; Total giving, $302,928; Grants to individuals, 186 grants totaling $302,928 (high: $4,500, low: $133).
Fields of interest: Native Americans/American Indians.
Type of support: Technical education support; Undergraduate support.
Application information: Application form required.
  Deadline(s): Contact trust for deadline
  Applicants should submit the following:
    1) Transcripts
    2) Letter(s) of recommendation
    3) Essay
  Additional information: Application must also include bio, and proof of enrollment.
EIN: 943116762

2944
Marie Newmeyer Trust

P.O. Box 722
Harlan, IA   51537   (712) 755-5257
Contact: William T. Early, Tr.

Foundation type: Independent foundation
Limitations: Scholarships to financially needy graduates of Shelby County, IA, high schools for study at The University of Iowa, Iowa State University, or local vocational and technical schools.
Financial data: Year ended 08/31/2005. Assets, $250,976 (M); Expenditures, $54,097; Total giving, $48,455; Grants to individuals, totaling $48,455.
Fields of interest: Vocational education.
Type of support: Support to graduates or students of specific schools; Technical education support; Undergraduate support.
Application information: Applications accepted. Application form required.
  Deadline(s): May
  Applicants should submit the following:
    1) Transcripts
    2) Essay
    3) Financial information
Program description:
  Scholarship Program: One student will receive funds for four years of undergraduate work at either The University of Iowa or Iowa State University, including room, board, tuition, and books. One other student will receive funds for room, board, tuition, and books for attendance at vocational and technical schools in the Council Bluffs, IA and Omaha, NE, area. If living at home, the student will receive transportation expenses instead of room and board.
EIN: 426385108

2945
Newspaper Association of America Foundation

(also known as NAA Foundation)
1921 Gallows Rd., Ste. 600
Vienna, VA   22182-3900   (703) 902-1600
Contact: Margaret Vassilikos, Sr. V.P. and Treas.
FAX: (703) 902-1751; E-mail: laws@naa.org;
URL: http://www.naafoundation.org

Foundation type: Public charity
Limitations: Awards for students and fellowships by nomination only for student newspaper writing and journalism.
Publications: Annual report; Newsletter.
Financial data: Year ended 12/31/2004. Assets, $22,303,962 (M); Expenditures, $1,180,095; Total giving, $163,631.
Fields of interest: Journalism/publishing.
Type of support: Fellowships.
Application information: Application form required. Application form available on the grantmaker's Web site.
  Deadline(s): Feb. 29
Program descriptions:
  Fellowship Program: Fellowships, by nomination only by newspaper executives and journalism educators, are awarded to individuals who demonstrate managerial potential. Self-nomination with a supervisor's approval is also encouraged. A panel of judges determines recipients based on an assessment of the application and the most qualified candidates.
  McCormick Fellowships: Fellowships to 10 individuals based on the quality of their applications and recommendations. A panel of five judges from both print and broadcast media determines the recipients of the fellowship.
EIN: 136161165

2946
Horace & Letitia Newton Scholarship Fund

c/o KeyBank N.A.
P.O. Box 10099
Toledo, OH   43699-0099
Contact: Diane Ohns

Foundation type: Independent foundation
Limitations: Scholarships primarily to residents of Lucas County, OH, who are graduates or students of Toledo, OH, area schools.
Financial data: Year ended 12/31/2004. Assets, $5,149,868 (M); Expenditures, $276,760; Total giving, $229,700; Grants to individuals, 134 grants totaling $229,700 (high: $2,400, low: $500).
Type of support: Scholarships—to individuals; Support to graduates or students of specific schools.
Application information: Applications accepted. Application form required.
  Deadline(s): None
EIN: 346502592

2947
Bobe Ngwebifor Foundation

10 Saddleback Rd.
Rolling Hills, CA   90274-5141
Contact: Ngwebifor Fobi-Walker, Admin. Asst.
FAX: (562) 207-1587;
E-mail: info@bobengwebifor.org

Foundation type: Independent foundation

Limitations: Scholarship grants to people of Cameroon nationality.
Publications: Informational brochure.
Financial data: Year ended 12/31/2004. Assets, $0 (M); Expenditures, $205,190; Total giving, $205,190.
Fields of interest: Cameroon.
Type of support: Undergraduate support.
Application information: Contact foundation for current application deadline/guidelines.
EIN: 330924127

2948
Niagara Falls Rotary Foundation, Inc.

4998 Sweet Home Rd.
Niagara Falls, NY   14305-1449   (716) 298-8000
Contact: Harold C. Brown, Treas.

Foundation type: Public charity
Limitations: Scholarships to individuals residing in the Niagara Falls, NY area, for undergraduate education.
Financial data: Year ended 06/30/2003. Assets, $34,441 (M); Expenditures, $15,821; Total giving, $12,100; Grants to individuals, totaling $10,250.
Type of support: Undergraduate support.
Application information:
  Initial approach: Letter.
  Additional information: Contact foundation for current application guidelines.
EIN: 223017523

2949
Niccum Educational Trust Foundation

c/o JPMorgan Chase Bank, N.A.
P.O. Box 1308
Milwaukee, WI   53201
Contact: Mary Harder

Foundation type: Independent foundation
Limitations: Scholarships to graduates of public high schools in the IN counties of Elkhart, Kosciusko, LaGrange, Marshall, Noble, and St. Joseph.
Publications: Application guidelines; Program policy statement.
Financial data: Year ended 12/31/2004. Assets, $548,512 (M); Expenditures, $31,922; Total giving, $26,000.
Type of support: Support to graduates or students of specific schools; Undergraduate support.
Application information: Application form required.
  Initial approach: Letter.
  Deadline(s): Apr. 15
  Applicants should submit the following:
    1) Financial information
    2) Transcripts
    3) Letter(s) of recommendation
  Additional information: Application must also include three references, and a letter from applicant.
Program description:
  Scholarship Program: Scholarships awarded to students of merit and promise who need financial assistance to matriculate in and pursue higher education. Applicants must be U.S. citizens.
EIN: 356017515

2950
Howard & Mamie Nichols Scholarship Trust

c/o Wells Fargo Bank, N.A.
P.O. Box 63954
San Francisco, CA 94163-0001
Application address: c/o Arthur G. Parrot, Office of the Kern City Superintendent of Schools, 5801 Sundale Ave. Bakersfield, CA 93309-7908, tel.: (805) 398-3772

Foundation type: Independent foundation
Limitations: Scholarships to graduates of high schools in Kern County, CA, for higher education or vocational training.
Publications: Annual report.
Financial data: Year ended 09/30/2004. Assets, $447,935 (M); Expenditures, $62,316; Total giving, $41,950; Grants to individuals, 67 grants totaling $22,000 (high: $300, low: $225).
Fields of interest: Vocational education.
Type of support: Support to graduates or students of specific schools; Technical education support; Undergraduate support.
Application information: Application form required.
Deadline(s): Feb. 28
Applicants should submit the following:
1) Transcripts
Additional information: Application must also include confidential statement from an advisor or teacher, and a letter outlining applicant's goals; Applications available at Kern County, CA, high school offices.
Program description:
Scholarship Program: Recipients must maintain at least a 2.0 GPA and full-time status.
EIN: 956679686

2951
Mary Nichols Trust

c/o Eastern Bank & Trust Co.
605 Broadway, LF41
Saugus, MA 01906 (781) 581-4220
Contact: Shawn McCarthy, Trust Off., Eastern Bank & Trust Co.

Foundation type: Independent foundation
Limitations: Scholarships to residents of the Salem, MA, area.
Financial data: Year ended 12/31/2004. Assets, $193,868 (M); Expenditures, $10,413; Total giving, $7,500; Grants to individuals, 9 grants totaling $7,500 (high: $1,000, low: $500).
Type of support: Scholarships—to individuals.
Application information: Application form required.
Deadline(s): June 30
EIN: 046342221

2952
Robert L. Nichols, Jr. Scholarship Foundation

1 S. Main St., Apt. 1
Webb City, MO 64870
Contact: Scholarship: Robert L. Nichols
Application address: c/o Principal, Terrell Texas High School, Terrell, TX 75160

Foundation type: Operating foundation
Limitations: Scholarships to female graduating seniors of Terrell High School, TX.
Financial data: Year ended 12/31/2003. Assets, $153,564 (M); Expenditures, $3,265; Total giving, $3,000; Grant to an individual, 1 grant totaling $3,000.
Fields of interest: Women.

Type of support: Support to graduates or students of specific schools; Undergraduate support.
Application information: Applications accepted. Application form required.
Additional information: Interviews required.
EIN: 756081322

2953
L. E. Nicklies Scholarship Fund

c/o PNC Advisors
2 PNC Plz.
Pittsburgh, PA 15222

Foundation type: Independent foundation
Limitations: Scholarships to graduates of high schools in the City of Louisville and Jefferson County, KY, for attendance at an accredited college or university in the same location.
Publications: Application guidelines.
Financial data: Year ended 07/31/2003. Assets, $634,869 (M); Expenditures, $38,942; Total giving, $37,000.
Fields of interest: Law school/education; Medical school/education; Teacher school/education; Engineering school/education; Theological school/education.
Type of support: Support to graduates or students of specific schools; Undergraduate support.
Application information: Applications accepted. Application form required.
Deadline(s): Apr. 21
Additional information: Applications are mailed to Jefferson County Schools financial aid office.
Program description:
Scholarship Fund: The purpose of the fund is to make grants of up to $3,000 per year to any approved student of law, engineering, teaching, medicine, or Christian ministry at any accredited college, university, or school of divinity located in Jefferson County, KY. Applicants must exhibit some financial need and be recommended by a school official.
EIN: 610902261

2954
Anna Niconchuk Scholarship Trust

c/o Eastern Bank & Trust Co.
605 Broadway, LF41
Saugus, MA 01906
Application address: c/o Peabody Veterans Memorial High School, Attn.: School Comm. of the Principal, 485 Lowell St., Peabody, MA 01960

Foundation type: Independent foundation
Limitations: Scholarships to graduates of Peabody Veterans Memorial High School, MA, who are attending accredited colleges and universities.
Financial data: Year ended 12/31/2004. Assets, $103,785 (M); Expenditures, $6,794; Total giving, $5,000; Grants to individuals, 5 grants totaling $5,000 (high: $1,000, low: $1,000).
Type of support: Support to graduates or students of specific schools; Undergraduate support.
Application information: Applications accepted. Application form required.
EIN: 042775813

2955
William J. & Myra L. Niederkorn Scholarship Trust

206 N. Franklin St.
Port Washington, WI 53074
Application address: c/o Port Washington High School, Attn.: Scholarship Comm., 427 W. Jackson St., Port Washington, WI 53074

Foundation type: Independent foundation
Limitations: Scholarships to graduating seniors from Port Washington High School, WI.
Financial data: Year ended 05/31/2005. Assets, $381,584 (M); Expenditures, $26,496; Total giving, $22,000; Grants to individuals, 12 grants totaling $22,000 (high: $2,000, low: $1,000).
Type of support: Support to graduates or students of specific schools; Undergraduate support.
Application information: Contact scholarship committee for current application deadline/guidelines.
EIN: 396297158

2956
Nielson Scholarship Fund

(formerly Karl A. Nielson and Karen J. Nielson Scholarship Fund)
P.O. Box 247
Spearman, TX 79081
Application addresses: c/o Spearman High School, Attn.: Glenda Guthrie, Counselor, 403 E. 11th St., Spearman, TX 79081, tel.: (806) 659-2584, c/o Gruver High School, Attn.: Wendy Branstine, P.O. Box 747, Gruver, TX 79040, tel.: (806) 733-2477, c/o Tekamah-Herman Community Schools, Attn.: Bill Anderson, Principal, 112 N. 13th St., Tekamah, NE 68601

Foundation type: Independent foundation
Limitations: Scholarships to graduates of Spearman High School, TX, Gruver High School, TX, and Tekamah-Herman Community Schools, NE, who have been accepted to approved, postsecondary educational institutions.
Financial data: Year ended 12/31/2004. Assets, $220,004 (M); Expenditures, $8,908; Total giving, $6,517; Grants to individuals, 20 grants totaling $6,517 (high: $700, low: $95).
Type of support: Support to graduates or students of specific schools; Undergraduate support.
Application information: Application form required.
Deadline(s): Contact fund for application deadline
EIN: 752065409

2957
U. W. Nikkei Alumni Association

(formerly University Students Club, Inc.)
1414 S. Weller St.
Seattle, WA 98144-2053
Application address: c/o Scholarship Comm., 2703 36th Ave. S.W., Seattle, WA 98126, tel.: (206) 932-8051

Foundation type: Independent foundation
Limitations: Scholarships to students of Japanese ancestry who attend the University of Washington on a full-time basis.
Financial data: Year ended 06/30/2002. Assets, $215,473 (M); Expenditures, $13,777; Total giving, $9,500; Grants to individuals, totaling $9,500.
Fields of interest: Asians/Pacific Islanders.
Type of support: Support to graduates or students of specific schools; Undergraduate support.

Application information: Application form required.
Deadline(s): Apr. 15
Additional information: Application form available from the University of Washington.
Program description:
Scholarship Program: In addition to customary awards offered to students on the basis of their financial need, academic achievement, and community service, one or more scholarships will be granted to individuals who have the potential for college success, but who have not distinguished themselves academically.
EIN: 916035190

2958
Freda Nishan Scholarship Trust
c/o U.S. Bank, N.A.
P.O. Box 7900
Madison, WI 53707-7900
Application address: c/o Reedsburgh School District, Attn.: Nishan Scholarship Comm., 710 N. Webb Ave., Reedsburg, WI 53959-1198, tel.: (608) 524-2401

Foundation type: Independent foundation
Limitations: Scholarships to graduates of Reedsburg Webb High School, WI, and The Sauk County Normal School, WI.
Financial data: Year ended 12/31/2004. Assets, $1,108,127 (M); Expenditures, $67,399; Total giving, $57,855; Grants to individuals, 71 grants totaling $57,855 (high: $920, low: $275).
Type of support: Support to graduates or students of specific schools; Undergraduate support.
Application information:
Initial approach: Letter or telephone.
Additional information: Contact trust for current application deadline/guidelines.
EIN: 396038664

2959
Nixon Memorial Education Fund
c/o PNC Advisors
620 Liberty Ave., P2-PTPP-10-2
Pittsburgh, PA 15222-2705 (412) 762-7645
Contact: Susan Blake, V.P., PNC Bank, N.A.

Foundation type: Independent foundation
Limitations: Educational loans to residents of Penn Township in Butler County, PA.
Financial data: Year ended 12/31/2002. Assets, $222,959 (M); Expenditures, $12,797; Total giving, $12,000; Grants to individuals, 5 grants totaling $12,000 (high: $2,400, low: $2,400).
Type of support: Undergraduate support.
Application information: Application form required.
Initial approach: Letter.
Deadline(s): Before start of fall semester
EIN: 256072006

2960
Noble County Community Foundation
1599 Lincolnway S.
Ligonier, IN 46767 (260) 894-3335
Contact: Dave Knopp, Exec. Dir.; For grant applications: Jennifer Myers, Prog. Off.
FAX: (260) 894-9020; E-mail: nccf@ligtel.com; E-mail for grants applications: grants@ligtel.com; URL: http://www.noblecounty.org/cf_about_it.html

Foundation type: Community foundation

Limitations: Scholarships to eligible residents of Noble County, IN.
Publications: Annual report; Informational brochure (including application guidelines); Newsletter.
Financial data: Year ended 12/31/2004. Assets, $18,072,354 (M); Expenditures, $2,074,856; Total giving, $1,100,417; Grants to individuals, 93 grants totaling $143,343 (high: $2,390, low: $5).
Type of support: Undergraduate support.
Application information: Application form required.
Deadline(s): Mar. 2, May 2, July 2 and Nov. 2.
EIN: 351827247

2961
The Samuel Roberts Noble Foundation, Inc.
2510 Sam Noble Pkwy.
P.O. Box 2180
Ardmore, OK 73402 (580) 223-5810
Contact: Michael A. Cawley, C.E.O. and Pres.
Additional tel.: (866) 223-5810; URL: http://www.noble.org

Foundation type: Independent foundation
Limitations: Four-year scholarships to children of OK employees of Noble-affiliated companies and the Noble Foundation.
Publications: Application guidelines; Annual report; Grants list; Informational brochure.
Financial data: Year ended 12/31/2004. Assets, $1,161,500,185 (M); Expenditures, $47,546,854; Total giving, $6,674,662; Grants to individuals, 86 grants totaling $313,500 (high: $5,000, low: $1,250).
Type of support: Employee-related scholarships.
Application information: Application form required.
Deadline(s): Mar. 1
Additional information: Applications available through parents' employers only.
EIN: 730606209

2962
Robert J. Nolan Foundation, Inc.
P.O. Box 765
Glens Falls, NY 12801 (518) 793-6611
Contact: John C. Mannix, Pres.

Foundation type: Independent foundation
Limitations: Undergraduate and graduate scholarships to graduates of nine school districts in the Glens Falls, NY, area who plan to participate in organized team sports during college.
Financial data: Year ended 09/30/2005. Assets, $854,567 (M); Expenditures, $20,576; Total giving, $8,500; Grants to individuals, 4 grants totaling $8,500 (high: $2,500, low: $1,000).
Fields of interest: Athletics/sports, school programs.
Type of support: Graduate support; Undergraduate support.
Application information: Applications accepted. Application form required.
Deadline(s): June 1
Applicants should submit the following:
1) Essay
2) Letter(s) of recommendation
3) Transcripts
4) SAR
Additional information: Application must also include letter of acceptance from college.
Program description:
Scholarship Program: The foundation considers the following criteria equally in awarding scholarships:

· academic achievement
· participation in high school varsity athletic teams
· participation in extracurricular and civic activities
· religious organization participation
· financial need
A recipient may attend any accredited college or university. Once in college the recipient must make an attempt to join a varsity athletic team in any sport. Although a try-out attempt is required, success is not. Scholarships are renewable for up to four years. Children and descendants of the directors of the foundation are ineligible during the time of the director's service.
EIN: 222826285

2963
John H. Noll Foundation
c/o National City Bank of Indiana
110 W. Berry St.
Fort Wayne, IN 46802 (260) 461-6218
Contact: Denise Andorfer, Asst. V.P.

Foundation type: Independent foundation
Limitations: Scholarships to graduating seniors of the Fort Wayne public and parochial high schools and Homestead High School, IN.
Financial data: Year ended 09/30/2004. Assets, $3,508,495 (M); Expenditures, $187,298; Total giving, $165,250; Grants to individuals, 85 grants totaling $165,250 (high: $3,000, low: $750).
Type of support: Support to graduates or students of specific schools; Undergraduate support.
Application information: Application form required.
Deadline(s): Mar. 31
Additional information: Application forms are available from guidance counselors of participating high schools.
EIN: 237082877

2964
Gilbert and Evelyn Nolley Educational Scholarship Fund
c/o KeyBank N.A., Trust Div.
127 Public Sq., 16th Fl.
Cleveland, OH 44114 (216) 689-7777
Contact: Cynthia Clifton

Foundation type: Independent foundation
Limitations: Scholarships to residents of the Manchester, OH, school district who are also attending schools within the district.
Financial data: Year ended 12/31/2004. Assets, $236,838 (M); Expenditures, $16,352; Total giving, $12,000; Grants to individuals, 12 grants totaling $12,000 (high: $1,000, low: $1,000).
Type of support: Scholarships—to individuals; Support to graduates or students of specific schools.
Application information:
Initial approach: Letter or telephone.
Deadline(s): May 1
Applicants should submit the following:
1) Transcripts
2) Financial information
3) Essay
Additional information: Applications must include college exam scores.
EIN: 346981666

2965
Swan C. Norby Scholarship Fund
c/o Bank of America, N.A.
P.O. Box 831041
Dallas, TX 75283-1041
Application address: c/o Grandview High School,
2300 High Grove Rd., Grandview, MO 64030,
tel.: (816) 316-5800

Foundation type: Independent foundation
Limitations: Scholarships to graduating students
attending Grandview High School, MO.
Financial data: Year ended 12/31/2004.
Assets, $380,147 (M); Expenditures, $22,308;
Total giving, $16,800; Grants to individuals, 18
grants totaling $16,800 (high: $1,000, low: $500).
Type of support: Support to graduates or students
of specific schools; Undergraduate support.
Application information: Applications accepted.
Application form required.
   Additional information: Applications available
     through Grandview High School, MO.
EIN: 431763633

2966
Nordic Educational Trust
P.O. Box 895
Shelburne, VT 05482-0895
Contact: Ross R. Anderson, Pres.

Foundation type: Independent foundation
Limitations: Scholarships to residents of
Chittenden and adjacent counties, VT, for study
toward degrees in technical trades and professions
at regional colleges and technical schools.
Financial data: Year ended 12/31/2004.
Assets, $316,920 (M); Expenditures, $37,525;
Total giving, $31,000; Grants to individuals, 7
grants totaling $31,000 (high: $8,000, low:
$1,500).
Fields of interest: Vocational education.
Type of support: Technical education support;
Undergraduate support.
Application information: Application form required.
   Deadline(s): Jan. through Apr.
EIN: 222975012

2967
Amos Nordman Foundation Charitable Trust
(also known as Amos Nordman Charitable Trust)
P.O. Box 1242
Muskegon, MI 49443-1242
Contact: Charles E. Silky, Jr., Tr.

Foundation type: Independent foundation
Limitations: Scholarships to individuals attending
colleges and universities in the Muskegon, MI,
area. See program description for a complete list of
participating schools.
Financial data: Year ended 12/31/2004.
Assets, $484,227 (M); Expenditures, $82,350;
Total giving, $12,952; Grants to individuals, 5
grants totaling $3,202 (high: $889, low: $417).
Type of support: Support to graduates or students
of specific schools; Undergraduate support.
Application information: Applications accepted.
Application form required.
   Additional information: Contact participating
     college or university for application form.
Program description:
   Scholarship Program: Recipients receive a
maximum of $500 per semester, for study at the
following participating, MI, schools: Albion College;
Alma College; Andrews University; Aquinas College;
Butler University; Calvin College; Ferris State

University; Grand Valley State University; Hillsdale
College; Hope College; and Muskegon Community
College. Recipients are chosen by their schools, in
accordance with the foundation's guidelines.
EIN: 237251583

2968
The Norfolk Foundation
1 Commercial Pl., Ste 1410
Norfolk, VA 23510-2103 (757) 622-7951
Contact: Angelica D. Light, C.E.O.; For grants: Leigh
Evans Davis, Dir., Prog. and Donor Svcs.
FAX: (757) 622-1751;
E-mail: info@norfolkfoundation.org; Additional
E-mails: alight@norfolkfoundation.org and
ldavis@norfolkfoundation.org; URL: http://
www.norfolkfoundation.org

Foundation type: Community foundation
Limitations: Scholarships to financially needy
residents of Norfolk, VA, and the area within fifty
miles of its boundaries.
Publications: Application guidelines; Annual report
(including application guidelines); Financial
statement; Grants list; Informational brochure;
Newsletter.
Financial data: Year ended 12/31/2004.
Assets, $180,029,007 (M); Expenditures,
$7,794,718; Total giving, $6,898,792. Subtotal for
student loans—to individuals: 330 loans totaling
$800,000.
Type of support: Scholarships—to individuals;
Support to graduates or students of specific
schools; Graduate support; Undergraduate
support.
Application information: Applications accepted.
Application form required.
   Initial approach: Letter.
   Deadline(s): Mar. 1
   Applicants should submit the following:
     1) Transcripts
     2) SAT
     3) SAR
     4) Letter(s) of recommendation
     5) Financial information
   Additional information: Application must also
     include family income tax returns, home
     address, high school attended, choice of
     college, and field of study.
Program description:
   Scholarship Program: The foundation
administers several funds that have additional
limitations as specified by the donors. For these, an
applicant must qualify as to residence, secondary
school, college attended, or course of study
chosen.
EIN: 542035996

2969
The Kathleen Norman Trust for Visually Impaired Students
265 Sunrise Hwy., Ste. 65
Rockville Centre, NY 11570-4912
Contact: Jack D. Matza, Tr.

Foundation type: Independent foundation
Limitations: Scholarships to visually-impaired
undergraduate students.
Financial data: Year ended 12/31/2004.
Assets, $77,403 (M); Expenditures, $5,806; Total
giving, $3,808; Grants to individuals, 2 grants
totaling $3,808 (high: $2,500, low: $1,308).
Fields of interest: Disabilities, people with.
Type of support: Undergraduate support.

Application information: Applications by letter
accepted throughout the year.
EIN: 137221435

2970
Shelley R. and Alice S. Norris Fund, Inc.
c/o Harlan E. Judd, Jr.
P.O. Box 415
Burkesville, KY 42717-0415
Application address: c/o Bank of Cumberland,
Attn.: Vickie Wells, Trust Off., Burkesville, KY
42717, tel.: (270) 864-3144

Foundation type: Independent foundation
Limitations: Scholarships to individuals for medical
or nursing education who wish to practice in KY.
Financial data: Year ended 12/31/2004.
Assets, $255,023 (M); Expenditures, $13,099;
Total giving, $10,097; Grant to an individual, 1
grant totaling $10,097.
Fields of interest: Medical school/education;
Nursing school/education.
Type of support: Graduate support.
Application information:
   Initial approach: Letter.
   Deadline(s): Aug.
EIN: 311497834

2971
North Attleboro Scholarship Foundation, Inc.
P.O. Box 926
North Attleboro, MA 02761-0926

Foundation type: Independent foundation
Limitations: Scholarships to graduating seniors of
North Attleboro High School MA.
Financial data: Year ended 06/30/2005.
Assets, $1,784,562 (M); Expenditures, $96,542;
Total giving, $85,000; Grants to individuals, 31
grants totaling $85,000 (high: $5,000, low: $150).
Type of support: Support to graduates or students
of specific schools; Undergraduate support.
Application information: Applications not
accepted.
EIN: 046056778

2972
North Carolina Community Foundation
4601 Six Forks Rd., Ste. 524
Raleigh, NC 27609 (919) 828-4387
Contact: Elizabeth C. Fentress, Pres.
FAX: (919) 828-5495;
E-mail: general@nccommf.org; Additional tel.:
(800) 201-9533; Western Regional Office: P.O. Box
2148, Sylva, NC 28779, tel.: (828) 586-4616, FAX:
(828) 631-3951, E-mail: slelievre@nccommf.org;
Northeastern Regional Office: Harbinger Ctr., Ste.
4, Point Harbor, NC 27964, tel.: (252) 491-8166,
FAX: (252) 491-5714, E-mail: pbirk@nccommf.org;
Central and Western Piedmont Regional Office: P.O.
Box 2851, Hickory, NC 28603, tel.: (828)
328-1237, FAX: (828) 328-3948, E-mail:
jcorrell@nccommf.org; New Bern Office: P.O. Box
13276, New Bern, NC 28651, tel.: (252)
635-1001; FAX: (252) 635-3265; E-mail:
jalcock@nccommf.org; URL: http://
www.nccommunityfoundation.org

Foundation type: Community foundation
Limitations: Scholarships to North Carolina high
school students in pursuit of higher education.
Publications: Annual report; Informational
brochure; Newsletter.

Financial data: Year ended 03/31/2005.
Assets, $85,307,887 (M); Expenditures,
$4,499,029; Total giving, $2,179,761.
Fields of interest: Education.
Type of support: Scholarships—to individuals.
Application information:
Initial approach: Letter, telephone or fax.
Additional information: See web site for
application information and guidelines.
EIN: 581661700

2973
North Central Massachusetts Community Foundation, Inc.

285 John Fitch Hwy., Ste. 1
Fitchburg, MA   01420-5998   (978) 345-8383
Contact: Philip M. Grzewinski, Pres.
FAX: (978) 345-1459; E-mail: info@cfncm.org;
URL: http://www.cfncm.org

Foundation type: Community foundation
Limitations: Scholarships to individuals for higher
education.
Publications: Annual report; Informational
brochure; Newsletter.
Financial data: Year ended 06/30/2005.
Assets, $5,079,844 (M); Expenditures,
$1,176,925; Total giving, $976,410.
Fields of interest: Education.
Type of support: Scholarships—to individuals.
Application information: See web site for further
information.
EIN: 043537449

2974
North Dakota Community Foundation

P.O. Box 387
Bismarck, ND   58502-0387   (701) 222-8349
Contact: Kevin J. Dvorak, C.E.O.; Valerie M. Bren,
Administrator
E-mail: kdvorak@ndcf.net; E-mail: valerie@ndcf.net;
URL: http://www.ndcf.net

Foundation type: Community foundation
Limitations: Scholarships for higher education,
including vocational education, to high school
graduates in ND only.
Publications: Application guidelines; Annual report;
Informational brochure; Newsletter.
Financial data: Year ended 12/31/2005.
Assets, $27,291,653 (L); Expenditures,
$1,559,483; Total giving, $992,422; Grants to
individuals, 161 grants totaling $116,748.
Application information: Application form required.
Deadline(s): Contact foundation for deadline
Additional information: Applications available
through local high school guidance counselor
who provides names of candidates to the
foundation, which in turn selects recipients.
EIN: 450336015

2975
North Fork Foundation

(formerly The GreenPoint Foundation, Inc.)
c/o North Fork Bancorporation, Inc.
275 Broad Hollow Rd., M.C. 40700
Melville, NY   11747   (212) 834-1215
Contact: Gwen Perry, Mgr.
Scholarship application address: c/o GreenPoint
Achievers Scholarship Prog., Scholarship America,
Inc., 1505 Riverview Rd., P.O. Box 297, St. Peter,

MN 56082, tel.: (507) 931-1682, fax: (507)
931-9278, E-mail: gmiller@csfa.org
FAX: (212) 834-1406;
E-mail: gperry@northfork.com

Foundation type: Company-sponsored foundation
Limitations: Undergraduate scholarships to high
school students who reside in one of the five
boroughs of New York City, or in Westchester,
Nassau, or Suffolk counties, NY.
Financial data: Year ended 09/30/2004.
Assets, $47,094,123 (M); Expenditures,
$4,873,123; Total giving, $4,200,688.
Type of support: Undergraduate support.
Application information: Application form required.
Deadline(s): Mar. 1.
Additional information: Applications are available
at all Greenpoint Bank branches, listed on the
Greenpoint Web site, and from high school
counselors at participating schools.
Program description:
Greenpoint Achiever Scholarship Program:
Scholarships are up to $10,000 over a four-year
period. Winners will be selected based on their
academic performance, financial need, and future
potential, as reflected by their participation in
school and neighborhood community service, work
experience, and educational goals. Applicants must
have a cumulative GPA of 3.0, and minimum SAT
score of 1000.
EIN: 113276603

2976
North Haven Foundation

c/o Collins, Crandall, Hanscom
P.O. Box 664
Rockland, ME   04841

Foundation type: Community foundation
Limitations: Scholarships to residents of North
Haven, ME for higher education.
Publications: Annual report.
Financial data: Year ended 06/30/2005.
Assets, $1,534,096 (M); Expenditures,
$111,715; Total giving, $106,470; Grants to
individuals, 20 grants totaling $98,470 (high:
$6,350, low: $425).
Type of support: Undergraduate support.
Application information: Application form required.
Deadline(s): Contact foundation for current
application deadline
EIN: 016022839

2977
North Orange Memorial Hospital Tax District Trust

c/o SunTrust Bank
P.O. Box 1908
Orlando, FL   32802-1908
Application address: c/o North Orange, Tax District
Scholarship Comm., Attn.: Floride J. Nelson, 201
Park Ave., Apopka, FL 32703, tel.: (401) 886-2384

Foundation type: Independent foundation
Limitations: Scholarships to individuals who have
resided in the Orange County, FL, tax district for at
least one year, for study in a medical-related field.
Financial data: Year ended 09/30/2004.
Assets, $458,038 (M); Expenditures, $23,427;
Total giving, $19,782; Grants to individuals, 21
grants totaling $19,782 (high: $3,500, low: $250).
Fields of interest: Medical school/education.
Type of support: Scholarships—to individuals.
Application information: Applications accepted.
Application form required.
Deadline(s): Mar. 31

Applicants should submit the following:
1) Transcripts
2) Letter(s) of recommendation
EIN: 596730137

2978
North Valley Health Education Foundation

(formerly Chico Community Hospital Foundation)
1354 East Ave., Ste. R
Chico, CA   95926-7383   (530) 332-6182
Contact: Craig Ahlswede, Treas. and C.F.O.

Foundation type: Public charity
Limitations: Scholarships to medical students,
nursing students, and allied health professionals in
Chico, CA.
Publications: Informational brochure.
Financial data: Year ended 12/31/2004.
Assets, $594,152 (M); Expenditures, $37,846;
Total giving, $25,895; Grants to individuals,
totaling $25,895.
Fields of interest: Medical school/education;
Nursing school/education.
Type of support: Graduate support; Undergraduate
support.
Application information: Application form required.
Deadline(s): Mar. 1
Additional information: Contact financial aid
office of participating institution. Interviews
required for finalists.
Program description:
Scholarship Program: Awards two $2,000
scholarships to Butte County residents enrolled in
medical schools anywhere in the U.S.; four $2,000
scholarships to students enrolled in University of
California at Davis Medical School; $1,000
scholarships to nursing students enrolled in Chico
State University; and $500 to $750 scholarships to
those enrolled in Butte County Community
Colleges. Applicants must demonstrate scholastic
achievement, community involvement, and
financial need.
EIN: 237280072

2979
Northeast High School Alumni Foundation

c/o Northeast High School
Cottman & Algon Aves., Rm. 141
Philadelphia, PA   19111   (215) 728-5018
Contact: B.K. Barton, Principal, Northeast High
School

Foundation type: Independent foundation
Limitations: Scholarships and awards to graduating
seniors of Northeast High School, PA.
Financial data: Year ended 06/30/2004.
Assets, $719,717 (M); Expenditures, $24,445;
Total giving, $24,225; Grants to individuals,
totaling $22,375.
Type of support: Support to graduates or students
of specific schools; Awards/prizes; Undergraduate
support.
Application information:
Initial approach: Letter.
Deadline(s): End of school year for current
graduating class
Additional information: Application must also
include financial need and scholastic record.
EIN: 236463349

2980
Northeast Iowa Charitable Foundation
14 East Charles
Oelwein, IA   50662
Contact: Char DeHaven, Dir.

Foundation type: Independent foundation
Limitations: Scholarships to graduates of Oelwein Community Schools, Oelwein, IA.
Financial data: Year ended 12/31/2004.
Assets, $7,301,672 (M); Expenditures, $384,308; Total giving, $350,655; Grants to individuals, totaling $45,250.
Type of support: Support to graduates or students of specific schools.
Application information:
   Initial approach: Letter or telephone.
   Deadline(s): Contact foundation for current application deadline/guidelines
EIN: 421341188

2981
Northeastern New York Community Trust
c/o KeyBank N.A.
800 Superior, TR TX 4
Cleveland, OH   44114
Application address: c/o KeyBank N.A., 54 State St., Albany, NY 12207, tel.: (518) 486-8734

Foundation type: Independent foundation
Limitations: Scholarships to residents of northeastern NY who are children of employees of Albany or state agencies, or KeyCorp and its subsidiaries.
Financial data: Year ended 12/31/2004.
Assets, $2,384,074 (M); Expenditures, $140,623; Total giving, $120,500; Grants to individuals, totaling $120,500.
Type of support: Employee-related scholarships.
Application information:
   Initial approach: Letter.
   Deadline(s): Nov.
EIN: 146030063

2982
The Northern California Scholarship Foundation
(formerly The Northern California Scholarship Foundation and the Scaife Scholarship Foundation)
1547 Lakeside Dr.
Oakland, CA   94612-4520
Contact: Clyde Minar, Secy.-Treas.

Foundation type: Independent foundation
Limitations: Scholarships by recommendation only to northern CA public high school seniors with clear career goals (excluding medicine and the ministry) and American-born parents. Some grants for graduate study and alumni awards.
Publications: Application guidelines; Informational brochure; Program policy statement.
Financial data: Year ended 05/30/2004.
Assets, $13,315,293 (M); Expenditures, $720,950; Total giving, $619,090; Grants to individuals, 129 grants totaling $619,090 (high: $5,000, low: $1,250).
Fields of interest: Education.
Type of support: Graduate support; Undergraduate support.
Application information: Application form required.
   Deadline(s): Mar. 15
   Applicants should submit the following:
      1) Financial information
      2) Transcripts
   Additional information: Applicants must be recommended to the foundation by a principal

or senior counselor before an application form is mailed; college entrance exam scores must also be included.
Program description:
   Scholarship Program: Good health, excellent moral character, and high scholastic achievement are necessary. Candidates must be unable to meet the expenses of a higher education without financial help, and be willing to earn a portion of their expenses while in college. Students of medicine or the ministry are ineligible. Scholarships are renewable for up to four years of undergraduate study contingent upon maintenance of at least a "B" average. Final selections are made by May 10.
EIN: 941540333

2983
Northern Chautauqua Community Foundation, Inc.
212 Lake Shore Dr. W.
Dunkirk, NY   14048   (716) 366-4892
Contact: Diane Hannum, Exec. Dir.; Nancy Mosier;
For grants: Rich Ryan, Grants Coord.
FAX: (716) 366-3905;
E-mail: info@nccfoundation.org; Grant application
E-mail: rryan@nccfoundation.org; URL: http://www.nccfoundation.org

Foundation type: Community foundation
Limitations: Scholarships to high school graduates of over 15 high schools in northern Chautauqua County, NY.
Publications: Application guidelines; Annual report (including application guidelines); Financial statement; Newsletter.
Financial data: Year ended 12/31/2004.
Assets, $11,118,896 (M); Expenditures, $542,729; Total giving, $362,710; Grants to individuals, 189 grants totaling $119,319 (high: $3,500, low: $15).
Type of support: Undergraduate support.
Application information:
   Initial approach: Letter or telephone.
   Deadline(s): Contact foundation for deadline
   Additional information: Applications available from local high schools.
EIN: 161271663

2984
Northern Indiana Fuel and Light Company, Inc. Fund and Trust, Inc.
c/o National City Bank of Indiana
P.O. Box 94651
Cleveland, OH   44101-4651
Contact: Denise Andorfer
Application address: c/o National City Bank of Indiana, P.O. Box 110, Fort Wayne, IN 46801, tel.: (219) 460-6218

Foundation type: Company-sponsored foundation
Limitations: Scholarships to children of employees of Northern Indiana Fuel & Light Company, Inc.
Financial data: Year ended 12/31/2004.
Assets, $310,511 (M); Expenditures, $21,213; Total giving, $20,000; Grants to individuals, 9 grants totaling $20,000 (high: $2,500, low: $2,000).
Type of support: Employee-related scholarships.
Application information: Application form required.
   Deadline(s): June 1
   Applicants should submit the following:
      1) Transcripts
   Additional information: Application form may be obtained from the company.
EIN: 311030243

2985
Northern New York Community Foundation, Inc.
(formerly Watertown Foundation, Inc.)
120 Washington St., Ste. 400
Watertown, NY   13601   (315) 782-7110
Contact: Alex C. Velto, Exec. Dir.
FAX: (315) 782-0047; E-mail: info@nnycf.org;
URL: http://www.nnycf.org

Foundation type: Community foundation
Limitations: Scholarships to legal residents of Jefferson and Lewis counties, NY, who are enrolled as full-time undergraduate students at accredited institutions in the U.S.
Publications: Annual report; Grants list; Newsletter.
Financial data: Year ended 12/31/2004.
Assets, $26,666,244 (M); Expenditures, $2,120,469; Total giving, $1,612,129.
Fields of interest: Higher education; Nursing school/education; Engineering school/education; Health sciences school/education; Engineering/technology.
Type of support: Scholarships—to individuals.
Application information: Application form required.
   Initial approach: Letter, telephone, or office visit.
   Deadline(s): Apr. 1.
   Additional information: Applications may be obtained after Mar. 1 from the foundation's office, the guidance offices of Jefferson and Lewis counties high schools, and the financial aid office of certain colleges in the region.
Program descriptions:
   Herring College Scholars Program: Provides scholarships to students enrolled in engineering, technology, certain fields of science, and related fields of study. First-time recipients are selected at the freshman and junior class levels, and non-traditional students, at any level. Selection of non-traditional students is based primarily upon financial need. Selection is made by the scholarship selection committee on the basis of regents average, class rank, and SAT score. While selection is independent of financial need, the amount of the grant is dependent upon the level of unmet financial need as confirmed by applicant's college. Scholarships are normally granted through completion of the program for which they are approved, provided student maintains academic requirements. Grants are issued directly to recipients.
   Visiting Nurse Association Program: Provides scholarships to students enrolled in health science fields. First-time recipients are selected at the freshman and junior class levels, and non-traditional students, at any level. Selection of non-traditional students is based primarily upon financial need. Selection is made by the scholarship selection committee on the basis of regents average, class rank, and SAT score. While selection is independent of financial need, the amount of the grant is dependent upon the level of unmet financial need as confirmed by applicant's college. Scholarships are normally granted through completion of the program for which they are approved, provided student maintains academic requirements. Grants are issued directly to recipients.
   Northern New York Community Foundation Scholarship Program: Provides scholarships to students enrolled in all academic disciplines except theology. First-time recipients are selected at the freshman and junior class levels, and non-traditional students, at any level. Selection of non-traditional students is based primarily upon financial need. Selection is made by the scholarship selection committee on the basis of

regents average, class rank, and SAT score. While selection is independent of financial need, the amount of the grant is dependent upon the level of unmet financial need as confirmed by applicant's college. Scholarships are normally granted through completion of the program for which they are approved, provided student maintains academic requirements. Grants are issued directly to recipients.
EIN: 156020989

2986
The Northern Palm Beach County Youth Foundation, Inc.
2000 PGA Blvd., Ste. 2204
North Palm Beach, FL 33408

Foundation type: Independent foundation
Limitations: Scholarships to students in the Riveria, FL, area, for higher education.
Financial data: Year ended 12/31/2004. Assets, $0 (M); Expenditures, $133,077; Total giving, $132,200; Grants to individuals, 15 grants totaling $14,200 (high: $1,000, low: $200).
Type of support: Undergraduate support.
Application information: Contact foundation for current application deadline/guidelines.
EIN: 311732652

2987
Northern Virginia Community Foundation
8283 Greensboro Dr.
McLean, VA 22102 (703) 917-2600
Contact: Janet Miller Kreutter, Pres.
FAX: (703) 902-3564;
E-mail: jmkreutter@novacf.org; URL: http://www.novacf.org

Foundation type: Community foundation
Limitations: Scholarships to residents of northern VA. Scholarships also to dependents of employees of PRC, Ogden, and Booz, Allen & Hamilton, subject to certain restrictions.
Publications: Annual report; Financial statement; Grants list; Informational brochure; Informational brochure (including application guidelines); Newsletter; Occasional report.
Financial data: Year ended 06/30/2004. Assets, $19,666,833 (M); Expenditures, $3,132,250; Total giving, $1,845,063; Grants to individuals, 52 grants totaling $74,193.
Type of support: Employee-related scholarships; Scholarships—to individuals.
Application information: Application form required.
Initial approach: Telephone.
Deadline(s): Contact foundation for current application deadline.
EIN: 510232459

2988
Northrup Educational Foundation, Inc.
2485 County Line Rd.
Watkins Glen, NY 14891-9512 (607) 535-7438
Contact: Marilyn W. Cross, Secy.-Treas.

Foundation type: Independent foundation
Limitations: Interest-free student loans to college students in good standing who have resided in Schuyler County, NY, for ten years. Scholarships to the students with the highest ACT and SAT scores from Watkins Glen Central School and Odessa-Montour Central School, NY.
Financial data: Year ended 08/31/2004. Assets, $314,769 (M); Expenditures, $8,113;

Total giving, $2,000; Grants to individuals, 2 grants totaling $2,000; Loans to individuals, totaling $1,263.
Type of support: Support to graduates or students of specific schools; Undergraduate support.
Application information: Application form required.
Deadline(s): Apr. 1 to June 10
Applicants should submit the following:
1) SAT
2) ACT
Additional information: Application must also include statement of ten-year residency in Schuyler County, other tuition resources, unpaid debts, and grades from prior year.
Program description:
Student Loan Program: If a student remains in school and maintains satisfactory educational progress, the loan does not become due until graduation. Applicants are notified of decision by July 15.
EIN: 156020359

2989
Northwest Bancorp, Inc. Charitable Foundation
c/o Northwest Bancorp, Inc.
Liberty at 2nd Ave.
Warren, PA 16365 (814) 728-7261
Contact: Vicki Stec, Secy.

Foundation type: Company-sponsored foundation
Limitations: Scholarships to Northwest Bancorp, Inc. employees and their children for undergraduate education.
Financial data: Year ended 06/30/2005. Assets, $1,479,437 (M); Expenditures, $83,913; Total giving, $71,258; Grants to individuals, 21 grants totaling $48,300.
Type of support: Employee-related scholarships.
Application information: Application form required.
Additional information: Contact foundation for current application deadlines/guidelines.
EIN: 251819537

2990
Northwest Danish Foundation
c/o Scholarship Comm.
1833 N. 105th St., Ste. 203
Seattle, WA 98133-8973 (206) 523-3263
Contact: Scott Ryan Moore, Exec. Dir.
FAX: (206) 729-6997; E-mail: danesnw@aol.com; Additional address: 9500 S.W. Barbur Blvd., Ste. 302, Portland, OR 97219, tel.: (503) 452-9667; E-mail: nwdf@aol.com; URL: http://www.nwdanish.org

Foundation type: Public charity
Limitations: Scholarships only to WA and OR residents, who are either of Danish descent or married to someone of Danish descent, and have shown exceptional involvement in the Danish community. Consideration is also given to those who are not of Danish descent, but only if they have been exceptionally involved in the Danish community.
Publications: Application guidelines; Annual report; Newsletter.
Financial data: Year ended 06/30/2003. Assets, $2,281,133 (M); Expenditures, $514,871; Total giving, $14,785; Grants to individuals, totaling $14,785.
Fields of interest: Language (foreign); Arts; Vocational education.
Type of support: Scholarships—to individuals.
Application information: Application form required.

Initial approach: Letter, telephone, or e-mail.
Deadline(s): Apr. 1
Applicants should submit the following:
1) Transcripts
2) Essay
Additional information: Application must include information on Danish background, a character reference, educational reference, and Danish community reference.
Program description:
Scholarship Program: Scholarships may be used in seeking academic or vocational degrees, re-training for employment possibilities, training for legitimate artistic careers that enrich and/or entertain, or for participation in Danish activities such as language lessons, folk dancing, literary symposia, or any other program designated for advancement of the Danish culture.
EIN: 910565541

2991
Northwest Health Foundation
1500 S.W. 1st Ave., Ste. 850
Portland, OR 97201-5884 (503) 220-1955
Contact: Thomas Aschenbrener, Pres.
FAX: (503) 220-1335; E-mail: nwhf@nwhf.org; URL: http://www.nwhf.org

Foundation type: Public charity
Limitations: Grants to students in OR, or Clark, Cowlitz, Pacific, Skamania and Wahkiakum counties in WA, to engage in research related to health and medicine. Average grants range from $100 to $3,000.
Financial data: Year ended 12/31/2004. Assets, $61,286,389 (M); Expenditures, $4,436,347; Total giving, $2,815,502.
Fields of interest: Health care.
Type of support: Stipends.
Application information:
Initial approach: E-mail.
Additional information: Contact foundation for application guidelines.
EIN: 911854545

2992
The Norwegian Children's Home Association of New York, Inc.
P.O. Box 280104
Brooklyn, NY 11228-0104 (718) 238-4326
Contact: John Nersten, Jr., Pres.

Foundation type: Operating foundation
Limitations: Scholarships to students who are of at least 25 percent Norwegian ancestry, or who have a significant Norwegian affiliation, for higher education.
Financial data: Year ended 12/31/2002. Assets, $3,182,939 (M); Expenditures, $23,322; Total giving, $100.
Fields of interest: Norway.
Type of support: Undergraduate support.
Application information:
Initial approach: Letter.
Deadline(s): Mar. 10
EIN: 111666853

2993
Novi Educational Foundation
25345 Taft Rd.
Novi, MI 48374 (248) 449-1205
Contact: Bob Schram, Exec. Dir.

Foundation type: Public charity

Limitations: Grants to students of the Novi Community School District, MI, to broaden and enrich their experiences.
Publications: Informational brochure.
Financial data: Year ended 06/30/2005. Assets, $55,304 (M); Expenditures, $51,228; Total giving, $38,050; Grants to individuals, 13 grants totaling $38,050 (high: $3,500, low: $175).
Type of support: Support to graduates or students of specific schools; Precollege support.
Application information: Applications not accepted.
EIN: 382665305

2994
NRC Foundation, Inc.
c/o Seaview House
70 Seaview Ave.
Stamford, CT   06902-6040   (203) 964-5200
Contact: Michael Zauderer

Foundation type: Independent foundation
Limitations: Scholarships to family members of XL America employees.
Financial data: Year ended 12/31/2004. Assets, $200,043 (M); Expenditures, $15,057; Total giving, $15,000; Grants to individuals, 3 grants totaling $15,000 (high: $6,000, low: $4,000).
Type of support: Employee-related scholarships.
Application information: Application form required.
Deadline(s): June 30
Applicants should submit the following:
1) Letter(s) of recommendation
2) Transcripts
3) Essay
EIN: 061559574

2995
Nucor Foundation
2100 Rexford Rd.
Charlotte, NC   28211-3418
Contact: James M. Coblin, Dir.

Foundation type: Company-sponsored foundation
Limitations: Undergraduate and vocational education scholarships to children and stepchildren of employees of Nucor Corporation who have been employed for at least two years, or who are disabled or deceased. See program description for further employee qualifications.
Publications: Application guidelines.
Financial data: Year ended 12/31/2004. Assets, $18,760 (M); Expenditures, $992,277; Total giving, $991,609; Grants to individuals, 444 grants totaling $991,609 (high: $5,250, low: $120).
Fields of interest: Vocational education.
Type of support: Employee-related scholarships.
Application information: Application form required.
Deadline(s): Mar. 1
Applicants should submit the following:
1) Transcripts
2) Financial information
3) Letter(s) of recommendation
4) GPA
Additional information: Recipients notified late May.
Program description:
Scholarship Program: Scholarships are provided to children and stepchildren of qualified Nucor employees. Qualified employees include:
• Full-time, active Nucor employees who have been employed by Nucor for at least two years, who continue to work for Nucor until after the scholarship is disbursed, and who

are not Nucor executive officers or directors, or officers or directors of the foundation
• Nucor employees who have died, or became totally and permanently disabled while working full-time for Nucor
Scholarships are granted based on the applicant's personal background, academic abilities, leadership traits, character, and financial need. Scholarships are awarded for up to four years of study and must be applied for within four years of high school graduation. Scholarships are generally $2,000 per year, although children of qualified employees who died in a workplace incident are eligible for twice the normal maximum scholarship amount. In order to continue receiving annual scholarship renewals, recipients must maintain at least a 2.0 GPA and continue as full-time students.
EIN: 237318064

2996
Adaline C. Nugent Educational Fund
c/o United Bank, Inc.
514 Market St.
Parkersburg, WV   26101-5144

Foundation type: Independent foundation
Limitations: Scholarship to a financially needy student attending Parkersburg High School, WV, who might otherwise be forced to drop out.
Financial data: Year ended 12/31/2004. Assets, $206,885 (M); Expenditures, $10,125; Total giving, $7,000; Grant to an individual, 1 grant totaling $7,000.
Type of support: Support to graduates or students of specific schools; Undergraduate support.
Application information: Applications not accepted.
Additional information: The principals of Parkersburg High School, WV, and the four junior high schools feeding it, select the most deserving student for financial aid.
EIN: 237425082

2997
S. T. & Mabel I. Nuttycomb Charitable Trust No. 2
302 Holland St.
Prairie View, KS   67664

Foundation type: Independent foundation
Limitations: Scholarships to students from Phillips and Norton Counties, KS.
Financial data: Year ended 09/30/2005. Assets, $730,051 (M); Expenditures, $39,301; Total giving, $30,500; Grants to individuals, 32 grants totaling $30,500.
Type of support: Scholarships—to individuals.
Application information: Applications not accepted.
EIN: 481027799

2998
Grace Swift Nye & Alfred Gibbs Nye Scholarship Trust
c/o Elaine H. LeLaurin, Admin.
P.O. Box 271369
West Hartford, CT   06127-1369
(860) 521-5694
FAX: (860) 521-7247

Foundation type: Independent foundation

Limitations: Scholarships to graduating high school seniors in Bourne, Plymouth, Sandwich, and Wareham, MA.
Publications: Application guidelines.
Financial data: Year ended 12/31/2004. Assets, $5,321,751 (M); Expenditures, $407,363; Total giving, $320,497; Grants to individuals, totaling $320,497.
Type of support: Undergraduate support.
Application information: Application form required.
Deadline(s): Apr. 1
Additional information: Contact trust for current application guidelines.
EIN: 066421534

2999
NYS Fraternal Order of Police Foundation
(formerly NYS Fraternal Order of Police Empire State Foundation)
911 Police Plz.
Hicksville, NY   11801   (516) 433-4455
Contact: Frank Ferrerya, Pres.
URL: http://www.nysfop.org

Foundation type: Public charity
Limitations: Scholarships to high school seniors residing in NY.
Publications: Financial statement.
Financial data: Year ended 12/31/2004. Assets, $9,889,053 (M); Expenditures, $613,407.
Type of support: Undergraduate support.
Application information: Application form required.
Deadline(s): Apr. 7
Program description:
Scholarship Program: Recipients will be chosen by a lottery drawing and will be presented at the NYSFOP headquarters on the annual scholarship awards night.
EIN: 113207296

3000
The O'Brien-VRBA Scholarship Trust
c/o National City Bank
P.O. Box 94651
Cleveland, OH   44101-4651
Application address: c/o Jo Ann Harlan, National City Bank, P.O. Box 749, Peoria, IL 61652-0749, tel.: (309) 655-5000

Foundation type: Independent foundation
Limitations: Scholarships to Catholic residents of IA, IL, IN, MI and WI for higher education.
Financial data: Year ended 12/31/2004. Assets, $3,698,282 (M); Expenditures, $291,431; Total giving, $248,000; Grants to individuals, 236 grants totaling $232,000 (high: $1,000, low: $1,000).
Fields of interest: Roman Catholic agencies & churches.
Type of support: Undergraduate support.
Application information: Application form required.
Initial approach: Letter.
Deadline(s): Apr. 1
EIN: 376277500

3001
Frank O'Brion Trust
c/o Bank of America, N.A., Charitable Asset Div.
77 Main St., CTEN4022C
Hartford, CT   06115
Application address: c/o Anne Zartarian, Office of Financial Aid., P.O. Box 248, Cortland, NY 13045

Foundation type: Independent foundation

Limitations: Scholarships to financially needy children of employees of Bank of America, N.A. or any of its subsidiaries located in CT.
Financial data: Year ended 10/31/2004.
Assets, $1,330,852 (M); Expenditures, $96,399; Total giving, $74,000; Grants to individuals, totaling $74,000.
Fields of interest: Financial services.
Type of support: Employee-related scholarships.
Application information: Application form required.
　Deadline(s): Mar. 30
　Applicants should submit the following:
　　1) FAFSA
EIN: 066154532

3002
Charles D. & Gertrude H. O'Connor Educational Trust
8333 N. 700 W.
Earl Park, IN　47942　(219) 474-6674
Contact: Bruce Illingworth, Chair.

Foundation type: Independent foundation
Limitations: Scholarships to students residing in White and Benton counties, IN.
Financial data: Year ended 12/31/2004.
Assets, $268,101 (M); Expenditures, $18,973; Total giving, $14,000; Grants to individuals, 6 grants totaling $14,000.
Type of support: Scholarships—to individuals.
Application information: Application form required.
　Deadline(s): Apr. 1
　Applicants should submit the following:
　　1) Transcripts
　Additional information: Application must also include a listing of high school activities.
EIN: 311012552

3003
John and Blanche O'Hara Trust
c/o Marshall & Ilsley Bank
P.O. Box 2980
Milwaukee, WI　53201

Foundation type: Independent foundation
Limitations: Scholarships to graduating seniors of Superior High School, WI, who have been accepted to a junior college or university.
Financial data: Year ended 12/31/2004.
Assets, $692,985 (M); Expenditures, $42,124; Total giving, $37,201; Grants to individuals, 32 grants totaling $37,201 (high: $2,701; low: $1,000).
Type of support: Support to graduates or students of specific schools; Undergraduate support.
Application information: Contact high school guidance counselor for current application deadline/guidelines.
EIN: 946659540

3004
Catherine G. O'Leary Scholarship Fund Trust
c/o Joseph G. Prone
P.O. Box 3007
Andover, MA　01810-0801

Foundation type: Independent foundation
Limitations: Scholarships to the top ten students of Lawrence High School, MA.
Financial data: Year ended 12/31/2004.
Assets, $246,636 (M); Expenditures, $10,483; Total giving, $10,000.

Type of support: Scholarships—to individuals; Support to graduates or students of specific schools.
Application information: Applications not accepted.
EIN: 046307098

3005
The O'Meara Foundation, Inc.
P.O. Box 290157
Wethersfield, CT　06109-0157　(860) 563-2918
Contact: Martin O'Meara, Pres.
E-mail: BPINCMAX@aol.com; Application address: 1900 Berlin Tpke., Wethersfield, CT 06109

Foundation type: Independent foundation
Limitations: Scholarships to financially needy residents of Hartford County, CT, for higher education.
Publications: Annual report.
Financial data: Year ended 06/30/2005.
Assets, $4,441,912 (M); Expenditures, $201,897; Total giving, $160,000.
Type of support: Scholarships—to individuals.
Application information: Applications accepted. Application form required.
　Initial approach: Letter.
　Deadline(s): June 1
　Applicants should submit the following:
　　1) Letter(s) of recommendation
　　2) Transcripts
　Additional information: Application must include federal tax returns.
EIN: 066034580

3006
L. Arthur O'Neill, Jr. Education Fund
P.O. Box 1798
Sumter, SC　29151-1798　(803) 469-6137
Contact: Vivian Brogdon
Application address: P.O. Box 2091, Sumter, SC 29151

Foundation type: Independent foundation
Limitations: Student loans to residents of Sumter County, SC, to attend SC colleges and universities full-time.
Financial data: Year ended 04/30/2005.
Assets, $2,172,720 (M); Expenditures, $49,468; Total giving, $0; Loans to individuals, totaling $113,610.
Type of support: Student loans—to individuals.
Application information: Application form required.
　Deadline(s): May 1 and Nov. 1
　Applicants should submit the following:
　　1) Transcripts
　　2) Letter(s) of recommendation
　　3) FAFSA
　Additional information: Application must also include character reference.
EIN: 237227009

3007
Oak Park/River Forest Community Foundation
1049 Lake St., No. 204
Oak Park, IL　60301　(708) 848-1560
Contact: For grants: David Weindling, Donor Svcs. Dir.
FAX: (708) 848-1531;
E-mail: advisors@oprfcommfd.org; URL: http://www.oprfcommfd.org

Foundation type: Community foundation

Limitations: Scholarships to graduating high school seniors in the Oak Park and River Forest, IL, area. Camperships to children from low-income families in metropolitan Chicago.
Publications: Application guidelines; Annual report (including application guidelines); Grants list; Informational brochure; Newsletter; Occasional report.
Financial data: Year ended 12/31/2004.
Assets, $8,986,824 (M); Expenditures, $935,917; Total giving, $644,493.
Fields of interest: Recreation, community facilities; Children/youth, services.
Type of support: Support to graduates or students of specific schools; Undergraduate support; Grants for special needs.
Application information: Application form required.
　Initial approach: Letter.
　Deadline(s): Apr. for scholarships, None for camperships
　Additional information: See Web site for additional information.
Program descriptions:
　Kathy McMahon Adams Scholarship Fund: Provides scholarships to students who attend Ascension School and parishioners at Ascension Catholic Church, in Oak Park, IL, for undergraduate study.
　Crystal Scholarship Fund: Provides camperships to 11- to 18-year-old children from metropolitan Chicago low-income families to access "away from home" residential programs in order to help break the cycle of poverty.
　19th Century Woman's Club: Provides four-year scholarships to graduating senior women from Oak Park and River Forest High School.
　Oak Park/River Forest High School Scholarship Fund: Provides scholarships to graduating seniors at the high school.
　Rotary Scholarship Fund: Provides undergraduate scholarships to Oak Park and River Forest, IL, graduating seniors.
EIN: 364150724

3008
Frank L. Oakes Foundation
c/o JPMorgan Chase Bank, N.A.
P.O. Box 1308
Milwaukee, WI　53201
Application address: c/o Kathy Whitney, JPMorgan Chase Bank, N.A., 111 Monument Cir., Indianapolis, IN 46277-0115, tel.: (317) 321-8189

Foundation type: Independent foundation
Limitations: Scholarships by nomination only to graduates of Marion County, IN, high schools for college or other postsecondary education.
Financial data: Year ended 05/31/2005.
Assets, $454,791 (M); Expenditures, $27,535; Total giving, $25,660.
Fields of interest: College.
Type of support: Support to graduates or students of specific schools; Awards/grants by nomination only; Undergraduate support.
Application information: Application form required.
　Deadline(s): Apr. 30.
EIN: 356015133

3009
Oakland County Community Trust
c/o Comerica Bank
P.O. Box 75000, MC 3302
Detroit, MI　48275-3317

Foundation type: Public charity

Limitations: Scholarships to financially needy Oakland County, MI, residents.
Financial data: Year ended 12/31/2004.
Assets, $408,378 (M); Expenditures, $15,213; Total giving, $8,000.
Type of support: Scholarships—to individuals.
Application information: Contact trust for current application deadline/guidelines.
EIN: 386102697

3010

Oakland Foundation, Inc.
P.O. Box 491
Stowe, VT 05672-0491 (802) 253-5115
Contact: Scholarships: Katherine Lutz Coppock
FAX: (802) 253-6877; E-mail: oakland@oak.org;
Additional address: P.O. Box 3680, Parkersburg, VA 26103

Foundation type: Independent foundation
Limitations: Scholarships to individuals to attend college in WV.
Publications: Application guidelines; Annual report.
Financial data: Year ended 12/31/2004.
Assets, $3,826,585 (M); Expenditures, $199,746; Total giving, $139,375.
Fields of interest: Education.
Type of support: Scholarships—to individuals.
Application information:
  Initial approach: Telephone or e-mail.
  Additional information: Contact foundation for current application deadlines/guidelines.
EIN: 550754353

3011

L. R. Oates Scholarship Fund
c/o Wachovia Bank, N.A.
100 N. Maint St., 13th Fl.
Winston-Salem, NC 27150 (800) 576-5135
Contact: K. Mair, Account Mgr.
FAX: (336) 732-6537

Foundation type: Independent foundation
Limitations: Student loans to financially needy high school graduates for higher education.
Financial data: Year ended 05/31/2005.
Assets, $885,412 (M); Expenditures, $27,892; Total giving, $12,000; Grants to individuals, totaling $12,000.
Fields of interest: Higher education.
Type of support: Undergraduate support.
Application information: Applications accepted. Application form required.
  Initial approach: Letter.
  Applicants should submit the following:
    1) Transcripts
  Additional information: Application must also include a copy of driver's license.
EIN: 596672364

3012

Forrest C. Oates & Minnie Less Oates Scholarship Trust
c/o Wachovia Bank, N.A.
P.O. Box 830804
Birmingham, AL 35283-0804
Application address: c/o Scholarship Comm., First Baptist Church of Pelham, Pelham, AL 35124

Foundation type: Independent foundation
Limitations: Scholarships to residents of Pelham, AL, who attend or plan to attend a college or university in AL.

Financial data: Year ended 12/31/2004.
Assets, $242,495 (M); Expenditures, $13,437; Total giving, $9,781; Grants to individuals, 7 grants totaling $9,781 (high: $2,181, low: $1,000).
Type of support: Scholarships—to individuals.
Application information: Applications by letter, outlining financial need, accepted throughout the year.
EIN: 636166146

3013

Julia S. Oberdorfer Scholarship Trust Fund
c/o The Citizens State Bank
P.O. Box C
New Castle, IN 47362-1045
Application address: c/o Evelyn Rentchler, Counselor, New Castle Chrysler High School, 801 Parkview Dr., New Castle, IN 47362

Foundation type: Independent foundation
Limitations: Scholarships to graduating seniors of New Castle Chrysler High School, IN.
Financial data: Year ended 12/31/2004.
Assets, $432,329 (M); Expenditures, $19,973; Total giving, $16,500; Grants to individuals, 15 grants totaling $16,500 (high: $2,000, low: $500).
Type of support: Support to graduates or students of specific schools; Undergraduate support.
Application information: Application form required.
  Deadline(s): Feb. 15
  Applicants should submit the following:
    1) Transcripts
    2) SAT
    3) ACT
  Additional information: Application must also include PSAT test scores, attendance records, and name of college to attend.
EIN: 356238626

3014

Ocean State Power Scholarship Foundation, Ltd.
62 Capron St.
Uxbridge, MA 01569 (508) 278-6943

Foundation type: Operating foundation
Limitations: Scholarships to students of Uxbridge, MA, to attend four-year colleges.
Financial data: Year ended 12/31/2003.
Assets, $576,942 (M); Expenditures, $48,947; Total giving, $37,100; Grants to individuals, 16 grants totaling $37,100 (high: $13,975, low: $500).
Type of support: Scholarships—to individuals.
Application information: Applications accepted. Application form required.
  Deadline(s): Contact foundation for deadline
EIN: 222908697

3015

Ochoco Charitable Fund
(formerly Ochoco Scholarship Fund)
P.O. Box 668
Prineville, OR 97754
Contact: Vivian Stock, Tr.
Application address: c/o Crook County High School, 1100 S.E. Lynn Blvd., Prineville, OR 97754, tel.: (541) 416-6900

Foundation type: Company-sponsored foundation
Limitations: Scholarships to residents of the Prineville (Crook County), OR, area.
Financial data: Year ended 12/31/2002.
Assets, $495,516 (M); Expenditures, $33,389;

Total giving, $31,560; Grants to individuals, 60 grants totaling $31,560 (high: $900, low: $280).
Type of support: Undergraduate support.
Application information: Application form not required.
  Deadline(s): Contact fund for current application deadline
  Applicants should submit the following:
    1) GPA
  Additional information: Application by letter, including name of college attended and credit hours. Recipients are selected on the basis of academic standing, financial need, character, personality, and social adjustment. Grants are not usually given for the first college semester. Exceptions are made in cases where the applicant has shown marked ability in high school and is financially unable to enter college without a grant.
EIN: 936024014

3016

Ogden College Foundation
c/o Daryl Greattinger, Regent
1994 N. Main St.
Monticello, KY 42633
Contact: Daryl Greattinger, Regent
Application address: c/o Leigh Jones, Tr., P.O. Box 610, Madison, TN 37116-0610, tel.: (615) 868-9391; E-mail: ljones@tpac.org

Foundation type: Independent foundation
Limitations: Scholarships to graduates of KY public and private high schools who have a grade average of "B" or better and who intend to pursue a major or minor at the Ogden College of Science, Technology and Health at Western Kentucky University. Professorships, fellowships, and science awards are also granted.
Publications: Informational brochure (including application guidelines).
Financial data: Year ended 06/30/2005.
Assets, $2,613,960 (M); Expenditures, $139,208; Total giving, $96,640; Grants to individuals, 82 grants totaling $96,640 (high: $3,770, low: $100).
Fields of interest: Health sciences school/education; Science; Engineering/technology.
Type of support: Undergraduate support.
Application information: Applications accepted. Application form required.
  Deadline(s): None, however, scholarships are awarded on a first-come, first-served basis, so submission by at least Jan. 1 is encouraged
  Additional information: Interviews required.
EIN: 237078715

3017

Robert and Willora Oglesby Foundation, Inc.
1409 N. Waterview Dr.
Richardson, TX 75080-3904
Contact: Robert K. Oglesby, Dir.

Foundation type: Independent foundation
Limitations: Scholarships are awarded to private Christian colleges and universities on behalf of deserving but needy student pulpit preachers.
Financial data: Year ended 12/31/2004.
Assets, $312,258 (M); Expenditures, $16,919; Total giving, $16,150.
Fields of interest: Theological school/education; Christian agencies & churches.
Type of support: Scholarships—to individuals.

Application information: Applications not accepted.
EIN: 752468388

3018
Jean Paul Ohadi Memorial Foundation
1500 N. Skokie Blvd., No. 420
Northbrook, IL 60062 (972) 881-5399
Contact: Cynthia Drey, Secy.
Application address: 4333 Tall Oak Ln., Plano, TX 75074; Email: texnbell@mac.com

Foundation type: Independent foundation
Limitations: Scholarships to gay and lesbian individuals in IL, who are 17 years of age or older, who wish to attend an institution of higher learning.
Financial data: Year ended 06/30/2004.
Assets, $461,626 (M); Expenditures, $84,928; Total giving, $84,750; Grants to individuals, 2 grants totaling $10,000 (high: $2,000, low: $2,000).
Fields of interest: LGBTQ.
Type of support: Scholarships—to individuals.
Application information: Application form required.
Initial approach: Letter or e-mail.
Deadline(s): Feb. 15
Applicants should submit the following:
1) Work samples
2) Transcripts
3) Letter(s) of recommendation
4) Essay
Additional information: Contact foundation for current application guidelines.
EIN: 364240821

3019
Ohio County Community Foundation, Inc.
215 Main St.
P.O. Box 170
Rising Sun, IN 47040 (812) 438-9401
Contact: Peggy Dickson, Exec. Dir.
Email address for scholarships:
pdickson@occfrisingsun.com
FAX: (812) 438-9488;
E-mail: ohioccf@seidata.com; URL: http://www.occfrisingsun.com

Foundation type: Community foundation
Limitations: Scholarships to graduates of Rising Sun High School, IN.
Publications: Application guidelines; Annual report; Informational brochure; Newsletter.
Financial data: Year ended 12/31/2004.
Assets, $15,931,818 (M); Expenditures, $476,530; Total giving, $126,692; Grants to individuals, totaling $95,071.
Type of support: Support to graduates or students of specific schools.
Application information:
Initial approach: Letter.
Additional information: Contact foundation for current application deadline/guidelines.
EIN: 352038531

3020
Oilgear Ferris Foundation
P.O. Box 343924
Milwaukee, WI 53234-3924
Contact: Thomas Price, Treas.
Application address: 2300 S. 51st St., Milwaukee, WI 53219

Foundation type: Company-sponsored foundation

Limitations: Scholarships to children of active employees of The Oilgear Company.
Financial data: Year ended 12/31/2004.
Assets, $713,596 (M); Expenditures, $11,740; Total giving, $9,575.
Type of support: Employee-related scholarships.
Application information: Application form not required.
Deadline(s): Mar. 31.
Additional information: Interviews required.
EIN: 396050126

3021
Oklahoma Elks Major Project, Inc.
4232 Epperly Dr.
Del City, OK 73115-3726 (405) 672-2987
Contact: Richard Medlin, Pres.

Foundation type: Public charity
Limitations: Scholarships to high school graduates in OK for higher education.
Financial data: Year ended 03/31/2002.
Assets, $257,692 (M); Expenditures, $122,620; Total giving, $116,329; Grants to individuals, totaling $16,000.
Type of support: Undergraduate support.
Application information: Contact foundation for current application deadline/guidelines.
EIN: 237210114

3022
Oklahoma Scholarship Fund
3030 N.W. Expressway, Ste. 1313
Oklahoma City, OK 73112 (405) 942-5489
Contact: Karen Horton, Exec. Dir.

Foundation type: Independent foundation
Limitations: Scholarships to financially needy OK residents attending second through eighth grade.
Financial data: Year ended 11/30/2004.
Assets, $977 (M); Expenditures, $154,408; Total giving, $154,243; Grants to individuals, 137 grants totaling $154,243 (high: $9,024, low: $270).
Type of support: Scholarships—to individuals.
Application information: Applications accepted. Application form required.
Initial approach: Letter or telephone.
Deadline(s): Contact fund for current application deadline/guidelines
EIN: 731484452

3023
Old Harbor Scholarship Foundation
P.O. Box 71
Old Harbor, AK 99643

Foundation type: Company-sponsored foundation
Limitations: Scholarships to Old Harbour Native Corporation shareholders, their dependents, and descendants. Applicants must be either Alaska Natives or descendants thereof.
Financial data: Year ended 12/31/2004.
Assets, $12,378 (M); Expenditures, $20,000; Total giving, $20,000; Grants to individuals, 20 grants totaling $20,000 (high: $1,000, low: $1,000).
Type of support: Undergraduate support.
Application information: Applications accepted. Application form required.
Applicants should submit the following:
1) Letter(s) of recommendation
Additional information: Applications must include proof of college enrollment.
EIN: 920154160

3024
Olds Foundation, Inc.
P.O. Box 114
Amity, AR 71921
Contact: Millard Aud, Chair. and Mgr.

Foundation type: Independent foundation
Limitations: Scholarships to undergraduate college students in AR.
Financial data: Year ended 11/30/2004.
Assets, $11,986,215 (M); Expenditures, $646,875; Total giving, $551,506; Grants to individuals, 36 grants totaling $55,756 (high: $2,500, low: $750).
Type of support: Undergraduate support.
Application information: Application form required.
Deadline(s): Two months prior to start of college term
Additional information: Interviews required.
EIN: 710747091

3025
Jack H. & Lovell R. Olender Foundation
888 17th St. N.W., 4th Fl.
Washington, DC 20006
Contact: Jack H. Olender, Pres.; Lovell R. Olender, Secy.

Foundation type: Independent foundation
Limitations: Scholarships to students from low-income families living in Washington, DC.
Financial data: Year ended 12/31/2004.
Assets, $430,904 (M); Expenditures, $245,890; Total giving, $238,065; Grants to individuals, 12 grants totaling $12,000 (high: $1,000, low: $1,000).
Fields of interest: Economically disadvantaged.
Type of support: Scholarships—to individuals.
Application information:
Deadline(s): Before start of fall term
Applicants should submit the following:
1) Letter(s) of recommendation
2) Essay
Additional information: Application must also include a copy of senior year high school grades, and a copy of parents' tax return. Contact foundation for guidelines.
EIN: 521622462

3026
Matred Carlton Olliff Foundation
P.O. Box 995
Wauchula, FL 33873-0995
Application address: c/o Doyle E. Carlton, P.O. Box 144, Wauchula, FL 33873

Foundation type: Independent foundation
Limitations: Scholarships only to graduates of Hardee High School, Wauchula, FL.
Financial data: Year ended 08/31/2005.
Assets, $4,973,450 (M); Expenditures, $198,659; Total giving, $165,237; Grants to individuals, 52 grants totaling $54,638 (high: $4,473, low: $60).
Type of support: Support to graduates or students of specific schools; Undergraduate support.
Application information: Applications accepted.
Initial approach: Letter.
Deadline(s): July 1
EIN: 592241303

3027
C. P. & Irene Olson Trust
c/o Bremer Bank, N.A., Trust Dept.
1100 W. St. Germain St.
St. Cloud, MN 56302

Foundation type: Independent foundation
Limitations: Scholarships to students attending any college or university in ND, and to students at Concordia College-Moorhead and the University of Minnesota, MN.
Financial data: Year ended 12/31/2004. Assets, $250,249 (M); Expenditures, $15,611; Total giving, $12,800; Grants to individuals, 16 grants totaling $12,800 (high: $800; low: $800).
Type of support: Support to graduates or students of specific schools; Undergraduate support.
Application information: Applications not accepted.
EIN: 456076668

3028
Iona Olson Trust
4647 Thistle Mill Ct.
Kalamazoo, MI 49006 (269) 544-2946
Contact: Ronald Olson, Tr.

Foundation type: Independent foundation
Limitations: Scholarships to male students graduating from any high school in Potwin, KS, and who attend Potwin Christian Church.
Financial data: Year ended 12/31/2004. Assets, $391,945 (M); Expenditures, $18,324; Total giving, $11,577; Grants to individuals, 2 grants totaling $7,866 (high: $3,933; low: $3,933).
Fields of interest: Protestant agencies & churches.
Type of support: Undergraduate support.
Application information:
Deadline(s): None
Additional information: Recipients must have the most outstanding academic record of any male graduating high school senior who attends Potwin Christian Church and who plans to attend a qualifying education institution. If there is no male graduating high school senior who attends Potwin Christian Church and plans to attend a qualifying institution, scholarships will be awarded to female graduating high school seniors who attend Potwin Christian Church and who plan to attend a qualifying institution of higher learning. Application by letter.
EIN: 486328340

3029
Omaha Volunteers for Handicapped Children
10842 John Galt Blvd.
Omaha, NE 68137 (402) 553-0378
Contact: Lois M. Carlson, Pres.

Foundation type: Independent foundation
Limitations: Scholarships to individuals in Omaha, NE, who are pursuing careers in the education or care of handicapped children.
Financial data: Year ended 12/31/2004. Assets, $265,624 (M); Expenditures, $10,318; Total giving, $10,000; Grants to individuals, 10 grants totaling $10,000 (high: $1,000; low: $1,000).
Fields of interest: Education, special; Teacher school/education; Disabilities, people with.
Type of support: Undergraduate support.

Application information: Applications accepted. Application form required.
Deadline(s): July 15
Applicants should submit the following:
1) Transcripts
Additional information: Application must also include acceptance to institution.
EIN: 363958269

3030
The OMC Foundation
(formerly The Ole Evinrude Foundation)
P.O. Box 580692
Pleasant Prairie, WI 53158-8081

Foundation type: Independent foundation
Limitations: Undergraduate scholarships to children of employees of Outboard Marine Corporation in AR, FL, GA, IL, IN, MI, MO, NC, NY, OR, SC, TN, TX, and WI.
Financial data: Year ended 09/30/2004. Assets, $2,976,957 (M); Expenditures, $1,932,484; Total giving, $1,839,000; Grants to individuals, 18 grants totaling $19,000 (high: $2,000; low: $500).
Type of support: Employee-related scholarships.
Application information:
Initial approach: Letter.
Deadline(s): Sept. 15
Additional information: Interviews required.
EIN: 396037139

3031
Omega Charitable Foundation
(formerly Raymond A. Rich Charitable Foundation)
P.O. Box 241
Esopus, NY 12429
Contact: Claire W. Carlson, Secy.

Foundation type: Independent foundation
Limitations: Scholarships to students for higher education.
Financial data: Year ended 12/31/2004. Assets, $30,618 (M); Expenditures, $6,789; Total giving, $6,500; Grants to individuals, 2 grants totaling $6,500 (high: $5,500; low: $1,000).
Type of support: Undergraduate support.
Application information: Applications by letter accepted throughout the year.
EIN: 860659431

3032
Ontario Children's Home
P.O. Box 82
Canandaigua, NY 14424
Application address: c/o Mrs. Richard Ogden, 210 W. Gibson St., Canadaigua, NY 14424

Foundation type: Independent foundation
Limitations: Student loans to residents of Ontario County, NY, who are under the age of 21.
Financial data: Year ended 09/30/2004. Assets, $3,155,790 (M); Expenditures, $153,246; Total giving, $136,926; Loans to individuals, 50 loans totaling $74,492.
Type of support: Student loans—to individuals.
Application information:
Initial approach: Letter.
Deadline(s): Mar. 15
Additional information: Ineligible applications will not be considered or acknowledged; Interviews required.
EIN: 166028318

3033
The Ontonagon Area Scholarship Foundation
P.O. Box 92
Ontonagon, MI 49953

Foundation type: Public charity
Limitations: Scholarships to graduates of Ontonagon Area High School, MI.
Financial data: Year ended 05/31/2004. Assets, $411,264; Expenditures, $14,437; Total giving, $11,250; Grants to individuals, 15 grants totaling $11,250 (high: $750; low: $750).
Type of support: Support to graduates or students of specific schools.
Application information:
Initial approach: Letter.
Additional information: Contact foundation for further application information.
EIN: 383525614

3034
Oocea Foundation, Inc.
525 S. Magnolia Ave.
Orlando, FL 32801-4414 (407) 316-3800
Contact: Terri Slack, Pres.

Foundation type: Public charity
Limitations: Scholarships to residents of FL who are minorities and/or disadvantaged, for the study of engineering.
Financial data: Year ended 12/31/2004. Assets, $19,232 (M); Expenditures, $31,514; Total giving, $30,750.
Fields of interest: Engineering school/education.
Type of support: Undergraduate support.
Application information: Applications accepted. Application form required.
Initial approach: Letter.
Additional information: Contact foundation for further information.
Program description:
Engineering Scholarship: The criteria used to select recipients are as follows:
· Attend full-time (12 credit hours per semester)
· Be a minority or disadvantaged
· Enroll in a pre-engineering or an engineering technology program
· Demonstrate financial need
· A minimum GPA of 2.5 on a 4.0 scale
· Graduate from high school or receive their GED in Orange County, Seminole County, or in FL
EIN: 593262247

3035
Open Society Institute
400 W. 59th St.
New York, NY 10019 (212) 548-0600
Contact: Inquiry Mgr.
FAX: (212) 548-4600; URL: http://www.soros.org

Foundation type: Operating foundation
Limitations: Scholarships to students from Burma, Central and Eastern Europe, and the former Soviet Union to study at postsecondary institutions in the U.S. and Europe.
Publications: Annual report; Newsletter; Program policy statement.
Financial data: Year ended 12/31/2004. Assets, $329,344,522 (M); Expenditures, $124,835,453; Total giving, $83,470,616; Grants to individuals, 1,194 grants totaling $13,052,819 (high: $107,920; low: $44).

Fields of interest: Humanities; Environment, public policy; Environment, reform; Environment, legal rights; Social sciences.
Application information: Application form required.
Deadline(s): Varies by program
Additional information: See Web site or contact foundation for detailed application information and additional programs.
Program descriptions:

Faculty Development Fellowship Program: Each year, for up to three years, participants from Azerbaijan, Georgia, Kazakstan, Kyrgystan, and Uzbekistan spend one semester at a U.S. university and one semester teaching at their home universities. Deadline Apr. 19.

Undergraduate Exchange Program: Students aged 18 to 23 years from Eastern and Central Europe participate in a one-year, non-degree exchange program. Applicants must be from Azerbaijan, Belarus, Bulgaria, Croatia, Georgia, Kazakhstan, Kyrgyzstan, Latvia, Lithuania, Macedonia, Moldova, Mongolia, Romania, Russia (only for students from Nizhniy, Novgorod, Novosibirsk, and Vladivostok), Slovakia, Tajikistan, Ukraine, and Uzbekistan. The grant is available to students enrolled in an accredited university in their home country and studying American Studies, Art History, Classical Studies, Comparative Literature, Cultural Anthropology, Economic Theory, Fine or Performing Arts, Journalism, Philosophy, International Relations, History, Political Science, or Sociology at the undergraduate level. Students come to the U.S. for the equivalent of their junior year and are required to return home to complete their degrees. The program is designed to introduce students to a liberal arts curriculum and to give them exposure to subjects outside their area of study and potentially unavailable at their home universities. Deadline Dec. 1.

Supplementary Grants Program—Burma: This program provides grants to Burmese students to complete their education, and to students who are just beginning their academic careers. To be eligible, students must:
· be Burmese nationals
· be living in the country in which they want to study
· be proficient in the spoken and written language of the host country
· have already received scholarships or other financial aid prior to application
Deadline Mar. 15 for those studying in Asia and May 15 for those studying in North America, Europe and India. Completion of formal application required, including financial information, essay, and academic record. Contact Vera Djomparin at the institute. E-mail: vdjmparin@sorosny.org.

Social Work Fellowship Program: Fellowships to provide training in social work for students from Azerbaijan, Georgia, Kazakhstan, Kyrgyzstan, Mongolia, Tajikistan, and Uzbekistan. Fellows will be placed at U.S. universities for a two-year graduate program. Deadline Oct. 26.

Georgian Scholarship Program for Education Professionals: The program offers up to six awards per year for study in the United States leading to a Master's degree in education. Funded jointly by OSI and the Georgian Ministry of Education and Science, the program supports Georgian scholars and professionals in early or mid-career who demonstrate both academic excellence and the potential to become leaders, decision-makers and opinion-formers.
EIN: 137029285

3036
Operafestival Roma, Inc.
1445 Willow Lake Dr.
Charlottesville, VA 22902 (434) 984-4945
Contact: William H. Welty Ph.D., Pres.
FAX: (434) 984-5220; E-mail: operafest@aol.com;
URL: http://www.operafest.com

Foundation type: Public charity
Limitations: Scholarships to students for music education.
Financial data: Year ended 11/30/2003. Assets, $7,070 (M); Expenditures, $242,746; Total giving, $30,500; Grants to individuals, 16 grants totaling $30,500.
Fields of interest: Arts education; Music; Opera.
Type of support: Scholarships—to individuals.
Application information: Application form required.
Deadline(s): Contact foundation for deadline
Additional information: Application must also include a $50 application fee; See Web site for further information.
EIN: 431686401

3037
Optical Society of America
2010 Massachusetts Ave. N.W.
Washington, DC 20036-1023 (202) 223-8130
Contact: Elizabeth A. Rogan, Exec. Dir.
FAX: (202) 223-1096; E-mail: info@osa.org;
URL: http://www.osa.org

Foundation type: Public charity
Limitations: Travel grants for students presenting papers at conferences.
Financial data: Year ended 12/31/2004. Assets, $50,311,616 (M); Expenditures, $22,453,724; Total giving, $590,917; Grants to individuals, 93 grants totaling $96,527 (high: $10,000, low: $100).
Type of support: Travel grants.
Application information: Application form required.
Deadline(s): Contact foundation for current application deadline
Program description:

New Focus Travel Grants: Provides 20 travel grants annually of $500 each. These grants help to defer the travel expenses incurred by students who present papers at either CLEO or the OSA annual meeting. Grants are awarded to the presenter who must be the first author of the paper. All of the following information MUST be included in a grant application: a letter of support from the student, a letter of support from the student's advisor, an estimated budget for the trip, and a copy of the paper abstract. Both letters of support should describe the importance of the applicant's work and must clearly demonstrate the need for the grant. Incomplete applications will not be accepted. Applicants must submit the grant application materials on or before the posted deadline. Funds are distributed at the conference.
EIN: 530259696

3038
Orange County Community Foundation
30 Corporate Park, Ste. 410
Irvine, CA 92606 (949) 553-4202
Contact: Todd Hanson, V.P., Donor Rels. and Comm. Partnerships
FAX: (949) 553-4211; E-mail: occf@oc-cf.org;
Additional E-mail: thanson@oc-cf.org; URL: http://www.oc-cf.org

Foundation type: Community foundation

Limitations: Scholarships to residents of Orange County, CA, and to students of Orange County high schools.
Publications: Annual report; Informational brochure; Newsletter.
Financial data: Year ended 06/30/2004. Assets, $58,217,839 (M); Expenditures, $9,415,874; Total giving, $7,175,154; Grants to individuals, totaling $353,143.
Fields of interest: Law school/education; Teacher school/education; Business/industry; Hispanics/Latinos.
Type of support: Undergraduate support.
Application information: Application form required.
Deadline(s): Late Feb. to July for applications; Jan. 31 for concept proposal; early Apr. for full proposal
Additional information: Contact high schools for current application guidelines. See Web site for additional program information.
Program descriptions:

Kayla L. Aasgard Scholarship Fund: Provides a scholarship to a Trona High School graduating student.

Larry Ackerman Public Education Award: Provides a scholarship for an outstanding student from the Long Beach Unified School District pursuing a career as a public school teacher.

Always Helping Friends Fund; Eric Dostie Scholarships: Provides scholarships to high school graduates who have hemophilia.

Andrews Family Scholarship Fund: Provides scholarships to members of the sailing team at Newport Harbor High School in Newport Beach, CA.

Justice John A. Arguelles Scholarship Fund: Provides scholarships to local Latino youth who show potential for success in higher education.

Anna Mary Beck Fund: Provides scholarships to graduates of Laguna Beach High School to study business administration.

Richard Bermudez/Friends of Cal. State Fullerton Scholarship Fund: Provides scholarships for incoming Cal. State Fullerton Latino students who have graduated from an Orange County high school.

Frank and Ruth Bila Scholarships: Provides a scholarship every 3rd year for students from 17-30 years of age who are pursuing a career in the restaurant/hotel management field.

Case-Swayne Company Scholarship Fund: Provides a scholarship to a graduating senior with academic ability, scholarship, leadership, and financial need.

Community College Scholarships: Provides scholarships for Latino students who are currently enrolled at a community college and plan to transfer to a four-year institution.

Wally Davis Scholarship: Provides scholarships to Latino youths who eventually plan to attend law school.

Eisner Foundation Fund: Provides scholarships to Latino students who are active participants of the nonprofit organization Disney Goals.

David H. Fliegelman Fund: Provides scholarships to financially needy high school graduates who were students of American history classes at Lathrop Intermediate School in Santa Ana, for attendance at community colleges.

Joshua Dean Hall Memorial Scholarship Fund: Provides scholarships to seniors at Huntington Beach High School who are members of the surfing team.

Arthur Jackman Scholarship Fund: Provides scholarships to graduating Garden Grove seniors for technical training.
EIN: 330378778

3039

Orange Foundation

P.O. Box 729
Orange, CT 06477-0729 (203) 795-3716
Contact: Robert E. Archambault, Chair.
FAX: (203) 795-3716

Foundation type: Community foundation
Limitations: Scholarships and grants to residents of Orange, CT.
Publications: Application guidelines; Annual report; Grants list; Informational brochure; Informational brochure (including application guidelines); Newsletter (including application guidelines); Occasional report.
Financial data: Year ended 12/31/2004.
Assets, $584,335 (M); Expenditures, $22,365; Total giving, $17,766; Grants to individuals, 13 grants totaling $11,500 (high: $1,500; low: $500).
Type of support: Grants to individuals; Scholarships—to individuals; Student loans—to individuals; Support to graduates or students of specific schools; Postgraduate support; Grants for special needs; Project support.
Application information: Application form required.
Initial approach: Letter.
Copies of proposal: 1
Deadline(s): Apr. 30
Applicants should submit the following:
1) Letter(s) of recommendation
2) Transcripts
3) SAT
4) Proposal
5) Financial information
Additional information: Applications should be sent by mail; Recipients notified within one to two months.
Program description:
Scholarships:
· Thomas F. Birmingham, Jr. Scholarship Fund
· Charles L. Flynn Scholarship Fund
· William Knight Scholarship Fund
· Mary L. Tracy Memorial Scholarship Fund
· Edgar L. Vaughn Scholarship Fund
· Harry Haynes Scholarship Fund
· Elizabeth C. and John W. Povilaitis Community Fund
· Officer Robert F. Stanley Fund
· O'Sullivan Family Fund.
EIN: 060955006

3040

Orange Memorial Hospital Corporation

P.O. Box 2954
Orange, TX 77631-2954
Application address: c/o Robert A. Walker, V.P., 1502 Stickland, Ste. 7, Orange, TX 77630, tel.: (409) 886-3848

Foundation type: Independent foundation
Limitations: Scholarships to residents of Orange County, TX, who are pursuing medical degrees.
Financial data: Year ended 12/31/2003.
Assets, $4,845,597 (M); Expenditures, $478,206; Total giving, $436,168; Grants to individuals, 42 grants totaling $342,000.
Fields of interest: Medical school/education.
Type of support: Graduate support.
Application information: Applications accepted. Application form required.
Deadline(s): Mar. 15
Applicants should submit the following:
1) Class rank
2) Transcripts
3) SAT
4) GPA

Additional information: Application must include three references, and for high school students, a copy of college acceptance letter.
EIN: 741303719

3041

Orange Scholarship Foundation

P.O. Box 298
Orange, MA 01364-0298 (978) 544-6304

Foundation type: Independent foundation
Limitations: Scholarships to graduates of Ralph C. Mahar Regional High School, Orange, MA.
Financial data: Year ended 12/31/2004.
Assets, $484,213 (M); Expenditures, $28,295; Total giving, $26,800; Grants to individuals, 49 grants totaling $26,800 (high: $1,000; low: $400).
Type of support: Support to graduates or students of specific schools; Undergraduate support.
Application information: Application form required.
Deadline(s): May 27
Applicants should submit the following:
1) Transcripts
2) Financial information
Additional information: Selection is based on scholarship, citizenship, initiative, and financial need. Graduates of Franklin County Technical School, who are residents of Orange, New Salem, and Wendell, are eligible to apply for Orange High School Alumni Scholarships. Home school students who otherwise would have graduated from Ralph C. Mahar Regional High School are eligible to apply when they have completed one semester of college.
EIN: 046138742

3042

Order of the Alhambra Charity Fund, Inc.

4200 Leeds Ave.
Baltimore, MD 21229-5496
Contact: Roger Reid, Exec. Dir.
FAX: (410) 536-5729;
E-mail: hq@orderAlhambra.org; URL: http://www.OrderAlhambra.org

Foundation type: Public charity
Limitations: Scholarships to individuals who are entering their junior or senior year of college or to students of religious studies in schools in CA, VA, or Canada, for post-graduate study.
Financial data: Year ended 06/30/2005.
Assets, $3,066,509 (M); Expenditures, $1,380,062; Total giving, $14,000; Grants to individuals, 35 grants totaling $14,000 (high: $400, low: $400).
Fields of interest: Education, special; Theological school/education.
Type of support: Graduate support; Postgraduate support.
Application information: Applications accepted. Application form required.
Deadline(s): Contact foundation for current application deadline.
EIN: 521571850

3043

Oregon Association of Public Accountants Scholarship Foundation

1804 N.E. 43rd Ave.
Portland, OR 97213-1404
Contact: Susan G. Robertson, Treas.

Foundation type: Operating foundation

Limitations: Scholarships to residents of OR who are majoring in accounting at OR schools.
Financial data: Year ended 06/30/2004.
Assets, $0 (M); Expenditures, $8,603; Total giving, $7,500; Grants to individuals, 5 grants totaling $7,500 (high: $1,500, low: $1,500).
Fields of interest: Vocational education; Business school/education; Business/industry.
Type of support: Undergraduate support.
Application information: Applications accepted. Application form required.
Initial approach: Letter.
Deadline(s): Apr. 1
EIN: 930765047

3044

The Oregon Community Foundation

1221 S.W. Yamhill, Ste. 100
Portland, OR 97205 (503) 227-6846
Contact: Gregory A. Chaille, Pres.; For scholarships: Dianne Causey, Prog. Assoc.
FAX: (503) 274-7771; E-mail: info@ocf1.org; URL: http://www.ocf1.org

Foundation type: Community foundation
Limitations: Scholarships to students attending specific schools in OR, scholarships to residents of OR and WA for postsecondary education and vocational training, and Company-related scholarships to OR residents.
Publications: Application guidelines; Annual report; Informational brochure; Newsletter; Occasional report; Program policy statement.
Financial data: Year ended 12/31/2004.
Assets, $742,207,820 (M); Expenditures, $40,436,455; Total giving, $34,598,363; Grants to individuals, totaling $1,742,962.
Type of support: Undergraduate support.
Application information: Application form required.
Deadline(s): Mar. 1
Additional information: See Web site for current application guidelines; Interviews required; Applications available from Oregon State Scholarship Commission at http://www.osac.state.or.us.
EIN: 237315673

3045

Oregon Council for the Humanities

812 S.W. Washington St., Ste. 225
Portland, OR 97205-3210 (503) 241-0543
Contact: Christopher Zinn, Exec. Dir.
FAX: (503) 241-0024; E-mail: och@oregonhum.org; Additional tel.: (800) 735-0543; URL: http://www.oregonhum.org

Foundation type: Public charity
Limitations: Grants to OR high school students for humanities research.
Publications: Application guidelines; Annual report; Newsletter.
Financial data: Year ended 10/31/2004.
Assets, $463,173 (M); Expenditures, $757,542; Total giving, $94,453; Grants to individuals, 9 grants totaling $21,000 (high: $5,000, low: $2,000).
Fields of interest: Humanities.
Type of support: Awards/prizes; Precollege support.
Application information:
Initial approach: Statement of interest and intent.
Deadline(s): Mar. 22
Additional information: See Web site for further application information.

Program description:

Young Scholar Awards: Awards grants of $2,000 to OR high school students for the purpose of crafting and completing humanities research project of their own design. These grants encourage students to see themselves as scholars of their venture and of their community.
EIN: 930716419

3046
Oregon Trail Community Foundation, Inc.
115 Railway Plz.
P.O. Box 1344
Scottsbluff, NE   69361-1344   (308) 635-3393
Contact: Bev Overman, Exec. Secy.
FAX: (308) 635-3393; E-mail: info@otcf.org;
URL: http://www.otcf.org

Foundation type: Community foundation
Limitations: Scholarships to individuals from the Scottsbluff, NE, area, for undergraduate education at American colleges and universities.
Publications: Grants list; Informational brochure (including application guidelines); Newsletter.
Financial data: Year ended 12/31/2004.
Assets, $2,440,855 (M); Expenditures, $249,211; Total giving, $213,307; Grants to individuals, totaling $16,221.
Fields of interest: Arts, formal/general education; Dance; Theater; Music; College (community/junior); Journalism school/education.
Type of support: Support to graduates or students of specific schools; Technical education support; Undergraduate support.
Application information: Applications accepted. Application form required.
Additional information: Contact foundation for current application deadlines/guidelines.
Program descriptions:

Dorothy Bronson Memorial Scholarship: Funds 15 small scholarships for area students of music, theater, or dance.

CSI Scholarship Fund: Awarded to graduates of Scottsbluff High School. Three separate scholarships are awarded each year; two are for 4-year college or university studies and one is for 2-year technical or vocational training. Award is for 2 or 4 years, depending on which scholarship it is, $1,000 per year, paid to the college or university in the fall upon proof of registration. Minimum GPA and ACT requirements are included in application qualification and annual renewal. Applications and interviews are handled by Scottsbluff High School guidance and counseling staff, which also notes recipients and alternates.

Dill Scholarship: Available to Scotts Bluff County graduate attending Western Nevada Community College.

Lawrence and Pauline Lemons Scholarship: Two $4,000 scholarships per year given to a Scotts Bluff County graduate under 30 years of age. Preference is given to lineal descendants of Harry Wisner and Mabel Wisner and of Guy Lemons and Florence Lemons if such descendants meet all other criteria for eligibility.

Lovercheck Scholarship: Awarded to graduates of Gering High School to be used at a four-year institution for the study of art, music, theater, drama, or journalism. One award per year. Award is for 4 years, $500/semester, paid to the college or university upon receipt of grades for the preceding semester. Minimum GPA of 3.0 must be maintained. Applications are received and reviewed by GHS guidance and counseling staff.
EIN: 470596705

3047
Organization of American Historians
112 N. Bryan Ave.
P.O. Box 5457
Bloomington, IN   47408-5457   (812) 855-7311
Contact: Lee W. Formwalt, Exec. Dir.
FAX: (812) 855-0696; E-mail: oah@oah.org;
URL: http://www.oah.org

Foundation type: Public charity
Limitations: Fellowships to students of color in the Ph.D. program in U.S. History at Indiana University, IN.
Financial data: Year ended 06/30/2005.
Assets, $2,227,457 (M); Expenditures, $2,842,495.
Fields of interest: Historical activities; American studies; Minorities.
Type of support: Fellowships; Support to graduates or students of specific schools; Graduate support.
Application information: Application form required.
Deadline(s): Jan. 2
Additional information: Awards tuition and fees for six years of Ph.D. study including $18,000 for years one and two, $19,000 for years three and four, and $20,000 for years five and six. Students from underrepresented groups (including African American, Latino/a, Asian American, or Native American), who have not begun graduate research are eligible to apply.
EIN: 470426520

3048
Organization of Black Airline Pilots
8630 Fenton St., Ste. 126
Silver Spring, MD   20910   (800) 538-6227
URL: http://www.obap.org

Foundation type: Public charity
Limitations: Scholarships and fellowships to African American pilots for advanced training.
Financial data: Year ended 06/30/2003.
Assets, $365,105 (M); Expenditures, $179,205; Total giving, $19,462; Grants to individuals, 3 grants totaling $6,498 (high: $3,847, low: $151).
Fields of interest: Space/aviation; African Americans/Blacks.
Type of support: Fellowships; Undergraduate support.
Application information: Contact foundation for current application deadline/guidelines.
Program descriptions:

Airline Type Rating Scholarship Program: Provides scholarships for advanced training to improve pilots' employment potential. Winners spend four to six weeks training at the training facilities at the major airline that made the donation.

Fellowship Program: Provides financial assistance to pilots who hold a private pilot's license and instrument rating. OBAP will provide one half of the financial assistance for its members to complete Commercial Pilot Training, Certified Flight Instructor (CFI), Certified Flight Instructor-Instruments (CFII), Multi-Engine Instructor (MEI), and Airline Transport Pilot (ATP). The program will also provide financial assistance for interview preparation and simulator training.
EIN: 133061012

3049
Oro Grande Foundation
P.O. Box 3523
Apple Valley, CA   92307-0069

Foundation type: Independent foundation

Limitations: Scholarships are for Apple Valley, CA, local area residents.
Financial data: Year ended 12/31/2004.
Assets, $668,208 (M); Expenditures, $33,407; Total giving, $19,000; Grants to individuals, 23 grants totaling $19,000 (high: $1,000, low: $500).
Type of support: Scholarships—to individuals.
Application information: Application form required.
Deadline(s): Contact foundation for current application deadline
Applicants should submit the following:
1) Transcripts
EIN: 952106478

3050
Orphan Foundation of America
21351 Gentry Dr., Unit 130
Sterling, VA   20166   (571) 203-0270
Contact: Eileen McCaffrey, Exec. Dir.
FAX: (571) 203-0273; E-mail: help@orphan.org;
URL: http://www.orphan.org

Foundation type: Public charity
Limitations: Scholarships and loans to parentless students pursuing a two- or four-year degree or a certificate in vocational training.
Publications: Annual report.
Financial data: Year ended 12/31/2004.
Assets, $3,130,558 (M); Expenditures, $5,616,531; Total giving, $4,720,488; Grants to individuals, totaling $4,720,488.
Fields of interest: Foster care; Young adults, female.
Type of support: Technical education support; Undergraduate support.
Application information: Application form required.
Deadline(s): Apr. 1 for scholarships and June 1 for loans
Additional information: See Web site for complete guidelines.
Program descriptions:

Casey Family Scholarship Program: Awards $1,500-$10,000 to individuals under age 25 who have spent at least one year in foster care and were not subsequently adopted. Scholarships are awarded for the pursuit of post-secondary education, including vocational/technical training, and are renewable annually based on satisfactory progress and financial need.

Hildegard Lash Merit Scholarship: Provides $5,000 per academic year, paid in two installments, to college students who have no family supporting their goals and efforts. Students must be currently in foster care at the time of their high school graduation and/or 18th birthday, or entering their sophomore, junior or senior year as a full-time student at a four-year college or university. Recipients must maintain at least a 3.2 GPA. Scholarships may be used toward tuition costs or living expenses.

Burtrez Morrow Educational Loan Program: Provides student loans of up to $5,000 per year for up to two years to young women currently in foster care at the time of their high school graduation. Recipients must be enrolled full-time at a four-year college or university, and entering her junior or senior year of college. Loans may be used toward tuition costs, books and living expenses. Recipients must maintain at least a 2.0 GPA to be eligible for further loans.
EIN: 521238437

3051
The Orr Foundation
c/o Bank of America, N.A.
P.O. Box 1802
Providence, RI 02901-1802
Application addresses: c/o Newton North High
School, Attn.: Guidance Counselor, 360 Lowell
Ave., Newtonville, MA 02660-1831, c/o Newton
South High School, Attn.: Guidance Counselor, 140
Brandeis Rd., Newton Centre, MA 02459-2745

Foundation type: Independent foundation
Limitations: Scholarships to high school graduates
of Newton North High School, MA, and Newton
South High School, MA, for higher education.
Financial data: Year ended 12/31/2004.
Assets, $797,837 (M); Expenditures, $51,166;
Total giving, $46,000; Grants to individuals, 41
grants totaling $46,000 (high: $3,000, low: $500).
Type of support: Support to graduates or students
of specific schools; Undergraduate support.
Application information: Application form required.
Deadline(s): Apr.
Additional information: Application forms
available in guidance departments at Newton
North and South high schools.
EIN: 046034509

3052
Dr. Donald J. Orris Memorial Scholarship Trust Fund
c/o Comerica Bank
P.O. Box 75000
Detroit, MI 48275-3302
Application addresses: c/o Central Christian High
School, Attn.: Principal, 204 Hospital Ave., Du Bois,
PA 15801, c/o Du Bois Area Senior High School,
Attn.: Principal, 500 Liberty Blvd., Du Bois, PA
15801, c/o Punxytawney Area High School,
Attn.: Principal, 600 N. Findley St., Punxytawney, PA
15767, c/o Brookville Area High School,
Attn.: Principal, P.O. Box 479, Brookville, PA 15825

Foundation type: Independent foundation
Limitations: Scholarships to graduates of the
following PA schools: Central Christian High School,
Dubois Area High School, Punxytawney Area High
School, and Brookville Area High School.
Financial data: Year ended 12/31/2004.
Assets, $42,784 (M); Expenditures, $22,250;
Total giving, $19,500; Grants to individuals, 20
grants totaling $19,500 (high: $1,000, low: $500).
Type of support: Support to graduates or students
of specific schools; Undergraduate support.
Application information: Application form required.
Deadline(s): May 22
Additional information: Applications available
through high school principals.
EIN: 383406443

3053
Orscheln Industries Foundation, Inc.
P.O. Box 280
Moberly, MO 65270 (660) 263-4377

Foundation type: Company-sponsored foundation
Limitations: Scholarships only to graduates of
Cairo, Higbee, Moberly, and Westran high schools,
all in Randolph County, MO.
Publications: Application guidelines; Informational
brochure; Program policy statement.
Financial data: Year ended 09/30/2004.
Assets, $12,689,545 (M); Expenditures,
$759,902; Total giving, $699,593; Grants to
individuals, totaling $131,450.

Fields of interest: Business/industry; Computer
science; Engineering.
Type of support: Employee-related scholarships;
Support to graduates or students of specific
schools; Undergraduate support.
Application information: Application form required.
Deadline(s): Apr. 1
Applicants should submit the following:
1) Transcripts
Additional information: Scholarship application
address: c/o R. Brent Bradshaw, Scholarship
Comm., P.O. Box 266, Moberly, MO 65270,
tel.: (816) 263-8300.
Program description:
Orscheln Industries Scholarship Award: In Sept.,
high school students will be sent brochures
outlining the Orscheln Industries Scholarship
Award. Scholarships are awarded to those
graduating high school students who are seeking
degrees in accounting, engineering, drafting,
business administration, computer science, and
other business-related areas of study approved by
the foundation. Candidates must have a GPA of at
least 3.5 and demonstrate participation and
leadership in school and community activities.
Candidates are judged solely on their
achievements. Financial need is not a factor in
awarding scholarships. Each award is for $500 per
semester for eight semesters. One or two awards
go to children of Orscheln employees.
EIN: 237115623

3054
Orson A. Hull & Minnie E. Hull Educational Foundation
c/o Nancy Frankenberry
U.S. Bank, N.A., EP-MN-514
St. Paul, MN 55101
Application address: c/o Thomas Farrell, P.O. Box
18581, Minneapolis, MN 55418

Foundation type: Independent foundation
Limitations: Scholarships to graduating seniors of
certain St. Paul, MN, high schools.
Financial data: Year ended 06/30/2005.
Assets, $4,691,726 (M); Expenditures,
$488,871; Total giving, $426,544; Grants to
individuals, 54 grants totaling $426,544 (high:
$11,723, low: $1,447).
Type of support: Support to graduates or students
of specific schools; Undergraduate support.
Application information: Completion of formal
application required; Applications must be
submitted to and approved by school counselors.
Program description:
Scholarship Program: Scholarships are awarded
for up to four years. Scholarships used at private
schools are limited to the average amounts charged
at MN state-operated schools. A nominal book
allowance is paid to each student each year.
Notification by May 1.
EIN: 416019516

3055
Ortega Charitable Foundation
2000 N.W. 92nd Ave.
Miami, FL 33172

Foundation type: Independent foundation
Limitations: Scholarships to employees and
children of employees of Latino ancestry in FL and
PR who are dependents of brokers of Goya Foods,
Inc.
Financial data: Year ended 12/31/2004.
Assets, $6,542,681 (M); Expenditures,
$322,990; Total giving, $267,382; Grants to

individuals, 21 grants totaling $98,382 (high:
$9,890, low: $577).
Fields of interest: Hispanics/Latinos.
Type of support: Employee-related scholarships.
Application information: Applications accepted.
Application form required.
Initial approach: Letter.
Deadline(s): May 31
Applicants should submit the following:
1) GPA
EIN: 650014714

3056
Stig P. Orum Memorial Foundation, Inc.
P.O. Box 384
St. Charles, IL 60174-0384 (847) 742-1790
Contact: Irma B. Orum, Pres.

Foundation type: Independent foundation
Limitations: Scholarships to high school students
for higher education.
Financial data: Year ended 12/31/2004.
Assets, $193,121 (M); Expenditures, $9,674;
Total giving, $8,500; Grants to individuals, 5 grants
totaling $5,000 (high: $1,000, low: $1,000).
Type of support: Undergraduate support.
Application information: Application form required.
Additional information: Applications accepted
throughout the year.
EIN: 363727759

3057
Louise & Lane Osborn Memorial Trust
c/o Fifth Third Bank, Tax Dept.
38 Fountain Sq. Plz., MD 1COM31
Cincinnati, OH 45263
Application address: c/o Fifth Third Bank, Trust &
Investment Mgmt. Div., P.O. Box 719, Evansville, IN
47705-0719

Foundation type: Independent foundation
Limitations: Scholarships to graduates of Central
High School, IN. Scholarships are limited to $2,000
per year, per student.
Financial data: Year ended 07/31/2004.
Assets, $1,855,095 (M); Expenditures,
$107,635; Total giving, $85,200; Grants to
individuals, 18 grants totaling $30,500 (high:
$2,000, low: $500).
Type of support: Support to graduates or students
of specific schools; Undergraduate support.
Application information: Application form required.
Deadline(s): Apr. 15
EIN: 356561029

3058
Joyce L. Osborn Scholarship Trust
c/o U.S. Bank, N.A.
P.O. Box 64713
St. Paul, MN 55164-0713

Foundation type: Independent foundation
Limitations: Scholarships to Rochester, MN, high
school graduates to attend colleges and
universities in the U.S.
Financial data: Year ended 12/31/2004.
Assets, $173,174 (M); Expenditures, $11,129;
Total giving, $8,000; Grants to individuals, 8 grants
totaling $8,000 (high: $1,000, low: $1,000).
Type of support: Support to graduates or students
of specific schools; Undergraduate support.
Application information: Application form required.
Deadline(s): Apr. 1
Applicants should submit the following:

1) Transcripts
Additional information: Applications available from high school counselors in Rochester, MN.
EIN: 416293028

3059
Lawrence L. Osborn Scholarship Trust
c/o CentreBank
126 N. Main St.
Veedersburg, IN 47987
Application address: c/o Southeast Fountain School District, Dr. Gilbert, Superintendent, R.R. 2, Box 10A, Veedersburg, IN 47987

Foundation type: Independent foundation
Limitations: Scholarships to graduates of high schools in the Southeast Fountain School District, Veedersburg, IN.
Financial data: Year ended 09/30/2004. Assets, $315,679 (M); Expenditures, $6,928; Total giving, $5,875; Grants to individuals, 15 grants totaling $5,875 (high: $500, low: $375).
Type of support: Support to graduates or students of specific schools; Undergraduate support.
Application information: Application form required.
Deadline(s): Apr. 1
Applicants should submit the following:
1) Financial information
Additional information: Applications available from trustee or superintendent of schools.
EIN: 311020161

3060
Oshkosh Area Community Foundation
(formerly Oshkosh Foundation)
404 N. Main St., Ste. 205
Oshkosh, WI 54901 (920) 426-3993
Contact: Eileen Connolly-Keesler, Exec. Dir.
FAX: (920) 426-6997;
E-mail: info@oshkoshareaf.org; URL: http://www.oshkoshareacf.org

Foundation type: Community foundation
Limitations: Four-year scholarships to graduating seniors of high schools in Winnebago County, WI.
Publications: Application guidelines; Annual report; Financial statement; Informational brochure; Newsletter.
Financial data: Year ended 06/30/2005. Assets, $52,239,822 (M); Expenditures, $4,450,070; Total giving, $3,724,435.
Type of support: Support to graduates or students of specific schools; Technical education support; Undergraduate support.
Application information: Application form required.
Deadline(s): Mar. 31
Additional information: See Web site for programs and application guidelines.
EIN: 396041638

3061
Oshkosh B'Gosh Foundation, Inc.
c/o U.S. Bank, N.A.
P.O. Box 300
Oshkosh, WI 54902 (920) 231-8800
Contact: David Omachinski, V.P.
Application address: c/o Cheryl Fowler, Prog. Dir., Oshkosh Area Community Fdn., 404 N. Main St., Ste. 205, Oshkosh, WI 54901; tel.: (920) 426-3993, FAX: (920) 426-6997

Foundation type: Company-sponsored foundation

Limitations: Undergraduate scholarships to children of employees of Oshkosh B'Gosh.
Financial data: Year ended 12/31/2003. Assets, $889,946 (M); Expenditures, $333,986; Total giving, $329,933; Grants to individuals, 47 grants totaling $33,750 (high: $1,500, low: $750).
Type of support: Employee-related scholarships; Technical education support; Undergraduate support.
Application information: Application form required.
Deadline(s): Jan.
Applicants should submit the following:
1) FAF
Additional information: Each high school sets its own deadline; Completion of formal application required, including financial aid form, record of extracurricular activities, two short essays, and two letters of reference.
Program description:
Scholarship Program: High school students or graduates must:
· have had no previous full-time enrollment at a college
· have a GPA of at least 2.5 (or its equivalent)
· enroll in a beginning course of study at a college within eight months of high school graduation.
Continuing college students must:
· be pursuing a degree at an accredited college as a full-time undergraduate student and have at least one full year of study remaining
· maintain a minimum GPA of 2.5
· continue their course of study at a college within three months of the date of notification of continuation of the scholarship award
All applicants must submit evidence of enrollment in an educational institution to the scholarship committee before the award payment is made. Children of Oshkosh B'Gosh, Inc. officers and of the foundation's officers are ineligible.
EIN: 391525020

3062
Otero County Electric Education Foundation
P.O. Box 227
Cloudcroft, NM 88317-0227 (505) 682-2521
Contact: Jimmy Capps

Foundation type: Independent foundation
Limitations: Scholarships to active members of Otero County Electric Cooperative and to their immediate families to attend recognized NM institutions of higher education.
Financial data: Year ended 12/31/2004. Assets, $248,494 (M); Expenditures, $11,602; Total giving, $10,500; Grants to individuals, 12 grants totaling $10,500 (high: $1,000, low: $500).
Type of support: Undergraduate support.
Application information: Application form required.
Deadline(s): Apr. 1
Applicants should submit the following:
1) Transcripts
2) Letter(s) of recommendation
Additional information: The foundation awards a one-year, $1,000 scholarship, $500 to be paid at the start of each semester on confirmation that the applicant has maintained at least a 2.5 GPA on a 4.0 scale, and is a full-time student. Applicants must be of good character, demonstrate a coherent degree plan, and a willingness to pursue a course of higher learning. Economic need of the applicant is given secondary

consideration. Recipients must reapply each year.
EIN: 850374112

3063
Richard F. Ott Scholarship Foundation
c/o AmSouth Bank
P.O. Box 2918
Clearwater, FL 33757-2918 (727) 592-6907
Contact: Laura Papasergi, Trust Off., AmSouth Bank

Foundation type: Independent foundation
Limitations: Scholarships, which are renewable for up to four years of undergraduate study, to financially needy graduates of Clearwater High School, FL, who graduated in the top 25 percent of their classes and display qualities of a high moral character, scholastic achievement, and leadership ability.
Financial data: Year ended 10/31/2004. Assets, $1,416,617 (M); Expenditures, $92,627; Total giving, $55,250; Grants to individuals, 15 grants totaling $55,250 (high: $3,750, low: $1,750).
Type of support: Support to graduates or students of specific schools; Undergraduate support.
Application information: Application form required.
Deadline(s): Deadline May 1.
Applicants should submit the following:
1) Financial information
EIN: 596833432

3064
Raymond J. Ott Scholarship Fund
221 N. LaSalle St., Ste. 3200
Chicago, IL 60601-1512
Contact: David B. Pogrund, Tr.

Foundation type: Independent foundation
Limitations: Scholarships to financially needy full-time students with at least a 3.0 GPA to study toward one of the following degrees: bachelor's, master's, Ph.D., M.D., Doctor of Law, or D.V.M.
Financial data: Year ended 12/31/2004. Assets, $410,622 (M); Expenditures, $27,485; Total giving, $10,000; Grants to individuals, 2 grants totaling $10,000 (high: $5,000, low: $5,000).
Fields of interest: Law school/education; Medical school/education; Veterinary medicine.
Type of support: Fellowships; Graduate support; Undergraduate support; Doctoral support.
Application information:
Initial approach: Letter or telephone.
Additional information: Contact fund for current application deadline/guidelines.
EIN: 366742652

3065
Harlan, Ruby & Phil E. Ott Scholarship Trust
(also known as Phil E. Ott Scholarships)
c/o JPMorgan Chase Bank, N.A.
P.O. Box 1308
Milwaukee, WI 53201-1308
Application address: c/o George Stone, Superintendent, Central Noble, 200 E. Main St., Albion, IN 46701, tel.: (219) 636-2175

Foundation type: Independent foundation
Limitations: Scholarships to financially needy graduates of Central Noble High School, IN, to attend accredited colleges.

Financial data: Year ended 12/31/2004.
Assets, $860,696 (M); Expenditures, $65,552;
Total giving, $39,708; Grants to individuals, 31
grants totaling $39,708 (high: $900, low: $100).
Type of support: Support to graduates or students
of specific schools; Undergraduate support.
Application information:
   Deadline(s): Apr. 28
   Applicants should submit the following:
      1) Transcripts
      2) FAF
EIN: 356455490

3066
Outer Banks Community Foundation, Inc.
P.O. Box 1100
Kill Devil Hills, NC   27948-1100
(252) 261-8839
Contact: Barbara A. Bingham, Exec. Dir.
FAX: (252) 261-0371; E-mail: info@obcf.org;
URL: http://www.obcf.org

Foundation type: Community foundation
Limitations: Scholarships to residents of Dare
County, NC. The foundation manages many
scholarship funds, each of which has its own
criteria for selection, such as academic ability,
career choice, financial need, athletic interests, or
geographic location. Contact the foundation for
specific information about the funds.
Publications: Application guidelines; Annual report;
Financial statement; Grants list; Informational
brochure; Newsletter.
Financial data: Year ended 12/31/2004.
Assets, $5,373,388 (M); Expenditures,
$282,375; Total giving, $150,408; Grants to
individuals, 49 grants totaling $54,050 (high:
$5,000, low: $500, average grant: $500-$5,000).
Type of support: Undergraduate support.
Application information: Application form required.
   Initial approach: Application.
   Copies of proposal: 1
   Deadline(s): Apr. 15
   Applicants should submit the following:
      1) SAT
      2) GPA
      3) Transcripts
      4) Letter(s) of recommendation
EIN: 581516313

3067
Jack & Charlotte Owen Educational
Scholarship Trust
c/o Hibernia National Bank
P.O. Box 451
Texarkana, TX   75504

Foundation type: Independent foundation
Limitations: Scholarships to high school graduates
in Bowie County, TX.
Financial data: Year ended 12/31/2004.
Assets, $1,608,332 (M); Expenditures,
$102,269; Total giving, $77,845; Grants to
individuals, 44 grants totaling $77,845 (high:
$5,500, low: $750).
Type of support: Scholarships—to individuals.
Application information: Application form required.
   Deadline(s): Apr.
   Applicants should submit the following:
      1) Transcripts
      2) SAT
      3) ACT
   Additional information: Application must also
      include a signature letter; Application forms
      available from high school counselors.
EIN: 756414441

3068
Elizabeth Anne Owens Foundation
P.O. Box 1229
Brewton, AL   36427-1229
Application address: c/o Scholarship Selection
Comm., 315 Belleville Ave., Brewton, AL 36426

Foundation type: Independent foundation
Limitations: Scholarships to residents of Escambia
County, AL, students at Jefferson Davis Community
College, the University of Alabama, and Auburn
University, and women who are attending or are
graduates of Westover School in Middlebury, CT, for
higher education.
Financial data: Year ended 12/31/2004.
Assets, $603,858 (M); Expenditures, $27,027;
Total giving, $27,000; Grants to individuals, 10
grants totaling $27,000 (high: $3,000, low:
$1,500).
Fields of interest: Women.
Type of support: Support to graduates or students
of specific schools; Graduate support;
Undergraduate support; Postgraduate support.
Application information: Application form required.
   Initial approach: Letter.
   Deadline(s): Feb. 1; Applications accepted Oct.
      through Jan
   Applicants should submit the following:
      1) Letter(s) of recommendation
      2) Transcripts
      3) SAT
      4) ACT
Program description:
   Scholarship Program: Scholarships are awarded
   to:
   · Men and women residing in Escambia
      County, AL who are attending an accredited
      preparatory school and who are attending
      Jefferson Davis Community College,
      Brewton, AL, or pursuing undergraduate or
      postgraduate degrees at recognized
      four-year colleges or universities.
   · Men and women who reside outside
      Escambia County, AL, who are pursuing
      undergraduate or graduate degrees at
      Jefferson Davis Community College, the
      University of Alabama, or Auburn
      University.
   · Women who are attending or have
      graduated from The Westover School
      located in Middlebury, CT, and are pursuing
      undergraduate or graduate degrees at
      recognized four-year colleges or
      universities, wherever located.
Scholarships are awarded on the basis of prior
academic performance, performance on aptitude
and achievement tests, recommendations from
instructors, financial need, and the committee's
evaluation of the applicant's motivation, character,
ability, and potential. Scholarships are granted for
one year of study, however, they may be renewable
for applicants who have maintained satisfactory
progress in school.
EIN: 631058213

3069
Owens Scholarship Trust Co.
c/o BB&T, Trust Dept.
P.O. Box 2907
Wilson, NC   27894-2907
Application address: c/o Larry Price,
Superintendent, Wilson County Schools, 117 N.
Tarboro St., Wilson, NC 27893

Foundation type: Independent foundation
Limitations: Scholarships to graduates of Wilson
County, NC, public schools, primarily to those who

commit to teach in the Wilson County, NC, public
schools for a minimum of four years.
Publications: Application guidelines.
Financial data: Year ended 08/31/2004.
Assets, $2,821,653 (M); Expenditures,
$237,027; Total giving, $214,975; Grants to
individuals, 31 grants totaling $214,975 (high:
$13,000, low: $3,250).
Fields of interest: Teacher school/education;
Education.
Type of support: Support to graduates or students
of specific schools; Undergraduate support.
Application information: Application form required.
   Deadline(s): Apr. 1
   Additional information: Applicants must have at
      least a 3.0 GPA; Applications available from
      high school guidance counselors in Wilson
      County, NC.
EIN: 566532306

3070
Owenton Rotary Student Loan Fund
P.O. Box 296
Owenton, KY   40359
Application Address: c/o Gary Gibson, 825 Green
Acres Dr., Owenton KY 40359

Foundation type: Operating foundation
Limitations: Student loans to individuals in
Owenton, KY.
Financial data: Year ended 12/31/2003.
Assets, $69,245 (M); Expenditures, $2,800; Total
giving, $2,800; Loans to individuals, 3 loans
totaling $2,800.
Type of support: Student loans—to individuals.
Application information: Applications accepted.
   Initial approach: Letter.
   Deadline(s): None
   Additional information: Contact foundation for
      current application guidelines.
EIN: 311533803

3071
The Oyster Bay Sailing Foundation
P.O. Box 720
Oyster Bay, NY   11771   (516) 922-7136
Contact: Thomas H. Josten, Pres. and Secy.
E-mail: vonet@pb.net

Foundation type: Public charity
Limitations: Grants to individuals for training and
preparation for local, regional, national, world or
Olympic sailing events.
Financial data: Year ended 12/31/2004.
Assets, $56,161 (M); Expenditures, $336,038;
Total giving, $23,305; Grants to individuals, 4
grants totaling $12,090 (high: $10,000, low:
$300).
Fields of interest: Athletics/sports, water sports;
Athletics/sports, amateur competition; Athletics/
sports, Olympics.
Type of support: Grants to individuals.
Application information: Contact foundation for
current application deadline/guidelines.
EIN: 112839663

3072
Janet Ozinga Memorial Scholarship
Foundation
c/o Barry N. Voorn
15959 S. 108th Ave.
Orland Park, IL   60467-5301   (708) 479-0787
Contact: Martin Ozinga, Jr., Tr.

Foundation type: Independent foundation
Limitations: Scholarships to high school seniors residing in the Southwest Chicagoland area, IL.
Financial data: Year ended 12/31/2004. Assets, $489,993 (M); Expenditures, $52,815; Total giving, $40,000; Grants to individuals, 8 grants totaling $40,000 (high: $5,000, low: $5,000).
Type of support: Scholarships—to individuals.
Application information: Application form required.
   Deadline(s): Varies
EIN: 363554481

3073
Pace 8-591 Fallen Workers Memorial Scholarship
c/o Scholarship Comm.
P.O. Box 483
Anacortes, WA   98221-0483

Foundation type: Independent foundation
Limitations: Scholarships to students attending high schools in Island, Skagit, Snohomish and Whatcom counties, WA, and to children of Pace Union members.
Financial data: Year ended 06/30/2005. Assets, $1,010,697 (M); Expenditures, $53,170; Total giving, $47,700; Grants to individuals, 51 grants totaling $47,700 (high: $1,000, low: $100).
Type of support: Support to graduates or students of specific schools; Undergraduate support.
Application information: Application form required.
   Deadline(s): Mar. 30.
   Additional information: Application should include an essay of 700 words or less about an influential person who has shaped labor history.
EIN: 911986402

3074
Pacers Foundation, Inc.
(formerly Pacers Basketball Corporation Foundation, Inc.)
125 S. Pennsylvania St.
Indianapolis, IN   46204-2603   (317) 917-2864
Contact: Dale Ratermann, Exec. Dir.
FAX: (317) 917-2599;
E-mail: foundation@pacers.com; URL: http://www.nba.com/pacers/news/Foundation_Index.html

Foundation type: Public charity
Limitations: Undergraduate scholarships to students residing in IN who are interested in medicine, sports medicine, physical therapy or a related discipline.
Publications: Application guidelines; Annual report; Grants list; Newsletter.
Financial data: Year ended 06/30/2004. Assets, $1,018,966 (L); Expenditures, $897,414; Total giving, $261,175; Grants to individuals, totaling $16,000.
Fields of interest: Medical school/education; Athletics/sports, training.
Type of support: Undergraduate support.
Application information: Applications accepted. Application form required.
   Initial approach: E-mail.
   Deadline(s): Mar. 1 for TeamUp, Nov. 1 for Linda Craig Memorial Scholarships.
Program descriptions:
   Linda Craig Memorial Scholarship: This $1,000 scholarship is awarded to undergraduate college students presently enrolled in an Indiana college or university interested in pursuing sports medicine,

medicine, physical therapy and/or other related disciplines. The applicant must be outstanding in character, integrity, and leadership.
   TeamUp Scholarship: This $2,000 scholarship is awarded to five high school seniors in Indiana on the basis of service to the community. It's purpose is to encourage young people to develop an understanding of critical issues facing society and propose ways to address the needs of others. The award is applied to the student's college freshman year only.
EIN: 351908365

3075
Pacific N.W. Kiwanis Foundation
P.O. Box 747
Beaverton, OR   97005
Contact: John Frucci, Pres.

Foundation type: Public charity
Limitations: Scholarships to individuals for higher education.
Financial data: Year ended 09/30/2003. Assets, $479,292 (M); Expenditures, $45,541; Total giving, $15,125; Grants to individuals, totaling $10,125.
Type of support: Scholarships—to individuals.
Application information: Application form required.
   Deadline(s): Before High School graduation
EIN: 930900103

3076
PacifiCare Health Systems Foundation
5995 Plaza Dr., MS CY20-326
Cypress, CA   90630   (714) 825-5233
Contact: Bill Wood, Pres.; Scholarship Prog.: Riva Gibal
Application address: P.O. Box 25186, Santa Ana, CA 92799

Foundation type: Company-sponsored foundation
Limitations: Scholarships to Latino high school seniors in areas of PacifiCare operations who will major in a health care program.
Publications: Annual report; Informational brochure (including application guidelines).
Financial data: Year ended 12/31/2004. Assets, $1,652,956 (M); Expenditures, $5,246,672; Total giving, $4,346,845.
Fields of interest: Nursing school/education; Health sciences school/education; Hispanics/Latinos.
Type of support: Technical education support; Undergraduate support.
Application information: Applications accepted. Application form required. Application form available on the grantmaker's Web site.
   Deadline(s): June 30.
   Applicants should submit the following:
      1) Letter(s) of recommendation
      2) Transcripts
   Additional information: Application should include a personal essay in Spanish, and copy of birth certificate. See Website for further information.
Program description:
   Latino Health Scholars Program: Awards 70 scholarships of $2,000 each to high school seniors of Latino descent who are entering community college or an accredited technical college and majoring in one of the following approved health care programs:
      · Nursing (R.N., L.V.N.)
      · Medical Interpretation
      · Health Claims Examiner
      · Health Information Technology Programs

      · Pharmacy Technician
      · Public Health
      · Pre-med.
Recipients must be fluent in Spanish and carry a minimum GPA of 3.0.
EIN: 330473608

3077
Paddington Foundation
(formerly Beard Family Foundation)
125 1st Ave.
Pittsburgh, PA   15222-1590   (412) 391-8510
Contact: Philip E. Beard, Tr.

Foundation type: Independent foundation
Limitations: Scholarships to individuals, primarily in PA, for undergraduate education.
Financial data: Year ended 12/31/2004. Assets, $187,224 (M); Expenditures, $55,458; Total giving, $52,500; Grants to individuals, 15 grants totaling $52,500 (high: $5,000, low: $1,250).
Type of support: Undergraduate support.
Application information: Applications accepted.
   Initial approach: Letter.
   Applicants should submit the following:
      1) Letter(s) of recommendation
      2) Financial information
   Additional information: Application must also include biographical record, academic history and goals.
EIN: 256742854

3078
Arline P. Padelford Scholarship Trust Fund
c/o U.S. Trust Co., N.A.
P.O. Box 55122
Boston, MA   02205-8670
Application address: c/o Guidance Counselor, Taunton High School, 50 Williams St., Taunton, MA 02780, tel.: (617) 823-8181

Foundation type: Independent foundation
Limitations: Scholarships to graduates of Taunton High School, MA, only.
Financial data: Year ended 12/31/2004. Assets, $353,043 (M); Expenditures, $24,703; Total giving, $18,500.
Type of support: Support to graduates or students of specific schools; Undergraduate support.
Application information: Application form required.
   Additional information: Application form and current deadline available from Taunton High School Guidance Counselor.
EIN: 046096792

3079
Lou & Lillian Padolf Foundation
c/o AmSouth Bank, Trust Dept.
P.O. Box 2918
Clearwater, FL   33757-2918
Contact: J. Michael Chapman, Trust Off., AmSouth Bank

Foundation type: Independent foundation
Limitations: Undergraduate scholarships only to graduates of Pinellas County, FL, high schools for attendance at FL colleges and junior colleges. Permanent residence must be maintained in mid-Pinellas County, FL, north of Walshingham Rd. and south of Klosterman Rd.
Financial data: Year ended 12/31/2004. Assets, $843,494 (M); Expenditures, $45,318; Total giving, $37,250.

Type of support: Support to graduates or students of specific schools; Undergraduate support.
Application information: Application form required.
  Initial approach: Letter.
  Deadline(s): May 1
  Additional information: Scholarships are awarded on the basis of financial need and academic performance. Applicants must rank in the top twenty-five percent of their high school classes. Renewal of the scholarship also depends upon financial need and academic achievement, which must reflect at least a cumulative "C" average for all college work. Generally, grants are awarded to students each year in amounts of less than $1,500 per person, per year.
EIN: 596190737

3080

Page Education Foundation
P.O. Box 581254
Minneapolis, MN 55458-1254 (612) 332-0406
Contact: Ramona Harristhal, Admin. Dir.
FAX: (612) 332-0403; E-mail: info@page-ed.org;
URL: http://www.page-ed.org

Foundation type: Public charity
Limitations: Scholarships for postsecondary education in MN to financially needy MN residents of color who demonstrate positive attitudes toward education and community service.
Financial data: Year ended 06/30/2005.
Assets, $2,069,138 (M); Expenditures, $992,071; Total giving, $734,200; Grants to individuals, 570 grants totaling $734,200.
Fields of interest: Vocational education; Community development, volunteer services.
Type of support: Graduate support; Technical education support; Undergraduate support.
Application information: Application form required.
  Deadline(s): May 1
  Applicants should submit the following:
    1) Financial information
    2) Letter(s) of recommendation
    3) Transcripts
    4) Essay
  Additional information: Scholarships range from $900 to $2,500 per year and are renewable. As part of the program, recipients must fulfill a community service contract working with K-8th grade students. Examples of typical projects include tutoring or volunteering in schools. In addition, the foundation offers adult mentors to recipients to encourage them in this service component.
EIN: 363605013

3081

Frank E. Page Trust
c/o Bank of America, N.A.
10 Light St., MD4-302-17-06
Baltimore, MD 21202
Application address: c/o Secy., The Frank E. Page Scholarship Committee, P.O. Box 29, Christiansburg, VA 24073, tel.: (540) 382-4901

Foundation type: Independent foundation
Limitations: Scholarships to graduates of public high schools in Montgomery County, VA.
Financial data: Year ended 12/31/2004.
Assets, $2,328,891 (M); Expenditures, $162,902; Total giving, $132,100; Grants to individuals, 27 grants totaling $132,100 (high: $41,950, low: $100).
Type of support: Support to graduates or students of specific schools; Undergraduate support.

Application information: Application form required.
  Deadline(s): Apr. 15
  Applicants should submit the following:
    1) Transcripts
  Additional information: Application must also include three letters of reference, all from non-related persons and only one from a faculty member. Applications available from high school guidance counselors.
EIN: 546035807

3082

The Pagliara Charitable Foundation
P.O. Box 608
Dunedin, FL 34697

Foundation type: Independent foundation
Limitations: Scholarships to individuals for higher education.
Financial data: Year ended 12/31/2004.
Assets, $755,861 (M); Expenditures, $151,122; Total giving, $120,791; Grants to individuals, 7 grants totaling $12,787 (high: $4,500, low: $212).
Type of support: Scholarships—to individuals.
Application information: Application form not required.
  Initial approach: Letter.
  Additional information: Contact foundation for current application deadline/guidelines; Application by letter of proposal.
EIN: 596978261

3083

Charles J. Paine Scholarship Fund Trust
c/o Taylor, Ganson & Perrin, LLP
160 Federal St.
Boston, MA 02110 (617) 951-2777
Contact: Charles M. Ganson, Jr., Tr.

Foundation type: Independent foundation
Limitations: Scholarships to residents of Weston, MA, attending Harvard University or Massachusetts Institute of Technology.
Financial data: Year ended 12/31/2004.
Assets, $237,048 (M); Expenditures, $11,000; Total giving, $7,500; Grants to individuals, 6 grants totaling $7,500 (high: $1,500, low: $1,000).
Type of support: Support to graduates or students of specific schools; Undergraduate support.
Application information: Application form required.
  Initial approach: Letter stating need and personal background.
  Additional information: Applications accepted throughout the year.
EIN: 046028710

3084

The John and Lucia Pais Family Educational Foundation, Inc.
c/o First Century Bank, N.A.
500 Federal St.
Bluefield, WV 24701 (304) 324-3262

Foundation type: Independent foundation
Limitations: Scholarships to graduating students attending McDowell County, WV, public high schools.
Publications: Application guidelines.
Financial data: Year ended 06/30/2005.
Assets, $255,679 (M); Expenditures, $38,875; Total giving, $34,100; Grants to individuals, 10 grants totaling $34,100 (high: $5,600, low: $1,600).

Type of support: Scholarships—to individuals; Support to graduates or students of specific schools; Graduate support; Undergraduate support.
Application information: Application form required.
  Initial approach: Application.
  Deadline(s): Apr. 15
  Applicants should submit the following:
    1) Transcripts
    2) Letter(s) of recommendation
    3) GPA
    4) Financial information
    5) FAFSA
    6) Essay
    7) Budget Information
    8) ACT
  Additional information: Applications available at school; Interviews required.
EIN: 311561732

3085

Countess Frances Thorley Palen-Klar Scholarship Fund
c/o Bank of America, N.A.
P.O. Box 1802
Providence, RI 02901-1802
Application address: c/o Greenwich Scholarship Assoc., United Way of Greenwich, 1 Lafayette Ct., Greenwich, CT 06830, tel.: Beth Bean, (203) 625-8093; John Whalon, (203) 625-8097; Sharon Vacchiolla, (203) 531-4229

Foundation type: Independent foundation
Limitations: Scholarships to graduates of Greenwich High School, CT, to attend accredited colleges and universities.
Financial data: Year ended 12/31/2004.
Assets, $486,895 (M); Expenditures, $30,113; Total giving, $23,000; Grants to individuals, 12 grants totaling $23,000 (high: $2,000, low: $1,000).
Type of support: Support to graduates or students of specific schools; Undergraduate support.
Application information: Application form required.
  Deadline(s): Mar. 15
EIN: 066033692

3086

Ann Palmer Foundation
1400 Colorado St., Ste. C
Boulder City, NV 89005-2448 (702) 293-6076
URL: http://www.annpalmerfoundation.org

Foundation type: Independent foundation
Limitations: Scholarships to individuals for undergraduate education.
Financial data: Year ended 12/31/2004.
Assets, $297,509 (M); Expenditures, $271,825; Total giving, $256,027; Grants to individuals, 159 grants totaling $256,027 (high: $5,000, low: $220).
Type of support: Undergraduate support.
Application information: Applications accepted. Application form required. Application form available on the grantmaker's Web site.
  Initial approach: letter.
  Deadline(s): Aug. 1 for Fall/Winter granting, Dec. 1 for Spring/Summer granting
  Applicants should submit the following:
    1) Essay
  Additional information: Applicants must be accepted to a college or university.
EIN: 330934523

3087
Isaac E. Palmer Fund Trust
c/o Bank of America, N.A.
P.O. Box 6767
Providence, RI 02940-6767
Application address: c/o Bank of America, N.A.,
Attn.: Tina Hamilton, 777 Main St., CT2-102-22-02,
Hartford, CT 06115

Foundation type: Independent foundation
Limitations: Scholarships to residents of Montville,
CT, who are under the age of 25 and have graduated
from Montville High School, CT.
Financial data: Year ended 12/31/2003.
Assets, $1,482,037 (M); Expenditures, $79,706;
Total giving, $63,318; Grants to individuals, 57
grants totaling $63,318 (high: $2,500, low: $500).
Type of support: Scholarships—to individuals;
Support to graduates or students of specific
schools.
Application information:
Initial approach: Letter.
Deadline(s): First week of Apr.
Additional information: Contact trust for current
application guidelines.
EIN: 066026227

3088
C. Paul Palmer Memorial Scholarship Fund
P.O. Box 120
Findlay, OH 45839 (419) 422-4341
Contact: Deb Montooth

Foundation type: Independent foundation
Limitations: Scholarships to children and
grandchildren of National Lime and Stone Co.
employees.
Financial data: Year ended 12/31/2004.
Assets, $217,397 (M); Expenditures, $15,761;
Total giving, $14,000; Grants to individuals, 7
grants totaling $14,000 (high: $2,000, low:
$2,000).
Type of support: Employee-related scholarships.
Application information: Application form required.
Initial approach: Letter or telephone.
Deadline(s): Mar. 15
EIN: 341759012

3089
Walter Curtis Palmer Scholarship Trust
c/o JPMorgan Chase Bank, N.A.
P.O. Box 1308
Milwaukee, WI 53201

Foundation type: Independent foundation
Limitations: Scholarships to residents of Racine
City, WI who are graduating seniors.
Financial data: Year ended 12/31/2004.
Assets, $204,064 (M); Expenditures, $10,645;
Total giving, $7,734.
Type of support: Undergraduate support.
Application information: Contact trust for current
application deadline/guidelines.
EIN: 396037713

3090
Marvin O. Palmer Trust
c/o U.S. Bank, N.A.
P.O. Box 3168
Portland, OR 97208
Application address: c/o Park High School,
Attn.: Principal, 102 Vista View Dr., Livingston, MT
59407, tel.: (408) 222-0448

Foundation type: Independent foundation
Limitations: Scholarships to graduates of Park High
School, MT, for higher education.
Financial data: Year ended 12/31/2004.
Assets, $741,891 (M); Expenditures, $46,539;
Total giving, $36,632.
Type of support: Support to graduates or students
of specific schools; Undergraduate support.
Application information: Contact trust for current
application deadline/guidelines.
EIN: 816079218

3091
Palos Bank Foundation, Inc.
12600 S. Harlem Ave.
Palos Heights, IL 60463

Foundation type: Company-sponsored foundation
Limitations: Scholarships to graduating seniors
from eight local area high schools, IL.
Financial data: Year ended 12/31/2004.
Assets, $353 (M); Expenditures, $20,020; Total
giving, $20,000; Grants to individuals, 10 grants
totaling $20,000 (high: $2,000, low: $2,000).
Type of support: Support to graduates or students
of specific schools; Technical education support;
Undergraduate support.
Application information: Application form required.
Deadline(s): Mar. 1
Additional information: Scholarships are $2,000
each and are annually awarded to one
recipient at each of the following schools:
Amos Alonzo Stagg High School; Carl
Sandburg High School; Alan B. Shepard High
School; Marist High School; Mother McAuley
High School; Providence Catholic High School;
Chicago Christian High School; and Lockport
High School. Recipients must maintain a "B"
average or better throughout seven terms of
high school and plan to enroll full-time at an
accredited college, university or trade/
vocational school.
EIN: 364443693

3092
Irene A. Paltz Memorial Scholarship Trust
c/o Wells Fargo Bank Nebraska, N.A.
1919 Douglas St., MAC N8000-027
Omaha, NE 68102-1310
Application address: c/o Wells Fargo Bank Indiana,
N.A., P.O. Box 370, Peru, IN 46970

Foundation type: Independent foundation
Limitations: Scholarships to graduates of
Rochester Community High School, IN.
Financial data: Year ended 12/31/2004.
Assets, $28,977 (M); Expenditures, $10,211;
Total giving, $8,200; Grants to individuals, 20
grants totaling $8,200 (high: $410, low: $410).
Type of support: Support to graduates or students
of specific schools; Undergraduate support.
Application information: Contact foundation for
current application deadline/guidelines.
EIN: 356490966

3093
Pan-Icarian Foundation
P.O. Box 79037
Pittsburgh, PA 15216-0037 (412) 563-0547
Contact: Konstantinos Mavrikis, Scholarship Chair.
URL: http://www.pan-icarian.com/foundation

Foundation type: Public charity

Limitations: Undergraduate and graduate
scholarships.
Financial data: Year ended 06/30/2004.
Assets, $2,500,496 (M); Expenditures,
$126,985; Total giving, $37,100; Grants to
individuals, 29 grants totaling $37,100.
Type of support: Graduate support; Undergraduate
support.
Application information: Contact foundation for
current application deadline/guidelines.
EIN: 256085664

3094
Panasonic Tennessee-Japan Cultural Exchange Foundation
(formerly ACOM Tennessee-Japan Cultural
Exchange Foundation)
5105 S. National Dr.
Knoxville, TN 37914

Foundation type: Company-sponsored foundation
Limitations: Scholarships by nomination only to
students of Knox County High School, TN, for travel
to Japan.
Financial data: Year ended 02/28/2005.
Assets, $411,324 (M); Expenditures, $30,619;
Total giving, $30,529; Grants to individuals, 5
grants totaling $30,529.
Type of support: Exchange programs; Support to
graduates or students of specific schools; Awards/
grants by nomination only; Undergraduate support.
Application information: Applications not
accepted.
EIN: 621558047

3095
Panizza Family Foundation
101 Marchwood Rd.
Exton, PA 19341 (610) 363-6003
Contact: John E. Panizza, Pres.

Foundation type: Operating foundation
Limitations: Scholarships to students in PA, for
higher education.
Financial data: Year ended 12/31/2002.
Assets, $73,622 (M); Expenditures, $108,546;
Total giving, $108,364; Grants to individuals, 13
grants totaling $76,089 (high: $27,069, low: $25).
Type of support: Undergraduate support.
Application information: Applications accepted.
Deadline(s): None
EIN: 232986055

3096
Robert Pape Charitable Foundation
c/o Bank of America, N.A.
P.O. Box 1802
Providence, RI 02901-1802
Contact: James R. Degiacomo, Tr.
Application address: 1 Post Office Sq., Boston, MA
02109

Foundation type: Independent foundation
Limitations: Scholarships to graduates of Cohasset
High School, MA, for college or technical school.
Financial data: Year ended 12/31/2004.
Assets, $417,409 (M); Expenditures, $22,174;
Total giving, $15,500; Grants to individuals, 4
grants totaling $15,500 (high: $4,000, low:
$3,500).
Fields of interest: Vocational education.
Type of support: Support to graduates or students
of specific schools; Technical education support;
Undergraduate support.

Application information: Application form required.
Initial approach: Letter or telephone.
Deadline(s): May 1
EIN: 046692518

3097
Arthur F. Pape Educational Fund Trust
c/o United Bank & Trust
P.O. Box 150
Marysville, KS   66508-0150   (785) 562-2344

Foundation type: Independent foundation
Limitations: Student loans to graduates of high schools in Marshall County, KS, to attend trade schools, and two- and four-year colleges.
Financial data: Year ended 07/31/2005.
Assets, $702,665 (M); Expenditures, $16,429; Total giving, $0; Loans to individuals, 33 loans totaling $45,600.
Fields of interest: Vocational education.
Type of support: Student loans—to individuals; Support to graduates or students of specific schools; Technical education support.
Application information: Application form required.
Deadline(s): July 1
Applicants should submit the following:
  1) Financial information
Additional information: Loans are limited to $1,500 per semester, or $3,000 per year. The maximum loan is $12,000 over a period of six years. The interest on the loan must be repaid semi-annually while the student is in school. The principal must be repaid on an amortized basis after graduation, termination of schooling, or six years from the time of the initial loan. The minimum monthly payment is $75. The maximum repayment term for a loan of $9,001 to $12,000 is ten years; for a loan of $6,001 to $9,000 is eight years; and for a loan of less than $6,000, up to six years. The current interest rate is 6.5 percent. The parents of the recipients must co-sign the loan.
EIN: 480941171

3098
John A. & Irene Papines Scholarship Trust
c/o Bank of America, N.A.
P.O. Box 441, NJ6-219-02-03
Ridgefield Park, NJ   07660-9984

Foundation type: Independent foundation
Limitations: Scholarships to residents of Atlantic, Cape May, Cumberland, and Ocean counties, NJ, who are of Greek descent.
Financial data: Year ended 12/31/2004.
Assets, $749,618 (M); Expenditures, $47,280; Total giving, $40,425; Grants to individuals, 64 grants totaling $40,425 (high: $1,350, low: $600).
Fields of interest: Greece.
Type of support: Scholarships—to individuals.
Application information: Application form required.
Deadline(s): May 1
EIN: 226321385

3099
Paris Education Foundation
P.O. Box 356
Paris, TX   75461-0356   (903) 782-0251
Contact: Sandra Holt, Exec. Dir.

Foundation type: Public charity
Limitations: Scholarships to students of Paris High School for higher education.

Financial data: Year ended 06/30/2005.
Assets, $1,003,263 (M); Expenditures, $96,389; Total giving, $48,686; Grants to individuals, totaling $48,686.
Fields of interest: Higher education.
Type of support: Scholarships—to individuals.
Application information: Applications accepted. Application form required.
Program description:
  Post High School Scholarships: Available to Paris High School graduating seniors who plan to enter a college, university or vocational/technical school. Scholarships are competitive with consideration given to each applicant's financial need; academic performance; teacher evaluations; community and school involvement and work activities.
EIN: 752294089

3100
Park Foundation
c/o The Huntington National Bank
P.O. Box 1558, EA4E86
Columbus, OH   43216
Application address: c/o Bank of Corning, Attn.: Kathy Colvin, Secy. and Trust Off., P.O. Box 428, Corning, OH 43730

Foundation type: Independent foundation
Limitations: Scholarships to high school seniors who reside in Perry County, OH, and attend Southern Local High School their entire senior year.
Financial data: Year ended 06/30/2005.
Assets, $614,971 (M); Expenditures, $36,087; Total giving, $27,800; Grants to individuals, 15 grants totaling $27,800 (high: $9,800, low: $200).
Type of support: Support to graduates or students of specific schools; Undergraduate support.
Application information: Application form required.
Deadline(s): Apr. 30
Applicants should submit the following:
  1) Transcripts
Additional information: Application must also include two character reference letters, and biographical statements; New applicants must include a letter of acceptance from college or university.
EIN: 316207775

3101
Willis H. Park Technical Student Fund
c/o National City Bank
P.O. Box 94651
Cleveland, OH   44101-4651
Contact: Myra Vitto, Trust Off., National City Bank
Application address: P.O. Box 450, Youngstown, OH 44501, tel.: (330) 742-4289

Foundation type: Independent foundation
Limitations: Scholarships for undergraduate and graduate study to financially needy graduates of Rayen High School and South High School in Youngstown, OH.
Financial data: Year ended 12/31/2004.
Assets, $122,452 (M); Expenditures, $3,511; Total giving, $2,500; Grant to an individual, 1 grant totaling $2,500.
Type of support: Support to graduates or students of specific schools; Graduate support; Undergraduate support.
Application information: Application form required.
Deadline(s): Contact fund for current application deadline
Applicants should submit the following:
  1) Letter(s) of recommendation
  2) Financial information
  3) Transcripts

Additional information: Scholarships are renewable if a cumulative GPA of at least 2.5 is maintained. Maximum scholarship for any given year shall be $500.
EIN: 346515519

3102
Parke County Community Foundation, Inc.
P.O. Box 276
Rockville, IN   47872   (765) 569-7223
E-mail: pccf@abcs.com

Foundation type: Community foundation
Limitations: Scholarships to students in the Parke County, IN, area.
Financial data: Year ended 06/30/2004.
Assets, $8,240,084 (M); Expenditures, $566,839; Total giving, $346,337; Grants to individuals, 122 grants totaling $57,107 (high: $1,500, low: $30).
Type of support: Scholarships—to individuals.
Application information: Contact foundation for current application deadline/guidelines.
EIN: 351881810

3103
Winston E. Parker Scholarship Foundation
(formerly Winston E. Parker Scholarship Fund)
22 N. Main St.
Medford, NJ   08055
Contact: Jack Henderson
Application address: c/o G. Anderson Agency, 509 S. Lenola Rd., Moorestown, NJ, 08057

Foundation type: Independent foundation
Limitations: Scholarships to full-time college juniors, seniors, and graduate students studying arboriculture, forestry, ornamental horticulture, and related fields. Applicants from Rotary Districts 7500 and 7640 (southern NJ) are preferred. The fund is administered by the Rotary Club of Moorestown, NJ.
Publications: Informational brochure.
Financial data: Year ended 12/31/2004.
Assets, $466,808 (M); Expenditures, $67,850; Total giving, $48,708.
Fields of interest: Environment, forests; Horticulture/garden clubs; Biological sciences.
Type of support: Graduate support; Undergraduate support.
Application information: Application form required.
Deadline(s): May 1 for fall semester
Additional information: Interviews required.
EIN: 223069120

3104
Henry & Louise Parker Scholarship Trust
c/o Comerica Bank
P.O. Box 75000
Detroit, MI   48275
Application addresses: c/o Santa Cruz High School, Attn: Principal, 415 Walnut Ave., Santa Cruz, CA 95060, c/o Harbor High School, Attn: Principal, 300 LaFonda Ave., Santa Cruz, CA 95062, c/o Soquel High School, Attn: Principal, 401 Old San Jose Rd., Soquel, CA 95073

Foundation type: Independent foundation
Limitations: Scholarships to students from Santa Cruz High School and Harbor High School in Santa Cruz, CA, and Soquel High School in Soquel, CA. Recipients are chosen by a scholarship committee

made up of the principals of Santa Cruz, Harbor, and Soquel high schools.
Financial data: Year ended 12/31/2004. Assets, $296,961 (M); Expenditures, $14,468; Total giving, $10,800; Grants to individuals, 2 grants totaling $10,800 (high: $5,500, low: $5,300).
Type of support: Support to graduates or students of specific schools; Undergraduate support.
Application information: Application form required.
Deadline(s): Contact trust for current application deadline
EIN: 946347991

3105
Pauline R. Parker Trust
c/o Chemung Canal Trust Co.
P.O. Box 1522
Elmira, NY 14902-1522   (607) 737-3896

Foundation type: Independent foundation
Limitations: Interest-free student loans to financially needy residents of Broome County, NY, attending Broome Community College or State University of New York at Binghamton.
Financial data: Year ended 12/31/2004. Assets, $288,373 (M); Expenditures, $14,189; Total giving, $8,822; Grant to an individual, 1 grant totaling $6,822; Loan to an individual, 1 loan totaling $2,000.
Type of support: Student loans—to individuals; Support to graduates or students of specific schools; Undergraduate support.
Application information: Application form required.
Deadline(s): None
Applicants should submit the following:
1) Financial information
Additional information: The maximum loan amount is $2,500 per student. Repayment begins immediately after graduation.
EIN: 166095226

3106
Parkersburg Area Community Foundation
501 Avery St.
P.O. Box 1762
Parkersburg, WV 26102-1762   (304) 428-4438
Contact: Judy Sjostedt, Exec. Dir.; Mariam Clowes, Prog. and Devel. Off.; Sarah Holt, Prog. and Devel. Off.
FAX: (304) 428-1200; E-mail: info@pacfwv.com; Additional tel.: (866) 428-4438; Additional E-mails: marian.clowes@pacfwv.com and sarah.holt@pacfwv.com; URL: http://www.pacfwv.com

Foundation type: Community foundation
Limitations: Scholarships to residents of the Parkersburg/Mid-Ohio Valley area, primarily those who are students or graduates of Wood County, WV, high schools. All grants to individuals are prize awards or scholarships to individuals, as directed by specific scholarship endowment agreements.
Publications: Application guidelines; Annual report; Informational brochure; Newsletter.
Financial data: Year ended 06/30/2004. Assets, $17,708,608 (M); Expenditures, $1,033,740; Total giving, $704,099; Grants to individuals, 233 grants totaling $193,634 (high: $2,750, low: $75).
Fields of interest: Arts; Elementary school/education; Secondary school/education; Education, special; Reading; Health care; Athletics/sports, training; Human services; Children/youth, services.

Type of support: Support to graduates or students of specific schools; Awards/prizes; Undergraduate support.
Application information: Applications not accepted.
Additional information: Unsolicited requests for funds not considered or acknowledged.
EIN: 556027764

3107
Ruth Parks Trust for the Education of Nurses
c/o United Bank of Iowa
501 2nd St.
Ida Grove, IA 51445-1305

Foundation type: Independent foundation
Limitations: Scholarships to individuals pursuing an education in nursing. Preference is given to individuals living within 20 miles of Ida Grove, IA, and/or those who are seeking an R.N. degree.
Financial data: Year ended 12/31/2004. Assets, $149,976 (M); Expenditures, $6,810; Total giving, $5,250; Grants to individuals, totaling $5,250.
Fields of interest: Nursing school/education.
Type of support: Scholarships—to individuals.
Application information: Applications accepted. Application form required.
Deadline(s): May 31
Applicants should submit the following:
1) Class rank
2) Financial information
3) GPA
Additional information: Application must also include a statement of career plans.
EIN: 426378004

3108
Arthur and Doreen Parrett Scholarship Trust Fund
(also known as Parrett Scholarship Fund)
c/o U.S. Bank, N.A., Trust Div.
P.O. Box 3169
Portland, OR 97208
Contact: Scholarship: Katherine K. West
Application address: c/o U.S. Bank, N.A., Attn.: Paul Schneider, Trust Off., P.O. Box 720, Seattle, WA 88111-0720

Foundation type: Independent foundation
Limitations: Scholarships to WA residents for study in schools of engineering, science, medicine, and dentistry. Applicant must have completed one year of college by July 31 and be enrolled full-time.
Financial data: Year ended 11/30/2002. Assets, $453,605 (M); Expenditures, $22,276; Total giving, $14,500; Grants to individuals, totaling $14,500.
Fields of interest: Dental school/education; Medical school/education; Science; Engineering.
Type of support: Undergraduate support.
Application information: Application form required.
Initial approach: Letter.
Deadline(s): July 31
Additional information: Applications are mailed to eligible students in Jan.
EIN: 916228230

3109
W. N. Parsons Scholarship Foundation
c/o Peoples Bank
P.O. Box C
Pratt, KS 67124
Application address: c/o The Peoples Bank, Attn.: Wyan Alexander, Coldwater, KS, 67029

Foundation type: Independent foundation
Limitations: Scholarships to residents of Commanche, Kiowa, and Clark counties, KS, for attendance at vocational and trade schools, and community colleges.
Financial data: Year ended 12/31/2004. Assets, $605,372 (M); Expenditures, $32,421; Total giving, $27,000; Grants to individuals, 11 grants totaling $27,000 (high: $3,000, low: $1,500).
Fields of interest: Vocational education.
Type of support: Technical education support; Undergraduate support.
Application information: Applications accepted. Application form required.
Applicants should submit the following:
1) GPA
Additional information: Application must also include a personal statement.
EIN: 481086241

3110
Trustees of Partridge Academy in Duxbury
P.O. Box 92
Duxbury, MA 02331-0092
Application address: c/o Guidance Dir., Duxbury High School, Duxbury, MA 02332, tel.: (781) 934-7661

Foundation type: Independent foundation
Limitations: Scholarships to graduates of Duxbury Junior and Senior High School, MA.
Financial data: Year ended 12/31/2004. Assets, $1,860,258 (M); Expenditures, $82,158; Total giving, $78,800; Grants to individuals, 40 grants totaling $78,800 (high: $7,000, low: $300).
Type of support: Support to graduates or students of specific schools; Undergraduate support.
Application information:
Deadline(s): Spring of senior year
Additional information: Applicants should contact guidance counselors for specific application guidelines.
EIN: 222838857

3111
William G. & Rhoda B. Partridge Memorial Scholarship Fund
c/o NBT Bank, N.A.
52 S. Broad St.
Norwich, NY 13815
Contact: Sandra E. Colton, Trust Off., NBT Bank, N.A.

Foundation type: Independent foundation
Limitations: Scholarships to graduates of Northville High School or residents of Edinburg in Saratoga County, NY to pursue a medical degree.
Publications: Application guidelines.
Financial data: Year ended 06/30/2005. Assets, $842,003 (M); Expenditures, $39,168; Total giving, $36,000; Grants to individuals, 4 grants totaling $36,000 (high: $15,000, low: $4,000).
Fields of interest: Medical school/education.
Type of support: Support to graduates or students of specific schools; Undergraduate support.

Application information: Application form required.
  Deadline(s): May 15
  EIN: 141597911

3112
PARTS Scholarship Foundation
(formerly Pennsylvania Auto & Truck Salvage
Association Scholarship Foundation)
1200 Camp Hill Bypass, Ste. 101
Camp Hill, PA   17011
Application address: c/o Harrisburg Area
Community College, Office of Financial Aid, 1 HACC
Dr., Harrisburg, PA 17110, tel.: (717) 780-2300

Foundation type: Independent foundation
Limitations: Scholarships to members, employees,
and their families, of Pennsylvania Automotive
Recycling Trade Society (PARTS) for undergraduate
or technical school education.
Financial data: Year ended 09/30/2004.
Assets, $47,993 (M); Expenditures, $40,732;
Total giving, $22,000; Grants to individuals, 8
grants totaling $22,000 (high: $4,000, low:
$1,000).
Type of support: Employee-related scholarships;
Technical education support.
Application information: Application form required.
  Deadline(s): Apr. 1
  EIN: 232361314

3113
Grace Patch Scholarship Trust
c/o Wells Fargo Bank Nevada, N.A.
P.O. Box 95021, MAC 54035-014
Henderson, NV   89009

Foundation type: Independent foundation
Limitations: Scholarships to graduates of Sweet
Home High School, OR, for education at
Linn-Benton Community College in Albany, OR.
Financial data: Year ended 03/31/2005.
Assets, $222,551 (M); Expenditures, $12,760;
Total giving, $8,875; Grant to an individual, 1 grant
totaling $8,875.
Type of support: Support to graduates or students
of specific schools; Undergraduate support.
Application information: Applications not
accepted.
EIN: 936181508

3114
Charles A. & Odette W. Patterson
Charitable Trust
c/o Bank of America, N.A.
P.O. Box 40200, MC FL9-100-10-19
Jacksonville, FL   32203-0200
Application addresses: c/o Chief of Police, City of
St. Petersburg, St. Petersburg, FL 33731, or c/o
Chief of Fire Dept., City of St. Petersburg, St.
Petersburg, FL 33731

Foundation type: Independent foundation
Limitations: Scholarships and awards to
employees of the St. Petersburg, FL, police and/or
fire department(s).
Financial data: Year ended 09/30/2004.
Assets, $459,123 (M); Expenditures, $18,691;
Total giving, $15,526; Grants to individuals, 37
grants totaling $10,526 (high: $500, low: $31).
Fields of interest: Crime/law enforcement.
Type of support: Employee-related scholarships;
Awards/prizes.
Application information: Applications accepted.
Application form required.

Additional information: Contact St. Petersburg
Chief of Police or Chief of Fire Dept. for
application materials.
Program description:
  Scholarship Program: Scholarship applicants
must be enrolled at or accepted by an accredited
college or university and pursue a degree deemed
appropriate for a law enforcement career. In
addition, applicants must maintain at least a 3.0
GPA and remain in service.
EIN: 596953716

3115
Father Joseph Patterson Foundation, Inc.
P.O. Box 25407
Tempe, AZ   85285-5407   (480) 838-8777
Contact: Erin Patterson, V.P.

Foundation type: Independent foundation
Limitations: Scholarships primarily to residents of
AZ.
Financial data: Year ended 07/31/2005.
Assets, $747,850 (M); Expenditures, $56,955;
Total giving, $56,250; Grants to individuals, 68
grants totaling $56,250 (high: $1,000, low: $500).
Type of support: Scholarships—to individuals.
Application information: Application form required.
  Deadline(s): June 15
  EIN: 953325958

3116
Nicholas Patterson Perpetual Fund
P.O. Box 887
Buffalo, NY   14205-0887
Contact: Frederick B. Cohen, Tr.
E-mail: pattersonfund@aol.com; URL: http://
www.pattersonfund.org

Foundation type: Independent foundation
Limitations: Scholarships to residents of Erie
County, NY, for college and graduate school.
Financial data: Year ended 12/31/2004.
Assets, $512,001 (M); Expenditures, $34,027;
Total giving, $25,000; Grants to individuals, 20
grants totaling $20,000 (high: $1,000, low:
$1,000).
Fields of interest: Economically disadvantaged.
Type of support: Graduate support; Undergraduate
support.
Application information: Application form required.
  Initial approach: Letter, telephone or e-mail.
  Copies of proposal: 5
  Deadline(s): May 1
  Applicants should submit the following:
    1) Letter(s) of recommendation
    2) Financial information
    3) Budget Information
  Additional information: Application must also
    include tuition costs and personal statement.
  EIN: 222806714

3117
Frances Patterson Trust
P.O. Box 332
Fredonia, KS   66736   (620) 378-4177

Foundation type: Independent foundation
Limitations: Scholarships to graduates of Fredonia
High School, KS.
Financial data: Year ended 12/31/2004.
Assets, $117,773 (M); Expenditures, $10,730;
Total giving, $10,730; Grants to individuals, 5
grants totaling $4,600 (high: $1,125, low: $500).

Type of support: Support to graduates or students
of specific schools; Undergraduate support.
Application information: Applications accepted
throughout the year; Submit three-page letter with
appropriate attachments.
EIN: 446008159

3118
G. F. Patterson Trust
c/o Citizens National Bank
P.O. Box 790
Paris, IL   61944   (217) 465-7641
Contact: Chris Hollowell, Trust Off., Citizens
National Bank

Foundation type: Independent foundation
Limitations: Scholarships to residents of Edgar
County, IL.
Financial data: Year ended 12/31/2004.
Assets, $700,891 (M); Expenditures, $31,338;
Total giving, $19,800; Grants to individuals, 6
grants totaling $19,800 (high: $3,300, low:
$3,300).
Type of support: Undergraduate support.
Application information: Applications accepted.
Application form required.
  Initial approach: Letter.
  Deadline(s): May 15
  Additional information: Applications are available
    at the Citizens National Bank of Paris.
  EIN: 376343185

3119
Minnie Patton Scholarship Foundation
Trust
c/o Bank of America, N.A.
P.O. Box 831041
Dallas, TX   75283-0241   (214) 209-1905
Application address: c/o Cindy Miller, Bank of
America, N.A., P.O. Box 832408, Dallas, TX
75283-2408, tel.: (214) 209-1905

Foundation type: Independent foundation
Limitations: Scholarships to individuals to attend
any college or university in Dallas County, TX.
Publications: Program policy statement.
Financial data: Year ended 01/31/2003.
Assets, $903,941 (M); Expenditures, $88,932;
Total giving, $48,000; Grants to individuals,
totaling $48,000.
Type of support: Scholarships—to individuals.
Application information: Applications accepted.
Application form required.
  Applicants should submit the following:
    1) Class rank
    2) Financial information
  Additional information: Application must also
    include two personal references, and
    signature of notary public.
  EIN: 756318876

3120
George W. & Mary B. Patton Scholarship
Fund
(formerly Patton Scholarship Fund)
c/o Wells Fargo Bank Minnesota, N.A.
625 Marquette Ave., N9311-142
Minneapolis, MN   55402
Application address: c/o Lincoln High School,
Independent School District 813, Attn.: Thomas
Boe, Lake City, MN 55041

Foundation type: Independent foundation

Limitations: Scholarships to graduating seniors of Lake City High School, MN, who are members of the honor society.
Financial data: Year ended 12/31/2004.
Assets, $170,274 (M); Expenditures, $8,454; Total giving, $6,000.
Type of support: Support to graduates or students of specific schools; Undergraduate support.
Application information: Applications accepted throughout the year; Completion of formal application required.
EIN: 416059300

3121
Patton Scholarship Trust
c/o Wells Fargo Bank, N.A.
4707 S. 96th St.
Phoenix, AZ 85072
Application address: c/o Superintendent, Twin Lakes School Corp., 565 S. Main St., Monticello, IN 47960

Foundation type: Independent foundation
Limitations: Scholarships to graduating seniors of Twin Lakes High School, IN.
Financial data: Year ended 02/28/2005.
Assets, $314,224 (M); Expenditures, $17,910; Total giving, $14,000.
Type of support: Support to graduates or students of specific schools; Undergraduate support.
Application information: Application form required.
Deadline(s): Mar. 1
EIN: 356570391

3122
Thomas M. Paul Memorial Trust
c/o U.S. Bank, N.A.
P.O. Box 308
St. Joseph, MO 64502-0308 (816) 233-2000

Foundation type: Independent foundation
Limitations: Scholarships to students of Missouri Western State College who have graduated from St. Joseph, MO, high schools and who are preparing for careers in the medical field.
Financial data: Year ended 12/31/2002.
Assets, $872,863 (M); Expenditures, $44,486; Total giving, $30,825; Grants to individuals, 46 grants totaling $30,825 (high: $2,000, low: $250).
Fields of interest: Medical school/education.
Type of support: Support to graduates or students of specific schools; Undergraduate support.
Application information:
Initial approach: Telephone.
Additional information: Contact foundation for current application deadline/guidelines.
EIN: 436009612

3123
PAULA Difference Scholarship Fund
87 E. Green St., Ste. 206
Pasadena, CA 91105 (626) 304-0401
Contact: Debbie Maddocks, C.F.O.

Foundation type: Company-sponsored foundation
Limitations: Scholarships to individual dependents of farm workers.
Financial data: Year ended 12/31/2004.
Assets, $537 (M); Expenditures, $9,250; Total giving, $9,250; Grants to individuals, totaling $9,250.
Fields of interest: Agriculture/food.
Type of support: Undergraduate support.

Application information: Applications accepted. Application form required.
Deadline(s): Apr. 30
Additional information: Completion of formal application required including personal statement.
EIN: 954643798

3124
Paulsen Trust
5230 Village Dr. S.W.
Wyoming, MI 49509-5147
Contact: Nelson R. Allen, Tr.
Application address: 2121 Pantano Rd., No. 267, Tucson, AZ 85710, tel.: (520) 751-7897

Foundation type: Independent foundation
Limitations: Scholarships to graduating high school seniors in MI who plan to attend any postsecondary institution in MI, regardless of degrees offered.
Financial data: Year ended 12/31/2004.
Assets, $195,502 (M); Expenditures, $9,886; Total giving, $9,000; Grants to individuals, 6 grants totaling $9,000 (high: $2,000, low: $1,000).
Fields of interest: Vocational education.
Type of support: Scholarships—to individuals.
Application information: Applications accepted throughout the year; Contact trust for current application guidelines; Completion of formal application required.
EIN: 386537948

3125
Jack Paxton Memorial Scholarship Fund, Inc.
555 Jefferson St.
Paducah, KY 42001
Contact: Bill Bartleman, Secy.
Application address: P.O. Box 2300, Paducah, KY 42001-2300

Foundation type: Independent foundation
Limitations: Scholarships to residents of western KY.
Financial data: Year ended 12/31/2004.
Assets, $491,276 (M); Expenditures, $16,757; Total giving, $15,250; Grants to individuals, 14 grants totaling $15,250 (high: $1,500, low: $350).
Type of support: Scholarships—to individuals.
Application information: Application form required.
Deadline(s): Apr. 15
EIN: 611093502

3126
Charles K. Payne Scholarship Fund, Inc.
P.O. Box 125
Butler, NJ 07405 (973) 492-0101
Contact: Timothy L. Hammond, Exec. Dir.

Foundation type: Independent foundation
Limitations: Scholarships to high school graduates from Butler, Bloomingdale, and Kinnelon areas in NJ.
Financial data: Year ended 12/31/2004.
Assets, $415,902 (M); Expenditures, $24,616; Total giving, $21,000; Grants to individuals, 19 grants totaling $21,000 (high: $2,000, low: $1,000).
Type of support: Support to graduates or students of specific schools; Undergraduate support.
Application information: Application form required.
Deadline(s): Apr. 15
EIN: 226207012

3127
The Grace & Bill Peabody Foundation, Inc.
69 E. Housatonic St.
Pittsfield, MA 01201
Contact: William S. Peabody, Pres.
Application address: 53 Walker Rd., Atkinson, NH 03811, tel.: (603) 362-4003

Foundation type: Operating foundation
Limitations: Scholarships to children of staff and employees of Wilmington, MA schools.
Financial data: Year ended 12/31/2003.
Assets, $8,938 (M); Expenditures, $10,252; Total giving, $10,000; Grants to individuals, 3 grants totaling $10,000 (high: $5,000, low: $2,500).
Type of support: Employee-related scholarships.
Application information:
Initial approach: Letter.
Additional information: Contact foundation for further information.
EIN: 043571773

3128
Louise Peacock Educational Trust
c/o Fifth Third Bank
200 S. Riverside Ave.
St. Clair, MI 48079
Application address: c/o Corunna High School, Guidance Office, 417 E. King St., Corunna, MI 48817

Foundation type: Independent foundation
Limitations: Interest-free student loans to financially needy, graduating seniors in Corunna High School District, MI, for study at two- and four-year colleges.
Financial data: Year ended 04/30/2002.
Assets, $219,428 (M); Expenditures, $17,142; Total giving, $14,000; Loans to individuals, 14 loans totaling $14,000.
Type of support: Support to graduates or students of specific schools; Undergraduate support.
Application information: Application form required.
Deadline(s): May 15
EIN: 386215314

3129
Walter G. and Ella M. Peak Scholarship Fund
c/o FirstMerit Bank, N.A.
106 S. Main St., Ste. 1600
Akron, OH 44308

Foundation type: Independent foundation
Limitations: Scholarships to graduating residents of the Elyria Central School District, OH.
Financial data: Year ended 12/31/2003.
Assets, $122,173 (M); Expenditures, $7,084; Total giving, $5,000; Grants to individuals, totaling $5,000.
Type of support: Support to graduates or students of specific schools; Undergraduate support.
Application information: Application form required.
Deadline(s): Mar. 1
Additional information: Application may be obtained from and returned to school counselor.
EIN: 341776865

3130

Jack & Katherine Pearce Educational Foundation

c/o Frost National Bank
P.O. Box 8210
Galveston, TX   77553-8210   (409) 770-5665
Contact: Janet L. Bertolino, Admin., Frost National Bank

Foundation type: Independent foundation
Limitations: Interest-free student loans to academically worthy young residents of the city of Galveston, TX, who have graduated from Galveston schools. Loans may be used for undergraduate, graduate, postgraduate, or professional education.
Publications: Informational brochure (including application guidelines).
Financial data: Year ended 12/31/2004.
Assets, $1,898,119 (M); Expenditures, $167,567; Total giving, $138,000; Loans to individuals, 34 loans totaling $138,000.
Type of support: Student loans—to individuals; Support to graduates or students of specific schools.
Application information: Applications accepted. Application form required.
  Initial approach: Letter or telephone.
  Deadline(s): Mar. 31
  Applicants should submit the following:
    1) Letter(s) of recommendation
    2) Essay
    3) Budget Information
    4) Transcripts
    5) SAT
    6) ACT
    7) Financial information
  Additional information: Application must also include references, recent photograph, and two co-signatures.
Program description:
  Student Loan: Loans assist full-time students with a maximum amount of $4,000 per year for up to four years. Loans may be renewed on a yearly basis. Recipients are required to send monthly payments of at least $35 while in school. Recipients are allowed up to six years after graduation or termination of schooling to pay off the loan in full. Two co-signatures are required, one of which must be from a resident of TX. Applicants who are entering college freshmen must achieve a minimum score on the ACT or SAT. Students who graduate in the lower three-quarters of their high school class must score at least 25 on the ACT or 1050 on the SAT. Students in the next 15 percent of their class must score at least 24 on the ACT or 1000 on the SAT. There is no minimum test score requirement for the top 10 percent of the class. College upperclassmen must maintain a GPA of at least 2.75.
EIN: 746035546

3131

Pearce Foundation

c/o Sky Bank
P.O. Box 479
Youngstown, OH   44501-0479   (330) 742-7035
Contact: Carol Chamberlain, V.P. and Trust Off., Sky Bank

Foundation type: Independent foundation
Limitations: Scholarships for higher education.
Financial data: Year ended 12/31/2004.
Assets, $2,369,922 (M); Expenditures, $159,287; Total giving, $133,329; Grants to individuals, 4 grants totaling $12,000 (high: $3,000, low: $3,000).
Type of support: Scholarships—to individuals.

Application information:
  Initial approach: Letter or telephone.
  Additional information: Contact foundation for current application deadline/guidelines.
EIN: 346572300

3132

George & Belle Pearce Trust

P.O. Box 913
Hutchinson, KS   67504-0913   (620) 663-1521
Contact: Donald D. Adams, Exec. V.P. and Trust Off., First National Bank

Foundation type: Independent foundation
Limitations: Scholarships only to residents of Hutchinson and Reno County, KS, who are attending Hutchinson Community College, KS.
Financial data: Year ended 12/31/2004.
Assets, $632,915 (M); Expenditures, $83,875; Total giving, $75,600; Grants to individuals, 8 grants totaling $12,500 (high: $2,000, low: $500).
Type of support: Support to graduates or students of specific schools; Undergraduate support.
Application information: Applications accepted throughout the year; Contact Hutchinson Community College for current application guidelines; Initial approach by letter.
EIN: 486186188

3133

Edwin & Gladys Pearson Scholarship Trust

c/o 1st Source Bank
100 N. Michigan Ave.
South Bend, IN   46601

Foundation type: Independent foundation
Limitations: Scholarships to graduates of Argos High School, IN, for full-time study at postsecondary institutions.
Financial data: Year ended 09/30/2004.
Assets, $188,729 (M); Expenditures, $11,389; Total giving, $8,000; Grants to individuals, totaling $8,000.
Type of support: Support to graduates or students of specific schools; Undergraduate support.
Application information: Applications accepted. Application form required.
  Applicants should submit the following:
    1) Essay
    2) FAFSA
  Additional information: Application must also include teacher evaluations, test scores, and employment record.
EIN: 356400471

3134

Viola Pearson Scholarship Trust

c/o American National Bank
P.O. Box 1528
Cheyenne, WY   82003
Contact: Dersnie R. Barber, V.P. and Trust Off., American National Bank

Foundation type: Operating foundation
Limitations: Scholarships to graduates of East High School, Cheyenne, WY.
Financial data: Year ended 12/31/2003.
Assets, $162,751 (M); Expenditures, $6,809; Total giving, $4,083; Grants to individuals, 19 grants totaling $4,083.
Type of support: Support to graduates or students of specific schools; Undergraduate support.

Application information: Applications accepted.
  Initial approach: Letter.
  Applicants should submit the following:
    1) Transcripts
  Additional information: Applications outlining financial need, accompanied by letter of reference from a faculty member, accepted throughout the year.
EIN: 836031271

3135

Abel E. Peck Memorial Fund

c/o The National Bank of Delaware County
P.O. Box 389
Walton, NY   13856
Application address: c/o Guidance Dept., Walton Central High School, Walton, NY 13856, tel.: (607) 865-4116

Foundation type: Independent foundation
Limitations: Scholarships to students of Walton Central School District No. 1, NY.
Financial data: Year ended 11/30/2002.
Assets, $749,017 (M); Expenditures, $32,867; Total giving, $29,984; Grants to individuals, 7 grants totaling $29,984.
Type of support: Scholarships—to individuals; Support to graduates or students of specific schools.
Application information: Application form required.
  Initial approach: Letter requesting application.
  Deadline(s): Apr. 1
EIN: 166254479

3136

Katherine L. Peck Trust

c/o Bank of America, N.A.
P.O. Box 6767
Providence, RI   02940-6767
Application address: c/o First Congregational Church Scholarship Comm., 222 W. Main St., Waterbury, CT 06708, tel.: (203) 757-0331

Foundation type: Independent foundation
Limitations: Scholarships to Protestant girls in the Waterbury, CT, area.
Financial data: Year ended 12/31/2002.
Assets, $363,291 (M); Expenditures, $27,820; Total giving, $21,000; Grants to individuals, 12 grants totaling $21,000 (high: $2,000, low: $1,000).
Fields of interest: Protestant agencies & churches; Women.
Type of support: Scholarships—to individuals.
Application information: Applications accepted.
  Initial approach: Letter.
  Deadline(s): Apr. 15
  Applicants should submit the following:
    1) Transcripts
    2) Financial information
  Additional information: Application must also include activities, and grades.
EIN: 066024593

3137

Hattie M. Peckitt Scholarship Trust

(formerly Leonard Carlton Peckitt Scholarship Trust)
c/o Wachovia Bank, N.A.
100 N. Main St., 13th Fl.
Winston-Salem, NC   27150

Foundation type: Independent foundation

Limitations: Scholarships are granted for one to four years of study to graduates of Catasauqua High School, PA.
Financial data: Year ended 12/31/2004.
Assets, $312,706 (M); Expenditures, $14,116; Total giving, $10,500.
Fields of interest: Education.
Type of support: Support to graduates or students of specific schools.
Application information: Applications not accepted.
EIN: 236611993

3138
Marion A. & Eva S. Peeples Trust
c/o JPMorgan Chase Bank, N.A.
P.O. Box 1308
Milwaukee, WI 53201
Application address: c/o Elizabeth Schlueter, JPMorgan Chase Bank, N.A., 111 Monument Cir., IN1-0150, Indianapolis, IN 46204-5100

Foundation type: Independent foundation
Limitations: Scholarships for studies in nursing or dietetics, or to obtain training in teaching industrial arts in IN.
Financial data: Year ended 06/30/2005.
Assets, $1,754,455 (M); Expenditures, $132,429; Total giving, $81,750; Grants to individuals, totaling $81,750.
Fields of interest: Design; Nursing school/education; Teacher school/education; Nutrition.
Type of support: Support to graduates or students of specific schools; Undergraduate support.
Application information: Applications accepted. Application form required.
  Initial approach: Letter.
  Deadline(s): Mar. 20; Notification before June 30.
  Applicants should submit the following:
    1) Financial information
    2) Letter(s) of recommendation
  Additional information: Interviews required.
Program description:
  Scholarship Program: In awarding scholarships, preference is given first to graduates of Franklin Community High School, IN, and then graduates of Johnson county schools, and all Indiana high school graduates who plan to attend an IN college or university. The recipients will be students wishing to pursue a course of study leading to a degree in nursing (B.S., R.N., L.P.N. or an approved hospital nursing program), dietetics (B.S.) or Industrial Arts Education (B.S.). All grants are for one year only, but at the discretion of the scholarship committee, grants may be awarded for up to four years. The amount of the grant is determined by the scholarship committee. The criteria used by the scholarship committee include:
  · prior academic performance
  · performance on college board tests
  · recommendation from instructors and other responsible persons
  · financial need
  · applicant's motivation, character, ability, and potential, as apparent in a personal interview.
EIN: 356306320

3139
Bulah Peery Memorial Scholarship Fund
Box 515
Booker, TX 79005-0515 (806) 658-4551
Contact: Daryl Pitts, Dir.

Foundation type: Independent foundation

Limitations: Scholarships to graduates of Booker High School, TX, who attended the school for at least two years, including senior year.
Financial data: Year ended 07/31/2004.
Assets, $360,726 (M); Expenditures, $17,374; Total giving, $16,200; Grants to individuals, 26 grants totaling $16,200 (high: $1,000, low: $300).
Type of support: Support to graduates or students of specific schools; Undergraduate support.
Application information: Applications accepted throughout the year; Application must include proof of college enrollment at a U.S. institution.
EIN: 756038523

3140
Charles Pehna Scholarship Trust
c/o National City Bank
P.O. Box 94651
Cleveland, OH 44101

Foundation type: Independent foundation
Limitations: Scholarships to students, primarily in PA, for higher education.
Financial data: Year ended 12/31/2004.
Assets, $340,391 (M); Expenditures, $16,202; Total giving, $12,000; Grants to individuals, 12 grants totaling $12,000 (high: $1,000, low: $1,000).
Type of support: Undergraduate support.
Application information: Applications not accepted.
EIN: 527155874

3141
Andrew Pekema Memorial Scholarships
P.O. Box 937
Ferndale, WA 98248-0937
Contact: Rikki Thompson, Secy.

Foundation type: Independent foundation
Limitations: Scholarships to children of active and retired employees of Intalco Aluminum Corp. in Ferndale, WA.
Financial data: Year ended 12/31/2004.
Assets, $20,738 (M); Expenditures, $21,677; Total giving, $21,677; Grants to individuals, 21 grants totaling $21,677 (high: $1,332, low: $333).
Type of support: Employee-related scholarships.
Application information: Application form required.
  Initial approach: Letter.
  Deadline(s): Apr. 21
  Applicants should submit the following:
    1) Transcripts
    2) Essay
EIN: 911346995

3142
Pella Rolscreen Foundation
c/o Pella Corp.
102 Main St.
Pella, IA 50219 (641) 621-6224
Contact: Mary A. Van Zante, Dir.
FAX: (641) 621-6950;
E-mail: mavzants@pella.com; URL: http://www.pellarolscreen.org

Foundation type: Company-sponsored foundation
Limitations: Scholarships only to children of employees of Pella Corporation, IA.
Publications: Application guidelines; Annual report.
Financial data: Year ended 12/31/2004.
Assets, $16,419,636 (M); Expenditures, $1,997,364; Total giving, $1,830,448; Grants to

individuals, 97 grants totaling $183,000 (high: $6,000, low: $1,500).
Fields of interest: Education.
Type of support: Employee-related scholarships.
Application information:
  Initial approach: Letter.
  Deadline(s): None
  Additional information: Inappropriate applications not considered or acknowledged.
EIN: 237043881

3143
Willis & Mildred Pellerin Foundation
P.O. Box 400
Kenner, LA 70063-0400 (504) 467-9591
Contact: Lynne Hotfelter, Admin. Asst.

Foundation type: Independent foundation
Limitations: Scholarships to highly qualified and financially needy residents of LA who are enrolled in a LA college or university for full-time undergraduate study.
Financial data: Year ended 05/31/2005.
Assets, $1,576,413 (M); Expenditures, $83,055; Total giving, $76,750; Grants to individuals, totaling $76,750.
Type of support: Undergraduate support.
Application information: Application form required.
  Initial approach: Letter requesting application and guidelines after Oct. 1, but before Feb. 1.
  Deadline(s): Mar. 1
  Applicants should submit the following:
    1) Photograph
    2) Transcripts
    3) Letter(s) of recommendation
  Additional information: Application must also include a handwritten explanation of need, and certification of acceptance for enrollment. Applicants are required to repay one-half of the grant in equal weekly installments. The grants will be repaid without interest except for an 8 percent per annum charge on late payments. Immediate descendants of Willis and Mildred Pellerin, the members of the board of trustees, or the members of the advisory board are ineligible.
EIN: 510166877

3144
PEMCO Foundation
325 Eastlake Ave. E.
Seattle, WA 98109
Contact: Stan W. McNaughton, Treas.

Foundation type: Company-sponsored foundation
Limitations: Scholarships to individuals residing in WA for undergraduate education.
Financial data: Year ended 06/30/2005.
Assets, $3,153,303 (M); Expenditures, $573,956; Total giving, $571,958; Grants to individuals, 246 grants totaling $156,600 (high: $2,500, low: $200).
Type of support: Undergraduate support.
Application information: Application form required.
  Deadline(s): None
  Applicants should submit the following:
    1) Transcripts
    2) Letter(s) of recommendation
  Additional information: Applicants are generally notified within two months.
EIN: 916072723

3145
Penasco Valley Telephone Education Foundation
4011 W. Main St.
Artesia, NM 88210-9566   (505) 748-1241

Foundation type: Company-sponsored foundation
Limitations: Scholarships to members of Penasco Valley Telephone Cooperative and dependents of active members of the Cooperative for higher education.
Financial data: Year ended 12/31/2004. Assets, $551,659 (M); Expenditures, $32,517; Total giving, $31,500; Grants to individuals, 26 grants totaling $31,500 (high: $1,500, low: $750).
Type of support: Employee-related scholarships.
Application information: Application form required.
  Deadline(s): Mar. 15
  Applicants should submit the following:
    1) Transcripts
    2) Essay
  Additional information: Applications are available at high schools as well as through the foundation.
EIN: 850422272

3146
Peninsula Community Foundation
1700 S. El Camino Real, Ste. 300
San Mateo, CA 94402-3049   (650) 358-9369
Contact: For grants: Ellen Clear, V.P., Community Progs.
FAX: (650) 358-9817; E-mail: inquiry@pcf.org; Grant application E-mails: ellen@pcf.org or grants@pcf.org; URL: http://www.pcf.org

Foundation type: Community foundation
Limitations: Scholarships to residents of San Mateo County and northern Santa Clara County, CA. Support also to employee's of Mervyn's and Una Mas, and their families, residing in CA.
Publications: Application guidelines; Annual report; Financial statement; Grants list; Informational brochure; Newsletter.
Financial data: Year ended 12/31/2004. Assets, $611,716,329 (M); Expenditures, $119,524,673; Total giving, $110,910,875; Grants to individuals, 786 grants totaling $444,637 (high: $15,000, low: $250).
Fields of interest: Literature; Medical school/education; Education; Women.
Type of support: Employee-related scholarships; Graduate support; Undergraduate support.
Application information:
  Deadline(s): Vary
  Additional information: See Web site for further application information.
Program descriptions:
  Crain Educational Grant Program: Awards up to 10 $5,000 undergraduate and graduate scholarships to financially needy Peninsula High School graduates who have demonstrated academic and extracurricular excellence.
  Curry Award for Girls and Young Women: Awards up to seven $1,000 scholarships to self-motivated young women between the ages of 16 and 26 who are San Mateo County residents.
  Ruppert Educational Grants: Awards up to 30 $1,000 scholarships to young people who are "late bloomers".
  Dr. Mary Finegold Scholarship: One $1,000 scholarship is awarded to a senior girl graduating from a public or private high school in San Mateo or Northern Santa Clara County (Daly City through Mountain View)

  Sand Hill Scholars Program: Awards up to 10 $2,500 scholarships to graduates of the Ravenswood City School District in East Palo Alto.
  Bobette Bibo Gugliotta Memorial Scholarship for Creative Writing: Awards one $2,000 scholarship to an undergraduate or graduate student, and one $500 scholarship to a graduating high school senior who aspire to become writers.
  Dr. James L. Hutchinson and Evelyn Ribbs Hutchinson Scholarship Fund: Awards one scholarship of up to $2,000 to a Peninsula student to attend medical school.
  James A. McCavitt and Annie Lepors McCavitt Scholarship: Awards Mervin G. Morris Educational Scholarship: Awards up to 16 $1,000 to $5,000 scholarships to children and grandchildren of Mervin's employees.
  Hua Chien Tang Memorial Scholarship: Awards up to two $1,000 to $2,000 scholarships to seniors graduating from Redwood High School in Redwood City.
  Roantree Family Scholarship Program: Awards up to three $2,500 scholarships to eighth-grade graduates of the Ravenwood City School District, and graduating seniors attending high school in San Mateo County or Santa Clara County.
  Woodlake Scholarship Fund: Awards 10 to 12 scholarships of $1,000 to $3,000 to young women of color who are residents of East Palo Alto or East Menlo Park, and who are graduating from high school with a GPA of less than 3.0, but have a strong desire to attend college.
  Kilmartin Educational Scholarship: Awards approximately 30 $1,000 scholarships to employees of Mervyn's stores who have accumulated at least 1,000 hours of employment service. Deadline early Mar.
EIN: 942746687

3147
The Peninsula Foundation
c/o Scholarship Comm.
1512 Pacheco St., Ste. D-203
Santa Fe, NM 87505   (505) 986-6874
Application address: c/o Guidance Dept., Menominee High School, 2101 18th St., Menominee, MI 49858; tel.: (906) 863-7814

Foundation type: Independent foundation
Limitations: Scholarships to graduating seniors at Menominee High School, MI for higher education.
Financial data: Year ended 12/31/2004. Assets, $29,459 (M); Expenditures, $11,074; Total giving, $10,000; Grants to individuals, 4 grants totaling $10,000 (high: $2,500, low: $2,500).
Type of support: Support to graduates or students of specific schools; Undergraduate support.
Application information: Applications accepted. Application form required.
  Deadline(s): Feb. 1
  Applicants should submit the following:
    1) Transcripts
    2) Letter(s) of recommendation
    3) Essay
  Additional information: Contact Guidance Department for application form.
EIN: 742028228

3148
Penn Jersey Youth Umpires School, Inc.
60 Temple Ave.
Stratford, NJ 08084-2017

Foundation type: Public charity

Limitations: Scholarships to individuals who demonstrate merit and need eligibility.
Financial data: Year ended 01/31/2005. Assets, $445,549 (M); Expenditures, $46,327; Total giving, $45,710; Grants to individuals, 27 grants totaling $45,710 (high: $4,676, low: $325).
Fields of interest: College; Education.
Type of support: Scholarships—to individuals.
Application information: Applications accepted.
  Applicants should submit the following:
    1) SAR
    2) Transcripts
  Additional information: Application must also include a full time four-year college term bill.
Program description:
  Scholarships: Scholarships are awarded to college bound students who demonstrate merit and need eligibility, and maintains a B minus GPA for the preceding full-time term.
EIN: 222430620

3149
Pennsylvania Industrial Chemical Corporation-Chester High School Scholarship Fund
c/o Wachovia Bank, N.A.
100 N. Main St., 13th Fl.
Winston-Salem, NC 27150
Application address: c/o Center For Scholarship Admin., Inc., P.O.Box 1465, Taylors, SC 29687-0031, tel.: (864) 268-3363

Foundation type: Independent foundation
Limitations: Scholarships to graduates and graduating seniors of Chester High School, PA.
Financial data: Year ended 12/31/2004. Assets, $1,618,124 (M); Expenditures, $123,778; Total giving, $124,170.
Type of support: Scholarships—to individuals; Support to graduates or students of specific schools.
Application information:
  Initial approach: Letter.
  Deadline(s): Apr. 15
  Applicants should submit the following:
    1) Letter(s) of recommendation
  Additional information: Application must also include personal information, and participation in curricular activities.
EIN: 236233922

3150
Pennsylvania Industrial Chemical Corporation-Clairton High School Scholarship Fund
c/o National City Bank of PA
P.O. Box 94651
Cleveland, OH 44101-4651
Application address: c/o Richard A. Bertini, Principal, Clarion Senior High School, 5th St., Clarion, PA 15025

Foundation type: Independent foundation
Limitations: Scholarships to graduates of Clarion High School, PA, to attend accredited colleges and universities, and business, nursing, technical, and trade schools.
Financial data: Year ended 06/30/2005. Assets, $558,074 (M); Expenditures, $32,358; Total giving, $26,500; Grants to individuals, 26 grants totaling $26,500 (high: $1,200, low: $500).
Fields of interest: Vocational education; Business school/education; Nursing school/education.
Type of support: Support to graduates or students of specific schools; Undergraduate support.

Application information:
Deadline(s): Apr. 1
Additional information: Contact fund for current application guidelines. Scholarships will be awarded on the basis of financial need, proficiency of scholastic work, character qualifications, future promise, and the overall contribution by the student to Clarion High School.
EIN: 256032785

3151

Penrose Foundation
c/o Patricia Schieffer
777 Main St., Ste. 3250 CT2-102-22-02
Fort Worth, TX 76102 (817) 332-1328
Contact: Sharon Schieffer Mayes, Dir.

Foundation type: Independent foundation
Limitations: Scholarships to students of Latino descent who maintain a 3.0 GPA each semester.
Financial data: Year ended 12/31/2004. Assets, $1,055,112 (M); Expenditures, $70,061; Total giving, $40,000; Grants to individuals, 17 grants totaling $40,000 (high: $3,000, low: $1,500).
Fields of interest: Hispanics/Latinos.
Type of support: Scholarships—to individuals.
Application information: Applications accepted.
Initial approach: Letter.
Deadline(s): Apr. 1
Applicants should submit the following:
1) Essay
2) Transcripts
3) SAT
4) Letter(s) of recommendation
5) ACT
Additional information: Application must also include a copy of parents' last three income tax returns.
EIN: 752456902

3152

People to People International
501 E. Armour Blvd.
Kansas City, MO 64109-2200 (816) 531-4701
Contact: Mary Eisenhower, Pres. and C.E.O.
FAX: (816) 561-7502; E-mail: ptpi@ptpi.org;
URL: http://www.ptpi.org

Foundation type: Public charity
Limitations: Scholarships to students for higher education who are involved in any of the organizations' programs.
Financial data: Year ended 12/31/2004. Assets, $3,888,605 (M); Expenditures, $3,249,406; Total giving, $138,469; Grants to individuals, totaling $138,469.
Fields of interest: Higher education.
Type of support: Scholarships—to individuals.
Application information: Applications accepted. Application form required. Application form available on the grantmaker's Web site.
Deadline(s): Oct. 15
Applicants should submit the following:
1) Financial information
2) Transcripts
3) Letter(s) of recommendation
4) Essay
Program descriptions:
Joyce C. Hall College Scholarship: Scholarships are $2,000 each and up to five will be selected annually. Each award will be sent directly to the students university for the benefit of the named student. The scholarship must be used to pay tuition first, then books and supplies. Applicants

must have had experience with People to People International through participation in one of their various programs, such as the Student Ambassador Program, student or adult chapter activities, School and Classroom Program, Global Youth Forum, etc.. This experience must have been within the past four years. Applicants must be a current member of People to People International. The applicant must currently be a high school senior or a full-time college or university student and maintain a 3.0 GPA on a 4.0 scale.
James & Eunice Doty PTP/Congressional Award Scholarship: Four scholarships are awarded to junior high and high school students (college students are not eligible) who have earned the Congressional Award that year. Applicants must currently be a junior high school or high school student. Applicants must be at least fourteen years of age and cannot be older than 18 by July 15, 2006.
EIN: 440659517

3153

H. Stanley & Marie Percival Scholarship Fund
c/o Wells Fargo Bank West, N.A.
P.O. Box 21927
Seattle, WA 98111
Application addresses: c/o Capital High School, Attn: Principal, 100 Valley Dr., Helena, MT 59601 or c/o Helena High School, Attn: Principal, 1300 Billings Ave., Helena, MT 59601

Foundation type: Independent foundation
Limitations: Scholarships to graduating seniors from Capital High School and Helena High School, MT.
Financial data: Year ended 03/31/2005. Assets, $232,494 (M); Expenditures, $12,304; Total giving, $10,000; Grants to individuals, 2 grants totaling $10,000.
Type of support: Support to graduates or students of specific schools; Undergraduate support.
Application information: Application form required.
Initial approach: Letter.
Deadline(s): Apr. 1
Additional information: Completion of formal application required, including statement of background, activities and achievements, goals and need for assistance.
EIN: 816052962

3154

The Percy Franklin Lucas Memorial Student Loan Fund
(formerly Lottie King Lucas Percy Memorial Trust)
c/o Bank of America, N.A.
P.O. Box 831041
Dallas, TX 75283-1041
Contact: David P. Ross, Sr. V.P. and Trust Off., Bank of America, N.A.
Application address: P.O. Box 419119, Kansas City, MO 84141-6119, tel.: (818) 878-7481

Foundation type: Independent foundation
Limitations: Student loans to financially needy students at the University of Missouri in Kansas City, MO.
Financial data: Year ended 12/31/2004. Assets, $491,874 (M); Expenditures, $7,815; Total giving, $0; Loans to individuals, 24 loans totaling $36,000.
Type of support: Student loans—to individuals; Support to graduates or students of specific schools.

Application information: Applications accepted.
Initial approach: Letter or telephone.
Additional information: Contact foundation for current application guidelines.
EIN: 446008488

3155

Evelyn Perdue Education Fund
c/o Peoples Bank
P.O. Box 20
Ottawa, KS 66067
Application address: c/ o Louisburg High School, Attn: Don Meek, Principal, 505 E. Amity, Louisburg, KS 66053, tel.: (913) 837-2941

Foundation type: Independent foundation
Limitations: Scholarships to students and graduates of Unified School District No. 416, Louisburg, KS, for attendance at colleges, universities, and vocational schools.
Financial data: Year ended 09/30/2004. Assets, $561,858 (M); Expenditures, $28,406; Total giving, $20,000; Grants to individuals, totaling $20,000.
Fields of interest: Vocational education.
Type of support: Support to graduates or students of specific schools; Technical education support; Undergraduate support.
Application information: Application form required.
Deadline(s): May 1
Applicants should submit the following:
1) Transcripts
Additional information: Application may also include three letters of reference; Interviews may be required; Scholarships are renewable.
EIN: 486297052

3156

Performing Arts Foundation, Inc.
2600 W. Olive Ave., 8th Fl.
Burbank, CA 91505 (818) 238-6604
Contact: Charisse Browner, Pres. and Exec. Dir.
FAX: (818) 846-4106;
E-mail: kipfund106@aol.com; URL: http://www.power106.fm/knowledgeispower/foundation.aspx

Foundation type: Public charity
Limitations: Scholarships to financially-needy residents of CA.
Financial data: Year ended 12/31/2003. Assets, $187,998 (M); Expenditures, $183,610; Total giving, $84,350.
Type of support: Scholarships—to individuals; Support to graduates or students of specific schools; Postdoctoral support; Graduate support; Technical education support; Undergraduate support; Postgraduate support.
Application information: Applications accepted. Application form required. Application form available on the grantmaker's Web site.
Initial approach: Letter or e-mail.
Deadline(s): Dec. 15
Applicants should submit the following:
1) Essay
Additional information: Application should also include proof of CA residency and proof of enrollment.
Program description:
Knowledge Is Power: Each scholarship is valued up to $1,000.00 each. Five scholarships will be awarded each month (January to December) to applicants who are interested in pursuing education at a trade school, city college, 2- or 4-year college or university. Scholarships are also available to graduating high school students who will

successfully enroll in either of the aforementioned institutions. Applicants may reapply annually to renew their scholarship application throughout their education, but no more than once every 12 months. Funds may be used for tuition, textbooks, fees and learning materials. Knowledge Is Power Educational Scholarships are not available to individuals receiving a full scholarship from another source.
EIN: 954459369

3157

The Pergo Foundation
(formerly The Andrew and Denise Goldfarb Family Foundation)
14170 Chandler Blvd.
Sherman Oaks, CA 91401
Contact: Andrew Goldfarb, Pres.; Denise Goldfarb, Secy.

Foundation type: Independent foundation
Limitations: Scholarships to individuals residing in the Sherman Oaks, CA, area.
Financial data: Year ended 06/30/2004.
Assets, $4,544,396 (M); Expenditures, $259,965; Total giving, $214,850; Grants to individuals, 122 grants totaling $116,750 (high: $2,000, low: $125).
Type of support: Undergraduate support.
Application information: Applications accepted.
  Initial approach: Letter.
  Additional information: Applications by letter accepted throughout the year.
EIN: 954610805

3158

Mary Perisho - Nina Rall McConkey Scholarship Trust
c/o The Edgar County Bank & Trust Co.
P.O. Box 400
Paris, IL 61944-0400 (217) 465-4154
Contact: John D. Carrington, Trust Off., The Edgar County Bank & Trust Co.

Foundation type: Independent foundation
Limitations: Scholarships to home economics students of Paris High School, IL, to further their education in home economics.
Financial data: Year ended 04/30/2005.
Assets, $161,161 (M); Expenditures, $6,916; Total giving, $3,950.
Fields of interest: Home economics.
Type of support: Scholarships—to individuals; Support to graduates or students of specific schools.
Application information: Application form required.
  Deadline(s): May 18
EIN: 371248386

3159

B. F. & Rose H. Perkins Foundation
P.O. Box 1064
Sheridan, WY 82801-1064 (307) 674-8871
FAX: (307) 674-8803

Foundation type: Independent foundation
Limitations: Student loans to graduates of high schools in Sheridan County, WY. First-time applicants must be under 20 years of age and residents of Sheridan County for at least one year.
Financial data: Year ended 12/31/2004.
Assets, $9,834,276 (M); Expenditures, $340,640; Total giving, $213,124; Grants to individuals, 109 grants totaling $208,124 (high:

$5,710, low: $42); Loans to individuals, 119 loans totaling $472,150.
Type of support: Student loans—to individuals; Support to graduates or students of specific schools.
Application information: Application form required.
  Deadline(s): June 1
  Applicants should submit the following:
    1) Transcripts
EIN: 830138740

3160

The James W. Perkins Memorial Trust
c/o Payne, Gates, Farthing and Rodd, PC
999 Waterside Dr., Ste. 1515
Norfolk, VA 23510-3309 (757) 640-1500
Contact: C. Arthur Robinson II, Tr.

Foundation type: Independent foundation
Limitations: Scholarships to residents of VA.
Publications: Annual report.
Financial data: Year ended 12/31/2004.
Assets, $314,610 (M); Expenditures, $47,297; Total giving, $33,000; Grants to individuals, totaling $33,000.
Type of support: Graduate support; Technical education support; Precollege support; Undergraduate support.
Application information: Application form required.
  Initial approach: Letter.
  Deadline(s): July 1
EIN: 546271058

3161

Trustees of the Perley Free School
101 W. Main St.
Georgetown, MA 01833-1525 (978) 352-2168
Contact: T. Louis Hamelin, Treas.

Foundation type: Independent foundation
Limitations: Scholarships to residents of Georgetown, MA.
Financial data: Year ended 04/30/2005.
Assets, $1,233,676 (M); Expenditures, $57,429; Total giving, $26,650; Grants to individuals, totaling $26,300.
Type of support: Scholarships—to individuals.
Application information: Deadline May 15; Completion of formal application required, including secondary school record, estimated college expenses, and work experience.
EIN: 046032270

3162

Permanent Endowment Fund for Martha's Vineyard
c/o Dukes County Savings Bank
P.O. Box 602
West Tisbury, MA 02575-0602 (508) 693-8850
Contact: Deborah L. Hale, Chair.
FAX: (508) 693-0171

Foundation type: Community foundation
Limitations: Scholarships primarily to graduates of Martha's Vineyard Regional High School, MA, Martha's Vineyard Charter School, MA, and residents of Martha's Vineyard.
Publications: Application guidelines; Annual report.
Financial data: Year ended 12/31/2004.
Assets, $3,393,756 (M); Expenditures, $236,475; Total giving, $197,935; Grants to individuals, totaling $86,250.
Fields of interest: Nursing school/education; Natural resources; Dental care.

Type of support: Support to graduates or students of specific schools; Awards/prizes; Graduate support; Undergraduate support.
Application information: Application form required.
  Initial approach: letter outlining financial need.
  Deadline(s): Mar. 15
  Additional information: Applications for scholarships accepted in accord with Martha's Vineyard Regional High School Scholarship schedule; Awards made in mid-June; Interviews required; Martha's Vineyard Regional High School students apply through the Guidance Dept.
EIN: 042774790

3163

Permian Basin Area Foundation
550 W. Texas Ave., Ste. 1260
Midland, TX 79701 (432) 682-4704
Contact: John D. Swallow, C.E.O. and Pres.; Guy McCrary, V.P. and C.O.O.
FAX: (432) 617-0151; E-mail: gmccrary@pbaf.org; URL: http://www.pbaf.org

Foundation type: Community foundation
Limitations: Academic scholarships to students pursuing higher education, and vocational education from the Permian Basin region, TX.
Publications: Application guidelines; Annual report; Newsletter.
Financial data: Year ended 12/31/2004.
Assets, $34,418,989 (M); Expenditures, $2,848,479; Total giving, $2,178,686.
Fields of interest: Vocational education, post-secondary; Education.
Type of support: Scholarships—to individuals.
Application information: Applications accepted. Application form required.
  Initial approach: Telephone or letter.
  Deadline(s): Varies
  Applicants should submit the following:
    1) Transcripts
    2) Letter(s) of recommendation
    3) Essay
EIN: 752295008

3164

Charles & Olivina Perron Memorial Trust
(also known as Charles A. Perron Memorial Trust f/b/o Graduates of High School Serving the City of North Adams)
c/o TD Banknorth, N.A., Wealth Mgmt. Group
178 Main St.
P.O. Box 174
New Britain, CT 06050
Application address: c/o TD Banknorth, N.A., Wealth Mgmt. Group, 99 West St., Pittsfield, MA 01201, tel.: (413) 445-8249

Foundation type: Independent foundation
Limitations: Scholarships to graduates of high schools in North Adams, MA.
Financial data: Year ended 12/31/2004.
Assets, $164,315 (M); Expenditures, $10,551; Total giving, $7,697; Grants to individuals, 13 grants totaling $7,697.
Type of support: Support to graduates or students of specific schools; Undergraduate support.
Application information: Contact trust for current application deadline.
EIN: 222672860

3165
Perry Memorial Scholarship Fund
(formerly Frank H. & Annie Belle Whilhelm Perry Memorial Scholarships)
c/o Bank of America, N.A.
100 N. Main St., 13th Fl.
Winston-Salem, NC 27150
Contact: Nancy Truitt, V.P., Bank of America, N.A.

Foundation type: Independent foundation
Limitations: Scholarships to students of Lees-McRae College and Montreat College in NC, and Kings College in Kingston, TN.
Financial data: Year ended 01/31/2005. Assets, $482,787 (M); Expenditures, $27,787; Total giving, $20,775.
Type of support: Support to graduates or students of specific schools; Undergraduate support.
Application information:
Deadline(s): Contact trust for current application deadline
Additional information: Application by letter.
EIN: 566290640

3166
Perry Scholarship Foundation
(formerly Nathan F. & Edna L. Perry Scholarship)
c/o KeyBank N.A., Trust Div.
800 Superior Ave., 4th Fl.
Cleveland, OH 44114

Foundation type: Independent foundation
Limitations: Scholarships to graduates of Presque Isle High School who are residents of Presque Isle, ME.
Financial data: Year ended 05/31/2005. Assets, $463,400 (M); Expenditures, $23,301; Total giving, $17,250; Grants to individuals, 63 grants totaling $17,250 (high: $500, low: $250).
Type of support: Support to graduates or students of specific schools; Undergraduate support.
Application information: Applications not accepted.
EIN: 510158963

3167
Mildred R. Perry Scholarship Trust
c/o Baraboo National Bank
P.O. Box 50
Baraboo, WI 53913
Application address: c/o Webb High School, Attn: Principal, 707 N. Webb Ave., Reedsburg, WI 53959

Foundation type: Independent foundation
Limitations: Scholarships to graduates of Reedsburg Webb High School, WI.
Financial data: Year ended 12/31/2004. Assets, $141,306 (M); Expenditures, $4,644; Total giving, $2,100; Grants to individuals, 2 grants totaling $2,100.
Type of support: Support to graduates or students of specific schools; Undergraduate support.
Application information: Application form required.
Deadline(s): July 1
Applicants should submit the following:
1) SAT
2) ACT
3) Financial information
4) Essay
EIN: 391437634

3168
The Perry-Griffin Foundation
P.O. Box 82
Oriental, NC 28571 (252) 249-0227
Contact: Edward D. Lupton, Mgr.

Foundation type: Independent foundation
Limitations: Educational loans to individuals in Pamlico and Jones counties, NC, seeking higher education.
Financial data: Year ended 08/31/2004. Assets, $2,227,465 (M); Expenditures, $126,694; Total giving, $23,500; Grants to individuals, 11 grants totaling $23,500.
Type of support: Student loans—to individuals.
Application information: Application form required.
Deadline(s): May 16
Applicants should submit the following:
1) Transcripts
2) Letter(s) of recommendation
EIN: 560860864

3169
The Herman & Katherine Peters Foundation Corp.
67 E. Madison St., Ste. 1515
Chicago, IL 60603-3014 (312) 782-4415
Contact: Scot A. Leonard, Pres.

Foundation type: Independent foundation
Limitations: Scholarships to students from AZ, CO, IL, MI, and WI for higher education in the fields of forestry/conservation or Christian-based religious instruction.
Financial data: Year ended 12/31/2004. Assets, $9,800,669 (M); Expenditures, $211,685; Total giving, $157,200; Grants to individuals, 32 grants totaling $84,000.
Fields of interest: Environmental education; Religion, formal/general education.
Type of support: Undergraduate support.
Application information: Application form required.
Additional information: Applications accepted throughout the year.
EIN: 364180010

3170
Ruth R. Peters Scholarship B Fund
c/o Sky Bank
P.O. Box 479
Youngstown, OH 44501-0479
Application address: c/o Brookfield High School, Attn.: Superintendent, 7000 Grove St., Brookfield, OH 44403-9505, tel.: (330) 448-3001

Foundation type: Independent foundation
Limitations: Scholarships to graduates of Brookfield High School, OH, who will study mathematics at Oberlin College, OH.
Financial data: Year ended 12/31/2004. Assets, $356,126 (M); Expenditures, $20,292; Total giving, $15,504.
Fields of interest: Mathematics.
Type of support: Support to graduates or students of specific schools; Undergraduate support.
Application information: Applications accepted throughout the year; Completion of formal application required.
EIN: 237872473

3171
Glenn D. Peters Trust
c/o Calumet National Bank
5231 Hohman Ave.
Hammond, IN 46320-1790 (219) 932-6900
Contact: Sheilia Hayden, Exec. V.P., Calumet National Bank

Foundation type: Independent foundation
Limitations: Scholarships to law students who are residents of IN.
Financial data: Year ended 09/30/2004. Assets, $731,324 (M); Expenditures, $29,555; Total giving, $21,500; Grants to individuals, 20 grants totaling $21,500.
Fields of interest: Law school/education.
Type of support: Graduate support.
Application information: Application form required.
Initial approach: Letter requesting application.
Deadline(s): May 2
EIN: 356218833

3172
Peters Valley Craftsman, Inc.
19 Kuhn Rd.
Layton, NJ 07851 (973) 948-5200
Contact: Jimmy Clark, Exec. Dir.
FAX: (973) 948-0011; E-mail: pv@warwick.net;
URL: http://www.pvcrafts.org

Foundation type: Public charity
Limitations: Scholarships to college students to attend the Center's workshops and classes.
Financial data: Year ended 09/30/2003. Assets, $182,115 (M); Expenditures, $865,736.
Fields of interest: Folk arts; Visual arts; Ceramic arts; Arts.
Type of support: Precollege support; Undergraduate support.
Application information: Application form required.
Initial approach: E-mail.
Deadline(s): Apr. 1
Applicants should submit the following:
1) SASE
2) Work samples
3) Letter(s) of recommendation
Additional information: Application must also include letter of intent.
Program descriptions:
Tuition Scholarship for College Students: Peters Valley will offer 5 full-tuition scholarships and 10 half-tuition scholarships to matriculated college students. The 5 college students who are awarded the full scholarship will receive free workshop tuition for a single workshop during the summer. The students who are awarded the 50% scholarship will receive 1/2 off the workshop tuition for a single workshop during the summer. These awards are for the summer workshop programs only, and can not be carried over to any future programs. All scholarship recipients will be responsible for all other applicable costs such as housing, meals, and material fees.
Tuition Scholarship for High School Students: Peters Valley will offer tuition scholarship to four high school students. Applicants must be at least 17 years old to be considered. These four students will receive free workshop tuition and free housing for a workshop of their choice during the summer. Recipients will be responsible for all other associated costs such as material fees and meals.
EIN: 221920050

3173
Petersburg Methodist Home for Girls
P.O. Box 1688
Petersburg, VA 23805-1688
Contact: Barbara W. Moore, Secy.-Treas.

Foundation type: Independent foundation
Limitations: Scholarships to residents of Southside, VA.
Financial data: Year ended 12/31/2004.
Assets, $3,374,292 (M); Expenditures, $188,083; Total giving, $149,000; Grants to individuals, 29 grants totaling $45,000 (high: $3,000, low: $1,000).
Type of support: Scholarships—to individuals.
Application information: Application form required.
  Deadline(s): July and Feb.
EIN: 540542500

3174
Alan & Mildred Peterson Charitable Foundation
150 S. Wacker Dr., Ste. 500
Chicago, IL 60606 (312) 849-9000
Contact: Alan E. Peterson, Dir.

Foundation type: Independent foundation
Limitations: Scholarships to individuals for higher education.
Financial data: Year ended 12/31/2004.
Assets, $1,376,796 (M); Expenditures, $351,792; Total giving, $335,910; Grants to individuals, 17 grants totaling $60,000 (high: $4,000, low: $3,000).
Type of support: Graduate support; Undergraduate support.
Application information: Applications accepted throughout the year; Completion of formal application required, including transcript, letter, recommendations, and proof of tuition.
Program description:
  Scholarship Program: Applicant must already be accepted at an undergraduate or graduate institution, and must enroll as a full-time student. Applicant must obtain a 3.0 GPA upon high school graduation and must maintain a 3.0 GPA in college. Most grants are for students attending institutions in the Midwest.
EIN: 363355444

3175
John P. Peterson Foundation
c/o Rick Burn Park
359 McLean Blvd.
Paterson, NJ 07513 (973) 684-1782
Contact: James Burnes III, Tr.

Foundation type: Independent foundation
Limitations: Undergraduate scholarships to high school seniors in NJ who are financially needy or who have a mental or physical disability.
Publications: Financial statement.
Financial data: Year ended 12/31/2004.
Assets, $1,658,065 (M); Expenditures, $93,008; Total giving, $68,320; Grants to individuals, 21 grants totaling $68,320.
Fields of interest: Physically disabled; Mentally disabled.
Type of support: Undergraduate support.
Application information: Application form required.
  Deadline(s): Contact foundation for current application deadline
  Applicants should submit the following:
    1) Letter(s) of recommendation
    2) Transcripts
    3) SAR

4) Essay
Additional information: Application should include summary of activities and estimate of school costs No grants are given for graduate study or to international students. No loans are given. New awards are limited to five or fewer undergraduates per year.
EIN: 222147375

3176
Petoskey-Harbor Springs Area Community Foundation
616 Petoskey St., Ste. 100
Petoskey, MI 49770 (231) 348-5820
Contact: Maureen M. Nicholson, Exec. Dir.
FAX: (231) 348-5883; E-mail: info@phsacf.org; Additional E-mails: mnicholson@phsacf.org and lwendland@phsacf.org; URL: http://www.petoskey-harborspringsfoundation.org

Foundation type: Community foundation
Limitations: Scholarships to individuals residing in the Emmet County, MI, area for undergraduate education at institutions in the U.S.
Publications: Application guidelines; Annual report; Financial statement; Informational brochure.
Financial data: Year ended 03/31/2005.
Assets, $10,166,572 (M); Expenditures, $745,296; Total giving, $441,144; Grants to individuals, 18 grants totaling $32,000.
Fields of interest: Vocational education, post-secondary; Business school/education; Law school/education; Medical school/education; Nursing school/education; Engineering school/education; Health sciences school/education; Agriculture/food, formal/general education; Mathematics; Computer science; Science.
Type of support: Support to graduates or students of specific schools; Graduate support; Technical education support; Undergraduate support; Doctoral support.
Application information: Applications accepted. Application form required.
  Initial approach: Telephone.
  Copies of proposal: 1
  Deadline(s): Varies; Generally in Mid-Apr.
  Applicants should submit the following:
    1) ACT
    2) SAT
    3) Letter(s) of recommendation
    4) Financial information
    5) Essay
  Additional information: Most scholarship applications require a $5 fee; See Web site for complete scholarship and program information.
EIN: 383032185

3177
Hans & Thora Petraborg Educational Trust Fund
c/o Paul R. Beyreuther
38 Minnesota Ave. S.
Aitkin, MN 56431 (218) 927-2115
Contact: Edward Anderson, Tr.

Foundation type: Operating foundation
Limitations: Interest-free loans to graduates of Aitkin High School, MN, for higher education.
Financial data: Year ended 12/31/2003.
Assets, $330,003 (M); Expenditures, $32,308; Total giving, $32,050; Loans to individuals, 28 loans totaling $32,050.
Type of support: Support to graduates or students of specific schools; Undergraduate support.

Application information: Applications accepted. Application form required.
  Deadline(s): Contact fund for deadline
  Additional information: Application forms available upon request.
EIN: 411360435

3178
Pettee-Chace Memorial Scholarship Fund
c/o E.E. Wiesner, Jr.
P.O. Box 694
Sandwich, MA 02563-0694
Contact: Thomas Sampson, Pres.
Application address: 309 Main St., Brockton, MA 02401, tel.: (508) 586-0399

Foundation type: Operating foundation
Limitations: Scholarships to students of Abington High School, MA and Brockton High School, MA, for higher education.
Financial data: Year ended 12/31/2004.
Assets, $205,290 (M); Expenditures, $11,326; Total giving, $9,500; Grants to individuals, totaling $9,500.
Type of support: Support to graduates or students of specific schools; Undergraduate support.
Application information: Application form required.
  Deadline(s): Mar. 31
  Applicants should submit the following:
    1) Transcripts
    2) SAT
    3) Financial information
    4) Essay
EIN: 223051579

3179
The Mary L. Peyton Foundation
Bassett Tower, Ste. 908
303 Texas Ave.
El Paso, TX 79901-1456
Contact: James M. Day, Exec. Admin.

Foundation type: Operating foundation
Limitations: Scholarships for vocational training to legal residents of El Paso County, TX, who are unable to earn a livelihood due to age, physical or mental disability, or other hardship. Some recipients receive more than one grant.
Financial data: Year ended 05/31/2005.
Assets, $3,970,107 (M); Expenditures, $263,443; Total giving, $150,404.
Fields of interest: Vocational education.
Type of support: Technical education support.
Application information: Applications accepted. Application form required.
  Additional information: Application should be made through social service agencies.
EIN: 741276102

3180
Pfister & Vogel Tanning Company, Inc. Foundation
c/o U.S. Bank, N.A.
P.O. Box 2043, LC4NE
Milwaukee, WI 53201-9116
Application address: Pfister & Vogel Tanning Co., Inc., 1531 N. Water St., Milwaukee, WI 53202

Foundation type: Company-sponsored foundation
Limitations: Scholarships to children of employees of Pfister & Vogel Tanning Company, Inc.
Financial data: Year ended 05/31/2005.
Assets, $463,840 (M); Expenditures, $28,940; Total giving, $24,000.

Type of support: Employee-related scholarships.
Application information:
Deadline(s): None
Additional information: Applications by letter.
EIN: 396036556

3181
Pflughaupt Charitable Foundation, Inc.
(formerly Eugene B. and Margery Ames Pflughaupt
Charitable Foundation, Inc.)
c/o Ernestine Jennings
6336 Finchville Rd.
Shelbyville, KY 40065

Foundation type: Independent foundation
Limitations: Scholarship to a graduating senior at
Shelby County High School, Shelby County, KY.
Financial data: Year ended 12/31/2004.
Assets, $144,066 (M); Expenditures, $20,929;
Total giving, $20,000; Grants to individuals, 4
grants totaling $20,000.
Type of support: Support to graduates or students
of specific schools.
Application information: Applications not
accepted.
EIN: 611274891

3182
The Pharmacy Network Foundation, Inc.
4020 Old Wake Forest Rd., Ste. 102
Raleigh, NC 27609 (919) 772-4371
Contact: J. Andrew Barrett, Exec. V.P.
Application address: Jimmy S. Jackson, V.P. and
Secy., 2015 Navan Ln., Garner, NC 27529

Foundation type: Company-sponsored foundation
Limitations: Scholarships only to students at the
University of North Carolina at Chapel Hill and
Campbell University, NC, who are studying to
become pharmacists.
Financial data: Year ended 12/31/2004.
Assets, $22,107,859 (M); Expenditures,
$1,093,879; Total giving, $756,380.
Fields of interest: Pharmacy/prescriptions.
Type of support: Support to graduates or students
of specific schools; Undergraduate support.
Application information:
Deadline(s): Mar. 15
Additional information: Application by two-page
essay, explaining why applicant wants to be a
retail pharmacist.
EIN: 561690027

3183
Winifred Y. Phelps Trust
c/o Comerica Bank
P.O. Box 75000
Detroit, MI 48275
Application address: c/o Antioch High School,
Attn.: Scholarship Comm., 700 W. 18th St.,
Antioch, CA 94509, tel.: (415) 757-6560

Foundation type: Independent foundation
Limitations: Scholarships to graduates of Antioch
and San Lorenzo Valley high schools, CA.
Financial data: Year ended 12/31/2004.
Assets, $321,682 (M); Expenditures, $26,400;
Total giving, $22,500.
Type of support: Support to graduates or students
of specific schools; Undergraduate support.
Application information: Contact scholarship
committee for current application deadline/
guidelines.
EIN: 946087426

3184
Phi Delta Theta Educational Foundation
2 S. Campus Ave.
Oxford, OH 45056 (513) 523-6966
Contact: William R. Richardson, Pres.
FAX: (513) 523-9200;
E-mail: foundation@phideltatheta.org

Foundation type: Public charity
Limitations: Undergraduate scholarships and
graduate fellowships by nomination only, primarily
to members of Phi Delta Theta Fraternity.
Publications: Newsletter.
Financial data: Year ended 12/31/2003.
Assets, $10,545,360 (M); Expenditures,
$1,731,180; Total giving, $518,374; Grants to
individuals, totaling $183,540 (high: $4,000).
Type of support: Awards/grants by nomination only.
Application information: Application form required.
Deadline(s): Apr. 1
Additional information: See Web site for
complete program listing.
EIN: 346539803

3185
Phi Kappa Tau Foundation
5221 Morning Sun Rd.
Oxford, OH 45056-1304 (513) 523-4193
Contact: John Green, Exec. Dir.
FAX: (513) 523-9325; Additional tel.: (800)
758-1906; URL: http://www.phikappatau.org

Foundation type: Public charity
Limitations: Scholarships to alumni and
undergraduate members of Phi Kappa Tau
Fraternity.
Financial data: Year ended 06/30/2004.
Assets, $9,506,280 (M); Expenditures,
$1,082,907; Total giving, $325,078; Grants to
individuals, totaling $54,120.
Fields of interest: Students, sororities/fraternities;
Adults, men.
Type of support: Grants to individuals;
Undergraduate support.
Application information: Applications accepted.
Application form required. Application form
available on the grantmaker's Web site.
Initial approach: Letter or telephone.
Deadline(s): Vary
Applicants should submit the following:
1) Transcripts
2) Letter(s) of recommendation
3) Financial information
4) GPA
5) Essay
Additional information: See Web site for
additional application guidelines.
Program descriptions:
Paul A. Elfers Omega Scholarship: Six $2,250
scholarships are available.
Named Scholarship: For outstanding
undergraduate members, nine $1,000
scholarships are available.
Foundation Scholarship: This scholarship is for
initiated members of Phi Kappa Tau who are
returning to school.
Parents Fund Scholarship: Provided by parents of
initiated members, two $1,000 scholarships are
available.
Scholastic Honor Society Rebates: These rebates
are for reimbursement of initiation fees for those
members who join the Phi Beta Kappa and/or Phi
Kappa Phi academic honor societies.
Heidi Kahle Memorial Scholarship: For members
of chapters at Nebraska Wesleyan, Iowa State or
the University of Nebraska at Kearney.
EIN: 316024975

3186
Phi Mu Foundation
400 Westpark Dr.
Peachtree City, GA 30269 (770) 632-2090
Contact: Shellye Stanley McCarty, Pres.
FAX: (770) 632-2135; E-mail: nwalls@phimu.org;
URL: http://www.phimu.org/foundation

Foundation type: Public charity
Limitations: Scholarships to graduate and
undergraduate students who are members of Phi
Mu.
Publications: Application guidelines.
Financial data: Year ended 08/31/2004.
Assets, $7,544,069 (M); Expenditures,
$704,179; Total giving, $127,857; Grants to
individuals, 104 grants totaling $82,050 (high:
$2,500, low: $250).
Fields of interest: Students, sororities/fraternities;
Women.
Type of support: Internship funds; Student loans—
to individuals; Graduate support; Undergraduate
support.
Application information: Application form required.
Deadline(s): Mar. 1 for scholarships
Additional information: See Web site for
application information.
Program descriptions:
Lewis Hughes Memorial Loan: Loans for
emergency educational aid, professional
advancement and technological enhancement. A
maximum of $1,500 may be borrowed at an interest
rate of five percent. Repayment begins one year
after funds are disbursed. Alumnae in good
standing who are members of Phi Mu Foundation
may apply.
Project HOPE Internship: Awards a $500 stipend
with a summer internship for a rising senior for a
four to six week period at Project HOPE's
Headquarters in Millwood, VA and/or any domestic
HOPE location. Contact Project HOPE, P.O. Box
250, Millwood, VA 22646, or call 800-544-4673 for
more information.
Scholarships: Awards over 85 scholarships
totaling $85,000 to qualified Phi Mu undergraduate
and graduate students. See Web site for specific
scholarship information.
EIN: 626042543

3187
Philips Electronics North American
Foundation
(formerly North American Philips Foundation)
c/o Scholarship Prog. Admin.
1251 Ave. of the Americas, 20th Fl.
New York, NY 10020-1104

Foundation type: Company-sponsored foundation
Limitations: Scholarships to the children of current,
retired, or deceased employees of Philips
Electronics North America.
Financial data: Year ended 12/31/2004.
Assets, $30,000 (M); Expenditures, $305,250;
Total giving, $305,250; Grants to individuals, 230
grants totaling $305,250 (high: $3,500, low:
$500).
Type of support: Employee-related scholarships.
Application information: Application form required.
Initial approach: Letter requesting application.
Deadline(s): Mar. 1
Program description:
Scholarship Program: Scholarship awards are
made on the basis of:
· academic performance and potential as
shown by applicant's high school record
and college entrance tests

- participation and leadership roles in extracurricular activities and sports
- evidence of strong character and motivation as seen in applicant's life outside of school.

EIN: 132961300

3188

Phillips Foundation, Inc.

1 Massachusetts Ave. N.W., Ste. 620
Washington, DC 20001
Contact: John W. Farley, Secy.
Contact for scholarships: D. Jeffrey Hollingsworth, Asst. Secy., tel.: (202) 250-3887, ext. 628, E-mail: jhollingsworth@phillips.com
FAX: (202) 216-9188; E-mail: jfarley@phillips.com; Additional tel.: (202) 250-3887; URL: http://www.thephillipsfoundation.org

Foundation type: Company-sponsored foundation
Limitations: Scholarships to undergraduates attending four-year colleges who demonstrate leadership on behalf of the cause of freedom, American values, and constitutional principles.
Financial data: Year ended 09/30/2004. Assets, $11,205,349 (M); Expenditures, $661,734; Total giving, $372,500; Grants to individuals, 60 grants totaling $372,500 (high: $35,000, low: $1,000).
Type of support: Fellowships; Scholarships—to individuals; Undergraduate support.
Application information: Application form required. Application form available on the grantmaker's Web site.
Deadline(s): Jan. 15
Applicants should submit the following:
  1) GPA
  2) Essay
  3) Resume
Additional information: Application should also include narrative, supporting documentation, two letters of recommendation, and Dean's or Registrar's certification of full-time enrollment in good standing; See Web site for further information.
Program description:
Ronald Reagan Future Leaders Scholarship Program: Awards a minimum of two $10,000 grants annually to outstanding young people who are promoting freedom, constitutional principles and American values on college campuses. Winners will receive the grant for their junior year and may apply for renewal before their senior year. The grant may be used to defray college expenses, including tuition and fees, room and board, and related costs. Students may apply directly or be nominated by a third party.
EIN: 521707001

3189

Stephen Phillips Memorial Charitable Trust

P.O. Box 870
Salem, MA 01970
Contact: Karen Emery, Scholarship Coord.
Additional E-mail: kemery@spscholars.org
FAX: (978) 744-0456;
E-mail: info@phillips-scholarship.org; URL: http://www.phillips-scholarship.org/

Foundation type: Independent foundation
Limitations: Scholarships to individuals for undergraduate study at colleges and universities. Scholarships are renewable.

Publications: Application guidelines; Informational brochure (including application guidelines).
Financial data: Year ended 12/31/2004. Assets, $59,961,761 (M); Expenditures, $3,718,860; Total giving $2,856,254; Grants to individuals, 642 grants totaling $2,856,254 (high: $10,000, low: $1,500).
Type of support: Undergraduate support.
Application information: Application form required.
Deadline(s): May 1
Additional information: See Web site for complete application information.
EIN: 237235347

3190

The V. E. & Betty Phillips Scholarship Fund

c/o National City Bank
P.O. Box 94651
Cleveland, OH 44101-4651
Application address: c/o Michael L. Stahlman, Corry Area High School, 534 E. Pleasant St., Corry, PA 16407, tel.: (814) 665-8297

Foundation type: Independent foundation
Limitations: Scholarships to graduates of Corry area high schools, PA.
Financial data: Year ended 04/30/2003. Assets, $863,668 (M); Expenditures, $74,568; Total giving, $64,500; Grants to individuals, 57 grants totaling $64,500 (high: $1,500, low: $400).
Type of support: Support to graduates or students of specific schools; Undergraduate support.
Application information: Application form required.
Deadline(s): Mar. 1
EIN: 237418046

3191

Russell Phillips Trust

c/o Marshall & Ilsley Bank
P.O. Box 2980
Milwaukee, WI 53201-2980
Application address: c/o Marshall & Ilsley Bank, Attn.: Robert F. Penn, Stevens Point, WI, 54481, tel.: (715) 342-3250

Foundation type: Independent foundation
Limitations: Scholarships to residents of Portage County, WI, who are studying agriculture, forestry, or conservation at a college in WI.
Financial data: Year ended 12/31/2004. Assets, $122,785 (M); Expenditures, $8,543; Total giving, $5,845; Grants to individuals, 4 grants totaling $5,845.
Fields of interest: Natural resources; Environment, forests; Agriculture.
Type of support: Scholarships—to individuals.
Application information:
Initial approach: Letter specifying amount of tuition needed.
Deadline(s): Mar. 1
EIN: 396276572

3192

Phillips-Hernandez Scholarship Foundation

P.O. Box 645
Pampa, TX 79066-0645
Contact: John W. Warner, Secy.-Treas.
Application address: 309 W. Foster, Pampa, TX 79065, tel.: (806) 699-3397

Foundation type: Operating foundation

Limitations: Scholarships to graduates of Pampa High School, TX, for higher education, with preference given to minority females.
Financial data: Year ended 12/31/2003. Assets, $84,097 (M); Expenditures, $3,532; Total giving, $3,500; Grants to individuals, totaling $3,500.
Fields of interest: Minorities; Women.
Type of support: Support to graduates or students of specific schools; Undergraduate support.
Application information:
Deadline(s): Apr. 15
Additional information: Contact foundation for current application guidelines.
EIN: 752227488

3193

Phoenix Foundation Trust Fund

c/o Most Worshipful Grand Lodge F&AM of Arizona
345 W. Monroe St.
Phoenix, AZ 85003-1617 (602) 252-1924
Contact: George H. Stablein, Sr., Grand Secy.

Foundation type: Independent foundation
Limitations: Scholarships to individuals attending public colleges and universities in AZ.
Financial data: Year ended 05/31/2004. Assets, $1,250,233 (M); Expenditures, $72,860; Total giving, $51,000; Grants to individuals, 28 grants totaling $51,000.
Type of support: Support to graduates or students of specific schools; Undergraduate support.
Application information: Application form required.
Initial approach: Letter.
Deadline(s): Feb. 1
EIN: 959013325

3194

Phoenix Scholarship Foundation, Inc.

3261 Old Washington Rd., Ste. 3021
Waldorf, MD 20602
Contact: Parran Foster, Dir.

Foundation type: Operating foundation
Limitations: Scholarships to individuals for higher education.
Financial data: Year ended 09/30/2003. Assets, $292,617 (M); Expenditures, $83,695; Total giving, $82,000; Grants to individuals, 107 grants totaling $82,000 (high: $5,000, low: $500).
Type of support: Scholarships—to individuals.
Application information: Contact foundation for current application deadlines/guidelines.
EIN: 311490141

3195

Phoenix Suns Charities, Inc.

P.O. Box 1369
Phoenix, AZ 85001-1369 (602) 379-7900
Contact: Thomas P. Ambrose, Exec. Dir.
E-mail: phoneixsunscharities@suns.com; URL: http://www.nba.com/suns/news/charities_index.html

Foundation type: Public charity
Limitations: Scholarships to graduating high school seniors in AZ.
Publications: Application guidelines; Grants list.
Financial data: Year ended 06/30/2003. Assets, $343,899 (M); Expenditures, $529,151; Total giving, $505,991; Grants to individuals, 16 grants totaling $15,000 (high: $5,000, low: $1,000).
Fields of interest: Higher education.

Type of support: Scholarships—to individuals.
Application information:
Initial approach: Letter or telephone.
Deadline(s): Contact foundation for deadline
Applicants should submit the following:
1) Letter(s) of recommendation
2) Essay
Program description:
Sun Students College Scholarship Program: The program provides 10 college scholarships of $1,000 and one $5,000 scholarship every year to AZ high school students. To be eligible the applicant must have at least a 2.5 GPA and provide evidence of regular involvement in charitable and/or volunteer services at school, churches or community organizations.
EIN: 860633919

3196
Phoenixville Community Health Foundation
1260 Valley Forge Rd., Ste. 102
Phoenixville, PA 19460 (610) 917-9890
Contact: Louis J. Beccaria, Pres. and C.E.O.
FAX: (610) 917-9861; E-mail: pchfl@juno.com;
URL: http://www.pchf1.org/

Foundation type: Public charity
Limitations: Undergraduate scholarships to students from the greater 17 Township/Borough Phoenixville area who plan to pursue careers in health care.
Publications: Application guidelines; Annual report; Financial statement; Grants list; Informational brochure (including application guidelines); Newsletter; Program policy statement.
Financial data: Year ended 06/30/2005.
Assets, $50,456,856 (M); Expenditures, $2,260,761; Total giving, $1,618,159.
Fields of interest: Health sciences school/education.
Type of support: Undergraduate support.
Application information:
Initial approach: Letter, telephone or office visit.
Deadline(s): None
Applicants should submit the following:
1) Essay
2) FAFSA
3) Financial information
4) GPA
5) Letter(s) of recommendation
6) Transcripts
Additional information: Interviews required.
EIN: 232912035

3197
Photronics Scholarship Foundation, Inc.
1061 E. Indiantown Rd., Ste. 310
Jupiter, FL 33477

Foundation type: Company-sponsored foundation
Limitations: Scholarships to children of employees of Phototronics, Inc., for higher education.
Financial data: Year ended 10/31/2004.
Assets, $399,236 (M); Expenditures, $54,127;
Total giving, $53,957; Grants to individuals, 36 grants totaling $53,957 (high: $4,000, low: $500).
Type of support: Employee-related scholarships.
Application information:
Deadline(s): Apr. 15
Applicants should submit the following:
1) Transcripts
2) Letter(s) of recommendation

Additional information: Application by letter, also including test scores.
EIN: 061462843

3198
Physicians' Relief Fund
c/o Glenmeade Trust Co., N.A.
1650 Market St., Ste. 1200
Philadelphia, PA 19103-7391
Contact: Virginia Kanick M.D.
Application address: 560 Riverside Dr., Ste. 17B, New York, NY 10027

Foundation type: Independent foundation
Limitations: Interest-free loans to medical school students in New York City who have at least one parent who is a physician.
Financial data: Year ended 12/31/2003.
Assets, $1,751,713 (M); Expenditures, $96,550;
Total giving, $40,130; Grants to individuals, 15 grants totaling $35,130 (high: $5,400, low: $750).
Fields of interest: Medical school/education.
Type of support: Graduate support.
Application information:
Initial approach: Letter.
Deadline(s): Applications accepted throughout the year
Additional information: Application outlining financial need attested to by the financial office of the medical school.
EIN: 237426275

3199
Pi Beta Phi Educational Foundation, Inc.
c/o Mrs. Douglas Miller
5735 High Dr.
Shawnee Mission, KS 66208
Scholarship address: c/o University of Kansas, Attn.: Mandy Peterson, Office of Student Financial Aid, 50 Strong Hall, Lawrence, KS 66045-7535

Foundation type: Independent foundation
Limitations: Scholarships to female students at the University of Kansas who have had a 2.21 GPA for the previous two years.
Financial data: Year ended 09/30/2004.
Assets, $398,520 (M); Expenditures, $66,078;
Total giving, $63,039; Grants to individuals, 7 grants totaling $19,046 (high: $4,418, low: $2,168).
Fields of interest: Women.
Type of support: Support to graduates or students of specific schools; Undergraduate support.
Application information: Applications accepted throughout the year; Contact foundation for current application guidelines.
EIN: 486111427

3200
The Vernon J. Pick Foundation
5815 W. Main St.
Maple Plain, MN 55359
Contact: Frederick A. Pick, Pres.
Application address: 8136 Long Lake Dr. N.E., Bemidji, MN 56601

Foundation type: Independent foundation
Limitations: Scholarships to MN high school seniors majoring in science or engineering.
Financial data: Year ended 12/31/2004.
Assets, $769,784 (M); Expenditures, $52,475;
Total giving, $38,487; Grants to individuals, 9 grants totaling $38,487.

Fields of interest: Engineering school/education; Science.
Type of support: Undergraduate support.
Application information: Application form required.
Deadline(s): Mar. 1
EIN: 411733851

3201
Pickett & Hatcher Educational Fund, Inc.
P.O. Box 8169
Columbus, GA 31908-8169 (706) 327-6586
Contact: Scholarships: Kenneth R. Owens
FAX: (706) 324-6788; E-mail: info@phef.org; E-mail for Scholarships: kenowens@phef.org; Additional tel.: (800) 864-8308; URL: http://www.phef.org

Foundation type: Independent foundation
Limitations: Undergraduate student loans to residents of the U.S. Recipients must attend four-year colleges and universities. No loans are given to students planning to enter fields of medicine, law, or the ministry, or for vocational studies.
Publications: Informational brochure (including application guidelines).
Financial data: Year ended 09/30/2005.
Assets, $34,893,636 (M); Expenditures, $2,972,618; Total giving, $2,301,356; Loans to individuals, 643 loans totaling $2,301,356.
Type of support: Undergraduate support.
Application information: Applications accepted. Application form required.
Initial approach: Letter or telephone.
Additional information: Application must include test scores, and endorsement from a credit-worthy individual; see Web site for latest application guidelines and procedures.
Program description:
Student Loan: Applicants must be U.S. citizens and should be of good character, have a good academic record, and demonstrate financial need. Loans are made to undergraduates. However, exceptions may be made for graduate students who received fund assistance as undergraduates in order that they will not be forced to borrow from two or more sources. The directors consider such requests individually. Students pursuing courses in colleges and universities offering broad liberal education and degrees are eligible for assistance, but students enrolled in vocational or business schools are not eligible. Loans carry a two-percent interest rate while in college, and a rate of six percent after college. Interest is payable quarterly while in college and monthly thereafter. Repayment of the principal begins six months after leaving college. Consideration is given to applications for the amount required for fees, tuition, room and board up to a maximum of $5,500 per academic year. Students attending summer school may receive an additional amount. The total amount which may be borrowed is $22,000.
EIN: 580566216

3202
Elva and Herbert Pickle Memorial Scholarship Fund
c/o Wells Fargo Bank, N.A.
P.O. Box 63954
San Francisco, CA 94163
Application address: c/o Potter Valley High School, Attn.: Brent Russert, Counselor, P.O. Box 219, Potter Valley, CA 95469, tel.: (707) 743-2101

Foundation type: Independent foundation

Limitations: Scholarships to graduates of Potter Valley High School, CA, to attend accredited junior colleges, universities, and trade schools.
Financial data: Year ended 03/31/2005.
Assets, $466,769 (M); Expenditures, $26,677; Total giving, $19,400; Grants to individuals, 20 grants totaling $19,400.
Fields of interest: Vocational education; College; University.
Type of support: Support to graduates or students of specific schools.
Application information: Application form required.
  Deadline(s): None
  Applicants should submit the following:
    1) Letter(s) of recommendation
    2) Essay
  Additional information: Applicant must show completion of one semester of full-time undergraduate study with at least a 2.0 GPA.
EIN: 946616460

3203
Mills O. Pierce & Mount Vernon Pierce Charitable Foundation
22530 Cove Creek S.
Prairie Grove, AR 72753-9230
Contact: Delma D. Dunn, Tr.

Foundation type: Independent foundation
Limitations: Scholarships to graduates of Prairie Grove High School, AR.
Financial data: Year ended 12/31/2004.
Assets, $132,111 (M); Expenditures, $7,285; Total giving, $6,800; Grants to individuals, 22 grants totaling $6,800.
Type of support: Support to graduates or students of specific schools; Undergraduate support.
Application information: Application form required.
  Deadline(s): June 30
Program description:
  Scholarships: Scholarships are granted for one year only, but are renewable by re-application each year. Scholarship funds are provided in two increments. To obtain the second increment, students must have achieved a minimum GPA of 3.2 (12 hours) for the fall semester and be enrolled in a minimum of 12 hours (undergraduate) or 6 hours (graduate) for the spring semester.
EIN: 710526830

3204
Beatrice D. Pierce Trust
c/o Bank of America, N.A.
P.O. Box 6767
Providence, RI 02940-6767

Foundation type: Independent foundation
Limitations: Scholarships to individuals who are graduates of Lebanon, NH, high schools.
Financial data: Year ended 09/30/2002.
Assets, $503,958 (M); Expenditures, $29,059; Total giving, $23,250; Grants to individuals, 31 grants totaling $23,250 (high: $750, low: $750).
Type of support: Support to graduates or students of specific schools; Undergraduate support.
Application information: Applications accepted throughout the year; Contact trust for current application guidelines.
EIN: 046089261

3205
Frank Pierce Trust
102 E. Church St.
Marshalltown, IA 50158 (641) 752-4507

Foundation type: Independent foundation
Limitations: Low-interest loans to individuals who are students at or graduates of Marshalltown Community High School, or students attending an IA college or university and have been residents of the Marshalltown Community School District for the last six years for undergraduate or professional study.
Financial data: Year ended 12/31/2004.
Assets, $2,571,919 (M); Expenditures, $36,617; Total giving, $0; Loans to individuals, 97 loans totaling $249,585.
Type of support: Support to graduates or students of specific schools; Undergraduate support.
Application information: Application form required.
  Deadline(s): May 1
  Applicants should submit the following:
    1) Photograph
    2) Transcripts
  Additional information: Application must also include test scores, a completed Educational Finance Planner, and the consent of co-signer. Loans are not granted for graduate study.
EIN: 420737535

3206
Julia Pierson Trust
P.O. Box 29
Carrollton, IL 62016-1015 (217) 942-5244

Foundation type: Operating foundation
Limitations: Scholarships to graduates of Carrollton Community Unit School District No. 1, IL.
Financial data: Year ended 12/31/2003.
Assets, $2,081,128 (M); Expenditures, $56,632; Total giving, $52,996; Grants to individuals, 91 grants totaling $52,996 (high: $960, low: $200).
Type of support: Support to graduates or students of specific schools; Undergraduate support.
Application information:
  Initial approach: Letter.
  Deadline(s): May 1
EIN: 376321165

3207
Paul Pigott Scholarship Foundation
P.O. Box 1518
Bellevue, WA 98009
Contact: G. V. Huffman, Mgr.

Foundation type: Independent foundation
Limitations: Scholarships only to dependents of employees of PACCAR, Inc. and its subsidiaries, for the first college year or grades 9-12 at non-tax supported secondary schools.
Financial data: Year ended 07/31/2004.
Assets, $2,318,818 (M); Expenditures, $26,284; Total giving, $25,146.
Type of support: Employee-related scholarships; Precollege support; Undergraduate support.
Application information: Application form required.
  Deadline(s): Nov. 1
  Applicants should submit the following:
    1) SAT
    2) Transcripts
  Additional information: Application must also include school report. Scholarships are not renewable.
EIN: 916030639

3208
Walt and Olga Pilch Foundation
c/o Thomas J. Pilch
P.O. Box 6498
Sheridan, WY 82801 (307) 674-7491
Contact: Cindy L. Pilch, Dir.

Foundation type: Independent foundation
Limitations: Educational loans to students attending Colorado State University, CO, Sheridan College or the University of Wyoming, WY.
Financial data: Year ended 06/30/2004.
Assets, $302,434 (M); Expenditures, $24,227; Total giving, $19,500; Grants to individuals, 5 grants totaling $4,500; Loans to individuals, 3 loans totaling $15,000.
Type of support: Support to graduates or students of specific schools; Undergraduate support.
Application information: Application form required.
  Deadline(s): Contact foundation for deadline
  Applicants should submit the following:
    1) Transcripts
    2) Financial information
EIN: 830323151

3209
A. Franklin Pilchard Foundation
508 N. Plum Grove Rd.
Palatine, IL 60067
Contact: Robert C. Pacilio, Treas.

Foundation type: Independent foundation
Limitations: Scholarships to students attending specific educational institutions in IL.
Financial data: Year ended 06/30/2005.
Assets, $20,925,215 (M); Expenditures, $1,098,387; Total giving, $922,225; Grants to individuals, 138 grants totaling $922,225 (high: $15,407, low: $325).
Type of support: Scholarships—to individuals; Support to graduates or students of specific schools.
Application information: Application form required.
  Deadline(s): Oct. 31
Program description:
  Scholarships: Applicants must be graduating from one of the following IL high schools: Brother Rice High School, Chicago; Genoa Kingston High School; Josephinum High School, Chicago; King High School, Chicago; Lane Technical High School, Chicago; Lemont Township High School; Maine East High School, Park Ridge; Maine West High School, Des Plaines; Mother McAuley Liberal Arts High School, Chicago; Spaulding High School, Chicago; Sycamore High School; or Whitney Young Magnet School, Chicago. Applicants must also attend a college or university located in IL.
EIN: 363723290

3210
The Pilgrim Foundation
P.O. Box 3400
Brockton, MA 02303 (508) 588-6100

Foundation type: Independent foundation
Limitations: Scholarships to residents of Brockton, MA.
Financial data: Year ended 12/31/2004.
Assets, $4,401,588 (M); Expenditures, $222,236; Total giving, $177,082; Grants to individuals, 97 grants totaling $81,632 (high: $1,000, low: $90).
Type of support: Scholarships—to individuals.
Application information: Applications accepted. Application form required.

Initial approach: Telephone.

Deadline(s): Apr. 1 for graduating high school seniors and May 1 for returning college students

Additional information: Application must include name of college or university attending, courses of study, education history, parents' history, financial information, and a copy of applicant's federal aid forms or parents' federal income tax return.

EIN: 042104834

3211

Pilot International Foundation, Inc.

P.O. Box 5600

Macon, GA 31208-5600 (478) 743-2245

Contact: Frank Soldovere, Exec. Dir.

FAX: (478) 743-2482; E-mail: pifinfo@pilothq.org; URL: http://www.pilotinternational.org/html/foundation/overview.shtml

Foundation type: Public charity

Limitations: Scholarships to undergraduate and graduate students who will pursue careers helping the disabled. Preference is given to those specializing in brain disorders.

Financial data: Year ended 06/30/2005. Assets, $1,846,737 (M); Expenditures, $470,934; Total giving, $77,655; Grants to individuals, totaling $77,655.

Fields of interest: Business school/education; Teacher school/education; Social work school/education; Public health school/education; Journalism school/education; Organ diseases; Brain disorders; Pediatrics; Agriculture/food, formal/general education; Agriculture, livestock issues; Home economics; Computer science; Psychology/behavioral science; Religion, formal/general education; Disabilities, people with.

Type of support: Foreign applicants; Graduate support; Undergraduate support.

Application information: Applications accepted. Application form available on the grantmaker's Web site.

Initial approach: E-mail.

Deadline(s): Feb. 15; Applicants are notified by June 30.

Additional information: Only Pilot Club members are eligible to apply.

Program descriptions:

Ruby Newhall Memorial Scholarship: Scholarships of up to $1,500 to international students for undergraduate and Master's study in agriculture, business administration, computer information management, education, guidance counseling, healing arts and services, social service, the livestock industry, political science, psychology, public health, religion, home economics or journalism. Applicants must have spent at least one full semester in a college in the U.S. or Canada and have a 3.0 GPA. Deadline Dec. 1.

Maria Newton Sepia Memorial Scholarship: Awards up to $1,000 to graduate students planning careers with children with brain-related disorders or disabilities.

Pilot International Foundation Scholarship: Provides assistance to undergraduate students preparing for careers working directly with people with disabilities or training those who will.

Pilot International/Lifeline Scholarship: Awards up to $500 to part-time students and up to $1,000 to full-time students preparing for a second career, re-entering the labor market or obtaining additional training in their current fields. Applicants must

intend to assist those with brain-related disorders or brain-related disabilities.

EIN: 237443190

3212

The Edward H. Pingel & Cora W. Pingel Educational Fund

c/o Harris Bank, N.A.

P.O. Box 755

Chicago, IL 60690

Application address: c/o Marengo Community High School, Attn: Board of Education, 110 Franks Rd., Marengo, IL 60152

Foundation type: Independent foundation

Limitations: Student loans to graduates of Marengo Community High School, IL, for associate and baccalaureate degree programs.

Financial data: Year ended 12/31/2004. Assets, $410,664 (M); Expenditures, $29,217; Total giving, $14,000; Loans to individuals, 7 loans totaling $14,000.

Type of support: Support to graduates or students of specific schools; Undergraduate support.

Application information: Application form required.

Deadline(s): May 15

Program description:

Pingel Loan: Students who have graduated from Marengo Community High School may apply for this $2,000 loan. Two graduates will be selected each year. Loans are renewable provided that the recipient continues as a full-time student leading to termination of education or graduation. No interest will be charged while full-time student status continues. Loans have a four percent per annum charge commencing one month after graduation or termination of schooling.

EIN: 366910594

3213

Pioneer Natural Resources Scholarship Foundation

(formerly Parker & Parsley Scholarship Foundation)

c/o Larry N. Paulsen

5205 N. O'Connor Blvd., Ste. 900

Irving, TX 75039 (972) 444-9001

Foundation type: Company-sponsored foundation

Limitations: Scholarships to children of full-time employees who have been employed by Pioneer Natural Resources Company or its subsidiaries for a minimum of one year.

Financial data: Year ended 12/31/2004. Assets, $8,200 (M); Expenditures, $16,750; Total giving, $16,750; Grants to individuals, 25 grants totaling $16,750 (high: $1,000; low: $250).

Type of support: Employee-related scholarships.

Application information: Application form required.

Initial approach: Letter or telephone.

Deadline(s): May 31

Additional information: Contact foundation for current application guidelines.

EIN: 752443728

3214

Pipe Line Contractors Association Scholarship Foundation

1700 Pacific Ave., Ste. 4100

Dallas, TX 75201-4675

Application address: c/o Scholarship Management Svcs., 1505 Riverview Rd., P.O. Box 297, St. Peter, MN 56082, tel.: (507) 931-1682

Foundation type: Independent foundation

Limitations: Scholarships to children and grandchildren of full-time employees of regular and associate members of the Pipe Line Contractors Assn.

Financial data: Year ended 12/31/2004. Assets, $759,208 (M); Expenditures, $99,488; Total giving, $85,000; Grants to individuals, 17 grants totaling $85,000.

Type of support: Employee-related scholarships.

Application information: Application form required.

Deadline(s): Jan. 7

Program description:

Scholarships: Scholarships are $5,000 each and are renewable. Recipients must be high school seniors or graduates who plan to enroll or students who are already enrolled in a full-time undergraduate course of study at an accredited four-year college or university. Recipients must be 25 years of age or younger.

EIN: 752744096

3215

Piper Foundation, Inc.

32 Dover Rd.

Wellesley, MA 02482

Foundation type: Independent foundation

Limitations: Scholarships to graduating students attending high schools in the Keystone Central School District, PA.

Publications: Annual report.

Financial data: Year ended 12/31/2004. Assets, $1,108,637 (M); Expenditures, $59,067; Total giving, $42,133; Grants to individuals, 7 grants totaling $17,500.

Type of support: Support to graduates or students of specific schools; Undergraduate support.

Application information:

Deadline(s): Contact foundation for current application deadline.

Additional information: Application by letter outlining financial need and achievements, after having been selected by a high school administrator.

EIN: 240863140

3216

Minnie Stevens Piper Foundation

1250 N.E. Loop 410, Ste. 810

San Antonio, TX 78209-1539 (210) 525-8494

Contact: Joyce M. Ellis, Secy. and Exec. Dir.

FAX: (210) 341-6627; E-mail: mspf@mspf.org; URL: http://www.mspf.org

Foundation type: Independent foundation

Limitations: Student loans to full-time undergraduate juniors and seniors, and graduate students, who are U.S. citizens or permanent residents, and who are residents of TX, attending TX colleges and universities.

Publications: Application guidelines; Occasional report; Program policy statement.

Financial data: Year ended 12/31/2004. Assets, $22,952,803 (M); Expenditures, $1,872,923; Total giving, $588,500.

Type of support: Graduate support; Undergraduate support.

Application information: Application form required.

Deadline(s): Contact foundation for current application deadline

Applicants should submit the following:

1) Letter(s) of recommendation

2) Transcripts

Additional information: Recommendation must be from head of department of student's major or Dean of Students.

Program description:
Student Loan: Undergraduate recipients may receive up to $1,000 each per semester except during summer semesters, when $500 is available per summer session. Graduate recipients may receive up to $2,000 each per semester, except in the summer, when they may receive up to $1,000. A maximum of $10,000 may be loaned to any one student. Loans are due for repayment one year after graduation. If at that time the recipient is unable to repay the full amount, a repayment schedule may be requested. If approved, the loan will be repaid in monthly installments at an interest rate of six percent, over a four-year period. Students who already have a bachelor's degree are not eligible if they are pursuing an additional bachelor's degree. Likewise, students with master's degrees will not be eligible for a loan to pursue a second degree.
EIN: 741292695

3217
The Piqua Community Foundation
P.O. Box 226
Piqua, OH 45356-0226 (937) 615-9080
Contact: Karen S. Wendeln, Exec. Dir.

Foundation type: Community foundation
Limitations: Scholarships to high school graduates in Piqua County, OH, for higher education.
Publications: Application guidelines; Annual report; Informational brochure; Newsletter.
Financial data: Year ended 12/31/2004.
Assets, $3,606,892 (M); Expenditures, $1,038,474; Total giving, $982,355; Grants to individuals, totaling $82,700.
Type of support: Undergraduate support.
Application information: Contact foundation for current application deadline/guidelines.
EIN: 311391908

3218
Pitcairn High School Alumni - R. J. Conrad Scholarship Fund
P.O. Box 144
Oakmont, PA 15139
Contact: Robert J. Conrad, Chair.
Application address: R.R. 2, Box 85, Ford City, PA 16226

Foundation type: Independent foundation
Limitations: Scholarships to alumni and descendents of alumni of Pictairn High School, PA, for undergraduate education.
Financial data: Year ended 12/31/2003.
Assets, $19,045 (M); Expenditures, $10,100; Total giving, $10,000; Grants to individuals, 10 grants totaling $10,000 (high: $1,000, low: $1,000).
Type of support: Support to graduates or students of specific schools; Undergraduate support.
Application information: Applications by letter accepted throughout the year, including letter outlining financial need , proof of alumni status or that of a relative, and transcripts.
EIN: 251799746

3219
The Pittsburgh Foundation
1 PPG Pl., 30th Fl.
Pittsburgh, PA 15222-5401 (412) 391-5122
Contact: For grant applications: Dr. William E. Trueheart, C.E.O.; For scholarships: Debra Turner
FAX: (412) 391-7259; E-mail: email@pghfdn.org;
Grant application E-mail: trueheartw@pghfdn.org;
URL: http://www.pittsburghfoundation.org

Foundation type: Community foundation
Limitations: Scholarships, awards, research grants, internships, camperships, and financial assistance to residents of Pittsburgh and Allegheny County, PA.
Publications: Application guidelines; Annual report; Informational brochure (including application guidelines); Newsletter.
Financial data: Year ended 12/31/2004.
Assets, $617,284,142 (M); Expenditures, $30,352,653; Total giving, $23,124,555.
Type of support: Internship funds; Research; Scholarships—to individuals; Camperships.
Application information: Applications accepted. Application form required.
Initial approach: E-mail or telephone for application information.
Additional information: See web site for additional application information and program description. Scholarship application information, tel.: (412) 394-2649, e-mail: turnerD@pghfdn.org.
EIN: 250965466

3220
John Pitzer Trust
c/o First National Bank & Trust Co.
P.O. Box 9012
Kokomo, IN 46904-9012

Foundation type: Independent foundation
Limitations: Scholarships to graduates of Kokomo High School, IN, to attend Indiana University.
Financial data: Year ended 12/31/2004.
Assets, $76,409 (M); Expenditures, $34,998; Total giving, $28,000; Grants to individuals, 17 grants totaling $28,000.
Type of support: Support to graduates or students of specific schools; Undergraduate support.
Application information: Application form required.
Deadline(s): Mar. 31
EIN: 356563238

3221
Elsie L. Plank Trust f/b/o C. Plank Scholarship Trust
c/o Mellon Financial Corp.
P.O. Box 185
Pittsburgh, PA 15230-9897
Application address: Peg Watson, c/o Mellon Bank, N.A., 1735 Market St., 3rd Fl., Philadelphia, PA 19101

Foundation type: Independent foundation
Limitations: Scholarships to graduates of Conestoga Valley High School, for higher education at F&M College, PA.
Financial data: Year ended 12/31/2003.
Assets, $122,320 (M); Expenditures, $7,206; Total giving, $5,500; Grants to individuals, totaling $5,500.
Type of support: Support to graduates or students of specific schools; Undergraduate support.
Application information: Application form required.
Deadline(s): Aug. 1
EIN: 236241620

3222
Plexus Corp. Charitable Foundation, Inc.
(formerly Plexon Corp. Charitable Foundation, Inc.)
55 Jewelers Park Dr.
Neenah, WI 54956 (920) 722-3451
Contact: Jo Lemoine, Pres.

Foundation type: Company-sponsored foundation
Limitations: Scholarships to children of employees of Plexus Corporation, WI and its related subsidiaries.
Financial data: Year ended 06/30/2005.
Assets, $108,346 (M); Expenditures, $158,396; Total giving, $158,385; Grants to individuals, 9 grants totaling $20,000 (high: $4,000, low: $764).
Type of support: Employee-related scholarships.
Application information:
Deadline(s): None
Additional information: Contact foundation for current application guidelines.
EIN: 391828689

3223
Alice H. Plimpton Educational Fund
c/o State Street Bank and Trust Co.
P.O. Box 55122
Boston, MA 02101

Foundation type: Independent foundation
Limitations: Scholarships to students of Norwood High School, MA.
Financial data: Year ended 09/30/2005.
Assets, $1,190,537 (M); Expenditures, $77,036; Total giving, $55,200; Grants to individuals, 48 grants totaling $55,200.
Type of support: Scholarships—to individuals; Support to graduates or students of specific schools.
Application information: Applications not accepted.
Additional information: Recipients are selected by the faculty of Norwood High School, MA.
EIN: 046013418

3224
Peter & Masha Plotkin Memorial Foundation
c/o Peter Plotkin
9700 Aviation Blvd., Ste. 1
Los Angeles, CA 90045

Foundation type: Independent foundation
Limitations: Scholarships to students in CA for higher education and to travel overseas.
Financial data: Year ended 12/31/2004.
Assets, $0 (M); Expenditures, $281,997; Total giving, $37,800; Grants to individuals, 15 grants totaling $37,800.
Type of support: Undergraduate support; Travel grants.
Application information: Applications not accepted.
EIN: 954394293

3225
Plummer Scholarship Fund
c/o KeyBank N.A., Trust Div.
202 S. Michigan St.
South Bend, IN 46601-2021
Application address: c/o KeyBank N.A., Trust Div., Linda Baitz, Trust. Off., P.O. Box 9001, Kokomo, IN 46904, tel.: (765) 868-6022

Foundation type: Independent foundation

Limitations: Scholarships to financially needy graduates of Howard County, IN, high schools to pursue studies in medicine or nursing at accredited colleges and universities in the U.S.
Financial data: Year ended 10/31/2004. Assets, $340,636 (M); Expenditures, $21,800; Total giving, $16,500; Grants to individuals, 7 grants totaling $16,500.
Fields of interest: Medical school/education; Nursing school/education.
Type of support: Support to graduates or students of specific schools; Undergraduate support.
Application information: Application form required.
  Deadline(s): Mar. 26
EIN: 356510973

3226

PLUS Foundation
5353 Wayzata Blvd., Ste.600
Minneapolis, MN 55416 (952) 746-2590
Contact: Daniel Jenney, Assoc. Dir.
FAX: (952) 746-2599;
E-mail: djenney@plusweb.org; Additional tel.: (800) 845-0778; URL: http://www.plusfoundation.org/

Foundation type: Public charity
Limitations: Grants for the study of insurance. General scholarships only to members, member companies and their families.
Publications: Annual report.
Financial data: Year ended 12/31/2004. Assets, $560,099 (M); Expenditures, $248,806; Total giving, $93,210.
Fields of interest: Business school/education.
Type of support: Scholarships—to individuals; Graduate support.
Application information: Application form required. Application form available on the grantmaker's Web site.
  Initial approach: Letter.
  Additional information: See Web site for further information and limitations.
EIN: 411903374

3227

The PMC Foundation
12243 Branford St.
Sun Valley, CA 91352

Foundation type: Company-sponsored foundation
Limitations: Scholarships to eligible individuals.
Financial data: Year ended 10/31/2003. Assets, $33 (M); Expenditures, $103,044; Total giving, $100,593; Grants to individuals, 23 grants totaling $97,807 (high: $5,700, low: $193).
Type of support: Scholarships—to individuals.
Application information:
  Initial approach: Letter.
  Additional information: Contact foundation for current application deadline/guidelines.
EIN: 954194948

3228

PMMI Education and Training Foundation
(formerly Packaging Machinery Manufacturers Institute)
4350 N. Fairfax Dr., Ste. 600
Arlington, VA 22203-1620 (703) 243-8555
Contact: Glen A. Long, Chair.
FAX: (703) 243-8556; E-mail: education@pmmi.org

Foundation type: Public charity

Limitations: Scholarships to individuals who work for PMMI member companies for one job-related course per semester, not to exceed $500.
Publications: Annual report.
Type of support: Employee-related scholarships.
Application information:
  Initial approach: Letter or telephone.
  Deadline(s): Dec. 15 for Spring
  Additional information: Completion of formal application required, including recommendations from immediate supervisor and company-designated PMMI executive representative.
Program description:
  PMMI Member Employee Scholarships: This program supports employees who wish to further their education. Members must:
  · attend an accredited institution
  · take a job-related course
  · achieve a final grade of "B" or above in the course, or (for seminars) obtain a certificate of completion
  · be employed at a PMMI member company at the time of application as well as at the end of the semester/time or reimbursement.
EIN: 541820667

3229

PNC Memorial Foundation
c/o PNC Advisors
620 Liberty Ave., P2-PTPP-10-2
Pittsburgh, PA 15222-2705
Contact: R. Bruce Bickel, Sr. V.P. and Trust Off., PNC Bank, N.A.

Foundation type: Company-sponsored foundation
Limitations: Scholarships only to children of current or deceased employees of PNC Bank, N.A.
Financial data: Year ended 12/31/2004. Assets, $202,875 (M); Expenditures, $11,369; Total giving, $9,000; Grants to individuals, 6 grants totaling $9,000 (high: $1,500, low: $1,500).
Type of support: Employee-related scholarships.
Application information: Application form required.
  Deadline(s): May 31
EIN: 256487950

3230

The Podiatry Foundation of Pittsburgh
405 Rosslyn Rd.
Carnegie, PA 15106-1057
E-mail: info@podiatryplace.com; Application address: c/o Nicki Nigro, 1601 Union Ave., Natrona Heights, PA 15065, tel.: (412) 276-4568; URL: http://www.podiatryplace.org

Foundation type: Independent foundation
Limitations: Scholarships to podiatry students to further them in their studies.
Financial data: Year ended 06/30/2005. Assets, $2,416,354 (M); Expenditures, $429,407; Total giving, $366,202; Grants to individuals, 13 grants totaling $144,000 (high: $15,000, low: $8,000).
Fields of interest: Education; Podiatry.
Type of support: Scholarships—to individuals.
Application information: Applications accepted throughout the year; Completion of formal application required, including letter.
EIN: 251024331

3231

Bess R. Poff Scholarship Foundation
P.O. Box 842
Floyd, VA 24091
Contact: Robert G. Nester, Jr., Pres.

Foundation type: Independent foundation
Limitations: Scholarships to graduates of Floyd County High School, Floyd County, VA, for undergraduate education.
Financial data: Year ended 12/31/2004. Assets, $154,138 (M); Expenditures, $9,587; Total giving, $8,000; Grants to individuals, 7 grants totaling $8,000 (high: $2,000, low: $500).
Type of support: Support to graduates or students of specific schools.
Application information: Application form required.
  Deadline(s): Apr. 1
  Additional information: Completion of formal application required, including GPA, extracurricular activities, and college choice.
EIN: 541867764

3232

John Polakovic Charitable Trust
32100 Telegraph Rd., Ste. 200
Bingham Farms, MI 48025
Contact: James B. Tintera, Tr.
Application address: 117 Scissortail Trail, Georgetown, TX 78628

Foundation type: Independent foundation
Limitations: Scholarships to individuals attending J. Sterling Morton high schools in Berwyn, Cicero, Stickney IL, for undergraduate education.
Financial data: Year ended 12/31/2004. Assets, $137,424 (M); Expenditures, $13,588; Total giving, $12,000; Grants to individuals, 8 grants totaling $12,000.
Type of support: Support to graduates or students of specific schools; Awards/grants by nomination only; Graduate support; Undergraduate support.
Application information: Applications accepted through high schools only; Contact schools for current application deadline; Completion of formal application required, including high school academic information.
EIN: 386390004

3233

Polish American Board of Education of Berks County, PA
38 N. 6th St.
Reading, PA 19603
Contact: Eleanor Parker, Treas.
Application address: 311 Mifflin Blvd., Shillington, PA 19607, tel.: (610) 777-2770

Foundation type: Independent foundation
Limitations: Scholarships only to high school students who have at least 25 percent Polish heritage, and who are residents of Berks County, PA.
Financial data: Year ended 12/31/2003. Assets, $382,089 (M); Expenditures, $20,783; Total giving, $18,125; Grants to individuals, 32 grants totaling $18,125 (high: $1,875, low: $125).
Fields of interest: Poland.
Type of support: Undergraduate support.
Application information: Application form required.
  Deadline(s): Mar. 5
  Additional information: Initial approach by letter with completed application (available from Berks County high school offices).
EIN: 232061281

3234
The Polk County Community Foundation, Inc.
255 S. Trade St.
Tryon, NC 28782-3707 (828) 859-5314
Contact: Elizabeth Nager, Exec. Dir.
FAX: (828) 859-6122;
E-mail: foundation@polkccf.org; URL: http://www.polkccf.org

Foundation type: Community foundation
Limitations: Awards and scholarships to graduating seniors of Polk county, NC, and surrounding areas.
Publications: Application guidelines; Annual report; Financial statement; Informational brochure (including application guidelines); Occasional report.
Financial data: Year ended 12/31/2004. Assets, $19,452,429 (M); Expenditures, $1,174,060; Total giving, $776,851.
Fields of interest: Higher education.
Type of support: Scholarships—to individuals.
Application information: Applications accepted. Application form required.
Initial approach: Telephone, letter, or e-mail.
Deadline(s): Jan. and Sept.
Applicants should submit the following:
1) Pell Grant
2) Class rank
3) Transcripts
4) SAT
5) Letter(s) of recommendation
6) Financial information
7) Essay
Additional information: Interviews may be required. See web site for additional application information.
EIN: 510168751

3235
Annie M. & Clarke A. Polk Foundation
P.O. Box 399
Chappell Hill, TX 77426-0399 (979) 836-3499

Foundation type: Independent foundation
Limitations: Scholarships to full-time undergraduate students, primarily those residing in Washington County, TX.
Financial data: Year ended 06/30/2004. Assets, $709,402 (M); Expenditures, $58,692; Total giving, $58,250; Grants to individuals, 61 grants totaling $58,250.
Type of support: Undergraduate support.
Application information: Application form required.
Initial approach: Letter.
Deadline(s): Apr. 30
Applicants should submit the following:
1) Transcripts
2) Financial information
Additional information: Interviews required.
EIN: 742293811

3236
The Polonsky Brothers Foundation
P.O. Box 821
Red Bank, NJ 07701-0821 (732) 741-8438
Application address: c/o Ivan Polonsky, 151 Harding Rd., Red Bank, NJ 07701-0821

Foundation type: Operating foundation
Limitations: Scholarships to disadvantaged urban youths who are high school juniors in selected schools in NJ and NY to help cover tuition, books, travel, and fees for summer educational enrichment programs.

Financial data: Year ended 12/31/2003. Assets, $105,188 (M); Expenditures, $75,917; Total giving, $56,603; Grants to individuals, 12 grants totaling $56,603 (high: $7,417, low: $990).
Fields of interest: Youth, services.
Type of support: Scholarships—to individuals.
Application information: Application form required.
Additional information: Applications accepted throughout the year.
Program description:
Scholarship Program: The program selects high school juniors from pre-selected public high schools in NY or NJ for summer enrichment programs. The foundation hopes that this experience will stimulate the student in his senior year to apply for college placement.
EIN: 136169593

3237
Harriet & Fred Pomeroy Scholarship Fund Trust
c/o KeyBank N.A.
800 Superior Ave., 4th Fl.
Cleveland, OH 44114-1306
Application address: c/o Bates College, 2 Andrews Rd., Lewiston, ME 04240

Foundation type: Independent foundation
Limitations: Scholarships to biology students of Bates College, ME, for the continuation of biology studies at the graduate level.
Financial data: Year ended 06/30/2005. Assets, $381,592 (M); Expenditures, $35,097; Total giving, $30,000; Grants to individuals, 6 grants totaling $30,000.
Fields of interest: Graduate/professional education; Science, formal/general education; Biological sciences.
Type of support: Support to graduates or students of specific schools; Graduate support.
Application information: Applications by letter outlining financial need and stating qualifications accepted throughout the year.
EIN: 016008640

3238
Pomona Valley Community Hospital LTD-Womens Auxiliary
1798 N. Garey Ave.
Pomona, CA 91767 (909) 865-9668
Contact: Celeste Palmer, Pres.

Foundation type: Public charity
Limitations: Scholarships to active auxiliary junior volunteers residing in CA for undergraduate education. Preference is given to those planning to pursue health care education.
Financial data: Year ended 12/31/2004. Assets, $382,364; Expenditures, $242,509; Total giving, $18,000; Grants to individuals, totaling $18,000.
Fields of interest: Health sciences school/education; Health organizations, volunteer services.
Type of support: Undergraduate support.
Application information: Application form required.
Deadline(s): First week of Apr.
Additional information: Interviews required.
EIN: 956053224

3239
Ida M. Pope Memorial Scholarship Fund
c/o Bank of Hawaii
P.O. Box 3170
Honolulu, HI 96802-3170
Application address: Hawaii Community Foundation, 1164 Bishop St., Ste. 800, Honolulu, HI 96813, tel.: (808) 537-6333

Foundation type: Independent foundation
Limitations: Scholarships to financially needy female residents of HI who are of Hawaiian or part-Hawaiian ancestry for undergraduate or graduate study. Recipients must attend or have been admitted to an accredited graduate or undergraduate institution and have a satisfactory GPA.
Publications: Informational brochure.
Financial data: Year ended 06/30/2004. Assets, $1,100,947 (M); Expenditures, $82,917; Total giving, $63,000; Grants to individuals, 66 grants totaling $63,000.
Fields of interest: Asians/Pacific Islanders; Native Americans/American Indians; Women.
Type of support: Graduate support; Undergraduate support.
Application information: Applications accepted. Application form required.
Deadline(s): Mar. 1
Additional information: Scholarships are renewable provided the recipient maintains full-time status and a 2.0 cumulative GPA.
EIN: 996003339

3240
Thomas H. Pope Scholarship Fund
c/o James Porath
20 Cloutman's Ln.
Marblehead, MA 01945

Foundation type: Independent foundation
Limitations: Scholarships to residents of Danvers, MA, for higher education.
Financial data: Year ended 06/30/2005. Assets, $165,048 (M); Expenditures, $15,120; Total giving, $15,000; Grants to individuals, 3 grants totaling $15,000.
Type of support: Undergraduate support.
Application information: Applications not accepted.
EIN: 046850495

3241
Port Arthur Higher Education Foundation, Inc.
1500 Procter St.
Port Arthur, TX 77641 (409) 984-6100
Contact: Jack Verret, Chair. and Pres.

Foundation type: Public charity
Limitations: Scholarships to students at Lamar State College- Port Arthur.
Financial data: Year ended 12/31/2004. Assets, $2,347,434 (M); Expenditures, $401,837; Total giving, $249,064; Grants to individuals, totaling $249,064.
Type of support: Support to graduates or students of specific schools.
Application information: Contact foundation for current application deadline/guidelines.
EIN: 237272448

3242
Porter Art Foundation
c/o Wells Fargo Bank Indiana, N.A.
P.O. Box 370
Peru, IN 46970
Application address: c/o Janey Borden, 2526 Wolf Point Dr., Rochester, IN 46975-8685, tel.: (574) 223-8494

Foundation type: Independent foundation
Limitations: Scholarships to graduates of high schools in Miami County, IN, for higher education in performing arts.
Financial data: Year ended 12/31/2004. Assets, $1,604 (M); Expenditures, $16,700; Total giving, $13,750; Grants to individuals, 6 grants totaling $13,750.
Fields of interest: Performing arts, education.
Type of support: Support to graduates or students of specific schools; Undergraduate support.
Application information: Application form required.
  Deadline(s): Contact foundation for current application deadline
  Additional information: Interviews required.
EIN: 356067146

3243
Edwin M. Porter Educational Fund
c/o U.S. Bank, N.A.
P.O. Box 387
St. Louis, MO 63166
Application address: c/o Bowling Green R-1 High School, Attn: Guidance Counselor, 700 W. Adams., Bowling Green, MO 63334

Foundation type: Independent foundation
Limitations: Scholarships and loans to students from the Bowling Green R-1 School District, MO.
Financial data: Year ended 03/31/2005. Assets, $305,775 (M); Expenditures, $16,860; Total giving, $11,000; Grants to individuals, 25 grants totaling $11,000.
Type of support: Support to graduates or students of specific schools; Undergraduate support.
Application information: Application form required.
  Deadline(s): Applications accepted throughout the year
  Additional information: Application forms are available from the guidance counselor and principal of Bowling Green high schools, MO.
EIN: 436225390

3244
Laura E. Porter Trust
P.O. Box H
Pratt, KS 67124-1108 (620) 672-5533
Contact: Bill Hampton, Jr., Tr.

Foundation type: Independent foundation
Limitations: Student loans and scholarships to men graduating from Pratt County Community College, KS, to further their education at universities approved by the trustees.
Financial data: Year ended 12/31/2004. Assets, $904,744 (M); Expenditures, $39,811; Total giving, $21,950; Grants to individuals, 19 grants totaling $21,950; Loans to individuals, 16 loans totaling $59,100.
Fields of interest: Men.
Type of support: Student loans—to individuals; Support to graduates or students of specific schools; Undergraduate support.
Application information: Applications accepted.
  Deadline(s): None

Additional information: Interviews granted upon request.
EIN: 486105318

3245
The Portland Foundation
112 E. Main St.
Portland, IN 47371 (260) 726-4260
Contact: Douglas L. Inman, Exec. Dir.
FAX: (260) 726-4273; E-mail: portfoun@jayco.net; URL: http://www.portlandfoundation.org

Foundation type: Community foundation
Limitations: Scholarships to residents of Jay County, IN.
Publications: Application guidelines; Annual report; Newsletter.
Financial data: Year ended 12/31/2004. Assets, $16,795,760 (M); Expenditures, $1,024,471; Total giving, $740,337; Grants to individuals, 77 grants totaling $156,800 (high: $12,000, low: $100, average grant: $2,000-$2,000).
Fields of interest: Language (foreign); Vocational education; Business school/education; Nursing school/education; Teacher school/education; Engineering school/education; Health sciences school/education; Agriculture; Protestant agencies & churches.
Type of support: Support to graduates or students of specific schools; Technical education support; Undergraduate support.
Application information: Applications accepted. Application form required.
  Initial approach: E-mail or telephone.
  Deadline(s): Feb. 28
  Additional information: Contact foundation for current application guidelines.
EIN: 356028362

3246
Leslie T. & Frances U. Posey Foundation
1800 2nd St., Ste. 750
Sarasota, FL 34236 (941) 957-0442
FAX: (941) 957-3135; URL: http://www.selbyfdn.org/sarasotaCounty.html

Foundation type: Independent foundation
Limitations: Graduate scholarships for art education, especially painting and sculpture of the traditional kind.
Financial data: Year ended 08/31/2004. Assets, $357,146 (M); Expenditures, $17,555; Total giving, $8,000; Grants to individuals, 2 grants totaling $8,000 (high: $4,000, low: $4,000).
Fields of interest: Arts education; Sculpture; Painting; Arts.
Type of support: Graduate support.
Application information: Application form required.
  Deadline(s): Mar. 1
  Additional information: Completion of formal application required, including essays, slides, and photographs.
EIN: 596832335

3247
POSSCA, Inc.
P.O. Box 7615
Olympia, WA 98507-7615 (360) 754-6050
Contact: Trent K.D. Hart, Pres.

Foundation type: Public charity

Limitations: Scholarships to high schools seniors in Olympia, WA, who demonstrate artistic ability, for undergraduate education.
Financial data: Year ended 12/31/2003. Assets, $50,561 (M); Expenditures, $48,819; Total giving, $35,750; Grants to individuals, 11 grants totaling $13,750 (high: $1,750, low: $1,200).
Fields of interest: Arts.
Type of support: Undergraduate support.
Application information: Application form required.
  Deadline(s): Contact foundation for current application deadline
EIN: 910828618

3248
Ralph B. Post Trust
c/o Alliance Bank, N.A.
241 Main St.
Buffalo, NY 14203

Foundation type: Independent foundation
Limitations: Scholarships to pre-selected female residents of NY who are pursuing nursing degrees.
Financial data: Year ended 09/30/2004. Assets, $2,626,251 (M); Expenditures, $223,353; Total giving, $193,792; Grants to individuals, 48 grants totaling $193,792 (high: $19,923, low: $70).
Fields of interest: Nursing school/education; Women.
Type of support: Scholarships—to individuals.
Application information: Applications not accepted.
EIN: 146052967

3249
Howard and Edna Postles Scholarship Fund
c/o PNC Advisors
1600 Market St.
Philadelphia, PA 19103-7240
Application address: c/o PNC Advisors, 22 Delaware Ave., Wilmington, DE 19899

Foundation type: Independent foundation
Limitations: Scholarships to financially needy high school seniors who are in the top ten percent of their class and who live within a 15-mile radius of Milford, DE, for attendance at any postsecondary institution.
Financial data: Year ended 12/31/2004. Assets, $988,039 (M); Expenditures, $53,683; Total giving, $44,000; Grants to individuals, 41 grants totaling $44,000.
Fields of interest: Vocational education.
Type of support: Undergraduate support.
Application information: Application form required.
  Copies of proposal: 6
  Deadline(s): None
  Applicants should submit the following:
    1) Transcripts
    2) Letter(s) of recommendation
  Additional information: Selection is based on academic performance, extracurricular activities, community service, and financial need. Scholarships are renewable.
EIN: 516169946

3250

Potlatch Foundation for Higher Education

601 W. Riverside Ave., Ste. 1100
Spokane, WA 99201 (509) 835-1515
Contact: Sharon Pegau, Admin., Corp. Progs. and Board
E-mail: foundation@potlatchcorp.com; URL: http://www.potlatchcorp.com/scholarship

Foundation type: Company-sponsored foundation
Limitations: Scholarships to undergraduates who reside within a 30-mile radius of Potlatch Corporation operations, primarily in ID, AR, and MN.
Publications: Informational brochure.
Financial data: Year ended 12/31/2005.
Assets, $201,531 (M); Expenditures, $344,730; Total giving, $327,658; Grants to individuals, totaling $327,658.
Type of support: Undergraduate support.
Application information: Application form required.
   Initial approach: Letter or e-mail.
   Deadline(s): Feb. 1
   Applicants should submit the following:
      1) Financial information
      2) GPA
      3) Transcripts
      4) SAT
      5) Letter(s) of recommendation
      6) ACT
   Additional information: Request application no later than Dec. 1 preceding the year for which the scholarship is sought.
Program description:
   Scholarships: The foundation awards scholarships to individuals graduating from high schools or having a permanent residence within 30 miles of major Potlatch facilities. The majority of Potlatch Foundation scholarships are awarded to students residing near major Potlatch operating facilities in ID, MN, and AR. Applicants need not be related to a company employee. Recipients are selected on the basis of character, personality, leadership qualities, scholastic achievement and ability, and financial need. Scholarships are subject to annual renewal during the course of a four-year program leading to a bachelor's or other degree approved by the foundation's trustees. Approximately 75 new awards are made each year.
EIN: 826005250

3251

The Philip E. Potter Foundation

6 Ford Ave.
Oneonta, NY 13820 (607) 432-6720
Contact: Henry L. Hulbert, Mgr.

Foundation type: Independent foundation
Limitations: Scholarships primarily to graduates of Oneonta High School, NY.
Financial data: Year ended 10/31/2004.
Assets, $10,900,492 (M); Expenditures, $696,802; Total giving, $562,500; Grants to individuals, totaling $562,500.
Type of support: Support to graduates or students of specific schools; Undergraduate support.
Application information: Deadline May 15; Completion of formal application required, including high school evaluation form and financial information; Application forms available from local high school and foundation office.
EIN: 166169167

3252

Stephen J. Potter Memorial Foundation, Inc.

47 Sunnyside E.
Queensbury, NY 12804 (518) 761-7695
Contact: John Austin, Jr., Secy.-Treas.
Application address: c/o Ticonderoga Senior High School, Attn: Principal, 5 Calkins Pl., Ticonderoga, NY 12883

Foundation type: Independent foundation
Limitations: Scholarships to graduating seniors of Ticonderoga High School, NY.
Financial data: Year ended 09/30/2004.
Assets, $570,528 (M); Expenditures, $49,615; Total giving, $41,000; Grants to individuals, 34 grants totaling $32,250.
Type of support: Support to graduates or students of specific schools; Undergraduate support.
Application information:
   Deadline(s): Apr. 1
   Additional information: Contact foundation for current application guidelines.
EIN: 146016858

3253

The Greater Pottstown Foundation

P.O. Box 696
934 High St.
Pottstown, PA 19464-0696
Contact: Harold H. Prince, Secy.
Application address: P.O. Box 85, Pottstown, PA 19464

Foundation type: Independent foundation
Limitations: Scholarships to seniors graduating from The Hill School, Owen J. Roberts High School, Pottsgrove High School, Pottstown High School or St. Pius X High School, PA.
Financial data: Year ended 12/31/2004.
Assets, $1,906,872 (M); Expenditures, $54,764; Total giving, $18,555.
Type of support: Scholarships—to individuals; Support to graduates or students of specific schools.
Application information: Application form required.
   Deadline(s): May 1
   Applicants should submit the following:
      1) Essay
EIN: 232568998

3254

Frank C. Poucher and Lillian S. Poucher Memorial Fund

506 Poplar Ave.
Linwood, NJ 08221-2211
Application address: c/o Atlantic County Vocational Technical School, Attn.: William J. Flynn, 5080 Atlantic Ave., Mays Landing, NJ 08330-2098

Foundation type: Independent foundation
Limitations: Scholarships to financially needy students of the Atlantic County Vocational and/or Atlantic City public school systems, NJ.
Financial data: Year ended 12/31/2004.
Assets, $1,206,339 (M); Expenditures, $28,714; Total giving, $21,000; Grants to individuals, 7 grants totaling $21,000.
Type of support: Support to graduates or students of specific schools; Technical education support; Undergraduate support.
Application information: Applications accepted. Application form required.

Additional information: Applications accepted throughout the year.
EIN: 223579083

3255

The Poujol Foundation

8733 Daffodil St.
Houston, TX 77063 (713) 977-0610
Contact: Micheal A. Poujol, Pres.

Foundation type: Independent foundation
Limitations: Scholarships to children of employees of Anderson Wire Works, Inc., for higher education.
Financial data: Year ended 06/30/2003.
Assets, $30,631 (M); Expenditures, $120,909; Total giving, $120,909; Grants to individuals, 15 grants totaling $83,909 (high: $7,500, low: $632).
Type of support: Employee-related scholarships.
Application information:
   Applicants should submit the following:
      1) Financial information
      2) Letter(s) of recommendation
   Additional information: Contact foundation for current application deadline/guidelines. Assistance for higher education is limited to $5,000 per recipient per year, with 80% of scholarships going to children of employees of Anderson Wire Works, Inc. The remaining 20% will be available to the general public.
EIN: 311562146

3256

Howard A. Power Scholarship Fund

c/o PNC Advisors
620 Liberty Ave., P2-PTPP-10-2
Pittsburgh, PA 15222-2705
Application address: c/o Univ. of Pittsburgh, Attn: School of Medicine, Scaife Hall, Terrace St., Pittsburgh, PA 15261

Foundation type: Independent foundation
Limitations: Scholarships to students attending the University of Pittsburgh School of Medicine.
Publications: Application guidelines.
Financial data: Year ended 12/31/2004.
Assets, $746,022 (M); Expenditures, $42,649; Total giving, $35,000; Grants to individuals, 4 grants totaling $35,000.
Fields of interest: Medical school/education.
Type of support: Support to graduates or students of specific schools; Graduate support.
Application information: Application form required.
   Applicants should submit the following:
      1) Financial information
   Additional information: Applications accepted throughout the year.
EIN: 256234582

3257

Greater Poweshiek Community Foundation

833 4th Ave.
P.O. Box 538
Grinnell, IA 50112
Contact: Tom Marshall, Pres.

Foundation type: Community foundation
Limitations: Scholarships to residents of Poweshiek County, IA, for post-secondary education.
Financial data: Year ended 12/31/2004.
Assets, $1,600,225 (M); Expenditures, $48,104; Total giving, $34,250; Grants to individuals, 102 grants totaling $32,650 (high: $4,000, low: $175).

Type of support: Undergraduate support.
Application information: Application form required.
  Deadline(s): Contact foundation for current
    application deadline
EIN: 421298055

3258
Guy and Nyda Prater Scholarship Fund
c/o Bank of America, N.A.
P.O. Box 34345
Seattle, WA   98124-1345

Foundation type: Independent foundation
Limitations: Scholarships to graduates of Dayton
High School, Dayton, WA for higher education.
Financial data: Year ended 06/30/2005.
Assets, $318,936 (M); Expenditures, $16,402;
Total giving, $12,500; Grants to individuals, 9
grants totaling $12,500.
Type of support: Scholarships—to individuals;
Support to graduates or students of specific
schools.
Application information: Application form required.
  Deadline(s): Apr. 30
  Additional information: Contact fund for current
    application guidelines. Completion of formal
    application including transcript of all grades
    from grade nine and higher, and completion of
    the confidential rating sheet (supplied by the
    selection committee) from two teachers and
    two adults who are not relatives.
EIN: 916305003

3259
Precision Rubber Products Foundation, Inc.
104 Hartmann Dr.
Lebanon, TN   37087-8401

Foundation type: Company-sponsored foundation
Limitations: Scholarships to high school seniors
who are children and grandchildren of employees of
Parker Seals at Lebanon and Livingston,
Tennessee.
Financial data: Year ended 06/30/2005.
Assets, $1,313,616 (M); Expenditures, $56,073;
Total giving, $53,750; Grants to individuals, 7
grants totaling $18,000 (high: $3,000, low:
$2,000).
Type of support: Employee-related scholarships.
Application information:
  Deadline(s): Nov. 30
  Applicants should submit the following:
    1) Transcripts
  Additional information: Applications are available
    at the Human Resources Office of Parker
    Seals.
EIN: 310503347

3260
Preferred Mutual Insurance Company Foundation
c/o Preferred Mutual Insurance Co.
1 Preferred Way
New Berlin, NY   13411   (607) 847-6161
Contact: John G. Frisch, Advisory Comm. Member
E-mail: info@pminsco.com

Foundation type: Company-sponsored foundation
Limitations: Scholarships to students in Chenango,
Delaware, and Otsego counties, NY.
Financial data: Year ended 12/31/2004.
Assets, $463,368 (M); Expenditures, $26,864;

Total giving, $26,500; Grants to individuals, 9
grants totaling $9,500 (high: $2,000, low: $500).
Type of support: Scholarships—to individuals.
Application information: Application form required.
  Deadline(s): May 1
  Additional information: Interviews required.
EIN: 226423721

3261
Prescott Christian School Scholarship Foundation
2126 W. Charteroak Dr.
Prescott, AZ   86305-7711
Contact: William Warren, Pres.

Foundation type: Independent foundation
Limitations: Scholarships to graduating seniors of
Christian Academy of Prescott and Prescott
Christian High School, AZ.
Financial data: Year ended 12/31/2004.
Assets, $226,620 (M); Expenditures, $188,693;
Total giving, $180,471; Grants to individuals, 138
grants totaling $180,471 (high: $2,888, low:
$323).
Type of support: Support to graduates or students
of specific schools; Undergraduate support.
Application information: Application form required.
  Deadline(s): Contact foundation for current
    application deadline
  Additional information: Applications available at
    local schools.
EIN: 860947958

3262
William Pressman Foundation
c/o M&T Bank
21 E. Market St.
York, PA   17401-1205
Application address: c/o M&T Trust Co., 110 S.
Paca St., Baltimore, MD 21201

Foundation type: Independent foundation
Limitations: Scholarships to graduates of
Wicomico High School, Wicomico Junior High, and
Parkside High School, all in MD, to participate in
their school's marching and concert band.
Financial data: Year ended 06/30/2005.
Assets, $425,864 (M); Expenditures, $23,960;
Total giving, $20,880; Grants to individuals, 4
grants totaling $18,270.
Fields of interest: Music.
Type of support: Undergraduate support.
Application information: Contact foundation for
current application deadline/guidelines. Applicant
must have participated in band throughout high
school. The scholarship is available for the
attendance of a college of his or her choice with a
major chosen by the recipient, provided the
recipient continues in both marching and concert
bands in college.
EIN: 521885294

3263
Joe Prest Educational Trust Fund
P.O. Box 819
300 Sinclair Bldg.
Steubenville, OH   43952   (740) 282-5353
Contact: Michael J. Calabria, Tr.

Foundation type: Independent foundation
Limitations: Scholarships to individuals from the
Steubenville, OH, area for undergraduate education
at U.S. universities and colleges.

Financial data: Year ended 12/31/2004.
Assets, $98,814 (M); Expenditures, $12,401;
Total giving, $12,215; Grants to individuals, 12
grants totaling $12,000.
Type of support: Undergraduate support.
Application information:
  Deadline(s): None
  Additional information: Applicants must
    demonstrate participation in athletics,
    extracurricular activities, and, when
    appropriate, financial need. Minimum 2.75
    GPA.
EIN: 341742248

3264
The Presto Foundation
1011 Centre Rd.
Wilmington, DE   19805
Contact: Norma Jaenke
Application address: 3925 N. Hastings Way, Eau
Claire, WI 54703, tel.: (715) 839-2119

Foundation type: Company-sponsored foundation
Limitations: Scholarships to children of employees
of National Presto Industries, Inc., with preference
given to those in northwestern WI, especially Eau
Claire and Chippewa counties.
Financial data: Year ended 05/31/2005.
Assets, $15,420,915 (M); Expenditures,
$743,024; Total giving, $682,458; Grants to
individuals, 31 grants totaling $310,208 (high:
$11,000, low: $522).
Type of support: Employee-related scholarships.
Application information:
  Initial approach: Letter including proposed
    budget.
  Deadline(s): None
  Additional information: Contact foundation for
    current application guidelines.
EIN: 396045769

3265
Elmer O. & Ida Preston Educational Trust
c/o Monica Morgan
801 Grand Ave., Ste. 3700
Des Moines, IA   50309-2727   (515) 243-4191

Foundation type: Independent foundation
Limitations: Scholarships and student loans
limited to worthy and financially needy young
Protestants residing in IA to pursue collegiate or
professional studies in IA in preparation for a career
in Christian service.
Publications: Annual report.
Financial data: Year ended 12/31/2004.
Assets, $2,512,040 (M); Expenditures,
$102,550; Total giving, $50,000; Grants to
individuals, 34 grants totaling $50,000.
Fields of interest: Protestant agencies & churches.
Type of support: Scholarships—to individuals;
Student loans—to individuals.
Application information: Application form required.
  Initial approach: Letter or telephone.
  Deadline(s): June 30
  Additional information: Interviews required.
    Applicants are required to furnish academic
    background and qualifications and
    demonstrate financial need. Awards are given
    in the form of half grant and half loan.
EIN: 426053621

3266

A. A. Previti Family Charitable Foundation, Inc.

23 Vreeland Rd., Ste. 120
Florham Park, NJ 07932
Contact: Lucille P. Lupton, V.P.
Application address: 908 Shore Rd., Somers Point, NJ 08244, tel.: (609) 927-2759

Foundation type: Operating foundation
Limitations: Scholarships to graduates of Florham Park, NJ, area high schools for undergraduate education.
Financial data: Year ended 12/31/2002. Assets, $550,519 (M); Expenditures, $36,401; Total giving, $32,450; Grants to individuals, 15 grants totaling $18,050 (high: $2,000, low: $100).
Type of support: Support to graduates or students of specific schools.
Application information:
  Initial approach: Applications by letter including brief outline of academic qualifications.
  Deadline(s): None
  Additional information: Contact guidance office for further application information.
EIN: 223633945

3267

Price Chopper's Golub Foundation

(formerly Golub Foundation)
501 Duanesburg Rd.
Schenectady, NY 12306 (518) 356-9450
Scholarship application address: c/o Price Chopper Scholarship Office, P.O. Box 1074, Schenectady, NY 12301
FAX: (518) 374-4259; Application address: P.O. Box 1074, Schenectady, NY 12301; Additional tel.: (877) 877-0870; URL: http://www.pricechopper.com/GolubFoundation/GolubFoundation_S.las?-token.S=0C2T9R7F62211b8P73922412RLWN6L5J64CA5D|24634|0507251403||||

Foundation type: Company-sponsored foundation
Limitations: Scholarships to residents of areas served by Price Chopper Supermarkets, including upstate NH, NY, MA, PA, VT, and northwestern CT, who are entering two- or four-year colleges or graduate schools in NY, MA, PA, VT, NH, or CT. See program description for further limitations.
Publications: Informational brochure (including application guidelines).
Financial data: Year ended 03/31/2005. Assets, $70,608 (M); Expenditures, $776,824; Total giving, $739,345; Grants to individuals, 54 grants totaling $59,000 (high: $3,000, low: $500).
Fields of interest: Education, research; Health care; Business/industry; Computer science; Minorities; Asians/Pacific Islanders; African Americans/Blacks; Hispanics/Latinos; Native Americans/American Indians.
Type of support: Employee-related scholarships; Graduate support; Undergraduate support.
Application information: Applications accepted. Application form required.
  Initial approach: Letter.
  Deadline(s): Mar. 15
  Applicants should submit the following:
    1) Transcripts
    2) SAT
    3) Letter(s) of recommendation
  Additional information: To qualify for the scholarships applicants must live in the Price Chopper marketing area. Application must include an original essay of less than 1,000 words on why the Golub Foundation should award the scholarship; Graduate scholarship applicants must also supply GRE and/or LSAT or MCAT test scores, if applicable; Finalists notified by Apr. 10; Recipients notified by May 22. Interviews required; See Web site for further application and program information.
Program description:
  Golub Scholarship Program: The foundation administers the following scholarship programs:
  · The Founders' Scholarships: $8,000 each to be awarded over four years to two graduating high school seniors, entering the first year of college, who have demonstrated outstanding leadership and scholastic abilities
  · The Educators' Scholarship: $8,000 to be awarded over four years to a graduating high school senior, entering the first year of college, who has demonstrated scholastic ability and has chosen to enter into the field of education
  · The Tillie Golub-Schwartz Memorial Scholarship for Minorities: $8,000 to be awarded over four years to a graduating high school senior, entering the first year of college, who has shown a commitment to humanity through demonstrated activities in school, community, or religious organizations. Scholastic ability will also be considered. Eligible minorities are: Native Americans or Alaskan Natives, Asians or Pacific Islanders, African Americans, Puerto Ricans, Mexican Americans, and other Latinos
  · The Charles Pierce Memorial Scholarship: $8,000 to be awarded over four years to a graduating high school senior, entering the first year of college, who has demonstrated scholastic ability. Eligible applicants are: A. active Price Chopper associates B. children of active, retired, and deceased Price Chopper associates C. children of active, retired, and deceased members of the Grocery Manufacturers' Representatives
  · The Two Year Scholarship: $2,000 to be awarded over two years to a graduating high school senior, entering the freshman year of a degree-granting community college or junior college. The applicant must have demonstrated either outstanding leadership, entrepreneurial ability, or a commitment to humanity, as well as scholastic ability
  · The Graduate or Professional School Scholarship: $4,000 to be awarded over two years to a graduating college senior or a college graduate who has demonstrated scholastic ability and plans to attend graduate school as a fully-matriculated first-year student
  · The Two Year Health Care Scholarship: $2,000 to be awarded over two years to a graduating high school senior, entering the freshman year of a degree-granting community college or junior college. The applicant must have demonstrated scholastic ability and have chosen to enter the health care field
  · The Computer Studies Scholarship: $8,000 to be awarded over 4 years to a graduating high school senior, entering the freshman year of a degree-granting college or university. Applicants must have demonstrated scholastic ability and have chosen to enter the Computer Science, Computer Information Systems, Electronic Arts, or Graphic Design fields
  · The Junior College Transfer Scholarship: $4,000 to be awarded over 2 years to a graduating community/junior college or a community/junior college graduate who is entering the sophomore year of a degree-granting community college. Applicants must have chosen to enter the Tourism, Hospitality, or Culinary fields.
EIN: 222341421

3268

Herschel C. Price Educational Foundation

P.O. Box 412
Huntington, WV 25708-0412 (304) 529-3852
Contact: Jonna L. Hughes, Dir.

Foundation type: Independent foundation
Limitations: Scholarships to students residing in WV and/or attending WV colleges and universities.
Financial data: Year ended 04/30/2005. Assets, $5,027,910 (M); Expenditures, $327,033; Total giving, $282,900; Grants to individuals, 186 grants totaling $272,900 (high: $5,000, low: $400).
Type of support: Graduate support; Undergraduate support.
Application information: Application form required.
  Initial approach: Letter stating current address and college attending.
  Deadline(s): Apr. 1 for Fall semester and Oct. 1 for Spring semester
  Additional information: Submit application from Jan. to Mar., or from Aug. to Sept.; Interviews required.
Program description:
  Scholarship Program: Scholarships are given directly to deserving candidates who demonstrate both scholastic achievement and financial need, and who meet the residency qualifications. WV undergraduate residents who attend an accredited educational institution in the state of WV are shown preference. However, graduate students, residents of another state who attend a WV college, and WV residents who choose an out-of-state school are also eligible for consideration. U.S. citizenship is required. Recipients are notified of final action regarding their application by May 15 and Nov. 15 respectively. Grants may range anywhere from $250 to a maximum of $2,500 per semester. Each applicant and recipient may reapply each subsequent semester by updating his or her file for any change in financial status and submitting continuously current transcripts, other required data, and updated additional pertinent information. The trustees of the foundation feel that it is an improper expenditure of foundation funds to answer all requests and inquiries from students residing in areas outside the foundation's main focus of attention, and/or those requests and inquiries from students that obviously do not fit the basic guidelines and policies of the foundation.
EIN: 556076719

3269

Price Foundation, Inc.

P.O. Box 672
Upland, CA 91785

Foundation type: Independent foundation
Limitations: Interest-free student loans to residents of the west end of San Bernardino County, CA, only.
Financial data: Year ended 12/31/2004. Assets, $1,287,479 (M); Expenditures, $96,709; Total giving, $80,060; Loans to individuals, 6 loans totaling $22,360.
Fields of interest: Vocational education.
Type of support: Student loans—to individuals.

Application information: Applications accepted. Application form required.
Initial approach: Letter.
Applicants should submit the following:
1) GPA
Additional information: Application must also include personal statement, and three letters of reference; Interviews required.
EIN: 956069011

3270
Joseph R. and Florence A. Price Scholarship Fund
c/o Hyde Park School
655 Metropolitan Ave.
Hyde Park, MA   02136
Contact: Linda Cabral

Foundation type: Independent foundation
Limitations: Scholarships only to seniors of Hyde Park High School, MA.
Financial data: Year ended 12/31/2004. Assets, $389,821 (M); Expenditures, $20,172; Total giving, $14,080.
Type of support: Support to graduates or students of specific schools; Undergraduate support.
Application information: Applications accepted. Application form required.
Deadline(s): Apr. 15
Applicants should submit the following:
1) Financial information
2) Letter(s) of recommendation
EIN: 046031925

3271
Albert M. Price Trust
c/o Unizan Bank, N.A.
P.O. Box 393
Charleston, WV   25392
Application address: c/o Unizan Bank, N.A., Attn: Linda Richards, P.O. Box 1508, Parkersburg, WV 26101

Foundation type: Independent foundation
Limitations: Scholarships primarily to Boone County, WV, residents for higher education. The trust will also consider other WV residents and U.S. residents.
Financial data: Year ended 12/31/2004. Assets, $1,247,685 (M); Expenditures, $104,815; Total giving, $53,000; Grants to individuals, 80 grants totaling $53,000.
Type of support: Scholarships—to individuals.
Application information: Application form required.
Deadline(s): Mar. 1
Additional information: Applications available Dec. to Feb.; Completion of formal application required, including GPA, ACT and/or SAT scores, and recommendations from instructors.
Program description:
Jackson Newcomb Scholarship: The trust gives to Boone County, WV, residents as a first priority, WV residents outside of Boone County as a second priority, and U.S. residents outside of WV only as a last priority. In all cases, the student may attend any participating educational institution. Scholarships are renewable, provided the recipient maintains at least a 2.0 GPA. If a recipient changes schools second semester, the scholarship is canceled. Scholarships are granted based on prior academic performance, performance on aptitude tests, recommendations, and financial need.
EIN: 556081789

3272
The Pride Foundation
1122 E. Pike St., No. 1001
Seattle, WA   98122-3934   (206) 323-3318
Contact: Audrey Haberman, Exec. Dir.
FAX: (206) 323-1017;
E-mail: info@pridefoundation.org; Application address: 2150 N. 107th St., Ste. 205, Seattle, WA 98133; Additional tel.: (800) 735-7287; E-mail: scholarhips@pridefoundation.org; URL: http://www.pridefoundation.org

Foundation type: Public charity
Limitations: Scholarships to lesbian, gay, bisexual or transgender students, family members, or allies residing in AK, ID, MT, OR, and WA.
Publications: Application guidelines; Financial statement; Grants list; Newsletter.
Financial data: Year ended 03/31/2004. Assets, $5,389,154 (M); Expenditures, $1,657,541; Total giving, $725,848; Grants to individuals, 69 grants totaling $95,978 (high: $4,828, low: $500).
Type of support: Scholarships—to individuals.
Application information: Applications accepted. Application form required. Application form available on the grantmaker's Web site.
Copies of proposal: 7
Deadline(s): Jan. 20
Applicants should submit the following:
1) Transcripts
2) Letter(s) of recommendation
Additional information: See web site for complete program listing and application information.
EIN: 911325007

3273
Nathan D. Prince Trust No. 2
c/o Bank of America, N.A.
777 Main St., CT2-102-22-02
Hartford, CT   06115
Application address: c/o David Cressy, Killingly High School, 190 Main St., Danielson, CT 06239-2823

Foundation type: Independent foundation
Limitations: Scholarships to financially needy graduates of Killingly High School, Danielson, CT.
Financial data: Year ended 09/30/2004. Assets, $781,058 (M); Expenditures, $42,258; Total giving, $33,500; Grants to individuals, 49 grants totaling $33,500 (high: $1,100, low: $500).
Type of support: Support to graduates or students of specific schools; Undergraduate support.
Application information:
Deadline(s): None
EIN: 066031329

3274
Princeton Area Community Foundation, Inc.
(formerly The Princeton Area Foundation, Inc.)
15 Princess Rd.
Lawrenceville, NJ   08648   (609) 219-1800
Contact: Nancy W. Kieling, Pres. and Exec. Dir.
FAX: (609) 219-1850; E-mail: info@pacf.org;
URL: http://www.pacf.org

Foundation type: Community foundation
Limitations: Scholarships to residents of NJ for higher education.
Publications: Application guidelines; Annual report; Grants list; Informational brochure; Newsletter.
Financial data: Year ended 12/31/2004. Assets, $34,355,979 (M); Expenditures, $6,988,120; Total giving, $6,407,110; Grants to

individuals, 25 grants totaling $40,750 (high: $5,000, low: $500).
Fields of interest: Higher education; College; University; Teacher school/education; Health sciences school/education.
Type of support: Scholarships—to individuals.
Application information: Applications accepted. Application form required. Application form available on the grantmaker's Web site.
Deadline(s): June 10 for the Glazier Scholarship; May 2nd for the Clark Memorial, Hensor Teaching, Maas Allied Health Professions, and Wislar Memorial Scholarships
Applicants should submit the following:
1) Transcripts
2) SAR
3) Letter(s) of recommendation
4) Financial information
5) FAFSA
6) Essay
Program descriptions:
Frank Clark Memorial Scholarship: Awards $800 annually to a student beginning his or her freshman year of college. The grant is for one year only and is not renewable. Awardee must be a graduating resident of Mercer County planning to enter a four-year college or university. Awards are made on the basis of achievement, character, motivation, and financial need. It is very important that the student has demonstrated a strong commitment to community service.
Sandra M. Glazier Scholarship Fund: One scholarship totaling up to $20,000 is awarded annually to a graduating senior from high school in Ocean or Monmouth County, NJ. The award will be paid out in amounts of $5,000 per year for up to four years. The award is not renewable or transferable. A "C+" (2.5 g.p.a.) average or better must be achieved throughout the term of the scholarship. The student must be enrolled full-time at an accredited college, university or vocational school.
A. Myrtle Hensor Teaching Scholarship: Awards a $1,000 scholarship to any female graduating from Princeton High School who is planning to pursue a career in education. One award will be available annually to a student beginning her freshman year of college and is not renewable.
Louise Maas Allied Health Professions Scholarship: Awards a $1,000 scholarship to any female graduating from Princeton High School of good character and warm personality with a desire to pursue a career in the allied health professions. One award will be available annually to a student beginning her freshman year of college, and it is not renewable.
Mary Elliot Wislar Memorial Scholarship: Awards a $5,000 scholarship to a graduating resident of Mercer County who is going on to post-secondary education. The grant is for one year only and is not renewable.
EIN: 521746234

3275
Princeton High School Class of 1926 Scholarship Fund
c/o First Community Bank, Inc.
P.O. Box 5939
Princeton, WV   24740   (304) 487-9000
Contact: Ronda Lilly, Trust Off., First Community Bank, Inc.

Foundation type: Independent foundation
Limitations: Scholarships to students of Princeton Senior High School, WV.
Financial data: Year ended 12/31/2004. Assets, $103,527 (M); Expenditures, $12,070;

Total giving, $11,500; Grants to individuals, 11 grants totaling $11,500.
Type of support: Support to graduates or students of specific schools; Undergraduate support.
Application information: Application form required.
Deadline(s): None
Additional information: Awards restricted to $6,000 over four years per recipient. Recipients are chosen by Princeton Senior High School staff and the foundation's trustees.
EIN: 310889436

3276
C. Pringle Charitable Foundation
(formerly Charles G. Pringle Foundation)
c/o Bank of America, N.A.
P.O. Box 6767
Providence, RI 02940-6767
Contact: Patricia F. Karl, Tr.
Application address: 11 Lawrence St., 6th Fl., Lawrence, MA 01840-1423

Foundation type: Independent foundation
Limitations: Scholarships and exam fees paid for residents of Lawrence, MA.
Financial data: Year ended 10/31/2004. Assets, $3,027,724 (M); Expenditures, $190,694; Total giving, $152,838.
Type of support: Scholarships—to individuals.
Application information: Applications by letter outlining financial need accepted throughout the year.
EIN: 046020426

3277
Beatrice Prior Memorial Scholarship Trust
146 E. Center St.
Marion, OH 43302

Foundation type: Independent foundation
Limitations: Scholarships by nomination only to graduates of Marion Harding High School, OH.
Financial data: Year ended 12/31/2004. Assets, $322,366 (M); Expenditures, $16,821; Total giving, $12,746; Grants to individuals, 7 grants totaling $12,746.
Type of support: Support to graduates or students of specific schools; Awards/grants by nomination only; Undergraduate support.
Application information: Applications not accepted.
EIN: 316637737

3278
Pritchard Educational Fund
c/o Cherokee State Bank
212 W. Willow St.
Cherokee, IA 51012-1857
FAX: (712) 225-4185; E-mail: chstbk@ncn.net

Foundation type: Independent foundation
Limitations: Educational loans to students of the Cherokee Community School District, IA, for undergraduate or graduate education.
Publications: Annual report.
Financial data: Year ended 12/31/2004. Assets, $6,908,471 (M); Expenditures, $60,498; Total giving, $246,465; Loans to individuals, 122 loans totaling $246,465.
Type of support: Student loans—to individuals; Support to graduates or students of specific schools; Graduate support; Undergraduate support.

Application information: Application form required.
Deadline(s): July 15
Additional information: Interviews required for first-year applicants.
EIN: 426051872

3279
Scott R. Pritchett Trust
c/o Wells Fargo Bank, N.A., Trust Tax Dept.
P.O. Box 63954
San Francisco, CA 94163
Application address: c/o Los Molinos Unified School District, Attn: A.R. Tolman, District Supt., P.O. Box 88, Los Molinos, CA 96055, tel.: (530) 384-2107

Foundation type: Independent foundation
Limitations: Scholarships to residents of Vina, CA.
Financial data: Year ended 12/31/2004. Assets, $841,829 (M); Expenditures, $39,062; Total giving, $28,525; Grants to individuals, 22 grants totaling $28,525.
Type of support: Undergraduate support.
Application information: Application form required.
Deadline(s): Apr. 15
Additional information: Applications available at Los Molinos High School.
Program description:
S.R. Pritchett Scholarship: The scholarship may be used upon graduation from high school by students from the Vina area to enable them to pursue their studies, or develop their talents in schools, colleges or universities anywhere in the world. The recipient shall not be determined solely by academic standing but should have at least average grades.
EIN: 946060240

3280
Private Colleges and Universities Foundation
2 Lan Dr., Ste. 100
Westford, MA 01886
Contact: Paul D. Adams

Foundation type: Operating foundation
Limitations: Scholarships to high school seniors of color involved in community service activities to pursue higher education at private colleges and universities.
Financial data: Year ended 12/31/2002. Assets, $62,565 (M); Expenditures, $30,308; Total giving, $30,000; Grants to individuals, totaling $30,000.
Fields of interest: Community development, volunteer services; Minorities.
Type of support: Scholarships—to individuals.
Application information: Application form required.
Deadline(s): Nov. 1.
Additional information: Application should include class rank, transcripts, equivalency diploma (if applicable), recommendations from teachers, employers, or other individuals familiar with your recent activities, and personal statement.
EIN: 061280421

3281
Professional Horsemen's Scholarship Fund, Inc.
202 Old Sleepy Hollow Rd.
Pleasantville, NY 10570-3806 (914) 769-1493
Contact: Ann Grenci, Pres.
Application address: 20 Via del Corso, Palm Beach Gardens, FL 33418, tel.: (407) 694-6893

Foundation type: Operating foundation
Limitations: Scholarships to members of the Professional Horsemen's Association for higher education.
Financial data: Year ended 12/31/2003. Assets, $138,702 (M); Expenditures, $10,500; Total giving, $10,500; Grants to individuals, 10 grants totaling $10,500 (high: $1,500, low: $1,000).
Type of support: Scholarships—to individuals.
Application information: Application form required.
Initial approach: Letter or telephone.
Deadline(s): July 1
Additional information: Completion of formal application required, including letter outlining financial need and proof of professional membership in Professional Horsemen's Association.
EIN: 066086137

3282
Progressive Business Publications Foundation
370 Technology Dr.
Malvern, PA 19355-0719
Contact: Len Fesi

Foundation type: Company-sponsored foundation
Limitations: Scholarships to employees of Progressive Business Publications, Malvern, PA.
Financial data: Year ended 12/31/2004. Assets, $0 (M); Expenditures, $24,113; Total giving, $24,113; Grants to individuals, 10 grants totaling $24,113 (high: $2,500, low: $1,613).
Type of support: Employee-related scholarships.
EIN: 256665358

3283
Prohaska Scholarship Foundation
c/o Selection Comm.
134 S. 8th St.
Medford, WI 54451

Foundation type: Independent foundation
Limitations: Scholarships to graduating seniors of Medford Senior High School, WI.
Financial data: Year ended 12/31/2002. Assets, $362,938 (M); Expenditures, $30,848; Total giving, $28,750; Grants to individuals, 15 grants totaling $28,750 (high: $2,500, low: $1,250).
Type of support: Scholarships—to individuals; Support to graduates or students of specific schools.
Application information: Contact foundation for current application deadline/guidelines; Application by letter, including personal essay.
EIN: 391712984

3284
Project Reach Youth, Inc.
199 14th St.
Brooklyn, NY 11215 (718) 768-0778
Contact: Robert T. Madison, Exec. Dir.
URL: http://www.pry.org/

Foundation type: Public charity
Limitations: Scholarships to students from the Park Slope, Sunset Park, Red Hook, Fort Greene, Prospect Heights, and Flatbush areas of Brooklyn, NY, for college expenses.
Financial data: Year ended 06/30/2004. Assets, $887,518 (M); Expenditures, $4,335,623; Total giving, $1,945; Grants to individuals, totaling $1,945.
Fields of interest: Children, services; Economically disadvantaged.
Type of support: Scholarships—to individuals.
Application information: Contact foundation for current application deadline/guidelines.
EIN: 112331112

3285
Promotional Products Education Foundation

3125 Skyway Cir. N.
Irving, TX   75038-3526   (972) 258-3097
Contact: Sara Keller, Mgr.
FAX: (972) 258-3092; E-mail: ppef@ppa.org; URL: http://www.ppa.org/ppef

Foundation type: Public charity
Limitations: Scholarships to dependents of and/or employees in the promotional products industry.
Publications: Application guidelines; Financial statement.
Financial data: Year ended 12/31/2004. Assets, $1,476,075 (M); Expenditures, $175,251; Total giving, $36,000; Grants to individuals, 33 grants totaling $36,000 (high: $2,500, low: $1,000).
Type of support: Undergraduate support.
Application information: Applications accepted. Application form required. Application form available on the grantmaker's Web site.
  Initial approach: Web site or telephone.
  Copies of proposal: 1
  Deadline(s): Mar. 15
  Applicants should submit the following:
    1) Transcripts
    2) SAT
    3) Resume
    4) ACT
    5) Letter(s) of recommendation
    6) GPA
    7) Essay
  Additional information: See Web site for additional application information.
Program descriptions:
  4-Year Scholarships: Awards $1000 each year. The scholarships are renewable for the full four years of college, provided the student demonstrates satisfactory progress toward the degree and meets the required criteria for scholarship renewal. Scholarships will be awarded on the basis of the student's GPA, a letter from the candidate, financial need and ACT/SAT scores, as well as other pertinent information concerning the student, submitted to the Foundation's Scholarship Committee. Students eligible for scholarships during the forthcoming academic year must be entering a four-year college or university as a freshman and must be employed in or dependents of employees in the promotional products industry.
  Chairman's Scholarship: Awards $2,500 each year to students entering their junior years of college, and will be renewable for their senior years of college. To be eligible, a student must be entering his or her junior year in college, pursuing a bachelor's degree in an academic field related to promotional products, and express a clear intent to enter the field of promotional products as a career. The scholarships will be awarded on the basis of

the student's college GPA, a student position paper, letter of recommendation, and extra curricular activities and/or work experience.
EIN: 751714221

3286
John and Elizabeth Pryde Scholarship Fund

c/o Bank of America, N.A.
10 Light St.
Baltimore, MD   21202
Application addresses: c/o Principal, Suitland Senior High School, 5200 Silver Hill Rd., Forestville, MD 20747, c/o Principal, Surrattsville Senior High School, 6101 Garden Dr., Clinton, MD 20735

Foundation type: Independent foundation
Limitations: Scholarships to graduates of Sutland High School, in Clinton, MD, and Surrattsville Senior High School, in Forestville, MD, for the study of education.
Financial data: Year ended 12/31/2002. Assets, $181,802 (M); Expenditures, $12,388; Total giving, $9,500; Grants to individuals, 11 grants totaling $9,500 (high: $1,000, low: $500).
Fields of interest: Teacher school/education.
Type of support: Scholarships—to individuals; Support to graduates or students of specific schools.
Application information: Application form required.
  Deadline(s): Apr. 1
EIN: 526143655

3287
Mark R. Pryor Foundation, Inc.

P.O. Box 889
Winona, MN   55987-0889   (507) 454-4124
Contact: Barbara J. Pryor, Pres.

Foundation type: Independent foundation
Limitations: Scholarships to students who are residents of Winona, MN.
Financial data: Year ended 12/31/2004. Assets, $290,317 (M); Expenditures, $15,157; Total giving, $14,325; Grants to individuals, 10 grants totaling $14,325.
Type of support: Scholarships—to individuals.
Application information: Contact foundation for current application deadline; Completion of formal application required, including a letter of recommendation from an educator or other community leader.
EIN: 411637603

3288
Public Interest Law Foundation at Columbia

(formerly Columbia Foundation for Public Interest Law, also known as PILF)
435 W. 116 St., Box C-26
New York, NY   10027-7201   (212) 854-5917
Contact: Steve Krause, V.P., Comm. Grants
FAX: (212) 854-8873;
E-mail: pilf@law.columbia.edu; URL: http://www.columbiaPILF.org

Foundation type: Public charity
Limitations: Fellowships to provide supplementary support for Columbia Law School, NY, students engaged in public interest law summer internships.
Publications: Newsletter.
Financial data: Year ended 01/31/2004. Assets, $13,734 (M); Expenditures, $94,312;

Total giving, $90,545; Grants to individuals, totaling $45,545.
Fields of interest: Legal services, public interest law.
Type of support: Fellowships; Internship funds; Graduate support.
Application information: Applications accepted. Application form required.
  Initial approach: Telephone or e-mail.
  Copies of proposal: 15
  Deadline(s): Dec. 8
  Applicants should submit the following:
    1) Budget Information
    2) Letter(s) of recommendation
  Additional information: Proposals must be a maximum of ten double-spaced typed pages. Application must also include a project description and timetable.
Program description:
  Fellowship Funds: Stipends to Columbia Law School students engaging in public interest legal work over the summer. These grants allow students to accept internships at governmental agencies and non-profit organizations, which typically do not have the resources to pay students for their summer work.
EIN: 133007632

3289
Puckett Foundation

c/o Fairfield National Bank, Advisory Comm.
P.O. Box 429
Fairfield, IL   62837-0429   (618) 842-2107

Foundation type: Independent foundation
Limitations: Scholarships to graduating seniors at Fairfield Community High School, IL, who have a minimum ACT score of 19, a 4.0 GPA, and a class rank in the upper 25 percent of their classes.
Publications: Application guidelines.
Financial data: Year ended 12/31/2004. Assets, $1,674,644 (M); Expenditures, $77,319; Total giving, $68,697; Grants to individuals, 6 grants totaling $17,000.
Type of support: Support to graduates or students of specific schools; Undergraduate support.
Application information:
  Initial approach: Letter or telephone.
  Deadline(s): Mar. 1
  Additional information: Scholarships of $2,000 per year are awarded for up to four years based on scholarship, ability, industry and integrity. The scholarship will be terminated if the recipient does not maintain a passing average. In case the student must discontinue schooling, for unavoidable reasons, during the four-year period, the scholarship may be reinstated at the discretion of the foundation.
EIN: 136115138

3290
Leta Potter Puckett Memorial Fund

c/o Wells Fargo Bank, N.A.
P.O. Box 63954
San Francisco, CA   94163
Application addresses: c/o Betty Barnett, Guidance Dean, Roosevelt High School, Fresno, CA 93727, tel.: (559) 431-3777 (science and pre-med scholarship), or c/o Richard Brown, Pastor, Belmont Christian Church, 4974 N. Fresno, Ste. 325, Fresno, CA 93726-0387, tel.: (559) 222-6561 (Chapman Scholarship address)

Foundation type: Independent foundation

Limitations: Science and pre-med scholarships to graduates of Roosevelt High School in Fresno, CA. Chapman Scholarships for religious education to graduates of high schools in Fresno County, CA.
Financial data: Year ended 03/31/2003. Assets, $906,579 (M); Expenditures, $47,530; Total giving, $34,844; Grants to individuals, 5 grants totaling $34,844.
Fields of interest: Medical school/education; Theological school/education; Science.
Type of support: Support to graduates or students of specific schools; Undergraduate support.
Application information:
  Deadline(s): Jan. 1 for Chapman Scholarships, Spring for science and pre-med scholarships
  Additional information: Completion of formal application required, including a resume, statement of goals, name of college, financial information, and transcripts.
EIN: 956731500

3291

Pugh Foundation Scholarship Fund

(formerly Hazel & Ben Pugh Foundation Scholarship Fund)
c/o JPMorgan Chase Bank, N.A
P.O. Box 1308
Milwaukee, WI 53201-1308
Application address: c/o Rick Colbo, School Counselor, Mukwonago High School, W. School Rd., Mukwonago, WI 53149

Foundation type: Independent foundation
Limitations: Scholarships to graduating seniors of Mukwonago High School, WI, for undergraduate studies at any college or university.
Financial data: Year ended 09/30/2004. Assets, $316,117 (M); Expenditures, $16,585; Total giving, $13,112.
Type of support: Support to graduates or students of specific schools; Undergraduate support.
Application information: Application form required.
  Deadline(s): May 1
EIN: 396452749

3292

Pulaski County Community Foundation

105 E. Main St.
P.O. Box 407
Winamac, IN 46996-0407   (574) 946-0906
Contact: Wendy Rose, Exec. Dir.
FAX: (574) 946-0971; E-mail: pccf@pwrtc.com;
URL: http://pccf.pulaskionline.org

Foundation type: Community foundation
Limitations: Scholarships to individuals residing in the Pulaski County, IN, area for undergraduate education.
Financial data: Year ended 12/31/2004. Assets, $5,493,997 (M); Expenditures, $349,187; Total giving, $168,323; Grants to individuals, 61 grants totaling $101,598 (high: $9,730, low: $150, average grant: $150-$9,580).
Type of support: Undergraduate support.
Application information: Applications accepted. Application form required.
  Additional information: Contact foundation for current application deadlines/guidelines.
EIN: 352127564

3293

George M. Pullman Educational Foundation

39 S. LaSalle St., Ste. 718
Chicago, IL   60603-1621   (312) 422-0444
FAX: (312) 422-0448; URL: http://www.pullmanfoundation.org

Foundation type: Independent foundation
Limitations: Scholarships by nomination only to residents of Cook County, IL, and to children and grandchildren of graduates of Pullman Free School of Manual Training. Grants are for undergraduate or vocational-technical studies.
Publications: Informational brochure.
Financial data: Year ended 07/31/2005. Assets, $26,955,435 (M); Expenditures, $1,399,306; Total giving, $806,909.
Fields of interest: Vocational education.
Type of support: Awards/grants by nomination only; Technical education support; Undergraduate support.
Application information:
  Deadline(s): Jan. 5 for first-year students, May 1 for new upper class students, and June 1 for renewal students
  Additional information: Individual applications not accepted. All candidates must be nominated by their high schools; Completion of formal nomination required.
EIN: 362216171

3294

Pursuit of Excellence

1795 Hamilton Ave.
Palo Alto, CA 94303   (650) 322-9417
Contact: Marjorie Hopkins Smallwood, Pres.

Foundation type: Independent foundation
Limitations: Scholarships to financially needy high school seniors in Palo Alto and the Sequoia Union High School District, CA. Family income must be under $20,000.
Financial data: Year ended 09/30/2004. Assets, $598,726 (M); Expenditures, $89,965; Total giving, $83,842; Grants to individuals, totaling $83,842.
Type of support: Support to graduates or students of specific schools; Undergraduate support.
Application information: Application form required.
  Deadline(s): Mar. 1
  Additional information: Initial approach by letter requesting application, including a SASE.
EIN: 770054289

3295

The Putnam County Community Foundation

2 S. Jackson St.
P.O. Box 514
Greencastle, IN 46135-0514   (765) 653-4978
Contact: M. Elaine Peck, Exec. Dir.; For grant applications: Nelda Shoemaker, Asst. to Exec. Dir.
FAX: (765) 653-6385;
E-mail: info@pcfoundation.org; Additional E-mail: epeck@pcfoundation.org; E-mail for grant applications: nshoemaker@pcfoundation.org;
URL: http://www.pcfoundation.org

Foundation type: Community foundation
Limitations: Scholarships to residents of Putnam County, IN.
Publications: Application guidelines; Annual report (including application guidelines).

Financial data: Year ended 12/31/2004. Assets, $15,951,035 (M); Expenditures, $529,101; Total giving, $282,128; Grants to individuals, 51 grants totaling $66,461 (high: $14,560, low: $70).
Type of support: Scholarships—to individuals; Undergraduate support.
Application information: Application form required.
  Initial approach: One-page letter of inquiry.
  Deadline(s): Vary
  Additional information: See Web site for specific deadlines and further information.
Program description:
  Lilly Endowment Community Scholarships: The foundation offers numerous scholarships in the Putnam County, IN, area. See Web site for further details pertaining to each scholarship fund.
EIN: 311159916

3296

Oscar Lee Putnam Cultural Endowment

c/o Hibernia National Bank
P.O. Box 61540
New Orleans, LA 70161
Application address: c/o Tulane University, Attn: Anthony M. Cummings, Dean of Arts & Sciences, 6823 St. Charles Ave., New Orleans, LA 70118, tel.: (504) 865-5720

Foundation type: Independent foundation
Limitations: Scholarships to residents of LA for higher education.
Financial data: Year ended 12/31/2004. Assets, $332,088 (M); Expenditures, $23,850; Total giving, $18,600; Grants to individuals, totaling $18,600.
Type of support: Scholarships—to individuals.
Application information: Applications accepted. Application form not required.
  Deadline(s): June 15
  Additional information: Application by letter outlining financial need and high school academic record.
EIN: 726022138

3297

Trustees of the Putnam Free School

P.O. Box 562
Newburyport, MA 01950   (978) 462-2197

Foundation type: Independent foundation
Limitations: Scholarships to residents of the following towns in MA: Georgetown, West Newbury, Amesbury, Merrimac, Newburyport, Newbury, Salisbury, Rowley, Boxford, and Topsfield. Applicants must take courses in English and mathematics during their first year of college.
Financial data: Year ended 10/31/2004. Assets, $1,317,405 (M); Expenditures, $53,791; Total giving, $43,779; Grants to individuals, totaling $43,779.
Type of support: Undergraduate support.
Application information: Application form required.
  Deadline(s): July 1
  Additional information: Completion of formal application required, including proof of college acceptance and financial need.
EIN: 046040535

3298

William Lowell Putnam Prize Fund for the Promotion of Scholarship

c/o Ropes & Gray
1 International Pl.
Boston, MA   02110-2624

Foundation type: Independent foundation
Limitations: Awards to individuals who compete in the fund's mathematics competition.
Financial data: Year ended 12/31/2004. Assets, $9,888,800 (M); Expenditures, $749,888; Total giving, $581,000; Grants to individuals, 33 grants totaling $36,000 (high: $3,500, low: $200).
Fields of interest: Mathematics.
Type of support: Awards/prizes.
Application information: Applications not accepted.
EIN: 043414102

3299

Franklin H. Putnam Trust

c/o Bank of America, N.A.
P.O. Box 6768
Providence, RI   02940-6768
Contact: Nora Lynch, Trust Off., Bank of America, N.A.
Application address: 100 Federal St., Boston, MA 02105

Foundation type: Independent foundation
Limitations: Scholarships to residents of MA based on financial need, academic excellence, and involvement in extracurricular activities.
Financial data: Year ended 12/31/2003. Assets, $856,079 (M); Expenditures, $42,202; Total giving, $35,000; Grants to individuals, 9 grants totaling $35,000 (high: $4,500, low: $3,000).
Type of support: Scholarships—to individuals.
Application information:
  Deadline(s): Aug. 1
  Additional information: Completion of formal application required, including financial information and transcripts; Recipients notified by mid-July.
EIN: 046009430

3300

Joseph P. Pyle Trust

c/o PNC Advisors
1600 Market St.
Philadelphia, PA   19103-7240
Application address: c/o PNC Bank, 222 Delaware Ave., Wilmington, DE 19899, tel.: (302) 429-1338

Foundation type: Independent foundation
Limitations: Scholarships to residents in the corporate city limits of Wilmington, DE, who are between the ages of 17 and 21, and are entering their first year of college.
Financial data: Year ended 08/31/2004. Assets, $705,320 (M); Expenditures, $28,198; Total giving, $24,625; Grants to individuals, 8 grants totaling $24,625 (high: $5,000, low: $1,250).
Type of support: Undergraduate support.
Application information: Application form required.
  Deadline(s): Mar. 1
  Applicants should submit the following:
    1) Letter(s) of recommendation
    2) Transcripts
    3) SAT
    4) Financial information

Additional information: Application must also include a list of extracurricular activities and honors. Interviews required.
EIN: 516010048

3301

Quad City Osteopathic Foundation

P.O. Box 1245
Bettendorf, IA   52722-0021
Contact: Eugene R. Holst, Pres.
Tel.: (563) 570-8156; FAX: (309) 797-2662; E-mail: geneholst@mcleodusa.net

Foundation type: Independent foundation
Limitations: Scholarships, internships, loans, and residencies to students in IA and IL pursuing a degree in the field of osteopathy.
Publications: Annual report.
Financial data: Year ended 11/30/2004. Assets, $4,274,219 (L); Expenditures, $267,306; Total giving, $97,505; Grants to individuals, 7 grants totaling $11,000 (high: $3,500, low: $500).
Fields of interest: Medical school/education; Health organizations.
Type of support: Fellowships; Internship funds; Scholarships—to individuals; Student loans—to individuals.
Application information: Application form required.
  Initial approach: Letter.
  Deadline(s): Mar. 15
  Additional information: Interviews required.
EIN: 420666790

3302

The Quaker Chemical Foundation

Elm & Lee Sts.
Conshohocken, PA   19428   (610) 832-4301
Contact: Shirley Widdoes

Foundation type: Company-sponsored foundation
Limitations: Scholarships only to CA, MI, and PA employees of Quaker Chemical Corporation.
Publications: Application guidelines.
Financial data: Year ended 06/30/2002. Assets, $346,799 (M); Expenditures, $235,990; Total giving, $214,754; Grants to individuals, totaling $20,000.
Type of support: Employee-related scholarships.
Application information: Contact foundation for current application deadline/guidelines. Only one scholarship per year is awarded.
EIN: 236245803

3303

Thomas P. Quinn Scholarship Fund

c/o Bank of America, N.A.
P.O. Box 1802
Providence, RI   02901-1802
Application address: c/o Bank of America, N.A., Attn.: Majorie Alexandre Davis, 777 Main St., CT2-102-22-02, Hartford, CT 06115

Foundation type: Independent foundation
Limitations: Scholarships to students graduating from New London, CT, high schools who are in the top ten percent of their classes.
Financial data: Year ended 12/31/2004. Assets, $355,000 (M); Expenditures, $21,901; Total giving, $16,000.
Type of support: Support to graduates or students of specific schools; Undergraduate support.
Application information:
  Deadline(s): June 1

Additional information: Contact fund for current application guidelines.
EIN: 223003812

3304

The R.O.S.E. Fund, Inc.

(formerly Ryka Rose Foundation)
175 Federal St., Ste. 455
Boston, MA   02110   (617) 482-5400
Contact: Barbara J. Wandyes, Exec. Dir.
FAX: (617) 482-3443; E-mail: rosefund@ici.net;
URL: http://www.rosefund.org

Foundation type: Public charity
Limitations: Scholarships and awards to women who have survived violent crimes and are now serving as role models for others.
Publications: Application guidelines; Financial statement; Grants list; Informational brochure; Newsletter.
Financial data: Year ended 12/31/2003. Assets, $210,146 (M); Expenditures, $374,800; Total giving, $106,473; Grants to individuals, totaling $106,473.
Fields of interest: Domestic violence; Civil rights, women; Women.
Type of support: Scholarships—to individuals; Support to graduates or students of specific schools; Undergraduate support.
Application information: Application form required.
  Initial approach: Telephone or e-mail.
  Deadline(s): Vary
Program descriptions:
  R.O.S.E. Scholarship: Scholarships of up to $10,000 to women and children who are survivors of abuse to be used toward education at any college or university, preferably in the state of MA. All final applicants may be requested to participate in an interview. Deadlines Mar. 15 and Aug. 31.
  R.O.S.E. Scholarship at Pine Manor College: Awards one scholarship to a Pine Manor student who will be enrolled in a minimum of twelve credits per semester. Deadline Mar. 15.
  R.O.S.E. Scholarship at UMASS Boston: Two $2,500 scholarships awarded annually to current or future UMASS Boston students who are or will be enrolled in a minimum of nine credits per semester. Deadlines June 15 and Nov. 15.
EIN: 043154445

3305

Herbert and Gwendolyn Raab Educational Trust

428 E. National Ave.
Brazil, IN   47834

Foundation type: Independent foundation
Limitations: Scholarships to students in IN.
Financial data: Year ended 06/30/2004. Assets, $991,389 (M); Expenditures, $59,860; Total giving, $48,074; Grants to individuals, 6 grants totaling $48,074 (high: $5,000, low: $5,000).
Type of support: Scholarships—to individuals.
Application information: Contact trust for current application deadline/guidelines.
EIN: 356645581

3306
Omer E. Rabideau Education Scholarship Fund
(formerly REO Education Fund)
P.O. Box 38
Clifton, IL 60927
Contact: Arlyn Rabideau, Tr.
Application address: c/o Central High School, 1134 E. 3100 N. Rd., Clifton, IL 60927

Foundation type: Independent foundation
Limitations: Scholarships to graduates and graduating seniors of Clifton Central High School, IL.
Financial data: Year ended 12/31/2004.
Assets, $477,094 (M); Expenditures, $14,331; Total giving, $14,000; Grants to individuals, 7 grants totaling $14,000.
Type of support: Support to graduates or students of specific schools; Undergraduate support.
Application information:
   Deadline(s): Apr. 1
   Additional information: Application by letter outlining financial need and listing qualifications.
EIN: 363553408

3307
J. L. & Helen B. Racey Foundation, Inc.
P.O. Box 864
Bassett, VA 24055-0864 (276) 629-5381
Contact: Betty H. Wright, Secy.-Treas.

Foundation type: Independent foundation
Limitations: Scholarships to individuals from the Bassett, VA, area for undergraduate education at U.S. universities and colleges.
Financial data: Year ended 12/31/2004.
Assets, $75,425 (M); Expenditures, $22,659; Total giving, $22,000; Grants to individuals, 6 grants totaling $22,000.
Type of support: Undergraduate support.
Application information: Applications accepted. Application form not required.
   Deadline(s): None
   Additional information: Contact foundation for current application guidelines.
EIN: 541605493

3308
Rachor Family Foundation, Ltd.
(formerly Michael Garry Rachor Professional School Scholarship Fund, Ltd.)
P.O. Box 320100
Flint, MI 48532-0002

Foundation type: Independent foundation
Limitations: Scholarships to individuals, with emphasis on law and medicine.
Financial data: Year ended 12/31/2004.
Assets, $1,792,168 (M); Expenditures, $69,682; Total giving, $56,775; Grants to individuals, 5 grants totaling $31,100.
Fields of interest: Law school/education; Medical school/education.
Type of support: Scholarships—to individuals.
Application information: Application form required.
   Initial approach: Letter.
   Deadline(s): None.
EIN: 383264828

3309
Racine Community Foundation, Inc.
(formerly Racine County Area Foundation, Inc.)
245 Main St., Ste. L-2
Racine, WI 53403 (262) 632-8474
Contact: Margaret L. Kozina, Exec. Dir.
FAX: (262) 632-3739; *E-mail:* info@racinecf.org;
URL: http://www.racinecf.org

Foundation type: Community foundation
Limitations: Scholarships by nomination only to residents of Racine County, WI.
Publications: Application guidelines; Annual report; Informational brochure; Newsletter.
Financial data: Year ended 12/31/2004.
Assets, $29,148,862 (M); Expenditures, $1,475,566; Total giving, $1,177,129.
Type of support: Support to graduates or students of specific schools; Awards/grants by nomination only.
Application information:
   Initial approach: Letter or telephone.
   Deadline(s): Contact foundation for current nomination deadlines.
   Additional information: Completion of formal nomination required; See Web site for complete program listing.
EIN: 510188377

3310
Radio and Television News Directors Foundation
1600 K St., N.W., Ste. 700
Washington, DC 20006-2838 (202) 659-6510
Contact: Barbara Cochran, Pres.; For Scholarships: Irving Washington
E-mail for scholarships: irvingw@rtndf.org
FAX: (202) 223-4007; *E-mail:* rtndf@rtndf.org;
URL: http://www.rtndf.org

Foundation type: Public charity
Limitations: Scholarships and internship opportunities to U.S. residents who are undergraduate or graduate students pursuing radio and television news careers.
Publications: Application guidelines; Annual report.
Financial data: Year ended 12/31/2004.
Assets, $3,757,134 (M); Expenditures, $2,499,317; Total giving, $263,010.
Fields of interest: Media/communications; Journalism/publishing.
Type of support: Internship funds; Graduate support; Undergraduate support.
Application information: Application form required.
   Initial approach: Letter, e-mail, or telephone.
Program description:
   Scholarships and Internships: The foundation administers the following scholarship and internship programs:
   · Jane Pauley Internship
   · Scholarship Program
   · Radio and TV Minority News Management Internships
   · Capitol Hill Internships.
EIN: 381860090

3311
Robert L. Ragel Scholarship Fund
c/o Schwabe, Williamson, & Wyatt
1211 S.W. 5th Ave., Ste. 1800
Portland, OR 97204-3795
Contact: Nikki C. Hatton

Foundation type: Independent foundation
Limitations: Scholarships to graduates of Tigard High School, OR, for higher education.

Financial data: Year ended 12/31/2004.
Assets, $1,093,893 (M); Expenditures, $48,539; Total giving, $45,000; Grants to individuals, 4 grants totaling $45,000.
Type of support: Support to graduates or students of specific schools; Undergraduate support.
Application information: Application form required.
   Deadline(s): Feb. 1
   Additional information: Applications available from Tigard High School guidance counselors.
EIN: 931254085

3312
Rahr Foundation
P.O. Box 15186
Minneapolis, MN 55415-0186 (612) 332-5161
Contact: Frederich W. Rahr, Pres.
FAX: (612) 332-6841

Foundation type: Company-sponsored foundation
Limitations: Scholarships only to children of employees of Rahr Malting Company and its affiliates.
Financial data: Year ended 12/31/2003.
Assets, $4,898,486 (M); Expenditures, $390,289; Total giving, $265,435; Grants to individuals, totaling $21,000.
Type of support: Employee-related scholarships.
Application information:
   Initial approach: Letter.
   Deadline(s): Mar. 15.
   Additional information: Interviews required.
EIN: 396046046

3313
Helen Raider Memorial Trust
c/o Burlington Bank & Trust
222 N. Main St.
P.O. Box 728
Burlington, IA 52601-5214 (319) 753-9130

Foundation type: Independent foundation
Limitations: Scholarships to graduates of Des Moines County, IA, high schools for undergraduate education at U.S. universities and colleges.
Financial data: Year ended 12/31/2004.
Assets, $409,583 (M); Expenditures, $25,601; Total giving, $22,600; Grants to individuals, 25 grants totaling $22,600.
Type of support: Support to graduates or students of specific schools; Undergraduate support.
Application information: Contact trust for current application deadlines/guidelines.
EIN: 426372386

3314
The Raies-Murr Educational Trust
315 Arden Ave., Ste. 18
Glendale, CA 91203

Foundation type: Operating foundation
Limitations: Scholarships to financially needy public high school students residing in the greater Los Angeles, CA, area.
Financial data: Year ended 12/31/2003.
Assets, $359,438 (M); Expenditures, $20,878; Total giving, $17,350; Grants to individuals, 22 grants totaling $17,350 (high: $1,250; low: $400).
Type of support: Undergraduate support.
Application information: Applications not accepted.
EIN: 956932192

3315
Bish Rainey Memorial Trust
c/o Bank of America, N.A.
231 LaSalle St.
Chicago, IL   60697
Contact: John C. McMullan
Application address: c/o Kennett Public Schools, Kennett, MO 63857

Foundation type: Independent foundation
Limitations: Scholarships to graduates of Kennett Public Schools, MO, for postsecondary education.
Financial data: Year ended 01/31/2004. Assets, $382,811 (M); Expenditures, $18,613; Total giving, $12,250; Grants to individuals, 4 grants totaling $12,250 (high: $3,500, low: $1,750).
Fields of interest: Vocational education.
Type of support: Support to graduates or students of specific schools; Undergraduate support.
Application information: Application form required.
Deadline(s): Apr. 15
EIN: 431223959

3316
Micki Rainey Scholarship Fund, Inc.
P.O. Box 5
Martinez, CA   94553

Foundation type: Independent foundation
Limitations: Scholarships to individuals for higher education.
Financial data: Year ended 04/30/2005. Assets, $360,344 (M); Expenditures, $16,238; Total giving, $16,000; Grants to individuals, 16 grants totaling $16,000 (high: $1,000, low: $1,000).
Fields of interest: Higher education.
Type of support: Scholarships—to individuals.
Application information: Applications not accepted.
Additional information: Unsolicited requests for funds not considered or acknowledged.
EIN: 680097366

3317
Agustin A. Ramirez, Jr. Family Foundation
411 E. Wisconsin Ave., Ste. 2040
Milwaukee, WI   53202-4497
Application address: c/o Scholarship Prog. Coord., P.O. Box 257, Waukesha, WI 53187-0257

Foundation type: Independent foundation
Limitations: Scholarships to individuals to attend a fully accredited four-year college or university for higher education.
Financial data: Year ended 12/31/2004. Assets, $374,382 (M); Expenditures, $149,152; Total giving, $134,750; Grants to individuals, 202 grants totaling $134,750 (high: $5,000, low: $500).
Type of support: Employee-related scholarships; Scholarships—to individuals; Undergraduate support.
Application information: Application form required.
Deadline(s): Apr.
Program description:
Scholarships: Applicants must be enrolled in a fully accredited four-year college or university and be in at least one of the following categories:
- Latino student of Greater Milwaukee Standard Metropolitan Statistical Area or Waukesha County High School
- Graduate of the Bruce-Guadalupe School
- Student of a public high school in the Elmbrook School District

- Child of a full-time employee of HUSCO International
- Other foundation-eligible category as determined by the trustees of the foundation.
EIN: 396626017

3318
Ramona's Mexican Food Products Scholarship Foundation
13633 S. Western Ave.
Gardena, CA   90249   (310) 323-1950

Foundation type: Company-sponsored foundation
Limitations: Scholarships to financially needy students of Mexican descent from Garfield, Roosevelt, and Lincoln high schools in Los Angeles, CA.
Financial data: Year ended 09/30/2004. Assets, $407,995 (M); Expenditures, $95,657; Total giving, $94,075; Grants to individuals, 15 grants totaling $94,075 (high: $18,579, low: $1,358).
Fields of interest: Mexico.
Type of support: Support to graduates or students of specific schools; Undergraduate support.
Application information: Applications accepted throughout the year at the specified high schools; Completion of formal application required.
EIN: 237425268

3319
Edward Ramsdale Scholarship Fund, Inc.
1150 Alturas Dr., Ste. 104
Moscow, ID   83843
Application address: c/o Troy High School, Attn: Vickie Bledsoe, Counselor, 101 S. Main St., Troy, ID 83871, tel.: (208) 835-2361

Foundation type: Independent foundation
Limitations: Scholarships only to graduating seniors of Troy High School, ID.
Financial data: Year ended 12/31/2004. Assets, $588,317 (M); Expenditures, $28,001; Total giving, $26,775; Grants to individuals, totaling $26,775.
Type of support: Support to graduates or students of specific schools; Undergraduate support.
Application information: Applications not accepted.
EIN: 841398428

3320
Ayn Rand Institute/The Center for the Advancement of Objectivism
2121 Alton Pkwy., Ste. 250
Irvine, CA   92606-4926   (949) 222-6550
Contact: Yaron Brook, Pres. and Exec. Dir.
Application address for individuals: The Ayn Rand Institute, P.O. Box 6099, Inglewood, CA 90312; Tel.: (949) 222-6550 ext. 209;
E-mail: essay@aynrand.org (for Anthem and Fountainhead contests)
FAX: (949) 222-6558; E-mail: mail@aynrand.org; URL: http://www.aynrand.org

Foundation type: Public charity
Limitations: Awards to high school, undergraduate, and graduate students for critical analysis of Ayn Rand's novels.
Publications: Annual report; Financial statement; Informational brochure (including application guidelines).

Financial data: Year ended 07/30/2004. Assets, $2,211,898 (L); Expenditures, $3,481,837; Total giving, $202,162; Grants to individuals, totaling $202,162.
Fields of interest: Literature; Philosophy/ethics.
Type of support: Awards/prizes; Graduate support; Precollege support; Undergraduate support.
Application information:
Deadline(s): Sept.16 for Atlas Shrugged, Mar. 18 for Anthem, and Apr. 15 for Fountainhead
Additional information: Contact institute for current application guidelines.
Program descriptions:
Annual Essay Contest on Ayn Rand's Novel Atlas Shrugged: Awards given to graduate and undergraduate students in business degree programs for exemplary essays on the novel, Atlas Shrugged, discussing specific topics selected by the institute. Prizes range from $400 to $5,000 each.
Annual Essay Contest on Ayn Rand's Novel The Fountainhead: Awards given to 11th and 12th grade students for exemplary essays on the novel, The Fountainhead, answering specific questions posed by the institute. Prizes range from $1,000 to $10,000 each.
Annual Essay Contest for Ayn Rand's Novelette Anthem: Awards given to 9th and 10th grade students for exemplary essays on the novel, Anthem, answering specific questions posed by the institute. Prizes range from $30 to $1,000 each.
EIN: 222570926

3321
John Randolph Foundation
112 N. Main St., Ste. B
P.O. Box 1606
Hopewell, VA   23860   (804) 458-2239
Contact: Lisa H. Sharpe, Exec. Dir.
FAX: (804) 458-3754;
E-mail: jrfoundation@covad.net; URL: http://johnrandolphfoundation.org

Foundation type: Public charity
Limitations: Scholarships to local students for higher education in professional health fields who reside in the city of Hopewell, Colonial Heights, Petersburg, Emporia, Ft. Lee, Prince George, Dinwiddie, Chesterfield, Charles City, Sussex, Surry, Greensville, Charles City and Varina, Southeast Henrico, and South of I-64 in VA.
Publications: Application guidelines; Informational brochure; Newsletter.
Financial data: Year ended 12/31/2004. Assets, $4,066,199 (M); Expenditures, $629,323; Total giving, $170,644.
Fields of interest: Health sciences school/education.
Type of support: Graduate support; Technical education support; Undergraduate support.
Application information: Deadline Mar. 1; Initial approach by letter or telephone; Completion of formal application required.
Program description:
John Randolph Foundation Scholarship Program: Applicants must express an interest in attending college as a full- or part-time student, show strong academic capabilities, meet and maintain at least a 3.0 GPA, and demonstrate financial need. Various scholarships are awarded each spring to local students.
EIN: 541649268

3322

The Randolph Foundation
P.O. Box 283
Gorham, NH 03581
Contact: John Mudge, Pres.

Foundation type: Public charity
Limitations: Scholarships to students who are residents of Randolph, NH, and have satisfactory grades.
Publications: Annual report; Newsletter.
Financial data: Year ended 06/30/2005. Assets, $465,022 (M); Expenditures, $32,773; Total giving, $22,525; Grants to individuals, totaling $17,025.
Type of support: Scholarships—to individuals.
Application information: Contact foundation for current application deadline/guidelines.
EIN: 026009502

3323

Randolph Memorial Scholarship Trust
c/o Old National Bank
P.O. Box 207
Evansville, IN 47702
Additional address: c/o Henderson County High School, Attn: Phyllis Ware, Sr., Counselor, 2424 Zion Rd., Henderson, KY 42420

Foundation type: Independent foundation
Limitations: Scholarships to graduates of Henderson County High School, KY, based on character, industry, integrity, and academic achievement.
Financial data: Year ended 12/31/2004. Assets, $104,011 (M); Expenditures, $11,394; Total giving, $8,772; Grants to individuals, 3 grants totaling $8,772.
Type of support: Support to graduates or students of specific schools; Undergraduate support.
Application information: Applications accepted. Application form required.
  Deadline(s): Apr. 1
  Additional information: Applications are made through the high school guidance office.
EIN: 616114750

3324

Rangeley Educational Fund
c/o SunTrust Bank
P.O. Box 1908
Orlando, FL 32802-1908
Contact: Gladys Setliff, Trust Off., SunTrust Bank

Foundation type: Independent foundation
Limitations: Student loans to financially needy individuals primarily residing in the City of Martinsville, VA, and Henry and Franklin counties, VA, for technical, vocational, academic, and professional degrees.
Publications: Application guidelines.
Financial data: Year ended 10/31/2004. Assets, $3,521,020 (M); Expenditures, $40,311; Total giving, $0; Loans to individuals, totaling $207,453.
Fields of interest: Vocational education.
Type of support: Graduate support; Technical education support; Undergraduate support.
Application information: Applications accepted. Application form required.
  Initial approach: Letter.
  Deadline(s): May 31
  Applicants should submit the following:
    1) Transcripts
    2) SAT

Additional information: Application may also include college readiness test scores.
Program description:
  Student Loan: Loans will be based on scholastic ability and financial need. The maximum loan amount is $5,000 per year for a total of up to $25,000 per applicant. Loan repayments must begin within six months after completion of course of study and must be paid in full within ten years from the time repayment commences. No interest accrues while the recipient is in college. Five percent interest begins accruing five months after college graduation or termination. Recipients are notified by the end of June. Loans may be given for the duration of the course of study.
EIN: 546077906

3325

Ranger-Ryan Scholarship Foundation
10777 Westheimer Rd., Ste. 5N
Houston, TX 77042 (800) 537-4180
Contact: Mary Ploog
Application address: 1505 Riverview Rd., P.O. Box 297, St. Peter, MN 56082

Foundation type: Company-sponsored foundation
Limitations: Scholarships to financially needy graduates of Ryan Middle School, Houston, TX.
Financial data: Year ended 12/31/2004. Assets, $213,439 (M); Expenditures, $199,293; Total giving, $198,000; Grants to individuals, 297 grants totaling $198,000 (high: $500, low: $500).
Type of support: Scholarships—to individuals; Support to graduates or students of specific schools.
Application information: Applications not accepted.
EIN: 760266492

3326

The Bill Raskob Foundation, Inc.
P.O. Box 507
Crownsville, MD 21032-0507 (410) 879-0500
Contact: Edward H. Robinson, Corp. Secy.
E-mail: info@billraskob.org; Additional E-mail: ed@billraskob.org; URL: http://www.billraskob.org

Foundation type: Independent foundation
Limitations: Undergraduate and graduate interest-free student loans to American citizens enrolled at accredited institutions within the U.S.
Publications: Application guidelines; Program policy statement.
Financial data: Year ended 12/31/2004. Assets, $5,314,637 (L); Expenditures, $435,078; Total giving, $310,250.
Type of support: Graduate support; Undergraduate support.
Application information: Application form required.
  Initial approach: Letter.
  Deadline(s): May 1
  Applicants should submit the following:
    1) Transcripts
    2) Letter(s) of recommendation
    3) Essay
    4) Financial information
  Additional information: Application must also include a copy of applicant's or parents' tax return, copy of financial aid award letter from school, and a brochure, booklet, or letter from school indicating costs of tuition, room and board, and other expenses; Interviews may be required; Loan recipients will be notified in Aug.

Program description:
  Student Loan: The foundation strongly recommends that all applicants first apply for government loans or grants. If funds are not available, or only a portion of the amount needed can be granted, then application can be made to the foundation. The foundation does not accept applications from incoming students on any level (undergraduate or medical), or from foreign students. It is not the policy of the foundation to fund a student through more than one degree. Repayment must begin six months after graduation, except for medical, dental, and veterinarian students, who may begin repayment within 12 months. Deferments are not granted.
EIN: 510110185

3327

Edward F. Rathke Irrevocable Scholarship Trust
c/o Marshall & Isley Bank
P.O. Box 2427
Green Bay, WI 54306-2427 (920) 432-6361

Foundation type: Independent foundation
Limitations: Scholarships to high school seniors attending schools in Brown and Oconto counties, WI.
Financial data: Year ended 12/31/2004. Assets, $93,938 (M); Expenditures, $10,770; Total giving, $8,500; Grants to individuals, 17 grants totaling $8,500.
Type of support: Support to graduates or students of specific schools; Undergraduate support.
Application information: Applications accepted throughout the year; Completion of formal application required, including name of school and applicant's and parents' financial information.
EIN: 510187617

3328

The Ratner, Miller, Shafran Foundation
50 Public Sq., Ste. 1600
Cleveland, OH 44113-2295 (216) 267-1200
Contact: Albert Ratner, Secy.
Application address: 1100 Terminal Twr., 50 Public Sq., Cleveland, OH 44113-2203

Foundation type: Independent foundation
Limitations: Scholarships to residents of Cuyahoga County, OH.
Financial data: Year ended 11/30/2004. Assets, $141,587 (M); Expenditures, $254,545; Total giving, $249,903; Grants to individuals, totaling $35,236.
Application information: Application form required.
  Deadline(s): May 1
  Applicants should submit the following:
    1) Transcripts
    2) Letter(s) of recommendation
EIN: 346521216

3329

Alexander and Cassia Rau Trust
c/o M&T Trust Co.
21 E. Market St., M/C 402-130
York, PA 17401-1500
Application address: c/o St. Mark's Lutheran Church Council, Attn: Pres., 700 E. Market St., York, PA 17403

Foundation type: Independent foundation
Limitations: Student loans for higher education, primarily in PA.

Financial data: Year ended 12/31/2004. Assets, $297,284 (M); Expenditures, $15,968; Total giving, $12,545; Loans to individuals, 4 loans totaling $12,545.
Type of support: Student loans—to individuals.
Application information: Contact trust for current application deadline/guidelines; Applications available from the Church Council.
EIN: 236417951

3330
Rauch Family Foundation II, Inc.
1705 2nd Ave., Ste. 424
Rock Island, IL   61201-8718   (309) 788-2300
Contact: Samuel Gilman, Tr.
FAX: (309) 788-3298;
E-mail: day.rauch@sbcglobal.net

Foundation type: Independent foundation
Limitations: Grants to programs and projects for the enhancement of Judaism, its traditions and people.
Publications: Annual report (including application guidelines).
Financial data: Year ended 12/31/2004. Assets, $1,366,176 (M); Expenditures, $65,568; Total giving, $54,114.
Fields of interest: Camps; Jewish agencies & temples.
Type of support: Undergraduate support; Travel grants; Camperships.
Application information: Application form not required.
    Initial approach: Letter or telephone.
    Deadline(s): None
    Applicants should submit the following:
        1) Proposal
    Additional information: Applications should outline financial need.
EIN: 363570748

3331
Walter C. & Ella Rawls Educational Trust
P.O. Box 1908
Orlando, FL   32802-1908

Foundation type: Independent foundation
Limitations: Scholarships to graduating high school seniors who reside in Suffolk, Forest Glen, Kennedy, and Sussex, VA, and Gates, NC.
Financial data: Year ended 06/30/2005. Assets, $405,410 (M); Expenditures, $38,585; Total giving, $11,690; Grants to individuals, 7 grants totaling $11,690.
Fields of interest: Vocational education.
Type of support: Undergraduate support.
Application information: Contact local high schools for current application deadline/guidelines.
EIN: 546053305

3332
The Jerry S. Rawls Scholarship Foundation
1107 Homestead Ave.
Lubbock, TX   79416

Foundation type: Independent foundation
Limitations: Scholarships to students who attend Texas Tech University.
Financial data: Year ended 06/30/2005. Assets, $4,898,754 (M); Expenditures, $360,974; Total giving, $290,500; Grants to individuals, 112 grants totaling $290,000 (high: $7,000, low: $1,000).

Fields of interest: Men.
Type of support: Scholarships—to individuals.
Application information: Unsolicited requests for funds not considered or acknowledged.
EIN: 916530654

3333
Ray-Carroll County Grain Growers Scholarship Fund, Inc.
P.O. Box 158
Richmond, MO   64085-0158   (816) 776-2291
Contact: Mike Nordwald

Foundation type: Company-sponsored foundation
Limitations: Scholarships to graduating seniors residing in the Ray-Carroll Cooperative service area to attend colleges in MO. Scholarships must be used within two years of graduation from high school.
Financial data: Year ended 09/30/2005. Assets, $156,123 (M); Expenditures, $11,877; Total giving, $11,250; Grants to individuals, 25 grants totaling $11,250 (high: $750, low: $375).
Type of support: Undergraduate support.
Application information: Applications accepted. Application form required.
    Deadline(s): Six weeks after application form is sent out.
    Applicants should submit the following:
        1) Transcripts
    Additional information: Application must include teacher evaluation, a statement of plans, goals, and the college to be attended.
EIN: 431244005

3334
The Rayni Foundation, Inc.
c/o Raul F. Rodriguez
300 S.W. 124 Ave.
Miami, FL   33184

Foundation type: Operating foundation
Limitations: Scholarships by nomination only to graduates of Archbishop Carroll Catholic High School and the Belen Jesuit School, FL.
Financial data: Year ended 12/31/2004. Assets, $3,630,374 (M); Expenditures, $277,351; Total giving, $209,818.
Fields of interest: Roman Catholic agencies & churches.
Type of support: Support to graduates or students of specific schools; Awards/grants by nomination only; Undergraduate support.
Application information: Unsolicited requests for funds not accepted.
EIN: 650838191

3335
The Rayonier Foundation
(formerly The ITT Rayonier Foundation)
50 N. Laura St., Ste. 1900
Jacksonville, FL   32202   (904) 357-9100
Contact: Jay A. Fredericksen, V.P.

Foundation type: Company-sponsored foundation
Limitations: Scholarships to students residing in Nassau County, FL, Wayne County, GA, and Clallam, Grays Harbor, and western Jefferson counties, WA.
Financial data: Year ended 12/31/2002. Assets, $4,311,554 (M); Expenditures, $857,674; Total giving, $851,215; Grants to individuals, totaling $115,914.

Fields of interest: Science; Chemistry; Physics; Computer science; Engineering; African Americans/ Blacks.
Type of support: Undergraduate support.
Application information: Application form required.
    Deadline(s): Nov. 30.
    Applicants should submit the following:
        1) Transcripts
        2) SAT
        3) ACT
        4) Letter(s) of recommendation
    Additional information: Application must also include personal statement and employment history; Interviews required; Applications available from high school principals in the eligible counties.
Program descriptions:
    Timber County Scholarship Program: Provides scholarships to students graduating from high schools and residing in states where Rayonier, Inc., has significant timberland ownership: FL, GA, and WA. Three $1,000 scholarships are awarded for the Northeast and six $1,500 scholarships are awarded for the Southeast. Recipients may attend two- or four-year institutions and major in any subject. Selection is based on scholarship, leadership, and financial need, and scholarships are not renewable.
    The Black Scholar Awards: Provides an $8,000, four-year scholarship to an outstanding African American student residing in, and graduating from, a high school in Wayne County, GA, or Nassau County, FL. The winner will receive $2,000 per school year, to attend any accredited college, and major in any subject leading to a Bachelor's degree, providing the student maintains a satisfactory level of achievement. Recipients may not rely on any additional scholarships of equal or higher value.
    Engineering and Science Four Year Scholarship: Provides an $8,000, four-year scholarship to a high school student residing and attending school in Wayne County, GA, pursuing a bachelor's degree in chemical, mechanical, electrical, civil, or industrial engineering. Other technical fields such as physics, chemistry, or computer science may be considered.Recipients receive $2,000 per school year providing they maintain satisfactory college records, good personal behavior, and a reasonable amount of extracurricular activity. Selections are based on scholarship, personality, leadership, and to some extent, financial need. Persons related to selection committee members are not eligible to receive a foundation scholarship.
EIN: 136064462

3336
RCL Foundation
(formerly Richard S. Staley Foundation)
1805 Industrial St.
Los Angeles, CA   90021   (213) 627-0972
Contact: Angela Tan, Secy.-Treas.

Foundation type: Operating foundation
Limitations: Scholarships and student loans primarily to residents of CA who are graduate students in the medical field.
Financial data: Year ended 04/30/2004. Assets, $2,744,768 (M); Expenditures, $91,768; Total giving, $56,413.
Fields of interest: Medical school/education.
Type of support: Graduate support.
Application information: Applications accepted throughout the year; Completion of formal application required, including GPA; Recipients generally notified within two months.
EIN: 953387067

3337
Reaching Up, Inc.
c/o Citrin Cooperman and Co., LLP
529 5th Ave.
New York, NY   10017   (212) 827-0660

Foundation type: Public charity
Limitations: Scholarships and career mentoring to paraprofessionals, who are enrolled at a City University of New York School, or a State University of New York School.
Financial data: Year ended 12/31/2004. Assets, $64,854 (M); Expenditures, $93,865; Total giving, $37,228; Grants to individuals, totaling $37,228.
Type of support: Support to graduates or students of specific schools; Undergraduate support.
Application information: Applications not accepted.
Program description:
  Kennedy Fellows Mentoring Program: Provides scholarships and career mentoring to paraprofessionals who are enrolled for at least six credits at a CUNY or SUNY college. Recipients must be committed to completing several years of specialized course work in the field of disabilities. They must be enrolled in such degree programs as special education, psychology, social work, nursing, speech-language (pathology), occupational therapy, recreation, human services, child care and gerontology.
EIN: 133577206

3338
Reader's Digest Foundation
Reader's Digest Rd.
Pleasantville, NY   10570-7000   (914) 244-5370
Contact: Janis L. Braun, Secy.
FAX: (914) 238-7642;
E-mail: carolyn.malile@readersdigest.com;
URL: http://www.readersdigest.com/corporate/rd_foundation.html

Foundation type: Company-sponsored foundation
Limitations: Undergraduate scholarships to children of NY employees of Reader's Digest Association, Inc. Scholarships are not available to children of foundation managers.
Publications: Annual report (including application guidelines).
Financial data: Year ended 06/30/2004. Assets, $14,237,259 (M); Expenditures, $1,701,182; Total giving, $1,465,119; Grants to individuals, 53 grants totaling $162,600 (high: $10,000, low: $1,000).
Type of support: Employee-related scholarships.
Application information: Contact foundation for current application deadline/guidelines.
EIN: 136120380

3339
Reading Musical Foundation
P.O. Box 14835
Reading, PA   19612-4835   (610) 376-3395
Contact: Tammy K. Mitgang, Exec. Dir.
URL: http://www.readingmusicalfoundation.org/

Foundation type: Public charity
Limitations: Scholarships and awards to music students in Berks County, PA.
Financial data: Year ended 06/30/2003. Assets, $4,763,749 (M); Expenditures, $604,244; Total giving, $313,740.
Fields of interest: Music; Performing arts, education; Education; Women.
Type of support: Scholarships—to individuals.

Application information: Contact foundation for current application deadline/guidelines.
Program descriptions:
  Elaine Bausher Post Scholarship: Three scholarships awarded annually for the first, second, and third place winners. Tuition assistance is provided for each of the four years a student is enrolled as a music major.
  David Bilger Woodwind Scholarship: Three scholarships are awarded for extended music study at qualified workshops, summer schools, or camps.
  Mildred Mogel Engle Scholarship: One scholarship is awarded every four years to a worthy and needy student. The amount of the scholarship will be determined by the amount of total interest accumulated during the four year period immediately preceding. Scholarship funds will be prorated over the four years the student is enrolled in an accredited college or university.
  Katherine N. Quartner-Rita Quartner Kerman String Scholarship: Nine scholarships are awarded for extended music study at qualified workshops, summer schools, or camps, such as Congress of String, Tanglewood, or Youth Symphony camp.
  Charlotte B. Wicklein Scholarship: One scholarship is awarded annually to a female student. Tuition assistance is provided for each of the four years a student is enrolled as a music major.
EIN: 231472487

3340
The Ronald Reagan Presidential Foundation
40 Presidential Dr., Ste. 200
Simi Valley, CA   93065-0600   (805) 522-2977
Contact: Mark M. Burson, Exec. Dir.
FAX: (805) 520-9702;
E-mail: info@reaganfoundation.org; URL: http://www.reaganlibrary.com

Foundation type: Public charity
Limitations: Scholarships to high school students in Ventura, CA, for higher education.
Financial data: Year ended 09/30/2003. Assets, $108,343,015 (M); Expenditures, $9,596,223; Total giving, $20,000; Grants to individuals, 5 grants totaling $20,000 (high: $5,000, low: $2,500).
Fields of interest: Higher education.
Type of support: Scholarships—to individuals.
Application information:
  Initial approach: Letter.
  Additional information: Selection is based on recommendations from school principals, teachers, and an essay written about American government judged by a panel of community leaders.
EIN: 770054631

3341
Real Colegio Complutense, Inc.
26 Trowbridge St.
Cambridge, MA   02138-5326   (617) 495-3536
FAX: (617) 496-6880;
E-mail: rcc-info@camail.harvard.edu; URL: http://www.realcolegiocomplutense.harvard.edu

Foundation type: Independent foundation
Limitations: Scholarships to students, scholars, and researchers from Spanish universities for study and research in any discipline at Harvard University.
Financial data: Year ended 06/30/2004. Assets, $1,577,567 (M); Expenditures, $698,492; Total giving, $291,534; Grants to

individuals, 41 grants totaling $241,534 (high: $20,000, low: $600).
Fields of interest: Spain.
Type of support: Fellowships; Research; Scholarships—to individuals; Foreign applicants.
Application information: Applications accepted.
  Initial approach: Letter or telephone.
  Deadline(s): Jan. 10
  Applicants should submit the following:
    1) Resume
    2) Letter(s) of recommendation
    3) Financial information
EIN: 043134531

3342
The Real Estate Educational Foundation, Inc.
West Bldg., Lower level
127 Washington Ave.
North Haven, CT   06473-1715   (203) 234-7700

Foundation type: Operating foundation
Limitations: Scholarships to residents of the greater New Haven, CT, area, who are active in community service.
Financial data: Year ended 12/31/2002. Assets, $144,247 (M); Expenditures, $10,849; Total giving, $8,800; Grants to individuals, totaling $4,800.
Fields of interest: Community development.
Type of support: Scholarships—to individuals.
Application information: Applications accepted throughout the year; Contact foundation for current application guidelines; Initial approach by letter.
EIN: 061062962

3343
Realize Your Dream Foundation
235 Alpha Dr., Ste. 300
Pittsburgh, PA   15238   (412) 967-6200
Contact: Kathleen A. Santelli, Scholarship Coord.

Foundation type: Independent foundation
Limitations: Scholarships to high school seniors attending private and public high schools within the city of Pittsburgh, PA, and those geographic boundaries surrounding the Pittsburgh area: as far east as Lower Burrell, west to Sewickley, north to Butler, and south to the Allegheny and Ohio rivers.
Financial data: Year ended 12/31/2003. Assets, $381,091 (M); Expenditures, $127,588; Total giving, $117,286.
Type of support: Support to graduates or students of specific schools; Undergraduate support.
Application information: Application form required.
  Initial approach: Telephone.
  Deadline(s): Feb. 28
  Applicants should submit the following:
    1) Essay
    2) Letter(s) of recommendation
    3) GPA
    4) SAT
    5) Transcripts
  Additional information: Contact foundation for current application guidelines; Application must also include total custodial family income, and specific outline of community service projects.
Program description:
  Scholarship Program: Applicants must have a 3.2 GPA or higher.
EIN: 232884514

3344
Realty Foundation of New York
551 5th Ave., Ste. 415
New York, NY 10176 (212) 697-3943
Contact: Scholarship and Aid Comm.
FAX: (212) 949-9319

Foundation type: Independent foundation
Limitations: Scholarships for full-time
undergraduate and graduate-level study to
employees and children of employees of the
foundation's member firms in the real estate
industry in the five boroughs of New York City.
Publications: Informational brochure.
Financial data: Year ended 06/30/2005.
Assets, $1,798,336 (M); Expenditures,
$470,428; Total giving, $258,468; Grants to
individuals, 62 grants totaling $254,068 (high:
$20,000, low: $750).
Fields of interest: Business/industry; Community
development, real estate.
Type of support: Employee-related scholarships;
Undergraduate support.
Application information: Application form required.
  Initial approach: Letter or telephone.
  Deadline(s): None
  Applicants should submit the following:
    1) Letter(s) of recommendation
    2) FAF
Program description:
  Scholarship Program: Candidates who are
  graduate students must be enrolled for a minimum
  of 12 credit hours and working towards a master's
  or doctoral degree. Students on institutional
  fellowships, graduate assistantships, or research
  grants are ineligible. Thesis work and exam
  programs for credit are also ineligible.
EIN: 136016622

3345
George J. Record School Foundation
P.O. Box 581
Conneaut, OH 44030
Contact: Charles N. Lafferty, Pres.

Foundation type: Independent foundation
Limitations: Scholarships to legal residents of
Ashtabula County, OH, for tuition and fees at
approved private colleges and universities.
Financial data: Year ended 12/31/2004.
Assets, $3,237,501 (M); Expenditures,
$308,162; Total giving, $227,708; Grants to
individuals, 86 grants totaling $227,708 (high:
$3,500, low: $1,750).
Fields of interest: Religion.
Type of support: Undergraduate support.
Application information: Application form required.
  Deadline(s): May 20 for first-year students, June
  20 for upper class students
  Applicants should submit the following:
    1) Photograph
    2) Class rank
    3) Letter(s) of recommendation
    4) Transcripts
    5) SAT
    6) GPA
  Additional information: Applicants must attend
    approved private colleges and complete the
    equivalent of six semester hours or nine
    quarter-hours of religious study. Interviews
    required.
EIN: 340830818

3346
Recreational Boating Industries Educational Foundation
32398 Five Mile Rd.
Livonia, MI 48154-6109 (734) 261-0123
Contact: Van W. Snider, Jr., Dir.

Foundation type: Independent foundation
Limitations: Scholarships to permanent residents
of MI pursuing a career in the recreational boating
industry, including marketing, service, facilities
design for boat stores and marinas, and
manufacturing.
Financial data: Year ended 12/31/2004.
Assets, $78,231 (M); Expenditures, $128,471;
Total giving, $37,400; Grants to individuals, 14
grants totaling $15,000 (high: $2,000, low: $500).
Fields of interest: Recreation; Marine science.
Type of support: Undergraduate support.
Application information:
  Deadline(s): Apr. 20
  Additional information: Application by letter
    outlining financial need and academic and
    work-related performance. Recipients are
    chosen based on merit and financial need. In
    addition to scholarship money, recipients
    receive summer placements with members of
    the Michigan Boating Industries Association.
    Up to thirty percent of scholarships may be
    granted to employees and family members of
    Michigan Boating Industries Association
    members. The same selection criteria applies
    to these grants.
EIN: 382704909

3347
Redding Family Foundation
2530 Atlantic Ave., Ste. B
Long Beach, CA 90806 (562) 490-2488
Contact: Sandra Redding, Secy.-Treas.

Foundation type: Independent foundation
Limitations: Scholarships to students in Granville
County, NC.
Financial data: Year ended 12/31/2004.
Assets, $64,354 (M); Expenditures, $10,308;
Total giving, $9,000; Grants to individuals, totaling
$9,000.
Type of support: Undergraduate support.
Application information: Contact foundation for
current application deadline/guidelines; Initial
approach by telephone.
EIN: 330210244

3348
John A. Reddington Scholarship Fund & Trust
c/o Genesee Valley Trust Co.
50 Office Park Way
Pittsford, NY 14534-1796 (585) 586-6900
Contact: John A. Reddington, Scholarship Fund
Committee

Foundation type: Operating foundation
Limitations: Scholarships to students in NY who
are attending or planning to attend Catholic school.
Financial data: Year ended 08/31/2004.
Assets, $584,693 (M); Expenditures, $39,868;
Total giving, $29,800; Grants to individuals, 73
grants totaling $29,800 (high: $1,000, low: $75).
Fields of interest: Roman Catholic agencies &
churches.
Type of support: Precollege support.
Application information: Application form required.
  Deadline(s): Apr. 30

Additional information: Scholarships are limited
  to students who attend, or are registered to
  attend Catholic school, or who qualify for
  admission to college. Recipients must
  demonstrate a financial need using criteria
  normally utilized by institutions to which
  admission is sought.
EIN: 161555796

3349
Dr. Prem Reddy Charitable Foundation
(formerly Desert Valley Charitable Foundation)
16850 Bear Valley Rd.
Victorville, CA 92392

Foundation type: Operating foundation
Limitations: Scholarships to High Desert, CA,
residents planning to enroll in an accredited
program in health care or a medical-related field.
Publications: Application guidelines; Financial
statement; Informational brochure.
Financial data: Year ended 12/31/2002.
Assets, $3,243,092 (M); Expenditures,
$115,511; Total giving, $22,350; Grants to
individuals, totaling $8,000.
Fields of interest: Medical school/education;
Health sciences school/education; Health care.
Type of support: Scholarships—to individuals.
Application information: Deadline July 14;
Completion of formal application required, including
at least two references from school or work
supervisors, official high school transcript and other
supporting scholastic data, personal statement of
plans and goals, and documentation of individual's
or parent/guardian's personal financial condition.
Program description:
  Scholarship Program: The scholarship program
  awards students who have achieved academic
  excellence while being involved in school and
  community activities. Recipients are notified of
  their award by July 28 of each year. Award checks
  must be used for tuition, books, lab fees or other
  related costs. The recipient will be required to
  submit quarterly transcripts of grades to continue
  to be eligible.
EIN: 330486173

3350
Richard F. Redfield Trust
4390 Hwy. 8 E.
Rhinelander, WI 54501

Foundation type: Independent foundation
Limitations: Scholarships to graduates of
Rhinelander High School, WI, for higher education.
Financial data: Year ended 05/31/2005.
Assets, $913,215 (M); Expenditures, $103,931;
Total giving, $75,851; Grants to individuals, 6
grants totaling $61,513.
Type of support: Support to graduates or students
of specific schools; Undergraduate support.
Application information: Deadline Mar. 31;
Completion of formal application required;
Applications can be obtained from Rhinelander Area
Scholarship Foundation or Rhinelander High
School.
EIN: 396694213

3351
Redwood Area Communities Foundation, Inc.

P.O. Box 127
Redwood Falls, MN   56283   (507) 637-4004
Contact: Patricia Dingels
Application address: 200 S. Mills St., Redwood Falls, MN 56283
FAX: (507) 637-4082;
E-mail: radc@redwoodfalls.org; URL: http://radc.org/foundation.html

Foundation type: Independent foundation
Limitations: Loans and scholarships to needy students graduating from high schools in or within a ten-mile radius of Redwood County, MN.
Publications: Application guidelines; Informational brochure.
Financial data: Year ended 12/31/2004.
Assets, $0 (M); Expenditures, $319,032; Total giving, $40,000; Grants to individuals, totaling $40,000.
Fields of interest: Mathematics; Science.
Type of support: Student loans—to individuals; Undergraduate support.
Application information: Applications accepted. Application form required.
  Initial approach: Letter, telephone, or e-mail.
  Deadline(s): Apr. 2 for Grefe Scholarship, May 15 for Ehlers Student Fund
  Additional information: Application should include transcripts, photocopy of parents' tax form, two recommendations, and proof of enrollment.
Program descriptions:
  Martin and Winifred Ehlers Student Fund: Provides interest-free student loans to individuals who have graduated from area high schools who plan to continue their education by attending college, vocational school, or trade school. Eligible applicants will live within Redwood County or a 10-mile radius of Redwood County. Loans will be made on the basis of need, character, and academic ability. The maximum loan amount that can be received during any one school year is $4,500 per student.
  Ray and Joan Grefe Scholarship Fund: Provides $5,000 scholarships to two high school seniors who will major in math or natural sciences in college, and have three years of math or natural science course work in high school. Applications will be accepted from individuals living within or attending school within the following MN counties: Brown, Chippewa, Cottonwood, Jackson, Lac Qui Parle, Lincoln, Lyon, Martin, Murray, Nobles, Pipestone, Redwood, Renville, Rock, Watonwan, and Yellow Medicine. Scholarships will be made on the basis of need, character, and academic ability, and are renewable for up to four years.
EIN: 363611923

3352
The Donna Reed Foundation for the Performing Arts

1305 Broadway
Denison, IA   51442   (712) 263-3334
Contact: Gwen Ecklund, Exec. Dir.
FAX: (712) 263-8026; E-mail: info@donnareed.org;
URL: http://www.donnareed.org

Foundation type: Public charity
Limitations: Scholarships to students who are U.S. residents for further education in the performing arts.
Publications: Application guidelines; Informational brochure (including application guidelines); Newsletter.

Financial data: Year ended 09/30/2004.
Assets, $700,072 (M); Expenditures, $121,032; Total giving, $23,750; Grants to individuals, 51 grants totaling $23,750 (high: $1,000, low: $31).
Fields of interest: Performing arts; Dance; Theater; Music; Performing arts, education.
Type of support: Undergraduate support.
Application information:
  Deadline(s): Mar. 15
  Additional information: Completion of formal application required, including video and/or audio tapes, depending on category, and $30 per category for National Scholarships or $10 per category for State of Iowa Scholarships; Auditions required for finalists; Consult Web site for application forms.
Program descriptions:
  Crawford County, Iowa Scholarship: Three $500 scholarships are given to Crawford County, IA, residents who are graduating high school seniors to pursue higher education at a college or an approved program of study of their choice. Applicants must also be U.S. citizens or permanent residents. Applications are accepted for the following disciplines: acting, dance, instrumental music, musical theater, and vocals. Each category has separate application materials that must be submitted. Applicants for this scholarship may simultaneously apply for the National Scholarship, the State of Iowa Scholarship, or both, however each competition requires a separate application form and fee. There is no fee for this program. Five recipients in each category will receive all-expenses paid, full-tuition scholarships to the Donna Reed Festival and Workshop for the Performing Arts in June.
  National Scholarships: Six $4,000 scholarships are given each year to graduating high school seniors who are U.S. citizens or permanent residents for higher education in the performing arts at a college of the recipient's choice or an approved program of study. One scholarship is awarded to the top applicant in each of the following five categories: acting, dance, musical theatre and vocal. In addition, three $500 awards will be given to finalists not receiving the aforementioned $4,000 scholarships. Each finalist will have a live audition in front of a panel of judges to decide the undergraduate scholarship winners. Finalist awards include transportation, lodging, food, and full tuition for the workshops of the winner's choice. Finalists are selected based on audio/video taped recordings by a panel of expert judges in each division. Three finalists in each category will receive all-expenses paid, full-tuition scholarships to the Donna Reed Festival and Workshop for the Performing Arts in June.
  State of Iowa Scholarships: Three $1,000 scholarships are awarded to graduating high school seniors who are both residents of IA and U.S. citizens or permanent residents. Scholarships may be applied to a college or to an approved program of study of their choice. Applicants apply in the categories of acting, vocals, and musical theater. Recipients are selected by a panel of expert judges in each category on the basis of audio/video recordings. The five recipients, one in each category, will also receive all-expenses paid, full-tuition scholarships to the Donna Reed Festival and Workshop for the Performing Arts in June.
EIN: 421285098

3353
Joanna F. Reed Medical Scholarship Trust

c/o BancTrust Co.
P.O. Box 469
Brewton, AL   36427-0469   (251) 867-3231

Foundation type: Independent foundation
Limitations: Medical school scholarships to residents of AL or northwest FL, who will attend a private university. (Northwest FL is defined as all counties west of the Apalachicola River.)
Publications: Application guidelines.
Financial data: Year ended 12/31/2004.
Assets, $434,098 (M); Expenditures, $23,714; Total giving, $19,000; Grants to individuals, 3 grants totaling $19,000.
Fields of interest: Medical school/education.
Type of support: Graduate support.
Application information: Deadline May 15; Completion of formal application required, including transcripts, MCAT scores, and two letters of recommendation from former academic instructors.
EIN: 630805093

3354
Spence Reese Foundation

c/o Bank of America, N.A., Trust Tax Div.
P.O. Box 830259
Dallas, TX   75283-0259
Contact: Audrey Mandeville
Application address: c/o Jeff Miller, V.P., Boys & Girls Clubs of Greater San Diego, 4635 Clairemont Mesa Blvd., San Diego, CA 92117

Foundation type: Independent foundation
Limitations: Scholarships given on a national basis to males currently in their senior year of high school who will major in medicine, law, engineering, or political science.
Financial data: Year ended 04/30/2003.
Assets, $645,594 (M); Expenditures, $52,245; Total giving, $27,000; Grants to individuals, 15 grants totaling $27,000 (high: $3,000, low: $1,000).
Fields of interest: Law school/education; Medical school/education; Engineering; Political science; Men.
Type of support: Undergraduate support.
Application information: Application form required. Application form available on the grantmaker's Web site.
  Initial approach: Letter.
  Deadline(s): Apr. 15
  Applicants should submit the following:
    1) SASE
    2) SAT
    3) Letter(s) of recommendation
    4) GPA
    5) ACT
  Additional information: Interviews required.
Program description:
  Scholarships: Scholarships are generally renewable for up to four years. Four new scholarships are awarded each year.
EIN: 510203269

3355
Reeves Foundation

c/o Old National Bank
P.O. Box 207
Evansville, IN   47702
Application address: c/o University of Evansville, P.O. Box 329, Evansville, IN 47714, tel.: (812) 479-2149

Foundation type: Independent foundation
Limitations: Student loans to financially needy residents of Vanderburgh County, IN, who are studying full-time at the University of Evansville and have completed two years of academic work in good standing.

Financial data: Year ended 05/31/2005. Assets, $327,665 (M); Expenditures, $6,543; Total giving, $0; Loans to individuals, totaling $15,600.
Type of support: Support to graduates or students of specific schools; Undergraduate support.
Application information: Applications accepted throughout the year; Initial approach by letter; Completion of formal application required.
EIN: 356077653

3356
Sophia K. Reeves Foundation Trust
c/o Mellon Financial Corp.
P.O. Box 185
Pittsburgh, PA 15230-9897
Application address: c/o Mellon Bank, N.A., Attn: Annamaria C. Lyles, P.O. Box 7236, Philadelphia, PA 19101, tel.: (215) 553-2596

Foundation type: Independent foundation
Limitations: Scholarships to children of employees of Philadelphia Gas Works, to residents of Laurel Springs, NJ, and to Protestant residents of the part of Camden County that is contingent to Laurel Springs.
Financial data: Year ended 06/30/2005. Assets, $1,535,447 (M); Expenditures, $102,631; Total giving, $69,440; Grants to individuals, 28 grants totaling $69,440.
Fields of interest: Protestant agencies & churches.
Type of support: Employee-related scholarships.
Application information: Deadline Mar. 10; Completion of formal application required; Applications available Jan. and Mar.
EIN: 236226072

3357
Reeves Foundation, Inc.
9405 W. US Hwy. 40
Knightstown, IN 46148-9507
Application address: c/o Counselor's Office, Knightstown High School, Knightstown, IN 46148

Foundation type: Independent foundation
Limitations: Scholarships to students attending Knightstown High School, IN.
Financial data: Year ended 12/31/2004. Assets, $939,362 (M); Expenditures, $52,070; Total giving, $46,000; Grants to individuals, 13 grants totaling $46,000.
Type of support: Support to graduates or students of specific schools; Undergraduate support.
Application information: Deadline May; Completion of formal application required, including autobiographical information.
EIN: 311175067

3358
Edgar and Lois Reich Education Foundation
c/o Wachovia Bank, N.A.
P.O. Box 3099
Winston-Salem, NC 27150-6732
Scholarship URL: http://www.wachoviascholars.com/ereic/csaw_reich_deadline.php

Foundation type: Independent foundation
Limitations: Scholarships to individuals residing in Forsyth or Davidson counties, NC, for the study of dentistry or teaching.
Financial data: Year ended 12/31/2004. Assets, $577,841 (M); Expenditures, $44,187;

Total giving, $35,059; Grants to individuals, 21 grants totaling $29,801 (high: $4,000, low: $500).
Fields of interest: Dental school/education; Teacher school/education.
Type of support: Undergraduate support.
Application information: Application form required.
Initial approach: Letter or telephone.
Deadline(s): Apr. 1
Additional information: See web site for further application information: http://www.wachoviascholars.com/ereic/csaw_reich_deadline.php.
EIN: 582245280

3359
M. C. & A. A. Reid Educational Trust
c/o Citizens Bank Wealth Mgmt., N.A.
328 S. Saginaw St., M/C 002072
Flint, MI 48502
Application address: c/o Helen James, Citizens Bank Wealth Mgmt., N.A., 101 N. Washington Ave., Saginaw, MI 48607, tel.: (989) 776-7368

Foundation type: Independent foundation
Limitations: Student loans to residents of Saginaw County, MI, who are between the ages of 15 and 30.
Financial data: Year ended 08/31/2004. Assets, $482,526 (M); Expenditures, $11,988; Total giving, $0; Loans to individuals, 12 loans totaling $42,000.
Type of support: Student loans—to individuals.
Application information: Deadline June 1; Completion of formal application required.
EIN: 386347006

3360
The W. Scott Reid Scholarship Fund
c/o IOOF Grand Lodge of Maine
80 Caron Ln.
Auburn, ME 04210 (207) 786-3638

Foundation type: Independent foundation
Limitations: Scholarships to residents of ME who are pursuing a nursing degree from an institution of higher learning in ME.
Financial data: Year ended 12/31/2004. Assets, $433,619 (M); Expenditures, $30,066; Total giving, $26,300; Grants to individuals, 23 grants totaling $26,300.
Fields of interest: Nursing school/education.
Type of support: Scholarships—to individuals.
Application information: Deadline Mar. 1; Completion of formal application required, including family information, statement of preparation, employment while in school, transcript, and agreement to advise of academic progress at end of each semester.
EIN: 016141002

3361
Olive Rice Reierson Foundation
c/o Wells Fargo Bank Montana, N.A.
P.O. Box 597
Helena, MT 59624 (406) 447-2050
Contact: Martin J. Lewis

Foundation type: Operating foundation
Limitations: Scholarships to Powell County, MT, residents who graduated from a Powell County high school.
Publications: Application guidelines.
Financial data: Year ended 09/30/2003. Assets, $1,207,328 (M); Expenditures, $81,981;

Total giving, $68,500; Grants to individuals, 20 grants totaling $68,500 (high: $6,000, low: $1,500).
Type of support: Support to graduates or students of specific schools; Undergraduate support.
Application information: Deadline Apr. 1; Completion of formal application required.
EIN: 363463190

3362
Reifel-Ellwood Education Trust
1023 Corning St.
Red Oak, IA 51566-2001 (712) 623-3218
Contact: Kenneth Rech, Tr.

Foundation type: Independent foundation
Limitations: Scholarships to high school seniors who are residents of Montgomery County, IA.
Financial data: Year ended 01/31/2005. Assets, $97,507 (M); Expenditures, $4,318; Total giving, $3,200; Grant to an individual, 1 grant totaling $3,200.
Type of support: Technical education support; Undergraduate support.
Application information: Deadline May 25; Completion of formal application required.
EIN: 426149714

3363
The Reilly Family Foundation
c/o The Ballpark
1017 S. FM Road 5
Aledo, TX 76008 (817) 265-2364
FAX: (817) 265-0537

Foundation type: Independent foundation
Limitations: Scholarships to individuals, primarily in TX, for higher education.
Financial data: Year ended 12/31/2004. Assets, $527,521 (M); Expenditures, $160,806; Total giving, $146,344; Grants to individuals, totaling $46,561 (high: $15,058).
Type of support: Undergraduate support.
Application information: Contact foundation for current application deadline; Completion of formal application required.
EIN: 752366809

3364
Reilly Foundation
300 N. Meridian St., Ste. 1500
Indianapolis, IN 46204-1761
Contact: Rand Brooks, Tr.

Foundation type: Company-sponsored foundation
Limitations: Scholarships to children of employees of Reilly Industries, Inc.
Financial data: Year ended 12/31/2003. Assets, $591,069 (M); Expenditures, $329,552; Total giving, $323,350.
Type of support: Employee-related scholarships.
Application information:
Initial approach: Letter.
Deadline(s): None.
Additional information: Contact foundation for current application guidelines.
EIN: 352061750

3365
The Reinhardt Family Scholarship Trust
1207 Delaware Ave., Ste. 208
Buffalo, NY   14209-1401
Application address: c/o Holland Central High School, Attn: Selection Comm., 103 Canada St., Holland, NY 14080, tel.: (716) 537-2231

Foundation type: Independent foundation
Limitations: Scholarships to students of Holland Central High School, NY.
Financial data: Year ended 12/31/2004. Assets, $124,293 (M); Expenditures, $11,933; Total giving, $9,250; Grants to individuals, 6 grants totaling $9,000.
Type of support: Support to graduates or students of specific schools; Undergraduate support.
Application information: Applications accepted throughout the year; Completion of formal application required; Applications available from high school.
EIN: 161512484

3366
Floyd J. Reinhart Memorial Scholarship Foundation
256 Locust Ave.
Amsterdam, NY   12010-2628
Contact: Frances Allen, Tr.

Foundation type: Independent foundation
Limitations: Scholarships to current graduates of Canajoharie, Fort Plain, and St. Johnsville high schools, all in Montgomery County, NY.
Financial data: Year ended 06/30/2005. Assets, $3,046,147 (M); Expenditures, $144,993; Total giving, $116,000; Grants to individuals, 101 grants totaling $116,000 (high: $3,000, low: $500).
Type of support: Support to graduates or students of specific schools; Undergraduate support.
Application information: Contact foundation for current application deadline/guidelines.
EIN: 141605307

3367
Mildred Reinheimer Trust
33 S. 4th St.
Pekin, IL   61554-4202
Application address: c/o Walter Dare, Scholarship Comm., Delavan High School, Delavan, IL 61734, tel.: (309) 244-8285

Foundation type: Independent foundation
Limitations: Scholarships to graduates of Delavan High School, IL.
Financial data: Year ended 05/31/2005. Assets, $0 (M); Expenditures, $10,143; Total giving, $6,541.
Type of support: Support to graduates or students of specific schools; Undergraduate support.
Application information: Deadline May 1; Completion of formal application required; Applications available from Delavan High School.
EIN: 376154891

3368
William M. Reiss Foundation
c/o Bank of America, N.A.
231 S. LaSalle St.
Chicago, IL   60697
Application address: c/o Bank of America, N.A., 100 N. Broadway, P.O. Box 14737, St. Louis, MO 63178, tel.: (314) 466-9067

Foundation type: Independent foundation
Limitations: Scholarships to financially needy students at Belleville, IL, area public schools. Students pursuing degrees in medicine are ineligible.
Financial data: Year ended 12/31/2004. Assets, $956,320 (M); Expenditures, $35,167; Total giving, $22,500.
Type of support: Support to graduates or students of specific schools; Undergraduate support.
Application information: Applications accepted. Application form required.
> *Deadline(s):* May 1
> *Applicants should submit the following:*
> 1) Transcripts
> 2) Financial information
> 3) FAF
> 4) FAFSA
EIN: 237056642

3369
Henry K. & Evelyn Reitnauer Scholarship Fund
c/o Investors Trust Co.
2201 Ridgewood Rd., No. 180
Wyomissing, PA   19610
Application address: c/o Boyertown Area School District, Attn: Guidance Dept., 911 Montgomery Ave., Boyertown, PA 19512, tel.: (610) 369-7436

Foundation type: Independent foundation
Limitations: Scholarships to financially needy graduates of Boyertown Area Senior High School, PA, pursuing a teaching degree in special education or another degree that relates to special education.
Financial data: Year ended 12/31/2004. Assets, $1,364,072 (M); Expenditures, $73,214; Total giving, $60,888; Grants to individuals, 26 grants totaling $60,888.
Fields of interest: Education, special; Teacher school/education.
Type of support: Scholarships—to individuals; Support to graduates or students of specific schools.
Application information: Application form required.
> *Deadline(s):* Apr. 15
> *Applicants should submit the following:*
> 1) Financial information
Program description:
> *Scholarship Program:* Scholarships are in amounts of up to 80 percent of the recipient's total school costs, with a limit of $5,000 per year. Scholarships are awarded for the entire length of the recipient's period of study. Recipients are chosen by a committee made up of the Superintendent of Schools, the High School Principal, the Director of Pupil Services, and the Senior High School Guidance Department Chairperson.
EIN: 232214468

3370
The Relevance Foundation
P.O. Box 5447
Sacramento, CA   95817-0448
Contact: Patience Crowder
URL: http://www.sthope.com

Foundation type: Independent foundation
Limitations: Scholarships to financially needy students for higher education.
Financial data: Year ended 06/30/2003. Assets, $1,536,038 (L); Expenditures, $39,879; Total giving, $15,550; Grants to individuals, 5 grants totaling $15,550 (high: $7,000, low: $500).
Type of support: Scholarships—to individuals.
Application information: Contact foundation for current application deadline; Application by letter demonstrating purpose, qualification, and need.
EIN: 943192757

3371
Elizabeth Reller Memorial Scholarship Fund
c/o First National Bank, Trust Dept.
300 Washington St.
Beardstown, IL   62618   (217) 323-4105

Foundation type: Independent foundation
Limitations: Loans to financially needy graduates of Beardstown High School, IL, for higher education.
Financial data: Year ended 12/31/2004. Assets, $1,243,673 (M); Expenditures, $5,527; Total giving, $0; Loans to individuals, totaling $51,217.
Type of support: Student loans—to individuals; Support to graduates or students of specific schools.
Application information: Application form required.
> *Deadline(s):* July 15 and Dec. 15
> *Applicants should submit the following:*
> 1) Essay
> 2) Transcripts
> 3) Letter(s) of recommendation
> 4) Financial information
> *Additional information:* Recipients are required to begin repayment of their loans 30 days after discontinuation of studies or one year after graduation, if they have completed their studies. Interest begins accruing the first day after education ceases, and will accrue at a rate equal to one half the prime rate published daily in the Wall Street Journal. Interest rates will be fixed at the date of loan. Repayment is generally over a 120-month period, and there is no penalty for early pay off.
EIN: 371337146

3372
Remmele Foundation
c/o Human Resources Dept.
10 Old Hwy. 8 S.W.
New Brighton, MN   55112-7709
Contact: Scott Furey, Treas.

Foundation type: Company-sponsored foundation
Limitations: Scholarships to children of employees (excluding company officers) of Remmele Engineering, Inc., MN. Awards up to $5,000 per year for up to four years for college or university students, and up to $2,000 per year for up to two years for vocational students.
Financial data: Year ended 12/31/2004. Assets, $12,950 (M); Expenditures, $43,004; Total giving, $42,842; Grants to individuals, 9 grants totaling $42,842 (high: $7,076, low: $3,200).
Fields of interest: Vocational education.
Type of support: Employee-related scholarships.
Application information: Application form required.
> *Deadline(s):* Apr. 15
> *Applicants should submit the following:*
> 1) Photograph
> 2) Transcripts
> *Additional information:* Application should also include personal essay, three references, results of any aptitude, intelligence, or achievement tests taken, and scholastic record form completed by principal or high school counselor.
EIN: 411356088

3373
Waldo E. Rennie Scholarship Fund
c/o Wells Fargo Bank West, N.A.
P.O. Box 53436
Phoenix, AZ   85072
Loan application address: c/o Wells Fargo Bank
West, N.A., 633 17th St., Denver, CO 80270

Foundation type: Independent foundation
Limitations: Loans to financially needy students to
study physics, geology, or engineering at a college
or university which receives its principal support
directly from the state of CO. Recipients must be
pursuing a four-year degree.
Publications: Informational brochure.
Financial data: Year ended 09/30/2005.
Assets, $4,969,177 (M); Expenditures,
$256,163; Total giving, $157,602; Loans to
individuals, totaling $157,602.
Fields of interest: Education; Physics; Geology;
Engineering/technology.
Type of support: Loans—to individuals.
Application information: Application form required.
  Deadline(s): None.
  Additional information: Contact school's financial
    aid office for application.
EIN: 846138107

3374
The Brent & Helen Rentschler Scholarship Fund
c/o First National Bank & Trust Co.
P. O. Box 9012
Kokomo, IN   46904-9012
Application address: c/o First National Bank & Trust
Co., Trust Dept., P.O. Box 70, Sullivan, IN
47882-0070

Foundation type: Independent foundation
Limitations: Scholarships to high school graduates
of Clay County, IN, for higher education.
Financial data: Year ended 12/31/2004.
Assets, $386,203 (M); Expenditures, $21,531;
Total giving, $19,000; Grants to individuals, 19
grants totaling $19,000.
Type of support: Scholarships—to individuals.
Application information: Applications accepted
throughout the year; Application by letter, including
school attended, leadership abilities,
extracurricular activities, and scholastic standing.
EIN: 316261269

3375
Research & Education Foundation of the American Association for the Surgery of Trauma
5323 Harry Hines, Ste. E-5.514
Dallas, TX   75390-9158   (214) 648-3531
Contact: Frank L. Mitchell M.D., Pres.

Foundation type: Public charity
Limitations: Scholarships to individuals for
research and education in the field of trauma.
Financial data: Year ended 12/31/2003.
Assets, $2,248,196 (M); Expenditures,
$156,026; Total giving, $132,500; Grants to
individuals, 4 grants totaling $132,500 (high:
$40,000, low: $17,500).
Fields of interest: Medical school/education;
Health sciences school/education.
Type of support: Scholarships—to individuals.
Application information: Applications accepted.
  Initial approach: Letter.
  Additional information: Interviews required.
EIN: 561918296

3376
The Research Foundation of CFA Institute
560 Ray C. Hunt Dr.
P.O. Box 3668
Charlottesville, VA   22903   (434) 951-5362
Contact: Katrina F. Sherrerd, Exec. Dir.
FAX: (434) 951-5370; E-mail: rf@cfainstitute.org;
URL: http://www.cfainstitute.org/research/
index.html

Foundation type: Public charity
Limitations: Scholarships to individuals who were
either permanently disabled in the September 11th
terrorist attacks or who are closely related to
someone who was killed or permanently disabled in
the attacks.
Financial data: Year ended 08/31/2003.
Assets, $7,927,995; Expenditures, $409,587;
Total giving, $179,000; Grants to individuals,
totaling $89,000.
Fields of interest: Safety/disasters; Disabilities,
people with.
Type of support: Undergraduate support.
Application information: Contact foundation for
current application deadline/guidelines.
Program description:
  11 September Memorial Scholarship Fund:
  Provides scholarships of up to $25,000 each to
  individuals who were permanently disabled in the
  attacks or were the spouse, domestic partners or
  dependents of anyone killed or permanently
  disabled in the attacks and who will pursue
  university-level education in finance, economics or
  health-related fields.
EIN: 546063408

3377
Research Foundation of The City University of New York
230 W. 41st St., 7th Fl.
New York, NY   10036   (212) 417-8300
Contact: Richard F. Rothbard, Pres.
E-mail: questions@rfcuny.org; URL: http://
www.rfcuny.org

Foundation type: Public charity
Limitations: Scholarships to undergraduate and
graduate students attending City University of New
York, NY.
Publications: Annual report.
Financial data: Year ended 06/30/2004.
Assets, $157,042,833 (M); Expenditures,
$320,013,268; Total giving, $40,947,755; Grants
to individuals, totaling $40,947,755.
Type of support: Support to graduates or students
of specific schools.
Application information:
  Initial approach: Letter or e-mail.
  Additional information: Scholarships based on
    various sets of criteria established by the
    restricted projects and by type of awards
    listed in the CUNY catalogue. Contact
    foundation for program descriptions and
    application procedures.
EIN: 131988190

3378
Walter and May Reuther Memorial Fund
c/o Comerica Bank
P.O. Box 75000 MC 3430
Detroit, MI   48275-3430   (313) 222-4085
Contact: Stephen P. Yokish, Pres.

Foundation type: Public charity
Limitations: Scholarships for the study of
educational services in the fields of labor, human
relations, and the betterment of mankind.
Applicants must be a member, or be the dependent
of a member of the UAW or of some other labor
organization.
Financial data: Year ended 12/31/2003.
Assets, $770,549 (M); Expenditures, $87,947;
Total giving, $81,578; Grants to individuals, 30
grants totaling $50,084 (high: $24,360, low: $24).
Type of support: Undergraduate support.
Application information:
  Initial approach: Letter.
  Additional information: Contact organization for
    further application guidelines.
EIN: 237067164

3379
Reverend Boutin Brothers Trust
135 Nichols St.
Gardner, MA   01440
Application addresses: c/o Rev. Joseph Sirois, 51
Illinois St., Worcester, MA 01610, tel.: (508)
799-2792; c/o Henri Sans, 21 Pleasant St.,
Gardner, MA 01440, tel.: (508) 632-0011; c/o
Rev. Andrew Guenette, 135 Nichols St., Gardner,
MA 01440, tel.: (508) 632-0285

Foundation type: Independent foundation
Limitations: Scholarships to young men of
Franco-American extraction studying for the
priesthood and ultimately serving the Worcester
Diocese. Applicants must be from The Holy Name
of Jesus Parish, in Worcester, MA, or The Holy
Rosary Parish, in Gardner, MA.
Financial data: Year ended 12/31/2004.
Assets, $199,473 (M); Expenditures, $10,822;
Total giving, $8,000; Grants to individuals, totaling
$8,000.
Fields of interest: Theological school/education;
Men.
Type of support: Scholarships—to individuals.
Application information: Applications accepted
throughout the year; Completion of formal
application required; Interviews required.
Program description:
  Scholarship Program: The trust provides
  educational assistance to young men of the Holy
  Name of Jesus and Holy Rosary parishes, who are
  of Franco-American extraction, studying for the
  priesthood and ultimately serving in the Worcester,
  MA, diocese. If no applications are received from
  these parishes, the trustees will consider
  applications from other Franco-American parishes
  within the diocese of Worcester.
EIN: 046197940

3380
The Rexam Foundation
(formerly Rexam Corporation Foundation)
4201 Congress St., Ste. 340
Charlotte, NC   28209
Contact: Marsha McMurray

Foundation type: Company-sponsored foundation
Limitations: Scholarships to children of Rexam
employees for higher education.
Financial data: Year ended 12/31/2004.
Assets, $1,350 (M); Expenditures, $29,033; Total
giving, $28,618.
Type of support: Employee-related scholarships.
EIN: 136165669

3381
Rexnord Foundation Inc.
P.O. Box 2191
Milwaukee, WI 53201-2191 (414) 643-3000
Scholarship application address: c/o Scholarship
Admin., Rexnord Industries, Inc., 4701 W.
Greenfield Ave., Milwaukee, WI 53214

Foundation type: Company-sponsored foundation
Limitations: Scholarships to children and
dependents of Rexnord Corporation employees,
including employees of subsidiary companies.
Applicants must have a minimum ACT score of 20
or SAT score of 1,000.
Publications: Application guidelines.
Financial data: Year ended 10/31/2003.
Assets, $3,843,813 (M); Expenditures,
$400,423; Total giving, $397,846.
Type of support: Employee-related scholarships.
Application information: Application form not
required.
> *Deadline(s):* May 14.
> *Additional information:* Application by letter,
> including photocopy of test scores.
EIN: 396042029

3382
Edith Grace Reynolds Estate
(formerly Edith Grace Reynolds Estate Residuary
Trust)
c/o KeyBank N.A.
800 Superior Ave., 4th Fl.
Cleveland, OH 44114-1306
Application address: Stanley Lepkowski, Trust Off.,
c/o KeyBank N.A., 33 State St., Albany, NY 12207

Foundation type: Independent foundation
Limitations: Scholarships to individuals residing in
School District No. 1, Rensselaer County, NY.
Financial data: Year ended 03/31/2005.
Assets, $1,163,803 (M); Expenditures, $76,380;
Total giving, $63,000; Grants to individuals, 106
grants totaling $53,000 (high: $500, low: $500).
Type of support: Scholarships—to individuals.
Application information: Application form required.
> *Deadline(s):* Feb. 15
> *Applicants should submit the following:*
> 1) Transcripts
> 2) Financial information
EIN: 237170056

3383
Dr. & Mrs. Charles O. Reynolds Medical
Scholarship Fund
c/o City National Bank of WV
1900 3rd Ave.
Huntington, WV 25703

Foundation type: Independent foundation
Limitations: Scholarships to first-year Marshall
University medical students who are residents of
WV.
Financial data: Year ended 12/31/2004.
Assets, $98,573 (M); Expenditures, $6,559; Total
giving, $5,000; Grant to an individual, 1 grant
totaling $5,000.
Fields of interest: Medical school/education.
Type of support: Support to graduates or students
of specific schools; Undergraduate support.
Application information: Applications accepted
throughout the year; Contact fund for current
application guidelines; Initial approach by letter.
EIN: 556097807

3384
Harry Bertram Reynolds Trust
c/o U.S. Bank, N.A.
P.O. Box 387
St. Louis, MO 63166-0387
Contact: Tom Feig, Trust Off., U.S. Bank, N.A.
Application address: 235 N. Elm, P.O. Box 709,
Centralia, Il 62801, tel.: (618) 545-1217

Foundation type: Independent foundation
Limitations: Student loans to residents of Jefferson
County, IL, for high school, trade school, and higher
education.
Financial data: Year ended 12/31/2004.
Assets, $87,686 (M); Expenditures, $5,085; Total
giving, $2,800; Grants to individuals, 7 grants
totaling $2,800.
Fields of interest: Vocational education.
Type of support: Technical education support;
Precollege support; Undergraduate support.
Application information: Applications accepted.
Application form required.
> *Additional information:* Interviews required.
EIN: 376027000

3385
Reynolds-Barwick Scholarship Fund
2931 E. 1300 N. Rd.
Sheldon, IL 60966

Foundation type: Independent foundation
Limitations: Scholarships to one graduate at each
of the ten high schools in Iroquois County, IL.
Financial data: Year ended 12/31/2004.
Assets, $1,459,377 (M); Expenditures,
$138,377; Total giving, $75,000; Grants to
individuals, 10 grants totaling $75,000 (high:
$7,500, low: $7,500).
Type of support: Support to graduates or students
of specific schools; Undergraduate support.
Application information: Application form required.
> *Initial approach:* Through the high school.
> *Deadline(s):* Feb. 15
> *Additional information:* Applicants must rank in
> the upper 30 percent of their classes.
> Candidates are evaluated on scholarship,
> character, citizenship, honesty, dedication,
> and financial need.
EIN: 376245457

3386
Robert L. Rhoad Testamentary Trust
c/o Drake, Phillips, Kuenzli & Clark
301 S. Main St., Ste. 3
Findlay, OH 45840 (419) 423-0242
Contact: William E. Clark, Tr.

Foundation type: Independent foundation
Limitations: Scholarships to residents of Hancock
County, OH, who are pursuing higher education.
Financial data: Year ended 12/31/2002.
Assets, $1,021,104 (M); Expenditures, $96,000;
Total giving, $62,000; Grants to individuals, 39
grants totaling $62,000 (high: $2,000, low:
$1,000).
Type of support: Undergraduate support.
Application information: Deadline Apr. 1; Initial
approach by letter, including scholastic and
extracurricular activities; Completion of formal
application required.
EIN: 346959896

3387
T. L. Rhoads Foundation
(formerly Leidy-Rhoads Foundation Trust)
c/o Mellon Financial Corp.
P.O. Box 185
Pittsburgh, PA 15230-9897
Application address: c/o Boyertown Area School
District, Attn: Jean Butt, 911 Montgomery Ave.,
Boyertown, PA 19512, tel.: (610) 367-6031

Foundation type: Independent foundation
Limitations: Scholarships to residents of
Boyertown, PA, primarily for higher education at
colleges, universities, and trade schools.
Financial data: Year ended 12/31/2004.
Assets, $1,657,343 (M); Expenditures, $96,493;
Total giving, $86,100; Grants to individuals, 30
grants totaling $86,100.
Fields of interest: Vocational education.
Type of support: Technical education support;
Undergraduate support.
Application information: Application form required.
> *Deadline(s):* Early Spring
EIN: 236227398

3388
Rhoads Scholarship Trust
c/o Kentucky Trust Bank
1042 Fairview Ave.
Bowling Green, KY 42103

Foundation type: Independent foundation
Limitations: Scholarships to financially needy
female graduating seniors with at least a 3.0 GPA.
Financial data: Year ended 12/31/2004.
Assets, $268,323 (M); Expenditures, $11,870;
Total giving, $10,000; Grants to individuals, 10
grants totaling $10,000 (high: $1,000, low:
$1,000).
Fields of interest: Vocational education; Women.
Type of support: Scholarships—to individuals.
Application information: Deadline Mar. 15; Initial
approach by letter or telephone; Application by
letter, including biographical sketch, transcripts,
and ACT scores.
EIN: 611089770

3389
Rhode Island Building Industry
Scholarship Fund
29 New York Ave.
Cumberland, RI 02864

Foundation type: Independent foundation
Limitations: Scholarships to RI residents pursuing
education related to the building industry.
Financial data: Year ended 12/31/2004.
Assets, $100,258 (M); Expenditures, $8,981;
Total giving, $8,000; Grants to individuals, 4 grants
totaling $8,000.
Type of support: Support to graduates or students
of specific schools; Undergraduate support.
Application information:
> *Deadline(s):* Mar. 1
> *Additional information:* Application by letter
> outlining financial need with resume;
> Interviews required for finalists; Notification
> within twenty days after application deadline.
> Students may attend school full- or part-time
> at colleges, junior colleges, night school,
> technical school, professional society
> seminars, or trade school classes in
> engineering, architecture, drafting, blueprint
> reading, estimating, construction-related
> programs, surveying, etc.
EIN: 050375250

3390
The Rhode Island Foundation
(also known as The Rhode Island Community Foundation)
1 Union Station
Providence, RI   02903   (401) 274-4564
Contact: Karen Voci, Sr. V.P., Prog.; For artists: Claude Elliott
FAX: (401) 331-8085; Artist grants E-mail: celliott@rifoundation.org; URL: http://www.rifoundation.org

Foundation type: Community foundation
Limitations: Scholarships to residents of RI.
Publications: Application guidelines; Annual report (including application guidelines); Grants list; Informational brochure; Newsletter; Occasional report; Program policy statement.
Financial data: Year ended 12/31/2004. Assets, $428,970,585 (M); Expenditures, $26,734,100; Total giving, $22,400,000.
Fields of interest: Folk arts; Arts education; Film/video; Design; Music; Performing arts, education; Students, sororities/fraternities; Nursing care; Disasters, fire prevention/control; Community development, volunteer services; Business/industry; Financial services.
Type of support: Employee-related scholarships; Support to graduates or students of specific schools; Awards/prizes; Graduate support; Precollege support; Undergraduate support; Travel grants; Grants for special needs.
Application information: Application form required. Application form available on the grantmaker's Web site.
   Initial approach: Telephone or letter.
   Deadline(s): Contact foundation for current application deadline
Program description:
   Scholarship Program: The foundation provides scholarships through the following funds:
   · Edward R. Anderson Scholarship Trust Fund
   · A.T. Cross Scholarship Fund
   · Karl Augenstein Memorial Fund: For study in the jewelry-making field
   · Bach Organ Scholarship Fund: For organ and keyboard students
   · Frederick J. Benson Scholarship Fund: For residents of Block Island, RI
   · Bristol Children's Home Scholarship Fund: For residents of Bristol, RI
   · Ladies Auxiliary of the Bristol Volunteer Fire Department Fund: For children of Bristol firefighters
   · James J. Burns & C.A. Haynes Scholarship Fund
   · Cataract Fire Company No. 2 Scholarship Fund: For Warwick, RI, residents
   · Antonio Cirino Memorial Fund: For fellowships in arts education training
   · John and Lori Anne Corbiskley Fund: For inner-city RI children
   · Corning Glass Works Scholarship Fund: For students in Blackstone Valley, RI
   · Edward Leon Duhamel Scholarship Fund: For dependents of Westerly Free Masons
   · J.D. Edsal Scholarship Fund: For the study of filmmaking, television, and advertising
   · Patricia W. Edwards Memorial Fund: For high school students studying painting
   · George R. Frankovich Scholarship Fund: For students pursuing jewelry careers
   · Dominic Gencarelli Family Trust Fund: For graduates of Westerly High School who plan to attend Providence College
   · Jewelry Foundation Scholarship Fund: For study in the jewelry field

   · Johnston Lions Armand Muto Scholarship Fund: For residents of Johnston, RI
   · Jennie M. Kiernan Fund: For students at Blackstone Valley high schools, RI
   · Fordyce Remsen Lozier & Mary Williams Horr Lozier Fund: For Sigma Chi fraternity members
   · Michael Marcogliese Scholarship Fund: For study in the jewelry field
   · Michael P. Metcalf Memorial Fund: For individuals in RI for personal growth through travel
   · Judy Morse Scholarship Fund
   · Albert E. & Florence W. Newton Fund: For practicing nurses
   · Pawtucket East High School, Class of '42 Scholarship Fund: For graduating seniors at Tolman High School
   · Rhode Island Association of Former Legislators: For graduating high school seniors from RI who have engaged in significant community service during their school years
   · Andrew & Frances Salvadore Scholarship Fund: For study in the jewelry field
   · Lily & Catello Sorrentino Memorial Fund: For undergraduate students under the age of 45
   · Stone Bridge Volunteer Fire Department Scholarship Fund: For residents of Tiverton
   · Bruce and Marjorie Sundlun Scholarship Fund: For single parents returning to school
   · Raymond H. Trott Scholarship Fund: For study in the banking field
EIN: 222604963

3391
William B. Rice Aid Fund, Inc.
c/o Hudson Savings Bank
P.O. Box 868
Hudson, MA   01749-0868   (978) 562-7994
Contact: George Sousa, Tr.

Foundation type: Independent foundation
Limitations: Scholarships and loans to residents of the Hudson, MA, area.
Financial data: Year ended 12/31/2004. Assets, $1,139,070 (M); Expenditures, $60,176; Total giving, $24,000; Grants to individuals, 12 grants totaling $24,000; Loans to individuals, 4 loans totaling $4,000.
Type of support: Scholarships—to individuals; Student loans—to individuals.
Application information: Deadline Apr. 1; Completion of formal application required.
EIN: 046058104

3392
James C. & Irene M. Rice Trust
c/o Wells Fargo Bank Nevada, N.A.
3800 Howard Hughes Pkwy., Ste. 300
Las Vegas, NV   89109

Foundation type: Independent foundation
Limitations: Scholarships to high school seniors attending Elko High School, NV. One recipient is selected each year.
Financial data: Year ended 12/31/2004. Assets, $22,224 (M); Expenditures, $16,706; Total giving, $13,000; Grants to individuals, 7 grants totaling $13,000 (high: $2,000, low: $1,000).
Type of support: Support to graduates or students of specific schools; Undergraduate support.

Application information:
   Deadline(s): Contact trust for current application deadline/guidelines.
EIN: 886031782

3393
Richard Richardi Scholarship Trust
501 S. Ridgewood Ave.
Daytona Beach, FL   32114

Foundation type: Independent foundation
Limitations: Scholarships to graduates of Walpole High School, MA, who are second-year college students.
Financial data: Year ended 05/31/2005. Assets, $2,154,220 (M); Expenditures, $145,283; Total giving, $100,000; Grants to individuals, 34 grants totaling $100,000.
Type of support: Support to graduates or students of specific schools; Undergraduate support.
Application information: Application form required.
   Deadline(s): Apr. 1
EIN: 597062049

3394
The Mabel Wilson Richards Scholarship Fund
4712 Admiralty Way, No. 227
Marina Del Rey, CA   90292
Contact: Joanie C. Freckman, Tr.

Foundation type: Independent foundation
Limitations: Scholarships to female U.S. citizens residing in the greater Los Angeles, CA, area, for undergraduate or graduate study at specific CA colleges and universities.
Publications: Application guidelines; Program policy statement.
Financial data: Year ended 06/30/2005. Assets, $13,700,425 (M); Expenditures, $864,489; Total giving, $543,119.
Fields of interest: Women.
Type of support: Support to graduates or students of specific schools; Graduate support; Undergraduate support.
Application information: Application form required.
   Deadline(s): Oct. 31 and Feb. 15
   Additional information: Application forms available from financial aid offices of participating colleges.
Program description:
   Scholarship Program: Scholarships are awarded to provide financial assistance for the education of worthy and financially needy females. Applications are accepted only through the financial aid offices of approximately 40 CA colleges. The financial aid offices make recommendations to the fund's trustees, who make the final selection of recipients. All grants are made on a competitive basis, with consideration to scholastic achievement, financial need, high moral character, and good citizenship. Applicants must already be accepted for admission by one of the following CA colleges: Art Center College of Design; California State University, Long Beach; California State University, Los Angeles; California State University, Northridge; Claremont McKenna College; Compton Community College; Loma Linda University School of Medicine; Los Angeles City College; Los Angeles County Medical Center School for Nursing; Los Angeles Mission College; Los Angeles Southwest College; Los Angeles Trade-Technical College; Loyola Marymount University; Loyola Marymount University School of Law; Mount Saint Mary's College, CA; Harvey Mudd College; Occidental College; Pacific Oaks College; Pepperdine University; Pitzer College;

Pomona College; Santa Monica College; Scripps College; Southwestern University, School of Law; Stanford University; University of California, Berkeley; University of California, Davis; University of California, Irvine; University of California, Los Angeles; University of California, Riverside; University of California, San Diego; University of California, Santa Barbara; University of Southern California; University of Southern California Law Center; University of Southern California School of Medicine; University of the Pacific; or Woodbury University.

EIN: 956021322

3395
Clarence & Olive Richards Scholarship Trust

c/o U.S. Bank, N.A.
P.O. Box 2043
Milwaukee, WI 53201-9116

Foundation type: Independent foundation
Limitations: Scholarships to high school graduates of the Washington, Iowa School District and high school graduates residing in Oregon Township, Washington County, Iowa.
Financial data: Year ended 12/31/2004.
Assets, $707,522 (M); Expenditures, $44,641; Total giving, $38,000; Grants to individuals, 20 grants totaling $38,000.
Type of support: Support to graduates or students of specific schools; Undergraduate support.
Application information: Application form required.
   Deadline(s): Mar. 31
EIN: 396672759

3396
Mary T. & William A. Richardson Fund Corporation

c/o Eastern Bank
605 Broadway, LF41
Saugus, MA 01906 (781) 581-4274
Contact: Robert M. Wallask, Clerk

Foundation type: Independent foundation
Limitations: Scholarships to graduating high school seniors who are residents of Massachusetts.
Financial data: Year ended 12/31/2004.
Assets, $35,043 (M); Expenditures, $21,862; Total giving, $21,000; Grants to individuals, 19 grants totaling $21,000.
Type of support: Scholarships—to individuals.
Application information: Deadline Apr. 15; Completion of formal application required, including high school transcripts, financial aid information, and letters of recommendation.
EIN: 510152650

3397
Sid Richardson Memorial Fund

309 Main St.
Fort Worth, TX 76102 (817) 336-0494
Contact: Peggy Laskoski, Coord.
FAX: (817) 332-2176;
E-mail: plaskoski@sidrichardson.org; *URL:* http://www.sidrichardson.org

Foundation type: Independent foundation
Limitations: Scholarships to direct descendants (children and grandchildren) of persons presently employed or retired with a minimum of three years' full-time service at one or more of the following: Sid Richardson Carbon & Gasoline, Bass Enterprises Production Co., Bass Bros. Enterprises, Richardson

Oils, Perry R. Bass, Sid W. Richardson Fdn., San Jose Cattle Co., City Center Development, Richardson Aviation.
Financial data: Year ended 12/31/2005.
Assets, $6,117,319 (M); Expenditures, $332,145; Total giving, $209,100; Grants to individuals, 76 grants totaling $209,100 (high: $6,000, low: $500).
Type of support: Employee-related scholarships; Scholarships—to individuals; Graduate support; Technical education support; Undergraduate support.
Application information: Application form required.
   Initial approach: Letter.
   Copies of proposal: 1
   Deadline(s): Mar. 31
   Additional information: Applications may be submitted from Jan. to Mar.; Application should include name, place, and dates of service of qualifying employee.
Program description:
   Scholarships: On the average, 18 new scholarships are awarded annually for one year of graduate, undergraduate, or college or vocational study. Acceptance is based on academic achievement and financial need. Renewal applications accepted.
EIN: 751220266

3398
Bob Richardson Memorial Trust

c/o U.S. Bank, N.A.
P.O. Box 3168
Portland, OR 97208
Contact: Marilyn Norquist
Scholarship application address: c/o Richardson Scholarship Comm., Toledo High School, 1800 N.E. Sturdevant Rd., Toledo, OR 97391, tel.: (503) 336-1046

Foundation type: Independent foundation
Limitations: Scholarships to residents of the city of Toledo, OR, and Lincoln County, OR.
Financial data: Year ended 06/30/2005.
Assets, $2,962,027 (M); Expenditures, $200,869; Total giving, $154,038.
Type of support: Scholarships—to individuals.
Application information: Contact trust for current application deadline/guidelines.
EIN: 943101770

3399
Richardson Musical Education Scholarship Fund

c/o Baker Boyer National Bank
7601 W. Clearwater Ave., Ste. 404
Kennewick, WA 99336-1677 (509) 783-6800
Contact: C. Wayne May, Trust Off., Baker Boyer National Bank

Foundation type: Independent foundation
Limitations: Music scholarships to graduating seniors in the Richland, Pasco, Kennewick, Finley, Burbank, and Kiona-Benton school districts, WA, and to students of Columbia Basin College, Pasco, WA.
Financial data: Year ended 10/31/2004.
Assets, $362,178 (M); Expenditures, $10,788; Total giving, $5,000; Grants to individuals, 2 grants totaling $5,000.
Fields of interest: Music; Performing arts, education.
Type of support: Support to graduates or students of specific schools; Undergraduate support.

Application information: Deadline Jan. 5; Completion of formal application required, including music instructor's recommendation, transcripts, supplementary background material, and an eight-minute audition cassette tape; Interviews and auditions required; See program description for further information.
Program description:
   Robert W. Richardson Musical Education Scholarship: There are three awards available to cover the costs of tuition and books: the Robert W. Richardson Award, the Leone J. Richardson Award, and the Virginia Richardson Stanton Award. Applicants need not be music majors. They must, however, have a GPA of at least 2.0 and demonstrate talent and potential in either instrumental or vocal music. Career orientation, academic excellence, and social, civic, and personal responsibility will also be considered. Applicants must submit four copies of identical, eight-minute audition cassette tapes. Only side A may be used. Name and school must be marked on the tape, and must be stated along with the type of instrument at the beginning of the tape. Each excerpt must be introduced on the tape by title and composer. Solo works are preferred, but if a group performance is used, applicant's part must be identified and other performers credited. Selected students will be requested, before Feb. 4, to attend an interview. Those who are successful in the interview stage will then be required to perform at the Robert W. Richardson Annual Recital in March.
EIN: 916326487

3400
Richardson Scholarship Foundation, Inc.

P.O. Box 370
Vero Beach, FL 32961
Application address: P.O. Box 339, Vero Beach, FL 32961-0339

Foundation type: Operating foundation
Limitations: Graduate scholarships primarily to Indian River County, FL, residents. Recipients are selected on the basis of recommendation solicited by the foundation from educational institutions and other parties.
Financial data: Year ended 12/31/2004.
Assets, $121,827 (M); Expenditures, $34,598; Total giving, $33,975; Grants to individuals, 2 grants totaling $2,000 (high: $1,000, low: $1,000).
Type of support: Graduate support.
Application information: Application form required.
   Deadline(s): May 10
   Additional information: Application must include ACT student data form, family financial statement, high school transcripts, and SAT or ACT scores; Interviews required.
EIN: 650064113

3401
Charlotte M. Richardt Charitable Trust

c/o Ronald G. Keeping
P.O. Box 5
Henderson, KY 42419-0005

Foundation type: Independent foundation
Limitations: Scholarships to students of Central High School, IN, for higher education.
Financial data: Year ended 12/31/2002.
Assets, $325,404 (M); Expenditures, $378,821; Total giving, $368,600; Grants to individuals, 4 grants totaling $18,600 (high: $5,000, low: $3,600).

Type of support: Support to graduates or students of specific schools; Undergraduate support.
Application information: Unsolicited requests for funds not accepted.
EIN: 616233945

3402
Richland County Foundation

(formerly The Richland County Foundation of Mansfield, Ohio)
24 W. 3rd St., Ste. 100
Mansfield, OH   44902-1209   (419) 525-3020
Contact: Pamela H. Siegenthaler, C.E.O.
FAX: (419) 525-1590;
E-mail: info@rcfoundation.org; URL: http://www.rcfoundation.org

Foundation type: Community foundation
Limitations: Scholarships to financially needy residents of Richland County, OH, with at least a 2.5 GPA, for full-time undergraduate study.
Publications: Application guidelines; Annual report (including application guidelines); Informational brochure; Newsletter.
Financial data: Year ended 12/31/2004.
Assets, $60,542,628 (M); Expenditures, $2,660,571; Total giving, $2,098,918; Grants to individuals, 344 grants totaling $281,745 (high: $1,200, low: $15).
Type of support: Undergraduate support.
Application information: Application form required.
  Initial approach: Letter or telephone.
  Deadline(s): First Fri. of Jan., Mar., May, July, Sept. and Nov.
  Applicants should submit the following:
    1) FAFSA
    2) Transcripts
EIN: 340872883

3403
Richmond Educational Foundation

P.O. Box 460129
Escondido, CA   92046-0129
Application address: c/o James L. Richmond, Tr., 427 Washingtonia Dr., San Marcos, CA 92078-5033

Foundation type: Operating foundation
Limitations: Scholarships to residents of CA for higher education.
Financial data: Year ended 12/31/2003.
Assets, $267,002 (M); Expenditures, $37,865; Total giving, $9,635; Grants to individuals, totaling $9,635.
Fields of interest: Higher education.
Type of support: Scholarships—to individuals.
Application information: Application form required.
  Deadline(s): Apr. 15
  Applicants should submit the following:
    1) Letter(s) of recommendation
    2) Transcripts
  Additional information: Recipients must have applied for any available FASFA to be eligible for scholarships. They must be willing to work part-time and/or take out student loans in their name. Scholarships will not be renewed for recipients who do not work (after their first semester) unless they notify the selection committee in writing, or extenuating circumstances prevent their employment.
EIN: 330638221

3404
Ricker College Endowment Fund

c/o Ricker College Trustees
P.O. Box 1016
Houlton, ME   04730
Contact: Gary Bossie, Exec. Dir.
E-mail: rickerscholarship@verizon.net

Foundation type: Independent foundation
Limitations: Scholarships to graduates of high schools in Aroostook and Washington counties, ME, who are in the top 25 percent of their classes. Preference is shown to descendants of graduates of Ricker Classical Institute, Ricker Junior College, Ricker College, and to descendants of longtime Ricker teachers and staff. Scholarships are generally in the amount of $1,500 per year and are renewable for up to four years.
Publications: Informational brochure (including application guidelines).
Financial data: Year ended 12/31/2004.
Assets, $2,793,302 (M); Expenditures, $204,998; Total giving, $155,800; Grants to individuals, totaling $155,800.
Type of support: Support to graduates or students of specific schools; Undergraduate support.
Application information: Application form required.
  Deadline(s): Fourth Fri. of Apr.
  Applicants should submit the following:
    1) Transcripts
    2) Financial information
  Additional information: Application must also include proof of acceptance in a baccalaureate program.
EIN: 222709285

3405
Gladys & Evelyn Rickert Memorial Scholarship Fund

c/o National City Bank of Pennsylvania
P.O. Box 94651
Cleveland, OH   44101-4651
Application address: c/o Greenville Area High School, Attn: Principal, 9 Donation Rd., Greenville, PA 16125

Foundation type: Independent foundation
Limitations: Scholarships to students from Greenville Area Senior High School for higher education. Recipients are selected based on financial need, scholastic aptitude and academic performance.
Financial data: Year ended 12/31/2004.
Assets, $294,104 (M); Expenditures, $15,617; Total giving, $11,900; Grants to individuals, 14 grants totaling $11,900.
Type of support: Support to graduates or students of specific schools; Undergraduate support.
Application information: Applications accepted throughout the year; Contact fund for current application guidelines; Initial approach by letter.
EIN: 237876237

3406
Raymond and Helen Ricketts Scholarship Fund

P.O. Box 88
State Line, IN   47982-0088   (765) 793-2293
Contact: Donald L. Fowler, Tr.

Foundation type: Independent foundation
Limitations: Scholarships to graduates of Covington School Corporation and Metropolitan School District of Warren County, IN.
Financial data: Year ended 12/31/2004.
Assets, $204,234 (M); Expenditures, $11,650;

Total giving, $10,500; Grants to individuals, totaling $10,500.
Type of support: Scholarships—to individuals; Support to graduates or students of specific schools.
Application information: Deadline May 1; Completion of formal application required.
EIN: 356583846

3407
Faye Riddleberger Scholarship Trust

2114 North St.
Logansport, IN   46947-3750   (574) 722-3254
Contact: Jan M. Blackburn, Tr.

Foundation type: Independent foundation
Limitations: Scholarships to graduates of high schools in Cass County, IN, and to current students at Ivy Tech, Logansport, or Indiana University, Kokomo, IN.
Financial data: Year ended 12/31/2004.
Assets, $619,651 (M); Expenditures, $45,496; Total giving, $34,000; Grants to individuals, 15 grants totaling $34,000.
Type of support: Scholarships—to individuals; Support to graduates or students of specific schools.
Application information: The committee solicits applications for scholarships during the first quarter of each calendar year; Completion of formal application required, including completed FAF and letter of recommendation from school administration or teacher.
EIN: 356596875

3408
The Ridgefield Scholarship Group, Inc.

P.O. Box 823
Ridgefield, CT   06877
Contact: Linda Maggs, Treas.
Application address: 118 Ramapoo Rd., Ridgefield, CT 06877

Foundation type: Operating foundation
Limitations: Scholarships primarily to graduates of Ridgefield High School, CT, who are Ridgefield, CT, residents.
Financial data: Year ended 12/31/2003.
Assets, $174,248 (M); Expenditures, $36,820; Total giving, $27,500; Grants to individuals, 11 grants totaling $27,500 (high: $6,000, low: $1,000).
Type of support: Support to graduates or students of specific schools; Undergraduate support.
Application information: Deadline Apr. 15; Completion of formal application required; Contact Ridgefield High School Guidance Dept. for application form.
EIN: 061010124

3409
Albert Rieben Memorial Scholarship Fund, Inc.

c/o A.R. Rieben
11200 Albert Rieben Rd.
Bay Minette, AL   36507   (251) 937-7017

Foundation type: Operating foundation
Limitations: Scholarships to students residing in AL.
Financial data: Year ended 12/31/2002.
Assets, $21,010 (M); Expenditures, $18,127; Total giving, $18,000; Grants to individuals, 18

grants totaling $18,000 (high: $1,000, low: $1,000).

Type of support: Scholarships—to individuals.

Application information:

Deadline(s): May 1

Additional information: Application by letter including referrals from teachers and guidance counselors.

EIN: 630011787

3410

Herman Rieger Foundation

P.O. Box 169
Forrest, IL   61741-0169
Contact: Scholarship: Kay Crane
Application address: P.O. Box 541, Forrest, IL 61741

Foundation type: Independent foundation

Limitations: Scholarships to individuals from the Forrest, IL, area for undergraduate education.

Financial data: Year ended 01/31/2004. Assets, $112,280 (M); Expenditures, $5,395; Total giving, $12,550; Grants to individuals, 21 grants totaling $12,550 (high: $4,000, low: $250).

Type of support: Undergraduate support.

Application information: Application form required.

Deadline(s): Mar. 1.

Additional information: Contact foundation for current application guidelines.

EIN: 371206579

3411

Carl and Camilla Rietman Charitable Foundation

P.O. Box D
Lakeside, OR   97449-0803
Scholarship address: c/o Alfred C. Walsh Jr., 280 N. Collier St., Coquille, OR 97423, tel.: (541) 396-2169

Foundation type: Independent foundation

Limitations: Scholarships to graduates of Coquille High School, OR.

Financial data: Year ended 09/30/2004. Assets, $3,782,162 (M); Expenditures, $243,986; Total giving, $204,834; Grants to individuals, 51 grants totaling $128,334 (high: $5,000, low: $2,500).

Type of support: Support to graduates or students of specific schools; Undergraduate support.

Application information: Deadline Apr. 15; Completion of formal application required, including references.

EIN: 931221623

3412

Rigorous Educational Assistance for Deserving Youth Foundation, Inc.

(also known as READY Foundation, Inc.)
310 South St.
P.O. Box 1975
Morristown, NJ   07962-1975
Contact: Donald R. Smith

Foundation type: Independent foundation

Limitations: Scholarships to students in Newark, NJ, for higher education.

Financial data: Year ended 09/30/2004. Assets, $52,960 (M); Expenditures, $1,049,108; Total giving, $485,213; Grants to individuals, totaling $485,213.

Type of support: Undergraduate support.

Application information: Unsolicited requests for funds not accepted.

EIN: 222815535

3413

The Grace O. & Harry D. Riley Foundation

936 S. 111th Plz.
Omaha, NE   68154-3306   (402) 334-9118
Application addresses: c/o Randolph High School, Attn.: Scholarship Comm., 207 N. Pierce, P.O. Box 755, Randolph, NE 68771, tel.: (402) 337-0252; or c/o Omaha North High School, Attn.: Scholarship Comm., 4323 N. 37th St., Omaha, NE 68111, tel.: (402) 554-6506

Foundation type: Independent foundation

Limitations: Scholarships to high school students of Randolph and Omaha North high schools, NE for higher education.

Financial data: Year ended 12/31/2004. Assets, $262,521 (M); Expenditures, $13,644; Total giving, $11,800; Grants to individuals, 9 grants totaling $10,800.

Type of support: Support to graduates or students of specific schools; Undergraduate support.

Application information: Application form required.

Deadline(s): Apr.1.

EIN: 470697802

3414

Robert Rimmele Scholarship Fund

c/o Bank of America, N.A.
P.O. Box 1802
Providence, RI   02901-1802
Application address: c/o Susana Forster-Castillo, Bank of America, N.A., 100 Federal St., Boston, MA 02110

Foundation type: Independent foundation

Limitations: Scholarships to graduating high school students who are residents of Needham, MA.

Financial data: Year ended 12/31/2004. Assets, $318,236 (M); Expenditures, $16,221; Total giving, $11,000; Grants to individuals, 9 grants totaling $11,000.

Type of support: Scholarships—to individuals.

Application information: Deadline end of Feb.; Completion of formal application required, including financial and educational information.

EIN: 046712607

3415

Lila Rinker Trust

(also known as Dr. E. B. Rinker Medical Scholarship Fund)
c/o JPMorgan Chase Bank, N.A
P.O. Box 1308
Milwaukee, WI   53201

Foundation type: Independent foundation

Limitations: Scholarships to students of the School of Medicine, Indiana University, IN.

Financial data: Year ended 06/30/2005. Assets, $944,236 (M); Expenditures, $52,582; Total giving, $43,808.

Fields of interest: Medical school/education.

Type of support: Support to graduates or students of specific schools; Graduate support.

Application information: Applications not accepted.

EIN: 356262657

3416

Ripley County Community Foundation, Inc.

132 S. Main St.
P.O. Box 279
Batesville, IN   47006   (812) 933-1098
Contact: Sally Morris, Exec. Dir.
FAX: (812) 933-0096; E-mail: rccfound@nalu.net; Additional tel.: (887) 234-5220; Additional E-mail: smorris@rccfonline.org; URL: http://www.rccfonline.org

Foundation type: Community foundation

Limitations: Scholarships to residents of Ripley County, IN, for higher education.

Financial data: Year ended 12/31/2004. Assets, $6,451,059 (M); Expenditures, $579,622; Total giving, $357,415; Grants to individuals, totaling $103,017.

Type of support: Scholarships—to individuals.

Application information: Contact foundation for current application deadline/guidelines; Interviews required.

EIN: 352048001

3417

Jean Risley Educational Trust

c/o Wells Fargo Bank Northwest, N.A.
P.O. Box 21927
Seattle, WA   98111

Foundation type: Independent foundation

Limitations: Student loans to senior-year law students in OR. Preference is given to individuals in Benton, Linn, and Marion counties.

Financial data: Year ended 11/30/2004. Assets, $833,623 (M); Expenditures, $45,146; Total giving, $25,000; Grants to individuals, 7 grants totaling $25,000.

Fields of interest: Law school/education.

Type of support: Graduate support.

Application information: Application form required.

Deadline(s): Contact trust for current application deadline

Applicants should submit the following:

1) Transcripts

Program description:

Loan Program: Applicants must provide letter from registrar's office stating that they have successfully completed their junior year and are enrolled full-time for the senior year. Loans may be extended by determination of need. The maximum loan per student is $5,000. The interest rate is six percent which accrues from the date the student completes school. Repayment of the loan begins six months after graduation. Minimum payment amount is $50 per month including interest. Maximum loan term is ten years.

EIN: 943117918

3418

Lois E. Riss Trust

c/o Wayne Kjeldgaard
P.O. Box 436
Big Springs, NE   69122-0436   (308) 889-3681

Foundation type: Independent foundation

Limitations: Scholarships to high school seniors and graduates of high schools in the cities of Big Spring, Chappell, and Brule, NE for higher education.

Financial data: Year ended 12/31/2004. Assets, $412,523 (M); Expenditures, $28,988; Total giving, $20,550; Grants to individuals, 19 grants totaling $18,500.

Type of support: Scholarships—to individuals.

Application information: Application by letter including ambitions, objectives and references.
EIN: 476199355

3419
Lieutenant Robert Bolenius Ritchie Memorial Fund
c/o Wachovia Bank, N.A.
100 N. Main St., 13th Fl.
Winston-Salem, NC 27150

Foundation type: Independent foundation
Limitations: Scholarships by nomination only to financially needy graduates of public high schools in Lancaster City and County, PA.
Financial data: Year ended 12/31/2004.
Assets, $954,323 (M); Expenditures, $46,402; Total giving, $38,500; Grants to individuals, 20 grants totaling $38,500.
Fields of interest: Public affairs, citizen participation.
Type of support: Support to graduates or students of specific schools; Awards/grants by nomination only; Undergraduate support.
Application information: Application form required.
Additional information: Students are nominated by school officials; Contact high school for current nomination guidelines.
Program description:
Scholarships: Scholarships are awarded on the basis of scholastic achievement, financial need, results of interview, and patriotism and leadership. Recipients must support the ideals of Lt. Ritchie's Alma Mater, West Point, that is Duty, Honor, and Country. Nominees are selected by the superintendents, principals, and guidance counselors of Lancaster city and county high schools and are presented to the fund for final selection. Scholarships are renewable.
EIN: 236718706

3420
Riverwood International Corporation Philanthropic Fund
814 Livingston Ct.
Marietta, GA 30067   (770) 644-3000
Contact: Patricia Szall

Foundation type: Company-sponsored foundation
Limitations: Scholarships to the children and legal dependents of Riverwood International employees who have been with the company at least one year for higher education.
Publications: Informational brochure.
Financial data: Year ended 12/31/2002.
Assets, $10,130 (M); Expenditures, $53,524; Total giving, $53,509.
Type of support: Employee-related scholarships.
Application information: Application form required.
Deadline(s): Apr. 1.
Applicants should submit the following:
1) Transcripts
2) Letter(s) of recommendation
EIN: 582059854

3421
Rixstine Charitable Trust
(formerly Mary Amanda Hawke Rixstine Charitable Trust)
c/o Wachovia Bank, N.A.
100 N. Main St., 13th Fl.
Winston-Salem, NC 27150
Application address: c/o Wachovia Bank, N.A., Trust Dept., 123 S. Broad St., Philadelphia, PA 19109-9989

Foundation type: Independent foundation
Limitations: Scholarships to graduates of schools in the Phoenixville, PA, area.
Financial data: Year ended 12/31/2004.
Assets, $183,231 (M); Expenditures, $8,049; Total giving, $7,000; Grants to individuals, 5 grants totaling $7,000.
Type of support: Support to graduates or students of specific schools; Undergraduate support.
Application information: Deadline Apr. 29; Contact trust for current application guidelines.
EIN: 236242481

3422
Ruth E. Roach Memorial Scholarship Fund
1150 S. McCord Rd., Ste. 601
Holland, OH 43528   (419) 865-4480
Contact: Rochelle Bartlett

Foundation type: Independent foundation
Limitations: Scholarships to high school graduates residing in OH, for undergraduate education at U.S. institutions.
Financial data: Year ended 12/31/2004.
Assets, $338,720 (M); Expenditures, $17,443; Total giving, $16,750; Grants to individuals, totaling $16,750.
Type of support: Undergraduate support.
Application information: Applications accepted. Application form required.
Deadline(s): Apr. 15 for Fall semester and Sept. 15 for Spring semester
EIN: 341799826

3423
Mary E. Roark Scholarship Fund Trust
123 Public Sq.
Gallatin, TN 37066   (615) 452-4611
Contact: Nathan Harsh, Tr.

Foundation type: Independent foundation
Limitations: Scholarships to financially needy graduates of Gallatin High School and Westmoreland High School, TN.
Financial data: Year ended 12/31/2004.
Assets, $352,521 (M); Expenditures, $15,762; Total giving, $14,572; Grants to individuals, 11 grants totaling $14,572 (high: $7,360; low: $51).
Type of support: Support to graduates or students of specific schools; Undergraduate support.
Application information: Application by letter including personal life history, resume, grades, and work background.
EIN: 626289349

3424
Fred L. Robbins Trust
c/o U.S. Trust Co., N.A.
P.O. Box 55122
Boston, MA 02205
Application address: c/o Acton-Boxborough Regional High School, Attn: Stephen Donovan Jr., Principal, Acton, 96 Hayward Rd., Acton, MA 01720

Foundation type: Independent foundation
Limitations: Scholarships to student residents of Acton, MA.
Financial data: Year ended 12/31/2004.
Assets, $436,060 (M); Expenditures, $18,913; Total giving, $13,000; Grants to individuals, 9 grants totaling $13,000.
Type of support: Scholarships—to individuals.
Application information: Deadline Apr. 1; Completion of formal application required.
EIN: 046095991

3425
Louis A. Roberg Endowment Trust
P.O. Box 682
Litchfield, MN 55355-0682

Foundation type: Independent foundation
Limitations: Scholarships to financially needy graduating seniors residing in Meeker, McLeod, or Kandiyohi counties, MN, and graduating from one of six participating high schools, to attend agricultural and vocational schools located anywhere, and public colleges and universities in MN.
Financial data: Year ended 09/30/2004.
Assets, $1,437,387 (M); Expenditures, $74,755; Total giving, $48,408.
Fields of interest: Vocational education; Agriculture.
Type of support: Technical education support; Undergraduate support.
Application information: Application form required.
Deadline(s): Apr.
Applicants should submit the following:
1) Class rank
2) Letter(s) of recommendation
3) Financial information
4) Essay
Additional information: Scholarships and loans are based on financial need, scholastic ability and achievement, extracurricular participation, community service, and likelihood of success in chosen field. Grants are renewable.
EIN: 416223072

3426
Mary K. Roberts Scholarship Foundation
c/o National Bank & Trust Co.
230 W. State St., MSC M-300
Sycamore, IL 60178
Contact: Marilyn Knetsch, V.P. and Trust Off., National Bank & Trust Co.

Foundation type: Independent foundation
Limitations: Scholarships to graduates of Sycamore High School, IL, who are pursuing degrees in social work, sociology, nursing, or special education at four-year colleges and universities.
Financial data: Year ended 12/31/2004.
Assets, $494,630 (M); Expenditures, $30,249; Total giving, $22,820; Grants to individuals, totaling $22,820.
Fields of interest: Education, special; Nursing school/education; Reading; Human services; Anthropology/sociology.
Type of support: Support to graduates or students of specific schools; Undergraduate support.
Application information: Deadline Apr. 1; Completion of formal application required.
EIN: 366868922

3427
Roberts Student Aid Fund
c/o Bank of America, N.A.
P.O. Box 441, NJ6-219-02-03
Ridgefield Park, NJ 07660-9984
Application address: c/o Bank of America, N.A.,
Attn.: Cindy Leip, Trust Off., 1125 Rte. 22 W.,
Bridgewater, NJ 08807, tel.: (908) 253-4863

Foundation type: Independent foundation
Limitations: Scholarships to high school seniors in
Bethlehem, PA, for undergraduate education.
Financial data: Year ended 12/31/2002.
Assets, $126,140 (M); Expenditures, $21,032;
Total giving, $18,400; Grants to individuals, 4
grants totaling $18,400 (high: $4,600, low:
$4,600).
Type of support: Undergraduate support.
Application information: Application form required.
  Deadline(s): Mar. 31
  Additional information: See high school guidance
  counselor for application.
EIN: 246020452

3428
A. F. Robertson Family Memorial Fund
c/o National City Bank
P.O. Box 94651
Cleveland, OH 44101-4651
Contact: Tim Ueber, Tr. Off.
Application address: c/o National City Bank of
Indiana, Trust Dept., P.O. Box 5031, Indianapolis,
IN 46255, tel.: (317) 267-7288

Foundation type: Independent foundation
Limitations: Scholarships to students of Seymour
High School and Brownstown Central High School,
both in IN. Preference is given to residents of
Brownstown and Hamilton Townships.
Financial data: Year ended 12/31/2004.
Assets, $606,619 (M); Expenditures, $43,138;
Total giving, $31,525; Grants to individuals, 30
grants totaling $31,525 (high: $1,650, low: $400).
Type of support: Scholarships—to individuals;
Support to graduates or students of specific
schools.
Application information: Application form required.
  Deadline(s): Mar. 1
  Applicants should submit the following:
    1) Transcripts
    2) Letter(s) of recommendation
    3) FAFSA
    4) FAF
  Additional information: Application must also
  include an appraisal of qualifications by
  principal or counselor. Applications may be
  obtained from guidance counselors of
  Seymour High School and Brownstown Central
  High School, both in IN. Interviews required.
EIN: 356057077

3429
The Beatrice & Samuel Robins
Educational Scholarship Foundation
70 Marcus Dr.
Melville, NY 11747-4210

Foundation type: Independent foundation
Limitations: Scholarships to individuals in NY.
Financial data: Year ended 06/30/2004.
Assets, $25,659 (M); Expenditures, $18,649;
Total giving, $18,500; Grants to individuals, 13
grants totaling $18,500 (high: $3,000, low: $500).
Type of support: Scholarships—to individuals.

Application information: Applications not
accepted.
EIN: 113268877

3430
Jackie Robinson Foundation, Inc.
c/o Scholarship Prog.
3 W. 35th St., 11th Fl.
New York, NY 10001-2204   (212) 290-8600
FAX: (212) 290-8081;
E-mail: general@jackierobinson.org; URL: http://
www.jackierobinson.org

Foundation type: Public charity
Limitations: Four-year college scholarships to
financially needy minority students who are high
school graduates.
Publications: Biennial report; Financial statement;
Informational brochure.
Financial data: Year ended 06/30/2003.
Assets, $10,781,311 (M); Expenditures,
$3,095,654; Total giving, $1,220,104; Grants to
individuals, 202 grants totaling $1,220,104.
Fields of interest: Minorities.
Type of support: Undergraduate support.
Application information:
  Deadline(s): Apr. 2
  Additional information: Contact foundation for
  current application guidelines; Candidates are
  recruited through various print media,
  mailings to counselors, teachers and
  principals, and JRF's network of concerned
  community leaders, and then screened by
  corporate, academic, and civic leaders who
  constitute the national selection committee in
  New York City, and five regional committees
  in Atlanta, Boston, Chicago, Los Angeles, and
  Stamford.
Program description:
  *JRF Education and Leadership Development
  Program:* The program helps promising students to
  obtain college degrees and pursue successful
  careers by providing scholarships of up to $6,000
  annually for four consecutive years. JRF also
  provides mentoring, counseling, career and
  leadership development, summer jobs, and
  placement assistance after graduation.
  Scholarships are awarded on the basis of academic
  achievement, leadership potential, financial need,
  and the results of the personal interview. The
  majority of JRF scholars are sponsored by
  corporations, philanthropic organizations, and
  private individuals. During their undergraduate
  years, JRF scholars are expected to engage in
  significant community service efforts.
EIN: 132896345

3431
Fred L. Robinson Fund
c/o First State Bank of Malta
P.O. Box 910
Malta, MT 59538-0910

Foundation type: Independent foundation
Limitations: Scholarships to Phillips County, MT,
high school seniors.
Financial data: Year ended 12/31/2004.
Assets, $0 (M); Expenditures, $3,000; Total giving,
$3,000; Grant to an individual, 1 grant totaling
$3,000.
Type of support: Support to graduates or students
of specific schools; Undergraduate support.
Application information: Deadline Jan. 15;
Application by letter.
EIN: 237079421

3432
Florence M. Robinson Scholarship Trust
c/o Peoples Bank
P.O. Box 20
Ottawa, KS 66067-0020
Application address: c/o Darren Dennis, Principal,
Ottawa High School, 11th & Ash Sts., Ottawa, KS
66067, tel.: (785) 229-8020

Foundation type: Independent foundation
Limitations: Scholarships to students of Unified
School District No. 290, Ottawa, KS.
Financial data: Year ended 08/31/2004.
Assets, $385,038 (M); Expenditures, $17,501;
Total giving, $12,050; Grants to individuals,
totaling $12,050.
Fields of interest: Vocational education; Teacher
school/education.
Type of support: Support to graduates or students
of specific schools; Undergraduate support.
Application information: Application form required.
  Deadline(s): May 1
  Applicants should submit the following:
    1) Transcripts
    2) GPA
    3) Letter(s) of recommendation
Program description:
  Scholarships: Academic scholarships are for four
  years. Vocational scholarships may be for one- or
  two-year programs. Proof of enrollment is required
  each year before scholarship is disbursed.
  Recipients must maintain at least a 2.0 GPA.
  Scholarships are granted in semester payments.
  Scholarships are awarded in the following
  categories:
  · students entering the field of education
  · students with financial need
  · students who are leaders involved in the
    community, and are academic achievers
  · students enrolling in vocational programs.
EIN: 486295973

3433
Harry W. and Virginia Robinson Trust
c/o Bank of America, N.A.
P.O. Box 513189, GMF
Los Angeles, CA 90051

Foundation type: Independent foundation
Limitations: Scholarships to students attending
California Institute of Technology and Pitzer
College.
Financial data: Year ended 05/31/2005.
Assets, $4,921,473 (M); Expenditures,
$274,042; Total giving, $221,449; Grants to
individuals, totaling $221,449.
Type of support: Scholarships—to individuals;
Support to graduates or students of specific
schools.
Application information: Application form not
required.
EIN: 956648391

3434
Mary H. Robinson Trust
c/o Bank of America, N.A.
231 S. LaSalle St., IL1-231-14-19
Chicago, IL 60697

Foundation type: Independent foundation
Limitations: Scholarships to students or graduates
of Bolivar public schools, MO.
Financial data: Year ended 12/31/2004.
Assets, $623,532 (M); Expenditures, $28,605;
Total giving, $22,295; Grants to individuals,
totaling $22,295.

Fields of interest: Vocational education.
Type of support: Support to graduates or students of specific schools; Technical education support; Undergraduate support.
Application information: Applications not accepted.

Additional information: Scholarships are awarded for higher education, including trade and vocational education. Scholarships are renewable, providing the recipient maintains a good scholastic average.
EIN: 436260501

3435
John W. Robinson Welfare Trust
P.O. Box 101
Gardiner, ME 04345-0026
Contact: Glenna Nowell, Tr.

Foundation type: Independent foundation
Limitations: Scholarships to financially needy residents of Gardiner, ME, and the surrounding area, who are graduating seniors of Gardiner Area High School, ME, to attend accredited universities, colleges, junior colleges, vocational/technical schools, and professional schools. Scholarships may be used for professional programs such as nursing and legal studies.
Financial data: Year ended 12/31/2003.
Assets, $1,332,748 (M); Expenditures, $55,513; Total giving, $35,400; Grants to individuals, 14 grants totaling $13,500 (high: $1,000, low: $500).
Fields of interest: Vocational education; College; University.
Type of support: Support to graduates or students of specific schools.
Application information: Applications not accepted.

Additional information: Contact Gardiner Area High School for application guidelines.
EIN: 016009329

3436
Angus Robinson, Jr. Memorial Foundation, Inc.
c/o Odyssey American
300 First Stamford Pl.
Stamford, CT 06902
Contact: Pat Robinson, Pres.

Foundation type: Independent foundation
Limitations: Scholarships to students attending or planning to attend an accredited four-year college or university with an insurance-related degree program and with at least a "B" average in high school, 1050 SAT score, and involvement in extracurricular or community activities.
Financial data: Year ended 12/31/2004.
Assets, $784,276 (M); Expenditures, $52,886; Total giving, $49,500; Grants to individuals, totaling $49,500.
Fields of interest: Business school/education.
Type of support: Undergraduate support.
Application information:

Deadline(s): Contact foundation for current application deadline
Applicants should submit the following:
1) Transcripts
2) Financial information
3) FAF
Additional information: Recipients must maintain a 2.75 GPA, provide verification of good standing from the college or university, and submit annually a 5-page paper detailing the event which the applicant deems to have had

the most significant impact on the insurance industry during the previous year.
EIN: 061300536

3437
Robustelli Family Foundation
118 St. Nicholas Ave.
South Plainfield, NJ 07080
Contact: Jonathan Robustelli, Tr.

Foundation type: Company-sponsored foundation
Limitations: Scholarships to residents of the South Plainfield, NJ, area.
Financial data: Year ended 12/31/2004.
Assets, $187,940 (M); Expenditures, $28,655; Total giving, $28,600; Grants to individuals, 4 grants totaling $13,300 (high: $5,000, low: $600).
Type of support: Undergraduate support.
Application information: Applications not accepted.

Additional information: Unsolicited requests for funds not considered or acknowledged.
EIN: 223341755

3438
The Rochetta-Wessies Scholarship Foundation
c/o Carleton M. Tower & Co., Ltd.
10 S. LaSalle St., No. 3450
Chicago, IL 60603
Contact: Rev. John McGivern, Pres.
Application address: c/o St. Edmund Church, 188 S. Oak Park Ave., Oak Park, IL 60302

Foundation type: Independent foundation
Limitations: Scholarships to graduates of St. Edmund's Grade School, IL.
Financial data: Year ended 12/31/2004.
Assets, $911,265 (M); Expenditures, $46,223; Total giving, $44,125; Grants to individuals, 15 grants totaling $44,125 (high: $5,125, low: $1,000). Subtotal for support to graduates or students of specific schools: 15 grants totaling $44,125 (high: $5,125, low: $1,000).
Type of support: Support to graduates or students of specific schools; Undergraduate support.
Application information:

Deadline(s): June 15
Additional information: Contact foundation for current application guidelines.
EIN: 363853007

3439
Rockford Health Careers Foundation
c/o WCMS
6991 Redansa Dr.
Rockford, IL 61108
Contact: Terry Rifkin, Pres.; for scholarship application: Kathy White
Scholarship application address: 1419 National Ave., Rockford, IL 61103
Application address: 2193 Dior Dr., Rockford, IL 61107

Foundation type: Independent foundation
Limitations: Scholarships to residents of Winnebago County, IL, and to individuals who have been accepted at professional schools in the health care field in Winnebago County, IL. Students attending the following schools are eligible: University of Illinois College of Medicine, Rock Valley College, and Northern Illinois University.
Financial data: Year ended 09/30/2004.
Assets, $333,683 (M); Expenditures, $16,613;

Total giving, $13,000; Grants to individuals, totaling $13,000.
Type of support: Support to graduates or students of specific schools.
Application information: Application form required.

Initial approach: Letter.
Deadline(s): Applications accepted throughout the year.
EIN: 366115620

3440
Rocky Mountain Elk Foundation, Inc.
5705 Grant Creek Rd.
P.O. Box 8249
Missoula, MT 59807   (406) 523-4500
Contact: Sara Dexter, Grants Admin.
FAX: (404) 523-4550; *E-mail:* info@rmef.org;
Additional tel.: (800) 225-5355; *URL:* http://www.rmef.org

Foundation type: Public charity
Limitations: Scholarships to college juniors and seniors with wildlife-related majors.
Publications: Application guidelines; Annual report.
Financial data: Year ended 12/31/2004.
Assets, $44,758,397 (M); Expenditures, $31,634,704.
Fields of interest: Animals/wildlife, preservation/protection.
Type of support: Undergraduate support.
Application information: Application form required.

Deadline(s): Mar. 1
Applicants should submit the following:
1) Letter(s) of recommendation
2) Essay
Program description:

Wildlife Leadership Awards: Ten $2,000 undergraduate scholarship awards are given to junior- and senior-year college students in recognized U.S. or Canadian wildlife programs with at least one semester or two quarters remaining in their degree programs. Previous recipients are ineligible. Applicants must be enrolled as a full-time student for the following fall semester/quarter. Recipients also receive engraved wall plaques and free one-year memberships in RMEF along with their cash awards. Recipients are announced in Apr. and scholarships are paid at the beginning of the fall semester/quarter.
EIN: 810421425

3441
Roddick Fund
390 Mentor Ave.
Painesville, OH 44077
Contact: R. Johnson, Tr.

Foundation type: Independent foundation
Limitations: Scholarships to residents of the greater Painesville, OH, community.
Financial data: Year ended 12/31/2004.
Assets, $1,175,816 (M); Expenditures, $60,809; Total giving, $58,921; Grants to individuals, totaling $58,921.
Type of support: Scholarships—to individuals.
Application information: Deadline Apr. 1; Initial approach by letter; Completion of formal application required.
EIN: 346793439

3442
Polly W. Roesch Vocal Scholarship Trust
c/o JPMorgan Chase Bank, N.A.
P.O. Box 1308
Milwaukee, WI 53201
Contact: JoAnn Ley, Trust Off., JPMorgan Chase
Bank, N.A.
Application address: 1 E. Old Capital Plz., 3rd Fl.,
Springfield, IL 62701-1320, tel.: (217) 525-9745

Foundation type: Independent foundation
Limitations: Scholarships to Sangamon County, IL,
residents who are planning to be vocal music
majors.
Financial data: Year ended 12/31/2004.
Assets, $197,024 (M); Expenditures, $7,549;
Total giving, $6,000; Grants to individuals, totaling
$6,000.
Fields of interest: Music; Performing arts,
education.
Type of support: Scholarships—to individuals.
Application information: Application form required.
Deadline(s): Mar. 1
Program description:
Scholarship Fund: In addition to a standard
scholarship application form, applicants must
participate in a vocal audition. Material to be
covered may include:
  · A performance (prepared piece) not longer
    than 10 minutes
  · Sight reading
Students are encouraged to perform from memory
and must provide their own accompanists.
EIN: 376234631

3443
Rogers Brothers Foundation
c/o The Bank of Commerce
P.O. Box 1887
Idaho Falls, ID 83403

Foundation type: Company-sponsored foundation
Limitations: Scholarships to children of current
employees or retirees of Rogers Brothers Company,
or Rogers NK Seed Company, or their subsidiaries,
who have completed at least 3,000 hours of
service.
Financial data: Year ended 06/30/2005.
Assets, $2,078 (M); Expenditures, $9,050; Total
giving, $8,550; Grants to individuals, 10 grants
totaling $8,550 (high: $2,000, low: $100).
Type of support: Employee-related scholarships.
Application information: Contact foundation for
current application deadline/guidelines.
EIN: 826012018

3444
Ada M. Rogers Trust
(also known as Bruce & Mary Rogers Memorial
Student Loan Fund)
c/o Sky Bank
P.O. Box 479
Youngstown, OH 44501-0479
Application address: c/o Rev. James L. Unger,
Western Reserve Baptist Church, 8590 Hitchcock
Rd., Youngstown, OH 44512

Foundation type: Independent foundation
Limitations: Student loans to members or children
of members of the Western Reserve Baptist
Church, Trumbull Baptist Association of Churches,
Ohio Baptist Convention, and American Baptist
Church USA. Loans are interest-free if repaid within
five years of graduation.
Financial data: Year ended 08/31/2004.
Assets, $270,557 (M); Expenditures, $87,006;

Total giving, $71,000; Grants to individuals,
totaling $71,000.
Fields of interest: Christian agencies & churches;
Religion.
Type of support: Student loans—to individuals.
Application information: Deadline Feb. 15;
Completion of formal application required, including
a complete biographical record, a statement of
plans after graduation, transcripts, two letters of
recommendation, and a statement of financial
need.
EIN: 346631957

3445
The Rogow Greenberg Foundation, Inc.
(formerly The Rogow Birken Foundation, Inc.)
c/o Birken Manufacturing Co.
3 Old Windsor Rd.
Bloomfield, CT 06002
Contact: Gary Greenberg, V.P.

Foundation type: Independent foundation
Limitations: Scholarships to residents of CT, FL,
MA, and NY.
Financial data: Year ended 12/31/2004.
Assets, $8,596,358 (M); Expenditures,
$544,044; Total giving, $393,324; Grants to
individuals, 26 grants totaling $125,124 (high:
$25,000, low: $400).
Type of support: Scholarships—to individuals.
Application information: Applications by letter
accepted throughout the year.
EIN: 061051591

3446
William G. Rohrer, Jr. Educational Foundation
c/o PNC Advisors
1600 Market St., 4th Fl.
Philadelphia, PA 19103-7240
Contact: John C. Watson, V.P., PNC Advisors
Application address: c/o PNC Advisors, Rte. 38 at
Eastgate Dr., Morristown, NJ 08057, tel.: (856)
638-4906

Foundation type: Independent foundation
Limitations: Scholarships to financially needy
residents of the Haddon Township, NJ, area.
Financial data: Year ended 12/31/2004.
Assets, $1,004,590 (M); Expenditures, $55,246;
Total giving, $36,000; Grants to individuals,
totaling $36,000.
Type of support: Scholarships—to individuals.
Application information: Deadline Mar. 31; Initial
approach by letter; Completion of formal application
required, including personal essay and financial
information.
EIN: 226070758

3447
Rolfs Educational Foundation, Ltd.
c/o U.S. Bank
P.O. Box 2043
Milwaukee, WI 53201-9116 (414) 287-5668

Foundation type: Independent foundation
Limitations: Scholarships to students who are
residents of West Bend, WI. Also, awards to
teachers in the West Bend, WI, area.
Financial data: Year ended 12/31/2004.
Assets, $768,672 (M); Expenditures, $57,620;
Total giving, $56,500; Grants to individuals,
totaling $56,500.

Type of support: Awards/prizes; Undergraduate
support.
Application information: Applications not
accepted.
EIN: 391651525

3448
Mars & Verna Rolfson Scholarship Trust
c/o First Interstate Bank
P.O. Box 1299
Polson, MT 59860-1299

Foundation type: Independent foundation
Limitations: Scholarships to seniors and graduates
of Polson High School, MT, for higher education or
Vocational/Technical.
Financial data: Year ended 12/31/2004.
Assets, $549,730 (M); Expenditures, $23,569;
Total giving, $17,750; Grants to individuals,
totaling $17,750.
Type of support: Support to graduates or students
of specific schools; Undergraduate support.
Application information:
Deadline(s): Apr. 1
Additional information: Completion of formal
application required, including transcripts,
FAF, and three references.
EIN: 363677368

3449
John W. Rollison Educational Scholarship Trust
c/o Wachovia Bank, N.A.
100 N. Main St., 13th Fl.
Winston-Salem, NC 27150

Foundation type: Independent foundation
Limitations: Scholarships to students of Franklin
and Southampton counties, VA.
Financial data: Year ended 12/31/2004.
Assets, $1,061,538 (M); Expenditures, $58,463;
Total giving, $44,345; Grants to individuals,
totaling $44,345.
Type of support: Scholarships—to individuals.
Application information: Application form not
required.
Deadline(s): None
Additional information: Applications by letter.
EIN: 546485419

3450
Ronald McDonald House Charities of Greater Washington, DC, Inc.
1326 Quincy St., N.E.
Washington, DC 20017 (202) 529-8204
Additional tel.: Grants Coord. (703) 698-7080 for
applications; URL: http://www.rmhc.greaterdc.org

Foundation type: Public charity
Limitations: Scholarships to residents of DC, MD,
VA, and WV who have health-related issues.
Publications: Financial statement; Grants list;
Informational brochure (including application
guidelines); Newsletter.
Financial data: Year ended 12/31/2004.
Assets, $10,969,797 (L); Expenditures,
$1,230,063; Total giving, $239,202; Grants to
individuals, 24 grants totaling $48,000 (high:
$2,000, low: $2,000).
Type of support: Undergraduate support.
Application information: Applications accepted.
Initial approach: Letter.

Additional information: Contact foundation for further program guidelines.
EIN: 521132262

3451
Ronald McDonald House Charities of New Mexico

1011 Yale N.E.
Albuquerque, NM   87106   (505) 842-8960
Contact: Sandra Mann, Exec. Dir.
FAX: (505) 764-0412;
E-mail: smann7@comcast.net; URL: http://www.rmhc-nm.org/

Foundation type: Public charity
Limitations: Undergraduate scholarships to Latino students graduating from NM high schools.
Publications: Application guidelines; Annual report; Financial statement; Informational brochure (including application guidelines); Newsletter.
Financial data: Year ended 12/31/2003. Assets, $3,054,836 (M); Expenditures, $465,094; Total giving, $67,597; Grants to individuals, 35 grants totaling $35,000 (high: $1,000, low: $1,000).
Fields of interest: Hispanics/Latinos; Economically disadvantaged.
Type of support: Undergraduate support.
Application information: Application form required.
Deadline(s): Feb. 1
Additional information: Applications are sent to schools, and are available at McDonald's Restaurants.
Program description:
Hispanic American Commitment to Education Resources (RMHC/HACER) Scholarship Program: These $1,000 scholarships are awarded to Latino students based on academic achievement, financial need, and involvement in their community. To be eligible, students must have at least one parent of Hispanic origin, be eligible to enroll in and attend a two- or four-year college with a full course of study in the U.S., and reside in a participating area. Most scholarships are in the amount of $1,000 and are designed for graduating seniors, but some local programs may award different scholarship amounts. See Web site for full listing of participating areas.
EIN: 850283204

3452
Freda T. Roof Memorial Scholarship Fund

c/o Wells Fargo Bank West, N.A.
P.O. Box 5825
Denver, CO   80274
Contact: Mary Jane Simmons, Trust Off., Wells Fargo Bank West, N.A.

Foundation type: Independent foundation
Limitations: Scholarships to financially needy and worthy students in CO obtaining a professional education at nonprofit and accredited colleges and universities in CO.
Financial data: Year ended 12/31/2004. Assets, $1,534,913 (M); Expenditures, $96,160; Total giving, $81,400; Grants to individuals, 37 grants totaling $81,400 (high: $2,200, low: $2,200).
Type of support: Undergraduate support.
Application information: Students must apply to their school's financial aid office, and not directly to the bank.
EIN: 846016684

3453
Rooke Foundation, Inc.

P.O. Box 610
Woodsboro, TX   78393-0610
Contact: Robert E. Rooke, Jr., V.P.
Application address: P.O. Box 7, Woodsboro, TX 78393

Foundation type: Independent foundation
Limitations: Scholarships to graduates of high schools in Refugio County, TX.
Financial data: Year ended 12/31/2004. Assets, $183,025 (M); Expenditures, $8,025; Total giving, $8,000; Grants to individuals, totaling $8,000.
Type of support: Support to graduates or students of specific schools; Undergraduate support.
Application information: Deadline Apr. 1; Completion of formal application required; Applications available from Refugio County high schools; Interviews required.
EIN: 746003460

3454
Art Rooney Scholarship Fund

1 Oxford Ctr., 40th Fl.
Pittsburgh, PA   15219-6498   (412) 392-2000
Contact: Arthur J. Rooney II, Dir.

Foundation type: Public charity
Limitations: Scholarships to graduates of Oliver High School, Perry High School, or North Catholic High School, all in Pittsburgh, PA.
Financial data: Year ended 12/31/2003. Assets, $125,138 (M); Expenditures, $61,981; Total giving, $32,500; Grants to individuals, 13 grants totaling $32,500 (high: $2,500, low: $2,500).
Type of support: Support to graduates or students of specific schools.
Application information: Applications accepted.
Initial approach: Letter.
Deadline(s): June 1
Applicants should submit the following:
1) Letter(s) of recommendation
Additional information: Contact foundation for further application information.
EIN: 251605932

3455
Roosevelt County Electric Education Foundation

P.O. Box 389
Portales, NM   88130-0389   (505) 356-4491
Contact: Robin Inge
E-mail: rcec@rcec.org; URL: http://www.rcec.org/rcechome/scholars.htm

Foundation type: Company-sponsored foundation
Limitations: Scholarships to members and their immediate families who receive services from Roosevelt County Electric Cooperative, Inc.
Financial data: Year ended 12/31/2004. Assets, $364,814 (M); Expenditures, $31,166; Total giving, $31,035; Grants to individuals, 56 grants totaling $31,035 (high: $1,767, low: $500).
Type of support: Employee-related scholarships.
Application information: Application form required.
Deadline(s): Feb. 1
Applicants should submit the following:
1) Photograph
2) Transcripts
Additional information: Application should also include three letters of recommendation; Recipients must re-apply annually.
EIN: 850350615

3456
The Roothbert Fund, Inc.

475 Riverside Dr., Rm. 252
New York, NY   10115   (212) 870-3116
Contact: Blake T. Newton III, Pres.
E-mail: office@roothbertfund.org; URL: http://www.roothbertfund.org

Foundation type: Independent foundation
Limitations: Graduate and undergraduate scholarships to students who are primarily motivated by spiritual values, with preference to those considering teaching as a profession.
Publications: Application guidelines; Annual report; Informational brochure.
Financial data: Year ended 12/31/2004. Assets, $4,655,191 (M); Expenditures, $269,472; Total giving, $179,500.
Fields of interest: Education, research.
Type of support: Scholarships—to individuals; Graduate support; Technical education support; Undergraduate support.
Application information: Application form required.
Deadline(s): Feb. 1
Additional information: Initial approach by letter after Dec. 1 requesting application; Application must include SAT and/or GRE scores, personal statement, references, photograph, and transcripts; Interviews are held during Mar. of each year at fund headquarters in New York City and currently also in Washington, DC, Philadelphia, PA, and New Haven, CT.
Program description:
Roothbert Fund Grants Program: The fund assists college or university students who are primarily motivated by spiritual values, with preference to those of high scholastic achievement who are considering teaching as a vocation. The term "spiritual" is intended to reflect a personal commitment or direct awareness of a spiritual Force or Being in the universe to which the individual feels responsive rather than affiliation with a particular established religious dogma or group. The fund also makes grants to help pay the cost of independent study for nondegree-granting programs that may enhance the spiritual qualities that the fund seeks in young people. Application procedures, including interviews, are the same as those required for scholarships. Grants are small and meant to be supplementary. Aid is given for the ensuing school year, and is dependent upon individual need and circumstances. Renewals, considered in light of achievement during the previous years, may be applied for by writing for the fund's renewal form. Acceptance of an award requires the recipient to maintain a high standard of work and conduct, to have transcripts sent by his or her school after each semester, to keep a close relationship with the fund through correspondence and visits, and to advise the fund promptly of any change in his or her academic or financial situation. Every award is subject to revocation if, in the opinion of the fund, the holder fails to live up to these requirements.
EIN: 136162570

3457
Max C. Rosenfeld Trust

c/o Mellon Financial Corp.
P.O. Box 185
Pittsburgh, PA   15230-0185
Application address: c/o Ruth S. Wolf, 41 New Chardon St., Boston, MA 02114

Foundation type: Independent foundation

Limitations: Scholarships to financially needy young Jewish women living in Boston, MA, and its suburbs.
Financial data: Year ended 08/31/2004. Assets, $962,886 (M); Expenditures, $95,570; Total giving, $70,700.
Fields of interest: Jewish agencies & temples; Women.
Type of support: Scholarships—to individuals.
Application information: Deadline May 15; Initial approach by letter requesting application; Completion of formal application required.
EIN: 046044784

3458
John M. Ross Foundation
c/o Bank of Hawaii
P.O. Box 3170, Dept. 758
Honolulu, HI 96802-3170
Scholarship address: c/o Hawaii Community Fdn., 1164 Bishop St., Ste. 800, Honolulu, HI 96813, tel.: (808)537-6333, FAX: (808) 521-6286

Foundation type: Independent foundation
Limitations: Scholarships to financially needy residents of the Island of Hawaii, HI, for full-time study at accredited two- and four-year undergraduate or graduate institutions primarily in HI.
Financial data: Year ended 06/30/2004. Assets, $761,228 (M); Expenditures, $42,052; Total giving, $33,000; Grants to individuals, totaling $33,000.
Fields of interest: Higher education.
Type of support: Graduate support; Undergraduate support.
Application information: Application form required.
Deadline(s): Mar. 1.
Applicants should submit the following:
1) SAR
2) Transcripts
3) Letter(s) of recommendation
4) Essay
Program description:
Ross Foundation Program: Preference is shown to renewal applicants, those who plan to remain in or return to the Island of Hawaii after graduation, and to undergraduates. Applicants are notified of the foundation's decision within three months of the application deadline.
EIN: 996007327

3459
The Ross Loan Fund
c/o M&T Bank
P.O. Box 459
Chambersburg, PA 17201 (717) 261-2833
Contact: Alan B. Rhinehart, M&T Investment Group, M&T Bank

Foundation type: Independent foundation
Limitations: Low-interest student loans to graduates of Chambersburg Area Senior High School. Graduates from other high schools in Franklin County, PA, will be considered as funds permit.
Financial data: Year ended 12/31/2004. Assets, $3,531,466 (M); Expenditures, $471,373; Total giving, $437,500; Loans to individuals, 91 loans totaling $437,500.
Type of support: Student loans—to individuals; Support to graduates or students of specific schools; Undergraduate support.
Application information: Application form required.
Deadline(s): Apr. 15
Applicants should submit the following:

1) Transcripts
Additional information: Also include a copy of the first page of parents' 1040 tax return.
Program description:
Jane R. Ross Student Loan Fund: To receive funds the borrower and a parent or legal guardian with good credit standing must both sign a note in the amount of the loan. Additionally, the borrower must agree to carry life insurance with the trustee as beneficiary in the amount of the loan. The borrower must start monthly payments on the loan no later than one year after graduation. Rate of interest is two percent per year while the student is still in school, and for one year after graduation. The second year after graduation, the loan, principal, and interest is amortized over a seven-year period at a rate of eight percent per year. Completion of repayment shall not exceed eight years from the date of graduation or withdrawal. Funds are renewable if a GPA of at least 2.0 is maintained.
EIN: 236262609

3460
Charles M. Ross Trust
c/o Weeks & Brucker, Ltd.
P.O. Box 288, 606 W. Oak St.
Fairbury, IL 61739 (815) 692-2302
Contact: Thomas Brucker

Foundation type: Independent foundation
Limitations: Graduate scholarships to financially needy students at participating schools studying in the fields of religion, sociology, medicine, and teaching. Applicants must be active members of a local church, possess a good understanding of the world mission of the church, and have graduated in the top ten percent of their undergraduate classes.
Financial data: Year ended 06/30/2005. Assets, $439,044 (M); Expenditures, $26,567; Total giving, $18,000; Grants to individuals, totaling $18,000.
Fields of interest: Medical school/education; Teacher school/education; Theological school/education; Human services; Anthropology/sociology; Religion, formal/general education; Religion.
Type of support: Support to graduates or students of specific schools; Graduate support.
Application information: Application form required.
Initial approach: Letter.
Deadline(s): Deadline Aug. 1
Additional information: Applications not accepted by the trust, but are accepted by the schools with which the trust has established a working relationship ; Applications available from eligible schools; Each educational institution recommends no more than three students each year. The eligible institutions are: Lexington Theological Seminary, Vanderbilt University, University of Chicago, Marquette University, Brite Divinity School at Texas Christian University, and Centenary College of Louisiana. Grants range from $500 to $1,200 per year.
EIN: 376075511

3461
George Rossman Fund for Pacific University
c/o U.S. Bank, N.A.
P.O. Box 3168
Portland, OR 97208-3168
Application address: c/o Robert L. Macy, Dir. of Financial Aid, Pacific University, Forest Grove, OR 97116

Foundation type: Independent foundation
Limitations: Scholarships to students of Pacific University, OR.
Financial data: Year ended 12/31/2004. Assets, $581,890 (M); Expenditures, $31,835; Total giving, $25,000; Grants to individuals, totaling $25,000.
Type of support: Scholarships—to individuals; Support to graduates or students of specific schools.
Application information: Contact fund for current application deadline/guidelines.
EIN: 936051550

3462
Albert J. and Susan E. Rot Foundation
P.O. Box 222
Naperville, IL 60565-0222 (630) 369-8383
Contact: Albert J. Rot, Pres.

Foundation type: Independent foundation
Limitations: Scholarships to individuals for higher education. Students throughout the U.S. may apply, though students from local high schools are given priority.
Financial data: Year ended 12/31/2004. Assets, $1,569,327 (M); Expenditures, $81,488; Total giving, $77,000; Grants to individuals, totaling $77,000.
Type of support: Scholarships—to individuals.
Application information: Completion of formal application required, including a student needs analysis service of ACT.
EIN: 363653679

3463
Rotalia Foundation
1407 N.W. 191st St.
Shoreline, WA 98177-2737
Application address: 11045 Alton Ave. N.E., Seattle, WA 98125

Foundation type: Operating foundation
Limitations: Scholarships and research grants to individuals in the U.S. and abroad who read, speak, and understand Estonian.
Financial data: Year ended 12/31/2003. Assets, $300,825 (M); Expenditures, $20,202; Total giving, $18,000; Grants to individuals, 18 grants totaling $18,000 (high: $1,000, low: $1,000).
Fields of interest: Language (foreign); International exchange, students.
Type of support: Research; Exchange programs; Foreign applicants; Graduate support; Undergraduate support; Postgraduate support.
Application information: Application form required.
Deadline(s): Contact foundation for deadline
Applicants should submit the following:
1) Essay
2) Letter(s) of recommendation
3) Financial information
Additional information: Applications must be submitted in Estonian.
Program description:
Undergraduate and Graduate Scholarships: Grants are given at all levels—undergraduate, graduate, postgraduate, and for research. The foundation is particularly interested in supporting qualified individuals in the U.S. to study in Estonia, and individuals in Estonia to study in the U.S.
EIN: 911409344

3464
Rotary Club Education Fund of Framingham
c/o Tim Sullivan, Sullivan and Shuman, P.C.
P.O. Box 3030, Three Tech Cir.
Natick, MA   01760

Foundation type: Public charity
Limitations: Scholarships to seniors of Ashland, Framingham, Holliston or Hopkinton high schools, MA.
Financial data: Year ended 06/30/2004. Assets, $810,385 (M); Expenditures, $57,056; Total giving, $54,500; Grants to individuals, 16 grants totaling $54,500 (high: $3,500, low: $2,000).
Type of support: Support to graduates or students of specific schools; Undergraduate support.
Application information: Applications not accepted.
  Additional information: Unsolicited requests for funds not accepted.
EIN: 046136783

3465
Rotary Club of Marshall Finney Educational Trust Fund
c/o Miller & Meehling
115 S. 6th St.
Marshall, IL   62441-0100
Contact: Karen Keim
Application address: Court House, Marshall, IL 62441, tel.: (217) 826-6201

Foundation type: Independent foundation
Limitations: Scholarships to graduating seniors from the Marshall, IL, School District Unit C-2 for educational expenses. Close relatives of current Rotary Club members are not eligible.
Financial data: Year ended 12/31/2002. Assets, $11,542 (M); Expenditures, $3,013; Total giving, $3,000; Grants to individuals, totaling $3,000 (high: $1,000, low: $1,000).
Type of support: Support to graduates or students of specific schools; Undergraduate support.
Application information: Deadline May 1; Completion of formal application required, including academic and financial information.
EIN: 237454972

3466
The Rotary Foundation of Rotary International
1 Rotary Ctr.
1560 Sherman Ave.
Evanston, IL   60201-3698   (847) 866-3000
Contact: Edwin H. Futa, Genl. Secy.
FAX: (847) 328-8554; URL: http://www.rotary.org/foundation

Foundation type: Public charity
Limitations: Scholarships to qualified students who have completed at least two years of college or university work, for study in a country other than their own, where they serve as unofficial "ambassadors of goodwill.".
Publications: Annual report.
Financial data: Year ended 06/30/2005. Assets, $674,700,000 (M); Expenditures, $128,100,000; Total giving, $94,500,000.
Fields of interest: International exchange, students.
Type of support: Scholarships—to individuals; Exchange programs; Awards/prizes; Graduate

support; Undergraduate support; Postgraduate support; Travel grants; Doctoral support.
Application information: Application form required.
  Initial approach: Letter or Web site.
  Deadline(s): Applications accepted from Jan. through June for two years of study in the future
  Additional information: Interviews required.
EIN: 363245072

3467
Rotary Service Foundation of San Mateo
P.O. Box 95
San Mateo, CA   94401   (650) 343-5900
Contact: Lynn Armenio, Pres.

Foundation type: Public charity
Limitations: Scholarships to students who are residents of the San Mateo, CA, area, for higher education.
Financial data: Year ended 06/30/2004. Assets, $1,033,013 (M); Expenditures, $208,539; Total giving, $204,542; Grants to individuals, totaling $107,766.
Type of support: Undergraduate support.
Application information: Contact foundation for current application deadline/guidelines.
EIN: 237101037

3468
Helen L. & Marie F. Rotterman Trust
1900 Kettering Twr.
Dayton, OH   45423   (937) 222-2500
Contact: Jeffrey B. Shulman, Tr.

Foundation type: Independent foundation
Limitations: Scholarships to young Catholic women primarily from the Dayton, OH, area to attend Trinity College, Washington, DC.
Financial data: Year ended 07/31/2005. Assets, $3,712,884 (M); Expenditures, $153,875; Total giving, $118,000; Grant to an individual, 1 grant totaling $10,000.
Fields of interest: Roman Catholic agencies & churches; Women.
Type of support: Scholarships—to individuals; Support to graduates or students of specific schools.
Application information: Deadline four to six months prior to school year; Application by letter, including a copy of Trinity College application, high school transcripts, and proof of Catholic Church affiliation.
EIN: 316236156

3469
Rouch Foundation
(formerly A. P. and Louise Rouch Boys Foundation)
c/o Wells Fargo Bank Arizona, N.A.
P.O. Box 21927, MAC U1828-011
Phoenix, AZ   85072
Application address: c/o Wells Fargo Bank Northwest, N.A., 102 Main Ave., South Twin Falls, ID 83303, tel.: (208) 736-1242

Foundation type: Independent foundation
Limitations: Scholarships to financially needy students attending college in the Twin Falls, ID, area, who are orphaned, poor, or underprivileged, and pursuing undergraduate, vocational, or graduate education.
Financial data: Year ended 12/31/2004. Assets, $244,380 (M); Expenditures, $15,805;

Total giving, $12,606; Grants to individuals, totaling $12,606.
Fields of interest: Vocational education; Residential/custodial care.
Type of support: Graduate support; Technical education support; Undergraduate support.
Application information: Contact foundation for current application deadline/guidelines.
Program description:
  Scholarship Program: The foundation provides college, vocational school, trade school, and university scholarships to high school graduates and individuals who have attained a GED, who are orphaned, poor, or underprivileged. Applicants must have demonstrated ability, industry, and a promise of useful citizenship. The scholarships are awarded on an annual basis for an amount that is approximately equal to the tuition charges for a year at the College of Southern Idaho or the University of Idaho. The foundation grants scholarships only to undergraduate students. However, by unanimous consent, the Advisory Committee may grant scholarships to students seeking advanced degrees, providing that undergraduate work that has been completed has been done expeditiously, insofar as possible. Each student must submit a grade transcript one month after the conclusion of the academic year. Additional progress reports are encouraged, but not required.
EIN: 826005152

3470
Rowan Family Foundation
P.O. Box 992335
Redding, CA   96099-2335
Contact: Richard E. Rowan, Pres.

Foundation type: Independent foundation
Limitations: Scholarships to individuals for higher education.
Financial data: Year ended 12/31/2004. Assets, $784,606 (M); Expenditures, $65,664; Total giving, $44,700; Grants to individuals, totaling $44,700.
Type of support: Undergraduate support.
Application information: Applications by letter accepted throughout the year.
EIN: 943162645

3471
Pleasant T. Rowland Foundation, Inc.
3415 Gateway Rd., Ste. 200
Brookfield, WI   53045-5111
Contact: Marti Sebree, Grants Mgr.
Application address: 1 S. Pinckney St., No. 810, Madison, WI 53703

Foundation type: Independent foundation
Limitations: Scholarships to students, primarily in Dane County, WI.
Publications: Application guidelines.
Financial data: Year ended 12/31/2004. Assets, $111,203,802 (M); Expenditures, $16,048,790; Total giving, $14,831,944; Grants to individuals, 8 grants totaling $67,820 (high: $14,000, low: $1,500).
Fields of interest: Arts.
Type of support: Fellowships; Graduate support; Undergraduate support.
Application information: Applications not accepted.
EIN: 391868295

3472
Roy Scholarship Fund
c/o JPMorgan Chase Bank
P.O. Box 31412
Rochester, NY   14603
Contact: Sonia Garza
Application addresses: c/o Senior Counselor, Westlake High School, 4100 Westbank Dr., Austin, TX 78746, tel.: (512) 328-4100; c/o Senior Counselor, Stephen F. Austin High School, 1715 W. 1st St., Austin, TX 78703, tel.: (512) 474-5977

Foundation type: Independent foundation
Limitations: Scholarships to graduating seniors from Stephen F. Austin and Westlake high schools, both in Austin, TX, to attend accredited colleges in TX.
Financial data: Year ended 10/31/2004. Assets, $697,172 (M); Expenditures, $34,753; Total giving, $26,500; Grants to individuals, totaling $26,500.
Type of support: Support to graduates or students of specific schools; Undergraduate support.
Application information:
  Deadline(s): May. 31.
  Additional information: Contact counselors at high schools for current application guidelines.
EIN: 746086969

3473
Mildred C. Roy Scholarship Fund
211 E. 2nd St.
Port Clinton, OH   43452-1116   (419) 734-4060
Contact: George C. Wilbur, Tr.

Foundation type: Operating foundation
Limitations: Scholarships to graduates of Port Clinton High School, OH.
Financial data: Year ended 12/31/2003. Assets, $83,823 (M); Expenditures, $7,178; Total giving, $6,750; Grants to individuals, totaling $6,750.
Type of support: Support to graduates or students of specific schools; Undergraduate support.
Application information: Deadline Feb. 1; Completion of formal application required; Applications available from Port Clinton High School Counselor.
EIN: 341325350

3474
Royal Oak Foundation
26 Broadway, Ste. 950
New York, NY   10004   (212) 480-2889
Contact: Damaris S. Horan, Exec. Dir.
FAX: (212) 785-7234;
E-mail: general@royal-oak.org; Additional tel.: (800) 913-6565; URL: http://www.royal-oak.org

Foundation type: Public charity
Limitations: Grants to U.S. students for study and travel who are interested in working on architecture, landscape architecture, or interior design projects in Great Britain.
Publications: Application guidelines; Financial statement; Grants list; Informational brochure; Newsletter.
Financial data: Year ended 12/31/2003. Assets, $3,155,826 (M); Expenditures, $1,520,760; Total giving, $178,700; Grants to individuals, 6 grants totaling $25,000 (high: $5,000, low: $4,000).
Fields of interest: Architecture; Design; Landscaping.

Type of support: Scholarships—to individuals; Travel grants.
Application information: Applications accepted throughout the year; Contact foundation for current application deadline/guidelines.
Program description:
  Royal Oak Architectural Competition: Awards of $15,000 are given biannually to U.S. citizens and permanent residents for study and travel in Great Britain to resolve hypothetical architectural projects created by a professional architect or designer. The focus of the competition is on architecture, landscape architecture, and interior design. The winner will be able to enrich his/her professional and intellectual development and bring this knowledge to design professionals in the U.S. The applicant must be a current student or have graduated from an accredited architecture, landscape architecture, or design school within the past five years. The competition entry must be the original work of the applicant.
EIN: 237349380

3475
The Rachel Royston Permanent Scholarship Foundation of Alpha Sigma State of the Delta Kappa Gamma Society International
1501 4th Ave., Ste. 2880
Seattle, WA   98101-1631
Contact: Carol Clarke, Tr.
Application address: 1203 W. 4th St., Grandview, WA 98930-1121, tel.: (509) 882-2731

Foundation type: Operating foundation
Limitations: Scholarships for graduate study to female educators who are residents of WA.
Financial data: Year ended 06/30/2004. Assets, $527,607 (M); Expenditures, $37,804; Total giving, $10,000; Grants to individuals, 4 grants totaling $10,000 (high: $3,000, low: $1,000).
Fields of interest: Teacher school/education; Education; Women.
Type of support: Graduate support.
Application information:
  Deadline(s): Dec. 1
  Additional information: Completion of formal application required, including letter of acceptance to special project or degree program, three recommendations, progress statement from advisor for doctoral students, budget, and personal statement; Interviews required.
Program description:
  Scholarship Program: Recipients may work toward a master's or doctorate degree, or work in a field of special interest. Awards may only be made for one year or a portion thereof, however additional applications may be requested and submitted in later years. Applicants are judged on the basis of their project, its significance to the field of education, and evidence of the candidate's ability to pursue it. Applicants must be residents of WA, must be doing graduate work in an approved institution of higher learning which has been accredited by a regional and/or national accrediting association, and must show promise in a particular field. Recipients are required to submit copies of any written materials produced during the period of the scholarship to the foundation's resource center. Applicants will be notified of the board's decision to be selected for interviews by March of the following year. Finalists will be notified within two weeks of the required interview.
EIN: 916060790

3476
RPW Foundation, Inc.
(formerly Wurster Foundation)
c/o Russel P. Wurster
Royal Pin Leisure Centers
8463 Castlewood Dr., 2nd Fl.
Indianapolis, IN   46250-1534

Foundation type: Operating foundation
Limitations: Scholarships to participants of the Royal Pin Leisure Centers youth league bowling program in IN.
Financial data: Year ended 12/31/2004. Assets, $278,302 (M); Expenditures, $101,886; Total giving, $101,154; Grants to individuals, 24 grants totaling $98,154 (high: $19,040, low: $20).
Fields of interest: Recreation.
Type of support: Scholarships—to individuals.
Application information: Applications accepted throughout the year; Completion of formal application required, including high school transcripts and letters of recommendation.
EIN: 351778480

3477
J. M. Rubin Foundation, Inc.
505 S. Flagler Dr., Ste. 1320
West Palm Beach, FL   33401   (561) 833-3309
FAX: (561) 833-2258; E-mail: info@jmrf.org;
URL: http://www.jmrf.org

Foundation type: Independent foundation
Limitations: Scholarships to residents of Palm Beach County, FL, for higher education.
Publications: Application guidelines.
Financial data: Year ended 11/30/2004. Assets, $29,559,399 (M); Expenditures, $1,971,047; Total giving, $1,049,525; Grants to individuals, 190 grants totaling $528,525 (high: $5,750, low: $150).
Type of support: Scholarships—to individuals.
Application information: Application form required.
  Initial approach: Letter.
  Deadline(s): Mar. 1
  Applicants should submit the following:
    1) Letter(s) of recommendation
    2) Financial information
    3) Essay
  Additional information: Application must also include test scores, and intended major. Interviews may be required.
EIN: 591958240

3478
Lillian & Harold Rudy Scholarship Fund
1701 Golf Rd., Ste. 800
Rolling Meadows, IL   60008
Application address: c/o Wauconda School District, Attn.: Dr. John Barbini, Superintendent, 555 N. Main St., Wauconda, IL 60084-1299

Foundation type: Independent foundation
Limitations: Scholarships to graduating students of Wauconda High School, IL.
Financial data: Year ended 12/31/2004. Assets, $607,012 (M); Expenditures, $40,601; Total giving, $33,000; Grants to individuals, totaling $33,000.
Type of support: Support to graduates or students of specific schools; Undergraduate support.
Application information: Application form required.
  Deadline(s): Apr. 1
  Additional information: Application should include proof of registration to an accredited two- or four-year college or university. Recipients must be in the upper 25 percent of

their graduating classes, participate in at least one extracurricular activity during their four years in high school and maintain good citizenship and attendance record. Students attending two-year colleges should have the intent of continuing his/her education at a four-year college or university.
EIN: 367168424

3479
Clara A. Ruf Scholarship Trust
207 S. Saginaw St.
St. Charles, MI 48655

Foundation type: Independent foundation
Limitations: Scholarships to graduates of St. Charles High School, MI.
Financial data: Year ended 12/31/2004. Assets, $89,507 (M); Expenditures, $3,547; Total giving, $3,000; Grants to individuals, 3 grants totaling $3,000.
Type of support: Support to graduates or students of specific schools; Undergraduate support.
Application information: Applications by letter accepted throughout the year.
EIN: 382587560

3480
Merlin & Ethyl Rufer Scholarship Trust
c/o United Bank of Iowa
501 2nd St.
Ida Grove, IA 51445-1304 (712) 364-3393
Contact: Gerald Schmidt, Trust Off., United Bank of Iowa
Additional application addresses: c/o Larry Lee, Scholarship Comm., First Presbyterian Church, 1111 5th Ave. N., Fort Dodge, IA 50501, tel.: (515) 576-2091, or c/o Dan Brown, Scholarship Comm., Masonic Temple Assoc., 1021 1st Ave. N., Fort Dodge, IA 50501, tel.: (515) 576-3201

Foundation type: Independent foundation
Limitations: Scholarships to children of members of Yorkrite Masons of the Masonic Temple Assn. or the First Presbyterian Church, Fort Dodge, IA.
Financial data: Year ended 12/31/2004. Assets, $280,117 (M); Expenditures, $20,865; Total giving, $19,020; Grants to individuals, 44 grants totaling $19,020.
Type of support: Undergraduate support.
Application information: Applications accepted throughout the year; Completion of formal application required.
EIN: 421350542

3481
Esther and Alcide Ruffini Charitable Foundation
(formerly Ruffini Charitable Foundation)
c/o Rockland Trust Co.
2036 Washington St.
Hanover, MA 02339 (781) 878-6100
Scholarship address: c/o Robert Holton, Chair., Scholarship Comm., Plymouth North High School, Plymouth, MA 02360

Foundation type: Independent foundation
Limitations: Scholarships to graduating seniors at North Plymouth High School, MA.
Financial data: Year ended 06/30/2004. Assets, $1,674,448 (M); Expenditures, $81,884; Total giving, $65,000; Grants to individuals, 2 grants totaling $2,000 (high: $1,000, low: $1,000).

Type of support: Support to graduates or students of specific schools; Undergraduate support.
Application information:
Initial approach: Letter or telephone.
Deadline(s): None.
Additional information: Contact foundation for current application guidelines.
EIN: 043030385

3482
Isabel R. Ruge Trust
(formerly Edgar G. W. Ruge Education Foundation)
c/o Wachovia Bank, N.A.
401 S. Tryon St., 4th Fl.
Charlotte, NC 28288-5709

Foundation type: Independent foundation
Limitations: Scholarships only to graduates of Appalachicola High School for study at FL colleges and universities.
Financial data: Year ended 12/31/2004. Assets, $404,446 (M); Expenditures, $24,102; Total giving, $19,800; Grants to individuals, totaling $19,800.
Type of support: Support to graduates or students of specific schools; Undergraduate support.
Application information: Applications accepted.
Initial approach: Letter.
Additional information: Contact foundation for current application guidelines.
EIN: 596527097

3483
Dr. Henry Hobert Ruger Trust
P.O. Box 838
Devils Lake, ND 58301-0838
Contact: John T. Traynor, Tr.

Foundation type: Independent foundation
Limitations: Scholarships to medical students at the University of North Dakota, Grand Forks, and the Park District of the city of Devils Lake, ND.
Financial data: Year ended 12/31/2004. Assets, $1,172,783 (M); Expenditures, $84,137; Total giving, $40,000; Grants to individuals, totaling $40,000.
Fields of interest: Medical school/education.
Type of support: Support to graduates or students of specific schools; Undergraduate support.
Application information: Contact trust for current application deadline; Completion of formal application required.
EIN: 456071291

3484
Constance H. Rumbough Trust
(formerly James Hickey Rumbough Fund)
c/o Wachovia Bank, N.A.
401 S. Tryon St., 4th Fl.
Charlotte, NC 28288-5709
Contact: Jane D. Hickey, Asst. Atty. General
Application address: Supreme Court Bldg., 101 N. 8th St., Richmond, VA 23219

Foundation type: Independent foundation
Limitations: Scholarships to residents of Lynchburg, VA, and the immediate surrounding area.
Financial data: Year ended 12/31/2004. Assets, $313,859 (M); Expenditures, $13,746; Total giving, $9,000; Grants to individuals, totaling $9,000.
Type of support: Scholarships—to individuals.
Application information: Application form required.

Initial approach: Letter.
Deadline(s): .
Additional information: Applications accepted throughout the year. Scholarships are awarded on the basis of financial need, character, citizenship, and motivation.
EIN: 546113973

3485
Rural American Scholarship Fund
P.O. Box 2674
Oak Harbor, WA 98277 (360) 679-1979
Contact: Ginny Thomas, Secy.
E-mail: ginnyrasf@aol.com

Foundation type: Operating foundation
Limitations: Scholarships for higher education only to students residing in rural areas of ID, OR, and WA.
Financial data: Year ended 12/31/2004. Assets, $26,063 (M); Expenditures, $177,331; Total giving, $172,000; Grants to individuals, 100 grants totaling $172,000 (high: $4,500, low: $27).
Type of support: Graduate support; Undergraduate support.
Application information: Applications not accepted.
Program description:
Scholarships: Applicants must meet the following requirements: at least 23 years of age by Sept. 1; missed opportunity for college attendance upon completion of high school; currently underemployed or holding an unfulfilling position; currently residing in or came from a rural community; legal resident of state in which you will be attending college, or as a reciprocal agreement with another university; accumulated 2.8 GPA. Master's candidates are eligible to apply.
EIN: 850386189

3486
The John Rusch Family Scholarship
126 W. Chicago Rd.
Sturgis, MI 49091 (269) 651-7861
Contact: Donald S. Eaton, Tr.

Foundation type: Independent foundation
Limitations: Scholarships only to graduates of Mason High School, MI.
Financial data: Year ended 04/30/2005. Assets, $25,308 (M); Expenditures, $11,908; Total giving, $10,500; Grants to individuals, totaling $10,500.
Type of support: Support to graduates or students of specific schools; Undergraduate support.
Application information: Deadline May; Contact foundation for current application guidelines; Initial approach by letter.
EIN: 386635264

3487
Rush County Community Foundation, Inc.
117 N. Main St.
Rushville, IN 46173 (765) 938-1177
Contact: Garry E. Cooley, Exec. Dir.
FAX: (765) 938-1719; E-mail: rccf@verizon.net; URL: http://www.rushcounty.com/foundation

Foundation type: Community foundation
Limitations: Scholarships to residents of Rush County, IN.
Publications: Annual report; Newsletter.

Financial data: Year ended 12/31/2004.
Assets, $6,105,017 (M); Expenditures,
$381,883; Total giving, $263,498.
Fields of interest: Vocational education.
Type of support: Scholarships—to individuals.
Application information: Application form required.
  Initial approach: Letter or telephone.
  Deadline(s): Apr. 1
EIN: 351835950

3488
David and Mary P. Rush Educational Trust
P.O. Box 579
Hays, KS   67601
Contact: Dennis Bieker, Tr.

Foundation type: Independent foundation
Limitations: Scholarships to financially needy
graduates of Graham County, KS, high schools who
are full-time students and have at least a 2.0 GPA.
Financial data: Year ended 01/31/2005.
Assets, $3,419,254 (M); Expenditures,
$216,377; Total giving, $142,500.
Type of support: Support to graduates or students
of specific schools; Undergraduate support.
Application information: Application form required.
  Deadline(s): May 1.
EIN: 486243254

3489
Lonza L. Rush Testamentary Trust
(formerly R. Roy Rush Trust)
c/o SunTrust Bank
P.O. Box 1908
Orlando, FL   32802-1908
Application address: c/o SunTrust Bank,
Attn.: Carolyn McCoy, P.O. Box 13888, Roanoke,
VA 24018, tel.: (540) 982-3014

Foundation type: Independent foundation
Limitations: Scholarships to residents of VA for
higher education.
Financial data: Year ended 02/28/2005.
Assets, $1,082,371 (M); Expenditures, $36,553;
Total giving, $22,500; Grants to individuals, 11
grants totaling $22,500 (high: $3,000, low:
$1,500).
Type of support: Scholarships—to individuals.
Application information: Applications by letter
accepted throughout the year.
EIN: 546138578

3490
Gertrude Marion Ruskin Trust
c/o Wachovia Bank, N.A.
P.O. Box 3099
Winston-Salem, NC   27150-6732
(336) 732-5912
Contact: Shane Thomas

Foundation type: Independent foundation
Limitations: Scholarships to residents of Madison,
Buncombe, and Haywood counties, NC, and
Cherokee Indian reservations in NC.
Financial data: Year ended 01/31/2005.
Assets, $461,727 (M); Expenditures, $21,267;
Total giving, $17,208; Grants to individuals,
totaling $17,208.
Fields of interest: Native Americans/American
Indians.
Type of support: Scholarships—to individuals.

Application information: Deadline June 1; Initial
approach by letter or telephone; Completion of
formal application required.
EIN: 586187363

3491
Benjamin and Roberta Russell Foundation
(formerly Benjamin and Roberta Russell
Educational and Charitable Foundation, Inc.)
P.O. Box 369
Alexander City, AL   35011-0369
Contact: James D. Nabors, Secy.-Treas.

Foundation type: Independent foundation
Limitations: Scholarships to residents of
Tallapoosa and Coosa counties, AL.
Financial data: Year ended 12/31/2004.
Assets, $17,382,257 (M); Expenditures,
$936,772; Total giving, $752,436.
Type of support: Scholarships—to individuals.
Application information: Applications not
accepted.
EIN: 630393126

3492
Russell Scholarship Fund
(formerly Helen B. & Robert H. Russell Scholarship
Fund)
c/o JPMorgan Chase Bank, N.A.
P.O. Box 1308
Milwaukee, WI   53201-1308
Contact: H. Edward Johnson, Sr. Trust Off.,
JPMorgan Chase Bank, N.A.
Application address: 1114 Market St., Wheeling,
WV 26003, tel.: (304) 234-4123

Foundation type: Independent foundation
Limitations: Scholarships to residents of Ohio and
Belmont counties, WV, and non-residents attending
high schools in those counties who are between the
ages of 17 and 25.
Financial data: Year ended 12/31/2004.
Assets, $802,270 (M); Expenditures, $48,974;
Total giving, $40,000.
Type of support: Scholarships—to individuals.
Application information: Applications accepted
throughout the year; Completion of formal
application required, including three references,
FAF, extracurricular activities, transcripts, and
recent photograph.
EIN: 556122686

3493
Clyde Russell Scholarship Fund
35 Community Dr.
Augusta, ME   04330
Contact: Ian D. Deming, Treas.

Foundation type: Public charity
Limitations: Scholarships to students residing in
ME for the study of teaching.
Fields of interest: Teacher school/education.
Type of support: Undergraduate support.
Application information: Applications accepted.
Application form required.
  Applicants should submit the following:
    1) Letter(s) of recommendation
  Additional information: Contact foundation for
    current application deadline/guidelines;
    Application must include biographical
    information; Interviews required.
EIN: 222535972

3494
Mary Rutan Foundation
205 Palmer Ave.
Bellefontaine, OH   43311-2298
(937) 592-4015
Contact: Dwight Spencer, Dir.
URL: http://www.maryrutan.org/html/
mary_rutan_foundation.html

Foundation type: Public charity
Limitations: Scholarships for medical school to
Logan County, OH, residents.
Financial data: Year ended 12/31/2003.
Assets, $4,223,573 (M); Expenditures,
$200,579; Total giving, $148,923; Grants to
individuals, 30 grants totaling $73,031 (high:
$11,069, low: $560).
Fields of interest: Medical school/education;
Nursing school/education; Health sciences
school/education.
Type of support: Graduate support.
Application information: Contact foundation for
current application deadline/guidelines.
Program description:
  Mary Rutan Scholarships: Applicants must be in
a medical, nursing, or allied health program, and be
a resident of Logan County. Scholarships are
awarded on the basis of GPA, financial need,
association with Mary Rutan Hospital, personality,
tuition costs and graduation date.
EIN: 341407262

3495
Rutherford Foundation
2720 Woodland Dr.
Lamar, CO   81052-0110   (719) 336-5600
Contact: Jan P. Hall, Tr.

Foundation type: Independent foundation
Limitations: Scholarships to students in the Baca
County school district, CO.
Financial data: Year ended 12/31/2004.
Assets, $1 (M); Expenditures, $26,836; Total
giving, $18,300; Grants to individuals, totaling
$18,300.
Type of support: Scholarships—to individuals;
Support to graduates or students of specific
schools.
Application information: Applications accepted.
Application form required.
  Deadline(s): None
EIN: 840751642

3496
Edward Rutledge Charity
P.O. Box 758
Chippewa Falls, WI   54729-0738
Contact: Betty Manning

Foundation type: Independent foundation
Limitations: Scholarships to high school graduates
who are residents of Chippewa County, WI.
Financial data: Year ended 05/31/2005.
Assets, $18,890,116 (M); Expenditures,
$436,569; Total giving, $247,275; Grants to
individuals, 86 grants totaling $74,500 (high:
$1,400, low: $300); Loans to individuals, 67 loans
totaling $3,291.
Type of support: Scholarships—to individuals;
Undergraduate support.
Application information: Applications accepted.
Application form required.
  Deadline(s): June 1
  Applicants should submit the following:
    1) SAR
    2) Transcripts

3) FAFSA
4) Financial information
Additional information: Application must include copy of award letter, and copy of parents' income tax returns; Interviews required.
EIN: 390806178

3497
The Dorothy and Robert Ryan Charitable Foundation
715 S.W. Morrison St., No. 1000
Portland, OR 97205-3122

Foundation type: Independent foundation
Limitations: Scholarships to individuals in Vancouver, WA, for higher education.
Financial data: Year ended 12/31/2004. Assets, $1 (M); Expenditures, $11,925; Total giving, $11,275; Grants to individuals, totaling $11,275.
Type of support: Undergraduate support.
Application information: Unsolicited requests for funds not considered or acknowledged.
EIN: 911837467

3498
H. L. and K. G. Ryan County Scholarship Fund
(formerly Katherine G. Ryan County Scholarship Fund)
c/o Wachovia Bank, N.A.
401 S. Tryon St., 4th Fl.
Charlotte, NC 28288-5709

Foundation type: Independent foundation
Limitations: Scholarships to financially needy residents of Bucks County, PA, who rank in the upper third of their class.
Financial data: Year ended 03/31/2005. Assets, $105,819 (M); Expenditures, $7,891; Total giving, $5,100; Grants to individuals, 17 grants totaling $5,100 (high: $300, low: $300).
Type of support: Undergraduate support.
Application information: Application form required.
Deadline(s): Apr. 1
Applicants should submit the following:
1) Letter(s) of recommendation
2) Transcripts
Additional information: Recipients must have already been accepted by their chosen college and must submit proof of admission. The maximum grant will not exceed $1,500 per student per year. Scholarships are renewable.
EIN: 232164671

3499
V. Gerard Ryan Fund
(formerly V. Gerard Ryan Fund f/b/o Portland High School)
c/o Bank of America, N.A.
P.O. Box 6767
Providence, RI 02940-6767
Application address: c/o Portland High School, 95 High St., Portland, CT 06480

Foundation type: Independent foundation
Limitations: Scholarships by nomination only to graduates of Portland High School, CT.
Financial data: Year ended 06/30/2002. Assets, $88,480 (M); Expenditures, $6,251; Total giving, $4,025; Grants to individuals, totaling $4,025.

Type of support: Support to graduates or students of specific schools; Awards/grants by nomination only; Undergraduate support.
Application information: Applications not accepted.
Additional information: Recipients are nominated by Portland High School faculty and selected by the fund's trustees.
EIN: 066214894

3500
The Ryder System Charitable Foundation, Inc.
c/o Corp. Tax
11690 N.W. 105th St.
Miami, FL 33178 (305) 500-3031

Foundation type: Company-sponsored foundation
Limitations: Scholarships to individuals in CA, FL, GA, MI, MO, OH, and TX for higher education.
Publications: Corporate giving report.
Financial data: Year ended 12/31/2004. Assets, $133,383 (M); Expenditures, $1,287,089; Total giving, $1,287,089; Grants to individuals, 44 grants totaling $25,275 (high: $1,850, low: $150).
Type of support: Undergraduate support.
Application information:
Initial approach: Letter.
Deadline(s): June 30
Additional information: Contact foundation for current application deadline/guidelines.
EIN: 592462315

3501
Rye Rotary Foundation, Inc.
c/o Frank J. LaRusso, C.P.A.
P.O. Box 736
Harrison, NY 10528
Contact: Allan Winston, Pres.
Application address: P.O. Box 404, Rye, NY 10580

Foundation type: Independent foundation
Limitations: Scholarships to graduates of Rye High School, Rye, NY, for higher education. Selection is based on leadership, academic achievement, and financial need.
Financial data: Year ended 09/30/2004. Assets, $96,147 (M); Expenditures, $25,267; Total giving, $25,000; Grants to individuals, totaling $25,000.
Type of support: Support to graduates or students of specific schools; Undergraduate support.
Application information: Contact foundation for current application deadline; Completion of formal application required.
EIN: 133041401

3502
The Ryrie Foundation
3310 Fairmount St., Apt. 5D
Dallas, TX 75201-1232
Contact: Charles C. Ryrie, Tr.

Foundation type: Independent foundation
Limitations: Scholarships primarily to residents of TX.
Financial data: Year ended 12/31/2004. Assets, $2,302,782 (M); Expenditures, $116,720; Total giving, $113,400.
Type of support: Scholarships—to individuals.
Application information: Applications accepted.
Deadline(s): None

Additional information: Completion of formal application required, including educational background, goals, current school enrollment status, financial need, statement of doctrinal compatibility, brief autobiography, and a recent photograph.
EIN: 752001540

3503
Ryu Family Foundation, Inc.
901 Murray Rd.
East Hanover, NJ 07936-2200 (973) 560-9696
Contact: Suk Tae Limb, Exec. Dir.
Additional tel.: (973) 560-0667
FAX: (973) 560-0661

Foundation type: Independent foundation
Limitations: Scholarships to U.S. citizens or permanent residents of Korean ancestry who are legal residents of ten northeastern states and who will study within those ten states.
Financial data: Year ended 06/30/2005. Assets, $1,112,849 (M); Expenditures, $81,867; Total giving, $62,000.
Type of support: Scholarships—to individuals; Graduate support.
Application information: Applications accepted. Application form required.
Deadline(s): Nov. 15
Applicants should submit the following:
1) Letter(s) of recommendation
2) Transcripts
3) Essay
Additional information: Application must include proof of enrollment.
Program description:
Seol Bong Scholarship: Applicants must be full-time students working toward an advanced degree at an approved institution of higher education in CT, DE, ME, MA, NH, NJ, NY, PA, RI, or VT. In addition, applicants must be residents of one of the aforementioned states and have at least a 3.5 GPA.
EIN: 223319101

3504
S.D. Scholarship Fund
(formerly Champion International Corporation)
c/o Abitibi-Consolidated
P.O. Box 1149
Lufkin, TX 75902-1149
Contact: Glynda Holland

Foundation type: Company-sponsored foundation
Limitations: Scholarships to children of employees of the Champion International Corporation, Lufkin Mill, TX.
Financial data: Year ended 08/31/2004. Assets, $5,640 (M); Expenditures, $105,000; Total giving, $105,000; Grants to individuals, 24 grants totaling $73,000 (high: $4,000, low: $1,000).
Fields of interest: Higher education.
Type of support: Employee-related scholarships.
Application information:
Deadline(s): Oct. 1
Additional information: Deadline for submission of transcripts, ACT or SAT scores, personal essay of less than 300 words, and class rank Apr. 1; Application forms are available from the Employee Relations Dept. after Sept. 1.
Program description:
Scholarship Fund: Applicants must, at the time they enter their senior year in high school, have a parent who has been an employee of Champion International Corporation for one year, or for two

years if that parent was disabled, retired, or died during the student's high school attendance. Children of members of the Scholarship Fund Administration Committee are ineligible. Applicants must maintain an average of at least 80 percent during high school. Applicants will be judged on a weighted scale of academic achievement (65 percent), character (20 percent), and citizenship (15 percent). Each scholarship is for a total of $4,000, payable at the rate of $1,000 per year for four years, provided the student remains eligible. Absence from college for two years will terminate a recipient's eligibility.

EIN: 742077273

3505
Charles E. Saak Trust

c/o Wells Fargo Bank, N.A., Fdns. Dept
P.O. Box 20160
Long Beach, CA 90802
Contact: Jennifer M. Thompson, Trust Off.
Telephone: (800) 352-3705

Foundation type: Independent foundation
Limitations: Scholarships to underprivileged students under 21 years of age residing in the Porterville/Poplar area, CA.
Publications: Application guidelines.
Financial data: Year ended 01/31/2005. Assets, $1,733,993 (M); Expenditures, $118,093; Total giving, $85,158; Grants to individuals, 71 grants totaling $77,858.
Type of support: Undergraduate support.
Application information: Applications accepted. Application form required.
Deadline(s): Mar. 31
Applicants should submit the following:
1) Financial information
2) Transcripts
Program description:
Scholarships: Recipients must carry a course load of at least 12 credits and maintain at least a 2.0 GPA. Scholarships are renewable. The majority of recipients attend Porterville College.
EIN: 946076213

3506
Sabatini Family Foundation

120 S.W. 6th St.
Topeka, KS 66603-3806 (785) 274-5761

Foundation type: Independent foundation
Limitations: Scholarships to students from the Topeka, KS, area to attend the University of Kansas, Washburn University, and St. Mary College.
Financial data: Year ended 03/31/2004. Assets, $1,991,922 (M); Expenditures, $375,382; Total giving, $373,956.
Type of support: Scholarships—to individuals; Support to graduates or students of specific schools.
Application information: Contact foundation for application deadline/guidelines; Application by letter to the school.
EIN: 480966619

3507
Joseph Sacco Scholarship Fund

(formerly SIU Scholarship Foundation and Trust)
5201 Auth Way
Suitland, MD 20746 (301) 899-0675
Contact: David Heindel, Mgr.

Foundation type: Operating foundation
Limitations: Scholarships to children of SIU employees residing in FL and MD.
Financial data: Year ended 12/31/2002. Assets, $153,563 (M); Expenditures, $9,871; Total giving, $9,750; Grants to individuals, totaling $9,750.
Type of support: Employee-related scholarships.
Application information: Deadline Apr. 15; Completion of formal application required, including transcripts, reference letters, SAT/ACT scores, autobiographical statement, photograph, and birth certificate.
EIN: 521642751

3508
Sachs Foundation

90 S. Cascade Ave., Ste. 1410
Colorado Springs, CO 80903 (719) 633-2353
Contact: Morris A. Esmiol, Jr., Pres.
E-mail: sachs@frii.com; URL: http:// sachsfoundation.net/index.htm

Foundation type: Independent foundation
Limitations: Undergraduate and graduate scholarships to African American high school seniors who have been residents of CO for at least five years and who have at least a 3.6 GPA.
Publications: Application guidelines; Financial statement.
Financial data: Year ended 12/31/2004. Assets, $8,533,070 (M); Expenditures, $1,248,403; Total giving, $873,569; Grants to individuals, 291 grants totaling $860,700 (high: $10,000, low: $66).
Fields of interest: African Americans/Blacks.
Type of support: Graduate support; Undergraduate support.
Application information:
Initial approach: Letter.
Copies of proposal: 2
Deadline(s): Mar. 1
Additional information: Application should include photograph, references, financial history, and SASE; Interviews required; Applications may be submitted online from Jan. 1 through Mar. 1.
Program description:
Scholarships: Scholarships are awarded to African American high school seniors who have been residents of CO for at least five years, to obtain undergraduate or graduate degrees. Recipients must maintain a 2.5 GPA average or better without incompletes or failures and be enrolled for a minimum of 12 credit hours. Awards are made for a maximum of four years. Graduate scholarships are considered on a case-by-case basis only to previous recipients of Sachs undergraduate scholarships. Recipients may attend educational institutions in any state.
EIN: 840500835

3509
Sacramento Mountain Scholarship Fund, Inc.

P.O. Box 900
Artesia, NM 88211-0900 (505) 746-0018
Contact: Lester Rinderknecht, Tr.

Foundation type: Independent foundation
Limitations: Scholarships to graduates of Weed or Cloudcroft High Schools, NM, with a GPA above 2.5, to attend an accredited educational institution.
Financial data: Year ended 12/31/2004. Assets, $195,865 (M); Expenditures, $44,893;

Total giving, $44,875; Grants to individuals, totaling $44,875.
Type of support: Support to graduates or students of specific schools; Undergraduate support.
Application information: Applications accepted. Application form required.
Deadline(s): Apr. 1
EIN: 850347084

3510
Sacramento Region Community Foundation

(formerly Sacramento Regional Foundation)
555 Capitol Mall, Ste. 550
Sacramento, CA 95814 (916) 492-6510
Contact: Ruth Blank, C.E.O.
FAX: (916) 492-6515;
E-mail: srf@sacregfoundation.org; Field-of-Interest grant application E-mail: applications@sacregcf.org; URL: http:// www.sacregcf.org

Foundation type: Community foundation
Limitations: Scholarships to residents of Sacramento, Yolo, Placer, and El Dorado counties, CA.
Publications: Annual report; Financial statement; Informational brochure; Newsletter.
Financial data: Year ended 12/31/2004. Assets, $68,223,184 (M); Expenditures, $7,877,759; Total giving, $6,658,810.
Type of support: Scholarships—to individuals.
Application information: Applications accepted throughout the year; Completion of formal application required, including FAFSA, essay, list of activities, transcript, two letters of reference, and additional materials as required by the individual scholarships; Interviews required.
EIN: 942891517

3511
Saddle River Valley Lions Charities, Inc.

P.O. Box 333
Saddle River, NJ 07458 (201) 825-0383
Contact: James Murphy, Jr., Pres.

Foundation type: Public charity
Limitations: Scholarships to individuals, primarily legally blind residents of Bergen County, NJ.
Financial data: Year ended 06/30/2004. Assets, $63,581; Expenditures, $61,277; Total giving, $57,610; Grants to individuals, totaling $15,000.
Fields of interest: Disabilities, people with.
Type of support: Undergraduate support.
Application information: Contact foundation for current application deadline/guidelines.
EIN: 222051734

3512
Saginaw Community Foundation

100 S. Jefferson Ave., Ste. 201
Saginaw, MI 48607 (989) 755-0545
Contact: Renee S. Johnston, Pres.
FAX: (989) 755-6524;
E-mail: info@saginawfoundation.org; URL: http:// www.saginawfoundation.org

Foundation type: Community foundation
Limitations: Scholarships primarily to Saginaw, MI, residents.
Publications: Application guidelines; Annual report (including application guidelines); Occasional report.

Financial data: Year ended 12/31/2004. Assets, $30,044,660 (M); Expenditures, $3,034,803; Total giving, $1,817,251.
Type of support: Scholarships—to individuals.
Application information:
  Initial approach: Letter or telephone.
  Deadline(s): Feb. 15
  Additional information: Interviews required; Contact foundation for current application guidelines; See Web site for complete program listing.
EIN: 382474297

3513

Sailfish Point Foundation, Inc.

2201 SE Sailfish Point Blvd.
Stuart, FL   34996   (772) 225-6689
Contact: John J. Kelleher III, Pres.
Nursing Scholarship: c/o Rachel Perkins, Martin Memorial Medical Center, 300 SE Hospital Ave., Stuart, FL 34994

Foundation type: Public charity
Limitations: Scholarships to needy children and adult residents of Martin County, FL to pursue a career in nursing.
Financial data: Year ended 12/31/2004. Assets, $221,521 (M); Expenditures, $347,228; Total giving, $340,765; Grants to individuals, totaling $331,765.
Fields of interest: Nursing school/education.
Type of support: Graduate support; Undergraduate support.
Application information: Applications accepted. Application form required.
  Initial approach: Letter.
  Deadline(s): Aug. 26
  Applicants should submit the following:
   1) Letter(s) of recommendation
   2) Financial information
   3) Transcripts
   4) GPA
   5) Essay
EIN: 650978271

3514

The Saint Paul Foundation, Inc.

55 5th St. E., Ste. 600
St. Paul, MN   55101-1797   (651) 224-5463
Contact: Carleen Rhodes, Pres.
FAX: (651) 224-8123;
E-mail: inbox@saintpaulfoundation.org; Additional tel.: (800) 875-6167; Additional E-mails: ckr@saintpaulfoundation.org and lyp@saintpaulfoundation.org; URL: http://saintpaulfoundation.org

Foundation type: Community foundation
Limitations: Scholarships to residents of MN, primarily in the Saint Paul area.
Publications: Application guidelines; Annual report (including application guidelines); Financial statement; Grants list; Informational brochure; Newsletter.
Financial data: Year ended 12/31/2004. Assets, $594,648,660 (M); Expenditures, $39,065,856; Total giving, $27,990,733.
Fields of interest: Native Americans/American Indians.
Type of support: Support to graduates or students of specific schools; Undergraduate support.
Application information:
  Initial approach: Telephone or e-mail.
  Deadline(s): Vary.

Additional information: See Web site for complete list of scholarship programs and guidelines.
Program descriptions:
  Kleeker Scholarship: Scholarship available to graduating seniors residing in Fairfax, MN.
  Two Feathers Fund Scholarship: Applicant must belong to a Minnesota Indian Tribe and be on file with MN Indian Scholarship Application.
  Reuben W. Anderson Scholarship: Applicants must be seniors graduating from Stillwater High School.
  Anthony Garofal Scholarship: Applicants must be seniors graduating from Hill-Murray School, St. Paul, MN.
EIN: 416031510

3515

Saks Incorporated Foundation

750 Lakeshore Pkwy., Tax Dept.
Birmingham, AL   35211
Application address: c/o Ken Metzner, 12 E. 49th St., New York, NY 10017

Foundation type: Company-sponsored foundation
Limitations: Scholarships to employees of Saks Inc., only.
Financial data: Year ended 01/29/2005. Assets, $2,189,189 (M); Expenditures, $1,902,055; Total giving, $736,070.
Type of support: Employee-related scholarships.
EIN: 631207483

3516

Toyo Sakumoto Charitable Trust

c/o Bank of Hawaii
P.O. Box 3170
Honolulu, HI   96802-3170
Application address: c/o Hawaii Community Foundation, Scholarships, 1164 Bishop St., Ste. 800, Honolulu, HI 96813

Foundation type: Independent foundation
Limitations: Scholarships to students residing in HI who are of Japanese descent.
Publications: Informational brochure (including application guidelines).
Financial data: Year ended 03/31/2005. Assets, $800,611 (M); Expenditures, $47,266; Total giving, $35,500; Grants to individuals, totaling $35,500.
Type of support: Undergraduate support.
Application information:
  Deadline(s): Mar. 1
  Additional information: Completion of formal application required, including personal statement, transcript, and essay; Application available on Web site.
Program description:
  Scholarships: Applicants must have been born in Hawaii, and have at least a 3.5 GPA.
EIN: 996089401

3517

James and Beatrice Salah Family Foundation for the Town of Canton, Inc.

c/o Salah M. James
100 Hudson Rd.
Canton, MA   02021-1435

Foundation type: Independent foundation
Limitations: Scholarships to individuals of Canton, MA.

Financial data: Year ended 12/31/2004. Assets, $2,137,196 (M); Expenditures, $127,850; Total giving, $112,500; Grants to individuals, 17 grants totaling $85,000.
Type of support: Scholarships—to individuals.
Application information: Applications not accepted.
EIN: 043292638

3518

The Lucy Pannill Sale Foundation

231 E. Church St., 5th Fl.
Martinsville, VA   24112

Foundation type: Independent foundation
Limitations: Scholarships to residents of VA.
Financial data: Year ended 05/31/2005. Assets, $1,931,810 (M); Expenditures, $309,819; Total giving, $263,454; Grants to individuals, 7 grants totaling $54,563 (high: $20,000, low: $200).
Type of support: Scholarships—to individuals.
Application information: Applications by letter accepted throughout the year.
EIN: 541726783

3519

Salem Community Foundation, Inc.

713 E. State St.
Salem, OH   44460-2911   (330) 332-4021
Contact: John E. Tonti, Pres.
FAX: (330) 337-3474; E-mail: scf@salemohio.com; URL: http://www.salemohio.com/scf

Foundation type: Community foundation
Limitations: Scholarships primarily to residents of Salem, and Columbiana, OH, for undergraduate education.
Publications: Annual report; Newsletter.
Financial data: Year ended 12/31/2004. Assets, $12,746,095 (M); Expenditures, $1,014,855; Total giving, $958,883; Grants to individuals, 33 grants totaling $83,944 (high: $1,000, low: $200).
Type of support: Scholarships—to individuals; Undergraduate support.
Application information: Application form required.
  Initial approach: Letter outlining financial need.
  Deadline(s): May 1
  Additional information: Applications should be sent by mail.
EIN: 341001130

3520

The Salem Foundation

c/o Pioneer Trust Bank, N.A.
P.O. Box 2305
Salem, OR   97308   (503) 363-3136
Contact: Carol Herman
E-mail: salemfoundation@pioneertrustbank.com

Foundation type: Community foundation
Limitations: Scholarships to local students for undergraduate support who live in the Salem, OR, area.
Publications: Application guidelines; Financial statement; Informational brochure.
Financial data: Year ended 04/30/2005. Assets, $12,454,742 (M); Expenditures, $1,005,489; Total giving, $886,973; Grants to individuals, 29 grants totaling $19,715 (high: $1,700, low: $25).
Type of support: Undergraduate support.

Application information: Contact foundation for current application deadline/guidelines.
EIN: 936018523

3521
Salem Hospital Foundation
665 Winter St., S.E.
P.O. Box 14001
Salem, OR 97309-5014
Contact: Kent Aldrich, Secy.-Treas.
URL: http://www.salemhospital.org/foundation/index.htm

Foundation type: Public charity
Limitations: Scholarships to individuals residing in OR for undergraduate education leading to health care careers.
Financial data: Year ended 09/30/2003. Assets, $6,625,990 (M); Expenditures, $254,708; Total giving, $124,461.
Fields of interest: Health sciences school/education.
Type of support: Undergraduate support.
Application information: Deadline May 15; Completion of formal application required, including transcript, one-page narrative, three letters of recommendation, and resume; Application available on Web site.
Program description:
   Scholarships: Applicants must have a permanent residence in Marion, Polk or Yamhill County and at the time of the application must be accepted into or have applied to a formal training program in a health care field. Depending on the specific program of study, there may be a one to two year prerequisite course to complete prior to applying for the actual program; These prerequisite studies are not eligible for scholarship assistance. Students must be taking at least part-time class schedule to qualify.
EIN: 237002687

3522
Salem Lutheran Foundation
2700 E. Dublin-Granville Rd.
Columbus, OH 43231 (614) 863-3124
Contact: Terrie Rice, Secy.

Foundation type: Company-sponsored foundation
Limitations: Scholarships to men studying to become Lutheran ministers in the Wisconsin Evangelical Lutheran Synod.
Financial data: Year ended 12/31/2004. Assets, $2,752,987 (M); Expenditures, $209,919; Total giving, $194,900; Grants to individuals, 267 grants totaling $194,900 (high: $1,500, low: $200).
Fields of interest: Theological school/education; Protestant agencies & churches; Men.
Type of support: Scholarships—to individuals.
Application information: Application form required.
   Deadline(s): May 31 for requesting application, July 1 for submission
   Applicants should submit the following:
      1) Financial information
      2) Essay
      3) Transcripts
      4) Letter(s) of recommendation
   Additional information: Application must also include employment history; Analysis Report required from students of Northwestern University only; Recipients notified after Aug. 1.
EIN: 316084166

3523
Mary M. Saletra Scholarship Fund
c/o Pennsville National Bank
170 S. Broadway
P.O. Box 345
Pennsville, NJ 08070-0345 (856) 678-6006

Foundation type: Independent foundation
Limitations: Scholarships to current and former graduates of Penns Grove High School, NJ, and to residents of the Penns Grove-Carney's Point School District.
Financial data: Year ended 12/31/2004. Assets, $8,007 (M); Expenditures, $2,052; Total giving, $2,000; Grants to individuals, totaling $2,000.
Type of support: Support to graduates or students of specific schools; Undergraduate support.
Application information: Application form required.
   Deadline(s): Mar. 3
   Applicants should submit the following:
      1) Transcripts
Program description:
   Scholarship Fund: Preference is given to individuals who attend or have attended Penns Grove High School, NJ, are pursuing four-year degrees at Rowan University, NJ, and exhibit active involvement in school and extracurricular activities while maintaining a superior GPA. Scholarships are renewable each semester provided the student maintains satisfactory progress.
EIN: 226590422

3524
Salick Health Care Foundation
c/o Zeneca, Inc.
8201 Beverly Blvd.
Los Angeles, CA 90048-4505
E-mail: info@aptiumoncology.com

Foundation type: Company-sponsored foundation
Limitations: Scholarships and internship opportunities for students at Fremont High School, Los Angeles, CA.
Financial data: Year ended 12/31/2004. Assets, $18,964 (M); Expenditures, $13,561; Total giving, $13,500; Grants to individuals, 8 grants totaling $13,500 (high: $3,000, low: $1,500).
Fields of interest: Health care.
Type of support: Internship funds; Scholarships—to individuals; Support to graduates or students of specific schools.
Application information:
   Initial approach: Letter.
   Additional information: Contact foundation for current application deadline/guidelines.
Program description:
   Fremont High School Program: Under this two-part program, students at Fremont High School, Los Angeles, CA, receive a $1,250 scholarship to attend a college or university of their choice, after completing a brief internship at Salick Health Care during their school vacations. At the start of the internship component, students receive a $250 award. After the internship period, interns receive their scholarship money. In addition, some former interns may receive $100 honoraria if they return to their high school to promote this program.
EIN: 954382184

3525
Burl E. Salisbury Memorial Scholarship Fund
c/o Southern Michigan Bank & Trust
51 W. Pearl St.
Coldwater, MI 49036
Contact: Mary Guthrie, Trust Off., Southern Michigan Bank & Trust

Foundation type: Independent foundation
Limitations: Educational loans to students of Bronson High School, MI.
Financial data: Year ended 04/30/2005. Assets, $308,237 (M); Expenditures, $37,017; Total giving, $30,000; Grants to individuals, totaling $30,000.
Type of support: Support to graduates or students of specific schools; Undergraduate support.
Application information: Deadline May 1; Initial approach by letter; Completion of formal application required, including FAS and GPA.
EIN: 386429664

3526
Salisbury-Rowan Community Service Council, Inc.
P.O. Box 631
Salisbury, NC 28144 (704) 633-6633
Contact: Willette Johnson, Exec. Dir.
FAX: (704) 633-7814

Foundation type: Public charity
Limitations: Grants to economically disadvantaged residents of Rowan and Cabarrus counties, NC, for tuition, books, and supplies.
Publications: Application guidelines; Annual report; Financial statement; Grants list; Informational brochure; Newsletter; Program policy statement.
Financial data: Year ended 10/31/2003. Assets, $1,021,263 (M); Expenditures, $9,170,503.
Fields of interest: Economically disadvantaged.
Type of support: Scholarships—to individuals; Grants for special needs.
Application information: Contact council for current application deadline/guidelines.
Program description:
   Scholarships: Applicants must be high school graduates or the equivalent, meet Income Poverty Guidelines, and maintain a 2.5 GPA. Recipients will need to attend their classes regularly and furnish grades and other needed information to the council each semester or quarter.
EIN: 560840196

3527
Fritchof T. Sallness and Marian M. Sallness Memorial Scholarship Fund
c/o Citizens Bank
328 S. Saginaw St., M/C 002072
Saginaw, MI 48602
Application address: Helen James, 101 N. Washington Ave., Saginaw, MI 48607-1206, tel.: (989) 776-7368

Foundation type: Independent foundation
Limitations: Scholarships and student loans to residents of Saginaw County, MI, to attend a MI college or university.
Financial data: Year ended 12/31/2004. Assets, $221,497 (M); Expenditures, $6,262; Total giving, $1,000; Grants to individuals, 2 grants totaling $1,000 (high: $500, low: $500); Loans to individuals, 2 loans totaling $5,500.
Type of support: Undergraduate support.

Application information:
Deadline(s): May 1
Additional information: Application by letter.
EIN: 386565588

3528
Salute to Education, Inc.
100 N.E. Loop 410, No. 625
San Antonio, TX 78216-4742
Application address: 110 Broadway, Ste. 220, San Antonio, TX 78205, tel.: (210) 225-3353

Foundation type: Operating foundation
Limitations: Scholarships to high school seniors in CA, FL, and TX, interested in pursuing careers in automotive technology. Support also for undergraduate education in other academic subjects.
Financial data: Year ended 12/31/2004. Assets, $595,887 (M); Expenditures, $461,723; Total giving, $295,000; Grants to individuals, 125 grants totaling $190,000.
Fields of interest: Vocational education, post-secondary.
Type of support: Technical education support; Undergraduate support.
Application information: Application form required.
Deadline(s): Feb. 7
Applicants should submit the following:
1) Letter(s) of recommendation
2) Transcripts
3) Essay
EIN: 742661078

3529
Spero Samer Trust
c/o First Commonwealth Trust Co.
111 S. Main St.
Greensburg, PA 15601-3101 (724) 834-6062

Foundation type: Independent foundation
Limitations: Scholarships to seminarians or candidates for the priesthood from the Pittsburgh Diocese of the Greek Orthodox Church, PA.
Financial data: Year ended 12/31/2004. Assets, $2,167,712 (M); Expenditures, $138,942; Total giving, $118,334; Grants to individuals, 24 grants totaling $118,334 (high: $12,648, low: $1,000).
Fields of interest: Theological school/education; Christian agencies & churches.
Type of support: Scholarships—to individuals.
Application information: Applications accepted. Application form required.
Deadline(s): May 1 for fall semester, Nov. 1 for spring semester
EIN: 256175080

3530
Jerold J. & Margaret M. Samet Foundation
15022 Snowden Dr.
Silver Spring, MD 20905
Contact: Jerold J. Samet, Pres.

Foundation type: Independent foundation
Limitations: Scholarships to individuals who demonstrate the commitment to and idealism of freemasonry, and DeMolay & Youth Leaders International.
Financial data: Year ended 12/31/2004. Assets, $1,187,893 (M); Expenditures, $99,435; Total giving, $62,354.
Fields of interest: Fraternal societies.
Type of support: Undergraduate support.

Application information: Applications accepted.
Additional information: Application by letter accepted throughout the year.
EIN: 522128751

3531
Adrian M. Sample Scholarship Trust
P.O. Box 1908
Orlando, FL 32802-1908
Contact: Margaret G. Sample, Scholarship Coord.

Foundation type: Independent foundation
Limitations: Scholarships to Protestant residents of St. Lucie and Okeechobee counties, FL, planning to attend FL colleges and universities or Davidson College, NC.
Publications: Application guidelines; Program policy statement.
Financial data: Year ended 12/31/2004. Assets, $3,720,613 (M); Expenditures, $152,179; Total giving, $142,175.
Fields of interest: Protestant agencies & churches.
Type of support: Scholarships—to individuals.
Application information: Deadline Apr. 1; Initial approach by letter; Completion of formal application required including transcript; Application forms available only through high schools, Indian River Community College and local churches.
Program description:
Scholarships: Applicants must be active Protestant church members and unmarried. Funds are allocated directly to students.
EIN: 596490788

3532
R. E. & Catherine Woodson Sampley Educational Foundation, Inc.
P.O. Box 1147
Mount Ida, AR 71957
Contact: Frances Dobbs, Secy.

Foundation type: Operating foundation
Limitations: Renewable scholarships of $1,500 each semester for up to four years to Montgomery County, AR, students.
Financial data: Year ended 12/31/2002. Assets, $2,228,683 (M); Expenditures, $158,235; Total giving, $144,000; Grants to individuals, 43 grants totaling $144,000 (high: $4,500, low: $1,500).
Type of support: Scholarships—to individuals.
Application information:
Deadline(s): Contact foundation for current application deadline/guidelines.
EIN: 716156225

3533
Gordon Samstag Fine Arts Trust
c/o Bank of America, N.A.
P.O. Box 40200, FL9-100-10-19
Jacksonville, FL 32203-0200
E-mail: samstag@unisa.edu.au; Application address: c/o Ross Wolfe, Dir., Samstag Scholarship Program, University of South Australia, GPO Box 2471, Adelaide, South Australia 5001, tel.: (08) 8302-0865; FAX: (08) 8302-0866; International Code for Australia is 618; URL: http://www.unisa.edu.au/samstag

Foundation type: Independent foundation
Limitations: Support for Australian visual art students to study art abroad at an art institute or university.
Publications: Application guidelines.

Financial data: Year ended 12/31/2004. Assets, $10,186,761 (M); Expenditures, $661,898; Total giving, $363,065; Grants to individuals, 22 grants totaling $363,065 (high: $55,571, low: $139).
Fields of interest: Visual arts.
Type of support: Scholarships—to individuals; Foreign applicants.
Application information:
Deadline(s): June 30
Additional information: Completion of formal application required, including proof of Australian citizenship, financial information, sample works, curriculum vitae, transcripts, two references, and an applicant statement.
Program description:
Anne and Gordon Samstag International Visual Arts Scholarships: Grants of $30,000 (Australian) are available to Australian students who have completed at least the equivalent of two full years of full-time study and recent graduates (not more than five years since graduation) in the visual arts, to further study at an approved university or university-level school of visual arts in New York City, or elsewhere in the U.S. for one year. Applicants must be at least 18 years of age and hold Australian citizenship or permanent residency. Funds are meant to cover materials and equipment costs, reasonable living expenses, institutional fees, economy-class return airfare to Australia, and personal travel and medical insurance. Grants may be renewable for up to one half the original award amount, however this is only in extraordinary circumstances. Recipients are usually not allowed to receive other awards, grants, or paid leaves in conjunction with this grant. Applicants may submit videotapes, films, slides, or Mac-compatible CD-ROMs for their work samples. Recipients are selected on the basis of merit of their work, their potential for further advancement, and their current stage of development first, and then on the basis of academic achievement. In addition, according to the rules of the will of Mr. Samstag, in any year where more than one scholarship is given, at least one recipient must be either a resident of South Australia for at least two years, a graduate of a South Australian institution within the last five years, or a student studying at a South Australian institution for at least two years.
EIN: 656064217

3534
San Antonio A & M Club Foundation
6205 West Ave.
San Antonio, TX 78213-2315
Contact: Jim Whiteaker, Scholarship Admin.

Foundation type: Independent foundation
Limitations: Scholarships to Bexar County, TX, high school students to attend Texas A&M University.
Financial data: Year ended 12/31/2004. Assets, $629,913 (M); Expenditures, $193,518; Total giving, $16,400; Grants to individuals, totaling $16,400.
Type of support: Support to graduates or students of specific schools; Undergraduate support.
Application information: Application form required.
Deadline(s): Feb.
EIN: 742247729

3535
San Antonio Area Foundation
110 Broadway, Ste. 230
San Antonio, TX   78205   (210) 225-2243
Contact: Clarence R. "Reggie" Williams, C.E.O.; For grant applications: Lydia Rodriguez, Prog. Off., Discretionary Funds
FAX: (210) 225-1980; E-mail: info@saafdn.org; Grant application tel.: (210) 228-3753 and E-mail: lrodriguez@saafdn.org; URL: http://www.saafdn.org

Foundation type: Community foundation
Limitations: Scholarships primarily to high school seniors in Bexar County, TX.
Publications: Application guidelines; Annual report; Financial statement; Grants list; Informational brochure; Newsletter.
Financial data: Year ended 12/31/2005. Assets, $123,604,277 (M); Expenditures, $16,510,392; Total giving, $14,475,224; Grants to individuals, 329 grants totaling $658,876 (high: $25,310, low: $250).
Fields of interest: Education.
Type of support: Scholarships—to individuals.
Application information: Application form required.
   Deadline(s): Nov. 15.
   Additional information: Applications must be submitted to Bexar County Scholarship Clearing House.
EIN: 746065414

3536
The San Antonio Spurs Foundation
(formerly Spurs Foundation)
1 SBC Center
San Antonio, TX   78219   (210) 444-5862
Contact: Alison Fox, Exec. Dir.
FAX: (210) 444-5875; URL: http://www.nba.com/spurs/community/in_the_community.html

Foundation type: Public charity
Limitations: Scholarships to students in southern TX for higher education.
Financial data: Year ended 06/30/2003. Assets, $370,355 (M); Expenditures, $1,307,125; Total giving, $441,276; Grants to individuals, 47 grants totaling $66,380 (high: $11,380, low: $1,000).
Type of support: Undergraduate support.
Application information: Applications accepted. Application form required.
   Initial approach: Letter.
   Deadline(s): Feb.
EIN: 742509544

3537
San Diego County Citizens Scholarship Foundation
6401 Linda Vista Rd., Rm. 624
San Diego, CA   92111-7399

Foundation type: Independent foundation
Limitations: Scholarships to financially needy students enrolled in high schools in San Diego County, CA, who have been residents of San Diego County for at least one year, and plan to attend San Diego colleges and universities.
Financial data: Year ended 09/30/2003. Assets, $1,015,061 (M); Expenditures, $33,255; Total giving, $26,400.
Type of support: Scholarships—to individuals; Support to graduates or students of specific schools.
Application information: Contact fund for current application deadline; Completion of formal application required, including personal statement, financial information, high school transcripts, and a copy of the first page of parent's latest 1040 tax form; Interviews required.
EIN: 956111706

3538
San Diego County Salute to Education
4300 El Cajon Blvd.
San Diego, CA   92105   (619) 521-2404
FAX: (619) 283-1327;
E-mail: salute2education@aol.com; URL: http://www.salutetoeducation.com

Foundation type: Independent foundation
Limitations: Scholarships to high school students who reside in the San Diego, CA, area for undergraduate education.
Financial data: Year ended 12/31/2004. Assets, $83,921 (M); Expenditures, $369,751; Total giving, $265,648; Grants to individuals, 251 grants totaling $264,648 (high: $14,648, low: $1,000).
Fields of interest: Higher education.
Type of support: Undergraduate support.
Application information: Application form required. Application form available on the grantmaker's Web site.
   Deadline(s): Feb. 17
   Applicants should submit the following:
      1) Letter(s) of recommendation
      2) Essay
   Additional information: See Web site for additional application information.
EIN: 330773691

3539
The San Diego Foundation
(formerly San Diego Community Foundation)
1420 Kettner Blvd., Ste. 500
San Diego, CA   92101-9693   (619) 235-2300
Contact: Robert A. Kelly, C.E.O.; For scholarships and project grants: Valerie Attisha
FAX: (619) 239-1710;
E-mail: info@sdfoundation.org; Additional tel.: (858) 385-1595 (for North County); URL: http://www.sdfoundation.org

Foundation type: Community foundation
Limitations: Scholarships to students or adults residing in San Diego County, CA.
Publications: Annual report; Financial statement; Grants list; Informational brochure; Newsletter.
Financial data: Year ended 06/30/2005. Assets, $451,470,000 (M); Expenditures, $49,765,000; Total giving, $41,106,000; Grants to individuals, 444 grants totaling $1,890,700 (high: $156,000, low: $250).
Type of support: Undergraduate support.
Application information: Applications accepted. Application form required. Application form available on the grantmaker's Web site.
   Initial approach: E-mail.
   Deadline(s): Jan.
   Applicants should submit the following:
      1) Transcripts
      2) SAT
      3) Work samples
      4) Proposal
      5) Letter(s) of recommendation
      6) GPA
      7) Financial information
      8) Essay
      9) Budget Information
      10) ACT

Additional information: Contact foundation for further application guidelines.
EIN: 952942582

3540
San Diego Martin Luther King Jr. Foundation
3636 Fifth Ave., No. 300
San Diego, CA   92103   (619) 232-2200
Contact: Reese Jarrett, Dir.

Foundation type: Public charity
Limitations: Scholarships to residents of the San Diego, CA, area who demonstrate qualities reflecting the life and principles of Martin Luther King, Jr.
Financial data: Year ended 12/31/2003. Assets, $151,889 (M); Expenditures, $20,000; Total giving, $15,750; Grants to individuals, 9 grants totaling $15,750 (high: $5,000, low: $625).
Type of support: Undergraduate support.
Application information:
   Initial approach: Letter.
   Additional information: Contact foundation for further information.
EIN: 330736895

3541
San Felipe Humanitarian Alliance
(formerly San Felipe del Rio, Inc.)
9666 Business Park Ave., Ste. 102
San Diego, CA   92131
URL: http://sanfelipealliance.org/

Foundation type: Operating foundation
Limitations: Scholarships to dependent, neglected, or abused youths particularly from CA, NM, and OR. Preference is shown to former residents of San Felipe del Rio's Children's Group Home in Taos, NM.
Financial data: Year ended 06/30/2005. Assets, $3,814,339 (M); Expenditures, $384,062; Total giving, $131,879.
Fields of interest: Children/youth, services.
Type of support: Scholarships—to individuals.
Application information: Applications not accepted.
EIN: 237276447

3542
The San Francisco Foundation
225 Bush St., Ste. 500
San Francisco, CA   94104-4224
(415) 733-8500
Contact: Sandra R. Hernandez M.D., C.E.O. and Secy.
FAX: (415) 477-2783; E-mail: rec@sff.org; Intent to Apply E-mail: apps@sff.org; Additional E-mail: srh@sff.org; URL: http://www.sff.org

Foundation type: Community foundation
Limitations: Scholarships to residents of CA for upper level or graduate study at specific institutions. See program description for details.
Publications: Application guidelines; Annual report; Financial statement; Grants list; Informational brochure (including application guidelines); Newsletter; Program policy statement.
Financial data: Year ended 06/30/2004. Assets, $757,717,972 (M); Expenditures, $74,554,575; Total giving, $64,392,830.
Fields of interest: Arts education; Media/communications; Architecture; Design; Engineering school/education; Natural resources;

Environmental education; Hispanics/Latinos; LGBTQ.
Type of support: Awards/grants by nomination only; Graduate support; Undergraduate support.
Application information: Contact foundation for current application deadline/guidelines; See Web site for complete program listing.

3543
San Francisco Girls Chorus
44 Page St., No. 200
San Francisco, CA 94102 (415) 863-1752
FAX: (415) 934-0302;
E-mail: info@sfgirlschorus.org; URL: http://www.sfgirlschorus.org

Foundation type: Public charity
Limitations: Scholarships for girls and young women ages seven to eighteen for music education and choral training.
Financial data: Year ended 06/30/2004. Assets, $2,392,334 (M); Expenditures, $1,774,060; Total giving, $100,039; Grants to individuals, totaling $100,039.
Fields of interest: Music; Music (choral).
Type of support: Scholarships—to individuals.
Application information:
Initial approach: E-mail.
EIN: 942711726

3544
San Luis Obispo County Community Foundation
1401 Higuera St.
P.O. Box 1580
San Luis Obispo, CA 93406-1580
(805) 543-2323
Contact: David Edwards, Exec. Dir.; For grants: Janice Fong Wolf, Dir., Grants & Progs.
FAX: (805) 543-2346; E-mail: info@sloccf.org; Additional E-mails: dave@sloccf.org and jwolf@sloccf.org; URL: http://www.sloccf.org

Foundation type: Community foundation
Limitations: Scholarships to residents of San Luis Obispo County, CA.
Publications: Application guidelines; Annual report; Grants list; Informational brochure; Newsletter.
Financial data: Year ended 12/31/2004. Assets, $17,981,139 (M); Expenditures, $2,344,426; Total giving, $1,797,948.
Type of support: Undergraduate support.
Application information: Applications not accepted.
Additional information: Unsolicited requests for funds not considered or acknowledged.
EIN: 770496500

3545
Sandusky County Bar Association
802 Court St.
Fremont, OH 43420
Application address: c/o C. Westly Bristley, Trust Off., Croghan Colonial Bank, 323 Croghan St., Fremont, OH 43420, tel.: (419) 332-7301

Foundation type: Independent foundation
Limitations: Scholarships to individuals from Sandusky, OH, to attend law school.
Financial data: Year ended 12/31/2004. Assets, $251,836 (M); Expenditures, $12,622; Total giving, $11,000; Grants to individuals, totaling $11,000.
Fields of interest: Law school/education.

Type of support: Scholarships—to individuals.
Application information: Applications accepted throughout the year; Completion of formal application required.
EIN: 341894555

3546
Sandy Hill Foundation
P.O. Box 30
Hudson Falls, NY 12839 (518) 747-5805
Contact: Floyd H. Rourke, Tr.

Foundation type: Independent foundation
Limitations: Scholarships to residents of the greater Hudson Falls, NY, area.
Financial data: Year ended 08/31/2005. Assets, $8,724,601 (M); Expenditures, $553,210; Total giving, $496,053; Grants to individuals, 46 grants totaling $69,500 (high: $1,500, low: $100).
Type of support: Scholarships—to individuals.
Application information: Deadline Apr. 1; Completion of formal application required, including transcripts, essay, letter of recommendation from guidance counselor, standardized test results, and copy of parents' tax returns.
EIN: 146018954

3547
Andrew and Martha Sanford Scholarship Foundation
P.O. Box 1958
Kilmarnock, VA 22482-1958
Application address: P.O. Box 26311, Richmond, VA 23260-6311

Foundation type: Independent foundation
Limitations: Scholarships to residents of Westmoreland, Richmond, Lancaster, and Northumberland counties, VA, for attendance at colleges, universities, and trade schools. Preference is given to applicants from Westmoreland. Scholarships are awarded on the basis of financial need, academic achievement, character, and community and extracurricular activities.
Financial data: Year ended 12/31/2004. Assets, $445,325 (M); Expenditures, $22,640; Total giving, $17,299; Grants to individuals, totaling $17,299.
Fields of interest: Vocational education.
Type of support: Technical education support; Undergraduate support.
Application information:
Initial approach: Letter.
Deadline(s): Mar. 15
Additional information: Completion of formal application required, including transcripts, essays, GPA, and financial information; Recipients notified by May 15.
EIN: 546295578

3548
Joe & Babe Sanford Scholarship Foundation
c/o Pinnacle Bank
P.O. Box 127
Mitchell, NE 69357-0127 (308) 623-1611
Contact: Larry G. Janecek, Tr.

Foundation type: Independent foundation
Limitations: Scholarships primarily to graduates of Mitchell High School, NE, based on character, scholastic abilities, and financial need.

Financial data: Year ended 12/31/2004. Assets, $50,851 (M); Expenditures, $2,898; Total giving, $2,600; Grants to individuals, totaling $2,600.
Type of support: Support to graduates or students of specific schools; Undergraduate support.
Application information: Contact foundation for current application deadline/guidelines.
EIN: 470585538

3549
Sanilac County Community Foundation
47 Austin St.
P.O. Box 307
Sandusky, MI 48471-0307 (810) 648-3634
Contact: Joan Nagelkirk, Secy.
FAX: (810) 648-4418;
E-mail: director@sanilaccountycommunityfoundatio n.org; URL: http://www.sanilaccountycommunityfoundation.org

Foundation type: Community foundation
Limitations: Scholarships to graduating seniors of Sanilac County, MI, high schools.
Financial data: Year ended 12/31/2004. Assets, $2,333,633 (M); Expenditures, $201,477; Total giving, $159,480.
Type of support: Support to graduates or students of specific schools; Undergraduate support.
Application information:
Deadline(s): June 1 and Dec. 1
Additional information: Contact foundation for current application guidelines.
EIN: 383204484

3550
Santa Barbara Foundation
15 E. Carrillo St.
Santa Barbara, CA 93101 (805) 963-1873
Contact: Charles O. Slosser, C.E.O.
FAX: (805) 966-2345;
E-mail: cslosser@sbfoundation.org; URL: http://www.sbfoundation.org

Foundation type: Community foundation
Limitations: Student loans and scholarships to residents of Santa Barbara County, CA, who have attended grades 7-12 at Santa Barbara county schools. See program description for specific limitations.
Publications: Application guidelines; Annual report; Financial statement; Informational brochure; Newsletter; Occasional report.
Financial data: Year ended 12/31/2004. Assets, $222,388,000 (M); Expenditures, $12,614,067; Total giving, $8,602,456.
Fields of interest: Performing arts, education; Literature; Education, research; Vocational education; Medical school/education; Community development, volunteer services; Women.
Type of support: Support to graduates or students of specific schools; Undergraduate support.
Application information: Applications accepted. Application form required.
Initial approach: Letter with SASE.
Deadline(s): Vary
Additional information: See Web site for complete program listing.
EIN: 951866094

3551
The Sapelo Foundation, Inc.
(formerly Sapelo Island Research Foundation, Inc.)
1712 Ellis St., 2nd Fl.
Brunswick, GA 31520 (912) 265-0520
Contact: Phyllis Bowen, Exec. Dir.
FAX: (912) 265-1888;
E-mail: sapelofoundation@mindspring.com;
URL: http://www.sapelofoundation.org

Foundation type: Independent foundation
Limitations: Funding for scholarships to financially needy residents of McIntosh County, GA, to attend accredited colleges, universities, and technical schools. Funds are made available to schools on behalf of these recipients.
Publications: Application guidelines; Annual report; Grants list.
Financial data: Year ended 06/30/2004.
Assets, $34,942,159 (M); Expenditures, $1,803,468; Total giving, $1,441,505; Grants to individuals, totaling $138,125.
Fields of interest: Vocational education; Higher education.
Type of support: Scholarships—to individuals.
Application information: Applications accepted. Application form required. Application form available on the grantmaker's Web site.
   Initial approach: Online application.
   Deadline(s): Mar. 1
   Additional information: The Sapelo Foundation administers the Richard J. Reynolds, Jr. Scholarship Program.
EIN: 580827472

3552
Sarver Charitable Trust
c/o Smith County State Bank & Trust Co.
P.O. Box 307
Smith Center, KS 66967
Application address: c/o Paul S. Gregory, P.O. Box 345, Osborne, KS 67473

Foundation type: Independent foundation
Limitations: Scholarships to graduating high school students and current college students from Osborne County, KS.
Financial data: Year ended 12/31/2004.
Assets, $9,448,168 (M); Expenditures, $339,229; Total giving, $259,983; Grants to individuals, 183 grants totaling $23,514.
Type of support: Undergraduate support.
Application information: Deadline Apr. 1; Completion of formal application required, including transcripts and GPA.
EIN: 486298990

3553
Sasso Scholarship Fund Trust
(formerly Sasso Consolidation Fund Trust)
c/o Bank of America, N.A.
P.O. Box 6768
Providence, RI 02940-6768
Contact: Thomas N. James

Foundation type: Independent foundation
Limitations: Scholarships to Meriden High School, CT, graduates for higher education.
Financial data: Year ended 12/31/2004.
Assets, $159,614 (M); Expenditures, $11,313; Total giving, $7,000; Grants to individuals, totaling $7,000.
Type of support: Support to graduates or students of specific schools; Undergraduate support.

Application information: Application form required.
   Deadline(s): May 1
EIN: 066131106

3554
Walter H. Sauvain Trust
(formerly Sauvain Scholarship Fund)
c/o Wachovia Bank, N.A.
401 S. Tryon St., 4th Fl.
Charlotte, NC 28288-1159

Foundation type: Independent foundation
Limitations: Scholarships to residents of the Lewisburgh, PA, area.
Financial data: Year ended 12/31/2004.
Assets, $855,016 (M); Expenditures, $47,859; Total giving, $40,000; Grants to individuals, totaling $40,000.
Type of support: Undergraduate support.
Application information: Applications not accepted.
EIN: 236791852

3555
Lillie Murray Sawyer Teacher Scholarship Fund
8601 Manchester Rd., No. 312
Silver Spring, MD 20901 (301) 587-8175
Contact: Plugenia Smith Robinson, Tr.

Foundation type: Independent foundation
Limitations: Scholarships to high school seniors residing in DC, who are members of Mt. Airy Baptist Church and intend to become teachers.
Financial data: Year ended 12/31/2004.
Assets, $495,906 (M); Expenditures, $19,546; Total giving, $15,000; Grants to individuals, totaling $15,000.
Fields of interest: Teacher school/education.
Type of support: Scholarships—to individuals.
Application information: Applications accepted. Application form required.
   Deadline(s): July 1
EIN: 521794412

3556
Ryan W. Sayles Foundation
c/o UMB Bank, N.A.
P.O. Box 419692, M/S 1020305
Kansas City, MO 64141-6692
Application address: c/o UMB Bank, N.A., Patti Glass, 1010 Grand Ave, Kansas City, MO 64106

Foundation type: Independent foundation
Limitations: Scholarships to residents of MO for higher education.
Financial data: Year ended 12/31/2004.
Assets, $432,601 (M); Expenditures, $29,696; Total giving, $26,600; Grants to individuals, totaling $26,600.
Type of support: Undergraduate support.
Application information: Unsolicited requests for funds not accepted.
EIN: 431774887

3557
The Scaife Scholarship Foundation
1547 Lakeside Dr.
Oakland, CA 94612-4520
Contact: Clyde D. Minar, Secy.-Treas.

Foundation type: Independent foundation

Limitations: Scholarships to male graduates of public high schools in northern CA whose parents were born in the U.S.
Financial data: Year ended 05/31/2004.
Assets, $10,667,602 (M); Expenditures, $524,519; Total giving, $449,920; Grants to individuals, 92 grants totaling $449,920 (high: $6,250, low: $2,000).
Fields of interest: Men.
Type of support: Scholarships—to individuals; Support to graduates or students of specific schools.
Application information: Deadline Mar. 15; Completion of formal application required, including transcripts, College Board scores, and statement of financial need.
EIN: 943161402

3558
Scalp and Blade Scholarship Trust
c/o M&T Bank
1 M&T Plz., 8th Fl.
Buffalo, NY 14203

Foundation type: Independent foundation
Limitations: Scholarships to graduating men from high schools in Erie County, NY, who plan to attend schools outside Erie and Niagara counties. Scholarships are up to $750 annually for eligible applicants.
Financial data: Year ended 12/31/2004.
Assets, $91,776 (M); Expenditures, $6,225; Total giving, $6,025; Grants to individuals, totaling $6,025.
Fields of interest: Men.
Type of support: Scholarships—to individuals.
Application information:
   Deadline(s): May 31
   Additional information: Interviews granted upon request; Contact Erie County, NY, high school guidance counselors or principals for current application guidelines.
EIN: 166020842

3559
Scanlan Foundation
1403 Main St.
Rock Valley, IA 51247-1223 (712) 476-5411

Foundation type: Independent foundation
Limitations: Student loans to members of St. Mary's Catholic Church in Rock Valley, IA.
Financial data: Year ended 12/31/2004.
Assets, $430,106 (M); Expenditures, $1,167; Total giving, $0; Loans to individuals, 14 loans totaling $30,000.
Fields of interest: Roman Catholic agencies & churches.
Type of support: Student loans—to individuals.
Application information: Contact foundation for current application deadline; Initial approach by letter or telephone; Completion of formal application required.
EIN: 421373828

3560
Trusteeship of Emmett R. Scanlan & Catherine D. Scanlan Memorial Scholarship Fund
c/o Michele M. McGill
1403 Main St.
Rock Valley, IA 51247-1223 (712) 476-5411

Foundation type: Independent foundation

Limitations: Loans to financially needy high school seniors or graduates of Rock Valley Community School, IA, for postsecondary education.
Financial data: Year ended 12/31/2004.
Assets, $97,339 (M); Expenditures, $3,318; Total giving, $0; Loans to individuals, 12 loans totaling $12,000.
Type of support: Support to graduates or students of specific schools; Undergraduate support.
Application information: Contact foundation for current application deadline; Completion of formal application required.
EIN: 421453663

3561
Andrew J. Scarlett Scholarship Fund
c/o Clark A. Griffiths
74 Prospect St.
Lebanon, NH 03766

Foundation type: Independent foundation
Limitations: Student loans and scholarships to undergraduate members of the Sigma Alpha Epsilon Fraternity at Dartmouth College, NH.
Financial data: Year ended 06/30/2005.
Assets, $440,235 (M); Expenditures, $10,522; Total giving, $9,820; Grants to individuals, totaling $9,820.
Fields of interest: Students, sororities/fraternities.
Type of support: Support to graduates or students of specific schools; Undergraduate support.
Application information: Applications not accepted.
EIN: 026012571

3562
Scarsdale Foundation
P.O. Box 542
Scarsdale, NY 10583 (914) 725-5492
Contact: Barbara Jaffe, Pres.

Foundation type: Public charity
Limitations: Scholarships and awards to residents of Scarsdale, NY.
Publications: Financial statement.
Financial data: Year ended 06/30/2004.
Assets, $1,546,890 (M); Expenditures, $69,536; Total giving, $65,603.
Fields of interest: Education.
Type of support: Scholarships—to individuals; Awards/prizes.
Application information: Application form required.
  Initial approach: Telephone or letter.
  Applicants should submit the following:
    1) Transcripts
    2) GPA
    3) Financial information
    4) FAFSA
  Additional information: Contact foundation for current application deadline/guidelines.
Program description:
  Scholarships: Awards scholarships to seniors at Scarsdale High School, NY.
EIN: 136103826

3563
Margaret Lobdell Schack Memorial Scholarship Fund
c/o Union Bank of California, N.A.
P.O. Box 84495
Seattle, WA 98124-5795
Contact: Kim Cacace, Trust Off., Union Bank of California, N.A.
Application address: c/o Union Bank of California, N.A., P.O. Box 3123, Seattle, WA 98114

Foundation type: Independent foundation
Limitations: Scholarships to graduates and graduating seniors of Garfield High School, Seattle, WA.
Financial data: Year ended 03/31/2005.
Assets, $143,158 (M); Expenditures, $6,717; Total giving, $3,700; Grants to individuals, totaling $3,700.
Type of support: Support to graduates or students of specific schools; Undergraduate support.
Application information: Applications by letter accepted throughout the year.
EIN: 916240991

3564
Lewis G. Schaeneman, Jr. Memorial Scholarship Foundation, Inc.
c/o Peter M. Phillipes
1385 Hancock St.
Quincy, MA 02169-5100
Contact: Richard Picariello, Pres.

Foundation type: Independent foundation
Limitations: Scholarships to qualified Stop&Shop employees for undergraduate education.
Financial data: Year ended 12/31/2004.
Assets, $562,526 (M); Expenditures, $39,280; Total giving, $37,396; Grants to individuals, totaling $37,396.
Type of support: Employee-related scholarships; Undergraduate support.
Application information: Contact foundation for current application deadline/guidelines.
EIN: 043476066

3565
Frank and Elizabeth Schafer Scholarship Fund
c/o U.S. Bank, N.A.
P.O. Box 387
St. Louis, MO 63166-0387
Application address: c/o Gib Wamsley, Superintendent of Schools, P.O. Box 536, Owensville, MO 65066

Foundation type: Independent foundation
Limitations: Scholarships to financially needy graduates of Owensville High School, MO, who rank in the top third of their class and are pursuing two- or four-year college degrees, graduate degrees, or professional studies.
Financial data: Year ended 06/30/2005.
Assets, $604,756 (M); Expenditures, $35,317; Total giving, $23,250; Grants to individuals, totaling $23,250.
Fields of interest: Vocational education.
Type of support: Support to graduates or students of specific schools; Graduate support; Undergraduate support.
Application information: Deadline Jan. 31; Completion of formal application required, including transcripts and three letters of recommendation; Interviews required.

Program description:
  Scholarships: Scholarships are renewable and are limited to $5,000 per year per student. Recipients must carry a course load of at least 12 credits and maintain at least a 2.7 GPA.
EIN: 436294428

3566
The Schechter Foundation
P.O. Box 4822
New York, NY 10185-4822
Contact: Alfred Schechter, Pres.
E-mail: schechtertenrock@aol.com

Foundation type: Independent foundation
Limitations: Scholarships to graduate students studying occupational and physical therapy, as well as other graduate programs in health care and related fields.
Financial data: Year ended 12/31/2004.
Assets, $1,159,295 (M); Expenditures, $181,991; Total giving, $92,430; Grants to individuals, 28 grants totaling $52,000.
Fields of interest: Physical therapy; Health care.
Type of support: Graduate support.
Application information: Applications accepted. Application form required.
  Initial approach: Letter.
  Deadline(s): July 1
  Applicants should submit the following:
    1) Photograph
    2) Transcripts
    3) FAF
    4) Financial information
    5) SAT
    6) Resume
    7) Letter(s) of recommendation
    8) GPA
    9) Essay
  Additional information: Application should also include statement of financial need, goals, academic evaluation form, and signed copy of applicant or parents' most recent tax return.
EIN: 133157311

3567
Scheffler Family Foundation
2637 E. Mercer Ln.
Phoenix, AZ 85028-2531
Application address: c/o Scholarship Fund, P.O. Box 3731, Boca Raton, FL 33427

Foundation type: Independent foundation
Limitations: Scholarships to the residents of the Boca Raton, FL, area.
Financial data: Year ended 12/31/2004.
Assets, $984,529 (M); Expenditures, $65,290; Total giving, $44,175; Grants to individuals, 74 grants totaling $44,175 (high: $965; low: $195).
Type of support: Undergraduate support.
Application information: Applications accepted throughout the year; Completion of formal application required, including applicant's most recent grade report, a copy of parent's most recent income tax statement, and a letter of recommendation from high school (if applicable).
Program description:
  Scholarships: Applicant must be in financial need, and must currently have at least a 2.0 GPA. Handicapped students must submit a physician's report as to the extent and nature of their handicap. This scholarship is available for eligible high school seniors, and to college students continuing their study.
EIN: 592129811

3568
Jane Schenck Estate Trust
(formerly Jane Schenck Estate)
c/o NBT Bank, N.A.
52 S. Broad St.
Norwich, NY 13815-1646
Application addresses: c/o Superintendent, Greene Central School, Greene, NY 13778, c/o Superintendent, Afton Central School, Afton, NY 13730

Foundation type: Independent foundation
Limitations: Loans for higher education to graduates of Greene and Afton Central Schools, NY.
Financial data: Year ended 06/30/2005. Assets, $199,282 (M); Expenditures, $8,905; Total giving, $7,500; Grants to individuals, totaling $7,500.
Type of support: Support to graduates or students of specific schools; Undergraduate support.
Application information: Applications accepted throughout the year; Completion of formal application required; Applications available from schools.
EIN: 166052404

3569
The Schenectady Foundation
c/o United Way of Schenectady County
P.O. Box 916
Schenectady, NY 12301 (518) 272-6402
Contact: Robert A. Carreau, Secy. and Grant Prog. Mgr.
E-mail: racarreau@outcomeswork.com;
URL: http://www.schenectadyfoundation.org

Foundation type: Community foundation
Limitations: Scholarships to graduating seniors of high schools in Schenectady County, NY, pursuing a teaching career. Scholarships are renewable for four years of study provided students maintain full-time status and satisfactory academic performance.
Publications: Application guidelines; Annual report; Grants list; Informational brochure.
Financial data: Year ended 12/31/2003. Assets, $10,797,496 (M); Expenditures, $564,539; Total giving, $487,932.
Fields of interest: Teacher school/education.
Type of support: Undergraduate support.
Application information: Application form required.
  Deadline(s): Contact foundation for current application deadline.
EIN: 146019650

3570
Leopold Schepp Foundation
551 5th Ave., Ste. 3000
New York, NY 10176 (212) 692-0191
Contact: SuzanneClair Guard, Exec. Dir.
URL: http://www.scheppfoundation.org

Foundation type: Independent foundation
Limitations: Scholarships to students who are U.S. citizens enrolled on a full-time basis at accredited colleges and universities. Only one member of a family may apply at the same time. Four-year undergraduate scholarships to individuals under 30, graduate scholarships to individuals under 40, and a limited number of postdoctoral fellowships to individuals in the arts, literature, medicine, and oceanography.
Publications: Application guidelines; Informational brochure; Informational brochure (including application guidelines); Newsletter.

Financial data: Year ended 02/28/2005. Assets, $15,423,403 (M); Expenditures, $1,200,065; Total giving, $715,300; Grants to individuals, 157 grants totaling $715,300 (high: $8,000, low: $1,500).
Fields of interest: Literature; Arts; Medical school/education; Public health; Marine science.
Type of support: Grants to individuals; Scholarships—to individuals; Awards/prizes; Graduate support; Undergraduate support; Doctoral support.
Application information: Applications accepted. Application form required. Application form available on the grantmaker's Web site.
  Initial approach: Letter or Web site.
  Deadline(s): Contact foundation for current application deadline.
  Applicants should submit the following:
    1) Transcripts
    2) Letter(s) of recommendation
    3) GPA
    4) Financial information
    5) Essay
    6) Curriculum vitae
    7) Budget Information
    8) SASE
  Additional information: Interviews required; Applications distributed to eligible students. Lists close when a sufficient number of applications have been completed and received for committee decisions.
Program description:
  Schepp Foundation Scholarships: Scholarships are awarded to U.S. citizens of character and ability who have insufficient means to obtain or complete their formal education and who are already enrolled in college or preparing for graduate study. Preference is given to those with goals that show promise of future usefulness to society. Those who have only the doctoral dissertation to complete may not apply. A limited number of grants are made for independent study and research beyond the doctoral level to individuals in the fields of literature, the arts, oceanography, and medicine (including public health) upon the recommendation of a recognized institution. Research likely to improve the general welfare of humankind is particularly favored and encouraged.
EIN: 135562353

3571
The Karla Scherer Foundation
c/o Karla Scherer
737 N. Michigan Ave., Ste. 2330
Chicago, IL 60611-2680
URL: http://comnet.org/kschererf/

Foundation type: Independent foundation
Limitations: Scholarships only to women accepted into the Master of Arts Program in the Humanities at the University of Chicago.
Financial data: Year ended 12/31/2004. Assets, $6,008,772 (M); Expenditures, $298,609; Total giving, $193,370.
Fields of interest: Humanities; Women.
Type of support: Support to graduates or students of specific schools; Graduate support.
Application information: Application form required.
  Initial approach: Letter.
  Deadline(s): Mar. 1 written request for application form
  Applicants should submit the following:
    1) SASE
  Additional information: Application must also outline financial need and description of career plan, identity of college or university and courses of study; Applications by

international students must include evidence of a U.S. visa; Interviews required.
EIN: 382877392

3572
William J. Schiff and Elizabeth Schiff Scholarship Fund
c/o Bank of America, N.A.
P.O. Box 1802
Providence, RI 02901-1802
Application Address: c/o Bank of America, N.A., 1125 Route 22 W., Bridgewater, NJ 08807-2965

Foundation type: Independent foundation
Limitations: Scholarships to graduating seniors from Neptune, NJ, high schools who have been enrolled in the Neptune Township public schools for at least two years prior to graduation and intend to pursue full-time engineering or nursing curricula.
Financial data: Year ended 12/31/2004. Assets, $1,861,897 (M); Expenditures, $209,680; Total giving, $190,333; Grants to individuals, 34 grants totaling $190,333 (high: $14,894, low: $143).
Fields of interest: Nursing school/education; Engineering school/education.
Type of support: Support to graduates or students of specific schools; Undergraduate support.
Application information: Applications accepted. Application form required.
  Deadline(s): May 1
EIN: 226606811

3573
Helen M. Schiffner Scholarship Fund
c/o M&T Trust Co.
21 E. Market St., M/C 402-130
York, PA 17401-1500

Foundation type: Independent foundation
Limitations: Scholarships to the Wyomissing Area High School, PA, male and female graduates with the highest academic standing.
Financial data: Year ended 12/31/2004. Assets, $178,649 (M); Expenditures, $5,547; Total giving, $4,073; Grants to individuals, totaling $4,073.
Type of support: Support to graduates or students of specific schools; Undergraduate support.
Application information: Contact fund for current application deadline/guidelines.
EIN: 256641691

3574
Schilling Family Scholarship Fund
(also known as Schilling Family Foundation)
c/o U.S. Bank, N.A.
P.O. Box 3168
Portland, OR 97208
Application address: c/o Scholarship Selection Comm., Butte High School, Butte, MT 59701

Foundation type: Independent foundation
Limitations: Scholarships to graduates of Butte High School, MT, who have at least a 3.25 GPA and are full-time students.
Financial data: Year ended 03/31/2005. Assets, $401,458 (M); Expenditures, $26,708; Total giving, $15,000; Grants to individuals, totaling $15,000.
Type of support: Support to graduates or students of specific schools; Undergraduate support.

Application information: Application form required.
Deadline(s): Contact high school for current application deadline.
EIN: 816067894

3575
Marjorie Schlagenbusch Scholarship Trust
c/o Fort Madison Bank & Trust Co.
7th and Ave. G
Fort Madison, IA   52627   (319) 372-5164
Contact: Doyce Ruble

Foundation type: Independent foundation
Limitations: Scholarships to graduates of Ft. Madison High School, IA, who wish to pursue a teaching career.
Financial data: Year ended 12/31/2004. Assets, $626,802 (M); Expenditures, $53,168; Total giving, $46,204; Grants to individuals, totaling $46,204.
Fields of interest: Teacher school/education.
Type of support: Support to graduates or students of specific schools.
Application information: Applications accepted. Application form required.
Additional information: Application forms are available at local high schools and at the bank.
EIN: 426608574

3576
Earle J. Schlarb Scholarship Trust
c/o Jeffrey G. Lenhart
P.O. Box 1287
Harrisonburg, VA   22801

Foundation type: Independent foundation
Limitations: Scholarships to graduating seniors of each public high school in Shenandoah County, VA, for full-time higher education at a college, university or vocational/technical school.
Financial data: Year ended 12/31/2004. Assets, $739,412 (M); Expenditures, $42,890; Total giving, $27,427; Grants to individuals, totaling $27,427.
Type of support: Support to graduates or students of specific schools; Technical education support; Undergraduate support.
Application information: Applications accepted throughout the year; Contact trust for current application guidelines.
EIN: 546405104

3577
Raymond C. & Dorothy I. Schlotterer Memorial Education Fund
(formerly Raymond C. & Dorothy I. Schlotterer Trust)
c/o John Lyttle, Windels, Marx, et al.
156 W. 56th St.
New York, NY   10019

Foundation type: Independent foundation
Limitations: Interest-free loans of $3,000 to students pursuing an education at a pharmaceutical institution within a 100-mile radius of New York, NY. Recipients are chosen based upon financial need and academic performance.
Financial data: Year ended 12/31/2004. Assets, $139,876 (M); Expenditures, $38,099; Total giving, $0; Loan to an individual, 1 loan totaling $3,000.
Fields of interest: Pharmacy/prescriptions.
Type of support: Student loans—to individuals.

Application information: Applications accepted. Application form required.
Deadline(s): None
Program description:
Interest Free Loan: A $3,000 interest free loan is granted to a student who will pursue an education at a pharmaceutical institution within a 100 mile radius of New York City based upon financial need, academic performance and other criteria.
EIN: 136966814

3578
William E. Schmidt Foundation, Inc.
P.O. Box 160
Haubstadt, IN   47639-0160

Foundation type: Independent foundation
Limitations: Scholarships to individuals between ages 16 and 20 for part-time or full-time study at accredited U.S. colleges and universities.
Financial data: Year ended 12/31/2002. Assets, $2,340,631 (M); Expenditures, $231,874; Total giving, $205,963.
Type of support: Scholarships—to individuals.
Application information: Application form required.
Deadline(s): Mar. 31
Applicants should submit the following:
1) Essay
2) GPA
3) Letter(s) of recommendation
EIN: 351884241

3579
Walter C. and Marie C. Schmidt Foundation
c/o U.S. Bank, N.A., Trust Tax Svcs.
P.O. Box 3168
Portland, OR   97208-3168   (503) 275-4887
Contact: Matthew Rast, Trust Admin., U.S. Bank, N.A.

Foundation type: Independent foundation
Limitations: Scholarships to residents of OR to study nursing, particularly geriatric health care.
Financial data: Year ended 06/30/2004. Assets, $605,332 (M); Expenditures, $35,503; Total giving, $25,000; Grants to individuals, totaling $25,000.
Fields of interest: Nursing school/education; Health care; Gerontology.
Type of support: Scholarships—to individuals.
Application information: Contact foundation for current application deadline/guidelines.
Program description:
Nursing Scholarships: First priority given to students who intend to work in Lane County, OR. Second priority given to students who intend to work in other parts of OR.
EIN: 936267092

3580
Lee Schmidt Scholarship Trust Fund
c/o Mac Hatch, C.P.A.
834 Falls Ave., No. 1020D
Twin Falls, ID   83301
Application address: c/o Ray Strolberg, Tr., 1910 San LaRue Ave., Twin Falls, ID 83301

Foundation type: Operating foundation
Limitations: Scholarships to graduates of Kimberly High School, ID, for higher education.
Financial data: Year ended 12/31/2002. Assets, $415,941 (M); Expenditures, $22,556;

Total giving, $19,900; Grants to individuals, 18 grants totaling $19,900.
Type of support: Support to graduates or students of specific schools; Technical education support; Undergraduate support.
Application information: Deadline Apr. 1; Completion of formal application required.
Program description:
Scholarships: Recipients must be accepted to a college or training institute, show financial need and a desire to succeed in an institution of higher learning, and must maintain a GPA of 2.5 from high school or college.
EIN: 820497599

3581
Walter F. Schmidt Trust
c/o First Crawford State Bank, Trust Dept.
P.O. Box 8640
Robinson, IL   62454-8640   (618) 544-8666

Foundation type: Independent foundation
Limitations: Scholarships to graduates of Crawford County, IL, high schools for attendance at Lincoln Trail College, IL.
Financial data: Year ended 06/30/2004. Assets, $1,644,699 (M); Expenditures, $135,113; Total giving, $116,449; Grants to individuals, 124 grants totaling $116,449 (high: $2,736, low: $35).
Type of support: Support to graduates or students of specific schools; Undergraduate support.
Application information: Deadline July 15; Completion of formal application required, including essay and transcript.
EIN: 376311892

3582
Cecil Mae Schmoker Trust
c/o Wells Fargo Bank Nebraska, N.A.
1248 O St., 4th Fl., MAC N8032-04
Lincoln, NE   68508

Foundation type: Independent foundation
Limitations: Scholarships to high school seniors who reside in Webster County, IA.
Financial data: Year ended 12/31/2004. Assets, $885,435 (M); Expenditures, $36,925; Total giving, $24,328; Grants to individuals, totaling $24,328.
Type of support: Scholarships—to individuals.
Application information: Contact trust for current application deadline/guidelines; Scholarships are renewable.
EIN: 426446089

3583
Roland R. Schneider Memorial Scholarship Fund
P.O. Box M
Cortez, CO   81321-0678
Contact: Donald Haley, Tr.
Application address: P.O. Drawer A, Cortez, CO 81321, tel.: (970) 565-3781

Foundation type: Independent foundation
Limitations: Scholarships only to graduates of Montezuma-Cortez High School in Cortez, CO.
Financial data: Year ended 12/31/2004. Assets, $69,945 (M); Expenditures, $10,218; Total giving, $10,000; Grants to individuals, totaling $10,000.
Type of support: Support to graduates or students of specific schools; Undergraduate support.

Application information: Application form required.
 Deadline(s): Apr. 15.
 Additional information: Application by letter, including education and career plans, high school grades and activities, anticipated income, financial need, and expenses during college.
EIN: 510142447

3584

Scholarship America

(formerly Citizens' Scholarship Foundation of America)
1 Scholarship Way
P.O. Box 297
St. Peter, MN   56082   (800) 537-4180
FAX: (507) 931-9168; URL: http://www.scholarshipamerica.org

Foundation type: Public charity
Limitations: Scholarships to students at a wide variety of postsecondary institutions in the U.S.
Publications: Annual report (including application guidelines); Newsletter.
Financial data: Year ended 06/30/2003.
Assets, $279,505,771 (M); Expenditures, $154,667,066; Total giving, $137,866,170; Grants to individuals, totaling $137,866,170.
Fields of interest: Disasters, 9/11/01.
Type of support: Scholarships—to individuals; Undergraduate support.
Application information:
 Initial approach: Letter, telephone or see Web site for further information.
 Deadline(s): Contact foundation for current application deadline/guidelines;
 Additional information: See Web site for further information.
Program descriptions:
 Families of Freedom Scholarship Fund: The sole purpose of this fund is to provide financial assistance for postsecondary education to the spouses and children of individuals killed in the Sept. 11 terrorist attacks.
 Dollars for Scholars: Provide scholarships to graduating high school seniors planning to attend any accredited postsecondary educational institution.
EIN: 042296967

3585

Scholarship Foundation of Erie Scottish Rite

P.O. Box 1364
Erie, PA   16512   (814) 866-5382
Contact: Harold A. Durst, Treas.

Foundation type: Operating foundation
Limitations: Scholarships to financially needy high school graduates who are residents of northwest PA.
Financial data: Year ended 07/31/2002.
Assets, $1,120,087 (M); Expenditures, $75,658; Total giving, $74,500; Grants to individuals, 44 grants totaling $54,500 (high: $2,000, low: $500).
Type of support: Scholarships—to individuals.
Application information: Deadline Apr. 1; Application by letter outlining financial need, including SAT scores or transcripts.
EIN: 251710223

3586

Scholarship Foundation of Santa Barbara

P.O. Box 3620
Santa Barbara, CA   93130-3620
(805) 687-6065
Contact: Billie Maunz, Exec. Dir.
FAX: (805) 687-6031;
E-mail: info@sbscholarship.org; URL: http://www.sbscholarship.org

Foundation type: Public charity
Limitations: Scholarships and student loans to Santa Barbara County, CA, high school graduates for undergraduate, graduate, medical, and vocational study.
Publications: Financial statement; Informational brochure (including application guidelines).
Financial data: Year ended 06/30/2005.
Assets, $35,319,514 (M); Expenditures, $5,923,457; Total giving, $3,366,154; Grants to individuals, 1,370 grants totaling $3,366,154 (high: $35,000, low: $1,000); Loans to individuals, 1,237 loans totaling $2,082,195.
Fields of interest: Education.
Type of support: Scholarships—to individuals; Student loans—to individuals; Support to graduates or students of specific schools; Undergraduate support.
Application information: Application form required. Application form available on the grantmaker's Web site.
 Initial approach: Letter, telephone, fax or e-mail.
 Copies of proposal: 1
 Deadline(s): Jan. 31
 Applicants should submit the following:
  1) Transcripts
  2) SAT
  3) Resume
  4) Letter(s) of recommendation
  5) GPA
  6) Financial information
  7) Essay
  8) Budget Information
 Additional information: Application forms available online between Oct. 1 and Jan. 31; Interviews required.
Program descriptions:
 Loan Program: Student loans to individuals who have attended at least grades 9 to 12 in Santa Barbara County and have graduated from a Santa Barbara County high school. All applicants must attend full-time (12 units minimum per term) at an approved vocational school, two- or four-year college and maintain at least a 2.0 GPA to be eligible.
 Scholarship Program: Applicants must have attended at least grades 9 to 12 in Santa Barbara County and have graduated from a Santa Barbara County high school. All applicants must attend full-time (12 units minimum per term) at an approved vocational school or two- or four-year college and maintain at least a 2.0 GPA to be eligible.
EIN: 237087774

3587

The Scholarship Foundation of the Union League of Philadelphia

140 S. Broad St.
Philadelphia, PA   19102-3083   (215) 587-5568
Contact: Joseph A. Dubee, Fdn. Dir.
FAX: (215) 563-1198;
E-mail: youthwork@erols.com; URL: http://www.unionleague.org

Foundation type: Public charity

Limitations: Renewable scholarships to Union League Good Citizenship Awardees in NJ and PA for study at colleges, universities, and trade schools.
Publications: Informational brochure.
Financial data: Year ended 06/30/2003.
Assets, $1,512,340 (M); Expenditures, $143,333; Total giving, $97,000.
Fields of interest: Public affairs, citizen participation.
Type of support: Technical education support; Undergraduate support.
Application information: Application form required.
 Initial approach: Letter or telephone.
 Deadline(s): Contact fund for current application deadline.
 Additional information: Interviews required.
EIN: 236427434

3588

The Scholarship Foundation

307 Provincetown Rd.
Cherry Hill, NJ   08034   (856) 573-9400
Contact: Bernard T. Cote, Pres.

Foundation type: Independent foundation
Limitations: Scholarships to children of employees of various corporations.
Financial data: Year ended 12/31/2004.
Assets, $166,073 (M); Expenditures, $2,176,598; Total giving, $2,073,698; Grants to individuals, 824 grants totaling $2,073,698 (high: $79,140, low: $25).
Type of support: Employee-related scholarships.
Application information: Application form required.
 Deadline(s): Varies
 Applicants should submit the following:
  1) Class rank
  2) Letter(s) of recommendation
  3) GPA
 Additional information: Application must also include a written statement by the applicant on his/her desire for a college education; Application forms available only from the sponsoring companies. Do not contact the foundation.
EIN: 521560429

3589

Scholarship Fund of Flint Plumbing and Pipefitting Industry

6525 Centurion Dr.
Lansing, MI   48917
Application address: 906 Woodbridge, Flint, MI 48504

Foundation type: Independent foundation
Limitations: Scholarships to sons and daughters of Flint, MI, plumbing and pipefitting industry employers and employees.
Financial data: Year ended 04/30/2005.
Assets, $19,961 (M); Expenditures, $23,326; Total giving, $21,100; Grants to individuals, totaling $21,100.
Type of support: Employee-related scholarships; Scholarships—to individuals.
Application information: Deadline Mar. 1; Completion of formal application required, including transcripts.
EIN: 386522581

3590
Scholarship Fund of Kappa Sigma Fraternity
c/o John K. Stanchfield
P.O. Box 3592
Peabody, MA 01960-3592
Application address: Kappa Sigma Fraternity Scholarship Committee, P.O. Box 218, Wrentham, MA 02093

Foundation type: Independent foundation
Limitations: Undergraduate scholarships to individuals whose relatives are Kappa Sigma Fraternity alumni in MA.
Financial data: Year ended 12/31/2004.
Assets, $207,801 (M); Expenditures, $21,662; Total giving, $9,000; Grants to individuals, totaling $9,000.
Fields of interest: Students, sororities/fraternities.
Type of support: Undergraduate support.
Application information: Deadline June 1; Completion of formal application required, including recommendation letter from relative who attended University of Massachusetts, Amherst, and was a member of the Gamma Delta chapter of Kappa Sigma Fraternity, essay, proof of admission to college, and an additional reference who is a Kappa Sigma Fraternity alumnus.
EIN: 042986731

3591
Scholarship Fund, Inc.
3312 Corey Rd.
Toledo, OH 43615
Contact: J. A. Brunner, Treas.
Application address: University of Toledo, 2801 Bancroft St., Toledo, OH 43606

Foundation type: Independent foundation
Limitations: Undergraduate and graduate scholarships to residents of northwest OH, including nonresidents presently living on campus at the University of Toledo, OH, and Lourdes College, OH, to attend an area college.
Financial data: Year ended 12/31/2004.
Assets, $566,221 (M); Expenditures, $37,138; Total giving, $33,500; Grants to individuals, totaling $33,500.
Type of support: Support to graduates or students of specific schools; Graduate support; Undergraduate support.
Application information: Applications are received through the scholarship or financial aid offices at Lourdes College or the University of Toledo; Completion of formal application required; Interviews required.
EIN: 346533380

3592
The Scholarships Foundation, Inc.
P.O. Box 6020
New York, NY 10128

Foundation type: Independent foundation
Limitations: Scholarships to undergraduate and graduate students with priority given to those whose studies do not fit into defined scholarship categories. Applicants must have reached the age of 20 at the time of application, have two years or less remaining in their course of study, and pursue their education in NY. Grants are rarely made to high school students, to foreign students, or for study abroad.
Financial data: Year ended 06/30/2004.
Assets, $458,662 (M); Expenditures, $171,845; Total giving, $144,250; Grants to individuals, 52

grants totaling $144,250 (high: $4,000, low: $750).
Type of support: Graduate support; Undergraduate support.
Application information: Applications accepted throughout the year, however, letters received after May 1 cannot be considered in time for Sept. grants; Initial approach by letter, no longer than one typewritten page, including SASE; Completion of formal application required.
Program description:
  Scholarships: Awards are based on merit and need. The foundation is unable to reply to form letters or to those from computer/search companies.
EIN: 066043809

3593
Scholz Family Foundation
6195 Ridgeview Ct.
Reno, NV 89509
Contact: Genl. Martin Brandtner, Co-Treas.

Foundation type: Independent foundation
Limitations: Scholarships to individuals of La Crosse, WI, for theological education.
Financial data: Year ended 12/31/2002.
Assets, $1,434,972 (M); Expenditures, $2,681,679; Total giving, $2,372,828; Grants to individuals, 3 grants totaling $23,600 (high: $14,600, low: $1,000).
Fields of interest: Theological school/education.
Type of support: Scholarships—to individuals.
Application information: Applications accepted throughout the year; Contact foundation for current application guidelines; Initial approach by letter.
EIN: 880397940

3594
Karl Schooler Scholarship Trust Fund
P.O. Box K
Carlisle, IA 50047   (515) 989-0744
Contact: W.R. Schooler, Sr., Tr.

Foundation type: Independent foundation
Limitations: Scholarships to students who reside in Warren County, IA, based on financial need.
Financial data: Year ended 10/31/2004.
Assets, $608,231 (M); Expenditures, $53,460; Total giving, $48,700; Grants to individuals, totaling $48,700.
Type of support: Scholarships—to individuals.
Application information: Contact foundation for current application deadline; Completion of formal application required.
EIN: 421494825

3595
The Paul Schooley Trust Fund
c/o Counselor, Bolivar High School
1401 N. Hwy. D
Bolivar, MO 65613   (417) 326-5228
URL: http://www.bolivar.k12.mo.us

Foundation type: Independent foundation
Limitations: Scholarships to students of Bolivar High School, MO.
Financial data: Year ended 12/31/2002.
Assets, $452,219 (M); Expenditures, $28,295; Total giving, $26,432; Grants to individuals, 80 grants totaling $26,432.
Type of support: Support to graduates or students of specific schools; Undergraduate support.

Application information: Application form required.
Deadline(s): Apr. 15
EIN: 431243897

3596
Schowengerdt Family Scholarship Fund
c/o Edward Jones Trust Co.
12555 Manchester Rd.
St. Louis, MO 63131
Application address: c/o The Schowengerdt Family Scholarship Committee, P.O. Box 786, Warrenton, MO 63383

Foundation type: Independent foundation
Limitations: Scholarships to undergraduates to attend the University of Missouri-Columbia, MO.
Financial data: Year ended 12/31/2004.
Assets, $432,391 (M); Expenditures, $28,375; Total giving, $22,500; Grants to individuals, totaling $22,500.
Type of support: Support to graduates or students of specific schools; Undergraduate support.
Application information: Contact scholarship committee for current application deadline/ guidelines.
EIN: 376318007

3597
Schramm Foundation
800 E. Virginia Ave.
West Chester, PA 19380   (610) 696-2500

Foundation type: Independent foundation
Limitations: Scholarships to high school graduates living in the West Chester, PA, area to study business and engineering at trade schools, junior colleges, and four-year colleges.
Financial data: Year ended 12/31/2003.
Assets, $135,024; Expenditures, $10,411; Total giving, $10,100; Grants to individuals, 9 grants totaling $10,100 (high: $500, low: $300).
Fields of interest: Vocational education; Business school/education; Engineering school/education.
Type of support: Technical education support; Undergraduate support.
Application information: Applications not accepted.
  Additional information: Letters are sent to local high schools explaining the scholarships; Applicants must contact their counselors or principals for more information.
Program description:
  Scholarships: Recipients are selected based on the likelihood of the student completing the degree program, financial need, and extracurricular activities. If satisfactory academic performance is maintained, scholarships are renewable for up to the number of years necessary to complete the program of study.
EIN: 236291235

3598
Jake J. Schreibman Foundation
208 Weymouth St.
Cambria, CA 93428-2348
Contact: Marlene S. Bernstein, Pres.

Foundation type: Operating foundation
Limitations: Scholarships to students of Omaha public schools, NE, for higher education.
Financial data: Year ended 12/31/2003.
Assets, $300,122 (M); Expenditures, $64,022; Total giving, $35,500; Grants to individuals, 5

grants totaling $35,500 (high: $26,000, low: $500).

Fields of interest: Jewish agencies & temples.

Type of support: Undergraduate support.

Application information: Applications accepted. Application form required.

Additional information: Interviews required.

Program description:

Jake J. Schreibman Freshman Year Scholarship: Preference is given to Jewish students connected to or who are members of an Omaha, NE, synagogue, with at least a 3.0 GPA, have work experience, and participate in team sports or a Jewish community center.

EIN: 470790155

3599
J. P. and Maude V. Schroeder Memorial Trust

c/o U.S. Bank, N.A.
P.O. Box 3168
Portland, OR   97208

Foundation type: Independent foundation

Limitations: Scholarships to graduating high school seniors who are residents of Grant County, WA.

Financial data: Year ended 12/31/2004. Assets, $963,542 (M); Expenditures, $66,334; Total giving, $46,000; Grants to individuals, totaling $46,000.

Type of support: Scholarships—to individuals.

Application information: Applications accepted. Application form required.

Deadline(s): May 1

Applicants should submit the following:
1) Transcripts
2) Letter(s) of recommendation

EIN: 916306402

3600
William Archie Schroeder Scholarship Trust

c/o National Bank of Petersburg
P.O. Box 470
Petersburg, IL   62675-0470   (217) 632-3241
Contact: Lew Hultgren, Trust Off., National Bank of Petersburg

Foundation type: Independent foundation

Limitations: Scholarships to financially needy students and graduates of Menard County, IL, high schools. Scholarships are renewable.

Financial data: Year ended 04/30/2005. Assets, $243,847 (M); Expenditures, $11,336; Total giving, $8,500; Grants to individuals, totaling $8,500.

Type of support: Support to graduates or students of specific schools; Undergraduate support.

Application information: Applications accepted. Application form required.

Deadline(s): May 15.

Applicants should submit the following:
1) Financial information
2) Transcripts
3) Letter(s) of recommendation

EIN: 376267162

3601
Maude M. Schuetze Foundation

c/o American State Bank & Trust Co.
P.O. Box 1446
Williston, ND   58802-1446

Foundation type: Operating foundation

Limitations: Scholarships for high school graduates of Culbertson, Westby, Plentywood, Medicine Lake, Froid, and Bainville, MT.

Financial data: Year ended 04/30/2005. Assets, $337,454 (M); Expenditures, $18,288; Total giving, $12,875; Grants to individuals, totaling $12,475.

Type of support: Graduate support; Technical education support; Precollege support; Undergraduate support.

Application information: Applications accepted Feb. through Apr.; Completion of formal application required.

EIN: 456063398

3602
Kate W. Schultz Trust

c/o Old National Bank
P.O. Box 746
Mount Vernon, IN   47620-0746
Application address: c/o Old National Bank, 420 Main St., Mt. Vernon, IN 47620, tel.: (812) 838-8018

Foundation type: Independent foundation

Limitations: Scholarships to residents of Posey County, IN, for the study of veterinary medicine or engineering.

Financial data: Year ended 12/31/2003. Assets, $227,918 (M); Expenditures, $34,068; Total giving, $8,833; Grants to individuals, totaling $8,833.

Fields of interest: Veterinary medicine; Engineering.

Type of support: Graduate support; Undergraduate support.

Application information: Applications accepted. Application form required.

Initial approach: Letter.

Applicants should submit the following:
1) Photograph
2) Class rank
3) Transcripts
4) SAT
5) Financial information

Additional information: Application must also include proof of acceptance to college.

EIN: 356024699

3603
Irmgard Schulz Trust

c/o Wells Fargo Bank Nevada, N.A.
P.O. Box 95021
Henderson, NV   89009-5021
Contact: Leslie Young, Trust Off., Wells Fargo Bank Northwest, N.A.
Application address: P.O. Box 1067, Medford, OR 97501

Foundation type: Independent foundation

Limitations: Scholarships to high school graduates of Jackson County, OR, to pursue advanced degrees at accredited colleges, universities, and schools of art and music.

Financial data: Year ended 10/31/2002. Assets, $93,114 (M); Expenditures, $14,528; Total giving, $11,300; Grants to individuals, 4 grants totaling $11,300 (high: $11,000, low: $100).

Fields of interest: Arts education; Music; Performing arts, education.

Type of support: Scholarships—to individuals; Support to graduates or students of specific schools.

Application information: Applications by letter accepted throughout the year.

EIN: 936273775

3604
Herman Oscar Schumacher School Fund

(formerly Herman Oscar Schumacher Scholarship Fund for Men)
c/o Washington Trust Bank
717 W. Sprague Ave.
Spokane, WA   99201
Application address: c/o Washington Trust Bank, WM&AS, P.O. Box 2127, Spokane, WA 99210-2127
E-mail: clegate@watrust.com

Foundation type: Independent foundation

Limitations: Scholarships to male Christian residents of Spokane County, WA, who have completed one year of study at an accredited college. Preference is given to orphans and the financially needy. Applicants must be loyal to the principles of democracy and support the Constitution of the U.S.

Financial data: Year ended 06/30/2005. Assets, $540,410 (M); Expenditures, $14,132; Total giving, $5,500; Grants to individuals, totaling $5,500.

Type of support: Undergraduate support.

Application information: Application form required.

Deadline(s): Oct. 1

Additional information: Application should also include college transcripts and proof of enrollment.

EIN: 916237367

3605
Byron S. Schuyler Child Educational Fund Trust

c/o Bank of America, N.A.
P.O. Box 6768
Providence, RI   02940-6768
Application Address: c/o Judith A. Lee, Columbia Mgmt., 1 E. Ave., 3rd Fl., NYUT37603D, Rochester, NY 14604

Foundation type: Independent foundation

Limitations: Scholarships to residents of Fulton County, NY.

Financial data: Year ended 01/31/2005. Assets, $182,261 (M); Expenditures, $10,463; Total giving, $8,000; Grants to individuals, totaling $8,000.

Type of support: Scholarships—to individuals.

Application information: Deadline June 1; Completion of formal application required, including letter of acceptance from college, high school class rank, and recommendation from guidance counselor.

EIN: 146083934

3606
Schuylkill Area Community Foundation

(formerly Ashland Trusts)
101 N. Centre St., 2nd Fl., Ste. A
Pottsville, PA   17901   (570) 624-1580
Contact: Therese "Terry" Sadusky, Exec. Dir.
FAX: (570) 624-1581; E-mail: tsadusky@uplink.net

Foundation type: Community foundation

Limitations: Scholarships to undergraduate students in the Pottsville, PA, area.

Financial data: Year ended 12/31/2004.
Assets, $7,146,025 (M); Expenditures,
$696,413; Total giving, $417,196.
Application information: Contact foundation for
current application deadline/guidelines; See Web
site for complete list of programs.
EIN: 236422789

3607
John Schwab Foundation
c/o SunBank
P.O. Box 57
Selinsgrove, PA   17870-0057
Application address: 2 E. 4th St., Emporium, PA
15834

Foundation type: Independent foundation
Limitations: Scholarships to financially needy
residents of Cameron County, PA.
Financial data: Year ended 12/31/2004.
Assets, $487,818 (M); Expenditures, $38,165;
Total giving, $34,090; Grants to individuals,
totaling $34,090.
Type of support: Scholarships—to individuals.
Application information: Deadline June 10;
Completion of formal application required, including
transcript and financial information.
EIN: 256029493

3608
Schwab-Rosenhouse Memorial
Foundation
c/o Wells Fargo Bank, N.A.
P.O. Box 63954
San Francisco, CA   94163
Contact: Connie Grueter
Scholarship address: P.O. Box 4004, Concord, CA
94524-4004, tel.: (925) 808-2034

Foundation type: Independent foundation
Limitations: Scholarships to residents of the five
counties in and around Sacramento, CA, to enroll
at a postsecondary school located within a
100-mile radius of Sacramento.
Financial data: Year ended 12/31/2002.
Assets, $7,918,037 (M); Expenditures,
$920,507; Total giving, $751,416; Grants to
individuals, 381 grants totaling $738,916 (high:
$5,000, low: $1,000).
Type of support: Scholarships—to individuals.
Application information: Deadline Feb.1;
Completion of formal application required, including
transcript and personal recommendations.
EIN: 686136241

3609
Elmer & Ruth Schwantes Scholarship
Fund
550 W. 7th Ave., Ste. 705
Anchorage, AK   99501   (907) 276-6015

Foundation type: Independent foundation
Limitations: Undergraduate scholarships to
graduates of Alaska high schools, and from
Spencer High School in WI.
Financial data: Year ended 12/31/2004.
Assets, $294,741 (M); Expenditures, $19,570;
Total giving, $5,500; Grants to individuals, totaling
$5,500.
Type of support: Support to graduates or students
of specific schools; Undergraduate support.
Application information: Contact foundation for
current application deadline/guidelines; Initial

approach by letter requesting application;
Completion of formal application required.
EIN: 920151161

3610
Ernie P. Schwartz Foundation
c/o Wells Fargo Bank Iowa, N.A.
625 Marquette Ave.
Minneapolis, MN   55402

Foundation type: Independent foundation
Limitations: Scholarships primarily to residents of
Des Moines, IA.
Financial data: Year ended 09/30/2004.
Assets, $253,412 (M); Expenditures, $18,257;
Total giving, $15,820; Grants to individuals,
totaling $15,820.
Type of support: Scholarships—to individuals.
Application information: Contact foundation for
current application deadline/guidelines.
EIN: 426277194

3611
A. J. Schwartze Linn High School
Scholarship Fund Trust I
c/o Central Bank
P.O. Box 779
Jefferson City, MO   65102-0779
Application address: Superintendent of the Osage
County R-II School District, 1212 E. Main St., Linn,
MO 65051

Foundation type: Independent foundation
Limitations: Scholarships to graduates of Linn High
School, MO, for higher education. Recipients must
be in the top 20 percent of their graduating class.
Financial data: Year ended 12/31/2004.
Assets, $585,090 (M); Expenditures, $41,538;
Total giving, $35,505; Grants to individuals,
totaling $35,505.
Type of support: Support to graduates or students
of specific schools; Undergraduate support.
Application information: Contact trust for current
application deadline; Completion of formal
application required, including essay; Interviews
required.
EIN: 436816359

3612
A. J. Schwartze Scholarship Fund Trust II
c/o Central Bank
P.O. Box 779
Jefferson City, MO   65102
Application address: c/o Superintendent Osage
County R-III School Dist., P.O. Box 37, 143 E. Main
St., Westphalia, MO 65085, tel.: (573) 455-2375

Foundation type: Independent foundation
Limitations: Scholarships to graduates of Fatima
High School, MO, ranking in the upper third of their
graduating class who plan to attend a university,
college, or vocational/technical school in MO.
Financial data: Year ended 12/31/2004.
Assets, $574,914 (M); Expenditures, $60,456;
Total giving, $54,451; Grants to individuals,
totaling $54,451.
Type of support: Support to graduates or students
of specific schools; Technical education support;
Undergraduate support.
Application information: Applications accepted.
Application form required.
Initial approach: Letter.
Deadline(s): Mar. 15.
EIN: 436685932

3613
A. J. Schwartze Scholarship Fund Trust III
c/o Central Bank
P.O. Box 779
Jefferson City, MO   65102   (573) 455-2375
Application address: c/o Superintendent Osage
County R-III School Dist., P.O. Box 37, 143 E. Main
St., Westphalia, MO 65085, tel.: (573) 455-2375

Foundation type: Independent foundation
Limitations: Scholarships only to students in the
top 20 percent of their graduating class at Fatima
High School, Westphalia, MO.
Financial data: Year ended 12/31/2004.
Assets, $557,146 (M); Expenditures, $52,050;
Total giving, $46,239; Grants to individuals,
totaling $46,239.
Type of support: Support to graduates or students
of specific schools; Undergraduate support.
Application information: Contact fund for current
application deadline; Completion of formal
application required, including essay; Interviews
required.
EIN: 436804089

3614
A. J. Schwartze Scholarship Fund Trust IV
c/o Central Bank
P.O. Box 779
Jefferson City, MO   65102
Application address: c/o Osage County R-III School
Dist., Superintendent, 143 E. Main St., P.O. Box
37, Westphalia, MO 65085, tel.: (573) 455-2375

Foundation type: Independent foundation
Limitations: Scholarships to graduates of Osage
County high schools, MO, for higher education.
Financial data: Year ended 12/31/2004.
Assets, $629,033 (M); Expenditures, $60,575;
Total giving, $54,149; Grants to individuals,
totaling $54,149.
Type of support: Support to graduates or students
of specific schools; Undergraduate support.
Application information: Contact trust for current
application deadline; Completion of formal
application required.
EIN: 436804090

3615
A. J. Schwartze Scholarship Fund Trust
c/o Central Bank
P.O. Box 779
Jefferson City, MO   65102
Application address: c/o Osage County R-III School
Dist., Dan Johnson, Superintendent, P.O. Box 37,
143 E. Main St., Westphalia, MO 65085, tel.: (573)
455-2375

Foundation type: Independent foundation
Limitations: Scholarships to graduates of Fatima
High School, MO who are in the top twenty percent
of their class.
Financial data: Year ended 12/31/2004.
Assets, $498,755 (M); Expenditures, $59,088;
Total giving, $53,560; Grants to individuals,
totaling $53,560.
Type of support: Support to graduates or students
of specific schools; Undergraduate support.
Application information: Deadline Apr. 1;
Completion of formal application required, including
essay; Interviews required.
EIN: 436550546

3616
A. J. Schwartze Seminary Scholarship Fund

c/o Central Bank
P.O. Box 779
Jefferson City, MO   65102-0779

Foundation type: Independent foundation
Limitations: Scholarships to Catholic priesthood seminary school students within the boundaries of the Jefferson City, MO, diocese.
Financial data: Year ended 12/31/2004.
Assets, $1,160,257 (M); Expenditures, $62,847; Total giving, $52,740.
Fields of interest: Theological school/education; Religion, formal/general education; Roman Catholic agencies & churches.
Type of support: Scholarships—to individuals.
Application information: Application form required.
   Deadline(s): Contact fund for current application deadline.
   Applicants should submit the following:
      1) Essay
   Additional information: Interviews required.
EIN: 436700318

3617
A. J. Schwartze Trust Helias High School Scholarship Fund II

c/o Central Bank
P.O. Box 779
Jefferson City, MO   65102-0779
Application address: c/o Helias High School, Scholarship Comm., 1305 Swifts Hwy., Jefferson City, MO 65101

Foundation type: Independent foundation
Limitations: Scholarships to graduating seniors of Helias High School, MO, for higher education.
Financial data: Year ended 12/31/2004.
Assets, $318,615 (M); Expenditures, $37,122; Total giving, $33,531.
Type of support: Support to graduates or students of specific schools; Undergraduate support.
Application information: Contact trust for current application deadline; Completion of formal application required, including essay; Interviews required.
EIN: 436804088

3618
A. J. Schwartze Trust Helias High School Scholarship Fund III

c/o Central Bank
P.O. Box 779
Jefferson City, MO   65102
Application address: c/o Helias High School, Scholarship Comm., 1305 Swifts Hwy., Jefferson City, MO 65101

Foundation type: Independent foundation
Limitations: Scholarships to graduates of Helias High School, MO, for undergraduate education primarily at MO colleges and universities.
Financial data: Year ended 12/31/2004.
Assets, $615,860 (M); Expenditures, $41,753; Total giving, $35,537.
Type of support: Support to graduates or students of specific schools; Undergraduate support.
Application information:
   Applicants should submit the following:
      1) Transcripts
   Additional information: Contact foundation for current application deadlines/ guidelines;

Scholarships are renewable for up to seven additional semesters.
EIN: 436837622

3619
A. J. Schwartze Trust Helias High School Scholarship Fund

c/o Central Trust Bank
P.O. Box 779
Jefferson City, MO   65102-0779
Application address: c/o Helias High School, Selection Comm., 1305 Swifts Hwy., Jefferson City, MO 65102; tel.: (573) 635-6139

Foundation type: Independent foundation
Limitations: Scholarships to graduating students attending Helias High School, MO, who will receive a degree from a vocational/technical school within four years.
Financial data: Year ended 12/31/2004.
Assets, $302,505 (M); Expenditures, $32,421; Total giving, $28,956; Grants to individuals, totaling $28,956.
Fields of interest: Vocational education, post-secondary.
Type of support: Support to graduates or students of specific schools; Technical education support; Undergraduate support.
Application information: Completion of formal application required, including an essay; Interviews required.
EIN: 436700316

3620
A. J. Schwartze Trust Linn High School Scholarship Fund II

c/o Central Bank
P.O. Box 779
Jefferson City, MO   65102-0779
Application address: c/o Superintendent, Osage County R-II School District, Linn, MO 65051

Foundation type: Independent foundation
Limitations: Scholarships to graduates of Linn High School, MO, for higher education.
Financial data: Year ended 12/31/2004.
Assets, $713,361 (M); Expenditures, $58,025; Total giving, $50,997; Grants to individuals, totaling $50,997.
Type of support: Support to graduates or students of specific schools; Undergraduate support.
Application information: Application form required.
   Deadline(s): Feb. 1
   Applicants should submit the following:
      1) Essay
   Additional information: Interviews required.
EIN: 436816360

3621
The Evalee C. Schwarz Charitable Trust for Education

c/o JPMorgan Chase Bank
P.O. Box 2558
Houston, TX   77252-2558
Contact: Jennifer Grosvenor, V.P. and Trust Off., JPMorgan Chase Bank

Foundation type: Independent foundation
Limitations: Interest-free student loans to individuals for the pursuit of undergraduate or graduate degrees at a school in the state where student resides.
Financial data: Year ended 08/31/2004.
Assets, $15,178,429 (M); Expenditures,

$276,391; Total giving, $0; Loans to individuals, 68 loans totaling $460,000.
Type of support: Graduate support; Undergraduate support.
Application information: Application form required. Application form available on the grantmaker's Web site.
   Deadline(s): Apr. 15
   Applicants should submit the following:
      1) Letter(s) of recommendation
Program description:
   Student Loans: Loan applicant must be a U.S. citizen at the time of application. Qualify for financial need in the form of government aid. Be enrolled in a school in the state in which the student resides. Demonstrate an outstanding combination of standardized test scores and class rank. Test scores must be in the top 10 percent of nation-wide scores. Not be seeking a law degree. Loans range from $5,000 to $15,000 per year. Each recipient has a lifetime maximum cap of $50,000.
EIN: 766129622

3622
Faythe Schwarz Trust f/b/o Stockbridge High School

c/o State Bank of Chilton
P.O. Box 149
Chilton, WI   53014-0149
E-mail: phugo@charter.net

Foundation type: Independent foundation
Limitations: Scholarships to individuals residing in the Chilton WI, area.
Financial data: Year ended 12/31/2004.
Assets, $298,418 (M); Expenditures, $11,359; Total giving, $9,496; Grants to individuals, totaling $9,496.
Type of support: Undergraduate support.
Application information: Unsolicited requests for funds not accepted.
EIN: 806026133

3623
Science Scholarship Foundation

c/o A.B. Jacobs
P.O. Box 9175
Laguna Beach, CA   92652-7160

Foundation type: Independent foundation
Limitations: Scholarships to students at Saddleback Community College, CA, who are U.S. citizens and have at least a 3.5 GPA in chemistry, mathematics, physics, or allied science courses. Relatives of selection committee members are ineligible.
Financial data: Year ended 05/31/2005.
Assets, $2,309 (M); Expenditures, $50,595; Total giving, $50,000; Grants to individuals, totaling $50,000.
Fields of interest: Science; Chemistry; Mathematics; Physics.
Type of support: Support to graduates or students of specific schools; Undergraduate support.
Application information: Application form required.
   Deadline(s): Mar.
   Additional information: Applications available from Saddleback Community College.
EIN: 953646338

3624
Science Service, Inc.
1719 N. St., N.W.
Washington, DC 20036 (202) 785-2255
Contact: Larry Sigler, Business Mgr.
FAX: (202) 785-1243; URL: http://www.sciserv.org

Foundation type: Public charity
Limitations: Scholarships to graduating high school seniors for original research projects in mathematics, science, or engineering.
Financial data: Year ended 12/31/2004.
Assets, $40,949,359 (M); Expenditures, $14,486,896; Total giving, $2,122,548; Grants to individuals, totaling $2,122,548.
Fields of interest: Engineering school/education; Science, formal/general education; Mathematics; Engineering.
Type of support: Awards/prizes; Undergraduate support.
Application information: Application form required.
  Deadline(s): Nov. 19
  Applicants should submit the following:
    1) ACT
    2) Transcripts
    3) Letter(s) of recommendation
    4) GPA
    5) Essay
  Additional information: Application must also include research plan, and statement from supervising scientist. See Web site for further application information.
Program description:
  Science Scholarships: Awards one first place scholarship of $100,000 for four years, and numerous smaller scholarships.
EIN: 530196483

3625
Scotch Plains Fanwood Scholarship Foundation
P.O. Box 123
Fanwood, NJ 07023-0123 (908) 889-7646
Contact: Eleanor Kramps, Pres.

Foundation type: Public charity
Limitations: Scholarships to graduates of Scotch Plains-Fanwood High School, NJ.
Financial data: Year ended 12/31/2003.
Assets, $429,187 (M); Expenditures, $110,200; Total giving, $105,800; Grants to individuals, 90 grants totaling $105,800.
Type of support: Support to graduates or students of specific schools; Undergraduate support.
Application information: Applications accepted. Application form required.
  Initial approach: Letter.
  Applicants should submit the following:
    1) Letter(s) of recommendation
    2) Transcripts
  Additional information: Application by letter.
EIN: 226105926

3626
Scots' Charitable Society
P.O. Box 863
4 Buchan Rd.
Andover, MA 01810
Contact: Douglas Smith
Application address: c/o Alan M. Kelly, Chair., 222 Normandy Dr., Norwood, MA 02062, tel.: (617) 551-9709

Foundation type: Independent foundation
Limitations: Scholarships to individuals of verifiable Scottish descent pursing vocational education, including secretarial and nursing school, or other undergraduate studies.
Financial data: Year ended 10/31/2002.
Assets, $1,579,702 (M); Expenditures, $143,040; Total giving, $99,950; Grants to individuals, totaling $99,950.
Fields of interest: Vocational education; Nursing school/education.
Type of support: Technical education support; Undergraduate support.
Application information: Applications accepted. Application form required.
  Initial approach: Letter requesting application by Mar. 20.
  Deadline(s): Apr. 4
  Additional information: Application must include proof of Scottish lineage, parents' and student's most recent tax returns, and transcripts.
Program description:
  Scholarships: A letter of verification from a member of the Society or The Women's Auxiliary Society is sufficient proof of Scottish lineage. Scholarships are not awarded for graduate or part-time studies.
EIN: 046040091

3627
Scott & Stringfellow Educational Foundation
P.O. Box 1575
Richmond, VA 23218-1575 (800) 552-7757
Contact: Bradley H. Gunter, Secy.
FAX: (804) 643-3718; Application address: c/o Elizabeth Ronston, 909 E. Main St., Richmond, VA 23219, tel.: (804) 782-7757; URL: https://www.scottstringfellow.com/ss/about-us-serving-our-communities.asp

Foundation type: Company-sponsored foundation
Limitations: Scholarships to spouses and dependents of employees of Scott & Stringfellow, Inc. and others in the surrounding areas of company business offices.
Publications: Informational brochure.
Financial data: Year ended 12/31/2004.
Assets, $1,171,552 (M); Expenditures, $61,906; Total giving, $56,626; Grants to individuals, 40 grants totaling $55,426 (high: $5,000, low: $300).
Type of support: Employee-related scholarships.
Application information:
  Deadline(s): Mar.
  Applicants should submit the following:
    1) Transcripts
  Additional information: Application should also include letter of recommendation from principal, guidance counselor, or a teacher, and copy of parents' or guardian's federal tax return.
EIN: 541669283

3628
Richard L. & F. Annette Scott Foundation
700 11th St. S., Ste. 101
Naples, FL 34102

Foundation type: Independent foundation
Limitations: Scholarships to graduates of North Kansas City High School, MO, for higher education.
Financial data: Year ended 09/30/2004.
Assets, $2,358,603 (M); Expenditures, $48,952; Total giving, $426,500; Grants to individuals, totaling $426,500.
Type of support: Support to graduates or students of specific schools; Undergraduate support.

Application information: Applications not accepted.
EIN: 621646107

3629
Olin Scott Fund, Inc.
407 Main St.
P.O. Box 1208
Bennington, VT 05201 (802) 447-1096
Contact: Melinda L. Dickie, Exec. Dir.
FAX: (802) 447-8560

Foundation type: Independent foundation
Limitations: Student loans to young men from Bennington County, VT, planning to attend VT colleges and universities.
Financial data: Year ended 06/30/2005.
Assets, $3,208,690 (M); Expenditures, $89,499; Total giving, $12,000; Grants to individuals, totaling $12,000.
Fields of interest: Men.
Type of support: Undergraduate support.
Application information: Applications accepted throughout the year; Initial approach by letter or telephone; Completion of formal application required, including application fee of $25 for initial loan and for each renewal; Interviews required.
Program description:
  Student Loans: Applicants must have at least a 2.5 GPA to receive and to renew a student loan. The maximum amount of each loan is $3,000 per year, $12,000 maximum over four years.
EIN: 036005697

3630
The Arthur H. Scott Memorial Trust
c/o Chittenden Bank, Trust Dept.
2 Burlington Sq., P.O. Box 820
Burlington, VT 05402

Foundation type: Independent foundation
Limitations: Scholarships to graduating seniors of Champlain Valley Union High School, Hinesburg, VT, Northfield High School, VT, and Chelsea High School, VT, who are majoring in education or the performing arts.
Financial data: Year ended 12/31/2004.
Assets, $1,474,087 (M); Expenditures, $97,492; Total giving, $82,731; Grants to individuals, totaling $82,731.
Fields of interest: Performing arts, education; Teacher school/education.
Type of support: Support to graduates or students of specific schools; Undergraduate support.
Application information: Applications not accepted.
EIN: 036047004

3631
M. M. Scott Scholarship Fund - Gertrude S. Straub Trust Estate
c/o Bank of Hawaii
P.O. Box 3170
Honolulu, HI 96802-3170
Contact: Meleen P. Corenevsky, Asst. V.P., Bank of Hawaii
Scholarship address: c/o Hawaii Community Fdn., 1164 Bishop St., Ste. 800, Honolulu, HI 96813, tel.: (808) 537-6333

Foundation type: Independent foundation
Limitations: Scholarships to HI public high school graduates to attend mainland U.S. colleges and universities, with a major in a subject relating to

better understanding of peace and the promotion of international peace.

Publications: Informational brochure (including application guidelines).

Financial data: Year ended 03/31/2004. Assets, $8,466,901 (M); Expenditures, $431,814; Total giving, $379,350; Grants to individuals, 247 grants totaling $379,350 (high: $2,800, low: $450).

Fields of interest: History/archaeology; Philosophy/ethics; International peace/security; International affairs; Anthropology/sociology; Economics; Psychology/behavioral science; Political science; Law/international law; Government/public administration.

Type of support: Graduate support; Undergraduate support.

Application information: Application form required.

Initial approach: Letter or telephone.

Deadline(s): Mar. 1

Applicants should submit the following:
1) Transcripts
2) SAR
3) Letter(s) of recommendation
4) Essay

Additional information: Application must also include a personal statement.

Program description:

Marion Maccarrell Scott Scholarship Fund: Applicants must be residents of HI, graduates of a HI public high school, plan to attend a two- or four-year mainland accredited college or university on a full-time basis, demonstrate financial need, meet a standard of academic performance, and demonstrate good character and motivation towards achieving educational goals. Applicants must be studying at the undergraduate or graduate level. They must also plan to enroll in one of the following courses: history, government, political science, anthropology, economics, geography, international relations, law, psychology, philosophy, or sociology. Scholarships are awarded annually and are renewable for up to four years. Renewals are given preference as long as the student's academic work is satisfactory. Awards are not intended to cover all expenses. Applicants to this foundation may automatically be considered for other scholarship programs administered by the Hawaii Community Foundation. Employees or direct relatives of employees of Bancorp Hawaii and the Hawaii Community Foundation are ineligible.

EIN: 996003243

3632
Ethel Voris Scott Trust

c/o JPMorgan Chase Bank, N.A.
P.O. Box 1308
Milwaukee, WI 53201
Application address: JPMorgan Chase Bank, N.A., Attn.: Dennis S. Hickle, Trust Off., 111 Monument Cir., IN1-0169, Indianapolis, IN 46277, tel.: (317) 756-1362

Foundation type: Independent foundation

Limitations: Scholarships to dependent orphan children in Montgomery County, IN.

Financial data: Year ended 12/31/2004. Assets, $1,121,559 (M); Expenditures, $48,107; Total giving, $36,000.

Fields of interest: Residential/custodial care.

Type of support: Scholarships—to individuals.

Application information: Applications by letter, with sufficient proof of need, accepted throughout the year.

EIN: 356011994

3633
Gordon and Ann Scott Trust

c/o Daniel C. Blaney
P.O. Box 500
Morocco, IN 47963-0500

Foundation type: Independent foundation

Limitations: Scholarships to graduates of North Newton High School, IN, and residents of Washington Township, IN.

Financial data: Year ended 12/31/2004. Assets, $443,748 (M); Expenditures, $57,317; Total giving, $25,350; Grants to individuals, totaling $25,350.

Type of support: Support to graduates or students of specific schools; Undergraduate support.

Application information: Applications accepted throughout the year; Completion of formal application required, including financial information, post-high school plans, high school transcript and extracurricular activities.

EIN: 356681290

3634
Scott-Jenkins Fund

c/o Wilber National Bank
245 Main St.
Oneonta, NY 13820
Application address: c/o Financial Aid Office, Netzer Administration Building, SUCO Oneonta, NY 13820, tel.: (607) 436-2532

Foundation type: Independent foundation

Limitations: Scholarships and work-grants to foreign and minority students attending State University of New York College at Oneonta.

Financial data: Year ended 06/30/2005. Assets, $755,906 (M); Expenditures, $42,097; Total giving, $38,011; Grants to individuals, totaling $38,011.

Fields of interest: Education; International exchange, students; Minorities.

Type of support: Support to graduates or students of specific schools; Foreign applicants; Undergraduate support; Workstudy grants.

Application information: Contact fund for current application deadline; Completion of formal application required.

Program descriptions:

Scott-Jenkins Work-Grants: Grants of $750 each are available to students who work a minimum of 11 hours per week on average for 30 weeks. Students will be paid every two weeks for hours worked the previous two weeks.

Scott-Jenkins Foreign Student Scholarships: Available to any foreign student, and are to be used for room and board and maintenance expenses in a campus residence hall. Candidates must be recommended by the Director of International Education.

Scott-Jenkins Memorial Scholarship: A renewable award for minority students in good academic standing. Candidates are recommended by the Office of Special Programs and the Financial Aid Office.

Scott-Jenkins Foreign Study Scholarships: Available to students in a foreign study program sponsored by State University of New York College at Oneonta, or Hartwick College. The scholarship covers the program costs over and above those which are not already covered by financial aid, but not to exceed $500 per student. Candidates are recommended by the Director of International Education and the Financial Aid Office.

EIN: 166199427

3635
Scottish Rite Foundation in Kentucky

200 E. Gray St.
Louisville, KY 40202

Foundation type: Independent foundation

Limitations: Fellowships to residents of KY who are pursuing a doctorate in Public Education Administration at the University of Louisville.

Financial data: Year ended 06/30/2005. Assets, $883,445 (M); Expenditures, $40,720; Total giving, $32,584; Grants to individuals, totaling $32,584.

Fields of interest: Education, administration/regulation; Education, public education.

Type of support: Fellowships; Doctoral support.

Application information: Contact foundation for current application deadline; Completion of formal application required; Applications are available at the University of Louisville.

EIN: 616036090

3636
Scotts Miracle-Gro Foundation

c/o Rob McMahon
800 Port Washington Blvd.
Port Washington, NY 11050

Foundation type: Independent foundation

Limitations: Scholarships to children enrolled in the Miracle-Gro Kids Program in Columbus, OH.

Financial data: Year ended 12/31/2004. Assets, $421,214 (M); Expenditures, $162,620; Total giving, $160,000.

Fields of interest: Youth development, adult & child programs.

Type of support: Scholarships—to individuals.

Application information:

Initial approach: Letter.

Additional information: Contact foundation for additional application information.

Program description:

Miracle-Gro Kids Program: The Miracle-Gro Kids Program was launched in September 2002, and originally encompassed both 4th grade classes of Trevitt Elementary School in Columbus, Ohio. This select group of children, which now includes students from additional schools, is being followed through high school. Their after-school activities, academic tutoring and social support are all structured toward the goal of college graduation. College tuition is ensured for each Miracle-Gro Kid who graduates from high school. Each of the Miracle-Gro Kids is paired with a Scotts mentor who meets each week during the school year with their Miracle-Gro Kid, providing the consistent friendship and encouragement that every child needs to succeed in life.

EIN: 311799491

3637
The Screen Actors Guild Foundation

5757 Wilshire Blvd., 7th Fl.
Los Angeles, CA 90036 (323) 549-6708
Contact: Marcia Smith, Exec. Dir.
E-mail: msmith@sag.org; FAX: (323) 549-6710; URL: http://www.sagfoundation.org

Foundation type: Public charity

Limitations: Scholarships to Guild members and their dependents for higher education.

Financial data: Year ended 09/30/2003. Assets, $15,072,481 (M); Expenditures, $2,139,507; Total giving, $612,448.

Fields of interest: Performing arts.

Type of support: Undergraduate support.

Application information: Applications accepted. Application form required.
Deadline(s): Mar. 15
Program description:
John L. Dales Scholarship Fund: The awards apply only to accredited and licensed universities, colleges, junior colleges, adult specialty schools or trade/vocational schools. The number and amount of the awards to be given are determined annually.
EIN: 953967876

3638
The Scudder Association, Inc.
Tinywood Rd.
Darien, CT 06820
Application address: c/o Pam Nothacker, Chair., Scudder Educational Grant Comm., 6328 North Fairhill St., Philadelphia, PA 19126;
E-mail: nothacker5@aol.com; URL: http://www.scudder.org/philanthropy.html

Foundation type: Independent foundation
Limitations: Scholarships to financially needy undergraduate and graduate students from the U.S. and India who are studying for the ministry or in the fields of medicine, nursing, or other medically-related careers, teaching, or social services. Preference is shown to renewal applicants and individuals recommended by Scudder Association members or by the financial aid office of Cornell Medical College, NY. Scholarships are renewable for up to a total of four years of undergraduate and/or graduate support.
Financial data: Year ended 12/31/2004. Assets, $2,141,715 (M); Expenditures, $95,346; Total giving, $40,950; Grants to individuals, totaling $40,950.
Fields of interest: Medical school/education; Teacher school/education; Theological school/education; Social work school/education; India.
Type of support: Graduate support; Undergraduate support.
Application information: Application form required.
Deadline(s): July 15.
Additional information: Application must include two letters of recommendation from faculty members, personal statement of 500 words or less, official transcripts, and verification of financial need from college.
EIN: 135647705

3639
SDMS Educational Foundation
2745 Dallas Pkwy., Ste. 350
Plano, TX 75093-8730 (214) 473-8057
Contact: Dawn Sanchez, Exec. Dir.
FAX: (214) 473-8563;
E-mail: foundation@sdms.org; URL: http://www.sdms.org/foundation/gems.asp

Foundation type: Public charity
Limitations: Scholarships to financially needy students with scholastic merit who are enrolled in CAAHEP or CMA accredited diagnostic medical sonography programs, and grants to practicing sonographers. The maximum scholarship amount is $500 per calendar year.
Financial data: Year ended 12/31/2003. Assets, $562,186 (M); Expenditures, $106,484; Total giving, $24,155; Grants to individuals, 81 grants totaling $24,155 (high: $1,500, low: $150).
Fields of interest: Health sciences school/education.
Type of support: Scholarships—to individuals.

Application information: Application form required.
Deadline(s): Applications accepted three times per year.
Applicants should submit the following:
1) Financial information
2) Transcripts
3) Essay
EIN: 752262610

3640
Seabee Memorial Scholarship Association
P.O. Box 6574
Silver Spring, MD 20916-6574 (301) 570-2850
Contact: Sheryl Chiogioji, Admin. Asst.
FAX: (301) 570-2873; E-mail: smsa@erols.com;
URL: http://www.seabee.org

Foundation type: Public charity
Limitations: Scholarships to deserving children and grandchildren of the men and women who have comprised the Naval Construction Force, also known as Seabees.
Publications: Informational brochure; Newsletter.
Financial data: Year ended 12/31/2003. Assets, $2,894,427 (M); Expenditures, $259,959; Total giving, $157,500; Grants to individuals, totaling $157,500.
Type of support: Undergraduate support.
Application information: Deadline Apr. 15; Completion of formal application required.
EIN: 520910325

3641
Sealaska Heritage Institute
(formerly Sealaska Heritage Foundation)
1 Sealaska Plz., Ste. 201
Juneau, AK 99801-1249 (907) 463-4844
Contact: Rosita Worl, Pres.
FAX: (907) 586-9293; URL: http://www.sealaskaheritage.org

Foundation type: Public charity
Limitations: Scholarships and apprenticeships to Alaskan Native Americans and Sealaska Corporation shareholders. Giving primarily in AK, but giving also in lower 48 states.
Publications: Informational brochure; Newsletter.
Financial data: Year ended 12/31/2003. Assets, $1,285,218 (M); Expenditures, $2,372,578; Total giving, $694,724; Grants to individuals, totaling $694,724.
Fields of interest: Native Americans/American Indians.
Type of support: Technical education support; Undergraduate support.
Application information: Deadlines vary; Initial approach by letter or telephone; Completion of formal application required.
Program description:
Scholarships/Heritage Study: Scholarships are provided for postsecondary education and apprenticeships to young Native people seeking to further their knowledge of traditional culture and art forms in order to create a living resource serving Alaska's native cultures and all of Alaska as well. Applicants for scholarships must be a Sealaska Corporation shareholder, a native descendant of a shareholder, or a Native American residing in south Alaska, attending, or planning to attend, college or vocational/technical training on a full-time basis. Students are selected for awards based on their application form, academic achievement, and letters of recommendation.
EIN: 920081844

3642
Seamen's Long Point Charitable Foundation, Inc.
c/o Seamen's Bank
221 Commercial St.
Provincetown, MA 02657 (508) 487-0035

Foundation type: Company-sponsored foundation
Limitations: Scholarships to residents of the Provincetown, MA, area.
Financial data: Year ended 03/31/2005. Assets, $494,441 (M); Expenditures, $87,636; Total giving, $87,421; Grants to individuals, 9 grants totaling $9,000 (high: $1,000, low: $1,000).
Type of support: Undergraduate support.
Application information: Application form required.
Initial approach: Letter.
Additional information: Contact foundation for further program information.
EIN: 043368515

3643
William Searls Scholarship Foundation
c/o First National Bank of Bar Harbor
102 Main St.
Bar Harbor, ME 04609
Contact: Margo Stanley, Trust Off., First National Bank of Bar Harbor; Donald Worcester, Trust Off., First National Bank of Bar Harbor

Foundation type: Independent foundation
Limitations: Scholarships to graduates of Pemetic High School in Southwest Harbor, ME.
Financial data: Year ended 12/31/2004. Assets, $406,991 (M); Expenditures, $12,707; Total giving, $8,000; Grants to individuals, totaling $8,000.
Type of support: Support to graduates or students of specific schools; Undergraduate support.
Application information: Deadlines Apr. 15 for June graduates, May 1 for all others; Completion of formal application required, including elementary school record, birth certificate, parents' confidential financial statement and income tax return for the current year.
Program description:
Scholarships: Recipients are chosen on the basis of character, ambition, financial need, and academic achievement. Scholarships are disbursed after completion of one semester and enrollment in the second semester. Applicant must notify the foundation in writing of enrollment in the second semester. Recipients failing to complete a semester in which funds have been disbursed will be required to return the unused portion of those funds.
EIN: 016009698

3644
Greater Seattle Business Association Scholarship Fund
(also known as GSBA)
2150 N. 107th St., Ste. 205
Seattle, WA 98133-9009 (206) 363-9188
Contact: Louise Chernin, Exec. Dir.
FAX: (206) 367-8777; E-mail: office@thegsba.org;
URL: http://www.thegsba.org

Foundation type: Public charity
Limitations: Scholarships of up to $5,000 to students in the Pacific Northwest who demonstrate community leadership potential and who foster the understanding and diversity of the sexual minority community.

Publications: Application guidelines; Annual report; Informational brochure; Newsletter.
Financial data: Year ended 12/31/2003.
Assets, $576,194 (M); Expenditures, $48,878; Total giving, $48,875; Grants to individuals, 25 grants totaling $48,875 (high: $4,000, low: $500).
Fields of interest: LGBTQ.
Type of support: Scholarships—to individuals.
Application information: Application form required.
Deadline(s): Feb. 4.
EIN: 943138514

3645
Seay Foundation
c/o American National Bank, Trust Div.
P.O. Box 9250
Colorado Springs, CO 80932
Application address: c/o American National Bank, 102 N. Cascade Ave., Colorado Springs, CO 80903

Foundation type: Independent foundation
Limitations: Scholarships by nomination only to students for higher education.
Financial data: Year ended 12/31/2004.
Assets, $19,699,717 (M); Expenditures, $752,273; Total giving, $616,202; Grants to individuals, 22 grants totaling $159,202 (high: $18,000, low: $1,000).
Type of support: Awards/grants by nomination only; Undergraduate support.
Application information: Deadline May 1; Completion of formal nomination required, including transcript, photo and three reference forms.
Program description:
Scholarships: Scholarships are for attendance at any college or university in the U.S. Minimum GPA requirement is 2.5. Recipients must be nominated by a member of the foundation's advisory committee or an adult who knows the student.
EIN: 436055549

3646
Security Benefit Group Charitable Trust
c/o Security Benefit Life Insurance Co.
1 Security Benefit Pl.
Topeka, KS 66636-1000 (785) 438-3000
Contact: DeeAnn Hurla

Foundation type: Company-sponsored foundation
Limitations: Scholarships primarily to individuals for attendance at colleges and universities in FL, IL, KS, NE, and TX.
Financial data: Year ended 12/31/2004.
Assets, $8,707 (M); Expenditures, $88,750; Total giving, $88,750.
Type of support: Undergraduate support.
Application information: Applications accepted. Application form required.
Deadline(s): Apr., Aug., and Oct.
Additional information: Contact trust for application form.
EIN: 046962651

3647
Theodore H. Sedler Scholarship Fund
c/o Community First Bank
520 Main Ave.
Fargo, ND 58124-0001

Foundation type: Independent foundation
Limitations: Scholarships to graduating seniors at high schools in Richland County, ND.

Financial data: Year ended 12/31/2004.
Assets, $743,403 (M); Expenditures, $51,913; Total giving, $36,593; Grants to individuals, 7 grants totaling $36,593 (high: $6,250, low: $1,250).
Fields of interest: Education.
Type of support: Support to graduates or students of specific schools; Graduate support; Undergraduate support.
Application information: Applications accepted. Application form required.
Deadline(s): Mar. 31
Additional information: Application must include letters of reference.
EIN: 456091443

3648
Seed Money for Growth Foundation, Inc.
(also known as SMFG Foundation, Inc.)
4716 N. Dromedary Rd.
Phoenix, AZ 85018-2939 (602) 840-7841

Foundation type: Operating foundation
Limitations: Scholarships to financially needy residents of AZ for attendance at "AMI approved" Montessori schools, Montessori teacher training, development of special talents at the graduate level in the arts and sciences at an AZ institution, and for nurses of free-standing ambulatory surgical centers (FSASC).
Publications: Informational brochure (including application guidelines).
Financial data: Year ended 07/31/2004.
Assets, $905,362 (M); Expenditures, $105,568; Total giving, $60,273; Grants to individuals, 72 grants totaling $60,271 (high: $2,800, low: $125).
Fields of interest: Arts; Elementary school/education; Education; Health care; Science.
Type of support: Graduate support; Undergraduate support.
Application information: Application form required.
Initial approach: Telephone.
Copies of proposal: 1
Deadline(s): None
Applicants should submit the following:
1) Financial information
2) Budget Information
Additional information: Application should also include W-2 copies and a copy of previous year's IRS filing for income verification.
EIN: 942919372

3649
R. Q. & L. A. Seely Charitable Trust
(formerly Roger Q. & Lovye A. Seely Trust)
c/o Corsicana National Bank
P.O. Box 624
Corsicana, TX 75151
Application address: c/o C.T. Griffin, Superintendent, Wortham Independent School District, P.O. Box 247, Wortham, TX 76695, tel.: (817) 765-3678

Foundation type: Independent foundation
Limitations: Scholarships to high school graduates of the Wortham, TX, area to attend Navarro College. Loans to high school graduates of the Wortham, TX, area to attend colleges and universities in TX.
Financial data: Year ended 02/28/2005.
Assets, $609,410 (M); Expenditures, $22,906; Total giving, $15,288.
Type of support: Support to graduates or students of specific schools; Undergraduate support.
Application information: Application form required.
Deadline(s): May 10.
Applicants should submit the following:

1) Financial information
2) Essay
3) Letter(s) of recommendation
Additional information: Interviews required; Applications available at Wortham High School.
Program description:
Seely Charitable Trust Program: Children and grandchildren of the trust's board members are ineligible. Awards are renewable. Interest on loans must be paid annually. Repayment of principal begins upon graduation or termination of education. Loans and scholarships will be terminated if applicant enters the armed forces, withdraws from a majority of enrolled classes, or joins a social fraternity or sorority.
EIN: 756069098

3650
The Abe and Annie Seibel Foundation
c/o Frost National Bank
P.O. Box 179
Galveston, TX 77553 (409) 770-5665
Contact: Janet L. Bertiolino, V.P. and Trust Off., Frost National Bank
FAX: (409) 770-7166

Foundation type: Independent foundation
Limitations: Interest-free undergraduate student loans to TX residents and graduates of TX high schools for full-time attendance at TX colleges and universities.
Publications: Application guidelines; Informational brochure (including application guidelines).
Financial data: Year ended 07/31/2004.
Assets, $41,036,681 (M); Expenditures, $4,288,019; Total giving, $3,568,670; Loans to individuals, totaling $3,468,670.
Fields of interest: Higher education.
Type of support: Undergraduate support.
Application information: Application form required.
Initial approach: Letter or telephone.
Deadline(s): Feb. 28
Applicants should submit the following:
1) SAT
2) Letter(s) of recommendation
3) GPA
4) Financial information
5) Essay
6) Budget Information
7) ACT
8) Transcripts
Program description:
Seibel Foundation Loan Program: Recipients are selected on the basis of need and GPA and SAT scores. Minimum SAT scores of 1000 (for top 25 percent of the class) or 1100-1200 (for bottom 75 percent of the class) are required. Maximum loan amount is $4,000. Loans must be co-signed. A minimum monthly payment of $35 must be made while in school. Funds are usually made to the student in two disbursements, half of the approved amount for each semester. Upon completion of an undergraduate degree, students will have six years to repay the loan. College students must maintain a 2.75 overall GPA.
EIN: 746035556

3651
Selah Charitable Trust
P.O. Box 732
Lakeside, MT 59922-0732

Foundation type: Independent foundation
Limitations: Scholarships for graduate school.

Financial data: Year ended 12/31/2004. Assets, $3,005,930 (M); Expenditures, $176,514; Total giving, $174,170; Grants to individuals, 4 grants totaling $51,040 (high: $20,040, low: $5,000).
Type of support: Graduate support.
Application information:
Initial approach: Letter.
Additional information: Contact foundation for further guidelines.
EIN: 376393903

3652
William G. Selby and Marie Selby Foundation
1800 2nd St., Ste. 750
Sarasota, FL 34236 (941) 957-0442
Contact: Debra M. Jacobs, Pres.
FAX: (941) 957-3135; URL: http://www.selbyfdn.org/selby.html

Foundation type: Independent foundation
Limitations: Scholarships to graduating seniors at high schools in Sarasota, Manatee, Charlotte, and DeSoto counties, FL.
Publications: Informational brochure (including application guidelines).
Financial data: Year ended 05/31/2005. Assets, $71,198,434 (M); Expenditures, $4,668,051; Total giving, $3,842,616; Grants to individuals, totaling $454,000.
Type of support: Support to graduates or students of specific schools; Undergraduate support.
Application information: Contact foundation for current application deadline/guidelines.
EIN: 596121242

3653
Ben Selling Scholarship Loan Fund
c/o Wells Fargo Bank Northwest, N.A.
P.O. Box 21927
Seattle, WA 98111

Foundation type: Independent foundation
Limitations: Low-interest student loans to financially needy and worthy students of any OR school, or of any rabbinical college in the U.S. Priority is given to students of Oregon Health Sciences University, Reed College, Portland State University, Portland Community College, and Mt. Hood Community College, all in OR.
Financial data: Year ended 09/30/2004. Assets, $601,935 (M); Expenditures, $21,120; Total giving, $12,322; Grants to individuals, totaling $12,322.
Fields of interest: Theological school/education.
Type of support: Student loans—to individuals; Support to graduates or students of specific schools.
Application information: Applications accepted throughout the year; Initial approach by letter requesting application; Completion of formal application required, including transcripts, proof of enrollment, financial aid information, and a processing fee of $30 which will be refunded if application is declined; Interviews granted upon request.
EIN: 936017158

3654
Sells Foundation, Inc.
215 E. 9th Ave.
Johnson City, TN 37601
Contact: Ellen Sells, V.P.

Foundation type: Independent foundation
Limitations: Grants to financially needy theological students in TN attending seminaries or other educational institutions. Recipients must adhere to the theological views of the foundation.
Financial data: Year ended 10/31/2004. Assets, $3,418,150 (M); Expenditures, $206,107; Total giving, $199,735; Grants to individuals, 12 grants totaling $199,735 (high: $26,400, low: $7,800).
Fields of interest: Theological school/education.
Type of support: Scholarships—to individuals.
Application information: Potential applicants are contacted by the foundation and furnished with forms to complete; Completion of formal application required.
EIN: 237322421

3655
SEMA Memorial Scholarship Fund
P.O. Box 4910
Diamond Bar, CA 91765-0910 (909) 396-0289
Contact: Christopher J. Kersting, Pres.
Scholarship address: 1575 S. Valley Vista Dr., Diamond Bar, CA 91765, Attn. Education Department
E-mail: education@sema.org; URL: http://www.sema.org/scholarship

Foundation type: Public charity
Limitations: Scholarships to students engaged in studies which will lead to a career in the automotive aftermarket or a related field.
Financial data: Year ended 06/30/2004. Assets, $1,633,131 (M); Expenditures, $101,038; Total giving, $100,802; Grants to individuals, 71 grants totaling $100,802 (high: $2,000, low: $802).
Type of support: Undergraduate support.
Application information: Applications accepted. Application form required. Application form available on the grantmaker's Web site.
Initial approach: E-mail or letter.
Deadline(s): May 15
Applicants should submit the following:
1) Photograph
2) Letter(s) of recommendation
3) Transcripts
4) Essay
Program description:
SEMA Memorial Scholarship Fund: Student Qualification Requirements:
· Minimum 2.5 GPA
· Applicant must be enrolled in a full-time program with an accredited university, college, or proprietary program in the United States or Canada
· Pursuing studies leading to a career in the automotive aftermarket or related field
EIN: 954131888

3656
Sequim Masonic Lodge Foundation
c/o Lewis W. Kastner
P.O. Box 1500
Sequim, WA 98382-1500
Contact: Glenn Greathouse, Secy.
Application address: 306 Reservoir Rd., Sequim, WA 98382

Foundation type: Independent foundation
Limitations: Scholarships to graduates of the Sequim, WA, school district who are members of recognized youth organizations.
Financial data: Year ended 06/30/2005. Assets, $425,766 (M); Expenditures, $36,794;

Total giving, $36,000; Grants to individuals, totaling $36,000.
Fields of interest: Youth development, centers/clubs.
Type of support: Support to graduates or students of specific schools; Undergraduate support.
Application information: Deadline Mar. 31; Applications by letter, including resume outlining participation in youth organizations.
EIN: 910987628

3657
Sertoma Foundation
1912 E. Meyer Blvd.
Kansas City, MO 64132 (816) 333-8300
Contact: Steven Murphy, Exec. Dir.
FAX: (816) 333-4320;
E-mail: infosertoma@sertoma.org; URL: http://www.sertoma.org

Foundation type: Public charity
Limitations: Undergraduate and graduate scholarships to students who are hard-of-hearing, or students studying pathology and audiology.
Publications: Application guidelines; Annual report.
Financial data: Year ended 08/31/2003. Assets, $7,907,988 (M); Expenditures, $790,606; Total giving, $190,636.
Fields of interest: Speech/hearing centers; Ear & throat diseases; Pathology; Disabilities, people with.
Type of support: Graduate support; Undergraduate support.
Application information: Applications accepted. Application form required. Application form available on the grantmaker's Web site.
Deadline(s): Vary.
Program descriptions:
Communicative Disorders Scholarship: Twenty to thirty $2,500 scholarships are awarded annually to students already accepted in graduate level classes in speech pathology and audiology. Deadline Mar. 31.
Scholarship for Hearing-Impaired Students: Twenty to thirty $1,000 scholarships are awarded annually to hard-of-hearing students pursuing a bachelor's degree at any four year college. The scholarship is renewable up to four times with the annual submission of an application. Students must have a 3.2 GPA or at least 85 percent in all high school and college classes. Deadline May 1.
EIN: 630655922

3658
Servant-Leader Scholarship Trust
42 Woodberry Rd.
Little Rock, AR 72212

Foundation type: Independent foundation
Limitations: Scholarships by nomination only to children of ministers and Christian leaders, in AR, for higher education.
Financial data: Year ended 06/30/2004. Assets, $930 (M); Expenditures, $17,332; Total giving, $16,416.
Fields of interest: Religion.
Type of support: Graduate support; Undergraduate support.
Application information: Applications not accepted.
EIN: 716182280

3659
Servco Foundation
P.O. Box 2788
Honolulu, HI 96803
Contact: Sandra C.H. Wong, Secy.
FAX: (808) 523-3937

Foundation type: Company-sponsored foundation
Limitations: Scholarships to spouses and children of Servco Pacific Inc. employees to pursue studies at any accredited college.
Publications: Application guidelines.
Financial data: Year ended 06/30/2004. Assets, $6,172,090 (M); Expenditures, $355,635; Total giving, $297,590; Grants to individuals, 15 grants totaling $36,250 (high: $1,250, low: $833).
Type of support: Employee-related scholarships; Scholarships—to individuals.
Application information: Application form required.
Deadline(s): Mar. 1
Applicants should submit the following:
1) Class rank
2) Transcripts
3) SAT
4) SAR
5) GPA
Additional information: Application should also include two letters of recommendation; Interviews required for semifinalists.
Program description:
Scholarship Program: Applicants must have demonstrated leadership and responsibility through participation in school activities and community service. Upon completion of studies, recipients must plan to return to HI or to the Pacific Island region to contribute to its growth and development.
EIN: 990248256

3660
Service League of Cherokee County
P.O. Box 1132
Canton, GA 30114-1132 (770) 479-2368
Contact: Vicki Smith, Pres.

Foundation type: Public charity
Limitations: Scholarships to residents of GA, for higher education.
Financial data: Year ended 03/31/2003. Assets, $213,000 (M); Expenditures, $134,570; Total giving, $64,444; Grants to individuals, totaling $13,950.
Fields of interest: Higher education.
Type of support: Scholarships—to individuals.
Application information: Contact foundation for current application deadline/guidelines.
EIN: 581685138

3661
Seven Oaks Foundation, Inc.
225 Peachtree St. N.E., Ste. 1200
Atlanta, GA 30303-1729

Foundation type: Independent foundation
Limitations: Scholarships by nomination only to graduating high school seniors who are U.S. citizens, or noncitizens currently working towards citizenship.
Financial data: Year ended 12/31/2004. Assets, $22,872 (M); Expenditures, $33,385; Total giving, $33,284; Grants to individuals, totaling $33,284.
Fields of interest: Education.
Type of support: Awards/grants by nomination only.
Application information: Applications not accepted.

Additional information: High school counselors nominate students to compete; Completion of formal application required by nominees only. Scholarship recipients are chosen biannually by competition.
EIN: 581828554

3662
Seymour Community School Scholarship Trust
P.O. Box 67
Seymour, WI 54165-0067 (920) 833-2356
Contact: Vernon Lubinski, Tr.

Foundation type: Independent foundation
Limitations: Scholarships to graduating seniors of the Seymour Community School District, WI, who exhibit leadership abilities and will be attending college.
Financial data: Year ended 12/31/2004. Assets, $670,511 (M); Expenditures, $29,749; Total giving, $28,497; Grants to individuals, totaling $28,497.
Type of support: Support to graduates or students of specific schools; Undergraduate support.
Application information: Contact trust for current application deadline/guidelines. Recipients must complete the first semester of their freshman year to receive the scholarship.
EIN: 391769065

3663
Greater Seymour Trust Fund
c/o Jacqueline F. Sciarra
P.O. Box 1001
Seymour, IN 47274

Foundation type: Independent foundation
Limitations: Scholarships to students of Seymour High School, IN, and Washington High School in Milwaukee, WI.
Publications: Annual report; Informational brochure.
Financial data: Year ended 06/30/2005. Assets, $5,495,905 (M); Expenditures, $288,951; Total giving, $244,166; Grants to individuals, 124 grants totaling $214,186 (high: $6,986, low: $300).
Fields of interest: Vocational education.
Type of support: Support to graduates or students of specific schools; Precollege support.
Application information: Application form required.
Additional information: Applications available from school guidance offices.
EIN: 356208884

3664
Allen J. Shafer Trust
c/o U.S. Bank, N.A.
P.O. Box 7900
Madison, WI 53707-7900

Foundation type: Independent foundation
Limitations: Scholarships to graduates of West High School, Madison, WI. Recipients are selected by West High School committee.
Financial data: Year ended 12/31/2004. Assets, $176,790 (M); Expenditures, $10,967; Total giving, $9,120; Grants to individuals, totaling $9,120.
Type of support: Support to graduates or students of specific schools; Undergraduate support.

Application information:
Deadline(s): Contact trust for current application deadline/guidelines.
EIN: 396140024

3665
Moses and Caroline Shallow Scholarship Foundation, Inc.
P.O. Box 375
Wausaukee, WI 54177
Contact: William Pickett, Pres.

Foundation type: Independent foundation
Limitations: Scholarships to residents of Marinette County, WI.
Financial data: Year ended 12/31/2004. Assets, $1,205,534 (M); Expenditures, $72,901; Total giving, $61,400; Grants to individuals, totaling $61,400.
Type of support: Scholarships—to individuals; Awards/grants by nomination only; Undergraduate support.
Application information:
Initial approach: Letter or telephone.
EIN: 391336290

3666
The M. L. Shanor Foundation
P.O. Box 2370
Wichita Falls, TX 76307 (940) 761-2401
Contact: Frank W. Jarratt, Pres.

Foundation type: Independent foundation
Limitations: Student loans to residents of Cherokee, Wichita, and Wilbarger counties, TX.
Financial data: Year ended 12/31/2004. Assets, $4,086,249 (M); Expenditures, $260,509; Total giving, $183,325; Grants to individuals, 104 grants totaling $160,825 (high: $3,300, low: $350).
Type of support: Student loans—to individuals.
Application information: Deadline Aug. 1; Completion of formal application required, including GPA, student's financial information, and two high school references from either two teachers or a teacher and a principal.
EIN: 756012834

3667
Ida Shapiro Testamentary Scholarship Trust
c/o First National Bank of Decatur
130 N. Water St.
Decatur, IL 62523

Foundation type: Independent foundation
Limitations: Scholarship awards to four deserving college students: a graduate from Decatur Dist. 61 high schools, a graduate of Clinton Community Unit No. 15 High School, a student attending Illinois Wesleyan University, Bloomington, and a student attending the School of Journalism at Northwestern University.
Financial data: Year ended 12/31/2004. Assets, $368,172 (M); Expenditures, $22,690; Total giving, $16,536; Grants to individuals, totaling $16,536.
Type of support: Support to graduates or students of specific schools; Undergraduate support.
Application information:
Initial approach: Letter.
EIN: 367383601

3668
Share the Dream Foundation
P.O. Box 1497
Santa Rosa, CA 95402
Contact: Mickey Freeman
Application address: 3100 Five Forks Trilkum Rd.,
Ste. 401, Liburn, GA 30047, tel.: (770) 736-9383
ex.200
E-mail: info@share-the-dream.org; URL: http://
www.share-the-dream.org/

Foundation type: Independent foundation
Limitations: Scholarships to individuals who are
currently attending an elementary or high school
that has been an active customer of National Scrip
Center for at least three academic years.
Scholarships also to students who are served by a
nonprofit youth organization, such as a soccer club
or Boys and Girls Club, which has been an active
customer of National Scrip Center for three years.
Financial data: Year ended 12/31/2003.
Assets, $5,082 (M); Expenditures, $80,442; Total
giving, $54,000; Grants to individuals, 35 grants
totaling $54,000 (high: $9,000, low: $500).
Type of support: Technical education support;
Precollege support; Undergraduate support.
Application information: Applications accepted.
Application form required. Application form
available on the grantmaker's Web site.
> *Additional information:* See Web site for current
> application information.

EIN: 680413769

3669
Robert G. Sharp Trust
2781 Queen Ann Ct.
Green Bay, WI 54304

Foundation type: Independent foundation
Limitations: Scholarships to high school graduates
of Oconto and Brown counties, WI, for attendance
at Marquette University, Lawrence University, St.
Norbert College, Beloit College, and any university
in the WI system: Eau Claire, Green Bay, La Crosse,
Madison, Milwaukee, Oshkosh, Parkside,
Platteville, River Falls, Stevens Point, Stout,
Superior, and Whitewater.
Publications: Application guidelines.
Financial data: Year ended 08/31/2005.
Assets, $655,341 (M); Expenditures, $55,334;
Total giving, $28,500; Grants to individuals,
totaling $28,500.
Type of support: Support to graduates or students
of specific schools; Undergraduate support.
Application information: Application form required.
> *Deadline(s):* Apr. 15
> *Additional information:* Application forms and FAF
> available from high school counselors in Dec.
> of each year; Applications should be
> submitted to the high school guidance
> counselors.

Program description:
> *Scholarship Program:* Recipients are chosen
> based on scholarship, character, and financial
> need. Scholarship winners are announced in May
> and a $500 award is then submitted to the
> respective university or college the first weeks of
> Sept. and Jan. To be eligible for continued grants,
> recipients are required to attend a university or
> college as a full-time student, report grades each
> semester, give immediate notice upon
> discontinuation or transferring schools, notify the
> trustee of any change in financial need, and advise
> trustee of full-time attendance for the following
> semester. Should a recipient of a Sharp Trust award
> receive assistance from other sources, all or some
> of the aid from Sharp may be withdrawn or

discontinued, depending upon the financial needs
of the student at that time.
EIN: 396084979

3670
Helen B. Shartzer Scholarship Fund
c/o PNC Advisors
620 Liberty Ave., 10th Fl.
Pittsburgh, PA 15222-2705
Application address: c/o Scholarship Comm.,
Norristown Area High School, Norristown, PA 19401

Foundation type: Independent foundation
Limitations: Undergraduate scholarships to worthy
residents of Norristown, PA.
Financial data: Year ended 12/31/2004.
Assets, $145,366 (M); Expenditures, $10,485;
Total giving, $8,400; Grants to individuals, totaling
$8,400.
Type of support: Undergraduate support.
Application information: Contact foundation for
current application deadline/guidelines.
EIN: 236398364

3671
Shasta Regional Community Foundation
1335-B Arboretum Dr., Ste. B
Redding, CA 96002 (530) 244-1219
Contact: Kathy Ann Anderson, C.E.O.; For
scholarships: Alisha Walsh
FAX: (530) 244-0905; E-mail: info@shastarcf.org;
URL: http://www.shastarcf.org

Foundation type: Community foundation
Limitations: Scholarships to individuals from
Shasta and Sishiyou counties, CA, for
undergraduate education at American colleges and
universities.
Publications: Application guidelines; Annual report;
Grants list; Informational brochure.
Financial data: Year ended 06/30/2005.
Assets, $3,693,961 (M); Expenditures,
$1,060,836; Total giving, $484,851.
Fields of interest: Music; Business school/
education; Law school/education; Crime/law
enforcement, formal/general education; Athletics/
sports, racquet sports; Science; Women.
Type of support: Scholarships—to individuals;
Support to graduates or students of specific
schools; Undergraduate support.
Application information: Applications accepted.
Application form required.
> *Initial approach:* Letter or fax.
> *Deadline(s):* Varies
> *Applicants should submit the following:*
> 1) Letter(s) of recommendation
> 2) GPA
> 3) Essay
> *Additional information:* Contact high school
> counselor or the foundation for current
> application deadlines/guidelines.

EIN: 680242276

3672
J. D. Shatford Memorial Trust
c/o JPMorgan Chase Bank
345 Park Ave., 4th Fl.
New York, NY 10154 (212) 464-2441
Contact: Edward L. Jones, V.P., JPMorgan Chase
Bank
FAX: (212) 464-2305;
E-mail: jones_ed_l@JPMorgan.com; Additional tel.:
(212) 464-2470 (Rohit Burman, Prog. Off.)

Foundation type: Independent foundation
Limitations: Scholarships to residents of
Hubbards, Nova Scotia, Canada.
Publications: Grants list; Informational brochure.
Financial data: Year ended 12/31/2004.
Assets, $7,589,062 (M); Expenditures,
$420,718; Total giving, $344,825; Grants to
individuals, 104 grants totaling $344,825 (high:
$15,000, low: $1,250).
Type of support: Foreign applicants; Graduate
support; Undergraduate support.
Application information: Applications accepted
throughout the year; Completion of formal
application required.
EIN: 136029993

3673
The Fred S. Shaulis Foundation, Inc.
c/o Donald R. Mering
120 E. Baltimore St., 8th Fl.
Baltimore, MD 21202-1643
Contact: Randell L. Urban, V.P.
Application address: P.O. Box 121, Friedens, PA
15541, tel.: (814) 445-9534

Foundation type: Independent foundation
Limitations: Student loans for college or other
post-high school education in the Somerset County
PA, area.
Financial data: Year ended 02/28/2005.
Assets, $571,548 (M); Expenditures, $6,190;
Total giving, $0; Loans to individuals, 18 loans
totaling $72,450.
Fields of interest: Vocational education.
Type of support: Student loans—to individuals.
Application information: Application form required.
> *Deadline(s):* Jan. 5 for spring semester and Aug.
> 5 for fall semester
> *Additional information:* Interviews required.

Program description:
> *Student Loan Program:* There are no minimum
> GPA requirements, however, well-rounded students
> who display evidence of hard-working principals,
> both scholastically and personally, are considered
> the highest priority for awarding loans. Loans must
> be repaid. The longest term for repayment is ten
> years and loans provide for equal quarterly
> installments.

EIN: 521382605

3674
Clyde L. and Mary C. Shaull Education
Foundation
c/o PNC Advisors
1600 Market St.
Philadelphia, PA 19103-7240
Contact: James Best, Trust Off., PNC Advisors
Application address: P.O. Box 308, Camp Hill, PA
17001

Foundation type: Independent foundation
Limitations: Scholarships to graduates of
Mechanicsburg High School, PA, who are enrolled
in postsecondary schools.
Financial data: Year ended 12/31/2004.
Assets, $680,478 (M); Expenditures, $26,735;
Total giving, $8,000; Grants to individuals, totaling
$8,000.
Type of support: Scholarships—to individuals;
Support to graduates or students of specific
schools.
Application information: Deadline June 1;
Completion of formal application required, including
financial statement; Initial approach by letter;

Application forms available from Mechanicsburg High School guidance counselors.
EIN: 237101845

3675

John P. Sheehan Scholarship Fund
c/o Bank of America, N.A.
P.O. Box 6768
Providence, RI 02940-6768
Application address: c/o Bank of America, N.A., TSU-268, Genesee St., 2nd Fl., Utica, NY 13502, tel.: (315) 798-2553

Foundation type: Independent foundation
Limitations: Scholarships to financially needy graduates of public and parochial high schools in Utica, NY, based on moral fitness, likelihood for success in college, high school academic performance, and financial need.
Financial data: Year ended 12/31/2004. Assets, $361,293 (M); Expenditures, $26,228; Total giving, $20,400; Grants to individuals, totaling $20,400.
Type of support: Support to graduates or students of specific schools; Undergraduate support.
Application information: Application form required.
  Deadline(s): Apr. 30
  Applicants should submit the following:
    1) Financial information
EIN: 156014981

3676

Howard J. & Ruth H. Sheen Scholarship Fund
c/o PNC Advisors
620 Liberty Ave., P2-PTPP-10-2
Pittsburgh, PA 15222-2705
Application address: c/o Michael L. Stahlman, Principal, Corry Area High School, 534 E. Pleasant St., Corry, PA 16407

Foundation type: Independent foundation
Limitations: Scholarships to graduates of Corry Area High School, PA, who wish to enter medical related fields.
Financial data: Year ended 12/31/2004. Assets, $146,115 (M); Expenditures, $7,867; Total giving, $6,075; Grants to individuals, totaling $6,075.
Fields of interest: Medical school/education.
Type of support: Support to graduates or students of specific schools; Undergraduate support.
Application information: Deadline May 15; Completion of formal application required.
EIN: 256257707

3677

Edward J. & Lavelette Rockwell Sheil Memorial Fund
c/o National City Bank of Pennsylvania
P.O. Box 94651
Cleveland, OH 44101
Application address: c/o Paul N. Shaler, Head Counselor, Coronado High School, 650 D Ave., Coronado, CA 92118, tel.: (714) 435-3172

Foundation type: Independent foundation
Limitations: Scholarships primarily to young men who have graduated from Coronado High School, CA.
Financial data: Year ended 12/31/2003. Assets, $255,736 (M); Expenditures, $17,173; Total giving, $14,625; Grants to individuals, 5

grants totaling $14,625 (high: $3,250, low: $1,625).
Fields of interest: Men.
Type of support: Support to graduates or students of specific schools; Undergraduate support.
Application information: Applications accepted. Application form required.
  Additional information: Applications accepted throughout the year and are available upon request. Recipients are usually notified in June of each year of their application's approval.
EIN: 256081887

3678

Shelby Foundation
142 N. Gamble St., Ste. F
Shelby, OH 44875 (419) 342-3686
Contact: Cheryl A. Schumacher, Chair.
E-mail: administrator@shelbyfoundation.com;
URL: http://www.shelbyfoundation.com/

Foundation type: Independent foundation
Limitations: Scholarships to individuals residing in the city of Shelby and Richland County, OH.
Financial data: Year ended 12/31/2004. Assets, $3,075,530 (M); Expenditures, $212,119; Total giving, $139,872.
Type of support: Scholarships—to individuals.
Application information: Applications by letter accepted throughout the year.
EIN: 346710288

3679

Shelter Insurance Foundation
1817 W. Broadway
Columbia, MO 65218 (573) 214-4290
Contact: Raymond E. Jones, Secy.

Foundation type: Company-sponsored foundation
Limitations: Scholarships to high school seniors who are residents of AR, CO, IA, IL, IN, KS, KY, LA, MO, MS, NE, OK, and TN.
Financial data: Year ended 06/30/2005. Assets, $8,395,112 (M); Expenditures, $583,182; Total giving, $576,760; Grants to individuals, totaling $463,500.
Type of support: Undergraduate support.
Application information: Applications accepted.
  Deadline(s): None
Program description:
  Shelter Insurance Awards: The foundation also granted the:
    · Lang Award of $250
    · WJHS Teacher Award of $1,000 to two residents of MO.
EIN: 431224155

3680

Shenango Valley Community Foundation
(formerly Shenango Valley Foundation)
33 Chestnut St.
Sharon, PA 16146 (724) 981-5882
Contact: Larry Haynes, Exec. Dir.
FAX: (724) 983-9044;
E-mail: larrysvf@adelphia.net; URL: http://www.sv-foundation.org

Foundation type: Community foundation
Limitations: Scholarships, student loans, and other grants to individuals residing in Mercer County and Lawrence County, PA, and Trumbull County, OH, areas.

Publications: Application guidelines; Annual report; Informational brochure.
Financial data: Year ended 12/31/2004. Assets, $25,169,744 (M); Expenditures, $1,984,470; Total giving, $1,611,402; Loans to individuals, 230 loans totaling $1,241,814.
Type of support: Conferences/seminars; Scholarships—to individuals; Student loans—to individuals.
Application information: Contact foundation for current application deadline; Initial approach by letter or telephone; Completion of formal application required; Interviews required.
EIN: 251407396

3681

Leon and Josephine Wade Shepard Scholarship Fund Foundation, Inc.
c/o National City Bank
171 Monroe Ave. N.W., KC17063
Grand Rapids, MI 49503-2634
Application address: c/o Alan Hogenmiller, 4 Memorial Dr., Fennville, MI 49408

Foundation type: Independent foundation
Limitations: Scholarships to needy, qualified graduates of Fennville High School, MI, enrolled in institutions of higher learning in MI that are approved by the Michigan Dept. of Public Instruction.
Financial data: Year ended 03/31/2004. Assets, $827,001 (M); Expenditures, $92,126; Total giving, $77,650; Grants to individuals, totaling $77,650.
Type of support: Support to graduates or students of specific schools; Undergraduate support.
Application information: Deadline late Feb. to early Mar.; Completion of formal application required; Applications available from Fennville High School.
Program description:
  Scholarship Program: Students must be enrolled in 12 or more credit hours. Grants are awarded for two years, not to exceed $1,000 per year.
EIN: 386101349

3682

Elizabeth Buford Shepherd Scholarship Committee
c/o AmSouth Bank
315 Deaderick St., 4th Fl.
Nashville, TN 37237-0401
Contact: Joseph Chickey, Trust Off., AmSouth Bank

Foundation type: Independent foundation
Limitations: Undergraduate scholarships to high school graduates who are residents of TN and live within a 250-mile radius of Nashville, TN.
Financial data: Year ended 12/31/2004. Assets, $1,835,169 (M); Expenditures, $121,449; Total giving, $95,000; Grants to individuals, 100 grants totaling $95,000.
Type of support: Undergraduate support.
Application information: Application form required.
  Deadline(s): Mar. 1 for first-time applicants, Jan. 15 for renewals
EIN: 626047221

3683
Sheridan County Memorial Educational Trust

P.O. Box 1827
Williston, ND 58802-1827
Application address: c/o Weldon Richardson, P.O. Box 697, Blaine, WA 98230

Foundation type: Independent foundation
Limitations: Scholarships to graduates of Sheridan County high schools, MT, who have made a significant impact on the community.
Financial data: Year ended 12/31/2002.
Assets, $215,609 (M); Expenditures, $14,856; Total giving, $12,500; Grants to individuals, 25 grants totaling $12,500 (high: $500, low: $500).
Fields of interest: Community development.
Type of support: Support to graduates or students of specific schools.
Application information: Applications accepted throughout the year; Initial approach by letter; Completion of formal application required.
EIN: 363479962

3684
Harry R. Sheridan Memorial Scholarship

P.O. Box 820
Burlington, VT 05402-0820

Foundation type: Public charity
Limitations: Scholarships to students from the Monpelier School District and Union 32 School District, VT.
Financial data: Year ended 02/28/2004.
Assets, $889,242 (M); Expenditures, $58,041; Total giving, $48,000; Grants to individuals, 17 grants totaling $48,000 (high: $5,000, low: $1,000).
Type of support: Support to graduates or students of specific schools; Undergraduate support.
Application information: Applications accepted throughout the year; Completion of formal application required.
EIN: 036048570

3685
Sherman Educational Fund

c/o First National Bank & Trust Co.
P.O. Box 9012
Kokomo, IN 46904-9012
Contact: Joseph W. Cartledge
Application address: c/o First National Bank & Trust Co., P.O. Box 70, Sullivan, IN 47882-0070, tel.: (812) 268-4377

Foundation type: Independent foundation
Limitations: Scholarships to graduates of IN high schools.
Financial data: Year ended 12/31/2004.
Assets, $3,501,414 (M); Expenditures, $204,623; Total giving, $189,500; Grants to individuals, 90 grants totaling $189,500 (high: $5,000, low: $650).
Type of support: Scholarships—to individuals.
Application information: Deadline Apr. 1; Contact fund for current application guidelines.
EIN: 356020497

3686
Mabel E. Sherman Educational Fund

c/o Citizens First National Bank
P.O. Box 1227
Storm Lake, IA 50588 (712) 732-5440

Foundation type: Independent foundation
Limitations: Student loans to residents of Ida and Cherokee counties, IA, who attend Buena Vista University, Cornell College, or Morningside College, all in IA. If funds allow, residents of other parts of IA may be considered.
Publications: Annual report.
Financial data: Year ended 06/30/2005.
Assets, $3,841,166 (M); Expenditures, $139,604; Total giving, $88,093; Loans to individuals, totaling $88,093.
Type of support: Support to graduates or students of specific schools; Undergraduate support.
Application information: Contact the financial aid offices of fund-supported colleges for current application deadline/guidelines.
Program description:
Student Loans: Due dates of loans are not to exceed ten years from the date the loan is made. Loans are interest-free until due date, at which time an interest rate of seven percent per annum is added. Loans are given only if all other means are exhausted.
EIN: 426278859

3687
The John F. & Mary E. Shiel Trust

c/o Jackson County Bank, Trust Dept.
P.O. Box 1001
Seymour, IN 47274
Contact: Jackie Sciarra, Trust Off., Jackson County Bank

Foundation type: Independent foundation
Limitations: Scholarships to graduates of Seymour High School, IN, to attend colleges and universities full-time.
Publications: Application guidelines; Annual report.
Financial data: Year ended 09/30/2004.
Assets, $108,954 (M); Expenditures, $4,624; Total giving, $3,000; Grants to individuals, totaling $3,000.
Type of support: Support to graduates or students of specific schools; Undergraduate support.
Application information: Application form required.
Deadline(s): Apr. 1
Applicants should submit the following:
1) Transcripts
2) SAT
3) GPA
Additional information: Applications are available from the Jackson County Bank Trust Dept.
Program description:
Scholarship Program: Scholarships are only awarded for the first year of college. Selection is based on academic achievement and school and community involvement.
EIN: 316260142

3688
Howard & Christine Shifler Memorial Foundation

c/o Bank of America, N.A.
P.O. Box, 441 NJ6-219-02-03
Ridgefield Park, NJ 07660-9984

Foundation type: Independent foundation
Limitations: Scholarships to graduates of Southern Regional High School, Manahawkin, NJ, to attend colleges and trade schools.
Financial data: Year ended 12/31/2004.
Assets, $255,444 (M); Expenditures, $13,843; Total giving, $11,000; Grants to individuals, 16 grants totaling $11,000 (high: $1,000, low: $500).
Fields of interest: Vocational education.

Type of support: Support to graduates or students of specific schools; Technical education support; Undergraduate support.
Application information: Application form required.
Deadline(s): Feb. 28
Applicants should submit the following:
1) Financial information
EIN: 226403942

3689
William M. Shinnick Educational Fund

601 Underwood St.
Zanesville, OH 43701 (740) 452-2273
Contact: Barbara Cornell, Admin. Asst.

Foundation type: Independent foundation
Limitations: Scholarships to financially needy graduates of high schools in Muskingum County, OH. Student loans to financially needy residents of Muskingum County, OH.
Financial data: Year ended 06/30/2005.
Assets, $3,045,032 (M); Expenditures, $296,751; Total giving, $229,917; Grants to individuals, 27 grants totaling $89,667 (high: $4,000, low: $2,000); Loans to individuals, 103 loans totaling $140,250.
Type of support: Student loans—to individuals; Undergraduate support.
Application information: Deadline June 30; Initial approach by telephone; Completion of formal application required, including financial statement; Interviews required.
Program description:
Scholarship and Loan Program: Scholarships are for four years, providing recipient maintains at least a 2.0 GPA. Maximum scholarship per year is $5,000. Apart from scholarships and loans, the fund may make additional awards to some loan recipients.
EIN: 314394168

3690
Joseph Shinoda Memorial Scholarship Foundation

234 Via La Paz
San Luis Obispo, CA 93401-6960
URL: http://www.shinodascholarship.org

Foundation type: Independent foundation
Limitations: Scholarships to students for the study of floriculture at accredited colleges and universities.
Financial data: Year ended 12/31/2004.
Assets, $629,588 (M); Expenditures, $43,226; Total giving, $19,300; Grants to individuals, 12 grants totaling $17,500.
Fields of interest: Botanical/horticulture/ landscape services.
Type of support: Undergraduate support.
Application information: Deadline Mar. 30; Completion of formal application required; Applications available on Web site.
EIN: 237213289

3691
Ray S. Shoemaker Trust for Shoemaker Scholarship Fund

c/o Mellon Financial Corp.
2 N. 2nd St., 12th Fl.
Harrisburg, PA 17108
Scholarship application address: c/o Dir. of Admissions, Harrisburg Area Community College,

Cameron St., Harrisburg, PA 17108, tel.: (717) 780-2400

Foundation type: Independent foundation
Limitations: Undergraduate and graduate scholarships to graduates of high schools in the greater Harrisburg, PA, area.
Financial data: Year ended 09/30/2004. Assets, $5,657,864 (M); Expenditures, $324,980; Total giving, $320,472; Grants to individuals, totaling $320,472.
Type of support: Support to graduates or students of specific schools; Graduate support; Undergraduate support.
Application information: Deadline Apr. 1; Completion of formal application required, including financial statement and high school transcripts.
EIN: 236237250

3692

Shoppers Village/Maureen Nolan Memorial Fund

877 N. Corona Ave.
Valley Stream, NY 11580-1549
Contact: Robert W. O'Brien, Secy.
Application address: 138 Woodfield Rd., West Hempstead, NY 11552, tel.: (516) 538-0800

Foundation type: Independent foundation
Limitations: Scholarships to high school students who are members of St. Thomas the Apostle Parish, West Hempstead, NY, or of West Hempstead School District No. 27.
Financial data: Year ended 07/31/2004. Assets, $27,931 (M); Expenditures, $3,000; Total giving, $3,000; Grants to individuals, totaling $3,000.
Fields of interest: Christian agencies & churches.
Type of support: Undergraduate support.
Application information: Deadline Nov. 25; Completion of formal application required.
EIN: 112617929

3693

J. Leo Short Scholarship Fund

c/o JPMorgan Chase Bank, N.A
P.O. Box 1308
Milwaukee, WI 53201
Application address: JPMorgan Chase Bank, N.A., 8111 Preston Rd., Dallas, TX 75255, tel.: (214) 360-4373

Foundation type: Independent foundation
Limitations: Scholarships to graduating seniors of Denison High School, TX.
Financial data: Year ended 12/31/2004. Assets, $262,923 (M); Expenditures, $17,575; Total giving, $13,000.
Type of support: Support to graduates or students of specific schools; Undergraduate support.
Application information: Application form required.
Deadline(s): Mar. 31.
Program description:
Scholarship Program: Selection is based on scholarship, citizenship, seriousness of educational purpose, school attendance record, and financial need.
EIN: 756097737

3694

Helen Shacklet Shouse Memorial Scholarship Trust

c/o Bank of America, N.A.
P.O. Box 831041
Dallas, TX 75283-1041
Application address: c/o Bank of America, N.A., Attn: David P. Ross, Sr. V.P., P.O. Box 419119, Kansas City, MO 64141-6119, tel.: (816) 979-7481

Foundation type: Independent foundation
Limitations: Scholarships to high school graduates who reside in Lafayette County, MO, for attendance at any accredited MO college.
Financial data: Year ended 12/31/2004. Assets, $299,582 (M); Expenditures, $18,646; Total giving, $12,700; Grants to individuals, 2 grants totaling $12,000.
Type of support: Undergraduate support.
Application information: Deadline Apr. 1; Completion of formal application required, including financial need demonstration.
EIN: 431764196

3695

Victoria Livestock Show Foundation, Inc.

209 Dundee St.
Victoria, TX 77904
Contact: Randy Crow, Secy.-Treas.

Foundation type: Independent foundation
Limitations: Scholarships to high school students who reside in Victoria Court, TX, for higher education.
Financial data: Year ended 04/30/2005. Assets, $1 (M); Expenditures, $10,964; Total giving, $10,000; Grants to individuals, totaling $10,000.
Type of support: Undergraduate support.
Application information: Application form required.
Deadline(s): Feb. 15
Applicants should submit the following:
1) SAT
2) GPA
3) Transcripts
Program description:
Scholarship Awards: The foundation administers the following scholarships:
· Dan McCue Memorial Scholarships: Two $1,500 scholarships.
· Dennis Williams Memorial Scholarship: Awards one $1,000 scholarship.
· Victoria Livestock Show Scholarships: Awards six $1,000 scholarships.
All candidates must meet the following criteria:
· The candidate must be a Victoria Court resident and enrolled as a student in any accredited high school which include but are not limited to the following high schools: Bloomington, Industrial, St. Joseph, Memorial High or Profit High
· The candidate must be a high school senior who has achieved the equivalent of either of the following academic credentials: a 3.0 GPA on a 4.0 scale or an 85 GPA on a 100 point scale as of the completion of the candidate's first semester of the senior year, or its equivalent; or a 2.5 GPA on a 4.0 point scale or an 80 point average on a 100 point scale, as of the completion of candidate's senior year, or its equivalent, and a minimum score of 950 on the SAT or a minimum score of 20 on the ACT
· The candidate must enroll in a Texas college or university

· The candidate must have been a member either of the Texas FFA or a Texas 4-H Club for at least two years
· The candidate must have participated in a Victoria Livestock Show activity in at least two of the four years immediately preceding the filing of the candidate's application
· The candidate must graduate from one of the above listed high schools by the end of the spring semester following the presentation of the scholarship.
EIN: 742712669

3696

William A. & Mary A. Shreve Foundation, Inc.

25 Abe Voorhees Dr.
Manasquan, NJ 08736
Contact: Peter T. Broege, Tr.
Application address: 2517 Hwy. 35, Manasquan, NJ 08736

Foundation type: Independent foundation
Limitations: Scholarships primarily to students in NJ.
Financial data: Year ended 12/31/2004. Assets, $694,072 (M); Expenditures, $63,052; Total giving, $36,200; Grants to individuals, 12 grants totaling $36,200.
Type of support: Scholarships—to individuals.
Application information: Contact foundation for current application deadline/guidelines.
EIN: 226054057

3697

Benjamin F. & Emma B. Shroyer Scholarship Fund

c/o First Merchants Bank, N.A.
200 E. Jackson St.
Muncie, IN 47305

Foundation type: Independent foundation
Limitations: Scholarships to children of employees of First Merchants Bank and American National Bank.
Financial data: Year ended 12/31/2004. Assets, $1,198,826 (M); Expenditures, $96,485; Total giving, $85,320; Grants to individuals, 36 grants totaling $85,320.
Type of support: Employee-related scholarships.
Application information: Deadline Mar. 21; Completion of formal application required.
EIN: 356017466

3698

Bernard E. Shultz Eagle Scout Foundation

c/o Larry Bledsoe
200 W. 10th St.
Aberdeen, WA 98520-2423
Contact: Trustees

Foundation type: Independent foundation
Limitations: Scholarships to students from Nampa High School or Skyview High School, ID.
Financial data: Year ended 12/31/2003. Assets, $1,366,664 (M); Expenditures, $52,245; Total giving, $52,100; Grants to individuals, totaling $48,600.
Type of support: Support to graduates or students of specific schools; Undergraduate support.
Application information: Deadline Apr. 15; Application available through the foundation or at

Nampa High School or Skyview High School in Nampa, ID.
EIN: 820446208

3699
Ruth A. Shultz Scholarship Fund
c/o Legacy Portfolio Mgmt.
99 North St.
P.O. Box 1759
Pittsfield, MA 01201
Contact: Eugene D. Cornell, V.P., Berkshires, N.A.

Foundation type: Operating foundation
Limitations: Scholarships to high school graduates of the Caanan, CT, area.
Financial data: Year ended 12/31/2003. Assets, $169,519 (M); Expenditures, $9,731; Total giving, $6,500; Grants to individuals, totaling $6,500.
Type of support: Undergraduate support.
Application information: Contact fund for current application deadline; Completion of formal application required, including transcript and parents' financial information.
EIN: 066205123

3700
The Paul and Adelyn C. Shumaker Foundation
c/o JPMorgan Chase Bank, N.A.
P.O. Box 1308
Milwaukee, WI 53201
Application address: c/o JPMorgan Chase Bank, N.A., 28 Park Ave. W., Mansfield, OH 44901-1616, tel.: (419) 525-5517

Foundation type: Independent foundation
Limitations: Scholarships to residents of Richland County, OH, for medical education.
Financial data: Year ended 12/31/2004. Assets, $1,461,126 (M); Expenditures, $16,841; Total giving, $0; Loans to individuals, totaling $92,000.
Fields of interest: Medical school/education.
Type of support: Scholarships—to individuals.
Application information: Applications accepted throughout the year; Completion of formal application required.
EIN: 346621245

3701
John Q. Shunk Association
P.O. Box 625
Bucyrus, OH 44820-0625
Contact: Jane C. Peppard, Secy.-Treas.
FAX: (740) 386-6134;
E-mail: pepspatch@marion.net; Application address: 1201 Timber Ln., Marion, OH 43302-5739, tel.: (614) 389-3132

Foundation type: Independent foundation
Limitations: Scholarships only to graduates of four specified high schools in Crawford County, OH, for attendance at accredited colleges and universities.
Financial data: Year ended 12/31/2004. Assets, $2,022,694 (M); Expenditures, $93,849; Total giving, $55,425; Grants to individuals, 23 grants totaling $55,425.
Type of support: Support to graduates or students of specific schools; Undergraduate support.
Application information: Application form required.
Initial approach: Letter.
Deadline(s): Feb. 15

Additional information: Completion of formal application required, including parents' financial statement and recommendation from a high school representative; Annual interviews required; Application forms may be obtained from guidance offices of the specified high schools.
Program description:
John Q. Shunk Scholarship Program:
Scholarships to graduates of the following Crawford County, OH, schools: Bucyrus High School, Colonel Crawford High School, Wynford High School, and Buckeye Central High School. Scholarships are awarded on the basis of need, attitude, and worthiness. There are no stipulations concerning a required GPA. If recipient is suspended for any reason, including grades, the scholarship is automatically terminated and will not be reinstated. Scholarship checks are given directly to the individual recipient, however, the check is made payable to the educational institution. Recipients must reapply for renewal each year.
EIN: 340896477

3702
Agnes Cecelia J. Siebenthal Scholarship Charitable Trust
c/o National City Bank
P.O. Box 94651
Cleveland, OH 44101-4651
Application address: c/o Manual High School, Attn: Principal, 811 S. Griswold, Peoria, IL 61605, tel.: (309) 672-6600

Foundation type: Independent foundation
Limitations: Scholarships to Peoria, IL, area students who have graduated from Manual High School, IL, to pursue teaching careers.
Financial data: Year ended 09/30/2004. Assets, $687,737 (M); Expenditures, $36,220; Total giving, $34,269; Grants to individuals, 18 grants totaling $34,269.
Fields of interest: Teacher school/education.
Type of support: Support to graduates or students of specific schools; Undergraduate support.
Application information: Contact school for current application deadline/guidelines; Initial approach by letter.
EIN: 376193766

3703
Siemens Foundation
170 Wood Ave. S.
Iselin, NJ 08830 (877) 822-5233
FAX: (732) 603-5890;
E-mail: foundation@sc.siemens.com; URL: http://www.siemens-foundation.org

Foundation type: Company-sponsored foundation
Limitations: Scholarships to high school students who excelled in advanced mathematics and physics and were competitive with the best mathematics and science students in the world. Awards also to teachers for exemplary teaching of mathematics and/or science.
Financial data: Year ended 09/30/2003. Assets, $6,284,407 (L); Expenditures, $3,766,058; Total giving, $799,126; Grants to individuals, 120 grants totaling $452,676 (high: $103,000, low: $166).
Fields of interest: Mathematics; Physics; Engineering/technology.
Type of support: Awards/prizes; Undergraduate support.
Application information: Application form required.

Initial approach: Proposal of no more than 10 pages.
Deadline(s): Mar. 1
Additional information: See Web site for further information.
Program description:
Siemens Award for Advanced Placement:
· Students: Awards scholarships of $3,000, plus an expense-paid trip to DC in Dec. for recognition in a ceremony at the Smithsonian, to the top 24 students, two females and two males in each of the six College Board regions, who have earned the highest and next-to-highest number of AP scores in five of seven exams. The exams are Biology, Calculus BC, Chemistry, Computer Science AB, Environmental Science, Physics C (Physics C Mechanics and Physics C Electricity and Magnetism each count as half) and Statistics. At the ceremony at the Smithsonian, the top male and top female students are announced as National Winners and each receive an additional $5,000 scholarship.
· Teachers: Awards of $1,000, a lapel pin and a plaque to 18 full-time teachers for exemplary teaching and enthusiastic dedication to both students and the subject. Twelve teachers, two in each of the College Board's six regions, are selected for their commitment to students and the AP program. Six additional teachers, one in each region, are recognized because they successfully teach AP mathematics and/or science to underrepresented minority students in non-magnet urban schools. Teachers are honored at a ceremony in Nov. at the Georgia Institute of Technology.
EIN: 522136074

3704
Sierra Pacific Foundation
P.O. Box 496028
Redding, CA 96049-6028 (530) 378-8000
Contact: Carolyn Emmerson Dietz, Pres.
FAX: (530) 378-8109;
E-mail: foundation@spi-ind.com; URL: http://www.spi-ind.com/Company/SPFoundation.htm

Foundation type: Company-sponsored foundation
Limitations: Scholarships to dependent children of Sierra Pacific Industries employees who reside in CA.
Publications: Grants list.
Financial data: Year ended 06/30/2005. Assets, $372,164 (M); Expenditures, $1,208,216; Total giving, $1,199,701; Grants to individuals, 252 grants totaling $268,275 (high: $1,750, low: $375).
Type of support: Employee-related scholarships.
Application information: Application form required.
Initial approach: Letter requesting application.
Deadline(s): Mar. 31
EIN: 942574178

3705
Sierra Pacific Soroptimist Foundation
2150 Lanai Ct.
Tulare, CA 93274
Application address: 534 Molino Dr., San Francisco, CA 94127

Foundation type: Operating foundation
Limitations: Scholarships to individuals in CA for higher education.

Financial data: Year ended 06/30/2002.
Assets, $204,594 (M); Expenditures, $37,000;
Total giving, $32,000; Grants to individuals, 7
grants totaling $26,000 (high: $5,000, low:
$1,000).
Type of support: Undergraduate support.
Application information: Application form required.
Initial approach: Letter.
Additional information: Contact foundation for
current application deadline.
EIN: 770415014

3706
Philip and Aida Siff Educational Foundation

(formerly Philip Francis Siff Educational Foundation)
222 E. Anapamu St., Ste. 25
Santa Barbara, CA 93101

Foundation type: Independent foundation
Limitations: Scholarships to graduate students of
University of California, Los Angeles, and to full-time
students of Hunter College of the City University of
New York, University of California, Santa Barbara,
and Santa Barbara City College, CA.
Financial data: Year ended 06/30/2005.
Assets, $2,201,244 (M); Expenditures,
$142,514; Total giving, $117,000.
Fields of interest: Humanities; Science.
Type of support: Support to graduates or students
of specific schools; Graduate support;
Undergraduate support.
Application information: Applications not
accepted.
Program description:
Scholarship Program: The following scholarships
are awarded on an annual basis:
· One grant of $4,000 to a graduate student
enrolled at University of California, Los
Angeles
· Five grants of up to $2,000 each to full-time
students enrolled at Hunter College
· Seven grants of up to $3,000 each to
full-time students majoring in science or
humanities at the University of California,
Santa Barbara
· Eight grants of up to $1,000 each to
students enrolled at Santa Barbara City
College.
EIN: 770165960

3707
Sigma Alpha Iota Philanthropies, Inc.

1 Tunnel Rd.
Asheville, NC 28805   (828) 251-0606
Contact: Ruth Sieber Johnson, Exec. Dir.
FAX: (828) 251-0644; E-mail: nh@sai-national.org;
URL: http://www.sai-national.org

Foundation type: Public charity
Limitations: Scholarships to members of the Sigma
Alpha Iota fraternity, and non-members, primarily
for music study.
Financial data: Year ended 06/30/2004.
Assets, $2,537,769 (M); Expenditures,
$329,731; Total giving, $99,114; Grants to
individuals, totaling $99,114.
Fields of interest: Music; Students, sororities/
fraternities.
Type of support: Awards/prizes; Graduate support;
Undergraduate support; Doctoral support.
Application information: Applications accepted.
Application form required. Application form
available on the grantmaker's Web site.
Deadline(s): Varies

Program description:
Scholarship and Loan Program: The foundation
administers numerous scholarships and student
loans to music students. See Web site for further
information.
EIN: 237391912

3708
Sigma Chi Foundation

1714 Hinman Ave.
P.O. Box 469
Evanston, IL 60204   (847) 869-3655
Contact: Frank Raymond, Pres.
Application address: c/o Scholarship Comm., 1714
Hinman Ave., Evanston, IL, 60201;
E-mail: scholarship@sigmachi.org
FAX: (847) 869-4906;
E-mail: foundation@sigmachi.org; URL: http://
www.sigmachi.org/foundation

Foundation type: Public charity
Limitations: Scholarships and fellowships to
individuals for higher education.
Publications: Annual report; Grants list;
Newsletter.
Financial data: Year ended 06/30/2005.
Assets, $20,695,131 (M); Expenditures,
$6,087,796; Total giving, $2,746,255.
Fields of interest: Business school/education;
Engineering; Economics; Political science;
International studies.
Type of support: Fellowships; Graduate support;
Undergraduate support.
Application information: Application form required.
Initial approach: Telephone, FAX, or e-mail.
Additional information: Contact foundation for
current application deadline/guidelines.
Program descriptions:
Balfour Fellowship Program: Fellowships to
graduate students who will serve as educational
advisors at undergraduate chapters to enhance the
educational and cultural environment as well as
lend their leadership and attention to
underachieving students to accelerate their
progress toward a degree.
Denton Scholarship Award: Scholarship to a
deserving graduating senior or current graduate
student in the field of international affairs, with
emphasis on world trade, economics, business or
political science.
Mark P. Herschede Engineering Award: Provides
scholarships of $2,500 or more to Sigma Chi
graduate students in engineering, for tuition and
fees to come in future years.
Grace and Jack D. Madson Graduate Scholarship:
Scholarships on a one-time basis to first year
graduate students with a minimum 3.0 GPA for
tuition and fees.
Scholarship Grants: Scholarships to deserving
undergraduate students in any field with a minimum
GPA of 3.0 who have completed at least three
semesters of study.
EIN: 362208386

3709
John J. Signer Memorial Trust Fund

c/o Union Bank of California, N.A.
400 California St.
San Francisco, CA 94104
Contact: Douglas G. Moore, Tr.
Application address: 166 Geary St., Ste. 702, San
Francisco, CA 94108, tel.: (415) 392-5248

Foundation type: Independent foundation
Limitations: Scholarships to graduates of Lick
Wilmerding High School, San Francisco, CA, who

are planning to study electricity, electronics, or
electrical engineering.
Financial data: Year ended 04/30/2005.
Assets, $782,428 (M); Expenditures, $69,849;
Total giving, $27,890; Grants to individuals, 3
grants totaling $27,890 (high: $11,195, low:
$6,250).
Fields of interest: Business/industry; Engineering.
Type of support: Support to graduates or students
of specific schools; Undergraduate support.
Application information: Deadline two months
before commencement; Application by thoughtful,
comprehensive letter about applicant's personality,
character, accomplishments, awards, ratings on
tests, and other pertinent information.
EIN: 946288204

3710
Silver Shield Foundation, Inc.

720 Fifth Ave., 10th Fl.
New York, NY 10019   (212) 572-6334
Contact: James E. Fuchs, Pres.
FAX: (212) 572-6419;
E-mail: moreinfo@silvershieldfoundation.org;
URL: http://www.silvershieldfoundation.org

Foundation type: Public charity
Limitations: Scholarships to surviving dependents
of New York City police officers and firefighters in
New York, New Jersey and Connecticut State
Troopers and members of other law enforcement
agencies within an approximate 50 mile radius of
the borough of Manhattan, NY are also eligible.
Publications: Annual report; Informational
brochure.
Financial data: Year ended 12/31/2003.
Assets, $5,272,352 (M); Expenditures,
$984,721; Total giving, $678,696; Grants to
individuals, totaling $678,696.
Type of support: Employee-related scholarships;
Awards/grants by nomination only; Undergraduate
support.
Application information: Applications not
accepted.
Additional information: The foundation will
contact the surviving family following official
notice of relative's death.
EIN: 133120746

3711
Rose Silverthorne Foundation

2940 N. O'Connor Rd., Ste. 125
Irving, TX 75062   (972) 252-4200
Contact: William B. Driscoll, Treas.

Foundation type: Independent foundation
Limitations: Scholarships to individuals in TX for
higher education.
Publications: Application guidelines.
Financial data: Year ended 12/31/2002.
Assets, $2,105,560 (M); Expenditures,
$147,988; Total giving, $131,727; Grants to
individuals, 34 grants totaling $131,727 (high:
$11,747, low: $37).
Type of support: Undergraduate support.
Application information: Applications accepted.
Application form required.
Initial approach: Letter.
Copies of proposal: 1
Deadline(s): Mar.
EIN: 752669407

3712
Esther N. Simmons Charitable Trust
c/o National City Bank
P.O. Box 94651
Cleveland, OH 44101-4651
Application address: c/o National City Bank,
Attn.: M. Vito, 20 Federal Plz., Youngstown, OH
44503, tel.: (330) 742-4289

Foundation type: Independent foundation
Limitations: Music scholarships to students of
Steubenville High School, OH.
Financial data: Year ended 05/31/2005.
Assets, $2,827,640 (M); Expenditures,
$186,222; Total giving, $163,860.
Fields of interest: Music; Performing arts,
education.
Type of support: Support to graduates or students
of specific schools; Undergraduate support.
Application information:
Deadline(s): None.
Additional information: Contact trust for current
application guidelines.
EIN: 346743541

3713
Ralph & Mary Simmons Welfare Fund
c/o KeyBank N.A.
800 Superior Ave., 4th Fl.
Cleveland, OH 44114-2601
Contact: Mr. Mulford, Trust Off., KeyBank N.A.
Application address: P.O. Box 1054, Augusta, ME
04332-1054

Foundation type: Independent foundation
Limitations: Scholarships to financially needy
residents of Kingfield, ME.
Financial data: Year ended 08/31/2003.
Assets, $0 (M); Expenditures, $22,566; Total
giving, $20,706; Grants to individuals, 27 grants
totaling $20,706 (high: $2,736, low: $100).
Type of support: Scholarships—to individuals.
Application information: Application form not
required.
Additional information: Applications by letter,
outlining need and purpose of grant, accepted
throughout the year.
EIN: 016007242

3714
Simon Educational Trust Foundation
c/o Wells Fargo Bank Arizona, N.A.
P.O. Box 53456, MAC S4035-014
Phoenix, AZ 85072

Foundation type: Independent foundation
Limitations: Scholarships to students graduating
from high schools in South Bend, IN, and other
schools located in St. Joseph County, IN.
Preference is given to graduates of public schools
and those who plan to attend Brandeis University in
MA.
Financial data: Year ended 12/31/2004.
Assets, $305,412 (M); Expenditures, $11,418;
Total giving, $6,800.
Type of support: Support to graduates or students
of specific schools; Undergraduate support.
Application information: Application form not
required.
Deadline(s): Feb. 15 for FAF, Mar. 31 for
application letter.
Applicants should submit the following:
1) GPA
2) Class rank
3) SAT
4) Transcripts

Additional information: Application by letter to
school principal, which should also include
three character references, IQ rating,
attendance record, school activity record, and
FAF, Program No. 0346.
Program description:
Scholarship Program: Awards are based upon
scholastic achievement, general moral character,
industry and tenacity of academic purpose, and
financial need. Recipients are selected by a
committee made up of a person associated with the
South Bend, IN, public school system, a judge, a
rabbi, members of the Simon family, and a
representative of the trustee. Scholarships are
renewable for up to four years of study.
EIN: 356012970

3715
The Simon Family Foundation
c/o Rita Simon
110 Primrose St.
Chevy Chase, MD 20815

Foundation type: Independent foundation
Limitations: Scholarship awards to residents of
Israel.
Financial data: Year ended 12/31/2004.
Assets, $67,238 (M); Expenditures, $55,569;
Total giving, $49,975; Grants to individuals, 37
grants totaling $49,975 (high: $7,275, low: $500).
Type of support: Foreign applicants.
Application information:
Initial approach: Letter.
Additional information: Contact foundation for
further information.
EIN: 521928868

3716
Simon Youth Foundation, Inc.
115 W. Washington St., Ste. 1325
Indianapolis, IN 46204 (317) 263-2361
Contact: Richard M. Markoff Ph.D., Exec. Dir.
FAX: (317) 263-2371; E-mail: syf@simon.com;
Scholarship address: Scholarship America, c/o SYF
Scholarship Programs, P.O. BOX 297, St. Peter, MN
56082; tel.: (800) 537-4180; Additional E-mail (for
Richard M. Markoff, Ph.D.): markoff@simon.com;
URL: http://syf.org

Foundation type: Public charity
Limitations: Awards scholarships of $1,500 each
to deserving high school seniors who plan to enroll
in a full-time undergraduate course of study at an
accredited two- or four-year college, university or
technical school.
Publications: Annual report.
Financial data: Year ended 12/31/2004.
Assets, $6,631,580 (M); Expenditures,
$1,697,081; Total giving, $382,390; Grants to
individuals, totaling $382,390.
Type of support: Technical education support;
Undergraduate support.
Application information: Deadline Feb. 15;
Completion of formal application required; See Web
site for additional information.
EIN: 352035269

3717
The Simpson Foundation
c/o Regions Bank
P.O. Box 2450
Montgomery, AL 36102-2450

Foundation type: Independent foundation

Limitations: Scholarships to students of Wilcox
County, AL, high schools.
Financial data: Year ended 04/30/2005.
Assets, $5,690,258 (M); Expenditures,
$296,227; Total giving, $264,200.
Type of support: Support to graduates or students
of specific schools; Undergraduate support.
Application information: Application form required.
Deadline(s): Jan. 1 to Mar. 31.
Applicants should submit the following:
1) Transcripts
2) Letter(s) of recommendation
Additional information: Interviews required.
EIN: 630925496

3718
The William G. & M. Virginia Simpson Foundation
c/o William S. Kistler
208 Spencer Ct.
Moon Township, PA 15108

Foundation type: Independent foundation
Limitations: Scholarships to students attending
Lehigh University, University of Pittsburgh, or
University of Pennsylvania, all in PA, who are either
from, or presently living in, western PA or parts of
OH, WV, and MD. Applicants must have had
experience working in business or finance, or
demonstrated significant interest in working in
these areas.
Financial data: Year ended 06/30/2005.
Assets, $1,675,700 (M); Expenditures,
$170,760; Total giving, $98,000; Grants to
individuals, 18 grants totaling $22,200 (high:
$8,000, low: $750).
Fields of interest: Business school/education;
Economics.
Type of support: Support to graduates or students
of specific schools; Undergraduate support.
Application information: Applications not
accepted.
Additional information: Recipients are nominated
by participating universities.
EIN: 251488701

3719
Joseph J. Sinek Scholarship Trust
c/o Citizens State Bank
200 N. Main St.
Pocahontas, IA 50574
Application address: c/o Kate Schiek, Guidance
Counselor, Pocahontas Area Community School,
Pocahontas, IA 50574, tel.: (712) 335-4848

Foundation type: Independent foundation
Limitations: Undergraduate scholarships only to
graduates of Pocahontas Area Community High
School, IA.
Financial data: Year ended 12/31/2004.
Assets, $1,389,438 (M); Expenditures, $63,394;
Total giving, $45,110; Grants to individuals, 160
grants totaling $45,110.
Type of support: Support to graduates or students
of specific schools; Undergraduate support.
Application information: Application form required.
Deadline(s): Apr. 1
Applicants should submit the following:
1) Class rank
2) Transcripts
3) Essay
4) ACT
5) Financial information
EIN: 426336481

3720
Bertha P. Singer Student Nurses Fund
c/o U.S. Bank, N.A.
P.O. Box 3168
Portland, OR 97208
Application address: c/o Oregon Student
Assistance Commission, 1500 Valley Dr., Ste. 100,
Eugene, OR 97401

Foundation type: Independent foundation
Limitations: Scholarships to financially needy
graduates of OR high schools and residents of OR
who have been accepted at accredited OR graduate
or undergraduate nursing programs.
Financial data: Year ended 06/30/2005.
Assets, $478,872 (M); Expenditures, $32,261;
Total giving, $23,000.
Fields of interest: Nursing school/education.
Type of support: Graduate support; Undergraduate
support.
Application information: Applications accepted Jan
1. to Mar. 15; Completion of formal application
required, including transcripts, SAT scores, GPA,
FAFSA, and proof of acceptance to a nursing
program; Applications available from high schools,
college financial aid offices, and the OR State
Scholarship Commission; Interviews required for
finalists.
Program description:
Scholarship Program: Applicants selected for
interviews must supply a Student Aid Report (SAR)
and their financial aid award letter to the
committee. Students are interviewed in June at the
U.S. Bank Trust Dept. in Portland, OR. Conference
calls are accepted in lieu of personal appearances.
Generally, 25 scholarships, ranging from $300 to
$1,500 are awarded each year. Applicants must
maintain at least a 3.0 GPA. Scholarships are
renewable.
EIN: 510181219

3721
Single Parent Scholarship Fund of Washington County, Inc.
(formerly Arkansas Single Parent Scholarship Fund,
Inc.)
614 E. Emma St., Ste. 103
Springdale, AR 72764 (479) 750-4971
Contact: Jean Kebis, Exec. Dir.

Foundation type: Public charity
Limitations: Scholarships to single parents who are
residents of Washington County, AR.
Financial data: Year ended 12/31/2004.
Assets, $533,655 (M); Expenditures, $260,698;
Total giving, $135,600; Grants to individuals,
totaling $135,600.
Fields of interest: Single parents.
Type of support: Technical education support;
Undergraduate support.
Application information: Application form required.
Initial approach: Letter.
Deadline(s): Mar. 15, June 15 and Oct. 15
Applicants should submit the following:
1) Transcripts
2) Letter(s) of recommendation
3) Financial information
EIN: 680498770

3722
M. E. Singleton Scholarship Trust
P.O. Box 717
Waxahachie, TX 75168
Contact: George H. Singleton, Pres.

Foundation type: Independent foundation

Limitations: Scholarships to financially needy
students who graduate from high schools in Ellis
County, TX.
Financial data: Year ended 07/31/2005.
Assets, $2,324,510 (M); Expenditures,
$126,065; Total giving, $118,800; Grants to
individuals, 62 grants totaling $118,800 (high:
$2,000, low: $400).
Type of support: Support to graduates or students
of specific schools; Undergraduate support.
Application information: Applications accepted.
Application form required.
Initial approach: Letter requesting application.
Deadline(s): None
Program description:
Scholarship Program: Students are
recommended for scholarship assistance by the
principals of Ellis County high schools. The board
chooses applicants with the greatest financial
need.
EIN: 756037399

3723
Sioux Falls Area Community Foundation
300 N. Phillips Ave., Ste. 102
Sioux Falls, SD 57104-6035 (605) 336-7055
Contact: Candy Hanson, C.E.O. and Pres.; For
grants: Patrick Gale
FAX: (605) 336-0038; E-mail: chanson@sfacf.org;
URL: http://www.sfacf.org

Foundation type: Community foundation
Limitations: Scholarships primarily to students
from the Sioux Falls, SD, area, and secondarily to
northwest IA, and southeast MN area residents to
attend postsecondary schools. Some funding is
provided to employees of Citibank (SD) NA/Dakota
King for emergency assistance.
Publications: Application guidelines; Annual report
(including application guidelines); Financial
statement; Grants list; Informational brochure;
Informational brochure (including application
guidelines); Newsletter.
Financial data: Year ended 06/30/2005.
Assets, $48,728,191 (M); Expenditures,
$6,529,700; Total giving, $5,803,788; Grants to
individuals, 20 grants totaling $19,000 (high:
$3,000, low: $200).
Fields of interest: Vocational education; Natural
resources; Athletics/sports, training; Business/
industry; Christian agencies & churches; Protestant
agencies & churches; Native Americans/American
Indians; Norway.
Type of support: Support to graduates or students
of specific schools; Awards/prizes;
Employee-related welfare; Graduate support;
Technical education support; Undergraduate
support.
Application information: Application form required.
Initial approach: Contacting college financial aid
office or high school counselor's office.
Copies of proposal: 1
Deadline(s): Varies
Additional information: Applications should be
sent by mail.
EIN: 311748533

3724
Siouxland Community Foundation
(formerly Siouxland Foundation)
505 5th St., Ste. 412
Sioux City, IA 51101-1507
Contact: Debbie Hubbard, Exec. Dir.
E-mail: office@siouxlandcommunityfoundation.org;
Tel./Fax: (712) 293-3303; URL: http://
www.siouxlandcommunityfoundation.org

Foundation type: Community foundation
Limitations: Scholarships to graduating seniors
who attend high school within a 50-mile tri-state
radius of Sioux City, IA.
Publications: Application guidelines; Annual report
(including application guidelines); Informational
brochure (including application guidelines);
Newsletter.
Financial data: Year ended 12/31/2004.
Assets, $5,910,698 (M); Expenditures,
$348,272; Total giving, $212,392; Grants to
individuals, 25 grants totaling $26,895 (high:
$12,000).
Type of support: Scholarships—to individuals.
Application information: Application form required.
Application form available on the grantmaker's Web
site.
Initial approach: Letter or telephone.
Copies of proposal: 1
Deadline(s): Feb. 15
Applicants should submit the following:
1) Transcripts
2) Resume
3) Letter(s) of recommendation
4) GPA
5) Essay
6) ACT
EIN: 421323904

3725
Bedford W. Sipes Memorial Student Loan Fund
c/o Wells Fargo Bank Texas, N.A.
P.O. Box 41629
Austin, TX 78704
Contact: Lauren Ranly, Trust Off., Wells Fargo Bank,
N.A.

Foundation type: Independent foundation
Limitations: Student loans to students and
graduates of Sinton High School, TX, for higher
learning at TX institutions.
Financial data: Year ended 02/28/2005.
Assets, $269,214 (M); Expenditures, $22,661;
Total giving, $13,000; Loans to individuals, 6 loans
totaling $13,000.
Type of support: Support to graduates or students
of specific schools; Undergraduate support.
Application information: Applications accepted.
Application form required.
Initial approach: Letter outlining financial need.
Deadline(s): None
EIN: 746321954

3726
Clara Lou Vena Siros Foundation
c/o Laredo National Bank, Trust Dept.
P.O. Box 59
Laredo, TX 78042-0059 (956) 723-1151

Foundation type: Independent foundation
Limitations: Scholarships to financially needy
students at Laredo Community College, TX, who
reside in either Webb County or Laredo, TX.
Applicants with family incomes above $60,000 will
not be considered.

Financial data: Year ended 12/31/2004. Assets, $867,739 (M); Expenditures, $63,355; Total giving, $50,000; Grants to individuals, 73 grants totaling $50,000.
Type of support: Support to graduates or students of specific schools; Undergraduate support.
Application information: Application form required.
Initial approach: Letter or telephone.
Deadline(s): Apr. 27
Applicants should submit the following:
1) Letter(s) of recommendation
2) Transcripts
Additional information: Application must also include photograph, parents' and student's tax returns, and copy of financial aid award letter.
EIN: 742574458

3727
Sitnasuak Foundation
c/o Board of Directors
P.O. Box 905
Nome, AK 99762

Foundation type: Independent foundation
Limitations: Scholarships, stipends, grants, student aid, and other means of support to students for educational training at colleges and other institutions.
Financial data: Year ended 12/31/2004. Assets, $10,634 (M); Expenditures, $15,778; Total giving, $12,355.
Type of support: Scholarships—to individuals.
Application information: Applications by letter accepted throughout the year.
EIN: 920148088

3728
Ida M. Sivyer Trust for Boys Trade Technical High School
c/o Stephen Knox, U.S. Bank, N.A.
P.O. Box 3194, MK-WI-TWPT
Milwaukee, WI 53201-2043

Foundation type: Independent foundation
Limitations: Scholarships by nomination only to students at Milwaukee Technical High School, WI.
Financial data: Year ended 06/30/2005. Assets, $256,311 (M); Expenditures, $13,032; Total giving, $10,360; Grants to individuals, 5 grants totaling $10,360.
Type of support: Support to graduates or students of specific schools; Awards/grants by nomination only; Undergraduate support.
Application information: Applications not accepted.
EIN: 396035625

3729
Joan Skahan Memorial Fund
c/o NBT Bank, N.A.
52 S. Broad St.
Norwich, NY 13815-6073

Foundation type: Independent foundation
Limitations: Scholarships by nomination only to graduating seniors at Whitesboro Senior High School, NY.
Financial data: Year ended 10/31/2004. Assets, $55,207 (M); Expenditures, $2,700; Total giving, $2,300.
Type of support: Support to graduates or students of specific schools; Awards/grants by nomination only; Undergraduate support.

Application information: Application form required.
Deadline(s): Mid-May for faculty nominations
Additional information: Faculty reviews school records of all graduating seniors and selects them to be nominated; Another committee selects the recipients; Applications obtained through school.
EIN: 166238801

3730
Skandalaris Family Foundation
P.O. Box 2061
Venice, FL 34284   (941) 544-8659
FAX: (941) 408-9526;
E-mail: info@skandalaris.com; Application address for Future Leaders Merit Scholarship: 33 Bloomfield Hills Pkwy., Ste. 240, Bloomfield Hills, MI 48304;
URL: http://www.skandalaris.com

Foundation type: Independent foundation
Limitations: Scholarships to individuals, primarily in FL, MI and NY, for higher education.
Financial data: Year ended 12/31/2004. Assets, $23,374 (M); Expenditures, $211,575; Total giving, $175,000; Grants to individuals, 86 grants totaling $175,000 (high: $2,500, low: $2,000).
Type of support: Undergraduate support.
Application information: Contact foundation or see Web site for current application deadline/guidelines.
EIN: 383394567

3731
SKB Foundation
1247 Elko Dr.
Sunnyvale, CA 94089-2211
Contact: Ho-Tzu Yen, Pres.; Yung-Tsai Yen, Secy.

Foundation type: Independent foundation
Limitations: Student loans to individuals of Taiwanese or Chinese origin residing in the CA Bay Area for undergraduate education.
Financial data: Year ended 11/30/2004. Assets, $6,373,653 (M); Expenditures, $196,967; Total giving, $152,150; Loans to individuals, 10 loans totaling $31,235.
Fields of interest: Asians/Pacific Islanders; China; Taiwan.
Type of support: Student loans—to individuals; Undergraduate support.
Application information: Applications by letter accepted throughout the year.
EIN: 943024121

3732
Homer Skelton Charitable Foundation
4225 State Line Rd.
Olive Branch, MS 38654-7087
Contact: Homer D. Skelton, Tr.

Foundation type: Independent foundation
Limitations: Scholarships to individuals, primarily in TN, for higher education.
Financial data: Year ended 12/31/2004. Assets, $2,210,856 (M); Expenditures, $1,059,423; Total giving, $1,058,223; Grants to individuals, 16 grants totaling $62,140 (high: $13,528, low: $35).
Fields of interest: Higher education.
Type of support: Scholarships—to individuals.
Application information: Applications accepted.
Initial approach: Letter.
EIN: 621578268

3733
Skelton Scholarship Fund
(formerly Ila M. Skelton Trust Fund)
c/o JPMorgan Chase Bank, N.A.
P.O. Box 1308
Milwaukee, WI 53201-1308

Foundation type: Independent foundation
Limitations: Scholarships to residents for attendance at one of IL colleges or universities.
Financial data: Year ended 07/31/2005. Assets, $333,573 (M); Expenditures, $20,478; Total giving, $15,100; Grants to individuals, 13 grants totaling $15,100 (high: $1,500, low: $900).
Type of support: Scholarships—to individuals.
Application information: Applications not accepted.
Additional information: Unsolicited requests for funds not considered or acknowledged.
EIN: 371297171

3734
The Thomas J. Skeuse and Rita T. Skeuse Scholarship Fund, Inc.
115 Rte. 202-31 S.
Ringoes, NJ 08551

Foundation type: Company-sponsored foundation
Limitations: Scholarships to employees of Reagent and Chemical Research, Inc., NJ.
Financial data: Year ended 12/31/2004. Assets, $343 (M); Expenditures, $11,353; Total giving, $11,186; Grants to individuals, 7 grants totaling $11,186 (high: $2,500, low: $1,250).
Type of support: Employee-related scholarships.
Application information: Unsolicited requests for funds not considered or acknowledged.
EIN: 223741423

3735
Chris A. Skillman Scholarship Fund
P.O. Box 380
Platte City, MO 64079
Contact: John W. Coots, Jr., Tr.
Application address: P.O. Box 368, Platte City, MO 64079, tel.: (816) 858-2121

Foundation type: Independent foundation
Limitations: Student loans to deserving and needy students of Platte County, MO.
Financial data: Year ended 12/31/2004. Assets, $588,046 (M); Expenditures, $34,832; Total giving, $33,524; Loans to individuals, 14 loans totaling $33,524.
Type of support: Student loans—to individuals.
Application information: Applications accepted throughout the year; Initial approach by letter; Completion of formal application required, including resume.
EIN: 436188683

3736
Frank Foster Skillman Scholarship
c/o PNC Advisors
620 Liberty Ave., PTTP-10-2
Pittsburgh, PA 15222-2705
Contact: James D. Huizenga, Trust Off., PNC Advisors

Foundation type: Independent foundation
Limitations: Scholarships to full-time students who are residents of Cincinnati, OH.
Financial data: Year ended 09/30/2004. Assets, $523,929 (M); Expenditures, $21,236;

Total giving, $6,916; Grants to individuals, totaling $6,916.
Type of support: Scholarships—to individuals.
Application information: Deadline May 15; Completion of formal application required.
EIN: 316018084

3737
SLA Foundation
c/o John G. Wethey
1575 Vine St.
Denver, CO   80206-1309   (303) 331-9399

Foundation type: Independent foundation
Limitations: Scholarships to full-time students who are CO high school graduates, majoring in business education or a related subject at accredited colleges and universities in CO.
Financial data: Year ended 12/31/2004. Assets, $712,752 (M); Expenditures, $42,652; Total giving, $38,000; Grants to individuals, 30 grants totaling $38,000 (high: $2,500, low: $1,000).
Fields of interest: Business school/education; Computer science.
Type of support: Scholarships—to individuals.
Application information:
Initial approach: Letter including college name and address.
Deadline(s): Apr. 21
Applicants should submit the following:
1) Class rank
2) Transcripts
3) GPA
4) Resume
5) Letter(s) of recommendation
Additional information: Application must also include college name and address, major field of study, high school information, personal information, and work history.
Program description:
Scholarship Program: Acceptable majors include accounting, actuarial science, business, computer science, finance, insurance, and other such fields. Applicants must have a minimum GPA of 2.5 to be eligible.
EIN: 841329138

3738
The Slemp Foundation
c/o U.S. Bank, N.A., Trust Tax Dept.
P.O. Box 1118, ML CN-OH-W10X
Cincinnati, OH   45201-1118
Grant and scholarship application address: c/o Patricia L. Durbin, Tr. Off., U.S. Bank, N.A., P.O. Box 5208, ML CN-OH-W7PT, Cincinnati, OH 45201-5208; URL: http://www.slempfoundation.org

Foundation type: Independent foundation
Limitations: Undergraduate scholarships limited to individuals residing in Lee and Wise counties, VA, or to individuals who are descendants of residents.
Publications: Application guidelines.
Financial data: Year ended 06/30/2005. Assets, $20,159,044 (M); Expenditures, $1,125,021; Total giving, $976,382; Grants to individuals, 244 grants totaling $244,000 (high: $1,000, low: $1,000).
Type of support: Undergraduate support.
Application information: Applications accepted. Application form required.
Initial approach: Letter.
Program description:
Scholarship Program: Approximately 25 new college scholarships are granted each year to

qualified individuals. Applications should be made during student's senior year in high school.
EIN: 316025080

3739
V. M. Slipher Testamentary Trust
c/o JPMorgan Chase Bank, N.A
P.O. Box 1308
Milwaukee, WI   53201
Application addresses: c/o University of Arizona, Head of Science Dept., Tucson, AZ 85721, c/o Arizona State University, Head of Science Dept., Tempe, AZ 85287, or c/o Northern Arizona University, Head of Science Dept., S. San Francisco St. Flagstaff, AZ 86011

Foundation type: Independent foundation
Limitations: Scholarships to third- and fourth-year physics and astronomy undergraduates who are recommended by their department heads and attend Northern Arizona University, Arizona State University, or the University of Arizona.
Financial data: Year ended 12/31/2004. Assets, $594,366 (M); Expenditures, $14,996; Total giving, $8,000; Grants to individuals, totaling $8,000.
Fields of interest: Science; Physics.
Type of support: Support to graduates or students of specific schools; Awards/grants by nomination only; Undergraduate support.
Application information: Applications not accepted.
Additional information: Contact scholarship office of one of the three participating universities listed above for nomination guidelines.
EIN: 866065266

3740
Slippery Rock University Foundation, Inc.
(formerly Slippery Rock Foundation, Inc.)
P.O. Box 233
Slippery Rock, PA   16057-0233
(724) 738-2047
Contact: Edward R. Bucha, Exec. Dir.

Foundation type: Public charity
Limitations: Scholarships to students at Slippery Rock University, PA.
Financial data: Year ended 06/30/2003. Assets, $15,026,554 (M); Expenditures, $5,475,696; Total giving, $1,122,769; Grants to individuals, 1,475 grants totaling $1,122,769 (high: $10,946, low: $7).
Type of support: Support to graduates or students of specific schools; Graduate support; Undergraduate support.
Application information: Deadline Feb. 15; Application by letter.
Program description:
Scholarship Program: Scholarships eligibility is based on diverse criteria, including academic scores, talent, place of residence and/or major. Eligibility criteria is specific to each scholarship.
EIN: 237093388

3741
O. Temple Sloan, Jr. Foundation
P.O. Box 26006
Raleigh, NC   27611   (919) 573-3211
Contact: Carol Sloan, Tr.
Additional tel.: (919) 573-3000

Foundation type: Independent foundation

Limitations: Scholarships and loans to graduating high school seniors, primarily in MT and NC, for higher education.
Financial data: Year ended 12/31/2003. Assets, $31,760 (M); Expenditures, $277,963; Total giving, $267,842; Grants to individuals, 12 grants totaling $73,652 (high: $20,862, low: $1,500).
Type of support: Undergraduate support.
Application information: Applications accepted throughout the year; Completion of formal application required, including references; Interviews required.
EIN: 561870844

3742
Slowinski Charitable Foundation
(also known as Slowinski Estate Fund Trust)
c/o Bank of America, N.A.
P.O. Box 6768
Providence, RI   02940-6768
Scholarship application address: c/o Bank of America, N.A., Attn.: Marjorie A. Davis, Trust Off., 777 Main St., CT2-102-22-02, Hartford, CT 06115, tel.: (860) 986-7696

Foundation type: Independent foundation
Limitations: Scholarships to females attending Columbia University, NY, who have completed their third year of study.
Financial data: Year ended 12/31/2004. Assets, $210,960 (M); Expenditures, $16,118; Total giving, $12,000; Grant to an individual, 1 grant totaling $12,000.
Type of support: Support to graduates or students of specific schools.
Application information: Applications accepted. Application form required.
Initial approach: Letter.
Deadline(s): None
EIN: 066314132

3743
SMACNA College of Fellows Foundation
c/o J. Robert Roach
P.O. Box 221230
Chantilly, VA   20151-1230   (703) 803-2980

Foundation type: Independent foundation
Limitations: Scholarships to children of the owners and employees of SMACNA firms who are pursuing studies related to the sheet metal industry at an accredited U.S. college or university.
Financial data: Year ended 12/31/2004. Assets, $328,244 (M); Expenditures, $28,850; Total giving, $28,800; Grants to individuals, 16 grants totaling $28,800.
Fields of interest: Engineering/technology.
Type of support: Employee-related scholarships.
Application information: Deadline Apr. 30; Completion of formal application required.
EIN: 521538775

3744
Smalley Foundation, Inc.
P.O. Box 1385
Brookline, MA   02445
Contact: Ellin Smalley, Pres.

Foundation type: Independent foundation
Limitations: Scholarships to public high school graduates from Worcester, MA, and Yonkers, NY, who have been accepted to institutions where the foundation has established scholarships.

Financial data: Year ended 12/31/2003. Assets, $1,090,992 (M); Expenditures, $150,208; Total giving, $110,000; Grants to individuals, totaling $110,000.
Type of support: Support to graduates or students of specific schools; Undergraduate support.
Application information: Contact schools for current application deadline; Completion of formal application required.
EIN: 136225947

3745
Smallwood Scholarship Foundation
812 Main Ave. N.
Twin Falls, ID 83301-5742
Contact: Kendal F. Egbert, Tr.

Foundation type: Independent foundation
Limitations: Scholarships to graduates of Twin Falls County high schools, ID, for higher education.
Financial data: Year ended 12/31/2004. Assets, $265,488 (M); Expenditures, $9,884; Total giving, $3,750; Grants to individuals, 5 grants totaling $3,750.
Type of support: Support to graduates or students of specific schools; Undergraduate support.
Application information: Deadline Jan. 1 to Apr. 1; Completion of formal application required.
Program description:
 Scholarship Program: Recipients must be residents of Twin Falls, ID. Scholarships are limited to cost of books, tuition and supplies.
EIN: 820504275

3746
Hazel Dell Neff Smelser Scholarship Fund
c/o 1st Source Bank, Trust Dept.
1 1st Source Ctr.
South Bend, IN 46601

Foundation type: Independent foundation
Limitations: Scholarships to high school graduates of Marshall or St. Joseph counties, IN, for music study.
Financial data: Year ended 12/31/2004. Assets, $563,339 (M); Expenditures, $52,915; Total giving, $44,900; Grants to individuals, 18 grants totaling $44,900.
Fields of interest: Performing arts, education.
Type of support: Support to graduates or students of specific schools; Undergraduate support.
Application information: Deadline Apr. 11 for summer study, Jan. 15 for regular study; Completion of formal application required, including brief personal statement, three letters of recommendation from a music instructor, a teacher, and a community member, transcripts, PSAT or SAT results, photograph, and financial information; Interviews and auditions required.
Program description:
 Scholarship Program: Scholarships are awarded for the study of voice, piano, organ, orchestral string instruments, or other recognized musical instruments. Recipients are determined by academic record, financial need, musical ability, and character. Awards are available to graduating seniors, or students involved in college or university musical training and private study. The scholarship may be renewed by the committee dependent upon available funds, the student's academic record, and evidence of progress in development of student's talent.
EIN: 310884462

3747
Smick Memorial Loan Fund
(formerly Citizens Scholarship Foundation)
P.O. Box 263
Oberlin, KS 67749-0263
Contact: Ken Shobe, Treas.

Foundation type: Independent foundation
Limitations: Interest-free loans to students graduating from high schools in Decatur County, KS, to attend colleges or other approved postsecondary schools.
Financial data: Year ended 12/31/2004. Assets, $162,415 (M); Expenditures, $387; Total giving, $0; Loans to individuals, totaling $18,775.
Type of support: Support to graduates or students of specific schools; Undergraduate support.
Application information: Deadline July 1; Initial approach by letter; Completion of formal application required.
EIN: 237121059

3748
Jean and Verne Smith Charitable Trust
119 Peachtree Dr.
Greer, SC 29651
Contact: Carole S. Olmert, Tr.

Foundation type: Independent foundation
Limitations: Scholarships to individuals for higher education.
Financial data: Year ended 12/31/2004. Assets, $531,842 (M); Expenditures, $137,320; Total giving, $134,500; Grants to individuals, 9 grants totaling $34,500 (high: $11,000; low: $500).
Type of support: Undergraduate support.
Application information: Applications accepted throughout the year; Initial approach by letter or telephone; Completion of formal application required, including personal and financial need information, educational background, work experience, extracurricular activities, desire for education and career goals, and basis of worthiness and scholarship.
EIN: 586404187

3749
William Harold Smith Charitable Trust
1105 Airport Rd.
Marion, NC 28752
Contact: Matt Smith, Tr.

Foundation type: Independent foundation
Limitations: Scholarships to financially needy graduates of McDowell High School, NC.
Financial data: Year ended 12/31/2004. Assets, $4,598,281 (M); Expenditures, $224,977; Total giving, $210,475; Grants to individuals, 80 grants totaling $210,475 (high: $6,000, low: $200).
Type of support: Support to graduates or students of specific schools; Undergraduate support.
Application information:
 Deadline(s): Mar. 15
 Additional information: Completion of formal application required, including two recommendations, (one from school personnel and one from a member of the community), personal essay, list of extracurricular activities, copy of parents' and student's tax returns; Applications can be obtained from high school guidance counselors.
EIN: 566526359

3750
Jennie Smith Education Fund
(formerly Smith Educational Fund)
c/o Bank of America, N.A.
P.O. Box 1802
Providence, RI 02940-1802
Application address: c/o South Hadley School District, Attn: Superintendent, 116 Main St., South Hadley, MA 01075

Foundation type: Independent foundation
Limitations: Scholarships to residents of South Hadley, MA.
Financial data: Year ended 12/31/2004. Assets, $456,133 (M); Expenditures, $21,640; Total giving, $18,375; Grants to individuals, 23 grants totaling $18,375.
Type of support: Scholarships—to individuals.
Application information: Deadline June 10; Completion of formal application required.
EIN: 046033742

3751
Charles C. Smith Educational Foundation
P.O. Box 310
Washington, NJ 07882-0310
Contact: Lori Fitzgibbon, Secy.-Treas.
Application address: 12 Perry Ln., Ridgefield, CT 06877

Foundation type: Independent foundation
Limitations: Scholarships to high school seniors in the Washington and North Hunterdon, NJ, areas.
Financial data: Year ended 10/31/2004. Assets, $301,223 (M); Expenditures, $24,713; Total giving, $24,000; Grants to individuals, 10 grants totaling $24,000.
Type of support: Undergraduate support.
Application information: Deadline Apr. 1; Completion of formal application required.
EIN: 222186867

3752
Smith Educational Memorial Fund
(also known as Earl E. & Marie M. Smith Educational Memorial Fund)
c/o National City Bank
P.O. Box 94651
Cleveland, OH 44101-4651
Application address: c/o National City Bank of Indiana, Attn.: Denise Andorfer, P.O. Box 110, Fort Wayne, IN 46802, tel.: (260) 461-6218

Foundation type: Independent foundation
Limitations: Educational loans to residents of Kosciusko County, IN, only, with preference given to applicants in the fields of medicine, nursing, and related clinical pursuits.
Financial data: Year ended 12/31/2004. Assets, $168,684 (M); Expenditures, $7,453; Total giving, $0; Loans to individuals, totaling $10,000.
Fields of interest: Medical school/education; Nursing school/education.
Type of support: Student loans—to individuals.
Application information: Applications accepted throughout the year; Completion of formal application required.
Program description:
 Loan Program: Candidates must have been accepted for enrollment at an eligible school and furnish a high school transcript to trustees. After training is complete, the recipient has four months to arrange for repayment. Loans are interest-free up to this time. During the repayment period, loan recipients pay a simple rate of interest with a

minimum monthly payment of $25. Recipients have ten years from the beginning of repayment to complete repayment of the loan.
EIN: 510174338

3753
The McGregor & Elizabeth Wilson Smith Foundation, Inc.

(formerly The McGregor Smith Foundation)
200 S. Biscayne Blvd., 40th Fl.
Miami, FL 33131-2310 (305) 667-4952
Contact: Wilson Smith, Pres.

Foundation type: Independent foundation
Limitations: Scholarships and loans to individuals for higher education in Dade County, FL.
Financial data: Year ended 12/31/2004.
Assets, $1,609,802 (M); Expenditures, $97,718; Total giving, $71,206; Grants to individuals, 10 grants totaling $48,007.
Type of support: Scholarships—to individuals; Student loans—to individuals.
Application information: Application form required.
  Initial approach: Letter.
  Deadline(s): Aug. 1.
  Applicants should submit the following:
    1) Letter(s) of recommendation
    2) Transcripts
    3) Financial information
EIN: 591038572

3754
Jean M. R. Smith Foundation

c/o Robert A. Sajdak
1200 Earhart Rd., No. 506
Ann Arbor, MI 48105-2768 (734) 663-4385
Contact: Edward J. Moore, Treas.
Application address: 64 Westland Dr., Bad Axe, MI 48413, tel.: (989) 269-9909

Foundation type: Independent foundation
Limitations: Scholarships primarily to graduating students attending Huron County, MI, high schools.
Financial data: Year ended 12/31/2004.
Assets, $1,139,348 (M); Expenditures, $45,628; Total giving, $30,977; Grants to individuals, 11 grants totaling $30,977 (high: $5,000, low: $1,000).
Type of support: Support to graduates or students of specific schools; Undergraduate support.
Application information: Contact foundation for current application deadline/guidelines; Applicants should submit academic records and two letters of reference.
EIN: 383323030

3755
Marguerite Carl Smith Foundation

c/o Wachovia Bank, N.A.
100 N. Main St., 13th Fl.
Winston-Salem, NC 27150

Foundation type: Independent foundation
Limitations: Scholarships to financially needy graduates of Jersey Shore area school district, PA.
Financial data: Year ended 05/31/2005.
Assets, $2,576,544 (M); Expenditures, $150,449; Total giving, $123,000; Grants to individuals, 43 grants totaling $107,500 (high: $2,500, low: $2,500).
Type of support: Support to graduates or students of specific schools; Undergraduate support.

Application information: Contact foundation for current application deadline/guidelines; Initial approach by letter or telephone.
EIN: 232564406

3756
William & Anna Smith Foundation

(also known as W. F. & Anna Smith Foundation)
c/o KeyBank N.A.
800 Superior Ave., 4th Fl.
Cleveland, OH 44114

Foundation type: Independent foundation
Limitations: Scholarships to residents of the Wendover, UT, area.
Financial data: Year ended 12/31/2004.
Assets, $626,576 (M); Expenditures, $108,128; Total giving, $101,750; Grants to individuals, 10 grants totaling $26,750 (high: $4,000, low: $1,500).
Type of support: Scholarships—to individuals.
Application information: Applications by letter, outlining financial need, accepted throughout the year.
EIN: 942728399

3757
Horace Smith Fund

1441 Main St., 8th Fl.
P.O. Box 3034
Springfield, MA 01103 (413) 739-4222
Contact: Benjamin Bump, Exec. Secy.

Foundation type: Independent foundation
Limitations: Scholarships and fellowships to financially needy residents and secondary school graduates of Hampden County, MA.
Financial data: Year ended 03/31/2005.
Assets, $6,879,378 (M); Expenditures, $426,529; Total giving, $277,110; Grants to individuals, totaling $277,110.
Fields of interest: Education.
Type of support: Fellowships; Undergraduate support.
Application information: Application form required.
  Deadline(s): Jan. 10 for scholarships; Feb. 1 for fellowships
  Additional information: Applications available after Sept. 1 for fellowships; See program description for further information.
Program descriptions:
  Walter S. Barr Scholarships: Awarded to seniors in secondary schools in Hampden County, MA, for undergraduate education. Application forms are available in the guidance offices of these schools. Recipients are selected on the basis of school records, college entrance exams, general attainment, and financial need. Scholarships are renewable for up to four years.
  Walter S. Barr Fellowships: Awarded to Hampden County residents for full-time graduate study and are determined on the basis of scholastic record and financial need. Applicants must include high school and college transcripts, parents' or student's financial statement, and three reference forms, at least two of which must be from college professors. All materials should be addressed to the Barr Fellowship Committee, care of the Horace Smith Fund. Applicants must also arrange for their GRE scores or appropriate professional school test scores (e.g. MCAT, LSAT) to be sent by the Educational Testing Service to the fund. The ETS code for Barr Fellowships is 0017. Recipients will be notified by Apr. 15.
EIN: 042235130

3758
Everett Smith Group Foundation, Ltd.

(formerly Maysteel Foundation, Ltd.)
800 N. Marshall St.
Milwaukee, WI 53202-3911 (414) 273-3421
Contact: Elizabeth H. Perry, Pres.

Foundation type: Independent foundation
Limitations: Undergraduate scholarships to children of employees of Maysteel Corporation.
Financial data: Year ended 11/30/2004.
Assets, $60,724 (M); Expenditures, $186,310; Total giving, $185,250; Grants to individuals, 6 grants totaling $8,750 (high: $2,500, low: $1,250).
Type of support: Employee-related scholarships; Undergraduate support.
Application information: Contact foundation for current application deadline; Completion of formal application required.
EIN: 391480641

3759
Arthur Albert Smith Memorial Fund

c/o KeyBank N.A.
800 Superior Ave. E, 4th Fl.
Cleveland, OH 44114-2601
Application address: Mrs. Brown, c/o KeyBank N.A., P.O. Box 1054, Augusta, ME 04332-1054

Foundation type: Independent foundation
Limitations: Scholarships to male graduates of Freeport High School, ME.
Financial data: Year ended 08/31/2004.
Assets, $263,847 (M); Expenditures, $7,845; Total giving, $3,740; Grants to individuals, totaling $3,740.
Fields of interest: Men.
Type of support: Support to graduates or students of specific schools; Undergraduate support.
Application information: Applications accepted.
  Initial approach: Letter.
  Deadline(s): None
  Additional information: Contact fund for current application guidelines.
EIN: 016079294

3760
Mace C. & Dee Smith Memorial Scholarship Fund

c/o Wood & Huston Bank
P.O. Box 40
Marshall, MO 65340 (660) 886-6825

Foundation type: Independent foundation
Limitations: Scholarships to graduates of Sweet Springs High School, MO.
Financial data: Year ended 12/31/2004.
Assets, $310,081 (M); Expenditures, $15,674; Total giving, $11,516; Grants to individuals, 11 grants totaling $11,516.
Type of support: Support to graduates or students of specific schools; Undergraduate support.
Application information: Contact foundation for current application deadline; Initial approach by letter; Completion of formal application required.
EIN: 436455069

3761
Norman W. Smith Revolving Loan Trust

c/o The Huntington National Bank
P.O. Box 633, WE3013
Charleston, WV 25322-0633
Contact: Carla Parsons, Trust Admin.

Foundation type: Independent foundation
Limitations: Student loans to residents of Berkeley County, WV, for study at an accredited seminary or medical school.
Publications: Application guidelines; Informational brochure (including application guidelines).
Financial data: Year ended 12/31/2004. Assets, $1,012,244 (M); Expenditures, $69,690; Total giving, $58,000; Grants to individuals, totaling $58,000.
Fields of interest: Medical school/education; Theological school/education.
Type of support: Student loans—to individuals.
Application information: Application form not required.
   Deadline(s): None
   Additional information: Applications by letter, including proof of school attendance and evidence of residence.
Program description:
   Scholarship Program: Recipients will begin to pay back the loan, with interest, one year after graduation or one year after student ceases full-time enrollment.
EIN: 556084952

3762
Gerald F. Smith Scholarship Foundation
P.O. Box 3588
Winchester, VA   22604-2586

Foundation type: Independent foundation
Limitations: Scholarships to residents of PA, VA, and VT.
Financial data: Year ended 12/31/2004. Assets, $4,007 (M); Expenditures, $31,331; Total giving, $30,000; Grants to individuals, 6 grants totaling $30,000.
Type of support: Scholarships—to individuals.
Application information: Applications not accepted.
EIN: 541725608

3763
Ellen V. and Robert H. Smith Scholarship Fund
c/o Bank of America, N.A.
P.O. Box 1802
Providence, RI   02901-1802
Contact: Beth Kernan, Trust Admin., Bank of America, N.A.
Application address: c/o The Smith Scholarship Selection Committee, P.O. Box 2483, East Side Sta., Providence, RI 02906

Foundation type: Independent foundation
Limitations: Scholarships to residents of South Kingston, RI, who are between the ages of 15 and 23 years, to attend programs at accredited colleges, universities, and graduate professional schools leading to a bachelor's degree or doctorate. Scholarships are awarded on the basis of need, and are renewable.
Financial data: Year ended 12/31/2004. Assets, $1,774,202 (M); Expenditures, $91,405; Total giving, $76,003; Grants to individuals, 37 grants totaling $76,003.
Type of support: Graduate support; Undergraduate support.
Application information: Application form required.
   Deadline(s): Dec. 15 for preliminary application and Feb. 15 for biographical questionnaire and secondary school report or college transcript.
   Applicants should submit the following:

1) FAF
2) SAT
EIN: 056069745

3764
J. A. & Flossie Mae Smith Scholarship Fund
c/o U.S. National Bank, Trust Dept.
P.O. Box 1335
Rancho Santa Fe, CA   92067-1335
(858) 756-4884
Contact: R.D. Taramasco, Tr.
Application address: c/o Curtis Darling, P.O. Box 2411, Bakersfield, CA 93303, tel.: (661) 325-5075

Foundation type: Independent foundation
Limitations: Scholarships to graduate and undergraduate students who demonstrate academic ability and financial need and who intend to pursue a full-time academic program, with emphasis on agriculture at an accredited, tax-exempt CA college.
Financial data: Year ended 12/31/2004. Assets, $335,673 (M); Expenditures, $16,625; Total giving, $13,500; Grants to individuals, totaling $13,500.
Fields of interest: Agriculture.
Type of support: Graduate support; Undergraduate support.
Application information: Applications accepted. Application form required.
   Deadline(s): None
   Additional information: Interviews required.
Program description:
   Scholarship Program: Scholarships are to help cover the costs of tuition, books, and living expenses. Scholarships are limited to $2,500 per student, per year, and are renewable for up to six years.
EIN: 956432440

3765
Kathleen A. Smith Scholarship Fund
c/o Wachovia Bank, N.A.
100 N. Main St., 13th Fl.
Winston-Salem, NC   27150

Foundation type: Independent foundation
Limitations: Scholarships to graduates of Warren Hills Regional Senior High School, NJ, for higher education.
Financial data: Year ended 03/31/2005. Assets, $273,556 (M); Expenditures, $15,509; Total giving, $10,313.
Type of support: Support to graduates or students of specific schools; Undergraduate support.
Application information: Applications not accepted.
EIN: 237773022

3766
Elmer Smith Scholarship Trust
c/o Bank of America, N.A.
P.O. Box 6768
Providence, RI   02940-6767

Foundation type: Independent foundation
Limitations: Scholarships to students at Cape May County and Holy Spirit high schools, NJ.
Financial data: Year ended 12/31/2004. Assets, $688,253 (M); Expenditures, $30,131; Total giving, $23,000; Grants to individuals, 30 grants totaling $23,000.

Type of support: Support to graduates or students of specific schools; Undergraduate support.
Application information: Deadline May 1; Completion of formal application required; Applications available from high schools.
EIN: 226213088

3767
Zella M. Smith Scholarship Trust
c/o Bank of America, N.A.
P.O. Box 513189, GMF
Los Angeles, CA   90051-1189
Application address: c/o Fallbrook Union High School District, Attn: Gayle Olsen, Dir. of Student Svcs., 2234 South Stage Coach Ln., Fallbrook, CA 92028, tel.: (760) 723-6402

Foundation type: Independent foundation
Limitations: Scholarships to graduating seniors of the Fallbrook Union High School District, CA, for higher education.
Financial data: Year ended 02/28/2005. Assets, $335,399 (M); Expenditures, $18,586; Total giving, $14,800; Grants to individuals, 20 grants totaling $14,800.
Type of support: Scholarships—to individuals.
Application information: Application form required.
   Initial approach: Letter.
   Deadline(s): Apr. 15
   Additional information: Unsolicited requests for applications not accepted.
EIN: 953653710

3768
The Alice Aber Smith Scholarship
c/o First Banking Center
P.O. Box 660
Burlington, WI   53105
Contact: Rev. Clarence Cheever, Chair.
Application address: 455 S. Jefferson St., Waterford, WI 53185

Foundation type: Independent foundation
Limitations: Scholarships to graduates of Racine County, WI, high schools for attendance at colleges and universities that are affiliated with, or governed by a Christian religious organization.
Financial data: Year ended 12/31/2004. Assets, $924,048 (M); Expenditures, $55,105; Total giving, $45,000; Grants to individuals, 15 grants totaling $45,000.
Fields of interest: Christian agencies & churches.
Type of support: Support to graduates or students of specific schools; Undergraduate support.
Application information: Application form required.
   Deadline(s): May 1
   Applicants should submit the following:
   1) Transcripts
   Additional information: Completion of formal application required, including two references (one from a teacher), and a form to be filled in by the high school guidance counselor.
Program description:
   The Alice Aber Smith Scholarship: Determination of awards will be made based on the following qualifications:
   · high scholarship; general good character; poise and conduct; ability to impart acquired knowledge and advance original ideas; a desire for further education, and financial need
   · scholarships are renewable for up to three years beyond the initial award year, provided that the recipient has used all previous funds to finance his or her education at an appropriate institution;

continues to be of general good character, poise, and conduct; and submits prior May 31 a request for continued support and evidence of satisfactory completion of his or her coursework

· in addition, the committee requires students to maintain fellowship within their churches and maintain a 3.0 GPA.

EIN: 396628593

3769
Charles & Charlotte Bissell Smith Scholarship

c/o KeyBank N.A.
800 Superior Ave., 4th Fl.
Cleveland, OH 44114
Application address: c/o KeyBank N.A., P.O. Box 22042, Albany, NY 12201

Foundation type: Independent foundation
Limitations: Scholarships to U.S. citizens who are graduates of Oneonta High School, NY, with good scholastic standing and citizenship, who are involved in two or more extracurricular activities, and who plan to attend two- and four-year colleges.
Financial data: Year ended 02/28/2005. Assets, $2,649,155 (M); Expenditures, $192,169; Total giving, $169,400; Grants to individuals, 170 grants totaling $169,400 (high: $2,000, low: $1,000).
Fields of interest: Public affairs, citizen participation.
Type of support: Support to graduates or students of specific schools; Undergraduate support.
Application information: Deadline Feb. 15; Completion of formal application required.
EIN: 146105261

3770
Mabel Glidden Smith Trust f/b/o Williams School Loan Fund

c/o Bank of America, N.A.
P.O. Box 6767
Providence, RI 02940-6767
Application address: c/o Bank of America, N.A., 777 Main St., CT2-102-22-02, Hartford, CT 06115

Foundation type: Independent foundation
Limitations: Loans to graduates of The Williams School, CT, for higher education.
Financial data: Year ended 12/31/2003. Assets, $375,866 (M); Expenditures, $22,645; Total giving, $16,000; Grants to individuals, 6 grants totaling $16,000 (high: $5,000, low: $1,500); Loans to individuals, totaling $25,500.
Type of support: Support to graduates or students of specific schools; Undergraduate support.
Application information: Application form required.
   Deadline(s): June 1
EIN: 066060068

3771
Arline J. Smith Trust

c/o JPMorgan Chase Bank
P.O. Box 31412
Rochester, NY 14603-1412
Application address: c/o Dir. of Financial Aid, Juilliard School of Music, 60 Lincoln Ctr. Plz., Rm. 235, New York, NY 10023-6591, tel.: (212) 799-5000, Ext. 211

Foundation type: Independent foundation

Limitations: Scholarships to financially needy residents of specific towns in western CT to attend The Juilliard School, NY.
Financial data: Year ended 08/31/2004. Assets, $579,521 (M); Expenditures, $63,962; Total giving, $55,700; Grants to individuals, totaling $55,700.
Fields of interest: Music; Performing arts, education.
Type of support: Scholarships—to individuals; Support to graduates or students of specific schools.
Application information:
   Initial approach: Letter or telephone.
   Deadline(s): Jan., Apr., and June.
EIN: 066246639

3772
Elva S. Smith Trust

c/o Citizens Bank
870 Westminster St.
Providence, RI 02903
Application address: c/o Toni Carbo Bearman, Dean, University of Pittsburgh, 509 School of Library and Sciences Building, Pittsburgh, PA 15260, tel.: (412) 624-5230

Foundation type: Independent foundation
Limitations: One full scholarship awarded annually for attendance at the School of Library and Information Science at the University of Pittsburgh, PA.
Financial data: Year ended 12/31/2004. Assets, $2,196,244 (M); Expenditures, $145,958; Total giving, $129,082.
Fields of interest: Libraries/library science.
Type of support: Scholarships—to individuals; Support to graduates or students of specific schools.
Application information:
   Initial approach: Letter or telephone.
   Deadline(s): None.
   Additional information: Contact trust for current application guidelines.
EIN: 026014169

3773
The Freda B. & William H. Smith Trust

c/o First State Bank of Conrad
P.O. Box 10
Conrad, IA 50621-0010 (641) 366-2165

Foundation type: Operating foundation
Limitations: Scholarships to graduates of Beaman-Conrad-Liscomb-Union-Whitten schools, IA.
Financial data: Year ended 12/31/2004. Assets, $542,267 (M); Expenditures, $25,357; Total giving, $17,010; Grants to individuals, 21 grants totaling $17,010.
Type of support: Undergraduate support.
Application information: Deadline Mar. 31; Completion of formal application required.
EIN: 426478959

3774
The Smithfield Township College Assistance Fund

(formerly Jessie B. Kautz Trust)
c/o Mellon Financial Corp.
P.O. Box 185
Pittsburgh, PA 15230
Application address: c/o Stephen Carey, Mellon Bank, N.A., 15 Public Sq., Wilkes-Barre, PA 18701-1702, tel.: (570) 424-7180

Foundation type: Independent foundation
Limitations: Scholarships to residents of Smithfield Township, PA, who are graduates of the Smithfield Township Public School and the East Stroudsburg Area High School to attend a non-sectarian college or university. See program description for a list of eligible areas of study.
Financial data: Year ended 12/31/2004. Assets, $194,256 (M); Expenditures, $7,666; Total giving, $4,900; Grants to individuals, 10 grants totaling $4,900.
Fields of interest: Journalism/publishing; Agriculture; Business/industry; Science; Physical/earth sciences; Chemistry; Mathematics; Physics; Engineering; Biological sciences; Economics; Political science.
Type of support: Support to graduates or students of specific schools; Undergraduate support.
Application information: Applications by letter, with brief request, accepted throughout the year.
Program description:
   Scholarship Program: Scholarships are awarded for study in the following fields: Agriculture, Atomic Science, Biology, Business Administration, Chemistry, Economics, Electronics, Engineering, Geology, Journalism, Mathematics, Metallurgy, Mining, Physics, Political Science, and Pre-medicine.
EIN: 236720230

3775
Smolin-Melin Scholarship Fund Trust

(formerly Antonia Smolin and Victor Smolin Scholarship Fund Charitable Trust)
c/o Bank of America, N.A.
P.O. Box 513189
Los Angeles, CA 90051-1189
Application address: c/o Richard Zuckerman, 1188 Franklin St., Ste. 201, San Francisco, CA 94109, tel.: (415) 771-6400

Foundation type: Independent foundation
Limitations: Scholarships to children of members of Local 10 of the International Longshoremen's and Warehousemen's Union.
Financial data: Year ended 12/31/2004. Assets, $560,792 (M); Expenditures, $28,859; Total giving, $18,325; Grants to individuals, 11 grants totaling $18,325.
Fields of interest: Labor unions/organizations.
Type of support: Undergraduate support.
Application information: Applications by letter accepted throughout the year.
EIN: 943070732

3776
Helen F. Smucker Memorial Scholarship Trust

c/o National City Bank
P.O. Box 94651
Cleveland, OH 44101-4651
Application address: c/o Guidance Dir., Orrville High School, 841 N. Ella, Orrville, OH 44667, tel.: (330) 682-4661

Foundation type: Independent foundation
Limitations: Scholarships to graduates of Orrville High School, OH.
Financial data: Year ended 12/31/2004.
Assets, $295,173 (M); Expenditures, $15,085; Total giving, $12,040; Grants to individuals, 4 grants totaling $12,040.
Type of support: Support to graduates or students of specific schools; Undergraduate support.
Application information: Deadline May 1; Application by letter.
EIN: 341296818

3777
Harry L. & John L. Smysor Memorial Fund
c/o First Mid-Illinois Bank & Trust
P.O. Box 499
Mattoon, IL 61938-3932
Application address: c/o Gary Kuhns, First Mid-Illinois Bank & Trust, 1515 Charleston Ave., Mattoon, IL 61938, tel.: (217) 234-7454

Foundation type: Independent foundation
Limitations: Scholarships to students of Windsor High School, IL, for higher education.
Financial data: Year ended 05/31/2005.
Assets, $4,711,898 (M); Expenditures, $457,065; Total giving, $257,100; Grants to individuals, 179 grants totaling $257,100 (high: $3,400, low: $600).
Type of support: Support to graduates or students of specific schools; Undergraduate support.
Application information: Deadline Apr. 15; Completion of formal application required; Application form available from Windsor, IL, high schools or from trustee bank.
EIN: 371160678

3778
Henry Herbert Smythe Trust
c/o Bank of America, N.A.
P.O. Box 6767
Providence, RI 02940-6767
Contact: Emma Greene, Acct. Mgr.

Foundation type: Independent foundation
Limitations: Scholarships to students from Falmouth High School and Hoosac High School, MA.
Financial data: Year ended 09/30/2004.
Assets, $1,758,445 (M); Expenditures, $86,013; Total giving, $79,281; Grants to individuals, 63 grants totaling $79,281 (high: $850, low: $655).
Type of support: Scholarships—to individuals; Support to graduates or students of specific schools.
Application information: Applications not accepted.
EIN: 046008387

3779
The SNA Foundation
P.O. Drawer L
Seldovia, AK 99663-0250 (907) 234-7625
Contact: Don Kashevaroff, Pres.
FAX: (907) 234-7637; Additional tel.: (800) 478-7898; URL: http://www.snai.com/foundation.htm

Foundation type: Company-sponsored foundation
Limitations: Scholarships to AK natives, their children and spouses who are enrolled at Seldonia Native Association, Inc.
Financial data: Year ended 12/31/2004.
Assets, $203,848 (M); Expenditures, $15,868;

Total giving, $14,500; Grants to individuals, 9 grants totaling $14,500 (high: $2,500, low: $500).
Fields of interest: Native Americans/American Indians.
Type of support: Graduate support; Undergraduate support.
Application information: Deadline July 1; Completion of formal application required.
EIN: 920157596

3780
Harry E. and Florence W. Snayberger Memorial Foundation
(also known as Snayberger Memorial Foundation)
c/o M&T Bank
1 S. Center St.
Pottsville, PA 17901
Contact: Carolyn Bernatonis, Trust Dept.
FAX: (570) 622-1306;
E-mail: cbernationis@mandtbank.com

Foundation type: Independent foundation
Limitations: Scholarships to financially needy residents of Schuylkill County, PA, for undergraduate, graduate, and vocational study. Preference is shown to the children and grandchildren of employees of the Walkin Shoe Company who were employed prior to Sept. 1974.
Financial data: Year ended 03/31/2005.
Assets, $4,177,747 (M); Expenditures, $224,643; Total giving, $192,405; Grants to individuals, 318 grants totaling $166,505 (high: $2,000, low: $200).
Fields of interest: Vocational education.
Type of support: Employee-related scholarships; Graduate support; Technical education support; Undergraduate support.
Application information: Application form required.
Initial approach: Letter.
Copies of proposal: 1
Deadline(s): Last Fri. of Feb.
Applicants should submit the following:
1) Financial information
Additional information: Application should also include a signed notarized affidavit for applicants claiming preferential status; Recipients notified by mid-Oct.; Scholarships are renewable.
EIN: 232056361

3781
W. B. and Mary W. Snow No. 5 Scholarship Fund
c/o FirstMerit Bank, N.A.
106 S. Main St., Ste. 1600
Akron, OH 44308
Application address: c/o Phyllis Bernel, Office of Career Education, 65 Steiner Ave., Rm. 210, Akron, OH 44301

Foundation type: Independent foundation
Limitations: Scholarships to residents of Summit County, OH, for education and training in the manual skills and trades.
Financial data: Year ended 08/31/2003.
Assets, $262,360 (M); Expenditures, $21,548; Total giving, $11,234; Grants to individuals, 8 grants totaling $11,234 (high: $1,500, low: $884).
Type of support: Technical education support.
Application information: Deadline Jan. 25; Initial approach by letter; Completion of formal application required.
EIN: 311564522

3782
Burt Snyder Educational Foundation
c/o Wells Fargo Bank Northwest, N.A.
P.O. Box 21927
Seattle, WA 98111
Application address: c/o Jim Lynch, 620 N. 1st St., Lake View, OR 97630-1506, tel.: (541) 947-2196

Foundation type: Independent foundation
Limitations: Scholarships to graduates of public high schools in Lake County, OR.
Financial data: Year ended 06/30/2005.
Assets, $523,127 (M); Expenditures, $34,087; Total giving, $23,766; Grants to individuals, 2 grants totaling $8,800.
Type of support: Support to graduates or students of specific schools; Undergraduate support.
Application information: Applications accepted throughout the year; Contact foundation for current application guidelines.
EIN: 936033286

3783
The Harold B. and Dorothy A. Snyder Foundation, Inc.
P.O. Box 671
Moorestown, NJ 08057-0671
Contact: Joseph A. Vallone III, Exec. Dir.

Foundation type: Independent foundation
Limitations: Scholarships primarily to residents of NJ for college education, with emphasis on business, ministry, and engineering students.
Financial data: Year ended 09/30/2005.
Assets, $12,069,666 (M); Expenditures, $1,104,635; Total giving, $881,703.
Fields of interest: Business school/education; Nursing school/education; Housing/shelter, development; Engineering; Protestant agencies & churches.
Type of support: Technical education support; Undergraduate support.
Application information: Applications not accepted.
EIN: 222316043

3784
Fred C. Snyder Fund
(formerly Elizabeth P. Snyder Trust)
c/o Bank of America, N.A.
P.O. Box 1802
Providence, RI 02940-6767
Application address: c/o Dolgeville Central School, 38 Slawson St., Dolgeville, NY 13329

Foundation type: Independent foundation
Limitations: Scholarships to financially needy graduates of Dolgeville Central School, NY.
Financial data: Year ended 12/31/2004.
Assets, $643,822 (M); Expenditures, $30,063; Total giving, $25,500; Grants to individuals, 14 grants totaling $25,500.
Type of support: Support to graduates or students of specific schools; Undergraduate support.
Application information: Deadline July 31; Completion of formal application required.
EIN: 156021382

3785
H. L. Snyder Medical Research Institute
1407 Wheat Rd.
Winfield, KS 67156 (620) 221-4080
Contact: Toya Smith, Admin.
FAX: (620) 221-2684;
E-mail: tsmith@snydermri.org; URL: http://
www.snydermri.org/sp.html

Foundation type: Operating foundation
Limitations: Scholarships to residents of Winfield, KS, who are seeking education in the medical and biomedical fields.
Financial data: Year ended 06/30/2004. Assets, $7,586,962 (M); Expenditures, $335,309; Total giving, $10,615; Grants to individuals, totaling $10,615.
Fields of interest: Health care, formal/general education.
Type of support: Undergraduate support.
Application information: Applications accepted. Application form required. Application form available on the grantmaker's Web site.
Initial approach: Letter.
Deadline(s): May 1
Applicants should submit the following:
1) Letter(s) of recommendation
2) Financial information
3) Essay
Program description:
Healthcare Scholarship: Students must be a resident of Winfield, KS for the last 3 years or a graduate of Winfield High School-USD 465 and enrolled full time (12 hours or more) per semester in an accredited university or college program in the healthcare field. Scholarships will be available to students who are starting their junior year in college with a 3.0 GPA or higher and are entering the healthcare or bioscience field.
EIN: 480622380

3786
Franklin C. Snyder/Longue Vue Club Employee Scholarship Foundation
400 Longue Vue Dr.
Verona, PA 15147 (412) 793-2375
Contact: Kenneth R. Pizzica, V.P.

Foundation type: Independent foundation
Limitations: Scholarships to employees of Longue Vue Club.
Financial data: Year ended 12/31/2004. Assets, $144,861 (M); Expenditures, $38,624; Total giving, $35,000; Grants to individuals, 23 grants totaling $35,000.
Type of support: Employee-related scholarships.
Application information: Applications accepted throughout the year; Initial approach by letter; Completion of formal application required.
EIN: 251715070

3787
Harry L. & Ruby T. Soames Educational Foundation
c/o Wells Fargo Bank Nevada, N.A.
P.O. Box 95021
Henderson, NV 89009-5021
Application address: c/o George Daniel, Sr. Principal, Kent High School, 12033 S.E. 256th St., Kent, WA 98031-6503, tel.: (206) 859-7201

Foundation type: Independent foundation
Limitations: Scholarships to graduates of Kent School District high schools, WA, who meet entrance requirements for the University of

Washington even if this is not the institution they will be attending.
Financial data: Year ended 09/30/2004. Assets, $689,023 (M); Expenditures, $43,523; Total giving, $33,129; Grants to individuals, 7 grants totaling $18,625 (high: $7,875, low: $875).
Type of support: Support to graduates or students of specific schools; Undergraduate support.
Application information:
Deadline(s): June 1
Additional information: Application by letter outlining grades and reasons for wanting a higher education.
EIN: 916281207

3788
Social Science Research Council
(also known as SSRC)
810 7th Ave.
New York, NY 10019 (212) 377-2700
Contact: Gail Kovach, Dir., Admin. Svcs.
FAX: (212) 377-2727; E-mail: info@ssrc.org; URL: http://www.ssrc.org

Foundation type: Public charity
Limitations: Fellowships to students at specific schools for interdisciplinary research and training.
Publications: Application guidelines; Informational brochure; Newsletter.
Financial data: Year ended 06/30/2004. Assets, $36,267,050 (M); Expenditures, $16,063,786; Total giving, $2,820,881; Grants to individuals, totaling $2,820,881.
Type of support: Fellowships; Support to graduates or students of specific schools.
Application information: Applicants must contact their school for current application deadline/guidelines.
EIN: 131325070

3789
Societe des Professeurs Francais et Franophones d'Amerique
(formerly Societe des Professeurs Francais en Amerique)
c/o F.D.R. Station
P.O. Box 6026
New York, NY 10150-6026
Contact: Gerard Roubichou, Pres.
FAX: (212) 996-2367

Foundation type: Independent foundation
Limitations: Scholarships to researchers, graduate and undergraduate students, and high school students studying French in the U.S., France, or Quebec, Canada.
Publications: Grants list; Informational brochure.
Financial data: Year ended 12/31/2002. Assets, $2,957,814 (M); Expenditures, $138,996; Total giving, $84,500; Grants to individuals, 28 grants totaling $84,500 (high: $10,000, low: $1,500).
Fields of interest: Language (foreign); International exchange, students.
Type of support: Research; Graduate support; Precollege support; Undergraduate support; Travel grants.
Application information:
Deadline(s): Jan. 1 for Marandon Scholarship, Feb. 23 for New York City Public High School Competition, July 1 for Dufrenoy Scholarship, and Nov. 15 for Quebec Scholarship
Additional information: See program description for further application information.

Program descriptions:
Jeanne Marandon Scholarship: This fund provides scholarships to researchers, graduate students, undergraduate students enrolled in a study abroad program, and students enrolled for M.A., M.H.A., or M.A.T. degrees studying in France or Quebec. Applicants must have sufficient knowledge of oral and written French to continue study. Researchers must submit a resume, proposal, bibliography, and three letters of recommendation. Graduate students must submit a thesis proposal, resume, transcripts, and three letters of recommendation, one of which is from the dissertation director. Beginning master's students must submit transcripts and three letters of recommendation. Undergraduate students must submit transcripts, financial data, proof of matriculation, and three letters of recommendation, one from the head of the department and, if possible, one from a society member. Application address: c/o Bourses Marandon, SPFFA, P.O. Box 6641, Yorkville Finance Sta., New York, NY 10128.
Jean et Marie-Louis Dufrenoy Scholarship: This fund provides scholarships to first-year graduate students who possess a knowledge of French at a level that allows studies to be undertaken at a university in France. Applicants must submit a letter in French stating reason for studying at a French university, with two copies of transcripts, and three letters of recommendation. Application address: SPFFA, Commission de la Bourse Dufrenoy, P.O. Box 6641, Yorkville Finance Sta., New York, NY 10128.
New York City Public High School Written Competition: This competition is open to students enrolled in level III, IV, or V French classes in a New York City public high school. Up to eight students per school are selected each year. Prior recipients are ineligible. Students are preselected by their schools.
Quebec Scholarship: This scholarship is awarded to college students studying at a Quebec university. Applicants must submit a transcript, a letter of recommendation, an essay written under the supervision of a teacher, and a letter in French stating reasons for studying at a Quebec university. Application address: SPFFA, Quebec Scholarship, P.O. Box 6641, Yorkville Finance Sta., New York, NY 10128.
EIN: 133150248

3790
Society for Analytical Chemists of Pittsburgh
300 Penn Ctr. Blvd., Ste. 332
Pittsburgh, PA 15235-5503 (412) 825-3220
Contact: Charles L. Holifield, Chair.
FAX: (412) 825-3224; E-mail: sacpinfo@pitton.org; URL: http://www.sacp.org/

Foundation type: Independent foundation
Limitations: Awards to individuals by nomination only in recognition of work in the field of analytical chemistry, primarily in PA. Also, scholarships to high school seniors and summer internships to college juniors and seniors who are chemistry majors and plan to pursue graduate education in analytical chemistry.
Publications: Informational brochure.
Financial data: Year ended 06/30/2005. Assets, $174,764 (M); Expenditures, $478,723; Total giving, $330,086; Grants to individuals, 75 grants totaling $56,834 (high: $5,000, low: $69).
Fields of interest: Science; Chemistry.
Type of support: Awards/grants by nomination only; Awards/prizes.

Application information: Contact society or consult Web site for current application deadline/guidelines.

Program descriptions:

High School Science Essay Contest: Prizes of varying cash amounts given to high school students for winning essays on science topics.

Keene Dimick Award: $5,000 cash award presented annually for noteworthy accomplishments in the area of gas and supercritical fluid chromatography (GC,SFC). Awards are presented at a symposium arranged by the awardee during the Pittsburgh Conference.

Middle School Science Essay Contest: Prizes of varying cash amounts given to middle school students for winning essays on science topics.

Pittsburgh Analytical Chemistry Award: $2,000 award given in recognition of outstanding research in the field of analytical chemistry.

Waters Instrumentation Symposium: Honoraria are paid to participants in this symposium, which recognizes pioneers in the development of scientific instrumentation.

EIN: 256072976

3791
The Society for the Increase of the Ministry

920 Farmington Ave., Ste. 202
West Hartford, CT   06107   (860) 233-1732
Contact: John L.C. Mitman, Exec. Dir.
FAX: (860) 233-2644;
E-mail: simministry@earthlink.net

Foundation type: Public charity
Limitations: Scholarships for theological education to students preparing for ordination in the Episcopal Church.
Publications: Application guidelines; Informational brochure; Newsletter.
Financial data: Year ended 08/31/2003. Assets, $3,922,136 (M); Expenditures, $409,896; Total giving, $178,000; Grants to individuals, totaling $178,000 (average grant: $1,500-$3,000).
Fields of interest: Theological school/education; Protestant agencies & churches.
Type of support: Scholarships—to individuals.
Application information: Application form required.
Deadline(s): Mar. 1
Additional information: Contact financial aid officer of seminary or the society for current application guidelines.
EIN: 066053077

3792
Society of Kastorians "Omonoia", Inc.

150-28 14th Ave.
Whitestone, NY   11357   (718) 746-4505

Foundation type: Operating foundation
Limitations: Scholarships to financially needy individuals in NJ and NY, who are of Kastorian, Greek or Macedonian descent, for higher education.
Financial data: Year ended 12/31/2004. Assets, $3,723,798 (M); Expenditures, $526,902; Total giving, $109,406; Grants to individuals, totaling $57,950.
Fields of interest: Greece; Macedonia.
Type of support: Undergraduate support.
Application information:
Deadline(s): Aug. 31
Additional information: Application by typed letter, including academic achievements,

schools attended and all academic and professional goals.
EIN: 133000517

3793
Society of Manufacturing Engineers Education Foundation

(also known as SME Education Foundation)
1 SME Dr.
P.O. Box 930
Dearborn, MI   48121-0930   (313) 425-3300
Contact: Sherril K. West, Pres.
FAX: (313) 425-3411;
E-mail: foundation@sme.org; URL: http://www.sme.org/foundation

Foundation type: Public charity
Limitations: Scholarships to full-time undergraduate students in manufacturing engineering programs at specifically approved schools.
Publications: Application guidelines; Annual report; Grants list; Program policy statement.
Financial data: Year ended 12/31/2004. Assets, $23,309,005 (M); Expenditures, $1,651,514; Total giving, $729,302; Grants to individuals, totaling $218,330.
Fields of interest: Engineering school/education.
Type of support: Support to graduates or students of specific schools; Undergraduate support.
Application information: Application form required.
Initial approach: Telephone.
Deadline(s): Contact foundation for current application deadline
Additional information: See program descriptions for names of specific schools providing scholarships.

Program descriptions:

PACCAR Scholarship Award Fund: Supports three scholarships of $2,000 each for students enrolled in manufacturing engineering technology or mechanical engineering technology at the University of North Texas. This is a one-time award. Applicants must have an overall minimum GPA of 3.0 on a 4.0 scale, or 2.5 minimum if working 30 hours a week while attending school.

Boeing/SME-EF at California State University Long Beach: Applicants must be undergraduate students enrolled in the Manufacturing Option within the Aerospace Engineering Program at CSULB, or in other CSULB Manufacturing degreed programs. Applicants must possess an overall minimum GPA of 3.0 on a 4.0 scale. Applications are available through CSULB.

Albert E. Wischmeyer Memorial Scholarship Award: Supports two scholarships of at least $1,900 each. Applicants must be residents of western New York state (west of Interstate 81) and graduating high school seniors or current undergraduate students enrolled in an accredited degree program in manufacturing engineering, manufacturing engineering technology, or mechanical technology. Applicants must have an overall minimum GPA of 3.0 on a 4.0 scale and plan to attend a college or university in New York state.

Milwaukee Chapter 4 Lawrence A. Wacker Memorial Scholarship Award: Supports two scholarships of $1,500 each for students enrolled in a degree program in manufacturing, mechanical, or industrial engineering at a college or university in the state of Wisconsin. Applicants must attend school in Wisconsin and have an overall minimum GPA of 3.0 on a 4.0 scale.

Detroit Chapter 1 Scholarships: Funds three scholarships of at least $1,000 each. One award will be available to a student member of the SME chapters sponsored by Detroit Chapter 1 in each of

the following three academic levels: associate degree or equivalent, baccalaureate degree, and graduate degree program. Applicants must be undergraduate or graduate students enrolled in a manufacturing engineering, manufacturing engineering technology, or closely related degree or certificate program at one of five approved schools and have an overall minimum GPA of 3.0 on a 4.0 scale.

Edward S. Roth Manufacturing Engineering Scholarship: Supports one scholarship of $2,500 for a student enrolled in an accredited four-year degree program in manufacturing engineering in the U.S. Contact SME-EF for a list of accredited programs. All applicants must have and maintain a GPA of 3.0 or better on a 4.0 scale and must be U.S. citizens. Preference will be given to students demonstrating financial need, minority students, and students participating in a co-op program.

Oswald Boehme Scholarship Award Fund: One $250 undergraduate scholarship is given to a student enrolled in a manufacturing engineering or manufacturing engineering technology program at Marquette University or Valparaiso University.

Clinton Helton Scholarship Award Fund: Two $1,200 undergraduate scholarships are available to students enrolled in a manufacturing engineering or manufacturing engineering technology program at Colorado State University or University of Colorado at Boulder.

Connie and Robert T. Gunter Scholarship Award Fund: One $750 undergraduate scholarship is given to a student enrolled in a manufacturing engineering or manufacturing engineering technology program at Georgia Institute of Technology, Georgia Southern University, or Southern Polytechnic State University, GA.

Kalamazoo Chapter No. 116 - Roscoe Douglas Scholarships Award Fund: One $1,500 undergraduate scholarship is given to a student enrolled in a manufacturing engineering or manufacturing engineering technology program at one of the following schools: Glen Oaks Community College, MI; Jackson Community College, MI; Kalamazoo Valley Community College, MI; Kellogg Community College, MI; Lake Michigan College, MI; Southwestern Michigan College; or Western Michigan University.

St. Louis Chapter 17 Scholarship Fund: Six $1,000 undergraduate scholarships are provided to students enrolled in manufacturing engineering, industrial technology, or other manufacturing-related programs at one of the following two- or four-year schools: Jefferson College, MO; Mineral Area College, MO; St. Louis Community College at Florissant Valley, MO; Southeast Missouri State University; Southern Illinois University at Carbondale; or University of Missouri—Rolla.
EIN: 382746841

3794
Elizabeth H. Soeder Scholarship Trust

c/o Wachovia Bank, N.A.
100 N. Main St., 13th Fl.
Winston-Salem, NC   27150-6732
(800) 576-5135
Contact: Scholarships: Martha Johnson
Scholarship URL: http://www.wachoviascholars.com/sodr/csaw_soeder_deadline.php

Foundation type: Independent foundation
Limitations: Scholarships to graduating seniors in Cape May County, NJ.
Financial data: Year ended 04/30/2005. Assets, $516,343 (M); Expenditures, $49,280;

Total giving, $42,250; Grants to individuals, totaling $42,250.
Type of support: Support to graduates or students of specific schools; Undergraduate support.
Application information: Applications accepted. Application form required.
Additional information: See Web site for additional information.
EIN: 226082438

3795
Soldwedel Foundation
c/o Commerce Bank, N.A.
416 Main St.
Peoria, IL 61602

Foundation type: Independent foundation
Limitations: Scholarships to financially needy Pekin High School, IL, graduates who meet certain field of study and academic expectations for study at a college or university.
Financial data: Year ended 12/31/2004.
Assets, $383,440 (M); Expenditures, $36,141; Total giving, $34,000; Grants to individuals, 8 grants totaling $34,000.
Type of support: Support to graduates or students of specific schools; Undergraduate support.
Application information: Contact foundation for current application deadline; Application form can be obtained from guidance counselor.
EIN: 376296318

3796
John E. Solem Scholarship Trust
c/o First National Bank of Sioux Falls, Trust Dept.
P.O. Box 5186
Sioux Falls, SD 57117-5186
Application addresses: c/o Baltic High School, Attn: Leonard Bettnemg, 500 3rd St., Baltic, SD 57003, tel.: (605) 529-5466; c/o Dell Rapids High School, Attn: George Henry, 1216 N. Garfield Ave., Dell Rapids, SD 57002, tel.: (605) 428-5473; c/o Garretson High School, Attn: Clarence Kooistra, 505 2nd St., Garretson, SD 57030; tel.: (605) 594-3452

Foundation type: Independent foundation
Limitations: Scholarships to high school graduates of Baltic, Dell Rapids, and Garretson, SD, only.
Financial data: Year ended 12/31/2004.
Assets, $147,918 (M); Expenditures, $14,850; Total giving, $11,750; Grants to individuals, 12 grants totaling $11,750.
Type of support: Support to graduates or students of specific schools; Undergraduate support.
Application information: Deadline Apr. 1; Initial approach through local high school counselor; Completion of formal application required; Interviews required.
EIN: 466010949

3797
Soli Deo Gloria Foundation
P.O. Box 17452
San Antonio, TX 78217

Foundation type: Operating foundation
Limitations: Awards to student winners of an essay contest in MS, and their English teachers. Award of $1,500 presented to first place essay winner, $1,000 to second, $500 to third, and awards of $200 each are awarded to honorable mention recipients.

Financial data: Year ended 12/31/2004.
Assets, $2,078,885 (M); Expenditures, $40,493; Total giving, $26,840; Grants to individuals, 10 grants totaling $4,350 (high: $1,000, low: $300).
Fields of interest: Literature.
Type of support: Awards/prizes; Precollege support.
Application information: Applications not accepted.
EIN: 640864685

3798
Gerald B. H. Solomon Freedom Foundation, Inc.
P.O. Box 1246
South Glens Falls, NY 12803

Foundation type: Independent foundation
Limitations: Scholarships for higher education to Eagle Scouts who have achieved the gold star award and who reside in the Glens Falls, NY, area.
Financial data: Year ended 09/30/2004.
Assets, $427,235 (M); Expenditures, $19,500; Total giving, $18,750; Grants to individuals, 35 grants totaling $17,500.
Fields of interest: Boy scouts.
Type of support: Scholarships—to individuals.
Application information: Applications not accepted.
EIN: 223246773

3799
Somerville Scholarship Foundation
(formerly Grahame and Thelma Somerville Scholarship Foundation)
c/o National City Bank of Indiana
110 W. Berry St.
Fort Wayne, IN 46802 (260) 461-6218
Contact: Denise Andorfer, V.P., National City Bank of Indiana

Foundation type: Independent foundation
Limitations: Scholarships to nontraditional-aged students of the Fort Wayne, IN, area, who seek an undergraduate degree or vocational training.
Financial data: Year ended 10/31/2004.
Assets, $2,430,664 (M); Expenditures, $138,431; Total giving, $124,820; Grants to individuals, 250 grants totaling $124,820 (high: $2,700, low: $20).
Fields of interest: Vocational education.
Type of support: Undergraduate support.
Application information: Application form required.
Deadline(s): July 15
Program description:
Support to Nontraditional Students: The foundation aims to address the needs of nontraditional students who wish to further their education or training as a means of entering or advancing within the employment market. Preference will be given to applicants who desire further education as a result of divorce, the death of a spouse, loss of existing employment, or some similar misfortune. Scholarships may be applied to a degree or nondegree program at an accredited college, university, or vocational institution. Members of the scholarship committee and employees or relatives of employees of National City Bank are ineligible.
EIN: 356547210

3800
Jason C. Somerville Trust
P.O. Box 299
Bethlehem, NH 03574-0299
Contact: John Stevenson, Tr.; Nancy Stevenson, Tr.

Foundation type: Independent foundation
Limitations: Scholarships for full-time study to residents of Bethlehem, NH, who attended Profile High School for four years and graduated.
Financial data: Year ended 12/31/2004.
Assets, $1,863,412 (M); Expenditures, $126,562; Total giving, $110,400; Grants to individuals, 59 grants totaling $110,400 (high: $3,800, low: $800).
Type of support: Support to graduates or students of specific schools; Undergraduate support.
Application information: Application form required.
Deadline(s): July 31
Applicants should submit the following:
1) Pell Grant
2) Financial information
3) Transcripts
4) SAT
Additional information: Application must also include PSAT scores, and FAS from the college. Interviews required.
Program description:
Scholarships: Applications are screened by the Bethlehem Profile School Board and then passed on to the Trustees with the board's recommendations. The Trustees select recipients based on standardized test scores, high school grades, attitude toward school authorities, participation in extracurricular activities, family income, number of family members attending college, and the character and reputation of the applicant within the community, with stress placed on good morals. Scholarships are:
- for tuition, room, board, books, and educational supplies for full-time study. Travel expenses are not covered. Trustees meet with the applicant and guidance counselor at least once each year
- renewable for up to four years or eight semesters, providing a GPA of at least 2.0 is maintained
Applicants must:
- have resided with their parents, single parent, or close relative in the town of Bethlehem, NH, during their entire, four-year education at Profile High School
- not have been involved with drugs or alcohol.
EIN: 026033716

3801
Nicholas A. Somma Scholarship Fund
9023 Forest Hill Ave.
Richmond, VA 23235-3054
Application address: c/o Chair., Scholarship Comm., Highland Springs High School, 15 S. Oak Ave., Highland Springs, VA 23075, tel.: (804) 737-6681

Foundation type: Independent foundation
Limitations: Scholarships for attendance at four-year colleges and universities to graduates of Highland Springs High School, VA, who are planning a career in education and are from a family with a deceased parent.
Financial data: Year ended 06/30/2002.
Assets, $472,206 (M); Expenditures, $27,142; Total giving, $16,300; Grants to individuals, 9 grants totaling $16,300 (high: $6,000, low: $501).
Fields of interest: Teacher school/education.

Type of support: Support to graduates or students of specific schools; Undergraduate support.
Application information: Deadline Jan. 15; Completion of formal application required, including transcript, GPA, class rank, and SAT scores.
EIN: 541393792

3802
Walter & Anna Soneson Scholarship Fund Trust

c/o U.S. Bank, N.A.
P.O. Box 64713
St. Paul, MN 55164-0713

Foundation type: Independent foundation
Limitations: Scholarships for high school seniors in Duluth, MN, with a 2.0 GPA who will attend college in MN, MI, IA, IN, IL, WI, ND or SD.
Financial data: Year ended 12/31/2004. Assets, $801,021 (M); Expenditures, $59,116; Total giving, $50,000; Grants to individuals, 24 grants totaling $50,000.
Type of support: Support to graduates or students of specific schools; Undergraduate support.
Application information: Application form required.
Additional information: Contact trust for current application deadline; Applications available through high school counselors.
EIN: 416018233

3803
Sonlight Curriculum Foundation

c/o Scholarship Comm.
8042 S. Grant Way
Littleton, CO 80122-2705
Contact: John Holzmann, Pres.
FAX: (303) 795-8668;
E-mail: scholarship@sonlight.com; URL: http://www.sonlight.com/scholarships.html

Foundation type: Company-sponsored foundation
Limitations: Scholarships to students who have purchased and used three full Sonlight Curriculum Core programs over three years.
Financial data: Year ended 12/31/2004. Assets, $223,993 (M); Expenditures, $44,740; Total giving, $44,740; Grants to individuals, 26 grants totaling $44,740 (high: $5,000, low: $240).
Fields of interest: Christian agencies & churches.
Type of support: Undergraduate support.
Application information: Application form required.
Deadline(s): Dec. 15
Applicants should submit the following:
  1) Essay
  2) ACT
  3) SAT
Additional information: Application must include extracurricular activities, three reference letters, and photograph; See Web site for further application information.
Program description:
Scholarships: Awards one $5,000 scholarship, two $2,500 scholarships, and four $1,000 scholarships annually. All scholarships are renewable for four years, provided student maintains a 3.0 GPA or "B" average. Special attention is also paid to the student's dedication to "seeking God's Kingdom.".
EIN: 841521871

3804
Sonora Area Foundation

20100 Cedar Rd., No. E
P.O. Box 577
Sonora, CA 95370-0577   (209) 533-2596
Contact: Mick Grimes, Exec. Dir.
FAX: (209) 533-2412;
E-mail: acorn@sonara-area.org; Grant application E-mail: leaf@sonara-area.org; URL: http://www.sonora-area.org

Foundation type: Community foundation
Limitations: Scholarships to Tuolumne County, CA, residents.
Publications: Application guidelines; Annual report; Biennial report; Financial statement; Grants list; Informational brochure; Informational brochure (including application guidelines); Newsletter; Occasional report.
Financial data: Year ended 12/31/2004. Assets, $8,841,502 (L); Expenditures, $980,261; Total giving, $738,177; Grants to individuals, 64 grants totaling $65,550 (high: $3,600, low: $125).
Type of support: Precollege support; Undergraduate support.
Application information: Application form required. Application form available on the grantmaker's Web site.
Initial approach: Letter or telephone.
Deadline(s): Contact foundation for current application deadline/guidelines
EIN: 931023051

3805
Sons of Italy Foundation

219 E St. N.E.
Washington, DC 20002   (202) 547-2900
Contact: Philip R. Piccigallo, Natl. Exec. Dir.
FAX: (202) 547-0121;
E-mail: scholarships@osia.org; URL: http://www.osia.org

Foundation type: Public charity
Limitations: Scholarships to U.S. citizens of Italian-American descent enrolled full-time in undergraduate or graduate programs at accredited schools, colleges, and universities.
Publications: Application guidelines; Biennial report; Newsletter.
Financial data: Year ended 09/30/2004. Assets, $1,448,960 (L); Expenditures, $2,162,442; Total giving, $527,867.
Type of support: Graduate support; Undergraduate support.
Application information:
Initial approach: E-mail.
Deadline(s): Feb. 28
Applicants should submit the following:
  1) Essay
  2) Letter(s) of recommendation
  3) Transcripts
  4) SAT
  5) ACT
Additional information: Completion of formal application required, including extracurricular activities, and a $25 processing fee. See Web site for further application and program information.
Program description:
National Leadership Grant Competition (NLGC):
· Pietro Secchia Scholarship: Undergraduate students entering their sophomore, junior, or senior year of college are eligible for this scholarship for study abroad at John Cabot University in Rome, Italy.
· Sons of Italy Foundation/George L. Graziadio Scholarship: Students at the

George L. Graziadio School of Business and Management at Pepperdine University are eligible for this scholarship. Contact the school at (310) 568-5500 or http://www.bschool.pepperdine.edu for more information.
· Henry Salvatori Scholarship: Provides a $5,000 grant to a college-bound high school senior who has demonstrated exceptional leadership, distinguished scholarship, and a deep understanding and respect for the principles on which our nation was founded - liberty, freedom and equality.
EIN: 236276526

3806
Madeleine H. Soren Trust

c/o Mellon Financial Corp.
P.O. Box 185
Pittsburgh, PA 15230-0185
Contact: Sandra Brown-McMullen, Trust Off., Mellon Financial Corp.
tel.: (617) 722-3881

Foundation type: Independent foundation
Limitations: Scholarships to financially needy female graduates of MA high schools for studies in music and music education at MA colleges, universities, and conservatories.
Financial data: Year ended 08/31/2002. Assets, $369,089 (M); Expenditures, $27,785; Total giving, $19,800; Grants to individuals, 4 grants totaling $19,800 (high: $7,000, low: $2,000).
Fields of interest: Music; Performing arts, education; Women.
Type of support: Undergraduate support.
Application information: Deadline May 1; Initial approach by letter; Completion of formal application required.
EIN: 046092280

3807
Paul & Daisy Soros Foundation

400 W. 59th St.
New York, NY 10019   (212) 547-6926
Contact: For fellowships: Carmel Geraghty
FAX: (212) 548-4623;
E-mail: pdsoros_fellows@sorosny.org; URL: http://www.pdsoros.org

Foundation type: Independent foundation
Limitations: Fellowships to graduate students who are new Americans for study in any graduate program.
Publications: Application guidelines.
Financial data: Year ended 12/31/2004. Assets, $3,193,880 (M); Expenditures, $2,457,388; Total giving, $1,790,628; Grants to individuals, 70 grants totaling $1,624,953 (high: $55,935, low: $2,000).
Fields of interest: Education; Immigrants/refugees.
Type of support: Fellowships; Graduate support.
Application information: Applications accepted. Application form required. Application form available on the grantmaker's Web site.
Deadline(s): Nov. 1
Applicants should submit the following:
  1) Essay
  2) Letter(s) of recommendation
  3) Transcripts
  4) Resume

Additional information: Application should include proof of eligibility for fellowship; See Web site for further information.
Program descriptions:
Paul & Daisy Soros Fellowships for New Americans: Thirty fellowships of $20,000 per year and half of tuition for up to two years are awarded to individuals for graduate study in the U.S. Recipients are chosen on a national competitive basis. New Americans are described as: 1) resident aliens who hold Green Cards, or 2) have been naturalized as U.S. citizens, or 3) are children of parents who are both naturalized citizens. Recipients must not be older than 30 years of age as of application deadline. Fellows may pursue a graduate degree in any professional field (e.g., engineering, medicine, law, social work, etc.) or scholarly discipline in the arts, humanities, or social sciences (the fine and performing arts are included).
New Americans Program: The Program is open to individuals who retain loyalty and a sense of commitment to their country of origin as well as to the United States, but is intended to support individuals who will continue to regard the United States as their principal residence and focus of national identity. The applicant must either have a bachelor's degree or be in her/his final year of undergraduate study. Those who have a bachelor's degree may already be pursuing graduate study and may receive Fellowship support to continue that study. Individuals who are in the third, or subsequent, year of study in the same graduate program are not, however, eligible for this competition. Students who have received a master's degree in a program and are continuing for a doctoral degree in the same program are considered to have been in the same program from the time they began their work on their master's degree. To be eligible you must not be older than thirty years of age. Contact cgeraghty@sorosny.org or visit URL: http://www.pdsoros.org/requirements.html#question1 for more information.
EIN: 137057096

3808
South Butler County School District Foundation
328 Knoch Rd.
Saxonburg, PA 16056
Application address: c/o Counseling Center, Knoch Senior High School, 345 Knoch Rd., Saxonburg, PA 16056

Foundation type: Independent foundation
Limitations: Scholarships to students of the South Butler County School District, PA.
Financial data: Year ended 06/30/2004. Assets, $1,663,118 (M); Expenditures, $167,552; Total giving, $60,600; Grants to individuals, 44 grants totaling $60,600 (high: $2,200, low: $300).
Type of support: Support to graduates or students of specific schools; Undergraduate support.
Application information: Deadline Mar. 15; Contact foundation for current application guidelines.
EIN: 251735818

3809
South Dakota Community Foundation
207 E. Capitol Ave.
P.O. Box 296
Pierre, SD 57501-0296 (605) 224-1025
Contact: Bob Sutton, Secy. and Exec. Dir.
FAX: (605) 224-5364;
E-mail: bsutton44@sdcommunityfoundation.org;
Additional tel.: (800) 888-1842; Additional E-mail: stephj16@sdcommunityfoundation.org;
URL: http://www.sdcommunityfoundation.org

Foundation type: Community foundation
Limitations: Undergraduate scholarships to graduates of SD high schools for higher education.
Publications: Application guidelines; Annual report; Financial statement; Grants list; Informational brochure; Newsletter; Program policy statement.
Financial data: Year ended 12/31/2004. Assets, $46,464,530 (M); Expenditures, $4,426,436; Total giving, $3,964,815; Grants to individuals, 311 grants totaling $234,649 (high: $6,665, low: $5).
Type of support: Undergraduate support.
Application information: Applications accepted. Application form required.
Initial approach: Telephone.
Deadline(s): None
Additional information: The foundation provides numerous scholarships throughout SD; See Web site for further information.
EIN: 460398115

3810
South Eden Foundation
7814 S. Pheasant Wood Dr.
Sandy, UT 84093-6291 (801) 532-1500
Contact: Jane A. Kennedy, Pres.

Foundation type: Independent foundation
Limitations: Scholarships to residents of UT for attendance at high schools, vocational schools, colleges and universities in the U.S. and South America.
Financial data: Year ended 12/31/2004. Assets, $8,678 (M); Expenditures, $18,486; Total giving, $17,080; Grants to individuals, 2 grants totaling $15,580.
Fields of interest: South America.
Type of support: Foreign applicants; Technical education support; Precollege support; Undergraduate support.
Application information: Applications by letter accepted throughout the year, including prior academic performance, test scores, proposed academic institution, recommendations and financial need.
EIN: 870579749

3811
South Madison Community Foundation
102 W. State St.
Pendleton, IN 46064 (765) 778-8444
Contact: Richard Creger, C.E.O.
FAX: (765) 778-9144; E-mail: smcfed@msn.com;
URL: http://www.smcfdn.org

Foundation type: Community foundation
Limitations: Scholarships to residents of the South Madison, IN, area.
Publications: Application guidelines; Annual report; Financial statement; Grants list; Informational brochure; Newsletter; Occasional report.
Financial data: Year ended 06/30/2004. Assets, $3,679,720 (M); Expenditures,

$151,526; Total giving, $67,992; Grants to individuals, totaling $50,789.
Type of support: Undergraduate support.
Application information: Deadlines July 1 and Dec. 1; Initial approach by letter or telephone; Completion of formal application required.
EIN: 351839759

3812
South Mountain Association
P.O. Box 23
Pittsfield, MA 01202-0023
Contact: Lou R. Steigler, Exec. Dir.

Foundation type: Operating foundation
Limitations: Scholarships to residents or students in Berkshire County, MA, who are pursuing careers in music (violin, viola, and cello players only). Preference is given to high school seniors, but candidates may apply up to their 25th birthday.
Financial data: Year ended 12/31/2003. Assets, $2,234,063 (M); Expenditures, $192,182; Total giving, $16,000; Grants to individuals, 6 grants totaling $16,000 (high: $4,000, low: $1,500).
Fields of interest: Music; Performing arts, education.
Type of support: Undergraduate support.
Application information:
Initial approach: Letter.
Deadline(s): May 1
Additional information: Completion of formal application required, including two letters of recommendation, an essay on the applicant's reasons for pursuing music, and a recorded sample of the applicant's recent playing; Recipients notified by June 1.
Program description:
Musical Training: Awards are granted solely on the basis of musical proficiency. Grants are made in amounts of up to $10,000 per year and are renewable for up to four years of training.
EIN: 046049419

3813
South St. Paul Educational Foundation
521 Marie Ave.
South St. Paul, MN 55075-2049
(651) 457-9440
Contact: Cari Vujovich, Exec. Dir.
FAX: (651) 552-5586;
E-mail: foundation@sspps.org; URL: http://www.sspps.org/index.asp?Type=B_DIR&SEC={047B587E-F496-4FDE-99BD-A643FF8D500D}

Foundation type: Public charity
Limitations: Scholarships to graduating high school seniors in South St. Paul Public School District No. 6, MN.
Publications: Annual report.
Financial data: Year ended 06/30/2005. Assets, $2,926,224 (M); Expenditures, $329,977; Total giving, $205,334; Grants to individuals, 137 grants totaling $144,802 (high: $13,500, low: $255).
Type of support: Scholarships—to individuals.
Application information: Application form required.
Deadline(s): contact foundation for current application deadline
EIN: 411494597

3814
South Washington County Scholarship Committee
944 Portland Ave.
St. Paul Park, MN 55071

Foundation type: Operating foundation
Limitations: Scholarships to individuals attending Park High School, MN, and Woodbury High School, MN for higher education.
Financial data: Year ended 12/31/2003. Assets, $75,985 (M); Expenditures, $23,559; Total giving, $23,000; Grants to individuals, 18 grants totaling $23,000 (high: $1,500, low: $1,000).
Type of support: Support to graduates or students of specific schools; Undergraduate support.
Application information: Deadline May 1; Completion of formal application required; Applications available from high school counselors at Woodbury and Park high schools.
EIN: 411433314

3815
Southeast Texas A & M Foundation
P.O. Box 22902
Beaumont, TX 77720-2902
Application address: c/o Leonard Forey, 1429 Graham Ln., Port Neches, TX 77651, tel.: (409) 721-6400

Foundation type: Independent foundation
Limitations: Scholarships to residents of Jefferson, Hardin or Chambers counties, TX, who are attending Texas A&M University.
Financial data: Year ended 12/31/2004. Assets, $76,177 (M); Expenditures, $29,747; Total giving, $17,700; Grants to individuals, 21 grants totaling $17,700.
Type of support: Support to graduates or students of specific schools; Undergraduate support.
Application information: Deadline Mar. 22; Completion of formal application required.
EIN: 760300907

3816
Southeastern Michigan Chapter NECA Educational and Research Foundation
25180 Lahser Rd.
Southfield, MI 48037 (248) 355-3500
Scholarship application address: c/o Scholarship Committee, P.O. Box 385, Southfield, MI 48037

Foundation type: Independent foundation
Limitations: Scholarship to employees and relatives of employees of SMC/NECA.
Financial data: Year ended 12/31/2004. Assets, $71,551 (M); Expenditures, $43,066; Total giving, $34,281; Grants to individuals, 10 grants totaling $14,900.
Type of support: Employee-related scholarships.
Application information: Applications accepted. Application form required.
  Initial approach: Letter.
  Deadline(s): Apr. 15
  Additional information: Contact foundation for further program information.
EIN: 300134735

3817
Southeastern Wyoming Home Builders Scholarship Trust
P.O. Box 2066
Cheyenne, WY 82003 (307) 778-8222

Foundation type: Independent foundation
Limitations: Scholarships to individuals studying courses related to construction management, primarily in WY.
Financial data: Year ended 12/31/2004. Assets, $208,632 (M); Expenditures, $14,510; Total giving, $14,500; Grants to individuals, 15 grants totaling $14,500.
Type of support: Technical education support; Undergraduate support.
Application information: Applications by letter accepted throughout the year.
EIN: 943161079

3818
The Southwest Florida Community Foundation, Inc.
8260 College Pkwy., Ste. 101
Fort Myers, FL 33919 (239) 274-5900
Contact: For grants: Carol McLaughlin, Chief Prog. Off.
FAX: (239) 274-5930;
E-mail: info@floridacommunity.com; URL: http://www.floridacommunity.com

Foundation type: Community foundation
Limitations: Scholarships to students from high schools in Lee, Charlotte, Hendry, Glades and Collier counties, FL.
Publications: Application guidelines; Annual report (including application guidelines); Financial statement; Grants list; Informational brochure; Newsletter.
Financial data: Year ended 06/30/2005. Assets, $45,698,864 (M); Expenditures, $5,069,795; Total giving, $4,431,847; Grants to individuals, 165 grants totaling $397,190.
Fields of interest: Historic preservation/historical societies; Arts; Environment; Health care; Human services; Physically disabled.
Type of support: Awards/grants by nomination only; Undergraduate support.
Application information: Application form required. Application form available on the grantmaker's Web site.
  Copies of proposal: 1
  Deadline(s): Contact foundation for current deadline/guidelines.
  Applicants should submit the following:
    1) Transcripts
    2) SAT
    3) Letter(s) of recommendation
    4) GPA
    5) Financial information
    6) Essay
    7) Curriculum vitae
    8) ACT
  Additional information: The foundation administers a variety of scholarship programs. Interviews may be required; See Web site for program information.
EIN: 596580974

3819
Southwest School of Art and Craft
300 Augusta St.
San Antonio, TX 78205 (210) 224-1848
FAX: (210) 224-9337; E-mail: info@swschool.org;
URL: http://www.swschool.org

Foundation type: Public charity
Limitations: Scholarships to those enrolled at Southwest School or Art and Craft, TX.
Financial data: Year ended 07/31/2004. Assets, $14,880,237 (M); Expenditures,

$2,928,095; Total giving, $24,195; Grants to individuals, 159 grants totaling $24,195 (high: $315).
Fields of interest: Arts.
Type of support: Undergraduate support.
Application information:
  Initial approach: Telephone or e-mail.
  Deadline(s): Contact foundation for current application deadline/guidelines
Program descriptions:
  Young Artist Programs Scholarships: Provides scholarships based on merit and need. Written recommendations for scholarship must come from a classroom teacher, or qualified professional, and parent or guardian. Direct letters of application to Young Artists Prog. Dir. Jim LaVilla-Havelin.
  Special Scholarship Opportunity for Adults: Awards scholarships of $250 each to a limited number of deserving students.
  Adult Scholarship Program: Awards a limited number of scholarships for adult programs. Scholarships are awarded on the basis of merit and need. Application forms can be obtained from the Registration Office or Department Chairs. Scholarships are granted on a first-come, first-served basis, and are dependent upon availability of funds.
EIN: 746068932

3820
Southwestern Oregon Community College Foundation
1988 Newmark
Coos Bay, OR 97420 (541) 888-7210
Contact: Mike Gaudette, Exec. Dir.
Additional tel.: (800) 962-2838, ext. 7210;
FAX: (541) 888-7239;
E-mail: foundation@southwestern.cc.or.us;
URL: http://www.socc.edu/foundation/index.html

Foundation type: Public charity
Limitations: Scholarships to students at Southwestern Oregon Community College, OR.
Financial data: Year ended 06/30/2003. Assets, $1,800,658 (M); Expenditures, $377,891; Total giving, $182,987; Grants to individuals, 163 grants totaling $182,987 (high: $8,687, low: $67).
Type of support: Support to graduates or students of specific schools; Undergraduate support.
Application information: Deadline Mar. 5; Completion of formal application required; See Web site for application.
EIN: 936031563

3821
Bessie Sparks Scholarship Fund
c/o Peoples Bank & Trust Co.
P.O. Box 8
101 N. Main St.
Owenton, KY 40359
Additional application address: c/o Owen County High School, 2060 Hwy. 22 E., Owenton, KY 40359

Foundation type: Independent foundation
Limitations: Scholarships to students of Owen County High School, KY.
Financial data: Year ended 12/31/2004. Assets, $219,068 (M); Expenditures, $7,142; Total giving, $5,000; Grants to individuals, 10 grants totaling $5,000.
Type of support: Support to graduates or students of specific schools; Precollege support.

Application information: Deadline May; Completion of formal application required; Contact fund for application information.
EIN: 616143459

3822
SPE Foundation
c/o Society of Petroleum Engineers
222 Palisades Creek Dr.
Richardson, TX 75080-2040   (972) 952-9393
Contact: T. Don Stacy, Pres.

Foundation type: Public charity
Limitations: Scholarships to undergraduates studying petroleum engineering or a related science.
Financial data: Year ended 11/30/2003. Assets, $9,339,652 (M); Expenditures, $1,086,829; Total giving, $643,317; Grants to individuals, 9 grants totaling $643,317 (high: $5,000, low: $2,500).
Fields of interest: Engineering school/education; Physical/earth sciences; Mathematics; Physics.
Type of support: Undergraduate support.
Application information: Contact foundation for current application deadline/guidelines.
Program description:
Archie Scholarship Fund: Awards $5,000 per year for four years to a freshman student enrolled in an accredited college offering a petroleum engineering or other major engineering curriculum, or curriculum in earth sciences, physics, or mathematics.
EIN: 751575590

3823
John and L. A. Spears Foundation, Inc.
c/o R. Terry Pate
706 Holcomb Bridge Rd.
Norcross, GA 30071   (770) 368-8081

Foundation type: Independent foundation
Limitations: Scholarships to individuals in GA for higher education.
Financial data: Year ended 12/31/2004. Assets, $18,872 (M); Expenditures, $14,498; Total giving, $14,000; Grants to individuals, 2 grants totaling $14,000.
Type of support: Scholarships—to individuals.
Application information: Contact foundation for current application deadline; Completion of formal application required.
EIN: 582448721

3824
Special Libraries Association
(also known as SLA)
331 S. Patrick St.
Alexandria, VA 22314-3501   (703) 647-4900
Contact: Janice R. Lachance, C.E.O.
FAX: (703) 647-4901; E-mail: sla@sla.org;
URL: http://www.sla.org

Foundation type: Public charity
Limitations: Graduate scholarships to individuals for the study of library science.
Publications: Application guidelines; Annual report; Financial statement; Informational brochure; Newsletter.
Financial data: Year ended 12/31/2004. Assets, $14,233,375 (M); Expenditures, $6,733,548; Total giving, $30,500; Grants to individuals, 6 grants totaling $30,500 (high: $6,000, low: $500).

Fields of interest: Libraries/library science; Minorities.
Type of support: Postdoctoral support; Graduate support; Doctoral support.
Application information: Application form required.
  Initial approach: letter.
  Deadline(s): Oct. 31
  Additional information: See Web site for further information.
Program descriptions:
Affirmative Action Scholarship: A $6,000 scholarship is awarded each year for graduate study in librarianship leading to a master's degree at a recognized school of library or information science. Applicants must be a member of a minority group, defined by the U.S. Government as: Black (not of Latino origin), Latino (regardless of race), Asian, Pacific Islander, Native American, or Alaskan Native.
Institute for Scientific Information: One $1,000 ISI scholarship is available each year for beginning graduate study leading to a Ph.D. from a recognized program in a library science, information science or related fields of study. Applicants must be members of the Special Libraries Association and have worked in a special library. Applicants must be beginning doctoral candidates enrolled in a course of study by the time the award is given.
Plenum Scholarship: One $7,000 scholarship is available each year for graduate study leading to a Ph.D. from a recognized program in library science, information science or related fields of study. Applicants must be members of the Special Libraries Association and have worked in a special library. Applicants must be doctoral candidates who have dissertation topic approval and are enrolled in a course of study by the time the award is given.
SLA Scholarship: Up to three $6,000 scholarships are available each year for graduate study in librarianship leading to a master's degree at a recognized school of library or information science. Applicants must be college graduates or college seniors with an interest in special librarianship.
EIN: 135404745

3825
Special People in Need
500 W. Madison St., Ste. 3700
Chicago, IL 60661   (312) 715-5019
Contact: Irene S. Peterson, Asst. to Secy.
Irene S. Peterson tel: (312) 715-5235

Foundation type: Independent foundation
Limitations: Scholarships to financially needy residents of IL and grants to physically disabled residents of IL to engage in productive activity.
Publications: Annual report.
Financial data: Year ended 12/31/2004. Assets, $4,629,858 (M); Expenditures, $229,017; Total giving, $164,950; Grants to individuals, 23 grants totaling $50,100 (high: $4,000, low: $350).
Fields of interest: Arts education; Education, research; Disabilities, people with; Economically disadvantaged.
Type of support: Undergraduate support; Grants for special needs.
Application information: Applications accepted.
  Initial approach: Letter.
  Copies of proposal: 1
  Deadline(s): Contact foundation for current application deadline
  Applicants should submit the following:
    1) Letter(s) of recommendation
    2) Financial information
    3) Essay

    4) Transcripts
  Additional information: Letter of acceptance from college or university, financial statement, biographical data, and letter of recommendation from an educator who is familiar with applicant's qualifications.
Program description:
  Grants to the Disabled: In general, grants will not be made with respect to postgraduate study. Grants may be made to pay the costs of special equipment for handicapped individuals to pursue study, hold a job, or to improve or enhance a literary, artistic, musical, scientific, teaching, or other similar capacity, skill, or talent.
EIN: 581483651

3826
Specialized Carriers & Rigging Foundation
2750 Prosperity Ave., Ste. 620
Fairfax, VA 22031-4312   (703) 698-0291

Foundation type: Independent foundation
Limitations: Scholarships to children and grandchildren of Specialized Carriers & Rigging Assoc. employees, who are junior and senior high school students pursuing studies in transportation, cable and rigging, and millwright fields.
Financial data: Year ended 12/31/2004. Assets, $1,106,926 (M); Expenditures, $68,358; Total giving, $21,000; Grants to individuals, 7 grants totaling $21,000.
Fields of interest: Engineering/technology; Transportation.
Type of support: Employee-related scholarships.
Application information: Applications accepted throughout the year; Completion of formal application required.
EIN: 521272278

3827
Peter and Evelyn Speerstra Scholarship Fund Trust
c/o Fifth Third Bank
P.O. Box 3636
Grand Rapids, MI 49501-3636
Application address: c/o Lowell High School, Attn: Barbara Pierce, 750 Foreman St., Lowell, MI 49331, tel.: (616) 897-4125

Foundation type: Independent foundation
Limitations: Scholarships to graduates of the Lowell, MI, Public School District for study at colleges, universities, and technical schools.
Financial data: Year ended 02/28/2005. Assets, $262,495 (M); Expenditures, $17,406; Total giving, $14,000; Grants to individuals, 22 grants totaling $14,000.
Fields of interest: Vocational education.
Type of support: Support to graduates or students of specific schools; Technical education support; Undergraduate support.
Application information:
  Deadline(s): Apr. 1
  Additional information: Completion of formal application required, including transcripts and a statement of educational goals.
EIN: 386480250

3828
Spencer Community School Foundation
23 E. 7th St.
Spencer, IA 51301   (712) 262-8950
Contact: Glen Lohman, Secy.

Foundation type: Operating foundation
Limitations: Scholarships to current and former Spencer School District, IA, students for undergraduate education.
Financial data: Year ended 12/31/2002. Assets, $942,918 (M); Expenditures, $80,384; Total giving, $66,584; Grants to individuals, 64 grants totaling $59,397 (high: $3,750, low: $200).
Fields of interest: Education.
Type of support: Support to graduates or students of specific schools; Undergraduate support.
Application information: Applications accepted. Application form required.
  Deadline(s): Apr. 1
  Applicants should submit the following:
    1) Letter(s) of recommendation
    2) Financial information
    3) Essay
  Additional information: See Web site for further application and scholarship information.
EIN: 421306327

3829

Spencer Education Foundation

(formerly George and Marie G. Spencer Education Foundation and Trust)
c/o National City Bank
P.O. Box 94651
Cleveland, OH 44101-4651
Scholarship application addresses: c/o Tipton High School, 619 S. Main St., Tipton, IN 46072, tel.: (317) 675-7431; c/o Tri-Central High School, R.R. No. 2, Sharpesville, IN 46068, tel.: (317) 963-2560

Foundation type: Independent foundation
Limitations: Scholarships to graduates of Tipton High School, IN, and Tri-Central High School, Sharpsville, IN.
Financial data: Year ended 12/31/2004. Assets, $3,363,112 (M); Expenditures, $226,185; Total giving, $198,508; Grants to individuals, totaling $198,508.
Type of support: Support to graduates or students of specific schools; Undergraduate support.
Application information: Application form required.
  Deadline(s): Oct. 1
  Additional information: Scholarships are renewable.
EIN: 356072759

3830

Spencer Educational Foundation, Inc.

c/o RIMS
1065 Ave. of the Americas, 13th Fl.
New York, NY 10018 (212) 655-6223
Contact: Angela Sabatino, Admin. Mgr.
FAX: (212) 655-6044; E-mail: Asabatino@rims.org;
URL: http://www.spencered.org

Foundation type: Public charity
Limitations: Scholarships to undergraduate, graduate, and doctoral students pursuing a career related to risk management.
Publications: Annual report; Informational brochure; Newsletter.
Financial data: Year ended 12/31/2004. Assets, $4,471,656 (M); Expenditures, $578,156; Total giving, $378,090; Grants to individuals, 32 grants totaling $159,840 (high: $10,000, low: $2,500).
Fields of interest: Business school/education.
Type of support: Graduate support; Undergraduate support; Doctoral support.

Application information: Applications accepted. Application form required. Application form available on the grantmaker's Web site.
  Deadline(s): Jan. 30 for Full-time scholarships; none for Part-time MBA scholarships
  Applicants should submit the following:
    1) Transcripts
    2) GPA
    3) Resume
    4) Letter(s) of recommendation
    5) Essay
Program descriptions:
  Full-time Scholarships: Awards scholarships to full-time students who are undergraduate juniors or seniors, Master's degree candidates, or teaching oriented, pre-dissertation, Ph.D. candidates. Minimum 3.3 GPA. Applicants must focus academically on an area related to risk management.
  Part-time MBA Scholarships: Awards up to $10,000 to part-time MBA candidates. Executive MBA students are eligible.
EIN: 581420617

3831

Spencer Scholarship Foundation

503 N. Ferndale Rd.
Wayzata, MN 55391-1008 (952) 476-1072
Contact: Dale A. Spencer, Pres.

Foundation type: Independent foundation
Limitations: Scholarships to undergraduate students at accredited colleges and universities, or technical and vocational schools.
Financial data: Year ended 12/31/2004. Assets, $178,844 (M); Expenditures, $75,122; Total giving, $66,266; Grants to individuals, 31 grants totaling $66,266.
Fields of interest: Vocational education.
Type of support: Technical education support.
Application information: Application form required.
  Deadline(s): Feb. 28.
  Additional information: Scholarship amounts are up to $3,000 for college or university, and up to $1,000 for vocational/technical school.
EIN: 411843693

3832

John W. Spencer Trust

c/o Mechanics Bank of Richmond
3170 Hilltop Mall Rd.
Richmond, CA 94806 (510) 262-7200
Contact: Ruth Byrone
Additional tel.: Diana McClelland, Spencer Schol. Admin., (510) 232-0459

Foundation type: Independent foundation
Limitations: Scholarships to financially needy Richmond and El Cerrito, CA, residents for full-time study at any campus of the University of California or Leland Stanford Junior University, CA.
Financial data: Year ended 11/30/2003. Assets, $1,686,581 (M); Expenditures, $116,752; Total giving, $94,550; Grants to individuals, 68 grants totaling $94,550 (high: $3,150, low: $300).
Type of support: Support to graduates or students of specific schools; Undergraduate support.
Application information: Application form required.
  Deadline(s): Apr. 1
  Applicants should submit the following:
    1) Class rank
    2) Transcripts
    3) Resume
    4) Letter(s) of recommendation
    5) GPA

    6) Financial information
    7) Essay
  Additional information: Application must also include a copy of letter of acceptance from university, and verification of address. Interviews required.
Program description:
  Scholarships: If the amount of the scholarship is $600 or more per year, payments will be made in nine equal monthly installments starting on Sept. 1. If the award is less than $600 per year, the entire award will be paid on Sept. 1. Scholarships are renewable.
EIN: 946055547

3833

The Sperry Fund

99 Park Ave., Ste. 2220
New York, NY 10016-1601
Contact: Thomas L. Parkinson Ph.D., Prog. Dir.
Application address: c/o Beinecke Scholarship Prog., Box 125, Fogelsville, PA 18051-0125, tel.: (610) 395-5560
FAX: (610) 625-7919;
E-mail: BeineckeScholarship@earthlink.net

Foundation type: Independent foundation
Limitations: Scholarships to college juniors who are U.S. citizens and are nominated by the presidents or deans of accredited colleges and universities, primarily in NY.
Publications: Informational brochure.
Financial data: Year ended 06/30/2005. Assets, $16,582,685 (M); Expenditures, $1,055,513; Total giving, $882,168; Grants to individuals, 92 grants totaling $650,168 (high: $20,000, low: $2,000).
Type of support: Awards/grants by nomination only; Undergraduate support.
Application information: Applications not accepted.
  Additional information: Individual applications not accepted; College or university must be invited to nominate an applicant.
Program description:
  Beinecke Memorial Scholarships: These scholarships were established to support men and women of exceptional ability and achievement. Since 1975, the program has selected college juniors for support during their senior year and two subsequent years of graduate study at a university or professional school. It seeks to encourage and enable highly motivated students to take fullest advantage of the opportunities available during senior year and to be courageous in the selection of graduate study programs. Each scholar receives $2,000 in the senior year of college and support of up to $15,000 for each of two years in graduate school. Beinecke scholars are nominated by their colleges and universities. Only one nominee may be submitted each year by an institution. Once an institution's nominee has been awarded a Beinecke scholarship, the institution may not submit another nomination for two years. Nominees are considered for superior strength of character, intellectual ability, and sense of purpose. Sixteen new awards are given each year.
EIN: 136114308

3834
The Sphinx Organization
(formerly Concert Competitions & Musical Development, Inc.)
400 Renaissance Ctr., Ste. 2120
Detroit, MI   48243   (313) 877-9100
Contact: Aaron Dworkin, Pres.
FAX: (313) 877-9145;
E-mail: info@sphinxmusic.org; URL: http://www.sphinxmusic.org

Foundation type: Public charity
Limitations: Prizes and scholarships to African American and Latino classical music students who are winners of the annual Sphinx Competition.
Financial data: Year ended 12/31/2003.
Assets, $1,171,300 (M); Expenditures, $845,918; Total giving, $57,035; Grants to individuals, totaling $57,035.
Fields of interest: Orchestra (symphony); Minorities.
Type of support: Awards/prizes; Undergraduate support.
Application information:
Deadline(s): Dec. 1
Additional information: Completion of formal application required, including copy of birth certificate, biography and photo, $35 application fee, and audition tape/CD.
Program description:
Sphinx Competition: All 18 Semi-Finalists will receive a full scholarship to attend a Summer Music or Artistic Sponsor Music Institution. Incoming first year students may be eligible for scholarships in partner institutions. In addition, all 18 Semi-Finalists will receive a Sphinx Music Assistance Fund scholarship which they can apply towards their musical development. Senior Division Prizes: 1st Place-$10,000 cash prize, solo appearances with major orchestras, performance with the Sphinx Symphony. 2nd Place-$5,000 cash prize, performance with Sphinx Symphony. 3rd Place-$3,500 cash prize, performance with the Sphinx Symphony. Junior Division Prizes: 1st Place-$5,000 cash prize, solo appearances with major orchestras, performances with the Sphinx Symphony, national radio debut. 2nd Place-$3,500 cash prize, performance with the Sphinx Symphony, national radio debut. 3rd Place-$2,000 cash prize, performance with the Sphinx Symphony, national radio debut.
EIN: 383283759

3835
Kathleen C. Spicer Scholarship Fund
c/o Bank of America, N.A.
NC1-002-11-18, Bank of America Plz.
Charlotte, NC   28255
Application address: c/o Bank of America, N.A., Attn.: Kim Sexton, 600 Peachtree St., Ste. 1100, Atlanta, GA 30308

Foundation type: Independent foundation
Limitations: Scholarships to residents of Cobb County, GA, to attend two- and four-year colleges.
Publications: Application guidelines.
Financial data: Year ended 06/30/2005.
Assets, $925,873 (M); Expenditures, $57,851; Total giving, $42,000; Grants to individuals, totaling $42,000.
Type of support: Undergraduate support.
Application information:
Deadline(s): Apr. 20
Additional information: Completion of formal application required, including two reference letters and a personal essay.

Program description:
Scholarships: Selection criteria include a minimum SAT score of 1200, a minimum GPA of 3.65 for high school applicants and 3.5 for college applicants, interscholastic activities, extracurricular activities, community involvement, course of study, and attendance record. No grants are awarded for postgraduate study.
EIN: 581448686

3836
The Anthony Spinazzola Foundation, Inc.
Cabot Executive Park
5 Cabot Pl.
Stoughton, MA   02072   (781) 344-4413
Contact: Claire H. Murtha, Exec. Dir.
FAX: (781) 344-4586; E-mail: info@spinazzola.org;
URL: http://www.spinazzola.org/

Foundation type: Public charity
Limitations: Scholarships to students aspiring for careers in the food and wine industry in MA and NH. Also gives grants for hunger relief.
Financial data: Year ended 12/31/2004.
Assets, $1,108,611 (M); Expenditures, $904,582; Total giving, $210,019; Grants to individuals, totaling $135,019.
Fields of interest: Agriculture/food, formal/general education.
Type of support: Undergraduate support; Grants for special needs.
Application information:
Initial approach: Proposal.
Deadline(s): Apr. 1
Additional information: See Web site for current application guidelines.
EIN: 043161888

3837
Abigail L. Spire Foundation, Inc.
1645 Country Club Rd.
Wilmington, NC   28403
Contact: Scholarships: Abigail L. Spire

Foundation type: Independent foundation
Limitations: Scholarships to individuals for attendance at Cape Fear Community College, NC, or University of North Carolina at Wilmington, NC.
Financial data: Year ended 07/31/2005.
Assets, $345,216 (M); Expenditures, $116,082; Total giving, $61,242.
Type of support: Support to graduates or students of specific schools; Undergraduate support.
Application information: Applications accepted. Application form required.
Deadline(s): Feb. 28
Additional information: Contact foundation for current application guidelines. Scholarships are renewable for a total of four years.
EIN: 562358231

3838
Spivey Scholarship Trust
c/o First Citizens Bank & Trust Dept.
P.O. Box 29522
Raleigh, NC   27626   (919) 357-0720
Contact: Linda F. Hofler, Tr.
Application address: Rte. 1, Box 95, Hobbsville, NC 27946, tel.: (919) 465-8621

Foundation type: Independent foundation
Limitations: One-year scholarships to seniors in Gates County High School, NC, starting with the top male and top female in the graduating class.

Publications: Annual report.
Financial data: Year ended 11/30/2004.
Assets, $840,962 (M); Expenditures, $47,709; Total giving, $41,500; Grants to individuals, 5 grants totaling $41,500 (high: $11,540, low: $3,018).
Type of support: Support to graduates or students of specific schools; Undergraduate support.
Application information: Applications accepted throughout the year; Initial approach by letter; Completion of formal application required.
EIN: 566235902

3839
The Don H. Splawn Charitable Foundation
P.O. Box 1705
Pleasanton, CA   94566-0170
Contact: Phillips Yee, Tr.

Foundation type: Independent foundation
Limitations: Scholarships to individuals for higher education, primarily in CA.
Financial data: Year ended 12/31/2002.
Assets, $2,595,816 (M); Expenditures, $246,178; Total giving, $216,000; Grants to individuals, 170 grants totaling $194,000 (high: $3,000, low: $250).
Type of support: Undergraduate support.
Application information: Deadline varies; Application by letter.
EIN: 770420822

3840
Roy L. Splawn Charitable Foundation
P.O. Box 1705
Pleasanton, CA   94566-0170
Contact: Phillips Yee, Tr.

Foundation type: Independent foundation
Limitations: Scholarships to individuals for higher education.
Financial data: Year ended 12/31/2003.
Assets, $1,060,621 (M); Expenditures, $164,631; Total giving, $153,903; Grants to individuals, 29 grants totaling $35,500 (high: $3,000, low: $250).
Type of support: Scholarships—to individuals.
Application information: Applications accepted.
Initial approach: Letter.
Additional information: Contact foundation for current application deadline/guidelines.
EIN: 943276752

3841
The Harper W. Spong Family Scholarship Foundation
(also known as Spong Family Foundation)
c/o M&T Trust Co.
21 E. Market St., M/C402-130
York, PA   17401-1500
Application address: c/o M&T Bank, P.O. Box 2961, Harrisburg, PA 17105

Foundation type: Independent foundation
Limitations: Scholarships to full-time Allfirst Bank employees and their dependent children for study at postsecondary educational institutions. Employees must have worked three or more years in Dauphin, Cumberland, Lancaster, York, or Lebanon counties, PA.
Financial data: Year ended 12/31/2002.
Assets, $104,184 (M); Expenditures, $43,704; Total giving, $39,750; Grants to individuals, 23 grants totaling $39,750.

Type of support: Employee-related scholarships.
Application information: Applications accepted. Application form required.
   Deadline(s): None
EIN: 232247380

3842
Ralph & Bernice Sprehe Scholarship Trust
c/o U.S. Bank, N.A.
P.O. Box 387
St. Louis, MO   63166

Foundation type: Independent foundation
Limitations: Scholarships to individuals who are members of the parish of St. Mary's Roman Catholic Church in Centralia, IL who are graduates of Centralia High School, IL, and who are enrolled in Kaskaskia College, IL. Occasionally, scholarship recipients may also be members of any Roman Catholic Church in Marion County, IL.
Financial data: Year ended 01/31/2005. Assets, $531,632 (M); Expenditures, $43,862; Total giving, $35,860; Grants to individuals, totaling $35,860.
Fields of interest: Roman Catholic agencies & churches.
Type of support: Support to graduates or students of specific schools; Undergraduate support.
Application information:
   Applicants should submit the following:
      1) Letter(s) of recommendation
      2) GPA
      3) Financial information
      4) Essay
   Additional information: If the recipient maintains a 'C' average, the scholarship is renewable for up to four semesters.
EIN: 371369459

3843
The Springfield Foundation
4 W. Main St., Ste. 825
Springfield, OH   45502-1323   (937) 324-8773
Contact: Robin Atwood Pfeil, C.E.O.; For grant application: Ed Baker, Prog. Off.
FAX: (937) 324-1836;
E-mail: robin@springfieldfoundation.org; E-mail for grant application: ed@springfieldfoundation.org;
URL: http://www.springfieldfoundation.org

Foundation type: Community foundation
Limitations: Scholarships to residents of Clark County, OH.
Publications: Application guidelines; Annual report; Financial statement; Grants list; Informational brochure (including application guidelines); Newsletter; Program policy statement.
Financial data: Year ended 03/31/2005. Assets, $31,150,487 (M); Expenditures, $1,989,717; Total giving, $1,237,536.
Type of support: Employee-related scholarships; Scholarships—to individuals.
Application information: Application form required.
   Deadline(s): Mar. 15
   Applicants should submit the following:
      1) Letter(s) of recommendation
      2) ACT
   Additional information: Each scholarship has different guidelines according to each individual donor's wishes; See Web site for complete program listing.
EIN: 316030764

3844
The Springfield Teachers' Club, Inc.
195 State St.
Springfield, MA   01103
Application address: c/o Margaret Scanlon, 75 Terrace Ln., Springfield, MA 01118

Foundation type: Independent foundation
Limitations: Scholarships to seniors of Springfield, MA, public high schools for attendance at accredited institutions of higher learning.
Financial data: Year ended 05/31/2005. Assets, $136,009 (M); Expenditures, $12,407; Total giving, $11,014; Grants to individuals, 9 grants totaling $4,500.
Type of support: Support to graduates or students of specific schools; Undergraduate support.
Application information: Applications accepted. Application form required.
   Deadline(s): Apr. 13
EIN: 046065091

3845
Mabel W. Springfield Trust
c/o Superintendant of Sayre Public Schools
716 N.E. 66th St.
Sayre, OK   73662
Application address: c/o Principal, Sayre High School, 600 E. Hanna, Sayre, OK 73662, tel.: (580) 928-5576

Foundation type: Operating foundation
Limitations: Scholarships to students who have attended Sayre High School, OK, for three consecutive years and will graduate in the top 80 percent of their class.
Financial data: Year ended 02/28/2005. Assets, $809,364 (M); Expenditures, $19,975; Total giving, $18,750.
Type of support: Support to graduates or students of specific schools; Undergraduate support.
Application information: Application form required.
   Deadline(s): Mar. 1
EIN: 736101794

3846
Springman Scholarship Fund
c/o Fifth Third Bank
P.O. Box 630858
Cincinnati, OH   45263-0858   (513) 579-5237

Foundation type: Independent foundation
Limitations: Scholarships to graduates of Goshen High School, OH.
Financial data: Year ended 09/30/2004. Assets, $1,060,442 (M); Expenditures, $67,165; Total giving, $56,499; Grants to individuals, 16 grants totaling $56,499.
Type of support: Support to graduates or students of specific schools; Undergraduate support.
Application information: Applications not accepted.
EIN: 316455677

3847
The Springs Close Foundation, Inc.
(formerly Springs Foundation, Inc.)
1826 Second Baxter Crossing
Fort Mill, SC   29708   (803) 548-2002
Contact: Angela H. McCrae, Exec. Dir.
FAX: (803) 548-1797; URL: http://www.thespringsclosefoundation.org

Foundation type: Independent foundation

Limitations: Student loans to residents of Lancaster County or the townships of Fort Mill and Chester, SC, for undergraduate study, or medical or dental school.
Publications: Application guidelines; Annual report; Annual report (including application guidelines).
Financial data: Year ended 12/31/2005. Assets, $41,359,032 (M); Expenditures, $3,575,626; Total giving, $2,928,430.
Fields of interest: Dental school/education; Medical school/education.
Type of support: Student loans—to individuals; Graduate support; Undergraduate support.
Application information: Application form required. Application form available on the grantmaker's Web site.
   Initial approach: Letter or telephone.
   Copies of proposal: 1
   Deadline(s): May 1 and Dec. 1.
   Applicants should submit the following:
      1) ACT
      2) GPA
      3) Letter(s) of recommendation
      4) SAT
      5) Transcripts
   Additional information: Interviews required.
Program description:
   Leroy Springs Student Loan Program:
Interest-free student loans are made on the basis of financial need to individuals attending four-year, accredited colleges in SC. Loans to undergraduate students may not exceed $14,000 over a four-year period, and loans to medical and dental school students may not exceed $18,000 over a four-year period. Participants must live in or their parents must work in Lancaster County, Chester, or Fort Mill, SC. Interest-free loans of up to $1,500 are available to students attending York Technical College; same restrictions apply. Applicants must be in the upper 50 percent of their high school graduating class and must score at least 820 on the SAT. Upperclassmen must maintain a cumulative GPA of at least 2.5 to remain eligible and be enrolled full-time.
EIN: 570426344

3848
Rose Spurrier Scholarship Fund
P.O. Box 473
Kingman, KS   67068-0473   (620) 532-3108
Contact: Robert S. Wunsch, Tr.

Foundation type: Independent foundation
Limitations: Scholarships to qualified graduates of Kingman City High School, KS.
Financial data: Year ended 12/31/2004. Assets, $2,256,291 (M); Expenditures, $104,081; Total giving, $70,959; Grants to individuals, totaling $70,959.
Type of support: Support to graduates or students of specific schools; Undergraduate support.
Application information: Contact fund for current application deadline/guidelines.
EIN: 480978238

3849
The William D. Squires Educational Foundation
10950 W. Union Hills Dr., Ste. 408
Sun City, AZ   85373
Application address: c/o Cynthia Squires Gross, P.O. Box 2940, Jupiter, FL 33468-2940

Foundation type: Independent foundation
Limitations: Scholarships to students in OH for higher education.

Financial data: Year ended 12/31/2004. Assets, $1,108,667 (M); Expenditures, $196,633; Total giving, $130,300; Grants to individuals, 101 grants totaling $130,300 (high: $15,000, low: $800).
Type of support: Undergraduate support.
Application information: Deadline Apr. 5; Application by eight-page letter, including at least two letters of recommendation, transcript, short essay and SAR from the FAFSA.
EIN: 860946058

3850

St. Clair County Scholarship Trust Fund

c/o Martha Omalley
500 Wilshire Dr.
Belleville, IL 62223-1149
Contact: Rosella Wamser, Regional Superintendent

Foundation type: Independent foundation
Limitations: Scholarships to graduates of high schools in St. Clair County, IL.
Financial data: Year ended 12/31/2004. Assets, $597,354 (M); Expenditures, $38,813; Total giving, $33,250; Grants to individuals, 26 grants totaling $33,250.
Type of support: Support to graduates or students of specific schools; Undergraduate support.
Application information: Application form required.
Deadline(s): Mar. 1.
Applicants should submit the following:
1) SAT
2) ACT
3) Financial information
4) Transcripts
5) Letter(s) of recommendation
6) GPA
7) Essay
Program descriptions:
Constant J. and Mary Lenore Comment Scholarship: Scholarships are renewable for up to four years. Each scholarship is $1,500.
St. Clair County Scholarship: Scholarships are $250 each and cover one year of study only.
EIN: 371286750

3851

St. Elmo Foundation

(formerly Delta Phi Educational Fund, Inc.)
174 Old Pascack Rd.
Pearl River, NY 10965-1553
Contact: Gregory E. McElroy, Exec. Dir.
Application address: P.O. Box 81521, Athens, GA 30608-1521; Tel./Fax: (845) 735-3278; E-mail: St.Elmo@DeltaPhi.org; URL: http://www.st-elmo.net/foundation/

Foundation type: Public charity
Limitations: Scholarships to Delta Phi members and other students for undergraduate and graduate education. Some grants also to members, students, and faculty or staff for special projects.
Financial data: Year ended 12/31/2003. Assets, $1,868,541 (M); Expenditures, $75,701; Total giving, $13,697; Grants to individuals, 9 grants totaling $4,400.
Fields of interest: Education.
Type of support: Grants to individuals; Undergraduate support.
Application information: Applications accepted. Application form required.
Applicants should submit the following:
1) Letter(s) of recommendation
2) Transcripts
3) Financial information
4) Essay

Additional information: Application must also include income tax returns; See Web site for further application and scholarship information.
EIN: 136170013

3852

St. Joseph Kiwanis Foundation

c/o Jonathan B. Sauer
414 Main St.
St. Joseph, MI 49085-1235

Foundation type: Independent foundation
Limitations: Scholarships to students from Lakeshore High School, St. Joseph High School, and Lake Michigan Catholic High School, all in MI.
Financial data: Year ended 12/31/2004. Assets, $519,518 (M); Expenditures, $25,938; Total giving, $19,000; Grants to individuals, 23 grants totaling $19,000.
Type of support: Support to graduates or students of specific schools; Undergraduate support.
Application information: Applications accepted.
Deadline(s): None
Additional information: Completion of formal application required, including financial statement, photograph, two references, and personal statement; Interviews required.
Program description:
Scholarship Program: In selecting recipients, the foundation will consider:
· expectation of remaining in school and meeting the standards of the school
· past conduct and present attitude indicating a reasonable chance of attaining educational and sociological benefits
· facts indicating that applicant will be unable to attend the institution selected without financial assistance.
EIN: 386117678

3853

St. Jude Foundation

c/o Sheila Zipse
P.O. Box 279
Grand Junction, CO 81502-0279
Application address: c/o IHM Church, Scholarship Comm., 790 26 1/2 Rd., Grand Junction, CO 81506

Foundation type: Independent foundation
Limitations: Scholarships to high school graduates under 25 years of age who are active members of the Catholic Church in Mesa County, CO, pursuing a degree at an accredited college or university.
Financial data: Year ended 12/31/2004. Assets, $235,344 (M); Expenditures, $13,977; Total giving, $12,150; Grants to individuals, 22 grants totaling $12,150.
Fields of interest: Roman Catholic agencies & churches.
Type of support: Scholarships—to individuals.
Application information: Deadline Mar. 31; Completion of formal application required; Applications may be obtained at Catholic churches in Mesa County, CO.
EIN: 841276940

3854

St. Louis Auto Dealers Charities, Inc.

10730 Manchester Rd.
Kirkwood, MO 63122
Contact: David Crafton

Foundation type: Independent foundation
Limitations: Scholarships to St. Louis, MO, area students to study automotive industry-related fields.
Financial data: Year ended 12/31/2003. Assets, $256 (M); Expenditures, $40,672; Total giving, $40,000; Grants to individuals, 45 grants totaling $40,000 (high: $1,000, low: $500).
Type of support: Scholarships—to individuals.
Application information:
Initial approach: Letter or telephone.
Deadline(s): None
Additional information: Contact foundation for current application guidelines.
EIN: 431400990

3855

St. Louis Carpenters District Council Scholarship Fund, Inc.

c/o Scholarship Comm.
1401 Hampton Ave.
St. Louis, MO 63139 (314) 644-4800
Contact: Terry Nelson, Pres.

Foundation type: Public charity
Limitations: Scholarships to high school seniors who are dependents of members in good standing of the United Brotherhood of Carpenters of St. Louis, MO.
Financial data: Year ended 12/31/2003. Assets, $105,790 (M); Expenditures, $26,000; Total giving, $26,000; Grants to individuals, 52 grants totaling $26,000 (high: $500, low: $500).
Type of support: Scholarships—to individuals.
Application information: Contact fund for current application deadline; Initial approach by letter or telephone; Completion of formal application required.
EIN: 431812440

3856

St. Luke's Nurses' Benefit Fund

P.O. Box 250892, Columbia Station
New York, NY 10025
Contact: Barbara Edwards Dennis
Application address: 3 Leewald Ln., City Island, NY 10464

Foundation type: Independent foundation
Limitations: Grants to needy graduates of St. Luke's School of Nursing, NY.
Financial data: Year ended 06/30/2002. Assets, $431,718 (M); Expenditures, $13,750; Total giving, $11,000; Grants to individuals, totaling $11,000 (high: $6,000, low: $5,000).
Fields of interest: Nursing care.
Type of support: Support to graduates or students of specific schools; Undergraduate support.
Application information: Applications accepted throughout the year; Completion of formal application required.
EIN: 136164433

3857

St. Mary's High School Trust No. 3

c/o JPMorgan Chase Bank, N.A
P.O. Box 1308
Milwaukee, WI 53201
Application address: c/o Fr. Daniel Divis, 309 7th St., Lorain, OH 44052, tel.: (440) 245-5283

Foundation type: Independent foundation

Limitations: Scholarships to parishioners of St. Mary's Church and to students of St. Mary's High School, both in Lorain, OH.
Financial data: Year ended 12/31/2004. Assets, $562,062 (M); Expenditures, $17,290; Total giving, $8,900.
Fields of interest: Christian agencies & churches.
Type of support: Support to graduates or students of specific schools; Undergraduate support.
Application information: Application form required.
Deadline(s): Apr. 15
Program description:
Scholarship Program: Selection is based on need, scholastic record, and community involvement.
EIN: 346631616

3858
St. Marys Community Foundation
146 E. Spring St.
St. Marys, OH   45885   (419) 394-5693
Contact: Darwin D. Zeigler, Admin.
FAX: (419) 394-7694; E-mail: smcf@bright.net;
URL: http://www.ridertown.com/community/foundation.html

Foundation type: Community foundation
Limitations: Grants and loans to students of the St. Marys city schools, who reside in St. Marys, OH, area.
Publications: Annual report; Informational brochure; Occasional report.
Financial data: Year ended 06/30/2005. Assets, $4,058,323 (M); Expenditures, $224,245; Total giving, $195,563; Grants to individuals, totaling $35,000.
Type of support: Support to graduates or students of specific schools; Undergraduate support.
Application information: Contact foundation for current application deadline/guidelines.
EIN: 237372270

3859
St. Paul College Club, Inc. - AAUW Scholarship Trust
990 Summit Ave.
St. Paul, MN   55105-3033   (651) 227-4477
Contact: Billy Franey, Chair.

Foundation type: Independent foundation
Limitations: Scholarships limited to area high school seniors in MN, attending an AAUW approved college or university.
Financial data: Year ended 06/30/2005. Assets, $430,412 (M); Expenditures, $50,397; Total giving, $31,000; Grants to individuals, 11 grants totaling $31,000 (high: $3,000, low: $1,500).
Type of support: Undergraduate support.
Application information: Deadline Mar. 15; Completion of formal application required; Applications available from area high school counseling offices.
EIN: 411373110

3860
St. Paul's Church Home
c/o St. Paul's Episcopal Church
815 E. Grace St.
Richmond, VA   23218-1535

Foundation type: Independent foundation

Limitations: Educational grants to persons between the ages of 17 and 25 who reside in the Richmond, VA, metropolitan area.
Publications: Application guidelines.
Financial data: Year ended 12/31/2004. Assets, $1,065,682 (M); Expenditures, $58,994; Total giving, $56,097; Grants to individuals, totaling $17,580.
Type of support: Undergraduate support.
Application information: Applications accepted. Application form required.
Initial approach: Letter outlining financial need.
Deadline(s): None
Applicants should submit the following:
1) Letter(s) of recommendation
2) Transcripts
3) Financial information
Additional information: Application should also include two references, and personal letter outlining educational and academic goals.
EIN: 546048630

3861
St. Petersburg Times Scholarship Fund
(formerly The Poynter Fund)
P.O. Box 1121
St. Petersburg, FL   33731-1121
Application address: c/o Andrew Corty, 490 First Ave. S., St. Petersburg, FL 33701

Foundation type: Independent foundation
Limitations: Undergraduate scholarships and fellowships to journalism students residing in west central FL.
Financial data: Year ended 12/31/2003. Assets, $13,511,660 (M); Expenditures, $1,017,879; Total giving, $773,093; Grants to individuals, totaling $320,800.
Fields of interest: Education.
Type of support: Graduate support; Undergraduate support.
Application information: Application form required.
Deadline(s): Varies
Additional information: Interview required.
Program descriptions:
St. Petersburg Times Scholarships: Awarded to high school seniors from Hillsborough, Pinellas, Pasco, Citrus and Hernando counties, FL. Deadline Nov. 16.
Career Journalism Scholarships: Awarded to high school seniors from the Hillsborough, Pinellas, Pasco, Citrus and Hernando counties, FL. Deadline Feb. 1.
Intern Scholars: Awarded to full-time undergraduate and graduate students employed as interns. Deadline July 1.
EIN: 596142547

3862
Henry P. and Mary B. Stager Memorial Nursing Scholarship
c/o Fulton Financial Advisors, N.A.
P.O. Box 3215
Lancaster, PA   17604-3215
Application address: c/o Financial Aid Admin., 145 E. Lemon St., Lancaster, PA 17602

Foundation type: Independent foundation
Limitations: Scholarships to students at the Lancaster Institute for Health Education, School of Nursing.
Financial data: Year ended 10/31/2004. Assets, $1,656,156 (M); Expenditures, $114,052; Total giving, $101,250; Grants to

individuals, 128 grants totaling $101,250 (high: $1,500, low: $250).
Fields of interest: Nursing school/education.
Type of support: Support to graduates or students of specific schools; Undergraduate support.
Application information: Deadline May 1; Completion of formal application required.
EIN: 232821372

3863
Mabel Stagner Charitable Trust
c/o Wells Fargo Bank, N.A., Trust Tax Dept.
P.O. Box 63954
San Francisco, CA   94163
Application address: c/o Wells Fargo Bank, N.A., Attn.: Helen Robideaux, P.O. Box 20160, Long Beach, CA 90802

Foundation type: Independent foundation
Limitations: Scholarships to graduating seniors of Fort Bragg High School, CA, for full-time study at a college or university.
Financial data: Year ended 05/31/2005. Assets, $179,909 (M); Expenditures, $7,022; Total giving, $4,000.
Type of support: Support to graduates or students of specific schools; Undergraduate support.
Application information: Applications accepted.
Deadline(s): None
Additional information: Recipients must maintain at least a 2.0 GPA.
EIN: 956795944

3864
Mildred T. Stahlman Education Foundation
c/o Vanderbilt University
1125-B Light Hall
Nashville, TN   37232-0001

Foundation type: Independent foundation
Limitations: Scholarships to students or graduates of high schools in Humphreys County, TN.
Financial data: Year ended 12/31/2004. Assets, $17,698 (M); Expenditures, $17,180; Total giving, $15,500; Grants to individuals, 13 grants totaling $15,500.
Type of support: Support to graduates or students of specific schools; Undergraduate support.
Application information: Contact foundation for current application deadline; Completion of formal application required, including letters of recommendation, transcripts, and personal and financial information.
EIN: 621379222

3865
Stained Glass Players
1996 W. Evangel St.
Ozark, MO   65721-9166   (417) 581-9192
Contact: Ron Boutwell, Exec. Dir.

Foundation type: Public charity
Limitations: Scholarships to college students with a demonstrated commitment to Christian theater, including past involvement with the Stained Glass Theater in MO.
Financial data: Year ended 12/31/2004. Assets, $624,052 (M); Expenditures, $261,318; Total giving, $9,978; Grants to individuals, 6 grants totaling $2,160 (high: $1,000, low: $50).
Fields of interest: Theater; Protestant agencies & churches.
Type of support: Undergraduate support.

Application information: Contact foundation for current application deadline; Completion of formal application required.
EIN: 431326065

3866
The Richard Seth Staley Educational Foundation
(formerly Richard Seth Staley Foundation for Psychological Development)
P.O. Box 4129
Aspen, CO 81612
Contact: Donald H. Keltner, Pres.

Foundation type: Operating foundation
Limitations: Scholarships to individuals for attendance at U.S. colleges and universities. Some preference is given to individuals attending CA institutions.
Financial data: Year ended 09/30/2004. Assets, $12,522,808 (M); Expenditures, $516,990; Total giving, $324,384.
Type of support: Undergraduate support.
Application information: Applications accepted. Application form required.
Deadline(s): None
Applicants should submit the following:
1) Letter(s) of recommendation
2) Transcripts
EIN: 953532336

3867
Stamford Rotary Trust Fund
P.O. Box 8026
Stamford, CT 06905-8026 (203) 325-0003

Foundation type: Public charity
Limitations: Scholarships to residents of Stamford, CT.
Financial data: Year ended 06/30/2005. Assets, $238,428 (M); Expenditures, $17,387; Total giving, $16,500; Grants to individuals, 7 grants totaling $10,500 (high: $1,500, low: $1,500).
Type of support: Scholarships—to individuals.
Application information: Contact foundation for current application deadline/guidelines.
EIN: 066068805

3868
Stamford Woman's Club, Inc.
P.O. Box 16793
Stamford, CT 06905
Contact: Roseanne DeCamillo, Dir.

Foundation type: Operating foundation
Limitations: Scholarships to residents of Stamford, CT.
Financial data: Year ended 04/30/2004. Assets, $1,247,567 (M); Expenditures, $133,167; Total giving, $67,657; Grants to individuals, 34 grants totaling $36,000 (high: $1,500, low: $1,000).
Type of support: Scholarships—to individuals.
Application information: Application form required.
Deadline(s): Mar. 1
EIN: 060653184

3869
Arnold P. Stamm Scholarship Trust
c/o Marshall & Ilsley Bank
P.O. Box 2980
Milwaukee, WI 53201
Application address: c/o Rick Altendorf, Weyauwega-Fremont High School, 500 E. Ann St., Weyauwega, WI 54983

Foundation type: Independent foundation
Limitations: Scholarships to individuals who reside in the Weyauwega-Fremont School District, WI.
Financial data: Year ended 03/31/2005. Assets, $594,938 (M); Expenditures, $31,906; Total giving, $28,250; Grants to individuals, 30 grants totaling $28,250 (high: $2,000, low: $300).
Type of support: Scholarships—to individuals.
Application information: Deadline May 1; Contact trust for current application guidelines.
EIN: 396582045

3870
Eugene & Florence O. Stanley Scholarship Trust
c/o 1st Source Bank, Trust Dept.
100 N. Michigan St.
South Bend, IN 46601 (574) 235-2790
Application address: c/o 1st Source Bank, Trust Dept., P.O. Box 1602, South Bend, IN 46634

Foundation type: Independent foundation
Limitations: Scholarships to graduates of Plymouth Community Schools, IN, who are in the top 30 percent of their classes based on seven semester rankings.
Financial data: Year ended 12/31/2004. Assets, $1,854,542 (M); Expenditures, $78,403; Total giving, $59,334; Grants to individuals, 81 grants totaling $59,334.
Type of support: Support to graduates or students of specific schools; Undergraduate support.
Application information: Deadline Mar. 25 for first-time applicants, Mar. 1 for renewals; Completion of formal application required, including transcripts, financial information, PSAT or SAT scores (if applicable), letter of recommendation, essay, completed confidential sheet, and photograph of self.
EIN: 356375193

3871
Charles E. Stanley Scottish Rite Memorial Fund
c/o Bank of Stockton
P.O. Box 1110
Stockton, CA 95201
Application address: c/o Scottish Rite Office, 33 W. Alpine St., Stockton, CA 95204

Foundation type: Independent foundation
Limitations: Educational loans to students residing in the area served by the Scottish Rite Temple, CA.
Financial data: Year ended 12/31/2004. Assets, $1,573,332 (M); Expenditures, $15,565; Total giving, $0; Loans to individuals, 20 loans totaling $80,000.
Type of support: Student loans—to individuals.
Application information: Application form required.
Deadline(s): June 1
Applicants should submit the following:
1) Transcripts
Additional information: Include three references.
EIN: 946220263

3872
Clarence Elbert Stanton Memorial Scholarship Foundation
523 N. Broadway St.
Lake Orion, MI 48362
Contact: Bert Quinn, Secy.-Treas.
Application address: c/o Jim Bushman, 46 Elizabeth St., Lake Orion, MI 48362, tel.: (248) 693-1208

Foundation type: Independent foundation
Limitations: Scholarships to residents of the Oxford-Orion, MI, community.
Financial data: Year ended 12/31/2003. Assets, $586,759 (M); Expenditures, $105,180; Total giving, $102,100; Grants to individuals, 128 grants totaling $102,100 (high: $900, low: $500).
Type of support: Scholarships—to individuals.
Application information: Application form required.
Initial approach: Letter or telephone.
Deadline(s): Apr. 1
Additional information: Contact foundation for current application guidelines.
EIN: 382962898

3873
Stanwood-Camano Area Foundation
P.O. Box 1209
Stanwood, WA 98292 (360) 629-6878
E-mail: info@s-caf.org; URL: http://www.s-caf.org

Foundation type: Community foundation
Limitations: Scholarships to individuals residing in the Stanwood-Camano area, WA for undergraduate education.
Publications: Application guidelines; Annual report; Informational brochure.
Financial data: Year ended 12/31/2004. Assets, $80,075 (M); Expenditures, $133,786; Total giving, $129,302; Grants to individuals, totaling $58,444.
Fields of interest: Visual arts; Music; Vocational education, post-secondary; Journalism school/education; Adult/continuing education.
Type of support: Undergraduate support.
Application information: Applications accepted. Application form required. Application form available on the grantmaker's Web site.
Deadline(s): Apr. 15
Additional information: See Web site for complete program information.
EIN: 916036846

3874
The Stanzel Family Foundation, Inc.
P.O. Box 6
Schulenburg, TX 78956
Contact: Robert R. Stanzel, Pres.

Foundation type: Independent foundation
Limitations: Scholarships to graduating high school seniors who live in the Schulenburg or Weimar Independent school districts or are enrolled in Schulenburg or Weimar high schools, TX. Graduate scholarships may also be available to previous graduates of Schulenburg or Weimar high schools.
Financial data: Year ended 12/31/2004. Assets, $16,482,455 (M); Expenditures, $1,012,613; Total giving, $507,328; Grants to individuals, 124 grants totaling $307,925 (high: $3,000, low: $117).
Type of support: Support to graduates or students of specific schools; Undergraduate support; Postgraduate support.
Application information: Application form required.
Deadline(s): Mar. 31
EIN: 742579827

3875

Staples Free School Trust

c/o Barbara Broderick
P.O. Box 425
Easton, CT   06612-0425

Foundation type: Independent foundation
Limitations: Loans to residents of Easton, CT, to attend accredited colleges and universities. One-half of the amount must be repaid to the trust within 7 years of disbursement.
Financial data: Year ended 06/30/2005. Assets, $443,217 (M); Expenditures, $34,715; Total giving, $27,400; Grants to individuals, 7 grants totaling $27,400.
Type of support: Student loans—to individuals.
Application information: Application form required.
   Deadline(s): May 1
EIN: 066038707

3876

Star Foundation, Inc.

30 Bethany Church Rd.
Tallapoosa, GA   30176   (770) 574-7157
Contact: Jessie L. Newman, Pres.

Foundation type: Independent foundation
Limitations: Scholarships to dependents of workers employed at the American Thread Company, Tallapoosa, GA, for study at an accredited four-year institution.
Financial data: Year ended 12/31/2004. Assets, $39,226 (M); Expenditures, $2,626; Total giving, $2,500; Grants to individuals, 5 grants totaling $2,500.
Type of support: Employee-related scholarships.
Application information: Applications accepted throughout the year; Completion of formal application required.
EIN: 586043712

3877

Genevieve Starcher Educational Foundation

c/o United Bank, N.A.
P.O. Box 393
Charleston, WV   25322-0393
Contact: Kathryn Goodwin, Pres.
Application address: P.O. Box 266, Ripley, WV 25271

Foundation type: Independent foundation
Limitations: Scholarships to Jackson County, WV, residents to attend colleges and trade schools. Preference is given to graduates of Ripley High School, WV, and underprivileged students.
Financial data: Year ended 12/31/2004. Assets, $540,214 (M); Expenditures, $23,448; Total giving, $15,500; Grants to individuals, 20 grants totaling $13,500.
Fields of interest: Vocational education.
Type of support: Scholarships—to individuals.
Application information: Deadline May 31; Completion of formal application required.
EIN: 510159560

3878

Stark Community Foundation

(formerly The Stark County Foundation, Inc.)
400 Market Ave., N. Ste. 200
Canton, OH   44702-2107   (330) 454-3426
Contact: James A. Bower, Pres.; For grants: Cynthia M. Lazor, V.P., Progs.
FAX: (330) 454-5855; E-mail: jbower@starkcf.org; Additional E-mail: cmlazor@starkcf.org; URL: http://www.starkcommunityfoundation.org

Foundation type: Community foundation
Limitations: Scholarships and student loans only to students who are residents of Stark County, OH.
Publications: Application guidelines; Annual report (including application guidelines); Financial statement; Grants list; Informational brochure; Newsletter; Program policy statement.
Financial data: Year ended 12/31/2004. Assets, $137,086,201 (M); Expenditures, $6,778,515; Total giving, $5,682,172.
Type of support: Scholarships—to individuals; Student loans—to individuals.
Application information: Application form required.
   Initial approach: Letter or telephone.
   Deadline(s): Mar. 1 to May 30
   Applicants should submit the following:
      1) GPA
      2) Letter(s) of recommendation
   Additional information: Applications not reviewed by foundation, separate board reviews and interviews applicants; Contact foundation for individuals who are on the board.
Program description:
   Scholarships and Loan Program: Student aid and loans made on the basis of financial need and ability to complete college. No restrictions are made on the basis of race, religion, or creed.
EIN: 340943665

3879

Nelda C. and H. J. Lutcher Stark Foundation

P.O. Box 909
Orange, TX   77631-0909   (409) 883-3513
Contact: Grant Dept.
FAX: (409) 883-3530;
E-mail: stark@starkadmin.org; Address for physical delivery: 601 W. Green Ave. Orange, TX 77630-5718; URL: http://www.starkfoundation.org

Foundation type: Independent foundation
Limitations: Scholarships limited to students graduating from Orange County, TX, high schools, who are winners in a reading and declamation contest.
Publications: Application guidelines; Annual report.
Financial data: Year ended 12/31/2004. Assets, $346,968,630 (M); Expenditures, $14,533,912; Total giving, $4,307,219; Grants to individuals, 21 grants totaling $48,138 (high: $7,000, low: $888).
Type of support: Support to graduates or students of specific schools.
Application information:
   Deadline(s): Contact foundation for current application deadline/guidelines.
   Additional information: Scholarship awards are paid directly to the educational institution.
EIN: 746047440

3880

Jasper Stark Trust Fund

305 Poplar View Pkwy.
Collierville, TN   38017-3111
Contact: Pam Wilson, Tr.
Application address: 305 Poplar View, Collierville, TN 38017, TL.: (901) 853-4781

Foundation type: Independent foundation
Limitations: Scholarships to graduates of Collierville High School, TN.
Financial data: Year ended 12/31/2004. Assets, $76,069 (M); Expenditures, $3,640; Total giving, $3,000; Grants to individuals, 5 grants totaling $3,000.
Type of support: Support to graduates or students of specific schools; Undergraduate support.
Application information: Deadline Apr. 1; Completion of formal application required; Applications available from the high school.
EIN: 237378290

3881

Starks Charitable Foundation

P.O. Box 170103
Hialeah, FL   33017-0103   (888) 541-9774
Contact: Duane L. Starks, Pres.
E-mail: info@starksfoundation.org; URL: http://www.starksfoundation.org

Foundation type: Public charity
Limitations: Scholarships to economically disadvantaged residents of FL.
Financial data: Year ended 12/31/2004. Assets, $6,866 (M); Expenditures, $73,061; Total giving, $17,352; Grants to individuals, 11 grants totaling $13,300.
Type of support: Undergraduate support.
Application information: Applications accepted. Application form required. Application form available on the grantmaker's Web site.
   Initial approach: E-mail.
   Deadline(s): Apr. 15
   Applicants should submit the following:
      1) Financial information
      2) Letter(s) of recommendation
      3) Transcripts
      4) GPA
      5) Essay
Program description:
   Quest for Success: Applicants must have a minimum of 2.5 GPA, and a minimum of 6 hours volunteer work at SCF Football Clinic.
EIN: 650864604

3882

William F. Starr Fellowship Fund

c/o Bank of America, N.A.
P.O. Box 1802
Providence, RI   02901-1802

Foundation type: Independent foundation
Limitations: Fellowships to financially needy students attending the University of Connecticut School of Law in Hartford, CT.
Financial data: Year ended 06/30/2005. Assets, $750,707 (M); Expenditures, $41,969; Total giving, $33,044.
Fields of interest: Law school/education; Law/international law.
Type of support: Fellowships; Awards/grants by nomination only; Graduate support.
Application information: Application form not required.

Additional information: Board of trustees chooses award recipients according to merit.
EIN: 066024050

3883
State Employees Association of North Carolina Scholarship Fund, Inc.
P.O. Drawer 27727
Raleigh, NC 27611
Contact: Mitch Leonard, Dir.
E-mail: mleonard@seanc.org; URL: http://www.seanc.org/site/index.cfm?fuseaction=page&filename=scholarshipprogram.html

Foundation type: Independent foundation
Limitations: Scholarships for family members of members of the State Employees Association of North Carolina, Inc. (SEANC).
Publications: Informational brochure (including application guidelines).
Financial data: Year ended 09/30/2004. Assets, $352,171 (M); Expenditures, $83,220; Total giving, $50,000; Grants to individuals, 57 grants totaling $50,000.
Type of support: Scholarships—to individuals.
Application information: Applications by letter accepted throughout the year.
EIN: 561436745

3884
The Stateline Community Foundation
(formerly The Greater Beloit Community Foundation)
121 W. Grand Ave.
Beloit, WI 53511 (608) 362-4228
Contact: Tara Tinder, Exec. Dir.
FAX: (608) 362-0056;
E-mail: tara@statelinecf.com; Additional E-mail: statelinecf@aol.com; URL: http://www.statelinecf.com

Foundation type: Community foundation
Limitations: Scholarships to residents of the greater Beloit, WI, area.
Publications: Application guidelines; Annual report; Grants list; Informational brochure; Newsletter.
Financial data: Year ended 12/31/2004. Assets, $5,942,124 (M); Expenditures, $330,835; Total giving, $139,661; Grants to individuals, totaling $28,356.
Fields of interest: Education.
Type of support: Graduate support; Undergraduate support.
Application information: Contact foundation for current application deadline/guidelines; Initial approach by letter or telephone.
EIN: 391585271

3885
The Statler Foundation
107 Delaware Ave., Ste. 680
Buffalo, NY 14202 (716) 852-1104
Contact: Herb M. Siegel, Chair.
FAX: (716) 852-3928

Foundation type: Independent foundation
Limitations: Scholarships only to students of hotel management and culinary arts who are residents of Buffalo, NY.
Financial data: Year ended 12/31/2004. Assets, $33,314,389 (M); Expenditures, $1,963,242; Total giving, $1,399,210; Grants to individuals, totaling $745,044.
Fields of interest: Vocational education.

Type of support: Scholarships—to individuals.
Application information: Application form required.
Initial approach: Letter.
Deadline(s): Apr. 30.
EIN: 131889077

3886
Gladys Staufenbeil Student Loan Trust
c/o Bank of America, N.A.
P.O. Box 34345
Seattle, WA 98124-1345
Application addresses: c/o Univ. of Washington, School of Medicine, Seattle, WA 98195, c/o Univ. of Idaho, School of Medicine, Moscow, ID 83843

Foundation type: Independent foundation
Limitations: Student loans to medical students attending the University of Washington, WA, and the University of Idaho. No loans for transportation.
Financial data: Year ended 12/31/2003. Assets, $298,395 (M); Expenditures, $17,411; Total giving, $13,779; Loans to individuals, totaling $13,779.
Type of support: Support to graduates or students of specific schools; Graduate support.
Application information: Application form required.
Deadline(s): Applications accepted throughout the year.
EIN: 916031720

3887
Virginia E. Stauffer Scholarship Fund
c/o KeyBank N.A.
800 Superior Ave., 4th Fl.
Cleveland, OH 44114-2601

Foundation type: Independent foundation
Limitations: Scholarships to graduates of high schools within a ten-mile radius of the Exchange Bank of Olean, NY, including Allegany Central School, Hinsdale Central School, Olean High School, Portville Central School, and Walsh (Archbishop) High School.
Financial data: Year ended 08/31/2005. Assets, $469,033 (M); Expenditures, $22,645; Total giving, $15,500; Grants to individuals, 11 grants totaling $15,500.
Type of support: Support to graduates or students of specific schools.
Application information: Applications accepted. Application form required.
Deadline(s): None
EIN: 133143537

3888
Staunton Augusta Waynesboro Community Foundation
(also known as SAW Community Foundation)
100 Lucy Ln.
Waynesboro, VA 22980 (540) 932-7878
Contact: Joi E. Brown, Exec. Dir.
FAX: (540) 932-7539;
E-mail: communityfoundation@ntelos.net;
URL: http://www.cfw.com/~sawfdtn
Additional URL: http://www.communityfoundationCBR.org

Foundation type: Community foundation
Limitations: Scholarships and awards to improve the quality of life in Staunton, Waynesboro, Augusta and Nelson counties, VA.
Publications: Application guidelines; Annual report; Grants list; Informational brochure.

Financial data: Year ended 12/31/2004. Assets, $7,285,812 (M); Expenditures, $481,599; Total giving, $398,609; Grants to individuals, 23 grants totaling $95,000 (high: $74,250, low: $80).
Type of support: Awards/prizes; Technical education support; Undergraduate support.
Application information: Application form required.
Initial approach: telephone.
Deadline(s): Apr. 15
EIN: 541647385

3889
Alexander William Stearn Foundation, Inc.
8 Treadwell Ct.
Lutherville, MD 21093

Foundation type: Independent foundation
Limitations: Scholarships by nomination only to financially needy graduating seniors of Lake Clifton Senior High School, Baltimore, MD.
Financial data: Year ended 06/30/2003. Assets, $632,337 (M); Expenditures, $31,041; Total giving, $24,500; Grants to individuals, totaling $24,500.
Type of support: Support to graduates or students of specific schools; Awards/grants by nomination only; Undergraduate support.
Application information: Applications not accepted.
Additional information: Recipients are nominated by the school.
EIN: 521457719

3890
Teresa Treat Stearns Trust
P.O. Box 798
Fort Dodge, IA 50501-0798 (515) 832-1133
Application address: c/o First American Bank, 1207 Central Ave., Fort Dodge, IA 50501

Foundation type: Independent foundation
Limitations: Scholarships to residents of the Webster City, IA, area.
Financial data: Year ended 06/30/2005. Assets, $796,272 (M); Expenditures, $34,956; Total giving, $29,066; Grants to individuals, 7 grants totaling $21,066 (high: $5,000, low: $1,200).
Type of support: Scholarships—to individuals.
Application information:
Initial approach: Letter or telephone.
Deadline(s): Contact trust for current application deadline.
Additional information: Application should include three references (at least one teacher and one former employer).
EIN: 426099826

3891
J. C. Steele, Jr. Scholarship Foundation
P.O. Box 1834
Statesville, NC 28687-1834
Contact: John S. Steele, Tr.

Foundation type: Operating foundation
Limitations: Scholarships to children of J. C. Steele & Sons, Inc. employees.
Financial data: Year ended 12/31/2003. Assets, $22,019 (M); Expenditures, $6,000; Total giving, $6,000; Grants to individuals, totaling $6,000.
Type of support: Employee-related scholarships.

Application information: Application form required.
Deadline(s): May 17
EIN: 581530789

3892
Fred T. & John H. Steffens Scholarship Trust

c/o First National Bank & Trust Co.
P.O. Box 627
Phillipsburg, KS 67661
Contact: Cy Moyer, Tr.

Foundation type: Independent foundation
Limitations: Student loans to graduates of Phillipsburg High School, KS, for postsecondary education at KS institutions.
Financial data: Year ended 12/31/2004.
Assets, $376,429 (M); Expenditures, $18,684; Total giving, $14,750; Grants to individuals, 27 grants totaling $14,750.
Type of support: Support to graduates or students of specific schools; Technical education support; Undergraduate support.
Application information: Application form required.
Deadline(s): Apr. 1.
Applicants should submit the following:
1) Transcripts
EIN: 486346084

3893
Phyllis H. Steigler Trust

c/o KeyBank N.A.
800 Superior Ave., 4th Fl.
Cleveland, OH 44114-2601
Application address: c/o KeyBank N.A., Cristina Cook, Trust Off., P.O. Box 1054, Augusta, ME 04330

Foundation type: Independent foundation
Limitations: Scholarships to residents of ME.
Financial data: Year ended 06/30/2005.
Assets, $518,123 (M); Expenditures, $35,529; Total giving, $28,000.
Type of support: Scholarships—to individuals.
Application information: Applications by letter, outlining financial need and qualifications, accepted throughout the year.
EIN: 016109107

3894
J. B. Steinbach Scholarship Fund

(formerly Steinbach Foundation)
c/o U.S. Bank, N.A.
P.O. Box 3168
Portland, OR 97208-3168

Foundation type: Independent foundation
Limitations: Scholarships and loans to residents of OR.
Financial data: Year ended 06/30/2005.
Assets, $1,298,285 (M); Expenditures, $86,423; Total giving, $62,100; Grants to individuals, totaling $62,100.
Fields of interest: Vocational education.
Type of support: Undergraduate support.
Application information: Applications accepted Jan. 1 through Apr. 1 for scholarships; Completion of formal application required; Application forms available from local area high schools, college financial aid offices, and U.S. Bank branches; Interviews required in May for scholarship finalists.
Program description:
Jerome B. Steinbach Scholarship: Awarded to OR residents for full-time undergraduate study. Eligible

schools include accredited colleges, universities, and trade schools located in the U.S. Required minimum cumulative GPA is 3.5 for a high school senior, and 3.25 for a college student. Award is based on academic achievement, financial need, personality, and the ability to utilize the educational advantages offered. Notification is June 30 for scholarships, July 15 for loans.
EIN: 936020885

3895
Sophie & William Steinkamp Education Trust

c/o Bank of America, N.A.
P.O. Box 831041, TX1-492-12-01
Dallas, TX 75283-1041
Application address: c/o Trust Admin., Bank of America, N.A., P.O. Box 1681, Little Rock, AR 72203

Foundation type: Independent foundation
Limitations: Scholarships to orphans of Pulaski County, AR.
Financial data: Year ended 03/31/2005.
Assets, $152,425 (M); Expenditures, $10,932; Total giving, $6,400; Grants to individuals, 8 grants totaling $6,400.
Fields of interest: Residential/custodial care.
Type of support: Scholarships—to individuals.
Application information: Applications accepted throughout the year; Application by letter, including transcripts, college board scores, financial statements, essay on desire for college education, and letters of recommendation.
EIN: 716123582

3896
Albert L. Steinke Trust

c/o U.S. Bank, N.A., Trust Tax Svcs.
P.O. Box 64713
St. Paul, MN 55164-0713
Application address: c/o Stan Gaffin, U.S. Bank, N.A., 225 S. 6th St., Minneapolis, MN 55402

Foundation type: Independent foundation
Limitations: Scholarships to financially needy students who have completed four years of regular high school in Pipestone County, MN.
Financial data: Year ended 12/31/2004.
Assets, $1,185,648 (M); Expenditures, $72,019; Total giving, $62,900; Grants to individuals, totaling $62,900.
Type of support: Support to graduates or students of specific schools; Undergraduate support.
Application information: Applications accepted.
Deadline(s): None
Program description:
Scholarship Program: The minimum scholarship amount is $1,000 per person. The total amount available depends on income generated by trust assets.
EIN: 416045691

3897
James Hale Steinman Foundation

8 W. King St.
P.O. Box 128
Lancaster, PA 17608-0128
Contact: Christine Mellinger
E-mail: cmellinger@lnpnews.com

Foundation type: Independent foundation

Limitations: Scholarships to newspaper carriers and children of employees of Steinman Enterprises, primarily in Lancaster, PA.
Financial data: Year ended 12/31/2004.
Assets, $31,666,512 (M); Expenditures, $1,590,256; Total giving, $1,476,126; Grants to individuals, totaling $97,500.
Type of support: Employee-related scholarships.
Application information: Application form required.
Initial approach: Letter.
Deadline(s): Feb. 28.
EIN: 236266377

3898
John Frederick Steinman Foundation

P.O. Box 128
Lancaster, PA 17608-0128
Contact: Christine Mellinger
E-mail: cmellinger@lnpnews.com; Additional address: 8 W. King St., Lancaster, PA 17603

Foundation type: Independent foundation
Limitations: Fellowships primarily to residents of Lancaster, PA, for graduate study in mental health and related fields.
Publications: Informational brochure.
Financial data: Year ended 12/31/2004.
Assets, $29,851,327 (M); Expenditures, $1,121,574; Total giving, $994,529; Grants to individuals, totaling $32,904.
Fields of interest: Mental health/crisis services, research.
Type of support: Fellowships; Graduate support.
Application information: Application form required.
Deadline(s): Feb. 1.
EIN: 236266378

3899
The Stensrud Foundation

P.O. Box 501035
San Diego, CA 92150-1035 (858) 513-1245
Contact: Carol Stensrud, Secy.-Treas.
E-mail: carols@adnc.com

Foundation type: Independent foundation
Limitations: Scholarships to individuals residing in the San Diego, CA, area for undergraduate education. Applicants must be referred by local 501 (c)(3) organizations such as the YMCA or Boys and Girls Clubs.
Financial data: Year ended 12/31/2004.
Assets, $473,451 (M); Expenditures, $285,550; Total giving, $282,777.
Type of support: Undergraduate support.
Application information: Application form required.
Deadline(s): May 15
EIN: 330757049

3900
A. K. Stephenson Foundation Charitable Trust

c/o First Financial Bank
300 High St.
Hamilton, OH 45011
Contact: Thomas E. Humbach, Tr.

Foundation type: Independent foundation
Limitations: Scholarships primarily to financially needy residents of Butler County, OH, to pursue undergraduate degrees at any accredited U.S. college or university.
Financial data: Year ended 12/31/2004.
Assets, $1,155,014 (M); Expenditures, $128,509; Total giving, $74,000; Grants to

individuals, 99 grants totaling $74,000 (high: $2,000, low: $500).
Type of support: Undergraduate support.
Application information:
Initial approach: Letter or telephone.
Additional information: Contact trust for current application deadline/guidelines.
EIN: 311386444

3901
Stephenson-Beelard Scholarship Foundation
(formerly Stephenson Scholarship Foundation)
500 Main St.
Vacaville, CA 95688-3989 (707) 448-6894
Contact: Donald P. Stephenson, Pres.

Foundation type: Independent foundation
Limitations: Scholarships to graduating seniors who are residents of Vacaville, CA, at the time that they graduate from a public high school, and/or college undergraduates who resided in Vacaville at the time that they graduated from a public high school. Applicants must have been involved in athletics for at least two years while in high school.
Financial data: Year ended 06/30/2005. Assets, $206,708 (M); Expenditures, $7,885; Total giving, $7,500; Grants to individuals, 10 grants totaling $7,500.
Fields of interest: Athletics/sports, training.
Type of support: Undergraduate support.
Application information: Application form required.
Initial approach: Letter requesting application guidelines.
Deadline(s): Early Aug.
Additional information: Interviews required.
Program description:
Scholarship Program: Applicants must demonstrate financial responsibility through savings accounts and wise spending. College students must have at least a 3.0 GPA.
EIN: 237412597

3902
Sterling-Rock Falls Community Trust
P.O. Box 1000
Sterling, IL 61081
Application address: c/o Amcore Trust Co., Trust Dept., 302 1st Ave., Sterling, IL 61081

Foundation type: Independent foundation
Limitations: Scholarships to graduating seniors of Newman Central Catholic High School and Sterling High School, both in Sterling, IL, and Rock Falls High School in Rock Falls, IL. Recipients must live within the boundaries of the Sterling and Rock Falls school districts.
Financial data: Year ended 12/31/2004. Assets, $1,728,107 (M); Expenditures, $97,002; Total giving, $81,612; Grants to individuals, 36 grants totaling $42,094.
Type of support: Support to graduates or students of specific schools; Undergraduate support.
Application information: Application form required.
Deadline(s): Apr. 1
Program description:
Scholarship Program: Financial need criteria vary each year, based on funds available. The trust's board determines the maximum family income of eligible students.
EIN: 366217952

3903
Steuben County Community Foundation
207 S. Wayne, Ste. A
Angola, IN 46703 (260) 665-6656
Contact: Sharon E. Stroh, C.E.O.
FAX: (260) 665-8420; E-mail: sccf@locl.net;
URL: http://www.steubenfoundation.org

Foundation type: Community foundation
Limitations: Scholarships to designated Steuben County, IN, high school students.
Publications: Application guidelines; Annual report; Financial statement; Informational brochure (including application guidelines); Newsletter; Occasional report.
Financial data: Year ended 06/30/2005. Assets, $13,139,264 (M); Expenditures, $813,722; Total giving, $430,644.
Type of support: Scholarships—to individuals; Support to graduates or students of specific schools; Technical education support; Undergraduate support.
Application information: Application form required.
Initial approach: Telephone.
Copies of proposal: 1
Deadline(s): Mar. 15
Applicants should submit the following:
1) Financial information
2) Budget Information
3) Transcripts
4) SAT
5) Letter(s) of recommendation
6) GPA
7) Essay
8) ACT
Additional information: Contact foundation for current application guidelines.
EIN: 351857065

3904
James W. & Cecile I. Steven Scholarship Trust
c/o Commerce Bank
P.O. Box 1119
St. Joseph, MO 64502-1119
Contact: Glen Zahnd, Tr.
Application address: c/o Glen Zahnd, 104 S. 14th, Savannah, MO 64485, tel.: (816) 324-3083

Foundation type: Independent foundation
Limitations: Scholarships to financially needy high school students from Buchanan County and Andrew County, MO, for undergraduate education.
Financial data: Year ended 06/30/2004. Assets, $198,477 (M); Expenditures, $12,139; Total giving, $9,650; Grants to individuals, totaling $9,650.
Type of support: Support to graduates or students of specific schools; Undergraduate support.
Application information:
Deadline(s): Apr. 1
Applicants should submit the following:
1) GPA
2) Transcripts
Additional information: Completion of formal application required, including financial information, and two references, one from high school counselor. Applicants must have at least a 2.5 GPA.
EIN: 436633578

3905
Jess L. and Miriam B. Stevens Foundation
3700 First Place Twr.
15 E. 5th St.
Tulsa, OK 74103-4344
Contact: Joseph J. McCain, Jr., Tr.

Foundation type: Independent foundation
Limitations: Scholarships to individuals residing in northeastern OK and St. Louis, MO, for undergraduate education.
Financial data: Year ended 07/31/2005. Assets, $13,434,342 (M); Expenditures, $830,745; Total giving, $672,500; Grants to individuals, 8 grants totaling $45,000 (high: $10,000, low: $5,000).
Type of support: Undergraduate support.
Application information: Applications by letter accepted throughout the year.
EIN: 731557364

3906
Harley and Mertie Stevens Memorial Fund
c/o U.S. Bank, N.A.
P.O. Box 3168
Portland, OR 97208-3168
Contact: Marlyn Norquist, V.P., U.S. Bank, N.A.
Application address: c/o Oregon State Scholarship Commission, 1500 Valley River Dr., No. 100, Eugene, OR 97401, tel.: (800) 452-8807;
URL: http://www.osca.state.or.us/

Foundation type: Independent foundation
Limitations: Scholarships to OR residents who are graduates of accredited Clackamas County, OR, high schools for their first and fourth full-time undergraduate years at public or private, Protestant-owned and operated, two- or four-year colleges or universities in OR. Loans are granted only to second- and third-year students who previously received scholarships.
Financial data: Year ended 06/30/2005. Assets, $1,260,988 (M); Expenditures, $86,166; Total giving, $61,050.
Fields of interest: Protestant agencies & churches.
Type of support: Support to graduates or students of specific schools; Undergraduate support.
Application information: Application form required.
Deadline(s): Jan. 1 and Mar. 15 for scholarships and June 1 and June 15 for loans
Additional information: Interviews for scholarship finalists required.
Program description:
Mertie and Harley Stevens Memorial Scholarship: Presented to graduates from accredited high schools in Clackamas County, OR, for their first and fourth year of schooling, who enroll as full-time undergraduate students. Award recipients are also eligible for loans for their sophomore and junior years. Eligible schools include accredited, state supported or private, Protestant-owned and operated colleges or universities in OR. Required minimum cumulative GPA for high school seniors is 3.50 and for college students 3.25. For loans the minimum is 2.75. Loans are awarded at three percent interest for the sophomore and junior years of schooling.
EIN: 936053655

3907
Stevenson Foundation Trust
c/o JPMorgan Chase Bank
P.O. Box 31412
Rochester, NY 14603-1412

Foundation type: Independent foundation

Limitations: Scholarships to deserving and financially needy students in the Canandaigua, NY, area who are currently enrolled in a recognized college of medicine.
Financial data: Year ended 12/31/2004. Assets, $141,350 (M); Expenditures, $18,622; Total giving, $15,000; Grants to individuals, 2 grants totaling $15,000.
Fields of interest: Medical school/education.
Type of support: Graduate support.
Application information: Contact trust for current application deadline; Application by letter outlining financial need, as well as pertinent information regarding current enrollment in medical school, including name of school and year of study.
EIN: 166102231

3908
J. C. Stewart Memorial Trust
7718 Finns Ln.
Lanham, MD 20706-1320 (301) 459-4200
Contact: Robert S. Hoyert, Tr.

Foundation type: Independent foundation
Limitations: Scholarships and student loans to MD residents.
Financial data: Year ended 11/30/2004. Assets, $1,015,188 (M); Expenditures, $63,168; Total giving, $15,500.
Type of support: Scholarships—to individuals; Student loans—to individuals.
Application information: Deadlines Aug. 15 for Grants in Aid, Nov. 1 for others; Applications accepted throughout the year for student loans; Completion of formal application required.
EIN: 237357104

3909
Marie Palmer Stewart Scholarship Trust
c/o Wachovia Bank, N.A.
100 N. Main St., 13th Fl.
Winston-Salem, NC 27150
Application address: c/o Franklin High School, Attn: Carolyn Patillon, Guidance Counselor, 23 School Dr., Franklin, NC 28734, tel.: (704) 524-6467

Foundation type: Independent foundation
Limitations: Scholarships to female students of Franklin High School, Franklin, NC, to attend the University of North Carolina at Greensboro. If no one from Franklin High School is eligible, other students from western NC will be considered.
Financial data: Year ended 12/31/2004. Assets, $191,168 (M); Expenditures, $13,667; Total giving, $9,529; Grants to individuals, 2 grants totaling $9,279.
Fields of interest: Race/intergroup relations; Women.
Type of support: Support to graduates or students of specific schools; Undergraduate support.
Application information: Applications accepted throughout the year; Contact trust for current application guidelines; Initial approach by letter; Interviews required.
EIN: 566194108

3910
Ross W. Stice Trust
103 N. Union St.
P.O. Box 212
Council Grove, KS 66846 (620) 767-6825
Contact: D. Randall Heilman, Tr.

Foundation type: Independent foundation
Limitations: Scholarships to students of Council Grove High School, KS, who have resided within the former Alta Vista, KS, school district, to attend Kansas State University, University of Kansas, or Emporia State University, KS.
Financial data: Year ended 06/30/2005. Assets, $367,459 (M); Expenditures, $14,643; Total giving, $11,850; Grants to individuals, totaling $11,650.
Type of support: Support to graduates or students of specific schools; Undergraduate support.
Application information: Applications accepted. Application form required.
> *Deadline(s):* July 15 for fall semester and Dec. 31 for spring semester
EIN: 480874854

3911
Carl Dee Stickley Educational Fund
c/o The Bank of Romney
P.O. Box 876
Romney, WV 26757
Contact: Lawrence Foley, Tr.

Foundation type: Independent foundation
Limitations: Scholarships to financially disadvantaged graduates of secondary schools in Hampshire County, WV, including Hampshire High School, the West Virginia School for the Blind, and the West Virginia School for the Deaf.
Financial data: Year ended 03/31/2004. Assets, $160,761 (M); Expenditures, $8,615; Total giving, $7,800; Grants to individuals, totaling $7,800.
Fields of interest: Disabilities, people with.
Type of support: Support to graduates or students of specific schools; Undergraduate support.
Application information: Applications accepted throughout the year; Completion of formal application required, including financial information.
Program description:
> *Scholarship Program:* The parents of recipients must have an annual income of less than $25,000. No scholarship is awarded to an individual who has used alcohol, tobacco, or narcotics, or who has been associated with any person who uses narcotics. Recipients must provide the board of trustees with written certification from the college which they are attending that they are maintaining at least a "C+" grade average. Recipients must attend a college in WV, unless they are graduates of the schools for the blind and deaf. Scholarships will not exceed $1,500 per year, per student. They may be used to pay tuition, fees, books, and room and board.
EIN: 550682624

3912
The Stickney Educational Trust
P.O. Box 101
Twin Mountain, NH 03595-0101
(603) 846-5725
Contact: George E. Brodeur, Sr., Tr.

Foundation type: Independent foundation
Limitations: Scholarships to individuals for higher education.
Financial data: Year ended 12/31/2004. Assets, $149,667 (M); Expenditures, $4,474; Total giving, $4,000; Grants to individuals, 3 grants totaling $4,000.
Type of support: Scholarships—to individuals.
Application information: Deadline July 30; Completion of formal application required, including

name of school or university applicant will be attending.
EIN: 026088650

3913
Robert F. Stiens and Glenda M. Stiens Trust
c/o U.S. Bank, N.A.
P.O. Box 818
Richmond, IN 47374-0818 (765) 965-2293

Foundation type: Independent foundation
Limitations: Scholarships to graduating students attending Randolphe Southern High School, Union High School, and Northeastern High School, IN.
Financial data: Year ended 12/31/2004. Assets, $368,519 (M); Expenditures, $33,190; Total giving, $28,633; Grants to individuals, 15 grants totaling $10,995 (high: $733, low: $733).
Type of support: Support to graduates or students of specific schools; Undergraduate support.
Application information:
> *Deadline(s):* Contact foundation for deadline
> *Additional information:* Application must also include information on family income, course of study, student income, and degree.
EIN: 356332467

3914
George E. Stifel Endowment Fund
c/o JPMorgan Chase Bank, N.A.
P.O. Box 1308
Milwaukee, WI 53201 (414) 977-1210
Contact: Ed Johnson

Foundation type: Public charity
Limitations: Prizes to students of the fifth grade or higher at the public schools within the city limits of Wheeling, WV.
Financial data: Year ended 12/31/2004. Assets, $3,030,517 (M); Expenditures, $86,030; Total giving, $61,645; Grants to individuals, 189 grants totaling $61,645 (high: $1,800, low: $30).
Type of support: Support to graduates or students of specific schools; Awards/prizes; Precollege support.
Application information: Contact foundation for current application deadline/guidelines.
EIN: 556018247

3915
George E. Stifel Scholarship Fund
c/o JPMorgan Chase Bank, N.A.
P.O. Box 1308
Milwaukee, WI 53201
Application address: c/o JP Morgan Chase Bank, N.A., Tr. Dept., 1114 Market St., Wheeling, WV 26003

Foundation type: Independent foundation
Limitations: Scholarships to graduates of Ohio County, WV, high schools.
Financial data: Year ended 04/30/2005. Assets, $1,723,984 (M); Expenditures, $98,129; Total giving, $76,800; Grants to individuals, 41 grants totaling $76,800 (high: $3,500, low: $500).
Type of support: Undergraduate support.
Application information: Application form required.
> *Deadline(s):* Contact fund for current application deadlines
> *Additional information:* In awarding the scholarships, the trustees consider the personality of each applicant, academic achievement, extracurricular activities,

deportment, spirit of cooperation with school authorities, and the general promise the applicant shows of becoming a better citizen if given the opportunity of a college education. Scholarships are renewable for up to four years; Interviews required.

EIN: 556018248

3916
Stillwater Medical Center Foundation, Inc.

604 S. Walnut St.
Stillwater, OK   74076-2408   (405) 742-5387
Contact: Teresa Hopkins, Exec. Dir.
Additional tel.: (405) 742-5738;
E-mail: trennie@stillwater-medical.org;
URL: http://www.smc-foundation.org/

Foundation type: Public charity
Limitations: Scholarships to employees of Stillwater Medical Center, OK, for enhancement of their professional growth, and a summer program to high school students contemplating a career in health care.
Publications: Annual report; Biennial report; Informational brochure; Newsletter.
Financial data: Year ended 12/31/2003. Assets, $1,667,255 (M); Expenditures, $308,614; Total giving, $252,065; Grants to individuals, 6 grants totaling $6,577 (high: $1,500, low: $477).
Fields of interest: Health care.
Type of support: Employee-related scholarships.
Application information: Applications accepted. Application form available on the grantmaker's Web site.
Additional information: Not all application forms are available online; See Web site for additional scholarships and complete program guidelines.
Program description:
Summer Scholar Program: Three awards of $1,500 each are awarded to area high school students who participate in a six-week summer program through a healthcare internship. Applications are available in early spring.
· Rippy Fellowship
· Franklin Fellowship
· Breedlove Externship.
EIN: 731173571

3917
Dr. W. C. Stillwell Foundation

c/o Philip Wold
25 Browns Ct.
Mankato, MN   56001
Contact: John Hoines M.D., Secy.
Application address: 1630 Adams St., Mankato, MN 56001, tel.: (507) 345-6151

Foundation type: Operating foundation
Limitations: Four-year scholarships to full-time medical students from 22 counties in the southcentral and southwestern MN areas who are enrolled in their first year at an accredited medical school.
Financial data: Year ended 12/31/2002. Assets, $537,549 (M); Expenditures, $29,070; Total giving, $27,000; Grants to individuals, 9 grants totaling $27,000 (high: $3,000, low: $3,000).
Fields of interest: Medical school/education.
Type of support: Graduate support.

Application information: Deadline Aug. 31; Initial approach by letter; Completion of formal application required.
Program description:
Scholarship Program: Scholarships available to first-year medical school students from the following counties in MN: Lincoln, Lyon, Redwood, Renville, Sibley, Nicollet, LeSueur, Brown, Rice, Steele, Waseca, Blue Earth, Watonwan, Cottonwood, Murray, Pipestone, Rock, Nobles, Jackson, Martin, Faribault, and Freeborn.
EIN: 411423785

3918
Anna D. Stinson Trust

c/o KeyBank N.A.
800 Superior Ave., 4th Fl.
Cleveland, OH   44114-1306
Application address: c/o KeyBank N.A., Ellsworth, ME 04605

Foundation type: Independent foundation
Limitations: Scholarships to high school graduates from Ellsworth and Surrey, ME, for higher education.
Financial data: Year ended 04/30/2005. Assets, $0 (M); Expenditures, $11,225; Total giving, $7,000; Grants to individuals, 7 grants totaling $7,000.
Type of support: Undergraduate support.
Application information: Applications by letter accepted throughout the year.
EIN: 016057075

3919
Paul Stock Foundation

P.O. Box 2020
Cody, WY   82414-2020
Contact: Charles G. Kepler, Pres.

Foundation type: Independent foundation
Limitations: Scholarships to WY residents of at least one year, primarily from the Cody, WY, area. GPA awards to students of Cody High School, Meeteetse High School, and Powell High School, all in Park County, WY. Writing awards to students of Cody High School, WY.
Financial data: Year ended 12/31/2004. Assets, $1,402,136 (M); Expenditures, $693,510; Total giving, $664,186; Grants to individuals, totaling $250,000.
Fields of interest: Literature.
Type of support: Support to graduates or students of specific schools; Awards/prizes; Undergraduate support.
Application information:
Deadline(s): None
Additional information: Contact foundation for current application guidelines.
Program descriptions:
Scholarship: The largest individual grants program administered by the foundation is the scholarships to WY residents. The foundation also awards four-year scholarships of $3,000 each to students with the highest GPAs in the graduating classes of Cody High School, Powell High School, and Meeteetse High School.
Stock Lockhart Writing Awards: Given to students of Cody High School in the amount of $100.
EIN: 830185157

3920
Stockard Charitable Trust

c/o United Bank & Trust
1016 Broadway
P.O. Box 150
Marysville, KS   66508   (785) 562-2344

Foundation type: Independent foundation
Limitations: Scholarships to graduates of Marysville High School, KS, for undergraduate education.
Financial data: Year ended 12/31/2004. Assets, $956,556 (M); Expenditures, $53,646; Total giving, $44,396; Grants to individuals, 13 grants totaling $44,396.
Type of support: Support to graduates or students of specific schools.
Application information:
Deadline(s): July 1
Additional information: Completion of formal application required, including financial information; Guidance counselor distributes applications to eligible applicants.
Program description:
Stockard Scholars: Males in the top 25 percent of each graduating class and females in the top 20 percent of each graduating class are eligible. The scholarship committee selects one male and one female for each years graduating seniors to be named as Stockard Scholars and receive annual renewable scholarship grants of not less than $440 nor more than $2,000 per years for up to five years of education at an institution of higher education or vocational school. Provided recipients maintain a GPA of "C+" or better.
EIN: 746452154

3921
Tom Stockert Foundation

c/o JPMorgan Chase Bank, N.A.
P.O. Box 1308
Milwaukee, WI   53201
Application address: c/o JPMorgan Chase Bank, N.A., Attn.: Tom Teter, 229 W. Main St., Clarksburg, WV 26301, tel.: (304) 624-3443

Foundation type: Operating foundation
Limitations: Scholarships primarily to WV residents for attendance at the University of Virginia College of Law.
Financial data: Year ended 12/31/2004. Assets, $763,086 (M); Expenditures, $56,769; Total giving, $29,000; Grants to individuals, 36 grants totaling $29,000 (high: $1,500, low: $250).
Fields of interest: Law school/education.
Type of support: Support to graduates or students of specific schools.
Application information:
Deadline(s): Last week in Apr.
Additional information: Application by letter including academic history and extracurricular activities.
EIN: 546423244

3922
Stockton Fire Fighters Gladys Benerd Memorial Trust

P.O. Box 692201
Stockton, CA   95269-2201   (209) 937-8024
Contact: Ed Nevill

Foundation type: Operating foundation
Limitations: Scholarships to individuals for higher education who are dependents of firefighters.
Financial data: Year ended 12/31/2003. Assets, $913,865 (M); Expenditures, $53,362;

Total giving, $49,925; Grants to individuals, 32 grants totaling $49,925 (high: $2,400, low: $1,325).
Type of support: Scholarships—to individuals.
Application information: Contact trust for current application deadline/guidelines; Initial approach by letter or telephone.
EIN: 686117555

3923
Harry T. Stoddart Trust
c/o Mellon Bank, N.A.
P.O. Box 185
Pittsburgh, PA 15230-0185

Foundation type: Independent foundation
Limitations: Scholarships to female residents of Luzerne County, PA.
Financial data: Year ended 09/30/2004. Assets, $1,059,686 (M); Expenditures, $97,176; Total giving, $96,000; Grants to individuals, 26 grants totaling $26,000 (high: $1,000, low: $1,000).
Fields of interest: Women; Adults, women.
Type of support: Scholarships—to individuals; Undergraduate support.
Application information: Applications not accepted.
Program description:
  Elizabeth Stoddart Fund: Scholarships do not exceed $1,500 each per year. Recipients are selected by a panel of superintendents and principals of schools in Luzerne County, PA.
EIN: 236224343

3924
Freddie Lewis Stoepler Trust
P.O. Box 915
Eden, TX 76837
Application address: c/o High School counselor, Eden High School, Eden, TX 76837

Foundation type: Independent foundation
Limitations: Student loans primarily to residents of the Eden, TX, area.
Financial data: Year ended 12/31/2004. Assets, $1 (M); Expenditures, $4,334; Total giving, $0; Loans to individuals, 4 loans totaling $3,000.
Type of support: Student loans—to individuals.
Application information: Applications accepted throughout the year; Completion of formal application required; Applications available from counselor.
EIN: 752387244

3925
Stokes Scholarship Trust
c/o Bank of America, N.A.
P.O. Box 1802
Providence, RI 02901-1802
Contact: Michael Wrenn

Foundation type: Independent foundation
Limitations: Scholarships to residents of Langdon, NH, to attend accredited colleges, universities, vocational schools, or two-year colleges in the U.S. Preference is given to nursing students pursuing the degree of Bachelor of Arts or Bachelor of Sciences.
Financial data: Year ended 12/31/2004. Assets, $1,450,050 (M); Expenditures, $53,449; Total giving, $39,000; Grants to individuals, 24 grants totaling $39,000 (high: $3,000, low: $1,500).

Fields of interest: Vocational education; Nursing school/education.
Type of support: Technical education support; Undergraduate support.
Application information: Deadline July 1; Completion of formal application required, including financial information, recommendations, and essay; Interviews required.
Program description:
  Scholarship Program: Scholarships are awarded on the basis of financial need, industry, character, merit, and academic achievement. Awards are disbursed in two equal payments. Recipients are notified at the time of graduation. The trust also gives smaller grants to aged and indigent individuals residing in Langdon and Alstead, NH, to help cover the costs of medical expenses and fuel.
EIN: 026092657

3926
Olive A. Stokes Scholarship Trust
c/o Comerica Bank
P.O. Box 75000, M/C 3302
Detroit, MI 48275-3302
Application address: c/o RBC Centura Bank, Attn.: Sharon Stephens, P.O. Box 1220, Rocky Mount, NC 27804, tel.: (252) 454-4025

Foundation type: Independent foundation
Limitations: Scholarships to individuals for higher education, NC.
Financial data: Year ended 09/30/2004. Assets, $518,688 (M); Expenditures, $29,359; Total giving, $18,610; Grants to individuals, 17 grants totaling $18,610 (high: $1,750, low: $400).
Type of support: Undergraduate support.
Application information: Contact trust for current application deadline/guidelines.
EIN: 316646001

3927
Albert H. & Ruben S. Stone Fund
c/o Bowditch & Dewey
311 Main St.
Worcester, MA 01608
Contact: Carlton E. Nichols, Jr., Tr.
Scholarship application address: c/o Nicholas & Stone, 232 Sherman St., Gardner, MA 01440, tel.: (978) 632-2770

Foundation type: Independent foundation
Limitations: Scholarships only to residents of Gardner, MA, who are full-time students.
Financial data: Year ended 12/31/2004. Assets, $3,838,786 (M); Expenditures, $255,904; Total giving, $233,575; Grants to individuals, 257 grants totaling $223,575 (high: $10,000, low: $125).
Type of support: Scholarships—to individuals.
Application information: Deadline early in second semester; Initial approach by letter; Applications may be obtained personally through group appointments set with guidance department of high school or by mail; Past recipients of grants receive applications automatically each spring; Completion of formal application required; Interviews required.
EIN: 046050419

3928
Stonecutter Foundation, Inc.
300 Dallas St.
Spindale, NC 28160
Contact: Van H. Lonon, Treas.
Application address: P.O. Box 157, Spindale, NC 28160

Foundation type: Company-sponsored foundation
Limitations: Undergraduate student loans to financially needy residents of the Rutherford and Polk County, NC, area.
Financial data: Year ended 03/31/2004. Assets, $8,904,714 (M); Expenditures, $361,430; Total giving, $274,350; Loans to individuals, 118 loans totaling $63,000.
Type of support: Undergraduate support.
Application information: Applications accepted throughout the year; Completion of formal application required, including transcripts and proof of acceptance at an institution of higher education.
EIN: 566044820

3929
Katherine M. Stoner Trust
c/o M&T Bank
21 E. Market St.
York, PA 17401-1205
Application address: c/o M&T Bank, Attn: John Schall, 14 N. Main St., Chambersburg, PA 17201, tel.: (717) 267-7625

Foundation type: Independent foundation
Limitations: Educational loans only to nursing students enrolled at Franklin County Vo-Tech, PA.
Financial data: Year ended 12/31/2004. Assets, $92,151 (M); Expenditures, $3,500; Total giving, $2,200; Grants to individuals, 4 grants totaling $2,200.
Fields of interest: Nursing school/education.
Type of support: Support to graduates or students of specific schools; Technical education support; Undergraduate support.
Application information: Applications accepted throughout the year; Completion of formal application required.
EIN: 256266025

3930
I. F. Doug Stonier and Ella Stonier Educational Trust
c/o Granville National Bank
328 S. McCoy St.
P.O. Box 344
Granville, IL 61326
Contact: Philip C. Carlson, Trust Off., Granville National Bank

Foundation type: Independent foundation
Limitations: Scholarships to high school graduates in the Putnam County Community Unit School District.
Financial data: Year ended 04/30/2005. Assets, $275,181 (M); Expenditures, $12,549; Total giving, $11,550; Grants to individuals, 6 grants totaling $11,550.
Type of support: Scholarships—to individuals.
Application information: Deadline June 30; Completion of formal application required, including financial information.
EIN: 363204200

3931
Stony Wold-Herbert Fund, Inc.
136 E. 57th St., Rm. 1705
New York, NY 10022 (212) 753-6565
Contact: Cheryl S. Friedman, Exec. Dir.
FAX: (212) 753-6053;
E-mail: director@stonywold-herbertfund.com;
URL: http://www.stonywold-herbertfund.com

Foundation type: Independent foundation
Limitations: Undergraduate and vocational school scholarships to financially needy students living in the greater New York, NY, area who are at least 16 years old, and who suffer from a documented respiratory or pulmonary problem.
Publications: Application guidelines; Annual report; Informational brochure; Newsletter.
Financial data: Year ended 12/31/2004. Assets, $6,679,346 (M); Expenditures, $391,610; Total giving, $241,311; Grants to individuals, totaling $46,125.
Fields of interest: Vocational education; Lung diseases.
Type of support: Undergraduate support.
Application information: Applications accepted. Application form required.
  Deadline(s): None
  Additional information: Application must include applicant's medical profile completed by a doctor, proof of residence, W-2 form, transcripts, one letter of recommendation, and a brief personal history; Interviews required.
Program description:
  Direct Service Grants: These grants serve as supplemental financial aid to eligible students of at least 16 years of age to help them meet the peripheral expenses involved in attending school. The grants average $250 monthly during the educational or vocational training period of selected students, who suffer from a documented pulmonary problem. The grants are based on the financial need of the recipient, as well as his or her educational goals.
EIN: 132784124

3932
Oliver W. Storer Scholarship Foundation
c/o JPMorgan Chase Bank, N.A.
P.O. Box 1308
Milwaukee, WI 53202
Contact: Charles E. Retherford
Application address: c/o Beasley, Glickison, Retherford & Buckles, 110 E. Charles St., Muncie, IN 47305, tel.: (317) 289-0661

Foundation type: Independent foundation
Limitations: Scholarships to graduating seniors of Delaware County, IN.
Financial data: Year ended 02/28/2005. Assets, $5,313,858 (M); Expenditures, $356,202; Total giving, $313,373; Grants to individuals, 67 grants totaling $313,373 (high: $7,733, low: $1,293).
Type of support: Support to graduates or students of specific schools; Undergraduate support.
Application information: Deadline 60 days prior to start of school year; Application by letter, stating purpose and need.
EIN: 356012044

3933
The Stork Charitable Trust
5727 Twin Silo Rd.
Doylestown, PA 18901
Application address: c/o Erica Zoino Curran, 146 Cockle Cove Rd., S. Chatham, MA 02659

Foundation type: Independent foundation
Limitations: Scholarships to financially needy graduating seniors of Brockton High School, MA, who have been accepted to four-year colleges and universities.
Financial data: Year ended 09/30/2004. Assets, $511,030 (M); Expenditures, $35,375; Total giving, $35,000.
Type of support: Support to graduates or students of specific schools; Undergraduate support.
Application information: Application form required.
  Deadline(s): Mar. 15
  Applicants should submit the following:
    1) Transcripts
    2) FAF
    3) Financial information
  Additional information: Application must also include personal statement. Applications available at the school's guidance office.
Program description:
  Scholarship Programs: Selection is based on financial need, academic ability, personal qualities, and educational goals. Only one application is necessary to be considered for all scholarships. Each scholarship is $7,000.
EIN: 236951762

3934
Lottie D. Stoudenmire Education Fund
c/o Wachovia Bank, N.A.
100 N. Main St., 13th Fl.
Winston-Salem, NC 27150
Application address: c/o Financial Aid Dir., Newberry College, 2100 College St., Newberry, SC 29108

Foundation type: Independent foundation
Limitations: Scholarships to students of all majors at Newberry College, SC, who indicate an intent to enter the ministry.
Financial data: Year ended 04/30/2005. Assets, $239,380 (M); Expenditures, $12,761; Total giving, $7,400; Grants to individuals, totaling $7,400.
Fields of interest: Theological school/education.
Type of support: Support to graduates or students of specific schools; Undergraduate support.
Application information: Applications by letter accepted throughout the year.
EIN: 576087466

3935
C. B. Stout Foundation
c/o Old National Bank
P.O. Box 550
Jasper, IN 47547-0550
Application address: c/o Paoli Community Schools, Attn: Leslie Hash, Guidance Counselor, 501 Elm St., Paoli, IN 47454, tel.: (812) 723-3905

Foundation type: Independent foundation
Limitations: Scholarships to graduates of high schools in Orange County, IN, with preference shown to students of Paoli High School.
Financial data: Year ended 12/31/2004. Assets, $107,949 (M); Expenditures, $11,320; Total giving, $9,825; Grants to individuals, 64 grants totaling $9,825.
Type of support: Support to graduates or students of specific schools; Undergraduate support.

Application information: Application form required.
  Deadline(s): May 1.
  Applicants should submit the following:
    1) Financial information
    2) Transcripts
    3) SAT
    4) GPA
EIN: 356211379

3936
O. J. Stout Scholarship Fund
c/o Unizan Bank, N.A.
P.O. Box 1508
Parkersburg, WV 26102
Contact: Seth Cumberledge, Trust Off., Unizan Bank, N.A.
Application address: c/o Unizan Bank N.A., Trust Dept., 514 Market St., Parkersburg, WV 26101

Foundation type: Independent foundation
Limitations: Scholarships and student loans to financially needy, male high school graduates in Wood County, WV, and adjacent WV counties for undergraduate and graduate study. Preference is given to students studying to become ministers at West Virginia Wesleyan College, Buckhannon, WV.
Financial data: Year ended 12/31/2004. Assets, $11,917,537 (M); Expenditures, $518,605; Total giving, $367,000; Grants to individuals, 161 grants totaling $293,600 (high: $3,600, low: $800); Loans to individuals, 161 loans totaling $73,400.
Fields of interest: Protestant agencies & churches; Men.
Type of support: Support to graduates or students of specific schools; Graduate support; Undergraduate support.
Application information: Application form required.
  Deadline(s): Apr. 1
  Applicants should submit the following:
    1) FAF
    2) Transcripts
  Additional information: Application must also include first page of parents' 1040, and three reference letters. Each recipient is given a scholarship and a student loan. The loan is equivalent to 20 percent of the scholarship amount. Recipients must maintain at least a 2.0 GPA in order to be eligible for additional scholarships and loans. Repayment of loans begins five years after completion or termination of education. Interest rate is 3 percent annually.
EIN: 556029015

3937
Ralph Stowers Scholarship
c/o Bank of Tazewell County Trust
P.O. Box 687
Tazewell, VA 24651

Foundation type: Independent foundation
Limitations: Scholarships to students graduating from a high school in Tazewell County, VA.
Financial data: Year ended 12/31/2003. Assets, $2,154,992 (M); Expenditures, $114,367; Total giving, $100,703; Grants to individuals, 19 grants totaling $100,703 (high: $15,451, low: $983).
Type of support: Support to graduates or students of specific schools; Undergraduate support.
Application information: Applications accepted throughout the year; Contact foundation for current application guidelines.
EIN: 546309437

3938
The David L. Strahan Educational Foundation, Inc.
17967 S.E. 87th St., Melrose Ct.
The Villages, FL 32162-4825
Application address for individuals: c/o Principal,
Wirt County High School, Mulberry St., Elizabeth,
WV 26143, tel.: (304) 275-4241

Foundation type: Independent foundation
Limitations: Scholarships to graduates of Wirt
County High School, WV.
Financial data: Year ended 06/30/2005.
Assets, $213,481 (M); Expenditures, $13,268;
Total giving, $12,500; Grants to individuals, 5
grants totaling $12,500 (high: $2,500, low:
$2,500).
Type of support: Support to graduates or students
of specific schools; Undergraduate support.
Application information: Applications accepted.
Application form required.
Initial approach: Letter.
Deadline(s): June
EIN: 550752363

3939
Leland & Lucille Strahl Educational Trust
c/o Dacotah Bank
P.O. Box 1210
Aberdeen, SD 57402-1210
Application address: c/o Leland Strahl, 26 W. 6th
Ave., No. 306, Redfield, SD 57469, tel.: (605)
472-0425

Foundation type: Operating foundation
Limitations: Undergraduate scholarships to
graduates of Redfield and Northwestern school
districts, SD.
Financial data: Year ended 06/30/2004.
Assets, $388,775 (M); Expenditures, $21,241;
Total giving, $18,000; Grants to individuals, 17
grants totaling $18,000 (high: $1,500, low:
$1,000).
Type of support: Support to graduates or students
of specific schools; Undergraduate support.
Application information: Contact foundation for
current application deadline; Initial approach by
letter; Completion of formal application required.
EIN: 460412852

3940
Gladys Stratton Trust
c/o The Citizens National Bank of Paris
P.O. Box 790
Paris, IL 61944
Contact: Chris Hollowell, Trust Off., The Citizens
National Bank of Paris

Foundation type: Independent foundation
Limitations: Educational loans to residents of
Edgar County, IL, and children of tenants of any land
held in the Gladys Stratton Trust.
Financial data: Year ended 12/31/2002.
Assets, $1,655,594 (M); Expenditures, $30,807;
Total giving, $0; Loans to individuals, 19 loans
totaling $30,250.
Type of support: Student loans—to individuals.
Application information: Application form required.
Deadline(s): Apr. 15
Additional information: Contact trust for current
application deadline/guidelines and forms.
EIN: 376164685

3941
Straub Family Foundation
(formerly Straub Foundation)
7306 Oliver Smith Dr.
Des Moines, IA 50322-3126 (515) 276-9143
Contact: Tim Lockner, Pres.

Foundation type: Independent foundation
Limitations: Scholarships to residents of IA.
Financial data: Year ended 12/31/2004.
Assets, $192,399 (M); Expenditures, $23,188;
Total giving, $7,250; Grants to individuals, 11
grants totaling $7,250.
Type of support: Scholarships—to individuals.
Application information: Applications accepted
throughout the year; Completion of formal
application required.
EIN: 426059605

3942
Helaine & Edgar Strauss Opportunity Trust
154 Maple Ave.
Wilmette, IL 60091
Contact: Ronald Strauss, Tr.

Foundation type: Independent foundation
Limitations: Scholarships to minorities and women.
Giving to graduating seniors in the top ten percent
of their class from selected Chicago high schools.
Financial data: Year ended 12/31/2004.
Assets, $445,635 (M); Expenditures, $41,710;
Total giving, $39,200; Grants to individuals, 17
grants totaling $39,200 (high: $4,800, low: $800).
Fields of interest: Higher education.
Type of support: Undergraduate support.
Application information: Application form required.
Additional information: Applications accepted
throughout the year.
EIN: 363976041

3943
Donald A. Strauss Scholarship Foundation
201 Shipyard Way, Cabin E
Newport Beach, CA 92663 (949) 723-0459
Contact: Ann Mellini
FAX: (949) 673-7371;
E-mail: dastraus@pacbell.net; URL: http://
www.straussfoundation.org

Foundation type: Independent foundation
Limitations: Scholarships by nomination only to
full-time juniors for senior year of study at four-year
colleges or universities in CA.
Financial data: Year ended 06/30/2005.
Assets, $3,596,991 (M); Expenditures,
$201,345; Total giving, $136,250; Grants to
individuals, 26 grants totaling $116,250 (high:
$8,000, low: $2,000).
Type of support: Awards/grants by nomination only;
Undergraduate support.
Application information: Deadline 2nd week of
Mar.; Completion of formal nomination required,
including 3 letters of recommendation, resume,
transcript, and proposal.
Program description:
Scholarship Program: Recipient must be
expecting that a significant part of his or her life will
be devoted to public services and in the upper third
of their class. Students must submit applications
to their schools. A faculty committee on each
campus will select three finalists, whose
applications will then be forwarded to the
foundation for the final selection process.
EIN: 330734363

3944
Nadie E. Strayer Scholarship Fund
2495 Resort St.
Baker City, OR 97814
Contact: Ruth Whitnah, Tr.
Application address: 1995 3rd St., Baker City, OR
97814, tel.: (541) 523-2162

Foundation type: Independent foundation
Limitations: Scholarships to graduates of Baker
County, OR, high schools.
Financial data: Year ended 12/31/2004.
Assets, $62,675 (M); Expenditures, $4,044; Total
giving, $4,000.
Type of support: Support to graduates or students
of specific schools; Undergraduate support.
Application information: Deadline May 1;
Completion of formal application required, including
two letters of reference, SAR form and official
transcripts.
EIN: 931137546

3945
Strayer University Educational Foundation
2121 15th St. N., Ste. 300
Arlington, VA 22201 (703) 558-7055
Contact: Roger Brown, Exec. Dir.
E-mail: roger.brown@strayer.edu; URL: http://
www.strayerfoundation.org

Foundation type: Public charity
Limitations: Scholarships to students attending
Strayer University campuses in DC, MD, and VA.
Financial data: Year ended 12/31/2003.
Assets, $2,334,899 (M); Expenditures,
$135,455; Total giving, $75,500; Grants to
individuals, 97 grants totaling $75,500 (high:
$1,500, low: $500).
Type of support: Support to graduates or students
of specific schools.
Application information: Applications accepted.
Application form required. Application form
available on the grantmaker's Web site.
Deadline(s): May 31 and Nov. 30
Additional information: Completion of formal
application required, including 250-word
essay.
Program descriptions:
High School Grant: Awards scholarship grants to
students selected by high schools in the general
geographic area of the individual campuses of
Strayer University. The individual high schools are
provided specific criteria for the award of a
scholarship (usually a single $1,000 scholarship
for study in a degree program at any Strayer
Campus). The high school then selects the
scholarship recipient who meets those criteria.
Community College Grants: Awards scholarship
grants to students at community colleges with
articulation agreements with Strayer University.
Each community college selects recipients from
among its student body who meet specific criteria
for the awarding of scholarships. The scholarships
(usually two $1,000 grants) are awarded for
continuing college study at Strayer University.
Strayer Scholarships: Awards approximately
$100,000 in scholarship grants each year to
students at Strayer University. Typical grants are
from $500 to $1,000. The grant program is made
available to the general student body through
Strayer's Web site. Strayer University and Strayer
University Educational Foundation employees and
their immediate family members are not eligible to
apply for the Strayer Scholarship.
EIN: 521720424

3946
Charles A. Strickland Memorial Fund

c/o Wachovia Bank, N.A.
100 N. Main St., 13th Fl.
Winston-Salem, NC 27150

Foundation type: Independent foundation
Limitations: Scholarships to students, primarily attending Wake Forest University and Duke University, both in NC.
Financial data: Year ended 12/31/2004. Assets, $2,701,204 (M); Expenditures, $75,104; Total giving, $61,125; Grants to individuals, 69 grants totaling $61,125.
Type of support: Support to graduates or students of specific schools; Undergraduate support.
Application information: Applications not accepted.
  Additional information: Unsolicited requests for funds not accepted.
EIN: 566050004

3947
Evelyn E. Stricklin Scholarship Foundation

(formerly Evelyn E. Stricklin Scholarship Fund)
c/o PNC Advisors, Delaware
1600 Market St., Tax Dept.
Philadelphia, PA 19103-7240
Application address: c/o Donald W. Davis, PNC Bank, Delaware, N.A., 222 Delaware Ave., 16th Fl., Wilmington, DE 19801, tel.: (302) 429-1338

Foundation type: Independent foundation
Limitations: Scholarships to residents of DE for attendance at the University of Delaware, DE.
Financial data: Year ended 09/30/2004. Assets, $1,595,530 (M); Expenditures, $116,576; Total giving, $97,328; Grants to individuals, 20 grants totaling $97,328.
Type of support: Support to graduates or students of specific schools.
Application information: Applications accepted. Application form required.
  Initial approach: Letter.
  Additional information: Contact foundation for further application guidelines.
EIN: 016173503

3948
Strive, Inc.

P.O. Box 23371
Hilton Head Island, SC 29925-3371
Contact: Susan Carter Barnwell, Dir.

Foundation type: Operating foundation
Limitations: Scholarships to individuals who were in STRIVE during their high school years.
Publications: Newsletter.
Financial data: Year ended 06/30/2005. Assets, $2,957 (M); Expenditures, $19,735; Total giving, $19,127; Grants to individuals, 10 grants totaling $19,127 (high: $5,222, low: $247).
Type of support: Technical education support; Undergraduate support.
Application information:
  Initial approach: Letter.
  Deadline(s): None
  Additional information: contact foundation for current application guidelines.
EIN: 570935388

3949
Hattie M. Strong Foundation

1620 Eye St. N.W., Ste. 700
Washington, DC 20006-2402 (202) 331-1619
Contact: Judith B. Cyphers, Secy. and Dir. of Grants
FAX: (202) 466-2894;
E-mail: hmsf@hmstrongfoundation.org;
URL: http://www.hmstrongfoundation.org/

Foundation type: Independent foundation
Limitations: Interest-free loans to U.S. citizens who are entering their final year of a baccalaureate or graduate degree program at an accredited four-year college or graduate school. Foreign students temporarily in this country do not qualify for loans.
Publications: Application guidelines; Annual report; Grants list; Informational brochure.
Financial data: Year ended 08/31/2004. Assets, $31,451,087 (M); Expenditures, $1,659,401; Total giving, $818,810; Loans to individuals, 118 loans totaling $497,420.
Type of support: Graduate support; Undergraduate support.
Application information: Applications accepted Jan. 1 to Mar. 31; Initial approach by letter requesting application form, and including SASE; Completion of formal application required, including letter outlining financial aid; Recipients notified in July; See program description for further details.
Program description:
  Interest-Free Student Loans: Application letter should include a brief personal history, institution attended, subjects studied, amount of funds needed, and the expected date for completion of studies. Application forms are then sent to eligible students. Loan recipients are selected on the basis of motivation, financial need, self-reliance, and scholastic record. The maximum loan amount available is $5,000 per year. The terms of repayment are based upon monthly income after graduation and are arranged on an individual basis.
EIN: 530237223

3950
The Carol Dimaiti Stuart Foundation

c/o Brown Rudnick Berlack Isreals
One Financial Ctr.
Boston, MA 02111
Contact: Carl Dimaiti, Pres.

Foundation type: Public charity
Limitations: Scholarships to individuals for higher education.
Financial data: Year ended 12/31/2003. Assets, $591,484 (M); Expenditures, $121,002; Total giving, $113,750; Grants to individuals, 40 grants totaling $113,750 (high: $5,000, low: $200).
Fields of interest: Higher education.
Type of support: Scholarships—to individuals.
Application information:
  Initial approach: Letter.
EIN: 223026439

3951
R. L. and Ethel Stubbs Scholarship Trust

c/o Security National Bank
P.O. Box 147
Sioux City, IA 51102-0147

Foundation type: Independent foundation
Limitations: Scholarships to students in the Galva-Holstein Community School District, IA.
Financial data: Year ended 12/31/2004. Assets, $979,166 (M); Expenditures, $51,085;

Total giving, $39,342; Grants to individuals, 41 grants totaling $39,342.
Type of support: Support to graduates or students of specific schools.
Application information: Contact high school for current application deadline/guidelines; Initial approach by letter.
EIN: 421386035

3952
The Clair E. Stuck and Flora E. Stuck Foundation, Inc.

7958 U.S. Hwy. 522 S.
McVeytown, PA 17051-7457 (717) 248-8245
Contact: Gloria A. Shank, Pres.

Foundation type: Independent foundation
Limitations: Scholarships to graduates of high schools in Mifflin and Juniata counties, PA, who have maintained at least a "C" average in high school.
Financial data: Year ended 12/31/2004. Assets, $177,313 (M); Expenditures, $21,084; Total giving, $19,825; Grants to individuals, 27 grants totaling $19,825.
Type of support: Support to graduates or students of specific schools; Undergraduate support.
Application information: Deadline prior to end of school year; Application by essay of at least 300 words, describing need and reason for furthering education, including copy of grades and list of courses studied.
Program description:
  Scholarship Program: Recipients are chosen by a selection committee made up of teachers, counselors, and principals of high schools in Juniata and Mifflin counties. Selection is based on financial need and academic achievement. Scholarships are granted for tuition only. Recipients of scholarships from other foundations are ineligible.
EIN: 251709803

3953
Student Aid Foundation Enterprises

800 Commerce St.
Houston, TX 77002

Foundation type: Independent foundation
Limitations: Scholarships principally to younger students who are residents of Houston, TX, are underprivileged, have learning disabilities or are victims of drug abuse. Students must be nominated by local agencies. College students are eligible only if they are either prior recipients of secondary school assistance or are nominated by a particular college at which the Student Aid Foundation has a program.
Financial data: Year ended 06/30/2005. Assets, $1,280,983 (M); Expenditures, $242,024; Total giving, $174,571; Grants to individuals, 3 grants totaling $26,086 (high: $9,875, low: $6,892).
Fields of interest: Substance abuse, treatment; Learning disorders; Children/youth, services.
Type of support: Awards/grants by nomination only.
Application information: Applications not accepted.
  Additional information: Direct applications not accepted.
Program description:
  Memorial Hall School Scholarships: The scholarships are given at the secondary school level to disadvantaged children with learning

disabilities and/or to dysfunctional foreign students.
EIN: 746060745

3954
Student Aid Foundation, Inc.
1393 Sheffield Pkwy.
Marietta, GA 30062 (770) 973-7077
Contact: Catherine W. Reynolds, Exec. Secy.
FAX: (770) 973-2220;
E-mail: studentaid@bellsouth.net; URL: http://www.studentaidfoundation.org

Foundation type: Independent foundation
Limitations: Student loans to financially needy females who are either legal residents of GA, or nonresidents attending GA schools.
Financial data: Year ended 03/31/2005.
Assets, $1,640,105 (M); Expenditures, $60,612; Total giving, $0; Loans to individuals, totaling $255,500.
Fields of interest: Vocational education; Medical school/education; Women.
Type of support: Student loans—to individuals; Graduate support; Undergraduate support.
Application information:
Deadline(s): Apr. 15
Additional information: Completion of formal application required, including outline of financial need, transcripts, and loan amount needed.
Program description:
Loan Program: Funds are loaned for regular college work and for most specialized training programs. Loans are for one academic year and are limited to $3,500-$4,500 for undergraduate and $5,000 for graduate students. Recipients may reapply for loans for each year of study. All promissory notes must be co-signed or endorsed. Loans are interest-free while the student is still in college or training full-time. Interest at six percent begins three months after the student completes her studies or leaves school for any reason. If the loan is not repaid within four years of completion of studies, interest at twelve percent is charged on the remaining unpaid balance.
EIN: 580612611

3955
Stueven Charitable Foundation
5251 W. Husker Hwy.
Alda, NE 68810-9610 (308) 382-8113
Contact: Delbert G. Stueven, Pres.

Foundation type: Independent foundation
Limitations: Scholarships to residents of Hall County, NE, and individuals attending high school there.
Financial data: Year ended 12/31/2004.
Assets, $205,880 (M); Expenditures, $10,688; Total giving, $9,000; Grants to individuals, 12 grants totaling $9,000.
Type of support: Precollege support; Undergraduate support.
Application information: Deadline Feb. 15; Completion of formal application, including transcripts, extracurricular activities, essay, support letter from parent or guardian, and three letters of recommendation.
EIN: 470732885

3956
CDR William S. Stuhr Scholarship Fund for Military Sons and Daughters
c/o Walter Loving
74 S. Dogwood Tr.
Southern Shores, NC 27949 (252) 255-3013
Contact: Joseph La Riviere, Exec. Dir.

Foundation type: Public charity
Limitations: Scholarships to dependents of active and retired members of the U.S. Armed Services.
Financial data: Year ended 12/31/2003.
Assets, $224,130 (M); Expenditures, $59,146; Total giving, $24,000; Grants to individuals, 5 grants totaling $24,000 (high: $4,800, low: $4,800).
Type of support: Scholarships—to individuals.
Application information: Contact fund for current application deadline/guidelines.
EIN: 133187922

3957
Jacob Stump, Jr. and Clara Stump Memorial Scholarship Fund
c/o First National Bank
P.O. Box 685
Mattoon, IL 61938 (217) 234-6430
Contact: Tabby Bell

Foundation type: Independent foundation
Limitations: Scholarships to high school graduates from Mattoon, Charleston, Arcola, and Neoga, IL, to attend any IL tax-supported college or university.
Financial data: Year ended 07/31/2004.
Assets, $1,304,021 (M); Expenditures, $141,730; Total giving, $95,000; Grants to individuals, 142 grants totaling $95,000 (high: $1,000, low: $500).
Type of support: Undergraduate support.
Application information: Deadline Apr. 15; Completion of formal application required; Applications available from high schools and The First National Bank.
EIN: 376064295

3958
E. Isabella Stupfel Trust
7535 E. Hampden Ave., Ste. 305
Denver, CO 80231-4840
Contact: David J. Kloepfer, Chair.

Foundation type: Independent foundation
Limitations: Scholarships to financially needy residents of CO.
Financial data: Year ended 06/30/2005.
Assets, $459,282 (M); Expenditures, $5,209; Total giving, $4,259.
Type of support: Scholarships—to individuals.
Application information: Applications accepted throughout the year; Completion of formal application required, including references, reports, and transcripts.
EIN: 742439595

3959
The Stephen H. Sturges & Rose P. Sturges Charitable Trust
P.O. Box 4997
Yuma, AZ 85366
Application address: 2260 S. 4th Ave., Yuma, AZ 85364, tel.: (928) 783-8321

Foundation type: Independent foundation
Limitations: Scholarships to residents of Yuma, AZ.

Financial data: Year ended 11/30/2004.
Assets, $5,122,919 (M); Expenditures, $174,128; Total giving, $106,250; Grants to individuals, totaling $56,250.
Type of support: Undergraduate support.
Application information: Application form required.
Additional information: Applications are made to individuals' high schools, which then forward the applications to the foundation, along with their recommendations.
Program description:
Scholarship Program: The maximum scholarship amount per individual per year is $2,500. Generally, no more than two grants will be approved annually from each Yuma County high school.
EIN: 860427923

3960
W. P. Sturgis Foundation
P.O. Box 394
Arkadelphia, AR 71923 (870) 246-6514
Contact: June Anthony, Secy.-Treas.

Foundation type: Independent foundation
Limitations: Scholarships to AR students with at least a 2.0 GPA. Students who have completed eight or more semesters of undergraduate study will not be considered.
Financial data: Year ended 12/31/2004.
Assets, $3,256,390 (M); Expenditures, $214,237; Total giving, $185,773; Grants to individuals, totaling $138,211.
Type of support: Undergraduate support.
Application information: Application form required.
Deadline(s): June 1 for fall and Dec. 1 for spring
Applicants should submit the following:
1) Financial information
2) Photograph
3) Transcripts
4) GPA
Additional information: Application must also include personal statement, and most recent federal tax return.
EIN: 716057063

3961
Seg and Harty Suarez Charitable Foundation
23 Public Sq., Ste. 440
Belleville, IL 62220 (618) 233-0480
Contact: M. Lee Suarez, V.P.
FAX: (618) 233-0601

Foundation type: Independent foundation
Limitations: Scholarships to economically disadvantaged youths in the Fairmont City, IL, area.
Financial data: Year ended 12/31/2004.
Assets, $8,460 (M); Expenditures, $257,634; Total giving, $257,588; Grants to individuals, 93 grants totaling $62,700 (high: $1,320, low: $660).
Type of support: Scholarships—to individuals.
Application information: Applications accepted throughout the year; Contact foundation for current application guidelines.
EIN: 431545390

3962
Sudbury Foundation
278 Old Sudbury Rd.
Sudbury, MA 01776 (978) 443-0849
Contact: Fredericka Tanner, Exec. Dir.
FAX: (978) 579-9536;
E-mail: contact@sudburyfoundation.org;
URL: http://www.sudburyfoundation.org

Foundation type: Independent foundation
Limitations: Scholarships to graduating seniors who are residents of Sudbury, MA, or the descendents of residents, students of Lincoln-Sudbury Regional High School, and dependents of full-time employees of the Town of Sudbury, MA, or Lincoln-Sudbury Regional High School.
Publications: Application guidelines; Biennial report; Informational brochure; Program policy statement.
Financial data: Year ended 12/31/2004. Assets, $29,531,256 (M); Expenditures, $1,342,464; Total giving, $992,450; Grants to individuals, 59 grants totaling $281,750 (high: $5,000, low: $300).
Fields of interest: Vocational education.
Type of support: Employee-related scholarships; Technical education support; Undergraduate support.
Application information: Deadline Feb. 1; Initial approach by letter or telephone; Completion of formal application required, including official transcript, standardized test scores, letters of recommendation, and personal statement; Interviews may be required; Recipients notified in mid-Mar.
Program description:
Atkinson Scholarship Program: Scholarships may be used to attend accredited two- and four-year colleges and universities, and approved vocational and professional programs. Recipients are chosen on the basis of academic achievement, financial need, future potential, and the desire and ability to contribute to society through community service, the advancement of a field of interest, or the sharing of a special skill or talent. Scholarships are awarded in amounts of up to $5,000 per year, and are renewable annually for a total of $20,000 based on continued financial need and acceptable academic performance.
EIN: 046037026

3963
Rudy Suden Scholarship Trust Fund
c/o First Interstate Bank
P.O. Box 5010
Great Falls, MT 59403-5010
Application addresses: For Stanford students: Attn.: Mike Zacher, c/o Basin State Bank, P.O. Box 428, Stanford, MT 59479, tel.: (406) 566-2238, for Denton students: Attn.: Peter Moe, c/o Farmers State Bank, P.O. Box 1047, Denton, MT 59430, tel.: (406) 567-2226

Foundation type: Independent foundation
Limitations: Scholarships to graduates and graduating seniors of Denton High School, MT, and Stanford High School, MT.
Financial data: Year ended 03/31/2005. Assets, $2,107,412 (M); Expenditures, $99,577; Total giving, $88,421; Grants to individuals, 55 grants totaling $88,421.
Fields of interest: Vocational education.
Type of support: Support to graduates or students of specific schools; Technical education support; Undergraduate support.
Application information: Application form required.
Deadline(s): Apr. 1
Applicants should submit the following:
1) Transcripts
2) GPA
3) Financial information
Program description:
Scholarship Program: Applicants must have attended Denton or Stanford high schools for the two academic years preceding graduation. Applications must be made within two years of graduation, unless the individual enters military service during that time. Scholarships are renewable for up to four years provided recipient has maintained at least a 2.5 GPA and has completed at least 45 credit hours per year.
EIN: 816063733

3964
Suder-Pick Foundation, Inc.
777 E. Wisconsin Ave.
Milwaukee, WI 53202 (414) 297-5748
Contact: Harrold J. McComas, V.P.

Foundation type: Independent foundation
Limitations: Scholarships to graduating seniors of West Bend high schools, WI.
Financial data: Year ended 12/31/2004. Assets, $24,606 (M); Expenditures, $74,445; Total giving, $69,000; Grants to individuals, 30 grants totaling $45,000.
Type of support: Support to graduates or students of specific schools; Undergraduate support.
Application information: Applications by letter accepted throughout the year.
EIN: 396048255

3965
James A. Suffridge UFCW Scholarship Fund
1775 K St., N.W.
Washington, DC 20006 (202) 223-3111
Contact: Joseph T. Hansen, Pres.
URL: http://www.UFCW.org

Foundation type: Public charity
Limitations: Scholarships to persons affiliated with UFCW.
Financial data: Year ended 04/30/2005. Assets, $439,910 (M); Expenditures, $32,441; Total giving, $29,000; Grants to individuals, 28 grants totaling $29,000 (high: $2,000, low: $1,000).
Fields of interest: Labor unions/organizations.
Type of support: Scholarships—to individuals.
Application information: Deadline Mar. 15; Completion of formal application required, including high school transcript and copy of SAT scores. Contact foundation for geographic limitations.
EIN: 526033919

3966
Ray & Pauline Sullivan Foundation
c/o Bank of America, N.A.
777 Main St. CT2-102-22-02
Hartford, CT 06115 (860) 952-7412

Foundation type: Independent foundation
Limitations: Scholarships and student loans primarily to graduates of St. Bernard High School, CT, and other area schools to acquire educational advantages that might otherwise not be available to them.
Financial data: Year ended 01/31/2005. Assets, $13,959,252 (M); Expenditures, $646,306; Total giving, $553,571.
Type of support: Student loans—to individuals; Support to graduates or students of specific schools; Undergraduate support.
Application information: Application form required.
Deadline(s): May 1.
EIN: 066141242

3967
Bob Sullivan Memorial Foundation
41 Accord Park Dr.
Norwell, MA 02061 (781) 871-2260
Contact: Paul Sullivan, Pres.

Foundation type: Public charity
Limitations: Scholarships and grants to individuals to pursue their educational goals.
Financial data: Year ended 12/31/2003. Assets, $221,650 (M); Expenditures, $18,120; Total giving, $17,177; Grants to individuals, 13 grants totaling $17,177 (high: $2,000, low: $500).
Fields of interest: Higher education.
Type of support: Grants to individuals; Scholarships—to individuals.
Application information:
Initial approach: Letter.
EIN: 043214451

3968
Sulphur Springs Valley Electric Cooperative Foundation
(also known as SSVEC Foundation)
P.O. Box 820
Willcox, AZ 85644 (520) 384-2221
Contact: Brian Fickett
E-mail: brianf@ssvec.com

Foundation type: Company-sponsored foundation
Limitations: Awards and prizes by nomination only given to support science and other educational activities in the Sulphur Springs Valley Electric Cooperative, Inc. service area within Cochise and Santa Cruz counties, AZ.
Financial data: Year ended 12/31/2003. Assets, $472,638 (M); Expenditures, $97,968; Total giving, $81,002; Grants to individuals, totaling $55,062.
Fields of interest: Science; Science.
Type of support: Conferences/seminars; Awards/grants by nomination only; Awards/prizes; Travel grants.
Application information:
Initial approach: Letter, e-mail, or telephone.
Deadline(s): Oct. 31
Program descriptions:
International Science Fair: Two grand prize winners, their advisors, and two adults in charge receive an all expenses paid trip to compete in the International Fair.
Washington Youth Tour: Selected students attend a one-week educational program in Washington, DC.
Youth Engineering Science (YES) Fair: Students compete to receive awards for science projects, to be used to purchase computers, software, science equipment, or educational materials.
EIN: 860488826

3969
Sunburst Foundation, Inc.
P.O. Box 812155
Boca Raton, FL 33481-2155
Contact: James M. Hankins, Pres.
E-mail: sunfound@bellsouth.net; *URL:* http://www.sunburst-foundation.org

Foundation type: Independent foundation
Limitations: Scholarships to graduating seniors of specific FL high schools who are majoring in the physical sciences.
Financial data: Year ended 06/30/2004. Assets, $2,227,956 (M); Expenditures, $116,539; Total giving, $82,000; Grants to

individuals, 32 grants totaling $82,000 (high: $5,500, low: $1,000).
Fields of interest: Dental school/education; Medical school/education; Veterinary medicine; Physical/earth sciences; Chemistry; Mathematics; Physics; Engineering; Biological sciences.
Type of support: Support to graduates or students of specific schools; Undergraduate support.
Application information: Deadline Feb.; Completion of formal application required; Applications available through guidance counselors.
Program description:
Scholarship Program: Awards are based on economic need and academic requirements. Student must have a cumulative high school G.P.A. of 3.0 or above, and must intend to declare a major in engineering, computer science, chemistry, physics, biology, botany, mathematics, oceanography, geology, pre-dental, pre-medical, or pre-veterinarian studies. The estimated range of the amount of the individual's scholarship will be between $1,000 and $6,000 per recipient per academic year which may be applied toward tuition, laboratory, books, and room and board expenses only. Students at the following schools are eligible to apply: Atlantic High School, Boca Raton High School, Deerfield Beach High School, Ely High School, Olympic High School, and Spanish River High School.
EIN: 592637289

3970
Sunnyside Foundation, Inc.
(formerly Sunnyside, Inc.)
8222 Douglas Ave., Ste. 501
Dallas, TX 75225 (214) 692-5686
Contact: Peggy Hueffner, Exec. Dir.
FAX: (214) 692-1968;
E-mail: sunnysidetexas@sbcglobal.net

Foundation type: Independent foundation
Limitations: Scholarships to underprivileged Christian Science children under the age of 20 residing in TX who regularly attend Christian Science Sunday schools, to provide for their intellectual needs.
Publications: Application guidelines; Informational brochure (including application guidelines); Program policy statement (including application guidelines).
Financial data: Year ended 12/31/2004.
Assets, $27,223,095 (M); Expenditures, $1,174,691; Total giving, $832,878; Grants to individuals, totaling $832,878.
Fields of interest: Christian agencies & churches.
Type of support: Scholarships—to individuals.
Application information: Applications accepted. Application form required.
Deadline(s): Applications accepted throughout the year
EIN: 756037004

3971
Support Network, Inc.
15 E. 40th St.
New York, NY 10010-0000 (212) 685-8503
Contact: Ruth Clark, Pres.

Foundation type: Public charity
Limitations: Scholarships to low-income individuals.
Financial data: Year ended 06/30/2004.
Assets, $30,478 (M); Expenditures, $200,846; Total giving, $18,116.
Fields of interest: Economically disadvantaged.

Type of support: Scholarships—to individuals.
Application information: Contact foundation for current application deadline/guidelines.
EIN: 133549282

3972
Supreme Council Education and Charity Fund
P.O. Box 519
Lexington, MA 02420 (781) 862-4410
Contact: Walter E. Webber, Pres.
Fax: (781) 274-7319

Foundation type: Public charity
Limitations: Scholarships to residents of the 15 states which comprise the Scottish Rite Northern Masonic Jurisdiction.
Financial data: Year ended 07/31/2003.
Assets, $5,921,586 (M); Expenditures, $400,000; Total giving, $400,000; Grants to individuals, 400 grants totaling $400,000 (high: $2,350, low: $200).
Fields of interest: Fraternal societies.
Type of support: Scholarships—to individuals.
Application information: Contact foundation for current application deadline; Completion of formal application required.
EIN: 046116087

3973
Edna Bailey Sussman Fund
c/o Boyce, Hughes & Farrell, LLP
1025 Northern Blvd., Ste. 300
Roslyn, NY 11576-1506
Contact: Dorothy Bertine, Admin.

Foundation type: Independent foundation
Limitations: Internships by nomination only to individuals who have completed at least one year of college and are enrolled in an environmental studies program as an undergraduate or graduate student at a university.
Financial data: Year ended 04/30/2005.
Assets, $5,896,433 (M); Expenditures, $264,608; Total giving, $225,847.
Fields of interest: Natural resources; Environment; Animals/wildlife, preservation/protection.
Type of support: Internship funds; Awards/grants by nomination only; Graduate support; Undergraduate support.
Application information: Applications not accepted.
Additional information: The fund only accepts nominations of students from colleges and universities with which it has established relationships.
Program description:
Internships: The program furthers the preservation of wildlife, the control of pollution, and the preservation of natural land and resources. Weekly or monthly stipends are disbursed to the institution on behalf of the intern selected by the fund's trustees. The length of internships is no less than one year. Institutions that have established relations with the fund are: Colorado School of Mines; University of Colorado; Cornell University; Duke University; University of Michigan; Pennsylvania State University; State University of New York College of Environmental Science and Forestry; Virginia Polytechnic Institute and State University; and Yale University.
EIN: 133187064

3974
Otto Sussman Trust
1025 Northern Blvd., Ste. 300
Roslyn, NY 11576-1506
Contact: Edward S. Miller, Tr.
Application address: P.O. Box 1374, Trainsmeadow Sta., Flushing, NY 11370-0998

Foundation type: Independent foundation
Limitations: Scholarships to financially needy residents of NJ, NY, OK, and PA who are in need due to illness or death in their immediate family or some other unusual or unfortunate circumstance.
Financial data: Year ended 12/31/2004.
Assets, $5,320,457 (M); Expenditures, $248,497; Total giving, $183,421; Grants to individuals, 105 grants totaling $183,421 (high: $4,970, low: $300).
Type of support: Scholarships—to individuals; Grants for special needs.
Application information: Application form required.
Deadline(s): Applications accepted throughout the year
Additional information: Applicants must be recommended by and submit applications through educational agencies known to the trustees.
Program description:
Scholarship Program: Applications for scholarship grants are considered only if all other kinds of aid available to students, including student loans, have been explored and proven fruitless.
EIN: 136075849

3975
The Sutcliffe Foundation
2236 Encinitas Blvd., Ste. A
Encinitas, CA 92024
Contact: Barry Axelrod, Dir.

Foundation type: Independent foundation
Limitations: Scholarships to students, primarily in MO, for higher education.
Financial data: Year ended 11/30/2003.
Assets, $521,576 (M); Expenditures, $18,344; Total giving, $12,650; Grants to individuals, 24 grants totaling $12,650 (high: $6,000, low: $125).
Type of support: Undergraduate support.
Application information: Contact foundation for current application deadline; Application by letter.
EIN: 330072137

3976
Gerald Sutliff Trust f/b/o Hofstra University
c/o The Bank of New York, Tax Dept.
1 Wall St., 28th Fl.
New York, NY 10286
Application address: Alfred E. Urban, Jr., c/o Wm. Bradford Turner Post 265, P.O. Box 8, Garden City, NY, 11530-0008

Foundation type: Independent foundation
Limitations: Scholarships to graduates of Garden City High School, NY, who will attend Hofstra University.
Financial data: Year ended 09/30/2004.
Assets, $256,047 (M); Expenditures, $9,388; Total giving, $8,000; Grants to individuals, 8 grants totaling $8,000.
Type of support: Support to graduates or students of specific schools; Undergraduate support.
Application information: Applications accepted throughout the year; Completion of formal application required.
EIN: 133543303

3977

Svarre Foundation

101 S. Central Ave.
Sidney, MT 59270-4123   (406) 433-8600
Contact: Robert J. Gross, Chair.

Foundation type: Independent foundation
Limitations: Scholarships to residents of Richland County, MT.
Financial data: Year ended 12/31/2004.
Assets, $567,340 (M); Expenditures, $22,470; Total giving, $22,000; Grants to individuals, 6 grants totaling $12,000.
Type of support: Scholarships—to individuals.
Application information: Applications accepted throughout the year; Completion of formal application required, including the purpose of the grant, reason needed, resume, and high school transcripts.
EIN: 816013673

3978

John Steven Svehla Foundation, Inc.

1721 Edmondson Ave.
Catonsville, MD 21228

Foundation type: Independent foundation
Limitations: Scholarships to individuals residing in MD for undergraduate education.
Financial data: Year ended 12/31/2004.
Assets, $27,971 (M); Expenditures, $40,976; Total giving, $15,800; Grants to individuals, 4 grants totaling $12,000.
Type of support: Undergraduate support.
Application information: Contact foundation for current application deadline/guidelines.
EIN: 522269164

3979

SVI Scholarship Fund

831 Summit St.
Glen Ellyn, IL 60137
Contact: Jack W. Fiene, Treas.
Application address: 1245 Executive Pl., Geneva, IL 60134

Foundation type: Independent foundation
Limitations: Scholarships to high school seniors for higher education who are high school seniors at the time of the grant receipt.
Financial data: Year ended 10/31/2004.
Assets, $212,095 (M); Expenditures, $14,473; Total giving, $12,000; Grants to individuals, 5 grants totaling $10,000.
Type of support: Undergraduate support.
Application information: Applications accepted.
Initial approach: Letter.
Applicants should submit the following:
    1) Letter(s) of recommendation
    2) Class rank
    3) Transcripts
Additional information: Appplication must also include verification by principal of enrollment and residence, scores on scholastic aptitude or other tests measuring aptitude for higher education, statement of extracurricular activities, proof of expenses and copy of parents' and student's income tax returns for previous two years.
EIN: 363995732

3980

Ernest and Lillian Swanson Memorial Scholarship Trust

c/o Judy Sheets
2626 Brune Rd.
Farmington, MO 63640
E-mail: JusyS@i1.net

Foundation type: Operating foundation
Limitations: Scholarships to MO residents enrolled in botany, plant genetics and related programs at accredited universities or community colleges.
Publications: Application guidelines.
Financial data: Year ended 12/31/2003.
Assets, $297,380 (M); Expenditures, $12,933; Total giving, $8,200; Grants to individuals, 6 grants totaling $8,200 (high: $2,000, low: $700).
Fields of interest: Botany.
Type of support: Graduate support; Undergraduate support.
Application information: Application form required. Application form available on the grantmaker's Web site.
Initial approach: Application.
Copies of proposal: 1
Deadline(s): Mar. 1
Applicants should submit the following:
    1) Transcripts
    2) Letter(s) of recommendation
    3) GPA
    4) Financial information
Additional information: Contact trust for current application guidelines; Applications can be obtained from community colleges or universities.
Program description:
Ernest and Lillian Swanson Scholarship: Awarded to any high school senior, undergraduate or graduate student who is majoring in botany, agriculture, environmental science, plant genetics, or related fields. Applicants must be a resident of MO. Scholarships are awarded in March the following semester.
EIN: 431713377

3981

Swasey Fund, Inc.

c/o Riley & Associates
P.O. Box 157
Newburyport, MA 01950-0157

Foundation type: Independent foundation
Limitations: Scholarships to financially needy residents of Newburyport, Newbury, Byfield, West Newbury, and Salisbury, MA, for study in a health-oriented field.
Financial data: Year ended 03/31/2005.
Assets, $617,525 (M); Expenditures, $41,603; Total giving, $32,850.
Fields of interest: Medical school/education; Health sciences school/education.
Type of support: Graduate support; Undergraduate support.
Application information: Application form required.
Deadline(s): Second Thurs. in Apr.
Additional information: Application should include class rank, standardized test scores, and personal and academic references.
Program description:
Scholarship Program: Awards of $500 each are made to qualified high school seniors with the remaining amount made available to qualified graduate and undergraduate students. Recipients are selected on the basis of academic achievement, financial need, and character. Scholarships are renewable.
EIN: 046051742

3982

Lloyd D. Sweet Educational Foundation

P.O. Box 638
Chinook, MT 59523-0638
Contact: Debra Davies, Foundation Mgr.
E-mail: info@chinookmontana.com; URL: http://www.chinookmontana.com/Sweetscholar/Default.htm

Foundation type: Independent foundation
Limitations: Scholarships only to graduates of Chinook High School, MT, who maintain at least a 2.0 GPA and carry at least 12 college credits.
Financial data: Year ended 12/31/2003.
Assets, $2,519,686 (M); Expenditures, $129,179; Total giving, $107,675; Grants to individuals, 68 grants totaling $107,675 (high: $2,800, low: $525).
Type of support: Support to graduates or students of specific schools; Undergraduate support.
Application information: Applications accepted. Application form required.
Deadline(s): Mar. 1
EIN: 237131688

3983

Harry B. Sweet Foundation, Inc.

c/o Michael L. Johnson
145 E. 4th St.
Superior, NE 68978-1707   (402) 879-3251

Foundation type: Independent foundation
Limitations: Scholarships to residents or graduates of high schools in Smith, Jewell, and Republic counties, KS, or Nuckolls County, NE. Award must be used for tuition and other college-related expenses.
Financial data: Year ended 12/31/2004.
Assets, $370,990 (M); Expenditures, $5,164; Total giving, $4,600; Grants to individuals, 14 grants totaling $4,600.
Type of support: Support to graduates or students of specific schools; Undergraduate support.
Application information: Application form required.
Applicants should submit the following:
    1) Transcripts
    2) Letter(s) of recommendation
Additional information: Contact school counselor by Mar. 1 for current application deadline; Application should be sent through counselor, not directly to the foundation.
EIN: 470634034

3984

Willard Sweitzer American Legion Trust Fund

130 S. Main St.
Washington, IL 61571   (309) 444-3131
Contact: Carol A. Madden, Tr.

Foundation type: Independent foundation
Limitations: Scholarships to graduates of Washington Community High School, IL, who rank in the top ten percent of their class.
Financial data: Year ended 12/31/2004.
Assets, $161,233 (M); Expenditures, $6,239; Total giving, $5,000; Grants to individuals, 4 grants totaling $5,000.
Type of support: Support to graduates or students of specific schools; Undergraduate support.
Application information: Deadline within 180 days of trust publication notice; Completion of formal application required.
EIN: 376127123

3985
Sidney A. Swensrud Scholarship Fund
P.O. Box 167
Northwood, IA   50459-0167

Foundation type: Independent foundation
Limitations: Scholarships to graduating seniors of Northwood-Kensett High School in Northwood, IA.
Financial data: Year ended 12/31/2004.
Assets, $2,685,788 (M); Expenditures, $94,500; Total giving, $92,850; Grants to individuals, 59 grants totaling $92,850 (high: $3,400, low: $750).
Type of support: Support to graduates or students of specific schools; Undergraduate support.
Application information: Application form required.
  Deadline(s): May 1
EIN: 426061933

3986
Wesley H. and Barbara Duer Swiler Memorial Scholarship Trust Fund
c/o Burlington Bank & Trust
P.O. Box 728
Burlington, IA   52601   (319) 753-9130
Contact: Frank Delaney, Trust Off., Burlington Bank & Trust

Foundation type: Independent foundation
Limitations: Scholarships to students at Burlington Community High School, IA, and Notre Dame High School, Burlington, IA.
Financial data: Year ended 02/28/2005.
Assets, $298,722 (M); Expenditures, $19,629; Total giving, $17,000; Grants to individuals, 8 grants totaling $17,000 (high: $3,000, low: $2,000).
Type of support: Support to graduates or students of specific schools; Undergraduate support.
Application information: Deadline Mar. 15; Completion of formal application required, including photograph, ACT scores, GPA, class rank, essay, and three references from high school faculty.
EIN: 426485815

3987
Edward F. Swinney Student Loan Fund
c/o Bank of America, N.A.
P.O. Box 831041
Dallas, TX   75283-1041
Contact: David P. Ross, Sr. V.P., Bank of America, N.A.
Application address for individuals: P.O. Box 419119, Kansas City, MO 84141-6119, tel.: (816) 979-7481

Foundation type: Independent foundation
Limitations: Student loans to MO residents with financial need who are attending colleges in MO.
Financial data: Year ended 12/31/2004.
Assets, $899,944 (M); Expenditures, $12,363; Total giving, $0; Loans to individuals, 5 loans totaling $46,000.
Type of support: Student loans—to individuals.
Application information: Applications accepted throughout the year; Completion of formal application required.
EIN: 446009266

3988
Swiss Benevolent Society of Chicago
P.O. Box 2137
Chicago, IL   60690
E-mail: president@sbschicago.org/; URL: http://www.sbschicago.org

Foundation type: Independent foundation
Limitations: Undergraduate scholarships to full-time students of Swiss descent residing in IL and southern WI.
Financial data: Year ended 12/31/2004.
Assets, $1,749,565 (M); Expenditures, $115,962; Total giving, $77,516; Grants to individuals, 39 grants totaling $54,464. Subtotal for scholarships—to individuals: 37 grants totaling $41,980.
Type of support: Undergraduate support.
Application information: Application form required.
  Deadline(s): Contact foundation for current application deadline
  Applicants should submit the following:
    1) Class rank
    2) ACT
    3) Essay
    4) GPA
    5) SAT
    6) Transcripts
Program description:
  Scholarship Program: Scholarships are granted as full ($2,500), half ($1,250), or one-fourth ($750) awards, depending on the applicants' overall rating and tuition charged. Financial need is not a requirement. Applicants must be Swiss nationals or of documented Swiss descent, and have GPAs of at least 3.5 (in high school or college), and ACT scores of at least 26 or SAT scores of at least 1050. Students who have completed any kind of a bachelor's degree are not eligible for scholarships.
EIN: 366076395

3989
Charles S. Swope Memorial Scholarship Trust
c/o First National Bank of Chester County
P.O. Box 3105
West Chester, PA   19381

Foundation type: Independent foundation
Limitations: Scholarships to full-time students in their junior year who have completed 64 to 96 credit hours of course work at West Chester University, PA, and to students who have received a B.A. from West Chester University and are enrolled full-time in graduate school. Students must be U.S. citizens and residents. Scholarships are awarded on the basis of academic achievement, leadership, service, character, industry, and financial need.
Financial data: Year ended 12/31/2004.
Assets, $635,907 (M); Expenditures, $41,949; Total giving, $29,000; Grants to individuals, 29 grants totaling $29,000.
Type of support: Support to graduates or students of specific schools; Undergraduate support.
Application information: Deadline Apr. 1; Completion of formal application required, including transcripts, financial statement, personal statement, and two letters of recommendation from West Chester University faculty members; Recipients notified in May.
EIN: 236390730

3990
Gerald Swope Trust
c/o U.S. Bank, N.A.
P.O. Box 387
St. Louis, MO   63166-0387
Application address: c/o Financial Aid Office, Washington University, Box 1041, St. Louis, MO 63130

Foundation type: Independent foundation

Limitations: Scholarships and student loans to graduates of St. Louis, MO, city and county public high schools.
Financial data: Year ended 09/30/2003.
Assets, $369,846 (M); Expenditures, $25,813; Total giving, $23,000; Grants to individuals, 9 grants totaling $23,000 (high: $5,000, low: $700).
Type of support: Student loans—to individuals; Support to graduates or students of specific schools; Undergraduate support.
Application information: Applications accepted throughout the year; Initial approach by letter.
EIN: 436019071

3991
Edward Syder Trust
c/o Bank of America, N.A.
P.O. Box 1802
Providence, RI   02901-1802
Application address: P.O. Box 360, Ramsey, NJ 07446

Foundation type: Independent foundation
Limitations: Scholarships to residents of Ramsey, NJ, who have completed their first year of college, graduate or undergraduate, and demonstrated academic accomplishment, community involvement, and good character.
Financial data: Year ended 12/31/2004.
Assets, $600,994 (M); Expenditures, $38,460; Total giving, $25,000.
Type of support: Graduate support; Undergraduate support.
Application information: Deadline Oct. 15; Applications available after Aug. 15; Completion of formal application required; Awards announced by Dec. 3.
EIN: 226513992

3992
T.I.S.-Tichenor Foundation, Inc.
P.O. Box 1525
Pennington, NJ   08534-1525
Contact: Martha B. Tichenor, Pres.
Application address: P.O. Box 669, Bloomington, IN 47402

Foundation type: Independent foundation
Limitations: Scholarships to financially needy, single residents of IN who are full-time junior or senior undergraduate students at Indiana University in Bloomington or Ball State University in Muncie. Leadership scholarships by nomination only to undergraduates at the University of Illinois at Urbana-Champaign, who have demonstrated leadership abilities and have maintained a "B" average.
Financial data: Year ended 03/31/2004.
Assets, $310,434 (M); Expenditures, $85,809; Total giving, $80,750.
Type of support: Support to graduates or students of specific schools; Awards/grants by nomination only; Undergraduate support.
Application information: Application form required.
  Deadline(s): None.
  Additional information: See program description for further information.
Program descriptions:
  Indiana Scholarships: Applicant must be a junior or senior who is single and enrolled at one of the two schools on a full-time basis for a minimum of two semesters. A financial need of $4,000 or more to meet total costs of yearly enrollment is necessary to apply. Applicants from Ball State University must have at least a 3.0 GPA. Applicants

from Indiana University must have at least a 3.25 GPA.

T.I.S. Bookstore Student Leadership Scholarships: Recipients must demonstrate leadership qualities that inspire and serve others. A GPA of 4.0 on a 5.0 scale is also required. One freshman, one junior, and one sophomore are chosen each year. Recipients must be nominated by peers, faculty, or staff. Nominations are solicited through "The Daily Illini" newspaper and through college administrative offices. Each recipient receives $1,500 and a commemorative plaque.
EIN: 351761666

3993
Betsey W. Taber Trust
(formerly Taber Scholarship Fund)
c/o Bank of America, N.A.
P.O. Box 1802
Providence, RI 02901-1802
Application address: c/o Bank of America, N.A., Attn.: Carol V. Grey, Trust Off., 100 Federal St., Boston, MA 02110

Foundation type: Independent foundation
Limitations: Scholarships to high school students of the greater New Bedford, MA, area.
Financial data: Year ended 09/30/2005. Assets, $612,866 (M); Expenditures, $34,167; Total giving, $27,000; Grants to individuals, 42 grants totaling $27,000.
Type of support: Undergraduate support.
Application information: Applications accepted throughout the year; Completion of formal application required.
EIN: 046418554

3994
The Salvatore Taddonio Family Foundation
5139 Arbutus St.
Arvada, CO 80002-1719
Contact: Sandra Madsen, Secy.

Foundation type: Independent foundation
Limitations: Scholarships to residents of CO who are of twenty-five percent Italian-American heritage to attend accredited universities or colleges in CO.
Financial data: Year ended 12/31/2004. Assets, $89,191 (M); Expenditures, $18,687; Total giving, $18,000; Grants to individuals, 12 grants totaling $18,000.
Fields of interest: Italy.
Type of support: Scholarships—to individuals.
Application information: Deadline Aug. 15; Contact foundation for application guidelines.
EIN: 841158317

3995
Tahquamenon Education Foundation
P.O. Box 482
Newberry, MI 49868
E-mail: teflil@lighthouse.net

Foundation type: Public charity
Limitations: Scholarships to graduating seniors of the Tahquamenon Area School District, MI, for undergraduate education.
Financial data: Year ended 06/30/2005. Assets, $551,764 (M); Expenditures, $86,453; Total giving, $42,500; Grants to individuals, 42 grants totaling $42,500 (high: $2,000, low: $500).
Type of support: Support to graduates or students of specific schools.

Application information: Contact foundation for current application deadline/guidelines.
EIN: 382744932

3996
Mamoru and Aiko Takitani Foundation, Inc.
(formerly Takitani Foundation, Inc.)
c/o Pacific Tower
1001 Bishop St., Ste. 1700
Honolulu, HI 96813   (808) 247-6085
Application address: P.O. Box 10687, Honolulu, HI 96816-0687

Foundation type: Independent foundation
Limitations: Scholarships to high school graduates in HI.
Financial data: Year ended 12/31/2004. Assets, $1,442,645 (M); Expenditures, $99,689; Total giving, $75,000; Grants to individuals, 49 grants totaling $75,000.
Type of support: Undergraduate support.
Application information: Applications accepted throughout the year; Contact foundation for current application guidelines.
Program description:
Scholarship Program: Scholarships are generally $1,000 each, but some recipients will be eligible for scholarships of $5,000 to $10,000. Recipients are selected based on academics, need and community service.
EIN: 510212114

3997
Mr. & Mrs. Harley Talley Scholarship Fund
c/o Irwin Union Bank & Trust Co.
P.O. Box 929
Columbus, IN 47202-0929   (812) 376-1918
Additional tel.: (812) 376-1883

Foundation type: Independent foundation
Limitations: Scholarships for students from Columbus East, Columbus North, and Hauser high schools. Students must be Bartholomew County, IN, residents.
Financial data: Year ended 12/31/2004. Assets, $55,330 (M); Expenditures, $11,167; Total giving, $9,205; Grants to individuals, totaling $7,940.
Type of support: Support to graduates or students of specific schools; Undergraduate support.
Application information: Application form required.
Initial approach: Letter with recommendations from high school principal.
Deadline(s): May 31
Applicants should submit the following:
1) Financial information
2) Transcripts
Program description:
Scholarship Program: Student scholarship eligibility is based on financial need, scholarship records, capabilities, mental attitude, and a sincere interest in advanced education. Students must have at least a 2.0 GPA to be eligible. Grants are for a four-year maximum. The maximum amount per year is $1,500.
EIN: 356388000

3998
Tamer Foundation
56 S. Groesbeck Hwy.
Clinton Township, MI 48036

Foundation type: Independent foundation

Limitations: Scholarships to residents of MI for higher education.
Financial data: Year ended 04/30/2005. Assets, $10,966,925 (M); Expenditures, $617,831; Total giving, $585,950; Grants to individuals, 24 grants totaling $64,400 (high: $6,008, low: $691).
Type of support: Scholarships—to individuals.
Application information: Contact foundation for current application deadline/guidelines.
EIN: 382679633

3999
Tanaq Foundation
c/o Frankie Mack
2600 Denali St., Ste. 300
Anchorage, AK 99503   (907) 272-9886

Foundation type: Independent foundation
Limitations: Scholarships to Native St. George Tanaq Corp. shareholders or their children for undergraduate education.
Financial data: Year ended 12/31/2004. Assets, $1,621 (M); Expenditures, $8,909; Total giving, $5,250; Grants to individuals, 4 grants totaling $5,250.
Fields of interest: Native Americans/American Indians.
Type of support: Undergraduate support.
Application information: Deadline June 30; Completion of formal application required, including transcript, proof of postsecondary enrollment, essay, and letter or recommendation.
EIN: 920150959

4000
Jane and Tom Tang Foundation for Education, Inc.
c/o Tom Tang
800 Palisades Ave., Ste. 23C
Fort Lee, NJ 07024

Foundation type: Operating foundation
Limitations: Scholarships to individuals for medical degrees.
Financial data: Year ended 12/31/2004. Assets, $17,648 (M); Expenditures, $256,315; Total giving, $251,705; Grants to individuals, totaling $42,356.
Fields of interest: Medical school/education.
Type of support: Graduate support; Doctoral support.
Application information: Contact foundation for current application deadlines/guidelines.
EIN: 223693816

4001
Tannenbaum-Sternberger Foundation, Inc.
(formerly Sigmund Sternberger Foundation, Inc.)
600 Bank of America Bldg.
P.O. Box 3112
Greensboro, NC 27402   (336) 373-1500
Contact: Sally B. Cone, Exec. Dir.
FAX: (336) 272-8258;
E-mail: scone@sternlawnc.com; URL: http://www.TSFoundation.com

Foundation type: Independent foundation
Limitations: Scholarships to children and grandchildren of members of the Revolution Masonic Lodge, Greensboro, NC.
Publications: Application guidelines.

Financial data: Year ended 03/31/2005. Assets, $16,656,769 (M); Expenditures, $777,794; Total giving, $665,058; Grants to individuals, 15 grants totaling $26,100 (high: $3,000, low: $1,000).
Fields of interest: Vocational education; Fraternal societies.
Type of support: Scholarships—to individuals.
Application information: Application form required. Application form available on the grantmaker's Web site.
Initial approach: Letter.
Copies of proposal: 1
Deadline(s): Varies
Applicants should submit the following:
1) Transcripts
2) Letter(s) of recommendation
3) Budget Information
4) Financial information
EIN: 566045483

4002
Eva March Tappan Trust
c/o Bank of America, N.A.
P.O. Box 6767
Providence, RI 02940-6767
Contact: Michelle Neubauer-Pinkett, Trust Off., Bank of America, N.A.
Application address: 100 Federal St., Boston, MA 02110

Foundation type: Independent foundation
Limitations: Scholarships to graduates of Worcester County high schools, MA, to attend Vassar College.
Financial data: Year ended 10/31/2004. Assets, $800,358 (M); Expenditures, $42,215; Total giving, $31,510; Grants to individuals, 7 grants totaling $31,510 (high: $4,510, low: $4,500).
Type of support: Support to graduates or students of specific schools; Undergraduate support.
Application information: Deadline Jan. 31; Application by letter, including transcripts, SAT scores, and a letter of recommendation from the principal of any Worcester County high school.
EIN: 046023587

4003
TAPPI Foundation, Inc.
15 Technology Pkwy. S.
Norcross, GA 30092-2928 (770) 209-7289
Contact: Mary Lynn Miller, Exec. Dir.
FAX: (770) 446-6947;
E-mail: foundation@tappi.org; URL: http://www.tappi.org/index.asp?pid=16129&ch=15

Foundation type: Public charity
Limitations: Scholarships to students who are TAPPI members at Auburn University, AL, Miami University, OH, Mississippi State University, North Carolina State University, State University of New York, University of Maine, University of Minnesota, University of Washington, University of Wisconsin-Stevens Point, and Western Michigan University.
Publications: Annual report.
Financial data: Year ended 08/31/2005. Assets, $3,523,535 (M); Expenditures, $210,108; Total giving, $181,729; Grants to individuals, 38 grants totaling $180,729 (high: $74,695, low: $48).
Type of support: Support to graduates or students of specific schools; Undergraduate support.
Application information: Application form required.
Deadline(s): Deadline May 1.

Applicants should submit the following:
1) Transcripts
2) Letter(s) of recommendation
Program description:
William L. Cullison Scholarship: The award of $4,000 per academic year provides an incentive for students entering their third year of college to pursue an academic path related to the pulp and paper industry. Potential candidates must maintain a 3.5 GPA or better through freshman and sophomore years; demonstrate outstanding leadership abilities; and demonstrate significant interest in the pulp and paper industry. Financial need is not a requirement.
EIN: 581886221

4004
The Leslie E. Tassell Foundation
3439 Quiggle Ave. S.E.
Ada, MI 49301-9237
Contact: Joyce Wisner, Tr.

Foundation type: Independent foundation
Limitations: Scholarships to students in MI for higher education.
Financial data: Year ended 12/31/2003. Assets, $8,992,127 (M); Expenditures, $214,314; Total giving, $170,286; Grants to individuals, 14 grants totaling $47,866 (high: $7,214, low: $1,500).
Type of support: Undergraduate support.
Application information: Applications accepted throughout the year; Initial approach by letter; Completion of formal application required.
EIN: 383186818

4005
Tate Family Foundation, Inc.
(formerly Joseph P. Tate Foundation)
3252 N. Lake Dr., Ste. 300
Milwaukee, WI 53211-3124
Application address: c/o Fort Atkinson High School, Attn: Guidance Dept., 310 E. SE 4, Fort Atkinson, WI 53538, tel.: (920) 563-7814

Foundation type: Independent foundation
Limitations: Scholarships to students attending Fort Atkinson High School, WI, who are related to an employee of Superior Services.
Financial data: Year ended 12/31/2004. Assets, $514,674 (M); Expenditures, $38,955; Total giving, $15,000.
Type of support: Employee-related scholarships.
Application information:
Deadline(s): June 1
Additional information: Contact foundation for current application guidelines.
EIN: 391790720

4006
Tau Delta Phi Scholarship Fund, Inc.
c/o Ronald S. Katch
191 Waukegan Rd., Ste. 103
Northfield, IL 60093
Contact: Alan J. Freeman, Dir.
Application address: 9560 Grosse Point Rd., Skokie, IL 60076, tel.: (312) 360-0080

Foundation type: Independent foundation
Limitations: Scholarships to students who are residents of IL for higher education.
Financial data: Year ended 12/31/2004. Assets, $14,512 (M); Expenditures, $27,294;

Total giving, $26,500; Grants to individuals, 9 grants totaling $26,500.
Type of support: Technical education support; Undergraduate support.
Application information: Contact fund for current application deadline; Application by letter, including personal essay.
EIN: 363849823

4007
The Taubman Foundation
(formerly Arthur & Grace W. Taubman Foundation, Inc.)
2965 Colonnade Dr., Ste. 300
Roanoke, VA 24018

Foundation type: Independent foundation
Limitations: Scholarships primarily to residents of PA and VA.
Financial data: Year ended 12/31/2004. Assets, $96,527 (M); Expenditures, $520,637; Total giving, $520,557.
Type of support: Scholarships—to individuals.
Application information: Applications not accepted.
EIN: 546052861

4008
Taunton Family Children's Home, Inc.
P.O. Box 870
Wewahitchka, FL 32465-0870

Foundation type: Operating foundation
Limitations: Scholarships to students in FL, primarily in Wewahitchka, for higher education.
Financial data: Year ended 12/31/2003. Assets, $811,424 (M); Expenditures, $265,976; Total giving, $38,494; Grants to individuals, 7 grants totaling $38,494 (high: $13,978, low: $1,356).
Type of support: Undergraduate support.
Application information: Applications not accepted.
EIN: 592335556

4009
TAV Foundation
P.O. Box 952
Daphne, AL 36526-0952
Contact: Y. Charles Earle, Jr., Pres.
Application address: P.O. Box 778, Daphne, AL 36526, tel.: (251) 621-4140

Foundation type: Independent foundation
Limitations: Scholarships to graduates of public and private high schools in Baldwin County, AL.
Financial data: Year ended 12/31/2004. Assets, $1,439,967 (M); Expenditures, $43,269; Total giving, $41,500; Grants to individuals, 21 grants totaling $41,500.
Type of support: Support to graduates or students of specific schools; Undergraduate support.
Application information: Deadline Mar. 15; Initial approach by letter; Completion of formal application required, including GPA, ACT scores, three references, financial information, and personal statement.
EIN: 630919414

4010

Tavitian Foundation, Inc.

c/o Syncsort Inc.
50 Tice Blvd.
Woodcliff Lake, NJ 07677

Foundation type: Independent foundation
Limitations: Scholarships primarily to individuals who are natural or adoptive children, grandchildren, or great-grandchildren of an Armenian or Eastern European parent, grandparent, or great-grandparent.
Financial data: Year ended 12/31/2004. Assets, $13,046,013 (M); Expenditures, $1,264,430; Total giving, $1,167,671.
Type of support: Scholarships—to individuals; Undergraduate support.
Application information: Contact foundation for current application deadline/guidelines.
Program description:
 Scholarship Program: Recipients may use their award at any approved institution for any course of study. Recipients are called upon to make non-binding moral commitment to assist needy students in the future, if they are ever in the position to do so. Recipients are selected on the basis of standardized test scores, recommendations, financial need, and personal interviews, and strong preference to those of Armenian or Eastern European descent.
EIN: 521939275

4011

Taylor Community Foundation

300 Johnson Ave.
P.O. Box 227
Ridley Park, PA 19078 (610) 461-6571
Contact: William T. Skinner, Pres.
FAX: (610) 521-6057;
E-mail: info@taylorcommfdn.org; URL: http://www.taylorcommfdn.org

Foundation type: Public charity
Limitations: Scholarships to individuals residing in the Ridley Park, PA, area for undergraduate education in health professions.
Publications: Grants list.
Financial data: Year ended 06/30/2005. Assets, $10,756,103 (M); Expenditures, $3,485,271; Total giving, $603,686; Grants to individuals, 55 grants totaling $137,500 (high: $2,500, low: $2,500).
Fields of interest: Health sciences school/education.
Type of support: Undergraduate support.
Application information: Contact foundation for current application guidelines.
EIN: 232354770

4012

Frank C. Taylor & Helen M. Taylor Education Fund

c/o Welby Law Offices, PC
13 Ventura Dr.
North Dartmouth, MA 02747 (508) 998-6152

Foundation type: Operating foundation
Limitations: Scholarships to graduating seniors of New Bedford High School, Dartmouth High School, Bishop Stang High School, Greater New Bedford Vocational Technical High School, and Fairhaven High School, all in MA.
Financial data: Year ended 12/31/2003. Assets, $79,223 (M); Expenditures, $8,175; Total giving, $7,000; Grants to individuals, totaling $7,000.

Fields of interest: Vocational education.
Type of support: Support to graduates or students of specific schools; Undergraduate support.
Application information: Contact fund for current application deadline; Completion of formal application required, including transcripts and essay.
EIN: 046071778

4013

The Jack L. Taylor Education Trust

c/o JPMorgan Chase Bank, N.A.
P.O. Box 1308
Milwaukee, WI 53201
Application address: c/o JP Morgan Chase Bank, N.A., Attn: Gail Randall, 111 Monument Cir., IN1-0150, Indianapolis, IN 46277-0115

Foundation type: Independent foundation
Limitations: Scholarships to Whiting High School, IN, graduates with at least a "C" average for study at four-year colleges. No scholarships will be given for athletics.
Financial data: Year ended 09/30/2004. Assets, $62,268 (M); Expenditures, $11,798; Total giving, $9,000; Grants to individuals, totaling $9,000.
Type of support: Support to graduates or students of specific schools; Undergraduate support.
Application information:
 Initial approach: Initial approach by letter.
 Deadline(s): Deadline Mar. 1.
 Additional information: Contact trust for current application guidelines.
EIN: 356549775

4014

Robert B. Taylor Educational Trust

P.O. Box 28629
San Antonio, TX 78228-0629
Application address: c/o Financial Aid Off., St. Phillip's College, San Antonio, TX 78228, tel.: (210) 531-3272

Foundation type: Independent foundation
Limitations: Scholarships to full-time allied health majors at St. Philip's College, TX, who have completed at least 12 hours and possess a 3.0 GPA.
Financial data: Year ended 12/31/2002. Assets, $525,440 (M); Expenditures, $11,344; Total giving, $10,500; Grants to individuals, 8 grants totaling $10,500 (high: $1,500, low: $750).
Fields of interest: Health sciences school/education.
Type of support: Support to graduates or students of specific schools; Undergraduate support.
Application information: Contact college financial aid dept. for current application deadline/guidelines; Initial approach by letter or telephone.
EIN: 746365869

4015

Mr. & Mrs. George W. Taylor Foundation

c/o Wachovia Securities
6810 Spring Creek Rd., Ste. 2B
Rockford, IL 61104 (815) 637-6363
Contact: James Thiede, Tr.

Foundation type: Independent foundation
Limitations: Scholarships to students in the Rockford, IL, community to participate in the engineering program at the University of Minnesota Institute of Technology.

Financial data: Year ended 12/31/2003. Assets, $2,705,119 (M); Expenditures, $286,216; Total giving, $221,724; Grants to individuals, 6 grants totaling $23,200 (high: $9,613, low: $1,050).
Fields of interest: Engineering school/education.
Type of support: Support to graduates or students of specific schools; Technical education support; Undergraduate support.
Application information: Contact foundation for current application deadline/guidelines; Initial approach by letter; Scholarship applicants are reviewed by a scholarship committee and selection is based on academic and leadership qualifications.
EIN: 363321315

4016

The Patrick F. Taylor Foundation

1 Lee Cir.
New Orleans, LA 70130 (504) 581-5491
Contact: Phyllis M. Taylor, Pres.

Foundation type: Independent foundation
Limitations: Scholarships by nomination only to U.S. citizens for undergraduate education.
Financial data: Year ended 12/31/2003. Assets, $924,621 (M); Expenditures, $811,941; Total giving, $739,873; Grants to individuals, 28 grants totaling $43,682 (high: $5,000, low: $500).
Type of support: Awards/grants by nomination only.
Application information: Nominations by letter accepted throughout the year.
Program description:
 Taylor Scholarship: Applicants must be citizens of the US who are attending or who will attend on a full-time basis (12 semester hours or more) an accredited institution of higher learning. There are no restrictions or limitations of any kind relating to race or employment status.
EIN: 581686754

4017

Brent Taylor Perpetual Charitable Trust

c/o Mercantile Trust & Savings Bank
133 N. 33rd St.
P.O. Box 371
Quincy, IL 62306-0371 (217) 221-4489

Foundation type: Independent foundation
Limitations: Scholarships to residents of Quincy, IL, Ellsworth, MI, and Saltville, VA.
Financial data: Year ended 12/31/2004. Assets, $33,916 (M); Expenditures, $33,142; Total giving, $31,814; Grants to individuals, 30 grants totaling $31,814 (high: $2,680, low: $1,000).
Type of support: Undergraduate support.
Application information: Applications accepted. Application form required.
 Initial approach: Letter.
 Additional information: Contact trust for current application guidelines.
EIN: 376353965

4018

TDX Foundation

4300 B St., Ste. 402
Anchorage, AK 99503-5946

Foundation type: Company-sponsored foundation
Limitations: Educational support to Aluets residing in AK, and their descendants that are record or beneficial owners of TDX common stock.

Financial data: Year ended 09/30/2004. Assets, $45,007 (M); Expenditures, $84,294; Total giving, $27,800; Grants to individuals, 22 grants totaling $27,800 (high: $2,000, low: $300).
Fields of interest: Native Americans/American Indians.
Type of support: Scholarships—to individuals.
Application information: Deadline Aug. 1; Application by letter of intent, including transcripts and a letter of acceptance.
EIN: 920144730

4019
Teamsters BBYO Scholarship Fund
45 E. 33rd St., Ste. 601
New York, NY 10016-5336 (212) 696-9020
Contact: Martin Adelstein, Tr.

Foundation type: Operating foundation
Limitations: Grants to members of B'nai B'rith Youth Organization in the Northeast region to attend B'nai B'rith Youth Organization Summer Programs.
Financial data: Year ended 07/31/2004. Assets, $77,393 (M); Expenditures, $5,051; Total giving, $5,000; Grants to individuals, totaling $5,000.
Fields of interest: Children/youth, services; Jewish agencies & temples.
Type of support: Grants to individuals.
Application information: Application form required.
  Deadline(s): Mar. 30
  Additional information: Contact fund or nearest B'nai B'rith chapter for current application guidelines.
EIN: 237383406

4020
Teamsters Local 830 Scholarship Fund
12298 Townsend Rd.
Philadelphia, PA 19154 (215) 969-1012
Contact: Joe Brock, Jr. C.M.S., Pres.
Scholarship application address: P.O. Box 6040, Philadelphia, PA 19114
FAX: (215) 969-3205

Foundation type: Public charity
Limitations: Scholarships to dependent children of Teamsters Local 830 Scholarship Fund who are in their senior year of high school. Application forms are mailed out to all employers who participate in the fund.
Publications: Application guidelines; Annual report; Financial statement.
Financial data: Year ended 12/30/2003. Assets, $166,633 (M); Expenditures, $80,499; Total giving, $64,000; Grants to individuals, 8 grants totaling $64,000 (high: $8,000, low: $8,000).
Fields of interest: Labor unions/organizations.
Type of support: Undergraduate support.
Application information:
  Deadline(s): Feb. 1
  Additional information: Completion of formal application required, including college entrance examination board scores, general scholastic achievements, and transcripts.
EIN: 232003122

4021
Technical Training Foundation
1551 Osgood St.
North Andover, MA 01845
Contact: Ibrahim Hefni, Tr.

Foundation type: Independent foundation
Limitations: Scholarships for scientific and technical training.
Financial data: Year ended 08/31/2003. Assets, $48,534,925 (M); Expenditures, $1,753,023; Total giving, $992,325; Grants to individuals, 67 grants totaling $643,325 (high: $128,334, low: $287).
Fields of interest: Vocational education; Science; Engineering/technology.
Type of support: Technical education support.
Application information: Application form not required.
  Deadline(s): Contact foundation for current application deadline.
  Additional information: Application by letter.
EIN: 042864138

4022
Fred M. Teel Charitable Trust
c/o NBT Bank, N.A.
52 S. Broad St.
Norwich, NY 13815
Application address: c/o Guidance Dept., Afton Central School, 29 Academy St., Afton, NY 13733

Foundation type: Independent foundation
Limitations: Scholarships to Afton Central School, NY, graduates.
Financial data: Year ended 12/31/2004. Assets, $73,092 (M); Expenditures, $3,526; Total giving, $3,000; Grants to individuals, 2 grants totaling $3,000. Subtotal for scholarships—to individuals: 2 grants totaling $3,000.
Type of support: Support to graduates or students of specific schools; Undergraduate support.
Application information: Deadline May 15; Applications obtained through Afton Central school; Initial approach by letter, including financial status, goals, career to be pursued, and grades; Completion of formal application required; Interviews required.
EIN: 156020508

4023
Teen Mania Ministries, Inc.
P.O. Box 2000
Lindale, TX 75771-2000 (903) 324-8000
Contact: Ron Luce, Pres.

Foundation type: Public charity
Limitations: Fellowships, scholarships and loans to individuals for short-term missionary trips to Latin America, Europe, Africa and Asia.
Financial data: Year ended 08/31/2004. Assets, $18,435,452 (M); Expenditures, $24,971,371; Total giving, $86,280; Grants to individuals, 13 grants totaling $11,200 (high: $5,000, low: $50).
Fields of interest: Religion.
Type of support: Fellowships; Scholarships—to individuals; Student loans—to individuals.
Application information: Contact foundation for current application deadline/guidelines.
EIN: 731284606

4024
Walter Telfer & Everett Improvement Company Scholarship Trust
(formerly Everett Improvement Company Scholarship Trust)
c/o Wells Fargo Bank Northwest, N.A.
P.O. Box 21927, MAC P6540-144
Seattle, WA 98111
Application address: c/o Everett Community College, Office of Financial Aid, 801 Wetmore Ave., Everett, WA 98201-1327

Foundation type: Independent foundation
Limitations: Scholarships to students and graduates of Everett Community College, WA, who are residents of Snohomish County, WA.
Financial data: Year ended 06/30/2005. Assets, $86,606 (M); Expenditures, $13,052; Total giving, $10,000; Grants to individuals, totaling $10,000.
Type of support: Support to graduates or students of specific schools; Undergraduate support.
Application information: Applications accepted.
  Initial approach: Letter.
  Deadline(s): May 1
EIN: 916231655

4025
William F. Temple Memorial Foundation
c/o Market Day Corp.
555 W. Pierce Rd., Ste. 200
Itasca, IL 60143-2647

Foundation type: Company-sponsored foundation
Limitations: Scholarships only to dependents of employees of the Market Day Corp.
Financial data: Year ended 12/31/2004. Assets, $6,250 (M); Expenditures, $20,250; Total giving, $20,250; Grants to individuals, 18 grants totaling $20,250 (high: $1,500, low: $750).
Type of support: Employee-related scholarships.
EIN: 364222360

4026
Temple-Inland Foundation
1300 S. Mopac
Austin, TX 78749 (936) 829-1721
Contact: M. Richard Warner, V.P.

Foundation type: Company-sponsored foundation
Limitations: Undergraduate scholarships to children of employees of Temple-Inland, Inc. and its subsidiaries (except Inland Container Corporation). The employee must have completed three years of continuous full-time service as of Apr. 1 of the year of application.
Financial data: Year ended 06/30/2004. Assets, $954,267 (M); Expenditures, $5,032,249; Total giving, $5,003,550; Grants to individuals, totaling $2,041,763.
Type of support: Employee-related scholarships.
Application information: Contact foundation for current application deadline/guidelines.
Program description:
  Employee Scholarship Program: Relatives of officers or directors of Temple-Inland, Inc., its subsidiaries, the foundation, or its substantial contributors are ineligible. Grants are for four years.
EIN: 751977109

4027
Temple-Krick YFU Scholarship Fund, Inc.
2345 Delaware Dr.
Ann Arbor, MI 48103-6170 (734) 663-6472
Contact: Barbara T. Krick, Pres.

Foundation type: Independent foundation
Limitations: Scholarships to high school students residing in MI who have been accepted to participate in Youth For Understanding, an international student exchange program.
Financial data: Year ended 03/31/2005. Assets, $8,505 (M); Expenditures, $3,869; Total giving, $3,848; Grant to an individual, 1 grant totaling $3,848.
Fields of interest: International exchange, students.
Type of support: Exchange programs; Precollege support.
Application information: Applications by letter accepted throughout the year; Completion of formal application required; Interviews required.
EIN: 382808315

4028
John B. Templeton Trust Foundation
1105 35th St.
Oak Brook, IL 60521-4439
Application address: c/o Templeton, Kenly & Co., Attn: S. Ruksana, 2525 Gardner Rd., Broadview, IL 60153

Foundation type: Independent foundation
Limitations: Scholarships based on leadership qualities, past and present scholastic achievement, personal character and integrity, and financial need to IL employees and children of employees of Templeton, Kenly & Co., Inc., who are currently enrolled in an accredited collegiate program.
Financial data: Year ended 12/31/2004. Assets, $215,147 (M); Expenditures, $13,279; Total giving, $11,500; Grants to individuals, 15 grants totaling $11,500.
Type of support: Employee-related scholarships.
Application information: Application form required.
   Deadline(s): June 1
   Applicants should submit the following:
      1) Transcripts
      2) Resume
      3) Essay
EIN: 366891453

4029
Tenenbaum Educational Trust
P.O. Box 15128 G.M.F.
Little Rock, AR 72231 (501) 945-0881
Contact: R.J. Wills, Tr.

Foundation type: Independent foundation
Limitations: Scholarships to high school graduates who are residents of AR for medical education expenses.
Financial data: Year ended 12/31/2004. Assets, $102,453 (M); Expenditures, $39,569; Total giving, $39,466; Grants to individuals, 12 grants totaling $39,466.
Fields of interest: Medical school/education.
Type of support: Undergraduate support.
Application information: Applications accepted throughout the year; Initial approach by letter; Completion of formal application required.
EIN: 710705223

4030
Richard J. & Florence J. Tenholder Trust
(also known as The Griffis Memorial Scholarship in Art and Theatre)
801 S. 8th St.
Atchison, KS 66002 (913) 360-6200
Contact: Mary Collins, Tr.
Application address: c/o Benedictine College, Attn: Financial Aid Office, 1020 N. Second St., Atchison, KS 66002

Foundation type: Independent foundation
Limitations: Scholarships and achievement awards to women seeking a degree in art or theater at Benedictine College, KS.
Financial data: Year ended 12/31/2004. Assets, $437,022 (M); Expenditures, $21,978; Total giving, $18,500; Grants to individuals, 13 grants totaling $18,500.
Fields of interest: Arts education; Theater; Women.
Type of support: Support to graduates or students of specific schools; Awards/prizes; Undergraduate support.
Application information: Applications accepted. Application form required.
   Deadline(s): None
   Applicants should submit the following:
      1) Letter(s) of recommendation
      2) Financial information
   Additional information: Application must also include a Family Financial Statement or financial aid form; Art applicants must submit a portfolio; Theatre applicants must have an audition or interview; Notice of approval or rejection usually sent in two months.
Program description:
   The Griffis Memorial Scholarship or Achievement Award in Art and Theatre: Scholarship awards are $3,000 per year and are renewable for up to four years for a total of $12,000. Applicants must have a high school or college GPA of 3.0 or higher. A limited number of $1,000 Achievement Awards are made depending on the availability of funds. Priority is given to the Benedictine Sisters of Mount St. Scholastica, to women students attending Benedictine College, to Catholics, and to residents of Atchison, KS. Only women majoring in theater or art at Benedictine College in Atchison, KS, will be considered.
EIN: 481061565

4031
Tenneco Foundation
c/o Bank of America, N.A.
P.O. Box 831041
Dallas, TX 75283-1041

Foundation type: Company-sponsored foundation
Limitations: Scholarships primarily to residents of Houston, TX.
Financial data: Year ended 12/31/2004. Assets, $479,921 (M); Expenditures, $22,672; Total giving, $4,500.
Type of support: Scholarships—to individuals.
Application information: Contact foundation for current application deadline/guidelines.
EIN: 746037919

4032
Tenney Educational Fund, Inc.
c/o Oakley, O'Sullivan, & Eaton, PC
89 Main St.
Andover, MA 01810 (978) 474-4447
Contact: John C. Oakley, Treas.

Foundation type: Operating foundation

Limitations: Scholarships to graduates of Methuen High School, MA.
Financial data: Year ended 04/30/2003. Assets, $499,404 (M); Expenditures, $32,133; Total giving, $29,250; Grants to individuals, 15 grants totaling $29,250 (high: $2,500, low: $1,000).
Type of support: Support to graduates or students of specific schools; Undergraduate support.
Application information: Deadline May 15; Completion of formal application required.
EIN: 046038700

4033
Terplan Family Foundation, Inc.
25 Summit Ave.
Hackensack, NJ 07601

Foundation type: Independent foundation
Limitations: Scholarships and grants for related educational expenses to foreign students for undergraduate study in the U.S.
Financial data: Year ended 12/31/2002. Assets, $49,045 (M); Expenditures, $54,536; Total giving, $35,085; Grants to individuals, 3 grants totaling $35,085 (high: $21,521, low: $8,472).
Type of support: Foreign applicants; Undergraduate support.
Application information: Contact foundation for current application deadline/guidelines.
EIN: 233789231

4034
Ronald Terrill Memorial Fund, Inc.
P.O. Box 265
Morrisville, VT 05661
Contact: Robert Magoon, Secy.-Treas.

Foundation type: Operating foundation
Limitations: Scholarships to graduates of Lamoille Union High School, and Peoples Academy, VT, for higher education at two- and four-year colleges and technical schools.
Financial data: Year ended 04/30/2003. Assets, $685,868 (M); Expenditures, $35,891; Total giving, $33,000; Grants to individuals, 9 grants totaling $33,000 (high: $5,000, low: $2,000).
Type of support: Support to graduates or students of specific schools; Technical education support; Undergraduate support.
Application information: Deadline May 10; Application by letter, including FAF, educational and vocational goals, need for financial aid, school or community service, work experience, transcripts, class rank, college entrance scores, and recommendation letter.
EIN: 030213310

4035
Blanche G. Terry Educational Trust
c/o Citizens National Bank
400 W. Collin St.
Corsicana, TX 75110-5124 (903) 874-1700

Foundation type: Independent foundation
Limitations: Scholarships to residents of Navarro County, TX.
Financial data: Year ended 05/31/2005. Assets, $635,259 (M); Expenditures, $36,817; Total giving, $30,550; Grants to individuals, 36 grants totaling $30,550.
Type of support: Scholarships—to individuals.

Application information: Deadline Apr. 15;
Completion of formal application required;
Applicants are notified within two months.
EIN: 756173637

4036
Seymour Terry Memorial Scholarship Trust Fund

c/o Regions Bank
P.O. Box 1471
Little Rock, AR 72203-1471 (501) 371-7000
Contact: Lee Price, Trust Off., Regions Bank

Foundation type: Independent foundation
Limitations: Scholarships to graduates of Little
Rock Central High School, AR, who will attend
University of Arkansas, in Fayetteville.
Financial data: Year ended 06/30/2005.
Assets, $639,357 (M); Expenditures, $39,668;
Total giving, $30,000; Grants to individuals, 6
grants totaling $30,000.
Type of support: Support to graduates or students
of specific schools; Undergraduate support.
Application information: Applications by letter,
including scholastic record, general records, and
financial need, accepted throughout the year.
EIN: 716050556

4037
C. D. Terry, Jr. Scholarship Foundation

c/o Brotherhood Bank & Trust
2649 S. 142nd St.
Bonner Springs, KS 66012

Foundation type: Company-sponsored foundation
Limitations: Scholarships to full-time employees,
spouses, children and grandchildren of Berkel and
Co. Contractors, Inc., for college or vocational
schools.
Financial data: Year ended 12/31/2004.
Assets, $27,677 (M); Expenditures, $30,000;
Total giving, $29,860; Grants to individuals, 42
grants totaling $29,860 (high: $1,000, low: $415).
Fields of interest: Vocational education,
post-secondary.
Type of support: Employee-related scholarships.
Application information:
Deadline(s): None
Additional information: Application should also
include transcript of last semester's grades;
Application address: c/o Berkel & Co.
Contractors, Inc., P.O. Box 335, Bonner
Springs, KS 66012.
EIN: 486316064

4038
The Texas Area Fund Foundation, Inc.

P.O. Box 283
Palestine, TX 75802
E-mail: txfoundation@goquest.com; URL: http://
www.tourism-tools.com/TAFF.htm

Foundation type: Community foundation
Limitations: Scholarships to individuals in the
Palestine Independent School District, TX.
Financial data: Year ended 12/31/2004.
Assets, $1,951,046 (M); Expenditures, $82,137;
Total giving, $60,564; Grants to individuals, 12
grants totaling $19,000 (high: $4,000, low: $500).
Type of support: Scholarships—to individuals;
Support to graduates or students of specific
schools.

Application information: Contact fund for current
application deadline/guidelines.
EIN: 752834546

4039
Texas Industries Foundation

c/o Texas Industries Scholarship Coord.
1341 W. Mockingbird Ln., Ste. 700
Dallas, TX 75247-6913 (972) 647-6700

Foundation type: Company-sponsored foundation
Limitations: Scholarships to LA, MS and TX
dependents of employees of Texas Industries, Inc.
for study at accredited institutions.
Financial data: Year ended 12/31/2004.
Assets, $6,953 (M); Expenditures, $30,000; Total
giving, $30,000; Grants to individuals, 6 grants
totaling $30,000 (high: $5,000, low: $5,000).
Type of support: Employee-related scholarships.
Application information: Application form required.
Deadline(s): Mar. 31
Applicants should submit the following:
1) SAT
2) ACT
Additional information: Application should also
include grade reports, acceptance letter to
accredited college, and 1000-word statement
describing college plans and career
intentions.
EIN: 756043179

4040
Texas Knights Templar Educational Foundation

(formerly Templar Educational Foundation)
c/o Lloyd L. Chance
2013 Young St.
Dallas, TX 75201-5719 (214) 651-6070

Foundation type: Independent foundation
Limitations: Scholarships and student loans to
students who need assistance for postsecondary
studies, primarily in TX.
Financial data: Year ended 12/31/2004.
Assets, $108,697 (M); Expenditures, $53,652;
Total giving, $39,000; Grants to individuals, 39
grants totaling $39,000.
Type of support: Scholarships—to individuals;
Student loans—to individuals.
Application information: Contact foundation for
current application deadline; Initial approach by
letter or telephone; Completion of formal
application required, including transcripts, three
personal reference letters, three instructor
references, SAT and ACT scores, GPA, and recent
photograph.
EIN: 752234779

4041
Texas Nursery and Landscape Association Education and Research Foundation

7730 S. IH-35
Austin, TX 78745 (512) 280-5182
FAX: (512) 280-3012; E-mail: info@txnla.org;
URL: http://www.tnlafoundation.com/index.html

Foundation type: Public charity
Limitations: Scholarships to TX residents pursuing
higher education in horticulture at pre-approved TX
institutions. See program description for list of
eligible schools.
Publications: Application guidelines.

Financial data: Year ended 06/30/2004.
Assets, $639,075 (M); Expenditures, $33,001;
Total giving, $25,200; Grants to individuals, 8
grants totaling $15,200 (high: $2,100, low: $500).
Fields of interest: Horticulture/garden clubs.
Type of support: Scholarships—to individuals;
Support to graduates or students of specific
schools.
Application information: Application form required.
Initial approach: Letter or telephone.
Deadline(s): June 1
Applicants should submit the following:
1) Photograph
2) Transcripts
3) Letter(s) of recommendation
Additional information: Recommendations must
be from two of the following: a member of the
TNLA, most recent employer, horticulture
instructor, counselor, club advisor, church
leader, or other persons qualified to attest to
applicant's abilities, character, and
scholastic ability.
Program description:
Scholarship Program: Scholarships are allotted
for one year, for up to $2,100 each. Awards are paid
out as $100 cash awards upon notification and
$1,000 per semester for the next four consecutive
semesters. Applicants must attend one of the
following TX institutions: Collin County Community
College, Houston Community College, Richland
College, Sam Houston State University, Southwest
Texas State University, Stephen F. Austin State
University, Tarleton University, Tarrant County
Junior College, Texas A&M University, Texas Tech
University, Texas State Technical College, Trinity
Valley College, Tyler Junior College, Central Texas
College, Northeast Texas Community College, Palo
Alto College, Wharton Junior College or Western
Texas College. Grants are also awarded for applied
and basic research which add to the industry's body
of knowledge. Grants that address specific industry
needs are preferred.
EIN: 742637783

4042
Texas Rangers Baseball Foundation

P.O. Box 90111
Arlington, TX 76004-3111 (817) 273-5222
URL: http://texas.rangers.mlb.com/NASApp/mlb/
tex/community/tex_foundation_programs.jsp

Foundation type: Public charity
Limitations: Scholarships to students in the
Dallas-Fort Worth, TX, area.
Financial data: Year ended 12/13/2003.
Assets, $1,095,251 (M); Expenditures,
$650,089; Total giving, $277,834; Grants to
individuals, 94 grants totaling $13,000 (high:
$1,000, low: $100).
Type of support: Employee-related scholarships;
Support to graduates or students of specific
schools; Precollege support; Undergraduate
support.
Application information:
Initial approach: Telephone.
Additional information: Contact foundation for
current application deadline/guidelines.
Program descriptions:
Texas Rangers Wells Fargo Teens on the Ball:
Three scholarships of $2,000 are awarded to
students recommended by high school principals
and guidance counselors. Recipients must have at
least a 3.0 GPA and an interest in community
service. Members meet with professionals in
various careers and industries in order to increase
their knowledge of the wide variety of career choices

available to them and the educational requirements necessary.

Richard Greene Scholarships: Scholarships of $2,500 per year for four years are awarded to high school juniors at each of the five high schools in the Arlington School District, which allows them to have a mentorship program. Each school selects the top three students, whose names are then forwarded to the Richard Greene Scholarship Program.
EIN: 752404714

4043
The Reuben E. Thalberg Foundation, Inc.
P.O. Box 272
Southington, CT   06489-0272
Contact: Genevieve B. Thalberg, Secy.-Treas.

Foundation type: Independent foundation
Limitations: Scholarships to students of Southington High School, CT.
Financial data: Year ended 11/30/2004. Assets, $350,054 (M); Expenditures, $17,187; Total giving, $14,500; Grants to individuals, 33 grants totaling $13,500.
Type of support: Support to graduates or students of specific schools; Undergraduate support.
Application information: Deadline Mar. 31; Completion of formal application required.
EIN: 066034447

4044
The Tharpe Foundation
(formerly The Robert H. and Kathryne B. Tharpe Foundation)
c/o Wachovia Bank, N.A.
191 Peachtree St. N.E., 24th Fl.
Atlanta, GA   30303

Foundation type: Independent foundation
Limitations: Scholarships to residents of Moultrie, GA.
Financial data: Year ended 12/31/2004. Assets, $1,379,086 (M); Expenditures, $75,552; Total giving, $55,000.
Type of support: Undergraduate support.
Application information: Applications not accepted.
EIN: 581858404

4045
Muriel Thauer Scholarship Fund
c/o Marshall & Ilsley Bank
P.O. Box 2980
Milwaukee, WI   53201
Application address: c/o Watertown High School, 825 Endeavor Dr., Watertown, WI 53098, tel.: (920) 262-7500

Foundation type: Independent foundation
Limitations: Scholarships to graduates of Watertown High School, WI, to attend an accredited college or university.
Financial data: Year ended 12/31/2004. Assets, $604,543 (M); Expenditures, $42,886; Total giving, $37,500; Grants to individuals, 16 grants totaling $37,500.
Type of support: Support to graduates or students of specific schools; Undergraduate support.
Application information: Applications by letter accepted throughout the year.
EIN: 396057804

4046
Thayer Family Scholarship Trust
c/o KeyBank N.A.
800 Superior Ave., 4th Fl.
Cleveland, OH   44114

Foundation type: Independent foundation
Limitations: Scholarships to graduates of Cooperstown High School, NY, to pursue postsecondary study in nature, the environment, wildlife conservation, or veterinary science.
Financial data: Year ended 07/31/2005. Assets, $2,308,497 (M); Expenditures, $134,830; Total giving, $126,050; Grants to individuals, 14 grants totaling $126,050 (high: $15,000, low: $5,750).
Fields of interest: Vocational education; Natural resources; Environment; Animals/wildlife, preservation/protection; Veterinary medicine.
Type of support: Support to graduates or students of specific schools; Undergraduate support.
Application information: Applications accepted throughout the year; Completion of formal application required.
EIN: 146134451

4047
Oscar and Hildegard Thiele Scholarship Fund
c/o FirstMerit Bank, N.A.
106 S. Main St., 16th Fl.
Akron, OH   44308   (330) 722-5555
Application address: c/o Firstmerit Bank, N.A., P.O. Box 725, Medina, OH 44258

Foundation type: Independent foundation
Limitations: Scholarships to graduating seniors of Buckeye High School, OH, other than the valedictorian or salutatorian, who have at least a "B" average and demonstrate maturity and common sense.
Financial data: Year ended 12/31/2004. Assets, $151,769 (M); Expenditures, $12,099; Total giving, $9,125; Grants to individuals, 25 grants totaling $9,125.
Type of support: Support to graduates or students of specific schools; Undergraduate support.
Application information: Application form required.
Deadline(s): Apr. 30
Additional information: Application available at Buckeye High School, OH.
EIN: 346854105

4048
The Thoburn Foundation for Education
c/o Tina Thoburn
466 Freeman Rd.
Ligonier, PA   15658

Foundation type: Independent foundation
Limitations: Scholarships to graduates of Ligonier Valley School District, PA, area for attendance at colleges, universities, technical and vocational schools.
Financial data: Year ended 05/31/2004. Assets, $531,675 (M); Expenditures, $41,925; Total giving, $32,780; Grants to individuals, 31 grants totaling $30,900 (high: $1,750, low: $500).
Type of support: Support to graduates or students of specific schools; Undergraduate support.
Application information:
Deadline(s): Mar. 31
Applicants should submit the following:
1) Letter(s) of recommendation
2) Transcripts

3) Financial information
EIN: 251494744

4049
The Carl and Elinor Glyn Thom Charitable Foundation
206 Bridge St.
Charlevoix, MI   49720-1404

Foundation type: Independent foundation
Limitations: Scholarships to residents of MI for higher education.
Financial data: Year ended 12/31/2003. Assets, $1,540,943 (M); Expenditures, $367,253; Total giving, $102,000; Grants to individuals, 28 grants totaling $87,000 (high: $6,000, low: $1,000).
Type of support: Scholarships—to individuals.
Application information: Applications not accepted.
EIN: 383105784

4050
Douglas A. Thom Memorial Corporation
c/o Bank of America, N.A.
P.O. Box 780
Camden, ME   04843
Contact: Sara K. Montgomery, V.P.
Application address for individuals: c/o Allen Agency, 34-36 Elm St., Camden, ME 04843

Foundation type: Independent foundation
Limitations: Loans for scholarships to residents of Camden, ME.
Financial data: Year ended 12/31/2004. Assets, $438,604 (M); Expenditures, $660; Total giving, $0; Loans to individuals, totaling $15,000.
Type of support: Student loans—to individuals.
Application information: Deadline July 1; Completion of formal application required, including recommendation letter from school guidance counselor or advisor, transcripts, and personal letter describing goals and objectives.
EIN: 016019126

4051
Albert L. & Ivy B. Thomas Educational Fund
c/o U.S. Bank, N.A.
P.O. Box 3168
Portland, OR   97208-3168
Application address: 1530 Monmouth St., Independence, OR 97351, tel.: (503) 838-0480

Foundation type: Independent foundation
Limitations: Scholarships to graduates of the Independence-Monmouth School District 13J in OR.
Financial data: Year ended 12/31/2004. Assets, $1,282,685 (M); Expenditures, $84,196; Total giving, $54,635; Grants to individuals, totaling $54,635.
Type of support: Support to graduates or students of specific schools; Undergraduate support.
Application information: Application form required.
Deadline(s): Feb.
EIN: 936196091

4052
Harvey Thomas Estate Student Aid Trust
c/o Wachovia Bank, N.A.
100 N. Main St., 13th Fl.
Winston-Salem, NC 27150-6732
Contact: Martha Johnson, Trust Off., Wachovia
Bank, N.A.

Foundation type: Independent foundation
Limitations: Student loans to residents of Chester
County, PA.
Financial data: Year ended 09/30/2004.
Assets, $1,254,958 (M); Expenditures, $49,175;
Total giving, $43,300; Loans to individuals, 24
loans totaling $43,300.
Fields of interest: Higher education.
Type of support: Student loans—to individuals.
Application information: Applications accepted.
Application form required.
Deadline(s): None.
EIN: 236215693

4053
Godfrey Thomas Foundation
623 S. Tyler St.
DeWitt, AR 72042-2319 (870) 946-1982
Contact: Mary B. Carr, Tr.

Foundation type: Independent foundation
Limitations: Scholarships to residents of DeWitt,
AR, for higher education.
Financial data: Year ended 12/31/2004.
Assets, $1,885,491 (M); Expenditures, $71,561;
Total giving, $54,350; Grants to individuals, 25
grants totaling $21,200.
Type of support: Scholarships—to individuals.
Application information: Application form required.
Deadline(s): May 15 for fall semester and Dec. 1
for spring semester
Additional information: Contact foundation for
current application guidelines.
EIN: 716065971

4054
J and K Thomas Foundation
619 Chimney Sweep Hill
Glastonbury, CT 06033
Contact: Karl M. Thomas, Tr.

Foundation type: Independent foundation
Limitations: Scholarships primarily to residents of
Hartford and East Hartford, CT. Also awards smaller
grants to economically disadvantaged individuals.
Publications: Annual report (including application
guidelines).
Financial data: Year ended 06/30/2005.
Assets, $899,737 (M), Expenditures, $64,466;
Total giving, $72,425; Grants to individuals, 11
grants totaling $44,600.
Fields of interest: Economically disadvantaged.
Type of support: Undergraduate support.
Application information: Application form required.
Deadline(s): Apr. 30
Additional information: Time for response to an
application is one month; Applications should
be sent by mail.
EIN: 061528257

4055
John J. Thomas Foundation
c/o PNC Advisors
620 Liberty Ave., P2-PTPP-10-2
Pittsburgh, PA 15222-2705 (412) 768-8360

Foundation type: Independent foundation

Limitations: Scholarships to men from PA studying
for the priesthood of the Roman Catholic Church
and to women from PA studying nursing.
Financial data: Year ended 09/30/2004.
Assets, $563,553 (M); Expenditures, $29,399;
Total giving, $23,002; Grants to individuals, 5
grants totaling $23,002.
Fields of interest: Nursing school/education;
Theological school/education; Roman Catholic
agencies & churches.
Type of support: Scholarships—to individuals;
Support to graduates or students of specific
schools.
Application information: Applications by letter
accepted throughout the year.
Program description:
Scholarship Program: In recent years, all
recipients have attended Duquesne University or
Carlow College, both in Pittsburgh, PA.
EIN: 251381212

4056
Russ Thomas Scholarship Fund
3707 W. Maple St., Ste. 13
Bloomfield Hills, MI 48301-3212
(248) 216-4050
Contact: Dorothy S. Thomas, Tr.

Foundation type: Independent foundation
Limitations: Undergraduate scholarships to
residents of the greater Detroit, MI, area who are
graduating high school seniors.
Financial data: Year ended 11/30/2004.
Assets, $812,492 (M); Expenditures, $62,616;
Total giving, $55,000; Grants to individuals, 17
grants totaling $50,000 (high: $6,000, low:
$1,000).
Type of support: Scholarships—to individuals;
Undergraduate support.
Application information: Applications not
accepted.
EIN: 382984958

4057
David E. Thomas Trust
c/o Louise Policello
W7364 Creek Rd.
Wausaukee, WI 54177

Foundation type: Independent foundation
Limitations: Scholarships to graduates of
Wausaukee, Pembine and Crivitz high schools, WI.
Financial data: Year ended 12/31/2004.
Assets, $1,442,994 (M); Expenditures, $78,904;
Total giving, $71,294; Grants to individuals,
totaling $66,250.
Type of support: Support to graduates or students
of specific schools; Undergraduate support.
Application information: Applications not
accepted.
EIN: 396156536

4058
The Thomasson Foundation
(formerly Oxford Foundation, Inc.)
11711 N. Meridian St., Ste. 600
Carmel, IN 46032 (317) 843-5678
Contact: Jeffrey H. Thomasson, Pres. and Treas.
Application Address: P.O. Box 80238, Indianapolis,
IN 46280-0238

Foundation type: Independent foundation

Limitations: Undergraduate scholarships to
financially needy children of Christian missionaries
in the U.S. and elsewhere.
Financial data: Year ended 12/31/2003.
Assets, $20,499 (M); Expenditures, $366,485;
Total giving, $361,679; Grants to individuals,
totaling $361,679.
Fields of interest: Christian agencies & churches.
Type of support: Undergraduate support.
Application information: Contact foundation for
current application deadline; Initial approach by
letter; Application by letter outlining financial need,
including transcripts, standardized test scores,
essay, and recommendation letter.
EIN: 351870799

4059
Thomasville Furniture Industries Foundation
c/o Wachovia Bank of North Carolina, N.A.
P.O. Box 3099
Winston-Salem, NC 27150-1022
(336) 732-6010
Contact: Sherald Cratch
Application address: c/o Vickie Holder, Thomasville
Furniture Industries, Inc., P.O. Box 339,
Thomasville, NC 27360

Foundation type: Company-sponsored foundation
Limitations: Scholarships only to children of
employees of Thomasville Furniture Industries, Inc.
Financial data: Year ended 12/31/2002.
Assets, $3,645,483 (M); Expenditures,
$333,629; Total giving, $301,932; Grants to
individuals, 36 grants totaling $57,583 (high:
$2,000, low: $250).
Type of support: Employee-related scholarships.
Application information:
Deadline(s): None
Additional information: Applications by letter;
Applications available through employee's
supervisor.
EIN: 566047870

4060
Bessie & Godfrey Thompson Charitable Foundation
c/o Bank of America, N.A.
P.O. Box 34345
Seattle, WA 98124-1345

Foundation type: Independent foundation
Limitations: Scholarships to individuals in WA.
Financial data: Year ended 06/30/2005.
Assets, $1,306,286 (M); Expenditures, $59,177;
Total giving, $43,396; Grants to individuals, 57
grants totaling $20,828.
Type of support: Scholarships—to individuals.
Application information: Applications not
accepted.
EIN: 957078668

4061
Edgel Paul and Garnet E. Thompson Charitable Trust
c/o Fifth Third Bank
38 Fountain Square Plz., MD 1090FA
Cincinnati, OH 45263-0001
Application address: c/o Fifth Third Bank of Ohio
Valley, Attn. Audrey Bailey, 999 4th Ave.,
Huntington, WV 25701, tel.: (304) 691-6634

Foundation type: Independent foundation

Limitations: Scholarships to individuals residing in Boyd and Lawrence counties, KY, for tuition, books, room, and board. Preference to individuals attending Christian colleges.
Financial data: Year ended 02/28/2005. Assets, $460,229 (M); Expenditures, $19,972; Total giving, $15,000; Grants to individuals, 10 grants totaling $15,000 (high: $3,750, low: $400).
Fields of interest: Religion, formal/general education; Christian agencies & churches.
Type of support: Undergraduate support.
Application information:
  Initial approach: Letter.
  Deadline(s): None
EIN: 616206389

4062
Willard E. & Ella P. Thompson Educational Fund

c/o LaSalle Bank, N.A.
135 S. LaSalle St., Ste. 2060
Chicago, IL 60603

Foundation type: Independent foundation
Limitations: Scholarships to graduates of Iowa High School in Algona School District, Algona, IA.
Financial data: Year ended 12/31/2004. Assets, $5,035,422 (M); Expenditures, $285,600; Total giving, $252,653; Grants to individuals, 342 grants totaling $252,653 (high: $1,120, low: $210).
Type of support: Support to graduates or students of specific schools; Undergraduate support.
Application information: Applications accepted throughout the year; Initial approach by letter detailing need.
EIN: 366028029

4063
Mary & Perry Thompson Educational Trust

c/o BB&T
P.O. Box 5228
Martinsville, VA 24115
Application address: c/o First Virginia Bank, Trust Dept., P.O. Box 638, Fredericksburg, VA 22404

Foundation type: Independent foundation
Limitations: Scholarships to legal residents of the city of Fredericksburg, and the counties of Stafford and Spotsylvania, VA.
Financial data: Year ended 10/31/2003. Assets, $868,242 (M); Expenditures, $65,295; Total giving, $51,500; Grants to individuals, 47 grants totaling $51,500 (high: $2,000, low: $500).
Type of support: Scholarships—to individuals.
Application information: Deadline Sept. 30; Initial approach by letter; Completion of formal application required, including transcripts, teacher evaluations, and financial information.
EIN: 546330780

4064
The Donald E. Thompson Family Charitable Foundation

P.O. Box G
Troy, MO 63379-0167
Contact: David W. Thompson, Tr.

Foundation type: Independent foundation
Limitations: Scholarships to individuals residing in the Troy, MO, area for undergraduate education.
Financial data: Year ended 12/31/2004. Assets, $449,818 (M); Expenditures, $57,715;

Total giving, $55,700; Grants to individuals, 23 grants totaling $41,000.
Type of support: Undergraduate support.
Application information: Contact foundation for current application deadline/guidelines; Completion of formal application required, including transcript and financial information.
EIN: 436816074

4065
Frank G. Thompson Foundation

c/o Donald O'Connor
1120 Bloomfield Ave., No. 101
West Caldwell, NJ 07006
Contact: Mark Mongon, Secy.
Application address: 11 Foxcroft Dr., Livingston, N.J. 07039, tel.: (973) 535-8000

Foundation type: Independent foundation
Limitations: Scholarships to residents of Livingston, North Caldwell, West Caldwell, and Essex Falls, NJ.
Financial data: Year ended 12/31/2004. Assets, $367,731 (M); Expenditures, $19,862; Total giving, $15,000; Grants to individuals, 9 grants totaling $15,000.
Type of support: Scholarships—to individuals.
Application information: Deadline Feb. 28; Completion of formal application required.
EIN: 222245964

4066
Jack W. Thompson Foundation

c/o Wells Fargo Bank Northwest, N.A.
P.O. Box 21927
Seattle, WA 98111
Application address: c/o Wells Fargo Bank Montana, N.A., P.O. Box 597, Helena, MT 59624

Foundation type: Independent foundation
Limitations: Scholarships to financially needy college students from Dawson County, MT, whose academic standing is in the middle one-third of their class.
Financial data: Year ended 10/31/2004. Assets, $324,864 (M); Expenditures, $18,929; Total giving, $16,000; Grants to individuals, 22 grants totaling $16,000.
Type of support: Undergraduate support.
Application information:
  Deadline(s): Apr. 1
  Additional information: Completion of formal application required, including three references, transcripts, FAF, and a personal statement of 200 words or less; Applications can be obtained from Glendine High School.
Program description:
  Scholarship Program: Scholarships are for one year and are for the payment of tuition, fees, room and board, and books and other study materials.
EIN: 816010360

4067
Thompson Scholarship Fund

c/o William W. Corcoran
P.O. Box 389
Newport, RI 02840
Application address: c/o Guidance Office, Rogers High School, Wickham Rd., Newport, RI 02840, tel.: (401) 849-3585

Foundation type: Independent foundation

Limitations: Scholarships to graduating seniors at Rogers High School, Newport, RI, for study at four-year colleges.
Financial data: Year ended 12/31/2003. Assets, $2,005,606 (M); Expenditures, $115,753; Total giving, $100,410; Grants to individuals, 51 grants totaling $100,410 (high: $2,500, low: $1,000).
Type of support: Support to graduates or students of specific schools; Undergraduate support.
Application information: Contact fund for current application deadline; Initial approach by letter or telephone; Completion of formal application required, including copy of most recent tax return; handwritten essay, two letters of recommendation (one from a teacher), and transcripts.
EIN: 056012968

4068
Viola Thompson Student Nurses Fund

200 Health Care Dr.
Greenville, IL 62246-1156

Foundation type: Independent foundation
Limitations: Loans for scholarships to nursing students who wish to continue their education in health care and are employed or placed in the care of a facility owned or operated by Edward A. Utlaut Memorial Hospital, Inc. in IL.
Financial data: Year ended 12/31/2004. Assets, $7,555,563 (M); Expenditures, $61,587; Total giving, $48,524; Grants to individuals, 12 grants totaling $19,680.
Fields of interest: Nursing school/education.
Type of support: Student loans—to individuals.
Application information: Contact the fund for current application deadline; Completion of formal application required; Interviews required.
Program description:
  Nursing School Loan Program: These loans provide financial aid to students of Edward A. Utlaut Memorial Hospital who meet specific qualifications. The recipient is then required to work for the hospital upon graduating assuming the hospital needs help. After the service requirement has been completed (or if the hospital does not need the recipient's services upon graduation), the recipient is free to work wherever he/she chooses. If the recipient withdraws from the program or refuses to complete the service requirement, the scholarship money must be repaid at an appropriate rate of interest.
EIN: 436249005

4069
Frank Thomson Scholarship Trust

c/o Wachovia Bank, N.A.
Broad & Walnut Sts., 5th Fl.
Philadelphia, PA 19109 (215) 670-4226
Contact: Reginald Middleton

Foundation type: Independent foundation
Limitations: Scholarships to high school seniors who are sons of active, retired, or deceased employees of Conrail, Penn Central, and Amtrak who were employed by the Penn Central Transportation Company or Pennsylvania Railroad Company before June 1976.
Financial data: Year ended 12/31/2004. Assets, $2,545,490 (M); Expenditures, $254,447; Total giving, $214,750; Grants to individuals, 410 grants totaling $214,750 (high: $1,750, low: $250).
Fields of interest: Education.
Type of support: Employee-related scholarships.
Application information: Application form required.

Initial approach: Letter.
Deadline(s): Mar. 31
EIN: 236217801

4070
Thorbeck Foundation
R.R. 1, Box 30
Gonvick, MN 56644

Foundation type: Operating foundation
Limitations: Scholarships to graduates of high schools in the northern Clearwater County, MN, area, to attend four-year colleges and universities.
Financial data: Year ended 12/31/2003.
Assets, $195,663 (M); Expenditures, $13,251; Total giving, $13,000; Grants to individuals, 13 grants totaling $13,000 (high: $1,000, low: $1,000).
Type of support: Support to graduates or students of specific schools; Undergraduate support.
Application information: Applications not accepted.
EIN: 363487775

4071
Columbus W. Thorn, Jr. Foundation
109 E. Main St.
Elkton, MD   21921   (410) 398-0611
Contact: Trustees

Foundation type: Independent foundation
Limitations: Student loans to worthy and financially needy high school graduates who are residents of Cecil County, MD, for undergraduate, graduate, and technical education.
Financial data: Year ended 12/31/2005.
Assets, $16,784,668; Expenditures, $882,564; Total giving, $741,418; Loans to individuals, 126 loans totaling $741,418.
Type of support: Graduate support; Technical education support; Undergraduate support.
Application information: Contact foundation for current application deadline; Initial approach by telephone; Completion of formal application required.
Program description:
 Loan Program: Repayment of the loan is required within four years after completion or discontinuation of student's advanced education. Repayment is guaranteed by student's parents. Interest rate on the loan is five percent from graduation or discontinuation of study.
EIN: 237153983

4072
John M. Thorne & Ethel C. Thorne Foundation, Inc.
66 Thorne Rd.
Bourne, MA 02532-5415

Foundation type: Independent foundation
Limitations: Scholarships to residents of Bourne, Falmouth, Sandwich, and Wareham, MA.
Financial data: Year ended 04/30/2005.
Assets, $508,044 (M); Expenditures, $30,083; Total giving, $19,600; Grants to individuals, 20 grants totaling $10,000.
Type of support: Scholarships—to individuals.
Application information: Contact foundation for current application deadline/guidelines.
EIN: 046047689

4073
Haywood R. Thornton III Memorial Scholarship Trust
702 Delaware Ave.
St. Cloud, FL 34769
Contact: Elizabeth Abshier, Tr.

Foundation type: Independent foundation
Limitations: Scholarships to graduates of Saint Cloud High School, FL, for higher education.
Financial data: Year ended 12/31/2004.
Assets, $335,690 (M); Expenditures, $21,598; Total giving, $20,000; Grants to individuals, 4 grants totaling $20,000.
Type of support: Support to graduates or students of specific schools; Undergraduate support.
Application information: Application form required.
 Deadline(s): Apr. 15
EIN: 596839701

4074
Thorntown Businessmen's Educational Foundation, Inc.
1201 Indianapolis Ave.
Lebanon, IN 46052

Foundation type: Independent foundation
Limitations: Scholarships to residents of Thorntown, IL.
Financial data: Year ended 12/31/2004.
Assets, $191,521 (M); Expenditures, $6,890; Total giving, $6,300; Grants to individuals, 3 grants totaling $6,300.
Type of support: Undergraduate support.
Application information: Unsolicited requests for funds not accepted.
EIN: 351939684

4075
Charles Thorwelle Foundation
c/o Rouis and Co., LLP
P.O. Box 209
Wurtsboro, NY   12790
Contact: Robert C. Curtis, Tr.
Application address: c/o Bank of America, N.A., Curtis Bldg., Callicoon, NY 12723, tel.: (845) 887-4400

Foundation type: Independent foundation
Limitations: Scholarships to graduates of Delaware Valley Central High School in Callicoon, NY.
Financial data: Year ended 12/31/2004.
Assets, $1,619,567 (M); Expenditures, $80,614; Total giving, $56,662; Grants to individuals, totaling $38,750.
Type of support: Support to graduates or students of specific schools; Undergraduate support.
Application information: Deadline May 1; Completion of formal application required; Applications available from school guidance director.
EIN: 146047928

4076
Robert A. Thrush Charitable Trust
2810 E. Oakland Park Blvd.
Fort Lauderdale, FL 33306-1801
(954) 563-1000
Contact: James L. Case, Tr.

Foundation type: Independent foundation
Limitations: Scholarships for higher education, primarily to residents of OH.

Financial data: Year ended 12/31/2004.
Assets, $343,987 (M); Expenditures, $91,147; Total giving, $23,700; Grants to individuals, 15 grants totaling $22,700.
Type of support: Scholarships—to individuals.
Application information: Contact trust for current application deadline; Application by letter, including transcript.
EIN: 650136688

4077
Rabbi Samuel Thurman Educational Foundation
15332 Braefield Dr.
Chesterfield, MO 63017

Foundation type: Operating foundation
Limitations: Scholarships and student loans to individuals in St. Louis, MO, pursuing higher education.
Financial data: Year ended 05/31/2004.
Assets, $154,381 (M); Expenditures, $8,211; Total giving, $8,000; Grants to individuals, totaling $8,000.
Type of support: Scholarships—to individuals; Student loans—to individuals.
Application information: Applications not accepted.
EIN: 431063744

4078
Harlan R. Thurston Foundation
420 E. Main St., Ste. 203
Anoka, MN 55303
Contact: Erling O. Johnson, Pres.
Application address: 832 Eastwood Ln., Anoka, MN 55303, tel.: (612) 427-1442

Foundation type: Independent foundation
Limitations: Student loans to graduates of Anoka-Hennepin Independent School District No. 11, MN, for undergraduate study.
Financial data: Year ended 12/31/2004.
Assets, $239,916 (M); Expenditures, $30,007; Total giving, $1,500; Grants to individuals, 5 grants totaling $1,500; Loans to individuals, totaling $16,535.
Type of support: Support to graduates or students of specific schools; Undergraduate support.
Application information: Applications accepted. Application form required.
 Deadline(s): None
 Additional information: Contact foundation for current application deadline.
EIN: 416043390

4079
Tidewater Builders Association Scholarship Foundation, Inc.
c/o Mary Hearring
2117 Smith Ave.
Chesapeake, VA   23320   (757) 420-2434
URL: http://www.tbaonline.org/scholarships.php

Foundation type: Independent foundation
Limitations: Scholarships to financially needy high school seniors residing in Chesapeake, Norfolk, Portsmouth, Suffolk, Franklin, Southampton, Virginia Beach, VA, or the Eastern Shore of VA. Awards also given to young designers from VA enrolled in drafting and design classes. See program description for further information.
Financial data: Year ended 12/31/2004.
Assets, $1,020,726 (M); Expenditures,

$124,550; Total giving, $94,238; Grants to individuals, totaling $94,238.
Fields of interest: Arts education; Visual arts; Design.
Type of support: Awards/prizes; Undergraduate support.
Application information: Application form required.
  Initial approach: Letter or telephone.
  Deadline(s): Mar. 23 for scholarships and Apr. 28 for Young Designers' program
  Applicants should submit the following:
  1) Financial information
  2) SAT
  3) Transcripts
  Additional information: Application should also include teacher and counselor evaluations and recommendations, and a copy of parents' federal income tax return, W-2 forms, and other income statements.
Program description:
  Scholarship Program: The foundation also sponsors The Young Designers' Scholarship Competition for students currently enrolled in drafting and design classes in public and private secondary schools in Chesapeake, Franklin, Norfolk, Portsmouth, Southampton County, Suffolk, Virginia Beach, VA, and the Eastern Shore of VA. The contest challenges high school designers to create a house to meet a fictional family's needs. Family profile, design specifications, and contest rules are available from the foundation. First place award is a $1,500 scholarship. Second place award is $1,000. Third place award is $500. There are two different categories of awards, CAD and Hand-drawn, each with a first and second place award. Scholarships may be used to study any field, but a GPA of at least 2.0 must be maintained.
EIN: 546057730

4080

The Tilles Fund
(formerly Rosalie Tilles Nonsectarian Charity Fund)
c/o U.S. Bank, N.A.
SL-MO-T14E, Private Client Group
P.O. Box 387
St. Louis, MO   63166
Contact: Garth Silvey, V.P.
URL: http://www.thetillesfund.com

Foundation type: Independent foundation
Limitations: Scholarships to recent high school graduates who are residents of the city or county of St. Louis, MO, and who have been nominated by their financial aid officers, to attend colleges and universities in MO.
Publications: Application guidelines.
Financial data: Year ended 06/30/2005.
Assets, $13,223,494 (M); Expenditures, $703,957; Total giving, $585,817; Grants to individuals, 52 grants totaling $375,817 (high: $14,850, low: $734).
Type of support: Scholarships—to individuals; Undergraduate support.
Application information:
  Initial approach: Letter to the financial aid dept. at the participating college or university.
  Copies of proposal: 7
  Deadline(s): May 1
  Additional information: Awards are granted after May 1, and payment is made directly to the college.
Program description:
  The Tilles Fund for Full-Tuition Undergraduate Scholarships: Scholarships are awarded to residents of St. Louis, MO, to attend MO universities and colleges. Applicants must be first-year students directly out of high school.

Scholarships are renewable for four years and cover full tuition, provided a 3.0 cumulative GPA is maintained for the semester. Transcripts must be provided after each semester to verify compliance with the GPA criteria. Recipients are chosen by the student financial aid officer or scholarship coordinator at the student's school. The officer must submit the name of one scholar and one alternate to the Tilles Trustees for selection. Recipients are selected on the basis of secondary school academic record, class rank, test scores, major academic interest, extracurricular activity, and financial need (based on previous year's family income and parent(s) occupation(s)
EIN: 436020833

4081

Margaret B. Tilt Scholarship Trust
c/o Orange County Trust Co.
75 North St.
Middletown, NY   10940-5022
Application address: c/o Warwick Valley Central School District, Attn: Allan Newton, Supervising Principal, Warwick, NY 10990, tel.: (914) 986-1181

Foundation type: Independent foundation
Limitations: Scholarships to graduates of Warwick Valley Central School District, NY, who are pursuing a bachelor's or master's degree.
Financial data: Year ended 12/31/2004.
Assets, $146,051 (M); Expenditures, $6,513; Total giving, $4,200; Grants to individuals, 14 grants totaling $4,200.
Type of support: Support to graduates or students of specific schools; Graduate support; Undergraduate support.
Application information: Applications accepted throughout the year; Completion of formal application required.
EIN: 146086361

4082

The Timken Company Educational Fund, Inc.
1835 Dueber Ave. S.W.
Canton, OH   44706
E-mail: palomba@timken.com

Foundation type: Company-sponsored foundation
Limitations: Scholarships to children and dependent stepchildren of employees and retirees of The Timken Company.
Financial data: Year ended 12/31/2003.
Assets, $931,914 (M); Expenditures, $665,733; Total giving, $634,050; Grants to individuals, 46 grants totaling $634,050 (low: $135).
Type of support: Employee-related scholarships.
Application information: Application form required.
  Additional information: Contact fund for current application deadline.
EIN: 346520257

4083

Tipton County Foundation, Inc.
1020 W. Jefferson St.
P.O. Box 412
Tipton, IN   46072-0412   (765) 675-8480
Contact: Frank M. Giammarino, Exec. Dir.
FAX: (765) 675-8488; *E-mail:* tcf@tiptontel.com;
URL: http://www.tiptoncf.org

Foundation type: Community foundation

Limitations: Scholarships to residents of Tipton County, IN.
Publications: Annual report; Financial statement; Grants list; Informational brochure; Newsletter; Occasional report.
Financial data: Year ended 12/31/2004.
Assets, $17,477,155 (M); Expenditures, $762,850; Total giving, $536,158; Grants to individuals, 17 grants totaling $142,825 (high: $23,312).
Type of support: Scholarships—to individuals.
Application information:
  Initial approach: E-mail or telephone.
  Deadline(s): Contact foundation for current deadline.
  Additional information: See Web site for application guidelines.
EIN: 311175045

4084

The Tiscornia Foundation, Inc.
1010 Main St., Ste. A
St. Joseph, MI   49085   (269) 983-4711
Contact: Laurianne T. Davis, Pres.
FAX: (269) 983-6959

Foundation type: Independent foundation
Limitations: Scholarships to graduating seniors of high schools in Northern Berrien County, MI.
Publications: Annual report (including application guidelines).
Financial data: Year ended 12/31/2004.
Assets, $3,862,702 (M); Expenditures, $451,339; Total giving, $263,964; Grants to individuals, 27 grants totaling $108,000 (high: $4,000, low: $4,000).
Type of support: Support to graduates or students of specific schools; Undergraduate support.
Application information:
  Deadline(s): Apr. 1
  Additional information: Application by letter; Recipients notified in May; See Scholarship program for a list of participating schools.
Program description:
  Scholarship Program: Graduating seniors of the following MI schools may apply: Northern Berrien County High School, Lakeshore High School, St. Joseph High School, Coloma High School, Benton Harbor High School, Watervliet High School, Lake Michigan Lutheran High School, and Lake Michigan Catholic High School.
EIN: 381777343

4085

Evelyn K. Titus Trust
200 E. Broadway
Monmouth, IL   61462-0440
Contact: Alan Kulczewski, Tr.
Application address: 1000 N. Main St., Monmouth, IL 61462, tel.: (309) 734-5161, FAX: (309) 734-5532

Foundation type: Independent foundation
Limitations: Scholarships to Warren County, IL, residents who major in agriculture or home economics.
Financial data: Year ended 12/31/2004.
Assets, $317,745 (M); Expenditures, $15,769; Total giving, $12,000; Grants to individuals, 8 grants totaling $12,000.
Fields of interest: Agriculture; Home economics.
Type of support: Scholarships—to individuals.
Application information: Applications accepted.
  Initial approach: Letter.
  Deadline(s): Contact trust for deadline
  Applicants should submit the following:

1) Transcripts
2) Financial information
Additional information: Application must also include educational interest in agricultural or related fields.
EIN: 366982233

4086
TLB Foundation, Inc.
(formerly Great Commission Foundation, Inc.)
P.O. Box 991
Findlay, OH 45839-0991   (419) 420-0419
Contact: Jack W. Ridge, Pres.

Foundation type: Independent foundation
Limitations: Project support and educational grants primarily to residents of Hancock County, OH. Recipients must agree with and strive to uphold the statement of Christian faith set forth by the foundation.
Financial data: Year ended 11/30/2004. Assets, $24,148 (M); Expenditures, $223,981; Total giving, $220,571; Grants to individuals, 2 grants totaling $57,000 (high: $43,000, low: $14,000).
Fields of interest: Theological school/education; Christian agencies & churches.
Type of support: Program development; Grants to individuals; Scholarships—to individuals.
Application information: Applications only received through local contacts.
Program description:
Christian Faith Statement: The foundation's statement of Christian faith has seven parts. These parts state the foundation's specific beliefs in, and approaches toward:
 · the Holy Trinity
 · the Bible
 · the birth, life, and death of Jesus Christ
 · the power and divinity of the Holy Spirit
 · the creation of man and his salvation
 · the Church
 · the proclamation of the Gospel and a complete commitment to Christ.
EIN: 341648111

4087
The Vera H. and William R. Todd Foundation
c/o Bank of America, N.A.
P.O. Box 1802
Providence, RI 02901-1802
Application address: c/o Bank of America, N.A., Attn.: Marjorie Alexandre Davis, 777 Main St., CT2-102-22-02, Hartford, CT 06115

Foundation type: Independent foundation
Limitations: Scholarships to residents of Derby or Shelton, CT.
Financial data: Year ended 12/31/2004. Assets, $229,415 (M); Expenditures, $13,726; Total giving, $10,000.
Type of support: Scholarships—to individuals.
Application information: Deadline Apr. 22; Initial approach by letter requesting application guidelines.
EIN: 066031931

4088
Tokushukai International Foundation
4510 Aukai Ave.
Honolulu, HI 96816
Contact: Ruth M. Ono, Pres.

Foundation type: Independent foundation
Limitations: Scholarships to individuals in HI for higher education.
Financial data: Year ended 06/30/2003. Assets, $86,939 (M); Expenditures, $50,415; Total giving, $45,745; Grants to individuals, 5 grants totaling $10,000 (high: $3,000, low: $1,000).
Type of support: Undergraduate support.
Application information: Applications by letter accepted throughout the year; Applicant must show financial need.
EIN: 990322920

4089
Tomara Corporation
120 W. Main St.
P.O. Box 985
Collinsville, IL 62234   (618) 344-0484
Contact: Robert W. Karrer, Dir.

Foundation type: Independent foundation
Limitations: Scholarships to residents of Collinsville, IL, for higher education.
Financial data: Year ended 12/31/2004. Assets, $54,546 (M); Expenditures, $65,780; Total giving, $57,500; Grants to individuals, 12 grants totaling $25,000.
Type of support: Undergraduate support.
Application information: Applications accepted throughout the year; Contact foundation for current application guidelines.
EIN: 371193115

4090
The William J. Tomasso Foundation, Inc.
(formerly The Tomasso Family Foundation, Inc.)
c/o David Findley
P.O. Box 488
New Britain, CT 06050   (860) 224-9977

Foundation type: Independent foundation
Limitations: Scholarships to financially needy students graduating from public, private, and parochial schools in New Britain, Plainville, and Berlin, CT, to attend accredited two- or four-year colleges, or technical or vocational schools.
Financial data: Year ended 03/31/2005. Assets, $400,816 (M); Expenditures, $23,801; Total giving, $23,000; Grants to individuals, 6 grants totaling $23,000.
Fields of interest: Vocational education.
Type of support: Technical education support; Undergraduate support.
Application information: Application form required.
 Deadline(s): Mar. 1
 Additional information: Selection is based on financial need, academic performance, and performance on ability and aptitude tests.
EIN: 060991847

4091
Tomorrow Scholarship Fund Trust
28 W. 5th St.
Crossville, TN 38555   (931) 484-3556
Contact: Vivian E. Warner, Tr.

Foundation type: Operating foundation
Limitations: Scholarships to graduates of Cumberland County, TN, high schools.
Financial data: Year ended 12/31/2002. Assets, $88,106 (M); Expenditures, $11,538; Total giving, $11,000; Grants to individuals, 11

grants totaling $11,000 (high: $1,000, low: $1,000).
Type of support: Support to graduates or students of specific schools; Undergraduate support.
Application information: Deadline May 1; Completion of formal application required, including essay.
EIN: 621747882

4092
Martin L. & Mary Ellen Tompkins & John A. Tompkins Trust
c/o First National Bank
P.O. Box 388
Nevada, MO 64772-0388   (417) 667-3057
Contact: David J. Swearingen, Tr.

Foundation type: Independent foundation
Limitations: Scholarships to graduates of Oernon County high schools, MO, to attend the School of Agriculture at the University of Missouri.
Financial data: Year ended 12/31/2004. Assets, $165,717 (M); Expenditures, $8,558; Total giving, $7,841; Grants to individuals, 2 grants totaling $7,841.
Fields of interest: Agriculture.
Type of support: Support to graduates or students of specific schools; Undergraduate support.
Application information: Contact foundation for current application deadline; Application by letter including name of applicant, name of parents, their occupation and financial condition, transcript, and details of what the applicant plans to do after graduation.
EIN: 436121395

4093
Almeda Leake Toomey Trust f/b/o Dover High School & Central Catholic High School
c/o The Huntington National Bank
P.O. Box 1558, EA4E86
Columbus, OH 43216

Foundation type: Independent foundation
Limitations: Scholarships to graduates of Dover, Central Catholic and New Philadelphia high schools, OH.
Financial data: Year ended 06/30/2005. Assets, $301,955 (M); Expenditures, $18,767; Total giving, $14,699; Grants to individuals, 7 grants totaling $14,699 (high: $2,450, low: $1,633).
Type of support: Support to graduates or students of specific schools; Undergraduate support.
Application information: Application form required.
 Initial approach: Letter.
 Deadline(s): None.
 Additional information: Applications can be obtained at each school.
EIN: 316630558

4094
Willis & Imogene Toothaker Trust
P.O. Box 235
Hoxie, KS 67740
Contact: Scholarship Prog.: Michael H. Haas

Foundation type: Independent foundation
Limitations: Scholarships to individuals in Hoxie, KS, for undergraduate or vocational education.
Financial data: Year ended 12/31/2004. Assets, $1,386,656 (M); Expenditures, $73,573;

Total giving, $67,200; Grants to individuals, totaling $67,200.
Fields of interest: Vocational education, post-secondary.
Type of support: Technical education support; Undergraduate support.
Application information: Applications accepted. Application form required.
> *Deadline(s):* Application must be submitted before high school graduation; Additional information must be submitted by Jan. 7.

EIN: 486363592

4095
Tourism Cares for Tomorrow

(formerly National Tourism Foundation)
585 Washington St.
Canton, MA   02021   (781) 821-5990
Contact: Carolyn Viles, Prog. Mgr.
FAX: (781) 821-8949;
E-mail: carolynv@tourismcares.org; URL: http://www.tourismcares.org

Foundation type: Public charity
Limitations: Scholarships to North American college juniors or seniors pursuing degrees in tourism or travel-related fields.
Publications: Application guidelines; Grants list; Informational brochure; Newsletter.
Financial data: Year ended 12/31/2005. Total giving, $242,300; Grants to individuals, 34 grants totaling $48,300 (high: $10,000, low: $500).
Type of support: Conferences/seminars; Internship funds; Research; Scholarships—to individuals; Support to graduates or students of specific schools; Awards/grants by nomination only; Awards/prizes; Graduate support; Technical education support; Undergraduate support; Doctoral support.
Application information: Applications accepted. Application form required. Application form available on the grantmaker's Web site.
> *Initial approach:* Application.
> *Copies of proposal:* 1
> *Deadline(s):* Apr. 1
> *Applicants should submit the following:*
> 1) Resume
> 2) GPA
> *Additional information:* Each program has its own set of specific requirements. See Web site for additional application guidelines.

Program description:
> *Tourism Cares for Tomorrow:* The foundation administers scholarships to full-time students at two- and four-year colleges and universities in North America. Applicants must also be entering their junior or senior year of study and have a degree emphasis in a travel and tourism-related field. See Web site for further details about the amount of each award and its criteria.

EIN: 202013457

4096
Pierre Toussant/Roger Radloff Foundation

10017 S.W. 41st Rd.
Gainesville, FL   32608-4361
Contact: Vincent D. McInerney, Tr.

Foundation type: Independent foundation
Limitations: Scholarships and grants to needy students, primarily talented and artistic Haitians in FL.
Financial data: Year ended 12/31/2004.
Assets, $269,860 (M); Expenditures, $65,112;

Total giving, $60,937; Grants to individuals, totaling $60,937.
Fields of interest: Haiti.
Type of support: Scholarships—to individuals.
Application information: Contact foundation for current application deadline; Completion of formal application required; Applications must be submitted by the institution which the applicant is attending or plans to attend.
EIN: 656083720

4097
Frank L. Touvelle Trust

c/o Wells Fargo Bank Northwest, N.A.
P.O. Box 21927
Seattle, WA   98111
Application address: Frank C. Bash, Chair., c/o Sam Harbison, Attorney at Law, P.O. Box 1583, Medford, OR 97501

Foundation type: Independent foundation
Limitations: Scholarships to male residents of Jackson County, OR, who have had difficulties in their personal lives, and need financial assistance to attend secondary school.
Financial data: Year ended 12/31/2003.
Assets, $704,484 (M); Expenditures, $29,064; Total giving, $18,275; Grants to individuals, totaling $18,275.
Fields of interest: Secondary school/education; Men.
Type of support: Precollege support.
Application information: Applications not accepted.
EIN: 936018391

4098
Mildred Towle Scholarship Trust Fund

c/o First Hawaiian Bank
P.O. Box 3708
Honolulu, HI   96811

Foundation type: Independent foundation
Limitations: Scholarships to HI residents studying overseas or at Boston University, and to African Americans studying in HI. Also, scholarships to international students with student visas (F or J) for study in HI.
Financial data: Year ended 09/30/2004.
Assets, $1,301,586 (M); Expenditures, $82,716; Total giving, $71,090; Grants to individuals, totaling $71,090.
Fields of interest: African Americans/Blacks.
Type of support: Support to graduates or students of specific schools; Undergraduate support.
Application information: Special consideration is given to applicants who pursue studies in the social sciences relating to international understanding and interracial fellowship. Applicants to this foundation may automatically be considered for other scholarship programs administered by the Hawaii Community Foundation. Employees and direct relatives of employees of First Hawaiian Bank and the Hawaii Community Foundation are ineligible. Overseas study is not funded during the summer term.
EIN: 996050638

4099
Town & Country Community Foundation, Inc.

c/o Wells Fargo Bank Wisconsin, N.A.
636 Wisconsin Ave., P.O. Box 171
Sheboygan, WI   53082-0171
Application address: c/o Judy Konecki, Trust Off., Wells Fargo Bank IL, N.A., 121 W. First St., Geneseo, IL, 61254

Foundation type: Independent foundation
Limitations: Scholarships to nursing students in the Geneseo, IL, area.
Financial data: Year ended 12/31/2002.
Assets, $263,458 (M); Expenditures, $18,278; Total giving, $14,598; Grants to individuals, totaling $8,598.
Fields of interest: Nursing school/education.
Type of support: Scholarships—to individuals.
Application information: Applications accepted throughout the year; Contact foundation for current application guidelines.
EIN: 363696115

4100
C. E. Towne Scholarship Fund

c/o Wells Fargo Bank, N.A., Trust Tax Dept.
P.O. Box 63954
San Francisco, CA   94163
Contact: Judy Lang
Application address: c/o California Masonic Foundation, 1111 California St., San Francisco, CA 93108, tel.: (415) 292-9196; FAX: (415) 776-7170; URL: http://www.freemason.org

Foundation type: Independent foundation
Limitations: Scholarships to children of Protestant Masonic families, for higher education.
Financial data: Year ended 06/30/2003.
Assets, $7,252,879 (M); Expenditures, $579,498; Total giving, $514,000; Grants to individuals, 44 grants totaling $514,000 (high: $16,000, low: $12,000).
Fields of interest: Protestant agencies & churches.
Type of support: Undergraduate support.
Application information: Application form required.
> *Deadline(s):* Feb. 28.

EIN: 946705897

4101
Henry Towne Scholarship Fund

c/o KeyBank N.A.
800 Superior Ave., 4th Fl.
Cleveland, OH   44114-2601

Foundation type: Company-sponsored foundation
Limitations: Scholarships to high school students who are children of regular, full-time employees of Eaton Corporation.
Financial data: Year ended 12/31/2003.
Assets, $410,812 (M); Expenditures, $98,457; Total giving, $93,860.
Type of support: Employee-related scholarships.
Application information:
> *Initial approach:* Letter or telephone.
> *Deadline(s):* Jan. 1.
> *Additional information:* Contact fund for current application guidelines; Application address: Melanie Maloney, c/o Human Resources Dept., Eaton Corp., Eaton Ctr., Cleveland, OH 44114, tel.: (216) 534-4353.

EIN: 136104340

4102
Harry and Minerva Townley Educational Trust
P.O. Box 313
Wibaux, MT 59353
Contact: Connie J. Chaffee, Tr.
Application address: P.O. Box 124, Wibaux, MT 59353

Foundation type: Independent foundation
Limitations: Scholarships to graduates of Wibaux County High School, MT.
Financial data: Year ended 12/31/2004. Assets, $287,387 (M); Expenditures, $21,408; Total giving, $20,150; Grants to individuals, 34 grants totaling $20,150.
Type of support: Support to graduates or students of specific schools; Undergraduate support.
Application information: Application form required.
   Deadline(s): May 1
EIN: 816082126

4103
The Townsend Foundation
58 Holly Oak Dr.
Voorhees, NJ 08043-1538 (856) 772-9570
Contact: John Langan, Tr.

Foundation type: Independent foundation
Limitations: Scholarships to full- and part-time Bachelor's and Associates students enrolled in a developmental reading or writing course. Award amount is based upon number books read.
Financial data: Year ended 12/31/2004. Assets, $417,284 (M); Expenditures, $21,000; Total giving, $21,000; Grants to individuals, totaling $21,000.
Fields of interest: Adult education—literacy, basic skills & GED.
Type of support: Undergraduate support.
Application information: Applications accepted.
   Initial approach: E-mail.
   Additional information: Awards $100 for every ten books read, for a total of $300 for thirty books read.
EIN: 223435514

4104
Tozer Foundation, Inc.
P.O. Box 64713
St. Paul, MN 55164
Contact: Cheryl Nelson
Application address for grants: c/o U.S. Bank, 101 E. 5th St., Saint Paul, MN 55101

Foundation type: Independent foundation
Limitations: Scholarships to graduating high school students in Pine, Kanabec, and Washington counties, MN.
Financial data: Year ended 10/31/2004. Assets, $27,459,680 (M); Expenditures, $1,859,673; Total giving, $1,597,335.
Type of support: Support to graduates or students of specific schools; Undergraduate support.
Application information:
   Initial approach: Letter or telephone.
   Deadline(s): None.
   Additional information: Candidates must apply for scholarships through selected high schools.
EIN: 416011518

4105
Gladys Tozier Memorial Scholarship Trust
c/o M&T Bank
21 E. Market St.
York, PA 17401-1205
Contact: Evan Rosser, Jr., Tr.
Application address: 1400 Woodmont Ave., Williamsport, PA 17701

Foundation type: Independent foundation
Limitations: Scholarships to residents of Lycoming, Elk, and Clearfield counties, PA.
Financial data: Year ended 12/31/2004. Assets, $475,010 (M); Expenditures, $31,718; Total giving, $25,000; Grants to individuals, 14 grants totaling $25,000.
Type of support: Scholarships—to individuals.
Application information: Applications accepted throughout the year; Completion of formal application required, including transcripts.
EIN: 232650705

4106
The Dennis and Sara Trachsel Foundation
2034 Matheny Ave.
Marion, OH 43302 (740) 382-1771
Contact: Sam Sparling, Tr.
Application address: c/o James Waddell, 1111 Mt. Vernon St., Marion, OH 43302

Foundation type: Independent foundation
Limitations: Scholarships to graduates of Ridgedale and River Valley high schools, OH, for attendance at a college, university or technical school.
Financial data: Year ended 12/31/2004. Assets, $3,721,746 (M); Expenditures, $661,142; Total giving, $211,110; Grants to individuals, 22 grants totaling $194,110 (high: $17,406, low: $514).
Type of support: Support to graduates or students of specific schools; Technical education support; Undergraduate support.
Application information: Application form required.
   Deadline(s): Apr. 15
EIN: 311472824

4107
The Tractor & Equipment Company Foundation
5336 Airport Hwy.
Birmingham, AL 35212
Contact: Lloyd Adams, Secy.-Treas.

Foundation type: Company-sponsored foundation
Limitations: Scholarships only to children of Tractor & Equipment Company, Inc. employees residing in AL to attend accredited institutions of higher education.
Financial data: Year ended 12/31/2004. Assets, $278,515 (M); Expenditures, $110,080; Total giving, $110,043; Grants to individuals, 9 grants totaling $41,993 (high: $22,386, low: $500).
Type of support: Employee-related scholarships.
Application information: Application form required.
   Additional information: Applications from individuals who are not within the stated recipient restriction are not accepted. Scholarship application address: c/o James W. Waitzman, Jr., Pres., Tractor & Equipment Co., Inc., P.O. Box 12326, Birmingham, AL 35201.
EIN: 630718825

4108
James & Phyllis Tracy Scholarship Foundation
c/o Bank of America, N.A.
P.O. Box 1802
Providence, RI 02901-1802
Application address: c/o Bank of America, N.A., Attn.: Peter Weston, 777 Main St., CT2-102-22-02, Hartford, CT 06115

Foundation type: Independent foundation
Limitations: Scholarships to students from Waterbury High School, CT, who have been Waterbury residents for the past five years.
Financial data: Year ended 12/31/2004. Assets, $143,295 (M); Expenditures, $11,090; Total giving, $9,000; Grants to individuals, 3 grants totaling $9,000.
Type of support: Support to graduates or students of specific schools; Precollege support; Undergraduate support.
Application information: Applications accepted. Application form required.
   Deadline(s): Apr. 1.
   Applicants should submit the following:
      1) SAT
      2) Letter(s) of recommendation
      3) GPA
      4) FAFSA
      5) Transcripts
      6) Financial information
Program description:
   Scholarship Program: Students must be enrolled in a college or trade school; demonstrate financial need, and have satisfactory scholarship and good character. Applicants who attend college should provide final high school transcripts.
EIN: 066025726

4109
Perry S. and Stella H. Tracy Scholarship Fund
c/o Wells Fargo Bank, N.A.
P.O. Box 63954, MAC A0330-011
San Francisco, CA 94163
Application address: Beverly Garcia, Tracy Trust Off., c/o Bank of America, Tracy Memorial Scholarship, 3044 Sacramento St., Placerville, CA 95667, tel.: (530) 622-5919

Foundation type: Independent foundation
Limitations: Scholarships for full-time study to graduating seniors of El Dorado, Independence, Oak Ridge, and Ponderosa high schools, CA, who have lived in and attended high school in El Dorado County for at least two years and have a GPA of at least 3.0.
Financial data: Year ended 05/31/2005. Assets, $1,267,342 (M); Expenditures, $75,592; Total giving, $52,145; Grants to individuals, 154 grants totaling $52,145 (high: $500, low: $300).
Type of support: Support to graduates or students of specific schools; Undergraduate support.
Application information: Deadline Apr. 19 for first-time applicants, Apr. 30 for renewals; Completion of formal application required, including transcripts and personal statement; Applications available through El Dorado County high schools.
Program description:
   Tracy Scholarship Fund: The completed application should be submitted to the principal of applicant's high school, who will then forward it to the scholarship selection committee. The selection committee consists of the principals of El Dorado County high schools, mayors of the towns within the

county, and the managers of the Bank of America branches in the county.
EIN: 946203372

4110
Brig. Gen. Edward Dorr Tracy, CFSA and 1st Lt. William G. Burt, Jr., USAF Fund
c/o Bank of America, N.A.
487 Cherry St., Ste. 200
Macon, GA 31201

Foundation type: Independent foundation
Limitations: Scholarships to male residents of Macon County, GA, who attend the University of Georgia.
Financial data: Year ended 12/31/2004. Assets, $1,765,157 (M); Expenditures, $100,691; Total giving, $80,322; Grants to individuals, 21 grants totaling $80,322.
Fields of interest: Men.
Type of support: Support to graduates or students of specific schools.
Application information: Applications accepted. Application form required.
    Deadline(s): Contact foundation for current application guidelines.
EIN: 527077420

4111
Transit Mix Concrete Company Trust
(formerly Transmix Concrete Company Trust)
c/o Wells Fargo Bank
P.O. Box 53456
Phoenix, AZ 85072

Foundation type: Company-sponsored foundation
Limitations: Scholarships to children of employees of Transit Mix Concrete Co. who are graduates of area high schools and who have resided in El Paso County, CO, for at least two years.
Financial data: Year ended 12/31/2004. Assets, $15,707 (M); Expenditures, $20,008; Total giving, $18,000; Grants to individuals, 18 grants totaling $18,000 (high: $1,000, low: $1,000).
Type of support: Employee-related scholarships.
EIN: 846042789

4112
Louis D. Traurig Scholarship Trust
c/o Lawrence H. Engelman
P.O. Box 369
Middlebury, CT 06762
Contact: Rabbi Eric Polokoff, Tr.
Application address: 82 Hampton Rd., Southbury, CT 06488

Foundation type: Independent foundation
Limitations: Scholarships to residents of the greater Waterbury, CT, area.
Financial data: Year ended 12/31/2004. Assets, $679,411 (M); Expenditures, $34,567; Total giving, $30,000; Grants to individuals, 14 grants totaling $30,000.
Type of support: Scholarships—to individuals.
Application information:
    Initial approach: Letter or telephone.
    Deadline(s): Feb. 15
    Additional information: Completion of formal application required, including transcripts.
EIN: 222936329

4113
Travel Industry Association of America Foundation
1100 New York Ave., N.W., Ste. 450
Washington, DC 20005-3934   (202) 408-8422
Contact: Robert C. McClure, V.P., Membership and Devel.
FAX: (202) 408-1255; URL: http://www.tia.org/about/Foundation.html

Foundation type: Public charity
Limitations: Scholarships to graduates who have been nominated to participate in travel and tourism programs.
Financial data: Year ended 12/31/2003. Assets, $477,360 (M); Expenditures, $36,931; Total giving, $35,000; Grants to individuals, 10 grants totaling $35,000 (high: $4,000, low: $3,000).
Type of support: Scholarships—to individuals; Awards/grants by nomination only.
Application information:
    Deadline(s): Mar. and Oct.
    Additional information: Completion of formal nomination required; Applications are only accepted from students nominated by schools.
EIN: 520231139

4114
Treacy Company
P.O. Box 1479
Helena, MT 59624
Contact: James O'Connell, Chair.

Foundation type: Independent foundation
Limitations: Scholarships to financially needy freshmen and sophomore college students who are residents of ID, MT, ND, and SD.
Publications: Annual report.
Financial data: Year ended 12/31/2004. Assets, $2,479,358 (M); Expenditures, $159,437; Total giving, $118,303; Grants to individuals, 74 grants totaling $27,300.
Type of support: Undergraduate support.
Application information: Application form required.
    Initial approach: Letter.
    Deadline(s): June 15
    Applicants should submit the following:
        1) Transcripts
    Additional information: Applications should be sent by mail.
Program description:
    Scholarship Program: Recipients are chosen by the Scholarship Selection Committee on the basis of personal motivation and financial need. Scholarships are renewable for up to four years. Grants are paid directly to the institution to be applied to the student's account. The company awards approximately 60 scholarships each year, the number of new awards depending on the number of renewals.
EIN: 810270257

4115
William F. Treacy Scholarship Fund
115-06 Myrtle Ave.
Richmond Hill, NY 11418   (718) 847-8484
Contact: John T. Ahern, Tr.; Ed Ford, Tr.

Foundation type: Independent foundation
Limitations: Scholarships to sons, daughters, and grandchildren of members of the International Union of Operating Engineers (IUOE) Local 30, in NY.

Financial data: Year ended 12/31/2004. Assets, $9,849 (M); Expenditures, $43,428; Total giving, $36,000; Grants to individuals, totaling $36,000.
Fields of interest: Labor unions/organizations; Engineering.
Type of support: Undergraduate support.
Application information: Deadline June 1; Completion of formal application required, including essay, high school transcripts, SAT scores, and letters of recommendation.
Program description:
    Scholarship Program: Generally, awards do not exceed $1,000 per recipient, per school year, and are renewable for up to four years of study at any accredited college or university.
EIN: 237442878

4116
Jane & Gunby Treakle Charitable & Educational Foundation, Inc.
P.O. Box 420
Irvington, VA 22480-0420
Application address: c/o Director, P.O. Box 1419, Kilmarnock, VA 22482

Foundation type: Independent foundation
Limitations: Scholarships to residents of the Irvington, VA, area.
Financial data: Year ended 11/30/2004. Assets, $951,400 (M); Expenditures, $48,228; Total giving, $22,350; Grants to individuals, totaling $22,350.
Type of support: Scholarships—to individuals.
Application information: Contact foundation for current application deadline; Completion of formal application required.
EIN: 510215563

4117
Trefler Foundation
233 Needham St., Rm. 420
Newton, MA 02464   (617) 454-1135
Contact: Pamela Trefler, Tr.

Foundation type: Independent foundation
Limitations: Scholarships to individuals for higher education.
Financial data: Year ended 12/31/2004. Assets, $520,732 (M); Expenditures, $1,244,953; Total giving, $647,838.
Type of support: Graduate support; Undergraduate support.
Application information: Contact foundation for current application deadline/guidelines.
EIN: 043369962

4118
John E. Trembly Foundation
P.O. Box 274
Council Grove, KS 66846
Scholarship address: c/o Council Grove High School, 129 Hockaday St., Council Grove, KS 66846, tel.: (620) 767-5149

Foundation type: Independent foundation
Limitations: Scholarships to KS students attending a KS college other than Kansas State University or Emporia State University.
Financial data: Year ended 12/31/2004. Assets, $1,331,031 (M); Expenditures, $79,713; Total giving, $70,734; Grants to individuals, 12 grants totaling $6,125.
Type of support: Scholarships—to individuals.

Application information: Application form required.
   Deadline(s): Apr. 15
Program description:
   Scholarship Program: Scholarships are paid directly to the school. Priority is given to renewal scholarships.
EIN: 486106606

4119
Trial Lawyers Foundation for Youth Education
c/o Merrill Lynch Trust Co.
1300 Merrill Lynch Dr., 3rd Fl.
Pennington, NJ   08534
Application address: c/o Robstown High School, Financial Aid Office, Hwy. 44, Robstown, TX 78380, tel.: (361) 387-5999

Foundation type: Independent foundation
Limitations: Scholarships to full-time students attending, or registered to attend, a college or university, who graduated, or are graduating from, Robstown High School, TX.
Financial data: Year ended 12/31/2002. Assets, $1,064,371 (M); Expenditures, $182,409; Total giving, $155,150; Grants to individuals, 252 grants totaling $155,150 (high: $1,200, low: $250).
Type of support: Support to graduates or students of specific schools; Undergraduate support.
Application information: Deadlines Mar. 19 for graduating seniors, June 4 for in-college applicants; Completion of formal application required, including transcripts and a letter of recommendation.
EIN: 866267254

4120
Triangle Community Foundation
4813 Emperor Blvd., Ste. 130
P.O. Box 12834
Research Triangle Park, NC   27709
(919) 474-8370
Contact: Krystin Jorgenson, Cont.
FAX: (919) 941-9208; E-mail: info@trianglecf.org; Additional E-mails: krystin@trianglecf.org and cathy@trianglecf.org; URL: http://www.trianglecf.org

Foundation type: Community foundation
Limitations: Grants and scholarships to residents of Durham, Wake, Orange, and Chatham counties, NC., and one scholarship per year is awarded to a child of a Newton Instrument Co. employee.
Publications: Annual report; Newsletter.
Financial data: Year ended 06/30/2005. Assets, $100,752,459 (M); Expenditures, $10,417,732; Total giving, $9,115,831.
Fields of interest: Medical school/education; Women.
Type of support: Employee-related scholarships; Undergraduate support.
Application information: Applications accepted. Application form required. Application form available on the grantmaker's Web site.
   Applicants should submit the following:
      1) Transcripts
   Additional information: See Web site for additional programs and application information.
Program descriptions:
   GlaxoSmithKline Opportunity Scholarships: Awards scholarships of up to $5,000 per year for up to four years to legal residents of the U.S. who maintain permanent residence in Durham, Orange, Wake or Chatham counties, NC, for at least six

months. Recipients must demonstrate the potential to succeed despite adversity as well as an exceptional desire to improve himself or herself through further education or training. The award covers tuition, required fees, and books for a maximum of four years.
   Robert Franklin Black Scholarship: Awards two annual scholarships to students who demonstrate academic achievement, financial need, participation in school and community activities, work experience and educational goals. Preference is given to students interested in pursuing their education in a public university or college in NC. However, if NC institutions do not offer a degree program for which student is interested, institutions out-of-state will be considered.
   Gertrude B. Elion Mentored Medical Student Research Awards: One-year awards to female medical students attending NC-based medical schools, allowing them time from their studies to pursue health-related interests under the guidance of a mentor.
   George and Mary Newton Scholarship: One scholarship per year is awarded to a child of a Newton Instrument Company employee. Applications are available at Newton Instruments.
EIN: 561380796

4121
Tribble Foundation
P.O. Box 796
Seneca, SC   29679-0796   (864) 882-9440
Contact: Robert N. McLellan, Tr.
Application address: P.O. Box 794, Seneca, SC 29678-0794

Foundation type: Independent foundation
Limitations: Scholarships of a minimum of $1,000 to residents of Oconee County, SC.
Financial data: Year ended 06/30/2005. Assets, $1,002,603 (M); Expenditures, $37,110; Total giving, $35,730; Grants to individuals, totaling $21,480.
Type of support: Scholarships—to individuals.
Application information: Application form required.
   Deadline(s): Apr. 1.
   Additional information: Applications available from guidance counselors at local high schools.
EIN: 237023624

4122
The Trico Foundation
c/o Trico Electric Cooperative, Inc.
P.O. Box 930
Marana, AZ   85653-0930

Foundation type: Company-sponsored foundation
Limitations: Scholarships to Trico Electric Cooperative consumers, and their dependent children, who reside in Pima, Pinal, and Santa Cruz counties, AZ.
Financial data: Year ended 12/31/2004. Assets, $973,401 (M); Expenditures, $83,210; Total giving, $66,700; Grants to individuals, 37 grants totaling $66,700 (high: $4,600, low: $460).
Type of support: Technical education support; Undergraduate support.
Application information: Application form required.
   Applicants should submit the following:
      1) Transcripts
      2) Letter(s) of recommendation
   Additional information: Contact foundation for current application deadline; Application should also include outline of financial need; Application address: c/o Trico Electric

Cooperative, Inc., 5100 W. Ina Rd., Tucson, AZ 85743-9746.
Program description:
   Trico Foundation Scholarship Program: Applicants must have at least a 2.5 GPA and plan to be full-time undergraduates with a minimum of 12 units. The average amount for a two-year scholarship is $1,840, and for a four-year scholarship, it is $4,600.
EIN: 942941045

4123
George Trimble Special Need Trust
c/o Bank of America, N.A.
P.O. Box 831041
Dallas, TX   75283-1041
Application address: c/o Bank of America, N.A., Attn.: Julie Dalton, P.O. Box 1122, Wichita, KS 67201-1122, tel.: (316) 216-4097

Foundation type: Independent foundation
Limitations: Scholarships to graduates of El Dorado High School, KS.
Financial data: Year ended 12/31/2004. Assets, $386,507 (M); Expenditures, $20,739; Total giving, $17,500; Grants to individuals, 27 grants totaling $13,500.
Type of support: Support to graduates or students of specific schools; Undergraduate support.
Application information: Application form required.
   Deadline(s): May 1
   Applicants should submit the following:
      1) Letter(s) of recommendation
      2) Essay
      3) Transcripts
   Additional information: Applications may be obtained from the principal or counselors at El Dorado High School; Interviews required.
Program descriptions:
   Good Citizen Scholarships: Grants shall be made for one academic year (grants may be renewed for up to four years) and shall be in such amounts as the Selection Committee shall determine up to the full cost of tuition, books and lodging for attending an accredited institution of higher learning. Each applicant shall have graduated from El Dorado High School and, in addition, shall:
   · have maintained at least a "B" average in high school
   · have completed an application form
   · have submitted a written memorandum to the Trust concerning his or her desire to continue his or her studies at an accredited institution of higher learning and why, with such additional education, he or she can become a more productive and useful citizen.
The Selection Committee shall consider financial need and support, moral and leadership qualities, scholastic achievement, diligence toward chosen tasks and other personal objectives in determining to whom to make awards. Grantees shall attend the two or four-year accredited college or university of their choice on a full-time basis. To be considered for a scholarship for a subsequent year, an individual must provide evidence that such individual is making satisfactory progress towards a degree.
   Opportunity for Advancement Scholarships: Grants are determined by the Selection Committee and shall be made to selected graduates of El Dorado High School to attend technical training and vocation schools, renewable for one year upon satisfactory completion of the first year of work. Applicants shall have attended secondary education schools for no more than two years prior

to the date of application hereunder. Applicants shall:

· have completed an application form
· have submitted a written memorandum to the Trust concerning his or her desire to pursue the training indicated and why with such training he or she can become a more productive and useful citizen.

The Selection Committee shall judge applicants upon consideration of their financial need and support; any statement of indicated experience; any statement of objectives; character references and a statement concerning the applicant's reasons for believing that vocational or technical education would be advantageous to him or her and to society. Grantees shall attend an approved vocational or technical school of his or her choice on a full-time basis.
EIN: 486319821

4124
Trinity Community Services & Educational Foundation
1050 Porter St.
Detroit, MI 48226 (313) 965-4450
Contact: Fr. Russell Kohler, Pres.

Foundation type: Public charity
Limitations: Scholarships to individuals in public schools in MI, with emphasis on Most Holy Trinity Elementary School and St. Vincent's School.
Financial data: Year ended 12/31/2003. Assets, $695,439 (M); Expenditures, $130,603; Total giving, $30,109; Grants to individuals, totaling $13,890.
Fields of interest: Elementary/secondary education.
Type of support: Support to graduates or students of specific schools; Precollege support.
Application information: Contact foundation for current application deadline/guidelines.
EIN: 383129349

4125
Trinity Foundation
P.O. Box 7008
Pine Bluff, AR 71611-7008
Contact: Drew Atkinson, Secy.

Foundation type: Independent foundation
Limitations: Scholarships to graduating high school seniors at specific high schools in Pine Bluff, Little Rock, Benton, and Bauxite, AR.
Financial data: Year ended 09/30/2004. Assets, $18,603,421 (M); Expenditures, $1,227,580; Total giving, $1,118,700; Grants to individuals, totaling $139,150.
Type of support: Support to graduates or students of specific schools; Undergraduate support.
Application information: Application form required.
Deadline(s): Apr. 10.
Additional information: Applications available only at the guidance offices of eligible public high schools.
EIN: 716050288

4126
Dr. H. A. Trippeer Charitable Foundation
925 4th Ave., Ste. 2900
Seattle, WA 98104-1158
Contact: John A. Gose, Tr.

Foundation type: Independent foundation

Limitations: Scholarships to graduates of high schools in Walla Walla County, WA, who are attending or who have been accepted to attend four-year undergraduate degree programs at accredited colleges or universities.
Financial data: Year ended 12/31/2004. Assets, $1,546,762 (M); Expenditures, $66,823; Total giving, $58,900; Grants to individuals, totaling $58,900.
Type of support: Support to graduates or students of specific schools; Undergraduate support.
Application information:
Initial approach: Letter or telephone.
Deadline(s): Apr. 25
Additional information: Completion of formal application required, including transcript, PSAT score, biography, essay, and three recommendations; Interviews required.
EIN: 916371911

4127
Carl W. Troedson Educational Fund
c/o Wells Fargo Bank Nevada, N.A.
P.O. Box 95021
Henderson, NV 89009
Application address: c/o Morrow County School District, P.O. Box 368, Lexington, OR 92835

Foundation type: Independent foundation
Limitations: Scholarships to students of the Morrow County School District, OR.
Financial data: Year ended 06/30/2005. Assets, $654,564 (M); Expenditures, $64,656; Total giving, $57,667; Grants to individuals, totaling $57,667.
Type of support: Scholarships—to individuals; Support to graduates or students of specific schools.
Application information: Deadline first Fri. in May; Completion of formal application required; Forms available from Morrow County School District.
EIN: 936087212

4128
Barbara Davies Troisi Foundation
230 Park Ave.
New York, NY 10169
Contact: Frank X. Troisi, Tr.

Foundation type: Independent foundation
Limitations: Scholarships to individuals with reading and learning disabilities, primarily in NJ and NY.
Financial data: Year ended 12/31/2004. Assets, $469,740 (M); Expenditures, $32,654; Total giving, $26,013; Grants to individuals, 7 grants totaling $16,000.
Fields of interest: Learning disorders.
Type of support: Scholarships—to individuals.
Application information: Applications by letter accepted throughout the year.
EIN: 133534989

4129
Blanche Barr Trone Scholarship Trust
20152 East Ave. N.
Battle Creek, MI 49017 (269) 964-7348
Contact: Stig Renstrom, Tr.

Foundation type: Independent foundation
Limitations: Scholarships to financially needy high school graduates of the Battle Creek, MI, area. Preference is shown to those studying pharmacy, or other medical fields.

Financial data: Year ended 12/31/2004. Assets, $598,607 (M); Expenditures, $22,841; Total giving, $18,000; Grants to individuals, totaling $18,000.
Fields of interest: Medical school/education; Pharmacy/prescriptions.
Type of support: Undergraduate support.
Application information: Deadline June; Completion of formal application required, including high school transcripts, three personal and educational references, parents' tax return, and financial information.
EIN: 386500164

4130
Esther L. Trotter Charitable Trust
c/o U.S. Bank, N.A.
415 Francis St.
P.O. Box 308
St. Joseph, MO 64503-0308 (816) 364-7235
Contact: Sonya Flanders, Trust Off., U.S. Bank, N.A.

Foundation type: Independent foundation
Limitations: Grants to St. Joseph or Buchanan County, MO, residents who are physically handicapped and require educational assistance at any academic level. Grants may be used for tuition, specialized equipment, transportation costs, and/or other items related to the individual's educational pursuits.
Financial data: Year ended 10/31/2004. Assets, $181,071 (M); Expenditures, $10,604; Total giving, $7,544; Grants to individuals, totaling $7,544.
Fields of interest: Vocational education; Disabilities, people with.
Type of support: Grants for special needs.
Application information: Applications accepted. Application form required.
Deadline(s): July 1
Additional information: Include description of handicap from physician, and parents' or student's tax return.
EIN: 436436638

4131
Paul A. Troutman Foundation
c/o Community Bank, N.A.
9 N. Centre St.
Pottsville, PA 17901
Contact: Kimberly Arthur-Tressler, V.P. and Trust Off., Community Banks
Application address: 201 St. Johns Church Rd., Camphill, PA 17011

Foundation type: Independent foundation
Limitations: Scholarships to graduating seniors of Millersburgh School District, Millersburgh, PA.
Financial data: Year ended 11/30/2004. Assets, $876,318 (M); Expenditures, $53,700; Total giving, $44,250; Grants to individuals, totaling $14,000.
Type of support: Support to graduates or students of specific schools; Undergraduate support.
Application information: Applications accepted throughout the year; Contact foundation for current application guidelines; Completion of formal application required.
EIN: 232086508

4132
Florence B. Trueman Educational Trust
401 Fairleigh Ct.
Tracys Landing, MD 20779 (410) 859-5699
Contact: J. Scott Whitney, Tr.

Foundation type: Independent foundation
Limitations: Scholarships to graduates of public high schools in Calvert County, MD, who are also residents of the county.
Financial data: Year ended 06/30/2004.
Assets, $837,035 (M); Expenditures, $73,985; Total giving, $37,500; Grants to individuals, totaling $37,500.
Type of support: Support to graduates or students of specific schools; Undergraduate support.
Application information: Applications accepted. Application form required.
  Initial approach: Letter.
  Deadline(s): None
  Additional information: Application forms available from school guidance offices.
EIN: 521649301

4133
The Trumansburg Charitable Trust
P.O. Box 368
Trumansburg, NY 14886-0368

Foundation type: Operating foundation
Limitations: Scholarships to graduates of Charles O. Dickerson High School, Trumansburg, NY, pursuing careers as primary or secondary school teachers.
Financial data: Year ended 12/31/2002.
Assets, $640,840 (M); Expenditures, $68,526; Total giving, $58,000; Grants to individuals, 14 grants totaling $58,000 (high: $5,000, low: $1,000).
Fields of interest: Elementary school/education; Secondary school/education; Teacher school/ education; Education.
Type of support: Support to graduates or students of specific schools; Undergraduate support.
Application information: Deadline Feb. 28; Completion of formal application required.
EIN: 161422770

4134
Trump Indiana Foundation
6012 W. Industrial Hwy.
Gary, IN 46406

Foundation type: Operating foundation
Limitations: Undergraduate scholarships to high school seniors from Gary, IN.
Financial data: Year ended 12/31/2003.
Assets, $1,532,870 (M); Expenditures, $139,036; Total giving, $128,009; Grants to individuals, 97 grants totaling $128,009 (high: $25,000, low: $10).
Type of support: Undergraduate support.
Application information: Deadline Apr. 15; Contact foundation for current application guidelines; Completion of formal application required.
EIN: 351989786

4135
Paul and Ida Trump Scholarship Fund
c/o Valley View Fin. Group
5901 College Blvd., Ste. 100
Overland, KS 66211 (913) 319-0350

Foundation type: Independent foundation

Limitations: Scholarships to graduates of Osawatomie High School, KS.
Financial data: Year ended 04/30/2005.
Assets, $251,415 (M); Expenditures, $21,258; Total giving, $18,000; Grants to individuals, totaling $18,000.
Type of support: Support to graduates or students of specific schools; Undergraduate support.
Application information: Contact fund for current application deadline; Application by letter.
EIN: 481240121

4136
Truscott Family Scholarship Fund
c/o JPMorgan Chase Bank, N.A.
P.O. Box 1308
Milwaukee, WI 53201
Application address: c/o JPMorgan Chase Bank, N.A., 1800 Broadway, Boulder, CO 80302, tel.: (303) 245-6703

Foundation type: Independent foundation
Limitations: Scholarships to promising students in the Thompson School District R2-J, CO, for college expenses.
Financial data: Year ended 12/31/2004.
Assets, $34,207 (M); Expenditures, $11,075; Total giving, $6,500; Grants to individuals, totaling $6,500.
Type of support: Support to graduates or students of specific schools; Undergraduate support.
Application information: Contact fund for current application deadline/guidelines; Initial approach by letter or telephone.
EIN: 846192161

4137
Allene S. Trushel Scholarship Trust
c/o Citizens Trust Co.
10 N. Main St.
Coudersport, PA 16915 (814) 274-9150
Application address: c/o Superintendent, Oswayo Valley School District, P.O. Box 610, Shinglehouse, PA 16478, tel.: (814) 697-7175

Foundation type: Independent foundation
Limitations: Scholarships to graduates of Oswayo Valley School District, PA, schools who have completed their entire senior year while residing within the district.
Publications: Application guidelines.
Financial data: Year ended 12/31/2004.
Assets, $757,553 (M); Expenditures, $41,113; Total giving, $35,817; Grants to individuals, 7 grants totaling $35,817 (high: $12,033, low: $337).
Fields of interest: Medical school/education; Nursing school/education; Veterinary medicine.
Type of support: Support to graduates or students of specific schools; Undergraduate support.
Application information: Deadline Apr. 15; Completion of formal application required, including transcripts and proof of enrollment or acceptance; Applications available from the guidance counselor at Oswayo Valley Junior-Senior High School, PA.
Program description:
  Trushel Scholarship Program: Primary consideration will be given to applicants attending medical school, veterinary school, or nursing school. Secondary consideration will be given to applicants entering their junior year of a pre-medical or pre-veterinary undergraduate program or those attending a one-year LPN program. Scholarships are renewable, but applications must be submitted each year for consideration.
EIN: 251419907

4138
Trust for Higher Education of Graduates of Accredited Fillmore County, Nebraska High Schools
c/o Geneva State Bank
896 G. St.
P.O. Box 313
Geneva, NE 68361-0313
Contact: Evelyn M. Volkmer, Trust. Off., Geneva State Bank

Foundation type: Independent foundation
Limitations: Scholarships to students of Fillmore County, NE, high schools, for higher education in NE.
Publications: Annual report.
Financial data: Year ended 11/30/2004.
Assets, $392,775 (M); Expenditures, $24,289; Total giving, $20,250; Grants to individuals, 24 grants totaling $20,250 (high: $1,500, low: $750).
Type of support: Support to graduates or students of specific schools; Undergraduate support.
Application information: Deadline Apr. or May; Completion of formal application required, including essay, class rank, and GPA.
EIN: 237159935

4139
Florence J. Tryon Trust
c/o Bank of America, N.A.
P.O. Box 6767
Providence, RI 02940-6767
Application addresses: c/o Guidance Dept., Westfield Vocational High School, Westfield, MA 01085 or c/o Guidance Dept., St. Mary's High School, Westfield, MA 01085

Foundation type: Independent foundation
Limitations: Scholarships only to male residents of Westfield, MA, between the ages of 16 and 22, who have graduated from the following MA schools: St. Mary's High School, Westfield, Westfield High School, or Westfield Technical Vocational High.
Financial data: Year ended 10/31/2004.
Assets, $377,528 (M); Expenditures, $18,895; Total giving, $13,800; Grants to individuals, 8 grants totaling $10,800 (high: $2,000, low: $1,000).
Fields of interest: Men.
Type of support: Support to graduates or students of specific schools; Undergraduate support.
Application information: Deadline Apr. 30; Completion of formal application required.
EIN: 046033568

4140
Grace F. Tschirgi Scholarship Fund
c/o U.S. Bank, N.A.
P.O. Box 2043, LC4NE
Milwaukee, WI 53201-9116
Application address: c/o Tom Collins, Advisory Comm., Shuttleworth & Ingersoll, U.S. Bank Bldg., 5th Fl., Cedar Rapids, IA 52401

Foundation type: Independent foundation
Limitations: Scholarships to residents of Linn County, IA.
Financial data: Year ended 05/31/2005.
Assets, $936,457 (M); Expenditures, $49,322; Total giving, $40,000; Grants to individuals, totaling $40,000.
Type of support: Scholarships—to individuals.
Application information:
  Deadline(s): Applications accepted throughout the year.

Additional information: Contact foundation for current application guidelines; Personal interview optional.
EIN: 426054236

4141
TSTE Foundation
301 Mamon Dr.
Longview, TX   75604-5411   (903) 237-3493

Foundation type: Independent foundation
Limitations: Scholarships for the study of engineering at schools primarily in TX.
Financial data: Year ended 12/31/2004. Assets, $3,096 (M); Expenditures, $8,750; Total giving, $8,750; Grants to individuals, totaling $8,750.
Type of support: Undergraduate support.
Application information: Applications not accepted.
Additional information: Unsolicited requests for funds not accepted.
EIN: 760637320

4142
Tucson Osteopathic Medical Foundation
(formerly Tucson Osteopathic Foundation)
3182 N. Swan Rd.
Tucson, AZ   85712   (520) 299-4545
Contact: Susan Henderson, Assoc. Dir.
FAX: (520) 299-4609; E-mail: info@tomf.org; Additional tel.: (800) 201-8663; URL: http://www.tomf.org/

Foundation type: Operating foundation
Limitations: Scholarships and student loans to AZ residents pursuing D.O. degrees at AOA-accredited colleges of osteopathic medicine. Preference is given to residents of the seven southernmost counties of AZ: Cochise, Graham, Greenlee, Pima, Pinal, Santa Cruz, and Yuma.
Publications: Application guidelines.
Financial data: Year ended 06/30/2004. Assets, $11,018,165 (M); Expenditures, $813,809; Total giving, $66,730; Grants to individuals, 4 grants totaling $50,000 (high: $12,500, low: $12,500).
Fields of interest: Medical school/education; Health organizations.
Type of support: Graduate support.
Application information: Application form required.
Initial approach: Letter.
Deadline(s): Dec. 1
Applicants should submit the following:
1) FAF
2) GPA
Additional information: Applicant should include two letters of recommendation (one of which must be from an osteopathic physician), personal statement; Interviews required; Recipients notified by Apr. 30.
Program description:
Founders' Awards Program: Grants are initially made in the form of a scholarship but become a loan if the recipient does not establish a primary practice in southern AZ (Cochise, Graham, Greenlee, Pima, Pinal, Santa Cruz, and Yuma counties). If the recipient maintains his/her principal medical practice in one of the seven counties then 20 percent of the scholarship is forgiven for each year of practice. If the recipient does not set up his/her principal medical practice in one of the seven counties then the scholarship becomes a loan at an interest rate comparable to currently available educational loan programs. The loan is interest-free through the time of residency.

Loan payments can be deferred during other advanced professional training and military service at the foundation's discretion. After deferment period, if recipient has not established a primary practice in southern AZ, full repayment of the loan will be required within a maximum schedule of five years. Recipients are chosen with special consideration of county of residence, academic record and activities, financial need, statement of goals on application form and first-time personal interview.
EIN: 742449503

4143
Tudor Foundation
c/o Roger A. Rieger
411 University St., Ste. 1200
Seattle, WA   98101

Foundation type: Operating foundation
Limitations: Scholarships to post high school students for tuition, books, and related expenses.
Financial data: Year ended 12/31/2003. Assets, $57,556,277 (M); Expenditures, $9,014,125; Total giving, $269,459; Grants to individuals, totaling $26,895.
Type of support: Graduate support; Undergraduate support.
Application information: Applications not accepted.
EIN: 911708176

4144
T. J. Tufts Charitable Foundation
P.O. Box 422
Wilbur, WA   99185-0422
Contact: Charles Wyborney, Tr.

Foundation type: Independent foundation
Limitations: Scholarships to students of Wilbur Public Schools, WA, who have at least a 3.0 GPA.
Financial data: Year ended 12/31/2003. Assets, $695,608 (M); Expenditures, $47,465; Total giving, $29,982; Grants to individuals, totaling $17,000.
Type of support: Support to graduates or students of specific schools; Undergraduate support.
Application information: Application form required.
Deadline(s): Apr. 1
EIN: 911489095

4145
Berndine MacMullen Tuohy-University of Michigan Student Loan Fund
c/o West Michigan National Bank & Tr.
120 Cypress St., Trust Off.
Manistee, MI   49660   (231) 723-8867

Foundation type: Independent foundation
Limitations: Student loans to residents of Manistee, Mason, Wexford, and Benzie counties, MI, who have attended the University of Michigan for at least one year.
Financial data: Year ended 12/31/2004. Assets, $1,031,321 (M); Expenditures, $32,197; Total giving, $18,277; Grants to individuals, 3 grants totaling $18,277.
Type of support: Support to graduates or students of specific schools; Undergraduate support.
Application information: Applications accepted throughout the year; Completion of formal application required, including GPA, financial

budget, and copy of University of Michigan Student Acceptance Form or current academic record.
EIN: 382528185

4146
Olive Tupper Foundation
1210 1/2 Arkansas St.
Lake Charles, LA   70605

Foundation type: Independent foundation
Limitations: Scholarships to financially needy full-time undergraduate and graduate nursing students who have graduated from an accredited high school and plan to attend McNeese State University, LA, or other qualified schools.
Financial data: Year ended 08/31/2004. Assets, $2,443,416 (M); Expenditures, $135,392; Total giving, $119,690; Grants to individuals, 45 grants totaling $79,690 (high: $5,000, low: $1,000).
Fields of interest: Nursing school/education.
Type of support: Support to graduates or students of specific schools; Graduate support; Undergraduate support.
Application information: Application form required.
Deadline(s): 60 days prior to start of the semester
Applicants should submit the following:
1) Essay
2) ACT
3) GPA
4) Letter(s) of recommendation
5) Transcripts
Additional information: High school students should provide evidence of college acceptance; all applicants should provide most recent tax return.
Program description:
Nursing School Scholarship Program: Applicants must possess good character, ambitious purpose, and positive qualities, and should be capable of using educational opportunities to enhance personal excellence and to contribute to his/her community. Residents of Allen and Jefferson Davis parishes, LA, will be given priority. Applicants must also be nursing students accepted to or currently attending McNeese State University, LA, except in the case where enrollment precludes the applicant's admission to McNeese. In this case, the student may enroll at any educational organization which provides a curriculum in nursing (with the exception of pass/fail and remedial courses). In addition, applicants must have a maximum adjusted gross income, (as determined by the federal tax return) of $20,000 plus $3,000 for each child under the age of 23 residing at home or in school. Recipients are selected on the basis of academic achievement and financial need, and are notified by letter. As a condition of the award, recipients must furnish a copy of the courses taken and grade records to the foundation and submit current year tax returns every year.
EIN: 721277047

4147
The Turco Foundation
1101 Moore Rd.
Avon, OH   44011
Application addresses: c/o Loreto Turco, Jr., 1784 Arabian Ln., Palm Harbor, FL 34685, tel.: (440) 934-1902, c/o Tracey Lynne McIntosh, 2855 Harwick Dr., Dunwoody, GA 30350

Foundation type: Independent foundation

Limitations: Scholarships to students accepted for enrollment or currently enrolled at an accredited educational institution.
Financial data: Year ended 12/31/2004.
Assets, $2,034,217 (M); Expenditures, $76,426; Total giving, $76,181; Grants to individuals, totaling $55,000.
Type of support: Undergraduate support.
Application information:
Deadline(s): June 1 and Dec. 1
Additional information: Completion of formal application required, including 500-word essay, two letters of recommendation, transcript and ACT or SAT scores if available. Recipients must maintain academic records that place them in good standing with institutions.
EIN: 341942938

4148
Sam and Ida Turken Charitable Foundation
1015 Gayley Ave., No. 1264
Los Angeles, CA 90024

Foundation type: Independent foundation
Limitations: Scholarships for higher education, primarily to residents of MO and TN.
Financial data: Year ended 12/31/2003.
Assets, $310,330 (M); Expenditures, $781,972; Total giving, $777,900.
Type of support: Scholarships—to individuals.
Application information: Applications accepted. Application form required.
Deadline(s): None
EIN: 431431267

4149
Marie R. & Ervine Turner Educational Foundation, Inc.
P.O. Box 620
Jackson, KY 41339 (606) 666-9366
Contact: Lesley Warrix-Allen, Exec. Secy.

Foundation type: Operating foundation
Limitations: Scholarships to residents of KY, primarily in Breathitt County, for higher education.
Financial data: Year ended 12/31/2004.
Assets, $0 (M); Expenditures, $230,963; Total giving, $147,210; Grants to individuals, 218 grants totaling $147,210 (high: $1,575, low: $135).
Type of support: Scholarships—to individuals.
Application information: Contact foundation for current application deadline; Completion of formal application required; Applications available at foundation office or schools in Breathitt County, KY.
EIN: 611333558

4150
Lena & Harry Turner Foundation
c/o Bank of America, N.A.
P.O. Box 831041
Dallas, TX 75283-1041
Contact: Marshall Sutton, Tr.
Application address for individuals: 110 S.W. 2nd St., Grand Prairie, TX 75050-5603

Foundation type: Independent foundation
Limitations: Scholarships to residents of Grand Prairie, TX.
Financial data: Year ended 12/31/2004.
Assets, $678,166 (M); Expenditures, $43,945; Total giving, $23,540; Grants to individuals, totaling $20,540.

Type of support: Scholarships—to individuals.
Application information: Applications accepted throughout the year; Contact foundation for current application guidelines.
EIN: 237416737

4151
Mark E. & Emily Turner Foundation
P.O. Box 149
Presque Isle, ME 04769-2524
Contact: Marcus J. Barresi, Chair.
Application address: P.O. Box 807, Presque Isle, ME 04769, tel.: (207) 764-5639

Foundation type: Independent foundation
Limitations: Scholarships to Presque Isle, ME, area residents, primarily for the first year of college.
Financial data: Year ended 12/31/2004.
Assets, $3,948 (M); Expenditures, $38,321; Total giving, $38,100; Grants to individuals, totaling $38,100.
Type of support: Undergraduate support.
Application information: Applications by letter, including course of study and qualifications of applicant, accepted throughout the year.
EIN: 016019456

4152
Bismarck H. Turner Scholarship Trust
c/o U.S. Bank, N.A.
P.O. Box 3168
Portland, OR 97208
Application address: c/o Helene Paroif, Educational Svc. District No. 101, W. 1025 Indiana Ave., Spokane, WA 99205

Foundation type: Independent foundation
Limitations: Scholarships to graduates of high schools in Spokane or Pend Oreille counties, WA, or Bonner or Kootenai counties, ID.
Financial data: Year ended 03/31/2005.
Assets, $486,041 (M); Expenditures, $30,406; Total giving, $23,347; Grants to individuals, totaling $23,347.
Type of support: Support to graduates or students of specific schools; Undergraduate support.
Application information: Application form required.
Initial approach: Letter.
Deadline(s): Apr. 15.
Applicants should submit the following:
1) Transcripts
2) FAF
Additional information: Application must be submitted to the superintendent of qualified school district.
Program description:
Scholarship Program: Selection is based on scholastics, character, and financial need. Recipients may reapply for subsequent years if they maintain at least a "B" average.
EIN: 916254764

4153
Turning Leaf Foundation, Inc.
16 Highland Ave.
Cambridge, MA 02139

Foundation type: Independent foundation
Limitations: Scholarships to individuals in WI.
Financial data: Year ended 12/31/2004.
Assets, $1,094,735 (M); Expenditures, $40,184; Total giving, $35,357; Grants to individuals, totaling $35,357.
Type of support: Scholarships—to individuals.

Application information: Applications not accepted.
EIN: 043397818

4154
Tuscora Park Health & Wellness Foundation
460 W. Paige Ave.
Barberton, OH 44203 (330) 745-5995
Scholarship application address: c/o Barbara Berlin, Nursing Office, Barberton Citizens Hospital, Nursing Scholarship Comm., 155 5th St. N.E., Barberton, OH 44203, tel.: (330) 745-1611, ext. 3352
FAX: (330) 745-3990;
E-mail: tuschealthfdn@yahoo.com; URL: http://www.bcfcharity.org/bcf/tuscorapark_txt.html

Foundation type: Independent foundation
Limitations: Scholarships to residents of southern Summit County, OH, as well as the Barberton, Kenmore, Manchester, Coventry, Norton, Doylestown, Rittman, Canal Fulton, Green, and Clinton areas, OH, for nursing education. Applicants must be currently enrolled or accepted for enrollment in an accredited school of higher education, leading to a diploma or degree in professional nursing.
Financial data: Year ended 12/31/2004.
Assets, $4,194,167 (M); Expenditures, $307,286; Total giving, $157,003; Grants to individuals, 18 grants totaling $157,003 (high: $45,000, low: $3,962).
Fields of interest: Nursing school/education.
Type of support: Undergraduate support.
Application information: Applications accepted. Application form required.
Deadline(s): Mar. 13
Applicants should submit the following:
1) Transcripts
Additional information: Interviews required.
EIN: 341193807

4155
The Jay Lloyd and Corrine Tuthill Memorial Scholarship Trust
P.O. Box 250
Hayden, AL 35079

Foundation type: Independent foundation
Limitations: Scholarships primarily to residents of Birmingham, AL.
Financial data: Year ended 12/31/2004.
Assets, $562,328 (M); Expenditures, $19,004; Total giving, $15,075; Grants to individuals, totaling $15,075.
Type of support: Scholarships—to individuals.
Application information: Applications not accepted.
EIN: 636138369

4156
Two Harbors High School Senior Scholarship Fund
c/o Wells Fargo Bank Minnesota, N.A.
230 W. Superior St., Ste. 400
Duluth, MN 55802
Application address: c/o Two Harbors High School, 405 4th Ave., Two Harbors, MN 55616

Foundation type: Independent foundation
Limitations: Scholarships to graduates of Two Harbors High School, MN.
Financial data: Year ended 06/30/2005.
Assets, $340,815 (M); Expenditures, $20,721;

Total giving, $16,000; Grants to individuals, totaling $16,000.
Type of support: Support to graduates or students of specific schools; Undergraduate support.
Application information: Application form required.
Deadline(s): Contact foundation for current application deadline.
EIN: 416395607

4157
John Tyndale Scholarship Fund
(also known as John Tyndale Testamentary Trust)
c/o Mellon Financial Corp.
P.O. Box 185
Pittsburgh, PA 15230-9897

Foundation type: Independent foundation
Limitations: Scholarships to Tyndale family members and graduates of Central High School, PA.
Financial data: Year ended 09/30/2004.
Assets, $244,332 (M); Expenditures, $11,805; Total giving, $11,800; Grants to individuals, totaling $11,800.
Type of support: Scholarships—to individuals; Support to graduates or students of specific schools.
Application information: Applications accepted throughout the year; Contact fund for current application guidelines.
EIN: 236223859

4158
Tyson Foundation, Inc.
2210 W. Oaklawn Dr.
Springdale, AR 72762-6999   (479) 290-4955
Contact: Shelby Rogers, Pres.
FAX: (479) 290-7984

Foundation type: Independent foundation
Limitations: Scholarships to Tyson Foods Inc. employees and dependents of employees or growers, who are majoring in certain areas of business, agriculture, engineering, computer science, or nursing.
Financial data: Year ended 12/31/2004.
Assets, $28,386,296 (M); Expenditures, $1,005,894; Total giving, $753,283; Grants to individuals, totaling $594,783.
Fields of interest: Business school/education; Nursing school/education; Engineering school/education; Agriculture; Computer science.
Type of support: Internship funds; Undergraduate support.
Application information: Application form required.
Initial approach: Letter or telephone.
Deadline(s): Aug. 1
Additional information: Applications must be requested by last day of Feb.
Program description:
Scholarship Program: Applicants must earn a part of his or her school expenses by working in the summer and/or during the school year. In addition, applicants should demonstrate financial need, be U.S. citizens, attend school full-time, and maintain a 2.5 GPA. Scholarships are renewable provided the recipient can continue to meet all application requirements.
EIN: 237087948

4159
Maoz Tzur Foundation, Inc.
1860 Flatbush Ave.
Brooklyn, NY 11210
Contact: Charles Neiss, Pres.

Foundation type: Operating foundation
Limitations: Grants and scholarships, primarily in Israel, for religious and educational purposes.
Financial data: Year ended 12/31/2002.
Assets, $157,458 (M); Expenditures, $755,073; Total giving, $753,794; Grants to individuals, 50 grants totaling $402,865 (high: $94,050, low: $50).
Fields of interest: Jewish agencies & temples.
Type of support: Scholarships—to individuals.
Application information: Applications not accepted.
EIN: 113423569

4160
U.S. Navy Warner Trust
262 S. Chestnut St.
Fremont, IA 52561   (641) 933-4832
Contact: Susan Sieran, Tr.

Foundation type: Independent foundation
Limitations: Scholarships to high school graduates residing in the Fremont School District of IA, who meet minimum GPA requirements and maintain at least three-quarter credit hour schedules each semester.
Financial data: Year ended 12/31/2004.
Assets, $367,150 (M); Expenditures, $21,735; Total giving, $19,600; Grants to individuals, totaling $19,600.
Type of support: Scholarships—to individuals.
Application information: Applications by letter, including college choice, accepted throughout the year.
EIN: 426348143

4161
U.S.D. No. 380 Endowment Association
c/o Superintendent of Schools
P.O. Box 107
Vermillion, KS 66544-0107   (785) 382-6216

Foundation type: Independent foundation
Limitations: Scholarships to students in KS for higher education.
Financial data: Year ended 12/31/2004.
Assets, $1,162,736 (M); Expenditures, $34,400; Total giving, $8,691; Grants to individuals, totaling $8,691.
Type of support: Undergraduate support.
Application information:
Deadline(s): May 1
Additional information: Completion of formal application required, including transcript, two letters of recommendation, essay and list of other scholarships received.
EIN: 481122532

4162
UFA Widow's and Children's Fund
204 E. 23rd St
New York, NY 10010   (212) 683-4832
URL: http://www.ufalocal94.org

Foundation type: Public charity
Limitations: Scholarships to individuals who are surviving dependants of UFA members who were killed in the line of duty. Giving primarily in NY.
Financial data: Year ended 07/31/2003.
Assets, $24,266,670 (M); Expenditures, $46,015,203; Total giving, $45,972,724; Grants to individuals, totaling $21,284,456.
Fields of interest: Safety, education.
Type of support: Undergraduate support.

Application information: Contact fund for current application information.
EIN: 133047544

4163
UFCW Region 5 Educational Trust
(formerly Meat Cutters Educational Trust)
c/o UFCW, Region 5
1701 W. Northwest Hwy., Ste. 200
Grapevine, TX 76051-8107
Application address: c/o UFCW Scholarship Prog., Office of Education, 1775 K St., N.W., Washington, DC 20006

Foundation type: Independent foundation
Limitations: Scholarships to members and children of members of various UFCW Local Unions in TX, LA, OK, KS, MO, and AR. Applicants must be high school seniors who will graduate the following spring, be under 20 years of age as of Mar. 15 of their graduating year, and plan to enter college in the fall. Scholarships are $1,500 for one year.
Publications: Informational brochure (including application guidelines).
Financial data: Year ended 12/31/2004.
Assets, $210,507 (M); Expenditures, $19,226; Total giving, $13,500; Grants to individuals, 9 grants totaling $13,500 (high: $1,500, low: $1,500).
Application information: Application form required.
Deadline(s): Dec. 31
Additional information: Application must include SAT or ACT scores.
EIN: 752035368

4164
UIC Foundation, Inc.
P.O. Box 890
Barrow, AK 99723-0890   (907) 852-4460
Contact: Mabel J. Kaleak
FAX: (907) 852-4459; *E-mail:* mkaleak@ukpik.com

Foundation type: Company-sponsored foundation
Limitations: Scholarships to UIC shareholders and their children to attend any university, college, or training institute.
Publications: Application guidelines; Financial statement.
Financial data: Year ended 12/31/2004.
Assets, $7,447 (M); Expenditures, $50,016; Total giving, $49,484; Grants to individuals, 59 grants totaling $49,484 (high: $3,921, low: $120).
Type of support: Fellowships; Scholarships—to individuals.
Application information: Application form required. Application form available on the grantmaker's Web site.
Initial approach: Letter.
Copies of proposal: 1
Deadline(s): Mar. 1, June 1, Aug. 1, and Dec. 1
Applicants should submit the following:
1) Transcripts
2) SAT
3) Letter(s) of recommendation
4) GPA
5) Financial information
6) FAFSA
7) Essay
8) Curriculum vitae
9) Budget Information
10) ACT
Additional information: Applications should be sent by mail or fax; Recipients notified in two weeks.
EIN: 920157584

4165
Ukiah Educational Foundation
925 N. State St.
Ukiah, CA 95482   (707) 463-5201
Contact: Kristi Duncan, Pres.

Foundation type: Public charity
Limitations: Scholarships to students in the Ukiah, CA, area for higher education.
Financial data: Year ended 07/31/2004. Assets, $1,388,777 (M); Expenditures, $30,867; Total giving, $29,462; Grants to individuals, 17 grants totaling $22,000 (high: $2,000, low: $500).
Type of support: Undergraduate support.
Application information: Application form required.
Deadline(s): May 1 for fall semester and Nov. 1 for spring semester
EIN: 680288281

4166
Ukrop's Educational Foundation
c/o Select. Comm.
2001 Maywill St., Ste. 100
Richmond, VA 23230   (804) 340-3000

Foundation type: Independent foundation
Limitations: Scholarships to employees and children of VA employees of Ukrop's for attendance at colleges, universities, or vocational schools.
Financial data: Year ended 03/31/2005. Assets, $3,811,705 (M); Expenditures, $214,876; Total giving, $187,500; Grants to individuals, 125 grants totaling $187,500 (high: $1,500, low: $1,500).
Fields of interest: Vocational education.
Type of support: Employee-related scholarships.
Application information: Application form required.
Deadline(s): Mar. 1
Applicants should submit the following:
1) Letter(s) of recommendation
2) SAT
3) Transcripts
Additional information: Eligible associates must have worked 500 hours in the past year, with one year of service.
EIN: 541777866

4167
Ullery Charitable Trust
(formerly Jimmie Ullery Charitable Trust)
c/o JPMorgan Chase Bank, N.A.
P.O. Box 1308
Milwaukee, WI 53201
Contact: Bruce Currie, Trust Off.
Application address: c/o JPMorgan Chase Bank, N.A., 15 E. 5th St., Tulsa, OK 74103, tel.: (918) 586-5273

Foundation type: Independent foundation
Limitations: Scholarships to individuals contemplating full-time Christian service, primarily for study at Presbyterian theological seminaries.
Financial data: Year ended 01/31/2005. Assets, $498,310 (M); Expenditures, $38,457; Total giving, $31,876.
Fields of interest: Theological school/education; Christian agencies & churches.
Type of support: Scholarships—to individuals.
Application information: Application form required.
Deadline(s): June 1
EIN: 736142334

4168
Ulster Savings Charitable Foundation
c/o Jeff Wood
180 Schwenk Dr.
Kingston, NY 12401   (845) 338-6322
Contact: Jeffrey D. Wood, Dir.
E-mail: humanresources@ulstersavings.com

Foundation type: Company-sponsored foundation
Limitations: Scholarships to residents of Ulster and Duchess counties, NY, to attend schools in those same counties.
Publications: Application guidelines; Financial statement.
Financial data: Year ended 12/31/2004. Assets, $0 (M); Expenditures, $110,998; Total giving, $110,900.
Type of support: Undergraduate support.
Application information: Applications accepted. Application form required.
Initial approach: E-mail.
Deadline(s): Mar. 15
Applicants should submit the following:
1) Letter(s) of recommendation
2) Essay
3) GPA
4) Transcripts
EIN: 562307217

4169
Unaka Scholarship Foundation, Inc.
c/o Unaka Co., Inc.
P.O. Box 877
Greeneville, TN 37744-0877
Contact: Dominick Jackson, Pres.
Application address: 1500 Industrial Rd., Greeneville, TN 37745, tel.: (423) 639-1171

Foundation type: Company-sponsored foundation
Limitations: Scholarships to children of Unaka Group employees who have worked at least 10 weeks for five seasons with the company, primarily in SC and TN.
Financial data: Year ended 06/30/2002. Assets, $78,344 (M); Expenditures, $60,641; Total giving, $59,260; Grants to individuals, 58 grants totaling $51,721 (high: $1,500, low: $500).
Type of support: Employee-related scholarships.
Application information: Application form required.
Deadline(s): None
EIN: 621530053

4170
Unanue Lopez Family Foundation
P.O. Box 1467
Bayamon, PR 00960-1467
Contact: Diana Lopez, Tr.

Foundation type: Operating foundation
Limitations: Scholarships to individuals in PR for higher education.
Financial data: Year ended 12/31/2004. Assets, $775,685 (M); Expenditures, $38,090; Total giving, $28,940; Grants to individuals, totaling $19,960.
Type of support: Support to graduates or students of specific schools; Awards/grants by nomination only; Undergraduate support.
Application information: Contact foundation for current application deadline/guidelines.
EIN: 660572018

4171
The Minnie Quickenstedt Underwood Foundation
c/o Bank of America, N.A.
P.O. Box 831041
Dallas, TX 75283-1041
Application address: c/o Trinity University, Scholarship Board, 715 Stadium Dr., San Antonio, TX 78284

Foundation type: Independent foundation
Limitations: Scholarships to junior, senior, and graduate ministerial students at Trinity University, San Antonio, TX.
Financial data: Year ended 08/31/2004. Assets, $226,841 (M); Expenditures, $15,068; Total giving, $11,000; Grants to individuals, 2 grants totaling $11,000 (high: $5,500, low: $5,500).
Fields of interest: Theological school/education.
Type of support: Support to graduates or students of specific schools; Graduate support; Undergraduate support.
Application information: Application form required.
Deadline(s): Aug. 1
EIN: 756049861

4172
UniGroup, Inc. Scholarship Foundation
1 United Dr.
Fenton, MO 63026-2535   (636) 349-3947
FAX: (314) 349-2503

Foundation type: Operating foundation
Limitations: Scholarships and honorariums to the children of employees of UniGroup, Inc. and its affiliated companies in MO.
Financial data: Year ended 12/31/2003. Assets, $114,562 (M); Expenditures, $129,001; Total giving, $70,000; Grants to individuals, 24 grants totaling $70,000 (high: $5,000, low: $2,500).
Type of support: Employee-related scholarships.
Application information: Deadline Mar. 17; Completion of formal application required.
EIN: 431806966

4173
Union County Community Foundation, Inc.
P.O. Box 148
El Dorado, AR 71731-0148
Contact: Elise Drake, Dir.

Foundation type: Community foundation
Limitations: Scholarships for higher education to students of El Dorado High School, Smackover High School, Norphlet High School, Union County high schools, South Arkansas Community College, and University of the South at Sawannee, TN, and to residents of Union County, AR.
Publications: Financial statement; Grants list; Newsletter.
Financial data: Year ended 09/30/2004. Assets, $10,117,860 (M); Expenditures, $496,978; Total giving, $387,911; Grants to individuals, 41 grants totaling $107,656 (high: $30,650, low: $100).
Fields of interest: Nursing school/education; Teacher school/education; Education; Engineering.
Type of support: Support to graduates or students of specific schools; Undergraduate support.
Application information: Contact foundation for current application deadline/guidelines.

Program description:

Scholarships: The foundation administers the following funds:

- Dr. Carl F. Hartmann Engineering Scholarship Fund: The fund offers scholarships to promising students entering the educational field of engineering.
- Olin C. and Marjorie H. Bailey Scholarship Fund: The fund offers scholarships to worthy graduates of El Dorado High School.
- Kimberly Wood Memorial Nursing Scholarship Fund: The fund assists local students with tuition assistance to the South Arkansas Community College Nursing Program.
- The Union County Farm Bureau Scholarship Fund: The fund provides scholarships to students of Union County Farm Bureau families as a service to their membership.
- The Proctor Hill Memorial Educational Fund: The fund provides renewable scholarships for full tuition, room, and board to students of El Dorado High School who attend the University of the South at Sawanee, TN.
- The Ricky Sewell Memorial Fund: The fund provides scholarships, supports educational programs, and assists charitable organizations.
- The Jodie Mahoney Fund: The fund provides tuition assistance to students of South Arkansas Community.
- Smackover High School Education Fund: The fund promotes and furthers educational opportunities, including scholarship, for Smackover High School students and teachers.
- Gloria Flenniken Calhoun Fund: The fund provides scholarships to students of Norphlet High School.
- The Thomas F. Meeks, Jr. Scholarship Fund: The fund provides tuition assistance to students who are graduates of Union County high schools.
- Lacy Kathryn Allen Memorial Fund: The fund primarily funds scholarships.

EIN: 311500805

4174

Union County CPA Scholarship Fund
c/o Philip J. Kinzel
195 Fairfield Ave., Ste. 1D
West Caldwell, NJ   07006
Contact: Dale Nelson, Chair.
Application address: 64 Post Rd., Clark, NJ 07066,
tel.: (973)504-6467

Foundation type: Independent foundation
Limitations: Scholarships to Union County, NJ, residents majoring in accounting.
Financial data: Year ended 05/31/2005.
Assets, $60,925 (M); Expenditures, $9,224; Total giving, $9,000; Grants to individuals, totaling $9,000.
Fields of interest: Business school/education.
Type of support: Scholarships—to individuals.
Application information: Contact foundation for current application deadline/guidelines.
EIN: 222377473

4175

Union County Foundation, Inc.
404 Eaton St.
Liberty, IN   47353   (765) 458-7664

Foundation type: Community foundation

Limitations: Scholarships to residents of Union County, IN.
Financial data: Year ended 12/31/2004.
Assets, $4,932,672 (M); Expenditures, $224,961; Total giving, $131,992; Grants to individuals, 33 grants totaling $39,528 (high: $1,000, low: $50).
Type of support: Undergraduate support.
Application information: More than 100 scholarships were provided in the last fiscal year. Contact foundation for current application deadlines/guidelines.
EIN: 351769294

4176

Union League Civic & Arts Foundation
(also known as Union League Club)
65 W. Jackson Blvd.
Chicago, IL   60604-3598   (312) 427-7800
Contact: Anne Shea, Exec. Dir.
FAX: (312) 427-9177;
E-mail: civicandarts@aol.com; URL: http://www.civicandarts.org/

Foundation type: Public charity
Limitations: Scholarships to pre-professional musicians and visual arts students in the metropolitan Chicago, IL, area.
Financial data: Year ended 12/31/2004.
Assets, $1,211,483 (M); Expenditures, $465,525; Total giving, $164,737; Grants to individuals, 83 grants totaling $91,111 (high: $12,000, low: $50).
Fields of interest: Arts education; Visual arts; Music; Performing arts, education.
Type of support: Scholarships—to individuals; Undergraduate support.
Application information: Contact foundation for current application deadline/guidelines.
Program descriptions:

Music Scholarship Competition: Each year, ten outstanding, pre-professional musicians receive awards totaling $38,000.

Visual Arts Scholarship Competition: Each year, ten students enrolled full-time in visual arts degree programs at metropolitan Chicago, IL, schools receive awards totaling $20,000. In addition, recipients' artwork will be displayed.
EIN: 362446421

4177

United Cancer Research Society, Inc.
P.O. Box 271
Redlands, CA   92373-0081
Contact: Robert Earhart, Dir., Devel.

Foundation type: Public charity
Limitations: Scholarships to graduates studying in the medical field.
Financial data: Year ended 12/31/2003.
Assets, $28,231 (M); Expenditures, $203,836; Total giving, $37,686; Grants to individuals, totaling $37,686.
Fields of interest: Medical school/education.
Type of support: Graduate support.
Application information: Unsolicited requests for funds not accepted.
EIN: 237376161

4178

United Conveyor Foundation
2100 Norman Dr. W.
Waukegan, IL   60085   (847) 473-5900
Contact: Gloria A. Smiley

Foundation type: Company-sponsored foundation
Limitations: Scholarships for students whose parents have been employed at United Conveyor Corporation, IL, for at least three years.
Financial data: Year ended 12/31/2004.
Assets, $4,515,237 (M); Expenditures, $171,471; Total giving, $168,875; Grants to individuals, 7 grants totaling $21,000 (high: $3,000, low: $3,000).
Type of support: Employee-related scholarships.
Application information: Application form required.
Deadline(s): July 1
Applicants should submit the following:
  1) Letter(s) of recommendation
  2) SAT
  3) ACT
  4) Transcripts
Additional information: Application should include evidence of acceptance at an institution of higher learning.
EIN: 366033638

4179

United Help, Inc.
520 8th Ave., 5th Fl.
New York, NY   10018   (212) 971-7600
Contact: Eric S. Sondheimer, Pres.

Foundation type: Public charity
Limitations: Scholarships to survivors of the Holocaust and their families, primarily in NY.
Financial data: Year ended 06/30/2004.
Assets, $996,121 (M); Expenditures, $910,582; Total giving, $902,350.
Fields of interest: Jewish agencies & temples.
Type of support: Undergraduate support.
Application information:
Initial approach: Letter.
Additional information: Contact foundation for current application deadline/guidelines.
EIN: 135654450

4180

United Negro College Fund, Inc.
8260 Willow Oaks Corp. Dr.
P.O. Box 10444
Fairfax, VA   22031-8044   (800) 331-2244
Contact: Michael Lomax Ph.D., Pres. and C.E.O.
URL: http://www.uncf.org

Foundation type: Public charity
Limitations: Scholarships to individuals for undergraduate and graduate study at institutions of their choice.
Financial data: Year ended 03/31/2005.
Assets, $964,297,881 (M); Expenditures, $139,592,820; Total giving, $100,788,490; Grants to individuals, totaling $74,885,172.
Fields of interest: Asians/Pacific Islanders; African Americans/Blacks; Hispanics/Latinos; Native Americans/American Indians.
Type of support: Graduate support; Undergraduate support.
Application information: Completion of formal application required; See Web site for deadlines and further information.
Program description:

Gates Millenium Scholars Program: Awards scholarships with the purpose of expanding access and the opportunity for higher education to citizens who help reflect the diverse society in which we live. The program seeks to increase the number of African Americans, Native Americans/Alaska Natives, Asians/Pacific Americans and Latino Americans enrolling in and completing undergraduate and graduate degree programs. The

goal is to promote academic excellence and to provide an opportunity for thousands of outstanding students to reach their fullest potential. Administered by the Bill & Melinda Gates Foundation, this program seeks to encourage and support students in completing college and in continuing to earn masters and doctorate degrees in disciplines where ethnic and racial groups are currently underrepresented. The awards will enable thousands of young Americans to attend undergraduate and graduate institutions of their choice and be prepared to assume important roles as leaders in their professions and in their communities.
EIN: 131624241

4181
United Society of Friends Women Trust
5135 Southland Dr.
Archdale, NC   27263
Application address: c/o Leanna Roberts, 3702 E. 196th St., Westfield, IN 46074, tel.: (317) 896-3380

Foundation type: Independent foundation
Limitations: Scholarships to active Quaker students, primarily for study at a seminary.
Publications: Informational brochure (including application guidelines).
Financial data: Year ended 12/31/2004. Assets, $1,696,118 (M); Expenditures, $88,742; Total giving, $65,110; Grants to individuals, totaling $65,110.
Fields of interest: Theological school/education.
Type of support: Graduate support; Undergraduate support.
Application information: Application form required.
Initial approach: Letter.
Additional information: Application should include references.
Program description:
John Sarrin Scholarship Fund: Recipients must not use alcohol, tobacco, or harmful drugs, not join the combatant military forces of any country, be moral and upright, and maintain a satisfactory standard of work and conduct. If the recipient fails to live up to these requirements, the grant may be cancelled.
EIN: 237089265

4182
United States Steel Foundation, Inc.
(formerly USX Foundation, Inc.)
600 Grant St., Rm. 639
Pittsburgh, PA   15219-2800   (412) 433-5237
Contact: Susan M. Kapusta, Genl. Mgr.
FAX: (412) 433-2792; URL: http://www.ussteel.com/corp/ussfoundation/ussfound.htm

Foundation type: Company-sponsored foundation
Limitations: Scholarships to children of United States Steel Corporation employees.
Publications: Application guidelines; Annual report (including application guidelines).
Financial data: Year ended 11/30/2004. Assets, $2,790,243 (M); Expenditures, $2,082,590; Total giving, $1,989,296.
Type of support: Employee-related scholarships.
Application information: Application form required.
Initial approach: Letter.
Deadline(s): Apr. 15
Additional information: Application available through Grantmakers of Western Pennsylvania at http://www.gwpa.org.
EIN: 136093185

4183
United Student Aid Funds, Inc.
P.O. Box 6028
Indianapolis, IN   46206
Contact: Henry L. Fernandez, Exec. Dir.
E-mail: contact@usafunds.org; URL: http://www.usafunds.org

Foundation type: Public charity
Limitations: Scholarships and grants to deserving low-income students.
Publications: Newsletter.
Financial data: Year ended 09/30/2004. Assets, $744,960,140 (M); Expenditures, $367,127,499; Total giving, $13,448,622; Grants to individuals, 4 grants totaling $10,294 (high: $4,933, low: $1,048).
Fields of interest: Higher education.
Type of support: Scholarships—to individuals.
Application information: Applications accepted. Application form required. Application form available on the grantmaker's Web site.
Deadline(s): Feb. 28
Additional information: See Web site for application deadlines and guidelines.
Program descriptions:
Access to Education Scholarships: Assists students in achieving their higher-education goals by awarding scholarships to qualified students who demonstrate financial need, according to the following criteria:
· Plan to enroll or be enrolled in full- or half-time undergraduate or full-time graduate coursework at an accredited two- or four-year college, university or vocational/technical school. Eligible applicants include students attending or planning to attend law school, medical school, or other professional-degree programs. GED recipients also are eligible
· Have an annual adjusted gross family income of $35,000 or less
· Be a U.S. citizen or eligible noncitizen
Arizona Silver Anniversary Scholarships: Awards to Arizona residents from households with annual incomes of $35,000 or less. Full-time undergraduate, graduate and professional students may apply to receive $1,500 awards. Half-time undergraduates will be eligible for $750 scholarships. The scholarships may be renewed annually, provided that the student meets academic qualifications, until the recipient completes a degree or certificate or accumulates $6,000 in scholarship awards.
Scholarships: Grants are awarded to postsecondary institutions that are declared disaster areas due to hurricanes Dennis and Katrina. Assistance of up to $750 per student may be used for tuition, fees, books, room and board or other education-related expenses. Further details can be obtained through the Web site of the program administrator Scholarship America at www.scholarshipamerica.org.
EIN: 946050341

4184
United Telephone Educational Foundation, Inc.
P.O. Box 729
Langdon, ND   58249-0729   (701) 256-5156
Contact: Kenneth Carlson, Secy.-Treas.
E-mail: utcfound@utma.com; URL: http://scholarship.utma.com

Foundation type: Company-sponsored foundation
Limitations: Scholarships to children of members of United Telephone Mutual Aid Corporation.

Financial data: Year ended 12/31/2004. Assets, $614,148 (M); Expenditures, $20,445; Total giving, $19,400; Grants to individuals, 46 grants totaling $19,400 (high: $1,500, low: $300).
Type of support: Scholarships—to individuals.
Application information: Application form required.
Deadline(s): Mar. 30
Program description:
Scholarship Program: Applicants must have maintained at least a 2.5 GPA in high school.
EIN: 450414760

4185
Unity Foundation of La Porte County, Inc.
619 Franklin St.
P.O. Box 527
Michigan City, IN   46360-0527   (219) 879-0327
Contact: Margaret A. Spartz, Pres.
FAX: (219) 873-2416; E-mail: unity@uflc.net; Additional tel.: (888) 89-UNITY; URL: http://www.uflc.net

Foundation type: Community foundation
Limitations: Scholarships to students in LaPorte County, IN.
Publications: Application guidelines; Annual report; Annual report (including application guidelines); Financial statement; Grants list; Newsletter.
Financial data: Year ended 12/31/2004. Assets, $16,429,012 (M); Expenditures, $1,127,438; Total giving, $511,276; Grants to individuals, 106 grants totaling $267,182 (high: $21,000, low: $100).
Type of support: Scholarships—to individuals; Precollege support; Undergraduate support.
Application information: Application form required. Application form available on the grantmaker's Web site.
Initial approach: Telephone.
Copies of proposal: 1
Deadline(s): April
Applicants should submit the following:
1) Transcripts
2) SAT
3) SAR
4) GPA
5) Financial information
6) Budget Information
7) ACT
Additional information: Applications should be sent by mail; Recipients notified within 90 days.
EIN: 351658674

4186
Universal Forest Products Education Foundation
(formerly Universal Companies, Inc. Education Foundation)
2801 E. Beltline N.E.
Grand Rapids, MI   49525-9600   (616) 364-6161
Contact: Nancy DeGood

Foundation type: Company-sponsored foundation
Limitations: Scholarships to employees of Universal Forest Products, Inc. and its subsidiaries who have 12 months of seniority prior to June 1st of the scholarship year, and to their natural and adopted children under the age of 25 for postsecondary education at colleges, universities, community colleges, and accredited two-year vocational schools.
Financial data: Year ended 12/31/2004. Assets, $536,451 (M); Expenditures, $28,707;

Total giving, $28,400; Grants to individuals, 47 grants totaling $28,400 (high: $1,200, low: $400).
Fields of interest: Vocational education.
Type of support: Employee-related scholarships.
Application information: Application form required.
   Initial approach: Letter or telephone.
   Deadline(s): May 31
EIN: 382945715

4187
University Club Scholarship Fund
426 Stuart St.
Boston, MA 02116

Foundation type: Independent foundation
Limitations: Scholarships to graduates of the Boston, MA, public school system for undergraduate education.
Financial data: Year ended 12/31/2003. Assets, $178,473 (M); Expenditures, $20,059; Total giving, $13,750; Grants to individuals, 11 grants totaling $13,750 (high: $2,000, low: $1,000).
Type of support: Support to graduates or students of specific schools; Undergraduate support.
Application information: Applications not accepted.
EIN: 042618671

4188
University of California Chinese Alumni Foundation
5484 Fernhoff Rd.
Oakland, CA 94619
Application address: c/o Dean of Studies, Univ. of CA Berkeley, Berkeley, CA 94720
E-mail: cf_xdirect@netzero.net

Foundation type: Independent foundation
Limitations: Scholarships to students attending the University of California, Berkeley, CA.
Financial data: Year ended 12/31/2004. Assets, $1,023,654 (M); Expenditures, $66,407; Total giving, $60,300; Grants to individuals, 2 grants totaling $60,300.
Type of support: Support to graduates or students of specific schools; Undergraduate support.
Application information: Contact foundation for current application deadline/guidelines.
EIN: 237375387

4189
University of Phoenix Alumni Network
(formerly University of Phoenix Network for Professional Development)
4615 E. Elwood St.
Phoenix, AZ 85040-1958 (800) 795-2586
Contact: Carrie Fries, Dir.; Destany Schreiber

Foundation type: Operating foundation
Limitations: Scholarships for students of the University of Phoenix.
Financial data: Year ended 08/31/2004. Assets, $301,365 (M); Expenditures, $695,502; Total giving, $354,338; Grants to individuals, 316 grants totaling $354,338 (high: $2,500, low: $1,000).
Type of support: Support to graduates or students of specific schools.
Application information: Applications not accepted.
Program description:
   Scholarships: The foundation administers the following scholarship funds:

- HMS Scholarship
- Farmers Insurance Scholarship
- Patty Hardman Scholarship
- Shirley Eisenach Scholarship.

EIN: 953366652

4190
Unocal Foundation
14141 Southwest Fwy.
Sugar Land, TX 77478
Contact: Laurie Regelbrugge, Mgr.
Application address: 1150 Connecticut Ave. N.W., Ste. 1025, Washington, DC 20036, tel.: (202) 367-2782, FAX: (202) 367-2790,
E-mail: laurier@unocal.com

Foundation type: Company-sponsored foundation
Limitations: Graduate study grants and industry-related scholarships in areas of company operations in CA, IL, and TX.
Publications: Annual report.
Financial data: Year ended 12/31/2004. Assets, $2,319,466 (M); Expenditures, $3,495,548; Total giving, $3,495,038.
Fields of interest: Engineering school/education; Science; Engineering/technology.
Type of support: Scholarships—to individuals; Graduate support.
Application information: Contact foundation for current application deadline/guidelines.
Program description:
   Unocal Scholarship Program: The foundation operates two programs for individual applicants. Graduate study grants provide opportunities for selected students to pursue studies beyond the undergraduate level in disciplines related to the petroleum industry. Industry-related scholarships assist in strengthening student interest in the disciplines vital to the future of the petroleum industry. Both programs prefer students of the sciences, technology, and engineering.
EIN: 956071812

4191
Darryl E. Unruh Foundation, Inc.
68 Orange St.
Asheville, NC 28801-2341
Contact: Darryl E. Unruh, Pres.

Foundation type: Operating foundation
Limitations: Scholarships to high school seniors graduating from the City of Asheville, NC, and Buncombe County, NC, school systems, who plan to enroll in a four-year college or university in the North Carolina State University system.
Financial data: Year ended 12/31/2002. Assets, $36,988 (M); Expenditures, $20,968; Total giving, $19,593; Grants to individuals, 8 grants totaling $19,593 (high: $6,469, low: $350).
Type of support: Support to graduates or students of specific schools; Undergraduate support.
Application information: Application form required.
   Deadline(s): Mar. 15
   Applicants should submit the following:
     1) Photograph
     2) Class rank
     3) Transcripts
     4) SAT
     5) Letter(s) of recommendation
     6) GPA
     7) ACT
   Additional information: Application must also include a 750-word statement of plans, career goals, and reasons for wanting and needing a scholarship; Interviews required.

Program description:
   Unruh Scholarship Program: Applicants must be accepted to a NC state college or university, be in the top 20 percent of their classes, have a minimum SAT score of 900 or an ACT score of 20, have good character, have participated in extracurricular activities, and show evidence of financial need. Recipients must be enrolled in at least 15 credit hours per semester. Scholarships are renewable for up to four years, covering full tuition, room/board, and books each year, plus a summer internship program. A GPA of at least 3.0 must be maintained to remain eligible for the scholarship.
EIN: 561570954

4192
Urann Foundation
c/o Bank of America, N.A.
P.O. Box 1802
Providence, RI 02901-1802
Application address: P.O. Box 1788, Breckton, MA 02403, tel.: (617) 588-7744

Foundation type: Independent foundation
Limitations: Scholarships to members of families living in MA who are engaged in the production of cranberries.
Financial data: Year ended 12/31/2004. Assets, $3,294,922 (M); Expenditures, $206,691; Total giving, $168,000; Grants to individuals, 19 grants totaling $126,000 (high: $4,000, low: $500).
Fields of interest: Agriculture.
Type of support: Scholarships—to individuals; Graduate support; Undergraduate support.
Application information: Application form required.
   Initial approach: Letter.
   Deadline(s): Apr. 15.
   Additional information: Applications also available at guidance departments of high schools.
Program description:
   Scholarship Program: The foundation makes scholarship grants to provide assistance for postsecondary education. Scholarships granted may be for a single semester or for a full year. Additional grants may be made on a yearly basis for continuation in undergraduate or graduate school. Applicants must show financial need.
EIN: 046115599

4193
Urbanek-Levy Education Fund
19800 Glen Una Dr.
Saratoga, CA 95070

Foundation type: Independent foundation
Limitations: Scholarships to children of KLA-Tencor employees, primarily in CA, for undergraduate education.
Financial data: Year ended 12/31/2004. Assets, $1,466,117 (M); Expenditures, $209,357; Total giving, $194,500; Grants to individuals, 63 grants totaling $194,500 (high: $5,000, low: $1,000).
Type of support: Employee-related scholarships.
Application information: Unsolicited requests for funds not considered or acknowledged.
EIN: 943372793

4194
US Airways Education Foundation
(formerly America West Airlines Education Foundation, Inc.)
c/o Community Rels.
4000 E. Sky Harbor Blvd.
Phoenix, AZ   85034   (480) 693-3652
Contact: Win Holden, Pres.
FAX: (480) 693-3715;
E-mail: community.relations@usairways.com;
URL: http://www2.usairways.com/awa/content/aboutus/corporategiving/education.aspx

Foundation type: Public charity
Limitations: Scholarships to children of employees of America West Airlines.
Publications: Application guidelines.
Financial data: Year ended 12/31/2004.
Assets, $257,211 (M); Expenditures, $150,418; Total giving, $150,000; Grants to individuals, 90 grants totaling $90,000 (high: $1,000, low: $1,000).
Type of support: Employee-related scholarships.
Application information: Application form required.
Initial approach: Letter.
Deadline(s): 1st Friday in Mar.
Applicants should submit the following:
   1) Essay
   2) GPA
   3) Letter(s) of recommendation
   4) Transcripts
   5) SAT
   6) ACT
Additional information: See Web site for further information.
EIN: 860670438

4195
USAWOA Scholarship Foundation
462 Herndon Pkwy., Ste. 207
Herndon, VA   20170-5235   (703) 742-7727
Contact: Robert D. Scott, Pres. and Exec. Dir.
FAX: (703) 742-7728;
E-mail: usawoasf@cavetel.net; URL: http://www.usawoa.org/woasf

Foundation type: Public charity
Limitations: Scholarships to qualified family members of warrant officers serving in or retired from the U.S. Army, the U.S. Army Reserve and the Army National Guard of the various states and territories.
Financial data: Year ended 12/31/2004.
Assets, $18,398 (M); Expenditures, $11,680; Total giving, $11,000; Grants to individuals, totaling $11,000.
Fields of interest: Military/veterans' organizations.
Type of support: Undergraduate support.
Application information: Applications accepted. Application form required. Application form available on the grantmaker's Web site.
Initial approach: E-mail or telephone.
Deadline(s): Jan. 1 and May 1
Additional information: See Web site for additional application information.
EIN: 861055533

4196
Curt & Margaret Uschmann Memorial Scholarship Fund
1211 S.W. 5th Ave., Ste. 560
Portland, OR   97204

Foundation type: Independent foundation
Limitations: Scholarships to graduates of Lebanon High School, OR, for college or technical schools.

Financial data: Year ended 03/31/2005.
Assets, $660,580 (M); Expenditures, $53,855; Total giving, $39,000; Grants to individuals, totaling $39,000.
Fields of interest: Vocational education.
Type of support: Support to graduates or students of specific schools; Undergraduate support.
Application information: Application form required.
Initial approach: Letter.
Deadline(s): Apr. 30
EIN: 936146393

4197
Vacaville Community Foundation
3170 Hilltop Mall Rd.
Richmond, CA   94806-6069

Foundation type: Independent foundation
Limitations: Scholarships to residents of Vacaville, CA.
Financial data: Year ended 12/31/2003.
Assets, $2,552,820 (M); Expenditures, $168,688; Total giving, $142,500; Grants to individuals, 29 grants totaling $142,500 (high: $5,000, low: $2,500).
Type of support: Scholarships—to individuals.
Application information: Applications accepted.
Deadline(s): None
EIN: 237087582

4198
Mabel Vacek Scholarship Trust
c/o Remley, Willems, McQuillen, & Voss
209 E. Main St.
Anamosa, IA   52205-0228

Foundation type: Operating foundation
Limitations: Scholarships to individuals, primarily in Oxford Junction, IA.
Financial data: Year ended 12/31/2003.
Assets, $255,023 (M); Expenditures, $11,559; Total giving, $9,122; Grants to individuals, totaling $9,122.
Type of support: Scholarships—to individuals.
Application information: Contact foundation for current application deadline/guidelines.
EIN: 426580517

4199
Erral A. Vaile & Evelyn L. Cleaveland Scholarship Fund
c/o Chittenden Bank
P.O. Box 820
Burlington, VT   05402
Application address: c/o Bertie Sprague, Principal, Brattleboro Union District No. 6 High School, Fairground Rd., Brattleboro, VT 05301

Foundation type: Independent foundation
Limitations: Scholarships to graduating seniors at Brattleboro Union High School, VT, who have spent their junior and senior years at that school, for higher education leading to a bachelor of arts or bachelor of science degree.
Financial data: Year ended 12/31/2004.
Assets, $376,422 (M); Expenditures, $32,741; Total giving, $32,741; Grants to individuals, totaling $32,741.
Type of support: Support to graduates or students of specific schools; Undergraduate support.
Application information:
Deadline(s): May 12
Additional information: Application by letter including parents' and student's financial

statements, transcripts, and two letters of recommendation.
EIN: 030343444

4200
Valero Scholarship Trust
P.O. Box 696000
San Antonio, TX   78269-6000

Foundation type: Company-sponsored foundation
Limitations: Scholarships to dependents of employees of Valero Energy Corp., or one of its wholly-owned subsidiaries for higher education.
Financial data: Year ended 12/31/2004.
Assets, $166,607 (M); Expenditures, $213,362; Total giving, $197,750; Grants to individuals, 78 grants totaling $197,750 (high: $5,000, low: $1,250).
Type of support: Employee-related scholarships.
Application information:
Deadline(s): Mar. 1
Additional information: Contact trust for current application guidelines.
EIN: 746437579

4201
The Valley Foundation
4729 E. Sunrise Dr., Ste. 307
Tucson, AZ   85718   (520) 777-3622

Foundation type: Independent foundation
Limitations: Scholarships to residents of Tucson, AZ.
Financial data: Year ended 12/31/2004.
Assets, $1,410,471 (M); Expenditures, $62,302; Total giving, $50,000; Grants to individuals, totaling $50,000.
Type of support: Scholarships—to individuals.
Application information: Application form required.
Deadline(s): Mar. 1
EIN: 931228513

4202
Valley Telephone Cooperative Foundation
752 E. Maley St.
P.O. Box 970
Willcox, AZ   85644-0970   (520) 384-2231
Contact: Judy Smith
FAX: (520) 384-2831

Foundation type: Company-sponsored foundation
Limitations: Scholarships to member-patrons and family members of patrons of Valley Telephone Cooperative, Inc. in AZ and NM.
Financial data: Year ended 12/31/2004.
Assets, $806,899 (M); Expenditures, $35,262; Total giving, $32,000; Grants to individuals, 31 grants totaling $28,000 (high: $2,500, low: $500).
Type of support: Undergraduate support.
Application information: Application form required.
Deadline(s): Contact foundation for current application deadline
EIN: 742613547

4203
The Valspar Foundation
4900 IDS Ctr.
80 S. 8th St., Ste. 4900
Minneapolis, MN   55402-2226   (612) 337-5903
Contact: Gwen Leifeld, Mgr.
FAX: (612) 337-5904

Foundation type: Company-sponsored foundation

Limitations: Scholarships to children of employees of the Valspar Corporation.
Publications: Application guidelines; Program policy statement.
Financial data: Year ended 09/30/2003. Assets, $428,658 (M); Expenditures, $867,040; Total giving, $864,932; Grants to individuals, 80 grants totaling $120,000 (high: $1,500, low: $1,500).
Type of support: Employee-related scholarships.
Application information: Application form required.
Deadline(s): June 9
Program description:
Valspar Scholarship Program: Applicant must be a child of a Valspar Corporation employee and enter a postsecondary educational institution as a full-time student. Selection is based on financial need and record of achievement.
EIN: 411363847

4204

Scott Van Doren Memorial Scholarship Fund
60 Deerhill Rd.
Lebanon, NJ   08833

Foundation type: Operating foundation
Limitations: Four-year scholarships to wrestlers at North Hunterdon High School, Annandale, NJ, for postsecondary education.
Financial data: Year ended 06/30/2004. Assets, $68,338 (M); Expenditures, $7,051; Total giving, $7,000; Grants to individuals, totaling $7,000.
Fields of interest: Athletics/sports, training.
Type of support: Support to graduates or students of specific schools; Undergraduate support.
Application information: Contact fund for current application deadline; Initial approach by letter or telephone.
EIN: 223117696

4205

Peter Ellis Van Doren Scholarship Fund
c/o Peapack-Gladstone Bank
P.O. Box 178
Gladstone, NJ   07934-0178
Application address: P.O. Box 584, Peapack, NJ 07977

Foundation type: Independent foundation
Limitations: Scholarships to graduating seniors who are residents of Somerset County, NJ, with preference to the boroughs of Peapack and Gladstone.
Financial data: Year ended 12/31/2004. Assets, $1,046,512 (M); Expenditures, $59,340; Total giving, $48,500; Grants to individuals, totaling $48,500.
Type of support: Support to graduates or students of specific schools; Undergraduate support.
Application information: Application form required.
Deadline(s): Feb. 20
Additional information: Forms are available at all public and private secondary school guidance departments in Somerset County, NJ.
EIN: 226666043

4206

Homer J. Van Hollenbeck Foundation
13231 23 Mile Rd.
Shelby Township, MI   48315   (586) 726-4300
Contact: Stefan Wanczyk, Pres.

Foundation type: Independent foundation
Limitations: Scholarships to Macomb County, MI, area high school seniors who are financially needy and have at least a 2.5 GPA. Scholarships are limited to $2,000 per year, with a maximum total award of $6,000 per student.
Financial data: Year ended 12/31/2004. Assets, $1,116,575 (M); Expenditures, $41,932; Total giving, $36,000; Grants to individuals, totaling $36,000.
Type of support: Support to graduates or students of specific schools; Undergraduate support.
Application information: Application form required.
Deadline(s): May 31.
Applicants should submit the following:
1) Letter(s) of recommendation
EIN: 383085929

4207

Isabel Van Horn Scholarship Trust
c/o JPMorgan Chase Bank, N.A
P.O. Box 1308
Milwaukee, WI   53201
Contact: Rev. Mark Richardson
Application address: c/o Central Christian Church, 587 Mount Vernon Rd., Newark, OH 43055

Foundation type: Independent foundation
Limitations: Scholarships to men and women entering the seminary in preparation for ministry in the Central Christian Church in Newark, OH.
Financial data: Year ended 12/31/2004. Assets, $1,295,306 (M); Expenditures, $97,890; Total giving, $86,956; Grants to individuals, totaling $86,956.
Fields of interest: Theological school/education; Christian agencies & churches.
Type of support: Graduate support.
Application information:
Deadline(s): Applications by letter accepted throughout the year.
Additional information: Recipients are approved by a majority of the elders of the Church.
EIN: 316464732

4208

E. Van Horne Educational Fund
c/o Mellon Financial Corp.
P.O. Box 185
Pittsburgh, PA   15230-9897
Contact: Laurie Moritz, Trust Off., Mellon Financial Corp.
Application address: 3 Mellon Bank Ctr., Rm. 4130, Pittsburgh, PA 15259, tel.: (412) 234-0023

Foundation type: Independent foundation
Limitations: Scholarships to financially needy graduating seniors at Crawford County, PA, high schools, primarily to attend colleges and universities in PA.
Financial data: Year ended 12/31/2004. Assets, $862,836 (M); Expenditures, $41,322; Total giving, $36,100.
Type of support: Support to graduates or students of specific schools; Undergraduate support.
Application information: Application form required.
Additional information: Contact fund for current application deadline.
EIN: 256220814

4209

Virginia W. Van Hyning Scholarship Fund
c/o The Huntington National Bank
P.O. Box 1558, EA4E86
Columbus, OH   43216

Foundation type: Independent foundation
Limitations: Scholarships to graduates of Benjamin Logan High School, Zanesfield, OH.
Financial data: Year ended 12/31/2004. Assets, $275,682 (M); Expenditures, $13,743; Total giving, $11,000; Grants to individuals, totaling $11,000.
Type of support: Support to graduates or students of specific schools; Undergraduate support.
Application information: Applications not accepted.
EIN: 316258749

4210

The Van Wert County Foundation
138 E. Main St.
Van Wert, OH   45891   (419) 238-1743
Contact: Larry L. Wendel, Exec. Secy.
FAX: (419) 238-3374; E-mail: vwcf@bright.net; URL: http://www.vanwert.com/foundation

Foundation type: Community foundation
Limitations: Scholarships to graduates of high schools in Paulding and Van Wert counties, OH.
Publications: Application guidelines; Informational brochure; Informational brochure (including application guidelines); Newsletter.
Financial data: Year ended 12/31/2004. Assets, $35,283,741 (M); Expenditures, $1,759,889; Total giving, $1,187,114; Grants to individuals, 343 grants totaling $319,150 (high: $2,850).
Fields of interest: Arts education; Architecture; Music; Performing arts, education; Literature; Education, research; Medical school/education; Nursing school/education; Theological school/education; Environment, forests; Horticulture/garden clubs; Veterinary medicine; Agriculture; Nutrition; Home economics; Business/industry; Engineering; Christian agencies & churches; Women; Men.
Type of support: Scholarships—to individuals; Support to graduates or students of specific schools; Awards/grants by nomination only; Awards/prizes; Undergraduate support.
Application information: Application form required.
Initial approach: Letter or telephone.
Copies of proposal: 1
Deadline(s): June 1
Applicants should submit the following:
1) Transcripts
2) GPA
3) Curriculum vitae
Additional information: Application should include a photograph for first-time applicants; Interviews required.
Program description:
Scholarship Programs: No graduate scholarships are awarded. Students who have completed their first year of college must have a 2.75 GPA or better. Scholarships, in general, will not be awarded to applicants whose family income exceeds $55,000. These figures may be modified depending upon the number of children in school. Scholarships are available as follows for attendance at any recognized college or university:
· Wassenberg Art and Architecture Scholarships for students majoring in art or architecture.
· Ault Agriculture, Home Economics, or Teaching Scholarships for females who

wish to be teachers or students who wish to study home economics, the science of nutrition, dietetics, home demonstration or related subjects, or students who wish to attend a school of agriculture for the sciences of agronomy, animal husbandry, dairying, poultry raising, veterinary medicine, horticulture, forestry, and related subjects.

- Saltzgaber Scholarships for students majoring in music.
- Koehler, Bair, Wolfe, Wild, Eggers Scholarships for students majoring in any area. Preference will be given to males.
- Matthys Scholarships for applicants majoring in any area of study. One-third of income must be used for pre-med students.
- Thatcher Scholarships for male students majoring in agriculture. First preference must be to a graduate of Lincolnview High School, OH.
- Gilliland Scholarships for students majoring in any area of study.
- Myers Scholarships for students majoring in a church-related activity such as ministry, music, counseling, etc. Applicant may attend any recognized college or university that grants at least an associate degree.
- Culler Scholarships for students majoring in pre-med who attend any recognized college or university that grants at least an associate degree.
- Games Scholarship for students majoring in English who attend any recognized college or university that grants at least an associate degree.
- Eirich Scholarships for females majoring in any course. Preference will be given to those attending either Ohio Wesleyan University or the University of Michigan.
- Kiwanis Club Scholarships for students majoring in education.
- Kennedy Scholarships for students majoring in agriculture.
- Gearhiser Scholarships and Neubrecht Scholarships for students majoring in nursing.
- Lippi Scholarships for students majoring in any area of study.
- Jones Scholarships for students majoring in accounting.
- Fox Scholarships for students majoring in elementary education.
- Rasor Scholarships for students majoring in medicine or related fields.
- Knittle Scholarships for students majoring in music.
- Gordon Scholarships for students majoring in any area of study.
- Scott Scholarships for students majoring in any area of study.
- Stittsworth Scholarships for students majoring in any area of study.
- Flickinger Scholarships for students majoring in any area of study.

EIN: 340907558

4211
J. A. Van Wynen, Jr. & W. F. Van Wynen Trust A

(also known as The John A. & Winnifred F. Van Wynen Scholarship Fund)
c/o PNC Bank, N.A.
1600 Market St., 4th Fl.
Philadelphia, PA 19103-7240

Foundation type: Independent foundation
Limitations: Scholarships to graduates of Immaculate Conception High School, Montclair, NJ, and Glen Ridge High School, Glen Ridge, NJ, to attend accredited colleges or trade schools.
Financial data: Year ended 12/31/2004. Assets, $1,053,333 (M); Expenditures, $50,389; Total giving, $40,750; Grants to individuals, totaling $40,750.
Fields of interest: Vocational education.
Type of support: Support to graduates or students of specific schools; Technical education support; Undergraduate support.
Application information: Application form required.
  Deadline(s): Feb. 15 for first-time applicants, Mar. 15 for renewals
  Applicants should submit the following:
   1) Transcripts
   2) Letter(s) of recommendation
Program description:
  Scholarship Program: Recipients are chosen based on the following criteria:
   · Scholastic record
   · Financial need
   · Acceptance at an accredited college or trade school
  Amount of scholarship is dependent on financial need. Providing the continuance of financial need, scholarships are for the duration of attendance until a degree is obtained or student discontinues education.
EIN: 226502704

4212
Fred N. VanBuren Scholarship Fund

107 N. Main St.
Baltimore, OH 43105 (740) 862-4191
Contact: Richard Miller, Tr.; James Keller, Tr.; G. Gene Jackson, Tr.

Foundation type: Independent foundation
Limitations: Scholarships to financially needy Liberty Union-Thurston High School students residing in Liberty Township or Liberty Union School District, OH, who are seeking degrees in agriculture or home economics.
Financial data: Year ended 06/30/2005. Assets, $0 (M); Expenditures, $94,194; Total giving, $82,000; Grants to individuals, totaling $82,000.
Fields of interest: Agriculture; Home economics.
Type of support: Support to graduates or students of specific schools; Undergraduate support.
Application information:
  Deadline(s): Apr. 15
  Additional information: Completion of formal application required, including transcripts, GPA, statement of financial need, and a recent photograph. Applicants cannot be users of tobacco, alcoholic beverages, or abusive drugs.
EIN: 311117779

4213
Vancouver Methodist Foundation

401 E. 33rd St.
Vancouver, WA 98663-2203

Foundation type: Independent foundation
Limitations: Scholarships and study grants primarily to residents of WA.
Financial data: Year ended 12/31/2003. Assets, $892,591 (M); Expenditures, $127,238; Total giving, $125,072; Grants to individuals, 30 grants totaling $41,109 (high: $4,000, low: $500).
Fields of interest: Theological school/education.
Type of support: Scholarships—to individuals.
Application information:
  Deadline(s): Apr. 1 for Clark County Scholarship; Contact foundation for other program deadlines/guidelines
  Additional information: Completion of formal application required, including transcripts, three letters of reference, and a financial statement.
Program description:
  Scholarship Program: The foundation has several programs, including scholarships specifically for residents of Clark County, WA, and scholarships for seminary students.
EIN: 910850194

4214
Helen Vandenbark Scholarship Fund

c/o Unizan Financial Svcs. Group
P.O. Box 2307
Zanesville, OH 43702-2307 (740) 455-7060

Foundation type: Independent foundation
Limitations: Scholarships to graduates of Zanesville High School, OH, who are majoring in education.
Financial data: Year ended 12/31/2004. Assets, $125,839 (M); Expenditures, $6,531; Total giving, $5,800; Grants to individuals, totaling $5,800.
Fields of interest: Teacher school/education.
Type of support: Support to graduates or students of specific schools; Undergraduate support.
Application information:
  Deadline(s): May 1
  Additional information: Completion of formal application required, including recent grades, financial statement, and at least two letters of recommendation.
EIN: 316226483

4215
William Vanderhout Trust

c/o TD Banknorth, N.A., Wealth Mgmt. Group
P.O. Box 1180
South Yarmouth, MA 02664-0180
Application address: c/o Nauset Regional High School, Attn: Principal, 100 Cable Rd., North Eastham, MA 02651, tel.: (508) 255-1505

Foundation type: Independent foundation
Limitations: Scholarships to graduates of Nauset Regional High School, North Eastham, MA, residing in the towns of Brewster, Eastham, Orleans, and Wellfleet, MA, to attend accredited colleges.
Financial data: Year ended 07/31/2005. Assets, $1,751,102 (M); Expenditures, $106,306; Total giving, $85,000; Grants to individuals, totaling $85,000.
Type of support: Support to graduates or students of specific schools; Undergraduate support.
Application information:
  Deadline(s): Apr. 15

Additional information: Application by letter.
EIN: 046753154

4216

Dr. Lavern and Betty VanKley Educational Foundation

20 Princeton Ct.
Zeeland, MI 49464

Foundation type: Independent foundation
Limitations: Student loans to members and children of members of the First Reformed Church of Zeeland, MI.
Financial data: Year ended 12/31/2004. Assets, $337,659 (M); Expenditures, $2,041; Total giving, $0; Loans to individuals, 8 loans totaling $20,500.
Fields of interest: Protestant agencies & churches.
Type of support: Student loans—to individuals.
Application information: Applications not accepted.
EIN: 386500707

4217

VARA Educational Foundation, Inc.

619 Varney Hill Rd.
Starksboro, VT 05487 (802) 453-2755
Contact: Steven P. Kelly, Treas.

Foundation type: Independent foundation
Limitations: Scholarships to residents of VT who are students of skiing academies or skiing clubs.
Financial data: Year ended 07/31/2004. Assets, $174,543 (M); Expenditures, $19,995; Total giving, $19,180; Grants to individuals, 11 grants totaling $11,750.
Fields of interest: Athletics/sports, academies.
Type of support: Undergraduate support.
Application information:
  Initial approach: Letter.
EIN: 237336991

4218

Varflex Educational Foundation

512 W. Court St.
Rome, NY 13440
Contact: Dorothy G. Griffin, Tr.

Foundation type: Independent foundation
Limitations: Scholarships to children of Varflex Corporation employees and to graduates of specified high schools.
Financial data: Year ended 12/31/2004. Assets, $231,453 (M); Expenditures, $17,078; Total giving, $15,500; Grants to individuals, totaling $15,500.
Fields of interest: Disabilities, people with.
Type of support: Employee-related scholarships; Support to graduates or students of specific schools; Undergraduate support.
Application information:
  Deadline(s): Apr. 14
  Additional information: Completion of formal application required, including a photocopy of SAR, school/college certification form, optional letters of recommendation; Interviews may be required.
Program description:
  Scholarship Program: Applicants who are not children of Varflex Corporation employees must be candidates for graduation or have graduated from the following schools: Adirondack Central High School, Camden High School, New York State School for the Deaf in Rome, NY, Oriskany Central

School, Rome Catholic High School, Rome Free Academy, Verona-Vernon-Sherrill High School, and Westmoreland High School. Candidates will be notified of the Committee's decision on or about June 15.
EIN: 161471541

4219

Otto Ruth Varner-Seneca Valley High School Scholarship Fund

c/o Mellon Financial Corp.
P.O. Box 185
Pittsburgh, PA 15230-0185
Contact: Laurie Moritz, Trust Off., Mellon Bank, N.A.
Application address: c/o Seneca Valley High School, Attn.: Guidance Counselor, 128 Seneca School Rd., Harmony, PA 16037

Foundation type: Independent foundation
Limitations: Scholarships to residents of Butler, PA, who attend Seneca Valley High School.
Financial data: Year ended 05/31/2005. Assets, $1,268,326 (M); Expenditures, $60,303; Total giving, $56,750; Grants to individuals, 40 grants totaling $56,750 (high: $2,000, low: $1,000).
Type of support: Scholarships—to individuals; Support to graduates or students of specific schools.
Application information: Application form required.
  Additional information: Contact high school guidance counselor for current application deadline.
Program description:
  Scholarship Program: Scholarships of $2,000 each are one-time grants. Some recipients receive one-time grants of $1,000, while others receive four-year scholarships of $1,000 per year.
EIN: 256292867

4220

George J. & Margaret I. Vasset Memorial Foundation

(formerly George J. & Margaret I. Vasset Memorial Fund)
c/o Wachovia Bank, N.A.
1819 Main St.
Sarasota, FL 34236

Foundation type: Independent foundation
Limitations: Scholarships to members of First Presbyterian Church, Bradenton, FL, for religious education.
Financial data: Year ended 03/31/2005. Assets, $230,197 (M); Expenditures, $14,231; Total giving, $10,235; Grants to individuals, totaling $10,235.
Fields of interest: Theological school/education.
Type of support: Scholarships—to individuals.
Application information: Applications accepted throughout the year.
EIN: 237320718

4221

Elizabeth Boone Vastine & Katherine Vastine Bernheimer Memorial Fund

c/o Fulton Financial Advisors, N.A.
P.O. Box 3215
Lancaster, PA 17604-3215
Application address: c/o Carl Marrara, Guidance Counselor, Danville Senior High School, Northumberland Rd., Danville, PA 17821, tel.: (570) 275-4113

Foundation type: Independent foundation
Limitations: Scholarships to seniors at Danville Senior High School, PA, and other Danville area seniors who are residents of Montour County, PA.
Financial data: Year ended 12/31/2004. Assets, $244,752 (M); Expenditures, $17,359; Total giving, $14,000; Grants to individuals, totaling $14,000.
Type of support: Support to graduates or students of specific schools; Undergraduate support.
Application information:
  Deadline(s): May 1
  Additional information: Completion of formal application required, including FAFSA and class rank.
Program description:
  Scholarship Program: Scholarships are awarded on the basis of financial need, mental ability, attitude toward school, and reputation and standing in the community. Scholarships are for four years of study.
EIN: 232120313

4222

Ruth Veasey Educational Foundation, Inc.

P.O. Box 326
Dermott, AR 71638
Contact: David Holt, Dir.
Application address: P.O. Box 3, Dermott, AR 71638, tel.: (870) 538-5221

Foundation type: Operating foundation
Limitations: Student loans to graduates of Dermott High School, AR, for education at an accredited college, technical institute or university. If funds permit, loans are also given to other residents of AR.
Financial data: Year ended 05/31/2004. Assets, $1,042,237 (M); Expenditures, $32,251; Total giving, $23,625; Loans to individuals, totaling $23,625.
Type of support: Support to graduates or students of specific schools; Undergraduate support.
Application information:
  Deadline(s): Apr. 30
  Additional information: Completion of formal application required, including three references, one from a local business person if possible.
EIN: 716051103

4223

Rino & Ruth Della Vedova Scholarship Trust

c/o U.S. Bank, N.A.
123 E. 3rd St.
Ottumwa, IA 52501-2904 (641) 683-1641

Foundation type: Independent foundation
Limitations: Scholarships to graduates of Albia Community High School, IA, who are pursuing an engineering degree.
Financial data: Year ended 06/30/2005. Assets, $735,400 (M); Expenditures, $16,983; Total giving, $9,500; Grants to individuals, totaling $9,500.
Fields of interest: Engineering school/education.
Type of support: Support to graduates or students of specific schools; Undergraduate support.
Application information: Application form required.
  Deadline(s): Apr. 1
EIN: 421368808

4224
Peter Simon Veeder Scholarship Fund
c/o JPMorgan Chase Bank
P.O. Box 31412
Rochester, NY 14603
Contact: Robert Baker
Application address: c/o Southeast Fountain High School, 744 E. U.S. 136, Veedersburg, IN 47987

Foundation type: Independent foundation
Limitations: Scholarships to students from Southeast Fountain High School, IN.
Financial data: Year ended 12/31/2004. Assets, $834,007 (M); Expenditures, $53,143; Total giving, $36,835; Grants to individuals, totaling $36,835.
Type of support: Support to graduates or students of specific schools; Undergraduate support.
Application information: Applications accepted.
  Initial approach: Letter or telephone.
  Deadline(s): None
  Additional information: Application by letter.
EIN: 066115230

4225
The Evelyn Vellguth Foundation, Inc.
3484 Carrick Cir.
Snellville, GA 30039 (770) 978-9470
Contact: William E. Oliver, Pres.

Foundation type: Operating foundation
Limitations: Scholarships to high school graduates who are residents of Fayette, GA.
Financial data: Year ended 12/31/2002. Assets, $833,572 (M); Expenditures, $172,466; Total giving, $109,565; Grants to individuals, 13 grants totaling $109,565 (high: $26,976, low: $894).
Type of support: Scholarships—to individuals.
Application information:
  Deadline(s): Contact foundation for current application deadline
  Additional information: Application by typewritten letter, including list of educational courses currently studied or that will be studied, and name of educational institution.
EIN: 582522659

4226
Austin L. and Nell S. Venable Educational Trust
c/o Regions Bank
P.O. Box 2450
Montgomery, AL 36102-2450 (334) 230-6109
Contact: Elaine Ward, Trust Off., Regions Bank

Foundation type: Independent foundation
Limitations: Scholarships to individuals who are at least second-generation natives of Elmore County, AL, and who are in the top 25 percent of their high school graduating class.
Financial data: Year ended 06/30/2005. Assets, $723,346 (M); Expenditures, $44,183; Total giving, $35,100; Grants to individuals, totaling $35,100.
Type of support: Undergraduate support.
Application information: Application form required.
  Deadline(s): Jan. 1 and Mar. 1.
  Additional information: Application forms available from Elmore County, AL, high schools.
EIN: 636158945

4227
Venango Area Community Foundation
213 Seneca St.
P.O. Box 374
Oil City, PA 16301 (814) 677-8687
Contact: Steven P. Kosak, Exec. Dir.
E-mail: jeanne_vacf@verizon.net; URL: http://www.ocasd.org/vacf

Foundation type: Community foundation
Limitations: Scholarships to graduates of Oil City High School, Cranberry Area High School, Franklin High School, Keystone High School and Christian Life Academy, PA.
Publications: Application guidelines; Annual report; Informational brochure.
Financial data: Year ended 08/31/2004. Assets, $4,432,153 (M); Expenditures, $275,887; Total giving, $174,368; Grants to individuals, 115 grants totaling $84,335 (high: $2,075, low: $50).
Type of support: Support to graduates or students of specific schools; Technical education support; Undergraduate support.
Application information: Contact foundation for current application deadline/guidelines.
EIN: 251292553

4228
Doris M. Vennard Residual Trust
c/o Wells Fargo Bank Nebraska, N.A.
P.O. Box 2999
Minneapolis, MN 55402

Foundation type: Independent foundation
Limitations: Scholarships to high school graduate residents of Chippewa County, WI, who will be pursuing a career in nursing.
Financial data: Year ended 12/31/2003. Assets, $69,234 (M); Expenditures, $5,243; Total giving, $3,050; Grants to individuals, 13 grants totaling $3,050.
Fields of interest: Nursing school/education.
Type of support: Scholarships—to individuals.
Application information: Applications accepted.
  Deadline(s): None
  Additional information: Application by resume of academic qualifications.
EIN: 396376718

4229
Ventura County Community Foundation
1317 Del Norte Rd., Ste. 150
Camarillo, CA 93010 (805) 988-0196
Contact: Hugh J. Ralston, C.E.O.
FAX: (805) 485-5537; E-mail: vccf@vccf.org;
URL: http://www.vccf.org

Foundation type: Community foundation
Limitations: Scholarships to individuals in Ventura County, CA.
Publications: Application guidelines; Annual report (including application guidelines); Financial statement; Informational brochure; Newsletter.
Financial data: Year ended 09/30/2004. Assets, $51,198,402 (M); Expenditures, $4,824,871; Total giving, $2,935,779.
Fields of interest: Vocational education.
Type of support: Graduate support; Technical education support; Undergraduate support.
Application information: Applications accepted. Application form required. Application form available on the grantmaker's Web site.
  Deadline(s): Feb. 20.
  Additional information: Interviews required.
EIN: 770165029

4230
Vermillion County Community Foundation
P.O. Box 532
Clinton, IN 47842 (765) 832-8665
Contact: Steve Paloncy, Exec. Dir.
E-mail: director@thevccf.org; URL: http://www.thevccf.org

Foundation type: Community foundation
Limitations: Scholarships to high school seniors of North Vermillion and South Vermillion counties, IN for attendance at IN colleges.
Publications: Biennial report; Financial statement; Grants list; Informational brochure.
Financial data: Year ended 06/30/2003. Assets, $2,754,395 (M); Expenditures, $310,579; Total giving, $211,264; Grants to individuals, 10 grants totaling $180,938 (high: $32,051, low: $4,916).
Type of support: Awards/prizes; Technical education support; Undergraduate support.
Application information: Contact foundation for current application deadline/guidelines; Initial approach by letter.
EIN: 351998550

4231
Vermont Community Foundation
3 Court St.
P.O. Box 30
Middlebury, VT 05753 (802) 388-3355
Contact: Julie Cadwallader-Staub, V.P., Community Grantmaking; For artist grants: Mary Conlon
FAX: (802) 388-3398; E-mail: info@vermontcf.org; Additional E-mails: jcstaub@vermontcf.org and mconlon@vermontcf.org; URL: http://www.vermontcf.org

Foundation type: Community foundation
Limitations: Scholarships to students in VT for higher education.
Publications: Application guidelines; Annual report; Financial statement; Grants list; Informational brochure; Informational brochure (including application guidelines); Multi-year report; Newsletter; Occasional report; Program policy statement.
Financial data: Year ended 12/31/2004. Assets, $110,314,471 (M); Expenditures, $10,766,535; Total giving, $8,276,588.
Type of support: Undergraduate support.
Application information: Applications not accepted.
  Additional information: Application by proposal.
EIN: 222712160

4232
Vermont Student Opportunity Scholarship Fund, Inc.
P.O. Box 232
Williston, VT 05495 (888) 558-8883
Contact: Ruth Stokes, Exec. Dir.

Foundation type: Public charity
Limitations: Scholarships to residents of VT for K-8 education; Eligibility for scholarships is limited to those students who qualify for participation in the Federal Free and Reduced Lunch program.
Financial data: Year ended 06/30/2005. Assets, $37,926 (M); Expenditures, $218,720; Total giving, $171,662; Grants to individuals, 112 grants totaling $171,662 (high: $2,000, low: $371).
Type of support: Precollege support.
Application information: Application form required.
  Deadline(s): Apr. 1

Additional information: Selection is determined by a lottery drawing.
EIN: 030358908

4233
Carrol C. Vernon Scholarship Fund
c/o Bank of America, N.A.
10 Light St., MD4-302-17-06
Baltimore, MD 21202
Application addresses for individuals: c/o Bank of America, N.A., P.O. Box 351, Charlottesville, VA 22902, tel.: (804) 977-2148; c/o Greene County School Board Office, Vice-Chair., P.O. Box 98, Stanardsville, VA 22973

Foundation type: Independent foundation
Limitations: Scholarships to graduates of William Monroe High School in Greene County, VA, for study at a four-year college or university.
Financial data: Year ended 12/31/2004.
Assets, $67,632 (M); Expenditures, $17,375; Total giving, $15,416; Grants to individuals, totaling $15,416.
Type of support: Support to graduates or students of specific schools; Undergraduate support.
Application information: Applications accepted. Application form required.
  Deadline(s): June 1
  Applicants should submit the following:
    1) Financial information
    2) Transcripts
  Additional information: Application should include extracurricular activities and class rank.
EIN: 546277310

4234
Vernon A. & Ada L. Vesper Educational Trust
c/o First State Bank
101 E. Cherry St.
Hill City, KS 67642-1707 (785) 421-2168
Contact: Dexter Potter, Tr.

Foundation type: Independent foundation
Limitations: Student loans to graduates of high schools in Graham County, KS. Preference is given to students of medicine, dentistry, nursing, medical technology, and related courses of study. Students attending schools of osteopathic, chiropractic, and naturopathic study are ineligible.
Financial data: Year ended 10/31/2004.
Assets, $316,523 (M); Expenditures, $93,269; Total giving, $90,750; Grants to individuals, totaling $90,750.
Fields of interest: Dental school/education; Medical school/education; Nursing school/education; Health sciences school/education.
Type of support: Support to graduates or students of specific schools; Undergraduate support.
Application information: Applications accepted throughout the year; Application by letter, including name of high school, date of graduation, intended college or university, and course of study.
EIN: 486121219

4235
Adolph and Esther Vestergaard Memorial Scholarship Fund
c/o Lawrence S. Harden
P.O. Box 908
Spencer, IA 51301-0908 (712) 262-1500
Contact: Selection Comm.

Foundation type: Independent foundation
Limitations: Scholarships to residents of Clay and Dickinson counties, IA, for higher education.
Financial data: Year ended 12/31/2004.
Assets, $786,890 (M); Expenditures, $38,498; Total giving, $30,000; Grants to individuals, totaling $30,000.
Type of support: Scholarships—to individuals.
Application information: Deadline May 15; Completion of formal application required, including college student will attend, extracurricular activities, and other scholarships.
EIN: 421369816

4236
Vetowich Family Foundation
c/o William Felosak
26026 Telegraph Rd., Ste. 200
Southfield, MI 48034

Foundation type: Independent foundation
Limitations: Soccer scholarships, by nomination only, to individuals residing in the Southfield, MI, area.
Financial data: Year ended 08/31/2004.
Assets, $259,862 (M); Expenditures, $15,343; Total giving, $12,500; Grants to individuals, 4 grants totaling $12,500.
Fields of interest: Athletics/sports, soccer.
Type of support: Awards/grants by nomination only; Undergraduate support.
Application information: Unsolicited requests for funds not considered or acknowledged.
EIN: 386750824

4237
Frances S. Viele Scholarship Trust
170 E. 78th St., Ste. 8B
New York, NY 10021 (212) 608-1080
Application address: Attn.: William Brennan, c/o Morea Financial Svcs., 120 Broadway, Ste. 101, New York, NY 10271

Foundation type: Independent foundation
Limitations: Scholarships to members of Sigma Phi Society.
Financial data: Year ended 05/31/2005.
Assets, $3,602,543 (M); Expenditures, $181,004; Total giving, $148,674; Grants to individuals, 42 grants totaling $148,674 (high: $7,500, low: $1,000).
Fields of interest: Students, sororities/fraternities.
Type of support: Scholarships—to individuals.
Application information: Contact trust for current application deadline; Completion of formal application required, including complete financial statement, two essays, and transcripts.
EIN: 953285561

4238
Vietnamese American Scholarship Fund
8021 Golfers Oasis Dr.
Las Vegas, NV 89149
Contact: Doan L. Phung, Tr.

Foundation type: Independent foundation
Limitations: Scholarships, based on merit and need, to students and teachers of American or Vietnamese origin.
Financial data: Year ended 12/31/2004.
Assets, $3,372,234 (M); Expenditures, $139,087; Total giving, $136,585.
Fields of interest: Education; Asians/Pacific Islanders; Vietnam.

Type of support: Scholarships—to individuals.
Application information:
  Initial approach: Letter.
  Deadline(s): None
  Additional information: Application should include documents supporting merit.
EIN: 621336969

4239
Viles Foundation, Inc.
c/o Bank of America, N.A.
P.O. Box 26900
Albuquerque, NM 87125-6900
Application address for individuals: P.O. Box 1177, Las Vegas, NM 87701-1117

Foundation type: Independent foundation
Limitations: Scholarships to financially needy residents of San Miguel and Mora counties, NM, for attendance at colleges, universities, and vocational-technical schools. Funds are very limited.
Financial data: Year ended 12/31/2002.
Assets, $46,554 (M); Expenditures, $106,290; Total giving, $104,450; Grants to individuals, 55 grants totaling $104,450.
Fields of interest: Vocational education; Residential/custodial care; Women.
Type of support: Technical education support; Undergraduate support.
Application information: Unsolicited applications not considered or acknowledged.
EIN: 856011506

4240
Villa Park Bank Foundation
10 S. Villa Ave.
Villa Park, IL 60181 (630) 834-0800

Foundation type: Operating foundation
Limitations: Scholarships to high school or preparatory school seniors only in the foundation's immediate area, with preference given to residents of Villa Park, IL, and the areas juxtaposed to Villa Park. Applicants must reside in the 60101, 60126, 60148, or 60181 ZIP codes.
Financial data: Year ended 12/31/2003.
Assets, $63,971 (M); Expenditures, $32,470; Total giving, $32,450; Grants to individuals, totaling $24,350.
Fields of interest: Vocational education.
Type of support: Technical education support; Undergraduate support.
Application information: Applications accepted. Application form required.
  Deadline(s): Early Jan.; Contact foundation for current application deadline.
  Additional information: Application forms available at Villa Park area high schools or at Villa Park Trust & Savings Bank; Interviews required for finalists.
Program descriptions:
Villa Park Bank Foundation Vocational Scholarship: Awards $3,000 annually divided between one to four scholarships to individuals attending a two-year college or trade school. Scholarships are paid directly to the institution.
Villa Park Academic Scholarship: Awards three scholarships, of $4,000, $3,000, and $2,00 each, annually, to individuals attending four-year colleges and universities. Scholarships are paid directly to the institution.
EIN: 366198333

4241
Maurice Villency Foundation, Inc.
c/o American Express Tax & Business Services, Inc.
1185 Ave. of the Americas
New York, NY 10036-2602
Contact: Robert Villency, Dir.
Application address: c/o Maurice Villency Fdn., Inc., 950 3rd Ave., New York, NY 10022

Foundation type: Company-sponsored foundation
Limitations: Scholarships to deserving homeless or otherwise financially needy individuals to help them to get off public assistance through educational advancement.
Financial data: Year ended 05/31/2004.
Assets, $1,303 (M); Expenditures, $12,752; Total giving, $12,447; Grant to an individual, 1 grant totaling $12,447.
Fields of interest: Economically disadvantaged.
Type of support: Scholarships—to individuals.
Application information: Applications accepted throughout the year; Completion of formal application required, including transcripts, two letters of recommendation (one from a teacher), and 500-word essay on why applicant deserves a scholarship.
EIN: 133487733

4242
Otto Villwock Medical Educational Scholarship Fund
c/o JPMorgan Chase Bank, N.A
P.O. Box 1308
Milwaukee, WI 53201-1308
Application address: c/o Financial Aid Offices at Case Western Reserve University, University of Wisconsin Medical School, and University of Cincinnati Medical School

Foundation type: Independent foundation
Limitations: Scholarships to financially needy students whose fathers are deceased and who have been admitted to Case Western Reserve University, University of Wisconsin—Madison Medical School, or University of Cincinnati Medical School.
Financial data: Year ended 05/31/2005.
Assets, $393,454 (M); Expenditures, $21,786; Total giving, $17,520; Grants to individuals, 8 grants totaling $17,520.
Fields of interest: Medical school/education.
Type of support: Scholarships—to individuals; Support to graduates or students of specific schools.
Application information: Deadline Mar. 31; Application by letter.
EIN: 510172011

4243
Anna M. Vincent Trust
c/o Mellon Financial Corp.
P.O. Box 185
Pittsburgh, PA 15230-9897
Application address: c/o Michael L. McGrath, P.O. Box 7899, Philadelphia, PA 19101-7899, tel.: (215) 553-1825

Foundation type: Independent foundation
Limitations: Scholarships to long-term residents of the five-county Philadelphia area, PA (Delaware Valley area), for graduate or undergraduate study at recognized colleges, universities, and other institutions of higher learning.
Publications: Application guidelines.

Financial data: Year ended 06/30/2005.
Assets, $7,582,300 (M); Expenditures, $461,389; Total giving, $394,000; Grants to individuals, 117 grants totaling $394,000 (high: $5,000, low: $1,000).
Type of support: Graduate support; Undergraduate support.
Application information: Application form required.
Initial approach: Letter.
Deadline(s): Mar. 1
Additional information: Application forms available at local high schools.
Program description:
Scholarship Program: Most recipients are seniors in high school. The trust also awards multiple-year grants, renewable for up to five years.
EIN: 236422666

4244
Francois Vinecore Memorial Fund
(formerly Francios Vinecore Scholarship Foundation)
c/o Bank of America, N.A.
P.O. Box 34345
Seattle, WA 98124-1345
Application address: c/o Mike Tabler, P.O. Box 1230, Ephrata, WA 98823-1230

Foundation type: Independent foundation
Limitations: Scholarships to students of Douglas County, WA, who attend Washington State University and are majoring in horticulture, business administration, or any degree associated with tree fruit research.
Financial data: Year ended 03/31/2005.
Assets, $374,879 (M); Expenditures, $17,592; Total giving, $13,750; Grants to individuals, 4 grants totaling $13,750 (high: $3,438, low: $3,427).
Fields of interest: Business school/education; Horticulture/garden clubs; Agriculture.
Type of support: Scholarships—to individuals; Support to graduates or students of specific schools.
Application information: Applications accepted. Application form required.
Applicants should submit the following:
1) Transcripts
2) Financial information
3) Essay
Additional information: Application must also include extracurricular activities.
EIN: 916307756

4245
Dolly Vinsant Memorial Foundation
c/o McAllen National Bank
P.O. Box 5555
McAllen, TX 78502-5555
Application address: c/o Richard H. Welch, P.O. Box 711, Route 6, San Benito, TX 78586, tel.: (956) 399-2491

Foundation type: Independent foundation
Limitations: Scholarships to graduating students attending high school in Cameron County, TX, to attend a two- or four-year college, university, or vocational-technical school, and pursue a career in the medical field.
Financial data: Year ended 09/30/2004.
Assets, $1,153,968 (M); Expenditures, $117,940; Total giving, $100,000; Grants to individuals, 58 grants totaling $100,000 (high: $4,500, low: $500).
Fields of interest: Vocational education; Medical school/education.

Type of support: Support to graduates or students of specific schools; Technical education support; Undergraduate support.
Application information: Applications accepted throughout the year; Completion of formal application required, including an official transcript, an essay, and two letters of recommendation.
Program description:
Scholarship Program: Applicants must be in the top 25 percent of their graduating class. Recipients must maintain a 2.0 GPA in all classes.
EIN: 741143136

4246
Vinson & Elkins L.L.P. Scholarship Foundation
2300 First City Tower
1001 Fannin St., Ste. 2300
Houston, TX 77002-6760
Contact: Sandra McCaffety

Foundation type: Company-sponsored foundation
Limitations: Scholarships to financially needy graduating high school seniors at public high schools in the greater Houston, TX, area, who are of African American or Latino origin, plan to pursue law at U.S. universities, are in the top 20th percentile of their graduating classes, and have received at least a 1000 combined SAT score.
Financial data: Year ended 12/31/2004.
Assets, $0 (M); Expenditures, $55,000; Total giving, $55,000; Grants to individuals, 22 grants totaling $55,000 (high: $2,500, low: $2,500).
Fields of interest: Law school/education; African Americans/Blacks; Hispanics/Latinos.
Type of support: Support to graduates or students of specific schools; Undergraduate support.
Application information: Deadline Mar. 3; Completion of formal application required, including SAT and ACT scores and class rank; Applications available only through high school counselors.
Program description:
Scholarship Program: Applicants must meet all of the stated criteria. Scholarships are renewable.
EIN: 760428361

4247
Visible Changes Educational Foundation
1303 Campbell Rd.
Houston, TX 77055

Foundation type: Independent foundation
Limitations: Scholarships only to children of employees of Visible Changes Educational Foundation.
Financial data: Year ended 12/31/2004.
Assets, $602,253 (M); Expenditures, $56,354; Total giving, $55,407; Grants to individuals, totaling $55,407.
Type of support: Employee-related scholarships.
Application information: Applications not accepted.
EIN: 760303682

4248
The Visiting Nurse Association of Rye, Inc.
c/o Bryon Hawkins
131 Old Post Rd.
Rye, NY 10580-1401
Contact: Frances T. Wiener, Pres.
Application address: 7 Pine Island Rd., Rye, NY 10580, tel.: (914) 967-5718

Foundation type: Independent foundation
Limitations: Scholarships only to residents of Rye, NY, pursuing degrees in medicine, nursing, or related fields.
Financial data: Year ended 12/31/2004. Assets, $265,899 (M); Expenditures, $47,467; Total giving, $44,200; Grants to individuals, totaling $44,200.
Fields of interest: Medical school/education; Nursing school/education; Health sciences school/education.
Type of support: Scholarships—to individuals.
Application information: Deadline Apr. 15; Completion of formal application required; Application forms available at all Rye public and parochial schools; Interviews required.
EIN: 131825945

4249
Visitor Industry Human Resource Development Council
701 Brickell Ave., Ste. 2700
Miami, FL 33131-2847 (305) 539-3032
Contact: Stuart L. Blumberg, Chair.

Foundation type: Public charity
Limitations: Scholarships to minority students in the hospitality field.
Financial data: Year ended 09/30/2003. Assets, $236,183 (M); Expenditures, $163,211; Total giving, $23,642; Grants to individuals, 18 grants totaling $23,642.
Fields of interest: Agriculture/food, formal/general education; Minorities.
Type of support: Scholarships—to individuals.
Application information: Contact foundation for current application deadline/guidelines.
EIN: 650329273

4250
Visual Arts Foundation, Inc.
15 Grammercy Park S.
New York, NY 10003 (212) 260-7607
Contact: Silas Rhodes, Pres.
E-mail: rdouglas@sva.edu

Foundation type: Public charity
Limitations: Scholarships, grants and awards to deserving students pursuing courses in the field of art.
Financial data: Year ended 12/31/2003. Assets, $896,404 (M); Expenditures, $474,007; Total giving, $230,310; Grants to individuals, totaling $230,310.
Fields of interest: Visual arts.
Type of support: Scholarships—to individuals; Awards/prizes.
Application information: Application form required.
  Deadline(s): Apr. 15
EIN: 136261474

4251
The VM Family Foundation
1135 Rivergate Dr.
Lodi, CA 95240

Foundation type: Independent foundation
Limitations: Scholarships to economically challenged high school students in San Joaquin County, CA, for higher education.
Financial data: Year ended 12/31/2004. Assets, $220,768 (M); Expenditures, $64,337; Total giving, $62,715; Grants to individuals, 21 grants totaling $15,500 (high: $2,000, low: $250).

Type of support: Scholarships—to individuals.
Application information: Applications not accepted.
  Additional information: Unsolicited requests for funds not acknowledged or considered.
EIN: 680400296

4252
Theodore Vodgis Charitable Trust
766 Old Hammonds Ferry Rd.
Linthicum, MD 21090
Application address: Denise S. Fargo, Principal, c/o Frederick High School, 650 Carroll Pkwy., Frederick, MD 21701, tel.: (301) 694-1367

Foundation type: Independent foundation
Limitations: Scholarships to graduates of Frederick High School, MD.
Financial data: Year ended 12/31/2004. Assets, $1,396,183 (M); Expenditures, $251,157; Total giving, $236,268; Grants to individuals, 9 grants totaling $236,268 (high: $69,547, low: $223).
Type of support: Support to graduates or students of specific schools; Undergraduate support.
Application information: Application form required.
  Deadline(s): May
  Applicants should submit the following:
    1) FAFSA
    2) Essay
EIN: 526101497

4253
T. Vogeley Memorial Trust
c/o Mellon Financial Corp.
P.O. Box 185
Pittsburgh, PA 15230-9897 (412) 234-0023
Application address: c/o Vogaley Scholarship Committee, 165 New Castle Rd., Butler, PA 16001

Foundation type: Independent foundation
Limitations: Scholarships to graduates of Butler High School, PA.
Financial data: Year ended 09/30/2004. Assets, $3,301,632 (M); Expenditures, $168,808; Total giving, $165,415; Grants to individuals, totaling $165,415.
Type of support: Support to graduates or students of specific schools; Undergraduate support.
Application information: Contact high school guidance counselor for current application deadline; Completion of formal application required.
EIN: 256235851

4254
Mary G. Voght Trust
(formerly Voght Scholarship Fund)
c/o TD Banknorth, N.A., Investment Mgmt. Group
178 Main St.
P.O. Box 174
New Britain, CT 06050

Foundation type: Independent foundation
Limitations: Scholarships to individuals for higher education.
Financial data: Year ended 12/31/2004. Assets, $184,447 (M); Expenditures, $9,981; Total giving, $7,200; Grants to individuals, 9 grants totaling $7,200.
Type of support: Scholarships—to individuals.
Application information: Contact trust for current application deadline/guidelines.
EIN: 046555019

4255
Volz Foundation Charitable Trust
10849 Indian Head Industrial Blvd.
St. Louis, MO 63132-1166

Foundation type: Independent foundation
Limitations: Scholarships to underprivileged individuals.
Financial data: Year ended 12/31/2004. Assets, $1 (M); Expenditures, $7,897; Total giving, $7,447; Grants to individuals, totaling $6,647.
Type of support: Scholarships—to individuals.
Application information: Contact trust for current application deadline; Application by letter.
EIN: 431427425

4256
The Vomberg Foundation
c/o Olivet College
320 S. Main St.
Olivet, MI 49076-9406 (269) 749-7585
Contact: Maria Beam

Foundation type: Independent foundation
Limitations: Scholarships to financially needy high school seniors who are residents of Eaton County, MI.
Financial data: Year ended 12/31/2004. Assets, $624,603 (M); Expenditures, $36,653; Total giving, $29,225; Grants to individuals, totaling $29,225.
Type of support: Undergraduate support.
Application information: Deadline Dec. 1 of senior year; Completion of formal application required; Interviews required.
EIN: 386072845

4257
Flora Von der Ahe School Trust
c/o U.S. Bank, N.A., Trust Tax Svcs.
P.O. Box 3168
Portland, OR 97208-3168

Foundation type: Independent foundation
Limitations: Scholarships to graduates of Umatilla County, OR, high schools, who have at least a 2.5 GPA, for full-time undergraduate or graduate study at accredited colleges, universities, and technical schools in OR.
Financial data: Year ended 06/30/2005. Assets, $255,185 (M); Expenditures, $20,500; Total giving, $12,200; Grants to individuals, totaling $12,200.
Fields of interest: Vocational education.
Type of support: Support to graduates or students of specific schools; Graduate support; Technical education support; Undergraduate support.
Application information: Applications accepted. Application form required.
  Deadline(s): Jan. 1 to Apr. 1.
  Applicants should submit the following:
    1) Transcripts
    2) FAF
  Additional information: Interviews required; Application forms are available from U.S. National Bank branches, high school guidance offices, and the College Financial Aid Office in OR.
Program description:
  Scholarship Program: Scholarships are renewable. Generally 20 to 22 scholarships ranging from $200 to $750 are awarded each year. Awards are based on scholastic achievement, financial need, responsibility, and ambition. Applicants are notified of decision by June 30.
EIN: 936066821

4258
The Von Rosenberg Foundation
8502 Dashwood Dr.
Houston, TX 77036-4716

Foundation type: Independent foundation
Limitations: Scholarships to individuals, primarily in Longview, TX.
Financial data: Year ended 10/31/2004. Assets, $45,344 (M); Expenditures, $31,107; Total giving, $29,700; Grants to individuals, totaling $29,700.
Type of support: Scholarships—to individuals.
Application information: Contact foundation for current application deadline/guidelines.
EIN: 760520143

4259
Roger L. VonAmelunxen Foundation, Inc.
83-21 Edgerton Blvd.
Jamaica, NY 11432 (718) 641-4800
Contact: Karen Donnelly, V.P.
FAX: (718) 641-4802;
E-mail: rogerfoundation@aol.com; URL: http://rogerfoundation.org

Foundation type: Independent foundation
Limitations: Scholarships to children of employees of the U.S. Customs Service for attendance at accredited institutions of higher learning.
Financial data: Year ended 07/31/2004. Assets, $583,882 (M); Expenditures, $331,960; Total giving, $325,883; Grants to individuals, 146 grants totaling $325,883 (high: $6,000, low: $350).
Type of support: Employee-related scholarships.
Application information:
Deadline(s): Aug. 1
Additional information: Application by letter, including proof of relationship to U.S. Customs employee.
EIN: 112583014

4260
VSA arts
1300 Connecticut Ave., N.W., Ste. 700
Washington, DC 20036 (202) 628-2800
Contact: Soula Antoniou, Pres.; GTI: Elena Widder
FAX: (202) 737-0725; E-mail: info@vsarts.org; Additional tel.: (800) 933-8721; E-mail for Elena Widder: elenaw@vsarts.org; URL: http://www.vsarts.org/

Foundation type: Public charity
Limitations: Awards to outstanding young musicians, ages 25 and under, who are disabled. Also awards to teachers and students for plays related to disabilities.
Financial data: Year ended 06/30/2003. Assets, $1,535,518 (M); Expenditures, $6,972,168; Total giving, $2,628,108; Grants to individuals, totaling $14,250.
Fields of interest: Theater; Music; Disabilities, people with.
Type of support: Awards/prizes.
Application information: Applications accepted. Application form required. Application form available on the grantmaker's Web site.
Program descriptions:
Playwright Discovery Award: Awards $1,000 to challenge middle and high school students of all abilities to take a closer look at the world around them, examine how disability affects their lives and the lives of others, and express their views through the art of playwriting.

Playwright Discovery Teacher Award: Awards middle and high school teachers who creatively bring disability awareness to the classroom through the art of playwriting. One teacher will be selected to receive funds to purchase playwriting resources.
Young Soloists Award: Awards outstanding young musicians with disabilities, ages 25 and under, who have exhibited exceptional talents as vocalists or instrumentalists. Awards are made in two categories: the Panasonic Young Soloists Award for musicians who reside in the U.S.; and the Rosemary Kennedy International Young Soloists Award for musicians who reside outside the U.S.
EIN: 521065313

4261
Vulcan Scholarships, Inc.
P.O. Box 1850
Foley, AL 36536-1850 (251) 943-2645
Contact: Thomas M. Lee, Secy.
URL: http://www.vulcaninc.com/plt0p04.htm

Foundation type: Company-sponsored foundation
Limitations: Undergraduate scholarships to residents of Baldwin County, AL, and to students at Foley High School, AL, Gulf Shores High School, AL, and Robertsdale High School, AL, for study in engineering.
Financial data: Year ended 10/31/2005. Assets, $257,083 (M); Expenditures, $14,703; Total giving, $14,550; Grants to individuals, 11 grants totaling $14,550 (high: $2,100, low: $750).
Fields of interest: Engineering school/education.
Type of support: Support to graduates or students of specific schools; Undergraduate support.
Application information: Application form required.
Deadline(s): Mid-Feb.
Applicants should submit the following:
1) Transcripts
2) SAT
3) GPA
4) ACT
Additional information: See web site for scholarship awards.
EIN: 630887786

4262
W & G Scholarship Trust
c/o Karen Gates Hildt
P.O. Box 277
Port Townsend, WA 98368

Foundation type: Independent foundation
Limitations: Scholarships to residents of Port Townsend, WA, for higher education.
Financial data: Year ended 12/31/2004. Assets, $452,241 (M); Expenditures, $14,120; Total giving, $10,000; Grants to individuals, totaling $10,000.
Type of support: Undergraduate support.
Application information: Applications not accepted.
EIN: 911941288

4263
Wabash Magnetics Scholarship Foundation
c/o DKM Corp.
565 5th Ave., 4th Fl.
New York, NY 10017

Foundation type: Company-sponsored foundation
Limitations: Scholarships to children of employees of Wabash, Inc., its divisions and subsidiaries,

including IPM and Wabash Automotive Components Division.
Financial data: Year ended 12/31/2004. Assets, $78,747 (M); Expenditures, $21,393; Total giving, $20,650; Grants to individuals, 24 grants totaling $20,650 (high: $1,875, low: $500).
Type of support: Employee-related scholarships.
Application information: Application form required.
Initial approach: Letter.
Deadline(s): None
Additional information: Scholarships are renewable.
EIN: 356205883

4264
Wabash Valley Community Foundation, Inc.
2901 Ohio Blvd., Ste. 153
Terre Haute, IN 47803-2239 (812) 232-2234
Contact: Beth A.A. Tevlin, Exec. Dir.
FAX: (812) 234-4853; E-mail: info@wvcf.com; Additional E-mails: beth@wvcf.com and rose@wvcf.com; URL: http://www.wvcf.com

Foundation type: Community foundation
Limitations: Scholarships to students in Clay, Sullivan and Vigo counties, IN.
Publications: Application guidelines; Annual report; Grants list; Informational brochure; Newsletter.
Financial data: Year ended 09/30/2005. Assets, $22,223,214 (M); Expenditures, $1,123,607; Total giving, $671,772; Grants to individuals, 62 grants totaling $78,454.
Fields of interest: Business school/education; Nursing school/education; Science; Mathematics; Engineering/technology.
Type of support: Technical education support; Undergraduate support.
Application information: Applications accepted. Application form required.
Initial approach: Letter.
Deadline(s): Dec. 15
Applicants should submit the following:
1) Letter(s) of recommendation
2) FAFSA
Additional information: See Web site for further program and application information.
Program description:
Scholarship Awards: The foundation offers numerous scholarships to students in the Clay, Sullivan and Vigo county areas, IN. See Web site for a full listing of scholarships offered.
EIN: 351848649

4265
Verneda A. and Leo J. Wachter, Sr. Foundation
19514 Orrick Trail
Kirksville, MO 63501
Contact: Therese A. Wachter Ream, Pres.

Foundation type: Operating foundation
Limitations: Scholarships to deserving and/or needy students who attend Blair County, PA high schools, for higher education.
Publications: Application guidelines.
Financial data: Year ended 12/31/2004. Assets, $420,917 (M); Expenditures, $44,406; Total giving, $43,450; Grants to individuals, 7 grants totaling $10,500 (high: $1,500, low: $1,500).
Type of support: Scholarships—to individuals.
Application information: Applications accepted. Application form required.
Initial approach: Application.

Copies of proposal: 6
Deadline(s): Mid-Jan.
Applicants should submit the following:
1) Transcripts
2) SAT
3) Letter(s) of recommendation
4) GPA
5) Essay
Additional information: Contact Blair County, PA high schools guidance office for application.
EIN: 251531899

4266

Edwin J. Wadas Foundation, Inc.

c/o Feldman, Domagal and Kupiec
246 Genesse St.
Utica, NY 13502-4325
Application address: c/o Edwin J. Wadas, 22 Greenman Ave., New York Mills, NY 13417-1004

Foundation type: Independent foundation
Limitations: Scholarships to graduates of Clinton, New York Mills, Sauquoit, Whitesboro and Whitestown school districts, NY.
Financial data: Year ended 12/31/2004. Assets, $2,636,001 (M); Expenditures, $151,242; Total giving, $143,415; Grants to individuals, 10 grants totaling $13,000.
Type of support: Support to graduates or students of specific schools; Undergraduate support.
Application information: Contact foundation for current application deadline; Completion of formal application required.
EIN: 161361881

4267

Frank C. Wagenknecht Scholarship Trust

c/o LaSalle Bank, N.A.
105 Marquette St.
P.O. Box 461
La Salle, IL 61301

Foundation type: Independent foundation
Limitations: Scholarships to the top two (or more if funds permit) GPA students from LaSalle-Peru High School, IL.
Financial data: Year ended 05/31/2005. Assets, $1,788,431 (M); Expenditures, $79,606; Total giving, $65,007; Grants to individuals, totaling $65,007.
Type of support: Support to graduates or students of specific schools; Undergraduate support.
Application information: Applications not accepted.
Additional information: Applicants are determined by grade-points only; Selections are made by the school.
EIN: 936122496

4268

The Wagnalls Memorial

P.O. Box 217
150 E. Columbus St.
Lithopolis, OH 43136-0217 (614) 837-4765
Contact: Carl A. Spencer, Exec. Dir.
E-mail: caspencer@wagnalls.org; URL: http://wagnalls.org/

Foundation type: Independent foundation
Limitations: Graduate and undergraduate scholarships to graduates of high schools in the Lithopolis and Bloom Township areas of Fairfield County, OH.

Publications: Application guidelines; Annual report; Financial statement; Informational brochure; Newsletter.
Financial data: Year ended 12/31/2004. Assets, $18,933,808 (M); Expenditures, $1,027,805; Total giving, $24,261; Grants to individuals, 17 grants totaling $18,725 (high: $1,000, low: $500).
Type of support: Graduate support; Undergraduate support.
Application information: Application form required.
Initial approach: Letter or telephone.
Copies of proposal: 1
Deadline(s): May 1
Applicants should submit the following:
1) Photograph
2) GPA
3) Financial information
4) Transcripts
Additional information: Application must also include a signed and notarized affidavit certifying Bloom Township residency; Interviews required.
Program description:
Scholarships: To be eligible to receive the scholarship, applicant and his or her parent or guardian must have moved into Bloom Township before Sept. 1 of the year the student enters the first grade of school. Students cease to be eligible ten years from the date of high school graduation. Applicants must have at least a 2.25 GPA. They can enroll in part-time or full-time programs. Scholarship awards are $500 to $1,000 for the first year of college. Scholarships are not given for vocational studies.
EIN: 314379589

4269

Edward Wagner and George Hosser Scholarship Fund Trust

c/o Citizens Bank of NH
870 Westminster St.
Providence, RI 02903
Application address: c/o Citizens Bank New Hampshire, Attn.: Renee Hall, 1 Capital Plz., Concord, NH 03301, tel.: (603) 229-3573

Foundation type: Independent foundation
Limitations: Undergraduate scholarships to male residents of Manchester, NH.
Financial data: Year ended 06/30/2005. Assets, $5,670,990 (M); Expenditures, $475,142; Total giving, $393,500; Grants to individuals, 97 grants totaling $393,500 (high: $8,000, low: $3,500).
Fields of interest: Men.
Type of support: Undergraduate support.
Application information: Deadline May 31; Completion of formal application required.
EIN: 026005491

4270

Kathryn & Otto H. Wagner Charitable Trust

c/o Bank of America, N.A.
P.O. Box 34345
Seattle, WA 98124-1345
Contact: Jodi Gardner, Tr.
Application address for individuals: P.O. Box 128, Township, WA 99856-0128

Foundation type: Independent foundation
Limitations: Scholarships for higher education in Seattle, WA.

Financial data: Year ended 12/31/2004. Assets, $842,090 (M); Expenditures, $40,474; Total giving, $14,962; Grants to individuals, totaling $14,962.
Type of support: Scholarships—to individuals.
Application information: Contact trust for current application deadline/guidelines.
EIN: 916103623

4271

Claire Wagner Estate Heinbach-Wagner Trust

c/o Deutsche Trust Co. of NY
P.O. Box 829, Church St. Sta.
New York, NY 10008
Application address: c/o David Wolkenbrod, Deutsche Trust Co. of NY, 280 Park Ave., New York, NY 10017

Foundation type: Independent foundation
Limitations: Scholarships to students at The Albert Einstein College of Medicine of Yeshiva University for medical education, NY.
Financial data: Year ended 12/31/2004. Assets, $1,177,703 (M); Expenditures, $55,076; Total giving, $38,677; Grants to individuals, 9 grants totaling $18,677 (high: $3,750, low: $1,250).
Fields of interest: Medical school/education.
Type of support: Support to graduates or students of specific schools; Graduate support.
Application information: Applications accepted.
Deadline(s): None
Additional information: Contact trust for current application guidelines.
EIN: 136182244

4272

Elizabeth C. Wagner Trust

c/o SunTrust Bank
P.O. Box 1908
Orlando, FL 32802-1908

Foundation type: Independent foundation
Limitations: Scholarships to high school graduates for higher education, primarily in VA.
Financial data: Year ended 02/28/2005. Assets, $1,171,333 (M); Expenditures, $56,003; Total giving, $51,162.
Type of support: Undergraduate support.
Application information: Contact trust for current application deadline/guidelines.
EIN: 546374333

4273

Harold Wahala Scholarship Fund

c/o Pennsville National Bank
P.O. Box 345
Pennsville, NJ 08070-0345

Foundation type: Independent foundation
Limitations: Scholarships to graduating seniors of Pennsville Memorial High School or residents of Pennsville Township, NJ.
Financial data: Year ended 12/31/2004. Assets, $60,759 (M); Expenditures, $31,555; Total giving, $30,000; Grants to individuals, totaling $30,000.
Type of support: Support to graduates or students of specific schools; Undergraduate support.
Application information: Deadline Mar. 7; Completion of formal application required.

Program description:

Scholarship Program: Preference is given to students seeking a four-year bachelor's degree or a two-year associate degree at a NJ college or an institution within 200 miles of Pennsville Township. Emphasis is placed on financial need, active involvement in a school and extracurricular activities and/or having a superior GPA.
EIN: 226805185

4274
Leo J. Wahl Foundation

c/o Wahl Clipper Corp., Personnel Dept.
2902 N. Locust St.
P.O. Box 578
Sterling, IL   61081   (815) 625-6525

Foundation type: Company-sponsored foundation
Limitations: Scholarships to dependents of Wahl Clipper Corporation employees, primarily in IL.
Financial data: Year ended 12/31/2004. Assets, $207,172 (M); Expenditures, $17,170; Total giving, $17,150; Grants to individuals, 22 grants totaling $17,150 (high: $1,200, low: $500).
Type of support: Employee-related scholarships.
Application information: Application form required.
Deadline(s): None
Applicants should submit the following:
1) Transcripts
2) GPA
EIN: 363447061

4275
William F. & Gertrude Wahl Scholarship Fund

c/o Heritage Community Bank
P.O. Box 176
Vevay, IN   47043-0176

Foundation type: Independent foundation
Limitations: Scholarships to graduating seniors of Switzerland County High School, IN, who are in the upper quarter of their graduating classes, demonstrate financial need, and are of good standing in the community and school.
Financial data: Year ended 12/31/2004. Assets, $715,151 (M); Expenditures, $29,402; Total giving, $20,245; Grants to individuals, totaling $20,245.
Type of support: Support to graduates or students of specific schools; Undergraduate support.
Application information: Applications accepted throughout the year; Initial approach by unsigned letter to selection committee.
EIN: 311014220

4276
Waimea Educational & Cultural Association

P.O. Box 595
Waimea, HI   96796-0595
Application address: P.O. Box 236, Waimea, HI 96796, tel.: (808) 338-1425

Foundation type: Independent foundation
Limitations: Scholarships primarily to students who reside in HI.
Financial data: Year ended 06/30/2005. Assets, $354,218 (M); Expenditures, $24,810; Total giving, $19,000; Grants to individuals, totaling $19,000.
Type of support: Scholarships—to individuals.

Application information: Applications by letter accepted throughout the year.
EIN: 996005136

4277
Wake Charitable Foundation

203 S. 6th St.
Seward, NE   68434-2401   (402) 643-3602
Contact: James S. Wake

Foundation type: Independent foundation
Limitations: Scholarships to graduates of the following NE high schools: Seward High School in Seward, East Butler High School in Brainard, Aquinas High School in David City, and Centennial High School in Utica.
Financial data: Year ended 12/31/2004. Assets, $1,886,682 (M); Expenditures, $112,182; Total giving, $100,875; Grants to individuals, 63 grants totaling $33,500 (high: $1,000, low: $500).
Type of support: Support to graduates or students of specific schools; Undergraduate support.
Application information: Deadline Apr.; Completion of formal application required.
EIN: 476038985

4278
Carlos E. Wakefield and Beatrice E. Wakefield Scholarship Trust

c/o KeyBank N.A.
800 Superior Ave., 4th Fl.
Cleveland, OH   44114-1306
Application address: Freda Wortman, Chair., c/o Scholarship Comm., Highland Ave., Dexter, ME 04930

Foundation type: Independent foundation
Limitations: Scholarships to residents of Dexter and Ripley, ME.
Financial data: Year ended 08/31/2004. Assets, $765,891 (M); Expenditures, $63,474; Total giving, $54,910; Grants to individuals, totaling $54,910.
Type of support: Scholarships—to individuals.
Application information: Applications accepted throughout the year; Completion of formal application required.
EIN: 222929235

4279
Wal-Mart Foundation

(also known as SAM'S CLUB Foundation)
702 S.W. 8th St.
Bentonville, AR   72716-0150   (800) 530-9925
Contact: Brad Fisher, Dir.
FAX: (479) 273-6850; URL: http://www.walmartfoundation.org

Foundation type: Company-sponsored foundation
Limitations: Scholarships to employees and children of employees of Wal-Mart/Sam's Club, general offices, distribution centers, or other facilities. Scholarships also to graduating high school seniors in areas where Wal-Mart Stores, Inc., or Sam's Club stores are located.
Publications: Informational brochure.
Financial data: Year ended 01/31/2005. Assets, $18,881,075 (M); Expenditures, $155,212,734; Total giving, $154,537,406; Grants to individuals, 98 grants totaling $503,501 (high: $100,000, low: $1).
Type of support: Employee-related scholarships; Scholarships—to individuals.

Application information: Application form required.
Deadline(s): Feb. 1 and Mar. 1 for Walton and Associate Scholarships.
Additional information: Applications available late Nov. and early Jan. from a member of store management or the home office.
Program descriptions:

Wal-Mart Associate Scholarship: This $2,000 scholarship, payable over one year, is open to graduating high school seniors who are current associates of Wal-Mart Stores, Inc. Applicants must plan to attend accredited institutions. Selection is based on academic achievement, ACT or SAT scores, extracurricular activities, leadership qualities, and financial need.

Sam Walton Community Scholarship: Each Wal-Mart and Sam's Club store can award up to two $1,000 scholarships, payable over one year, to local high school graduating seniors. The program is administered through the participating high schools. All scholarship recipients will automatically be entered into a state competition for a chance to win an additional $4,000 scholarship, for a total award of $5,000. All state winners will then be automatically entered into a national competition, with a chance to win an additional $20,000 scholarship, for a total scholarship award of $25,000. Applicants must plan to attend accredited institutions. Students must not be Wal-Mart associates, or have parents who work for Wal-Mart Stores, Inc. Selection is based on academic achievement, ACT/SAT scores, community/extracurricular involvement, work experience, and financial need.

Walton Foundation Scholarship: This $8,000 scholarship, payable over four years, is open to the children of Wal-Mart Stores associates. Associate must have been employed full-time for a full year prior to the application deadline. Any associate not meeting the terms of employment may qualify their student for the Wal-Mart Associate Scholarship as a nonqualifying Walton applicant. (See the following program.) Applicants must plan to attend accredited institutions. Selection is based on academic achievement, ACT/SAT scores, extracurricular activities, leadership qualities, and financial need.
EIN: 716107283

4280
Anna Marie & Russel Waldron Scholarship Fund

c/o The Huntington National Bank
P.O. Box 1558, EA4E86
Columbus, OH   43216

Foundation type: Independent foundation
Limitations: Scholarships to students of Rutherford B. Hayes High School, who attended Conger Elementary School, OH.
Financial data: Year ended 06/30/2005. Assets, $204,744 (M); Expenditures, $11,783; Total giving, $9,000; Grants to individuals, 7 grants totaling $9,000 (high: $1,800, low: $900).
Type of support: Support to graduates or students of specific schools; Undergraduate support.
Application information: Applications not accepted.
EIN: 311415607

4281
Harold B. Walker Charitable Trust
c/o Bank of America, N.A.
P.O. Box 1802
Providence, RI 02901-1802
Application address: c/o Carol M. Brewster, Ashland High School, 87 W. Union St., Ashland, MA 01721

Foundation type: Independent foundation
Limitations: Scholarships to graduates of Ashland High School, MA, for higher education.
Financial data: Year ended 12/31/2004. Assets, $512,982 (M); Expenditures, $31,201; Total giving, $24,000; Grants to individuals, 27 grants totaling $24,000 (high: $1,250, low: $250).
Type of support: Support to graduates or students of specific schools; Undergraduate support.
Application information: Contact trust for current application deadline/guidelines.
EIN: 046633929

4282
Charles M. Walker Foundation, Inc.
416 S. Broad St.
P.O. Box 1764
Monroe, GA 30655-6764
Contact: Agnes Shackleford, Secy.-Treas.
Loan Application address: 401 Woodlawn Rd., Monroe, GA 30655, tel.: (770) 267-3001

Foundation type: Independent foundation
Limitations: Educational loans to students in Walton County, GA.
Financial data: Year ended 12/31/2004. Assets, $1,810,293 (M); Expenditures, $78,410; Total giving, $60,100; Loans to individuals, totaling $60,675.
Type of support: Student loans—to individuals.
Application information: Deadline July 31; Completion of formal application required.
Program description:
Loan Program: The purpose of the loan is to achieve a specific objective, produce a report, or other similar project, or to improve or enhance a literary, artistic, musical, scientific, teaching, or other similar capacity, skill, or talent of the student. Applicant must have better than a "C" average. A transcript of grades and courses completed or an acceptable certificate giving the same information must be submitted with the application for a loan. Application will state how much is desired per quarter or semester, inasmuch as loans are disbursed for only one quarter at a time. Applicant must show evidence of successful completion of the previous quarter before additional funds will be released. Within the last quarter of graduation a loan repayment plan must be presented. Interest will begin the day the student leaves school. If the borrower and parents move from Walton County, the loan will become due at once.
EIN: 586036759

4283
N. Tracy Walker Scholarship Fund
5612 S. Kingston Ave.
Lisle, IL 60532
Contact: Paul S. Perkins, Dir.

Foundation type: Independent foundation
Limitations: Scholarships to students of Lisle Senior High School, IL, for higher education.
Financial data: Year ended 12/31/2002. Assets, $76,081 (M); Expenditures, $4,020; Total giving, $4,000; Grants to individuals, totaling $4,000.

Type of support: Support to graduates or students of specific schools; Undergraduate support.
Application information: Unsolicited requests for funds not accepted.
EIN: 364058285

4284
Walker Scholarship Grant
c/o U.S. Bank, N.A.
P.O. Box 1880
Iowa City, IA 52244-1880
Application address: c/o School of Religion, Univ. of Iowa, Iowa City, IA 52242

Foundation type: Operating foundation
Limitations: Scholarships to residents of IA attending a seminary or engaged in religious training in order to become a minister, priest, or rabbi.
Financial data: Year ended 08/31/2003. Assets, $7,754 (M); Expenditures, $7,587; Total giving, $7,500; Grants to individuals, totaling $7,500.
Fields of interest: Theological school/education; Religion.
Type of support: Scholarships—to individuals.
Application information: Deadline Feb. 15; Completion of formal application required.
EIN: 237435737

4285
James P. and Mary E. Walker Scholarship
1477 W. Main St.
Livingston, TN 38570

Foundation type: Operating foundation
Limitations: Scholarships to students of Livingston Academy High School, TN.
Financial data: Year ended 12/31/2002. Assets, $556,811 (M); Expenditures, $20,000; Total giving, $20,000; Grants to individuals, 4 grants totaling $20,000 (high: $5,000, low: $5,000).
Type of support: Support to graduates or students of specific schools; Undergraduate support.
Application information: Applications accepted. Application form required.
   Additional information: Applications are available at Livingston Academy High School.
EIN: 626363028

4286
Walkling Memorial Trust
(formerly Ben & Myrtle Walkling Memorial Trust)
P.O. Box 1588
Port Angeles, WA 98362 (360) 582-3801
Contact: Karen Yakovich

Foundation type: Independent foundation
Limitations: Scholarships to graduates of Port Angeles High School and other Clallam County schools, WA.
Financial data: Year ended 12/31/2004. Assets, $2,409,329 (M); Expenditures, $111,322; Total giving, $66,400; Grants to individuals, totaling $26,150.
Fields of interest: Vocational education; Medical school/education; Health sciences school/education.
Type of support: Support to graduates or students of specific schools; Undergraduate support.
Application information: Contact foundation for current application deadline/guidelines.

Program descriptions:
Physicians Community Benefit Fund: Provides medical related scholarships to residents of Clallam County.
Vocational Scholarship Fund: Provides vocational scholarships to graduates of Port Angeles High School.
Academic Scholarship Fund: Provides academic scholarships to graduates of Port Angeles High School.
Outlying Scholarship Fund: Provides academic scholarships to graduates of other Clallam County high schools.
EIN: 943166048

4287
Wallace Trust Foundation
209 W. Oak St.
McGehee, AR 71654 (870) 222-6660
Contact: Gibbs Ferguson, Tr.

Foundation type: Independent foundation
Limitations: Scholarships to residents of McGehee, AR, for higher education.
Financial data: Year ended 12/31/2003. Assets, $2,065 (M); Expenditures, $102,156; Total giving, $102,156; Grants to individuals, 23 grants totaling $67,914 (high: $13,440, low: $50).
Type of support: Undergraduate support.
Application information: Applications by letter accepted throughout the year.
EIN: 710754251

4288
The Marcus Wallenberg Foundation
c/o Sullivan & Cromwell, LLP
125 Broad St.
New York, NY 10004-2498 (212) 558-4000

Foundation type: Independent foundation
Limitations: Scholarships to students from Scandinavian countries, in particular Sweden, for study in the U.S. in the fields of international enterprise and commerce. Grants to U.S. citizens intending to live and work in Sweden.
Financial data: Year ended 03/31/2005. Assets, $2,162,175 (M); Expenditures, $146,439; Total giving, $110,000; Grants to individuals, 3 grants totaling $110,000 (high: $40,000, low: $30,000).
Fields of interest: Business school/education; International exchange, students; International affairs; Business/industry.
Type of support: Publication; Fellowships; Scholarships—to individuals; Foreign applicants.
Application information:
   Initial approach: Letter.
   Deadline(s): None
   Applicants should submit the following:
      1) Transcripts
   Additional information: Application should also include a complete biographical record, reports on applicant's careers, details of applicant's future plans, a list of published works, and letters of reference; Interviews may be required.
Program description:
Scholarship Program: Any of the following may apply: a person who is enrolled as a graduate or undergraduate student; a person participating in a fellowship program, writing program or field research under the auspices of a university; a college graduate working on a book or research paper relating to aspects of international trade or business; a professional or someone employed in international trade or business seeking to further

his or her education whether it leads to a degree or not. Grants are renewable for up to four years.
EIN: 133176307

4289

Walters Scholarship Fund

c/o Marshall & Ilsley Bank
P.O. Box 2980
Milwaukee, WI 53201-2980
Contact: Carolie Balder Kuehn
Application address: c/o Marshall & Ilsley Bank, Attn.: Carolie B. Kuehn, 500 3rd St., Wausau, WI 54402

Foundation type: Independent foundation
Limitations: Scholarships to members of the graduating class of Rhinelander High School, Milwaukee, WI, who are in the top 25 percent of their class and are planning to pursue a full-time engineering course of study in college.
Financial data: Year ended 09/30/2004. Assets, $267,248 (M); Expenditures, $16,564; Total giving, $13,029; Grants to individuals, 4 grants totaling $13,029.
Fields of interest: Engineering school/education.
Type of support: Support to graduates or students of specific schools; Undergraduate support.
Application information: Applications accepted throughout the year; Contact fund for current application guidelines.
EIN: 930834256

4290

Walther Cancer Institute and Foundation, Inc.

3202 N. Meridian St.
Indianapolis, IN 46208-4646 (317) 921-2040
Contact: Fred Haslam, Exec. V.P.
For fellowships: Peggy Weber, Dir. of Prog. Devel., Tel.: (317) 274-7563, E-mail: bcog@walther.org
FAX: (317) 924-4688;
E-mail: fhaslam@walther.org; URL: http://www.walther.org

Foundation type: Public charity
Limitations: Scholarships to medical students who express an interest in conducting cancer research.
Publications: Annual report; Newsletter; Program policy statement.
Financial data: Year ended 06/30/2005. Assets, $54,754,154 (M); Expenditures, $4,946,422; Total giving, $3,179,147; Grants to individuals, 16 grants totaling $164,050 (high: $30,000, low: $750).
Fields of interest: Cancer; Cancer research.
Type of support: Graduate support.
Application information:
  Initial approach: E-mail.
  Additional information: Contact foundation for further application guidelines.
EIN: 351650570

4291

Charles & Alberta Walther Scholarship Fund

c/o Wells Fargo Bank Nebraska, N.A.
1248 O St., 4th Fl.
Lincoln, NE 68508
Scholarship information address: c/o Scholarship Mgmt. Svcs., CSFA, 1505 Riverview Road, P.O. Box 297, St. Peter, MN 56082, tel.: (507) 931-1682

Foundation type: Independent foundation

Limitations: Scholarships to dependent children of Omaha, NE, firefighters for attendance in college or vocational school programs.
Financial data: Year ended 12/31/2004. Assets, $227,550 (M); Expenditures, $17,670; Total giving, $15,095.
Fields of interest: Vocational education, post-secondary; Disasters, fire prevention/control.
Type of support: Employee-related scholarships.
Application information: Deadline Mar. 1; Completion of formal application required.
EIN: 470806637

4292

Lillian Waltom Foundation

901 Oak St.
Jourdanton, TX 78026 (830) 769-2001
Contact: W.F. Zuhlke, Jr., Tr.

Foundation type: Independent foundation
Limitations: Scholarships to financially needy students in Atascosa County, TX.
Financial data: Year ended 12/31/2004. Assets, $1,433,528 (M); Expenditures, $79,073; Total giving, $54,250; Grants to individuals, totaling $43,750.
Type of support: Scholarships—to individuals.
Application information: Applications accepted throughout the year; Initial approach by letter requesting application; Completion of formal application required.
EIN: 742509618

4293

Walton Central School District Trust No. 1

c/o The National Bank of Delaware County
P.O. Box 389
Walton, NY 13856
Application address: c/o Guidance Dept., Walton High School, Walton, NY 13856

Foundation type: Independent foundation
Limitations: Scholarships to graduating seniors of Walton Central High School, NY.
Financial data: Year ended 12/31/2004. Assets, $96,918 (M); Expenditures, $5,766; Total giving, $5,333; Grants to individuals, totaling $5,333.
Type of support: Support to graduates or students of specific schools; Undergraduate support.
Application information: Deadline Apr. 15; Completion of formal application required.
EIN: 166280038

4294

Walton Family Foundation, Inc.

P.O. Box 2030
Bentonville, AR 72712 (479) 464-1570
Contact: Buddy D. Philpot, Exec. Dir.
FAX: (479) 464-1580; URL: http://www.wffhome.com

Foundation type: Independent foundation
Limitations: Scholarships to children of Wal-Mart employees residing in AR and MS, who are high school seniors who demonstrate high academic achievement and have been active in positions of leadership and responsibility.
Financial data: Year ended 12/31/2004. Assets, $1,129,770,302 (M); Expenditures, $103,500,243; Total giving, $101,240,263; Grants to individuals, totaling $627,015.
Fields of interest: Education.
Type of support: Employee-related scholarships.

Application information: Contact foundation for current application deadline/guidelines.
EIN: 133441466

4295

Rew & Edna Walz Scholarship Trust

c/o Wells Fargo South Dakota, N.A.
P.O. Box 1040
Rapid City, SD 57709-1040
Application address: c/o First Presbyterian Church, Rew and Edna Walz Scholarship Comm., 710 Kansas City St., Rapid City, SD 57701

Foundation type: Independent foundation
Limitations: Scholarships to students pursuing careers in Presbyterian Church-related vocations such as pastor, church music director, Christian education director, missionary, or other church-related positions in SD.
Financial data: Year ended 12/31/2004. Assets, $187,224 (M); Expenditures, $19,605; Total giving, $17,000; Grants to individuals, totaling $12,000.
Fields of interest: Theological school/education; Christian agencies & churches; Protestant agencies & churches; Religion.
Type of support: Scholarships—to individuals.
Application information: Deadline Apr. 15; Completion of formal application required, including at least three letters of recommendation and essays.
EIN: 466093427

4296

The Wapakoneta Area Community Foundation

10 W. Auglaize St.
P.O. Box 1957
Wapakoneta, OH 45895-1957 (419) 739-9223
Contact: Larry R. Tester, Exec. Dir.
FAX: (419) 739-9220;
E-mail: ltesterwacf@brightohio.net; URL: http://www.wapakacf.org

Foundation type: Community foundation
Limitations: Scholarships to high school seniors in Wapakoneta, OH, for higher education.
Publications: Annual report; Informational brochure; Newsletter.
Financial data: Year ended 05/31/2005. Assets, $1,393,853 (M); Expenditures, $130,830; Total giving, $107,388; Grants to individuals, totaling $14,500.
Type of support: Scholarships—to individuals.
Application information: Contact foundation for current application deadline/guidelines.
EIN: 341615229

4297

The Ella Tomlinson Ward Charitable Foundation, Inc.

1411 Hudson Ln.
Monroe, LA 71201

Foundation type: Independent foundation
Limitations: Scholarships to residents of Monroe, LA.
Financial data: Year ended 06/30/2004. Assets, $871,563 (M); Expenditures, $256,071; Total giving, $114,933; Grants to individuals, 11 grants totaling $64,933 (high: $22,159, low: $1,444).
Type of support: Undergraduate support.

Application information:
Initial approach: Letter.
Additional information: Contact foundation for further information.
EIN: 470920358

4298
Ward Educational Scholarship
c/o U.S. Bank Corp.
4387 N. Illinois St.
Swansea, IL 62226-1836
Application address: c/o Board of Directors, Community Dist. 3, Pleasant, IL 62366

Foundation type: Independent foundation
Limitations: Scholarships to individuals residing within ten miles of Pleasant Hill, IL.
Financial data: Year ended 12/31/2004.
Assets, $196,214 (M); Expenditures, $10,048; Total giving, $7,120; Grants to individuals, 3 grants totaling $7,120.
Type of support: Undergraduate support.
Application information: Contact foundation for current application deadlines/guidelines; Initial approach by letter.
EIN: 431835410

4299
Wilbur H. Ward Educational Trust
437 Main St.
Amherst, MA 01002-2313
Application address: c/o University of Massachusetts, Attn.: M. Markwell, Registar's Office, Amherst, MA 01003

Foundation type: Independent foundation
Limitations: Scholarships to young male residents of Hampshire County, MA, for study at the University of Massachusetts.
Financial data: Year ended 12/31/2003.
Assets, $401,712 (M); Expenditures, $22,904; Total giving, $17,000; Grants to individuals, totaling $17,000.
Fields of interest: Men.
Type of support: Support to graduates or students of specific schools; Undergraduate support.
Application information: Application form required.
Deadline(s): July 1.
EIN: 046047818

4300
Jeanne Ward Foundation
(formerly Jeanne Ward Faith Foundation)
2425 Mission St., Ste. 1
San Marino, CA 91108   (626) 799-5655
Contact: Timothy J. McKnight, Secy.-Treas.
FAX: (626) 799-0225

Foundation type: Independent foundation
Limitations: Scholarships to high school seniors in the Pasadena Community College District and Glendale School District, CA. Scholarships also to students at Glendale Community College and Pasadena City College, CA, for study in the visual arts.
Publications: Application guidelines.
Financial data: Year ended 01/31/2005.
Assets, $1,968,159 (M); Expenditures, $129,860; Total giving, $70,000; Grants to individuals, 12 grants totaling $21,000.
Fields of interest: Visual arts.
Type of support: Support to graduates or students of specific schools; Awards/grants by nomination only; Graduate support; Undergraduate support.

Application information: Application form not required.
Initial approach: Letter.
Copies of proposal: 1
Deadline(s): Oct. 31
Applicants should submit the following:
  1) Work samples
  2) Proposal
Additional information: Interviews may be required.
Program description:
Scholarships: Nominated applicants must have successfully completed at least two courses in the arts. The foundation will invite educational institutions to nominate two students per institution and encourage the students to submit an application with two personal references. Applicants are required to submit samples or photographs of their art work for evaluation by a committee selected by the board. Students of photography, video, cinematography, and music are ineligible. Officers, board members, employees of the foundation, and their relatives are ineligible. Scholarships are renewable.
EIN: 953761013

4301
Warman Scholarship Trust
c/o KeyBank N.A.
800 Superior Ave., 4th Fl.
Cleveland, OH 44114

Foundation type: Independent foundation
Limitations: Scholarships to graduates of ME secondary schools.
Financial data: Year ended 03/31/2005.
Assets, $551,350 (M); Expenditures, $32,987; Total giving, $27,000; Grants to individuals, totaling $27,000.
Type of support: Undergraduate support.
Application information: Applications not accepted.
EIN: 046731724

4302
Mary Ellen Warner Educational Trust
P.O. Box 30
Beverly Hills, CA 90213
Contact: Stephen Petty, Tr.
FAX: (310) 274-0422; URL: http://www.mewtrust.com

Foundation type: Independent foundation
Limitations: Student loans to graduate students and upper division undergraduate students who are permanent CA residents and are attending fully accredited colleges or universities in CA. No support for the study of social welfare, social work, psychology, or therapy.
Publications: Informational brochure.
Financial data: Year ended 10/31/2004.
Assets, $599,920 (M); Expenditures, $11,849; Total giving, $0; Loan to an individual, 1 loan totaling $10,000.
Type of support: Graduate support; Technical education support; Undergraduate support.
Application information: Applications accepted throughout the year; Initial approach by letter outlining financial need; Completion of formal application required; Interview in southern CA required.
Program description:
Loan Program: Loans to students whom the trustees deem needy and deserving. Repayment must begin not more than 36 months from date of

loan. Maximum loan is $10,000. The trust makes no awards for scholarships or grants.
EIN: 956037882

4303
Warner Home for Little Wanderers
4 Forest Hill Dr.
St. Albans, VT 05478
Contact: Donna Roby, Treas.

Foundation type: Independent foundation
Limitations: Scholarships to financially needy residents of Franklin County, VT, aged 21 and under.
Financial data: Year ended 04/30/2005.
Assets, $1,624,641 (M); Expenditures, $158,573; Total giving, $142,948; Grants to individuals, 392 grants totaling $142,948 (high: $3,000, low: $25).
Type of support: Scholarships—to individuals.
Application information: Contact foundation for current application deadline/guidelines.
EIN: 030179439

4304
Charles Warnken, Sr. Memorial College Scholarship Fund
P.O. Drawer B
Pleasanton, TX 78064
Contact: Catherine W. Bertrand, Mgr.
Application address: P.O. Box 276, Poth, TX 78147

Foundation type: Independent foundation
Limitations: Undergraduate scholarships to graduating seniors at Poth High School, TX.
Financial data: Year ended 06/30/2005.
Assets, $250,122 (M); Expenditures, $17,727; Total giving, $14,000; Grants to individuals, 2 grants totaling $14,000.
Type of support: Support to graduates or students of specific schools; Undergraduate support.
Application information: Deadline Apr. 15; Application by letter, including SAT scores.
EIN: 742213880

4305
Warren Academy
P.O. Box 305
Wilmington, MA 01887-0305
Contact: Phyllis M. Jensen, Tr.

Foundation type: Independent foundation
Limitations: Scholarships to graduates of Woburn High School, MA, who are in the high honors group.
Financial data: Year ended 02/28/2005.
Assets, $179,186 (M); Expenditures, $6,258; Total giving, $6,000; Grants to individuals, 4 grants totaling $6,000.
Type of support: Support to graduates or students of specific schools; Undergraduate support.
Application information: Applications not accepted.
Additional information: Recipients are chosen on the basis of class rank.
EIN: 046032875

4306
Warren Benevolent Fund, Inc.
P.O. Box 114
Ashland, MA   01721-0114
Contact: Geoffrey Wells, Treas.
Application address: 194 Winter St., Ashland, MA 01721, tel.: (508) 881-5633

Foundation type: Independent foundation
Limitations: Scholarships and student loans to graduates of Ashland High School, MA.
Financial data: Year ended 12/31/2004.
Assets, $1 (M); Expenditures, $16,892; Total giving, $10,187; Grants to individuals, 3 grants totaling $10,187.
Type of support: Support to graduates or students of specific schools; Undergraduate support.
Application information: Applications by letter accepted throughout the year.
EIN: 042309470

4307
Dement & Mabel Warren Educational Foundation
c/o AmSouth Bank
P.O. Box 23100
Jackson, MS   39225-3100   (601) 354-8107
Contact: Faison Campbell, Trust Off., AmSouth Bank

Foundation type: Independent foundation
Limitations: Student loans to financially needy undergraduates in MS.
Financial data: Year ended 12/31/2003.
Assets, $217,921 (M); Expenditures, $31,678; Total giving, $0; Loans to individuals, totaling $14,568.
Type of support: Undergraduate support.
Application information: Contact foundation for current application deadline; Completion of formal application required, including two personal references and a confidential statement from parents.
EIN: 237318072

4308
Earl Warren Legal Training Program, Inc.
99 Hudson St. 1600
New York, NY   10013-2815   (212) 965-2200
Contact: Elaine R. Jones Esq., Pres.
URL: http://www.naacpldf.org

Foundation type: Public charity
Limitations: Scholarships to law students who intend to practice civil rights law, as well as to undergraduate students who plan careers serving communities of color.
Financial data: Year ended 12/31/2003.
Assets, $814,037 (M); Expenditures, $106,730; Total giving, $67,500; Grants to individuals, 15 grants totaling $67,500 (high: $6,750, low: $3,000).
Fields of interest: Law school/education; Civil rights, formal/general education; African Americans/Blacks.
Type of support: Graduate support; Undergraduate support.
Application information:
  Initial approach: Letter.
  Deadline(s): Apr. 30
  Additional information: Applicants must contact the program between Nov. 30 and Feb. 15 requesting application.
Program descriptions:
  Herbert Lehman Education Fund: Awards $2,000 to full-time students entering college as first-year

students. Scholarships are renewable if the recipient maintains good academic and social standing.
  Earl Warren Civil Rights Training Scholarships: Awards up to $3,000 to students whose community involvement activities and leadership qualities demonstrate outstanding potential for training as civil rights and public interest attorneys.
  Earl Warren Shearman & Sterling Scholarships: Awards two special stipends annually to African American students who are entering law school. Each annual $15,000 grant includes a $13,500 scholarship and a $1,500 allowance to meet the costs of attending LDF's yearly Civil Rights Institute. Scholarships are renewable for the second and third years of law school provided the scholar maintains an acceptable academic record and makes normal progress toward obtaining a law degree within three consecutive academic years.
EIN: 132695683

4309
The Grace High Washburn Trust
1520 Melody Ln.
Bucyrus, OH   44820
Contact: John R. Clime, Secy.-Treas.
Application address: P.O. Box 389, Bucyrus, OH 44820

Foundation type: Independent foundation
Limitations: Scholarships to female Protestant residents of Bucyrus, OH, and vicinity to attend Ohio State University and its branch schools. Scholarships are not to exceed four years.
Financial data: Year ended 12/31/2004.
Assets, $2,451,761 (M); Expenditures, $113,283; Total giving, $100,949; Grants to individuals, totaling $100,949.
Fields of interest: Protestant agencies & churches; Adults, women.
Type of support: Support to graduates or students of specific schools; Undergraduate support.
Application information: Applications accepted. Application form required.
  Deadline(s): Deadline May 31.
  Applicants should submit the following:
    1) Letter(s) of recommendation
    2) Financial information
EIN: 346521078

4310
Elda Washer Scholarship Fund
c/o Wells Fargo Bank Nevada, N.A.
P.O. Box 95021
Henderson, NV   89009-5021
Application addresses: c/o Jean Frost; Cleveland High School, 3400 S.E. 26th, Portland, OR 97202, or c/o Barbara Ward, Jefferson High School, 5210 N. Kirby, Portland, OR 97208

Foundation type: Independent foundation
Limitations: Scholarships to graduates of Cleveland and Jefferson high schools, OR.
Financial data: Year ended 07/31/2004.
Assets, $606,605 (M); Expenditures, $24,917; Total giving, $17,334; Grants to individuals, 14 grants totaling $17,334 (high: $2,000, low: $500).
Type of support: Support to graduates or students of specific schools; Undergraduate support.
Application information: Application form required.
  Additional information: Contact fund for current application deadline; Application forms available at Cleveland and Jefferson high schools, OR.
EIN: 936178135

4311
Washington Apple Education Foundation
P.O. Box 3720
Wenatchee, WA   98807-3720   (509) 663-7713
Contact: Jennifer Whitney, Exec. Dir.
FAX: (509) 682-1293; *E-mail:* info@waef.org;
URL: http://www.waef.org

Foundation type: Public charity
Limitations: Scholarships to students who are residents of WA for higher education.
Financial data: Year ended 12/31/2004.
Assets, $915,877 (M); Expenditures, $296,308; Total giving, $172,066; Grants to individuals, totaling $141,097 (high: $10,000).
Type of support: Undergraduate support.
Application information: Deadline generally Apr. 1; Contact foundation for current application deadline; Initial approach by letter; Completion of formal application required; See Web site for further application information and for application forms.
Program description:
  Scholarship Program: Scholarships range from $250 to full-tuition. Qualifications vary greatly, from those growing up in farming families, those wishing to study commodity-related trade, and some for simply showing potential.
EIN: 911638890

4312
Washington DC Chapter, Continental Societies, Inc.
P.O. Box 91294
Washington, DC   20090
Contact: Barbara Morgan, Pres.

Foundation type: Public charity
Limitations: Scholarships to students attending high school in Washington, DC.
Financial data: Year ended 06/30/2005.
Assets, $74,944 (M); Expenditures, $27,873; Total giving, $15,822; Grants to individuals, totaling $4,500.
Type of support: Support to graduates or students of specific schools; Undergraduate support.
Application information: Contact foundation for current application deadline/guidelines.
EIN: 237408604

4313
Washington Education Foundation
1605 NW Sammamish Rd., Ste. 100
Issaquah, WA   98027   (425) 416-2000
Contact: Tanguy Martin, Exec. Dir.
FAX: (425) 416-2001;
E-mail: info@waedfoundation.org; *URL:* http:// www.waedfoundation.org

Foundation type: Public charity
Limitations: Scholarships to financially needy residents of WA, and to wards of the court or those aging out of foster care.
Financial data: Year ended 12/31/2003.
Assets, $107,928,619 (M); Expenditures, $10,015,731; Total giving, $7,383,196; Grants to individuals, totaling $7,383,196.
Type of support: Undergraduate support.
Application information: Applications accepted. Application form required.
  Initial approach: E-mail.
  Deadline(s): Vary
  Applicants should submit the following:
    1) GPA
    2) Transcripts
    3) Essay

Additional information: Contact foundation for further application guidelines.

Program descriptions:

Washington State Achievers Scholarship: Awards an average of $20,000 for four years to students in WA. Students must be in their junior year, plan on attending a four-year college in WA, and have an income that is in the lowest 35 percent of WA state income levels.

Governor's Scholarship for Foster Youth: Awards twenty to thirty scholarships ranging between $1,000 to $5,000 per year for up to five years to WA high school students. Applicants must be a ward of the court, or who is aging out of foster care.

EIN: 912036088

4314

The George Washington Foundation

403 E. E St.
Yakima, WA 98901
Contact: James R. Sharples, Secy.-Treas.
Application address: 2581 Mapleway Rd., Yakima, WA 98908, tel.: (509) 965-0706

Foundation type: Independent foundation
Limitations: Scholarships to graduating local high school seniors in eastern Washington for undergraduate study primarily at Yakima Valley College. Scholarships are available, however, for study at institutions nationwide.
Financial data: Year ended 06/30/2005.
Assets, $1,313,478 (M); Expenditures, $70,422; Total giving, $58,950; Grants to individuals, totaling $58,950.
Type of support: Undergraduate support.
Application information: Application form required.
   Deadline(s): Apr. 1
   Applicants should submit the following:
      1) Photograph
      2) Transcripts
      3) Financial information
      4) Essay
      5) Letter(s) of recommendation
   Additional information: Applications available from local public high school principals or counselors. Applications must also include student's personal and family data sheet; high school principal's data sheet. See web site for additional information.
EIN: 916024141

4315

The Washington Post Company Educational Foundation

1150 15th St. N.W.
Washington, DC 20071
Contact: Tito Tolentino, Grants Coord.
Note: Applications not accepted

Foundation type: Company-sponsored foundation
Limitations: Scholarships for pre-college and higher education.
Financial data: Year ended 12/31/2004.
Assets, $44,799 (M); Expenditures, $599,271; Total giving, $236,932; Grants to individuals, 58 grants totaling $65,800 (high: $3,000, low: $400).
Type of support: Precollege support; Undergraduate support.
Application information: Applications not accepted.
EIN: 521545926

4316

The Washington Scholarship Fund

1133 15th St. NW, Ste. 550
Washington, DC 20005 (202) 293-5560
Contact: Sally J. Sachar, Pres. and C.E.O.
FAX: (202) 293-7893;
E-mail: arobinson@washingtonscholarshipfund.org
; URL: http://www.washingtonscholarshipfund.org

Foundation type: Public charity
Limitations: Scholarships to low-income students who reside in Washington, DC, for private K-8 education.
Financial data: Year ended 06/30/2004.
Assets, $2,273,135 (M); Expenditures, $2,601,188; Total giving, $1,695,597; Grants to individuals, totaling $1,695,597.
Fields of interest: Economically disadvantaged.
Type of support: Precollege support.
Application information: Application form required.
   Deadline(s): Contact foundation for deadline
   Additional information: Application must also include tax forms and proof of public assistance status; See Web site for further application information.
Program description:
   Scholarship Program: Funds 30-60 percent of tuition based on household size and income. Scholarship recipients are selected at random.
EIN: 521808833

4317

Washington Tennis & Education Foundation

William H.G. FitzGerald Tennis Ctr.
16th & Kennedy Sts., N.W.
Washington, DC 20011 (202) 291-9888
Contact: Eleni A. Rossides, Exec. Dir.
E-mail: wtef@wtef.org; URL: http://www.wtef.org/

Foundation type: Public charity
Limitations: Scholarships to lower-income residents of Washington DC who are enrolled in the Foundation's Center for Excellence Program.
Financial data: Year ended 08/31/2004.
Assets, $2,245,396 (M); Expenditures, $1,431,375; Total giving, $10,605; Grants to individuals, 12 grants totaling $10,605 (high: $1,908, low: $235).
Type of support: Undergraduate support.
Application information:
   Initial approach: E-mail or letter.
   Additional information: Contact foundation for further application information.
EIN: 526046504

4318

Washington Women in Need

1849 114th Ave. N.E.
Bellevue, WA 98004 (425) 451-8838
Contact: Colleen M. Crowley, Exec. Dir.

Foundation type: Operating foundation
Limitations: Educational assistance to financially needy women who reside in WA.
Financial data: Year ended 06/30/2004.
Assets, $1,812,870 (M); Expenditures, $993,895; Total giving, $622,333; Grants to individuals, totaling $622,333.
Fields of interest: Women.
Type of support: Scholarships—to individuals.
Application information: Applications accepted. Application form required.
   Deadline(s): Applications accepted throughout the year

Additional information: Individuals apply to the organization but payment is made directly to the service providers for the benefit of the client.
EIN: 911559848

4319

David Wasserman Scholarship Fund, Inc.

Adirondack Ctr.
4722 State Hwy. 30
Amsterdam, NY 12010 (518) 843-2800
Contact: Norbert J. Sherbunt, Pres.

Foundation type: Independent foundation
Limitations: Scholarships to undergraduate students residing in Montgomery County, NY.
Financial data: Year ended 04/30/2003.
Assets, $713 (M); Expenditures, $42,088; Total giving, $17,250; Grants to individuals, 66 grants totaling $17,250 (high: $600, low: $150).
Type of support: Undergraduate support.
Application information: Deadline Apr. 15; Initial approach by letter; Completion of formal application required.
EIN: 146030181

4320

Waterford Foundation for Public Education

P.O. Box 300681
Waterford, MI 48330-0681
Contact: Mary Lou Simmons, Pres.
URL: http://www.waterford.k12.mi.us/foundation/

Foundation type: Public charity
Limitations: Scholarships to graduates of Waterford public high schools, MI.
Publications: Annual report; Financial statement.
Financial data: Year ended 06/30/2005.
Assets, $1,001,858 (M); Expenditures, $125,359; Total giving, $55,613; Grants to individuals, 3 grants totaling $7,500 (high: $2,500, low: $2,500).
Type of support: Support to graduates or students of specific schools.
Application information: Applications accepted. Application form required. Application form available on the grantmaker's Web site.
   Initial approach: Letter.
   Deadline(s): Mar. 1
   Applicants should submit the following:
      1) Transcripts
      2) Letter(s) of recommendation
      3) Essay
   Additional information: See Web site for additional application guidelines.
EIN: 382528009

4321

Watertown Foundation, Inc.

P.O. Box 117
Watertown, CT 06795 (860) 274-4288
Contact: Stedman Sweet, Pres.
E-mail: wttnfoundation@sheglobal.net

Foundation type: Public charity
Limitations: Scholarships only to residents of Watertown, CT for higher education.
Publications: Annual report; Grants list; Informational brochure; Occasional report.
Financial data: Year ended 08/31/2005.
Assets, $2,306,193 (M); Expenditures, $96,695; Total giving, $75,742; Grants to individuals, 15 grants totaling $22,500.

Type of support: Scholarships—to individuals; Undergraduate support.
Application information: Applications accepted. Application form required.
>   *Copies of proposal:* 1
>   *Deadline(s):* Apr. 1
>   *Applicants should submit the following:*
>   1) Essay
>   2) FAFSA
>   3) GPA
>   4) Letter(s) of recommendation
>   5) SAT
>   6) Transcripts
>   *Additional information:* Contact foundation for further information.
EIN: 066064660

4322
Hattie G. Watkins Educational Fund
c/o Union Planters Bank, Trust Dept.
P.O. Box 387
Memphis, TN   38147   (901) 580-5383
Contact: Steve Spencer, Trust Off., Union Planters Bank

Foundation type: Independent foundation
Limitations: Scholarships of up to $750 per semester to individuals for undergraduate education, primarily in TN.
Financial data: Year ended 10/31/2004. Assets, $260,412 (M); Expenditures, $16,943; Total giving, $12,600; Grants to individuals, totaling $12,600.
Type of support: Undergraduate support.
Application information: Applications accepted. Application form required.
>   *Deadline(s):* May 31
>   *Additional information:* Application should include a brief resume of academic qualifications, transcripts and financial statements.
EIN: 626051024

4323
Watson Family Foundation
6301 N. Western Ave., Ste. 250
Oklahoma City, OK   73118
Contact: H.B. Watson, Jr., Pres.

Foundation type: Independent foundation
Limitations: Scholarships to residents of OK for higher education.
Financial data: Year ended 12/31/2004. Assets, $500,212 (M); Expenditures, $126,576; Total giving, $123,350; Grants to individuals, 16 grants totaling $66,000 (high: $8,500, low: $2,500).
Type of support: Undergraduate support.
Application information: Application form required.
>   *Initial approach:* Letter.
>   *Additional information:* Applications accepted throughout the year.
EIN: 731512470

4324
John W. and Rose E. Watson Foundation
c/o Citizens Bank Wealth Mgmt., N.A.
328 S. Saginaw St., MC 002072
Flint, MI   48502
Application address: c/o Jean Seman, 5800 Weiss St., Saginaw, MI 48602

Foundation type: Independent foundation

Limitations: Scholarships to Saginaw County, MI, residents graduating from Catholic high schools.
Financial data: Year ended 12/31/2004. Assets, $7,121,623 (M); Expenditures, $394,656; Total giving, $324,500; Grants to individuals, totaling $310,000.
Fields of interest: Roman Catholic agencies & churches.
Type of support: Undergraduate support.
Application information: Deadline one month prior to beginning of academic year; Completion of formal application required; Interviews required.
EIN: 386091611

4325
Raymond E. & Evona Watson Foundation
c/o Comerica Bank, Tr.
P.O. Box 75000, MC 3302
Detroit, MI   48275-3302
Application address: c/o Colorado School of Mines, Attn.: Financial aid Office, 1500 Illinois St., Golden, CO 80401, tel.: (800) 446-9488

Foundation type: Independent foundation
Limitations: Scholarships to student attending or who plan to attend the Colorado School of Mines, CO.
Financial data: Year ended 12/31/2004. Assets, $203,163 (M); Expenditures, $26,088; Total giving, $18,000; Grants to individuals, totaling $18,000.
Type of support: Support to graduates or students of specific schools; Undergraduate support.
Application information: Deadline prior to end of term or semester; Completion of formal application required; Applications can be requested from the Colorado School of Mines and must be pre-approved by the school's financial aid office.
EIN: 383493259

4326
C. S. Watson Scholarship Foundation
(also known as Clara Stewart Watson Foundation)
c/o Bank of America, N.A.
P.O. Box 831041
Dallas, TX   75283-1041

Foundation type: Independent foundation
Limitations: Scholarships to graduates of high schools in Dallas and Tarrant counties, TX, for undergraduate study at colleges and universities in TX.
Financial data: Year ended 08/31/2004. Assets, $726,936 (M); Expenditures, $24,444; Total giving, $17,500; Grants to individuals, 21 grants totaling $12,500 (high: $1,000, low: $500).
Fields of interest: Vocational education.
Type of support: Technical education support; Undergraduate support.
Application information: Contact fund for current application deadline/guidelines.
Program description:
>   *Scholarship Program:* Applicants must be of good moral character, have above average grades, need financial assistance to attend college, and seriously intend to pursue and complete an academic or technical education. The maximum amount for each grant is $1,500 per academic year.
EIN: 756064730

4327
Watson-Brown Foundation, Inc.
310 Tom Watson Way
Thomson, GA   30824-0037   (706) 595-8886
Contact: Mary Anne Coussons, Dir.
FAX: (706) 595-3948; E-mail: mcoussons@bellsouth.net; URL: http://www.watson-brown.org/

Foundation type: Independent foundation
Limitations: Scholarships to residents of the Central Savannah River Area (CSRA) of GA and SC for undergraduate education.
Financial data: Year ended 12/31/2004. Assets, $128,358,577 (M); Expenditures, $4,693,670; Total giving, $2,654,920; Grants to individuals, totaling $1,073,500.
Type of support: Undergraduate support.
Application information: Applications accepted. Application form required. Application form available on the grantmaker's Web site.
>   *Initial approach:* Telephone or e-mail.
>   *Copies of proposal:* 1
>   *Deadline(s):* Apr. 15
>   *Applicants should submit the following:*
>   1) Transcripts
>   2) SAT
>   3) Letter(s) of recommendation
>   4) GPA
>   5) Financial information
>   6) Essay
>   7) ACT
Program description:
>   *Scholarship Program:* Recipients must maintain at least a 3.0 GPA in both high school and college, attend a four-year accredited college or university, demonstrate financial need and be a resident of GA or SC.
EIN: 237097393

4328
Watt Brothers Scholars Trust
P.O. Box 999
Tillamook, OR   97141-0999
Contact: Phyllis Wustenberg, Chair.
Application address: P.O. Box 3312, Bay City, OR 97107

Foundation type: Operating foundation
Limitations: Scholarships to seniors graduating from Tillamook County high schools, OR.
Financial data: Year ended 12/31/2002. Assets, $1,733,438 (M); Expenditures, $116,622; Total giving, $111,108; Grants to individuals, 34 grants totaling $89,139 (high: $4,000, low: $666).
Type of support: Support to graduates or students of specific schools; Undergraduate support.
Application information: Deadline June 1; Completion of formal application required, including handwritten letter of no more than 300 words explaining college plans, high school transcripts, and senior photograph.
EIN: 931224469

4329
Grace Margaret Watterson Trust
c/o Wachovia Bank, N.A.
100 N. Main St., 13th Fl.
Winston-Salem, NC   27150-6732
(800) 576-5135
Contact: A. Shane Thomas, A.V.P.
Additional tel.: (336) 732-5912; E-mail: Shane Thomas@wachovia.com

Foundation type: Independent foundation

Limitations: Scholarships to financially needy graduating seniors from high schools in Daytona Beach and Ormond Beach, FL, and Peterborough, Ontario, Canada. Applicants must have at least a 3.0 GPA.
Financial data: Year ended 02/28/2003. Assets, $2,246,348 (M); Expenditures, $200,710; Total giving, $173,512; Grants to individuals, totaling $173,512.
Fields of interest: Education.
Type of support: Support to graduates or students of specific schools.
Application information: Application form required.
   Deadline(s): Feb. 28
   Additional information: Application information will be available in the administrative offices of the qualifying high schools by Nov. Scholarships are renewable each year for a maximum of four years.
EIN: 596807104

4330
J. Watumull Fund
(formerly J. Watumull Estate, Inc.)
c/o Watumull Bros., Ltd.
P.O. Box 88296
Honolulu, HI 96830-8296   (808) 971-8800
Contact: Gulab Watumull, Pres.
Application address: Watumull Bldg., 307 Lewers St., 6th Fl., Honolulu, HI 96815; FAX: (808) 971-8824

Foundation type: Independent foundation
Limitations: Scholarships to individuals of Indian ancestry, with preference to HI residents.
Financial data: Year ended 12/31/2002. Assets, $8,136,004 (M); Expenditures, $445,141; Total giving, $309,000; Grants to individuals, 28 grants totaling $28,000 (high: $1,000, low: $1,000).
Type of support: Fellowships.
Application information: Applications by letter accepted throughout the year.
EIN: 510205431

4331
Waverly Community Foundation
c/o State Bank of Waverly
P.O. Box 58
Waverly, IA 50677

Foundation type: Independent foundation
Limitations: Scholarships only to graduates of high schools, in Bremer County, IA.
Financial data: Year ended 12/31/2004. Assets, $2,516,933 (M); Expenditures, $137,550; Total giving, $115,020.
Type of support: Support to graduates or students of specific schools; Undergraduate support.
Application information: Deadline Apr. 1; Application by letter, including current resume.
EIN: 426058774

4332
Waverly Community House, Inc.
1115 N. Abington Rd.
P.O. Box 142
Waverly, PA 18471   (570) 586-8191
Contact: Kathleen Keating, Exec. Dir.
FAX: (570) 586-0185;
E-mail: info@waverlycomm.com; URL: http://www.waverlycomm.com/

Foundation type: Public charity

Limitations: Scholarships awarded to qualifying individuals or groups on a non-discriminatory basis.
Financial data: Year ended 12/31/2004. Assets, $3,093,937 (M); Expenditures, $504,244; Total giving, $20,000; Grants to individuals, 4 grants totaling $20,000 (high: $5,000, low: $5,000).
Fields of interest: Arts education.
Type of support: Scholarships—to individuals.
Application information:
   Deadline(s): Dec. 15
EIN: 240798358

4333
Way Foundation
510 Pat Way Dr.
Fairview, OK 73737-2704   (580) 227-3337
Contact: Howard W. Way III, Tr.

Foundation type: Independent foundation
Limitations: Scholarships primarily to Fairview, OK, students.
Financial data: Year ended 12/31/2004. Assets, $0 (M); Expenditures, $16,189; Total giving, $13,124; Grants to individuals, 11 grants totaling $13,124 (high: $2,000, low: $124).
Type of support: Scholarships—to individuals.
Application information: Application form required.
   Initial approach: Letter or telephone.
   Deadline(s): Mar. 31
EIN: 731553537

4334
Wayne County Community Foundation
(formerly Greater Wayne County Foundation, Inc.)
517 N. Market St.
P.O. Box 201
Wooster, OH 44691   (330) 262-3877
Contact: B. Diane Gordon, Exec. Dir.
FAX: (330) 262-8057; E-mail: info@gwcf.net; Additional E-mail: gwcf@gwcf.net; URL: http://www.gwcf.net

Foundation type: Community foundation
Limitations: Scholarships to individuals residing in the Wooster, OH, area for undergraduate education at U.S. colleges and universities. The foundation administers approximately 60 scholarships to residents of Akron, Ashland, Dalton, Doylestown, Norwayne, Orrville, Rittman, Triway, Wayne County, Waynedale, and Wooster, OH.
Publications: Application guidelines; Annual report; Financial statement; Informational brochure (including application guidelines).
Financial data: Year ended 06/30/2005. Assets, $27,132,212 (M); Expenditures, $1,467,019; Total giving, $1,270,263; Grants to individuals, 128 grants totaling $266,390 (high: $5,000, low: $100).
Type of support: Undergraduate support.
Application information: Applications accepted. Application form required. Application form available on the grantmaker's Web site.
   Deadline(s): Vary
EIN: 341281026

4335
Wayne County, Indiana Foundation, Inc.
33 S. 7th St., Ste. 1
Richmond, IN 47374   (765) 962-1638
Contact: Steven C. Borchers, Exec. Dir.
FAX: (765) 966-0882;
E-mail: info@waynecountyfoundation.org;
Additional E-mail:

steve@waynecountyfoundation.org; URL: http://www.waynecountyfoundation.org

Foundation type: Community foundation
Limitations: Scholarships and awards to residents of Wayne County, IN.
Publications: Annual report; Informational brochure (including application guidelines); Newsletter.
Financial data: Year ended 12/31/2004. Assets, $27,864,807 (M); Expenditures, $1,226,929; Total giving, $818,920; Grants to individuals, 206 grants totaling $300,206 (high: $26,878, low: $100).
Fields of interest: Education.
Type of support: Scholarships—to individuals.
Application information: Application form required.
   Initial approach: Letter.
   Deadline(s): Feb. 1 and Aug. 1
   Additional information: See web site for listing of various scholarships.
Program description:
   Component Funds: This endowment holds the following component funds:
   · Charles P. & Sylvia D. Bane Memorial Fund
   · James & Margaret Gibbons Memorial Fund
   · Elizabeth Jay Memorial Fund
   · Frances Mayhew Memorial Fund
   · John & Katherine Miller Scholarship Fund
   · Fred Nottingham Memorial Fund.
EIN: 351406033

4336
John Wayne Scholarship Trust
127 S. Side Sq.
Macomb, IL 61455   (309) 833-4551

Foundation type: Public charity
Limitations: Scholarships to graduates of McDonough and Fulton county high schools, IL.
Financial data: Year ended 12/31/2004. Assets, $364,940 (M); Expenditures, $20,090; Total giving, $17,200; Grants to individuals, 19 grants totaling $17,200 (high: $1,800, low: $500).
Type of support: Scholarships—to individuals.
Application information: Contact foundation for current application deadline/guidelines; Initial approach by letter.
EIN: 376187937

4337
Weaver-Fagan Memorial Fund
1 W. Queens Way, Ste. 200
Hampton, VA 23669-3593
Contact: Patrick B. McDermott, Tr.

Foundation type: Independent foundation
Limitations: Scholarships to graduating seniors of Hampton, VA, public high schools, who have at least a 2.5 GPA, for study at four-year accredited VA colleges and universities.
Financial data: Year ended 12/31/2004. Assets, $1,522,780 (M); Expenditures, $79,064; Total giving, $66,000; Grants to individuals, totaling $66,000.
Type of support: Support to graduates or students of specific schools; Undergraduate support.
Application information: Deadline Mar. 1; Completion of formal application required, including a typed, personal essay, two letters of recommendation, transcripts, and completed Hampton City Schools Activities Data Sheet.
EIN: 541560569

4338
Benjamin N. Webber Charitable Private Foundation

(also known as Benjamin N. Webber Scholarship Fund)
c/o Wells Fargo Bank Arizona, N.A., Tax Dept.
P.O. Box 53456, MAC 54101-182
Phoenix, AZ 85072
Application address: c/o Webber Educational Grants Comm., Arizona Home Economics, 7030 E. Bonnie Brae Dr., Tucson, AZ 85710

Foundation type: Independent foundation
Limitations: Scholarships in home economics and nutrition to Mexican-American bilingual females from mining towns in AZ. Recipients must attend undergraduate programs in AZ colleges and maintain at least a 2.0 GPA. Preference is given to nutrition majors.
Publications: Informational brochure (including application guidelines).
Financial data: Year ended 09/30/2005. Assets, $1,611,135 (M); Expenditures, $32,232; Total giving, $13,308; Grants to individuals, 4 grants totaling $13,308 (high: $5,977, low: $1,529).
Fields of interest: Nutrition; Home economics; Women; Mexico.
Type of support: Undergraduate support.
Application information: Applications accepted throughout the year; Completion of formal application required, including letter outlining financial need, educational and professional goals, three letters of recommendation, and transcripts.
EIN: 866136517

4339
Jacques Weber Foundation, Inc.

c/o Scholarship Comm.
P.O. Box 420
Bloomsburg, PA 17815
Contact: Sandra Grasley, Asst. Secy.

Foundation type: Independent foundation
Limitations: Scholarships to residents of Bloomsburg, PA, and Monroe, NC, who are children of employees of Bloomsburg Mills Inc.
Financial data: Year ended 09/30/2004. Assets, $3,411,261 (M); Expenditures, $155,395; Total giving, $146,750; Grants to individuals, 19 grants totaling $76,250 (high: $5,000, low: $2,500).
Type of support: Employee-related scholarships.
Application information: Application form required.
Additional information: Contact foundation for current application deadline; Interview required.
EIN: 136101161

4340
William Webermeier Scholarship Trust

c/o Wells Fargo Bank Nebraska, N.A.
1248 O St., 4th Fl.
Lincoln, NE 68508-1423
Application address: c/o Superintendent of Schools, Milford, NE 68405

Foundation type: Independent foundation
Limitations: Scholarships only to graduates of Milford High School, NE.
Financial data: Year ended 09/30/2004. Assets, $529,318 (M); Expenditures, $24,858; Total giving, $22,151; Grants to individuals, totaling $22,151.
Type of support: Support to graduates or students of specific schools; Undergraduate support.

Application information: Contact superintendent of Milford School District for current application deadline/guidelines.
EIN: 476062610

4341
WEDC Foundation, Inc.

(also known as Women's Economic Development Council)
P.O. Box 4761
Huntsville, AL 35815 (256) 885-3731
Contact: Cindi C. Branham, Pres.
E-mail: info@wedcfoundation.org; URL: http://www.wedc-online.com/foundation.html

Foundation type: Public charity
Limitations: Scholarships to economically disadvantaged women residing in Madison County, AL.
Financial data: Year ended 09/30/2004. Assets, $95,331 (M); Expenditures, $18,101; Total giving, $12,527; Grants to individuals, totaling $12,527.
Fields of interest: Women; Economically disadvantaged.
Type of support: Undergraduate support.
Application information:
Initial approach: Letter.
Deadline(s): Apr. 1
Additional information: Contact foundation for additional application information.
EIN: 631207448

4342
J.A. Wedum Foundation

2537 University Ave. S.E.
Minneapolis, MN 55414 (612) 789-3363
Contact: Kathleen Hansen, Pres.
E-mail: kathleenhansen@wedum.org; URL: http://www.wedum.org

Foundation type: Independent foundation
Limitations: Student aid primarily to residents of the Midwest.
Publications: Application guidelines; Annual report; Informational brochure.
Financial data: Year ended 12/31/2003. Assets, $162,915,223 (M); Expenditures, $25,745,547; Total giving, $272,662; Grants to individuals, 2 grants totaling $49,367 (high: $48,367, low: $1,000).
Type of support: Student loans—to individuals; Graduate support.
Application information: Application form required.
Deadline(s): None
Additional information: Application should also include resume of academic qualifications.
EIN: 416025661

4343
G. H. Weems Educational Fund

126 E. Main St.
Waverly, TN 37185
Contact: William M. Slayden III, Exec. Dir.

Foundation type: Independent foundation
Limitations: Scholarships and interest-free student loans to residents of Montgomery, Dickson, and Humphreys counties, TN, for study in education-related fields.
Publications: Newsletter.
Financial data: Year ended 12/31/2004. Assets, $1,092,607 (M); Expenditures, $103,298; Total giving, $59,063; Grants to

individuals, totaling $59,063; Loans to individuals, totaling $5,000.
Fields of interest: Teacher school/education.
Type of support: Scholarships—to individuals; Student loans—to individuals.
Application information: Applications accepted throughout the year; Initial approach by letter; Completion of formal application required.
EIN: 626047271

4344
Edna Weigel Scholarship Fund

c/o Marshall & Ilsley Bank
P.O. Box 2980
Milwaukee, WI 53201
Application address: c/o Guidance Off., Watertown High School, 825 Endeavour Dr., Watertown, WI 53098, tel.: (414) 262-7500

Foundation type: Independent foundation
Limitations: Scholarships to financially needy graduates of Watertown Senior High School for full-time enrollment in Wisconsin institutions with accredited baccalaureate programs.
Financial data: Year ended 05/31/2005. Assets, $438,926 (M); Expenditures, $39,972; Total giving, $34,500; Grants to individuals, totaling $34,500.
Type of support: Support to graduates or students of specific schools; Undergraduate support.
Application information: Contact fund for current application deadline; Completion of formal application required.
EIN: 396618926

4345
Charles & Dorothy Wein Charitable Fund

c/o National City Bank
P.O. Box 94651
Cleveland, OH 44101-4651
Contact: Steven P. Kosak, Trust Off., National City Bank
Application address: P.O. Box 374, Oil City, PA 16301, tel.: (814) 676-1600

Foundation type: Independent foundation
Limitations: Scholarships for higher education to residents of Clarion County, PA.
Financial data: Year ended 06/30/2005. Assets, $733,408 (M); Expenditures, $40,468; Total giving, $31,150; Grants to individuals, 11 grants totaling $31,150 (high: $3,500, low: $100).
Type of support: Scholarships—to individuals.
Application information: Applications accepted throughout the year; Application by letter stating purpose of funds requested.
EIN: 256225347

4346
James Weir Memorial Fund-Bigelow District

P.O. Box 325
Wasco, OR 97065-0325 (541) 442-5086
Contact: Trena Gray
Additional tel.: (541) 565-3502

Foundation type: Independent foundation
Limitations: Scholarships and other educational grants to students and residents of the Bigelow District in Sherman County, OR.
Financial data: Year ended 06/30/2004. Assets, $793,814 (M); Expenditures, $36,183; Total giving, $19,551; Grants to individuals, 11 grants totaling $19,551 (high: $5,000, low: $5).

Type of support: Scholarships—to individuals; Support to graduates or students of specific schools.
Application information: Contact foundation for current application deadline; Application by letter, including purpose and amount of funds desired.
EIN: 936041768

4347
Weiss Education Foundation
(also known as Weiss Scientific Foundation)
c/o Admissions Comm.
14380 N.W. Science Park Dr.
Portland, OR 97229-5419 (503) 643-5674
Contact: Robert Jarrett, Dir., Finance

Foundation type: Company-sponsored foundation
Limitations: Scholarships to children of Tosoh Quartz Portland employees residing in CA, OR and TX, with at least four years seniority for higher education.
Financial data: Year ended 12/31/2004.
Assets, $249,180 (M); Expenditures, $163,491; Total giving, $161,806; Grants to individuals, 11 grants totaling $161,806 (high: $42,122, low: $1,477).
Type of support: Employee-related scholarships.
Application information:
  Deadline(s): July 1
  Applicants should submit the following:
    1) Resume
    2) Transcripts
  Additional information: Application by letter, also including description of extra-curricular and community activities.
EIN: 930879802

4348
Ella Weiss Educational Fund
c/o FirstMerit Bank, N.A.
106 S. Main St., Ste. 1600
Akron, OH 44308 (330) 384-7320
Contact: Ronald B. Tynan, V.P. and Sr. Trust Off., FirstMerit Bank, N.A.
FAX: (330) 849-8992

Foundation type: Independent foundation
Limitations: Scholarships to residents of OH under 23 years old who are attending educational institutions in OH.
Financial data: Year ended 11/30/2004.
Assets, $679,920 (M); Expenditures, $47,391; Total giving, $33,000; Grants to individuals, totaling $33,000.
Type of support: Scholarships—to individuals.
Application information: Deadline Mar. 31; Initial approach by letter requesting application and providing stamped business-size, self-addressed envelope; Completion of formal application required, including recommendations and high school and college transcripts.
EIN: 237133041

4349
Evelyn & Fredrick Weissman Education and Charitable Foundation
30238 Spring River Dr.
Southfield, MI 48076-1047 (248) 203-9270
Contact: Rebecca Weissman, Dir.

Foundation type: Operating foundation
Limitations: Scholarships to individuals. Grants also given for speech and physical therapy to mentally disabled individuals.

Financial data: Year ended 12/31/2003.
Assets, $157,178 (M); Expenditures, $43,045; Total giving, $37,625; Grants to individuals, 5 grants totaling $6,000.
Fields of interest: Physical therapy; Speech/hearing centers; Disabilities, people with.
Type of support: Scholarships—to individuals; Grants for special needs.
Application information: Applications accepted throughout the year; Completion of formal application required, including transcript and essay.
EIN: 383196147

4350
Lorna A. Welch Charitable Foundation
P.O. Box 390
Flushing, MI 48433

Foundation type: Operating foundation
Limitations: Scholarships to residents of Flushing, MI, for higher education.
Financial data: Year ended 12/31/2002.
Assets, $240,432 (M); Expenditures, $14,250; Total giving, $14,000; Grants to individuals, 4 grants totaling $14,000 (high: $3,500, low: $3,500).
Type of support: Undergraduate support.
Application information: Contact foundation for current application deadline/guidelines.
EIN: 383553903

4351
The Sara & Warren Welch Foundation
P.O. Box 125
Newville, PA 17241-0125

Foundation type: Independent foundation
Limitations: Student loans to graduates of Big Spring School District, PA.
Financial data: Year ended 04/30/2005.
Assets, $260,259 (M); Expenditures, $9,734; Total giving, $0; Loans to individuals, 14 loans totaling $24,000.
Type of support: Support to graduates or students of specific schools; Undergraduate support.
Application information: Deadline June 1; Initial approach by letter requesting application; Completion of formal application required.
Program description:
  Loan Program: Loans are interest-free while recipient is in school. Upon graduation, the loan begins to amortize with interest and principal payments.
EIN: 232130843

4352
Anna B. Welch Memorial Trust
c/o First Mid-Illinois Bank & Trust
P.O. Box 499
Mattoon, IL 61938 (217) 234-7454
Contact: Gary Kuhns, V.P.

Foundation type: Independent foundation
Limitations: Scholarships to residents of Coles and Cumberland counties, IL. Preference is given to students who are financially needy and to those enrolled in medical fields of study, including nursing and medical technology.
Financial data: Year ended 02/28/2005.
Assets, $1,604,830 (M); Expenditures, $95,546; Total giving, $67,950; Grants to individuals, totaling $66,750.
Fields of interest: Medical school/education; Nursing school/education.

Type of support: Scholarships—to individuals; Graduate support.
Application information: Deadline Apr. 15; Completion of formal application required, including tax returns.
Program description:
  Welch Memorial Scholarship Program: Applicants must have been residents of Coles or Cumberland counties, IL, for at least the past five consecutive years in order to qualify. Scholarships are renewable.
EIN: 376284353

4353
George T. Welch Testamentary Trust
c/o Baker Boyer National Bank
P.O. Box 1796
Walla Walla, WA 99362 (509) 525-2000
Contact: Sandra Bradley, Trust Off., Baker Boyer National Bank

Foundation type: Independent foundation
Limitations: Scholarships for three undergraduate years to unmarried, financially needy students who are residents of Walla Walla County, WA, and are enrolled in four-year colleges.
Publications: Application guidelines; Program policy statement.
Financial data: Year ended 09/30/2005.
Assets, $4,340,813 (M); Expenditures, $254,028; Total giving, $205,395; Grants to individuals, 78 grants totaling $114,945 (high: $2,500, low: $5).
Type of support: Undergraduate support.
Application information: Applications accepted. Application form required.
  Deadline(s): May 1
  Additional information: Forms available by Jan. 1; Interviews required.
EIN: 916024318

4354
Weller Foundation, Inc.
P.O. Box 636
Atkinson, NE 68713 (402) 925-2803

Foundation type: Independent foundation
Limitations: Scholarships to financially needy high school graduates of Boyd, Brown, Garfield, Holt, Keya Paha, and Rock counties, NE. Applicants must be U.S. citizens attending one of the approved technical community colleges in NE or other vocational education institutions. See program description for a list of approved schools and additional limitations.
Publications: Application guidelines.
Financial data: Year ended 10/31/2004.
Assets, $4,225,780 (M); Expenditures, $266,658; Total giving, $170,344; Grants to individuals, totaling $170,344.
Fields of interest: Vocational education; Business school/education; Nursing school/education; Engineering school/education; Computer science.
Type of support: Support to graduates or students of specific schools; Technical education support; Undergraduate support.
Application information:
  Deadline(s): Apr. 1 and June 1 for new applicants, June 1 and Nov. 1 for renewal applicants
  Additional information: Completion of formal application required, including parents' and student's financial information, and copy of GED or diploma; Recipients notified within 30 days of applying.

Program description:

Scholarship Program: Applicants must be 40 or under as of July 1, be high school graduates or have their GED, and be full-time students without bachelor's degrees. Grants are renewable provided the recipient maintains a 2.0 GPA. The scholarship is not intended to assist students in bachelor's degree programs, however there are some exceptions to this rule, such as for nursing programs. Scholarships range from $300 to $1,500 per year and cover two semesters of study. Students of the following schools are eligible: Bellvue College; Bryan Memorial Hospital School of Nursing; Chadron State College; Clarkson College; College of St. Mary; Central Community College; McCook Community College; Metropolitan Community College; Mid-Plains Community College; Northeast Community College; Platte Community College; Southeast Community College; University of Nebraska; Western Nebraska Community College; Concordia Teachers College; Creighton University Mary Lanning Memorial Hospital School of Nursing; Creighton University; Doane College; Midland Lutheran College; Nebraska Methodist College; Nebraska Wesleyan University; Peru State College; Union College; Wayne State College; West Nebraska General Hospital School of Nursing; Career Institute of Omaha; Electronic Computer Programming Institute of Omaha; Lincoln School of Commerce; Spencer School of Business; Gateway Electronics Institute; and Universal Technical Institute.
EIN: 470611350

4355

The Weller Foundation, Inc.
P.O. Box 1145
Woodbury, CT 06798 (203) 263-0229
Contact: JoAnn E. Davies, Mgr.

Foundation type: Independent foundation
Limitations: Scholarships and awards to high school students in Newtown, Monroe, Trumbull, Shelton, and Easton-Redding, CT, as well as grants to outstanding teachers.
Financial data: Year ended 12/31/2004.
Assets, $2,522,986 (M); Expenditures, $130,789; Total giving, $79,918; Grants to individuals, totaling $63,318.
Fields of interest: Science.
Type of support: Support to graduates or students of specific schools; Undergraduate support.
Application information: Applications accepted.
Additional information: Deadlines and procedures vary; See program description for more information. All applications must be mailed.

Program descriptions:

Barton L. Weller Scholarship: Available to senior-year students attending one of the following CT high schools: Joel Barlow High School, Masuk High School, Newtown High School, Shelton High School, or Trumbull High School. The award is determined by a regional competition designed to encourage academic excellence in a substantial independent six-month research or study project of the student's choosing. Sample topics include the fine arts, computer projects, economics, science or engineering, mathematics, or political or environmental factors affecting the immediate geographic area. Deadline Oct. 22 for project proposal. Contact foundation for specific proposal-writing guidelines. Five finalists are selected by Nov. 1 and are given $100 to help defray project expenses. These finalists then have from Nov. 1 to Apr. 21 to complete their proposed projects. Finalists are interviewed in May and then

the winner is announced at an awards dinner for the finalists. The winner receives a scholarship of $10,000, payable in four annual increments of $2,500. Runners-up receive $400. Recent winning projects include a computer game for elementary students, a high school humor magazine, and an analysis of bilingual education.

Senior Science Award, Eleanor F. Moor Business Award, Paul W. Broggi Communications Award: Presented annually in each of the five high schools honoring students who have excelled in science, business studies, and communications. The recipients are chosen by the faculties of the individual high schools. No application is required.

Vincent Voccia Vocational Awards: Provide financial assistance to students at Masuk, Newtown, Trumbull, Joel Barlow, and Shelton high schools to prepare for vocational or technical careers. Correspondence schools and four-year degree programs are not acceptable under this program. One winner is chosen from each school. Financial need is not a factor. Winners receive an award equal to the lesser of $2,500 or 50 percent of the cost of tuition and fees of the vocational-technical program proposed. Payment is made directly to the institution, one half upon enrollment and one half after satisfactory completion of the first half of the program. The program must begin within nine months of the award date. Application forms are available from the schools' guidance offices. Deadline Apr. 29. Recipients notified on or near May 16.

Weller Entrepreneurial Scholarship: Presented through Junior Achievement of Western CT, Inc. and is given to a high school senior who has demonstrated entrepreneurial characteristics and has a class rank within the range of 30 to 70 percent. All student members of a Junior Achievement company who are not related to the judges and who are enrolled in a four-year degree program are eligible. Applicants must also teach at least one J.A. Business Basic Course to a fifth or sixth grade class, be recommended by their adult company advisors, and display leadership, reliability, teamwork, job attitude, and job performance. Financial need is not a consideration. Completion of formal application required, including recommendations from school (to verify class rank), and from J.A. staff. A maximum award of $8,000 will be given to each winner in annual installments of $2,000. Verification of college enrollment is necessary for first payment. Recipients must maintain at least a "C" average to continue receiving payments.

Weller Collegiate Scholarships: Presented annually to incoming freshmen at local colleges who are from one of the foundation's five communities. The recipients are chosen by the local colleges based on financial need. No application form is required.

Weller Instrumental Music Scholarship: Presented annually to high school students who have enrolled in conservatories or colleges as music majors with a concentration in instrumental music. Applicants must be full-time senior-year students at Joel Barlow, Masuk, Newton, Shelton, and Trumbull high schools and not be related to the foundation's trustees or judges. Financial need is not a consideration. A formal application is due Apr. 1. Finalists will be selected by the Director of Instrumental Music at each school and must audition before a panel of judges on Apr. 26. The winner must start a formal education program within six months from the date of receiving the scholarship. The award is payable in four annual installments of $1,000. Proof of enrollment is required for first payment. Recipients must maintain at least a 2.5 GPA to continue receiving payments.

Weller Eighth Grade Scholastic Achievement Awards: Presented annually to eighth grade students with outstanding scholastic achievement in each of the six middle schools in the foundation's five-town area. Participating schools are Clark Hill Middle School in Monroe, Newtown Middle School, John Read Middle School in Redding, Intermediate Middle School in Shelton, and Hillcrest and Madison middle schools, both in Trumbull. The recipients are full-time eighth grade students who have achieved the highest final GPA in their classes. The recipients are announced in June, and receive a $200 U.S. Savings Bond and a certificate of honor.

Weller Outstanding Teacher Award: Presented annually in recognition of the teaching quality and innovation exhibited by classroom teachers of grades K-5. Teachers currently teaching in the Monroe, Trumbull, and Newtown public school systems who developed a successful curriculum project that was implemented during the current or previous academic year may apply. The winner receives $1,000 and a certificate. Deadline Apr. 1. Completion of formal application required. Form is available from the Office of the Asst. Superintendent of Schools or the foundation. Completed forms should be mailed to: Dr. Kenneth R. Freeston, Assistant Superintendent, Newtown Public Schools, 11 Queen St., Newtown, CT 06470. The winner will be selected by a panel of judges from the Instructional Coordinating Council.
EIN: 066068987

4356

John H. Wellons Foundation, Inc.
(formerly Wellons Foundation, Inc.)
P.O. Box 1254
Dunn, NC 28335-1254 (910) 892-0436
Contact: John H. Wellons Sr., Pres.

Foundation type: Public charity
Limitations: Student loans for higher education only to local Dunn, NC, students.
Financial data: Year ended 12/31/2003.
Assets, $5,603,925 (M); Expenditures, $745,172; Total giving, $9,925.
Type of support: Student loans—to individuals.
Application information: Application form required.
Deadline(s): None.
Additional information: Loans only for Dunn, NC, students; Others need not apply.
EIN: 566061476

4357

The Wells County Foundation, Inc.
109 N. Scott St.
Bluffton, IN 46714-0060
Contact: Bette Erxleben, C.E.O.
E-mail: wellscountyfound@wellscountyfound.org;
Additional E-mail: berxleben@parlorcity.com;
URL: http://www.wellscountyfound.org

Foundation type: Community foundation
Limitations: Scholarships to individuals residing in Wells County, IN.
Publications: Application guidelines; Annual report; Informational brochure.
Financial data: Year ended 12/31/2004.
Assets, $13,501,400 (M); Expenditures, $1,081,070; Total giving, $865,757; Grants to individuals, totaling $249,947.
Fields of interest: Education.
Type of support: Scholarships—to individuals.
Application information: Application form required.
Deadline(s): Vary

Additional information: See Web site for additional application information and scholarship listings.
EIN: 356042815

4358

Glen, Frieda and John Wells Education Fund

P.O. Box 70
Hartford, KY 42347

Foundation type: Independent foundation
Limitations: Scholarships to graduates of Ohio County High School, KY, for higher education.
Financial data: Year ended 12/31/2004. Assets, $1,186,483 (M); Expenditures, $57,150; Total giving, $57,150; Grants to individuals, totaling $57,150.
Type of support: Support to graduates or students of specific schools; Undergraduate support.
Application information: Contact fund for current application deadline; Completion of formal application required.
Program description:
   Wells Scholarship Fund Program: Recipients must be enrolled full-time, for their first year, at Wesleyan College or Western Kentucky University, KY.
EIN: 611362784

4359

Wells Family Foundation

P.O. Box 3207
Sioux City, IA 51102
Application addresses: c/o Guidance Counselor, Gehlen High School, 709 Plymouth St. N.E., Le Mars, IA 51031; or c/o Daniel W. Wells, Pres., P.O. Box 1310, Le Mars, IA 51031

Foundation type: Independent foundation
Limitations: Scholarships to graduates of LeMars Community and Gehlen Catholic high schools, LeMars, IA.
Financial data: Year ended 12/31/2003. Assets, $0 (M); Expenditures, $19,877; Total giving, $19,875; Grants to individuals, 22 grants totaling $17,875 (high: $1,000, low: $750).
Type of support: Support to graduates or students of specific schools; Undergraduate support.
Application information: Deadline Apr. 14; Completion of formal application required, including field of study, community service, awards, goals and other pertinent information.
EIN: 421453884

4360

Julia O. Wells Memorial Educational Foundation, Inc.

P.O. Box 1931, Apt. 2
Albany, NY 12201

Foundation type: Independent foundation
Limitations: Scholarships to students at participating colleges.
Financial data: Year ended 12/31/2004. Assets, $2,001,328 (M); Expenditures, $180,169; Total giving, $147,000; Grants to individuals, 44 grants totaling $24,500 (high: $750, low: $250).
Type of support: Undergraduate support.
Application information: Unsolicited requests for funds not considered or acknowledged.
EIN: 222921430

4361

Loretta A. Wells Nursing Scholarship Trust

c/o JPMorgan Chase Bank, N.A.
P.O. Box 1308
Milwaukee, WI 53201
Application address: c/o JPMorgan Chase Bank, N.A., 200 W. College Ave., Appleton, WI 54911, tel.: (414) 735-1382

Foundation type: Independent foundation
Limitations: Scholarships to Brown County, WI, nursing students.
Financial data: Year ended 07/31/2005. Assets, $158,338 (M); Expenditures, $112,745; Total giving, $96,386; Grants to individuals, totaling $96,386.
Fields of interest: Nursing school/education.
Type of support: Undergraduate support.
Application information: Deadline Apr. 30; Completion of formal application required; Interviews required.
EIN: 396364734

4362

Lucile Wells Scholarship Fund

c/o Marshall & Ilsley Bank
P.O. Box 2977
Milwaukee, WI 53201
Application address: c/o Rev. George H. McKillingin, 919 N. Wuthering Hills Dr., Janesville, WI 53546

Foundation type: Independent foundation
Limitations: Scholarships to high school graduates who are members of the Trinity Episcopal Church, Janesville, WI.
Financial data: Year ended 07/31/2005. Assets, $1,047,751 (M); Expenditures, $64,132; Total giving, $52,978; Grants to individuals, totaling $52,978.
Fields of interest: Protestant agencies & churches.
Type of support: Undergraduate support.
Application information: Applications accepted throughout the year; Completion of formal application required.
EIN: 396694943

4363

Wells Trust Fund

c/o The Citizens National Bank of Paris
P.O. Box 790
Paris, IL 61944-0279
Contact: Chris Hollowell, Trust Off., The Citizens National Bank of Paris

Foundation type: Independent foundation
Limitations: Undergraduate scholarships to Protestant residents of Edgar County, IL, attending Depauw University, Eastern Illinois University, Millikin University, and the University of Illinois.
Financial data: Year ended 12/31/2004. Assets, $1,063,217 (M); Expenditures, $54,109; Total giving, $38,000; Grants to individuals, totaling $38,000.
Fields of interest: Protestant agencies & churches.
Type of support: Support to graduates or students of specific schools; Undergraduate support.
Application information: Deadline June 1; Completion of formal application required.
EIN: 376115126

4364

Fred W. Wells Trust Fund

c/o Bank of America, N.A.
465 Colrain Rd.
Greenfield, MA 01301
Contact: Cynthia Nims, Tr.
Application address: c/o Bank of America, N.A., Attn.: Admin., 100 Federal St., Boston, MA 02109

Foundation type: Independent foundation
Limitations: Scholarships to residents of the following towns in Franklin County, MA: Greenfield, Deerfield, Shelburne, Ashfield, Montague, Buckland, Charlemont, Heath, Leyden, Gill, Northfield, Conway, Bernardston, Hawley, Rowe, and Monroe.
Publications: Application guidelines.
Financial data: Year ended 06/30/2005. Assets, $4,756,363 (M); Expenditures, $254,657; Total giving, $219,479; Grants to individuals, 353 grants totaling $186,479 (high: $1,400, low: $110).
Application information: Application form required.
   Initial approach: Letter.
   Deadline(s): Apr. 15
   Additional information: Scholarships are renewable for up to four years with a limit of $1,000 per student, per year.
EIN: 046412350

4365

Horace Wells Trust Fund

100 Sherman St.
Norwich, CT 06360

Foundation type: Independent foundation
Limitations: Scholarships to dental students.
Financial data: Year ended 10/31/2005. Assets, $250,990 (M); Expenditures, $12,013; Total giving, $6,000; Grants to individuals, 6 grants totaling $6,000 (high: $1,000, low: $1,000).
Fields of interest: Dental school/education.
Type of support: Scholarships—to individuals.
Application information: Contact foundation for current application deadline/guidelines.
EIN: 066037032

4366

Leon Wells Trust

c/o Monroe Bank & Trust
102 E. Front St.
Monroe, MI 48161-2162

Foundation type: Independent foundation
Limitations: Scholarships by nomination only to financially needy graduating seniors of Dundee and Summerfield community schools who are residents of Dundee or Summerfield townships, Monroe County, MI.
Financial data: Year ended 05/31/2005. Assets, $333,855 (M); Expenditures, $38,451; Total giving, $34,104; Grants to individuals, totaling $34,104.
Type of support: Support to graduates or students of specific schools; Awards/grants by nomination only; Undergraduate support.
Application information: Application form required.
   Deadline(s): May 1
   Applicants should submit the following:
      1) Financial information
   Additional information: Application must include an affidavit of residency; Applications for continuing awards must include college transcripts; Application forms are available from the qualifying high schools, and are to be submitted to the high school principal.

Applicants must have maintained a GPA of at least 3.0 over the first seven semesters of high school. Applicants for continuing awards must have maintained at least a 2.5 GPA in college. Students are nominated by a five-member committee consisting of the high school principal, counselors, and tenured teachers. Recipients are chosen by a committee consisting of the superintendents of the two schools and the Judge of Probate of Monroe County. The minimum amount for an initial scholarship is $400, for a renewal, $200. The maximum amount is one-half of the estimated average expenses for full-time study. Scholarships are renewable for up to four years.
EIN: 386146348

4367
Wellstar Foundation, Inc.
(formerly Kennestone Regional Foundation, Inc.)
680 Church St., Ste. 100
Marietta, GA   30060   (770) 793-7026
Contact: Sandy White, Exec. Dir.
FAX: (770) 793-7983;
E-mail: wellstar@wellstar.org; URL: http://www.wellstar.org

Foundation type: Public charity
Limitations: Scholarships to employees, dependents and residents of the Wellstar service area, primarily in GA, for undergraduate education. Preference is given to applicants pursuing a health care related course of study.
Financial data: Year ended 06/30/2003. Assets, $1,401,117 (M); Expenditures, $1,936,177; Total giving, $28,000; Grants to individuals, 42 grants totaling $28,000 (high: $1,000, low: $500).
Fields of interest: Health sciences school/education.
Type of support: Employee-related scholarships; Scholarships—to individuals; Undergraduate support.
Application information:
Initial approach: Letter or e-mail.
Deadline(s): Contact foundation for current application deadline/guidelines
Additional information: Scholarships up to $2,500 are awarded.
EIN: 581627413

4368
Frank A. & M. Esther Wenstrom Foundation
c/o American State Bank & Trust Co.
P.O. Box 1446, 223 Main St.
Williston, ND   58802-1446

Foundation type: Operating foundation
Limitations: Scholarships to residents of ND.
Financial data: Year ended 09/30/2004. Assets, $426,340 (M); Expenditures, $13,755; Total giving, $9,500; Grants to individuals, totaling $9,500.
Type of support: Scholarships—to individuals.
Application information: Applications accepted throughout the year; Completion of formal application required, including college transcript.
EIN: 450447357

4369
West Bend Clinic Foundation, Inc.
1700 W. Paradise Dr.
West Bend, WI   53095

Foundation type: Independent foundation
Limitations: Scholarships by nomination only to graduating seniors of West Bend East or West Bend West high schools, WI.
Financial data: Year ended 06/30/2004. Assets, $226,037 (M); Expenditures, $21,660; Total giving, $20,000; Grants to individuals, 4 grants totaling $20,000 (high: $5,000, low: $5,000).
Type of support: Support to graduates or students of specific schools; Awards/grants by nomination only; Undergraduate support.
Application information: Unsolicited requests for funds not accepted.
Program description:
West Bend Clinic Scholarship Program: Scholarships are $5,000 each for one year only, but may be continued throughout recipient's 4-year college career if activities and conduct are satisfactory to scholarship committee. Recipient must maintain a 3.0 GPA or better.
EIN: 391833049

4370
W. F. & Blanche E. West Educational Fund
c/o Wells Fargo Bank Northwest, N.A.
P.O. Box 21927
Seattle, WA   98111
Contact: Jodi Bruns
Application address: c/o Scholarship America, 1 Scholarship Way, P.O. Box 297, St. Peter, MN 56082

Foundation type: Independent foundation
Limitations: Scholarships to graduates of W.F. West High School, Chehalis, WA, who have lived in Lewis County, WA, for at least two years. Some recipients receive more than one grant.
Financial data: Year ended 12/31/2004. Assets, $2,695,124 (M); Expenditures, $156,317; Total giving, $119,042; Grants to individuals, totaling $119,042.
Fields of interest: Education.
Type of support: Support to graduates or students of specific schools.
Application information: Application form required.
Deadline(s): July 1 for new applicants
Additional information: Applications accepted throughout the year for renewals; Application forms available at school.
EIN: 916101769

4371
The H. O. West Foundation
101 Gordon Dr.
Exton, PA   19341-0645   (610) 594-2900
Contact: Richard D. Luzzi, Tr.; Maureen B. Goebel, Admin.

Foundation type: Company-sponsored foundation
Limitations: Scholarships only for dependent children of employees of West Pharmaceutical Services, Inc.
Publications: Application guidelines.
Financial data: Year ended 12/31/2004. Assets, $1,209,597 (M); Expenditures, $428,292; Total giving, $423,930; Grants to individuals, 44 grants totaling $55,345 (high: $2,500, low: $533).
Type of support: Employee-related scholarships.

Application information: Application form required.
Deadline(s): Feb. 28
Applicants should submit the following:
1) Transcripts
2) SAT
3) Letter(s) of recommendation
4) GPA
5) Essay
6) ACT
Program description:
H.O. West Foundation Scholarship Program: Seven college scholarships of up to $2,500 per year for four successive years are awarded for a baccalaureate program at an accredited college or university. Winners are selected on the basis of character, maturity, leadership, extra-curricular activities, motivation, interest and desire, patriotism, predicted success in college and academic achievement. Recipients must enter college in the fall of the year the award is given and continue full-time for four years.
EIN: 383674460

4372
West Hudson Foundation
206 Bergen Ave.
Kearny, NJ   07032   (201) 955-7054
Contact: John Magullian, Pres.

Foundation type: Public charity
Limitations: Scholarships to postsecondary students within the West Hudson Hospital, NJ, service area who are interested in the medical field.
Financial data: Year ended 12/31/2003. Assets, $423,069 (M); Expenditures, $56,229; Total giving, $23,200; Grants to individuals, 21 grants totaling $23,200 (high: $2,000, low: $200).
Fields of interest: Medical school/education.
Type of support: Graduate support; Undergraduate support.
Application information: Deadline mid-May; Completion of formal application required, including essay, recommendations, transcripts, and GPA.
EIN: 222311645

4373
Dudley R. West Memorial Scholarship Foundation
c/o Wachovia Bank, N.A.
100 N. Main St, 13th Fl.
Winston-Salem, NC   27150
Application address: c/o Wachovia Bank, N.A., Box 26311, Richmond, VA, 23260

Foundation type: Independent foundation
Limitations: Scholarships to graduates of high schools in Buckingham County, VA.
Financial data: Year ended 12/31/2004. Assets, $218,844 (M); Expenditures, $8,901; Total giving, $7,000; Grants to individuals, totaling $7,000.
Type of support: Support to graduates or students of specific schools; Undergraduate support.
Application information: Deadline Apr. 15; Completion of formal application required, including transcripts, GPA, and outline of financial need.
Program description:
Memorial Scholarship Program: Recipients are selected on the basis of character, intelligence, scholastic record, financial need, and community and extracurricular activities. The minimum scholarship award is set at $1,000.
EIN: 541672687

4374
Marion Huxley West Scholarship Fund
c/o Rockland Trust Co.
2036 Washington St.
Hanover, MA   02339
Application address: c/o Principal, Middleboro High School, 71 E. Grove St., Middleboro, MA 02346-1847

Foundation type: Independent foundation
Limitations: Scholarships only to graduates of Middleboro High School, MA, to attend a four-year college or university.
Financial data: Year ended 06/30/2003. Assets, $155,568 (M); Expenditures, $8,374; Total giving, $6,500; Grants to individuals, 2 grants totaling $6,500 (high: $5,000, low: $1,500).
Type of support: Support to graduates or students of specific schools; Undergraduate support.
Application information: Applications accepted throughout the year; Completion of formal application required.
EIN: 043397114

4375
Merle S. & Emma J. West Scholarship Fund
c/o U.S. Bank, N.A.
P.O. Box 3168
Portland, OR   97208
Scholarship application address: c/o Jamie M. Fabian, West Scholarship Comm., 3720 S. 6th St., Klamath Falls, OR 97603, tel.: (503) 883-3857

Foundation type: Independent foundation
Limitations: Scholarships to graduates of high schools in Klamath County, OR, for postsecondary and vocational education.
Financial data: Year ended 12/31/2004. Assets, $3,925,204 (M); Expenditures, $243,292; Total giving, $178,324; Grants to individuals, 42 grants totaling $178,324 (high: $52,962, low: $350).
Fields of interest: Vocational education.
Type of support: Support to graduates or students of specific schools; Technical education support; Undergraduate support.
Application information: Applications accepted. Application form required.
  Deadline(s): Feb. 15 to Apr. 15
  Additional information: Interviews required.
Program description:
  West Scholarship Program: The required minimum GPA for college students is 2.35 for freshmen and sophomores, and 2.50 for juniors and seniors.
EIN: 936160221

4376
Westchester Foundation
P.O. Box 3009
Champaign, IL   61826   (217) 352-6000
Contact: Richard J. Baker, Exec. Dir.

Foundation type: Independent foundation
Limitations: Scholarships to individuals, primarily in IL and OR, for higher education.
Financial data: Year ended 12/31/2004. Assets, $392,291 (M); Expenditures, $15,808; Total giving, $14,000; Grants to individuals, totaling $14,000.
Type of support: Scholarships—to individuals.
Application information: Contact foundation for current application deadlines; Completion of formal

application required, including transcript and two letters of reference.
EIN: 364149509

4377
Westendorf Family Foundation
P.O. Box 147
Sioux City, IA   51102-0147

Foundation type: Independent foundation
Limitations: Scholarships to IA residents for higher education.
Financial data: Year ended 10/31/2004. Assets, $651,779 (M); Expenditures, $58,697; Total giving, $58,445; Grants to individuals, totaling $16,000.
Type of support: Scholarships—to individuals.
Application information: Contact foundation for current application deadline/guidelines; Initial approach by letter.
EIN: 426373031

4378
Ward W. and Norabelle Wester Memorial Charitable Foundation
c/o National City Bank
P.O. Box 94651
Cleveland, OH   44101-4651
Application address: c/o Youngstown Shrine Club, P.O. Box 302, North Lima, OH 44452

Foundation type: Independent foundation
Limitations: Scholarships to needy individuals who have received treatment at the Shriners Hospital for Crippled Children, Cincinnati, OH, Burn Institute or who have received treatment at the Shriners Hospital for Crippled Children, Erie, PA, Unit.
Financial data: Year ended 09/30/2004. Assets, $1,073,135 (M); Expenditures, $54,045; Total giving, $41,285; Grants to individuals, totaling $41,285.
Fields of interest: Children/youth, services.
Type of support: Scholarships—to individuals.
Application information: Contact foundation for current application deadline; Application by letter, including social security number and proof of treatment or benefits from the Shriners Hospitals of Cincinnati, OH, or Erie, PA.
EIN: 346998992

4379
Western Lane Community Foundation
(formerly Western Lane County Foundation)
1525 W. 12th St., Ste. 18
P.O. Box 1589
Florence, OR   97439
E-mail: wlcf@oregonfast.net; Tel./Fax: (541) 997-1274; URL: http://www.wlcfonline.com

Foundation type: Community foundation
Limitations: Scholarships to graduates of Sinslaw High School, OR, and Mapleton High School, OR for undergraduate education.
Publications: Application guidelines; Annual report; Informational brochure; Newsletter; Program policy statement.
Financial data: Year ended 12/31/2004. Assets, $2,574,206 (M); Expenditures, $135,247; Total giving, $102,406; Grants to individuals, totaling $51,881.
Type of support: Support to graduates or students of specific schools; Undergraduate support.
Application information: Applications accepted. Application form required.

Additional information: Contact foundation or high school guidance office for further application information.
EIN: 237438503

4380
Western Minnesota Masonic Foundation
101 S. 1st St.
P.O. Box 658
Montevideo, MN   56265
Contact: Ralph Lunde, Secy.
Application address: 121 N. 6th St., Montevideo, MN 56265

Foundation type: Operating foundation
Limitations: Scholarships to graduates of Monterideo High School, MN, for attendance at colleges or universities in the United States.
Financial data: Year ended 12/31/2003. Assets, $146,860 (M); Expenditures, $12,307; Total giving, $12,188; Grants to individuals, 4 grants totaling $12,188 (high: $3,250, low: $938).
Type of support: Support to graduates or students of specific schools; Undergraduate support.
Application information: Applications accepted. Application form required.
  Deadline(s): Apr. 1
  Additional information: Application should include class rank and anticipated college major.
EIN: 411570211

4381
Peter V. Westhaysen Medical Education Trust
c/o Bank Calumet
P.O. Box 69
Hammond, IN   46325

Foundation type: Independent foundation
Limitations: Scholarships to residents of Lake County, IN, for medical and nursing education at accredited colleges and universities.
Financial data: Year ended 12/31/2004. Assets, $1,227,381 (M); Expenditures, $69,712; Total giving, $59,700; Grants to individuals, totaling $59,700.
Fields of interest: Medical school/education; Nursing school/education.
Type of support: Graduate support; Undergraduate support.
Application information: Deadline June 1; Completion of formal application required.
EIN: 316290396

4382
James L. & Nellie M. Westlake Scholarship Fund
c/o U.S. Bank, N.A.
P.O. Box 387
St. Louis, MO   63166
Contact: Angela Pearson
Scholarship application address: c/o Scholarship Management Svcs., 1 Scholarship Way, P.O. Box 297, St. Peter, MN 56082

Foundation type: Independent foundation
Limitations: Scholarships only to high school seniors who are residents of MO.
Publications: Application guidelines.
Financial data: Year ended 06/30/2005. Assets, $22,092,420 (M); Expenditures, $996,939; Total giving, $867,220; Grants to

individuals, 73 grants totaling $867,220 (high: $30,200, low: $3,800).
Type of support: Undergraduate support.
Application information: Application form required.
  Initial approach: Letter.
  Deadline(s): Mar. 1
  Additional information: Scholarships are awarded on the basis of financial need, academic potential, good character, school/community leadership, ambition to succeed, and present and future useful citizenship. Renewals may be made for up to eight semesters.
EIN: 436248269

4383
Westmoreland Coal Company and Penn Virginia Corporation Foundation
2 N. Cascade Ave., 3rd Fl.
Colorado Springs, CO   80903   (719) 442-5854
Contact: Nancy Bielaski, Admin.

Foundation type: Company-sponsored foundation
Limitations: Scholarships to children of employees of Westmoreland Coal Company and Penn Virginia Corporation and their subsidiaries. Scholarships also to individuals who reside in Albermarle, Lee, Scott, and Wise counties, VA; Boone, Kanowa, Logan, Raleigh, Wyoming, and Wayne counties, WV; Harlan, Martin, and Pike counties, KY; El Paso County, CO; and Big Horn County, MT.
Publications: Informational brochure (including application guidelines).
Financial data: Year ended 12/31/2004.
Assets, $407,314 (M); Expenditures, $33,663; Total giving, $12,820; Grants to individuals, 35 grants totaling $12,820 (high: $500, low: $250).
Fields of interest: Vocational education; Nursing school/education; Business/industry.
Type of support: Employee-related scholarships.
Application information: Application form required.
  Deadline(s): Dec. 1
  Additional information: Applications accepted beginning in the fall; Contact high school for application.
Program description:
  Scholarship Program: Recipients may attend junior colleges, community colleges, four-year colleges and universities, schools of nursing, and technical programs related to mining.
EIN: 237398163

4384
The Westport-Weston Foundation Trust
c/o Hudson United Bank, Wealth Mgmt. Group
90 Post Rd. E., 3rd Fl.
Westport, CT   06880
Contact: Mark Brennan, V.P., TD Banknorth, N.A., Wealth Mgmt. Group

Foundation type: Independent foundation
Limitations: Undergraduate scholarships to financially needy residents of Westport and Weston, CT, only.
Financial data: Year ended 12/31/2004.
Assets, $858,223 (M); Expenditures, $34,638; Total giving, $24,513; Grants to individuals, 3 grants totaling $6,000.
Type of support: Undergraduate support.
Application information: Applications accepted. Application form required.
  Initial approach: Letter.
  Deadline(s): None
  Additional information: Interviews may be required.
EIN: 066035931

4385
Harold and Sara Wetherbee Foundation
c/o Regions Bank
P.O. Box 8
Albany, GA   31702-0008
Contact: James Reynolds, Trust Off.; Debbie Chambless, Trust Off.

Foundation type: Independent foundation
Limitations: Scholarships to graduating seniors of Dougherty County and Lee County high schools, GA. Scholarships are made on the basis of grades, financial need, and extracurricular activities.
Financial data: Year ended 11/30/2004.
Assets, $1,594,542 (M); Expenditures, $97,891; Total giving, $80,794; Grants to individuals, totaling $80,794.
Fields of interest: Education.
Type of support: Support to graduates or students of specific schools.
Application information: Application form required.
  Deadline(s): Apr. 15
  Additional information: Interviews required.
EIN: 586068645

4386
Marian J. Wettrick Charitable Foundation
c/o City Trust Company Trustee
10 N. Main St.
Coudersport, PA   16915   (814) 274-9150
FAX: (814) 274-0401

Foundation type: Independent foundation
Limitations: Scholarships to female graduates of a PA college who have been accepted to a medical school in PA.
Financial data: Year ended 12/31/2004.
Assets, $1,546,826 (M); Expenditures, $89,880; Total giving, $80,000; Grants to individuals, totaling $80,000.
Fields of interest: Medical school/education; Women.
Type of support: Graduate support.
Application information: Deadline May 15; Completion of formal application required.
Program description:
  Wettrick Charitable Scholarship Program: Recipients must be planning to practice medicine at Charles Cole Memorial Hospital in Coudersport, PA.
EIN: 256545149

4387
Wesley Weyman Trust
c/o Welch & Forbes
45 School St., 5th Fl.
Boston, MA   02108
Contact: Christoph Wolff, Tr.
Application address: The Graduate School of Arts and Sciences, Harvard University, University Hall 18, Cambridge, MA 02138

Foundation type: Independent foundation
Limitations: Scholarships to students enrolled in qualified institutions for study in the field of music.
Financial data: Year ended 01/31/2005.
Assets, $231,108 (M); Expenditures, $15,433; Total giving, $10,765; Grants to individuals, totaling $10,765.
Fields of interest: Music; Performing arts, education.
Type of support: Scholarships—to individuals.
Application information: Contact trust for current application deadline/guidelines.
EIN: 046118681

4388
WGR Employee Scholarship Fund Trust
1099 18th St., Ste. 1200
Denver, CO   80202-1955
Contact: John C. Walter, Tr.

Foundation type: Company-sponsored foundation
Limitations: Scholarships to children of Western Gas Resources, Inc. Consolidated employees.
Financial data: Year ended 11/30/2004.
Assets, $2 (M); Expenditures, $24,305; Total giving, $24,000; Grants to individuals, 12 grants totaling $24,000 (high: $2,000, low: $2,000).
Type of support: Employee-related scholarships.
Application information: Application form required.
  Initial approach: Letter.
  Deadline(s): None
EIN: 846246472

4389
Whatcom Community Foundation
119 Grand Ave., Ste. A
Bellingham, WA   98225   (360) 671-6463
Contact: Sue Sharpe, Interim Dir.
FAX: (360) 671-6437; *E-mail:* wcf@whatcomcf.org; *URL:* http://www.whatcomcf.org

Foundation type: Community foundation
Limitations: Scholarships by nomination only, to residents of Whatcom, WA who have graduated from Bellingham high schools.
Publications: Application guidelines; Annual report; Financial statement; Grants list; Informational brochure; Newsletter.
Financial data: Year ended 06/30/2005.
Assets, $4,665,696 (M); Expenditures, $829,487; Total giving, $308,456.
Type of support: Support to graduates or students of specific schools; Awards/grants by nomination only.
Application information: Applications not accepted.
  Additional information: Unsolicited requests for funds not considered or acknowledged.
EIN: 911726410

4390
Wheelwright Scientific School
Sagamore Tax Group
27 School St., Rm. 201
Boston, MA   02108
Application address: John H. Pramberg, Jr., P.O. Box 625, Newburyport, MA 01950

Foundation type: Independent foundation
Limitations: Scholarships to Protestant young men who are residents of Newburyport, MA, to pursue higher education in the sciences.
Financial data: Year ended 06/30/2005.
Assets, $4,054,297 (M); Expenditures, $264,445; Total giving, $169,050; Grants to individuals, 18 grants totaling $169,050.
Fields of interest: Science; Protestant agencies & churches; Men.
Type of support: Scholarships—to individuals.
Application information: Applications accepted. Application form required.
  Deadline(s): Feb.
  Additional information: Application must include the names of references, one of whom must be the minister of the applicant's church; Scholarships are renewable.
EIN: 046004390

4391
Whirlpool Foundation
2000 N. M-63
Benton Harbor, MI 49022-2692
(269) 923-5580
Contact: Barbara Hall, Exec. Dir.
FAX: (269) 925-0154; URL: http://whirlpoolcorp.com/social_responsibility/whirlpoolfoundation/default.asp

Foundation type: Company-sponsored foundation
Limitations: Scholarships to children of employees of the Whirlpool Corporation.
Publications: Annual report (including application guidelines).
Financial data: Year ended 03/31/2004. Assets, $257,343 (M); Expenditures, $8,902,630; Total giving, $8,486,000; Grants to individuals, 211 grants totaling $747,736 (high: $14,500, low: $900).
Type of support: Employee-related scholarships.
Application information: Application form required.
Initial approach: Letter or telephone.
Deadline(s): Mar. 1
Additional information: Interviews required.
Program description:
Sons and Daughters Scholarship Program: Offers four-year $16,000 scholarships, one-time honor awards of $2,500, and one-time incentive awards of $1,000 to U.S. employees' children every year.
EIN: 386077342

4392
Doris Whisnant Memorial Foundation, Inc.
P.O. Box 15
Hickory, NC 28603
Contact: Alfred N. Whisnant, Dir.

Foundation type: Independent foundation
Limitations: Scholarships to individuals, primarily in NC.
Financial data: Year ended 06/30/2002. Assets, $10,792 (M); Expenditures, $234,602; Total giving, $233,724; Grants to individuals, 12 grants totaling $10,600.
Type of support: Scholarships—to individuals.
Application information: Applications accepted throughout the year; Completion of formal application required.
EIN: 237318076

4393
Peter N. Whitcher Trust
c/o Scolaro, Shulman, Cohen, et al.
507 Plum St., Ste. 300
Syracuse, NY 13204
Contact: Daniel C. Labelle, Exec. Dir.
Application address: P.O. Box 259, Skaneateles, NY

Foundation type: Independent foundation
Limitations: Scholarships to children of members in good standing of the Iron Workers District Council of Western NY and vicinity. The parent of the applicant, if deceased, must have been a member in good standing at the time of death.
Financial data: Year ended 12/31/2004. Assets, $218,716 (M); Expenditures, $21,707; Total giving, $11,500; Grants to individuals, totaling $11,500.
Fields of interest: Labor unions/organizations.
Type of support: Scholarships—to individuals.
Application information: Deadline Feb. 1; Completion of formal application required, including letter of recommendation.

Program description:
Whitcher Trust Scholarship Program: Selection is based on financial need, academic performance, extracurricular activities, and College Entrance Examination Board tests. Scholarships are renewable.
EIN: 112552891

4394
The White Beeches Country Club Caddy Scholarship Fund, Inc.
c/o Caddy Scholarship Fund, Inc.
53 Grove St.
Lodi, NJ 07644

Foundation type: Independent foundation
Limitations: Scholarships to students for higher education who have participated in the Caddy Scholarship program.
Financial data: Year ended 12/31/2004. Assets, $11,304 (M); Expenditures, $45,675; Total giving, $20,750; Grants to individuals, totaling $20,750.
Fields of interest: Athletics/sports, golf.
Type of support: Undergraduate support.
Application information: Contact fund for current application deadline/guidelines.
EIN: 222918973

4395
Grant T. White Foundation
c/o First National Bank, Trust Dept.
P.O. Box 7
Fort Smith, AR 72902 (479) 788-4343
Contact: Brian Schneider, Trust Off., First National Bank

Foundation type: Independent foundation
Limitations: Scholarships primarily to high school graduates of Fort Smith, AR. Scholarships are renewable.
Financial data: Year ended 05/31/2005. Assets, $679,155 (M); Expenditures, $60,240; Total giving, $47,000; Grants to individuals, 92 grants totaling $47,000 (high: $1,000, low: $250).
Type of support: Undergraduate support.
Application information: Application form required.
Deadline(s): Apr. 10
EIN: 710561239

4396
The Mahlon Thatcher White Foundation
(formerly The Thatcher Foundation)
P.O. Box 2097
Pueblo, CO 81004
Contact: Valeri Hardin

Foundation type: Independent foundation
Limitations: Giving limited to residents of Pueblo county, CO.
Financial data: Year ended 12/31/2004. Assets, $4,135,090 (M); Expenditures, $387,711; Total giving, $348,573; Grants to individuals, 8 grants totaling $39,473 (high: $12,140, low: $1,431).
Application information: Deadline Nov. 1; Initial approach by letter; Application by letter outlining financial need.
EIN: 840581724

4397
The Marvin White Foundation
1 N. Main Pl.
P.O. Box 913
Hutchinson, KS 67504-0913
Application address: Jeffrey W. Smith, Secy., White Scholarship Foundation, 717 4th Ave., Inman, KS 67546-8041

Foundation type: Operating foundation
Limitations: Scholarships to residents of McPherson County, KS, and to individuals who attend colleges in McPherson County to study music, math, or science. See program description for further limitations.
Financial data: Year ended 12/31/2004. Assets, $156,144 (M); Expenditures, $9,242; Total giving, $7,400; Grants to individuals, 18 grants totaling $7,400 (high: $500, low: $300).
Fields of interest: Music; Science; Mathematics.
Type of support: Undergraduate support.
Application information: Applications accepted. Application form required.
Deadline(s): Mar. 2.
Applicants should submit the following:
1) Transcripts
2) Letter(s) of recommendation
Additional information: Application should include a personal statement describing talent, training, goals, and what additional education is needed; Interviews required for Math and Science Scholarships; Auditions required for Music Scholarships; Application forms are available from high school guidance offices and the music, science, and math departments of McPherson County colleges.
Program descriptions:
Scholarship Program: Scholarships are awarded regardless of financial need. Scholarship amounts range from $250 to $800 per academic year, and are renewable.
White Music Scholarships: Applicants must be college music majors or high school students planning to major in music, and must be pursuing or planning to pursue careers in music. Auditions of 10 to 15 minutes are required. Applicants must furnish their own accompanists. Vocalists are expected to have all music memorized. Instrumentalists must have a significant portion of their performance memorized.
White Math and Science Scholarships: Applicants must be college math or science majors or high school students planning to major in math or science, and must be pursuing or planning to pursue a career in math or science. Applicants will be screened and finalists will be invited to appear before a selection committee. Students of dentistry and medicine are eligible.
EIN: 486244419

4398
G. & M. White Scholarship Fund
c/o KeyBank N.A.
800 Superior Ave., 4th Fl.
Cleveland, OH 44114
Application address: c/o Cooperstown High School, Cooperstown, NY 13326

Foundation type: Independent foundation
Limitations: Scholarships to graduating students of Cooperstown High School, NY.
Financial data: Year ended 12/31/2004. Assets, $203,184 (M); Expenditures, $12,413; Total giving, $10,000; Grants to individuals, totaling $10,000.
Type of support: Support to graduates or students of specific schools; Undergraduate support.

Application information: Contact fund for current application deadline; Completion of formal application required.
EIN: 156026002

4399
Eleanor White Trust
c/o TD Banknorth, N.A., Investment Mgmt. Group
P.O. Box 595
Williston, VT 05495-0595

Foundation type: Independent foundation
Limitations: Scholarships to residents of Fair Haven, VT, for attendance at technical schools, colleges, and universities.
Financial data: Year ended 12/31/2004. Assets, $478,000 (M); Expenditures, $71,509; Total giving, $57,500; Grants to individuals, 19 grants totaling $57,500.
Fields of interest: Vocational education.
Type of support: Technical education support; Undergraduate support.
Application information: Application form required.
Deadline(s): July 31
EIN: 036004915

4400
Elizabeth White Trust
c/o KeyBank N.A.
800 Superior Ave., 4th Fl.
Cleveland, OH 44114
Application address: c/o KeyBank N.A., 35 State St., Albany, NY 12207

Foundation type: Independent foundation
Limitations: Scholarships to graduates of Cooperstown High School, NY, who are studying education in college.
Financial data: Year ended 12/31/2004. Assets, $145,718 (M); Expenditures, $8,275; Total giving, $6,410; Grants to individuals, totaling $6,410.
Fields of interest: Teacher school/education.
Type of support: Support to graduates or students of specific schools; Undergraduate support.
Application information: Applications accepted throughout the year; Contact foundation for current application guidelines.
EIN: 146179502

4401
White-Williams Scholars
215 S. Broad St., 5th Fl.
Philadelphia, PA 19107 (215) 735-4480
Contact: Amy T. Holdsman, Exec. Dir.
FAX: (215) 735-4485;
E-mail: info@wwscholars.org; URL: http://www.wwscholars.org

Foundation type: Public charity
Limitations: Grants to economically disadvantaged Philadelphia, PA, public high school students for school-related expenses such as supplies, books, transportation and food.
Publications: Annual report; Newsletter.
Financial data: Year ended 06/30/2004. Expenditures, $1,687,502; Total giving, $779,540; Grants to individuals, totaling $779,540.
Fields of interest: Education.
Type of support: Precollege support.
Application information: Applications accepted. Application form required. Application form available on the grantmaker's Web site.

Initial approach: Letter.
Copies of proposal: 1
Deadline(s): None
Applicants should submit the following:
  1) Transcripts
  2) GPA
  3) Financial information
Additional information: Application should include a copy of recent grades and proof of family income.
Program description:
White-Williams Scholarship Program: Students must have all A's and B's in major subjects. Students may have one C, but it must be balanced by an A in another major subject. Students may not have any D's in major subjects. Family income should not exceed the income limits of the free lunch program. Students must show good citizenship demonstrated by student conduct.
EIN: 231365983

4402
Helen E. Davis Whitefield Trust
(formerly Thomas & Helen Davis Memorial Foundation)
c/o Fulton Financial Advisors, N.A.
P.O. Box 3215
Lancaster, PA 17604-3215
Application address: c/o Supervisor of Guidance, Woodstown High School, East Ave., Woodstown, NJ 08098

Foundation type: Independent foundation
Limitations: Scholarships to graduates of Woodstown High School, NJ.
Publications: Application guidelines.
Financial data: Year ended 02/28/2005. Assets, $239,974 (M); Expenditures, $27,644; Total giving, $22,500; Grants to individuals, 5 grants totaling $22,500 (high: $4,500, low: $4,500).
Type of support: Support to graduates or students of specific schools; Undergraduate support.
Application information: Application form required.
Deadline(s): May 1
EIN: 222764049

4403
Lee Whitehall Educational Trust
121 W. Main St.
Attica, IN 47918 (765) 762-6741
Contact: Thomas P. O'Connor, Tr.

Foundation type: Independent foundation
Limitations: Scholarships to residents of Fountain and Warren counties, IN.
Financial data: Year ended 12/31/2004. Assets, $365,704 (M); Expenditures, $12,660; Total giving, $11,910; Grants to individuals, totaling $11,910.
Type of support: Scholarships—to individuals.
Application information: Deadline Apr. 15; Completion of formal application required.
EIN: 356560882

4404
The John and Elizabeth Whiteley Foundation
c/o Hubbard, Fox, White, & Bengston, LLC
5801 W. Michigan Ave.
P.O. Box 80857
Lansing, MI 48908-0857 (517) 886-7176
Contact: Donald B. Lawrence, Jr., Secy.
FAX: (517) 886-1080;
E-mail: mstray@hubbardlaw.com

Foundation type: Independent foundation
Limitations: Scholarships to financially needy and deserving students whose parents live in Ingham County, MI, and who are studying business education.
Financial data: Year ended 12/31/2004. Assets, $0 (M); Expenditures, $99,242; Total giving, $39,000; Grants to individuals, 21 grants totaling $21,000 (high: $1,000, low: $1,000).
Fields of interest: Business school/education.
Type of support: Undergraduate support.
Application information: Applications accepted throughout the year; Completion of formal application required, including transcripts, financial statement, letter of admission from college or university applicant is attending, and letter of recommendation from high school principal or scholarship office representative of the college or university applicant is attending.
EIN: 381558108

4405
Whiteside Scholarship Fund Trust
(formerly Robert B. and Sophia Whiteside Scholarship Fund)
c/o U.S. Bank, N.A.
P.O. Box 64713
St. Paul, MN 55164-0713

Foundation type: Independent foundation
Limitations: Scholarships to graduates of Duluth, MN, high schools who rank in the top ten percent of their classes.
Financial data: Year ended 12/31/2004. Assets, $1,598,162 (M); Expenditures, $290,873; Total giving, $231,666; Grants to individuals, totaling $231,666.
Type of support: Support to graduates or students of specific schools; Undergraduate support.
Application information: Application form required.
Deadline(s): Fall of senior year in high school
Additional information: Application through local high school counselors; Interviews required.
Program description:
Whiteside Scholarship Fund: Applicants are interviewed and selected by a scholarship committee in the spring of their senior year. Awards are renewable for up to four years providing recipients maintain at least a 3.0 GPA.
EIN: 411288761

4406
Howard Whitfield Foundation
P.O. Box 336
Red Bank, NJ 07701
Contact: Willis M. Sisson
Application address: P.O. Box 220, Fair Haven, NJ 07704-0220, tel.: (732) 643-0300

Foundation type: Independent foundation
Limitations: Scholarships to graduating seniors of Red Bank Regional High School, NJ. Graduates from public schools in Monmouth County, NJ, are eligible for awards as funds permit. Six types of scholarships are awarded by the foundation:

medical, legal, commercial, liberal arts, religious, and journalism.
Financial data: Year ended 12/31/2004.
Assets, $3,691 (M); Expenditures, $27,297; Total giving, $9,900.
Fields of interest: Journalism/publishing; Law school/education.
Type of support: Support to graduates or students of specific schools; Undergraduate support.
Application information: Applications accepted. Application form required.
> *Deadline(s):* Deadline May 1.
> *Additional information:* Application and financial statement forms are available from the guidance offices of all public schools in Monmouth County, NJ.

EIN: 210593879

4407
Whitley County Community Foundation

400 N. Whitley St.
P.O. Box 527
Columbia City, IN   46725-0527   (260) 244-5224
Contact: September McConnell, Exec. Dir.; For grant applications: John Slavich, Prog. Off.
FAX: (260) 244-5724; E-mail: wccf@kconline.com;
URL: http://whitleycountycommunityfoundation.org

Foundation type: Community foundation
Limitations: Scholarships to graduates of Whitley County high schools, IN.
Publications: Application guidelines; Biennial report; Informational brochure (including application guidelines); Newsletter.
Financial data: Year ended 12/31/2004.
Assets, $13,774,470 (M); Expenditures, $1,346,072; Total giving, $929,058; Grants to individuals, 49 grants totaling $217,780; Loans to individuals, 87 loans totaling $390,947.
Type of support: Support to graduates or students of specific schools.
Application information: Applications accepted. Application form required. Application form available on the grantmaker's Web site.
> *Initial approach:* E-mail.
> *Deadline(s):* Apr. 15
> *Applicants should submit the following:*
> 1) Transcripts
> 2) Letter(s) of recommendation
> 3) Financial information
> *Additional information:* See Web site for full program listing and descriptions. Scholarship applications are also available in high school guidance offices.

EIN: 351860518

4408
David M. Whitmore & Glenna M. Whitmore Memorial Scholarship Endowment Fund

P.O. Box 910
Piqua, OH   45356
Contact: Larry Householder, Superintendent
Application address: c/o Upper Valley Joint Vocational School, 8811 Career Dr., Piqua, OH 45356, tel.: (937) 778-1980

Foundation type: Independent foundation
Limitations: Scholarships to graduating seniors from Miami County, OH, who have completed a one- or two-year program at Upper Valley Joint Vocational School.
Financial data: Year ended 04/30/2004.
Assets, $101,191 (M); Expenditures, $7,606;

Total giving, $4,750; Grants to individuals, totaling $4,750.
Fields of interest: Vocational education.
Type of support: Support to graduates or students of specific schools; Technical education support; Undergraduate support.
Application information: Deadline Apr. 14; Completion of formal application required.
EIN: 316224298

4409
Whitney Benefits, Inc.

245 Broadway
P.O. Box 5085
Sheridan, WY   82801   (307) 674-7303
Contact: Patrick Henderson, Exec. Dir.
FAX: (307) 674-4335;
E-mail: info@whitneybenefits.org; URL: http://www.whitneybenefits.org

Foundation type: Independent foundation
Limitations: Interest-free student loans for undergraduate study to graduates of high schools in Sheridan and Johnson counties, WY, and to GED recipients from Sheridan County, WY.
Publications: Annual report.
Financial data: Year ended 12/31/2005.
Assets, $109,351,973 (M); Expenditures, $1,978,303; Total giving, $1,527,220; Loans to individuals, totaling $1,214,092.
Type of support: Support to graduates or students of specific schools; Undergraduate support.
Application information: Application form required.
> *Initial approach:* Letter or telephone.
> *Additional information:* Applications accepted throughout the year, preferably between Mar. and June; Interviews required.

Program description:
> *Loan Program:* When funds are available, applicants from other parts of WY, outside Sheridan and Johnson counties, are also eligible. Basic loan requirements for all recipients are:
> · Family income under $40,000 (for one child; adjustments made for larger families)
> · Family income must be supported by copy of federal tax return for last year
> · Applicants must be under the age of 25.

EIN: 830168511

4410
Edna May Whittemore Trust

c/o Eastern Bank & Trust Co.
94 Pleasant St.
Malden, MA   02148   (781) 388-3062
Contact: Deborah Gaff, Asst. V.P., Eastern Bank & Trust Co.

Foundation type: Independent foundation
Limitations: Scholarships to graduates of secondary schools in the Malden, MA, area.
Financial data: Year ended 06/30/2005.
Assets, $196,993 (M); Expenditures, $26,209; Total giving, $23,350; Grants to individuals, totaling $12,350.
Type of support: Support to graduates or students of specific schools; Undergraduate support.
Application information: Deadline June 1; Completion of formal application required, including transcripts.

Program description:
> *Whittemore Scholarship Program:* Recipients are chosen on the basis of financial need, grades, and character. Scholarships are renewable for up to four years. Recipients are announced in early July.

Grants are paid in two installments directly to the college on behalf of the student.
EIN: 046045950

4411
Ivie Frances Wickam Scholarship Trust

c/o Wells Fargo Bank, N.A., Trust Tax Dept.
P.O. Box 63954
San Francisco, CA   94163

Foundation type: Independent foundation
Limitations: Scholarships only to financially needy female graduates of Escondido High School, CA, and Palomar College, CA.
Financial data: Year ended 05/31/2005.
Assets, $839,708 (M); Expenditures, $46,013; Total giving, $25,000; Grants to individuals, totaling $25,000.
Fields of interest: Women.
Type of support: Support to graduates or students of specific schools; Undergraduate support.
Application information: Completion of formal application required; Interviews required; Contact Palomar College or Escondido High School for application information.
EIN: 956530377

4412
Phyllis A. Widding Foundation for Women

(formerly Phyllis A. Browne Foundation for Women)
32 Bretagne Cir.
Little Rock, AR   72223
Application address: c/o University of Arkansas, Attn: Mary C. Boaz, Dev. Dept., 2801 S. University Ave., Little Rock, AR 72204-1099

Foundation type: Independent foundation
Limitations: Scholarships to single women, with dependent children, who are students at the University of Arkansas at Little Rock.
Financial data: Year ended 12/31/2004.
Assets, $23,517 (M); Expenditures, $22,804; Total giving, $19,272; Grants to individuals, totaling $19,272.
Fields of interest: Women.
Type of support: Support to graduates or students of specific schools; Undergraduate support.
Application information: Deadline Mar. 1; Initial approach by letter; Completion of formal application required, including needs and future goals.
EIN: 716168654

4413
The Elie Wiesel Foundation for Humanity

529 5th Ave., Ste. 1802
New York, NY   10017   (212) 490-7777
Contact: Alexandrea J. Ravenelle, Dir.
FAX: (212) 490-6006;
E-mail: info@eliewieselfoundation.org; URL: http://www.eliewieselfoundation.org

Foundation type: Public charity
Limitations: Prizes to full-time undergraduate juniors and seniors at accredited four-year colleges and universities during the fall semester for winning essays on ethics.
Publications: Application guidelines; Informational brochure; Newsletter.
Financial data: Year ended 12/31/2003.
Assets, $2,530,272 (M); Expenditures, $774,256; Total giving, $425,563.
Fields of interest: Philosophy/ethics; Religion.
Type of support: Awards/prizes.
Application information: Application form required.

Initial approach: Letter, telephone or fax.
Deadline(s): 1st Mon. in Dec.
Additional information: See Web site for application.

Program description:
Elie Wiesel Prize in Ethics: A first prize of $5,000, second prize of $2,500, third prize of $1,500 and two honorable mentions of $500 each awarded to undergraduates who are or will be registered as full-time juniors or seniors at accredited four-year colleges or universities in the U.S. and Canada. All entries must be in the form of informal voice, ranging from 3,000 to 4,000 words, and may take the form of an analysis that is biographical, historical, literary, philosophical, psychological, sociological or theological. All candidates must be sponsored by a faculty member.
EIN: 133398151

4414
Barbara Thorndike Wiggin Fund

c/o Bank of America, N.A.
P.O. Box 1802
Providence, RI 02901-1802
Application address: c/o Bank of America, N.A., P.O. Box 9791, Portland, ME 04104

Foundation type: Independent foundation
Limitations: Scholarships to financially needy female graduates of high schools in Knox County, ME, who are pursuing careers in nursing or teaching. Preference is given to graduates of Rockland District High School.
Financial data: Year ended 12/31/2004. Assets, $633,106 (M); Expenditures, $28,320; Total giving, $19,500; Grants to individuals, 27 grants totaling $19,500 (high: $1,500, low: $250).
Fields of interest: Nursing school/education; Teacher school/education; Women.
Type of support: Support to graduates or students of specific schools; Undergraduate support.
Application information: Applications accepted throughout the year; Completion of formal application required; Interviews recommended.
EIN: 016013826

4415
J. J. Wiggins Memorial Trust

P.O. Box 1111
Moore Haven, FL 33471 (863) 946-3400

Foundation type: Independent foundation
Limitations: Scholarships to individuals who have been residents of Glades County, FL, for at least one year, and who are under 21 years old.
Financial data: Year ended 04/30/2005. Assets, $0 (L); Expenditures, $289,479; Total giving, $65,000; Grants to individuals, totaling $65,000.
Fields of interest: Vocational education; Business school/education.
Type of support: Technical education support; Undergraduate support.
Application information: Application form required.
Initial approach: Letter.
Deadline(s): Contact trust for deadline
Applicants should submit the following:
1) SAT
2) GPA
3) ACT

Program description:
Wiggins Memorial Scholarship Program: Scholarships may be used for attendance at an accredited college, university, vocational/technical center, or business school. All applicants must have at least a 2.25 GPA, and college students must also have completed at least 12 credit hours. Recipients must maintain at least a 2.5 GPA in college. Scholarships are awarded for one semester, and are renewable for up to a total of four years of study. Applicants must submit requests prior to their 21st birthday, or 24th birthday if they have served in the military.
EIN: 592675273

4416
Wigginton Educational Foundation

c/o Fifth Third Bank
233 Washington Ave.
Grand Haven, MI 49417
Contact: Lisa Danicek, Treas.
Application address: 1415 S. Beachtree St., Grand Haven, MI 49417, tel.: (616) 842-6760

Foundation type: Independent foundation
Limitations: Scholarships to worthy, financially needy residents of school districts in Ottawa and Muskegon counties, MI, and in the city of Grand Haven, MI.
Financial data: Year ended 12/31/2004. Assets, $447,444 (M); Expenditures, $17,835; Total giving, $13,629; Grants to individuals, 35 grants totaling $13,629 (high: $3,500, low: $4).
Type of support: Scholarships—to individuals.
Application information: Applications accepted throughout the year; Initial approach by letter or telephone; Completion of formal application required.
EIN: 382388277

4417
The Wight Foundation, Inc.

60 Park Pl., 17th Fl.
Newark, NJ 07102 (973) 824-1195
Contact: Rhonda Auguste, Exec. Dir.
FAX: (973) 824-1199; E-mail: wightfdn@aol.com; URL: http://www.wightfoundation.org

Foundation type: Independent foundation
Limitations: Scholarships by nomination only for private high school education at specific boarding schools to residents of the greater Newark, NJ, area. Students currently in the seventh grade who attend public, private, or parochial schools are eligible.
Publications: Informational brochure (including application guidelines); Newsletter.
Financial data: Year ended 12/31/2004. Assets, $12,639,477 (M); Expenditures, $996,353; Total giving, $345,713; Grants to individuals, 96 grants totaling $281,213 (high: $11,250, low: $25).
Fields of interest: Secondary school/education.
Type of support: Support to graduates or students of specific schools; Awards/grants by nomination only; Precollege support.
Application information:
Deadline(s): For preliminary applications Jan. 25; approved students are sent final applications, which are due Feb. 15
Additional information: Application should include recommendations, essays, report from the School and Student Services for Financial Aid (SSS), and SAT scores; Students must apply directly to the foundation; Interviews required.

Program description:
Wight Scholarship Program: To qualify, students must maintain a "B" average and score above grade level in standardized tests in reading, language, and math. Scholars are expected to complete 20 hours of community service annually in the greater Newark area. All finalists must compete in STEP, a 14-month enrichment program taught by Wight Foundation alumni, which prepares them for the boarding school experience. The following boarding schools participate in the program: Blair Academy, NJ; Canterbury School, CT; Cheshire Academy, CT; Episcopal High School, VA; George School, PA; Hill School, PA; Kent School, CT; Lawrenceville School, NJ; Marvelwood School, CT; Miss Porter's School, CT; Peddie School, NJ; Perkiomen School, PA; Phillip Exeter Academy, NH; Purnell School, NJ; Solebury School, PA; South Kent School, CT; St. Andrew's School, DE; St. Paul's School, NH; St. Timothy's School, MD; Stoneleigh-Burnham School, MA; Taft School, CT; Trinity-Pawling School, NY; Westminster School, CT; Westover School, CT; Westtown School, PA.
EIN: 222743349

4418
Charles Joseph Wilber Educational Scholarship Trust

c/o Marshall & Ilsley Bank
P.O. Box 2980
Milwaukee, WI 53201-2980
Application address: c/o Superintendent of Schools, Tomahawk High School, 1048 E. Kings Rd., Tomahawk, WI 54487

Foundation type: Independent foundation
Limitations: Scholarships to graduates of Tomahawk High School, WI. Preference is given to applicants studying law or medicine.
Financial data: Year ended 10/31/2004. Assets, $128,440 (M); Expenditures, $8,320; Total giving, $6,250; Grants to individuals, 13 grants totaling $6,250 (high: $750, low: $375).
Fields of interest: Law school/education; Medical school/education.
Type of support: Support to graduates or students of specific schools; Undergraduate support.
Application information: Contact Tomahawk High School for current application deadline; Completion of formal application required.
EIN: 396371278

4419
The Wilbur Foundation

(formerly Marguerite Eyer Wilbur Foundation)
P.O. Box 3370
Santa Barbara, CA 93130-3370
Contact: Gary R. Ricks, Pres.
FAX: (805) 563-1082;
E-mail: Info@WilburFoundation.org; URL: http://www.wilburfoundation.org

Foundation type: Independent foundation
Limitations: Resident fellowships, research grants, and support for writing projects to individuals in the areas of humane literature. The Foundation will be phasing out grants to individuals in the near future.
Publications: Application guidelines; Program policy statement.
Financial data: Year ended 12/31/2003. Assets, $3,121,864 (M); Expenditures, $221,616; Total giving, $129,000. No monetary support given for residencies.
Fields of interest: Humanities; History/archaeology; Literature; Philosophy/ethics; Religion.
Type of support: Fellowships; Research.
Application information: Contact foundation for current application deadlines/guidelines.
Program description:
Wilbur Fellowship Program: Resident fellowships are awarded at Mecosta, MI, where writers of

promise live, work, and write under the supervision of Dr. Russell Kirk, with preference given to writers in the areas of history, religion, or philosophy. Grants to individuals are provided to those who have demonstrated unique accomplishments or promise in humane literature, particularly in history, religion and philosophy.
EIN: 510168214

4420

Penelope Jackson & Ralph O. Wilcox Foundation

3301 Celinda Dr.
Carlsbad, CA 92008

Foundation type: Independent foundation
Limitations: Scholarships to graduating seniors from Carlsbad, El Camino and Oceanside high schools, CA.
Financial data: Year ended 12/31/2004. Assets, $260,579 (M); Expenditures, $244,568; Total giving, $154,950; Grants to individuals, 18 grants totaling $37,350 (high: $6,000; low: $50).
Type of support: Support to graduates or students of specific schools; Undergraduate support.
Application information:
  Initial approach: Letter or telephone.
  Additional information: Contact foundation for current application deadline/guidelines.
EIN: 330841274

4421

The Nettie L. Wiley and Charles L. Wiley Foundation

P.O. Box 126
Irvington, VA 22480
Application address: c/o Thomas A. Gosse, P.O. Box 420, Irvington, VA 22480-0420

Foundation type: Independent foundation
Limitations: Scholarships to students in northern VA who are interested in teaching.
Financial data: Year ended 12/31/2004. Assets, $9,059,972 (M); Expenditures, $414,441; Total giving, $340,100; Grants to individuals, 9 grants totaling $17,600 (high: $3,000, low: $600).
Fields of interest: Teacher school/education.
Type of support: Undergraduate support.
Application information: Applications accepted throughout the year; Completion of formal application required.
EIN: 521231771

4422

Wilkerson Scholarship Fund

7-9 Issac St.
Norwalk, CT 06852-0511
Application address: P.O. Box 511, Norwalk, CT 06852-0511, tel.: (203) 853-3030

Foundation type: Independent foundation
Limitations: Scholarships to individuals residing in the Norwalk, CT, area for undergraduate education.
Financial data: Year ended 12/31/2004. Assets, $479,669 (M); Expenditures, $27,978; Total giving, $26,500; Grants to individuals, totaling $26,500.
Type of support: Undergraduate support.
Application information: Contact foundation for current application deadline/guidelines.
EIN: 061617537

4423

Ted and Betty Williams Charitable Trust

c/o Gwynne R. Hinterthuer
400 W. Captiol Ave., Ste. 2000
Little Rock, AR 72201-3493

Foundation type: Independent foundation
Limitations: Scholarships to needy students for higher education, primarily in AL.
Financial data: Year ended 12/31/2004. Assets, $2,587,012 (M); Expenditures, $598,628; Total giving, $580,000; Grants to individuals, totaling $575,000.
Type of support: Undergraduate support.
Application information: Contact trust for current application deadline/guidelines.
EIN: 716172017

4424

Don E. & Charlotte J. Williams Foundation

1000 36th Ave., Ste. 100
Moline, IL 61265-7126

Foundation type: Independent foundation
Limitations: Scholarships to children of deWco employees for elementary, secondary, and undergraduate education, primarily in IL and WI.
Financial data: Year ended 12/31/2004. Assets, $1,306,508 (M); Expenditures, $58,879; Total giving, $40,000; Grants to individuals, totaling $40,000.
Fields of interest: Elementary school/education; Secondary school/education.
Type of support: Employee-related scholarships.
Application information: Application form required.
  Deadline(s): Contact foundation for current application deadline.
  Applicants should submit the following:
    1) Transcripts
    2) Financial information
Program description:
  Williams Scholarship Program: Grants may cover travel, study, apprenticeships, trade schools, or other similar purposes. The purpose of this support is to achieve a specific objective, produce a report or similar product, or to improve or enhance a literary, artistic, musical, scientific, teaching, or other similar capacity, skill, or talent of the recipient. Elementary and secondary scholarships are non-renewable. Postsecondary scholarships are renewable for up to $10,000 total, provided that the recipient maintains a 2.0 GPA on a 4.0 scale and that she/he has not yet attained a baccalaureate degree.
EIN: 363611702

4425

Horace Williams Memorial Fund

c/o KeyBank N.A.
800 Superior Ave., 4th Fl.
Cleveland, OH 44114-2601
Application address: c/o William Pelletier, Trust Off., Kennebec Savings Bank, P.O. Box 108, Augusta, ME 04330

Foundation type: Independent foundation
Limitations: Scholarships to residents of ME.
Financial data: Year ended 08/31/2003. Assets, $271,620 (M); Expenditures, $8,659; Total giving, $6,500; Grants to individuals, totaling $6,500.
Type of support: Scholarships—to individuals.
Application information: Applications accepted throughout the year; Initial approach by letter.
EIN: 016008547

4426

Howell and Lois Williams Memorial Fund

c/o National City Bank of Pennsylvania
P.O. Box 94651
Cleveland, OH 44101-4651
Contact: Donald E. Hollerman
Application address: c/o Lincoln High School, 501 Crescent Ave., Ellwood City, PA 16117

Foundation type: Independent foundation
Limitations: Scholarships to students of the Ellwood City Area School District, PA, who excel in biology or English.
Financial data: Year ended 04/30/2005. Assets, $335,141 (M); Expenditures, $6,688; Total giving, $3,000; Grants to individuals, totaling $3,000.
Fields of interest: Literature; Biological sciences.
Type of support: Support to graduates or students of specific schools; Undergraduate support.
Application information: Deadline Mar. 1; Completion of formal application required.
EIN: 251671119

4427

Charles and Ada Williams Memorial Scholarship Fund, Inc.

P.O. Box 342
Salem, IN 47167-0342
Application address: c/o West Washington High School, Campbellsburg, IN 47108

Foundation type: Independent foundation
Limitations: Scholarships to graduates of West Washington High School, IN, for undergraduate education.
Financial data: Year ended 08/31/2004. Assets, $250,011 (M); Expenditures, $16,743; Total giving, $16,000; Grants to individuals, totaling $16,000.
Type of support: Support to graduates or students of specific schools; Undergraduate support.
Application information: Contact fund for current application deadline; Applicants must write an essay on soil and water conservation, school administration, or local government.
EIN: 351708866

4428

George B. Williams Scholarship Foundation

c/o Bank of America, N.A.
P.O. Box 1802
Providence, RI 02901-1802
Application address: c/o Newington High School, Att.: Guidance Office, 605 Willard Ave., Newington, CT 06111

Foundation type: Independent foundation
Limitations: Scholarships to graduates of Newington High School, CT.
Financial data: Year ended 04/30/2005. Assets, $309,510 (M); Expenditures, $19,444; Total giving, $15,000; Grants to individuals, 15 grants totaling $15,000 (high: $1,000, low: $1,000).
Type of support: Support to graduates or students of specific schools; Undergraduate support.
Application information: Applications accepted. Application form required.
  Initial approach: Letter.
  Additional information: Applications are available at Newington High School guidance office.
EIN: 020682841

4429
The Frank O. and Clara R. Williams Scholarship Fund

c/o Kosak & Assocs.
P.O. Box 374
Oil City, PA   16301
Contact: Stephen P. Kosak

Foundation type: Independent foundation
Limitations: Grants and scholarships to graduates of Venango County, PA, high schools. Dependents of National City Bank employees are not eligible.
Publications: Application guidelines.
Financial data: Year ended 12/31/2004. Assets, $6,468,997 (M); Expenditures, $260,610; Total giving, $199,175; Grants to individuals, 280 grants totaling $199,175 (high: $5,500, low: $50).
Type of support: Support to graduates or students of specific schools; Undergraduate support.
Application information:
  Initial approach: Letter.
  Additional information: Applications accepted throughout the year; Completion of formal application required, including letter outlining financial need and/or CSS profile; Interviews required.
EIN: 256031440

4430
Gwilym T. Williams Scholarship Fund

c/o PNC Advisors
620 Liberty Ave, No. P2-PTPP
Pittsburgh, PA   15222-2705

Foundation type: Independent foundation
Limitations: Scholarships to students who belong to a church of the Penn Northeast Conference of the United Church of Christ and who plan to become ordained ministers, enter the field of education, or become physicians.
Financial data: Year ended 12/31/2004. Assets, $1,017,300 (M); Expenditures, $45,744; Total giving, $43,000.
Fields of interest: Medical school/education; Teacher school/education; Theological school/education; Christian agencies & churches; Protestant agencies & churches.
Type of support: Scholarships—to individuals.
Application information: Application form required.
  Initial approach: Letter.
  Deadline(s): July 1 and Dec. 1.
EIN: 236420348

4431
Williams Scholarship Loan Fund, Inc.

c/o J. Hammond
501 Indiana Ave.
Indianapolis, IN   46202
Application address: c/o John E. Shelton, Marian College Office of Financial Aid, 3200 Cold Spring Rd., Indianapolis, IN 46222

Foundation type: Independent foundation
Limitations: Loans to students at Marian College, IN, who are majoring in dentistry, education, nursing, medicine or veterinary medicine.
Financial data: Year ended 12/31/2004. Assets, $485,443 (M); Expenditures, $15,626; Total giving, $8,143; Grants to individuals, totaling $8,143.
Fields of interest: Dental school/education; Medical school/education; Nursing school/education; Teacher school/education; Veterinary medicine.

Type of support: Student loans—to individuals; Support to graduates or students of specific schools; Graduate support; Undergraduate support.
Application information: Application form required.
  Deadline(s): Contact fund for current application deadline.
  Applicants should submit the following:
    1) FAF
  Additional information: Application should include proof of enrollment.
EIN: 352071999

4432
Milton L. Williams Trust

c/o Eastern Bank & Trust Co.
605 Broadway, Ste. LF41
Saugus, MA   01906
Contact: Robert W. Welch, Tr.
Application address: 18 Brown St., Salem, MA 01970

Foundation type: Independent foundation
Limitations: Scholarships by nomination only to graduates of high schools in Salem, MA.
Financial data: Year ended 12/31/2004. Assets, $428,066 (M); Expenditures, $25,840; Total giving, $19,000; Grants to individuals, totaling $19,000.
Type of support: Support to graduates or students of specific schools; Awards/grants by nomination only; Undergraduate support.
Application information: Deadline June 1; Applicants must be nominated by a high school principal; Completion of formal nomination required.
EIN: 046016107

4433
Mary Williamson Educational Loan Fund

P.O. Box 810
New Market, VA   22844-0810   (540) 740-3636
Contact: Allen D. Johnson, Tr.

Foundation type: Independent foundation
Limitations: Student loans to residents of the New Market, VA, area.
Financial data: Year ended 12/31/2004. Assets, $903,248 (M); Expenditures, $43,771; Total giving, $0; Loans to individuals, totaling $50,100.
Type of support: Student loans—to individuals.
Application information: Applications accepted throughout the year; Completion of formal application required, including financial information and three personal references.
EIN: 546043362

4434
Philip S. Willis Student Loan Trust

c/o KeyBank N.A., Trust Div.
P.O. Box 10099
Toledo, OH   43699-0099

Foundation type: Independent foundation
Limitations: Educational loans to residents of Lucas County, OH.
Financial data: Year ended 12/31/2002. Assets, $1,158,224 (M); Expenditures, $30,910; Total giving, $0; Loans to individuals, totaling $6,000.
Type of support: Student loans—to individuals.

Application information: Applications not accepted.
EIN: 346518056

4435
James Worthington Willmott Memorial Trust II

c/o National City Bank of Kentucky
P.O. Box 94651
Cleveland, OH   44101-4651
Application address: c/o John Cheshire, 301 E. Main St., Lexington, KY 40507, tel.: (859) 281-5248

Foundation type: Independent foundation
Limitations: Scholarships to residents of Bourbon County, KY, and adjacent counties.
Financial data: Year ended 12/31/2004. Assets, $2,370,459 (M); Expenditures, $107,043; Total giving, $88,675; Grants to individuals, 118 grants totaling $88,675 (high: $1,400, low: $300).
Type of support: Scholarships—to individuals.
Application information: Applications accepted throughout the year; Completion of formal application required, including complete biographical record, current academic transcripts, statement of educational plans, letters of reference, report on aptitude test results, evidence of financial need, and a statement of residency.
EIN: 616174229

4436
Veronica Willo Scholarship Fund

c/o JPMorgan Chase Bank, N.A.
P.O. Box 1308
Milwaukee, WI   53201-0013
Application address: c/o Robert Clark, Admin., JPMorgan Chase Bank, N.A., 100 E. Broad St., Columbus, OH 43271

Foundation type: Independent foundation
Limitations: Undergraduate scholarships by nomination only to graduating seniors of Mahoning County, OH, high schools.
Financial data: Year ended 12/31/2004. Assets, $242,602 (M); Expenditures, $10,595; Total giving, $9,579.
Type of support: Support to graduates or students of specific schools; Awards/grants by nomination only; Undergraduate support.
Application information: Individual applications not accepted; Nominations are made by Mahoning County, OH, high school principals.
Program description:
  Scholarship Program: The fund requests all high school principals in Mahoning County, OH, to submit the name of a graduating student deserving of a scholarship based on financial need and academic ability. The winners of the scholarships are selected by a committee consisting of the Bishop of the Catholic Dioceses of Youngstown, the President of the Mahoning Valley Association of Churches, and the President of the Mahoning Valley Bar Association. Scholarships are renewable for up to four years of study.
EIN: 346577619

4437
Wills Memorial Foundation

c/o County Executive
1 N. Washington St.
Brownsville, TN   38012

Foundation type: Independent foundation
Limitations: Scholarships to residents of Haywood County, TN, for study in a health-related field.
Financial data: Year ended 06/30/2005.
Assets, $435,617 (M); Expenditures, $6,918; Total giving, $4,750; Grants to individuals, totaling $4,750.
Fields of interest: Medical school/education; Nursing school/education; Health sciences school/education.
Type of support: Scholarships—to individuals.
Application information: Deadline last Fri. in June; Completion of formal application required.
EIN: 620973997

4438
J. B. Wilson & Garnet A. Wilson Charitable Trust
P.O. Box 686
Waverly, OH   45690-0686   (740) 947-2727
Contact: Billy S. Moore, Tr.

Foundation type: Independent foundation
Limitations: Scholarships for studies at OH colleges and universities.
Financial data: Year ended 12/31/2004.
Assets, $5,992,659 (M); Expenditures, $566,843; Total giving, $535,750; Grants to individuals, 129 grants totaling $535,750 (high: $6,900, low: $500).
Type of support: Scholarships—to individuals.
Application information: Contact trust for current application deadline; Completion of formal application required.
EIN: 310983188

4439
Wilson Family Memorial Scholarship
c/o Wachovia Bank, N.A.
100 N. Main St., 13th Fl.
Winston-Salem, NC   27150

Foundation type: Independent foundation
Limitations: Scholarships by nomination only to individuals.
Financial data: Year ended 12/31/2004.
Assets, $2,377,187 (M); Expenditures, $219,739; Total giving, $202,010; Grants to individuals, 18 grants totaling $202,010 (high: $29,649, low: $2,299).
Type of support: Awards/grants by nomination only.
Application information: Unsolicited requests for funds not considered or acknowledged.
EIN: 237787902

4440
John & Mary Wilson Foundation
c/o Wells Fargo Bank Northwest, N.A.
P.O. Box 21927
Seattle, WA   98111   (206) 685-9229

Foundation type: Independent foundation
Limitations: Scholarships only to undergraduate or graduate medical students attending the University of Washington.
Financial data: Year ended 12/31/2004.
Assets, $7,021,061 (M); Expenditures, $398,387; Total giving, $336,500; Grants to individuals, 114 grants totaling $332,000 (high: $7,000, low: $600).
Fields of interest: Medical school/education.
Type of support: Support to graduates or students of specific schools; Graduate support; Undergraduate support.

Application information: Application form required.
Initial approach: Letter.
Additional information: Contact foundation for current application deadline.
EIN: 237425273

4441
Patti Johnson Wilson Foundation
c/o The Trust Co. of Oklahoma
1924 S. Utica Ave., Ste. 500
Tulsa, OK   74104-6540   (918) 745-2400
Contact: Paul Kallenberger, Tr.

Foundation type: Independent foundation
Limitations: Scholarships to worthy students in the fields of music, engineering, and liberal arts, primarily for attendance at state-sponsored universities in OK, KS, and AR.
Publications: Application guidelines.
Financial data: Year ended 08/31/2004.
Assets, $869,745 (M); Expenditures, $59,763; Total giving, $49,000; Grants to individuals, 31 grants totaling $39,000 (high: $2,500, low: $750).
Fields of interest: Music; Performing arts, education; Humanities; Engineering school/ education.
Type of support: Undergraduate support.
Application information:
Deadline(s): Mar. 1
Additional information: Completion of formal application required, including recommendations and standardized test scores; Interviews required.
Program description:
Scholarship Program: Eligible students may request the financial aid office at their university to contact the foundation. All scholarships will be awarded on the basis of information contained in the Financial Aid Application form furnished by the Trust Company of OK. Scholarships are awarded on the basis of the following criteria: academic achievement, performance on college aptitude tests, recommendations from instructors, financial need, and any summation of the candidate's motivation and character. The selection committee prefers students who supplement their educational expenses with part-time employment of at least ten hours per week during the school year.
EIN: 736156280

4442
Warren and Velda Wilson Foundation
747 N. Burlington Ave.
Hastings, NE   68901-4421
Contact: Jennifer Fleischer, Dir.
Application address: P.O. Box 121, Clay Center, NE 68933

Foundation type: Operating foundation
Limitations: Scholarships to individuals residing in the Hastings, NE, area for undergraduate education.
Financial data: Year ended 12/31/2002.
Assets, $2,863,197 (M); Expenditures, $24,413; Total giving, $11,000; Grants to individuals, 11 grants totaling $11,000 (high: $1,000, low: $1,000).
Type of support: Undergraduate support.
Application information: Application form required.
Deadline(s): Apr. 24
Additional information: Contact foundation for current application guidelines.
EIN: 470741012

4443
The Woodrow Wilson National Fellowship Foundation
P.O. Box 5281
Princeton, NJ   08543-5281   (609) 452-7007
FAX: (609) 452-0066; E-mail: jlp@woodrow.org;
URL: http://www.woodrow.org

Foundation type: Public charity
Limitations: Fellowships and grants to individuals in various disciplines.
Publications: Annual report; Newsletter.
Financial data: Year ended 06/30/2005.
Assets, $20,737,668 (M); Expenditures, $15,097,337; Total giving, $10,155,178.
Fields of interest: Humanities; Language (foreign); Health sciences school/education; Health care; Children/youth, services; International affairs; Business/industry; Social sciences; Anthropology/ sociology; Economics; Political science; Women's studies; Public policy, research; Government/ public administration; Leadership development; Religion; Women.
Type of support: Fellowships; Internship funds; Graduate support; Undergraduate support; Doctoral support.
Application information: Applications accepted. Application form required.
Initial approach: Letter or telephone.
Deadline(s): Contact foundation for current application deadlines
Program descriptions:
Thomas R. Pickering/Foreign Affairs Fellowship Program: College sophomores may apply for this fellowship, sponsored by the U. S. Department of State, the fellowship includes junior- and senior-year scholarships, attendance at a junior-year, seven-week summer institute for preparation for graduate schools, participation in two summer internships in the State Department, and first-year graduate funding at a school of international affairs, (second-year graduate funding is provided by participating schools and is based on need). Women, members of groups historically underrepresented in the Foreign Service, and qualified applicants with financial need are encouraged to apply. Recipients are obligated to work four and a half years as Foreign Service Officers in the Department of State.
Thomas R. Pickering/Graduate Foreign Affairs Fellowship Program: Individuals who will be enrolled in the first year of a two-year master's degree program in international affairs, public administration, public policy, or academic fields such as business, economics, foreign languages, political science, or sociology may apply for this renewable fellowship. Applicants should be interested in pursuing a Foreign Service career with the U.S. Department of State, and they must be applying to or enrolled in graduate school and have an undergraduate GPA of at least 3.2 in order to qualify. Recipients are chosen on the basis of outstanding leadership skills, academic achievement, and financial need. Women, minorities historically underrepresented in the Foreign Service, and students with financial need are encouraged to apply. Applicants must be U.S. citizens. Fellowship includes tuition, room, board, and mandatory fees for each year of the fellowship; reimbursement for books; one round-trip travel; mentoring from a Foreign Service Officer; and participation in a paid internship program each summer. The first summer internship will be domestic and the second summer internship will take place overseas. All recipients must meet Department of State Foreign Service entry requirements. Recipients are obligated to work

three years as Foreign Service Officers in the Department of State.
EIN: 210703075

4444

Ralph Wilson Plastics Employees Scholarship Fund

600 General Bruce Dr.
Temple, TX 76504

Foundation type: Company-sponsored foundation
Limitations: Scholarships to dependents of TX employees of Ralph Wilson Plastics who are full-time students at a college or university. Scholarships are renewable.
Financial data: Year ended 06/30/2005. Assets, $1,197,823 (M); Expenditures, $47,207; Total giving, $39,750; Grants to individuals, 27 grants totaling $39,750.
Type of support: Employee-related scholarships.
Application information: Application form required.
Deadline(s): Apr. 1
Applicants should submit the following:
1) Transcripts
2) SAT
3) ACT
Additional information: Application should also include copy of letter of acceptance to college or university; Letters of recommendation are optional; Application address for scholarships: c/o Selection Comm., P.O. Box 625, Temple, TX 76503-0625, tel.: (254) 207-6360.
EIN: 746245026

4445

Ralph Wilson Plastics Scholarship Fund, Inc.

P.O. Box 1118
Fletcher, NC 28732

Foundation type: Company-sponsored foundation
Limitations: Scholarships to dependents of employees of Ralph Wilson Plastics Co. in NC.
Financial data: Year ended 12/31/2004. Assets, $749,365 (M); Expenditures, $37,241; Total giving, $36,461; Grants to individuals, 19 grants totaling $36,461 (high: $2,084; low: $1,043).
Type of support: Employee-related scholarships.
EIN: 581576914

4446

E. E. Wilson Scholarship Fund Foundation

c/o U.S. Bank, N.A.
P.O. Box 3168
Portland, OR 97208
Application address: c/o Oregon State Univ., Frank Ragulsky, Student Media Center, 118 MU East, Corvallis, OR 97331-1617, tel.: (541) 737-3374

Foundation type: Independent foundation
Limitations: Scholarships based on character and scholastic ability to financially needy Benton County, OR, residents of two years or more, to attend Oregon State University.
Financial data: Year ended 06/30/2005. Assets, $912,082 (M); Expenditures, $60,169; Total giving, $47,675; Grants to individuals, totaling $47,675.
Type of support: Support to graduates or students of specific schools; Undergraduate support.

Application information: Contact fund for current application deadline/guidelines.
EIN: 936022322

4447

John R. Wilson Scholarship Trust

c/o TD Banknorth, N.A., Investment Mgmt. Group
P.O. Box 595
Williston, VT 05495-0595
Application address: c/o D. Rodman Thomas, Trust Off., 500 Main St., Bennington, VT 05201

Foundation type: Independent foundation
Limitations: Scholarships by school recommendation only to female students from Bennington County high schools, VT, who would otherwise have little opportunity for further education.
Financial data: Year ended 12/31/2004. Assets, $475,814 (M); Expenditures, $25,761; Total giving, $20,000; Grants to individuals, totaling $20,000.
Fields of interest: Women.
Type of support: Support to graduates or students of specific schools; Awards/grants by nomination only; Undergraduate support.
Application information:
Deadline(s): May 1
Additional information: Individual applications not accepted.
EIN: 036016072

4448

Wimmer Scholarship Fund

(formerly George G., Elma & Ruth M. Wimmer Scholarship Fund)
c/o National City Bank
P.O. Box 94651
Cleveland, OH 44101-4651
Scholarship application address: c/o William Gordon, Sr., 533 Warren St., Huntington, IN 46750-2723, tel.: (219) 356-4100

Foundation type: Independent foundation
Limitations: Scholarships to students of Fort Wayne Elmhurst High School and Huntington North High School, IN, to pursue careers in medicine, nursing, and science.
Financial data: Year ended 08/31/2005. Assets, $2,403,401 (M); Expenditures, $123,657; Total giving, $108,000; Grants to individuals, 54 grants totaling $108,000 (high: $3,000, low: $1,000).
Fields of interest: Medical school/education; Nursing school/education; Science.
Type of support: Support to graduates or students of specific schools; Technical education support; Undergraduate support.
Application information: Deadline Mar. 31; Completion of formal application required; Applications are made through high school guidance offices.
EIN: 311036448

4449

The Winchester Foundation

112 1/2 W. Washington
P.O. Box 27
Winchester, IN 47394 (765) 584-2523
Contact: Chris Talley, Chair.

Foundation type: Independent foundation
Limitations: Scholarships to residents of Randolph County, IN, and to graduates of Winchester

Community High School, IN, who attended the school for the last two years.
Financial data: Year ended 12/31/2004. Assets, $7,124,973 (M); Expenditures, $332,276; Total giving, $248,550; Grants to individuals, 35 grants totaling $118,550 (high: $21,800, low: $300).
Type of support: Scholarships—to individuals; Support to graduates or students of specific schools; Undergraduate support.
Application information:
Deadline(s): Spring
Additional information: Completion of formal application required, including transcripts, list of extracurricular activities, four personal essays, photograph, and three letters of reference, including one from a high school teacher and one from a citizen of Randolph County, IN.
Program description:
Scholarship Funds: The foundation administers eight scholarship funds:
· Richard and Mamie Fields Scholarship Fund
· Ruth Bales Fisch Memorial Scholarship Fund
· Ralph W. Stuck, Jr. Memorial Fund
· Winchester Athena Club Scholarship Fund
· Wallace and Edna Fields Scholarship Fund
· Virginia Davis Crew Weber Scholarship Fund
· Robert G. Jones Scholarship Fund
Contact the fund for specific limitations.
EIN: 237422941

4450

The Windham Foundation, Inc.

P.O. Box 70
Grafton, VT 05146 (802) 843-2211
Contact: Stephan A. Morse, C.E.O.
Application address for VSAC: Vermont Student Assistance Corp., P.O. Box 2000, Winooski, Vermont 05404-2601, Attn: Grant Program
FAX: (802) 843-2205; E-mail: winfound@sover.net; URL: http://www.windham-foundation.org

Foundation type: Operating foundation
Limitations: Undergraduate and technical school scholarships to Windham County, VT, residents only.
Publications: Application guidelines; Annual report; Informational brochure; Informational brochure (including application guidelines).
Financial data: Year ended 10/31/2005. Assets, $59,087,070 (M); Expenditures, $3,458,115; Total giving, $183,275.
Fields of interest: Vocational education.
Type of support: Technical education support; Undergraduate support.
Application information: Applications accepted. Application form required. Application form available on the grantmaker's Web site.
Initial approach: E-mail.
Copies of proposal: 1
Deadline(s): Apr. 1
Applicants should submit the following:
1) FAFSA
2) Transcripts
EIN: 136142024

4451
Windhover Foundation, Inc.
c/o Quad/Graphics, Inc.
N63 W23075 Main St.
Sussex, WI 53089-2827
Contact: Eileen T. Graves
URL: http://www.qg.com/whoarewe/windhover.html

Foundation type: Company-sponsored foundation
Limitations: Company-related employee scholarships for higher education.
Financial data: Year ended 12/31/2004. Assets, $13,163,098 (M); Expenditures, $2,412,671; Total giving, $2,321,000; Grants to individuals, 158 grants totaling $263,000 (high: $2,500, low: $1,250).
Type of support: Employee-related scholarships.
Application information: Contact foundation for current application deadline/guidelines.
EIN: 391482470

4452
Windsor Foundation
104 Ronsard Ln.
Cary, NC 27511-6019

Foundation type: Independent foundation
Limitations: Scholarships to individuals for higher education.
Financial data: Year ended 12/31/2004. Assets, $546,469 (M); Expenditures, $210,715; Total giving, $208,325; Grants to individuals, 27 grants totaling $208,325 (high: $48,906, low: $649).
Fields of interest: Higher education.
Type of support: Scholarships—to individuals.
Application information: Contact foundation for current application deadline/guidelines.
EIN: 562226375

4453
Windsor High School Alumni Scholarship Fund
c/o RF Carroll C.P.A.
43 Poquonock ave.
Windsor, CT 06095
Application address: c/o Guidance Office, Windsor High School, 50 Sage Park Rd., Windsor, CT 06095

Foundation type: Independent foundation
Limitations: Scholarships to students of Windsor High School, CT, for higher education.
Financial data: Year ended 06/30/2005. Assets, $178,634 (M); Expenditures, $5,554; Total giving, $5,000; Grants to individuals, totaling $5,000.
Type of support: Support to graduates or students of specific schools; Undergraduate support.
Application information: Deadline Apr. 5; Application by letter, including financial need established by FAFSA.
EIN: 066026061

4454
Wine & Spirits Wholesalers of Georgia Foundation, Inc.
5 Piedmont Ctr.
3525 Piedmont Rd., Ste. 710
Atlanta, GA 30305
Application address: c/o Ray Tripp, Dir. of Student Financial Aid, University System of Georgia Schools, 220 Academic Bldg., Athens, GA 30602

Foundation type: Independent foundation
Limitations: Undergraduate scholarships to GA residents, enrolled full-time in the University of Georgia or the University of Georgia school system.
Financial data: Year ended 12/31/2004. Assets, $865,665 (M); Expenditures, $49,758; Total giving, $47,308; Grants to individuals, 24 grants totaling $46,808 (high: $2,940, low: $1,000).
Type of support: Support to graduates or students of specific schools; Undergraduate support.
Application information: Deadline May 1; Completion of formal application required.
EIN: 586047788

4455
The Wine and Food Foundation of Texas
(formerly Texas Hill County Wine and Food Foundation)
1006 Mopac Cir., No. 102
Austin, TX 78746
Contact: Rebecca Robinson, Exec. Dir.
FAX: (512) 327-7551;
E-mail: robinson@winefoodfoundation.org;
URL: http://www.winefoodfoundation.org

Foundation type: Public charity
Limitations: Scholarships to residents of TX, for higher education in the culinary arts.
Publications: Informational brochure; Newsletter.
Financial data: Year ended 12/31/2004. Assets, $531,286 (M); Expenditures, $314,734; Total giving, $117,284.
Fields of interest: Vocational education.
Type of support: Conferences/seminars; Research; Grants to individuals; Scholarships—to individuals; Undergraduate support.
Application information: See Web site for current application deadline/guidelines.
EIN: 742846361

4456
Wine Spectator California Scholarship Foundation
387 Park Ave. S.
New York, NY 10016 (212) 684-4224

Foundation type: Public charity
Limitations: Grants and scholarships to graduating secondary, college or graduate students, or students enrolled in adult education classes, who reside in the U.S. pursuing careers in wineblending, or other wine industry or hospitality industry-related vocations.
Financial data: Year ended 06/30/2004. Assets, $4,565,421 (M); Expenditures, $1,987,336; Total giving, $340,231; Grants to individuals, totaling $18,231.
Fields of interest: Vocational education; Business/industry.
Type of support: Graduate support; Doctoral support.
Application information: Contact foundation for current application deadline/guidelines.
EIN: 133129027

4457
Winegardner Community Foundation, Inc.
8275 Tournament Dr., Ste. 144
Memphis, TN 38125
Contact: Roy E. Winegardner, Pres.

Foundation type: Independent foundation
Limitations: Scholarships primarily to residents of Memphis, TN.
Financial data: Year ended 08/31/2005. Assets, $777,145 (M); Expenditures, $157,805; Total giving, $157,775; Grants to individuals, totaling $10,000.
Type of support: Scholarships—to individuals.
Application information: Application form required.
Deadline(s): None.
Applicants should submit the following:
  1) GPA
  2) Letter(s) of recommendation
  3) SAT
  4) ACT
Program description:
Winegardner Community Scholarship Program: Each scholarship recipient is expected to contribute towards their own financial support by maintaining employment of at least ten hours per week during the school year, and forty hours per week during summer vacation.
EIN: 581487801

4458
Wing-Benjamin Trust Fund
c/o KeyBank N.A.
800 Superior Ave., 4th Fl.
Cleveland, OH 44114-1306
Contact: Cris Cook, Trust Off., KeyBank N.A.
Application address: 286 Water St., Augusta, ME 04330

Foundation type: Independent foundation
Limitations: Scholarships to residents of ME.
Financial data: Year ended 04/30/2004. Assets, $904,869 (M); Expenditures, $50,643; Total giving, $39,230.
Type of support: Scholarships—to individuals.
Application information: Applications by letter accepted throughout the year.
EIN: 016007288

4459
Wingaris Scholarship Fund
c/o Wachovia Bank, N.A.
401 S. Tryon St., 4th Fl.
Charlotte, NC 28288-5709

Foundation type: Independent foundation
Limitations: Scholarships to residents of Minersville Borough, PA or Brauch Township, PA.
Financial data: Year ended 06/30/2002. Assets, $253,016 (M); Expenditures, $18,564; Total giving, $17,050; Grants to individuals, 11 grants totaling $17,050 (high: $1,950, low: $1,850).
Type of support: Undergraduate support.
Application information: Unsolicited requests for funds not accepted.
EIN: 236790141

4460
Winged Foot Scholarship Foundation
2640 Golden Gate, No. 305
Naples, FL 34105-3203
Application address: c/o Collier Athletic Club, P.O. Box 8808, Naples, FL 34101

Foundation type: Independent foundation
Limitations: Scholarships to athletic students in Collier County (Naples area), FL, for higher education.
Financial data: Year ended 12/31/2004. Assets, $0 (M); Expenditures, $100,047; Total

giving, $28,500; Grants to individuals, 10 grants totaling $28,500 (high: $3,000, low: $2,500).
Fields of interest: Athletics/sports, training.
Type of support: Scholarships—to individuals.
Application information: Deadline May 1; Initial approach by letter or telephone; Completion of formal application required, including transcripts and two letters of recommendation, one from a teacher and one from a coach.
EIN: 650227001

4461
The Ernest & Maxine Wingett Memorial Education Trust
P.O. Box 78
Syracuse, OH   45779-0078
Contact: Robert Wingett, Dir.

Foundation type: Independent foundation
Limitations: Scholarships to residents of Sutton Township and Meigs County, OH, and to local descendants of Ernest and Maxine Wingett.
Financial data: Year ended 06/30/2004. Assets, $242,245 (M); Expenditures, $7,215; Total giving, $7,000; Grants to individuals, totaling $7,000.
Type of support: Scholarships—to individuals.
Application information: Deadline Mar. 15; Initial approach by letter or telephone; Completion of formal application required.
EIN: 316411166

4462
Walter Winkenhofer Foundation
c/o Old National Bank
P.O. Box 207
Evansville, IN   47702
Application address: c/o Peter F. Murphy, 305 N. Geieger St., Huntingburg, IN 47542

Foundation type: Independent foundation
Limitations: Scholarships to students graduating from Southridge High School in Huntingburg, IN.
Financial data: Year ended 04/30/2005. Assets, $48,743 (M); Expenditures, $4,280; Total giving, $3,250.
Type of support: Support to graduates or students of specific schools; Undergraduate support.
Application information: Applications accepted by letter throughout the year, including grades, goals, parents' income, and number of people dependent on family income.
EIN: 356311887

4463
C. D. Winning Scholarship Fund
(formerly Kiwanis Scholarship Fund)
c/o National City Bank
P.O. Box 94651
Cleveland, OH   44101-4651
Application address: c/o Edward Hack, Egert, Schneider, Mayer, & Hack, Lakewood Ctr. N., 14600 Detroit Ave., Ste. 1300, Lakewood, OH 44107, tel.: (216) 228-4400

Foundation type: Independent foundation
Limitations: Scholarships to young single men graduating from high schools in the City of Lakewood, OH, to study government, civil affairs, foreign languages, public relations, the humanities, or related fields at four-year colleges or universities.
Financial data: Year ended 12/31/2004. Assets, $346,645 (M); Expenditures, $20,402;

Total giving, $17,000; Grants to individuals, totaling $17,000.
Fields of interest: Humanities; Language (foreign); Political science; Public policy, research; Government/public administration; Men.
Type of support: Support to graduates or students of specific schools; Undergraduate support.
Application information: Deadline early Mar.; Completion of formal application required; Completed application forms should be returned to the school's guidance office.
Program description:
   Scholarship Program: Applicants must be at least 17 years of age prior to July 1 of graduating year, and not over age 21. Applicants are judged on leadership potential, community service, and scholastic ability. Scholarships are $1,000 each and are renewable for one year.
EIN: 346902315

4464
WinShape Centre, Inc.
5200 Buffington Rd.
Atlanta, GA   30349-2998   (800) 448-6955
Scholarship application address: Winshape Centre, Berry College, P.O. Box 490009, Mount Berry, GA 30149-0009, tel.: (706) 238-7718
FAX: (706) 238-7742;
E-mail: dvance@winshape.com; URL: http://www.winshape.com

Foundation type: Operating foundation
Limitations: Scholarships to unmarried undergraduate students attending Berry College in Mount Berry, GA.
Publications: Application guidelines; Informational brochure (including application guidelines).
Financial data: Year ended 12/31/2004. Assets, $37,659,572 (M); Expenditures, $10,685,319; Total giving, $770,651.
Type of support: Support to graduates or students of specific schools; Undergraduate support.
Application information: Application form required.
   Initial approach: Letter.
   Deadline(s): None.
   Additional information: Application should include list of honors.
EIN: 581595471

4465
Winship Memorial Scholarship Foundation
c/o Comerica Bank, Trust Div.
49 W. Michigan Ave.
Battle Creek, MI   49017-3603   (269) 966-6340
Contact: Lori A. Hill, Secy.

Foundation type: Independent foundation
Limitations: Scholarships to graduates of Battle Creek, MI, area public high schools, including those in the school systems of Battle Creek/Springfield, Climax-Scotts, Galesburg-Augusta, Harper Creek, Lakeview, and Pennfield.
Publications: Application guidelines; Annual report; Informational brochure.
Financial data: Year ended 12/31/2004. Assets, $3,759,877 (M); Expenditures, $234,034; Total giving, $182,605; Grants to individuals, 98 grants totaling $182,605 (high: $3,300, low: $550).
Type of support: Support to graduates or students of specific schools; Undergraduate support.
Application information: Deadline Mar. 1; Completion of formal application required;

Interviews required; Applications available through local high schools.
Program description:
   Winship Memorial Scholarship Program: Scholarships are awarded for recipient's entire college education, including postgraduate. Applicants must be enrolled full-time in accredited institutions of higher education.
EIN: 386092543

4466
The Lloyd E. & Katherine S. Winslow Education Trust
P.O. Box 327
Iola, KS   66749-0327
Application address: c/o Superintendent of Schools, Dotson Bradbury, P.O. Box 35, Moran, KS 66755, tel.: (620) 237-4250

Foundation type: Independent foundation
Limitations: Scholarships to residents of Moran, Marmaton Township, and Allen County, KS, for higher education. Scholarships are renewable.
Financial data: Year ended 12/31/2004. Assets, $841,457 (M); Expenditures, $69,308; Total giving, $54,750; Grants to individuals, totaling $54,750.
Type of support: Scholarships—to individuals.
Application information:
   Deadline(s): July 1
   Additional information: Completion of formal application required, including SAT/ACT scores, transcripts, and financial information.
EIN: 481060065

4467
Winslow Foundation
5301 W. Highwood Dr.
Edina, MN   55436
Contact: Daniel A. Boeckermann
Application address: 7900 Xerxes Ave. S., Ste. 1200, Bloomington, MN 55431

Foundation type: Independent foundation
Limitations: Scholarships to financially disadvantaged minorities attending North High School, MN, only.
Financial data: Year ended 12/31/2004. Assets, $3,417 (M); Expenditures, $4,370; Total giving, $3,000; Grants to individuals, 3 grants totaling $3,000.
Fields of interest: Minorities.
Type of support: Support to graduates or students of specific schools.
Application information: Application by letter outlining financial need and educational background.
EIN: 411670398

4468
The Winston-Salem Foundation
860 W. 5th St.
Winston-Salem, NC   27101-2506
(336) 725-2382
Contact: Scott F. Wierman, Pres.
FAX: (336) 727-0581;
E-mail: info@wsfoundation.org; Additional tel.: (866) 227-1209; Additional E-mail: swierman@wsfoundation.org; URL: http://www.wsfoundation.org

Foundation type: Community foundation
Limitations: Student loans to residents of Forsyth, Davie, Davidson, Surry, Stokes, and Yadkin

counties, NC, and scholarships primarily to residents of Forsyth County, NC. Some loans are also given to residents of other parts of NC.

Publications: Application guidelines; Annual report (including application guidelines); Grants list; Newsletter.

Financial data: Year ended 12/31/2004. Assets, $197,225,243 (M); Expenditures, $22,446,845; Total giving, $18,689,671.

Fields of interest: Law school/education; Medical school/education; Nursing school/education; Students, sororities/fraternities; Education; Health care; Athletics/sports, training; Science; Mathematics; Biological sciences; Military/veterans' organizations; Christian agencies & churches; Disabilities, people with.

Type of support: Employee-related scholarships; Student loans—to individuals; Graduate support; Undergraduate support.

Application information: Applications accepted. Application form required. Application form available on the grantmaker's Web site.

  Initial approach: Letter or telephone.

  Additional information: Applications distributed between Jan. and beginning of the fall semester for next academic year; a $20 application fee is required. For Student Aid Loan/Grant Program, see Web site for complete program listing and guidelines.

EIN: 566037615

4469
David and Eula Wintermann Foundation

P.O. Box 337
Eagle Lake, TX   77434-0337   (979) 234-5551
Contact: Jack Johnson, Pres.
Additional tel.: (713) 228-7273

Foundation type: Independent foundation

Limitations: Scholarships to seniors at Rice High School, Eagle Lake, TX, to pursue studies in the medical field.

Financial data: Year ended 09/30/2002. Assets, $285,407 (M); Expenditures, $31,504; Total giving, $15,000; Grants to individuals, 5 grants totaling $15,000 (high: $4,000, low: $1,000).

Fields of interest: Medical school/education; Nursing school/education.

Type of support: Support to graduates or students of specific schools; Undergraduate support.

Application information: Deadline Apr. 1; Initial approach by letter; Completion of formal application required, including high school transcripts, statement of financial need, field of intended study, and a character reference.

EIN: 760082100

4470
Nels and Lucille Winther Foundation

P.O. Box 110
Minden, NE   68959
Application address: c/o Ray Van Norman, P.O. Box 179, Minden, NE 68959

Foundation type: Operating foundation

Limitations: Scholarships to individuals for higher education in the areas of Minden, Kearney County, and Blue Hill, NE.

Financial data: Year ended 12/31/2003. Assets, $301,869 (M); Expenditures, $122,184; Total giving, $121,000; Grants to individuals, 20 grants totaling $21,000 (high: $2,250, low: $750).

Type of support: Scholarships—to individuals.

Application information: Contact foundation for current application deadline/guidelines; Application by letter.

EIN: 363737675

4471
Evelyn and Ronald Wirick Foundation

504 Maple Dr.
Morenci, MI   49256-1222   (517) 458-7189
Contact: Ralph R. Ferris, Pres.

Foundation type: Independent foundation

Limitations: Scholarships to graduates of the Morenci Public School District, MI.

Financial data: Year ended 12/31/2004. Assets, $1,182,399 (M); Expenditures, $29,945; Total giving, $12,900; Grants to individuals, totaling $12,900.

Type of support: Support to graduates or students of specific schools; Undergraduate support.

Application information: Contact foundation for current application deadline/guidelines.

EIN: 382700421

4472
Wisconsin Institute of Certified Public Accountants Educational Foundation, Inc.

235 N. Executive Dr., Ste. 200
Brookfield, WI   53008-1010   (262) 785-0445
Contact: Joan Phillips, Pres.
FAX: (262) 785-0838;
E-mail: comments@wicpa.org; Additional tel.: (800) 772-6939; URL: http://www.wicpa.org

Foundation type: Public charity

Limitations: Scholarships to students studying accounting at WI universities.

Financial data: Year ended 04/30/2004. Assets, $1,259,980 (M); Expenditures, $53,181; Total giving, $41,000; Grants to individuals, 16 grants totaling $41,000 (high: $5,000, low: $500).

Fields of interest: Business school/education.

Type of support: Scholarships—to individuals.

Application information:

  Deadline(s): Contact funds for deadline

  Additional information: See web site for guidelines and various scholarship listings.

EIN: 237109897

4473
Wisconsin Medical Society Foundation, Inc.

(formerly State Medical Society Foundation)
330 E. Lakeside St.
P.O. Box 1109
Madison, WI   53701   (608) 442-3720
Contact: Renee Reback, Exec. Dir.
URL: http://www.wisconsinmedicalsociety.org/physician_resources/foundation

Foundation type: Public charity

Limitations: Scholarships and student loans to medical school students in WI.

Publications: Application guidelines; Newsletter.

Financial data: Year ended 12/31/2004. Assets, $7,749,797 (M); Expenditures, $378,318; Total giving, $48,350; Grants to individuals, 31 grants totaling $48,350; Loans to individuals, 64 loans totaling $320,000.

Fields of interest: Medical school/education; Native Americans/American Indians.

Type of support: Program development; Fellowships; Research; Grants to individuals;

Scholarships—to individuals; Student loans—to individuals; Support to graduates or students of specific schools; Awards/prizes; Graduate support; Undergraduate support; Postgraduate support.

Application information: Application form required. Application form available on the grantmaker's Web site.

  Initial approach: Letter.

  Copies of proposal: 7

  Deadline(s): Contact foundation for current application guidelines

Program descriptions:

  Victor C. Baylor, M.D. Memorial Scholarship: Available to medical students, medical technologists, and clinical laboratory scientists in Racine and Milwaukee counties.

  Student Loans: Provides needy, deserving medical students with $1,000 (for first and second year) and $3,000 (for third and fourth year) loans which are interest-free until the student graduates. Students attending either medical school, nursing or allied health care programs in the state of WI are eligible.

  Goodman-Goodell Scholarship Fund: Awarded to a second-year medical student from the Portage area planning to specialize in pulmonary or in general or family practice.

  Hoyton Award: Two scholarships are presented each year to the outstanding seniors at the University of Wisconsin-Madison Medical School and the Medical College of Wisconsin.

  Amy Louise Hunter-Wilson, M.D. Scholarship: Assists American Indians who pursue a training or advanced education as doctors of medicine, nurses, technicians or in a related health field.

  Jefferson County Allied Health Career Scholarship Fund: Provides scholarships to students of Jefferson County interested in allied health careers who are attending either medical school or technical school in the Madison area.

  NMC Projects: Nelson Industries provides a scholarship to an outstanding medical student from an area in which their plant facilities are located.

  Edward M. Vetter, M.D. Medical Education Scholarship Fund: Awards scholarships to medical students in all specialty fields of medicine.

EIN: 396045649

4474
Wisconsin Troopers Association Scholarship Fund

2099 Ironwood Dr.
Green Bay, WI   54304
Contact: Gwen Schneider, Dir.
Application address: 600 S. Main St., Deerfield, WI 53531, tel.: (608) 764-8306
URL: http://www.wi-troopers.org

Foundation type: Independent foundation

Limitations: Scholarships primarily to members of the Wisconsin Troopers Association and their relatives to pursue higher education at colleges, universities, and technical schools.

Financial data: Year ended 12/31/2004. Assets, $0 (L); Expenditures, $12,450; Total giving, $12,300; Grants to individuals, 19 grants totaling $12,300 (high: $1,000, low: $300).

Fields of interest: Vocational education.

Type of support: Technical education support; Undergraduate support.

Application information: Application form required.

  Initial approach: Letter.

  Deadline(s): Mar. 15

EIN: 391606135

4475
Erbon & Marie Wise Educational Trust
1235 Peachtree Rd.
Sulphur, LA   70663-3802
Contact: Scholarships: E.C. Gensheimer

Foundation type: Independent foundation
Limitations: Scholarships to residents of south and central LA.
Financial data: Year ended 12/31/2004.
Assets, $116,969 (M); Expenditures, $8,616; Total giving, $8,000; Grants to individuals, totaling $8,000.
Type of support: Undergraduate support.
Application information: Applications accepted.
Additional information: Contact foundation for current application deadlines/guidelines.
EIN: 726137018

4476
Dr. L. G. Wisner & Winfred T. Wisner Scholarship Trust Fund
c/o National City Bank
P.O. Box 94651
Cleveland, OH   44101-4651
Application address: c/o Wisner Selection Board, Herscher C.U.S.D. No. 2 Office, P.O. Box 504, Herscher, IL 60941-0504

Foundation type: Independent foundation
Limitations: Scholarships to financially needy graduating seniors and graduates from Herscher High School, IL.
Financial data: Year ended 04/30/2005.
Assets, $209,714 (M); Expenditures, $8,150; Total giving, $6,300; Grants to individuals, totaling $6,300.
Type of support: Support to graduates or students of specific schools; Undergraduate support.
Application information: Application form required.
Deadline(s): Apr. 22
Applicants should submit the following:
1) GPA
2) ACT
Additional information: Application should include class rank. Recipients are selected on the basis of character, citizenship, leadership qualities, financial need, and academic achievement. Applicants who are current Herscher High School students must obtain and complete their application forms in the guidance office. Graduates can secure their application materials from the school district office.
EIN: 366872997

4477
Mabel M. Witmer Trust
c/o M&T Bank
21 E. Market St.
York, PA   17401-1205
Application address: c/o M&T Bank, Attn.: John Schall, 14 N. Main St., Chambersburg, PA 17201, tel.: (717) 267-7625

Foundation type: Independent foundation
Limitations: Scholarships based on financial need and academic standing, to students from Franklin and Cumberland counties, PA.
Financial data: Year ended 12/31/2004.
Assets, $89,697 (M); Expenditures, $1,976; Total giving, $700.
Type of support: Technical education support.

Application information: Contact trust for current application deadline; Completion of formal application required.
EIN: 256183584

4478
WKBJ Partnership Foundation
(formerly The Made in Dover Foundation)
50 Smith Rd.
Denville, NJ   07834-9405   (973) 328-0303
Contact: Bob Howitt
FAX: (973) 328-0388

Foundation type: Operating foundation
Limitations: Scholarships to financially disadvantaged students residing in the northeastern U.S.
Financial data: Year ended 12/31/2004.
Assets, $5,767,579 (M); Expenditures, $937,700; Total giving, $668,855; Grants to individuals, 20 grants totaling $56,855 (high: $8,882, low: $100).
Fields of interest: Economically disadvantaged.
Type of support: Undergraduate support.
Application information:
Initial approach: Letter.
Additional information: Applications by letter accepted throughout the year; Contact foundation for current application guidelines.
EIN: 223000244

4479
Wolf Foundation for Education Trust
c/o The Ephrata National Bank
47 E. Main St.
Ephrata, PA   17522-0457   (717) 733-4181
Contact: Carl Brubaker, Trust Off., The Ephrata National Bank

Foundation type: Independent foundation
Limitations: Scholarships to students who graduated from high schools in Ephrata Township and Ephrata Borough, PA. Scholarships are renewable for up to four years of study.
Financial data: Year ended 12/31/2004.
Assets, $428,490 (M); Expenditures, $23,778; Total giving, $20,000; Grants to individuals, totaling $20,000.
Type of support: Support to graduates or students of specific schools; Undergraduate support.
Application information: Applications accepted. Application form required.
Deadline(s): Contact trust for current application deadline.
Applicants should submit the following:
1) SAT
2) ACT
3) Financial information
EIN: 236750958

4480
The Loretta Frances Wolf Foundation
c/o Merrill Lynch Trust Co.
P.O. Box 1525, MSC 06-03
Pennington, NJ   08534-1525

Foundation type: Independent foundation
Limitations: Scholarships to individuals, primarily in NJ, for undergraduate education.
Financial data: Year ended 10/31/2004.
Assets, $519,038 (M); Expenditures, $54,861; Total giving, $44,375; Grants to individuals, totaling $25,625.
Type of support: Undergraduate support.

Application information: Contact foundation for current application deadlines/guidelines.
EIN: 251880485

4481
Benjamin & Fredora K. Wolf Memorial Foundation
621 Pemberton St.
Philadelphia, PA   19147
Contact: Thomas Ginsberg, Treas.

Foundation type: Independent foundation
Limitations: Scholarships based on merit to residents of the Philadelphia, PA, area.
Financial data: Year ended 05/31/2005.
Assets, $3,225,911 (M); Expenditures, $160,389; Total giving, $134,000; Grants to individuals, 269 grants totaling $134,000 (high: $500, low: $300).
Type of support: Scholarships—to individuals.
Application information: Applications accepted.
Deadline(s): None
EIN: 236207344

4482
Charles F. Wolf Scholarship Fund
c/o Pagones, Cross & VanTuyl
355 Main St.
Beacon, NY   12508

Foundation type: Independent foundation
Limitations: Scholarships to students accepted to the New York University School of Medicine, NY.
Financial data: Year ended 05/31/2005.
Assets, $2,463,721 (M); Expenditures, $122,085; Total giving, $79,831; Grants to individuals, totaling $79,831.
Fields of interest: Medical school/education.
Type of support: Support to graduates or students of specific schools; Graduate support.
Application information: Contact fund for current application deadline/guidelines.
EIN: 141580597

4483
Elizabeth Wolf Scholarship Fund
c/o Pagones, Cross & VanTuyl, PC
355 Main St.
Beacon, NY   12508
Application address: c/o Nick Coto, Principal, Beacon High School, Beacon, NY 12508, tel.: (914) 838-6950

Foundation type: Independent foundation
Limitations: Scholarships to graduates of Beacon High School, NY.
Financial data: Year ended 05/31/2005.
Assets, $126,660 (M); Expenditures, $15,201; Total giving, $11,845; Grants to individuals, totaling $11,845.
Type of support: Support to graduates or students of specific schools; Undergraduate support.
Application information: Deadline June; Completion of formal application required, including biographical and scholastic information, and references.
EIN: 141580472

4484
Walter J. Wolf Trust
c/o PNC Advisors
620 Liberty Ave., 10th Fl.
Pittsburgh, PA 15222-2705

Foundation type: Independent foundation
Limitations: Scholarships to graduates of Potts Grove High School, PA.
Financial data: Year ended 12/31/2003. Assets, $315,855 (M); Expenditures, $20,573; Total giving, $16,750; Grants to individuals, 29 grants totaling $16,750 (high: $500, low: $250).
Type of support: Support to graduates or students of specific schools; Undergraduate support.
Application information: Applications accepted throughout the year; Contact trust for current application guidelines; Recipients are chosen by Potts Grove High School, PA.
EIN: 236429959

4485
The O. G. Wollman, Dorothy Armstrong Wollman and Ella Armstrong Scholarship Fund
c/o AmSouth Bank
315 Deaderick St., 4th Fl.
Nashville, TN 37237-0401
Application address: c/o First National Bank, Attn.: Beth Welsh, P.O. Box 520, Tullahoma, TN 37388

Foundation type: Independent foundation
Limitations: Scholarships to students of the senior class of Tullahoma High School, TN, for higher education.
Financial data: Year ended 01/31/2005. Assets, $276,172 (M); Expenditures, $18,040; Total giving, $15,050; Grants to individuals, totaling $15,050.
Type of support: Support to graduates or students of specific schools; Undergraduate support.
Application information: Applications accepted throughout the year; Initial approach by letter; Completion of formal application required.
EIN: 626266551

4486
Gus & Ethel Wolters Foundation Trust
c/o Frost National Bank
P.O. Box 2950
San Antonio, TX 78299 (210) 220-4457
Contact: Steve W. Barker, V.P., Frost National Bank

Foundation type: Independent foundation
Limitations: Scholarships to graduates of Shriner High School and St. Paul's Catholic High School in Shriner, TX, who reside in Lavaca County, TX.
Financial data: Year ended 08/31/2004. Assets, $5,774,995 (M); Expenditures, $187,163; Total giving, $140,400; Grants to individuals, totaling $140,400.
Type of support: Support to graduates or students of specific schools; Undergraduate support.
Application information: Applications accepted. Application form required.
Deadline(s): None
Additional information: Application should also include complete biographical data, a report of high school performance, a statement of an academic plan, and a letter of reference; Applications available from the above named schools.
EIN: 742335544

4487
B. M. Woltman Foundation
2525 N. Loop W., Ste. 102
Houston, TX 77008
Contact: Rev. Kenneth Hennings, Exec. Dir
Application address: c/o Lutheran Church, Missouri Synod, 7900 East Hwy. 290, Austin, TX 78724-2499

Foundation type: Independent foundation
Limitations: Scholarships to students who are from TX or studying in TX, and preparing for the Lutheran ministry or for teaching in Lutheran schools.
Financial data: Year ended 12/31/2004. Assets, $6,128,260 (M); Expenditures, $317,351; Total giving, $257,038; Grants to individuals, 39 grants totaling $75,773 (high: $2,241, low: $991).
Fields of interest: Education, research; Theological school/education; Protestant agencies & churches.
Type of support: Scholarships—to individuals.
Application information: Deadline prior to school term; Initial approach by letter; Completion of formal application required; Interviews required.
EIN: 741402184

4488
Mildred and Charles Wolverton Scholarship Trust
c/o Bank of America, N.A.
P.O. Box 513189 GMF
Los Angeles, CA 90051-1189
Application address: c/o Robert Britton, 555 S. Flower St., 11th Fl., Los Angeles, CA 90071, tel.: (213) 345-5845

Foundation type: Independent foundation
Limitations: Scholarships to residents of at least two years of CA who are completely visually impaired, for study at California Polytechnic College in San Luis Obispo, CA.
Financial data: Year ended 06/30/2005. Assets, $457,067 (M); Expenditures, $27,250; Total giving, $22,664; Grants to individuals, totaling $22,664.
Fields of interest: Disabilities, people with.
Type of support: Scholarships—to individuals; Support to graduates or students of specific schools.
Application information: Applications accepted throughout the year; Initial approach by letter requesting information.
EIN: 956855392

4489
Womack Foundation
513 Wilson St.
Danville, VA 24541
Contact: James A.L. Daniel, Chair.
Application address: c/o Louise Wright, Secy.-Treas., P.O. Box 521, Danville, VA 24543

Foundation type: Operating foundation
Limitations: Student loans to residents of the city of Danville and Pittsylvania County, VA and Caswell County, NC.
Financial data: Year ended 03/31/2005. Assets, $615,456 (M); Expenditures, $83,275; Total giving, $66,206; Loans to individuals, totaling $13,952.
Fields of interest: Vocational education; Nursing school/education.
Type of support: Graduate support; Technical education support; Undergraduate support.

Application information: Applications accepted throughout the year; Completion of formal application required; Interviews required.
Program description:
Womack Scholarship Program: Any student who has not been able to get sufficient funds from his/her family or other sources may apply. Grants may be used for college, vocational school, nursing school, or any formal educational program. Loan interest is 10 percent. The student is to keep the foundation informed of his/her progress.
EIN: 546053255

4490
The Woman's Literary Union
904 Washington Ave.
Portland, ME 04103 (207) 797-6333

Foundation type: Independent foundation
Limitations: Scholarships to students of greater Portland, ME, high schools.
Financial data: Year ended 03/31/2005. Assets, $731,053 (M); Expenditures, $50,942; Total giving, $4,000; Grants to individuals, 2 grants totaling $4,000.
Type of support: Support to graduates or students of specific schools; Undergraduate support.
Application information: Deadline end of academic year; Seniors are recommended by high school guidance counselors.
EIN: 010220139

4491
Woman's Seamen's Friend Society of Connecticut, Inc.
c/o New Alliance Bank Trust Dept.
P.O. Box 302
New Haven, CT 06502
Application address: 291 Whitney Ave., Ste. 203, New Haven, CT 06511-3724

Foundation type: Independent foundation
Limitations: Scholarships for the study of marine sciences in CT or for CT residents at any approved institution, and for dependents of CT merchant marine seamen pursuing any course of study.
Financial data: Year ended 12/31/2004. Assets, $5,275,657 (M); Expenditures, $200,539; Total giving, $100,615; Grants to individuals, totaling $13,775.
Fields of interest: Marine science; Military/veterans' organizations.
Type of support: Undergraduate support.
Application information: Application form required.
Initial approach: Letter.
Deadline(s): Apr. 1 for summer term, May 15 for academic year.
Additional information: The Scholarship Committee makes awards after considering financial need, academic achievement, letters of recommendation, and proposed program of study. The awards are supplemental and are not intended to be the primary source of financial assistance.
EIN: 060655133

4492
Women's Aid of Penn Central School
(formerly Women's Aid Scholarship)
c/o Wachovia Bank, N.A.
123 S. Broad St., 5th Fl.
Philadelphia, PA 19109 (215) 209-5054
Contact: Reginald Middleton, V.P.

Foundation type: Company-sponsored foundation
Limitations: Scholarships to children of employees of Conrail, employees of its predecessor roads (Penn Central or PRR) now employed by Amtrak or Penn Central Corporation, and former employees of Penn Central or PRR who have retired because of age or disability, or who have died.
Financial data: Year ended 12/31/2003. Assets, $2,008,889 (M); Expenditures, $372,734; Total giving, $340,575; Grants to individuals, 308 grants totaling $340,575 (high: $1,750, low: $125).
Type of support: Employee-related scholarships.
Application information:
 Deadline(s): Apr. 1
 Additional information: Scholarship application address: c/o Conrail, 6 Penn Ctr., Rm. 1010, Philadelphia, PA 19102.
EIN: 236232572

4493
The Women's Council of the Brain Research Foundation

5812 S. Ellis Ave., MC 7112-J141
Chicago, IL 60637 (773) 834-6754

Foundation type: Public charity
Limitations: Scholarships to female graduate and post-doctoral students for study of neuroscience at the University of Chicago, IL.
Fields of interest: Medical school/education; Neuroscience; Women.
Type of support: Program development; Research; Support to graduates or students of specific schools; Postdoctoral support; Graduate support; Undergraduate support.
Application information: Contact foundation for current application deadline; Completion of formal application required, including proposal for research.
EIN: 237004230

4494
Women's Sports Foundation

Eisenhower Park
East Meadow, NY 11554 (516) 542-4700
Contact: Donna A. Lopiano Ph.D., Exec. Dir.
FAX: (516) 542-4716; E-mail: wosport@aol.com; Additional tel.: (800) 227-3988; URL: http://www.womenssportsfoundation.org

Foundation type: Public charity
Limitations: Educational support to women and girls interested in sports.
Publications: Application guidelines; Annual report; Financial statement; Grants list; Informational brochure; Newsletter.
Financial data: Year ended 12/31/2003. Assets, $5,517,332 (L); Expenditures, $4,370,568; Total giving, $787,728.
Fields of interest: Higher education; Minorities; Women.
Type of support: Internship funds; Scholarships—to individuals.
Application information:
 Deadline(s): Vary
 Additional information: See Web site for further information.
Program descriptions:
 Zina Garrison/Visa Minority Internship: Women of color are provided with internship opportunities in sports-related careers and stipends of up to $5,000. Applicants may be in school to apply.
 Dorothy Harris Endowed Scholarship: Full-time female graduate students in physical education,

sports management, sports psychology, or sports sociology are provided with a $1,500 scholarship to attend an accredited graduate school in the fall. Deadline Dec. 31.
 Jackie Joyner-Kersee/Ray Ban Minority Internship: Women of color are given an opportunity to gain experience in a sports-related career and interact in the sports community. Applicants may be undergraduate, college graduates, graduate students or women in career change. Internships include $4,000 to $5,000 in stipends.
 Linda Riddle/SGMA Endowed Scholarship: Provides $1,500 scholarships are awarded to young female athletes of limited financial means to provide the opportunity to pursue a college education as well as continue their sports participation. Applicants must be seniors who will pursue a full-time course of study at an accredited two- or four-year college in the fall.
 RYKA Women's Fitness Grant: Provides $5,000 in financial assistance to women aged 25 and over. Grants are to promote women's health and fitness. Deadline Aug. 15. See Web site for further information.
EIN: 237380557

4495
L. S. Wood Charitable Trust

c/o Bank of America, N.A.
231 S. LaSalle St.
Chicago, IL 60697 (312) 828-1785
Application address: c/o Donald H. Parkison, Admin., 1317 Grand Ave., Ste. 228, Glenwood Springs, CO 81601, tel.: (970) 945-4952, FAX: (970) 947-9215, E-mail: parkison@sopris.net

Foundation type: Independent foundation
Limitations: Undergraduate scholarships to individuals studying at accredited colleges and universities.
Financial data: Year ended 12/31/2004. Assets, $8,797,351 (M); Expenditures, $723,420; Total giving, $579,380; Grants to individuals, totaling $579,380.
Type of support: Undergraduate support.
Application information: Contact trust for current application deadline; Initial approach by letter or telephone; Completion of formal application required.
Program description:
 L.S. Wood Scholarship Program: Recipients must maintain at least a 2.0 GPA.
EIN: 366146230

4496
A. R. Wood Educational Trust

c/o Wells Fargo Bank South Dakota, N.A.
230 W. Superior St., Ste. 40
Duluth, MN 55802
Contact: Robin Aden, Trust Off., Wells Fargo Bank South Dakota, N.A.

Foundation type: Independent foundation
Limitations: Scholarships only to graduates of Luverne High School, MN, who are in the top 20 percent of their class, and have at least a 3.0 GPA.
Financial data: Year ended 12/31/2004. Assets, $197,803 (M); Expenditures, $10,629; Total giving, $7,000.
Type of support: Support to graduates or students of specific schools; Undergraduate support.
Application information: Applications not accepted.
EIN: 416023357

4497
The Jim and Marie Wood Foundation

c/o Alan Anderson
110 N. 2nd Ave.
Logan, IA 51546

Foundation type: Independent foundation
Limitations: Scholarships to residents of the Logan, IA, area.
Financial data: Year ended 12/31/2004. Assets, $3,733,179 (M); Expenditures, $118,960; Total giving, $118,548; Grants to individuals, 8 grants totaling $30,000 (high: $5,000, low: $2,500).
Type of support: Scholarships—to individuals.
Application information: Contact foundation for current application deadline/guidelines.
EIN: 931044500

4498
Alice Louise Ridenour Wood Scholarship Fund

c/o National City Bank
P.O. Box 94651
Cleveland, OH 44101

Foundation type: Independent foundation
Limitations: Scholarships to graduating seniors at specific OH high schools for undergraduate and technical/vocational school studies.
Financial data: Year ended 12/31/2004. Assets, $1,659,742 (M); Expenditures, $79,386; Total giving, $63,036; Grants to individuals, 44 grants totaling $63,036 (high: $3,700, low: $276).
Fields of interest: Vocational education.
Type of support: Support to graduates or students of specific schools; Technical education support; Undergraduate support.
Application information: Application form required.
 Initial approach: Letter or telephone.
 Deadline(s): Contact fund for current application deadline
Program descriptions:
 Jonathan Alder High School Scholarships: Scholarships are awarded to students of Jonathan Alder High School, Plain City, OH, who are ranked in the top 18th percentile of all graduating seniors. Funds must be used for two- or four-year colleges, two-year technical schools, or nursing schools. Applicants must complete their senior years at Jonathan Alder High School and reside within the boundaries of the school system.
 London High School Scholarships: Applicants must have at least a 2.8 cumulative GPA and must plan to pursue postsecondary education at either a junior college, two-year community college, four-year public or private university, technical college/school, or accredited proprietary school. Recipients are chosen on the basis of merit. A minimum of two scholarships per award year will be awarded to qualified London High School students who attend Tolles Technical School. Scholarships are awarded for one year only and they are not renewable.
 Madison Plains High School Scholarships: Scholarships are awarded to graduates of Madison Plains High School, London, OH, to attend postsecondary schools. At least one half of the scholarships must be awarded on the basis of merit alone, as determined by grades, teacher evaluations, and student essays. In addition financial need is a criteria.
 West Jefferson High School Scholarships: Scholarships are awarded to residents of the Jefferson Local School District who are currently in

their senior years at West Jefferson High School, OH. Scholarships are renewable.
EIN: 316395426

4499
Cora W. Wood Scholarship Fund
c/o JPMorgan Chase Bank, N.A.
P.O. Box 1308
Milwaukee, WI 53201
Contact: Julie Birdwell, Trust Off., JPMorgan Chase Bank, N.A.
Application address: 1125 17th St., Denver, CO 80202

Foundation type: Independent foundation
Limitations: Scholarships to graduating high school seniors residing in the Pike's Peak region, CO, to attend state-supported colleges and universities in CO.
Financial data: Year ended 12/31/2004. Assets, $185,608 (M); Expenditures, $9,614; Total giving, $4,400; Grants to individuals, 2 grants totaling $4,400.
Type of support: Undergraduate support.
Application information: Deadline Apr. 30; Application by letter, including resume, photograph, financial statement, and letter of recommendation from teacher or counselor for verification and comments.
EIN: 237169976

4500
Ethel Arnold Wood Scholarship Fund
c/o Bank of America, N.A.
P.O. Box 6767
Providence, RI 02940-6767
Application addresses: c/o John C. Newburn, Principal, Fairhaven High School, 12 Huttleston Ave., Fairhaven, MA 02719, tel.: (617) 997-2971; c/o Joseph Didato, Guidance Counselor, Martha's Vineyard High School, Oak Bluffs, MA 02557, tel.: (617) 693-1033

Foundation type: Independent foundation
Limitations: Scholarships to graduates of Fairhaven High School and Martha's Vineyard Regional High School, MA.
Financial data: Year ended 09/30/2004. Assets, $175,135 (M); Expenditures, $8,803; Total giving, $5,600; Grants to individuals, 5 grants totaling $5,600.
Type of support: Support to graduates or students of specific schools; Undergraduate support.
Application information: Application form required.
   Deadline(s): Apr. 15 for Martha's Vineyard Regional High School, and May 1 for Fairhaven High School
   Applicants should submit the following:
     1) Financial information
     2) Transcripts
   Additional information: Application by letter stating past and current activities, and future plans.
EIN: 046332654

4501
Woodbury Educational Foundation
P.O. Box 320
Woodbury, TN 37190-0320 (615) 563-2431
Contact: Russell E. Myers, Secy.-Treas.

Foundation type: Independent foundation

Limitations: Scholarships to students of Cannon County, TN, high schools for undergraduate and vocational study.
Financial data: Year ended 05/31/2005. Assets, $0 (M); Expenditures, $40,156; Total giving, $36,693; Grants to individuals, 23 grants totaling $36,693 (high: $2,000, low: $193).
Fields of interest: Vocational education, post-secondary.
Type of support: Support to graduates or students of specific schools; Technical education support.
Application information: Contact foundation for current application deadline/guidelines.
EIN: 620470043

4502
Woodbury Foundation
c/o Christine M. Rhode
222 N. LaSalle St., 24th Fl.
Chicago, IL 60601
Application address: c/o Dean of Admissions, Warren Wilson College, Swannanoa, NC 28778, tel.: (704) 298-3325

Foundation type: Independent foundation
Limitations: Scholarships to individuals for attendance at Warren Wilson College, NC.
Financial data: Year ended 05/31/2004. Assets, $18,275,004 (M); Expenditures, $887,473; Total giving, $816,500.
Type of support: Support to graduates or students of specific schools.
Application information: Contact foundation for current application deadline/guidelines.
EIN: 363715828

4503
Ward & Mary Wooddell Scholarship Trust
c/o Janet Dixon, National Bank & Trust Co.
P.O. Box 711
Wilmington, OH 45177 (937) 382-1441

Foundation type: Independent foundation
Limitations: Scholarships to graduating seniors from Clinton County, OH, high schools. Scholarships are renewable for up to four years of study.
Financial data: Year ended 09/30/2004. Assets, $201,177 (M); Expenditures, $23,162; Total giving, $17,499; Grants to individuals, totaling $17,499.
Type of support: Support to graduates or students of specific schools; Undergraduate support.
Application information:
   Deadline(s): Apr. 1
   Additional information: Completion of formal application required, including financial statement.
EIN: 316368376

4504
L. Dexter Woodman Scholarship, Inc.
P.O. Box 81
Essex, MA 01929
Application addresses: c/o Guidance Dept., Hamilton-Wenham Regional High School, 775 Bay Rd., South Hamilton, MA 01930, c/o Manchester Jr., Sr. High School Guidance Dept., Lincoln St., Manchester, MA 01930

Foundation type: Independent foundation
Limitations: Scholarships to students from Hamilton-Wenham Regional High School and Manchester by the Sea High School, MA.

Financial data: Year ended 06/30/2004. Assets, $304,422 (M); Expenditures, $80,907; Total giving, $50,182; Grants to individuals, totaling $48,182.
Type of support: Support to graduates or students of specific schools; Undergraduate support.
Application information: Deadline Apr. 15; Completion of formal application required.
EIN: 222925975

4505
The Woodmansee Scholarship Fund
c/o Pioneer Trust Bank, N.A.
P.O. Box 2305
Salem, OR 97308

Foundation type: Independent foundation
Limitations: Scholarships to graduating seniors from OR high schools to attend institutions of higher learning in OR.
Financial data: Year ended 05/31/2005. Assets, $119,839 (M); Expenditures, $15,539; Total giving, $12,592; Grants to individuals, totaling $12,592.
Type of support: Undergraduate support.
Application information: Deadline Mar. 15; Initial approach by letter with SASE; Completion of formal application required.
EIN: 936195941

4506
Woodrow Foundation
c/o U.S. Bank, N.A.
P.O. Box 3168
Portland, OR 97208

Foundation type: Independent foundation
Limitations: One scholarship annually to a student of Whitworth College, Spokane, WA.
Financial data: Year ended 06/30/2005. Assets, $935,862 (M); Expenditures, $49,558; Total giving, $37,904; Grants to individuals, totaling $21,724.
Type of support: Support to graduates or students of specific schools; Undergraduate support.
Application information: Application form required.
   Deadline(s): Contact foundation for current application deadline.
EIN: 916326014

4507
Woodrow W. Woods Educational Trust
c/o JPMorgan Chase Bank, N.A.
P.O. Box 1308
Milwaukee, WI 53201
Application address: c/o JPMorgan Chase Bank, N.A., 229 W. Main St., Clarksburg, WV 26301, tel.: (304) 624-3443

Foundation type: Independent foundation
Limitations: Loans to graduating seniors from Harrison County high schools, WV for higher education.
Financial data: Year ended 12/31/2004. Assets, $1,349,668 (M); Expenditures, $15,962; Total giving, $0; Loans to individuals, 24 loans totaling $37,500.
Type of support: Support to graduates or students of specific schools; Undergraduate support.
Application information: Deadline May 30; Contact trust for current application guidelines.
EIN: 546409374

4508
Tiger Woods Foundation, Inc.
4281 Katella Ave., Ste. 111
Los Alamitos, CA 90720-3588 (714) 816-1806
Contact: Gregory T. McLaughlin, Pres.
FAX: (714) 816-1869; URL: http://
www.tigerwoodsfoundation.org

Foundation type: Public charity
Limitations: Scholarships to graduating seniors, one male and one female, who attend Minerva High School in Ohio.
Financial data: Year ended 09/30/2003. Assets, $33,341,870 (M); Expenditures, $3,263,707; Total giving, $1,519,099.
Fields of interest: Athletics/sports, golf; Civil rights, minorities; Minorities.
Type of support: Support to graduates or students of specific schools; Precollege support; Undergraduate support.
Application information: Contact foundation for current application deadline/guidelines.
Program descriptions:
William and Marcella Powell Scholarship: Awards $1,000 annually to one male and one female graduating senior at Minerva High School in OH who has overcome significant challenges while achieving academic excellence.
Alfred "Tup" Holmes Memorial Scholarship: Established to honor the civil-rights pioneer who paved the way for desegregating Atlanta's public golf courses in the 1950's.
National Minority Junior Golf Scholarship: Five $2,000 scholarships are awarded to minority golfers attending college.
Start Something Scholarship Program: This program is designed to help students ages 8 to 17 figure out what they want to do with their life, and what steps they should take to pursue their interests and reach their goals. Students may work in groups with a teacher or group leader. The group leader will coordinate sessions and activities and provide supervision for students in their group. Students can work on their own, following the curriculum online. Younger students may find it helpful to have a parent or another adult guide them through activities. The program is set up as a series of 10 two-hour sessions. Each session has several activities to do, such as: reading, thinking about goals and dreams, reflecting and writing about ideas, and doing an outside project. It is designed to be completed over 10 weeks, but it can be done in a few weeks or several months- the schedule is completely up to recipients.
EIN: 061468499

4509
Valeria Walton Woods Scholarship Fund Trust
c/o Fulton Financial Advisors, N.A.
P.O. Box 3215
Lancaster, PA 17604-3215
Application address: c/o Guidance Counselor, Danville Senior High School, Northumberland Rd., Danville, PA 17821, tel.: (570) 275-4113

Foundation type: Independent foundation
Limitations: Scholarships to financially needy graduates of Danville Senior High School, PA.
Financial data: Year ended 12/31/2004. Assets, $63,435 (M); Expenditures, $3,484; Total giving, $2,250; Grants to individuals, totaling $2,250.
Type of support: Support to graduates or students of specific schools; Undergraduate support.

Application information: Deadline May 1; Completion of formal application required, including FAFSA and class rank.
Program description:
Scholarship Fund Program: The maximum amount awarded is $500 per student, per year for four years. Applicants are automatically considered for all scholarships awarded by the Comprehensive Scholarship Committee.
EIN: 246015619

4510
Marlow & Vella Woodward Foundation, Inc.
675 N. Main St.
North Salt Lake, UT 84054-0298

Foundation type: Operating foundation
Limitations: Scholarships and grants to individuals, primarily in UT.
Financial data: Year ended 12/31/2002. Assets, $225,741 (M); Expenditures, $25,975; Total giving, $25,871; Grants to individuals, 5 grants totaling $25,871 (high: $16,106, low: $665).
Type of support: Scholarships—to individuals.
Application information: Application form required.
Additional information: Applications accepted throughout the year.
EIN: 870616969

4511
Woodward/Graff Wine Foundation
(formerly Chalone Wine Foundation)
27 E. Napa St., Ste. S
Sonoma, CA 95476 (707) 935-2100
Contact: W. Philip Woodward, Pres.
URL: http://
www.woodward-graffwinefoundation.org/

Foundation type: Public charity
Limitations: Scholarships to students interested in the study of wine and food and who are residents of CA.
Financial data: Year ended 03/31/2004. Assets, $853,676 (M); Expenditures, $193,079; Total giving, $43,392.
Fields of interest: Agriculture/food, formal/general education.
Type of support: Undergraduate support.
Application information: Contact foundation for current application deadline/guidelines.
EIN: 943297049

4512
Woolworth Scholarship Fund
P.O. Box 729
San Angelo, TX 76902-0729
Application addresses: c/o Counselor's Office, San Angelo Central High School, 100 Cottonwood St., San Angelo, TX 76901, tel.: (915) 658-3511; or c/o Lakeview High School, 900 E. 43 St., San Angelo, Texas 76903, tel.: (915) 659-3500

Foundation type: Independent foundation
Limitations: Scholarships to male high school seniors, primarily in TX, who are math/science majors and are in the top 10 percent of their classes, for higher education.
Financial data: Year ended 12/31/2004. Assets, $269,492 (M); Expenditures, $14,261; Total giving, $9,750; Grants to individuals, totaling $9,750.
Fields of interest: Science; Mathematics; Men.

Type of support: Scholarships—to individuals.
Application information:
Deadline(s): Five months before graduation
Additional information: Contact fund for current application guidelines.
EIN: 756185995

4513
Greater Worcester Community Foundation, Inc.
370 Main St., Ste. 650
Worcester, MA 01608-1738 (508) 755-0980
Contact: Ann T. Lisi, Exec. Dir.; For grant information: Debra Medeiros, Sr. Prog. Off.
FAX: (508) 755-3406;
E-mail: gwcf@greaterworcester.org; Additional E-mail: atlisi@greaterworcester.org; Grant application E-mail:
dmedeiros@greaterworcester.org; URL: http://
www.greaterworcester.org

Foundation type: Community foundation
Limitations: Scholarships to students who are residents of Worcester County, MA.
Publications: Application guidelines; Annual report; Newsletter.
Financial data: Year ended 12/31/2004. Assets, $103,277,292 (M); Expenditures, $5,521,904; Total giving, $4,490,807; Grants to individuals, 245 grants totaling $338,103 (high: $5,000, low: $100).
Type of support: Support to graduates or students of specific schools; Undergraduate support.
Application information: Applications accepted. Application form required. Application form available on the grantmaker's Web site.
Initial approach: Telephone.
Copies of proposal: 2
Deadline(s): Early Mar.
Applicants should submit the following:
1) Transcripts
2) SAT
3) Letter(s) of recommendation
4) GPA
5) Financial information
6) Budget Information
Additional information: Applications available at Worcester County high schools; Interviews required for finalists; Inappropriate requests not considered or acknowledged.
EIN: 042572276

4514
Corale B. Workum Trust
c/o Fifth Third Bank
MD 1090C8, Trust Tax Dept.
Cincinnati, OH 45263 (513) 579-5310

Foundation type: Public charity
Limitations: Scholarships primarily to students at the University of Cincinnati, OH.
Financial data: Year ended 03/31/2004. Assets, $4,313,866 (M); Expenditures, $322,643; Total giving, $286,235.
Fields of interest: Jewish agencies & temples.
Type of support: Scholarships—to individuals.
Application information: Contact trust for current application deadline/guidelines.
EIN: 316019902

4515
World Affairs Council of Northern California
312 Sutter St., Ste. 200
San Francisco, CA 94108 (415) 293-4600
Contact: Jane Wales, Pres. and C.E.O.
FAX: (415) 982-5028; URL: http://
www.itsyourworld.org

Foundation type: Public charity
Limitations: Scholarships to high school students residing in CA for study abroad, and also to teachers and high school undergraduate, and graduate students for attendance at the Asilomar Conference.
Publications: Application guidelines; Informational brochure; Newsletter (including application guidelines).
Financial data: Year ended 12/31/2004. Assets, $6,317,506 (M); Expenditures, $2,662,572; Total giving, $42,760; Grants to individuals, 90 grants totaling $42,760 (high: $3,500, low: $220).
Fields of interest: International affairs, formal/ general education.
Type of support: Exchange programs; Graduate support; Precollege support; Travel grants.
Application information: Deadlines vary; Completion of formal application required; See Web site for further application information.
Program descriptions:
Asilomar Scholarship: Awards ten $350 scholarships to pre-collegiate teachers and 80 $375 scholarships to high school, undergraduate and graduate students for attendance at the Asilomar Conference. Deadline Feb. 26.
Study Abroad Scholarship: At least one scholarship of $3,000 or more every year to high school students for the Youth for Understanding (YFU) study abroad program. The scholarship covers a portion of the cost of spending a summer, semester, or academic year with a host family in Chile, France, Thailand, or any of the other 35 participating countries worldwide. Sophomores, juniors, or seniors who attend Northern California high schools and have a cumulative GPA of 3.0 or above are eligible to apply (in special circumstances, students with a cumulative GPA of 2.5 or above will be considered for summer programs only.) Deadline Dec.
EIN: 943053917

4516
WPS Foundation, Inc.
(formerly Wisconsin Public Service Foundation, Inc.)
700 N. Adams St.
Green Bay, WI 54301
Contact: P.J. Reinhard
Scholarship application address: c/o Scholarship Prog., Scholarship Assessment Svc., P.O. Box 5189, Appleton, WI 54912-5189
Application address: P.O. Box 19001, Green Bay, WI 54307-9001; URL: http://www.wpsr.com/ community/solarwise.asp

Foundation type: Company-sponsored foundation
Limitations: Scholarships to children of employees and customers of Wisconsin Public Service Corp. in WI and upper MI.
Publications: Application guidelines; Informational brochure.
Financial data: Year ended 12/31/2004. Assets, $19,161,797 (M); Expenditures, $1,034,328; Total giving, $1,017,726; Grants to individuals, totaling $171,700.

Fields of interest: Vocational education; Adult/ continuing education; Environment, forests; Agriculture; Agriculture/food; Minorities; Women.
Type of support: Employee-related scholarships; Support to graduates or students of specific schools; Technical education support; Undergraduate support.
Application information: Application form required.
Initial approach: Letter.
Deadline(s): Contact foundation for current application deadlines
Additional information: Contact foundation for more information about employee-related scholarships.
Program descriptions:
Agribusiness Scholarship Program: The program offers financial assistance to young people in the company's service territory who will enter a WI technical college or agribusiness degree program, or the Farm Short course offered at University of Wisconsin-Madison, Michigan Technological University, or Michigan State University. Ten $700 scholarships will be awarded. Information regarding the program can be obtained from the vocational/ technical college, county agricultural agent, vocational agriculture instructor, high school guidance counselor or principal, or local Public Service office. Completed forms should be mailed to the company.
Four-Year College Scholarship Program: Applicants must be sons or daughters of customers with voting residence in the retail territory of Wisconsin Public Service Corp. or Upper Peninsula Power Co. or sons or daughters of employees. Applicants must attend one of the approved colleges and rank in the upper 15 percent of their graduating classes. Scholarship award winners can receive a maximum award of $1,500 per year for four years. The amount is based on financial need. Combined scholarships must not exceed the student's financial need. Awards may be used at an approved college in WI or upper MI.
Technical Scholarship Program: The program provides graduating high school seniors with financial assistance to continue their education through enrollment in certain WI vocational and technical colleges. Recipients may pursue any one-year vocational diploma or two-year associate degree program. Each scholarship is a one-year nonrenewable scholarship of $400. Applicants must be graduating from high school in the current academic year, have applied to attend one of the participating colleges, and be residents in Wisconsin Public Service Corp. utility territory. The application must be filled out and presented to the high school principal or guidance counselor. The school sends the completed form to the school to be attended. The participating schools are: Fox Valley Technical College; Lake Shore Technical College; Mid-State Technical College, WI; Nicolet Technical College; North Central Technical College, WI; and Northeast Wisconsin Technical College. Only high school students should apply.
Minority/Female Technical College Scholarship Program: Three $400 non-renewable scholarships are awarded annually to minority or female students who enroll in non-traditional technical programs at Northeast Wisconsin Technical College.
Linus M. Stoll Technical College Scholarship: Two $1,000 renewable scholarships are awarded annually to eligible students in the service area.
Adult Student Technical College Scholarship: Awards ten $400 non-renewable scholarships for adults who have been in the workforce and are now returning to school. Applicants must be at least 25 years of age.
EIN: 396075016

4517
Bruce & Gladys Wright Charitable Trust
P.O. Box 596
309 North Allen
Edna, TX 77957
Application address: c/o Peggy Burnside, Edna High School Counselor, 1307 W. Gayle St., Edna, TX 77957, tel.: (361) 782-5255

Foundation type: Independent foundation
Limitations: Scholarships to graduates of Edna High School, TX, for undergraduate education at a college or university.
Financial data: Year ended 09/30/2005. Assets, $1,038,000 (M); Expenditures, $39,374; Total giving, $38,175; Grants to individuals, totaling $34,250.
Type of support: Support to graduates or students of specific schools; Undergraduate support.
Application information: Applications accepted. Application form required.
Deadline(s): May 1 and Dec. 1
Additional information: Applications are available at guidance counselor's office.
EIN: 316647955

4518
R. R. Wright Educational Fund
c/o Mellon Bank, N.A.
P.O. Box 185
Pittsburgh, PA 15230-9897 (412) 234-5524
Contact: Donna Bricker, Trust. Off., Mellon Financial Corp.
Application address: Donna Bricker, Mellon Bank, N.A., 1 Mellon Bank Ctr., Rm. 151-3835, Pittsburgh, PA 15258-0001

Foundation type: Independent foundation
Limitations: Scholarships to graduates of Mercer High School, PA.
Financial data: Year ended 04/30/2004. Assets, $321,374 (M); Expenditures, $24,184; Total giving, $20,850; Grants to individuals, 84 grants totaling $20,850 (high: $8,000, low: $100).
Type of support: Support to graduates or students of specific schools; Undergraduate support.
Application information: Application form required.
Additional information: Applications accepted throughout the year.
EIN: 236785914

4519
Charles L. Wright Foundation
c/o National City Bank of PA
P.O. Box 94651
Cleveland, OH 44101-4651
Application address: c/o Lisa Hibbs, Trust Off., National City Bank, 1900 E. 9th St., Cleveland, OH 44114, tel.: (216) 222-1087

Foundation type: Independent foundation
Limitations: Scholarships to seniors in the New Brighton School District, PA, for completion of a two-year degree or nursing program.
Financial data: Year ended 12/31/2004. Assets, $105,278 (M); Expenditures, $7,290; Total giving, $5,750; Grants to individuals, totaling $5,750.
Fields of interest: Nursing school/education.
Type of support: Support to graduates or students of specific schools; Undergraduate support.
Application information: Applications accepted throughout the year; Completion of formal application required.
EIN: 256217209

4520
Mae Belle Wright Trust
555 Center St.
Laguna Beach, CA 92651-1915
(949) 222-2930
Contact: Roger T. Stewart, Tr.

Foundation type: Independent foundation
Limitations: Scholarships to residents of Laguna Beach, CA.
Financial data: Year ended 06/30/2004.
Assets, $43,538 (M); Expenditures, $17,080; Total giving, $13,855; Grants to individuals, 4 grants totaling $12,855 (high: $5,000, low: $250).
Type of support: Scholarships—to individuals.
Application information: Applications accepted.
Deadline(s): None
Additional information: Contact foundation for current application guidelines.
EIN: 956053212

4521
Wu Zhong-Yi Scholarship Foundation, Inc.
15 Claremont Ave., Apt. 73
New York, NY 10027-6814
Contact: Luke C.L. Yuan, Pres.

Foundation type: Independent foundation
Limitations: Scholarships only to individuals at the Ming de School in Liu He, Jiangsu Province, China.
Financial data: Year ended 10/31/2004.
Assets, $1,018,170 (M); Expenditures, $34,753; Total giving, $28,125; Grants to individuals, totaling $28,125.
Type of support: Scholarships—to individuals; Support to graduates or students of specific schools.
Application information: Applications not accepted.
EIN: 133387111

4522
Wyandotte Public Schools Scholarship Foundation
(formerly Wyandotte Public Schools Foundation, also known as WPS Scholarship Foundation)
P.O. Box 412
Wyandotte, MI 48192-0012 (734) 246-1008
Application address: c/o Wyandotte Regional High School, Principal, 540 Eureka Rd., Wyandotte, MI 48192-5709, tel.: (734) 246-1000
E-mail: wpsf@wyandotte.org; URL: http://www.wyandotte.org/wpsf.html

Foundation type: Operating foundation
Limitations: Scholarships to students graduating from Wyandotte, MI, public high schools.
Financial data: Year ended 06/30/2003.
Assets, $414,674 (M); Expenditures, $54,185; Total giving, $51,316; Grants to individuals, 62 grants totaling $51,016 (high: $1,246, low: $100).
Type of support: Support to graduates or students of specific schools; Undergraduate support.
Application information: Deadline Apr. 28; Completion of formal application required; Application forms are available from qualifying high schools.
EIN: 382898957

4523
Helen F. Wylie Foundation
c/o Bank of America, N.A.
P.O. Box 6768
Providence, RI 02940-6768
Contact: Marilyn L. Hotch, Tr.
Application address: HC 32 Box 41C, Owls Head, ME 04854

Foundation type: Independent foundation
Limitations: Scholarships to students who have been residents of Owls Head in Knox County, ME, for at least three years prior to the date award is received.
Financial data: Year ended 12/31/2004.
Assets, $691,941 (M); Expenditures, $36,024; Total giving, $24,500; Grants to individuals, totaling $24,500.
Type of support: Technical education support; Undergraduate support.
Application information: Application form required.
Deadline(s): Apr. 30
Additional information: Application should include College Board examination scores, transcripts, three letters of reference, and a letter from the applicant.
Program description:
Wylie Scholarship Program: Candidates are recommended to the trustees by an award committee. Scholarships are for attendance at public or private colleges, universities, vocational schools, and trade schools on a full- or part-time basis. In making selections, character, citizenship, need, and ambition are considered. Awards may be by grant or loan. While it is not the intent of the trustees to award scholarships on a loan basis, it is hoped that in the years ahead recipients of scholarships will be sufficiently appreciative, successful, and motivated to ensure a continuance and expansion of this fund that they will, to the extent possible, return funds to the foundation. Recipients must be 35 years of age or under.
EIN: 010342663

4524
Eloise Strother Wyly Scholarship Trust
c/o Wachovia Bank, N.A.
100 N. Main St., 13th Fl.
Winston-Salem, NC 27150
Application address: c/o John Hostetler, Walhalla High School, Razorback Ln., Walhalla, SC 29691

Foundation type: Independent foundation
Limitations: Full-tuition scholarships to students from the Walhalla, SC, school district to attend Clemson University and Winthrop University.
Financial data: Year ended 07/31/2005.
Assets, $1,952,588 (M); Expenditures, $12,516; Total giving, $0.
Type of support: Support to graduates or students of specific schools; Undergraduate support.
Application information:
Deadline(s): Feb. 15
Additional information: Completion of formal application required, including FAF and 1040 tax return; Application forms available from Walhalla High School.
EIN: 570640726

4525
Kenneth B. Wyman Scholarship Trust
c/o KeyBank N.A.
800 Superior Ave., 4th Fl.
Cleveland, OH 44114-1306
Application address: P.O. Box 1054, Augusta, ME 04332

Foundation type: Independent foundation
Limitations: Scholarships to students who are residents of Northport, ME, for higher education.
Financial data: Year ended 04/30/2005.
Assets, $173,352 (M); Expenditures, $12,166; Total giving, $8,000; Grants to individuals, 9 grants totaling $8,000 (high: $1,000, low: $500).
Type of support: Undergraduate support.
Application information: Applications by letter accepted throughout the year.
EIN: 016075670

4526
Wyoming Community Foundation
221 Ivinson Ave., Ste. 202
Laramie, WY 82070-3038 (307) 721-8300
Contact: George H. Gault, Pres.; For grants: Samin Dadelahi, Sr. Prog. Off.
FAX: (307) 721-8333; E-mail: wcf@wycf.org; Additional tel.: (866) 708-7878; Grant application E-mail: samin@wycf.org; URL: http://www.wycf.org

Foundation type: Community foundation
Limitations: Scholarships to graduating seniors of specific WY high schools, and to nursing students in their junior or senior year at University of Wyoming.
Publications: Application guidelines; Annual report; Grants list; Informational brochure (including application guidelines); Newsletter; Program policy statement.
Financial data: Year ended 12/31/2005.
Assets, $49,340,813 (M); Expenditures, $2,093,788; Total giving, $1,931,866.
Fields of interest: Nursing school/education.
Type of support: Support to graduates or students of specific schools; Technical education support; Undergraduate support.
Application information: Applications accepted. Application form required. Application form available on the grantmaker's Web site.
Initial approach: Letter.
Deadline(s): Feb. 1.
Applicants should submit the following:
1) Transcripts
Program description:
Scholarship Program: The foundation offers numerous scholarships to students of the following WY schools: Big Piney High School, Campbell County High School, Cody High School, Evanston High School, Glenrock High School, Kemmerer High School, Niobrara County High School, Pinedale High School, Platte County High School, Rock Springs High School, St. Laurence School, and University of Wyoming. See the foundation's Web site for more information about these funds.
EIN: 830287513

4527
The Xerox Foundation
800 Long Ridge Rd.
P.O. Box 1600
Stamford, CT 06904 (203) 968-3445
Contact: Joseph M. Cahalan, V.P.
FAX: (203) 968-3330; Additional tel.: (203) 968-4416; URL: http://www.xerox.com/foundation

Foundation type: Company-sponsored foundation
Limitations: Undergraduate scholarships for minority students.
Publications: Application guidelines; Corporate giving report (including application guidelines); Informational brochure (including application guidelines); Program policy statement (including application guidelines).
Financial data: Year ended 12/31/2004. Assets, $4,294 (M); Expenditures, $605,000; Total giving, $605,000; Grants to individuals, 150 grants totaling $150,000 (high: $1,000, low: $1,000).
Fields of interest: Education; Minorities.
Type of support: Program development; Research; Technical education support; Undergraduate support; Project support.
Application information: Application form not required.
 Initial approach: Letter of request or proposal.
 Copies of proposal: 1
 Deadline(s): None
 Applicants should submit the following:
  1) Proposal
 Additional information: See Web site for further information.
EIN: 060996443

4528
Y.E.S. Opportunities, Inc.
13889 Del Webb Blvd.
Summerfield, FL 34491 (866) 297-7272
Contact: Dorothy Rice-Cobbs, Pres.
URL: http://www.yesopportunities.org

Foundation type: Independent foundation
Limitations: Scholarships of $1,000-$3,500 to individuals with a GPA of at least 2.5 who are attending or planning to attend a two- or four-year educational institution.
Publications: Informational brochure.
Financial data: Year ended 12/31/2004. Assets, $682,979 (M); Expenditures, $1,206,041; Total giving, $37,000; Grants to individuals, 37 grants totaling $37,000 (high: $1,000, low: $1,000).
Type of support: Scholarships—to individuals; Technical education support; Undergraduate support.
Application information: Application form required.
 Deadline(s): Contact foundation for application deadline
 Applicants should submit the following:
  1) Letter(s) of recommendation
  2) Financial information
  3) Transcripts
 Additional information: Application must also include SSDI verification or medical statement.
EIN: 593656796

4529
Yampa Valley Community Foundation
P.O. Box 881869
Steamboat Springs, CO 80488
(970) 879-8632
Contact: Linda Haltom, Exec. Dir.
FAX: (970) 871-0431; E-mail: donate@yvcf.org; Additional E-mail: Linda@yvcf.org; URL: http://www.yvcf.org

Foundation type: Community foundation
Limitations: Scholarships to local residents in Routt and Moffat counties, CO.

Publications: Application guidelines; Annual report; Financial statement; Grants list; Informational brochure; Newsletter.
Financial data: Year ended 12/31/2004. Assets, $5,369,533 (M); Expenditures, $1,176,458; Total giving, $649,621.
Type of support: Exchange programs; Graduate support; Technical education support; Undergraduate support; Travel grants.
Application information: Application form required.
 Additional information: Applications are available through the participating schools. See web site for various scholarship listings. Interviews required.
EIN: 840794536

4530
Marian Gaynor Yanamura Educational Fund
c/o C.O. McCawley, Jr.
P.O. Box 511
Fairhope, AL 36533-0511

Foundation type: Independent foundation
Limitations: Scholarships to graduating seniors from Fairhope and Daphne high schools, AL.
Financial data: Year ended 09/30/2004. Assets, $0 (M); Expenditures, $55,861; Total giving, $52,000; Grants to individuals, 26 grants totaling $52,000 (high: $2,000, low: $2,000).
Type of support: Support to graduates or students of specific schools; Undergraduate support.
Application information: Contact foundation for current application deadline; Completion of formal application required; Application forms are available from the two eligible high schools.
EIN: 721351380

4531
Charm & Goodloe Yancey Foundation
c/o SunTrust Bank
P.O. Box 1908
Orlando, FL 32802-1908
Contact: Blair Curtis, Chair.
Application address: P.O. Box 43326, Atlanta, GA 30336

Foundation type: Independent foundation
Limitations: Scholarships to children of employees of Yancey Brothers, Inc.
Financial data: Year ended 12/31/2004. Assets, $1,345,529 (M); Expenditures, $79,834; Total giving, $69,640; Grants to individuals, totaling $69,640.
Type of support: Employee-related scholarships.
Application information: Applications by letter accepted throughout the year.
EIN: 581413050

4532
Alice M. Yarnold and Samuel Yarnold Scholarship Trust
180 Locust St.
Dover, NH 03820
Contact: Stephen H. Roberts, Tr.

Foundation type: Independent foundation
Limitations: Scholarships to financially needy postsecondary students in the fields of nursing, medicine, and social work, who are also NH residents.
Financial data: Year ended 12/31/2004. Assets, $870,950 (M); Expenditures, $49,814;

Total giving, $42,786; Grants to individuals, totaling $42,786.
Fields of interest: Vocational education; Medical school/education; Nursing school/education; Human services.
Type of support: Graduate support; Technical education support; Undergraduate support.
Application information: Deadline May 14; Completion of formal application required, including transcripts, FAFSA, essay, and two letters of recommendation, at least one of which is from a professor or instructor at the applicant's school.
Program description:
 Scholarship Program: Applicants must already be studying at postsecondary institutions. Scholarships are renewable.
EIN: 020476417

4533
Charles F. & Mary M. Yeiser Foundation
c/o Carew Twr.
441 Vine St. Tower, Ste. 4001
Cincinnati, OH 45202 (513) 621-1384

Foundation type: Independent foundation
Limitations: Scholarships to residents of OH.
Financial data: Year ended 12/31/2004. Assets, $6,253 (M); Expenditures, $65,175; Total giving, $65,175; Grants to individuals, 19 grants totaling $65,175 (high: $3,500, low: $36).
Type of support: Scholarships—to individuals.
Application information: Applications accepted throughout the year; Initial approach by letter; Completion of formal application required.
EIN: 316033638

4534
Martha E. Yerkes Scholarship Trust
(formerly Martha E. Yerkes Scholarship Foundation)
c/o Wachovia Bank, N.A.
100 N. Main St., 13th Fl.
Winston-Salem, NC 27150
Scholarship URL: http://www.wachoviascholars.com/yerk/csaw_yerkes_deadline.php

Foundation type: Independent foundation
Limitations: Scholarships to high school graduates residing in Chester County, PA, for higher education.
Financial data: Year ended 12/31/2004. Assets, $211,294 (M); Expenditures, $6,698; Total giving, $5,500; Grants to individuals, totaling $5,500.
Type of support: Undergraduate support.
Application information: Deadline Apr. 4; Contact foundation for current guidelines.
EIN: 236441277

4535
W. T. Yett Charitable Foundation
c/o Frost National Bank, Trust Dept.
P.O. Box 2950
San Antonio, TX 78299-2950

Foundation type: Independent foundation
Limitations: Scholarships to high school graduates in Blanco County, TX.
Financial data: Year ended 12/31/2002. Assets, $798,183 (M); Expenditures, $72,337; Total giving, $43,650.
Type of support: Undergraduate support.
Application information:
 Deadline(s): None.

Additional information: Contact foundation for current application guidelines.
EIN: 742640368

4536
Yoder Brothers Memorial Scholarship Fund
(formerly Joshua Yoder Memorial Scholarship)
11952 Collier's Reserve Dr.
Naples, FL 34110
Contact: Timothy Yoder, Tr.; Kara Yoder, Tr.
Application address: 17460 Old State Rd., Middlefield, OH 44062

Foundation type: Independent foundation
Limitations: Scholarships to students at Cardinal High School and other Geauga County, OH, high schools.
Financial data: Year ended 12/31/2004. Assets, $423,778 (M); Expenditures, $79,304; Total giving, $45,000; Grants to individuals, totaling $45,000.
Type of support: Support to graduates or students of specific schools; Undergraduate support.
Application information: Contact fund for current application deadline; Completion of formal application required, including essay on applicant's activities, description of need for financial aid, transcripts, and two letters of recommendation (one from a teacher and the other from a minister, pastor, employer, or school guidance counselor).
EIN: 341848189

4537
Yopst Educational Loan Fund Trust
c/o Wells Fargo Bank Indiana, N.A.
841 N. Cass St.
Wabash, IN 46992 (260) 563-6378
Contact: William C. Coleman, Trust Off., Wells Fargo Bank Indiana, N.A.

Foundation type: Independent foundation
Limitations: Loans to residents of Wabash County or its five bordering counties for higher education.
Financial data: Year ended 08/31/2002. Assets, $2,185,208 (M); Expenditures, $115,102; Total giving, $91,111; Loans to individuals, 342 loans totaling $91,111.
Type of support: Support to graduates or students of specific schools; Undergraduate support.
Application information: Contact trust for current application deadlines; Completion of formal application required, including proof of residence, high school and college transcripts, and references.
EIN: 351971478

4538
York County Medical Society Educational Trust
c/o M&T Trust Co.
21 E. Market St., M/C 401-130
York, PA 17401-1500
Contact: Rhonda S. Renninger, Exec. Dir.
Application address: c/o York Hospital, 1001 S. George St., York, PA 17405, tel.: (717) 843-6744

Foundation type: Independent foundation
Limitations: Scholarships and student loans to financially needy residents of York County, PA, who are pursuing a medical education.
Financial data: Year ended 12/31/2004. Assets, $370,879 (M); Expenditures, $42,494; Total giving, $42,000; Loans to individuals, totaling $42,000.

Fields of interest: Medical school/education.
Type of support: Scholarships—to individuals; Student loans—to individuals.
Application information: Deadline June 30; Applicants should submit a brief resume including academic records, financial need, status, and intended goals in pursuing medical studies.
EIN: 236284266

4539
Ralph W. Young Family Foundation
108 W. Chevalier Ct.
Eighty Four, PA 15330

Foundation type: Independent foundation
Limitations: Scholarships primarily to individuals for attendance at PA colleges and universities, as well as for nursing education.
Financial data: Year ended 12/31/2004. Assets, $7,915,565 (M); Expenditures, $371,970; Total giving, $286,323; Grants to individuals, 10 grants totaling $49,780.
Fields of interest: Nursing school/education.
Type of support: Undergraduate support.
Application information:
   Deadline(s): Contact foundation for current application deadlines/guidelines
EIN: 306009141

4540
The Young Family Foundation
115 W. Putnam
Ganado, TX 77962
Application addresses: c/o Ganado High School, 510 W. Devers, Ganado, TX 77962; c/o Louise High School, 408 2nd St., Louise, TX 77455, c/o Tidehaven High School, P.O. Box 159, El Maton, TX 77440

Foundation type: Independent foundation
Limitations: Scholarships to graduates of Ganado High School, TX, Louise High School, TX, and Tidehaven High School, TX for attendance at a TX college or university.
Financial data: Year ended 09/30/2005. Assets, $1,142,741 (M); Expenditures, $57,029; Total giving, $53,351; Grants to individuals, 20 grants totaling $41,250 (high: $4,500, low: $750).
Type of support: Support to graduates or students of specific schools; Undergraduate support.
Application information: Applications accepted. Application form required.
   Initial approach: Contact high school guidance counselor.
   Deadline(s): May 1 for initial application and Jan. 1 for renewals
EIN: 742979295

4541
Coleman A. Young Foundation
2111 Woodward Ave., Ste. 600
Detroit, MI 48201 (313) 962-2200
Contact: Claudette Y. Smith Ph.D., Exec. Dir.
FAX: (313) 962-2208;
E-mail: claudettesmith@cayf.org; URL: http://www.cayf.org

Foundation type: Public charity
Limitations: Scholarships to residents of Detroit, MI, for higher education.
Publications: Application guidelines; Annual report; Financial statement; Informational brochure (including application guidelines); Newsletter.

Financial data: Year ended 12/31/2004. Assets, $2,201,719 (M); Expenditures, $614,738; Total giving, $174,274; Grants to individuals, 38 grants totaling $174,274 (high: $5,000, low: $4,000).
Type of support: Undergraduate support.
Application information: Application form required. Application form available on the grantmaker's Web site.
   Copies of proposal: 1
   Deadline(s): Apr. 1
   Applicants should submit the following:
      1) Transcripts
      2) SAT
      3) Letter(s) of recommendation
      4) GPA
      5) Financial information
      6) FAFSA
      7) FAF
      8) Essay
      9) Curriculum vitae
      10) Budget Information
      11) ACT
   Additional information: Contact foundation for current application deadline/guidelines.
Program description:
   Coleman A. Young Scholars Program: Awards four-year, renewable scholarships with a total value of $20,000, payable in annual $5,000 increments. Applicants must plan to attend one of the country's fully-accredited, historically- black colleges or universities, or an accredited, four-year college or university in Michigan.
EIN: 382400801

4542
Walter & Carole Young Foundation
P.O. Box 185
Woodsville, NH 03785 (603) 747-3351

Foundation type: Independent foundation
Limitations: Scholarships to students who have been legal residents of the towns of Bath, Benton, and Haverhill, NH, and Groton, Newbury, and Ryegate, VT, for at least three years prior to graduation. Recipients may attend accredited two- and four-year colleges, vocational/technical schools, trade schools, and short-term training programs.
Financial data: Year ended 12/31/2004. Assets, $163,115 (M); Expenditures, $59,222; Total giving, $59,000; Grants to individuals, totaling $59,000.
Fields of interest: Vocational education.
Type of support: Technical education support; Undergraduate support.
Application information:
   Deadline(s): Apr. 15
   Additional information: Initial approach by letter requesting application or through applicant's high school guidance counselor or principal; Completion of formal application required, including transcripts, financial information, letter of acceptance from an accredited school, and evaluation by a teacher, faculty advisor, or employer.
EIN: 020349358

4543
Judson Young Memorial Educational Foundation, Inc.
P.O. Box 459
100 W. 4th St.
Salem, MO 65560 (573) 729-3137
Contact: Geriann C. Ball, Secy.

Foundation type: Independent foundation
Limitations: Student loans to graduates in the Salem, MO, area. Preference is given to graduates of Salem High School, MO.
Financial data: Year ended 12/31/2004. Assets, $4,005,724 (M); Expenditures, $176,362; Total giving, $129,297; Loans to individuals, 18 loans totaling $31,467.
Type of support: Support to graduates or students of specific schools; Undergraduate support.
Application information: Deadlines Aug. 15 for fall term, Dec. 15 for winter term, and May 15 for summer term; Completion of formal application required with two copies.
EIN: 436061841

4544
John B. & Brownie Young Memorial Fund
c/o BB&T
230 Frederica St.
Owensboro, KY 42301 (270) 688-7878

Foundation type: Independent foundation
Limitations: Scholarships and awards to students in school districts of Owensboro, Daviess, and McLean counties, KY.
Financial data: Year ended 12/31/2004. Assets, $18,207,250 (M); Expenditures, $932,787; Total giving, $764,100; Grants to individuals, totaling $760,600.
Type of support: Support to graduates or students of specific schools; Undergraduate support.
Application information: Application form required.
  Deadline(s): Feb.
  Applicants should submit the following:
    1) Essay
    2) Financial information
    3) ACT
    4) GPA
EIN: 616025137

4545
Alden N. Young Trust
1500 Worcester Rd.
Framingham, MA 01702
Application address: c/o Nancy S. Smith, 2676 Wakefield Rd., Wakefield, NH 03872-4375, tel.: (603) 522-3373

Foundation type: Independent foundation
Limitations: Scholarships to individuals for higher education who are residents of Wakefield, NH.
Financial data: Year ended 12/31/2004. Assets, $3,385,847 (M); Expenditures, $203,606; Total giving, $159,420; Grants to individuals, 50 grants totaling $94,420 (high: $4,000, low: $39).
Type of support: Undergraduate support.
Application information: Applications accepted.
  Deadline(s): None
  Additional information: Contact trust for current application guidelines.
EIN: 026117755

4546
Youth Foundation, Inc.
36 W. 44th St., Ste. 716
New York, NY 10036-8144 (212) 840-6291
Contact: Johanna M. Lee
FAX: (212) 840-6747; E-mail: youthfdn@aol.com; URL: http://foundationcenter.org/grantmaker/youthfdn

Foundation type: Independent foundation

Limitations: Scholarships for undergraduate study to high school seniors who are U.S. citizens.
Publications: Application guidelines; Program policy statement.
Financial data: Year ended 12/31/2004. Assets, $10,463,169 (M); Expenditures, $588,109; Total giving, $346,500; Grants to individuals, 89 grants totaling $329,000 (high: $4,000, low: $2,500).
Type of support: Scholarships—to individuals; Undergraduate support.
Application information: Application form required.
  Initial approach: Letter or e-mail.
  Deadline(s): Feb. 28
  Applicants should submit the following:
    1) Transcripts
    2) SAT
    3) SASE
    4) GPA
    5) Financial information
    6) Essay
    7) Curriculum vitae
    8) ACT
  Additional information: Applicant must complete "request for application" form to receive application; Only "request for application" form available online; Application must also include SASE and two letters of recommendation; Final notification in May.
Program description:
  Alexander and Maude Hadden Scholarships: Awarded to secondary school seniors with a B+ average or better for undergraduate college education at a four-year college or university with need as well as ability. The scholarships are paid to the institution as tuition. Requests for application forms must be accompanied by a written recommendation from an administrative or faculty member of an educational institution. Approximately 25 new scholarships are awarded each year. Application for renewal of a scholarship will be considered upon filing a renewal application form no later than April 15th. No study abroad aid except "Junior Year Abroad," etc., where credit is given toward a degree from an American institution.
EIN: 136093036

4547
Youth Ministry, Inc.
3616 Wickersham Ln.
Winston-Salem, NC 27106 (336) 924-1505
Contact: Sarah K. Bush, Secy.-Treas.
E-mail: sbush513@earthlink.net

Foundation type: Independent foundation
Limitations: Scholarships to students pursuing biblical and theological studies, prior to their ordination.
Publications: Annual report; Informational brochure.
Financial data: Year ended 12/31/2004. Assets, $40,213 (M); Expenditures, $61,527; Total giving, $56,998; Grants to individuals, totaling $56,998.
Fields of interest: Theological school/education.
Type of support: Graduate support; Undergraduate support.
Application information: Contact foundation for current application deadline and for application form; Initial approach by e-mail; Completion of formal application required, including letter outlining academic standing, church affiliation, activities, and financial information.
EIN: 581366662

4548
Daniel Zaccheus Foundation
c/o PNC Advisors
620 Liberty Ave.
Pittsburgh, PA 15222-2705
Application address: c/o PNC Advisors, 2 PNC Plz., 5th Fl., Pittsburgh, PA 15222-2705

Foundation type: Independent foundation
Limitations: Scholarships to graduate students studying astronomy and astrophysics in PA.
Financial data: Year ended 12/31/2003. Assets, $586,890 (M); Expenditures, $33,135; Total giving, $27,000; Grants to individuals, 10 grants totaling $27,000 (high: $9,000, low: $400).
Fields of interest: Astronomy; Space/aviation; Physics.
Type of support: Graduate support.
Application information: Applications accepted throughout the year; Application by letter, including letter of recommendation from university department head outlining background and experience of applicant.
EIN: 256065413

4549
Edward B. Zahn FFA Scholarship Trust at the Iola High School
c/o Richard W. Zahn
P.O. Box 388
Oldwick, NJ 08858
Application address: c/o David South, Principal, Lola High School, 300 E. Jackson Ave., Iola, KS 66749

Foundation type: Operating foundation
Limitations: Scholarships to Iola High School FFA members to pursue postsecondary training in the agricultural field, KS.
Financial data: Year ended 12/31/2003. Assets, $32,870 (M); Expenditures, $10,200; Total giving, $10,000; Grants to individuals, 5 grants totaling $10,000 (high: $2,750, low: $500).
Fields of interest: Agriculture/food, formal/general education.
Type of support: Support to graduates or students of specific schools; Undergraduate support.
Application information: Applications accepted throughout the year; Completion of formal application required.
EIN: 486327729

4550
Angela M. Zampogna Scholarship Fund
c/o Enterprise Bank
222 Merrimack St.
Lowell, MA 01852
Contact: Raymond F. LaFond, Tr.
Application address: 333 Betty Spring Rd., Gardner, MA 01440, tel.: (978) 632-8558

Foundation type: Independent foundation
Limitations: Scholarships to graduates of Gardner High School, MA.
Financial data: Year ended 12/31/2004. Assets, $577,768 (M); Expenditures, $32,429; Total giving, $25,500; Grants to individuals, totaling $25,500.
Type of support: Support to graduates or students of specific schools; Undergraduate support.
Application information: Contact fund for current application deadline; Completion of formal application required, including transcript.
EIN: 223193009

4551
The Anne and Henry Zarrow Foundation
401 S. Boston, Ste. 900
Tulsa, OK 74103-4012 (918) 295-8004
Contact: Jeanne Gillert, Grants Mgr.
FAX: (918) 295-8049; E-mail (for Jeanne Gillert): jgillert@zarrow.com; URL: http://www.zarrow.com/ahz.htm

Foundation type: Independent foundation
Limitations: Scholarships to financially needy residents of the Tulsa, OK, area, who are under 28 years old.
Publications: Application guidelines.
Financial data: Year ended 12/31/2004. Assets, $96,864,858 (M); Expenditures, $5,788,486; Total giving, $5,440,247; Grants to individuals, 109 grants totaling $449,265 (high: $24,025, low: $121, average grant: $1,500-$7,500).
Type of support: Scholarships—to individuals.
Application information: Contact foundation for current application deadline; Initial approach by letter; Completion of formal application required, including student's and parents' latest tax returns and letter of recommendation.
EIN: 731286874

4552
Delyte K. Zearing and Robert I. Zearing Trust
c/o Citizens First National Bank
606 S. Main St.
Princeton, IL 61356-2013 (815) 875-4444
Contact: Robert B. Schneider
Application address: c/o Regional Office of Education, 313 N. Canal St., Annawn, IL 61234

Foundation type: Independent foundation
Limitations: Scholarships to students at Bureau County, IL, high schools to attend the University of Illinois at Urbana-Champaign.
Financial data: Year ended 12/31/2004. Assets, $1,143,412 (M); Expenditures, $94,221; Total giving, $65,500; Grants to individuals, totaling $65,500.
Type of support: Support to graduates or students of specific schools; Undergraduate support.
Application information: Deadline Mar. 31; Completion of formal application required, including three letters of support attesting to the applicant's scholarship, citizenship, leadership, and probability of success in college.
Program description:
Delyte K. and Robert I. Zearing Scholarships: Graduates of Bureau County, IL, high schools who rank in the top 10 percent of their graduating classes, have a minimum composite score of 24 on the ACT, and who have been accepted to University of Illinois at Urbana-Champaign may apply for these $2,500 per year scholarships. Scholarships are renewable provided that the recipient maintains a minimum GPA of 3.75 on the University of Illinois' five-point scale and provides evidence of earning a minimum of 15 credit hours per semester. Financial need is not a factor in determining eligibility.
EIN: 366980732

4553
Zeta Psi Educational Foundation
15 South Henry St.
Pearl River, NY 10965 (845) 735-1847
Contact: Richard Breeswine, Exec. Dir.
E-mail: exec.director@zetapsi.org; URL: http://www.zetapsi.org

Foundation type: Public charity
Limitations: Scholarships to members of Zeta Psi Fraternity.
Financial data: Year ended 05/31/2003. Assets, $2,636,861 (M); Expenditures, $719,015; Total giving, $238,595; Grants to individuals, 180 grants totaling $238,595 (high: $2,500, low: $250).
Fields of interest: Students, sororities/fraternities; Men.
Type of support: Undergraduate support.
Application information: Deadlines Feb. 15 and Oct. 15; Completion of formal application required, including financial information and biographical information; Application available on Web site.
Program description:
Zeta Psi Scholarship Program: Awards up to $1,400 per semester. Scholarships are renewable.
EIN: 131832953

4554
Olia & Michael Zetkin Memorial Scholarship
481 Carol Pl.
Pelham, NY 10803-2111 (914) 738-4998
Contact: Arthur Rabin, Pres.

Foundation type: Independent foundation
Limitations: Scholarships to students of classical vocal music who are NY residents, to pursue further studies.
Financial data: Year ended 05/31/2005. Assets, $385,316 (M); Expenditures, $17,634; Total giving, $17,000; Grants to individuals, totaling $17,000.
Fields of interest: Music; Performing arts, education.
Type of support: Undergraduate support.
Application information: Applications accepted.
Initial approach: Letter.
Deadline(s): None
Additional information: Applicants must apply through The Juilliard School.
EIN: 133010508

4555
Zichron Tzvi, Inc.
661 7th St.
Lakewood, NJ 08701 (732) 367-9497
Contact: Naphtali Bassman, Pres.

Foundation type: Independent foundation
Limitations: Educational grants to rabbis.
Financial data: Year ended 12/31/2004. Assets, $22,980 (M); Expenditures, $8,863; Total giving, $6,360; Grants to individuals, 2 grants totaling $6,360.
Fields of interest: Theological school/education; Jewish agencies & temples.
Type of support: Scholarships—to individuals.
Application information: Contact foundation for current application deadline; Initial approach by letter or telephone.
EIN: 223087544

4556
The Christopher Zider Scholarship Fund
c/o Marchon Eyewear, Inc.
3000 Sand Hill Rd., Bldg. 1, Ste. 235
Menlo Park, CA 94025 (650) 233-8700

Foundation type: Company-sponsored foundation
Limitations: Scholarships to residents of Atherton, East Palo Alto, Menlo Park, Palo Alto, Portola Valley, Stanford, and Woodside, CA, high schools, to be used in any of the next six years to attend public or private secondary schools or four-year colleges. Any student who attends Menlo School or Woodside High School is also eligible.
Financial data: Year ended 12/31/2004. Assets, $481,001 (M); Expenditures, $51,961; Total giving, $46,094; Grants to individuals, 11 grants totaling $44,094 (high: $15,000, low: $1,000).
Type of support: Support to graduates or students of specific schools; Precollege support; Undergraduate support.
Application information: Application form required.
Deadline(s): Mar. 23 (preliminary) and May 18 (full invited applications)
Additional information: Interviews required.
EIN: 946655102

4557
The Herbert C. Ziegler Foundation
4150 Millennium Blvd. S.E.
Massillon, OH 44646-7449 (330) 834-3332
Contact: William C. Ziegler, Tr.

Foundation type: Independent foundation
Limitations: Scholarships to OH employees of The Ziegler Tire and Supply Company and The Ziegler Oil Company, and to their children.
Financial data: Year ended 11/30/2004. Assets, $792,626 (M); Expenditures, $41,835; Total giving, $39,350.
Type of support: Employee-related scholarships.
Application information: Applications accepted throughout the year; Completion of formal application required, including four character references.
EIN: 341381823

4558
Fred B. and Ruth B. Zigler Foundation
P.O. Box 986
Jennings, LA 70546-0986 (337) 824-2413
Contact: Julie G. Berry, Pres.
FAX: (337) 824-2414

Foundation type: Independent foundation
Limitations: Scholarships to graduating seniors of Jefferson Davis Parish, LA, high schools.
Publications: Annual report.
Financial data: Year ended 12/31/2004. Assets, $8,031,266 (M); Expenditures, $558,077; Total giving, $374,437.
Type of support: Support to graduates or students of specific schools; Undergraduate support.
Application information: Application form required.
Initial approach: Letter.
Deadline(s): Contact foundation for current application deadline.
Applicants should submit the following:
   1) SAT
   2) ACT
   3) Financial information
   4) GPA
   5) Letter(s) of recommendation
   6) Transcripts
Additional information: Applications available at Jefferson Davis Parish High School; Scholarships are awarded on the basis of financial need and the ability to perform college-level work.
Program description:
Zigler Scholarship Program: Scholarships are awarded on the basis of financial need and the ability to perform college-level work.
EIN: 726019403

4559
Zimmer Family Foundation
5803 Glenmont Dr.
Houston, TX 77081-1701 (713) 295-7200
Contact: George Zimmer, Chair.

Foundation type: Independent foundation
Limitations: Scholarships primarily to residents of CA and TX.
Financial data: Year ended 12/31/2003.
Assets, $3,504,848 (M); Expenditures, $1,396,388; Total giving, $1,345,347; Grants to individuals, 139 grants totaling $588,607 (high: $9,843, low: $431).
Type of support: Scholarships—to individuals.
Application information: Applications by letter accepted throughout the year.
EIN: 760370782

4560
The Mabel Zimmerman and Adelia Klinger Scholarship Fund
(formerly The Mabel and Adelia Zimmerman Foundation)
c/o Fulton Financial Advisors, N.A.
P.O. Box 3215
Lancaster, PA 17604-3215
Application address: c/o Fulton Financial Advisors, N.A., 555 Willow St., Lebanon, PA 17042

Foundation type: Independent foundation
Limitations: Undergraduate and graduate scholarships to Pine Grove Area High School seniors and graduates who currently reside, and were born in, the Pine Grove Area High School District, PA, as it was constituted in 1981.
Financial data: Year ended 07/31/2005.
Assets, $1,269,960 (M); Expenditures, $84,745; Total giving, $72,015; Grants to individuals, totaling $72,015.
Type of support: Support to graduates or students of specific schools; Graduate support; Undergraduate support.
Application information: Deadline Apr. 30; Completion of formal application required.
Program description:
Scholarship Program: There is a limit of one award per individual, either as a high school senior or a college student, unless the individual is a native Ravine, PA, resident, in which case they are entitled to one additional award. At the time of application to the foundation, the student must be accepted into a baccalaureate or master's degree program at a college or university.
EIN: 236887468

4561
Hans and Clara Davis Zimmerman Foundation
c/o Bank of Hawaii
1164 Bishop St., Ste. 800
Honolulu, HI 96802-3170 (808) 537-6333

Foundation type: Independent foundation
Limitations: Scholarships to financially needy full-time students who are legal residents of HI for studies at accredited two- and four-year colleges and universities that would lead to careers in the fields of medicine, nursing, or other health-related fields.
Publications: Informational brochure (including application guidelines).
Financial data: Year ended 12/31/2004.
Assets, $13,983,711 (M); Expenditures, $778,307; Total giving, $653,025; Grants to

individuals, 327 grants totaling $653,025 (high: $6,000, low: $500).
Fields of interest: Medical school/education; Nursing school/education; Health sciences school/education.
Type of support: Undergraduate support.
Application information: Deadline Mar. 1; Initial approach by letter or telephone; Completion of formal application required, including transcripts, a personal statement, two letters of recommendation, and SAR.
Program description:
Hans & Clara Davis Zimmerman Foundation Health & Education Scholarships: The foundation awards these scholarships to students in the last year of a BSN or RN program in HI. To be considered for this scholarship, applicants must respond to the following two questions in their personal statements:
· Why did you choose nursing as a career?
· Who or what most influenced your decision to study nursing?
All scholarships are based on financial need and are renewable. Applicants to this foundation may automatically be considered for other scholarship programs administered by the Hawaii Community Foundation. Employees or direct relatives of employees of the Hawaii Community Foundation are ineligible.
EIN: 996006669

4562
Zimmerman Scholarship Fund
(formerly Martin H. Zimmerman Scholarship Trust)
c/o Wachovia Bank, N.A.
100 N. Main St., 13th Fl.
Winston-Salem, NC 27150 (800) 576-5135
Contact: Scholarships: Christopher W. Spaugh
Application address: 4259 W. Swamp Rd., Ste. 310, Doylestown, PA 18901

Foundation type: Independent foundation
Limitations: Scholarships to Pennridge High School graduates or other public school graduates living in the Pennridge, PA, area at the time of graduation.
Financial data: Year ended 06/30/2005.
Assets, $529,106 (M); Expenditures, $22,768; Total giving, $20,788; Grants to individuals, totaling $20,788.
Type of support: Support to graduates or students of specific schools; Undergraduate support.
Application information: Applications accepted. Application form required.
Deadline(s): Mar. 15.
EIN: 236688479

4563
The Father Joe Znotas Memorial Scholarship Fund
3010 Lyons Rd.
Austin, TX 78702-3639
Contact: Rev. Msgr. Lonnie Reyes, Pres.

Foundation type: Independent foundation
Limitations: Scholarships to graduates of high schools in Austin, TX.
Financial data: Year ended 12/31/2003.
Assets, $50,892 (M); Expenditures, $833,068; Total giving, $50,900; Grants to individuals, 52 grants totaling $50,900 (high: $2,000, low: $162).
Type of support: Undergraduate support.
Application information: Deadline Apr. 30; Completion of formal application required.
EIN: 742157960

4564
Don and Julia Zumwalt Scholarship Fund
c/o Wells Fargo Bank Nevada, N.A.
P.O. Box 95021
Henderson, NV 89009
Application address: Ted Gehrman, Secondary Supt., Klamath County School District, Veterans Memorial Bldg., Klamath Falls, OR 97601, tel.: (541) 882-7721

Foundation type: Independent foundation
Limitations: Scholarships to graduating seniors at Klamath County high schools, OR.
Financial data: Year ended 12/31/2004.
Assets, $181,336 (M); Expenditures, $10,871; Total giving, $7,500; Grants to individuals, 8 grants totaling $7,500 (high: $2,500, low: $500).
Type of support: Support to graduates or students of specific schools; Undergraduate support.
Application information: Application form required.
Initial approach: Letter.
Deadline(s): Prior to high school graduation
EIN: 936034766

4565
Hattie Zurfluh Scholarship Fund
c/o Wells Fargo Bank Texas, N.A.
P.O. Box 2626
Waco, TX 76702 (254) 714-6160

Foundation type: Independent foundation
Limitations: Scholarships for higher education to Waco, TX, high school seniors.
Financial data: Year ended 12/31/2004.
Assets, $492,349 (M); Expenditures, $24,551; Total giving, $19,500; Grants to individuals, totaling $19,500.
Type of support: Support to graduates or students of specific schools; Undergraduate support.
Application information: Application form required.
Deadline(s): Mar.
Applicants should submit the following:
1) Class rank
2) SAT
3) GPA
4) ACT
EIN: 746370513

4566
Harry R. & Gertrude Zweifel Trust
P.O. Box 584
Freeport, IL 61032

Foundation type: Independent foundation
Limitations: Scholarships for postsecondary education to residents of Orangeville, IL, Stephenson County, IL, and Green County, WI.
Financial data: Year ended 12/31/2004.
Assets, $434,140 (M); Expenditures, $26,687; Total giving, $12,361; Grants to individuals, 39 grants totaling $12,361 (high: $400, low: $200).
Type of support: Undergraduate support.
Application information: Application form required.
Deadline(s): Aug. 1
Program description:
Zweifel Scholarship Program: Support is only available in the first four years after high school graduation. Preference is given first to Orangeville, IL, residents, second to Stephenson County, IL, residents, and last to residents of Green County, WI.
EIN: 366063248

GENERAL WELFARE

This section lists sources for all types of grants, loans, and in-kind services provided by grantmakers on an emergency or long-term basis to individuals for personal, living, or medical expenses. Many of these grants are paid to the hospitals, doctors, or agencies that actually render the service rather than to the individuals. Some require a referral from a social service agency or a doctor; others accept direct applications by individuals.

Also included in this section are grants, loans, and in-kind services provided by grantmakers on an emergency or long-term basis to company employees, former employees, or families of employees for general welfare assistance.

Welfare programs that restrict their giving to artists or those involved in cultural endeavors are not included in this section; such programs may be found in the "Arts and Cultural Support" section.

Entries are arranged alphabetically by grantmaker name. Access to grants by specific subject areas, types of support, and geographic focus, is provided in the "Subject," "Types of Support," "Geographic Focus," and "International Giving" indexes in the back of the book.

Limitations on giving are indicated when available. *The limitations statement should be checked carefully as a grantmaker will reject any application that does not fall within the grantmaker's geographic area, recipient type, or field of interest.*

REMEMBER: IF YOU DON'T QUALIFY, DON'T APPLY.

4567
A Good Day Foundation
414 Walnut St., Ste. 1014
Cincinnati, OH   45202-3913
Contact: Michelle Kelley, Secy.-Treas.

Foundation type: Operating foundation
Limitations: Grants to economically disadvantaged individuals and victims of illness or emergencies, primarily in KY and OH.
Financial data: Year ended 06/30/2005.
Assets, $443,143 (M); Expenditures, $676,125; Total giving, $619,153; Grants to individuals, 94 grants totaling $619,153 (high: $26,000, low: $55).
Fields of interest: Human services, emergency aid; Human services, victim aid.
Type of support: Grants for special needs.
Application information: Applications by letter accepted throughout the year.
EIN: 223885978

4568
The Clara Abbott Foundation
1505 White Oak Dr.
Waukegan, IL   60085   (800) 972-3859
Contact: Glenn S. Warner, V.P. and Exec. Dir.
URL: http://clara.abbott.com

Foundation type: Independent foundation
Limitations: Special relief grants and loans, and aid for the aged and economically disadvantaged, only to children of employees and retirees who have worked at Abbott Laboratories for at least one year.
Publications: Annual report (including application guidelines); Financial statement; Informational brochure.
Financial data: Year ended 12/31/2004.
Assets, $274,447,766 (M); Expenditures, $22,380,946; Total giving, $13,613,681; Grants to individuals, totaling $13,613,681; Loans to individuals, totaling $417,000.
Fields of interest: Aging; Economically disadvantaged.
Type of support: Employee-related welfare.
Application information: Applications accepted throughout the year; Completion of formal application required.
EIN: 366069632

4569
ADA Foundation
(formerly American Dental Association Health Foundation)
211 E. Chicago Ave.
Chicago, IL   60611-2678   (312) 440-2547
Contact: Arthur A. Dugoni D.D.S., Pres.
FAX: (312) 440-3526; E-mail: adaf@ada.org;
URL: http://www.ada.org/ada/prod/adaf/index.asp

Foundation type: Public charity
Limitations: Financial assistance to dentists and their dependents who, because of accidental injury, a medical condition or advanced age, are not self-supporting. Grants also to members of the dental profession who are victims of disasters.
Publications: Application guidelines; Annual report; Informational brochure; Newsletter.
Financial data: Year ended 12/31/2004.
Assets, $22,713,944 (M); Expenditures, $6,374,074; Total giving, $645,778.
Type of support: Emergency funds; Grants for special needs.

Application information: Applications accepted. Application form required. Application form available on the grantmaker's Web site.
Initial approach): E-mail.
Deadline(s): Vary
Additional information: Contact foundation for application guidelines.
Program descriptions:
Relief Grant: All applications are initiated by either the dentist's component or constituent dental society. The application is investigated by the constituent society relief fund to ascertain the eligibility of the applicant, the amount of assistance required, and the duration of the grant. Once the application has been approved by the constituent society relief fund, it is forwarded, along with recommendations for action, to the ADAF for consideration. After the application is reviewed by the Charitable Assistance Programs Committee for completeness, it is voted upon. If approved, the constituent relief fund and ADA Foundation share equally in the funding of the grant. Individuals applying to the ADAF Relief Grant Program for the first time, apply for an initial grant, which can be given for a maximum of six months. The grant recipient receives a check each month from the ADAF Relief Grant Program. Subsequent extensions to an initial grant, a renewal grant, may be made for a maximum period of 12 months. Requests to renew either grant involve the same application process as an initial grant. An emergency grant can be made in cases of special emergency and is a single payment. An emergency grant can be given only once to an individual.
Disaster Assistance: The purpose of disaster grants is to provide a small measure of immediate financial assistance to needy eligible beneficiaries, as defined in this section, who are victims of a disaster. A disaster is defined as a "sudden occurrence which inflicts widespread catastrophic damage to a large geographic area and/or which generally affects a large number of individuals". Disasters can be both natural and caused by human conduct. Examples include, but are not necessarily limited to: civil disorders (excluding acts of war), explosions, fires, tornadoes, earthquakes, floods, tidal waves, forest fires and hurricanes. Any dentist who is a victim of a disaster may apply to the ADA Foundation for a grant. As a result of the disaster, the applicant must show that he or she suffered property damages. The grant amount for any disaster applicant shall be determined at the discretion of the Board based on applicant needs, but shall not exceed $2,500, depending on funds available.
EIN: 366132046

4570
Emma J. Adams Memorial Fund, Inc.
862 Park Ave.
New York, NY   10021
Contact: Edward R. Finch, Jr., Pres.
FAX: (212) 327-0593

Foundation type: Independent foundation
Limitations: Welfare assistance primarily through institutions to senior citizens and economically disadvantaged individuals residing in the greater New York, NY, metropolitan area.
Publications: Application guidelines.
Financial data: Year ended 12/31/2004.
Assets, $3,907,866 (M); Expenditures, $464,599; Total giving, $209,547; Grants to individuals, 35 grants totaling $209,547 (high: $10,000, low: $75).
Fields of interest: Aging; Economically disadvantaged.

Type of support: Emergency funds; Grants for special needs.
Application information: Applications accepted. Application form required.
Initial approach: Letter outlining financial need.
Deadline(s): Contact foundation for current application deadlines.
Applicants should submit the following:
1) Financial information
Additional information: Interviews required.
EIN: 136116503

4571
The Agape Foundation
3603 N. 7th Ave., Ste. 14
Phoenix, AZ   85013-3638
Contact: Ruth Flack

Foundation type: Operating foundation
Limitations: Awards to families with special needs children.
Financial data: Year ended 12/31/2003.
Assets, $4,153,971 (M); Expenditures, $154,647; Total giving, $139,325; Grants to individuals, 4 grants totaling $28,000 (high: $8,500, low: $6,500).
Fields of interest: Mental health, disorders; Residential/custodial care; Disabilities, people with.
Type of support: Grants for special needs.
Application information: Contact foundation for current application deadline; Applications by letter, including materials applicant feels are relevant.
EIN: 860840802

4572
Athas Zaharis Agoriani Trust
58-29 213th St.
Bayside, NY   11361   (718) 423-1732
Contact: John Zaharis, Tr.

Foundation type: Independent foundation
Limitations: Grants to indigent residents of the town of Agoriani in Sparta, Greece. Grants are given for rent, repairs, student aid, the disabled, and general support.
Financial data: Year ended 12/31/2004.
Assets, $365,925 (M); Expenditures, $34,175; Total giving, $27,858; Grants to individuals, totaling $27,858.
Fields of interest: Disabilities, people with; Economically disadvantaged.
Type of support: Foreign applicants; Grants for special needs.
Application information: Applications by letter accepted throughout the year including the reason for and amount of request.
EIN: 112801980

4573
AIDS Alabama, Inc.
(formerly AIDS Task Force of Alabama, Inc)
3521 7th Ave. S.
Birmingham, AL   35222   (205) 324-9822
Contact: Kathie Hiers, C.E.O.
FAX: (205) 324-9311;
E-mail: kathie@aidsalabama.org; URL: http://www.aidsalabama.org/

Foundation type: Public charity
Limitations: Grants for housing assistance for persons in AL who test positive for HIV/AIDS and who are homeless. Referrals must be submitted by a third party.

Financial data: Year ended 09/30/2003. Assets, $2,644,164 (M); Expenditures, $3,810,104; Total giving, $528,027; Grants to individuals, totaling $528,027.
Fields of interest: Homeless, human services; AIDS, people with.
Type of support: Grants for special needs.
Application information: Contact foundation for current application deadlines; Applications must be submitted by third party referrals.
EIN: 581727755

4574
The Alexander Foundation
P.O. Box 1995
Denver, CO   80201   (303) 331-3377
Contact: Jack Heruska, Pres.
URL: http://www.thealexanderfoundation.org

Foundation type: Public charity
Limitations: Grants for individuals with illnesses such as cancer and other catastrophic assistance who reside in CO.
Financial data: Year ended 12/31/2003. Assets, $275,113 (M); Expenditures, $141,636; Total giving, $128,924; Grants to individuals, totaling $128,924.
Fields of interest: Medical care, outpatient care.
Type of support: Grants for special needs.
Application information:
Initial approach: Letter.
Program description:
Grants:
· Emergency Grants: Provides basic assistance for housing, utilities, and food
· Medical Insurance Grants: Covers the monthly premiums for individuals with HIV/AIDS who already have insurance, but who can no longer afford payments
· Holiday Season Grants: Assists deserving individuals with ongoing needs
· Educational Scholarship Grants: Assists students working towards degree in higher education and at trade schools
EIN: 742243837

4575
Allgemeiner Deutscher Frauen-Hilfsverein
(also known as German Ladies General Benevolent Society)
P.O. Box 27101
San Francisco, CA   94127   (415) 391-9947
Contact: Jutta Kiel, Treas.

Foundation type: Operating foundation
Limitations: Temporary assistance to financially needy women and children of German descent who reside in the greater San Francisco Bay Area, CA.
Publications: Annual report.
Financial data: Year ended 12/31/2003. Assets, $2,174,074 (M); Expenditures, $104,786; Total giving, $55,951; Grants to individuals, totaling $55,951.
Fields of interest: Children/youth, services; Race/intergroup relations; Women; Germany.
Type of support: Grants for special needs.
Application information: Applications accepted throughout the year; Completion of formal application required.
EIN: 941528193

4576
Alpha Omicron Pi Foundation
(formerly Alpha Omicron Pi Philanthropic Foundation)
P.O. Box 395
Brentwood, TN   37024-0395   (615) 370-0920
Contact: Bobby Stanton, Exec. Dir.
E-mail: foundation@alphaomicronpi.org;
URL: http://www.aoiifoundation.org

Foundation type: Public charity
Limitations: Grants to economically disadvantaged members of Alpha Omicron Pi to help them through times of financial crisis.
Publications: Biennial report; Grants list; Informational brochure.
Financial data: Year ended 06/30/2005. Assets, $3,267,819 (M); Expenditures, $628,847; Total giving, $344,725; Grants to individuals, 40 grants totaling $77,500.
Fields of interest: Students, sororities/fraternities; Women.
Type of support: Grants for special needs.
Application information: Application form required.
Additional information: Contact foundation for current application deadline/guidelines.
Program description:
Ruby Fund: The fund helps sisters in time of extreme financial need when no other resources are available for support. All requests and awards remain confidential and are handled by the Ruby Fund Committee. Senior collegians may be considered for fund assistance, although alumnae are the main recipients.
EIN: 581343315

4577
American Association of University Women Legal Advocacy Fund
1111 16th St., N.W.
Washington, DC   20036-4873   (800) 326-2289
Contact: Michele Wetherald, Pres.
E-mail: laf@aauw.org; TDD: (202) 785-7777;
URL: http://www.aauw.org/laf/index.cfm

Foundation type: Public charity
Limitations: Grants to women seeking judicial redress for sex discrimination in higher education.
Publications: Application guidelines; Informational brochure; Newsletter; Occasional report.
Financial data: Year ended 06/30/2004. Assets, $217,625 (M); Expenditures, $1,027,342; Total giving, $97,087; Grants to individuals, 23 grants totaling $97,087 (high: $10,000, low: $161).
Fields of interest: Courts/judicial administration; Women.
Type of support: Grants for special needs.
Application information: Application form required.
Initial approach: Telephone or e-mail.
Deadline(s): Apr. 15, Aug. 15, and Dec. 15
Additional information: Consult Web site for additional information.
Program description:
AAUW Legal Advocacy Fund Case Support: The program provides funding and a support system for women seeking judicial redress for sex discrimination in higher education. To be considered for support, a case must have been filed in state or federal court and demonstrate the following:
· potential significance for women in higher education
· the plaintiff's need for financial aid
· a high probability of success on the merits.
EIN: 521232075

4578
American Federation of Riders
(also known as A.F.R., Inc.)
3646 Glenmore Ave.
Cincinnati, OH   45211-4730   (513) 661-6080
Contact: Dan Lintz, Treas.
E-mail: afr@afr1982.org; URL: http://www.afr1982.org/

Foundation type: Public charity
Limitations: Medical assistance, trust funds, and scholarships to economically disadvantaged, orphaned, handicapped, abused and neglected children.
Financial data: Year ended 10/31/2003. Assets, $77,801 (M); Expenditures, $25,832; Total giving, $17,686.
Fields of interest: Disabilities, people with; Economically disadvantaged.
Type of support: Undergraduate support; Grants for special needs.
Application information: Contact foundation for current application deadline/guidelines.
EIN: 311041172

4579
American Health Assistance Foundation
22512 Gateway Center Dr.
Clarksburg, MD   20871   (301) 948-3244
Contact: Brian K. Regan Ph.D., Pres.
FAX: (301) 258-9454; E-mail: jwilson@ahaf.org;
Additional tel.: (800) 437-2423; URL: http://www.ahaf.org

Foundation type: Public charity
Limitations: Grants to Alzheimer's patients and caregivers to help ease financial burdens.
Financial data: Year ended 03/31/2005. Assets, $36,706,118 (M); Expenditures, $30,106,080; Total giving, $6,017,789; Grants to individuals, totaling $5,117,789.
Fields of interest: Health care, patient services; Health care; Alzheimer's disease.
Type of support: Grants for special needs.
Application information: Applications accepted. Application form required.
Initial approach: E-mail or telephone.
Deadline(s): Oct. 16
Additional information: Application must include physician's statement indicating "Alzheimer's disease," "probable Alzheimer's disease" or "dementia of the Alzheimer's type.".
Program description:
Alzheimer's Family Relief Program: Emergency grants of up to $500 are provided for expenses such as short-term nursing care, home health care, respite care, adult day care, medication, medical or personal hygiene supplies, transportation, and other expenses. Grants are not provided for pay of nursing home fees. Candidates may apply more than once.
EIN: 237337229

4580
American Psychiatric Foundation, Inc.
1000 Wilson Blvd., Ste. 1825
Arlington, VA   22209-3901   (703) 907-7300
Contact: Steven A. Rubloff, Exec. Dir.
FAX: (703) 907-7851; E-mail: apf@psych.org;
URL: http://www.psychfoundation.org

Foundation type: Public charity
Limitations: Financial assistance of up to $2,500 to psychiatrists and psychiatric residents who have been affected by natural disasters such as hurricanes.

Financial data: Year ended 12/31/2003. Assets, $2,656,481 (M); Expenditures, $2,880,272; Total giving, $2,136,484; Grants to individuals, 4 grants totaling $46,200 (high: $20,000, low: $600).
Type of support: Emergency funds.
Application information: Applications accepted. Application form required. Application form available on the grantmaker's Web site.
Initial approach: E-mail.
Deadline(s): Jan. 1
Additional information: Contact foundation for program guidelines.
EIN: 521773663

4581
D. Baker Ames Charitable Foundation
c/o SunTrust Bank
P.O. Box 1908
Orlando, FL 32802-1908
Application address: c/o Nancy Shumadine, Trust Off., SunTrust Bank, P.O. Box 2642, Norfolk, VA 23501, tel.: (757) 624-5524

Foundation type: Independent foundation
Limitations: Grants to financially needy superannuated employees of Ames & Brownley, Inc., VA, for basic needs.
Financial data: Year ended 05/31/2005. Assets, $743,016 (M); Expenditures, $27,348; Total giving, $19,900; Grants to individuals, totaling $15,000.
Type of support: Employee-related welfare.
Application information: Applications by letter outlining financial need accepted throughout the year.
EIN: 546034951

4582
Dorothy Ames Trust
c/o KeyBank N.A.
800 Superior Ave., 4th Fl.
Cleveland, OH 44114
Application address: c/o Chris Cook, P.O. Box 1054, Augusta, ME 04332-1054

Foundation type: Independent foundation
Limitations: Grants only to hearing-impaired children from New England, primarily in MA and ME. Assistance is given for hearing aids, auditory trainers, and other expenses related to hearing-impairment.
Financial data: Year ended 08/31/2004. Assets, $603,810 (M); Expenditures, $38,820; Total giving, $30,594; Grants to individuals, 25 grants totaling $19,094 (high: $4,500, low: $375).
Fields of interest: Children/youth, services; Disabilities, people with.
Type of support: Grants for special needs.
Application information: Applications accepted throughout the year; Initial approach by letter stating need.
EIN: 016065594

4583
AMJ Trust
(formerly Addie M. Jones Trust)
c/o Wells Fargo Bank Minnesota, N.A.
625 Marquette Ave., N9311-142
Minneapolis, MN 55402

Foundation type: Independent foundation
Limitations: Grants to retired MPLS teachers in MN for nursing and hospital expenses.

Financial data: Year ended 12/31/2002. Assets, $271,451 (M); Expenditures, $18,950; Total giving, $16,144; Grants to individuals, 24 grants totaling $16,144 (high: $3,000, low: $144).
Fields of interest: Education; Health care.
Type of support: Grants for special needs.
Application information: Applications not accepted.
EIN: 416011959

4584
Ralph W. Anderson Veterans Trust
27 Mayridge Dr.
Shenandoah, IA 51601-2233
Contact: Janice J. Billings, Secy.-Treas.

Foundation type: Independent foundation
Limitations: General welfare support and grants for medical expenses to needy war veterans residing in the Northboro, Farragut, and Shenandoah areas of IA, and to their spouses, children, and grandchildren.
Financial data: Year ended 06/30/2005. Assets, $91,920 (M); Expenditures, $21,719; Total giving, $20,662; Grants to individuals, totaling $20,662.
Fields of interest: Health care; Military/veterans' organizations.
Type of support: Grants for special needs.
Application information: Applications accepted. Application form required.
Deadline(s): None
Additional information: Completion of formal application required, including copy of veteran's DD-214 military service release or its equivalent.
Program description:
Veteran Grants Program: To be eligible, the veteran must have served active duty in the U.S. Armed Forces and have received an honorable or medical discharge from the military.
EIN: 426523038

4585
Anverse, Inc.
P.O. Box 3248
Cartersville, GA 30120
Contact: Patsy Wade
Application address: P.O. Box 3188, Cartersville, GA 30120, tel.: (770) 607-8870

Foundation type: Operating foundation
Limitations: Grants to individuals residing in GA, MD, NC, PR, and VA for medical, fire, or other disaster expenses.
Financial data: Year ended 06/30/2004. Assets, $159,394,430 (M); Expenditures, $8,422,706; Total giving, $10,217.
Type of support: Emergency funds.
Application information: Applications by letter outlining financial need accepted throughout the year.
EIN: 582507031

4586
Arizona Kidney Foundation
4203 E. Indian School Rd., Ste. 140
Phoenix, AZ 85018 (602) 840-1644
Contact: Glenna Jones Shapiro, C.E.O.
FAX: (602) 840-2360; E-mail: info@azkidney.org;
URL: http://www.azkidney.org

Foundation type: Public charity

Limitations: Financial assistance to kidney patients residing in AZ, for dental needs, food, medications, transportation and utilities.
Financial data: Year ended 06/30/2003. Assets, $2,617,920 (M); Expenditures, $1,821,400; Total giving, $24,751; Grants to individuals, totaling $24,751.
Fields of interest: Kidney diseases.
Type of support: Grants for special needs.
Application information: Contact foundation for current application deadline; Completion of formal application required; See Web site for further information.
Program description:
Arizona Kidney Foundation Program: Applications are to be reviewed by and submitted by the patient's renal social worker only.
EIN: 866052343

4587
Arkansas Human Development Corporation
300 S. Spring St., Ste. 800
Little Rock, AR 72201-2424 (501) 374-1103
Contact: Clevon Young, Exec. Dir.
FAX: (501) 374-1413

Foundation type: Public charity
Limitations: Grants to economically disadvantaged individuals in rural AR to improve their standards of living and quality of life.
Publications: Annual report; Informational brochure; Newsletter.
Financial data: Year ended 06/30/2004. Assets, $1,211,753 (M); Expenditures, $2,692,419; Total giving, $446,471; Grants to individuals, totaling $346,462.
Fields of interest: Economically disadvantaged.
Type of support: Grants for special needs.
Application information: Contact foundation for current application deadline/guidelines.
EIN: 237248955

4588
Arvac, Inc.
P.O. Box 808
Dardanelle, AR 72834 (479) 229-4861
Contact: Bob Adkison, Exec. Dir.

Foundation type: Public charity
Limitations: Grants to economically disadvantaged residents of AR for food, shelter, energy and other types of assistance.
Financial data: Year ended 06/30/2003. Assets, $1,386,378 (M); Expenditures, $2,507,780; Total giving, $741,443; Grants to individuals, 27 grants totaling $741,443 (high: $450, low: $100).
Fields of interest: Economically disadvantaged.
Type of support: Grants for special needs.
Application information: Contact foundation for current application deadline/guidelines.
EIN: 710386402

4589
Assistance League of Newport-Mesa California
c/o David A. Brounstein, C.P.A.
P.O. Box 7669
Newport Beach, CA 92658-7669

Foundation type: Public charity
Limitations: Dental and health care services, clothing distribution, financial support for day care,

and other services to underprivileged children living in the Newport-Mesa, CA, school district.
Financial data: Year ended 05/31/2005.
Assets, $3,748,831 (M); Expenditures, $886,164; Total giving, $51,722; Grants to individuals, totaling $51,722.
Fields of interest: Dental care; Human services; Day care; Children, services.
Type of support: Grants for special needs.
Application information: Contact foundation for current application deadline/guidelines.
EIN: 951942148

4590
Assistance League of Pueblo, Inc.
515 N. Chester Ave.
Pueblo, CO 81003-3312 (719) 543-1383
Contact: Mildred Elkins, Pres.

Foundation type: Public charity
Limitations: Grants for clothing and other aid to needy children in the Pueblo, CO area.
Financial data: Year ended 05/31/2005.
Assets, $870,536 (M); Expenditures, $204,624; Total giving, $62,235; Grants to individuals, totaling $62,235.
Fields of interest: Children, services.
Type of support: Grants for special needs.
Application information: Contact foundation for current application deadline/guidelines.
EIN: 237127355

4591
Associated Charities of Findlay, Ohio
233 S. Main St.
Findlay, OH 45840 (419) 423-2021
Contact: Peggy Wood, Exec. Secy.

Foundation type: Independent foundation
Limitations: Emergency financial assistance by referral only to families and individuals living in Findlay, OH, and Hancock County, OH.
Publications: Annual report.
Financial data: Year ended 12/31/2004.
Assets, $4,372,394 (M); Expenditures, $266,042; Total giving, $209,473.
Fields of interest: Human services, emergency aid.
Type of support: Awards/grants by nomination only; Grants for special needs.
Application information: Applicants must be referred by a social services agency; The majority of aid is given as a result of personal interviews; In extreme cases, aid may be given as a result of a telephone call.
Program description:
  Associated Charities of Findley, Ohio Program: Aid is given for shelter, utilities, clothing, repairs, medicine, medical expenses, dental expenses, and other emergency needs.
EIN: 346400067

4592
Association for the Relief of Aged Women of New Bedford
1140 State Rd.
P.O. Box 819
Westport, MA 02790

Foundation type: Operating foundation
Limitations: Relief assistance to needy, aged women in New Bedford, Dartmouth, Fairhaven, and Acushnet, MA.
Financial data: Year ended 03/31/2004.
Assets, $17,068,320 (M); Expenditures,

$471,236; Total giving, $357,915; Grants to individuals, 117 grants totaling $244,572 (high: $10,193, low: $42).
Fields of interest: Aging; Women.
Type of support: Grants for special needs.
Application information: Applications not accepted.
  Additional information: Recipients are nominated by nonprofit agencies.
EIN: 046056367

4593
Athanasiades Cultural Foundation, Inc.
30-96 42nd St.
Astoria, NY 11103-3031 (718) 278-3014

Foundation type: Operating foundation
Limitations: Grants to needy individuals for medical expenses and general welfare, primarily in NY.
Financial data: Year ended 12/31/2003.
Assets, $2,029,429 (M); Expenditures, $66,958; Total giving, $13,567; Grants to individuals, 21 grants totaling $11,100.
Fields of interest: Health care; Economically disadvantaged.
Type of support: Grants for special needs.
Application information: Deadline Oct. 31; Initial approach by telephone; Application by letter.
EIN: 133614414

4594
Athena Charitable Trust
5411 Bahia Ln.
La Jolla, CA 92037-7020

Foundation type: Operating foundation
Limitations: Support to individuals for a variety of needs, including educational assistance, general welfare, and medical expenses, primarily in MI.
Financial data: Year ended 06/30/2003.
Assets, $0 (M); Expenditures, $76,099; Total giving, $11,300; Grants to individuals, 6 grants totaling $4,900.
Fields of interest: Scholarships/financial aid; Health care.
Type of support: Scholarships—to individuals; Grants for special needs.
Application information: Unsolicited requests for funds not considered or acknowledged.
EIN: 336211470

4595
ATP Tour Charities, Inc.
201 ATP Tour Blvd.
Ponte Vedra Beach, FL 32082-3211
(904) 285-8000
Contact: Philip Galloway, C.F.O.

Foundation type: Public charity
Limitations: Grants to members or former members for medical and dental assistance, and for hospital expenses.
Financial data: Year ended 12/31/2003.
Assets, $113,017 (M); Expenditures, $68,438; Total giving, $67,900; Grants to individuals, totaling $42,000.
Fields of interest: Dental care; Health care.
Type of support: Grants for special needs.
Application information: Contact foundation for current application deadline/guidelines.
EIN: 593046932

4596
Aurora Ministries, Inc.
(formerly Bible Alliance, Inc.)
P.O. Box 1848
Bradenton, FL 34206 (941) 748-4100
FAX: (941) 748-2625;
E-mail: aurora@auroraministries.org; URL: http://www.auroraministries.org

Foundation type: Operating foundation
Limitations: Grants of cassette tape recordings of the Bible made to the visually impaired and physically disabled.
Financial data: Year ended 12/31/2004.
Assets, $5,029,724 (M); Expenditures, $3,908,511; Total giving, $2,642,654; Grants to individuals, totaling $2,642,654.
Fields of interest: Christian agencies & churches; Religion; Disabilities, people with.
Type of support: Grants for special needs.
Application information: Contact foundation for current application deadline/guidelines.
EIN: 237178299

4597
Aventis Pharmaceuticals Health Care Foundation
(formerly Hoechst Marion Roussel Health Care Foundation for the Ill)
P.O. Box 6912
Bridgewater, NJ 08807

Foundation type: Company-sponsored foundation
Limitations: Prescription drugs to individuals who fall below the federal poverty level and who have no prescription reimbursement coverage. Applicants must also be ineligible for third party medication payments.
Financial data: Year ended 12/31/2004.
Assets, $0 (M); Expenditures, $114,668,984; Total giving, $114,668,984; Grants to individuals, totaling $114,668,984.
Fields of interest: Pharmacy/prescriptions; Aging; Economically disadvantaged.
Type of support: Grants for special needs.
Application information: Applications accepted.
  Initial approach: Letter.
  Deadline(s): None
  Additional information: Completion of formal application required, including physician's certification of patient's medical and financial needs.
Program description:
  Aventis Pharmaceutical Program: The program supplies pharmaceuticals manufactured by Hoechst Marion Roussel. No monetary grants are given. Initial inquiry may be made by the patient, patient's family, social service worker, or physician. However, each applicant must have a physician's endorsement. Most recipients are elderly, though there is no age requirement. Once accepted to the program, individuals may continue indefinitely, provided they are still in severe financial and medical need.
EIN: 431614543

4598
Avery-Fuller-Welch Children's Foundation
(formerly Avery-Fuller Children's Center)
500 Sutter St., Ste. 401
San Francisco, CA 94102
Contact: Nancy J. Lobaugh, Exec. Dir.

Foundation type: Independent foundation
Limitations: Financial assistance to mentally and physically disabled children in San Francisco,

Alameda, Contra Costa, San Mateo, and Marin counties, CA, to increase their self-sufficiency. See program description for further limitations.
Publications: Application guidelines; Informational brochure (including application guidelines); Program policy statement.
Financial data: Year ended 06/30/2005. Assets, $5,931,728 (M); Expenditures, $321,170; Total giving, $259,952; Grants to individuals, 62 grants totaling $259,952 (high: $9,300, low: $550).
Fields of interest: Physical therapy; Youth development; Children/youth, services; Disabilities, people with.
Type of support: Grants for special needs.
Application information: Application form required.
Initial approach: Letter or telephone.
Deadline(s): Feb. 15, May 15, Aug. 15, and Nov. 15
Additional information: See program description for further application information.
Program description:
Childrens Aid Program: Funds are available to pay for medical services, physical and occupational therapy, psychotherapy, special school or remedial education, prosthetics, appliances, prescriptions, and related services for disabled children. Grants are not made for groups of children, preliminary evaluations, orthodontia, eyeglasses, or routine eye care. Recipients are chosen on the basis of evidence of strong motivation in the child, the therapist, and the family, favorable prognosis for achieving independence or progress toward that goal, and the inability to obtain support elsewhere. The application must be submitted by the professional who has the primary case responsibility (a social worker, teacher, physician, or therapist). Both the professional and the child must reside within the geographic specifications. Specific forms are required for:
· remedial therapy or schooling
· renewal applications
· medical services, prosthetics, appliances, and prescriptions (this form must include a physician's detailed report on the child and a financial plan)
All applications must include a monthly family expense report if the family's income is more than $2,000 per month for one child or more than $2,500 per month for two children. Double grants are made in special circumstances when there is a professional collaboration, which must be detailed in the application. Evaluations of the project that detail the progress of the child are required. One evaluation is required if the project lasts eight months or less. Two are required for projects nine months to a year in duration. Evaluations are due one month after project completion. The typical length of a grant is six months to a year. Priority is given to cases with concrete short-term goals. Grants are renewable for up to a year. Extended treatment projects are not supported. Recipients are notified within four weeks of the deadline. Rejected applications will be reconsidered once at the next review date, provided the applicant requests so in writing. Funds are generally disbursed directly to the service provider and/or organization on behalf of the recipients.
EIN: 941243657

4599
Aysr Foundation
1388 State Rte. 487
Bloomsburg, PA 17815
For Individuals: John D. Klingerman, Orangeville, PA 17859, Tel.: (570) 784-0111

Foundation type: Independent foundation
Limitations: Grants to economically disadvantaged individuals.
Financial data: Year ended 12/31/2004. Assets, $67,978 (M); Expenditures, $53,626; Total giving, $53,133; Grants to individuals, totaling $53,133.
Type of support: Grants for special needs.
Application information: Applications by letter accepted throughout the year.
EIN: 232966353

4600
William Babcock Memorial Endowment
305 San Anselmo Ave., Ste. 219
San Anselmo, CA 94960
Contact: Lynne Walsh, Exec. Dir.

Foundation type: Independent foundation
Limitations: Grants and loans for medical costs not covered by insurance or other community agencies, only to financially needy residents of Marin County, CA.
Publications: Application guidelines.
Financial data: Year ended 02/28/2005. Assets, $4,845,790 (L); Expenditures, $841,068; Total giving, $620,685; Grants to individuals, 309 grants totaling $620,685 (high: $75,000, low: $34).
Fields of interest: Health care; Economically disadvantaged.
Type of support: Grants for special needs.
Application information: Applications accepted. Application form required.
Deadline(s): None
Additional information: Inappropriate applications will not be considered or acknowledged. Interviews required.
EIN: 941367170

4601
The Bagby Foundation for the Musical Arts, Inc.
501 5th Ave., Ste. 801
New York, NY 10017 (212) 986-6094
Contact: J. Andrew Lark, Exec. Dir.

Foundation type: Independent foundation
Limitations: Grants for pensions and emergency aid to aged needy individuals who have aided the world of music.
Financial data: Year ended 12/31/2004. Assets, $2,118,090 (M); Expenditures, $141,316; Total giving, $70,705; Grants to individuals, totaling $55,706.
Fields of interest: Music; Aging.
Type of support: Grants for special needs.
Application information: Applications by letter, outlining financial need, accepted throughout the year.
EIN: 131873289

4602
Rudy Balke Trust, Inc.
530 S. Nevada Ave.
Colorado Springs, CO 80903-3985
Contact: Kenneth W. Geddes, Tr.

Foundation type: Independent foundation
Limitations: Grants to economically disadvantaged individuals in the Colorado Springs, CO, area, for medical care.
Financial data: Year ended 12/31/2004. Assets, $645,266 (M); Expenditures, $45,841;

Total giving, $32,895; Grants to individuals, totaling $32,895.
Fields of interest: Health care.
Type of support: Grants for special needs.
Application information: Applications by proposal accepted throughout the year.
EIN: 846044826

4603
Bangor Fuel Society
Eaton Peabody
P.O. Box 1210
Bangor, ME 04402
Contact: Calvin True, Pres.

Foundation type: Operating foundation
Limitations: Deliveries of home heating fuel to low-income residents of Bangor, ME.
Financial data: Year ended 10/31/2004. Assets, $783,854 (M); Expenditures, $51,876; Total giving, $50,187; Grants to individuals, totaling $50,187.
Fields of interest: Housing/shelter, services; Economically disadvantaged.
Type of support: Grants for special needs.
Application information: Applications available through local services agencies.
EIN: 016010608

4604
Baseball Assistance Team
245 Park Ave., 34th Fl.
New York, NY 10167 (866) 605-4594
Contact: James Martin, Exec. Dir.

Foundation type: Public charity
Limitations: Grants to former Major League Baseball players, employees, and their families for living expenses and other financial needs.
Publications: Informational brochure.
Financial data: Year ended 12/31/2003. Assets, $9,332,643 (M); Expenditures, $1,601,335; Total giving, $845,207; Grants to individuals, totaling $845,207.
Fields of interest: Athletics/sports, baseball.
Type of support: Employee-related welfare.
Application information: Contact foundation for current application deadline/guidelines.
EIN: 133355155

4605
Battered Women's Assistance
P.O. Box 1119
Santa Cruz, CA 95061-1119

Foundation type: Operating foundation
Limitations: Financial assistance and volunteer guidance to battered women and children in Santa Cruz County, CA.
Financial data: Year ended 12/31/2003. Assets, $0 (M); Expenditures, $24,722; Total giving, $24,550; Grants to individuals, 19 grants totaling $24,550 (high: $3,500, low: $283).
Fields of interest: Crime/violence prevention; Domestic violence; Children/youth, services; Domestic violence; Women.
Type of support: Grants for special needs.
Application information: Applications accepted throughout the year; Completion of formal application required. Applicants must be referred by another 501(c)(3) agency.
EIN: 770167239

4606
The James Gordon Bennett Memorial Corporation
c/o John Campbell
100 Bertwell Rd.
Lexington, MA 02420-3313

Foundation type: Independent foundation
Limitations: Pecuniary aid to needy journalists who have been employees for 10 or more years of a New York, NY, daily newspaper.
Financial data: Year ended 12/31/2004.
Assets, $5,450,612 (M); Expenditures, $261,842; Total giving, $211,950; Grants to individuals, 97 grants totaling $211,950 (high: $12,000, low: $250).
Fields of interest: Journalism/publishing.
Type of support: Employee-related welfare.
Application information: Applications accepted. Application form required.
   Initial approach: Letter requesting application.
   Deadline(s): None
Program description:
   Journalism Program: The foundation gives first priority to journalists who have worked in the borough of Manhattan, NY. Remaining funds are used to assist journalists who worked in the other boroughs of New York City. Acceptance is based on need and aid is to be used for "the physical needs of persons, who, by reason of old age, accident or bodily infirmity, or through lack of means, are unable to care for themselves".
EIN: 136150414

4607
Frank C. & Georgia M. Bentley Charitable Trust
3394 W. Farm Rd. 178
Springfield, MO 65810-1165

Foundation type: Independent foundation
Limitations: Financial assistance to individuals residing in Springfield, MO, who are at least 60 years of age.
Financial data: Year ended 12/31/2004.
Assets, $2,034,473 (M); Expenditures, $124,267; Total giving, $89,966; Grants to individuals, 75 grants totaling $89,966 (high: $6,000, low: $38).
Fields of interest: Aging.
Type of support: Grants for special needs.
Application information: Applications accepted throughout the year; Initial approach by telephone; Completion of formal application required.
EIN: 436050610

4608
Bible Students Aid Foundation
c/o Stock Yard Bank & Trust Co.
P.O. Box 34290
Louisville, KY 40232-4290

Foundation type: Independent foundation
Limitations: Emergency aid for Bible students for utilities, groceries, prescriptions, rent or mortgage payments, etc.
Financial data: Year ended 07/31/2003.
Assets, $848,700 (M); Expenditures, $67,434; Total giving, $61,846; Grants to individuals, 10 grants totaling $28,079 (high: $7,301, low: $800).
Fields of interest: Theological school/education.
Type of support: Grants for special needs.
Application information: Applications by letter, including a supporting letter from a Bible student elder, accepted throughout the year.
EIN: 616176491

4609
Mary L. C. Biddle Foundation
c/o PNC Advisors
620 Liberty Ave., P2-PTPP-10-2
Pittsburgh, PA 15222-2705 (800) 762-2272

Foundation type: Independent foundation
Limitations: Financial assistance to women in the Philadelphia, PA, area.
Financial data: Year ended 12/31/2003.
Assets, $323,971 (M); Expenditures, $23,075; Total giving, $19,800; Grants to individuals, 10 grants totaling $19,800 (high: $1,980, low: $1,980).
Fields of interest: Women.
Type of support: Grants for special needs.
Application information: Applications by letter accepted throughout the year.
Program description:
   Biddle Foundation Program: Grants are usually paid in monthly installments.
EIN: 236205851

4610
Ingeborg A. Biondo Memorial Foundation
(formerly Ingeborg A. Biondo Memorial Trust)
221 Broad St.
Milford, PA 18337
Application address: c/o Trudy Derse, Tr., 4040 Sumerset Ct., Milford Landing, Milford, PA 18337

Foundation type: Operating foundation
Limitations: Grants to orphaned and physically, mentally, and emotionally handicapped individuals in NY and PA.
Financial data: Year ended 12/31/2003.
Assets, $2,664,412 (M); Expenditures, $170,099; Total giving, $18,690; Grants to individuals, totaling $7,590.
Fields of interest: Residential/custodial care; Disabilities, people with.
Type of support: Grants for special needs.
Application information: Applications accepted. Application form required.
   Deadline(s): None
EIN: 112801015

4611
Philo and Sarah Blaisdell Foundation
410 Seneca Bldg.
Bradford, PA 16701 (814) 362-6340
Contact: Howard Fesenmyer, Exec. Secy.
Scholarship application address: c/o Office of Financial Aid, Univ. of Pittsburgh at Bradford, Bradford, PA 16701, tel.: (814) 362-3801

Foundation type: Independent foundation
Limitations: Grants for medical, educational and other support to economically disadvantaged residents of McKean County, PA.
Financial data: Year ended 12/31/2003.
Assets, $3,880,264 (M); Expenditures, $324,127; Total giving, $263,655; Grants to individuals, 18 grants totaling $9,358 (high: $2,000, low: $80).
Fields of interest: Education; Economically disadvantaged.
Type of support: Emergency funds; Employee-related scholarships; Grants to individuals; Employee-related welfare; Undergraduate support.
Application information: Contact foundation for current application deadline/guidelines.
EIN: 256035748

4612
Blue Horizon Health & Welfare Trust
c/o Salisbury Bank & Trust Co.
19 Bissell St.
Lakeville, CT 06039 (860) 435-4809
Contact: Judith W. McKernon, Trust Off., Salisbury Bank & Trust Co.
Application address: P.O. Box 1944, Lakeville, CT 06039

Foundation type: Independent foundation
Limitations: Assistance in paying medical expenses for needy residents of the townships of Salisbury and Sharon, CT.
Financial data: Year ended 12/31/2004.
Assets, $203,516 (M); Expenditures, $10,499; Total giving, $8,372; Grants to individuals, totaling $8,372.
Fields of interest: Health care.
Type of support: Grants for special needs.
Application information: Applications accepted.
   Initial approach: Letter.
   Deadline(s): None
EIN: 066032105

4613
Boeing Employees Emergency Aid Fund
(also known as EFAF)
c/o The Boeing Co.
P.O. Box, MC S100-3478
St. Louis, MO 63166
Application address: c/o Angela Most, P.O. Box 516, MC 2100-3478, St. Louis, MO 63166-0516

Foundation type: Independent foundation
Limitations: Grants to employees of Boeing Co. for emergency assistance, MO.
Publications: Informational brochure.
Financial data: Year ended 12/31/2003.
Assets, $17,148 (M); Expenditures, $20,346; Total giving, $20,346; Grants to individuals, 6 grants totaling $11,392 (high: $2,222, low: $1,526).
Type of support: Grants for special needs.
Application information: Application form required. Application form available on the grantmaker's Web site.
   Initial approach: Telephone.
   Copies of proposal: 1
   Deadline(s): None
EIN: 431554300

4614
The Bone Marrow Foundation, Inc.
337 E. 88th St., Ste. 1B
New York, NY 10128 (212) 838-3029
Contact: Christina Merrill, Exec. Dir.
E-mail: info@bonemarrow.org; Toll-free tel.: (800) 365-1336; URL: http://www.bonemarrow.org

Foundation type: Public charity
Limitations: Grants to bone marrow transplant patients for medical and other related expenses.
Publications: Newsletter.
Financial data: Year ended 12/31/2004.
Assets, $324,330 (M); Expenditures, $434,273; Total giving, $64,430; Grants to individuals, totaling $64,430.
Fields of interest: Nerve, muscle & bone diseases.
Type of support: Grants for special needs.
Application information: Application form required.
   Initial approach: E-mail.
   Additional information: Contact foundation for current application deadline.

Program description:

Patient Aid Program: This program covers the cost for donor searches, compatibility testing, bone marrow procurement, medication, transportation, housing expenses and many other ancillary costs associated with a transplant. The application requires information about diagnosis, treatment, financial status information from the social worker and physician. The social worker must be contacted to apply for the Patient Aid Program grant. Applications are only accepted from affiliated institutions. See Web site for affiliated centers.

EIN: 133674198

4615
Boogies Diner Foundation

(formerly The Weinglass Foundation, Inc.)
P.O. Box 11509
Aspen, CO   81612

Foundation type: Independent foundation
Limitations: Grants to economically disadvantaged residents of Aspen County, CO, primarily for medical treatment and related expenses. Scholarships are also awarded.
Financial data: Year ended 12/31/2004. Assets, $2,568,180 (M); Expenditures, $568,622; Total giving, $528,163; Grants to individuals, totaling $168,330. Subtotal for grants for special needs: grants totaling $106,334 (high: $21,317, low: $200).
Fields of interest: Economically disadvantaged.
Type of support: Grants for special needs.
Application information: Applications not accepted.
   Additional information: Contributes only to preselected individuals.
EIN: 521307628

4616
Borders Group Foundation

100 Phoenix Dr.
Ann Arbor, MI   48108   (734) 477-1100
E-mail: bgf@bordersgroupinc.com; URL: http://www.bordersgroupinc.com/community/foundation.htm

Foundation type: Public charity
Limitations: Short-term financial assistance to employees and the immediate families of Borders Group, Inc. or its subsidiaries who have demonstrated financial need arising from severe hardship and/or emergency circumstances including diaster relief.
Financial data: Year ended 12/31/2004. Assets, $2,878,749; Expenditures, $422,495; Total giving, $396,717; Grants to individuals, totaling $396,717. Subtotal for employee-related welfare: 271 grants totaling $342,217.
Type of support: Employee-related welfare.
Application information: Application form required.
   Additional information: Contact foundation for current application deadline.
Program description:
   Borders Group Foundation Program: Full-time and part-time employees are eligible to apply if they have been on the payroll for at least 90 days. Grants are for basic living expenses as well as diaster relief.
EIN: 383279018

4617
Boston Fatherless & Widows Society

c/o Goodwin Procter LLP
Exchange Pl., Ste. 2200
Boston, MA   02109-2881   (617) 570-1130
Contact: George W. Butterworth III, Treas.

Foundation type: Independent foundation
Limitations: Grants to economically disadvantaged widows who are residents of the greater Boston, MA, area, to cover expenses for food, housing, clothing, and medical treatment.
Financial data: Year ended 11/30/2004. Assets, $7,050,807 (M); Expenditures, $449,588; Total giving, $395,807; Grants to individuals, 100 grants totaling $273,807 (high: $5,500, low: $1,000).
Fields of interest: Housing/shelter; Residential/custodial care; Women.
Type of support: Grants for special needs.
Application information:
   Initial approach: Referral from agencies and other nonprofits.
   Additional information: Applications by letter, outlining financial needs accepted throughout the year.
EIN: 046006506

4618
Boston Leather Trade Benevolent Society

532 E. Broadway
South Boston, MA   02127-4407
(617) 268-3939
Contact: Daniel D. Gallagher, Secy.

Foundation type: Independent foundation
Limitations: Grants to financially needy individuals who have been affiliated with the leather trade in New England.
Financial data: Year ended 12/31/2004. Assets, $241,196 (M); Expenditures, $31,535; Total giving, $20,800; Grants to individuals, totaling $20,800.
Fields of interest: Business/industry.
Type of support: Grants for special needs.
Application information: Applications by letter, outlining financial need, background, and references, accepted throughout the year.
EIN: 237219487

4619
Bridgeport Ladies Charitable Society

c/o People's Bank, Trust Dept.
850 Main St.
Bridgeport, CT   06604

Foundation type: Independent foundation
Limitations: Grants by referral only to financially needy residents of the greater Bridgeport, CT, area only, for health care and home assistance.
Publications: Informational brochure.
Financial data: Year ended 09/30/2004. Assets, $998,047 (M); Expenditures, $72,672; Total giving, $62,124; Grants to individuals, totaling $62,124.
Fields of interest: Health care; Housing/shelter; Economically disadvantaged.
Type of support: Grants for special needs.
Application information: Unsolicited requests for funds not considered or acknowledged; Recipients are referred by Family Services-Woodfield in Bridgeport, CT, and other community agencies in CT.
EIN: 066068224

4620
Greater Bridgeport Retired Teachers Building Fund

P.O. Box 1802
Providence, RI   02901-1802
Application address: c/o Barbara Surina, 2401 Huntington Rd., Trumbull, CT 06611

Foundation type: Independent foundation
Limitations: Grants to retired teachers of the greater Bridgeport, CT, area.
Financial data: Year ended 06/30/2005. Assets, $1,077,140 (M); Expenditures, $115,278; Total giving, $107,045; Grants to individuals, 289 grants totaling $107,045 (high: $2,639, low: $9).
Fields of interest: Education.
Type of support: Grants for special needs.
Application information: Applications accepted.
   Deadline(s): None
   Additional information: Applications by letter, outlining reason for financial need and doctor's statement.
EIN: 237258527

4621
British Charitable Society

c/o Charles C.J. Platt
125 Farm St.
Dover, MA   02030
Application address: c/o Exec. Secy., 342 Bunker Hill St., Charlestown, MA 02129

Foundation type: Independent foundation
Limitations: Assistance to British individuals who hold a passport from the U.K. or its dependencies, and their children and grandchildren. Applicants must be residents of one of the six New England states.
Financial data: Year ended 12/31/2002. Assets, $655,415 (M); Expenditures, $40,015; Total giving, $36,863; Grants to individuals, totaling $36,863.
Type of support: Emergency funds; Grants for special needs.
Application information: Applications by letter, outlining financial need, accepted throughout the year; Interviews may be required; The society prefers to receive applications through social service agencies.
Program description:
   British Charitable Society Relief Program: The average amount of relief is $500 to $1,500. Grants do not exceed $3,000 per applicant or family. Relief is generally given for emergency care, support during transition periods without income, and airfare home for emergencies or permanent resettlement.
EIN: 046054689

4622
Broadcasters Foundation, Inc.

7 Lincoln Ave.
Greenwich, CT   06830
Contact: Gordon Hastings, C.E.O. and Pres.

Foundation type: Independent foundation
Limitations: Financial assistance to needy members of the broadcast industry.
Publications: Newsletter.
Financial data: Year ended 12/31/2004. Assets, $1,437,324 (M); Expenditures, $1,146,751; Total giving, $240,521; Grants to individuals, totaling $240,521 (high: $15,000).
Fields of interest: Media/communications; Journalism/publishing.

Type of support: Grants for special needs.
Application information: Applications accepted. Application form required.
  Initial approach: Letter.
  Deadline(s): None
  Additional information: Grants are paid directly to the individual, for his or her general welfare. The foundation does not pay any bills directly.
EIN: 131975618

4623
Brockway Foundation for the Needy of the Village and Township of Homer, New York
c/o KeyBank N.A.
25 S. Main St.
Homer, NY   13077-1314
Contact: Kevin Crosley, Pres.
Application address: c/o Key Bank, 24 N. Main St., Homer, NY 13077

Foundation type: Independent foundation
Limitations: Financial assistance only to needy residents of the Homer, NY, area.
Financial data: Year ended 12/31/2004.
Assets, $575,736 (M); Expenditures, $31,124; Total giving, $23,825; Grants to individuals, 13 grants totaling $21,725 (high: $1,950, low: $600).
Fields of interest: Economically disadvantaged.
Type of support: Grants for special needs.
Application information: Applications by letter accepted throughout the year.
EIN: 156021436

4624
Marshall and Mary Brondum Special Assistance Foundation, Inc.
P.O. Box 3106
Missoula, MT   59806-3106

Foundation type: Independent foundation
Limitations: Financial assistance to needy residents primarily from the northwestern U.S.
Financial data: Year ended 03/31/2005.
Assets, $3,540,137 (M); Expenditures, $176,371; Total giving, $125,828; Grants to individuals, 39 grants totaling $125,828 (high: $2,700, low: $111).
Fields of interest: Health care; Human services.
Type of support: Grants for special needs.
Application information: Deadline 45 days prior to quarterly meetings - Apr., July, Oct., Jan.; Completion of formal application required, including a brief description of purpose and need.
EIN: 363700887

4625
Buchly Charity Fund
8105 Lakenheath Way
Potomac, MD   20854-2739
Contact: Paul D. Dolinsky, Tr.
Application address: 1200 N. Nash St., No. 246, Arlington, VA 22209-1439

Foundation type: Independent foundation
Limitations: Welfare assistance to widows and orphans of deceased members of Federal Lodge No. 1 of the Masons, primarily in AZ, DC, MD and VA.
Financial data: Year ended 09/30/2004.
Assets, $1,272,789 (M); Expenditures, $73,882; Total giving, $63,700; Grants to individuals, totaling $40,700.

Fields of interest: Residential/custodial care; Fraternal societies; Women.
Type of support: Grants for special needs.
Application information:
  Initial approach: Letter.
  Additional information: Unsolicited applications not accepted.
Program description:
  Buchly Charity Fund Program: Upon the death of a Federal Lodge No. 1 member, one of the trustees of the fund contacts the widow in writing to express condolences and encloses a check to assist the widow with her immediate needs. If the widow needs further assistance, she must write to the trustees, who will evaluate her needs and determine whether or not to fund them. The trustees re-evaluate each widow's needs annually.
EIN: 520943739

4626
Laura A. Burgess Fund
c/o Bank of America, N.A., P.C. Group
P.O. Box 1802
Providence, RI   02940-1802
Application address: c/o Bank of America, N.A., Attn.: Emma Greene, 100 Federal St., Boston, MA 02110, tel.: (617) 434-4644

Foundation type: Independent foundation
Limitations: Financial assistance to economically disadvantaged elderly Protestant women in specified area of southeastern Massachusetts.
Financial data: Year ended 12/31/2004.
Assets, $1,015,053 (M); Expenditures, $55,563; Total giving, $42,500.
Fields of interest: Protestant agencies & churches; Women; Economically disadvantaged.
Type of support: Grants for special needs.
Application information: Applications by letter, outlining financial need, accepted throughout the year.
EIN: 056004330

4627
Thomas C. Burke Foundation
804 Cherry St., Ste. B
Macon, GA   31201   (478) 738-9955
Contact: Carolyn P. Griggers, R.N.
FAX: (478) 738-0618

Foundation type: Independent foundation
Limitations: Medical assistance to cancer patients in the Macon-Bibb County, GA, area, who are under the care of a Macon, GA, physician.
Financial data: Year ended 09/30/2004.
Assets, $5,691,222 (M); Expenditures, $318,027; Total giving, $201,140.
Fields of interest: Cancer.
Type of support: Grants for special needs.
Application information: Applications accepted.
  Initial approach: Telephone or in person.
  Deadline(s): None
  Additional information: Applicants must be referred by their physicians.
Program description:
  Burke Foundation Program: The foundation has a nurse available for assessment evaluation of personal needs. The foundation gives financial assistance for the following medical services: drugs, food supplement, supplies, equipment, and oxygen.
EIN: 586047627

4628
Burks Charitable Trust f/b/o Fresno Lodge No. 247, F. & A. M.
c/o Fresno Lodge No. 247, F. & A.M.
3444 E. Shields Ave.
Fresno, CA   93726-6919   (559) 222-8565

Foundation type: Independent foundation
Limitations: Financial assistance, including medical expenses, to needy families who are residents of CA.
Financial data: Year ended 10/31/2004.
Assets, $70,849 (M); Expenditures, $3,912; Total giving, $3,413; Grants to individuals, totaling $3,413.
Fields of interest: Health care; Family services; Economically disadvantaged.
Type of support: Grants for special needs.
Application information: Applications by letter, outlining financial need and reason for request, accepted throughout the year; Committee interviews and investigation of all applicants required.
Program description:
  Burks Charitable Trust Program: No grants are made without a personal interview at the trust's Fresno, CA, office. Applicants must have resided in CA for at least 12 months prior to application.
EIN: 946362466

4629
Burlington Cancer Relief Association, Inc.
c/o Elizabeth Van Buren
7492 Spear St.
Shelburne, VT   05482-6573   (802) 899-4083
Contact: Edwarda DuBrul Aiken

Foundation type: Operating foundation
Limitations: Financial assistance to low-income cancer patients in Chittenden County, VT, who are referred to the association, as noted in the application procedures below.
Financial data: Year ended 09/30/2003.
Assets, $371,411 (M); Expenditures, $20,769; Total giving, $15,885; Grants to individuals, 18 grants totaling $15,885 (high: $2,175, low: $125).
Fields of interest: Cancer.
Type of support: Emergency funds; Stipends.
Application information: Applications not accepted.
Program description:
  Cancer Relief Program: Assistance includes monthly stipends to lower-income cancer patients to help them meet their medical and other needs as determined by the Association's visiting agent, a registered nurse. Other forms of assistance may be considered as well. Individuals must be referred through appropriate channels in order to be considered.
EIN: 237422919

4630
Burlington Industries Foundation
804 Green Valley Rd., Ste. 300
Greensboro, NC   27408
Contact: Delores C. Sides, Exec. Dir.

Foundation type: Company-sponsored foundation
Limitations: Emergency aid for disaster relief to employees of Burlington Industries and their families residing in NC, SC and VA. The employee must have suffered a severe loss due to a disaster such as a fire or flood.
Publications: Application guidelines.
Financial data: Year ended 09/30/2004.
Assets, $2,161,781 (M); Expenditures,

$200,672; Total giving, $189,396; Grants to individuals, 4 grants totaling $5,000 (high: $1,500, low: $1,000).
Fields of interest: Disasters, preparedness/ services.
Type of support: Emergency funds; Employee-related welfare.
Application information:
  Initial approach: Telephone or letter.
  Deadline(s): None
  Additional information: Interviews granted upon request.
EIN: 566043142

4631
Butler Manufacturing Company Foundation
P.O. Box 419917
Kansas City, MO 64141-0917   (816) 968-3208
Contact: Pamela Bird Yeater, Dir.
FAX: (816) 627-8946;
E-mail: psbirdyeater@butlermfg.com; URL: http:// www.butlermfg.com/faq/Foundationguidelines.pdf

Foundation type: Company-sponsored foundation
Limitations: Hardship grants to financially needy employees of the Butler Manufacturing Co. and their dependents, who reside in IL, MO and TX.
Publications: Application guidelines; Informational brochure (including application guidelines).
Financial data: Year ended 12/31/2004.
Assets, $6,166,062 (M); Expenditures, $295,049; Total giving, $275,201; Grants to individuals, 3 grants totaling $4,000 (high: $2,000, low: $1,000).
Type of support: Employee-related welfare.
Application information:
  Deadline(s): None
  Additional information: Applications accepted throughout the year from corporate and division executives.
Program description:
  Butler Manufacturing Employee Program: Grants are given only to employees of Butler Manufacturing Co. and its wholly-owned subsidiaries who are in financial distress because of serious illness, accidents, or loss or damage to property from weather or fire.
EIN: 440663648

4632
Butterworth Foundation, Inc.
75 Butterworth Rd.
Orange, MA 01364
Contact: Allen Young, Treas.

Foundation type: Independent foundation
Limitations: Grants to fulfill the wishes of residents of Worcester and Franklin counties, MA, who are diagnosed with AIDS. As funds are available, applications will also be considered from residents of Hampshire County, MA (Amherst-Northampton area), Cheshire County, NH (Keene area), and Windham County, VT (Brattleboro area).
Financial data: Year ended 06/30/2005.
Assets, $70,508 (M); Expenditures, $5,105; Total giving, $3,577; Grants to individuals, totaling $3,577.
Fields of interest: AIDS.
Type of support: Grants for special needs.
Application information: Applications accepted throughout the year; Application by letter, outlining wish, including documentation from a health care provider or other qualified individual, indicating that the applicant has not been an active drug abuser

for at least the past six months; Recipients notified within eight weeks.
Program description:
  AIDS Relief Program: The purpose of the foundation is to grant wishes to individuals diagnosed with AIDS (rather than individuals who are healthy, but have tested positive for the HIV virus), so that they may live a fuller, more complete, and enjoyable life. The foundation defines a wish as something the individual wants, but has never had the time or resources to attain since contracting AIDS. The grant is intended to satisfy a one-time occurrence or need, rather than an ongoing need such as medical care, rent, or food. It should be something primarily for enjoyment, and related to the quality of life of the applicant. Examples of wishes that the foundation has granted in the past include travel for enjoyment or to visit a relative or loved one; airfare for a relative or loved one to visit the person with AIDS; gift certificates for movies, books, art supplies, theatre or concert tickets, and restaurants; tuition or fees for educational programs or self-improvement courses and seminars, exercise programs, massage therapy, or legitimate alternative therapies not usually covered by health insurance.
EIN: 043147430

4633
Gertrude Butts Memorial Home Association
31 Mulberry St.
Newark, NJ 07102   (973) 622-4306
Contact: Rt. Rev Jack M. McKelvey, Exec. Secy.

Foundation type: Independent foundation
Limitations: General welfare support to children of urban clergy in NJ.
Financial data: Year ended 12/31/2004.
Assets, $2,274,445 (M); Expenditures, $70,754; Total giving, $61,000; Grants to individuals, totaling $60,000.
Fields of interest: Christian agencies & churches.
Type of support: Grants for special needs.
Application information: Applications accepted. Application form required.
  Deadline(s): None
EIN: 226043630

4634
Californian Humanitarian Foundation for Holocaust Survivors
4640 Admiralty Way, No. 216
Marina del Rey, CA 90292
Contact: Arthur P. Stern, Chair.

Foundation type: Independent foundation
Limitations: Grants to needy, elderly Holocaust survivors who are residents of CA.
Financial data: Year ended 12/31/2004.
Assets, $267,613 (M); Expenditures, $1,141,285; Total giving, $1,086,850; Grants to individuals, totaling $1,086,850.
Type of support: Grants for special needs.
Application information: Contact foundation for current application deadline/guidelines.
EIN: 954831848

4635
Camden Home for Senior Citizens
c/o Adele Hopkins
66 Washington St.
Camden, ME 04843   (207) 236-2087

Foundation type: Operating foundation
Limitations: Financial assistance with a maximum amount of $300 per month is granted to residents of Camden, Rockport, Hope, and Lincolnville, ME, for heating, food, rent, real estate taxes, medication, and other medical needs.
Financial data: Year ended 05/31/2004.
Assets, $3,051,632 (M); Expenditures, $109,439; Total giving, $81,568; Grants to individuals, 315 grants totaling $81,568 (high: $2,500, low: $60).
Application information: Applications accepted throughout the year; Completion of formal application required.
EIN: 010248064

4636
Cancer Aid and Research Fund
21208 N. 52nd Ave.
Glendale, AZ 85308   (623) 561-5893
Contact: Larry MacKay, Pres.
FAX: (602) 674-5254;
E-mail: lmackay106@aol.com; URL: http:// www.canceraidresearch.org

Foundation type: Public charity
Limitations: Grants to cancer patients and their families for medical assistance.
Financial data: Year ended 09/30/2004.
Assets, $377,839 (M); Expenditures, $3,201,679; Total giving, $2,900,596.
Fields of interest: Cancer.
Type of support: Grants for special needs.
Application information: Contact foundation for current application deadline/guidelines.
EIN: 742520175

4637
Cape Cod Times Needy Fund, Inc.
P.O. Box 36
Hyannis, MA 02601   (508) 778-5661
Contact: Betsey Sethares, Exec. Dir.
E-mail: fund-drive@needyfund.org; URL: http:// www.needyfund.org

Foundation type: Public charity
Limitations: Grants to economically disadvantaged individuals in the Cape Cod, MA, area.
Financial data: Year ended 11/30/2004.
Assets, $207,629 (M); Expenditures, $457,022; Total giving, $368,910; Grants to individuals, totaling $368,910.
Fields of interest: Economically disadvantaged.
Type of support: Grants for special needs.
Application information: Contact fund for current application deadline/guidelines.
EIN: 222480332

4638
Capital Newspapers Public Benefit Fund, Inc.
New Plz., Box 15000
Albany, NY 12212   (518) 454-5660

Foundation type: Public charity
Limitations: Grants to economically disadvantaged senior citizens residing in the Albany, NY, area.
Financial data: Year ended 12/31/2003.
Assets, $170 (M); Expenditures, $165,200; Total giving, $165,200; Grants to individuals, totaling $165,200.
Fields of interest: Aging; Economically disadvantaged.
Type of support: Grants for special needs.

Application information: Contact foundation for current application deadline/guidelines.
Program description:
Capital Newspaper Public Benefit Fund Program: Awards up to $50 per person. Recipients must be 60 years old.
EIN: 141536782

4639
Care Consistency Foundation, Inc.
7761 Meadow Cir.
Meridian, MS 39305
Contact: Gay Whitworth, Pres.

Foundation type: Public charity
Limitations: Grants to disabled individuals in Meridian, MS, for medical and other types of assistance.
Financial data: Year ended 12/30/2003.
Assets, $3,713,281 (M); Expenditures, $177,709; Total giving, $123,030; Grants to individuals, totaling $47,003.
Fields of interest: Disabilities, people with.
Type of support: Grants for special needs.
Application information: Unsolicited requests for funds not accepted.
EIN: 640730846

4640
Care To Share
P.O. Box 397
Beaverton, OR 97075-0397 (503) 292-4415
Contact: Dorie Horne, Exec. Dir.
FAX: (503) 292-1496;
E-mail: caretoshare@quest.net; Additional tel.: (503) 292-4094

Foundation type: Public charity
Limitations: Emergency assistance to economically disadvantaged individuals residing in the 97005, 97006, 97008, 97225, and 97229 ZIP codes, OR. Assistance includes food, as well as rent and utility assistance.
Publications: Informational brochure; Newsletter.
Financial data: Year ended 12/31/2003.
Assets, $131,059 (M); Expenditures, $191,047; Total giving, $105,254; Grants to individuals, totaling $105,254.
Fields of interest: Human services; Economically disadvantaged.
Type of support: Emergency funds; Grants for special needs.
Application information: Applications accepted.
Initial approach: Telephone.
Deadline(s): None
Additional information: Maximum grant amount is $250; Interviews required.
EIN: 930900348

4641
Amory S. Carhart Memorial Fund Trust
c/o Warrenton Hunt
P.O. Box 972
Warrenton, VA 20188
Contact: For general welfare: Mrs. F.B. Higginson

Foundation type: Independent foundation
Limitations: Financial assistance to persons who have incurred injury, illness, or disability following activities in a fox hunt, hunter trail, horse show, hound trail, field trail, steeplechase, point to point, hunt race, pony rally, or any similar activity. Applicants must be residents or visitors within the area registered as the Warrenton Hunt Country, VA, by the Master Fox Hound Assn.
Financial data: Year ended 12/31/2004.
Assets, $509,911 (M); Expenditures, $18,422; Total giving, $17,459; Grants to individuals, totaling $17,459.
Fields of interest: Athletics/sports, training; Athletics/sports, equestrianism.
Type of support: Grants for special needs.
Application information: Applications by letter accepted throughout the year.
EIN: 237418084

4642
Caring Foundation for Children
(formerly The Caring Foundation, Inc.)
P.O. Box 25185
Salt Lake City, UT 84125-0185
(801) 972-5437
Contact: Kathleen Pitcher, Exec. Dir.
FAX: (801) 333-6563; Toll-free tel.: (800) 589-5437; Additional address: P.O. Box 2560, Boise, ID 83701, tel.: (208) 395-7741, FAX: (208) 333-6563, Toll-free tel.: (866) 938-0084;
URL: http://www.caringfoundationforchildren.org

Foundation type: Public charity
Limitations: Dental and health insurance to uninsured children residing in UT and ID.
Publications: Application guidelines; Annual report.
Financial data: Year ended 12/31/2003.
Assets, $596,935 (M); Expenditures, $313,830; Total giving, $311,159; Grants to individuals, 949 grants totaling $311,159.
Fields of interest: Dental care.
Type of support: Grants to individuals.
Application information: Applications accepted throughout the year; Completion of formal application required, including copies of two most recent paystubs, copy of the first page of last year's tax return or W-2 form; See Web site for further application information.
Program description:
Caring Foundation for Children Program: The maximum income for recipients is $24,240 for a family of two and $6,280 more for each additional family member over the age of eight. Children must be younger than 19 years of age, and cannot be eligible to receive any public or private dental plan.
EIN: 870490448

4643
Caring Foundation of Wyoming
P.O. Box 2266
Cheyenne, WY 82003
Toll-free tel.: (888) 556-8074; URL: http://www.bcbswy.com/insurance/foundations.html

Foundation type: Public charity
Limitations: Grants to economically disadvantaged residents of WY for health care.
Financial data: Year ended 12/31/2004.
Assets, $323,806 (M); Expenditures, $85,230; Total giving, $85,230; Grants to individuals, totaling $85,230.
Fields of interest: Health care; Economically disadvantaged.
Type of support: Grants for special needs.
Application information: See Web site for application information.
EIN: 830292601

4644
Alice L. Carlisle Trust for Children of Goshen Trust
c/o Bank of America, N.A.
P.O. Box 6768
Providence, RI 02940-6768
Contact: Peter Weston
Application address: c/o Bank of America, N.A., P.O. Box 2210, Waterbury, CT 06722-2210

Foundation type: Independent foundation
Limitations: Medical expenses for children living in Goshen, CT.
Financial data: Year ended 12/31/2003.
Assets, $1,554,099 (M); Expenditures, $95,892; Total giving, $79,974; Grants to individuals, 85 grants totaling $79,974 (high: $5,200, low: $25).
Fields of interest: Health care; Children, services.
Type of support: Grants for special needs.
Application information: Application by letter, outlining financial need, accepted throughout the year.
EIN: 066115749

4645
Charles Wentz Carter Memorial Foundation
74 Pasture Ln., Ste. 120
Bryn Mawr, PA 19010-1766 (610) 527-3303
Contact: Eleanor Wentz, Pres.

Foundation type: Independent foundation
Limitations: Grants for education and health of children in PA.
Publications: Application guidelines.
Financial data: Year ended 12/31/2004.
Assets, $870,232 (M); Expenditures, $32,052; Total giving, $30,750.
Fields of interest: Environment; Health care; Learning disorders.
Type of support: Grants for special needs.
Application information: Application form required.
Initial approach: Telephone.
Deadline(s): Dec. 1
EIN: 236395203

4646
Amon G. Carter Star-Telegram Employees Fund
P.O. Box 17480
Fort Worth, TX 76102 (817) 332-3535
Contact: Nenetta Carter Tatum, Pres.

Foundation type: Company-sponsored foundation
Limitations: Pension supplements and medical and hardship assistance to employees of the Fort Worth Star-Telegram, KXAS-TV, and WBAP-Radio, all in TX.
Financial data: Year ended 04/30/2005.
Assets, $25,929,797 (M); Expenditures, $1,202,457; Total giving, $1,065,072; Grants to individuals, 227 grants totaling $416,092 (high: $7,352, low: $70).
Type of support: Employee-related welfare.
Application information:
Initial approach: Letter.
Applicants should submit the following:
1) Proposal
EIN: 756014850

4647
The CB Trust
1177 Rockingham Dr., Ste. 200
Richardson, TX 75080

Foundation type: Operating foundation
Limitations: Grants to qualified players and coaches, and their spouses, who are now or were at one time on the active roster of a member team of the National Football League, and do not have any pension or retirement benefits.
Financial data: Year ended 12/31/2003. Assets, $3,701 (M); Expenditures, $4,404; Total giving, $4,036; Grant to an individual, 1 grant totaling $4,036.
Fields of interest: Athletics/sports, training; Athletics/sports, football.
Type of support: Grants for special needs.
Application information: Applications by letter, outlining financial need, accepted throughout the year.
EIN: 751815162

4648
CCBCC Relief Foundation, Inc.
P.O. Box 31487
Charlotte, NC   28231-1487
Contact: Caroline S. Umberger, Secy.

Foundation type: Company-sponsored foundation
Limitations: Grants to current and retired employees of Coca-Cola Bottling Co. Consolidated for natural disaster relief and to alleviate hardship caused by permanent disability and destitute circumstances.
Publications: Annual report; Financial statement.
Financial data: Year ended 12/31/2004. Assets, $202,215 (M); Expenditures, $38,059; Total giving, $38,000; Grants to individuals, 11 grants totaling $38,000 (high: $7,000, low: $1,500).
Fields of interest: Safety/disasters; Disabilities, people with.
Type of support: Emergency funds; Employee-related welfare.
Application information: Application form required.
   Additional information: Applications accepted throughout the year from current or retired employees of Coca-Cola Bottling Co. Consolidated.
Program description:
   CCBCC Relief Program: Provides emergency and natural disaster relief to current and retired employees of Coca-Cola Bottling Co. Employees who encounter permanent disability and destitute circumstances may also receive some assistance.
EIN: 561927278

4649
Central Missouri Counties Human Development Corporation
807B N. Providence Rd.
Columbia, MO   65203   (573) 443-8706
Contact: Tandy Florence, Exec. Dir.
FAX: (573) 875-2689; URL: http://www.cmchdc.org/

Foundation type: Public charity
Limitations: Grants to needy individuals residing in Audrain, Boone, Callaway, Cole, Cooper, Howard, Moniteau, and Osage counties, MO, to help with rental utilities, and weatherization assistance.
Financial data: Year ended 09/30/2003. Assets, $3,509,044 (M); Expenditures, $9,131,712; Total giving, $2,935,081; Grants to individuals, totaling $2,923,757.
Type of support: Grants for special needs.
Application information:
   Initial approach: Letter.

Additional information: See Web site for additional information.
EIN: 430835026

4650
Chadwell-Townsend Private Foundation
159 W. Franklin St.
Bellbrook, OH   45305
Contact: Mark Bertke, Mgr.
FAX: (937) 848-3323

Foundation type: Operating foundation
Limitations: Grants to economically disadvantaged individuals residing in the Dayton, OH, area, for mortgages.
Financial data: Year ended 09/30/2005. Assets, $2,806,983 (M); Expenditures, $157,887; Total giving, $154,882; Grants to individuals, 2 grants totaling $154,882 (high: $90,000, low: $64,882).
Fields of interest: Housing/shelter, expense aid; Economically disadvantaged.
Type of support: Grants for special needs.
Application information:
   Initial approach: Fax.
   Additional information: Applications by letter accepted throughout the year.
Program description:
   Chandwell-Townsend Program: Applicants do not need to be U.S. citizens.
EIN: 912158710

4651
The Roy Chambers Foundation
1358 National Rd.
Wheeling, WV   26003   (304) 242-8410
Contact: Linda M. Bordas, Tr.

Foundation type: Independent foundation
Limitations: Grants to needy children of Ohio County, WV, for general welfare, including eye care, clothing, school supplies, and sports camp.
Financial data: Year ended 12/31/2004. Assets, $1,302,323 (M); Expenditures, $115,218; Total giving, $47,408; Grants to individuals, totaling $35,881.
Fields of interest: Optometry/vision screening; Athletics/sports, training; Children/youth, services; Economically disadvantaged.
Type of support: Grants for special needs.
Application information: Applications accepted throughout the year; Completion of formal application required.
EIN: 556113902

4652
Charitable Society in Hartford
c/o Bank of America, N.A.
777 Main St., CT2-102-22-02
Hartford, CT   06115
Contact: Raymond S. Andrews, Jr., Pres.
Application address: 18 N. Main St., West Hartford, CT 06117, tel.: (860) 561-9011

Foundation type: Independent foundation
Limitations: Small grants to needy residents of Hartford, CT, to meet emergency needs (e.g., food, shelter, clothing, heat).
Financial data: Year ended 08/31/2004. Assets, $799,803 (M); Expenditures, $32,787; Total giving, $21,667; Grants to individuals, totaling $21,667.
Fields of interest: Human services, emergency aid.
Type of support: Grants for special needs.

Application information: Applications accepted throughout the year; Applicants must be referred by recognized social service agencies, churches, or schools.
EIN: 066026007

4653
The Cherokee & Walker Foundation
6440 Wasatch Blvd., Ste. 200
Salt Lake City, UT   84121-3515
(801) 278-7800
Contact: Shane R. Peery, Tr.

Foundation type: Independent foundation
Limitations: Grants to residents of UT.
Financial data: Year ended 12/31/2004. Assets, $44,485 (M); Expenditures, $173,748; Total giving, $171,867.
Fields of interest: Human services.
Type of support: Grants for special needs.
Application information: Applications by letter accepted throughout the year.
EIN: 870635720

4654
Chest and Foundation of the Fur Industry of the City of New York, Inc.
1359 Broadway, Ste. 1206
New York, NY   10018-7102
Contact: Harold A. Schwartz, Pres.

Foundation type: Public charity
Limitations: Grants to economically disadvantaged former members of the fur industry.
Financial data: Year ended 12/31/2004. Assets, $195,742 (M); Expenditures, $57,049; Total giving, $51,820; Grants to individuals, totaling $40,820.
Fields of interest: Economically disadvantaged.
Type of support: Grants for special needs.
Application information: Applications accepted.
   Additional information: Contact foundation for current application deadline/guidelines.
EIN: 135631505

4655
Children's Oncology Services, Inc.
500 N. Michigan Ave., No. 300
Chicago, IL   60611
Contact: Jacob Drescher, Exec. Dir.
FAX: (312) 924-4222; URL: http://www.onestepcamp.org/

Foundation type: Public charity
Limitations: Grants to children with cancer or leukemia to allow them to lead "normal" lives by providing camping and other experiences.
Publications: Annual report; Informational brochure; Newsletter.
Financial data: Year ended 09/30/2003. Assets, $1,989,229 (M); Expenditures, $567,601; Total giving, $214,774; Grants to individuals, totaling $214,774.
Fields of interest: Cancer; Leukemia; Camps; Children/youth, services.
Type of support: Grants for special needs.
Application information: Contact foundation or see Web site for current application information.
EIN: 364263831

4656
Christian BusinessCares Foundation
137 S. Main St.
Akron, OH 44308
Application address: P.O. Box 219, Peninsula, OH
44264-0219

Foundation type: Operating foundation
Limitations: Grants to residents of northeast OH for one-time needs which are life-threatening or are emergencies, such as children and families with medical needs, single moms working to support their children, and the elderly with critical needs.
Financial data: Year ended 10/31/2004.
Assets, $94,211 (M); Expenditures, $61,558; Total giving, $59,431; Grants to individuals, 27 grants totaling $57,776 (high: $7,912, low: $19).
Type of support: Grants for special needs.
Application information: Applications accepted throughout the year; Initial approach by letter or telephone; Completion of formal application required; Interviews required.
Program description:
  Christian BusinessCares Grant Program: Grants are determined on the basis of the impact they would have on the applicant's overall condition. A grant must make a difference. Therefore, persons in a deteriorated economic condition are generally not eligible. Types of grants include assistance for rent, medical expenses, utilities, and other urgent needs.
EIN: 341377938

4657
Christian Services, Inc.
P.O. Box 720
Winsted, MN 55395 (320) 485-7496
Contact: Barbara Moore, Pres.

Foundation type: Public charity
Limitations: Support and assistance to missionaries, missionary children, and individuals in financial, physical, or otherwise needy circumstances.
Financial data: Year ended 12/03/2003.
Assets, $21,060 (M); Expenditures, $253,359; Total giving, $205,713; Grants to individuals, 2 grants totaling $8,092.
Fields of interest: Christian agencies & churches; Religion; Economically disadvantaged.
Type of support: Grants for special needs.
Application information: Applications not accepted.
EIN: 237304856

4658
CIACO, Inc.
4563 W. 200 N.
Anderson, IN 46011-8788 (317) 637-2050
Contact: Nancy M. Arellano, Dir.

Foundation type: Independent foundation
Limitations: Grants to economically disadvantaged individuals residing in IN for medical expenses, food, shelter, and clothing.
Financial data: Year ended 12/31/2004.
Assets, $742 (M); Expenditures, $33,104; Total giving, $32,090; Grants to individuals, 15 grants totaling $29,712 (high: $6,371, low: $250). Subtotal for grants for special needs: 2 grants totaling $1,528.
Fields of interest: Health care; Nutrition; Housing/shelter; Economically disadvantaged.
Type of support: Grants for special needs.
Application information: Application form required.

Additional information: Contact foundation for current application deadline.
EIN: 351756007

4659
Bish & Frannie Cismoski Foundation
350 N. LaSalle St., Ste. 900
Chicago, IL 60610

Foundation type: Independent foundation
Limitations: Grants to priests and pastors.
Financial data: Year ended 12/31/2004.
Assets, $357,272 (M); Expenditures, $67,509; Total giving, $58,000; Grants to individuals, totaling $10,000.
Fields of interest: Christian agencies & churches.
Type of support: Grants to individuals.
Application information: Applications not accepted.
  Additional information: Unsolicited requests for funds not considered or acknowledged.
EIN: 364434359

4660
Civitan Child Welfare Auxiliary, Inc.
3712 Anderson Ave.
Chattanooga, TN 37412
Contact: Hunter D. Heggle, Chair.; For General Welfare: Henry Crine
Application address: P.O. Box 339, Signal Mountain, TN 3737, E-mail: hheggie830327@comcast.net

Foundation type: Independent foundation
Limitations: Support to disabled children 16 years old or under who live in the immediate Chattanooga, TN, area.
Financial data: Year ended 12/31/2004.
Assets, $1,507,144 (M); Expenditures, $61,325; Total giving, $60,127; Grants to individuals, 15 grants totaling $51,477 (high: $6,200, low: $350). Subtotal for grants for special needs: 15 grants totaling $51,477 (high: $6,200, low: $350).
Fields of interest: Children, services; Disabilities, people with.
Type of support: Grants for special needs.
Application information: Applications accepted. Application form not required.
  Initial approach: Letter.
  Copies of proposal: 1
  Deadline(s): None
  Applicants should submit the following:
    1) Proposal
    2) Curriculum vitae
    3) Budget Information
  Additional information: Applications accepted throughout the year; Initial approach by letter or telephone.
EIN: 626036153

4661
The Clark Foundation
1 Rockefeller Plz., 31st Fl.
New York, NY 10020-2102
Contact: Charles H. Hamilton, Exec. Dir.

Foundation type: Independent foundation
Limitations: Grants for medical and convalescent care to financially needy individuals who are patients at the Mary Imogene Bassett Hospital in Cooperstown, NY.
Publications: Application guidelines; Program policy statement.
Financial data: Year ended 06/30/2005.
Assets, $544,631,091 (M); Expenditures,

$28,821,942; Total giving, $21,603,356; Grants to individuals, 4 grants totaling $37,462 (high: $18,600, low: $262).
Fields of interest: Nursing home/convalescent facility; Health care.
Type of support: Grants for special needs.
Application information: Applications accepted.
  Initial approach: Letter.
EIN: 135616528

4662
Louis G. & Elizabeth L. Clarke Endowment Fund
c/o U.S. Bank, N.A.
P.O. Box 3168
Portland, OR 97208
Application address: c/o Walter L. Peters, Exec. Secy., Scottish Rite Temple, 709 S.W. 15th Ave., Portland, OR 97205, tel.: (503) 228-9405

Foundation type: Independent foundation
Limitations: Financial assistance to economically disadvantaged Masons and their immediate families requiring hospitalization in Multnomah, Clackamas, and Washington counties, OR.
Financial data: Year ended 12/31/2004.
Assets, $1,559,853 (M); Expenditures, $88,740; Total giving, $65,682; Grants to individuals, totaling $65,682.
Fields of interest: Economically disadvantaged.
Type of support: Grants for special needs.
Application information: Applications accepted.
  Initial approach: Letter.
  Deadline(s): None
EIN: 936020655

4663
The Elizabeth Church Clarke Testamentary Trust/Fund Foundation
c/o Citibank, N.A.
153 E. 53rd St., 23rd Fl.
New York, NY 10022-0000
Application address for individuals: c/o Scottish Rite Temple, Attn.: G.L. Selmyhr, Exec. Secy., 709 S.W. 15th Ave., Portland, OR 97205, tel.: (503) 228-9405

Foundation type: Independent foundation
Limitations: Grants to OR residents for medical assistance and bodily rehabilitation. Medical assistance payments may be made directly to the individual recipient, or to the doctors and hospitals providing medical services.
Financial data: Year ended 12/31/2004.
Assets, $2,004,714 (M); Expenditures, $113,192; Total giving, $90,397; Grants to individuals, totaling $90,397.
Fields of interest: Medical care, rehabilitation; Health care.
Type of support: Grants for special needs.
Application information: Applications accepted.
  Deadline(s): None
  Additional information: Applications by letter, including complete details of needs and costs.
EIN: 936024205

4664
Clemson Community Care, Inc.
P. O. Box 271
Clemson, SC   29633-0271   (864) 653-4460
Contact: Joe Dickerson, Pres.
FAX: (864) 639-0999;
E-mail: ccccare@bellsouth.net; URL: http://www.clemsoncommunitycare.org

Foundation type: Public charity
Limitations: Financial assistance to economically disadvantaged residents of Clemson County, SC, to help with rent, food, utilities, and medical bills.
Publications: Application guidelines.
Financial data: Year ended 12/31/2004.
Assets, $46,194 (M); Expenditures, $280,027; Total giving, $93,919; Grants to individuals, totaling $93,919.
Type of support: Grants for special needs.
Application information:
  Initial approach: Letter.
  Additional information: Contact foundation for further application guidelines and program information.
EIN: 570868065

4665
Clergy Society
(formerly Society for the Relief of the Widows, Orphans, Aged and Disabled Clergy Diocese of South Carolina)
314 Mill Creek Dr.
Charleston, SC   29407
Contact: G.B. Danich, Pres.
Application address: P.O. Box 640 Charleston, SC 29402, tel.: (843) 577-9700

Foundation type: Operating foundation
Limitations: Grants to clergy and their dependents or survivors, primarily in SC, for medical expenses, living expenses, and children's education.
Financial data: Year ended 12/31/2002.
Assets, $1,316,418 (M); Expenditures, $71,186; Total giving, $69,171; Grants to individuals, 14 grants totaling $67,846 (high: $21,196, low: $400).
Fields of interest: Christian agencies & churches.
Type of support: Grants for special needs.
Application information: Applications by letter outlining financial need accepted throughout the year.
EIN: 576021772

4666
Cloud County Children's Trust
c/o Citizens National Bank
115 W. 6th St., Box 409
Concordia, KS   66901-2815   (785) 243-3211
Contact: Marcy Johnson, Trust Off., Citizens National Bank

Foundation type: Independent foundation
Limitations: Grants to Cloud County, KS, children age 12 and under with special needs, and their families. Needs and expenses must not be covered by insurance or other programs and charities. See program description for strict financial eligibility limits.
Financial data: Year ended 06/30/2005.
Assets, $573,458 (M); Expenditures, $36,116; Total giving, $29,142; Grants to individuals, totaling $29,142.
Fields of interest: Education, special; Reading; Physical therapy; Mental health, counseling/support groups; Disabilities, people with.
Type of support: Grants for special needs.

Application information: Applications accepted.
  Deadline(s): None
  Additional information: Completion of formal application required, including first two pages of last year's federal income tax return, current financial statement, and signature of a health official (county nurse, child's doctor or therapist, or school director of special education) who is acquainted with child's needs and resources.
Program description:
  Special Education Awards: Grants are intended for special education expenses, therapy, and equipment. Net worth of families cannot exceed $10,000, excluding cost of home and one vehicle. Income cannot exceed the following levels of household size and corresponding income:
  · 1 - $16,768
  · 2 - $22,507
  · 3 - $28,246
  · 4 - $33,985
  · 5 - $39,723
  · 6 - $45,462
  · 7 - $51,201
  · 8 - $56,939
  · 9 - $62,678
  · 10 - $68,417
  · 11 - $74,155
  · 12 - $79,894.
EIN: 510196634

4667
Club of Hearts, Inc.
241 Ralph McGill Blvd., Rm. 10131
Atlanta, GA   30308-3374   (404) 506-6709
Contact: Audra Adair, Chair.

Foundation type: Public charity
Limitations: Emergency grants to Southern Company/Georgia Power employees, contractors, retirees, and transferred employees and their family members. A person or family may not approach the organization more than twice in one calendar year.
Financial data: Year ended 12/31/2003.
Assets, $157,105 (M); Expenditures, $1,035,641; Total giving, $1,035,641; Grants to individuals, totaling $82,815.
Fields of interest: Human services, emergency aid.
Type of support: Employee-related welfare.
Application information: Application form required.
  Initial approach: Initial approach by letter.
  Deadline(s): Applications accepted throughout the year.
EIN: 586056698

4668
Coast Guard Foundation, Inc.
394 Taugwonk Rd.
Stonington, CT   06378-1807   (860) 535-0786
Contact: James C. Link, Pres.
FAX: (860) 535-0944; E-mail: info@cgfdn.org;
URL: http://www.cgfdn.org

Foundation type: Public charity
Limitations: Financial assistance to Coast Guard personnel who had lost their homes and possessions in natural disasters.
Financial data: Year ended 12/31/2003.
Assets, $5,392,760 (M); Expenditures, $2,924,021; Total giving, $412,510; Grants to individuals, totaling $412,510.
Fields of interest: Military/veterans' organizations.
Type of support: Emergency funds.
Application information:
  Initial approach: Telephone or e-mail.

  Additional information: Contact foundation for application guidelines.
EIN: 042899862

4669
Coastal Jewish Foundation, Inc.
400 Mall Blvd., Ste. M
Savannah, GA   31406-4820
Contact: Charles Garfunkel, Treas.

Foundation type: Operating foundation
Limitations: Grants to individuals in the metropolitan New York, NY, area as well as in Jerusalem for general welfare.
Financial data: Year ended 08/31/2003.
Assets, $13,911 (M); Expenditures, $23,311; Total giving, $23,221; Grants to individuals, 6 grants totaling $22,246 (high: $13,726, low: $260).
Fields of interest: Jewish agencies & temples.
Type of support: Foreign applicants; Grants for special needs.
Application information: Application form not required.
  Deadline(s): June 1
  Additional information: Application by letter outlining purpose of grant and other grants received.
EIN: 581053510

4670
Marion Isabelle Coe Fund
c/o Bank of America, N.A.
777 Main St., CT2-102-22-02
Hartford, CT   06115   (860) 952-7392
Contact: Amy R. Lynch, V.P., Bank of America, N.A.

Foundation type: Independent foundation
Limitations: Relief assistance to worthy adult residents of Goshen, Litchfield, Morris, and Warren, CT, for general living and medical expenses.
Financial data: Year ended 12/31/2004.
Assets, $674,652 (M); Expenditures, $34,356; Total giving, $28,000.
Fields of interest: Health care, financing.
Type of support: Grants for special needs.
Application information: Applications by letter accepted throughout the year.
Program description:
  Marion Isabelle Coe Fund Program: Grants are awarded to provide continuing assistance to needy men and women to enable them to live in their own homes. Most awards are paid in monthly installments and renewed annually. Grants are also given to pay for insurance, taxes, car repairs, and to provide domestic companions.
EIN: 066040150

4671
Regina Coeli Foundation, Inc.
739 N. Lake St.
Mundelein, IL   60060
Contact: Rev. John R. Hoffman, Pres.

Foundation type: Independent foundation
Limitations: Financial assistance to disadvantaged individuals residing in the Chicago, IL, area.
Financial data: Year ended 05/31/2005.
Assets, $13,338 (M); Expenditures, $13,174; Total giving, $13,120; Grants to individuals, totaling $7,420.
Fields of interest: Mental health, counseling/support groups; Economically disadvantaged.
Type of support: Grants for special needs.

Application information: Applications by letter outlining financial need accepted throughout the year.
Program description:
Regina Coeli Foundation Program: In the past, grants have been given for medical assistance, hardship assistance, and special counseling.
EIN: 366126117

4672
Colorado Legal Services
(formerly Legal Aid Society of Metropolitan Denver)
c/o Billie Hall
1905 Sherman St., Ste. 400
Denver, CO 80203-1181   (303) 866-9358
URL: http://www.coloradolegalservices.org

Foundation type: Public charity
Limitations: Civil legal services to the economically disadvantaged residents of CO, and grants to offset the costs of court filing fees, process service and witness fees, and miscellaneous litigation expenses.
Financial data: Year ended 12/31/2004.
Assets, $941,404 (M); Expenditures, $6,417,931; Total giving, $17,874; Grants to individuals, totaling $17,874.
Fields of interest: Legal services; Economically disadvantaged.
Type of support: Grants for special needs.
Application information:
Initial approach: Letter.
Additional information: Contact the local branch for further information.
EIN: 840402702

4673
Colorado Masons Benevolent Fund Association
c/o Scottish Rite Masonic Center
1370 Grant St., Ste. 212
Denver, CO 80203-2347
Contact: Robert L. Bartholic, Exec. Secy.

Foundation type: Operating foundation
Limitations: Relief assistance to distressed members of Colorado Masonic lodges, their wives, widows, mothers, sisters, and dependent minor children. Scholarships also to graduating high school seniors for undergraduate studies at CO institutions.
Financial data: Year ended 10/30/2004.
Assets, $11,216,093 (M); Expenditures, $762,103; Total giving, $642,621; Grants to individuals, totaling $591,501.
Fields of interest: Human services, emergency aid; Fraternal societies.
Type of support: Emergency funds; Undergraduate support; Grants for special needs.
Application information: Applications accepted. Application form required.
Initial approach: Letter outlining financial need.
Additional information: Contact lodge in CO where applicant has membership relationship;.
EIN: 840406813

4674
Columbus Female Benevolent Society
1234 E. Broad St.
Columbus, OH 43205-1453
Contact: Duane M. Campbell
Application address: 158 S. Roosevelt Ave., Columbus, OH 43209

Foundation type: Operating foundation
Limitations: Direct aid on a regular, special, or temporary basis to pensioned widows who are residents of Franklin County, OH.
Financial data: Year ended 12/31/2003.
Assets, $25,669 (M); Expenditures, $34,902; Total giving, $34,385; Grants to individuals, 17 grants totaling $27,875.
Application information: Applications by letter accepted throughout the year.
EIN: 316042036

4675
Common Grace Ministries, Inc.
3800 Commerce St., Ste. 217
Dallas, TX 75226   (214) 370-5750
Contact: Martin Hironaga, Exec. Dir.

Foundation type: Operating foundation
Limitations: Grants to individuals or families who reside in East Dallas, TX, who have a financial or emergency need.
Financial data: Year ended 12/31/2004.
Assets, $161,621 (M); Expenditures, $435,359; Total giving, $127,952.
Fields of interest: Economically disadvantaged.
Type of support: Grants for special needs.
Application information:
Deadline(s): None.
Additional information: Contact foundation for current application guidelines.
EIN: 752727006

4676
Communications Workers of America Disaster Relief Fund
501 3rd St., N.W.
Washington, DC 20001-2797   (202) 797-8700
Contact: Morton Bahr, Pres.
URL: http://www.cwa-union.org

Foundation type: Public charity
Limitations: Emergency grants to Communication Workers of America members and their families who are victims of declared federal, state, or local disasters.
Financial data: Year ended 12/31/2003.
Assets, $197,288 (M); Expenditures, $42,033; Total giving, $41,328; Grants to individuals, totaling $41,328.
Fields of interest: Labor unions/organizations; Safety/disasters.
Type of support: Emergency funds; Grants for special needs.
Application information:
Initial approach: Letter.
Additional information: Contact foundation for current application deadline/guidelines.
EIN: 522128973

4677
The Community Foundation for the Alleghenies
(also known as The Community Foundation of Greater Johnstown)
116 Market St., Ste. 4
Johnstown, PA 15901   (814) 536-7741
Contact: Mike E. Kane, Exec. Dir.
FAX: (814) 536-5859;
E-mail: cfalleghenies@atlanticbb.net; Additional tel.: (888) 280-7741; URL: http://www.cfalleghenies.org

Foundation type: Community foundation

Limitations: Grants to individuals who are residents of Bedford, Cambria, Indiana and Somerset counties, PA. Scholarships are also provided.
Publications: Annual report; Grants list; Informational brochure; Newsletter.
Financial data: Year ended 06/30/2004.
Assets, $23,139,993 (M); Expenditures, $2,028,001; Total giving, $1,452,724; Grants to individuals, 121 grants totaling $71,199 (high: $1,269, low: $50).
Type of support: Undergraduate support; Grants for special needs.
Application information: Application form required.
Deadline(s): Last Fri. in Jan and Aug.
EIN: 251637373

4678
Community Foundation of Boone County, Inc.
60 E. Cedar St.
P.O. Box 92
Zionsville, IN 46077   (317) 873-0210
Contact: Lisa Latz John, Exec. Dir.
FAX: (317) 873-0219; E-mail: cfbc@in-motion.net; Additional tel.: (765) 482-0024; URL: http://www.bccn.boone.in.us/cf

Foundation type: Community foundation
Limitations: Assistance to senior citizens residing in Boone County, IN.
Publications: Application guidelines; Annual report; Informational brochure; Newsletter.
Financial data: Year ended 12/31/2004.
Assets, $13,945,414 (M); Expenditures, $799,043; Total giving, $481,266; Grants to individuals, 13 grants totaling $9,740 (high: $1,200, low: $100).
Type of support: Grants for special needs.
Application information: Contact foundation or see Web site for further application information.
EIN: 351829585

4679
Community Foundation of Gaston County, Inc.
P.O. Box 123
Gastonia, NC 28053   (704) 864-0927
Contact: John A. Edgerton, Exec. Dir.
FAX: (704) 869-0222; E-mail: info@cfgaston.org; Additional E-mail: jedgerton@cfgaston.org; URL: http://www.cfgaston.org

Foundation type: Community foundation
Limitations: Grants for medical expenses only to children, 18 years of age or younger, in Gaston County, NC.
Publications: Annual report; Informational brochure; Newsletter.
Financial data: Year ended 12/31/2004.
Assets, $85,165,926 (M); Expenditures, $6,837,266; Total giving, $6,349,836.
Type of support: Grants for special needs.
Application information: Application form required.
Initial approach: Letter.
Deadline(s): Applications accepted throughout the year
Additional information: Interviews required.
EIN: 581340834

4680
Community Foundation of the Florida Keys, Inc.

P.O. Box 162
Key West, FL   33041   (305) 292-1502
Contact: Ann Storandt, Secy.
FAX: (305) 292-1598; E-mail: cffk@bellsouth.net;
Additional contact address: 614 Whitehead St., Ste. 200, Key West, FL 33040

Foundation type: Community foundation
Limitations: Grants to individuals in Key West, FL. Scholarships are also given to students of Key West High School.
Publications: Annual report; Newsletter.
Financial data: Year ended 06/30/2003. Assets, $3,118,874 (M); Expenditures, $683,642; Total giving, $594,527; Grants to individuals, 17 grants totaling $45,500 (high: $5,000, low: $1,500).
Type of support: Research; Scholarships—to individuals; Undergraduate support; Grants for special needs.
Application information: Applications accepted. Application form required.
   Initial approach: Letter.
   Copies of proposal: 1
   Deadline(s): Contach foundation for deadline
   Additional information: Application must also include proposal.
EIN: 650648968

4681
Community Foundation of the Lowcountry

(formerly Hilton Head Island Foundation, Inc.)
4 Northridge Dr., Ste. A
P.O. Box 23019
Hilton Head Island, SC   29925-3019
(843) 681-9100
Contact: Dianne K. Garnett, C.E.O.
FAX: (843) 681-9101;
E-mail: foundation@cf-lowcountry.org; Additional Address: Oakwood Professional Bldg., 15 Sam's Point Rd., Ste. 103, Beaufort, SC 29907, tel: (843) 525-1325, FAX: (843) 522-3471; URL: http://www.cf-lowcountry.org

Foundation type: Community foundation
Limitations: General welfare grants to residents of Beaufort, Colleton, Hampton and Jasper Counties, SC.
Publications: Application guidelines; Annual report; Financial statement; Grants list; Informational brochure; Informational brochure (including application guidelines); Newsletter.
Financial data: Year ended 06/30/2005. Assets, $34,552,307 (L); Expenditures, $3,591,632; Total giving, $2,525,562.
Type of support: Grants for special needs.
Application information: Applications accepted. Application form required.
   Initial approach: Letter or telephone.
   Deadline(s): None
   Additional information: Applications should be sent by mail; Recipients notified within 3 months.
EIN: 570756987

4682
Community Service Society of New York

105 E. 22nd St.
New York, NY   10010   (212) 254-8900
Contact: David R. Jones, Pres. and C.E.O.
FAX: (212) 614-5515; E-mail: info@cssny.org;
URL: http://www.cssny.org

Foundation type: Public charity
Limitations: Grants to economically disadvantaged families and individuals in New York City, NY.
Financial data: Year ended 06/30/2003. Assets, $156,147,703 (M); Expenditures, $19,646,259; Total giving, $3,711,831; Grants to individuals, totaling $3,711,831.
Fields of interest: Economically disadvantaged.
Type of support: Grants for special needs.
Application information:
   Initial approach: E-mail.
   Additional information: Contact organization for current application deadline/guidelines.
EIN: 135562202

4683
Copley Fund

29 Birge St.
Morrisville, VT   05661
Application address: c/o Richard C. Sargent, P.O. Box 696, Morrisville, VT 05661, tel.: (802) 888-2000

Foundation type: Independent foundation
Limitations: Housing assistance for elderly residents of Lamoille County, VT.
Financial data: Year ended 12/31/2004. Assets, $4,995,279 (M); Expenditures, $191,509; Total giving, $172,700.
Fields of interest: Housing/shelter; Aging.
Type of support: Grants for special needs.
Application information:
   Initial approach: Letter.
   Deadline(s): Dec. 31
EIN: 036006013

4684
Bill & Hazel Cordell Foundation

P.O. Box 179
Quitman, TX   75783   (903) 763-1226
Contact: Jesse A. Cordell, Tr.

Foundation type: Independent foundation
Limitations: Grants to economically disadvantaged individuals in TX.
Financial data: Year ended 11/30/2004. Assets, $385,632 (M); Expenditures, $24,310; Total giving, $20,579; Grants to individuals, 3 grants totaling $9,250 (high: $8,500, low: $350).
Fields of interest: Economically disadvantaged.
Type of support: Grants for special needs.
Application information:
   Deadline(s): Contact foundation for current application deadline.
   Additional information: Application by letter outlining needs.
EIN: 760330598

4685
Maxwell M. Corpening, Jr. Memorial Foundation

P.O. Box 2400
Marion, NC   28752
Contact: Terri Laws
Additional address: c/o YMCA, 1388 Sugar Hill Rd., Marion, NC 28752

Foundation type: Operating foundation
Limitations: Grants for rent, utilities, medicine, and other necessities to financially needy, long-term residents of McDowell County in Marion, NC.
Financial data: Year ended 12/31/2004. Assets, $137,302 (M); Expenditures, $632,967;

Total giving, $621,072; Grants to individuals, totaling $115,495.
Fields of interest: Health care; Housing/shelter, expense aid; Economically disadvantaged.
Type of support: Grants for special needs.
Application information: Application form required.
   Initial approach: By appointment only.
   Additional information: Interviews required.
EIN: 237201488

4686
Corporal Works of Mercy Society of St. Mary's Church

c/o Craig R. Burgess
101 Centre St.
Bath, ME   04530-2551

Foundation type: Independent foundation
Limitations: Grants to economically disadvantaged individuals residing in Bath, ME.
Financial data: Year ended 12/31/2004. Assets, $53,948 (M); Expenditures, $5,387; Total giving, $5,000; Grants to individuals, totaling $5,000.
Fields of interest: Economically disadvantaged.
Type of support: Grants for special needs.
Application information: Applications accepted throughout the year; Contact the society for current application guidelines.
EIN: 237218514

4687
The Correspondents Fund

c/o Barbara Baumgarten
229 W. 43rd St.
New York, NY   10036-3959
Contact: James L. Greenfield, Pres.

Foundation type: Independent foundation
Limitations: Grants for temporary emergency relief aid to men and women and their spouses and children who have served in the U.S. press, television, radio, news, film, and other U.S. organizations within or outside the U.S., or who have served the foreign press or other foreign news organizations.
Financial data: Year ended 04/30/2004. Assets, $825,535 (M); Expenditures, $49,325; Total giving, $31,500.
Application information: Applications by letter, including details of circumstances for which aid is being requested, accepted throughout the year.
EIN: 136100568

4688
The Costco Foundation

999 Lake Dr.
Issaquah, WA   98027
Contact: John Matthews, Pres.

Foundation type: Operating foundation
Limitations: Grants to employees of Costco Wholesale Corp. and its subsidiaries for emergency relief.
Financial data: Year ended 08/29/2004. Assets, $2,260 (M); Expenditures, $49,551; Total giving, $49,541; Grants to individuals, 23 grants totaling $49,541 (high: $6,500, low: $1,000).
Type of support: Employee-related welfare.
Application information: Applications accepted throughout the year; Contact foundation for current application guidelines.
EIN: 911799391

4689
Robert B. Cranston/Theophilus T. Pitman Fund

55 Memorial Blvd.
Newport, RI 02840   (401) 847-0217
Contact: Vernon A. Harvey, Tr.
Application address: c/o John Grant, 18 Market Sq., Newport, RI 02840, tel.: (401) 847-4260

Foundation type: Independent foundation
Limitations: Aid to aged and economically disadvantaged people of Newport, RI.
Financial data: Year ended 12/31/2003. Assets, $2,306,920 (M); Expenditures, $99,345; Total giving, $82,062; Grants to individuals, totaling $82,062.
Fields of interest: Aging; Economically disadvantaged.
Type of support: Grants for special needs.
Application information: Applications accepted throughout the year; Personal appearance or reference from local welfare agencies required.
Program description:
  Special Needs Program: The fund provides grants for medical assistance, food, utilities, clothing, housing, and travel expenses for residents of Newport, RI.
EIN: 056008897

4690
Luther E. Crist and Phyllis C. Crist Trust

c/o Charles L. Park, Jr.
150 Second Rd.
Marlboro, MA 01752

Foundation type: Independent foundation
Limitations: Grants to residents of Marlsborough, MA, for medical expenses.
Financial data: Year ended 12/31/2004. Assets, $329,354 (M); Expenditures, $16,977; Total giving, $11,500; Grants to individuals, totaling $11,500.
Fields of interest: Health care; Economically disadvantaged.
Type of support: Grants for special needs.
Application information: Applications not accepted.
  Additional information: Contact foundation for additional information.
EIN: 046802292

4691
The Cultural Society, Inc.

200 W. 19th St.
Panama City, FL 32405

Foundation type: Independent foundation
Limitations: Relief assistance to financially needy Muslims, primarily in FL.
Financial data: Year ended 06/30/2004. Assets, $0 (M); Expenditures, $51,170; Total giving, $50,000.
Fields of interest: Islam.
Type of support: Grants for special needs.
Application information: Applications by letter accepted throughout the year.
EIN: 510183515

4692
Effie H. and Edward H. Curtis Trust Fund

c/o Wells Fargo Bank West, N.A.
1740 Broadway, No. 8681
Denver, CO 80274
Application address: Jean DeGrave, Trust Off. c/o Wells Fargo Bank West, N.A., 401 S. College, Fort Collins, CO 80522

Foundation type: Independent foundation
Limitations: Grants to permanent residents of Larimer County, CO, who are under 18 years of age and in need of emergency medical and dental assistance.
Publications: Occasional report.
Financial data: Year ended 12/31/2004. Assets, $1,100,078 (M); Expenditures, $60,298; Total giving, $44,453; Grants to individuals, totaling $44,453.
Fields of interest: Dental care; Health care; Children/youth, services.
Type of support: Grants for special needs.
Application information: Application form required.
  Deadline(s): 20th of each month
  Additional information: Application must include itemized bills and estimates on pre-approvals from the attending physician, and a copy of applicant's latest tax return.
EIN: 846019933

4693
Albert B. Cutter Memorial Trust Fund

c/o Bank of America, N.A.
3650 14th St.
Riverside, CA 92501
Application address: c/o Bank of America, N.A., Attn.: Bruce Dunlap, Trust Off., 74-785 Hwy. 111, Ste. 211, Indian Wells, CA 92210, tel.: (760) 341-4773

Foundation type: Independent foundation
Limitations: Limited emergency grants only to persons who have been permanent residents of Riverside, CA, for a minimum of one year and have been referred by local agencies.
Financial data: Year ended 12/31/2003. Assets, $949,287 (M); Expenditures, $41,568; Total giving, $22,892; Grants to individuals, 12 grants totaling $6,142 (high: $1,715; low: $200).
Type of support: Grants for special needs.
Application information: Applications accepted from local agencies throughout the year; Completion of formal application required; Interviews required; Individuals are referred by local agencies.
Program description:
  Cutter Memorial Trust Fund Program: Limited funds are available to assist permanent residents of Riverside, CA, who find themselves in distressing circumstances largely through no fault of their own, yet are ineligible for the usual sources of help. Grant payments are made to those providing the services for the individual. Individuals and agencies must be from Riverside, CA.
EIN: 956112842

4694
Samuel S. Dale Trust

c/o U.S. Trust
P.O. Box 55122
Boston, MA 02205

Foundation type: Independent foundation
Limitations: Grants to individuals in Herkimer County, NY, for medical assistance.

Financial data: Year ended 12/31/2004. Assets, $1,291,466 (M); Expenditures, $98,801; Total giving, $78,856; Grants to individuals, totaling $3,687.
Fields of interest: Health care.
Type of support: Grants for special needs.
Application information: Applications not accepted.
EIN: 046489258

4695
Josiah H. Danforth Memorial Fund

52 S. Broad St.
Norwich, NY 13815
Application address: 8 Fremont St., Gloversville, NY 12078, tel.: (518) 725-0653

Foundation type: Independent foundation
Limitations: Medical assistance grants only to residents of Fulton County, NY.
Financial data: Year ended 12/31/2004. Assets, $628,960 (M); Expenditures, $37,351; Total giving, $29,794; Grants to individuals, totaling $29,794.
Fields of interest: Health care.
Type of support: Grants for special needs.
Application information: Applications accepted throughout the year; Completion of formal application required.
Program description:
  Danforth Memorial Fund Program: Grants are awarded for the payment of medical expenses in times of illness, need, and misfortune. Generally, the maximum grant per year, per individual, is $500.
EIN: 146023489

4696
George W. Davenport Charitable Trust

c/o Bank of America, N.A., P.C. Group
P.O. Box 6767
Providence, RI 02940-6767
Application address: c/o Bank of America, N.A., Attn.: Thea Katsounakis, Trust Admin., 1 Monarch Pl., Springfield, MA 01101, tel.: (413) 787-8524

Foundation type: Independent foundation
Limitations: Provides assistance to needy, elderly women or couples residing in Bernardston, Leyden, or Greenfield, MA.
Financial data: Year ended 12/31/2003. Assets, $527,529 (M); Expenditures, $17,465; Total giving, $8,757.
Fields of interest: Aging; Women.
Type of support: Grants for special needs.
Application information: Applications accepted throughout the year; Completion of formal application required.
EIN: 046312563

4697
R. L. Davis Charitable Trust Fund, Inc.

P.O. Box 806
Farmville, NC 27828-0806   (252) 753-4520
Contact: Cedric Davis, Secy.
Application address: 110 W. Wilson St., Ste. 6, Farmville, NC 27828, tel.: (919) 753-4520

Foundation type: Independent foundation
Limitations: Medical assistance to financially needy individuals who live within a five-mile radius of Farmville, NC, or on land owned by heirs of R.L. Davis.

Financial data: Year ended 10/31/2004. Assets, $670,978 (M); Expenditures, $32,075; Total giving, $14,818; Grants to individuals, totaling $14,818.
Fields of interest: Health care; Economically disadvantaged.
Type of support: Grants for special needs.
Application information: Applications accepted throughout the year; Initial approach by telephone; Interviews required; Applications must be made in person; Information requested includes the nature of the health problem, extent of financial resources, marital and dependent status, and place of residence.
EIN: 566045863

4698
Daystar Northwest
P.O. Box 46261
Seattle, WA 98146

Foundation type: Independent foundation
Limitations: General welfare support to elderly residents of Daystar Retirement Village, WA.
Financial data: Year ended 12/31/2004. Assets, $235,883 (M); Expenditures, $97,648; Total giving, $95,180; Grants to individuals, 4 grants totaling $95,180.
Fields of interest: Aging.
Type of support: Grants to individuals.
Application information: Applications not accepted.
EIN: 910782369

4699
The de Kay Foundation
c/o JPMorgan Chase Bank
345 Park Ave., 4th Fl.
New York, NY 10154
Contact: Yvette Boisnier MSW, Prog. Dir.
Application address: 1211 6th Ave., 34th Fl., New York, NY 10036

Foundation type: Independent foundation
Limitations: Financial assistance to needy individuals over the age of 65 in NY, NJ, and CT.
Publications: Application guidelines.
Financial data: Year ended 02/28/2005. Assets, $37,651,604 (M); Expenditures, $2,238,456; Total giving, $1,848,614.
Application information: Application form required.
Initial approach: Letter.
Additional information: Direct applications from individuals not accepted; Applications only accepted from social service agency representatives which must include age, budget, personal history, and needs of client. Grants are awarded to promote the well-being of men and women of culture or refined heritage who are over age 65, and in need of financial assistance.
EIN: 136203234

4700
Colleen DeCrane Family Foundation
17209 Bradgate Ave.
Cleveland, OH 44111   (216) 252-8324
Contact: Kevin A. Decrane, Pres.

Foundation type: Public charity
Limitations: Grants to seriously ill residents of the Cleveland, OH, metropolitan area for general welfare and medical expenses.

Financial data: Year ended 12/31/2003. Assets, $44,858 (M); Expenditures, $12,970; Total giving, $9,816; Grants to individuals, 6 grants totaling $9,056 (high: $3,150, low: $500).
Fields of interest: Economically disadvantaged.
Type of support: Emergency funds; Grants for special needs.
Application information:
Initial approach: Letter.
Deadline(s): Contact foundation for current application deadline/guidelines
EIN: 341912789

4701
Delaware Foundation for Retarded Children, Inc.
640 Plaza Dr.
Newark, DE 19702   (302) 454-2730
Contact: Anthony Glenn, Exec. Dir.

Foundation type: Public charity
Limitations: Financial assistance to residents of DE with children who are mentally disabled.
Financial data: Year ended 12/31/2003. Assets, $1,303,259 (M); Expenditures, $454,297; Total giving, $229,572; Grants to individuals, totaling $229,572.
Fields of interest: Children; Disabilities, people with.
Type of support: Grants for special needs.
Application information:
Initial approach: Letter.
Additional information: Contact foundation for further application information.
EIN: 510102390

4702
Wayne M. Densch Charities, Inc.
P.O. Box 536845
Orlando, FL 32853
Contact: Application Committee

Foundation type: Operating foundation
Limitations: Grants to economically disadvantaged individuals, primarily in FL, for medical and food assistance.
Financial data: Year ended 12/31/2004. Assets, $17,083,509 (M); Expenditures, $950,757; Total giving, $177,543; Grants to individuals, totaling $177,543.
Fields of interest: Health care; Food services; Economically disadvantaged.
Type of support: Grants for special needs.
Application information: Applications by letter accepted throughout the year.
EIN: 582013696

4703
Dorothy Dickinson Trust
c/o NBT Bank, N.A.
52 S. Broad St.
Norwich, NY 13815-1646

Foundation type: Independent foundation
Limitations: Grants to residents of Bainbridge, NY for assistance with medical bills.
Publications: Application guidelines.
Financial data: Year ended 10/31/2004. Assets, $188,177 (M); Expenditures, $9,114; Total giving, $8,100; Grants to individuals, 11 grants totaling $8,100 (high: $2,000, low: $100).
Fields of interest: Health care.
Type of support: Grants for special needs.

Application information: Applications accepted. Application form required.
Copies of proposal: 1
Deadline(s): None
Additional information: Applications by grantee form, including medical bill.
EIN: 166130872

4704
Diema's Dream Foundation
9103 Dellwood Dr.
Vienna, VA 22180   (703) 319-9164
Contact: Debra Cockrell, C.F.O. and Exec. Dir.
FAX: (703) 319-0011;
E-mail: debra@diemasdream.com; URL: http://www.diemasdream.com

Foundation type: Public charity
Limitations: Grants to mentally and/or physically disabled children in Eastern Europe and Russia for educational, medical, and other types of support.
Publications: Financial statement; Informational brochure; Newsletter; Program policy statement.
Financial data: Year ended 12/31/2003. Assets, $158,069 (M); Expenditures, $146,387; Total giving, $84,594.
Fields of interest: Children, services; Disabilities, people with.
Type of support: Grants for special needs.
Application information: Contact foundation for current application deadline/guidelines.
EIN: 364254630

4705
Disabled American Veterans Charities of Los Angeles
13550 E. Ramona Blvd.
Baldwin Park, CA 91706-3903   (626) 960-5429
Contact: Charles "Karl" Cade, Genl. Mgr.
FAX: (626) 472-0192;
E-mail: dvc.california@verizon.net; URL: http://www.disabledveteranscharities.com

Foundation type: Public charity
Limitations: Small loans to impoverished veterans residing in the Los Angeles, CA area.
Financial data: Year ended 12/31/2003. Assets, $4,238,558 (M); Expenditures, $4,456,677; Total giving, $693,782; Loans to individuals, totaling $4,605.
Fields of interest: Adult/continuing education; Health care; Employment, services; Human services; Military/veterans' organizations; Disabilities, people with.
Type of support: Loans—to individuals.
Application information: Unsolicited requests for loans not considered or acknowledged.
EIN: 952593421

4706
District Lodge No. 3, Sons of Norway Foundation
(formerly District Lodge No. 3, Sons of Norway Charitable Trust)
c/o Robert E. Norton
922 Dellwood Dr.
Vienna, VA 22180-6121

Foundation type: Independent foundation
Limitations: Grants to indigent individuals of "Sons of Norway," who are members in good standing of District Lodge No. 3 in FL and NY.
Financial data: Year ended 12/31/2002. Assets, $244,082 (M); Expenditures, $25,536;

Total giving, $24,910; Grants to individuals, 9 grants totaling $24,910 (high: $3,910, low: $600).
Fields of interest: Fraternal societies; Economically disadvantaged; Norway.
Type of support: Grants for special needs.
Application information: Applications accepted throughout the year; Initial approach by letter; Completion of formal application required, including 1040 tax return.
EIN: 237150690

4707
The Dixie Group Foundation, Inc.
(formerly Dixie Yarns Foundation, Inc.)
c/o The Dixie Group, Inc.
P.O. Box 25107
Chattanooga, TN 37422-5107
Contact: Starr T. Klein, Secy.-Treas.

Foundation type: Company-sponsored foundation
Limitations: Financial assistance to indigent employees of The Dixie Group, Inc., Chattanooga, TN.
Financial data: Year ended 12/31/2004.
Assets, $834,190 (M); Expenditures, $119,810; Total giving, $119,331; Grants to individuals, 48 grants totaling $39,031.
Type of support: Employee-related welfare.
Application information: Applications not accepted.
   Additional information: Unsolicited requests for funds not considered or acknowledged.
EIN: 620645090

4708
Dove Givings Foundation
222 Purchase St.
P.O. Box 316
Rye, NY 10580 (914) 460-4040
Contact: Rich Cayne
Application addresses: c/o John A. Heneghan, Pres., 125 Freeport Ave., Point Lookout, NY 11569, c/o Kevin Heneghan, Secy.-Treas., 177 Bayside Dr., Point Lookout, NY 11569, c/o Betty Heneghan, V.P., 417 Manning Blvd., Albany, NY 12206; Additional tel.: (516) 889-3530

Foundation type: Operating foundation
Limitations: Financial assistance to needy children and families.
Financial data: Year ended 12/31/2003.
Assets, $3,442,682 (M); Expenditures, $2,611,802; Total giving, $2,606,643; Grants to individuals, 31 grants totaling $433,137 (high: $76,500, low: $500).
Fields of interest: Children/youth, services; Family services; Christian agencies & churches; Economically disadvantaged.
Type of support: Grants for special needs.
Application information: Applications accepted.
   Initial approach: Letter or telephone.
EIN: 133795957

4709
Baron & Emilie Dow Home, Inc.
c/o Wells Fargo Bank South Dakota, N.A.
101 N. Phillips Ave., P.O. Box 5953
Sioux Falls, SD 57117-5953
Application address: c/o Ralph Jenson, 1000 N. Lake, Sioux Falls, SD 57104, tel.: (605) 336-1490

Foundation type: Independent foundation

Limitations: General welfare assistance to financially needy residents of Dow Rummel Village, SD.
Financial data: Year ended 12/31/2004.
Assets, $1,740,303 (M); Expenditures, $192,265; Total giving, $182,667; Grants to individuals, totaling $182,667.
Fields of interest: Economically disadvantaged.
Type of support: Grants to individuals.
Application information: Applications accepted.
   Initial approach: Letter.
EIN: 466018386

4710
Drag Racing Association of Women
(also known as DRAW)
3221 Rosewood Ct.
Davie, FL 33328-6759

Foundation type: Public charity
Limitations: Grants and services to economically disadvantaged or distressed professional race car drivers, crew and family members resulting from death, disability or injury suffered by race car drivers and their crew in the course of racing activities.
Financial data: Year ended 12/31/2003.
Assets, $1,015,036 (M); Expenditures, $333,592; Total giving, $166,000; Grants to individuals, 40 grants totaling $166,000.
Fields of interest: Health care; Athletics/sports, professional leagues; Recreation; Disabilities, people with.
Type of support: Grants for special needs.
Application information: Contact foundation for current application deadline/guidelines.
EIN: 953950424

4711
Leva & Frank Duclos Foundation
c/o Citizens National Bank
115 W. 6th St.
P.O. Box 409
Concordia, KS 66901-0409 (785) 243-3211
Contact: Amy DeGraff, Trust Off., Citizens National Bank
FAX: (785) 243-1833

Foundation type: Independent foundation
Limitations: Emergency assistance to individuals and families in Cloud, Republic, and adjacent KS counties for medical hardship and loss due to a natural disaster.
Financial data: Year ended 12/31/2004.
Assets, $1,221,811 (M); Expenditures, $82,288; Total giving, $64,016.
Fields of interest: Health care; Safety/disasters; Economically disadvantaged.
Type of support: Emergency funds; Grants for special needs.
Application information: Applications accepted. Application form required.
   Deadline(s): Apr. 30 and Nov. 30.
EIN: 237222272

4712
Alfred I. duPont Foundation, Inc.
4600 Touchton Rd. E., Bldg. 200, Ste. 120
Jacksonville, FL 32246 (904) 232-4123
Contact: Rosemary C. Wills, Secy.

Foundation type: Independent foundation
Limitations: Relief assistance to the economically disadvantaged elderly who reside in the southeastern U.S.

Financial data: Year ended 12/31/2004.
Assets, $36,001,162 (M); Expenditures, $1,614,668; Total giving, $1,384,325; Grants to individuals, 184 grants totaling $473,500 (high: $6,500, low: $150).
Fields of interest: Aging; Economically disadvantaged.
Type of support: Grants for special needs.
Application information: Applications accepted. Application form required.
   Initial approach: Letter.
   Deadline(s): None
Program description:
   duPont Foundation Program: Grants are awarded to the needy elderly whose other sources of income are inadequate. The majority of those receiving grants are experiencing extreme hardship and require health, economic, or educational assistance. Grants are primarily distributed on a regular, monthly basis, and each case is reviewed periodically throughout the year. The foundation also awards both temporary grants and special grants.
EIN: 591297267

4713
Eagles Memorial Foundation, Inc.
4710 14th St. S. W.
Bradenton, FL 34207 (941) 755-1976
Contact: Thomas J. McGriff, Exec. Secy.
Additional tel.: (941) 758-4042; Application address for individuals: c/o Richard J. Steinberg, Golden Eagle Fund, P.O. Box 25916, Milwaukee, WI 53225-0916
E-mail: memorial@foe.com; URL: http://www.foe.com/memorial/index.html

Foundation type: Public charity
Limitations: Medical and dental expense assistance to children of deceased Eagle servicemen and women, law officers, and firefighters.
Publications: Financial statement; Informational brochure.
Financial data: Year ended 05/31/2004.
Assets, $12,582,388 (M); Expenditures, $1,745,005; Total giving, $670,150.
Fields of interest: Dental care; Health care; Disasters, fire prevention/control; Military/veterans' organizations.
Type of support: Grants for special needs.
Application information: Contact foundation for current application deadline/guidelines.
Program description:
   Eagles Memorial Foundation Program: Medical assistance includes doctor, dentist, and hospital bills, and the cost of eyeglasses, drugs, and medical and dental devices. Assistance is paid retroactive to the time of the Eagle member's death. Individuals are eligible up to the age of 18 unless married or self-supporting by that time. Total payments for psychiatric, hospital, and orthodontic bills combined are limited to $10,000. The foundation pays the total bill if individual is uninsured, and pays the excess if the individual has insurance. No benefits are available for any injury or illness resulting from the unlawful use of drugs, the excessive use of alcohol, the commission or attempted commission of a crime, or any self-inflicted injury.
EIN: 396126176

4714
Eastern Star Charity Foundation of New Jersey
111 Finderne Ave.
Bridgewater, NJ 08807-3100
Contact: Lynn Billingham, Pres.

Foundation type: Public charity
Limitations: Grants to economically disadvantaged members of the Eastern Star of NJ.
Financial data: Year ended 05/31/2003. Assets, $1,694,604 (M); Expenditures, $178,405; Total giving, $165,734; Grants to individuals, totaling $64,416.
Fields of interest: Human services; Scotland.
Type of support: Grants for special needs.
Application information: Applications accepted. Application form required.
  Additional information: Contact foundation for current application deadline; Interviews required.
EIN: 221613650

4715
Eastern West Virginia Community Foundation
229 E. Martin St., Ste. 4
Martinsburg, WV 25401 (304) 264-0353
Contact: Amy E. Owen, Exec. Dir.
FAX: (888) 507-8375; E-mail: info@ewvcf.org; Additional E-mail: aowen@ewvcf.org; URL: http://www.ewvcf.org

Foundation type: Community foundation
Limitations: Grants and scholarships to improve the quality of life for children in Jefferson, Hampshire, Berkeley and Morgan counties, WV.
Publications: Application guidelines; Annual report; Financial statement; Grants list; Informational brochure; Newsletter.
Financial data: Year ended 12/31/2004. Assets, $3,198,733 (M); Expenditures, $90,172; Total giving, $57,665.
Fields of interest: Children/youth, services.
Type of support: Graduate support; Undergraduate support; Grants for special needs.
Application information:
  Initial approach: Letter or proposal.
  Additional information: Contact foundation for current application deadline.
EIN: 550742377

4716
The Eaton Fund, Inc.
c/o Mercantile-Safe Deposit & Trust Co.
766 Old Hammonds Ferry Rd.
Linthicum, MD 21090-1323
Application address: c/o Blanche Roche, Mercantile-Safe Deposit & Trust Co., 2 Hopkins Plz., Baltimore, MD 21201, tel.: (410) 237-4545

Foundation type: Independent foundation
Limitations: Relief assistance to women 60 years of age or older who are residents of Baltimore, MD, and its vicinity.
Financial data: Year ended 12/31/2004. Assets, $139,595 (M); Expenditures, $27,727; Total giving, $24,000; Grants to individuals, totaling $24,000.
Fields of interest: Health care; Housing/shelter; Aging; Disabilities, people with; Women.
Type of support: Grants for special needs.
Application information: Applications by letter accepted throughout the year.

Program description:
  Eaton Fund Program: Grants are awarded to women who, due to physical infirmity or other special disability, are unable to provide themselves with the necessities of life. The duration of the grant depends on the particular situation and need of the recipient. Grants are given to provide health care, adequate housing, and other critical services.
EIN: 526034106

4717
Georgiana Goddard Eaton Memorial Fund
c/o Welch & Forbes LLC
45 School St.
Boston, MA 02108
Contact: Philip Hall, Admin.
Application address: c/o Grants Mgmt. Assocs., 77 Summer St., 8th Fl., Boston, MA 02110-1006; tel.: (617) 426-7080, FAX: (617) 426-7087; E-mail: phall@grantsmanagement.com; URL: http://www.grantsmanagement.com/eatonguide.html

Foundation type: Independent foundation
Limitations: Pensions to former employees of Community Workshops, Inc.
Publications: Application guidelines.
Financial data: Year ended 06/30/2005. Assets, $11,459,734 (M); Expenditures, $759,233; Total giving, $320,418; Grants to individuals, 3 grants totaling $44,418 (high: $20,328, low: $7,247).
Type of support: Employee-related welfare.
Application information: Applications accepted.
EIN: 046112820

4718
The Annie Eaton Society, Inc.
c/o Suzanne May
500 E. 83 St.
New York, NY 10028 (212) 734-8695
FAX: (212) 535-5641

Foundation type: Public charity
Limitations: Awards child care grants to graduate students in social work.
Financial data: Year ended 07/31/2004. Assets, $728,940 (M); Expenditures, $38,703; Total giving, $29,300; Grants to individuals, 6 grants totaling $10,000 (high: $2,500, low: $1,200).
Fields of interest: Human services; Day care.
Type of support: Grants for special needs.
Application information: Applications not accepted.
EIN: 136112113

4719
Edmondson-Telford Foundation
P.O. Box 3430
Gainesville, GA 30503 (770) 532-3228
Contact: William M. House, Tr.

Foundation type: Independent foundation
Limitations: Grants to financially needy residents of the Hall County, GA, area, for medical expenses and general welfare assistance. A small amount is also given for educational expenses.
Financial data: Year ended 03/31/2005. Assets, $102,385 (M); Expenditures, $12,499; Total giving, $11,620; Grants to individuals, 20 grants totaling $6,547 (high: $1,200).
Fields of interest: Education; Health care; Economically disadvantaged.

Type of support: Scholarships—to individuals; Grants for special needs.
Application information: Unsolicited applications not considered or acknowledged.
EIN: 237062020

4720
El Monte-South El Monte Emergency Resources Association
2645 N. Lee Ave., Ste. 6
South El Monte, CA 91733-1499
(626) 444-7269
Contact: Hector Delgado, Pres.

Foundation type: Public charity
Limitations: Emergency assistance to residents in the El Monte, CA, community for basic necessities and living expenses, including food, shelter, transportation, rent, utilities, clothing, furniture, car repair, medical assistance, and holiday gift distribution.
Financial data: Year ended 06/30/2004. Assets, $44,253 (M); Expenditures, $245,591; Total giving, $113,077; Grants to individuals, totaling $113,077.
Fields of interest: Health care; Food distribution, groceries on wheels; Housing/shelter, temporary shelter; Housing/shelter, expense aid; Housing/shelter; Human services, transportation; Human services, gift distribution; Human services, emergency aid.
Type of support: Grants for special needs.
Application information: Applications accepted throughout the year; Initial approach by telephone; Completion of formal application required.
Program description:
  Emergency Resources Program: Assistance is paid only to the vendor (landlord, medical provider, etc.) for the benefit of the individual, not directly to the individual.
EIN: 956097318

4721
El Puente Charitable Foundation
4370 Doyle Dr.
San Jose, CA 95129

Foundation type: Independent foundation
Limitations: Temporary financial assistance to economically disadvantaged individuals for housing, education, medical expenses and living expenses.
Financial data: Year ended 12/31/2004. Assets, $519,165 (M); Expenditures, $31,258; Total giving, $10,484; Grants to individuals, totaling $10,484.
Fields of interest: Economically disadvantaged.
Type of support: Emergency funds; Grants for special needs.
Application information: Unsolicited requests for funds not considered or acknowledged.
EIN: 770557020

4722
Ahmed M. & Fawzia A. El-Mahdawy Foundation, Inc.
4421 S.W. 85th Way
Gainesville, FL 32608
Contact: Ahmed M. El-Mahdawy, Pres.

Foundation type: Independent foundation
Limitations: Grants to economically disadvantaged individuals in the U.S. and Egypt.

Financial data: Year ended 10/31/2004. Assets, $3,288,014 (M); Expenditures, $99,715; Total giving, $22,537; Grants to individuals, totaling $6,167.
Fields of interest: Economically disadvantaged.
Type of support: Foreign applicants; Grants for special needs.
Application information: Applications accepted. Application form required.
Initial approach: Letter.
EIN: 593412308

4723
Elderhostel, Inc.
11 Ave. de Lafayette
Boston, MA   02111-1746   (617) 426-7788
E-mail: Registration@elderhostel.org; Toll-free tel.: (800) 454-5768; URL: http://www.elderhostel.org

Foundation type: Public charity
Limitations: Grants to senior citizens for educational purposes.
Publications: Annual report; Financial statement; Informational brochure; Newsletter.
Financial data: Year ended 09/30/2004. Assets, $81,140,863 (M); Expenditures, $180,286,176; Total giving, $256,027; Grants to individuals, 554 grants totaling $256,027.
Fields of interest: Education; Aging.
Type of support: Grants to individuals.
Application information:
Initial approach: E-mail.
Additional information: Contact foundation for current application deadline/guidelines.
EIN: 042632526

4724
Elfarouq Foundation
1207 Conrad Sauer Dr.
Houston, TX   77043   (713) 465-2020
FAX: (713) 467-0044;
E-mail: Administrators@masjidelfarouq.org; Application address: c/o Admin. Office, 1207 Conrad Sauer, Houston, TX 77043, tel.: (713) 465-2020; FAX: (713) 476-004.; URL: http://elfarouq.org

Foundation type: Independent foundation
Limitations: Grants to individuals of Arabic descent, primarily in TX, for Ramadan.
Financial data: Year ended 12/31/2002. Assets, $6,227,629 (M); Expenditures, $716,478; Total giving, $36,884; Grants to individuals, totaling $21,884 (high: $21,109).
Fields of interest: Religion, formal/general education; Islam.
Type of support: Grants to individuals.
Application information: Applications accepted. Application form required.
Initial approach: Letter or e-mail.
Additional information: Applications accepted throughout the year.
EIN: 760527335

4725
Mary E. Elliott Trust Fund
c/o Anthony R. Walker
93 Woodland Dr.
Contoocook, NH   03229

Foundation type: Independent foundation
Limitations: Grants to economically disadvantaged citizens of Contoocook and Hopkinton, NH.

Financial data: Year ended 12/31/2003. Assets, $546,456 (M); Expenditures, $26,625; Total giving, $21,090; Grants to individuals, 5 grants totaling $14,990 (high: $3,500, low: $990).
Fields of interest: Economically disadvantaged.
Type of support: Grants for special needs.
Application information: Applications not accepted.
Additional information: The town of Hopkinton advises trustees of needy residents.
EIN: 026010880

4726
Rudolph Ellis Gratuity Fund
c/o Wachovia Bank, N.A.
100 N. Main St., 13th Fl.
Winston-Salem, NC   27150

Foundation type: Independent foundation
Limitations: Assistance to financially needy families of non-office holding retirees of First Fidelity Bank, PA.
Financial data: Year ended 12/31/2004. Assets, $2,736,839 (M); Expenditures, $615,306; Total giving, $592,182; Grants to individuals, totaling $592,182.
Type of support: Employee-related welfare.
Application information: Applications not accepted.
EIN: 236220273

4727
Emergency Fund
(formerly Emergency Fund for the Needy People)
208 S. Lasalle St., Ste. 776
Chicago, IL   60604   (312) 379-0301
Contact: Nonie Brennan, Exec. Dir.
FAX: (312) 379-0304;
E-mail: info@emergencyfund.org; URL: http://www.emergencyfund.org

Foundation type: Public charity
Limitations: Financial assistance to low-income families residing in Chicago, IL.
Financial data: Year ended 12/31/2004. Assets, $1,332,661 (M); Expenditures, $787,585; Total giving, $482,644; Grants to individuals, totaling $482,644.
Fields of interest: Economically disadvantaged; Homeless.
Type of support: Grants for special needs.
Application information:
Initial approach: E-mail or telephone.
Additional information: Contact fund for further application guidelines.
Program description:
Crisis Solution Fund: The Emergency Fund distributes assistance on behalf of low-income Chicago residents facing emergency situations. At each agency, a volunteer Fund Manager disburses anywhere between $1000 and $2500 per month to eliminate these crises and help families get back on their feet. Rather than responding with cash, fund managers give transportation passes and food vouchers, make direct payments to landlords and utility companies and purchase money orders to be used toward the purchase of items such as clothing and furniture. Assistance is limited to once per 12-month period for each client for short-term crisis situations and up to three months of financial support to help families on the road to self-sufficiency. An average crisis solution grant is about $100, while an average self-sufficiency grant is about $500.
EIN: 237359890

4728
Emmons County Sports Alumni, Inc.
c/o Terry Gimbel
420 N. Broadway
Linton, ND   58552

Foundation type: Independent foundation
Limitations: Emergency assistance to needy individuals residing in Emmons County, ND.
Financial data: Year ended 12/31/2004. Assets, $11,082 (M); Expenditures, $8,277; Total giving, $2,500; Grants to individuals, totaling $2,500.
Fields of interest: Economically disadvantaged.
Type of support: Grants for special needs.
Application information: Applications accepted. Application form required.
Deadline(s): Apr. 15
EIN: 363442049

4729
Empty Stocking Fund
c/o Southeastern Newspapers
P.O. Box 936
Augusta, GA   30903-0936   (703) 823-3356
Contact: William S. Morris III, Pres.

Foundation type: Public charity
Limitations: Financial assistance to indigents residing in Augusta, GA, primarily during the Christmas holiday season.
Financial data: Year ended 12/31/2004. Assets, $566,402 (M); Expenditures, $407,746; Total giving, $407,485; Grants to individuals, totaling $251,591.
Type of support: Grants for special needs.
Application information:
Initial approach: Letter.
Additional information: Contact fund for application guidelines.
Program description:
General Welfare: Examples of giving include assistance with rent, utilities, prescriptions, doctor bills, food, clothing, toys, and meals during the Christmas season.
EIN: 586045083

4730
Energy Assistance Foundation
P.O. Box 1758
Decatur, IL   62525   (217) 422-3203
Contact: Phillip Beach, Exec. Dir.
E-mail: Phil_Beach@illinoispower.com

Foundation type: Public charity
Limitations: Grants to elderly and disabled individuals for home weatherization and heating bill payment assistance to individuals who reside within Illinois Power's service territory.
Financial data: Year ended 12/31/2003. Assets, $1,179,727 (M); Expenditures, $661,309; Total giving, $572,011; Grants to individuals, totaling $445,075.
Fields of interest: Housing/shelter, expense aid; Aging; Disabilities, people with.
Type of support: Emergency funds; Grants for special needs.
Application information: Contact foundation for current application deadline/guidelines.
Program descriptions:
Warm Neighbors Bill Payment Program: Applicants must be in danger of losing their primary source of heating, and, if eligible, have already applied for federal and/or state fuel assistance. Applicants must also meet one of the following requirements: total household income at or below

200 percent of poverty level; primary wage earner is unemployed; or demonstrate personal or family crisis. This program runs from Nov. 1 through May 31.

Weatherization Program: Provides home weatherization to the elderly and disabled who do not qualify for other programs. Thirteen volunteer agencies help to approve grantees for this purpose.
EIN: 363216406

4731
Estonian Relief Committee, Inc.
243 E. 34 St.
New York, NY   10016-4852   (212) 685-7467
Contact: Endel Reinpoid, Pres.

Foundation type: Public charity
Limitations: Giving primarily to Estonian individuals and families in need. Some support also for scholarships.
Financial data: Year ended 12/31/2003. Assets, $540,875 (M); Expenditures, $183,616; Total giving, $156,419; Grants to individuals, 11 grants totaling $17,395.
Fields of interest: Human services.
Type of support: Scholarships—to individuals; Grants for special needs.
Application information:
  Initial approach: Letter.
  Additional information: Contact foundation for additional application information.
EIN: 135576607

4732
Ethnic Voice of America
4606 Bruening Dr.
Parma, OH   44134-4640

Foundation type: Public charity
Limitations: Financial assistance to families residing in OH, for the benefit of children requiring medical treatment.
Financial data: Year ended 10/31/2004. Assets, $1,751,914 (M); Expenditures, $502,891; Total giving, $51,110; Grants to individuals, 2 grants totaling $10,500 (high: $10,000, low: $500).
Type of support: Grants for special needs.
Application information:
  Initial approach: Letter.
  Additional information: Contact foundation for program information.
EIN: 341649643

4733
Euro Brokers Relief Fund, Inc.
c/o Applications Off.
1 Seaport Plz., 19th Fl.
New York, NY   10038   (646) 346-7000
Contact: Brian G. Clark, Pres.
Additional tel.: (646) 346-7208; URL: http://relief.ebi.com

Foundation type: Public charity
Limitations: Financial assistance to the surviving dependents of Euro Brokers staff killed in the Sept. 11th attack.
Financial data: Year ended 06/30/2005. Assets, $2,152,871 (M); Expenditures, $834,822; Total giving, $834,272; Grants to individuals, 67 grants totaling $572,276 (high: $13,600, low: $571).

Application information: Application form required. Application form available on the grantmaker's Web site.
  Applicants should submit the following:
    1) Financial information
  Additional information: Applications accepted throughout the year.
EIN: 134191859

4734
Ezer M'Zion, Inc.
1281 49th St.
Brooklyn, NY   11219   (718) 853-8400
Contact: Chananya Cholak, Pres.
FAX: (718) 437-4683;
E-mail: EZERMIZION@aol.com; URL: http://www.ezer-mizion.org.il/index.htm

Foundation type: Public charity
Limitations: Grants to individuals in Israel for medical expenses.
Financial data: Year ended 12/31/2003. Assets, $437,549 (M); Expenditures, $4,128,403; Total giving, $4,128,403; Grants to individuals, totaling $4,128,403.
Fields of interest: Health care; Israel.
Type of support: Foreign applicants; Grants for special needs.
Application information: Contact foundation for current application deadline/guidelines.
EIN: 133660421

4735
The Fabela Family Foundation
2835 Aurora Ave., Ste. 115-383
Naperville, IL   60540
Contact: Marcela D. Jones, Prog. Dir.

Foundation type: Operating foundation
Limitations: Assistance to families in IL who demonstrate financial need, and have a child under the age of six.
Financial data: Year ended 12/31/2004. Assets, $2,345,172 (M); Expenditures, $321,914; Total giving, $145,715; Grants to individuals, 44 grants totaling $145,715 (high: $5,936, low: $100).
Fields of interest: Children/youth, services; Economically disadvantaged.
Type of support: Grants for special needs.
Application information: Applications accepted throughout the year; Completion of formal application required.
EIN: 364144423

4736
The Elssy Fabela Foundation
501 E. College Ave., Ste. 308
Aurora, IL   60505   (630) 820-0400
Contact: Elssy Fabela, Chair. and V.P.
FAX: (630) 820-0904; E-mail: salvaladez@aol.com

Foundation type: Operating foundation
Limitations: Assistance to families with disadvantaged children and teens in Aurora, IL, to aid them in completing their education and become productive adults in the community.
Publications: Informational brochure.
Financial data: Year ended 12/31/2003. Assets, $3,765,224 (L); Expenditures, $317,569; Total giving, $73,704; Grants to individuals, 72 grants totaling $42,144.
Fields of interest: Children/youth, services; Economically disadvantaged.

Type of support: Grants for special needs.
Application information: Applications accepted. Application form required.
  Deadline(s): None
  Additional information: Application must include tax forms, public aid documents, check stubs, information on social security and disability awards, and children's grade reports.
Program description:
  Elssy Fabela Foundation Program: The foundation primarily accepts referrals from community leaders who know of disadvantaged families who appear to need assistance. The family must then formally apply. Education on many levels is provided, including language classes. Family members may be asked to assist the foundation in providing other services to other families if they possess an appropriate skill level. Qualified applicants also receive aid in the form of clothing, shoes, personal care products, and expenses for emergency needs.
EIN: 364144368

4737
Fairfield County Community Foundation, Inc.
(also known as FCCF)
523 Danbury Rd.
Wilton, CT   06897   (203) 834-9393
Contact: Letter of inquiry guidelines: Jeanette Allam, Prog. Asst.; For scholarships: Karen R. Brown
FAX: (203) 834-9996;
E-mail: info@fccfoundation.org; E-mail for guidelines: jallam@fccfoundation.org; URL: http://www.fccfoundation.org

Foundation type: Community foundation
Limitations: Grants to individuals residing in Fairfield County, CT, for health, cultural, and housing expenses. Scholarships also to area students for undergraduate education.
Publications: Application guidelines; Annual report; Financial statement; Grants list; Informational brochure; Newsletter; Occasional report.
Financial data: Year ended 06/30/2004. Assets, $54,935,183 (M); Expenditures, $8,255,493; Total giving, $7,201,431.
Fields of interest: Education; Health care; Housing/shelter; Human services.
Type of support: Scholarships—to individuals; Undergraduate support; Grants for special needs.
Application information: Applications accepted. Application form required.
  Initial approach: Letter of Inquiry.
  Deadline(s): Contact foundation for current application deadlines.
Program description:
  Fairfield County Community Foundation Program: FCC staff will respond to letter of inquiry with a preliminary assessment of proposed project. If approved, applicant will receive a full grant application.
EIN: 061083893

4738
The Family Outreach Foundation
5 Wilson St.
Mendham, NJ   07945   (973) 543-1292
Contact: Grants: Nicholas Cusano

Foundation type: Independent foundation
Limitations: Medical assistance to financially needy children.
Financial data: Year ended 12/31/2004. Assets, $0 (M); Expenditures, $63,451; Total

giving, $55,311; Grants to individuals, 24 grants totaling $55,311 (high: $8,470, low: $275).
Fields of interest: Medical care, outpatient care; Children; Economically disadvantaged.
Type of support: Grants for special needs.
Application information: Applications accepted. Application form required.
  Initial approach: Letter.
  Additional information: Application must state child's medical condition and purpose of contribution.
EIN: 223788982

4739
The Fant Foundation
9219 Katy Fwy., Ste. 161
Houston, TX   77024
Contact: Kelley Williams, Dir.

Foundation type: Operating foundation
Limitations: Assistance to financially needy residents of Houston, TX. The foundation helps cover the costs of food, clothing, transportation, guidance, medical expenses, and counseling to impoverished, distressed, and disadvantaged individuals.
Financial data: Year ended 12/31/2003.
Assets, $845,186 (M); Expenditures, $350,288; Total giving, $339,727; Grants to individuals, 7 grants totaling $46,177.
Type of support: Grants for special needs.
Application information: Application form required.
  Initial approach: Initial approach by letter.
  Deadline(s): Applications accepted throughout the year.
EIN: 760443413

4740
Farm Income Improvement Foundation, Inc.
9201 Bunsen Pkwy.
P.O. Box 20700
Louisville, KY   40220
Contact: Carol Finney
Application address: P.O. Box 20700, Louisville, KY 40250-0700, tel.: (502) 495-5101

Foundation type: Independent foundation
Limitations: Grants to farmers in KY for various types of equipment and services.
Financial data: Year ended 12/31/2003.
Assets, $225,821 (M); Expenditures, $491,692; Total giving, $474,666; Grants to individuals, 7 grants totaling $21,180 (high: $10,000, low: $300).
Fields of interest: Agriculture, farm bureaus/granges.
Type of support: Grants for special needs.
Application information: Deadlines Apr. 1 and May 1; Initial approach by letter; Completion of formal application required; Applications postmarked prior to Feb. 1 not accepted; Application must be mailed individually and not hand-delivered or sent by FAX.
EIN: 311525389

4741
E. D. Farmer Relief Fund
c/o County Judge's Office
1 Courthouse Sq.
Weatherford, TX   76086
Contact: Don Duffield, Tr.

Foundation type: Independent foundation

Limitations: Grants to economically disadvantaged individuals residing in Parker County, TX, for medical expenses, supplies, utilities, transportation, and shelter.
Financial data: Year ended 12/31/2004.
Assets, $0 (M); Expenditures, $4,040; Total giving, $3,538; Grants to individuals, totaling $3,538.
Fields of interest: Health care; Housing/shelter; Economically disadvantaged.
Type of support: Grants for special needs.
Application information: Contact fund for current application deadline/guidelines; Initial approach by letter.
EIN: 756027759

4742
Edwin S. Farmer Trust
c/o Simonds, Winslow, Willis & Abbott
50 Congress St., No. 925
Boston, MA   02109
Contact: John L. Worden III, Tr.

Foundation type: Independent foundation
Limitations: Grants to aged, economically disadvantaged women and married couples who are residents of Arlington, MA.
Financial data: Year ended 12/31/2004.
Assets, $764,152 (M); Expenditures, $33,113; Total giving, $22,371; Grants to individuals, 18 grants totaling $22,371 (high: $4,650, low: $200).
Fields of interest: Health care; Aging; Women; Economically disadvantaged.
Type of support: Grants for special needs.
Application information: Applications accepted throughout the year; Application by letter stating marital status, gender, age, and financial circumstances.
Program description:
  Farmer Trust Program: Financial aid, recurring or one-time for elderly, impoverished women or couples in Arlington, MA. A letter describing need usually comes from Council on Aging social worker, Arlington Housing Authority or clergy. Most grants are only a few hundred dollars.
EIN: 046257543

4743
Henry Farnam Trust
c/o Day, Berry & Howard
1 International Pl.
Boston, MA   02110
Contact: Beverly J. Goulet, Tr.
Application address: c/o City of Norwich, Dept. of Social Services, City Hall Annex, Union Sq., Norwich, CT 06360, tel.: (860) 823-3781

Foundation type: Independent foundation
Limitations: Assistance to poor and meritorious widows who reside in the City of Norwich, CT.
Financial data: Year ended 06/30/2005.
Assets, $362,406 (M); Expenditures, $25,215; Total giving, $19,800; Grants to individuals, totaling $19,800.
Fields of interest: Women.
Type of support: Grants for special needs.
Application information: Applications accepted throughout the year; Contact foundation for current application guidelines.
EIN: 046057931

4744
The Female Association of Philadelphia
630 Carisbrooke Rd.
Bryn Mawr, PA   19010

Foundation type: Independent foundation
Limitations: Relief assistance to women over 60 years of age in the Philadelphia, PA, area with income under $10,000 annually.
Financial data: Year ended 09/30/2005.
Assets, $3,314,439 (M); Expenditures, $215,577; Total giving, $189,852; Grants to individuals, 422 grants totaling $189,852 (high: $450, low: $402).
Fields of interest: Aging; Women.
Type of support: Grants for special needs.
Application information: Applications not accepted.
EIN: 236214961

4745
Feng Li Li Foundation
180 W. Laurel Ave.
Lake Forest, IL   60045

Foundation type: Independent foundation
Limitations: Grants to individuals for expenses relating to the adoption of children.
Financial data: Year ended 12/31/2004.
Assets, $10,200 (M); Expenditures, $38,475; Total giving, $29,950; Grants to individuals, totaling $29,950.
Fields of interest: Adoption.
Type of support: Grants for special needs.
Application information: Applications accepted throughout the year; Completion of formal application required.
EIN: 364266091

4746
The Arch L. Ferguson Foundation
601 E. Abram St.
Arlington, TX   76010

Foundation type: Independent foundation
Limitations: Grants to financially needy Protestants primarily in Arlington, TX. Aid is also given to ministers and retired ministers.
Financial data: Year ended 12/31/2004.
Assets, $7,454,486 (M); Expenditures, $386,689; Total giving, $169,934; Grants to individuals, 11 grants totaling $13,400 (high: $1,500, low: $500).
Fields of interest: Christian agencies & churches; Protestant agencies & churches.
Type of support: Grants for special needs.
Application information: Applications not accepted.
EIN: 237103241

4747
The FesteCapital Foundation
(formerly The Malachi Foundation)
12400 Hwy. 71 W., Ste. 350
P.O. Box 246
Austin, TX   73738
Application address: c/o Joe Feste, 8226 Bee Caves Rd., Austin, TX 78746, FAX: (512) 402-0482

Foundation type: Independent foundation
Limitations: Support to Christian ministers and for religious ministry to individuals in need in OK, TN and TX.
Financial data: Year ended 12/31/2004.
Assets, $257,047 (M); Expenditures, $282,062; Total giving, $151,490; Grants to individuals, 33 grants totaling $126,290 (high: $19,603, low: $1,000).

Fields of interest: Christian agencies & churches; Religion.
Type of support: Grants for special needs.
Application information: Contact foundation with specific request; Initial approach by letter.
EIN: 760439471

4748
First Brokers Good Samaritan Fund
Harborside Financial Ctr.
Plz. 5, Ste. 1500
Jersey City, NJ 07311
Contact: Robert F. Cudeguest, Tr.
New York, NY tel.: (212) 513-4466

Foundation type: Operating foundation
Limitations: Grants primarily to individuals affected by September 11, 2001. Some support also to economically disadvantaged individuals.
Financial data: Year ended 12/31/2003.
Assets, $446,739 (L); Expenditures, $462,841; Total giving, $456,017.
Fields of interest: Human services; Economically disadvantaged.
Type of support: Grants for special needs.
Application information: Application by letter accepted throughout the year.
EIN: 137298341

4749
Blanche Fischer Foundation
1509 S.W. Sunset Blvd., Ste. 1-B
Portland, OR 97201
FAX: (503) 246-4941; E-mail: bff@bff.org;
URL: http://www.bff.org

Foundation type: Operating foundation
Limitations: General welfare assistance to financially needy, physically disabled residents of OR.
Financial data: Year ended 12/31/2003.
Assets, $1,776,025 (M); Expenditures, $149,875; Total giving, $40,914.
Fields of interest: Disabilities, people with.
Type of support: Grants for special needs.
Application information: Application form required.
Initial approach: Letter.
Deadline(s): Contact foundation for current application deadline
Applicants should submit the following:
1) Financial information
Additional information: Applicants should not contact the foundation by telephone.
EIN: 930790099

4750
Fisher and Fuel Society of Beverly
240 Cabot St.
Beverly, MA 01915 (978) 922-2100
Contact: Avis A. Beaulieu, Treas.

Foundation type: Independent foundation
Limitations: Grants to residents of Beverly, MA, for special assistance in times of illness or misfortune.
Financial data: Year ended 09/30/2003.
Assets, $1,577,662 (M); Expenditures, $98,645; Total giving, $81,839; Grants to individuals, 96 grants totaling $71,939 (high: $2,600, low: $58).
Type of support: Grants for special needs.
Application information: Applications accepted.
Additional information: Individual applications not accepted; Applications by written appeal from clergy, social welfare agency, or other recognized agency attesting to the need of the

person(s) requesting aid accepted throughout the year.
EIN: 046039361

4751
Fleetwood Memorial Foundation, Inc.
501 S. Fielder Rd.
Arlington, TX 76013
Contact: Tom Cravens, Chair.

Foundation type: Operating foundation
Limitations: Support to certified TX law enforcement officers and fire protection personnel, and their families, who were injured or killed in the line of duty. Some funds are available for retraining if the injury prevents the individual from continuing to work in the police force or the fire department.
Publications: Application guidelines; Informational brochure.
Financial data: Year ended 10/31/2004.
Assets, $4,411,234 (M); Expenditures, $296,935; Total giving, $212,650; Grants to individuals, 61 grants totaling $212,650 (high: $10,000, low: $500).
Application information: Application form required.
Deadline(s): None
EIN: 510163324

4752
Floor Covering Industry Foundation
2211 E. Howell Ave.
Anaheim, CA 92806 (714) 634-0302
Contact: D. Christopher Davis, Pres.
FAX: (714) 978-6745; E-mail: info@fcif.org;
URL: http://www.fcif.org

Foundation type: Public charity
Limitations: Financial assistance to individuals who have been affiliated with the floor covering industry and who experience catastrophic illness, severe disabilities, or other life-altering hardships.
Financial data: Year ended 12/31/2003.
Assets, $418,654 (M); Expenditures, $221,901; Total giving, $141,502; Grants to individuals, 16 grants totaling $141,502 (high: $21,000, low: $1,000).
Fields of interest: Health care; Housing/shelter; Human services.
Type of support: Grants for special needs.
Application information: Applications accepted. Application form required. Application form available on the grantmaker's Web site.
Additional information: See Web site for complete application guidelines.
EIN: 521238188

4753
Florida Endowment Foundation for Vocational Rehabilitation
(also known as The Able Trust)
106 E. College, Ste. 820
Tallahassee, FL 32301-2808 (850) 224-4493
Contact: Sharon Griffith M.B.A., Pres.
FAX: (850) 224-4496; E-mail: info@abletrust.org;
URL: http://www.abletrust.org/

Foundation type: Public charity
Limitations: Grants to disabled FL residents to become independent, productive, and self-supporting members of society.
Publications: Application guidelines; Annual report; Informational brochure; Newsletter.
Financial data: Year ended 06/30/2004.
Assets, $17,659,961 (L); Expenditures,

$3,144,196; Total giving, $1,847,734; Grants to individuals, 119 grants totaling $1,847,734.
Fields of interest: Disabilities, people with.
Type of support: Grants for special needs.
Application information: Application by proposal or telephone accepted throughout the year.
Program description:
Able Trust Grants to Individuals: Grants are made in a variety of areas including equipment needed for employment, education where federal or state financial aid is not available, and assistance with small business start up costs that could not be provided by an agency of the state of Florida or in emergency situations. Grants for job accommodation average $2,000 to $3,000; grants for small business start up average $5,000.
EIN: 593052307

4754
The Forbes Kirkside Foundation, Inc.
(formerly The Kirkside, Inc.)
P.O. Box 855
Westborough, MA 01581-3346
Contact: Bruce Lopatin, Treas.

Foundation type: Operating foundation
Limitations: Personal aid grants to residents and former residents of Westboro, MA.
Financial data: Year ended 12/31/2002.
Assets, $510,941 (M); Expenditures, $33,547; Total giving, $13,499; Grants to individuals, 20 grants totaling $13,499 (high: $2,087, low: $120).
Type of support: Grants for special needs.
Application information: Applications by proposal accepted throughout the year.
EIN: 042311010

4755
The S. N. Ford and Ada Ford Fund
c/o KeyBank N.A
P.O. Box 10099
Toledo, OH 43699
Contact: Nick Gesouras, Trust Off., KeyBank N.A
Application address: c/o KeyBank N.A., 42 N. Main St., Mansfield, OH 44902, tel.: (419) 525-7665

Foundation type: Independent foundation
Limitations: Relief and medical expense assistance to aged and incurably ill residents of Richland County, OH.
Publications: Annual report.
Financial data: Year ended 12/31/2004.
Assets, $11,811,909 (M); Expenditures, $578,966; Total giving, $541,500.
Fields of interest: Aging.
Type of support: Grants for special needs.
Application information: Application form required.
Initial approach: Telephone.
Deadline(s): None
EIN: 340842282

4756
Fore-Christ, Inc.
2618 New Village Way
Wilmington, NC 28405 (910) 251-8543
Contact: Decarol Williamson, Pres.
URL: http://www.forechrist.com

Foundation type: Operating foundation
Limitations: Grants to individuals for religious support.
Financial data: Year ended 12/31/2004.
Assets, $12,538,703 (M); Expenditures,

$204,785; Total giving, $45,943; Grant to an individual, 1 grant totaling $2,893.
Fields of interest: Religion.
Type of support: Grants to individuals.
Application information: Contact foundation for current application deadline; Application by letter.
EIN: 561988905

4757
Donald J. Foss Memorial Employees Trust
604 Madison Ave.
Wooster, OH   44691-4764
Contact: Woodrow J. Zook, Tr.

Foundation type: Independent foundation
Limitations: Financial assistance to employees of Wooster Brush Co., Wooster, OH, and their immediate families in time of sickness, death, or other unfortunate circumstances. Officers and directors of the company are ineligible.
Financial data: Year ended 04/30/2005.
Assets, $8,287,753 (M); Expenditures, $440,013; Total giving, $439,813; Grants to individuals, 111 grants totaling $220,313 (high: $11,670, low: $250).
Type of support: Employee-related welfare.
Application information: Applications accepted throughout the year; Completion of formal application required.
EIN: 346517801

4758
Foundation for the Carolinas
217 S. Tryon St.
Charlotte, NC   28202   (704) 973-4500
Contact: Donald K. Jonas Ph.D., Sr. V.P., Community Philanthropy
FAX: (704) 973-4599; E-mail: infor@fftc.org; Additional tel.: (800) 973-7244; Additional E-mail: djonas@fftc.org; URL: http://www.fftc.org

Foundation type: Community foundation
Limitations: Medical expense assistance to financially needy children who are residents of NC and SC.
Publications: Application guidelines; Annual report (including application guidelines); Newsletter.
Financial data: Year ended 12/31/2004.
Assets, $349,127,277 (M); Expenditures, $92,191,230; Total giving, $82,821,824.
Fields of interest: Health care; Children/youth, services; Disabilities, people with; Economically disadvantaged.
Type of support: Grants for special needs.
Application information: Application form required.
Initial approach: Letter.
Deadline(s): Varies
Program description:
Children's Welfare: The foundation administers the following funds for children:
· Children's Medical Fund: Provides assistance for the medical needs of children, age 17 and under, that are beyond the means of the family income
· E.F. Hutton Fund: Provides assistance to children under age 18 of NC who are disabled and in need of braces, corrective shoes, wheelchairs, and other orthopedic appliances.
EIN: 566047886

4759
The Foundation for Visions
2601 N.W. Expwy., Ste. 612
Oklahoma City, OK   73112
Contact: Donna Kay Harrison, Pres.

Foundation type: Independent foundation
Limitations: Medical and educational grants to people in need who have come to the attention of the foundation from a report published in the media.
Financial data: Year ended 12/31/2004.
Assets, $203,025 (M); Expenditures, $78,189; Total giving, $77,763; Grants to individuals, totaling $10,659.
Type of support: Scholarships—to individuals; Grants for special needs.
Application information: Unsolicited applications not accepted.
Program description:
Foundation for Vision Program: Generally, the foundation learns of a prospective grantee from a media report, and then obtains additional information and/or recommendations from one or more adults who know the prospective grantee. In some years, the foundation will solicit applications for scholarships by notifying principals and/or counselors of one or more schools.
EIN: 731412490

4760
The Foundation
c/o Chapman Bird & Grey
1990 Bundy Dr., Ste. 200
Los Angeles, CA   90025
Contact: Jim McDuffie
Application address: 13 Kastor Ln., West Long Branch, NJ 07764

Foundation type: Independent foundation
Limitations: Grants for home repairs to low-income homeowners in Monmouth County, NJ. Maximum grant is generally $10,000.
Financial data: Year ended 12/31/2004.
Assets, $46,706 (M); Expenditures, $60,051; Total giving, $43,550; Grants to individuals, 7 grants totaling $43,550 (high: $15,300, low: $1,500).
Fields of interest: Housing/shelter, repairs; Housing/shelter, expense aid; Housing/shelter; Economically disadvantaged.
Type of support: Grants for special needs.
Application information: Applications by letter accepted throughout the year.
EIN: 222995739

4761
Hugh A. Fraser Fund
c/o The Huntington National Bank
P.O. Box 1558, EA4E86
Columbus, OH   43216
Contact: Richard L. Stephenson, Chair.
Application address: c/o New Philadelphia Lions Club, 206 W. High Ave., New Philadelphia, OH 44663

Foundation type: Independent foundation
Limitations: Grants to financially needy children for speech therapy, medicine, hospital costs, shoes, summer camp and other expenses, who are residents of Tuscarawas County, OH.
Financial data: Year ended 06/30/2003.
Assets, $1,910,453 (M); Expenditures, $116,165; Total giving, $98,998; Grants to individuals, 46 grants totaling $98,998 (high: $24,000, low: $90).

Application information: Application form not required.
Deadline(s): None
Additional information: Application by letter.
EIN: 346622461

4762
Lena P. Frederick Trust Fund
c/o KeyBank N.A., Trust Div.
800 Superior Ave., 4th Fl.
Cleveland, OH   44114
Application address: c/o Christina Cook, KeyBank N.A., 286 Water St., Augusta, ME 04330

Foundation type: Independent foundation
Limitations: Grants to needy persons of Belfast, ME, for medical and general assistance.
Financial data: Year ended 04/30/2003.
Assets, $0 (M); Expenditures, $16,117; Total giving, $11,027.
Fields of interest: Health care.
Type of support: Grants for special needs.
Application information: Applications accepted.
Deadline(s): None
EIN: 016010164

4763
The French Benevolent Society of Philadelphia
c/o Clairmont Paciello & Co.
250 Tanglewood Ln.
King of Prussia, PA   19406-2365
Application address: c/o Directors or Scholarship Comm., 1301 Medical Arts Bldg., 1601 Walnut St., Philadelphia, PA 19102, tel.: (215) 563-3276

Foundation type: Independent foundation
Limitations: Aid to persons of French extraction in need due to misfortune, age, or illness. Preference is given in the following order: persons of French birth, of French-born parents, and persons of French extraction. Limited to residents of the Philadelphia, PA, metropolitan area.
Publications: Informational brochure (including application guidelines).
Financial data: Year ended 10/31/2004.
Assets, $1,187,792 (M); Expenditures, $76,953; Total giving, $38,410; Grants to individuals, 6 grants totaling $38,410 (high: $9,900, low: $939).
Fields of interest: Aging; France.
Type of support: Grants for special needs.
Application information: Applications accepted.
Deadline(s): None
EIN: 231401532

4764
Friends Neighborhood Guild, Inc.
704 W. Girard Ave.
Philadelphia, PA   19123-1313   (215) 923-1544
Contact: Felicia Coward, Exec. Dir.
FAX: (215) 923-2502; URL: http:// www.friendsneighborhoodguild.org

Foundation type: Public charity
Limitations: Emergency funds to needy individuals in the eastern north central Philadelphia, PA, area.
Publications: Application guidelines; Annual report; Informational brochure; Newsletter.
Financial data: Year ended 05/31/2003.
Assets, $1,078,142 (M); Expenditures, $1,239,822; Total giving, $1,039,708; Grants to individuals, totaling $9,065.

Fields of interest: Housing/shelter, services; Housing/shelter, expense aid; Human services, emergency aid.
Type of support: Grants for special needs.
Application information: Applications accepted throughout the year; Completion of formal application required; Visit office for initial assessment.
Program description:
Assistance Program: Limited funds are available to clients for oil, gas, electric and water assistance. Eligible applicants must have an income level of 150 percent of poverty level or below. Oil clients will be eligible for 100 gallons of oil and will be asked to join the Energy Cooperative Association of Philadelphia (ECAP), a fuel oil co-op. Assistance will be provided to restore gas and electric service, to prevent termination of services or to avoid default on payment agreements up to $250.
EIN: 231424024

4765
The Fulton School Employees Charitable Fund, Inc.
554 Parkway Dr.
Hapeville, GA 30354
Contact: Christine Estelle, Secy.

Foundation type: Public charity
Limitations: Grants to current Fulton County school employees and children who at the time of the financial emergencies were students in the Fulton County school district.
Publications: Informational brochure.
Financial data: Year ended 12/31/2003.
Assets, $232,221 (M); Expenditures, $367,555; Total giving, $364,754; Grants to individuals, totaling $18,207.
Fields of interest: Economically disadvantaged.
Type of support: Emergency funds; Grants for special needs.
Application information: Applications not accepted.
Additional information: Unsolicited requests for funds not considered or acknowledged.
EIN: 581852091

4766
The Fund for the Diaconate of the Episcopal Church in the United States
(formerly Retiring Fund for the Women in the Diaconate of the Episcopal Church)
33 Old Ford Dr.
Hilton Head Island, SC 29926-2601

Foundation type: Public charity
Limitations: Grants to deacons who have served the Episcopal Church and have insufficient funds for their needs in retirement.
Financial data: Year ended 07/31/2003.
Assets, $5,118,704; Expenditures, $139,178; Total giving, $85,155; Grants to individuals, 11 grants totaling $85,155.
Fields of interest: Protestant agencies & churches; Economically disadvantaged.
Type of support: Grants for special needs.
Application information: Contact fund for current application deadline/guidelines.
EIN: 237125960

4767
G.M.L. Foundation, Inc.
P.O. Box 916
Port Angeles, WA 98362-0158

Foundation type: Operating foundation
Limitations: Medical expense assistance limited to residents of Clallam County, WA.
Financial data: Year ended 12/31/2003.
Assets, $463,182 (M); Expenditures, $24,365; Total giving, $17,648; Grants to individuals, totaling $17,648.
Fields of interest: Health care.
Type of support: Grants for special needs.
Application information: Applications not accepted.
EIN: 916030844

4768
Alice G. Gadd & F. Frederick Romanow, Jr. Charitable Foundation
(formerly Alice G. Gadd Charitable Foundation)
c/o Nickerson
11 Market St.
P.O. Box 211
Belfast, ME 04915-1712

Foundation type: Independent foundation
Limitations: Grants to individuals with diabetes residing in Waldo County, ME.
Financial data: Year ended 12/31/2004.
Assets, $346,053 (M); Expenditures, $32,057; Total giving, $14,404; Grants to individuals, totaling $14,404.
Fields of interest: Diabetes.
Type of support: Grants for special needs.
Application information: Applications accepted throughout the year; Contact foundation for current application guidelines; Initial approach by letter.
Program description:
Diabetes Assistance Program: Grants are for the purchase of supplies, equipment or services used to facilitate the treatment of diabetes.
EIN: 223177652

4769
Annie Gardner Foundation
620 S. 6th St.
Mayfield, KY 42066-2316
Contact: Nancy H. Sparks, Dir., Education

Foundation type: Operating foundation
Limitations: Financial assistance to indigent residents of Graves County, KY, to help pay for rent, utilities, medical bills, and clothing.
Financial data: Year ended 05/31/2005.
Assets, $9,979,771 (M); Expenditures, $543,029; Total giving, $278,529; Grants to individuals, totaling $278,529; Loans to individuals, totaling $297,250.
Type of support: Grants for special needs.
Application information:
Initial approach: Letter.
Deadline(s): July 1
Additional information: Contact foundation for further application guidelines.
EIN: 610564889

4770
Virginia Gay Fund
c/o National City Bank, Columbus
P.O. Box 94651
Cleveland, OH 44101-4651
Application address: 750 Brooksedge Blvd., Ste. 104, Westerville, OH 43081-2881

Foundation type: Independent foundation
Limitations: Relief assistance to retired women who have been school teachers in OH for at least

20 years, and who are aged 55 or over or who have been permanently disabled.
Financial data: Year ended 12/31/2004.
Assets, $1,968,506 (M); Expenditures, $194,788; Total giving, $175,938; Grants to individuals, 61 grants totaling $175,938 (high: $7,776, low: $100).
Fields of interest: Education; Aging; Disabilities, people with; Women.
Type of support: Grants for special needs.
Application information: Applications accepted throughout the year; Completion of formal application required, including financial statement and three references.
Program description:
Virgina Gay Fund Program: Awards are paid either in monthly installments or in a lump sum. Monthly awards may be used for medical, nursing, dental, and other expenses as determined by the individual's specific circumstances. Grants are determined by comparing average monthly income with average monthly expenses. Lump-sum grants are to be used for those services and items directly related to the physical and mental well-being of the applicant. To be eligible, candidates must have a minimum of 20 years of service as an OH public school teacher and be at least 55 years old, unless prevented from continuing to teach by a disability.
EIN: 314379588

4771
General Charitable Society of Newburyport
P.O. Box 365
Newburyport, MA 01950
Contact: Sara-Anne Eames, Pres.

Foundation type: Independent foundation
Limitations: Financial assistance only to residents of Newburyport, MA.
Financial data: Year ended 10/31/2004.
Assets, $1,216,544 (M); Expenditures, $79,357; Total giving, $53,961.
Type of support: Grants for special needs.
Application information: Applications not accepted.
Program description:
Assistance Program: The society assists individuals by providing a monthly allowance, or by other aid the board of directors deems advisable. Types of aid include rent, fuel assistance, telephone and electric bills, groceries, and medical expenses.
EIN: 042589680

4772
Genzyme Charitable Foundation, Inc.
15 Pleasant St. Connector
Framingham, MA 01701
Application address: 500 Kendall St., Cambridge, MA 02142, tel.: (617) 768-9009

Foundation type: Operating foundation
Limitations: Grants to individuals of Ceredase/Cerezyme prescription medication based on both financial and medical need for the treatment of Gaucher disease and lysosomal storage disorders.
Financial data: Year ended 12/31/2004.
Assets, $0 (M); Expenditures, $43,275,974; Total giving, $43,275,709; Grants to individuals, totaling $43,275,709.
Fields of interest: Health care, patient services.
Type of support: Grants for special needs.
Application information: Application form required.
Initial approach: Letter.

Applicants should submit the following:
1) Financial information
Additional information: Patients must be referred by a physician recommending treatment based on medical need. Interviews required.
Program description:
CAP: This program is a temporary source of funding. In order to maintain eligibility, patients and their families are expected to continue to explore other funding options, including private insurance, government programs and charitable sources. The program simultaneously assists the uninsured patient/family to find insurance coverage so that access to other medical services is available.
EIN: 043236375

4773
German Aid Society of Boston, Inc.
8 County St.
P.O. Box 207
Walpole, MA   02081
Application address: c/o Gustav Scheer, Agentment, 115 Stanford Dr., Westwood, MA 02090, tel.: (508) 668-8827

Foundation type: Independent foundation
Limitations: Financial assistance to needy individuals and families in the Boston, MA, area.
Financial data: Year ended 04/30/2005.
Assets, $645,376 (M); Expenditures, $81,817; Total giving, $58,987; Grant to an individual, 1 grant totaling $28,837.
Fields of interest: Economically disadvantaged.
Type of support: Grants for special needs.
Application information: Applications accepted throughout the year; Completion of formal application required; Interviews required.
EIN: 046038293

4774
Daniel & Flavia Gernatt Family Foundation
Richardson Rd.
Collins, NY   14034

Foundation type: Independent foundation
Limitations: Grants to individuals and families in Collins, North Collins and Gowanda, NY.
Financial data: Year ended 12/31/2004.
Assets, $3,016,841 (M); Expenditures, $138,986; Total giving, $133,000.
Type of support: Grants for special needs.
Application information: Applications accepted. Application form required.
Deadline(s): None
Additional information: Contact foundation for current application guidelines.
EIN: 222914177

4775
A. P. Giannini Foundation for Employees
c/o Bank of America, N.A., Trust Dept.
P.O. Box 513189 GMF
Los Angeles, CA   90051
Application address: c/o Bank of America, N.A., Personnel Dept., Bank of America Ctr., San Francisco, CA 94111

Foundation type: Company-sponsored foundation
Limitations: Relief assistance to employees and their families of the Bank of America and its subsidiaries for medical bills or other emergencies.
Financial data: Year ended 12/31/2004.
Assets, $1,606,202 (M); Expenditures, $85,643;

Total giving, $25,458; Grants to individuals, 21 grants totaling $25,458 (high: $3,713, low: $5).
Type of support: Employee-related welfare.
Application information:
Deadline(s): None
Additional information: Application should include reason for grant request, amount requested, and applicant's financial status.
EIN: 946089550

4776
Clorinda Giannini Memorial Benefit Fund
c/o Bank of America, N.A.
P.O. Box 513189 GMF
Los Angeles, CA   90051-1189   (213) 345-5136

Foundation type: Company-sponsored foundation
Limitations: Relief assistance to employees, their dependents, and retirees of the Bank of America National Trust and Savings Association who are residents of CA, for illness, accident disability, surgery, medical and nursing care, hospitalization, financial difficulties, loss of income, and other emergencies.
Financial data: Year ended 04/30/2005.
Assets, $1,350,251 (M); Expenditures, $106,648; Total giving, $105,247; Grants to individuals, 119 grants totaling $105,247 (high: $5,000, low: $20).
Fields of interest: Health care.
Type of support: Employee-related welfare.
Application information:
Deadline(s): None
Additional information: Applications should be sent by letter.
EIN: 946073513

4777
C. E. Gibbs Memorial Fund Trust
c/o The Honesdale National Bank
733 Main St.
Honesdale, PA   18431   (570) 253-3355
Contact: Mary McNichols, Trust Off., The Honesdale National Bank

Foundation type: Operating foundation
Limitations: Medical expense assistance to residents of Wayne County, PA.
Financial data: Year ended 12/31/2002.
Assets, $203,408 (M); Expenditures, $7,555; Total giving, $2,006; Grants to individuals, totaling $2,006.
Fields of interest: Health care.
Type of support: Grants for special needs.
Application information: Applications by letter outlining financial needs accepted throughout the year; Initial approach by letter; Interviews required.
EIN: 236496941

4778
Addison H. Gibson Foundation
1 PPG Pl., Ste. 2230
Pittsburgh, PA   15222-5401   (412) 261-1611
Contact: Rebecca Wallace, Exec. Dir.
FAX: (412) 261-5733;
E-mail: rwallace@gibson-fnd.org; URL: http://www.gibson-fnd.org

Foundation type: Independent foundation
Limitations: Financial assistance for hospital and medical costs to self-supporting residents of Allegheny, Armstrong, Beaver, Butler, Clarion, Crawford, Erie, Fayette, Forest, Greene, Lawrence, Mercer, Venango, Warren, Washington, and

Westmoreland counties, PA, and the westernmost portions of Cambria, Elk, Indiana, Jefferson, and Somerset counties, PA, who have correctable medical conditions but do not have the ability to pay for the necessary treatment.
Financial data: Year ended 12/31/2004.
Assets, $27,584,622 (M); Expenditures, $1,451,079; Total giving, $1,009,665; Grants to individuals, 104 grants totaling $1,009,665 (high: $30,000, low: $1,000); Loans to individuals, 138 loans totaling $791,415.
Fields of interest: Health care.
Type of support: Student loans—to individuals; Graduate support; Undergraduate support; Grants for special needs.
Application information: Applications accepted. Application form required.
Initial approach: Letter, telephone, e-mail or referral from physician or social service officer.
Additional information: Applications can only be submitted by physicians and social workers; Contact foundation for current application deadline.
Program description:
Health Care Assistance Program: Without exception, all applicants must be referred to the foundation by an attending physician or social service officer prior to treatment. Grants are paid directly to the physician, hospital, or medical provider rendering the services, and never to the applicant. Grants are made at the sole discretion of the trustees. The foundation does not reimburse applicants or providers for previously incurred expenses.
EIN: 250965379

4779
Gift of Adoption Fund
(formerly The JSW Adoption Foundation, Inc.)
101 E. Pier St., 1st Fl.
Port Washington, WI   53074   (262) 268-1386
Contact: Debra Fulton, C.E.O.
E-mail: info@giftofadoption.org; URL: http://www.giftofadoption.org/

Foundation type: Public charity
Limitations: Grants to individuals who adopt children through an agency program, independent adoption agency, or international adoption agency.
Publications: Informational brochure (including application guidelines); Newsletter.
Financial data: Year ended 06/30/2004.
Assets, $562,646 (M); Expenditures, $417,087; Total giving, $39,300; Grants to individuals, 12 grants totaling $39,300 (high: $5,000, low: $300).
Fields of interest: Adoption.
Type of support: Grants for special needs.
Application information: Applications accepted. Application form required. Application form available on the grantmaker's Web site.
Initial approach: Web site.
Copies of proposal: 1
Deadline(s): Last day of each month
Additional information: .
Program description:
Gift of Adoption Fund Program: Grant amounts are usually between $2,000 and $5,000. Criteria include homestudy approval, financial need, and hardship.
EIN: 391863217

4780
Charles D. Gilfillan Memorial, Inc.
332 Minnesota St., Ste. 2200
St. Paul, MN 55101
Contact: Leah Slye
Application address: 3537 Edward St. N.E.,
Minneapolis, MN 55418, tel.: (612) 788-9010

Foundation type: Independent foundation
Limitations: Grants to individuals in MN for medical
assistance.
Financial data: Year ended 03/31/2005.
Assets, $319,482 (M); Expenditures, $155,330;
Total giving, $106,340; Grants to individuals,
totaling $106,340 (high: $3,000, low: $41).
Fields of interest: Health care.
Type of support: Grants for special needs.
Application information: Applications accepted
throughout the year; Contact foundation for current
application guidelines.
EIN: 416028756

4781
Fanny S. Gilfillan Memorial, Inc.
c/o Arliss Becker
P.O. Box 68
Morgan, MN 56266
Application address: c/o Redwood County Human
Svcs. Office, P.O. Box 27, Redwood Falls, MN
56283

Foundation type: Independent foundation
Limitations: Medical expense assistance only to
financially needy residents of Redwood County, MN,
who are otherwise unable to pay, yet who are
ineligible for government-sponsored medical
assistance.
Financial data: Year ended 12/31/2004.
Assets, $877,283 (M); Expenditures, $19,634;
Total giving, $18,014; Grants to individuals,
totaling $18,014.
Fields of interest: Health care.
Type of support: Grants for special needs.
Application information: Applications accepted
throughout the year; Completion of formal
application required; Application forms available at
Redwood County Human Services.
Program description:
Special Needs Grants: The foundation helps
needy people who cannot receive aid by other
means, frequently not even through the county
welfare office. Individuals who are not eligible for
county welfare may apply to the foundation through
the welfare office. Grants are to be used to help pay
the costs of hospitalization, and medical and dental
bills.
EIN: 410892731

4782
Gilmore Foundation
c/o Fifth Third Bank
P.O. Box 4019
Kalamazoo, MI 49003

Foundation type: Independent foundation
Limitations: Financial assistance to extremely
low-income residents of the Kalamazoo, MI, area
who are unable to care for themselves due to
physical limitations or advanced age.
Financial data: Year ended 12/31/2004.
Assets, $41,684 (M); Expenditures, $38,959;
Total giving, $35,134; Grants to individuals,
totaling $35,134.
Application information: Applications not
accepted.
EIN: 386052803

4783
Sidney and Lisa Glenner Foundation
5454 W. Fargo Ave.
Skokie, IL 60077 (847) 674-5454
Contact: Sidney Glenner, Pres.

Foundation type: Independent foundation
Limitations: Grants for medical expenses and other
general welfare support.
Financial data: Year ended 11/30/2004.
Assets, $1,422,066 (M); Expenditures,
$2,272,266; Total giving, $2,256,716.
Fields of interest: Health care.
Type of support: Grants for special needs.
Application information:
Initial approach: Letter or telephone.
Deadline(s): Contact foundation for current
application deadline.
EIN: 363557155

4784
God's Gift Foundation, Inc.
P.O. Box 5605
Columbus, GA 31906-5605
Contact: Paul S. Amos, Pres.

Foundation type: Independent foundation
Limitations: Grants to economically disadvantaged
individuals in GA for housing and medical
assistance.
Financial data: Year ended 12/31/2004.
Assets, $1,453,556 (M); Expenditures,
$117,909; Total giving, $110,286; Grants to
individuals, 46 grants totaling $91,547 (high:
$24,000, low: $200).
Fields of interest: Health care; Housing/shelter;
Economically disadvantaged.
Type of support: Grants for special needs.
Application information: Contact foundation for
current application deadline/guidelines.
EIN: 582486355

4785
Goldstein Family Foundation
6 Vincent Rd.
Spring Valley, NY 10977 (212) 239-7500

Foundation type: Independent foundation
Limitations: General welfare grants to Jewish
indigent individuals residing in NY, primarily in
Brooklyn.
Financial data: Year ended 12/31/2004.
Assets, $586,539 (M); Expenditures, $65,450;
Total giving, $65,450; Grants to individuals,
totaling $55,350.
Type of support: Grants for special needs.
Application information:
Initial approach: Letter.
Additional information: Contact foundation for
further information.
EIN: 020581239

4786
Good Neighbor Foundation
(formerly Cosgrave Foundation)
P.O. Box 98805
Des Moines, WA 98198

Foundation type: Operating foundation
Limitations: Grants to economically disadvantaged
individuals, primarily in Seattle, WA.
Financial data: Year ended 12/31/2003.
Assets, $1,114,728 (M); Expenditures, $34,254;
Total giving, $550.
Fields of interest: Economically disadvantaged.

Type of support: Grants for special needs.
Application information: Applications not
accepted.
EIN: 911021848

4787
Good Shepherd Foundation, Inc.
6244 Hwy. 55 W.
Kinston, NC 28504-7435 (252) 569-3241
Contact: Sue White, Secy.-Treas.

Foundation type: Independent foundation
Limitations: Assistance in paying medical
expenses for needy residents of Trent Township,
NC.
Financial data: Year ended 11/30/2004.
Assets, $10,945 (M); Expenditures, $12,110;
Total giving, $10,000; Grants to individuals,
totaling $10,000.
Fields of interest: Health care.
Type of support: Grants for special needs.
Application information: Applications accepted.
Application form required.
Initial approach: Letter.
Additional information: Unsolicited applications
not accepted or acknowledged.
EIN: 510175676

4788
The Good Shepherd Foundation, Inc.
37110 St. Andrews Fwy.
Prairieville, LA 70769
Contact: Louis J. Lambert, Pres.
Application address: P.O. Box 1648, Gonzales, LA
70708-1648, tel.: (225) 673-8708

Foundation type: Operating foundation
Limitations: Grants to child cancer patients,
primarily those who are LA residents, for travel and
treatment expenses.
Financial data: Year ended 12/31/2002.
Assets, $41,230 (M); Expenditures, $2,100; Total
giving, $2,100; Grants to individuals, totaling
$2,100.
Fields of interest: Cancer; Children/youth,
services.
Type of support: Grants for special needs.
Application information: Applications by letter
accepted throughout the year; Initial approach by
letter or telephone.
EIN: 721231453

4789
**Gary Goodgear Emergency Assistance
Foundation, Inc.**
4444 W. 147th St.
Midlothian, IL 60445 (708) 389-5922
Contact: Cecilia Moran, Treas.

Foundation type: Independent foundation
Limitations: Grants to economically disadvantaged
residents of IL, primarily for medical expenses.
Financial data: Year ended 06/30/2005.
Assets, $482,062 (M); Expenditures, $46,627;
Total giving, $45,450; Grants to individuals,
totaling $6,100.
Fields of interest: Health care; Economically
disadvantaged.
Type of support: Grants for special needs.
Application information: Applications by letter
accepted throughout the year.
EIN: 363924161

4790
Goodwill Industries of North Florida, Inc.
4526 Lenox Ave.
Jacksonville, FL   32205   (904) 384-1361
Contact: Robert H. Thayer, Pres.
URL: http://www.goodwilljax.org/

Foundation type: Public charity
Limitations: Grants to economically disadvantaged individuals for housing assistance in northern FL. Also provides job training and placement.
Financial data: Year ended 12/31/2004. Assets, $11,686,378 (M); Expenditures, $11,643,238; Total giving, $1,102,577; Grants to individuals, totaling $2,577.
Fields of interest: Employment, services; Employment, training; Housing/shelter.
Type of support: Grants for special needs.
Application information: Contact foundation for current application deadline/guidelines.
EIN: 590637858

4791
Gore Family Memorial Foundation
c/o SunTrust Bank
P.O. Box 14728
Fort Lauderdale, FL   33302
Application address: 4747 N. Ocean Dr., Ste. 204, Fort Lauderdale, FL 33308

Foundation type: Independent foundation
Limitations: Relief assistance to financially needy and physically disabled residents of Broward County, FL.
Financial data: Year ended 01/31/2005. Assets, $20,528,309 (M); Expenditures, $1,343,113; Total giving, $761,302.
Fields of interest: Housing/shelter; Transportation; Disabilities, people with; Physically disabled.
Type of support: Grants for special needs.
Application information:
  Initial approach: Letter.
  Deadline(s): Applications accepted throughout the year.
Program description:
  Assistance Program: Grants are awarded to assist individuals with medical expenses, equipment for the physically disabled, and housing and transportation costs. Most grants are in the form of one-time or short-term assistance.
EIN: 596497544

4792
Charles N. Gorham Memorial Fund
c/o JPMorgan Chase Bank, N.A.
P.O. Box 1308
Milwaukee, WI   53201
Application address: c/o Brian Debenedetto, JPMorgan Chase Bank, N.A., 6000 E. State St., IL 61108, tel.: (815) 394-4616

Foundation type: Independent foundation
Limitations: Support to physically disabled children under the age of 15 who are residents of Winnebago County, IL.
Financial data: Year ended 12/31/2004. Assets, $964,549 (M); Expenditures, $40,198; Total giving, $28,381; Grants to individuals, totaling $28,381.
Fields of interest: Children/youth, services; Disabilities, people with.
Type of support: Grants for special needs.
Application information: Application form required.
  Initial approach: Letter or telephone.

Additional information: Applications accepted throughout the year.
EIN: 366032552

4793
Grand Rapids Area Community Foundation
201 N.W. 4th St., Central Sq. Mall
Grand Rapids, MN   55744   (218) 327-8855
Contact: Wendy Roy, Exec. Dir.
FAX: (218) 327-8865; *E-mail:* info@gracf.org; Grant application E-mail: wroy@gracf.org; *URL:* http://www.gracf.org

Foundation type: Community foundation
Limitations: Financial assistance to economically disadvantaged residents of Grand Rapids and Itasca, MN,.
Publications: Application guidelines; Annual report; Informational brochure; Newsletter.
Financial data: Year ended 12/31/2004. Assets, $6,670,295 (L); Expenditures, $1,992,371; Total giving, $1,772,645; Grants to individuals, 300 grants totaling $90,000 (high: $5,000, low: $50). Subtotal for grants for special needs: 250 grants totaling $40,000 (high: $350, low: $50).
Type of support: Grants for special needs.
Application information:
  Initial approach: Letter or e-mail.
  Additional information: Contact foundation for program guidelines.
EIN: 411761590

4794
Nora Greenwalt Trust
(formerly Nora Greenwalt Foundation)
c/o The Huntington National Bank
P.O. Box 1558, EA4E86
Columbus, OH   43216
Contact: Don W. Zimmerman, Chair.
Application address: 140 E. Fair Ave., New Philadelphia, OH 44663, tel.: (216) 364-1614

Foundation type: Independent foundation
Limitations: Grants to disabled children in need of financial assistance in the New Philadelphia, OH, area.
Financial data: Year ended 06/30/2003. Assets, $149,856 (M); Expenditures, $8,678; Total giving, $8,000.
Fields of interest: Health care; Youth, services; Disabilities, people with; Economically disadvantaged.
Type of support: Grants for special needs.
Application information: Contact trust for current application deadline; Completion of formal application required.
EIN: 346521347

4795
Abbie M. Griffin Hospital Fund
c/o The William Mann Co.
378 Main St.
Nashua, NH   03060   (603) 881-5633
Contact: William M. Prizer, Tr.

Foundation type: Independent foundation
Limitations: Grants to financially needy residents of Merrimack in Hillsborough County, NH, for the payment of hospital bills.
Financial data: Year ended 06/30/2005. Assets, $399,108 (M); Expenditures, $21,464;

Total giving, $12,816; Grants to individuals, totaling $12,816.
Fields of interest: Health care.
Type of support: Grants for special needs.
Application information: Applications by letter accepted throughout the year.
EIN: 026021464

4796
Group Health Community Foundation
(formerly The Group Health Foundation)
1730 Minor Ave., Ste. 1500
Seattle, WA   98101-1404   (206) 287-4645
Contact: Laura Rehrmann, Pres. and C.E.O.
FAX: (206) 287-4710;
E-mail: foundation.ghc@ghc.org; Additional address: 950 Pacific Ave., Ste. 900, Tacoma, WA 98402, tel.: (253) 383-7891, fax: (253) 383-5981; *URL:* http://www.ghcfoundation.org

Foundation type: Public charity
Limitations: Financial assistance to employees of Group Health residing in ID, OR and WA.
Publications: Application guidelines; Annual report; Financial statement; Grants list; Informational brochure; Newsletter; Program policy statement.
Financial data: Year ended 12/31/2004. Assets, $12,287,954 (M); Expenditures, $1,376,771; Total giving, $1,069,996.
Type of support: Employee-related scholarships; Employee-related welfare; Grants for special needs.
Application information: Application form required.
  Deadline(s): Contact the foundation for current application deadline
  Additional information: Applications available from personnel office or foundation.
EIN: 911246278

4797
Growing Family Foundation, Inc.
4203 Earth City Expwy.
St. Louis, MO   63045   (314) 702-3272
Contact: Candy Shelley, Secy.
URL: http://www.growingfamily.com/gf_professional/gff_home_new.html

Foundation type: Company-sponsored foundation
Limitations: Grants to economically disadvantaged individuals for the care of newborns.
Financial data: Year ended 12/31/2004. Assets, $121,726 (M); Expenditures, $38,571; Total giving, $33,350; Grants to individuals, 146 grants totaling $33,350 (high: $700, low: $50).
Fields of interest: Children, services; Economically disadvantaged.
Type of support: Grants for special needs.
Application information: Deadline varies; Completion of formal application required; Application must be completed and submitted online by a professional healthcare provider.
Program description:
  Growing Family Foundation Program: Recipients' children must be under the age of one. Grants are no more than $1,000.
EIN: 431877493

4798
Stephen R. Grubb Charitable Foundation, Inc.
475 S. 50th St., Ste. 100
West Des Moines, IA   50265
Contact: Stephen R. Grubb, Pres.

Foundation type: Company-sponsored foundation

Limitations: Grants to residents of the Des Moines, IA, area for medical and other expenses.
Financial data: Year ended 12/31/2002. Assets, $11,164 (M); Expenditures, $106,457; Total giving, $105,917; Grants to individuals, 4 grants totaling $7,447 (high: $3,600, low: $111).
Type of support: Grants for special needs.
Application information: Contact foundation for current application deadline; Application by letter.
EIN: 391901112

4799
Louise H. Haeseler Memorial Fund
c/o Wachovia Bank, N.A.
100 N. Main St., 13th Fl.
Winston-Salem, NC 27150
Application address: c/o Philadelphia High School for Girls, Bread and Olney Sts., Philadelphia, PA 19141

Foundation type: Independent foundation
Limitations: Grants are awarded to past or present employees of Philadelphia School District, PA, who are in need.
Financial data: Year ended 12/31/2004. Assets, $778,323 (M); Expenditures, $23,635; Total giving, $20,257.
Type of support: Employee-related welfare.
Application information: Application form required.
Deadline(s): None
EIN: 236428035

4800
F. V. Hall, Jr. & Marylou Hall Children's Crisis Foundation
c/o Bank of America, N.A.
P.O. Box 831041
Dallas, TX 75283-1041
Application address: P.O. Box 60163, San Angelo, TX 76906-0163

Foundation type: Independent foundation
Limitations: Financial assistance to infants and children under 12 years of age residing in Tom Green County, TX, who are in a situation of crisis, critical need, or critical want.
Financial data: Year ended 04/30/2004. Assets, $1,422,300 (M); Expenditures, $60,506; Total giving, $48,443.
Fields of interest: Children/youth, services.
Type of support: Emergency funds; Grants for special needs.
Application information: Applications accepted. Application form required.
Deadline(s): None
Additional information: Interviews required.
Program description:
Children's Crisis Aid Program: Eligibility for assistance is limited to children who were born in Tom Green County, TX, or who have been physically in residence in the county for more than 12 consecutive months, and whose parents, or those persons responsible for them, have no financial sources available to satisfy the particular critical want or need of the child.
EIN: 756260350

4801
Hall Family Foundation
P.O. Box 419580, Dept. 323
Kansas City, MO 64141-6580
Contact: Tracy McFerrin Foster, V.P.; Jeanne Bates, V.P.; Sally Groves, Prog. Off.
FAX: (816) 274-8547; URL: http://www.hallfamilyfoundation.org

Foundation type: Independent foundation
Limitations: Emergency relief assistance only to employees of Hallmark Cards, Inc.
Publications: Annual report; Grants list; Informational brochure (including application guidelines).
Financial data: Year ended 12/31/2004. Assets, $785,079,156 (M); Expenditures, $41,330,373; Total giving, $35,588,948; Grants to individuals, 325 grants totaling $243,000 (high: $750, low: $750).
Type of support: Employee-related welfare.
Application information: Applications by letter accepted from Hallmark employees only.
EIN: 446006291

4802
James T. Hambay Foundation
c/o M&T Bank
P.O. Box 6361
Harrisburg, PA 17112 (717) 652-7911
Contact: Dolores Macri, Exec. Dir.

Foundation type: Independent foundation
Limitations: Medical expense assistance to blind, physically disabled, and economically disadvantaged children under the age of 18, who reside in Dauphin, Cumberland and Perry counties.
Financial data: Year ended 12/31/2004. Assets, $2,785,355 (M); Expenditures, $93,977; Total giving, $68,750; Grants to individuals, 11 grants totaling $28,109 (high: $6,435, low: $125).
Fields of interest: Health care; Children/youth, services; Disabilities, people with; Economically disadvantaged.
Type of support: Grants for special needs.
Application information: Application form required.
Initial approach: Letter, telephone, or referrals from doctors.
Deadline(s): None
Applicants should submit the following:
1) Proposal
2) Financial information
Program description:
Hambay Foundation Program: Assistance is primarily given for medical expenses. Support also includes camperships. Grants are usually paid directly to the organization providing services to the individual.
EIN: 236243877

4803
Hana Maui Trust
P.O. Box 463
Kula, HI 96790

Foundation type: Community foundation
Limitations: Grants to residents of the Hana, HI, community who have special needs.
Financial data: Year ended 12/31/2004. Assets, $1,169,174 (M); Expenditures, $25,730; Total giving, $9,250.
Type of support: Grants for special needs.
Application information:
Initial approach: Letter.

Additional information: Contact trust for current application deadline/guidelines.
EIN: 996011303

4804
The Marion D. and Maxine C. Hanks Foundation, Inc.
Judge Bldg.
8 E. Broadway, Ste. 520
Salt Lake City, UT 84111
Contact: Phyllis Warnick

Foundation type: Independent foundation
Limitations: General welfare grants and support for medical expenses to needy residents of UT.
Financial data: Year ended 12/31/2004. Assets, $1,589,876 (M); Expenditures, $243,428; Total giving, $206,050; Grants to individuals, 20 grants totaling $53,400 (high: $12,000, low: $200).
Fields of interest: Health care; Economically disadvantaged.
Type of support: Grants for special needs.
Application information: Contact foundation for current application deadline/guidelines; Initial approach by letter.
EIN: 870503758

4805
Harbert Employees Reaching Out Foundation
(formerly Hero Foundation)
c/o Harbert Management Corporation
1 Riverchase Pkwy. S.
Birmingham, AL 35244 (205) 987-5500
Contact: For general welfare: Sonja Keeton
FAX: (205) 987-5568;
E-mail: skeeton@harbert.net; E-mail: lgriggs@harbert.net

Foundation type: Public charity
Limitations: Grants to needy individuals residing in AL to restore financial independence when there is hardship caused by natural disaster, medical condition or other temporary financial hardship.
Publications: Application guidelines; Financial statement; Newsletter.
Financial data: Year ended 12/31/2003. Assets, $201,044; Expenditures, $124,583; Total giving, $96,025; Grants to individuals, 42 grants totaling $96,025.
Type of support: Emergency funds.
Application information: Applications accepted. Application form required.
Initial approach: Initial approach by letter.
Deadline(s): None
Additional information: Application must include financial information for requests of more than $2,500; Interviews required.
EIN: 631202843

4806
James H. Harless Foundation, Inc.
P.O. Box 1210
Gilbert, WV 25621 (304) 664-3227
Contact: Sharon Murphy

Foundation type: Independent foundation
Limitations: Loans to distressed families in the Gilbert, WV, area.
Financial data: Year ended 12/31/2004. Assets, $524,047 (M); Expenditures, $114,201; Total giving, $50,060; Grants to individuals, totaling $10,775.

Fields of interest: Family services.
Type of support: Emergency funds.
Application information: Applications accepted. Application form required.
Deadline(s): None
EIN: 237093387

4807
Harrison & Conrad Memorial Trust
c/o Bank of America, N.A.
10 Light St., MD4-302-17-06
Baltimore, MD 21202
Application address: c/o Loudoun Memorial Hospital, Admin. Office, 70 W. Cornwall St., Leesburg, VA 22075, tel.: (703) 777-3300

Foundation type: Operating foundation
Limitations: Grants only to children of Leesburg and Loudoun County, VA, who are suffering from polio, muscular dystrophy or any other crippling disease, and whose families cannot afford treatment.
Financial data: Year ended 01/31/2005.
Assets, $3,261,835 (M); Expenditures, $207,668; Total giving, $129,936.
Fields of interest: Health care; Muscular dystrophy; Children/youth, services; Disabilities, people with.
Type of support: Grants for special needs.
Application information: Applications accepted.
Deadline(s): Apr. 1
Applicants should submit the following:
1) Financial information
Additional information: Interviews required.
EIN: 521300410

4808
The Havens Relief Fund Society
475 Riverside Dr., Rm. 1940
New York, NY 10115
Contact: Joyce R. Willis, Exec. Dir.

Foundation type: Operating foundation
Limitations: Financial assistance to needy residents of greater New York City.
Financial data: Year ended 12/31/2004.
Assets, $25,170,749 (M); Expenditures, $1,213,749; Total giving, $770,085; Grants to individuals, totaling $770,085.
Fields of interest: Economically disadvantaged.
Type of support: Emergency funds; Awards/grants by nomination only; Grants for special needs.
Application information: Individual applications not accepted.
Program description:
Assistance Program: Funds are distributed to Almoners, appointed by the foundation, who are responsible for distributing them to individuals who meet the Havens guidelines and are residents of New York City.
EIN: 135562382

4809
Haverhill Female Benevolent Society
58 Marshland St.
Haverhill, MA 01830-3317
Contact: Meredith Germinara, Pres.; Grants: C. Mandel

Foundation type: Independent foundation
Limitations: Grants to economically disadvantaged individuals in the Haverhill, MA, area for food, clothing and utility assistance.
Financial data: Year ended 09/30/2004.
Assets, $464,747 (M); Expenditures, $53,906;

Total giving, $8,126; Grants to individuals, totaling $8,126.
Fields of interest: Economically disadvantaged.
Type of support: Grants for special needs.
Application information: Applications accepted throughout the year; Application by letter outlining financial need.
EIN: 046047957

4810
Hawaii Community Foundation
(formerly The Hawaiian Foundation)
1164 Bishop St., Ste. 800
Honolulu, HI 96813 (808) 537-6333
Contact: Kelvin H. Taketa, C.E.O. and Pres.
FAX: (808) 521-6286; E-mail: info@hcf-hawaii.org; Additional tel.: (888) 731-3863; Scholarship inquiry E-mail: scholarships@hcf-hawaii.org; URL: http://www.hawaiicommunityfoundation.org

Foundation type: Community foundation
Limitations: Grants to economically disadvantaged senior citizens living in HI.
Publications: Application guidelines; Annual report; Informational brochure; Newsletter; Program policy statement.
Financial data: Year ended 12/31/2004.
Assets, $263,717,137 (M); Expenditures, $23,951,706; Total giving, $18,130,056; Grants to individuals, totaling $2,627,817.
Fields of interest: Aging; Economically disadvantaged.
Type of support: Grants for special needs.
Application information: Applications accepted. Application form required.
Initial approach: Telephone or letter, the foundation will submit application to appropriate fund.
Deadline(s): None.
Program description:
Financial Assistance: The foundation administers the following seven funds for residents of HI in need:
· May Templeton Hopper Fund: Provides assistance to HI's aged men and women in order to help them maintain independence and dignity
· Abraham & Annie Lau Children's Fund: Provides support to needy children in HI
· James & Winifred D. Robertson Fund: Provides assistance for the comfort and relief of needy individuals on Oahu
· Irving L. Singer Fund: Provides assistance to needy and poor people of Hawaiian descent
· Alice M. G. Soper Fund: Provides assistance to defray all reasonable expenses of the aged who are sick, infirm, or helpless and without adequate means
· Kitaro Watanabe Fund: Provides assistance to needy children in HI, particularly those who are sick or in life-threatening situations
· Lillian K. Wilder Fund: Provides assistance to residents of HI with preference to native Hawaiians.
EIN: 990261283

4811
Health Education Resource Organization, Inc.
(also known as HERO)
1734 Maryland Ave.
Baltimore, MD 21201 (410) 685-1180
Contact: Leonardo R. Ortega, C.E.O. and Exec. Dir.
Additional tel.: (800) 376-HERO; FAX: (410) 685-3101; E-mail: HEROCEO@aol.com; URL: http://www.hero-mcrc.org

Foundation type: Public charity
Limitations: Grants and social support services for HIV-positive residents of MD. Money can go toward emergency financial needs, including housing, transportation and food.
Publications: Annual report; Financial statement; Informational brochure; Newsletter.
Financial data: Year ended 06/30/2003.
Assets, $2,658,597 (L); Expenditures, $4,439,788; Total giving, $449,418; Grants to individuals, totaling $449,418.
Fields of interest: AIDS, people with.
Type of support: Emergency funds; Grants for special needs.
Application information: Contact foundation for current application deadline/guidelines; Initial approach by telephone or in person; See Web site for full description of services and more information.
EIN: 521291470

4812
The Gary & Diane Heavin Community Fund Inc.
(formerly The Curves Community Fund, Inc.)
400 Schroeder Dr.
Waco, TX 76710

Foundation type: Company-sponsored foundation
Limitations: Grants to individuals.
Financial data: Year ended 04/30/2002.
Assets, $2,171,437 (M); Expenditures, $1,256,494; Total giving, $1,256,494; Grants to individuals, 19 grants totaling $44,109 (high: $16,967, low: $380).
Type of support: Grants to individuals.
Application information: Unsolicited requests for funds not accepted.
EIN: 743003293

4813
Hegeman Memorial Trust Fund
c/o MetLife, Inc.
27-01 Queens Plz. N., Fl. 5
Long Island City, NY 11101 (212) 578-6953
Contact: Ben LoCasto, Dir., Employee Assistance Dept.

Foundation type: Company-sponsored foundation
Limitations: General welfare grants to U.S. residents who are present and former employees of Metropolitan Life Insurance Company and to their spouses, dependents, and survivors.
Financial data: Year ended 12/31/2004.
Assets, $1,016,713 (M); Expenditures, $40,668; Total giving, $38,568; Grants to individuals, 11 grants totaling $38,568 (high: $10,000, low: $1,000).
Type of support: Employee-related welfare.
Application information: Application form required.
Initial approach: Letter or telephone.
Applicants should submit the following:
1) Financial information
Additional information: Applications from anyone other than MetLife employees will not be

considered or acknowledged; Interviews
required.
EIN: 133043763

4814

Hemophilia Outreach of Wisconsin, Inc.
1794 E. Allouez Ave.
Green Bay, WI 54311-6236 (920) 965-0606

Foundation type: Operating foundation
Limitations: Grants to economically disadvantaged
individuals in WI affected by hemophilia or other
severe bleeding disorders for medical, living and
funeral expenses. Funding for medical expenses is
up to $1,500 per individual per calendar year, for
living expenses $500 per individual per calendar
year, and for funeral expenses $1,000 per
individual per calendar year.
Financial data: Year ended 12/31/2003.
Assets, $6,241,658 (M); Expenditures,
$674,194; Total giving, $55,342; Grants to
individuals, 15 grants totaling $45,342 (high:
$5,000, low: $88).
Fields of interest: Hemophilia.
Type of support: Grants for special needs.
Application information: Application form required.
Deadline(s): May 1
EIN: 391858104

4815

Elizabeth A. Herdegen Trust
c/o Comerica Bank
P.O. Box 75000
Detroit, MI 48275 (313) 222-9067
Application address: c/o Taylor Statten Camps, 59
Hoyle Ave., Toronto, Canada M4S 2X5, tel.: (416)
486-6959

Foundation type: Independent foundation
Limitations: Camperships to financially needy
individuals aged seven to seventeen.
Financial data: Year ended 12/31/2004.
Assets, $179,689 (M); Expenditures, $11,540;
Total giving, $8,500; Grants to individuals, totaling
$8,500.
Fields of interest: Children/youth, services;
Economically disadvantaged.
Type of support: Precollege support.
Application information:
Deadline(s): Feb. 15
Additional information: Contact foundation for
current application guidelines.
EIN: 386461176

4816

Herschend Family Foundation
c/o Jack R. Herschend
Silver Dollar City Inc.
100 Corporate Pl., Corp. Offices
Branson, MO 65616

Foundation type: Independent foundation
Limitations: Fund ministries in Stone and Taney
counties that help those in need.
Financial data: Year ended 12/31/2004.
Assets, $3,694,822 (M); Expenditures,
$248,651; Total giving, $245,894.
Type of support: Grants for special needs.
Application information: Applications not
accepted.
Additional information: Unsolicited applications
not accepted or acknowledged.
EIN: 431391940

4817

William Higgins Trust for Avelena Fund
c/o JPMorgan Chase Bank, N.A
P.O. Box 1308
Milwaukee, WI 53201-1308
Application address: c/o: National City Bank,
Attn.: Robert A. Duff, P.O. Box 849, Anderson, IN
46015

Foundation type: Independent foundation
Limitations: Financial assistance to aged, indigent
residents of IN.
Financial data: Year ended 10/31/2004.
Assets, $458,993 (M); Expenditures, $32,229;
Total giving, $23,828.
Fields of interest: Aging; Economically
disadvantaged.
Type of support: Grants for special needs.
Application information: Applications accepted.
Applicants should submit the following:
1) Financial information
EIN: 356009209

4818

His Helping Hand Foundation
P.O. Box 1119
Goldendale, WA 98620
Contact: Corinne Fuller, Pres.

Foundation type: Operating foundation
Limitations: Provides partial financial assistance to
supplement funds of parents residing in OR and WA
who want to enroll their children in Christian
schools.
Financial data: Year ended 06/30/2005.
Assets, $201,630 (M); Expenditures, $79,741;
Total giving, $78,433.
Fields of interest: Elementary/secondary
education.
Type of support: Grants to individuals.
Application information: Applications accepted.
Application form required.
Initial approach: Letter.
Applicants should submit the following:
1) Financial information
EIN: 911791444

4819

Cathy L. Hodges Memorial Cancer Foundation
9724 Kingston Pike, Ste. 1000
Knoxville, TN 37922 (865) 690-5346
Contact: Bill A. Hodges, Pres.

Foundation type: Independent foundation
Limitations: Grants to economically disadvantaged
individuals for medical expenses.
Financial data: Year ended 06/30/2005.
Assets, $1,073 (M); Expenditures, $34,498; Total
giving, $32,628; Grants to individuals, totaling
$32,628.
Fields of interest: Health care; Economically
disadvantaged.
Type of support: Emergency funds; Grants for
special needs.
Application information:
Deadline(s): 10th of each month
Additional information: Application from health
care professionals only.
Program description:
Health Care Assistance Program: Grants not
exceeding $500 must be submitted by health care
professionals. Limited to cancer patients in East
Tennessee.
EIN: 621620282

4820

Hoellen Foundation
(formerly Hoellen Family Foundation)
1940 Irving Park Rd.
Chicago, IL 60613-2498 (773) 327-4700
Contact: R. Hoellen, Dir.

Foundation type: Independent foundation
Limitations: Grants to individuals residing in the
Ravenswood area, Chicago, IL.
Financial data: Year ended 12/31/2003.
Assets, $6,420,256 (M); Expenditures,
$322,591; Total giving, $249,000.
Type of support: Grants to individuals.
Application information:
Initial approach: Letter.
Deadline(s): Oct.
Additional information: Contact foundation for
current application deadline/guidelines.
EIN: 363209348

4821

Holland Lodge Foundation, Inc.
71 W. 23rd St., Ste. 701
New York, NY 10010-4102 (212) 675-0323
FAX: (212) 675-8730; E-mail: office@holland8.org

Foundation type: Independent foundation
Limitations: Relief grants to the elderly and young,
primarily in New York, NY.
Financial data: Year ended 09/30/2004.
Assets, $1,765,397 (M); Expenditures,
$144,080; Total giving, $98,540; Grants to
individuals, 3 grants totaling $31,500 (high:
$20,000, low: $1,500).
Fields of interest: Children/youth, services; Aging.
Type of support: Grants for special needs.
Application information: Applications by letter,
outlining financial need and reason for assistance,
accepted throughout the year.
EIN: 136126132

4822

Home Team Foundation
6103 Hidden Lakes Dr.
Kingwood, TX 77345 (281) 540-5603
Contact: Sherri Hutcheon, Secy.

Foundation type: Independent foundation
Limitations: Grants to economically disadvantaged
individuals. Applicants must be single parents not
receiving financial support from their ex-spouses.
Financial data: Year ended 12/31/2003.
Assets, $8,689 (M); Expenditures, $44,639; Total
giving, $31,507; Grants to individuals, totaling
$31,507.
Fields of interest: Single parents; Economically
disadvantaged.
Type of support: Grants for special needs.
Application information: Applications accepted.
Deadline(s): None
Additional information: Contact foundation for
further application information.
EIN: 742903875

4823

The Homer Family Foundation
c/o Foundation Source
501 Silverside Rd.
Wilmington, DE 19809-1377

Foundation type: Independent foundation
Limitations: Grants to severely or profoundly
hearing impaired individuals using auditory verbal
as their primary mode of communication.

Recipients must be residents of the U.S. and attending school.
Financial data: Year ended 06/30/2005.
Assets, $1,009,445 (M); Expenditures, $51,496; Total giving, $39,250; Grants to individuals, 16 grants totaling $26,750.
Fields of interest: Disabilities, people with.
Type of support: Grants for special needs.
Application information: Application form required.
Initial approach: Letter.
Deadline(s): Mar. 31
EIN: 010449273

4824
Housing Industry Foundation
1845 S. Bascom Ave., The Annex
Campbell, CA 95008 (408) 369-9900
Contact: Deborah Wade, Exec. Dir.
FAX: (408) 369-9763; E-mail: debbie@HIFinfo.org;
URL: http://www.hifinfo.org

Foundation type: Public charity
Limitations: Grants to low-income families in San Mateo and Santa Clara counties, CA, who are at risk of losing their housing or having to relocate due to an unavoidable crisis.
Publications: Informational brochure; Newsletter.
Financial data: Year ended 06/30/2003.
Assets, $643,308 (M); Expenditures, $468,770; Total giving, $301,116; Grants to individuals, totaling $14,371.
Fields of interest: Housing/shelter.
Type of support: Grants for special needs.
Application information: Applications accepted from partner agencies throughout the year.
Program description:
Housing Industry Projects:
· Emergency Housing Fund
· Shelter Rehab Projects: HIF will make needed repairs and improvements to housing provided by nonprofit organizations to low-income households and special population groups.
EIN: 943100671

4825
Howard Benevolent Society
14 Beacon St., Rm. 804
Boston, MA 02108-3704 (617) 747-2952
Contact: Marcia T. Burley
FAX: (617) 723-8248; E-mail: hbsboston@aol.com

Foundation type: Operating foundation
Limitations: Welfare assistance to sick and destitute residents of the Boston, MA, area.
Publications: Informational brochure.
Financial data: Year ended 09/30/2004.
Assets, $4,038,801 (M); Expenditures, $236,581; Total giving, $88,279; Grants to individuals, totaling $88,279.
Fields of interest: Human services.
Type of support: Grants for special needs.
Application information: Applications by letter or telephone accepted throughout the year.
EIN: 042129132

4826
Howland Fund for Aged Women
c/o Child & Family Svcs.
1061 Pleasant St.
New Bedford, MA 02740-6728

Foundation type: Independent foundation

Limitations: Relief assistance by referral only to financially needy, aged women residing in New Bedford, MA.
Financial data: Year ended 02/28/2005.
Assets, $809,231 (M); Expenditures, $35,040; Total giving, $34,425; Grants to individuals, totaling $34,425.
Fields of interest: Aging; Women.
Type of support: Grants for special needs.
Application information: Unsolicited requests for funds not considered or acknowledged.
EIN: 046050865

4827
Hudson-Webber Foundation
333 W. Fort St., Ste. 1310
Detroit, MI 48226-3149 (313) 963-7777
Contact: David O. Egner, Pres.
URL: http://www.hudson-webber.org

Foundation type: Independent foundation
Limitations: Grants to qualified employees and former employees of the J.L. Hudson Company ("Hudsonians") and their dependents for dental and medical expenses, primarily in MI.
Publications: Biennial report (including application guidelines); Financial statement; Grants list.
Financial data: Year ended 12/31/2005.
Assets, $150,376,115 (M); Expenditures, $8,608,489; Total giving, $7,299,369.
Application information: Applications not accepted.
EIN: 386052131

4828
Huen Foundation, Inc.
1801 W. 16th St.
Broadview, IL 60155
Contact: Michael F. Hughes, Dir.

Foundation type: Operating foundation
Limitations: Medical expense assistance to financially needy families residing in Illinois.
Financial data: Year ended 12/31/2004.
Assets, $285,259 (M); Expenditures, $38,015; Total giving, $38,000; Grants to individuals, 4 grants totaling $33,000 (high: $20,000, low: $3,000).
Fields of interest: Human services.
Type of support: Grants for special needs.
Application information:
Initial approach: Letter describing need.
EIN: 200196993

4829
Teresa F. Hughes Trust
P.O. Box 3170
Honolulu, HI 96802-3170
Application address: c/o Grants Admin., Hawaii Community Foundation, 1164 Bishop St., Ste. 800, Honolulu, HI 96813, tel.: (808) 537-6333

Foundation type: Independent foundation
Limitations: Grants to financially needy HI residents who are orphans, half-orphans, social orphans (neglected or abused), children born out-of-wedlock, or indigent or infirmed adults age 50 or over.
Financial data: Year ended 03/31/2004.
Assets, $9,373,224 (M); Expenditures, $426,842; Total giving, $367,400.
Fields of interest: Residential/custodial care; Aging; Economically disadvantaged.
Type of support: Grants for special needs.

Application information: Applications accepted. Application form required.
Deadline(s): None
Additional information: Application must include a social summary from a professional in the community that describes the applicant and his/her need.
Program description:
Assistance Program: In the past, assistance has been given for income supplements, clothing, utility payments, food, rent, other living expenses, travel expenses, child care, adult day health care, medical expenses, dental expenses, medication, tax assistance, and therapy.
EIN: 990042494

4830
Human Aid Society of Iowa
1601 W. Lakes Pkwy., Ste. 300
West Des Moines, IA 50266

Foundation type: Operating foundation
Limitations: Relief assistance to residents of Polk County, IA, who demonstrate immediate need in acquiring food, clothing, and other items of subsistence. Assistance is generally limited to $200 per individual per year.
Financial data: Year ended 12/31/2003.
Assets, $30,817 (M); Expenditures, $4,960; Total giving, $4,598; Grants to individuals, totaling $4,598.
Type of support: Grants for special needs.
Application information: Applications not accepted.
EIN: 426075775

4831
Humane Society of the Commonwealth of Massachusetts
c/o Mellon Financial Corp.
P.O. Box 185
Pittsburgh, PA 15230-0185

Foundation type: Independent foundation
Limitations: Grants, medals and, certificates, by nomination only, to individuals residing in MA who have heroically saved or attempted to save someone's life.
Financial data: Year ended 02/28/2005.
Assets, $4,696,718 (M); Expenditures, $199,317; Total giving, $132,000; Grants to individuals, 22 grants totaling $92,000 (high: $10,000, low: $500).
Fields of interest: Safety/disasters, ethics; Disasters, search/rescue.
Type of support: Awards/grants by nomination only; Awards/prizes.
Application information: Unsolicited requests for funds not considered or acknowledged.
EIN: 042104291

4832
Orion L. & Emma B. Hurlbut Memorial Fund
701 Market St.
Chattanooga, TN 37402
Application address: c/o Kathy Wood, 975 E. 3rd St., Chattanooga, TN 37403, tel.: (423) 778-7503

Foundation type: Independent foundation
Limitations: Financial assistance for medical expenses to economically disadvantaged cancer patients at Erlanger Hospital, outside of Hamilton

County, TN. Payments are made directly to the physicians and health facilities providing treatment.
Financial data: Year ended 04/30/2005. Assets, $20,291,738 (M); Expenditures, $956,156; Total giving, $724,843.
Fields of interest: Cancer; Economically disadvantaged.
Type of support: Grants for special needs.
Application information: Applications accepted.
Additional information: Applications by letter accepted throughout the year, including physician's detailed expense vouchers.
EIN: 626034546

4833
Horace C. Hurlbutt Memorial Fund
90 Post Rd. E., 3rd Fl.
Westport, CT 06880

Foundation type: Independent foundation
Limitations: Grants to financially needy individuals of Westport, CT.
Financial data: Year ended 12/31/2004. Assets, $681,642 (M); Expenditures, $24,414; Total giving, $14,508; Grants to individuals, 39 grants totaling $8,500.
Fields of interest: Education; Housing/shelter; Economically disadvantaged.
Type of support: Grants for special needs.
Application information: Applications not accepted.
Program description:
Hurlbutt Memorial Foundation Program: Previous grants have been given for attendance at after-school programs, medical expenses, and rent assistance.
EIN: 066035912

4834
Mary J. Hutchins Foundation, Inc.
50 E. 42nd St., 19th Fl.
New York, NY 10017 (212) 599-2234

Foundation type: Independent foundation
Limitations: Welfare assistance to economically disadvantaged individuals, primarily in the New York, NY, metropolitan area.
Financial data: Year ended 12/31/2004. Assets, $37,327,319 (M); Expenditures, $2,055,399; Total giving, $1,772,607.
Fields of interest: Economically disadvantaged.
Type of support: Grants for special needs.
Application information: Applications not accepted.
EIN: 136083578

4835
Hynd Blind Fund of the James Hynd Trust
c/o JPMorgan Chase Bank, N.A
P.O. Box 1308
Milwaukee, WI 53201
Application address: Attn: Brian J. Pieper, 1800 Broadway, Boulder, CO 80302, tel.: (303) 245-6701

Foundation type: Independent foundation
Limitations: Eyeglasses to financially needy residents of Boulder County, CO.
Financial data: Year ended 06/30/2005. Assets, $1,518,760 (M); Expenditures, $93,333; Total giving, $66,587; Grants to individuals, totaling $66,587.
Fields of interest: Optometry/vision screening; Disabilities, people with.

Type of support: Grants for special needs.
Application information: Applications not accepted.
EIN: 846022973

4836
I Care Foundation
496 N. 80 W.
Lindon, UT 84042
Contact: Ilene Olsen, Tr.

Foundation type: Operating foundation
Limitations: Grants to economically disadvantaged individuals and families in the Wasatch Front, UT, area, for food, clothing, educational support and other necessities.
Financial data: Year ended 12/31/2002. Assets, $6,334 (M); Expenditures, $60,141; Total giving, $59,668; Grants to individuals, totaling $46,725.
Fields of interest: Education; Food services; Economically disadvantaged.
Type of support: Grants for special needs.
Application information:
Deadline(s): Applications accepted throughout the year.
Additional information: Contact foundation for current application guidelines.
EIN: 870653978

4837
IAFF Disaster Relief Fund
1750 New York Ave., N.W., Ste. 300
Washington, DC 20006-5395 (202) 737-8484

Foundation type: Public charity
Limitations: Grants to aid the recovery of fire fighters who have suffered large natural disasters.
Financial data: Year ended 12/31/2003. Assets, $1,949,953; Expenditures, $3,164,522; Total giving, $13,000; Grants to individuals, 26 grants totaling $13,000.
Fields of interest: Safety/disasters.
Type of support: Emergency funds.
Application information: Contact fund for current application deadline/guidelines.
EIN: 521846252

4838
Leonard & Mildred Igstaedter Foundation, Inc.
15 Serfilippi Dr.
Ridgefield, CT 06877

Foundation type: Independent foundation
Limitations: Financial assistance to needy individuals residing in CT.
Financial data: Year ended 12/31/2004. Assets, $299,459 (M); Expenditures, $18,647; Total giving, $14,665; Grants to individuals, totaling $11,690.
Type of support: Grants for special needs.
Application information: Unsolicited requests for funds not considered or acknowledged.
EIN: 061399555

4839
International Medical Outreach, Inc.
915 Gessner Rd., Ste. 620
Houston, TX 77024
Contact: Todd Price, Pres.

Foundation type: Independent foundation

Limitations: Grants to individuals for medicine, food, and other necessities, for distribution on international Christian missions.
Financial data: Year ended 12/31/2004. Assets, $251,315 (M); Expenditures, $86,881; Total giving, $37,245; Grants to individuals, totaling $37,245.
Fields of interest: Christian agencies & churches.
Type of support: Travel grants; Grants for special needs.
Application information: Application form required.
Deadline(s): None
Additional information: Application must include affiliation with Christian organization and need, location, and purpose of medical mission.
EIN: 760392915

4840
The Ioan Foundation
14010 Columbet Ave.
San Martin, CA 95046-9710
Contact: Lloyd Martin, Pres.

Foundation type: Independent foundation
Limitations: Grants to individuals in CA and WA who demonstrate a need for public or private charitable support.
Financial data: Year ended 12/31/2004. Assets, $33,378 (M); Expenditures, $11,285; Total giving, $10,700; Grants to individuals, totaling $9,000.
Type of support: Grants for special needs.
Application information:
Initial approach: Letter.
Additional information: Contact foundation for current application deadline.
EIN: 770559484

4841
Iowa P.E.O. Project Fund, Inc.
(formerly Sarah Porter Beckwith Fund)
P.O. Box 1006
Dubuque, IA 52004-1006
Application address: c/o Kimberly R. Baudino, 3826 Grand Ave., Des Moines, IA 50312

Foundation type: Independent foundation
Limitations: Grants to individuals in IA for medical and other living expenses.
Publications: Annual report; Financial statement.
Financial data: Year ended 03/31/2005. Assets, $3,002,670 (M); Expenditures, $149,864; Total giving, $141,940.
Fields of interest: Health care.
Type of support: Seed money; Travel grants; Grants for special needs.
Application information: Applications accepted. Application form required.
Deadline(s): None
Additional information: Applicants must be recommended by local IA P.E.O. chapters.
EIN: 420722695

4842
Italian American Delegates, Inc.
15985 Canal Rd., Ste. 5
Clinton Township, MI 48038-5021
(586) 228-5800
Contact: Vito Tocco, Pres.

Foundation type: Public charity

Limitations: Assistance to the disadvantaged in MI, primarily to children and senior citizens of Italian American heritage, for medical and burial costs.
Financial data: Year ended 10/31/2004.
Assets, $19,122 (M); Expenditures, $78,243; Total giving, $76,750; Grants to individuals, 4 grants totaling $6,500 (high: $2,000, low: $500).
Fields of interest: Disabilities, people with; Economically disadvantaged; Italy.
Type of support: Grants to individuals.
Application information: Contact foundation for current application deadline/guidelines.
EIN: 382840038

4843
Italian-American Community Services Agency
(formerly Italian Welfare Agency, Inc.)
678 Green St.
San Francisco, CA 94133-3896
URL: http://italiancommunityservices.org/

Foundation type: Operating foundation
Limitations: Assistance to economically disadvantaged individuals, including senior citizens.
Financial data: Year ended 12/31/2003.
Assets, $3,589,111 (M); Expenditures, $413,107; Total giving, $19,239; Grants to individuals, totaling $19,239.
Fields of interest: Aging; Economically disadvantaged.
Type of support: Grants for special needs.
Application information: Contact agency for current application deadline/guidelines.
EIN: 941196199

4844
Ittleson-Beaumont Fund
1211 Ave. of the Americas
New York, NY 10036

Foundation type: Independent foundation
Limitations: Relief assistance primarily to needy current and former employees, and their families, of C.I.T. Financial Corporation and its affiliates.
Financial data: Year ended 12/31/2004.
Assets, $2,539,240 (M); Expenditures, $61,345; Total giving, $61,345; Grants to individuals, totaling $27,503.
Type of support: Employee-related welfare.
Application information: Applications accepted.
Initial approach: Letter stating reason for request and detailing applicant's financial status.
Deadline(s): None
Program description:
Financial Assistance Program: All applicants in need of assistance are considered by the fund. However, preference may be given to current or former employees of C.I.T. Financial Corporation and its affiliates. The purpose of the grants is to provide supplemental income to persons demonstrating continuing hardship and financial need.
EIN: 136083909

4845
Jack in the Box Foundation
c/o Tax Dept.
9330 Balboa Ave.
San Diego, CA 92123-1516
URL: http://www.jackinthebox.com/foundation/

Foundation type: Company-sponsored foundation

Limitations: Grants to employees of Jack in the Box who are victims of natural or personal disasters.
Financial data: Year ended 10/03/2004.
Assets, $217,403 (M); Expenditures, $1,150,015; Total giving, $931,549; Grants to individuals, totaling $118,860.
Fields of interest: Safety/disasters.
Type of support: Emergency funds; Employee-related welfare.
EIN: 330776076

4846
Clive T. Jaffray Employees Trust
c/o U.S. Bank, N.A.
P.O. Box 64713
St. Paul, MN 55164-0713 (612) 303-3209
Contact: Joyce James, Fund Admin., U.S. Bank, N.A.

Foundation type: Independent foundation
Limitations: Financial assistance to employees of U.S. Bank, N.A. for extraordinary purposes, primarily in MN.
Financial data: Year ended 12/31/2004.
Assets, $184,789 (M); Expenditures, $12,800; Total giving, $9,675; Grants to individuals, totaling $9,675.
Type of support: Employee-related welfare.
Application information: Contact trust for current application deadline/guidelines.
EIN: 416015737

4847
The James 1:27 Foundation
12173 Network Blvd., Ste. 150
San Antonio, TX 78249-3359 (210) 561-5360
Contact: General Welfare: Kay King

Foundation type: Operating foundation
Limitations: Grants to economically disadvantaged individuals residing in the San Antonio, TX area based on spiritual, emotional, physical, and security needs. Priority is given to single mothers.
Financial data: Year ended 12/31/2004.
Assets, $909,939 (M); Expenditures, $230,354; Total giving, $165,439; Grants to individuals, 102 grants totaling $165,439 (high: $41,396, low: $15).
Fields of interest: Women; Single parents.
Type of support: Grants for special needs.
Application information: Application form required.
Deadline(s): None
EIN: 742959955

4848
Janssen Ortho Patient Assistance Foundation, Inc.
1 Johnson & Johnson Plz.
New Brunswick, NJ 08933 (800) 652-6227

Foundation type: Operating foundation
Limitations: Pharmaceutical products to needy persons on a nondiscriminating basis without charge.
Financial data: Year ended 12/31/2004.
Assets, $5,364,051 (M); Expenditures, $323,753,737; Total giving, $289,783,393; Grants to individuals, 193,499 grants totaling $289,783,393.
Fields of interest: Health care; Human services; Economically disadvantaged.
Type of support: Grants for special needs.

Application information: Applications accepted.
Application form required.
Initial approach: Letter.
EIN: 311520982

4849
Tom Coughlin Jay Fund Foundation, Inc.
P.O. Box 50798
Jacksonville Beach, FL 32240-0798
(904) 465-4044
Contact: Keli Coughlin, Exec. Dir.

Foundation type: Public charity
Limitations: Assistance to families with individuals suffering from Leukemia and other cancers. Aid includes travel, special medical procedures, equipment and living expenses while undergoing treatment.
Financial data: Year ended 12/31/2003.
Assets, $222,196 (M); Expenditures, $175,142; Total giving, $139,161; Grants to individuals, 48 grants totaling $63,998 (high: $15,120, low: $257).
Fields of interest: Cancer; Leukemia.
Type of support: Grants for special needs.
Application information:
Initial approach: Letter.
EIN: 593426937

4850
John Percival and Mary C. Jefferson Endowment Fund
P.O. Box 99
Santa Barbara, CA 93102
Application address: c/o Patricia Allen, 114 E. De La Guerra St., Studio 3, Santa Barbara, CA 93101, tel.: (805) 963-8822

Foundation type: Independent foundation
Limitations: Relief assistance to Santa Barbara County, CA, residents of limited means for medical, dental, and living expenses.
Financial data: Year ended 03/31/2005.
Assets, $4,244,693 (M); Expenditures, $274,248; Total giving, $137,766; Grants to individuals, 36 grants totaling $57,766 (high: $6,500, low: $330).
Fields of interest: Dental care; Health care; Economically disadvantaged.
Type of support: Grants for special needs.
Application information: Applications accepted throughout the year; Initial approach by letter; Completion of formal application required; Interviews required.
EIN: 956005231

4851
Jewish Family Assistance Fund
5743 Bartlett St.
Pittsburgh, PA 15217
Contact: James Reich, Pres.

Foundation type: Independent foundation
Limitations: Financial assistance to needy Jewish families for living, personal, food, and medical expenses.
Financial data: Year ended 12/31/2004.
Assets, $266,968 (M); Expenditures, $177,272; Total giving, $168,404; Grants to individuals, totaling $91,869.
Fields of interest: Health care; Jewish agencies & temples.
Type of support: Grants for special needs.

Application information: Applications by letter accepted throughout the year.
EIN: 251512726

4852
Jewish Family Services, Inc.
6560 Poplar Ave.
Memphis, TN   38138   (901) 767-8511
Contact: Robert Silver, Exec. Dir.
FAX: (901) 763-2348; E-mail: jfsmem@aol.com;
URL: http://jewishfamilyservicememphis.org

Foundation type: Public charity
Limitations: Grants to families in the Memphis, TN, area.
Publications: Financial statement; Newsletter.
Financial data: Year ended 12/31/2003.
Assets, $897,785 (M); Expenditures, $754,688;
Total giving, $21,059.
Fields of interest: Family services.
Type of support: Grants for special needs.
Application information: Contact foundation for current application deadline/guidelines.
EIN: 620199430

4853
Jewish Federation of Galveston County, Inc.
P.O. Box 146
Galveston, TX   77553   (409) 763-5241
Contact: Charlotte Levy, Pres.

Foundation type: Public charity
Limitations: Assistance to economically disadvantaged members of the Galveston, TX, Jewish community.
Financial data: Year ended 12/31/2004.
Assets, $272,941 (M); Expenditures, $61,219;
Total giving, $47,287; Grants to individuals, totaling $18,787.
Fields of interest: Jewish agencies & temples; Economically disadvantaged.
Type of support: Grants for special needs.
Application information: Contact foundation for current application deadline/guidelines.
EIN: 741257017

4854
The Jockey Club Foundation
40 E. 52nd St.
New York, NY   10022-5911
Contact: Nancy Kelly, Secy.

Foundation type: Independent foundation
Limitations: Relief assistance to financially needy individuals who are licensed and legitimately connected with thoroughbred breeding and racing.
Financial data: Year ended 12/31/2004.
Assets, $9,477,278 (M); Expenditures, $698,911; Total giving, $589,162; Grants to individuals, 85 grants totaling $523,287 (high: $36,774, low: $150).
Fields of interest: Athletics/sports, equestrianism.
Type of support: Grants for special needs.
Application information: Applications accepted.
Initial approach: Letter.
Additional information: Inappropriate applications will not be considered or acknowledged.
EIN: 136124094

4855
Dexter G. Johnson Educational and Benevolent Trust
P.O. Box 1620
Tulsa, OK   74101-1620
Contact: Betty Crews
Application address: P.O. Box 850250, Oklahoma City, OK 73085

Foundation type: Independent foundation
Limitations: Medical expenses to physically disabled children and young men and women of OK.
Financial data: Year ended 12/31/2003.
Assets, $3,864,936 (M); Expenditures, $239,817; Total giving, $145,385; Grants to individuals, totaling $145,385.
Fields of interest: Health care; Disabilities, people with.
Type of support: Grants for special needs.
Application information: Applications accepted throughout the year; Completion of formal application required, including financial information, family history, physical condition, age, education goals, and other data necessary to show need.
Program description:
Health Care Assistance Program: Assistance includes corrective surgery and hospitalization and the necessities of life while in convalescence. Past grants have been for ear and eye surgery, prosthesis, and skin surgery.
EIN: 237389204

4856
Journal Publishing Company Employees Welfare Fund, Inc.
c/o U.S. Bank, N.A.
P.O. Box 3168
Portland, OR   97208-3168

Foundation type: Independent foundation
Limitations: Welfare assistance to retired employees of Journal Publishing Co.
Financial data: Year ended 06/30/2005.
Assets, $300 (M); Expenditures, $11,150; Total giving, $9,900; Grants to individuals, totaling $9,900.
Type of support: Employee-related welfare.
Application information: Applications accepted throughout the year; Contact foundation for current application guidelines.
EIN: 237066006

4857
The Joyard Foundation
2056 Lyans Dr.
La Canada Flintridge, CA   91011-1537

Foundation type: Independent foundation
Limitations: Grants to individuals for medical and living expenses.
Financial data: Year ended 12/31/2003.
Assets, $1,188,195 (M); Expenditures, $411,391; Total giving, $405,048; Grants to individuals, 10 grants totaling $305,048 (high: $55,508).
Fields of interest: Health care.
Type of support: Grants for special needs.
Application information: Contact foundation for current application deadline/guidelines.
EIN: 954636168

4858
Loris and Pauline Keen Charitable Trust
P.O. Box 404
Blackwell, OK   74631-0404   (580) 363-2659
Contact: Daniel C. McClung, Tr.

Foundation type: Independent foundation
Limitations: Support for medical expenses for financially needy children with eye problems living in OK. Some assistance is also available for children in OK in need of dental care. Assistance includes exams, screenings, and lenses.
Financial data: Year ended 12/31/2004.
Assets, $764,305 (M); Expenditures, $40,029; Total giving, $23,100; Grants to individuals, totaling $20,494.
Fields of interest: Eye diseases; Children/youth, services.
Type of support: Grants for special needs.
Application information: Application form required.
Deadline(s): Applications accepted throughout the year.
Applicants should submit the following:
1) Financial information
EIN: 736252829

4859
Kellogg Company 25-Year Employees Fund, Inc.
c/o Kellogg Co.
1 Kellogg Sq.
P.O. Box 3599
Battle Creek, MI   49016-3599   (269) 961-2000
Contact: Timothy S. Knowlton, Pres.
Application address: c/o Managing Decisions, Inc., 400 Orchard Ave., Battle Creek, MI 49017

Foundation type: Company-sponsored foundation
Limitations: Supplemental living expense grants to financially needy individuals who have been employed by Kellogg Company or any of its subsidiaries for at least 25 years or who are spouses of such a person.
Publications: Application guidelines; Program policy statement.
Financial data: Year ended 12/31/2003.
Assets, $52,455,658 (M); Expenditures, $1,431,402; Total giving, $1,198,088; Grants to individuals, 177 grants totaling $1,198,088 (high: $35,500, low: $135).
Fields of interest: Economically disadvantaged.
Type of support: Employee-related welfare.
Application information: Applications accepted. Application form required.
Deadline(s): None
Program description:
Assistance Program: Supplemental living expense grants are made to individuals who have been Kellogg Company or its subsidiaries employees for at least 25 years, and their spouses. In order to qualify, applicants must meet the following minimum financial need requirements:
· qualifying income dependent on number in household
· liquid assets of less than $20,000
· no significant property assets beyond primary residence.
EIN: 386039770

4860
Keren America
245 S. Benton St., Ste. 100
Lakewood, CO   80226

Foundation type: Independent foundation

Limitations: Assistance to economically disadvantaged individuals for living expenses.
Financial data: Year ended 11/30/2004. Assets, $0 (M); Expenditures, $187,769; Total giving, $185,810; Grants to individuals, totaling $185,810.
Fields of interest: Economically disadvantaged.
Type of support: Grants for special needs.
Application information: Contact foundation for current application deadline/guidelines.
EIN: 841527140

4861
Keren Keshet - The Rainbow Foundation
1015 Park Ave.
New York, NY   10028   (212) 396-8800
Contact: Linda Sakacs, Secy.

Foundation type: Independent foundation
Limitations: Hardship grants to economically disadvantaged Israelis.
Financial data: Year ended 12/31/2004. Assets, $253,005,275 (M); Expenditures, $9,732,222; Total giving, $4,699,925; Grants to individuals, 4 grants totaling $155,000 (high: $100,000, low: $2,500).
Fields of interest: Jewish agencies & temples; Economically disadvantaged.
Type of support: Emergency funds; Foreign applicants.
Application information: Applications accepted.
Deadline(s): None
EIN: 134069592

4862
Kerman Bible Studies
7033 W. Rialto Ave.
Fresno, CA   93727

Foundation type: Independent foundation
Limitations: Grants to economically disadvantaged Christian individuals, primarily in Fresno, CA. Also giving to Russian missionaries.
Financial data: Year ended 12/31/2004. Assets, $0 (M); Expenditures, $53,846; Total giving, $42,762.
Fields of interest: Christian agencies & churches; Economically disadvantaged; Russia.
Type of support: Grants for special needs.
Application information: Applications accepted.
Additional information: Contact foundation for current application deadline/guidelines.
EIN: 770386371

4863
Keshet Foundation
c/o Abraham Family
200 W. 57th St., Ste. 1005
New York, NY   10019

Foundation type: Independent foundation
Limitations: Grants to economically disadvantaged individuals of Jewish faith in NY.
Financial data: Year ended 11/30/2003. Assets, $304,101 (M); Expenditures, $1,943,080; Total giving, $1,940,710; Grants to individuals, 27 grants totaling $1,165,800.
Fields of interest: Jewish agencies & temples; Economically disadvantaged.
Type of support: Grants for special needs.
Application information: Applications not accepted.
EIN: 137132997

4864
Kids Campaign, Inc.
3800 Hooper Ave.
Baltimore, MD   21211-1313   (410) 467-3000
Contact: Edward C. Kiernan, Pres.

Foundation type: Public charity
Limitations: General welfare grants to residents of Baltimore, MD.
Financial data: Year ended 12/31/2003. Assets, $505,377 (M); Expenditures, $171,000; Total giving, $167,925; Grants to individuals, totaling $50,000.
Type of support: Grants for special needs.
Application information:
Initial approach: Letter.
Additional information: Recipients receive gift certificates to enable their families to celebrate the holiday season.
EIN: 521304326

4865
King Benevolent Fund, Inc.
(formerly King Pharmaceuticals Benevolent Fund)
1119 Commonwealth Ave.
Bristol, VA   24201   (276) 466-3014
Contact: Mary Ann Blessing, Secy.-Treas.
FAX: (276) 466-0108; Toll-free tel.: (800) 321 9234; URL: http://www.kingbf.org

Foundation type: Public charity
Limitations: Grants for distributions of food and medical supplies to needy widows in the local Bristol, VA, community; and medication and medical supplies to medical mission teams traveling to Third World countries.
Publications: Annual report; Informational brochure; Newsletter.
Financial data: Year ended 12/31/2004. Assets, $63,223,146 (M); Expenditures, $351,142,890; Total giving, $348,437,324.
Fields of interest: Pharmacy/prescriptions; Health care; Aging, centers/services; Women, centers/services; International relief; Aging; Women; Economically disadvantaged.
Type of support: Grants for special needs.
Application information: Contact foundation for current application deadline/guidelines.
EIN: 541668650

4866
The Larry King Cardiac Foundation
15720 Crabbs Branch Way
Rockville, MD   20855   (866) 302-5523
Contact: Larry King, Jr., Pres.
URL: http://www.lkcf.org

Foundation type: Public charity
Limitations: Assistance with medical and hospital expenses for economically disadvantaged individuals requiring cardiac surgery.
Financial data: Year ended 12/31/2004. Assets, $559,196 (M); Expenditures, $1,560,297; Total giving, $571,000; Grants to individuals, 27 grants totaling $471,000.
Fields of interest: Heart & circulatory diseases.
Type of support: Grants for special needs.
Application information:
Deadline(s): Contact foundation for current application deadline/guidelines.
Additional information: Application by biographical letter including physician's letter, financial statement, and health insurance documentation.

Program description:
Surgery Program: Procedures are performed in one of the foundation's affiliate care centers located in CA, DC, and NY.
EIN: 521563547

4867
Arlen Francis Klein Trust Fund
903 N. Dunlap Ave.
Savoy, IL   61874-9611   (217) 359-2497
Contact: Richard Woodworth, Secy.

Foundation type: Operating foundation
Limitations: Grants to disabled children (under the age of 21) and their families, primarily in IL.
Financial data: Year ended 09/30/2002. Assets, $472,319 (M); Expenditures, $25,696; Total giving, $20,978; Grants to individuals, 9 grants totaling $13,197 (high: $5,192, low: $300).
Fields of interest: Disabilities, people with.
Type of support: Grants for special needs.
Application information: Applications accepted. Application form required.
Additional information: Contact foundation for current application guidelines.
EIN: 371284503

4868
Elsie Kohen Non-Exempt Charitable Trust
c/o Quad City Bank & Trust Co.
3551 7th St., Ste. 100
Moline, IL   61265-6156
Application address: c/o Joel Deutsch, 1825 3rd Ave., Rock Island, IL 61201

Foundation type: Independent foundation
Limitations: Grants to economically disadvantaged residents of Rock Island or Moline, IL, who are of the Jewish faith.
Financial data: Year ended 03/31/2005. Assets, $442,737 (M); Expenditures, $19,637; Total giving, $13,313; Grants to individuals, 6 grants totaling $12,700 (high: $3,700, low: $1,200).
Fields of interest: Jewish agencies & temples; Economically disadvantaged.
Type of support: Grants for special needs.
Application information: Applications accepted throughout the year; Contact trust for current application guidelines.
EIN: 366616802

4869
Ida C. Koran Trust
c/o U.S. Bank, N.A.
P.O. Box 64713
St. Paul, MN   55164-0704

Foundation type: Independent foundation
Limitations: Hardship grants and loans to dependents of Ecolab, Inc. employees.
Financial data: Year ended 12/31/2004. Assets, $39,764,035 (M); Expenditures, $1,983,499; Total giving, $1,667,266; Grants to individuals, totaling $1,635,266; Loans to individuals, totaling $339,654.
Fields of interest: Economically disadvantaged.
Type of support: Employee-related welfare.
Application information: Applications not accepted.
EIN: 416124022

4870
The Krempels Brain Injury Foundation
(formerly 2001 Brain Injury Support Fund, Inc.)
P.O. Box 4388
Portsmouth, NH 03802 (603) 433-9821
Contact: Lisa Hanson
URL: http://www.krempelsfoundation.org/

Foundation type: Operating foundation
Limitations: Grants to NH residents who suffered severe traumatic brain injury, brain tumor, or stroke.
Financial data: Year ended 12/31/2004.
Assets, $120,760 (M); Expenditures, $263,649; Total giving, $77,852; Grants to individuals, totaling $77,852.
Fields of interest: Disabilities, people with.
Type of support: Grants for special needs.
Application information: Applications accepted.
Deadline(s): None
Additional information: Completion of formal application required, including medical and financial information; Applications accepted from families and friends of survivors, New Hampshire Brain Injury Association, hospitals, rehab facilities, social workers, and therapists.
Program description:
Krempels Grants Program: Awards are up to $5,000.
EIN: 020499997

4871
George S. Ladd Memorial Fund
c/o Wells Fargo Bank, N.A.
P.O. Box 63954
San Francisco, CA 94163

Foundation type: Independent foundation
Limitations: Financial assistance, including medical treatment, to elderly and retired employees of Pacific Bell, Nevada Bell, and Pacific Northwest Bell, primarily in CA and NV.
Financial data: Year ended 12/31/2004.
Assets, $1,129,676 (M); Expenditures, $42,198; Total giving, $20,100; Grants to individuals, totaling $20,100.
Fields of interest: Health care; Aging.
Type of support: Employee-related welfare.
Application information: Contact fund for current application deadline; Completion of formal application required.
EIN: 376070933

4872
Ladies of the Grand Army of the Republic
(also known as George H. Thomas Circle No. 32, Ladies of the Grand Army of the Republic)
1500 Grant Ave., Ste. 200
Novato, CA 94945

Foundation type: Operating foundation
Limitations: Assistance to financially needy individuals, primarily in CA.
Financial data: Year ended 12/31/2002.
Assets, $30,372 (M); Expenditures, $55,179; Total giving, $49,100; Grants to individuals, 13 grants totaling $46,426 (high: $5,570, low: $600).
Fields of interest: Economically disadvantaged.
Type of support: Grants for special needs.
Application information: Applications not accepted.
EIN: 946138985

4873
William B. Lake Foundation
c/o Wachovia Bank, N.A.
401 S. Tryon St., NC119
Charlotte, NC 28288
Application address: c/o Elizabeth K. Deegan, 214 W. Maury St., Chester, PA, 19013

Foundation type: Independent foundation
Limitations: Assistance to residents of Philadelphia, PA, and environs suffering from diseases of the respiratory tract, or pulmonary disease.
Publications: Application guidelines.
Financial data: Year ended 05/31/2005.
Assets, $1,021,085 (M); Expenditures, $41,648; Total giving, $32,140; Grants to individuals, totaling $32,140.
Application information: Deadlines May 1 and Nov. 1; Initial approach by letter with full medical details and supporting documents; Completion of formal application required; Interviews required.
EIN: 236266137

4874
Della Lamb Community Services
(formerly Della C. Lamb Neighborhood House)
500 Woodland Ave.
Kansas City, MO 64106-1361 (816) 842-8040
Contact: William F. Ross, Pres.
FAX: (816) 842-7727; URL: http://www.dellalamb.org

Foundation type: Public charity
Limitations: Emergency assistance to needy residents of Kansas City, MO.
Financial data: Year ended 12/31/2003.
Assets, $3,333,390 (M); Expenditures, $7,287,696; Total giving, $514,525; Grants to individuals, totaling $514,525.
Fields of interest: Human services.
Type of support: Grants for special needs.
Application information: Applications accepted.
Initial approach: Letter.
EIN: 440549931

4875
Larrabee Fund Association
c/o Bank of America, N.A.
777 Main St., CT2-102-22-02
Hartford, CT 06115

Foundation type: Independent foundation
Limitations: Relief to women receiving assistance cannot be on welfare and must have an assigned social worker, in the Hartford, CT, area.
Financial data: Year ended 10/31/2003.
Assets, $4,279,474 (M); Expenditures, $433,587; Total giving, $396,502; Grants to individuals, totaling $396,135.
Application information: Applications accepted throughout the year; Completion of formal application required; Applications must be submitted through social worker.
EIN: 066038638

4876
George A. Laughlin Trust
c/o WesBanco Bank, Inc., Trust Dept.
1 Bank Plz.
Wheeling, WV 26003 (304) 234-9428
Contact: Lea Ridenhour, Trust Off., WesBanco Bank, Inc.

Foundation type: Independent foundation

Limitations: Interest-free home loans to Ohio County, WV, families with three or more children to purchase homes.
Financial data: Year ended 12/31/2004.
Assets, $13,700,524 (M); Expenditures, $831,259; Total giving, $725,403; Loans to individuals, 108 loans totaling $725,403.
Fields of interest: Housing/shelter.
Type of support: Grants for special needs.
Application information:
Deadline(s): May 1 through 31
Additional information: Completion of formal application required, including financial statement and four references; Interviews required.
Program description:
Laughlin Plan: To be eligible for assistance from the Laughlin Plan, an applicant must:
- not presently own a home or other real estate
- be a resident of Ohio County, WV
- be steadily employed, industrious, and of good character
- have at least three dependent children living at home
- be insurable for life insurance
- not be in a position, under present circumstances, to obtain a home through any other means

Applicants are not required to have a down payment. No interest will be charged on the loan. Monthly payments are approximately the same as rent for property. The trustee will consult with the successful applicant and as far as possible will assist in buying a house in the location and of the type that the applicant desires. The cost of the house should be no more than can be repaid in a 20-year period in monthly installments. Each payment will not exceed a fair monthly rental rate of the property. The home selected for purchase must be located in Ohio County and may not be used as a rental property throughout the term of the loan.
EIN: 556016889

4877
Laurendeau Foundation for Cancer Care
P.O. Box 157
Bellingham, WA 98227-0157 (360) 676-8779
Contact: Jeanie Schneider, V.P.

Foundation type: Operating foundation
Limitations: Grants to individuals residing in Bellingham, WA, for outpatient cancer care.
Financial data: Year ended 09/30/2004.
Assets, $98,766 (M); Expenditures, $47,388; Total giving, $37,859; Grants to individuals, 28 grants totaling $37,859.
Fields of interest: Medical care, outpatient care; Cancer.
Type of support: Grants for special needs.
Application information: Application form required.
Deadline(s): Monthly
EIN: 911121989

4878
Lavoie Foundation
P.O. Box 12
Barnstead, NH 03218 (603) 435-7583
Contact: Patricia Sanborn, Dir.

Foundation type: Independent foundation
Limitations: Financial assistance to economically disadvantaged individuals, primarily in NH, for medical expenses, rent, and some scholarships.
Financial data: Year ended 12/31/2004.
Assets, $3,282,617 (M); Expenditures,

$191,192; Total giving, $174,853; Grants to individuals, 7 grants totaling $14,069 (high: $5,462, low: $288).
Fields of interest: Economically disadvantaged.
Type of support: Scholarships—to individuals; Grants for special needs.
Application information: Applications by letter accepted throughout the year.
EIN: 020502244

4879
The Lazarus Foundation, Inc.
340 Edgemont Ave., Ste. 500
Bristol, TN   37620
Contact: Mary Ann Blessing, Treas.

Foundation type: Operating foundation
Limitations: Grants by referral only to financially needy individuals, primarily in TN, NC, and VA.
Financial data: Year ended 12/31/2004.
Assets, $30,517,659 (M); Expenditures, $14,874,729; Total giving, $14,061,326; Grants to individuals, 43 grants totaling $291,304.
Type of support: Grants for special needs.
Application information: Individual applications not accepted; Referrals accepted throughout the year.
EIN: 541654943

4880
Leary Firefighters Foundation
594 Broadway, Ste. 409
New York, NY   10012   (212) 343-0240
Contact: Lys Hopper, Exec. Dir.
E-mail: info@learyfirefightersfoundation.org;
URL: http://www.learyfirefightersfoundation.org

Foundation type: Public charity
Limitations: Grants to the families of firefighters who have perished or been injured in the line of duty.
Financial data: Year ended 12/31/2003.
Assets, $875,274 (M); Expenditures, $2,410,859; Total giving, $1,788,007; Grants to individuals, 343 grants totaling $307,490.
Fields of interest: Disasters, fire prevention/control; Disasters, 9/11/01.
Type of support: Grants for special needs.
Application information:
   Initial approach: E-mail.
   Additional information: Contact foundation for further application information. Grant seekers are invited to review Foundation guidelines and if appropriate, send a letter of inquiry.
EIN: 134125074

4881
Cora Lembke Trust
c/o First National Bank
P.O. Box 2147
Valparaiso, IN   46384-2147

Foundation type: Independent foundation
Limitations: Financial assistance to elderly women who are residents of Porter County, IN.
Financial data: Year ended 09/30/2004.
Assets, $76,649 (M); Expenditures, $16,625; Total giving, $15,600; Grants to individuals, totaling $15,600.
Fields of interest: Aging; Women.
Type of support: Grants for special needs.
Application information: Applications by letter outlining financial need accepted throughout the year.
EIN: 356043012

4882
Lend A Hand Society
175 Federal St.
Boston, MA   02110
Contact: Melania Smith

Foundation type: Independent foundation
Limitations: Relief assistance to financially needy individuals for food, rent, clothing, medicine, utilities, and camperships in the Boston, MA, area.
Financial data: Year ended 12/31/2004.
Assets, $2,174,366 (M); Expenditures, $83,869; Total giving, $46,773; Grants to individuals, totaling $46,773.
Type of support: Grants for special needs.
Application information:
   Deadline(s): Mar. 31 for camperships; Applications accepted throughout the year for other types of grants.
   Additional information: Application by letter submitted by licensed social worker.
EIN: 042104384

4883
Mosette Levin Trust
c/o Horizon Trust & Investment Mgmt.
515 Franklin Sq.
P.O. Box 1125
Michigan City, IN   46360   (219) 873-2629
Contact: Brenda Smythe

Foundation type: Operating foundation
Limitations: Medical assistance to residents of LaPorte County, IN, who have cancer and to those under the age of 16 suffering from any childhood illnesses and life-threatening diseases.
Financial data: Year ended 12/31/2002.
Assets, $775,651 (M); Expenditures, $45,460; Total giving, $33,924; Grants to individuals, 24 grants totaling $33,924 (high: $3,379, low: $105).
Fields of interest: Pharmacy/prescriptions; Cancer; Children/youth, services.
Type of support: Grants for special needs.
Application information: Applications accepted throughout the year; Initial approach by letter, outlining financial need and medical condition, and requesting application form; Completion of formal application required; Interviews required.
Program description:
   Mosette Levin Trust Program: The trust assists recipients in all aspects of medical treatment, including the purchase of medication, transportation to receive treatment, and physicians' bills. All payments are made directly to the medical provider.
EIN: 356031456

4884
Randolph Lewisohn Fund
c/o JPMorgan Chase Bank
1211 6th Ave., 34th Fl.
New York, NY   10036
Application address: c/o Presbytery of N.Y.C., 7 W. 11th St., New York, NY 10011, tel.: (212) 691-9650

Foundation type: Independent foundation
Limitations: Loans to Presbyterian ministers.
Financial data: Year ended 12/31/2003.
Assets, $1,532,065 (M); Expenditures, $93,387; Total giving, $73,635; Grants to individuals, totaling $73,635.
Fields of interest: Protestant agencies & churches.
Type of support: Grants for special needs.

Application information: Applications accepted throughout the year; Contact foundation for current application guidelines.
EIN: 133408705

4885
The Lexington Foundation
P. O. Box 445
Lexington, MS   39095
Contact: Peggy Garrison
Application address: 102 Andrews St., Lexington, MS 39095, tel.: (662) 834-0288

Foundation type: Independent foundation
Limitations: Grants to residents of MS for medical, educational and emergency support.
Financial data: Year ended 12/31/2003.
Assets, $1,002,545 (M); Expenditures, $113,370; Total giving, $88,638; Grants to individuals, 12 grants totaling $13,654 (high: $4,500, low: $150).
Fields of interest: Education; Health care; Safety/disasters; Economically disadvantaged.
Type of support: Emergency funds; Grants for special needs.
Application information: Applications accepted throughout the year; Initial approach by letter; Completion of formal application required.
EIN: 640912814

4886
Lifelong AIDS Alliance
(formerly Northwest AIDS Foundation-Chicken Soup Brigade)
1002 E. Seneca St.
Seattle, WA   98122   (206) 328-8979
FAX: (206) 325-2689; TDD: (206) 323-2685;
URL: http://www.lifelongaidsalliance.org

Foundation type: Public charity
Limitations: Emergency assistance for people living with HIV/AIDS in King County, WA.
Publications: Annual report.
Financial data: Year ended 06/30/2005.
Assets, $3,775,624 (M); Expenditures, $11,365,893; Total giving, $3,393,375; Grants to individuals, totaling $3,355,962.
Fields of interest: AIDS.
Type of support: Grants for special needs.
Application information: Deadline fall; Contact King Co. Case Manager for current application guidelines; Initial approach by letter or telephone.
EIN: 911215715

4887
Limiar U.S.A., Inc.
111 Broken Bough
San Antonio, TX   78231   (210) 479-0300
Contact: Nancy L. Cameron, Pres.
FAX: (210) 479-3835; E-mail: limiarusa@aol.com;
URL: http://www.limiar.org

Foundation type: Public charity
Limitations: Grants to provide for medical expenses, education, and financial support to Brazilian orphans.
Financial data: Year ended 12/31/2003.
Assets, $19,783 (M); Expenditures, $233,317; Total giving, $188,018; Grants to individuals, totaling $188,018.
Type of support: Grants for special needs.
Application information:
   Initial approach: E-mail.

Additional information: Contact foundation for further information.
EIN: 341461670

4888
The Lion's Pride Foundation, Inc.
P.O. Box 1330
Salisbury, NC   28145
Contact: Alicia Howard, Coord.
Tel.: (704) 633-8250, ext. 2974, 3385; FAX: (704) 656-4162

Foundation type: Public charity
Limitations: Grants to individuals in times of crisis.
Financial data: Year ended 12/31/2003.
Assets, $535,733 (M); Expenditures, $71,353; Total giving, $42,258; Grants to individuals, totaling $42,258.
Fields of interest: Safety/disasters.
Type of support: Emergency funds; Grants for special needs.
Application information: Applications accepted throughout the year; Initial approach by telephone; Completion of formal application required.
Program description:
   Assistance Program: Awards of up to $500 per year are given to individuals who provide sufficient evidence of need (e.g. water, electricity, mortgage bills).
EIN: 561895601

4889
The Lissak Foundation, Inc.
175 South St.
Morristown, NJ   07960   (973) 898-9494
Contact: Kenneth Lissak, Mgr.

Foundation type: Independent foundation
Limitations: Grants to individuals.
Financial data: Year ended 11/30/2004.
Assets, $0 (M); Expenditures, $1,248,775; Total giving, $1,247,801; Grants to individuals, 16 grants totaling $273,049 (high: $50,383, low: $1,000).
Type of support: Grants to individuals.
Application information: Contact foundation for current application deadline/guidelines.
EIN: 061468915

4890
Lockheed Martin Aeronautics Employees Reaching Out Club
(formerly General Dynamics Employees Contribution Club Fort Worth Texas)
P.O. Box 748
Fort Worth, TX   76101-0748   (817) 777-2715
Contact: Kathy Luper, Exec. Dir.

Foundation type: Public charity
Limitations: General welfare grants to employees of Lockheed Martin and their dependants for emergency aid.
Financial data: Year ended 12/31/2003.
Expenditures, $2,751,059; Total giving, $2,751,039; Grants to individuals, totaling $366,765.
Type of support: Employee-related welfare; Grants for special needs.
Application information:
   Initial approach: Letter or telephone.
   Additional information: Contact foundation for further application information.
EIN: 756036122

4891
Lockheed Martin Missiles and Fire Control Employee Charity Fund
(formerly Lockheed Martin Vought Systems Employee Charity Fund)
P.O. Box 650003, PT 42
Dallas, TX   75265-0003
Contact: Brent Berryman, Treas.

Foundation type: Company-sponsored foundation
Limitations: Individual grants to AR and TX employees of Lockheed Martin Missiles and Fire Control in need due to illness, injury, or other catastrophe.
Financial data: Year ended 12/31/2004.
Assets, $363,692 (M); Expenditures, $469,004; Total giving, $469,004; Grants to individuals, 25 grants totaling $44,000 (high: $5,000, low: $500).
Fields of interest: Health care.
Type of support: Emergency funds; Employee-related welfare.
Application information: Contact fund for current application deadline; Applications by letter; Must demonstrate financial need.
EIN: 752528901

4892
Loeb Foundation
c/o Lebanon Citizens National Bank
P.O. Box 59
Lebanon, OH   45036-0059   (513) 932-1414
Contact: B.H. Wright, Jr., Tr.
FAX: (513) 932-1492; E-mail: bwright@lcnb.com

Foundation type: Independent foundation
Limitations: Grants and loans to indigent individuals over the age of 60 to allow them to remain in their own homes. Limited to Warren County, OH, residents.
Publications: Annual report.
Financial data: Year ended 09/30/2005.
Assets, $7,810,884 (M); Expenditures, $478,141; Total giving, $359,179; Grants to individuals, 30 grants totaling $92,592 (high: $3,000, low: $450).
Fields of interest: Aging; Economically disadvantaged.
Type of support: Grants for special needs.
Application information: Applications accepted. Application form required.
   Initial approach: Contact Warren County Community Services.
   Copies of proposal: 1
   Deadline(s): None
   Applicants should submit the following:
      1) Financial information
   Additional information: Interviews required.
EIN: 316225986

4893
Mary Jane Luick Trust
c/o Old National Bank
P.O. Box 207
Evansville, IN   47702   (800) 468-0347
Application address: c/o Old National Bank, 320 S. High St., Muncie, IN 47305

Foundation type: Independent foundation
Limitations: Grants to needy elderly women of Delaware County, IN for medical expenses and monthly living allowances.
Financial data: Year ended 12/31/2004.
Assets, $96,044 (M); Expenditures, $5,378; Total giving, $3,400; Grants to individuals, totaling $3,400.

Fields of interest: Aging; Women; Economically disadvantaged.
Type of support: Grants for special needs.
Application information: Applications accepted throughout the year; Contact trust for current application guidelines.
EIN: 356009785

4894
Mac, Incorporated
1504 Riverside Dr.
Salisbury, MD   21801-6740   (410) 742-0505
Contact: Margaret A. Bradford, Exec. Dir.

Foundation type: Public charity
Limitations: Rent assistance, meals, and transportation to the elderly.
Financial data: Year ended 06/30/2004.
Assets, $940,157 (M); Expenditures, $3,907,639; Total giving, $1,643,379; Grants to individuals, totaling $216,344.
Fields of interest: Aging.
Type of support: Grants for special needs.
Application information: Contact foundation for current application deadline/guidelines.
EIN: 520992005

4895
Mary W. MacKinnon Fund
c/o Wilber National Bank, Trust Dept.
245 Main St., P.O. Box 430
Oneonta, NY   13820-2502   (607) 432-1700

Foundation type: Independent foundation
Limitations: Medical, hospital, rehabilitation, and nursing home expenses paid for elderly and economically disadvantaged residents of Sidney, NY.
Financial data: Year ended 12/31/2004.
Assets, $2,221,812 (M); Expenditures, $140,573; Total giving, $127,669; Grants to individuals, totaling $106,669 (high: $5,260).
Fields of interest: Medical care, in-patient care; Medical care, outpatient care; Medical care, rehabilitation; Aging; Economically disadvantaged.
Type of support: Grants for special needs.
Application information: Applications accepted. Application form required.
   Copies of proposal: 1
   Deadline(s): None
   Applicants should submit the following:
      1) Financial information
   Additional information: Requests for assistance must be submitted through doctor or hospital on behalf of the patient; Requests by medical professionals accepted throughout the year.
EIN: 237234921

4896
A. F. MacPherson Trust
(also known as Anonymous Fund)
c/o U.S. Bank, N.A.
P.O. Box 7900
Madison, WI   53707-7900
Application address: c/o Atty. Roger Gierhart, Bell, Metzner, Gierhart, & Moore, S.C., 44 E. Mifflin St., P.O. Box 1807, Madison, WI 53701

Foundation type: Independent foundation
Limitations: Assistance to financially needy Protestants in the U.S. and Canada, with preference shown to residents of WI.
Publications: Application guidelines.

Financial data: Year ended 12/31/2004.
Assets, $544,990 (M); Expenditures, $29,811;
Total giving, $18,731; Grants to individuals,
totaling $18,731.
Fields of interest: Protestant agencies & churches;
Economically disadvantaged.
Type of support: Grants for special needs.
Application information: Application form required.
Initial approach: letter.
Deadline(s): Mar. 31, June 30, Sept. 30, and
Dec. 31
Additional information: Application should
include a letter from clergy, doctor, or social
worker regarding need, and detailed financial
information.
Program description:
MacPherson Trust Program: Previous types of
assistance given include bill payments, utility
payments, dental work, clothing, rent, daycare, and
medical equipment. The maximum any individual
may receive is $5,000 in total. Funds are
distributed directly to creditor or retailer.
Applications are reviewed in Jan., Apr., July, and
Oct., with payments made on or about the 30th of
each of these months.
EIN: 396038607

4897
Majid Family Foundation
2325 Delaney Dr.
Ottawa, IL   61350

Foundation type: Operating foundation
Limitations: Grants to individuals for medical
assistance and other needs.
Financial data: Year ended 12/31/2003.
Assets, $51,942 (M); Expenditures, $56,063;
Total giving, $56,025; Grants to individuals, 5
grants totaling $38,044 (high: $16,944, low:
$2,000).
Fields of interest: Health care.
Type of support: Grants for special needs.
Application information: Applications not
accepted.
EIN: 364183120

4898
Mallory-Taylor Foundation, Inc.
115 W. Main St.
P.O. Box 229
La Grange, KY   40031-0229
Contact: Barry D. Moore, Chair.

Foundation type: Operating foundation
Limitations: Health care assistance to residents of
Oldham County, KY, who do not have any other form
of medical coverage.
Financial data: Year ended 12/31/2003.
Assets, $649,366 (M); Expenditures, $33,942;
Total giving, $20,887; Grants to individuals, 6
grants totaling $20,887 (high: $5,291, low: $951).
Fields of interest: Health care, financing; Health
care.
Type of support: Grants for special needs.
Application information: Application form required.
Deadline(s): Applications accepted throughout
the year.
Additional information: Applicants must have
been residents of Oldham County, KY, for at
least six months prior to submission of
application.
EIN: 611187509

4899
Karl Malone Foundation for Kids
P.O. Box 520640
Salt Lake City, UT   84152-0640
(801) 944-4032
Contact: Kerry Rupp, Tr.

Foundation type: Public charity
Limitations: Grants to needy families for special
needs.
Financial data: Year ended 12/31/2003.
Assets, $790,475 (M); Expenditures, $148,976;
Total giving, $65,015; Grants to individuals,
totaling $65,015.
Fields of interest: Human services.
Type of support: Grants for special needs.
Application information: Applications accepted.
Initial approach: Letter.
EIN: 870569257

4900
Rema Hort Mann Foundation, Inc.
155 Hudson St.
New York, NY   10013   (212) 431-1622
Contact: Susan Hart, Pres.
FAX: (212) 431-2634;
E-mail: cancergrant@remahortmannfoundation.org;
URL: http://www.remahortmannfoundation.org

Foundation type: Public charity
Limitations: Grants by nomination only to cancer
patients, primarily in the New York, NY metropolitan
area, to pay for expenses that allow their friends
and family to be with them.
Financial data: Year ended 12/31/2004.
Assets, $107,355 (M); Expenditures, $116,585;
Total giving, $106,210; Grants to individuals,
totaling $106,210.
Fields of interest: Cancer.
Type of support: Emergency funds; Awards/grants
by nomination only; Travel grants; Grants for special
needs.
Application information:
Deadline(s): Contact foundation for current
nomination deadline/guidelines; Nominees
are chosen by hospital social workers.
EIN: 133879538

4901
Mary Mansfield Fund for the Aged
c/o Fifth Third Bank
38 Fountain Sq. Plz., Dept. 00858
Cincinnati, OH   45263
Application address: 269 W. Main St., Lexington, KY
40507

Foundation type: Independent foundation
Limitations: Grants for medical expenses to
indigent residents of Bourbon County, KY.
Financial data: Year ended 12/31/2003.
Assets, $409,862 (M); Expenditures, $20,409;
Total giving, $15,955; Grants to individuals,
totaling $15,955.
Type of support: Grants for special needs.
Application information: Applications accepted
throughout the year; Completion of formal
application required.
EIN: 616021948

4902
Marblehead Female Humane Society, Inc.
P.O. Box 425
Marblehead, MA   01945
Contact: Lee Weed, Pres.

Foundation type: Operating foundation
Limitations: Financial assistance to residents of
Marblehead, MA.
Financial data: Year ended 09/30/2002.
Assets, $2,393,945 (M); Expenditures,
$124,024; Total giving, $47,606; Grants to
individuals, totaling $21,535.
Fields of interest: Economically disadvantaged.
Type of support: Grants for special needs.
Application information: Applications by letter
accepted throughout the year; Applicants notified
usually within 60 days.
EIN: 042104694

4903
The Marguerite Home, a Charitable Trust
(formerly The Marguerite Home Association)
400 Capital Mall, Ste. 2200
Sacramento, CA   95814-4557
Contact: Lawrence A. Schei, Pres.

Foundation type: Independent foundation
Limitations: Financial assistance to a group of
pre-selected women who live in the Sacramento,
CA, area, and are needy, elderly, and single.
Financial data: Year ended 06/30/2005.
Assets, $1,481,574 (M); Expenditures, $62,811;
Total giving, $52,539; Grants to individuals,
totaling $52,539.
Fields of interest: Aging; Women.
Type of support: Grants for special needs.
Application information: Applications not
accepted.
Additional information: Contributes only to
pre-selected individuals.
EIN: 946065622

4904
Glenn L. Martin Foundation
c/o Bruce T. Hyland
4503 Coulbourn Mill Rd.
Salisbury, MD   21804

Foundation type: Independent foundation
Limitations: Financial assistance to retired
employees of the Martin Marietta Corporation, MD,
who are suffering hardship.
Financial data: Year ended 12/31/2004.
Assets, $3,202,726 (M); Expenditures,
$228,103; Total giving, $204,777; Grants to
individuals, 19 grants totaling $143,000 (high:
$9,000, low: $2,500).
Type of support: Employee-related welfare.
Application information: Applications not
accepted.
EIN: 136086736

4905
Henry B. Martin Fund, Inc.
c/o Russell, Brier & Co.
50 Congress St., Rm. 900
Boston, MA   02109

Foundation type: Independent foundation
Limitations: Relief assistance to financially needy
elderly citizens who currently or previously have had
a connection to the town of Milton, MA.
Financial data: Year ended 12/31/2004.
Assets, $1,793,941 (M); Expenditures,
$121,639; Total giving, $81,500; Grants to
individuals, totaling $81,500.
Fields of interest: Aging; Economically
disadvantaged.
Type of support: Grants for special needs.

Application information: Applications not accepted.
EIN: 046031995

4906

Martin Memorial Foundation, Inc.

P.O. Box 9033
Stuart, FL 34995-9033 (772) 223-5634
Contact: Alan Woodruff, Chair.
E-mail: info@mmhs.com; URL: http://www.mmhs.com/content/Donate.asp

Foundation type: Public charity
Limitations: Medical and dental expense aid to economically disadvantaged children in the communities served by Martin Memorial Health Systems (Martin and St. Lucie counties, FL).
Financial data: Year ended 09/30/2003.
Assets, $8,384,358 (M); Expenditures, $3,538,644; Total giving, $2,866,768.
Fields of interest: Dental care; Health care; Children, services.
Type of support: Grants for special needs.
Application information: Contact foundation for current application deadline/guidelines.
EIN: 592343938

4907

Mary R. Martin Trust 1

P.O. Box 1739
Wolfeboro, NH 03894
Contact: G. Thomas Bickford, Tr.

Foundation type: Independent foundation
Limitations: Assistance with bills and living expenses to economically disadvantaged residents of Wolfeboro, NH.
Financial data: Year ended 12/31/2004.
Assets, $429,092 (M); Expenditures, $12,479; Total giving, $8,975; Grants to individuals, 42 grants totaling $8,974 (high: $500, low: $50).
Fields of interest: Economically disadvantaged.
Type of support: Grants for special needs.
Application information: Application form required.
  Initial approach: Telephone.
  Copies of proposal: 1
  Deadline(s): None
  Additional information: Interviews required.
EIN: 026009373

4908

Masonic Grand Lodge Charities of Rhode Island, Inc.

222 Taunton Ave.
East Providence, RI 02914 (401) 435-4650
Contact: John M. Faulhaber, Secy.

Foundation type: Independent foundation
Limitations: Grants to members and widows and children of members of the Masonic Lodge, who are RI residents.
Financial data: Year ended 10/31/2004.
Assets, $1,812,524 (M); Expenditures, $291,488; Total giving, $221,634; Grants to individuals, totaling $209,122.
Fields of interest: Children/youth, services; Fraternal societies; Women.
Type of support: Grants for special needs.
Application information:
  Deadline(s): May 1
  Additional information: Applications should be made through the local masonic lodge.
EIN: 056014340

4909

Massachusetts Charitable Fire Society

c/o J.M. Forbes & Co.
3 Post Office Sq., Ste. 1000
Boston, MA 02109 (617) 423-5705
Contact: G. West Saltonstall, Treas.

Foundation type: Independent foundation
Limitations: Giving limited to individuals in the Boston, MA, area, who have suffered loss due to fire and require assistance in replacing necessities.
Financial data: Year ended 07/31/2003.
Assets, $1,836,930 (M); Expenditures, $109,095; Total giving, $99,871.
Fields of interest: Housing/shelter, expense aid; Safety/disasters.
Type of support: Emergency funds.
Application information: Applications by letter, including a description of the event giving rise to the need and the specific items for which relief is requested, accepted throughout the year.
EIN: 042305919

4910

David May Employees Trust Fund

c/o The May Department Stores Co., Tax Dept.
611 Olive St.
St. Louis, MO 63101

Foundation type: Company-sponsored foundation
Limitations: Financial assistance to employees and former employees of the May Department Stores Company.
Financial data: Year ended 12/31/2004.
Assets, $192,452 (M); Expenditures, $139,877; Total giving, $135,266; Grants to individuals, 103 grants totaling $135,266 (high: $7,500, low: $300).
Type of support: Employee-related welfare.
EIN: 436027540

4911

Kate McClintock Home

P.O. Box 341
Paris, KY 40362-0341

Foundation type: Operating foundation
Limitations: Grants for living expenses to elderly women residing in Bourbon County, KY, who are independently financed and not receiving any state assistance, such as TANF or Section 8.
Financial data: Year ended 08/31/2003.
Assets, $246,191 (M); Expenditures, $29,865; Total giving, $28,680; Grants to individuals, 18 grants totaling $28,680 (high: $2,700, low: $400).
Fields of interest: Aging; Women.
Type of support: Grants for special needs.
Application information: Application form required.
  Additional information: Applications accepted throughout the year; Grants are paid in monthly installments of $100 to $225.
EIN: 610458372

4912

Sophia Byers McComas Foundation

c/o U.S. Bank, N.A.
P.O. Box 3168
Portland, OR 97208-3168 (503) 275-5929
Contact: William Dolan
FAX: (503) 275-4177

Foundation type: Independent foundation
Limitations: Financial assistance by recommendation only to aged and indigent persons

who are residents of OR and who are not on welfare assistance.
Financial data: Year ended 06/30/2004.
Assets, $1,907,367 (M); Expenditures, $128,139; Total giving, $110,150; Grants to individuals, totaling $110,150.
Fields of interest: Aging; Economically disadvantaged.
Type of support: Awards/grants by nomination only; Grants for special needs.
Application information: Individual applications not accepted; Applicants are recommended to the trustees by various church groups and service agencies.
Program description:
  Assistance Program: Approximately 40 individuals receive monthly grants from the foundation.
EIN: 936019602

4913

Merchants Fund

(formerly Merchants-Oliver Fund)
P.O. Box 668
Narberth, PA 19072 (610) 949-9270
Contact: Dorothy Darragh, Exec. Dir.
FAX: (610) 949-9412;
E-mail: merchantsfund@comcast.net

Foundation type: Operating foundation
Limitations: Relief assistance to economically disadvantaged merchants, business owners and former business owners, and widows and families in the Philadelphia, PA, area.
Financial data: Year ended 12/31/2004.
Assets, $7,924,522 (M); Expenditures, $584,018; Total giving, $435,907; Grants to individuals, 76 grants totaling $435,907 (high: $10,800, low: $494).
Fields of interest: Business/industry; Women.
Type of support: Grants for special needs.
Application information: Applications accepted. Application form required.
  Initial approach: Letter or telephone requesting application.
  Deadline(s): None
  Additional information: Completion of formal application required, including tax returns, general circumstances of financial need, and proof of business ownership in Philadelphia; Interview required.
Program description:
  Merchants Fund: This program provides relief to struggling merchants of the city of Philadelphia, especially if aged or infirm. It also provides temporary financial assistance to businesses in financial difficulty due to medical crisis or family emergency. When in the judgment of the Board of Directors, the corporation has sufficient assets to do so, it will extend relief to the widows of deceased beneficiaries.
EIN: 231584975

4914

Charles Meyer Trust

c/o U.S. National Bank
P.O. Box 179
Galveston, TX 77553
Application address: c/o Rabbi, Temple B'nai Israel, 3008 Ave. O, Galveston, TX 77550

Foundation type: Independent foundation
Limitations: Grants to underprivileged Jewish residents of Galveston, TX.
Financial data: Year ended 05/31/2005.
Assets, $628,979 (M); Expenditures, $35,885;

Total giving, $27,800; Grants to individuals, totaling $27,800.
Fields of interest: Jewish agencies & temples; Economically disadvantaged.
Type of support: Grants for special needs.
Application information: Applications accepted.
Deadline(s): None
Additional information: Applications by letter outlining financial need and indicating Jewish faith.
EIN: 746035534

4915
The Robert Benson Meyer, Jr. Foundation, Inc.

c/o RGND
9800 Sotweed Dr.
Potomac, MD 20854
Contact: Maria Teresa De Z. Meyer, Pres.

Foundation type: Independent foundation
Limitations: Assistance to individuals for travel expenses, immigration expenses, and for housing.
Financial data: Year ended 12/31/2004.
Assets, $1,100,325 (M); Expenditures, $102,855; Total giving, $100,548.
Fields of interest: Housing/shelter, expense aid; Immigrants/refugees.
Type of support: Grants to individuals; Travel grants.
Application information: Contact foundation for current application deadline/guidelines.
EIN: 522104075

4916
Michigan Dental Association Relief Fund

230 N. Washington Ave., Ste. 208
Lansing, MI 48933-1302   (517) 372-9070
Contact: Gerri Cherney, Exec. Dir.
E-mail: deason@michigandental.org

Foundation type: Public charity
Limitations: Financial assistance to economically disadvantaged dentists and their spouses or survivors, primarily in MI.
Financial data: Year ended 12/31/2004.
Assets, $316,090 (M); Expenditures, $23,787; Total giving, $17,569; Grants to individuals, totaling $17,569.
Fields of interest: Economically disadvantaged.
Type of support: Grants for special needs.
Application information: Application form required.
Initial approach: Telephone.
Copies of proposal: 1
Applicants should submit the following:
   1) Financial information
Additional information: Contact foundation for current application deadline/guidelines.
EIN: 386112478

4917
Kate Kinloch Middleton Fund

c/o Regions Bank
P.O. Box 2527
Mobile, AL 36622
Application address: c/o Lola Melton, Merchants National Bank Bldg., Rm. 1507, Mobile, AL 36602, tel.: (251) 438-9597

Foundation type: Independent foundation
Limitations: Grants to financially needy residents of Mobile County, AL, to help cover the cost of medical expenses.

Financial data: Year ended 01/31/2005.
Assets, $2,981,507 (M); Expenditures, $152,887; Total giving, $107,314; Grants to individuals, 28 grants totaling $98,083 (high: $26,784, low: $508).
Fields of interest: Health care.
Type of support: Grants for special needs.
Application information: Applications accepted throughout the year; Completion of formal application required, including copies of medical bills and proof of income and expenses; Interviews required.
EIN: 636018539

4918
Ambrose Middleton Trust

c/o KeyBank N.A.
800 Superior Ave., 4th Fl.
Cleveland, OH 44114
Application address: Billy T. White, c/o Distrib. Comm., First National Bank, McConnellsville, OH 43756, tel.: (614) 962-3911

Foundation type: Independent foundation
Limitations: Food, clothing, and medical assistance to financially needy individuals residing in Morgan County, OH.
Financial data: Year ended 08/31/2004.
Assets, $300,434 (M); Expenditures, $10,780; Total giving, $9,921; Grants to individuals, totaling $9,921.
Fields of interest: Health care; Economically disadvantaged.
Type of support: Grants for special needs.
Application information: Applications accepted throughout the year; Contact trust for current application guidelines.
EIN: 346513420

4919
Military Women In Need

(formerly California Soldiers' Widows Home Association)
11693 San Vicente Blvd., Ste. 122
Los Angeles, CA 90049
Contact: grants for special needs: Ranlyn Hill
FAX: (310) 441-1619;
E-mail: info@militarywomeninneed.org;
URL: http://www.militarywomeninneed.org

Foundation type: Independent foundation
Limitations: Grants to female residents of southern CA who are widows of U.S. Armed Forces veterans and are in need of housing assistance. Recipients must be at least 50 years of age, have resided in CA for the past five years, have assets of $20,000 or less (excluding one car), be able to live independently, and have an annual income of less than $25,000.
Publications: Application guidelines.
Financial data: Year ended 06/30/2004.
Assets, $2,785,116 (M); Expenditures, $228,506; Total giving, $115,224; Grants to individuals, 35 grants totaling $115,224 (high: $6,445, low: $275).
Fields of interest: Housing/shelter, expense aid; Women.
Type of support: Grants for special needs.
Application information: Applications accepted.
Deadline(s): Contact association for current application deadline;
Additional information: Application by letter including copy of latest payroll, SSA or other check, income and expense documentation

for verification and budget purposes, and documents verifying assets.
EIN: 953533990

4920
Millard Foundation

c/o John Irwin
P.O. Box 8303
Radnor, PA 19087
Application address: c/o Marion M. Thompson, 44 Pembroke Rd., Mendham, NJ 07945

Foundation type: Independent foundation
Limitations: Grants for case management services to elderly and disabled residents of PA.
Financial data: Year ended 12/31/2003.
Assets, $326,516 (M); Expenditures, $141,373; Total giving, $140,002; Grants to individuals, 40 grants totaling $95,002 (high: $7,980, low: $378).
Fields of interest: Aging; Disabilities, people with.
Type of support: Grants for special needs.
Application information: Application by letter accepted throughout the year.
EIN: 232452507

4921
Miracle-Ear Children's Foundation

5000 Cheshire Ln. N., Ste. 1
Plymouth, MN 55446-3715   (763) 268-4000
Contact: Kitty Curran, Dir.
Additional tel.: (800) 234-5422; URL: http://www.miracle-ear.com/resources/children_request.asp

Foundation type: Company-sponsored foundation
Limitations: Contributions of hearing aids to hearing-impaired children ages 16 and younger from families with income levels which do not allow them to receive public support.
Publications: Annual report; Informational brochure; Program policy statement.
Financial data: Year ended 12/31/2004.
Assets, $38,150 (M); Expenditures, $73,676; Total giving, $73,676; Grants to individuals, totaling $73,676.
Fields of interest: Children/youth, services; Disabilities, people with.
Type of support: Grants for special needs.
Application information: Application form required.
Deadline(s): Applications accepted throughout the year.
Additional information: Application must also include a dated, recent audiogram and medical clearance.
EIN: 411677967

4922
Miracles of Mitch Foundation

105 Peavey Rd., Ste. 190
Chaska, MN 55318   (952) 361-9600
Contact: Ronald M. Stanchfield, Exec. Dir.
E-mail: rmsassoc@usinternet.com; URL: http://www.miraclesofmitchfoundation.org

Foundation type: Public charity
Limitations: Financial support to families with children living with cancer.
Financial data: Year ended 06/30/2004.
Assets, $34,842 (M); Expenditures, $22,761; Total giving, $10,738; Grants to individuals, totaling $10,738.
Fields of interest: Cancer; Children.
Type of support: Grants for special needs.

Application information:
Initial approach: E-mail or telephone.
Additional information: Requests directly from families is prohibited. All requests must come from the Hospital Social Worker or the Treating Physician.
Program description:
Financial Assistance: Grants go towards mortgage assistance, emergency housing assistance, food and clothing, automobile payments, household utility assistance, or counseling and guidance referral.
EIN: 562384527

4923
The Mirror Foundation
13907 Ventura Blvd., Ste. 104
Sherman Oaks, CA   91423   (818) 506-5973
Contact: Nicole P. Johnson, Secy.

Foundation type: Independent foundation
Limitations: Emergency housing assistance to individuals in need, primarily in CA. Grants will normally not exceed $1,000 each.
Financial data: Year ended 12/31/2004. Assets, $0 (M); Expenditures, $441,005; Total giving, $32,579; Grants to individuals, totaling $32,579.
Fields of interest: Housing/shelter.
Type of support: Grants for special needs.
Application information:
Initial approach: Letter or telephone.
Additional information: Contact foundation for current application deadline/guidelines.
EIN: 954201793

4924
Missionary Enterprises
P.O. Box 2127
La Habra, CA   90632-2127

Foundation type: Independent foundation
Limitations: Grants to Christian missionaries.
Financial data: Year ended 12/31/2004. Assets, $16,681 (M); Expenditures, $98,486; Total giving, $83,880.
Fields of interest: Christian agencies & churches.
Application information: Applications not accepted.
EIN: 952152466

4925
Monahan-Laighton Memorial Fund
(formerly Margaret B. Monahan and Alberta W. Laighton Memorial Fund)
P.O. Box 788
Pawling, NY   12564-0788

Foundation type: Independent foundation
Limitations: Grants to economically disadvantaged individuals residing in Pawling, NY, town and village.
Financial data: Year ended 12/31/2004. Assets, $515,575 (M); Expenditures, $31,530; Total giving, $30,300; Grants to individuals, 12 grants totaling $28,600 (high: $3,700, low: $500).
Fields of interest: Economically disadvantaged.
Type of support: Emergency funds; Grants for special needs.
Application information: Application form not required.
Initial approach: Letter or telephone.
Deadline(s): None

Additional information: Contact fund for current application deadline/guidelines; Applicants must demonstrate financial need.
EIN: 146022154

4926
Charles E. Montague Charitable Trust
c/o Bank of America, N.A.
P.O. Box 6768
Providence, RI   02940-6768
Application address: c/o Bank of America, N.A., 100 Federal St., Boston, MA 02110

Foundation type: Independent foundation
Limitations: Assistance to financially needy residents of Wakefield, MA, to help cover hospital bills, including psychotherapy.
Financial data: Year ended 09/30/2004. Assets, $1,455,129 (M); Expenditures, $72,824; Total giving, $56,618; Grants to individuals, totaling $56,618.
Fields of interest: Medical care, in-patient care; Psychology/behavioral science; Economically disadvantaged.
Type of support: Grants for special needs.
Application information: Applications accepted.
Deadline(s): None
Additional information: Contact trust for current application guidelines.
EIN: 046047134

4927
Montgomery Child Care Association, Inc.
(also known as MCCA)
2730 University Blvd. W., Ste. 616
Wheaton, MD   20902-1949   (301) 946-1213
Contact: Christina Giovinazzo, Exec. Dir.
FAX: (301) 949-6726; E-mail: info@mccaedu.org;
URL: http://www.mccaedu.org

Foundation type: Public charity
Limitations: Grants to economically disadvantaged families residing in Montgomery County, MD, for assistance with caring for children.
Publications: Financial statement; Newsletter.
Financial data: Year ended 08/31/2004. Assets, $2,013,047 (M); Expenditures, $6,124,584; Total giving, $19,029; Grants to individuals, 7 grants totaling $19,029 (high: $12,036, low: $286). Subtotal for emergency funds: 8 grants totaling $19,029 (high: $12,036, low: $286).
Fields of interest: Children/youth, services; Family services; Economically disadvantaged.
Type of support: Grants for special needs.
Application information: Application form required.
Initial approach: Letter.
Copies of proposal: 1
Deadline(s): Rolling
Applicants should submit the following:
1) Financial information
Additional information: Application by letter outlining financial need; Interviews may be required.
EIN: 520880656

4928
Anita Card Montgomery Foundation
c/o Fran Moore
P.O. Box 815
Camden, ME   04843
Application address: c/o Julia L. Libby, P.O. Box 190, Camden, ME 04843, tel.: (207) 763-4220

Foundation type: Independent foundation
Limitations: Assistance to financially needy individuals of Camden, Rockport, Lincolnville, and Hope, ME, including medical, dental, and eyecare expenses.
Financial data: Year ended 12/31/2004. Assets, $0 (M); Expenditures, $28,422; Total giving, $27,594; Grants to individuals, 25 grants totaling $27,594 (high: $3,677, low: $15).
Fields of interest: Dental care; Optometry/vision screening; Health care; Economically disadvantaged.
Type of support: Grants for special needs.
Application information: Applications accepted throughout the year; Completion of formal application required, including copies of bills and estimated costs from medical professionals.
EIN: 237091570

4929
William A. Morse Fund
c/o TD Banknorth, N.A., Investment Mgmt. Group
P.O. Box 595
Williston, VT   05495
Application address: c/o Dora Powers, R.R. 2, Box 239-D, West Brattleboro, VT 05301

Foundation type: Independent foundation
Limitations: Grants to financially needy children under age 16 from Brattleboro, Williamsville, and South Newfane, VT, only, with preference given to Brattleboro residents.
Financial data: Year ended 12/31/2004. Assets, $311,795 (M); Expenditures, $33,092; Total giving, $27,938; Grants to individuals, totaling $14,881.
Fields of interest: Pharmacy/prescriptions; Children/youth, services; Day care.
Type of support: Grants for special needs.
Application information: Applications accepted throughout the year; Completion of formal application required, including financial information, tax return, and medical insurance information.
Program description:
Children Assistance Program: Grants are given to help pay for temporary family assistance for children under the age of 16. Seventy-five percent of funds are allocated to Brattleboro, VT, residents and 25 percent to Newfane, South Newfane, and Williamsville VT, residents.
EIN: 036004778

4930
Mark Morton Memorial Fund
123 N. Wacker Dr.
Chicago, IL   60606-1743

Foundation type: Independent foundation
Limitations: Grants to needy LA and TX individuals who are verifiable employees of the Morton Salt Company on or before June 30, 1971, to assist with hospital, medical, and surgical expenses, as well as assistance for those who are aged or disabled.
Financial data: Year ended 12/31/2004. Assets, $22,252,403 (M); Expenditures, $1,653,478; Total giving, $1,308,443; Grants to individuals, 153 grants totaling $608,443 (high: $26,029, low: $52).
Fields of interest: Health care; Aging; Disabilities, people with.
Type of support: Employee-related welfare; Grants for special needs.
Application information: Applications not accepted.
EIN: 237181380

4931
Paul Motry Memorial Fund
c/o John R. Ball
P.O. Box 929
Sandusky, OH 44870-0357 (419) 625-0515

Foundation type: Independent foundation
Limitations: Grants for medical expenses to physically disabled children who are residents of Erie and Eastern Ottawa counties, OH.
Financial data: Year ended 12/31/2004. Assets, $527,597 (M); Expenditures, $22,342; Total giving, $13,513; Grants to individuals, totaling $13,513.
Fields of interest: Physical therapy; Children/youth, services; Disabilities, people with.
Type of support: Grants for special needs.
Application information: Applications accepted. Application form required.
  Deadline(s): None
  Additional information: Application should include a letter from the doctor, proving need.
Program description:
  Medical Assistance Program: Grants are given for hospital and doctor bills, dental expenses, therapy, and rental of medical equipment. Some recipients receive more than one award during the same year.
EIN: 237420173

4932
Marilyn Moyer Charitable Trust
805 S.W. Broadway, Ste. 2020
Portland, OR 97205 (503) 241-1111
Contact: Thomas Paul Moyer, Tr.

Foundation type: Independent foundation
Limitations: Grants to individuals who have lived in OR, or in Clark County, WA for at least 18 months, to help cover medical expenses not covered by insurance, or social or governmental agencies.
Publications: Application guidelines.
Financial data: Year ended 07/31/2004. Assets, $1,088,090 (M); Expenditures, $55,273; Total giving, $48,851; Grants to individuals, 12 grants totaling $26,551.
Fields of interest: Health care.
Type of support: Grants for special needs.
Application information: Applications accepted. Application form required.
EIN: 936238025

4933
Multiple Sclerosis Foundation, Inc.
(also known as MS Foundation)
6350 N. Andrews Ave.
Fort Lauderdale, FL 33309-2130
(954) 776-6805
Contact: Alan Segaloff, Exec. Dir.
FAX: (954) 351-0630;
E-mail: support@msfocus.org; Additional tel.: (888) 673-6287; URL: http://www.msfacts.org/

Foundation type: Public charity
Limitations: Programs and services to individuals with multiple sclerosis for goods to improve the quality of their lives by enhancing safety, self-sufficiency, comfort or well-being.
Publications: Application guidelines; Financial statement; Newsletter.
Financial data: Year ended 12/31/2004. Assets, $1,058,347 (M); Expenditures, $4,728,344; Total giving, $550,764.
Fields of interest: Multiple sclerosis.
Type of support: Grants for special needs.

Application information:
  Initial approach: A 100 word essay, describing how the grant would help applicant have "A Brighter Tomorrow".
  Additional information: See Web site for further guidelines and deadline.
Program description:
  Brighter Tomorrow Grants: Provides grants of up to $1,000 per recipient to individuals with multiple sclerosis. Recipients must be 18 years of age or older and diagnosed with MS, or the parent of a minor child diagnosed with MS, and be a permanent resident of the U.S. They must not have any other means of fulfilling the need they express. For further information, call the Program Services Dept. at (888) MSFOCUS or contact by e-mail: support@msfocus.org.
EIN: 592792934

4934
William J. Munson Fund
c/o Bank of America, N.A.
P.O. Box 6768
Providence, RI 02940-6768
Contact: Alfred Morency, Chair.
Application address: 71 Scott Rd., Watertown, CT 06795, tel.: (203) 274-4288

Foundation type: Independent foundation
Limitations: Medical expense assistance to residents of Watertown, CT.
Financial data: Year ended 12/31/2003. Assets, $1,773,312 (M); Expenditures, $107,297; Total giving, $80,648; Grants to individuals, 87 grants totaling $80,648 (high: $3,261, low: $8).
Fields of interest: Health care.
Type of support: Grants for special needs.
Application information:
  Applicants should submit the following:
    1) Financial information
EIN: 066024564

4935
Nagel Family Foundation
310 Jamieson Dr.
Fort Pierre, SD 57532
Contact: John E. Nagel, Co-Chair.

Foundation type: Independent foundation
Limitations: Financial assistance primarily to residents of the Pierre, SD, area. Giving also in NE.
Financial data: Year ended 12/31/2003. Assets, $0 (M); Expenditures, $30,000; Total giving, $30,000; Grants to individuals, 3 grants totaling $30,000 (high: $25,000, low: $2,000).
Fields of interest: Economically disadvantaged.
Type of support: Grants for special needs.
Application information: Applications accepted. Application form not required.
  Deadline(s): None
  Additional information: Applicant must demonstrate his or her financial need.
EIN: 200203023

4936
National Children's Cancer Society, Inc.
1015 Locust Bldg., Ste. 600
St. Louis, MO 63101 (314) 241-1600
Contact: Mark Stolze, Pres. and C.E.O.
FAX: (314) 241-1996; Additional tel.: (800) 532-6459; URL: http://www.nationalchildrenscancersociety.org

Foundation type: Public charity
Limitations: Financial and in-kind assistance for children with cancer and their families.
Publications: Annual report; Informational brochure; Newsletter.
Financial data: Year ended 09/30/2004. Assets, $1,938,624 (M); Expenditures, $37,962,740; Total giving, $28,819,057.
Fields of interest: Health care, patient services; Health care; Cancer.
Type of support: Grants for special needs.
Application information: Application form required.
  Initial approach: Letter.
  Deadline(s): None
  Additional information: Interviews required.
EIN: 371227890

4937
National Foundation, Inc.
2925 Professional Pl., Ste. 201
Colorado Springs, CO 80904-8105
E-mail: nfi@thefoundations.org; URL: http://www.thefoundations.org

Foundation type: Public charity
Limitations: Financial assistance to individuals who reside in Nepal for medical expenses.
Publications: Financial statement; Informational brochure; Newsletter; Program policy statement.
Financial data: Year ended 12/31/2003. Assets, $14,919,378 (M); Expenditures, $918,083; Total giving, $693,081.
Type of support: Foreign applicants; Grants for special needs.
Application information: Applications not accepted.
EIN: 541230512

4938
National Kidney Foundation of Alabama
5735 Carmichael Pkwy., Ste. 200
Montgomery, AL 36117 (334) 396-9870
Contact: Barbara A. Jackson, Exec. Dir.
FAX: (334) 396-9872; E-mail: nkfal@bellsouth.net; Additional tel.: (888) 533-1981; URL: http://www.kidney.org/affiliate/al/index.html

Foundation type: Public charity
Limitations: Financial assistance to individuals residing in AL who are afflicted with kidney or urinary tract-related disease, to assist with medications, transportation and living expenses.
Financial data: Year ended 06/30/2004. Assets, $389,091 (M); Expenditures, $273,901.
Fields of interest: Kidney diseases.
Type of support: Grants for special needs.
Application information: Application form required.
  Initial approach: Letter or e-mail.
  Deadline(s): Contact foundation for current application deadline
EIN: 630810007

4939
National Kidney Foundation of Connecticut
2139 Silas Deane Hwy., Ste. 208
Rocky Hill, CT 06067-2336 (860) 257-3770
Contact: Kimberly Hathaway, C.E.O.
FAX: (860) 257-3429; E-mail: info@kidneyct.org; URL: http://www.kidneyct.org

Foundation type: Public charity

Limitations: Financial assistance to kidney patients residing in CT for utilities, medications and transportation.
Financial data: Year ended 06/30/2005.
Assets, $660,178 (M); Expenditures, $103,253; Total giving, $40,062; Grants to individuals, totaling $40,062.
Fields of interest: Kidney diseases.
Type of support: Grants for special needs.
Application information: Contact foundation for current application deadline/guidelines.
Program description:
  NKF Program: Applications are to be submitted by the patient's social worker.
EIN: 060792956

4940
National Kidney Foundation of East Tennessee
4450 Walker Blvd., Ste. 2
Knoxville, TN 37917 (865) 688-5481
Contact: Helen Harb, C.E.O.
FAX: (865) 688-5495; URL: http://www.kidneyetn.org

Foundation type: Public charity
Limitations: Financial assistance to residents of eastern TN who are low-income kidney patients, for help with expenses such as medication, utilities, transportation, doctors' bills or nutritional supplements.
Publications: Annual report; Financial statement; Informational brochure; Newsletter.
Financial data: Year ended 06/30/2004.
Assets, $430,315 (M); Expenditures, $747,912; Total giving, $111,960; Grants to individuals, totaling $111,960 (high: $1,200, low: $875).
Fields of interest: Kidney diseases.
Type of support: Grants for special needs.
Application information: Application form required.
  Initial approach: E-mail.
  Deadline(s): Contact foundation for current application deadline
EIN: 620886595

4941
National Kidney Foundation of Eastern Missouri and Metro East, Inc.
1423 Hanley Industrial Ct.
St. Louis, MO 63144 (314) 961-2828
Contact: Barbara McQuitty, C.E.O.
FAX: (314) 961-0888; E-mail: mail@nkfstl.com; URL: http://www.nkfstl.com

Foundation type: Public charity
Limitations: Financial assistance to renal patients residing in MO and the Metro East region for emergency needs.
Publications: Annual report; Informational brochure; Newsletter; Occasional report.
Financial data: Year ended 06/30/2004.
Assets, $1,017,099 (M); Expenditures, $841,974; Total giving, $167,254; Grants to individuals, totaling $107,237.
Fields of interest: Health care, organ/tissue banks; Kidney diseases.
Type of support: Emergency funds; Research; Grants for special needs.
Application information: Application form required.
  Additional information: Applications accepted throughout the year.

Program description:
  NKF Program: Each patient's grant request must be submitted by the patient's Renal Social Worker. Requests are evaluated by a review panel.
EIN: 436066368

4942
National Kidney Foundation of Florida
1040 Woodcock Rd., Ste. 119
Orlando, FL 32803-3510 (407) 894-7325
Contact: Gregory Ward, Interim Exec. Dir.
FAX: (407) 895-0051; E-mail: nkf@kidneyfla.org; Toll-free tel.: (800) 927-9659; URL: http://www.kidneyfla.org

Foundation type: Public charity
Limitations: Financial assistance to kidney patients in FL for medication, transportation and other related expenses.
Financial data: Year ended 06/30/2005.
Assets, $316,913 (M); Expenditures, $1,092,847; Total giving, $51,221; Grants to individuals, totaling $51,221.
Fields of interest: Kidney diseases.
Type of support: Grants for special needs.
Application information: Contact foundation for current application deadline/guidelines.
EIN: 592190073

4943
National Kidney Foundation of Georgia
2951 Flowers Rd. S., Ste. 211
Atlanta, GA 30341 (770) 452-1539
Contact: Charles C. Starr, C.E.O.
E-mail: info@kidney.org; Toll-free tel.: (800) 633-2339; URL: http://www.nkfg.org

Foundation type: Public charity
Limitations: Financial assistance to kidney dialysis and transplant patients residing in GA.
Financial data: Year ended 06/30/2004.
Assets, $989,833 (M); Expenditures, $1,387,332; Total giving, $97,658; Grants to individuals, totaling $15,158.
Fields of interest: Kidney diseases.
Type of support: Grants for special needs.
Application information: Contact foundation for current application deadline/guidelines.
Program description:
  NKF Program: Applications are to be submitted only by the social worker or physician.
EIN: 237077237

4944
National Kidney Foundation of Hawaii
1314 S. King St., Ste. 305
Honolulu, HI 96814 (808) 593-1515
Contact: Glen Hayashida, Exec. Dir.
Additional tel.: (800) 488-2277; FAX: (808) 593-8096; E-mail: info@kidney.org; URL: http://www.kidneyhi.org

Foundation type: Public charity
Limitations: Financial assistance to renal patients residing in HI, for medical equipment, medication, transportation, food, rent and utilities.
Financial data: Year ended 06/30/2003.
Assets, $2,479,459; Expenditures, $1,573,830; Total giving, $16,703; Grants to individuals, 29 grants totaling $5,311.
Fields of interest: Kidney diseases.
Type of support: Grants for special needs.
Application information: Contact foundation for current application deadline/guidelines.

Program description:
  NKF Program: Applications are to be submitted by the social worker or physician only.
EIN: 990266733

4945
National Kidney Foundation of Indiana, Inc.
911 E. 86th St., Ste. 100
Indianapolis, IN 46240-1840 (317) 722-5640
Contact: Margie Fort, Exec. Dir.
FAX: (317) 722-5650; E-mail: nkfi@myvine.com; Additional tel.: (800) 382-9971; URL: http://www.kidneyindiana.org

Foundation type: Public charity
Limitations: Financial assistance to kidney patients residing in IN, for help with expenses, such as utilities, transportation and medication.
Financial data: Year ended 06/30/2005.
Assets, $623,717 (M); Expenditures, $1,215,100; Total giving, $425,506; Grants to individuals, totaling $425,506.
Fields of interest: Kidney diseases.
Type of support: Grants for special needs.
Application information: Application form required.
  Initial approach: E-mail.
  Deadline(s): Contact foundation for current application deadline
EIN: 351180274

4946
National Kidney Foundation of Iowa
P.O. Box 1364
Cedar Rapids, IA 52403 (319) 369-4474
Contact: Diane Hagarty, Exec. Dir.
Additional address: c/o Mercy Medical Center, 701 10th St., S.E., Ste. 5618, Cedar Rapids, IA 52406; additional tel.: (800) 369-3619; FAX: (319) 369-4419

Foundation type: Public charity
Limitations: Financial assistance to residents of IA, who are low-income kidney patients, for help with expenses such as wheelchair ramps, medical equipment, special food, or utilities.
Financial data: Year ended 06/30/2004.
Assets, $891,193; Expenditures, $370,721; Total giving, $30,000.
Fields of interest: Kidney diseases.
Type of support: Grants for special needs.
Application information: Contact foundation for current application deadline; Initial approach by telephone; Completion of formal application required.
Program description:
  NKF Program: The maximum grant to any needy individual is $100 or less per year. The application for the funds must be made by a licensed social worker.
EIN: 237094979

4947
National Kidney Foundation of Kansas and Western Missouri
1900 W. 47th Pl., Ste. 310
Westwood, KS 66205 (913) 262-1551
Contact: Ahmed Awad D.O.
FAX: (913) 722-4841; E-mail: info@kidneyksmo; Additional tel: (800) 444-8113; URL: http://www.kidneyksmo.org

Foundation type: Public charity

Limitations: Grants to individuals who are residents of KS or western MO for dialysis treatment.
Publications: Annual report; Informational brochure; Newsletter.
Financial data: Year ended 06/30/2004. Assets, $666,507 (M); Expenditures, $1,095,082; Total giving, $97,694; Grants to individuals, 4,000 grants totaling $97,694.
Fields of interest: Kidney diseases.
Type of support: Grants for special needs.
Application information: Contact foundation for current application deadline/guidelines.
EIN: 480756377

4948
National Kidney Foundation of Louisiana
8200 Hampson St., Ste. 425
New Orleans, LA 70118 (504) 861-4500
Contact: K. Trevor From M.D., Pres.
FAX: (504) 861-1976; E-mail: info@kidneyla.org; Toll-free tel.: (800) 462-3694; URL: http://www.kidneyla.org

Foundation type: Public charity
Limitations: Financial assistance to kidney patients residing in LA, for dialysis treatment and transportation.
Financial data: Year ended 06/30/2004. Assets, $605,839 (M); Expenditures, $655,308; Total giving, $37,863; Grants to individuals, totaling $37,863.
Fields of interest: Kidney diseases.
Type of support: Grants for special needs.
Application information: Contact foundation for current application deadline/guidelines.
EIN: 720649707

4949
National Kidney Foundation of Maine
630 Congress St.
P.O. Box 1134
Portland, ME 04104 (207) 772-7270
Contact: Tammy Atwood, Exec. Dir.
FAX: (207) 772-4202; E-mail: info@kidneyme.org; Toll-free tel.: (800) 639-7220; URL: http://www.kidneyme.org

Foundation type: Public charity
Limitations: Financial assistance to renal patients residing in ME, for medication, transportation, housing, food and other material needs.
Publications: Newsletter.
Financial data: Year ended 06/30/2005. Assets, $124,854 (M); Expenditures, $495,376; Total giving, $62,813; Grants to individuals, totaling $62,813.
Fields of interest: Kidney diseases.
Type of support: Grants for special needs.
Application information:
Deadline(s): Contact foundation for current application deadline/guidelines.
Program description:
NKF Program: Patient assistance grants are available as a one-time emergency request. Patients must contact their dialysis center social worker to apply for funds.
EIN: 010318150

4950
National Kidney Foundation of North Carolina
5950 Fairview Rd., Ste. 550
Charlotte, NC 28210-2102 (704) 552-1351
FAX: (704) 552-7870; E-mail: info@kidney.org; Toll-free tel.: (800) 356-5362; URL: http://www.nkfnc.org

Foundation type: Public charity
Limitations: Financial assistance to renal patients residing in NC for rent, transportation, utilities and medications.
Publications: Application guidelines.
Financial data: Year ended 06/30/2005. Assets, $1,249,627 (M); Expenditures, $1,895,688; Total giving, $272,270; Grants to individuals, totaling $252,125.
Fields of interest: Kidney diseases.
Type of support: Grants for special needs.
Application information: Contact foundation for current application deadline/guidelines.
Program description:
NKF Program: Applications are to be submitted by the social worker only.
EIN: 237055496

4951
National Kidney Foundation of Northern California
611 Mission St., 3rd Fl.
San Francisco, CA 94105 (415) 543-3303
Contact: Christopher Kelley, C.E.O.
E-mail: melanie@kidneynca.org; FAX: (415) 543-3331; E-mail: info@kidneyca.org; URL: http://www.kidneynca.org

Foundation type: Public charity
Limitations: Financial assistance to dialysis patients residing in northern CA for transportation, medication, housing, food or utilities.
Publications: Application guidelines; Annual report; Financial statement; Informational brochure (including application guidelines); Newsletter.
Financial data: Year ended 06/30/2003. Assets, $663,559 (M); Expenditures, $1,253,452; Total giving, $265,154; Grants to individuals, totaling $75,256.
Fields of interest: Kidney diseases.
Type of support: Grants for special needs.
Application information: Contact foundation for current application deadline/guidelines.
EIN: 946130713

4952
National Kidney Foundation of Ohio, Inc.
1373 Grandview Ave., Ste. 200
Columbus, OH 43212-2804 (614) 481-4030
Contact: Orelle Jackson, Exec. Dir.
E-mail: info@nkfofohio.org; Additional tel.: (800) 242-2133; URL: http://www.nkfofohio.org

Foundation type: Public charity
Limitations: Financial assistance to renal patients in OH for medication, transportation, and nutritional supplements.
Financial data: Year ended 06/30/2003. Assets, $787,096 (M); Expenditures, $729,828; Total giving, $62,703; Grants to individuals, totaling $56,103.
Fields of interest: Kidney diseases.
Type of support: Grants for special needs.
Application information: Contact foundation for current application deadline/guidelines.
EIN: 311197264

4953
National Machinery Foundation, Inc.
161 Greenfield St.
P.O. Box 747
Tiffin, OH 44883
Contact: Larry F. Baker, Pres.

Foundation type: Company-sponsored foundation
Limitations: Relief assistance to former employees of National Machinery Company and other needy individuals in Seneca County, OH.
Financial data: Year ended 12/31/2003. Assets, $12,794,671 (M); Expenditures, $330,420; Total giving, $248,005; Grants to individuals, 190 grants totaling $73,450 (high: $8,000, low: $55).
Type of support: Employee-related welfare; Grants for special needs.
Application information:
Deadline(s): None
Additional information: Applications by letter, outlining financial need and purpose of grant.
EIN: 346520191

4954
National Multiple Sclerosis Society Michigan Chapter, Inc.
21311 Civic Center Dr.
Southfield, MI 48076-3911 (248) 350-0020
FAX: (248) 350-0029; E-mail: info@mig.nmss.org; Additional tel.: (800) 243-5767; URL: http://www.nmssmi.org

Foundation type: Public charity
Limitations: Grants to individuals in MI afflicted with multiple sclerosis, for medical equipment.
Publications: Annual report; Newsletter.
Financial data: Year ended 09/30/2004. Assets, $1,642,211 (M); Expenditures, $3,914,761; Total giving, $694,864; Grants to individuals, totaling $29,571.
Fields of interest: Multiple sclerosis research.
Type of support: Grants for special needs.
Application information: Applications accepted throughout the year; Initial approach by telephone; Completion of formal application required.
EIN: 381410476

4955
National Multiple Sclerosis Society, North Central Texas Chapter
4086 Sandshell Dr.
Fort Worth, TX 76137 (817) 306-7003
FAX: (817) 306-7055; E-mail: nms@ncfms.org; Additional tel.: (800) FIGHT-MS; URL: http://www.nationalmssociety.org/TXT/home/

Foundation type: Public charity
Limitations: Assistance to residents of north central TX with Multiple Sclerosis.
Financial data: Year ended 09/30/2005. Assets, $422,059 (M); Expenditures, $796,277.
Fields of interest: Multiple sclerosis.
Type of support: Grants for special needs.
Application information:
Initial approach: Letter or e-mail.
Additional information: Contact foundation for current application deadline/guidelines; Initial approach by letter or e-mail.
EIN: 751803731

4956
National Transplant Assistance Fund (NTAF)
150 N. Radnor-Chester Rd.
Radnor, PA   19087
Contact: Lynne Coughlin Samson
FAX: (610) 535-6106; Additional tel.: (800) 642-8399; FAX: (610) 353-1616; E-mail: NTAF@transplantfund.org; URL: http://www.transplantfund.org

Foundation type: Public charity
Limitations: Financial assistance grants to transplant and catastrophic injury patients.
Publications: Annual report; Financial statement; Newsletter.
Financial data: Year ended 09/30/2004. Assets, $9,001,858 (M); Expenditures, $3,776,514; Total giving, $3,077,947; Grants to individuals, totaling $3,077,947.
Fields of interest: Organ diseases; Surgery.
Type of support: Grants for special needs.
Application information: Applications not accepted.
Program description:
Assistance: Transplant and catastrophic injury patients were assisted with grants for uninsured medically related expenses including, but not limited to, physician fees, hospital charges, home health care expenses, medical insurance, medication costs, transportation expenses, dental costs, funeral costs, and hardship expenses.
EIN: 521322317

4957
Nebraska Friends of Foster Children Foundation
P.O. Box 31142
Omaha, NE   68131-0142
Contact: Mickey Dodson, Pres.

Foundation type: Independent foundation
Limitations: Grants to children of NE who are wards of the state.
Financial data: Year ended 06/30/2005. Assets, $34,768 (M); Expenditures, $54,928; Total giving, $51,651; Grants to individuals, totaling $47,542.
Fields of interest: Children/youth, services; Foster care.
Type of support: Grants for special needs.
Application information: Applications accepted throughout the year; Completion of formal application required.
EIN: 363926272

4958
Netzach Foundation
200 W. 57th St., Ste. 1005
New York, NY   10019

Foundation type: Independent foundation
Limitations: Grants to individuals for religious and literary tutoring, and general welfare.
Financial data: Year ended 03/31/2004. Assets, $8,050,414 (M); Expenditures, $2,476,050; Total giving, $2,447,715; Grants to individuals, 18 grants totaling $72,585 (high: $25,190, low: $625).
Fields of interest: Education, services; Jewish agencies & temples; Religion.
Type of support: Scholarships—to individuals; Grants for special needs.

Application information: Applications not accepted.
EIN: 136967224

4959
New Horizons Foundation
c/o Gifford & Dearing, LLP
700 S. Flower St., Ste. 1222
Los Angeles, CA   90017-4114
Contact: Henry H. Dearing, Pres.

Foundation type: Independent foundation
Limitations: Financial assistance to needy Christian Scientists who are over 65 years of age and are residents of Los Angeles County, CA.
Financial data: Year ended 05/31/2005. Assets, $1,090,511 (M); Expenditures, $88,690; Total giving, $79,362; Grants to individuals, 7 grants totaling $65,600.
Fields of interest: Christian agencies & churches; Aging.
Type of support: Grants for special needs.
Application information:
Initial approach: Letter.
Program description:
New Horizons Foundation Program: Applicants must be members of The First Church of Christ, Scientist, in Boston, MA, or an authorized branch thereof. They must also have run out of all conventional means of support, public or otherwise, prior to seeking assistance from the foundation.
EIN: 956031571

4960
New York Stock Exchange Fallen Heroes Fund
11 Wall St.
New York, NY   10005
Contact: David L. Schuler, Secy.
URL: http://www.nyse.com/about/corpcitizenship/1091792165924.html#heroes

Foundation type: Public charity
Limitations: Grants to surviving spouses or children of New York, NY police officers and firefighters killed in the line of duty.
Financial data: Year ended 12/31/2004. Assets, $2,923,567 (M); Expenditures, $200,000; Total giving, $200,000; Grants to individuals, 12 grants totaling $200,000 (high: $20,000, low: $6,667).
Fields of interest: Crime/law enforcement, police agencies; Safety/disasters.
Type of support: Employee-related welfare.
Application information: Contact foundation for current application deadline/guidelines.
EIN: 134048148

4961
Newaygo County Community Services
4 W. Oak St.
Fremont, MI   49412   (231) 924-0641
Contact: Beverly Cassidy, Exec. Dir.

Foundation type: Public charity
Limitations: Grants to residents of Newaygo County, MI, for child care, food, housing and other assistance.
Financial data: Year ended 12/31/2003. Assets, $3,769,362; Expenditures, $2,633,245; Total giving, $1,326,547; Grants to individuals, totaling $1,269,789.
Fields of interest: Food services; Housing/shelter; Children/youth, services.

Type of support: Grants for special needs.
Application information: Contact foundation for current application deadline/guidelines.
EIN: 386158533

4962
Newburyport Howard Benevolent Society
P.O. Box 9
Newburyport, MA   01950

Foundation type: Independent foundation
Limitations: Financial assistance to low-income families in Newburyport, MA.
Financial data: Year ended 09/30/2004. Assets, $2,644,142 (M); Expenditures, $106,534; Total giving, $80,685; Grants to individuals, totaling $43,885.
Fields of interest: Economically disadvantaged.
Type of support: Grants for special needs.
Application information: Applications not accepted.
EIN: 046041304

4963
Nicholas Family Foundation
119 Valley View Dr.
Edinboro, PA   16412-2316   (814) 734-5001
Contact: Donna Nicholas, Dir.

Foundation type: Independent foundation
Limitations: Grants to residents of Erie County, PA, for expenses pertaining to medical, housing and educational needs.
Financial data: Year ended 12/31/2003. Assets, $7,465 (M); Expenditures, $24,670; Total giving, $24,670; Grants to individuals, 2 grants totaling $24,670 (high: $20,632, low: $4,038).
Fields of interest: Health care; Housing/shelter, repairs.
Type of support: Grants for special needs.
Application information: Application form required.
Additional information: Contact foundation for current application deadline.
EIN: 251855273

4964
James R. Nicholl Memorial Foundation
c/o JPMorgan Chase Bank, N.A.
P.O. Box 1308
Milwaukee, WI   53201   (216) 781-2386

Foundation type: Independent foundation
Limitations: Medical and surgical expense assistance to needy children (2 to 21 years of age) who have been residents of Lorain County, OH, for at least two years.
Publications: Informational brochure.
Financial data: Year ended 12/31/2004. Assets, $1,258,159 (M); Expenditures, $63,634; Total giving, $47,233; Grants to individuals, totaling $47,233.
Fields of interest: Health care; Children/youth, services.
Type of support: Grants for special needs.
Application information: Application form required.
Deadline(s): None.
Additional information: Application should include a letter indicating the medical need.
Program description:
Health Care Assistance Program: Grants are paid directly to health care providers. Some recipients receive more than one grant.
EIN: 346574742

4965
North Fork Women for Women Fund, Inc.
P.O. Box 804
Greenport, NY 11944-0924 (631) 477-8464
Contact: Phyllis Zwarych, Pres.
E-mail: nfwfwfmail@igc.org; URL: http://
www.nfwfwf.org

Foundation type: Public charity
Limitations: Grants for health care costs to
lesbians residing on the North Fork of Long Island,
NY, and on Shelter Island, NY.
Publications: Application guidelines; Annual report;
Informational brochure; Newsletter.
Financial data: Year ended 12/31/2003.
Assets, $169,266 (L); Expenditures, $46,844;
Total giving, $34,617; Grants to individuals, 34
grants totaling $34,617 (high: $4,799, low: $300).
Fields of interest: Health care; Women; LGBTQ.
Type of support: Grants for special needs.
Application information: Applications accepted
throughout the year; Completion of formal
application required; Consult the fund's Web site
for further information.
Program description:
   Financial Assistance Program: Provides financial
   assistance to lesbians on the North Fork of Long
   Island, NY, who are facing emergency health
   situations, difficulties caused by aging, illness,
   disability, or disruptions of physical or mental
   well-being. Also supports those with inadequate or
   no health insurance. Membership in NFWFWF is
   free and open to any self-identified lesbian who
   resides on a permanent or part-time basis in the
   geographical area from Riverhead Township to
   Orient Point and on Shelter Island. Members must
   register for the Corporation's mailing list, support
   our goals, and volunteer time, participate in a
   sponsored program, or contribute to the
   Corporation's efforts in some way. Members may
   apply for grants and/or reimbursements to cover
   the costs of health care needs such as
   mammograms and other diagnostic tests, annual
   physicals, dental and eye care, health insurance,
   psychotherapy, physical therapy, home care and
   assistive devices.
EIN: 113116020

4966
Northern Virginia Family Service
100 N. Washington St., Ste. 400
Falls Church, VA 22046 (703) 533-9727
Contact: Mary B. Agee, Exec. Dir.
E-mail: info@nvfs.org; URL: http://www.nvfs.org/

Foundation type: Public charity
Limitations: Interest-free loans to economically
disadvantaged families in northern VA for housing,
day care and other expenses. Loans are for
$3,000, and are to repaid within two years.
Financial data: Year ended 06/30/2004.
Assets, $6,450,005; Expenditures, $16,597,418;
Total giving, $1,492,469; Grants to individuals,
totaling $631,632.
Fields of interest: Housing/shelter; Family
services; Economically disadvantaged.
Type of support: Student loans—to individuals;
Loans—to individuals.
Application information: Deadline July 12; Initial
approach by letter, telephone or e-mail; Completion
of formal application required; See Web site for
additional information.
Program description:
   Loan Program: Recipients receive up to $3,000
   and are expected to pay back the loan within two
   years.
EIN: 540791977

4967
Northwest Lions Foundation for Sight & Hearing
(formerly Lions Sight and Hearing Foundation of
Washington & Northern Idaho)
901 Boren Ave., Ste. 810
Seattle, WA 98104-3534 (800) 847-5786
Contact: Monty Montoya, Pres. and C.E.O.
FAX: (206) 682-8504;
E-mail: info@nlfoundation.org; URL: http://
www.nlfoundation.org

Foundation type: Public charity
Limitations: Grants for blind and deaf patient care
in WA and northern ID, including surgical costs,
purchase of hearing aids, and guide dog training
fees.
Publications: Application guidelines; Informational
brochure (including application guidelines);
Newsletter.
Financial data: Year ended 06/30/2004.
Assets, $6,513,151 (M); Expenditures,
$5,000,475; Total giving, $274,911.
Fields of interest: Health care; Disabilities, people
with.
Type of support: Grants for special needs.
Application information: Contact foundation for
current application deadline; Initial approach by
letter; Completion of formal application required;
Applicants must be sponsored by a local Lions Club
or Lions organization.
EIN: 237051021

4968
Nurses House, Inc.
2113 Western Ave., Ste. 2
Guilderland, NY 12084-9501 (518) 456-7858
Contact: Susan Fraley

Foundation type: Operating foundation
Limitations: Short-term assistance to ill and
economically disadvantaged registered nurses in
the U.S. who are in need of financial assistance to
help meet basic living expenses. Costs of medical
care and education are not funded.
Publications: Application guidelines; Informational
brochure; Newsletter.
Financial data: Year ended 12/31/2002.
Assets, $276,413 (M); Expenditures, $361,170;
Total giving, $135,898; Grants to individuals,
totaling $135,898.
Fields of interest: Nursing care.
Type of support: Grants for special needs.
Application information: Application form required.
   Initial approach: Letter.
   Copies of proposal: 1
   Deadline(s): None
Program description:
   Financial Assistance Program: Program intent is
   to provide financial assistance for registered or
   formerly registered nurses who may require
   assistance by reason of age, illness, disability,
   destitution, or otherwise, as well as to provide
   guidance, information and referral, as needed.
   Services are given regardless of race, creed, color,
   or sex.
EIN: 131927913

4969
NYS Fraternal Order of Police Foundation
(formerly NYS Fraternal Order of Police Empire State
Foundation)
911 Police Plz.
Hicksville, NY 11801 (516) 433-4455
Contact: Frank Ferrerya, Pres.
URL: http://www.nysfop.org

Foundation type: Public charity
Limitations: Financial assistance to family
members of police officers killed in the line of duty,
primarily in NY.
Publications: Financial statement.
Financial data: Year ended 12/31/2004.
Assets, $9,889,053 (M); Expenditures, $613,407.
Fields of interest: Crime/law enforcement, police
agencies; Crime/law enforcement.
Type of support: Emergency funds; Undergraduate
support; Grants for special needs.
Application information: Applications accepted.
   Additional information: Applications accepted
   throughout the year; Contact foundation for
   current application guidelines.
EIN: 113207296

4970
The Mary Oakley Foundation, Inc.
585 Tree Top Ln.
Thousand Oaks, CA 91360-2455
Application address: c/o Dir. of Patient and Family
Svcs., Alzheimer's Assoc. of Santa Barbara, 2024
De La Vina, Santa Barbara, CA 93105

Foundation type: Independent foundation
Limitations: Grants to economically disadvantaged
individuals who are residents of the Tri-Counties of
Santa Barbara, San Luis Obispo and Ventura, CA,
who suffer from Alzheimer's disease.
Financial data: Year ended 12/31/2004.
Assets, $8,134,220 (M); Expenditures,
$405,668; Total giving, $356,129; Grants to
individuals, 8 grants totaling $238,129.
Fields of interest: Alzheimer's disease; Aging;
Economically disadvantaged.
Type of support: Grants for special needs.
Application information: Contact foundation for
current application deadline; Initial approach by
letter; Completion of formal application required.
EIN: 770391113

4971
Office Depot Disaster Relief Foundation
2200 Old Germantown Rd.
Delray Beach, FL 33445 (561) 438-4800
Contact: Charles Patton, Pres.
E-mail: CommunityRelations@officedepot.com;
URL: http://www.community.officedepot.com

Foundation type: Public charity
Limitations: Emergency aid to employees of Office
Depot who have suffered loss due to a natural
disaster such as fire, flood, hurricane or tornado.
Financial data: Year ended 12/27/2003.
Assets, $2,418,320 (M); Expenditures,
$276,783; Total giving, $227,528; Grants to
individuals, totaling $16,614.
Fields of interest: Safety/disasters.
Type of support: Emergency funds;
Employee-related welfare.
Application information: Contact foundation for
current application deadline/guidelines;
Completion of formal application required.
Program description:
   Assistance Program: All current employees of
   Office Depot who have completed 90 days of active

service with the company are eligible for disaster relief. The first and most common type of Internal Assistance is an interest-free loan to cover expenses relating to natural disaster. The amount of each loan is determined on the basis of need, but generally may not exceed $2,000 per employee. All loans are repaid through weekly payroll deductions within a 52-week period. The second, rarely awarded type of Internal Assistance is money to help pay for service needed by an employee suffering from a personal disaster (i.e. funeral, health care, hotel, etc.). The maximum amount of this type of Internal Assistance is generally also $2,000.

EIN: 650596803

4972
Ontario Children's Home

P.O. Box 82
Canandaigua, NY 14424
Application address: c/o Mrs. Richard Ogden, 210 W. Gibson St., Canandaigua, NY 14424

Foundation type: Independent foundation
Limitations: Grants restricted to children under 21 years of age in Ontario County, NY, for child day care, youth organization memberships, children's medical and dental expenses, day camp, field trips, and participation in the Special Olympics.
Financial data: Year ended 09/30/2004. Assets, $3,155,790 (M); Expenditures, $153,246; Total giving, $136,926; Loans to individuals, 50 loans totaling $74,492.
Fields of interest: Education; Children/youth, services; Day care; Disabilities, people with.
Type of support: Scholarships—to individuals; Grants for special needs.
Application information: Ineligible applicants will not be considered or acknowledged.
EIN: 166028318

4973
Louis S. Oppenheim Trust

c/o National City Bank
P.O. Box 94651
Cleveland, OH 44101-4651
Contact: JoAnn Harlan, V.P., National City Bank
Application address: 301 S.W. Adams St., Peoria, IL 61652, tel.: (309) 655-5385

Foundation type: Operating foundation
Limitations: Medical and living expenses to financially needy, blind residents of Peoria County, IL.
Financial data: Year ended 12/31/2003. Assets, $1,442,718 (M); Expenditures, $71,595; Total giving, $68,123; Grants to individuals, 6 grants totaling $19,403 (high: $6,525; low: $291).
Fields of interest: Disabilities, people with; Economically disadvantaged.
Type of support: Grants for special needs.
Application information: Applications by letter or telephone, outlining financial need, accepted throughout the year.
EIN: 376030392

4974
Oregon Lions Sight and Hearing Foundation, Inc.

1410 S.W. Morrison, Ste. 760
Portland, OR 97205 (503) 827-6952
Contact: Amber Kern, Exec. Dir.
Additional tel.: (800) 635-4667; FAX: (503) 827-6958; E-mail: amber.kern@orlions.org; URL: http://www.orlions.org

Foundation type: Public charity
Limitations: Grants to economically disadvantaged residents of OR in need of eyeglasses, eyecare, or hearing loss treatments. Also awards scholarships and research grants for sight, hearing and diabetes research.
Publications: Application guidelines; Annual report; Financial statement; Grants list; Informational brochure; Newsletter.
Financial data: Year ended 06/30/2003. Assets, $4,721,696 (M); Expenditures, $2,363,992; Total giving, $100,626; Grants to individuals, totaling $19,088 (high: $2,000; low: $100).
Fields of interest: Optometry/vision screening; Health care; Ear & throat diseases; Eye research; Ear & throat research; Diabetes research; Children/youth, services; Disabilities, people with; Deaf/hearing impaired; Economically disadvantaged.
Type of support: Research; Undergraduate support; Grants for special needs.
Application information: Applications accepted throughout the year; Initial approach by letter or e-mail; Completion of formal application required; Interviews required. Financially challenged OR children with chronic low vision may apply to receive low-vision devices.
Program descriptions:
Lions Hearing Aid Bank of Oregon: Low-income OR residents can apply through their local Lions Clubs to receive rebuilt hearing aids that they could not otherwise afford. Interested applicants should call the foundation in order to be put in contact with their local Lions Clubs.
Lions Indigent Patient Care: Indigent individuals who have been residents of OR for at least six months can apply for a medical grant to pay for eye and ear surgery required by the applicant. Federal poverty guidelines are used in determining financial need. Recipients receive their grants as a direct payment to the eye/ear surgeons, hospitals, and anesthesiologists providing the service.
Small Grants Program: Through this program, individuals in OR may apply for funds to help with sight, hearing or diabetes research.
EIN: 936041506

4975
The Ostberg Foundation, Inc.

87 Ruckman Rd.
P.O. Box 1098
Alpine, NJ 07620-1098
Contact: Charles Borhan

Foundation type: Independent foundation
Limitations: Financial aid to elderly and ill individuals, regardless of country of residence.
Financial data: Year ended 11/30/2004. Assets, $1,154,530 (M); Expenditures, $116,244; Total giving, $112,850.
Fields of interest: Aging.
Type of support: Foreign applicants; Grants for special needs.
Application information: Applications accepted. Application form required.
EIN: 132963335

4976
Herman & Hazel Owen Foundation

490 Eubanks Dr.
Columbus, MS 39702
Contact: Marjorie Robertson, Secy.-Treas.

Foundation type: Independent foundation
Limitations: Welfare assistance to indigent residents of Lowndes County, MS, and to individuals residing within 50 miles of Columbus, MS, for medical expenses.
Financial data: Year ended 01/31/2005. Assets, $1,098,977 (M); Expenditures, $60,428; Total giving, $48,184; Grants to individuals, 6 grants totaling $2,269 (high: $819, low: $200).
Fields of interest: Health care; Economically disadvantaged.
Type of support: Grants for special needs.
Application information: Applications accepted.
Deadline(s): None
Additional information: Applications by letter, including biographical and financial information.
EIN: 640601824

4977
Palmetto Electric Trust

P.O. Box 820
Ridgeland, SC 29936

Foundation type: Public charity
Limitations: Grants to economically disadvantaged individuals in the tri-county coastal Lowdown area of SC, for food, clothing, shelter, medical and educational costs.
Financial data: Year ended 12/31/2003. Assets, $137,278 (M); Expenditures, $231,944; Total giving, $229,079; Grants to individuals, totaling $229,079.
Fields of interest: Economically disadvantaged.
Type of support: Scholarships—to individuals; Grants for special needs.
Application information: Application form required.
Initial approach: Letter.
Additional information: Contact foundation for current application deadline.
EIN: 570931978

4978
Pardee Cancer Treatment Association of Greater Brazosport

490 This Way, Ste. 220
Lake Jackson, TX 77566
Application address: c/o Desiree Pearson, 710 N. Gulf Blvd., Freeport, TX 77541, tel.: (979) 233-1426

Foundation type: Independent foundation
Limitations: Grants for cancer treatment to individuals who have lived in southern Brazoria County, TX, within one year of being diagnosed with cancer. Grants are for hospital, clinical, and doctor expenses, and for prescription drugs.
Financial data: Year ended 12/31/2003. Assets, $211,256 (M); Expenditures, $118,993; Total giving, $100,902; Grants to individuals, 3 grants totaling $100,902.
Type of support: Grants for special needs.
Application information: Application form required.
Additional information: Applications accepted throughout the year.
EIN: 510169385

4979
Pardee Cancer Treatment Fund of Bay County

c/o Vicki Place
P.O. Box 541
Bay City, MI   48707   (989) 891-8815

Foundation type: Operating foundation
Limitations: Payment of medical bills for cancer patients who are residents of Bay County, MI.
Financial data: Year ended 12/31/2003. Assets, $152,842 (M); Expenditures, $73,317; Total giving, $65,263; Grants to individuals, totaling $65,263.
Fields of interest: Health care; Cancer.
Type of support: Grants for special needs.
Application information: Applications by in-person visit with list of expenses incurred and other financial information accepted throughout the year; Interviews required.
EIN: 382877951

4980
Parsons Community Foundation

1405 Morgan Ave.
Parsons, KS   67357   (620) 421-3453
Contact: W.D. Hughes, Pres.

Foundation type: Community foundation
Limitations: Grants to residents of the Parsons, KS, area for emergency assistance and for special needs.
Publications: Annual report; Informational brochure; Occasional report.
Financial data: Year ended 05/31/2005. Assets, $3,026,682 (M); Expenditures, $247,478; Total giving, $230,421; Grants to individuals, totaling $8,000.
Fields of interest: Safety/disasters.
Type of support: Emergency funds; Grants for special needs.
Application information: Contact foundation for current application deadline/guidelines.
EIN: 481152358

4981
Pearle Vision Foundation, Inc.

2465 Joe Field Rd.
Dallas, TX   75229   (972) 277-6191
Contact: Trina Parasiliti, Admin.
FAX: (972) 277-6422;
E-mail: trinaparasiliti@pearlevision.com;
URL: http://www.pearlevision.com/webapp/wcs/stores/servlet/PearleVision/StoreContent/about/community.jsp

Foundation type: Operating foundation
Limitations: Grants to U.S. residents for low-vision equipment aids.
Publications: Application guidelines; Newsletter.
Financial data: Year ended 01/01/2005. Assets, $658,072 (M); Expenditures, $465,169; Total giving, $414,080; Grants to individuals, 19 grants totaling $38,660 (high: $3,274, low: $820).
Fields of interest: Optometry/vision screening; Eye diseases; Health organizations.
Type of support: Grants for special needs.
Application information: Contact foundation for current application deadline; Initial approach by letter or telephone; Completion of formal application required, including financial information and letter from sponsor.
Program description:
Vision Assistance Program: Grants are not given for routine eye exams, eyeglasses or eye surgeries but rather for low-vision equipment aids only.

Application must be made prior to the purchase of equipment.
EIN: 752173714

4982
People in Business Care, Inc.

P.O. Box 977
Chanhassen, MN   55317

Foundation type: Company-sponsored foundation
Limitations: Grants for medical assistance and emergency aid primarily to residents of CA and MN.
Financial data: Year ended 07/31/2004. Assets, $1,682,128 (M); Expenditures, $385,280; Total giving, $384,754.
Fields of interest: Health care.
Type of support: Grants for special needs.
Application information: Applications by letter outlining financial need and reason for application accepted throughout the year.
EIN: 363261419

4983
B. F. & Rose H. Perkins Foundation

P.O. Box 1064
Sheridan, WY   82801-1064   (307) 674-8871
FAX: (307) 674-8803

Foundation type: Independent foundation
Limitations: Medical assistance include dental care, orthodontia, medical care, surgery and eyeglasses to individuals who are from 2 to 20 years of age and have been residents of Sheridan County, WY, for one year.
Financial data: Year ended 12/31/2004. Assets, $9,834,276 (M); Expenditures, $340,640; Total giving, $213,124; Grants to individuals, 109 grants totaling $208,124 (high: $5,710, low: $42); Loans to individuals, 119 loans totaling $472,150.
Application information: Deadline to submit completed form from individual and doctor is the first week of the month prior to treatment; Completion of formal application required; Application forms available from the above address, including form to be sent by foundation to doctor for estimate of charges prior to treatment; Interviews required.
EIN: 830138740

4984
The Perot Foundation

P.O. Box 269014
Plano, TX   75026   (972) 788-3000
Contact: Carolyn P. Rathjen, V.P.

Foundation type: Independent foundation
Limitations: Grants for emergency needs, including legal fees, burial costs and medical care to soldiers, veterans, police officers and humanitarian workers.
Financial data: Year ended 12/31/2004. Assets, $47,205,698 (M); Expenditures, $7,969,844; Total giving, $7,816,923; Grants to individuals, 42 grants totaling $243,616 (high: $44,803; low: $10, average gift: $159-$8,762).
Fields of interest: Human services, emergency aid; International relief; Foundations (non-grantmaking, non-operating); Military/veterans' organizations; Cemeteries/burial services.
Type of support: Grants for special needs.
Application information: Contact foundation for current application deadlines/guidelines.
EIN: 756093258

4985
The Perpetual Benevolent Fund

c/o Bank of America, N.A.
39 Main St.
Watertown, MA   02472
Contact: Darlene G. Furbush, Secy.
Application address: Nathaniel Murphy, c/o Bank of America, N.A., 100 Federal St., Boston, MA 02110
FAX: (617) 923-4623

Foundation type: Independent foundation
Limitations: Assistance to financially needy individuals in the greater Boston, MA, area, with preference to residents of Newton and Waltham.
Publications: Application guidelines.
Financial data: Year ended 12/31/2004. Assets, $6,399,846 (M); Expenditures, $313,503; Total giving, $242,251; Grants to individuals, 293 grants totaling $144,949 (high: $850, low: $35).
Fields of interest: Pharmacy/prescriptions; Housing/shelter; Day care; Human services, emergency aid.
Type of support: Grants for special needs.
Application information: Applications accepted. Application form required.
   Applicants should submit the following:
      1) Financial information
   Additional information: Application must include applicant's social history. Direct applications by individuals not accepted.
Program description:
Financial Assistance Program: Financial assistance is given to those who have no other resources and who need emergency aid as payment for security deposits, last and first month's rent, overdue utility bills, apartment de-leading costs, family clothing grants, household furnishings, day care, overdue rent to prevent eviction, emergency food and shelter costs, oil deliveries, prescription medicines, washing machines and refrigerators, and emergency dental work. Formal applications are submitted through social agencies, schools, hospitals, and health and welfare departments. Each application is reviewed on the basis of financial need, income, one-time crisis, emergency, and priority factors.
EIN: 237011723

4986
The Mary L. Peyton Foundation

Bassett Tower, Ste. 908
303 Texas Ave.
El Paso, TX   79901-1456
Contact: James M. Day, Exec. Admin.

Foundation type: Operating foundation
Limitations: Grants for medical and living expenses and emergency assistance to legal residents of El Paso County, TX, who are unable to earn a livelihood due to age, physical or mental disability, or other hardship.
Financial data: Year ended 05/31/2005. Assets, $3,970,107 (M); Expenditures, $263,443; Total giving, $150,404.
Fields of interest: Vocational education; Optometry/vision screening; Health care; Food services; Housing/shelter, expense aid; Human services, transportation; Aging, centers/services; Disabilities, people with.
Type of support: Grants for special needs.
Application information: Applications accepted throughout the year; Applications should be made through social service agencies; Initial approach by letter explaining economic situation causing the need for assistance and itemization of those services for which assistance is requested.

Program description:

Assistance Program: Grants are given to those legal residents who have no other resources on which to depend and cannot obtain funds elsewhere. Types of assistance include medical attention and equipment, prescriptions, eyeglasses, hearing aids, clothing, food, transportation, rent, and utilities. Some recipients receive more than one grant.

EIN: 741276102

4987
Pfaffinger Foundation
316 W. Second St., Ste. PH-C
Los Angeles, CA   90012   (213) 680-7460
Contact: Mary Tower, Pres.
FAX: (213) 680-7474

Foundation type: Independent foundation
Limitations: Relief assistance to employees and retirees of the former Times Mirror Co., and employees and retirees of the Los Angeles Times.
Financial data: Year ended 12/31/2004. Assets, $90,584,689 (M); Expenditures, $5,236,865; Total giving, $3,529,963; Grants to individuals, totaling $2,702,963.
Type of support: Employee-related welfare.
Application information: Application form required.
   Initial approach: Letter.
   Deadline(s): None
   Additional information: Interviews required; Final notification usually one week after receipt of application.
EIN: 951661675

4988
The Philadelphia Foundation
1234 Market St., Ste. 1800
Philadelphia, PA   19107-3794   (215) 563-6417
Contact: R. Andrew Swinney, Pres.
FAX: (215) 563-6882;
E-mail: parkow@philafound.org; URL: http://www.philafound.org

Foundation type: Community foundation
Limitations: Grants to individuals residing in Philadelphia, PA, for emergency needs.
Publications: Newsletter.
Financial data: Year ended 12/31/2004. Assets, $277,295,464 (M); Expenditures, $19,881,412; Total giving, $15,024,991; Grants to individuals, 29 grants totaling $35,013 (high: $6,000, low: $467).
Type of support: Emergency funds.
Application information: Contact foundation for current application deadlines/guidelines.
EIN: 231581832

4989
Philanthropic Ventures Foundation
1222 Preservation Pkwy.
Oakland, CA   94612-1201   (510) 645-1890
Contact: Bill Somerville, Pres. and Exec. Dir.
FAX: (510) 645-1892;
E-mail: info@venturesfoundation.org; URL: http://www.venturesfoundation.org/

Foundation type: Public charity
Limitations: Financial assistance to individuals 18 years or younger who have congenital health problems referred by designated professionals.
Publications: Annual report; Informational brochure; Newsletter.

Financial data: Year ended 12/31/2004. Assets, $11,416,897 (L); Expenditures, $5,892,859; Total giving, $5,400,812.
Fields of interest: Health care.
Type of support: Grants for special needs.
Application information: Applications accepted only through designated professionals.
Program description:
   Youth Health Fund: This program provides financial assistance to persons 18 years or younger who have congenital health problems and whose financial circumstances cannot cover the entire cost of treatment. These grants are one-time only and are up to $4,000.
EIN: 943136771

4990
Phillips Foundation
P.O. Box 471
Columbus, MS   39703
Application address: c/o Betty Miller, 116 5th St. N., Columbus, MS 39701, tel.: (662) 327-8401

Foundation type: Operating foundation
Limitations: General welfare grants primarily to economically disadvantaged residents of Lowndes County, MS, for medical, surgical, and hospital attention and services other than doctors' bills or surgical fees.
Financial data: Year ended 12/31/2003. Assets, $4,245,177 (M); Expenditures, $183,238; Total giving, $150,066; Grants to individuals, totaling $150,066.
Type of support: Grants for special needs.
Application information: Applications accepted. Application form required.
   Additional information: Application should include referral.
EIN: 646020136

4991
Edwin Phillips Foundation
P.O. 610075
Newton Highlands, MA   02461

Foundation type: Independent foundation
Limitations: Medical equipment primarily to financially needy, physically and mentally disabled children residing in Marshfield, MA.
Financial data: Year ended 12/31/2004. Assets, $11,986,214 (M); Expenditures, $609,244; Total giving, $465,028; Grants to individuals, totaling $302,607.
Fields of interest: Health care, patient services; Children/youth, services; Disabilities, people with.
Type of support: Grants for special needs.
Application information: Applications accepted throughout the year; Completion of formal application required in duplicate, including financial statement, doctor's letter, tax returns, and other sources of funding received or sought.
Program description:
   Assistance Program: The foundation makes grants to help individuals to live in their own homes. Grants are used to provide prosthetic appliances, wheelchairs, beds, or other forms of physical assistance. First priority is given to children in the town of Marshfield, MA. Only one proposal for funds per applicant may be submitted at a time. Applicants must wait one year after a proposal has been rejected to reapply. Grants are renewable in exceptional circumstances.
EIN: 046025549

4992
Physicians Aid Association
10937 Hillhaven Ave.
Tujunga, CA   91042-1417
Contact: Bonnie L. Ferris, Exec. Dir.

Foundation type: Independent foundation
Limitations: Medical and financial assistance to physicians living or working in Los Angeles County, CA, who are disabled or retired, and to their immediate families.
Financial data: Year ended 12/31/2004. Assets, $3,599,213 (M); Expenditures, $226,302; Total giving, $90,492; Grants to individuals, 16 grants totaling $90,492 (high: $19,819, low: $450).
Fields of interest: Health care, association; Disabilities, people with.
Type of support: Grants for special needs.
Application information: Application form required.
   Initial approach: Letter or telephone.
   Additional information: Applications accepted throughout the year.
EIN: 951660852

4993
The Physicians Aid Association of the Delaware Valley
(formerly Aid Association of the Phila County Medical Society)
684 Ridge Rd.
Spring City, PA   19475   (610) 469-9241
Contact: Charles T. Lee, Jr. M.D., Pres.

Foundation type: Public charity
Limitations: Grants to needy physicians and their families who practice in the Philadelphia, PA, area and hold an M.D. or D.O. degree.
Financial data: Year ended 12/31/2004. Assets, $7,831,893 (M); Expenditures, $270,528; Total giving, $216,700; Grants to individuals, totaling $216,700.
Fields of interest: Health care.
Type of support: Grants for special needs.
Application information: Contact association for current application deadline/guidelines.
EIN: 236266619

4994
Physicians' Relief Fund
c/o Glenmeade Trust Co., N.A.
1650 Market St., Ste. 1200
Philadelphia, PA   19103-7391
Contact: Virginia Kanick M.D.
Application address: 560 Riverside Dr., Ste. 17B, New York, NY 10027

Foundation type: Independent foundation
Limitations: Loans and grants to financially needy physicians and their families in the New York, NY, area.
Financial data: Year ended 12/31/2003. Assets, $1,751,713 (M); Expenditures, $96,550; Total giving, $40,130; Grants to individuals, 15 grants totaling $35,130 (high: $5,400, low: $750).
Fields of interest: Health care, association.
Type of support: Grants for special needs.
Application information: Applications accepted. Application form required.
   Initial approach: Letter.
   Deadline(s): Applications accepted throughout the year
EIN: 237426275

4995
S. S. Pierce Company Employees Aid Fund
c/o Mellon Trust of New England
P.O. Box 185
Pittsburgh, PA 15230-0185

Foundation type: Company-sponsored foundation
Limitations: Supplements to retirement income
only for needy former employees of S.S. Pierce
Company who reside in MA.
Financial data: Year ended 08/31/2005.
Assets, $22,788 (M); Expenditures, $3,716; Total
giving, $2,991; Grants to individuals, 56 grants
totaling $2,991.
Type of support: Employee-related welfare.
Application information: Applications not
accepted.
Additional information: Contributes only to
pre-selected individuals.
EIN: 046092670

4996
Katharine C. Pierce Trust
c/o U.S. Trust Co., N.A.
225 Franklin St.
Boston, MA 02110
Contact: Amy F. Sahler

Foundation type: Operating foundation
Limitations: Financial assistance to needy and
deserving gentlewomen residing in MA. Preference
is shown to the elderly.
Publications: Application guidelines; Annual report.
Financial data: Year ended 12/31/2003.
Assets, $5,540,322 (M); Expenditures,
$316,020; Total giving, $264,275; Grants to
individuals, 13 grants totaling $30,000 (high:
$1,200, low: $200).
Fields of interest: Aging; Women.
Type of support: Grants for special needs.
Application information: Applications accepted.
Application form required.
Initial approach: Letter.
Applicants should submit the following:
1) Letter(s) of recommendation
Additional information: Applications from outside
the state of MA will not be considered.
EIN: 046095694

4997
The Pilgrim Foundation
P.O. Box 3400
Brockton, MA 02303 (508) 588-6100

Foundation type: Independent foundation
Limitations: Welfare assistance to economically
disadvantaged families and children who are
residents of Brockton, MA.
Financial data: Year ended 12/31/2004.
Assets, $4,401,588 (M); Expenditures,
$222,236; Total giving, $177,082; Grants to
individuals, 97 grants totaling $81,632 (high:
$1,000, low: $90).
Fields of interest: Family services; Economically
disadvantaged.
Type of support: Grants for special needs.
Application information: Contact foundation for
current application deadline/guidelines.
EIN: 042104834

4998
The Pitney Bowes Relief Fund Charitable Trust
c/o Arlen Hencock
1 Elmcroft Rd., Ste. 6101
Stamford, CT 06926-0700 (203) 356-5000
URL: http://www.pb.com/communityinvestments

Foundation type: Public charity
Limitations: Financial assistance to individuals who
have experienced natural disasters or catastrophic
events. Examples of support include housing
assistance, medical expenses, funeral expenses,
daycare, house fires, etc.
Financial data: Year ended 08/31/2003.
Assets, $465,332; Expenditures, $175,820; Total
giving, $175,760; Grants to individuals, totaling
$135,760.
Type of support: Emergency funds; Grants for
special needs.
Application information:
Initial approach: Letter.
Additional information: Contact foundation for
further application guidelines.
EIN: 223198214

4999
Plitt Southern Theatres, Inc. Employees Fund
7502 Greenville Ave., Ste. 500
Dallas, TX 75231

Foundation type: Company-sponsored foundation
Limitations: Financial assistance to employees of
Plitt Southern Theatres, Inc.
Financial data: Year ended 12/31/2004.
Assets, $2,293,758 (M); Expenditures,
$336,545; Total giving, $286,452.
Type of support: Employee-related welfare.
EIN: 756037855

5000
Plymouth Fragment Society Trust
P.O. Box 6386
Plymouth, MA 02362-6386

Foundation type: Independent foundation
Limitations: Grants to senior citizens and
economically disadvantaged individuals residing in
MA for fuel, medical, food and other needs.
Financial data: Year ended 09/30/2004.
Assets, $194,097 (M); Expenditures, $7,438;
Total giving, $6,591.
Fields of interest: Health care; Aging; Economically
disadvantaged.
Type of support: Grants for special needs.
Application information:
Deadline(s): None.
Additional information: Contact trust for current
application guidelines.
EIN: 046043957

5001
The Polaris Foundation
c/o Dir., Progs.
2100 Hwy. 55
Medina, MN 55340-9770

Foundation type: Company-sponsored foundation
Limitations: Disaster relief grants to employees of
Polaris Industries, Inc.
Financial data: Year ended 12/31/2004.
Assets, $60,908 (M); Expenditures, $71,271;
Total giving, $71,000.

Type of support: Emergency funds;
Employee-related welfare.
Application information: Application form required.
Deadline(s): None
EIN: 411828276

5002
Police Officer Assistance Trust
2634 N.W. 97th Ave.
Miami, FL 33172 (305) 594-6662
Contact: Chief Steve Rothlein, Pres.
FAX: (305) 594-0997; E-mail: office@poat.org;
URL: http://www.poat.org

Foundation type: Public charity
Limitations: Grants to police officers and their
families residing in FL, for expenses arising as a
result of death, disability, illness, injury or some
other catastrophic circumstance.
Financial data: Year ended 09/30/2004.
Assets, $1,146,404; Expenditures, $406,986;
Total giving, $311,712; Grants to individuals,
totaling $311,712.
Type of support: Grants for special needs.
Application information: Contact trust for current
application deadline/guidelines.
EIN: 650164129

5003
Portland Female Charitable Society
149 Allen Ave., Ste. 122
Portland, ME 04103-4426 (207) 775-1377
Contact: Jean Leighton, Treas.

Foundation type: Independent foundation
Limitations: Aid limited to financially needy
residents of the City of Portland, ME, for dental
care, prescriptions, hearing aids, glasses, or other
needs having to do with health, food, or shelter,
with emphasis on the needs of children, the elderly,
and the ill.
Financial data: Year ended 09/30/2004.
Assets, $176,231 (M); Expenditures, $9,180;
Total giving, $7,011; Grants to individuals, totaling
$7,011.
Fields of interest: Dental care; Optometry/vision
screening; Health care; Housing/shelter; Children/
youth, services; Aging; Disabilities, people with.
Type of support: Grants for special needs.
Application information: Applications from
individuals residing outside of stated geographic
restriction not accepted; Requests accepted
throughout the year; No formal applications;
Requests usually presented by social workers,
public health nurses, counselors, etc.; Interviews
required.
EIN: 010370961

5004
Portland Seamen's Friend Society
14 Lewis St.
Westbrook, ME 04092 (207) 854-4308
Contact: Lewis G. Emery, Treas.

Foundation type: Independent foundation
Limitations: Financial assistance in the form of a
small monthly stipend to indigent seamen who
reside in the state of ME.
Financial data: Year ended 12/31/2003.
Assets, $244,294 (M); Expenditures, $76,698;
Total giving, $66,584; Grants to individuals,
totaling $8,219.
Fields of interest: Military/veterans' organizations.
Type of support: Grants for special needs.

Application information:
Initial approach: Letter or telephone.
Deadline(s): Contact society for current application deadline
Additional information: Applications by letter outlining financial need and including references accepted throughout the year; Interviews required.
EIN: 010211545

5005
Portland Valley Acacia Fund, Inc.
(formerly Scottish Rite Oregon Consistory Almoner Fund, Inc.)
709 S.W. 15th Ave.
Portland, OR 97205-1995 (503) 226-7827
Contact: Allen Kirk

Foundation type: Independent foundation
Limitations: Relief assistance with medical, hospital, or emergency sustenance to distressed Masons, their widows and orphans, and other worthy recipients living in the state of OR.
Financial data: Year ended 12/31/2004.
Assets, $21,474 (M); Expenditures, $34,025; Total giving, $20,245; Grants to individuals, totaling $4,820.
Application information:
Initial approach: Letter or telephone.
Additional information: Applications by letter, indicating reason for request, accepted throughout the year.
EIN: 237154746

5006
Positive Impact, Inc.
711 N. Tamarisk St.
Chandler, AZ 85224 (480) 963-0393
Contact: Renee M. Villa, V.P.

Foundation type: Public charity
Limitations: Grants to individuals and families in AZ for medical and temporary living expenses.
Financial data: Year ended 12/31/2003.
Assets, $90,221 (M); Expenditures, $71,365; Total giving, $64,460; Grants to individuals, totaling $64,460.
Fields of interest: Human services.
Type of support: Grants for special needs.
Application information:
Initial approach: Letter.
EIN: 860920583

5007
Mary E. Powell Trust
c/o Citizens Federal Bldg.
112 N. Main St.
Bellefontaine, OH 43311
Contact: D. Fred Burton, Pres.

Foundation type: Independent foundation
Limitations: Financial assistance to elderly ladies who are residents of Logan County, OH.
Financial data: Year ended 12/31/2004.
Assets, $86,462 (M); Expenditures, $10,366; Total giving, $6,840; Grants to individuals, totaling $6,840.
Fields of interest: Aging; Women.
Type of support: Grants for special needs.
Application information: Applications accepted throughout the year.
EIN: 346532522

5008
Ross Powers Foundation
c/o Peter Carlisle
P.O. 17574
Portland, ME 04112 (207) 775-1500
E-mail: info@rosspowersfoundation.org;
URL: http://www.rosspowersfoundation.org/

Foundation type: Public charity
Limitations: Financial assistance to VT athletes who have resided in VT or who have attended school there for at least the past two years.
Financial data: Year ended 06/30/2005.
Assets, $95,025 (M); Expenditures, $22,380; Total giving, $14,450; Grants to individuals, 8 grants totaling $14,450 (high: $5,000, low: $500).
Fields of interest: Athletics/sports, training; Athletics/sports, winter sports.
Type of support: Grants for special needs.
Application information: Applications accepted. Application form required. Application form available on the grantmaker's Web site.
Initial approach: Letter.
Applicants should submit the following:
1) Budget Information
EIN: 010541580

5009
Fannie B. Pratt Trust
c/o Dane & Howe
45 School St., 4th Fl.
Boston, MA 02108-3204 (617) 227-3600
Contact: Marion K. Daley, Tr.

Foundation type: Operating foundation
Limitations: Grants to economically disadvantaged widows of Boston, MA.
Financial data: Year ended 12/31/2003.
Assets, $1,237,011 (M); Expenditures, $83,292; Total giving, $64,043; Grants to individuals, 27 grants totaling $17,424 (high: $2,450, low: $50).
Fields of interest: Women; Economically disadvantaged.
Type of support: Grants for special needs.
Application information: Applications not accepted.
Additional information: Recipients are chosen by referral and evaluation only.
EIN: 046027727

5010
The Price Family Charitable Foundation, Inc.
c/o Foundation Source
501 Silverside Rd., Ste. 123
Wilmington, DE 19809-1377

Foundation type: Independent foundation
Limitations: Short-term emergency assistance grants to economically disadvantaged residents of the Gulf Breeze, FL, region.
Financial data: Year ended 12/31/2004.
Assets, $545,161 (M); Expenditures, $180,400; Total giving, $178,000; Grants to individuals, 118 grants totaling $122,000 (high: $5,000, low: $1,000).
Type of support: Grants for special needs.
Application information: Applications not accepted.
Additional information: Unsolicited requests for funds not considered or acknowledged.
EIN: 200768318

5011
Procrit Foundation, Inc.
1 Johnson & Johnson Plz.
New Brunswick, NJ 08933 (800) 553-3851
FAX: (800) 987-5572

Foundation type: Operating foundation
Limitations: Grants to economically disadvantaged individuals for pharmaceutical products.
Financial data: Year ended 12/31/2003.
Assets, $21,649 (M); Expenditures, $175,240; Total giving, $172,515; Grants to individuals, 230 grants totaling $172,515.
Fields of interest: Pharmacy/prescriptions; Health care; Economically disadvantaged.
Type of support: Grants for special needs.
Application information: Applications accepted throughout the year; Completion of formal application required.
EIN: 311756693

5012
Professional Athletes Foundation
2021 L St. N.W., 6th Fl.
Washington, DC 20036

Foundation type: Independent foundation
Limitations: Assistance for former professional and amateur athletes who are faced with unusual financial problems, whether due to medical, educational, or catastrophic events. Grants are available up to $10,000 per recipient.
Financial data: Year ended 12/31/2004.
Assets, $11,868,935 (M); Expenditures, $989,391; Total giving, $873,170; Grants to individuals, 115 grants totaling $571,970 (high: $15,000, low: $154).
Fields of interest: Athletics/sports, amateur leagues; Athletics/sports, professional leagues.
Type of support: Scholarships—to individuals; Grants for special needs.
Application information:
Deadline(s): Contact foundation for current application deadline/guidelines.
EIN: 521205920

5013
Project Single Parent, Inc.
(formerly Single Parent Assistance Fund, Inc.)
c/o Sharon Pens
6120 S. Yale Ave., Ste. 700
Tulsa, OK 74136 (918) 488-0999

Foundation type: Independent foundation
Limitations: Grants to single parents who are OK residents.
Financial data: Year ended 12/31/2004.
Assets, $104,745 (M); Expenditures, $54,914; Total giving, $54,630; Grants to individuals, totaling $54,630.
Fields of interest: Single parents.
Type of support: Grants for special needs.
Application information: Applications by letter, including name, address, telephone number and brief background, including work history, accepted throughout the year.
EIN: 731531820

5014
Protein Foundation
56 Ivy St.
Greenwich, CT 06830
Contact: Carol Fuchella, Tr.

Foundation type: Independent foundation

Limitations: Assistance to economically disadvantaged individuals.
Financial data: Year ended 12/31/2004. Assets, $3,697 (M); Expenditures, $4,628; Total giving, $4,628; Grants to individuals, totaling $4,628.
Fields of interest: Economically disadvantaged.
Type of support: Emergency funds; Grants for special needs.
Application information: Applications by letter outlining financial need accepted throughout the year.
EIN: 061046591

5015
Providence Female Charitable Society
P.O. Box 829
Rumford, RI 02916
Contact: Mrs. Charles E. Gross, Treas.

Foundation type: Independent foundation
Limitations: Assistance by referral only to economically disadvantaged women who are residents of RI. Types of assistance include the purchase of clothing and furniture, income supplement, medical expenses, sending children to summer camp, and payment of rent and utilities.
Financial data: Year ended 03/31/2005. Assets, $622,315 (M); Expenditures, $40,393; Total giving, $32,450; Grants to individuals, totaling $32,450.
Fields of interest: Women; Economically disadvantaged.
Type of support: Grants for special needs.
Application information: Applicants must be referred to the Society, in most cases. Unsolicited requests for funds not considered or acknowledged.
EIN: 056008631

5016
Allen B. Puckett, Jr. Family Foundation, Inc.
P.O. Box 9630
Columbus, MS 39705
Contact: Allen B. Puckett III, Tr.

Foundation type: Independent foundation
Limitations: Grants to needy individuals residing in MS for general welfare and medical expenses.
Financial data: Year ended 12/31/2004. Assets, $233,924 (M); Expenditures, $56,395; Total giving, $53,109; Grants to individuals, totaling $32,346.
Fields of interest: Health care.
Type of support: Grants for special needs.
Application information: Applications not accepted.
EIN: 640732703

5017
Sarah L. Pugliese Medical Foundation
c/o Commercial Bank & Trust Co.
P.O. Box 1090
Paris, TN 38242-1090 (731) 642-3341

Foundation type: Operating foundation
Limitations: Grants to residents of TN, who are under 30 years of age, for medical expenses.
Financial data: Year ended 12/31/2003. Assets, $446,218 (M); Expenditures, $8,294; Total giving, $4,252; Grants to individuals, totaling $4,252.
Fields of interest: Health care.

Type of support: Grants for special needs.
Application information: Contact foundation for current application deadline; Application by letter, including medical condition, age and address.
EIN: 621763873

5018
Robert D. & Margaret W. Quin Foundation
c/o Northeast PA Trust Co
31 W. Broad St.
Hazleton, PA 18201

Foundation type: Independent foundation
Limitations: Grants to financially needy individuals who are 19 years old or younger, and who have been residents for at least one year of an area within a ten-mile radius of Hazleton City Hall, PA.
Financial data: Year ended 12/31/2004. Assets, $4,912 (M); Expenditures, $8,052; Total giving, $6,915; Grants to individuals, totaling $6,915.
Fields of interest: Education, services; Optometry/vision screening; Children/youth, services; Day care; Economically disadvantaged.
Type of support: Grants for special needs.
Application information: Applications accepted throughout the year; Completion of formal application required.
Program description:
Assistance Program: In the past, grants have been given for medical and dental expenses, day care, tutoring, camperships, furniture, utility payments, and talent advancement.
EIN: 222439876

5019
Raleigh County Community Action Association, Inc.
P.O. Box 3066
Beckley, WV 25801 (304) 252-6396
Contact: Barbara Thomas-Bailey, Exec. Dir.
URL: http://www.rccaa.org

Foundation type: Public charity
Limitations: Financial assistance to homeless persons residing in Raleigh County, WV to pay for medical, dental, and hospital expenses.
Financial data: Year ended 12/31/2004. Assets, $1,473,315 (M); Expenditures, $3,934,215; Total giving, $117,014; Grants to individuals, totaling $117,014.
Type of support: Grants for special needs.
Application information:
Initial approach: Letter.
Additional information: Contact foundation for further application guidelines.
EIN: 550480001

5020
Reade Industrial Fund
c/o Harris Trust and Savings Bank
P.O. Box 755
Chicago, IL 60690

Foundation type: Independent foundation
Limitations: Emergency grants to financially needy individuals who are employed or have been employed in industry in the state of IL. Preference is shown to those in the Chicago area.
Financial data: Year ended 12/31/2004. Assets, $4,010,504 (M); Expenditures, $183,181; Total giving, $157,000.
Type of support: Grants for special needs.

Application information: Applications accepted.
Initial approach: Letter from social service agency.
Additional information: Candidates are preselected by local social service agencies; Nominations accepted throughout the year; Completion of formal nomination required.
Program description:
Financial Assistance Program: Grants of up to $5,000 are given only to individuals of good moral character, who are or have been employed in industry in IL. Recipients must require financial assistance due to an emergency beyond their control, such as accidental injury, illness of themselves or family members, inability to obtain employment, or sudden and involuntary cessation of employment.
EIN: 366048673

5021
Realty Foundation of New York
551 5th Ave., Ste. 415
New York, NY 10176 (212) 697-3943
Contact: Scholarship and Aid Comm.
FAX: (212) 949-9319

Foundation type: Independent foundation
Limitations: Assistance to financially needy employees of the real estate industry in the five boroughs of New York City.
Publications: Informational brochure.
Financial data: Year ended 06/30/2005. Assets, $1,798,336 (M); Expenditures, $470,428; Total giving, $258,468; Grants to individuals, 62 grants totaling $254,068 (high: $20,000, low: $750).
Fields of interest: Business/industry; Community development, real estate; Economically disadvantaged.
Type of support: Employee-related welfare.
Application information: Applications accepted. Application form required.
Deadline(s): Applications accepted throughout the year
Applicants should submit the following:
1) Letter(s) of recommendation
2) Financial information
EIN: 136016622

5022
Peter S. Reed Foundation, Inc.
(formerly The Concrete Foundation, Inc.)
Watts St.
New York, NY 10013

Foundation type: Independent foundation
Limitations: Grants to individuals in NY for religious and other assistance.
Financial data: Year ended 06/30/2004. Assets, $2,213,013 (M); Expenditures, $157,611; Total giving, $98,500; Grants to individuals, 18 grants totaling $93,500.
Type of support: Grants for special needs.
Application information: Unsolicited requests for funds not accepted.
EIN: 133036536

5023
The Reiner Foundation, Inc.
855 S. Cedar Ln.
Valparaiso, IN 46383-4380
Contact: Walter M. Reiner, Pres.

Foundation type: Independent foundation

Limitations: Grants for academic assistance, insurance, and home repairs and improvements, and low-income housing provided to low-income children and families residing in IN, who are referred by churches and other nonprofit benevolent organizations.
Financial data: Year ended 12/31/2003. Assets, $4,385 (M); Expenditures, $29,155; Total giving, $25,143; Grants to individuals, 5 grants totaling $6,623 (high: $2,333, low: $633).
Fields of interest: Housing/shelter, repairs; Housing/shelter; Economically disadvantaged.
Type of support: Grants for special needs.
Application information: Application form not required.
EIN: 351685765

5024
Relief Association Trust
(formerly Relief Association, Inc)
c/o Bank of America, N.A.
P.O. Box 1802
Providence, RI 02940-1802

Foundation type: Independent foundation
Limitations: Welfare assistance to the aged and indigent of Nantucket, MA, who are recommended by the Center of Elderly Affairs.
Financial data: Year ended 12/31/2004. Assets, $783,052 (M); Expenditures, $36,706; Total giving, $29,735; Grants to individuals, totaling $29,735.
Fields of interest: Aging; Economically disadvantaged.
Type of support: Grants for special needs.
Application information: Applications not accepted.
  Additional information: Recipients are recommended by the Center of Elderly Affairs.
EIN: 046066321

5025
Renal Assistance, Inc.
4401 Hollywood Blvd.
Hollywood, FL 33021 (954) 962-2211
Contact: Deborah Kostner, V.P.

Foundation type: Independent foundation
Limitations: Grants to residents of FL who require hemodialysis therapy or have received a renal transplant, for the purpose of medical assistance, travel assistance, and emergency assistance.
Financial data: Year ended 01/31/2005. Assets, $232,943 (M); Expenditures, $12,484; Total giving, $9,335; Grants to individuals, totaling $9,335.
Fields of interest: Health care; Kidney diseases.
Type of support: Grants for special needs.
Application information: Applications not accepted.
  Additional information: The foundation contributes only to preselected individuals.
EIN: 591429145

5026
Rest Haven Preventorium for Children, Inc.
(also known as Children's Health Fund)
P.O. Box 420369
San Diego, CA 92142-0369

Foundation type: Operating foundation
Limitations: Grants to financially needy children only in San Diego County and Imperial County, CA, for medical, dental, optical, therapy, hearing, childcare, and nutritional expenses.
Financial data: Year ended 12/31/2004. Assets, $7,540,722 (L); Expenditures, $262,275; Total giving, $183,226.
Fields of interest: Optometry/vision screening; Pharmacy/prescriptions; Mental health/crisis services; Nutrition; Children/youth, services; Disabilities, people with.
Type of support: Grants for special needs.
Application information: Applications not accepted.
EIN: 952128344

5027
Richman Brothers Foundation
P.O. Box 657
Chagrin Falls, OH 44022
Contact: Raymond J. Novak, Pres.

Foundation type: Independent foundation
Limitations: Grants primarily to pensioners of Richman Brothers Co. and their surviving spouses.
Financial data: Year ended 12/31/2005. Assets, $2,902,503 (M); Expenditures, $147,352; Total giving, $147,352; Grants to individuals, 64 grants totaling $37,252 (high: $1,000, low: $300).
Type of support: Employee-related welfare.
Application information:
  Initial approach: Letter.
  Additional information: Contact foundation for current application guidelines.
EIN: 346504927

5028
Frank Rider Trust
7451 Garfield-Farmington Rd.
Garfield, WA 99130-8723 (509) 534-4005
Contact: Hollis Jamison, Secy.-Treas.

Foundation type: Independent foundation
Limitations: Assistance only to indigent Freemasons in Whitman, Lincoln, Adams, Franklin, and Grant counties, WA, for medical and other expenses.
Financial data: Year ended 12/31/2004. Assets, $1,515,334 (M); Expenditures, $100,836; Total giving, $39,150; Grants to individuals, 8 grants totaling $39,150.
Fields of interest: Health care; Economically disadvantaged.
Type of support: Grants for special needs.
Application information: Application form required.
  Initial approach: Letter.
  Deadline(s): Applications accepted throughout the year
  Additional information: Grants are renewable.
EIN: 910641308

5029
Rivendell Stewards' Trust
735 State St., Ste. 632
Santa Barbara, CA 93101
Contact: Amity Wicks, Admin.
FAX: (805) 564-7137; *E-mail:* info@rstrust.org;
URL: http://www.rstrust.org

Foundation type: Independent foundation
Limitations: Grants to individuals for Christian ministry projects in developing countries.
Publications: Application guidelines.
Financial data: Year ended 12/31/2004. Assets, $5,478,957 (M); Expenditures,
$867,371; Total giving, $723,947; Grants to individuals, 4 grants totaling $25,000 (high: $10,000, low: $5,000).
Fields of interest: Christian agencies & churches; Developing countries.
Type of support: Program development.
Application information:
  Initial approach: Letter.
  Deadline(s): July 1
EIN: 776016389

5030
Charlotte M. Robbins Trust
c/o State Street Bank and Trust Co.
P.O. Box 351, M-10
Boston, MA 02101
Contact: Amy F. Sahler, Trust Off.
Application address: 225 Franklin St., Boston, MA 02110

Foundation type: Independent foundation
Limitations: Financial assistance limited to aged couples and aged women who are residents of the towns of Ayer, Groton, Harvard, Littleton, and Shirley, MA.
Financial data: Year ended 12/31/2002. Assets, $413,787 (M); Expenditures, $28,407; Total giving, $22,157; Grants to individuals, totaling $22,157.
Fields of interest: Aging; Women.
Type of support: Grants for special needs.
Application information: Applications by letter, including applicant's income and expenses, assets, and reason for request, accepted throughout the year.
EIN: 046096044

5031
Rochester Female Charitable Society
c/o JPMorgan Chase Bank
P.O. Box 31412
Rochester, NY 14603 (716) 258-9796
Contact: Margaret Trevett
Application address: c/o Mrs. Peter E. Baltzer, 56 Oak Ln., Rochester, NY 14610, tel.: (585) 381-0436

Foundation type: Independent foundation
Limitations: Giving restricted to the greater Rochester, NY, area. Individuals must be referred by greater Rochester area social workers.
Publications: Grants list.
Financial data: Year ended 03/31/2005. Assets, $2,896,358 (M); Expenditures, $151,133; Total giving, $126,272.
Fields of interest: Disabilities, people with.
Type of support: Grants for special needs.
Application information:
  Initial approach: Initial approach by letter, including copy of I.R.S. exemption letter.
  Deadline(s): None.
  Additional information: Application form is printed in the Guide for Grantmakers, Rochester Grantmakers Forum.
Program description:
  Assistance Program: The foundation's purpose is "to provide aid for relief of the sick and needy poor." Giving is directed primarily to physically/mentally ill and financially needy people of any age; also, support for summer camperships and Christmas giving.
EIN: 237166180

5032
Scott Rose Foundation, Inc.
P.O. Box 5001
London, KY 40745-5001 (606) 862-4221
Contact: Lawrence Kuhl, Treas.

Foundation type: Independent foundation
Limitations: Support for medical and general welfare needs of disabled and disadvantaged children and young adults living in southeastern KY.
Financial data: Year ended 06/30/2005.
Assets, $779,616 (M); Expenditures, $43,921; Total giving, $35,495; Grants to individuals, totaling $35,495.
Fields of interest: Children/youth, services; Disabilities, people with.
Type of support: Grants for special needs.
Application information: Applications accepted.
  Initial approach: Letter or telephone.
  Additional information: Contact foundation for current application guidelines.
EIN: 611048189

5033
Rose Ladies Aid Society
1925 Wabash Ave.
P.O. Box 330
Terre Haute, IN 47807

Foundation type: Independent foundation
Limitations: Financial assistance to low-income families in Vigo County, IN, for medical, dental, educational, and emergency living expenses.
Financial data: Year ended 04/30/2005.
Assets, $1,241,705 (M); Expenditures, $64,710; Total giving, $54,835; Grants to individuals, totaling $54,835.
Fields of interest: Dental care; Health care; Economically disadvantaged.
Type of support: Grants for special needs.
Application information: Applications not accepted.
  Additional information: Recipients are referred by schools.
EIN: 350911948

5034
Rostra Engineered Component Sunshine Fund
(formerly Century Brass Sunshine Fund)
P.O. Box 1802
Providence, RI 02901-1802

Foundation type: Company-sponsored foundation
Limitations: Emergency grants and loans and gift baskets for funerals and illnesses to Rostra Engineered Components employees.
Financial data: Year ended 12/31/2004.
Assets, $56,917 (M); Expenditures, $8,590; Total giving, $7,400.
Type of support: Employee-related welfare.
Application information: Contact Sunshine Fund secretary for current application guidelines.
EIN: 066219258

5035
Herman & Lenore Rottenberg Foundation, Inc.
c/o Spitz & Greenstein, C.P.A.
21 E. 40th St., No. 1006
New York, NY 10016-0501
Application address: c/o Herman Rottenberg, 115 Central Park West, New York, NY 10023

Foundation type: Independent foundation
Limitations: Grants to individuals, primarily in NY, to talented young performing artists for assistance in helping them achieve their goals which brought them to New York City.
Financial data: Year ended 01/31/2005.
Assets, $2,197,407 (M); Expenditures, $208,433; Total giving, $205,015; Grants to individuals, totaling $11,425 (high: $2,750).
Type of support: Grants to individuals.
Application information: Applications by letter accepted throughout the year including complete background information.
EIN: 136132611

5036
Russian Children's Welfare Society, Inc.
200 Park Ave. S., Ste. 1617
New York, NY 10003-1503 (212) 473-6263
Contact: Vladimer P. Fekula, Pres.
FAX: (212) 473-6301; E-mail: main@rcws.org;
Additional tel.: (888) 732-7297; URL: http://www.rcws.org

Foundation type: Public charity
Limitations: Grants to economically disadvantaged children of Russian descent, both in Russia and in other countries.
Financial data: Year ended 12/31/2003.
Assets, $6,199,724; Expenditures, $573,626; Total giving, $353,047; Grants to individuals, totaling $353,047.
Fields of interest: Children/youth, services; Economically disadvantaged; Russia.
Type of support: Grants for special needs.
Application information: Contact foundation for current application deadline/guidelines.
EIN: 135562332

5037
Edward Rutledge Charity
P.O. Box 758
Chippewa Falls, WI 54729-0738
Contact: Betty Manning

Foundation type: Independent foundation
Limitations: Charitable gifts and loans of up to $50 in value to worthy needy residents of Chippewa County, WI.
Financial data: Year ended 05/31/2005.
Assets, $18,890,116 (M); Expenditures, $436,569; Total giving, $247,275; Grants to individuals, 86 grants totaling $74,500 (high: $1,400, low: $300); Loans to individuals, 67 loans totaling $3,291.
Type of support: Grants for special needs.
Application information: Application form required.
  Initial approach: In person.
  Additional information: Applications accepted throughout the year; Interviews required.
EIN: 390806178

5038
The Ryder System Charitable Foundation, Inc.
c/o Corp. Tax
11690 N.W. 105th St.
Miami, FL 33178 (305) 500-3031

Foundation type: Company-sponsored foundation
Limitations: Grants to individuals in CA, FL, GA, MI, MO, OH, and TX for disaster relief.
Publications: Corporate giving report.

Financial data: Year ended 12/31/2004.
Assets, $133,383 (M); Expenditures, $1,287,089; Total giving, $1,287,089; Grants to individuals, 44 grants totaling $25,275 (high: $1,850, low: $150).
Fields of interest: Safety/disasters.
Type of support: Emergency funds; Grants for special needs.
Application information:
  Initial approach: Letter.
  Deadline(s): June 30
  Additional information: Contact foundation for current application deadline/guidelines.
EIN: 592462315

5039
Charles E. Saak Trust
c/o Wells Fargo Bank, N.A., Fdns. Dept
P.O. Box 20160
Long Beach, CA 90802
Contact: Jennifer M. Thompson, Trust Off.
Telephone: (800) 352-3705

Foundation type: Independent foundation
Limitations: Dental and emergency medical assistance to children under 21 years of age from low-income families residing in the Porterville/Poplar area, CA.
Publications: Application guidelines.
Financial data: Year ended 01/31/2005.
Assets, $1,733,993 (M); Expenditures, $118,093; Total giving, $85,158; Grants to individuals, 71 grants totaling $77,858.
Fields of interest: Dental care; Health care; Children/youth, services.
Type of support: Grants for special needs.
Application information: Applications accepted. Application form required.
  Deadline(s): Mar. 31
  Applicants should submit the following:
    1) Financial information
Program description:
  Health Care Assistance Program: Medical and dental grants are awarded on a one-time basis only. One award will cover the total cost up to the foundation's limit for one injury, sickness, or dental treatment. Additional unpredicted costs related to the same injury, sickness, or dental treatment must be pre-approved by the trustee.
EIN: 946076213

5040
Salem Female Charitable Society
c/o Fiduciary Trust Co.
P.O. Box 1647
Boston, MA 02105-1647
Application address: c/o Rosamond Dennis, 33 Warren St., Salem, MA 01970

Foundation type: Independent foundation
Limitations: Assistance to aged and indigent women of Salem, MA, only. Aid is forfeited if resident moves to another town.
Financial data: Year ended 04/30/2005.
Assets, $948,951 (M); Expenditures, $57,599; Total giving, $43,100; Grants to individuals, totaling $43,100.
Fields of interest: Aging; Women; Economically disadvantaged.
Type of support: Grants for special needs.
Application information: Application form not required.
  Initial approach: Letter.
  Copies of proposal: 1

Additional information: Applications by letter, outlining financial need, accepted throughout the year.
EIN: 046014190

5041
The Samaritan Society
c/o Cabot Farm
Orne St. Extension
Salem, MA 01970-2421   (978) 745-5532

Foundation type: Independent foundation
Limitations: Grants to economically disadvantaged residents of Salem, MA, for rent, medications, fuel, and emergencies.
Financial data: Year ended 11/30/2004. Assets, $37,658 (M); Expenditures, $20,527; Total giving, $18,401; Grants to individuals, totaling $18,401.
Fields of interest: Economically disadvantaged.
Type of support: Grants for special needs.
Application information: Application form not required.
Additional information: Maximum grant is $100 per month.
EIN: 046062897

5042
The San Francisco Family Foundation
P.O. Box 6886
San Rafael, CA 94903   (415) 922-4091
Contact: Beryl C.D. Kay, Exec. Dir.
FAX: (415) 922-5717; Application address: 2269 Chestnut St., Ste. 255, San Francisco, CA 94123

Foundation type: Independent foundation
Limitations: General welfare assistance, including food, clothing, medical, dental, and housing expenses, to elderly individuals residing in CA. Applicants must apply through an appropriate agency.
Publications: Application guidelines; Financial statement; Informational brochure; Program policy statement.
Financial data: Year ended 12/31/2004. Assets, $1,314,258 (M); Expenditures, $139,583; Total giving, $43,467; Grants to individuals, 51 grants totaling $40,467.
Fields of interest: Dental care; Aging.
Type of support: Grants for special needs.
Application information:
Initial approach: Initial approach by letter or telephone.
Deadline(s): Contact foundation for current application deadline/guidelines.
Additional information: Application address: c/o Beryl Kay, 2269 Chestnut St., Ste. 255, San Francisco, CA 94123.
EIN: 680217117

5043
Sanders Fund, Inc.
50 Congress St., Ste. 800
Boston, MA 02109
Contact: Diana Satterfield

Foundation type: Independent foundation
Limitations: Grants to economically disadvantaged individuals in Boston, Cambridge, and Salem, MA.
Financial data: Year ended 12/31/2004. Assets, $295,376 (M); Expenditures, $278,445; Total giving, $275,895; Grant to an individual, 1 grant totaling $2,945.
Fields of interest: Economically disadvantaged.

Type of support: Grants for special needs.
Application information: Unsolicited applications not accepted.
EIN: 042265212

5044
Saranac Lake Voluntary Health Association, Inc.
75 Main St.
Saranac Lake, NY 12983

Foundation type: Operating foundation
Limitations: Grants for dental assistance to students attending schools in the Saranac Lake School District, NY, and for visiting nurse services for the elderly in Saranac Lake, NY.
Financial data: Year ended 03/31/2004. Assets, $2,828,692 (M); Expenditures, $100,399; Total giving, $76,582; Grants to individuals, totaling $35,305.
Fields of interest: Dental care; Health care, home services; Aging.
Type of support: Grants for special needs.
Application information: Applications not accepted.
EIN: 150532253

5045
Savannah Widows Society
3025 Bull St.
Savannah, GA 31405-2016   (912) 232-6312
Contact: Rosetta Sellers, Pres.

Foundation type: Operating foundation
Limitations: Grants primarily to single women, 55 or older, residing in Chatham County, GA. Also, aid to seriously disabled or handicapped persons, residing in Chatham County, GA, whose income from other sources is insufficient to provide their care in a reasonably comfortable manner.
Financial data: Year ended 08/31/2002. Assets, $0 (M); Expenditures, $71,312; Total giving, $40,933; Grants to individuals, 77 grants totaling $40,933 (high: $1,575, low: $99).
Fields of interest: Aging; Disabilities, people with; Women.
Type of support: Grants for special needs.
Application information: Contact society for current application deadline; Completion of formal application required.
EIN: 580603157

5046
Virginia Scatena Memorial Fund for San Francisco School Teachers
c/o Bank of America, N.A.
P.O. Box 513189 GMF
Los Angeles, CA 90051-1189
Application address: c/o Bank of America, N.A., Attn.: R. Britton, 600 Wilshire Blvd., 6th Fl., Los Angeles, CA 90017, tel.: (213) 345-5236

Foundation type: Independent foundation
Limitations: Financial assistance to retired teachers of the San Francisco Public School District who are needy, sick, or disabled.
Financial data: Year ended 12/31/2004. Assets, $165,556 (M); Expenditures, $2,550; Total giving, $2,540; Grants to individuals, totaling $2,540.
Fields of interest: Disabilities, people with; Economically disadvantaged.
Type of support: Employee-related welfare.

Application information: Applications accepted throughout the year; Completion of formal application required.
EIN: 946073769

5047
Cornelia Schnurmann Foundation
P.O. Box 398
Novelty, OH 44072-0398
Contact: Gabi W. Hays, Exec. Dir.
E-mail: schnrmnn@stratos.net

Foundation type: Public charity
Limitations: Grants for medical and housing assistance to economically disadvantaged individuals, and services for senior citizens.
Financial data: Year ended 12/31/2003. Assets, $1,240,418 (M); Expenditures, $94,905; Total giving, $15,111.
Fields of interest: Aging; Economically disadvantaged.
Type of support: Grants for special needs.
Application information:
Initial approach: E-mail.
Additional information: Contact foundation for current application deadline/guidelines.
EIN: 346567496

5048
J. F. Schoellkopf Silver Wedding Fund
c/o M&T Bank
1 M&T Plz., 8th Fl.
Buffalo, NY 14203
Application Address: c/o Buffalo Color Corp., Attn.: Paul Gilmour, 100 Lee St., P.O. Box 7027, Buffalo, NY 14210-2100, tel.: (716) 827-4636

Foundation type: Independent foundation
Limitations: Welfare assistance to residents of Buffalo, NY, who are members, or spouses or children of members, of the Mutual Aid Society.
Financial data: Year ended 12/31/2004. Assets, $1,535,548 (M); Expenditures, $94,489; Total giving, $82,000; Grants to individuals, totaling $2,000.
Fields of interest: Mutual aid societies.
Type of support: Grants for special needs.
Application information: Applications accepted throughout the year; Completion of formal application required.
Program description:
Assistance Program: Grants are awarded for the most part on an ongoing basis to indigent families, as well as to individuals, as temporary aid.
EIN: 166030147

5049
Theodore & Catherine Schulte Foundation
c/o JPMorgan Chase Bank, N.A.
P.O. Box 1308
Milwaukee, WI 53201-1308
Application address: c/o Robert Sharp, 610 Main St., Racine, WI 53403

Foundation type: Independent foundation
Limitations: Housing allowances for retired Catholic priests from Racine, WI.
Financial data: Year ended 09/30/2004. Assets, $883,460 (M); Expenditures, $85,424; Total giving, $72,498.
Fields of interest: Housing/shelter; Christian agencies & churches; Roman Catholic agencies & churches.
Type of support: Grants for special needs.

Application information: Applications accepted throughout the year; Contact foundation for current application guidelines.
EIN: 396222864

5050
SCI Special Fund
30398 Esperanza
Rancho Santa Margarita, CA 92688
(949) 635-1970
Contact: Helen Alonso, C.F.O.

Foundation type: Independent foundation
Limitations: Supporting apparatuses, free rehabilitative care, and equipment to qualified patients with spinal cord injuries residing in CA.
Financial data: Year ended 12/31/2004. Assets, $1,023,643 (M); Expenditures, $222,513; Total giving, $176,287; Grants to individuals, 30 grants totaling $156,287 (high: $16,500, low: $613).
Fields of interest: Medical care, rehabilitation; Spine disorders.
Type of support: Grants for special needs.
Application information: Applications not accepted.
Additional information: Unsolicited requests for funds not considered or acknowledged.
Program description:
Assistance Program: The fund will seek reports from the patient's physical therapist and/or social worker.
EIN: 330310017

5051
Scots' Charitable Society
P.O. Box 863
4 Buchan Rd.
Andover, MA 01810
Contact: Douglas Smith
Application address: c/o Alan M. Kelly, Chair., 222 Normandy Dr., Norwood, MA 02062, tel.: (617) 551-9709

Foundation type: Independent foundation
Limitations: Relief assistance to financially needy individuals of verifiable Scottish descent in the greater Boston, MA, area.
Financial data: Year ended 10/31/2002. Assets, $1,579,702 (M); Expenditures, $143,040; Total giving, $99,950; Grants to individuals, totaling $99,950.
Fields of interest: Economically disadvantaged; Scotland.
Type of support: Grants for special needs.
Application information: Applications by letter accepted throughout the year.
EIN: 046040091

5052
The Screen Actors Guild Foundation
5757 Wilshire Blvd., 7th Fl.
Los Angeles, CA 90036 (323) 549-6708
Contact: Marcia Smith, Exec. Dir.
E-mail: msmith@sag.org; FAX: (323) 549-6710; URL: http://www.sagfoundation.org

Foundation type: Public charity
Limitations: Grants to economically disadvantaged members of the guild for expenses due to illness and other situations.
Financial data: Year ended 09/30/2003. Assets, $15,072,481 (M); Expenditures, $2,139,507; Total giving, $612,448.

Fields of interest: Performing arts; Health care; Economically disadvantaged.
Type of support: Grants for special needs.
Application information: Contact foundation for current application deadline/guidelines.
Program description:
Screen Actors Guild Foundation Program: The foundation administers the following programs:
· Membership Assistance
· Catastrophic Health Fund.
EIN: 953967876

5053
Bette Lou Seidner Charitable Foundation
1900 Lake St.
Dyer, IN 46311
Contact: Bette Lou Seidner, Pres.

Foundation type: Independent foundation
Limitations: Financial assistance to individuals for psychiatric care.
Financial data: Year ended 12/31/2002. Assets, $47,133 (M); Expenditures, $48,428; Total giving, $40,675; Grants to individuals, 3 grants totaling $21,575 (high: $7,965, low: $6,920).
Fields of interest: Mental health, treatment.
Type of support: Grants for special needs.
Application information: Applications not accepted.
EIN: 363857046

5054
Selah Charitable Trust
P.O. Box 732
Lakeside, MT 59922-0732

Foundation type: Independent foundation
Limitations: Grants to provide medical, travel, and housing assistance to the ill or homeless.
Financial data: Year ended 12/31/2004. Assets, $3,005,930 (M); Expenditures, $176,514; Total giving, $174,170; Grants to individuals, 4 grants totaling $51,040 (high: $20,040, low: $5,000).
Type of support: Grants for special needs.
Application information:
Initial approach: Letter.
Additional information: Contact foundation for guidelines.
EIN: 376393903

5055
Senior Services of Stamford, Inc.
945 Summer St.
Stamford, CT 06905-5519
Contact: John Atkinson, Treas.

Foundation type: Independent foundation
Limitations: General welfare assistance and financial aid for medical, dental, and housing expenses to elderly individuals in Stamford, CT.
Publications: Annual report; Informational brochure.
Financial data: Year ended 02/29/2004. Assets, $12,941,281 (M); Expenditures, $814,389; Total giving, $414,564; Grants to individuals, totaling $406,064.
Fields of interest: Dental care; Health care; Housing/shelter, expense aid; Aging.
Type of support: Grants for special needs.
Application information: Applications accepted throughout the year; Initial approach by letter or

telephone; Completion of formal application required.
EIN: 060646916

5056
Serbian Brothers Help, Inc.
19697 W. Grand Ave.
P.O. Box 6008
Lindenhurst, IL 60046-6008 (847) 356-1809
FAX: (847) 265-7079; URL: http://www.sbhusa.org

Foundation type: Public charity
Limitations: Grants to individuals of Serbian origin residing in the U.S. or Canada who are disabled, elderly, or ill.
Financial data: Year ended 03/31/2004. Assets, $813,449 (M); Expenditures, $52,253; Total giving, $7,050; Grants to individuals, totaling $7,050.
Fields of interest: Aging; Disabilities, people with; Economically disadvantaged; Serbia.
Type of support: Grants for special needs.
Application information: Contact foundation for current application deadline/guidelines.
EIN: 366094578

5057
Sexton Can Company Employees Aid Fund
23 East St., Ste. 301
Cambridge, MA 02141

Foundation type: Company-sponsored foundation
Limitations: Emergency aid to present or former employees of Sexton Can Company or their dependents who reside in MA.
Financial data: Year ended 12/31/2003. Assets, $60,670 (M); Expenditures, $15,750; Total giving, $15,750; Grants to individuals, 10 grants totaling $15,750 (high: $3,550, low: $700).
Type of support: Employee-related welfare.
Application information:
Deadline(s): None
Additional information: Application by letter outlining financial need.
EIN: 046087676

5058
Shaklee Cares
4747 Willow Rd.
Pleasanton, CA 94588 (925) 924-2003
Contact: Sibylle Whittam, Pres.
FAX: (925) 925-2303;
E-mail: shakleecares@shaklee.com; URL: http://www.shakleecares.org/index.html

Foundation type: Public charity
Limitations: Grants to families for natural disasters relief.
Financial data: Year ended 03/31/2005. Assets, $174,961 (M); Expenditures, $516,106; Total giving, $516,036.
Fields of interest: Disasters, floods.
Type of support: Emergency funds.
Application information: Contact foundation for current application deadline/guidelines.
EIN: 943169989

5059
Jasper H. Sheadle Trust
c/o KeyBank N.A.
800 Superior Ave., 4th Fl.
Cleveland, OH 44114

Foundation type: Independent foundation
Limitations: Annuities to American-born aged couples or aged women (60 and over) of good character residing in Cuyahoga or Mahoning counties, OH.
Financial data: Year ended 12/31/2004. Assets, $2,519,789 (M); Expenditures, $128,947; Total giving, $110,900; Grants to individuals, 21 grants totaling $110,900 (high: $7,500, low: $1,500).
Fields of interest: Aging; Women.
Type of support: Grants for special needs.
Application information: Applications not accepted.
Program description:
   Assistance Program: Applicants for pension assistance are usually nominated by institutions through letters to the trust managers. Information required includes current income, expenses, and assets. Grants are given in monthly installments.
EIN: 346506457

5060
Nellie R. Sherwood Trust
1026 A Ave. N.E.
Cedar Rapids, IA   52402

Foundation type: Public charity
Limitations: Grants to retired teachers of the Cedar Rapids Community School District, IA, to pay medical, dental and hospital bills.
Financial data: Year ended 12/31/2003. Assets, $503,408; Expenditures, $87,485; Total giving, $85,741; Grants to individuals, totaling $45,222.
Type of support: Grants for special needs.
Application information: Unsolicited requests for funds not considered or acknowledged.
EIN: 426061621

5061
Shiloh Ministries International, Inc.
5991 Edmondson Pike
Nashville, TN   37211

Foundation type: Operating foundation
Limitations: Grants to ministers of the Gospel of Jesus Christ to support widows, orphans, or single parents.
Financial data: Year ended 12/31/2003. Assets, $7,240 (M); Expenditures, $92,533; Total giving, $89,086.
Fields of interest: Religion; Economically disadvantaged.
Type of support: Grants for special needs.
Application information: Applications not accepted.
EIN: 621768267

5062
The Ronald Shingu Foundation
8920 Wilshire Blvd., Ste. 310
Beverly Hills, CA   90211

Foundation type: Independent foundation
Limitations: Assistance to individuals living with AIDS.
Financial data: Year ended 12/31/2004. Assets, $1,344 (M); Expenditures, $97,334; Total giving, $95,904; Grants to individuals, totaling $95,904.
Fields of interest: AIDS, people with.
Type of support: Grants for special needs.

Application information: Applications not accepted.
   Additional information: Unsolicited requests for funds not considered or acknowledged.
EIN: 954617743

5063
Shriners of Rhode Island Charities Trust
(formerly Palestine Temple Charities Trust)
1 Rhodes Pl.
Cranston, RI   02905   (401) 737-7100
Contact: A. Sheffield Reynolds, Treas.

Foundation type: Independent foundation
Limitations: Medical expense assistance primarily to financially needy individuals living in RI.
Financial data: Year ended 12/31/2004. Assets, $23,507,086 (M); Expenditures, $1,296,692; Total giving, $1,137,542.
Fields of interest: Health care; Economically disadvantaged.
Type of support: Grants for special needs.
Application information: Applications by letter, including medical information, accepted throughout the year.
Program description:
   Health Care Assistance Program: Grants help cover the costs of health care providers, doctors' bills, hospital stays, drugs, and medical supplies.
EIN: 223191072

5064
Sidwell Charitable Trust
P.O. Box 754
Winfield, KS   67156-0754
Contact: Kay Roberts Light, Dir.

Foundation type: Operating foundation
Limitations: Grants to financially needy individuals over the age of 60 who reside in Winfield, KS.
Financial data: Year ended 12/31/2003. Assets, $353,283 (M); Expenditures, $22,586; Total giving, $18,651; Grants to individuals, 35 grants totaling $18,651 (high: $2,100, low: $15).
Fields of interest: Aging; Economically disadvantaged.
Type of support: Grants for special needs.
Application information: Applications accepted throughout the year; Completion of formal application required, including personal statement.
EIN: 486290978

5065
The Fred B. Sieber Foundation
119 N. 11th St.
Tampa, FL   33602-4201

Foundation type: Independent foundation
Limitations: Grants to provide temporary financial assistance to HIV positive individuals residing in FL who do not qualify for federal or state assistance because they continue to work, and those who cannot work and have applied for assistance but have not yet been approved.
Financial data: Year ended 03/31/2005. Assets, $2,629,010 (M); Expenditures, $103,349; Total giving, $66,500; Grants to individuals, totaling $66,500.
Fields of interest: AIDS.
Type of support: Grants for special needs.
Application information: Contact your local HIV case manager, Pinellas County, FL for application deadline/guidelines.
EIN: 593281642

5066
Sightless Children Club, Inc.
3700 Braddock St.
Dayton, OH   45420   (937) 671-9171
Contact: Randy Phipps, Treas.
E-mail: lisab@sightlesschildren.org; URL: http://www.sightlesschildren.org

Foundation type: Independent foundation
Limitations: Educational equipment, equipment repairs, and seminars for the educational and social development of sightless individuals residing in the Dayton metropolitan, OH, area.
Publications: Informational brochure (including application guidelines); Newsletter.
Financial data: Year ended 10/31/2004. Assets, $2,250,749 (M); Expenditures, $2,944,451; Total giving, $261,539; Grants to individuals, 23 grants totaling $121,215 (high: $18,932, low: $79).
Fields of interest: Disabilities, people with.
Type of support: Grants for special needs.
Application information: Applications accepted. Application form required.
   Copies of proposal: 3
   Deadline(s): May
   Applicants should submit the following:
      1) Proposal
      2) Letter(s) of recommendation
   Additional information: Applications by letter, including a description of equipment required, estimated cost, and how the equipment will be used.
EIN: 316006092

5067
Sioux Falls Area Community Foundation
300 N. Phillips Ave., Ste. 102
Sioux Falls, SD   57104-6035   (605) 336-7055
Contact: Candy Hanson, C.E.O. and Pres.; For grants: Patrick Gale
FAX: (605) 336-0038; E-mail: chanson@sfacf.org; URL: http://www.sfacf.org

Foundation type: Community foundation
Limitations: Grants to economically disadvantaged residents of Sioux Falls, SD, and to employees of Citibank (SD) NA/Dakota King for emergency assistance such as medical bills.
Publications: Application guidelines; Annual report (including application guidelines); Financial statement; Grants list; Informational brochure; Informational brochure (including application guidelines); Newsletter.
Financial data: Year ended 06/30/2005. Assets, $48,728,191 (M); Expenditures, $6,529,700; Total giving, $5,803,788; Grants to individuals, 20 grants totaling $19,000 (high: $3,000, low: $200).
Type of support: Grants for special needs.
Application information: Applications not accepted.
   Additional information: Unsolicited requests for funds not considered or acknowledged.
EIN: 311748533

5068
Homer Skelton Charitable Foundation
4225 State Line Rd.
Olive Branch, MS   38654-7087
Contact: Homer D. Skelton, Tr.

Foundation type: Independent foundation
Limitations: Financial assistance to individuals for child care, primarily in TN.

Financial data: Year ended 12/31/2004. Assets, $2,210,856 (M); Expenditures, $1,059,423; Total giving, $1,058,223; Grants to individuals, 16 grants totaling $62,140 (high: $13,528, low: $35).
Fields of interest: Day care.
Type of support: Grants to individuals.
Application information: Applications accepted.
Initial approach: Letter.
EIN: 621578268

5069
Josiah Sleeper & Lottie S. Hill Fund
c/o PNC Advisors
620 Liberty Ave., P2-PTPP-10-2
Pittsburgh, PA 15222-2705

Foundation type: Independent foundation
Limitations: Grants to women and children, primarily in PA, to cover rehabilitative and convalescent expenses.
Financial data: Year ended 03/31/2005. Assets, $818,261 (M); Expenditures, $46,348; Total giving, $40,000; Grants to individuals, totaling $40,000.
Fields of interest: Medical care, rehabilitation; Nursing home/convalescent facility; Children/youth, services; Women.
Type of support: Grants for special needs.
Application information: Applications accepted throughout the year; Completion of formal application required.
EIN: 232120878

5070
Slovak Catholic Charitable Organization
2900 Williams Dr.
Woodridge, IL 60517 (630) 963-4483
Contact: John Koys, Treas.

Foundation type: Independent foundation
Limitations: Support to parishioners in need residing in IL.
Financial data: Year ended 12/31/2004. Assets, $0 (M); Expenditures, $7,749; Total giving, $6,300; Grants to individuals, totaling $2,300.
Fields of interest: Roman Catholic agencies & churches.
Type of support: Grants for special needs.
Application information:
Initial approach: Letter or telephone.
Additional information: Contact foundation for current application deadline/guidelines.
EIN: 362523541

5071
SMF Foundation, Inc.
1185 Ave. of the Americas, 5th Fl.
New York, NY 10036

Foundation type: Independent foundation
Limitations: Grants to economically disadvantaged individuals in Brooklyn, NY.
Financial data: Year ended 12/31/2002. Assets, $114,329 (M); Expenditures, $194,030; Total giving, $188,717; Grants to individuals, totaling $45,192 (high: $3,400).
Fields of interest: Economically disadvantaged.
Application information:
Initial approach: Letter or telephone.
Additional information: Contact foundation for current application deadline/guidelines.
EIN: 136113805

5072
Tom C. Smith Charitable Trust
P.O. Box 1216
Huntington, WV 25714-1216 (304) 523-3424
Contact: George Sinkewitz, Tr.

Foundation type: Independent foundation
Limitations: Emergency aid and assistance to financially needy residents of Chesapeake, OH, and Huntington, WV.
Financial data: Year ended 03/31/2005. Assets, $188,604 (M); Expenditures, $60,490; Total giving, $24,239; Grants to individuals, totaling $24,239.
Fields of interest: Economically disadvantaged.
Type of support: Grants for special needs.
Application information:
Initial approach: Letter or telephone.
Additional information: Applications accepted throughout the year.
EIN: 550570334

5073
Winthrop H. Smith Memorial Foundation, Inc.
c/o Merrill Lynch & Co.
100 Union Ave.
Cresskill, NJ 07626 (201) 871-0350
Contact: Westina M. Shatteen, Pres.
FAX: (201) 871-7434; Application address: Lisa Applegate, 800 Scudders Hill Rd., CTC 3, Plainsboro, NJ 08536, tel.: (609) 282-3692, fax: (609) 282-3672, e-mail: lisa_applegate@ml.com; URL: http://www.ml.com/philanthropy/winsmith/

Foundation type: Public charity
Limitations: Grants in aid and loans to needy individuals for emergency relief of personal or family misfortune.
Financial data: Year ended 12/31/2003. Assets, $8,925,573 (M); Expenditures, $587,918; Total giving, $387,905; Grants to individuals, 78 grants totaling $387,905 (high: $21,600, low: $365).
Type of support: Grants for special needs.
Application information: Contact foundation for current application deadline/guidelines.
EIN: 136160365

5074
Frank L. and Laura L. Smock Foundation
c/o Wells Fargo Bank Indiana, N.A.
4704 S. 96th St.
Omaha, NE 68127

Foundation type: Independent foundation
Limitations: Medical and nursing care assistance to ailing, needy, crippled, blind, or elderly residents of IN who are members of Presbyterian churches and who have less than $3,000 in assets.
Financial data: Year ended 12/31/2004. Assets, $16,390,456 (M); Expenditures, $755,817; Total giving, $723,885; Grants to individuals, 19 grants totaling $410,152 (high: $57,457).
Application information: Applications not accepted.
EIN: 356011335

5075
Nancy and John Snyder Foundation
(formerly Nancy and John Foundation)
201 Main St., Ste. 1450
Fort Worth, TX 76102-3105

Foundation type: Independent foundation
Limitations: Grants primarily to residents of Fort Worth, TX, to alleviate personal hardship.
Financial data: Year ended 12/31/2003. Assets, $9,408,405 (M); Expenditures, $353,879; Total giving, $250,426; Grants to individuals, 16 grants totaling $7,171 (high: $2,000).
Fields of interest: Christian agencies & churches.
Type of support: Grants for special needs.
Application information: Applications not accepted.
EIN: 751737014

5076
The Society for Organizing Charity of the City of Salem, New Jersey, Inc.
c/o Annabelle D. Williams
118 Washington St.
Woodstown, NJ 08098

Foundation type: Operating foundation
Limitations: Emergency aid and assistance, including medical expenses, to economically disadvantaged individuals residing in Salem, NJ.
Financial data: Year ended 09/30/2003. Assets, $720,441 (M); Expenditures, $30,940; Total giving, $28,772.
Fields of interest: Optometry/vision screening; Pharmacy/prescriptions; Economically disadvantaged.
Type of support: Grants for special needs.
Application information: Applications by letter accepted throughout the year.
Program description:
Society for Organizing Charity: Assistance includes food bills, clothing, rent, utilities, eye exams and glasses, and prescription medication.
EIN: 216015103

5077
Society for the Relief of Families of Deceased & Disabled Indigent Members of the Medical Profession of the State of South Carolina
c/o J. Ray Ivester, M.D.
19 Guerard Road
Charleston, SC 29407

Foundation type: Operating foundation
Limitations: Grants to families of deceased and disabled SC physicians.
Financial data: Year ended 11/30/2004. Assets, $694,057 (M); Expenditures, $45,251; Total giving, $22,000; Grants to individuals, 4 grants totaling $21,000.
Fields of interest: Health care, association; Disabilities, people with; Economically disadvantaged.
Type of support: Grants for special needs.
Application information: Applications not accepted.
Additional information: The Benevolent Committee evaluates potential recipients throughout the year.
EIN: 576021204

5078
Society for the Relief of Women & Children
c/o McLaughlin & Stern
260 Madison Ave., 18th Fl.
New York, NY 10116-2404   (212) 448-1100
Contact: Elizabeth J. Scott
E-mail: hheld@mclaughlinstern.com

Foundation type: Independent foundation
Limitations: Grants to women in New York, NY, who after leading productive lives, are unable, because of circumstances beyond their control, to adequately support themselves.
Financial data: Year ended 10/31/2004. Assets, $2,746,348 (M); Expenditures, $137,877; Total giving, $98,744; Grants to individuals, 64 grants totaling $98,744 (high: $4,200, low: $186).
Fields of interest: Women.
Type of support: Awards/grants by nomination only; Grants for special needs.
Application information: Individual applications not accepted; Grants made only on recommendation of church or a social service agency.
EIN: 136161272

5079
Society of St. Vincent de Paul Manitowoc, Inc.
P.O. Box 692
Manitowoc, WI 54221-0692   (920) 683-3487
Contact: William V. Geigel, Treas.

Foundation type: Public charity
Limitations: Grants to economically disadvantaged individuals in WI for medical care, rent, food, lodging and other expenses.
Financial data: Year ended 09/30/2004. Assets, $998,073; Expenditures, $284,840; Total giving, $119,839; Grants to individuals, totaling $192.
Fields of interest: Health care; Food services; Housing/shelter; Economically disadvantaged.
Type of support: Grants for special needs.
Application information: Contact foundation for current application deadline/guidelines.
EIN: 391096113

5080
Someone Cares Charitable Trust
P.O. Box 2062
Wheat Ridge, CO 80034
Contact: Philip Yancey, Pres.
FAX: (303) 670-6803

Foundation type: Independent foundation
Limitations: Grants to economically disadvantaged individuals for education, medical and other support.
Financial data: Year ended 05/31/2004. Assets, $483,738 (M); Expenditures, $497,319; Total giving, $486,704; Grants to individuals, 6 grants totaling $19,000 (high: $5,000, low: $3,000).
Fields of interest: Education; Health care; Economically disadvantaged.
Type of support: Grants for special needs.
Application information: Applications not accepted.
  Additional information: Unsolicited requests for funds not considered or acknowledged.
EIN: 363415880

5081
South Shore Community Action Council, Inc.
265 S. Meadow Rd.
Plymouth, MA 02360-4782   (508) 747-7575
Contact: Patricia Daly, Exec. Dir.
FAX: (508) 747-1250

Foundation type: Public charity
Limitations: Grants to economically disadvantaged residents of the South Shore, MA, area, for fuel and weatherization assistance as well as food, shelter and clothing.
Financial data: Year ended 09/30/2003. Assets, $4,133,920; Expenditures, $10,604,010; Total giving, $5,024,641; Grants to individuals, totaling $5,024,641.
Fields of interest: Food services; Housing/shelter; Human services; Economically disadvantaged.
Type of support: Grants for special needs.
Application information: Contact foundation for current application deadline/guidelines.
EIN: 046125732

5082
Southern Oregon Lions Sight & Hearing Center, Inc.
228 N. Holly St.
Medford, OR 97501   (541) 779-3653
Contact: Sherrie Messer, Exec. Dir.
FAX: (541) 857-0747

Foundation type: Operating foundation
Limitations: Grants to residents of southern OR, particularly Jackson County, for vision and hearing medical care, including exams, surgery, eyeglasses, hearing aids, and travel expenses.
Publications: Application guidelines; Informational brochure.
Financial data: Year ended 06/30/2003. Assets, $1,217,446 (M); Expenditures, $284,111; Total giving, $57,633; Grants to individuals, 23 grants totaling $14,427 (high: $2,790, low: $35).
Fields of interest: Optometry/vision screening; Health care; Disabilities, people with.
Type of support: Grants for special needs.
Application information: Applications by letter outlining sight and hearing impairments accepted throughout the year.
EIN: 936042046

5083
Southwest Michigan Rehab Foundation
100 Peet's Cove
Battle Creek, MI 49015
Contact: Cheryl Humbarger, Grant Coord.

Foundation type: Independent foundation
Limitations: Payment of medical equipment expenses for patient rehabilitation to financially needy residents of the Battle Creek, MI, area only. Recipient's income must not exceed two and one-half times the poverty rate.
Publications: Informational brochure.
Financial data: Year ended 12/31/2005. Assets, $2,064,978 (M); Expenditures, $435,699; Total giving, $427,570; Grants to individuals, 45 grants totaling $22,699 (high: $2,000, low: $30). Subtotal for grants for special needs: 45 grants totaling $22,699 (high: $2,000, low: $30).
Fields of interest: Physical therapy; Health care; Economically disadvantaged.
Type of support: Grants for special needs.

Application information: Application form required.
  Initial approach: Letter or telephone.
  Copies of proposal: 1
  Deadline(s): Fri. before 3rd Thurs. of month, throughout the year
  Applicants should submit the following:
    1) Financial information
  Additional information: Application should include doctor's prescription; Interviews required.
EIN: 382939930

5084
Isabel M. Spackman Foundation
c/o PNC Advisors
620 Liberty Ave., 10th Fl
Pittsburgh, PA 15222-2705

Foundation type: Independent foundation
Limitations: General welfare support primarily to financially needy Episcopalians, primarily in PA.
Financial data: Year ended 12/31/2004. Assets, $1,058,568 (M); Expenditures, $81,429; Total giving, $71,565.
Fields of interest: Protestant agencies & churches; Economically disadvantaged.
Type of support: Grants for special needs.
Application information:
  Deadline(s): None
  Additional information: Applications by letter.
EIN: 237226511

5085
The Sparrow Foundation
101 Winners Cir.
P.O. Box 5085
Brentwood, TN 37024-5085
Contact: Holly Hearn-Whaley, Exec. Dir.

Foundation type: Company-sponsored foundation
Limitations: Grants to children for medical needs.
Publications: Informational brochure.
Financial data: Year ended 06/30/2005. Assets, $940,041 (M); Expenditures, $106,312; Total giving, $58,700; Grants to individuals, 3 grants totaling $6,000 (high: $3,000, low: $1,000).
Fields of interest: Health care.
Type of support: Grants for special needs.
Application information: Applications accepted throughout the year; Application by letter outlining financial need.
EIN: 621516024

5086
Hans & Anna Spartvedt Testamentary Trust
c/o Marshall & Ilsley Bank
P.O. Box 2980
Milwaukee, WI 53201
Application address: c/o Marshall & Ilsley Trust Co., 401 N. Segoe Rd., Ste. 2N, Madison, WI 53705

Foundation type: Independent foundation
Limitations: Grants to economically disadvantaged individuals, who are residents of WI and under the age of 21, for medical expenses.
Financial data: Year ended 12/31/2004. Assets, $133,377 (M); Expenditures, $17,572; Total giving, $14,700; Grants to individuals, totaling $14,700.
Fields of interest: Health care; Children/youth, services; Disabilities, people with; Economically disadvantaged.

Type of support: Grants for special needs.
Application information: Applications by letter, including medical information and family data, accepted throughout the year.
EIN: 396266732

5087
Inez Sprague Trust
c/o Bank of America, N.A.
P.O. Box 1802
Providence, RI 02901-1802
Application address: c/o Bank of America, N.A., Attn: Charitable Trust, 100 Federal St., Boston, MA 02110

Foundation type: Independent foundation
Limitations: Welfare assistance and medical expenses to needy residents of Narragansett, RI.
Financial data: Year ended 06/30/2005. Assets, $810,485 (M); Expenditures, $35,157; Total giving, $23,799; Grants to individuals, totaling $23,799.
Fields of interest: Health care; Economically disadvantaged.
Type of support: Grants for special needs.
Application information: Applications accepted throughout the year; Contact trust for current application guidelines.
EIN: 056067971

5088
The Springfield Teachers' Club, Inc.
195 State St.
Springfield, MA 01103
Application address: c/o Margaret Scanlon, 75 Terrace Ln., Springfield, MA 01118

Foundation type: Independent foundation
Limitations: Eye exams and eyeglasses to needy students of the Springfield, MA, public school system, and small gifts to retired teachers.
Financial data: Year ended 05/31/2005. Assets, $136,009 (M); Expenditures, $12,407; Total giving, $11,014; Grants to individuals, 9 grants totaling $4,500.
Fields of interest: Education; Optometry/vision screening.
Type of support: Grants for special needs.
Application information:
  Deadline(s): Apr. 13
  Additional information: Contact club for current application guidelines.
EIN: 046065091

5089
St. George's Society of New York
216 E. 45th St., Ste. 901
New York, NY 10017-3304 (212) 682-6110
Contact: John Shannon, Exec. Dir.
FAX: (212) 682-3465;
E-mail: info@stgeorgessociety.org; URL: http://www.stgeorgessociety.org

Foundation type: Operating foundation
Limitations: Financial assistance to elderly or infirm natives of the United Kingdom or the British Commonwealth and their children, who find themselves in need, trouble, sickness, or other adversity in the CT, NJ and NY area.
Publications: Application guidelines; Annual report; Informational brochure; Newsletter.
Financial data: Year ended 12/31/2004. Assets, $9,195,881 (M); Expenditures,

$913,762; Total giving, $365,840; Grants to individuals, 61 grants totaling $365,840.
Fields of interest: Aging.
Type of support: Grants to individuals; Foreign applicants; Grants for special needs.
Application information: Applications accepted. Application form required.
  Copies of proposal: 1
  Applicants should submit the following:
    1) Financial information
  Additional information: Applications by letter, including proof of need and British background, accepted throughout the year; Visits from the society's social worker and interviews required.
Program description:
  St. George Society Assistance Program: Help is given only to natives of the United Kingdom and of other countries within the Commonwealth, those who served in His/Her Britannic Majesty's Armed Forces, and their wives and/or widows. Assistance takes the form of allowances for pension supplements, funeral expenses, emergency loans, and at the recommendation of the British Consulate, visitors' aid for those in the U.S. on visitors visas who suddenly find themselves in need. Average grant is $432 per month.
EIN: 237426425

5090
St. John's Mite Association
5428 MacArthur Blvd. N.W.
Washington, DC 20016
Contact: George J. Stoklas, Pres.
Application address: 11004 Wickshire Way, North Bethesda, MD 20852

Foundation type: Independent foundation
Limitations: Grants to masons, their widows and children under the age of 18 who are residents of the Washington, DC, metropolitan area.
Financial data: Year ended 10/31/2004. Assets, $172,329 (M); Expenditures, $14,853; Total giving, $12,680; Grants to individuals, 4 grants totaling $12,680 (high: $4,500, low: $1,200).
Type of support: Grants for special needs.
Application information: Applications by letter accepted throughout the year.
EIN: 526051971

5091
St. Paul's Church Home
c/o St. Paul's Episcopal Church
815 E. Grace St.
Richmond, VA 23218-1535

Foundation type: Independent foundation
Limitations: Grants to students from the Richmond, VA, metropolitan area for care, maintenance, and education, and to destitute, sick individuals of any age in the Richmond, VA, area for care, maintenance, and medical and hospital expenses.
Publications: Application guidelines.
Financial data: Year ended 12/31/2004. Assets, $1,065,682 (M); Expenditures, $58,994; Total giving, $56,097; Grants to individuals, totaling $17,580.
Fields of interest: Health care; Children/youth, services; Economically disadvantaged.
Type of support: Undergraduate support; Grants for special needs.
Application information: Applications accepted. Application form required.
  Initial approach: Letter outlining financial need.
  Deadline(s): None

  Applicants should submit the following:
    1) Financial information
EIN: 546048630

5092
The Steeplechase Fund
c/o Peter McGivney
400 Fair Hill Dr.
Elkton, MD 21921

Foundation type: Independent foundation
Limitations: Financial assistance and medical expenses only to former steeplechase jockeys and their widows and families.
Financial data: Year ended 12/31/2004. Assets, $711,077 (M); Expenditures, $40,971; Total giving, $16,796; Grants to individuals, totaling $16,796.
Fields of interest: Athletics/sports, equestrianism; Women.
Type of support: Grants for special needs.
Application information:
  Initial approach: Letter.
  Additional information: Application must include information about when applicant was disabled and medical bills accepted throughout the year; Inappropriate applications will not be considered or acknowledged.
EIN: 136067724

5093
Helen Wolcott Stockwell Trust
c/o Mellon Financial Corp.
P.O. Box 185
Pittsburgh, PA 15230-0185

Foundation type: Independent foundation
Limitations: Grants to economically disadvantaged individuals of Stoneham, MA for medical aid.
Financial data: Year ended 08/31/2002. Assets, $973,715 (M); Expenditures, $64,402; Total giving, $51,620; Grants to individuals, totaling $49,296.
Fields of interest: Health care.
Type of support: Grants for special needs.
Application information: Contact trust for current application deadline/guidelines.
EIN: 046092050

5094
Stolberg Foundation for Preschool Childcare
(also known as The Children's Seedling Fund)
370 17th St., Ste. 3650
Denver, CO 80202
Contact: Ted Stolberg, Tr.

Foundation type: Operating foundation
Limitations: Grants to individuals for adoption services, tuition and other expenses, primarily in NY and OH.
Financial data: Year ended 12/31/2003. Assets, $980,736 (M); Expenditures, $67,381; Total giving, $52,030.
Fields of interest: Education; Adoption.
Type of support: Grants for special needs.
Application information: Applications accepted throughout the year; Completion of formal application required.
EIN: 341780793

5095
Hill Stump Disaster Charitable Trust
c/o First Community Bank, Inc.
P.O. Box 5939
1001 Mercer St.
Princeton, WV 24740
Application address: c/o Trust Dept., First
Community Bank, Inc., P.O. Box 280, Buckhannon,
WV 26201

Foundation type: Independent foundation
Limitations: Emergency aid to residents of Upshur
County, WV, who have suffered loss due to a natural
disaster such as fire, flood, or storm.
Financial data: Year ended 12/31/2004.
Assets, $727,670 (M); Expenditures, $39,837;
Total giving, $37,000; Grants to individuals,
totaling $17,940.
Fields of interest: Disasters, floods; Disasters, fire
prevention/control; Safety/disasters.
Type of support: Emergency funds.
Application information: Application form required.
Applicants should submit the following:
   1) Financial information
Additional information: Applications accepted
      throughout the year.
EIN: 556104851

5096
Sunnyside Foundation, Inc.
(formerly Sunnyside, Inc.)
8222 Douglas Ave., Ste. 501
Dallas, TX 75225 (214) 692-5686
Contact: Peggy Hueffner, Exec. Dir.
FAX: (214) 692-1968;
E-mail: sunnysidetexas@sbcglobal.net

Foundation type: Independent foundation
Limitations: Grants and camperships to
underprivileged Christian Science children under
the age of 20, who regularly attend Christian
Science Sunday schools and reside in TX, to provide
for their physical, moral, and spiritual needs.
Publications: Application guidelines; Informational
brochure (including application guidelines);
Program policy statement (including application
guidelines).
Financial data: Year ended 12/31/2004.
Assets, $27,223,095 (M); Expenditures,
$1,174,691; Total giving, $832,878; Grants to
individuals, totaling $832,878.
Fields of interest: Camps; Children/youth,
services; Christian agencies & churches.
Type of support: Grants for special needs.
Application information: Applications accepted.
Application form required.
Deadline(s): Applications accepted throughout
   the year
Additional information: Application must include
   Sunday school information and parents'
   financial information.
EIN: 756037004

5097
Otto Sussman Trust
1025 Northern Blvd., Ste. 300
Roslyn, NY 11576-1506
Contact: Edward S. Miller, Tr.
Application address: P.O. Box 1374, Trainsmeadow
Sta., Flushing, NY 11370-0998

Foundation type: Independent foundation
Limitations: Assistance to residents of NJ, NY, OK,
and PA in need due to death or illness in their
immediate families or some other unusual or
unfortunate circumstance.

Financial data: Year ended 12/31/2004.
Assets, $5,320,457 (M); Expenditures,
$248,497; Total giving, $183,421; Grants to
individuals, 105 grants totaling $183,421 (high:
$4,970, low: $300).
Application information: Applications accepted.
Application form required.
Initial approach: Letter requesting application
   and stating circumstances of need.
Deadline(s): Applications accepted throughout
   the year
Additional information: Applications must come
   from individuals who are recommended by
   selected educational, medical, social service,
   and similar entities with whom the trust has a
   working relationship; Applications must be
   submitted through those organizations.
EIN: 136075849

5098
Swan Society in Boston
(formerly Widows Society in Boston)
581 Boylston St., Ste. 705
Boston, MA 02116 (617) 536-7951
Contact: Jackie Husid, Exec. Dir.
FAX: (617) 536-0725

Foundation type: Operating foundation
Limitations: Financial assistance to widowed,
divorced, and single women who are over 65 years
old and who live within 25 miles of the
Massachusetts State House in Boston, MA, so that
they may continue to live independently.
Publications: Application guidelines; Annual report;
Informational brochure.
Financial data: Year ended 10/31/2004.
Assets, $4,525,969 (M); Expenditures,
$178,604; Total giving, $122,620; Grants to
individuals, totaling $122,620.
Fields of interest: Aging; Women; Economically
disadvantaged.
Type of support: Emergency funds; Grants for
special needs.
Application information: Application form required.
Initial approach: Letter or telephone.
Copies of proposal: 1
Applicants should submit the following:
   1) Budget Information
Additional information: Applications accepted
   throughout the year; Initial approach by letter
   or telephone; Completion of formal
   application required; The society's licensed
   social worker screens recommended
   applicants.
EIN: 042306840

5099
Swift Charity, Inc.
c/o Russell, Brier & Co.
10 Post Office Sq., 6th Fl.
Boston, MA 02109

Foundation type: Independent foundation
Limitations: Grants to financially needy, elderly
citizens of the town of Milton, MA.
Financial data: Year ended 12/31/2004.
Assets, $917,399 (M); Expenditures, $73,549;
Total giving, $41,500; Grants to individuals,
totaling $41,500.
Fields of interest: Aging; Economically
disadvantaged.
Type of support: Grants for special needs.
Application information: Contact charity for current
application deadline/guidelines.
EIN: 046052150

5100
Edward F. Swinney Foundation
c/o Bank of America, N.A.
P.O. Box 831041
Dallas, TX 75283-1041
Application address: c/o Spence Heddens, Bank of
America, N.A., P.O. Box 419119, Kansas City, MO
64141-6119, tel.: (816) 979-7304

Foundation type: Independent foundation
Limitations: Grants to financially needy employees
of Bank of America, N.A., MO.
Financial data: Year ended 12/31/2004.
Assets, $964,109 (M); Expenditures, $163,255;
Total giving, $128,479; Grants to individuals, 42
grants totaling $15,189 (high: $600, low: $300).
Type of support: Employee-related welfare.
Application information: Applications accepted
throughout the year; Completion of formal
application required; Applications are available
from the personnel department of Bank of America,
N.A., MO.
EIN: 446009677

5101
Swiss Benevolent Society of Chicago
P.O. Box 2137
Chicago, IL 60690
E-mail: president@sbschicago.org/; URL: http://
www.sbschicago.org

Foundation type: Independent foundation
Limitations: Relief assistance to financially needy
or elderly Chicago, IL, residents of Swiss descent
or nationality.
Financial data: Year ended 12/31/2004.
Assets, $1,749,565 (M); Expenditures,
$115,962; Total giving, $77,516; Grants to
individuals, 39 grants totaling $54,464. Subtotal
for grants for special needs: 2 grants totaling
$12,484 (average grant: $6,242).
Fields of interest: Aging; Switzerland.
Type of support: Grants for special needs.
Application information: Applications accepted.
Application form required.
Initial approach: Letter or e-mail.
Deadline(s): None
Additional information: Application must include
   proof of Swiss citizenship; Interviews
   required.
EIN: 366076395

5102
Tarboro Community Outreach, Inc.
701 Cedar Ln.
P.O. Box 445
Tarboro, NC 27886-0445
Contact: Sr. Mary Ann Czaja, Exec. Dir.

Foundation type: Public charity
Limitations: Grants to residents of Edgecombe
County, NC, to pay for utility bills, rent, and
prescription drugs. Support also to people in need
of food, counseling, or shelter.
Financial data: Year ended 12/31/2004.
Assets, $213,852 (M); Expenditures, $925,447;
Total giving, $815,117; Grants to individuals,
totaling $815,117.
Fields of interest: Health care; Mental health,
counseling/support groups; Housing/shelter;
Human services; Poverty studies.
Type of support: Grants for special needs.
Application information: Contact foundation for
current application deadline/guidelines.
EIN: 561557200

5103
Nathaniel Taylor Fund, Inc.
c/o Rockland Trust Co.
2036 Washington St.
Hanover, MA   02339
Contact: Sheila Atwater, Treas.
Application address: P.O. Box 693, Marshfield, MA 02050

Foundation type: Independent foundation
Limitations: Financial assistance to residents of Marshfield, MA, who are in need due to sickness or other unfortunate circumstances. A small amount for scholarships is also given to local high school graduates to study nursing or a related subject.
Financial data: Year ended 09/30/2005.
Assets, $419,692 (M); Expenditures, $34,117; Total giving, $28,700; Grants to individuals, totaling $28,700.
Fields of interest: Nursing school/education.
Type of support: Undergraduate support; Grants for special needs.
Application information: Applications accepted throughout the year; Contact fund for current application guidelines.
EIN: 046065495

5104
Thomas Taylor Poor Fund
c/o PNC Advisors
620 Liberty Ave., P2-PTPP-10-2
Pittsburgh, PA   15222

Foundation type: Independent foundation
Limitations: Assistance to the most worthy and deserving of the borough of Pottstown, PA.
Financial data: Year ended 09/30/2002.
Assets, $769,707 (M); Expenditures, $44,569; Total giving, $35,616.
Type of support: Grants for special needs.
Application information: All requests for assistance must come through a social agency or church.
Program description:
Assistance Program: Assistance is not provided on an ongoing basis. Total assistance for any one individual is generally no more than $200 per year.
EIN: 236249419

5105
Texas Star Oaks Fund, Inc.
29406 Summit Ridge Dr.
Fair Oaks, TX   78015
Application address: c/o Sally Eaves, General Welfare Div., 3304 W. 18th St., Plainview, TX 79072-3634

Foundation type: Operating foundation
Limitations: Financial assistance only to needy TX residents. Grants are given as one-time support or on a monthly basis for ongoing financial needs.
Financial data: Year ended 03/31/2004.
Assets, $1,659,367 (M); Expenditures, $58,760; Total giving, $77,025; Grants to individuals, 37 grants totaling $77,025 (high: $6,000, low: $1,000).
Type of support: Grants for special needs.
Application information: Applications accepted. Application form required.
  Initial approach: Letter or telephone.
  Deadline(s): None
  Applicants should submit the following:
    1) Letter(s) of recommendation

Additional information: Contact fund for current application guidelines; Application must also include case history.
EIN: 746047454

5106
Pauline Revere Thayer Memorial Pension Fund
c/o U.S. Trust Co., N.A.
P.O. Box 55122
Boston, MA   02205

Foundation type: Independent foundation
Limitations: Pension assistance to financially needy and deserving employees of the Chilton Club of Boston, MA.
Financial data: Year ended 12/31/2004.
Assets, $601,062 (M); Expenditures, $51,266; Total giving, $43,300; Grants to individuals, totaling $42,800.
Type of support: Employee-related welfare.
Application information: Applications not accepted.
EIN: 046096055

5107
The Thomley Foundation, Inc.
P.O. Box 1562
Brentwood, TN   37024-1562

Foundation type: Operating foundation
Limitations: Grants to economically disadvantaged individuals in the U.S. and Italy for medical and other assistance.
Financial data: Year ended 12/31/2003.
Assets, $27,891 (M); Expenditures, $106,975; Total giving, $46,725; Grants to individuals, 5 grants totaling $45,525 (high: $32,400, low: $900).
Fields of interest: Health care; Economically disadvantaged; Italy.
Type of support: Foreign applicants; Grants for special needs.
Application information: Applications not accepted.
EIN: 631207742

5108
Wm. B. Thompson Fund
c/o Cusack & Stiles, LLP
61 Broadway, Ste. 2100
New York, NY   10006

Foundation type: Independent foundation
Limitations: Grants only to individuals specified in the trust instrument.
Financial data: Year ended 11/30/2004.
Assets, $442,287 (M); Expenditures, $13,398; Total giving, $9,350; Grants to individuals, totaling $9,350.
Type of support: Grants for special needs.
Application information: Applications not accepted.
EIN: 136089682

5109
Ella B. Thompson Trust
c/o Bank of America, N.A.
P.O. Box 831041
Dallas, TX   75283-1041

Foundation type: Independent foundation

Limitations: Financial assistance to retired school teachers of the Galveston Public School System, TX.
Financial data: Year ended 12/31/2004.
Assets, $640,684 (M); Expenditures, $38,857; Total giving, $31,400; Grants to individuals, totaling $31,400.
Fields of interest: Pensions, teacher funds.
Type of support: Employee-related welfare.
Application information: Applications not accepted.
EIN: 746082981

5110
The Annie Tinker Association for Women, Inc.
(formerly Annie Rensselaer Tinker Memorial Fund)
12 W. 11 St.
New York, NY   10011
Contact: Isabel B. Spencer, Mgr.

Foundation type: Operating foundation
Limitations: Monthly assistance to financially needy retired women who are living independently and have worked in the arts or within the arts professions, primarily in NY.
Publications: Newsletter.
Financial data: Year ended 06/30/2004.
Assets, $2,427,874 (M); Expenditures, $307,764; Total giving, $174,897; Grants to individuals, 151 grants totaling $174,897 (high: $26,210, low: $120).
Fields of interest: Arts; Aging; Women; Economically disadvantaged.
Type of support: Grants for special needs.
Application information: Applications accepted. Application form required.
  Initial approach: Letter.
  Deadline(s): None
Program description:
  Assistance Program: The main focus of the fund is to encourage the emotional, social, and financial well-being of its beneficiaries. Beneficiaries are women over 65 years of age who are able to live independently and are able to benefit from the interaction with others in the Tinker Fund and their community.
EIN: 136405671

5111
TLB Foundation, Inc.
(formerly Great Commission Foundation, Inc.)
P.O. Box 991
Findlay, OH   45839-0991   (419) 420-0419
Contact: Jack W. Ridge, Pres.

Foundation type: Independent foundation
Limitations: Financial assistance to individuals in severe need, primarily those in northwestern OH.
Financial data: Year ended 11/30/2004.
Assets, $24,148 (M); Expenditures, $223,981; Total giving, $220,571; Grants to individuals, 2 grants totaling $57,000 (high: $43,000, low: $14,000).
Fields of interest: Christian agencies & churches; Economically disadvantaged.
Type of support: Grants for special needs.
Application information: Applications accepted only through local contacts.
Program description:
  TLB Foundation Program: The foundation is a Christian organization. While it seeks to serve those who are in agreement with the foundation's specific beliefs, it does not restrict its giving to those in

severe need to Christians only. The foundation's beliefs are centered on:
- The Holy Trinity
- The birth, life, and death of Jesus Christ
- The power and divinity of the Holy Spirit
- The creation of man and his salvation
- The Church
- The proclamation of the Gospel and a complete commitment to Christ.

EIN: 341648111

5112
Randall L. Tobias Foundation, Inc.
500 E. 96th St., Ste. 110
Indianapolis, IN 46240
E-mail: snh@rltfound.org

Foundation type: Independent foundation
Limitations: Grants to enrich learning for children of all ages from infancy through twelfth grade, IN.
Financial data: Year ended 12/31/2004.
Assets, $1,943,504 (M); Expenditures, $5,494,397; Total giving, $5,270,000.
Fields of interest: Children/youth, services.
Type of support: Grants for special needs.
Application information: Application form required.
Initial approach: Telephone or e-mail.
Deadline(s): Mar. 1 and Sept. 1
Program description:
Assistance Program: Grants generally range between $5,000 and $50,000 although requests for lesser or greater amounts may be considered. Some grants may be paid over a multi-year period.
EIN: 351938355

5113
Townsend Aid for the Aged
43 Benedict Ave.
Portsmouth, RI 02871
Contact: Caroline Kaull, Pres.
Application address: c/o Janice Barrows, 12 Madeline Dr., Newport, RI 02840

Foundation type: Independent foundation
Limitations: Grants to financially needy, elderly residents of Newport, RI, to provide the necessities of life.
Financial data: Year ended 04/30/2005.
Assets, $2,640,937 (M); Expenditures, $151,161; Total giving, $127,000; Grants to individuals, totaling $127,000.
Fields of interest: Aging; Economically disadvantaged.
Type of support: Grants for special needs.
Application information: Applications not accepted.
Additional information: Grants are awarded to worthy individuals as directed by an advisory committee, which initiates the application process.
EIN: 056009549

5114
Treehouse
2100 24th Ave. S., Rm 220
Seattle, WA 98144 (206) 767-7000
Contact: Kim Eiring, Pres.
URL: http://www.treehouse4kids.org

Foundation type: Public charity
Limitations: Grants to foster children for developmental opportunities and educational support.

Financial data: Year ended 09/30/2003.
Assets, $4,576,919; Expenditures, $2,867,658; Total giving, $1,153,077.
Fields of interest: Children/youth, services; Foster care.
Type of support: Undergraduate support; Grants for special needs.
Application information: Contact fund for current application deadline/guidelines.
EIN: 911425676

5115
Trolinger Trust
c/o SunTrust Bank
P.O. Box 1908
Orlando, FL 32802-1908
Application address: c/o John I. Barton, P.O. Box 3064, 1st St. Sta., Radford, VA 24141

Foundation type: Independent foundation
Limitations: Financial assistance to residents of Montgomery County and Radford, VA, and other southwestern VA counties and cities.
Financial data: Year ended 06/30/2005.
Assets, $1,851,640 (M); Expenditures, $113,532; Total giving, $93,000; Grants to individuals, totaling $6,850.
Type of support: Grants for special needs.
Application information: Applications by letter, including statement of financial need, accepted throughout the year.
EIN: 546110451

5116
Jeremiah Tumey Fund
(also known as Jeremiah Tumey & Grand Lodge)
c/o Comerica Bank
P.O. Box 75000, MC 3302
Detroit, MI 48275-3302

Foundation type: Independent foundation
Limitations: Grants to economically disadvantaged members of Masons or their spouses in MI.
Financial data: Year ended 12/31/2004.
Assets, $213,862 (M); Expenditures, $15,279; Total giving, $12,053; Grants to individuals, totaling $12,053.
Fields of interest: Economically disadvantaged.
Type of support: Grants for special needs.
Application information: Unsolicited requests for funds not accepted.
EIN: 386043299

5117
The Turnbow Foundation, Inc.
7619 E. Tasman Cir.
Mesa, AZ 85207

Foundation type: Operating foundation
Limitations: Grants to economically disadvantaged individuals and families.
Financial data: Year ended 12/31/2002.
Assets, $0 (M); Expenditures, $204,265; Total giving, $190,838; Grants to individuals, 3 grants totaling $8,988.
Fields of interest: Family services.
Type of support: Grants for special needs.
Application information: Applications not accepted.
EIN: 860732335

5118
Isaac H. Tuttle Fund
1155 Park Ave.
New York, NY 10128-1209 (212) 831-0429
Contact: Stephanie A. Raneri, Exec. Dir.
FAX: (212) 426-5684; *E-mail:* info@tuttlefund.org;
URL: http://www.tuttlefund.org

Foundation type: Independent foundation
Limitations: Direct financial assistance to elderly individuals, 65 years of age or older, who live in Manhattan (New York, NY), with the goal of enabling them to continue living in their own homes so long as they are physically and mentally able to do so.
Publications: Application guidelines; Financial statement.
Financial data: Year ended 12/31/2005.
Assets, $52,130,849 (M); Expenditures, $2,571,604; Total giving, $1,698,664; Grants to individuals, 129 grants totaling $563,664.
Fields of interest: Aging; Economically disadvantaged.
Type of support: Grants for special needs.
Application information: Applicants must be referred by social service agencies, hospital social work depts., private social workers, or similar organizations; No self-referrals are accepted.
EIN: 135628325

5119
The Twenty First Century Foundation
P.O. Box 543
Norwalk, OH 44857
Contact: Thomas W. McLaughlin

Foundation type: Independent foundation
Limitations: Grants by nomination only to economically disadvantaged parents of Huron, Erie or Seneca counties, OH for emergencies, disasters and medical expenses.
Financial data: Year ended 06/30/2005.
Assets, $6,567,064 (M); Expenditures, $267,619; Total giving, $233,839.
Fields of interest: Health care; Housing/shelter; Safety/disasters.
Type of support: Emergency funds; Grants to individuals; Awards/grants by nomination only; Grants for special needs; Project support.
Application information: Applications not accepted.
Additional information: Unsolicited requests for funds not considered or acknowledged.
EIN: 341852806

5120
Two Ten International Footwear Foundation, Inc.
1466 Main St.
Waltham, MA 02451 (781) 736-1522
Contact: Peggy K. Meill, Pres.
FAX: (781) 736-1555;
E-mail: scholarship@twoten.org; Additional tel.: (800) FIND-210; URL: http://www.twoten.org

Foundation type: Public charity
Limitations: Assistance and resources to needy individuals in the shoe industry, leather trade, and allied trades.
Publications: Application guidelines; Annual report; Informational brochure; Newsletter.
Financial data: Year ended 06/30/2004.
Assets, $27,417,985 (M); Expenditures, $3,379,048; Total giving, $1,128,167; Grants to individuals, 774 grants totaling $1,128,167.
Subtotal for scholarships—to individuals: 541

grants totaling . Subtotal for emergency funds: 233 grants totaling .
Fields of interest: Economically disadvantaged.
Type of support: Scholarships—to individuals; Grants for special needs.
Application information: Application form required.
Initial approach: Telephone.
Deadline(s): Contact foundation for current application deadline
Additional information: See Web site for further information.
EIN: 222579809

5121
Marion C. Tyler Foundation
c/o KeyBank N.A.
127 Public Sq., 16th Fl.
Cleveland, OH 44114-2601
Contact: Toby Blossom

Foundation type: Company-sponsored foundation
Limitations: Pension supplements to retired employees of W.S. Tyler, Inc.
Financial data: Year ended 12/31/2004.
Assets, $1,097,322 (M); Expenditures, $34,245; Total giving, $22,992; Grants to individuals, 14 grants totaling $22,992 (high: $3,600, low: $60).
Type of support: Employee-related welfare.
Application information: Application form required.
Initial approach: Letter requesting application.
Deadline(s): None
Applicants should submit the following:
1) Financial information
Additional information: Application address: c/o Don Whitehouse, 3200 Bessemer City Rd., Box 8900, Gastonia, NC 28053, tel.: (704) 629-2214.
EIN: 346525274

5122
UFA Widow's and Children's Fund
204 E. 23rd St
New York, NY 10010 (212) 683-4832
URL: http://www.ufalocal94.org

Foundation type: Public charity
Limitations: Scholarships, memorial service, and other financial assistance to the surviving dependents of UFA members who passed away in the line of duty. Giving primarily in NY.
Financial data: Year ended 07/31/2003.
Assets, $24,266,670 (M); Expenditures, $46,015,203; Total giving, $45,972,724; Grants to individuals, totaling $21,284,456.
Fields of interest: Disasters, fire prevention/control.
Type of support: Undergraduate support; Grants for special needs.
Application information: Contact fund for further application information.
EIN: 133047544

5123
The Van Dam Foundation
P.O. Box 41
Okabena, MN 56161
Contact: William Vangsness, Tr.

Foundation type: Independent foundation
Limitations: Grants to physically disabled individuals residing in Jackson, Martin, Watonwan, Cottonwood, Nobles, Murray, Rock, and Pipestone Counties, MN, for medical bills.

Financial data: Year ended 02/28/2003.
Assets, $901,382 (M); Expenditures, $24,022; Total giving, $15,522; Grants to individuals, 11 grants totaling $15,522 (high: $2,577, low: $385).
Fields of interest: Physically disabled.
Type of support: Grants for special needs.
Application information: Applications by letter accepted throughout the year.
EIN: 411350271

5124
Vang Memorial Foundation
P.O. Box 11727
Pittsburgh, PA 15228-0727 (412) 563-0261
Contact: E.J. Hosko, Treas.

Foundation type: Independent foundation
Limitations: Grants to economically disadvantaged past and present employees, and their dependents, of George Vang, Inc. and related companies.
Financial data: Year ended 12/31/2004.
Assets, $1,453,131 (M); Expenditures, $120,070; Total giving, $97,529; Grants to individuals, 18 grants totaling $67,479 (high: $14,269, low: $699).
Fields of interest: Economically disadvantaged.
Type of support: Employee-related welfare.
Application information: Applications accepted throughout the year; Application by letter, including copies of previous year's federal and state income tax returns, type of grant requested, and basis of need.
EIN: 256034491

5125
Vermont Community Foundation
3 Court St.
P.O. Box 30
Middlebury, VT 05753 (802) 388-3355
Contact: Julie Cadwallader-Staub, V.P., Community Grantmaking; For artist grants: Mary Conlon
FAX: (802) 388-3398; E-mail: info@vermontcf.org; Additional E-mails: jcstaub@vermontcf.org and mconlon@vermontcf.org; URL: http://www.vermontcf.org

Foundation type: Community foundation
Limitations: Grants to residents of VT for medical assistance.
Publications: Application guidelines; Annual report; Financial statement; Grants list; Informational brochure; Informational brochure (including application guidelines); Multi-year report; Newsletter; Occasional report; Program policy statement.
Financial data: Year ended 12/31/2004.
Assets, $110,314,471 (M); Expenditures, $10,766,535; Total giving, $8,276,588.
Type of support: Grants for special needs.
Application information: Applications not accepted.
Additional information: Application by proposal.
EIN: 222712160

5126
Vero Beach Foundation for the Elderly
c/o Wachovia Wealth Mgmt.
3601 PGA Blvd., Ste. 200
Palm Beach Gardens, FL 33410
Contact: Richard L. Mead, Chair.
Application address: 2800 Indian River Blvd., Apt. U-2, Vero Beach, FL 32960, tel.: (772) 770-0044

Foundation type: Independent foundation

Limitations: Relief assistance only to economically disadvantaged residents of Indian River County, FL, who are at least 65 years old.
Publications: Informational brochure.
Financial data: Year ended 12/31/2003.
Assets, $1,024,094 (M); Expenditures, $127,920; Total giving, $82,271; Grants to individuals, 11 grants totaling $6,681 (high: $1,500, low: $40).
Fields of interest: Aging; Economically disadvantaged.
Type of support: Grants for special needs.
Application information: Applications accepted throughout the year; All applications must come through Indian River County Council of Aging; Completion of formal application required, including financial and family information.
Program description:
Elderly Assistance Program: Grants and loans are made for medical and convalescent care of indigent individuals, as well as for food and general assistance. Direct payments are also made to physicians and medical facilities.
EIN: 596214870

5127
VFW Charitable Trust
4605 E. Roundup Rd.
Bismarck, ND 58501 (701) 258-5016
Contact: Wallace Bolte, Dir.

Foundation type: Independent foundation
Limitations: Medical assistance to veterans from ND.
Financial data: Year ended 06/30/2005.
Assets, $66,946 (M); Expenditures, $16,749; Total giving, $13,050; Grants to individuals, totaling $13,050.
Fields of interest: Health care; Military/veterans' organizations.
Type of support: Grants for special needs.
Application information: Applications by letter, outlining financial need, accepted throughout the year; Financial need must be verified by Post Commander.
EIN: 456056378

5128
Mary Beth and James C. Vogelzang Foundation
c/o Mary Beth Vogelzang
1231 State St., No. 203
Santa Barbara, CA 93101

Foundation type: Independent foundation
Limitations: Grants to the economically disadvantaged.
Financial data: Year ended 12/31/2003.
Assets, $1,638,159 (M); Expenditures, $196,973; Total giving, $173,193; Grant to an individual, 1 grant totaling $13,125.
Fields of interest: Economically disadvantaged.
Application information: Applications not accepted.
Additional information: Unsolicited requests for funds not considered or acknowledged.
EIN: 841314262

5129
Voice in the Wilderness, Inc.
204 N. Main St., Ste. 102
Duncanville, TX 75116
Contact: Rev. Ronnie Williamson, Exec. Dir.

Foundation type: Public charity
Limitations: Grants to individuals for medical, religious and educational support.
Financial data: Year ended 04/30/2005. Assets, $353,930 (M); Expenditures, $209,422; Total giving, $42,140; Grants to individuals, totaling $42,140.
Fields of interest: Education; Health care; Religion.
Type of support: Scholarships—to individuals; Grants for special needs.
Application information: Contact foundation for current application deadline/guidelines.
EIN: 736102847

5130
Roger L. VonAmelunxen Foundation, Inc.
83-21 Edgerton Blvd.
Jamaica, NY   11432   (718) 641-4800
Contact: Karen Donnelly, V.P.
FAX: (718) 641-4802;
E-mail: rogerfoundation@aol.com; *URL:* http://rogerfoundation.org

Foundation type: Independent foundation
Limitations: Assistance to financially needy and distressed families of U.S. Customs Service employees.
Financial data: Year ended 07/31/2004. Assets, $583,882 (M); Expenditures, $331,960; Total giving, $325,883; Grants to individuals, 146 grants totaling $325,883 (high: $6,000, low: $350).
Fields of interest: Economically disadvantaged.
Type of support: Employee-related welfare.
Application information:
  Deadline(s): Aug. 1
  Additional information: Application by letter, including proof of relationship to U.S. Customs employee.
EIN: 112583014

5131
Vonder Linden Charitable Trust
c/o Leonard Rachmilowitz, C.P.A.
P.O. Box 334
Rhinebeck, NY   12572-0334
Application address: c/o Fund Admin., P.O. Box 572, Rhinebeck, NY 12572

Foundation type: Independent foundation
Limitations: Assistance to financially needy residents of Ulster and Dutchess counties, NY, to cover the costs of rent, bills, and other expenses.
Financial data: Year ended 06/30/2004. Assets, $481,514 (M); Expenditures, $34,692; Total giving, $23,608; Grants to individuals, totaling $23,608.
Fields of interest: Housing/shelter, expense aid; Economically disadvantaged.
Type of support: Grants for special needs.
Application information: Applications by letter accepted throughout the year.
EIN: 146102155

5132
Herbert E. Wadsworth Fund
c/o Bank of America, N.A.
P.O. Box 1802
Providence, RI   02901

Foundation type: Independent foundation
Limitations: Assistance for citizens of Winthrop, ME, when in the ward of a well-regulated and recognized hospital outside the town of Winthrop.

Financial data: Year ended 11/30/2004. Assets, $290,424 (M); Expenditures, $10,160; Total giving, $6,090; Grants to individuals, totaling $6,090.
Fields of interest: Medical care, in-patient care.
Type of support: Grants for special needs.
Application information: Applications accepted throughout the year; Contact trust for current application guidelines.
EIN: 016017480

5133
Walgreen Benefit Fund
200 Wilmot Rd., Ste. 2270
Deerfield, IL   60015
Contact: E.H. King, V.P.
Application address: Ruth D. Crane, Corp. 104, Wilmot Rd., M.S. 1444, Deerfield, IL 60015, tel.: (847) 315-4663,
E-mail: ruth.crane@walgreen.com

Foundation type: Company-sponsored foundation
Limitations: Welfare assistance to financially needy Walgreen employees and retirees and their families.
Publications: Application guidelines; Annual report.
Financial data: Year ended 04/30/2005. Assets, $21,150,048 (M); Expenditures, $1,610,521; Total giving, $1,586,306; Grants to individuals, 1,804 grants totaling $1,586,306 (high: $8,284, low: $10).
Type of support: Employee-related welfare.
Application information:
  Deadline(s): None
  Additional information: Applications by letter.
EIN: 366051130

5134
Wallace Trust Foundation
209 W. Oak St.
McGehee, AR   71654   (870) 222-6660
Contact: Gibbs Ferguson, Tr.

Foundation type: Independent foundation
Limitations: Grants to residents of McGehee, AR, for hardship assistance.
Financial data: Year ended 12/31/2003. Assets, $2,065 (M); Expenditures, $102,156; Total giving, $102,156; Grants to individuals, 23 grants totaling $67,914 (high: $13,440, low: $50).
Type of support: Grants for special needs.
Application information: Applications by letter accepted throughout the year.
EIN: 710754251

5135
Anna Emory Warfield Memorial Fund, Inc.
P.O. Box 674
Riderwood, MD   21139
Contact: Braxton D. Mitchell, Pres.

Foundation type: Independent foundation
Limitations: Relief assistance to aged and dependent women in the Baltimore, MD, area.
Publications: Application guidelines.
Financial data: Year ended 12/31/2004. Assets, $5,763,421 (M); Expenditures, $295,532; Total giving, $243,900; Grants to individuals, 38 grants totaling $243,900 (high: $9,150, low: $2,250).
Fields of interest: Aging; Women; Economically disadvantaged.
Type of support: Grants for special needs.

Application information: Applications by letter, including financial information, accepted throughout the year.
EIN: 520785672

5136
Warner Home for Little Wanderers
4 Forest Hill Dr.
St. Albans, VT   05478
Contact: Donna Roby, Treas.

Foundation type: Independent foundation
Limitations: Financial assistance to needy residents, aged 21 and under, from Franklin County, VT, to help defray costs of summer camp; musical instrument rental, purchase, and lessons; art lessons; equipment; and other extracurricular activities.
Financial data: Year ended 04/30/2005. Assets, $1,624,641 (M); Expenditures, $158,573; Total giving, $142,948; Grants to individuals, 392 grants totaling $142,948 (high: $3,000, low: $25).
Fields of interest: Arts education; Performing arts, education; Camps; Children/youth, services.
Type of support: Scholarships—to individuals; Grants for special needs.
Application information: Contact foundation for current application deadline/guidelines.
EIN: 030179439

5137
Washington Group Foundation
(formerly Morrison Knudsen Corporation Foundation)
P.O. Box 73
Boise, ID   83729
Contact: Marlene M. Puckett, Secy.
Application address: 1 Morrison Knudsen Plz., Boise, ID 83729

Foundation type: Operating foundation
Limitations: Welfare assistance to financially needy individuals and families, including employees and former employees, only in specific locations where Washington Group International has operations.
Financial data: Year ended 12/31/2003. Assets, $5,950,392 (M); Expenditures, $251,878; Total giving, $212,785; Grants to individuals, 160 grants totaling $156,778 (high: $9,500, low: $22).
Type of support: Grants for special needs.
Application information: Applications accepted throughout the year; Completion of formal application required, including financial statement; Interviews required.
EIN: 826005410

5138
Washington Women in Need
1849 114th Ave. N.E.
Bellevue, WA   98004   (425) 451-8838
Contact: Colleen M. Crowley, Exec. Dir.

Foundation type: Operating foundation
Limitations: Grants to financially needy women who reside in WA, for health care and emergency services.
Financial data: Year ended 06/30/2004. Assets, $1,812,870 (M); Expenditures, $993,895; Total giving, $622,333; Grants to individuals, totaling $622,333.
Fields of interest: Health care; Women.
Type of support: Grants for special needs.

Application information: Applications accepted. Application form required.

Deadline(s): Applications accepted throughout the year

Additional information: Individuals apply to the organization but payment is made directly to the service providers for the benefit of the client.

EIN: 911559848

5139
We Deliver Dreams Foundation
(formerly MBE Foundation for Children's Initiatives)
6060 Cornerstone Ct. W.
San Diego, CA 92121-3795 (858) 455-8918
E-mail: foundation@mbe.com; URL: http://www.mbe.com/wddf/

Foundation type: Public charity
Limitations: Grants by nomination only to children who are victims of severe abuse, poverty or illness.
Publications: Financial statement.
Financial data: Year ended 12/31/2003.
Assets, $99,084 (M); Expenditures, $184,471; Total giving, $127,938; Grants to individuals, totaling $79,094.
Fields of interest: Children, services.
Type of support: Awards/grants by nomination only.
Application information: Nominations accepted throughout the year; Completion of formal nomination required; See Web site to download nomination form.
Program description:

Children's Dream Program: The foundation funds one-time, life-enhancing requests to children who are victims of tragedy. Dream requests are sponsored by local MBE (Mail Boxes Etc.) centers. Requests must be submitted with an MBE franchisee nomination.

EIN: 311616081

5140
Weather Shield LITE Foundation
P.O. Box 309
Medford, WI 54451 (715) 748-2100
Contact: Kevin Schield, Pres.
URL: http://www.weathershield.com/aboutUs.jsp?tier1=15&tier2=5&subNav=6

Foundation type: Public charity
Limitations: General welfare grants to employees of Weather Shield for assistance with medical bills and expenses due to catastrophic events such as fires and tornadoes.
Financial data: Year ended 12/31/2003.
Assets, $136,788 (M); Expenditures, $175,793; Total giving, $173,793; Grants to individuals, 41 grants totaling $12,443 (high: $500, low: $150).
Type of support: Emergency funds; Employee-related welfare; Grants for special needs.
Application information:

Initial approach: Letter.
Additional information: See Web site for further information.

EIN: 391978784

5141
Emma Reed Webster Aid Association, Inc.
5140 Angevine Rd.
Albion, NY 14411-9417
Contact: Frances Peglow, Treas.

Foundation type: Operating foundation

Limitations: Financial assistance only to indigent individuals and families in Orleans County, NY. Awards are granted in monthly payments.
Financial data: Year ended 05/31/2004.
Assets, $153,203 (M); Expenditures, $65,893; Total giving, $57,787; Grants to individuals, 57 grants totaling $43,070 (high: $1,560, low: $50).
Fields of interest: Economically disadvantaged.
Type of support: Grants for special needs.
Application information: Application form required.

Initial approach: Letter.
Applicants should submit the following:
1) SASE
Additional information: Applications accepted throughout the year.

EIN: 166031485

5142
Hamilton Fish Webster Medical Fund
c/o Bank of America, N.A.
P.O. Box 1802
Providence, RI 02901-1802
Contact: Virginia B. Samson, Chair.
Application address: 114 Bayview Ave., Portsmouth, RI 02871

Foundation type: Independent foundation
Limitations: Financial assistance for medical care to needy residents of Aquidnick Island, RI, who are retired or members of the business or professional community.
Financial data: Year ended 12/31/2004.
Assets, $1,170,742 (M); Expenditures, $42,111; Total giving, $27,664.
Fields of interest: Health care; Business/industry; Economically disadvantaged.
Type of support: Grants for special needs.
Application information: Application form required.

Deadline(s): None

EIN: 056007212

5143
George S. Weeks Trust
c/o JPMorgan Chase Bank, N.A.
P.O. Box 1308
Milwaukee, WI 53201

Foundation type: Independent foundation
Limitations: Financial assistance to needy, legally blind individuals of Fayette and Bourbon Counties, KY, for equipment, supplies, and training.
Financial data: Year ended 12/31/2004.
Assets, $684,149 (M); Expenditures, $32,387; Total giving, $27,786.
Fields of interest: Disabilities, people with; Economically disadvantaged.
Type of support: Grants for special needs.
Application information: Applications not accepted.

EIN: 616208193

5144
George T. Welch Testamentary Trust
c/o Baker Boyer National Bank
P.O. Box 1796
Walla Walla, WA 99362 (509) 525-2000
Contact: Sandra Bradley, Trust Off., Baker Boyer National Bank

Foundation type: Independent foundation
Limitations: Medical and welfare assistance to financially needy residents of Walla Walla County, WA.

Publications: Application guidelines; Program policy statement.
Financial data: Year ended 09/30/2005.
Assets, $4,340,813 (M); Expenditures, $254,028; Total giving, $205,395; Grants to individuals, 78 grants totaling $114,945 (high: $2,500, low: $5).
Fields of interest: Health care; Economically disadvantaged.
Type of support: Grants for special needs.
Application information: Applications accepted. Application form required.

Deadline(s): Feb. 20, May 20, Aug. 20, and Nov. 20
Additional information: Completion of formal application required.

EIN: 916024318

5145
Carrie Welch Trust
P.O. Box 1234
Walla Walla, WA 99362
Contact: Phelps Gose, Tr.

Foundation type: Independent foundation
Limitations: Financial assistance to financially needy and/or worthy aged persons residing in WA, with preference to those in the Walla Walla area.
Financial data: Year ended 10/31/2005.
Assets, $1,252,754 (M); Expenditures, $137,144; Total giving, $64,890; Grants to individuals, totaling $9,207.
Fields of interest: Aging.
Type of support: Grants for special needs.
Application information: Applications presently not accepted; Funds are fully committed.
EIN: 916030361

5146
Welfare Trust Fund of the Twenty-Five Year Club
c/o The Bank of New York, Tax Dept.
1 Wall St., 28th Fl.
New York, NY 10286

Foundation type: Independent foundation
Limitations: Grants to aged, infirm, and otherwise needy persons who are connected with the independent distribution of magazines, small-sized books, and newspapers.
Financial data: Year ended 12/31/2002.
Assets, $120,535 (M); Expenditures, $104,647; Total giving, $103,200; Grants to individuals, 169 grants totaling $103,200 (high: $1,000, low: $2).
Fields of interest: Media/communications; Journalism/publishing; Business/industry; Aging.
Type of support: Grants for special needs.
Application information: Applications not accepted.
EIN: 136064124

5147
West Side Ecumenical Ministry
5209 Detroit Ave.
Cleveland, OH 44102 (216) 651-2037
Contact: Judith Z. Peters, Pres. and C.E.O.
FAX: (216) 651-4145; URL: http://www.wsem.org

Foundation type: Public charity
Limitations: Grants to assist individuals and families for basic necessities, including food and clothing, Cleveland, OH.
Publications: Annual report; Informational brochure; Newsletter.

Financial data: Year ended 12/31/2004. Assets, $6,533,446 (M); Expenditures, $7,203,151; Total giving, $183,271; Grants to individuals, totaling $183,271.
Fields of interest: Food services; Human services.
Type of support: Grants for special needs.
Application information: Contact foundation for current application deadline/guidelines.
EIN: 237034175

5148
Western Association of Ladies for the Relief and Employment of the Poor
c/o Wachovia Bank
Broad and Walnut Sts., PA1210
Philadelphia, PA   19109
Contact: Marlane Bohon, Exec. Secy.; Reginald Middleton
Application address: 240 Chatham Way, West Chester, PA 19380

Foundation type: Independent foundation
Limitations: Relief to the poor and aged of Philadelphia County, PA. Candidates must be referred by a social service agency and not be covered by government programs or other funding sources.
Financial data: Year ended 12/31/2004. Assets, $2,852,520 (M); Expenditures, $167,175; Total giving, $99,736.
Fields of interest: Aging; Economically disadvantaged.
Type of support: Grants for special needs.
Application information: Applications accepted.
  Deadline(s): None
  Additional information: Application must be submitted in writing through a social worker from an approved organization.
EIN: 231353393

5149
Westminster Canterbury Foundation
1600 Westbrook Ave.
Richmond, VA   23227-3337   (804) 264-6000

Foundation type: Public charity
Limitations: Fellowships to financially needy elderly individuals.
Fields of interest: Aging; Economically disadvantaged.
Type of support: Fellowships.
Application information: Unsolicited requests for funds not accepted.
EIN: 521189655

5150
The Westport-Weston Foundation Trust
c/o Hudson United Bank, Wealth Mgmt. Group
90 Post Rd. E., 3rd Fl.
Westport, CT   06880
Contact: Mark Brennan, V.P., TD Banknorth, N.A., Wealth Mgmt. Group

Foundation type: Independent foundation
Limitations: Grants for assistance with medical and basic living expenses and Christmas presents to financially needy residents of Westport and Weston, CT, only.
Financial data: Year ended 12/31/2004. Assets, $858,223 (M); Expenditures, $34,638; Total giving, $24,513; Grants to individuals, 3 grants totaling $6,000.
Fields of interest: Health care; Human services, gift distribution; Economically disadvantaged.

Type of support: Grants for special needs.
Application information: Applications accepted. Application form required.
  Initial approach: Letter.
  Deadline(s): Applications accepted throughout the year
EIN: 066035931

5151
Charles & Elizabeth Wetmore Foundation
1101 Dealers Ave.
New Orleans, LA   70123
Application address: c/o Keta Lowe, Exec. Dir., 4700 Hessmer Ave., Metairie, LA 70002, tel.: (504) 779-1888; FAX: (504) 779-1830

Foundation type: Operating foundation
Limitations: Grants to economically disadvantaged individuals who suffer from tubercular disease and other respiratory diseases and disorders in the metropolitan New Orleans, LA, area.
Financial data: Year ended 12/31/2002. Assets, $201,843 (M); Expenditures, $579,387; Total giving, $509,643; Grants to individuals, totaling $143,869.
Fields of interest: Lung diseases; Economically disadvantaged.
Type of support: Grants for special needs.
Application information: Applications accepted throughout the year; Application by referral from physician or treatment center outlining the individual's qualification for aid.
EIN: 237120743

5152
The George Whitefield Society
14000 Parkway Commons
Oklahoma City, OK   73134   (405) 607-7000

Foundation type: Operating foundation
Limitations: Benevolence grants to individuals, primarily in Oklahoma City, OK.
Financial data: Year ended 12/31/2004. Assets, $83,742 (M); Expenditures, $167,212; Total giving, $132,882; Grants to individuals, 49 grants totaling $129,304 (high: $21,500, low: $100).
Type of support: Grants for special needs.
Application information: Applications not accepted.
EIN: 731492931

5153
Burt Whiteley Charity Fund Trust
c/o Old National Bank
P.O. Box 207
Evansville, IN   47702

Foundation type: Independent foundation
Limitations: Grants for general welfare to individuals in Delaware County, IN, referred by social welfare agencies.
Financial data: Year ended 12/31/2004. Assets, $83,357 (M); Expenditures, $7,700; Total giving, $6,738; Grants to individuals, totaling $6,738.
Type of support: Grants for special needs.
Application information: Applications accepted throughout the year; Contact fund for current application guidelines; Initial approach by letter or telephone; Applicant must include referral from welfare agency.
EIN: 356009797

5154
Whitley County Community Foundation
400 N. Whitley St.
P.O. Box 527
Columbia City, IN   46725-0527   (260) 244-5224
Contact: September McConnell, Exec. Dir.; For grant applications: John Slavich, Prog. Off.
FAX: (260) 244-5724; E-mail: wccf@kconline.com;
URL: http://whitleycountycommunityfoundation.org

Foundation type: Community foundation
Limitations: Financial assistance to economically disadvantaged residents of Whitley County, IN, who are referred by their local church or social service agency. Examples of assistance include prescription medication, travel expenses related to care, and burial costs.
Publications: Application guidelines; Biennial report; Informational brochure (including application guidelines); Newsletter.
Financial data: Year ended 12/31/2004. Assets, $13,774,470 (M); Expenditures, $1,346,072; Total giving, $929,058; Grants to individuals, 49 grants totaling $217,780; Loans to individuals, 87 loans totaling $390,947.
Type of support: Grants for special needs.
Application information: Applications accepted.
  Initial approach: Letter or e-mail.
  Additional information: Contact foundation for further program guidelines.
EIN: 351860518

5155
Wichita Consistory Midian Temple Crippled Children's Fund
c/o Jim Davenport
332 E. 1st St. N.
Wichita, KS   67202-2402   (316) 263-4945

Foundation type: Independent foundation
Limitations: Grants to economically disadvantaged individuals in KS.
Publications: Occasional report.
Financial data: Year ended 12/31/2004. Assets, $328,978 (M); Expenditures, $7,489; Total giving, $7,320; Grants to individuals, totaling $7,320.
Fields of interest: Economically disadvantaged.
Type of support: Grants for special needs.
Application information: Contact fund for current application deadline; Application by letter, outlining financial need.
EIN: 481117049

5156
Widows Society
c/o Bank of America, N.A.
777 Main St., CT2-102-22-03
Hartford, CT   06115
Contact: Pat Staffaroni, Trust Off., Bank of America, N.A.

Foundation type: Independent foundation
Limitations: Loans to financially needy women who reside in the Hartford, CT, area.
Financial data: Year ended 08/31/2005. Assets, $4,568,810 (M); Expenditures, $221,594; Total giving, $180,740; Grants to individuals, totaling $180,740.
Fields of interest: Women.
Type of support: Grants for special needs.
Application information:
  Initial approach: Letter.
  Additional information: Applications accepted throughout the year; Applicants are generally

referred through public or private social service agencies.
EIN: 066026060

5157
The Craig D. Wiesberg & Calvin P. Ranney Children's Foundation
21555 S.W. Hells Canyon Rd.
Sherwood, OR 97140-8500
Contact: Steven W. Wiesberg, Dir.
Application address for individuals: Lee Zumwalt, 619 S.E. 12th Ave., Portland, OR 97214; Tel.: (503) 235-4627; Fax: (503) 235-4625

Foundation type: Independent foundation
Limitations: Grants and special medical equipment to low-income families in OR.
Publications: Application guidelines; Informational brochure.
Financial data: Year ended 12/31/2004. Assets, $31,076 (M); Expenditures, $65,308; Total giving, $45,931; Grants to individuals, 90 grants totaling $45,931 (high: $5,000, low: $24).
Type of support: Grants for special needs.
Application information: Application form required.
 Initial approach: Letter or telephone.
 Deadline(s): Contact foundation for current application deadline
 Applicants should submit the following:
  1) Proposal
  2) Letter(s) of recommendation
 Additional information: Applications should be sent by fax; Time for response to an application is 1-3 days.
EIN: 931228840

5158
The R. H. Wilkin Charitable Trust
P.O. Box 76561
Oklahoma City, OK 73147
Contact: Paul A. Porter, Tr.
Application address: P.O. Box 23374, Oklahoma City, OK 73123

Foundation type: Independent foundation
Limitations: Assistance to needy, crippled children of Oklahoma County, OK, for medical care and treatment.
Financial data: Year ended 12/31/2003. Assets, $320,121 (M); Expenditures, $15,334; Total giving, $4,883; Grants to individuals, totaling $4,883.
Fields of interest: Children/youth, services; Disabilities, people with.
Type of support: Grants for special needs.
Application information: Applications accepted.
 Initial approach: Letter.
 Applicants should submit the following:
  1) Financial information
 Additional information: Application must include professional recommendation for special care and treatment of applicant's handicap required. Unsolicited applications not considered or acknowledged.
EIN: 736157614

5159
A. F. Williams Fund for Teachers
(formerly A. F. Williams Fund for Barnard School for Girls)
c/o Citibank, N.A., C.D.S. Tax Dept.
153 E. 53rd St., 23rd Fl.
New York, NY 10022-0000
Application address: c/o Citibank, N.A., Attn., Mike Festa, PBG Trust Off., 153 E. 53rd St., 5th Fl., New York, NY 10043

Foundation type: Independent foundation
Limitations: Emergency grants to retired teachers, primarily in NY.
Financial data: Year ended 12/31/2004. Assets, $749,975 (M); Expenditures, $33,740; Total giving, $32,010; Grants to individuals, totaling $32,010.
Fields of interest: Education.
Type of support: Grants for special needs.
Application information: Application form not required.
 Deadline(s): Dec. 31.
 Additional information: Application by letter.
EIN: 136054008

5160
Winnett Foundation
c/o Macy's West
2850 N. Main St.
Santa Ana, CA 92705-6601 (714) 569-9852

Foundation type: Independent foundation
Limitations: Aid to financially needy employees and retirees of Bullock's Department Store, CA, for medical, hospital, and other expenses.
Financial data: Year ended 12/31/2004. Assets, $596,425 (M); Expenditures, $27,935; Total giving, $24,700; Grants to individuals, totaling $24,700.
Fields of interest: Health care; Economically disadvantaged.
Type of support: Employee-related welfare.
Application information: Contact foundation for current application deadline/guidelines.
EIN: 952036597

5161
Winterhaven, Inc.
119 19th St., Ste. 206
West Des Moines, IA 50265

Foundation type: Independent foundation
Limitations: Grants to economically disadvantaged individuals in IA for housing assistance.
Financial data: Year ended 12/31/2002. Assets, $668 (M); Expenditures, $482,960; Total giving, $234,178; Grants to individuals, 62 grants totaling $234,178.
Fields of interest: Housing/shelter.
Type of support: Grants for special needs.
Application information: Contact foundation for current application deadline/guidelines.
EIN: 421278027

5162
Wisconsin Eastern Star Foundation, Inc.
4528 N. 72nd St.
Milwaukee, WI 53218-5422
Contact: Mary Jane Kimber, Board Member
Application address: c/o J. Paul Trugleth, S3919A Hwy. 12, Baraboo, WI 53913, tel.: (262) 950-2200

Foundation type: Independent foundation

Limitations: Relief assistance only to members of Eastern Star chapters in WI.
Financial data: Year ended 12/31/2004. Assets, $228,899 (M); Expenditures, $12,851; Total giving, $7,851; Grants to individuals, totaling $7,351.
Type of support: Grants for special needs.
Application information: Applications accepted throughout the year; Completion of formal application required.
EIN: 396059144

5163
The Frank M. Wolfe Foundation, Inc.
505 N. Orlando Ave., Ste. 304
Cocoa Beach, FL 32931 (321) 783-2834
Contact: Frank M. Wolfe, Pres.

Foundation type: Operating foundation
Limitations: Grants to economically disadvantaged residents of FL for tuition, books, living assistance and other fees.
Financial data: Year ended 12/31/2003. Assets, $819,723 (M); Expenditures, $8,392; Total giving, $4,995; Grants to individuals, totaling $4,995.
Fields of interest: Economically disadvantaged.
Type of support: Grants for special needs.
Application information: Applications accepted throughout the year; Contact foundation for current application guidelines.
EIN: 593482977

5164
The Woman's Club of Minneapolis
410 Oak Grove St.
Minneapolis, MN 55403-3225 (612) 870-8001
Contact: Kevin J. Ehlert, Gen'l. Mgr.
URL: http://www.womansclub.org

Foundation type: Public charity
Limitations: Grants to individuals for food, educational, civic and social services in Minneapolis, MN.
Financial data: Year ended 04/30/2004. Assets, $10,408,713 (M); Expenditures, $2,733,733; Total giving, $60,300.
Fields of interest: Education; Food services; Human services; Community development.
Type of support: Grants for special needs.
Application information: Contact foundation for current application deadline/guidelines.
EIN: 410618870

5165
Woman's Seamen's Friend Society of Connecticut, Inc.
c/o New Alliance Bank Trust Dept.
P.O. Box 302
New Haven, CT 06502
Application address: 291 Whitney Ave., Ste. 203, New Haven, CT 06511-3724

Foundation type: Independent foundation
Limitations: Assistance to widows of merchant seamen in CT.
Financial data: Year ended 12/31/2004. Assets, $5,275,657 (M); Expenditures, $200,539; Total giving, $100,615; Grants to individuals, totaling $13,775.
Fields of interest: Military/veterans' organizations; Women.
Type of support: Grants for special needs.

Application information: Contact society for current application deadline/guidelines.
EIN: 060655133

5166
The Woodhill Foundation
11767 Katy Fwy., Ste. 375
Houston, TX   77079

Foundation type: Independent foundation
Limitations: Grants primarily to individuals residing in TX.
Financial data: Year ended 12/31/2003.
Assets, $119,606 (M); Expenditures, $211,008;
Total giving, $113,471.
Type of support: Grants for special needs.
Application information: Contact foundation for current application deadline/guidelines.
EIN: 760644277

5167
World-Herald Goodfellows Charities, Inc.
World-Herald Sq.
Omaha, NE   68102-0000   (402) 444-1388
Contact: Elizabeth C. Terry, Goodfellows Prog. Coord.
FAX: (402) 348-1828

Foundation type: Public charity
Limitations: Food certificates and other emergency assistance to financially needy individuals and families who are referred by human services agencies, primarily in western NE.
Publications: Informational brochure.
Financial data: Year ended 02/28/2004.
Assets, $320,156 (M); Expenditures, $307,174;
Total giving, $307,174; Grants to individuals, totaling $77,100.
Fields of interest: Economically disadvantaged.
Type of support: Grants to individuals.
Application information: Applicants must be referred by local partnering or human services agencies; Interviews required.
EIN: 476000559

5168
Wright Charities Corp.
(formerly Easthampton Home for Aged Women, Inc.)
P.O. Box 36
Easthampton, MA   01027-2011

Foundation type: Operating foundation
Limitations: Subsidies to elderly residents of Easthampton, Southampton, and Westhampton, MA, to reside in Loomis House, Holyoke, MA.
Financial data: Year ended 09/30/2002.
Assets, $732,752 (M); Expenditures, $20,407;
Total giving, $18,338; Grants to individuals, 2 grants totaling $18,338.
Fields of interest: Senior continuing care.
Type of support: Grants to individuals.
Application information:
Initial approach: Letter.
Additional information: Contact foundation for current application deadline/guidelines.
EIN: 042104166

5169
Virginia Wright Mothers Guild, Inc.
c/o Marjorie Courtwright
426 E. Clinton St.
Columbus, OH   43202-2741

Foundation type: Independent foundation
Limitations: Assistance to aged, financially needy women of the Columbus, OH, area to allow them to live at home.
Financial data: Year ended 06/30/2005.
Assets, $43,623 (M); Expenditures, $3,944; Total giving, $3,100; Grants to individuals, 3 grants totaling $3,100 (high: $1,300, low: $500).
Fields of interest: Aging; Women; Economically disadvantaged.
Type of support: Grants for special needs.
Application information: Contact guild for current application deadline/guidelines.
EIN: 316034381

5170
Yankama Feed the Children Charitable Foundation
601 S. Shore Dr.
Battle Creek, MI   49015

Foundation type: Independent foundation
Limitations: Grants to economically disadvantaged individuals for food and other basic necessities.
Financial data: Year ended 12/31/2002.
Assets, $39,500 (M); Expenditures, $20,128;
Total giving, $22,707; Grants to individuals, 23 grants totaling $14,898 (high: $100, low: $25).
Fields of interest: Food services; Human services; Economically disadvantaged.
Type of support: Grants for special needs.
Application information: Contact foundation for current application deadline/guidelines.
EIN: 383219667

5171
The Leonard Young Memorial Foundation, Inc.
c/o Cole, Samuel & Bernstein, LLC
72 Essex St.
Lodi, NJ   07644
FAX: (201) 356-1910;
E-mail: gyoung@imresearch.com

Foundation type: Independent foundation
Limitations: Financial assistance to cancer patients and their families, primarily in NJ, to pay for psychological counseling to help them cope with the illness.
Financial data: Year ended 12/31/2004.
Assets, $0 (M); Expenditures, $18,260; Total giving, $18,260; Grants to individuals, totaling $18,260.
Fields of interest: Mental health, counseling/support groups; Cancer.
Type of support: Grants for special needs.
Application information:
Initial approach: Letter or telephone.
Additional information: Contact foundation for current application deadline/guidelines.
EIN: 223006817

5172
Horace L. Young Trust
c/o Wachovia Bank, N.A.
401 S. Tryon St., 4th Fl.
Charlotte, NC   28288-1159

Foundation type: Independent foundation
Limitations: Grants, paid in monthly installments, to former employees of J.B. Davis Co.
Financial data: Year ended 12/31/2004.
Assets, $958,052 (M); Expenditures, $55,720;

Total giving, $43,989; Grants to individuals, totaling $43,989.
Type of support: Employee-related welfare.
Application information: Applications not accepted.
EIN: 236218857

5173
Youth Service America
1101 15th St., Ste. 200
Washington, DC   20005   (202) 296-2992
Contact: Steven A. Culbertson, Pres. and C.E.O.
FAX: (202) 296-4030; URL: http://www.ysa.org

Foundation type: Public charity
Limitations: Grants of $1,000 to young people who wish to implement hurricane-relief projects.
Publications: Application guidelines; Grants list.
Financial data: Year ended 12/31/2004.
Assets, $462,078 (M); Expenditures, $1,969,030; Total giving, $264,891; Grants to individuals, 256 grants totaling $264,891 (high: $2,000, low: $500).
Fields of interest: Safety/disasters, public education; Disasters, floods; Disasters, Hurricane Katrina.
Type of support: Grants to individuals.
Application information: Applications accepted. Application form required. Application form available on the grantmaker's Web site.
Initial approach: Letter or e-mail.
Deadline(s): Mar. 3
Additional information: See Web site for application guidelines.
Program description:
Katrina's Kids Community Service Grants: The Katrina's Kids Community Service Grant is open to all U.S. citizens between the ages of 5 and 25. Applicants will be expected to develop and implement a sustainable relief project that supports hurricane-relief efforts in the Gulf Coast region. The program welcomes projects in which children and youth work in partnership with adults (parents, coaches, teachers, youth leaders, etc.); however, projects should be youth-led and created, and must take place on National and Global Youth Service Day. For questions e-mail myoung@ysa.org.
EIN: 521500870

5174
Zichron Sholom Shraga Foundation
4915 16th Ave.
Brooklyn, NY   11204   (718) 436-9500
Contact: Warren Edelman, Pres.; Elisheva Edelman, Dir.
Application address: c/o Warren & Elisheva Edelman, 18 Zabriskie Terr., Monsey, NY 10952

Foundation type: Operating foundation
Limitations: Grants to individuals for hardship including food subsidies, and medical expenses.
Financial data: Year ended 12/31/2003.
Assets, $612 (M); Expenditures, $17,456; Total giving, $15,487; Grants to individuals, 39 grants totaling $9,647 (high: $400, low: $50).
Type of support: Grants for special needs.
Application information: Applications by letter accepted throughout the year.
EIN: 133900515

ARTS AND CULTURAL SUPPORT

This section lists sources of support for individuals involved in the arts and cultural fields, including visual artists, performing artists, and writers.

The main types of support available include the following:

- **Fellowships**—includes grants awarded for independent cultural and artistic projects

- **Residencies**—includes awards of studio, work, or living space, equipment, materials, etc. that enable individuals to pursue creative endeavors

- **Arts-related Welfare Assistance and Emergency Aid**—includes all types of grants provided by grantmakers on an emergency or long-term basis to artists or those involved in cultural endeavors for personal, living, or medical expenses

- **Awards and Prizes**—includes grants, awards and prizes given in recognition to winners of competitions sponsored by the grantmaker or an affiliated organization

- **By Nomination Only**—includes fellowships, residencies, and awards for which application must be made by an institution or a separate individual, on behalf of the applicant

Entries are arranged alphabetically by grantmaker name. Access to grants by the above types of support, as well as by specific subject areas and geographic focus, is provided in the "Subject," "Types of Support," "Geographic Focus," and "International Giving" indexes in the back of the book.

Limitations on grantmaking are indicated in the entry when available. *The limitations statement should be checked carefully as a grantmaker will reject any application that does not fall within its stated geographic area, recipient type, or area of interest.*

REMEMBER: IF YOU DON'T QUALIFY, DON'T APPLY.

5175
18th Street Arts Complex
1639 18th St.
Santa Monica, CA 90404 (310) 453-3711
Contact: Clayton Campbell, Co-Exec. Dir.
E-mail: 18thstreet@18thstreet.org; URL: http://
www.18thstreet.org

Foundation type: Public charity
Limitations: Residencies to Los Angeles, CA,
emerging and mid-career contemporary artists.
Financial data: Year ended 06/30/2003.
Assets, $4,229,246 (M); Expenditures,
$731,507. No monetary support given for
residencies.
Fields of interest: Visual arts; Arts, artist's
services.
Type of support: Residencies.
Application information: Applications accepted.
Deadline(s): Contact foundation for current
application deadline
Additional information: Application should
include biography, work samples and
personal statement.
Program description:
Residencies: This program provides studio
space, housing, administrative and fundraising
consultation services, and audio/visual equipment.
Residencies last for three years.
EIN: 953825203

5176
911 Media Arts Center
402 9th Ave., N.
Seattle, WA 98109 (206) 682-6552
Contact: Heather Dew-Oaksen, Pres.
FAX: (206) 682-7422; E-mail: info@911media.org;
URL: http://www.911media.org

Foundation type: Public charity
Limitations: Residencies to digital media artists
residing in the Seattle, WA area.
Financial data: Year ended 12/31/2003.
Assets, $98,615; Expenditures, $514,959; Total
giving, $0. No monetary support given for
residencies.
Fields of interest: Media/communications; Film/
video; Visual arts; Performing arts (multimedia).
Type of support: Residencies; Stipends.
Application information: Applications accepted.
Application form required.
Deadline(s): Nov. 29
Additional information: Completion of formal
application required, including letter of
interest, project description, project budget,
resume, work samples and SASE; See Web
site for further application information.
Program description:
Residency Program: This program provides
production and editing equipment, technical
support, production budget of up to $4,000, and
artist honorarium of $1,000 upon completion of
project. Applicants may be emerging or established
artists using digital media as an art form
(filmmakers, animators, installation artists,
performers, etc.)
EIN: 911271691

5177
Academy Foundation
8949 Wilshire Blvd.
Beverly Hills, CA 90211 (310) 247-3000
Contact: Bruce Davis, Exec. Dir.
FAX: (310) 859-9351; E-mail: ampas@oscars.org;
URL: http://www.oscars.org/foundation/
index.html

Foundation type: Public charity
Limitations: Fellowships to screenwriters for
completion of their original works.
Financial data: Year ended 06/30/2003.
Assets, $69,160,334 (M); Expenditures,
$13,377,294; Total giving, $914,000; Grants to
individuals, 22 grants totaling $184,000 (high:
$18,000, low: $1,000).
Fields of interest: Film/video.
Type of support: Fellowships.
Application information: Application form required.
Deadline(s): May 1
Additional information: See Web site for further
information.
Program description:
Don and Gee Nicholl Fellowship in Screenwriting:
Awards fellowships of $25,000 on a quarterly basis
for one year to screenplay writers. First payments
will be made before end of the calendar year,
second, third and final will be subject to satisfactory
progress of recipient's work. Recipients will be
expected to complete at least one original
screenplay of 100 to 103 pages in length, written
in standard screenplay format.
EIN: 952243698

5178
Academy of American Poets, Inc.
588 Broadway, Ste. 604
New York, NY 10012 (212) 274-0343
Contact: Ryan Murphy, Awards Coord.
FAX: (212) 274-9427; E-mail: academy@poets.org;
URL: http://www.poets.org/

Foundation type: Public charity
Limitations: Fellowships and prizes by nomination
only, with the exception of the Walt Whitman Prize,
to American poets at all stages of their careers.
Publications: Financial statement; Informational
brochure; Newsletter.
Financial data: Year ended 06/30/2004.
Assets, $6,818,993 (M); Expenditures,
$1,520,129; Total giving, $235,125; Grants to
individuals, totaling $235,125 (high: $150,000).
Fields of interest: Literature.
Type of support: Publication; Fellowships; Awards/
grants by nomination only; Awards/prizes;
Residencies.
Program descriptions:
Academy Fellowship: $135,000 is awarded for
distinguished poetic achievement.
Wallace Stevens Award: $100,000 is awarded to
recognize outstanding and proven mastery in the art
of poetry.
Lenore Marshall Poetry Prize: $10,000 is
awarded for the best book of poetry published in the
previous year.
James Laughlin Award: $5,000 to recognize and
support a poet's second book.
Walt Whitman Award: First book publication.,
$5,000, and one-month residency at the Vermont
Studio Center for an American who has not yet
published a book of poetry.
Raiziss/de Palchi Translation Awards: $5,000
book prize and $20,000 fellowship to recognize
outstanding translation into English of modern
Italian poetry.

Harold Morton Landon Translation Award:
$1,000 for a published translation of poetry from
any language into English.
University & College Poetry Prizes: Annual prizes
at more than 160 schools around the country.
EIN: 131879953

5179
ACMP Foundation
1123 Broadway, Rm. 304
New York, NY 10010-2007 (212) 645-7424
Contact: Daniel Nimetz, Exec. Dir.
FAX: (212) 741-2678; E-mail: office@acmp.net;
URL: http://www.acmp.net

Foundation type: Public charity
Limitations: Grants to amateur musicians who
meet regularly in groups to hire professional
coaches.
Publications: Application guidelines; Grants list;
Occasional report; Program policy statement.
Financial data: Year ended 07/31/2004.
Assets, $8,091,308 (M); Expenditures,
$313,882; Total giving, $236,674; Grants to
individuals, 97 grants totaling $15,137 (high:
$300, low: $50).
Fields of interest: Music ensembles/groups.
Type of support: Fellowships.
Application information: Application form required.
Application form available on the grantmaker's Web
site.
Initial approach: Telephone.
Copies of proposal: 1
Deadline(s): Varies
Additional information: Applications by e-mail not
accepted; See Web site for further application
information.
Program description:
ACMP Member Grants: This program will pay up
to 50 percent of the coach's fee. Applicant must be
an ACMP member.
EIN: 954437773

5180
Actors' Fund of America
729 7th Ave., 10th Fl.
New York, NY 10019 (212) 221-7300
FAX: (212) 764-0238; URL: http://
www.actorsfund.org/about/

Foundation type: Public charity
Limitations: Emergency assistance grants to
entertainment industry professionals for essentials
such as food, rent and medical care.
Financial data: Year ended 12/31/2004.
Assets, $45,618,505 (M); Expenditures,
$20,385,502; Total giving, $2,672,344; Grants to
individuals, totaling $2,672,344.
Fields of interest: Performing arts; Arts, artist's
services.
Type of support: Grants for special needs.
Application information:
Initial approach: Telephone or letter.
Additional information: Contact foundation for
application guidelines.
EIN: 131635251

5181
Alaska Humanities Forum
421 W. 1st St., Ste. 300
Anchorage, AK 99501 (907) 272-5341
FAX: (907) 272-3979; E-mail: info@akhf.org; E-mail
(for grants information): grants@akhf.org;
URL: http://www.akhf.org

Foundation type: Public charity
Limitations: Grants to AK residents to use the humanities to promote the civic, intellectual, and cultural life of all Alaskans.
Publications: Application guidelines; Biennial report; Financial statement; Grants list; Informational brochure; Newsletter.
Financial data: Year ended 09/30/2004. Assets, $996,764 (M); Expenditures, $2,128,735; Total giving, $137,715.
Fields of interest: Humanities; Arts; Community development.
Type of support: Conferences/seminars; Research.
Application information: Application form required.
  Initial approach: Telephone.
  Deadline(s): Contact foundation for current application deadline
Program description:
  Grants Program: Makes possible innovative humanities-based projects across the state, including publications, films, lectures, exhibits, conferences, scholarly research, and public gatherings to discuss social, cultural, and other community issues. Potential grantees are encouraged to consult with the form staff as they write their proposal.
EIN: 920042123

5182
Edward Albee Foundation, Inc.
c/o A. Kozak & Co., LLP
192 Lexington Ave., Ste. 1100
New York, NY 10016
Application address: c/o Edward Albee, 14 Harrison St., New York, NY 10013; URL: http://www.albeefoundation.org

Foundation type: Operating foundation
Limitations: One-month residencies to sculptors, visual artists, writers, and composers.
Financial data: Year ended 12/31/2004. Assets, $489,865 (M); Expenditures, $31,930; Total giving, $0. No monetary support given for residencies.
Fields of interest: Visual arts; Sculpture; Theater (playwriting); Music composition; Literature.
Type of support: Residencies.
Application information: Applications accepted.
  Initial approach: Letter to request application and guidelines.
  Deadline(s): Jan. 1 to Apr. 1
  Additional information: See program description for further application information.
Program description:
  Residencies: The foundation maintains the William Flanagan Memorial Center for Creative Persons where talented sculptors, visual artists, and writers may receive a grant for a free room for one month in order to allow them to work free from financial pressure. Applicants for grants of a room are recommended by well-known persons in the arts as well as by application. The residency period is from June to Oct. Each residency is for one month. The standards for admission are talent and need. To apply, applicants should complete the forms and include:
  · six to 12 slides of their work if they are painters or sculptors
  · a manuscript if they are playwrights or screenwriters
  · 12 poems if they are poets
  · one short story or two chapters from a novel if they are fiction writers
  · three essays or articles if they are nonfiction writers

· a recording of at least two original compositions if they are composers
Writers who write in a foreign language should include English translations of their work. Applicants must also include a resume, two letters of recommendation from professionals familiar with the applicant and his or her work, a letter of intent outlining the applicant's proposed project while in residence, two mailing labels bearing the applicant's name only (last name first), and a SASE for return of materials. Applications lacking any of the above items will be returned, unprocessed. Applicants should request a specific month for residency, but should also include one or two alternate choices. The foundation is often unable to accommodate first choices. Applicants should alert the foundation if they are applying to more than one foundation for the same period of time, or if they will be unavailable for any particular month.
EIN: 136168827

5183
The Herb Alpert Foundation
c/o Rona Sebastian, Pres.
1414 6th St.
Santa Monica, CA 90401

Foundation type: Independent foundation
Limitations: Fellowships and residencies by nomination only to U.S. artists.
Financial data: Year ended 12/31/2004. Assets, $43,503,849 (M); Expenditures, $4,052,395; Total giving, $3,101,547.
Fields of interest: Film/video; Visual arts; Dance; Theater; Music.
Type of support: Fellowships; Awards/grants by nomination only; Awards/prizes; Residencies.
Application information: Applications not accepted.
EIN: 954191227

5184
Alpha Delta Kappa Foundation
1615 W. 92nd St.
Kansas City, MO 64114 (816) 363-5525
Contact: Janice M. Estell, Exec. Admin.
FAX: (816) 363-4010;
E-mail: headquarters@alphadeltakappa.org;
Additional tel.: (800) 363-5525; URL: http://www.alphadeltakappa.org

Foundation type: Public charity
Limitations: Awards to individuals pursuing a career in the fine arts fields of painting and music with string instruments.
Financial data: Year ended 05/31/2003. Assets, $1,520,429 (M); Expenditures, $228,293; Total giving, $167,361; Grants to individuals, totaling $72,000 (high: $10,000).
Fields of interest: Visual arts; Music composition.
Type of support: Awards/prizes; Graduate support.
Application information: Application form required.
  Initial approach: Telephone, fax, or e-mail.
  Deadline(s): Apr. 1
  Additional information: Awards are in the amounts of $5,000, $3,000, and $1,000 biennially to individuals with bachelor's degrees in the fine arts to promote further study in their fields. See Web site for additional information.
EIN: 431280111

5185
The Amadeus Fund, Inc.
1114 Ave. of the Americas, Ste. 3400
New York, NY 10036

Foundation type: Independent foundation
Limitations: Limited financial assistance to vocalists and instrumentalists of classical music who are U.S. residents aged 35 or younger.
Financial data: Year ended 08/31/2004. Assets, $1,591 (M); Expenditures, $5,095; Total giving, $5,000; Grants to individuals, totaling $5,000.
Fields of interest: Music.
Type of support: Awards/grants by nomination only.
Application information: Unsolicited applications not considered or acknowledged.
EIN: 133545537

5186
American Academy in Berlin
14 E. 60th St., Ste. 604
New York, NY 10022 (212) 588-1755
Contact: Gary Smith, Exec. Dir.
FAX: (212) 588-1758;
E-mail: nyoffice@americanacademy.de;
URL: http://www.americanacademy.de

Foundation type: Public charity
Limitations: Fellowships for scholars of the fine arts, scholarly disciplines and professional fields to study at the American Academy in Berlin, Germany.
Publications: Application guidelines; Newsletter.
Financial data: Year ended 12/31/2004. Assets, $28,701,264 (M); Expenditures, $3,811,021; Total giving, $501,782; Grants to individuals, totaling $501,782.
Fields of interest: Film/video; Sculpture; Drawing; Theater; Opera; Music (choral); Art history; Arts.
Type of support: Fellowships; Exchange programs.
Application information: Applications accepted. Application form required.
  Deadline(s): Dec. 1
  Additional information: Contact foundation for current application guidelines; See Web site for further information.
Program description:
  Fellowship Program: The fellowship includes round-trip airfare, room and board and a stipend of $5,000 during the semester or year-long duration.
EIN: 521726273

5187
American Academy of Arts and Letters
(formerly American Academy & Institute of Arts and Letters)
633 W. 155th St.
New York, NY 10032-7501 (212) 368-5900
Contact: Virginia Dajani, Exec. Dir.

Foundation type: Operating foundation
Limitations: Prizes to artists, architects, writers, and composers who are not members of the Academy, for exceptional artistic achievement. Candidates for prizes must be nominated by members.
Publications: Informational brochure.
Financial data: Year ended 12/31/2002. Assets, $52,603,395 (M); Expenditures, $2,350,824; Total giving, $907,400; Grants to individuals, 89 grants totaling $798,200 (high: $50,000, low: $4,800).
Fields of interest: Theater (musical); Arts.
Type of support: Awards/grants by nomination only; Awards/prizes.

Application information: With the exception of the Richard Rodgers Awards in Musical Theater, applications for awards or financial assistance are not accepted.

Program descriptions:

The Richard Rogers Awards for Readings, Workshops, and Productions: These awards subsidize workshops, readings, and productions of original musical theatre works in nonprofit, off-Broadway theatres.

Awards and Prizes: Recipients are nominated by the 250 members of the Academy. Prizes are given annually to artists, architects, writers, and composers for exceptional artistic achievement. An exhibition of prize winners' works—painting, sculpture, models, manuscripts, books, and scores —is mounted in the spring. Several music award winners also receive a subsidized recording.

EIN: 130429640

5188

The American Berlin Opera Foundation, Inc.

Scholarship Competition (GACC)
6 E. 87th St.
New York, NY 10128
Contact: Amy R. Sperling, Scholarship Chair.
E-mail: gala@operafoundation.org; Tel./FAX: (212) 534-5383; URL: http://www.operafoundation.org

Foundation type: Public charity
Limitations: Scholarships to young American singers to study and perform in Berlin, Germany, and thereafter to pursue career opportunities in Europe.
Publications: Application guidelines.
Financial data: Year ended 06/30/2003. Assets, $11,756 (M); Expenditures, $54,720; Total giving, $36,652; Grants to individuals, 3 grants totaling $36,652 (high: $18,461, low: $300).
Fields of interest: Opera; Performing arts, education.
Type of support: Scholarships—to individuals.
Application information: Application form required.
Deadline(s): Feb. 5
Additional information: Audition required.

Program description:

A.B.O.F.: Awards two scholarships which include a $15,000 stipend and a round-trip flight to Berlin for a ten-month training at the Deutsche Opera. The competition is open to American citizens or permanent residents between the ages of 18 and 30 who are at the beginning of their professional careers.

EIN: 133377138

5189

American Composers Forum

332 Minnesota St., Ste. E-145
St. Paul, MN 55101-1300 (651) 228-1407
Contact: Julie Stroud, Dir., Devel.
FAX: (651) 291-7978;
E-mail: mail@composersforum.org; URL: http://www.composersforum.org

Foundation type: Public charity
Limitations: Fellowships and grants to composers to support their creative work.
Publications: Application guidelines; Annual report; Newsletter.
Financial data: Year ended 06/30/2003. Assets, $6,161,788 (M); Expenditures, $2,886,231; Total giving, $678,289; Grants to individuals, totaling $678,289.

Fields of interest: Music composition; Religion, interfaith issues.
Type of support: Fellowships; Grants to individuals; Residencies; Loans—to individuals.
Application information: Application form required.
Initial approach: Telephone or e-mail.
Deadline(s): Vary
Additional information: Applications accepted throughout the year.

Program descriptions:

Community Partners Projects: Residencies for composers to partner with local educational, cultural, and social institutions in the creation and presentation of new music. Calls for projects are made annually to members in each chapter. Awards are in the $1,500 to $4,000 range.

Composers Commissioning Program (CCP): Supports creation of new works by emerging composers by underwriting the composers' commissioning fees. Composers apply to CCP in conjunction with a performing organization (a soloist or a group). Alternatively, composer-performer-improvisers may apply in conjunction with a presenting organization. CCP welcomes applicants working in all musical genres, including jazz, experimental, contemporary classical, improvised, and international styles, and seeks to expand new music culture beyond the conventional venues. Grants range from $2,500 to $8,000, with an average grant amount of $5,500. An additional $1,000 per grantee is available to subsidize performance of new pieces. Since CCP rarely covers the entire cost of a commission, performers are encouraged to pursue other funding sources to supplement the composer's fee. Grantees are chosen by a three-member panel that changes annually. Applications are due in Aug. and recipients are notified in Oct.

Continental Harmony: Takes the form of community-designed and managed composer residencies, culminating in premieres of new works. Projects will be selected in all 50 states over a three-year cycle. Qualifying states and calls for composers will be listed on ACF's Web site.

Faith Partners Residency Program: Funds two-year-long composer residencies in consortia of three congregations of different faiths. Each composer creates a total of six works during the course of the residency: three to be shared by all members of the consortium, and one for each consortium member individually. Each composer receives $8,000. ACF composer members in the upper Midwest and selected chapter areas of the U.S. may apply.

McKnight Composer Fellowships: Awards $25,000 fellowships annually to four Minnesota composers who are ACF members and have resided in Minnesota for the past 12 months. These prestigious fellowships are intended to reward artistic excellence and to support composers who have reached a critical point in their career development. The $25,000 award provides for both an unrestricted portion to be used for any purpose, such as "buying" compositional time, acquisition of equipment, travel, and private study, as well as a portion to support self-designed community projects that enable the composer to work outside the conventional new music orbit for at least 25 days. Residencies in schools, rural areas, neighborhood organizations, or any other setting where the composer acts as facilitator and educator will be especially encouraged. Fellows are selected by a three-member panel consisting of nationally recognized composers and other musicians familiar with a wide spectrum of musical styles. Deadline Mar.

McKnight Visiting Composer Program: Underwrites a Minnesota residency of two months

or longer for two non-Minnesota composers, including $14,000 fellowships. While in residence, the visiting fellow collaborates on a project with Minnesota performing, presenting, and/or community organizations. The program encourages interaction with a variety of audiences, including rural populations and students; the selection process favors projects that promise to have considerable impact on the host community. Applications with detailed descriptions of the proposed residency activities are reviewed by a three-member panel. Visiting composers should complete their projects within one year of receiving the award. ACF composer-members residing outside Minnesota may apply by Mar., and recipients will be notified in May.

Recording Assistance Program: Through this program, ACF members enter into a collaboration with the Forum to produce and distribute a compact disc of their work on the Innova Recordings label. ACF makes a low-interest loan (six percent APR) to cover the costs of manufacturing 1,000 CDs and of designing and printing booklets and tray cards, along with national distribution, marketing assistance, and help in choosing and approaching appropriate media targets. Members supply a complete and compelling tape and agree to assume a key role in promoting the project. The program enables the forum's professional members to obtain a crucial "calling card" that helps advance their careers, and provides valuable experience in dealing with retailers, press, radio, and others in the music business. The application process is competitive: judgments are based on musical and audio quality, a detailed marketing plan prepared by the applicant, a credit check, and the applicant's willingness to join actively with ACF in promoting the recording. Application can be made with a cassette mock-up of the disc, but a finished digital tape must be presented before the project is approved for production. Loans made under the program may not be used to cover costs incurred in the recording process itself. Money loaned is paid not to the applicant, but directly to vendors contracted by ACF for manufacturing and other services. Loans generally vary between $4,000 and $6,000. Once the costs associated with the loan are fully repaid, the applicant collects all profits from further sales. If re-issue is warranted, a second loan may be made.

EIN: 237452688

5190

American Institute of Indian Studies

1130 E. 59th St.
Chicago, IL 60637-1539 (773) 702-8638
Contact: Elise Auerbach, Admin.
E-mail: aiis@uchicago.edu; URL: http://www.indiastudies.org

Foundation type: Public charity
Limitations: Grants to performing artists for study in India.
Publications: Application guidelines; Informational brochure; Newsletter.
Financial data: Year ended 06/30/2003. Assets, $5,285,732 (M); Expenditures, $2,295,705.
Fields of interest: Performing arts; Arts, artist's services.
Type of support: Fellowships.
Application information: Applications accepted. Application form required.
Deadline(s): July 1
Additional information: Application must include a $25 application fee.

Program description:

Senior Performing and Creative Arts Fellowships: Available to accomplished practitioners of performing arts of India who demonstrate that study in India would enhance their skills, develop their capabilities to teach or perform in the U.S., enhance American involvement with India's artistic traditions, and strengthen their links with peers in India.
EIN: 236297039

5191
American Music Center, Inc.

30 W. 26th St., Ste. 1001
New York, NY 10010-2011 (212) 366-5260
Contact: Anna Smith, Grants Mgr.
FAX: (212) 366-5265; E-mail: center@amc.net;
URL: http://www.amc.net

Foundation type: Public charity
Limitations: Grants to disseminate the work of contemporary American composers.
Publications: Application guidelines; Grants list; Informational brochure.
Financial data: Year ended 06/30/2004.
Assets, $3,480,903 (M); Expenditures, $1,535,693; Total giving, $355,824; Grants to individuals, 103 grants totaling $82,324 (high: $2,500, low: $250).
Fields of interest: Music; Music composition.
Type of support: Program development; Grants to individuals.
Application information: Application form required. Application form available on the grantmaker's Web site.
  Initial approach: Telephone or e-mail.
  Copies of proposal: 1
  Deadline(s): Feb. 1, May 1, Oct. 1
  Applicants should submit the following:
    1) SASE
    2) Work samples
    3) Resume
    4) Proposal
    5) Essay
    6) Curriculum vitae
    7) Budget Information
  Additional information: Applications should be sent by mail; Response to application given within six weeks.
Program description:

Composer Assistance Program: Provides support to American composers who are members of the American Music Center for the expenses of preparing for a premiere performance. Eligible preparation costs include: copy, extraction, reproduction of parts; purchase of computer hardware, software and/or office supplies for copying purposes; hiring a copyist; hiring an engineer to prepare electronic materials to be used in a live performance premiere; studio time to record for a live performance premiere; permission to use copyright material. On the average, the program awards between $40,000 and $80,000 annually; previous grants to composers have ranged from $1,000 to $2,000. Priority is given to composers who have not received significant amounts from the program in the past.
EIN: 130432981

5192
American String Teachers, Inc.

4153 Chain Bridge Rd.
Fairfax, VA 22030 (703) 279-2113
Contact: Elizabeth Bookwalter, Development Mgr.
FAX: (703) 279-2114; E-mail: liz@astaweb.com;
URL: http://www.astaweb.com

Foundation type: Public charity
Limitations: Prizes to composers who win the Merle J. Isaac Composition Contest.
Financial data: Year ended 06/30/2004.
Assets, $703,588 (M); Expenditures, $1,461,666; Total giving, $155,000.
Fields of interest: Music composition.
Type of support: Awards/prizes.
Application information: Applications accepted. Application form required. Application form available on the grantmaker's Web site.
  Deadline(s): Apr. 1
  Additional information: Application must include six copies of the score and a $25 application fee.
Program description:

Merle J. Isaac Composition Contest: Composers are invited to submit an original, unpublished composition for string orchestra suitable for the elementary, middle/junior high school, or high school orchestra levels. Compositions written for commission and composition that have been submitted for publication will not be accepted. Winner receives national publicity, aid in publication of the work, and $1,500.
EIN: 226080964

5193
American Symphony Orchestra League

33 W. 60th St., 5th Fl.
New York, NY 10023-7905 (212) 262-5161
Contact: Henry Fogel, Pres. and C.E.O.
FAX: (212) 262-5198;
E-mail: league@symphony.org; Additional address: 910 17th St., N.W., Washington, DC 20006, tel.: (202) 776-0215, fax: (202) 776-0224; e-mail: pkahn@symphony.org; URL: http://www.symphony.org

Foundation type: Public charity
Limitations: Scholarships to gifted, young African American musicians who intend to pursue professional careers in American symphonies or orchestras.
Financial data: Year ended 09/30/2004.
Assets, $6,573,133 (M); Expenditures, $5,587,247; Total giving, $15,400; Grants to individuals, 19 grants totaling $15,400 (high: $1,000, low: $800).
Fields of interest: Music.
Type of support: Fellowships; Awards/prizes.
Application information: Contact foundation for current application deadline; Initial approach by e-mail; Completion of formal application required.
Program descriptions:

Music Assistance Fund: Scholarship awards range from $500 to $3,500 each. Awards are based on a live audition and recommendations from teachers and orchestra conductors. Recipients range in age from 12 through college-age, and funds are primarily used for tuition expenses at music schools and summer programs in North America which provide concentrated study and performance opportunities.

Orchestra Management Fellowship Program: This comprehensive management training program offers a $25,000 stipend to a limited number of highly qualified individuals who aspire to be executive directors of American orchestras. In

addition, fellows participate in residencies with orchestras of all sizes, and intensive orientation to the music industry, and course work in relevant topics. Qualified applicants should be strong leaders who are committed to pursuing a career as an executive director.
EIN: 237300636

5194
Amy Foundation

c/o The Amy Writing Awards
P.O. Box 16091
Lansing, MI 48901-6091

Foundation type: Independent foundation
Limitations: Awards to authors of published articles on biblical interpretations of topical social issues.
Publications: Informational brochure; Newsletter.
Financial data: Year ended 12/31/2004.
Assets, $309,106 (M); Expenditures, $204,823; Total giving, $115,705; Grants to individuals, totaling $66,900.
Fields of interest: Literature; Religion.
Type of support: Awards/prizes.
Application information: Applications not accepted.
  Additional information: The foundation contributes only to preselected individuals. Unsolicited applications not accepted or acknowledged.
Program description:

AMY Writing Awards: The award recognizes creative, skillful writing that presents in a sensitive, thought-provoking manner the biblical position on issues affecting the world today. To be eligible, articles must be published in a secular publication. The author should present biblical truth as quoted from an accepted and popular edition of the Bible such as the New International Version, The Living Bible, the King James, or the Revised Standard Version. The article should deal with the Bible's position on current and provocative issues such as divorce, moral values, family, abortion, and addiction to drugs and alcohol. In addition to content, articles will be judged on their persuasive power, the author's skill in relating the Bible to contemporary issues, and the author's sensitivity in relating the biblical position to the search for the meaning of life. Typically, awards are made in the following manner: a $10,000 1st prize, a $5,000 2nd prize, a $4,000 3rd prize, a $3,000 4th prize, a $2,000 5th prize, and ten prizes of $1,000 each. Recipients are notified by May 1.
EIN: 237044543

5195
Anchor Graphics, Inc.

119 W. Hubbard St.
Chicago, IL 60610 (312) 595-9598
Contact: David Jones, Exec. Dir.
E-mail: print@anchorgraphics.org; URL: http://www.anchorgraphics.org

Foundation type: Public charity
Limitations: Residencies to printmaking artists.
Publications: Newsletter.
Financial data: Year ended 12/31/2003.
Assets, $50,871 (M); Expenditures, $151,190. No monetary support given for residencies.
Fields of interest: Visual arts.
Type of support: Residencies.
Application information: Applications accepted.
  Initial approach: E-mail.
  Deadline(s): July 9
  Additional information: Application by letter should also include ten slides, SASE,

curriculum vitae, artist statement, choices for dates of residency.

Program description:

Residency Program: Four to six residents will have access to printmaking facilities for two weeks. Artists will interact with visitors to the printshop and share their work with printmaking students.
EIN: 363617905

5196

Anderson Center for Interdisciplinary Studies, Inc.

163 Tower View Dr.
P.O. Box 406
Red Wing, MN 55066 (651) 388-2009
Contact: Robert Hedin, Dir.
E-mail: laura@andersoncenter.com; URL: http://www.andersoncenter.org

Foundation type: Public charity
Limitations: Residencies to MN artists and writers, who will reside at the Anderson Center.
Publications: Application guidelines; Annual report.
Financial data: Year ended 06/30/2004.
Assets, $1,602,963 (M); Expenditures, $300,645. No monetary support given for residencies.
Fields of interest: Literature; Arts.
Type of support: Residencies.
Application information: Applications accepted. Application form required.
Deadline(s): Feb. 1
Program description:
Residency Program: Residencies last from two weeks to one month and will include meals, studio space, and lodging. Residents are expected to work on a clearly defined project and to make a contribution to the community in the form of a talk, class, or a performance of their work.
EIN: 411792770

5197

Sherwood Anderson Foundation

1108 Satinwood Dr.
Greensboro, NC 27410
Contact: Karlyn Shankland, Dir.
URL: http://oncampus.richmond.edu/academics/journalism/comp.html

Foundation type: Independent foundation
Limitations: Awards to individuals who have published at least one book of fiction or a collection of short stories in a major literary or commercial publication.
Financial data: Year ended 12/31/2004.
Assets, $477,437 (M); Expenditures, $18,698; Total giving, $16,100; Grants to individuals, totaling $15,000.
Fields of interest: Journalism/publishing; Literature.
Type of support: Scholarships—to individuals.
Application information: Applications accepted.
Deadline(s): Apr. 1
Additional information: Application by resume, including bibliography of works published, cover letter, work samples, and $20 application fee; Applications by e-mail not accepted.
Program description:
The Sherwood Anderson Foundation Fiction Award: Applicant should have published at least one book of fiction or have had several short stories published in major literary and/or commercial publications. A detailed resume that provides a bibliography of applicant's publication, a history of

writing experience and future plans for writing projects, two or three examples of applicant's best work. Manuscripts are accepted only in English.
EIN: 581717970

5198

Angels Gate Cultural Center, Inc.

3601 S. Gaffey St.
San Pedro, CA 90731 (310) 519-0936
Contact: Juliann Wolfgram, Pres.; Residencies: Marshall Astor
E-mail address for M. Astor (GTI):
marshall@angelsgateart.org
FAX: (310) 519-8698;
E-mail: info@angelsgateart.org; URL: http://angelsgateart.org/

Foundation type: Public charity
Limitations: Studio space to professional artists of various disciplines.
Financial data: Year ended 12/31/2003.
Assets, $111,317 (M); Expenditures, $256,303.
Fields of interest: Visual arts; Literature.
Type of support: Residencies.
Application information: Applications accepted. Application form required.
Initial approach: E-mail, telephone or letter.
Deadline(s): None
Applicants should submit the following:
1) Curriculum vitae
2) Work samples
Additional information: Application must also include letter of intent, as well as hard copies of work samples, preferably in CD format.
EIN: 953688214

5199

Ann Arbor Film Festival

203 E. Ann St.
Ann Arbor, MI 48104 (734) 995-5356
Contact: Christen McArdle, Exec. Dir.
FAX: (734) 995-5396; E-mail: info@aafilmfest.org; URL: http://aafilmfest.org

Foundation type: Public charity
Limitations: Awards to winners of the Ann Arbor Film Festival, held in MI.
Publications: Informational brochure (including application guidelines); Newsletter.
Financial data: Year ended 10/31/2004.
Assets, $47,095 (M); Expenditures, $174,113.
Fields of interest: Film/video.
Type of support: Awards/prizes.
Application information: Applications accepted. Application form required. Application form available on the grantmaker's Web site.
Initial approach: E-mail.
Deadline(s): Sept. 1 and Nov. 1
Applicants should submit the following:
1) SASE
2) Work samples
Additional information: There is an application fee of $30. Applications are available in PDF format on the site, or applicants may submit via www.withoutabox.com.
Program descriptions:
Between The Lines Award Best Gay/Lesbian Film: This $500 award honors the film that best deals with gay/lesbian issues.
Chris Frayne Award Best Animated Film: This $500 award is given for the best animated film in the festival in memory of Chris Frayne, a key participant in the festival's early years, whose spirit and approach was reminiscent of his cartoon characters.

Doug Wandrei Award Best Lighting Design: This $500 award recognizes the most creative use of lighting in a film in which mood and atmosphere of the environment are greatly enhanced through lighting design.
Griot Editorial Best Editing Award: This $500 award is given to a film entry that demonstrates outstanding creativity and technical excellence in the art of motion picture editing.
Gus Van Sant Best Experimental Film Award: This $1,000 award goes to the film that best represents the use of experimental processes, forms, and topics.
Isabella Liddell Art Award: This award of $400 is given to the film(s) that best deal with women's issues.
Kodak/Film Craft Lab Award for Best Cinematography: This award is for $1,500 worth of 16mm or 35mm film stock donated by Kodak, and the processing donated by Film Craft Lab. For the film that demonstrates the highest excellence and creativity in cinematography.
Lawrence Kasdan Award Best Narrative Film: This $1,000 award is given to recognize works which make use of the film medium's unique ability to convey striking and original stories.
Marvin Felheim Award Special Jury Prize: This $500 prize is awarded to a work of film art that extends the range of subject matter traditionally dealt with in the film medium, while at the same time transcending standard genre categorization.
Michael Moore Award Best Documentary Film: This $1,000 award is given for the best documentary film in the festival.
Michigan Vue Magazine Award Best Michigan Filmmaker: This award of $500 is given to support and encourage the local filmmaking community by rewarding excellence in a Michigan-produced film within any genre.
Peter Wilde Award Most Technically Innovative Film: This award of $500 goes to the film that most respects the integrity of the projected image and celebrates the indelible beauty of metallic silver-based images.
Prix DeVarti Funniest Film: Awards $1,000 to the funniest film in the festival in memory of Dominick and Alice DeVarti.
The EMPA Work Life Award (Employee Motivation Performance Assessment): This award of $1,200 goes to the film that best addresses issues that pertain to careers, the workplace, job hunting, employment, co-workers, job responsibilities, or the impact of employment on the individual's personal life.
The Ken Burns Best of the Festival Award: This top award of $3,000 recognizes the filmmaker with the most outstanding entry award honors the film that best represents the artistic and creative standards of the festival.
Tio's Red Hot & Spicy Award: This $500 award is awarded to any film considered "red hot and spicy" based on form, flavor, or content.
Tom Berman Most Promising Filmmaker Award: This award of $1,000 supports a young filmmaker that the Awards Jury expects will make a significant contribution to the art of film in the course of his/her filmmaking career.
Vicki Honeyman Award for Best 16mm Film: This $500 award is intended for the 16mm film that best embodies the spirit of the films that rock her world: technically challenging, innovative, quirky and unique, with a strong respect and passion for film as an art form.
EIN: 382379836

5200
Anodyne Artist Company
825 Carleton St.
St. Paul, MN 55114 (651) 642-1684
Contact: Mary Pendergast, Exec. Dir.
E-mail: anodyneart@aol.com

Foundation type: Public charity
Limitations: Studio space to handicapped and non-traditional artists residing in the St. Paul, MN area, who specialize in visual and performing arts.
Financial data: Year ended 06/30/2003. Assets, $45,380 (M); Expenditures, $187,568. No monetary support given for residencies.
Fields of interest: Visual arts; Performing arts; Disabilities, people with.
Type of support: Residencies.
Application information:
Initial approach: Letter and telephone.
Additional information: Contact foundation for further information.
EIN: 411951094

5201
The Antonovych Foundation, Inc.
5143 Cathedral Ave. N.W.
Washington, DC 20016
Application address: P.O. Box 40818, Washington, DC 20011

Foundation type: Independent foundation
Limitations: Awards for achievement in Ukrainian literature and science.
Financial data: Year ended 11/30/2004. Assets, $1,683,870 (M); Expenditures, $869,657; Total giving, $865,000.
Fields of interest: Literature; Science; Ukraine.
Type of support: Awards/prizes.
Application information: Deadline Oct.; Application by letter, including applicant's published materials.
EIN: 521224032

5202
The Arrowhead Regional Arts Council
1301 Rice Lake Rd., Ste. 111
Duluth, MN 55811 (218) 722-0952
Contact: Robert DeArmond, Exec. Dir.
FAX: (218) 722-4459; *E-mail:* aracouncil@aol.com;
Additional tel.: (800) 569-8134; URL: http://www.aracouncil.org

Foundation type: Public charity
Limitations: Grants to artists in Aitkin, Carlton, Cook, Itasca, Koochiching, Lake and St. Louis counties, MN.
Publications: Application guidelines; Annual report; Biennial report; Informational brochure; Newsletter.
Financial data: Year ended 06/30/2005. Assets, $64,467 (M); Total giving, $131,850; Grants to individuals, 17 grants totaling $30,000 (high: $4,000, low: $500). Subtotal for fellowships: 6 grants totaling $20,000 (high: $4,000, low: $2,000). Subtotal for project support: 11 grants totaling $10,000 (high: $1,000, low: $500).
Fields of interest: Arts.
Type of support: Fellowships; Residencies; Travel grants; Project support.
Application information: Application form required. Application form available on the grantmaker's Web site.
Initial approach: Letter, telephone or e-mail.
Copies of proposal: 1
Deadline(s): Contact foundation for current application deadlines
Applicants should submit the following:
1) Work samples
2) Resume
3) Proposal
4) Budget Information
Additional information: Applications should be sent by mail; Time for response to an application is 6-8 weeks.
Program descriptions:
Artist of Color Career Development Grant Program: Provide financial support to developing and established regional artists of color wishing to take advantage of impending concrete opportunities that will advance their work or careers. An applicant may request up to $1,000 per application and grant round.
McKnight/ARAC Fellowship Grants: Recognize, reward, and encourage outstanding individual artists at various stages in their careers. The program awards 7 fellowships annually; five of $4,000 each and two of $2,000 each for emerging artists.
McKnight/ARAC Individual Career Development Grants: Provide financial support to developing and established regional artists wishing to take advantage of impending, concrete opportunities that will advance their work or careers. An applicant may request up to $1,000 per application and grant round.
EIN: 411358639

5203
Art in General, Inc.
79 Walker St.
New York, NY 10013-3523 (212) 219-0473
Contact: Holly Block, Exec. Dir.
FAX: (212) 219-0511;
E-mail: info@artingeneral.org; URL: http://www.artingeneral.org

Foundation type: Public charity
Limitations: Residencies to artists.
Financial data: Year ended 07/31/2004. Assets, $298,948 (M); Expenditures, $755,169. No monetary support given for residencies.
Fields of interest: Visual arts.
Type of support: Residencies.
Application information: Applications accepted. Application form required.
Initial approach: Letter.
Deadline(s): Jan. 10, Apr. 10, and Oct. 4
Additional information: Formal application should also include ten slides, resume, artist statement, and project outline.
Program description:
Residency Program: The residency program provides a public exhibition space for six to eight weeks. The proposed project should include a public aspect. The residents also work with the foundation's Education Department to develop programs for school-age children.
EIN: 133472869

5204
Art Omi International Art Center
(formerly Art/Omi, Inc.)
55 5th Ave., 15th Fl.
New York, NY 10003-4398 (212) 206-5684
Contact: Ruth Adams, Exec. Dir.
FAX: (212) 206-6023; *E-mail:* artists@artomi.org;
URL: http://www.artomi.org

Foundation type: Public charity
Limitations: Fellowships and residencies to visual artists, writers and musicians.
Publications: Informational brochure; Newsletter.
Financial data: Year ended 12/31/2003. Assets, $18,013,539 (M); Expenditures, $710,793. No monetary support given for residencies.
Fields of interest: Visual arts; Music; Literature.
Type of support: Fellowships; Residencies.
Application information: Applications accepted.
Deadline(s): Feb. 1 for visual artists, Nov. 30 for writers, May 1 for musicians
Additional information: See Web site for complete application guidelines.
Program description:
Residency Program:
· International Artists Colony: A three-week residency program for visual artists. Artist receives a studio, living quarters, and meals
· Ledig House International Writers Residency: Residencies can last from one week to two months for writers and translators from all fields. Residency includes housing and meals
· International Musicians' Residency Program: Twelve music performers and composers from around the world will receive residencies for two and a half weeks. Residency includes full room and board.
EIN: 133641616

5205
Artist Trust
1835 12th Ave.
Seattle, WA 98122-2437 (206) 467-8734
Contact: Fidelma McGinn, Exec. Dir.
FAX: (206) 467-9633; *E-mail:* info@artisttrust.org;
Additional tel.: (866) 21TRUST; URL: http://www.artisttrust.org

Foundation type: Public charity
Limitations: Awards and fellowships to professional artists in WA.
Publications: Application guidelines; Annual report; Informational brochure; Newsletter.
Financial data: Year ended 06/30/2004. Assets, $2,522,679 (M); Expenditures, $691,358; Total giving, $209,775; Grants to individuals, 62 grants totaling $190,525 (high: $10,000, low: $1,400).
Fields of interest: Visual arts; Arts; Aging; Women.
Type of support: Fellowships; Grants to individuals; Awards/prizes; Project support.
Application information: Application form required. Application form available on the grantmaker's Web site.
Initial approach: Letter, telephone or e-mail.
Applicants should submit the following:
1) Work samples
2) Resume
3) Proposal
4) Budget Information
Additional information: Contact foundation for current application deadlines.
Program descriptions:
Artist Trust/WSAC Fellowships: Fellowships of $6,000 to practicing professional artists of exceptional talent and demonstrated ability. Fellowships are merit-based and not project-based.
Grants for Artists Projects (GAP): Awards a maximum of $1,400 to artists for projects, which can include, but are not limited to, the development, completion or presentation of new work. Projects created in all disciplines are welcome.
Twining Humber Award for Lifetime Artistic Achievement: Annual award of $10,000 to a female visual artist, 60 years or older, who has dedicated a lifetime to her work.
EIN: 911353974

5206
Artists Fellowship, Inc.
c/o Salmagundi Club
47 5th Ave.
New York, NY   10003   (646) 230-9833
Contact: Richard Pionk, Tr.
URL: http://www.artistsfellowship.com

Foundation type: Independent foundation
Limitations: Emergency aid to American professional visual artists and their families for relief of financial distress due to disability, age, or bereavement. Preference is shown to those living in the U.S.
Financial data: Year ended 10/31/2004. Assets, $3,013,331 (M); Expenditures, $186,903; Total giving, $156,375; Grants to individuals, 44 grants totaling $156,375 (high: $11,100, low: $300).
Fields of interest: Visual arts; Arts, artist's services.
Type of support: Grants for special needs.
Application information: Applications accepted throughout the year; Completion of formal application required.
EIN: 136122134

5207
Artists Space, Inc.
38 Greene St., 3rd Fl.
New York, NY   10013-2505   (212) 226-3970
Contact:
FAX: (212) 966-1434;
E-mail: artspace@artistsspace.org; URL: http://www.artistsspace.org

Foundation type: Public charity
Limitations: Grants to artists and groups of artists who live and work in the five boroughs of New York City.
Publications: Application guidelines; Annual report.
Financial data: Year ended 06/30/2004. Assets, $1,891,118 (M); Expenditures, $694,883; Total giving, $6,857; Grants to individuals, totaling $6,857.
Fields of interest: Arts, artist's services; Arts.
Type of support: Grants to individuals.
Application information: Application form required.
Initial approach: In person only.
Deadline(s): Jan. 15 and Sept. 15
Additional information: Application should also include confirmed exhibition or event dates.
Program description:
Independent Project Grants: Twenty $500 grants are awarded on a lottery basis to help realize projects, including visual arts, film and video, new media and performance pieces, in nontraditional, nonprofit public venues. An ongoing initiative, the IPG revives Artists Space's previous grants programs and is conceived to support independent arts projects that bypass or are ineligible for presentation within the commercial gallery structure.
EIN: 132749632

5208
Arts & Cultural Council for Greater Rochester, Inc.
277 N. Goodman St.
Rochester, NY   14607   (585) 473-4000
Contact: Sarah Lentini, Pres. & C.E.O.
FAX: (585) 473-4051;
E-mail: mfutter@artsrochester.org; URL: http://www.artsrochester.org

Foundation type: Public charity

Limitations: Grants to artists in all disciplines, who are Rochester, NY, area residents.
Publications: Application guidelines; Annual report; Grants list; Newsletter.
Financial data: Year ended 12/31/2004. Assets, $870,480 (M); Expenditures, $764,754; Total giving, $213,722.
Fields of interest: Arts.
Type of support: Fellowships; Stipends; Project support.
Application information:
Initial approach: Letter or telephone.
Deadline(s): Feb., May 21, and Sept. for Special Opportunity Stipends, Oct. 28 for Artist Projects, and NYSCA Decentralization Project Support
Additional information: Contact Council for application guidelines or consult Web site for additional information.
Program descriptions:
Artist Projects: $2,500 grants are given to individual artists to create new work and share the process or results with the community through artist-initiated public activities such as exhibits, lectures, performances, readings, residencies, etc.
NYSCA Decentralization Fund Project Support: Grants of up to $5,000 are available to individual artists in Monroe County, NY, for arts-related projects and programs in all disciplines that serve Monroe County residents.
Special Opportunity Stipends: Stipends of $100 to $600 are given to artists in all media to take advantage of opportunities that may benefit their work or career development. Eligible artists must be residents of one of the following NY counties for the past year: Cayuga, Genesee, Livingston, Monroe, Ontario, Orleans, Seneca, Wayne, Wyoming, or Yates.
EIN: 222309669

5209
Arts Alive Fort Collins
P.O. Box 739
Fort Collins, CO   80522   (970) 482-2232
Contact: Terry Stanfill, Treas.
E-mail: info@artsalivefc.org; URL: http://artsalivefc.org

Foundation type: Public charity
Limitations: Fellowships to artists residing in Fort Collins, CO.
Financial data: Year ended 06/30/2004. Assets, $51,989 (M); Expenditures, $169,994; Total giving, $85,971; Grants to individuals, totaling $85,971.
Fields of interest: Film/video; Performing arts; Choreography; Music; Literature.
Type of support: Fellowships; Stipends.
Application information: Applications accepted. Application form required.
Initial approach: E-mail.
Applicants should submit the following:
1) SASE
2) Essay
3) Resume
Additional information: Application must also include work samples.
Program description:
Artistic Fellowships: These fellowships support artists in the development and creation of art, believing that their work is essential to the creative vitality of Fort Collins. This award recognizes artistic innovation, integrity and quality among Fort Collins' artists, and promotes public awareness of their work. Up to four outstanding local artists may receive $1,000 fellowships. They will be chosen from, but not restricted to, visual arts, music,

literary arts, choreography, film arts, and new genres and improvisational forms.
EIN: 846048890

5210
Arts and Humanities Council of Montgomery County
801 Ellsworth Dr.
Silver Spring, MD   20910-4438   (301) 565-3805
Contact: Theresa A. Cameron, Exec. Dir.
FAX: (301) 565-3809;
E-mail: info@creativemoco.com; URL: http://www.creativemoco.com/

Foundation type: Public charity
Limitations: Awards a maximum of $3,000 to six individual artists or scholars for their artistic or scholarly development.
Publications: Application guidelines; Annual report; Financial statement; Grants list; Informational brochure.
Financial data: Year ended 06/30/2005. Assets, $397,761 (M); Expenditures, $1,642,955; Total giving, $1,177,760; Grants to individuals, 51 grants totaling $96,279 (high: $3,000, low: $500).
Fields of interest: Media/communications; Visual arts; Performing arts; Humanities.
Type of support: Grants to individuals; Awards/prizes.
Application information: Applications accepted. Application form required. Application form available on the grantmaker's Web site.
Initial approach: Telephone.
Copies of proposal: 6
Deadline(s): June 27
Applicants should submit the following:
1) Work samples
2) Resume
3) Essay
4) Curriculum vitae
5) Budget Information
Additional information: See Web site for additional application information.
Program description:
Awards: Program is intended to recognize the outstanding work of artists and scholars in Montgomery County and to support the development of Montgomery County's finest artists and humanities scholars. Each award provides direct support and may be spent in any way the individual chooses. Art and humanities disciplines for these awards alternate each year. An individual may submit only one application in one discipline each year. See Web site for additional information.
EIN: 521086825

5211
Arts and Humanities Council of Southwest Louisiana, Inc.
809 Kirby St., Ste. 202
P.O. Box 1437
Lake Charles, LA   70602   (337) 439-2787
Contact: Margaret Chalfant, Exec. Dir.
FAX: (337) 439-8009;
E-mail: jfisher@artsandhumanitieswla.org;
URL: http://www.artsandhumanitieswla.org

Foundation type: Public charity
Limitations: Grants to artists in the five-parish southwest LA regions of Allen, Beauregard, Calcasieu, Cameron and Jeff Davis.

Publications: Application guidelines; Annual report; Financial statement; Grants list; Informational brochure; Newsletter.
Financial data: Year ended 08/31/2004. Assets, $267,933 (M); Expenditures, $327,871; Total giving, $170,210.
Fields of interest: Arts.
Type of support: Awards/prizes.
Application information: Application form required. Application form available on the grantmaker's Web site.

> *Deadline(s):* Contact foundation for current application deadline
> *Additional information:* See Web site for further information.

EIN: 720860898

5212

Arts Council of Greater Kalamazoo

359 S. Kalamazoo Mall
Kalamazoo, MI   49007   (269) 342-5059
FAX: (269) 342-6531;
E-mail: info@kalamazooarts.com; URL: http://www.kalamazooarts.com

Foundation type: Public charity
Limitations: Grants to local artists in Kalamazoo County, MI, for innovative projects.
Publications: Application guidelines; Annual report; Biennial report; Grants list; Informational brochure; Informational brochure (including application guidelines); Multi-year report; Newsletter; Program policy statement.
Financial data: Year ended 09/30/2004. Assets, $312,464 (M); Expenditures, $792,714.
Fields of interest: Arts, artist's services; Arts.
Type of support: Program development.
Application information:

> *Initial approach:* Letter or telephone.
> *Additional information:* Contact council for current application deadline/guidelines.

Program descriptions:

Arts Fund of Kalamazoo County: This fund supports organizations and individual artists in Kalamazoo County, MI, through funding for a wide variety of arts projects. Applications are reviewed with artistic quality as the top priority and inclusion of rural/ethnic/minority/tribal emphasis as a special mandate.

Pharmacia & Upjohn Community Arts Grant Program: This program regrants monies to individual artists and organizations of Kalamazoo County, MI, for innovative arts projects which will benefit the community.
EIN: 386121183

5213

Arts Council of Indianapolis, Inc.

20 N. Meridian St., Ste. 500
Indianapolis, IN   46204-3040   (317) 631-3301
Contact: Gregory Charleston, Pres.
FAX: (317) 624-2559;
E-mail: indyarts@indyarts.org; URL: http://www.indyarts.org

Foundation type: Public charity
Limitations: Fellowships to individual artists and arts administrators in IN.
Publications: Application guidelines; Annual report; Informational brochure; Newsletter.
Financial data: Year ended 12/31/2004. Assets, $12,071,592 (M); Expenditures, $4,882,552; Total giving, $2,331,675; Grants to individuals, 30 grants totaling $82,500 (high: $2,750, low: $2,750).
Fields of interest: Arts.

Type of support: Fellowships.
Application information: Application form required. Application form available on the grantmaker's Web site.

> *Initial approach:* Telephone or e-mail.
> *Deadline(s):* Dec.
> *Additional information:* See Web site for further information.

Program description:

Creative Renewal Arts Fellowships Program for Professional Individuals Artists and Arts Administrators: Provides 50 fellowships of $7,500 to professional individual artists and arts administrators. To qualify, arts administrators must be employed by nonprofit arts organizations in central IN (Marion, Boone, Hamilton, Hendricks, Hancock, Morgan, Johnson and Shelby counties).
EIN: 311225893

5214

Arts Council Silicon Valley

4 N. 2nd St., Ste. 210
San Jose, CA   95113   (408) 998-2787
Contact: Diem Jones, Dir., Grant Progs.
FAX: (408) 971-9458;
E-mail: djones@artscouncil.org; URL: http://www.artscouncil.org

Foundation type: Public charity
Limitations: Fellowships to visual and performing artists who are residents of the Silicon Valley, CA, area.
Financial data: Year ended 06/30/2003. Assets, $1,328,012 (M); Expenditures, $1,490,351; Total giving, $412,843; Grants to individuals, 6 grants totaling $18,000 (high: $3,000, low: $3,000).
Fields of interest: Visual arts; Performing arts.
Type of support: Fellowships.
Application information: Applications accepted.

> *Initial approach:* Telephone or e-mail.
> *Deadline(s):* Contact foundation for current application deadline/guidelines

Program description:

Artist Fellowships: Up to six fellowships of $4,000 each are given annually in rotating artistic categories, including visual arts (sculpture and crafts), performing arts (theatre directors and set designers), installation art, literary art and poetry. See Web site for current categories.
EIN: 942825213

5215

Arts International, Inc.

526 W. 26th St., Ste. 516
New York, NY   10001   (212) 924-0771
Contact: Noreen Tomassi, Pres. and C.E.O.
FAX: (212) 924-0773

Foundation type: Public charity
Limitations: Project grants, travel grants, fellowships, and residencies to performing and visual artists, and arts administrators, to promote global connections and interchange.
Financial data: Year ended 09/30/2003. Assets, $1,511,990 (M); Expenditures, $3,946,752; Total giving, $2,033,865.
Fields of interest: Arts, administration/regulation; Arts, research; Cultural/ethnic awareness; Visual arts; Performing arts; Arts, artist's services; Arts.
Type of support: Program development; Fellowships; Exchange programs; Residencies; Travel grants.
Application information: Contact foundation for current program information.

Program descriptions:

Artists at Giverny: Supports three-month residencies for U.S. visual artists to live, study, research, and create work at Claude Monet's residence and gardens in Giverny, France. Three artists are awarded per year and receive round-trip airfare, a $20,000 fellowship, studio apartment, and shared studio space. For more information, e-mail giverny@artsinternational.org.

Artists' Exploration Fund: Enables individual performing artists to pursue opportunities abroad that further their artistic development. Grant decisions will be based on artistic excellence, the applicant's reasons for wanting to travel to a particular country, and the scope and feasibility of the work to be done there. Grants, ranging from $1,000 to $3,000, will support a variety of activities including development of relationships with artists and organizations, research of significant artistic expression, participation in international conferences and seminars, or creation of new work. Grants will not support travel costs related to touring. Eligible expenses may include international and in-country travel, food and lodging, and other essential costs. Applicants must be U.S. residents or permanent residents. Students, scholars, curators, critics, presenters, and administrators are not eligible.

California Presenters Initiative: Irvine Presenter Fellowships: Supports the professional advancement of individual leaders who have substantial responsibility for program decision-making within a performing arts presenting organization in CA. Fellowship activities may include research involving outside experts, participation in meetings, conferences or classes, or travel that advances artistic understanding. Applicants must be sponsored by non-profit organizations, and must be an established resident of CA. Deadlines vary.

FACE Croatia: U.S./Croatian Cultural Exchange Grants: Aims to increase awareness and appreciation for Croatian arts and culture through exchange opportunities. The program is restricted to professional artists and/or arts administrators and does not include education initiatives for students. Applications by proposal are accepted throughout the year. For more information, e-mail facecroatia@artsinternational.org.

Fund for U.S. Artists: Provides up to $25,000 to U.S. artists invited to participate in major international performing arts festivals and recurring visual arts exhibitions. Applicants must be performing artists working at a professional level who are U.S. citizens or permanent residents. Preference will be given to applicants invited to festivals in areas where U.S. work is not frequently seen, such as Africa, Asia, and Latin America. Support generally ranges from $1,000 to $15,000.

International Touring Pilot Program: Awards $1,000 to $10,000 to American performing artists to travel to places where U.S. work is less frequently seen, such as Africa, Latin America, and Asia.
EIN: 133084708

5216

The Arts Partnership of Greater Spartanburg

385 S. Spring St.
Spartanburg, SC   29306   (864) 542-2787
Contact: Everett G. Powers, Pres.
FAX: (864) 948-5353;
E-mail: epowers@spartanarts.org; URL: http://www.spartanarts.org

Foundation type: Public charity

Limitations: Grants to artists in SC for travel, educational, and other expenses to enhance their careers and promote professional artistic development.
Financial data: Year ended 06/30/2004. Assets, $32,867,990 (M); Expenditures, $1,406,414; Total giving, $761,186.
Fields of interest: Arts.
Type of support: Fellowships; Residencies; Travel grants.
Application information: Applications accepted. Application form required.
   Initial approach: Telephone.
   Deadline(s): Jan. 2, Apr. 1, July 1 and Oct. 1;
Program description:
   Professional Artists: Awards from $100 to $1,000 to artists in support of travel, registration fees, educational expenses or other costs directly associated with general cultural programming within the context of career enhancement, professional artistic development, business or management skills development, artistic fellowships or residencies.
EIN: 570986224

5217

The ASCAP Foundation

1 Lincoln Plz.
New York, NY   10023-7142
Contact: Colleen McDonough, Dir.
FAX: (212) 595-3342;
E-mail: ascpfoundation@ascap.com; URL: http://www.ascapfoundation.org

Foundation type: Public charity
Limitations: Awards to new and established composers.
Publications: Application guidelines; Annual report; Informational brochure; Newsletter.
Financial data: Year ended 12/31/2003. Assets, $4,999,605 (M); Expenditures, $714,384; Total giving, $407,039; Grants to individuals, totaling $60,550.
Fields of interest: Theater (musical); Orchestra (symphony); Music composition.
Type of support: Awards/grants by nomination only; Awards/prizes.
Application information: Applications accepted. Application form required. Application form available on the grantmaker's Web site.
   Initial approach: Letter or telephone.
   Deadline(s): Dec. 1
Program descriptions:
   Sammy Cahn Award: Given by nomination only to a promising lyricist from the ASCAP Songwriter Workshop Series.
   Morton Gould Young Composer Awards: Cash prizes are awarded to composers who are U.S. residents under 30 years of age. Music submitted may be in any genre, but it must be a complete score.
   Rudolf Nissim Prize: Awards a cash prize annually to an ASCAP member composer for an orchestral work written for a large ensemble, requiring a conductor, which has not been performed professionally.
   Richard Rodgers Award: Given by nomination only to a veteran composer or lyricist of musical theater.
   Richard Rodgers New Horizons Award: Given by nomination only to recognize and encourage promising young composers or lyricists of musical theater.
EIN: 510181769

5218

The Asia Society

725 Park Ave.
New York, NY   10021-5088   (212) 288-6400
Contact: Nicholas Platt, Pres.
FAX: (212) 517-8315; E-mail: info@asiaoc.org;
Additional tel.: (888) ASK-ASIA; (888) FAX-ASIA;
URL: http://www.asiasociety.org/education/programs.html

Foundation type: Public charity
Limitations: Prizes awarded annually to a writer who has produced the best example of journalism about Asia in print or online during the calendar year.
Financial data: Year ended 12/31/2003. Assets, $107,766,074 (M); Expenditures, $18,450,755; Total giving, $208,850.
Fields of interest: Journalism/publishing.
Type of support: Awards/prizes.
Application information:
   Initial approach: Letter or e-mail.
   Deadline(s): Mar. 1
   Additional information: Contact foundation for application guidelines and complete program information.
Program description:
   Osborn Elliott Prize: The $10,000 prize is awarded annually to a writer who has produced the best example of journalism about Asia in print or online during the calendar year. Criteria for the prize include consideration for the impact of the work, its originality, creativity, depth of research, and educational value in informing the public about Asia. An independent jury of distinguished writers, award-winning journalists, and Asia-hands will review nominations for the prize from both media organizations and journalists. All nominations or direct applications are limited to one per organization or journalist. For the purposes of this award, "Asia" is termed as defined by the Asia Society, comprising countries from Iran eastward to and including Australia and New Zealand. It does not include the Arab Middle East.
EIN: 133234632

5219

Asian Cultural Council

437 Madison Ave., 37th Fl.
New York, NY   10022-7001   (212) 812-4300
Contact: Ralph Samuelson, Dir.
FAX: (212) 812-4299; E-mail: acc@accny.org;
URL: http://www.asianculturalcouncil.org

Foundation type: Public charity
Limitations: Fellowships and residencies for cultural research and study on topics relating to Asian art and religion and the humanities.
Publications: Application guidelines; Annual report; Informational brochure.
Financial data: Year ended 12/31/2004. Assets, $36,099,285 (M); Expenditures, $4,001,358; Total giving, $1,319,821; Grants to individuals, 136 grants totaling $1,319,821 (high: $32,300, low: $1,000).
Fields of interest: Cultural/ethnic awareness; Film/video; Visual arts; Architecture; Photography; Art conservation; Performing arts; Dance; Theater; Music; Humanities; Art history; History/archaeology; Arts, artist's services; Arts; International studies; Religion.
Type of support: Program development; Conferences/seminars; Professorships; Fellowships; Research; Grants to individuals; Exchange programs; Foreign applicants; Residencies; Travel grants; Doctoral support.
Application information: Application form required.

   Initial approach: Letter or telephone.
   Deadline(s): Feb. 1 (and Aug. 1 for a small number of requests)
   Additional information: Application by letter outlining project; Applications not accepted by FAX or e-mail.
Program descriptions:
   ACC Residency Program: Assists individual American artists, scholars, and professionals undertaking research, teaching and creative residencies at cultural and educational institutions in East and Southeast Asia. Projects supported demonstrate close collaboration in design and execution between the visiting American specialist and the host organization, and produce tangible results such as publication, course development, or the creation of new artistic work.
   Asian Art and Religion Fellowships: Research fellowships, visiting professorships, and travel grants are awarded to American scholars, specialists, and artists wishing to conduct research and undertake projects in South, Southeast, and East Asia. The focus of the recipient's project should be on the relationship between artistic and religious traditions in Asia. Fellowships range in duration from one to six months.
   Humanities Fellowships: This program provides support to American scholars, doctoral students, and specialists in the humanities for research, and specialists in the humanities for research and study in South, Southeast, and East Asia in the following fields: archaeology; art conservation; musicology; and the theory, history, and criticism of architecture, art, dance, design, film, music, photography, and theater. Support is also provided to American and Asian scholars participating in conferences, exhibitions, visiting professorships, and similar projects. Fellowships range in duration from one to nine months.
   Japan-United States Arts Program Fellowships: Fellowships to encourage the study and understanding of the art and culture of Japan and the U.S. are available to American and Japanese artists, scholars, and specialists in the visual and performing arts. Recipients receive support to travel to the U.S. (if Japanese) or to Japan (if American) for research, observation, and creative work for a period ranging from one to six months.
EIN: 133018822

5220

Association of Performing Arts Presenters

1112 16th St., N.W., Ste. 400
Washington, DC   20036   (202) 833-2787
Contact: Prog. Assoc.: Rachel Ferrara
FAX: (202) 833-1543;
E-mail: theatretravel@artspresenters.org;
URL: http://www.artspresenters.org/

Foundation type: Public charity
Limitations: Travel grants to theater directors, producers, presenters, managers, artists, and agents to see work by ensemble theatre companies who have initiated a dialogue with them about a long-term partnership.
Publications: Application guidelines.
Financial data: Year ended 06/30/2004. Assets, $2,553,773 (M); Expenditures, $3,092,020; Total giving, $46,206.
Fields of interest: Arts, management/technical aid; Theater.
Type of support: Travel grants.
Application information: Applications accepted. Application form required. Application form available on the grantmaker's Web site.

Initial approach: E-mail.
Deadline(s): April 4 for travel during June-Dec., Sept. 9 for travel during Oct.-Apr.
Applicants should submit the following:
1) Resume
2) Essay
3) Budget Information

Program description:
Travel Subsidy Grants: In addition, artistic, production, education, publicity, or marketing staff at ensemble theater companies are also eligible for funds to visit a potential host theater or arts presenter in order to effectively prepare for an engagement at least 6-12 months in advance. The travel must have educational purposes that will assist the individual traveling in making more informed decisions in communicating about and/or managing an existing project or collaboration between an ensemble theatre and a theatre partner, or an arts presenter partner or consortia of theatres and arts presenters. The travel fund will reimburse up to $2,000 to cover the real cost of one roundtrip airfare and per diem, not to exceed $40 per day for up to 10 days. Per diems will be based on the total amount of days traveled. Maximum subsidy per person is $2,000 annually. See http://www.artspresenters.org/services/travelgrants.cfm for further details.
EIN: 391131995

5221
Association of Writers and Writing Programs

c/o Carty House, Mail Stop 1E3
George Mason University
Fairfax, VA   22030-4444   (703) 993-4301
Contact: Matt Burriesci, Assoc. Dir.
FAX: (703) 993-4302;
E-mail: chronicle@awpwriter.org; URL: http://www.awpwriter.org

Foundation type: Public charity
Limitations: Awards to writers and poets. Also, scholarships for emerging writers to attend a writer's conference.
Publications: Application guidelines; Annual report; Informational brochure; Informational brochure (including application guidelines); Newsletter.
Financial data: Year ended 06/30/2005. Assets, $1,283,637 (M); Expenditures, $1,304,950.
Fields of interest: Literature.
Type of support: Conferences/seminars; Scholarships—to individuals; Awards/prizes; Workstudy grants.
Application information: Applications accepted. Application form required.
Initial approach: E-mail.
Deadline(s): Aug. 1 for George Garrett Award, Mar. 1 for scholarships
Applicants should submit the following:
1) SASE
Additional information: Applications should also include entry fee and manuscripts. See Web site for additional application information.

Program descriptions:
Donald Hall Prize for Poetry: An award of $4,000 and publication for the best book-length manuscript of poetry. This competition is open to published and unpublished poets alike.
Grace Paley Prize in Short Fiction: Awards the winner $4,000 and publication.
Novel and Creative Nonfiction: Awards $2,000 cash honorarium from AWP and publication by a participating press.
George Garrett Award for Outstanding Community Service in Literature: The award will be given to a

nominated individual who has demonstrated exceptional generosity to writers by excellent work in one or more of the following activities: teaching creative writing and literature; serving as a mentor, supporter, or guide to writers; publishing or editing literature, especially works by emerging or neglected talents; building new resources that benefit writers (reading series, presses, awards, endowments, fellowships, stipends, programs, community centers, foundations, etc.); administering to programs or institutions that benefit writers or that expand audiences for contemporary authors; working generally to make North America a more supportive place for contemporary literature and its makers. The award will include a $1,000 honorarium from AWP in addition to travel, accommodations, and registration for attending the AWP Annual Conference, where the award will be publicly announced and conferred.
WC&C Scholarship Competition: Writers' Conferences & Centers is conducting its annual competition to provide scholarships for emerging writers who wish to attend a writer's conference. The scholarships will be applied to fees to attend any of the member conferences of WC&C, an association of outstanding conferences, colonies, and festivals for writers. The competition is open to all writers who would like to attend a member conference of WC&C. Two scholarships of $500 will be awarded.
EIN: 050314999

5222
The Astraea Lesbian Foundation for Justice, Inc.

(formerly ASTRAEA, National Lesbian Action Foundation)
116 E. 16th St., 7th Fl.
New York, NY   10003-2112   (212) 529-8021
Contact: Katherine T. Acey, Exec. Dir.
FAX: (212) 982-3321;
E-mail: info@astraeafoundation.org; URL: http://www.astraeafoundation.org/

Foundation type: Public charity
Limitations: Grants to emerging lesbian writers and scholarships to female undergraduate activists.
Publications: Application guidelines; Annual report; Grants list; Informational brochure; Newsletter.
Financial data: Year ended 06/30/2004. Assets, $4,570,521 (M); Expenditures, $3,059,451; Total giving, $996,169; Grants to individuals, 24 grants totaling $75,907 (high: $10,000, low: $100).
Fields of interest: Visual arts; Literature; Women; LGBTQ.
Type of support: Support to graduates or students of specific schools; Awards/grants by nomination only; Awards/prizes; Undergraduate support.
Application information: Applications accepted. Application form required.
Initial approach: Letter, telephone, or e-mail.
Deadline(s): June 30 for Lesbian Writer's Fund; Mar. 31 for Lesbian Visual Artists; Nov. 15 for Karle Scholarships
Additional information: Guidelines can be downloaded from Web site.

Program description:
Artist Fund: The foundation provides support to individuals through the following funds:
· Lesbian Writers Fund: One grant of $10,000 and two grants of $1,500 are awarded to emerging lesbian writers in each of the fields of poetry and fiction
· Margot Karle Scholarship: One $1,000 grant is awarded to a full-time female

undergraduate activist attending a City University of New York (CUNY) school
· Lesbian Visual Artists: Two grants of $2,500 each to lesbian visual artists. Applicants must be U.S. citizens.
EIN: 132992977

5223
Atlantic Center for the Arts, Inc.

1414 Art Center Ave.
New Smyrna Beach, FL   32168   (386) 427-6975
Contact: Ann Brady, Exec. Dir.
FAX: (386) 427-5669;
E-mail: program@atlanticcenterforthearts.org;
URL: http://www.atlanticcenterforthearts.org

Foundation type: Public charity
Limitations: Residencies to artists of all disciplines for participation in the Atlantic Center for the Arts program.
Publications: Application guidelines; Annual report; Informational brochure; Newsletter.
Financial data: Year ended 12/31/2003. Assets, $8,148,514 (M); Expenditures, $1,369,929. No monetary support given for residencies.
Fields of interest: Visual arts; Performing arts; Literature; International exchange.
Type of support: Exchange programs; Residencies.
Application information: Application form required.
Initial approach: E-mail.
Deadline(s): Varies

Program description:
Residency Program: Residencies provide housing, studio space and meals. The program includes master classes, individual critiques and opportunities for collaboration with artists of varied disciplines. The Atlantic Center also has an international exchange program with France, Japan, Italy and Mexico. Average length of residency is three weeks.
EIN: 591998321

5224
Aurora Project, Inc.

RR 1, Box 224
Aurora, WV   26705   (304) 735-6344
Contact: David King, Pres.
FAX: (304) 735-6643;
E-mail: auroraproject@frontiernet.net

Foundation type: Public charity
Limitations: Residencies to artists specializing in visual arts, film, video, music, and writing, to stay in WV.
Financial data: Year ended 12/31/2003. Assets, $294,639 (M); Expenditures, $8,508; Total giving, $100.
Fields of interest: Film/video; Visual arts; Architecture; Art conservation; Music; Literature.
Type of support: Residencies.
Application information: Applications accepted.
Initial approach: Letter or e-mail.
Deadline(s): Mar. 1 and Sept. 1
Additional information: There is a $20 application fee. Contact foundation for further program information.

Program description:
Aurora Project Residency: This residency is geared towards artists working in visual arts, music, writing, film and video. Architects and historic preservationist will be considered for exploration of new ideas, research and writing residencies. The program includes housing, studio space, and meals. Repeat residencies every three years.

Average length of residencies is 3-6 weeks. The average number of artists present at one time is 7-14. There is a suggested residency fee of $25, but no one will be turned down due to inability to pay.
EIN: 550783568

5225

Austin Film Society
1901 E. 51st St.
Austin, TX 78723 (512) 322-0145
Contact: Rebecca Campbell, Exec. Dir.
FAX: (512) 322-5192; E-mail: afs@austinfilm.org;
URL: http://www.austinfilm.org

Foundation type: Public charity
Limitations: Awards to film and video artists in TX.
Publications: Application guidelines; Grants list; Informational brochure; Newsletter (including application guidelines); Program policy statement.
Financial data: Year ended 08/31/2003.
Assets, $686,973 (M); Expenditures, $894,803; Total giving, $60,525; Grants to individuals, totaling $60,525.
Fields of interest: Film/video.
Type of support: Internship funds; Awards/prizes.
Application information: Deadline July 1; Completion of formal application required; See Web site for guidelines and application forms.
Program description:
  Texas Filmmakers' Production Fund: Awards one-year grants of up to $15,000 to emerging film and video artists in the state of TX. The foundation has awarded $403,000 to over 140 individuals for film and video projects. Awards are provided to artists whose work shows promise, skill and creativity.
EIN: 742433823

5226

The Authors League Fund
31 E. 28th St., 10th Fl.
New York, NY 10016
E-mail: authlgfund@aol.com

Foundation type: Operating foundation
Limitations: Loans, which do not have to be repaid, to authors with immediate need.
Financial data: Year ended 12/31/2002.
Assets, $5,478,502 (M); Expenditures, $323,243; Total giving, $186,420; Loans to individuals, 60 loans totaling $186,420.
Fields of interest: Literature.
Type of support: Loans—to individuals.
Application information: Application form required.
  Deadline(s): Applications accepted throughout the year.
  Applicants should submit the following:
    1) Financial information
EIN: 131966496

5227

The George Balanchine Foundation, Inc.
161 W. 61st St., Ste. 1N
New York, NY 10023-7400 (212) 262-0700
FAX: (212) 262-2892;
E-mail: information@balanchine.org; URL: http://www.balanchine.org

Foundation type: Public charity
Limitations: Support to dancers participating in The Interpretive Archives of George Balanchine and The Balanchine Essays programs, as well as occasional

grants to individuals working on projects related to the foundation's mission.
Publications: Informational brochure.
Financial data: Year ended 12/31/2004.
Assets, $516,085 (M); Expenditures, $473,498; Total giving, $187,107.
Fields of interest: Dance; Choreography.
Type of support: Program development.
Application information: Unsolicited applications not accepted for most grants.
EIN: 133180628

5228

Ballet Hispanico of New York, Inc.
167 W. 89th St.
New York, NY 10024-1904 (212) 362-6710
Contact: Thomas W. Ostrander, Pres.
FAX: (212) 362-7809;
E-mail: info@ballethispanico.org; URL: http://www.ballethispanico.org

Foundation type: Public charity
Limitations: Scholarships to students at the Ballet Hispanico School of Dance, NY.
Financial data: Year ended 06/30/2004.
Assets, $6,593,088 (M); Expenditures, $3,127,906; Total giving, $118,400; Grants to individuals, 142 grants totaling $118,400 (high: $2,240, low: $200).
Fields of interest: Dance; Performing arts, education.
Type of support: Scholarships—to individuals.
Application information: Contact foundation for current application deadline/guidelines.
EIN: 132685755

5229

Baltimore Clayworks, Inc.
5707 Smith Ave.
Baltimore, MD 21209 (410) 578-1919
Contact: Deborah Bedwell, Exec. Dir.; fellowships: Karen Moreau Ceballos
FAX: (410) 578-0058;
E-mail: karen.ceballos@baltimoreclayworks.org;
URL: http://www.baltimoreclayworks.org

Foundation type: Public charity
Limitations: Residencies to clay artists.
Financial data: Year ended 12/31/2003.
Assets, $2,414,839 (M); Expenditures, $1,030,033.
Fields of interest: Sculpture.
Type of support: Residencies; Stipends.
Application information: Applications accepted. Application form required. Application form available on the grantmaker's Web site.
  Initial approach: E-mail.
  Deadline(s): June 15
  Applicants should submit the following:
    1) SASE
    2) Letter(s) of recommendation
    3) Resume
  Additional information: See Web site for additional program information.
Program description:
  Lorimina Salter Fellowship: Residency includes a year of studio space, a $100/month stipend, a solo exhibition, and access to facilities.
EIN: 521409133

5230

The Barakat Foundation
6892 S. Yosemite Ct., Ste. 2-105
Centennial, CO 80112 (303) 770-0187
Contact: Mohannad S. Malas, Pres.
FAX: (720) 489-6052; E-mail: mmalas@msn.com

Foundation type: Independent foundation
Limitations: Scholarships and other support to graduate students in specified fields of Islamic art, who have been accepted to any accredited university.
Financial data: Year ended 12/31/2004.
Assets, $126,043 (M); Expenditures, $31,071; Total giving, $30,520; Grants to individuals, 4 grants totaling $30,520 (high: $17,520, low: $1,500).
Fields of interest: Arts education; Art conservation; Art history; Islam.
Type of support: Program development; Conferences/seminars; Publication; Research; Graduate support; Travel grants; Workstudy grants.
Application information: Applications accepted. Application form required.
  Initial approach: Letter outlining financial need.
  Additional information: Applications accepted throughout the year, which must include academic and financial information and two references. Interviews required.
EIN: 752249402

5231

Barbershop Harmony Society
(formerly Society for the Preservation & Encouragement of Barbershop Quartet Singing in America, also known as SPEBSQSA - Far Western District)
313 Hash Ct.
Petaluma, CA 94952
Contact: Robb Ollett

Foundation type: Public charity
Limitations: Travel assistance to district quartets and chorus representatives to attend international conventions, primarily in AZ, CA, HI, and NV.
Financial data: Year ended 12/31/2004.
Assets, $115,801 (M); Expenditures, $123,946; Total giving, $11,879; Grants to individuals, totaling $11,879.
Fields of interest: Music (choral); Music ensembles/groups.
Type of support: Conferences/seminars; Travel grants.
Application information: Contact foundation for current application deadline/guidelines.
Program description:
  Youth Harmony: Send students to workshops sponsored by SPEBSQSA, paying for housing, tuition and travel.
EIN: 956085839

5232

Robert T. Bates Foundation
c/o First Iowa State Bank
19 Benton Ave. E.
Albia, IA 52531 (641) 932-2144
Contact: Raymond H. Davis, Pres., First Iowa State Bank

Foundation type: Independent foundation
Limitations: Grants to individuals for historic preservation projects in Albia, IA.
Financial data: Year ended 12/31/2004.
Assets, $2,696,111 (M); Expenditures, $88,434; Total giving, $26,924; Grants to individuals, totaling $12,201.

Fields of interest: Historic preservation/historical societies.
Type of support: Grants to individuals.
Application information: Applications by letter accepted throughout the year.
EIN: 421392613

5233
Frank Huntington Beebe Fund for Musicians
c/o Welch & Forbes
45 School St.
Boston, MA 02108 (617) 585-1267
Contact: Carol B. Woodworth, Exec. Secy.
Application address: 290 Huntington Ave., Boston, MA 02115

Foundation type: Independent foundation
Limitations: Travel grants to talented, advanced-level musicians to pursue music study abroad, primarily in Europe.
Financial data: Year ended 11/30/2004. Assets, $1,360,930 (M); Expenditures, $49,579; Total giving, $25,400; Grants to individuals, 3 grants totaling $25,400 (high: $9,300; low: $8,000).
Fields of interest: Music.
Type of support: Travel grants.
Application information: Application form required. Application form available on the grantmaker's Web site.
   Initial approach: Letter requesting application after Oct. 1.
   Deadline(s): Dec. 15
   Applicants should submit the following:
   1) Letter(s) of recommendation
   2) Transcripts
   3) Proposal
   Additional information: Semifinalists notified in Feb.
Program description:
   Fellowship Fund: Provides fellowships for gifted young musicians, generally performers and composers in classical disciplines, who wish to pursue advanced music study and performance abroad, usually in Europe. Fellowships are awarded to musicians at the outset of their professional lives, for whom this would be the first extended period of study abroad. Applicants must demonstrate a solid base of accomplishment in order to be considered and are generally not older than their mid-twenties. A strong, well-planned project of study will enhance the applicant's life in music must be proposed. Enrollment in a school or university is not required unless such study is an essential part of the project. The fund provides financial support and transportation, living and other expenses, approximately $16,000. Fellowships are for one year and are generally not renewable.
EIN: 046112830

5234
The Behnke Foundation
(formerly Skinner Foundation)
601 Union St., Ste. 3016
Seattle, WA 98101 (206) 623-5449
Contact: Michelle McBride
FAX: (206) 623-6138;
E-mail: behnkefoundation@aol.com

Foundation type: Company-sponsored foundation
Limitations: Fellowships by nomination only to artists residing in the greater Seattle, WA, area.

Publications: Application guidelines; Annual report; Informational brochure (including application guidelines).
Financial data: Year ended 12/31/2004. Assets, $2,529,544 (M); Expenditures, $125,979; Total giving, $96,925.
Fields of interest: Visual arts; Painting.
Type of support: Fellowships; Awards/grants by nomination only.
Application information: Application form required.
   Initial approach: E-mail.
   Deadline(s): Contact foundation for current application deadline.
Program description:
   The Neddy Artist Fellowship: Two $10,000 fellowships are given, one for painting and one in a rotating discipline. Additionally, each nominated artist receives $1,000.
EIN: 916025144

5235
Bemis Center for Contemporary Arts, Inc.
724 S. 12th St.
Omaha, NE 68102 (402) 341-7130
Contact: Mark Masuoka, Exec. Dir.
FAX: (402) 341-9791;
E-mail: info@bemiscenter.org; URL: http://www.bemiscenter.org

Foundation type: Public charity
Limitations: Residencies to visual artists for a period of three to six months.
Financial data: Year ended 12/31/2003. Assets, $2,006,063; Expenditures, $620,557. No monetary support given for residencies.
Fields of interest: Visual arts; Disabilities, people with.
Type of support: Residencies.
Application information: Applications accepted.
   Deadline(s): Sept. 30 and Apr. 30
   Additional information: Contact foundation for current application guidelines; Application fee of $35 is required; See Web site for complete program guidelines.
Program description:
   Residency Program: Artists may be eligible for $750 per month stipends. Residencies usually last three to six months. Artists are provided with living quarters and studio space. Artists in wheelchairs can be accommodated.
EIN: 470653927

5236
Birmingham-Bloomfield Symphony Orchestra
1592 Buckingham
Birmingham, MI 48009 (248) 645-2276
Contact: Carla D. Lamphere, Exec. Dir.
Application address: c/o Millicent Berry, 25435 Wareham, Huntington Woods, MI 48070;
URL: http://www.bbso.org/pages/9/index.htm

Foundation type: Public charity
Limitations: Awards to MI musicians in grades 6-12 who win the Instrument & Piano Young Artist Concerto Competition.
Publications: Informational brochure; Informational brochure (including application guidelines).
Financial data: Year ended 06/30/2004. Assets, $28,770 (M); Expenditures, $114,321.
Fields of interest: Orchestra (symphony).
Type of support: Awards/prizes.
Application information: Applications accepted. Application form required.
   Deadline(s): Feb. 28

   Applicants should submit the following:
   1) SASE
   Additional information: Application should also include $35 application fee.
Program description:
   Instrument & Piano Young Artist Concerto Competition: The Senior Division is for grades 9-12 and the Junior Division is for grades 6-8. Note that Piano Competition is for Senior Division Only. Senior winner in both categories performs at BBSO concert with orchestra and receives $750. Junior winner in instrument category receives $200.
EIN: 382088537

5237
Black Rock Arts Foundation
1900 3rd St., 2nd Fl.
San Francisco, CA 94158 (415) 626-1248
Contact: Leslie Pritchett, Exec. Dir.
E-mail: info@blackrockarts.org; URL: http://www.blackrockarts.org

Foundation type: Public charity
Limitations: Grants to artists for the creation of community-based interactive art projects.
Financial data: Year ended 12/31/2003. Assets, $26,655 (M); Expenditures, $38,336; Total giving, $18,750; Grants to individuals, 5 grants totaling $18,750 (high: $15,000; low: $500).
Fields of interest: Visual arts.
Type of support: Seed money.
Application information: Applications accepted. Application form required.
   Initial approach: E-mail.
   Additional information: Contact foundation for further application information.
EIN: 912130056

5238
Blacklock Nature Sanctuary
P.O. Box 426
Moose Lake, MN 55767-0426 (612) 802-6155
Contact: Harriet Barlow, Exec. Dir.
URL: http://www.blacklock.org

Foundation type: Public charity
Limitations: Residencies to emerging artists residing in MN and to female nature photographers.
Publications: Application guidelines.
Financial data: Year ended 12/31/2004. Assets, $1,315,385 (M); Expenditures, $42,794; Total giving, $8,300; Grants to individuals, totaling $8,300.
Fields of interest: Media/communications; Visual arts; Photography; Sculpture; Painting; Performing arts; Theater (playwriting); Literature; Women.
Type of support: Residencies.
Application information: Deadline Jan. 31; Completion of formal application required, including samples, resume, proposal and SASE.
Program descriptions:
   Emerging Artists Residency: Four positions are available to MN emerging artists who wish to work solo or in collaboration with others, or with a mentor (defined as an established or mid-career artist) on an artistic project may apply for the month-long residency. A stipend of $2,000 to cover food & supplies may be offered. Two positions are available to MN emerging artists who wish to work alone, in collaboration, or with a mentor for two weeks. Stipend includes $1,000 to cover food or supplies.
   Nadine Blacklock Nature Photography Residency for Women: One woman nature photographer will be selected for a month-long residency. The purpose

of the program is to give recognition to women working in the nature photography genre and allow them access to the subject matter found at the Blacklock Nature Sanctuary. Successful proposals will connect and build upon Nadine Blacklock's aesthetic sensibilities. Housing is included but there is no stipend.

EIN: 411794361

5239
Leni Fe Bland Foundation
2059 Boundary Dr.
Santa Barbara, CA 93108
Application address: P.O. Box 41114, Santa Barbara, CA 93140

Foundation type: Independent foundation
Limitations: Awards of merit and encouragement to instrumentalists and vocalists who are U.S. citizens and residents of CA. Recipients must use their awards to further their musical knowledge and careers.
Financial data: Year ended 12/31/2004. Assets, $6,923 (M); Expenditures, $77,136; Total giving, $74,750; Grants to individuals, totaling $74,750.
Fields of interest: Music; Performing arts, education.
Type of support: Awards/prizes.
Application information:
  Deadline(s): Apr.
  Additional information: Completion of formal application required, including performance tape; Auditions required for finalists.
EIN: 330451431

5240
BMI Foundation, Inc.
320 W. 57th St.
New York, NY 10019-3705
Contact: Ralph N. Jackson, Pres.
E-mail: info@bmifoundation.org; TN tel.: (615) 401-2411; URL: http://www.bmifoundation.org

Foundation type: Public charity
Limitations: Awards, commissions, and fellowships to music composers.
Financial data: Year ended 12/31/2003. Assets, $1,476,769 (M); Expenditures, $138,248; Total giving, $135,450; Grants to individuals, 29 grants totaling $57,450 (high: $7,500, low: $100).
Fields of interest: Theater (musical); Music; Music composition.
Type of support: Fellowships; Awards/grants by nomination only; Awards/prizes.
Application information:
  Initial approach: E-mail.
  Deadline(s): May 31 for Woody Gunthrie Fellowship
  Additional information: See Web site for additional program information and eligibility.
Program descriptions:
  The Woody Guthrie Fellowship: This program includes short-term fellowships to support scholarly use of the Woody Guthrie Archives Research Collection. A limited number of fellowships will be selected with a value of up to $2,500 per recipient to help defray travel to New York City and residence expenses for the duration of the fellowship. The length of the fellowship will depend on the applicant's research proposal, but is normally limited from one to six months. The Woody Guthrie Fellowship program invites applicants who are pursuing research topics or themes related to Woody Guthrie which explore his creative work and

contribution to American music and culture. Disciplines may include, but are not limited to American Musicology, Historical Musicology, Ethnomusicology, Cultural Studies, Social Sciences, Humanities, and American History. The application must include a C.V. and proposal. See Web site for additional application information.
  The Pete Carpenter Fellowship: This fellowship gives aspiring TV and film composers the opportunity to work with the eminent composer Mike Post at his studio in Los Angeles. The fellowship, which usually runs 4-5 weeks, includes a $2,000 stipend for travel and expenses and there are opportunities to meet with other distinguished theatrical, film and television composers and leaders in the entertainment industry. The fellowships are presented annually and are open to any composer under the age of 35. There is no citizenship requirement. Questions may be directed to carpenterfellowship@bmifoundation.org.
  The Charlie Parker Jazz Composition Prize: This prize is awarded annually to the best new work created in the BMI Jazz Composers Workshop and is named for the jazz legend, Charlie Parker. The winner is chosen by a distinguished panel of judges at the annual workshop showcase concert, held each year in New York City. Included in the prize is a $3,000 commission to write a new work to be premiered at the following years showcase concert.
  The Carlos Surinach Commissioning Program: This program funds the creation of new works by former winners of the BMI Student Composer Awards. Established by a generous bequest from the late classical composer Carlos Surinach, the program identifies orchestras, chamber music groups and classical soloists with a strong record of performing contemporary music. For each commission, the selected performer or organization chooses a former BMI Student Composer Award-winning composer and premieres the commissioned work. This program is by invitation only, no applications accepted.
  The Boudleaux Bryant Commissioning Program: This program funds the creation of new chamber works by former winners of the BMI Student Composer Awards. Awarded on a regular basis, these commissions were established through the generosity of the family and friends of the late celebrated songwriter, Boudleaux Bryant. For each commission, the BMI Foundation chooses a prominent contemporary music performer or organization and they in turn select a former BMI Student Composer Award-winning composer to write the commissioned work. This program is by invitation only, no applications accepted.
  The Jerry Bock Award for Excellence in Musical Theatre: The Jerry Bock Award for Excellence in Musical Theatre is given to a project developed in the BMI Lehman Engel Musical Theatre Workshop. The Award is a $2,000 grant split between the composer and lyricist of the project. The finalists for the Award are recommended by the Workshop Steering Committee and the winner(s) chosen by Mr Bock. This program is by nomination only, no applications accepted.
  The Jerry Harrington Award: The Jerry Harrington Awards For Outstanding Creative Achievement in Musical Theatre are presented annually to a writer in each of the BMI Lehman Engel Musical Theatre Workshop groups - First Year $500, Second Year $600, Advanced $1000 and Librettist $500. The awardees are selected by the moderators of the workshop groups. The award is by nomination only, no applications accepted.
EIN: 133249311

5241
The Bogliasco Foundation, Inc.
885 2nd Ave., Rm. 3100
New York, NY 10017 (212) 940-8204
E-mail: MAU@bfny.org; URL: http://www.liguriastudycenter.org

Foundation type: Operating foundation
Limitations: Residential fellowships at the Liguria Study Center in Bogliasco, Italy, for individuals doing advanced creative or scholarly work in the arts and humanities.
Financial data: Year ended 12/31/2003. Assets, $2,524,204 (M); Expenditures, $810,314; Total giving, $4,199; Grants to individuals, 2 grants totaling $4,199 (high: $3,000, low: $1,199).
Fields of interest: Film/video; Visual arts; Architecture; Dance; Theater; Music; History/archaeology; Language (classical); Literature; Philosophy/ethics; Landscaping.
Type of support: Fellowships; Residencies.
Application information: Applications accepted. Application form required. Application form available on the grantmaker's Web site.
  Initial approach: Letter or e-mail.
  Deadline(s): Jan.15 and Apr.15
  Additional information: Application should include letters of recommendation, a project description and curriculum vitae.
Program description:
  Bogliasco Fellowships: Fellowships are granted to qualified persons for residencies at the Liguria Study Center in Italy doing advanced creative work or scholarly research in the following disciplines: archaeology, architecture, classics, dance, film or video, history, landscape architecture, literature, music, philosophy, theater, and visual arts. An approved project is presumed to lead to the completion of a major work followed by publication, performance, production, or exhibition. Fellowships are scheduled during the two semesters of the academic year, and usually have a duration of either one month or a half semester. See Web site for further information.
EIN: 133632296

5242
Bossak-Heilbron Charitable Foundation, Inc.
720 Milton Rd.
Rye, NY 10580
Contact: Jane Heilbron, Pres.

Foundation type: Independent foundation
Limitations: Project grants to dancers in NY, Seattle, WA, and the DC area.
Publications: Application guidelines.
Financial data: Year ended 10/31/2004. Assets, $1,696,185 (M); Expenditures, $82,770; Total giving, $77,950; Grants to individuals, totaling $29,500.
Fields of interest: Dance.
Type of support: Program development; Grants to individuals; Awards/prizes.
Application information: Application form required.
  Initial approach: Letter.
  Copies of proposal: 3
  Deadline(s): Mar. 31
  Applicants should submit the following:
    1) Work samples
    2) Proposal
EIN: 133862827

5243
Boulder County Arts Alliance
2590 Walnut St., Ste. 9
Boulder, CO   80302-5700
Contact: Alison Moore, Exec. Dir.
E-mail: info@bouldercountyarts.org; URL: http://
www.bouldercountyarts.org

Foundation type: Public charity
Limitations: Grants and awards for projects and
equipment to artists in Boulder County, CO.
Publications: Application guidelines; Annual report;
Grants list; Informational brochure; Newsletter.
Financial data: Year ended 12/31/2004.
Assets, $1,548,114 (M); Expenditures,
$236,221; Total giving, $100,540.
Fields of interest: Visual arts; Performing arts; Arts,
artist's services; Arts.
Type of support: Program development; Awards/
prizes.
Application information: Applications accepted.
Application form required.
  Initial approach: Letter.
  Additional information: Contact foundation for
    current application deadlines.
Program descriptions:
  AHAB/Addison Mini-Grant Program: Provides
support for individual artist projects, including
equipment purchases. Awards will not exceed
$500, and are given in Jan. and July.
  AHAB/Milash Award: Awards $1,000 to a
representational painter annually.
  AHAB/Neodata Endowment Grant Program:
Supports artistic excellence and promotes stability
among individual artists. Grants range from $1,000
to $2,500, and are given in the categories of
projects/equipment and fellowships.
  AHAB/Tesser Award: For collaborative,
multi-disciplinary performance art. At least two
artists of different disciplines must come together
to create a truly collaborative performance that is a
unique synthesis and new for both the artists and
for Boulder. At least one award, of a minimum of
$2,500, is given annually.
EIN: 840566939

5244
Archie Bray Foundation
2915 Country Club Ave.
Helena, MT   59602   (406) 443-3502
Contact: Josh DeWeese, Resident Dir.
FAX: (406) 443-0934;
E-mail: archiebray@archiebray.org; Contact info. for
Josh DeWeese: tel.: (406) 443-3502, ext. 12,
E-mail: Josh@archiebray.org; URL: http://
www.archiebray.org

Foundation type: Public charity
Limitations: Fellowships to clay artists.
Scholarships are also available to fund three-month
summer residencies.
Financial data: Year ended 12/31/2004.
Assets, $3,639,459 (M); Expenditures,
$635,907; Total giving, $34,721; Grants to
individuals, totaling $34,721.
Fields of interest: Sculpture; Ceramic arts.
Type of support: Fellowships.
Application information: Deadlines Feb. 1 and Mar.
1; Contact foundation for current application
guidelines; Initial approach by letter, telephone, FAX
or e-mail.
Program description:
  Fellowship Fund: One-year residential fellowships
provide a stipend of $5,000. See Web site for
further information.
EIN: 810284022

5245
Brooklyn Arts Exchange, Inc.
421 5th Ave., 3rd Fl.
Brooklyn, NY   11215   (718) 832-0018
Contact: Marya Warshaw, Exec. Dir.
FAX: (718) 832-9189; E-mail: info@bax.org;
URL: http://www.bax.org

Foundation type: Public charity
Limitations: Residencies to dance and theater
artists residing in New York, NY.
Publications: Grants list; Newsletter.
Financial data: Year ended 12/31/2003.
Assets, $74,505 (M); Expenditures, $514,932. No
monetary support given for residencies.
Fields of interest: Dance; Theater.
Type of support: Residencies.
Application information: Applications accepted.
Application form required.
  Initial approach: Letter, telephone or e-mail.
  Deadline(s): Contact foundation for current
    application deadline
Program description:
  AIR Program: Residency includes 200 hours of
studio space, a stipend and an opportunity to
present works in progress.
EIN: 113071458

5246
Buffalo Bayou ArtPark
P.O. Box 70260
Houston, TX   77270-0260   (713) 520-0152
Contact: Kevin Jefferies, Dir.
E-mail: bbap@bbap-houston.org; URL: http://
www.bbap-houston.org

Foundation type: Public charity
Limitations: One residency to an international
artist. Grants also to Houston, TX, artists to develop
local public art projects.
Financial data: Year ended 12/31/2003.
Assets, $24,749 (M); Expenditures, $40,326;
Total giving, $17,500; Grants to individuals, 31
grants totaling $17,500.
Fields of interest: Visual arts; Arts.
Type of support: Foreign applicants; Residencies;
Stipends.
Application information:
  Initial approach: E-mail or telephone.
  Additional information: Application by proposal.
    Contact foundation for application deadlines/
    guidelines.
Program description:
  Artist in Residence and Public Art Projects: The
program seeks to create public art projects in the
Houston, TX, area. The residency provides a stipend
and housing. The size of the stipend depends on
the nature of the proposal and the artist. Stipends
usually start at $1,000. Hand-picked artists must
recently have developed projects over a two-year
period. Also offered are exhibition opportunities on
a rotating basis.
EIN: 760401057

5247
Bush Foundation
E-900 First National Bank Bldg.
332 Minnesota St.
St. Paul, MN   55101   (651) 227-0891
Contact: Anita M. Pampusch, Pres.
FAX: (651) 297-6485;
E-mail: info@bushfoundation.org; URL: http://
www.bushfoundation.org

Foundation type: Independent foundation

Limitations: Fellowships to selected writers,
choreographers, composers, and visual artists
residing in MN, ND, SD, and the 26 counties in
western WI which make up the Ninth Federal
Reserve District. Applicants must be at least 25
years old and have lived in the foundation's area for
12 of the 36 months preceding the application
deadline.
Publications: Application guidelines; Annual report;
Financial statement; Grants list; Informational
brochure; Occasional report; Program policy
statement.
Financial data: Year ended 11/30/2004.
Assets, $732,455,635 (M); Expenditures,
$39,422,963; Total giving, $31,047,370; Grants
to individuals, totaling $2,503,116.
Fields of interest: Folk arts; Film/video; Visual arts;
Photography; Sculpture; Design; Choreography;
Theater (playwriting); Music composition;
Literature; Arts, artist's services; Arts.
Type of support: Program development;
Fellowships; Research.
Application information: Applications accepted.
Application form required. Application form
available on the grantmaker's Web site.
  Initial approach: Letter or telephone.
  Deadline(s): Oct. 22 for Literature, Oct. 29 for
    Film Video and Scriptworks, and Nov. 5 for
    Music Composition
  Additional information: Interviews required;
    Students are ineligible; See Web site for
    complete application and program
    information.
Program description:
  Bush Artist Fellowships Program: The program
provides artists with significant financial support
that enables them to further their work and their
contribution to their communities. Grants of up to
$44,000 each are awarded to visual artists,
writers, composers, film/video artists,
choreographers, multimedia artists, traditional and
folk artists and performance artists who are at least
25 years old and whose work reflects any of the
region's diverse geographic, racial, and aesthetic
communities. The selected counties in western WI
are: Ashland, Barron, Bayfield, Buffalo, Burnett,
Chippewa, Douglas, Dunn, Eau Claire, Florence,
Forest, Iron, La Crosse, Lincoln, Oneida, Pepin,
Pierce, Polk, Price, Rusk, Saint Croix, Sawyer,
Taylor, Trempealeau, Vilas, and Washburn. Up to
15 artists are selected each year. The categories
for 2006 are visual arts, two- and three-dimensional
visual arts, choreography, multimedia, and
performance art. Artists may be at any stage of their
life work from early to mature. Among the qualities
sought in a Fellow are strong vision, creative energy,
and perseverance. Applicants propose a fellowship
plan for 12 to 18 continuous months. Fellowships
must be completed within four years of the award.
Panelists consider the artist's past endeavors and
current work, the impact the fellowship may have on
the applicant's life work and future directions, and
the difference the artist may make in the region as
a result of the fellowship. Recipients may use their
fellowship in many ways in order to further their
work and their contribution to their communities,
including artistic experimentation, continuing a
work-in-progress, accomplishing work not financially
feasible without the fellowship, or for solitary work
and reflection, collaborations, community projects,
travel, research, or any other activity that
contributes to their lives as artists. However,
recipients are expected to devote extended periods
of focused time to the work supported by the
fellowship, which they may define based on their
individual circumstances.
EIN: 416017815

5248

Ella Lyman Cabot Trust, Inc.

c/o Edwards Angell Palmer & Dodge, LLP
111 Huntington Ave., 19th Fl.
Boston, MA   02199
Contact: Mary Jane Gibson, Exec. Secy.
Application address: c/o Brooks Thompson, 109 Rockland St., Holliston, MA 01746

Foundation type: Independent foundation
Limitations: Grants for individual projects of personal significance with a promise of good to others.
Publications: Application guidelines.
Financial data: Year ended 12/31/2004. Assets, $3,334,093 (M); Expenditures, $171,357; Total giving, $135,907; Grants to individuals, 13 grants totaling $135,907 (high: $21,000; low: $2,008).
Fields of interest: Human services.
Type of support: Program development.
Application information: Applications accepted. Application form required.
  Deadline(s): Feb. 15 and Sept. 15
  Applicants should submit the following:
    1) Budget Information
  Additional information: Application proposal must include description of the project, amount of grant requested, and qualifications of the applicant.

Program description:
  Project Support Grant: The trust is interested in giving help to individuals at critical points in their lives in the development of projects which have personal significance to them and, at the same time, show some promise of making a contribution to other people. A project must be strategic and in some way unique for the individual, a turning point perhaps, and not a part of his or her routine professional or occupational efforts. The trust does not give grants for scholarships or fellowships in support of a regular part of a person's academic education; nor are academic research projects pursued as a regular part of a professional career appropriate to this trust. The trust seldom supports the writing and/or publication of a book, the production of a film, or the completion of an artistic work; however, this does not mean that an artist or writer may not submit a proposal if it is unique and has a special humanitarian objective. An artistic project must meet the same criteria as all other projects, with a specific aim of making a contribution for the good of others. The trust is relatively small, and the grants, given twice yearly (May and Nov.), are modest: $1,000-$20,000, most often in the range of $7,000-$12,000. They are typically awarded on a one-time, nonrenewable basis. The recipient of a grant is required to submit a Report of Progress and Expenditure when the project has been completed or the grant expended. The letter of proposal should be typewritten on standard 8.5" x 11" white paper and should not be longer than five pages. It should include:
  · description of the project. Applicant should include desired accomplishment, why it is significant at this particular time in life, and what are the benefits to others
  · amount of grant requested. The budget must declare and justify the amount of the grant requested with an honest, realistic, and detailed account of exactly how the grant will be spent. Bear in mind that the trust does not give grants for salaries or replacement thereof during sabbatical leaves. It does, however, help with living expenses, etc.
  · qualifications of applicant. This need not be a formal curriculum vitae, but applicant must give an explanation of why he/she is

particularly capable of carrying out the project successfully - i.e., skills, talents, training brought to the task
The published closing deadlines are Feb. 15 and Sept. 15, but these deadlines are for completed final applications (after initial approval of the letter of proposal). Letters of proposal should be sent in well before those dates, to allow time for review by the screening committee and for completion of formal application requirements, if the proposal is accepted for consideration. If a proposal comes too late for one period, it can be carried over to the next. The receipt of the letter of proposal will be acknowledged by postcard. After acknowledgement is received, no further action is required until applicant hears from the trust. If that time is extended, the trust regrets any anxiety this delay may cause. Applicants are requested not to send cassettes, videos, and other illustrative materials, unless specifically requested by the trust. These materials will not be returned.
EIN: 042111393

5249

Caldera

224 N.W. 13th Ave., Ste. 304
Portland, OR   97209-2953
FAX: (503) 937-8594; *URL:* http://www.calderaarts.org

Foundation type: Public charity
Limitations: Residencies to artists and writers to foster creativity and a deeper appreciation for the environment.
Publications: Application guidelines; Annual report; Informational brochure.
Financial data: Year ended 12/31/2004. Assets, $8,988,027 (M); Expenditures, $611,218.
Fields of interest: Arts.
Type of support: Residencies.
Application information: Application form required.
  Initial approach: Letter or telephone.
  Copies of proposal: 3
  Deadline(s): June 1
  Applicants should submit the following:
    1) Work samples
    2) Resume
    3) Proposal
    4) Letter(s) of recommendation
  Additional information: Professional non-student applicants are welcomed; Applicants must cover all transportation, supplies and food costs.
EIN: 943235649

5250

California Community Foundation

445 S. Figueroa St., Ste. 3400
Los Angeles, CA   90071   (213) 413-4130
Contact: Alvertha Penny, V.P., Progs.; Catherine Stringer, Dir., Comms.; For grants: Cindy DiGiampaolo, Sr. Prog. Asst.
FAX: (213) 383-2046; *E-mail:* info@ccf-la.org; *URL:* http://www.calfund.org

Foundation type: Community foundation
Limitations: Grants to artists in the greater Los Angeles County, CA, area.
Publications: Application guidelines; Annual report (including application guidelines); Financial statement; Informational brochure; Newsletter.
Financial data: Year ended 06/30/2005. Assets, $762,726,071 (M); Expenditures, $103,547,825; Total giving, $91,295,121.
Fields of interest: Visual arts; Performing arts; Literature; Arts, artist's services.

Type of support: Program development; Awards/ grants by nomination only.
Application information: Applications accepted. Application form required.
  Initial approach: Letter or telephone requesting application.
  Additional information: See program description for more information.
Program descriptions:
  J. Paul Getty Trust Fund for the Visual Arts: This program is for established, mid-career visual artists in the greater Los Angeles area who have worked at least ten years in their field outside of school. Arts organizations in Los Angeles are contacted and asked to nominate one artist.
  Brody Arts Fund: This program is for emerging artists in the greater Los Angeles area who promote cultural diversity. Applications are accepted and are available in Jan. Deadline is in Mar. There are three arts programs that rotate on a three-year cycle: Visual Arts, Performing Arts, and Literary/Media.
EIN: 953510055

5251

California Council for the Humanities

312 Sutter St., Ste. 601
San Francisco, CA   94108-4371
(415) 391-1474
Contact: James Quay, Exec. Dir.
FAX: (415) 391-1312; *E-mail:* info@calhum.org; *URL:* http://www.californiastories.org

Foundation type: Public charity
Limitations: Awards for projects that document aspects of life in CA in film, photography or story form.
Publications: Application guidelines; Biennial report; Financial statement; Informational brochure; Newsletter.
Financial data: Year ended 10/31/2003. Assets, $1,692,640 (L); Expenditures, $2,428,061; Total giving, $916,553.
Fields of interest: Film/video; Photography; Literature; Historical activities.
Type of support: Program development; Grants to individuals.
Application information: Applications accepted. Application form required.
  Initial approach: Proposal.
  Deadline(s): Aug. 1 for California Story Fund, others vary
  Additional information: See Web site for complete listing and information about other projects.
Program description:
  California Story Fund: Awards up to $5,000 for projects that provide opportunities for individual Californians to contribute their stories to the evolvement of the state of CA.
EIN: 942952469

5252

California Institute of Contemporary Arts

c/o F. Klein
4545 Park Blvd., No. 206
San Diego, CA   92116

Foundation type: Independent foundation
Limitations: Grants to CA individuals who have the support of an organization for projects in the arts, including theater, music, visual arts, and cultural education.
Financial data: Year ended 06/30/2005. Assets, $79,405 (M); Expenditures, $14,828; Total giving, $14,500; Grants to individuals, totaling $14,500.

Fields of interest: Visual arts; Performing arts; Theater; Music; Arts, artist's services; Arts.
Type of support: Program development.
Application information: Applications not accepted.
Additional information: Unsolicited requests for funds not considered or acknowledged.
EIN: 330094053

5253
The Camargo Foundation
400 Sibley St., Ste. 125
St. Paul, MN 55101-1928
URL: http://www.camargofoundation.org

Foundation type: Operating foundation
Limitations: Fellowships to scholars, visual artists, photographers, video artists, filmmakers, media artists, composers and writers to stay at the foundation's study center in Cassis, France.
Publications: Biennial report; Informational brochure (including application guidelines).
Financial data: Year ended 12/31/2004.
Assets, $22,753,050 (M); Expenditures, $784,215; Total giving, $715,596; Grants to individuals, 25 grants totaling $87,500.
Fields of interest: Media/communications; Film/video; Visual arts; Photography; Music composition; Literature.
Type of support: Fellowships; Residencies; Stipends.
Application information: Applications accepted. Application form required. Application form available on the grantmaker's Web site.
Deadline(s): Jan. 15
Applicants should submit the following:
1) Curriculum vitae
2) Work samples
3) Resume
4) Proposal
5) Letter(s) of recommendation
Additional information: Application should also include project description; See Web site for further application information.
Program description:
Residential Grants: The program provides free housing, reference library, darkroom, artist's studio, music composition studio, and a $3,500 stipend. A visa is required for a stay in France of more than three months. Residential grants last from three to four months.
EIN: 132622714

5254
Capezio/Ballet Makers Dance Foundation, Inc.
1 Campus Rd.
Totowa, NJ 07512   (973) 595-9000
Contact: Jane Remer, Exec. Dir.
E-mail: dfiorenzi@balletmakers.com

Foundation type: Company-sponsored foundation
Limitations: Awards by nomination only to individuals who contribute to dance and public awareness of dance as an art form.
Publications: Application guidelines; Grants list; Informational brochure (including application guidelines).
Financial data: Year ended 12/31/2004.
Assets, $25,639 (M); Expenditures, $101,088; Total giving, $100,000.
Fields of interest: Dance.
Type of support: Awards/grants by nomination only; Awards/prizes.

Application information: Applications not accepted.
Program description:
Capezio Award: This program awards $10,000 to one individual, company, or organization per year, who has made a significant contribution to the field of American dance. Recipient must be a U.S. citizen. Awardees are chosen by the trustees on the advice of national advisors.
EIN: 136161198

5255
Career Transition for Dancers
c/o C & T Newhouse Center for Dancers
165 W. 46th St., Ste. 701
Actor's Bldg.
New York, NY 10036-2501   (212) 764-0172
Contact: Alexander J. Dube, Exec. Dir.
FAX: (212) 764-0343;
E-mail: info@careertransition.org; URL: http://www.careertransition.org

Foundation type: Public charity
Limitations: Scholarships to current and former dancers for education, career transitions, and entrepreneurial endeavors.
Financial data: Year ended 12/31/2004.
Assets, $2,162,025 (M); Expenditures, $891,757; Total giving, $259,297; Grants to individuals, 177 grants totaling $259,297.
Fields of interest: Dance.
Type of support: Seed money; Undergraduate support.
Application information: Applications accepted.
Initial approach: Telephone.
Deadline(s): Jan. 14, Mar. 17, May 19, July 14, Sept. 15, and Nov. 10.
Additional information: Contact foundation to determine eligibility.
Program description:
Caroline H. Newhouse Scholarship Fund:
EIN: 133488203

5256
Carnegie Fund for Authors
1 Old Country Rd.
Carle Place, NY 11514

Foundation type: Independent foundation
Limitations: Emergency assistance to financially needy writers who have commercially published at least one book of reasonable length which has received reader acceptance.
Financial data: Year ended 12/31/2004.
Assets, $958,377 (M); Expenditures, $18,701; Total giving, $5,500; Grants to individuals, totaling $5,500.
Fields of interest: Literature.
Type of support: Grants for special needs.
Application information: Applications accepted throughout the year; Application by letter, including the author's credentials, their circumstances, and reason why assistance is needed.
Program description:
Emergency Grant: Applicants must have suffered a financial emergency as a result of illness or injury to self, spouse, or dependent child, or some other misfortune that has placed the applicant in pressing, substantial, and verifiable need. The fund does not make loans or grants to permit an applicant to complete a projected or unfinished work for publication.
EIN: 136084244

5257
The Carving Studio & Sculpture Center
636 Marble St.
P.O. Box 495
West Rutland, VT 05777   (802) 438-2097
Contact: Carol Driscoll, Exec. Dir.
FAX: (802) 438-2020;
E-mail: carving@vermontel.net; URL: http://www.carvingstudio.org

Foundation type: Public charity
Limitations: Residencies to sculptors.
Financial data: Year ended 12/31/2004.
Assets, $345,213 (M); Expenditures, $201,417; Total giving, $20,995; Grants to individuals, totaling $20,995.
Fields of interest: Sculpture.
Type of support: Foreign applicants; Residencies.
Application information: Contact foundation for current application deadline/guidelines; Initial approach by letter or e-mail.
Program description:
Residency Program: A typical residency lasts for one month. U.S. and international applicants are eligible. One-week residencies are also available to sculpture artists residing in VT.
EIN: 030325486

5258
Cave Canem Foundation, Inc.
584 Broadway, Ste. 508
New York, NY 10012   (212) 941-5720
Contact: Carolyn Micklem, Exec. Dir.
FAX: (212) 941-5724;
E-mail: cavecanempoets@aol.com; Application address: c/o Cave Canem Poetry Prize, P.O. Box 4286, Charlottesville, VA 22905, tel.: (434) 979-8825; URL: http://www.cavecanempoets.org

Foundation type: Public charity
Limitations: Prizes to African American poets who have not been published by a professional press.
Publications: Application guidelines; Annual report; Informational brochure (including application guidelines).
Financial data: Year ended 12/31/2003.
Assets, $54,058 (M); Expenditures, $165,017.
Fields of interest: Literature.
Type of support: Awards/prizes.
Application information:
Initial approach: Letter, including two copies of manuscript.
Deadline(s): May 15
Program description:
Poetry Prize: A prize of $500 is awarded to an African American poet who has not been published by a professional press. The prize also includes publication by University of Georgia Press, and 50 copies of their book.
EIN: 133932909

5259
The Celebration Foundation
3234 N.E. 62nd Ave.
Portland, OR 97213   (503) 493-9770
Contact: Alan Toribio, Secy.-Treas.

Foundation type: Independent foundation
Limitations: Grants to individuals involved in the arts, primarily in OR, to further their artistic development.
Financial data: Year ended 06/30/2005.
Assets, $80,948 (M); Expenditures, $89,702; Total giving, $72,500; Grants to individuals, totaling $59,500.
Fields of interest: Arts.

Type of support: Grants for special needs.
Application information: Applications accepted throughout the year; Completion of formal application required; Applicant must supply four copies of application plus original.
EIN: 931312787

5260
Center for Alternative Media and Culture

c/o CRM Mgmt.
P.O. Box 778
New York, NY 10013

Foundation type: Operating foundation
Limitations: Grants to filmmakers whose projects focus on civil justice issues.
Financial data: Year ended 12/31/2003.
Assets, $439,855 (M); Expenditures, $43,651; Total giving, $36,000.
Fields of interest: Film/video.
Type of support: Program development.
Application information: Applications accepted.
  Initial approach: Letter.
  Deadline(s): None
EIN: 382415253

5261
Center for Book Arts, Inc.

28 W. 27th St., 3rd Fl.
New York, NY 10001-2609 (212) 481-0295
Contact: Alexander Campos, Exec. Dir.
FAX: (212) 481-9853;
E-mail: info@centerforbookarts.org; URL: http://www.centerforbookarts.org

Foundation type: Public charity
Limitations: Residencies to writers and artists who practice the craft of bookmaking, all of whom are residents of NY.
Financial data: Year ended 12/31/2004.
Assets, $568,084 (M); Expenditures, $451,215.
Fields of interest: Arts.
Type of support: Residencies; Stipends.
Application information:
  Initial approach: Telephone or e-mail.
  Deadline(s): Oct. 1
  Applicants should submit the following:
    1) Resume
  Additional information: Application must also include personal statement and 10 slides of recent work. See Web site for complete application guidelines.
Program descriptions:
  Emerging Artist Program: This program includes studio space, a $500 stipend, materials budget, and a reception and presentation of artist's work.
  Sally Bishop Artist's Residency: The recipient of this award will create a limited edition book and will teach a workshop at The Center during a six-week residency. The residency includes travel expenses, housing a $1,500 stipend, studio space, an assistant and materials budget.
EIN: 132842726

5262
The Center for Photography of Woodstock, Inc.

59 Tinker St.
Woodstock, NY 12498-1236 (845) 679-9957
Contact: Colleen Kenyon, Exec. Dir.
FAX: (845) 679-6337; E-mail: info@cpw.org;
URL: http://cpw.org/

Foundation type: Public charity

Limitations: Fellowships to photographers and artists who use photography and reside in NY state. Full-time students are ineligible.
Publications: Application guidelines; Informational brochure; Program policy statement.
Financial data: Year ended 09/30/2003.
Assets, $371,772; Expenditures, $397,605.
Fields of interest: Visual arts; Photography.
Type of support: Fellowships.
Application information: Applications accepted.
  Deadline(s): Varies
  Additional information: Ten slides or prints of photographs should be submitted; Resume and statement optional; Contact foundation for current application guidelines.
Program description:
  Photographers' Fund Fellowships: Two $1,000 fellowships are given each year for photographers and artists who use the photographic process and reside in the following counties in NY: Albany, Clinton, Columbia, Delaware, Dutchess, Essex, Franklin, Fulton, Greene, Hamilton, Montgomery, Orange, Otsego, Rensselaer, Saratoga, Schenectady, Schohar, Sullivan, Ulster, Warren, and Washington.
EIN: 141592639

5263
Center on Contemporary Art

410 Dexter Ave. N.
Seattle, WA 98109 (206) 728-1980
Contact: Don Hudgins, Exec. Dir.
E-mail: info@cocaseattle.org; URL: http://www.cocaseattle.org

Foundation type: Public charity
Limitations: Awards to artists who win the Northwest Annual Juried Show, held in Seattle, WA.
Financial data: Year ended 12/31/2004.
Assets, $100,080 (M); Expenditures, $214,710.
Fields of interest: Media/communications; Film/video; Photography; Sculpture; Painting; Arts.
Type of support: Awards/prizes.
Application information: Applications accepted. Application form required. Application form available on the grantmaker's Web site.
  Deadline(s): Aug. 15
  Additional information: Application must also include SASE, slides/digital images of recent work and a $25 application fee.
Program description:
  Northwest Annual Juried Show: The competition is open to all professional artists residing in the U.S., Canada, and Mexico who specialize in painting, drawing, photography, sculpture, mixed media, and video. First place winner receives $1,000 and second place winner receives $500.
EIN: 911222655

5264
Central Minnesota Arts Board

114 Fourth Ave. N.
P.O. Box 458
Foley, MN 56329 (320) 968-4290
Contact: Leslie Schumacher, Exec. Dir.
FAX: (320) 968-4291;
E-mail: mail@centralmnartsboard.org; Toll-free tel.: (866) 345-7140; URL: http://www.centralmnartsboard.org

Foundation type: Public charity
Limitations: Awards to outstanding individual artists residing in Benton, Sherburne, Stearns and Wright counties, MN, as well as scholarships to graduating high school seniors in the region who want to further their education in the arts.

Publications: Application guidelines; Newsletter.
Financial data: Year ended 06/30/2004.
Assets, $93,360 (M); Expenditures, $251,195; Total giving, $184,783.
Fields of interest: Arts education; Visual arts; Performing arts; Dance; Music; Performing arts, education; Literature.
Type of support: Awards/prizes; Graduate support; Undergraduate support.
Application information: Applications accepted. Application form required. Application form available on the grantmaker's Web site.
  Initial approach: Letter or telephone.
  Additional information: See Web site or contact foundation for current application deadline.
Program descriptions:
  Individual Artist Awards: These awards are intended to recognize, reward, and encourage outstanding individual artists in central MN; up to four awards, ranging from $2,625 to $3,500 each, are awarded annually. Awards may be used any way the artist wishes. Deadline May 6.
  Scholarships: Support ranging from $1,000 to $1,500 is available to graduating high school seniors who want to further their education in the areas of music, dance, literature, visual arts, and performance art. These are one-time awards. Deadline May 10.
EIN: 411349992

5265
Centrum Foundation

P.O. Box 1158
Port Townsend, WA 98368-0958
(360) 385-3102
FAX: (360) 385-2470; E-mail: info@centrum.org;
URL: http://www.centrum.org

Foundation type: Public charity
Limitations: Residencies to creative thinkers and artists from all genres.
Publications: Application guidelines; Grants list; Newsletter.
Financial data: Year ended 12/31/2004.
Assets, $741,019 (M); Expenditures, $1,881,287. No monetary support given for residencies.
Fields of interest: Film/video; Photography; Sculpture; Performing arts; Theater (playwriting); Music; Opera; Music composition; Literature; Arts; Science; Social sciences.
Type of support: Residencies.
Application information: Applications accepted. Application form required.
  Initial approach: E-mail.
  Deadline(s): Oct. 1
  Applicants should submit the following:
    1) Proposal
    2) Resume
    3) Work samples
  Additional information: Contact foundation for current application guidelines.
Program description:
  Centrum Creative Residency Program: Residencies can last from one week to one month, during Jan. through May, or Sept. through Dec. Studio space and housing are provided.
EIN: 237348302

5266
Chamber Music America
305 7th Ave., 5th Fl.
New York, NY   10001-6008   (212) 242-2022
Contact: Al Pryor, Prog. Off.
E-mail: sdadian@chamber-music.org; FAX: (212)
242-7955; E-mail: info@chamber-music.org;
URL: http://www.chamber-music.org

Foundation type: Public charity
Limitations: Grants and awards to individuals
performing in chamber music ensembles, who are
members of the Chamber Music America
organization.
Publications: Application guidelines; Financial
statement; Grants list; Informational brochure;
Newsletter.
Financial data: Year ended 06/30/2003.
Assets, $8,006,319 (M); Expenditures,
$2,023,286; Total giving, $320,151; Grants to
individuals, 14 grants totaling $152,000 (high:
$12,000, low: $10,000).
Fields of interest: Music; Music ensembles/
groups; Music composition.
Type of support: Conferences/seminars; Awards/
prizes.
Application information: Applications accepted.
Application form required.
  Deadline(s): Vary
  Additional information: Applications must include
    work samples; See Web site for further
    application information.
Program descriptions:
  *New Works: Creation & Presentation Grant
  Program:* Provides $10,000 to $15,000 for the
creation and presentation of original jazz music.
Applicants must be Chamber Music America
organization members. Deadline Feb. 26.
  Opportunity Awards: Grants to Chamber Music
America organization members for assistance in
defraying the cost of attending conferences,
workshops, seminars and training opportunities. Up
to $1,000 is available for the payment of
registration fees and/or tuition.
EIN: 132934575

5267
Chamber Music Northwest, Inc.
522 S.W. 5th Ave., Ste. 920
Portland, OR   97204   (503) 223-3202
Contact: Linda Magee, Exec. Dir.
FAX: (503) 294-6400; E-mail: info@cmnw.org;
URL: http://www.cmnw.org

Foundation type: Public charity
Limitations: Fellowships to classical musicians
aged 12 to 22.
Financial data: Year ended 09/30/2004.
Assets, $3,251,360 (M); Expenditures,
$1,010,706.
Fields of interest: Music; Music ensembles/
groups.
Type of support: Fellowships.
Application information: Deadline Dec. 31; Initial
approach by e-mail; Completion of formal
application required, including biography, 15
minute audition cassette/CD and
recommendations; See Web site for further
application information.
Program description:
  Young Artist Fellowship: Fellowship can last up to
12 months, with one or two positions per year.
String and wind players, pianists, and pre-formed
chamber ensembles can apply. Fellowships provide
opportunities for mentoring master classes, and
community outreach.
EIN: 237355562

5268
chashama, Inc.
201 E. 42nd St.
New York, NY   10036   (212) 391-8151
Contact: Anita Durst, Pres.
E-mail: chashama@info.org; Additional tel.: (212)
391-8152; URL: http://www.chashama.org

Foundation type: Public charity
Limitations: Residencies, technical support,
administrative support, and stipends to performing
and visual artists residing in the New York, NY
metropolitan area.
Publications: Informational brochure.
Financial data: Year ended 06/30/2004.
Assets, $9,193 (M); Expenditures, $237,728. No
monetary support given for residencies.
Fields of interest: Visual arts; Performing arts.
Type of support: Awards/prizes; Residencies;
Stipends.
Application information:
  Initial approach: Telephone or e-mail.
  Deadline(s): Contact foundation for current
    proposal deadline
  Additional information: See Web site for further
    proposal information; Sample proposals
    available on Web site. Interviews required.
Program description:
  Theater Incubator Program: Awards work space,
technical and administrative support, and a
production stipend to early and mid-career visual
and theater artists.
EIN: 133862422

5269
Chester Springs Studio
1671 Art School Rd.
P.O. Box 329
Chester Springs, PA   19425   (610) 827-7277
Contact: Dorothy Manou, Dir.
FAX: (610) 827-7157; E-mail: drbmanou@aol.com;
URL: http://www.chestersspringsstudio.org

Foundation type: Public charity
Limitations: Residencies to visual and ceramic
artists.
Financial data: Year ended 08/31/2003.
Assets, $368,183 (M); Expenditures, $407,500.
No monetary support given for residencies.
Fields of interest: Visual arts; Ceramic arts.
Type of support: Residencies.
Application information: Applications accepted.
  Initial approach: E-mail.
  Deadline(s): Apr. 30
  Additional information: Application by letter
    including resume, SASE, and ten slides.
Program descriptions:
  Artist Residency Program: The program offers
short and long-term residencies up to a year.
Residencies include a stipend, studio space,
materials, a model or firing allowance, room and
board, and in some cases, a final exhibition.
Residents lead classes and workshops at Chester
Springs.
  Ceramics Residency: The one-year residency
includes studio space, materials, the opportunity of
a paid teaching position, a solo exhibition, and a
$650 monthly stipend.
EIN: 232098526

5270
The Chinati Foundation
1 Cavalry Row
P.O. Box 1135
Marfa, TX   79843   (432) 729-4362
Contact: Rob Weiner, Assoc. Dir.
FAX: (432) 729-4597;
E-mail: information@chinati.org; URL: http://
www.chinati.org

Foundation type: Public charity
Limitations: Residencies to artists of diverse ages,
backgrounds, and disciplines.
Financial data: Year ended 12/31/2003.
Assets, $13,912,714 (M); Expenditures,
$952,675. No monetary support given for
residencies.
Fields of interest: Visual arts.
Type of support: Foreign applicants; Residencies.
Application information:
  Initial approach: Letter.
  Deadline(s): Apr. 1
  Additional information: Application must include
    resume. Slides of recent work, and sufficient
    return postage for materials.
Program description:
  Artist in Residence Program: The program
provides housing, studio space, access to Chinati's
collection and archives, a stipend of $1,000, and
an opportunity to hold an exhibition at the
conclusion of the residency. The average residency
lasts from two to three months.
EIN: 742340423

5271
Cintas Foundation, Inc.
c/o Hannah W. Mensch
1301 Ave. of the Americas
New York, NY   10019-6092   (212) 259-8498
Application address: The Frost Art Museum at
Florida International University, c/o Jose W. Perez,
Cintas Fellows Collection Manager, 11200 SW 8th
St., PC110, Miami, FL 33199,
E-mail: perezjos@fiu.edu, tel: (305) 348-6086;
URL: http://www.spliteye.com/cintas/fellowship

Foundation type: Independent foundation
Limitations: Fellowships to individuals of Cuban
citizenship or lineage for continuing work outside
Cuba in the arts, including the fine arts, music, and
literature. A committee appointed by the Institute of
International Education awards nominees.
Publications: Application guidelines.
Financial data: Year ended 08/31/2005.
Assets, $2,157,435 (M); Expenditures,
$114,207; Total giving, $36,400.
Fields of interest: Visual arts; Architecture; Music
composition; Literature; Arts.
Type of support: Fellowships; Foreign applicants.
Application information: Application form required.
  Initial approach: Telephone or e-mail.
  Deadline(s): Feb. 16
  Additional information: See Web site for further
    information.
Program description:
  Fellowship Program: Cintas Fellowships are
intended to acknowledge demonstrated creative
accomplishments and to encourage the
professional development of talented creative
artists in the fields of architecture, literature, music
composition, and the visual arts. Eligibility is limited
to professionals in these arts who are living outside
Cuba, who are of Cuban citizenship or direct
lineage, and who have completed their academic
and technical training. Fellowships are awarded
annually in the amount of $10,000 each, and are
paid in quarterly stipends. The fellowships are not

awarded toward the furtherance of academic study, research, or writing, nor to performing artists. Fellows are free to pursue their arts activities as they wish, either in the U.S. or in other countries approved by the foundation. Fellows will be asked to submit interim and final reports to the U.S. Student Programs division of the Institute of International Education and to contribute or dedicate work done during the fellowship year to the foundation. Applicants may request additional information and application materials from the Institute of International Education.
EIN: 131980389

5272

Blanche E. Colman Trust

c/o Mellon Financial Corp.
P.O. Box 185
Pittsburgh, PA   15230-0185
Contact: Sandra Brown-McMullen, V.P., Mellon Financial Corp.

Foundation type: Independent foundation
Limitations: Grants by recommendation to worthy artists residing in New England (including CT, MA, ME, NH, RI, and VT).
Financial data: Year ended 08/31/2004. Assets, $534,891 (M); Expenditures, $22,662; Total giving, $16,500; Grants to individuals, 9 grants totaling $16,500 (high: $2,500, low: $1,000).
Fields of interest: Arts, artist's services.
Type of support: Awards/grants by nomination only.
Application information: Deadline Mar. 1; Completion of formal application required, including financial information and two letters of recommendation from recognized art professionals.
Program description:
  Artist Grant: Artists should have completed their formal education and have exhibited considerable potential in the art world. Recipients are selected solely at the discretion of a jury of professional artists for their creative work and study in the field of art.
EIN: 046094293

5273

Committee on Poetry, Inc.

P.O. Box 582 Stuyvesant Sta.
New York, NY   10009-0582
Contact: Robert Rosenthal, Pres.
E-mail: info@committeeOnPoetry.org

Foundation type: Public charity
Limitations: Grants to writers, artists and poets to aid in their artistic endeavors.
Financial data: Year ended 05/31/2002. Assets, $46,501 (M); Expenditures, $16,080; Total giving, $11,840; Grants to individuals, 2 grants totaling $11,840 (high: $10,000, low: $1,840).
Fields of interest: Arts, artist's services.
Type of support: Grants for special needs.
Application information: Applications not accepted.
EIN: 136205445

5274

Community Arts Partnership of Tompkins County, Inc.

116 N. Cayuga St.
Ithaca, NY   14850   (607) 273-5072
Contact: Richard Driscoll, Exec. Dir.
FAX: (607) 273-4816;
E-mail: director@artspartncr.org; URL: http://www.artspartner.org

Foundation type: Public charity
Limitations: Grants to individual artists in Ithaca and Tompkins County, NY, for the development of arts in the community.
Publications: Application guidelines; Newsletter.
Financial data: Year ended 12/31/2003. Assets, $314,573 (M); Expenditures, $432,363; Total giving, $78,346; Grants to individuals, 10 grants totaling $13,750 (high: $2,500, low: $1,000).
Fields of interest: Arts, artist's services.
Type of support: Grants to individuals.
Application information: Contact foundation for current application deadline/guidelines.
EIN: 161384455

5275

The Community Foundation in Jacksonville

(also known as The Community Foundation)
121 W. Forsyth St., Ste. 900
Jacksonville, FL   32202   (904) 356-4483
Contact: Judy Herrin, V.P., Professional Svcs.; For grants: Cheryl Riddick, V.P., Grantmaking Svcs.
FAX: (904) 356-7910; E-mail: jherrin@jaxcf.org; Additional E-mails: jzell@jaxcf.org and nwaters@jaxcf.org; Grant application E-mail: applications@jaxcf.org; URL: http://www.jaxcf.org

Foundation type: Community foundation
Limitations: Grants to emerging artists in the visual, literary, and performing arts who are legal residents of Nassau, Baker, Duval, Clay and St. Johns counties in northeastern FL.
Publications: Application guidelines; Annual report; Informational brochure; Newsletter.
Financial data: Year ended 12/31/2004. Assets, $105,025,898 (M); Expenditures, $11,213,095; Total giving, $9,546,937; Grants to individuals, totaling $170,606.
Fields of interest: Visual arts; Performing arts; Literature; Arts, artist's services; Arts.
Type of support: Program development; Stipends.
Application information: Application form required. Application form available on the grantmaker's Web site.
  Initial approach: Letter or telephone.
  Copies of proposal: 1
  Deadline(s): Mar. 1
  Applicants should submit the following:
    1) Proposal
    2) Resume
    3) Work samples
Program description:
  Foster Vitality in the Arts: Through grants in this area, the foundation seeks to support the artistic development of individual artists. Applicants must be at least 18 years of age, legal residents of counties of the First Coast region of northeastern FL, and must have resided in one of these counties for at least 12 months at the time of application.
EIN: 596150746

5276

Cornucopia Art Center, Inc.

103 Parkway Ave. N.
P.O. Box 152
Lanesboro, MN   55949   (507) 467-2446
Contact: Nancy Martinson, Exec. Dir.
URL: http://www.lanesboroarts.org

Foundation type: Public charity
Limitations: Residencies to emerging artists, primarily in the disciplines of sculpture, painting, poetry, and writing.
Financial data: Year ended 12/31/2003. Assets, $27,858 (M); Expenditures, $113,659. No monetary support given for residencies.
Fields of interest: Sculpture; Painting; Literature.
Type of support: Residencies.
Application information: Deadline June 15 and Oct. 15; Initial approach by e-mail; Completion of formal application required, including work samples, proposal, references, artist statement and SASE.
Program description:
  Lanesboro Residency: Residencies range from two to four weeks, with four to six artists each year. Housing and studio space are provided. Artists will receive stipends ranging from $1,250 for a two-week residency to $2,500 for a four-week residency.
EIN: 411731338

5277

The Corporation of Yaddo

Union Ave.
P.O. Box 395
Saratoga Springs, NY   12866-0395
(518) 584-0746
Contact: Elaina Richardson, Pres.
FAX: (518) 584-1312; E-mail: chwait@yaddo.org; URL: http://www.yaddo.org

Foundation type: Public charity
Limitations: Residencies to professional writers, visual artists, composers, choreographers, performance artists, and film and video artists.
Publications: Annual report; Informational brochure (including application guidelines); Newsletter.
Financial data: Year ended 12/31/2003. Assets, $38,617,851 (M); Expenditures, $2,108,300. No monetary support given for residencies.
Fields of interest: Film/video; Visual arts; Choreography; Music composition; Performing arts (multimedia); Literature.
Type of support: Foreign applicants; Residencies.
Application information: Deadlines Jan. 1 and Aug. 1; Initial approach by e-mail, telephone, or fax; Completion of formal application required, including resume, work samples and references; See Web site for application.
Program description:
  Residency Program: Residencies last from two weeks to two months. Residency supplies meals, housing, and studio space. A small fund exists to provide limited help towards the expenses of travel or renting equipment to invited artists of any discipline who otherwise might not be able to visit. In addition, up to $1,000 in financial aid is available to writers who might otherwise be unable to accept an invitation to visit Yaddo.
EIN: 141343055

5278
Craft Emergency Relief Fund, Inc.
P.O. Box 838
Montpelier, VT   05601-0838   (802) 229-2306
Contact: Cornelia Carey, Exec. Dir.
FAX: (802) 223-6484;
E-mail: info@craftemergency.org; URL: http://
www.craftemergency.org

Foundation type: Public charity
Limitations: Loans and grants to professional crafts artists who have suffered career-threatening emergencies.
Publications: Application guidelines; Financial statement; Informational brochure (including application guidelines); Newsletter.
Financial data: Year ended 09/30/2003. Assets, $611,174 (L); Expenditures, $282,780; Total giving, $17,000; Grants to individuals, 9 grants totaling $8,000 (high: $1,000, low: $500).
Fields of interest: Folk arts; Arts, artist's services; AIDS.
Type of support: Emergency funds; Grants for special needs.
Application information: Applications accepted. Application form required.
> *Initial approach:* Letter, FAX, phone, e-mail or visit.
> *Deadline(s):* None

Program description:
> *Emergency Fund for Artists:* The fund administers the following restricted funds:
> · American Association of Woodturners Fund (AAW): Funds are available to AAW members who suffer emergencies
> · California Fund: Funds are available to eligible CA craft artists
> · G.A.S. Fund: Funds are available to Glass Art Society members who suffer emergencies
> · HIV/AIDS Fund: Funds are available to craft artists living with HIV/AIDS
> · Society of American Silversmiths Fund (SAS): Funds are available to SAS members who suffer emergencies
> · TACA Fund: Funds are available to members of the Tennessee Association of Craft Artists who suffer emergencies
> · Vermont Fund: Funds are available to eligible VT craftspeople suffering career-threatening emergencies
> · Disaster Recovery Fund: Funds are available for craft artists who have suffered from a natural disaster or terrorist attack.

EIN: 133273980

5279
Creative Capital Foundation
65 Bleecker St., 7th Fl.
New York, NY   10012-2420   (212) 598-9900
Contact: Sean Elwood, Dir., Grantmaking and Artists Svcs.
FAX: (212) 598-4934;
E-mail: info@creative-capital.org; URL: http://
www.creative-capital.org/

Foundation type: Public charity
Limitations: Project grants to artists in media, performing, and visual arts, for work that has the potential for significant artistic and cultural impact.
Publications: Application guidelines; Biennial report; Grants list.
Financial data: Year ended 12/31/2004. Assets, $4,279,808 (M); Expenditures, $3,312,368; Total giving, $1,689,034; Grants to individuals, 41 grants totaling $1,689,034 (high: $40,000, low: $10,000).

Fields of interest: Media/communications; Film/video; Visual arts; Performing arts; Theater; Music; Performing arts (multimedia); Computer science.
Type of support: Program development.
Application information: Application form required.
> *Initial approach:* Letter of inquiry.
> *Deadline(s):* Mar. 14
> *Additional information:* See Web site for further application information and letter of inquiry form.

Program description:
> *Artist Grants:* Grants are given in four categories: Performing Arts includes dance, music theater, experimental music performance, experimental opera, spoken word, theater/performance art, and interdisciplinary projects; Emerging Fields includes computer-based artwork, new media, audio work, interactive installations, experimental literature, and interdisciplinary projects. The foundation rotates disciplines each cycle. Applicant must be a U.S. citizen or permanent legal resident, at least 25 years old, and a working artist with at least 5 years of experience. Full-time students in degree-granting programs are NOT eligible. The program will support approximately 20 projects in each of the four categories, with awards ranging from $5,000 to $20,000 each.

EIN: 311605982

5280
Cultural Arts Council of Houston/Harris County
3201 Allen Pkwy., Ste. 250
Houston, TX   77019-1800   (713) 527-9330
Contact: Joseph R. Wilson, Interim Exec. Dir.
FAX: (713) 630-5210; E-mail: info@cachh.org;
URL: http://www.cachh.org/home.html

Foundation type: Public charity
Limitations: Fellowships and awards to artists in Houston and Harris County, TX.
Publications: Application guidelines; Newsletter.
Financial data: Year ended 06/30/2005. Assets, $2,657,253 (M); Expenditures, $8,899,623; Total giving, $7,446,963; Grants to individuals, 33 grants totaling $130,500 (high: $5,000, low: $2,500).
Fields of interest: Arts, artist's services; Arts.
Type of support: Fellowships; Awards/prizes.
Application information: Application form required.
> *Deadline(s):* Dec. 3
> *Additional information:* Application workshops will be held to assist artists in preparing their materials.

Program descriptions:
> *Fellowships:* Cash awards of $2,500 and $5,000 to artists who have resided in Houston for at least two full years in dance, choreography, music composition, literature, and visual arts in alternating years. Please see web site for further deadline information.
> *Artist Project Awards:* Cash awards of up to $5,000 for innovative arts projects. The awards are open to artists who have resided in the city of Houston for at least two full years. Applicants may work in any art discipline, including visual arts, music, dance, theater, and writing.

EIN: 741946756

5281
Cuyahoga Valley National Park Association
15610 Vaughn Rd.
Brecksville, OH   44141   (216) 524-1497
Contact: Deborah Yandala, C.E.O.
Additional tel.: (800) 445-9667; Application address: 3675 Oak Hill Rd., Peninsula, OH 44264;
URL: http://www.nps.gov/cuva/culturalarts/
artistinresidence

Foundation type: Public charity
Limitations: Residencies to artists who will integrate their art with the environment in a national park, and share it with park visitors.
Financial data: Year ended 08/31/2003. Assets, $923,147 (M); Expenditures, $1,895,099; Total giving, $135,133.
Fields of interest: Arts.
Type of support: Residencies.
Application information: Applications accepted. Application form required.
> *Initial approach:* Letter.
> *Applicants should submit the following:*
> 1) SASE
> 2) Letter(s) of recommendation
> 3) Resume
> *Additional information:* Application must also include work samples.

Program description:
> *Residency Program:* Artists selected for the residency will develop and implement curriculum activities and theme-based arts experiences for fourth through ninth graders participating in the residential program of Cuyahoga Valley National Park. Residencies last from six to eight weeks. The program provides housing, studio space and an $800/week stipend.

EIN: 341917257

5282
Dance/USA
1156 15th St., N.W., Ste. 820
Washington, DC   20005-1726   (202) 833-1717
Contact: Andrea Snyder, Pres. and Exec. Dir.
FAX: (202) 833-2686;
E-mail: asnyder@danceusa.org; URL: http://
www.danceusa.org

Foundation type: Public charity
Limitations: Awards to professional dancers and choreographers residing in CA.
Publications: Application guidelines; Financial statement; Grants list; Newsletter; Occasional report.
Financial data: Year ended 06/30/2004. Assets, $2,912,692 (M); Expenditures, $17,880,808; Total giving, $377,500; Grants to individuals, 15 grants totaling $160,000 (high: $15,000, low: $10,000).
Fields of interest: Dance.
Type of support: Awards/prizes.
Application information: Deadline Apr. 6; Completion of formal application required, including detailed budget, biography, artist's statement, project summary, proof of CA residence, and videotape of work; Submit two copies of all information (except videotape); See Web site for further application information.

Program description:
> *Dance: Creation to Performance:* Awards 11 grants of $5,000 to $20,000 to individuals residing in CA who have demonstrated experience in concert, dance/theater or traditional dance choreography. Grants are to be used for three years

and applicants who receive less than $20,000 are eligible to re-apply for up to a total of $20,000.
EIN: 521253457

5283
The Dayton Foundation
2300 Kettering Twr.
Dayton, OH 45423-1395 (937) 222-0410
Contact: Michael M. Parks, Pres.; For discretionary grants: Marilyn Shannon, Sr. Prog. Off.
FAX: (937) 222-0636;
E-mail: info@daytonfoundation.org; Additional tel.: (877) 222-0410; Additional E-mails: Dtimmons@daytonfoundation.org and Mshannon@daytonfoundation.org; URL: http://www.daytonfoundation.org

Foundation type: Community foundation
Limitations: Annual salary bonuses to enhance the lives of dancers in the Dayton Ballet, Dayton Contemporary Dance Company, and Rhythm in Shoes.
Publications: Application guidelines; Financial statement; Newsletter; Program policy statement.
Financial data: Year ended 06/30/2005. Assets, $260,578,404 (M); Expenditures, $40,716,582; Total giving, $30,381,725; Grants to individuals, 1,063 grants totaling $1,532,936.
Fields of interest: Ballet.
Type of support: Stipends.
Application information:
Initial approach: Letter.
Additional information: Contact foundation for further program information.
EIN: 316027287

5284
Dedalus Foundation, Inc.
(formerly Motherwell Foundation, Inc.)
555 W. 57th St., Ste. 1222
New York, NY 10019
Contact: Richard Rubin, Chair.

Foundation type: Operating foundation
Limitations: Graduate fellowships by nomination only to aid students of painting and/or sculpture, or those preparing a dissertation on some aspect of the modernist tradition. Also, fellowship to an art historian, critic, or curator pursuing a project related to the study of modern art and modernism.
Publications: Informational brochure (including application guidelines).
Financial data: Year ended 12/31/2003. Assets, $48,106,632 (M); Expenditures, $3,067,651; Total giving, $740,679; Grants to individuals, 9 grants totaling $114,000 (high: $30,000, low: $1,000).
Fields of interest: Visual arts; Art history.
Type of support: Fellowships; Awards/grants by nomination only; Graduate support; Doctoral support.
Application information: Deadlines Oct. 1 for Senior Fellowship Program, Dec. 1 for Ph.D. Dissertation Fellowship, July 1 for M.F.A. Fellowship; Contact foundation for current nomination guidelines; Initial approach by letter.
Program descriptions:
Ph.D. Dissertation Fellowship: Provides $15,000 worth of support for a graduate student studying any aspect of the modernist tradition. Departments of art history at colleges and universities within the U.S. are invited to nominate one student. Nominees must have completed all course requirements and examinations and must have advanced candidacy for the Ph.D. Announcement of award made in Apr.

M.F.A. Fellowship: Provides $12,500 worth of support for graduate students of painting and sculpture who are about to enter their last year of candidacy for the M.F.A. degree at an American college, university, or art school. Graduate departments of art are invited to nominate one student for consideration. Announcement of award made in Dec.
Senior Fellowship Program: One grant of up to $25,000 awarded annually. Applicant need not be affiliated with an educational institution or museum, and cannot be a candidate for a degree. Grant only available to U.S. citizens.
EIN: 133091704

5285
Delaware Center for the Contemporary Arts, Inc.
200 S. Madison St.
Wilmington, DE 19801 (302) 656-6466
Contact: Neil Watson, Exec. Dir.
E-mail: info@thedcca.org; URL: http://www.thedcca.org

Foundation type: Public charity
Limitations: Residencies to visual artists.
Publications: Informational brochure.
Financial data: Year ended 07/31/2003. Assets, $5,325,520 (M); Expenditures, $977,970. No monetary support given for residencies.
Fields of interest: Visual arts.
Type of support: Residencies.
Application information: Applications accepted. Application form required.
Initial approach: E-mail.
Deadline(s): Apr.
Additional information: Contact foundation or call for submissions and current application information.
Program description:
Art and Community Residency: During this residency program, artists make a full-time commitment to collaborate with an under-served community group to create artwork based on issues relevant to the participants' lives. The residency is also geared to offering artists the time, space and financial assistance to work on their own independent projects. In addition to a stipend, the DCCA provides selected artists with an on-site apartment/studio space for eight weeks. U.S. citizens only may apply.
EIN: 510242942

5286
Dieu Donne Papermill
433 Broome St.
New York, NY 10013-2662 (212) 226-0573
Contact: Mina Takahashi, Exec. Dir., Prog.
FAX: (212) 226-6088;
E-mail: stacey@dieudonne.org; URL: http://www.Dieudonne.org

Foundation type: Public charity
Limitations: Awards of studio space to emerging artists who are NY residents for the opportunity to produce new projects in handmade paper.
Financial data: Year ended 12/31/2003. Assets, $332,058; Expenditures, $574,910.
Fields of interest: Visual arts; Arts.
Type of support: Awards/prizes; Residencies; Stipends.
Application information: Applications accepted. Application form required. Application form available on the grantmaker's Web site.

Initial approach: Telephone or e-mail.
Deadline(s): Jan. 15
Additional information: Application should include resume, 10 slides of current work, and a SASE.
Program descriptions:
Workspace Program: Three artists will each receive a $700 honorarium, materials and professional assistance for 7 days.
Lab Grant Program: Two artists nominated by outside advisors will each receive a $1,200 honorarium, 12 days of full technical assistance on the wet-floor studio, materials, and the option to present an exhibition at the Dieu Donne Gallery.
EIN: 222814886

5287
Diverseworks, Inc.
1117 East Freeway
Houston, TX 77002 (713) 223-8346
Contact: Sara Kellner, Exec. Dir.
FAX: (713) 223-4608;
E-mail: sixto@diverseworks.org; URL: http://www.diverseworks.org

Foundation type: Public charity
Limitations: Residencies to performing and visual artists with preference to residents of Houston, TX.
Financial data: Year ended 08/31/2003. Assets, $532,404; Expenditures, $832,200. No monetary support given for residencies.
Fields of interest: Visual arts; Performing arts.
Type of support: Residencies.
Application information: Applications accepted.
Deadline(s): Feb. 15 for Performing Arts, Nov. 1 for Visual Arts
Additional information: Application must include proposal, budget, resume, explanation of project, work samples, and technical/equipment requirements.
Program descriptions:
Performing Arts: Residents are chosen through a proposal review process. The program includes three to six weeks of access to a black box theater to construct, examine, and refine work.
Visual Arts: Emerging and under-recognized artists will show exhibits at the main galleries. Proposals from curators as well as artists are eligible. Inquiries should be addressed to Diane Barber, Visual Arts Director.
EIN: 760035355

5288
Do While Studio
122 South St.
Boston, MA 02111 (617) 338-9129
Contact: Jennifer Hall
FAX: (617) 338-8629;
E-mail: jenhall@massart.edu; URL: http://www.dowhile.org

Foundation type: Public charity
Limitations: Residencies to artists specializing in digital technology in concert with traditional forms of artistic expression such as painting, sculpture, poetry, choreography, storytelling, music, and design.
Financial data: Year ended 12/31/2003. Assets, $7,674 (M); Expenditures, $36,580. No monetary support given for residencies.
Fields of interest: Visual arts; Sculpture; Design; Painting; Choreography; Music; Literature; Computer science.
Type of support: Residencies.

Application information: Applications accepted.
Initial approach: E-mail.
Applicants should submit the following:
1) Resume
2) SASE
Additional information: Contact foundation for current application guidelines.
Program description:
Artist in Residence: Three month residencies are available with a maximum of three residencies per year. Studio space and equipment access are provided. Participants are required to present their work publicly and to document their work online.
EIN: 043134392

5289
Dramatists Guild Fund, Inc.
1501 Broadway
New York, NY 10036 (212) 391-8384
Contact: Susan Drury
FAX: (212) 391-8384;
E-mail: sdrury@dramaguild.com; URL: http://www.dramaguild.com

Foundation type: Independent foundation
Limitations: Grants-in-aid are made to needy U.S. playwrights who have had their works produced or published. Applicants are asked to restrict requests to their immediate needs.
Financial data: Year ended 12/31/2003.
Assets, $3,351,794 (M); Expenditures, $484,110; Total giving, $262,841; Loans to individuals, 17 loans totaling $31,591.
Fields of interest: Theater (playwriting); Literature.
Type of support: Grants for special needs.
Application information: Applications accepted. Application form required.
Initial approach: Letter or telephone.
Deadline(s): None
EIN: 136144932

5290
Dungannon Foundation, Inc.
c/o CPI Assocs., Inc.
32 E. 57th St., 14th Fl.
New York, NY 10022-2513

Foundation type: Operating foundation
Limitations: Awards to North American short story writers. Nominees are selected by a jury of three unrelated and independent experts.
Financial data: Year ended 12/31/2002.
Assets, $349,399 (M); Expenditures, $97,816; Total giving, $55,000; Grants to individuals, totaling $30,000.
Fields of interest: Literature.
Type of support: Awards/grants by nomination only; Awards/prizes.
Application information: Contact foundation for current nomination deadline/guidelines.
EIN: 133312300

5291
The Durfee Foundation
1453 3rd St. Promenade, Ste. 312
Santa Monica, CA 90401
Contact: Claire Peeps
FAX: (310) 899-5121; E-mail: admin@durfee.org;
Additional E-mail for Claire Peeps:
Claire@durfee.org; URL: http://www.durfee.org

Foundation type: Independent foundation
Limitations: Grants to artists and musicians residing in Los Angeles, CA.

Publications: Application guidelines; Annual report; Informational brochure.
Financial data: Year ended 12/31/2005.
Assets, $27,556,614 (M); Expenditures, $1,608,535; Total giving, $1,001,969; Grants to individuals, 50 grants totaling $243,484 (high: $15,000, low: $775).
Fields of interest: Music; Arts.
Type of support: Seed money.
Application information: Application form required.
Deadline(s): Jan. 20 for Master Musician Fellowships and Feb. 3, May 4, Aug. 3, and Nov. 3 for ARC
Applicants should submit the following:
1) Work samples
2) Resume
Additional information: Application should also include supporting information; See Web site for further application information.
Program descriptions:
Artists' Resource for Completion (ARC): Awards $3,500 to artists in any discipline for specific imminent opportunities that may significantly benefit their careers. The applicant must already have secured a commitment from a recognized institution to present his or her work. Grants may be used for materials, equipment, space, travel, shipping, or stipends to collaborating artists.
Master Musician Fellowships: Awards $15,000 per year for two years to established musicians to provide free weekly instruction to a qualified apprentice. Eligible applicants must:
· maintain a residence and live a substantial portion of each year in Los Angeles County
· be recognized as a master artist by virtue of performance history, community recognition and critical response
· have demonstrated teaching experience
· have identified a qualified apprentice who is willing and available to participate in the program
· have financial need
· not already be employed full-time at a teaching institution
· applicants may reapply for up to four additional years of support.
EIN: 954856207

5292
Dutchess County Arts Council, Inc.
9 Vassar St., Garden Level Ste.
Poughkeepsie, NY 12601-3211
(845) 454-3222
FAX: (845) 454-6902;
E-mail: info@artsmidhudson.org; URL: http://www.artsmidhudson.org

Foundation type: Public charity
Limitations: Fellowship to Dutchess and Ulster county, NY residents who are in the developmental phase of a career as a creative artist.
Financial data: Year ended 12/31/2004.
Assets, $251,063 (M); Expenditures, $618,151; Total giving, $281,638; Grants to individuals, totaling $3,000.
Fields of interest: Music composition.
Type of support: Fellowships.
Application information: Application form required. Application form available on the grantmaker's Web site.
Initial approach: Telephone.
Deadline(s): Apr. 30
Applicants should submit the following:
1) Work samples
2) Resume

Additional information: Application must also include proof of residency. See Web site for additional information.
Program description:
Fellowships: Provides $3,000 for a full fellowship in the area of music composition. All genres of music including jazz, folk, popular and electronic are eligible to apply. Full or partial fellowships may be awarded.
EIN: 146035153

5293
Joyce Dutka Arts Foundation, Inc.
P.O. Box 630053
Bronx, NY 10463 (718) 543-1567
Contact: Joyce Dutka, Pres.
E-mail: jdutka1999@cs.com

Foundation type: Operating foundation
Limitations: Prizes and awards to individuals in the performing or visual arts, primarily in NY.
Financial data: Year ended 06/30/2002.
Assets, $128,649 (M); Expenditures, $39,661; Total giving, $11,224; Grants to individuals, 10 grants totaling $10,499 (high: $2,000, low: $500).
Fields of interest: Music; Performing arts, education.
Type of support: Awards/prizes.
Application information: Application form required.
Initial approach: Letter.
Deadline(s): Dec. 1
Program description:
Arts Competition: Each year, the foundation sponsors a competition that focuses on one discipline in the arts. Prizes are awarded through a juried competition only.
EIN: 061551999

5294
Eastern Frontier Educational Foundation, Inc.
446 Long Ridge Rd.
Bedford, NY 10506
Contact: Stephen T. Dunn, Chair.
E-mail: webmaster@easternfrontier.com;
URL: http://www.easternfrontier.com

Foundation type: Public charity
Limitations: Residencies for visual artists, writers, and songwriter/composers to stay at Norton Island, ME.
Financial data: Year ended 05/31/2002.
Assets, $687,573 (M); Expenditures, $49,197. No monetary support given for residencies.
Fields of interest: Visual arts; Music composition; Literature.
Type of support: Residencies.
Application information: Application form required.
Initial approach: Letter or e-mail.
Deadline(s): Mar. 1
Additional information: Application must include $10 application fee, work samples, and choice of residency dates.
Program description:
Residency Program: The residency provides living space. The program takes place in the remote wilderness with limited, basic facilities. There are two sessions to choose from. The first session lasts for two weeks and the second is three weeks.
EIN: 010535353

5295

The Elizabeth Foundation for the Arts

P.O. Box 2670
New York, NY 10036 (212) 563-5855
Contact: Jane Stephenson, Pres.
FAX: (212) 563-1875; E-mail: grants@efal.org

Foundation type: Public charity
Limitations: Grants and residency support to qualified visual artists. Also, grants by nomination only to support elder artists with a mature body of work.
Publications: Application guidelines; Financial statement; Grants list.
Financial data: Year ended 12/31/2003. Assets, $11,684,679 (M); Expenditures, $1,412,832; Total giving, $82,712; Grants to individuals, 15 grants totaling $80,416 (high: $10,000, low: $1,600).
Fields of interest: Visual arts; Sculpture; Arts; Aging.
Type of support: Awards/grants by nomination only; Residencies.
Application information: Deadline May 1; Initial approach by letter after Jan. 1; Direct applications not accepted for nominations; Completion of formal application required, including up to ten slides of recent work, resume, and federal tax returns for the last two years.
Program descriptions:
EFA Studio Center: Partially subsidized studio work space and short-term exhibition space in Manhattan, NY, is provided to qualified visual artists.
Grants Program for Individuals in the Visual Arts: Visual artists who are at least 30 years old at the time of application or, if under 30, who have been working artists for at least six years since completion of formal schooling, may apply for grants to assist them in creating new work and/or in gaining recognition for their work. Selection is based on the artist's work as presented in ten slides, demonstrated financial need, background and dedication to career, and proposal for use of the grant. Artists working in photography, video, film, and crafts are not eligible for this program. In addition, recipients of the previous year's grant are not eligible for the current year.
Program for Senior Artists: This program provides multi-year funding and exhibition opportunities by nomination only to elder artists whose mature work, informed by a lifetime of experience, is being lost because of inadequate financial resources.
EIN: 061313662

5296

The Ensemble Studio Theatre, Inc.

549 W. 52nd St.
New York, NY 10019 (212) 247-4982
FAX: (212) 664-0041;
E-mail: sloanproject@ensemblestudiotheatre.org;
URL: http://www.ensemblestudiotheatre.org

Foundation type: Public charity
Limitations: Commission awards to artists, composers and choreographers whose winning proposals evolve into works presented at the Theater's First Light Festival.
Financial data: Year ended 06/30/2004. Assets, $2,020,729 (M); Expenditures, $1,319,048.
Fields of interest: Performing arts; Arts; Engineering/technology; Science.
Type of support: Awards/prizes; Residencies.
Application information:
Initial approach: Letter, fax or e-mail.
Deadline(s): Oct. 31

Additional information: Script submissions accepted throughout the year; Submit a one-page written proposal which includes a project description with a simple outline or synopsis, and a resume or biography.
Program description:
Artist Award: The Ensemble Studio Theatre/Alfred P. Sloan Foundation Science & Technology Project is designed to stimulate artists to create compelling work exploring the worlds of science and technology and to challenge the existing stereotypes of scientists and engineers in the popular imagination. Each season the EST/Sloan Project commissions develops new works, and then presents the results in a month-long festival called FIRST LIGHT. Commissions will be awarded to individuals, groups and creative teams for full-length plays or musicals, one-act plays or musicals, stand-up comedy, monologues, short pieces, dance or performance art. Commissions range from $500 to $10,000. The commitment to the amount will be tailored to the proposal and determined on a case-by-case basis.
EIN: 237150345

5297

The Entertainment Industry Foundation

11132 Ventura Blvd., Ste. 401
Studio City, CA 91604-3156 (818) 760-7722
Contact: Michael Balaoing
FAX: (818) 760-7898; URL: http://www.eifoundation.org

Foundation type: Public charity
Limitations: Awards by nomination only to dance, music, theatre and visual arts teachers for their school's art programs.
Publications: Application guidelines; Annual report; Financial statement; Grants list; Informational brochure; Informational brochure (including application guidelines); Newsletter; Program policy statement.
Financial data: Year ended 06/30/2003. Assets, $13,252,680 (L); Expenditures, $20,946,450; Total giving, $14,851,250.
Fields of interest: Arts; Education.
Type of support: Awards/grants by nomination only; Awards/prizes.
Application information: Application form required.
Deadline(s): Mar. 31
Additional information: Nominations available on Web site.
Program description:
Barbie Arts Teacher of the Year Award: Awards to 20 arts teachers in the amount of $5,000 for their school's arts programs. Students ages six to 12 who nominated the winning finalists will receive a $100 Mattel Toy prize package. The national Barbie Arts Teacher of the Year will receive an additional grant of $10,000 for his/her arts program.
EIN: 951644609

5298

Willard R. Espy Literary Foundation

P.O. Box 614
Oysterville, WA 98641 (360) 665-5220
Contact: Polly Friedlander, Pres.
FAX: (360) 665-5224;
E-mail: wrelf@willapabay.org; URL: http://www.espyfoundation.org

Foundation type: Public charity
Limitations: Residencies to writers of poetry, fiction, non-fiction, plays and screenplays.
Financial data: Year ended 12/31/2003. Assets, $157,408; Expenditures, $122,533; Total

giving, $1,000; Grant to an individual, 1 grant totaling $1,000.
Fields of interest: Theater (playwriting); Literature.
Type of support: Residencies.
Application information: Applications accepted. Application form required. Application form available on the grantmaker's Web site.
Initial approach: E-mail.
Deadline(s): Mar. 1 and July 1
Additional information: See Web site for additional application guidelines.
Program description:
Residency Program: Three writers will receive month-long residencies. Residents also receive weekly stipends for food. Residencies take place in June and Oct.
EIN: 911911141

5299

The Evergreen House Foundation, Inc.

c/o The Johns Hopkins University
4545 N. Charles St.
Baltimore, MD 21210-2693 (410) 516-0341
E-mail: joregan@jhu.edu; URL: http://www.jhu.edu/~evrgreen/internship.html

Foundation type: Public charity
Limitations: Residency to a visual artist residing outside of MD.
Financial data: Year ended 06/30/2004. Assets, $8,745,165 (M); Expenditures, $399,189; Total giving, $16,000.
Fields of interest: Visual arts.
Type of support: Residencies.
Application information:
Initial approach: Letter, telephone, or e-mail.
Deadline(s): Jan. 15
Applicants should submit the following:
1) Resume
2) SASE
Additional information: Application by letter, also including 20 slides of recent work, slide script, statement, and reviews.
Program description:
Residency Program: One residency is offered per year to a visual artist living outside of MD. The two-month summer residency provides housing, studio space, and a stipend. The art produced during the residency will form the basis of a solo exhibition scheduled at Evergreen House for the following year.
EIN: 520627782

5300

Experimental Sound Studio

5925 N. Ravenswood Ave.
Chicago, IL 60660 (773) 784-0449
Contact: Louis Mallozzi, Pres.
FAX: (773) 784-3087;
E-mail: ARP@expsoundstudio.org; URL: http://www.expsoundstudio.org

Foundation type: Public charity
Limitations: Residencies to Chicago area sonic artists and visual artists who wish to incorporate an audio element to their project.
Publications: Application guidelines.
Financial data: Year ended 12/31/2004. Assets, $30,344 (M); Expenditures, $90,441. No monetary support given for residencies.
Fields of interest: Visual arts.
Type of support: Residencies.
Application information: Application form required.
Deadline(s): Apr. 21

Additional information: Application must include work samples, SASE, proposal, resume, and preferred dates of residency; See Web site for further application information.

Program description:

Residency Program: 30-hour residencies includes access to the Studio's recording facilities with engineering assistance. Priority will be given to projects employing an innovative use of sound and the incorporation of sound with other media or disciplines.
EIN: 363482714

5301
Experimental Television Center, Ltd.
109 Lower Fairfield Rd.
Newark Valley, NY 13811
Contact: Ralph Hocking, Dir.
E-mail: etc@experimentaltvcenter.org; Tel./FAX: (607) 687-4341; URL: http://www.experimentaltvcenter.org

Foundation type: Public charity
Limitations: Awards and residencies to NY artists to support the creation of new media work.
Financial data: Year ended 06/30/2004. Assets, $508,501 (M); Expenditures, $261,431; Total giving, $172,583; Grants to individuals, totaling $170,983.
Fields of interest: Film/video; Arts.
Type of support: Awards/prizes; Residencies.
Application information: Application form required.
Initial approach: Initial approach by letter of inquiry.
Deadline(s): Deadlines Mar. 15 for Finishing Funds, July 15 and Dec. 15 for Residencies.
Additional information: Full-time students not eligible.

Program descriptions:

Finishing Funds: Provides awards of up to $1,500 annually to NY state's film and electronic media artists for the completion of new work.
Residencies: About 45 artists are awarded each year residencies that offer instruction, work space, and access to facilities for the study of analog and digital image processing. The program provides an estimated $50,000 in services to these artists each year. Each artist pays a $100 residency fee.
EIN: 160993211

5302
The Exploratorium
3601 Lyon St.
San Francisco, CA 94123 (415) 561-0309
Contact: Pamela Winfrey
E-mail: pamw@exploratorium.edu; URL: http://www.exploratorium.edu/arts

Foundation type: Public charity
Limitations: Residencies to visual and performing artists for the creation of art for the Exploratorium, a museum of science, art, and human perception located in San Francisco, CA.
Financial data: Year ended 05/31/2004. Assets, $62,634,802 (M); Expenditures, $23,471,386.
Fields of interest: Visual arts; Museums (art); Museums (science/technology); Performing arts.
Type of support: Residencies.
Application information: Application form not required.
Deadline(s): Quarterly.
Additional information: Application by letter, including background information, slides and other supporting materials; See Web site for complete application information.

Program description:

Artist in Residence Program: Residencies are focused around a formal proposal for a specific artwork or installation. Artists are expected to be in residence from one week to six months, to work closely with staff during the research development, and implementation of their projects, and to contribute to dialogue at the museum through staff presentations and talks with visitors. Residencies provide a stipend, travel and housing expenses, materials, workspace and staff support.
EIN: 941696494

5303
The Eyebeam Atelier
540 W. 21st St.
New York, NY 10011 (212) 937-6581
Contact: John S. Johnson, Chair.
FAX: (212) 937-6582; E-mail: info@eyebeam.org; URL: http://www.eyebeam.org

Foundation type: Public charity
Limitations: Residencies to artists for multi-disciplinary projects.
Financial data: Year ended 12/31/2003. Assets, $1,263,055 (M); Expenditures, $2,831,688. No monetary support given for residencies.
Fields of interest: Arts, formal/general education; Film/video; Visual arts; Arts.
Type of support: Residencies.
Application information: Applications accepted. Application form required. Application form available on the grantmaker's Web site.
Deadline(s): Vary
Additional information: Application should include proposal, timeline and resume.

Program descriptions:

Artist in Residence (AIR): Artists are encouraged to propose multi-disciplinary projects that make use of Eyebeam's studio space and classroom facilities at its gallery space as well as its moving image post-production studios. Artworks produced in the residency can take on a variety of forms, whether it be a finished work for exhibition, a public workshop, prototype, publishable materials or performance. Eyebeam provides a $1,000 stipend per artists' project, but does not provide a living or working stipend.
Education Residency: Residents work as After-School Atelier and Girls-Eye View teaching artists for three-11 week courses. Residents receive a teaching stipend, a technical assistant, a materials budget, and lab hours to work on independent projects. Deadlines Jan. 31 for Girls-Eye View and Feb. 1 for After-School Atelier. Contact Liz Slagus, Dir., Education.
Emerging Fields Residency: Space, technology, production support, and a stipend to artists, technologists, activists, and researchers. Deadline Feb. 10.

· Art Installation: Awards a $1,000 stipend plus limited production cost. Priority is given to a project that makes full use of a 500 square foot studio
· Engineering/Hacking: Awards a $5,000 stipend and the opportunity to work with several artists and contribute to in-house projects.

Moving Image Division Artist in Residency (MID AIR): Two five-month residencies annually, one from Sept.-Jan. and one from Mar.-July. Artists are given unlimited studio access, a small stipend, technical support, assistance from a production intern, and the ability to participate in an annual group

exhibition. See Web site for current application deadline and guidelines.
EIN: 133952075

5304
The Fabric Workshop and Museum
1315 Cherry St., 5th Fl.
Philadelphia, PA 19107 (215) 568-1111
FAX: (215) 568-8211;
E-mail: info@fabricworkshopandmuseum.org;
URL: http://www.fabricworkshop.org

Foundation type: Public charity
Limitations: Residencies by invitation only to contemporary artists for the creation of new work using experimental materials and techniques.
Financial data: Year ended 09/30/2004. Assets, $2,150,348 (M); Expenditures, $1,791,164; Total giving, $378,283; Grants to individuals, totaling $378,283.
Fields of interest: Visual arts; Design.
Type of support: Awards/grants by nomination only; Residencies.
Application information: Applications not accepted.
Additional information: Unsolicited requests for funds not considered or acknowledged.
EIN: 232018929

5305
FiftyCrows Foundation
5214-F Diamond Heights Blvd.
San Francisco, CA 94131
Contact: Andy Patrick, Exec. Dir.
FAX: (415) 551-0063; E-mail: info@fiftycrows.org; URL: http://www.fiftycrows.org

Foundation type: Public charity
Limitations: Grants to photographers for documentary photography projects that increase awareness of world events.
Financial data: Year ended 06/30/2004. Assets, $155,131 (M); Expenditures, $364,339.
Fields of interest: Cultural/ethnic awareness; Photography; International affairs.
Type of support: Awards/prizes.
Application information: Application form required.
Initial approach: E-mail.
Additional information: Contact foundation for current application guidelines; See Web site for further application information.

Program description:

International Fund for Documentary Photography: The Photo Fund supports emerging documentary photographers whose outstanding ability in visual storytelling leads us to a better understanding of our common humanity. Four winners will be selected for this competition. There will be two winners from each of the two categories. Each winner will receive the following:
· a monetary grant of $5,000 USD
· a FiftyCrows Media television short created with your images and voice-over
· a mini-website featured for two weeks on the home page of FiftyCrows.org and permanently archived within FiftyCrows.org including your entire photo essay, bio, written essay and associated information
· ongoing support and mentorship from FiftyCrows in the areas of marketing, publishing, exhibiting, building your successful career
· sales opportunities through FiftyCrows Fine Print program
· free lifetime Membership to FiftyCrows
· international press coverage

· one year of free service using Digital Railroad's suite of web-based applications for professional photographers
· free Adobe software

EIN: 912156051

5306
Film Arts Foundation

145 9th St., Ste. 101
San Francisco, CA 94103 (415) 552-8760
Contact: Janis Plotkin, Exec. Dir.
FAX: (415) 552-0882; E-mail: info@filmarts.org;
URL: http://www.filmarts.org

Foundation type: Public charity
Limitations: Grants to individual media artists who are residents of the ten Bay Area counties (Alameda, Contra Costa, Marin, Napa, San Francisco, Santa Clara, San Mateo, Santa Cruz, Sonoma, and Solano) of CA for their film and video projects.
Publications: Annual report; Grants list; Informational brochure.
Financial data: Year ended 12/31/2004. Assets, $816,374 (M); Expenditures, $2,053,551; Total giving, $22,500; Grants to individuals, totaling $22,500.
Fields of interest: Film/video.
Type of support: Program development; Awards/prizes.
Application information: Application form required.
Initial approach: Letter or telephone.
Additional information: Contact foundation for current application deadline.
Program descriptions:
Personal Works Grants: This program awards approximately five grants of $4,000 each for new short personal works in film or video. These grants are meant for artist-made films or videos which can be completed with this grant and in-kind contributions only. Priority is given to artistic concepts that challenge and expand the film/video art form.
Completion/Distribution Grants: Awards approximately five grants of $4,000 each for films or tapes that demonstrate a need of this amount to complete and/or distribute the project.
Development Grants: This program awards approximately five grants of $2,500 each for film/video projects in the development and fundraising stages. Priority is given to production of fundraising clips, research, and proposal/concept development. Recipients are required to submit periodic reports on the funding status of their projects.
Robin Eickman Feature Film Award: Awards approximately one award of $10,000 in cash and $40,000 in services for a feature-length narrative film budgeted under $200,000. Projects must be a completed screenplay and be at least 72 minutes in length. Priority is given to projects with financing for the balance of production or funds in place.
STAND 2000 (Support, Training and Access for New Directions): Awards approximately eight grants of $1,500 each to emerging film and videomakers from under-represented communities. The awards support the creation of a first film or video. Projects may not exceed six minutes. The awards consist of: orientations, training and access to production and post-production equipment available at Film Arts Foundation; four to six weeks of production primer and basic production class, and screenwriting workshop; 25 hours of project mentoring by an established director; a one year Film Art Foundation membership, and exhibition of completed works.
EIN: 942348632

5307
Fine Arts Work Center in Provincetown, Inc.

24 Pearl St.
Provincetown, MA 02657-1504
(508) 487-9960
Contact: Hunter O'Hanian, Exec. Dir.
FAX: (508) 487-8873; E-mail: general@fawc.org;
URL: http://www.fawc.org

Foundation type: Public charity
Limitations: Fellowships to visual artists and writers.
Publications: Application guidelines; Financial statement; Informational brochure (including application guidelines); Newsletter.
Financial data: Year ended 09/30/2003. Assets, $2,559,061 (M); Expenditures, $947,751.
Fields of interest: Visual arts; Literature; Arts, artist's services; Arts.
Type of support: Fellowships; Awards/prizes; Residencies.
Application information:
Initial approach: Letter, telephone, FAX, or e-mail.
Additional information: Feb 1 for visual artists and Dec. 1 for writers; Completion of formal application required, including work samples, application fee, self-addressed, stamped postcard, SASE, and other materials; Applications are available on Web site.
Program descriptions:
Visual Arts Fellowship: Available to artists in any of the visual arts media, however, facilities may limit certain types of work. Deadline Feb. 1.
Writing Fellowship: Available to fiction and poetry writers of merit. Deadline Dec. 1.
EIN: 042487373

5308
First Nations Development Institute

703 3rd. Ave., Ste. B.
Longmont, CO 80501 (303) 774-7841
Contact: Michael E. Roberts, Pres.
Additional address: 2300 Fall Hill Ave., Ste. 412, Fredericksburg. VA 22401; Additional tel.: (540) 371-5615; Additional FAX: (540) 371-3505;
URL: http://www.firstnations.org

Foundation type: Public charity
Limitations: Grants to Native American visual and graphic artists.
Publications: Biennial report; Grants list; Informational brochure; Newsletter; Occasional report.
Financial data: Year ended 06/30/2004. Assets, $2,162,783 (M); Expenditures, $3,209,580; Total giving, $1,047,043.
Fields of interest: Visual arts; Native Americans/American Indians.
Application information: Applications are currently not being accepted; See Web site for further application information.
Program description:
The Kookyangw Fund: Provides financial support, encouragement, and exposure to emerging Native American graphic and visual artists who have chosen a profession in graphic arts and/or fine arts. The goals of the fund are to increase knowledge, awareness and understanding of Native American arts; to encourage aesthetic expression by promoting the use of high-technology tools by Native American artists; and to enable their participation in the profession on a worldwide basis while maintaining their cultural integrity.
EIN: 541254491

5309
First People's Fund

P.O. Box 2977
Rapid City, SD 57709 (605) 348-0324
Contact: Lori Pourier, Pres.
FAX: (605) 348-6594;
E-mail: info@firstpeoplesfund.org; URL: http://www.firstpeoplesfund.org

Foundation type: Public charity
Limitations: Grants and fellowships to Native American artists.
Financial data: Year ended 12/31/2003. Assets, $55,388 (M); Expenditures, $260,082; Total giving, $25,500; Grants to individuals, 6 grants totaling $25,500 (high: $5,000, low: $500).
Fields of interest: Visual arts; Performing arts; Literature; Native Americans/American Indians.
Type of support: Fellowships.
Application information: Applications accepted.
Initial approach: E-mail.
Additional information: See Web site for further application information.
Program descriptions:
Community Spirit Awards: Community Spirit Awards are national fellowship awards for established artists practicing visual arts, performing arts and literary arts, who have demonstrated substantial contributions to their community through their careers as artists. In the spirit of giving, First Peoples Fund honors American Indian artists who exemplify their traditional cultural values and way of life through the sharing of their creative talents and skills with others in the community. Nominees must be:
· Practicing artists of demonstrated maturity in their field
· Continually practicing artists for a minimum of 10 years
· Documented affiliate of an United states tribe
· 25 years or older
Nominated candidates must be from an American Indian community. The completed application (nominator and artist) must include a resume, most recent examples of his or her artwork, 5 images on CD ROM or 5 photos. A national selection committee will review nominees and select four awardees from those that meet the outlined qualifications. Fellowship recipients will receive a $5,000 stipend, and will receive their award at a ceremony which is presented each year usually in December. An art exhibit is also usually held at the same location of previous year Community Spirit Award recipients. First Peoples Fund will provide travel and hotel accommodations.
Cultural Capital: This program provides up to five artists per year the opportunity to further their important cultural work in their respective communities. The program is designed to support previous year Community Spirit Award recipients, and engage them in reinforcing their unique cultural contribution. The aim is to develop local networks for leveraging other resources, and provide technical assistance training and capacity building.
Artists In Business: The program aims to cultivate entrepreneurial artists to a small business level (consistent and reliable income) where business concepts are understood and applied. First Peoples Fund finds and selects four "Fellows" per year based on demonstrated artistic talent, evidence of possessing the qualities of an entrepreneur, and indication of embodying the values of First Peoples Fund. Those selected are provided with a one year fellowship with one on one technical and business assistance, one year of group trainings, and access to national markets and shows.
EIN: 820583682

5310
Fleishhacker Foundation
1016 Lincoln Blvd., No. 12
San Francisco, CA 94129-1095
(415) 561-5350
Contact: Christine Elbel, Exec. Dir.
E-mail: info@fleishhackerfoundation.org;
URL: http://www.fleishhackerfoundation.org

Foundation type: Independent foundation
Limitations: One-year fellowships by nomination only to assist visual artists, 25 years of age or older, to residents of San Francisco, Marin, Sonoma, Alameda, Contra Costa, San Mateo, and Santa Clara counties, CA.
Publications: Application guidelines; Grants list; Program policy statement.
Financial data: Year ended 12/31/2004. Assets, $15,587,342 (M); Expenditures, $901,441; Total giving, $693,600; Grants to individuals, 5 grants totaling $99,500 (high: $25,000, low: $500).
Fields of interest: Visual arts.
Type of support: Fellowships; Awards/grants by nomination only; Awards/prizes.
Application information: Applications not accepted.
> *Additional information:* Artists are nominated by nonprofit art organizations; application cycle is every 3 years.

Program description:
> *Eureka Fellowship Program:* Grant recipients are selected once every three years, based on the nominations received from local nonprofit visual arts organizations. Each artist receives $25,000 for a one-year period.

EIN: 946051048

5311
Flintridge Foundation
1040 Lincoln Ave., Ste. 100
Pasadena, CA 91103 (626) 449-0839
Contact: Ms. J.L. Moseley, Managing Dir.
Application tel. for individuals: (800) 303-2139, e-mail: Awards@FlintridgeFoundation.org
FAX: (626) 585-0011;
E-mail: Jack@FlintridgeFoundation.org; Visual Arts Program toll-free tel.: (800) 303-2139; Visual Arts Program E-mail: Awards@FlintridgeFoundation.org;
URL: http://www.flintridgefoundation.org

Foundation type: Independent foundation
Limitations: Biennial awards to visual artists from CA, OR, and WA, for high artistic merit and maturity.
Publications: Application guidelines; Financial statement; Grants list; Informational brochure; Occasional report.
Financial data: Year ended 12/31/2004. Assets, $14,474,503 (M); Expenditures, $2,988,126; Total giving, $1,877,130; Grants to individuals, 10 grants totaling $250,000 (high: $25,000, low: $25,000, average grant: $25,000).
Fields of interest: Visual arts.
Type of support: Awards/prizes.
Application information: Applications accepted. Application form required. Application form available on the grantmaker's Web site.
> *Deadline(s):* Varies
> *Applicants should submit the following:*
>   1) Resume
> *Additional information:* Application should also include slides with an annotated slide script and artist's narrative.

Program description:
> *Awards for Visual Artists:* The program was established to recognize and support the unique contributions of visual artists in CA, OR, and WA.

The Awards honor outstanding artistic merit, a high level of serious, continued artistic exploration and a distinctive artistic voice that can be traced back twenty years, accompanied by a deepening of ideas, skills, and creativity. Based on independent panel recommendations, the foundation distributes biennial grants of $25,000 to five artists from CA, and five artists from OR and WA. The foundation selects two separate regional panels of arts professionals (artists, curators, etc.) who base their selection on high artistic merit and maturity of the applicants' work as demonstrated by the visual documentation submitted. Artists must maintain a nine-month-per year residency in the tri-state area for the last three years and may not have current national renown. Artists working in visual disciplines- fine arts, crafts, performance, and media work based in the visual arts traditions- are eligible. (Dance, theatre, independent film and video are not eligible). Recipients must have lived in CA, OR or WA at least nine months per year, for the last three years to present.
EIN: 953926331

5312
Forecast Public Artworks
2324 University Ave. W., Ste. 104
St. Paul, MN 55114-1843 (651) 641-1128
Contact: Nichole Alwell, Public Art Affairs Coord.
FAX: (651) 641-1983; E-mail: forecast@visi.com;
URL: http://www.forecastart.org

Foundation type: Public charity
Limitations: Grants to MN artists for the development and production of public art.
Publications: Application guidelines; Informational brochure; Informational brochure (including application guidelines); Newsletter.
Financial data: Year ended 09/30/2003. Assets, $89,612 (M); Expenditures, $322,049; Total giving, $30,800; Grants to individuals, 10 grants totaling $30,800 (high: $10,000, low: $800).
Fields of interest: Arts, artist's services; Arts.
Type of support: Awards/prizes; Project support.
Application information: Application form required. Application form available on the grantmaker's Web site.
> *Initial approach:* Must attend mandatory workshop before submitting proposal.
> *Copies of proposal:* 5
> *Deadline(s):* Nov. 15
> *Applicants should submit the following:*
>   1) Work samples
>   2) Proposal

Program description:
> *Public Art Affairs Programs:* Awards grants to MN artists in all disciplines. Grants are available in three categories: Research and Development Stipends ($1,000), Public Projects (up to $4,500), and University Avenue Commission (up to $14,000). Stipends fund development and design of public art installations and activities. Public Projects fund production costs and artist fees for publicly accessible temporary or permanent work in MN. Students are not eligible for the awards. Detailed program information is available at www.forecastART.org.

EIN: 411361351

5313
Olga Forrai Foundation, Inc.
c/o Oram, Yelon & Bernstein
420 Lexington Ave., Ste. 2150
New York, NY 10170
Contact: Erika Urbach, Treas.
Application address: 205 E. 82nd St., New York, NY 10028

Foundation type: Independent foundation
Limitations: Grants to singers and music conductors who are residents of New York City, to study and perform.
Financial data: Year ended 12/31/2004. Assets, $656,311 (M); Expenditures, $27,800; Total giving, $7,000; Grants to individuals, totaling $7,000.
Fields of interest: Music.
Type of support: Scholarships—to individuals.
Application information: Applications by letter accepted throughout the year.
EIN: 133182161

5314
Foundation for Contemporary Arts
820 Greenwich St.
New York, NY 10014 (212) 807-7077
Contact: Stacy Stark, Exec. Dir.
FAX: (212) 807-7177;
E-mail: info@contemporary-arts.org; URL: http://www.foundationforcontemporaryarts.org

Foundation type: Public charity
Limitations: Grants by nomination only to outstanding or unusually promising artists working in the areas of dance, music, performance art/theater, poetry, and the visual arts.
Publications: Grants list.
Financial data: Year ended 12/31/2004. Assets, $6,755,277 (M); Expenditures, $620,426; Total giving, $249,000; Grants to individuals, 25 grants totaling $198,150 (high: $20,000, low: $500).
Fields of interest: Visual arts; Performing arts; Dance; Theater; Music; Literature; Arts, artist's services.
Type of support: Program development; Awards/grants by nomination only; Awards/prizes.
Application information: Contact foundation for current nomination deadline/guidelines.
Program description:
> *John Cage Award for Music:* $50,000 awards are given biennially by nomination only to individual composers and musicians in recognition of outstanding achievement in contemporary music.

EIN: 131978163

5315
Foundation for the Art Renewal Center, Inc.
100 Markley St.
Port Reading, NJ 07064
Application address: P.O. Box 837, Glenham, NY, 12527
E-mail: scholarship@artrenewal.org; URL: http://www.artrenewal.org

Foundation type: Operating foundation
Limitations: Scholarships to artists whose work reflects traditional realism, for attendance at an approved program. Awards also to winners of the organization's Annual Open Competition.
Financial data: Year ended 12/31/2002. Assets, $3,513 (M); Expenditures, $79,188; Total giving, $18,983; Grants to individuals, 7 grants totaling $18,983 (high: $6,983, low: $800).

Fields of interest: Painting; Art history.
Type of support: Graduate support; Undergraduate support.
Application information: Application form required.
Deadline(s): May 31 for scholarships and Oct. 31 for Annual Open Competition
Additional information: Application must include five to ten work samples, three letters of recommendation, biography or C.V., and 250-word essay for scholarships. See Web site for further application information.
Program description:
Annual Open Competition: Awards one $2,000 Best in Show Award, three first place awards of $1,000, three second place awards of $500, and three third place awards of $100 plus online gallery space to representational visual artists.
EIN: 043598440

5316
The Foundation for the Jan Mitchell Prize, Inc.
595 Madison Ave.
New York, NY 10022 (212) 755-9760
Contact: Jan Mitchell, Pres.
Application address: 510 Park Ave., New York, NY 10022, tel.: (212) 755-9760

Foundation type: Independent foundation
Limitations: Prizes to authors of art history books written in English. Books must be published within the year prior to Sept. and submitted for competition.
Financial data: Year ended 03/31/2005.
Assets, $2,574 (M); Expenditures, $41,060; Total giving, $20,000; Grants to individuals, totaling $20,000.
Fields of interest: Art history; Literature.
Type of support: Awards/prizes.
Application information:
Deadline(s): Aug. 31
Additional information: Contact the foundation for current application guidelines.
EIN: 132898803

5317
The William and Eva Fox Foundation
c/o U.S. Trust
114 W. 47th St., 8th Fl.
New York, NY 10036
Contact: Andrew Lane
FAX: (212) 852-3377; E-mail: alane@ustrust.com;
URL: http://www.thefoxfoundation.org

Foundation type: Independent foundation
Limitations: Fellowships by nomination only to actors based on their artistic achievements, commitment to the stage and the strength of the fellowship proposal.
Publications: Grants list.
Financial data: Year ended 06/30/2005.
Assets, $5,893,138 (M); Expenditures, $328,715; Total giving, $250,000.
Fields of interest: Theater; Performing arts, education.
Type of support: Fellowships; Awards/grants by nomination only.
Application information: Applications not accepted.
EIN: 133497192

5318
Frameline
145 9th St., Ste. 300
San Francisco, CA 94103 (415) 703-8650
Contact: Jennifer Morris, Dir. Programming
FAX: (415) 861-1404; E-mail: info@frameline.org;
URL: http://www.frameline.org/fund/

Foundation type: Public charity
Limitations: Project support to gay, lesbian, bisexual and transgender media artists in their final stages of film and video production.
Publications: Application guidelines; Newsletter.
Financial data: Year ended 09/30/2004.
Assets, $284,128; Expenditures, $1,537,763; Total giving, $16,200; Grants to individuals, totaling $16,200.
Fields of interest: Film/video; Arts, artist's services; Arts; LGBTQ.
Type of support: Grants to individuals; Awards/prizes.
Application information: Applications accepted. Application form required. Application form available on the grantmaker's Web site.
Initial approach: Letter outlining financial need.
Copies of proposal: 7
Deadline(s): Oct. 1.
Applicants should submit the following:
1) Work samples
2) Proposal
3) Financial information
4) Essay
5) Budget Information
Additional information: Applications should be mailed; final decisions made 3 months from submission.
Program description:
Frameline Film and Video Completion Fund: This fund assists lesbian and gay media artists with the final stages of film and video productions by awarding completion funds ranging from $5,000 to $10,000. Submissions are accepted for documentary, educational, narrative, animation or experimental projects of any length or format. Women and people of color are encouraged to apply.
EIN: 942775772

5319
Franconia Sculpture Park
29815 Unity Ave.
Shafer, MN 55074
E-mail: info@franconia.org; Telephone/fax: (651) 465 3701; URL: http://www.franconia.org

Foundation type: Public charity
Limitations: Residencies to sculpture, installation and 3-D multimedia artists for the creation of a project in a public outdoor setting.
Publications: Application guidelines.
Financial data: Year ended 12/31/2004.
Assets, $1,098,970 (M); Expenditures, $292,418; Total giving, $28,429; Grants to individuals, 12 grants totaling $28,429 (high: $4,000).
Fields of interest: Media/communications; Sculpture.
Type of support: Residencies.
Application information:
Initial approach: E-mail.
Deadline(s): None
Additional information: Application by letter, including resume, slides of recent work, sketch or drawing of proposal, laser prints, budget, residency date preferences and SASE.

Program description:
FSP/Jerome Residency: Approximately 15 artists will be invited to the program, which can last from three days to three months. These artists may be eligible to apply for six to eight available stipends ranging from $3,000 to $5,000.
EIN: 411843609

5320
The Andrea Frank Foundation, Inc.
c/o Anchin, Block and Anchin LLP
1375 Broadway
New York, NY 10018

Foundation type: Independent foundation
Limitations: Grants to artists for the production of new work and teaching projects.
Financial data: Year ended 12/31/2004.
Assets, $4,765 (M); Expenditures, $81,982; Total giving, $75,000.
Fields of interest: Arts, artist's services.
Type of support: Program development.
Application information: Applications not accepted.
EIN: 133857299

5321
Franklin Furnace Archive, Inc.
c/o 80 Arts/The James E. Davis Arts Bldg.
80 Hanson Pl., Ste. 301
Brooklyn, NY 11217-1506 (718) 398-7255
Contact: Martha Wilson, Dir.
Application address: Franklin Furnace Archive, Inc., 45 John St., Rm. 611, New York, NY 10038-3706
FAX: (718) 398-7256;
E-mail: mail@franklinfurnace.org; URL: http://www.franklinfurnace.org

Foundation type: Public charity
Limitations: Residencies and grants to performance artists.
Publications: Application guidelines; Annual report; Newsletter.
Financial data: Year ended 07/31/2004.
Assets, $439,255 (M); Expenditures, $313,254; Total giving, $101,034; Grants to individuals, 26 grants totaling $101,034 (high: $32,184, low: $100).
Fields of interest: Visual arts; Performing arts.
Type of support: Awards/prizes; Residencies; Stipends.
Application information: Applications accepted. Application form not required. Application form available on the grantmaker's Web site.
Initial approach: E-mail.
Copies of proposal: 1
Deadline(s): Apr. 1
Applicants should submit the following:
1) Work samples
2) SASE
3) Budget Information
4) Resume
Additional information: Application must also include 100-word summary of proposed work and video/support materials; Fifty-one percent of recipients must now be from New York City.
Program descriptions:
The Future of the Present: Franklin Furnace offers artists an honorarium and a residency at a physical or online venue appropriate to the proposed work. Artists who are interested in developing "live art on the Internet" and engaging the Internet as an art medium and/or venue are encouraged to apply.
Franklin Furnace Fund for Performance Art: Franklin Furnace awards grants between $2,000

and $5,000 to performance artists, allowing them to produce major works in New York. Artists from all areas of the world are invited to apply.
EIN: 132879766

5322
French-American Foundation
28 W. 44th St., Ste. 1420
New York, NY 10036 (212) 829-8800
Contact: Nicholas W. F.R. Dungan, Pres.
FAX: (212) 829-8810;
E-mail: info@frenchamerican.org; URL: http://www.frenchamerican.org

Foundation type: Public charity
Limitations: Prizes to translators of French prose work into English.
Publications: Biennial report; Newsletter; Occasional report.
Financial data: Year ended 06/30/2004. Assets, $4,622,042 (M); Expenditures, $1,561,845; Total giving, $71,000; Grants to individuals, 4 grants totaling $71,000 (high: $55,000, low: $1,000).
Fields of interest: Language (foreign); Literature.
Type of support: Awards/prizes.
Application information: Unsolicited requests for funds not accepted.
Program description:
Translation Prize: A monetary prize is presented to a translator for the best published or to-be-published translation of a prose work from French to English.
EIN: 132847092

5323
Friends of the Schindler House
835 N. Kings Rd.
West Hollywood, CA 90069 (323) 651-1510
Contact: Robert L. Sweeney, Pres.
FAX: (323) 651-2340;
E-mail: office@makcenter.org; URL: http://www.makcenter.org

Foundation type: Public charity
Limitations: Residencies to free-lance artists and graduates of architecture.
Financial data: Year ended 12/31/2003. Assets, $397,668 (M); Expenditures, $672,913. No monetary support given for residencies.
Fields of interest: Architecture.
Type of support: Residencies.
Application information: Applications accepted. Application form required. Application form available on the grantmaker's Web site.
Initial approach: E-mail, telephone or letter.
Deadline(s): Mar. 6
Applicants should submit the following:
1) Proposal
Additional information: See Web site for additional application information.
Program description:
MAK Schindler Residency: Four scholarships each for projects in the fields of architecture and the fine arts respectively as part of the MAK Schindler Artists and Architects in Residence Program in Los Angeles, CA. The winners will stay at the Mackey House, one of the two locations of the MAK Center for Art and Architecture, Los Angeles, for six months, realizing the projects they have submitted. This program is open to free-lance artists, advanced students of architecture and graduates of architecture immediately after completion of their degree.
EIN: 953161402

5324
From the Heart Productions, Inc.
1455 Mandalay Beach Rd.
Oxnard, CA 93035 (805) 984-0098
Contact: Carole Dean, Pres.
E-mail: Caroleedean@att.net; URL: http://www.fromtheheartproductions.com

Foundation type: Public charity
Limitations: Grants to screenwriters and film makers.
Financial data: Year ended 12/31/2004. Assets, $9,056 (M); Expenditures, $71,935.
Fields of interest: Film/video.
Type of support: Residencies; Stipends.
Application information: Applications accepted. Application form required. Application form available on the grantmaker's Web site.
Initial approach: Letter or e-mail.
Deadline(s): May 30 and June 30
Applicants should submit the following:
1) Proposal
Additional information: Applications must include work samples, SASE, and preferred dates of stay. There is a suggested donation fee for all applications; See Web site for further information and guidelines.
Program descriptions:
Roy W. Dean Editing Grant: This award for film editing includes a residency in New Zealand and a living stipend.
New Zealand Film Grant: This film grant is for residents of New Zealand, who must film in the country. The grant includes goods and services from film companies.
Roy W. Dean Writing/Research Grant: This residency is for writers of screenplays, short films, and documentaries to stay in New Zealand for four to six weeks. The residency includes a stipend, supplies, and transportation costs.
EIN: 954445418

5325
The Gaea Foundation, Inc.
1611 Connecticut Ave. N.W., Rm. 200
Washington, DC 20009 (202) 232-0304
FAX: (202) 232-1651;
E-mail: info@gaeafoundation.org; URL: http://www.gaeafoundation.org

Foundation type: Independent foundation
Limitations: Residencies by nomination only to writers and to visual and performance artists who are engaged in social activism.
Financial data: Year ended 12/31/2004. Assets, $1,437,194 (M); Expenditures, $868,136; Total giving, $0.
Fields of interest: Visual arts; Performing arts; Literature.
Type of support: Awards/grants by nomination only; Residencies.
Application information: Unsolicited requests for funds not considered or acknowledged.
Program description:
Sea Change Residencies: Residencies last from four to eight weeks. Residents receive a stipend of $600 per week. A nominations committee consisting of accomplished artists, activists, non-profit leaders and academics submits candidates for Sea Change Residences to Gaea Foundation Staff.
EIN: 521858609

5326
Genesee Valley Council on the Arts
Livingston County Campus Bldg. 4, Apt. 1
Mount Morris, NY 14510 (585) 243-6785
Contact: Kathryn Hollinger, Exec. Dir.
FAX: (585) 243-6787; E-mail: mail@gvcaonline.org;
URL: http://www.gvcaonline.org

Foundation type: Public charity
Limitations: Grants to artists who are residents of Livingston County, NY.
Publications: Application guidelines; Annual report; Newsletter.
Financial data: Year ended 06/30/2005. Assets, $28,474 (M); Expenditures, $151,173; Total giving, $32,695; Grants to individuals, 8 grants totaling $7,575 (high: $2,000, low: $200).
Fields of interest: Media/communications; Visual arts; Performing arts; Literature; Arts, artist's services; Arts.
Type of support: Precollege support; Stipends.
Application information: Applications accepted. Application form required. Application form available on the grantmaker's Web site.
Deadline(s): Oct. 18
Additional information: Applicants must attend an application seminar or a private counseling session; Applications must include resume, SASE, letters of recommendation, and are available from the council's Web site.
Program description:
Individual Artist Grants: Three $2,500 grants are available to artists interested in creating new work within a community context. Applicants must be at least 18 years of age, have resided in Livingston County for at least six months, and not be enrolled in an undergraduate degree program. Visual, literary, media, and performing artists may apply.
EIN: 237171154

5327
The Elizabeth George Foundation
601 Belmont Ave. E., F-9
Seattle, WA 98102
Contact: Susan Elizabeth George, Dir.

Foundation type: Independent foundation
Limitations: Grants to unpublished fiction writers.
Financial data: Year ended 10/31/2004. Assets, $289,175 (M); Expenditures, $158,885; Total giving, $158,335; Grants to individuals, 2 grants totaling $44,335 (high: $41,250, low: $3,085).
Fields of interest: Literature.
Type of support: Conferences/seminars; Publication; Fellowships; Scholarships—to individuals; Support to graduates or students of specific schools; Graduate support; Travel grants; Grants for special needs; Project support.
Application information: Application form not required.
Initial approach: Letter.
Copies of proposal: 1
Deadline(s): July 15 for inquiry; Nov. 15 for final documents
Applicants should submit the following:
1) Work samples
2) Resume
3) Proposal
4) Letter(s) of recommendation
5) Financial information
6) Curriculum vitae
7) Budget Information
EIN: 330829947

5328
J. Paul Getty Trust
1200 Getty Ctr. Dr., Ste. 800
Los Angeles, CA 90049-1685 (310) 440-7320
Contact: The Getty Foundation
FAX: (310) 440-7703; URL: http://www.getty.edu

Foundation type: Operating foundation
Limitations: Support to scholars in the art history field, and internships to undergraduate and graduate students interested in exploring career possibilities in the visual arts, museum professions, and art history.
Publications: Application guidelines; Annual report; Grants list; Informational brochure.
Financial data: Year ended 06/30/2004. Assets, $9,642,414,092 (M); Expenditures, $278,649,757; Total giving, $22,671,156; Grants to individuals, 160 grants totaling $2,214,748 (high: $75,000, low: $500, average grant: $7,000-$60,000).
Fields of interest: Visual arts; Art conservation; Museums; Museums (art); Humanities; Art history; Arts; Science; Social sciences; Minorities; African Americans/Blacks; Hispanics/Latinos; Native Americans/American Indians.
Type of support: Fellowships; Internship funds; Research; Postdoctoral support; Postgraduate support.
Application information: Applications accepted. Application form required.
  Initial approach: Letter.
  Deadline(s): Nov. 1
  Additional information: See Web site for further application and program information.
Program descriptions:
  Curatorial Research Fellowships (Nonresidential): These fellowships provide support for the professional scholarly development of curators by providing them with time off from regular museum duties to undertake short-term research or study projects.
  Predoctoral and Postdoctoral Fellowships (Residential): Residential fellowships are offered to predoctoral and postdoctoral scholars at the Getty Research Institute in Los Angeles, CA. The fellowships provide the opportunity to pursue individual projects, take part in the intellectual life of the Research Institute, make use of its collections, and participate in a weekly seminar based upon the theme of the program that year. Applications for these fellowships—welcome from any discipline in the arts, humanities, or social sciences—are evaluated first and foremost in terms of how the proposed dissertation or book bears upon the year's theme.
  Postdoctoral Fellowships: These fellowships provide support for outstanding scholars in the early stages of their careers to pursue interpretive research projects that make a substantial and original contribution to the understanding of art and its history. Projects that explore connections between art history and other humanistic disciplines are especially encouraged. Postdoctoral fellowships are reserved for scholars who have earned a doctoral degree (or the equivalent in countries outside the U.S.) within the last six years. A maximum of 15 fellowships are awarded each year through an open competition. Fellowships provide a stipend of up to $22,000 for a period of 12 months.
  Collaborative Research Grants (Nonresidential): These grants are offered to teams of scholars to pursue interpretive research projects that offer new explanations of art and its history. Collaborations that foster a cross-fertilization of ideas and methodologies are particularly encouraged. Teams may consist of two or more art historians, or of an art historian and one or more scholars from other

disciplines. Funding is also available for the research and planning of scholarly exhibitions; teams for these projects should include scholars from both museums and universities.
  Getty Graduate Internships at the Getty Center: Full-time internships are offered to graduate students who intend to pursue careers in art museums and related fields of the visual arts, humanities, and sciences. Internships are full-time in various departments of the Getty Museum and other Getty programs located at the Getty Center in Los Angeles, California. Grant amounts are $17,800 for eight months and $25,000 for twelve months.
  Multicultural Undergraduate Internships at the Getty Center: Summer internships at the Getty Center are offered to outstanding students who are members of groups currently underrepresented in museum professions and fields related to the visual arts and humanities; individuals of African American, Asian, Latino, Native American, and Pacific Islander descent. Eligible applicants must be currently enrolled undergraduates who either reside or attend college in the Los Angeles area, who will have completed at least one semester of college by the summer of the internship, and will not graduate before Dec. of the year of the internship. The Getty internships provide stipends of $3,500 for a 10-week summer internship in specific departments of the Getty Museum and other Getty programs located at the Getty Center in Los Angeles, California. To be eligible, applicants must reside or have attended college in Los Angeles, CA. Housing and transportation are not provided.
  Fellowship Grants: Both the postdoctoral fellowships and senior research grants are open to scholars internationally. All of the grants, including the Central and Eastern European fellowships, are completely portable; that is, fellows pursue their research wherever necessary to complete their proposed projects. (CA residency is neither required nor provided.)
  Library Research Grants: Provides partial, short-term support for costs relating to travel and living expenses for scholars whose research requires use of specific collections housed in the Research Library at the Getty Research Institute. Grants are intended for scholars at any level who demonstrate a compelling need to use materials housed in the Research Library, and whose place of residence is more than eighty miles from the Getty Center. Library Research Grants range from $500 to $2,500. The research period may range from several days to a maximum of three months.
  Conservation Guest Scholars: Supports new ideas and perspectives in the field of conservation, this program provides an opportunity for professionals to pursue scholarly research in an interdisciplinary manner across traditional boundaries in areas of wide general interest to the international conservation community. Grants are for established conservators, scientists, and professionals who have attained distinction in conservation and allied fields. Conservation Guest Scholars are in residence at the Getty Center for three to nine consecutive months. A monthly stipend of $3,500 is awarded, up to a maximum of $31,500.
EIN: 951790021

5329
Gilman and Gonzalez-Falla Theatre Foundation, Inc.
P.O. Box 18925
Corpus Christi, TX 78480 (361) 937-2520
Contact: Celso M. Gonzales, V.P.
E-mail: celso@soncel.com

Foundation type: Independent foundation
Limitations: Awards by nomination only for recognition in American musical theater.
Financial data: Year ended 12/31/2003. Assets, $45,476 (M); Expenditures, $366,896; Total giving, $182,820; Grants to individuals, 10 grants totaling $38,000 (high: $12,500, low: $500).
Fields of interest: Theater.
Type of support: Awards/grants by nomination only; Awards/prizes.
Application information: Application form required.
  Deadline(s): None
EIN: 133463382

5330
Irving S. Gilmore International Keyboard Festival
359 S. Kalamazoo Mall, Ste. 101
Kalamazoo, MI 49007-4843 (269) 342-1166
Contact: Thomas W. Lambert, Pres.
FAX: (269) 342-0968; Toll-free tel.: (800) 347-4266; URL: http://www.gilmore.org/gilmore_festival/festival_2006.asp

Foundation type: Public charity
Limitations: Awards by nomination only to exceptional pianists who demonstrate the talent and drive to become successful concert artists.
Financial data: Year ended 08/31/2004. Assets, $1,788,924 (M); Expenditures, $2,552,533; Total giving, $78,315; Grants to individuals, totaling $78,315.
Fields of interest: Music.
Type of support: Awards/grants by nomination only; Foreign applicants; Awards/prizes.
Application information: Applications not accepted.
Program descriptions:
  Gilmore Young Artists Award: Awards of $15,000 are given every two years to a promising young American pianist 21 or younger. Nominations are made by leaders in the field of music, and nominees are not told their inclusion in this noncompetitive selection process. Final decisions are made by the Director of the Gilmore and an anonymous Artistic Advisory Committee.
  Gilmore Artists Award: Awards $300,000 every two years to an exceptional pianist who, regardless of age or nationality, is a superb pianist and profound musician, who desires and can sustain a career as a major international concert artist and whose developing career can be enhanced by the Award's money and prestige. Nominations are received from a wide range of sources, including a group of international musical performers and educators who are polled biennially for their suggestions. Recordings of those nominated, preferably made during concert performances, are then assessed by a Artistic Advisory Committee. After hearing the recordings, the Committee narrows down the field of nominees to several finalists. Committee members then travel to hear the artists in various performances that are part of the candidates' established concert schedule. Only then do they make their final choice. The next nomination will be in 2006.
EIN: 382868071

5331
The Dorothy and Lillian Gish Prize
c/o JPMorgan Chase Bank
345 Park Ave., 4th Fl.
New York, NY 10154
Contact: Edward L. Jones, V.P.
E-mail: jones_ed_l@JPMorgan.com; Tel./FAX: (212) 4642305

Foundation type: Independent foundation
Limitations: Annual prize awarded by nomination only to an individual who has made an outstanding contribution to the appreciation of the arts.
Financial data: Year ended 06/30/2005.
Assets, $8,226,392 (M); Expenditures, $424,468; Total giving, $250,000; Grant to an individual, 1 grant totaling $250,000.
Fields of interest: Arts.
Type of support: Awards/grants by nomination only; Awards/prizes.
Application information: Contact foundation for current nomination deadline/guidelines.
EIN: 133751413

5332
Glen Arbor Art Association
P.O. Box 305
Glen Arbor, MI 49636 (231) 334-6112
Contact: Shirley Hoagland, Pres.
E-mail: glenarborarts@yahoo.com; URL: http://www.glenarborart.org

Foundation type: Public charity
Limitations: Residencies to artists specializing in painting, photography, sculpture, fiber arts, ceramics, music, philosophy, and creative research.
Financial data: Year ended 12/31/2003.
Assets, $336,169 (M); Expenditures, $96,080; Total giving, $4,405. No monetary support given for residencies.
Fields of interest: Visual arts; Photography; Sculpture; Painting; Ceramic arts; Music; Philosophy/ethics.
Type of support: Residencies.
Application information:
  Initial approach: E-mail.
  Deadline(s): Apr. 15.
  Additional information: Application by letter including three work samples. Visual artists should send five slides of current work.
Program description:
  Residency Program: Residencies can last from one week to one month. Artists who are chosen will be asked to make a presentation to the community during their residency.
EIN: 382886660

5333
Sam and Adele Golden Foundation for the Arts
188 Bell Rd.
New Berlin, NY 13411 (607) 847-8158
Contact: Lucy Tower Funke, Dir.; Mark Golden, Pres.
FAX: (607) 847-8158;
E-mail: info@goldenfoundation.org; URL: http://www.goldenfoundation.org

Foundation type: Company-sponsored foundation
Limitations: Grants to professional artists, 25 years of age or older, working in paint who demonstrate exceptional creative ability.
Publications: Application guidelines.
Financial data: Year ended 12/31/2004.
Assets, $492,281 (M); Expenditures, $46,917; Total giving, $10,000.

Fields of interest: Painting.
Type of support: Awards/prizes; Stipends.
Application information: Applications accepted. Application form required. Application form available on the grantmaker's Web site.
  Initial approach: E-mail, telephone or letter.
  Copies of proposal: 1
  Deadline(s): Oct. 1
  Applicants should submit the following:
    1) Resume
    2) Proposal
    3) Budget Information
  Additional information: Application must also include one page typed narrative and six color slides in plastic sheet and slide list. Awards are intended for one year. Amounts range from $500 to $10,000.
EIN: 161523983

5334
Adolph and Esther Gottlieb Foundation, Inc.
380 W. Broadway
New York, NY 10012-5115 (212) 226-0581
Contact: Sheila Ross, Grants Mgr.
FAX: (212) 226-0584

Foundation type: Independent foundation
Limitations: Grants to painters, sculptors, and printmakers who have at least 20 years' experience in a mature phase of their art. Emergency assistance available for same visual artists who have at least ten years experience in a mature phase of their art and are in financial need as a result of an unexpected, catastrophic event.
Publications: Application guidelines; Informational brochure.
Financial data: Year ended 06/30/2005.
Assets, $28,778,366 (M); Expenditures, $891,471; Total giving, $461,505.
Fields of interest: Visual arts; Sculpture; Design; Arts, artist's services; Arts.
Type of support: Emergency funds; Grants for special needs.
Application information:
  Deadline(s): None
  Additional information: Applications by letter.
Program descriptions:
  Emergency Assistance Program: This program provides interim financial assistance to qualified artists whose needs are the result of an unforeseen, catastrophic incident, and who lack the resources to meet the situation. Each grant is given as one-time assistance for a specific emergency, such as fire, flood, or medical need. The maximum amount of this grant is $10,000. An award of $4,000 is typical. Applicants should note that there is a set amount appropriated for these grants each fiscal year. Once this budgetary limit has been reached, the foundation will not be able to consider any additional requests. Application forms for the Emergency Assistance Program are available from the foundation throughout the year and may be requested by telephone. Review procedures for applications begin as soon as they are received.
  Individual Support Program: "The foundation wishes to encourage those artists who have dedicated their lives to developing their art regardless of their level of commercial success. This program was conceived in order to recognize and support the serious, fully-committed artist." To be eligible for assistance under the Individual Support Program, the following criteria must be met:
    · Maturity: Successful applicants must demonstrate that they have been working in a mature phase of their art for at least

20 years. Maturity is based on the level of technical, intellectual, and creative development maintained over this period. Artists must show that their primary involvement has been with their artistic goals, regardless of other personal or financial responsibilities
    · Financial need: In addition to the maturity factor, eligibility for the Individual Support Grant is determined by the applicant's current financial need. A financial disclosure page, included in the application, must be completed and signed
The foundation does not fund organizations, projects of any type, educational institutions, students, graphic artists, or those working in crafts. The disciplines of photography, film, video, or related forms are ineligible unless the work directly involves, or can be interpreted as, painting or sculpture. Only written requests for application forms will be honored. The foundation will not mail out applications in response to telephone or second-party requests. Applicants must request a new application each year. Completed application materials must be postmarked no later than Dec. 15. Completed application materials consist of the following:
    · A current application form, available from the foundation
    · A written statement in a narrative format. This statement should include outside jobs which have helped support the artist's career, changes in artistic approach that have occurred, and other facts which can aid the review panel in forming an accurate picture of the applicant. All aspects of artistic history, i.e., education, exhibitions, etc., should be described, and dates must be provided for all information
    · A small group of slides of the artist's work which illustrates the progressive development of the art for at least a 20-year period. These slides must be labeled and dated
    · Financial information. Financial disclosure, which entails completing a disclosure page and submitting a copy of a recent federal tax return, is necessary in the determination of financial need
    · A self-addressed, stamped envelope for the return of supplementary materials.
EIN: 132853957

5335
Graham Foundation for Advanced Studies in the Fine Arts
4 W. Burton Pl.
Chicago, IL 60610-1416 (312) 787-4071
Contact: Patricia Snyder, Admin.
E-mail: info@grahamfoundation.org; URL: http://www.grahamfoundation.org

Foundation type: Independent foundation
Limitations: Project and publishing support, and travel grants to U.S. and Canadian residents working within the U.S. in the areas of contemporary architecture, design, and urban planning. Doctoral support by nomination only for Ph.D. candidates in the field of architecture through the Carter Manny Award.
Publications: Application guidelines; Annual report (including application guidelines); Grants list.
Financial data: Year ended 12/31/2004.
Assets, $37,657,188 (M); Expenditures, $2,189,177; Total giving, $1,181,699; Grants to individuals, 69 grants totaling $459,100 (high: $15,000, low: $2,000).

Fields of interest: Architecture; Design; Urban studies.
Type of support: Program development; Conferences/seminars; Publication; Fellowships; Research; Grants to individuals; Awards/prizes; Postdoctoral support; Travel grants; Doctoral support; Project support.
Application information: Application form not required.
  Initial approach: Proposal.
  Copies of proposal: 1
  Deadline(s): Jan. 15 and July 15
  Applicants should submit the following:
    1) Work samples
    2) Resume
    3) Proposal
    4) Letter(s) of recommendation
    5) Curriculum vitae
    6) Budget Information
  Additional information: Contact foundation for current application deadline; See program description for further details.
Program descriptions:
Graham Foundation Grants: Grants to individuals normally do not exceed $25,000. Applicants whose projects require more extensive support should indicate how the balance of funding is to be obtained. In most cases such additional support must be firmly obtained before a grant is released. Applications should contain:
- one-page summary of pertinent information (name and address of applicant, project title, concise abstract, amount of request, description of anticipated final products, names of people writing letters of support)
- proposal
- career resume
- work plan and schedule
- budget
- supplemental information (including visual information when appropriate)

In addition, applicants must request letters from three qualified references who are familiar with their ability and character and are knowledgeable in the area of the applicant's proposal. These letters are most helpful when they candidly assess the worthiness both of the individual and the project and are submitted by the reference person in confidence directly to the foundation without copies to the applicant. Reference letters must be postmarked within 15 days of the application deadline. No type smaller than ten points should be used in any application material. Applications sent by fax or e-mail will not be accepted. Send materials to the foundation by Jan. 15 or July 15. Awards are announced approximately 120 days after the application deadlines.
Carter Manny Award: The award is intended for scholars whose dissertations are directed towards architecture, landscape architecture, interior design, architectural history and theory, urban design and planning and—in some circumstances —the fine arts in relation to architectural topics. Applicants who have completed their course work and advanced to candidacy, and whose dissertation proposals have been approved by their academic departments, are eligible. Up to $10,000 will be awarded to one recipient per year. Applicants must submit a nomination letter from their department chair. Only one such nomination may be made annually by any one department. Applications are to include:
- cover sheet that states "Application for a Carter Manny Award" and provides the dissertation title; the applicant's name, address, and telephone numbers; and the name of the applicant's university and department

- one-page description of the dissertation project
- one-paragraph statement indicating amount requested and how funds would be applied
- brief resume
- no more than two pages of supplemental information (including visual information when appropriate)

In addition, applicants must request letters of recommendation from their thesis advisor, and from a specialist in the applicant's area of research who is not connected with the applicant's university. These must be sent directly to the foundation, and not via the applicant. No type smaller than ten points should be used in any application material. Applications sent by fax will not be accepted. Send materials to the Carter Manny Award Committee by Mar. 15. Recipients are notified no later than July 1.
EIN: 362356089

5336
Nancy Graves Foundation, Inc.
c/o Hecht and Company, PC
450 W. 31 St., 2nd Fl.
New York, NY 10001
E-mail: mail@nancygravesfoundation.org;
URL: http://www.nancygravesfoundation.org

Foundation type: Operating foundation
Limitations: Grants by nomination only to visual artists who wish to master a technique, medium, or discipline that is different from the one in which he or she is primarily recognized.
Publications: Grants list.
Financial data: Year ended 09/30/2004. Assets, $11,743,596 (M); Expenditures, $444,740; Total giving, $75,000; Grants to individuals, 3 grants totaling $75,000 (high: $25,000, low: $25,000).
Fields of interest: Visual arts.
Type of support: Awards/grants by nomination only.
Application information: Applications not accepted.
  Additional information: See Web site for complete nomination guidelines.
Program description:
Nancy Graves Grants for Visual Artist: Awards three grants of $25,000 each to visual artists who are residents of the U.S. who have been working as artists for at least five years beyond his or her schooling. Grants will not be awarded to students.
EIN: 133885307

5337
Virginia A. Groot Foundation
(formerly Candice B. Groot Foundation)
10750 55th Pl. N.
Plymouth, MN 55442-1930
Application address: c/o Patrice Olander-Quamme, Bookkeeper, P.O. Box 1050, Evanston, IL 60203-1050
E-mail: virginia@virginiaagrootfoundation.org;
URL: http://www.virginiaagrootfoundation.org

Foundation type: Independent foundation
Limitations: Grants to artists who have exceptional talent and demonstrated ability in ceramic arts in IA, IL, ND, SD, and WI.
Financial data: Year ended 12/31/2004. Assets, $621,336 (M); Expenditures, $68,167; Total giving, $35,000; Grants to individuals, 3 grants totaling $35,000 (high: $20,000, low: $5,000).
Fields of interest: Ceramic arts.

Type of support: Grants for special needs.
Application information: Applications accepted throughout the year; Completion of formal application required, including up to 20 35mm slides and SASE.
Program description:
Art Grants: Applicants may be at any stage of career development, from emerging through mature. Applicants must be 21 years of age or older at the time of the application deadline. Students enrolled or attending, either full-time or part-time, any institution of higher learning, are not eligible to apply. Teachers are eligible if their program plans are for their development as artists rather than as teachers. The grant is not for the support of continued academic training. Slides must be submitted in flat, transparent slide pages. Each slide must be numbered and labeled with the applicant's name and an arrow indicating the top of the slide. Accompanying the slides should be a typed or neatly printed sheet which corresponds with the numbered slides. For each slide the following information should be given: title, medium, size, and date completed. All application materials become the property of the foundation. Applicants who wish to have their slides returned after notification of the grant, must include a self-addressed, stamped envelope.
EIN: 411570531

5338
John Simon Guggenheim Memorial Foundation
90 Park Ave.
New York, NY 10016 (212) 687-4470
Contact: Edward Hirsch, Pres.
FAX: (212) 697-3248; E-mail: fellowships@gf.org;
URL: http://www.gf.org

Foundation type: Independent foundation
Limitations: Fellowships to published authors, exhibited artists, researchers, and others in the arts, humanities, social sciences, and natural sciences.
Publications: Annual report; Financial statement; Informational brochure (including application guidelines).
Financial data: Year ended 12/31/2004. Assets, $256,325,695 (M); Expenditures, $13,722,562; Total giving, $8,147,008; Grants to individuals, 399 grants totaling $8,147,008 (high: $50,000, low: $3,300, average grant: $10,000-$33,000).
Fields of interest: Humanities; Literature; Arts; Science, research; Mathematics; Social sciences.
Type of support: Fellowships; Foreign applicants.
Application information: Applications accepted. Application form required. Application form available on the grantmaker's Web site.
  Initial approach: E-mail.
  Deadline(s): Oct. 1 for the U.S. and Canada, Dec. 1 for Latin America and the Caribbean.
Program description:
Fellowship Awards: Fellowships are awarded to citizens and permanent residents of the U.S., Canada, Latin America, and the Caribbean who have already demonstrated exceptional capacity for productive scholarship or exceptional creative ability in the arts. Applicants are asked to show evidence of achievement through publication or exhibition and, if applying in the arts, submit examples of work. Individuals in all branches of the sciences and mathematics, all areas of the humanities, social sciences, and the creative arts, except for the performing arts may apply. The usual term of the fellowship is one year, but periods of a minimum of six months will be considered.

Amounts of the grants vary according to the needs of the individuals and their projects. Members of the teaching profession receiving sabbatical leave on full or part time salary are eligible for appointment, as are holders of other fellowships at other research centers. A list of the members of the Committee of Selection and Educational Advisory Board (which rotates about every four years) is available in the foundation's annual report, as are the biographies of the recipients of grants for each year. Numerous authorities and experts in each field serve as consultants.
EIN: 135673173

5339
The Gunk Foundation
P.O. Box 333
Gardiner, NY   12525   (845) 255-8252
Contact: Nadine Lemmon, Dir.
URL: http://www.gunk.org/

Foundation type: Operating foundation
Limitations: Grants to individual artists in CA, MA, NJ and NY for works of art.
Financial data: Year ended 12/31/2003.
Assets, $209,445 (M); Expenditures, $22,607; Total giving, $11,500; Grants to individuals, 6 grants totaling $10,500 (high: $3,000, low: $500).
Fields of interest: Arts.
Type of support: Program development; Grants to individuals.
Application information: Deadline Apr. 30; Application by letter, including examples of previous work (on slide sheet, one to two videos, CD-roms or DVDs); Application available on Web site; See Web site for further information.
EIN: 141777559

5340
The Hall Farm Center for Arts and Education
392 Hall Dr.
Townshend, VT   05353   (802) 365-4483
Contact: Scott Browning
E-mail: info@hallfarm.org; *URL:* http://www.hallfarm.org

Foundation type: Public charity
Limitations: Residencies to writers, visual artists and composers from the U.S. and abroad.
Publications: Newsletter.
Financial data: Year ended 12/31/2003.
Assets, $757,404 (M); Expenditures, $108,063. No monetary support given for residencies.
Fields of interest: Visual arts; Music composition; Literature.
Type of support: Foreign applicants; Residencies.
Application information: Applications accepted.
Application form required.
   Initial approach: E-mail.
   Deadline(s): Feb. 1.
   Additional information: Completion of formal application required, including work sample.
Program description:
   Residency Program: Residencies range from one week to one month. The residency season is divided into two sessions- applicants are asked to choose a period of time within a session. Housing, studios and meals are provided, but residents must supply their own transportation and materials.
EIN: 010526494

5341
Greater Hartford Arts Council, Inc.
P.O. Box 231436
Hartford, CT   06123-1436   (860) 525-8629
Contact: Kenneth Kahn, Exec. Dir.
E-mail: info@connectthedots.org; *URL:* http://www.connectthedots.org/

Foundation type: Public charity
Limitations: Fellowships to artists in the greater Hartford, CT, area.
Publications: Application guidelines; Annual report; Financial statement; Grants list; Informational brochure.
Financial data: Year ended 06/30/2004.
Assets, $2,320,484 (M); Expenditures, $4,599,661; Total giving, $1,501,669.
Fields of interest: Arts.
Type of support: Fellowships.
Application information: Applications accepted. Application form required. Application form available on the grantmaker's Web site.
EIN: 237111486

5342
Harvard Musical Association
c/o Chair., Awards Comm.
57A Chestnut St.
Boston, MA   02108   (617) 523-2897
FAX: (617) 523-2897;
E-mail: info@hmaboston.org; *URL:* http://www.hmaboston.org

Foundation type: Independent foundation
Limitations: Awards to secondary school students and conservatory students in MA, for recognition of artistic achievement.
Financial data: Year ended 06/30/2005.
Assets, $5,601,655 (M); Expenditures, $306,737; Total giving, $29,500; Grants to individuals, totaling $4,000.
Fields of interest: Performing arts; Music.
Type of support: Awards/prizes.
Application information: Applications accepted. Application form required.
   Initial approach: Letter.
   Deadline(s): Apr. 1
   Additional information: Contact association for current application guidelines.
EIN: 042104284

5343
Harvestworks, Inc.
596 Broadway, Ste. 602
New York, NY   10012   (212) 431-1130
Contact: Carol Parkinson
FAX: (212) 431-8473;
E-mail: hanst@harvestworks.org; *URL:* http://www.harvestworks.org

Foundation type: Public charity
Limitations: Residencies to artists for the creation of a new work of art that incorporates interactive technologies into the concept, design and presentation.
Publications: Application guidelines; Grants list; Informational brochure.
Financial data: Year ended 06/30/2003.
Assets, $95,104 (M); Expenditures, $529,341.
Fields of interest: Media/communications; Film/video; Visual arts; Music.
Type of support: Residencies.
Application information: Application form required.
   Initial approach: E-mail.
   Deadline(s): Jan. 15 for Interactive Technology AIR, Nov. 3 for New Works AIR

Applicants should submit the following:
   1) SASE
   2) Resume
Additional information: Application must also include description of project and audio/video work sample.
Program descriptions:
   New Works Residencies: The program offers commissions of up to $4,000 to make a new work in a state of the art digital media facility. Each artist receives $700 with the balance of the award posted in a "facilities account" which is used to manage and produce the work. The artist works with a team comprised of a project manager, engineer, and programmer.
   Residency Program: The Project offers a laboratory-like setting for the development of interactive computer environments, installations and instruments that foster new modes of perception and performance. National and international artists are invited to submit proposals for the creation of a new work of art that incorporates interactive technologies into the concept, design and presentation. Selected artists will be paired with a team of advisors that includes a project manager, programmers and designers. Two proposals will be chosen. Recipients will receive a $6,000 fee in addition to up to 100 hours in the facility with the technical team. Priority will be given to artists and/or collaborations already working in the field of interactive music and/or video technology who need technical assistance.
EIN: 132891159

5344
Hawaii Pacific Rim Society
P.O. Box 49
Honolulu, HI   96810

Foundation type: Independent foundation
Limitations: Grants to individuals involved in the arts, HI.
Financial data: Year ended 12/31/2003.
Assets, $2,770,024 (M); Expenditures, $175,822; Total giving, $142,500; Grant to an individual, 1 grant totaling $35,000.
Fields of interest: Arts.
Type of support: Grants for special needs.
Application information: Applications not accepted.
EIN: 990247100

5345
Headlands Center for the Arts
Bldg. 944
Fort Barry
Sausalito, CA   94965   (415) 331-2787
Contact: Kathryn Reasoner, Exec. Dir.
FAX: (415) 331-3857;
E-mail: staff@headlands.org; *URL:* http://www.headlands.org

Foundation type: Public charity
Limitations: Residencies to visual, literary, film/video and performing artists residing in CA, NJ, NC and OH.
Financial data: Year ended 12/31/2003.
Assets, $1,848,610 (M); Expenditures, $863,029; Total giving, $0. No monetary support given for residencies.
Fields of interest: Film/video; Visual arts; Performing arts; Literature.
Type of support: Foreign applicants; Residencies; Travel grants.
Application information: Applications accepted. Application form required.

Initial approach: Telephone.
Deadline(s): June 6.
Additional information: Headlands cannot accept unsolicited applications from artists from states or countries that do not currently have a formal sponsorship relationship with the Center.

Program description:
Residency Program: Thirty residencies are available for four weeks to eleven months, and include studio space, housing, travel costs, and meals. Artists must reside in CA, NC, NJ, and OH to be eligible. Currently, residencies are also being offered to artists from Taiwan, the Czech Republic and Slovakia.
EIN: 942817843

5346
The Ernest Hemingway Foundation, Inc.
c/o Fred Svoboda
2761 Roseland Ave.
East Lansing, MI   48823

Foundation type: Independent foundation
Limitations: Prizes and incentive awards for the best first novel by an American published in the previous year.
Financial data: Year ended 12/31/2004. Assets, $534,991 (M); Expenditures, $96,162; Total giving, $16,000; Grants to individuals, totaling $16,000.
Fields of interest: Literature.
Type of support: Awards/grants by nomination only; Awards/prizes.
Application information: No applications or nominations accepted; Recipients are pre-selected by a selection panel.
Program description:
Novelist Awards: The foundation awards a prize of $7,500 to the novelist whose work is chosen as the best first-time novel published in the preceding year. Recipients are chosen by a selection panel composed of members of P.E.N. Upon recommendation of the panel, the foundation may also award small prizes to one or two runners-up.
EIN: 136195832

5347
Henry Street Settlement
265 Henry St.
New York, NY   10002   (212) 766-9200
Contact: Robert Harrison, Chair.
FAX: (212) 505-8329;
E-mail: info@henrystreet.org; Residency application address: c/o Abrons Art Center, Attn: Artist-In-Residence Workspace Prog., 466 Grand St., New York, NY 10002; Additional tel.: (212) 598-0400; URL: http://www.henrystreet.org

Foundation type: Public charity
Limitations: Awards of studio space only to painters, printmakers, sculptors, installation artists and a clay artist, all of whom are residents of New York City.
Financial data: Year ended 06/30/2003. Assets, $30,425,587 (M); Expenditures, $35,134,651. No monetary support given for residencies.
Fields of interest: Visual arts; Sculpture; Painting.
Type of support: Awards/prizes; Residencies.
Application information: Application form required.
Initial approach: Telephone or e-mail.
Deadline(s): May 1
Applicants should submit the following:
1) Resume
2) Letter(s) of recommendation

Additional information: See Web site for current application guidelines; Applications must also include artist statement, slides of work, and references.
Program description:
Artist In Residence Workspace Program: Studio space at the Abrons Arts Center in NY is only provided to six New York City visual artists. Five of the artists selected will be painters, printmakers, sculptors or installation artists. One of the artists will be a clay artist. The program lasts for one year starting in late Sept. Each artist must make use of the collective workspace at least 20 hours per week. Residents are also required to provide a program of studio visits and an annual open house.
EIN: 131562242

5348
High Meadow Foundation, Inc.
c/o Country Curtains, Inc.
30 Main St.
Stockbridge, MA   01262   (413) 298-5565
Contact: Jane P. Fitzpatrick, Treas.; John H. Fitzpatrick, Pres.

Foundation type: Independent foundation
Limitations: Support primarily for the performing arts, especially theater and music; giving also for health, social services, and education. Giving primarily in Berkshire County, MA.
Financial data: Year ended 09/30/2004. Assets, $1,904,527 (M); Expenditures, $1,195,264; Total giving, $1,170,402.
Fields of interest: Performing arts; Theater; Music; Arts, artist's services; Arts; Education; Health care; Human services.
Type of support: Grants for special needs.
Application information: Applications accepted.
Initial approach: Letter.
Additional information: Contact foundation for current application guidelines.
EIN: 222527419

5349
Highpoint Center for Printmaking
2638 Lyndale Ave. S.
Minneapolis, MN   55408   (612) 871-1326
E-mail: info@highpointprintmaking.org;
URL: http://www.highpointprintmaking.org

Foundation type: Public charity
Limitations: Residencies to emerging printmaking artists residing in MN.
Publications: Application guidelines.
Financial data: Year ended 12/31/2004. Assets, $213,760 (M); Expenditures, $429,294. No monetary support given for residencies.
Fields of interest: Visual arts.
Type of support: Residencies.
Application information: Application form required.
Initial approach: E-mail.
Deadline(s): Mar. 26
Applicants should submit the following:
1) Resume
2) SASE
Additional information: Application must also include slides of recent work, letter of intent, and slide list.
Program description:
Residency Program: Three printmaking residencies are available to MN emerging artists. Residencies last for nine months. The program provides access to a printshop, technical support, storage space, use of supplies, discussions/

critiques, and a public show at the end of the residency.
EIN: 411977650

5350
Home for Contemporary Theater and Art
145 6th Ave.
New York, NY   10013-1548   (212) 647-0202
Contact: Kristin Marting, Exec. Dir.
FAX: (212) 647-0257; E-mail: info@here.org; Additional E-mail (for Kristin Marting): kristin@here.org; URL: http://www.here.org

Foundation type: Public charity
Limitations: Residencies to writers, performers, composers, directors, designers, puppeteers, dancers and singers in the live performance arts.
Financial data: Year ended 08/31/2004. Assets, $169,181 (M); Expenditures, $929,595.
Fields of interest: Film/video; Design; Performing arts; Performing arts centers; Dance; Theater; Music composition; Literature.
Type of support: Residencies.
Application information:
Initial approach: Letter.
Deadline(s): Jan. 2
Additional information: Application must also include, biography, resume, artist statement, work samples and project outline; Interviews required; See Web site for additional application information.
Program description:
Here Artist Residency Program (HARP): Each residency lasts a minimum of one year, for up to three years. Residencies begin on Mar. 1. The program nurtures the development of mid-career hybrid artists through cross-disciplinary exchange, peer-driven workshops, and panel discussions.
EIN: 133449416

5351
Houston Center for Contemporary Craft
4848 Main St.
Houston, TX   77002
Contact: Ann Lancaster, Exec. Dir.
E-mail: alancaster@crafthouston.org; URL: http://www.crafthouston.org

Foundation type: Public charity
Limitations: Residencies to artists working in craft media such as wood, glass, metal, fiber, and clay.
Publications: Informational brochure; Newsletter.
Financial data: Year ended 12/31/2003. Assets, $488,008 (M); Expenditures, $1,243,597. No monetary support given for residencies.
Fields of interest: Ceramic arts; Arts.
Type of support: Residencies.
Application information:
Deadline(s): Applications by letter accepted throughout the year
Applicants should submit the following:
1) Letter(s) of recommendation
2) Resume
Additional information: Application must also include 15-20 slides of recent work, personal statement and residency preference dates.
Program description:
Studio Residency: The program provides studio space and a $400 monthly stipend. The average length of stay is three to twelve months.
EIN: 760621817

5352
Richard Hugo House
1634 11th Ave.
Seattle, WA 98122 (206) 322-7030
Contact: Lyall Bush, Progs. and Educ. Mgr.
FAX: (206) 320-8767;
E-mail: programs@hugohouse.org; URL: http://www.hugohouse.org

Foundation type: Public charity
Limitations: Awards to winners of the Richard Hugo House New Works Competition who reside in AK, ID, MT, OR, and WA.
Financial data: Year ended 12/31/2003.
Assets, $947,002 (M); Expenditures, $728,557; Total giving, $9,150.
Fields of interest: Theater (playwriting); Literature.
Type of support: Awards/prizes.
Application information: Application form required.
Additional information: Contact foundation for current application guidelines; Interviews required.
Program description:
Awards: Applicants must be playwrights who submit original, unproduced, full-length plays. The award is $1,000 and a public reading of the play, to be staged at Hugo House.
EIN: 911718383

5353
Zora Neale Hurston & Richard Wright Foundation
6525 Belcrest Rd., Ste. 531
Hyattsville, MD 20782 (301) 683-2134
Contact: Marita Golden, Pres. and C.E.O.
E-mail: info@hurstonwright.org; URL: http://www.hurston-wright.org/

Foundation type: Public charity
Limitations: Awards to writers of African descent.
Financial data: Year ended 12/31/2003.
Assets, $12,036 (M); Expenditures, $296,070; Total giving, $64,500; Grants to individuals, totaling $64,500 (high: $10,000).
Fields of interest: Literature; African Americans/Blacks.
Type of support: Awards/prizes.
Application information: Applications accepted. Application form required. Application form available on the grantmaker's Web site.
Initial approach: E-mail.
Deadline(s): Oct. 19 for LEGACY Awards, and Dec. 31 for College Writers Awards
Additional information: Application must include entry fee and manuscript.
Program descriptions:
Hurston/Wright Award for College Writers: This award honors excellence in fiction writing by students of African descent enrolled full time as undergraduate or graduate students in any college or university in the United States. The first place award of $1,000 and two finalist awards of $500 will be presented at a ceremony in April to the writers of the best previously unpublished short story or novel excerpt. This ceremony will take place in Washington D.C.
Hurston/Wright LEGACY Award: This award is presented to published writers of African descent. There will be a first place winner in each category. Each first place winner will receive a cash award of $10,000. There will also be two finalists in each category. Each finalist will receive a cash award of $5,000. Full length books of fiction and nonfiction, collections of short stories and collections of essays by one author are eligible.
EIN: 521706969

5354
Independence Foundation
200 S. Broad St., Ste. 1101
Philadelphia, PA 19102 (215) 985-4009
Contact: Susan E. Sherman, C.E.O. and Pres.
FAX: (215) 985-3989;
E-mail: artfellowships@independencefoundation.org; URL: http://www.independencefoundation.org

Foundation type: Independent foundation
Limitations: Visual and performing arts fellowships by nomination only to residents of the Philadelphia, PA, area, including Bucks, Chester, Delaware, Montgomery, and Philadelphia counties.
Publications: Application guidelines; Annual report; Grants list; Occasional report.
Financial data: Year ended 12/31/2004.
Assets, $99,027,870 (M); Expenditures, $9,749,325; Total giving, $7,565,702; Grants to individuals, 20 grants totaling $156,200 (high: $10,000; low: $1,700, average grant: $7,500-$10,000).
Fields of interest: Visual arts; Performing arts; Arts, artist's services.
Type of support: Fellowships; Awards/grants by nomination only.
Application information:
Deadline(s): Mar. 26 for performing arts, and fall for visual arts
Additional information: Contact foundation for current nomination guidelines.
Program description:
Fellowships in the Arts: Originating artists include painters, sculptors, choreographers, playwrights, and composers. Interpretive artists include actors, dancers, and musicians. There are two grant cycles annually, one in the visual arts (spring), and one in the performing arts (fall). Applicants must have three to five years professional experience in the visual or performance arts; and must be nominated by an official nominating organization.
EIN: 231352110

5355
Independent Feature Project, Inc.
(also known as IFP)
104 W. 29th St.
New York, NY 10001 (212) 465-8200
Contact: Michelle Byrd, Exec. Dir.
FAX: (212) 465-8525; E-mail: mbyrd@ifp.org; URL: http://www.ifp.org

Foundation type: Public charity
Limitations: Grants to independent filmmakers.
Financial data: Year ended 12/31/2003.
Assets, $988,885 (M); Expenditures, $2,361,317; Total giving, $63,850; Grants to individuals, totaling $63,850.
Fields of interest: Film/video.
Type of support: Program development.
Application information: Application form required.
Deadline(s): Sept. 1 and Mar. 1
Additional information: See Web site for further application and program information.
Program description:
Anthony Radziwill Documentary Fund: Grants awarded to documentary artists who are seeking funds needed for research, treatment, and script development, initial interviews, and the production of trailers/clips for further funding needs. Proposed films and videos on the arts, humanities, societal issues, contemporary political issues, history, and personal documentaries are all encouraged. The fund supports a range of work, from the traditionally researched and structured to work that is more creatively risky and formally challenging. In all cases the fund looks to support work that will be artistically significant and culturally important. Grants are intended for feature-length nonfiction projects (more than fifty minutes) and are awarded to individuals with creative and financial control over the project. The grantee must be a legal resident of the U.S. and be 18 years of age or older. Projects should be intended for general audiences and for wide distribution via theatrical, television, and festival markets.
EIN: 133118525

5356
Independent Television Service
(also known as ITVS)
501 York St.
San Francisco, CA 94110 (415) 356-8383
FAX: (415) 356-8391; E-mail: itvs@itvs.org; URL: http://www.itvs.org

Foundation type: Public charity
Limitations: Grants to independent film and video artists to produce innovative television programming.
Publications: Application guidelines; Newsletter.
Financial data: Year ended 09/30/2004.
Assets, $18,278,606 (M); Expenditures, $10,092,056; Total giving, $32,272; Grants to individuals, totaling $32,272.
Fields of interest: Film/video; Arts.
Type of support: Program development; Grants to individuals.
Application information: Application form required.
Initial approach: Letter or telephone.
Deadline(s): Contact foundation for current application deadline
Program description:
Diversity Development Fund: Seeks talented minority producers to develop single programs for public television. Programs can be in any genre, including drama, documentary, docudrama, animation, experimental works or innovative combinations that will resound in multicultural communities. Deadline is Mar. 31.
EIN: 521654276

5357
International Association for Jazz Education
2803 Claflin Rd.
P.O. Box 724
Manhattan, KS 66505 (785) 776-8744
Contact: Bill McFarlin, Exec. Dir.
FAX: (785) 776-6190; E-mail: info@iaje.org; URL: http://www.iaje.org

Foundation type: Public charity
Limitations: Fellowships and commission awards to jazz composers.
Financial data: Year ended 06/30/2003.
Assets, $281,395 (M); Expenditures, $1,920,237; Total giving, $10,466; Grants to individuals, totaling $10,466.
Fields of interest: Music composition.
Type of support: Fellowships; Awards/prizes.
Application information:
Initial approach: E-mail.
Deadline(s): Apr. 1 for ASCAP/IAJE Commissions, Oct. 15 for Gil Evans Fellowship
Additional information: Application form required, including cassette recordings of original compositions, curriculum vitae, and biography; See Web site for further application information.

Program descriptions:

ASCAP/IAJE Commissions: Commissions for two works to be premiered at the annual IAJE Conference. Winners receive additional compensation for copying costs, travel and lodging for the conference. IAJE members are eligible for one of the following commissions:

· Established Jazz Composer commission-$7,500.

· Emerging Jazz Composer commission (who has not reached age 35 by time of application)-$3,000.

Gil Evans Fellowship: The fellowship recipient is commissioned to compose a work in the jazz idiom for performance during the International Association for Jazz Education Annual Conference. The commission range will be from $2,500 to $5,000. In addition, the fellowships recipient will be provided with all expenses to attend the IAJE International Conference for two years. All applicants shall be no older than 35 years of age.
EIN: 480794187

5358

International Reading Association, Inc.

800 Barksdale Rd.
P.O. Box 8139
Newark, DE   19714-8139   (800) 336-7323
Contact: Alan Farstrup, Exec. Dir.
FAX: (302) 731-1057;
E-mail: pubinfo@reading.org; Additional tel.: (302) 731-1600, outside of the U.S. and Canada;
URL: http://www.reading.org

Foundation type: Public charity
Limitations: Awards to writers for works aimed at children and young adults.
Financial data: Year ended 06/30/2004. Assets, $30,425,503 (M); Expenditures, $16,751,772; Total giving, $348,942; Grants to individuals, 37 grants totaling $50,746 (high: $6,000, low: $167).
Fields of interest: Literature.
Type of support: Awards/prizes.
Application information: Applications accepted. Application form required. Application form available on the grantmaker's Web site.
Initial approach: E-mail.
Deadline(s): Varies
Additional information: For further application guidelines, contact the foundation at: exec@reading.org.
Program descriptions:
IRA Children's Book Awards: Children's Book Awards are given for an author's first or second published book written for children or young adults (ages birth to 17 years). Awards are given for fiction and nonfiction in each of three categories: primary, intermediate, and young adult. Books from any country and in any language published for the first time during the current calendar year will be considered. Each award carries a monetary stipend.
Paul A. Witty Short Story Award: This award is given to the author of an original short story published for the first time during the current calendar year in a periodical for children. The award carries a $1,000 stipend. The short story should serve as a literary standard that encourages young readers to read periodicals.
Lee Bennett Hopkins Promising Poet Award: The Lee Bennett Hopkins Promising Poet Award is a $500 award given every three years to a promising new poet who writes for children and young adults, and who has published no more than two books of children's poetry. A book-length single poem may be submitted. ("Children's poetry" is defined as poetry, rather than light verse.) The award is for

published works only. Poetry in any language may be submitted; non-English poetry must be accompanied by an English translation.
EIN: 362364659

5359

Jacob's Pillow Dance Festival, Inc.

358 George Carter Rd.
Becket, MA   01223   (413) 243-9919
Contact: Ella Baff, Exec. Dir.
E-mail: info@jacobspillow.org; URL: http://www.jacobspillow.org

Foundation type: Public charity
Limitations: Scholarships to dancers in MA to attend the School at Jacob's Pillow.
Financial data: Year ended 11/30/2004. Assets, $11,820,272 (M); Expenditures, $3,753,525; Total giving, $71,260; Grants to individuals, totaling $71,260.
Fields of interest: Dance; Performing arts, education.
Type of support: Scholarships—to individuals.
Application information: Contact foundation for current application deadline; Completion of formal application required, including financial information; See Web site for application form.
Program description:
Scholarship Program: Scholarships are awarded on the basis of demonstrated financial need. In exchange for scholarships, recipients are assigned tasks which do not conflict with program participation. Recipients are expected to be exemplary Pillow community members. To assist as many students as possible, partial scholarships of varying amounts are awarded with full scholarships reserved for dancers of exceptional talent who strongly document their need for assistance.
EIN: 046002993

5360

The Rona Jaffe Foundation

P.O. Box 1847 Murray Hill Station
New York, NY   10156

Foundation type: Independent foundation
Limitations: Grants to writers in NY to support them in their works.
Financial data: Year ended 09/30/2002. Assets, $357,528 (M); Expenditures, $110,916; Total giving, $60,000; Grants to individuals, 6 grants totaling $60,000 (high: $10,000, low: $10,000).
Fields of interest: Journalism/publishing; Literature.
Type of support: Awards/prizes.
Application information: Unsolicited requests for funds not accepted.
EIN: 133383860

5361

Jentel Foundation

130 Lower Piney Creek Rd.
Banner, WY   82832   (307) 737-2311
FAX: (307) 737-2305;
E-mail: jentel@jentelarts.org; URL: http://www.jentelarts.org

Foundation type: Operating foundation
Limitations: Residencies to writers in all genres and to visual artists in all media over 25 years of age, for four weeks.

Publications: Application guidelines; Annual report; Informational brochure (including application guidelines).
Financial data: Year ended 12/31/2004. Assets, $2,966,693 (M); Expenditures, $409,583; Total giving, $0. No monetary support given for residencies.
Fields of interest: Visual arts; Literature.
Type of support: Residencies; Stipends.
Application information: Application form required. Application form available on the grantmaker's Web site.
Initial approach: E-mail.
Deadline(s): Jan. 15 and Sept. 15.
Applicants should submit the following:
1) Work samples
2) Proposal
3) Curriculum vitae
4) Letter(s) of recommendation
5) SASE
Additional information: Application must also include $20 application fee; See Web site for further information.
Program description:
Residencies: Awards around 66 one-month residencies to visual artists in all media and writers in all genres on a ranch twenty miles southeast of Sheridan, WY. Here a small group of artists and writers experience unfettered time to allow for thoughtful reflection on the creative process in a setting that preserves the agricultural and historical integrity of the land. The program provides each resident with a spacious private bedroom in a large comfortable house, and a private workspace. Applicants must bring their own materials. A monthly stipend of $400 is provided to defray personal expenses.
EIN: 830331644

5362

Jerome Foundation

400 Sibley St., Ste. 125
St. Paul, MN   55101-1928   (651) 224-9431
Contact: Cynthia A. Gehrig, Pres.
FAX: (651) 224-3439; E-mail: info@jeromefdn.org; Toll-free tel.: (800) 995-3766 (MN and New York City only); URL: http://www.jeromefdn.org

Foundation type: Independent foundation
Limitations: Grants for film, video, and interactive media projects to artists residing in New York City, NY, and the state of MN; and for travel and study to artists and nonprofit arts administrators in dance, literature, media arts, music, theater, and the visual arts residing in MN and New York City.
Publications: Application guidelines; Financial statement; Grants list; Informational brochure (including application guidelines).
Financial data: Year ended 04/30/2005. Assets, $77,092,175 (M); Expenditures, $4,298,797; Total giving, $3,130,060.
Fields of interest: Media/communications; Film/video; Visual arts; Dance; Theater; Music; Literature; Arts, artist's services.
Type of support: Travel grants; Project support.
Application information: Application form required. Application form available on the grantmaker's Web site.
Deadline(s): None for New York City Media Arts Program; Spring for Minnesota Media Arts Program; Jan. or Feb. for Travel and Study Grant Program
Applicants should submit the following:
1) Work samples
2) Resume
3) Proposal
4) Budget Information

Additional information: See program description for application information on specific programs.

Program descriptions:

New York City Media Arts Program: The foundation operates a special grant program for individual film and video artists living and working in New York City. This program awards production grants to emerging artists who make creative use of their respective media. The foundation supports artists whose work shows promise of excellence. These artists will most often be in the early stages of their careers and will not have had the support needed to fully display their work. Preference is given to personal, low-budget work in which the artist exercises complete creative control over all aspects of production. Applicants apply as individuals and are reviewed by an independent panel. This panel meets three times in the course of the fiscal year and makes recommendations to the foundation board which takes final action on all requests. Applications should include:

- American citizenship or legal permanent residency in the U.S. as well as residency in New York City.
- Completion of formal education or its equivalent (i.e., applicant need not hold a degree but must no longer be a student).
- Evidence that the applicant is an artist seriously striving toward professional status.
- Applicants should be able to submit work samples of up to 25 minutes in length. Student works are acceptable.

Travel and Study Grant Program: Awards grants of up to $1,200 for short-term travel and up to $5,000 for trips of one week or longer to artists and administrators in the fields of literature, media arts and music. Grants are for the purpose of professional development. Funding is available for activities such as dialogue on aesthetic issues, the experience of seeing artistic work outside of MN and New York City, time for reflection and individualized study, the development of collaborations, participation in specific training programs, and research leading to the creation of new work. Travel may be national or international.

Minnesota Media Arts Program: This program supports personally conceived independent film and video productions as well as other media forms, such as film/video installations, online projects, and interactive media created by residents of MN. Applicants must be residents of MN. Students are not eligible. Preference is given to personal work in which the artist exercises complete creative control over all aspects of production. The foundation considers requests for projects with total budgets of $175,000 or less. The level of support offered ranges from $8,000 to $20,000. The foundation places emphasis on funding projects in their early stages. Requests for productions that are more than half completed are eligible but represent a lower priority. No more than one grant will be awarded per project. A book of sample proposals and budgets, along with helpful application tips is available upon request. Completion of formal application is required, including work samples, a project budget, project description, current resume, list of submitted sample works, SASE for return of work samples, and if project is narrative, a ten-page excerpt of the script, storyboard, or detailed treatment. Applicants may submit up to three sample works with a maximum total viewing time of 20 minutes. Contact the foundation for detailed program description and application procedures. Questions should be directed to Robert Byrd, tel.: (651) 224-9431 or (800) 995-3766. Deadline May 23.
EIN: 416035163

5363
Joshua Tree National Park Association

74485 National Park Dr.
Twentynine Palms, CA   92277-3533
(760) 365-5537
Contact: Nancy Downer, Exec. Dir.
Residency application address: P.O. Box 1499, Joshua Tree, CA 92252;
E-mail: info@artmojave.org; URL: http://www.artmojave.org
E-mail: mail@joshuatree.org; URL: http://www.joshuatree.org

Foundation type: Public charity
Limitations: Residencies to visual artists and writers to stay at Joshua Tree National Park, CA.
Financial data: Year ended 09/30/2004. Assets, $306,815 (M); Expenditures, $317,375.
Fields of interest: Visual arts; Literature.
Type of support: Residencies.
Application information:
Deadline(s): Contact foundation for current application deadline.
Applicants should submit the following:
1) SASE
Additional information: Application by letter including 20 slides of work, exhibition record, and artist statement.
Program description:
Park Stewardship Through the Arts: The residency provides housing. The length of the program is four weeks, running from Jan. through May. Each artist will donate one example of work produced at the park.
EIN: 952312513

5364
Clarisse B. Kampel Foundation, Inc.

c/o Bruce MacCorkindale
3960 Merrick Rd.
Seaford, NY   11783
Contact: Carl Battaglia, Exec. Dir.
Application address: 330 E. 63rd St., New York, NY 10021

Foundation type: Independent foundation
Limitations: Project support to individuals primarily residing in New York, NY, who are aspiring to careers as vocal or instrumental artists.
Financial data: Year ended 06/30/2004. Assets, $154,760 (M); Expenditures, $25,599; Total giving, $25,000; Grants to individuals, 2 grants totaling $25,000 (high: $15,000, low: $10,000).
Fields of interest: Music.
Type of support: Program development.
Application information:
Initial approach: Letter.
Applicants should submit the following:
1) Resume
Additional information: Interviews required.
EIN: 133347805

5365
Kansas Cultural Trust

255 N. Roosevelt St.
Wichita, KS   67208-3720   (800) 666-9040
Contact: Howard W. Ellington, Tr.

Foundation type: Independent foundation

Limitations: Awards to promising painters, sculptors, musicians, dancers, and performing artists whose study has advanced beyond degree-granting programs and who are or were KS residents or graduates of KS universities and colleges.
Publications: Application guidelines.
Financial data: Year ended 12/31/2004. Assets, $33,877 (M); Expenditures, $156,650; Total giving, $96,115; Grants to individuals, 28 grants totaling $96,115 (high: $35,000, low: $400).
Fields of interest: Visual arts; Sculpture; Design; Painting; Performing arts; Dance; Music.
Type of support: Awards/prizes.
Application information: Deadlines vary; Completion of formal application required.
EIN: 480989992

5366
John F. Kennedy Center for the Performing Arts

2700 F St., N.W.
Washington, DC   20566-0001   (202) 416-8603
Contact: Michael M. Kaiser, Pres.
Tel.: (202) 416-8348 (Jazz Ahead Residency)
FAX: (202) 416-8205; E-mail:
rsfoster@kennedy-center.org (Fund for New American Plays), vilarinstitute@kennedy-center.org (internships), yfp@kennedy-center.org (Center for New Visions); URL: http://www.kennedy-center.org

Foundation type: Public charity
Limitations: Fellowships and residencies to artists.
Publications: Application guidelines.
Financial data: Year ended 09/30/2003. Assets, $344,282,110 (M); Expenditures, $112,097,169; Total giving, $694,394.
Fields of interest: Arts, management/technical aid; Performing arts; Performing arts centers; Music; Music composition.
Type of support: Fellowships; Residencies.
Application information: Application form required.
Deadline(s): Apr. 1. for Villar Fellowship, Dec. 17 for Jazz Ahead
Applicants should submit the following:
1) Resume
2) Transcripts
3) Letter(s) of recommendation
Additional information: See Web site for additional application information.
Program descriptions:
Vilar Institute Fellowships: Awards fellowships to individuals who aspire to manage performing arts institutions. The program includes extensive coursework in contemporary business practices management through the lens of planning, presenting and producing performing arts programming at an international performing arts institution. Fellows develop skills in working effectively with elected officials, business and community leaders and fellow arts professionals. The program emphasizes excellence, creativity, economic problem-solving, internationalism, and a commitment to new technologies. Fellows receive a stipend of $18,000 (paid bi-weekly).
Jazz Ahead: This residency program identifies emerging jazz artists in their mid-teens and twenties, and brings them together under the tutelage of experienced artist-instructors. The week-long program will include daily workshops and rehearsals, culminating in three concerts on the Kennedy Center's Millenium Stage. A travel and meal stipend, as well as housing, is included.
EIN: 530245017

5367

Kentucky Foundation for Women, Inc.
1215 Heyburn Bldg.
332 W. Broadway
Louisville, KY 40202-2184 (502) 562-0045
FAX: (502) 561-0420; E-mail: kfw@kfw.org; Toll
free:(866) 654-7564; URL: http://www.kfw.org/

Foundation type: Independent foundation
Limitations: Grants to feminist artists living in KY
with the mission of promoting social change
through varied feminist expressions in the arts.
Publications: Application guidelines; Annual report;
Grants list; Newsletter.
Financial data: Year ended 06/30/2005.
Assets, $12,802,795 (M); Expenditures,
$590,901; Total giving, $203,304; Grants to
individuals, 57 grants totaling $125,726 (high:
$6,260, low: $1,000).
Fields of interest: Arts; Civil rights, women.
Type of support: Program development.
Application information: Application form required.
Application form available on the grantmaker's Web
site.
  Initial approach: Letter or telephone requesting
    application.
  Deadline(s): Vary
  Additional information: Applicants must submit
    work samples that demonstrate high artistic
    merit. Residencies at Hopscotch House are
    currently available to Kentucky-based feminist
    artists and arts organizations by application.
    See Web site for further information.
Program descriptions:
  Artist Enrichment: This program provides grants
and opportunities for feminist artists and arts
organizations whose efforts promote social change
to enhance their abilities and skills to make art.
Deadline early Sept.
  Art Meets Activism: This program provides grants
and supports feminist artists and organizations in
developing and implementing work that is directly
focused on social change outcomes benefiting
Kentucky women and/or girls. Deadline Mar. 3.
EIN: 611070429

5368

**The Jack Kerouac Writers in Residence
  Project, Inc.**
P.O. Box 547477
Orlando, FL 32854
Contact: Bob Kealing, V.P.
E-mail: kerouacinflorida@hotmail.com;
URL: http://www.kerouacproject.org

Foundation type: Public charity
Limitations: Residencies to writers to stay at Jack
Kerouac's FL home.
Publications: Application guidelines.
Financial data: Year ended 06/30/2005.
Assets, $253,660 (M); Expenditures, $5,976. No
monetary support given for residencies.
Fields of interest: Literature.
Type of support: Residencies.
Application information:
  Deadline(s): Contact foundation for current
    application deadline/guidelines
  Additional information: Application by letter
    including resume, ten page manuscript, and
    time slot preference.
Program description:
  Writer in Residence: The residency lasts for three
months and includes housing as well as food gift
cards. The successful candidates and one spouse/
partner maximum can be accommodated upon

completion of the program, the resident will give a
reading at the Kerouac House.
EIN: 593531416

5369

John Anson Kittredge Educational Fund
c/o KeyBank N.A.
P.O. Box 1054
Augusta, ME 04330-1054
Contact: Ernest R. May
Travel grant application address: c/o Prof. Ernest R.
May, P.O. Box 2883, Cambridge, MA 02138
Application address: P.O. Box 382203, Cambridge,
MA 02238-2203

Foundation type: Independent foundation
Limitations: Grants awarded to artists and scholars
for travel to conferences, research, and other
artistic or scholarly projects. No scholarships are
awarded.
Financial data: Year ended 04/30/2004.
Assets, $0 (M); Expenditures, $144,145; Total
giving, $127,760; Grants to individuals, totaling
$127,760.
Application information:
  Deadline(s): None
  Additional information: Application by letter,
    including purpose, amount requested, period
    of funding, and supporting letters.
EIN: 016007180

5370

The Kleban Foundation, Inc.
345 E. 56th St., No. 10-J
New York, NY 10022 (212) 588-1145
Contact: Alan Stein, Secy.
URL: http://www.newdramatists.org/
kleban_award.htm

Foundation type: Independent foundation
Limitations: Support to promising theatrical
lyricists and librettists.
Financial data: Year ended 06/30/2005.
Assets, $2,470,071 (M); Expenditures,
$273,745; Total giving, $200,000; Grants to
individuals, 5 grants totaling $200,000 (high:
$50,000, low: $25,000).
Application information: Applications by letter
accepted throughout the year.
EIN: 133490882

5371

Koussevitzky Music Foundation, Inc.
c/o Anthony Schidt
475 Wall St.
Princeton, NJ 08540 (212) 895-2367
Contact: James M. Kendrick, Secy.
Application address: 900 3rd Ave., New York, NY
10036
FAX: (212) 895-2900;
E-mail: info@koussevitzky.org; URL: http://
www.koussevitzky.org/

Foundation type: Independent foundation
Limitations: Commissions based on merit to
composers of serious music who are over 25 years
of age, have completed formal conservatory studies
or have a B.A. from a recognized conservatory,
college, or university, or demonstrated equivalent,
and whose music has been published, recorded,
and/or performed in public, and are sponsored by
a performing organization. Composers who received
commission during the past ten years are ineligible.

Publications: Application guidelines; Informational
brochure (including application guidelines).
Financial data: Year ended 12/31/2004.
Assets, $1,608,817 (M); Expenditures,
$128,716; Total giving, $92,425; Grants to
individuals, totaling $92,425.
Application information: Application form required.
  Deadline(s): Mar. 1
EIN: 046128361

5372

**The Emory and Ilona E. Ladanyi
  Foundation, Inc.**
P.O. Box 6
Merrick, NY 11566-0006
Contact: Andrew S. Erdelyi, Pres.

Foundation type: Independent foundation
Limitations: Grants to young American artists.
Financial data: Year ended 10/31/2004.
Assets, $388,619 (M); Expenditures, $65,377;
Total giving, $41,835; Grants to individuals,
totaling $2,500.
Fields of interest: Arts, artist's services.
Type of support: Grants to individuals.
Application information: Contact foundation for
current application deadline; Application by
submission of a sample portfolio.
EIN: 133448832

5373

Lake Region Arts Council, Inc.
133 S. Mill St.
Fergus Falls, MN 56537-2578 (218) 739-5780
Contact: Maxine Adams, Exec. Dir.
E-mail: lrac4@charterinternet.com; Additional tel.:
(800) 262-2787; URL: http://
www.charterinternet.com/lrac4

Foundation type: Public charity
Limitations: Fellowships and grants to artists living
in the MN counties of Becker, Clay, Douglas, Grant,
Otter Tail, Pope, Stevens, Traverse and Wilkin.
Financial data: Year ended 06/30/2003.
Assets, $106,168 (M); Expenditures, $181,103;
Total giving, $75,580.
Fields of interest: Arts.
Type of support: Fellowships.
Application information: Application form required.
  Initial approach: Letter or telephone.
  Additional information: Contact foundation for
    current application deadline/guidelines.
Program description:
  Fellowship Program: Artist grants of up to $1,200
and arts fellowships of $5,000 are available to
artists residing in the MN counties of Becker, Clay,
Douglas, Grant, Otter Tail, Pope, Stevens, Traverse
and Wilkin.
EIN: 411430764

5374

Lannan Foundation
313 Read St.
Santa Fe, NM 87501-2628 (505) 986-8160
Contact: Ruth Simms, Cont.
FAX: (505) 986-8195; E-mail: info@lannan.org;
Additional contact information (for Ruth Simms):
FAX: (505) 954-5143, E-mail: ruth@lannan.org;
URL: http://www.lannan.org

Foundation type: Independent foundation
Limitations: Awards to writers writing in the English
language, and grants to visual artists from

indigenous communities promoting cultural freedom.

Financial data: Year ended 12/31/2004. Assets, $241,070,074 (M); Expenditures, $17,103,550; Total giving, $10,627,962; Grants to individuals, 23 grants totaling $1,068,250 (high: $125,000, low: $10,000, average grant: $25,000-$50,000).

Fields of interest: Visual arts; Literature.

Type of support: Program development; Publication; Awards/grants by nomination only; Awards/prizes.

Application information: Applications not accepted.

Program descriptions:

Art Program: Supports the creativity of exceptional contemporary visual artists. Funds are not available for documentary film or video projects, performing arts, theater, crafts, or decorative arts.

Lannan Literary Awards: Awards are given to encourage and support the creation of literature originally written in the English language, in order to help provide the greatest possible recognition for individual writers and their work, and to enhance the literary skills and talents of the recipients.

EIN: 366062451

5375
Larchmont Chamber Music Circle, Inc.

c/o American Express TBS
1185 Ave. of the Americas
New York, NY 10036-2602

Foundation type: Independent foundation

Limitations: Performance grants to individual musicians who display unusual talent and potential.

Financial data: Year ended 12/31/2004. Assets, $14,730 (M); Expenditures, $13,090; Total giving, $13,000; Grants to individuals, totaling $9,000.

Fields of interest: Performing arts; Music.

Type of support: Program development.

Application information: Applications by letter accepted throughout the year.

EIN: 136157956

5376
Jonathan Larson Performing Arts Foundation, Inc.

P.O. Box 672, Prince St. Station
New York, NY 10012 (212) 529-0814
FAX: (212) 253-7604; E-mail: JLPAF@aol.com;
URL: http://www.jlpaf.org/

Foundation type: Independent foundation

Limitations: Grants to composers, lyricists, and bookwriters working in musical theater.

Financial data: Year ended 12/31/2004. Assets, $841,067 (M); Expenditures, $326,372; Total giving, $47,700; Grants to individuals, 6 grants totaling $40,000.

Fields of interest: Theater (musical); Music composition; Literature.

Type of support: Program development.

Application information: Application form required. Application form available on the grantmaker's Web site.

Deadline(s): Mid-Sept.

Program description:

Larson Awards: Current priority is focused on composers, lyricists and bookwriters working in musical theatre. Awards are based on merit and need, with particular attention to commitment and dedication to an ongoing career in the performing arts. Grants range from $2,500 to $15,000.

Collaborators who work together may apply as a team. Recipients must be U.S. citizens.

EIN: 133902358

5377
The Leeway Foundation

c/o Wachovia Bank, N.A.
123 S. Broad St., Ste. 2040
Philadelphia, PA 19109 (215) 545-4078
Contact: Barbara Silzle, Exec. Dir.
FAX: (215) 545-4021; E-mail: info@leeway.org;
URL: http://www.leeway.org/

Foundation type: Independent foundation

Limitations: Grants to women artists 20 years of age and over who are residing in Bucks, Chester, Delaware, Montgomery, and Philadelphia counties, PA.

Publications: Application guidelines; Annual report; Grants list.

Financial data: Year ended 12/31/2004. Assets, $18,761,482 (M); Expenditures, $508,063; Total giving, $141,270; Grants to individuals, 83 grants totaling $141,270 (high: $2,000, low: $454).

Fields of interest: Visual arts; Sculpture; Arts; Women; Adults, women.

Type of support: Program development; Awards/prizes.

Application information: Applications accepted. Application form required.

Initial approach: Letter, telephone, or e-mail.

Deadline(s): Nov. 1 for Window of Opportunity Grants

Additional information: See Web site for further application information.

Program descriptions:

Art Program: Supports the creativity of exceptional contemporary visual artists. Funds are not available for documentary film or video projects, performing arts, theater, crafts, or decorative arts.

Window of Opportunity Grants: Awards project-specific grants of up to $2,000 to female artists working in any discipline. These grants help artists take advantage of unique, time-limited opportunities that could significantly benefit their work or increase its recognition. Grants are to finance needs such as travel for a residency, reading, performance, or exhibition; or rental of equipment or purchase of materials needed to complete a scheduled project; or support for a period of study with a significant mentor, and for other necessary items.

Transformation Award: This program awards $15,000 to women artists in the five-county Philadelphia region whose art engages in change and has an impact on the artist herself or a larger group, audience, or community; represents artistic excellence; and demonstrates continued growth and commitment. The Transformation Award application is a two-stage process: Stage 1: Open to all eligible women artists. After a review of applications (basic eligibility and five questions about their art and change work), all applicants will receive notification and selected artists will receive invitations to apply to Stage 2. Stage 2: By invitation. All invited applicants will receive a $150 application stipend to cover the costs of preparing work samples. In addition to the stipend, we will help lead applicants through Stage 2 with optional meetings, workshops, and so on.

EIN: 232727140

5378
LEF Foundation

1095 Lodi Ln.
St. Helena, CA 94574 (707) 963-9591
Contact: Marina Drummer, Grants Admin. (CA); Lyda Kuth, Dir. (New England)
FAX: (707) 963-2109;
E-mail: lyda@lef-foundation.org; New England address: P.O. Box 382066, Cambridge, MA 02238-2866, tel.: (617) 492-5333, FAX: (617) 868-5603; URL: http://www.lef-foundation.org

Foundation type: Independent foundation

Limitations: Grants that foster the creative development of artists including independent film and video, who are living and working in the six New England states.

Publications: Application guidelines; Grants list; Occasional report; Program policy statement.

Financial data: Year ended 06/30/2004. Assets, $14,117,004 (M); Expenditures, $2,156,119; Total giving, $1,894,737.

Fields of interest: Film/video; Visual arts.

Type of support: Stipends.

Application information: Applications accepted. Application form required.

Initial approach: Letter of inquiry.

Deadline(s): Sept. 23

Applicants should submit the following:
1) SASE
2) Resume
3) Proposal
4) Budget Information

Additional information: Application must also include work samples.

Program descriptions:

Contemporary Work Fund: The program supports innovative work of strong creative merit in all contemporary art disciplines, excluding filmmaking. Contemporary Work Fund grants are targeted primarily to the creation of new work and to projects that foster artists' creative development. Grantmaking is restricted to New England artists and nonprofit cultural organizations. Individual artists apply for project support through a nonprofit organization. In support of its goal to connect New England artists and audiences to the broader national and international landscape, the Foundation will also consider supporting a New England artist working with a cultural organization outside of the region. In addition, the Foundation will review proposals for the presentation of work by artists from outside the region for the benefit of New England artists and audiences. Grants range in size from $5,000 - $25,000, with the majority of grants awarded in the $12,000 - $15,000 range.

Moving Image Fund: The program supports independent film and video artists living and working in the six New England states. The grantmaking is targeted toward the production of work, with the larger goal of strengthening the voices of media artists and improving the overall environment for the production, exhibition, and distribution of their work. Grants are offered in two categories: Pre-production, with a maximum $5,000 grant, and Production, with a maximum $25,000 grant. Students are not eligible to apply. All applicants must have a fiscal sponsor in order to apply. The grantmaking program operates in two ways, with the majority of the funding awarded to artists for the production of new work. Artists at all career stages are eligible to apply for single channel film and video works. The fund supports work in all genres - documentary, animation, narrative, and experimental - and encourages projects that push the boundaries of these forms. In considering

projects, evidence of an authentic, original artistic voice is key.
EIN: 680070194

5379

Light Work Visual Studies, Inc.
c/o Robert P. Menschel Media Ctr.
316 Waverly Ave.
Syracuse, NY 13244 (315) 443-1300
FAX: (315) 443-9516; E-mail: info@lightwork.org;
URL: http://www.lightwork.org

Foundation type: Public charity
Limitations: Residencies to artists working in photography and related media.
Financial data: Year ended 06/30/2004.
Assets, $406,786 (M); Expenditures, $498,404.
No monetary support given for residencies.
Fields of interest: Photography.
Type of support: Residencies.
Application information:
   Deadline(s): Application accepted throughout the year
   Applicants should submit the following:
      1) SASE
      2) Resume
   Additional information: Applications by letter, including artist statement, and slides of recent work.
Program description:
   Residency Program: 12-15 artists will be selected to live in Syracuse for one month. The residency includes housing, a $2,000 stipend, private darkroom, and 24-hour access to facilities. Residents will be requested to donate a few samples of their work to Light Work's collection.
EIN: 237385641

5380

Gerda Lissner Foundation, Inc.
135 E. 55th St., 8th Fl.
New York, NY 10022-4049 (212) 826-6100
Contact: Betty Smith, Pres.
FAX: (212) 826-0366;
E-mail: gerdalissner@aol.com; URL: http://www.gerdalissner.org

Foundation type: Independent foundation
Limitations: Grants on an international basis for professional development to young operatic singers.
Publications: Application guidelines.
Financial data: Year ended 12/31/2004.
Assets, $14,428,242 (M); Expenditures, $758,270; Total giving, $244,224; Grants to individuals, 29 grants totaling $244,224 (high: $121,654, low: $1,000).
Fields of interest: Music; Opera.
Type of support: Grants to individuals.
Application information: Application form required. Application form available on the grantmaker's Web site.
   Initial approach: Application.
   Additional information: Contact foundation for current application deadline; Auditions required.
EIN: 133566516

5381

Literary Arts, Inc.
224 N.W. 13th Ave., Ste. 306
Portland, OR 97209 (503) 227-2583
Contact: Elizabeth Burnett, Exec. Dir.
FAX: (503) 243-1167; E-mail: la@literary-arts.org;
URL: http://www.literary-arts.org

Foundation type: Public charity
Limitations: Fellowships and awards to writers residing in OR.
Publications: Application guidelines.
Financial data: Year ended 05/31/2005.
Assets, $1,141,088 (M); Expenditures, $938,595; Total giving, $29,999; Grants to individuals, 25 grants totaling $25,001 (high: $1,634, low: $167).
Fields of interest: Literature.
Type of support: Fellowships; Awards/prizes.
Application information: Applications accepted. Application form required.
   Initial approach: E-mail, letter, or telephone.
   Deadline(s): May 30 for book Awards; June 27 for Fellowships.
   Applicants should submit the following:
      1) SASE
   Additional information: Applications must also include work samples and project description.
Program descriptions:
   Oregon Literary Fellowships: Fellowships to help Oregon writers initiate, develop or complete literary projects in the areas of poetry, fiction, literary nonfiction, drama and young readers literature. Applicants may request an amount between $500 and $3,000. The applicant's writing project must be described in detail. The main criterion will be literary merit, but financial need may also be considered. Applicants will be considered in two categories: Level I: Emerging Writer (never published a book before). Level II: Published Writer.
   Oregon Book Awards: Awards for original work published or produced in the following categories: Novel, Poetry, Short Fiction, Children's Literature, Young Adult Literature, Creative Nonfiction, General Nonfiction and Drama. Applicant must be a current full-time resident.
EIN: 930909494

5382

Living Archives, Inc.
262 W. 91st St.
New York, NY 10024 (212) 496-9195
Contact: D.A. Pennebaker, Pres.

Foundation type: Public charity
Limitations: Grants to artists for film production in NY.
Financial data: Year ended 10/31/2004.
Assets, $17,087 (M); Expenditures, $29,608; Total giving, $16,640; Grants to individuals, 3 grants totaling $16,640 (high: $11,500, low: $140).
Fields of interest: Film/video; Performing arts.
Type of support: Grants to individuals.
Application information: Contact foundation for current application deadline/guidelines.
EIN: 132896424

5383

The Loft Literary Center
c/o Open Book
1011 Washington Ave. S., Ste. 200
Minneapolis, MN 55415 (612) 215-2575
Contact: Linda Myers, Exec. Dir.
FAX: (612) 215-2576; E-mail: loft@loft.org;
URL: http://www.loft.org

Foundation type: Public charity
Limitations: Fellowships, awards, and prizes to writers of fiction, poetry, and creative nonfiction.
Publications: Annual report.
Financial data: Year ended 06/30/2004.
Assets, $2,466,178 (M); Expenditures, $1,699,085; Total giving, $125,000; Grants to individuals, totaling $125,000.
Application information: Deadline Jan. 28; Initial approach by telephone; Application guidelines are available six weeks prior to deadlines; Some programs have entry fees.
Program descriptions:
   Minnesota Writers Career Initiative: Awards of up to $8,000 each are given to two to four advanced writers with demonstrated records of publication and professional activities to pursue self-determined proposals that advance them toward the next stage of their careers. The participants are matched with consultants who provide advice and guidance.
   McKnight Artist Fellowships: Four $25,000 fellowships are awarded to writers of creative prose. These fellowships do not support the work of playwriting journalism or nonfiction that is written primarily for educational or technical use. A $25,000 fellowship is also awarded each year in children's literature, including poetry, fiction or creative nonfiction. All fellowship winners will be honored at receptions with the judges and will present their work in a public event.
EIN: 411297735

5384

Lower East Side Printshop, Inc.
59-61 E. 4th St., 6th Fl.
New York, NY 10003 (212) 673-5390
Contact: Dusica Kirjakovic, Exec. Dir.
E-mail: info@printshop.org; URL: http://www.printshop.org

Foundation type: Public charity
Limitations: Fellowships to artists who practice the art of printmaking.
Financial data: Year ended 08/31/2003.
Assets, $20,450; Expenditures, $255,926.
Fields of interest: Arts.
Type of support: Fellowships; Residencies.
Application information:
   Initial approach: Letter or e-mail.
   Deadline(s): None
   Additional information: Contact foundation for current application guidelines.
Program description:
   Artist Workspace Program: Fellowship offers emerging and underrepresented artists full access to professional printmaking facilities. The Printshop does not provide financial assistance or housing.
EIN: 132812419

5385

Lower Manhattan Cultural Council, Inc.

125 Maiden Ln., 2nd Fl.
New York, NY 10038 (212) 219-9401
Contact: Tom Healy, Pres.
FAX: (212) 219-2058; E-mail: info@lmcc.net;
Email: thealy@lmcc.net; URL: http://www.lmcc.net

Foundation type: Public charity
Limitations: Grants to artists who are residents of the borough of Manhattan, New York, and residencies in New York City open to artists throughout the world.
Financial data: Year ended 06/30/2003. Assets, $3,051,238 (M); Expenditures, $2,560,142; Total giving, $367,200; Grants to individuals, 87 grants totaling $72,000 (high: $2,000, low: $500).
Fields of interest: Visual arts; Photography; Sculpture; Painting; Performing arts (multimedia); Arts, artist's services.
Type of support: Program development; Residencies.
Application information: Application form required.
Initial approach: Letter or telephone.
Deadline(s): Vary
Additional information: Application should include printed materials, resume, biography, proposal, and SASE; See Web site for further application information.
Program descriptions:
Manhattan Community Arts Fund: Grants of up to $2,000 are awarded to individual artists and/or organizations who reside and complete their projects in Manhattan. Applicants who have received funds directly from NYSCA or NEA in the past two fiscal years are not eligible to apply.
LMCC/Workspace: Residencies and grants of $1,000 are awarded to emerging and mid-career artists working in all disciplines including painting, photography, sculpture, video, installation and new media. The five-month residency does not provide housing, but includes access to studios, opportunities to present work, and access to other LMCC services. Deadline Sept. 5.
Residency at the Cite Internationale des Arts, Paris, France: Residencies to emerging and mid-career American artists who are New York City residents, specializing in visual arts, photography, film/video, and multimedia. Artists will live and work at the Cite International des Arts in Paris, France. One artist will be selected to be in residence from Sept. to Feb.; and another from Jan. to June. The program provides each artist with live/work space and a monthly stipend of 1,296 Euros (approximately $1,400), the resident must pay a rent of 274 Euros (approximately $300) per month. Access is available to printmaking, photographic, and ceramics facilities, as well as to exhibition spaces. The French Consulate in New York will arrange six-month visas. Deadline for application materials for both sessions is Apr. 18. See Web site for further application information.
EIN: 237348782

5386

MacDowell Colony, Inc.

100 High St.
Peterborough, NH 03458-2442
(603) 924-3886
Contact: Cheryl Young, Exec. Dir.
FAX: (603) 924-9142;
E-mail: admissions@macdowellcolony.org;
Additional E-mail: info@macdowellcolony.org;
URL: http://www.macdowellcolony.org

Foundation type: Public charity
Limitations: Residencies to writers, composers, visual artists, photographers, printmakers, filmmakers, architects and those collaborating on creative works. Travel and Writers' aid grants are also offered.
Financial data: Year ended 03/31/2005. Assets, $25,402,888 (M); Expenditures, $2,503,031; Total giving, $52,846; Grants to individuals, 97 grants totaling $52,846 (high: $1,865, low: $53).
Fields of interest: Film/video; Visual arts; Architecture; Photography; Music composition; Literature.
Type of support: Foreign applicants; Residencies; Travel grants.
Application information: Application form required.
Deadline(s): Jan. 15, Apr. 15 and Sept. 15
Additional information: Application must include work samples and two references; See Web site for application form.
Program description:
Residency Program: Fellowships consist of residencies for up to two months. Financial aid to supplement fellowships is available for travel to and from the colony. Small stipends are available to writers only based on financial need.
EIN: 131592242

5387

Manhattan Neighborhood Network

(also known as Manhattan Community Access Corporation)
537 W. 59th St.
New York, NY 10019 (212) 757-2670
Contact: Dan Coughlin, Exec. Dir.
FAX: (212) 757-1603; URL: http://www.mnn.org

Foundation type: Public charity
Limitations: Project grants and travel grants to producers of successful cablecasts on Manhattan Neighborhood Network (MNN), NY.
Publications: Application guidelines; Financial statement; Newsletter.
Financial data: Year ended 12/31/2004. Assets, $13,089,816; Expenditures, $3,914,020.
Fields of interest: Film/video; Journalism/publishing; Community development; Computer science.
Type of support: Program development.
Application information: Deadlines July 31 and Oct. 31; Completion of formal application required.
Program descriptions:
Advanced Facilities Grant: Producers with successful cablecast of minimum two quarters of series programming or three specials on MNN to his/her credit may apply for subsidized use of advanced postproduction facilities in Manhattan. The program created must be cablecast on MNN when completed. Applicants must have the appropriate certificate of training for use of the facilities requested. Applications must include a clear description of the work to be done, the number of hours needed, how the work will improve the quality of the program, and other resources available.
Alliance for Community Media Conference Travel Grant: This program supports travel, accommodations, and registration at the Alliance's conference for producers with successful cablecast of a minimum of two quarters of series programming or two specials on MNN to their credit. Applicants with recommendation from at least one MNN staff member increase their chances for support. Recipients must submit reports after the conference and may be asked to participate on video crews at the conference.
Community Event Coverage: Support is provided to producers interested in coverage of community events for cablecast on MNN. Events include organized events such as parades, ethnic celebrations, street fairs, performances, etc. Events should be outdoors and admission free and open to the public. Special consideration will be given to the level of organization in the production and to the subject treatment. All applicants must have successful cablecast of minimum one quarter of series programming or two specials on MNN to his/her credit. MNN certification is required in appropriate categories if MNN facilities are to be used in production.
New Technologies Program: Support is available to producers with successful cablecast of a minimum one quarter of series programming or one special on MNN to his/her credit and to other producers by special consideration of MNN, for innovative use of new technologies of community media in the production of MNN programming. Possible technologies include Internet, video streaming, teleconferencing, public projection, and electronic signage. Special attention will be given to projects which bridge various forms of community media. Projects will be judged on creativity, reproducibility, and community accessibility. MNN certification in appropriate categories is required if MNN facilities are to be used. In addition, the applicant must demonstrate a working knowledge of the design and implementation of the technology to be utilized.
Processes of Dialogue Program: Producers with successful cablecast of a minimum of one quarter of series programming or two specials on MNN to their credit may apply for funding for programs which employ innovative use of video and MNN programming to establish dialogue between diverse or conflicting communities, interest groups, or philosophies. The end product should be the quality of the interaction between the groups involved, with the video being a medium of expression or documentation of the process. MNN certification in appropriate categories is required if MNN facilities are to be used.
Program Enhancement Grant: These grants may be used to add enhancements to a video program by producers who have a successful cablecast of a minimum one quarter of series programming on MNN to their credit. Eligible activities include: production of roll-in and/or credit video for series programs; production of video promos for use on MNN and/or other Time Warner cable channels; production of short-form pieces of 15 seconds to five minutes in length for fill between full-length programs; design and purchase of set materials or studio backdrops; express studio enhancements; rights to copyrighted music by local artists; or other approved enhancements.
Thematic Grants: Grants of up to $2,000 each are available to producers for the production of programming in predetermined themes around key cultural spaces and activities often overlooked in MNN programming. Projects may be documentaries, talk shows, or narrative pieces. To be eligible, producers must have successful cablecast of minimum of one quarter of series programming or two specials on MNN to his/her credit. MNN certification in appropriate categories is required if MNN facilities are to be used in production.
EIN: 133625426

5388
Rema Hort Mann Foundation, Inc.
155 Hudson St.
New York, NY 10013 (212) 431-1622
Contact: Susan Hart, Pres.
FAX: (212) 431-2634;
E-mail: cancergrant@remahortmannfoundation.org;
URL: http://www.remahortmannfoundation.org

Foundation type: Public charity
Limitations: Grants by nomination only to emerging artists, primarily in NY.
Financial data: Year ended 12/31/2004. Assets, $107,355 (M); Expenditures, $116,585; Total giving, $106,210; Grants to individuals, totaling $106,210.
Fields of interest: Visual arts.
Type of support: Awards/grants by nomination only.
Application information: Contact foundation for current nomination deadline/guidelines; Initial approach by e-mail.
EIN: 133879538

5389
Mari's Foundation
220 S. Morrison St.
Appleton, WI 54911-5739
Contact: Mari Taniguchi, Tr.

Foundation type: Independent foundation
Limitations: Grants to individuals for musical and artistic advancement.
Financial data: Year ended 12/31/2004. Assets, $152,567 (M); Expenditures, $10,613; Total giving, $9,874; Grants to individuals, totaling $9,874.
Fields of interest: Music; Arts.
Type of support: Scholarships—to individuals.
Application information: Applications accepted.
Deadline(s): None
Additional information: Application should include how the award will improve or enhance musical or artistic skills and dollar amount needed.
EIN: 396647866

5390
Mariachi Heritage Foundation
P.O. Box 925
Visalia, CA 93279 (559) 562-4963
Contact: Joaquin Garcia, Pres.

Foundation type: Public charity
Limitations: Grants for the training of students in the art and discipline of music in traditions of Hispanic culture.
Financial data: Year ended 12/31/2003. Assets, $44,857 (M); Expenditures, $27,659; Total giving, $140.
Fields of interest: Music; Hispanics/Latinos.
Type of support: Scholarships—to individuals.
Application information: Contact foundation for current application deadline/guidelines.
EIN: 770430212

5391
Peter and Madeleine Martin Foundation for the Creative Arts
466 Filbert St.
San Francisco, CA 94133-3024

Foundation type: Independent foundation
Limitations: Awards and project support to artists and writers in NM.

Financial data: Year ended 12/31/2004. Assets, $757,900 (M); Expenditures, $64,941; Total giving, $39,500; Grants to individuals, totaling $10,000.
Fields of interest: Literature; Arts, artist's services.
Type of support: Program development; Awards/prizes.
Application information: Applications not accepted.
EIN: 943113049

5392
Maryland Hall for the Creative Arts, Inc.
801 Chase St.
Annapolis, MD 21401 (410) 263-5544
Contact: Veronica Meneely, Pres.
E-mail: cmanucy@mdhallarts.org; *FAX:* (410) 263-5114; E-mail: info@mdhallarts.org;
URL: http://www.mdhallarts.org

Foundation type: Public charity
Limitations: Residencies to MD, NJ, NY and PA artists who specialize in the performing, visual, and language arts.
Financial data: Year ended 06/30/2004. Assets, $3,223,292 (M); Expenditures, $1,785,451. No monetary support given for residencies.
Fields of interest: Visual arts; Performing arts.
Type of support: Residencies; Stipends.
Application information: Applications accepted. Application form required.
Deadline(s): May 17 for Local AIR Program, June 1 for Visiting AIR Program
Applicants should submit the following:
1) Resume
2) Letter(s) of recommendation
3) Work samples
4) SASE
Program descriptions:
Local Artist-in-Residence Program: This program is designed to provide support of Maryland artists who wish to share their vision with the community in a specific manner. Accepted artists are reviewed on an annual basis for up to three years at which time artists may reapply to the program.
Visiting Artist-in-Residence Program: This program will consist of a residency taking place in a one to three month time period. Artist creating original work in any media, including visual, performing, and the language arts who live in New Jersey, New York, and Pennsylvania are eligible to apply. MHCA provides the accepted artist with administrative support, studio space at MHCA, housing, stipend, reasonable travel expenses to and from MHCA, and materials fee. Artists provide their own food and transportation while in Annapolis.
EIN: 521164469

5393
The Mattress Factory, Ltd.
500 Sampsonia Way
Pittsburgh, PA 15212 (412) 231-3169
Contact: Barbara Luderwoski, Pres.
FAX: (412) 322-2231; E-mail: info@mattress.org;
URL: http://www.mattress.org

Foundation type: Public charity
Limitations: Residencies to artists for the creation of new works by providing studio space for site-specific installations.
Financial data: Year ended 12/31/2003. Assets, $5,050,941 (M); Expenditures, $1,360,623. No monetary support given for residencies.
Fields of interest: Visual arts; Arts.

Type of support: Residencies.
Application information: Applications accepted.
Additional information: Applications in any form, including 35 millimeter slides, VHS video tapes, or CD-Rom that best represent the artists's work, accepted throughout the year.
Program description:
Residency Program: Residencies include studio space and housing, and range from one week to two months. The artist determines the specific length of time he or she will stay.
EIN: 251338941

5394
Israel Matz Foundation
14 E. 4th St., Ste. 403
New York, NY 10012 (212) 673-8142
Contact: Milton Arfa, Chair.

Foundation type: Independent foundation
Limitations: Relief assistance to economically disadvantaged Hebrew writers, scholars, public workers, and their dependents in Israel and the U.S.
Financial data: Year ended 12/31/2004. Assets, $1,296,575 (M); Expenditures, $108,747; Total giving, $26,500.
Fields of interest: Israel.
Application information:
Initial approach: Letter.
Deadline(s): None
Additional information: Application must include purpose of request, supporting documents such as curriculum vitae, and two letters of recommendation.
EIN: 136121533

5395
The Penny McCall Foundation, Inc.
c/o Jennifer McSweeney
170 E. 83rd St., Rm. 2M
New York, NY 10028
FAX: (212) 988-9714;
E-mail: info@pennymccallfoundation.org;
URL: http://www.pennymccallfoundation.org

Foundation type: Independent foundation
Limitations: Grants by nomination only to U.S. citizens for research of the visual arts. Awards are given biennially.
Financial data: Year ended 12/31/2003. Assets, $3,228,380 (M); Expenditures, $461,523; Total giving, $220,000; Grants to individuals, 10 grants totaling $220,000 (high: $30,000, low: $5,000).
Fields of interest: Arts, research.
Type of support: Research; Awards/grants by nomination only; Awards/prizes.
Application information: Applications not accepted.
Additional information: Candidates are nominated by an anonymous committee selected by the board.
EIN: 133376289

5396
McColl Center for Visual Arts
721 N. Tryon St.
Charlotte, NC 28202 (704) 332-5535
FAX: (704) 377-9808;
E-mail: dmcneil@mccollcenter.org; URL: http://www.mccollcenter.org

Foundation type: Public charity

Limitations: Residencies to artists in the following disciplines: sculpture, painting, technology/media, photography, ceramics, and installation.
Financial data: Year ended 06/30/2003. Assets, $14,472,536 (M); Expenditures, $1,436,457. No monetary support given for residencies.
Fields of interest: Media/communications; Photography; Sculpture; Painting; Ceramic arts.
Type of support: Residencies.
Application information: See Web site for programs and application guidelines.
Program description:
Residency Program: Residency includes housing, travel allowance, materials budget, and a monthly stipend. Residencies are from Sept.-Nov. and Jan.-Mar. Six positions are available for each residency.
EIN: 510195015

5397
The McKnight Foundation
710 S. 2nd St., Ste. 400
Minneapolis, MN 55401 (612) 333-4220
Contact: Peggy J. Birk, Interim Pres.
FAX: (612) 332-3833; E-mail: info@mcknight.org;
URL: http://www.mcknight.org

Foundation type: Independent foundation
Limitations: Awards to MN artists in recognition of their artistic excellence and significant impacts on the state's cultural life over several decades.
Publications: Application guidelines; Annual report; Financial statement; Grants list; Informational brochure; Informational brochure (including application guidelines); Newsletter; Occasional report.
Financial data: Year ended 12/31/2005. Assets, $2,050,595,000 (M); Expenditures, $106,510,176; Total giving, $90,710,176.
Fields of interest: Arts.
Type of support: Awards/grants by nomination only; Awards/prizes.
Application information: Application form required.
Deadline(s): Mar. 31 for Artist Awards
Additional information: Individual applications not accepted.
Program description:
McKnight Distinguished Artist Award: Each year, one artist is selected through a nomination process, to receive this $40,000 award. Artists in all disciplines, including ceramics, dance, film, literature, music, theater, and visual arts, whose careers have made a substantial impact on the arts in MN may be nominated. Artists must have worked in MN over a span of decades and have achieved their primary successes in MN, although they do not have to reside there at the time of nomination. Self-nominations and nominations by FAX, e-mail, or telephone are not accepted. Once an artist has been nominated, he/she will be considered each year for three years. No one artist may receive this award twice.
EIN: 410754835

5398
Meet The Composer, Inc.
75 Ninth Ave., Ste. 3RC
New York, NY 10011 (212) 645-6949
Contact: Edward Ficklin, Sr. Prog. Mgr.
FAX: (212) 645-9669;
E-mail: eficklin@meetthecomposer.org;
URL: http://www.meetthecomposer.org

Foundation type: Public charity

Limitations: Commissions, residencies and travel grants to talented composers.
Publications: Financial statement; Informational brochure (including application guidelines).
Financial data: Year ended 06/30/2004. Assets, $6,248,025 (M); Expenditures, $1,610,605; Total giving, $707,234. No monetary support given for residencies.
Fields of interest: Orchestra (symphony); Music composition.
Type of support: Residencies; Travel grants.
Application information: Applications accepted. Application form required.
Initial approach: Letter of intent.
Deadline(s): Feb. 13 for Extended Residencies, May 3 for Global Connections, Aug. 15 for Short-Term Residencies, and Oct. 1 for Extended Residencies
Additional information: Completion of formal application required, including work samples (for Research and Development), biographical essay and budget sheet; See Web site for further application information.
Program descriptions:
Global Connections: Awards grants of $500 to $5,000 to composers for travel, accommodation, and per diem costs related to travel abroad for the live performance of their work or for research and development. Applications are submitted by the composer and his or her sponsoring organization.
Music Alive: Offers support for composer residencies with professional and youth orchestras of all sizes.
• Short-Term Residencies: During two to eight week residencies, composers guide their host orchestra's presentation of new music and assist in the performance of their own works. Awards range from $7,000 to $28,000
• Extended Residencies: During one to three seasons, composers may organize one continuous stay or periodic visits over time to establish a structured relationship with the host orchestra. Awards range from $30,000 to $100,000.
EIN: 132928942

5399
Memorial Scholarship Foundation of the Music Teachers Association of California, Alemada County Branch
2908 Minna Ave.
Oakland, CA 94619-1712
Application address: c/o Paula Cekola, 7529 Valentine St., Oakland, CA 94605

Foundation type: Independent foundation
Limitations: Prizes to students of members of the Music Teachers Association of Alameda County, CA.
Financial data: Year ended 05/31/2005. Assets, $344,844 (M); Expenditures, $22,943; Total giving, $17,255; Grants to individuals, totaling $16,755.
Fields of interest: Music; Performing arts, education.
Type of support: Awards/grants by nomination only; Awards/prizes.
Application information: Contact foundation for current application deadline/guidelines; Auditions required.
EIN: 237165104

5400
The Millay Colony for the Arts, Inc.
454 E. Hill Rd.
P.O. Box 3
Austerlitz, NY 12017 (518) 392-3103
Contact: Drake Patten, Exec. Dir.
E-mail: application@millaycolony.org; URL: http://www.millaycolony.org

Foundation type: Public charity
Limitations: Residencies to writers, composers, visual artists, and filmmakers/video artists.
Financial data: Year ended 11/30/2003. Assets, $992,826; Expenditures, $225,083. No monetary support given for residencies.
Fields of interest: Film/video; Visual arts; Music composition; Literature.
Type of support: Foreign applicants; Residencies.
Application information: Application form required.
Initial approach: E-mail.
Deadline(s): Oct. 1.
Additional information: Application must include project description, work sample and SASE; See Web site for complete program guidelines.
Program description:
Residency Program: The residency accepts six to seven artists for one month between Apr.-Nov. The Colony provides housing, studio space, and meals.
EIN: 141556850

5401
Minnesota Center for Book Arts
1011 Washington Ave., S., Ste. 100
Minneapolis, MN 55415 (612) 215-2520
Contact: Dorothy Goldie, Exec. Dir.
FAX: (612) 215-2545;
E-mail: mcba@mnbookarts.org; URL: http://www.mnbookarts.org

Foundation type: Public charity
Limitations: Residencies to emerging printmaking, papermaking and bookbinding artists residing in MN.
Publications: Application guidelines.
Financial data: Year ended 12/31/2004. Assets, $307,203 (M); Expenditures, $666,649. No monetary support given for residencies.
Fields of interest: Arts.
Type of support: Residencies.
Application information: Contact foundation for current application deadline/guidelines; Initial approach by e-mail.
Program description:
Artists-in-Residence (AIR): This program is offered every other year to four to six emerging book artists residing in MN. The finished product, a new book work, is presented to the public in an exhibition and accompanying catalogue. Past residencies have lasted anywhere from three weeks to one year. Residents have access to facilities and equipment, although supplies and materials are not included. AIRs have the opportunity to teach one class, workshop or lecture during each MCBA class session, although a teaching component is not a requirement of the program. If you do choose to teach during your residency, you will be paid at a rate equal to that of other MCBA instructors. At this time a stipend is not available for the AIR program.
EIN: 411455905

5402
Minnesota Humanities Commission
987 E. Ivy Ave.
St. Paul, MN   55106-2046   (651) 774-0105
Contact: Jane Cunningham, Prog. Off.
FAX: (651) 774-0205;
E-mail: info@minnesotahumanities.org;
URL: http://www.thinkmhc.org

Foundation type: Public charity
Limitations: Prizes to winners of the annual
Minnesota Book Awards.
Publications: Annual report (including application
guidelines).
Financial data: Year ended 10/31/2004.
Assets, $4,853,034 (M); Expenditures,
$2,191,732; Total giving, $156,840; Grants to
individuals, totaling $17,500.
Fields of interest: Literature.
Type of support: Awards/prizes.
Application information: Applications accepted.
Application form required. Application form
available on the grantmaker's Web site.
Initial approach: E-mail or letter.
Deadline(s): Dec. 1
Additional information: See Web site for
application guidelines.
Program description:
Minnesota Book Awards: To be eligible for a
Minnesota Book Award, a book must be the work of
a Minnesota writer, anthology/collection editor, or
primary artistic creator such as an illustrator or
photographer whose work is integral to the project.
Current Minnesota residents are eligible, as are
individuals engaged in ongoing literary work in the
state and authors whose personal history, identity,
or literary work reflect a strong Minnesota influence.
EIN: 411322769

5403
Minnesota Music Teachers Association Foundation
(formerly Minnesota Music Teachers Association
Educational & Charitable Fund)
3200 Galleria
Edina, MN   55435
Contact: Leann House

Foundation type: Public charity
Limitations: Awards and prizes to exceptionally
talented young persons in MN to further promote
their musical education.
Publications: Application guidelines.
Financial data: Year ended 06/30/2003.
Assets, $273,353 (M); Expenditures, $12,718;
Total giving, $2,450; Grants to individuals, 42
grants totaling $2,450.
Fields of interest: Music.
Type of support: Awards/prizes; Travel grants;
Workstudy grants.
Application information: Contact foundation for
current application deadline/guidelines.
EIN: 237058157

5404
The Joan Mitchell Foundation, Inc.
c/o Carolyn Somers
155 Avenue of the Americas, 14th Fl.
New York, NY   10013   (212) 524-0100
FAX: (212) 524-0101;
E-mail: joanmitchellfdn@mindspring.com;
URL: http://foundationcenter.org/grantmaker/
joanmitchellfdn/

Foundation type: Independent foundation

Limitations: Grants to artists to further their
careers.
Financial data: Year ended 12/31/2003.
Assets, $615,027 (M); Expenditures, $697,689;
Total giving, $215,000; Grants to individuals, 31
grants totaling $200,000 (high: $7,500, low:
$3,750).
Fields of interest: Visual arts; Sculpture; Painting;
Arts.
Type of support: Grants to individuals; Stipends.
Application information: Contact foundation for
current deadline; Completion of formal nomination
required.
Program descriptions:
MFA Grant Program: Awards $10,000 annually to
ten artists who are about to receive their master's
degree in fine arts, to assist in furthering their
artistic careers and their transition from academic
to professional studio work. Recipients must
receive their degrees from a recognized art facility
in painting or sculpture.
Painters and Sculptors Grants Program: Awards
of $15,000 annually to 20 recipients to recognize
their artistic merit and to further their artistic
careers. Recipients must demonstrate financial
need.
EIN: 113161054

5405
Money for Women/Barbara Deming Memorial Fund, Inc.
P.O. Box 630125
Bronx, NY   10463-0805
Contact: Susan Pliner, Exec. Dir.

Foundation type: Independent foundation
Limitations: Project support to individual feminists
in the arts who are citizens of the U.S. or Canada.
Publications: Application guidelines; Informational
brochure; Newsletter.
Financial data: Year ended 07/31/2004.
Assets, $227,533 (M); Expenditures, $40,332;
Total giving, $16,400.
Fields of interest: Visual arts; Literature; Arts,
artist's services; Civil rights, minorities; Civil rights,
women; Women's studies; Minorities; Women;
LGBTQ.
Type of support: Program development.
Application information: Applications accepted.
Application form required.
Initial approach: Letter.
Deadline(s): Dec. 31 and June 30
Applicants should submit the following:
1) Work samples
2) Curriculum vitae
3) Resume
4) Budget Information
5) SASE
Additional information: Application must also
include a $10 processing fee, project
description, and work samples; Application
and supporting materials must be sent in
triplicate for writers.
Program description:
Artist Grants: The fund provides small grants to
individual feminists active in the following
categories of the arts: visual art, mixed genre,
fiction, poetry, and nonfiction. The work of these
women speaks for peace and social justice and in
some way sheds light upon the condition of women
or enhances self-realization. Applicants must be
citizens of the U.S. or Canada. The fund does not
give grants in the areas of dance, theater (play
scripts, performance art), film (screenplays), video
or music. The fund does not give loans or money for
educational assistance toward work on dissertation
projects or research (except to be used in writing a

book), or grants for business projects or funds for
self-publication. It also does not give emergency
money to people in need. The fund has two granting
cycles each year. Grant applications must be
mailed via regular first-class mail. Work samples
which support the application must be sent in the
following quantities:
· Art—four slides with name on each one
· Writing—three sets of six to twenty-five
pages maximum
All materials except writing samples will be returned
if a SASE is included. Notification of grant is within
five months of the deadline date. Those who have
applied previously must wait 2 years before
reapplying to the Fund. Grantees must wait 5 years
before reapplying. The fund has two special grants
that emphasize its longstanding commitment to
eliminating homophobia and racism: Gertrude Stein
Award is awarded to a lesbian whose work gives
voice to a lesbian sensibility or confronts
homophobia and Fannie Lou Hamer Grant is named
for the civil rights activist from MS who worked for
voter registration in the 1960s. It is awarded to a
woman whose work combats racism and celebrates
women of color. No special application need be
made for either grant. Recipients will be chosen
from all proposals received.
EIN: 510176956

5406
Thelonious Monk Institute of Jazz
5225 Wisconsin Ave., N.W., Ste. 605
Washington, DC   20015   (202) 364-7272
Contact: Thomas R. Carter, Pres.
FAX: (202) 364-0176;
E-mail: info@monkinstitute.com; URL: http://
www.monkinstitute.com

Foundation type: Public charity
Limitations: Awards to winners of the Thelonious
Monk International Jazz Competition.
Financial data: Year ended 12/31/2004.
Assets, $632,037 (M); Expenditures,
$1,556,089; Total giving, $247,576.
Fields of interest: Music.
Type of support: Foreign applicants; Awards/prizes;
Graduate support; Undergraduate support.
Application information:
Initial approach: E-mail.
Deadline(s): July 1 for Instrument Competition
and for Composers Competition
Additional information: Contact foundation for
current application guidelines; See Web site
for further application information.
Program description:
*Thelonious Monk International Jazz
Competition:* First place is a $20,000 scholarship,
second place is a $10,000 scholarship, and third
place is a $5,000 scholarship. The competition
finals will take place at the Kennedy Center Concert
Hall in Washington.
EIN: 521544030

5407
Montalvo Association
P.O. Box 158
Saratoga, CA   95071   (408) 961-5800
FAX: (408) 961-5850;
E-mail: general@villamontalvo.org; URL: http://
www.villamontalvo.org

Foundation type: Public charity
Limitations: Residencies to writers, poets,
playwrights, filmmakers, musicians, composers,
architects, and visual artists to stay at Montalvo, an
artists' retreat located in CA.

Financial data: Year ended 09/30/2004. Assets, $17,272,640 (M); Expenditures, $7,571,129.
Fields of interest: Film/video; Visual arts; Architecture; Theater; Theater (playwriting); Music; Music composition; Literature.
Type of support: Residencies.
Application information: Applications not accepted.
  Additional information: Applications by invitation only; Applicants are selected by an international pool of recommenders; See Web site for complete program description.
Program description:
  Residency Program: Residencies last from one to three months, and includes studio space and housing.
EIN: 941249283

5408
Movement Research
Old Chelsea Station
P.O. Box 49
New York, NY 10113 (212) 598-0551
Contact: Carla Peterson, Exec. Dir.
FAX: (212) 633-1974;
E-mail: info@movementresearch.org; Additional tel.: (212) 539-2611; URL: http://www.movementresearch.org

Foundation type: Public charity
Limitations: Residencies to dance and performance artists.
Publications: Newsletter.
Financial data: Year ended 06/30/2004. Assets, $41,297 (M); Expenditures, $292,315. No monetary support given for residencies.
Fields of interest: Dance.
Type of support: Residencies.
Application information: Applications accepted. Application form required.
  Initial approach: E-mail, telephone or letter.
  Deadline(s): Mar. 31
  Applicants should submit the following:
    1) SASE
    2) Work samples
    3) Resume
    4) Proposal
  Additional information: Applications must also include an artistic statement. See Web site for additional program information.
EIN: 133041403

5409
The Museum of Fine Arts, Houston
c/o Glassell School of Art
P.O. Box 6826
Houston, TX 77265-6826 (713) 639-7500
Additional address: 5101 Montrose Blvd., Houston, TX 77006-6534; URL: http://www.core.mfah.org

Foundation type: Public charity
Limitations: Residencies to visual artists and art critics.
Publications: Application guidelines; Annual report; Informational brochure; Program policy statement.
Financial data: Year ended 06/30/2004. Assets, $690,332,234 (M); Expenditures, $110,348,548; Total giving, $70,049; Grants to individuals, totaling $70,049.
Fields of interest: Visual arts.
Type of support: Fellowships; Postgraduate support; Residencies.
Application information:
  Deadline(s): Apr. 1

Additional information: Application by letter including 12 slides, resume, letters of recommendation, and SASE.
Program description:
  Core Program: The Core Program awards one- and two-year residencies to visual artists and art critics who have completed their undergraduate or graduate training but have not yet fully developed a professional career. Each resident is given a private studio space, 24-hour access to school facilities and equipment, and a $9,000 annual stipend. These residencies also include a $9,000 annual stipend and access to facilities, including borrowing privileges at the museum's Hirsch Library and nearby Rice University Fondren Library.
EIN: 741109655

5410
Museum of Glass
1801 E. Dock St.
Tacoma, WA 98402-3217 (253) 396-1768
FAX: (253) 396-1769;
E-mail: info@museumofglass.org; URL: http://www.museumofglass.org

Foundation type: Public charity
Limitations: Residencies by invitation only to glass artists.
Financial data: Year ended 06/30/2003. Assets, $31,818,811 (M); Expenditures, $3,093,226. No monetary support given for residencies.
Fields of interest: Visual arts.
Type of support: Residencies.
Application information: Applications not accepted.
Program descriptions:
  Visiting Artist Program: This program invites internationally known artists and emerging artists from the region and around the world to work with the Museum's resident Hot Shop Team to explore, invent and create with glass. Offering a diverse mixture of culture, style, focus and expertise, each artist creates a sense of excitement and wonder for visitors who are given the rare opportunity to witness art being made. Currently, the Visiting Artist residency program is by invitation only. Artists are invited in conjunction with an exhibition of their work in the galleries or by making a thematic connection with a current exhibition. During the Summer, the Museum partners with Pilchuck Glass School and invites both artists from the Pilchuck roster to participate in a residency here. The Summer Series runs 13 consecutive weeks and includes 13 artists.
  Hot Lunch Program: For local WA artists, the Museum hosts a Hot Lunch Program. Each Friday, just for the day, a local artist is invited to work in the hot shop, supported by the Museum's residency glassblowing team. The artists must be on the floor working during the hours that the Museum is open to the public. Artists keep the work they make. There is no compensation for this program.
EIN: 911669422

5411
Musicares Foundation, Inc.
3402 Pico Blvd.
Santa Monica, CA 90405-2118
(310) 392-3777
Contact: Kristen Madsen, Sr. V.P.
Application tel.: (800) 687-4227 free and confidential; URL: http://www.grammy.com/musicares

Foundation type: Public charity

Limitations: Assistance to economically disadvantaged individuals in the music recording community, including shelter, medical care, and substance abuse treatment.
Financial data: Year ended 07/31/2004. Assets, $5,077,429 (M); Expenditures, $3,568,042; Total giving, $1,369,485; Grants to individuals, totaling $1,365,335.
Fields of interest: Music; Arts, artist's services; Health care; Substance abuse, treatment; Housing/shelter.
Type of support: Grants for special needs.
Application information: Contact foundation for current application deadline/guidelines.
Program description:
  Special Needs Grant: Eligible individuals include singers, musicians, and technical, clerical, and unskilled labor personnel, who have been employed in the industry for at least five years. The grants are available to impoverished individuals who are unemployed or underemployed, frequently due to the sporadic nature of the industry.
EIN: 954470909

5412
Musicians Emergency Relief Fund-Local 802
322 W. 48th St.
New York, NY 10036 (212) 245-4802
Contact: David Lennon, Tr.

Foundation type: Operating foundation
Limitations: Relief assistance to sick, distressed, or economically disadvantaged musicians who have been union members for a minimum of three years and are in good standing (membership dues paid).
Publications: Application guidelines; Financial statement; Program policy statement.
Financial data: Year ended 12/31/2003. Assets, $388,470 (M); Expenditures, $121,245; Total giving, $91,221; Grants to individuals, 32 grants totaling $14,476 (high: $1,300, low: $32).
Fields of interest: Music; Disabilities, people with; Economically disadvantaged.
Type of support: Grants for special needs.
Application information: Applications accepted throughout the year; Initial approach in-person; Interviews required.
EIN: 136222619

5413
Musicians Foundation, Inc.
875 6th Ave., Ste. 2303
New York, NY 10001 (212) 239-9137
Contact: B.C. Vermeersch, Exec. Dir.
FAX: (212) 239-9138;
E-mail: info@musiciansfoundation.org;
URL: http://www.musiciansfoundation.org

Foundation type: Public charity
Limitations: Emergency financial assistance to professional musicians and their families.
Publications: Application guidelines.
Financial data: Year ended 04/30/2005. Assets, $2,797,302 (M); Expenditures, $189,668; Total giving, $107,110; Grants to individuals, 60 grants totaling $107,110 (high: $5,715, low: $230).
Fields of interest: Music.
Type of support: Grants for special needs.
Application information: Applications accepted. Application form required.
  Initial approach: Letter.
  Deadline(s): None

Additional information: Applications should be sent by mail.

EIN: 131790739

5414

Naftzger Fund for Fine Arts, Inc.

c/o Southwest National Bank
P.O. Box 1401
Wichita, KS 67201
Application address: c/o Naftzger Auditions, Century Concert Hall, 225 W. Douglas, Ste. 207, Wichita, KS 67202, tel.: (316) 267-5259

Foundation type: Independent foundation
Limitations: Awards to young KS, MO, or OK pianists, vocalists, and instrumentalists who are winners of the Naftzger Young Artist Competition.
Financial data: Year ended 12/31/2004. Assets, $834,253 (M); Expenditures, $23,735; Total giving, $18,473; Grants to individuals, 4 grants totaling $11,000.
Fields of interest: Performing arts; Music.
Type of support: Awards/prizes.
Application information: Applications accepted. Application form required.

Deadline(s): Mar.
Additional information: Application must also include tape recording; Auditions may be required for finalists.

EIN: 486106125

5415

The National Arts Club

15 Gramercy Park S.
New York, NY 10003 (212) 475-3424
Contact: O. Aldon James, Jr., Pres.
URL: http://www.nationalartsclub.org

Foundation type: Public charity
Limitations: Awards and scholarships by nomination only to artists, writers and singers.
Financial data: Year ended 03/31/2004. Assets, $3,629,381 (M); Expenditures, $2,063,740; Total giving, $46,900; Grants to individuals, totaling $46,900.
Fields of interest: Theater (playwriting); Music; Literature.
Type of support: Awards/grants by nomination only; Awards/prizes.
Application information: Applications not accepted.

Additional information: Unsolicited requests for funds not considered or acknowledged.

EIN: 135265900

5416

National Foundation for Advancement in the Arts

444 Brickell Ave., Ste. P-14
Miami, FL 33131 (305) 377-1140
Contact: William H. Banchs, Pres.
FAX: (305) 377-1149; E-mail: bill@nfaa.org;
URL: http://www.NFAA.ARTSawards.org

Foundation type: Public charity
Limitations: Grants to emerging artists, who are either U.S. citizens or resident aliens, to assist them at critical junctures in their educational and professional development.
Publications: Application guidelines; Annual report; Informational brochure; Newsletter.
Financial data: Year ended 06/30/2004. Assets, $13,629,499 (L); Expenditures,

$2,644,912; Total giving, $499,734; Grants to individuals, totaling $499,734.
Fields of interest: Visual arts; Arts, artist's services.
Type of support: Fellowships; Internship funds; Grants to individuals; Scholarships—to individuals; Awards/prizes; Travel grants; Stipends; Project support.
Application information: Application form required. Application form available on the grantmaker's Web site.

Initial approach: Online application.
Copies of proposal: 1
Deadline(s): Oct. 1
Applicants should submit the following:
1) Work samples
Additional information: Contact foundation for current application deadlines.

Program descriptions:
Arts Recognition and Talent Search (ARTS): Through this national program, 17- and 18-year-olds may apply for college scholarships. The most accomplished applicants are chosen to participate in the final adjudication process known as ARTS Week, a series of performances, master classes, seminars and readiness held in Jan. in Miami, FL. These 160 winners have the opportunity to earn cash awards of up to $10,000 each and be named Presidential Scholar in the ARTS. Artists in the categories of dance, jazz, film and video, music, photography, theater, visual arts, voice, and writing are eligible.

Astral Career Grants: These grants of up to $200 are awarded to meet modest expenses in response to external opportunities requiring timely action by an artist. Grants are only available in the fields of music (voice, piano and composition) and dance (ballet and choreography). The grant does not cover funds for medical care or general living support. Applicants must be U.S. citizens or permanent residents, and cannot be full-time students.

Fellowships in the Visual Arts: This program is conducted in collaboration with the Corcoran Gallery of Art in Washington, D.C., and provides a six-month residency that is renewable for two years. Each fellow receives round-trip transportation to Miami, FL; housing and studio space in Miami Beach; $1,000 monthly stipend; and funds for supplies. At the end of the residency, the Corcoran Gallery of Art hosts an exhibit and publishes a catalog of the show for distribution to museums, art dealers, curators and galleries. The program is not currently accepting applications.

EIN: 592141837

5417

National Foundation for Jewish Culture

330 7th Ave., 21st Fl.
New York, NY 10001-5010 (212) 629-0500
Contact: Richard Siegel, Exec. Dir.; For fellowships: Kristen L. Runk
FAX: (212) 629-0508;
E-mail: nfjc@jewishculture.org; URL: http://www.Jewishculture.org

Foundation type: Public charity
Limitations: Grants to individuals for creative projects involving Jewish cultural themes.
Publications: Newsletter.
Financial data: Year ended 12/31/2003. Assets, $3,757,603 (M); Expenditures, $2,984,045; Total giving, $385,870; Grants to individuals, 25 grants totaling $243,202 (high: $50,000, low: $1,500).
Fields of interest: Film/video; Visual arts; Theater; Literature; Jewish agencies & temples.

Type of support: Program development; Awards/prizes.
Application information: Applications accepted. Application form required.

Additional information: See Web site for each program's application guidelines and deadlines.

Program descriptions:
Fund for Jewish Documentary Filmmaking: The Fund for Jewish Documentary Filmmaking, currently in its fifth year, was developed with a lead grant of $650,000 from the Righteous Persons Foundation established by Steven Spielberg. The Fund is designed to support the creation of original documentary films and videos that promote thoughtful consideration of Jewish history, culture, identity, and contemporary issues among diverse public audiences.

The Samuel L. Goldberg & Sons Foundation Prize for Jewish Fiction by Emerging Writers: Awards $2,500 to an outstanding work of fiction relating to Jewish experience. The prize-winning writer cannot have published more than one previous work.

The New Play Commissions in Jewish Theater: Awards grants to new full-length plays or musicals dealing substantively with issues of Jewish history, tradition, values or contemporary life. The theater company must commit to presenting the play to the public in a workshop production and/or staged reading, including a forum for public discussion.

Ronnie Heyman Prize for an Emerging Artist: Recognizes and supports an emerging visual artist who is creating a body of work that reflects the Jewish experience. The $2,500 prize is awarded to a specific exhibited work of an artist who has been working in the field for less than ten years. Deadline Nov. 4.

EIN: 131927751

5418

National Sculpture Society, Inc.

237 Park Ave.
New York, NY 10017
Contact: Gwen Pier, Exec. Dir.
E-mail: info@nationalsculpture.org; FAX: (212) 764-5651; URL: http://www.nationalsculpture.org

Foundation type: Operating foundation
Limitations: Grants to encourage the creation and appreciation of sculpture throughout the U.S.
Publications: Financial statement; Informational brochure (including application guidelines).
Financial data: Year ended 09/30/2004. Assets, $5,289,860 (M); Expenditures, $585,301; Total giving, $26,950; Grants to individuals, 24 grants totaling $24,850 (high: $4,000, low: $1,000).
Fields of interest: Arts education; Sculpture.
Type of support: Internship funds; Scholarships—to individuals; Awards/prizes; Graduate support; Undergraduate support; Workstudy grants.
Application information: Application form not required. Application form available on the grantmaker's Web site.

Copies of proposal: 1
Deadline(s): Apr. 30 for scholarship; Varies for grants
Applicants should submit the following:
1) Resume
2) Work samples
Additional information: Initial approach by letter outlining background and including photographs of work.

Program description:
Educational Scholarships: Scholarships of $1,000 each are available for students of figurative or representational sculpture. Scholarships are

paid directly to the academic institution through which the student applies.
EIN: 131656673

5419
The Netherland-America Foundation, Inc.
82 Wall St., Ste. 1101
New York, NY 10005 (212) 825-1221
Contact: Joan Carolyn Kuyper, Exec. Dir.
FAX: (212) 825-9105; E-mail: info@TheNAF.org;
URL: http://www.thenaf.org/

Foundation type: Public charity
Limitations: Grants to young, beginning and aspiring visual and performing artists in the Netherlands and the U.S.
Publications: Application guidelines; Annual report; Financial statement; Grants list; Newsletter; Program policy statement.
Financial data: Year ended 12/31/2003. Assets, $4,034,915 (M); Expenditures, $513,612; Total giving, $443,335; Grants to individuals, 19 grants totaling $293,335 (high: $5,000, low: $500).
Fields of interest: Visual arts; Performing arts; Netherlands.
Type of support: Grants to individuals.
Application information: Contact foundation for current application deadline; Application by proposal.
EIN: 132989216

5420
New England Foundation for the Arts
(also known as NEFA)
145 Tremont St., 7th Fl.
Boston, MA 02111-1214 (617) 951-0010
Contact: Aria McElhenny, Comm., Research Dir.
FAX: (617) 951-0016; E-mail: info@nefa.org;
URL: http://www.nefa.org

Foundation type: Public charity
Limitations: Residencies and stipends to artists, primarily within New England, who seek to make vital connections between artists and audiences, and to build strength, knowledge and leadership of the region's creative sector. Also, grants by nomination only to artists to produce dance projects.
Publications: Annual report; Financial statement; Informational brochure (including application guidelines); Newsletter.
Financial data: Year ended 05/31/2003. Assets, $136,014,487 (M); Expenditures, $4,380,209; Total giving, $2,792,368.
Fields of interest: Dance; Arts; Environment.
Type of support: Program development; Awards/grants by nomination only; Residencies; Travel grants.
Application information: See Web site for complete program list and guidelines.
Program descriptions:
Art and Community Landscapes: Selected artists develop and implement projects to inspire greater involvement in protecting and enhancing rivers, trails, and greenways in collaboration with local communities. Projects may include temporary art installations, exhibitions, interpretive media, festivals, or other works informed by the sites and communities of the project's region. The project sites are Chelsea Creek Rail-Trail Project, East Boston, MA, and Perquimans County Greenways-Blueways Plan, Hertford. Applications are open to artists based in the United States (citizenship not required). Up to three finalist artists or artist teams per regional site will be awarded

$1,500 in planning grant funding to develop ideas, conceptual plans, and create an overall proposal for one or more candidate projects of the region. Based on project proposals, one artist or artist team will be selected per region for the residency and project implementation. Final implementation grants of up to $50,000 are awarded based on the project proposal's artistic merit, quality and feasibility.
Grants By Nomination: Grants generally range from $15,000 to $35,000 and are awarded to between 15 and 20 dance projects annually. Nominators may be artists, managers, presenters or agents, and choreographers or dance companies may self-nominate.
EIN: 042593591

5421
New Jersey Performing Arts Center, Corp.
1 Center St.
Newark, NJ 07102 (973) 642-8989
Telephone for Scholarships: (973) 353-8009
E-mail: artseducation@njpac.org; URL: http://www.njpac.org

Foundation type: Public charity
Limitations: Scholarships to high school students who are residents of Newark, NJ, and demonstrate the potential to become leading arts professionals.
Publications: Newsletter.
Financial data: Year ended 06/30/2004. Assets, $217,857,512 (M); Expenditures, $29,710,872; Total giving, $87,251; Grants to individuals, 21 grants totaling $87,251 (high: $11,385, low: $1,385).
Fields of interest: Arts education; Performing arts; Music; Music ensembles/groups.
Type of support: Scholarships—to individuals.
Application information: Applications accepted.
Initial approach: Letter, telephone or e-mail.
Program descriptions:
Jeffrey Carollo Music Scholarship: Scholarships awarded to twelve students who are enrolled in the after-school music programs at the Newark Community School of Arts. Classes include private lessons, music theory, music history and ensembles. Students must be referred by their private music teacher or public music teacher, and must go through an audition process in order to qualify for the scholarship.
Star Ledger Scholarship for the Performing Arts: This program identifies, trains, and cultivates gifted Newark high school seniors who are college-bound and who demonstrate the potential to become leading arts professionals. Three merit-based scholarships are awarded. These scholarships are among New Jersey's most prestigious scholastic awards. Scholarships awarded are $10,000 per year for four years, and $5,000 per year for four years. The scholarship supports a four-year education leading to the completion of a degree from an accredited undergraduate institution.
EIN: 222889703

5422
New York Foundation for the Arts
155 Ave. of the Americas, 14th Fl.
New York, NY 10013-1507 (212) 366-6900
FAX: (212) 366-1778; E-mail: nyfainfo@nyfa.org;
URL: http://www.nyfa.org

Foundation type: Public charity
Limitations: Fellowships and awards for artists who are NY state residents.
Publications: Application guidelines; Biennial report; Financial statement; Informational brochure; Newsletter.

Financial data: Year ended 06/30/2004. Assets, $4,171,216 (M); Expenditures, $8,733,703; Total giving, $5,011,609; Grants to individuals, totaling $3,890,587.
Fields of interest: Folk arts; Film/video; Visual arts; Architecture; Photography; Sculpture; Design; Painting; Performing arts; Choreography; Theater (playwriting); Music composition; Literature; Arts, artist's services; Arts; Computer science.
Type of support: Fellowships; Awards/prizes; Stipends.
Application information: Applications accepted. Application form required. Application form available on the grantmaker's Web site.
Initial approach: Telephone or e-mail.
Copies of proposal: 1
Deadline(s): Deadline Oct. 1 for Artists' Fellowship; Sept., Feb., and May for Strategic Opportunity
Applicants should submit the following:
1) Work samples
2) Curriculum vitae
Program descriptions:
Artists' Fellowships: Fellowships of $7,000 each are awarded each year to artists in specific disciplines. In even-numbered award years, artists in the following categories are eligible to apply: computer arts, crafts, performance art/multidisciplinary work, film, nonfiction literature, poetry, printmaking/drawing/artists' books, and sculpture. In odd-numbered years, artists in the following disciplines may apply: architecture/environmental structures, choreography, fiction, music composition, painting, photography, playwriting/screenwriting, and video. In order to be eligible for this program, the applicant must be over 18 and a resident of NY for at least two years, and not currently enrolled in any degree program.
Strategic Opportunity Stipends (SOS): This program provides cash stipends of $100 to $600 to artists who live in the state of NY and wish to take advantage of opportunities for significant career advancement. For more detailed information on applying for SOS funds, call the local arts service organization in your region. SOS is not yet available in the five boroughs of New York City. Applicants must be 18 years of age or older, and show proof of full-time NY state residency in a participating region for one year prior to the application date. Graduate, undergraduate and high school students enrolled in a degree program are ineligible to apply.
EIN: 237129564

5423
New York Mills Arts Retreat
24 N. Main Ave.
P.O. Box 246
New York Mills, MN 56567 (218) 385-3339
Contact: Lina Belar, Exec. Dir.
FAX: (218) 385-3366; E-mail: nymills@kulcher.org;
URL: http://www.kulcher.org

Foundation type: Public charity
Limitations: Residencies to artists, primarily to residents of MN and New York City, NY.
Publications: Application guidelines.
Financial data: Year ended 12/31/2004. Assets, $144,313 (M); Expenditures, $145,955.
Fields of interest: Sculpture; Arts; African Americans/Blacks.
Type of support: Residencies; Stipends.
Application information: Application form required.
Initial approach: E-mail.
Deadline(s): Apr. 1 and Oct. 1
Applicants should submit the following:
1) SASE
2) Letter(s) of recommendation

3) Work samples
4) Resume
Additional information: Application should also include biography.
Program description:
Residency Program: The residency includes housing and a stipend that will cover personal costs such as transportation, food, and supplies. A four-week stay carries a $1,500 stipend, while a two-week stay carries a $750 stipend. Residents will be expected to devote a portion of their stay to community outreach projects. The center reserves one fellowship annually to an artist of color and to a monumental sculptor.
EIN: 411690163

5424

The Newark Museum Association

49 Washington St.
Newark, NJ   07102-3176   (973) 596-6550
Contact: Mary Sue Sweeney Price, Secy.
URL: http://www.newarkmuseum.org

Foundation type: Public charity
Limitations: Prizes to winners of the Newark Museum's Paul Robeson Awards.
Financial data: Year ended 12/31/2003. Assets, $68,618,748 (M); Expenditures, $15,851,531.
Fields of interest: Film/video; African Americans/Blacks.
Type of support: Awards/prizes.
Application information: Application form required.
Initial approach: Telephone.
Deadline(s): Feb. 20
Additional information: Application should include a $35 entry fee, and film in VHS or DVD.
Program description:
Paul Robeson Awards: The Newark Museum organizes the Annual Newark Black Film Festival, a six-week long summer film festival that showcases the historic importance of the Black experience in the U.S. Original, non commercial 16mm optical track prints and videotapes. Cash awards will be distributed at the discretion of a panel of judges from the film industry.
EIN: 221487275

5425

Northern Clay Center

2424 Franklin Ave., E.
Minneapolis, MN   55406   (612) 339-8007
Contact: Emily Galusha, Exec. Dir.
FAX: (612) 339-0592;
E-mail: nccinfo@northernclaycenter.org;
URL: http://www.northernclaycenter.org

Foundation type: Public charity
Limitations: Project grants and fellowships to ceramic artists, primarily to MN residents.
Publications: Application guidelines; Annual report; Newsletter.
Financial data: Year ended 12/31/2004. Assets, $2,211,866 (M); Expenditures, $993,334.
Fields of interest: Ceramic arts.
Type of support: Fellowships; Residencies; Stipends.
Application information: Application form required.
Deadline(s): Feb. 23 for Project Grants, Mar. 26 for Fellowships
Applicants should submit the following:
1) SASE
2) Resume
3) Budget Information

Additional information: Application should also include project description and slides of recent work.
Program descriptions:
Jerome Projects Grants: This program is intended to help MN ceramic artists and potters, at early stages of their careers, to accomplish relatively short-term, specific objectives. Artists may request funds to explore new techniques, new forms, and/or new scale of work. Funds may also be used to purchase equipment specifically needed for the production of ceramic work or to rent studio space. Three $6,000 awards will be granted.
McKnight Artist Residencies for Ceramic Artists: This program provides individual, non-Minnesota, mid-career ceramic artists an opportunity to be in residence for three months at Northern Clay Center. Each resident artist receives a $5,000 award and is provided studio space, and glaze and firing allowances. At the end of the residency period, each artist will present a public workshop or lecture, for which he or she will receive a $300 honorarium. Four Residency grants are awarded annually. (Artists are responsible for making their own housing and travel arrangements during their residencies.)
McKnight Artist Fellowships for Ceramic Artists: This program provides support to Minnesota ceramic artists who have already proven their abilities and are at a career stage that is beyond emerging. Two grants of $25,000 each are awarded annually. Fellowship support may be used for, but is not limited to, buying time, experimenting with new techniques and materials, purchasing equipment, collaborating with other artists, and pursuing education, exhibition, or travel opportunities.
EIN: 411616650

5426

Ojai Film Festival

P.O. Box 1029
Ojai, CA   93024   (805) 640-1947
Contact: Barbara T. Hadley, Exec. Dir.
E-mail: info@ojaifilmfestival.com; *URL:* http://www.ojaifilmfestival.com

Foundation type: Public charity
Limitations: Trophies, certificates, and cash awards to winners of the Ojai Film Festival in CA.
Financial data: Year ended 12/31/2003. Assets, $17,623 (M); Expenditures, $55,813.
Fields of interest: Film/video.
Type of support: Awards/prizes.
Application information: Applications accepted. Application form required.
Initial approach: E-mail.
Applicants should submit the following:
1) SASE
Additional information: Applications must also include entry fee and film.
EIN: 460471403

5427

P.S. 1 Contemporary Art Center, Inc.

(formerly The Institute for Contemporary Art)
22-25 Jackson Ave.
Long Island City, NY   11101   (718) 784-2084
Contact: Alanna Heiss, Exec. Dir.
FAX: (718) 482-9454; *E-mail:* mail@ps1.org;
URL: http://www.ps1.org

Foundation type: Public charity
Limitations: Residencies by nomination only to artists from 14 specific countries. Also three-month residencies to visual artists who may apply directly.

Financial data: Year ended 06/30/2004. Assets, $3,613,287 (M); Expenditures, $3,848,629. No monetary support given for residencies.
Fields of interest: Visual arts; Arts.
Type of support: Awards/grants by nomination only; Foreign applicants; Awards/prizes; Residencies.
Application information: Applications accepted. Application form available on the grantmaker's Web site.
Initial approach: E-mail.
Deadline(s): Contact foundation for current application deadline.
Applicants should submit the following:
1) Resume
Additional information: Application should include slides or VHS of work and resume.
Program descriptions:
International Studio Program: Awards studio spaces to artists from Australia, Austria, Belgium (Flanders), Berlin, Croatia, France, Italy, Japan, Korea, The Netherlands, The Republic of Ireland, Spain, Switzerland, and Taiwan. This program is administered by P.S. 1 in cooperation with foreign governments and/or foundations. Only artists from the above-mentioned countries are eligible to apply to the International Studio Program. This program unites professional artists from varied cultural and aesthetic backgrounds. International artists are initially selected by a panel in their sponsoring country, and then by a second jury at P.S. 1. Each artist is responsible for supplying materials and equipment. This program offers no printing, photograph or welding facilities.
Clocktower/P.S. 1 Project: Provides studio space for the creation of specific projects, for three months or less.
EIN: 237379091

5428

Pacific Pioneer Fund

(formerly Pioneer Fund, Inc.)
P.O. Box 20504
Stanford, CA   94309
Contact: Armin Rosencranz, Secy.
E-mail: armin@stanford.edu; *URL:* http://www.pacificpioneerfund.com

Foundation type: Independent foundation
Limitations: Grants to emerging documentary filmmakers and videographers who live and work in CA, OR, or WA.
Publications: Application guidelines; Grants list; Program policy statement.
Financial data: Year ended 06/30/2004. Assets, $1,012,372 (M); Expenditures, $109,748; Total giving, $86,000.
Fields of interest: Film/video.
Type of support: Grants to individuals.
Application information: Applications accepted. Application form required.
Deadline(s): Feb. 1, May 15, and Oct. 1.
Program description:
Media Grants: Grants ranging from $1,000 to $10,000 are made to public charities which undertake to supervise any project from which individuals receive funds. The fund does not support instructional or performance documentaries, or student film projects. Filmmakers are eligible for only one grant from the fund during their careers.
EIN: 942614215

5429
Palm Beach County Cultural Council
1555 Palm Beach Lakes Blvd., No. 1414
West Palm Beach, FL 33401-2329
(561) 471-2901
Contact: Rena Minar, Exec. Dir.
FAX: (561) 687-9484; E-mail: grants@pbccc.org;
Additional tel.: (800) 882-ARTS; URL: http://
www.pbccc.org/

Foundation type: Public charity
Limitations: Residency grants to professional artists in Palm Beach County, FL in exchange for providing discipline-based arts education to children and their families living in neighborhoods in transition and redevelopment.
Publications: Application guidelines; Annual report; Financial statement; Grants list; Informational brochure (including application guidelines); Newsletter.
Financial data: Year ended 09/30/2003.
Assets, $112,443 (M); Expenditures, $37,150; Total giving, $37,150; Grants to individuals, totaling $37,150.
Fields of interest: Arts, public education; Arts, artist's services; Arts.
Type of support: Residencies.
Application information: Contact foundation for current application deadline/guidelines.
EIN: 591862336

5430
PEN American Center, Inc.
568 Broadway, Ste. 303
New York, NY 10012 (212) 334-1660
Contact: Peter Meyer, Devel. Assoc.
FAX: (212) 334-2181; E-mail: PEN@pen.org;
URL: http://www.pen.org

Foundation type: Public charity
Limitations: Awards by nomination only to writers, translators, editors, and book critics in various categories. Also, emergency assistance to published writers and editors for unexpected financial crises and HIV/AIDS-related emergencies.
Financial data: Year ended 06/30/2004.
Assets, $3,278,088 (M); Expenditures, $2,203,282; Total giving, $446,120; Grants to individuals, 6 grants totaling $139,384 (high: $35,000, low: $50).
Fields of interest: Journalism/publishing; Drawing; Theater (playwriting); Language (foreign); Literature; AIDS; International human rights.
Type of support: Awards/grants by nomination only; Awards/prizes; Grants for special needs.
Application information: Application form required.
Initial approach: Letter or telephone.
Deadline(s): Vary
Additional information: See programs for specific deadlines.
Program descriptions:
Freedom-to-Write Awards: Under this program, the PEN/Newman's Own First Amendment Award of $25,000 is given to an American who has courageously striven to safeguard the right to free expression. In addition, two PEN/Barbara Goldsmith Freedom-to-Write Awards of $3,000 each are given to foreign writers who are in prison or in danger as a consequence of their work. Applications are by nomination only.
Gregory Kolovakos Award for Commitment to Hispanic Literature: Awarded triennially, this $2,000 prize is given to an American literary translator, editor, or critic whose work, in meeting the challenge of cultural difference, extends Gregory Kolovakos' commitment to the richness of

Latino literature and to expanding its English-language audience. Deadline Jan. 1.
PEN Award for Poetry in Translation: This $3,000 award is given annually to the translator of an outstanding volume of poetry. Deadline Dec. 15.
PEN/Book-of-the-Month Club Translation Prize: This $3,000 prize is given for booklength translations from any language into English published during the current calendar year. Deadline Dec. 15.
PEN/Jerard Prize for Emerging Women Writers of Nonfiction: This $5,500 biennial award honors a work-in-progress of general nonfiction distinguished by high literary quality. Deadline Jan. 1.
PEN/Laura Pels Foundation Awards for Drama: American playwrights will be selected annually to receive honorary medals and cash prizes of $5,000 each. The medal goes to a master American dramatist, in recognition of his or her body of work. The cash prize is given to a mid-career American playwright whose literary achievements are vividly apparent in the rich and striking language of his or her work. Applications are by nomination only.
PEN/Martha Albrand Award: This $1,000 award is given for a first book of general nonfiction by an American writer, marked by qualities of literary excellence. Deadline Dec. 15.
PEN/Martha Albrand Award for the Art of the Memoir: This award of $1,000 is given to an American author for his or her first published memoir, distinguished by qualities of literary and stylistic excellence. Deadline Dec. 15.
PEN/Nora Magid Award for Distinguished Magazine Editor: This biennial award of $2,500 honors a magazine editor whose high literary standards and taste have, throughout his or her career, contributed significantly to the excellence of the publication he or she edits. Deadline Jan. 1.
PEN/Phyllis Naylor Working Writer Fellowship: This annual award of $5,000 is presented to a North American author of children's or young-adult fiction. The candidate must be nominated by an editor or fellow writer and demonstrate financial need. Deadline Jan. 15.
PEN/Spielvogel-Diamonstein Award for the Art of the Essay: This $5,000 award is given for a distinguished book of previously uncollected essays on any subject by an American writer, published in the previous year. Deadline is Dec. 15.
PEN/Voelcker Award for Poetry: This biennial award of $5,000 is presented to an American poet whose distinguished and growing body of work to date represents a notable and accomplished presence in American literature. Deadline Jan. 1.
PEN/Nabokov Award: This biennial award of $20,000 honors talented, living writers of works, either written in or translated into English, which evoke to some measure Nabokov's versatility and commitment to literature as a search for the deepest truth and the highest pleasure.
PEN Fund for Writers and Editors with HIV/AIDS: Grants of up to $1,000 each are provided to published professional writers and editors with serious unexpected financial difficulties due to HIV/AIDS-related illness.
PEN Writers Fund: This program provides grants and loans of up to $1,000 each to published professional literary writers or editors with serious financial difficulties.
EIN: 133447888

5431
PEN/Faulkner
c/o Folger Shakespeare Library
201 E. Capitol St., S.E.
Washington, DC 20003-1004 (202) 675-0345
Contact: Jessica Neely, Exec. Dir.
FAX: (202) 608-1719; URL: http://
www.penfaulkner.org

Foundation type: Public charity
Limitations: Awards only for peer-judged literary awards, and stipends only to authors and teachers who already participate in the Writers in Schools program.
Financial data: Year ended 06/30/2004.
Assets, $485,799 (M); Expenditures, $582,876; Total giving, $40,000; Grants to individuals, 7 grants totaling $40,000 (high: $5,000, low: $2,500).
Fields of interest: Literature; Arts.
Type of support: Awards/prizes.
Application information: Applications not accepted.
Program description:
Malamud Award: This award honors a short story writer for a body of work.
EIN: 521431622

5432
Peninsula Community Foundation
1700 S. El Camino Real, Ste. 300
San Mateo, CA 94402-3049 (650) 358-9369
Contact: For grants: Ellen Clear, V.P., Community Progs.
FAX: (650) 358-9817; E-mail: inquiry@pcf.org;
Grant application E-mails: ellen@pcf.org or grants@pcf.org; URL: http://www.pcf.org

Foundation type: Community foundation
Limitations: Grants to artists who are residents of San Mateo County and northern Santa Clara County, CA.
Publications: Application guidelines; Annual report; Financial statement; Grants list; Informational brochure; Newsletter.
Financial data: Year ended 12/31/2004.
Assets, $611,716,329 (M); Expenditures, $119,524,673; Total giving, $110,910,875; Grants to individuals, 786 grants totaling $444,637 (high: $15,000, low: $250).
Fields of interest: Visual arts; Performing arts; Dance; Music; Arts, artist's services.
Type of support: Program development.
Application information: Applications accepted. Application form required.
Initial approach: Letter or telephone.
Deadline(s): Nov. 30 and May 31
Applicants should submit the following:
1) Proposal
2) Budget Information
3) SASE
Additional information: .
Program description:
Grants to Individual Artists: Provides recipients with grants of up to $5,000 in total, and the artist is required to spend a matching amount on the project. Support is available for individual and collaborating artists for training and professional development, professional experiences, materials, and capital expenses. All media are eligible, including visual, performing, and horticultural arts. Applicants must be at least 19 years of age; actively working in the discipline of the application; and residing in San Mateo County or northern Santa Clara County for the last two years. Applicants are

encouraged to meet with a Program Officer about the application process before applying.
EIN: 942746687

5433

Pennsylvania Humanities Council

325 Chestnut St., Ste. 715
Philadelphia, PA 19106-2607 (215) 925-1005
Contact: Joseph J. Kelly, Exec. Dir.; Fellowships: Claire Lawrence
FAX: (215) 925-3054;
E-mail: phc@pahumanities.org; Additional tel.: (800) 462-0442 (for PA only); URL: http://www.pahumanities.org

Foundation type: Public charity
Limitations: Grants to PA media artists for works in film, video, radio, or slide projects which deal significantly with the humanities, particularly those of interest to PA residents.
Publications: Application guidelines; Annual report; Informational brochure; Newsletter.
Financial data: Year ended 10/31/2004. Assets, $759,082 (M); Expenditures, $1,249,756; Total giving, $385,445.
Fields of interest: Media/communications; Film/video; Radio; Humanities; Arts, artist's services.
Type of support: Fellowships.
Application information:
Initial approach: Letter or telephone.
Additional information: Contact the council for current application deadline/guidelines.
Program description:
Arts Commentary: Perspectives on the Arts: Fellowships to individuals for high-quality, nonfiction work which educates the general public about the contemporary arts. This fellowship recognizes work in all media and is open to the full range of Pennsylvanians producing arts commentary. Journalists, broadcast and electronic media professionals are encouraged to apply. This program awards $35,000 to individuals every two years.
EIN: 232007911

5434

Peters Valley Craftsman, Inc.

19 Kuhn Rd.
Layton, NJ 07851 (973) 948-5200
Contact: Jimmy Clark, Exec. Dir.
FAX: (973) 948-0011; E-mail: pv@warwick.net;
URL: http://www.pvcrafts.org

Foundation type: Public charity
Limitations: Residencies to artists specializing in blacksmithing, ceramics, fine metals, photography, surface design, weaving and woodworking.
Financial data: Year ended 09/30/2003. Assets, $182,115 (M); Expenditures, $865,736.
Fields of interest: Arts.
Type of support: Residencies.
Application information: Application form required.
Deadline(s): Mar. 17 for Summer Assistant Residency
Applicants should submit the following:
1) Letter(s) of recommendation
2) Resume
Additional information: Application must also include slides of recent work and letter of intent.
Program descriptions:
Summer Assistant Residency: Each year Peters Valley makes available the opportunity to participate in the summer program by assisting instructors and studio heads. There is no pay. Housing and most meals are provided. Heavy

emphasis will be placed on knowledge of studio operations. A letter of intent must state objectives for the summer and the outlines of a potential project to complete during class downtime. It is possible to apply for a time that is shorter than the full summer though the minimum time accepted will be one month. There will be opportunities to show and/or sell work in the store and gallery as well as to take a course as a student.
Associate Residency Program: Associates often come to Peters Valley to build a body of work for entry into graduate school or to explore a completely new phase in their artistic career. We will try to accommodate those who apply within the confines of available studio and housing space; but there is limited space available and limited space per discipline. Associates can stay at the Valley for periods up to 7 months during the "off-season". October through April. Shorter stays are possible, as well as interrupted stays. A furnished private room in a shared house with communal cooking and living areas is the norm. Our summer teaching studios are made available to two associates per discipline; our full-time resident artists share some of these spaces.
EIN: 221920050

5435

Pewabic Society, Inc.

10125 E. Jefferson Ave.
Detroit, MI 48214 (313) 822-0954
Contact: Terese Ireland, Exec. Dir.
FAX: (313) 822-6266;
E-mail: pewabic1@pewabic.com; URL: http://www.pewabic.com

Foundation type: Public charity
Limitations: Residencies to ceramic pottery artists who are interior design or BFA graduates.
Financial data: Year ended 09/30/2004. Assets, $1,776,782 (M); Expenditures, $1,901,528. No monetary support given for residencies.
Fields of interest: Sculpture; Ceramic arts.
Type of support: Residencies.
Application information:
Initial approach: E-mail.
Deadline(s): Contact foundation for current application deadline
Additional information: Application by letter, including six slides of recent work or URL address.
Program description:
Residency Program: Residencies last from six months to a year. Each Artist-in-Resident will work 30 hours/week in Pewabic's Design Studio assisting in-house designers with client projects. Must be proficient in CAD-based software and be strongly interested in ceramics and its use in architectural installations. Compensation includes an hourly wage of $9.00/hr, free studio space as well as free materials, kiln time and an opportunity to exhibit in Prewabic's Annual Student Staff Faculty Show.
EIN: 382277840

5436

Pittsburgh Glass Center, Inc.

5472 Penn Ave.
Pittsburgh, PA 15206 (412) 365-2145
Contact: Dyana Curreri-Ermatinger, Exec. Dir.
FAX: (412) 365-2140;
E-mail: heather@pittsburghglasscenter.org;
URL: http://www.pittsburghglasscenter.org

Foundation type: Public charity

Limitations: Grants to artists, primarily in PA, specializing in glassmaking.
Financial data: Year ended 12/31/2003. Assets, $2,936,842 (M); Expenditures, $844,781.
Fields of interest: Arts.
Type of support: Awards/prizes.
Application information:
Initial approach: Letter, telephone, or e-mail.
Additional information: Contact foundation for current application deadline/guidelines.
EIN: 251814656

5437

The Poetry Foundation

(formerly The Modern Poetry Association)
1030 N. Clark St., Ste. 420
Chicago, IL 60610-5412 (312) 787-7070
Contact: Deborah Cummins, Chair.
FAX: (312) 787-6650;
E-mail: mail@poetryfoundation.org; URL: http://www.poetryfoundation.org

Foundation type: Independent foundation
Limitations: Fellowships by nomination only to undergraduate and graduate students of creative writing or English.
Financial data: Year ended 12/31/2003. Assets, $168,512,730 (M); Expenditures, $1,911,430; Total giving, $604,851; Grants to individuals, 10 grants totaling $138,500 (high: $100,000, low: $500).
Fields of interest: Literature.
Type of support: Fellowships; Awards/grants by nomination only; Awards/prizes.
Application information:
Deadline(s): Apr. 15
Additional information: Completion of formal nomination required, including samples of candidate's work; Recipients must be nominated by program directors or department chairs.
Program descriptions:
Ruth Lilly Poetry Fellowships: Awards fellowships of $15,000 each to creative writing or English major students under 30 years old for further study of poetry.
Ruth Lilly Poetry Prize: Awards a $100,000 prize to a living U.S. poet whose lifetime accomplishments warrants extraordinary recognition.
EIN: 362490808

5438

The Pollock-Krasner Foundation, Inc.

863 Park Ave.
New York, NY 10021 (212) 517-5400
Contact: Caroline Black, Prog. Off.
FAX: (212) 288-2836; E-mail: grants@pkf.org;
URL: http://www.pkf.org

Foundation type: Independent foundation
Limitations: Grants based on financial need as well as merit to talented painters, sculptors, and artists who work on paper (including printmakers) in the U.S. and abroad, to further their artistic pursuits. The foundation does not provide scholarships, tuition reimbursement, or grants to students who have not been working artists.
Publications: Application guidelines; Annual report; Informational brochure (including application guidelines).
Financial data: Year ended 06/30/2005. Assets, $52,305,723 (M); Expenditures, $4,440,038; Total giving, $2,624,000; Grants to individuals, 139 grants totaling $2,624,000.

Fields of interest: Visual arts; Sculpture; Design; Painting; Arts, artist's services.
Type of support: Awards/grants by nomination only; Foreign applicants; Awards/prizes; Grants for special needs.
Application information: Application form required.
  Initial approach: Letter.
  Deadline(s): None
  Applicants should submit the following:
    1) Curriculum vitae
    2) Financial information
  Additional information: Application must include a biographical record, ten slides of recent work, and a cover letter stating the purpose of the grant and the amount requested.
Program descriptions:
  Special Needs Grant: The purpose of the foundation is to provide financial assistance to individual working artists of established ability through the generosity of the late Lee Krasner, one of the leading abstract expressionist painters and widow of Jackson Pollock. The foundation welcomes nominations and applications from painters, sculptors, graphic, mixed media, and installation artists of artistic merit. There is no age or geographic limitation. The foundation does not give grants to commercial artists, photographers, video artists, filmmakers, craft-makers, or students who are not or have not been working artists. Grants are not awarded as scholarships or for tuition reimbursements. Grants are intended for a one-year period. Legitimate expenditures relating to work, living, and medical care are considered, as is emergency assistance. Grants are not made for past debts, legal fees, the purchase of real estate, moves to other cities, or to pay for installations or projects ordered by others. Both recipients and those refused grants may reapply in 12 months.
  Lee Krasner Awards: Lee Krasner Awards are based on the same criteria as all regular Pollock-Krasner grants, but are given in recognition of a lifetime of artistic achievement. This honor is a tribute to and recognition of artists with long and distinguished careers. This award is by nomination only.
EIN: 133255693

5439
The Martha Boschen Porter Fund, Inc.
145 White Hollow Rd.
Sharon, CT 06069-2108
Contact: Robert Terrall, Treas.

Foundation type: Independent foundation
Limitations: Grants for projects to financially needy, working artists residing in northwest CT and adjacent areas in western MA and NY.
Financial data: Year ended 06/30/2004. Assets, $160,009 (M); Expenditures, $11,250; Total giving, $9,000; Grants to individuals, totaling $9,000.
Fields of interest: Dance; Choreography; Music; Literature; Arts.
Type of support: Program development.
Application information:
  Initial approach: Letter.
  Deadline(s): None.
  Applicants should submit the following:
    1) Budget Information
    2) Resume
    3) Proposal
Program description:
  Artists Program Development: Previous recipients include actors, musicians, writers, choreographers, and visual artists.
EIN: 061157164

5440
Portland Institute for Contemporary Art
224 NW 13th Ave., Ste. 305
Portland, OR 97209 (503) 242-1419
Contact: Erin Boberg, Asst. Curator, Perf. Arts
FAX: (503) 243-1167; E-mail: pica@pica.org; Additional E-mail: jacobs@pica.org; URL: http://www.pica.org

Foundation type: Public charity
Limitations: Six residencies are available each year to provide artists with materials and working space during a development stage in making a new project.
Financial data: Year ended 05/31/2003. Assets, $1,472,646 (M); Expenditures, $842,158. No monetary support given for residencies.
Fields of interest: Visual arts.
Type of support: Residencies.
Application information: Applications accepted. Application form not required.
  Initial approach: Letter.
  Deadline(s): None.
  Additional information: Submit work samples, biographic materials, work description, invitations to upcoming shows, and SASE.
EIN: 931177971

5441
Pottstown Symphony Orchestra
P.O. Box 675
Pottstown, PA 19464 (610) 323-2201
Contact: Kevin Wood, Exec. Dir.
For the Kathryn E. MacPhail Young Artist Competition: c/o Kathy Williams, 265 Old State Rd., Royersford, PA 19468; Tel.: (610) 948-4950
URL: http://www.pottstownsymphony.org

Foundation type: Public charity
Limitations: Prizes to winners of the Kathryn E. MacPhail Young Artist Competition for musicians, and an opportunity to perform in concert with the Pottstown Symphony.
Financial data: Year ended 06/30/2004. Assets, $111,018 (M); Expenditures, $230,413.
Fields of interest: Orchestra (symphony).
Type of support: Awards/prizes.
Application information: Applications accepted. Application form required. Application form available on the grantmaker's Web site.
  Initial approach: Letter.
  Deadline(s): Jan. 20
  Additional information: Applications must include a cassette/CD recording of the work to be performed at the audition, plus a $50 application fee.
EIN: 237050084

5442
The Presser Foundation
385 Lancaster Ave., No. 205
Haverford, PA 19041 (610) 658-9030
Contact: Edith A. Reinhardt, Pres.

Foundation type: Independent foundation
Limitations: Emergency aid to worthy music teachers in need.
Financial data: Year ended 06/30/2004. Assets, $55,632,794 (M); Expenditures, $2,371,772; Total giving, $2,115,888.
Fields of interest: Music; Education.
Type of support: Grants for special needs.
Application information: Applications accepted. Application form required.

Additional information: Application must also include financial statement, and three references.
EIN: 232164013

5443
Evelyn W. Preston Trust
c/o Bank of America, N.A.
777 Main St., CT2-102-22-02
Hartford, CT 06115 (860) 543-8874

Foundation type: Independent foundation
Limitations: Grants to musicians to perform free band and orchestral concerts in Hartford, CT, from June through Sept.
Financial data: Year ended 12/31/2004. Assets, $4,288,719 (M); Expenditures, $260,439; Total giving, $219,330; Grants to individuals, 22 grants totaling $83,715 (high: $6,000, low: $1,000).
Fields of interest: Music; Orchestra (symphony); Music ensembles/groups.
Type of support: Program development.
Application information: Applications accepted. Application form required.
  Additional information: Unsolicited requests for funding not considered or acknowledged.
EIN: 060747389

5444
Prince George's Arts Council, Inc.
Prince George's Metro Ctr.
6525 Belcrest Rd., Ste.132
Hyattsville, MD 20782 (301) 277-1402
Contact: Ethel Lewis, Acting Dir.
FAX: (301) 277-7215; E-mail: PGAC123@aol.com

Foundation type: Public charity
Limitations: Fellowships, awards, internships, residencies, and general grants to artists in Prince George's County, MD.
Publications: Application guidelines; Annual report (including application guidelines); Grants list; Informational brochure (including application guidelines); Newsletter.
Financial data: Year ended 06/30/2004. Assets, $195,026 (M); Expenditures, $237,979; Total giving, $149,595; Grants to individuals, 14 grants totaling $14,795 (high: $2,000, low: $150).
Fields of interest: Arts, artist's services.
Type of support: Fellowships; Internship funds; Awards/prizes; Residencies.
Application information: Contact council for current application deadline/guidelines; Initial approach by letter or telephone.
EIN: 521295007

5445
Princess Grace Foundation - U.S.A.
150 E. 58th St., 21st Fl.
New York, NY 10155 (212) 317-1470
Contact: Toby E. Boshak, Exec. Dir.
FAX: (212) 317-1473; E-mail: pgfusa@pgfusa.com; URL: http://www.pgfusa.com

Foundation type: Public charity
Limitations: Scholarships, apprenticeships, and fellowships to young artists in the fields of theater, dance, playwriting, and film who are U.S. citizens or permanent residents.
Publications: Application guidelines; Annual report; Financial statement; Grants list; Newsletter.
Financial data: Year ended 12/31/2004. Assets, $13,891,673 (M); Expenditures,

$1,023,698; Total giving, $363,361; Grants to individuals, 34 grants totaling $363,361 (high: $25,000, low: $1,000).
Fields of interest: Film/video; Dance; Theater; Theater (playwriting).
Type of support: Fellowships; Internship funds; Scholarships—to individuals.
Application information: Application form required.
Initial approach: Letter with SASE requesting guidelines.
Deadline(s): Mar. 31 for theater and playwriting, Apr. 30 for dance, and June 1 for film
Additional information: .
Program description:
Awards: Grants are offered as follows: scholarships, apprenticeships and fellowships in theater; scholarships and fellowships in dance; scholarships (undergraduate and graduate thesis support) in film; and fellowships in playwriting. Theater, dance, and film applicants must be nominated by deans/artistic directors. Playwrights may apply individually.
EIN: 232218331

5446
Puffin Foundation, Ltd.
20 E. Oakdene Ave.
Teaneck, NJ 07666
Contact: Gladys Miller-Rosenstein, Exec. Dir.
FAX: (201) 836-1734;
E-mail: puffingrant@mindspring.com; URL: http://www.puffinfoundation.org

Foundation type: Independent foundation
Limitations: Grants to emerging artists in the U.S. in the areas of music, literature, photography, and performing arts for projects that have social relevance.
Publications: Application guidelines; Informational brochure.
Financial data: Year ended 12/31/2003.
Assets, $14,421,182 (M); Expenditures, $946,545; Total giving, $354,221.
Fields of interest: Film/video; Photography; Performing arts; Music; Literature; Arts.
Type of support: Program development.
Application information: Application form required.
Initial approach: Letter/proposal.
Deadline(s): Dec. 31
Program description:
Artist Program Development: The foundation has two exhibition spaces for theater, art, and video performance of issues of social relevance, Puffin Room, Soho, NY, and Puffin Cultural Forum, Teaneck, NJ.
EIN: 133155489

5447
Pyramid Atlantic, Inc.
8230 Georgia Ave.
Silver Spring, MD 20910   (301) 608-9101
Contact: Helen C. Frederick, Exec. Artistic Dir.
FAX: (301) 608-9102;
E-mail: info@pyramid-atlantic.org; URL: http://www.pyramidatlanticartcenter.org

Foundation type: Public charity
Limitations: Residencies to artists who practice the disciplines of bookmaking, papermaking, and digital media.
Financial data: Year ended 06/30/2003.
Assets, $3,513,129 (M); Expenditures, $363,053.
Fields of interest: Media/communications; Visual arts.
Type of support: Residencies.

Application information:
Initial approach: Letter or e-mail.
Deadline(s): None.
Additional information: Contact foundation for current application guidelines.
Program description:
Residency Program: Residencies last from two weeks to one month. The facility supplies housing, meals, travel and studio space.
EIN: 521233802

5448
Queens Council on the Arts, Inc.
1 Forest Park at Oak Ridge
Woodhaven, NY 11421-1166   (718) 647-3377
Contact: Hoong Yee Lee Krakauer, Exec. Dir.
FAX: (718) 647-5036;
E-mail: qca@queenscouncilarts.org; URL: http://www.queenscouncilarts.org

Foundation type: Public charity
Limitations: Grants and technical assistance to artists who are residents of the borough of Queens in New York, NY.
Financial data: Year ended 06/30/2004.
Assets, $256,892 (M); Expenditures, $823,597; Total giving, $281,845.
Fields of interest: Arts, artist's services.
Type of support: Program development; Awards/prizes.
Application information: Applications accepted. Application form required.
Deadline(s): Mid-Sept.
EIN: 112219193

5449
The Ragdale Foundation
1260 N. Green Bay Rd.
Lake Forest, IL 60045   (847) 234-1063
Contact: Susan Page Tillet, Exec. Dir.
E-mail: eventsragdale@aol.com; Additional E-mail: sptil@aol.com; URL: http://www.ragdale.org

Foundation type: Public charity
Limitations: Fellowships to female writers and to visual artists residing in WI.
Financial data: Year ended 06/30/2004.
Assets, $3,661,670 (M); Expenditures, $696,725.
Fields of interest: Visual arts; Literature; Women.
Type of support: Fellowships; Residencies.
Application information: Applications accepted. Application form required. Application form available on the grantmaker's Web site.
Initial approach: E-mail.
Deadline(s): Vary
Applicants should submit the following:
1) Proposal
2) Resume
Additional information: A $20 application fee, and work sample must be included.
Program descriptions:
Frances Shaw Fellowship: Fellowships to women writers who began writing after age 55. Fellows are flown to Ragdale from anywhere and receive a free 6-week residency. Deadline Feb. 1.
Goberville Memorial Fellowship: Fellowship to a Wisconsin visual artist who is accepted for a residency. The fellowship covers all fees and a $250 stipend for travel and materials. Successful Wisconsin applicants will be automatically considered for this award upon acceptance to Ragdale's residency program. Artists should apply by submitting materials according to the regular Ragdale application guidelines.
EIN: 362937927

5450
Rasmuson Foundation
301 W. Northern Lights Blvd., Ste. 400
Anchorage, AK 99503   (907) 297-2700
Contact: Diane S. Kaplan, C.E.O. and Pres.
FAX: (907) 297-2770;
E-mail: rasmusonfdn@rasmuson.org; URL: http://www.rasmuson.org

Foundation type: Independent foundation
Limitations: Fellowships and awards to artists residing in AK.
Publications: Application guidelines; Grants list; Informational brochure (including application guidelines); Newsletter.
Financial data: Year ended 12/31/2004.
Assets, $513,459,645 (M); Expenditures, $26,359,024; Total giving, $22,555,934.
Fields of interest: Folk arts; Media/communications; Visual arts; Performing arts; Choreography; Music composition; Literature.
Type of support: Program development; Fellowships; Awards/prizes.
Application information: Applications accepted. Application form required. Application form available on the grantmaker's Web site.
Initial approach: Letter or telephone.
Deadline(s): Mar. 1 and Sept. 1 for Project Awards; Fellowship Awards and Distinguished Artist Awards deadline is Sept. 1
Applicants should submit the following:
1) Budget Information
2) SASE
3) Resume
Additional information: Application must also include project description, artist statement and work samples; See Web site for additional application information.
Program description:
Individual Artist Awards: The Rasmuson Foundation has created three award programs for individual artists living and working in Alaska: Project Awards: Awards of up to $5,000 for emerging, mid-career, and mature artists for specific, short-term projects that have a clear benefit to the artist and the development of his/her work. Artist Fellowships: $12,000 awards for mid-career or mature artists to focus their energy and attention for a one-year period on developing their creative work. Distinguished Artist: $25,000 annual award for an artist of recognized stature with a history of creative excellence and accomplishment in the arts.
EIN: 916340739

5451
REC Music Foundation
c/o Robert E. Crawford, Jr.
61 Crestwood Dr.
Clayton, MO 63105

Foundation type: Operating foundation
Limitations: Scholarships to individuals studying classical music.
Financial data: Year ended 12/31/2002.
Assets, $1,024,302 (M); Expenditures, $50,199; Total giving, $22,500; Grants to individuals, totaling $5,000.
Fields of interest: Performing arts; Music.
Type of support: Scholarships—to individuals.
Application information:
Deadline(s): Contact foundation for current application deadline
Additional information: See Web site for application guidelines.
EIN: 431607598

5452
Red Rock Mesa
P.O. Box 145
Springdale, UT 84767   (435) 772-0300
Contact: Fred Esplin
FAX: (435) 772-0303

Foundation type: Public charity
Limitations: Residencies to visual artists, composers and writers.
Financial data: Year ended 12/31/2003. Assets, $783,024 (M); Expenditures, $127,106. No monetary support given for residencies.
Fields of interest: Visual arts; Music composition; Literature.
Type of support: Residencies.
Application information: Applications accepted. Application form required.
   Initial approach: Letter or e-mail.
   Deadline(s): Contact foundation for current application deadline.
Program description:
   Residency Program: The Mesa accepts 12 artists at a time. Residency includes housing, studio space, and meals. The average length of a residency lasts from two weeks to three months.
EIN: 870509262

5453
Region 2 Arts Council
426 Bemidji Ave.
Bemidji, MN 56601   (218) 751-5447
Contact: Terri Widman, Exec. Dir.
E-mail: r2arts@paulbunyan.net; Additional tel.: (800) 275-5447; URL: http://www.r2arts.org

Foundation type: Public charity
Limitations: Project grants to artists who reside in the MN counties of Beltrami, Clearwater, Hubbard, Lake of the Woods and Mahnomen.
Financial data: Year ended 06/30/2005. Assets, $26,358 (M); Expenditures, $143,281; Total giving, $65,123; Grants to individuals, totaling $20,140.
Fields of interest: Arts.
Type of support: Seed money.
Application information: Deadlines Oct. 9 and Feb. 5; Completion of formal application required; See Web site for application form.
Program description:
   Artist Project Grant: Provides financial assistance to artists who show commitment to creative growth and career advancement. Artists may request up to $1,000 for expenses associated with a specific creative work or opportunity. These grants are only available to artists residing in the MN counties of Beltrami, Clearwater, Hubbard, Lake of the Woods and Mahnomen.
EIN: 411390021

5454
Regional Arts and Culture Council
108 NW 9th Ave., Ste. 300
Portland, OR 97209-3318   (503) 823-5111
Contact: Eloise Damrosch, Exec. Dir.; Fellowships: Lorin Schmit Dunlop
FAX: (503) 823-5432; E-mail for fellowships contact: lsdunlop@racc.org; Tel. for fellowships contact: (503) 823-5408; URL: http://www.racc.org

Foundation type: Public charity
Limitations: Project grants, fellowships, and professional development grants to artists residing in Clackamas, Multnomah, and Washington counties of OR.

Publications: Application guidelines; Annual report; Informational brochure; Newsletter.
Financial data: Year ended 06/30/2004. Assets, $2,006,666 (M); Expenditures, $4,100,047; Total giving, $2,013,298; Grants to individuals, 165 grants totaling $322,250 (high: $20,000, low: $100).
Fields of interest: Arts, management/technical aid; Arts, administration/regulation; Media/communications; Literature; Arts.
Type of support: Program development; Fellowships.
Application information: Applications accepted. Application form required. Application form available on the grantmaker's Web site.
   Initial approach: Telephone or e-mail.
   Deadline(s): Varies.
   Applicants should submit the following:
      1) Financial information
      2) Resume
      3) Letter(s) of recommendation
      4) Budget Information
      5) Proposal
   Additional information: Application must also include work samples.
Program descriptions:
   Individual Artist Fellowship: Awards to creative professional artists to help them sustain or enhance their artistic processes. Artists must have been working professionally in their discipline for ten years, been an Oregon resident for five years, and a current resident in Clackamas, Multnomah and Washington counties in Oregon. One literary arts and one media arts fellowship will be awarded. Deadline July 26.
   Professional Development Grants: Grants to administrators or individual artists to improve their business management development skills and/or rise to another level artistically. Proposals in the Professional Development Grant Program cannot be geared toward the creation of a specific art project, but must clearly demonstrate how the proposal will benefit the individual long-term. Available to artists in Clackamas, Multnomah and Washington counties in Oregon. Deadline October 25.
   Project Grants: Provides funding to artists who offer specific art programs or presentations to the general public. Projects can fall into one of three categories: Artistic Focus, Neighborhood Arts, and Arts in Schools. Applicants can apply in up to two different categories for separate projects. Available to artists in Clackamas, Multnomah and Washington counties in Oregon. Deadline August 16.
EIN: 931059037

5455
Heinz and Suze Rehfuss Memorial Fund
c/o Mark L. Stulmaker
42 Delaware Ave., Ste. 300
Buffalo, NY 14202-3901
Application address: c/o Melisse H. Pinto, 156 David Rd., Rutland, VT, 05701

Foundation type: Independent foundation
Limitations: Educational grants to young operatic and concert singers between 18 and 32 years of age who possess a high degree of motivation and musicianship and who show particular potential in voice quality and theatrical ability. Giving is limited to Buffalo, NY.
Financial data: Year ended 12/31/2004. Assets, $145,120 (M); Expenditures, $52,406; Total giving, $50,500; Grants to individuals, totaling $19,000.

Fields of interest: Music; Opera; Performing arts, education.
Type of support: Scholarships—to individuals.
Application information: Contact fund for current application deadline; Application by letter, including accomplishments to date, tape recordings, statement of career goals, intended use of award, and letters of recommendation; Auditions and interviews are required.
EIN: 166356877

5456
Renaissance Performing Arts Company
12601 E. Hwy. 60
Apache Junction, AZ 85218   (520) 463-2600
Contact: Jeff Siegel, Tr.

Foundation type: Company-sponsored foundation
Limitations: Grants to individuals for performance and education relating to the Carolina Renaissance Festival, NC.
Financial data: Year ended 12/31/2004. Assets, $1,893 (M); Expenditures, $22,112; Total giving, $20,716; Grants to individuals, 13 grants totaling $16,016 (high: $3,850, low: $100).
Fields of interest: Performing arts; Performing arts, education.
Type of support: Program development; Scholarships—to individuals.
Application information: Applications accepted throughout the year; Contact foundation for current application guidelines.
EIN: 411794770

5457
The Rhode Island Foundation
(also known as The Rhode Island Community Foundation)
1 Union Station
Providence, RI 02903   (401) 274-4564
Contact: Karen Voci, Sr. V.P., Prog.; For artists: Claude Elliott
FAX: (401) 331-8085; Artist grants E-mail: celliott@rifoundation.org; URL: http://www.rifoundation.org

Foundation type: Community foundation
Limitations: Fellowships and grants to RI artists.
Publications: Application guidelines; Annual report (including application guidelines); Grants list; Informational brochure; Newsletter; Occasional report; Program policy statement.
Financial data: Year ended 12/31/2004. Assets, $428,970,585 (M); Expenditures, $26,734,100; Total giving, $22,400,000.
Fields of interest: Film/video; Visual arts; Performing arts; Music composition; Literature.
Type of support: Fellowships; Stipends.
Application information: Applications accepted. Application form available on the grantmaker's Web site.
   Initial approach: Letter or e-mail.
   Deadline(s): Letter of Intent by May 2, Nov. 1 for Fellowships
   Applicants should submit the following:
      1) Proposal
      2) Budget Information
   Additional information: See Web site for a complete list of program guidelines and application forms.
Program descriptions:
   New Works: Visual, literary, performance, film and video artists who partner with nonprofit arts and/or community-based organizations will receive between $5,000 to $18,000.

Robert and Margaret MacColl Johnson Fellowships: The foundation will provide up to three $25,000 artist fellowships each year, rotating among three disciplines- music composition, creative writing, and visual arts.
EIN: 222604963

5458
The Rhythm and Blues Foundation, Inc.
253 W. 138 St.
New York, NY   10030   (212) 491-7700
Contact: Cecilia K. Carter, Exec. Dir.
FAX: (212) 491-7900; E-mail: RandBFdn@aol.com;
URL: http://www.rhythm-n-blues.org/

Foundation type: Public charity
Limitations: Awards by nomination only to pioneers in the Rhythm and Blues industry.
Publications: Application guidelines; Annual report; Financial statement; Informational brochure; Newsletter.
Financial data: Year ended 05/31/2003. Assets, $2,664,819 (M); Expenditures, $1,136,693; Total giving, $256,399; Grants to individuals, totaling $256,399.
Fields of interest: Music.
Type of support: Emergency funds; Awards/grants by nomination only; Awards/prizes; Grants for special needs.
Application information: Applications accepted. Application form required.
Initial approach: Telephone or e-mail.
Deadline(s): None
Program descriptions:
Pioneer Awards Program: This program recognizes legendary artists whose lifelong contributions have been instrumental in the development of rhythm and blues music. Award recipients are nominated by foundation trustees, advisory board and artist steering committee, and past Pioneer Award honorees, and are selected by the board of trustees. Awards are presented in the following categories: Individual, Group, Songwriter/ Sideperson/Entrepreneur, Lifetime Achievement and Legacy Tribute.
Doc Pomus Financial Assistance Grant Program: The program supports the current and specific financial needs of legendary rhythm and blues artists whose contributions have been seminal in the music's development and growth toward global popularity.
Gwendolyn B. Gordy Fugua Fund: This fund provides emergency financial assistance to living artists who performed R&B music of the 50's and 60's under the Motown label.
Motown/Universal Music Group Fund: This fund provides grants for health, welfare and related purposes to former R&B recording artists affiliated with the Universal Music Group or affiliated labels.
EIN: 521594184

5459
Roswell Museum and Art Center Foundation
400 N. Pennsylvania, No. 220
Roswell, NM   88201   (505) 627-0198
Contact: John W. Bassett, Pres.; For residencies: Stephen Fleming
E-mail: rswelair@dfn.com; URL: http://
www.roswellmuseum.org

Foundation type: Public charity
Limitations: Residencies to visual artists specializing in painting, drawing, sculpture,

printmaking, photography, installations and other fine art media.
Financial data: Year ended 12/31/2003. Assets, $483,943 (M); Expenditures, $56,911.
Fields of interest: Visual arts; Photography; Sculpture; Painting; Drawing.
Type of support: Residencies; Stipends.
Application information: Applications accepted. Application form required. Application form available on the grantmaker's Web site.
Applicants should submit the following:
1) Resume
2) SASE
Additional information: Applications must also include 15 slides of recent work, statement of intent, and an application fee of $25.
Program description:
Roswell Artist in Residence Program: The program provides artists a one-year residency which includes housing, studio space and a $500 monthly living stipend. The residency is located in Roswell, NM. Artists awarded a residency may receive an exhibition of their work at the Roswell Museum and Art Center. The program is not available to artists engaged in the disciplines of performance art or production crafts.
EIN: 850356617

5460
The Judith Rothschild Foundation
1110 Park Ave.
New York, NY   10128   (212) 831-4114
Contact: Elizabeth Slater, V.P., Grant Prog.
FAX: (212) 831-6222; E-mail: slatereliz@aol.com;
URL: http://www.judithrothschildfdn.org

Foundation type: Operating foundation
Limitations: Grants to individuals for projects that present, preserve, or interpret work by lesser known American artists who died after September 12, 1976.
Publications: Application guidelines; Grants list.
Financial data: Year ended 12/31/2002. Assets, $30,178,023 (M); Expenditures, $3,235,466; Total giving, $1,496,400; Grants to individuals, 2 grants totaling $30,000 (high: $15,000, low: $15,000).
Fields of interest: Arts, public education; Art conservation; Art history; Arts.
Type of support: Program development.
Application information: Applications accepted. Application form required. Application form available on the grantmaker's Web site.
Initial approach: 2- to 3-page letter.
Deadline(s): Between Apr. 15 and Sept. 15
Additional information: Applications by FAX not accepted.
Program description:
Artists Program Development: The primary emphasis is to promote public awareness of the scope of recently deceased American artist's achievements as well as direct aesthetic experience of their work. Independent curators, scholars, and historians, who have a direct recognized relationship to the artist's work, are eligible to apply.
EIN: 133736320

5461
Constance Saltonstall Foundation for the Arts, Inc.
435 Ellis Hollow Creek Rd.
Ithaca, NY   14850   (607) 539-3146
Contact: Laurel Guy, Prog. Dir.
FAX: (607) 539-3147; E-mail: info@saltonstall.org;
URL: http://www.saltonstall.org

Foundation type: Operating foundation
Limitations: Provides grants and art colony residencies to artists in NY.
Publications: Application guidelines; Informational brochure; Newsletter.
Financial data: Year ended 12/31/2004. Assets, $4,850,710 (M); Expenditures, $233,450; Total giving, $45,975; Grants to individuals, totaling $41,475.
Fields of interest: Photography; Painting; Literature; Arts, artist's services; Arts.
Type of support: Residencies.
Application information: Deadline Jan. 15; Completion of formal application required, including resume, statement of purpose and work samples.
Program descriptions:
Arts Colony: One-month residencies are available to painters, photographers, and writers of fiction, poetry, and creative nonfiction in NY state. Applicants must be at least 21 years old.
Grants: The foundation awards $5,000 grants to artists who are 21 or older, living in Allegany, Broome, Cattaraugus, Cayuga, Chautauqua, Chemung, Chenango, Cortland, Erie, Genesee, Jefferson, Lewis, Livingston, Madison, Monroe, Niagara, Oneida, Onondaga, Ontario, Orleans, Oswego, Schuyler, Seneca, Steuben, Tioga, Tompkins, Wayne, Wyoming, and Yates counties, NY. Arts categories for the grants change annually; see Web site for current categories. Recipients have used these grants in a variety of ways, including buying materials, preparing works for exhibit, and taking time off from non-arts jobs to create new work.
EIN: 161481219

5462
San Francisco Children's Art Center
Fort Mason Ctr., Bldg. C
San Francisco, CA   94123-1382
(415) 771-0292
E-mail: sfcac@childrensartcenter.org; URL: http://
www.childrensartcenter.org

Foundation type: Public charity
Limitations: Partial to full tuition assistance to children attending the Children's Art Center of San Francisco, CA.
Financial data: Year ended 08/31/2004. Assets, $18,151 (M); Expenditures, $118,789.
Fields of interest: Arts education.
Type of support: Scholarships—to individuals.
Application information: Applications accepted. Application form required. Application form available on the grantmaker's Web site.
Initial approach: Telephone or e-mail.
EIN: 942448876

5463
The San Francisco Foundation
225 Bush St., Ste. 500
San Francisco, CA   94104-4224
(415) 733-8500
Contact: Sandra R. Hernandez M.D., C.E.O. and
Secy.
FAX: (415) 477-2783; E-mail: rec@sff.org; Intent to
Apply E-mail: apps@sff.org; Additional E-mail:
srh@sff.org; URL: http://www.sff.org

Foundation type: Community foundation
Limitations: Awards to artists and community
leaders in the San Francisco, CA, area.
Publications: Application guidelines; Annual report;
Financial statement; Grants list; Informational
brochure (including application guidelines);
Newsletter; Program policy statement.
Financial data: Year ended 06/30/2004.
Assets, $757,717,972 (M); Expenditures,
$74,554,575; Total giving, $64,392,830.
Fields of interest: Arts, alliance; Film/video;
Journalism/publishing; Photography; Community
development, volunteer services.
Type of support: Awards/prizes.
Application information: Applications accepted.
Application form required.
Initial approach: Letter of intent.
Deadline(s): Vary
Program descriptions:
James D. Phelan Art Awards:
· Phelan Award in Photography:Three awards
of $2,500 are offered every odd year.
Winners participate in a group exhibition at
the San Francisco Camerawork gallery.
Deadline Oct.
· Phelan Award in Printmaking: Three awards
of $2,500 to artists. Recipients are invited
to participate in a group exhibition in the
Kala Art Institute's gallery. Deadline July 10
· Phelan Art Award in Filmmaking: An award
of $7,500 to a California-born artist
presented each even year. Deadline July 12
· Phelan Art Award in Video: Awards range
from $2,500 to $7,500 and are offered on
every even year. Deadline July
Community Leadership Awards: The award
recognizes individuals and organizations whose
leadership has made a significant impact in their
particular Bay Area communities. This work may
confront social or health problems, address
environmental concerns, or promote arts and
humanities. One of the four awards is designated
for an under-recognized, mature artist who has
made a significant and ongoing contribution in the
Bay Area. Artists from the performing, literary,
media, and visual arts, including craft, folk, and
traditional forms, will be considered. Individuals
receive $10,000 awards. Individuals in Alameda,
Contra Costa, Marin, San Francisco, and San Mateo
counties are eligible to apply.

5464
Santa Fe Jazz Foundation, Inc.
223 N. Guadalupe St. - PMB 288
Santa Fe, NM   87501-8582   (505) 989-8685
Contact: Robert H. Weil, Pres.

Foundation type: Independent foundation
Limitations: Scholarships and grants to jazz
musicians for emergency medical aid.
Financial data: Year ended 12/31/2004.
Assets, $277,310 (M); Expenditures, $43,874;
Total giving, $41,000; Grants to individuals,
totaling $13,850 (high: $1,000).
Fields of interest: Music; Health care.

Type of support: Scholarships—to individuals;
Grants for special needs.
Application information: Contact foundation for
current application deadline/guidelines;
Application by letter outlining financial need.
EIN: 850386250

5465
Damir I. Schmidek and Virginia A. Schmidek Charitable Foundation
15432 Banyan Ln.
Monte Sereno, CA   95030
Contact: Damir I. Schmidek, Pres.
Application address: c/o Ronald G. Coleman, PC, 99
Almaden Blvd., Ste. 500, San Jose, CA 95113, tel.
(408) 297-0700

Foundation type: Independent foundation
Limitations: Awards to individuals who are interns
at Opera San Jose, CA.
Financial data: Year ended 12/31/2004.
Assets, $873,090 (M); Expenditures, $69,616;
Total giving, $14,000; Grants to individuals,
totaling $14,000.
Fields of interest: Opera.
Type of support: Awards/prizes.
Application information: Deadline Apr. 1;
Application by letter.
EIN: 770520075

5466
School of American Research
P.O. Box 2188
Santa Fe, NM   87504   (505) 954-7200
Contact: Nancy Owen Lewis, Dir., Academic Progs.
FAX: (505) 954-7214; E-mail: info@sarsf.org;
URL: http://www.sarweb.org

Foundation type: Public charity
Limitations: Fellowships to female Native American
artists, Native American artists and artists who
specialize in Native American art. A prize is also
available to an author of anthropology.
Publications: Application guidelines; Annual report;
Informational brochure.
Financial data: Year ended 06/30/2004.
Assets, $31,738,505 (M); Expenditures,
$3,764,772; Total giving, $263,099.
Fields of interest: Arts; Anthropology/sociology;
Native Americans/American Indians; Women.
Type of support: Fellowships; Awards/prizes.
Application information:
Initial approach: E-mail.
Additional information: Contact foundation for
current application deadline/guidelines.
Program descriptions:
J.I. Staley Prize: A prize of $10,000 is awarded to
an author of anthropology.
King Fellowship: Provides financial assistance to
an artist specializing in Native American
Southwestern art.
Dobkin Fellowship: Provides financial assistance
to a Native American female artist specializing in
Native American Southwestern art.
Dubin Fellowship: Provides financial assistance
for a summer-long fellowship to a Native American
artist.
Branigar Fellowship: A nine-month tenure
provides a stipend, housing and travel funds to a
Native American specializing in Native American
curatorial work and art collection management.
EIN: 850125045

5467
The Schuylkill Center for Environmental Education
8480 Hagy's Mill Rd.
Philadelphia, PA   19128   (215) 482-7300
Contact: Tracy Kay, Exec. Dir.
FAX: (215) 482-5158; URL: http://
www.schuylkillcenter.org

Foundation type: Public charity
Limitations: Residencies to visual artists whose
projects include aspects of the environment and
ecology.
Financial data: Year ended 06/30/2003.
Assets, $10,808,035 (M); Expenditures,
$1,488,902.
Fields of interest: Visual arts; Environmental
education; Environment.
Type of support: Residencies.
Application information: Application form required.
Initial approach: Letter.
Deadline(s): Contact foundation for current
application deadline/guidelines.
Applicants should submit the following:
1) Resume
2) SASE
Additional information: Application must also
include proposals, slides of recent work, $15
application fee, and artist statement.
Program description:
Residency Program: The work can be for both
exterior and interior locations. Outdoor installations
are especially encouraged. Proposals should
indicate how the project relates to environment and
ecology academic subjects. Artists from all visual
arts backgrounds working with nontoxic materials
are eligible and include sculpture, painting, mixed
media, works on paper, fiber, etc. Selected artists
will receive an honorarium, studio space and a
housing stipend. The level and amount of stipends
are subject to availability of funding.
EIN: 231654975

5468
Sculpture Space, Inc.
12 Gates St.
Utica, NY   13502   (315) 724-8381
Contact: Sydney Waller, Exec. Dir.
FAX: (315) 797-6639;
E-mail: info@sculpturespace.org; URL: http://
www.sculpturespace.org

Foundation type: Public charity
Limitations: Residencies to professional artists
whose focus is sculpture.
Publications: Annual report; Informational
brochure; Newsletter.
Financial data: Year ended 06/30/2005.
Assets, $141,513 (M); Expenditures, $194,883.
Fields of interest: Sculpture.
Type of support: Residencies.
Application information: Application form required.
Initial approach: Letter, telephone, FAX, or e-mail.
Deadline(s): Dec. 1
Applicants should submit the following:
1) SASE
2) Resume
3) Letter(s) of recommendation
Additional information: Application must also
include slides of work and project description.
Program description:
Residency Program: Residents each receive a
$2,000 stipend. An average stay is two months.
Residencies provide studio space, equipment and
technical assistance.
EIN: 222197162

5469

Serpent Source Foundation for Women

2750 Lindsay Ave.
Louisville, KY 40206
Contact: Julia Youngblood, Pres.

Foundation type: Independent foundation
Limitations: Grants to economically disadvantaged, disabled female artists in the San Francisco Bay area, CA.
Financial data: Year ended 12/31/2004. Assets, $208 (M); Expenditures, $8,674; Total giving, $7,900; Grants to individuals, 7 grants totaling $7,900.
Fields of interest: Arts; Disabilities, people with; Women; Economically disadvantaged.
Type of support: Grants for special needs.
Application information: Application form required.
Initial approach: Letter.
Deadline(s): None.
Applicants should submit the following:
1) SASE
EIN: 943161163

5470

The Marie Walsh Sharpe Art Foundation

830 N. Tejon St., Ste. 120
Colorado Springs, CO 80903 (719) 635-3220
FAX: (719) 635-3018;
E-mail: sharpeartfdn@qwest.net; tel. for programs for individuals: (800) 232-2789; URL: http://www.sharpeartfdn.org

Foundation type: Independent foundation
Limitations: Grants for the following foundation programs: (1) Summer seminar for students gifted in the visual arts who have just completed their junior year of high school; (2) Artist studio spaces in New York, NY, to any nonstudent U.S. citizen or permanent U.S. resident aged 21 or over.
Financial data: Year ended 02/28/2003. Assets, $8,528,982 (M); Expenditures, $1,109,013; Total giving, $10,000.
Fields of interest: Arts education; Visual arts; Arts, artist's services.
Type of support: Precollege support; Residencies.
Application information: Application form required.
Deadline(s): Contact foundation for current application deadlines.
Additional information: All programs require representative slides of artwork; See program description for more information.
Program descriptions:
Summer Seminar Program: A seminar program open to artistically gifted high school juniors in the U.S., its territories, and the Department of Defense Schools Abroad. Recipients are chosen in the spring by jury selection from slide presentations of their artwork. Three seminars of two weeks each are held in the summer months for 20 students per session. The foundation invites a group of nationally prominent artists to instruct the students in drawing and painting, and to conduct critiques. The foundation hires a seminar faculty primarily from among interested art educators. The program uses a dormitory, art studio, cafeteria, and other facilities at Colorado College in Colorado Springs, CO. Accepted students are responsible only for their transportation to and from Colorado Springs, and their personal spending money. Applications must include a completed application form, six to ten slides of artwork in a vinyl slide sheet, a written personal statement, a letter of recommendation from a high school art teacher, and a SASE.
Studio Spaces: Fourteen free studio spaces in New York, NY are offered to visual artists 21 years and older. To be eligible, applicants must be U.S.

citizens or permanent U.S. residents and not in school at the time of residency. Studios are available for use for periods of up to one year. Studios are nonliving spaces for the making of new works of art. No stipend or equipment is provided. Proposals should include:
· eight slides (35mm) of recent work, one detail may be included (no glass slides are accepted), with the artist's name, arrow indicating the top of the work, and the slide number written on the slide. Or, if needed to portray work, a short video of three minutes or less
· an annotated list, including the slide number, title, size, date of work and medium used. Or, for video, a brief paragraph describing work
· a resume
· a concise statement of no more than one page, indicating why the studio space is needed
· a desired starting date and proposed length of stay. Date must be after Sept. 1 and may be for up to one year
· a SASE for the return of the slides
· all submissions will be juried by a panel of artists. Deadline Jan. 31.
EIN: 840956480

5471

The Shearwater Foundation, Inc.

12 E. 86th St., Apt. 1539
New York, NY 10028-0516
Contact: Joseph Arnold
Application address: c/o Andrew Pepper, 46 Crosby Rd., West Bridgford, Nottingham NG2 5GH England; E-mail: pepper@shearwaterfoundation.org

Foundation type: Operating foundation
Limitations: Annual grants of $10,000 each to four to eight art holographers residing in the U.S. and abroad. The foundation also supports activities that further the art of holography, through symposia, exhibitions, printed materials, and artist-in-residence programs.
Publications: Grants list; Program policy statement.
Financial data: Year ended 12/31/2004. Assets, $87 (M); Expenditures, $23,950; Total giving, $20,500.
Fields of interest: Arts, artist's services.
Type of support: Program development; Residencies.
Application information:
Deadline(s): None.
Additional information: Contact foundation for current application guidelines.
EIN: 133567898

5472

Shoshana Foundation, Inc.

251 W. 71st St., Ste. 3D
New York, NY 10023

Foundation type: Independent foundation
Limitations: Scholarships by nomination only, for the development of young men and women in the field of opera.
Financial data: Year ended 12/31/2003. Assets, $774,472 (M); Expenditures, $59,010; Total giving, $55,250; Grants to individuals, 20 grants totaling $55,250 (high: $4,000, low: $300).
Fields of interest: Opera; Performing arts, education.
Type of support: Scholarships—to individuals; Awards/grants by nomination only.

Application information: Applications not accepted.
Additional information: Recipients are nominated by 18 preselected institutions.
Program description:
Scholarship Program: Scholarships are awarded on the basis of promise and academic merit. The following institutions make recommendations: Central City Opera House Association, Denver, CO; Chautauqua Opera, Chautauqua, NY; Des Moines Metro Opera Inc., Indianola, IA; Houston Opera Studio, TX; Indiana University, Bloomington, IN; Juilliard School, New York, NY; Lake George Opera Festival, Glenns Falls, NY; Lyric Opera of Chicago, IL; Mannes College of Music, New York, NY; Manhattan School of Music, NY; New England Conservatory, Boston, MA; New York City Opera, NY; Pittsburgh Opera, PA; San Francisco Opera, CA; Sarasota Opera Association, FL; Summer Opera Theatre, Washington, DC; Tri-Cities Opera, Binghamton, NY; and the Wolf Trap Foundation, Vienna, VA.
EIN: 133317859

5473

Sitka Center for Art and Education

(also known as Neskowin Coast Foundation)
P.O. Box 65
Otis, OR 97368 (541) 994-5485
Contact: Laura Doyle, Acting Exec. Dir.
FAX: (541) 994-8024;
E-mail: info@sitkacenter.org; URL: http://www.sitkacenter.org

Foundation type: Public charity
Limitations: Residencies to musicians and artists whose works incorporate art and nature.
Financial data: Year ended 12/31/2003. Assets, $1,321,731 (M); Expenditures, $415,903.
Fields of interest: Visual arts; Music; Environment.
Type of support: Residencies.
Application information: Applications accepted. Application form required. Application form available on the grantmaker's Web site.
Deadline(s): Apr. 21
Applicants should submit the following:
1) Work samples
2) SASE
3) Letter(s) of recommendation
4) Resume
Additional information: Include preference for residency date.
Program descriptions:
Artist & Ecologist Residence Program: This program, which takes place in the Fall and Spring, provides housing and work space to artists in exchange for community outreach activities.
Recorder Residency: This residency lasts an average of two to three weeks each year or a month every other year. A studio and housing are provided. To be eligible for the residency, applicants are required to earn part of their income from recorder performance or composition. This is to indicate that applicants should have a degree of professionalism and people at the beginning of a career are as welcome as mature artists.
EIN: 237087718

5474

Smack Mellon Studios, Inc.

92 Plymouth St.
Brooklyn, NY 11201 (718) 422-0989
Contact: Kathleen Gilrain, Exec. Dir.
E-mail: info@smackmellon.org; URL: http://smackmellon.org/

Foundation type: Public charity
Limitations: Residencies and stipends for artists to work in Brooklyn, NY.
Financial data: Year ended 12/31/2003. Assets, $68,035 (M); Expenditures, $327,972.
Fields of interest: Media/communications; Film/video; Visual arts.
Type of support: Residencies; Stipends.
Application information: Applications accepted. Application form required. Application form available on the grantmaker's Web site.
  Initial approach: E-mail or telephone.
  Deadline(s): Oct. 22
  Applicants should submit the following:
    1) Resume
    2) Letter(s) of recommendation
    3) SASE
  Additional information: Application must also include work samples and artist statement.
Program description:
  Artist Studio Program: Smack Mellon offers free studio space to eligible artists for a one-year period. The program provides artists working in all visual arts media a free private studio space and a $5,000 stipend. The program does not provide living space. Artists also have access to shared facilities that include a fabrication shop, 2 G5 workstations for video editing, DVD burner and CD read/write capabilities, 2 emacs, flatbed and slide scanners, DVD players, projectors and monitors, wireless Internet access and technical support. Artists who are accepted into the program must be prepared to actively use their studio a minimum of 50 hours a month or they will lose it. The residency will run from April 1- March 1.
EIN: 113375393

5475
W. Eugene Smith Memorial Fund, Inc.
c/o Intl. Ctr. of Photography
1133 Ave. of the Americas
New York, NY   10036   (212) 857-0038
Contact: Helen Marcus, Pres.
Additional tel.: (212) 857-0000, ext. 138;
URL: http://www.smithfund.org

Foundation type: Company-sponsored foundation
Limitations: Competitive prizes for photojournalists whose work is based on a humanistic theme.
Publications: Informational brochure.
Financial data: Year ended 02/28/2005. Assets, $14,988 (M); Expenditures, $57,305; Total giving, $40,000; Grants to individuals, 3 grants totaling $40,000 (high: $30,000, low: $5,000).
Fields of interest: Journalism/publishing; Photography.
Type of support: Awards/prizes.
Application information: Application form required.
  Initial approach: Letter.
  Deadline(s): July 15
  Applicants should submit the following:
    1) Proposal
  Additional information: Finalists submit a comprehensive photographic portfolio in Aug.; Recipients notified by Oct. 15. A jury appointed by the fund's executive committee reviews applications and proposals.
EIN: 133060631

5476
Soapstone - A Writing Retreat for Women
622 S.E. 29th Ave.
Portland, OR   97214   (503) 233-3936
Contact: Ruth Gundle, Exec. Dir.
E-mail: mail@soapstone.org; URL: http://www.soapstone.org

Foundation type: Public charity
Limitations: Residencies to female writers.
Financial data: Year ended 12/31/2004. Assets, $154,947 (M); Expenditures, $26,906. No monetary support given for residencies.
Fields of interest: Literature; Women.
Type of support: Residencies.
Application information: Applications accepted. Application form required. Application form available on the grantmaker's Web site.
  Initial approach: E-mail.
  Deadline(s): Aug. 1.
  Additional information: Application should include writing sample and a $20 nonrefundable application fee.
Program description:
  Residency Program: Residencies are one to four weeks in length. Writers in residence must supply their own food, linens, and automobile due to Soapstone's isolated location.
EIN: 931072551

5477
Society of Singers, Inc.
6500 Wilshire Blvd., Ste. 640
Los Angeles, CA   90048   (323) 653-7672
Contact: Jerry Sharell, Pres. and C.E.O.
FAX: (323) 653-7675; E-mail: sos@singers.org;
Additional tel: (866) 767-7671, Help Line;
URL: http://www.singers.org

Foundation type: Public charity
Limitations: Grants to professional singers for financial assistance due to medical, family and other crises. Also provides scholarships to vocal students.
Publications: Application guidelines; Financial statement; Informational brochure (including application guidelines); Newsletter (including application guidelines).
Financial data: Year ended 12/31/2003. Assets, $1,271,619 (M); Expenditures, $1,219,786; Total giving, $246,780; Grants to individuals, 175 grants totaling $237,370.
Fields of interest: Music (choral); Economically disadvantaged.
Type of support: Emergency funds; Support to graduates or students of specific schools; Undergraduate support; Residencies; Grants for special needs.
Application information: Application form required.
  Initial approach: Telephone.
  Deadline(s): None
  Applicants should submit the following:
    1) Financial information
    2) Budget Information
  Additional information: Applicants must be professional singers of five or more years to be eligible. Interviews required.
Program description:
  Residency Program: The society provides confidential assistance to professional singers worldwide who are experiencing financial hardship due to an emergency or other circumstances. Charitable grants may be provided toward basic necessities of life such as food, shelter, utilities, medical/dental assistance, HIV/AIDS treatment, substance abuse rehab, psychotherapy and other basic expenses. Checks are always made payable

to creditors. SOS is unable to provide funds for personal loans, credit, tax debts, demos or headshots for music-related projects. Submission of an application is required with supporting documentation as follows: five years of singers' career documentation, latest tax return, bills for which one needs help, most current bank statements and proof of income for household members. In addition, vocal arts scholarships are granted to the National Foundation for Advancement in the Arts and students at local CA universities. Additional scholarships will be offered to master's level students who are attending vocal arts programs at accredited universities and who have demonstrated both financial need and talent.
EIN: 953903182

5478
Southwest School of Art and Craft
300 Augusta St.
San Antonio, TX   78205   (210) 224-1848
FAX: (210) 224-9337; E-mail: info@swschool.org;
URL: http://www.swschool.org

Foundation type: Public charity
Limitations: Residencies to artists specializing in letterpress, bookbinding and papermaking.
Financial data: Year ended 07/31/2004. Assets, $14,880,237 (M); Expenditures, $2,928,095; Total giving, $24,195; Grants to individuals, 159 grants totaling $24,195 (high: $315).
Fields of interest: Arts.
Type of support: Residencies.
Application information:
  Initial approach: E-mail.
  Deadline(s): Contact foundation for current application deadline
  Applicants should submit the following:
    1) Budget Information
    2) SASE
    3) Letter(s) of recommendation
    4) Work samples
    5) Proposal
    6) Resume
  Additional information: Application by letter.
Program descriptions:
  Book Arts & Papermaking Artist-in-Residence Program: Artists experienced in letterpress, book arts and/or papermaking spend up to three months working in the paper studio and the Book Arts Studio. The program includes access to facilities and possible housing, although it is not guaranteed.
  Residency for Letterpress & Book Arts Collaboration with Gemini Ink: Artists experienced in letterpress and bookbinding will work collaboratively with the winner of the Gemini Ink Award of Literary Excellence. Residency includes an honorarium of $800. The selected artist will complete a minimum of 40 copies. Housing may be available.
EIN: 746068932

5479
Southwestern Association for Indian Arts, Inc.
P.O. Box 969
Santa Fe, NM   87504-0969   (505) 983-5220
Contact: David Cloutier, Exec. Dir.
FAX: (505) 983-7647; E-mail: info@swaia.org;
URL: http://www.swaia.org

Foundation type: Public charity
Limitations: Fellowships to Native American artists, primarily in the southwest.

Financial data: Year ended 12/31/2003.
Assets, $614,097 (M); Expenditures, $977,025.
Fields of interest: Visual arts; Native Americans/
American Indians.
Type of support: Fellowships.
Application information: Applications accepted.
Application form required. Application form
available on the grantmaker's Web site.
  Initial approach: E-mail or letter.
  Deadline(s): Jan. 14
  Applicants should submit the following:
    1) Resume
    2) Essay
    3) Budget Information
  Additional information: Application must include
    slides of recent work. Six fellowships are
    awarded with a stipend of $3,000.
EIN: 850212504

5480

Staten Island Ballet Theater, Inc.

3081 Richmond Rd.
Staten Island, NY 10306-1941
(718) 980-0500
Contact: Paul Tharp, Exec. Dir.
E-mail: anbwilson@cs.com

Foundation type: Public charity
Limitations: Scholarships to individuals for ballet
arts training at the Staten Island Ballet Theater, NY.
Financial data: Year ended 05/31/2003.
Assets, $53,678 (M); Expenditures, $329,734;
Total giving, $58,900; Grants to individuals,
totaling $58,900.
Fields of interest: Dance; Ballet; Performing arts,
education.
Type of support: Scholarships—to individuals.
Application information: Contact foundation for
current application deadline/guidelines.
EIN: 133759761

5481

Jack Straw Foundation

4261 Roosevelt Way N.E.
Seattle, WA 98105-6999   (206) 634-0919
Contact: Joan Rabinowitz, Exec. Dir.
FAX: (206) 634-0925; E-mail: jsp@jackstraw.org;
E-mail (for Joan Rabinowitz): joan@jackstraw.org;
URL: http://www.jackstraw.org

Foundation type: Public charity
Limitations: Residencies to writers and artists
working with sound.
Financial data: Year ended 06/30/2004.
Assets, $1,325,168 (M); Expenditures,
$462,658. No monetary support given for
residencies.
Fields of interest: Music; Literature; Arts.
Type of support: Residencies.
Application information:
  Copies of proposal: 7
  Deadline(s): Vary.
  Applicants should submit the following:
    1) SASE
    2) Work samples
    3) Resume
  Additional information: Include project form.
Program descriptions:
  Artist Support: Each year, eight artists are
  awarded twenty hours of studio recording and
  production time with a Jack Straw engineer. An
  additional eight-ten artists will receive matching
  awards for studio time. Deadline Nov. 7.
  Writers Program: Aims to provide local writers
  with a new venue for the presentation of their work
  and to encourage the creation of new literary works.

Up to 14 authors are selected to participate
annually. The program features a series of three
public readings, half-hour radio programs
developed from recordings made of those readings,
a chapbook, and content for the Jack Straw
website. Other public events may also be organized.
During the program, writers are encouraged to write
a new piece to present to the public. Applicants in
all genres are welcomed. Deadline Nov. 14.
  New Media Gallery: Offers established and
  emerging artists of all disciplines the opportunity to
  create and present experimental work involving
  sound and technology, with the option of integrating
  any combination of other disciplines including
  visual and/or performance art. Up to three artists/
  artist teams are commissioned to create new works
  that include sound as a major component. Artists
  are encouraged to experiment and expand the
  artistic scope of their work by working with new
  technologies and artists from other disciplines.
  During the residency, artists work with a staff audio
  engineer to produce their work. Installations will be
  exhibited for up to three months and each
  installation will be accompanied by a reception and
  outreach programs. Deadline Nov. 21.
EIN: 910776606

5482

The Studio Museum in Harlem

144 W. 125th St.
New York, NY 10027   (212) 864-4500
FAX: (212) 864-4800; URL: http://
www.studiomuseum.org

Foundation type: Public charity
Limitations: Residencies to artists of African
descent as well as to African American artists.
Financial data: Year ended 06/30/2004.
Assets, $7,883,340 (M); Expenditures,
$4,902,183; Total giving, $43,269; Grants to
individuals, 6 grants totaling $43,269 (high:
$10,961, low: $3,462).
Fields of interest: Cultural/ethnic awareness;
African Americans/Blacks.
Type of support: Residencies.
Application information: Deadline Apr. 1; Initial
approach by letter; Completion of formal application
required, including work slides, letters of
recommendation, resume, artist statement, and
SASE.
Program description:
  Artist in Residence: Three emerging artists will be
  granted studio space, a $15,000 fellowship for a
  period of 12 months, and a $1,000 materials
  budget. An exhibition of the artist's work will be
  presented in the Museum's galleries.
EIN: 132590805

5483

The George Sugarman Foundation, Inc.

448 Ignacio Blvd., Ste. 329
Novato, CA 94949
Contact: Arden Sugarman, Pres. and Dir.
E-mail: sugarman@sonic.net; URL: http://
www.georgesugarman.com

Foundation type: Independent foundation
Limitations: Grants to working international artists
specializing in sculpture and painting.
Publications: Grants list; Program policy statement
(including application guidelines).
Financial data: Year ended 12/31/2004.
Assets, $723,580 (M); Expenditures, $120,700;
Total giving, $30,000; Grants to individuals,
totaling $30,000.
Fields of interest: Sculpture; Painting.

Type of support: Grants to individuals.
Application information: Applications accepted.
Application form required. Application form
available on the grantmaker's Web site.
  Deadline(s): June 30.
  Applicants should submit the following:
    1) SASE
    2) Work samples
    3) Resume
    4) Proposal
    5) Essay
    6) Budget Information
  Additional information: Applications should be
    sent by letter; Application should also include
    five to ten color slides or photos of their work
    and $25 application fee; See Web site for
    complete program descriptions and
    guidelines.
EIN: 134147012

5484

William Matheus Sullivan Musical Foundation, Inc.

P.O. Box 189
Kent, CT 06757   (860) 927-3572
Contact: Maggie Stearns, Exec. Dir.
FAX: (860) 927-1680;
E-mail: info@sullivanfoundation.org; Additional
e-mail: applications@sullivanfoundation.org;
URL: http://www.sullivanfoundation.org

Foundation type: Independent foundation
Limitations: Awards to gifted, operatically-trained
singers who have finished their basic studies.
Applicants must have had at least one professional
appearance with full orchestra and be engaged to
perform at least once after their audition.
Publications: Application guidelines; Informational
brochure.
Financial data: Year ended 12/31/2002.
Assets, $4,243,188 (M); Expenditures,
$231,699; Total giving, $134,350; Grants to
individuals, 57 grants totaling $129,350 (high:
$3,400, low: $400).
Fields of interest: Music; Opera.
Type of support: Awards/prizes.
Application information: Application form required.
  Initial approach: Letter or e-mail detailing musical
    experience and financial need.
  Deadline(s): May 15
  Applicants should submit the following:
    1) Financial information
    2) Resume
  Additional information: Application should also
    include requests for New York City auditions,
    and copy of contract for at least one
    engagement with full orchestra after Dec.;
    Auditions required.
Program description:
  Singing Grants: Grants of $7,500 are awarded to
  gifted young professional singers to advance any
  career-related purpose. In addition, for the next five
  years they may apply to the foundation for Role
  Preparation Grants to help defray expenses
  incurred in musical, dramatic, vocal and language
  coaching for specific professional engagements.
  Candidates should be able to supply the names of
  important conductors with whom they have sung or
  famous artists who have recognized their work.
  After initial screenings, international auditions are
  held in mid-Nov. or Dec. in New York City.
EIN: 136069096

5485
Summerfair, Inc.
2515 Essex Pl., Studio 243
Cincinnati, OH 45206 (513) 531-0050
Contact: Kevin Reynolds
FAX: (513) 531-0377;
E-mail: iinfo@summerfair.org; URL: http://
www.summerfair.org/

Foundation type: Public charity
Limitations: Grants to artists in the Cincinnati, OH, area.
Financial data: Year ended 09/30/2004.
Assets, $267,459 (M); Expenditures, $131,107;
Total giving, $50,500; Grants to individuals, totaling $32,950.
Fields of interest: Arts, artist's services.
Type of support: Grants to individuals.
Application information: Deadline third Fri. of Aug.; Completion of formal application required, including slides of artwork and SASE.
Program description:
Aid to Individual Artist (AIA): Awards four grants of $3,000 each to artists living within a 40-mile radius of Cincinnati. The artists may use the grant for any purpose as long as it helps advance their artistic vision. Past grants have been used to purchase supplies, rent studio space, or fund exhibits. Practicing artists and/or fine craftsmen, and art school students are eligible.
EIN: 237229462

5486
Sundance Institute
P.O. Box 3630
Salt Lake City, UT 84110-3630
(801) 328-3456
Contact: Kenneth Brecher, Exec. Dir.
FAX: (801) 575-5175;
E-mail: institute@sundance.org; Additional address: 8530 Wilshire Blvd., Beverly Hills, CA 90211; tel.: (310) 360-1981; fax: (310) 360-1969; e-mail: la@sundance.org; URL: http://
www.sundance.org

Foundation type: Public charity
Limitations: Awards and fellowships to film directors, artists, and writers that involve feature film script projects.
Financial data: Year ended 08/31/2004.
Assets, $26,585,091 (M); Expenditures, $13,814,381; Total giving, $1,475,688; Grants to individuals, totaling $1,469,688.
Fields of interest: Film/video; Literature; Arts; Science; Europe; Latin America; Japan.
Type of support: Fellowships; Awards/prizes; Residencies; Stipends.
Application information: Applications accepted. Application form required. Application form available on the grantmaker's Web site.
Initial approach: E-mail.
Deadline(s): June 27
Additional information: Application should include script, VHS videotape of director's previous work (preferably NTSC, with English subtitles if possible), recommendation forms, bios, and a logline and synopsis. See Web site for additional information.
Program descriptions:
NHK International Filmmakers Award: Includes a $10,000 prize, an invitation to attend the Sundance Film Festival in Park City, UT, and a purchase guarantee to acquire Japanese TV broadcast rights upon the film's completion. Submissions must be accompanied by a professional recommendation, and candidates must be emerging directors. Deadline June 30.

Arts Writing Fellowship: Fellowships to CA-based writers with a strong background in arts writing and who are interested in deepening their commitment to their writing. This fellowship is an opportunity to work intensively on a new and challenging arts writing project with the support of creative advisors, workshops, and participation in select Sundance programs such as the film festival. During the second year of the two-year fellowship, fellows have the opportunity to apply for funds to help provide the time and space they need to pursue their writing projects.
Alfred P. Sloan Fellowship: Support for a multi-year independent film project that explores science or technology themes or depicts scientists in engaging and innovative ways. Applicants must pay for a $30 non-refundable processing fee. Deadline May 1.
Annenburg Film Fellows Program: Personal stipends residencies and creative support to selected participants in the Feature Film Program. Fellowships are for two years.
Special Events Design Project: This program employs an artist to design the Sundance Film Festival's Official Parties program of the Sundance Institute. Each event will incorporate design, structure, lighting, and visual elements, with the intent of creating and enhancing the atmosphere of each individual Sundance Film Festival evening party. A total of $5,000 per event is available for all related expenses, including artist and design fees, fabrications, insurance, shipping, installation, documentation, etc. Sundance will provide artist transportation and lodging in Park City during the installation, and artists will receive recognition in the Sundance Film Festival Film Guide and other promotional materials.
EIN: 870361394

5487
Tanne Foundation
c/o Grants Mgmt. Assocs.
77 Summer St.
Boston, MA 02110 (617) 426-7172
Contact: Michelle Jenney
FAX: (617) 426-5441;
E-mail: mjenney@grantsmanagement.com;
URL: http://www.tannefoundation.org

Foundation type: Independent foundation
Limitations: Fellowships to artists who have demonstrated exceptional talent and creativity, for recognition of prior achievement, and to enrich their artistic lives.
Financial data: Year ended 06/30/2005.
Assets, $1,126,696 (M); Expenditures, $51,317;
Total giving, $28,000; Grants to individuals, 5 grants totaling $28,000.
Fields of interest: Arts.
Type of support: Fellowships.
Application information: Applications not accepted.
EIN: 020500550

5488
Terra Foundation for the Arts
(formerly Terra Museum of American Art)
664 N. Michigan Ave., 10th Fl.
Chicago, IL 60611 (312) 664-3939
Contact: Amy Zinck, V.P.
FAX: (312) 664-2052;
E-mail: grants@terraamericanart.org; Additional E-mail: contact@terraamericanart.org; URL: http://
www.terramuseum.org

Foundation type: Operating foundation

Limitations: Residencies by nomination only, to artists and scholars to study American art in Giverny, France.
Financial data: Year ended 06/30/2004.
Assets, $429,232,056 (M); Expenditures, $13,040,259; Total giving, $144,300; Grants to individuals, 12 grants totaling $53,800 (high: $4,700, low: $4,500).
Fields of interest: Visual arts; Painting; Art history.
Type of support: Awards/grants by nomination only; Residencies.
Application information: Applications accepted. Application form required. Application form available on the grantmaker's Web site.
Initial approach: E-mail.
Deadline(s): Jan. 23
Applicants should submit the following:
1) Work samples
2) Essay
3) Curriculum vitae
4) Letter(s) of recommendation
5) Proposal
Additional information: Application must also include artist statement.
Program description:
Terra Summer Residency in Giverny: The Terra Summer Residency in Giverny, France, provides artists and scholars with an opportunity for independent study of American art within a framework of interdisciplinary exchange and dialogue, and in a site rich in historical and cultural significance. The program's main aim is to foster an intercultural dialogue on American art. The eight-week residency, held in the Muse d'Art Amricain Giverny, seeks to widen the creative and research horizons of resident fellows, invites them to reflect on different methodologies and interpretive models and gives them the opportunity to create an intellectual network for lifelong exchange. Fellows receive a stipend of $4,500 and artists an additional $200 for purchase of materials. Studio space, meals and housing are included. Applicants must be nominated by a senior professor at an academic institution and must fall within one of the following categories:
· American and European doctoral candidates researching a subject that contains a significant American art component, or that examines artistic exchange between America and Europe. Candidates should be at an advanced stage of their doctoral research and writing
· American and European artists having completed a masters program (or its equivalent) in mixed media and/or painting
EIN: 362999442

5489
Theatre Bay Area
870 Market St., Ste. 375
San Francisco, CA 94102 (415) 430-1140
Contact: Brad Erickson, Exec. Dir.
FAX: (415) 430-1145;
E-mail: tba@theatrebayarea.org; URL: http://
www.theatrebayarea.org

Foundation type: Public charity
Limitations: Fellowships and grants to theatre and dance artists residing in the San Francisco Bay Area, CA. Financial assistance also to aforementioned artists with terminal or life-threatening illnesses who are in need of supplemental assistance to improve the quality of their lives as they deal with medical conditions.
Financial data: Year ended 06/30/2004.
Assets, $414,710 (M); Expenditures, $1,091,972; Total giving, $72,000; Grants to

individuals, 17 grants totaling $31,500 (high: $2,500, low: $1,500).

Fields of interest: Dance; Theater.

Type of support: Program development; Seed money; Fellowships; Grants for special needs.

Application information: Applications accepted. Application form required. Application form available on the grantmaker's Web site.

Initial approach: Letter or e-mail.

Deadline(s): Feb. 17 for Eric Landisman Fellowship, Aug. 19 and Sept. 30 for the CA $H Program

Additional information: See Web site for additional application information.

Program descriptions:

CA$H Program: This program was designed by artists for artists to support professionally oriented theatre and dance artists and small companies with budgets under $100,000. Its purpose is to spark a creative surge throughout Northern California's theatre and dance community by providing grants to artists ($1,500). Approximately $20,000 are awarded each round. Funding decisions are made by a rotating five-member panel. Artists must be at least 18 and be able to document at least one professionally oriented production that was presented publicly.

Eric Landisman Fellowship: This program supports the development of emerging Bay Area designers and technicians. Two fellowships of $2,000-$5,000 per year will be awarded. To be eligible, applicants must be training in an internship or mentorship or must have a commitment with a producer for an upcoming project or series of projects. The fellowship is to be awarded above and beyond the already agreed-on arrangement with the producer. The monies will go directly to the designer or technician and are not to go toward supplies or production expenses. E-mail dale@theatrebayarea.org for additional information.

Lemonade Fund: This program is eligible to theatre workers with terminal or life-threatening illnesses who are in need of supplemental financial assistance to improve the quality of their lives as they deal with medical conditions. Applicants must be a resident of the San Francisco Bay Area who has worked professionally or vocationally in local theatre, who has been an active participant in the theatre community; i.e., those whose life's work is the theatre, regardless of the income derived from work in the theatre (with two years' experience in the last five years), and has received a diagnosis of a terminal or life-threatening medical illness or condition. Requests for up to $1,000 may be submitted every six months. Repeated funding, however, is not guaranteed. If approved, the amount received may fluctuate according to how much is available in the Fund. The grant may be used for any need, excluding hospital expenses, that arises due to illness or intensive medical treatment. Eligible expenses may include activities or purchases that contribute to relieving stress or improving quality of life, e.g. alternative therapies, personal and home support, transportation costs, etc.

New Works Fund: Theatre Bay Area's New Works Fund seeks to provide local playwrights with new ways to establish relationships with local theatres and to encourage Bay Area theatre companies to foster and produce the work of local playwrights. The New Works Fund annually awards two grants of $10,000 each to a creative team composed of a Bay Area playwright and theatre company with $5,000 going to the playwrights and $5,000 to the theatre company. In fulfillment of the grant, the writer and company will develop and fully produce the awarded new work. Proposals are to be prepared jointly by a company and a playwright. Eligible companies must be members of Theatre Bay Area and have an annual operating budget between $50,000 and $750,000. Playwrights must be full time residents of the greater San Francisco Bay Area. For questions regarding the New Works Fund, contact Theatre Bay Area at (415) 430-1140 or members@theatrebayarea.org.

EIN: 942476071

5490
Theatre Communications Group

520 Eighth Ave., 24th Fl.
New York, NY   10018-4156   (212) 609-5900
Contact: Ben Cameron, Exec. Dir.
FAX: (212) 609-5901; E-mail: grants@tcg.org;
URL: http://www.tcg.org

Foundation type: Public charity

Limitations: Awards to theater directors and designers seeking a career in American nonprofit theater.

Publications: Annual report.

Financial data: Year ended 06/30/2004. Assets, $11,637,951 (M); Expenditures, $8,594,334; Total giving, $2,456,275.

Fields of interest: Theater; Theater (playwriting).

Type of support: Program development; Awards/prizes; Residencies; Travel grants.

Application information: Application form required.

Deadline(s): Varies

Additional information: See Web site for complete application and program information.

Program descriptions:

NEA/TCG Theatre Residency Program for Playwrights: This program gives 11 playwrights the opportunity to create a new work in residence at a host theatre. The playwrights become an integral part of the theatre's artistic life and community activities. Playwright receives $25,000 and host theatre a $4,500 Vivendi Universal Residency Award. To be eligible, a playwright's residency must be a minimum of six months in length (not necessarily consecutive); playwright must be a U.S. citizen; have had a full-length play either published and/or professionally produced in the U.S. at least once in the last five years. Deadline June 15 for Intent to Apply Card.

Alan Schneider Director Award: Awards by nomination only to assist mid-career freelance directors who have exhibited exceptional talent and established local or regional reputations. The award, which is presented biennially at the TCG National Conference, provides national visibility to the recipient as well as a grant to support activities specifically tied to the development of the craft of directing. Nominations for the award are made by artistic and administrative leaders of TCG theatres. The award is supported by proceeds from the Alan Schneider Memorial Fund. Nominees may not be employed as Artistic Director at a theatre and must be freelance mid-career artists with a commitment to work in the not-for-profit professional theatre. In addition, the panelists will consider each applicant's talent, professional experience and potential for future excellence. Deadline Feb. 28.

NEA/TCG Career Development Programs for Directors and Designers: Each year, six early directors and designers (costumes, scenic, lighting and sound) are chosen to participate in the National Endowment for the Arts/TCG Career Development Program for Directors and Designers. Recipients are given the opportunity to spend six months over a two-year period developing their skills through travel, research, observing and assisting. Program activity may also include directing or designing under the guidance of one or more designated mentors both nationally and internationally. Each recipient's program is hand-tailored and includes a $17,500 stipend distributed over the six-month period spent on the program. Recipients must: be a citizen or permanent resident of the U.S. at time of application; be prepared and able to relocate during the program period; have no professional or personal commitments that would prevent devoting six full months to program-related activities; and have directed at least three fully-staged professional productions or designed professionally for a minimum of two and no more than five years. Applicants are generally ineligible if they have not directed or designed professionally for at least one year after completing their academic training. Applicants must not: be enrolled in, or on leave from, university or conservatory programs at the commencements of the program period; maintain a salaried staff position during the program period; or be a previous recipient of NEA/TCG Director or Designer Fellowship or NEA/TCG Career Development Program for Directors or Designers. Deadline Jan. 5 for Career Development for Directors and Jan. 15 for Career Development for Designers.

Observership Program: Awards travel stipends of up to $2,000 for individuals to travel across the country and internationally. The program provides opportunities for key staff at TCG's Constituent Member Theatres to observe the administration and artistic work of other theatres and meet with colleagues. Eligibility requirements are as follows: key artistic and administrative personnel who hold salaried positions at TCG Constituent Theatres may apply; applicant theatres must be current on dues payments; no theatre will be awarded more than one Observership grant in a two-year period.

Travel Grant: Awards eight $2,500 travel stipends to theatre professionals (artists, administrators or educators) to support cultural exchange and artistic partnerships between professionals in the U.S. and their counterparts in Russia and Eastern and Central Europe. Funding may cover transportation, and out of town living expenses such as research materials, communication costs, theatre tickets and/or interpreter's services. Deadline Oct. 29.

EIN: 136160130

5491
The Thomas Charitable Foundation

c/o John C. Pretto & Karen Kriendler Nelson
P.O. Box 93
Berkeley Heights, NJ   07922

Foundation type: Independent foundation

Limitations: Awards of $15,000 to American-born or naturalized American opera singers of exceptional and undeniable promise for the furthering of their careers.

Financial data: Year ended 12/31/2002. Assets, $1,349,524 (M); Expenditures, $276,362; Total giving, $212,415; Grants to individuals, 3 grants totaling $45,000 (high: $15,000, low: $15,000).

Fields of interest: Opera.

Type of support: Awards/prizes.

Application information: Contact foundation for current application deadline; Application by letter of no more than two pages.

EIN: 066444610

5492
The Richard Tucker Music Foundation
1790 Broadway, Ste. 715
New York, NY   10019-1412   (212) 757-2218
Contact: Peter H. Carwell, Exec. Dir.
FAX: (212) 757-2347; E-mail: rtucker@rtucker.org;
URL: http://www.richardtucker.org

Foundation type: Public charity
Limitations: Awards and grants by nomination only
to American-born opera singers.
Financial data: Year ended 12/31/2003.
Assets, $226,712 (M); Expenditures, $646,159;
Total giving, $67,500; Grants to individuals, 7
grants totaling $67,500 (high: $30,000, low:
$5,000).
Fields of interest: Opera.
Type of support: Awards/grants by nomination only;
Awards/prizes.
Application information: Nominations of all
potential candidates are solicited from a national
panel of professionals in the field of opera;
Auditions required for nominees.
Program descriptions:
Richard Tucker Award: A cash prize of $30,000
is awarded to an American singer posed for the
start of a major national and international career.
The award recognizes and honors both the
accomplishments as well as the potential for such
an artist. In addition to the cash grant, the winner
has the opportunity to appear on the annual RTMF
Opera Gala, in concert with many of the
profession's major stars. The Gala is broadcast live
on WQXR in New York City, and is taped for telecast
nationally on the PBS network, providing substantial
exposure for the year's Richard Tucker award
winner.
Richard Tucker Career Grants: Four winners are
selected each year for a cash prize of $7,500 each.
Recipients are singers who have already amassed
substantial experience at well-known opera
companies, usually performing major roles. The
ideal candidates are those singers with potential for
a first-rate career, as the grant has sometimes been
followed by the renown Richard Tucker Award in
later years.
Sara Tucker Study Grants: Awarded annually with
a cash prize of $5,000. Recipients must be at the
start of their professional career, having just
completed a conservatory or graduate school
program, and the singer may still be at the
apprentice level in a company. Ideal candidates
have had performing opportunities, but in smaller
companies and usually not in major roles.
EIN: 237431029

5493
Union League Civic & Arts Foundation
(also known as Union League Club)
65 W. Jackson Blvd.
Chicago, IL   60604-3598   (312) 427-7800
Contact: Anne Shea, Exec. Dir.
FAX: (312) 427-9177;
E-mail: civicandarts@aol.com; URL: http://
www.civicandarts.org/

Foundation type: Public charity
Limitations: Awards to poets, writers, and
composers in the metropolitan Chicago, IL, area.
Financial data: Year ended 12/31/2004.
Assets, $1,211,483 (M); Expenditures,
$465,525; Total giving, $164,737; Grants to
individuals, 83 grants totaling $91,111 (high:
$12,000, low: $50).
Fields of interest: Music composition; Literature.
Type of support: Awards/prizes.

Application information: Contact foundation for
current application deadline/guidelines.
Program descriptions:
Piano Competition: A $2,000 award is given to an
aspiring young composer.
Young Writer's Short Story Competition: This
contest is open to any writer aged 18 to 22 living in
the metropolitan Chicago, IL, area. Each year, 10
winners each receive a $3,500 award and the
opportunity to have their work published in a
foundation-sponsored book.
Modern Poetry Prize Competition: A $2,000 prize
is awarded to the writer of the winning poem in this
annual event.
EIN: 362446421

5494
University Film & Video Association
c/o Peter J. Bukalski
P.O. Box 1777
Edwardsville, IL   62026   (618) 650-2249
Contact: Robert Johnson, Jr.
E-mail: ufva@smpte.org; Additional address:
Framingham State College, 100 State St.,
Framingham, MA 01701, tel.: (508) 626-4684;
URL: http://www.ufva.org

Foundation type: Public charity
Limitations: Project grants and scholarships to film,
video, multimedia, and cinematography students.
Financial data: Year ended 12/31/2003.
Assets, $41,479 (M); Expenditures, $85,936;
Total giving, $5,000; Grants to individuals, 4 grants
totaling $5,000 (high: $2,000, low: $500).
Fields of interest: Arts education; Media/
communications; Film/video.
Type of support: Program development; Research;
Awards/prizes; Graduate support; Undergraduate
support.
Application information: Application form required.
Deadline(s): Jan. 1 for Grants, June 15 for
Eastman Scholars Program
Additional information: Completion of formal
application required, including supporting
information; See Web site for complete
guidelines.
Program descriptions:
*Carole Fielding Student Production and Research
Grants:* Competitive awards presented annually to
students whose research and production projects
meet rigorous standards of academic scholarship.
Up to $4,000 is available for film, video, and
multimedia production, and up to $1,000 available
for research projects in historical, critical,
theoretical, and experimental studies of film and
video. An applicant must be enrolled as an
undergraduate or graduate student and must be
sponsored by a faculty person who is a member of
UFVA. Grant winners are required to attend and
present the completed work at a UFVA conference.
Eastman Scholars Program: Competitive awards
made to students in cinematography,
demonstrating overall academic excellence.
Colleges and universities may nominate up to two
students annually. Scholarships will not exceed
$5,000 and are paid directly to the student's
university.
EIN: 546055999

5495
UrbanGlass
(also known as NYContemporary Glass Center, Inc.)
647 Fulton St.
Brooklyn, NY   11217-1112   (718) 625-3685
Contact: Dawn Bennett, Exec. Dir.
FAX: (718) 625-3889; E-mail: info@urbanglass.org;
URL: http://www.urbanglass.org

Foundation type: Public charity
Limitations: Fellowships to artists specializing in
glass.
Financial data: Year ended 06/30/2004.
Assets, $1,152,752 (M); Expenditures,
$1,520,643.
Fields of interest: Ceramic arts.
Type of support: Fellowships; Foreign applicants.
Application information: Applications accepted.
Application form required.
Initial approach: E-mail.
Copies of proposal: 1
Deadline(s): Dec. 3
Applicants should submit the following:
1) SASE
2) Resume
3) Proposal
Additional information: Application should also
include two letters of recommendation, slides
of recent work, and biography.
Program description:
Glass Fellowships: Three fellowships to
international artists who wants to work in glass.
Two fellowships are offered to emerging artists and
one fellowship to an established artist. Fellowships
are for an eight week period and include access to
all areas of the studio on a scheduled basis,
technical support and materials as stipulated in the
fellowship agreement. The fellowship does not
include room and board. In addition, each visiting
artist may receive honorarium up to a maximum of
$2,500 for his/her discretionary use.
EIN: 133098471

5496
A. E. Ventures Foundation, Inc.
245 8th Ave., Ste. 194
New York, NY   10011

Foundation type: Independent foundation
Limitations: Grants by nomination only to mature
artists, primarily in NY.
Financial data: Year ended 12/31/2004.
Assets, $406,367 (M); Expenditures, $66,196;
Total giving, $50,500; Grants to individuals,
totaling $50,500.
Fields of interest: Arts.
Type of support: Awards/grants by nomination only.
Application information: Applications not
accepted.
Additional information: Nominations from
members of Board of Directors only.
EIN: 133999711

5497
Vermont Community Foundation
3 Court St.
P.O. Box 30
Middlebury, VT   05753   (802) 388-3355
Contact: Julie Cadwallader-Staub, V.P., Community
Grantmaking; For artist grants: Mary Conlon
FAX: (802) 388-3398; E-mail: info@vermontcf.org;
Additional E-mails: jcstaub@vermontcf.org and
mconlon@vermontcf.org; URL: http://
www.vermontcf.org

Foundation type: Community foundation

Limitations: Grants to support the development, completion and/or presentation of new work by VT artists.
Publications: Application guidelines; Annual report; Financial statement; Grants list; Informational brochure; Informational brochure (including application guidelines); Multi-year report; Newsletter; Occasional report; Program policy statement.
Financial data: Year ended 12/31/2004. Assets, $110,314,471 (M); Expenditures, $10,766,535; Total giving, $8,276,588.
Fields of interest: Arts.
Type of support: Grants to individuals.
Application information: Applications accepted. Application form required. Application form available on the grantmaker's Web site.
  Initial approach: Telephone.
  Copies of proposal: 6
  Deadline(s): May 1
  Applicants should submit the following:
    1) Proposal
    2) Work samples
    3) Financial information
    4) Resume
    5) SASE
  Additional information: Application by proposal; Application must also include project description and timeline, and supporting materials.
Program description:
  Artist Grants: All disciplines and media are eligible. Priority for new works funding will be given to projects which involve artists experimenting and/or proposing to move their work in new directions. Grant amounts range from $300 to $4,000.
EIN: 222712160

5498
Vermont Council on the Arts, Inc.
136 State St., Drawer 33
Montpelier, VT 05633-6001 (802) 828-3291
Contact: Alexander L. Aldrich, Exec. Dir.
FAX: (802) 828-3363;
E-mail: info@vermontartscouncil.org; URL: http://www.vermontartscouncil.org

Foundation type: Public charity
Limitations: Grants to artists in VT with demonstrated artistic merit.
Publications: Application guidelines; Annual report; Informational brochure.
Financial data: Year ended 06/30/2005. Assets, $910,460 (M); Expenditures, $1,521,743; Total giving, $590,137; Grants to individuals, 50 grants totaling $99,571 (high: $21,000, low: $185).
Fields of interest: Arts.
Type of support: Program development.
Application information: Applications accepted. Application form required. Application form available on the grantmaker's Web site.
  Initial approach: Telephone or e-mail.
  Deadline(s): Vary.
  Additional information: See Web site for further application information.
Program descriptions:
  Art in State Buildings Grants: Awards to artists commissioned to create work for state buildings through a state program administered by the council.
  Opportunity Grants: Awards from $250 to $7,000 to artists for projects and programs.
EIN: 030218115

5499
Vermont Studio Center, Inc.
P.O. Box 613
Johnson, VT 05656 (802) 635-2727
Contact: Jonathan T. Gregg, Pres.
FAX: (802) 635-2730;
E-mail: development@vermontstudiocenter.org;
URL: http://www.vermontstudiocenter.org

Foundation type: Public charity
Limitations: Fellowships to painters, printmakers, photographers, sculptors, and writers.
Publications: Application guidelines; Grants list; Informational brochure (including application guidelines).
Financial data: Year ended 12/31/2004. Assets, $4,638,233 (M); Expenditures, $3,187,157; Total giving, $34,500; Grant to an individual, 1 grant totaling $34,500.
Fields of interest: Photography; Sculpture; Painting; Literature.
Type of support: Fellowships.
Application information: Application form required.
  Initial approach: Letter or e-mail.
  Deadline(s): Feb. 15, June 15, and Oct. 1
  Applicants should submit the following:
    1) Work samples
    2) Resume
  Additional information: Application should also include $25 application fee, portfolio, first page of income tax return and references.
Program description:
  VSC Full Fellowships: 200 full fellowships based on merit are available for four weeks at no fee. Fellowship includes studio space and housing, and meals. Some fellowships include travel expenses.
EIN: 222478074

5500
Virginia Center for the Creative Arts
154 San Angelo Dr.
Amherst, VA 24521 (434) 946-7236
Contact: Charlene Monk, Exec. Dir.
FAX: (434) 946-7239; E-mail: vcca@vcca.com;
URL: http://www.vcca.com

Foundation type: Public charity
Limitations: Residency to a non-fiction writer.
Financial data: Year ended 06/30/2004. Assets, $2,504,657 (M); Expenditures, $815,138. No monetary support given for residencies.
Fields of interest: Literature.
Type of support: Residencies.
Application information: Applications accepted. Application form required.
  Initial approach: Telephone or e-mail.
  Deadline(s): May 15
  Applicants should submit the following:
    1) Work samples
    2) Letter(s) of recommendation
Program description:
  Goldfarb Family Fellowship for Nonfiction Writers: Residency includes housing, studio space and meals. The program lasts for two weeks.
EIN: 237136000

5501
Visual Aid
(formerly Visual Aid Artists for AIDS Relief)
116 New Montgomery, Ste. 640
San Francisco, CA 94105 (415) 777-8242
Contact: Julie Blankenship, Exec. Dir.
FAX: (415) 777-8240; E-mail: visaid@visualaid.org;
URL: http://www.visualaid.org

Foundation type: Public charity
Limitations: Support to seriously ill artists in Alameda, Contra Costa, Marin, Napa, San Francisco, San Mateo, Santa Clara, Solano and Sonoma counties, CA, in the form of vouchers redeemable at participating art supply stores in the San Francisco Bay area. Visual Aid also sponsors public exhibitions of art works by grant recipients.
Publications: Application guidelines; Informational brochure; Newsletter.
Financial data: Year ended 12/31/2003. Assets, $127,671 (M); Expenditures, $141,149; Total giving, $141,149; Grants to individuals, totaling $141,149.
Fields of interest: Arts, artist's services.
Type of support: Grants for special needs.
Application information: Application form required.
  Initial approach: Contact foundation before applying.
  Deadline(s): Contact foundation for current application deadline.
  Additional information: Application must also include slides or photographs of art work, three professional references, artistic statement, and proof of diagnosis of a life-threatening illness.
EIN: 943089742

5502
Visual Studies Workshop, Inc.
31 Prince St.
Rochester, NY 14607 (585) 442-8676
Contact: Robert Wilsey, Pres.
E-mail: info@vsw.org; URL: http://www.vsw.org

Foundation type: Public charity
Limitations: Residencies to artists specializing in photography, film, artists' books, digital video and multimedia.
Financial data: Year ended 06/30/2004. Assets, $1,329,649 (M); Expenditures, $417,998.
Fields of interest: Media/communications; Film/video; Photography; Literature.
Type of support: Residencies.
Application information: Applications accepted. Application form required.
  Initial approach: Telephone or e-mail.
  Copies of proposal: 1
  Deadline(s): Sept. 30
  Additional information: Application should include proposal, work samples and SASE; See Web site for further application information.
Program description:
  Residency Program: Residencies are project-based and last for one month. The program includes housing, access to facilities, and a $1,200 honorarium.
EIN: 160991020

5503
Ludwig Vogelstein Foundation, Inc.
P.O. Box 510
Shelter Island, NY 11964-0510
Contact: Diana Braunschweig, Exec. Dir.
E-mail: lvf@earthlink.net

Foundation type: Independent foundation
Limitations: Grants to financially needy individuals in the arts and humanities for specific projects. No scholarships, student aid, or faculty assistance granted.
Publications: Application guidelines.
Financial data: Year ended 12/31/2004. Assets, $643,859 (M); Expenditures, $145,800;

Total giving, $87,684; Grants to individuals, totaling $86,184.
Fields of interest: Sculpture; Theater (playwriting); Humanities; Literature.
Type of support: Program development.
Application information:
Initial approach: Letter requesting information and including SASE.
Applicants should submit the following:
1) Curriculum vitae
2) Work samples
3) SASE
4) Budget Information
Additional information: Initial letter requesting information should be sent between Jan. 1 and Mar. 15; Application by typewritten letter proposal describing project and financial need, also including copy of latest IRS return.
Program description:
Artist Program Development: Recipients are selected on the basis of merit and financial need, especially those with no other source of funding. Most grants range from $1,000 to $3,500. The categories are: prose, poetry, biography, playwriting, artists and sculptors in all media, and unaffiliated scholars. The foundation does not fund photographers.
EIN: 136185761

5504
VSA arts of Colorado, Inc.
909 Santa Fe Dr.
Denver, CO   80204   (303) 777-0797
Contact: Damon McLeese, Exec. Dir.
FAX: (303) 777-1188; E-mail: co@vsarts.org; TTY: (303) 777-0798; URL: http://co.vsarts.org/

Foundation type: Public charity
Limitations: Scholarships to disabled individuals in CO who wish to study art.
Publications: Newsletter.
Financial data: Year ended 09/30/2004. Assets, $59,937 (M); Expenditures, $178,529; Total giving, $14,619; Grants to individuals, totaling $14,619.
Fields of interest: Arts education; Arts; Disabilities, people with.
Type of support: Scholarships—to individuals.
Application information: See Web site for deadlines, guidelines and more information.
EIN: 742131682

5505
Washington Performing Arts Society
(also known as WPAS)
2000 L St., N.W., Ste. 510
Washington, DC   20036-4907   (202) 833-9800
Contact: Neale Perl, Pres.
FAX: (202) 331-7678; E-mail: info@wpas.org; URL: http://www.wpas.org

Foundation type: Public charity
Limitations: Scholarships to sixth through twelfth grade string students in the DC area for purchases of musical instruments, private music lessons or to attend summer music camp.
Publications: Application guidelines; Informational brochure.
Financial data: Year ended 08/31/2004. Assets, $8,477,532 (M); Expenditures, $6,631,876; Total giving, $17,703; Grants to individuals, 37 grants totaling $17,703 (high: $5,000, low: $50). Subtotal for awards/prizes: 37 grants totaling $17,703 (high: $5,000, low: $25).
Fields of interest: Music; Performing arts, education.

Type of support: Awards/prizes; Undergraduate support.
Application information: Application form required. Application form available on the grantmaker's Web site.
Initial approach: Telephone.
Copies of proposal: 1
Additional information: Contact foundation for current application deadline; Interviews required.
Program description:
Joseph & Goldie Feder Memorial String Competition: Awards cash prizes to students grades 6 through 12 in the DC area to purchase musical instruments or private lessons. Also awards scholarships for summer study programs.
EIN: 526062439

5506
Watershed Center for Ceramic Arts
19 Brick Hill Rd.
Newcastle, ME   04553   (207) 882-6075
Contact: Lynn Thompson, Exec. Dir.
FAX: (207) 882-6045;
E-mail: info@watershedceramics.org; URL: http://www.watershedcenterceramicarts.org

Foundation type: Public charity
Limitations: Residencies to ceramic artists.
Financial data: Year ended 12/31/2003. Assets, $1,033,930 (M); Expenditures, $285,497. No monetary support given for residencies.
Fields of interest: Ceramic arts.
Type of support: Residencies.
Application information: Applications accepted. Application form required.
Initial approach: E-mail.
Deadline(s): Apr. 1
Additional information: Application should include $25 application fee, slides of recent work, resume, SASE, cover letter and letters of recommendation.
Program description:
Residency Program: Artists may apply for fully and partially funded residency awards. Fully funded residents are given room, meals, and studio space. Four artists are chosen for the nine-month Winter Residency (Sept. through May). 20 artists are chosen for the Summer Residency.
EIN: 010427824

5507
Kurt Weill Foundation for Music, Inc.
7 E. 20th St.
New York, NY   10003   (212) 505-5240
Contact: Carolyn Weber, Dir.
FAX: (212) 353-9663; E-mail: cweber@kwf.org or kwfinfo@kwf.org; URL: http://www.kwf.org

Foundation type: Operating foundation
Limitations: Grants to individuals for projects which promote greater understanding of the musical works of Kurt Weill, and awards to singing competition winners.
Publications: Application guidelines; Informational brochure; Newsletter.
Financial data: Year ended 12/31/2004. Assets, $16,700,475 (M); Expenditures, $1,014,339; Total giving, $117,550; Grants to individuals, 17 grants totaling $30,550 (high: $6,000, low: $500).
Fields of interest: Music.

Type of support: Program development; Publication; Fellowships; Research; Awards/prizes; Travel grants.
Application information: Application form required.
Initial approach: Letter.
Deadline(s): Nov. 1
Additional information: See foundation's Web site for complete application guidelines and forms.
Program descriptions:
Research and Travel Grants: Applicants must be pursuing a research topic directly related to Kurt Weill and/or Lotte Lenya and must submit a detailed outline of the proposed project. Travel grants should be for travel to locations of primary source material.
Publication Assistance: Funding may be requested to assist in expenses related to preparing manuscripts relating to Kurt Weill for publication in a recognized scholarly medium. These expenses may include editing, indexing, design, reproduction fees, etc.
Dissertation Fellowships: Support is given to Ph.D. candidates conducting research on Kurt Weill. The application must include a copy of the dissertation proposal and two letters of recommendation, one of which is from the faculty advisor.
Professional Performance and Production Grants: Proposals are accepted for productions and performances of Kurt Weill's music in order to improve the musical qualities of the performance. Special guidelines apply to requests of over $5,000. If a significant portion of the performers are students or volunteers, applications must be submitted under the College/University category which has a limit of $5,000.
Recording Projects: Proposals requesting funds for artist and musician fees, rehearsal expenses, and mastertape production expenses are eligible. Priority is given to works by Weill that have not been recorded in their original form. Only projects with a commitment from a record company are eligible, and all financial arrangements with the record company must be disclosed.
Broadcasts: Proposals from independent producers are available to support post-production costs for special programs that feature primarily Kurt Weill and his music. A complete summary of the project must be submitted along with evidence of commitment for broadcast.
Lotte Lenya Competition for Singers: Recognizes excellence in the performance of music for the theater, in its broadest sense, including opera, operetta, and American musical theater. Criteria for adjudication include vocal beauty, technique, interpretation, acting, idiomatic performance of a varied repertoire, and stage presence. The competition is open to U.S. and Canadian residents under the age of 32 as of Dec. 31. See the foundation's Web site for additional information.
EIN: 136139518

5508
Weir Farm Trust, Inc.
735 Nod Hill Rd.
Wilton, CT   06897   (203) 761-9945
Contact: Constance Evans, Exec. Dir.
FAX: (203) 761-9116;
E-mail: evanswft@optonline.net; URL: http://www.nps.gov/wefa/Trust/Trust.htm

Foundation type: Public charity
Limitations: Residencies to advanced visual artists of all backgrounds.
Financial data: Year ended 06/30/2004. Assets, $498,137 (M); Expenditures, $355,159.

Fields of interest: Visual arts; Arts.
Type of support: Residencies; Stipends.
Application information: Applications accepted. Application form required.
  Initial approach: Telephone or e-mail.
  Deadline(s): Jan. 15 and July 15 for Artist-in-Residence Program, Apr. 30 for Visiting Artists Program
  Applicants should submit the following:
    1) SASE
    2) Resume
    3) Letter(s) of recommendation
    4) Work samples
  Additional information: Include a $25 non-refundable application fee for Artis-in-Residence and a $15 application fee for Visiting Artists Program; See Web site for complete application information.
Program descriptions:
  Visting Artists Program: Residency includes a $500 honorarium to help cover the cost of travel/supplies. The program begins in the summer and lasts for one year. Housing and studio space are not provided. Benefits of the program include an exhibition of work completed during the program, opening reception, and the opportunity to present a public lecture.
  Artist-in-Residence: Residency includes studio and living space. Artists will be given a monthly stipend of $500 to offset the cost of food, travel, supplies or other related needs. Residencies last from two weeks to one month.
EIN: 223035427

5509
Western Stage Auxiliary Corporation
156 Homestead Ave.
Salinas, CA 93901   (831) 755-6980
Contact: John Light, Mgr. Dir.
Additional information for scholarships: Melissa Chin Parker, Prog. Dir., FAX: (831) 755-6954
FAX: (831) 755-6954; URL: http://www.westernstage.org/Casting/auditionReqs.html

Foundation type: Public charity
Limitations: Grants for the promotion of theater arts in CA.
Financial data: Year ended 06/30/2004. Assets, $109,530; Expenditures, $1,075,854; Total giving, $119,135; Grants to individuals, totaling $119,135.
Fields of interest: Theater; Literature.
Application information: Contact foundation for current application deadline/guidelines.
EIN: 770273340

5510
Wexner Center Foundation
(formerly Wexner Center for the Arts)
c/o Ohio State Univ.
1871 N. High St.
Columbus, OH 43210   (614) 292-3535
Contact: C. Robert Kidder, Pres.
FAX: (614) 292-3369; URL: http://www.wexarts.org

Foundation type: Public charity
Limitations: Prize by nomination only to a major contemporary artist. Also, residencies to artists specializing in the performing arts, media arts (film/video), and visual arts.
Financial data: Year ended 06/30/2004. Assets, $6,224,400 (M); Expenditures, $2,839,233; Total giving, $2,239,200. No monetary support given for residencies.

Fields of interest: Film/video; Visual arts; Performing arts; Arts.
Type of support: Awards/grants by nomination only; Awards/prizes; Residencies.
Application information: See Web site for current application and program information.
Program descriptions:
  Artist Residency: Residencies support the creation or completion of new works by providing financial resources and technical support. Some residencies extend over several weeks of on-site creative development and/or community interaction. Other residencies involve hosting a preperformance discussion or meeting with a class.
  The Wexner Prize: The Wexner Prize is presented annually to a major contemporary artist whose work and career must exemplify the institution's goals of embracing exploration and innovation while upholding the highest standards of artistic quality and integrity. The recipient, who may be from any artistic field, is chosen by the trustees of the Wexner Center Foundation. Recipients are nominated by the center's International Arts Advisory Council, whose members are prominent artists and arts professionals from many disciplines. There is a $50,000 prize. There is no application process for this award.
EIN: 311306419

5511
Wheaton Village, Inc.
1501 Glasstown Rd.
Millville, NJ 08332   (856) 825-6800
Contact: Susan Gogan, Pres.
Additional tel.: (800) 998-4552;
E-mail: mail@wheatonvillage.org; URL: http://www.wheatonvillage.org

Foundation type: Public charity
Limitations: Fellowships to artists specializing in glass.
Financial data: Year ended 12/31/2003. Assets, $6,674,438 (M); Expenditures, $2,612,574. No monetary support given for residencies.
Fields of interest: Arts.
Type of support: Fellowships.
Application information: Application form required.
  Deadline(s): Sept. 20.
  Applicants should submit the following:
    1) Essay
    2) Resume
    3) Letter(s) of recommendation
  Additional information: Application should include ten slides of work, and a brief biographical statement.
Program description:
  Creative Glass Center of America Fellowship Program: Fellowship includes a monthly stipend, housing, and unlimited access to studio facilities. Applicant must be over 21 years of age, with knowledge of basic hot glassworking skills. The fellow will work in view of visitors 12 hours weekly, and must provide one work made during the fellowship to Wheaton Village.
EIN: 221849118

5512
Herbert and Irene Wheeler Foundation
(formerly The Wheeler Foundation, Inc.)
P.O. Box 300507
Brooklyn, NY 11230
Contact: Susan Stedman, Pres.
FAX: (718) 258-1157

Foundation type: Independent foundation

Limitations: Fellowships and emergency grants based on artistic merit, creative achievement, and future promise to visual artists of color who are residents of the New York City tri-state area and are over the age of 21.
Financial data: Year ended 05/31/2005. Assets, $10,406 (M); Expenditures, $38,290; Total giving, $27,726; Grants to individuals, totaling $27,726.
Fields of interest: Visual arts; Arts, artist's services; Minorities.
Type of support: Fellowships; Grants for special needs.
Application information:
  Initial approach: Letter.
  Additional information: Applications accepted throughout the year; Completion of formal application required for emergency grants, including resume, cover letter outlining financial need, recommendation of artistic merit from a member of the arts community, and a summary of the emergency situation; Applicants notified one month after application is completed.
Program description:
  Special Needs Grant: Emergency grants are given to financially needy visual artists of color for urgent needs involving housing, medical costs, fire and flood damage, etc. The foundation also awards fellowships to visual artists of color based on the merit of their work, creative achievements, and future promise. Artists from the following counties are eligible: Fairfield, CT; Bergen, Essex, Hudson, Middlesex, Morris, Passaic, Somerset, NJ; Nassau, Rockland, Suffolk, and Westchester, NY; and the New York City boroughs of the Bronx, Brooklyn, Manhattan, Queens, and Staten Island.
EIN: 133673063

5513
Mrs. Giles Whiting Foundation
1133 Ave. of the Americas, 22nd Fl.
New York, NY 10036-6710   (212) 336-2138
Contact: Robin Krause, Secy.
URL: http://www.whitingfoundation.org

Foundation type: Independent foundation
Limitations: Awards by nomination only to support emerging writers. Funds are currently committed for the foreseeable future.
Publications: Multi-year report.
Financial data: Year ended 11/30/2002. Assets, $51,985,228 (M); Expenditures, $2,621,564; Total giving, $1,622,675; Grants to individuals, 28 grants totaling $490,000 (high: $25,000, low: $10,000).
Fields of interest: Literature.
Type of support: Awards/grants by nomination only; Awards/prizes; Doctoral support.
Application information: Applications not accepted.
Program description:
  Whiting Writers' Awards: Made to support emerging writers. The program places special emphasis on exceptionally promising emerging talent. To qualify, writers need not be "young," given that new talent may emerge at any age. The foundation makes awards to individuals chosen by a Selection Committee drawn from a list of recognized writers, literary scholars, and editors. Recipients of the award are selected from nominations made by writers, educators, and editors from communities across the country whose experience and vocations bring them in contact with individuals of unusual talent. The nominators and selectors are appointed by the foundation and serve anonymously. Direct applications and

informal nominations are not accepted by the foundation. Nominated candidates may be writers of fiction, poetry, or nonfiction; they may be essayists, literary scholars, playwrights, novelists, poets, or critics. Selections are based on the quality of writing accomplishment and the likelihood of outstanding future work. Each artist receives $35,000.
EIN: 136154484

5514
The Woodrow Wilson National Fellowship Foundation
P.O. Box 5281
Princeton, NJ 08543-5281 (609) 452-7007
FAX: (609) 452-0066; E-mail: jlp@woodrow.org;
URL: http://www.woodrow.org

Foundation type: Public charity
Limitations: Grants to artists for social, cultural or educational projects.
Publications: Annual report; Newsletter.
Financial data: Year ended 06/30/2005.
Assets, $20,737,668 (M); Expenditures, $15,097,337; Total giving, $10,155,178.
Fields of interest: Humanities; Arts.
Type of support: Program development.
Application information: Applications accepted.
Deadline(s): Feb. 12
Additional information: Application by proposal; Applications may be submitted by e-mail via publicscholarship@woodrow.org with appropriate attachments.
Program descriptions:
Public Scholarship Partnership Grants: Awards of up to $10,000 for partnerships of arts and humanities faculty and community-based artists, humanists, educators and other individuals who have defined and designed a collaborative project in community creativity at the local, regional or national level. Up to seven awards will be granted.
Public Scholarship Curricular Design Grants: Awards of up to $10,000 for faculty teams to investigate ways to integrate public scholarship into doctoral curricula. Funds may be used to support planning and/or a small-scale pilot. Proposals should include evidence of institutional support, a record of engagement in public scholarship, and demonstrated experience in effective curricular design. Two or three awards will be granted.
EIN: 210703075

5515
Barbara & Howard Wise Endowment for the Arts, Inc.
110 W. 13th St.
New York, NY 10011-7802

Foundation type: Independent foundation
Limitations: Grants to NY artists to support their work.
Financial data: Year ended 12/31/2004.
Assets, $141,075 (M); Expenditures, $17,452; Total giving, $15,000; Grants to individuals, totaling $5,000.
Fields of interest: Arts, artist's services; Arts.
Type of support: Grants to individuals.
Application information: Unsolicited applications not accepted.
EIN: 133593706

5516
Wolf Trap Foundation for the Performing Arts
1645 Trap Rd.
Vienna, VA 22182 (703) 255-1900
Contact: Terrence D. Jones, Pres. and C.E.O.; For residencies: Kim Pensinger Witman
E-mail: wolftrap@wolftrap.org; URL: http://www.wolftrap.org

Foundation type: Public charity
Limitations: Residencies to emerging professional singers.
Financial data: Year ended 12/31/2003.
Assets, $38,553,952 (M); Expenditures, $24,803,956; Total giving, $50,200; Grants to individuals, 4 grants totaling $12,000 (high: $4,000, low: $2,000).
Fields of interest: Opera; Music (choral).
Type of support: Residencies; Stipends.
Application information: Applications accepted. Application form required.
Initial approach: Letter or e-mail.
Applicants should submit the following:
1) Resume
Additional information: Applications must also include photocopy of passport or birth certificate, $15 application fee, 8x10 black and white photograph, and audio recording.
Program description:
Filene Young Artists: This summer residency program is intended for aspiring singers who are at an interim point between academic training and full-time professional careers and who demonstrate career momentum in that critical period following advanced academic study. Most successful candidates are currently enrolled in or have recently completed graduate or professional degrees, and/or are not more than 2-3 years past completion of academic or apprenticeship training. Filene Young Artists receive a bi-weekly stipend, including the terms of a standard AGMA soloist contract for those artists cast in the opera presented at the Filene Center. Although housing expenses are not included in the compensation package, Wolf Trap Opera assists all incoming artists in locating housing with volunteer hosts within reasonable commuting distance. Access to a car is necessary since there is no public transportation.
EIN: 237011544

5517
Woman's Exchange, Inc. of Sarasota
539 S. Orange Ave.
Sarasota, FL 34236-0219 (941) 955-7859
Contact: Helen Maniscalco, Mgr.
FAX: (941) 955-0219

Foundation type: Public charity
Limitations: Support to individuals involved in theater and the performing arts located in Sarasota and Manatee counties, FL.
Publications: Application guidelines; Informational brochure.
Financial data: Year ended 05/31/2005.
Assets, $1,086,195 (M); Expenditures, $43,682.
Fields of interest: Performing arts; Theater.
Type of support: Grants to individuals.
Application information: Application form required.
Initial approach: Letter.
Copies of proposal: 10
Deadline(s): Feb. 1
EIN: 591109482

5518
Women in Film Foundation
8857 W. Olympic Blvd., Ste. 201
Beverly Hills, CA 90211 (310) 362-2694
Contact: Holly Thro, Fdn. Coord.
FAX: (310) 657-5154; E-mail: foundation@wif.org;
URL: http://wif.org/foundation

Foundation type: Public charity
Limitations: Project grants to women filmmakers.
Publications: Newsletter.
Financial data: Year ended 12/31/2003.
Assets, $395,356 (M); Expenditures, $732,576; Total giving, $10,000; Grants to individuals, totaling $10,000.
Fields of interest: Film/video; Arts, artist's services; Women.
Type of support: Grants to individuals.
Application information: Application form required.
Initial approach: Letter.
Deadline(s): Nov. 15
Additional information: Application must include a $20 application fee.
Program description:
Film Finishing Fund: Cash awards up to $5,000 to support independent and nonprofit women filmmakers in completing documentary, dramatic, educational, animated, or experimental films or videos which promote equal opportunities for women, enhance media images of women, and influence prevailing attitudes and practices regarding and on behalf of women. In some cases, the award will consist of in-kind support for post-production services, instead of or in addition to the cash award. In-kind awards include:
· Creative Cafe Sound Completion Grant, for post-production sound editing
· Hollywood Film and Video Grant, for film post-production services
· Liberty Live Wire Grant, for post-production services
· New York Women in Film and Television Grants, for post-production completion
· Women in Film and Television-Florida Independent Filmmaker Grant
Cash awards include:
· Dockers Khakis for Women Independent Vision Grant, an award of excellence for a woman filmmaker
· Loreen Arbus Focus on Disabilities Grant, for an exceptional film or television program featuring disabled performers and/or issues of disability
· Loreen Arbus Focus on Discrimination Grant, for an exceptional film or television program depicting discrimination of any kind
· Jose L. Nazar Grant for Latino Projects and/or Latino Filmmakers
No extra application is necessary for these awards.
EIN: 237322834

5519
Women's Studio Workshop, Inc.
P.O. Box 489
Rosendale, NY 12472-0489 (845) 658-9133
Contact: Ann Kalmbach, Exec. Dir.
FAX: (845) 658-9031;
E-mail: info@wsworkshop.org; Additional address: 722 Binnewater Ln., Rosendale, NY 12472;
URL: http://www.wsworkshop.org

Foundation type: Public charity
Limitations: Grants and residencies to printmakers, papermakers, photographers, and book artists.

Publications: Application guidelines; Informational brochure; Newsletter; Occasional report.
Financial data: Year ended 06/30/2005. Assets, $322,808 (L); Expenditures, $560,300; Total giving, $76,319.
Fields of interest: Arts, artist's services.
Type of support: Program development; Publication; Fellowships; Internship funds; Residencies.
Application information: Application form required. Application form available on the grantmaker's Web site.
    Initial approach: E-mail.
    Copies of proposal: 1
    Deadline(s): Vary
    Applicants should submit the following:
        1) Work samples
        2) Resume
        3) Proposal
        4) Letter(s) of recommendation
    Additional information: Contact foundation for current application deadline/guidelines; See Web site for additional information.
Program description:
    Residency Program: The workshop administers the following programs:
    · Artists Book Residency Grants: These awards enable artists to produce a limited edition bookwork at WSW. The grant includes a stipend of $2,000 for six weeks, materials up to $500, access to all studios, and on-site housing. Deadline Nov. 15.
    · Geraldine R. Dodge Foundation Residency Grants: These residencies are offered to two NJ artists to give them the time and resources to create a new body of work or to edition a new book work. These six-week residencies include a $2,000 artist's stipend, travel money, housing, and use of WSW's studios. Only NJ residents are eligible for this program. Deadline Apr. 1.
    · Hands-On-Art Visiting Artist Project: This program supports an emerging artist in an eight-week residency to produce a limited edition artists' book and work with young people in the arts-in-education program. The award includes a $3,200 stipend, a $500 materials budget, hours, and unlimited studio access. Deadline Apr.1.
    · WSW Internships: This program provides work opportunities to intern with WSW staff artists. Interns learn about papermaking, printmaking, book arts, and arts administration. They also assist WSW's Artist-in-Residence and work with artists/ educators in WSW's Art-in-Education program. Positions are full-time for six months. Off-site housing is provided, as well as a $150 per-month stipend. All meals and materials expenses are the responsibility of the intern. Deadlines Oct. 15 and Apr. 1.
EIN: 222147463

5520
Wood Turning Center, Inc.
501 Vine St.
Philadelphia, PA 19106 (215) 923-8000
Contact: Albert LeCoff, Exec. Dir.
FAX: (215) 923-4403;
E-mail: info@woodturningcenter.org; URL: http://www.woodturningcenter.org

Foundation type: Public charity

Limitations: Residencies to artists, scholars, furniture makers, educators and photojournalists interested in lathe-turned art.
Publications: Application guidelines; Annual report; Informational brochure; Newsletter (including application guidelines).
Financial data: Year ended 12/31/2004. Assets, $583,243 (M); Expenditures, $532,621; Total giving, $100. No monetary support given for residencies.
Fields of interest: Arts.
Type of support: Residencies.
Application information: Applications accepted. Application form required.
    Copies of proposal: 1
    Deadline(s): Oct. 1
    Additional information: Application should include a $25 application fee, slides of recent work, resume, project proposal.
Program description:
    Residencies: This 8-week residency program for four lathe artists, one scholar, one furniture maker/ educator, and one photojournalist, are selected to focus on advanced technical innovations, aesthetics, and techniques and for scholars to better understand the turning field and its practitioners. Residents will receive $350 per week, round-trip transportation to the residency location, and housing. In addition to helping with fundraising efforts prior to the residency, residents are asked to participate in two educational opportunities stemming from the International Turning Exchange: demonstrating turning techniques to the community and participating in a symposium on the philosophy and practice of lathe-turning.
EIN: 222806780

5521
Worldstudio Foundation, Inc.
200 Varick St., Ste. 507
New York, NY 10014 (212) 366-1317
Contact: David Sterling, Pres.
FAX: (212) 807-0024;
E-mail: info@worldstudio.org; Additional e-mail: scholarships@worldstudio.org; URL: http://www.worldstudio.org

Foundation type: Public charity
Limitations: Scholarships and mentoring for minority and disadvantaged undergraduate and graduate students of art, architecture and design, in cooperation with the design/arts industries.
Publications: Informational brochure; Newsletter.
Financial data: Year ended 12/31/2004. Assets, $115,294 (M); Expenditures, $145,088; Total giving, $69,975; Grants to individuals, 44 grants totaling $69,975 (high: $5,000, low: $100).
Fields of interest: Arts education; Architecture; Design; Arts, artist's services; Arts; Environment; Minorities; Economically disadvantaged.
Type of support: Graduate support; Undergraduate support.
Application information: Application form required.
    Deadline(s): Feb. 14
    Additional information: See Web site for further guidelines.
Program description:
    Scholarship Program: The scholarship program for minority and economically disadvantaged students of art, architecture, or design directly addresses the foundation's aim to increase diversity in the creative profession and its vision of a more responsible, sustainable future. Scholarship recipients not only exhibit talent and

need but also demonstrate a commitment to give back to the larger community through their work.
EIN: 133776523

5522
Abraham Woursell Foundation
c/o Citibank, N.A., Tax Dept.
125 Summer St., 17th Fl.
Boston, MA 02110

Foundation type: Independent foundation
Limitations: Literary prizes and fellowships to writers.
Financial data: Year ended 12/31/2002. Assets, $1,837,878 (M); Expenditures, $162,777; Total giving, $137,611; Grants to individuals, 6 grants totaling $125,513 (high: $26,100, low: $18,649).
Fields of interest: Literature.
Type of support: Fellowships; Awards/prizes.
Application information: Contact foundation for current application deadline/guidelines.
EIN: 136140514

5523
Writers Emergency Assistance Fund
(formerly The Llewellyn Miller Fund of the American Society of Journalists and Authors Charitable Trust)
1501 Broadway, Ste. 302
New York, NY 10036 (212) 997-0947
Contact: Patricia Schiff Estess, Chair.
FAX: (212) 937-2315; URL: http://www.asja.org/weaf.php

Foundation type: Independent foundation
Limitations: Relief assistance to financially needy, established, professional freelance writers of nonfiction books and magazine articles who are 60 years of age or older, disabled, or who are caught up in an extraordinary professional crisis.
Financial data: Year ended 08/31/2004. Assets, $140,441 (M); Expenditures, $32,876; Total giving, $31,850; Grants to individuals, 15 grants totaling $31,831 (high: $3,000, low: $1,000).
Fields of interest: Journalism/publishing; Literature; Aging; Disabilities, people with.
Type of support: Grants for special needs.
Application information: Applications accepted throughout the year; Initial approach by letter outlining financial need; Completion of formal application required, including financial records, references, and evidence of published works.
Program description:
    Writers Emergency Assistance Fund: This fund of the American Society of Journalists and Authors was established to help needy writers who have demonstrated their professionalism over a sustained period of years, but who have no pension from a former employer on which to rely. It also helps younger writers of demonstrated professionalism who have become disabled and thus unable to earn a living, or who are caught up in an extraordinary professional crisis such as a lawsuit. This fund is for professional writers only.
EIN: 136625578

5524
Writers' Colony at Dairy Hollow
515 Spring St.
Eureka Springs, AR   72632   (479) 253-7444
Contact: Rebecca Garner, Pres.
FAX: (479) 253-3859;
E-mail: director@writerscolony.org; URL: http://
www.writerscolony.org

Foundation type: Public charity
Limitations: Residencies to emerging and
experienced writers and songwriters at work on
specific projects.
Financial data: Year ended 12/31/2003.
Assets, $112,632; Expenditures, $194,864. No
monetary support given for residencies.
Fields of interest: Music composition; Literature.
Type of support: Residencies.
Application information: Application form required.
  Deadline(s): None
  Additional information: Application should
    include two work samples that are not
    returnable and a $35 non-refundable
    application fee. See Web site for complete
    application information.
Program description:
  Residency Program: The residency can range
  from two weeks to three months. Housing, food and
  studio space are provided. Residents must engage
  in one day of community service for every month of
  stay.
EIN: 731547467

5525
The Helene Wurlitzer Foundation of New Mexico
P.O. Box 1891
Taos, NM   87571   (505) 758-2413
Contact: Michael A. Knight, Exec. Dir.
FAX: (505) 758-2559; E-mail: hwf@taosnet.com

Foundation type: Operating foundation
Limitations: Residencies to creative (not
interpretive) artists in all media for rent- and
utilities-free housing in Taos, NM.
Financial data: Year ended 03/31/2004.
Assets, $3,654,620 (M); Expenditures,
$185,171; Total giving, $61,660; Grants to
individuals, totaling $61,460.
Fields of interest: Arts, artist's services.
Type of support: Residencies.
Application information: Application form required.
  Initial approach: Letter.
  Deadline(s): None
  Additional information: Application must include
    sample of work and description of project.
Program description:
  Residency Program: The foundation was
  established to encourage and stimulate creative
  work in the humanities, arts, and allied fields
  through the provision of rent- and utilities-free
  housing in Taos, NM. Eleven houses are available
  from Apr. through Sept. each year. Each house is
  used by one resident generally for a period of three
  months, although longer stays are sometimes
  granted. Recipient lists are made up to four years
  in advance.
EIN: 850128634

5526
Xeric Foundation
351 Pleasant St.
PMB 214
Northampton, MA   01060-3900
(413) 585-0671
E-mail: xericgrant@aol.com; URL: http://
www.xericfoundation.com

Foundation type: Independent foundation
Limitations: Awards by nomination only to
self-publishing comic book creators in the U.S. and
Canada.
Publications: Grants list; Informational brochure
(including application guidelines).
Financial data: Year ended 09/30/2004.
Assets, $2,491,833 (M); Expenditures,
$137,783; Total giving, $108,555; Grants to
individuals, 13 grants totaling $46,215 (high:
$5,796, low: $242). Subtotal for awards/prizes: 14
grants totaling $46,215 (high: $6,500, low:
$1,129).
Fields of interest: Drawing.
Type of support: Publication; Awards/grants by
nomination only.
Application information: Application form required.
Application form available on the grantmaker's Web
site.
  Initial approach: Telephone or e-mail.
  Copies of proposal: 6
  Deadline(s): Jan. 31 and July 31
  Applicants should submit the following:
    1) Work samples
    2) Resume
    3) Proposal
    4) Financial information
EIN: 223149258

5527
The Yard, Inc.
P.O. Box 405
Chilmark, MA   02535   (508) 645-9662
FAX: (508) 645-3176;
E-mail: admin@dancetheyard.org; URL: http://
www.dancetheyard.org

Foundation type: Public charity
Limitations: Residencies to choreographers and
dancers specializing in contemporary dance.
Publications: Application guidelines.
Financial data: Year ended 09/30/2004.
Assets, $54,613 (M); Expenditures, $326,684. No
monetary support given for residencies.
Fields of interest: Dance; Choreography.
Type of support: Residencies; Stipends.
Application information: Application form required.
  Initial approach: Letter or e-mail.
  Deadline(s): Jan. 7 for Dance Residencies, Nov.
    5 for Choreographer Residencies
  Additional information: Application should
    include letter of recommendation, $20
    application fee, VHS tape of recent work,
    SASE, headshot and resume.
Program descriptions:
  Patricia N. Nanon Residency: Patricia N. Nanon,
  Choreographer and Founder of the Yard, creates
  new work on an auditioned group of dances during
  this residency. Dancers receive housing and a
  stipend of $300 per week, from May 17 to June 27.
  Bessie Schonberg Dancers Residency: Eight
  dancers will be selected for this four-week
  residency, from July 12 to Aug. 7. This session
  gives independent choreographers an opportunity
  to work with an ad hoc company of professional
  dancers. Dancers for this residency are selected by
  the participating choreographers and the Artistic

Director of the Yard. Dancers receive housing and
a stipend of $300 per week.
  Bessie Schonberg Choreographers Residency:
  Four Modern Dance choreographers will be selected
  for this four-week residency to create, rehearse and
  present new work. In addition to housing, The Yard
  provides each choreographer with a stipend of
  $1,200, a production budget of up to $400, a photo
  shoot, video documentation and a critique by an
  outstanding professional in the field.
  Artist-In-The-Schools Program: One teaching
  artist/choreographer will be selected for each
  for-week residency to teach dance/movement in
  Martha's Vineyard public schools. The
  choreographer may bring up to three dancers, who
  may serve as teaching assistants. The Yard
  provides housing and studio space for the
  development of new work. The Artist-in-the-School
  residency requires a total of 36 hours of teaching.
  The teacher/choreographer receives a fee of
  $1,300 and up to three assistants/dancers receive
  a stipend of $100 per person, per week.
EIN: 237348937

5528
The Simon Yates and Kevin Roon Foundation
122 E. 25th St., 3rd Fl.
New York, NY   10010

Foundation type: Operating foundation
Limitations: Grants to individual musicians who
belong to pre-selected orchestras.
Financial data: Year ended 12/31/2002.
Assets, $0 (M); Expenditures, $58,655; Total
giving, $58,655; Grant to an individual, 1 grant
totaling $28,605.
Fields of interest: Music; Orchestra (symphony).
Type of support: Awards/grants by nomination only.
Application information: Unsolicited requests for
funds not considered or acknowledged.
EIN: 300106864

5529
Young Musicians Foundation
(also known as YMF)
195 S. Beverly Dr., Ste. 414
Beverly Hills, CA   90212   (310) 859-7668
Contact: Edye Rugolo, Exec. Dir.
FAX: (310) 859-1365; E-mail: info@ymf.org;
URL: http://ymf.org

Foundation type: Public charity
Limitations: Grants to young musicians residing in
southern CA, ages 9-25, to pay for private music
instruction. Prizes also to winners of the annual
National Debut Concerto Competition.
Financial data: Year ended 06/30/2003.
Assets, $1,400,767 (M); Expenditures,
$934,068; Total giving, $249,614; Grants to
individuals, totaling $249,614.
Fields of interest: Music; Orchestra (symphony).
Type of support: Scholarships—to individuals;
Awards/prizes.
Application information: Applications accepted.
Application form required. Application form
available on the grantmaker's Web site.
  Initial approach: E-mail.
  Deadline(s): May 18
  Applicants should submit the following:
    1) Letter(s) of recommendation
    2) Financial information
  Additional information: See Web site for
    additional program information.

Program descriptions:

YMF Scholarships: This program is geared towards young musicians, ages 9-25, selected during four days of county-wide auditions. As private music instruction becomes more expensive, YMF is one of the few places to which talented young musicians can apply for financial assistance. Students from all over Southern California audition for the prestigious awards. Scholarships ranging from $500 to $2,500 are granted to musicians demonstrating exceptional talent and financial need. Additionally, Honorary Certificates are awarded to encourage musicians who demonstrate exceptional talent but are not in need of financial assistance.

National Debut Concerto Competition: Current participants and alumni of all of YMF's programs through age 26 are eligible to audition for the annual National Debut Concerto Competition. A panel of professional musicians and the Music Director select young musicians to perform a concerto with the Debut Orchestra during the upcoming season. Eligibility: Current members and alumni of YMF's Debut orchestra, Scholarship Program, and Chamber Music Series through age 26 at the time of the auditions. Awards: Performance with the Debut Orchestra; $500-$2,500 honorariums.
EIN: 952250007

RESEARCH AND PROFESSIONAL SUPPORT

This section of the directory lists sources of support for those working at the postgraduate level and above, as well as those seeking support for projects within their professional careers.

Major types of assistance available include the following:

- **Fellowships**—grants awarded to doctoral students and researchers in colleges, universities, and other institutions

- **Project Support**—funding for specific proposed projects, generally conducted by highly qualified individuals

- **Research**—grants for investigative work, predominantly in specific areas of medicine, such as cancer research, but also in select areas of academia

- **Residencies**—grants for study or research, including advanced training in a medical specialty, or access to a particular library or institute for a specified period of time

- **Professional studies**—grants for continuing education to those already established in their careers, such as nurses and ministers

- **By Nomination Only**—includes fellowships, residencies, and awards for which application must be made by an institution or a separate individual, on behalf of the applicant

Not included are grants to individuals in the arts; such programs may be found in the "Arts and Cultural Support" section.

Entries are arranged alphabetically by grantmaker name. Access to grants by the above types of support, as well as specific subject areas and geographic focus, is provided in the "Subject," "Types of Support," "Geographic Focus," and "International Giving" indexes in the back of the book.

Limitations on grantmaking are indicated in the entry when available. *The limitations statement should be checked carefully, as a grantmaker will reject any application that does not fall within its stated geographic area, recipient type, or area of interest.*

REMEMBER: IF YOU DON'T QUALIFY, DON'T APPLY.

5530
A-T Medical Research Foundation
5241 Round Meadow Rd.
Hidden Hills, CA   91302-1163
Contact: Pamela J. Smith, Pres. and C.F.O.
FAX: (818) 704-8310

Foundation type: Operating foundation
Limitations: Grants to individuals in Canada, Costa Rica, the Netherlands, Poland, the U.S., Israel, Italy, and Turkey for medical research concerning ataxia-telangiectasia.
Publications: Annual report; Informational brochure; Newsletter.
Financial data: Year ended 09/30/2004. Assets, $168,688 (M); Expenditures, $743,422; Total giving, $412,500; Grants to individuals, 3 grants totaling $412,500 (high: $190,000, low: $35,000).
Fields of interest: Medical research, institute.
Type of support: Research.
Application information: Applications not accepted.
  Additional information: Unsolicited requests for funds not considered or acknowledged.
Program description:
  Medical Research Program: The foundation supports medical research in Canada, Costa Rica, the Netherlands, Poland, the U.S., Israel, Italy, and Turkey.
EIN: 953882022

5531
The Frederick B. Abramson Memorial Foundation
734 15th St., N.W., Ste. 502
Washington, DC   20005   (202) 463-6585
Contact: Lori Jackson, Exec. Dir.
FAX: (202) 828-6490;
E-mail: info@abramsonfoundation.org;
URL: http://www.abramsonfoundation.org

Foundation type: Public charity
Limitations: Fellowships of $5,000 to graduating law students or judicial law clerks in DC for one year's employment with either a public interest law firm or another nonprofit service organization.
Publications: Application guidelines; Informational brochure; Newsletter.
Financial data: Year ended 06/30/2003. Assets, $165,737 (M); Expenditures, $210,163; Total giving, $70,750; Grants to individuals, 32 grants totaling $70,750 (high: $5,000, low: $100).
Fields of interest: Legal services, public interest law.
Type of support: Fellowships.
Application information: Applications accepted. Application form required. Application form available on the grantmaker's Web site.
  Deadline(s): Apr. 15
EIN: 521800184

5532
Academic Distinction Fund
8550 United Plaza Blvd., Ste. 301
Baton Rouge, LA   70809   (225) 922-4560
Contact: Jan A. Melton, Exec. Dir.
FAX: (225) 922-4562; E-mail: info@adfbr.org;
URL: http://www.adfbr.org

Foundation type: Public charity
Limitations: Grants and fellowships to public school teachers in the East Baton Rouge Parish, LA, public school system.

Financial data: Year ended 07/31/2004. Assets, $497,695 (M); Expenditures, $441,753; Total giving, $162,456.
Fields of interest: Education.
Type of support: Program development; Fellowships; Awards/prizes; Travel grants.
Application information: Application form required.
  Deadline(s): Vary
Program descriptions:
  Grants for Teachers: Provides up to $1,000 each to teachers who want to implement new learning strategies in the classroom. These grants enable teachers to purchase materials that will enhance instruction. Through a competitive proposal process, teachers are challenged to improve student performance. Deadline Mar. 1.
  Teachers Learning Together: This program focuses on teacher collaboration and professional development and provides groups of two to four teachers up to $2,000 to attend professional conferences. Deadline Mar. 1.
  ADF Fellows: Fellowships of $2,500 plus an additional $1,000 for individual activities and/or travel to public school teachers to recognize their outstanding leadership. Deadline Sept. 10.
EIN: 721300995

5533
The ACVIM Foundation
1997 Wadsworth Blvd., Ste. A
Lakewood, CO   80214-5293   (303) 231-9933
Contact: Angela E. Frimberger D.V.M., Exec. Dir.
E-mail: foundation@acvim.org; URL: http://www.acvimfoundation.org

Foundation type: Public charity
Limitations: Grants to veterinarians for research on animal health, and support through grants and loans to veterinary residents in training.
Financial data: Year ended 09/30/2003. Assets, $137,896 (M); Expenditures, $114,648; Total giving, $40,225; Grants to individuals, 6 grants totaling $40,225 (high: $10,000, low: $3,800).
Fields of interest: Veterinary medicine.
Type of support: Research.
Application information: Applications accepted. Application form required. Application form available on the grantmaker's Web site.
  Copies of proposal: 1
  Deadline(s): Sept. 7 for Clinical Research
  Applicants should submit the following:
    1) Proposal
    2) Letter(s) of recommendation
    3) Curriculum vitae
    4) Budget Information
  Additional information: Applicants must also submit a proposal on a PC-formatted disk or CD; Please see Web site for further application information.
Program description:
  Clinical Investigation Grants: Awards up to $10,000 per year for three years to investigators who outline a project that has direct application to improving the diagnosis, treatment, or prevention of disease in animals.
EIN: 841541160

5534
ADA Foundation
(formerly American Dental Association Health Foundation)
211 E. Chicago Ave.
Chicago, IL   60611-2678   (312) 440-2547
Contact: Arthur A. Dugoni D.D.S., Pres.
FAX: (312) 440-3526; E-mail: adaf@ada.org;
URL: http://www.ada.org/ada/prod/adaf/index.asp

Foundation type: Public charity
Limitations: Grants for dental research.
Publications: Application guidelines; Annual report; Informational brochure; Newsletter.
Financial data: Year ended 12/31/2004. Assets, $22,713,944 (M); Expenditures, $6,374,074; Total giving, $645,778.
Fields of interest: Dental care.
Type of support: Research.
Application information:
  Initial approach: E-mail.
  Additional information: Contact foundation for application guidelines.
Program descriptions:
  American Association for Dental Research: Each fellowship position is provided $3,000 that includes a stipend, supplies and travel funds so that the recipient may present research results at the annual AADR meeting. Individuals interested in participating in this program should contact the AADR at www.dentalresearch.orplawards/studentresearch.html.
  Young Investigator Award: As a requirement of the Specialized Materials Science Research Grant from the National Institute of Dental Research, the ADAF Paffenbarger Research Center (PRC) annually appoints two young investigators to the industrial scholars program. The program brings industrial and dental research together in an environment outside the dental school. Individuals interested in learning more about the program, application process or deadlines are invited to contact PRC director of administration, Dr. Clifton M. Carey, at clif.carey@nist.gov.
  Research Training Fellowship: The Research Training Fellowship program is conducted at the ADAF Paffenbarger Research Center (PRC). The program includes a full-time fellow working in conjunction with the PRC's scientific research staff. Individuals interested in learning more about the program, application process or deadlines are invited to contact PRC director of administration, Dr. Clifton M. Carey, at clif.carey@nist.gov.
  Gold Medal Award: The Gold Metal Award for Excellence in Dental Research was established to honor individuals who through basic or clinical research contribute to the advancement of the profession of dentistry or to major improvement in the oral health of the community. The $25,000 and gold medallion award is presented every third year. Individuals interested in addition information concerning the award should contact: Ms. Marcia Greenberg at 312-440-2535 or at greenbergm@ada.org.
  Norton M. Ross Award: The Norton M. Ross Award for Excellence in Clinical Research acknowledges outstanding accomplishment in clinical investigation that has significantly contributed to the prevention of oral diseases. Individuals interested in additional information concerning the award should contact: Ms. Marcia Greenberg at 312-440-2535 or at greenbergm@ada.org.
EIN: 366132046

5535
Adopt an Orca, Inc.
c/o Thomas Newhof
6550 Old Darby Trail N.E.
Ada, MI 49301

Foundation type: Independent foundation
Limitations: Research grants to individuals for the study of the orca whale.
Financial data: Year ended 12/31/2004. Assets, $339 (M); Expenditures, $9,636; Total giving, $8,946.
Fields of interest: Animals/wildlife, research.
Type of support: Research.
Application information: Contact foundation for current application deadline/guidelines.
EIN: 383562103

5536
Aesthetic Surgery Education and Research Foundation
11081 Winners Cir., Ste. 200
Los Alamitos, CA 90720-2813 (562) 799-2356
Contact: Jeffrey Lang, Pres.
FAX: (562) 799-1098; E-mail: aserf@surgery.org;
URL: http://www.aserf.org

Foundation type: Public charity
Limitations: Research grants to plastic surgeons.
Financial data: Year ended 06/30/2004. Assets, $948,171 (M); Expenditures, $93,930; Total giving, $64,865; Grants to individuals, totaling $64,865.
Fields of interest: Surgery research.
Type of support: Research.
Application information: Contact foundation for current application deadline/guidelines.
EIN: 330613185

5537
AHP Foundation
313 Park Ave., Ste. 400
Falls Church, VA 22046-3303 (703) 532-6243
Contact: Nichole Sutton
FAX: (703) 532-7170; E-mail: nichole@ahp.org;
URL: http://www.ahp.org/

Foundation type: Public charity
Limitations: Educational scholarships to financially needy active AHP members and professional fundraisers for charitable hospitals, who could not attend a conference without scholarship aid.
Publications: Informational brochure; Newsletter.
Financial data: Year ended 06/30/2003. Assets, $290,000 (M); Expenditures, $300,000; Total giving, $200,000; Grants to individuals, 8 grants totaling $16,000 (high: $2,000, low: $2,000).
Fields of interest: Health care, formal/general education; Philanthropy/voluntarism, formal/general education.
Type of support: Conferences/seminars; Postgraduate support.
Application information: Applications accepted. Application form required.
  Deadline(s): Dec. 1
  Additional information: Completion of formal application required, including written statement of qualifications, brief history of professional fundraising experience, and any other supporting documentation.
Program description:
  Association for Healthcare Philanthropy Foundation Scholarships: Scholarships provide $2,000 in the following priority: covering registration, lodging and travel for attendance at

either the AHP Institute for Health Care Philanthropy in Madison, WI, or the AHP Annual International Educational Conference. The recipient is responsible for the balance of transportation and per diem expenses.
EIN: 237359389

5538
Air Force Association
(formerly Aerospace Education Foundation, Inc.)
1501 Lee Hwy.
Arlington, VA 22209-1198 (703) 247-5800
Contact: Donald L. Peterson, Exec. Dir.
FAX: (703) 247-5853; E-mail: afastaff@afa.org;
URL: http://www.afa.org

Foundation type: Public charity
Limitations: Grants to educators for the development of aerospace activities and programs.
Financial data: Year ended 12/31/2004. Assets, $4,428,849 (M); Expenditures, $1,651,536; Total giving, $350,706.
Fields of interest: Space/aviation.
Type of support: Grants to individuals.
Application information: Application form required.
  Deadline(s): Contact foundation for current application deadlines
  Additional information: See Web site for complete listings of guidelines and programs.
Program description:
  Professional Grants:
  · AFJROTC Instructor Grants: $250 grants are available to AFJROTC instructors for use in expanding aerospace and civics experiences for cadets
  · Civil Air Patrol Aerospace Education Instructor Grants: Grants of up to $250 are awarded to instructors of CAP cadet squadrons for new and innovative aerospace education programs
  · Educator Grants: Grants of up to $250 each are available to teachers for support of aerospace activities.
EIN: 526043929

5539
Airport High School Educational Foundation, Inc.
P.O. Box 2044
West Columbia, SC 29171 (803) 794-3712
Contact: Donald H. Burkett, Dir.

Foundation type: Public charity
Limitations: Grants to teachers to promote educational programs at Airport High School in SC.
Financial data: Year ended 06/30/2004. Assets, $47,747 (M); Expenditures, $27,283; Total giving, $21,068; Grants to individuals, 35 grants totaling $21,068 (high: $1,750, low: $31). Subtotal for program development: grants totaling (high: $800, low: $31).
Fields of interest: Secondary school/education.
Type of support: Program development.
Application information:
  Initial approach: Letter.
EIN: 562194610

5540
Alaska Conservation Foundation
441 W. 5th Ave., Ste. 402
Anchorage, AK 99501-2340 (907) 276-1917
Contact: Deborah L. Williams, Exec. Dir.; For grants: Julie Jessen, Assoc. Prog. Off.
FAX: (907) 274-4145; E-mail: acfinfo@akcf.org;
Grant request E-mail: jjessen@akcf.org;
URL: http://www.akcf.org

Foundation type: Community foundation
Limitations: Awards to environmentalists in AK. Also, scholarships to volunteer and professional environmental activists, primarily in AK, seeking to improve their leadership skills.
Publications: Application guidelines; Annual report; Financial statement; Grants list; Informational brochure; Newsletter; Program policy statement.
Financial data: Year ended 06/30/2004. Assets, $8,076,254 (M); Expenditures, $4,908,064; Total giving, $1,830,863; Grants to individuals, 6 grants totaling $8,145 (high: $3,000, low: $500).
Fields of interest: Film/video; Literature; Education; Natural resources; Environment; Youth development; Public affairs, government agencies; Leadership development; Native Americans/American Indians.
Type of support: Program development; Awards/prizes; Precollege support.
Application information: Application form required. Application form available on the grantmaker's Web site.
  Initial approach: Letter or telephone.
  Deadline(s): Mar. 15
Program descriptions:
  Jerry S. Dixon Award: This award is presented annually for excellence in environmental education. It rewards innovative educators who integrate stewardship of Alaska's vast and precious natural resources into their instructive efforts.
  Lowell Thomas Jr. Award for Outstanding Civil Service: This award recognizes a current, retired, or appointed public official who has demonstrated extraordinary commitment to conservation and building sustainable communities.
  Native Writing on the Environment Award: This award recognizes Native American writers who write about the importance of Alaska's natural environment in their lives and cultures and who reflect the need to protect Alaska's ecosystems.
  The Celia Hunter Award: This award is presented annually to honor AK's outstanding environmental volunteer activists. Recipients of the award designate the funds to an Alaskan environmental charity of their choosing.
  Daniel Housberg Wilderness Image Awards: These awards recognize outstanding photography and video projects which were designed to help advance protection of Alaska's wilderness environments.
  Olaus Murie Award: This award is presented annually to honor outstanding professional contributions to the AK conservation movement.
  Wilcher Award: This award honors senior high school students who have made a significant contribution to their community through activism.
  Alaska Environmental Leadership Scholarships: Volunteer and professional activists may apply for support to improve their leadership skills in the training course of their choice.
  Annual Awards: Awards by nomination only to individuals who have made outstanding contributions to Alaska's conservation movement. The awards include cash grants to the winners and/or grants to nonprofit organizations of the winner's choice. Deadline Mar. 15.
EIN: 920061466

5541
Consuelo Zobel Alger Foundation
110 N. Hotel St.
Honolulu, HI 96817
Contact: San Vuong, C.F.O.
FAX: (808) 532-3930; E-mail: info@consuelo.org;
URL: http://www.consuelo.org

Foundation type: Operating foundation
Limitations: Fellowships by nomination only to medical doctors in the Philippines and HI.
Publications: Annual report.
Financial data: Year ended 12/31/2004.
Assets, $132,593,764 (M); Expenditures,
$6,429,542; Total giving, $693,084.
Fields of interest: Health care.
Type of support: Fellowships; Awards/grants by nomination only; Foreign applicants.
Application information: Unsolicited requests for funds not considered or acknowledged.
EIN: 990266163

5542
Alliance for Cancer Gene Therapy, Inc.
96 Cummings Point Rd.
Stamford, CT 06902 (203) 358-8000
Contact: Edward Netter, Pres.
FAX: (203) 348-3103;
E-mail: aneslage@acgtfoundation.org; URL: http://www.acgtfoundation.org

Foundation type: Public charity
Limitations: Research grants to qualified scientists working in gene cancer therapy.
Publications: Application guidelines; Annual report; Financial statement; Grants list; Informational brochure; Newsletter; Occasional report.
Financial data: Year ended 04/30/2004.
Assets, $3,560,966 (M); Expenditures,
$2,283,548; Total giving, $2,239,948; Grants to individuals, 8 grants totaling $2,239,948 (high: $478,432, low: $15,414).
Fields of interest: Genetics/birth defects research; Cancer research; Leukemia research.
Type of support: Research; Awards/prizes; Postdoctoral support.
Application information: Applications accepted. Application form required. Application form available on the grantmaker's Web site.
  Deadline(s): Sept. 15 for Young Investigator Award
  Applicants should submit the following:
    1) Proposal
    2) Budget Information
Program descriptions:
  Gene Therapy Lymphoma and Leukemia Award: Provides up to $1,000,000 distributed over three to five years, inclusive of a maximum of ten percent indirect costs. The funds may be used at the recipient's discretion for salary, technical assistance, supplies, animals or capital equipment, but may not support staff not directly related to the project. Purchase of equipment is not allowed in the final year of the grant. Continued support is contingent upon submission and approval of a non-competitive renewal application each year. Candidates must hold an M.D., Ph.D., or equivalent degree and be a tenure-track or tenured faculty. The investigator must be conducting original research as an independent faculty member. There are no citizenship restrictions, but research supported by the award must be conducted at medical schools and research centers only in the U.S.
  Young Investigators Award: Provides up to $500,000 distributed over three years, inclusive of a maximum of ten percent indirect costs. The funds

may be used at the recipient's discretion for salary, technical assistance, supplies, animals or capital equipment, but may not support staff not directly related to the project. Purchase of equipment is not allowed in the third year of the grant. Continued support is contingent upon submission and approval of a non-competitive renewal application each year. Candidates must hold an M.D., M.P.H., Ph.D., or equivalent degree and be tenure-track Assistant Professors within five years of their initial appointment to this rank, at the time of award activation. The investigator must be conducting original research as an independent faculty member. There are no citizenship requirements, but research supported by the award must be conducted at medical schools and research institutions only in the U.S.
EIN: 061619523

5543
Alliance for Quality Education
P.O. Box 2264
Greenville, SC 29602-2264 (864) 233-4133
Contact: Grier Mullins, Exec. Dir.
E-mail: grier@afqe.org; URL: http://www.allianceforqualityed.org

Foundation type: Public charity
Limitations: Grants for teachers and administrators in the school district of Greenville County, SC.
Publications: Annual report; Grants list; Informational brochure; Newsletter; Occasional report.
Financial data: Year ended 12/31/2003.
Assets, $700,356 (M); Expenditures, $254,919; Total giving, $46,062; Grants to individuals, 82 grants totaling $46,062 (high: $1,500, low: $120).
Fields of interest: Education, management/technical aid.
Type of support: Grants to individuals.
Application information: Deadline May 15; Completion of formal application required.
Program description:
  Teacher Grants: Annually awards competitive grants to teachers for innovative classroom and school-wide projects. Funds are distributed to teachers each Aug. for projects they believe will increase their students' academic achievement. Grants are evaluated based on five factors: 1) cost-effectiveness; 2) ability to be replicated; 3) innovation; 4) benefit to students; and 5) potential to motivate students. The goal of the program is to enrich classroom instruction, recognize innovative teaching and enhance teacher morale by expressing community support.
EIN: 570769637

5544
Warren Alpert Foundation
27 Warren Way
P.O. Box 72743
Providence, RI 02907
E-mail: lvogel@thecastlegrp.com; URL: http://www.warrenalpert.org/home/

Foundation type: Independent foundation
Limitations: Medical research grants by nomination only in the form of annual prizes to medical doctors in the U.S. and abroad.
Publications: Grants list.
Financial data: Year ended 12/31/2004.
Assets, $856,070 (M); Expenditures, $405,388; Total giving, $305,425.
Fields of interest: Health care, association; Medical research, institute.

Type of support: Research; Awards/grants by nomination only; Foreign applicants; Awards/prizes.
Application information: Applications not accepted.
  Additional information: Recipients are chosen in consultation with a panel of medical experts and the faculties of Harvard Medical School and Albert Einstein School of Medicine.
EIN: 050426623

5545
Alpha Omicron Pi Foundation
(formerly Alpha Omicron Pi Philanthropic Foundation)
P.O. Box 395
Brentwood, TN 37024-0395 (615) 370-0920
Contact: Bobby Stanton, Exec. Dir.
E-mail: foundation@alphaomicronpi.org;
URL: http://www.aoiifoundation.org

Foundation type: Public charity
Limitations: Research grants in the field of arthritis to further efforts for improving the lives of those with arthritis. Grants are made for peer-reviewed projects.
Publications: Biennial report; Grants list; Informational brochure.
Financial data: Year ended 06/30/2005.
Assets, $3,267,819 (M); Expenditures, $628,847; Total giving, $344,725; Grants to individuals, 40 grants totaling $77,500.
Fields of interest: Students, sororities/fraternities; Arthritis research.
Type of support: Research.
Application information: Contact foundation for current application deadline/guidelines.
EIN: 581343315

5546
Alpha-1 Foundation, Inc.
2937 S.W. 27th Ave., Ste. 302
Miami, FL 33133 (305) 567-9888
Contact: John W. Walsh, Pres. and C.E.O.
FAX: (305) 567-1317;
E-mail: lrodriguez@alphaone.org; Toll-free tel.: (877) 228-7321; URL: http://www.alphaone.org

Foundation type: Public charity
Limitations: Fellowships, research, and travel grants in the area of Alpha-1 study.
Publications: Application guidelines; Financial statement.
Financial data: Year ended 06/30/2005.
Assets, $2,827,515 (M); Expenditures, $5,377,926; Total giving, $2,503,999.
Fields of interest: Ear & throat research; Lung research; Liver research; Medical research.
Type of support: Fellowships; Research; Postdoctoral support; Travel grants.
Application information: Contact foundation for current application deadline/guidelines.
Program descriptions:
  Fernandez Liver Research Initiative: Intended to stimulate research into the liver disease associated with AAT Deficiency. Four grants are awarded for the two years: two for studies of the treatment of Alpha-1 related liver disease, and two for the studies of the basic science of Alpha-1 related liver disease.
  Travel Awards: Gives $1,000 grants for travel to the American Thoracic Society/American Lung Association annual meeting.
  Young Investigator Fellowship Awards: Offers up to two postdoctoral fellowships for studies in the basic science or clinical investigation of Alpha-1.

Each grant provides for a maximum of $50,000 per year, renewable annually for up to an additional two years based upon documentation of progress. Applications evaluating hypothesis-driven proposals of all types are encouraged. Candidates must have at least one year of research experience, an M.D., Ph.D., or equivalent degree, and perform the work under the guidance of an established investigator. The award is intended primarily for salary support, and is not limited to U.S. citizens. Deadline Nov. 1.
EIN: 650585415

5547

Alternatives Research and Development Foundation

801 Old York Rd., Ste. 316
Jenkintown, PA   19046   (215) 887-8076
Contact: Sue A. Leary, Pres. and Exec. Dir.
FAX: (215) 887-0771; E-mail: info@ardf-online.org;
Additional E-mail: grants@ardf-online.org;
URL: http://www.ardf-online.org

Foundation type: Public charity
Limitations: Research grants to scientists who have an interest and expertise in alternative research investigation.
Financial data: Year ended 12/31/2004.
Assets, $7,620,855 (M); Expenditures, $272,477; Total giving, $161,790.
Fields of interest: Medical research.
Type of support: Research.
Application information:
   Initial approach: E-mail.
   Deadline(s): Apr. 30
   Additional information: Contact foundation for complete program information.
Program description:
   Alternatives Research Grant Program: Up to $40,000 in funding is available to support individual projects. Preferential consideration will be given to proposals that utilize human rather than non-human vertebrate tissue; do not involve the use of intact, non-human vertebrate or invertebrate animals; do not utilize serum or medium supplements obtained from non-human vertebrates; can be completed in one year; and are from individuals associated with U.S. institutions or organizations. The foundation does not provide funding for the use of monoclonal antibodies produced by in vivo methods. Source and production method for all antibodies must be clearly identified in the proposal.
EIN: 232740843

5548

Jenifer Altman Foundation

P.O. Box 29209
San Francisco, CA   94129   (415) 561-2182
Contact: Ashley Iwanaga
FAX: (415) 561-6480; E-mail: info@jaf.org;
URL: http://www.jaf.org

Foundation type: Independent foundation
Limitations: Awards to individuals who have made significant contributions to human health or the health of the earth.
Publications: Application guidelines; Grants list; Program policy statement.
Financial data: Year ended 06/30/2004.
Assets, $13,886,880 (M); Expenditures, $1,164,622; Total giving, $365,500.
Fields of interest: Environment; Health care.
Type of support: Awards/prizes.

Application information:
   Initial approach: Concept letter.
   Deadline(s): None
   Additional information: See Web site for further application information.
EIN: 943146675

5549

American Academy of Dermatology, Inc.

P.O. Box 4014
Schaumburg, IL   60168-4014   (847) 330-0230
Contact: Clay J. Cockerell M.D., Pres.
FAX: (847) 330-0050; URL: http://www.aad.org

Foundation type: Public charity
Limitations: Awards by nomination only to AAD members in accredited dermatology residency programs.
Financial data: Year ended 12/31/2003.
Assets, $49,975,874 (M); Expenditures, $18,290,121; Total giving, $374,835; Grants to individuals, totaling $374,835.
Fields of interest: Skin disorders research.
Type of support: Research; Awards/grants by nomination only; Awards/prizes.
Application information: Application form available on the grantmaker's Web site.
   Deadline(s): Dec. 12
   Applicants should submit the following:
      1) Letter(s) of recommendation
      2) Curriculum vitae
   Additional information: Only AAD members may be nominated; Completion of formal nomination required, including description of nominee's research, and residency. Nomination form available from Web site.
Program description:
   Awards for Young Investigators in Dermatology: Awards two young investigators in the U.S. and Canada with an engraved plaque and a $5,000 prize that is shared between the investigator and the nominating institution on a 40:60 basis. Nominations are accepted from either the head of the department of dermatology or the nominee's faculty advisor. For further information contact gmurphy@aad.org.
EIN: 410793046

5550

American Academy of Family Physicians Foundation

(also known as AAFP Foundation)
1140 Tomahawk Creek Pkwy., Ste. 440
Leawood, KS   66211-2627   (913) 906-6000
Contact: Sandra Panther; For Research: Susi Morantz
FAX: (913) 906-6095;
E-mail: foundation@aafp.org; Toll-free tel.: (800) 274-2237; Additional E-mail (for Susi Morantz): smorantz@aafp.org; URL: http://www.aafpfoundation.org

Foundation type: Public charity
Limitations: Grants to family physicians to support research projects on topics relevant to family medicine.
Publications: Application guidelines; Annual report; Informational brochure; Newsletter.
Financial data: Year ended 12/31/2004.
Assets, $11,419,865 (L); Expenditures, $3,235,560; Total giving, $1,343,748.
Fields of interest: Health care.
Type of support: Research.

Application information: Applications accepted. Application form required. Application form available on the grantmaker's Web site.
   Initial approach: Telephone.
   Copies of proposal: 1
   Deadline(s): June 1 and Dec. 1
   Applicants should submit the following:
      1) Proposal
Program description:
   Joint Grant Awards Program: This program supports research projects conducted by family physicians on topics relevant to family medicine. Funds are available for both formal grant proposals as well as less formal applications for research stimulation studies.
EIN: 446013671

5551

American Academy of Nurse Practitioners Foundation

P.O. Box 10729
Glendale, AZ   85318-0729   (623) 376-9467
Contact: Judith Dempster, Exec. Dir.
FAX: (623) 376-0369;
E-mail: foundation@aanp.org; URL: http://www.aanpfoundation.org

Foundation type: Public charity
Limitations: Research and project grants awarded to nurse practitioners.
Financial data: Year ended 12/31/2003.
Assets, $212,359 (M); Expenditures, $152,844; Total giving, $48,900; Grants to individuals, 29 grants totaling $45,950 (high: $6,000, low: $1,000).
Fields of interest: Nursing school/education; Allergies research; Asthma research; Alzheimer's disease research; Diabetes research.
Type of support: Research.
Application information: Applications accepted. Application form required.
   Initial approach: Telephone, E-mail, or Fax.
   Deadline(s): Apr. for 1st funding cycle; Oct. for 2nd funding cycle
   Additional information: Contact foundation to request application material; a $10 non refundable application/administration fee is due with each scholarship applied for.
Program description:
   Grants: Awards the following 8 project, student research and research grants:
      · AANP NP Project/Research Grant
      · Dempster NP Doctoral Dissertation Research Grant
      · NP Health Policy Internship Grant
      · Forest Laboratories NP Alzheimer's Grant
      · Novo Nordisk Pharmaceutical NP Diabetes Grant
      · Purdue Pharma NP Pain Management Grant
      · Ross Products Division NP Nutrition Grant
      · sanofi-aventis Group NP Allergy/Asthma Grant
EIN: 742861018

5552

American Anthropological Association

2200 Wilson Blvd., Ste. 600
Arlington, VA   22201   (703) 528-1902
Contact: Bill Davis, Exec. Dir.
FAX: (703) 528-3546; URL: http://www.aaanet.org

Foundation type: Public charity
Limitations: Awards grants to foster, support, and promote the professional interests of anthropologists and the field of anthropology.

Publications: Application guidelines; Annual report; Financial statement.
Financial data: Year ended 12/31/2004. Assets, $9,221,038 (M); Expenditures, $5,226,655; Total giving, $35,002; Grants to individuals, 54 grants totaling $35,002 (high: $5,000, low: $50).
Fields of interest: Anthropology/sociology.
Type of support: Fellowships; Research; Grants to individuals.
Application information: Applications accepted.
Initial approach: Letter.
Program description:
AAA Minority Dissertation Fellowship: Awards $10,000 to members of ethnic minorities to complete doctoral degress in anthropology, thereby increasing diversity in the discipline and/or promoting research on issues of concern among minority populations. An applicant must be: a US citizen; a member of an historically underrepresented ethnic minority group, including, but not limited to: African Americans, Alaskan Natives, American Indians or Native Americans, Asian Americans, Latinos/as, Chicano/as, and Pacific Islanders; enrolled in a full-time academic program leading to a doctoral degree in anthropology at the time of application; admitted to degree candidacy before the dissertation fellowship is awarded; and a member of the American Anthropology Association. The proposal must be approved by the applicant's committe prior to application. Students of any subfield or specialty in anthropology will receive equal consideration.
EIN: 530246691

5553
American Antiquarian Society
185 Salisbury St.
Worcester, MA 01609-1634 (508) 755-5221
Contact: Dir., Scholarly Progs.: Caroline F. Sloat
FAX: (508) 754-9069; E-mail: cfs@mwa.org; E-mail for Caroline F. Sloat: cloat@mwa.org; URL: http://www.americanantiquarian.org

Foundation type: Public charity
Limitations: Residency fellowships of one to twelve months at the American Antiquarian Society for research and writing in American history and culture through the year 1876.
Publications: Application guidelines; Annual report; Informational brochure (including application guidelines).
Financial data: Year ended 08/31/2005. Assets, $54,908,331 (M); Expenditures, $3,852,240; Total giving, $287,703; Grants to individuals, 35 grants totaling $287,703 (high: $40,000, low: $1,000).
Fields of interest: Media/communications; Visual arts; Performing arts; Humanities; Literature; Historical activities.
Type of support: Fellowships; Postdoctoral support; Residencies; Travel grants; Stipends.
Application information: Applications accepted. Application form required.
Initial approach: Letter, telephone, FAX, or e-mail requesting the specific program's application form.
Deadline(s): Vary
Applicants should submit the following:
1) Resume
Additional information: Application should also include two letters of reference and a personal statement.
Program descriptions:
AAS Short-term Fellowships: These fellowships provide support for one to three months' residence in the Society's library at stipends of $1000 per

month. Taken as a whole, AAS Short-term Fellowships are open to individuals who are engaged in scholarly research and writing in any field of American history and culture through 1876. This includes non-U.S. citizens and persons at work on doctoral dissertations. Specific eligibility requirements apply in certain categories, as detailed below.
· Kate B. and Hall J. Peterson Fellowships and Legacy Fellowship: These awards are the Society's broadest
· AAS-American Society for 18th-Century Studies Fellowship: These fellowships promote research in any area of American eighteenth-century studies. Degree candidates are not eligible. ASECS membership is required upon taking up an award, but not for making application
· Stephen Botein Fellowships and Reese Fellowship: These fellowships support research in the history of the book in American culture
· Joyce Tracy Fellowship: This fellowship is for research on newspapers and magazines or for projects using these resources as primary documentation. This award derives from an endowment established in memory of the Society's longtime curator of newspapers and periodicals
· American Historical Print Collectors Society Fellowship: This fellowship supports research on American prints of the 18th and 19th centuries for projects using prints as primary documentation
· "Drawn To Art" Fellowship: This fellowship supports research substantially using graphic materials as primary sources
· Legacy Fellowship: Fellowships for research on any topic supported by the collections, and is funded by the gifts of former fellows and research associates
· Reese Fellowship: Supports research in American bibliography and projects in the history of the book in America. Funding for this award is provided by the William Reese Co., New Haven, CT.
AAS-National Endowment for the Humanities Fellowships: at least three long-term fellowships, tenable for four to five or twelve months, will be awarded under a grant to the Society from the National Endowment for the Humanities. Normal tenure is six to twelve months, but new NEH guidelines permit the Society to arrange tenure of four or five months. These long-term fellowships are designed for both senior scholars working on sweeping subjects and younger scholars at work on more narrowly focused monographs. The maximum available stipend is $40,000. AAS-NEH Fellowships may not be awarded to degree candidates or for study leading to advanced degrees, nor may they be granted to non-U.S. citizens unless they have been residents in the U.S. for at least three years preceding their award. AAS-NEH Fellows must devote full-time to their studies, and may not accept teaching assignments or undertake any other major activities during the tenure of the award. Also, they may not hold any other fellowships, except sabbaticals or other grants from their own institutions. Deadline Jan. 15.
AAS Visiting Fellowships for Creative and Performing Artist & Writers: The fellowship provides a stipend of $1,200 for one month's residencies and use of the Society's library. An allowance for travel expenses is also provided. Recipients of these grants may be creative and performing artists, designers, illustrators, sculptors, painters, filmmakers, and journalists. Deadline in Oct.

Mellon Postdoctoral Research Fellowships: One fellowship will be awarded for an academic year (nine or ten months) in residence at the society's library. The maximum stipend is $35,000.
ACLS Frederick Burkhardt Fellowships: The American Council of Learned Societies will award these one-year residential fellowships for which recently tenured humanists may apply. The American Antiquarian society is one of nine major research libraries and interdisciplinary centers participating in this program.
Mellon Post-Dissertation Fellowship: This fellowship provides a $35,000, 12 month stipend to scholars who are no more than three years beyond receipt of their doctorates. The purpose of the fellowship is to provide time and resources to extend research and/or to revise the dissertation for publication. Any topic relevant to the Society's library collections and programmatic scope (American history and culture through 1876) is eligible. Applicants may come from such fields as history, literature, American studies, political science, art history, music history, and other fields relating to America in the period of the Society's coverage.
Fellowships: Selection is based on the applicant's scholarly qualifications, the general interest of the project, and the appropriateness of the inquiry to the Society's holdings.
Announcement of the awards is made by Mar. 30 for academic programs and by early Dec. for artists fellowships.
EIN: 042103652

5554
American Association for Cancer Research, Inc.
615 Chestnut St., 17th Fl.
Philadelphia, PA 19106 (215) 440-9300
E-mail: aacr@aacr.org; URL: http://www.aacr.org

Foundation type: Public charity
Limitations: Research grants and travel stipends to scientists for cancer research.
Financial data: Year ended 12/31/2003. Assets, $28,771,317 (M); Expenditures, $27,726,479; Total giving, $1,357,000; Grants to individuals, 31 grants totaling $1,357,000 (high: $200,000, low: $1,000).
Fields of interest: Cancer research.
Type of support: Fellowships; Research; Travel grants.
Application information: Applications accepted. Application form required. Application form available on the grantmaker's Web site.
Initial approach: E-mail.
Deadline(s): Varies
Additional information: See Web site for detailed program information.
Program descriptions:
Avon Foundation-AACR International Scholar Awards in Breast Cancer Research: Provides awards to junior faculty from countries where opportunities for scientific advancement are limited - such as those in Asia, Latin America, and Eastern Europe. The awards place scholars in U.S. institutions for two years and provide $50,000 in salary support per year, in addition to support for research expenses, income taxes, medical and other benefits, professional development opportunities, travel grants and more.
ACCR-Gertrude B. Elion Cancer Research Award: Awards grants to junior faculty at the level of Assistant Professor. One-year grant of $50,000 for salary, laboratory supplies, and limited domestic travel.

ACCR Career Development Awards: Awards grants to investigators at the level of Instructor, Research Assistant Professor, and Assistant Professor. Two-year grants of $50,000 per year for direct research expenses.

ACCR-Barletta Foundation Fellow Grant: Awards grants to postdoctoral fellows or clinical fellows in the 3rd, 4th, or 5th, year of by the start of the grant term. One-year grant of $35,000 to be used for direct research expenses associated with the Fellow's research proposal, which may be renewed for an additional year.

ACCR Research Fellowships: Awards grants to postdoctoral and clinical fellows who are in the 2nd, 3rd, or 4th year of their postdoctoral research training at the start of the award year. One-, two-, or three-year grants of $30,000 to $40,000 per year for salary support.
EIN: 236251648

5555
American Association for Clinical Chemistry

2101 L St., N.W., Ste. 202
Washington, DC 20037 (202) 857-0717
Contact: Mitchell G. Scott Ph.D., Pres.
FAX: (202) 887-5093; Additional tel.: (800) 892-1400; URL: http://www.aacc.org

Foundation type: Public charity
Limitations: Research grants and travel stipends by nomination only to clinical chemists and clinical scientists in the field of clinical laboratory science.
Financial data: Year ended 12/31/2004. Assets, $12,271,985 (M); Expenditures, $13,542,835; Total giving, $88,000; Grants to individuals, 55 grants totaling $86,050 (high: $5,000, low: $50).
Fields of interest: Medical research.
Type of support: Research; Awards/grants by nomination only; Travel grants.
Application information:
Initial approach: Nomination letter.
Applicants should submit the following:
1) Curriculum vitae
Additional information: See Web site for complete nomination guideline information.
Program description:
Nomination Awards: Presents the following awards to clinical chemists and scientist in the field of clinical laboratory science:
· Research Award
· International Travel Fellowship
· Young Investigator Award
· Ullman Award
· Journal Award
EIN: 390977801

5556
American Association for the Advancement of Science

(also known as AAAS)
1200 New York Ave., N.W.
Washington, DC 20005 (202) 326-6400
Contact: Alan Leshner, C.E.O.
URL: http://www.aaas.org

Foundation type: Public charity
Limitations: Awards to individuals in the scientific, science journalism, and engineering communities, as well as travel grants for research program development to scientists.
Publications: Annual report; Newsletter.

Financial data: Year ended 12/31/2004. Assets, $166,105,752 (M); Expenditures, $75,501,242; Total giving, $2,832,668.
Fields of interest: Engineering/technology; Science; Government/public administration; Minorities; Women.
Type of support: Awards/prizes.
Application information:
Deadline(s): Vary
Additional information: Nomination guidelines vary by program; See the association's Web site for complete guidelines and application forms.
Program descriptions:
Awards: All awards are presented at the AAAS annual meeting. All recipients receive a commemorative plaque, complimentary registration, and reimbursement for reasonable travel and hotel expenses, in addition to their monetary awards. Most awards are open to individuals regardless of nationality or citizenship.

Award for International Scientific Cooperation: This $2,500 award seeks to recognize an individual or a limited number of individuals working together in the scientific or engineering community for making an outstanding contribution to furthering international cooperation in science and engineering. Contact the Awards Coordinator of Directorate for International Programs at lstroud@aaas.org or (202) 326-6650 for more information. Deadline Aug. 1.

Awards for Public Understanding of Science and Technology: This $5,000 award recognizes scientists and engineers who make outstanding contributions to the popularization of science. Only materials produced for general audiences, as opposed to professional or trade audiences, will be considered. Contact the Public Understanding Awards Coord. at jkass@aaas.org or (202) 326-6670 for more information. Deadline Aug. 1.

Philip Hauge Abelson Prize: This $2,500 award is given either to: a public servant, in recognition of sustained exceptional contributions to advancing science; or a scientist, whose career has been distinguished both for scientific advancement and for other notable services to the scientific community. Contact the Abelson Prize Coord. at snelson@aaas.org or (202) 326-6600 for more information. Deadline Aug. 1.

Mentor Awards: These awards honor individuals who, during their careers, demonstrate extraordinary leadership to increase the participation of underrepresented groups in science and engineering fields and careers. These groups include: women of all racial and ethnic groups; African American, Native American, and Latino men; and people with disabilities. Two awards are given: Lifetime Mentor Award, a $5,000 prize to an individual who served as a mentor for 10 or more years; and Mentor Award, a $2,500 prize to an individual who has served as a mentor for less than 10 years. Contact the Awards Coord. at ygeorge@aaas.org or (202) 326-6670 for more information. Deadline July 31.

Newcomb Cleveland Award: This $5,000 award is given to the author or authors of an outstanding paper published in the research articles, reports, or reviews section of "Science." Contact the Awards Coord. of the "Science" Editorial Office at skihara@aaas.org or (202) 326-6507. Deadline June 30.

Scientific Freedom and Responsibility Award: This $2,500 award honors scientists and engineers whose exemplary actions have served to foster scientific freedom and responsibility. Contact Deborah Runkle at drunkle@aaas.org or (202) 326-6794. Deadline June 1.

AAAS Science Journalism Awards: Recognizes outstanding reporting for a general audience and honors individuals for their coverage of the sciences, engineering, or mathematics. Awards will be given in the following categories: large newspapers, small newspapers, magazines, television, radio, and on-line. Entries may include stories on life, physical, and social sciences; engineering and mathematics; and policy issues that are grounded in science or technology. Awards will be presented at the AAAS annual meeting. Reasonable travel and hotel expenses of the award winners will be reimbursed.

Women's International Science Collaboration (WISC) Program: Grants of $4,000 or $5,000 provide travel and living support for a U.S. scientist and, when appropriate, a co-PI, to visit a partner country to develop a research program. Funds can be used to support a second visit to the partner country or for a foreign partner to travel to the U.S. Applicants must be U.S. citizens or permanent residents who have their Ph.D. or equivalent experience. The following research fields are eligible: archaeology and anthropology; astronomy; biochemistry; biophysics and genetics; biological sciences; chemistry; computer science; earth sciences; economics; engineering; environmental sciences; geography; history and philosophy of science; linguistics; mathematics; physics; political science; non-clinically oriented psychology; science and technology policy; and sociology. See the association's Web site for contact information by region.
EIN: 530196568

5557
American Association of Museums

1575 Eye St., N.W., Ste. 400
Washington, DC 20005-1105 (202) 289-1818
Contact: Edward H. Able, Jr., Pres. and C.E.O.
FAX: (202) 289-6578;
E-mail: diversity@aam-us.org; URL: http://www.aam-us.org

Foundation type: Public charity
Limitations: Awards by nomination only for professional excellence and for the enhancement of accessibility in the museum field.
Publications: Annual report.
Financial data: Year ended 07/31/2003. Assets, $6,152,180 (M); Expenditures, $8,111,870; Total giving, $23,500; Grants to individuals, 26 grants totaling $16,150 (high: $1,000, low: $250).
Fields of interest: Museums; Disabilities, people with.
Type of support: Awards/grants by nomination only; Awards/prizes; Stipends.
Application information: Applications accepted. Application form required.
Initial approach: Telephone or e-mail.
Deadline(s): Jan. 15
Additional information: See Web site for additional information.
Program descriptions:
AAM Accessibility Award: Awards a stipend of $1,000, which is donated through the National Organization on Disability by Aetna and U.S. Healthcare to individuals by nomination only. Award is presented at the annual AAM meeting.

Nancy Hanks Memorial Award for Professional Excellence: Awards a stipend of $1,000 to an individual for the purpose of furthering his/her professional development with less than 10 years in the field. Application for award must be made by nominee's director. Museums of all types and sizes

are encouraged to nominate a candidate. Award is presented at the annual AAM meeting.
EIN: 530205889

5558
American Association of People with Disabilities

1629 K St., N.W., Ste. 503
Washington, DC 20006-3603 (202) 457-0046
Contact: Andrew Imparato, Pres. and C.E.O.
FAX: (202) 457-0473; E-mail: aapd@aol.com;
Additional tel.: (800) 840-8844; URL: http://www.aapd-dc.org

Foundation type: Public charity
Limitations: Awards by nomination only to disabled individuals, as well as fellowships to disabled individuals to offset costs associated with completing an internship.
Financial data: Year ended 12/31/2003.
Assets, $548,035 (M); Expenditures, $1,732,212.
Fields of interest: Disabilities, people with.
Type of support: Fellowships; Internship funds; Awards/prizes.
Application information: Application form required.
  Initial approach: Letter, telephone or e-mail.
  Deadline(s): Mar. 1 for spring and summer internships, Oct. 4 for Henry B. Betts Award and Nov. 1 for Paul G. Hearne Award.
  Additional information: Nominations must be submitted on official nomination form; See Web site for additional information.
Program descriptions:
  Henry B. Betts Award: Award of $50,000 annually to an individual whose work and scope of influence has significantly improved the quality of life for people with disabilities in the past, and will be a force for change in the future.
  Paul G. Hearne/AAPD Leadership Awards: Awards of $10,000 each to up to three individuals with disabilities who are emerging as leaders in their respective fields, to help them continue to progress as leaders. U.S. residents with any type of disability are eligible to apply.
  Exchange Pioneers Fellowships: Five $2,000 fellowships awarded to individuals with disabilities to offset costs associated with completing an internship. Internships must be between 25 and 40 hours per week for a minimum of three months in length during the summer. Interns should plan to support the organization's goals to increase their office and program accessibility. Each recipient will be required to write a publishable article about his/her experience and agree to be a peer mentor to others with disabilities seeking similar experiences. Recipients must have applied for internships prior to submitting application. Fellowships will be granted pending confirmation of internship acceptance.
EIN: 521930174

5559
American Association of Physics Teachers

1 Physics Ellipse
College Park, MD 20740-3845 (301) 209-3300
Address to mail Nomination: AAPT Awards Committee, c/o James Nelson, University High School, 11501 Eastwood Dr., Orlando, Fl 32817;
Additional tel. for scholarships: (301) 209-3344
FAX: (301) 209-0845; E-mail: aapt-prog@aapt.org;
URL: http://www.aapt.org

Foundation type: Public charity

Limitations: Scholarships and awards to teachers in the field of physics.
Financial data: Year ended 12/31/2004.
Assets, $8,076,004 (M); Expenditures, $5,417,513; Total giving, $471,786; Grants to individuals, totaling $471,786.
Fields of interest: Education; Physics.
Type of support: Scholarships—to individuals; Awards/prizes; Precollege support; Undergraduate support.
Application information: Application form required. Application form available on the grantmaker's Web site.
  Initial approach: Telephone.
  Additional information: See Web site for additional scholarship and awards information.
Program descriptions:
  Excellence in Pre-College Physics Teaching Award: An award of $3,000 is given in recognition of contributions to pre-college physics teaching. The AAPT member whose primary responsibility is teaching, is chosen to give a lecture at the AAPT Summer Meeting. A certificate and travel expenses to the meeting are also awarded. There are no self nominations.
  Excellence in Undergraduate Physics Teaching Award: This award recognizes significant contributions to undergraduate physics teaching by an AAPT member for whom teaching is a primary responsibility. Recipients present a lecture at the AAPT Summer Meeting and receive $3,000, travel expenses to the meeting, and a certificate. There are no self nominations.
  Paul Klopsteg Memorial Award: This $7,500 award is for recipients chosen to give a major lecture at the AAPT Summer Meeting on a topic of current significance suitable for nonspecialists. The award also includes travel expenses to the meeting, and a certificate.
  Robert A. Millikan Award: This $7,500 award recognizes teachers who have made notable and creative contributions to the teaching of physics. The recipient presents a lecture at the AAPT Summer Meeting. The award includes, an inscribed medal, travel expenses to the meeting, and a certificate.
  Oersted Award: This $10,000 award recognizes notable contributions to the teaching of physics. The recipient who need not be active in AAPT, presents an address at the Ceremonial Session of the AAPT Winter Meeting. Included in the award is, an inscribed medal, travel expenses to the meeting and a certificate.
  Melba Newell Phillips Award: A $7,500 award is given only occasionally to AAPT leaders who display a truly unique life of creative leadership, dedicated service, and exceptional contributions. The award also includes an inscribed medal, travel expenses to the meeting, and a certificate.
  Floyd K. Richtmyer Memorial Award: The recipient of this award presents a major address at the AAPT Winter Meeting on a topic of current significance suitable for nonspecialists. A $7,500 award, travel expenses to the meeting, and a certificate are presented.
  Barbara Lotze Scholarships: Two applicants will each receive a stipend of up to $2,000 to future high school physics teachers. Undergraduate students enrolled, or planning to enroll, in physics teacher preparation curricula and high school seniors entering such programs are eligible. The scholarship may be granted to an individual for each of years.
EIN: 520749775

5560
American Association of Plastic Surgeons

900 Cummings Ctr., Ste. 221-U
Beverly, MA 01915 (978) 927-8330
Contact: Paul N. Manson M.D., Pres.
FAX: (978) 524-8890; URL: http://www.aaps1921.org

Foundation type: Public charity
Limitations: Fellowships to individuals to pursue research in plastic surgery.
Financial data: Year ended 12/31/2003.
Assets, $2,037,816 (M); Expenditures, $297,610; Total giving, $62,000; Grants to individuals, 3 grants totaling $62,000 (high: $30,000, low: $2,000).
Fields of interest: Surgery research.
Type of support: Fellowships; Research.
Application information: Applications accepted. Application form required. Application form available on the grantmaker's Web site.
  Deadline(s): Dec. 1
Program description:
  John E. Hoopes Academic Scholar Program: Awards faculty research fellowships to surgeons entering academic careers in Plastic and Reconstructive Surgery. The award is to assist a surgeon in the establishment of a new and independent research program. Applicants should have demonstrated their potential to work as independent investigators. The fellowship award is $30,000 per year to provide salary and/or direct costs of the research. The applicant must submit a research plan and budget for the two-year period of the fellowship, even though Association approval is required for the second year. A minimum of 50% of the fellow's time will be spent in the research proposed in the application. Institutional support for this level of commitment must be evident in the supporting letters.
EIN: 946118700

5561
American Association of University Women Educational Foundation

1111 16th St. N.W.
Washington, DC 20036-4873 (202) 728-7602
Contact: Mary Ellen Smyth, Pres.
FAX: (202) 463-7169;
E-mail: foundation@aauw.org; Additional tel.: (319) 337-1716; URL: http://www.aauw.org/

Foundation type: Public charity
Limitations: Fellowships and grants to women for educational, project, and professional support, as well as for post-baccalaureate study or research in the U.S. Some awards allow for study in a country other than the applicant's own.
Publications: Annual report; Informational brochure (Including application guidelines).
Financial data: Year ended 06/30/2003.
Assets, $112,453,156 (M); Expenditures, $9,143,779; Total giving, $3,284,161; Grants to individuals, totaling $3,284,161 (high: $35,000).
Fields of interest: Elementary/secondary education; Elementary/secondary school reform; Civil rights, women; Mathematics; Engineering/technology; Science; Women's studies; Women; Girls.
Type of support: Program development; Seed money; Fellowships; Foreign applicants; Graduate support; Postgraduate support; Doctoral support.
Application information: Application form required.
  Initial approach: Telephone or e-mail.
  Deadline(s): Varies

Program descriptions:

American Fellowships: Support to women doctoral candidates completing dissertations or scholars seeking funds for post-doctoral research leave from accredited institutions. Applicants must be U.S. citizens or permanent residents. Candidates are evaluated on the basis of scholarly excellence, teaching experience, and active commitment to helping women and girls through service in their communities, professions, or other fields of research. The program offers three awards:

- Postdoctoral Research Leave Fellowships of $30,000. Deadline Nov. 15
- Dissertation Fellowships of $20,000. Deadline July 1
- Summer/Short-Term Research Publication Grants of $6,000. Deadline Nov. 15.

Career Development Grants: Grants ranging from $2,000 to $8,000 each are available to women who are in the early stages of their graduate study, in preparation for a change in career, to re-enter the work force, or advance their current careers. Applicants must be U.S. citizens or permanent residents who have earned a bachelor's degree, are enrolled in courses which are prerequisites for professional employment plans, and who are pursuing course work at an accredited two- or four-year college, university, or technical school. Deadline Dec. 15. Professional Development Institute Grants: These grants are also available under this program. The grants support women's participation in professional institutes that are academically based and have a focused program of study, a fixed schedule and short-term duration, and a selection process based on specified eligibility criteria. All above requirements for Career Development Grants also apply.

Community Action Grants: Two-year seed money grants of $5,000 to $10,000 are available to programs or nondegree research projects that promote education and equity for women and girls. Projects must focus on girls' achievement in math, science, or technology. Applicants must be women who are U.S. citizens or permanent residents with projects that will have direct public impact, be nonpartisan, and take place within the U.S. or its territories. Individuals may only submit one grant application per funding cycle; however, applicants may apply up to two times with the same project. Funds may support project-related expenses such as office and mailing costs, promotional materials, honoraria, and transportation. Funds cannot cover salaries/stipends for project directors, or regular, ongoing overhead costs for any organization. Deadline Jan. 15.

International Fellowships: These fellowships are only available for full-time study or research to women who are not U.S. citizens or permanent residents, and who have earned the equivalent of a U.S. bachelor's degree before Dec. 31. Both graduate and postgraduate study at accredited institutions are supported. Master's/First Professional Fellowships are $18,000, Doctorate Fellowships are $20,000, and Postdoctoral Fellowships are $30,000. Recipients are chosen on the basis of outstanding academic ability, professional potential, and importance of their studies to women and girls in their country of origin. Preference is given to women who have shown prior commitment to the advancement of women and girls through civic, community, or professional work. Recipients of six of the awards, jointly sponsored by the International Federation of University Women, may study in any country except their own.

Eleanor Roosevelt Teacher Fellowships: Full-time K-12 women teachers who are U.S. citizens or permanent residents may apply for these fellowships of up to $5,000 each. Fellowships are designed to promote gender equity in K-12 public schools and offer professional development support to individual teachers and teammates if applicable. All or part of the applicant's teaching assignments must be in math, science, or technology, (this includes elementary, special education, and gifted student education teachers). In addition, there must be a dedication to educational equity for girls and a commitment to teaching for three additional years, including the fellowship year. Successful applicants must attend a late July, five-day, all-expenses-paid teacher institute on gender equity and school reform issues. Limited technical assistance is available for proposal development. Deadline Jan. 10.

Selected Professions Fellowships: Fellowships range from $5,000 to $12,000 and are given to women in the following degree programs: architecture, computer/information sciences, engineering, and mathematics/statistics. Fellowships in the following degree programs are restricted to women of color: business administration (E.M.B.A., M.B.A.), law (J.D.), and medicine (M.D. or D.O.). Applicants must be entering the final year of study with two exceptions: women in an engineering master's program may apply for support for their first year and women in medical programs may apply for support for their third year. Applicants must be U.S. citizens or permanent residents, and special consideration is given to those who show professional promise in innovative or neglected areas of research and/or public interest concerns. Deadline Jan. 10 for Master's and First Professional Awards, and Nov. 20 for Engineering Dissertation Awards.

EIN: 526037388

5562
American College of Obstetricians and Gynecologists

(also known as A.C.O.G.)
409 12th St., S.W.
P.O. Box 96920
Washington, DC   20090-6920   (202) 638-5577
Contact: Ralph W. Hale M.D., Exec. V.P.
FAX: (202) 484-1595; E-mail: history@acog.org;
URL: http://www.acog.org

Foundation type: Public charity
Limitations: Fellowships to research the history of obstetrics and gynecology.
Financial data: Year ended 12/31/2004. Assets, $114,909,970 (M); Expenditures, $44,799,687; Total giving, $925,665.
Fields of interest: History/archaeology; Health sciences school/education; Reproductive health; Reproductive health, prenatal care; Women.
Type of support: Fellowships; Research; Postdoctoral support; Postgraduate support; Doctoral support.
Application information: Deadline Oct. 1; Completion of formal application required.
Program description:

ACOG-ORTHO Fellowship in the History of American Obstetrics and Gynecology: Awards one $5,000 fellowship each year. ACOG members and other qualified individuals are encouraged to apply. Recipients spend one month in the Washington, DC, area working full-time to complete their specific historical research project. Although the fellowships will be based in the ACOG History Library, the fellows are encouraged to use other national, historical and medical collections in the Washington, DC, area. The results of the research must be disseminated through either publication or presentation at a professional meeting.

EIN: 362217981

5563
American Council of Learned Societies

(also known as ACLS)
633 3rd Ave., Ste. 8C
New York, NY   10017-6795   (212) 697-1505
FAX: (212) 949-8058; E-mail: grants@acls.org;
URL: http://www.acls.org

Foundation type: Public charity
Limitations: Fellowships and grants to American and international scholars for advanced research and study in the humanities and social sciences.
Publications: Application guidelines; Annual report; Occasional report.
Financial data: Year ended 09/30/2004. Assets, $87,047,295 (M); Expenditures, $12,006,699; Total giving, $6,333,718.
Fields of interest: Arts, research; Architecture; Dance; Theater; Music; Humanities; Art history; History/archaeology; Language (foreign); Language/linguistics; Literature; Philosophy/ethics; Theology; Social sciences, research; Social sciences; Anthropology/sociology; Economics; Psychology/behavioral science; Political science; Law/international law; International studies; Religion, research.
Type of support: Fellowships; Research; Scholarships—to individuals; Awards/grants by nomination only; Foreign applicants; Postdoctoral support; Graduate support; Travel grants; Doctoral support; Stipends.
Application information: Applications accepted. Application form required.

Initial approach: Letter, FAX, or e-mail;.
Deadline(s): Varies

Program descriptions:

Dissertation Fellowships in East European Studies: Awards up to $17,000 to currently enrolled doctoral students for dissertations related to Albania, Bulgaria, the Czech Republic, Estonia, Hungary, Latvia, Lithuania, Poland, Romania, Slovakia, or the successor states of the former Yugoslavia.

East European Language Training Grants: Awards up to $2,500 to individuals for summer study of Albanian, Bosnian-Croatian-Serbian, Bulgarian, Czech, Estonia, Hungarian, Latvian, Lithuanian, Macedonian, Polish, Romanian, Slovak, or Slovene. Deadline Jan. 15.

Frederick Burkhardt Residential Fellowships for Recently Tenured Scholars: The fellowship is open to scholars engaged in long-term, unusually ambitious projects in the humanities and related social sciences. Appropriate fields of specialization include, but are not limited to, archaeology, anthropology, art history, economics, geography, history, language and literature, law, linguistics, musicology, philosophy, political science, psychology, religion, and sociology. Proposals in the social science fields listed above are eligible only if they employ predominantly humanistic approaches. Proposals in interdisciplinary and cross-disciplinary studies are welcome, as are proposals focused on any geographic region or any cultural or linguistic group. The ACLS will award approximately nine fellowships per year to recently tenured humanists at institutions in the U.S. and Canada. Each fellowship carries a stipend of $65,000.

ACLS Fellowships: These fellowships are available for full-time postdoctoral research in the humanities and social sciences lasting six to twelve consecutive months beginning between July and Feb. The program offers up to $50,000 for Full Professor and equivalent, $40,000 for Associate Professor and equivalent, and $30,000 for Assistant Professor and equivalent. Applicants must have received their Ph.D. at least two years prior to application, must be U.S. citizens or permanent legal residents, and may not be enrolled for any degree at the time of application. In addition, the applicant must not have received a supported research leave in less than five years prior to the beginning of this fellowship term. In some cases, established scholars without a Ph.D. may be eligible if they can establish the equivalent in professional experience and publications. Requests for applications to this program should include the following:

- highest academic degree held and date received
- country of citizenship or permanent legal residence
- academic or other position
- field of specialization
- proposed subject of research
- proposed date for beginning tenure of the award and duration requested
- specific ACLS program for which applicant is applying
- full name and mailing address.

ACLS/SSRC International Program:

- International Dissertation Field Research Fellowships: This program provides support for social scientists and humanists to conduct dissertation field research in all areas and regions of the world. It is open to full-time graduate students, regardless of citizenship, enrolled in doctoral programs in the U.S.
- International Predissertation Fellowship Program: This program is designed to encourage graduate students in the social sciences to specialize in areas of the developing world. It is available to students enrolled in Ph.D. programs in selected universities
- Abe Fellowship Program: The fellowships are designed to support Japanese and American scholars and research professionals who are conducting research in the social sciences and humanities relevant to matters of pressing worldwide concern, to problems common to advanced industrial societies, or to issues that relate to improving U.S.-Japan relations.

Henry Luce Foundation/ACLS Dissertation Fellowships in American Art: A stipend of $22,500 is awarded to U.S. citizens and permanent residents who will have met all requirements for the Ph.D. except the dissertation before beginning tenure of the award to support any phase of Ph.D. dissertation research or writing on any topic in the history of visual arts in the U.S. Stipends are given for one year only and may not be renewed. In addition, they may not be used for tuition costs. Students who will receive their Ph.D. degree from a department other than the art history department may be eligible if their principal dissertation advisors are in the department of art history. In all cases, the dissertation topic should be object-oriented. Application requests must contain the following:

- date all requirements for the Ph.D., except the dissertation were or will be completed
- department and institution that will grant the Ph.D. (If department is not art history, also give the name and department of principal dissertation advisor)
- topic of dissertation
- country of citizenship or permanent legal residence
- proposed date for beginning tenure of the award and duration requested
- specific program for which this request is made

- full name and mailing address

Deadline Nov. 10.

Contemplative Practice Fellowships: Under this program, approximately 10 fellowships of up to $20,000 each are offered to regular faculty members at U.S. academic institutions for the development of courses and teaching materials that explore contemplative practice from a variety of disciplinary and interdisciplinary perspectives over the summer. Applicants do not have to be U.S. citizens, and experience with contemplative practice is not a prerequisite. Acceptable disciplines include, but are not limited to, art, architecture, music, theater, dance, literature, philosophy, religious studies, history, and the humanistic social sciences. Of particular interest are imaginative teaching methodologies that include practical and experiential approaches to the subject matter. The inclusion of instruction in contemplative practice, either in or out of the classroom, is encouraged, though not required. Approval by the appropriate department head is required for all applicants. Recipients may be asked to share their experiences at future meetings and conferences. The fellowship stipend can be used for salary support and/or research expenses. Requests for applications must contain the following:

- academic position (rank, department, institution)
- field of specialization
- proposed subject of course/teaching materials to be developed
- highest academic degree held and date received
- country of citizenship or permanent legal residence
- proposed date for beginning tenure of the award and duration requested
- specific award program for which application is requested
- full name and mailing address.

Library of Congress Fellowships in International Studies: These are residential fellowships to support postdoctoral research in the humanities and social sciences using the foreign language collections at the Library of Congress. Approximately 10 fellowships will be available for four to nine months each, with a stipend of $3,000 per month.

National Program for Research in China: Research support including a monthly stipend and travel allowances is available to up to five U.S. citizens and permanent residents who are advanced graduate students or postdoctoral scholars in the humanities and social sciences for research in China. For graduate students, support is given for individuals enrolled in doctoral programs in social sciences or humanities to carry out 4 to 11 months of advanced study or dissertation research at Chinese universities or research institutes. Chinese language proficiency acquired through at least three years of college-level study or its equivalent is required. Applicants must demonstrate that they have fully utilized the available resources in the U.S. and are prepared by virtue of study and planning to take full advantage of an opportunity to do research in China. For postdoctoral scholars, support is given to individuals in the social sciences or humanities with the Ph.D. or equivalent to conduct in-depth research on China or the Chinese portion of a comparative study. Applicants must hold the Ph.D. degree by the application date. For all applicants, application requests must include the following:

- highest academic degree held and date received

- country of citizenship or permanent legal residence
- academic or other position
- field of specialization
- proposed subject of research
- proposed date for beginning tenure of the award and duration requested
- specific award program for which application is requested
- for graduate students only, include current level of graduate study, department and institution where enrolled, and where planned work would be conducted.

Fellowships for Postdoctoral Research in East European Studies: These fellowships of up to $25,000 each are offered to U.S. citizens and permanent legal residents for six to 12 consecutive months of full-time research in the social sciences and humanities relating to Albania, Bulgaria, the Czech Republic, Estonia, Hungary, Latvia, Lithuania, Poland, Romania, Slovakia, and the successor states of the former Yugoslavia. Proposals involving Albania, Bulgaria, Romania, and the former Yugoslavia are particularly encouraged. Research must begin between July and Sept. 1st after receiving the award. Support is intended for research taking place outside of East Europe, although short trips to the area may be proposed as part of a coherent program primarily undertaken elsewhere. Applicants must hold a Ph.D. degree by the time of application, or demonstrate the equivalent of the Ph.D. in publications and professional experience. Application requests must include the following:

- highest academic degree held and date received
- country of citizenship or permanent legal residence
- academic or other position
- field of specialization
- proposed subject of research
- proposed date for beginning tenure of the award and date requested
- specific award program for which application is requested
- for scholars who do not hold the Ph.D., current level of graduate study, department and institution where they are enrolled, and where the planned work will be conducted
- full name and mailing address

Deadline Nov. 3.

Chinese Fellowships for Scholarly Development: These fellowships are given to Chinese scholars in social sciences and humanities with the M.A., Ph.D., or equivalent from a Chinese institution to carry out one semester or one year of individual or collaborative research at the invitation of a U.S. host scholar. Candidates must be nominated by the U.S. host. Scholars who have previously visited the U.S. for five months or more, or who are enrolled in degree programs are not eligible. The postdoctoral fellowships provide for a modest living allowance, health insurance, and international airfare. The graduate fellowships offer a stipend to support the scholars' living expenses.

EIN: 131851145

5564
American Councils for International Education

1776 Massachusetts Ave., N.W., Ste. 700
Washington, DC 20036 (202) 833-7522
E-mail: general@actr.org; FAX: (202) 833-7523;
E-mail: general@americancouncils.org;
URL: http://www.americancouncils.org

Foundation type: Public charity

Limitations: Awards to teachers from the regions of the former Soviet Union.
Financial data: Year ended 06/30/2003. Assets, $6,855,858 (M); Expenditures, $49,447,769; Total giving $178,210; Grants to individuals, totaling $178,210.
Fields of interest: Humanities; Education, research; Elementary/secondary education; Social sciences, public education.
Type of support: Program development; Conferences/seminars; Foreign applicants; Awards/prizes; Travel grants.
Application information: Application form required.
Deadline(s): Vary
Additional information: See Web site for programs and application guidelines.
Program descriptions:
U.S.-NIS Awards for Excellence in Teaching Program: This program allows award-winning U.S. teachers to improve the quality of secondary schools in the New Independent States (NIS) of the former Soviet Union, to create learning partnerships between U.S. and NIS schools. U.S. middle school and high school teachers of humanities, social studies or language arts who have been recognized for excellence in teaching at the local, state or national level in the past year are welcome to apply.

Partners in Education: This program brings groups of approximately eight teachers and administrators from selected regions of Armenia, Azerbaijan, Georgia, Kyrgyzstan, Ukraine and Uzbekistan to school districts and universities in the U.S. Participants are assigned a host school and faculty mentor to learn about citizenship education in the U.S. and to observe and contribute to academic life at the host institutions. Upon their return to their home countries, participants are expected to provide a one- to two-week conference in civics curriculum development and evaluation. The program includes a reciprocal exchange that brings U.S. teachers to the schools of the participating NIS teachers for approximately two weeks.
EIN: 521067256

5565
American Dental Education Association
1400 K St., NW, Ste. 1100
Washington, DC 20005 (202) 289-7201
Contact: Richard Valachovic D.M.D., M.P.H., Exec. Dir.
FAX: (202) 289-7204;
E-mail: ValachovicR@adea.org; URL: http://www.adea.org

Foundation type: Public charity
Limitations: Grants to dental hygiene professionals, scholars, and administrators for advanced research. Also, scholarships by nomination only to predoctoral dental hygiene students.
Financial data: Year ended 06/30/2004. Assets, $7,887,996 (M); Expenditures, $10,798,192; Total giving, $1,735,838; Grants to individuals, 25 grants totaling $61,630 (high: $12,730, low: $250).
Fields of interest: Dental school/education; Dental care; Women.
Type of support: Fellowships; Research; Awards/grants by nomination only; Awards/prizes; Graduate support; Undergraduate support.
Application information: Application form required.
Deadline(s): Vary
Additional information: See Web site for further application and program information.

Program descriptions:
Professional Programs: The Association administers the following programs:
- Allied Dental Educators Fellowship
- Harry W. Bruce, Jr., Legislative Fellowship
- Crest Dental Hygiene Teaching Excellence Awards
- Dental Hygiene Development Grant
- Excellence in Teaching Award
- William J. Gies Foundation Educational Fellowship
- Higher Education Legislative Fellowship
- Junior Faculty Award
- Enid A. Neidle Scholar-in-Residence Program for Women.
ADEA/Listerine Preventive Dentistry Scholarships: Awards 12 $2,500 to predoctoral dental students who demonstrate academic excellence and who are members of the American Dental Education Association.
EIN: 911993281

5566
American Dental Hygienist Association Institute for Oral Health
444 N. Michigan Ave., Ste. 3400
Chicago, IL 60611 (312) 440-8900
Contact: Ann Battrell RDH, MSDH(c), Exec. Dir.
E-mail: institute@adha.net; Additional tel: (800) 243-2432; URL: http://www.adha.org/institute

Foundation type: Public charity
Limitations: Fellowships and research grants to individuals for excellence in dental hygiene.
Financial data: Year ended 06/30/2004. Assets, $879,516 (M); Expenditures, $242,490; Total giving, $94,631; Grants to individuals, 73 grants totaling $94,631.
Fields of interest: Dental school/education; Dental care; Human services.
Type of support: Program development; Research; Graduate support; Doctoral support.
Application information: Applications accepted. Application form required.
Deadline(s): Vary
Applicants should submit the following:
1) Transcripts
2) Letter(s) of recommendation
3) Curriculum vitae
Additional information: See Web site for further application information.
Program descriptions:
ADHA Institute Research Grant: Awards up to $10,000 to licensed dental hygienists and up to $5,000 to dental hygiene students for projects that advance public knowledge of dental hygiene and oral healthcare, and promote excellence in the field. Deadline Jan. 30.
Rosie Wall RDH Community Spirit Grant: Awards approximately $1,000 to licensed dental hygienists and dental hygiene students who integrate dental hygiene and community involvement. Deadline Feb. 28.
John C. Thiel Faculty Research Fellowship: Two fellowships of up to $5,000 each to faculty members pursuing either a Master's of science degree in dental hygiene education or related doctoral work. Applicants must be faculty at an accredited dental program in the U.S., licensed to practice dental hygiene and members of the American Dental Hygienist's Association. Deadline June 30.
EIN: 363468143

5567
American Diabetes Association
1701 N. Beauregard St.
Alexandria, VA 22311 (703) 549-1500
Contact: Caroline Stevens
FAX: (703) 549-1715;
E-mail: research@diabetes.org; Additional tel.: (800) 342-2383; URL: http://www.diabetes.org

Foundation type: Public charity
Limitations: Awards and fellowships for research on diabetes.
Publications: Application guidelines; Annual report; Corporate giving report; Financial statement; Informational brochure; Newsletter; Occasional report; Program policy statement.
Financial data: Year ended 06/30/2003. Assets, $106,866,844 (M); Expenditures, $183,641,147; Total giving, $26,710,635; Grants to individuals, 28 grants totaling $26,710,635.
Fields of interest: Eye research; Diabetes research.
Type of support: Professorships; Research; Awards/prizes; Postdoctoral support; Doctoral support.
Application information: Applications accepted. Application form required. Application form available on the grantmaker's Web site.
Initial approach: Website.
Deadline(s): Jan. 15 and July 15
Additional information: All applications require online electronic submission.
Program descriptions:
Junior Faculty Awards: Supports new investigators. Applicants must have a position at a university or other nonprofit research institution. The award provides $120,000 per year for three years. An additional 15 percent may be used for indirect costs.
Career Development Awards: Supports investigators establishing independent research careers. Applicants must hold an assistant professor or justified equivalent academic position within his/her institution. The award provides up to $150,000 per year for five years to be divided between salary and other grant support. An additional 15 percent may be used for indirect costs.
Clinical Research Awards: Supports investigators whose studies directly involve humans. Studies must focus on intact human subjects in which the effect of a change in the individual's external or internal environment is evaluated. Provides up to $100,000 per year for three years for the purchase of equipment, supplies, or technician salary support (up to $20,000 may be used for the investigator's salary). Up to 15 percent may be used for indirect costs.
Lions SightFirst Diabetic Retinopathy Research Awards: Supports clinical or applied research in diabetic retinopathy in the U.S. and abroad. Awards will be given to support new treatment regimens, epidemiology, and translation research. In addition, training and equipment grants will be considered.
Medical Scholars Program Awards and Physician-Scientist Training Awards: Provides one year of research support to students in medical school; the Physician-Scientist Award provides three years of support for the doctoral portion of an M.D./Ph.D. degree. Medical Scholars: up to $30,000 for one year; $20,000 for the student's stipend, and up to $10,000 for laboratory costs. Physician-Scientist: up to $30,000 per year for three years; $20,000 for the student, and $10,000 for tuition or lab costs.
Mentor-Based Postdoctoral Fellowships: Supports postdoctoral fellows working with established diabetes investigators. The investigator must meet citizenship and employment eligibility

requirements. The fellow must have an M.D. and Ph.D. degree, no more than three years of postdoctoral research experience, and cannot serve an internship or residency during the award period. Provides up to $45,000 per year for four years.

Research Awards: Provides grant support to both new and established investigators. Applications will be considered in any area that is relevant to the etiology or pathophysiology of diabetes and its complications. Funding of $20,000 to $100,000 per year for up to three years for the purchase of equipment, supplies, and salary for technical assistance; up to $20,000 may be used for the investigator's salary. Up to 15 percent may be used for indirect costs.
EIN: 131623888

5568

American Federation for Aging Research, Inc.

(also known as AFAR)
70 W. 40th St., 11th Fl.
New York, NY 10018 (212) 703-9977
Contact: Stephanie Lederman, Exec. Dir.; For Research: Odette van der Willik
E-mail address for GTI contact: grants@afar.org
FAX: (212) 977-0330; E-mail: info@afar.org;
URL: http://www.AFAR.org

Foundation type: Public charity
Limitations: Fellowships, scholarships and research grants for the study of aging.
Publications: Application guidelines; Annual report; Grants list; Informational brochure; Newsletter.
Financial data: Year ended 12/31/2004.
Assets, $28,134,998 (M); Expenditures, $7,856,999; Total giving, $6,079,950; Grants to individuals, 105 grants totaling $6,079,950.
Fields of interest: Geriatrics research.
Type of support: Research; Postdoctoral support; Graduate support; Undergraduate support; Stipends.
Application information: Application form required. Application form available on the grantmaker's Web site.
Initial approach: Letter of intent.
Deadline(s): Vary
Applicants should submit the following:
1) Proposal
2) Letter(s) of recommendation
3) GPA
4) Essay
5) Curriculum vitae
6) Budget Information
Additional information: See Web site for all deadlines and application details.
Program descriptions:
AFAR-Research Grants: Provides up to $60,000 for a one- to two-year award to junior faculty (M.D.s and Ph.D.s) to do research that will serve as the basis for longer-term research efforts. Investigators study a broad range of biomedical and clinical topics. Deadline Dec. 15.
Ellison Medical Foundation/AFAR Senior Postdoctoral Research Program: Provides up to three fellowships of $100,000 each to postdoctoral fellows (M.D.s and Ph.D.s) to encourage and further their careers in the fundamental mechanisms of aging. Fellows with at least three and no more than 5 years of prior postdoctoral training are eligible. Deadline Dec. 15.
AFAR Medical Student Summer Research Training in Aging Program: Awards short-term scholarships that provide an opportunity for students to train at an acclaimed center of excellence in geriatrics.

Beeson Career Development Award: The award is aimed at bolstering the current and severe shortage of academic physicians who have the combination of medical, academic and scientific training relative to caring for older people.
Glenn/AFAR Breakthroughs in Gerontology Awards: Support to a small number of pilot research programs that may be relatively high risk but which offer significant promise of yielding transforming discoveries in the fundamental biology of aging. The hope is that one or more of the funded projects will lead to major new insights into the molecular factors that coordinate aging in multiple cells and tissues, as well as the ways in which the aging process is differentially timed in long-lived species. To be eligible, applicants must be full-time faculty members at the rank of assistant professor or higher at the time they submit their proposal. Applications from individuals not previously engaged in aging research are particularly encouraged, as long as the research proposal shows high promise for leading to important new discoveries in biological gerontology. The proposed research must be conducted at any type of not-for-profit setting in the United States. Four one-year awards for $125,000. Awardees may be eligible to apply, on a competitive basis, for a second year of funding at the same level in subsequent years.
EIN: 133045282

5569

American Floral Endowment

P.O. Box 945
Edwardsville, IL 62025 (618) 692-0045
Contact: Sten Crissey, Secy.-Treas.
FAX: (618) 692-4045; E-mail: afe@endowment.org;
URL: http://www.endowment.org

Foundation type: Public charity
Limitations: Sabbatical leave grants for persons in research, extension, or teaching to leave the home university for professional development.
Publications: Application guidelines; Annual report; Informational brochure; Newsletter.
Financial data: Year ended 06/30/2004.
Assets, $10,850,210 (M); Expenditures, $1,048,324; Total giving, $677,828; Grants to individuals, 19 grants totaling $428,828 (high: $314,432, low: $400).
Fields of interest: Horticulture/garden clubs.
Type of support: Professorships; Research.
Application information: Completion of formal application required; Application must be submitted 12 to 24 months before sabbatical.
Program description:
American Floral Endowment Program: An award of $7,500 is available. Foreign sabbaticals are encouraged and given preference.
EIN: 236268380

5570

American Foundation for Pharmaceutical Education

1 Church St., Ste. 202
Rockville, MD 20850 (301) 738-2160
Contact: Robert Bachman, Pres. and Secy.
FAX: (301) 738-2161; E-mail: info@afpenet.org;
URL: http://www.afpenet.org

Foundation type: Public charity
Limitations: Fellowships and research grants for pharmaceutical studies.
Financial data: Year ended 12/31/2003.
Assets, $9,180,644 (M); Expenditures,

$1,204,218; Total giving, $748,451; Grants to individuals, 89 grants totaling $545,451 (high: $7,500, low: $3,000).
Fields of interest: Health sciences school/education; Pharmacy/prescriptions.
Type of support: Program development; Fellowships; Scholarships—to individuals.
Application information: Application form required.
Initial approach: Letter or telephone.
Additional information: Contact foundation for current application deadline.
Program descriptions:
Clinical Post-Pharm.D. Fellowships in the Biomedical Research Sciences: Awards $27,500 fellowships to Pharm.D. level clinical pharmacists.
Merck Research Scholar Program: Provides awards of $5,500 to students in a professional pharmacy degree program.
New Investigator Program for Pharmacy Faculty: Provides up to $10,000 to new faculty members to assist in establishing a research program.
EIN: 530214882

5571

American Foundation for Suicide Prevention

120 Wall St., 22nd Fl.
New York, NY 10005 (212) 363-3500
Contact: Robert Gebbia, Exec. Dir.
FAX: (212) 363-6237; E-mail: inquiry@afsp.org;
URL: http://www.afsp.org

Foundation type: Public charity
Limitations: Grants to investigators for suicide research.
Financial data: Year ended 06/30/2003.
Assets, $4,678,578 (M); Expenditures, $2,564,600; Total giving, $568,573; Grants to individuals, 10 grants totaling $568,573 (high: $98,099, low: $15,000).
Fields of interest: Suicide; Psychology/behavioral science.
Type of support: Program development; Seed money; Fellowships; Research; Awards/prizes; Postdoctoral support; Doctoral support.
Application information: Application form required.
Initial approach: Telephone or e-mail.
Deadline(s): Dec. 16
Additional information: See Web site for additional information and application form.
Program descriptions:
Distinguished Researcher Awards: Awards up to $100,000 over two years to investigators at the level of associate professor or higher with a proven history of research in the area of suicide.
Pilot Grants: Awards up to $20,000 over one to two years which provides seed money for new projects and are awarded to individual investigators without regard to academic work or previous research experience with suicide. Deadline Apr. 15, Aug. 15, and Dec. 15.
Postdoctoral Research Fellowships: Awards to investigators who have received a Ph.D. degree within the preceding three years for full-time training projects and have not had more than three years of fellowship support. Fellows receive a progressive stipend of $42,000 in the first year and $46,000 in the second year plus an institutional allowance of $6,000 per year.
Standard Research Grants: Grants of up to $60,000 over two years awarded to individual investigators for suicide research.
Young Investigator Award: Awards of up to $35,000 per year for a two-year period including the mentor fee of $5,000 (total of $70,000) are

awarded to investigators at the level of Assistant Professor or lower.
EIN: 133393329

5572
American Foundation for Urologic Disease, Inc

(also known as AFUD)
1000 Corporate Blvd.
Linthicum, MD 21090 (410) 689-3700
FAX: (410) 689-3800;
E-mail: auafoundation@auafoundation.org; Toll-free tel. (U.S. only): (866) 746-4282; URL: http://www.afud.org/auafhome.asp

Foundation type: Public charity
Limitations: Research grants for the prevention and cure of urologic disease.
Financial data: Year ended 12/31/2004. Assets, $6,039,310 (M); Expenditures, $3,125,353; Total giving, $822,500; Grants to individuals, totaling $822,500.
Fields of interest: Medical research.
Type of support: Research.
Application information: Applications accepted. Application form required. Application form available on the grantmaker's Web site.
Initial approach: Telephone or e-mail.
Deadline(s): Sept. 1
Program description:
A.F.U.D./AUA Research Scholar Program: Research grants to researchers in the U.S. and Canada studying urologic diseases affecting men, women and children.
EIN: 133396506

5573
American Geriatric Society, Inc.

350 5th Ave., Ste. 801
New York, NY 10118 (212) 308-1414
Contact: Meghan Gerety M.D., Pres.
FAX: (212) 832-8646;
E-mail: info@americangeriatrics.org; URL: http://www.americangeriatrics.org

Foundation type: Public charity
Limitations: Development awards by nomination only to young faculty in certain specialties within geriatrics.
Publications: Annual report; Financial statement; Newsletter.
Financial data: Year ended 12/31/2003. Assets, $3,647,884 (M); Expenditures, $7,673,087; Total giving, $15,735.
Fields of interest: Surgery; Anesthesiology research; Geriatrics research; Medical research; Orthopedics research.
Type of support: Program development; Conferences/seminars; Publication; Research; Awards/grants by nomination only; Awards/prizes.
Application information: Applications accepted. Application form required. Application form available on the grantmaker's Web site.
Initial approach: Letter, telephone, FAX or e-mail.
Deadline(s): Dec. 7
Additional information: See Web site for application.
Program descriptions:
Dennis W. Jahnigen Career Development Scholars Award Program: The two-year awards are designed to support young faculty in the specialties of anesthesiology, emergency medicine, general surgery, gynecology, ophthalmology, orthopaedic surgery, otolaryngology, physical medicine and rehabilitation, thoracic surgery, and urology, and

are intended to enable individuals in those specialties to initiate and sustain a career in their discipline. To that end, each award will provide $75,000 per year for salary and fringe benefits. The scholar's institution must provide $25,000 per year to support the costs of doing such research. Nominations for the awards are made by the individual's department chair. Departments may submit one application, while institutions may submit more than one application.
T. Franklin Williams Scholars Award: This program for is aimed at academic geriatricians who are conducting research on older patients that has applicability to the care provided by sub-specialists of internal medicine. The award provides $75,000 in project support over two years ($37,500/year) for a junior faculty member who is devoting 75% of his/her time to research. The award must be matched by support (either from the applicant's home institution or a grant-making agency) that provides for 75% protected time for research. For addition information, contact sreinthaler@americangeriatrics.org.
EIN: 131950856

5574
The American Head and Neck Society, Inc.

11300 W. Olympic Blvd., Ste. 600
Los Angeles, CA 90064 (310) 437-0559
Contact: John J. Coleman M.D., Pres.
FAX: (310) 437-0585; E-mail: admin@ahns.info;
URL: http://www.headandneckcancer.org

Foundation type: Public charity
Limitations: Research grants to individuals for the study of head and neck cancer.
Publications: Application guidelines.
Financial data: Year ended 12/31/2004. Assets, $880,763 (M); Expenditures, $901,463; Total giving, $73,651.
Fields of interest: Cancer research.
Type of support: Research.
Application information: Applications accepted. Application form required. Application form available on the grantmaker's Web site.
Deadline(s): Vary
Additional information: The complete listing of programs, as well as application guidelines, are available on the foundation's Web site.
Program descriptions:
AHNS-ACS Career Development Award: A two-year faculty career development award to head and neck surgeons. Must be a member or candidate member of ACS and AHNS. Must be within 5 years of completion of training, and be full-time faculty member. The award is to support clinical, basic science, or translational research in the study of neoplastic disease of the head and neck. The award is $40,000 per year for two years to support the research and is not renewable thereafter.
Ballantyne Resident Research Grant: Awards for best grant application by a resident utilizing the same forms and guidelines as the pilot grant. One year, non-renewable, $10,000 maximum total costs. One award available per year.
Pilot Research Grant: Open for residents, fellows, junior faculty for pilot research in head and neck related topics. One year, non-renewable, $10,000 maximum total costs. One award available per year.
Surgeon Scientist Career Development Award (with AAOHNS): Open to surgeons beginning a clinician-scientist career track to support research in the pathogenesis, pathophysiology, diagnosis, prevention, or treatment of head and neck neoplastic disease. Two year, nonrenewable

$70,000 maximum total costs ($35,000 per year). One award available per year.
Synthes Request for Applications - Head and Neck Reconstruction: Open to medical students, residents, fellows, and fulltime faculty at rank of Assistant Professor to conduct research related to reconstruction following ablative cancer surgery. One year with competitive renewal for a second year. $15,000 maximum total costs per year. One award available.
Young Investigator Award (with AAOHNS): Open to fellows and assistant professors. Must be AHNS member (may be candidate member). To support research in neoplastic disease of the head and neck. Up to two years, $10,000 per year. One award available per year.
EIN: 237323559

5575
American Health Assistance Foundation

22512 Gateway Center Dr.
Clarksburg, MD 20871 (301) 948-3244
Contact: Brian K. Regan Ph.D., Pres.
FAX: (301) 258-9454; E-mail: jwilson@ahaf.org;
Additional tel.: (800) 437-2423; URL: http://www.ahaf.org

Foundation type: Public charity
Limitations: Research grants for study of Alzheimer's disease, glaucoma, macular degeneration, heart disease and stroke.
Financial data: Year ended 03/31/2005. Assets, $36,706,118 (M); Expenditures, $30,106,080; Total giving, $6,017,789; Grants to individuals, totaling $5,117,789.
Fields of interest: Eye research; Heart & circulatory research; Alzheimer's disease research; Medical research.
Type of support: Research.
Application information: Applications accepted. Application form required.
Initial approach: E-mail.
Deadline(s): Vary
Program descriptions:
National Heart Foundation Starters Grants: Research grants of up to $25,000 for one year to assist young investigators who are beginning independent research careers at the assistant professor level. Recipients are evaluated on their potential to improve the understanding and therapy of the disease process in stroke or cardiovascular disease. Deadline Nov. 4.
Macular Degeneration Research: Grants for research into the cause(s) of and treatment(s) for macular degeneration. A maximum of $50,000 for one year of funding. Letter of Intent deadline July 16.
Alzheimer's Disease Research: Awards are given in two categories. Standard Awards have a maximum of $100,000 per year for up to two years, renewable on a competitive basis. Pilot Project Awards have a maximum of $50,000 per year for up to two years, and are especially geared toward junior scientists and established investigators who are new to the Alzheimer's field. Deadline Oct. 15.
National Glaucoma Research: Supports basic research into the causes and potential treatments of glaucoma. Grants are awarded for up to two years, for up to $35,000 per year, and may be renewed through the competitive review process. Deadline Nov. 18.
EIN: 237337229

5576
American Institute for Cancer Research
1759 R St., N.W.
Washington, DC 20009 (202) 328-7744
Contact: Helen Norman, Assoc. Dir., Research
FAX: (202) 328-7226; *E-mail:* research@aicr.org;
Additional tel.: (800) 843-8114; *URL:* http://
www.aicr.org

Foundation type: Public charity
Limitations: Research grants to investigators for
the study of diet and nutrition in the prevention and
treatment of cancer.
Publications: Application guidelines; Annual report;
Financial statement; Grants list; Informational
brochure; Newsletter.
Financial data: Year ended 09/30/2003.
Assets, $17,092,918 (M); Expenditures,
$33,444,733; Total giving, $3,507,193; Grants to
individuals, totaling $3,507,193.
Fields of interest: Cancer research; Nutrition.
Type of support: Research; Postdoctoral support.
Application information: Deadlines Dec. 17 and
July 1; Completion of formal application required;
Only one grant application per Principal Investigator
per grant cycle is permitted.
Program descriptions:
Investigator-Initiated Grants (IIG): Provides
$75,000 per year for two years plus 10 percent of
indirect costs to the awardee. It encourages
research on the dietary and nutritional means of
preventing and treating cancer. Innovative rather
than confirmatory programs are sought. Relevant
applications that are within the scope fall in these
general categories: 1) dietary factors and
prevention of cancer; and 2) dietary factors and
treatment of cancer.
Matching Grants: These grants fund, in
coordination with industry or individuals, research
projects in the area of diet, nutrition, and cancer
prevention and treatment. These projects will be
within the interest of AICR and the private sponsor.
Application should follow the guidelines and
application procedure of Investigator-Initiated
Grants.
Post-Doctoral Grant Awards (PDA): Provides
$25,000 per year for two years plus 10 percent of
indirect costs to the awardee. Grants provide
beginning investigators with funds to support
innovative research on the prevention, etiology, and
treatment of cancer by dietary or nutritional
methods. Applications should propose relevant
feasibility studies to obtain data in support of a new
hypothesis that then could be expanded to increase
understanding of the role of dietary and nutritional
factors in the etiology, pathogenesis, prevention, or
treatment of cancer. The Principal Investigator must
have a Ph.D. or equivalent degree or M.D. degree
that was awarded no more than three years prior to
the date of application, and must hold an academic
appointment no higher than Assistant Professor.
The applicant must be sponsored by a professor in
whose laboratory the applicant is to perform the
research. A letter of support from this individual
must be included in the Appendix section of the
application.
EIN: 521238026

5577
American Institute of Indian Studies
1130 E. 59th St.
Chicago, IL 60637-1539 (773) 702-8638
Contact: Elise Auerbach, Admin.
E-mail: aiis@uchicago.edu; *URL:* http://
www.indiastudies.org

Foundation type: Public charity

Limitations: Fellowships to doctoral candidates
and scholars for study in India.
Publications: Application guidelines; Informational
brochure; Newsletter.
Financial data: Year ended 06/30/2003.
Assets, $5,285,732 (M); Expenditures,
$2,295,705.
Type of support: Fellowships; Doctoral support.
Application information: Application form required.
Deadline(s): July 1
Additional information: Application should
include $25 application fee.
Program descriptions:
Junior Research Fellowships: Available to
doctoral candidates at U.S. colleges and
universities in all fields of study. The fellowships are
specifically designed to enable doctoral candidates
to pursue their dissertation research in India.
Fellows establish formal affiliations with Indian
universities and Indian research supervisors.
Awards are available for up to 11 months.
Fellowships for four months or less have significant
restrictions. Fellowships for six months or more
may include limited coverage for dependents if
funds are available.
Senior Research Fellowships: Available to
scholars who hold a Ph.D. or its equivalent and are
either U.S. citizens or resident aliens teaching
full-time at U.S. colleges and universities. The
fellowships are designed to enable scholars
specializing in South Asian studies to pursue
further research in India. Fellows establish formal
affiliations with Indian institutions. Awards are
available for up to nine months. Fellowships for four
months or less have significant travel restrictions.
EIN: 236297039

5578
American Institute of Physics, Inc.
1 Physics Ellipse
College Park, MD 20740-3843 (301) 209-3165
Contact: Marc H. Brodsky, C.E.O. and Exec. Dir.
FAX: (301) 209-0882; *E-mail:* aipinfo@aip.org;
URL: http://www.aip.org/aip/writing

Foundation type: Public charity
Limitations: Science writing awards to scientists,
journalists and broadcast media professionals for
published works on physics and astronomy.
Publications: Annual report; Informational
brochure.
Financial data: Year ended 12/31/2003.
Assets, $128,234,352 (M); Expenditures,
$70,961,208; Total giving, $215,270; Grants to
individuals, totaling $215,270.
Fields of interest: Journalism/publishing;
Astronomy; Physics.
Type of support: Awards/prizes.
Application information: Application form required.
Deadline(s): Mar. 31
Program description:
Science Reading Award: Awards of $3,000, plus
an engraved Windsor Chair and a certificate of
recognition to authors for exemplary writing in
Physics and Astronomy. Entries must be available
to, and intended for, the general public.
EIN: 131667053

5579
American Library Association
50 E. Huron St.
Chicago, IL 60611-2795 (800) 545-2433
Contact: Michael Gorman, Pres.
FAX: (312) 944-9374; *E-mail:* ala@ala.org; *TDD:*
(888) 814-7692; *URL:* http://www.ala.org

Foundation type: Public charity
Limitations: Awards to librarians, authors, and
other individuals for contributions to libraries and
librarianship. Also, research grants for the study of
library-related topics, and travel grants to attend
ALA's Annual Conference.
Financial data: Year ended 08/31/2004.
Assets, $50,503,470 (M); Expenditures,
$42,296,023; Total giving, $623,561; Grants to
individuals, 73 grants totaling $256,069 (high:
$5,000, low: $2,000).
Fields of interest: Libraries/library science.
Type of support: Research; Awards/grants by
nomination only; Awards/prizes; Travel grants.
Application information: Applications accepted.
Application form required.
Deadline(s): Varies
Program descriptions:
Awards Program: All awards carry the cash award
mentioned plus a 24K gold-framed citation.
 · Beta Phi Mu: $500 to a library school
   faculty member or to an individual for
   distinguished service to education in
   librarianship
 · William Young Boyd Literary Novel Award:
   $5,000 to an author for a military novel that
   honors service of American veterans during
   a time of war (1861-1865, 1914-1918,
   1939-1945)
 · Melvil Dewey Medal: A Dewey Medal
   awarded to an individual or group for recent
   creative professional achievement in
   library management, training, cataloging
   and classification, and the tools and
   techniques of librarianship
 · Equality Award: $500 to an individual or
   group for outstanding contribution that
   promotes equality in the library profession
 · Elizabeth Futas Catalyst for Change Award:
   $1,000 to make positive changes in the
   profession of librarianship
 · Grolier Foundation Award: $1,000 to a
   librarian whose "unusual contribution" to
   the stimulation and guidance of reading by
   children and young people exemplifies
   outstanding achievement in the profession
 · Highsmith Library Literature Award: $500
   to the author and/or co-authors who make
   an outstanding contribution to library
   literature issued during the three previous
   years
 · Paul Howard Award for Courage: $1,000
   awarded every two years to a librarian,
   library board, library group or an individual
   who has exhibited unusual courage for the
   benefit of library programs or services
 · Joseph W. Lippincott Award: $1,000 to a
   librarian for distinguished service to the
   profession, to include outstanding
   participation in professional library
   activities, notable published professional
   writing, or other significant activities on
   behalf of the profession.
ALA Research Grants: ALA Research Grant:
Awards up to $25,000 to support problem-based
research for the library and information science
profession. Research proposals should address
one of the following questions:
 · In what ways do the services of libraries
   have a positive impact on the lives of
   users?
 · What is/should be the role of librarians in
   adding value to electronic information?
   Deadline Dec.15.
Carroll Preston Baber Research Grant: Awards up
to $7,500 for innovative research that could lead to
an improvement in library services to any specified
group(s) of people. Librarians or library educators

who are ALA members are eligible. Deadline Dec. 14.

Diana V. Braddom FRDRS Scholarship: Awards to librarians and/or staff members from all types of libraries who have had no previous formal development training and have a genuine need for fundraising skills. Applicants must be employed by libraries, including but not limited to public, academic, multi-type, school and special libraries. Deadline Jan. 2.

EBSCO/ALA Conference Sponsorship: Awards ten $1,000 travel grants to allow librarians who are ALA members to attend ALA's Annual Conference in Atlanta, GA. Applicants must not supervise another professional librarian, and application is by essay. Deadline Dec. 1.

Loleta D. Fyan Public Library Research Grant: Provides up to $10,000 for the development and improvement of public libraries and the services they provide. Deadline Dec. 10.
EIN: 362166947

5580

American Lung Association of California
424 Pendleton Way
Oakland, CA 94621   (510) 638-5864
Contact: Ben Abate Ph.D., Pres. and C.E.O.
FAX: (510) 638-8984;
E-mail: contact@californialung.org; URL: http://www.californialung.org

Foundation type: Public charity
Limitations: Research grants, scholarships and fellowships to investigators for the study of lung disease, primarily in CA.
Financial data: Year ended 06/30/2004. Assets, $15,499,788 (M); Expenditures, $6,184,758; Total giving, $755,450; Grants to individuals, totaling $755,450.
Fields of interest: Nursing school/education; Lung research.
Type of support: Research; Postdoctoral support; Graduate support; Doctoral support.
Application information: Application form required.
   Deadline(s): Vary
   Additional information: See Web site for additional information.
Program descriptions:
Clinical Research Grant: Awards up to $50,000 per year for up to two years to an investigator who holds a doctoral degree, has an entry-level rank (instructor or assistant professor) and has completed two years of postdoctoral research training.
Research Grants: Awards up to $50,000 for two years to applicants who hold an M.D., D.O., Ph.D., ScD., DNSc. or comparable qualifications and have completed a minimum of two years of research training. Grant supports young investigators during the transition from research training to independent research as junior faculty.
Research Training Fellowships: Awards up to $50,000 for one year to applicants who hold an M.D., Ph.D. or equivalent, and doctoral nursing candidates seeking further training as scientific investigators.
Scholarships: Awards one-year scholarships of $6,000 each to graduate students enrolled in a master's program in nursing. Recipients must be committed to developing a specialty in pulmonary nursing, acute and/or chronic care.
EIN: 940362650

5581

American Lung Association of Eastern Missouri
1118 Hampton Ave.
St. Louis, MO 63139-3196   (314) 645-5505
Contact: Patricia Williams, Exec. Asst.
FAX: (314) 645-7128;
E-mail: pwilliams@lungmo.org; URL: http://www.lungusa2.org/missouri/

Foundation type: Public charity
Limitations: Research grants for the study of lung diseases, MO.
Financial data: Year ended 06/30/2003. Assets, $2,521,521 (M); Expenditures, $2,930,496; Total giving, $199,600; Grants to individuals, 3 grants totaling $191,025.
Fields of interest: Lung research.
Type of support: Research.
Application information: Contact foundation for current application deadline/guidelines.
EIN: 430662525

5582

American Lung Association of North Carolina
3801 Lake Boone Tr., Ste. 190
Raleigh, NC 27607   (919) 832-8326
Contact: Deborah Bryan, Pres. and C.E.O.
FAX: (919) 856-8530; E-mail: info@lungnc.org; Additional tel.: (800) LUNGUSA; E-mail (for Deborah Bryan): dbryan@lungnc.org; URL: http://lungnc.org/

Foundation type: Public charity
Limitations: Research grants to investigators for the correction, alleviation and elimination of diseases related to or associated with the human lungs.
Publications: Application guidelines; Annual report; Informational brochure; Newsletter.
Financial data: Year ended 06/30/2005. Assets, $2,487,735 (M); Expenditures, $1,874,968; Total giving, $89,265; Grants to individuals, totaling $33,310.
Fields of interest: Asthma; Lung research.
Type of support: Seed money; Fellowships; Research.
Application information:
   Initial approach: E-mail.
   Additional information: Contact foundation for current application deadline/guidelines.
Program descriptions:
Asthma Camps: Three-week long residential camps for children 8-15 years old diagnosed with asthma. Day camp opportunities also available.
Medical Fellowship: Seed grants for beginning researchers through the North Carolina Thoracic Society.
EIN: 560547515

5583

American Lung Association of the City of New York, Inc.
432 Park Ave. S., 8th Fl.
New York, NY 10016   (212) 889-3370
Contact: Louise A. Vetter, C.E.O.
FAX: (212) 889-3375; E-mail: info@alany.org; URL: http://www.lungusa.org/newyork/

Foundation type: Public charity
Limitations: Research grants and awards for basic and applied research in lung function and lung disease, primarily in NY.

Financial data: Year ended 06/30/2003. Assets, $6,353,922 (M); Expenditures, $3,243,276; Total giving, $215,000; Grants to individuals, totaling $215,000.
Fields of interest: Lung research; Asthma research.
Type of support: Research; Awards/prizes.
Application information: Contact foundation for current application deadline/guidelines.
EIN: 135563004

5584

American Lung Association of Vermont
30 Farrell St.
South Burlington, VT 05403-6196
(802) 863-6817
Contact: Robert C. Uerz, Exec. Dir.
FAX: (802) 863-6818; E-mail: info@vtlung.org; URL: http://www.lungusa.org/vermont

Foundation type: Public charity
Limitations: Grants to scientists residing in VT for lung research.
Financial data: Year ended 06/30/2003. Assets, $1,403,887 (M); Expenditures, $1,005,295; Total giving, $176,028; Grants to individuals, 2 grants totaling $20,000 (high: $10,000, low: $10,000).
Fields of interest: Lung research.
Type of support: Research.
Application information: See Web site for current application deadline/guidelines; Completion of formal application required.
EIN: 030185023

5585

American Lung Association of Wisconsin, Inc.
13100 W. Lisbon Rd., Ste. 700
Brookfield, WI 53005-2508   (262) 703-4200
Contact: Margaret MacLeod Brahm, Pres.
FAX: (262) 781-5180;
E-mail: amlung@lungwisconsin.org; URL: http://www.lungusa.org/wisconsin

Foundation type: Public charity
Limitations: Grants to scientists for lung research.
Financial data: Year ended 06/30/2003. Assets, $2,973,384 (M); Expenditures, $2,757,776; Total giving, $199,933; Grant to an individual, 1 grant totaling $67,933.
Fields of interest: Lung diseases.
Type of support: Research.
Application information: Completion of formal application required; See Web site for current application information.
EIN: 390806305

5586

American Medical Association Foundation
515 N. State St.
Chicago, IL 60610   (312) 464-4543
Contact: Krishna K. Sawhney M.D., Pres.
URL: http://www.ama-assn.org

Foundation type: Public charity
Limitations: Scholarships and grants by nomination only to medical students.
Financial data: Year ended 12/31/2003. Assets, $19,257,376 (M); Expenditures, $2,498,473; Total giving, $641,851.
Fields of interest: Medical school/education.
Type of support: Research; Awards/grants by nomination only; Awards/prizes; Doctoral support.

Application information:
Deadline(s): Varies
Additional information: Completion of formal nomination required; See Web site for further nomination information and for nomination forms.

Program descriptions:
Johnson F. Hammond, M.D., Memorial Scholarship: Awards $3,000 to a medical student of high moral character and outstanding academic achievement. Deadline May 1.

Jerry L. Pettis Memorial Scholarship: Awards $2,500 to a junior or senior medical student with a demonstrated interest and involvement in science communication. Deadline Feb. 13.

Rocky Sleyster, M.D., Memorial Scholarship: Awards $2,5000 to up to twenty fourth-year medical students enrolled in U.S. or Canadian medical schools and specializing in psychiatry. Nominees must be U.S. citizens. Deadline May 1.

Research Seed Grants: Awards $1,500-$2,500 to individuals conducting research in arthritis, rheumatism, cardiovascular/pulmonary diseases, HIV/AIDS, neoplastic diseases, neurological diseases, and leukemia. Deadline Nov. 15.

Arthur N. Wilson, M.D. Scholarship: Awards $3,000 to a medical student who is a graduate of a southeastern AK high school.

Health Literacy Grants: Provides $500 to $4,000 for programs that promote clearer communication between patients and their physicians and other healthcare providers. The grants are awarded to four groups: medical students; residents and fellows; physicians, hospital staffs, and medical societies; and AMA Alliance groups and community organizations. Deadline June 18.

EIN: 366080517

5587
American Meteorological Society

45 Beacon St.
Boston, MA 02108-3693 (617) 227-2425
Contact: Keith L. Seitter, Exec. Dir.
FAX: (617) 742-8718;
E-mail: amsinfo@ametsoc.org; Additional address: 1120 G. St., N.W., Ste. 800, Washington, DC 20005, tel.: (202) 737-9006, FAX: (202) 737-9050; URL: http://www.ametsoc.org/ams

Foundation type: Public charity
Limitations: Fellowships to individuals to enable them to work as legislative assistants.
Publications: Application guidelines; Annual report; Financial statement; Grants list; Informational brochure; Newsletter; Program policy statement.
Financial data: Year ended 12/31/2004.
Assets, $14,675,733 (M); Expenditures, $13,806,696.
Fields of interest: Physical/earth sciences; Government/public administration.
Type of support: Fellowships.
Application information:
Initial approach: Telephone or e-mail.
Deadline(s): Mar. 1
Program description:
AMS Congressional Science Fellowship: Provides a stipend of $47,000 and up to $10,000 for moving, travel, and other expenses to spend a year working as a legislative assistant to contribute scientific expertise to a member of Congress or a congressional committee. Applicants must have a Ph.D. or equivalent in the atmospheric or related sciences, be a member of AMS, and a U.S. citizen.
EIN: 042103657

5588
American Nurses Foundation, Inc.

(formerly American Nurses Association Foundation)
8515 Georgia Ave., Ste 400W
Silver Spring, MD 20910 (301) 628-5227
Contact: Leo Schargorodski, Exec. Dir.
E-mail: anf@ana.org; URL: http://www.ana.org/anf

Foundation type: Public charity
Limitations: Grants to beginning and experienced registered nurse researchers with a bachelor's or higher degree for the development of nursing research.
Publications: Application guidelines; Annual report; Informational brochure; Newsletter.
Financial data: Year ended 12/31/2004.
Assets, $9,871,722 (M); Expenditures, $2,390,193; Total giving, $262,440; Grants to individuals, 20 grants totaling $142,130 (high: $25,000, low: $3,145).
Fields of interest: Health care, research; Nursing care.
Type of support: Research.
Application information: Deadline 1st Mon. in May; Completion of formal application required.
EIN: 131893924

5589
American Osteopathic Association

142 E. Ontario St.
Chicago, IL 60611-2864 (312) 202-8000
Contact: Elizabeth Freeman
FAX: (312) 202-8200;
E-mail: research@osteopathic.org; Additional tel.: (800) 621-1773; URL: http://do-online.osteotech.org/index.cfm

Foundation type: Public charity
Limitations: Fellowships and grants to U.S. residents for osteopathic medical research.
Publications: Application guidelines.
Financial data: Year ended 05/31/2003.
Assets, $47,152,660 (M); Expenditures, $25,328,764; Total giving, $457,429; Grants to individuals, 16 grants totaling $28,000 (high: $4,000, low: $250).
Fields of interest: Health organizations; Medical research, institute.
Type of support: Fellowships; Research.
Application information: Application form required.
Initial approach: Telephone.
Deadline(s): Feb. 15 for research fellowships, Dec. 1 for others
Program descriptions:
Clinical Investigator Development Award: This program seeks to recruit and support osteopathic physicians for research and teaching careers in the medical sciences. The Bureau of Research awards an amount of $50,000 per year for a three-year period.

Grant Programs: The bureau will review grant applications for studies with budgets generally between $25,000 and $50,000 per year. Research studies that address the efficacy and outcomes of osteopathic principles and practices (OPP) and osteopathic manipulative treatment (OMT) may be funded at a higher level.

Research Fellowships: Sponsored by the Bureau of Research, this program supports the research training of an applicant and enables him/her to conduct a basic science or clinical research project. Four or five fellowships of $5,000 each are awarded annually.
EIN: 362170786

5590
American Otological Society

(formerly Research Fund of the American Otological Society, Inc.)
2720 Tartan Way
Springfield, IL 62707
Contact: Shirley Gossard
E-mail: segossard@aol.com; Application address: c/o Jeffrey P. Harris, M.D., 200 W. Arbor Dr., San Diego, CA 92103; Tel./FAX: (217) 483-6966

Foundation type: Public charity
Limitations: Grants to U.S. and Canadian citizens for research in the fields of otosclerosis, Meniere's disease, and related ear disorders.
Publications: Application guidelines.
Financial data: Year ended 06/30/2004.
Assets, $7,815,375 (M); Expenditures, $436,504; Total giving, $229,264; Grants to individuals, totaling $229,264.
Fields of interest: Medical research, institute; Ear & throat research; Medical research; Disabilities, people with.
Type of support: Fellowships; Research.
Application information: Application form required.
Deadline(s): Jan. 31
Additional information: Application must include description of research plan, researcher's background, and description of laboratory space and facilities.
Program descriptions:
Research Training Fellowships: Awards only to physicians, including residents and medical students. The fellowships support one to two years of full-time research conducted outside of residency training. Applications for fellowships must include documentation from the sponsoring institution stating that facilities and faculty are appropriate for requested research.

Research Grant Awards: Grants of $40,000 are available to physicians and nonphysician investigators and are renewable annually. Funding for investigator's salary is not offered.
EIN: 136131376

5591
American Parkinson's Disease Association

135 Parkinson Ave.
Staten Island, NY 10305-1946
(718) 981-8001
Contact: Paul Maestrone, Dir. of Scientific and Medical Affairs
FAX: (718) 981-4399; Additional tel.: (800) 223-2732; URL: http://www.apdaparkinson.org

Foundation type: Public charity
Limitations: Research grants and fellowships to doctors, medical students, and new investigators for the study of Parkinson's disease.
Publications: Application guidelines; Annual report; Grants list; Informational brochure; Newsletter.
Financial data: Year ended 08/31/2004.
Assets, $11,519,792 (M); Expenditures, $3,415,881; Total giving, $3,415,881; Grants to individuals, totaling $3,415,881.
Fields of interest: Nerve, muscle & bone research.
Type of support: Fellowships; Research.
Application information: Applications accepted. Application form required. Application form available on the grantmaker's Web site.
Initial approach: Telephone.
Copies of proposal: 3
Deadline(s): Mar. 1
Program description:
Fellowships:

- George C. Cotzias Memorial Fellowships: One or more three-year fellowships of $240,000 can be awarded each year to a medical doctor working on Parkinson's disease
- Medical Students Summer Fellowships: Provides stipends to enable medical students to perform active supervised laboratory or clinical research designed to clarify the understanding of Parkinson's disease, its nature, manifestations, etiology, or treatment
- Research Grants: One-year grants of $50,000 and more are awarded to investigators at the beginning of their scientific career to stimulate interest in Parkinson's disease research.

EIN: 131962771

5592

American Pharmacists Association Foundation

(also known as The APhA Foundation)
2215 Constitution Ave., N.W.
Washington, DC 20037-2985 (202) 429-7565
Contact: William Ellis, C.E.O. and Exec. Dir.
FAX: (202) 429-6300;
E-mail: info@aphafoundation.org; URL: http://www.aphafoundation.org

Foundation type: Public charity
Limitations: Grants and awards to practitioners in any pharmacy setting.
Publications: Annual report; Newsletter.
Financial data: Year ended 12/31/2003.
Assets, $6,782,938 (M); Expenditures, $1,366,684; Total giving, $37,750; Grants to individuals, 27 grants totaling $35,750 (high: $10,000, low: $500).
Fields of interest: Pharmacy/prescriptions; Medical research, institute.
Type of support: Program development; Research.
Application information: Applications accepted.
  Copies of proposal: 1
  Deadline(s): None
  Additional information: Applications by proposal.
Program description:
  Incentive Grants for Practitioner Innovation in Pharmaceutical Care: These grants of $1,000 each are awarded annually to help practitioners in any pharmacy setting try out novel approaches and services that enhance patient care. Practitioners can apply for a grant by submitting a brief proposal describing their intended project.
EIN: 526039142

5593

American Philosophical Society

104 S. 5th St.
Philadelphia, PA 19106-3387
Contact: H. Linda Musumeci, Research Admin.
E-mail: Hlmusumeci@amphilsoc.org; URL: http://www.amphilsoc.org

Foundation type: Public charity
Limitations: Grants to individual scholars for research.
Publications: Application guidelines.
Financial data: Year ended 12/31/2003.
Assets, $120,819,960 (M); Expenditures, $7,770,793; Total giving, $1,337,500; Grants to individuals, totaling $1,337,500.
Fields of interest: Humanities; Language/linguistics; Philosophy/ethics; Medical research; Social sciences, research; Ethnic studies.

Type of support: Fellowships; Research; Postdoctoral support.
Application information:
  Initial approach: Letter or e-mail.
  Additional information: Proposed use of funds must be stated. See Web site for all information and updates which are made annually in May.
Program descriptions:
  Franklin Research Grants: Applicants are normally expected to have a doctorate. Grants are rarely made to persons who have held the doctorate less than a year, and never for pre-doctoral study or research. It is the Society's long-standing practice to encourage younger scholars. The committee will seldom approve more than two grants to the same person within any five-year period. Grants are for research only, not for travel or expenses.
  Daland Fellowships for Research in Clinical Medicine: Fellowships are given for research in internal medicine, neurology, psychiatry, and pediatrics. Research must be patient-oriented. Candidates are expected to have held an M.D. degree for less than eight years. Applicants must expect to perform their research at an institution in the U.S. under the supervision of a scientific advisor. Deadline Sept. 1. Please consult the Web site for further information.
  Sabbatical Fellowship for the Humanities and Social Sciences: Fellowships awarded to mid-career faculty members of universities and four-year colleges in the U.S. who have been granted a sabbatical/research year, but for whom financial support from the parent institution is available for only part of the next academic year or the calendar year which begins 14 months after the deadline for receipt of proposals. Candidates must not have had a financially-supported leave at any time subsequent to Sept. 1 of the year which is three years prior to date of application. It is expected that the candidate's doctoral degree was conferred no fewer than seven years and no more than 23 years prior to date of application. Award is up to $40,000. Deadline Nov. 1.
  Phillips Fund Grants for Native American Research: Grants are awarded for research in North Native American linguistics and ethno history. Work in archaeology, ethnography, psycholinguistics, or pedagogy is ineligible. Applicants may be graduate students who have passed their qualifying examinations for either master's or doctorate degrees. Postdoctoral applicants are eligible. The maximum award is $3,000. Grants are ordinarily given for one year and cover travel, tapes, and informants' fees. Deadline Mar. 1.
  Library Resident Research Fellowships: $2,000 per month is awarded to support research in the American Philosophical Society's collections for a minimum of one month and a maximum of three months. Applications are accepted from persons whose normal place of residence is outside a 75-mile radius of Philadelphia. Applicants need not hold a doctorate. Deadline Mar. 1. Telephone inquiries to (215) 440-3443 for this program only.
EIN: 231353269

5594

American Physicians Fellowship for Medicine in Israel

(also known as APF)
2001 Beacon St., Ste. 210
Boston, MA 02135-7771 (617) 232-5382
Contact: I. Kelman Cohen M.D., Pres.
FAX: (617) 739-2616; E-mail: info@apfmed.org;
URL: http://www.apfmed.org

Foundation type: Public charity

Limitations: Fellowships to young Israeli physicians and nurses undertaking specialty training in North America who are committed to returning to Israel. Grants are also awarded to young Israelis for medical research.
Publications: Informational brochure; Newsletter.
Financial data: Year ended 12/31/2003.
Assets, $1,721,902 (M); Expenditures, $776,470; Total giving, $295,637; Grants to individuals, totaling $199,980.
Fields of interest: Medical school/education; Health care, association; Nursing care; Medical research, institute.
Type of support: Conferences/seminars; Fellowships; Research; Foreign applicants.
Application information: Applications accepted.
  Deadline(s): None
EIN: 042207701

5595

American Psychiatric Foundation, Inc.

1000 Wilson Blvd., Ste. 1825
Arlington, VA 22209-3901 (703) 907-7300
Contact: Steven A. Rubloff, Exec. Dir.
FAX: (703) 907-7851; E-mail: apf@psych.org;
URL: http://www.psychfoundation.org

Foundation type: Public charity
Limitations: Research grants for the study of psychiatry and mental illnesses.
Financial data: Year ended 12/31/2003.
Assets, $2,656,481 (M); Expenditures, $2,880,272; Total giving, $2,136,484; Grants to individuals, 4 grants totaling $46,200 (high: $20,000, low: $600).
Fields of interest: Mental health, disorders.
Type of support: Research.
Application information:
  Initial approach: E-mail or telephone.
  Additional information: Contact foundation for further program information.
EIN: 521773663

5596

American Psychiatric Publishing, Inc.

(formerly American Psychiatric Association)
1000 Wilson Blvd., Ste. 1825
Arlington, VA 22209-3901 (703) 907-7300
Contact: Thomas N. Wise M.D., Chair. and Pres.
FAX: (703) 907-1091; E-mail: appi@psych.org;
Additional tel.: (800) 368-5777; URL: http://www.appi.org

Foundation type: Public charity
Limitations: Fellowships and awards to outstanding members of the psychiatric community.
Financial data: Year ended 12/31/2003.
Assets, $33,195,800 (M); Expenditures, $10,402,875; Total giving, $1,677,076; Grants to individuals, 18 grants totaling $23,500 (high: $5,000, low: $500).
Fields of interest: Psychology/behavioral science; Government/public administration; Minorities.
Type of support: Fellowships; Research; Awards/prizes; Travel grants; Stipends.
Application information: Application form required.
  Deadline(s): Vary
  Additional information: See Web site for list of awards.
Program descriptions:
  APA/Avantis Travel Program for Women Residents in Psychiatry: Supports travel and related costs for female residents to attend the APA Annual Meeting. Candidates are selected based on their interest in future leadership positions in organized medicine and the APA. The program is open to

female residents who are APA members. Participants may be nominated by their training director, department chairperson, district branch officer or the chairperson of their district branch Committee on Women.

APA/Bristol-Myers Squibb Fellowship: Aims to heighten the awareness of psychiatry residents of the many activities of psychiatry in the public sector, the career opportunities in this area, and to provide experiences that will contribute to the professional development of those residents. Fellows participate in APA components and attend the Institute on Psychiatric Services twice. Psychiatry residents entering their PGY-III of training during the fellowship term are eligible. Deadline Apr. 1.

APA/Glaxo Wellcome Fellowship: Selects outstanding residents with a potential for leadership and assigns them to components of the APA where they may contribute the residents' point of view to the development of policy. Psychiatry residents who are PGY-III at the time of nomination, members-in-training of the APA, and have passed a national or state board exam are eligible for nomination. Deadline Mar. 31.

APA Minority Fellowships: Includes two groups of fellows: APA/CMHS Fellows and APA/AstraZeneca Fellows. Both offer the opportunity for minority residents to become part of the mainstream psychiatric leadership while learning about organized psychiatry. Applicants must be in at least their second year of training, and U.S. citizens or permanent residents. CMHS fellows receive government stipend support and incur a payback obligation. AstraZeneca fellows do not receive a stipend. Applications accepted between Nov. and Jan.

Daniel X. Freedman, M.D. Fellowship: Provides an educational opportunity in the area of federal health policy through work experience in a Congressional office. Residents in PGY-III and PGY-IV are eligible to apply. The program offers a $20,000 stipend plus corresponding benefits. Fellows serve a six-month term, from Jan. to June.

Program for Minority Research Training in Psychiatry: Designed to increase the number of underrepresented minority men and women in the field of psychiatric research. The program provides funding for short and long-term training opportunities at three levels: Medical School, Residency, and Post-Residency. Training takes place at research-intensive departments of psychiatry in major U.S. medical schools and other appropriate sites.

Van Ameringen Foundation/APA Health Services Research Scholars Program: The APA has accessed, catalogued, and begun to utilize several important data sets containing information on utilization, costs, and outcomes related to mental healthcare. This program's purpose is to make these data sets more widely available to the mental health research community. Psychiatry residents, fellows, and junior faculty in psychiatry departments are encouraged to propose specific analytic studies utilizing these large scale data sets to answer important mental health policy and services research questions.

APIRE/AstraZeneca Young Minds in Psychiatry Award: This program is a commitment by the American Psychiatric Institute for Research and Education (APIRE) and AstraZeneca Pharmaceuticals to recognize and promote promising work from young physicians (35 years of age or under) working in psychiatry. There are four USD $45,000 unrestricted career development awards (no additional overhead will be paid). Award proposals (which can cover a range of activities, including research, educational efforts, travel, salary support and materials) must demonstrate

how winning a Young Minds in Psychiatry Award till advance the applicant's career. Awards will be made to two promising physicians from the U.S. in Bipolar Disorder and Schizophrenia and two promising physicians from countries outside the U.S. in the same conditions. Recipients must be 35 years or under and working in bipolar disorder and schizophrenia. U.S. applicants must be members of the APA. International applicants need not be APA members before applying; awardees will receive international APA member benefits. Applications must be in proposal form and must demonstrate: evidence of academic promise; how the proposal will advance applicant's career; and innovative or original concepts, approaches or methods of developing applicant's career. Proposals should be printed in a minimum of 10-point type, with 1-inch (2.5 cm) margins on all sides and one full space between lines, no longer than three pages, including references.

Minority Mental Health Awards: Provides two awards of $5,000 each to psychiatrists and other mental health professionals who have undertaken innovative and supportive efforts to raise awareness of mental illness in minority communities, the need for early recognition, the availability of and cultural barriers to treatment; increase access to quality mental health services for minorities; and improve the quality of care for minorities, particularly those in the public health system or with severe mental illness. Deadline Nov. 1.

EIN: 130433740

5597

American Psychological Foundation

750 1st St. N.E.
Washington, DC 20002-4242 (202) 336-5843
Contact: Elizabeth H. Merck, Asst. Dir.
FAX: (202) 336-5812; E-mail: foundation@apa.org;
URL: http://www.apa.org/apf/

Foundation type: Public charity
Limitations: Research grants and awards to professionals in the field of psychology.
Publications: Annual report; Financial statement; Informational brochure (including application guidelines); Newsletter.
Financial data: Year ended 12/31/2004. Assets, $13,187,658 (M); Expenditures, $1,077,771; Total giving, $561,091; Grants to individuals, 82 grants totaling $546,091 (high: $30,000, low: $250).
Fields of interest: Psychology/behavioral science.
Type of support: Research; Awards/grants by nomination only; Awards/prizes; Graduate support.
Application information: Application form required.
Initial approach: Letter or telephone.
Deadline(s): Vary
Program descriptions:
APF/COGDOP Graduate Research Scholarships: $16,000 is available for graduate research scholarships. This includes up to 11 $1,000 awards; $3,000 for the top applicant, who will receive the Ruth G. and Joseph D. Matarazzo Scholarship; and $2,000, which is bestowed as the Clarence J. Rosecrans Scholarship. Students who would like to be considered for one of these awards should contact their department office to inquire about the nomination process. Applications are distributed each Mar. to all psychology departments that are members in good standing of the Council of Graduate Departments of Psychology (COGDOP). Deadline June 1.
Arthur Benton Lecture Series on Neuropsychology: The individual chosen to deliver the address at the APA annual convention must be

a distinguished figure in the field of neuropsychology, and will receive a $1,000 honorarium.

William Bevan Annual Lecture Series on Psychology and Public Policy: The individual selected should have demonstrated interest and research on how psychology shapes meaningful public policy. The individual will deliver the address at the APA annual convention, and will receive a $1,000 honorarium.

Lizette Peterson Homer Memorial Injury Research Grant: The Lizette Peterson Homer Memorial Injury Research Grant focuses on psychosocial research on injuries to children and young adults through accidents, violence, abuse, or suicide. A $1,000 annual award is given to the student whose research design best reflects this focus. The fund is administered by APA Division 54 (The Society of Pediatric Research), which solicits nominations and selects annual winners, subject to approval by the APF Board of Trustees.

Henry David International Travel Award: Award to a young psychologist for participation in an international congress of the individual's choice. Every third year the funds may be used to subsidize travel of one colleague from abroad to participate in the Psychosocial Workshop held in conjunction with the Population Association of America. The award is given each year in the amount of the candidate's expenses, up to a maximum of $1,000.

Distinguished Teaching in Psychology Award: Recognizes a significant career contribution to the teaching of psychology. The awardee receives a plaque, $2,000, and an all-expense paid round trip to the APA annual convention, where the award is presented. Deadline Dec. 1.

Distinguished Teaching in Psychology Lecture: This address is given in conjunction with the APF award that recognizes a significant career contribution to the teaching of psychology. The awardee receives a plaque, $2,000, and an all-expense paid round trip to the APA annual convention, where the award is presented.

Robert L. Fantz Memorial Award: Encourages and supports careers of promising young investigators in psychology or related disciplines. The foundation makes a $2,000 grant to the awardee's institution on behalf of the awardee for equipment purchases, travel, computer resources, etc., related to the work recognized by the award.

Gold Medal Awards: The following awards are given in recognition of a distinguished career and enduring contribution to psychology: Life Achievement in the Application of Psychology, Life Achievement in the Practice of Psychology, Life Achievement in the Science of Psychology, and Life Achievement in Psychology in the Public Interest. Each awardee receives a gold medal, $2,000 (given to the charity of the awardee's choice), and an all-expense paid trip to the APA annual convention, where the award is presented. Deadline Dec. 1.

Henry Hecaen and Manfred Meier Scholarships: Awards two $2,500 scholarships for neuropsychology graduate students who show evidence of need and a record of achievement that indicates a promising career in the field. The candidate's faculty mentor or director of training must approve and co-sign the application. Deadline June 1.

Esther Katz Rosen Lecture: The lecturer must be a distinguished individual in the field of psychological understanding of gifted children and adolescents. The individual will present the lecture at the APA annual convention, and will receive a $1,000 honorarium.

Spielberger EMPathy Symposium: The symposium is a forum for leading experts to present and discuss recent findings in the areas of Emotion,

Motivation, and Personality (EMPathy), in order to stimulate and facilitate the integration and dissemination of knowledge in these areas. The symposium is held at the APA annual convention, and each of three presenters receives a $500 honorarium.

Arthur W. Staats Lecture for Unifying Psychology: This lecture is presented at the APA annual convention by an individual whose work in a particular field has been judged to have great significance for other fields of psychology, or has the potential to be extrapolated to have unifying power within the discipline of psychology as a whole. The lecturer receives a $1,000 honorarium.

Lynn Stuart Weiss Lecture: Promotes psychology as a means of attaining peace through world law. The lecturer will present at the APA annual convention, and will receive a $1,000 honorarium.

Rosalee G. Weiss Lecture: The lecturer, who presents at the APA annual convention and receives a $1,000 honorarium, is an outstanding leader in psychology, or a leader in the arts or sciences whose work and activities has had an effect on psychology.

Randy Gerson Memorial Grant: Provides a $5,000 grant to advance the systemic understanding of couple and/or family dynamics and/or multi-generational processes. Work that advances theory, assessment, or clinical practice will be considered. Awards will be given on alternate years to students and professionals. Applicants for the professional-level award must have a doctorate (Ph.D., Psy.D., Ed.D., M.D., etc.). Deadline Feb. 1.

Evelyn Hooker Programs:
- Small Research Grants Program: Several grants of up to $5,000 are given to fund small-scale, pilot studies and to assist researchers in taking advantage of breaking opportunities for time-sensitive investigations. Deadline Jan. 29
- Large Research Grants Program: Two grants of up to $40,000 provide financial support to enable the most outstanding applicants to conduct their proposed research, and to give supportive and constructive feedback to all applicants. Deadline Mar. 14
- Roy Scrivner Research Grants: Supports empirical research, from all fields of the behavioral and social sciences, that focuses on lesbian, gay, and bisexual family psychology and family therapy. Up to two $4,000 awards for postdoctoral research and up to two $1,000 awards for predoctoral research will be given. Deadline Nov. 1
- Wayne F. Placek Research Grants: Supports individual research grants that will advance the goals of increasing the general public's understanding of gay men and lesbians.

F.J. McGuigan Lecture on Understanding the Human Mind: Lecturer must be a psychologist engaged in research that seeks to explicate the concept of the human mind. Research should be primarily psychophysiological, but physiological and behavioral research may also qualify for support. Dualistic approaches, such as those espoused by many contemporary cognitive psychologists, will not qualify. The lecturer will present at the APA convention on the human mind, and will receive a $1,000 honorarium.
EIN: 526051733

5598
American Skin Association, Inc.
346 Park Ave. S., 4th Fl.
New York, NY 10010 (212) 889-4858
Contact: Joyce Weidler, Managing Dir.
FAX: (212) 889-4959; Additional tel.: (800) 499-7546; URL: http://www.americanskin.org

Foundation type: Public charity
Limitations: Grants to researchers in the field of skin disease at major institutions in the country.
Publications: Informational brochure; Newsletter.
Financial data: Year ended 12/31/2004. Assets, $1,493,520 (M); Expenditures, $773,258; Total giving, $498,000; Grants to individuals, 15 grants totaling $313,000 (high: $50,000, low: $1,000).
Fields of interest: Skin disorders research.
Type of support: Research; Awards/prizes.
Application information: Deadlines Oct. 1 for Research Scholar Awards and Research Grants; See Web site to download application form.
Program descriptions:
Research Scholar Awards: This program awards $50,000 grants annually to individuals to foster the career development of young research investigators working in the fields of dermatology and cutaneous biology. Research must be focused on a categorical skin disorder or specific skin function.

Research Awards: These awards honor investigators for their original research in cutaneous biology in the fields of dermatitis, psoriasis, vitiligo, and skin cancer. The proposed research must be expected to make an impact on the lives of the people who have these disorders. Nominations are welcome.

Research Grants in Categorical Diseases: This program provides support for disease-specific research targeting five skin disorders: skin cancer/melanoma, lupus erythematosis, psoriasis, vitiligo, and childhood skin diseases/disfigurement. Grants $15,000 for one year.
EIN: 133401320

5599
American Society for Industrial Security Foundation
(also known as ASIS Foundation)
1625 Prince St.
Alexandria, VA 22314-2818 (703) 519-6200
Contact: Robert Rowe, Dir., Devel.
FAX: (703) 519-6299;
E-mail: foundation@asisonline.org; URL: http://www.asisonline.org/foundation/index.xml

Foundation type: Public charity
Limitations: Scholarships by nomination only to those who wish to be a Certified Protection Professional.
Publications: Application guidelines; Informational brochure; Newsletter.
Financial data: Year ended 12/31/2004. Assets, $784,746 (M); Expenditures, $318,926; Total giving, $128,167; Grants to individuals, 114 grants totaling $97,902 (high: $20,000, low: $128).
Fields of interest: Crime/law enforcement, association.
Type of support: Undergraduate support.
Application information: Application form required.
Deadline(s): June 1
Additional information: Application must be signed by ASIS chapter officer and faxed in.
Program description:
Alan J. Cross, CPP Award: A professional advancement scholarship that pays the cost of attending a CPP advancement course. The person

making use of the scholarship must be an ASIS International member and be nominated by the chapter. The scholarship is to be used specifically for the CPP review course that is offered just before the Annual Seminar in the host city. Twenty-five awards are given per year.
EIN: 520848090

5600
American Society of Consultant Pharmacists Research & Education Foundation
(also known as The ASCP Foundation)
1321 Duke St.
Alexandria, VA 22314-3563 (703) 739-1300
FAX: (703) 739-1500;
E-mail: info@ascpfoundation.org; Additional tel.: (800) 355-2727; URL: http://www.ascpfoundation.org/

Foundation type: Public charity
Limitations: Traineeships to individuals for pharmacy practice.
Publications: Annual report; Informational brochure; Newsletter.
Financial data: Year ended 12/31/2003. Assets, $2,104,936 (M); Expenditures, $957,848; Total giving, $10,000.
Fields of interest: AIDS research; Alzheimer's disease research.
Type of support: Research.
Application information: Application form required.
Initial approach: Telephone or e-mail.
Deadline(s): Varies by research category
Additional information: Application should include additional documents; See Web site for complete application and deadline information.
Program description:
Pharmacotherapy Traineeships: Five-day traineeships are open to pharmacists from all practice settings in the following categories: Disease Pharmacotherapy, Behavioral Disorders, HIV/AIDS Pharmacotherapy, Alzheimer's/Dementia, Parkinson's Disease, Pain Management, and Thrombosis Prevention and Management. Trainees are responsible for all expenses related to travel, meals, and incidental expenses. Hotel accommodation will be paid for by the foundation.
EIN: 541358129

5601
American Society of Health-System Pharmacists Research and Education Foundation
(also known as ASHP Research and Education Foundation)
7272 Wisconsin Ave., 2nd Fl.
Bethesda, MD 20814 (301) 657-3000
Contact: Henri R. Manasse, Jr., Pres.
FAX: (301) 664-8872;
E-mail: foundation@ashp.org; URL: http://www.ashpfoundation.org

Foundation type: Public charity
Limitations: Traineeships and grants for licensed pharmacists.
Publications: Application guidelines; Annual report; Newsletter.
Financial data: Year ended 05/31/2004. Assets, $9,755,618 (M); Expenditures, $1,251,747; Total giving, $277,775; Grants to individuals, 8 grants totaling $10,450 (high: $4,700, low: $250).

Fields of interest: Pharmacy/prescriptions.
Type of support: Fellowships.
Application information: Deadlines vary; Initial approach by e-mail; Completion of formal application required; See Web site for further application information.
Program descriptions:

Pharmacy Resident Grant Program: $12,000 available for 3-5 projects in medication safety. Program is offered to residents completing an ASHP-accredited residency program and is intended to support a research project devoted to improving medication safety. Funding will be provided for project-related expenses and may not be used for ongoing general operating expense, institutional overhead or indirect costs, projects conducted outside the U.S., individual stipends, and/or loans.

Diabetes Patient Care Traineeship: Grants funds cover the cost of registration, all educational materials, and travel expenses. The program is a 5-day experience-based program designed to train pharmacy practitioners to establish and maintain specialized services for the management of patients with diabetes mellitus.

Critical Care Patient Care Traineeship: Grants funds cover the cost of registration, all educational materials, and travel expenses. The program is a 10-day, experienced-based certificate program designed to train pharmacy practitioners to establish and maintain specialized services for the management of patients within the intensive care or critical care units.

Federal Services Junior Investigator Grant Program: Four to six grants available in the $10,000 to $25,000 range for each award. The research grant program is customed-designed to meet the needs of junior investigators or practitioners new to research in the federal services sector of health professionals. The program supports research efforts critical for the advancement of care and treatment of elderly patients in federal health care systems and aims to develop and strengthen the skills of newer researchers in the federal services and foster mentorship of these practioners by more experienced senior investigators.

Pharmacy/ Nursing Partnership for Medication Safety: $80,000 total is available for one to three grants awards. Grants awarded to provide funding for specific projects conducted by pharmacist/nursing research teams that address collaboration in the medication-use system to foster improvements in patient care and not intended for long-term support of research programs.

Junior Investigator in Critical Care Research Grant Program: $25,000 will be divided among three to five recipients. Grants are awarded to provide funding for specific projects conducted by junior investigators that address medication therapy issues in critically ill patients and not intended for long-term support.

Oncology Patient Care Traineeship: Grants funds cover the cost of registration, all educational materials, and travel expenses. The program is a 10-day, experience-based certificate program designed to train pharmacy practitioners to establish and maintain specialized services for the management of patients with cancer.
EIN: 237033369

5602
American Society of Newspaper Editors Foundation

11690B Sunrise Valley Dr.
Reston, VA 20191-1409 (703) 453-1122
Contact: Scott Bosley, Exec. Dir.
FAX: (703) 453-1133; E-mail: asne@asne.org;
URL: http://www.asne.org

Foundation type: Public charity
Limitations: Awards to recognize excellence in writing in American and Canadian daily newspapers and eligible wire services.
Financial data: Year ended 06/30/2003. Assets, $3,269,385 (M); Expenditures, $2,393,425; Total giving, $444,600; Grants to individuals, totaling $444,600.
Fields of interest: Journalism/publishing; Literature.
Type of support: Awards/prizes.
Application information: Application form required.
Initial approach: Telephone.
Deadline(s): Feb. 1
Additional information: Entries by FAX or e-mail not accepted.
Program descriptions:

Distinguished Writing Awards: Four $2,500 awards will be given per year for work done in these categories: 1) Non-Deadline Writing: focuses on writing not accomplished on deadline (except commentary), from any section of the newspaper. This category may include investigative and news-related material as well as any features material - profiles, interviews, trend stories, lifestyle, travel, etc.; 2) Commentary/Column Writing: encompasses any writing that expresses a personal point of view - columns and other forms of journalism opinion; 3) Editorial Writing: deals with editorials, signed or unsigned, written by one individual, that speak for the newspaper; and 4) Diversity: focuses on news and feature writing that helps readers understand how racial and ethnic diversity is changing their communities. Columns and editorials are not eligible in this category. In all categories, a minimum of three and a maximum of five articles will be accepted.

Jesse Laventhol Prizes for Deadline News Reporting: These prizes are awarded for breaking news events covered under deadline pressure. Entries will be evaluated in terms of descriptive power and literary style, depth and breadth of reporting, timeliness, completeness, and perspective. Two $10,000 awards are given, one for an individual and one for a team. One to three articles may be submitted in this category.
EIN: 239935413

5603
American Society of Safety Engineers Foundation

1800 Oakton St.
Des Plaines, IL 60018 (847) 699-2929
Contact: Fred J. Fortman, Exec. Dir.
URL: http://www.asse.org

Foundation type: Public charity
Limitations: Fellowships to researchers who have doctoral degrees for research on safety issues.
Publications: Annual report; Newsletter.
Financial data: Year ended 06/30/2003. Assets, $675,544 (M); Expenditures, $227,681; Total giving, $110,050; Grants to individuals, totaling $79,500.
Fields of interest: Safety/disasters, research.
Type of support: Fellowships; Research.

Application information: Applications accepted. Application form required. Application form available on the grantmaker's Web site.
Deadline(s): Deadlines Oct. 1 for Research Grants, Dec. 1 for Scholarships, and Apr. 15 for Research Fellowships.
Program descriptions:

Liberty Mutual Safety Research Fellowship Program: Fellowships of $2,000 for the first week and $1,000 per week thereafter to researchers with a Ph.D., or those who are working towards one or a master's, who are U.S. citizens to cover costs of transportation, room and board, rental cars and other expenses. Within eight weeks after the Fellowship, recipients must write an 800-word article for the ASSE Foundation Advocate explaining the results of the research, or an article for the Professional Safety magazine on the results of the safety research project and an outline for a proposal for a grant request for continuing research as an ongoing project if appropriate.

Research Grants: Awards up to $20,000 to a safety and health researcher to conduct applied research that would enhance management performance in reducing injuries and illness in the workplace.
EIN: 366145045

5604
American Society of Therapeutic Radiologists Education and Development Foundation

(also known as ASTRO)
12500 Fair Lakes Cir., No. 375
Fairfax, VA 22033-3882 (703) 502-1550
Contact: Laura Thevenot, C.E.O.
FAX: (703) 502-7852; Additional tel.: (800) 962-7876; E-mail: thevenot@astro.org;
URL: http://www.astro.org

Foundation type: Public charity
Limitations: Fellowships or scholarships, and awards for study of radiology and oncology to U.S. and foreign individuals. One-year fellowships for research in radiation oncology are available to qualified applicants.
Publications: Newsletter.
Financial data: Year ended 12/31/2004. Assets, $806,823 (M); Expenditures, $515,967; Total giving, $515,889.
Fields of interest: Diagnostic imaging research.
Type of support: Fellowships; Research.
Application information:
Initial approach: Letter or telephone.
Additional information: Contact foundation for current application deadline.
EIN: 510178702

5605
American Speech-Language-Hearing Association Foundation

10801 Rockville Pike
Rockville, MD 20852-3226 (301) 897-5700
Contact: Nancy J. Minghetti, Exec. Dir.
FAX: (301) 571-0457;
E-mail: foundation@asha.org; URL: http://www.ashfoundation.org

Foundation type: Public charity
Limitations: Research grants for study in the area of communication sciences.
Financial data: Year ended 12/31/2004. Assets, $4,389,743 (M); Expenditures, $458,443; Total giving, $148,000; Grants to

individuals, 36 grants totaling $107,500 (high: $10,000, low: $500).

Fields of interest: Ear & throat research.

Type of support: Research.

Application information: Applications accepted. Application form required.

Initial approach: Letter or FAX.

Additional information: Contact foundation for current application deadline.

Program descriptions:

Research Grant Competition for New Investigators: New researchers may submit proposals in competition for one of seven research grants of $5,000 each. The grants are designed to help further research activities of new investigators and should have particular clinical relevance to speech-language pathology and audiology. Proposals, while not limited in topic, are encouraged in the area of treatment research, particularly efficacy and outcome studies.

Research Grant in Speech Science: New researchers may submit proposals in competition for one $5,000 grant. The grant is designed to further research activities of new investigators and to promulgate the work of Dennis Klatt, noted speech communication researcher and scientist. It can be used to initiate new research or to supplement an existing research project. Funds may be requested for a variety of purposes; for example, equipment, subjects, research assistants, or research-related travel. Applicants must have received a doctoral degree within the last five years.

EIN: 526055761

5606
American-Italian Cancer Foundation

112 E. 71st. St., 2B
New York, NY 10021 (212) 628-9090
Contact: Dr. Esther R. Dyer, Exec. Dir.
FAX: (212) 517-6089; E-mail: aicf@aicfonline.org; URL: http://www.aicfonline.org

Foundation type: Public charity

Limitations: Grants and fellowships to physicians and researchers in the fight against cancer through research, training, and education.

Publications: Annual report; Financial statement; Informational brochure; Newsletter.

Financial data: Year ended 06/30/2003. Assets, $1,870,302 (M); Expenditures, $2,037,819; Total giving, $1,283,242; Grants to individuals, 25 grants totaling $590,000 (high: $30,000, low: $6,000).

Fields of interest: Cancer research.

Type of support: Conferences/seminars; Fellowships; Research; Awards/prizes.

Application information: Application form required. Application form available on the grantmaker's Web site.

Initial approach: Telephone or e-mail.

Deadline(s): Feb. 1 for fellowship programs

EIN: 133035711

5607
The American-Scandinavian Foundation

58 Park Ave.
New York, NY 10016 (212) 879-9779
Contact: Edward P. Gallagher, Pres.
E-mail: info@amscan.org; URL: http://www.amscan.org

Foundation type: Public charity

Limitations: Fellowships and grants to U.S. citizens or permanent residents for study in Scandinavian countries. Fellowships also for U.S. citizens or

permanent residents to study the arts in Scandinavia.

Publications: Newsletter.

Financial data: Year ended 06/30/2003. Assets, $46,348,930 (M); Expenditures, $4,022,696; Total giving, $888,183; Grants to individuals, 69 grants totaling $699,000 (high: $20,000, low: $2,500).

Fields of interest: Arts.

Type of support: Program development; Fellowships; Research; Awards/prizes; Postdoctoral support; Graduate support; Postgraduate support; Travel grants; Doctoral support.

Application information: Applications accepted. Application form required.

Deadline(s): Nov. 1

Applicants should submit the following:

1) Curriculum vitae

2) Budget Information

Additional information: Include fourteen copies of application and of project statement, three letters of recommendation. See Web site for further application information and for application form.

Program description:

Awards for Study in Scandanavia: Awards fellowships of up to $18,000 to graduate-level students for a year-long stay and grants of $3,000 to postgraduate students for one-three months of research. The award can be used for maintenance, travel, tuition and fees, and materials.

EIN: 131623897

5608
Ameritec Foundation

760 Arrow Grand Cir.
Covina, CA 91722
Contact: John Watson, Pres.
E-mail: ameritecprize@ameritec.com; URL: http://www.ameritec.com/ameritecfoundation/home.htm

Foundation type: Company-sponsored foundation

Limitations: Awards and prizes to researchers in Los Angeles, CA for basic (not clinical) research with the goal of finding a cure for spinal cord functional impairment (paralysis).

Publications: Informational brochure (including application guidelines).

Financial data: Year ended 12/31/2004. Assets, $1,549,587 (M); Expenditures, $86,922; Total giving, $74,500.

Fields of interest: Medical research, institute; Spine disorders research.

Type of support: Research; Awards/grants by nomination only; Awards/prizes.

Application information:

Initial approach: Letter.

Deadline(s): Oct. 15

Additional information: Contact foundation for current nomination guidelines.

EIN: 954147156

5609
Amgen Foundation, Inc.

1 Amgen Center Dr., M.S. 28-1-B
Thousand Oaks, CA 91320-1799
(805) 447-4056
FAX: (805) 449-6757;
E-mail: amgenfoundation@amgen.com;
URL: http://www.amgen.com/citizenship/foundation.html

Foundation type: Company-sponsored foundation

Limitations: Awards by nomination only to teachers of Ventura County, CA.

Publications: Application guidelines; Annual report.

Financial data: Year ended 12/31/2004. Assets, $99,227,433 (M); Expenditures, $16,560,662; Total giving, $16,279,383.

Fields of interest: Education.

Type of support: Awards/grants by nomination only; Awards/prizes.

Application information:

Deadline(s): Feb. 24

Additional information: Contact foundation for current nomination guidelines.

EIN: 770252898

5610
The Amyotrophic Lateral Sclerosis Association

(also known as The ALS Association)
27001 Agoura Rd., Ste. 150
Calabasas Hills, CA 91301-5104
(818) 880-9007
Contact: Gary A. Leo, Pres. and C.E.O.
Additional tel.: (800) 782-4747; URL: http://www.alsa.org/

Foundation type: Public charity

Limitations: Research grants to investigators to find a cure for ALS and to improve the standard of living for individuals with the disease.

Publications: Annual report; Informational brochure; Newsletter.

Financial data: Year ended 01/31/2005. Assets, $12,935,660 (M); Expenditures, $10,787,369; Total giving, $4,456,967; Grants to individuals, totaling $4,244,717.

Fields of interest: Nerve, muscle & bone research.

Type of support: Fellowships; Research.

Application information:

Initial approach: Proposal.

Deadline(s): Sept. 1 and Mar. 1

Additional information: Contact foundation for current application guidelines.

Program descriptions:

Multi-year Grants: Awards grants of up to $60,000 a year to researchers for projects of up to three years long. Funding is committed for one year only, with non-competitive renewals conditioned upon receipt of satisfactory interim progress reports.

Starter Grants: Awards one-year grants of a maximum of $35,000 to New Investigators entering the field of ALS proposing innovative and novel projects likely to provide important results relevant to ALS research. Alternately, they can be pilot studies by established ALS investigators. Applications do not require strong preliminary data, but must emphasize novelty, feasibility, innovation and relevance to ALS.

EIN: 133271855

5611
The Christina and John Anagnos Educational Foundation

c/o Helen Theodoropoulos
9217 N. Kenton Ave.
Skokie, IL 60076
Application address: c/o Eleni Andriotaki, Xanthou 5-Athens, Greece 10673, tel.: (011-30) 210-354-5862

Foundation type: Independent foundation

Limitations: Scholarships to medical students residing in Greece to attend a medical school in that country.

Financial data: Year ended 12/31/2004. Assets, $2,056,868 (M); Expenditures,

$149,783; Total giving, $104,300; Grants to individuals, 24 grants totaling $104,300.
Fields of interest: Medical school/education.
Type of support: Foreign applicants; Graduate support.
Application information:
Deadline(s): Dec. 16
Additional information: Completion of formal application required, including photocopy of identification, proof of medical school enrollment, proof of Greek residence, birth certificate and parents' and student's tax return; Applications in Greek accepted.
Program description:
Aganos Scholarships: Applicants must:
· be admitted to a medical school in Greece
· read a language in addition to Greek
· demonstrate financial need
· demonstrate capability to succeed in medical school
· demonstrate moral character and the promise of contributing to society.
Scholarships can be used for tuition or any living expenses incurred as a student. Scholarships are renewable if the student maintains satisfactory progress and does not transfer.
EIN: 306022912

5612
The Anderson Prize Foundation
2727 Vallejo St.
San Francisco, CA 94123 (773) 935-3963
Contact: Allen A. Schuh, Pres.

Foundation type: Independent foundation
Limitations: Awards by nomination only to individuals whose efforts have enhanced the quality of life for the gay and lesbian community.
Financial data: Year ended 12/31/2004.
Assets, $529,395 (M); Expenditures, $25,960; Total giving, $25,000; Grant to an individual, 1 grant totaling $25,000.
Application information:
Deadline(s): Dec. 15
Additional information: The Anderson Prize Foundation administers the Stonewall Awards program. Contact foundation for current nomination guidelines.
EIN: 363710311

5613
Anxiety Disorders Association of America
8730 Georgia Ave., Ste. 600
Silver Spring, MD 20910 (240) 485-1001
Contact: Jerilyn Ross, Pres. and C.E.O.
FAX: (240) 485-1035; E-mail: anxdis@adaa.org;
URL: http://www.adaa.org

Foundation type: Public charity
Limitations: Awards and research grants to professionals in the field of anxiety disorders.
Publications: Application guidelines.
Financial data: Year ended 12/31/2003.
Assets, $1,520,005 (M); Expenditures, $1,700,861; Total giving, $121,500; Grants to individuals, 16 grants totaling $121,500 (high: $31,000, low: $1,500).
Fields of interest: Mental health, disorders.
Type of support: Research; Awards/prizes; Postdoctoral support; Graduate support; Travel grants.
Application information: Application form required. Application form available on the grantmaker's Web site.
Deadline(s): Vary

Additional information: See Web site for deadlines for each specific program.
Program descriptions:
Trainee Travel Awards: Provides eight $1,500 awards to individuals to attend the ADAA Annual Conference and the invitation-only Scientific Satellite Meeting and Awards Luncheon. Applicants must be psychiatric residents or graduate students in neuroscience, psychology, social work or other related fields. They must have an interest in anxiety disorders and demonstrated previous relevant experience.
Career Development Travel Awards: Provides five $3,500 awards to attend and present a new research poster at the ADAA Annual Conference and the invitation-only Scientific Satellite Meeting and Awards Luncheon; and the annual meeting of the American College of Neuropsychopharmacology (ACNP) or of the Association for the Advancement of Behavior Therapy (AABT). Intended for young professionals with career interests in fields related to anxiety disorders, such as basic and clinical neuropsychopharmacology, clinical psychology, genetics, neuroimaging and epidemiology. The awards also include a one-year ADAA membership and personal profile in ADAA's newsletter, the Reporter. Winners must attend both the ADAA annual meeting and one other meeting of their choice. Applicants must be Ph.D-level scientists who have received their doctorates or completed a postdoctoral fellowship (whichever occurred last) within the past three years. Candidates will be judged on the following points: evidence of commitment to the field of anxiety disorders, strength of training and current program, quality and extent of relevant research, and a personal statement and professional reference.
Junior Faculty Research Grants: Provides two awards of $30,000 that are intended to provide partial salary support, with the possibility of a second year extension. The grants aim to increase the pool of independent investigators with interest and expertise in anxiety disorders research by assisting individuals in making the transition from trainee to junior faculty to independent investigator. In addition, grantees will receive: a complimentary registration to ADAA's Annual Conference and the invitation-only Scientific Satellite Meeting and Awards Luncheon; a travel stipend of up to $1,000 in order to attend the meeting; and a free one-year ADAA membership. Applicants who have completed at least one year of postdoctoral fellowship or postresidency research training by the time the grant is awarded. Investigators who have achieved the academic level of associate professor (or equivalent), or who are recipients of NIH/NIMH "K" or R01 grants, are not eligible. Recipients must have a mentor or senior research collaborator who is an established investigator in anxiety disorder research. Applications may cover a broad range of topics, including clinical epidemiological, basic science and health policy-related research, but they must contribute to the understanding of and/or treatment for anxiety disorders.
EIN: 521248820

5614
AO North America, Inc.
P.O. Box 1658
West Chester, PA 19380 (610) 344-2000
FAX: (610) 344-2001; E-mail: ellisa@aona.org;
Course Info.: c/o AO North America Continuing Medical Education, 1690 Russell Rd., Paoli, PA 19301, tel.: (800) 769-1391 or (610) 695-2459;
FAX: (610) 695-2420; E-mail: registrar@aona.org;
URL: http://www.aona.org

Foundation type: Independent foundation
Limitations: Fellowships to fully-trained orthopedic and general surgeons.
Financial data: Year ended 06/30/2005.
Assets, $3,354,034 (M); Expenditures, $3,671,060; Total giving, $1,150,646; Grants to individuals, 10 grants totaling $900,000 (high: $150,000, low: $75,000).
Fields of interest: Surgery; Nerve, muscle & bone research.
Type of support: Fellowships.
Application information: Application form required.
Initial approach: letter, telephone, or FAX.
Deadline(s): None
Additional information: Application should include curriculum vitae, copy of medical school diploma, copy of AO Basic Course certificate, two letters of recommendation, list of publications and/or lectures, and two photographs.
Program descriptions:
Standard AO Fellowship: Fellowships are awarded for a duration of one to three months to surgeons who are in their last year of residency or have just completed their residency training. Fellowships cover the cost of accommodations and meals in Canada, Austria, Belgium, France, Great Britain, Spain, Switzerland, Germany, Chile, Singapore, Australia and the U.S.
Jack McDaniel Memorial AO Fellowship: The award, given to one North American Resident, will consist of all travel expenses to the site of the fellowship, and the usual current monthly AO Fellowship stipend for a period of no more than three months ($2,000 per month). At the Annual North American Spring Basic & Advanced AO Course immediately after completion of the fellowship, the fellow will be invited to be a table instructor and travel expenses and lodging will be covered as for other faculty members. Support for family members is not included.
Martin Allgower Trauma Fellowship: The fellowship, to one practicing North American trauma surgeon, will be granted for three to six months, at a European AO trauma center. The award consists of round-trip travel expenses for the fellow to the site of the fellowship, living quarters for the fellow (and spouse), and a monthly stipend of $2,000 to cover meals and incidentals. Also included in the fellowship is an invitation as a faculty member to the annual AO ASIF Davos Course the year following completion of the fellowship, with the travel and lodging paid for by the course organization. During the course, the fellow may be asked to present a report on his/her fellowship experience.
John Border Memorial European Trauma Fellowship: Offered to a graduating North American trauma fellow who plans a career in academic trauma surgery. The award will consist of round-trip travel expenses to the site of the fellowship in Europe and a monthly stipend for up to three months to support living expenses at the fellowship site. Support for family members is not included. The fellowship will take place at major AO trauma centers in Europe. The recipient of the fellowship will be invited as a junior faculty member at a North American AO ASIF course in the year following his/her fellowship, with travel and lodging expenses paid by the AO Course organization.
EIN: 232701788

5615

Aorn Foundation
2170 S. Parker Rd., Ste. 300
Denver, CO 80231-5711 (303) 755-6300
Contact: Sheri J. Voss RN,MS,CNOR, Pres.
FAX: (303) 755-4219; E-mail: tbarlow@aorn.org;
Additional tel.: (800) 755-2676, ext. 8229;
URL: http://www.aorn.org

Foundation type: Public charity
Limitations: Grants to operating room nurses for research, continuing education, and other areas relevant to their work.
Publications: Annual report; Newsletter.
Financial data: Year ended 12/31/2003.
Assets, $1,456,484 (M); Expenditures, $447,384; Total giving, $322,195.
Fields of interest: Medical school/education; Adult/continuing education; Nursing care; Medical research, institute.
Type of support: Research; Postgraduate support.
Application information: Applications accepted.
Initial approach: Letter.
Deadline(s): Varies
Program descriptions:
AORN Foundation Research Grant Program: Provides funding opportunities for nurse researchers as well as chapters, specialty assemblies, state councils, and others engaged in collaborative research projects. For grants of $15,000 or more, indirect costs of 10 percent (maximum) may be requested; travel funds up to a maximum of $500, and funds to purchase computer software to be used as part of the research project may also be requested. Deadlines Nov. 1, Feb. 1, and June 1.
EAC Congress Grants: Awards thirty-one $1,710 grants to student nurses, international nurses, and AORN members to attend the AORN Congress. Deadline Dec. 31.
Ethicon Chapter Education Grants: Grants will be used to address the challenges nurses are facing as a result of the changes in the current health care environment, and how working together through teamwork can be a valuable way to address those changes.
Perioperative Clinical Improvement and Innovation Grant: Grants a maximum of $1,500 to assist clinicians who provide direct patient care with clinical improvement/innovation projects requiring an investment of personal time or other resources. The project must relate to the care of surgical patients, but need not be limited to only surgical patients.
Zimmerman Chapter Education Grants: Grants will be in the amount of $500, and must be used for continuing education activities hosted by the local chapter. Grants will be distributed equally per chapter size (15 per year in each category): small, 0-50 members; medium, 51-150 members; intermediate, 151-399 members; large, 400+ members.
EIN: 841193583

5616

APICS Educational & Research Foundation
5301 Shawnee Rd.
Alexandria, VA 22312-2317 (800) 444-2742
Contact: Florence Anderson, Interim Exec. Dir.
FAX: (703) 354-8106;
E-mail: foundation@apicshq.org; Additional tel.: (703) 354-8852; URL: http://www.apics.org

Foundation type: Public charity
Limitations: Grants to advance the identification, creation and dissemination of knowledge and

methodologies that encourage and support continual increases in the effective use of resources in manufacturing and service industries.
Publications: Application guidelines; Informational brochure; Newsletter.
Financial data: Year ended 12/31/2003.
Assets, $828,410 (M); Expenditures, $149,289; Total giving, $76,800.
Type of support: Grants to individuals.
Application information: Contact foundation for current application deadline/guidelines.
EIN: 366155750

5617

Aplastic Anemia & MDS International Foundation, Inc.
(formerly Aplastic Anemia Foundation of America, Inc.)
P.O. Box 613
Annapolis, MD 21404-0613 (410) 867-0242
Contact: Marilyn Baker M.S., Pres.
FAX: (410) 867-0240; E-mail: help@aamds.org;
Additional tel.: (800) 747-2820; URL: http://www.aamds.org/

Foundation type: Public charity
Limitations: Support for research into prevention and treatment of aplastic anemia, myelodysplastic syndromes, and other bone marrow failure.
Publications: Application guidelines; Annual report; Newsletter.
Financial data: Year ended 12/31/2004.
Assets, $2,236,885 (M); Expenditures, $872,840; Total giving, $168,750; Grants to individuals, 4 grants totaling $168,750 (high: $60,000, low: $22,500).
Fields of interest: Health care; Heart & circulatory diseases.
Type of support: Research.
Application information: Application form required.
Initial approach: Letter or telephone.
Deadline(s): Nov. 30
Program description:
New Researcher Awards: Awards to support research related to aplastic anemia, myelodysplastic syndromes, and other bone marrow failure are usually given in the amount of $30,000 and are renewable.
EIN: 521336903

5618

The Area Fund of Dutchess County
(formerly The Area Fund)
80 Washington St., Ste. 201
Poughkeepsie, NY 12601 (845) 452-3077
Contact: Andrea L. Reynolds, C.E.O.
FAX: (845) 452-3083;
E-mail: cfdc@communityfoundationdc.org;
Additional E-mail:
areynolds@communityfoundationdc.org;
URL: http://www.communityfoundationdc.org

Foundation type: Community foundation
Limitations: Grants to pre-kindergarten through 12th grade public, private, and parochial school teachers in Dutchess County, NY, for special projects and professional development.
Publications: Application guidelines; Annual report; Newsletter.
Financial data: Year ended 06/30/2004.
Assets, $19,924,579 (M); Expenditures, $2,861,454; Total giving, $1,185,480; Grants to individuals, 271 grants totaling $249,565 (high: $6,000, low: $20).
Fields of interest: Education.

Type of support: Program development.
Application information: Applications accepted.
Initial approach: Letter or telephone.
Additional information: Contact foundation for current application deadline/guidelines.
Program description:
Partnership in Education Grants: The program is open to classroom teachers of pre-kindergarten through 12th grade in public, private, and parochial schools in Dutchess County, NY.
EIN: 237026859

5619

Lance Armstrong Foundation, Inc.
P.O. Box 161150
Austin, TX 78716-1150 (512) 236-8820
Contact: Mitch Stoller, Pres.
URL: http://www.laf.org

Foundation type: Public charity
Limitations: Research grants to young investigators in the early stages of their careers for the study of cancer.
Publications: Application guidelines; Annual report; Newsletter.
Financial data: Year ended 12/31/2004.
Assets, $34,220,819 (M); Expenditures, $23,986,851; Total giving, $6,186,143.
Fields of interest: Cancer; Cancer research.
Type of support: Research.
Application information: Applications accepted. Application form required. Application form available on the grantmaker's Web site.
Initial approach: Letter.
Deadline(s): Apr. 24
Program descriptions:
Research Awards: Awards of up to $75,000 per year for one to three years (plus 10 percent indirect costs) to support research projects initiated by established investigators. Scientific and clinical research are focused on two key areas, cancer survivorship and the basic and clinical science of testicular cancer.
Young Investigator Research Awards: Awards of up to $50,000 per year for one to two years (plus 10 percent indirect costs) to support research to be carried out by investigators in the early stages of cancers dedicated to the study of cancer survivorship.
EIN: 742806618

5620

Arthritis Foundation, Inc.
1330 W. Peachtree St.
Atlanta, GA 30309 (404) 872-7100
Contact: John H. Klippel M.D., Pres.
FAX: (404) 872-0457; E-mail: kward@arthritis.org;
URL: http://www.arthritis.org

Foundation type: Public charity
Limitations: Grants to individuals conducting research on arthritis.
Publications: Annual report.
Financial data: Year ended 12/31/2003.
Assets, $66,519,154 (M); Expenditures, $69,236,889; Total giving, $20,706,270; Grants to individuals, totaling $20,706,270.
Fields of interest: Arthritis research.
Type of support: Research; Doctoral support.
Application information: Deadline Sept. 1; Initial approach by telephone; Completion of formal application required.
Program descriptions:
Arthritis Biomedical Science Grants: Awards $90,000 per year for three years to encourage and

support high quality, original biomedical research aimed at solving important scientific problems related to arthritis and rheumatic diseases. Individuals with doctoral degrees at the assistant professor level or higher, at any nonprofit institution in the U.S., are eligible to apply.

Arthritis Clinical Science Grants: Awards $90,000 per year for five years to encourage and support high quality original clinical research on problems related to the diagnosis, prognosis and management of adults and children with arthritis and related rheumatic diseases. Physicians or nonphysicians with doctoral degrees or the equivalent, who are associated with any nonprofit institution in the U.S., are eligible to apply.

Arthritis Investigator Award: Provides $74,000 plus a $1,000 institutional grant for three years, which may be renewed for two more years, to M.D.s, D.O.s, Ph.D.s, or equivalent who have a minimum of three years of research experience but are not yet established as an independent investigator. It requires an 80 percent time commitment in arthritis-related research.

Doctoral Dissertation Award for Arthritis Health Professionals: Awards $10,000 per year to provide for one or two years of salary and/or research support. The research project must be related to arthritis management and/or comprehensive patient care in rheumatology practice, research or education. Not for laboratory research.

New Investigator Grant for Arthritis Health Professionals: Awards $35,000 per year for two years, which may be renewed for a third year, to encourage individuals in health care to carry out innovative research projects in areas related to arthritis and the rheumatic diseases. Not for laboratory research. M.D.'s are not eligible.
EIN: 581341679

5621
Arthritis National Research Foundation
200 Oceangate, Ste. 830
Long Beach, CA 90802-4335
Contact: Helene F. Belisle, Exec. Dir.
FAX: (562) 983-1410; E-mail: anrf@ix.netcom.com;
URL: http://www.curearthritis.org

Foundation type: Public charity
Limitations: Research grants to newer postdoctoral investigators for the study of arthritis at a nonprofit U.S. institutions.
Publications: Application guidelines; Annual report; Financial statement; Grants list; Informational brochure (including application guidelines); Newsletter.
Financial data: Year ended 03/31/2005. Assets, $3,086,579 (M); Expenditures, $754,756; Total giving, $546,019; Grants to individuals, 10 grants totaling $546,019 (high: $100,000, low: $46,630).
Fields of interest: Arthritis research.
Type of support: Conferences/seminars; Fellowships; Research; Postdoctoral support; Travel grants.
Application information: Applications accepted. Application form required. Application form available on the grantmaker's Web site.
  Copies of proposal: 3
  Deadline(s): Jan. 16
  Applicants should submit the following:
    1) Resume
    2) Proposal
    3) Budget Information
  Additional information: One electronic copy and two hard copies of the proposal should be submitted; Application should include a letter of support from institution; Contact

foundation for current application guidelines or see Web site.
Program description:
  Arthritis National Research Foundation Grant: Grants between $20,000 and $50,000 to newer investigators holding an M.D. or Ph.D. for study into the causes of arthritis, with a general focus on high incidence of diseases. Salaries, supplies, and equipment directly related to the proposed studies are funded; overhead or indirect costs will not be funded.
EIN: 956043953

5622
The Ascension Fund, Inc.
P.O. Box 670
Gonzales, LA 70707-0670 (225) 647-0606
Contact: Mary Kruse, Exec. Dir.

Foundation type: Public charity
Limitations: Grants to teachers in Ascension Parish, LA, schools to enhance education.
Financial data: Year ended 03/31/2004. Assets, $1,159,806 (M); Expenditures, $60,352; Total giving, $35,111; Grants to individuals, totaling $35,111.
Fields of interest: Education.
Type of support: Program development.
Application information: Contact foundation for current application deadline; Application by proposal.
EIN: 721186479

5623
ASCO Foundation
1900 Duke St., Ste. 200
Alexandria, VA 22303 (703) 519-1456
Contact: Julia McCormack, Exec. Dir.
E-mail: mccormaj@asco.org; URL: http://www.ascofoundation.org

Foundation type: Public charity
Limitations: Grants for clinical research in the field of oncology.
Financial data: Year ended 08/31/2004. Assets, $8,538,243 (M); Expenditures, $18,488,865; Total giving, $17,013,246; Grants to individuals, 179 grants totaling $4,627,500 (high: $170,100, low: $1,500).
Fields of interest: Cancer; Cancer research.
Type of support: Research.
Application information: Applications accepted. Application form required. Application form available on the grantmaker's Web site.
  Deadline(s): Varies
  Additional information: See Web site for complete application information.
Program descriptions:
  Advanced Clinical Research Award: Awards up to $450,000 for three years for clinical oncology researchers involved in investigative work for 5 to ten years and intended to support original research not currently funded.
  Career Development Award: Awards up to $170,100 for three years to clinical investigators in their second, third or fourth year of a faculty appointment to establish an independent clinical cancer research program.
  Young Investigator Award: Awards up to $35,000 to a final year fellow or first year junior faculty, to encourage and promote quality research in clinical oncology.
  Merit Award: Awards $1,500 ($2,000 for international recipients attending a symposium) to oncology fellows who are first authors on abstracts selected for presentation at an ASCO scientific

meeting, including the Annual Meeting, and the prostate Cancer Symposium.
  International Development & Education Award: Provided to oncologists in developing countries to cover expenses associated with attending the ASCO Annual Meeting and visiting a cancer center.
EIN: 311667995

5624
Asian Cultural Council
437 Madison Ave., 37th Fl.
New York, NY 10022-7001 (212) 812-4300
Contact: Ralph Samuelson, Dir.
FAX: (212) 812-4299; E-mail: acc@accny.org;
URL: http://www.asianculturalcouncil.org

Foundation type: Public charity
Limitations: Fellowships to Asian artists, scholars, and specialists to conduct research, study, receive specialized training, undertake observation tours, or pursue creative activity in the U.S.
Publications: Application guidelines; Annual report; Informational brochure.
Financial data: Year ended 12/31/2004. Assets, $36,099,285 (M); Expenditures, $4,001,358; Total giving, $1,319,821; Grants to individuals, 136 grants totaling $1,319,821 (high: $32,300, low: $1,000).
Fields of interest: Arts, artist's services.
Type of support: Fellowships; Research; Foreign applicants; Undergraduate support.
Application information: Applications accepted. Application form required.
  Initial approach: Letter.
  Deadline(s): Feb. 1
Program description:
  Fellowship Grants to Asian Individuals: Full fellowships provide for round-trip international airfare, travel in the U.S., living expenses, medical insurance, and a miscellaneous expense allowance for books, supplies, and other grant-related costs for periods ranging from one to twelve months. Grant recipients are expected to return to their home countries at the conclusion of the fellowship period, using the training or experience acquired in the U.S. to fulfill professional responsibilities in their countries of origin. Support is not provided for undergraduate study, individual performance tours, or activities conducted by individuals within their own countries. Applicants seeking support to pursue graduate degrees in the U.S. must obtain tuition assistance from other sources.
EIN: 133018822

5625
The Aspen Institute
1 Dupont Cir., N.W., Ste. 700
Washington, DC 20036 (202) 736-5814
Contact: Winnifred Levy, Comms. Mgr.
FAX: (202) 293-0525; E-mail: info@aspeninst.org;
E-mail (for Winnifred Levy):
winnifred.levy@aspeninstitute.org; URL: http://www.nonprofitresearch.org
  http://www.aspeninstitute.org

Foundation type: Public charity
Limitations: General and doctoral dissertation research grants for study of nonprofit activities. Also provides limited undergraduate and graduate scholarships.
Publications: Application guidelines; Annual report; Grants list; Informational brochure; Newsletter.
Financial data: Year ended 12/31/2003. Assets, $75,312,572 (M); Expenditures, $35,673,968; Total giving, $1,047,725; Grants to individuals, totaling $119,463.

Fields of interest: Nonprofit management.
Type of support: Research; Doctoral support.
Application information: Application form required.
   Deadline(s): July 25 and Oct. 1
   Additional information: Application must also include brief project description, main research questions being addressed, populations being studied, methodology, data collection and analysis, schedule, budget, and additional materials required; See Web site for further application and program information. Additional e-mail for Research Fund: nsrf@aspeninstitute.org, and additional URL: www.nonprofitresearch.org.
Program descriptions:
   U.S. Community Foundations: Grants ranging from $10,000 to $125,000 are available to nonprofit practitioners, academic researchers, independent scholars, and policy analysts to support research on nonprofits. Areas of high priority are: the role of nonprofits and philanthropy in society; impact of public policy on nonprofits and their constituents; and nonprofit accountability, governance, and management. Amount of grant awarded is dependent on the scope of the project. See Nonprofit Sector Research Fund e-mail and web site for further information.
   Doctoral Dissertation Research: Provides grants of up to $20,000 to support graduate students engaged in doctoral dissertation research pertaining to nonprofit and philanthropic activities in the U.S. and other countries. To be eligible for funding, an applicant must have a university-approved doctoral prospectus or dissertation topic at the time grant is to be awarded. See Nonprofit Sector Research Fund e-mail and web site for further information.
   Nonprofit Sector Research Fund: The Nonprofit Sector Research Fund awards grants for: 1) Doctoral Dissertation Research. No grants for this program were awarded for the 2005-2006 academic year, and 2) the William Randolph Hearst Endowed Scholarship for Minority Students. This fund provides scholarships to undergraduate and graduate students to pursue research at the Nonprofit Sector Research Fund year-round for 10 to 15 weeks at the institute. Awards are between $2,500 and $5,000, depending on the recipient's educational level, financial need, and time commitment.
EIN: 840399006

5626

Association for Surgical Education Foundation

c/o SIU School of Medicine, Dept. of Surgery
P.O. Box 19655
Springfield, IL 62794
Contact: Susan Kepner, Exec. Dir.
Telephone for Susan Kepner: (212) 545-3835;
URL: http://www.surgicaleducation.com/asefounda/asefoundation.htm

Foundation type: Independent foundation
Limitations: Fellowships to researchers, educators, and clinicians investigating questions, issues and concerns that are integral to surgical education. Applicants must be Association for Surgical Education members.
Financial data: Year ended 06/30/2004. Assets, $0 (M); Expenditures, $246,872; Total giving, $157,020; Grants to individuals, 4 grants totaling $157,020 (high: $50,000, low: $17,000).
Fields of interest: Surgery research.
Type of support: Fellowships; Postdoctoral support.
Application information:
   Deadline(s): Dec. 15

Additional information: Completion of formal application required, including C.V., outline of prior medical research and published works, description of current research interests, and letter of support from Department Chair; See Web site for further application information.
Program description:
   Surgical Education Fellowship: Awards up to ten fellowships annually to spend a year studying under an advisor affiliated with the Foundation. Fellowships include $3,000 for tuition, travel to two seminars and costs associated with the Foundation's forum. Fellows are expected to submit the abstract or paper produced to a peer-reviewed forum or journal and to pass a final exam.
EIN: 371305690

5627

Association of Higher Education Facilities Officers

1643 Prince St.
Alexandria, VA   22314-2818   (703) 684-1446
Contact: Brooks H. Baker III, Pres.
FAX: (703) 549-2772; URL: http://www.appa.org

Foundation type: Public charity
Limitations: Awards by nomination only to APPA members.
Financial data: Year ended 03/31/2003. Assets, $4,051,045 (M); Expenditures, $3,153,046; Total giving, $25,050; Grants to individuals, 5 grants totaling $5,050 (high: $1,250, low: $950).
Type of support: Awards/grants by nomination only; Awards/prizes.
Application information: Application form required.
   Deadline(s): Vary
Program descriptions:
   Meritorious Service Award: Given to three individuals each year who have made significant, life-long contributions to the profession of higher education facilities management. Nominee must have been an active member of APPA for a minimum of five years, attended and participated in meetings and other functions at the international level, and demonstrated distinguished service to the association. Deadline Mar. 30.
   Pacesetter Award: Seven awards are given annually to individuals who have made significant contributions at the regions or chapters and have been active APPA members for a minimum of three years, continued service to the association through the task force, special project, authorship of publication, or presentation at a meeting, and other voluntary contribution of time, effort, and resources. Deadline Mar. 30.
   Rex Dillow Award: Presented to the author of the best article published in Facilities Manager during the previous calendar year. Eligible articles are those written by a full-time employee, from any department, of an APPA member institution of higher education.
EIN: 850211201

5628

Association of Theological Schools in the U.S. & Canada

10 Summit Park Dr.
Pittsburgh, PA   15275-1103   (412) 788-6505
Contact: Daniel O. Aleshire, Exec. Dir.
FAX: (412) 788-6510; E-mail: ats@ats.edu;
URL: http://www.ats.edu

Foundation type: Public charity

Limitations: Grants for the enhancement of theological studies to full-time faculty of accredited and candidate for member school.
Publications: Application guidelines; Grants list; Informational brochure (including application guidelines); Newsletter.
Financial data: Year ended 06/30/2004. Assets, $18,142,766 (M); Expenditures, $4,107,972; Total giving, $659,961; Grants to individuals, 30 grants totaling $659,961 (high: $74,174, low: $4,840).
Fields of interest: Theological school/education.
Type of support: Program development; Conferences/seminars; Fellowships; Research; Scholarships—to individuals; Travel grants.
Application information: Application form required.
   Initial approach: Letter, telephone, FAX or e-mail.
   Deadline(s): Jan 24
   Additional information: Inappropriate request for funding not considered or acknowledged; See Web site for further information.
Program descriptions:
   Faculty Fellowships: Up to five fellowships of no more than $25,000 awarded to individuals for substantial research projects reflecting high scholarly standards. Fellowships are designed to assist faculty members who offer well-developed plans for conducting significant research projects during an institutionally-approved research leave of six months or more. Awards will include salary and benefit replacement, and, if needed, funds for direct research expenses.
   Theological Scholars Grants: Provides up to $10,000 for as many as 10 grants to theological students. Faculty may request Theological Research Grants for three different patterns of work. Recipients can request or specify how the money can be used for research.
   Research Expenses Grants: Up to 10 grants of up to $5,000 each awarded to individuals in support of direct expenses for travel necessary to access material archived elsewhere, for research assistance in gathering or processing data, for essential specialized software or for similar direct expenses related to faculty research projects. Grants are awarded on the basis of a thoughtful and defensible project design that shows promise for valuable research and the necessity for the funds in order to undertake the project. The grants are designed to allow flexibility and to encourage creativity on the part of the recipients.
EIN: 310593259

5629

Atlas Economic Research Foundation

4084 University Dr., Ste. 103
Fairfax, VA   22030-6812   (703) 934-6969
Contact: Alejandro Chafuen, Pres. and C.E.O.
FAX: (703) 352-7530

Foundation type: Public charity
Limitations: Fellowships to individuals to inspire new intellectual entrepreneurs to dedicate themselves to the world of ideas in business and industry.
Financial data: Year ended 12/31/2003. Assets, $3,421,205 (M); Expenditures, $2,871,857; Total giving, $1,650,533.
Fields of interest: Business/industry.
Type of support: Fellowships; Foreign applicants.
Application information: Contact foundation for current application deadline/guidelines.
Program description:
   Atlas Fellowship Program: Fellowships of $1,000 per month to individuals to join Atlas for a three- to six-month period, to help with specific projects and to immerse themselves in the world of

market-oriented think tanks. Stipend is for travel expenses. Fellows are encouraged to purchase private health insurance before coming to the U.S.
EIN: 942763845

5630

Autism Society of America Foundation
7910 Woodmont Ave., Ste. 300
Bethesda, MD   20814-3015   (301) 657-0881
Contact: Rob Beck, Exec. Dir.
E-mail: asaf@autism-society.org; Additional tel.:
(800) 328-8476; URL: http://
www.autism-society.org

Foundation type: Public charity
Limitations: Research grants for the study of autism and the causes, cure and treatment thereof.
Financial data: Year ended 12/31/2004.
Assets, $492,716 (M); Expenditures, $256,837.
Fields of interest: Autism research.
Type of support: Research.
Application information: See web site for further application information.
EIN: 522007155

5631

Avatar Meher Baba Foundation, Inc.
P.O. Box 398
Mystic, CT   06355-0398
Contact: Emory Ayers, Pres.; Susan Ayers, Secy.-Treas.

Foundation type: Independent foundation
Limitations: Grants by nomination only to individuals to participate in the Avatar Meher Baba PPC Trust Spiritual Training Program in India.
Financial data: Year ended 03/31/2005.
Assets, $1,202,818 (M); Expenditures, $130,495; Total giving, $89,856; Grants to individuals, 10 grants totaling $12,000.
Fields of interest: Religion.
Type of support: Grants to individuals; Awards/ grants by nomination only.
Application information: Applications not accepted.
EIN: 061516691

5632

B'nai B'rith
2020 K St., N.W., 7th Fl.
Washington, DC   20006   (202) 857-6522
Contact: Richard D. Heideman, Pres.

Foundation type: Public charity
Limitations: Grants to researchers who reside in Israel or the U.S.
Financial data: Year ended 06/30/2003.
Assets, $15,437,885 (M); Expenditures, $17,444,888; Total giving, $3,613,865.
Type of support: Research.
Application information: Contact foundation for current application deadline/guidelines.
EIN: 530179971

5633

The Bachmann-Strauss Dystonia and Parkinson Foundation, Inc., Inc.
1 Gustave Levy Pl.
P.O. Box 1490
New York, NY   10029   (212) 241-5614
Contact: Helen H. Miller, Exec. Dir.
FAX: (212) 987-0662;
E-mail: bachmann.strauss@mssm.edu;
URL: http://www.dystonia-parkinsons.org

Foundation type: Public charity
Limitations: Research grants for the study of Dystonia and Parkinson's disease.
Financial data: Year ended 12/31/2003.
Assets, $2,384,295 (M); Expenditures, $1,344,310; Total giving, $885,865.
Fields of interest: Nerve, muscle & bone diseases; Parkinson's disease; Nerve, muscle & bone research; Parkinson's disease research.
Type of support: Research.
Application information: Applications accepted.
Initial approach: E-mail.
Deadline(s): Oct. 3
Additional information: Contact foundation for further application information.
EIN: 133804248

5634

Bainbridge Arts & Crafts, Inc.
151 Winslow Way E.
Bainbridge Island, WA   98110-2425
(206) 842-3132
Contact: Susan Jackson, Exec. Dir.
FAX: (206) 780-8149;
E-mail: info@bainbridgeartscrafts.org; URL: http://www.bainbridgeartscrafts.org

Foundation type: Public charity
Limitations: Grants to Bainbridge Island, WA, public school art teachers for the purchase of art materials which supplement the school district budget.
Financial data: Year ended 06/30/2004.
Assets, $113,911 (M); Expenditures, $316,090; Total giving, $7,179; Grants to individuals, totaling $7,179.
Fields of interest: Arts education.
Type of support: Grants to individuals.
Application information:
Initial approach: E-mail or letter.
Additional information: Contact foundation for further application information.
EIN: 910714664

5635

The Bakken
(formerly Bakken Library of Electricity in Life)
3537 Zenith Ave. S.
Minneapolis, MN   55416-4623
Contact: David J. Rhees, Exec. Dir.
URL: http://www.thebakken.org

Foundation type: Public charity
Limitations: Research grants and fellowships to individuals for work related to science, technology, medicine, and other related fields.
Financial data: Year ended 12/31/2003.
Assets, $11,169,412 (M); Expenditures, $1,776,399; Total giving, $45,971; Grants to individuals, totaling $45,971.
Fields of interest: Medical research; Science, research; Engineering/technology.
Type of support: Fellowships; Research; Travel grants.

Application information:
Deadline(s): Apr. 19 for Summer Graduate Fellowship; none for Research Travel Grants
Additional information: Application by letter outlining proposed research , including C.V. and two letters of recommendation; See Web site for further application information.
Program descriptions:
Summer Graduate Fellowship: Awards a stipend of $3,200 and for an eight-week period in the summer. The fellowship requires residence in the Twin Cities area. Approximately 40 percent of the fellow's time may be spent on his/her own research. (Research related to The Bakken's collections is encouraged but not required.) The remainder of the time will be spent working at The Bakken on projects that would benefit from the fellow's expertise in the history of science, technology, medicine, or cognate subjects. The main project for the fellowship is research and writing for a future exhibition; other minor projects may be pursued as time permits, such as bibliographical work; background research for K-12 education programs, etc.
Research Travel Grants: Awards research travel grants for the purpose of facilitating research in its collection of books, journals, manuscripts, prints, and instruments. $500 (domestic) and $750 (foreign) are available to help researchers to defray the expenses of travel, subsistence, and other direct costs of conducting research at The Bakken. The minimum period of residence is one week. For more information and application guidelines please contact Elizabeth Ihrig, Librarian.
EIN: 510175508

5636

Banner Health Foundation of Arizona
(formerly The Samaritan Foundation)
2025 N. Third St., Ste. 250
Phoenix, AZ   85004   (602) 495-4483
Contact: Andy Kramer, Pres. and C.E.O.
FAX: (602) 495-4539; URL: http://www.bannerhealth.com

Foundation type: Public charity
Limitations: Grants to AZ medical professionals for research that benefits the Banner Health System.
Publications: Financial statement; Newsletter.
Financial data: Year ended 12/31/2004.
Assets, $59,526,898 (M); Expenditures, $9,155,662; Total giving, $4,779,945; Grants to individuals, totaling $160,671.
Fields of interest: Medical research.
Type of support: Research.
Application information: Applications accepted.
Additional information: Contact foundation for current application deadlines/guidelines.
EIN: 942545356

5637

The Bantly Charitable Trust
806 Moss Creek Plantation
Duluth, GA   30097-5958   (770) 736-7534
Contact: Thomas W. Bantly, Tr.

Foundation type: Independent foundation
Limitations: Grants for religious study, missionary support, and medical research.
Financial data: Year ended 12/31/2004.
Assets, $437,704 (M); Expenditures, $25,129; Total giving, $19,500; Grants to individuals, totaling $19,500.
Fields of interest: Theological school/education; Medical research, institute; Biological sciences; Christian agencies & churches.

Type of support: Research.
Application information: Applications accepted. Application form required. Application form available on the grantmaker's Web site.
Initial approach: Letter.
Additional information: Applicants for medical research grants must also submit a memorandum outlining proposed medical research, approximate length of time the research will take, the specific issues the researcher will address or study, how the results will be used, and the applicant's overall assessment of the importance of the research to mental health in general. Interviews required.
Program description:
Medical Research Program: Medical research grants are for students interested in biochemical and molecular theories relating to the mind. Religious scholarships are for those intending a career in religious education or the ministry. The trust is presently localizing grants to the southeast and interviewing all grantseekers in person.
EIN: 581637392

5638
Baptist Health Care Foundation of Montgomery
P.O. Box 241647
Montgomery, AL 36124-1647 (334) 273-4567
Contact: Ben F. Kelley, V.P. and Exec. Dir.

Foundation type: Public charity
Limitations: Nursing and allied health scholarships to individuals.
Fields of interest: Nursing care; Health care.
Type of support: Scholarships—to individuals.
Application information: Unsolicited requests for funds not accepted.
EIN: 237281996

5639
Bartlesville Public School Foundation, Inc.
1100 S. Jennings
Bartlesville, OK 74003
Contact: Sherri Lynn

Foundation type: Independent foundation
Limitations: Grants to educators in the Bartlesville Public School System, OK.
Financial data: Year ended 06/30/2005. Assets, $1,079,275 (M); Expenditures, $289,646; Total giving, $276,887; Grants to individuals, 98 grants totaling $76,887.
Fields of interest: Education.
Type of support: Program development.
Application information: Deadline Oct. 1 and Feb. 1 for all but Professional Growth Program; Completion of formal application required.
Program descriptions:
Professional Growth for Teachers and Principals Program: Promotes growth in motivational and other techniques. Deadlines Sept. 17, Jan. 15, and Apr. 15.
Teacher Grants: For development of creative instructional techniques.
Experts in Residence: Exposes educators to experts in fields related to curriculum.
Field Trip Grants: Allows students the opportunity to enhance their education.
EIN: 731256865

5640
Bat Conservation International
P.O. Box 162603
Austin, TX 78716 (512) 327-9721
Contact: Emily Young, Dir. Devel.
FAX: (512) 327-9724; E-mail: info@batcon.org;
URL: http://www.batcon.org

Foundation type: Public charity
Limitations: Research grants and awards for the study and conservation of the bat.
Publications: Annual report; Informational brochure.
Financial data: Year ended 05/31/2004. Assets, $3,805,534 (M); Expenditures, $2,184,271; Total giving, $181,723.
Fields of interest: Animals/wildlife, preservation/protection.
Type of support: Research; Awards/prizes.
Application information: Contact foundation for current application deadline/guidelines.
EIN: 742553144

5641
The Bay and Paul Foundations, Inc.
(formerly Josephine Bay Paul and C. Michael Paul Foundation, Inc.)
17 W. 94th St., 1st Fl.
New York, NY 10025 (212) 663-1115
Contact: Frederick Bay, Exec. Dir.
FAX: (212) 932-0316;
E-mail: info@bayandpaulfoundations.org;
URL: http://www.bayandpaulfoundations.org

Foundation type: Independent foundation
Limitations: Awards by nomination only to researchers in the biodiversity conservation field.
Financial data: Year ended 12/31/2004. Assets, $73,879,324 (M); Expenditures, $3,841,382; Total giving, $2,648,817; Grants to individuals, 6 grants totaling $300,000 (high: $60,000, low: $30,000, average grant: $30,000-$60,000). Subtotal for awards/prizes: 6 grants totaling $300,000 (high: $60,000, low: $30,000).
Fields of interest: Natural resources; Biological sciences.
Type of support: Awards/grants by nomination only; Awards/prizes.
Application information: Applications not accepted.
Program description:
Biodiversity and Emerging Leadership Awards: Nomination and selection by an independent panel of scientists for early to middle career achievements in addressing the problems of conserving biological resources.
EIN: 131991717

5642
Arnold and Mabel Beckman Foundation
100 Academy Dr.
Irvine, CA 92617 (949) 721-2222
Contact: Jacqueline Dorrance, Exec. Dir.
FAX: (949) 721-2225; E-mail (for Kathlene Williams, Exec. Asst.): k.williams@beckman-foundation.com; URL: http://www.beckman-foundation.com

Foundation type: Independent foundation
Limitations: Research support to U.S. citizens and permanent residents with tenure-track appointments in academic and nonprofit organizations to fund research in the chemical and life sciences.

Publications: Application guidelines; Program policy statement.
Financial data: Year ended 08/31/2004. Assets, $373,405,000 (M); Expenditures, $17,185,044; Total giving, $15,644,933; Grants to individuals, 56 grants totaling $4,534,019 (high: $134,019, low: $80,000).
Fields of interest: Genetics/birth defects; Science, research; Science; Marine science; Chemistry; Biological sciences.
Type of support: Research; Awards/prizes.
Application information: Deadline Oct. 1; Completion of formal application required.
Program description:
Beckman Young Investigators: Research funding is available to U.S. citizens and permanent residents within the first three years of their tenure-track appointments in academic and nonprofit institutions conducting research in the chemical and life sciences, broadly interpreted. Projects should represent innovative departures in research rather than extensions of existing programs. Projects are normally funded for three years but may be funded for four-year periods. Grants are normally in the range of $240,000.
EIN: 953169713

5643
Berlex Foundation, Inc.
c/o Review Comm.
433 Hackensack Ave., 9th Fl.
Hackensack, NJ 07601 (201) 342-4441
E-mail: llisanti@berlex-foundation.org; Contact for Reproductive Scientist Development Prog.: Dr. Robert Jaffe, Univ. of California, San Francisco, Box 0922, San Francisco, CA 94143-0922, tel.: (415) 476-9047; URL: http://www.berlex-foundation.org/

Foundation type: Company-sponsored foundation
Limitations: Grants to medical doctors for research in the field of reproductive medicine. Doctors must be affiliated with a university or laboratory institution.
Publications: Application guidelines; Informational brochure (including application guidelines).
Financial data: Year ended 12/31/2002. Assets, $300,433 (M); Expenditures, $838,538; Total giving, $299,000; Grants to individuals, 8 grants totaling $299,000 (high: $50,000, low: $6,500).
Fields of interest: Medical research, institute; Biological sciences.
Type of support: Fellowships; Research.
Application information: Application form required.
Deadline(s): Oct. 1
Additional information: See program description for further information.
Program description:
Research Program: Scholar Award: Candidate must be an M.D. who:
· presents a research proposal of merit
· has a proven record of independent, fruitful investigation
· has assurance of an appropriate university faculty appointment
International Research Fellowship: Candidate must be a non-tenured faculty member of U.S. citizenship who has completed a residency in obstetrics and gynecology Reproductive Scientist Award: Candidate must have an M.D. and a career objective in academic obstetrics and gynecology with a major commitment to research. Applicants must send the following information:
· curriculum vitae
· present position and activities

- name of the director, institution, and laboratory in which the work will be conducted
- letter of endorsement from the program director, department chairman, and laboratory director at the institution where the work will be prepared
- statement of career goals
- research proposal not to exceed six typewritten pages prepared in the NIH format
- statement from the institution that a tenure-track faculty position will be offered by the end of the award year
- statement of any previous and current research funding.

EIN: 133359746

5644

Eric Berne Fund of the International Transactional Analysis Association

436 14th St., Ste. 1301
Oakland, CA 94612-2710 (510) 625-7720
Contact: Denton Roberts, Exec. Dir.
FAX: (510) 625-7725; E-mail: itaa@itaa-net.org;
URL: http://www.itaa-net.org

Foundation type: Public charity
Limitations: Project support for various evaluations and applications of transactional analysis theory to help fund program budgets.
Publications: Application guidelines; Informational brochure; Newsletter.
Financial data: Year ended 12/31/2003.
Assets, $1,118,462 (M); Expenditures, $373,399; Total giving, $13,250.
Fields of interest: Psychology/behavioral science.
Type of support: Program development; Research.
Application information:
Deadline(s): June 1
Additional information: Application by letter, including amount requested, problem for which funds are requested, program objectives, population to benefit from proposed project, plans for securing further financial support, applicant and staff qualifications, brief timetable, and statement of how and why success of program might be measured.
EIN: 946104066

5645

The Russell Berrie Foundation

300 Frank W. Burr Blvd., Bldg. E., 7th Fl.
Teaneck, NJ 07666-6704 (201) 928-1880
Contact: Robert Gordon, C.F.O.
URL: http://www.russberrie.com

Foundation type: Independent foundation
Limitations: Awards to NJ residents who have made a difference in the well-being of society.
Financial data: Year ended 12/31/2004.
Assets, $162,574,934 (M); Expenditures, $24,483,654; Total giving, $21,534,480; Grants to individuals, 19 grants totaling $150,000 (high: $50,000, low: $25,000).
Fields of interest: Social sciences.
Type of support: Awards/prizes.
Application information: Contact foundation for current application deadline/guidelines.
EIN: 222620908

5646

Bibliographical Society of America, Inc.

P.O. Box 1537
Lenox Hill Sta.
New York, NY 10021
E-mail: bsa@bibsocamer.org; Tel./FAX: (212) 452-2710; URL: http://www.bibsocamer.org

Foundation type: Public charity
Limitations: Fellowships and awards to applicants for various studies relating to bibliographical inquiries as well as research in the history of books and publishing.
Financial data: Year ended 12/31/2003.
Assets, $2,713,853 (M); Expenditures, $245,602; Total giving, $26,500; Grants to individuals, 12 grants totaling $26,500 (high: $4,500, low: $1,000).
Fields of interest: Literature.
Type of support: Fellowships; Research; Awards/prizes; Stipends.
Application information: Applications accepted. Application form required.
Initial approach: Letter or e-mail.
Deadline(s): Sept. 1 for Justin G. Schiller Prize, Dec. 1 for Fellowship, and Sept. 1, 2008 for William L. Mitchell Prize
Applicants should submit the following:
1) Letter(s) of recommendation
2) Curriculum vitae
Additional information: See Web site for additional awards information and guidelines.
Program descriptions:
Justin G. Schiller Prize: A cash award of $2,000 and a year's membership in the Society to a scholar whose works (includes theses, articles, books, or electronic resources) was published between Jan. 1, 2001 and Sept. 1, 2006. Submissions for the Prize may concentrate on any children's book printed before 1901 in any country or any language, but must be written in English. They should be based on investigations into bibliography and printing history broadly conceived and should focus on the physical aspects of the book as historical evidence for studying topics such as the history of book production, publication, distribution, collecting, or reading. Eligible scholarship may take the form of a book or article, as Master's thesis or doctoral dissertation defended and approved, or research results distributed in another manner such as on a World-Wide-Web site of CD-Rom.
William L. Mitchell Prize: A cash award of $1,000 and a year's membership in the Society to a scholar whose works (includes theses, articles, books, and electronics resources) was published after Dec. 31, 2004. Submissions for the Prize may concentrate on any periodicals or newspapers printed before 1800 in English-speaking countries, but should involve research into primary sources of historical evidence, such as the analysis of the physical objects, whether for establishing a text or understanding the history of the production, distribution, collecting, or reading of serial publications. Eligible scholarship may take the form of a book or article, a Master's thesis or doctoral dissertation defended and approved, or research results distributed in another manner, such as on a World-Wide-Web site of CD-Rom.
Fellowship Program: Fellows are paid a stipend of up to $2,000 per month (for up to two months) in support of travel, living and research expenses. Eligible topics may concentrate on books and documents in any field, but should focus on the book or manuscript (the physical object) as historical evidence. Such topics may include establishing a text or studying the history of book production, publication, distribution, collecting, or

reading. The program is open to applicants of any nationality.
EIN: 131632509

5647

Biegelsen Foundation, Inc.

740 S. Andrews Ave.
Fort Lauderdale, FL 33316
Contact: Jeffrey Biegelsen, V.P.
Application address: P.O. Box 210, Hollywood, FL 33022, tel.: (954) 463-6581

Foundation type: Independent foundation
Limitations: Grants to doctors for medical research at the University of Miami School of Medicine, FL.
Financial data: Year ended 09/30/2004.
Assets, $794,385 (M); Expenditures, $35,927; Total giving, $34,450.
Fields of interest: Heart & circulatory research; Arthritis research; Lupus research.
Type of support: Research; Postdoctoral support.
Application information: Applications accepted.
Deadline(s): None
Additional information: Contact foundation for current application guidelines.
EIN: 136103887

5648

Worth Bingham Memorial Fund

1616 H St. N.W., 3rd Fl.
Washington, DC 20006 (202) 737-3700
Contact: Susan Talalay
FAX: (202) 737-0530

Foundation type: Independent foundation
Limitations: Awards to honor newspaper and magazine investigative reporting of stories of national significance where the public interest is being ill-served.
Financial data: Year ended 12/31/2004.
Assets, $184,057 (M); Expenditures, $30,148; Total giving, $10,000; Grants to individuals, totaling $10,000.
Fields of interest: Journalism/publishing.
Type of support: Awards/prizes.
Application information:
Deadline(s): Jan. 3
Additional information: Completion of formal application required, including four copies of the completed application form and attached stories.
Program description:
Worth Bingham Prize: Entries may be a single story, a related series of stories, or up to three unrelated stories, and have a publish date of the year prior to application. Columns and editorials are eligible. Previous recipients are eligible for future awards without restriction.
EIN: 056020486

5649

The Black-Footed Ferret Recovery Foundation

P.O. Box 249
Wheatland, WY 82201
E-mail: wyoweasel@hotmail.com; URL: http://www.blackfootedferret.org

Foundation type: Independent foundation
Limitations: Grants to individuals who demonstrate an understanding of and commitment to the preservation of the black-footed ferret species.
Financial data: Year ended 12/31/2002.
Assets, $17,094 (M); Expenditures, $163,141;

Total giving, $128,322; Grants to individuals, 2 grants totaling $30,000 (high: $28,000, low: $2,000).
Fields of interest: Animal welfare; Animals/wildlife, preservation/protection; Animals/wildlife, endangered species.
Type of support: Research.
Application information: Applications by letter accepted throughout the year.
EIN: 841329767

5650
Blacklock Nature Sanctuary
P.O. Box 426
Moose Lake, MN 55767-0426 (612) 802-6155
Contact: Harriet Barlow, Exec. Dir.
URL: http://www.blacklock.org

Foundation type: Public charity
Limitations: Fellowships to administrators who manage MN arts organizations.
Publications: Application guidelines.
Financial data: Year ended 12/31/2004.
Assets, $1,315,385 (M); Expenditures, $42,794; Total giving, $8,300; Grants to individuals, totaling $8,300.
Fields of interest: Arts, administration/regulation.
Type of support: Internship funds.
Application information: Deadline Jan. 31; Completion of formal application required, including resume, proposal and SASE.
Program description:
Arts Administrator Renewal Fellowship: Administrators who manage Minnesota arts organizations or programs with budgets under $2 million may apply for a career renewal fellowship. Individuals or pairs of arts administrators may apply to spend one week at the residence to focus on career renewal activities. Stipend includes $300 per week for food or supplies.
EIN: 411794361

5651
Blakemore Foundation
c/o Perkins Coie LLP
1201 3rd Ave., Ste. 4800
Seattle, WA 98101-3266 (206) 359-8778
Contact: Griffith Way, Board Member; For inquiries: Cathy Scheibner, Admin. Asst.
FAX: (206) 359-9778;
E-mail: blackmore@perkinscoie.com; URL: http://www.blakemorefoundation.org

Foundation type: Independent foundation
Limitations: Fellowships to U.S. citizens and permanent U.S. residents studying languages in east and southeast Asia.
Financial data: Year ended 12/31/2004.
Assets, $12,481,927 (M); Expenditures, $1,717,466; Total giving, $1,459,122; Grants to individuals, 57 grants totaling $1,085,805 (high: $43,213, low: $255).
Fields of interest: Language (foreign).
Type of support: Fellowships.
Application information: Application form required. Application form available on the grantmaker's Web site.
Deadline(s): Jan. 15
Additional information: Application should include a three- to four-page proposal, college transcripts, and two letters of recommendation; Recipients notified in Mar.
Program description:
Blakemore Foundation Program: Grants are provided for a year of advanced language study at an institute in Asia. Applicants must be pursuing an

academic, professional, or business career that involves the regular use of a modern Asian language; have a bachelor's degree; be at or near an advanced level in the language; be a U.S. citizen or permanent resident; and be able to study the language full-time.
EIN: 911505735

5652
Blessed Hope Christian Mission Foundation
7114 Catlett St.
Springfield, VA 22151 (703) 256-6095
Contact: Robert J. Rooks, Pres.

Foundation type: Operating foundation
Limitations: Grants to individuals for missionary work.
Financial data: Year ended 06/30/2005.
Assets, $226,431 (M); Expenditures, $9,044; Total giving, $6,500; Grants to individuals, 3 grants totaling $6,500 (high: $4,000, low: $1,000).
Fields of interest: Protestant agencies & churches.
Type of support: Grants to individuals.
Application information:
Deadline(s): Contact foundation for current application deadline
Additional information: Completion of formal application required, including three written recommendations, one of which should be obtained from an ordained Christian minister.
EIN: 541691074

5653
Blue Cross and Blue Shield of Michigan Foundation
(formerly Michigan Health Care Education and Research Foundation/MHCERF)
600 Lafayette E., M.C. X520
Detroit, MI 48226-2928 (313) 225-8706
Contact: Ira Strumwasser Ph.D., C.E.O. and Exec. Dir.
FAX: (313) 225-7730;
E-mail: foundation@bcbsm.com; Additional tel.: (313) 225-7560; URL: http://www.bcbsm.com/foundation/

Foundation type: Public charity
Limitations: Research support and awards to MI residents who are health and medical researchers and students at MI universities.
Publications: Application guidelines; Annual report (including application guidelines); Informational brochure (including application guidelines).
Financial data: Year ended 12/31/2003.
Assets, $56,613,585 (M); Expenditures, $2,095,382; Total giving, $1,285,219; Grants to individuals, 41 grants totaling $987,970.
Fields of interest: Health sciences school/education; Health care; Medical research, institute.
Type of support: Fellowships; Research; Awards/prizes; Doctoral support.
Application information: Deadline Apr. 30 for Student Awards, Applications accepted throughout the year for other programs; Initial approach by letter; Completion of formal application required; See Web site for further application information.
Program descriptions:
Physician-Investigator Research Award: Provides seed money to physicians to explore the merits of a particular research idea for further study. Grants of up to $10,000 are offered for projects that include pilot studies, feasibility studies or small research studies in clinical or health services research. Recipient must submit a proposal.

Investigator-Initiated Research Program: Grants $50,000-$75,000 per year to researchers for studies in health services policy or clinical care. Grants over $75,000 are considered for exceptional projects. This program does not support basic or biomedical research, or research involving non-human subjects.
Student Awards Program: Awards $3,000 per year to students enrolled in medical or doctoral programs at MI universities for student research, pilot projects, interventions/evaluations, and demonstration projects.
Excellence in Research Award: Honors researchers, both physicians and those with terminal research degrees, who make a significant contribution to improving health care in MI.
Excellence in Research Award for Students: Designed to identify students at MI universities who have made contributions through their health and medical care research. Awards are presented to doctoral and medical students for contributions to health care research literature.
Frank J. McDevitt Excellence in Research Award for Health Services, Policy & Clinical Care: Four $10,000 awards annually for excellence in research to physician or doctoral-level researchers to conduct research on health services, policy, or clinical care. Deadline Jan. 1.
Men's Health Detection: Awards to Michigan-based physicians and doctoral-level researchers based at universities, academic medical settings, community hospitals, health systems, and community-based nonprofit organizations are invited to submit letters of interest to improve men's health through screening, referrals, and follow ups. Research projects should result in information that is directly applicable to the design of strategies to increase screening, referral, and follow-up care in Michigan. Deadline Jan. 15.
EIN: 382338506

5654
Boiron Research Foundation, Inc.
6 Campus Blvd., Bldg. A
Newtown Square, PA 19073
Contact: Thierry Boiron, Pres. and Secy.-Treas.

Foundation type: Company-sponsored foundation
Limitations: Grants only to professionals to conduct clinical studies using homeopathic medicines.
Financial data: Year ended 12/31/2004.
Assets, $256,898 (M); Expenditures, $30,732; Total giving, $24,000; Grant to an individual, 1 grant totaling $24,000.
Fields of interest: Medical research, institute.
Type of support: Research.
Application information: Contact foundation for current application deadline/guidelines; Ineligible applications not considered or acknowledged.
EIN: 521268329

5655
Bonfils-Stanton Foundation
Daniels and Fisher Twr.
1601 Arapahoe St., Ste. 500
Denver, CO 80202 (303) 825-3774
Contact: Dorothy A. Horrell Ph.D., C.E.O.
URL: http://www.bonfils-stanton.org

Foundation type: Independent foundation
Limitations: Annual awards by nomination only to individuals in CO who have made significant contributions in the fields of arts and humanities, community service, and science and medicine.

Publications: Annual report (including application guidelines); Grants list.
Financial data: Year ended 06/30/2005. Assets, $76,182,040 (M); Expenditures, $3,748,929; Total giving, $2,625,818; Grants to individuals, 3 grants totaling $75,000 (high: $25,000, low: $25,000).
Fields of interest: Humanities; Arts; Health care; Community development, volunteer services; Science; Science.
Type of support: Awards/grants by nomination only; Awards/prizes.
Application information: Nominations accepted throughout the year; Initial approach by letter.
EIN: 846029014

5656
The Ken Boxley Foundation
9894 Beverly Grove Dr.
Beverly Hills, CA   90210
Contact: Ken Boxley, Dir.

Foundation type: Independent foundation
Limitations: Scholarships by nomination only to individuals enrolled in advanced, postgraduate degree programs at accredited colleges and universities in the U.S. and abroad. Priority is given to applicants in exact sciences and business.
Financial data: Year ended 12/31/2004. Assets, $147,961 (M); Expenditures, $13,626; Total giving, $12,390; Grants to individuals, totaling $2,390.
Fields of interest: Business school/education; Science.
Type of support: Awards/grants by nomination only; Postgraduate support.
Application information: Unsolicited applications are not accepted; The foundation locates all candidates.
Program description:
Boxley Foundation Program: The selection committee will not seek unsolicited applications from graduate students. It may obtain recommendations from the faculties and deans of various universities and colleges and from leaders of various scientific and business communities. Once a recommendation is received, the selection committee will contact the proposed candidate and advise the individual that he or she has been recommended as a possible recipient. At that point, each proposed candidate will be required to complete an application form and submit the requested background information. Academic transcripts, financial need, character, and motivation are taken into account.
Recommendations are required and prospective grantees are interviewed. Recipients are usually able to renew their grants to complete their studies.
EIN: 954050419

5657
John Boyer First Troop
(formerly John Boyer First Troop Philadelphia City Cavalry Memorial Fund)
c/o Mellon Bank, N.A.
P.O. Box 185
Pittsburgh, PA   15230-9897

Foundation type: Independent foundation
Limitations: Scholarships by nomination only to members of the First Troop Philadelphia City Cavalry to study abroad for one year.
Financial data: Year ended 06/30/2005. Assets, $1,689,064 (M); Expenditures, $64,895; Total giving, $54,012; Grants to individuals, totaling $54,012.

Type of support: Awards/grants by nomination only; Travel grants.
Application information: Applications not accepted.
Additional information: Candidates must be nominated by a member of Cavalry.
EIN: 236227636

5658
Brewster Education Foundation, Inc.
P.O. Box 320
Brewster, NY   10509-0320   (845) 279-5051
Contact: Nicholas Simonelli, Pres.
URL: http://www.bef.org

Foundation type: Public charity
Limitations: Awards to teachers of the Brewster Central School District, NY, to develop innovative educational programs.
Publications: Application guidelines; Financial statement; Informational brochure.
Financial data: Year ended 06/30/2005. Assets, $460,897 (M); Expenditures, $72,296; Total giving, $65,686; Grants to individuals, 44 grants totaling $39,756 (high: $2,500, low: $500).
Fields of interest: Education.
Type of support: Program development; Awards/prizes.
Application information: Applications accepted throughout the year; Contact foundation for current application guidelines.
EIN: 222553348

5659
The Bristol-Myers Squibb Foundation, Inc.
(formerly The Bristol-Myers Fund, Inc.)
c/o Fdn. Coord.
345 Park Ave., 43rd Fl.
New York, NY   10154
Contact: Research by nomination only: Cindy Johnson
E-mail for Distinguished Achievement Awards: daa_admin@bms.com; URL: http://www.bms.com/aboutbms/founda/data

Foundation type: Company-sponsored foundation
Limitations: Research grants by nomination only to investigative scientists.
Publications: Corporate giving report.
Financial data: Year ended 12/31/2004. Assets, $32,119,565 (M); Expenditures, $21,965,242; Total giving, $21,955,431.
Fields of interest: Cancer research; Heart & circulatory research; Digestive disorders research; Diseases (rare) research; Neuroscience research; Nutrition.
Type of support: Research; Awards/grants by nomination only; Awards/prizes.
Application information: Application form required.
Deadline(s): Nov. 2 Cancer Award, Dec. 6 Cardiovascular, Jan. 14 Nutrition, Feb.7 Metabolics, Feb. 28 Neuroscience, Mar. 21 Infectious Diseases
Additional information: Nominations available on Web site or by request to application e-mail address.
Program description:
Distinguished Achievement Awards: These awards, which are a component of the Bristol-Myers Squibb Unrestricted Biomedical Research Grants Program, are presented annually to individuals for outstanding contributions in the fields of cancer, cardiovascular, infectious diseases, metabolic diseases, neuroscience and nutrition. Recipients in each field receive a $50,000 prize and a silver medallion. Independent peer-review committees,

comprised of the principal investigators of Bristol-Myers Squibb Unrestricted Research Grants, evaluate nominees and select the Distinguished Achievement Award recipients.
EIN: 133127947

5660
The Susan Thompson Buffett Foundation
(formerly The Buffett Foundation)
222 Kiewit Plz.
Omaha, NE   68131
Contact: Allen Greenberg, Pres.
Scholarship application address: c/o Devon Buffett, P.O. Box 4508, Decatur, IL 62525, tel.: (402) 451-6011
E-mail: scholarships@stbfoundation.org; Tel. for scholarship information: (402) 943-1383

Foundation type: Independent foundation
Limitations: Prizes by nomination only to winners of the Alice Buffett Outstanding Teacher Award, held in NE. Teachers must be nominated by members of the community.
Financial data: Year ended 12/31/2004. Assets, $5,052,931 (M); Expenditures, $36,704,755; Total giving, $35,644,506; Grants to individuals, 15 grants totaling $150,000 (high: $10,000, low: $10,000).
Type of support: Awards/grants by nomination only.
Application information: Individual applications not accepted. Contact foundation for current nomination deadline/guidelines.
EIN: 476032365

5661
Burroughs Wellcome Fund
21 T. W. Alexander Dr.
P.O. Box 13901
Research Triangle Park, NC   27709-3901
(919) 991-5100
Contact: Russ Campbell, Comms. Off.
FAX: (919) 991-5160; E-mail: info@bwfund.org; Contact info. for Russ Campbell III tel.: (919) 991-5119, FAX: (919) 991-5179, E-mail: rcampbell@bwfund.org; URL: http://www.bwfund.org

Foundation type: Independent foundation
Limitations: The fund emphasizes support for basic scientific research that has relevance to clinical medicine. Support is not provided for activities primarily clinical in nature or related to health care or health care policy; Grants are made to universities, medical schools, scientific institutions, and eligible nonprofit organizations on behalf of individual researchers.
Publications: Annual report (including application guidelines); Informational brochure (including application guidelines); Newsletter; Occasional report.
Financial data: Year ended 08/31/2004. Assets, $640,786,060 (M); Expenditures, $32,835,263; Total giving, $23,072,821.
Fields of interest: Medical school/education; Pharmacy/prescriptions; Parasitic diseases; Health organizations; Medical research, institute; Biomedicine research; Nutrition; Science, research; Science; Biological sciences; Psychology/behavioral science.
Type of support: Professorships; Publication; Fellowships; Research; Awards/grants by nomination only.
Application information: Application form required.

Initial approach: Letter or telephone requesting nomination guidelines.

Deadline(s): See program description for specific deadlines

Additional information: Interviews required; Nominations accepted only from organizations and not directly from individuals.

Program descriptions:

Scholar Awards: This award funds research and education in experimental therapeutics, toxicology, molecular parasitology, and molecular pathogenic mycology. Each award offers five years of support totaling $400,000. The award is made over a five-year period to cover the salary of the scholar involved in teaching, research, and/or further specialized training in the field, and incidental expenses such as supplies, publication costs, and travel. Candidates are generally expected to be at the associate professor level or its equivalent. Awards are available to U.S. and Canadian universities or scientific research institutes. Burroughs Wellcome Fund Experimental Therapeutics Awards provide an additional dimension to the fund's Clinical Pharmacology Award Program. The aim of the program is to identify and encourage the development of outstanding clinical scientists dedicated to improving the scientific basis of therapeutics. The awards are targeted primarily to physician scientists, to bring advanced scientific principles to the process of developing, studying, and using drugs in humans. It is hoped that such investigators will direct their careers to some aspects of the entire spectrum of inquiry from the molecular mechanisms of drug action, to the elucidation of the metabolism, distribution, targeting, binding and interaction of drugs with receptors or other targets, and exploration of the mechanisms of toxicity. The dean or other appropriate official of the medical school or university who sponsors the candidate must specify in his or her application the facilities for research and teaching which will be available, the role of the candidate within the experimental therapeutics program, and whether it is the medical school's purpose to initiate and develop a new section or division under the direction of the candidate or to provide the salary of the candidate as a faculty member in an established division of experimental therapeutics. Following review of the written applications, the Advisory Committee will interview some of the proposed candidates. Deadline Nov. 1.

Research Fellowships: These fellowships are competitive awards that enable researchers to pursue postdoctoral training programs. These two- and three-year fellowships are available to U.S. scientists at the postdoctorate level. The fund sponsors, in conjunction with outside organizations, the following programs:

· Research Fellowship in the Life Sciences: Three-year postdoctoral award administered by the Life Sciences Research Foundation. The award provides a stipend of $35,000 per year. Applications are available by calling (609) 258-3551. Deadline Oct. 1

· Obstetrics and Gynecology Fellowship: Two-year postdoctoral fellowship administered by the American Association of Obstetrics and Gynecology Foundation. The award provides a stipend of $40,000 per year. Applications are available by calling (713) 798-4717. Deadline Dec. 31

· Investigators in the Pathogenesis of Infectious Diseases: Awards up to ten awards of $400,000 over a period of three years to accomplished post-doctoral investigators for pathogenesis research. Deadline Nov. 1.

Visiting Professorships: These awards offer another kind of support for medical education. These grants bring leading researchers in the medical sciences to U.S. colleges and medical schools. Their lectures and tutorials introduce students to the newest ideas in their fields. Each grant is awarded to a host institution in support of its designated Visiting Professor. Visits are limited to one week. The dean of a medical school should send a letter indicating his or her choice for a Visiting Professor and include a curriculum vitae or information on his or her position and fields of interest, as well as a tentative program for his or her visit. Professors may be from the U.S. or abroad. Unsolicited applications from individual researchers are not accepted. Selection is made with the guidance of an Advisory Committee and is based on the needs of the applying medical school, suitable matching of the nominated professor and medical school based on those needs, and the total number of applications. Applications are encouraged from institutions with predominantly minority enrollments or newer campuses and from those located in less urban areas.

· Wellcome Visiting Professorships in the Basic Medical Sciences: Collaborative program with the Federation of American Societies for Experimental Biology (FASEB). FASEB members represent the disciplines of biophysics, anatomy, biological chemistry, immunology, nutrition, pathology, pharmacology, physiology and cell biology. Twenty-eight awards are given annually. Each Professorship award is $5,000. At least $2,000 of the award is given to the Visiting Professor. Deadline Mar. 1

· Wellcome Visiting Professorships in the Microbiological Sciences: Administered by the American Society for Microbiology. Five awards are given annually. Each Professorship award is $5,000. At least $2,000 of the award is given to the Visiting Professor. Deadline May 1.

Travel Programs:

· Wellcome Research Travel Grants: Support for travel by U.S. researchers who hold a doctorate degree and are working full-time in the health sciences or the history of medicine to the U.K. to learn new research techniques or to do collaborative research. Grants are for two weeks to six months and are not intended to support attendance at scientific meetings or extended sabbatical leaves. Approximately 45 grants are awarded each year, including 10 in the history of medicine. The Wellcome Trust in London sponsors visits to the U.S. by U.K. researchers. Applications are received and evaluated on an ongoing basis

· Hitchings-Elion Fellowships: Support for two years of postdoctoral training in the U.K. or Ireland, a transitional year to complete training abroad or to return to North America for a year of postdoctoral training, and two faculty years at a U.S. or Canadian university. It is expected that most fellows will obtain tenure-track faculty appointments. The awards provide a total of $325,000 over five years. Up to five fellowships will be awarded

Candidates must be citizens or permanent residents of the U.S. or Canada at the time of application. Persons who have applied for permanent residency but have not received their government documentation by the time of application are not eligible. Candidates must hold an M.D. or Ph.D. degree (including all types of medical and scientific doctoral degrees) at the time the award commences. Candidates generally must not have more than 24 months of postdoctoral experience by the application deadline. Candidates with more postdoctoral experience may be considered, if they can demonstrate a clear need to participate in training in the U.K. or Ireland; such candidates should contact the foundation before applying to determine whether they are eligible. Candidates in the behavioral sciences must be working in areas that have biomedical relevance; behavioral scientists should contact the foundation before applying to determine whether they are eligible. U.K. or Irish host institutions may include universities, medical or veterinary schools, scientific institutes, and government laboratories, but not industrial laboratories. Deadline Aug. 1.

New Investigator Program: The aim of the New Investigator Awards Program is to support research for beginning faculty. Applicants are generally expected to be at the early to middle assistant professor level or equivalent. Candidates must be U.S. citizens or permanent residents. Programs are as follows:

· New Investigator Awards in Molecular Parasitology: Three-year awards for individuals at the Instructor level or early Assistant Professor level who are committed to parasitology research. Three awards of $150,000 each are granted annually. Applications in letter form should be initiated jointly by such appropriate officials as the dean and head of the department in which the candidate holds his primary appointment. Deadline Jan. 15

· New Investigator Awards in the Basic Pharmacological Sciences: Three-year awards that give new investigators the freedom and flexibility to pursue higher-risk and longer-range basic pharmacological research at the beginning of their research careers. The awards are intended to catalyze the introduction of innovative research designs and approaches into basic pharmacological research. Four awards of $195,000 each are granted each year. Deadline Nov. 1

· New Initiatives in Malaria Research: Provides four-year awards to encourage work on fundamental biological questions about malaria and the parasites that cause the disease. The program's goals include encouraging more investigators to work on malaria, enhancing collaboration between investigators at the same or different institutions, and encouraging connections to field sites. Applicants must hold a doctorate degree in the sciences. Experience in malaria research is not a prerequisite, but such candidates will be required to explain how they intend to acquire the necessary expertise in working with the malaria-causing parasites as an experimental system. Applications from co-investigators with complementary expertise will be considered, generally collaborative projects should be limited to two principal investigators. Two awards of $400,000 are granted each year. Deadline Jan. 15

· New Investigator Awards in Molecular Pathogenic Mycology: Three-year awards that support research on the basic molecular biology of medically relevant fungi. The awards are intended to foster the use of a variety of modern scientific techniques—taken from molecular biology, biochemistry, immunology, pharmacology, and genetics—to advance knowledge of pathogenic fungi. Two awards of $150,000 each are granted each year. Deadline Jan. 15.

Career Awards in the Biomedical Sciences: These awards provide up to six years of stipend and research support during the advanced postdoctoral and beginning faculty years for outstanding young investigators in the basic biomedical sciences in the U.S. and Canada. Candidates must have completed at least one year, and not more than four years, of postdoctoral research training at the time of application. Individuals who hold tenure-track faculty appointments are not eligible. Recipients are expected to continue postdoctoral research training for at least one year after receipt of the award. At least one award will be allocated to the area of reproductive health. Twelve awards of approximately $500,000 each will be granted annually. Deadline Oct. 1.

Career Awards at the Scientific Interface: Grants of $500,000 over five years to support up to two years of advanced postdoctoral training and the first three years of a faculty appointment. Research proposals must address questions in any area of biomedical science. Research methods may include any combination of experiment, computation, mathematical modeling, statistical analysis, or computer simulation. Candidates for an award must hold a Ph.D. degree in mathematics, physics, chemistry (physical, theoretical, or computational), computer science, statistics, or engineering. Exceptions will be made only if the applicant can demonstrate significant expertise in one of these areas. Citizens of the United States and Canada are eligible to apply; non-citizen permanent residents and temporary residents holding H1B visas are also eligible. All candidates must be nominated by accredited, degree- granting institutions in the U.S. or Canada. Nomination deadline May 2.
EIN: 237225395

5662
Bush Foundation
E-900 First National Bank Bldg.
332 Minnesota St.
St. Paul, MN 55101 (651) 227-0891
Contact: Anita M. Pampusch, Pres.
FAX: (651) 297-6485;
E-mail: info@bushfoundation.org; URL: http://www.bushfoundation.org

Foundation type: Independent foundation
Limitations: Fellowships to residents of MN, ND, SD, and specified counties of western WI, for arts, leadership, and medicine.
Publications: Application guidelines; Annual report; Financial statement; Grants list; Informational brochure; Occasional report; Program policy statement.
Financial data: Year ended 11/30/2004. Assets, $732,455,635 (M); Expenditures, $39,422,963; Total giving, $31,047,370; Grants to individuals, totaling $2,503,116.
Fields of interest: Health organizations; Leadership development.
Type of support: Fellowships.
Application information: Applications accepted. Application form required.
　Initial approach: Letter or telephone.
　Deadline(s): Mid-Oct. Bush Leadership Fellows, Mar. 1 Medical Fellowships
　Additional information: Applications available in Aug.; Interviews may be required; see Web

site for complete eligibility information, application procedures and details on application workshops.

Program descriptions:

Bush Medical Fellows Program: Since 1979, Bush Medical Fellowships have been awarded to physicians in MN, ND, SD, and 26 counties in western WI. This program seeks to develop a physician's potential for increased competence and leadership in clinical medicine, health care delivery, administration, and education. It also seeks to improve linkages between rural physicians and metropolitan specialists. The program provides selected physicians in the designated geographical areas with an opportunity to pursue individually designed plans of study that take into account explicit health care needs in their communities. The strategy is to improve health care through the physician's personal and professional development. Approved plans range from three to 12 months. Plans usually include clinical study and/or studies to improve administrative, planning, and leadership skills. Fellows receive monthly stipends of $5,000 and tuition and travel allowances totaling $5,500 over the term of their fellowship. They may receive up to an additional $10,000 for tuition on a 50 percent basis. Stipends are intended to cover living expenses for the period of study during which income from medical practice will be reduced or nonexistent. Applicants must be currently practicing physicians, and at least 35 years of age with seven or more years of medical practice experience. They must be able to state clearly their needs and the opportunities available in their communities for the application of the new skills they seek. Special encouragement to apply is extended to physicians practicing in rural areas. Special consideration is given to applicants who seek training to assist underserved populations or provide services not currently available in the communities in which they practice. Inquiries about the program should be directed to Michael Wilcox, M.D., Prog. Dir., or Alice Sanborn, Asst. Dir., Bush Medical Fellows Program, 301 2nd St., NE, New Prague, MN 56071, tel.: (952) 442-2420, e-mail: bushmed@bushfound.org.

Bush Leadership Fellows Program: The program seeks accomplished, motivated individuals who are eager to prepare themselves for greater leadership responsibilities within their communities and professions. Fellowships support educational programs that may include academic course work, internships, self-designed study programs or various combinations of these and other kinds of learning experiences. Fellows are required to pursue their programs on a full-time basis, although they may design their programs to include two or three segments of full-time employment. The duration of fellowships range from a minimum of two months to a maximum of 18 months. Applicants for fellowships must be U.S. citizens or permanent residents. Applicants must be at least 28 years of age at the application deadline date. Applicants must have worked and lived for at least one continuous year immediately prior to the application deadline in MN, ND, SD, or the 26 counties of northwestern WI that are part of the 9th Federal Reserve District. At the time of application, applicants must be employed full-time, with a minimum of five years of work experience. Some experience in a policymaking or administrative capacity is desirable. Work experience may include part-time and volunteer work. Most successful applicants have B.A. degrees or the equivalent. Selection criteria include applicants' personal qualities, past work experiences, career goals, and the potential impact of their fellowships on their communities. Demonstrated leadership and

evidence of leadership potential are essential qualities. Selection committees review applicants' records for evidence of integrity, adaptability, intelligence, high energy, involvement in community activities, and professional competence. In fellowship plans, they look for clearly stated goals, carefully prepared educational plans, and reasonable assurance that those plans can be completed successfully.
EIN: 416017815

5663
C J Foundation for SIDS, Inc.
c/o Hackensack Univ. Medical Ctr.
30 Prospect Ave.
Hackensack, NJ 07601 (201) 996-5111
Contact: Barry A. Bornstein, Exec. Dir.
FAX: (201) 996-5326; E-mail: barry@cjsids.com; URL: http://www.cjsids.com

Foundation type: Public charity
Limitations: Grants to researchers specializing in Sudden Infant Death Syndrome (SIDS).
Publications: Application guidelines; Newsletter.
Financial data: Year ended 12/31/2004. Assets, $3,084,428 (M); Expenditures, $3,740,779; Total giving, $1,214,540; Grants to individuals, 11 grants totaling $451,790 (high: $150,000, low: $3,000).
Type of support: Research.
Application information: Contact foundation for current application deadline/guidelines; Initial approach by telephone or e-mail.
EIN: 223280254

5664
California HealthCare Foundation
476 9th St.
Oakland, CA 94607 (510) 238-1040
Contact: Beverly Wright, Dir., Grants Admin.
FAX: (510) 238-1388; E-mail: info@chcf.org; URL: http://www.chcf.org

Foundation type: Public charity
Limitations: A two-year fellowship (CHCF Health Care Leadership Program) to clinically trained health care professionals residing in CA.
Publications: Informational brochure (including application guidelines); Occasional report.
Financial data: Year ended 02/28/2005. Assets, $934,082,872 (M); Expenditures, $38,637,158; Total giving, $29,130,434; Grants to individuals, 37 grants totaling $1,231,685 (high: $164,375, low: $2,000).
Fields of interest: Health care.
Type of support: Fellowships.
Application information:
　Initial approach: Letter.
　Additional information: Contact foundation for further program guidelines.
EIN: 954523231

5665
The California Wellness Foundation
6320 Canoga Ave., Ste. 1700
Woodland Hills, CA 91367-7111
(818) 702-1900
Contact: Joan C. Hurley, Dir., Grants Mgmt.
FAX: (818) 702-1999; E-mail: tcwf@tcwf.org;
Branch Office address: 575 Market St., Ste. 1850, San Francisco, CA 94105, tel.: (415) 908-3000, FAX: (415) 908-3001; URL: http://www.tcwf.org

Foundation type: Independent foundation

Limitations: Fellowships, prizes, and awards to individuals by nomination only for health promotion, wellness education and disease prevention in CA.
Publications: Annual report; Annual report (including application guidelines); Informational brochure; Newsletter (including application guidelines); Occasional report.
Financial data: Year ended 12/31/2004. Assets, $1,095,660,990 (M); Expenditures, $53,874,302; Total giving, $40,505,102; Grants to individuals, 9 grants totaling $150,000 (high: $25,000, low: $12,500).
Fields of interest: Human services.
Type of support: Awards/prizes; Sabbaticals.
Application information:
Initial approach: Letter.
Additional information: Recipients notified within six to nine months after receipt of nomination letters. Unsolicited applications not considered or acknowledged.
Program description:
Sabbatical Program: The program offers grants of $30,000 to nonprofit health organizations to provide their executive directors with a paid leave of up to six months. The organizations will also receive up to $5,000 each for the professional development of managers and staff who will assume extra responsibilities in the absence of the sabbatical awardees. Only executive directors or their equivalents may apply. Candidates must have served in the executive role (though not necessarily for one organization) for the past six consecutive years (or more) without a significant leave of absence; have served in the current executive leadership role for a minimum of three years; and be employed full-time at the applicant organization. Candidates' organizations must be located in California and provide health services that directly benefit state residents; address the particular health needs of historically underserved populations, including low-income individuals, people of color, youth, and residents of rural areas; and be a nonprofit health organization. Deadline March 24.
EIN: 954292101

5666
The Trust for Fuller E. Callaway Professorial Chairs
c/o Bank of America, N.A.
101 S. Tryon St., NC1-002-11-18
Charlotte, NC 28255-0001 (404) 607-5307
FAX: (404) 607-4317

Foundation type: Public charity
Limitations: Grants for the benefit of named individuals for professorial chairs, primarily in GA.
Financial data: Year ended 06/30/2005. Assets, $22,839,872 (M); Expenditures, $1,022,308; Total giving, $902,900; Grants to individuals, 42 grants totaling $902,900 (high: $83,468, low: $1,829).
Type of support: Grants for special needs.
Application information: Applications not accepted.
EIN: 586075259

5667
Cancer Research Fund of the Damon Runyon-Walter Winchell Foundation
675 3rd Ave., 25th Fl.
New York, NY 10017 (877) 722-6237
Contact: Lorraine W. Egan, Exec. Dir.
E-mail: info@drcrf.org; Additional tel.: (212) 455-0500 (administration), (212) 455-0520

(awards); Additional e-mail for E. Bogert: elizabeth.bogert@drcrf.org; URL: http://www.drcrf.org

Foundation type: Public charity
Limitations: Fellowships to post-doctoral scientists and M.D.'s pursuing cancer research.
Publications: Application guidelines; Annual report; Newsletter.
Financial data: Year ended 06/30/2005. Assets, $85,011,254 (M); Expenditures, $12,557,759; Total giving, $10,181,288; Grants to individuals, totaling $10,181,288.
Fields of interest: Cancer research.
Type of support: Fellowships; Research; Postdoctoral support.
Application information: Applications accepted. Application form required. Application form available on the grantmaker's Web site.
Initial approach: Letter or telephone or Web site.
Deadline(s): Vary
Applicants should submit the following:
1) Letter(s) of recommendation
2) Proposal
3) Curriculum vitae
Additional information: See Web site for further application information.
Program description:
Cancer Research Program:
· Fellowship Award: Supports the training of the brightest young post-doctoral scientists as they embark upon their research careers. This funding enables them to be trained by established investigators in leading research laboratories across the country
· Clinical Investigator Award: 3-year Clinical Investigator Awards are granted each year for the development and training of young physicians conducting patient-oriented research. The goal is to increase the number of physician-scientists capable of connecting the laboratory and the bedside in search of breakthrough treatments. This funding will provide the resources and training structure essential to developing independent clinical investigators
EIN: 131933825

5668
Cancer Research Institute, Inc.
681 5th Ave., 12th Fl.
New York, NY 10022-4209 (212) 688-7515
Contact: Jill O'Donnell-Tormey, Exec. Dir.
FAX: (212) 832-9376;
E-mail: info@cancerresearch.org; Additional tel.: (800) 992-2623; URL: http://www.cancerresearch.org

Foundation type: Public charity
Limitations: Funding and fellowships to individuals for basic research in cancer immunology, immunotherapies, and other therapeutic areas that are synergistic with immunotherapy.
Publications: Application guidelines; Annual report; Financial statement; Grants list; Informational brochure; Newsletter; Program policy statement.
Financial data: Year ended 06/30/2005. Assets, $40,537,166 (L); Expenditures, $12,987,815; Total giving, $9,373,000; Grants to individuals, 62 grants totaling $9,373,000 (high: $739,745, low: $5,000).
Fields of interest: Immunology; Cancer research.
Type of support: Program development; Conferences/seminars; Fellowships; Research; Awards/grants by nomination only; Postdoctoral support; Graduate support.

Application information: Application form required. Application form available on the grantmaker's Web site.
Initial approach: Letter or e-mail.
Deadline(s): Varies
Applicants should submit the following:
1) Proposal
2) Letter(s) of recommendation
3) Curriculum vitae
Additional information: Applications should be sent by either mail or e-mail.
Program descriptions:
Pre-doctoral Emphasis Pathways in Tumor Immunology: Through this program, universities may apply for training grants establishing multi-year programs that support doctoral students interested in pursuing careers in cancer immunology. The grants provide the institution with $450,000 over a four-year period. Deadline Mar. 1.
Clinical Investigation Program: This program is comprised of three distinct funding mechanisms:
· Grants Program: Supports preclinical and clinical research in cancer antigen identification for vaccine and antibody therapies; characterization of the immune response to cancer antigens; and the fashioning of vaccine and antibody-based therapies for cancer. Grants provide a three-year commitment of $300,00 for preclinical research and $450,000 for clinical trial grants. Deadline Feb. 1
· Cancer Antigen Discovery Collaborative: Mobilizes experts who are invited to work cooperatively on defined tasks toward a common goal of identifying the targets on cancer cells that can serve as the basis for vaccines and antibody therapies. Participation in the program demands that the researchers involved collaborate and communicate, sharing reagents, data, and ideas. Collaboratives have been established in colon, breast and prostate cancer. Applications are by invitation only
· Cancer Vaccine Collaborative: This program was created in partnership with the Ludwig Institute for Cancer Research. It is a unique network of coordinated early-phase cancer vaccine trials at academic institutions, initially in New York City. These multiple, yet parallel trials, which use defined antigens, standardized treatment protocols, uniform monitoring methodologies, and centralized data collection, will provide comparable results that will teach us how to effectively immunize against cancer
Applications are by invitation only.
Investigator Awards: This program supports immunologists and cancer immunologists at the assistant professor level as they undertake their first independent investigations. Funds may be used at the recipient's discretion for salary, technical assistance, supplies or capital equipment. Investigator awards provide $50,000 per year for four years. Deadline Mar. 1.
Post-doctoral Fellowships: This program is designed to foster the training of qualified young immunologists and cancer immunologists at leading universities and research centers around the world. These three-year funding commitments have been raised to $40,000 in the first year, $42,000 in the second year, and $44,000 in the third year. Fellowships also include an institutional allowance of $1,500 per year. Deadlines Apr. 1 and Oct. 1.
EIN: 131837442

5669
Iris & B. Gerald Cantor Foundation
(formerly The B. G. Cantor Art Foundation)
1180 South Beverly Dr. Ste. 321
Los Angeles, CA 90035
Contact: Judith Sobol, Exec. Dir.
E-mail: jsobol@ibgcf.org; URL: http://
www.cantorfoundation.org

Foundation type: Independent foundation
Limitations: Grants to research the works and life
of Auguste Rodin, primarily to those in CA and NY.
Financial data: Year ended 04/30/2004.
Assets, $59,112,957 (M); Expenditures,
$3,445,559; Total giving, $2,925,995.
Type of support: Research.
Application information: Applications accepted.
Application form not required.
Initial approach: E-mail.
Copies of proposal: 10
Deadline(s): Quarterly
Applicants should submit the following:
1) Proposal
2) Curriculum vitae
3) Budget Information
Additional information: Contact foundation for
further program information.
EIN: 136227347

5670
Caring for Carcinoid Foundation, Inc.
1 Kendall Sq., PMB 180
Cambridge, MA 02139 (857) 222-5492
E-mail: info@caringforcarcinoid.org; URL: http://
www.caringforcarcinoid.org

Foundation type: Public charity
Limitations: Research grants to leading scientists
who undertake cutting-edge, genetically-based
carcinoid research.
Publications: Application guidelines.
Financial data: Year ended 12/31/2004.
Assets, $47,130; Expenditures, $20.
Fields of interest: Cancer research.
Type of support: Research.
Application information:
Initial approach: E-mail.
Additional information: Contact foundation for
further application information and program
guidelines.
EIN: 201945347

5671
Carlsbad Foundation, Inc.
116 S. Canyon St.
Carlsbad, NM 88220 (505) 887-1131
Contact: Jim Harrison, Exec. Dir.

Foundation type: Community foundation
Limitations: Awards by nomination only to residents
of Carlsbad and South Eddy County, NM.
Publications: Annual report (including application
guidelines); Newsletter.
Financial data: Year ended 06/30/2005.
Assets, $19,668,552 (M); Expenditures,
$760,828; Total giving, $480,704; Grants to
individuals, totaling $112,449.
Fields of interest: Humanities; Arts; International
affairs; Community development, volunteer
services.
Type of support: Awards/grants by nomination only;
Awards/prizes.
Application information: Applications accepted.
Initial approach: Nominating letter from members
of the local community.
Deadline(s): None

Additional information: Recipients are named at
the foundation's annual meeting in Sept.
Program descriptions:
A.J. Crawford Humanitarian Award: This $1,000
award is for excellence and compassion in
community service.
Special Recognition Award: Award of $250 for a
humanitarian who reflects outstanding qualities of
excellence and compassion, but whose humility or
low profile might cause him or her to be overlooked.
Pioneer Award: Award of $250 for long-term
humanitarian service.
Arts and Humanities Award: Award of $250 for
long-term community service in the arts and/or
humanities.
Good Samaritan Award: Award of $250 to an
individual whose single, meritorious act was
directed at protecting the life or health of another
or to an individual or family providing an outstanding
example of philanthropy at its finest.
EIN: 850206472

5672
Carlston Family Foundation
(formerly Broderbund Foundation)
P.O. Box 10162
San Rafael, CA 94912-0162 (415) 388-4763
Contact: Michele Samuels, Exec. Dir.
FAX: (415) 388-4769;
E-mail: CFF_Samuels@pacbell.net; URL: http://
www.carlstonfamilyfoundation.org

Foundation type: Independent foundation
Limitations: Awards by nomination only to
teachers, primarily in CA.
Publications: Annual report; Grants list; Program
policy statement.
Financial data: Year ended 12/31/2003.
Assets, $4,022,733 (M); Expenditures,
$195,675; Total giving, $111,896; Grants to
individuals, 5 grants totaling $75,000 (high:
$15,000, low: $15,000).
Fields of interest: Education.
Type of support: Awards/grants by nomination only;
Awards/prizes.
Application information: Nominations by letter
accepted throughout the year.
EIN: 680154752

5673
Carnegie Corporation of New York
437 Madison Ave.
New York, NY 10022 (212) 371-3200
Contact: Edward Sermier, V.P. and Corp. Secy.
FAX: (212) 754-4073; URL: http://
www.carnegie.org

Foundation type: Independent foundation
Limitations: Fellowships to individuals conducting
fundamental research.
Publications: Annual report; Grants list;
Informational brochure (including application
guidelines); Occasional report.
Financial data: Year ended 09/30/2005.
Assets, $2,244,208,247 (M); Expenditures,
$114,160,539; Total giving, $91,053,489; Grants
to individuals, 28 grants totaling $1,075,458.
Fields of interest: Elementary/secondary school
reform; International development; International
peace/security; Public affairs, reform; Islam.
Type of support: Conferences/seminars;
Publication; Fellowships; Research; Travel grants.
Application information: Applications not
accepted.

Program description:
Carnegie Corporation Scholars Program: Up to
twenty fellowships for one to two years of a
maximum of $100,000 awarded to scholars with
outstanding promise in fundamental research, as
well as established experts who stand to contribute
significantly to the advancement of knowledge and
understanding in the corporation's fields of
interest. Selection made on basis of nominations.
Nomination pool drawn from leading academics,
policy makers, and practitioners in the U.S. and a
few outside of the U.S. Recipients must be U.S.
citizens or permanent residents.
EIN: 131628151

5674
Carnegie Hero Fund Commission
425 6th Ave., Ste. 1640
Pittsburgh, PA 15219-1823 (412) 281-1302
Contact: Jeffrey A. Dooley, Investigations Mgr.
FAX: (412) 281-5751;
E-mail: carnegiehero@carnegiehero.org; Toll free
tel.: (800) 447-8900; URL: http://
www.carnegiehero.org/

Foundation type: Operating foundation
Limitations: Medals and grants awarded by
nomination only for acts of heroism voluntarily
performed by civilians within the U.S. and Canada
in saving or attempting to save the lives of others.
Publications: Annual report; Informational
brochure; Newsletter; Occasional report.
Financial data: Year ended 12/31/2004.
Assets, $33,529,062 (M); Expenditures,
$1,953,194; Total giving, $701,044; Grants to
individuals, totaling $701,044.
Type of support: Awards/grants by nomination only;
Awards/prizes.
Application information: Applications accepted.
Initial approach: Letter, including date, time, and
place of heroic actions, and addresses of hero
and witnesses.
Deadline(s): Within two years of the date of the
act for which individual is nominated;
Additional information: Completion of formal
nomination required.
Program description:
Carnegie Hero Fund Program: Medals and grants
of $3,500 each awarded in recognition of acts of
selfless heroism. Monetary assistance is given to
persons who have been awarded the Carnegie
Medal and who have need for financial aid as a
result of a disabling injury incurred. In addition,
grants may be given to the dependents of those who
have lost their lives in such heroic manner.
Recommendations for awards may be made by any
individual having knowledge of an outstanding act
of bravery. Scholarship aid is available to all medal
recipients as well as dependents of disabled and
posthumous awardees. There must be conclusive
evidence that the person performing a heroic act
voluntarily risked his or her life to an extraordinary
degree in saving or attempting to save the life of
another person, or voluntarily sacrificed himself or
herself in a heroic manner for the benefit of others.
The act of rescue must be one in which no full
measure of responsibility exists between the
rescuer and the rescued. The heroic act must have
been performed in the U.S., Canada, or the waters
thereof. The following types of people are ineligible
for an award:
· those whose regular vocations require
them to perform such acts, unless the
rescues are clearly beyond the line of duty
· members of the armed services

- children considered by the commission to be too young to comprehend the risks involved
- members of the same family, except in cases of outstanding heroism where the rescuer loses his or her life or is severely injured.

EIN: 251062730

5675
The Carter Center, Inc.
1 Copenhill
453 Freedom Pkwy.
Atlanta, GA 30307 (404) 420-5165
Contact: Thom Bornemann, Dir., Mental Health Program
FAX: (404) 420-5158; E-mail: ccmph@emory.edu;
URL: http://www.cartercenter.org

Foundation type: Public charity
Limitations: Grants to journalists to study selected topics of mental health or mental illness.
Publications: Informational brochure (including application guidelines).
Financial data: Year ended 08/31/2003.
Assets, $240,849,482 (M); Expenditures, $53,677; Total giving, $49,950; Grant to an individual, 1 grant totaling $10,000.
Fields of interest: Journalism/publishing; Mental health/crisis services, research; Mental health, disorders.
Type of support: Fellowships; Research.
Application information: Applications accepted. Application form not required.
  Deadline(s): May 3;
  Additional information: No standard application form is used. Instead, include objectives for fellowship and project description, samples of professional work, resume, and letter of support. See Web site for additional information.
Program description:
Rosalynn Carter Fellowships for Mental Health Journalism: Eligible applicants must have at least two years' experience in print or electronic journalism. Each year, six U.S. and four international fellows are awarded grants of $10,000 each to cover expenses during the fellowship project, including travel, materials, and other costs. Fellows also make two expense-paid visits to the Carter Center in Atlanta, Georgia. Fellows enjoy a great deal of flexibility scheduling their project work throughout the year. Projects do not require fellows to leave their jobs.
EIN: 581454716

5676
The Annie E. Casey Foundation
701 St. Paul St.
Baltimore, MD 21202 (410) 547-6600
Contact: Douglas W. Nelson, Pres.
FAX: (410) 547-6624; E-mail: webmail@aecf.org;
Additional address for Janice Nittoli (Advisory Board): c/o New York City Administration for Children's Services, 150 William St., 18th Fl., New York, NY 10038; tel.: (212) 788-2741; E-mail: jnittoli@aecf.org; URL: http://www.aecf.org

Foundation type: Independent foundation
Limitations: Fellowships to individuals to work and study at youth and family organizations and agencies.
Publications: Financial statement; Newsletter; Occasional report.
Financial data: Year ended 12/31/2004.
Assets, $3,295,299,665 (M); Expenditures,

$235,963,865; Total giving, $171,354,926; Grants to individuals, 4 grants totaling $4,969.
Fields of interest: Youth development; Human services; Family services; Public policy, research.
Type of support: Fellowships.
Application information: Applications accepted.
  Initial approach: Letter including a description of the project, objectives and plans, populations to be served, and amount requested.
  Additional information: After review, the foundation may request submission of a formal application and additional information.
Program description:
Casey Children and Family Fellowships: The fellowship program is intended to foster public policy and human service reforms that better meet the needs of today's disadvantaged children and families through the education of professional leaders. A full-time program, the fellowship initiative engages exceptional, mid- to senior-level professionals in an intensive 11-month course of study that includes field assignments at youth- and family-serving organizations and agencies, team and independent study projects, and a series of seminars. These seminars are coordinated and administrated by the Robert F. Wagner Graduate School of Public Service at New York University, which was awarded $209,000 for the design and implementation of this component of the fellowship program.
EIN: 521951681

5677
James McKeen Cattell Fund
c/o Duke Univ., Dept. of Psychology
Box 90086
Durham, NC 27708-0086 (919) 660-5726
Contact: Dr. Christina Williams, Secy.-Treas.
FAX: (919) 660-5726;
E-mail: williams@psych.duke.edu

Foundation type: Independent foundation
Limitations: Grants to supplement sabbatical allowances for psychologists teaching at universities in the U.S. and Canada.
Publications: Application guidelines; Annual report.
Financial data: Year ended 12/31/2004.
Assets, $2,575,784 (M); Expenditures, $129,825; Total giving, $91,604; Grants to individuals, 7 grants totaling $91,604 (high: $19,200, low: $6,704).
Fields of interest: Psychology/behavioral science.
Type of support: Research.
Application information: Application form required.
  Initial approach: Letter.
  Deadline(s): None
  Additional information: Applications must include a plan for the sabbatical period, bibliography, two references, and a form completed by the dept. chair or dean certifying applicant's eligibility.
Program description:
Psychology Research Grant Program: Grants are made to psychology department tenured faculty and non-tenured associate professors in tenure-track positions to enable them to take a sabbatical for a full year rather than for only half a year. Selection is based on evidence of scholarly productivity, the recommendation of notable colleagues, and the nature of the research proposed for the sabbatical year. Depending on the fund's budget, an average of five to six grants are awarded annually in amounts equal to half the individual's regular yearly salary to a maximum of $24,000. During the sabbatical the recipient must not engage in teaching or any other employment that may conflict

with accomplishing the endeavors for which the award was granted. Prior recipients are ineligible.
EIN: 136129600

5678
The CDC Foundation
(formerly National Fund for the CDC, Inc.)
50 Hurt Plz., Ste. 765
Atlanta, GA 30303 (404) 653-0790
Contact: Charles Stokes, Pres. and C.E.O.
FAX: (404) 653-0330; Additional tel.: (888) 880-4CDC; URL: http://www.cdcfoundation.org

Foundation type: Public charity
Limitations: Fellowships to third- and fourth-year medical and veterinary students to gain public health experience developing countries.
Financial data: Year ended 06/30/2003.
Assets, $31,384,465 (M); Expenditures, $9,907,039; Total giving, $7,643,228; Grants to individuals, totaling $499,582.
Fields of interest: Journalism/publishing; Medical school/education; Veterinary medicine; Public health; Health care; Medical research, public policy; Genetics/birth defects research; Medical specialty research.
Type of support: Conferences/seminars; Fellowships; Travel grants; Stipends.
Application information:
  Initial approach: Telephone.
  Additional information: Contact foundation for current application deadline/guidelines.
Program descriptions:
O.C. Hubert Student Fellowship in International Health: Awards up to seven fellowships of $7,000 to third- and fourth-year medical and veterinary students to gain public health experience in an international setting. Hubert fellows spend four to six weeks in a developing country working on a priority health problem in conjunction with CDC staff. Through these experiences, students establish relationships with, and receive training from, recognized experts from CDC and other national and international health agencies.
Applied Epidemiology Fellowship: Provides stipends to eight competitively selected third- and fourth-year medical students from around the U.S. to spend a year at the Center for Disease Control in Atlanta, GA. Areas of concentration for the fellowship include birth defects, injury, chronic disease, genomics, infectious disease, environmental health, public health policy, and reproductive health.
Knight Public Health Journalism Fellowship at CDC: A three-month, multi-faceted experience in research, field practice, and instruction. Six fellows will be selected to participate in the program, which takes place from June through Sept. Fellows receive a stipend to cover their living expenses. Journalists with a track record of accomplishment, a minimum of five years' reporting experience, and a desire to strengthen the reporting of public health are invited to apply.
Public Health Journalism Boot Camp at CDC: An intensive six-day seminar that provides training in statistics, epidemiology, bioterrorism, and other major public health topics. This year's program will take place June 19 - June 24. Approximately fifteen journalists will be selected for the program, which will provide housing, breakfast, and a per-diem stipend of $25 for other meals. The program is open to any journalist (whether print, online, or broadcast) interested in learning more about public health science. Deadline April 5.
EIN: 582106707

5679
CDS International, Inc.
871 United Nations Plz., 15th Fl.
New York, NY 10017 (212) 497-3500
Contact: Robert Fenstermacher, Exec. Dir.
FAX: (212) 497-3535; E-mail: info@cdsintl.org;
URL: http://www.cdsintl.org

Foundation type: Public charity
Limitations: Fellowships to professionals with graduate degrees in business administration, economics, journalism and mass communication, law, political science or public affairs to work in Germany.
Publications: Annual report; Informational brochure; Newsletter.
Financial data: Year ended 12/31/2003. Assets, $1,296,370 (M); Expenditures, $2,470,600.
Fields of interest: Media/communications; Journalism/publishing; Business/industry; Economics; Political science; Law/international law; Public affairs, administration/regulation.
Type of support: Fellowships; Internship funds; Exchange programs.
Application information:
  Initial approach: Letter or e-mail.
  Additional information: Contact foundation for current application deadline/guidelines.
Program description:
  Robert Bosch Fellowship Program: Fellowships last for nine months. Twenty Americans will be chosen for these fellowship positions. Fellows receive awards of EURO $1,800 or approximately $1,980 U.S. dollars at the current exchange rate.
EIN: 136275141

5680
Center for Research on Women and Newborn Health Foundation
c/o Beard Miller Co.
1685 Crown Ave.
Lancaster, PA 17601-6396
Contact: Daniel Kegel M.D., Treas.
Application address: 1059 Columbia Ave., Lancaster, PA 17603, tel.: (717) 393-1338

Foundation type: Independent foundation
Limitations: Medical research grants in the areas of women's health and obstetrics, primarily in CA and PA.
Financial data: Year ended 08/31/2005. Assets, $699,555 (M); Expenditures, $34,620; Total giving, $15,158; Grants to individuals, totaling $15,158.
Fields of interest: Reproductive health; Medical research, institute; Women.
Type of support: Research.
Application information: Contact center for current application deadline/guidelines.
EIN: 232744470

5681
Cervical Spine Research Society
6300 N. River Rd., Ste. 727
Rosemont, IL 60018-4226 (847) 698-1628
Contact: Bradford L. Currier M.D., Pres.; For Research Prog.: Peggy Wlezien
E-mail: wlezien@aaos.org
FAX: (847) 823-0536; URL: http://www.csrs.org

Foundation type: Public charity
Limitations: Awards for outstanding unpublished research papers of the cervical spine. In addition to grants for competitive research projects.
Publications: Application guidelines.

Financial data: Year ended 12/31/2004. Assets, $1,738,504 (M); Expenditures, $711,478; Total giving, $180,969; Grants to individuals, 8 grants totaling $23,500 (high: $16,000, low: $500).
Fields of interest: Spine disorders research.
Type of support: Research; Awards/prizes.
Application information: Applications accepted. Application form required. Application form available on the grantmaker's Web site.
  Initial approach: Abstract for Research awards.
  Deadline(s): June 15.
  Additional information: Research grant applications should include 13 copies of application, budget, proposal, and protocol statement. See Web site for further application information.
Program descriptions:
  Research Award: Monetary awards for outstanding unpublished papers on the cervical spine. Award categories are Clinical, Basic Science, and Resident/Fellow papers.
  Research Grants: Awards for basic science or clinical protocols with budgets of up to $30,000. The applicant should have completed his or her training and have a staff appointment at the institution where the research will be performed.
EIN: 521231718

5682
A Charitable Foundation Corporation
2657 Windmill Pkwy., Ste. 220
Henderson, NV 89014
Contact: Debra M. Foubert, V.P.

Foundation type: Independent foundation
Limitations: Research grants to individuals.
Financial data: Year ended 12/31/2004. Assets, $3,426,486 (M); Expenditures, $176,568; Total giving, $103,750; Grants to individuals, 2 grants totaling $46,000 (high: $36,000, low: $10,000).
Fields of interest: Brazil.
Type of support: Research.
Application information:
  Initial approach: Letter.
  Additional information: Contact foundation for application deadline/guidelines.
EIN: 880375802

5683
Charlotte Advocates for Education
(formerly Charlotte-Mecklenburg Education Foundation)
2 Wachovia Ctr.
301 S. Tryon St., Ste. 1725
Charlotte, NC 28282 (704) 335-0100
Contact: Allen Prichard, Chair.
FAX: (704) 334-3545;
E-mail: advocate@advocatesfored.org;
URL: http://www.advocatesfored.org

Foundation type: Public charity
Limitations: Awards by nomination only to individuals for exemplary service in the educational system in the Charlotte-Mecklenburg, NC, area.
Publications: Annual report; Informational brochure; Newsletter.
Financial data: Year ended 12/31/2004. Assets, $290,421 (M); Expenditures, $522,731.
Fields of interest: Education.
Type of support: Awards/grants by nomination only; Awards/prizes.
Application information: Individual applications not accepted; RFPs are sent to Charlotte-Mecklenburg public schools.

Program description:
  Harris Teacher of the Year Award: Honors exemplary teachers in Charlotte-Mecklenburg schools. The winner represents CMS in the regional Teacher of the Year competition with the possibility of advancing to the state and national competitions. The awards are underwritten by the James J. and Angelia M. Harris Foundation.
EIN: 561752043

5684
Chattanooga Orthopedic Educational and Research Foundation
975 E. 3rd St.
P.O. Box 260
Chattanooga, TN 37403 (423) 756-6623
Contact: Hugh P. Brown M.D., Pres.

Foundation type: Independent foundation
Limitations: Grants only to medical residents, primarily in TN, to enable them to attend the American Academy of Orthopedic Surgeons convention and for courses dealing with orthopedic training.
Financial data: Year ended 12/31/2004. Assets, $437,802 (M); Expenditures, $121,234; Total giving, $52,246; Grants to individuals, totaling $52,246.
Fields of interest: Orthopedics.
Type of support: Conferences/seminars; Fellowships; Travel grants.
Application information: Applications accepted. Application form required.
  Initial approach: Letter.
  Deadline(s): None
  Additional information: Applications not accepted from individuals who are not within the stated recipient restriction.
EIN: 237091528

5685
Chelonian Research Foundation
168 Goodrich St.
Lunenburg, MA 01462 (978) 582-9668
Contact: Anders G.J. Rhodin, Dir.

Foundation type: Operating foundation
Limitations: Research grants to individuals for the dissemination of information on turtles and tortoises.
Financial data: Year ended 12/31/2003. Assets, $168,475 (M); Expenditures, $139,625; Total giving, $18,000; Grants to individuals, totaling $18,000.
Fields of interest: Animals/wildlife, research.
Type of support: Research.
Application information: Deadline Nov. 15 for Linnaeus Fund Awards; Applications accepted throughout the year for general program funds; Completion of formal application required, including proposal.
EIN: 046705444

5686
Chemotherapy Foundation, Inc.
183 Madison Ave., Ste. 403
New York, NY 10016-4501 (212) 213-9292
Contact: Shirley Cox, Exec. Dir.
FAX: (212) 213-3831

Foundation type: Public charity
Limitations: Grants to researchers specializing in chemotherapy.

Financial data: Year ended 12/31/2004.
Assets, $9,660,769 (M); Expenditures,
$958,518; Total giving, $651,000; Grants to
individuals, 13 grants totaling $651,000 (high:
$100,000, low: $11,250).
Fields of interest: Cancer.
Type of support: Research.
Application information: Contact foundation for
current application deadline/guidelines.
EIN: 132622978

5687
Cherith Christian Private Foundation
4260 Newberry Ct.
Palo Alto, CA   94306

Foundation type: Independent foundation
Limitations: Grants to individuals involved with
full-time Christian work at churches and parachurch
organizations, and scholarships to individuals for
tuition at theological seminaries.
Financial data: Year ended 04/30/2005.
Assets, $291,653 (M); Expenditures, $95,237;
Total giving, $76,694.
Fields of interest: Theological school/education;
Christian agencies & churches.
Type of support: Scholarships—to individuals.
Application information: Applications accepted.
Deadline(s): None
Additional information: Contact foundation for
current application guidelines.
EIN: 954222174

5688
Chesed Avrhom Hacohn Foundation
c/o Staten Island Bank & Trust
1535 Richmond Rd.
Staten Island, NY   10304
Contact: A. Romi Cohn, Chair.
Application addresses: For America: 5312 17th
Ave., Brooklyn, NY 11204; For Israel: P.O. Box
91130, Jerusalem, Israel 13042

Foundation type: Independent foundation
Limitations: Awards for the continued education of
rabbinical scholars.
Financial data: Year ended 12/31/2003.
Assets, $551,696 (M); Expenditures, $122,697;
Total giving, $82,000; Grants to individuals, 13
grants totaling $82,000 (high: $14,000, low:
$2,200).
Fields of interest: Theological school/education;
Jewish agencies & temples; Religion.
Type of support: Postgraduate support.
Application information: Approximately Apr. 1
(Rosh Ha Chudesh Nissan).
Program description:
Award Programs: The Crown of Torah Award and
The Diadem of Jurisprudence Award were
established by Reb Avrohm Hacohn to assist those
of praiseworthy ability to advance their studies in
order to become rabbis, teachers, and leaders.
Each award recipient receives $25,000. Recipients
study for five years under the supervision of Roshei
Yeshiva and great rabbis. The recipient of The
Crown of Torah Award studies the Talmud, Rashi,
Tosefos, the Ri'f, and the Ro'sh intensively,
learning at least one page per day. Over the five
years, he must complete 800 folios. The recipient
of The Diadem of Jurisprudence Award studies the
Laws of Shabbos in Orach Chayim; the Laws of that
which is Forbidden and that which is Permitted;
Ritual Cleanliness and Interest in Yoreh Deah; and
the Laws of Judges in Choshen Hamishpat. He
must aspire to be ordained with the Ordination of
Scholars according to the Torah, and to be accepted

to the glorious position of a righteous judge. At the
end of each year, recipients are tested on their
cumulative learning of the past year and previous
years in this program. At the end of the five-year
program, they will be examined on the Talmudic and
other knowledge that they acquired during the entire
period.
EIN: 116313080

5689
Chest Foundation
3300 Dundee Road
Northbrook, IL   60062
Contact: Marilyn Lederer, V.P., and C.O.O.
FAX: (847) 498-5460;
E-mail: chestfoundation@chestnet.org; Additional
tel.: (847) 498-1400; URL: http://
www.chestfoundation.org

Foundation type: Public charity
Limitations: Research grants to individuals for
projects addressing chest diseases and their
prevention.
Publications: Application guidelines; Annual report.
Financial data: Year ended 06/30/2003.
Assets, $10,135,099 (M); Expenditures,
$2,235,066; Total giving, $672,171; Grants to
individuals, 39 grants totaling $57,500 (high:
$20,000, low: $1,000).
Fields of interest: Lung research; Asthma research;
Geriatrics research.
Type of support: Program development; Research;
Awards/prizes; Travel grants.
Application information: Deadlines Feb. 28 for
Clinical Research Trainee Awards and Apr. 30 for all
others; Initial approach by telephone or e-mail;
Completion of formal application required; See Web
site for additional information.
Program descriptions:
*Roger C. Bone Award for Advances in End-of-Life
Care:* Awards $2,500 to an individual for an
end-of-life care project/service, complimentary
registration to CHEST, and personalized crystal
plaque.
Clinical Research Trainee Awards: Awards
$10,000 each to eight qualified fellows who have
the best proposal for a clinical research project.
Geriatric Development Research Award: Awards a
$75,000 grant each year for two years to an
academic internist for a long-term career
development focus on integrating geriatrics into
subspecialties of internal medicine by developing
and implementing a basic, clinical, or health service
research project focused on a geriatric aspect of
chest medicine. Award includes a one-time travel
grant of $3,000 to attend the meetings of the
American Geriatrics Society and the American
College of Chest Physicians in the second year of
the award.
Governors Community Service Award: Awards
$2,500 to 30 recipients to support the project that
benefits from their volunteer efforts. Recipients
must be members of the ACCP.
*Eli Lilly & Co. Distinguished Scholar in Critical Care
Medicine:* Award of $50,000 annually over the
three-year term of the project to a distinguished
scholar to identify projects that will make an
outstanding contribution to critical care medicine;
assist in the college's development of these
projects to disseminate new knowledge and foster
the creation of best practices in patient care; and
represent the college as the distinguished expert in
the specialty area.
EIN: 363286520

5690
The Chicago Community Trust
111 E. Wacker Dr., Ste. 1400
Chicago, IL   60601   (312) 616-8000
Contact: For grants: Ms. Sandy Phelps, Grants Mgr.
FAX: (312) 616-7955; E-mail: info@cct.org; TDD:
(312) 856-1703; Grant inquiries E-mail:
grants@cct.org; URL: http://www.cct.org

Foundation type: Community foundation
Limitations: Fellowships to leaders of nonprofit or
public sector organizations serving residents of
Cook County, IL.
Publications: Application guidelines; Annual report;
Financial statement; Grants list; Informational
brochure (including application guidelines);
Newsletter.
Financial data: Year ended 09/30/2004.
Assets, $1,324,379,128 (M); Expenditures,
$72,982,300; Total giving, $61,677,060.
Fields of interest: Community development,
volunteer services; Leadership development.
Type of support: Fellowships; Research.
Application information: Applications accepted.
Application form required.
Initial approach: Letter of intent outlining
professional development activities to be
pursued and personal benefits that will be
received from fellowship year.
Deadline(s): Contact foundation for current
application deadline
Additional information: Interviews required.
Program description:
Community Leaders Fellowship: This program is
open to individuals working in nonprofit or public
sector entities serving the metropolitan Chicago
area to expand their knowledge base through a
self-directed course of learning, travel, observation,
and reflection. The program provides these
professionals with up to fifteen months of time off
from their day-to-day professional responsibilities.
The fellowship includes a stipend covering current
salary and benefits and associated expenses up to
$150,000.
EIN: 362167000

5691
Chicago Foundation for Education
400 N. Michigan Ave., Ste. 720
Chicago, IL   60611   (312) 670-2323
Contact: Kris Reichmann, Exec. Dir.
FAX: (312) 670-2029;
E-mail: cfe@chgofdneduc.org; URL: http://
www.chgofdneduc.org

Foundation type: Public charity
Limitations: Grants to Chicago, IL, elementary
public school teachers in grades pre-K through 8 to
improve and enhance the educational experience of
students.
Publications: Annual report; Informational
brochure; Newsletter.
Financial data: Year ended 06/30/2003.
Assets, $361,461 (M); Expenditures, $578,321;
Total giving, $221,238; Grants to individuals,
totaling $221,238.
Fields of interest: Early childhood education;
Elementary school/education; Education.
Type of support: Program development.
Application information: Deadlines Jan. for Study
Group Grants, Feb. for Mentor Grants, Sept./Oct.
for Small Grants; Initial approach by letter;
Completion of formal application required.
Program descriptions:
Small Grants: Awards grants of up to $400 to
teachers with innovative ideas for classroom
projects that can help students achieve. The

projects reflect the teachers' enthusiasm and offer students new, challenging instruction with the aim of making learning relevant, interesting and effective for the students. Individuals or teams of two or more teachers may apply.

IMPACT II Mentor Grants: Grants of $600 for individuals or $800 for teams of two or more are awarded to teachers with proven strategies to help students learn. The grants are available to teachers who have developed and successfully implemented classroom projects, and are prepared to share lessons and materials with other teachers across the city. Recipients' projects are published in an annual catalog which is distributed to all Chicago public elementary schools. Recipients also become part of the IMPACT II national teachers network.

Study Group Grants: Provides experienced teachers (Study Group Coaches) the opportunity to lead a Study Group around a proven Instructional Strategy with 4-6 teachers (Study Group Team Members) who are willing to adapt and implement the strategy in their own classrooms.
EIN: 363429023

5692
Child Nutrition Foundation
(formerly School Food Service Foundation)
700 S. Washington St., Ste. 300
Alexandria, VA 22314 (703) 739-3900
Contact: Barbara Belmont CAE, Exec. Dir.
FAX: (703) 739-3915; E-mail: cnf@asfsa.org;
URL: http://www.schoolnutrition.org/CNF.aspx?id=36

Foundation type: Public charity
Limitations: Fellowships and research grants in the areas of school food service and nutrition.
Publications: Application guidelines; Annual report; Informational brochure; Newsletter.
Financial data: Year ended 07/31/2003.
Assets, $3,513,630 (M); Expenditures, $1,172,396; Total giving, $155,114; Grants to individuals, totaling $155,114.
Fields of interest: Vocational education; Pediatrics; Nutrition; Business/industry; Biological sciences.
Type of support: Fellowships; Research.
Application information: Applications accepted. Application form required.
  Deadline(s): Apr. 30 for research grants and fellowships
  Additional information: See Web site for detailed application guidelines.
Program descriptions:
  Hubert Humphrey Research Grant: One research grant ranging from $2,500 to $5,000 is given annually to an active ASFSA member or school food service professional who will be supervised by active ASFSA members to conduct research which will advance the knowledge base of school food service and nutritional programs. Applicants must be currently enrolled in a graduate program majoring in food and nutrition, nutrition education, food service management, or a related field at an accredited institution. In addition, applicants must demonstrate evidence of good current or past academic standing (minimum GPA of 3.0) and research competency to conduct the proposed study. The proposed research must be applicable to school food service and child nutrition, and it must support the foundation's mission for the program. Application forms must be submitted with a letter of support from a major professor or advisor, and a full, detailed proposal.
  Lincoln Food Service Research Grant: One research grant ranging from $2,500 to $5,000 is given annually to an active ASFSA member or school food service professional who will be supervised by

active ASFSA members to conduct research which will advance the knowledge base of school food service and nutrition programs. Applicants must demonstrate research competency to conduct the proposed study and must submit a letter of support from an administrator who can address their ability to conduct the research, along with the required registration form. The proposed research must be applicable to school food service and child nutrition, and it must support the foundation's mission for the grant program.
EIN: 846039412

5693
Children for Children
335 Madison Ave., 24th Fl.
New York, NY 10017 (212) 708-0200
Contact: Maggie Jones, Exec. Dir.
FAX: (212) 688-7384;
E-mail: celebrate@childrenforchildren.org;
URL: http://www.childrenforchildren.org

Foundation type: Public charity
Limitations: Grants to New York City public school teachers who lack materials and resources needed to educate their students.
Publications: Annual report; Informational brochure; Newsletter.
Financial data: Year ended 12/31/2004.
Assets, $742,682 (M); Expenditures, $559,562; Total giving, $245,330.
Fields of interest: Education, public education.
Type of support: Program development.
Application information: Applications accepted. Application form required.
  Additional information: See Web site for further application information.
EIN: 133880287

5694
The Children's Heart Foundation
P.O. Box 244
Lincolnshire, IL 60069-0244 (847) 634-6474
Contact: Beth Linnen, Exec. Dir.
FAX: (847) 634-4988;
E-mail: sbilissis@childrensheart.com; URL: http://www.childrensheart.com/

Foundation type: Public charity
Limitations: Research grants to individuals for the study of causes of and improvement in the methods of diagnosing, treating and preventing congenital heart defects.
Publications: Annual report; Newsletter.
Financial data: Year ended 12/31/2003.
Assets, $145,000 (M); Expenditures, $315,000; Total giving, $105,000; Grants to individuals, 2 grants totaling $80,484 (high: $40,484, low: $40,000).
Fields of interest: Heart & circulatory research.
Type of support: Research.
Application information: Deadline June 30; Completion of formal application required; See Web site for additional information.
Program description:
  Medical Grants: Awards clinical and basic science research grants in congenital heart disease, including, but not limited to the following areas: molecular genetics, biochemistry, pharmacology, devices and procedural research (cardiac catherization and surgery) and long-term care of adults with congenital heart defects.
EIN: 364077528

5695
Children's Tumor Foundation
(formerly National Neurofibromatosis Foundation, Inc.)
95 Pine St., 16th Fl.
New York, NY 10005 (212) 344-6633
Contact: John River, Pres.
For research grants, contact Kim Hunter-Schaedle, Ph.D. Chief Scientific Officer, tel: 212-344-6633 x 231, e-mail: khunter-schaedle@ctf.org
FAX: (212) 747-0004; E-mail: info@ctf.org;
URL: http://www.ctf.org

Foundation type: Public charity
Limitations: Research grants to scientists for the development of therapies and cures for neurofibromatosis type 1 (NF1), neurofibromatosis type 2 (NF2), schwannomatosis and related disorders.
Publications: Annual report; Financial statement; Informational brochure; Newsletter.
Financial data: Year ended 12/31/2004.
Assets, $3,200,647 (M); Expenditures, $1,217,951; Total giving, $333,505.
Fields of interest: Nerve, muscle & bone diseases; Nerve, muscle & bone research.
Type of support: Research.
Application information: Applications accepted. Application form required. Application form available on the grantmaker's Web site.
  Initial approach: Letter or e-mail.
  Applicants should submit the following:
    1) Letter(s) of recommendation
    2) Proposal
    3) Budget Information
  Additional information: See Web site for application guidelines and complete program listing.
EIN: 132298956

5696
The Jane Coffin Childs Memorial Fund for Medical Research
333 Cedar St., SHM L300 MC 0191
P.O. Box 20800
New Haven, CT 06520-8000 (203) 785-4612
Contact: Kim Roberts, Admin. Dir.
FAX: (203) 785-3301; E-mail: jccFund@yale.edu

Foundation type: Independent foundation
Limitations: Postdoctoral fellowships to individuals with no more than one year of postdoctoral training for cancer research. See program description for further limitations.
Publications: Application guidelines; Annual report; Program policy statement.
Financial data: Year ended 06/30/2004.
Assets, $41,056,858 (M); Expenditures, $3,377,800; Total giving, $2,980,878; Grants to individuals, 75 grants totaling $2,920,504 (high: $47,250, low: $6,500).
Fields of interest: Cancer research.
Type of support: Fellowships; Postdoctoral support.
Application information: Application form required.
  Initial approach: Letter or telephone.
  Deadline(s): Feb. 1
  Additional information: Application must include proposal and previous work experience; Applicants must apply through the host institution; The fund does not give directly to individuals.
Program description:
  Cancer Research Fellowships: Fellowships are awarded for research into the causes, origins, and treatment of cancer. Fellowships are for full-time postdoctoral studies in the medical and related sciences bearing on cancer. Applicants in general

should not have more than one year of postdoctoral experience. They must hold either the M.D. degree or the Ph.D. degree in the field in which they propose to study, or furnish evidence of equivalent training and experience. The appointment will normally be for three years. Applicants may be citizens of any country, but for foreign nationals awards will be made only for study in the U.S. American citizens may hold a fellowship either in the U.S. or in a foreign country. The basic stipend at present is $37,000 the first year, $39,000 the second year, and $41,000 the third year, with an additional $750 for each dependent child. There is no dependency allowance for a spouse. An allowance of $1,500 a year toward the cost of the research usually will be made available to the laboratory sponsoring the Fellow. A travel award will be made to the Fellow and family for travel to the sponsoring laboratory. Applicants must apply through the host institution. The money is awarded to the host institution to be used by the Fellow at its facility. If the Fellow moves to another institution she or he must submit a request to transfer the fellowship money.
EIN: 066034840

5697
China Times Cultural Foundation
1499 Bayshore Hwy., No. 212
Burlingame, CA 94010 (718) 460-4900
Contact: Sophia Hsieh
E-mail: ctcfmail@yahoo.com

Foundation type: Independent foundation
Limitations: Scholarships to Ph.D. candidates in Chinese studies, and project support and travel grants to Chinese scholars to attend conferences relating to the history and development of China.
Financial data: Year ended 12/31/2004.
Assets, $2,246,653 (M); Expenditures, $123,638; Total giving, $27,500; Grants to individuals, 10 grants totaling $27,500 (high: $2,750, low: $2,750).
Fields of interest: International studies; China.
Type of support: Program development; Conferences/seminars; Fellowships; Research; Travel grants.
Application information:
Deadline(s): June 30
Additional information: Completion of formal application required, including report cards for previous four semesters, recent photographs, and parents' income.
EIN: 222711422

5698
Christian Community Foundation
2925 Professional Pl., Ste. 201
Colorado Springs, CO 80904-8105
E-mail: ccf@thefoundations.org; URL: http://www.thefoundations.org

Foundation type: Public charity
Limitations: Professional assistance and travel grants to Christian community leaders and missionaries.
Financial data: Year ended 12/31/2003.
Assets, $49,064,328 (M); Expenditures, $11,001,849; Total giving, $9,509,475.
Fields of interest: Religion.
Type of support: Awards/grants by nomination only; Travel grants.
Application information: Unsolicited requests for funds not considered or acknowledged.
EIN: 751750059

5699
Citizens United for Research in Epilepsy
720 N. Franklin St., Ste. 404
Chicago, IL 60610 (312) 255-1801
Contact: Susan Axelrod, Pres.
FAX: (312) 255-1809;
E-mail: info@cureepilepsy.org; URL: http://www.cureepilepsy.org

Foundation type: Public charity
Limitations: Medical research grants to investigators to aid in finding a cure for epilepsy.
Publications: Application guidelines; Newsletter.
Financial data: Year ended 12/31/2004.
Assets, $1,777,099 (M); Expenditures, $609,766; Total giving, $595,071; Grants to individuals, 8 grants totaling $398,544.
Fields of interest: Epilepsy research.
Type of support: Research.
Application information: Applications accepted.
Initial approach: Letter.
EIN: 364253176

5700
Clover Foundation
c/o William Orchard
420 Lexington Ave., Ste. 300
New York, NY 10170

Foundation type: Independent foundation
Limitations: Fellowships and publication grants to humanities scholars.
Financial data: Year ended 12/31/2003.
Assets, $30,654,728 (M); Expenditures, $343,943; Total giving, $197,000.
Fields of interest: Humanities.
Type of support: Publication; Fellowships.
Application information: Applications accepted throughout the year; Contact foundation for current application guidelines.
Program descriptions:
Clover Fellowships: Fellows are chosen by individual university departments for their extraordinary ability in the classroom and enthusiasm for Western texts. These post-doctoral fellows teach courses on the "Great Books" of Western culture to undergraduates at the most influential universities in the U.S.
Publications: Offers grants to support scholars who are preparing manuscripts regarding Western culture for publication.
EIN: 742390003

5701
The Club Foundation
1733 King St.
Alexandria, VA 22314 (703) 739-9500
Contact: Rhonda Schaver, Mgr., Admin. & Schol.
FAX: (703) 739-0124;
E-mail: rhonda.schaver@clubfoundation.org;
URL: http://www.clubfoundation.org/

Foundation type: Public charity
Limitations: Scholarships by nomination only to assist club managers interested in pursuing the Certified Club Manager (CCM) designation.
Financial data: Year ended 10/31/2004.
Assets, $3,294,711 (M); Expenditures, $1,117,917; Total giving, $391,149; Grants to individuals, 12 grants totaling $26,022 (high: $2,500, low: $117).
Fields of interest: Business school/education.
Type of support: Awards/grants by nomination only.
Application information: Applications accepted. Application form required.
Deadline(s): Nov. 3

Applicants should submit the following:
1) Letter(s) of recommendation
2) Essay
3) Resume
Program description:
Wilmoore H. Kendall Scholarship: Candidates must be a member of CMAA, an assistant manager, and actively pursuing the CCM designation. Candidates must be nominated for the scholarship by their chapter. The Club Foundation will award up to two scholarships annually. To help recipients meet certification requirements and prepare them for the CCM exam, each scholarship will include fees (except travel expenses) associated with the following programs: BMI II; BMI III; Certification Review Course (including Study Guide); and CCM Exam Fees.
EIN: 521642692

5702
The Common Wealth Trust
c/o PNC Bank, N.A.-Delaware
222 Delaware Ave.
Wilmington, DE 19899

Foundation type: Independent foundation
Limitations: Distinguished service awards by nomination only to prominent individuals in the dramatic arts, literature, public service, science, invention, government, and mass communications, primarily in OH.
Financial data: Year ended 12/31/2004.
Assets, $9,633,510 (M); Expenditures, $645,928; Total giving, $514,000; Grants to individuals, 4 grants totaling $200,000 (high: $50,000, low: $50,000).
Fields of interest: Media/communications; Theater; Science; Government/public administration; Leadership development.
Type of support: Awards/grants by nomination only; Awards/prizes.
Application information: Applications not accepted.
EIN: 510232187

5703
The Commonwealth Fund
1 E. 75th St.
New York, NY 10021-2692 (212) 606-3800
Contact: Andrea C. Landes, Dir., Grants Mgmt.
FAX: (212) 606-3500; E-mail: cmwf@cmwf.org;
URL: http://www.cmwf.org

Foundation type: Independent foundation
Limitations: Health policy fellowships to junior health policy researchers or practitioners from the United Kingdom, Australia, and New Zealand for research and training in the U.S., and also fellowships for the study of public policy in New Zealand.
Publications: Annual report (including application guidelines); Financial statement; Grants list; Informational brochure; Newsletter; Occasional report; Program policy statement.
Financial data: Year ended 06/30/2005.
Assets, $634,403,522 (M); Expenditures, $29,386,113; Total giving, $15,229,313; Grants to individuals, totaling $1,114,242.
Fields of interest: Health care, public policy; Health care; Public policy, research.
Type of support: Fellowships; Research; Foreign applicants; Travel grants.
Application information: Application form required.

Initial approach: Letter, telephone, or e-mail requesting application form and guidelines.

Deadline(s): Oct. 1 for Health Policy Fellowships, Nov. 1 for Ian Axford Fellowships.

Additional information: Application must include statement of professional objectives, curriculum vitae, preliminary proposal, and letters of reference; Interviews (in London, Sydney, and Wellington) required for short listed candidates; Application guidelines are also available on Web site.

Program descriptions:

Harkness Fellowships in Health Care Policy: Provides a unique opportunity for promising mid-career health policy researchers and practitioners (e.g., physicians, health services managers, government officials, and journalists) to spend six to 12 months in the U.S. conducting a policy-oriented research project and working with leading U.S. health policy experts. Up to nine fellows will be selected annually from the United Kingdom, Australia, or New Zealand. Fellowships are designed for professionals who are committed to advancing policy and practice in the Commonwealth Fund's principal areas of interest. Among the issues the fund addresses are improving the coverage of and access to health insurance and improving the quality of health care services. Its quality programs focus not only on general issues but also on the needs of specific groups, including underserved populations, young children, and frail elders. Studies that include comparisons between the U.S. and the applicant's home country are encouraged. All applicants must be citizens of the United Kingdom, Australia, or New Zealand. Applicants must hold a master's or doctoral degree (or equivalent thereof) in health care services, health policy research or a related discipline, and/or must show significant promise as a policy-oriented researcher or work as a practitioner with a demonstrated expertise in health policy issues as well as a track record in health policy analysis. If academically based, the applicant must be at the research fellow to senior lecturer level. The fund will provide extensive support to successful fellows to help them develop and shape their research proposals to fit the U.S. context. Through its extensive network of contacts, the fund will help identify and place fellows with a mentor who is an expert in the policy area to be studied. In collaboration with the U.K. Selection Committee, a home country mentor, who will act as a liaison with the U.S. mentor and supervise any cross-national comparisons that are to be conducted as part of the study, will also be identified after selection. Each fellowship will provide up to $75,000 (U.S.) in support, which includes round trip airfare to the U.S., a monthly stipend, support toward any portion of the study conducted in the home country, project-related travel and other research expenses, tuition for related academic courses, and health insurance. In addition, a family supplement is available to fellows accompanied by a spouse and/or children.

Ian Axford Fellowships in Public Policy: Fellowships to outstanding mid-career American professionals for an opportunity to study, travel and gain practical experience in public policy in New Zealand, including first-hand knowledge of economical, social and political reforms, and management of the government sector. Up to two fellowships per year are awarded for three to six months of study in New Zealand. Recipients must be U.S. citizens and must submit a formal application package. Fellowships are offered in any area of public policy.

EIN: 131635260

5704
The Community Foundation Serving Richmond & Central Virginia

(formerly Greater Richmond Community Foundation)

7325 Beaufant Springs Dr., Ste. 210
Richmond, VA   23225-5546   (804) 330-7400
Contact: Darcy S. Oman, C.E.O. and Pres.; For grants: Jill A. McCormick, Sr. Prog. Off.
FAX: (804) 330-5992;
E-mail: info@tcfrichmond.org; Additional E-mail: doman@tcfrichmond.org; Grant application E-mail: jmccormick@tcfrichmond.org; URL: http://www.tcfrichmond.org

Foundation type: Community foundation

Limitations: Professional development grants by nomination only to full-time K-12 teachers employed by the public school divisions of the City of Richmond, VA; Chesterfield, Hanover, and Henrico counties, VA; and the tri-cities area, including Hopewell, Colonial Heights, and Petersburg, VA. AIDS awards for outstanding service are also given.

Publications: Application guidelines; Annual report; Biennial report.

Financial data: Year ended 12/31/2004.
Assets, $161,627,393 (M); Expenditures, $13,927,079; Total giving, $11,935,299.

Fields of interest: Education; AIDS.

Type of support: Program development; Awards/grants by nomination only; Awards/prizes.

Application information:

Initial approach: Nomination letter.

Deadline(s): Deadlines are announced in Jan. of each year

Additional information: Completion of formal nomination required for teaching awards; Interviews required for teaching awards.

Program descriptions:

AIDS Awards: Two awards are given annually for outstanding humanitarian service and outstanding professional service to individuals working in the field of AIDS in Richmond and central VA. Awards are given each Apr.

R.E.B. Awards for Teaching Excellence: These awards identify, recognize, and support excellence in classroom teaching in area public schools. Grants are made to individual teachers to support development and enrichment activities, and to share educational ideas and experiences with teacher colleagues. Grants support projects of teachers' own designs, including world travel, advanced education, and on-site practice. Nominations are invited from parents, students, educators, and the community at large. After being nominated, teachers are invited to submit project proposals for review.

EIN: 237009135

5705
Compassion for Animals Foundation, Inc.

3962 Landmark St.
Culver City, CA   90232-2315
Contact: Gilbert N. Michaels, Pres.

Foundation type: Operating foundation

Limitations: Project support to individuals for the advancement of animal rights and the prevention of cruelty to animals through scientific research, and literary, educational, and charitable work.

Financial data: Year ended 11/30/2004.
Assets, $1,234,917 (M); Expenditures, $374,713; Total giving, $368,500.

Fields of interest: Animal welfare.

Type of support: Program development; Publication; Research.

Application information: Applications by letter, outlining project and stating how it relates to the protection or advancement of animal rights, accepted throughout the year.

EIN: 954082225

5706
Concern Foundation

8383 Wilshire Blvd., No. 337
Beverly Hills, CA   90211-2403   (323) 852-9844
Contact: Seunga Yu, Exec. Dir.
FAX: (323) 852-9873;
E-mail: info@concernfoundation.org; URL: http://www.concernfoundation.org

Foundation type: Public charity

Limitations: Grants to researchers in the field of cancer immunology, with particular interest in pediatric cancers and the molecular genetics of cancer.

Publications: Application guidelines; Grants list.

Financial data: Year ended 12/31/2004.
Assets, $4,566,845 (M); Expenditures, $1,648,687; Total giving, $1,312,435; Grants to individuals, 23 grants totaling $1,196,435 (high: $50,000; low: $22,914).

Fields of interest: Genetics/birth defects; Pediatrics; Cancer research; Immunology research.

Type of support: Research.

Application information: Deadline Dec.; Completion of formal application required; Applications by FAX not accepted; Consult Web site for additional information.

Program description:

Research Grants: Grants generally average $50,000 per year for two years and the foundation is especially interested in funding young researchers who may initially have difficulty obtaining funding from more traditional sources. Applicants must be independent investigators at the level of Assistant Professor or equivalent. Applicants at governmental agencies are not eligible. All funds are to be distributed only for salaries and supplies directly related to the funded research.

EIN: 237002878

5707
The Conservation Fund

1655 N. Fort Myer Dr., Ste. 1300
Arlington, VA   22209   (703) 525-6300
Contact: Jennifer Hauck, Sr. Admin. Asst.
FAX: (703) 525-4610;
E-mail: postmaster@conservationfund.org;
URL: http://www.conservationfund.org/

Foundation type: Public charity

Limitations: Awards by nomination only to Individuals for outstanding leadership and distinguished service for preserving and protecting the nation's natural and historic resources.

Publications: Application guidelines; Annual report; Corporate giving report; Newsletter.

Financial data: Year ended 12/31/2004.
Assets, $328,191,282 (M); Expenditures, $39,205,753; Total giving, $2,291,055; Grant to an individual, 1 grant totaling $10,000.

Fields of interest: Natural resources.

Type of support: Awards/grants by nomination only; Awards/prizes.

Application information:

Deadline(s): Apr. 17

Additional information: Nomination by letter; See Web site for complete nomination guidelines.

Program descriptions:

International Paper Environmental Awards: Awards of $10,000 to two individuals whose work demonstrates that a healthy environment and a healthy economy are mutually supportive. Awards are presented on an annual basis.

American Land Conservation Award: Award of $50,000 to a citizen conservationist to honor his or her outstanding leadership and distinguished service to preserving and protecting the nation's natural and historic resources for the benefit of their communities and future generations. Recipients of the award are recognized for building partnerships that lead to the preservation of open space, wildlife habitat and sites that preserve a sense of place. Recipients are honored for their work to protect coastlines, river corridors, forestlands, farmland, rangeland and historic sites.

International Paper Environmental Education Award: Awards of $10,000 by nomination only to educators who have shown special skills in giving their students a better understanding of the complex relationship between environmental protection and economic growth. Recipients must: demonstrate innovative approaches to environmental education that foster an understanding of the linkage between environmental protection and economic growth; and have achieved specific goals, demonstrate leadership, received national recognition and served as an example for others.

International Paper Conservation Partnership Award: Award by nomination only of $10,000 to an individual who has achieved significant results in the protection of terrestrial or wetland habitat in the U.S. and demonstrates positive value of cooperation partnerships between business and conservation.
EIN: 521388917

5708
Council for Advancement and Support of Education

1307 New York Ave. N.W., Ste. 1000
Washington, DC 20005-4701   (202) 328-5900
Contact: John Lippincott, Pres.
FAX: (202) 387-4973; E-mail: info@case.org;
URL: http://www.case.org

Foundation type: Public charity
Limitations: Fellowships to journalists to tap into cutting-edge ideas and gain perspectives away from daily pressures of the newsroom.
Financial data: Year ended 06/30/2003. Assets, $16,114,911 (M); Expenditures, $12,660,632; Total giving, $76,275; Grants to individuals, 9 grants totaling $17,000 (high: $5,000, low: $500).
Fields of interest: Journalism/publishing.
Type of support: Fellowships; Research.
Application information:
Deadline(s): July 11
Additional information: Contact foundation for current application guidelines; See Web site for further information.
Program description:
Media Fellowships: In recent years, fellowships have covered topics in business, education, the environment, family and social issues, health and medicine, international affairs, science, technology and more. Journalists discover the latest ideas being researched and explored at leading colleges and universities and interact with renowned scholars. They spend several days to a week in one-on-one meetings with senior faculty, engaging in hands-on research on campus and in the field.
EIN: 521012307

5709
Council of American Overseas Research Centers

(formerly Council of American Research Centers)
P.O. Box 37012, NHB Rm. CE-123, MRC 178
Washington, DC 20013-7012   (202) 633-1599
Contact: Lisa Rogers, Grants Admin.
FAX: (202) 786-2430;
E-mail: fellowships@caorc.org; URL: http://www.caorc.org

Foundation type: Public charity
Limitations: Fellowships to scholars for multi-country research.
Publications: Newsletter.
Financial data: Year ended 09/30/2003. Assets, $4,471,826 (M); Expenditures, $3,542,226; Total giving, $2,881,394; Grants to individuals, 22 grants totaling $122,193 (high: $9,000, low: $250).
Fields of interest: Humanities; International affairs; Social sciences.
Type of support: Fellowships; Research.
Application information: Deadline Dec. 31; Completion of formal application required, including project description, three letters of recommendation, and a transcript (for Ph.D. candidates) or curriculum vitae (for post-doctoral scholarships).
Program description:
Fellowships for Advanced Multi-Country Research: Ten awards of up to $9,000 each given to scholars who wish to carry out research on broad questions of multi-country significance in the fields of humanities, social sciences, and related natural sciences. The program is open to U.S. doctoral candidates and scholars who have earned their Ph.D. in fields of the humanities, social sciences, or allied natural sciences, and wish to conduct research in more than one country, at least one of which hosts a participating American Overseas Research Center. Scholars may apply individually or in teams. All applicants must be U.S. citizens.
EIN: 521395971

5710
The Covenant Foundation

1270 Avenue of the Americas, Ste. 304
New York, NY 10020   (212) 420-0604
Contact: Judith Ginsberg Ph.D., Exec. Dir.
FAX: (212) 245-3500; E-mail: info@covenantfn.org;
URL: http://www.covenantfn.org

Foundation type: Public charity
Limitations: Awards by nomination only to outstanding educators in the U.S. and Canada who perform exceptional work in any form of Jewish education.
Publications: Application guidelines; Grants list; Informational brochure; Program policy statement.
Financial data: Year ended 08/31/2004. Assets, $1,637,504 (M); Expenditures, $2,208,304; Total giving, $1,223,165.
Fields of interest: Secondary school/education; Theological school/education; Education; Jewish agencies & temples.
Type of support: Awards/grants by nomination only; Awards/prizes.
Application information:
Initial approach: Letter or telephone.
Deadline(s): Dec. 2 for nominations, Dec. 16 for supporting materials
Additional information: Nomination packets available after Sept.; Completion of formal nomination form required, including biographical information, three letters of support, statement of motivation, and statement of purpose; Recipients notified in May; See program description for additional information.
Program descriptions:
Teacher Awards: Selection Procedures and Notification of Covenant Award Winners: All completed nominations will be reviewed by the foundation staff and Selection Committee in Jan., Feb., and Mar. During the review process, candidates may be visited by members of the foundation staff. The foundation will notify award recipients in May. In addition, the Exec. Dir. of the foundation will advise all nominators and nominees of the final determinations. The awards will be presented at a ceremony. To be considered for a Covenant Award, a completed nomination must demonstrate the following:
· the candidate is an exceptional Jewish educator who has made a significant impact on others
· the candidate has contributed creatively to advancing the transmission of Jewish knowledge, values, and identity
· the candidate is a positive role model for other educators and for the Jewish community at large.
The Covenant Awards: These awards are designed to honor and thank outstanding teachers. They are presented to three educators each year. Each award will carry with it a prize of $20,000 for the individual educator, and an additional $5,000 for the educator's host institution. The awards seek to provide professional recognition and encouragement for singularly talented teachers whose role in transmitting Jewish knowledge, values, and identity is crucial to the continuity of the Jewish people. Despite the often overwhelming challenges of religious education today, the educators these awards seek to honor exemplify extraordinary dedication and proven success. Eligibility: Educators with significant achievements in the field of Jewish education are eligible recipients of Covenant Awards. These include professionals working in day schools, camps, informal programs, Hillel programs, family and adult programs, and other kinds of educational endeavors. All nominees must be currently working in the field of precollegiate or adult Jewish education in the U.S. or Canada. Nomination Procedures: Notices of the awards are sent to Jewish education institutions and organizations. Nominations for the Covenant Award are welcomed from anyone concerned with Jewish education in North America. Nominations from community members and professionals alike, from all religious denominations and institutional frameworks are encouraged. No one may nominate more than one person in any one year. Self-nomination is not considered appropriate. Those who wish to nominate an educator should complete the initial nomination form. The nominator is also requested to send the notice of nomination form to the nominee so that he or she has instructions on providing a nomination dossier. Nominators are also asked to solicit three letters of support for the nominee. These letters should be from colleagues, former or current students, or community members who have worked directly with the nominee. Ideally, there should be one letter from each category. All three letters should not come from one category. Nominees must provide: biographical data, a statement of motivation, and a statement of purpose.
EIN: 363722029

5711
Crohn's & Colitis Foundation of America, Inc.
386 Park Ave. S., 17th Fl.
New York, NY 10016-8804 (212) 685-3440
Contact: Richard Geswell, Pres. and C.E.O.
FAX: (212) 779-4098; E-mail: info@ccfa.org;
Toll-free tel.: (800) 923-2423; URL: http://www.ccfa.org

Foundation type: Public charity
Limitations: Research grants for the prevention and cure of Crohn's disease and ulcerative colitis.
Publications: Annual report; Financial statement; Informational brochure.
Financial data: Year ended 09/30/2003.
Assets, $636,549 (M); Expenditures, $24,065,737; Total giving, $6,400,401; Grants to individuals, 111 grants totaling $6,400,401 (high: $356,783, low: $581).
Fields of interest: Medical school/education; Digestive disorders research.
Type of support: Fellowships; Research; Awards/prizes; Postdoctoral support; Graduate support.
Application information: Applications accepted. Application form required.
> *Initial approach:* Telephone.
> *Deadline(s):* Jan 14 and July 1 for Senior Research, Research Fellowship Award and Career Development Awards; Mar. 15 for Student Research Fellowship Awards.
> *Additional information:* See Web site for additional information.
Program descriptions:
Basic and Clinical Career Development Awards: Awards of up to $52,000 for salary, plus fringe benefits (not to exceed 25 percent of the salary awarded) per year to researchers, with an additional stipend of up to $25,000 for supplies, technical support, travel, and other expenses. Total award must not exceed $90,000 and is renewable for up to three years. The awardee must devote a minimum of 80% of his/her time directly to the project. M.D. candidates must have at least five years postdoctoral experience (with two years of research relevant to IBD) prior to the beginning date of the award and generally not in excess of ten years beyond the attainment of the doctoral degree, and to Ph.D. candidates with two years of post doctoral research relevant to inflammatory bowel disease.
Research Fellowship Awards: Awards of $45,000 for one to three years salary plus fringe benefits (not to exceed 25 percent of the salary award) per year, with an additional stipend of up to $2,000 for expenses directly related to the project. Recipient must hold an M.D., Ph.D. or equivalent degree with at least two years of postdoctoral experience. Candidates who have obtained M.D. degrees must have at least two years of research experience, one year of which must be documented research experience relevant to IBD prior to the beginning date of the award. Candidates with Ph.D. degrees must have one year of research experience prior to the beginning date of the award.
Senior Research Awards: Awards a maximum of $100,000 per year in direct costs, and indirect costs at 15 percent (not to exceed $15,000). Awards are for one to two years with a third year by competitive renewal. Recipient must hold an M.D., Ph.D. or equivalent degree, and must be employed by an institution (public nonprofit, private nonprofit or government) engaged in health care and/or health-related research.
Student Research Fellowship Awards: Awards of up to 16 fellowships of $2,500 per year to undergraduate, medical or graduate students (not yet engaged in thesis research) in accredited North American institutions to conduct full-time research with a mentor investigating a subject relevant to IBD. Mentor may not be a relative of the applicant and may not work in their lab. The duration of the project is a minimum of ten weeks. Submission deadline is March 15 of each year; awards begin on or about June 15.
EIN: 136193105

5712
William Nelson Cromwell Foundation for the Research of the Law and Legal History of the Colonial Period of the U.S.A.
c/o Sullivan & Cromwell
125 Broad St.
New York, NY 10004-2498 (212) 558-4000
Contact: Henry Christensen III, Tr.

Foundation type: Independent foundation
Limitations: Project and publication support to individuals for research on American legal history with emphasis on the Colonial and early Federal periods.
Financial data: Year ended 12/31/2004.
Assets, $3,973,101 (M); Expenditures, $233,362; Total giving, $176,262.
Fields of interest: History/archaeology; Law/international law.
Type of support: Program development; Publication; Research.
Application information: Application form not required.
> *Deadline(s):* Nov. 15.
> *Additional information:* Application by letter outlining proposal briefly.
EIN: 136068485

5713
The Nicholas & Dorothy Cummings Foundation
4781 Caughlin Pkwy.
Reno, NV 89503-4331

Foundation type: Independent foundation
Limitations: Research grants to individuals for psychotherapy and the study of behavioral health, primarily in CA and NV.
Financial data: Year ended 12/31/2004.
Assets, $172,725 (M); Expenditures, $160,983; Total giving, $17,398; Grants to individuals, totaling $17,398.
Fields of interest: Medical specialty research.
Type of support: Research.
Application information: Applications not accepted.
EIN: 880321190

5714
Cure Autism Now
(also known as CAN)
5455 Wilshire Blvd., Ste. 715
Los Angeles, CA 90036-4234 (323) 549-0500
Contact: Peter Bell, Exec. Dir.
FAX: (323) 549-0547;
E-mail: info@cureautismnow.org; Additional tel.: (888) 828-8476; URL: http://www.cureautismnow.org

Foundation type: Public charity
Limitations: Research grants for the investigation of effective biological treatments, prevention and cure of autism and related disorders.

Publications: Application guidelines; Financial statement; Grants list; Informational brochure; Newsletter.
Financial data: Year ended 12/31/2003.
Assets, $1,550,741 (M); Expenditures, $5,637,127; Total giving, $2,301,995; Grants to individuals, totaling $2,034,871.
Fields of interest: Autism research.
Type of support: Research; Awards/prizes.
Application information: Initial approach by letter of intent; Completion of formal application required, including proposal; See Web site for additional application guidelines and deadline.
Program descriptions:
Bridge Grants: Grants of $1,000 to $20,000 to scientists for research projects. Time frames are determined on a case-by-case basis on an ad hoc basis with smaller, yet often crucial financial support when needed to complete an important research project.
Genius Grant: Awards $100,000 per year for two years to recruit the best minds in science to focus their attention on autism for a two-year period, devoting their laboratory, staff and brain power to the cause.
Pilot Award: Awards up to $60,000 per year for one or two years to help researchers investigate promising hypothesis, generate new hypotheses about the biology of autism, generate preliminary data leading to larger scale studies and federal funding and to replicate or expand previous findings. Deadline Mar. 1 for letter of intent.
Young Investigator Award: Awards $40,000 per year for one or two years to encourage the brightest new scientists to enter the field of autism research. Deadline Mar. 1 for letter of intent.
EIN: 954542637

5715
Cystic Fibrosis Foundation
6931 Arlington Rd.
Bethesda, MD 20814-5200 (301) 951-4422
Contact: Robert J. Beall Ph.D., Pres. and C.E.O.
FAX: (301) 951-6378; E-mail: info@cff.org;
Additional tel.: (800) 344-4823; URL: http://www.cff.org

Foundation type: Public charity
Limitations: Research grants and fellowships in the study of cystic fibrosis and related areas.
Publications: Annual report; Informational brochure; Newsletter.
Financial data: Year ended 12/31/2004.
Assets, $195,888,823 (M); Expenditures, $90,630,522; Total giving, $21,895,773.
Fields of interest: Cystic fibrosis research; Pediatrics research; Medical research.
Type of support: Fellowships; Research; Awards/prizes; Postdoctoral support.
Application information: Application form required.
> *Deadline(s):* Vary
Program descriptions:
CF Foundation/NIH Funding Award: Supports excellent CF-related research projects that have been submitted to and approved by the NIH, but cannot be supported by available NIH funds. Applications must fall within the upper 40th percentile with a priority score of 200 or better. CF Foundation support ranges from $75,000 to $125,000 per year for up to two years. Applications accepted throughout the year.
Clinical Fellowships: Encourages specialized training early in a physician's career and prepares candidates for careers in academic medicine. Training must take place in one of the foundation's care centers, and must encompass diagnostic and therapeutic procedures, comprehensive care, and

CF-related research. Applicants must be eligible for Board Certification in pediatrics or internal medicine by the time the fellowship begins. Awards are $36,000 (first year) and $37,500 (second year) for stipend. A third-year fellowship is also available for additional basic and/or clinical research training. Recipients are expected to be subspecialty Board eligible at the completion of the program. Applicants and sponsors must submit a proposal of the research studies to be undertaken and other specialized training that will be offered during this third year. Up to $55,000 may be awarded: $45,000 for stipend and $10,000 for research costs. A fourth year of support is available as an option to highly qualified candidates who have received foundation support as third-year fellows. The foundation will underwrite the interest payments for educational loans for up to $7,000 per year. Recipients who do not enter a career of academic medicine will be subject to payback provisions. U.S. citizenship or permanent resident status is required. Deadlines Oct. 1 for 1st and 2nd years, Sept. 1 for 3rd and 4th years.

Clinical Research Grants: Supports clinical research projects directly related to CF treatment and care. Projects may address diagnostic or therapeutic methods related to CF or the pathophysiology of CF. Applicants must demonstrate access to a sufficient number of CF patients from accredited CF Foundation care centers and appropriate controls. A letter of intent to apply must be submitted by potential applicants. Up to $80,000 per year for up to three years may be requested for single-center clinical research grants. For multi-center clinical research, the potential award is up to $150,000 per year for up to three years. Deadlines June 1 for letter of intent, Oct. 1 for application.

Leroy Matthews Physician/Scientist Award: Provides up to six years of support for outstanding, newly trained pediatricians and internists (M.D./Ph.D.s) to complete subspecialty training, develop into independent investigators, and initiate a research program. Support ranges from $36,000 (stipend) plus $10,000 (research and development) for year one, to $60,000 (stipend) plus $15,000 (research and development) for year six. The foundation will also underwrite the interest payments for educational loans for up to $7,000 per year. U.S. citizenship or permanent resident status is required. Deadline Sept. 1.

Pilot Feasibility Awards: For developing and testing new hypotheses and/or new methods, and to support promising new investigators as they establish themselves in research areas relevant to CF. Proposed work must be hypothesis driven and must reflect innovative approaches to critical questions in CF research. The award is not meant to support continuation of programs already begun under other granting mechanisms. Up to $40,000 per year for two years may be requested. Deadline Sept. 1, electronic submission only.

Post-Doctoral Research Fellowships: Offered to M.D.s, Ph.D.s, and M.D./Ph.D.s interested in conducting basic or clinical research related to CF. Awards are offered through the foundation's network of research centers or through individual applications submitted to the foundation. Stipends are $30,000 (first year), $31,000 (second year), and $33,000 (optional third year). U.S. citizenship or permanent resident status required. Deadline Sept. 1, electronic submission only.

Research Grants: Intended to encourage the development of new information that contributes to the understanding of the basic etiology and pathogenesis of CF. In addition, consideration will be given to those projects that provide insight into the development of information that may contribute to the development of new therapies of CF. All proposals must be hypothesis driven, and sufficient preliminary data must be provided to justify support. Support is available for $60,000 per annum for a period of two years, at which time a grant may be competitively renewed for an additional two years of funding. Deadline Sept. 1, electronic submission only.

Harry Shwachman Clinical Investigator Award: This three-year award provides the opportunity for clinically trained physicians to develop into independent biomedical research investigators who are actively involved in CF-related areas. It is also intended to facilitate the transition from post-doctoral training to a career in academic medicine. Support is available for up to $60,000 per year plus $15,000 for supplies. U.S. citizenship or permanent resident status required. Deadline Sept. 1.
EIN: 131930701

5716
George F. Dales Foundation
c/o James E. Reed
3 Altarinda Rd., Ste. 201
Orinda, CA 94563-2601
Application address: c/o Selection Comm., P.O. Box 7235, Berkeley, CA 94707

Foundation type: Independent foundation
Limitations: Scholarships to U.S. citizens enrolled in American universities and colleges which offer doctoral, master's, or professional degrees.
Financial data: Year ended 12/31/2004. Assets, $48,998 (M); Expenditures, $5,045; Total giving, $5,000; Grants to individuals, totaling $5,000.
Type of support: Graduate support; Doctoral support.
Application information: Deadline July 31; Completion of formal application required, including transcripts, official confirmation of enrollment, essay, two references, and five additional copies of all of the aforementioned materials.
EIN: 686083929

5717
The Dana Foundation
(formerly The Charles A. Dana Foundation, Inc.)
745 5th Ave., Ste. 900
New York, NY 10151-0799 (212) 223-4040
Contact: Burton M. Mirsky, V.P., Finance
FAX: (212) 317-8721; E-mail: danainfo@dana.org;
URL: http://www.dana.org

Foundation type: Independent foundation
Limitations: Awards by nomination only to scientists and educators who are making significant advances in the respective fields of neuroscience and pre-collegiate education.
Publications: Application guidelines; Annual report (including application guidelines); Financial statement; Informational brochure (including application guidelines); Newsletter; Occasional report.
Financial data: Year ended 12/31/2004. Assets, $314,755,556 (M); Expenditures, $23,486,878; Total giving, $14,944,641.
Fields of interest: Education, research; Brain research; Immunology research.
Type of support: Program development; Fellowships; Research; Awards/grants by nomination only; Postdoctoral support.
Application information:
   Initial approach: Letter of less than two pages, outlining financial need.
   Deadline(s): None.

Additional information: Grants require matching support from involved organizations.
Program descriptions:
Charles A. Dana Awards for Pioneering Achievements in Health and Education: These awards of up to $50,000 each, honor innovative ideas with demonstrated potential. The goals of the awards are to call attention to those ideas and to increase their impact by encouraging their development and dissemination. In health, the awards spotlight advances in neurosciences that can be applied to prevention and/or treatment of human brain disorders. In education, the awards focus on innovative ideas for improving precollegiate education.

Dana Program in Brain and Immuno-Imaging: Awards of up to $100,000, over a period of up to three years to investigators for study of the immune system and related disorders, or the interaction of the brain and immune system. Awards are by nomination only. Investigators using system neuroimaging, or molecular or cellular imaging of brain or immune cells, or their interactions, are invited to apply to this competitive program. Deadline May 27. See Web site for further information and complete guidelines.

Human Immunology Awards: Awards of $45,000 per year, for up to three years to investigators who are pursuing research in human immunology. Postdoctoral fellows (Junior/Senior), M.D.'s, and/or M.D./Ph.D.'s pursuing research in human immunology with direct emphasis on diabetes, HIV/AIDS, cancer, rheumatoid arthritis, lupus, and other diseases of the immune system are eligible. All research is to be conducted in a laboratory or hospital in the U.S.
EIN: 066036761

5718
Joseph and Sharon Darcey Foundation, Inc.
(formerly Joseph Darcey Foundation, Inc.)
314 W. Main St., Ste. 11
Watertown, WI 53094-7630
Contact: Claude Held

Foundation type: Independent foundation
Limitations: Awards to individuals for excellence in teaching in Watertown, WI.
Financial data: Year ended 12/31/2004. Assets, $1,620,911 (M); Expenditures, $80,024; Total giving, $70,220; Grants to individuals, 4 grants totaling $12,000.
Fields of interest: Education.
Type of support: Awards/prizes.
Application information: Applications not accepted.
   Additional information: Unsolicited requests for funds not considered or acknowledged.
EIN: 391715481

5719
Taraknath Das Foundation
c/o Southern Asian Institute, Columbia University
420 W. 118th St.
New York, NY 10027
Contact: Leonard A. Gordon, V.P.
URL: http://www.columbia.edu/cu/sipa/REGIONAL/SAI/tdas.html

Foundation type: Independent foundation
Limitations: Scholarships to Indian graduate students, scholars, writers, and researchers who are studying in the U.S. and have completed one year of study in the U.S.

Financial data: Year ended 05/31/2005.
Assets, $563,029 (M); Expenditures, $39,653;
Total giving, $30,075; Grants to individuals, 7
grants totaling $25,000 (high: $4,000, low:
$3,500).
Fields of interest: Literature; International
exchange, students.
Type of support: Foreign applicants; Graduate
support.
Application information: Deadline Aug. 1;
Completion of formal application required, including
academic transcript and letters of
recommendation.
EIN: 136161284

5720

James E. Davis, M.D. Education & Research Foundation
4200 Commerical Pkwy.
Glenview, IL 60025

Foundation type: Operating foundation
Limitations: Fellowships to medical doctors.
Financial data: Year ended 12/31/2002.
Assets, $2,100 (M); Expenditures, $60,115; Total
giving, $60,000; Grant to an individual, 1 grant
totaling $60,000.
Fields of interest: Health care.
Type of support: Fellowships; Postdoctoral support.
Application information: Contact foundation for
current application deadline/guidelines.
EIN: 364103325

5721

The Dayton Foundation
2300 Kettering Twr.
Dayton, OH 45423-1395 (937) 222-0410
Contact: Michael M. Parks, Pres.; For discretionary
grants: Marilyn Shannon, Sr. Prog. Off.
FAX: (937) 222-0636;
E-mail: info@daytonfoundation.org; Additional tel.:
(877) 222-0410; Additional E-mails:
Dtimmons@daytonfoundation.org and
Mshannon@daytonfoundation.org; URL: http://
www.daytonfoundation.org

Foundation type: Community foundation
Limitations: Awards to teachers in the greater
Dayton, OH, area and to City of Dayton employees.
Publications: Application guidelines; Financial
statement; Newsletter; Program policy statement.
Financial data: Year ended 06/30/2005.
Assets, $260,578,404 (M); Expenditures,
$40,716,582; Total giving, $30,381,725; Grants
to individuals, 1,063 grants totaling $1,532,936.
Fields of interest: Public affairs, government
agencies; Women.
Type of support: Awards/prizes.
Application information: Applications not
accepted.
  Additional information: Contact foundation for
  current nomination deadline.
Program descriptions:
  Paula J. MacIlwaine Award: Honors individuals
and organizations that have demonstrated
creativity in improving the quality of the lives of
women in the greater Dayton, OH, area through
self-sufficiency.
  Joseph T. Kline Award: Provides cash awards to
City of Dayton employees who exhibit excellence
and dedication in their work.
EIN: 316027287

5722

Dead Sea Scrolls Foundation
P.O. Box 1775
Warsaw, IN 46581-1775 (574) 269-5223
Contact: Weston W. Fields, Exec. Dir.

Foundation type: Public charity
Limitations: Research grants to individuals for the
translation of ancient scrolls and restoration and
conservation of original manuscripts.
Financial data: Year ended 12/31/2003.
Assets, $23,908 (M); Expenditures, $200,781;
Total giving, $41,800; Grants to individuals,
totaling $41,800 (high: $35,000).
Fields of interest: History/archaeology.
Type of support: Research.
Application information: Contact foundation for
current application deadline/guidelines.
EIN: 351855580

5723

Deafness Research Foundation
2801 M St., N.W.
Washington, DC 20007 (202) 719-8088
Contact: Jennifer Mottershead, Managing Dir.
FAX: (202) 338-8192; E-mail: info@drf.org;
Additional tel.: (866) 454-3924; URL: http://
www.drf.org

Foundation type: Public charity
Limitations: Research grants and fellowships to
third-year medical students studying hearing.
Publications: Application guidelines; Annual report;
Informational brochure (including application
guidelines); Newsletter; Program policy statement.
Financial data: Year ended 09/30/2004.
Assets, $1,349,666 (M); Expenditures,
$2,176,733; Total giving, $160,000.
Fields of interest: Ear & throat research.
Type of support: Research; Graduate support.
Application information: Contact foundation for
current application deadline/guidelines.
Program description:
  Research Grants: Research grants of up to
$20,000 are awarded annually to finance promising
research projects related to hearing problems that
show both high scientific merit and clear
importance for the advance of clinical medicine or
therapy.
EIN: 131882107

5724

Marion Park Deaver and Harry Gilbert Deaver Foundation
c/o Wachovia Bank, N.A.
975 S. Federal Hwy.
Boca Raton, FL 33432-6129

Foundation type: Independent foundation
Limitations: Awards by nomination only to K-12
teachers in FL, MN, and WI.
Publications: IRS Form 990-PF.
Financial data: Year ended 12/31/2003.
Assets, $18,253,971 (M); Expenditures,
$874,345; Total giving, $768,410; Grants to
individuals, 66 grants totaling $68,000.
Fields of interest: Elementary/secondary
education.
Type of support: Awards/grants by nomination only;
Awards/prizes.
Application information: Contact foundation for
current nomination deadlines/guidelines.
EIN: 656066225

5725

Christel DeHaan Family Foundation
(formerly RCI Foundation)
10 W. Market St., Ste. 1990
Indianapolis, IN 46204 (317) 464-2038
Contact: Karen K. Witt, Dir.
FAX: (317) 464-2039; E-mail: kwitt@cde-ltd.com

Foundation type: Independent foundation
Limitations: Awards to outstanding teachers of
K-12 education in IN.
Publications: Application guidelines.
Financial data: Year ended 12/31/2004.
Assets, $41,709,816 (M); Expenditures,
$3,917,093; Total giving, $2,914,363; Grants to
individuals, 25 grants totaling $88,350 (high:
$8,000, low: $50).
Fields of interest: Education.
Type of support: Awards/prizes.
Application information: Deadline varies; Contact
foundation for current application guidelines; Initial
approach by letter.
EIN: 351939960

5726

The Gladys Krieble Delmas Foundation
521 5th Ave., Ste. 1612
New York, NY 10175-1699 (212) 687-0011
Contact: Shirley Lockwood, Fdn. Admin.
FAX: (212) 687-8877; E-mail: info@delmas.org;
URL: http://www.delmas.org

Foundation type: Independent foundation
Limitations: Predoctoral and postdoctoral grants
for research in Venice and the Veneto, Italy.
Publications: Application guidelines; Financial
statement; Grants list; Informational brochure.
Financial data: Year ended 12/31/2004.
Assets, $55,554,542 (M); Expenditures,
$3,337,924; Total giving, $2,470,429; Grants to
individuals, 24 grants totaling $131,620.
Fields of interest: Architecture; Theater; Music; Art
history; History/archaeology; Literature; Science;
Economics; Political science; Law/international
law; United Kingdom.
Type of support: Fellowships; Research;
Postdoctoral support; Travel grants.
Application information: Application form required.
Application form available on the grantmaker's Web
site.
  Initial approach: Letter.
  Copies of proposal: 7
  Deadline(s): Dec. 15
  Applicants should submit the following:
    1) Proposal
    2) Letter(s) of recommendation
    3) Curriculum vitae
  Additional information: Recipients notified by Apr.
  1.
Program description:
  Venetian Research Program: This program
awards three types of support to individuals: Grants
for Independent Research on Venetian History and
Culture are pre-doctoral and post-doctoral grants for
travel and residence in Venice and the Veneto. The
grants support historical research on Venice, the
former Venetian empire, and contemporary Venice.
Grants for Venetian Research in European Libraries
and Archives outside Venice allow scholars who
have already received and accepted a Delmas grant
for work in Venice and the Venito to apply for a
one-time grant of $3,000, for one month only, to
work on Venetian materials in other European
libraries and archives. Publication Assistance
supports publications to help make possible the

dissemination of work accomplished through Delmas Grants for Independent Research.
EIN: 510193884

5727
Deloitte Foundation
(formerly Deloitte & Touche Foundation)
10 Westport Rd.
P.O. Box 820
Wilton, CT 06897-0820 (203) 761-3474
Contact: Janet Butchko, Mgr., Academic Devel.
URL: http://www.deloitte.com/dtt/section_node/0,1042,sid%253D2257,00.html

Foundation type: Company-sponsored foundation
Limitations: Fellowships to doctoral accounting students.
Publications: Informational brochure.
Financial data: Year ended 05/28/2005.
Assets, $6,970,259 (M); Expenditures, $3,943,507; Total giving, $3,902,494.
Fields of interest: Business school/education.
Type of support: Fellowships; Doctoral support.
Application information: Applications accepted. Application form required.
  Deadline(s): Oct. 16
  Applicants should submit the following:
    1) Transcripts
  Additional information: See Web site for program guidelines.
Program description:
  Doctoral Fellowship Program: Provides support to doctoral accounting candidates who have completed at least two semesters of the doctoral program. Up to ten $25,000 grants are awarded each year.
EIN: 136400341

5728
The Deseret Foundation
(formerly LDS Hospital-Deseret Foundation)
8th Ave. & C St.
Salt Lake City, UT 84143 (801) 408-1775
Contact: Lori T. Piscopo, Exec. Dir.
FAX: (801) 408-1663; *URL:* http://www.ihc.com/xp/ihc/lds/deseret/

Foundation type: Public charity
Limitations: Research grants for the study of the heart and lungs to investigators in the greater Salt Lake city, UT, area.
Financial data: Year ended 12/31/2004.
Assets, $49,797,956 (M); Expenditures, $1,977,994; Total giving, $258,878; Grants to individuals, 12 grants totaling $220,590 (high: $40,000, low: $2,750).
Fields of interest: Heart & circulatory research; Lung research.
Type of support: Research.
Application information: Contact foundation for current application deadline/guidelines; Initial approach by letter or telephone.
EIN: 237062016

5729
Detroit Golf Club Caddie Scholarship Foundation
201 W. Big Beaver Rd.
Troy, MI 48084

Foundation type: Independent foundation
Limitations: Scholarships toward college tuition to caddies at the Detroit Golf Club.

Financial data: Year ended 12/31/2004.
Assets, $111,045 (M); Expenditures, $16,858; Total giving, $14,000; Grants to individuals, 7 grants totaling $14,000 (high: $2,000, low: $2,000).
Fields of interest: Higher education.
Type of support: Scholarships—to individuals.
Application information: Applications accepted.
  Initial approach: Letter.
EIN: 300023878

5730
Dialysis Research Foundation
5575 S. 500 E.
Ogden, UT 84405 (801) 479-0351
FAX: (801) 476-1766

Foundation type: Independent foundation
Limitations: Research grants to individuals investigating renal disease, including research on dialysis treatment. Preference is given to applicants affiliated with the University of Utah.
Financial data: Year ended 12/31/2004.
Assets, $4,617,452 (M); Expenditures, $747,786; Total giving, $453,165; Grants to individuals, 23 grants totaling $62,051 (high: $9,355, low: $240).
Fields of interest: Kidney research.
Type of support: Research.
Application information: Applications accepted.
  Deadline(s): None
  Additional information: Contact foundation for current application guidelines.
EIN: 942819009

5731
Dibner Institute, Inc.
38 Memorial Dr., E56-100
Cambridge, MA 02139 (617) 253-8721
Contact: Bonnie Edwards, Exec. Dir.
FAX: (617) 253-9858; *E-mail:* dibner@mit.edu;
Additional tel.: (617) 253-6989; *URL:* http://dibinst.mit.edu

Foundation type: Public charity
Limitations: Fellowships to scholars specializing in the history of science and technology.
Financial data: Year ended 06/30/2003.
Assets, $6,519,173 (M); Expenditures, $2,617,483; Total giving, $964,125; Grants to individuals, 31 grants totaling $964,125 (high: $35,000, low: $16,500).
Fields of interest: Engineering/technology; Science.
Type of support: Fellowships; Foreign applicants; Postdoctoral support.
Application information: Applications accepted. Application form required.
  Initial approach: Letter, telephone or FAX.
  Deadline(s): Dec. 31
  Applicants should submit the following:
    1) Proposal
    2) Letter(s) of recommendation
    3) Curriculum vitae
Program descriptions:
  Postdoctoral Fellows Program: Fellowships are awarded to outstanding scholars of diverse countries of origin who have received the Ph.D. or equivalent within the previous five years. Fellowships provide office space, support facilities and full access of the Massachusetts Institute of Technology's library. There is a stipend of $35,000 and healthcare coverage. Fellowships last from Sept. 1 through Aug. 15 and may be extended for a second and final year at the discretion of the Dibner Insitute.

Senior Fellows Program: Candidates should have advanced degrees in disciplines relevant to their research. The Fall Term lasts from Aug. 1 through Dec. 31, and the Spring Term lasts from Jan. 1 through May 31. There is a stipend of $35,000, medical coverage, and one round-trip airfare for international fellows.
  Science Writer Fellowship: Fellowship is awarded to a senior science writer with a proven track record of writing and/or reporting for a general audience to pursue a substantial project of his or her own choosing that bears on history of science or technology. The Fellow will enjoy the camaraderie of the other Dibner Fellows and the opportunity to participate in the activities of MIT's Graduate Program in Science Writing and the Knight Science Journalism Program. There is a stipend of $35,000.
EIN: 043091094

5732
Joseph Z. & Agnes F. Dickson Trust for Dickson Prizes
c/o Mellon Finacial Group
500 Grant St., Ste. 3825
Pittsburgh, PA 15258-0001
Contact: Laurie Moritz

Foundation type: Independent foundation
Limitations: Prizes primarily to residents of PA.
Financial data: Year ended 09/30/2003.
Assets, $2,113,663 (M); Expenditures, $99,889; Total giving, $90,629; Grants to individuals, 3 grants totaling $90,429 (high: $44,000, low: $2,429).
Type of support: Awards/grants by nomination only; Awards/prizes.
Application information: Applications not accepted.
EIN: 256088346

5733
The Dixon Foundation
2830 Cahaba Rd.
Birmingham, AL 35223
Application address: P.O. Box 370928, Birmingham, AL 35237

Foundation type: Operating foundation
Limitations: Grants to ministers of the North Alabama Conference of United Methodist Church who are residents of AL and GA, for continuing study and programs beyond the graduate level. Three-year fellowships in pediatrics research at Children's Hospital, Birmingham, AL, are also awarded to residents of AL and GA.
Financial data: Year ended 12/31/2004.
Assets, $14,180,328 (M); Expenditures, $1,361,301; Total giving, $526,580.
Fields of interest: Theological school/education; Pediatrics research; Protestant agencies & churches.
Type of support: Fellowships; Research; Scholarships—to individuals; Postgraduate support.
Application information:
  Deadline(s): None
  Additional information: Application by letter, outlining financial need.
EIN: 630944809

5734

Geraldine R. Dodge Foundation, Inc.

163 Madison Ave., 6th Fl.
P.O. Box 1239
Morristown, NJ 07962-1239 (973) 540-8442
Contact: David Grant, C.E.O. and Pres.
FAX: (973) 540-1211; E-mail: info@grdodge.org;
URL: http://www.grdodge.org

Foundation type: Independent foundation
Limitations: Grants by invitation only to teachers in NJ and principals and vice principals in Newark, NJ, to enable them to pursue professional development; and fellowships for veterinary research projects in NJ.
Publications: Application guidelines; Annual report (including application guidelines); Grants list.
Financial data: Year ended 12/31/2004.
Assets, $295,393,959 (M); Expenditures, $25,288,384; Total giving, $21,025,856; Grants to individuals, totaling $438,310.
Fields of interest: Arts, artist's services; Education, research; Education; Veterinary medicine.
Type of support: Program development; Fellowships; Research; Scholarships—to individuals; Awards/grants by nomination only; Awards/prizes; Travel grants.
Application information: Applications not accepted.
 Additional information: Application by invitation from the foundation only; Unsolicited applications not considered or acknowledged.
Program description:
 Professional Support:
 · Summer Educational Opportunity Awards for Teachers: Provides $5,000 summer awards to middle and high school teachers from Atlantic, Cape May, Cumberland, and Salem counties, NJ, to pursue their educational goals
 · Dodge Awards for Artist/Educators: Provides $5,000 grants to NJ artist/educators whose students have excelled, to pursue their artistic interests and later implement visual arts projects in their schools
 · Frontiers for Veterinary Medicine Summer Grants: Provides $7,000 grants to North American veterinary students engaged in nontraditional research, including human-animal relations, veterinary ethics, international issues, and others. The program enables recipients to pursue a summer project of their own design in an area about which they are passionate, and which promises to advance the humane treatment of animals
 · Frontiers for Veterinary Medicine Fellowships: Provides awards of up to $6,500 to veterinary students to give them the opportunity to step outside of the traditional boundaries of veterinary education to explore and bring new, creative problem-solving perspectives to pressing animal-related issues. Proposals may be for work that is project-based (such as developing a humane education program) or research-based. See Web site for further information.
EIN: 237406010

5735

The Patrick and Catherine Weldon Donaghue Medical Research Foundation

18 N. Main St.
West Hartford, CT 06107-1919
Contact: Lynne Garner, Exec. Dir.
FAX: (860) 521-9018;
E-mail: office@donaghue.org; URL: http://www.donaghue.org

Foundation type: Independent foundation
Limitations: Grants and fellowships to scientific researchers in CT for clinical, preclinical, and biomedical research, as well as epidemiological, community health, and health services research.
Publications: Application guidelines; Annual report; Financial statement; Newsletter.
Financial data: Year ended 12/31/2004.
Assets, $67,245,326 (M); Expenditures, $4,169,606; Total giving, $3,466,942.
Fields of interest: Health care, research; Public health, epidemiology; Medical research.
Type of support: Fellowships; Research.
Application information: Application form required.
 Deadline(s): Vary
 Additional information: Applicants must apply jointly with their institution; See Web site for further information.
Program descriptions:
 Donaghue Investigator Grants: Supports particularly promising medical researchers holding faculty appointments at CT institutions. The funding emphasis is on the investigator and his or her program of research rather than upon a specific study. Approximately four to six awards will be made each year, of up to $100,000 each for up to five years. A prototypical Donaghue Investigator will 1) be committed to pursuing his or her career in CT for the foreseeable future, 2) show potential for an outstanding independent research career, and for leadership in his or her field(s) of research, 3) be accepting of the importance of earning support for research by actively explaining to the public his or her field of work and specific results and their value, 4) be enthusiastic about and committed to disciplinary and inter-institutional collaboration in integrative research, 5) be strongly supported by his or her institution, and 6) possess evidence of external recognition of his or her work. See Web site for deadline.
 Practical Benefit Initiatives: This program has no specific timeline for application or designated grant award amount. The foundation initiates research projects showing particular promise for producing practical benefit to human health. In areas the foundation wishes to pursue, an interactive process between the foundation and prospective investigators is used to develop projects for funding. Interested investigators should submit a short summary letter to the Dir. of Opers.
 Research in Clinical and Community Health Issues: Funds clinical, behavioral and other health-related research projects that address the major medical issues and social problems influencing the health of individuals, groups and communities. The foundation is especially interested in clinical, epidemiological and health service research studies that focus on the development and evaluation of more effective methods of preventing, diagnosing and treating illnesses and conditions that have a major impact on the people of CT. Each year the program awards several one-, two-, or three-year grants of up to $240,000 (including 20 percent indirect). See application for deadline.
EIN: 066348275

5736

Emily Dorfman Foundation for Children

c/o Rosen, Goltz & Assocs.
20 N. Wacker Dr., Ste. 2245
Chicago, IL 60606
Contact: Stephen M. Dorfman, Pres.

Foundation type: Independent foundation
Limitations: Grants to individuals for medical research on serious pediatric illnesses.
Financial data: Year ended 12/31/2003.
Assets, $346,440 (M); Expenditures, $195,982; Total giving, $173,528.
Fields of interest: Medical research, institute; Pediatrics research.
Type of support: Research; Grants to individuals.
Application information: Applications accepted.
 Initial approach: Letter.
 Additional information: Contact foundation for current application deadline.
EIN: 367092880

5737

Alden B. and Vada B. Dow Creativity Foundation

315 Post St.
Midland, MI 48640 (989) 837-4478
FAX: (989) 837-4468

Foundation type: Operating foundation
Limitations: Residencies to individuals in any field or profession who wish to pursue an innovative project or creative idea.
Financial data: Year ended 12/31/2004.
Assets, $1,589,062 (M); Expenditures, $672,883; Total giving, $0. No monetary support given for residencies.
Type of support: Residencies.
Application information: Applications accepted.
 Initial approach: Letter, telephone, FAX or e-mail.
 Deadline(s): Dec. 31.
 Additional information: Application by letter including $10 application fee, cover page, brief statement of project idea, resume, three references and support materials such as writing samples or slides.
Program description:
 Alden B. Dow Creativity Fellowship Program: The program is a ten-week residency from mid-June to mid-Aug. The residency includes a travel allowance, housing and studio space, and a stipend.
EIN: 382852321

5738

Dow Jones Newspaper Fund, Inc.

P.O. Box 300
Princeton, NJ 08543-0300 (609) 452-2820
Contact: Richard S. Holden, Exec. Dir.
FAX: (609) 520-5804;
E-mail: newsfund@wsj.dowjones.com; Street address: 4300 Rte. 1 N., South Brunswick, NJ 08852; URL: http://djnewspaperfund.dowjones.com

Foundation type: Independent foundation
Limitations: Fellowships to high school journalism teachers and newspaper advisors, and scholarships and internships to college sophomores, juniors, and seniors, and graduate students.
Publications: Application guidelines; Annual report; Grants list.
Financial data: Year ended 12/31/2003.
Assets, $492,975 (M); Expenditures, $551,507; Total giving, $475,414; Grants to individuals, 13

grants totaling $243,214 (high: $38,245, low: $167).

Fields of interest: Journalism/publishing; Education.

Type of support: Fellowships; Internship funds; Precollege support; Undergraduate support.

Application information:

Initial approach: Letter or telephone requesting guidelines.

Deadline(s): Vary

Additional information: Some programs require attendance at Dow Jones workshops.

Program descriptions:

Newspaper Fund: In addition to the programs listed, the fund sponsors workshops and training programs for minority high school students, college students, and high school journalism teachers through organizations, including colleges and universities. Schools and journalism related organizations interested in operating an intern program, training program, or journalism high school workshop should contact the fund for further information. Awards are made directly to the recipients' schools.

Newspaper Editing Intern Program for College Juniors, Seniors and Graduate Students: The purpose of the program is to encourage people to consider newspaper copy editing as a career by providing training, summer internships, and scholarship grants. All college juniors, seniors, and graduate students interested in pursuing careers in print journalism are eligible to apply. Students attend one- to two-week editing residencies and are placed as copy editors at daily newspapers, on-line newspapers and financial news services. Interns returning to school after the internship will receive $1,000 scholarships. Deadline Nov. 15.

High School Teachers Fellowship Program: This program awards $500 fellowships to high school journalism teachers and high school publications advisors to attend college or university-offered workshops. The purpose of the special summer workshops/programs is to enhance the ability of participants to teach students to write and edit more effectively, learn about the First Amendment and how it relates to scholastic journalism, and/or desktop publishing. High school teachers selected by the sponsors of the workshops and courses must teach journalism and/or advise the school newspaper. Additional information including a list of organizations sponsoring programs is available between Mar. 15 and July 1. Application deadlines vary.

EIN: 136021439

5739
Lily E. Drake Scholarship Trust

c/o KeyBank N.A.
800 Superior Ave., OH-01-02-0421
Cleveland, OH 44114
Application address: Key Trust Client Svcs., P.O. Box 89464, Cleveland, OH 44114

Foundation type: Independent foundation

Limitations: Scholarships to single female residents of OR who are registered nurses for further education.

Financial data: Year ended 12/31/2004. Assets, $259,214 (M); Expenditures, $7,220; Total giving, $2,953; Grants to individuals, totaling $2,953.

Fields of interest: Nursing school/education; Women.

Type of support: Postgraduate support.

Application information: Applications not accepted.

EIN: 936131516

5740
The Camille and Henry Dreyfus Foundation, Inc.

555 Madison Ave., 20th Floor
New York, NY 10022-3301 (212) 753-1760
Contact: Mark J. Cardillo Ph.D., Exec. Dir.
E-mail: admin@dreyfus.org; URL: http://www.dreyfus.org

Foundation type: Independent foundation

Limitations: Research and teaching grants by nomination only to young faculty members in chemistry, biochemistry, and chemical engineering departments of academic institutions in the U.S. See program description below for limitations on specific programs.

Financial data: Year ended 12/31/2004. Assets, $119,790,088 (M); Expenditures, $6,987,634; Total giving, $4,995,035; Grants to individuals, totaling $3,636,000.

Fields of interest: Engineering school/education; Education; Chemistry; Biological sciences.

Type of support: Professorships; Seed money; Fellowships; Research; Awards/grants by nomination only.

Application information: Application form required.

Deadline(s): July 1 for Scholar/Fellow, May 15 for Faculty Start-up and New Faculty, Nov. 15 for Teacher-Scholar

Applicants should submit the following:

1) Letter(s) of recommendation

Additional information: Direct applications from individuals not accepted; All applicants must be nominated by their departments.

Program descriptions:

Camille and Henry Dreyfus Faculty Start-up Grants for Undergraduate Institutions: The aims of this program are to provide funding for new faculty members establishing scholarly careers in chemistry at non-Ph.D.-granting institutions, and to broaden the role of undergraduates in chemical research. Grants of $12,500 are awarded to the institution for unrestricted use in support of the recipient's professional advancement. No more than $500 may be used for institutional administrative purposes. Funds may be used for any research or curriculum-related purpose considered appropriate for the recipient's professional activities, except to defray academic-year salary.

Camille and Henry Dreyfus New Faculty Awards: Academic research institutions in the U.S. are invited to nominate their best candidate who has recently accepted a faculty position in chemistry, biochemistry, or chemical engineering. Candidates are expected to have no more than three years of post-doctoral experience and be ready to begin their full-time tenure-track academic appointment at the time of the award. The grant funds are primarily for research purposes, particularly as seed money for new ideas and concepts, and not for salary during the regular academic year. The funds may also be used for student research stipends, for scientific equipment, and for other needs related to research or teaching. Ten awards of $25,000 each are made annually. Only one nomination from an institution will be considered per year.

Camille Dreyfus Teacher-Scholar Awards and The Henry Dreyfus Teacher-Scholar Awards: These two programs replaced the previously existing Camille and Henry Dreyfus Teacher-Scholar Awards. Institutions that grant a bachelor's or higher degree in chemistry, chemical engineering, or biochemistry may submit nominations to these programs. Both programs provide unrestricted grants of $60,000 each to academic leaders in chemical science research and education, usually at early stages of their careers. However, each program places a

different emphasis on the two components. The Camille Dreyfus program focuses primarily on research attainment and promise, although evidence of excellence in teaching is also expected. Nominees must hold a full-time tenure-track academic appointment and are normally expected to be within the first five years of their academic careers. 15 of these $60,000 awards are given annually. Of this amount, $5,000 is allocated to the Camille Dreyfus Teacher-Scholar's department for undergraduate educational purposes. The Henry Dreyfus program is directed to faculty whose predominant professional activity is with undergraduates, including teaching, mentorship, and research achievement. Nominees must hold a full-time tenure-track academic appointment. While the Henry Dreyfus program has no age limit, preference will be given to nominees who are at earlier stages of their academic careers. Ten of these $60,000 awards are given annually. Of this amount, $5,000 is allocated to the Henry Dreyfus Teacher-Scholar's department for undergraduate educational purposes.

Camille and Henry Dreyfus Scholar/Fellow Program for Undergraduate Institutions: This program places a teaching/research fellow in a non-Ph.D.-granting institution under the guidance of a nominated mentor. It is designed to attract talented Ph.D. recipients to careers in undergraduate colleges and universities and to recognize outstanding research accomplishments and/or potential in faculty members from predominantly undergraduate institutions. The dual purpose is integrated within a program that provides a grant to the institution on behalf of a selected faculty member, designated the Camille and Henry Dreyfus Scholar. The grant is to be used in part for the Scholar to recruit and appoint a recent Ph.D. recipient as a Camille and Henry Dreyfus Fellow. The Fellow will collaborate in research with the Scholar and will teach in the department. The program is open to all departments of chemistry, chemical engineering and biochemistry in public and private institutions that do not award Ph.D. degrees in these fields. Faculty proposed as Camille and Henry Dreyfus Scholars must hold full-time tenure-track positions. Ten new Scholars are chosen each year. Each recipient is granted a two-year program funded at $60,000, of which $25,000 the first year and $15,000 the next year is allocated as the Fellow's stipend, with $15,000 the first year and $5,000 the next year being allocated as research support. Institutional matching is required in the second year so that the Fellow's stipend is no less than that of the first year. A supplemental grant of $10,000 may be applied for by Fellows who complete the program and accept a full-time tenure-track faculty position at an undergraduate institution. Supplemental support up to $5,000 for institutional involvement with high school chemistry teaching by the Scholar or Fellow may be requested. A proposal of no more than ten pages, including a resume, and four copies of the application should be submitted by a department on behalf of a proposed Scholar. Each proposal should identify a candidate chosen on the basis of scholarly achievements and/or potential, and demonstrated dedication to undergraduate education. Contact foundation for complete proposal requirements.

EIN: 135570117

5741
Doris Duke Charitable Foundation
650 5th Ave., 19th Fl.
New York, NY 10019 (212) 974-7000
Contact: Betsy Fader, Dir., Strategy and Planning
FAX: (212) 974-7590; Additional tel.: (212)
974-7100; URL: http://www.ddcf.org

Foundation type: Independent foundation
Limitations: Research grants by nomination only to investigators to study cardiovascular disease and blood disorders.
Financial data: Year ended 12/31/2004.
Assets, $1,693,460,630 (M); Expenditures,
$77,397,265; Total giving, $59,167,979.
Fields of interest: Heart & circulatory research; Medical research.
Type of support: Fellowships; Research; Awards/grants by nomination only; Postdoctoral support.
Application information: Application form required. Application form available on the grantmaker's Web site.
Initial approach: Pre-proposal.
Deadline(s): Jan. 18
Additional information: See Web site for complete application information.
Program descriptions:
Doris Duke Clinical Research Fellowship (CRF) Program: Awards fellowships to medical students for a one-year experience in clinical research that includes both didactic and research components and matches students to outstanding clinical research mentors. Fellows will receive stipends of $23,000 plus health insurance to spend a year conducting clinical research and receiving didactic training. See Web site for complete information about the program and each institution at which it is eligible.
Innovation in Clinical Research Awards: Provides support to twelve research projects in cardiovascular disease and blood disorders. Six investigators and six pairs of investigators will each receive $200,000 in research funding over the next two years. Clinical researchers with an advanced degree (M.D., Ph.D., or M.D./Ph.D.) working in not-for-profit institutions are eligible to apply. Pairs of investigators from the same institution or different institutions working on new cross disciplinary innovative approaches are particularly encouraged to apply.
Clinical Scientist Development Awards: Provides support to 15 junior faculty-level physician-scientists as they establish independent clinical research careers. Awardees receive $100,000 annually for up to five years. The dean of a school or equivalent in eligible teaching hospitals and independent research institutions must nominate applicants. Deadline May 17 for letter of nomination.
Distinguished Clinical Scientist Award: Recognizes outstanding physician-scientists who are engaged in applying the latest basic science advances to the prevention, diagnosis, treatment, and cure of disease. Nominations for this award are solicited from academic medical centers and other research institutions. Deadline Apr. 25.
EIN: 137043679

5742
Duke Energy Foundation
(formerly Duke Power Company Foundation)
526 S. Church St., M.C. EC03ZJ
P.O. Box 1006
Charlotte, NC 28201-1006 (704) 382-7200
Contact: Kay Saville, Exec. Dir.
FAX: (704) 382-7600; URL: http://www.duke-energy.com/community/foundations/duke_foundation

Foundation type: Company-sponsored foundation
Limitations: Scholarships by nomination only to students whose parents live in Duke Power Company's areas in NC and SC, and to employees' and retirees' children.
Financial data: Year ended 12/31/2004.
Assets, $29,439,770 (M); Expenditures,
$14,751,718; Total giving, $14,739,126.
Fields of interest: Business school/education; Health sciences school/education; Science; Chemistry; Mathematics; Physics; Computer science; Engineering; Biological sciences; Economics; Minorities.
Type of support: Employee-related scholarships; Undergraduate support.
Application information:
Deadline(s): Mid-Oct. for Scholastic Awards Program, mid-Nov. for Minority Scholarship Program.
Applicants should submit the following:
1) ACT
2) Essay
3) GPA
4) SAT
5) Transcripts
6) Photograph
7) Letter(s) of recommendation
Additional information: Students must be nominated by school officials; Completion of formal nomination required and should also include signature of school principal or headmaster.
Program descriptions:
Duke Power Scholastic Awards Program: This program was established to help improve the quality of education in the region served by the company, to demonstrate Duke Power's commitment to higher education in NC and SC, and to recognize and reward individual merit and achievement by the region's young people. The foundation awards scholarships on a competitive basis to students whose parents live in company areas and to children of company employees and retirees.
Duke Power Minority Scholarship Program: This program was established to increase the number of minority students pursuing degrees in accounting, finance, mathematics, economics, computer science, chemistry, physics, biology, health physics, industrial hygiene, metallurgy, or one of the following types of engineering: mechanical, electrical, civil, nuclear, industrial, and chemical. Scholarships are awarded to minority high school seniors with outstanding records of academic excellence and school and community leadership, as well as on-the-job experience.
EIN: 581586283

5743
Danny M. Dunnaway Foundation
P.O. Box 545
Brookhaven, MS 39602
Contact: Danny M. Dunnaway, Pres.

Foundation type: Independent foundation

Limitations: Grants to domestic and foreign missionaries with whom a working relationship has been developed over the years.
Financial data: Year ended 12/31/2004.
Assets, $534,857 (M); Expenditures, $196,618; Total giving, $194,066; Grants to individuals, 8 grants totaling $16,885 (high: $5,725, low: $750).
Fields of interest: Christian agencies & churches; Religion; Global programs.
Type of support: Grants for special needs.
Application information: Applications not accepted.
EIN: 640847778

5744
Duplessis Scholarship Fund
P.O. Box 760
Damariscotta, ME 04543 (207) 563-8104
Contact: Robert B. Gregory, Tr.

Foundation type: Independent foundation
Limitations: Scholarships to women for doctoral studies, with preference given to graduates of ME colleges and universities.
Financial data: Year ended 04/30/2005.
Assets, $161,010 (M); Expenditures, $29,196; Total giving, $25,000; Grants to individuals, totaling $25,000.
Fields of interest: Women.
Type of support: Doctoral support.
Application information: Applications accepted. Application form required.
Initial approach: Letter or telephone.
Deadline(s): Feb. 5
Applicants should submit the following:
1) Curriculum vitae
2) Letter(s) of recommendation
EIN: 010490941

5745
The Durfee Foundation
1453 3rd St. Promenade, Ste. 312
Santa Monica, CA 90401
Contact: Claire Peeps
FAX: (310) 899-5121; E-mail: admin@durfee.org; Additional E-mail for Claire Peeps: Claire@durfee.org; URL: http://www.durfee.org

Foundation type: Independent foundation
Limitations: Paid sabbaticals to leaders in the Los Angeles, CA, nonprofit sector.
Publications: Application guidelines; Annual report; Informational brochure.
Financial data: Year ended 12/31/2005.
Assets, $27,556,614 (M); Expenditures, $1,608,535; Total giving, $1,001,969; Grants to individuals, 50 grants totaling $243,484 (high: $15,000, low: $775).
Type of support: Grants to individuals; Sabbaticals.
Application information: Application form required. Application form available on the grantmaker's Web site.
Deadline(s): May 30
Applicants should submit the following:
1) Budget Information
2) Resume
3) Essay
Additional information: Application should also include organizational information, three references, endorsement from Chair.; Interviews required.
Program description:
Professional Grants: Awards up to six grants of $30,000 each to individuals who are leaders in the Los Angeles nonprofit community. Applicants should:

- be outstanding leaders who have a demonstrated track record of contribution to the community
- work for a nonprofit social service or arts organization (employees of educational institutions and government agencies are not eligible for this program)
- hold primary or significant responsibility for management of the organizations' fund
- have worked a minimum of ten consecutive years in the nonprofit sector (though not necessarily for one organization) without significant leave
- be willing to participate in a peer network of program alumni
- be employed full-time at the applicant organization
- be recognized by their peers as exceptional individuals
- have financial need.

EIN: 954856207

5746
Dystonia Medical Research Foundation

1 E. Wacker Dr., Ste. 2430
Chicago, IL 60601-1905 (312) 755-0198
Contact: Janet Hieshetter, Exec. Dir.
FAX: (312) 803-0138;
E-mail: dystonia@dystonia-foundation.org;
URL: http://www.dystonia-foundation.org

Foundation type: Public charity
Limitations: Research grants, fellowships, and awards to those studying dystonia and related fields.
Publications: Application guidelines; Annual report; Grants list; Informational brochure; Newsletter.
Financial data: Year ended 12/31/2004.
Assets, $1,402,524 (M); Expenditures, $2,700,834; Total giving, $632,347; Grants to individuals, 10 grants totaling $632,347 (high: $75,000, low: $39,000).
Fields of interest: Genetics/birth defects; Neuroscience; Medical research, institute.
Type of support: Fellowships; Research; Awards/prizes.
Application information: Deadlines vary; Initial approach by letter, telephone, or e-mail; Completion of formal application required.
Program descriptions:
Fellowship Program: Assists postdoctoral students to establish careers in dystonia research. Fellowships provide $50,000 per year for two years. Deadline Dec. 30.
Grant and Contract Funding: Funding for research grants will be $40,000 for one-year pilot studies, and up to $75,000 per year for up to two years for other research grants. Applications will also be considered for larger projects, with funding up to $150,000 per year. Deadlines June 30 and Dec. 30.
New Millenium Dystonia Award Program for Young Investigators: Recognizes emerging medical professionals in neurology, otolaryngology, genetics, or other fields related to the study of dystonia. Applicants must be currently enrolled in an accredited medical school or graduate program (leading to an M.D., D.O., or Ph.D. degree), with an expressed interest in pursuing questions about pathophysiology and the genetics of, and new treatments for dystonia. The award includes a plaque, cash award of $1,000, and automatic eligibility for finalist prize of $2,000. Deadline June 30.
EIN: 953378526

5747
E & WG Foundation

(formerly Eleanor and Wilson Greatbatch Foundation)
8975 Main St.
Clarence, NY 14031
Contact: Richard K. Milewicz, Secy.

Foundation type: Independent foundation
Limitations: Research grants for the study of AIDS and cancer.
Financial data: Year ended 12/31/2004.
Assets, $1,623,054 (M); Expenditures, $207,292; Total giving, $200,205; Grants to individuals, 14 grants totaling $136,150 (high: $29,044, low: $100).
Fields of interest: Cancer research; AIDS research.
Type of support: Research.
Application information: Applications by letter, stating relevant facts and circumstances, accepted throughout the year.
EIN: 161065309

5748
Earhart Foundation

2200 Green Rd., Ste. H
Ann Arbor, MI 48105
Contact: Ingrid A. Gregg, Pres.

Foundation type: Independent foundation
Limitations: Fellowship research grants to individuals who have distinguished themselves professionally, generally in such disciplines as economics, history, international affairs, and political science. Some fellowships by nomination only.
Publications: Annual report (including application guidelines).
Financial data: Year ended 12/31/2004.
Assets, $73,066,351 (M); Expenditures, $6,342,409; Total giving, $5,085,788; Grants to individuals, 210 grants totaling $2,081,538 (high: $36,288, low: $400, average grant: $2,000-$15,000).
Fields of interest: Humanities; Social sciences, research.
Type of support: Fellowships; Research; Awards/grants by nomination only; Graduate support.
Application information:
Initial approach: Letter.
Deadline(s): Not less than 120 days before commencement of projected work period
Additional information: Applications must include personal history, three- to five-page description of proposed research, intended end use or publication of research, abstract of approximately one single-spaced page, budget, time schedule, list of five references, and statement about applications pending elsewhere; Interviews granted upon request.
Program descriptions:
Fellowship Research Grants: Applicants should be associated with educational and research institutions, and the effort supported should lead to the advancement of knowledge through teaching, lecturing, and publication. Each award is for a specific purpose and progress is monitored.
H.B. Earhart Fellowships: These fellowships are awarded to talented individuals for graduate study to embark upon careers in college or university teaching or in research in the social sciences and humanities. Candidates are nominated by faculty sponsors whose participation is invited annually. Sponsors also monitor the performance of the candidate.
EIN: 386008273

5749
Earthwatch Institute

(also known as Earthwatch Expeditions, Inc.)
3 Clock Tower Pl., Ste. 100
Maynard, MA 01754 (978) 461-0081
FAX: (978) 461-2332; E-mail: info@earthwatch.org;
Toll-free tel.: (800) 776-0188; URL: http://www.earthwatch.org

Foundation type: Public charity
Limitations: Fellowships and research grants to individuals for projects dealing with conservation of our natural resources and cultural heritage. Grants also to individual field researchers specializing in archaeology, marine ecology, and zoology.
Publications: Application guidelines; Grants list; Informational brochure; Newsletter.
Financial data: Year ended 09/30/2004.
Assets, $4,318,469 (M); Expenditures, $11,169,701; Total giving, $884,108; Grants to individuals, totaling $884,108.
Fields of interest: History/archaeology; Environment, research; Environment, formal/general education; Natural resources; Public health.
Type of support: Fellowships; Research; Awards/grants by nomination only; Awards/prizes; Travel grants.
Application information: Application form required.
Initial approach: Telephone.
Deadline(s): Vary
Additional information: See Web site for individual deadlines, applications and further information.
Program description:
Research Grants: Awards to researchers at the post-doctoral level, or the equivalent, for research pertaining to natural resource conservation. Funds are contributed by volunteers who enlist for the opportunity to join scientists in the field where they assist with data collection and other research tasks. Per capita grants average $800, and project grants average $16,000 to $32,000.
EIN: 237168440

5750
Eastern Scientific & Education Foundation

c/o Wachovia Bank, N.A.
100 N. Main St., 13th Fl.
Winston-Salem, NC 27150
Contact: Grants Program: Elizabeth Bradshaw

Foundation type: Independent foundation
Limitations: Grants to individuals for orthopedic research, primarily in PA.
Financial data: Year ended 12/31/2004.
Assets, $615,521 (M); Expenditures, $36,708; Total giving, $33,000.
Fields of interest: Orthopedics research.
Type of support: Research.
Application information: Applications accepted. Application form required.
Initial approach: Letter.
Additional information: Application must include financial information. Contact foundation for current application deadline/guidelines.
EIN: 236738070

5751
Echoing Green

(formerly Echoing Green Foundation)
60 E. 42nd St., Ste. 520
New York, NY   10165   (212) 689-1165
Contact: Cheryl L. Dorsey, Pres.
FAX: (212) 689-9010;
E-mail: info@echoinggreen.org; URL: http://
www.echoinggreen.org

Foundation type: Operating foundation
Limitations: Fellowships to visionary leaders
wishing to start their own organization to create
lasting social change.
Publications: Application guidelines; Grants list.
Financial data: Year ended 06/30/2004.
Assets, $1,531,819 (M); Expenditures,
$1,829,365; Total giving, $721,186; Grants to
individuals, totaling $721,186.
Fields of interest: Leadership development.
Type of support: Program development;
Conferences/seminars; Seed money; Fellowships.
Application information: Deadline Jan. 12;
Completion of formal application required; See Web
site for further application and program information;
Interviews required.
Program description:
Echoing Green Fellowship: All areas of public
service are eligible for consideration for this seed
money, including the environment, arts, education,
youth service, civil and human rights, and
community and economic development. Research
projects, staff positions, and positions to
implement another individual's or an organization's
idea are not eligible for support. Individual fellows
receive $30,000 per year for two years; partnership
fellowships of up to two members receive $45,000
per year for two years. All recipients must work
full-time (at least 35 hours per week) at their
organizations or on their projects as well as
participating in echoing green community events.
Fellowships are renewable.
EIN: 133424419

5752
Ecolab Foundation

370 Wabasha St.
St. Paul, MN   55102   (651) 293-2658
Contact: Kris J. Taylor, V.P.
E-mail: ecolabfoundation@ecolab.com;
URL: http://www.ecolab.com/CompanyProfile/
Foundation/default.asp

Foundation type: Company-sponsored foundation
Limitations: Grants to teachers for the
enhancement of their curriculum by providing more
exciting, challenging or accessible ways to learn.
This program is only available in 13 communities
across the nation, where Ecolab employees live.
Publications: Corporate giving report (including
application guidelines).
Financial data: Year ended 12/31/2004.
Assets, $6,653,214 (M); Expenditures,
$2,035,338; Total giving, $3,280,757.
Fields of interest: Education.
Type of support: Program development.
Application information:
Initial approach: E-mail.
Additional information: Contact foundation for
application guidelines.
EIN: 411372157

5753
Ecotrust Foundation

c/o Wells Fargo Bank Minnesota, N.A.
90 S. 7th St., Ste. 5300
Minneapolis, MN   55402

Foundation type: Independent foundation
Limitations: Fellowships by nomination only to
individuals whose activities demonstrate durable
qualities of leadership to improve the social,
economic, political and environmental conditions in
their homelands.
Financial data: Year ended 12/31/2004.
Assets, $2,404,111 (M); Expenditures,
$407,481; Total giving, $393,799.
Fields of interest: Environment, land resources;
Environment; Native Americans/American Indians.
Type of support: Fellowships; Awards/prizes.
Program description:
Buffett Award for Indigenous Leadership: A
$25,000 cash award will be presented to an
individual whose activities demonstrate durable
qualities of leadership to improve the social,
economic, political, and environmental conditions
in his or her homelands.Four honorees will receive
a $2,500 cash award. Deadline Sept. 31.
EIN: 411735062

5754
The Education Foundation of Palm Beach County

3306 Forest Hill Blvd., B-102
West Palm Beach, FL   33406   (561) 357-7659
Contact: Kelly Hurley, Exec. Dir.
FAX: (561) 434-8651; URL: http://
www.palmbeach.k12.fl.us/foundation/

Foundation type: Public charity
Limitations: Project grants to outstanding teachers
in Palm Beach County, FL.
Financial data: Year ended 06/30/2003.
Assets, $759,869 (M); Expenditures, $738,664;
Total giving, $318,301.
Fields of interest: Education.
Type of support: Program development.
Application information: Application form required.
Deadline(s): June 15 for Citibank, Mar. 31, July
31 and Nov. 30 for Mini-Grants
Program descriptions:
Citibank Success Fund: Provides small cash
grants to educators to support innovative
classroom learning projects which encourage "at
risk" students to stay in school. These mini-grants
average $500 each, and are awarded in the fall of
each school year.
Mini-Grant Program: Provides small grants to
teachers who develop innovative projects that
enhance the education opportunities for students
in Palm Beach County public schools. Awards to
individuals are up to $1,000; awards to teams are
up to $2,000.
EIN: 592420369

5755
Educational Theatre Association

2343 Auburn Ave.
Cincinnati, OH   45219-2815   (513) 421-3900
Contact: Michael J. Peitz, Exec. Dir.
FAX: (513) 421-7077; URL: http://www.edta.org

Foundation type: Public charity
Limitations: Grants to assist K-12 public or private
school teachers in the early stages of their careers
to cover the registration fee for attending the EdTA
Annual conference.
Publications: Annual report; Informational
brochure.
Financial data: Year ended 07/31/2004.
Assets, $4,774,193 (M); Expenditures,
$2,877,043; Total giving, $24,250; Grants to
individuals, 69 grants totaling $24,250 (high:
$2,500, low: $100).
Fields of interest: Theater; Performing arts,
education.
Type of support: Travel grants.
Application information: Applications accepted.
Application form required. Application form
available on the grantmaker's Web site.
Deadline(s): Aug. 21
Program description:
EdTA Annual Conference Grant: In order to
receive a grant, teachers must teach in grade K-12,
be a current member of EdTA or a Thespian sponsor
of record for a troupe, and have held a paid
membership status for at least one year. Teachers
must be in their second year of teaching and have
completed no more than six total years of teaching.
In addition, their school must be financially unable
to cover the registration fee. Applicants will be
responsible for their own travel and lodging. Grant
recipients may not apply for another scholarship.
EIN: 310743605

5756
EDUCAUSE

4772 Walnut St., Ste. 206
Boulder, CO   80301-2538   (303) 449-4430
Contact: Brian L. Hawkins, Pres.
FAX: (303) 440-0461; E-mail: info@educause.edu;
Additional address: 1150 18th St. NW, Ste.1010,
Washington, DC 20036, tel. (202) 872-4200, FAX:
(202) 872-4318; URL: http://www.educause.edu

Foundation type: Public charity
Limitations: Awards by nomination only to
professionals in higher education information
technology management, and to authors of articles
in EDUCAUSE Quarterly. Also, fellowships to staff at
institutions of higher education, and to information
technology professionals to attend EDUCAUSE
events.
Financial data: Year ended 12/31/2004.
Assets, $12,830,447 (M); Expenditures,
$12,094,402; Total giving, $141,587.
Fields of interest: Education, management/
technical aid; Education, research; Computer
science.
Type of support: Fellowships; Awards/grants by
nomination only; Awards/prizes.
Application information:
Deadline(s): Feb. 15 for Leadership Awards,
Sept. 6 for NLII and Dec. 1 for Ryland
Additional information: Completion of formal
nomination required for Leadership Awards;
Contact foundation for current application
deadline/guidelines for other program.
Program descriptions:
*National Learning Infrastructure Initiative (NLII)
Fellowship Program:* Offers two half-time, one-year
fellowships targeted toward faculty and teaching
and learning support staff at institutions of higher
education. Fellows will study, analyze, and assess
specific aspects of the transformation of teaching
and learning in higher education that are of
relevance to the NLII. Fellows will attend several
conferences, so they must be prepared for a
considerable amount of travel (averaging one week
per month). See Web site or e-mail
fellows@educause.edu for more information.
Leadership Awards: Recognizes prominent
leaders in the profession of higher education
information technology management. The awards

are given in four categories: Excellence in Leadership; Leadership in the Profession; Leadership in Information Technologies; and Leadership in Public Policy and Practice. Contributions are made to scholarship funds of the winner's choice in the amount of $5,000 for the Excellence in Leadership Award, and $2,000 for the other three awards. Award winners are also invited to present conference talks on a subject of their choice, reflecting their area of professional expertise and interest. Anyone, within or outside of higher education, may submit nominations.

EDUCAUSE Quarterly Contribution of the Year Award: To be considered for the award, the published article must be an original work that has been contributed by the author(s) and reviewed by the EDUCAUSE Quarterly Editorial Committee prior to publication as a feature article in the journal during the academic year previous to the award (between Sept. and June). All articles that meet the above criteria are automatically eligible. The winning author receives a $1,000 stipend (which is shared in the case of multiple authors), a commemorative plaque, a complimentary conference registration, and is invited to share the expertise represented by the article in an appropriate conference session.

Jane N. Ryland Fellowship Program: Expands opportunities for information technology professionals to attend EDUCAUSE events. Awards are made on an annual basis, and range from $500 to $3,000, depending on an applicant's educational goals and the needs of his or her institution. Fellowship monies are applied first to registration fees, then to transportation and housing costs. Applicants must demonstrate past achievement, personal and institutional commitment, potential benefit, and financial need.
EIN: 841455437

5757
Dr. Glenn G. Ehrler Foundation
c/o The Northern Trust Co.
50 S. LaSalle St., Ste. L-5
Chicago, IL 60675

Foundation type: Independent foundation
Limitations: Awards by nomination only to Nobel Prize winners in physiology and medicine.
Financial data: Year ended 03/31/2005.
Assets, $324,831 (M); Expenditures, $17,311; Total giving, $15,000; Grants to individuals, totaling $15,000.
Fields of interest: Medical research, institute; Biological sciences.
Type of support: Awards/grants by nomination only; Awards/prizes.
Application information: Contact foundation for current application deadline/guidelines; Initial approach by letter or telephone.
EIN: 366907152

5758
Eleutherian Mills-Hagley Foundation, Inc.
P.O. Box 3630
Wilmington, DE 19807 (302) 658-2400
Contact: George L. Vogt, Dir.

Foundation type: Public charity
Limitations: Fellowships to individuals researching the business, industrial and technological history of America's Middle Atlantic region.
Publications: Annual report; Informational brochure.
Financial data: Year ended 12/31/2004.
Assets, $142,368,406 (M); Expenditures,

$7,793,747; Total giving, $50,750; Grants to individuals, totaling $50,750.
Fields of interest: History/archaeology; Historical activities.
Type of support: Fellowships; Internship funds; Grants for special needs.
Application information: Application form required.
Initial approach: Letter.
Additional information: Contact foundation for current application deadline/guidelines.
EIN: 510070531

5759
The Ellison Medical Foundation
4710 Bethesda Ave., Ste. 204
Bethesda, MD 20814-5226 (301) 657-1830
Contact: Richard L. Sprott Ph.D., Exec. Dir.
FAX: (301) 657-1828;
E-mail: rsprott@ellisonfoundation.org; URL: http://www.ellisonfoundation.org

Foundation type: Independent foundation
Limitations: Research grants to U.S. nonprofit institutions and universities on behalf of emerging and senior investigators to study the basic biology of aging.
Publications: Informational brochure; Multi-year report; Newsletter.
Financial data: Year ended 12/31/2005.
Assets, $0 (M); Expenditures, $27,633,648; Total giving, $26,265,173; Grants to individuals, 134 grants totaling $20,294,068 (high: $697,268, low: $50,000).
Fields of interest: Medical research, institute; Geriatrics research.
Type of support: Research; Awards/prizes.
Application information: Application form required. Application form available on the grantmaker's Web site.
Initial approach: Letter of Intent.
Deadline(s): Mar. 8 for Letter of Intent
Additional information: Applicants for Senior Scholar Awards must complete and submit online Letter of Intent from foundation's Web site.
Program descriptions:
New Scholar Award in Aging: Supports new investigators to permit them to become established in the field of aging. Each award is for up to $50,000 per year for a four year period for successful candidates. including basic biology, basic biomedicine and epidemiology) on aging. Acceptable uses for award funds include salary, other personnel, equipment, supplies, resource acquisition and travel. The scholar's salary costs (including fringe benefits) may not exceed $10,000 per year. Carry-overs in excess of $25,000 must be approved by the Ellison Medical Foundation Scholars Program Office. Not more than eight percent of the total award may be deducted for overhead costs.
Senior Scholar Award in Aging: Awards are available to support established investigators, working at institutions in the U.S., to conduct research in the basic biological sciences relevant to understanding aging processes and age-related diseases and disabilities. Each award will be made for $150,000 per year direct cost, with indirect cost added to that, for up to four years. Contingent upon submission of acceptable progress reports.
EIN: 943269827

5760
Thomas H. Emerson Trust
c/o Wells Fargo Bank, N.A., Trust Tax Dept.
P.O. Box 63954
San Francisco, CA 94163-0001

Foundation type: Independent foundation
Limitations: Grants to pre-selected doctors in San Francisco, CA, so that they may provide medical care to arthritis patients.
Financial data: Year ended 09/30/2004.
Assets, $475,464 (M); Expenditures, $24,660; Total giving, $17,778; Grants to individuals, totaling $17,778.
Fields of interest: Health care, association; Health care, financing; Arthritis.
Type of support: Program development.
Application information: Applications not accepted.
EIN: 946058560

5761
Endowment for Biblical Research, Boston
2 Boulder Top
Rockport, MA 01966 (978) 546-5284
Contact: Virginia Stopfel, Secy.

Foundation type: Independent foundation
Limitations: Grants for research, travel, publishing, and lecture tours to individuals undertaking biblical and archaeological research, primarily in MA.
Publications: Informational brochure (including application guidelines).
Financial data: Year ended 12/31/2002.
Assets, $2,792,719 (M); Expenditures, $254,538; Total giving, $228,950.
Fields of interest: History/archaeology; Religion, research.
Type of support: Publication; Research; Travel grants.
Application information: Applications accepted.
Initial approach: Letter.
Deadline(s): Mar. and Sept.
Additional information: Applications are reviewed in Apr. and Oct.
EIN: 042104439

5762
Endowment of the U.S. Institute of Peace
1200 17th St., N.W., Ste. 200
Washington, DC 20036-3011 (202) 457-1700
Contact: Richard H. Solomon, Pres.
FAX: (202) 429-6063;
E-mail: grant_program@usip.org; URL: http://www.usip.org

Foundation type: Public charity
Limitations: Fellowships for scholars that address international conflict resolution.
Publications: Application guidelines; Annual report; Newsletter; Occasional report.
Financial data: Year ended 09/30/2004.
Assets, $6,034,134 (M); Expenditures, $9,415,453; Total giving, $6,576,209; Grants to individuals, totaling $6,576,209.
Fields of interest: International peace/security; International conflict resolution; International affairs.
Type of support: Fellowships.
Application information: Applications accepted. Application form required.
Initial approach: Letter, telephone, or e-mail.
Deadline(s): Sept. 17
Additional information: Interviews required.

Program description:

Jennings Rudolph Program - Senior Fellowships: Fellowships are undertaken in residence at the institute in Washington, D.C., ordinarily for 12 months beginning in Sept. Shorter-term fellowships are also available and may begin at any time of the year. Fellows come from a wide variety of professional levels and backgrounds. They address a range of topics related to the understanding, management, and resolution of violent international conflict. Women and members of minority groups are especially encouraged to apply. Stipends are based on the fellow's earned income for the preceding 12 months, up to a maximum equivalent of GS-15, step 6, on the federal pay scale. For fellows lasting less than 12 months, the stipends are pro-rated. Fellows are provided with contributions toward health insurance, use of an office, voicemail, Macintosh word processor, and part-time research assistance. The institute provides transportation to and from Washington, D.C., for the fellow and eligible family members at the beginning and end of the fellowship period. Housing is not provided.
EIN: 521503251

5763
The Enterprise Foundation
10227 Wincopin Cir., Ste. 500
Columbia, MD   21044-3400   (800) 624-4298
Contact: F. Barton Harvey, III, Chair. and C.E.O.
FAX: (410) 964-1918;
E-mail: mail@enterprisefoundation.org;
URL: http://www.enterprisefoundation.org

Foundation type: Public charity
Limitations: Fellowships to architects to encourage them to become lifelong leaders in public service and community development. Awards also to journalists for excellence in urban journalism.
Publications: Annual report; Financial statement; Informational brochure; Newsletter.
Financial data: Year ended 12/31/2004. Assets, $119,312,000 (M); Expenditures, $41,797,000; Total giving, $9,231,000.
Fields of interest: Journalism/publishing; Architecture; Housing/shelter, development; Urban/community development; Urban studies.
Type of support: Fellowships; Awards/prizes.
Application information: Applications accepted. Application form required. Application form available on the grantmaker's Web site.
Deadline(s): Mar. 28
Program description:
Frederick P. Rose Architectural Fellowship: Fellowships include an annual stipend of $40,000 for a period of three years. Fellows partner with a local Community Development Corporation (CDC), a local Community-Based Organization (CBO) or a Tribally-Designated Housing Entity (TDHE) for the duration of the Fellowship. The amount of the stipend is fixed at $120,000 for three years and cannot be augmented by the partner organization unless there are exceptional circumstances and there is a prior written approval of the Fellowship Director. Fellows are provided with an extensive orientation on Aug. 1 to 3 and participate in an annual symposium and Network Conference from Nov. 4 to 7. Attendance at the events is required.
EIN: 521231931

5764
Entomological Foundation
9332 Annapolis Rd., Ste. 210
Lanham, MD   20706-3115   (301) 459-9082
Contact: April Gower, Exec. Dir.
FAX: (301) 459-9084; E-mail: april@entfdn.org;
URL: http://www.entfdn.org/

Foundation type: Public charity
Limitations: Scholarships, fellowships, research grants and awards to entomology students in the U.S., Canada and Mexico.
Publications: Annual report; Newsletter.
Financial data: Year ended 12/31/2004. Assets, $660,013 (M); Expenditures, $147,157; Total giving, $13,100; Grants to individuals, 11 grants totaling $10,650 (high: $2,000, low: $300).
Fields of interest: Environment; Animals/wildlife, research; Agriculture.
Type of support: Fellowships; Research; Scholarships—to individuals; Support to graduates or students of specific schools; Awards/prizes; Postdoctoral support; Graduate support; Undergraduate support; Travel grants.
Application information: Application form required. Application form available on the grantmaker's Web site.
Initial approach: E-mail.
Copies of proposal: 1
Deadline(s): July 1
Applicants should submit the following:
1) Transcripts
2) Letter(s) of recommendation
3) Curriculum vitae
Additional information: See Web site for further guidelines.
Program descriptions:
Jeffery P. LaFage Graduate Student Research Award: Awards of up to $2,000 to graduate students for research in the field of the biology and control of termites or other insect pests of the urban environment.
Plant Resistance to Insects Graduate Student Research Award: Grants to graduate students to encourage research in the field of plant resistance to insects in entomology or plant breeding/ genetics. Award is made annually and consists of a plaque, and amount of grant is dependent on the interest earned from the endowment of Kenneth J. and Barbara Starks.
Henry and Sylvia Richardson Research Grant: Awards for research to postdoctoral members of the Entomological Society of America who have at least one year of promising work experience, are undertaking research in selected areas and have demonstrated a high level of scholarship. Amount to be determined by interest earned from the endowment fund.
Award for Excellence in Integrated Pest Management: Annual award an amount to be determined by the interest earned in the fund, along with an inscribed plaque, to recognize and encourage outstanding contributions to applied integrated pest management in North America and the U.S. territories.
Recognition Award in Urban Entomology: Award of an amount to be determined by the interest earned by the fund, and an inscribed plaque to recognize and encourage outstanding extension, research and teaching contributions in Urban Entomology, including the study of the biology and control of anthropods found in the home or surrounding landscape, structural and wood-destroying pests of ornamental plants, shade trees and turf.
The Larry Larson Graduate Student Award for Leadership in Applied Entomology: Leadership awards to master's students who exhibit exceptional interest in the study and application of

entomology through outstanding research and leadership skills. Amount to be determined by the interest earned in fund.
Snodgrass Memorial Research Award: Awards to graduate students who have completed investigations in selected areas of entomology. Recipient must have completed his or her research thesis or dissertation in related fields of entomology. Amount of award varies each year.
Thomas Say Award: Award to an individual for significant and outstanding work in the field of insect systematics, morphology or evolution. Amount to be determined by the interest earned by the fund. The recipient's work must have been published.
Joseph H. Camin Fellowship: Awards to graduate students attending the Acarology Summer Program at Ohio State University or an equivalent institution where they can obtain training in the systematics of acarines. Made annually, the value of the fellowship depends on interest earned from the endowment.
Stanley Beck Fellowship: Fellowships of varying amounts, to be determined by the interest earned in the fund, to students at the graduate or undergraduate level to assist them in education in entomology and related disciplines. The need may be based on physical limitations or economic, minority or environmental conditions.
Undergraduate Scholarships: Awards up to four scholarships annually to undergraduate students in an attempt to encourage interest in entomology. The amount must be determined by the interest earned by the fund.
Lillian and Alex Feir Graduate Student Travel Award: Travel award to graduate students working with insects or other anthropods in the broad areas of physiology, biochemistry and molecular biology to affiliate with the Entomological Society of America's section B and to attend the annual Entomological Society of America meeting or an international congress of Entomology. Amount to be determined by interest earned in the fund.
Pioneer Hi-Bred International Graduate Student Fellowship: Fellowship that sponsors a graduate student on the basis of recognizing and encouraging innovative research and graduate education in the area of entomology with a focus on key insects or complexes of insects that affect corn, soybeans, canola, alfalfa, or other significant commodity crops. This award is granted to one student over the next (up to) four years. The stipend will be $12,500 per year until completion of the graduate degree up to a limit of four years.
ICINN Student Recognition Award to Insect Physiology, Biochemistry, Toxicology, and Molecular Biology: The award shall be made on the basis of recognizing and encouraging innovative research in the areas of insect physiology, biochemistry, and toxicology in the broad sense. The amount varies depending upon the interest earned from the endowment.
EIN: 521756169

5765
Environmental Leadership Program, Inc.
132 Main St.
P.O. Box 446
Haydenville, MA   01039   (413) 268-0035
Contact: Paul Sabin, Exec. Dir.
FAX: (413) 268-0036; E-mail: info@elpnet.org;
Additional address: 258 Church St., Ste. 202, New Haven, CT 06510, tel.: (203) 624-9738, FAX: (203) 624-9732; URL: http://www.elpnet.org

Foundation type: Public charity
Limitations: Fellowships to individuals engaged in environmental and social change work.

Financial data: Year ended 12/31/2003. Assets, $628,829 (M); Expenditures, $657,507; Total giving, $29,533; Grants to individuals, 16 grants totaling $29,533.
Type of support: Fellowships.
Application information: Applications accepted. Application form required. Application form available on the grantmaker's Web site.
Initial approach: Letter or e-mail.
Deadline(s): Oct. 1
Applicants should submit the following:
1) Resume
2) Letter(s) of recommendation
3) Essay
Additional information: Applications must also include writing or work sample.
Program description:
Environmental Leadership Program: The program provides training, project support and a vibrant peer network to 20-25 talented and diverse individuals each year engaged in environmental and social change work. ELP fellows come from nonprofits, businesses, government, tribal government, and higher education, and include activists, artists, writers, lawyers, entrepreneurs, policy makers, and scientists. Applicants for the ELP Fellowship must commit to participating in four retreats over two years. In addition, each fellow has the opportunity to conduct a leadership building project of their design with support from the ELP Activity Fund. Fellows are given the opportunity to request a grant from the ELP Activity Fund which provides up to $10,000 per participant to support leadership-building activities through individual and collaborative projects. Grants typically average around $5000 per fellow. Fellows are encouraged to pursue activities that enhance their public leadership skills, reach diverse constituencies, build community, and strive for tangible environmental outcomes. The Activity Fund offers fellows the opportunity to collaborate with others within the ELP community to expand their work beyond their specific area of expertise. In addition to funding fellows' Activity Fund projects, ELP provides access to professional support services, such as consultation on writing, media, technical, legal, and financial issues.
EIN: 043521791

5766
Environmental Research and Education Foundation

(formerly EIA Research and Education Foundation)
901 N. Pitt St., Ste. 270
Alexandria, VA 22314 (703) 299-5139
Contact: Michael J. Cagney, Pres.
FAX: (703) 299-5145;
E-mail: mjcagney@erefdn.org; URL: http://www.erefdn.org

Foundation type: Public charity
Limitations: Three-year scholarships to doctoral candidates in the field of environmental science with an emphasis on the treatment of municipal solid waste.
Publications: Application guidelines; Annual report; Financial statement; Grants list; Informational brochure; Newsletter; Occasional report.
Financial data: Year ended 12/31/2004. Assets, $5,790,215 (L); Expenditures, $1,116,534; Total giving, $513,575; Grants to individuals, 6 grants totaling $48,000 (high: $12,000, low: $3,000).
Fields of interest: Environment, research; Waste management.
Type of support: Fellowships; Research; Postdoctoral support; Graduate support;

Postgraduate support; Doctoral support; Project support.
Application information: Applications accepted. Application form required. Application form available on the grantmaker's Web site.
Initial approach: Application.
Deadline(s): June 30
Applicants should submit the following:
1) Essay
2) Transcripts
3) Letter(s) of recommendation
Additional information: Application must also include relevant standardized test scores.
Program description:
Francois Fiessinger Environmental Scholarship and EREF Scholarships: Full-time Ph.D or post-Ph.D students with clearly demonstrated interests in the treatment of municipal solid waste research may apply for these three-year scholarships. Awards are based on academic or professional performance, relevance of the applicant's work to the advancement of environmental science, and potential for success. Recipients receive $12,000 per year, paid on a monthly basis, for a three-year period, to support their work in environmental science and research. Amounts awarded take into account the cost of tuition at the recipient's institution and any other funds received. Full scholarships cannot be awarded to students who will be receiving full-tuition scholarships from other sources (excluding direct university assistance such as tuition remission and/or income received from assistanceships), although such students may still be considered for partial awards.
EIN: 521804051

5767
Epilepsy Foundation of America
4351 Garden City Dr., Ste. 500
Landover, MD 20785-7223 (301) 459-3700
Contact: Jeanette Montgomery
FAX: (301) 577-2684; Additional tel.: (800) 332-1000; URL: http://www.efa.org

Foundation type: Public charity
Limitations: Fellowships and research grants to individuals for the study of epilepsy.
Publications: Application guidelines; Annual report; Informational brochure (including application guidelines).
Financial data: Year ended 06/30/2005. Assets, $21,625,672 (M); Expenditures, $15,868,923; Total giving, $2,007,765; Grants to individuals, 142 grants totaling $1,997,296 (high: $70,000, low: $32).
Fields of interest: Epilepsy research; Social sciences.
Type of support: Program development; Fellowships; Research; Postdoctoral support; Graduate support; Postgraduate support; Doctoral support.
Application information: Contact foundation for current application deadline/guidelines.
Program descriptions:
Behavioral Sciences Research Training Fellowship: Stipend of $30,000 to individuals who will have received their doctoral degree in a field of the social sciences by the time the fellowship commences, and who desire additional postdoctoral research experience. Deadline Mar. 3.
Research Grants Program: Provides funds to investigators in the early stages of their career by stimulating epilepsy research. Seed grants are awarded to clinical investigators or basic scientists for support of biological or behavioral research which will advance the understanding, treatment and prevention of epilepsy. Applications from

established investigators (Associate Professor level or above) are ineligible. Deadline Sept. 3.
Predoctoral Research Training Fellowship: Supports pre-doctoral students with dissertation research related to epilepsy, thus strengthening their interest in establishing epilepsy research as a career direction. Graduate students pursuing a Ph.D. degree in neuroscience, physiology, pharmacology, psychology, biochemistry, genetics, nursing, or pharmacy may apply. Deadline Sept. 3.
Postdoctoral Research Training Fellowship: Grants to individuals with an M.D. or D.O. who will have completed residency training in neurology, neurosurgery, pediatrics, internal medicine, or psychiatry by the time the fellowship commences and desires additional postdoctoral clinical research experience. Trains academic clinicians to teach patient care of persons with epilepsy and advance knowledge about epilepsy through research. Deadline Sept. 3.
Health Sciences Student Fellowships: Fellowships to individuals to pursue careers in epilepsy in either research or practice settings. Predoctoral training students in the health sciences may be accepted at any point in their schooling, following acceptance, but before beginning the first year, or in the period immediately following their final year. Deadline Mar. 3.
Fritz E. Dreifuss International Travel Program: Promotes the exchange of information and expertise on epilepsy between healthcare professionals of the U.S. and foreign countries. A qualified candidate may spend from 3 to 6 weeks at a host institution. At least one party in the exchange must be from the U.S.
EIN: 520856660

5768
The Eppley Foundation for Research, Inc.
c/o McLaughlin & Stern, LLP
260 Madison Ave.
New York, NY 10016
Contact: Huyler C. Held, Secy.-Treas.
FAX: (212) 448-6260;
E-mail: hheld@Mclaughlinstern.com

Foundation type: Independent foundation
Limitations: Grants for post-doctoral research in the physical and biological sciences. Grants are made only through recognized educational and research organizations.
Publications: Application guidelines; Informational brochure; Program policy statement.
Financial data: Year ended 12/31/2004. Assets, $2,296,163 (M); Expenditures, $343,241; Total giving, $322,471.
Fields of interest: Science, research; Physical/earth sciences; Biological sciences.
Type of support: Seed money; Research; Doctoral support.
Application information: Application form required.
Initial approach: Letter, including short statement of qualifications, proposed research, and an estimate of funding.
Deadline(s): Feb. 1, May 1, Aug. 1, and Nov.
Additional information: Grants are not made directly to individuals. Applicant must have a sponsoring institution.
Program description:
Research Grants: The foundation considers the most effective use of funds to be for research-initiation grants, with the understanding that sufficient work can be accomplished to enable the researcher to apply more readily for greater sums from other sources. It is important to the foundation that work proposed for support be original in its insights. Any applicant to the

foundation must be associated with a recognized educational or research institution; funds are not issued directly to individuals. Grant proposals from foreign countries are considered without prejudice, but such applicants must explain in a cover letter why they are unable to obtain research funds in their own countries.

EIN: 050258857

5769

Equipment Leasing and Finance Foundation, Inc.

4301 N. Fairfax Dr., Ste. 550
Arlington, VA   22203-1627   (703) 527-8655
Contact: Lisa A. Levine, Exec. Dir.
FAX: (703) 465-7488; E-mail: llevine@elamail.com;
URL: http://www.leasefoundation.org

Foundation type: Public charity
Limitations: Research grants for the study of topics of interest to the equipment leasing and finance industry.
Publications: Application guidelines; Grants list; Informational brochure; Newsletter; Occasional report.
Financial data: Year ended 12/31/2003. Assets, $1,044,537 (M); Expenditures, $347,198; Total giving, $4,000; Grants to individuals, 2 grants totaling $4,000 (high: $2,000, low: $2,000).
Fields of interest: Business school/education; Mathematics; Economics.
Type of support: Program development; Research.
Application information: Applications accepted throughout the year; Completion of formal application required; See Web site for guidelines and application forms.
Program description:
Research Grants: Awards research grants of $10,000 to encourage academics in all fields of scholarship to study topics of interest to the equipment leasing and finance industry. Projects should benefit a major segment of the lease finance industry, be broad based in geographical appeal, and contribute to the prosperity, vitality, and profitability of the industry. Higher grant amounts will be considered for exceptional projects.
EIN: 541527848

5770

Ernst & Young Foundation

5 Times Sq.
New York, NY   10036   (212) 773-3103
Contact: Ellen J. Glazerman, Dir.
FAX: (212) 773-6504; Additional tel.: (212) 773-5274; URL: http://www.ey.com/global/content.nsf/US/About_Ernst_Young_-_Foundation

Foundation type: Public charity
Limitations: Research grants, lectureships, and fellowships to faculty in the areas of tax research, accounting, and auditing.
Financial data: Year ended 06/30/2005. Assets, $12,512,171 (M); Expenditures, $9,067,470; Total giving, $8,968,953.
Fields of interest: Business/industry; Mathematics; Economics.
Type of support: Fellowships; Research.
Application information: Application form not required.
Additional information: Unsolicited applications not accepted; Applications accepted only from individuals affiliated with preselected educational institutions; scholarships are not granted.
EIN: 136094489

5771

The Eshe Fund

P.O. Box 65
Madison Sq. Station
New York, NY   10159-0065
Contact: Henry H. Steiner, Secy.

Foundation type: Independent foundation
Limitations: Grants for biomedical research, primarily in CT, MA and MO.
Financial data: Year ended 12/31/2004. Assets, $1,664,724 (M); Expenditures, $81,212; Total giving, $79,100; Grants to individuals, totaling $68,750.
Fields of interest: Biomedicine research.
Type of support: Research.
Application information: Applications accepted throughout the year; Initial approach by letter; Contact foundation for current application guidelines.
EIN: 133247309

5772

Esperantic Studies Foundation, Inc.

3900 Northampton St. N.W.
Washington, DC   20015   (202) 362-3963
Contact: Mark Fettes, Exec. Dir.
E-mail: admin@esperantic.com; Application address: Dr. Mark Fettes, Exec. Dir., Esperantic Studies Foundation, Faculty of Education, Simon Fraser University, 8888 University Dr., Burnaby, B.C., Canada V5A 1S6, tel.: (604) 434-2624, E-mail: mfettes@esperantic.org; Additional E-mail: EJL@Gwu.edu; URL: http://www.esperantic.org

Foundation type: Operating foundation
Limitations: Grants to individuals for research, teaching or publications dealing with interlinguistics.
Financial data: Year ended 12/31/2003. Assets, $3,185,400 (M); Expenditures, $257,499; Total giving, $77,941; Grants to individuals, 24 grants totaling $30,691 (high: $10,000, low: $450).
Fields of interest: Language/linguistics.
Type of support: Publication; Research.
Application information: Application form required.
Initial approach: Letter.
Deadline(s): None.
EIN: 520885287

5773

Everett McKinley Dirksen Endowment Fund

2815 Broadway
Pekin, IL   61554   (309) 347-7113
Contact: Frank Mackaman, Exec. Dir.
FAX: (309) 347-6432;
E-mail: info@dirksencenter.org; Additional e-mail: fmackaman@dirksencenter.org; URL: http://dirksencenter.org

Foundation type: Public charity
Limitations: Grants to fund research on congressional leadership and the U.S. Congress.
Financial data: Year ended 09/30/2004. Assets, $8,698,802 (M); Expenditures, $450,487; Total giving, $55,964; Grants to individuals, totaling $55,964.
Fields of interest: Political science.

Type of support: Research.
Application information: Applications accepted. Application form required. Application form available on the grantmaker's Web site.
Initial approach: Letter, telephone or e-mail.
Deadline(s): Feb. 1
Applicants should submit the following:
1) Letter(s) of recommendation
2) Proposal
3) Curriculum vitae
4) Budget Information
Additional information: See Web site for complete program information.
Program description:
Congressional Research Awards: The program is open to individuals with a serious interest in studying Congress. Political scientists, historians, biographers, scholars of public administration or American studies, and journalists are among those eligible. The Center encourages graduate students who have successfully defended their dissertation prospectus to apply and awards a significant portion of the funds for dissertation research. The awards program does not fund undergraduate or pre-Ph.D. study. Proposals should concentrate on leadership in the Congress, both House and Senate. Topics could include external factors shaping the exercise of congressional leadership, institutional conditions affecting it, resources and techniques used by leaders, or the prospects for change or continuity in the patterns of leadership. In addition, The Center invites proposals about congressional procedures, such as committee operation or mechanisms for institutional change, and Congress and the electoral process. The research for which assistance is sought must be original, culminating in new findings or new interpretation, or both. The awards program was developed to support work intended for publication in some form or for application in a teaching or policy-making setting. Awards range from a few hundred dollars to $3,500.
EIN: 366132816

5774

The Eye Research Foundation

1240 New Scotland Ave., Ste. 201
Slingerlands, NY   12159-9222

Foundation type: Operating foundation
Limitations: Grants to doctors to perform research on the eyes.
Financial data: Year ended 12/31/2002. Assets, $24,489 (M); Expenditures, $75,266; Total giving, $57,600; Grants to individuals, 7 grants totaling $39,600.
Fields of interest: Eye research.
Type of support: Research.
Application information: Contact foundation for current application deadline/guidelines.
EIN: 141768523

5775

Fannie Mae Foundation

4000 Wisconsin Ave., N.W.
N. Tower, Ste. 1
Washington, DC   20016-2804   (202) 274-8057
FAX: (202) 274-8100;
E-mail: grants@fanniemaefoundation.org;
Application addresses: Kennedy School Fellowships: Lisa Mallory-Hodge, Managing Dir., Policy and Consulting, Fannie Mae Foundation, 4000 Wisconsin Ave., N.W., N. Tower, Ste. 1, Washington, DC 20016-2804, tel.: (202) 274-8000, E-mail:

lmallory@fanniemaefoundation.org, James A. Johnson Fellowships: Wendy New,Dir., Policy and Leadership Devel., Fannie Mae Foundation, 4000 Wisconsin Ave., N.W., N. Tower, Ste. 1, Washington, DC 20016-2804, tel.: (202) 274-8043, FAX: (202) 274-8101, E-mail: wnew@fanniemaefoundation.org, Maxwell Awards: Maxwell Awards of Excellence, c/o Christine Tucker, Mgr., Policy and Leadership Devel., Fannie Mae Foundation, 4000 Wisconsin Ave., N.W., N. Tower, Ste. 1, Washington, DC 20016-2804, tel.: (202) 274-8044, E-mail: ctucker@fanniemaefoundation.org;; URL: http://www.fanniemaefoundation.org

Foundation type: Company-sponsored foundation
Limitations: Fellowships by nomination only and research support in the area of housing policy, finance, and community development.
Publications: Annual report; Financial statement.
Financial data: Year ended 12/31/2004. Assets, $178,738,695 (M); Expenditures, $122,462,544; Total giving, $47,742,454; Grants to individuals, 14 grants totaling $594,028 (high: $67,500, low: $14,300).
Fields of interest: Business school/education; Housing/shelter; Community development.
Type of support: Fellowships; Research; Awards/grants by nomination only.
Application information: Applications accepted. Application form required.
> *Deadline(s):* Nov. 1 for Feb. session and Apr. 1 for June and July sessions for Fellowships, and Dec.31 for Nominations.
> *Additional information:* Applications received after Oct. 1 may not receive a decision until the following calendar year; Unsolicited requests for application not accepted.

Program descriptions:
Kennedy School of Government Fellowships: The John F. Kennedy School of Government at Harvard University offers this program three times annually, in Feb., June, and July. Thirty-five senior managers and officials are selected annually to take part in one of the three-week sessions. The program is intended to enhance the management and decision-making skills of senior public and nonprofit officials committed to improving affordable housing opportunities in the U.S. Applicants must satisfy the requirements for admission to the Kennedy School. Fellowship funds cover the cost of the admission deposit, program tuition, and room and board for the session. Applicants must be able to attend the entire three-week session, and are responsible for their own transportation and other incidental costs.

James A. Johnson Fellowships: Recognizes and rewards urban and rural affordable housing and community development professionals for their work. Up to six seasoned professionals are chosen annually to design and pursue development plans that can include research, travel, study, self-designed internships, and other activities that enhance skills and knowledge. Fellows meet as a group four times during the fellowship, and may take as little or as much time away from their current positions as necessary. Each fellow receives a $70,000 grant and a stipend of up to $20,000 for travel and education-related expenses. Nominees must have a minimum of eight years in the affordable housing and community development field.

Research Support: The foundation funds policy analysis and empirical or theoretical research that makes significant contributions to the state of knowledge on housing policy, housing finance, and community development issues related to the foundation's focus areas. This research is intended to stimulate thoughtful and insightful discussion on a broad range of housing and community development topics, including barriers to decent and affordable housing, government housing policies, financial models, housing markets, housing demand and need, and other topics related to the provision of housing and the creation of healthy communities. The foundation expects both assignment of copyright to all products derived from the research it funds and the right of first refusal to publish. The foundation publishes its research in its scholarly journal, Housing Policy Debate, and occasional special publications. The foundation is liberal about giving special permission to organizations and individuals it funds to disseminate preliminary research reports and to republish copyrighted articles.
EIN: 521172718

5776

Anne & Jason Farber Foundation, Inc.
c/o Blanding Boyer & Rockwell
1676 N. California Blvd., 3rd Fl.
Walnut Creek, CA   94596
Contact: James A. Farber, Pres.

Foundation type: Independent foundation
Limitations: Research grants for the investigation of brain tumors.
Financial data: Year ended 11/30/2004. Assets, $4,602,055 (M); Expenditures, $137,466; Total giving, $56,500; Grants to individuals, totaling $15,000.
Fields of interest: Medical research, institute; Cancer research.
Type of support: Research.
Application information: Applications not accepted.
EIN: 942778778

5777

The Fashion Group Foundation of Chicago, Inc.
333 N. Michigan Ave., Ste. 2032
Chicago, IL   60601   (312) 527-7750
Contact: Sharon Tabaka, Pres.
FAX: (312) 726-9520

Foundation type: Public charity
Limitations: Grants to talented professionals in the field of fashion.
Financial data: Year ended 12/31/2004. Assets, $147,114 (M); Expenditures, $146,658; Total giving, $23,905; Grants to individuals, 6 grants totaling $15,000 (high: $5,000, low: $2,000).
Fields of interest: Design.
Type of support: Grants to individuals.
Application information: Deadline Sept. 1; Application by project description; Applications by FAX or e-mail not accepted.
Program description:
FGI Grant Program: Open to professionals working in fashion-related fields who are accomplished in their disciplines and/or who have proven ability to undertake and complete a project plan with defined, measurable results. Projects supported include program development, research initiatives, design initiatives, and innovation initiatives in technology. Grants are up to $15,000 for up to 12 months.
EIN: 363571476

5778

The Ferraro Foundation for Science and the Disabled, Inc.
77 Povershon Rd.
Nutley, NJ   07110
FAX: (201) 664-6693; URL: http://www.theferrarofoundation.org

Foundation type: Independent foundation
Limitations: Grants to recently disabled physicians needing to professionally re-establish themselves or retrain in another specialty, primarily in DC and NJ.
Financial data: Year ended 12/31/2004. Assets, $0 (M); Expenditures, $32,204; Total giving, $16,024; Grants to individuals, totaling $7,250.
Fields of interest: Science; Disabilities, people with.
Type of support: Doctoral support.
Application information: Contact foundation for current application deadline/guidelines.
EIN: 223537772

5779

John E. Fetzer Institute, Inc.
(formerly John E. Fetzer Foundation, Inc.)
9292 West KL Ave.
Kalamazoo, MI   49009-9398
Contact: Thomas F. Beech, C.E.O. and Pres.
FAX: (269) 372-2163; E-mail: info@fetzer.org; URL: http://www.fetzer.org

Foundation type: Operating foundation
Limitations: Research grants to individuals for the exploration of the integral relationships among the body, mind and spirit.
Publications: Informational brochure; Newsletter; Occasional report; Program policy statement.
Financial data: Year ended 07/31/2005. Assets, $374,178,286 (M); Expenditures, $14,140,624; Total giving, $751,945.
Fields of interest: Social sciences.
Type of support: Research.
Application information: Applications not accepted.
Program description:
End of Life and the Dying Process: the Role of Spirituality/Religiousness and Relationships: $1.3 million in funding is available for individual research projects ranging from one to two years in duration funded up to a total of $200,000 each. Toward understanding and improving the quality of life at the end of life, the Fetzer Institute invited research proposals from investigators at public or private nonprofit organizations, such as colleges, universities, hospitals, laboratories or research institutions. The principal investigator must have a doctoral degree with sufficient training and experience to accomplish the proposed work. Empirical research that links biological, clinical and/or social sciences with philosophical, ethical and religious understanding is encouraged. Preference will be given to innovative, interdisciplinary collaboration. Letters of intent due Jan. 10.
EIN: 386052788

5780
Fight for Sight, Inc.
381 Park Ave. S., Ste. 809
New York, NY   10016   (212) 679-6060
Contact: Mary Prudden, Exec. Dir.
FAX: (212) 679-4466;
E-mail: info@fightforsight.com; URL: http://
www.fightforsight.com

Foundation type: Public charity
Limitations: Research fellowships studies in
ophthalmology, vision, or related sciences.
Publications: Application guidelines; Financial
statement; Grants list; Informational brochure;
Newsletter.
Financial data: Year ended 03/31/2003.
Assets, $3,488,216 (M); Expenditures,
$1,117,797; Total giving, $502,786; Grant to an
individual, 1 grant totaling $51,796.
Fields of interest: Eye research.
Type of support: Fellowships; Graduate support;
Undergraduate support; Doctoral support.
Application information: Application form required.
Initial approach: Letter.
Deadline(s): Mar. 1
Additional information: Applications received by
FAX not accepted.
Program descriptions:
Post-Doctoral Support Research Fellowships:
Stipends of $5,000 to $14,000 per year to
individuals with doctorates who are interested in
academic careers involving basic or clinical
research in ophthalmology, vision, or related
sciences.
Student Fellowships: Awards $500 on a monthly
basis for 60 to 90 days of full-time research to
undergraduate, medical and graduate students
from the U.S. and Canada who are interested in
eye-related clinical or basic research.
EIN: 237085732

5781
James Marston Fitch Charitable Foundation
c/o The Neighborhood Preservation Center
232 E. 11th St.
New York, NY   10003   (212) 252-6809
Contact: Mary Dierickx, Chair.
FAX: (212) 471-9987;
E-mail: info@fitchfoundation.org; URL: http://
www.fitchfoundation.org

Foundation type: Independent foundation
Limitations: Research grants to U.S. citizens in the
field of historic preservation.
Publications: Application guidelines.
Financial data: Year ended 12/31/2004.
Assets, $243,547 (M); Expenditures, $31,971;
Total giving, $28,250; Grants to individuals,
totaling $28,250.
Fields of interest: Historic preservation/historical
societies.
Type of support: Research.
Application information: Deadline Sept. 7;
Application by proposal including three copies of
brief project description, schedule of work, budget,
curriculum vitae, past and present grants received,
and two letters of recommendation.
Program description:
Professional Research Grants: Awards $25,000
in research grants to mid-career professionals who
have an advanced or professional degree and at
least 10 years experience in historic preservation
or related fields, including architecture, landscape,
architecture, architectural conservation, urban
design, environmental planning, archaeology,
architectural history and the decorative arts. Other

smaller grants, up to $10,000 are made as well.
Grants are intended to support projects of
innovative original research or creative design that
advance the practice of historic preservation in the
U.S.
EIN: 133993856

5782
The Flinn Foundation
1802 N. Central Ave.
Phoenix, AZ   85004-1506   (602) 744-6800
Contact: John W. Murphy, C.E.O.
FAX: (602) 744-6815; E-mail: info@flinn.org; E-mail
for scholarship information: fscholars@flinn.org;
URL: http://www.flinn.org

Foundation type: Independent foundation
Limitations: Fellowships to AZ researchers involved
in clinical research and teaching.
Publications: Annual report; Financial statement;
Newsletter; Occasional report.
Financial data: Year ended 12/31/2004.
Assets, $178,440,413 (M); Expenditures,
$11,871,476; Total giving, $7,801,343.
Fields of interest: Education; Medical research.
Type of support: Fellowships.
Application information: Contact foundation for
current application deadline/guidelines.
Program description:
*Robert S. Flinn Clinical Faculty Research
Fellowship Program:* Awards up to $150,000
annually for a three-year period to researchers at
AZ-based institutions involved in clinical research
and teaching. The program aims to further the
career development and scientific competitiveness
of clinically-relevant research.
EIN: 860421476

5783
Gerald R. Ford Foundation
303 Pearl St., N.W.
Grand Rapids, MI   49504-5353
Contact: Diane Van Allsburg, Admin. Asst.; For
Journalism Prize: Barbara Packer; For Travel Grants:
Helmi Raaska
Additional tel.: (616) 254-0373, e-mail
address: barbara.packer@nara.gov (Barbara
Packer) and additional tel.: (734) 205-0555, e-mail
address: helmi.raaska@nara.gov (Helmi Raaska)
E-mail: geraldfordfoundation@nara.gov; Additional
address (for Prizes): Gerald R. Ford Foundation,
303 Pearl St., NW, Grand Rapids, MI 49504; (for
Travel Grants): Gerald R. Ford Presidential Library,
1000 Beel Ave., Ann Arbor, MI 48109; URL: http://
www.geraldrfordfoundation.org

Foundation type: Public charity
Limitations: Grants to journalists for reporting on
the presidency or national defense, and to
individuals for research at the Gerald R. Ford
Library.
Publications: Informational brochure.
Financial data: Year ended 12/31/2003.
Assets, $16,595,564 (M); Expenditures,
$1,083,518; Total giving, $34,908; Grants to
individuals, 25 grants totaling $34,908 (high:
$5,000, low: $549). Subtotal for travel grants:
grants totaling (high: $5,000). Subtotal for
research: grants totaling (high: $2,000, low: $500).
Fields of interest: Journalism/publishing; Political
science; American studies.
Type of support: Research; Awards/prizes; Travel
grants.
Application information: Applications accepted.
Application form required. Application form
available on the grantmaker's Web site.

Copies of proposal: 1
Deadline(s): Mar. 3 for Journalism Prize, Mar. 15
and Sept. 15 for Research Travel Grants
Applicants should submit the following:
1) Letter(s) of recommendation
2) Proposal
3) Curriculum vitae
Additional information: See Web site for further
application and program information.
Program descriptions:
Research Travel Grants: Awards grants of up to
$2,000 each to individuals to defray travel, living
and photocopy expenses of a research trip to the
Ford Library. Grants only cover travel within North
America. For further information, contact Helmi
Raaska, c/o Gerald R. Ford Presidential Library,
1000 Beal Ave., Ann Arbor, MI 48109-2114.
Journalism Prizes: Awards two $5,000 prizes to
print journalists for distinguished reporting on the
presidency or national defense. Journalists can
apply directly or be nominated, and must submit
seven copies of their portfolios, letters of
nomination, and biographical sketches. For further
information, contact Barbara Packer, c/o Gerald R.
Ford Foundation, 303 Pearl St., NW, Grand Rapids,
MI 49504-5353.
EIN: 382368003

5784
The Ford Foundation
320 E. 43rd St.
New York, NY   10017   (212) 573-5000
Contact: Secy.
FAX: (212) 351-3677;
E-mail: office-secretary@fordfound.org;
URL: http://www.fordfound.org

Foundation type: Independent foundation
Limitations: Fellowships, professorships, project
grants, internships and awards by nomination only
for advanced research, training, and other activities
related to urban poverty, rural poverty and
resources, rights and social justice, governance
and public policy, education and culture,
international affairs, and reproductive health and
population. No scholarships or loans to individuals.
Publications: Application guidelines; Annual report
(including application guidelines); Informational
brochure (including application guidelines);
Newsletter; Occasional report.
Financial data: Year ended 09/30/2005.
Assets, $11,570,213,000 (M); Expenditures,
$680,113,000; Total giving, $511,679,000.
Fields of interest: Public affairs, citizen
participation.
Type of support: Program development;
Conferences/seminars; Professorships;
Fellowships; Research; Awards/grants by
nomination only; Awards/prizes.
Application information: Applications accepted.
Application form not required.
Initial approach: Brief letter of inquiry.
Copies of proposal: 1
Deadline(s): None
Additional information: Grants to individuals are
few in number relative to demand, and are
limited to research, training, and other
activities related to the foundation's program
interests which generally focus on enhancing
the quality of life of disadvantaged groups in
the U.S. and the Third World. Undergraduate
scholarships or grants for purely personal or
local needs are not granted. Support for
graduate fellowships is generally provided
through grants to universities and other
organizations, who are responsible for
selecting the recipients. Grants are generally

awarded either through publicly announced competitions or on the basis of nominations from universities and other nonprofit institutions. The foundation generally makes awards to persons with advanced qualifications. Candidates from the U.S. and all over the world are eligible to apply. Recipients are selected on the basis of the merits of their proposals and their potential contribution to advancing the foundation's objectives. Foreign applicants should contact foundation for addresses of its overseas offices, through which they must apply; Applicants are advised to obtain a copy of "Current Interests of the Ford Foundation.".

Program descriptions:

Urban Poverty: The foundation's focus is on community and neighborhood development; strengthening children, youth, and families; and crosscutting research on poverty.

Rural Poverty and Resources: Support for community and economic development, environment and development, agricultural development, and women in development.

Education and Culture: Support for higher education, elementary and secondary education, and arts and culture.

Rights and Social Justice: Support for minority rights and opportunities, women's rights and opportunities, Latino public affairs, refugees and migrants' rights and opportunities, and legal services for the poor.

International Affairs: Support for peace and security, international law and organizations, international economics and development/ refugees and migration, international human rights, U.S. foreign policy and international relations, and the former Soviet Union and Central Europe.

Governance and Public Policy: Support for democratic institutions and state and local performance, philanthropy and the nonprofit sector, minority policy research and professional development, and immigration policy.

Reproductive Health and Population: Support for social sciences, women's empowerment and international networking, ethics, policy and law, new reproductive technologies, HIV/AIDS, and sexuality issues.

Leadership for a Changing World: Nominees must be U.S. residents working on U.S. issues, and must have been involved in the work for which they are being nominated for at least two years. Awardees will receive $100,000 over two years to support their program work, and will be provided an Independent Learning Account of $30,000 for supporting activities that will advance their efforts. Over the two-year program, awardees will participate in semi-annual program-wide meetings designed to provide opportunities for shared learning and collaboration among awardees and with other leaders.

EIN: 131684331

5785

Thomas B. Fordham Foundation

1701 K St. N.W., Ste. 1000
Washington, DC   20006   (202) 223-5452
Contact: Chester E. Finn, Jr., Pres.
FAX: (202) 223-9226;
E-mail: backtalk@edexcellence.net; URL: http://www.edexcellence.net

Foundation type: Independent foundation
Limitations: Awards, by nomination only to individual scholars who have made major contributions to education reform via research, analysis, and successful engagement in "the war of

ideas." Awards also to individuals who have made major contributions to education reform via noteworthy accomplishments at the national, state, local, and /or national levels.
Publications: Informational brochure.
Financial data: Year ended 12/31/2004. Assets, $43,989,468 (M); Expenditures, $2,284,808; Total giving, $850,500.
Fields of interest: Education, reform.
Type of support: Awards/prizes.
Application information:
   Deadline(s): May 13
   Applicants should submit the following:
      1) Essay
      2) Resume
   Additional information: Completion of formal nomination required; individuals may not apply directly.
EIN: 316032844

5786

Myron Jacob Foreman U.S. Scholarship Trust

560 Village Blvd., Ste. 335
West Palm Beach, FL   33409   (561) 964-9000
Contact: Rufus Lee Boozer, Tr.
Application address: 145 Bloomfield Dr., West Palm Beach, FL 33405, tel.: (561) 585-1938

Foundation type: Independent foundation
Limitations: Scholarships for Bahamian medical students.
Financial data: Year ended 06/30/2003. Assets, $916,701 (M); Expenditures, $59,250; Total giving, $37,585; Grants to individuals, 13 grants totaling $37,585 (high: $7,650, low: $1,200).
Fields of interest: Medical school/education; Bahamas.
Type of support: Foreign applicants; Graduate support.
Application information: Applications accepted. Application form required.
   Initial approach: Letter or telephone.
   Deadline(s): None
   Applicants should submit the following:
      1) Transcripts
   Additional information: Application must also include MedCat scores.
EIN: 656186928

5787

Fort Worth Police Officers' Award Foundation

P.O. Box 17659
Fort Worth, TX   76102

Foundation type: Independent foundation
Limitations: Monetary awards and grants to officers of the Fort Worth Police Department, TX, in recognition of their efficiency, skill, and devotion to the citizens of Fort Worth.
Financial data: Year ended 12/31/2004. Assets, $881,329 (M); Expenditures, $50,021; Total giving, $6,919; Grants to individuals, totaling $6,400.
Fields of interest: Crime/law enforcement, police agencies.
Type of support: Exchange programs; Awards/ grants by nomination only; Awards/prizes.
Application information: Applications not accepted.

Program description:
   Awards Program: The foundation gives monetary awards to top academy graduates, firing range awards, and prizes, including watches and trophies.
EIN: 751744211

5788

Foundation Fighting Blindness, Inc.

11435 Cronhill Dr.
Owings Mills, MD   21117-2220   (410) 568-0150
Contact: Edward H. Gollob, Pres.
E-mail: info@blindness.org; Toll-free tel.: (888) 394-3937; TDD: (800) 683-5555; URL: http://www.blindness.org

Foundation type: Public charity
Limitations: Research grants to Ph.D.s, M.D.s, D.O.s, and D.V.M.s at institutions to discover the causes, treatments, preventions and cures for retinal degenerative diseases.
Publications: Annual report; Financial statement; Informational brochure; Newsletter.
Financial data: Year ended 06/30/2005. Assets, $13,927,315 (M); Expenditures, $16,348,385; Total giving, $8,719,878; Grants to individuals, 45 grants totaling $2,927,987 (high: $594,023, low: $1,000).
Fields of interest: Pharmacy/prescriptions; Genetics/birth defects; Eye research.
Type of support: Research; Awards/prizes.
Application information: Applications not accepted.
Program descriptions:

Career Development Award: Emphasizes specialized and rigorous training in both research and clinical ophthalmology to be arranged at select locations. M.D.s, D.O.s, D.V.M.s, or equivalent foreign degrees are eligible. Candidates are usually post-residency fellows in ophthalmology. The foundation will undertake salary and research support. Awards may be made for up to three years.

Individual Research Award: Awards are currently available in the areas of genetics, gene therapy, transplantation, pharmaceutical therapy, cell biology, visual prosthesis, clinical studies, and medical therapy assessment (animal models). Ph.D.s, M.D.s, D.O.s, D.V.M.s or equivalent foreign degrees are eligible. An applicant who has not obtained his/her degree yet may apply provided he/ she obtains it by the date of activation of the award. Funding is provided based upon the needs of the proposal and may range from $20,000 to $150,000. Grants are normally funded for a three-year period.

Research Center Awards: Grants ranging from $50,000 to $500,000 are normally awarded for a five-year period. Preference will be given to applications with a strong clinical component that present an integrated program geared to achieve RD treatments and cures. Ph.D.s, M.D.s, D.O.s, D.V.M.s, or equivalent foreign degrees at accredited academic institutions are eligible.

Young Investigator Award: An average award of $50,000 per year for a three-year period is offered to junior basic and clinical scientists, to encourage the pursuit of studies in the field of retinal degeneration. Ph.D.s, M.D.s, D.O.s, D.V.M.s, or equivalent foreign degrees with a minimum of two and maximum of five years postdoctoral training and experience are eligible.
EIN: 237135845

5789
Foundation for a Christian Civilization, Inc.

P.O. Box 251
Spring Grove, PA 17362 (866) 661-0272
FAX: (717) 225-7382; E-mail: tfp@tfp.org;
URL: http://www.tfp.org/

Foundation type: Public charity
Limitations: Scholarships to individuals involved in the foundation's Exchange-Visitor program.
Financial data: Year ended 06/30/2005.
Assets, $4,162,626 (M); Expenditures,
$4,303,898; Total giving, $71,568; Grants to individuals, 3 grants totaling $8,278.
Fields of interest: International exchange; Roman Catholic agencies & churches.
Type of support: Exchange programs; Foreign applicants; Undergraduate support.
Application information: Contact foundation for current application deadline/guidelines.
EIN: 237325778

5790
The Foundation for AIDS Research, Inc.

(also known as amfAR & AIDS Research Foundation & American Foundation for AIDS Research)
120 Wall St., 13th Fl.
New York, NY 10005-3902 (212) 806-1600
Contact: Scott Newman, Asst. Treas., V.P., Fin. & Admin.
FAX: (212) 806-1601; E-mail: grants@amfar.org;
URL: http://www.amfar.org

Foundation type: Public charity
Limitations: Fellowships and travel grants to postdoctoral investigators specializing in AIDS research.
Publications: Application guidelines; Annual report; Financial statement; Informational brochure; Newsletter; Program policy statement.
Financial data: Year ended 09/30/2004.
Assets, $16,108,920 (M); Expenditures,
$15,776,280; Total giving, $2,410,539.
Fields of interest: AIDS research.
Type of support: Postdoctoral support; Travel grants.
Application information: Application form available on the grantmaker's Web site.
Initial approach: Letter of intent, including fact sheet, abstract, relevance description, biographical sketch(es), and research plan description; Submit letter of intent via e-mail with four additional copies, including signed original, by mail.
Deadline(s): Mar. 9 for e-mail submission and Mar. 12 for hard copy submission.
Program descriptions:
Collaboration: Awards up to $75,000 plus up to 20 percent of indirect costs for collaboration between two principal investigators.
Fellowships: Awards two-year fellowships providing $35,000 in salary support and $10,000 for supplies, plus up to 10 percent for indirect costs annually. Fellowships encourage the postdoctoral (M.D., Ph.D. or equivalent) investigator with limited experience in the field of HIV/AIDS to embark on or redirect a career in HIV/AIDS research.
Short-Term Travel Grants: Awards grants of $5,000 for short-term research, training, or study at another national or international institution by postdoctoral investigators affiliated with nonprofit institutions worldwide. Funds may be applied to the costs of transportation, housing, per-diem expenses, and payments to host institutions.
EIN: 133163817

5791
Foundation for Anesthesia Education and Research

200 First St., SW
Rochester, MN 55905 (507) 266-6866
Contact: Thomas M. Bruckman, Exec. Dir.
FAX: (507) 284-0291; URL: http://www.faer.org

Foundation type: Public charity
Limitations: Grants to individuals for clinical research related to anesthesiology.
Publications: Newsletter.
Financial data: Year ended 12/31/2003.
Assets, $17,737,306 (M); Expenditures,
$1,608,045; Total giving, $1,097,728; Grants to individuals, 88 grants totaling $1,097,728 (high: $99,658, low: $1,000).
Fields of interest: Anesthesiology research.
Type of support: Research; Postdoctoral support.
Application information: Applications accepted. Application form required. Application form available on the grantmaker's Web site.
Initial approach: Telephone.
Copies of proposal: 3
Deadline(s): Feb. 15 and Aug. 15
Program descriptions:
Research Starter Grant: Awards $35,000 for the first year of funding, and $50,000 for the second year of funding, to instructors of assistant professors for anesthesiology research.
Research Education Grant: Awards $50,000 per year for two years to individuals who have completed their clinical anesthesiology training and hold academic appointments.
EIN: 521494164

5792
The Foundation for Basic Cutaneous Research

210 W. Rittenhouse Sq., Apt. 3302
Philadelphia, PA 19103-5780
Contact: Lorraine H. Kligman, Pres.

Foundation type: Operating foundation
Limitations: Research grants for basic cutaneous research.
Financial data: Year ended 07/31/2003.
Assets, $837,688 (M); Expenditures, $309,680; Total giving, $9,625.
Fields of interest: Skin disorders research.
Type of support: Research.
Application information: Applications not accepted.
EIN: 232439001

5793
Foundation for Child Development

145 E. 32nd St., 14th Fl.
New York, NY 10016-6055
Contact: Mark Bogosian, Comms. and Grants Assoc.
FAX: (212) 213-5897;
E-mail: inforequest@fcd-us.org; URL: http://www.fcd-us.org

Foundation type: Independent foundation
Limitations: Fellowships to Ph.D. scholars for research on the health and education needs of young newcomer children, birth to age 10.
Publications: Annual report; Grants list; Informational brochure; Newsletter; Program policy statement.
Financial data: Year ended 03/31/2005.
Assets, $104,558,727 (M); Expenditures,
$4,634,715; Total giving, $2,769,674.
Fields of interest: Education; Children, services; Immigrants/refugees.
Type of support: Fellowships; Research.
Application information: Application form not required.
Initial approach: E-mail.
Deadline(s): Contact foundation for current application deadline.
Additional information: Application by proposal; See Web site for program information and guidelines.
Program description:
Changing Faces of America's Children Young Scholars Program: The FCD Young Scholars Program's goals are to:
· Stimulate both basic and policy-relevant research about the early education, health and well-being of immigrant children from birth to age 10, particularly those who are living in low-income families
· Support young investigators - from the behavioral and social sciences or in an allied professional field - to attain tenure or who have received tenure in the last four years from a college or university in the United States
Eligible researchers will have earned their doctoral degrees within the last 15 years, and be full-time, faculty members of a college or university in the United States. Applicants must hold a Ph.D. or its equivalent in one of the behavioral and social sciences or in an allied professional field (e.g., public policy, public health, education, social work, nursing, medicine). Three to four fellowships of up to $150,000 for use over one to three years (maximum) will be awarded competitively. Please note tenure equivalent positions are not eligible for the fellowship. Direct all questions to nac@fcd-us.org.
EIN: 131623901

5794
Foundation for Chiropractic Education & Research, Inc.

P.O. Box 400
Norwalk, IA 50211-0400 (515) 981-9888
Contact: DeAnna Beck, Dir., Admin.
Additional tel.: (800) 622-6309; FAX: (515) 981-9427; E-mail: FCER@fcer.org; URL: http://www.fcer.org

Foundation type: Public charity
Limitations: Research grants and postgraduate support to individuals primarily at chiropractic and non-chiropractic institutions.
Publications: Application guidelines; Financial statement; Grants list; Informational brochure; Newsletter.
Financial data: Year ended 03/31/2003.
Assets, $2,512,580 (M); Expenditures,
$1,356,260; Total giving, $203,175; Grants to individuals, 10 grants totaling $44,950 (high: $20,000, low: $1,067).
Fields of interest: Chiropractic research.
Type of support: Research; Postdoctoral support.
Application information: Deadlines Mar. 1 and Oct. 1; Completion of formal application required, including demographic and biological information, budget and narrative; See Web site for further application information.
EIN: 426085232

5795
Foundation for Deep Ecology

1062 Fort Cronkhite
Sausalito, CA 94965 (415) 229-9339
Contact: Lizzie Udwin, Prog. Admin.
FAX: (415) 229-9340;
E-mail: info@deepecology.org; URL: http://
www.deepecology.org

Foundation type: Independent foundation
Limitations: Awards to individuals in the U.S.,
Canada, Chile, Argentina and some of Europe for
research on biodiversity and wilderness, ecological
agriculture, and globalization and megatechnology.
Publications: Multi-year report.
Financial data: Year ended 06/30/2005.
Assets, $53,974,718 (M); Expenditures,
$4,066,455; Total giving, $2,732,181.
Fields of interest: Natural resources; Environment;
Animals/wildlife, preservation/protection;
Agriculture.
Type of support: Research; Awards/prizes.
Application information: Applications not
accepted.
EIN: 943106115

5796
Foundation for Digestive Health and Nutrition

(also known as American Digestive Health
Foundation)
4930 Del Ray Ave.
Bethesda, MD 20814-3015 (301) 222-4002
Contact: Carol Dreher, Exec. Dir.
FAX: (301) 222-4010; E-mail: info@fdhn.org;
URL: http://www.FDHN.org

Foundation type: Public charity
Limitations: Research grants and fellowships to
students and faculty specializing in
gastroenterological issues.
Publications: Application guidelines; Annual report;
Informational brochure; Newsletter.
Financial data: Year ended 12/31/2004.
Assets, $7,998,323 (M); Expenditures,
$3,430,295; Total giving, $1,923,500; Grants to
individuals, 22 grants totaling $57,000 (high:
$3,000, low: $500).
Fields of interest: Cancer research; Ear & throat
research; Liver research; Digestive disorders
research; Medical research; Science.
Type of support: Fellowships; Research; Awards/
prizes; Stipends.
Application information: Application form required.
Deadline(s): Vary
Additional information: For most programs,
membership in American Gastroenterological
Association is required. See Web site for
further application information and for
application forms.
Program descriptions:
AGA Research Scholarship Awards: A number of
awards at $65,000 per year for three years
($195,000 total) are made to support promising
junior faculty by protecting research time. Two of the
RSA's, sponsored by Roche Pharmaceuticals,
support liver disease research. All applications with
a focus on liver disease will be considered for this
award. Deadline Sept. 5.
*AGA Roche Research Scholar Award in Liver
Diseases:* Two awards of $65,000 per year for three
years ($195,000 total) are made to support
promising young investigators working towards
independent careers in liver disease research.
Deadline Sept. 5.
*AGA/AstraZeneca Fellowship/Faculty Transition
Awards:* Four awards at $40,000 per year for two

years ($80,000 total) are made to advanced
fellows/trainees, to provide salary support for
additional full-time research training in basic
science. Deadline Sept. 5.
*AGA/R. Robert and Sally D. Funderburg Research
Scholar Award in Gastric Cancer:* One award of
$25,000 per year for two years ($50,000 total) is
made to support the research of an established
investigator working on novel approaches to gastric
cancer. Deadline Sept. 5.
*AGA Centocor Excellence in IBD Clinical Research
Fellowship:* Four one-year awards of $70,000 each
to enable promising senior fellows to spend an
additional year of full-time clinical research in
inflammatory bowel diseases. Deadline Nov. 17.
*AGA Roche Junior Faculty Clinical Research
Awards in Hepatology:* Three two-year awards of
$70,000 per year (total $140,000 each) for young
investigators working toward independent clinical
research careers in hepatology. Deadline Nov. 17.
*AGA/June and Donald O. Castell, MD, Esophageal
Clinical Research Award:* One award of $35,000 is
made to provide research and/or salary support for
junior faculty involved in esophageal disease
clinical research. Deadline Jan. 14.
AGA/Elsevier Research Initiative Award: One
award of $25,000 is provided to an investigator to
support pilot research projects in GI- or
hepatology-related areas. Deadline Jan. 14.
*AGA/Miles and Shirley Fiterman Foundation Basic
Research Award:* Two awards of $35,000 each are
provided for research and/or salary support for
junior faculty involved in basic GI or liver disease
research. Deadline Jan. 4.
*AGA Solvay IBS/Motility Clinical Research
Award:* One award of $25,000 per year for three
years (total $75,000) to provide research and/or
salary support for junior faculty involved in clinical
research in irritable bowel syndrome (IBS) or
gastrointestinal motility. Deadline Feb. 14.
*AGA/Miles and Shirley Fiterman Foundation
Clinical Research in Gastroenterology (Joseph B.
Kirsner) or Hepatology/Nutrition (Hugh R. Butt)
Award:* Two awards of $35,000 each are given to
honor the individuals in whose names the awards
are given and to support the clinical
gastroenterology and hepatology/nutrition research
of the recipients. Deadline Feb. 14.
AGA Student Research Fellowships Awards: Up to
20 awards are made each year at a funding level
between $2,000-$3,000 per recipient to support
high school, college, medical, or graduate students
performing digestive disease or nutrition research
for a minimum of 10 weeks. Deadline Mar. 5.
EIN: 521764955

5797
Foundation for Eye Research

P.O. Box 8774
Rancho Santa Fe, CA 92067-8774

Foundation type: Independent foundation
Limitations: Research grants to individuals for the
study of the eye.
Financial data: Year ended 12/31/2004.
Assets, $797,692 (M); Expenditures,
$1,023,917; Total giving, $1,002,500.
Fields of interest: Eye research.
Type of support: Research; Postdoctoral support.
Application information: Applications not
accepted.
EIN: 330127290

5798
Foundation for Hand Research and Education

(formerly Foundation for Surgical Hand Research)
P.O. Box 80434
Indianapolis, IN 46280-0434
Contact: Richard Idler
Application address: 8501 Harcourt Rd.,
Indianapolis, IN 46280

Foundation type: Operating foundation
Limitations: Research grants to board-certified
physicians of orthopedics, plastic, or general
surgery, in IN.
Financial data: Year ended 12/31/2002.
Assets, $413,455 (M); Expenditures, $42,522;
Total giving, $25,140; Grants to individuals, 2
grants totaling $19,702 (high: $14,582, low:
$5,120).
Fields of interest: Surgery research; Orthopedics
research.
Type of support: Research.
Application information: Deadline Sept. 1; Initial
approach by letter; Completion of formal application
required.
EIN: 351728352

5799
Foundation for Improvement of Justice, Inc.

220 Roberts Rd.
Suwanee, GA 30024 (770) 831-9411
Contact: Malisa McOmber, Exec. Dir.
FAX: (770) 831-9896;
E-mail: info@justiceawards.com; URL: http://
justiceawards.com/

Foundation type: Independent foundation
Limitations: Awards by nomination only to
individuals for achievements in the field of justice.
Publications: Annual report; Informational brochure
(including application guidelines).
Financial data: Year ended 12/31/2004.
Assets, $1,312,074 (M); Expenditures,
$130,716; Total giving, $81,944; Grants to
individuals, 3 grants totaling $20,729.
Fields of interest: Crime/law enforcement; Law/
international law.
Type of support: Awards/grants by nomination only;
Awards/prizes.
Application information: Applications accepted.
Application form required.
Initial approach: Letter, telephone, or e-mail.
Deadline(s): June 1
Additional information: Completion of formal
nomination required; See program for further
nomination information.
Program description:
Improvement of Justice Program: The foundation
encourages improvement in local, state, and
federal systems of justice by recognizing and
rewarding accomplishment in the following
categories:
· simplification of the law
· crime prevention
· child protection
· speeding the process
· effecting restitution
· crime victims' rights
· alternative sentencing
· reducing recidivism
· lowering the cost
· other significant efforts
The foundation annually awards up to ten nominees
a certificate of appreciation, a commendation bar
pin, a medal, and a check for $10,000 presented

at an awards banquet in Atlanta. Formal nominations are required, including the following:
- a cover letter giving nominator's and nominee's name, position, address, and telephone number(s)
- a two-page, double-spaced, typewritten summary of nominee's accomplishment, with specific results. (Do not identify the nominee or nominator on this page in any manner. Refer only to "nominee." Information as to location, political affiliation, race, religion, etc. should be omitted in order that these may be judged without concern of prejudice; Judging is based on this paper)
- evidence of nominee's accomplishment such as commendations, endorsements, newspaper/magazine articles, TV clips, or other information. (The purpose of these is verification. An elaborate presentation is not necessary, substance counts)

A reference book describing successful programs that have been recognized is available for $5 shipping and handling cost. Mail request and payment to the foundation. Self-nominations are not accepted, and members, their relatives, and previous winners are ineligible.
EIN: 581593170

5800
The Foundation for Physical Therapy, Inc.
(formerly The Foundation for Physical Therapy Research)
1111 N. Fairfax St.
Alexandria, VA 22314 (703) 684-5984
Contact: Christine Williams, C.O.O.
FAX: (703) 706-8519;
E-mail: foundation@apta.org; URL: http://www.apta.org/Foundation

Foundation type: Public charity
Limitations: Research grants and doctoral support to students at regionally accredited postprofessional doctoral programs in physical therapy.
Publications: Application guidelines; Annual report; Financial statement; Grants list; Informational brochure; Multi-year report.
Financial data: Year ended 12/31/2004. Assets, $3,235,941 (M); Expenditures, $1,231,842; Total giving, $500,000; Grants to individuals, 23 grants totaling $500,000.
Fields of interest: Physical therapy.
Type of support: Program development; Fellowships; Research; Scholarships—to individuals; Postgraduate support; Doctoral support.
Application information: Applications accepted. Application form required. Application form available on the grantmaker's Web site.
Initial approach: Letter or e-mail.
Deadline(s): Contact foundation for current application deadline.
Applicants should submit the following:
1) Transcripts
2) Resume
3) Proposal
4) Letter(s) of recommendation
5) Curriculum vitae
6) Budget Information
Additional information: Five copies of scholarship applications and 15 copies of fellowship and research applications required; Applications should be mailed.

Program description:
Physical Therapy Research: The foundation offers the following programs of support for physical therapy research:
- Mary McMillan Doctoral Scholarships: Offers up to $5,000 to assist physical therapists with outstanding potential for doctoral studies in the first year of graduate studies toward a doctorate. Applicants will be notified in Dec. of award decisions
- Promotion of Doctoral Studies (PODS) Program: Offers $7,500 in support of doctoral students who, having completed two full semesters or three full quarters of coursework, wish to continue their studies, and up to $15,000 in support of doctoral students who have reached candidacy status. Applicants will be notified in June of award decisions
- New Investigator Fellowships Training Initiative: Offers a two year fellowship grant of $78,000 to doctorally prepared physical therapists as developing researchers to improve their competitiveness in securing external funding for future research. Applicants will be notified in June of award decisions
- Research Grants Program: Offers one-year, $40,000 research grants to emerging investigators for scientifically-based and clinically-relevant research related to the effectiveness of physical therapist practice. Applicants will be notified in Dec. of award decisions
EIN: 136161225

5801
Foundation for Saline Area Schools
P.O. Box 5
Saline, MI 48176 (734) 429-7378
Contact: Dan Ouellette, Pres.
E-mail: americandano@cs.com; URL: http://www.saline.lib.mi.us/fsas

Foundation type: Public charity
Limitations: Grants to teachers in Saline, MI, for projects and programs aimed at enhancing the quality of education and educational opportunities.
Financial data: Year ended 12/31/2003. Assets, $236,125 (M); Expenditures, $14,017; Total giving, $13,470; Grants to individuals, totaling $13,470.
Fields of interest: Education.
Type of support: Program development.
Application information: Application form required.
Deadline(s): 2nd Tues. of Apr. and Oct.
Additional information: See Web site for further information and guidelines.
EIN: 382733854

5802
Foundation for the Advancement of Mesoamerican Studies, Inc.
(also known as FAMSI)
268 S. Suncoast Blvd.
Crystal River, FL 34429
Contact: Sandra Noble, Ph.D., Exec. Dir.
FAX: (352) 795-1970; E-mail: famsi@famsi.org;
Additional E-mail: sandra@famsi.org; URL: http://www.famsi.org

Foundation type: Independent foundation
Limitations: Research grants to individuals studying the ancient cultures of Mexico,

Guatemala, Honduras, Belize and El Salvador (Pre-Columbian Mesoamerica).
Publications: Application guidelines; Grants list; Informational brochure; Informational brochure (including application guidelines); Occasional report; Program policy statement.
Financial data: Year ended 12/31/2003. Assets, $803,007 (M); Expenditures, $751,500; Total giving, $263,078; Grants to individuals, 35 grants totaling $263,078 (high: $10,000, low: $1,000).
Fields of interest: Cultural/ethnic awareness; History/archaeology; Language/linguistics; Historical activities; Anthropology/sociology; Mexico; Belize; El Salvador; Guatemala; Honduras.
Type of support: Seed money; Research; Grants to individuals; Foreign applicants; Awards/prizes; Postdoctoral support; Graduate support; Postgraduate support; Travel grants; Doctoral support; Project support.
Application information: Applications accepted. Application form required. Application form available on the grantmaker's Web site.
Initial approach: Letter, fax, or e-mail.
Copies of proposal: 2
Deadline(s): Sept. 30
Applicants should submit the following:
1) Resume
2) Proposal
3) Curriculum vitae
4) Budget Information
Additional information: Application should also include three letters of recommendation; Application brochures may be obtained through FAMSI Granting Comm. or Web site.
Program descriptions:
Award Program: The foundation supports projects in the disciplines of archaeology, art history, epigraphy, linguistics, ethnohistory, and sociology. The foundation encourages interdisciplinary projects. Awards go to the most qualified scholars regardless of degree level, although the foundation favors degree candidates, recent graduates, and professionals whose projects have not had extensive financial support.
Research Grants: Grants to scholars and other professionals for scholarly investigations of ancient cultures of Mesoamerica (limited to present Mexico, Guatemala, Belize, Honduras, and El Salvador). Applicants may be working in such fields as anthropology, archaeology, art history, ethnohistory, linguistics, and/or multidisciplinary studies involving combinations of these classifications. Research Grants support a wide variety of projects where financial needs range from $500 but do not usually exceed $10,000 per project. Deadline Sept. 15.
EIN: 593195520

5803
Foundation for the Future
123 105th Ave. S.E.
Bellevue, WA 98004 (425) 451-1333
Contact: Carol Johnson, Prog. Mgr.
FAX: (425) 688-1591;
E-mail: info@futurefoundation.org; URL: http://www.futurefoundation.org

Foundation type: Operating foundation
Limitations: Prizes by nomination only to individuals for outstanding achievement in identifying the genetic factors that may have a decisive impact on the survivability of a human population. Also, research grants awarded to scholars for study on humanity and related studies.
Financial data: Year ended 12/31/2004. Assets, $23,609,332 (M); Expenditures,

$1,139,799; Total giving, $116,000; Grants to individuals, 4 grants totaling $116,000 (high: $100,000, low: $1,000).
Fields of interest: Genetics/birth defects; Anthropology/sociology.
Type of support: Research; Awards/prizes.
Application information:
Initial approach: Proposal.
Additional information: Contact foundation for current application deadline/guidelines.
Program descriptions:
Kistler Prize: Award of $100,000 to an individual for international scholarship in the field of genetics. Prize is awarded for original, substantive and innovative contributions to the understanding of the relationship between genetics and human behavior, including intelligence. These contributions are of a scientific nature, employing scientific methods to establish the connections between genetics and human behavior.
Research Grants: Awards financial support to scholars undertaking research that is directly related to a better understanding of the factors affecting the quality of life for the long-term future of humanity. Individuals wishing to apply for grants in fields that are of interest to the foundation are welcome to submit a preliminary grant application. See Web site for application forms. The foundation provides funding for research but does not assume responsibility for findings and interpretations resulting from the research.
EIN: 911732102

5804
Foundation Francisco Marroquin
P.O. Box 2422
Stuart, FL   34995-2442   (772) 286-6450
Contact: Rosa Gutierrez, Adm.
FAX: (772) 288-0670; E-mail: rosa@ffmnet.org; Additional address: Paul V. Harberger, Pres., P.O. Box 1806, Santa Monica, CA 90406-1806, tel.: (310) 395-5047, FAX: (310) 395-5837, E-mail: pvh@ffmnet.org; URL: http://www.ffmnet.org

Foundation type: Public charity
Limitations: Fellowships by nomination only to Latin Americans who devote their lives to institutions that emphasize the ethics of a free society.
Publications: Newsletter.
Financial data: Year ended 03/31/2003.
Assets, $38,098 (M); Expenditures, $292,377; Total giving, $157,666; Grants to individuals, totaling $15,000.
Fields of interest: International development; International economic development.
Type of support: Fellowships; Awards/grants by nomination only.
Application information:
Initial approach: Letter.
Additional information: Applications accepted throughout the year.
Program description:
Francisco Marroquin Fellows: Provides a supplement to the low wages of key teachers and writers who are capable of educating Latin Americans about economics, and thereby to strengthen Latin America's free market think tanks. Each fellow receives $9,500 per year for up to two years, and remains a fellow for life.
EIN: 953303550

5805
Foundation of the Alumnae Association of Mount Sinai Hospital School of Nursing, Inc.
c/o Anne Taberna
1 Gustave L. Levy Pl.
New York, NY   10029   (212) 289-5566

Foundation type: Independent foundation
Limitations: Scholarship grants to registered professional nurses pursuing postgraduate studies in nursing and related fields only.
Financial data: Year ended 09/30/2004.
Assets, $158,117 (M); Expenditures, $40,774; Total giving, $29,122; Grants to individuals, totaling $29,122.
Fields of interest: Nursing school/education; Nursing care.
Type of support: Scholarships—to individuals; Postgraduate support.
Application information: Applications not accepted.
EIN: 136096777

5806
Foundation of the American College of Allergy, Asthma, and Immunology
85 W. Alonquin Rd., Ste. 550
Arlington Heights, IL   60005   (847) 427-1200
FAX: (847) 427-1294; E-mail: mail@acaai.org; URL: http://www.acaai.org

Foundation type: Public charity
Limitations: Clinical fellowship stipends, research grants, young faculty support awards, and scholars return awards to individuals specializing in asthma, immunology or allergies.
Financial data: Year ended 12/31/2004.
Assets, $1,468,710 (M); Expenditures, $401,340; Total giving, $213,000; Grants to individuals, totaling $212,000.
Fields of interest: Allergies research; Asthma research; Immunology research.
Type of support: Program development; Research; Awards/prizes.
Application information:
Deadline(s): Contact foundation for current application deadlines/guidelines
EIN: 364305678

5807
Michael J. Fox Foundation for Parkinson's Research
Grand Central Sta.
P.O. Box 4777
New York, NY   10163   (212) 509-0995
FAX: (212) 509-2390;
E-mail: research@michaeljfox.org; URL: http://www.michaeljfox.org

Foundation type: Public charity
Limitations: Research grants to investigators for the study and eventual cure of Parkinson's disease.
Publications: Application guidelines; Grants list; Informational brochure; Newsletter.
Financial data: Year ended 12/31/2004.
Assets, $13,600,446 (M); Expenditures, $15,431,736; Total giving, $11,607,858; Grants to individuals, totaling $11,607,858.
Fields of interest: Brain research; Parkinson's disease research.
Type of support: Research; Awards/prizes.
Application information:
Initial approach: July 27 for Letter of intent.

Program descriptions:
LEAPS (Linked Efforts to Accelerate Parkinson's Solutions): Awards for collaborative efforts by investigators that address questions that will have significant practical impact on the understanding and treatment of Parkinson's disease. The foundation believes the nature and scale of such projects will required coordinated, cross-disciplinary and often multi-institution approaches. The foundation expects that this mechanism is well-suited to projects that will translate into new treatments or otherwise have a tangible impact on Parkinson's disease. Examples of questions in the LEAPS program could be categorized under broad aims of:
  · Repairing of the PD brain
  · Slowing or halting the progression of PD
  · Preventing or controlling levodopa-induced dyskenesias
  · Identifying the cause of PD.
Research Grants: Awards grants to investigators with scientific interests and demonstrated success in the development, culture, and manipulation of individual cell lines are invited to direct their expertise to this RFA. The intent is to develop cell lines that will benefit researchers in their understanding of the causes of Parkinson's disease, to aid them in the developing of appropriate models relevant to understanding and treating the disease, and to assist them in developing innovative strategies to prevent, limit, or reverse the process of neuronal degeneration in Parkinson's disease.
EIN: 134141945

5808
Fraxa Research Foundation, Inc.
45 Pleasant St. 2nd Fl.
Newburyport, MA   01950   (978) 462-1866
Contact: Katherine Clapp, Pres.
FAX: (978) 463-9985; E-mail: info@fraxa.org; URL: http://www.fraxa.org

Foundation type: Public charity
Limitations: Fellowships and research grants for the study of Fragile X syndrome.
Publications: Application guidelines; Annual report; Financial statement; Grants list; Informational brochure; Newsletter.
Financial data: Year ended 12/31/2004.
Assets, $2,108,324 (M); Expenditures, $1,493,451; Total giving, $1,106,568; Grants to individuals, totaling $1,106,568.
Fields of interest: Genetics/birth defects research.
Type of support: Fellowships; Research; Postdoctoral support.
Application information:
Deadline(s): Dec. 1 and May 1.
Additional information: Contact foundation or see Web site for current application guidelines.
Program description:
Fellowships:
  · Postdoctoral Fellowships: Fellowships of up to $35,000 are provided for research aimed at finding a specific treatment and ultimate cure for Fragile X syndrome
  · Investigator-Initiated Grants: Grants are provided for innovative pilot studies aimed at developing and characterizing new therapeutic approaches for Fragile X syndrome. There is no funding limit for these grants, but typical grants range from $30,000-$50,000 per year
All fellowships are paid directly to the fellow's institution on his or her behalf.
EIN: 043222167

5809

The Freedom Forum, Inc.

1101 Wilson Blvd.
Arlington, VA   22209-2248   (703) 528-0800
Contact: Charles L. Overby, Chair.
FAX: (703) 284-3770;
E-mail: news@freedomforum.org; URL: http://www.freedomforum.org

Foundation type: Operating foundation
Limitations: Project support to journalists, professors, and other media professionals.
Publications: Annual report; Occasional report.
Financial data: Year ended 12/31/2004.
Assets, $924,229,500 (M); Expenditures, $57,848,576; Total giving, $23,152,188; Grants to individuals, 133 grants totaling $100,249 (high: $10,000, low: $25).
Application information: Applications not accepted.
EIN: 541604427

5810

The Alfred Friendly Foundation

c/o Susan Albrecht
1616 H St. N.W., 3rd Fl.
Washington, DC   20006
FAX: (202) 737-4416;
E-mail: info@pressfellowships.org; URL: http://www.pressfellowships.org

Foundation type: Operating foundation
Limitations: Fellowships to journalists from countries other than the U.S. to work as reporters for six months on publications so as to further understanding of the press.
Publications: Financial statement.
Financial data: Year ended 06/30/2005.
Assets, $2,113,873 (M); Expenditures, $287,048; Total giving, $132,611; Grants to individuals, 8 grants totaling $132,611 (high: $22,402, low: $14,015).
Fields of interest: Journalism/publishing.
Type of support: Fellowships; Foreign applicants.
Application information: Application form required. Application form available on the grantmaker's Web site.
Deadline(s): Sept. 1
Applicants should submit the following:
1) Work samples
2) Curriculum vitae
3) Letter(s) of recommendation
4) Essay
Additional information: Application must also include detailed biographical information, and samples of published work, with translations as necessary; Interviews required for finalists; English language proficiency exam required.
Program description:
Alfred Friendly Press Fellowships: Fellowships provide a working visit of approximately six months in the U.S. Fellows must be professional journalists, fluent in spoken and written English, with at least three years experience in the profession and an employer, preferably an independent publication, willing to endorse their application, to continue part of their salary during the fellowship, and to employ them when the fellowship ends. The fellowships cover all costs of international and national U.S. travel. A monthly stipend is provided to cover basic living expenses. The visit extends from Mar. to Sept. of each year, and is divided into three parts. The first two weeks are devoted to an orientation seminar in Washington, D.C., to ease the adjustment to a new cultural environment and to familiarize the fellows with media technology and journalistic practices in

the U.S. Sessions will also be held on the function of the free press in the U.S., political and social structure, the legal aspects of press freedom, and the problems and prospects of the media in the U.S. After their orientation, the fellows proceed directly to the media organizations that have agreed to be their hosts for the next five months. These work assignments are made with each fellow's career focus and interests in mind. During their job assignments, the fellows will be expected to contribute directly, as working reporters, to the routine output of their host publications. The fellowship requires fellows to write and submit, by Aug. 15, one short article, suitable for publication, evaluating their experience and its relevance to their interests and future career. In Sept., the fellows come together again in Washington, D.C., for a review of their experience, media visits, professional appointments, and a program of cultural activities before returning to their home countries.
EIN: 521307387

5811

Friends of Hama'ayan Institution, Inc.

c/o Paul Schwartz, C.P.A.
222 W. 83rd St., Ste. 4C
New York, NY   10024
Contact: Mordechai Krashinsky, Pres.
Application address: c/o Jacob Paskesz, 1353 56th St., Brooklyn, NY 11219

Foundation type: Independent foundation
Limitations: Scholarships to residents of Israel for postgraduate rabbinic and Talmudic research in Israel.
Financial data: Year ended 12/31/2004.
Assets, $113,965 (M); Expenditures, $52,145; Total giving, $43,700.
Fields of interest: Religion, research; Jewish agencies & temples; Israel.
Type of support: Research; Scholarships—to individuals; Foreign applicants; Postgraduate support.
Application information: Contact foundation for current application deadline/guidelines.
EIN: 112686188

5812

Friends of Jose Carreras International Leukemia Foundation

1100 Fairview Ave. N., Ste. D5-100
P.O. Box 19024
Seattle, WA   98109-1024   (206) 667-7108
Contact: Hon. Jose Carreras, Pres.
FAX: (206) 667-6498;
E-mail: friendsjc@carrerasfoundation.org;
URL: http://www.carrerasfoundation.org

Foundation type: Public charity
Limitations: Fellowships to individual M.D.'s and Ph.D.'s for research into the diagnosis, prevention, and cure of leukemia and related hematologic malignancies.
Publications: Newsletter.
Financial data: Year ended 06/30/2005.
Assets, $536,232 (M); Expenditures, $77,961; Total giving, $25,000; Grant to an individual, 1 grant totaling $25,000.
Fields of interest: Leukemia research.
Type of support: Fellowships; Postdoctoral support.
Application information: Application form required.
Deadline(s): Nov. 3
Additional information: Application must include C.V., abstract budget, and three letters of recommendation; Submit original and 11

copies of all information; See Web site for further application information.
Program description:
Fellowships: Awards fellowships of up to $50,000 for one year, renewable for two years upon satisfactory performance. Candidates must hold an M.D. or Ph.D. degree and have completed at least three years postdoctoral training but under ten years postdoctoral.
EIN: 911484924

5813

Friends United for Juvenile Diabetes Research

1700 Ryders Ln.
P.O. Box 585
Highland Park, IL   60035   (847) 831-5558
Contact: Susan Mandell, Pres.

Foundation type: Public charity
Limitations: Research grants to raise the awareness of juvenile diabetes.
Financial data: Year ended 12/31/2003.
Assets, $56,000 (M); Expenditures, $32,800; Total giving, $30,000; Grant to an individual, 1 grant totaling $30,000.
Fields of interest: Diabetes research.
Type of support: Research.
Application information: Contact foundation for current application deadline/guidelines.
EIN: 364256133

5814

Robert Frost Teaching Chairs Trust

c/o Bank of America, N.A., P.C. Group
P.O. Box 6767
Providence, RI   02940-6767

Foundation type: Independent foundation
Limitations: Awards by nomination only to teachers who have taught in a public high school in the town of Amherst, MA, for at least three years.
Financial data: Year ended 06/30/2005.
Assets, $120,932 (M); Expenditures, $6,621; Total giving, $5,400; Grants to individuals, totaling $5,400.
Fields of interest: Education.
Type of support: Awards/grants by nomination only; Awards/prizes.
Application information:
Deadline(s): June 1
Additional information: Contact trust for current nomination guidelines; Individual applications not accepted.
Program description:
Teaching Chairs Award Program: Awards are made to encourage excellence in teaching. Nominees are selected by secret ballot by a jury of their peers.
EIN: 046027359

5815

The Fund for American Studies

1706 New Hampshire Ave., N.W.
Washington, DC   20009   (202) 986-0384
Contact: Roger Ream, Pres.
FAX: (202) 986-0390; E-mail: info@tfas.org;
Additional tel.: (800) 741-6964; URL: http://www.tfas.org

Foundation type: Public charity
Limitations: Awards to magazine and newspaper reporters.

Publications: Annual report; Financial statement; Informational brochure; Newsletter.
Financial data: Year ended 09/30/2004. Assets, $20,747,114 (M); Expenditures, $5,901,260; Total giving, $1,161,002.
Fields of interest: Journalism/publishing; Economics; Political science.
Type of support: Awards/prizes.
Application information:
Initial approach: Letter, telephone, or e-mail.
Deadline(s): Mar. 1 for Mollenhoff Award and Mar. 15 for Economic Journalism Award
Additional information: See Web site for additional information.
Program descriptions:
Economic Journalism Award: A cash prize of $5,000 is awarded to a magazine or newspaper writer who has done the most to shape public opinion by giving a better understanding of economic theory and reality. More than one investigative series for a reporter, team or newspaper is permitted, but should be submitted as a separate entry. Stories must have been published after Mar. 1 of the previous year.
Clark-Mollenhoff Award for Excellence in Investigative Reporting: A cash award of $5,000 and a bronze award is presented to a newspaper reporter or team of reporters, showing initiative similar to Mollenhoff's. More than one investigative series for a reporter or team of reporters is permitted but each should be submitted as a separate entry. Stories must have been published after Mar. 1 of the previous year.
EIN: 136223604

5816
Fund for the City of New York, Inc.
121 Ave. of the Americas, 6th Fl.
New York, NY   10013-1590   (212) 925-6675
Contact: Mary McCormick, Pres.
FAX: (212) 925-5675; URL: http://www.fcny.org

Foundation type: Public charity
Limitations: Public service awards by nomination only to career public servants in New York City government.
Publications: Application guidelines; Informational brochure; Informational brochure (including application guidelines); Occasional report.
Financial data: Year ended 09/30/2004. Assets, $40,477,055 (M); Expenditures, $37,497,482; Total giving, $2,135,934.
Fields of interest: AIDS; Agriculture/food, reform; Housing/shelter, reform; Urban/community development; Community development; Government/public administration; Leadership development; Economically disadvantaged.
Type of support: Awards/grants by nomination only; Awards/prizes.
Application information: Nominations from all sources are accepted throughout the year, deadline Sept. 1 for Public Service Awards; Nominations are investigated by program staff; Final selections are made by an independent selection panel of citizens chosen on the basis of their standing in the community and their knowledge of government.
Program descriptions:
Public Service Awards: Annually presents cash payments to outstanding career public servants of the City of New York. The awards are intended to call public attention to superior work on behalf of the city and its people, raise the morale and effectiveness of the city's municipal work force, and encourage individuals to think of city service as a career. Any employee of the City of New York is eligible, including employees of the Transit and Housing Authorities, Health and Hospitals

Corporation, Board of Education, Board of Higher Education, and the public libraries.
Union Square Awards: Awards up to $50,000 to individuals who have initiated and developed projects/organizations in homelessness and hunger, HIV/AIDS prevention, education and treatment, conflict resolution, economic self-sufficiency, and youth and family development.
EIN: 132612524

5817
Galena Park ISD Education Foundation, Inc.
14705 Woodforest Blvd.
Houston, TX   77015   (832) 386-1000
Contact: Dr. Mark Henry, Superintendent
URL: http://www.galenaparkisd.com/foundati.htm

Foundation type: Public charity
Limitations: Career development scholarships to teachers at Galena Park Independent School District, TX.
Financial data: Year ended 12/31/2003. Assets, $224,005 (M); Expenditures, $170,069; Total giving, $117,418; Grants to individuals, totaling $117,418.
Type of support: Scholarships—to individuals.
Application information: Applications accepted. Application form required. Application form available on the grantmaker's Web site.
Initial approach: Letter or telephone.
Additional information: Contact foundation for application deadline/guidelines.
EIN: 760563596

5818
Gay and Lesbian Medical Association
459 Fulton St., Ste. 107
San Francisco, CA   94102   (415) 255-4547
Contact: Joel Ginsberg, Exec. Dir.
FAX: (415) 255-4784; E-mail: info@glma.org;
URL: http://www.glma.org

Foundation type: Public charity
Limitations: Grants for research projects in the area of lesbian health needs.
Publications: Application guidelines; Informational brochure (including application guidelines); Newsletter.
Financial data: Year ended 12/31/2004. Assets, $146,301 (M); Expenditures, $507,018; Total giving, $6,340; Grants to individuals, totaling $2,400.
Fields of interest: Health care; LGBTQ.
Type of support: Conferences/seminars; Research.
Application information: Application form required.
Initial approach: Letter or telephone.
Deadline(s): May 1 and Oct. 1.
Applicants should submit the following:
1) Proposal
Program descriptions:
Symposium Scholarships: The association offers several scholarships to enable medical students to attend the Annual Symposium of the Gay and Lesbian Medical Association.
Lesbian Health Fund: Grants range from $500 to $10,000 each.
EIN: 942901694

5819
General Motors Cancer Research Foundation, Inc.
300 Renaissance Ctr., M.C. 482-C27-D76
Detroit, MI   48265-3000
Contact: Samuel A. Wells, Jr., M.D., Pres.
URL: http://www.gm.com/company/gmability/
philanthropy/cancer_research/index.htm

Foundation type: Company-sponsored foundation
Limitations: Research prizes to individuals involved in cancer research from any part of the world. Candidates must be nominated by invited proposers.
Publications: Application guidelines.
Financial data: Year ended 12/31/2003. Assets, $1,237,644 (M); Expenditures, $2,765,712; Total giving, $1,742,000; Grants to individuals, 5 grants totaling $750,000 (high: $250,000, low: $125,000).
Fields of interest: Cancer research.
Type of support: Research; Awards/grants by nomination only; Awards/prizes.
Application information: Application form required.
Deadline(s): Oct. 3
Applicants should submit the following:
1) Curriculum vitae
Additional information: Individual applications are not considered; Invitations to nominate candidates are sent to individuals holding the rank of Professor or Associate Professor or its equivalent in universities and institutions selected for a given year's nominations; Final decisions made in Apr.
Program description:
GM Cancer Research Program: Annual awards are given to those who have made the most outstanding contributions in the field of cancer research. Contributions must be recent, generally within the last 15 years, with priority given to newer contributions. Each prize is awarded to a single individual who was clearly the principal investigator. In exceptional cases, prizes may be shared equally by two persons who worked together or who had significant interaction during the research. Nominators should keep the nominations confidential and refrain from informing the nominee. Each prize is a gold medal and $100,000.
EIN: 382219731

5820
Georgia Osteopathic Institute
2037 Grayson Hwy.
Grayson, GA   30017   (770) 908-3200
Contact: Barry Doublestein, Exec. Dir.
FAX: (770) 908-3210; Additional tel.: (800) 934-2495; URL: http://www.goi.org

Foundation type: Public charity
Limitations: Grants to third- and fourth-year osteopathic residents for training in local hospitals in GA.
Financial data: Year ended 08/31/2004. Assets, $3,673,875 (M); Expenditures, $385,781; Total giving, $16,236; Grants to individuals, totaling $16,236.
Fields of interest: Medical school/education.
Type of support: Postgraduate support.
Application information:
Initial approach: Telephone.
Deadline(s): Contact foundation for current application deadline/guidelines
Additional information: Residents needing reimbursement must submit an expense report to the director of the residency program.
EIN: 580683826

5821
The German Marshall Fund of the United States

1744 R St. N.W.
Washington, DC   20009   (202) 745-3950
Internship/Fellowships Contact: Abigail
Golden-Vazquez, Dir., Communications
FAX: (202) 265-1662; E-mail: info@gmfus.org;
European reps.: Heike MacKerron, Oranienburger
Strasse 13/14, Berlin, 10178, Germany (tel.:
493-0283-4902), and Amaya Bloch-Laine - 16, Rue
Paul Valery, 75016 Paris, France (tel.:
331-5628-0886); URL: http://www.gmfus.org

Foundation type: Public charity
Limitations: Fellowships and awards to U.S.
journalists, and research fellowships to U.S.
postdoctoral scholars for the study of transatlantic
issues. See program description for further
limitations.
Publications: Annual report.
Financial data: Year ended 05/31/2004.
Assets, $218,264,071 (M); Expenditures,
$18,051,591; Total giving, $5,818,402.
Fields of interest: Journalism/publishing;
Language (foreign); Education; Natural resources;
Energy; Environment; Agriculture; Foreign policy;
International affairs; Anthropology/sociology;
Economics; Political science; Government/public
administration.
Type of support: Program development;
Conferences/seminars; Fellowships; Internship
funds; Research; Exchange programs; Awards/
grants by nomination only; Foreign applicants;
Awards/prizes; Postdoctoral support; Travel grants.
Application information: Applications accepted.
Application form required.
  Deadline(s): Nov. 15 for Research Fellowship
    Program, contact fund for others.
  Additional information: See Web site for
    complete description of programs, and
    application information.
Program descriptions:
Research Program: This program offers grants for
advanced research to improve the understanding of
significant contemporary economic, political, and
social developments relating to Europe, European
integration, and relations between Europe and the
U.S. to graduate students, recent Ph.D. or L.L.M.
recipients, and more senior scholars. Projects
should involve either comparative analysis of a
specific issue in more than one country or the
exploration of an issue in a single country in ways
that can be expected to have relevance for other
countries. The geographic scope of the program
includes Western, Central, and Eastern Europe,
including Russia and Turkey, as they relate to
Europe, but not the Central Asian countries that
were formerly part of the Soviet Union. Special
consideration will be given to applicants seeking
support for dissertation fieldwork in one or more
European countries and to projects involving
parallel or collaborative research by both
established and younger scholars, including
projects designed on a transatlantic basis.
Marshall Memorial Fellowship (MMF): This
program provides a unique opportunity for young
policy and opinion leaders from 14 European
countries and the U.S. to gain an in-depth
understanding of societies, institutions and
peoples across the Atlantic. During the three- to
four-week traveling program, Fellows on both sides
of the Atlantic develop a broad knowledge of
political, economic, cultural and social issues in
their host countries through meetings with city
officials, schoolteachers, police officers,
government officials, business leaders, labor
organizers, farmers, activists, religious leaders,

academics and members of the community who
open their homes to Fellows. The foundation also
helps each Fellow set up a few personal
appointments that match his or her own expertise
and interest.
Transatlantic Environment Fellows Program:
Fellowships to younger-generation professionals
from Europe and the U.S. who are concerned with
environmental policies and sustainable change in
either government, non-government organizations,
business or think tanks. The goal of the program is
to further environmental leadership and encourage
sustained transatlantic cooperation and global
environment issues where the transatlantic
relationship is vital for progress. Awards range from
$9,000 to $40,000 depending on the length and
nature of Fellowship.
*Community Foundation Transatlantic
Fellowship:* Fellowships to five Europeans and five
Americans, beginning with a one-day orientation for
all Fellows in Washington, DC to sensitize
participants to transatlantic differences and
similarities to put the Fellowship into context.
Fellows then spend two and a half weeks in
residence at their host institution. At the conclusion
of the program, Fellows meet in Brussels, Belgium
to review and exchange the experiences and
impressions regarding community foundations on
the other side of the Atlantic.
Journalism Fellowship Program: Grants are
awarded each year to enable American journalists
to investigate and report on European subjects that
they would not otherwise have been able to cover.
The grants range from $2,000 for a feature-length
report to $25,000 for a book project, and include
funds for European travel, as appropriate. It is
expected that 20 to 30 fellowships will be awarded
each year to journalists from all regions of the U.S.
Internship Program in Berlin: Graduate students
and recent recipients of a B.A. are eligible for the
program, which offers an academic-year internship
in the fund's Berlin office. Strong research and
writing skills are important, as is the ability to work
independently. Preference is given to applicants
who have a demonstrated interest in U.S.-German
relations; whose academic work concentrates on
political science, public policy or history or whose
concentration on the German language is
complemented by courses in political science and
history; and who are U.S. citizens or permanent
residents. Fluency in written and spoken German is
required.
Peter Weitz Prize: Two awards are made to
promote the coverage of European issues by the
American media. A senior prize, worth $10,000, will
be open to all journalists covering European issues
for American newspapers and magazines, whether
they are based in Europe or the U.S. A $5,000
young journalist prize will be open only to journalists
who are U.S. citizens, based in the U.S. and under
35 years of age. Applicants may be nominated or
apply directly to be considered for the award. For
further information, e-mail Bridget Bodane, Asst.
Prog. Off. at: bbodane@gmfus.org.
Research Fellowship Program: Research
fellowships to academics (U.S. citizens and
permanent residents) to conduct research in
Europe. The program seeks to improve the
understanding of significant contemporary
economic, political and social developments
relating to Europe, European integration and
relations between Europe and the U.S. The program
is available for Dissertation and Advanced
Research. Deadline Nov. 15.
Transatlantic Fellowship: Fellowships to senior
policy-practitioners, journalists, analysts, business
people and academics undertaking original projects
that strengthen the transatlantic partnership.

Fellows work in residence at GMF's Transatlantic
Center in Brussels and/or at GMF's headquarters
in DC, where they have a bird's-eye view of
European and American policymaking processes,
as well as access to other fellows in both locations.
Depending on the nature of work, fellows may also
apply for travel stipends to conduct research at any
of GMF's five offices.
EIN: 520954751

5822
Giannini Family Foundation

57 Post St., Ste. 510
San Francisco, CA   94104   (415) 981-2966
Contact: John S. Blum, Admin.; Kenneth J. Blum,
Admin.
FAX: (415) 981-5218;
E-mail: info@gianninifamilyfoundation.org;
URL: http://www.gianninifamilyfoundation.org

Foundation type: Independent foundation
Limitations: Fellowships to promising young
postdoctoral investigators in the early stages of
their careers for research at one of the eight
medical schools in CA.
Publications: Financial statement.
Financial data: Year ended 12/31/2004.
Assets, $18,220,556 (M); Expenditures,
$1,004,450; Total giving, $574,500.
Fields of interest: Medical research, institute.
Type of support: Fellowships.
Application information: Application form required.
  Initial approach: Through any one of the
    accredited medical schools in CA.
  Deadline(s): Dec. 1
  Additional information: The applicant and his/her
    cooperating school should join in preparing
    information for presentation to the foundation
    in accordance with the instructions and
    application form; See Web site for further
    application information. Interviews required.
Program description:
Postdoctoral Research Fellowships: The
foundation considers applications from accredited
CA medical schools for grants to support a limited
number of annual fellowships. Awards are intended
primarily to help promising young postdoctoral
investigators in the early stages of their careers,
rather than to assist in the support of
well-established individuals to whom more general
sources of funds may be available. The area of the
proposed program of research may be related either
to basic science or to an applied field. It should in
some way lead to a better understanding of the
diagnosis, management, or prevention of disease.
Awards will be made for research work in any field
of medical science approved by the foundation and
a panel representing the research departments of
the participating medical schools. The research
project awarded must begin within the calendar year
it is granted. All research work by a Fellow is to be
conducted under the guidance of a qualified
investigator designated by the school. Fellows are
expected to devote the major portion of their time
to research, but may include some study and
clinical experience in allied fields. The medical
school must agree to supply adequate equipment,
laboratory facilities, and supplies. A report is to be
submitted to the foundation covering the principal
results of the research. All published papers should
carry a suitable footnote acknowledgement and one
reprint should be sent to the foundation.
Fellowships are open to U.S. citizens or permanent
residents who show promise of an unusual aptitude
and capacity for research. Applicants should have
M.D. or Ph.D. degrees, or be assured of receipt of
the degree prior to the beginning of the research

fellowship. Applicants must be sponsored by an accredited CA medical school. This fellowship cannot run concurrently with another federal or nonfederal fellowship. Applications for renewal of award will be competitive with all other applications.
EIN: 946089512

5823
The Gifford Foundation, Inc.
165 Farm Rd.
Woodside, CA   94062

Foundation type: Independent foundation
Limitations: Program development grants to individuals primarily in CA for community baseball programs.
Financial data: Year ended 05/31/2004. Assets, $18,354,600 (M); Expenditures, $1,054,892; Total giving, $918,759; Grants to individuals, 3 grants totaling $55,000 (high: $20,000, low: $15,000).
Fields of interest: Athletics/sports, baseball.
Type of support: Program development.
Application information: Contact foundation for current application deadlines, guidelines.
EIN: 943303273

5824
The Elizabeth Glaser Pediatric AIDS Foundation
(also known as Pediatric AIDS Foundation)
1140 Connecticut Ave. N.W., Ste. 200
Washington, DC   20036   (202) 296-9165
Contact: Pamela Barnes, Pres. and C.E.O.
FAX: (202) 296-9185;
E-mail: research@pedaids.org; URL: http://www.pedaids.org

Foundation type: Public charity
Limitations: Research grants and awards for the study of pediatric AIDS.
Publications: Annual report (including application guidelines); Informational brochure; Newsletter.
Financial data: Year ended 12/31/2004. Assets, $28,671,107 (M); Expenditures, $37,521,711; Total giving, $20,083,863; Grants to individuals, totaling $20,083,863.
Fields of interest: Pediatrics; AIDS research.
Type of support: Internship funds; Research; Awards/prizes.
Application information: Application form required.
Initial approach: Letter or telephone.
Deadline(s): June 13
Program descriptions:
Elizabeth Glaser Scientist Award: Given to a maximum of five scientists each year whose research will greatly impact children with HIV/AIDS. The award will provide $650,000 for a period of five years ($130,000 per year). Scientists are selected on the basis of their knowledge, innovation and ability to carry forward Elizabeth Glaser's vision of ending pediatric HIV/AIDS. The five-year duration of each award is designed to help build a network of scientists who will continue to impact pediatric HIV/AIDS research long after the individual grants have been utilized.
One-Year and Two-Year Pediatric Research Grants: Institutionally-affiliated investigators are provided with up to $80,000 in annual direct costs, for a period of performance not to exceed two years.
Short-Term Scientific Awards: Up to $5,000 is available for any project or portion of a project directly relevant to pediatric AIDS which can be completed in a short period of time.

Two-Year Renewable Scholars Awards: Provides up to $66,000 of salary support for two years to pediatric researchers with two to three years of postdoctoral research experience.
Student Intern Awards: These awards are intended to foster careers in pediatric HIV/AIDS research and care. The grants enable promising students to work with mentors who have extensive experience in the field.
EIN: 954191698

5825
The Glaucoma Foundation, Inc.
80 Maiden Ln., Ste. 1206
New York, NY   10038   (212) 285-0080
Contact: Scott R. Christensen, Pres. and C.E.O.
FAX: (212) 651-1888;
E-mail: info@glaucomafoundation.org; URL: http://www.glaucomafoundation.org/

Foundation type: Public charity
Limitations: Fellowships by nomination only to ophthalmologists and ophthalmology students in the last year of their residency who have recently completed a clinical glaucoma fellowship, and to ophthalmologists in developing countries for glaucoma research.
Publications: Annual report; Financial statement; Newsletter.
Financial data: Year ended 12/31/2004. Assets, $1,902,941 (M); Expenditures, $1,229,024; Total giving, $276,983; Grants to individuals, 13 grants totaling $276,983 (high: $50,708, low: $7,500).
Fields of interest: Eye diseases; Medical research, institute; Eye research.
Type of support: Fellowships; Research; Awards/grants by nomination only.
Application information:
Initial approach: Letter or telephone.
Deadline(s): July 15 for Shaffer Fellowship; for Clinical-Scientist Fellowships nominations accepted throughout the year including brief curriculum vitae and nomination letter from department chair
Additional information: Finalists are required to provide a detailed research proposal written jointly with their intended glaucoma mentor.
Program descriptions:
Clinician-Scientist Fellowship Program: These $75,000 one-year fellowships are provided to eligible individuals by nomination only to conduct a year of full-time laboratory research under the supervision of a glaucoma mentor. A portion of the fellowship will go to the institution to support the fellow's research. Applicants must submit a brief curriculum vitae and a letter of nomination from their departmental chair. Recipients are notified by Nov. 15 and fellowships commence on July 1.
Shaffer International Fellowship Program: Fellowships are given to ophthalmologists in developing countries to conduct glaucoma research at U.S. research centers where at least two-thirds of their time is spent in clinical or laboratory research. Applicants are usually assistant professors, and they must possess fluent written and spoken English abilities and be nominated by foreign department chairs who are their colleagues. Recipients receive a $25,000 stipend for living expenses, including health insurance and benefits. The host institution receives an additional $10,000 to support the individual's research efforts for one year. Recipients are notified by Aug. 15 and fellowships commence on July 1.
EIN: 133174839

5826
Glaucoma Research Foundation
251 Post St., Ste. 600
San Francisco, CA   94108   (415) 986-3162
Contact: Catalina San Agustin, Dir. Opers.
FAX: (415) 986-3763; E-mail: info@glaucoma.org;
Additional tel.: (800) 826-6693; URL: http://www.glaucoma.org

Foundation type: Public charity
Limitations: Research grants to individuals working on finding a cure for glaucoma. Fellowships by nomination only for study at a U.S. institution to ophthalmologists from developing countries who have been nominated by their department chairs.
Publications: Annual report; Grants list; Informational brochure (including application guidelines); Newsletter.
Financial data: Year ended 06/30/2004. Assets, $4,883,171 (M); Expenditures, $1,860,718; Total giving, $1,031,398.
Fields of interest: Eye diseases; Medical research, institute; Eye research.
Type of support: Fellowships; Research; Awards/grants by nomination only.
Application information: Application form required.
Initial approach: Proposal.
Deadline(s): Applications accepted between Jan. and July each year; Contact foundation for current application deadline
Applicants should submit the following:
1) Financial information
Additional information: Initial approach by letter for Shaffer International Fellowship contact Jennifer Rulon, Research Specialist.
Program descriptions:
Shaffer International Fellowship Program: Under this program, three ophthalmologists from developing countries are placed in academic institutions in the U.S. for one year, beginning in July. The foundation first selects five ophthalmologists who have been nominated by the department chairs in their countries. These individuals attend the American Academy of Ophthalmology's annual meeting under their Host-an-Ophthalmologist Program. During this one-week meeting, the candidates are interviewed by representatives from domestic ophthalmology departments at participating institutions. From this group, three recipients are selected. Upon completion of the fellowship period, the recipient returns to his/her country of origin to apply the research skills and knowledge they've obtained through clinical observation. Fellows each receive a $25,000 stipend and their participating academic institution receives $10,000 for required research materials and supplies for the fellow.
Clinician-Scientist Fellowship Program: Under this program, outstanding young ophthalmologists receive this one-year fellowship which provides a $75,000 stipend to the recipient to immerse him/herself full-time in basic science training through glaucoma research. A portion of the money will go towards research support. A maximum of one day per week must be set aside for clinical work. Candidates for this program should be in their last year of a medical residency. Preference is given to candidates looking at institutions that offer two-year fellowships, with the second year focused on basic research. Ophthalmologists currently in a clinical glaucoma fellowship or who have recently completed a clinical fellowship may also be considered. To apply, send a personal statement, a curriculum vitae and three letters of support. Finalists are chosen and invited to interview with members of the foundation's Scientific Advisor Committee, at the Association of Research in Vision and Ophthalmology (ARVO) meeting.

Pilot Project Grants Program: Grant money is provided to initiate new research in important areas of glaucoma research or to stimulate work examining critical issues in glaucoma. The primary focus is on funding collaborative pilot projects across disciplines. Typically, these grants range from $15,000 to $50,000 and may not be used for indirect costs or overhead. Researchers may receive support for up to two years, but a renewal application must be submitted. Any papers and abstracts resulting from research funded by the foundation must acknowledge this fact. Recipients are selected from proposals submitted in response to the foundation's periodic requests for proposals as well as from unsolicited proposals.
EIN: 942495035

5827

The Gleitsman Foundation

c/o Solomon, Ross, Grey & Co.
16633 Ventura Blvd., Ste. 600
Encino, CA 91436-1835
Application address: P.O. Box 6888, Malibu, CA 90264, tel.: (818) 995-0090; URL: http://www.gleitsman.org

Foundation type: Independent foundation
Limitations: Awards by nomination only to citizen activist leaders who confront, challenge and correct social injustice.
Financial data: Year ended 03/31/2005. Assets, $35,555 (M); Expenditures, $135,372; Total giving, $8,250; Grants to individuals, totaling $8,250.
Fields of interest: Human services; International human rights; Civil rights.
Type of support: Awards/grants by nomination only; Awards/prizes.
Application information: Application form required.
  Deadline(s): Nov. 5
  Additional information: Nomination available on Web site.
Program description:
  Gleitsman Foundation Program: Award recipients receive $100,000 to share, and each receive a specially commissioned sculpture.
Self-nominations are not accepted.
EIN: 954220291

5828

Glenn Foundation for Medical Research, Inc.

(formerly Paul F. Glenn Foundation for Medical Research, Inc.)
6187 Carpinteria Ave., Ste. 300
Carpinteria, CA 93014-5010
Contact: Mark R. Collins, Pres.
E-mail: mrc@glennfoundatlon.org; URL: http://www.glennfoundation.org

Foundation type: Independent foundation
Limitations: Grants for research on the biology of aging to those engaged in research on mechanisms of the aging process with one or more of the following objectives: delaying or preventing the onset of senility and prolonging the human life span, increasing the stature of the field of gerontology, broadening scientific understanding of the aging process, or advancing the field of biogerontology.
Publications: Grants list; Informational brochure; Program policy statement.
Financial data: Year ended 09/30/2004. Assets, $23,937,644 (M); Expenditures, $1,428,526; Total giving, $1,095,000.
Fields of interest: Biological sciences; Gerontology.

Type of support: Fellowships; Research; Awards/grants by nomination only.
Application information: Applications not accepted.
Program description:
  Research Program: Support programs are administered through internal recommendations or by anonymous outside advisors. No support is given for sociological, as opposed to biological, aging projects. All grants or awards must be free from allocations to administrative overhead by the recipient's institution.
EIN: 860710305

5829

Golden Apple Foundation for Excellence in Teaching

8 S. Michigan Ave., Ste. 700
Chicago, IL 60603-3463 (312) 407-0006
Contact: Greg Borkowski, Dir., Devel.
FAX: (312) 407-0344; Additional tel.: (312) 407-0433; URL: http://www.goldenapple.org

Foundation type: Public charity
Limitations: Awards by nomination only to full-time teachers at schools in Cook, Lake, and DuPage counties, IL, who spend the majority of their assignment time teaching one or more of grades 9 through 12, and student loans to nominated IL high school juniors to pursue teaching careers.
Publications: Annual report; Financial statement; Newsletter.
Financial data: Year ended 12/31/2004. Assets, $6,427,525 (M); Expenditures, $5,627,144; Total giving, $2,234,542; Grants to individuals, totaling $2,234,542.
Fields of interest: Education, research; Elementary school/education; Higher education; Education.
Type of support: Program development; Awards/grants by nomination only; Awards/prizes; Undergraduate support.
Application information: Application form required.
  Additional information: See Web site for further application information.
Program descriptions:
  Golden Apple Awards: Recipients receive paid full-term sabbatical at Northwestern University, IL, a $2,500 stipend, and an Apple computer system. While on their sabbatical at Northwestern University, recipients may take as many courses as they wish in any subjects they choose. As part of the sabbatical, the awardees design a seminar series as a group, to which they invite guest individuals who are making significant contributions in the field of education. Deadline Dec. 1.
  Golden Apple Scholars of Illinois: Juniors at IL high schools may be nominated by teachers, counselors, principals, or other non-family adults, to receive this renewable $5,000 student loan. Reclpients may use their loans for undergraduate tuition at any of the 27 participating IL colleges and universities. In addition, recipients participate in teaching internships and seminars at the Summer Institute. Scholars receive $2,000 each as a stipend during these summers. They also receive mentoring support from award-winning teachers. Loans are renewable for up to four years of study. The following are participating colleges and universities: Augustana College, Barat College, Benedictine College, Blackburn College, Bradley University, Chicago State University, Columbia College Chicago, DePaul University, Dominican University, Eastern Illinois University, Elmhurst College, Greenville College, Illinois College, Illinois State University, Illinois Wesleyan University, Knox College, Lake Forest College, Loyola University, Milliken University, Monmouth College,

National-Louis University, North Central College, Northeastern Illinois University, Northern University, Roosevelt University, Saint Xavier University, The School of the Art Institute of Chicago, Southern Illinois University-Carbondale, Southern Illinois University-Edwardsville, Trinity International University, University of Illinois at Urbana-Champaign, University of Illinois-Chicago, University of Francis, and Western Illinois University.
EIN: 363392992

5830

Goldman Environmental Foundation

The Presidio, 211 Lincoln Blvd.
P.O. Box 29924
San Francisco, CA 94129 (415) 345-6330
FAX: (415) 345-9686;
E-mail: info@goldmanprize.org; URL: http://www.goldmanprize.org

Foundation type: Independent foundation
Limitations: Awards by nomination only to individuals from six continents in recognition of significant achievement in the field of environmental protection.
Publications: Informational brochure; Newsletter; Occasional report.
Financial data: Year ended 12/31/2003. Assets, $31,455,437 (M); Expenditures, $3,225,187; Total giving, $823,000; Grants to individuals, 7 grants totaling $750,000 (high: $125,000, low: $62,500).
Fields of interest: Natural resources; Environment; Animals/wildlife, preservation/protection.
Type of support: Awards/grants by nomination only; Awards/prizes.
Application information: Unsolicited nominations not accepted; 21 organizations and a network of environmentalists are invited to submit nominations to the foundation.
EIN: 943094857

5831

Governor's Funding, Inc.

P.O. Drawer 730
Franklin, LA 70538

Foundation type: Independent foundation
Limitations: Awards to teachers and others in the LA public school system who have successfully implemented a character education curriculum or program within their classroom or school.
Financial data: Year ended 06/30/2005. Assets, $130,052 (M); Expenditures, $25,695; Total giving, $22,975.
Fields of interest: Education.
Type of support: Program development; Awards/prizes.
Application information: Applications accepted. Application form required.
  Deadline(s): Apr. 2
  Additional information: Applications available from public high school principals in LA.
EIN: 721428067

5832

William T. Grant Foundation

570 Lexington Ave., 18th Fl.
New York, NY 10022-6837 (212) 752-0071
Contact: Grants Coord.
FAX: (212) 752-1398; E-mail: info@wtgrantfdn.org; URL: http://www.wtgrantfoundation.org/

Foundation type: Independent foundation
Limitations: Research grants by nomination only to university faculty members in any medical or social-behavioral scientific discipline to study the development of school-age children, adolescents, and youth.
Publications: Application guidelines; Annual report; Financial statement; Grants list; Informational brochure; Informational brochure (including application guidelines).
Financial data: Year ended 12/31/2004. Assets, $262,365,521 (M); Expenditures, $12,634,629; Total giving, $7,019,240.
Fields of interest: Education, research; Mental health/crisis services; Pediatrics; Youth development; Children/youth, services; Social sciences, research; Psychology/behavioral science; Social sciences, interdisciplinary studies.
Type of support: Research; Awards/grants by nomination only.
Application information:
Deadline(s): July 1.
Additional information: Nominations from recipient's institution by proposal including supporting information; See Web site for further nomination information.
Program description:
William T. Grant Scholars Program: This program supports four to six talented junior investigators per year for five years to investigate topics relevant to the mental health of children, adolescents, and youth. Grants are by nomination only. Awards are made to institutions for support of selected faculty members for up to $60,000 per year for five years for a maximum total award of $300,000. This sum includes an indirect cost allowance not to exceed 7.5 percent of total direct costs. This money may be used only for the research efforts of the faculty member. Up to one-half of the faculty member's salary can be met by this grant, but it must not replace current university support for the faculty member's research efforts. In general, it is expected that a portion of this grant will be used for that percentage of the faculty member's salary equivalent to the time spent in research in this program area and the remainder used for support of the actual research. However, each institution will be free to propose how it will use the funds to best achieve the goals of the program. Faculty at all universities and nonprofit research institutions, both national and international, in any discipline are eligible. Only one candidate may be nominated from any department or research center of a university. Faculty so nominated usually should be in their first level or rank of appointment (usually at the assistant professor level). Support will be limited to faculty who are well-trained in research methods and wish to bring creative approaches to the study of problems relevant to the program interest of the foundation. They must demonstrate the ability to do sophisticated research in these areas rather than to pursue further training. Studies are sought that pursue creative and multi-method approaches, and/or that link behaviors and development during the school-age years to late adolescence and youth. The university must commit itself to the faculty member for the five-year period of appointment with space, remainder of salary support, and the free time to conduct the research. The setting in which the investigator will work should be thoroughly described. A mentor should be available to guide the research. Institutional resources must be available to conduct the research, and the setting in which the investigator can in turn influence colleagues and students should be outlined. The award should not duplicate other funding received or pending. A national selection committee will make recommendations for selection to the Board

of Trustees. After initial screening by the Selection Committee, finalists will be asked to come to New York for an interview with the Committee. Final selection will be made by the end of Mar.
EIN: 131624021

5833
The Grass Foundation
400 Franklin St., Ste. 302
Braintree, MA 02184
Contact: Steven J. Zottoli, Pres.
FAX: (781) 843-0474; E-mail: grassfdn@aol.com;
URL: http://www.grassfoundation.org

Foundation type: Independent foundation
Limitations: Fellowships to M.D.s and Ph.D.s, predoctoral and postdoctoral researchers in neurophysiology and allied fields of science and medicine.
Publications: Application guidelines; Informational brochure (including application guidelines); Program policy statement.
Financial data: Year ended 12/31/2003. Assets, $16,358,033 (M); Expenditures, $890,922; Total giving, $640,086.
Fields of interest: Biomedicine; Neuroscience; Medical research, institute; Medical research; Marine science; Biological sciences.
Type of support: Fellowships; Research; Postdoctoral support.
Application information: See program description for application information.
Program descriptions:
Grass Fellowships in Neuroscience: With these fellowships the foundation seeks to encourage independent research by young investigators, and to increase research opportunities for young persons trained for careers in neurophysiological investigation. These fellowships provide funds to support, for one summer, an investigator and his or her spouse and children at the Marine Biological Laboratory in Woods Hole, MA. Travel expenses are covered, unless the Fellow is coming from outside North America, in which case only the Fellow's, and not a spouse or children's, travel is funded. Laboratory research space rental, housing, and board are provided. Modest budgets for laboratory research expenses and personal expenses are also included. Normal tenure at MBL is 14 weeks. Applicants should be close to the award of a Ph.D. or M.D. Normally, persons continue to be eligible for the program through the third postdoctoral year. But exceptional circumstances in timing may be considered if fully documented in the application. Preference is given to those with no prior research experience at MBL and those who have demonstrated a commitment to a research career. Applicants should not try to combine the Fellowship with writing a dissertation. Applications must be received by Dec. 15 for candidates who wish to be considered for the coming summer. Successful candidates will be notified by Mar. 1. The application requires presentation of a research proposal, a budget (itemizing travel expenses, equipment shipping expenses, living accommodations), and a letter of recommendation from a senior investigator. Write in advance for more information.
Robert S. Morison Fellowship: The fellowship provides support for an outstanding young clinician who wishes to invest two years in basic science research training in preparation for an academic career. The program will be offered annually, but application for a second year will be reviewed on a competitive basis. Eligible applicants must be M.D.s who will have completed a residency in neurology, neurosurgery, or psychiatry prior to

beginning the fellowship; any concurrent clinical service responsibilities must be limited so as not to interfere with research training. The award provides for a yearly stipend of $40,000 with an additional $4,000 per year available for research expenses and travel to one scientific meeting. The application must be a joint statement from the candidate and sponsor that describes the proposed research. The sponsor is defined as an established investigator at a recognized institution who agrees to provide space and facilities within his laboratory and appropriate supervision for the accomplishment of the project. An additional letter of recommendation from the residency supervisor should be included, as well as the candidate's and sponsor's CVs. The research work must be done at a U. S. institution or other 501(c)(3) facility. Deadline for receipt of application in the foundation office is Nov. 1 fellowship will begin between July 1 and Dec. 1.
EIN: 046049529

5834
Gravity Research Foundation
41 Kirkland Cir.
Wellesley Hills, MA 02481-4812
Contact: Louis Witten, V.P.
Application address: c/o University of Cincinnati, 2600 Clifton Ave., Cincinnati, OH 45221

Foundation type: Operating foundation
Limitations: Awards to writers for the best essays on the subject of gravitation.
Publications: Application guidelines.
Financial data: Year ended 06/30/2002. Assets, $1,347,857 (M); Expenditures, $10,244; Total giving, $9,000; Grants to individuals, 9 grants totaling $9,000 (high: $3,000, low: $125).
Fields of interest: Physical/earth sciences.
Type of support: Awards/prizes.
Application information: Deadline Apr. 1; Applications must include three copies of a typewritten, double-spaced, English language essay and three copies of a summary paragraph of 125 words or less; Recipients notified after May 15.
Program description:
Awards for Essays on Gravitation: Five awards, ranging from $250 to $3,500 each, are given for short essays of 1,500 words or less. The organization holds an annual essay contest on the scientific study of gravity for the purpose of stimulating thought and encouraging work on gravitation. Cash awards are made for the best short essays, which are published in the Journal of General Relativity and Gravitation. Preference is given to essays written especially for these awards.
EIN: 046002754

5835
Great Basin Foundation for Biomedical Research
P.O. Box 3887
Reno, NV 89505-3887
Application address: 7350 Lakeside Dr., Reno, NV 89511-7608, tel.: (775) 853-2347

Foundation type: Independent foundation
Limitations: Grants primarily to individuals in NV for biomedical research.
Financial data: Year ended 07/31/2004. Assets, $442,666 (M); Expenditures, $312,658; Total giving, $105,038.
Fields of interest: Biomedicine; Biomedicine research.
Type of support: Research.

Application information: Applications accepted. Application form required.

Copies of proposal: 8

Deadline(s): Applications accepted throughout the year.

Additional information: Application by research proposal, not exceeding six pages, and including budget statement, biographical data of researchers, and evidence of approval by the relevant committee for human subjects or animal welfare.

Program description:

Biomedical Research Program: Applicants will be notified of funding decision within three months.

EIN: 943080694

5836

Peter Gruber Foundation

6000 Estate Charlotte Amalie, Ste. 4
St. Thomas, VI   00802   (340) 775-8035
Contact: Patricia Murphy Gruber, Pres.
Additional address: P.O. Box 503210, St. Thomas, VI 00805; FAX: (340) 775-8040;
E-mail: pat@petergruberfoundation.org;
URL: http://www.petergruberfoundation.org

Foundation type: Independent foundation

Limitations: Awards by nomination only to individuals for outstanding achievement in cosmology, genetics, justice, women's rights, and neuroscience.

Financial data: Year ended 12/31/2004. Assets, $23,861,375 (M); Expenditures, $1,782,004; Total giving, $1,225,788; Grants to individuals, 7 grants totaling $900,000 (high: $200,000, low: $100,000).

Fields of interest: Neuroscience; Genetics/birth defects research; International affairs; Civil rights, women; Astronomy; Law/international law.

Type of support: Awards/grants by nomination only; Awards/prizes.

Application information: Applications not accepted.

Additional information: See Web site for complete nomination guidelines; Deadline generally Sept. 30.

Program descriptions:

Cosmology Prize: Awards a gold medal and $200,000 cash prize to a leading cosmologist, astronomer, astrophysicist, or scientific philosopher in recognition of his or her ground-breaking theoretical, analytical, or conceptual discoveries. Nomination deadline Sept. 30.

Genetics Prize: Awards a gold medal and $200,000 cash prize to a leading scientist, or group of scientists working in genetics, in recognition of ground-breaking contributions in any realm of genetics research.

Justice Prize: Awards a gold medal and a $200,000 cash award. This is an international award given without respect to nationality, race, gender, ethnicity, or religious creed. Recipients are selected from the world community by a distinguished panel of international legal experts.

Women's Rights Prize: Awards a gold medal and an unrestricted cash award of $200,000, annually to an individual or group that has made significant contributions, often at great risk, to furthering the rights of women and girls and advancing public awareness of the necessity of these rights in achieving a just world. It may honor achievement in any area, including but not limited to, human rights, social welfare, education and the arts.

Neuroscience Prize: Awards an unrestricted cash award of $200,000, a gold medal inscribed with the recipient's name, and a citation describing the achievement for which the recipient is being honored, is awarded each year to a person or persons chosen by a distinguished advisory board of neuroscience experts. Nomination deadline to be announced.

EIN: 943185248

5837

The Harry Frank Guggenheim Foundation

25 W. 53rd St.
New York, NY   10019-5401   (212) 644-4907
Contact: Staff
FAX: (212) 644-5110; E-mail: info@hfg.org;
URL: http://www.hfg.org

Foundation type: Operating foundation

Limitations: Grants for doctoral and postdoctoral research in behavioral, social, and biological sciences, with the aim of providing a better understanding of dominance, aggression, and violence. Dissertation fellowship support in the same field is also available.

Publications: Application guidelines; Multi-year report; Occasional report.

Financial data: Year ended 12/31/2004. Assets, $85,618,206 (M); Expenditures, $2,347,839; Total giving, $887,853.

Fields of interest: Crime/violence prevention; Science; Social sciences; Psychology/behavioral science.

Type of support: Fellowships; Research; Postdoctoral support; Doctoral support.

Application information: Applications accepted. Application form required. Application form available on the grantmaker's Web site.

Initial approach: Letter or fax.

Deadline(s): Aug. 1 for postdoctoral research, Feb. 1 for dissertation support

Additional information: See Web site for complete guidelines.

Program descriptions:

Harry Frank Guggenheim Foundation Dissertation Fellowships: The dissertation fellowships of $15,000 are designed to enable the completion of the writing of the Ph.D. thesis within the award year. Awards are made for research clearly relevant to human dominance, aggression, and violence, but not necessarily restricted to studies of humans. Applications are evaluated in comparison with one another, but not with the postdoctoral research proposals. Applicants may be citizens of any country and studying at colleges or universities in any country. Final reports to the foundation are mandatory.

Harry Frank Guggenheim Foundation Grants for Research: The foundation sponsors an international program of scientific research and scholarly study concerning the causes and consequences of dominance, aggression, and violence. Awards will be made only for projects with well-defined aims clearly germane to the human case, but not necessarily restricted to studies of humans. The foundation will consider projects designed to reveal basic physiological mechanisms, to elucidate fundamental psychological processes, to analyze critical social interrelations, or otherwise advance knowledge from any discipline that will further the foundation's intellectual and practical objectives. Whatever the discipline and method, the principal criteria for support of a project proposed to the foundation are the same: excellence and relevance. While the average grant has been approximately $25,000 yearly, applications for greater or lesser sums will be judged on their merits. Most awards are in the range of $15,000-$30,000 per year. Proposals may be submitted for one-, two-, or three-year projects. All awards, however, are of one-year terms initially. Funding for second and third years of projects tentatively approved for more than one year will require annual applications for continuation and will depend upon evidence of satisfactory progress and an account of expenditures during the previous year. The principal objective of these short-term grants is to provide seed money to get new projects started rather then to lend continuing support to already well-established endeavors. Grants are made to individuals for individual projects either directly or to an institution on behalf of an individual. Requests will be considered for salaries, benefits, research assistantships, computer time, supplies and equipment, field work, secretarial and technical help, and other necessary items. Funds are not supplied for overhead costs of institutions, conferences, travel to professional meetings, or self-education. Final reports must be submitted to the foundation within six months after end of grant period.

EIN: 136043471

5838

The George Gund Foundation

1845 Guildhall Bldg.
45 Prospect Ave. W.
Cleveland, OH   44115-1018   (216) 241-3114
Contact: David T. Abbott, Exec. Dir.
Fellowship application address: c/o Robert Jaquay, Assoc. Dir., George Gund Foundation, 1845 Guildhall Bldg., 45 Prospect Ave., West Cleveland, Ohio 44115
FAX: (216) 241-6560; E-mail: info@gundfdn.org;
URL: http://www.gundfdn.org

Foundation type: Independent foundation

Limitations: Fellowships to promising professionals of the Cleveland metropolitan area, OH, to work inside the George Gund Foundation.

Publications: Application guidelines; Annual report (including application guidelines); Grants list; Informational brochure (including application guidelines).

Financial data: Year ended 12/31/2004. Assets, $484,344,362 (M); Expenditures, $25,635,725; Total giving, $20,822,137.

Fields of interest: Human services; Community development.

Type of support: Fellowships.

Application information:

Initial approach: E-mail.

Deadline(s): Jan. 3

Applicants should submit the following:

1) Essay

2) Letter(s) of recommendation

3) Resume

Additional information: Application by letter.

Program description:

George Gund Foundation Fellowship: This Fellowship provides an opportunity for promising professionals to work inside the Foundation, a philanthropic organization that plays a vital role in supporting the civic life of Greater Cleveland and in various national policy deliberations that impact our community. The Fellowship is a two-year, full-time commitment, requiring residence in Northeast Ohio during the term of engagement. The Fellowship experience will be tailored to the Foundation's needs and will include a wide range of substantive assignments including reviewing grant proposals, organizing and conducting site visits, and researching topics related to the Foundation's grantmaking interests. Each George Gund Foundation Fellow will receive a stipend of $40,000 per year. A full benefits package during the term of the Fellowship will also be provided by the

Foundation. Housing, transportation and other living arrangements are the responsibility of the Fellow. Successful candidates for this Fellowship will have a graduate degree and/or several years work experience in the nonprofit sector. Excellent writing skills and sufficient computer competency to carry out assigned projects are essential. A demonstrated desire to work in public service or the nonprofit sector is also important, as the Foundation views the Fellowship to be a valuable early career opportunity. The selection process is anticipated to be highly competitive.
EIN: 346519769

5839
James H. Hall Eye Foundation
P.O. Box 71288
Albany, GA 31708
Application e-mail for individuals:
dinorahh@bellsouth.net
URL: http://foundationcenter.org/grantmaker/jameshall/

Foundation type: Independent foundation
Limitations: Postdoctoral fellowships in pediatric ophthalmology and pediatric ophthalmology care for the indigent residing in GA.
Publications: Annual report; Financial statement.
Financial data: Year ended 09/30/2004.
Assets, $201,127 (M); Expenditures, $39,325; Total giving, $22,315; Grants to individuals, 3 grants totaling $22,315.
Fields of interest: Optometry/vision screening; Eye research; Children/youth.
Type of support: Fellowships; Research; Postdoctoral support; Grants for special needs.
Application information: Applications not accepted.
EIN: 510174948

5840
Donald D. Hammill Foundation
8700 Shoal Creek Blvd.
Austin, TX 78757-6816   (512) 451-0784
Contact: Cindy Thigpen, Secy.-Treas.
E-mail: ddhfound@aol.com

Foundation type: Independent foundation
Limitations: Research scholarships to financially needy individuals working at the dissertation level, in the field of special education, primarily in TX.
Publications: Informational brochure.
Financial data: Year ended 12/31/2004.
Assets, $4,489,471 (M); Expenditures, $243,174; Total giving, $174,503; Grants to individuals, 6 grants totaling $25,821 (high: $5,000, low: $1,000).
Fields of interest: Education, special.
Type of support: Fellowships; Research.
Application information: Deadline May 31; Initial approach by letter or telephone by Dec. 31 requesting application guidelines; Completion of formal application required, including letters of reference and proof of financial need; Interviews required; Recipients notified by end of June.
EIN: 742499947

5841
Hawaii Council for the Humanities
(formerly Hawaii Committee for the Humanities)
1st Hawaiian Bank Bldg.
3599 Wai'alae Ave., Rm. 23
Honolulu, HI 96816-2759
Contact: Robert G. Buss, Exec. Dir.
E-mail: info@hihumanities.org; *Tel./FAX:* (808) 732-5402; *URL:* http://www.hihumanities.org

Foundation type: Public charity
Limitations: Grants to Hiwaiian scholars to conduct research in the humanities.
Publications: Application guidelines; Annual report; Informational brochure; Newsletter.
Financial data: Year ended 10/31/2003.
Assets, $426,410 (M); Expenditures, $564,364; Total giving, $126,918; Grants to individuals, 5 grants totaling $10,310 (high: $2,500, low: $1,500).
Fields of interest: Humanities.
Type of support: Research.
Application information: Application form required. Application form available on the grantmaker's Web site.
> *Initial approach:* Letter, telephone or e-mail.
> *Copies of proposal:* 10
> *Deadline(s):* Varies
> *Applicants should submit the following:*
> 1) Resume
> 2) Proposal
> 3) Budget Information
> *Additional information:* See Web site for additional application information and programs.
EIN: 990153704

5842
Health Medicine Forum
3799 Mt. Diablo Blvd.
Lafayette, CA 94549

Foundation type: Operating foundation
Limitations: Awards a grant to a physician to assist in publishing a medical book.
Financial data: Year ended 12/31/2003.
Assets, $3,576 (M); Expenditures, $53,371; Total giving, $25,000; Grant to an individual, 1 grant totaling $25,000.
Fields of interest: Medical research, information services; Medical research, public education.
Type of support: Publication; Project support.
Application information: Applications not accepted.
> *Additional information:* Unsolicited requests for funds not considered or acknowledged.
EIN: 911858640

5843
Health Research and Educational Trust
1 N. Franklin, Ste. 2800
Chicago, IL 60606   (312) 422-2600
Contact: Mary A. Pittman Dr.P.H., Pres.
FAX: (312) 422-4568; *URL:* http://www.hret.org

Foundation type: Public charity
Limitations: Fellowships of $10,000 to individuals who have demonstrated a consistent pattern of leadership and innovation in healthcare.
Financial data: Year ended 12/31/2003.
Assets, $8,480,966 (M); Expenditures, $5,198,032; Total giving, $51,500; Grants to individuals, 11 grants totaling $25,500 (high: $10,000, low: $500).
Fields of interest: Health care.
Type of support: Fellowships.

Application information:
> *Initial approach:* Letter or telephone.
> *Additional information:* Contact foundation for application guidelines.
EIN: 362203931

5844
Healthtrac Foundation
135 Farm Rd.
Woodside, CA 94062   (650) 529-9533
Contact: Sarah Tilton Fries, Pres.
FAX: (650) 851-3830;
E-mail: sarafries@healthtracfoundation.org;
URL: http://www.healthtracfoundation.org

Foundation type: Operating foundation
Limitations: Prizes by nomination only to individuals who have greatly contributed to American health over the past decade.
Publications: Informational brochure (including application guidelines).
Financial data: Year ended 12/31/2004.
Assets, $1,673,497 (M); Expenditures, $136,097; Total giving, $86,500; Grants to individuals, 10 grants totaling $83,000 (high: $50,000, low: $1,000).
Fields of interest: Health care, formal/general education; Public health.
Type of support: Awards/prizes.
Application information:
> *Deadline(s):* May 15
> *Additional information:* Nominations from individuals not accepted; Nomination instructions can be requested by telephone, letter, or e-mail. Completion of formal, three-page nomination required, including: name, title, address, and telephone number of nominee and nominator with a summary of nominee's contribution; one-page description of the specific accomplishments of the individual; one-page summary of documentation; and names, titles and addresses of two references.
Program descriptions:
> *Fries Prize for Improving Health:* The foundation seeks to identify and honor individuals whose achievements have made the greatest contribution to the health of the public, to award accomplishment rather than promise, practicality rather than theory. One prize of $50,000 is awarded each year.
> *Health Education Award:* This $25,000 award is given to a health educator who has made a substantial contribution to advancing the fields of health education or health promotion through research, program development, or program delivery. Research is judged on the extent to which theoretical modes for changing health behavior, developed and applied in the research setting, demonstrate the potential to impact health outcomes in large populations. Criteria for program development include potential for broad applicability, quality of needs assessment and evaluation, and impact on the target population. Criteria for program delivery strategies include cost-effectiveness, penetration, and impact.
EIN: 943131228

5845
Heed Ophthalmic Foundation
c/o Cleveland Clinic Foundation
9500 Euclid Ave., Desk I-32
Cleveland, OH 44195 (216) 445-8145
Contact: Connie Gast, Admin.
FAX: (216) 444-8968; E-mail: fgutman@heed.org;
URL: http://www.heed.org/

Foundation type: Independent foundation
Limitations: Fellowships to U.S. citizens with exceptional ability to further their education in the fields of eye surgery and diseases of the eye, or to conduct research in ophthalmology.
Publications: Application guidelines; Program policy statement.
Financial data: Year ended 12/31/2004. Assets, $4,796,804 (M); Expenditures, $316,096; Total giving, $233,750; Grants to individuals, 84 grants totaling $165,417 (high: $3,333, low: $1,250).
Fields of interest: Eye diseases; Eye research.
Type of support: Fellowships; Research.
Application information: Applications accepted. Application form required.
  Deadline(s): Jan. 15
Program description:
  Research Grants: Applicants must be U.S. citizens and graduates of medical schools accredited by the AMA, and must agree to pursue education or research in the U.S. The fellowship is in the amount of $1,250 per month for up to one year of any one academic year. Preference is given to candidates who have completed the training requirements of the American Board of Ophthalmology and who wish additional training in a particular phase of their specialty. Special consideration is also given to candidates who plan to teach ophthalmology or conduct research in ophthalmology at medical schools on either a full- or part-time basis. This stipend may be augmented by funds from other sources.
EIN: 366012426

5846
Heinz Family Foundation
c/o Jeffrey R. Lewis
3200 Dominion Twr.
625 Liberty Ave.
Pittsburgh, PA 15222
FAX: (412) 497-5790; E-mail (for Jeffrey R. Lewis): jlewis@heinzoffice.org; URL: http://www.hfp.heinz.org/aboutus/philanthropies.html

Foundation type: Independent foundation
Limitations: Awards by nomination only to individuals for their contributions to the arts and humanities, the environment, the human condition, public policy, technology and the economy.
Financial data: Year ended 12/31/2003. Assets, $73,991,954 (M); Expenditures, $7,904,506; Total giving, $4,513,952; Grants to individuals, 24 grants totaling $877,360 (high: $250,000, low: $5,556).
Fields of interest: Humanities; Arts; Environment; Engineering/technology; Economics; Public policy, research.
Type of support: Awards/grants by nomination only; Awards/prizes.
Application information: Recipients are nominated by a foundation-appointed, anonymous council of nominators.
Program description:
  The Heinz Awards: Awards consisting of a medallion and $250,000 cash are given to individuals by nomination only, for their contributions in the areas of arts and humanities;

the environment; the human condition; public policy; and technology, the economy, and employment. Nominations are submitted by an anonymous Council of Nominators and are selected by the foundation's board of directors. In all categories, nominees must possess a passion for excellence, a concern for humanity, a knowledge of self, a "gritty" determination, and a broad vision. In addition, their accomplishments are significant; demonstrate an enduring and meaningful impact and aspect of a large, broad-based issue or problem; are appropriate and creative; and are replicable and replicated. The following are the specific criteria for each subject area: Arts and Humanities: Recognizes individual creators and thinkers who best preserve, teach, interpret, and advance the spirit of curiosity and faith in the power of the human mind. The Environment: Recognizes individuals who have confronted environmental concerns with a spirit of innovation and who demonstrate a blend of action and creativity. Human Condition: Recognizes individuals who have developed and implemented significant new programs to improve the human condition, and who have made outstanding efforts to protect and empower all individuals. Public Policy: Recognizes individuals who have had a positive impact on the process of public policy. Typically, recipients are elected or appointed officials; individuals who have significantly influenced the administrative, legislative, or regulatory process, including people who have identified, designed, and implemented changes to an area of public policy; or individuals whose impact on U.S. laws, regulations, and policies has resulted in the advancement of liberties and the betterment of society. Technology, the Economy, and Employment: Recognizes individuals who have created and implemented innovative yet practical programs to advance economic growth through job creation, technology advancement, competitiveness, and fair trade in a sustainable and environmentally safe manner.
EIN: 251689382

5847
Helmar Skating Fund
1515 Arapahoe St., Ste. 1525
Denver, CO 80202

Foundation type: Independent foundation
Limitations: Grants to U.S. Figure Skating Association recognized amateur ice skaters to help cover the costs of coaching fees and rink rental expenses. Grants are paid directly to specific coaches and rinks.
Financial data: Year ended 06/30/2005. Assets, $1,371,851 (M); Expenditures, $91,100; Total giving, $90,970; Grants to individuals, totaling $90,970.
Application information: Applications not accepted.
EIN: 841032757

5848
Drs. Henley & Smith Memorial Fund
c/o Wachovia Bank, N.A.
100 N. Main St., 13th Fl.
Winston-Salem, NC 27150

Foundation type: Independent foundation
Limitations: Scholarships by nomination only to medical students at the College of Medicine at Howard University, DC.
Financial data: Year ended 12/31/2004. Assets, $134,299 (M); Expenditures, $7,141;

Total giving, $4,000; Grants to individuals, totaling $4,000.
Fields of interest: Medical school/education.
Type of support: Support to graduates or students of specific schools; Awards/grants by nomination only; Graduate support.
Application information: Applications not accepted.
  Additional information: Scholarship recipients are recommended by the College.
EIN: 526061059

5849
Henrico Education Foundation
3820 Nine Mile Rd.
P.O. Box 23120
Richmond, VA 23223-0420 (804) 652-3869
Contact: Susan Stanley, Exec. Dir.
FAX: (804) 652-3856;
E-mail: sfstanle@henrico.k12.va.us; URL: http://www.cvco.org/education/henedf/about.htm

Foundation type: Public charity
Limitations: Grants to any teacher, guidance counselor, or school-level administrator employed by the Henrico County School Board for the creation of programs that address objectives or specific curriculum needs at their local school.
Financial data: Year ended 06/30/2004. Assets, $472,623 (M); Expenditures, $139,949; Total giving, $71,999; Grants to individuals, 28 grants totaling $56,750 (high: $5,000, low: $1,000).
Fields of interest: Education.
Type of support: Program development.
Application information: Applications accepted. Application form required.
  Initial approach: E-mail or letter.
  Copies of proposal: 5
  Deadline(s): July 14
  Applicants should submit the following:
    1) Budget Information
  Additional information: Application must also include proposal.
EIN: 541893274

5850
The Herbst Foundation, Inc.
30 Van Ness Ave., Ste. 3600
San Francisco, CA 94102 (415) 252-1220
Contact: Dwight L. Merriman, Jr., V.P.

Foundation type: Independent foundation
Limitations: Awards by nomination only to teachers in the San Francisco, CA, area.
Financial data: Year ended 07/31/2004. Assets, $59,218,480 (M); Expenditures, $3,454,498; Total giving, $2,997,057; Grants to Individuals, 8 grants totaling $16,000 (high: $2,000, low: $2,000).
Fields of interest: Education.
Type of support: Awards/grants by nomination only; Awards/prizes.
Application information: Unsolicited requests for funds not considered or acknowledged.
EIN: 946061680

5851
Hereditary Disease Foundation
3960 Broadway, 6th Fl.
New York, NY 10032 (212) 928-2121
FAX: (212) 928-2172;
E-mail: cures@hdfoundation.org; Additional address: 1303 Pico Blvd., Santa Monica, CA

90405; Tel.: (310) 450-9913; FAX: (310) 450-9532; URL: http://www.hdfoundation.org

Foundation type: Public charity
Limitations: Grants, fellowships, and awards for research on Huntington's disease.
Publications: Application guidelines; Grants list; Newsletter.
Financial data: Year ended 12/31/2004. Assets, $13,469,585 (M); Expenditures, $3,174,384; Total giving, $1,834,144; Grants to individuals, totaling $1,834,144 (high: $130,575).
Fields of interest: Genetics/birth defects research.
Type of support: Fellowships; Awards/prizes; Postdoctoral support.
Application information: Deadlines Feb. 15, June 15 and Oct. 15; Initial approach by letter; Completion of formal application required.
Program descriptions:
Research Grants: Grants of a maximum of $50,000 to individuals for research projects that contribute to identifying and understanding the basic defect in Huntington's disease. Grants are usually for one year with the possibility of renewal.
Milton Wexler Postdoctoral Fellowships: Fellowships, beginning at $43,000 salary, $12,000 for supply and $2,000 for travel expenses for first year, awarded to individuals conducting research that is highly relevant to curing Huntington's disease. Fellowships are provided for two years with the possibility of renewal for a third.
John J. Wasmuth Postdoctoral Fellowships: Fellowships to individuals for research projects dedicated to identifying and understanding the basic defect of Huntington's disease. Awards are based on a scale plus $5,000 for supplies.
Lieberman Award: Awards to individuals for innovative proposals leading to the treatment and cure of Huntington's disease. Awards can be funded for two years up to $75,000 per year. Areas of interest include trinucleotide expansions, animal models, gene therapy, neurobiology and development of the basal ganglia, cell survival and death, and intercellular signaling in striatal neurons.
EIN: 237376197

5852
The Heritage Foundation

214 Massachusetts Ave., N.E.
Washington, DC   20002   (202) 546-4400
Contact: Edwin J. Feulner, Pres.
Application contact for fellowships: Jonathan Butcher, Domestic Policy, tel.: (202) 608-6073, E-mail: FamilyDatabase@heritage.org
FAX: (202) 546-8328; E-mail: info@heritage.org; URL: http://www.heritage.org

Foundation type: Public charity
Limitations: Fellowships to candidates pursuing degrees in the social sciences.
Financial data: Year ended 12/31/2004. Assets, $151,065,828 (M); Expenditures, $35,829,107; Total giving, $42,898.
Type of support: Fellowships.
Application information:
Initial approach: E-mail or letter.
Additional information: See We site for further application information.
Program description:
Family and Society Database Fellowship: Up to ten fellowships are awarded each year to social scientists pursuing a Ph.D. Fellowships are approximately six months long with a stipend of $7,000. In addition, three fellowships are awarded each year (spring, summer, fall). These are

approximately three months long with a stipend of $2,000 per month.
EIN: 237327730

5853
Hellmuth Hertz Foundation

c/o The Northern Trust Co.
P.O. Box 803878
Chicago, IL   60680
Application address: c/o L.G. Harter, Baker & McKenzie, 815 Connecticut Ave. N.W., Washington, DC 20006-4078

Foundation type: Independent foundation
Limitations: Postdoctoral fellowships to individuals who have a doctoral degree from a Swedish university in the fields of natural science, medicine, or technology.
Financial data: Year ended 12/31/2004. Assets, $1,966,772 (M); Expenditures, $140,288; Total giving, $132,309; Grants to individuals, 3 grants totaling $132,309 (high: $44,103, low: $44,103).
Fields of interest: Medical school/education; Science; Engineering/technology.
Type of support: Fellowships; Postdoctoral support.
Application information: Applications not accepted.
Program description:
Fellowship Awards: Fellowships are given to individuals who have received their doctoral degrees from a Swedish university in the areas of natural science, medicine, or technology for further study and/or research in these fields. Eligible applicants are contacted directly by the foundation and given the opportunity to apply for funding. Solicited applicants must submit a detailed proposal of their planned research or course of study; a complete biographical record, including academic and professional history; a list of publications; date the Ph.D. exam will be taken, if not already completed; a reference letter from the institution where proposed research or study will occur; and an estimate of financial need. Grants are renewable, contingent upon satisfactory progress. Fellowship recipients are expected to embark upon careers in the stated fields.
EIN: 363741553

5854
The George E. Hewitt Foundation for Medical Research

16 Corporate Plaza Dr.
Newport Beach, CA   92660-7901
(949) 760-0554
Contact: George E. Hewitt, Pres.

Foundation type: Operating foundation
Limitations: Grants by nomination only to postdoctorates and M.D.s and Ph.D.s for medical research in CA.
Financial data: Year ended 12/31/2004. Assets, $9,490,741 (M); Expenditures, $243,994; Total giving, $201,041.
Fields of interest: Medical research, institute.
Type of support: Research; Awards/grants by nomination only; Postdoctoral support.
Application information: Applications not accepted. Applicants must be nominated by specific medical institutions in the southwest.
EIN: 953711123

5855
The Colin Higgins Foundation

P.O. Box 29903
San Francisco, CA   94129-0903
Contact: Vanessa Daniel, Admin.
FAX: (415) 561-6401;
E-mail: info@colinhiggins.org; URL: http://www.colinhiggins.org

Foundation type: Independent foundation
Limitations: Grants by nomination only for the foundation's Courage Awards, to individuals of the LGBTQ communities, who have endured overwhelming hostility and hate, yet have handled themselves with the utmost grace.
Publications: Application guidelines.
Financial data: Year ended 12/31/2005. Assets, $1,018,617 (M); Expenditures, $131,500; Total giving, $80,000; Grants to individuals, 3 grants totaling $15,000 (high: $5,000, low: $5,000).
Fields of interest: Youth development; Children/youth, services; Civil rights, gays/lesbians.
Type of support: Grants to individuals; Awards/grants by nomination only; Awards/prizes.
Application information: Application form required. Application form available on the grantmaker's Web site.
Initial approach: Online nomination.
Copies of proposal: 1
Deadline(s): See Web site for deadline
Applicants should submit the following:
   1) Letter(s) of recommendation
Additional information: Applications should be submitted online; Recipients notified within one to two months.
Program description:
Youth Courage Awards: Two to three annual awards by nomination only to recognize "ordinary but remarkable individuals who have endured overwhelming hostility and hate, yet have handled themselves with the utmost grace as they educate and enlighten others about the lesbian, gay, bisexual and transgender experience." Awards go to individuals in the following groups: 1) lesbian, gay, bisexual, transgender, queer and questioning youth who have stood up to hostility and intolerance based on their sexual orientation or gender and triumphed over bigotry; 2) lesbian, gay, bisexual, transgender and queer adults who have made a strong impact on the lives of LGBTQ youth or the overall LGBTQ movement; or 3) allies of any age working to end homophobia and discrimination against the LGBTQ communities. Awards are $10,000 each and include sponsorship to attend an LGBTQ conference.
EIN: 954084793

5856
Irma T. Hirschl Trust for Charitable Purposes

c/o JPMorgan Svcs. Inc.
P.O. Box 6089
Newark, DE   19714-6089

Foundation type: Independent foundation
Limitations: Awards to biomedical scientists in NY for careers in academic research.
Financial data: Year ended 10/31/2004. Assets, $58,627,036 (M); Expenditures, $2,886,888; Total giving, $2,661,000.
Fields of interest: Biomedicine research; Biological sciences.
Type of support: Research; Awards/prizes.
Application information: Deadline Oct. 15; Completion of formal application required; All

applications submitted by designated medical schools.

Program description:

Irma T. Hirschl and Monique Weill-Caulier Awards: Awards to talented biomedical scientists committed to careers in academic research, and in particular those who exhibit an exceptional potential for high quality productive research. Nominees are recommended by the Albert Einstein College of Medicine; Columbia University College of Physicians & Surgeons; Cornell Medical College; The Mount Sinai School of Medicine; New York University School of Medicine; and Rockefeller University.

EIN: 136356381

5857

Historical Research Foundation, Inc.

c/o Sanford Becker & Co.
1430 Broadway, 6th Fl.
New York, NY   10018   (212) 921-9000
Contact: Frances Bronson, Secy.
Application address: c/o National Review, 215 Lexington Ave., New York, NY 10016

Foundation type: Independent foundation
Limitations: Grants for historic and philosophic research and studies.
Financial data: Year ended 12/31/2004. Assets, $78,455 (M); Expenditures, $12,770; Total giving, $10,000.
Fields of interest: History/archaeology; Philosophy/ethics.
Type of support: Research.
Application information: Applications accepted throughout the year; Applications by letter including an informal description of the project, time of completion, and results anticipated.
EIN: 136059836

5858

The J. Edgar Hoover Foundation

P.O. Box 5914
Hilton Head Island, SC   29938-5914
(843) 671-5020
Contact: Cartha D. DeLoach, Chair.
Application address: 50 Gull Point Rd., Hilton Head Island, SC 29928

Foundation type: Independent foundation
Limitations: Awards to recognize individuals involved in law enforcement in the tradition of J. Edgar Hoover.
Financial data: Year ended 12/31/2003. Assets, $648,453 (M); Expenditures, $227,306; Total giving, $128,250; Grants to individuals, 65 grants totaling $78,250 (high: $25,000, low: $500).
Application information:

Deadline(s): Applications accepted throughout the year
Additional information: The J. Edgar Hoover Foundation administers the Law Enforcement Awards Program. Contact foundation for current application guidelines.
EIN: 526060988

5859

Hudson River Foundation

17 Battery Pl., Ste. 915
New York, NY   10004   (212) 483-7667
FAX: (212) 924-8325;
E-mail: info@hudsonriver.org; URL: http://www.hudsonriver.org

Foundation type: Public charity
Limitations: Research and travel grants restricted to projects for the study of the Hudson River.
Publications: Application guidelines.
Financial data: Year ended 12/31/2004. Assets, $33,105,529 (M); Expenditures, $5,175,031; Total giving, $2,577,946; Grants to individuals, 95 grants totaling $1,280,696 (high: $99,177, low: $401).
Fields of interest: Environment, research; Environment, water resources.
Type of support: Research; Graduate support; Undergraduate support; Travel grants; Doctoral support.
Application information: Deadlines vary; Initial approach by letter or telephone; Completion of formal application required.
Program descriptions:

Hudson River Graduate Fellowships: Awards up to six full-time research fellowships to advanced graduate students conducting research on the Hudson River system. A fellowship awarded to a doctoral student includes a stipend of up to $15,000 for one year, and an incidentals budget of $1,000. A master's level student fellowship includes a stipend of up to $11,000 for one year, and an incidentals budget of up to $1,000. The student's home university will be expected to be the primary source of support for materials and expenses required for the research. Deadline Mar. 5.

Tibor T. Polgar Fellowships: Provides eight summer grants of $3,500 and limited research funds to conduct research on the Hudson River. Undergraduate and graduate students are eligible, and each potential fellow must be sponsored by a primary advisor. Deadline Mar. 5.

Hudson River Research Grants: Awarded to researchers at colleges and universities. A preproposal consisting of a cover page, project description of no more than three single-spaced pages, and an estimated budget is due in early fall. Check Web site for current deadlines for both pre-proposals and full proposals.

Travel Grants: Available for travel related to the research goals of the fund. The foundation is particularly interested in visits by experts from outside the region to share new approaches to environmental questions about the Hudson River. Applications may be made at any time.

Expedited Grants: Available for the study of emergency situations affecting the Hudson River, such as unexpected natural or human-induced events, or research efforts for which additional funds are needed to enhance an existing research effort prior to the foundation's next formal funding cycle. Applications may be made at any time.
EIN: 133089956

5860

Howard Hughes Medical Institute

c/o Office of Grants and Special Progs.
4000 Jones Bridge Rd.
Chevy Chase, MD   20815-6789
(301) 215-8500
Contact: For general inquiries: Dr. Peter J. Bruns, V.P., Grants and Special Progs.; Dr. William R. Galey, Prog. Dir., Grad. Prog.; Stephen A. Barkanic, Prog. Dir., Undergrad Prog.; Dr. Jill G. Conley, Prog. Dir., International Prog., Precollege Prog., Research Resources Prog.; Dr. Dennis Liu, Prog. Dir., Educational Products
Additional tel.: (800) 448-4882
FAX: (301) 215-8888;
E-mail: grantswww@hhmi.org; URL: http://www.hhmi.org

Foundation type: Public charity
Limitations: Fellowships and research grants to medical students, graduate students, and non-U.S. scientists for the study of biology and related sciences. Academic institutions receive and administer these fellowships and grants on behalf of the individual recipients. Grants by nomination only to university science professors to create undergraduate science education initiatives.
Publications: Application guidelines; Annual report; Informational brochure (including application guidelines); Newsletter; Occasional report; Program policy statement.
Financial data: Year ended 08/31/2004. Assets, $15,396,735,408 (M); Expenditures, $640,853,700; Total giving, $57,627,987.
Fields of interest: Dental school/education; Medical school/education; Biomedicine research; Science, formal/general education; Biological sciences.
Type of support: Program development; Research; Awards/grants by nomination only; Foreign applicants.
Application information:

Deadline(s): Varies
Additional information: Competitions are announced on the institute's Web site and other sources; Interested parties should request program announcements for specific programs; Completion of formal application required for all fellowships; for HHMI Professors Program contact foundation for current nomination deadline/guidelines; Proposals required.
Program descriptions:

International Research Scholars Program: This program supports the research of outstanding biomedical scientists abroad. Each scientist receives research grants of $50,000 to $100,000 a year for five years. Recipients awarded grants in region-based competitions are in Canada and select countries in Latin America (Argentina, Brazil, Chile, Mexico and Venezuela) and in several countries of the Baltics, Central and Eastern Europe, and the former Soviet Union. Recipients awarded grants in a topic-based competition focused on infectious diseases and parasitology are located in 20 countries outside of the United States. For further information specific to this program and announcements of future competitions, consult the institute's Web site: http://www.hhmi.org/grants/funding/index.html.

HHMI-NIH Research Scholars Program (Cloister Program): Provides a year of basic research at the National Institutes of Health in Bethesda, MD, for U.S. medical or dental students. Students conduct research under the direct mentorship of senior NIH research scientists and live at the Cloister, the Research Scholars' residence on campus. Scholars receive an annual salary of $17,800; fully paid medical insurance; moving expense reimbursement; subsidized, furnished, on-campus housing; and an allowance for conference travel, related books and courses. Research areas include cell biology, epidemiology and biostatistics, genetics, immunology, neuroscience and structural biology. Deadline Jan. 10. Call the program's toll-free number, (800) 424-9924, for more information or see the institute's Web site: http://www.hhmi.org/cloister.

Research Training Fellowships for Medical Students: Provides funding for one year of full-time research for students enrolled in U.S. medical schools. Deadline early Nov. For further information specific to these programs, see the institute's Web site: http://www.hhmi.org/grants/funding/index.html.

HHMI Professors Program: This new program is designed to stimulate personalized undergraduate education by accomplished research scientists. For the first competition, individual four-year grants of $1 million were awarded to 20 faculty members for a total commitment of $20 million. Participation in this competition is by invitation only; each invited institution nominated up to two faculty members to compete for the awards. The focus of this competition is primarily on tenured faculty members with established research and educational programs in the biological sciences who are prepared to significantly expand their educational activities. For further information, see the institute's Web site: http://www.hhmi.org/grants/funding/index.html.
EIN: 590735717

5861
Humanities Tennessee
(formerly Tennessee Humanities Council)
306 Gay St., Ste. 306
Nashville, TN 37201 (615) 770-0006
Contact: Robert Cheatham, Pres.
FAX: (615) 770-0007; URL: http://www.humanitiestennessee.org

Foundation type: Public charity
Limitations: Awards by nomination to full-time public or private 3rd to 12th grade school teachers in Tennessee who have demonstrated excellence in teaching the humanities.
Financial data: Year ended 12/31/2004.
Assets, $411,343 (M); Expenditures, $1,093,323; Total giving, $123,195; Grants to individuals, 16 grants totaling $24,000 (high: $1,500, low: $1,500).
Fields of interest: Arts education; Music; Humanities.
Type of support: Fellowships; Awards/grants by nomination only; Awards/prizes.
Application information:
Initial approach: Letter or telephone.
Deadline(s): Jan. 31
Additional information: See web site for further nomination information.
Program description:
Teacher Awards: Awards of $2,000 fellowship to recipients to further their professional development in the humanities. Teachers of English, foreign language, history and social studies are eligible, as are teachers of art, drama and music, provided they employ a solid humanities approach to these subjects (as long as they emphasize the history, criticism and theory of the arts). The teacher's school will also receive a $1,500 grant to be used for the purchase of humanities instructional materials or for student humanities projects.
EIN: 620933337

5862
A. V. Hunter Trust, Inc.
650 S. Cherry St., Ste. 535
Glendale, CO 80246-1897 (303) 399-5450
Contact: Sharon Siddons, Secy.
Application address for individuals: P.O. Box 460668, Glendale, CO 80246-0668
FAX: (303) 399-5499; URL: http://www.avhuntertrust.org

Foundation type: Independent foundation
Limitations: Financial assistance by nomination from social service workers only for economically disadvantaged legal residents of CO. Grants assist case workers in acquiring durable medical equipments such as prosthesis, orthopedic braces, wheel chairs, eyeglasses and prescription drugs not covered by Medicare, Medicaid, or insurance for their clients, and for the working poor.
Publications: Application guidelines; Annual report (including application guidelines); Informational brochure (including application guidelines).
Financial data: Year ended 12/31/2004.
Assets, $62,964,966 (M); Expenditures, $3,214,978; Total giving, $2,391,234; Grants to individuals, 1,361 grants totaling $326,234.
Fields of interest: Human services.
Application information: Application form required. Application form available on the grantmaker's Web site.
Initial approach: Complete application.
Deadline(s): None
Applicants should submit the following:
1) Financial information
Additional information: Application should also include proof of CO residency and two forms of identification.
EIN: 840461332

5863
Hunter's Hope Foundation, Inc.
3859 N. Buffalo St.
P.O. Box 643
Orchard Park, NY 14127 (716) 667-1200
Contact: Debra Cagwin, Grants Admin.
Additional tel.: (877) 984-4673; FAX: (716) 667-1212; E-mail: hunters@huntershope.org; URL: http://www.huntershope.org

Foundation type: Public charity
Limitations: Research grants and fellowships for the study of Krabbe and other leukodystrophies.
Publications: Application guidelines; Annual report; Grants list; Newsletter; Program policy statement.
Financial data: Year ended 12/31/2003.
Assets, $1,136,657 (M); Expenditures, $909,360; Total giving, $317,127; Grants to individuals, totaling $317,127.
Fields of interest: Leukemia research.
Type of support: Fellowships; Research; Postdoctoral support.
Application information: Application form required.
Initial approach: Telephone.
Deadline(s): Apr. 15 and Sept. 15
Program descriptions:
Major Research Grants: $100,000 per year for two to three years will be awarded to senior investigators who are studying either basic mechanisms or treatment approaches to Krabbe disease or other leukodystrophies.
Pilot Studies: $30,000 awarded to researchers who wish to test new concepts or ideas related to Krabbe disease or ideas related to Krabbe or other leukodystrophies. Proposals will be funded at any time throughout the year.
Postdoctoral Fellowships: Awards to individuals who are within five years of receiving their terminal degree (M.D., D.V.M., Ph.D. or equivalent). Fellows will be working with senior investigators within their sponsoring institution on either basic mechanisms or treatment approaches to patients with Krabbe or other leukodystrophies. Fellowships will be awarded for two years with stipends ranging form $40,000 to $60,000 per year.
EIN: 161552315

5864
Huntington's Disease Society of America, Inc.
158 W. 29th St., 7th Fl.
New York, NY 10001-5300 (212) 242-1968
Contact: Barbara T. Boyle, C.E.O. and Natl. Exec. Dir.
FAX: (212) 239-3430; E-mail: rgraze@hdsa.org; Additional tel.: (800) 345-HDSA; Additional E-mail: jmurray@hdsa.org; URL: http://www.hdsa.org

Foundation type: Public charity
Limitations: Research grants and fellowships to investigators for research on Huntington's disease.
Publications: Application guidelines; Annual report; Newsletter.
Financial data: Year ended 09/30/2003.
Assets, $4,126,370 (L); Expenditures, $8,097,635; Total giving, $3,465,615; Grants to individuals, 40 grants totaling $3,465,615 (high: $100,000, low: $40,000).
Fields of interest: Genetics/birth defects research.
Type of support: Fellowships; Research; Postdoctoral support.
Application information: Application form required.
Initial approach: Letter, telephone, FAX or e-mail.
Deadline(s): Dec. 15
Program descriptions:
Research Grants: Awards a maximum of $40,000 for fellowships, $50,000 for grants, $100,000 for Coalition for the Cure grants. The grants go to investigators for new or innovative research projects on Huntington's disease. Awards are for one year and may be renewed for a second year contingent upon approval of required progress reports.
Initiative Grants: Awards of up to $20,000 for one year to investigators to support new and innovative work that may have relatively little preliminary data. The purpose of this program is to provide funding for time-sensitive projects that warrant immediate study.
EIN: 133349872

5865
Hyatt Foundation
71 S. Wacker Dr., Ste. 4600
Chicago, IL 60606
Contact: Carol A. Bock, Asst. Secy.

Foundation type: Independent foundation
Limitations: Annual awards to individuals for significant contribution to architecture. Posthumous awards are not given.
Financial data: Year ended 07/31/2004.
Assets, $14,507,008 (M); Expenditures, $662,412; Total giving, $546,325; Grants to individuals, totaling $511,325.
Fields of interest: Architecture.
Type of support: Awards/prizes.
Application information:
Deadline(s): Jan. 31.
Additional information: Contact foundation for current nomination guidelines.
EIN: 362981565

5866
IBM International Foundation
(formerly IBM South Africa Projects Fund)
New Orchard Rd.
Armonk, NY 10504-1709 (914) 765-1900
Contact: Ph.D. fellows: Prog. Mgr.
E-mail: phdfellow@us.ibm.com
URL: http://www.ibm.com/ibm/ibmgives/

Foundation type: Company-sponsored foundation

Limitations: Fellowships to Ph.D. students in areas of interest to IBM.
Publications: Application guidelines; Informational brochure.
Financial data: Year ended 12/31/2004. Assets, $164,195,806 (M); Expenditures, $11,918,255; Total giving, $10,505,172; Grants to individuals, totaling $1,632,437.
Fields of interest: Engineering/technology; Computer science; Engineering; Science.
Type of support: Fellowships; Awards/grants by nomination only; Doctoral support.
Application information: Applications accepted.
  Deadline(s): Nominations accepted from Oct. 15 to Dec. 14
  Additional information: Completion of formal nomination required; Nomination form available at foundation's Web site.
Program description:
  IBM Fellowship Grants: Provides funds for students pursuing Ph.D.s in areas of broad interest to IBM. Fellowships include a $15,000 stipend per academic year plus tuition and fees, with special fellowship stipends of $20,000 reserved for top finalists. Two types of fellowships are offered: Cooperative Fellowships are intended for students who wish to pursue a challenging technical career in advanced technology and product development as well as related research areas; Research Fellowships are intended for students wishing to pursue a career in research and will be administered by the IBM Research Division. Students receiving Research Fellowships will be offered an internship at one of the Research Division's laboratories; those with Cooperative Fellowships will be located at one of IBM's development laboratories.
EIN: 133267906

5867
IEEE Foundation, Inc.
445 Hoes Ln.
Piscataway, NJ   08854-4141   (732) 981-3435
Contact: Emerson W. Pugh Ph.D., Pres.
FAX: (732) 981-9019;
E-mail: foundation-office@ieee.org; URL: http://www.ieee.org

Foundation type: Public charity
Limitations: Awards by nomination only to technical professionals for exceptional achievements and outstanding contributions that have made a lasting impact on technology, society and the engineering profession.
Financial data: Year ended 12/31/2003. Assets, $23,830,330 (M); Expenditures, $2,461,243; Total giving, $1,735,923.
Fields of interest: Engineering school/education; Engineering.
Type of support: Awards/grants by nomination only; Awards/prizes.
Application information: Application form required.
  Initial approach: letter or e-mail.
  Deadline(s): Dec. 2, Mar. 14 and Aug. 15 for preliminary proposal, Jan. 13, Apr. 25 and Sept. 26 for full proposal
  Additional information: See Web site for further information.
EIN: 237310664

5868
The Illinois State Historical Society
210 1/2 S. 6th St., Ste. 200
Springfield, IL   62701-1503   (217) 525-2781
Contact: William Furry, Exec. Dir.
FAX: (217) 525-2783; E-mail: ISHS@eosinc.cm;
Application address: Tom Schwartz, Illinois Historic Preservation Agency, Old State Capitol Bldg., Springfield, IL 62701; URL: http://www.historyillinois.org

Foundation type: Public charity
Limitations: Awards to Ph.D. students for research in some part of Illinois history.
Publications: Informational brochure; Newsletter; Occasional report.
Financial data: Year ended 12/31/2003. Assets, $288,085 (M); Expenditures, $345,035; Total giving, $8,982; Grants to individuals, totaling $8,982.
Fields of interest: History/archaeology; Historical activities.
Type of support: Research; Awards/prizes.
Application information: Application form required.
  Initial approach: letter or telephone.
  Deadline(s): Feb. 1
Program description:
  King V. Hostick Research Awards: Awards are given to Ph.D. students doing research in any part of Illinois history, utilizing the Illinois State Historical Library collection.
EIN: 370767410

5869
Immune Deficiency Foundation, Inc.
40 W. Chesapeake Ave., Ste. 308
Towson, MD   21204   (800) 296-4433
Contact: Donald Weinapple, C.F.O.
FAX: (410) 321-9165;
E-mail: idf@primaryimmune.org; URL: http://www.primaryimmune.org/

Foundation type: Public charity
Limitations: Research grants and a fellowship for proposals focusing on primary immuno-deficiency diseases.
Publications: Application guidelines; Newsletter.
Financial data: Year ended 12/31/2003. Assets, $2,763,350 (M); Expenditures, $4,555,503; Total giving, $26,500; Grants to individuals, 34 grants totaling $26,500 (high: $1,000, low: $750).
Fields of interest: Medical school/education; AIDS; Medical research, institute.
Type of support: Fellowships; Research; Postgraduate support.
Application information: Application form required.
  Initial approach: Telephone or e-mail.
  Deadline(s): Nov. for research grants
Program description:
  Annual Fellowship: Provides a one-year stipend of $25,000 to qualified individuals (holding an M.D. or Ph.D. degree or equivalent) to pursue postdoctoral studies in the field of primary immune deficiency diseases. Deadline May 31.
EIN: 521214782

5870
Immunobiology Research Fund
828 Court St.
Woodland, CA   95695-3517   (530) 662-3911
Contact: Stephen C. Bick

Foundation type: Independent foundation
Limitations: Awards and travel grants to international researchers to attend institutions in the U.S. and for research in immunology, allergies, and rheumatology.
Financial data: Year ended 12/31/2004. Assets, $654,347 (M); Expenditures, $84,242; Total giving, $79,772; Grants to individuals, totaling $60,970.
Fields of interest: Allergies; Immunology research.
Type of support: Research; Foreign applicants; Awards/prizes; Travel grants.
Application information: Applications accepted.
  Deadline(s): None
  Additional information: Applications by letter, of no more than five pages.
EIN: 680070880

5871
The Impact Fund
125 University Ave.
Berkeley, CA   94710-1616   (510) 845-3473
Contact: Brad Seligman, Exec. Dir.
FAX: (510) 845-3654;
E-mail: impactfund@impactfund.org; URL: http://www.impactfund.org

Foundation type: Public charity
Limitations: Grants for the benefit of public interest in the areas of poverty law, environmental justice and civil human rights.
Publications: Application guidelines; Annual report.
Financial data: Year ended 06/30/2004. Assets, $633,786 (M); Expenditures, $1,140,934; Total giving, $242,000.
Fields of interest: Law/international law; Poverty studies.
Type of support: Grants to individuals.
Application information: Application form required. Application form available on the grantmaker's Web site.
  Initial approach: One to two page letter.
  Applicants should submit the following:
    1) Proposal
    2) Budget Information
  Additional information: See Web site for current application deadline and guideline information.
Program description:
  Impact Fund Program: Typically, no more than one outstanding major grant per grantee will be allowed, and $25,000 is the maximum amount for any one year. The majority of grants are in the $10,000 to $15,000 range.
EIN: 943161863

5872
Independence Foundation
200 S. Broad St., Ste. 1101
Philadelphia, PA   19102   (215) 985-4009
Contact: Susan E. Sherman, C.E.O. and Pres.
FAX: (215) 985-3989;
E-mail: artfellowships@independencefoundation.org; URL: http://www.independencefoundation.org

Foundation type: Independent foundation
Limitations: Fellowships for compensation and employment benefits to accomplished young lawyers, primarily in PA, employed in public interest service.
Publications: Application guidelines; Annual report; Grants list; Occasional report.
Financial data: Year ended 12/31/2004. Assets, $99,027,870 (M); Expenditures, $9,749,325; Total giving, $7,565,702; Grants to individuals, 20 grants totaling $156,200 (high: $10,000, low: $1,700, average grant: $7,500-$10,000).

Fields of interest: Legal services, public interest law.
Type of support: Fellowships.
Application information: Contact foundation for current application deadline/guidelines.
Program description:
Public Interest Law Fellowships: The fellowship assists the recipient in the repayment of their educational loans. The aim of the program is to enable some of the best and brightest law school graduates to come to the PA area and obtain employment with an organization based in the region that provides free legal services to poor and disadvantaged people.
EIN: 231352110

5873
Independent Sector
1200 18th St. NW, Ste. 200
Washington, DC 20036 (202) 467-6100
Contact: Diana Aviv, Pres.
FAX: (202) 467-6101;
E-mail: info@independentsector.org; URL: http://www.independentsector.org

Foundation type: Public charity
Limitations: Awards by nomination only to individuals who work in the nonprofit sector and to those who conduct research in that area.
Publications: Annual report.
Financial data: Year ended 12/31/2003.
Assets, $8,638,899 (M); Expenditures, $5,649,410; Total giving, $128,413.
Fields of interest: Community development; Philanthropy/voluntarism; Leadership development.
Type of support: Research; Awards/grants by nomination only; Awards/prizes.
Application information: Application form required.
Deadline(s): Jan. 31.
Additional information: See Web site for complete nomination guidelines.
Program descriptions:
Virginia A. Hodgkinson Research Prize: Awards in a first-place amount of $2,000 and second-place amount of $1,000 to individuals by nomination only for research on the nonprofit sector. Awards are presented to the author of a research report, book or article published in the last three years by researchers or practitioners from any discipline, nonprofit field or organization. All interested applicants should submit the official nomination form, which is available online, five copies of the research article, book or report, a brief biography of the author, and two letters of recommendation. Deadline June 18.
John W. Gardner Leadership Award: This award, given by nomination only, recognizes individuals working in or with the voluntary sector, who build, mobilize and unify people, institutions, or causes. The work of the Gardner Award recipient must have national or international impact, transform his/her chosen field and contribute to common good. Nominees may be of any age. Award is in the amount of $10,000 and is presented to recipient along with a statuette at the Independent Sector's annual conference.
EIN: 521081024

5874
The Infinity Foundation, Inc.
66 Witherspoon St., Ste. 400
Princeton, NJ 08542-3226 (609) 683-0548
Contact: Rajiv Malhotra, Pres.
FAX: (609) 683-0478;
E-mail: mail@infinityfoundation.com; URL: http://www.infinityfoundation.com

Foundation type: Independent foundation
Limitations: Research grants for scientific purposes to individuals, in the U.S., England, and India.
Financial data: Year ended 06/30/2005.
Assets, $4,122,107 (M); Expenditures, $255,203; Total giving, $107,310; Grants to individuals, 28 grants totaling $21,688 (high: $3,000, low: $100).
Type of support: Research.
Application information:
Initial approach: Proposal.
Deadline(s): None
Additional information: Contact foundation for current application guidelines.
EIN: 223339826

5875
Institut Francais de Washington
234 Dey Hall
Chapel Hill, NC 27599-3170 (919) 962-2032
Contact: Catherine A. Maley, Pres.
FAX: (919) 962-5457;
E-mail: cmaley@email.unc.edu; URL: http://www.unc.edu/depts/institut

Foundation type: Independent foundation
Limitations: Fellowships to individuals who are either in the final stage of their Ph.D. dissertation or who have held their Ph.D. for no longer than six years, for maintenance (not travel) during research in France for a period of at least two months. Research is limited to French studies in the areas of literature, art, economics, history, history of science, linguistics, social sciences and music.
Publications: Grants list; Informational brochure (including application guidelines).
Financial data: Year ended 12/31/2004.
Assets, $100,187 (M); Expenditures, $8,142; Total giving, $5,800; Grants to individuals, 5 grants totaling $5,800 (high: $1,500, low: $500).
Fields of interest: Art history; History/archaeology; Language (foreign); Language/linguistics; Literature; International affairs; Science; Social sciences; Economics.
Type of support: Fellowships; Research; Postdoctoral support; Doctoral support.
Application information:
Deadline(s): Jan. 15
Applicants should submit the following:
1) Curriculum vitae
2) Letter(s) of recommendation
Additional information: Application by two-page letter, including description of project, and research plans in France.
Program description:
Institut Francais de Washington: All awards are made through the Gilbert Chinard Fellowships, Harmon Chadbourn Rorison Fellowship and Edouard Morot-Sir Fellowship in Literature programs. Each year, three or four $1,500 fellowships are awarded for maintenance, not including travel expenses.
EIN: 526052929

5876
The Institute for Aegean Prehistory
3550 Market St., Ste. 100
Philadelphia, PA 19104 (215) 387-4911
Contact: Karen Velucci
FAX: (215) 387-4950; E-mail: instap@hotmail.com; URL: http://www.aegeanprehistory.net

Foundation type: Operating foundation
Limitations: Research grants to study Aegean prehistory with the expectation of research and publication under the direct supervision and control of the Institute.
Financial data: Year ended 06/30/2004.
Assets, $8,736,524 (M); Expenditures, $4,679,632; Total giving, $3,522,021; Grants to individuals, 155 grants totaling $1,977,934 (high: $60,000, low: $729, average grant: $5,000-$20,000).
Fields of interest: History/archaeology; Greece.
Type of support: Publication; Research.
Application information: Applications by letter, including resumes, project descriptions, relevance to Aegean prehistory, budgets, and references, accepted throughout the year.
EIN: 133137391

5877
Institute for Socioeconomic Studies, Inc.
20 New King St.
White Plains, NY 10604-1206 (914) 428-0400
Contact: Leonard M. Greene, Pres.

Foundation type: Operating foundation
Limitations: Research grants for study in socioeconomics and quality of life fields.
Financial data: Year ended 07/31/2002.
Assets, $1,693,883 (M); Expenditures, $746,247; Total giving, $41,000; Grants to individuals, 3 grants totaling $36,000 (high: $12,000, low: $12,000).
Fields of interest: Social sciences; Anthropology/sociology; Economics.
Type of support: Research.
Application information: Applications by letter, describing proposed research, accepted throughout the year.
EIN: 237167096

5878
Institute of Current World Affairs, Inc.
(also known as The Crane-Rogers Foundation)
4 W. Wheelock St.
Hanover, NH 03755 (603) 643-5548
Contact: Peter Bird Martin, Exec. Dir.
FAX: (603) 643-9599; E-mail: icwa@valley.net; URL: http://www.icwa.org

Foundation type: Operating foundation
Limitations: Fellowships to individuals 35 years or younger who have completed their formal education, for research outside of the U.S.
Publications: Application guidelines; Informational brochure.
Financial data: Year ended 12/31/2003.
Assets, $2,724,605 (M); Expenditures, $368,827; Total giving, $216,600; Grants to individuals, 9 grants totaling $216,600 (high: $51,252, low: $8,317, average grant: $23,000).
Fields of interest: International affairs.
Type of support: Fellowships; Research.
Application information: Application form required.
Initial approach: Letter or e-mail requesting brochure on current areas of interest.
Deadline(s): None
Additional information: Interviews required.

Program description:

Fellowship Awards: The purpose of the foundation is to identify areas or issues of the world in need of in-depth understanding and then to select young persons of outstanding character to study and write about those areas or issues for a minimum period of two years. Fellowships have been given—normally one or two a year—to men and women of varied academic and professional backgrounds. In keeping with its generalist and interdisciplinary approach, the institute's fellowships are not awarded to support work toward academic degrees, nor to underwrite specific studies, the writing of books, or programs of research as such. Full support, including living and travel expenses, is provided. In return, Fellows are required to write periodic reports to the Executive Director, which are circulated to persons in education, business, government, and the professions who are interested in the subject of the Fellow's inquiry. Applicants are invited to write to the Executive Director, explaining briefly the personal background and professional experience that would qualify them for the fellowship areas under consideration. If the candidates wish to have material returned, they should enclose a self-addressed, stamped envelope. Candidates may devise their own fellowships or request a list of the current areas of interest. For additional information and how to apply, consult Web site.
EIN: 131621044

5879

Institute of International Education, Inc.

809 United Nations Plz.
New York, NY   10017-3380   (212) 883-8200
Contact: Allan E. Goodman, Pres. and C.E.O.
FAX: (212) 984-5574;
E-mail: ainternational@iie.org; URL: http://www.iie.org/

Foundation type: Public charity
Limitations: Grants are administered for international educational exchange. Some grants included are for company employees. No loans are given.
Publications: Application guidelines; Annual report; Grants list; Informational brochure.
Financial data: Year ended 09/30/2004. Assets, $114,026,140 (M); Expenditures, $171,664,337; Total giving, $122,891,578; Grants to individuals, totaling $122,891,578.
Fields of interest: Visual arts; Architecture; Performing arts; Literature; Education.
Type of support: Conferences/seminars; Professorships; Publication; Fellowships; Internship funds; Research; Employee-related scholarships; Exchange programs; Awards/grants by nomination only; Awards/prizes; Postdoctoral support; Graduate support; Undergraduate support; Postgraduate support; Travel grants; Workstudy grants; Doctoral support.
Application information: Applications accepted. Application form required. Application form available on the grantmaker's Web site.
Deadline(s): Oct. 21
Additional information: See Web site for further information.
Program description:

Fulbright U.S. Student Program: Awards approximately 1,000 grants annually to American leaders for the opportunity to study and conduct research in other nations. Recipients aim to increase mutual understanding among nations through educational and cultural exchange while serving as catalysts for long-term leadership development. Grants generally provide funding for roundtrip travel, maintenance for one academic year, health and accident insurance, and full or partial tuition. Travel-only grants are also available to limited countries. Applicants must be U.S. citizens at the time of application and hold a bachelor's degree or the equivalent by the beginning of the grant period. In the creative and performing arts, four years of professional study and/or experience meets the basic eligibility requirement (Non-arts applicants lacking a degree but with extensive professional study and/or experience in fields in which they wish to pursue a project may also be considered).
EIN: 131624046

5880

Institute of Turkish Studies

c/o Georgetown Univ., Intercultural Ctr.
P.O. Box 571033
Washington, DC   20057-1033   (202) 687-0295
Contact: David C. Cuthell, Exec. Dir.
Application address: 1524 18th St., N.W., No. 1, Washington, DC 20036, tel.: (202) 328-6208
FAX: (202) 687-3780;
E-mail: institute_turkishstudies@yahoo.com;
URL: http://www.turkishstudies.org

Foundation type: Independent foundation
Limitations: Grants to the academic community of U.S. specialists in the field of Turkish studies.
Publications: Application guidelines; Grants list; Informational brochure; Multi-year report.
Financial data: Year ended 09/30/2004. Assets, $150,571 (M); Expenditures, $144,138; Total giving, $36,085; Grants to individuals, 12 grants totaling $25,050 (high: $5,000, low: $800).
Type of support: Research; Postdoctoral support; Travel grants; Doctoral support.
Application information:
Deadline(s): Mar. 1
Applicants should submit the following:
1) Letter(s) of recommendation
2) Proposal
3) Budget Information
Additional information: Typed letter not exceeding 12 pages.
Program description:

Travel Awards: Grants include matching travel awards to conferences for post-doctoral scholars (up to one-half of airfare), round-trip airfare to Turkey for post-doctoral scholars, dissertation writing grants (up to $3,000) for Ph.D. candidates who are teaching more than half-time, teaching aids grants, and matching post-doctoral released time grants.
EIN: 521294029

5881

Intel Foundation

5200 N.E. Elam Young Pkwy., AG6-601
Hillsboro, OR   97124-6497
Contact: Lisa Siewert, Admin.
FAX: (503) 456-1539;
E-mail: intel.foundation@intel.com; URL: http://www.intel.com/community/index.htm

Foundation type: Company-sponsored foundation
Limitations: Scholarships, research awards, and fellowships to American and Canadian doctoral and undergraduate students for research work in the sciences and engineering disciplines.
Publications: Corporate giving report.
Financial data: Year ended 12/31/2004. Assets, $83,912,682 (M); Expenditures, $34,561,326; Total giving, $34,561,326.

Fields of interest: Engineering; African Americans/Blacks; Hispanics/Latinos; Native Americans/American Indians; Women.
Type of support: Fellowships; Research; Awards/prizes; Postdoctoral support; Graduate support; Undergraduate support; Travel grants.
Application information: Application form required.
Program descriptions:

Graduate Fellowship Program: Fellowships, including a stipend of $1,800 per month for up to five years of doctoral study and an annual gift of $2,000 for travel, to graduate students at the doctoral level, to study science and technology, and who are interested in the semiconductor industry. Fellowships are open to students who are U.S. or Canadian citizens or permanent residents; are pursuing or planning to pursue a Ph.D. degree with research relevant to microelectronics under the guidance of an SRC- (Semiconductor Research Corporation) sponsored faculty member; will be performing research under an SRC-funded contract; and are willing to provide a copy of his/her Ph.D. dissertation to the SRC. It is expected, although not required, that GFP Fellows will complete the Ph.D. in an area relevant to microelectronics and that upon completion of the program, will secure employment with an SRC member or U.S. government agency, or a faculty position in an accredited four-year U.S. or Canadian college or university. Visit http://www.src.org for additional information.

Master's Scholarship Program: Awards scholarships to graduates in the microelectronics field who are studying for their master's degree, including stipend of $1,800 per month for up to two years and travel expenses for an annual conference. Scholarships are open to students who are women or members of an underrepresented minority category (African American, Hispanic or Native American); meet admission requirements for graduate school at an SRC-participating university; are U.S. or Canadian citizens or have permanent resident status; are planning to pursue a master's degree with research relevant to microelectronics under the guidance of an SRC-sponsored faculty member; will be performing research under an SRC-funded contract; and are willing to provide a copy of his/her master's thesis to the SRC. Scholarships are offered through a national competition and are awarded based on minority or female status and outstanding academic achievement.

International Graduate Fellowship Program: Awards fellowships to international doctoral students who are studying for their Ph.D. in the microelectronics field, including an $1,800 per month stipend and travel expenses to annual conference. Recipients must hold citizenship in a country other than the U.S. or Canada or countries defined by the U.S. as "export-controlled or embargoed countries"; meet the high academic standard set for all SRC Fellows; are pursuing or planning to pursue a Ph.D. degree with research relevant to microelectronics under the guidance of an SRC-sponsored faculty member; will be performing research defined in an SRC-funded contract; and are willing to provide a copy of his/her Ph.D. dissertation to the SRC. It is expected that IGFP Fellows will complete their Ph.D. in an area relevant to microelectronics and that upon completion of the program, will secure employment with an SRC member company or a faculty position in an accredited four-year college or university.

Intel Student Research Contest: This program gives undergraduates the opportunity to conduct research in the fields of science and engineering. Each researcher whose proposal is selected will receive up to $2,000 for their project. Winners will

present their results at the Intel Research Day event, held in Santa Clara, CA. Visit http://www.intel.com/research/awards/unitedstates.htm for more information. Deadline June 13. Send queries to researchawards@intel.com.
EIN: 943092928

5882

The International Association of Culinary Professionals Foundation

(formerly Cooking Advancement Research and Education Foundation)
304 W. Liberty St., Ste. 201
Louisville, KY   40202-3068   (502) 583-3783
Contact: Christopher Papagni, Secy.
FAX: (502) 589-3602;
E-mail: emcknight@hqtrs.com; URL: http://www.iacpfoundation.com/

Foundation type: Public charity
Limitations: Grants for research in the culinary arts and sciences.
Publications: Application guidelines; Annual report; Financial statement; Newsletter.
Financial data: Year ended 06/30/2004. Assets, $244,734 (M); Expenditures, $255,052; Total giving, $26,000; Grants to individuals, 6 grants totaling $26,000 (high: $5,000, low: $1,000).
Fields of interest: Business/industry.
Type of support: Research.
Application information:
Deadline(s): Dec. 1
Additional information: Contact foundation for current application guidelines.
EIN: 521333505

5883

International Association of Fire Fighters Burn Foundation

(also known as IAFF Burn Foundation)
1750 New York Ave., N.W., Ste. 300
Washington, DC   20006-5395   (202) 737-8484
FAX: (202) 737-8418;
E-mail: IAFFBurnFdn@aol.com; URL: http://www.iaff.org

Foundation type: Public charity
Limitations: Grants for burn injury research.
Publications: Annual report; Informational brochure; Program policy statement.
Financial data: Year ended 09/30/2004. Assets, $466,953 (M); Expenditures, $763,992; Total giving, $155,000.
Fields of interest: Burn centers; Medical research, institute.
Type of support: Research.
Application information:
Initial approach: Letter or telephone.
Deadline(s): Jan. 12
Additional information: See Web site for guideline information.
EIN: 521256006

5884

International Burn Foundation of the United States

P.O. Box 24386
Denver, CO   80224-0386

Foundation type: Independent foundation

Limitations: Awards by nomination only to individuals who have made an outstanding contribution to any aspect of the burn field.
Financial data: Year ended 12/31/2004. Assets, $820,740 (M); Expenditures, $45,895; Total giving, $35,000; Grants to individuals, totaling $35,000.
Fields of interest: Medical research, institute.
Type of support: Awards/grants by nomination only; Awards/prizes.
Application information:
Initial approach: Letter.
Deadline(s): Jan.
Additional information: Contact foundation for current application guidelines.
Program description:
Tanner-Vandeput-Boswick Burn Prize: The prize consists of a pin and a cash award. The prize is presented every four years.
EIN: 742345015

5885

The International Center for Journalists, Inc.

1616 H St. N.W., 3rd Fl.
Washington, DC   20006   (202) 737-3700
Contact: Susan Talalay, V.P., Devel. and Comms.
FAX: (202) 737-0530; E-mail: Stalalay@icfj.org; URL: http://www.icfj.org

Foundation type: Public charity
Limitations: Fellowships and internships to journalists who have exhibited outstanding personal and professional achievement, including technical, managerial and business aspects of a free press and who exhibit a spirit of adventure and willingness to face personal and professional hardships in the field.
Publications: Application guidelines.
Financial data: Year ended 12/31/2003. Assets, $10,454,287 (M); Expenditures, $5,623,249; Total giving, $761,948; Grants to individuals, 132 grants totaling $761,948.
Fields of interest: Journalism/publishing; Public affairs; Hispanics/Latinos.
Type of support: Fellowships; Internship funds; Research; Exchange programs; Foreign applicants; Travel grants.
Application information: Application form required.
Deadline(s): Varies
Additional information: See Web site for additional information and application forms.
Program descriptions:
World Affairs Journalism Program: This fellowship is aimed at news managers, editors, commentary writers and other gatekeepers of news. Twelve experienced media professionals are selected as recipients to travel overseas for one to three weeks on assignment and will explore issues of local importance and submit articles to their home newspapers for publication. Deadline June 28.
Knight International Press Fellowships: Annually awards fellowships to 22 American journalists and news executives to spend from two to nine months abroad in a variety of teaching, training, consulting and assistance roles, usually working in conjunction with overseas media centers. The program pays expenses and provides a stipend. Contact the Center by FAX or mail for detailed application and program guidelines. Applications are competitive and are reviewed on a rotating basis throughout the year. Deadlines Feb. 15 and Aug. 15.
McGee Journalism Fellowships in Southern Africa: Fellowship to a U.S. journalist each year to travel to one or more countries in southern Africa. For three to four months, the journalist will share his or her

expertise with colleagues in the region by consulting in newsrooms, leading workshops or teaching at a university. Deadline Apr. 16.
Arthur F. Bellows Fellowship Program: Fellowships for two months are awarded to young American and German print broadcast journalists. Ten participants from each country work at counterpart news organizations. Travel expenses and stipend are provided. Recipients should be working journalists in any news media, under the age of 35, with demonstrated journalistic talent and have an interest in U.S.-European affairs. Deadline Mar. 1.
ICFJ-KKC Journalism Fellowship in Japan: Fellowships to five selected American journalists each year to travel to Japan for a two-week working program in the fall that includes visits to news media, business leaders and government officials. The second week of the program is devoted to independent research and reporting projects designed by each participant. Applicants must be U.S. citizens with at least five years of media experience and no substantial previous travel to Japan.
Ford Environmental Journalism Fellowships: Fellowships to two U.S. environmental reporters to travel overseas to train journalists and to report on critical environmental issues. Fellows are posted, for up to three months, in the country of their choice, but preference is given to countries or regions in the developing world or with new democracies. On assignment, fellows work closely with host organizations, conduct workshops, seminars and lectures, and consult with local media organizations. Fellowships are open to U.S. environmental journalists and journalism teachers. The program pays a stipend plus travel expenses. Deadline Nov. 6.
Scripps Howard Internship for Latin American Journalism Students: Internships for ten to fourteen weeks to Latin American journalism students to work at the Scripps Howard News Service. The internship is designed to give students from Latin America and the Caribbean an opportunity to cover events in the U.S. capitol, as well as to report and write feature stories for the Scripps Howard Foundation wire. Interns must be journalism or communications students at Latin American or Caribbean universities and intend on pursuing careers in print journalism after graduation. Recipients must also be fluent in spoken and written English. Selected interns will work in one of three periods: Jan. to Apr.; June to Aug.; or Sept. to Dec. Internship pays for travel expenses to and from the U.S., an apartment, shared by interns, in Washington, DC, living and transportation costs and a health insurance policy. Deadlines Nov. 1 for Jan. to Apr.; Apr. 1 for June to Aug.; and July 1 for Sept. to Dec.
EIN: 112724905

5886

International Fellowships Fund

(also known as IFF)
809 United Nations Plz.
New York, NY   10017   (212) 984-5558
Contact: Joan Dassin, Exec. Dir.
FAX: (212) 984-5594; URL: http://www.fordifp.net

Foundation type: Public charity
Limitations: Fellowships to individuals from Africa, Asia, Latin America, the Middle East, and Russia for up to three years of graduate-level study.
Publications: Informational brochure.
Financial data: Year ended 09/30/2003. Assets, $298,820,593 (M); Expenditures,

$28,704,000; Total giving, $26,458,796; Grants to individuals, totaling $26,458,796.

Type of support: Fellowships; Foreign applicants; Graduate support.

Application information: Applications not accepted.

Additional information: See Web site for general guidelines and links to additional local guidelines at Web sites of partner organizations outside the United States where selections are managed and held.

Program description:

International Fellowships Program (IFP): Fellows are expected to use this education to become leaders in their respective fields, furthering development in their own countries and greater economic and social justice worldwide. Fellows may enroll in master's or doctoral programs and may pursue any academic discipline or field of study that is consistent with the interests of the Ford Foundation. Fellows receive placement guidance and may enroll in any university in the world to which they can gain admission up to approximately one year following selection. Funds are available for short-term pre-academic training, test and application fees, tuition and related fees, living expenses, health insurance, books, computer, travel, language training, professional development, and leadership development.

EIN: 134162722

5887

International Gospel Mission
15 Santa Rida
Irvine, CA   92606
Contact: Eugene J. Choy, Pres.

Foundation type: Operating foundation
Limitations: Grants to individuals for missions, primarily in CA.
Financial data: Year ended 12/31/2002. Assets, $679,321 (M); Expenditures, $41,979; Total giving, $36,300; Grants to individuals, 3 grants totaling $12,000 (high: $4,000, low: $4,000).
Fields of interest: Media/communications; Human services; Christian agencies & churches.
Type of support: Grants for special needs.
Application information:
Initial approach: Letter.
Additional information: Contact foundation for current application deadline/guidelines.
EIN: 953842453

5888

International Myeloma Foundation
12650 Riverside Dr., Ste. 206
North Hollywood, CA   91607-3421
(818) 487-7455
Contact: Susie Novis, Pres.
FAX: (818) 487-7454;
E-mail: TheIMF@myeloma.org; Additional tel.: (800) 452-2873; URL: http://www.myeloma.org

Foundation type: Public charity
Limitations: Research grants to investigators seeking methods of better treatments, management, prevention and a cure for myeloma.
Financial data: Year ended 12/31/2003. Assets, $1,047,886 (M); Expenditures, $2,850,794; Total giving, $160,000; Grants to individuals, 4 grants totaling $160,000 (high: $40,000, low: $40,000).
Fields of interest: Cancer research.
Type of support: Seed money; Internship funds; Research; Awards/prizes; Travel grants.

Application information: Application form required.
Deadline(s): Aug. 31
Additional information: See Web site for further information.
EIN: 954296919

5889

International Reading Association, Inc.
800 Barksdale Rd.
P.O. Box 8139
Newark, DE   19714-8139   (800) 336-7323
Contact: Alan Farstrup, Exec. Dir.
FAX: (302) 731-1057;
E-mail: pubinfo@reading.org; Additional tel.: (302) 731-1600, outside of the U.S. and Canada;
URL: http://www.reading.org

Foundation type: Public charity
Limitations: Research awards, grants, professional development awards, and fellowships to those in the fields of reading and reading education.
Financial data: Year ended 06/30/2004. Assets, $30,425,503 (M); Expenditures, $16,751,772; Total giving, $348,942; Grants to individuals, 37 grants totaling $50,746 (high: $6,000, low: $167).
Fields of interest: Language/linguistics; Elementary/secondary education; Elementary school/education; Adult education—literacy, basic skills & GED.
Type of support: Fellowships; Research; Awards/prizes.
Application information: Applications accepted. Application form required. Application form available on the grantmaker's Web site.
Initial approach: E-mail.
Deadline(s): Varies
Additional information: Full program listings can be found on the foundation's Web site. For additional application guidelines, contact the foundation at: research@reading.org.
Program descriptions:
Dina Feitelson Award: The Dina Feitelson Award is a $500 award established to honor the memory of Dina Feitelson by recognizing an outstanding empirical study published in English in a refereed journal. The work should report on one or more aspects of literacy acquisition, such as phonemic awareness, the alphabetic principle, bilingualism, or cross-cultural studies of beginning reading. Works may be submitted by the author or anyone else. Nomination for the Dina Feitelson Award is open to all literacy professionals. The deadline for submission is September 15.
Elva Knight Research Grant: The Elva Knight Research Grant provides up to $10,000 for research in reading and literacy. Contingent upon available funds in any given year, as many as four grants may be awarded. Projects should be completed within 2 years and may be carried out using any research method or approach so long as the focus of the project is on research in reading or literacy. Activities such as developing new programs or instructional materials are not eligible for funding except to the extent that these activities are necessary procedures for the conduct of the research. Each year, it is expected that at least one grant will be awarded to a researcher outside the United States and Canada and that one grant will be awarded to a teacher-initiated research project subject to being of high quality. Non-North Americans and classroom teachers are especially encouraged to apply. Deadline for submission is January 15.
Helen M. Robinson Grant: The Helen M. Robinson Grant is a $1,500 award given annually to assist doctoral students at the early stages of their

dissertation research in the area of reading and literacy. Applicants must be Association members. Completed applications must be received by January 15.
Jeanne S. Chall Research Fellowship: The Jeanne S. Chall Research Fellowship is a $6,000 grant established to encourage and support reading research by promising scholars. Its special emphasis is to support research efforts in the following areas: beginning reading (theory, research, and practice that improves the effectiveness of learning to read); readability (methods of predicting the difficulty of texts); reading difficulty (diagnosis, treatment, and prevention); stages of reading development; the relation of vocabulary to reading; and diagnosing and teaching adults with limited reading ability. The deadline for submission is January 15.
Nila Banton Smith Research Dissemination Support Grant: The Nila Banton Smith Research Dissemination Support Grant will provide funding of up to $5,000 to support a member of the International Reading Association in spending from 2 to 10 months working on a research dissemination activity. Completed applications must be received by January 15.
Outstanding Dissertation of the Year Award: The Outstanding Dissertation of the Year Award is a $1,000 award supported by a grant from Scott Foresman. Summaries of winning dissertations are published each year in Reading Research Quarterly. Dissertations in reading or related fields are eligible for the competition. Studies using any research approach (ethnographic, experimental, historical, survey, etc.) are encouraged. Each study is assessed in the light of this approach, the scholarly qualification of its report, and its significant contributions to knowledge within the reading field. The deadline for submission is October 1.
Reading/Literacy Research Fellowship: The Reading/Literacy Research Fellowship of $5,000 is given to a researcher outside the United States or Canada who has evidenced exceptional promise in reading research and deserves encouragement to continue working in the field of reading. Applicants must have received their doctorate or its equivalent within the past 5 years. Applicants must be Association members. Completed applications must be received by January 15.
Steven A. Stahl Research Grant: This $1,000 award was established to honor the memory and work of Steven A. Stahl by encouraging and supporting promising graduate students in their research. This grant will be awarded annually to a recipient with at least three years of teaching experience who is conducting classroom research (including action research) focused on improving reading instruction and children's reading achievement.
Teacher as Researcher Grant: This grant supports classroom teachers who undertake action research inquiries about literacy and instruction. Grants will be awarded up to $5,000, although priority will be given to smaller grants (e.g., $1,000 to $2,000) in order to provide support for as many teacher researchers as possible. Completed applications must be received by January 15.
EIN: 362364659

5890

International Women's Media Foundation
1625 K St., N.W., Ste. 1275
Washington, DC   20006   (202) 496-1992
Contact: Lisa Woll, Exec. Dir.
FAX: (202) 496-1977; E-mail: info@iwmf.org;
URL: http://www.iwmf.org

Foundation type: Public charity
Limitations: Awards by nomination only to women journalists who have shown extraordinary strength of character and integrity to report the news under dangerous and difficult circumstances.
Publications: Annual report; Informational brochure; Newsletter; Occasional report.
Financial data: Year ended 06/30/2003. Assets, $2,425,117 (M); Expenditures, $1,241,317; Total giving, $38,857; Grants to individuals, totaling $38,857.
Fields of interest: Journalism/publishing; Women.
Type of support: Fellowships; Awards/grants by nomination only; Foreign applicants; Awards/prizes; Stipends.
Application information: Application form required.
  Deadline(s): Mar. 15
  Additional information: See Web site for further nomination guidelines.
Program descriptions:
  Courage in Journalism Awards: Cash awards of no less than $2,000 are given to the winners.
  Fellowship Program for International Women Journalists: Airfare and stipends to international female journalists to spend four months with a U.S. media company.
EIN: 521648942

5891
International Youth Foundation

(also known as IYF)
32 South St., Ste. 500
Baltimore, MD   21202   (410) 951-1500
FAX: (410) 347-1188; E-mail: youth@iyfnet.org;
URL: http://www.iyfnet.org

Foundation type: Public charity
Limitations: Awards to individuals between 18 and 24 years of age who are working to bring a positive change in their communities.
Financial data: Year ended 12/31/2004. Assets, $36,734,829 (M); Expenditures, $22,172,720; Total giving, $11,533,679.
Fields of interest: Youth development; Community development.
Type of support: Awards/prizes.
Application information: Applications accepted. Application form required. Application form available on the grantmaker's Web site.
  Deadline(s): Apr. 15
  Applicants should submit the following:
    1) Essay
Program description:
  YouthActionNet Award: Awards of $500 each to youth leaders for emerging projects that promote social change and connect youth with local communities. Projects must have clearly defined goals and have potential for growth or further replication. Recipients also receive funds for a disposable camera to photo-document their project for an online photo gallery. They will also have the opportunity to take part in an online journal and contribute to a booklet of case studies highlighting the work of young people bringing positive change in their communities around the world. Applications must be written in English.
EIN: 382935397

5892
Agnes and Sophie Dallas Irwin Memorial Fund

c/o PNC Advisors
1600 Market St., 4th Fl.
Philadelphia, PA   19103-7240

Foundation type: Independent foundation
Limitations: Grants to retired secondary school teachers from private girls' schools primarily in the Philadelphia, PA, area, to cover the costs of study, research, and enjoyment of retirement.
Financial data: Year ended 12/31/2004. Assets, $1,179,104 (M); Expenditures, $53,994; Total giving, $53,000; Grants to individuals, totaling $43,000.
Fields of interest: Education, research; Education.
Type of support: Research.
Application information: Applications by letter accepted throughout the year.
EIN: 236207350

5893
James IV Association of Surgeons, Inc.

276 Hoffman St.
Franklin Square, NY   11010   (516) 775-3406
Contact: Murray Brennan M.D., Treas.
E-mail: jameslVassoc.surg@aol.com

Foundation type: Independent foundation
Limitations: Travel grants to American surgeons to teach new surgical skills and technologies in Australia, Hong Kong and Mexico.
Financial data: Year ended 12/31/2003. Assets, $1,068,046 (M); Expenditures, $74,209; Total giving, $24,000; Grants to individuals, 3 grants totaling $24,000 (high: $12,000, low: $6,000).
Fields of interest: Surgery; Mexico; Hong Kong; Australia.
Type of support: Travel grants.
Application information: Applications by letter accepted throughout the year.
EIN: 136138272

5894
The Martha Holden Jennings Foundation

The Halle Bldg.
1228 Euclid Ave. Ste. 710
Cleveland, OH   44115   (216) 589-5700
Contact: William T. Hiller, Exec. Dir.
FAX: (216) 589-5730; Business office: 20620 N. Park Blvd., No. 215, Cleveland, OH 44118, tel.: (216) 932-7337; URL: http://www.mhjf.org

Foundation type: Independent foundation
Limitations: Grants and awards to elementary and secondary educators and administrators in OH.
Publications: Application guidelines; Annual report; Newsletter; Program policy statement.
Financial data: Year ended 12/31/2004. Assets, $81,812,086 (M); Expenditures, $5,396,396; Total giving, $4,397,285; Grants to individuals, totaling $660,917.
Fields of interest: Education, administration/regulation; Elementary school/education; Secondary school/education; Education.
Type of support: Program development; Awards/grants by nomination only; Awards/prizes.
Application information: Application form required.
  Deadline(s): 20th of each month except June and Nov
  Additional information: Interviews granted upon request; See Web site for further information.
Program description:
  Jennings Grants-to-Educators Program: Allocates funds for separate grants of up to $3,000 to OH classroom teachers and administrators to test new methods, conduct classroom projects, or involve their students in extracurricular, enrichment, or summer programs. Specifically, these grants are awarded for curriculum enrichment, special education, reading, science, fine arts, community

interaction, writing, and outdoor education. Applications must be approved by the superintendent before being submitted to the foundation. In addition, the foundation sponsors a number of specialized workshops, seminars, lectures, and retreats for teachers and administrative personnel.
EIN: 340934478

5895
The Jerusalem Fund for Education and Community Development

(formerly The Jerusalem Fund)
2425 Virginia Ave., N.W.
Washington, DC   20037   (202) 338-1958
Contact: Samar Assad, Exec. Dir.
FAX: (202) 333-7742;
E-mail: info@palestinecenter.org; URL: http://www.palestinecenter.org

Foundation type: Public charity
Limitations: Scholarships, fellowships, and travel and research grants to residents of Palestinian communities in Israel, the West Bank, and Gaza.
Publications: Annual report; Financial statement; Grants list; Newsletter.
Financial data: Year ended 12/31/2004. Assets, $6,584,904 (M); Expenditures, $920,470; Total giving, $49,354; Grants to individuals, totaling $49,354.
Fields of interest: International exchange, students.
Type of support: Fellowships; Research; Scholarships—to individuals; Travel grants.
Application information:
  Initial approach: Letter.
  Deadline(s): Aug. 31 and Dec. 15
  Additional information: Completion of formal application required, including a biographical record, a report on academic and/or professional careers, and a statement of training plans; Interviews required; See program description below for application information on specific types of support.
Program descriptions:
  Scholarships: Applicants must produce official proof of enrollment in an academic or vocational school. There is a preliminary screening of all candidates, consisting of the executive director and three program assistants.
  Fellowships: Applicants must submit evidence of enrollment in an organized program accepted by a recognized academic institution in an area conforming to the purpose of the foundation. Letters of reference from academics may also be required as well as lists of publications, if any. There is a preliminary screening of all candidates, consisting of the executive director, three program assistants, and committee of the board of directors for applicants for fellowships.
  Travel Grants: Applicants must establish eligibility to attend the workshop, conference or similar program on a subject or topic matter that is consistent with the foundation's purposes. There is a preliminary screening of all candidates, consisting of the executive director, three program assistants, and a committee of the board of directors for applicants for travel grants.
  Research Grants: Applicants must furnish an outline of the research topic and budget for undertaking the research. Applicants must also demonstrate to the committee their ability to conduct and complete the proposed research, and the research topic must be germane to the foundation's purpose. There is a preliminary screening of all candidates, consisting of the executive director, three program assistants, and a

committee of the board of directors for applicants for research grants.
EIN: 521238142

5896

The Ji Ji Foundation
2730 Westlake Ave. N.
Seattle, WA 98109-1916
Contact: Margo Reich, Treas.
URL: http://www.jiji.org

Foundation type: Independent foundation
Limitations: Research grants to individuals for studies of human impact on the environment of the Pacific Coast.
Publications: Grants list.
Financial data: Year ended 09/30/2004. Assets, $868,214 (M); Expenditures, $72,186; Total giving, $66,778.
Fields of interest: Environment, research.
Type of support: Seed money; Research; Travel grants.
Application information: Applications accepted.
Initial approach: Letter.
Copies of proposal: 1
Deadline(s): None
Applicants should submit the following:
1) Budget Information
2) Curriculum vitae
3) Essay
4) Proposal
EIN: 911664723

5897

Barbara Piasecka Johnson Foundation
c/o Danser Balaam & Frank
5 Independence Way
Princeton, NJ 08540   (609) 688-1030
Contact: Beata Piasecka, Tr.

Foundation type: Independent foundation
Limitations: Fellowships to graduate, doctoral, and postgraduate students who are Polish or of Polish descent.
Publications: Application guidelines.
Financial data: Year ended 12/31/2004. Assets, $3,686,906 (M); Expenditures, $850,256; Total giving, $795,996; Grants to individuals, 16 grants totaling $82,737 (high: $20,000, low: $300).
Fields of interest: Poland.
Type of support: Foreign applicants; Graduate support; Postgraduate support; Doctoral support.
Application information: Application form required.
Initial approach: Letter or telephone.
Deadline(s): Mar. 30 and Sept. 1
Additional information: Contact foundation for current application guidelines.
EIN: 510201795

5898

The Robert Wood Johnson Foundation
Rte. 1 and College Rd. E.
P.O. Box 2316
Princeton, NJ 08543-2316   (888) 631-9989
Contact: Richard J. Toth, Dir., Office of Proposal Mgmt.
E-mail: mail@rwjf.org; *URL:* http://www.rwjf.org

Foundation type: Independent foundation
Limitations: Fellowships and grants to investigators for the study of substance abuse. Awards are also presented to teachers for epidemiology and public health issues, and by nomination only to community-based health providers and advocates or junior faculty in medical schools, and health policy fellowships to mid-career professionals.
Publications: Application guidelines; Annual report (including application guidelines); Grants list; Informational brochure; Newsletter; Occasional report.
Financial data: Year ended 12/31/2004. Assets, $8,991,086,132 (M); Expenditures, $498,867,828; Total giving, $359,500,275.
Fields of interest: Business school/education; Health care, management/technical aid; Health care, research; Health care, public policy; Medical care, community health systems; Public health, epidemiology; Nursing care; Health care; Substance abuse, services; Depression; Aging.
Type of support: Fellowships; Research; Awards/grants by nomination only; Awards/prizes.
Application information:
Deadline(s): Vary.
Additional information: Application by proposal, for awards by Nomination Only, nominations not accepted. See Web site of each program for application or nomination guidelines.
Program descriptions:
Clinical Scholars: Offers two years of graduate-level study and research as part of a university-based, post-residency training program. Applicants must be U.S. citizens training in any of the medical/surgical fields, including psychiatry, pediatrics, obstetrics/gynecology, and family medicine. Awards range from $45,000-$50,000. See the program's Web site (http://www.uams.edu/rwjcsp) for more information. Deadline Feb. 15. Candidates should begin the process 18 months before deadline.
Community Health Leadership Program: Honors 10 outstanding individuals who help expand access to health care and social services to underserved and isolated populations in communities across the U.S. Each honoree is awarded $120,000 ($105,000 for program support and $15,000 as a personal stipend). Community-based health providers and advocates in mid-career who have created or significantly improved health programs in local communities where health care needs have been ignored and unmet are eligible to be nominated. Nominees must be U.S. residents of one of the 50 states, DC, or PR and must be currently working in their own local community (not on a national or international level) in affiliation with a nonprofit or government agency on a three-quarter to full-time basis. Nominations are welcome from consumers, community leaders, health professionals, government officials, and others who have been personally inspired by people providing essential community health services. Nominations from development and public relations departments or professional grant writers cannot be accepted. See the program's Web site (http://www.communityhealthleaders.org) for more information. Deadline for letter of intent Sept. 22 and for nomination Nov. 10.
Developing Leadership in Reducing Substance Abuse: This program nurtures the next generation of public health leaders in substance abuse prevention. Each fellow receives $25,000 per year for three years to be used for a personalized program of career development. Each fellow will be paired with a senior person in the field as a mentor. Applications require a letter of sponsorship from applicant's institution. See the program's Web site (http://www.SALeaders.org) for more information. Deadline is usually in Feb.
Better Jobs Better Care: Better Jobs Better Care, a new four-year, $15.5 million research program which is funded by the Robert Wood Johnson Foundation and the Atlantic Philanthropies, offers grants with the goal of achieving changes in long-term policy and practices to help reduce the high vacancy and turnover rates of direct care staff across the spectrum of long-term care settings. The program offers Demonstration Grants to teams of long-term care providers, workers and consumers, working with state and local officials, to develop and implement policy changes and workplace interventions that affect the quality of direct care workforce. For more information, send e-mail to: bjbc@aahsa.org.
Harold Amos Medical Faculty Development Program: Offers 12 four-year postdoctoral research fellowships to minority physicians who have demonstrated superior academic and clinical skills and who are committed to careers in academic medicine. Each fellow receives a stipend of up to $65,000 per year, and a $26,350 grant toward the support of research activities. Applicants must be minority physicians who are U.S. citizens and are now completing or will have completed formal clinical training. See the program's Web site (http://www.mmfdp.org) for more information. Deadline usually in Mar.
Scholars in Health Policy Research: Enables up to 12 highly qualified individuals to undertake two-year fellowships at nationally prominent universities. Scholars will have access to the full range of university resources and will receive annual support of $71,000 for the first year and $74,000 for the second. Recent graduates of doctoral programs in economics, political science, and sociology, including junior faculty, are eligible. See the program's Web site (http://www.apsanet.org/PS/grants/rwjf.cfm) for more information. Deadline usually in Oct.
Executive Nurse Fellows Program: Each year, up to 20 highly qualified nurses in executive roles are selected to participate in this three-year fellowship. Awards up to $45,000 are to be paid over three years. Major components of the program include the completion of a core leadership curriculum, seminar and workshop sessions, pursuit of an individual learning plan, completion of an individual project and significant experience with a senior executive mentor. While this program is designed to allow fellows to remain at their home institutions, it will take fellows away from their regular duties a minimum of four weeks per year. Fellows will need to secure a commitment from their home institutions for release time and continued compensation while they attend all program activities. The program will focus on five key leadership competencies needed in the emerging health care system. All program activities will seek to enhance the following competencies of the fellows:
· Self-Knowledge - the ability to understand self in the context of organizational challenges, interpersonal demands and individual motivation
· Strategic Vision - the ability to connect broad social, economic and political changes to the strategic direction of institutions and organizations
· Risk-Taking and Creativity - the ability to transform self and organization by moving outside of the traditional patterned ways of success
· Interpersonal and Communication Effectiveness - the ability to translate strategic vision into compelling and motivating messages
· Managing Change - the ability to create, structure and effectively implement organizational change in a continuous manner. At the outset of the program,

fellows will work with program faculty and staff to prepare an individual learning plan to guide their leadership development activities over the three-year tenure of their appointment. Deadline Feb. 1.

Investigator Awards in Health Policy Research: Enables a select number of highly qualified individuals, from new investigators to distinguished senior scholars, to undertake research that will:

· explore underlying values, historical evolution and interplay among the social, economic and political forces that have shaped health, health care and health policy in the U.S.

· apply new perspectives from a variety of disciplines to the underlying principles, organization and functions of health care delivery systems

· analyze social and economic factors that hold promise for improving the performance of the health care system

· explore the policy significance of existing research concerning the function of the health care system and its participants.

Ideally, the research supported under this program should support development of creative solutions to critical health issues or make an enduring intellectual contribution. Traditional empirical data-driven health services research that focuses on a narrowly-defined research question, not a broad policy issue or problem, would not fit within the scope of this program. Depending on the specifics of a given proposal, grants are expected to range in size from $100,000 to $275,000 and in length from one to three years. Deadline Apr. 1 for Letter of Intent.

YES (Young Epidemiology Scholars) Teacher Competition: Awards $5,000 to individual high school teaching teams for innovative classroom curricula that incorporate epidemiological methods. Out of a maximum of 18 teachers or teaching teams, up to six are selected annually as national winners, and each receives an additional $15,000 award. Epidemiology curriculum should provide opportunities for students to:

· Learn and apply the scientific method. This includes the generation and testing of a hypothesis, the design of an empirical study, and the systematic collection and analysis of data.

· Learn and apply statistics used in epidemiology to assess the validity of their hypotheses.

· Demonstrate their understanding of non-statistical ideas, concepts, theories and principles in epidemiology.

· Apply the principles of epidemiology to problem-solving in other disciplines.

Deadline Oct. 15. See http://www.collegeboard.com/yes/ for more information.

Depression in Primary Care: Linking Clinical and System Strategies: Research grants to researchers or practitioners from nonprofit and for-profit managed-care organizations, office practices, delivery systems, academic institutions, and research organizations for projects that increase the use of effective treatment models in primary care settings for patients with depression. Smaller grants of less than $100,000 are available for projects to be completed within one to two years, and larger grants of $100,000-$300,000 are available for projects to be completed within two years. Deadline Nov. 3 for Larger Grants and Nov. 17 for Smaller Grants.

Health Policy Fellowships Program: Provides opportunities for mid-career professionals to gain an understanding of the health policy process and to contribute to the formulation of new policies and programs. Fellows are selected from academic facilities in medicine, dentistry, the biomedical sciences, nursing, public health, health services administration, the allied health professions, economics and other social sciences, and organized delivery systems such as HMOs and other community-based providers and institutions. Awards up to ten fellowships, each up to $155,000 for three years. Nominations are made by the C.E.O.s of the institutions. See the program's Web site (http://www.nas.edu/rwj) for more information. Deadline mid-Nov.

Generalist Physician Faculty Scholars Program: Offers four-year career development awards to outstanding junior faculty in medical school departments/divisions of family practice, general internal medicine, and general pediatrics. Four-year grants of up to $240,000 (60,000 annually) will be made to sponsoring institutions to help cover the scholar's salary and research costs. Scholars will be required to spend at least 40 percent of their time in research and other scholarly pursuits. Scholars must be nominated by medical school dean. See the program's Web site (http://www.gpscholar.uthsca.edu/) for more information. Deadline usually in Sept.

Nursing Policy and Philanthropy Program: Applications are being accepted for a joint fellowship position in Nursing Policy and Philanthropy. The fellow will work closely with senior leaders at the Robert Wood Johnson Foundation and serve as a faculty member at the Center for State Health Policy at Rutgers University. The fellowship helps the RWJF shape a Nursing Workforce agenda to support a hospital environment where patient safety and quality of care are assured and nurses are nurses are satisfied, supported, and energized to "transform care at the bedside." Candidates should have a strong background in nursing workforce management, research, and/or policy development.

Finding Answers: The Robert Wood Johnson Foundation is working to identify and implement real-world solutions to eliminating the gaps in care experienced by patients from racial and ethnic minority populations. The program is a research and tracking initiative that will focus on evaluating approaches already underway in the field to reduce racial and ethnic disparities in healthcare. While the existence of racial and ethnic disparities in health care is well documented, there is a shortage of practical and effective solutions. Finding Answers seeks to address this challenge by funding evaluations of efforts that target the treatment of cardiovascular disease, depression, and diabetes. These three diseases were selected because the racial and ethnic disparities in their treatment are significant and because there is general consensus about the right way to care for these illnesses. Six to eight grants ranging between $50,000 and $300,000 will be awarded. Deadline March 16, 2006 for brief proposals.
EIN: 226029397

5899
Marlene F. Johnson Memorial Fund for Scholarly Research on Christian Science

22 Concord Ave., Ste. 100
Cambridge, MA 02138
Contact: David Barrett Sand, Pres.
URL: http://www.johnsonfund.org

Foundation type: Independent foundation

Limitations: Grants and awards to individuals for research on Christian Science. Awards are for up to $40,000 per year, and are renewable.
Financial data: Year ended 04/30/2004. Assets, $916,798 (M); Expenditures, $86,715; Total giving, $24,546; Grants to individuals, 3 grants totaling $24,546 (high: $12,000, low: $2,546).
Fields of interest: Protestant agencies & churches.
Type of support: Research; Awards/prizes.
Application information: Applications accepted. Application form not required.
Deadline(s): Apr. 1 and Oct. 1
Applicants should submit the following:
1) Curriculum vitae
Additional information: Application by proposal of up to four pages, including published articles/work samples and two-three references.
EIN: 043453095

5900
The Jurassic Foundation, Inc.

Utah Museum of Natural History, University of Utah
1390 East Presidents Circle
Salt Lake City, UT 84112-0050
(801) 585-0561
Contact: Scott D. Sampson Ph.D., Pres.
FAX: (801) 585-3684;
E-mail: ssampson@umnh.utah.edu; URL: http://jurassicfoundation.org

Foundation type: Company-sponsored foundation
Limitations: Research grants to individuals for the study of dinosaur biology.
Financial data: Year ended 12/31/2004. Assets, $358,282 (M); Expenditures, $64,843; Total giving, $59,430; Grants to individuals, 29 grants totaling $59,430 (high: $3,500, low: $1,000).
Fields of interest: History/archaeology.
Type of support: Research.
Application information: Mar. 15 and Oct. 15.
Program description:
The Jurassic Foundation Program: Grants of $1,000 to $5,000 are awarded for the payment of field expenses, travel, materials, supplies, and support services. Purchase of equipment, payment of publication costs, and purchase of specimens will be considered under exceptional circumstances only. Institutional overheads, salaries and benefits for applicants, and meeting expenses will not be covered. Preference is given to international and non-tenured researchers.
EIN: 043448123

5901
Juvenile Diabetes Research Foundation International

120 Wall St., 19th Fl.
New York, NY 10005-4001   (212) 785-9500
Contact: William Ahearn, V.P., Strategic Comms.
FAX: (212) 785-9595; E-mail: info@jdrf.org;
Toll-free tel.: (800) 533-2873; URL: http://www.jdrf.org

Foundation type: Public charity
Limitations: Grants and fellowships for the study of juvenile (Type 1) diabetes.
Publications: Annual report; Informational brochure; Newsletter.
Financial data: Year ended 06/30/2004. Assets, $143,728,396 (M); Expenditures, $147,395,656; Total giving, $86,349,498.
Fields of interest: Diabetes research.

Type of support: Program development; Research; Awards/prizes; Postdoctoral support; Doctoral support.
Application information: Applications accepted. Application form required. Application form available on the grantmaker's Web site.
 Initial approach: Telephone or e-mail.
 Deadline(s): Jan. 15 and Aug. 15.
 Additional information: Letter of intent required for Special Grants.
Program descriptions:
 Clinical Investigation Research Grants: Awards up to $660,000 for up to five years to support early-stage clinical trials to test novel therapeutic approaches, or non-interventional patient-oriented studies that are intended to lead to the development of clinical interventions and monitoring tools for diabetes and its complications. These research grants must be goal-oriented and closely focused on JDRF's mission.
 Career Development Award: Provides up to $625,000 for a total of five years. The awards provide salary and research support for exceptional scientists in research related to diabetes who are beginning their careers as junior faculty. These prestigious awards provide support during the crucial first five years as an independent investigator.
 Clinical Scholars Award: Provides up to $750,000 for a total of five years. The award will foster the development and productivity of established, independent physician-scientists who will translate research from the laboratory to the clinic. The award is intended to give the recipients the freedom and flexibility to explore fundamental scientific questions, to apply the resulting knowledge at the bedside, and to bring insights from the clinical setting back to the laboratory for further exploration.
 Innovative Grants: Provides funds to develop preliminary data and/or test the feasibility of a promising new approach. Funding level is up to $55,000 for one year including indirect costs.
 Post-doctoral Fellowships: Provides $36,000 to $50,000 per year for two years. The fellowships provide crucial training support to M.D. or Ph.D recipients who will focus on research related to diabetes. Emphasis is placed on post-doctoral fellows whose focus is in clinical research. These awards are highly competitive and are focused toward recruiting outstanding junior scientists.
 Regular Research Grants: Awards up to $165,000 per year for three years to provide investigators with support to explore the feasibility and development of proposals that address JDRF research emphasis areas and are considered to be on the leading edge of diabetes research. Includes exploratory proposals that may not have substantial preliminary data but have a sound research development plan considered to be of high priority to the JDRF.
 Early Career Patient-Oriented Diabetes Research Awards: Awards up to $750,000 for five years plus medical debt reimbursement to support promising physicians or clinical doctoral recipients who pursue a career in patient-oriented, diabetes-related clinical investigation. These awards are made in the late stages of training and include the support for recipients to transition to independent faculty or research appointments. Additionally, this award allows for up to $100,000 in medical education loan reimbursement over the five-year award period.
EIN: 231907729

5902
The Henry J. Kaiser Family Foundation
2400 Sand Hill Rd.
Menlo Park, CA   94025   (650) 854-9400
Contact: Renee Wells, Grants and Contracts Mgr.
Additional E-mail: pduckham@kff.org; Washington, DC Office: 1330 G St., N.W., Washington, DC 20005, tel.: (202) 347-5270; FAX: (202) 347-5274
FAX: (650) 854-4800; E-mail: rwells@kff.org; URL: http://www.kff.org

Foundation type: Operating foundation
Limitations: Fellowships to media professionals and internship opportunities to young minority journalists in the area of health reporting.
Publications: Annual report; Informational brochure (including application guidelines).
Financial data: Year ended 12/31/2004. Assets, $547,983,207 (M); Expenditures, $66,214,838; Total giving, $839,393.
Fields of interest: Media/communications; Journalism/publishing; Minorities; AIDS, people with.
Type of support: Fellowships; Internship funds.
Application information:
 Initial approach: Letter.
 Deadline(s): Mar. for fellowships, Nov. for mini-fellowships, Dec. for internships.
 Applicants should submit the following:
  1) Resume
 Additional information: See Web site for complete application guidelines.
Program descriptions:
 Mini-Fellowship Awards: Awards up to ten mini-fellowships to print, television, and radio journalists to research and report on the health, social, economic, political and cultural implications of the global HIV/AIDS epidemic. Provides travel and research support to complete a specific project for publication or broadcast. Typically, grants are $10,000 each, for print and radio projects, or up to $20,000 for broadcast projects. Deadline Oct. 22.
 Media Fellowships in Health Program: Fellowships are awarded each year to up to six print, television, and radio health reporters, commentators, editors, and producers to provide them with time and travel opportunities to research specific topics, broaden their perspectives, and deepen their understanding of health policy, health financing, and public health issues. Fellows each receive a $55,000 stipend plus travel expenses for a 12-month period. As part of the program, fellows meet as a group five times during the year to participate in a series of seminars and site visits, in part designed by the fellows themselves. Deadline in Mar. See Web site for complete program information.
 Media Internships in Urban Health Reporting: Young minority journalists interested in reporting on urban public health issues may apply to participate in summer internships at 11 major metropolitan newspapers and at three local television stations. Internships begin with a week-long briefing on urban public health issues and health reporting in Washington, DC. Interns are then based for ten weeks at their newspaper or television station, typically under the direction of the health or metro editor/news director, where they report on health issues. The program ends with a three-day meeting and site visits in Boston. Interns receive a 12-week stipend and travel expenses. The foundation will provide a stipend matching the news' organizations own weekly rate, or $500 gross per week, minimum. Applicants are selected by the participating newspapers and television stations.

Deadline Dec. 3 for print applications and Jan. 7 for broadcast applications.
EIN: 946064808

5903
Kalamazoo Public Education Foundation
714 S. Westnedge Ave., Ste. 214
Kalamazoo, MI   49007-5094   (269) 337-0498
Contact: Pamela Kingery, Exec. Dir.
FAX: (269) 337-0496; E-mail: kpefcec@aol.com; URL: http://www.geocities.com/kpef_2000/

Foundation type: Public charity
Limitations: Grants to Kalamazoo Public School, MI, teachers for programs to benefit students.
Publications: Application guidelines; Grants list.
Financial data: Year ended 12/31/2005. Assets, $2,693,959 (M); Expenditures, $2,091,893; Total giving, $59,631.
Fields of interest: Education.
Type of support: Program development.
Application information:
 Deadline(s): Oct. 23
 Additional information: Application by proposal outlining project description, objectives, procedures, and budget; See Web site for further application information.
Program description:
 Mini-grants for Educators: Application is open to any Kalamazoo Public School employee, but the project must directly and actively involve students. Applicants may apply for grants up to $750. Grant recipients will be required to furnish a report at the end of the project which must contain an evaluation of the project and an itemized financial accounting including receipts for purchases/services.
EIN: 382873188

5904
Abraham J. & Phyllis Katz Foundation
303 Merrick Rd., Ste. 204
Lynbrook, NY   11563
Contact: Monica Pier

Foundation type: Operating foundation
Limitations: Grants for scientific research, with an emphasis on cancer research.
Financial data: Year ended 12/31/2003. Assets, $2,617,756 (M); Expenditures, $298,912; Total giving, $297,071; Grants to individuals, 4 grants totaling $20,000 (high: $4,000, low: $4,000).
Fields of interest: Cancer research; Medical research.
Type of support: Research.
Application information: Applications accepted throughout the year; Initial approach by letter; Completion of formal application required.
EIN: 116442077

5905
Ewing Marion Kauffman Foundation
4801 Rockhill Rd.
Kansas City, MO   64110-2046   (816) 932-1000
Contact: Joy Torchia, Comms. Mgr.
FAX: (816) 932-1100; E-mail: info@kauffman.org; URL: http://www.kauffman.org

Foundation type: Independent foundation
Limitations: The foundation rarely makes grants to individuals. Occasionally it provides funding by nomination only for leaders of grantee or key partner organizations to attend the Center for Creative Leadership.

Publications: Application guidelines; Annual report; Financial statement; Grants list; Informational brochure (including application guidelines); Newsletter.
Financial data: Year ended 06/30/2004. Assets, $1,774,756,631 (M); Expenditures, $107,613,216; Total giving, $58,043,698; Grants to individuals, 17 grants totaling $147,065 (high: $12,000, low: $1,700).
Type of support: Research.
Application information: Application form not required.
   Deadline(s): None
Program description:
   Kauffman Dissertation Fellowship Program: Fellowships are awarded to selected Ph.D. students completing a dissertation that focuses on entrepreneurship.
EIN: 436064859

5906
Keep North Carolina Clean and Beautiful, Inc.
(also known as NC Beautiful)
P.O. Box 12943
Raleigh, NC   27605-2943   (919) 787-1693
Contact: Stephen W. Earp, Pres.
E-mail: ncbeautiful@bellsouth.net

Foundation type: Public charity
Limitations: Fellowships to students residing in NC for education in environmental studies. Support also to NC K-12 teachers to develop environmental education programs.
Financial data: Year ended 12/31/2003. Assets, $444,441 (M); Expenditures, $264,996; Total giving, $38,881; Grants to individuals, 16 grants totaling $15,881 (high: $1,000, low: $830).
Fields of interest: Environment, formal/general education; Environmental education.
Type of support: Program development; Fellowships.
Application information: Deadlines vary; Contact foundation for current application deadline/guidelines; Initial approach by letter, telephone, or e-mail.
Program description:
   Windows of Opportunity Grants: Awards up to $1,000 to NC K-12 teachers to develop educational programs aimed at improving the environment while creating future environmental leaders. Deadline Sept. 19.
EIN: 560932528

5907
W. K. Kellogg Foundation
1 Michigan Ave. E.
Battle Creek, MI   49017-4058   (269) 968-1611
Contact: Debbie Rey, Supervisor of Proposal Processing
FAX: (269) 968-0413; URL: http://www.wkkf.org

Foundation type: Independent foundation
Limitations: Fellowships to Americans who are in their early years of professional activity, for personal and professional development. Individuals can be nominated by a national organization holding a 501(c)(3) tax status, or be self-nominated.
Publications: Application guidelines; Annual report (including application guidelines); Financial statement; Grants list; Informational brochure (including application guidelines); Newsletter; Occasional report; Program policy statement.

Financial data: Year ended 08/31/2005. Assets, $7,298,383,532 (M); Expenditures, $252,718,852; Total giving, $244,342,812.
Fields of interest: Leadership development.
Type of support: Fellowships.
Application information: Applications are temporarily not accepted; Consult Web site for current application guidelines.
EIN: 381359264

5908
John F. Kennedy Library Foundation, Inc.
Columbia Point
Boston, MA   02125-3313   (617) 514-1550
Contact: Sharon Kelly, Grant and Fellowship Coord.
Additional fax: (617) 514-1652
FAX: (617) 436-3395;
E-mail: kennedy.foundation@nara.gov;
URL: http://www.jfklibrary.org

Foundation type: Public charity
Limitations: Grants to scholars doing significant research using the holdings of the Library, and awards by nomination only to individuals in government to recognize political courage. Awards to secondary school students for essays on government.
Publications: Application guidelines; Grants list; Informational brochure; Newsletter.
Financial data: Year ended 12/31/2003. Assets, $23,005,956 (M); Expenditures, $3,382,350; Total giving, $176,662; Grants to individuals, totaling $176,662.
Fields of interest: Literature; Public policy, research; Government/public administration; Leadership development.
Type of support: Fellowships; Internship funds; Research; Awards/grants by nomination only; Awards/prizes; Precollege support; Undergraduate support.
Application information:
   Initial approach: Telephone or e-mail.
   Deadline(s): Mar.15, for spring and Aug. 15 for fall.
   Additional information: Completion of formal application required, including three- to four-page proposal describing the planned research, its significance, the intended audience, and expected outcome, project budget, curriculum vitae, and description of how funds will be applied, other funds available, qualifications, and similar projects undertaken, for Profiles in Courage award application by nominating letter, including any background materials; See program description for more information.
Program descriptions:
   Grant and Fellowship Programs: The foundation administers and funds a number of programs on behalf of the public John F. Kennedy Library, a presidential library under the National Archives and Records Administration. Only one grant or fellowship application per person may be submitted in a given year.
   · Majorie Kovler Fellowship: One fellowship of $2,500 is provided each year. Preference is given to research in the area of intelligence, foreign intelligence, and the presidency or a related topic. Deadline Mar. 15. Awards announced Apr. 20.
   · Arthur M. Schlesinger, Jr. Fellowship: Up to two fellowship awards of up to $5,000 are awarded each year. Preference is given to applicants specializing in Latin American or Western Hemisphere history or policy studies during the Kennedy administration or the period from the Roosevelt through

Kennedy presidencies. Deadline Aug. 15. Awards announced Oct. 15.
   · Abba Schwartz Fellowship: One fellowship of $3,100 is provided each year. Preference is given to research on immigration, naturalization, or refugee policy. Deadline Mar. 15. Awards announced Apr. 20.
   · Theodore C. Sorensen Fellowship: One fellowship of $3,600 is provided each year. Preference is given to research on domestic policy, political journalism, polling, or press relations. Deadline Mar. 15. Awards announced Apr. 20.
   · Kennedy Research Grants: Fifteen to 20 grants of between $500 and $1,500 are provided each year. Research may be on any topic relating to the Kennedy period or requiring use of the holdings. Preference is given to Ph.D. dissertation research, research in recently opened or relatively unused collections, and the preparation of recent dissertations for publication, but all proposals are welcome. Deadline Mar. 15 for spring grants, Aug. 15 for fall grants. Awards announced Apr. 20 and Oct. 20.
   · Hemingway Research Grants: Five to 10 grants of between $200 and $1,000 are provided each year. Grants are awarded to scholars requiring the use of the Hemingway Collection. Preference is given to dissertation research by Ph.D. candidates and research in recently opened or relatively unused portions of the collection, but all proposals are welcome. Deadline Mar. 15. Awards announced Apr. 20.
   · Archival Internships: Each year, the museum collections, as well as the textual and audiovisual branches of the archives at the Library offer a number of paid internships to students interested in working in the archival, manuscript, audiovisual, research library, or public history fields. Most interns are undergraduates in history, political science, journalism, communications, or English. A few are graduate students. Some have previous archives or library experience. Deadline Feb. 25 for immediate review. Notification of selection by Apr. 1.
A limited number of additional internships may open up during fall, winter, and spring as funds and positions become available. The library requires that interns make a minimum commitment of 12 hours per week. The library will also consider proposals for unpaid internships, independent study projects, work-study employment, and internships undertaken for academic credit. To apply, submit a completed application form (which can be obtained from the Intern Registrar) along with an unofficial copy of your current college transcript to the Intern Registrar at the foundation's address. Additional information on this program can be obtained by writing the Intern Registrar or calling (617) 514-1600.
   Profile in Courage Award: This award was created to recognize and promote the quality of political courage and leadership that Pres. Kennedy valued. The award is presented annually on or near May 29, the anniversary of Pres. Kennedy's birthday, to a current or former elected official whose actions best demonstrate the kind of political courage that Pres. Kennedy described in his Pulitzer Prize-winning book, "Profiles in Courage." The award can be made to municipal, state, or federal officials who have demonstrated an act of political

courage. The award consists of $25,000 and a silver lantern. With the establishment of the Profile in Courage Award Essay Contest and Scholarship, the foundation has further enhanced the scope of the award and its impact as an important educational tool for young people. The main purpose of this contest is to encourage students in grades 9-12 to work with elected officials to gain a greater understanding of the process of political decision-making and its integral role in the American democratic system. Judges by the same committee that selects the winner of the Profile in Courage Award, the winning essay is published in the John F. Kennedy Library Foundation Newsletter. The winner receives a $2,000 scholarship and is honored at the Profile in Courage Award Ceremony.
EIN: 046113130

5909
The Joseph P. Kennedy, Jr. Foundation
1133 19th St. N.W., 12th Fl.
Washington, DC 20036
Contact: Steven M. Eidelman
FAX: (202) 824-0351; E-mail: mancini@jpkf.org; URL: http://www.jpkf.org

Foundation type: Independent foundation
Limitations: Grants to individuals in the field of mental retardation to learn about public policy through work in government offices.
Publications: Application guidelines.
Financial data: Year ended 06/30/2004. Assets, $16,071,728 (M); Expenditures, $1,344,029; Total giving, $600,000.
Fields of interest: Youth development; Developmentally disabled, centers & services; Public policy, research; Disabilities, people with.
Type of support: Fellowships; Research.
Application information: Contact foundation for current application deadline/guidelines.
Program description:
  Public Policy Leadership Program: Grants are awarded to professionals in the field of mental retardation to come to Washington, D.C. to observe and understand public policy development through work on the staff of a congressional office committee or a federal agency working in the area of mental retardation and developmental disabilities.
EIN: 136083407

5910
The William F. Kerby and Robert S. Potter Fund
c/o Peter G. Skinner, Dow Jones & Co.
200 Liberty St.
New York, NY 10281

Foundation type: Independent foundation
Limitations: Grants by nomination only to individuals who are involved in criminal, civil, or administrative legal proceedings abroad involving freedom of expression. The grantee does not need to be a U.S. citizen or resident.
Financial data: Year ended 12/31/2003. Assets, $189,904 (M); Expenditures, $12,580; Total giving, $10,000; Grants to individuals, totaling $10,000.
Fields of interest: Journalism/publishing; International human rights; Civil rights, advocacy.
Type of support: Awards/grants by nomination only; Foreign applicants.
Application information: Individual applications not accepted; Potential recipients must be nominated by human rights and free speech groups;

Nominations accepted throughout the year; See program description for additional information.
Program description:
  Professional Grants Program: Recipients are chosen from lists sent to the fund from international human rights and free speech groups. The fund may then ask for additional information from the individual, including a career history, a sample of his or her work, information on the individual's area of expertise, financial status, and a summary of legal actions being taken against the individual. In choosing recipients, the selection committee considers the applicant's contributions to the profession, the severity of the action against the applicant, the importance of the cause, and the applicant's financial need.
EIN: 223021227

5911
Keren Keshet - The Rainbow Foundation
1015 Park Ave.
New York, NY 10028   (212) 396-8800
Contact: Linda Sakacs, Secy.

Foundation type: Independent foundation
Limitations: Grants to individuals in NY and Israel for research on Judaism.
Financial data: Year ended 12/31/2004. Assets, $253,005,275 (M); Expenditures, $9,732,222; Total giving, $4,699,925; Grants to individuals, 4 grants totaling $155,000 (high: $100,000, low: $2,500).
Fields of interest: Jewish agencies & temples; Israel.
Type of support: Research; Foreign applicants.
Application information: Applications accepted.
  Deadline(s): None
EIN: 134069592

5912
The Kerr Center for Sustainable Agriculture, Inc.
c/o The ASC
5101 N. Classen Blvd., Ste. 600
Oklahoma City, OK 73118
Application addresses: Farmer grants: c/o Alan Ware, Dir. of Farmer Grants; other grants: c/o Jim Horne, Pres., P.O. Box 588, Poteau, OK 74953, tel.: (918) 647-9123

Foundation type: Operating foundation
Limitations: Grants to individuals for agricultural projects and research, primarily in OK.
Publications: Informational brochure; Newsletter.
Financial data: Year ended 12/31/2003. Assets, $9,422,195 (M); Expenditures, $1,751,641; Total giving, $43,287; Grants to individuals, 7 grants totaling $10,982 (high: $2,850, low: $250).
Fields of interest: Agriculture.
Type of support: Program development; Research.
Application information: Applications accepted. Application form required.
  Copies of proposal: 1
  Deadline(s): Feb. 15 and Nov. 15
  Applicants should submit the following:
    1) Letter(s) of recommendation
    2) Proposal
  Additional information: Application should include detailed proposal of what agricultural practices will be demonstrated, budget and letter of support from agricultural professionals including university specialists.
EIN: 731256120

5913
Tai Soo Kim Architectural Fellowship Foundation, Inc.
41 Rear Concord St.
West Hartford, CT 06119   (860) 232-1719
Contact: Tai Soo Kim, Secy.-Treas.; Ryoung-Ja Kim, Dir.

Foundation type: Operating foundation
Limitations: Fellowships to individuals of Korean descent who are under the age of 35 and hold degrees in architecture.
Financial data: Year ended 12/31/2003. Assets, $474,270 (M); Expenditures, $38,847; Total giving, $35,550; Grants to individuals, 2 grants totaling $20,025 (high: $10,025, low: $10,000).
Fields of interest: Architecture; Korea.
Type of support: Fellowships.
Application information: Application form required.
  Deadline(s): Apr. 30.
  Additional information: Application must include portfolio of work.
EIN: 223136019

5914
The Sidney Kimmel Foundation
1650 Arch St., 22nd Fl.
Philadelphia, PA 19103-2097   (215) 977-2538
Contact: Matthew H. Kamens
Application address: Kimmel Scholars, Gary Cohen, M.D., Cancer Center GBMC, 6569 N. Charles St., Ste. 203 Baltimore, MD 21204, tel.: (443) 849-3729, E-mail: gcohen@gbmc.org
FAX: (215) 977-2644;
E-mail: mkamens@wolfblock.com; URL: http://www.kimmel.org

Foundation type: Independent foundation
Limitations: Research grants to physicians and young investigators for the study of cancer and translational science.
Financial data: Year ended 07/31/2004. Assets, $11,543,206 (M); Expenditures, $15,603,278; Total giving, $14,981,209; Grants to individuals, totaling $3,033,168.
Fields of interest: Cancer research; Medical research.
Type of support: Research; Awards/prizes.
Application information: Application form required.
  Deadline(s): Dec. 7 for Kimmel Scholar and , Dec. 31 for letters of reference
  Additional information: Application must include personal statement, research description, budget, three letters of reference, and appendix. Applications not accepted for Translational Science Program.
Program descriptions:
  Kimmel Scholar Award: Principally supports the research programs of accomplished young cancer investigators that emphasize basic cancer research, rapid translation of basic science concepts into potential therapeutic applications, and clinical research with novel or innovative treatment strategies. Ten recipients will receive $100,000 per year for two years. Qualified applicants must hold an M.D., Ph.D., or equivalent graduate degree, and must perform research in an American not-for-profit institution.
  Kimmel Translational Science Award: Provides five awards specifically for physicians engaged in translational science. Eligible applicants must hold an M.D. or equivalent degree, and must have achieved the rank of assistant professor. Applicants must demonstrate a significant personal involvement in the laboratory component of the

translational project described. The translational aspect may involve either animal or human studies.
EIN: 232698492

5915
Charles A. King Trust
c/o Bank of America, N.A.
100 Federal St., MADE10020B
Boston, MA 02110 (617) 434-4847
Contact: Kerry H. Sullivan, V.P.
Application address: Deborah Pearce, c/o Bank of America, N.A., 75 State St., Boston, MA 02109; tels.: (617) 451-0049 or (617) 434-4846

Foundation type: Independent foundation
Limitations: Postdoctoral fellowships for research in medicine and surgery at institutions within MA. Grants are paid to institutions on behalf of individuals.
Publications: Application guidelines.
Financial data: Year ended 12/31/2004. Assets, $20,485,233 (M); Expenditures, $1,105,100; Total giving, $925,251.
Fields of interest: Health care, association; Surgery; Medical research, institute; Medical research; Biomedicine research.
Type of support: Fellowships; Research; Postdoctoral support.
Application information: Deadline Oct. 15 for projects to start on or after Feb. 1 of the following year; Completion of formal application required.
Program description:
Medical Research Program: Grants are made for research in medicine or surgery as they are connected with the investigation of diseases of human beings and the alleviation of human suffering through improved methods of treatment. Support is for a postdoctoral research fellowship program in the biomedical sciences, including clinical investigation and problems of health in the community. Candidates are sought who have already completed a minimum of two or three years of postdoctoral research during which they have demonstrated competency and potential for a career in research. A primary goal of the fellowship program is to help assure future leadership of research in Boston area hospitals and other biomedical institutions. Reflecting this long-term objective, particular interest is taken in applicants whose sponsoring institutions indicate that a future career appointment is contemplated.
EIN: 046012742

5916
The Esther A. & Joseph Klingenstein Fund, Inc.
787 7th Ave., 6th Fl.
New York, NY 10019-6016 (212) 492-6181
Contact: John Klingenstein, Pres.; Kathleen Pomerantz
FAX: (212) 492-7007;
E-mail: kathleen.pomerantz@klingenstein.com;
URL: http://www.klingfund.org

Foundation type: Independent foundation
Limitations: Fellowships to young investigators for research in the neurosciences with emphasis on epilepsy.
Publications: Informational brochure.
Financial data: Year ended 09/30/2004. Assets, $124,448,967 (M); Expenditures, $6,110,015; Total giving, $4,493,623.
Fields of interest: Epilepsy; Neuroscience; Epilepsy research; Neuroscience research.
Type of support: Fellowships; Research.

Application information:
Initial approach: Letter or telephone.
Deadline(s): Dec.
Additional information: Completion of formal application required, including outline of research plans, abstracts from no more than four articles published by applicant, bibliography, and three letters of recommendation; Original plus eight copies of all materials must be submitted; Application form available from department heads or the fund; Awards will be announced in May to commence July 1.
Program description:
Klingenstein Fellowship Awards in the Neurosciences: Awards support young investigators in the early stages of their careers, who are engaged in basic or clinical research that may lead to a better understanding of the etiology, treatment, and prevention of epilepsy. The fund recognizes that to accomplish these goals, it is necessary to encourage a variety of approaches. These include studies at the molecular and cellular levels, research into the integrative function of the nervous system, and clinical investigations. Up to ten Fellows are appointed annually. Applications are reviewed, and selections are made by an Advisory Committee of distinguished neuroscientists. To qualify for an award investigators must hold the Ph.D. and/or M.D. degrees, and have completed all research training, including postdoctoral training. U.S. citizenship is not a requirement, but it is expected that candidates will be permanent residents of the U.S. Holding other fellowships concurrently with an award requires the approval of the Advisory Committee. The candidate should be an independent investigator, holding a tenure track academic rank (but not yet tenured) in a university or medical school, or the equivalent standing in a research institute or medical center. The award of $150,000 is payable over a three-year period and may be used for salary support, research assistants, equipment, or for any other purpose that promotes the scientific activities of the Fellow. An award is for the exclusive use of the Fellow and may not be used for institutional or departmental support. No provision is made for institutional overhead, but fringe benefits may be charged to the award. Payments will be made to the investigator's institution with the understanding that the total amount of the award is to be made available to the Fellow, and will be transferred should the Fellow change institutions. Annual reviews of the Fellow's activities and the funds disbursed will be required.
EIN: 136028788

5917
Ellen Beck Knox-MKB Foundation
(also known as MKB Foundation)
c/o Bank of America, N.A.
P.O. Box 831041
Dallas, TX 75283-1041
Application address: c/o Bank of America, N.A., Attn.: Susan Bullard, Trust Off., P.O. Box 830259, Dallas, TX 75283-0259, tel.: (214) 508-6674

Foundation type: Independent foundation
Limitations: Research grants to residents of Coleman County, TX, for the investigation of cancer or other health problems of the lungs, bronchial tubes, kidneys, blood, and teeth.
Financial data: Year ended 05/31/2004. Assets, $369,627 (M); Expenditures, $99,263; Total giving, $94,000; Grants to individuals, 83 grants totaling $94,000 (high: $15,000, low: $500).

Fields of interest: Vocational education; Medical research, institute; Cancer research; Kidney research; Lung research.
Type of support: Research.
Application information: Applications by letter accepted throughout the year.
EIN: 756233396

5918
Knoxville Christian Community Foundation
P.O. Box 1647
Knoxville, TN 37902
Tel.: (865) 523-5610, ext. 2

Foundation type: Public charity
Limitations: Grants to individuals in TN who promote peace and well-being in the community.
Financial data: Year ended 12/31/2003. Assets, $5,938,113 (M); Expenditures, $5,483,033; Total giving, $5,224,454.
Fields of interest: Community development; Christian agencies & churches.
Type of support: Program development.
Application information: Contact foundation for current application deadline/guidelines.
EIN: 621695494

5919
Dolores Kohl Education Foundation
825 Green Bay Rd., Ste. 130
Wilmette, IL 60091

Foundation type: Operating foundation
Limitations: Awards to elementary school teachers for exemplary teaching.
Financial data: Year ended 06/30/2002. Assets, $1,543,970 (M); Expenditures, $811,659; Total giving, $30,000; Grants to individuals, 5 grants totaling $25,000 (high: $5,000, low: $5,000).
Fields of interest: Education.
Type of support: Awards/grants by nomination only; Awards/prizes.
Application information: Contact foundation for current nomination deadline/guidelines.
EIN: 237206116

5920
Herb Kohl Educational Foundation
825 N. Jefferson St.
Milwaukee, WI 53202
Scholarship address: c/o Greg Doyle, Wisconsin Dept. of Public Instruction, P.O. Box 7841, Madison, WI 53707-7841, tel.: (608) 266-1098, E-mail: greg.doyle@dpi.state.wi.us
URL: http://www.kohleducation.org

Foundation type: Independent foundation
Limitations: Fellowships to K-12 teachers who are residents of WI.
Financial data: Year ended 12/31/2004. Assets, $2,776,677 (M); Expenditures, $409,427; Total giving, $388,157; Grants to individuals, 285 grants totaling $284,657 (high: $1,000, low: $657).
Fields of interest: Elementary school/education; Secondary school/education; Education; Leadership development.
Type of support: Program development; Fellowships.
Application information:
Deadline(s): Feb. 1

Additional information: Completion of formal application required, including several brief essays and four letters of recommendation, two of which come from individuals outside the immediate school community, such as former students, parents, community members, a college/university professor, or colleagues not directly linked to the school district.

Program description:

Kohl Teacher Fellowship Program: K-12 classroom teachers who are residents of WI and who plan on continuing to teach for at least one additional year may apply for this $1,000 fellowship to be used for unrealized classroom goals or toward professional development. Recipients are selected through a competitive process whereby teachers submit applications for review by regional nominating panels who then select a pre-determined number of nominees to receive this prestigious award. Recipients are chosen on the basis of the degree to which:
- students have benefited from their leadership
- professional colleagues, parents, the community, or the profession itself have benefited from their leadership
- they demonstrate and inspire a love of learning
- they have provided services above and beyond what was expected
- they have positively contributed to the improvement of education in general.

EIN: 391661743

5921

Komarek Charitable Trust

c/o Wells Fargo Bank Nebraska, N.A.
1248 O St., 4th Fl.
Lincoln, NE 68508

Foundation type: Independent foundation
Limitations: Scholarships by nomination only to students pursuing careers in the ministry of the Presbyterian and Methodist faiths and to students at the University of Nebraska College of Medicine.
Financial data: Year ended 05/31/2005. Assets, $1,597,853 (M); Expenditures, $100,566; Total giving, $77,000; Grants to individuals, totaling $23,100.
Fields of interest: Medical school/education; Theological school/education; Protestant agencies & churches.
Type of support: Awards/grants by nomination only; Graduate support.
Application information: Unsolicited requests for funds not considered or acknowledged.

Program description:

Scholarship Awards: Scholarships are made to further the education of deserving students who wish to pursue a career in the ministry of the Presbyterian and Methodist faiths and medical students enrolled in or accepted by the University of Nebraska College of Medicine. The trust selects recipients on the basis of character, financial need, and scholastic achievement. Ministerial and medical scholarship candidates are nominated by delegates of the Presbyterian and Methodist ministries of Omaha and by the scholarship committee of the College of Medicine, respectively. The trust's selection committee chooses the recipients and the scholarship amounts on the basis of the nominations received. No restrictions are placed on applicants with respect to age, sex, race, national origin, or religion (except for ministerial students who must be of the Methodist

or Presbyterian denominations). Scholarships are renewable.
EIN: 476141512

5922

Susan G. Komen Breast Cancer Foundation

Occidental Twr.
5005 Lyndon B. Johnson Freeway, Ste. 250
Dallas, TX 75244 (972) 855-1600
Contact: Patrice Tosl, C.O.O.
FAX: (972) 855-1605; E-mail: grants@komen.org; Additional tel.: (800) 462-9273; URL: http://www.komen.org

Foundation type: Public charity
Limitations: Awards to honor extraordinary achievement in research and clinical work specifically related to breast cancer survivorship.
Publications: Annual report; Grants list; Informational brochure; Newsletter.
Financial data: Year ended 03/31/2005. Assets, $116,598,410 (M); Expenditures, $95,390,752; Total giving, $53,323,199; Grants to individuals, 61 grants totaling $650,158 (high: $37,333, low: $1,530).
Fields of interest: Cancer research.
Type of support: Research.
Application information: Applications accepted. Application form required. Application form available on the grantmaker's Web site.
Initial approach: E-mail or letter.
Deadline(s): Mar. 1
Additional information: See Web site for application guidelines.

Program description:

Professor of Survivorship Award: The award is granted each year to two individuals who have distinguished themselves in research specific to long-term breast cancer survivor issues or in work with survivors that takes place in a clinical setting. Awardees are appointed Komen Professors of Survivorship for a one-year period, and each awardee receives a $20,000 honorarium to advance their work.
EIN: 751835298

5923

Kornberg Family Foundation

365 Golden Oak Dr.
Portola Valley, CA 94028
Application address: c/o Arthur Kornberg, Dept. of Biochemistry, Stanford University, Stanford, CA 94305, tel.: (650) 723-6988

Foundation type: Operating foundation
Limitations: Fellowships by nomination only to students of Stanford University and University of California at San Francisco for biomedical research.
Financial data: Year ended 12/31/2003. Assets, $428,047 (M); Expenditures, $30,046; Total giving, $27,500; Grants to individuals, 4 grants totaling $15,000.
Fields of interest: Chemistry; Biological sciences.
Type of support: Fellowships; Support to graduates or students of specific schools; Awards/grants by nomination only.
Application information: Nominations accepted throughout the year; Contact foundation for current nomination guidelines.
EIN: 943259687

5924

Emily Davie and Joseph S. Kornfeld Foundation

41 Schermerhorn St., Ste. 208
Brooklyn, NY 11201 (718) 624-7969
Contact: Bobye G. List, Exec. Dir.
FAX: (718) 834-1204;
E-mail: office@kornfeldfdn.org; URL: http://foundationcenter.org/grantmaker/kornfeld/
Additional URL: http://www.kornfeldfdn.org

Foundation type: Independent foundation
Limitations: Postgraduate fellowships, primarily to individuals residing in the New York, NY, metropolitan area for research in palliative care.
Publications: Annual report (including application guidelines); Grants list.
Financial data: Year ended 12/31/2004. Assets, $33,730,626 (M); Expenditures, $2,136,056; Total giving, $1,552,647; Grant to an individual, 1 grant totaling $3,647.
Fields of interest: Health care, ethics; Medical research, institute; Civil liberties, right to die.
Type of support: Fellowships.
Application information: Applications not accepted.
Additional information: No new Fellowships will be awarded. See Web site for further information.
EIN: 133042360

5925

Kosciuszko Foundation, Inc.

15 E. 65th St.
New York, NY 10021-6595 (212) 734-2130
Contact: Maryla Janiak, Dir., Educ. Progs.
Address in Poland: ul. Nowy Swiat 4, Rm. 118, 03-921 Warszawa, tel.: (48) (22) 21-7067
FAX: (212) 628-4552; E-mail: thekf@aol.com; URL: http://www.kosciuszkofoundation.org

Foundation type: Public charity
Limitations: Grants to Polish individuals who reside permanently in Poland for study in the U.S.
Publications: Annual report; Informational brochure (including application guidelines); Newsletter.
Financial data: Year ended 06/30/2003. Assets, $24,885,967 (M); Expenditures, $3,086,666; Total giving, $1,414,593; Grants to individuals, totaling $1,414,593.
Fields of interest: International exchange, students.
Type of support: Fellowships; Research; Scholarships—to individuals; Foreign applicants.
Application information: Application form required.
Initial approach: Letter.
Deadline(s): Oct. 15 for application or re-application
Additional information: Interviews required.

Program description:

Kosciuszko Foundation Program: Each year the foundation assists a number of Polish individuals in furthering their studies and research at accredited institutions of higher learning in the U.S. The foundation provides a stipend to cover housing, living costs, accident insurance, and when warranted, transatlantic and domestic transportation. (Note: a grant recipient is responsible for all travel arrangements.) Grants are for up to one academic year and are not renewable. The foundation does not pay for tuition; It can only assist an applicant in obtaining a tuition/fees waiver. Eligibility requirements are as follows:
- Polish citizens residing permanently in Poland. Those residing outside of Poland are not eligible for the exchange program

- Minimum completed M.A./M.S. degree. Priority is given to doctoral or postdoctoral students and scholars
- Excellent command of the English language. Only TOEFL/Cambridge Proficiency results are recognized by the Scholarship Committee

Application requirements are as follows:
- A thorough and well-reasoned typed proposal (not less than one page long) for conducting research/study in the U.S. with specific plans
- A reasonably current invitation from the American educational institution where the applicant plans to conduct research
- A list of important and most recent publications of which applicant is the principal author. All artists and authors must support their research proposal with examples of their work. Artists must submit catalogs, photographs, or slides. Materials submitted will not be returned.

EIN: 131628179

5926
The KPMG Foundation
(formerly The KPMG Peat Marwick Foundation)
3 Chestnut Ridge Rd.
Montvale, NJ 07645 (201) 307-7932
Contact: Tara Perino, Assoc. Dir.
Application address for Minority Accounting Doctoral Scholarships: KPMG Foundation Doctoral Scholarship Prog., c/o Anita C. English, Scholarship Admin., The KPMG Foundation, 3 Chestnut Ridge Rd., Montvale, NJ 07645
FAX: (201) 307-7093;
E-mail: kpmgfoundation-GM@kpmg.com; Additional E-mail: tperino@kpmg.com; URL: http://www.kpmgfoundation.org

Foundation type: Company-sponsored foundation
Limitations: Scholarships to full-time doctoral students of accounting who are African American, Latino, or Native American.
Publications: Annual report.
Financial data: Year ended 06/30/2004. Assets, $1,626,997 (M); Expenditures, $9,019,975; Total giving, $6,384,598; Grants to individuals, 42 grants totaling $645,000 (high: $10,000, low: $5,000).
Fields of interest: Business school/education; Business/industry; Minorities; African Americans/Blacks; Hispanics/Latinos; Native Americans/American Indians.
Type of support: Scholarships—to individuals; Doctoral support.
Application information: Application form required. Application form available on the grantmaker's Web site.
   Copies of proposal: 1
   Deadline(s): May 1
   Applicants should submit the following:
      1) Transcripts
      2) SAT
      3) Letter(s) of recommendation
      4) GPA
      5) Curriculum vitae
   Additional information: Application by letter; Recipients notified May 15.
Program description:
   Minority Accounting Doctoral Scholarship Program: The components of the program are as follows:
      • A $10,000 annual scholarship, renewable for a total of five years

- It is recommended that the institution provide annual stipend unrelated to the assistantships
- It is recommended that teaching and research assistanceships be made available by the institution as appropriate for their doctoral students
- It is recommended that the institution waive tuition and fees.

EIN: 136262199

5927
Samuel H. Kress Foundation
174 E. 80th St.
New York, NY 10021 (212) 861-4993
Contact: Lisa M. Ackerman, Exec. V.P.
FAX: (212) 628-3146; E-mail: lisa@shkf.org;
URL: http://www.kressfoundation.org

Foundation type: Independent foundation
Limitations: Fellowships for advanced training in art conservation and curation, and fellowships by nomination only for pre-doctoral candidates in art history.
Publications: Application guidelines; Annual report (including application guidelines).
Financial data: Year ended 06/30/2004. Assets, $97,441,123 (M); Expenditures, $5,694,793; Total giving, $3,750,579; Grants to individuals, 39 grants totaling $273,500 (high: $18,000, low: $1,500, average grant: $5,000-$18,000).
Fields of interest: Art conservation; Art history; History/archaeology.
Type of support: Fellowships; Awards/grants by nomination only.
Application information: Application form required.
   Deadline(s): Mar. 1 for Conservation Fellowships, Jan. 15 for Curatorial Fellowships and Nov. 30 for fellowships by nomination only
   Additional information: Application must be made by the museum or faculty at which the fellowship will be based; Candidates for fellowships by nomination only must be nominated by their art history department.
Program descriptions:
   Conservation Fellowships: Awards twelve $25,000 fellowships for one-year internships in advanced fine arts conservation at a museum or conservation research facility. The award is allocated as follows: $18,000 as a fellowship stipend; $2,000 for travel; and $5,000 toward administrative costs, benefits for the fellow, and other direct costs. Fellowships are restricted to individuals who have completed an M.A. degree in art conservation.
   Travel Fellowships in the History of Art: Awards 15 to 20 fellowships for travel required for the completion of dissertation research on European art. Stipends range from $1,000 to $5,000. Nominees must be pre-doctoral candidates in the history of art, who are U.S. citizens or individuals matriculated at an American university.
   Fellowships in Art History at Foreign Institutions: Awards four $22,500-per-year Institutional Fellowships in the History of European Art for a two-year research appointment in association with one of the following foreign institutes:
   - Kunsthistorishches Institut in Florence
   - Nelson Glueck School of Biblical Archaeology, Hebrew Union College in Jerusalem
   - Prentenkabinet/Kunsthistorisch Institut der Rijksuniversiteit in Leiden
   - Courtauld Institute of Art and Warburg Institute, University of London

   - Zentralinstitut fur Kunstgeschichte in Munich
   - Cyprus American Archaeological Research Institute in Nicosia
   - American University in Paris - Bibliotheca Hertziana in Rome
   - Swiss Institute for Art Research in Zurich
   Nominees must be pre-doctoral candidates in the history of art, who are U.S. citizens or individuals matriculated at an American university.
   Curatorial Fellowships: Awards six $25,000 fellowships for one-year internships for curatorial training in European art at an American museum. The award is allocated as follows: $18,000 as a fellowship stipend; $2,000 for travel; and $5,000 toward administrative costs, benefits the fellow, and other direct costs. Fellowships are restricted to individuals who have completed a Ph.D. in the history of European art.
EIN: 131624176

5928
Lafayette Education Foundation
4010 W. Congress; Ste. 104
Iberia Bank Bldg.
Lafayette, LA 70505 (337) 234-5383
Contact: Tina C. Broussard, Exec. Dir.
E-mail: lefabc@lefoundation.org; URL: http://www.lefoundation.org

Foundation type: Public charity
Limitations: Grants to any Lafayette Parish, LA, public school classroom or special education teacher, librarian, or guidance counselor, social worker, or other education professional directly involved in classroom instruction. Awards by nomination only to active academic educators.
Publications: Application guidelines; Grants list; Informational brochure; Newsletter.
Financial data: Year ended 12/31/2004. Assets, $1,713,401 (M); Expenditures, $207,639; Total giving, $73,854; Grants to individuals, 63 grants totaling $73,854 (high: $3,555, low: $107).
Fields of interest: Education.
Type of support: Program development; Awards/grants by nomination only; Awards/prizes.
Application information: Application form required.
   Initial approach: Telephone or e-mail.
   Deadline(s): Mar. 1 for Mini grants, Nov. 1 for grants by Nomination only
   Additional information: See Web site for application and/or nomination forms and guidelines.
Program descriptions:
   Mini Grants: Grants to individual teachers are up to $1,000 each. There is a limit of two applications per teacher. School impact grants, to teams of four or more teachers, are up to $5,000 each. There is a limit of one school impact grant application per school per year.
   LEF Teacher Awards: Awards by nomination only to active academic educators (i.e., teachers, counselors, librarians, or speech therapists) in the Lafayette Parish, LA, public, private, or parochial school systems in grades K-12.
EIN: 581849198

5929
Lake Travis Education Foundation
P.O. Box 340759
Austin, TX 78734 (512) 533-6095
Contact: Paula Baczewski, Admin. Dir.
FAX: (512) 261-5819;
E-mail: email@laketraviseducationfoundation.org;

URL: http://
www.laketraviseducationfoundation.org
Foundation type: Public charity
Limitations: Mini-grants to teachers, principals, and department heads for projects that enhance the learning environment for Lake Travis Independent School District, TX, students.
Publications: Grants list.
Financial data: Year ended 05/31/2004. Assets, $635,190 (M); Expenditures, $314,119; Total giving, $263,843; Grants to individuals, totaling $34,015.
Fields of interest: Elementary/secondary education.
Type of support: Program development.
Application information: Applications accepted. Application form required.
   Initial approach: Telephone or e-mail.
   Additional information: Contact foundation for current application deadline.
EIN: 742406134

5930

The Lalor Foundation

c/o Grants Mgmt. Assocs.
77 Summer St., 8th Fl.
Boston, MA   02110-1006   (617) 426-7080
Contact: Pamela Labonte Maksy, Admin.
FAX: (617) 426-7087;
E-mail: pmaksy@grantsmanagement.com;
URL: http://www.lalorfound.org

Foundation type: Independent foundation
Limitations: Postdoctoral research fellowship awards by nomination only in mammalian reproductive biology as related to the regulation of fertility.
Publications: Application guidelines; Grants list; Informational brochure (including application guidelines).
Financial data: Year ended 09/30/2005. Assets, $12,451,528 (M); Expenditures, $920,668; Total giving, $771,037.
Fields of interest: Science, research; Biological sciences.
Type of support: Fellowships; Research; Awards/grants by nomination only; Postdoctoral support.
Application information: Applications not accepted.
   Additional information: Recipients notified by Mar. 15; See Web site for application form.
Program description:
   Postdoctoral Research Fellowships: The individual nominated by the applicant institution for the postdoctoral fellowship may be a citizen of any country and should have training and experience at least equal to the Ph.D. or M.D. level. The foundation must approve both the nominee and the research contemplated. Those who have held doctoral degrees for less than five years are preferred. One nomination is to be made for each project. Grant payments are made to institutions on behalf of individuals. Grants range as high as $35,000 per year, and proportionately less for shorter time periods. Renewal of a grant is possible under special circumstances.
EIN: 516000153

5931

The LAM Foundation

10105 Beacon Hills Dr.
Cincinnati, OH   45241   (513) 777-6889
Contact: Sue Byrnes, Pres.
FAX: (513) 777-4109; E-mail: lam@one.net;
URL: http://lam.uc.edu/

Foundation type: Public charity
Limitations: Awards, fellowships and grants to investigators for research on lymphangioleiomatosis (LAM) to develop better methods of prevention, diagnosis and treatment of the disease.
Financial data: Year ended 12/31/2003. Assets, $703,281 (M); Expenditures, $875,589; Total giving, $459,703; Grants to individuals, totaling $459,703.
Fields of interest: Medical research; Immunology research.
Type of support: Research; Postdoctoral support.
Application information: Deadline Sept. 1; Completion of formal application required.
Program descriptions:
   Postdoctoral Fellowship Awards: Awards a maximum of $50,000 per year (renewable for up to two additional years) to postdoctoral fellows. More than 50 percent of the funds must be used for salary support. The balance of the funds may be used for fringe benefits, supplies or animal costs.
   Established Investigator Awards: Awards of a maximum of $50,000 per year (renewable for up to two additional years) to investigators. The structure and terms of award are identical to the Fellowship Award except that with this award, faculty level investigators are eligible to receive funding for technician support and supplies.
   Pilot Project Awards: Awards of up to $25,000 to investigators for the initiation of innovative research projects. Candidates must have at least two years of experience, an M.D., Ph.D., or equivalent degree, and perform the work in a laboratory with established expertise in smooth muscle biology or the genetics of tuberous sclerosis.
EIN: 311438001

5932

Albert and Mary Lasker Foundation, Inc.

110 E. 42nd St., Ste. 1300
New York, NY   10017   (212) 286-0222
Contact: Neen Hunt, Pres.
FAX: (212) 286-0924;
E-mail: info@laskerfoundation.org; Additional
E-mail for applications:
dkeegan@laskerfoundation.org; URL: http://
www.laskerfoundation.org

Foundation type: Operating foundation
Limitations: Awards by nomination only to medical researchers who have made significant contributions in basic or clinical research or to public servants who have advanced the cause of medical research.
Publications: Application guidelines.
Financial data: Year ended 12/31/2003. Assets, $1,743,593 (M); Expenditures, $630,559; Total giving, $100,000; Grants to individuals, 3 grants totaling $100,000 (high: $50,000, low: $25,000).
Fields of interest: Public health; Health care; Biomedicine research; Medical research; Science.
Type of support: Research; Awards/grants by nomination only; Awards/prizes.
Application information: Application form required.
   Deadline(s): Feb. 1
   Additional information: Nomination packets available on Web site between Nov. 1 and Feb. 1.
Program descriptions:
   Clinical Medical Research Awards: Awards of $50,000 to scientists whose contributions, directly or indirectly, have led to the improvement of the clinical management or treatment of patients and the alleviation or elimination of one of the major medical causes of disability or death.
   Special Achievement Award in Medical Science: Award of $25,000 to a scientist whose contributions to research are of unique magnitude and immeasurable influence on the course of science, health or biomedicine, and whose professional career has engendered within the biomedical community the deepest feelings of awe and respect.
   Public Service Award: This award will honor exceptional individuals whose public service has profoundly enlarged the possibilities for medical research and health sciences and their intended consequences. The award will be conferred on a winner annually selected from among policymakers, journalists, philanthropists, advocates and professional scientists. The winner's contribution to medical research and the health sciences will be judged by the standards that defined Mary Lasker's deep commitment and exemplary behavior: 1) an extraordinary dedication to the purposes of medical research and/or the health sciences extending beyond job performance exceptions; 2) exceptional fundraising or philanthropy in support of research or health and technology initiatives against disease; 3) unqualified success at creating important institutional or legislative changes, or knowledge contributions that speed the progress against disease and disability; or 4) compelling evidence of dramatically influencing the attitudes, expectations and understandings of leaders or the public toward medical research, medical practice or the health sciences. Recipients must meet at least one of these criteria.
   Basic Medical Research Awards: Awards of $50,000 to scientists who have made fundamental investigations that open new areas of biomedical science.
EIN: 131680062

5933

Dr. Henry P. and Marion Page Durkee Laughlin Foundation, Inc.

(formerly National Psychiatric Endowment Fund, Inc.)
4910 Ridgecrest Ct.
Frederick, MD   21702

Foundation type: Independent foundation
Limitations: Awards by nomination only to MD graduating psychiatric residency students in honor of their scholarship and academic leadership.
Financial data: Year ended 12/31/2004. Assets, $2,965,729 (M); Expenditures, $168,379; Total giving, $156,500; Grants to individuals, 27 grants totaling $13,500 (high: $750, low: $250).
Fields of interest: Health sciences school/education; Mental health, treatment.
Type of support: Awards/grants by nomination only; Graduate support; Doctoral support.
Application information: Applications not accepted.
EIN: 526080760

5934

L. S. B. Leakey Foundation for Research Related to Human Origins, Behavior and Survival

P.O. Box 29346
San Francisco, CA   94129-0346
(415) 561-4646
Contact: Robert W. Lasher, Exec. Dir.
FAX: (415) 561-4647;
E-mail: grants@leakeyfoundation.org; URL: http://
www.leakeyfoundation.org

Foundation type: Public charity
Limitations: Research grants and fellowships to scholars and students for the study of human origins.
Publications: Application guidelines; Financial statement; Grants list; Informational brochure; Newsletter.
Financial data: Year ended 08/31/2004. Assets, $13,950,015 (M); Expenditures, $1,664,066; Total giving, $642,614; Grants to individuals, 57 grants totaling $642,614.
Fields of interest: Science, research; Anthropology/sociology.
Type of support: Fellowships; Research; Foreign applicants; Postdoctoral support.
Application information: Application form required.
 Initial approach: Letter.
 Deadline(s): Jan. 5 and Aug. 15 for grants, Feb. 15 for fellowships for African scholars only.
 Additional information: See Web site for complete application guidelines.
Program descriptions:
 Franklin Mosher Baldwin Memorial Fellowships: Awards up to $12,000 per year for up to two years to scholars with African citizenship who seek an advanced degree or specialized training in an area related to human origin research.
 General Research Grants: Awards up to $12,000 to doctoral students and up to $20,000 to post-doctoral students and senior scientists for promising new research projects in the exploratory phases of understanding human origins. Grants are awarded twice annually, with no citizenship restrictions.
EIN: 952536475

5935
Manfred R. & Anne Lehmann Foundation
c/o Barry M. Strauss Assocs., Ltd.
307 5th Ave. 8th Fl.
New York, NY 10016-6517
Contact: Sara Anne Lehmann, Pres.

Foundation type: Independent foundation
Limitations: Research grants to scholars of Jewish history, primarily in NY.
Financial data: Year ended 09/30/2004. Assets, $1,705,737 (M); Expenditures, $433,815; Total giving, $252,003.
Fields of interest: History/archaeology; Jewish agencies & temples.
Type of support: Research.
Application information: Applications accepted.
 Initial approach: Letter.
 Deadline(s): None.
 Additional information: Interviews required.
EIN: 132918194

5936
The Leukemia & Lymphoma Society of America, Inc.
(formerly Leukemia Society of America, Inc.)
1311 Mamaroneck Ave.
White Plains, NY 10605 (914) 949-5213
Contact: Marshall Lichtman M.D., Exec. V.P., Research and Medical Progs.
FAX: (914) 949-6691;
E-mail: researchprograms@lls.org; Additional E-mail: researchprograms@leukemia-lymphoma.org; URL: http://www.lls.org

Foundation type: Public charity
Limitations: Grants for research on leukemia and related diseases.

Publications: Application guidelines; Annual report (including application guidelines); Grants list; Informational brochure; Program policy statement.
Financial data: Year ended 06/30/2004. Assets, $119,905,138 (M); Expenditures, $171,949,408; Total giving, $41,084,023; Grants to individuals, totaling $41,084,023.
Fields of interest: Cancer research; Leukemia research.
Type of support: Fellowships; Research; Doctoral support.
Application information: Application form required.
 Deadline(s): Varies
 Additional information: Preliminary application must be submitted on-line at Web site.
Program descriptions:
 Career Development Program: Four awards, Scholar, Scholar in Clinical Research, Special Fellow, and Fellow, provide stipends to investigators, allowing them to devote themselves to research bearing on leukemia, lymphoma, Hodgkin's disease, and myeloma. Scholar and Scholar in Clinical Research awards are $500,000 over five years; Special Fellows awards are $150,000 over three years; and Fellow awards are $120,000 over three years. Applicants must have a Ph.D., M.D., or equivalent degree, and must be conducting research at a nonprofit hospital, university, or research organization. Deadlines Sept. 15 for preliminary application and Oct. 1 for complete application.
 Specialized Center of Research: This program aims to bring together research teams that are focused on the cure or prevention of leukemia, Hodgkin's and non-Hodgkin's lymphoma, and myeloma in order to foster interdisciplinary and synergenetic research. Applicants may be individuals holding a M.D., Ph.D., or equivalent degree, working in domestic or foreign non-profit organizations. Applicants need not be U.S. citizens. Deadlines Nov. 1 for preliminary application and Mar. 15 for complete application. Grants are 1 million per year for up to five years.
 Translational Research Program: Provides early-stage support of up to $200,000 over three years for clinical research on leukemia, lymphoma, and myeloma, which is intended to develop innovative approaches to treatment, diagnosis, or prevention. Applications may be submitted by individuals working in domestic or foreign non-profit organizations. Applications from society scholars, investigators who are in an underrepresented minority, and women investigators are encouraged. Deadlines Mar. 1 for preliminary application and Mar. 15 for complete application.
EIN: 135644916

5937
Leukemia Research Foundation, Inc.
2700 Patriot Blvd., Ste. 100
Glenview, IL 60026 (847) 424-0600
Contact: Michael K. Murtagh, Sr. Dir., Mktg. & Devel.
FAX: (847) 424-0606; E-mail: info@lrfmail.org; Additional e-mail: mike@lrfmail.org; URL: http://www.leukemia-research.org

Foundation type: Public charity
Limitations: Grants and fellowships for the study of leukemia, lymphoma, and myelodysplastic diseases for researchers who meet eligibility requirements and for financial assistance to families where leukemia is present who reside in IL and/or within 100 mile radius of Chicago.
Publications: Annual report; Informational brochure (including application guidelines); Newsletter.

Financial data: Year ended 06/30/2005. Assets, $1,194,288 (M); Expenditures, $2,079,521; Total giving, $838,650; Grants to individuals, totaling $838,650.
Fields of interest: Leukemia research.
Type of support: Fellowships; Research; Postdoctoral support.
Application information: Application form required.
 Initial approach: Telephone.
 Deadline(s): Feb. 15
 Additional information: See Web site for further information.
Program descriptions:
 New Investigator Research Grants: Support research on leukemia and related subjects. Applicants for this grant must be investigators who are within five years of the end of their training or of their first faculty appointment at the time of the proposed starting date of the award. The award is a one-year, $75,000 grant. Principal investigators must be members of the staff of a university, hospital, or nonprofit research institute. Research fellows, residents, and other persons in training are not eligible for this funding.
 Physician-Scientist Postdoctoral Fellowships: This fellowship awards salary support of $45,000 per year for a two-year period totaling $90,000. The award helps physicians prepare for an independent career in research of leukemia and related disorders and obtain significant research results. The grant supports individuals involved in a clinical training program, not individuals with faculty rank. Persons with M.D., D.O., or D.V.M. degrees, or equivalent clinical degrees will be considered for a two-year period, nonrenewable salary support. The sponsor and the applicant must be members of a university, medical school, hospital, or research institute.
 Postdoctoral Fellowships: This fellowship provides salary support in the amount of $305,000 per year for a two-year period totaling $690,000. Persons with an M.D., Ph.D., or equivalent degree will be considered for a two-year period, nonrenewable salary support during their first to fourth years of postdoctoral training. Applicants must have at least one year of postdoctoral training remaining at the time the award is made.
EIN: 366102182

5938
Levin & Papantonio Family Foundation, Inc.
316 S. Baylen St., Ste. 600
Pensacola, FL 32502 (850) 944-5437
Contact: Suzie Page, Secy.-Treas.

Foundation type: Independent foundation
Limitations: Awards to teachers for exemplary work in the Pensacola, FL, area and Escambia and Santa Rosa counties, FL. Grants to individuals for medical assistance are also given.
Financial data: Year ended 12/31/2004. Assets, $858,124 (M); Expenditures, $361,177; Total giving, $343,991.
Fields of interest: Education; Health care; Children/youth.
Type of support: Emergency funds; Awards/prizes; Grants for special needs.
Application information: Application form required.
 Copies of proposal: 1
 Deadline(s): None.
 Additional information: Applications should be sent by mail.
EIN: 593107428

5939
Max and Anna Levinson Foundation
P.O. Box 6309
Santa Fe, NM 87502-6309 (505) 995-8802
Contact: Charlotte Talberth, V.P.
FAX: (505) 995-8982;
E-mail: info@levinsonfoundation.org; URL: http://www.levinsonfoundation.org

Foundation type: Independent foundation
Limitations: Grants to individuals who are committed to a more humane and rewarding society, in the areas of the environment, society, and Judaism/Israel.
Publications: Application guidelines; Grants list; Informational brochure (including application guidelines).
Financial data: Year ended 09/30/2004. Assets, $17,873,938 (M); Expenditures, $336,582; Total giving, $146,640.
Fields of interest: Natural resources; Environment; Human services; Jewish agencies & temples; Israel.
Type of support: Program development.
Application information: Application form required.
Deadline(s): Apr. 1.
Additional information: Grants are usually between $5,000 and $15,000.
EIN: 236282844

5940
Mabelle McLeod Lewis Memorial Fund
c/o Wells Fargo Bank, N.A.
P.O. Box 63954
San Francisco, CA 94163
Contact: Shirleyann Shyne
Application address: P.O. Box 3730, Stanford, CA 94305

Foundation type: Operating foundation
Limitations: Grants to humanities doctoral candidates in their last year of study or writing, who are attending a northern CA institution of higher learning. No grants for publication of dissertation.
Publications: Application guidelines; Program policy statement.
Financial data: Year ended 03/31/2005. Assets, $5,388,724 (M); Expenditures, $282,437; Total giving, $179,205; Grants to individuals, 7 grants totaling $179,205 (high: $28,084; low: $24,228).
Fields of interest: Humanities.
Type of support: Fellowships.
Application information: Deadline Jan. 15; Initial approach by letter; Completion of formal application required, including financial disclosure statement and resume and arrange for a recommendation from three recognized scholars.
EIN: 237079585

5941
Life Saving Benevolent Association of New York
c/o Helen Delaney
140 Broadway
New York, NY 10005-1101

Foundation type: Independent foundation
Limitations: Awards for life-saving heroism at sea and for training in seamanship, primarily to individuals living in NY.
Financial data: Year ended 12/31/2004. Assets, $726,374 (M); Expenditures, $50,405; Total giving, $13,120; Grants to individuals, totaling $13,120.
Fields of interest: Military/veterans' organizations.
Type of support: Awards/grants by nomination only; Awards/prizes.
Application information: Deadline Dec.; Initial approach by letter requesting nomination form; Completion of formal nomination required.
Program description:
Awards Program: Awards medals, pins, and sums of money to those individuals whose courage, skill, and seamanship saved a human life on the sea or any navigable waters (or lakes connected therewith). The association also gives medals and monetary awards to encourage training in seamanship, lifeboat work, methods of rescue in the water, and resuscitation.
EIN: 136104148

5942
The Lifebridge Foundation, Inc.
P.O. Box 327
High Falls, NY 12440
Contact: Barabra Valocore, Exec. Dir.
FAX: (845) 657-6849;
E-mail: lifebridgeinfo@aol.com; Additional E-mail: info@lifebridge.org; URL: http://www.lifebridge.org

Foundation type: Independent foundation
Limitations: Project support to individuals who have developed innovative, forward-looking, and unique approaches in the arts, the environment, education, and science. Grants are given to individuals on an international basis.
Publications: Informational brochure; Newsletter; Occasional report.
Financial data: Year ended 12/31/2004. Assets, $6,386,524 (M); Expenditures, $556,101; Total giving, $180,210; Grants to individuals, 3 grants totaling $19,500 (high: $15,000; low: $2,000).
Fields of interest: Arts; Education; Environment; Science.
Type of support: Program development; Conferences/seminars; Seed money; Research; Foreign applicants; Project support.
Application information: Applications not accepted.
Program description:
Lifebridge Foundation Program: The foundation supports individuals "who, through cultural, educational, and/or scientific means, are dedicated to creating bridges of understanding among all people by bringing to realization the concepts of one humanity and the interconnectedness of all life.".
EIN: 061356766

5943
Lighthouse International
111 E. 59th St.
New York, NY 10022-1202 (212) 821-9200
Contact: Tara A. Cortes R.N., Ph.D., Pres. and C.E.O.; Scholarships: Kelly Boyle
E-mail for scholarships: kboyle@lighthouse.org
FAX: (212) 821-9707; Additional tel.: (800) 829-0500; URL: http://www.lighthouse.org

Foundation type: Public charity
Limitations: Awards for eye research, by nomination only. Awards also to partially-sighted or blind employees who have overcome their vision limitations by acheiving gainful employment.
Financial data: Year ended 06/30/2004. Assets, $121,299,961 (M); Expenditures, $48,056,891; Total giving, $50,000; Grants to individuals, 5 grants totaling $50,000 (high: $30,000; low: $5,000).
Fields of interest: Eye diseases; Disabilities, people with.
Type of support: Research; Awards/prizes.
Application information:
Initial approach: E-mail or telephone.
Additional information: Contact foundation for further application information.
Program descriptions:
Career Awards for Employees and Employers: This award recognizes exceptional employees who are blind or partially sighted and have successfully overcome their vision limitations by achieving gainful employment. In addition, the awards acknowledge employers who demonstrate that people with impaired vision are a vital part of the workforce. The winning employee and self-employed individual will each receive a $1,000 prize.
Pisart Vision Award: This award of $30,000 is given by nomination only to people who have made a noteworthy contribution to the prevention, cure, or treatment of severe vision impairment or blindness. The award is open to citizens of any country.
EIN: 131096620

5944
The Lighthouse of the Lord, Inc.
13000 State Hwy. 20 E.
Freeport, FL 32439-2000 (850) 897-2752

Foundation type: Operating foundation
Limitations: Grants to missionaries for foreign travel.
Financial data: Year ended 12/31/2003. Assets, $836,485 (M); Expenditures, $352,408; Total giving, $61,893; Grants to individuals, totaling $29,125 (high: $8,640; low: $2,165).
Fields of interest: Christian agencies & churches; Religion.
Type of support: Travel grants.
Application information:
Initial approach: Letter.
Additional information: Contact foundation for further information.
EIN: 593756826

5945
Lilly Endowment Inc.
2801 N. Meridian St.
P.O. Box 88068
Indianapolis, IN 46208-0068 (317) 924-5471
Contact: Sue Ellen Walker, Comms. Assoc.
FAX: (317) 926-4431; URL: http://www.lillyendowment.org

Foundation type: Independent foundation
Limitations: Fellowships for professional and personal renewal to K-12 public and private school educators who are residents of IN.
Publications: Application guidelines; Annual report (including application guidelines); Program policy statement.
Financial data: Year ended 12/31/2004. Assets, $8,585,049,346 (M); Expenditures, $450,672,891; Total giving, $428,977,921; Grants to individuals, 120 grants totaling $900,000 (high: $7,500; low: $7,500).
Fields of interest: Education.
Type of support: Program development; Fellowships.
Application information: Application form required. Application form available on the grantmaker's Web site.
Copies of proposal: 2
Deadline(s): Dec. 1
Applicants should submit the following:

1) Proposal
2) Letter(s) of recommendation
3) Budget Information
Additional information: Application must include personal and professional information, description of project, and a six-week schedule of activities.

Program description:

Teacher Creativity Fellowship Program: The program aims to support a creative project that will personally revitalize and intellectually expand the individual educator. A secondary purpose is to extend the benefits of that educator's personal renewal to students. The grants are not intended for individuals who simply propose to develop new course outlines or lesson units in traditional ways. Personal and professional renewal of the educator is the primary focus of this program.

EIN: 350868122

5946
The Lincoln and Soldiers Institute

Campus Box 435
Gettysburg, PA 17325
Application address: c/o Tina Grim, 233 N. Washington St., Gettysburg, PA 17325, tel.: (717) 337-6590

Foundation type: Operating foundation
Limitations: Awards for published scholarly works related to the American Civil War.
Financial data: Year ended 12/31/2002. Assets, $201,035 (M); Expenditures, $168,826; Total giving, $50,000; Grant to an individual, 1 grant totaling $50,000.
Fields of interest: History/archaeology.
Type of support: Awards/prizes.
Application information: Initial approach by proposal describing completed scholarly work relating to the Civil War.
EIN: 061287456

5947
The James F. Lincoln Arc Welding Foundation

22801 St. Clair Ave.
Cleveland, OH 44117-1199 (216) 481-4300
Contact: Roy Morrow, Pres.
URL: http://www.jflf.org

Foundation type: Operating foundation
Limitations: Awards to professionals working in the fields of arc welding and engineering design for projects or papers dealing with problems relating to design or uses of arc welding.
Publications: Informational brochure (including application guidelines).
Financial data: Year ended 12/31/2003. Assets, $310,462 (M); Expenditures, $161,252; Total giving, $60,594; Grants to individuals, totaling $60,594.
Fields of interest: Business/industry; Mathematics.
Type of support: Awards/prizes.
Application information: Applications accepted. Application form required.
Deadline(s): May 1
Additional information: Application must include drawings, photographs, or sketches of applicant's project; See Web site for complete application guidelines.

Program descriptions:

Arc Welding Awards for Technicians, Craftsmen, and Users of Arc Welding: Given to teachers, technicians, shop and business owners, craftsmen,

farmers, ranchers, welders, or any other employed or self-employed person. Individual awards range from $150 to $2,000.

Professional Design Competition: Held for U.S. residents who are working, either individually or as part of a group, in the development or execution of an idea to reduce costs, conserve material, time or energy, increase production or improve quality, function, or appearance through the use of welded design, engineering fabrication, or research. Subject matter of entries may relate to any type of structure, product, or type of arc welding. These awards are granted biennially. Individual awards range from $500 to $10,000.

EIN: 346553433

5948
The Charles A. and Anne Morrow Lindbergh Foundation

(also known as Lindbergh Foundation)
2150 3rd Ave. N., Ste. 310
Anoka, MN 55303-2200 (763) 576-1596
Contact: Marlene White, Pres. and C.O.O.
FAX: (763) 576-1664;
E-mail: info@lindberghfoundation.org; *URL:* http://www.lindberghfoundation.org

Foundation type: Public charity
Limitations: Open to citizens of all countries, the Lindbergh Grants support research and educational projects that address the balance between technology and the environment. Scholarships, tuition, and fellowships are not supported.
Publications: Application guidelines; Annual report; Informational brochure; Newsletter.
Financial data: Year ended 12/31/2004. Assets, $1,524,002 (M); Expenditures, $364,197; Total giving, $80,075; Grants to individuals, 8 grants totaling $80,075 (high: $10,580, low: $8,100).
Fields of interest: Health sciences school/education; Natural resources; Energy; Animals/wildlife, preservation/protection; Medical research, institute; Biomedicine research; Agriculture; Science, research; Space/aviation; Engineering/technology; Population studies.
Type of support: Program development; Research; Foreign applicants.
Application information: Application form required. Application form available on the grantmaker's Web site.
Initial approach: Letter.
Copies of proposal: 8
Deadline(s): 2nd Tues. of June
Applicants should submit the following:
1) Proposal
2) Budget Information
3) SASE
Additional information: Application should also include statement, project summary, methodology, list of personnel, and two endorsers' reports; Faxed or e-mailed applications are not accepted; Recipients notified by Apr. 15.

Program description:

Lindbergh Grants Program: The foundation seeks to further the balance between technology and the natural environment. With this goal in mind, grants of up to $10,580 (a symbolic amount representing the cost of the "Spirit of St. Louis" in 1927) are given annually to individuals in a wide spectrum of disciplines. The foundation's fields of interest are: agriculture, aviation/aerospace, conservation, humanities, arts, intercultural communication, exploration, biomedical research, health and

population sciences, adaptive technology, and waste minimization and management.
EIN: 132882090

5949
G. and R. Loeb Foundation, Inc.

110 Westwood Plz., Rm. F412
Box 951481
Los Angeles, CA 90095-1481 (310) 206-1877
Application address: 110 Westwood Plz., Ste. B307, Box 951481, Los Angeles, CA 90095-1481
FAX: (310) 825-7977;
E-mail: loeb@anderson.ucla.edu; *URL:* http://www.anderson.ucla.edu/

Foundation type: Independent foundation
Limitations: Awards by nomination only to print and broadcast journalists who have made significant contributions to the understanding of business, finance, and economic issues.
Financial data: Year ended 09/30/2004. Assets, $562,891 (M); Expenditures, $205,738; Total giving, $22,000; Grants to individuals, totaling $22,000.
Fields of interest: Journalism/publishing; Business/industry; Economics.
Type of support: Awards/grants by nomination only; Awards/prizes.
Application information:
Initial approach: Telephone or e-mail.
Deadline(s): Feb. 15
Additional information: Contact Loeb Awards office for current application guidelines.

Program description:

Loeb Foundation Program: Winners in each category receive $2,000. If a winning entry has more than one author, authors divide the award equally. Honorable mentions in each category receive $500. Award winners are announced in late spring. Entry fees are:
· Print Media:$50 per entry for all categories except small newspapers; $25 per entry for small newspaper category submissions
· Broadcast Media:$100 per entry for television; $50 per entry for radio.
EIN: 136121546

5950
Terri Lynne Lokoff Child Care Foundation

320 S. Henderson Rd.
King of Prussia, PA 19406-2408
(610) 992-1140
Contact: Helene Marks, Exec. Dir.
FAX: (610) 992-1070;
E-mail: tllccf@childcareabc.org; *URL:* http://www.childcareabc.org

Foundation type: Public charity
Limitations: Project grants to early childhood education teachers in recognition of excellence in providing quality child care.
Publications: Application guidelines; Annual report; Financial statement; Grants list; Informational brochure; Newsletter.
Financial data: Year ended 12/31/2003. Assets, $237,806 (L); Total giving, $181,357; Grants to individuals, 50 grants totaling $50,000 (high: $1,000, low: $1,000).
Fields of interest: Early childhood education; Children/youth, services; Day care.
Type of support: Program development.
Application information: Applications accepted. Application form available on the grantmaker's Web site.
Deadline(s): Dec. 3
Applicants should submit the following:

1) Proposal

Additional information: See Web site for application information.

Program description:

National Child Care Teacher Awards: Applicants must have at least three years' experience in the same child care center or home child care facility. As part of the application process, applicants are asked to design an enhancement project with educational, social, and emotional benefits for the children in their classrooms. Fifty outstanding child care teachers will be honored with a $1,000 grant, $500 to implement their proposed project and $500 as a stipend to acknowledge the teacher's special dedication. One winner will be chosen from the pool of fifty award recipients to receive the Tylenol & Terri Lynne Lokoff Child Care Foundation National Child Care Teacher of the Year Award. Child care teachers from all fifty states and the District of Columbia are invited to apply for the award.

EIN: 222804790

5951

Love Family Foundation Incorporated

500 Grant St., Ste. 2715
Pittsburgh, PA   15219

Foundation type: Independent foundation
Limitations: Grants to doctors residing in the Pittsburgh, PA, area for pulmonary research.
Financial data: Year ended 12/31/2003. Assets, $1,814,508 (M); Expenditures, $133,014; Total giving, $119,500; Grant to an individual, 1 grant totaling $33,500.
Fields of interest: Lung research.
Type of support: Research.
Application information: Applications accepted.
Initial approach: Letter.
EIN: 331001484

5952

The Henry Luce Foundation, Inc.

111 W. 50th St., Ste. 4601
New York, NY   10020   (212) 489-7700
Contact: Michael Gilligan, Pres.
FAX: (212) 581-9541; E-mail: hlf@hluce.org;
URL: http://www.hluce.org

Foundation type: Independent foundation
Limitations: Fellowships by institutional nomination only to American citizens with a bachelor's degree who are no more than 29 years of age as of Sept. 1 of the year they enter the program.
Publications: Biennial report (including application guidelines); Grants list; Informational brochure; Newsletter.
Financial data: Year ended 12/31/2004. Assets, $780,692,462 (M); Expenditures, $41,911,447; Total giving, $33,603,688; Grants to individuals, 30 grants totaling $419,643.
Fields of interest: International studies.
Type of support: Fellowships; Internship funds; Awards/grants by nomination only.
Application information:
Deadline(s): First Mon. in Dec.
Additional information: Individual applications not accepted; Completion of formal nomination required; Awards based on nominations submitted by 67 participating colleges and universities; Interviews required.
Program description:
Luce Scholars Program: Grants made to individuals in a wide range of professional fields for participation in internships in East and Southeast Asia. The program enables 15 Americans under age 30 to spend approximately ten months in Asia from Sept. until July of the following year. The program is aimed at recent college graduates who are not Asian specialists and would not otherwise have the opportunity or incentive during the course of their careers to come to know Asia or their Asian colleagues. The program emphasizes experience rather than academic pursuits, and no academic credit is given. Candidates should have a record of the highest academic achievement and outstanding leadership qualities, either on campus or off. More important than any other single criterion is that candidates have a mature and clearly defined career interest in a specific field, and that they have evidenced a potential for professional accomplishment within that field as well as strong personal motivation. The amount of the fellowship is $22,000 for single and $27,000 for married scholars at many locations in East and Southeast Asia. The basic stipend is augmented by cost-of-living and/or housing allowances. The foundation administers the program with cooperation from the Asia Foundation, which arranges placements for the scholars and provides administrative support in Asia during the program year.
EIN: 136001282

5953

Lucent Technologies Foundation

600 Mountain Ave., Rm. 6F4
Murray Hill, NJ   07974   (908) 582-7906
Contact: Michele Donato, Mgr., Finance and Opers.
E-mail: foundation@lucent.com; Application address for Graduate Research Fellowships: Bell Labs Graduate Research Fellowship Prog., Scholarship Management Svcs., Scholarship America, 1 Scholarship Way, P.O. Box 297, St. Peter, MN 56082, E-mail: coopgraduate@lucent.com; Tel. for Conqueror of the Hill: (908) 582-7436; E-mail for Conqueror of the Hill: lucentcoh@lucent.com;; URL: http://www.lucent.com/social/foundation/home.html

Foundation type: Company-sponsored foundation
Limitations: Research fellowships to minorities and women to enhance their knowledge and to pursue a Ph.D. degree in science and engineering.
Publications: Application guidelines.
Financial data: Year ended 09/30/2005. Assets, $929,640 (M); Expenditures, $5,258,577; Total giving, $5,951,645.
Fields of interest: Engineering/technology; Minorities; Adults, women.
Type of support: Fellowships.
Application information:
Initial approach: E-mail.
Deadline(s): Jan. 13
Applicants should submit the following:
1) Essay
2) Transcripts
3) Letter(s) of recommendation
4) Resume
Additional information: See Web site for additional program information. Application address for Graduate Research Fellowships: Bell Labs Graduate Research Fellowship Prog., Scholarship Management Svcs., Scholarship America, 1 Scholarship Way, P.O. Box 297, St. Peter, MN 56082; E-mail: coopgraduate@lucent.com.
Program description:
Bell Labs Graduate Research Fellowship: Fellowships are awarded to women and members of a minority group currently underrepresented in the sciences who are U.S. citizens, permanent residents or non-residents here on an F1 student visa. The program is primarily directed to graduating college seniors, but applications from first-year graduate students will be considered. A maximum of ten (10) fellowships may be awarded each year. Candidates are selected on the basis of scholastic attainment in their fields of specialization, and other evidence of their ability and potential as research scientists. Students must be pursuing full-time doctorial studies in the following disciplines:

- Chemical Engineering
- Chemistry
- Communications Science
- Computer Science / Engineering
- Electrical Engineering
- Information Science
- Materials Science
- Mathematics
- Mechanical Engineering
- Operations Research/Industrial Engineering
- Physics
- Statistics

A distinctive feature of the program is the opportunity for fellowship participants to gain firsthand research and development experience, through on-site activities at Lucent Technologies Bell Labs, under the guidance of research scientists and engineers. Each participant is expected to spend the first summer working with their mentor at Bell Labs on a research project in their area of interest. During periods of internship at Bell Labs, participants receive salaries commensurate with their level of experience and training. The Fellowship provides full tuition to any appropriate, accredited, nonprofit United States institution of higher education offering advanced degrees in science, mathematics or engineering. An annual stipend of $25,000 which can be used for living expenses, books, and travel to conferences. Fellowships will be renewed on a yearly basis for up to four years of graduate study, subject to the participant's satisfactory progress toward the doctoral degree.
EIN: 223480423

5954

Commodore Thomas J. Lupo Foundation

145 Robert E. Lee Blvd., P.H. Ste.
New Orleans, LA   70124-2552

Foundation type: Independent foundation
Limitations: Awards by nomination only to individuals in the military for outstanding achievement in their respective areas of duty, FL and LA.
Financial data: Year ended 12/31/2004. Assets, $274,611 (M); Expenditures, $27,747; Total giving, $27,200.
Fields of interest: Military/veterans' organizations.
Type of support: Awards/grants by nomination only; Awards/prizes.
Application information: Applications by letter, stating qualifications, accepted throughout the year.
EIN: 720998028

5955
Lymphoma Research Foundation
(formerly Lymphoma Research Foundation of America, Inc.)
111 Broadway, 19th Fl.
New York, NY 10006 (212) 349-2910
Contact: Fran Morris, Dir., Research Admin.
FAX: (212) 349-2886;
E-mail: researchgrants@lymphoma.org; Additional tel.: (800) 235-6848; URL: http://www.lymphoma.org

Foundation type: Public charity
Limitations: Fellowships for research that will result in better, safer treatments and cures for lymphomas and awards by nomination only to researchers for lymphoma research.
Publications: Application guidelines; Annual report; Financial statement; Grants list; Informational brochure; Newsletter; Program policy statement.
Financial data: Year ended 12/31/2004.
Assets, $9,394,200; Expenditures, $10,074,748; Total giving, $6,382,784.
Fields of interest: Cancer research.
Type of support: Fellowships; Research; Awards/grants by nomination only; Awards/prizes.
Application information: Application form required.
Initial approach: Letter or telephone.
Deadline(s): Sept. 7
Additional information: For Saul Rosenberg Research grant contact foundation for current nomination deadline/guidelines.
Program descriptions:
Clinical Investigator Career Development Awards: Provides up to $225,000 to fund training of clinicians who will participate in developing new therapeutics and diagnostic tools for lymphoma. The focus of the training is to prepare clinicians to design and administer clinical studies in lymphoma and to take on the primary responsibilities for clinical trial design, protocol writing, Institutional Review Board (IRB) submission, and publication.
Saul Rosenberg Research Grant: Recognizes an individual who, through basic or clinical research, has made a major contribution to the treatment of patients with lymphoma. The $50,000 award must be used to support additional research into the diagnosis and treatment of lymphoma. Members of the foundation's Honorary Medical Board nominate candidates. The recipient may be a medical doctor, research scientist, senior or junior faculty member, or researcher in training.
Fellowships: Provides up to $105,000 in funds to encourage applicants to pursue careers in lymphoma basic, translational and clinical research. Research can be laboratory or clinic based, but the results and conclusions must be relevant to the treatment of lymphoma.
EIN: 954335088

5956
John D. and Catherine T. MacArthur Foundation
140 S. Dearborn St., Ste. 1200
Chicago, IL 60603-5285 (312) 726-8000
Contact: Richard J. Kaplan, Assoc. V.P., Institutional Research and Dir., Grants Mgmt.
FAX: (312) 920-6258;
E-mail: 4answers@macfound.org; TDD: (312) 920-6285; URL: http://www.macfound.org

Foundation type: Independent foundation
Limitations: MacArthur fellowships by nomination only to citizens and residents of the U.S.
Publications: Annual report; Newsletter.

Financial data: Year ended 12/31/2004.
Assets, $5,023,223,000 (M); Expenditures, $238,071,176; Total giving, $209,996,176.
Type of support: Fellowships; Awards/grants by nomination only.
Application information: MacArthur Fellows program individual applications and informal nominations not accepted. See program descriptions for detailed application and nomination information.
Program description:
MacArthur Fellows Program: Provides unrestricted fellowships of $500,000 over five years to exceptionally talented and promising individuals who have shown evidence of originality, dedication to creative pursuits, and capacity for self-direction. Fellows have the time and freedom to fulfill their potential by devoting themselves to their own endeavors at their own pace. Fellowships are intended to enhance the ability of recipients to pursue their work in accordance with their own inclinations. Fellowships are granted directly to individuals rather than through institutions. They are awarded without project proposals or applications, and no evaluations or specific products or reports are expected. Fellows are free to focus on more than one area through interdisciplinary work, to change fields if they wish, or even to alter the direction of their careers. They may be writers, scientists, artists, social scientists, humanists, activists, or workers in any other field or fields, with or without institutional affiliations. The MacArthur Fellows Program accepts nominations only from the more than 100 designated nominators across the country in a range of academic and professional fields. They are asked to propose extraordinarily creative and promising individuals who are at points in their careers when a fellowship could make a difference. Unsolicited requests are not accepted.
EIN: 237093598

5957
Edward Mallinckrodt, Jr. Foundation
8050 Watson Rd., No. 231
St. Louis, MO 63119
Contact: Oliver M. Langenberg, Chair. and Treas.
Application address: 1 N. Jefferson Ave., St. Louis, MO 63103-2205

Foundation type: Independent foundation
Limitations: Research grants to individuals in biomedical areas for start-up funds. Applicants must be connected with a U.S. university.
Financial data: Year ended 09/30/2005.
Assets, $40,945,721 (M); Expenditures, $1,930,293; Total giving, $1,663,424; Grants to individuals, 31 grants totaling $1,663,424 (high: $75,000, low: $12,224).
Fields of interest: Biomedicine research.
Type of support: Seed money; Research.
Application information:
Initial approach: Letter.
Deadline(s): None
Applicants should submit the following:
1) Budget Information
Additional information: Application by proposal, including project description; Interviews required.
Program description:
Medical Research Program: The aim of the foundation is to advance knowledge in the various fields of clinical and laboratory medical research. Contributions are confined to projects that are in need of initial start-up funding. Overhead is not funded. Proposals must be initiated by members of the faculties of accredited medical schools and

must be accompanied by letters of approval from the dean of said school and/or from the senior faculty member or members associated with the project and others acquainted with the qualifications of the applicant. Grants may be made for periods of one to three years and are contingent upon a yearly progress report by the applicant. Annual grants range in the $50,000 to $75,000 level, not to exceed $100,000. A grant is made on the assumption that the recipient will use the funds for the purpose indicated in the applications while serving on the faculty of the same institution as at the time the application is made.
EIN: 436030295

5958
So Mang Foundation
4538 Briney Point St.
La Verne, CA 91750

Foundation type: Independent foundation
Limitations: Grants by nomination only to Christian missionaries who need financial assistance in their theology study and pursuit of Christian world missions, and also grants to missionaries for theological study and pursuit of Christian world missions.
Financial data: Year ended 12/31/2004.
Assets, $4,019,073 (M); Expenditures, $186,819; Total giving, $62,800; Grants to individuals, totaling $22,500.
Fields of interest: Theological school/education; Protestant agencies & churches.
Type of support: Grants to individuals.
Application information: Applications not accepted.
EIN: 954658284

5959
MAP International
2200 Glynco Pkwy.
Brunswick, GA 31525-6800 (912) 265-6010
FAX: (912) 265-6170; E-mail: mapus@map.org;
Additional tel.: (800) 225-8550; URL: http://www.map.org

Foundation type: Public charity
Limitations: Support to North American senior medical students working with hospitals in developing countries.
Publications: Application guidelines; Annual report; Financial statement; Newsletter; Occasional report.
Financial data: Year ended 09/30/2004.
Assets, $61,102,146 (M); Expenditures, $239,682,886; Total giving, $29,466; Grants to individuals, 21 grants totaling $29,466 (high: $4,051, low: $872).
Fields of interest: Medical school/education; Health care, association.
Type of support: Fellowships.
Application information: Interviews required.
Program description:
Reader's Digest International Fellowship (MAP-RDIF): This fellowship provides a small stipend and 75 percent of approved round-trip airfare to a developing country for senior medical students in their third or fourth year of study or residency. The purpose is to encourage lifelong involvement in global issues. Applicants must have a hospital in a developing country willing to accept his/her "externship" and must commit to raise the other 25 percent of his/her travel expenses. Applicants are interviewed by a volunteer physician reviewer and, if passed on by the reviewer, their

applications are considered at the Mar. board meeting.
EIN: 362586390

5960
March of Dimes Birth Defects Foundation
c/o National Office
1275 Mamaroneck Ave.
White Plains, NY   10605   (914) 428-7100
Contact: Jane Massey, C.O.O. and Exec. V.P.
FAX: (914) 997-4560;
E-mail: researchgrants@marchofdimes.com;
Additional tel.: (914) 997-4555; Additional E-mail:
mktaz@marchofdimes.com; URL: http://
www.marchofdimes.com

Foundation type: Public charity
Limitations: Research grants by nomination only to investigators specializing in birth defects.
Publications: Application guidelines; Annual report; Financial statement; Grants list; Informational brochure.
Financial data: Year ended 12/31/2003. Assets, $129,558,866 (M); Expenditures, $205,978,454; Total giving, $34,877,797.
Fields of interest: Genetics/birth defects; Genetics/birth defects research.
Type of support: Awards/grants by nomination only; Awards/prizes.
Application information:
Deadline(s): Sept. 15.
Additional information: Completion of formal nomination required, including curriculum vitae; Nomination form available on Web site.
Program description:
Research Prize in Developmental Biology: Awards $250,000 and a medal to investigators whose research has profoundly advanced the science that underlies the understanding of birth defects.
EIN: 131846366

5961
Marijuana Policy Project Foundation
P.O. Box 77492
Washington, DC   20013-8492   (202) 462-5747
Contact: Rob Kampia, Exec. Dir.
FAX: (202) 232-0442; E-mail: info@mpp.org;
Additional e-mail: drosenthal@mpp.org;
URL: http://www.mpp.org

Foundation type: Public charity
Limitations: Research support to individuals for projects that seek to increase public understanding of or decriminalize marijuana.
Publications: Newsletter.
Financial data: Year ended 12/31/2003. Assets, $330,098 (M); Expenditures, $1,346,991; Total giving, $50,000.
Fields of interest: Crime/law enforcement, reform; Public affairs, reform.
Type of support: Research.
Application information: Applications accepted. Application form not required. Application form available on the grantmaker's Web site.
Deadline(s): Vary
Additional information: See Web site for complete application and program information.
Program descriptions:
Diagnostic and Statistical Manual: Grants to individuals to influence the American Psychiatric Association's definition of marijuana abuse and dependency in the forthcoming Diagnostic and Statistical Manual V.

Grassroots Organizing in Targeted States and Congressional Districts: Grants to individuals for comprehensive grass-roots organizing for marijuana policy reform in targeted states and congressional districts.
Marijuana Research: Grants of up to $60,000 to individuals for objective, publishable, scientifically rigorous research on marijuana and marijuana policy.
EIN: 521975211

5962
Marin Community Foundation
5 Hamilton Landing, Ste. 200
Novato, CA   94949   (415) 464-2500
Contact: Fred Silverman, V.P., Mktg. and Comms.
FAX: (415) 464-2555; E-mail: info@marincf.org;
URL: http://www.marincf.org

Foundation type: Community foundation
Limitations: Awards by nomination only to individuals in recognition of extraordinary achievement in building healthy and sustainable communities in Marin County, CA.
Publications: Application guidelines; Annual report; Informational brochure (including application guidelines); Newsletter.
Financial data: Year ended 06/30/2004. Assets, $1,153,585,937 (M); Expenditures, $86,083,264; Total giving, $49,224,806.
Fields of interest: Community development, volunteer services.
Type of support: Awards/grants by nomination only; Awards/prizes.
Application information: Nomination deadline June 1; Contact foundation for nomination guidelines; Recipients notified in the fall.
Program description:
Beryl H. Buck Awards for Achievement: Awards to individuals under this program are $10,000 each. Individuals must be nominated and only one individual per year receives the award.
EIN: 943007979

5963
Mary's Pence
402 Main St., Ste. 210
Metuchen, NJ   08840-1846   (732) 452-9611
Contact: Karen Flotte, Natl. Coord.
FAX: (732) 452-9612;
E-mail: mailbox@maryspence.org; URL: http://
www.maryspence.org

Foundation type: Public charity
Limitations: Grants to Catholic women who are creating or expanding a ministry in North, South and Central America, and the Caribbean.
Publications: Application guidelines; Annual report; Financial statement; Grants list; Informational brochure; Newsletter.
Financial data: Year ended 06/30/2004. Assets, $253,772 (L); Expenditures, $325,695; Total giving, $63,094; Grants to individuals, 7 grants totaling $11,094 (high: $2,594; low: $500).
Fields of interest: Roman Catholic agencies & churches; Orthodox Catholic agencies & churches; Religion; Women.
Type of support: Program development; Foreign applicants.
Application information: Application form required.
Initial approach: Letter or telephone.
Additional information: Contact foundation for current application deadline; Requests may be written in Spanish, English, or Haitian Creole.

Program description:
Mary's Pence Professional Program: An applicant must be a Catholic woman who is creating or expanding a ministry that will improve or empower the lives of women and/or women and children. Funds are usually given as one-time small grants of up to $5,000 to as many projects as possible. Special priority is given to requests that focus on the needs of economically disadvantaged women, as well as ministries created and managed by women of color.
EIN: 363556481

5964
Massachusetts Library Aid Association
c/o Thomas R. Clune
2 Memorial Dr.
Ashburnham, MA   01430
Application address: c/o Shelley Quezada, Dir., 648 Beacon St., 5th Fl., Boston, MA 02215

Foundation type: Independent foundation
Limitations: Grants of up to $550 to librarians and library assistants in MA, for traveling and training courses.
Financial data: Year ended 12/31/2004. Assets, $296,910 (M); Expenditures, $9,191; Total giving, $7,400; Grants to individuals, totaling $7,400.
Fields of interest: Libraries/library science.
Application information: Application form required.
Deadline(s): Applications accepted throughout the year.
EIN: 046038185

5965
Massage Therapy Foundation, Inc.
(formerly American Massage Therapy Association Foundation)
500 Davis St., Ste. 900
Evanston, IL   60201   (847) 869-5019
Contact: Elizabeth Lucas CAE, Exec. Dir.
FAX: (847) 869-1178;
E-mail: info@massagetherapyfoundation.org;
URL: http://www.amtafoundation.org/

Foundation type: Public charity
Limitations: Community service and research grants to individuals for the study of massage therapy.
Financial data: Year ended 02/28/2004. Assets, $434,480 (M); Expenditures, $199,725; Total giving, $65,930.
Fields of interest: Physical therapy; Community development.
Type of support: Program development; Research.
Application information: Mar. 1 and Apr. 1; Initial approach by proposal; Completion of formal application required.
Program descriptions:
Research Grants: Awards of between $1,000 and $20,000 to support highly-qualified investigators for research that contributes significantly and directly to the basic knowledge of massage therapy and/or its application, including applied research which investigates massage therapy as a health/mental health treatment and/or prevention modality. Deadline Mar. 1. See Web site for further information.
Community Service Grants: Awards up to $5,000 to support those providing massage to those who do not have access to it, and those in need.
EIN: 363735393

5966
Chaim Mayer Foundation, Inc.
80 Broad St., 29th Fl.
New York, NY 10004
Contact: Hirsch Wulliger, Cont.

Foundation type: Independent foundation
Limitations: Grants to financially needy rabbis and other persons for research and study of the Bible, the Talmud, and similar theological works at a Yeshiva, synagogue, or other such institutions.
Financial data: Year ended 04/30/2004.
Assets, $11,786 (M); Expenditures, $747,794; Total giving, $746,960.
Fields of interest: Theological school/education; Religion, research; Jewish agencies & temples; Economically disadvantaged.
Type of support: Research.
Application information: Applications by letter outlining financial need and full description of activities accepted throughout the year.
EIN: 133119407

5967
The McCarthey Dressman Education Foundation
610 E. South Temple, Ste. 110
Salt Lake City, UT 84102 (801) 578-1260
Application address: c/o Kristy Carson, 802 Boston Building, No. 9 Exchange Pl., Salt Lake City, UT 84111, tel.: (801) 320-0765
FAX: (801) 578-1261;
E-mail: info@mccartheydressman.org; URL: http://www.mccartheydressman.org

Foundation type: Operating foundation
Limitations: Grants to educators and licensed teachers employed by schools and nonprofit organizations for the creation of new curriculum.
Financial data: Year ended 12/31/2003.
Assets, $56,958 (M); Expenditures, $132,617; Total giving, $78,478; Grants to individuals, 13 grants totaling $78,478 (high: $10,000, low: $868).
Fields of interest: Elementary/secondary school reform.
Type of support: Program development.
Application information: Applications accepted. Application form required.
  Deadline(s): Apr. 20
  Applicants should submit the following:
    1) Essay
    2) Budget Information
    3) Letter(s) of recommendation
Program descriptions:
  Academic Enrichment: Awards two grants of $5,000-$10,000 each to educators to create enrichment programs that serve the intellectual, artistic, and creative development needs of children in grades Pre-K-12 from low-income households. Renewals may be available.
  Teacher Development Grant: Awards two grants of $5,000-$10,000 each to licensed Pre-K-12 teachers for innovative instruction. Grants are renewable for up to three years.
EIN: 870646265

5968
R. J. McElroy Trust
425 Cedar St., Ste. 312
Waterloo, IA 50701 (319) 287-9102
Contact: Linda L. Klinger, Exec. Dir.
FAX: (319) 287-9105;
E-mail: klinger@mcelroytrust.org; Additional E-mail: office@mcelroytrust.org; URL: http://www.mcelroytrust.org

Foundation type: Independent foundation
Limitations: Fellowships by nomination only to graduates of liberal arts colleges located within the KWWL viewing area in 22 counties in northeast IA. Candidates must be pursuing a Ph.D. and must be nominated by their college. The trust also awards Gold Star Awards to teachers in the same area.
Publications: Application guidelines; Grants list; Informational brochure; Informational brochure (including application guidelines); Program policy statement; Program policy statement (including application guidelines).
Financial data: Year ended 12/31/2004.
Assets, $48,071,087 (M); Expenditures, $2,159,694; Total giving, $1,816,929.
Fields of interest: Education.
Type of support: Fellowships; Awards/grants by nomination only; Awards/prizes; Graduate support.
Application information:
  Deadline(s): Feb.
  Additional information: Grants are by nomination only.
Program description:
  Mc Ellroy Scholarship: The president or dean of each college within the KWWL viewing area submits one nomination to the trust. A selection committee chooses two recipients to receive three-year fellowships. A statement regarding use of the fellowship and the progress being made by the fellow must be submitted to the trust by both the fellow and the dean.
EIN: 426173496

5969
The MCH Foundation, Inc.
300 N. Coit Rd., Ste. 820
Richardson, TX 75080-5430 (972) 231-4068
Contact: Gary R. Hoskins, Secy.-Treas.

Foundation type: Operating foundation
Limitations: Research grants to individuals for post-graduate study of East Asian art and artifacts.
Financial data: Year ended 05/31/2005.
Assets, $7,397,334 (M); Expenditures, $220,386; Total giving, $19,007; Grants to individuals, 2 grants totaling $19,007 (high: $13,414, low: $5,593).
Fields of interest: Arts, research; Art history; History/archaeology; Asia.
Type of support: Research; Postgraduate support.
Application information: Application by resume, including academic qualification and intended field of study, accepted throughout the year.
EIN: 752359010

5970
The McKnight Endowment Fund for Neuroscience
710 Second St. S., Ste. 400
Minneapolis, MN 55401 (612) 333-4220
Contact: Kathleen Rysted
FAX: (612) 332-2833; E-mail: info@mcknight.org; URL: http://www.mcknight.org/neuroscience

Foundation type: Independent foundation
Limitations: Grants for medical research in the neurosciences, especially as it pertains to memory and to a clearer understanding of diseases affecting memory and its biological substrates.
Publications: Application guidelines.
Financial data: Year ended 12/31/2004.
Assets, $9,437 (M); Expenditures, $4,244,615; Total giving, $3,775,000; Grants to individuals, 42 grants totaling $3,775,000 (high: $100,000, low: $75,000).
Fields of interest: Neuroscience research.
Type of support: Research; Awards/prizes.
Application information: Deadline Jan. 2 for the McKnight Scholar Award, May 1 for the McKnight Neuroscience of Brain Disorders Award, and Dec. 1 for the McKnight Technological Innovations in Neuroscience Award; Completion of formal application required; Letters of intent should not exceed two pages.
Program descriptions:
  McKnight Neuroscience of Brain Disorders Award: Up to six awards are made annually, each providing $100,000 per year for three years. This award helps translate laboratory discoveries about the brain into diagnoses and therapies to improve human health. Examples of projects include (but are not limited to): using a model organism to study the function of disease genes; applying novel technology (imaging, genomics, proteomics) to achieve early diagnosis, or to identify the pathogenesis of a brain disease; applying principles of gene transfer, stemcell biology, and axonal growth to neural repair and to the recovery from brain disorders.
  McKnight Technological Innovations in Neuroscience Award: Up to four awards are made annually, each providing $100,000 for two years. This award seeks to stimulate, encourage and support scientists working on the development of novel and creative approaches to understanding how the brain functions. The fund is especially interested in how technology may be used or adapted to monitor, manipulate and analyze brain function at any level, from the molecular to the entire organism. The program seeks to enlarge and advance the range of technologies available to the neurosciences and does not support research based primarily on existing techniques.
  McKnight Scholar Awards: McKnight Scholars are selected from among applicants who hold the M.D. and/or Ph.D. degree and who have completed formal postdoctoral training. Candidates should have demonstrated meritorious research in areas pertinent to the interests of the fund and should be in the early stages of establishing their own independent laboratory and research career. A candidate's record should provide evidence of a commitment to a career in neuroscience. Up to six McKnight Scholars are selected each year to receive support of $225,000 over a three-year period. Award funds may be used for salary and direct costs but not indirect costs.
EIN: 411563321

5971
The McKnight Foundation
710 S. 2nd St., Ste. 400
Minneapolis, MN 55401 (612) 333-4220
Contact: Peggy J. Birk, Interim Pres.
FAX: (612) 332-3833; E-mail: info@mcknight.org; URL: http://www.mcknight.org

Foundation type: Independent foundation
Limitations: Awards by nomination only to residents of MN who are direct-care personnel with minimum public recognition and minimum financial remuneration; and to MN artists and to individuals for preservation of natural areas and open space in the Twin Cities area.
Publications: Application guidelines; Annual report; Financial statement; Grants list; Informational brochure; Informational brochure (including application guidelines); Newsletter; Occasional report.

Financial data: Year ended 12/31/2005.
Assets, $2,050,595,000 (M); Expenditures,
$106,510,176; Total giving, $90,710,176.
Fields of interest: Arts; Botanical/horticulture/
landscape services; Human services.
Type of support: Awards/grants by nomination only;
Awards/prizes.
Application information:
 Deadline(s): July 11 for Human Services;
 Nominations for Champions of Open Space
 accepted throughout the year.
 Additional information: Individual applications
 not accepted; Completion of formal
 nomination required for named programs.
Program descriptions:
 McKnight Distinguished Artist Award: This award
is given to a MN artist in recognition of his/her
artistic excellence and significant impact on the
state's cultural life over several decades. Each
year, one artist is selected through a nomination
process, to receive this $40,000 award. Artists in
all disciplines, including ceramics, dance, film,
literature, music, theater, and visual arts, whose
careers have made a substantial impact on the arts
in MN may be nominated. Artists must have worked
in MN over a span of decades and have achieved
their primary successes in MN, although they do not
have to reside there at the time of nomination.
Self-nominations and nominations by FAX, e-mail, or
telephone are not accepted. Once an artist has
been nominated, he/she will be considered each
year for three years. No one artist may receive this
award twice.
 *Virginia McKnight Binger Awards in Human
Service:* Established in 1985 to honor Minnesotans
who are extraordinarily dedicated to meeting the
needs of others. Typical recipients of this award are
people who have worked quietly and selflessly, with
little or no recognition, taking action on their own
initiative with few resources. Each year, the
foundation presents ten awards of $7,500 each to
people who have helped others to become
productive, participating members of their
communities. Recipients are selected by a
committee of individuals active in human services
fields who review all nominations. Nominees should
demonstrate exceptional commitment to human
services in MN and address concerns in areas such
as adoption, chemical dependency, childcare,
corrections, counseling, employment, family
violence, foster care, geriatrics, disabilities,
healthcare, housing, mental health, neighborhood
or community involvement, and youth activities.
Deadline July 12.
 Champions of Open Space: Awards by
nominations only to individuals or groups that have
made extraordinary contributions to open-space
protection in the seven-county Twin Cities area by
engaging citizens and policymakers in decisions to
protect and preserve natural areas and open
spaces; and by providing leadership that has made
a difference in promoting the importance of natural
areas and open spaces. Nominations may be
submitted by Embrace Open Space partner
organizations, members of the public, public
officials, or others. Those nominated in one award
cycle will be considered for the other award
presentations. Everyone nominated for the award
will receive a certificate of nomination. See Web
site for the following complete nomination
guidelines and forms: http://
www.embraceopenspace.org/openspace/
champions/index.asp.
EIN: 410754835

5972
Medical Library Association

65 E. Wacker Pl., Ste. 1900
Chicago, IL 60601-7246 (312) 419-9094
Contact: For Scholarships: Lisa C. Fried
FAX: (312) 419-8950; E-mail: info@mlahq.org;
URL: http://www.mlanet.org

Foundation type: Public charity
Limitations: Research grants, scholarships and
fellowships to professionals in the health sciences
information field.
Publications: Application guidelines; Annual report.
Financial data: Year ended 12/31/2004.
Assets, $3,259,858 (M); Expenditures,
$3,004,194; Total giving, $69,563; Grants to
individuals, 33 grants totaling $69,563 (high:
$25,000, low: $66).
Fields of interest: Libraries/library science;
Libraries (school); Libraries (medical); Biomedicine
research; Minorities; Asians/Pacific Islanders;
African Americans/Blacks; Hispanics/Latinos;
Native Americans/American Indians.
Type of support: Fellowships; Research;
Scholarships—to individuals; Travel grants;
Doctoral support.
Application information: Applications accepted.
Application form required.
 Initial approach: Telephone.
 Deadline(s): Nov. 15 for Lindberg Research
 Fellowship, and Dec. 1 for scholarships
Program descriptions:
 *MLA Research, Development, and Demonstration
Project Grant:* Grants range from $100 to $1,000 to
provide support for research, development, or
demonstration projects that will help to promote
excellence in the field of health sciences
librarianship and information sciences.
 MLA Scholarship: A scholarship of up to $5,000
is granted to a student who is entering an
ALA-accredited library school or who has yet to
finish at least one half of the program's
requirements in the year following the granting of
the scholarship.
 MLA Scholarship for Minority Students: A
scholarship of up to $5,000 is granted to a minority
student who is entering an ALA-accredited library
school or has yet to finish at least one half of the
program's requirements in the year following the
granting of the scholarship. African American,
Hispanic, Asian, Native American, or Pacific
Islander American individuals who wish to study
health sciences librarianship are eligible to apply.
 David A. Kronick Traveling Fellowship: One
$2,000 fellowship is awarded each year to cover
expenses involved in traveling to three or more
medical libraries in the U.S. and Canada, for the
purpose of studying a specific aspect of health
information management.
 Donald A.B. Lindberg Research Fellowship: A
$25,000 grant is awarded annually by MLA through
a competitive grant process. This fellowship is to
fund research aimed at expanding the research
knowledgebase, linking the information services
provided by librarians to improved health care and
advances in biomedical research.
 Thomson Scientific/MLA Doctoral Fellowship: A
fellowship in the amount of $2,000 fosters and
encourages superior students to conduct doctoral
work in an area of health sciences librarianship or
information sciences and provides support to
individuals who have been admitted to candidacy.
The award supports research or travel applicable to
the candidate's study within a twelve-month period.
The award is given every other year and may not be
used for tuition.
EIN: 360540525

5973
MEEMIC Foundation for the Future of Education

691 N. Squirrel Rd., Ste. 100
Auburn Hills, MI 48326 (248) 375-7535
Contact: Kristy Mitchell, Dir.
FAX: (248) 375-7549;
E-mail: foundation@meemic.com; URL: http://
www.meemic.com/comfndoverCKR.htm

Foundation type: Company-sponsored foundation
Limitations: Mini-grants of up to $2,500 awarded
to MI educators in support of innovative programs
that enhance curriculum.
Financial data: Year ended 12/31/2004.
Assets, $1,739,659 (M); Expenditures, $72,812;
Total giving, $47,731; Grants to individuals, 31
grants totaling $47,731 (high: $2,500, low: $232).
Fields of interest: Education.
Type of support: Awards/prizes.
Application information: Contact foundation for
current application deadline/guidelines.
EIN: 383048526

5974
Melanoma Research Foundation

(also known as MRF)
24 Old Georgetown Rd.
Lake Forest, CA 92630 (800) 673-1290
Contact: Bill Marsch, Exec. Dir.
FAX: (732) 821-5955; E-mail: mrf@melanoma.org;
URL: http://www.melanoma.org

Foundation type: Public charity
Limitations: Research grants to scientists for the
study and eventual cure of melanoma.
Publications: Annual report; Newsletter.
Financial data: Year ended 12/31/2004.
Assets, $754,294 (M); Expenditures, $769,915;
Total giving, $350,000.
Fields of interest: Cancer research; Skin disorders
research.
Type of support: Research; Postdoctoral support;
Travel grants.
Application information: Application form required.
 Deadline(s): July 1
Program description:
 Young Investigator Awards: Awards $50,000 per
year for two years to researchers who are either
permanent residents or citizens of the U.S. and hold
a Ph.D. or M.D. degree and a title equivalent to
assistant professor or have at least four years of
postdoctoral experience and are eligible to apply.
Funds used for travel must be limited to $2,000 per
year and cannot be used for international travel.
EIN: 760514428

5975
Menlo Park-Atherton Education Foundation

P.O. Box 584
Menlo Park, CA 94026-0584 (650) 325-0100
Contact: Carol Fields, Co-Pres.
E-mail: mpaef@mpaef.org; URL: http://
www.mpaef.org

Foundation type: Public charity
Limitations: Grants to teachers who are employed
by the Menlo Park City School District, CA, to fund
classroom instructional programs.
Financial data: Year ended 06/30/2004.
Assets, $1,791,648 (M); Expenditures,
$1,039,658; Total giving, $953,734; Grants to
individuals, 19 grants totaling $29,864 (high:
$4,000, low: $106).

Fields of interest: Elementary/secondary education.
Type of support: Program development.
Application information: Deadline Oct. 15; Completion of formal application required, including detailed budget; See Web site for further application information.
EIN: 942871701

5976
Merck Institute for Science Education, Inc.
P.O. Box 100, WS2F-96
Whitehouse Station, NJ 08889-0100
Contact: Carlo Parravano, Exec. V.P.
URL: http://www.mise.org

Foundation type: Company-sponsored foundation
Limitations: Stipends to K-8 educators from Rahway, Linden, and Reddington Township public schools, NJ; and North Penn school district, PA, to attend peer teacher workshops for professional development.
Financial data: Year ended 12/31/2003.
Assets, $0; Expenditures, $3,054,468; Total giving, $1,331,900; Grants to individuals, 630 grants totaling $271,750 (high: $40,000, low: $50).
Fields of interest: Elementary school/education; Education.
Type of support: Program development.
Application information: Applications not accepted.
EIN: 223208944

5977
Messenger of Salvation
P.O. Box 624
Bethany, OK 73008

Foundation type: Operating foundation
Limitations: Grants to individuals in India for missionary work.
Financial data: Year ended 12/31/2003.
Assets, $2,173 (M); Expenditures, $17,805; Total giving, $17,755; Grants to individuals, totaling $17,755.
Fields of interest: Religion.
Type of support: Grants to individuals.
Application information: Applications not accepted.
EIN: 731361590

5978
The Metropolitan Museum of Art
1000 5th Ave.
New York, NY 10028-0198 (212) 879-5500
FAX: (212) 396-5168;
E-mail: education.grants@metmuseum.org;
URL: http://www.metmuseum.org/education/er_fellow.asp

Foundation type: Public charity
Limitations: Fellowships to graduate students and postdoctoral researchers who specialize in art history and conservation.
Financial data: Year ended 06/30/2004.
Assets, $2,483,852,019 (M); Expenditures, $256,149,551; Total giving, $916,342; Grants to individuals, 74 grants totaling $916,342 (high: $33,303, low: $1,375).
Fields of interest: Art conservation; Museums (art); Art history.
Type of support: Fellowships.

Application information:
Initial approach: E-mail.
Deadline(s): Jan. 9 for Conservation Fellowships, Nov. 7 for Art History Fellowships
Additional information: Application by letter including three letters of recommendation, resume, transcripts and work schedule; See Web site for further application information.
Program descriptions:
Bothmer Fellowship: Awarded to an outstanding graduate student who has been admitted to the doctoral program of a university in the U.S., and who has submitted an outline of a thesis dealing with either Greek or Roman art.
Chester Dale Fellowships: Intended for individuals whose fields of study are related to the fine arts of the western world and who are preferably American citizens under the age of 40. The grants which typically cover periods from three months to a year, are for research at the Metropolitan Museum.
Andrew W. Mellon Fellowships: For promising young scholars with commendable research projects related to the Museum's collections, as well as for distinguished visiting scholars from the U.S. and abroad who can serve as teachers and advisors and make their expertise available to catalogue and refine the collections.
J. Clawson Mills Fellowships: Awarded for up to one year's study or research at the Museum or abroad in any branch of the fine arts relating to the Metropolitan Museum's collection.
Polaire Weissman Fellowships: For qualified graduate students who preferably will have completed graduate studies in the fine arts or studies in costume, and who are interested in pursuing costume history in a museum or teaching career, or other career (including conservation) related to the field of costume.
Jane and Morgan Whitney Fellowship: Awarded for study, work, or research to students of the fine arts whose fields are related to the Museum's collections, with preference to be given to students in the decorative arts who are under 40 years of age.
Theodore Rousseau Fellowships: Awarded for the training of students whose goal is to enter museums as curators of painting. Applicants should have been enrolled for at least one year in an advanced degree program in the field of art history.
Annette Kade Fellowship: Awarded to French and German pre-doctoral art history students for one year's study or research at the Metropolitan Museum.
Douglass Foundation Fellowship in American Art: For one year's study or research in the American Wing (in either the Department of American Paintings and Sculpture or the Department of American Decorative Arts) on an aspect of the Museum's collection.
Andrew W. Mellon Conservation Fellowship: For training in one or more of the following Departments of the Museum: Paintings Conservation, Objects Conservation (including sculpture, metalwork, glass, ceramics, furniture, and archaeological objects), Musical Instruments, Arms and Armor, Paper Conservation, Textile Conservation, The Costume Institute, and Asian Art Conservation.
L.W. Frohlich Charitable Trust: Awards a fellowship in the Department of Objects Conservation. Applicants should be conservators, art historians or scientists.
Sherman Fairchild Fellowship: For study and training in the following Museum conservation departments: Paintings Conservation, Objects Conservation (including sculpture, metalwork, glass, ceramics, furniture, and archaeological objects), Musical Instruments, Arms and Armor,

Paper Conservation, Photograph Conservation, Textile Conservation, The Costume Institute, and Asian Art Conservation.
EIN: 131624086

5979
MFU Training Plan Trust
240 2nd St.
San Francisco, CA 94105

Foundation type: Operating foundation
Limitations: Training classes for members of the CA Pacific Coast Marine Fireman's Union, including travel expenses.
Financial data: Year ended 12/31/2003.
Assets, $0 (M); Expenditures, $138,866; Total giving, $99,596.
Type of support: Scholarships—to individuals; Travel grants.
Application information: Applications not accepted.
Program description:
MFU Training Plan: Training classes take place in either Oakland, CA, or Piney Point, MD. Approximately 400 members of the MFU participate. The trust is funded by American President Lines, Ltd. and Matson Navigation Company, Inc., the employers of MFU members.
EIN: 943058922

5980
Milheim Foundation for Cancer Research
c/o U.S. Bank, N.A.
8401 E. Belleview Ave., Ste. 200
Denver, CO 80237-2900 (303) 713-6466
Contact: Jennifer Lessard, Trust Account Rep., U.S. Bank, N.A.
E-mail: Jennifer.lessard@USBank.com; Additional tel.: (303) 713-6457

Foundation type: Independent foundation
Limitations: Grants for research on the prevention, treatment, or cure of cancer to residents of the continental U.S. No grants for travel to meetings or presentation of papers.
Publications: Application guidelines.
Financial data: Year ended 12/31/2003.
Assets, $1,405,066 (M); Expenditures, $124,569; Total giving, $103,300.
Fields of interest: Cancer research.
Type of support: Research.
Application information: Application form required.
Deadline(s): Mar. 15.
EIN: 846018431

5981
Minnesota American Legion, Auxiliary & The Sons of The American Legion Brain Science Foundation
(formerly Minnesota American Legion Auxiliary Brain Science Foundation)
c/o State Veterans Bldg.
20 W. 12th St., 3rd Fl.
St. Paul, MN 55155

Foundation type: Independent foundation
Limitations: Grants for the study of brain science research.
Financial data: Year ended 12/31/2004.
Assets, $1,340,161 (M); Expenditures, $93,797; Total giving, $78,231; Grants to individuals, totaling $10,000.
Fields of interest: Brain disorders.
Type of support: Research.

Application information: Applications not accepted.

> *Additional information:* Unsolicited requests for funds not accepted.

EIN: 411577513

5982

Missouri Chamber of Commerce Educational Foundation, Inc.

428 E. Capitol Ave.
Jefferson City, MO   65101   (573) 634-3511
Contact: Walter "Wally" A. Hellebusch, Chair.
FAX: (573) 634-8855;
E-mail: info@mochamber.com; URL: http://www.mochamber.org

Foundation type: Public charity
Limitations: Scholarships to MO teachers for enrollment in the Missourianna and Economic Study tours. Some support also to individual entrepreneurs.
Financial data: Year ended 09/30/2003. Assets, $963,503 (M); Expenditures, $306,030; Total giving, $15,036; Grants to individuals, 30 grants totaling $15,036 (high: $500, low: $450).
Fields of interest: Education; Economic development.
Type of support: Travel grants.
Application information: Contact foundation for current application deadline/guidelines; Initial approach by e-mail.
EIN: 436051487

5983

Morris Animal Foundation

45 Inverness Dr. E.
Englewood, CO   80112-5480   (303) 790-2345
Contact: Patricia N. Olson D.V.M., Ph.D., C.E.O. and Pres.
FAX: (303) 790-4066; Additional tel.: (800) 243-2345; URL: http://www.morrisanimalfoundation.org

Foundation type: Public charity
Limitations: Fellowships and awards, by nomination only, to researchers specializing in companion animal or wildlife research.
Publications: Annual report; Informational brochure; Newsletter (including application guidelines).
Financial data: Year ended 06/30/2005. Assets, $62,945,178 (M); Expenditures, $566,074.
Fields of interest: Veterinary medicine.
Type of support: Fellowships; Awards/grants by nomination only; Doctoral support.
Application information:

> *Initial approach:* Pre-proposal from applicant's institution.
> *Additional information:* See Web site for additional application information.

Program descriptions:

> *Established Investigator Grants:* Provides one to three years of funding for projects addressing animal health topics of significance to the Morris Animal Foundation. The average budget for health studies is $38,000 per year.
> *Fellowship Training Grants:* Provides training opportunities that will produce biomedical scientists (veterinarian and/or Ph.D.) committed to a career in companion animal and/or wildlife health research. The program provides two years of funding at a maximum $35,000 per year.
> *First Award Grants:* Provides doctoral (Ph.D.) investigators opportunities early in their career by:

- providing research funding for their "first" project in companion animal or wildlife research
- pairing them with an established researcher to facilitate launching a successful, long-term career in advancing companion animal and wildlife health.

The program provides two years of funding at $50,000 maximum per year.
EIN: 846032307

5984

Morrison Trust

c/o Frost National Bank Trust Dept.
P.O. Box 2950
San Antonio, TX   78299-2950   (210) 220-4991

Foundation type: Independent foundation
Limitations: Grants to support research, scientific study, development of methods of treatment, and the improvement of existing methods of treating and preventing human sickness in the fields of nutrition, blood chemistry, and radionics and electricity, primarily in TX.
Financial data: Year ended 09/30/2004. Assets, $3,363,522 (M); Expenditures, $212,532; Total giving, $178,875; Grants to individuals, 4 grants totaling $178,875 (high: $54,600, low: $35,734).
Fields of interest: Medical research, institute; Nutrition.
Type of support: Research.
Application information:

> *Deadline(s):* July 1
> *Additional information:* Contact trust for current application guidelines.

EIN: 746013340

5985

The Multiple Myeloma Research Foundation, Inc.

383 Main Ave., 5th Fl.
Norwalk, CT   06851   (203) 229-0464
Contact: Scott T. Santarella, Exec. Dir.
FAX: (203) 229-0572; E-mail: info@themmrf.org;
URL: http://www.multiplemyeloma.org

Foundation type: Public charity
Limitations: Grants to individuals for multiple myeloma research.
Publications: Application guidelines; Annual report; Financial statement; Informational brochure; Newsletter.
Financial data: Year ended 12/31/2004. Assets, $10,373,347 (M); Expenditures, $10,730,720; Total giving, $7,540,126; Grant to an individual, 1 grant totaling $1,000,000.
Fields of interest: Cancer research.
Type of support: Research; Awards/prizes.
Application information: Applications accepted. Application form required.

> *Initial approach:* Letter or telephone.
> *Deadline(s):* May 1 for Senior Research Awards and Mar. 1 for Fellows Awards
> *Additional information:* See Web site for additional application information/guidelines.

Program descriptions:

> *Fellows' Awards:* Awards $50,000 to researchers entering the field of multiple myeloma working under the direction of a research sponsor.
> *Senior Research Awards:* Awards $100,000 to investigators with an interest in myeloma who have been working in cancer research for a minimum of five years.

EIN: 061504413

5986

Muscular Dystrophy Association, Inc.

3300 E. Sunrise Dr.
Tucson, AZ   85718-3208   (520) 529-2000
Contact: Grants Mgr.
FAX: (520) 529-5454; E-mail: grants@mdausa.org;
Additional tel.: (800) 572-1717; URL: http://www.mdausa.org/research

Foundation type: Public charity
Limitations: Research grants to doctors specializing in muscular dystrophy.
Publications: Application guidelines; Annual report; Grants list; Informational brochure; Newsletter.
Financial data: Year ended 03/31/2003. Assets, $190,030,405 (M); Expenditures, $156,365,431; Total giving, $26,424,556; Grants to individuals, 337 grants totaling $26,424,556 (high: $1,058,325, low: $950).
Fields of interest: Nerve, muscle & bone diseases; Muscular dystrophy; Nerve, muscle & bone research; Muscular dystrophy research.
Type of support: Research; Postdoctoral support.
Application information: Application form required.

> *Initial approach:* Pre-proposal.
> *Deadline(s):* Jan. 15 and July 15
> *Additional information:* See Web site for further application information.

Program descriptions:

> *Development Grant:* Awards up to $45,000 per year for up to three years to individuals who hold an M.D., Ph.D. or equivalent degree for research into neuromuscular diseases. Grantees must have at least 18 months of postdoctoral research laboratory training at the time of application.
> *Research Grant:* Awards for up to three years to individuals who hold an M.D., Ph.D. or equivalent degree to conduct and supervise an original research program. Applicants must be professional or faculty members at appropriate educational, medical or research institutions. There is no maximum funding amount.

EIN: 131665552

5987

Musicares Foundation, Inc.

3402 Pico Blvd.
Santa Monica, CA   90405-2118
(310) 392-3777
Contact: Kristen Madsen, Sr. V.P.
Application tel.: (800) 687-4227 free and confidential; URL: http://www.grammy.com/musicares

Foundation type: Public charity
Limitations: Grants to individuals for projects that advance: the archiving and preservation of the music and recorded sound heritage of the Americas; research and research implementation projects related to music; and the medical and occupational well-being of music professionals.
Financial data: Year ended 07/31/2004. Assets, $5,077,429 (M); Expenditures, $3,568,042; Total giving, $1,369,485; Grants to individuals, totaling $1,365,335.
Fields of interest: Arts, research; Music.
Type of support: Program development; Research.
Application information: Applications accepted. Application form required.

> *Deadline(s):* Oct. 1;
> *Applicants should submit the following:*
> 1) Budget Information
> *Additional information:* Applications by fax not accepted.

Program description:

> *Musicares Professional Research Program:* Grant amounts generally range from $10,000 to $20,000

for 12 to 24 months. Priority is given to projects of national significance that achieve a broad reach and whose final results are accessible to the general public.
EIN: 954470909

5988
Muskingum County Community Foundation

534 Putnam Ave.
Zanesville, OH   43701   (740) 453-5192
Contact: David P. Mitzel, Exec. Dir.; For scholarships: Heather Sands, Prog. Coord.
Scholarship Central tel.: (740) 453-5192
FAX: (740) 453-5734; E-mail: giving@mccf.org;
URL: http://www.mccf.org

Foundation type: Community foundation
Limitations: Awards by nomination only to community volunteers from Muskingum County, OH.
Publications: Application guidelines; Annual report; Grants list; Informational brochure.
Financial data: Year ended 12/31/2004. Assets, $14,861,022 (M); Expenditures, $1,263,529; Total giving, $661,993; Grants to individuals, 58 grants totaling $48,595 (high: $2,000; low: $100).
Fields of interest: Philanthropy/voluntarism.
Type of support: Awards/grants by nomination only; Awards/prizes.
Application information: Deadline Apr. 1; Initial approach by letter or telephone; Completion of formal nomination required; Nomination form available online.
Program description:
Thomas Community Service Award: Individuals and organizations may nominate community volunteers from Muskingum County to receive this award, who then name a charitable organization to receive a $1,000 grant from the foundation.
EIN: 311147022

5989
Myasthenia Gravis Foundation of America, Inc.

1821 University Ave. W., Ste. S256
St. Paul, MN   55104   (800) 541-5454
Contact: L.J. Taugher, Chief Exec.
FAX: (651) 917-1835;
E-mail: mgfa@myasthenia.org; Additional tel.:
(651) 917-6256; URL: http://www.myasthenia.org

Foundation type: Public charity
Limitations: Fellowships to individuals in the U.S. or Canada for research on myasthenia gravis.
Publications: Application guidelines; Annual report; Grants list; Informational brochure; Newsletter.
Financial data: Year ended 12/31/2004. Assets, $953,015 (M); Expenditures, $351,434; Total giving, $64,597; Grants to individuals, totaling $64,597.
Fields of interest: Medical school/education; Nursing school/education; Myasthenia gravis; Myasthenia gravis research.
Type of support: Fellowships; Postdoctoral support; Graduate support; Doctoral support.
Application information: Application form required.
Deadline(s): Deadlines vary.
Additional information: See Web site for deadlines and application guidelines.
Program descriptions:
Henry R. Viets Medical/Graduate Student Research Fellowship: Fellowships of $3,000 on an annual basis awarded to current medical or

graduate students interested in the scientific basis of myasthenia gravis or related neuromuscular conditions, to further scientific inquiries into the nature of these disorders and encourage further research. To apply for this fellowship, submit eight copies of the following: letter of interest, summary of the research proposal and its significance to myasthenia gravis or related neuromuscular conditions, curriculum vitae of applicant and sponsoring preceptor, letter of recommendation from preceptor that indicates acceptance of the candidate and outlines the proposed work plan for the research study. Failure to include any of these items may delay review of the application. Incomplete applications will not be reviewed. Deadline Mar. 15.
Katharine M. Donohoe Nursing Research Fellowship: Fellowships of $3,000 on an annual basis are awarded to nurses or nursing students interested in studying problems encountered by patients with myasthenia gravis or related neuromuscular conditions. To apply, submit four copies of the following: cover letter, summary of the research proposal and its association to myasthenia gravis or related neuromuscular conditions, proposed budget, curriculum vitae of applicant and sponsoring preceptor (student only), letter of recommendation from preceptor that indicates acceptance of the candidate and outlines the proposed work plan for the research study. Incomplete applications will not be reviewed. Applications reviewed as received. No deadline.
Kermit E. Osserman/Hilbert Sosin/Blanche McClure Fellowship: Twelve-month postdoctoral fellowships to individuals for clinical or basic research pertinent to myasthenia gravis or related neuromuscular disorders. Research may be concerned with neuromuscular transmission, immunology, molecular or cell biology of the neuromuscular synapse; or the etiology/pathogenesis, diagnosis of myasthenia gravis. To apply, submit a proposal of no more than 10 pages in NIH format, providing a statement of specific aims, experimental design and research methods. Describe the research environment, including the educational opportunities available to the applicant. Submit a budget (stipend, supplies, travel and administrative lay support up to a maximum of $50,000). Also, submit a 250-word lay summary of proposed research, including hypotheses. Recipient must submit curriculum vitae and preceptor's curriculum vitae, letters of recommendation from preceptor and a past of current academic advisor. Deadline Oct. 1. Recipient must be a permanent resident of the U.S. or Canada who has been accepted to work in the laboratory of an established investigator at an institution in the U.S., Canada or abroad deemed appropriate by the Medical/Scientific Advisory Board of the Myasthenia Gravis Foundation of America, Inc.; or a foreign national who has been accepted to work in laboratory of an established investigator at an institution in the U.S. or Canada deemed appropriate by the Medical/Scientific Advisory Board of the Myasthenia Gravis Foundation of America, Inc.
EIN: 135672224

5990
Mycenaean Foundation, Inc.

c/o The Millburn Corp.
1270 Avenue of the Americas
New York, NY   10020
Application address: c/o Institute for Aegean Prehistory, Attn.: Philip Betancourt, 3550 Market St., Ste. 100, Philadelphia, PA 19104

Foundation type: Independent foundation
Limitations: Grants to support Mycenaean research.
Financial data: Year ended 12/31/2004. Assets, $559,701 (M); Expenditures, $31,792; Total giving, $18,000; Grants to individuals, totaling $18,000.
Fields of interest: History/archaeology; Greece.
Type of support: Research.
Application information: Contact foundation for current application deadline; Application by letter.
EIN: 436070522

5991
Myers Oceanographic & Marine Biology Trust

2600 Garden Rd., Ste. 320
Monterey, CA   93940
Contact: Stephen B. Ruth, V.P.
Application address: 129 Kailua Cir., Marina, CA 93933, tel.: (831) 645-1396

Foundation type: Operating foundation
Limitations: Research grants to marine biologists, primarily in CA.
Financial data: Year ended 12/31/2002. Assets, $646,819 (M); Expenditures, $35,819; Total giving, $35,000; Grants to individuals, 25 grants totaling $35,000.
Fields of interest: Marine science.
Type of support: Research.
Application information: Deadline Dec. 31; Application by letter.
Program description:
Marine Science Research Program: Grants are awarded through Moss Landing Marine Laboratories, Hopkins Marine Station, and the University of California at Santa Cruz.
EIN: 770094228

5992
NAPHCC Educational Foundation

180 S. Washington St
P.O. Box 6808
Falls Church, VA   22046   (703) 237-8100
Contact: Allen Inlow, C.E.O.

Foundation type: Public charity
Limitations: Research grants to individuals in the fields of engineering and corporate management.
Financial data: Year ended 12/31/2003. Assets, $8,161,446 (M); Expenditures, $724,352; Total giving, $60,000; Grants to individuals, 7 grants totaling $60,000 (high: $12,000, low: $1,250).
Fields of interest: Business school/education; Engineering.
Type of support: Research.
Application information: Contact foundation for current application deadline/guidelines.
EIN: 541396371

5993
NARSAD, The Mental Health Research Association

(formerly National Alliance for Research on Schizophrenia and Depression)
60 Cutter Mill Rd., Ste. 404
Great Neck, NY   11021   (516) 829-0091
FAX: (516) 487-6930; E-mail: grants@narsad.org;
URL: http://www.narsad.org

Foundation type: Public charity

Limitations: Research grants to scientists at all stages of their careers for neurobiological research, specifically severe psychiatric brain and behavior disorders.
Publications: Application guidelines; Annual report; Financial statement; Grants list; Informational brochure; Newsletter.
Financial data: Year ended 12/31/2004. Assets, $25,064,008 (M); Expenditures, $18,711,618; Total giving, $16,206,994; Grants to individuals, 460 grants totaling $16,206,994 (high: $100,000, low: $30,000).
Fields of interest: Schizophrenia; Neuroscience; Neuroscience research.
Type of support: Fellowships; Research; Awards/prizes; Postdoctoral support.
Application information: Applications accepted. Application form required. Application form available on the grantmaker's Web site.
  Initial approach: Application submission.
  Deadline(s): Varies
  Applicants should submit the following:
    1) Proposal
    2) Budget Information
    3) Curriculum vitae
  Additional information: Application must also include face sheet; See Web site for further application information and for application forms.
Program descriptions:
  Distinguished Investigator Award: A one-year award of $100,000 is provided for established scientists pursuing innovative projects in diverse areas of neurobiological research. Deadline May 15.
  Independent Investigator Award: A two-year award up to $50,000 per year (maximum of $100,000 for two years) is provided to scientists at the associate professor level or equivalent, who are clearly independent and who have won national competitive support as a principal investigator. Basic and/or clinical investigators are supported, but research must be relevant to schizophrenia, major affective disorders, or other serious mental illnesses. Deadline Mar. 5.
  Young Investigator Award: Provides support for the most promising young scientists conducting neurological research. One- and two-year awards up to $30,000 per year are provided to enable promising investigators to either extend research fellowship training or begin careers as independent research faculty. Basic and/or clinical investigators are supported, but research must be relevant to schizophrenia, major affective disorders, or other serious mental illnesses. Deadline July 25.
  Staglin Family Music Festival Award: Awards $250,000 for one investigator with an M.D., Ph.D., or doctoral degree and postdoctoral training applicable to schizophrenia, at assistant or associate professor level, age 45 or younger. The candidate should be nominated by the dean, department chair, or head of the scientific department of his/her university. Deadline Dec. 2.
EIN: 311020010

5994

The Nasdaq Stock Market Educational Foundation, Inc.

9513 Key West Ave.
Rockville, MD   20850-3389   (800) 842-0356
E-mail: foundation@nasdaq.com; Application address: 1801 K St., N.W., 8th Fl., Washington, DC 20006; URL: http://www.nasdaq.com/services/education_initiatives.stm

Foundation type: Company-sponsored foundation

Limitations: Fellowships to specifically qualified individuals for the purpose of conducting independent academic study or research on financial markets.
Financial data: Year ended 12/31/2003. Assets, $34,766,786 (M); Expenditures, $1,386,820; Total giving, $1,139,450.
Fields of interest: Economics.
Type of support: Fellowships.
Application information:
  Deadline(s): Vary
  Applicants should submit the following:
    1) Resume
    2) Curriculum vitae
    3) Budget Information
    4) Letter(s) of recommendation
  Additional information: Application by proposal; See Web site for further application information.
EIN: 521864429

5995

The National Academy of Education

500 5th St. N.W., No. 1030
Washington, DC   20001
Contact: Gregory White, Exec. Dir.
FAX: (202) 334-2350;
E-mail: info@naeducation.org; URL: http://www.naeducation.org

Foundation type: Operating foundation
Limitations: Fellowships to recent recipients of a Ph.D. or equivalent degree to promote scholarship in the U.S. and abroad on matters relevant to the improvement of education in all its forms.
Publications: Application guidelines; Informational brochure.
Financial data: Year ended 12/31/2004. Assets, $5,795,778 (M); Expenditures, $2,153,920; Total giving, $1,464,292; Grants to individuals, 61 grants totaling $1,464,292 (high: $50,000, low: $2,692, average grant: $12,500-$25,000).
Fields of interest: Humanities; Education, research; Social sciences; Psychology/behavioral science.
Type of support: Research; Postdoctoral support.
Application information: Applications accepted. Application form required. Application form available on the grantmaker's Web site.
  Initial approach: Telephone or e-mail.
  Copies of proposal: 6
  Deadline(s): Varies
  Applicants should submit the following:
    1) Letter(s) of recommendation
  Additional information: Applications should be sent by mail; Recipients notified in mid-May.
Program description:
  NAE/Spencer Postdoctoral Fellowship Program: Applicants must have received their Ph.D., Ed.D., or equivalent degree within the past five years. Applications from individuals in education, the humanities, or the social and behavioral sciences will be accepted. Applications must describe research relevant to education. No group applications will be accepted. Applications will be judged on the applicant's past research record, the promise of early work, and the quality of the project described in the application. Employees of the Spencer Foundation or the National Academy of Education are ineligible. Fellows receive $50,000 for one academic year of research, or $25,000 for each of two contiguous years, working half-time. Selection is made by a committee consisting of members of the National Academy of Education. Up to 20 fellowships are awarded each year.
EIN: 770415802

5996

National Alliance for Autism Research, Inc.

99 Wall St.
Research Park
Princeton, NJ   08540-1504   (609) 430-9160
FAX: (609) 430-9163; E-mail: naar@naar.org;
URL: http://www.naar.org

Foundation type: Public charity
Limitations: Research grants and fellowships to individuals for biomedical research into the causes, prevention, treatments, and cures for the autism spectrum disorders.
Publications: Application guidelines; Annual report; Financial statement; Grants list.
Financial data: Year ended 06/30/2005. Assets, $9,898,552 (M); Expenditures, $13,364,627; Total giving, $6,878,414; Grants to individuals, 110 grants totaling $6,878,414 (high: $75,000, low: $14,000).
Fields of interest: Autism research; Biomedicine research.
Type of support: Fellowships; Research.
Application information:
  Initial approach: Letter.
  Deadline(s): Dec. 15 for Letter of Interest and Feb.1 for Autism Research Awards
  Additional information: Contact alliance for current application guidelines.
Program descriptions:
  NAAR Autism Research Award: Investigators at established research institutions who require funds to develop concepts and obtain preliminary data may apply for up to $60,000 for a two-year award or up to $30,000 for a one-year award under this program. Interested applicants must submit a brief pre-proposal letter of no more than two pages to the alliance's Grants Office. The letter should describe the project, its relevance for advancing the scientific understanding of autism, where the research will be conducted, and the qualifications of the proposed investigators. Relevant scientific disciplines include: biochemistry, cellular physiology, clinically-based studies, developmental biology-teratology, genetics, immunology, language/neurocognitive development, molecular biology, neuroanatomy, neuroimaging, structural biology, toxicology, and virology.
  Bristol-Myers Squibb Fellowships in Autism Psychopharmacology: Fellowships are given to train clinician-researchers in the treatment and study of autism, with an emphasis on neuropharmacology.
EIN: 043246763

5997

National Alopecia Areata Foundation

14 Mitchell Blvd.
San Rafael, CA   94903   (415) 472-3780
Contact: Vicki Kalabokes, C.E.O.
FAX: (415) 472-5343; E-mail: info@naaf.org;
Additional Tel: (415) 456-4644; URL: http://www.naaf.org

Foundation type: Public charity
Limitations: Grants to medical professionals for research on alopecia areata.
Publications: Application guidelines; Annual report; Financial statement; Informational brochure; Newsletter.
Financial data: Year ended 12/31/2003. Assets, $1,371,370 (L); Expenditures, $1,342,349; Total giving, $306,250.
Fields of interest: Medical research, institute.
Type of support: Research.
Application information: Application form required.

Initial approach: Letter or FAX.
Deadline(s): Mar. 14.
Additional information: Recipients will be notified by June 30.
EIN: 942780249

5998
National Association of Insurance Women (International) Education Foundation

(also known as NAIW (International))
6528 E. 101st St.
PMB 750
Tulsa, OK 74182 (800) 766-6249
Contact: Billie Sleet, Exec. Dir.
Application address: P.O. Box 4410, Tulsa, OK 74159
FAX: (918) 743-1968; E-mail: joinnaiw@naiw.org; URL: http://www.naiw.org

Foundation type: Independent foundation
Limitations: Scholarships to those in the insurance industry for continued professional studies.
Financial data: Year ended 06/30/2004.
Assets, $833,053 (M); Expenditures, $256,882; Total giving, $42,425; Grants to individuals, 41 grants totaling $42,425 (high: $2,450, low: $78).
Type of support: Scholarships—to individuals.
Application information: Applications accepted. Application form required. Application form available on the grantmaker's Web site.
Initial approach: E-mail.
Deadline(s): Aug., Dec., and Apr.
Additional information: See Web site for full program descriptions.
EIN: 731429257

5999
National Association of Secondary School Principals

1904 Association Dr.
Reston, VA 20191-1537 (703) 860-0200
Contact: Gerald N. Tirozzi, Exec. Dir.; Awards and scholarships: Rosa Aronson
URL: http://www.nassp.org

Foundation type: Public charity
Limitations: Awards and scholarships by nomination only to individuals, and awards to outstanding 6th-12th grade principals who are members of the National Association of Secondary School Principals.
Financial data: Year ended 06/30/2004.
Assets, $15,978,118 (M); Expenditures, $19,575,999; Total giving, $602,732; Grants to individuals, totaling $485,507.
Fields of interest: Education, administration/regulation; Education; Recreation; Youth development, services; Youth development; Community development.
Type of support: Awards/grants by nomination only; Awards/prizes; Precollege support; Undergraduate support.
Application information: See Web site for deadlines, application and nomination forms for each program.
Program descriptions:
Assistant Principal of the Year Award: Annual awards by nomination only to outstanding secondary school assistant principals who have succeeded in providing high quality learning opportunities for students. These administrators have demonstrated excellent leadership to staff and students, service to their communities, and contributions to the overall profession of educational leadership. Each of the 50 states, DC

and the Department of Defense Education Activity selects one assistant principal. From these state winners, three finalists are selected and eligible for the National Assistant Principal of the Year award. National finalists are invited to attend the NASSP Annual Convention. The National Assistant Principal of the Year receives a $5,000 grant. Deadline is Oct. 1.
Principal of the Year Award: Annual awards by nomination only to outstanding middle-level and high school principals. Recipients have demonstrated extraordinary leadership, commitment to students and staff, service to communities, and contributions to the overall profession of educational leadership. Each of the 50 states, DC and the Dept. of Defense Education Activity selects one middle-level and one high school principal. From these state winners, six finalists (three middle and three high school) are selected and eligible for the National Principal of the Year award. Each finalist receives an award and a $1,500 grant. The National Principals of the Year receive awards and a $5,000 grant. These grants are used to improve learning at the recipient's school, including, but not limited to, a special school project and/or professional development opportunities. Deadline Jan. 10.
National Honor Society Scholarship: Awards scholarships, on an annual basis and by nomination only to high school seniors who demonstrate outstanding scholarship, leadership, service and character. Awards are in the amount of $1,000 each. Nominees are required to answer an essay question as part of the nomination form. Deadline Jan. 24.
Prudential Spirit of Community Award: This awards program recognizes students in grades 5 through twelve who have demonstrated exemplary community service. Schools and officially-designated organizations may select one middle-level and one high school Local Honoree for every 1,000 students. Local Honorees are judged at the state level and 104 State Honorees (including Honorees from PR and DC) receive $1,000 and an all-expenses-paid trip to DC in May, where ten National Honorees are chosen. Each recipient receives an additional $5,000, a gold medallion and a crystal trophy for his or her school. Applications can be obtained from every middle or high school, or from officially-designated local organizations across the country, including Girl Scout councils, county 4-H organizations, Campfire USA councils, American Red Cross chapters, YMCAs and Volunteer Center of Points of Light Foundation.
Wendy's High School Heisman Award: Awards to high school seniors who are recognized for their exceptional academics, athletic and community service efforts. Each year, two national winners, one male and one female, earn $2,500 each for their schools. From initial nominees, 1,020 students are selected as state finalists, and of those, 102 are named state winners. The competition continues with the selection of 12 national finalists, who receive $1,000 each for their schools. Deadline Oct. 1. Nomination material can be available online at http://www.wendyshighschoolheisman.com or call (800) 205-6367 or e-mail wendys@act.org. For more information e-mail frank_vamos@wendys.com.
TREE NLC Scholarships: Awards scholarships by nomination only to deserving student leaders or emerging leaders to participate in National Student Leadership Camp (NLC), as provided by the Trust to Reach Education Excellence (TREE). Thirty scholarships will be provided.
EIN: 526006937

6000
National Cancer Center, Inc.

88 Sunnyside Blvd.
Plainview, NY 11803-1507 (516) 349-0610
Contact: Regina English, Exec. Dir.

Foundation type: Public charity
Limitations: Fellowships for research into the causes and cure of cancer.
Financial data: Year ended 03/31/2004.
Assets, $1,806,035 (M); Expenditures, $34,091,171; Total giving, $215,529; Grants to individuals, totaling $215,529.
Fields of interest: Cancer research.
Type of support: Fellowships; Research.
Application information: Contact foundation for current application deadline/guidelines.
EIN: 131919715

6001
National Community Pharmacists Association Foundation

(formerly National Association of Retail Druggists)
100 Daingerfield Rd.
Alexandria, VA 22314-2885 (703) 683-8200
Contact: James R. Rankin P.D., Pres.
FAX: (703) 683-3619; E-mail: info@ncpanet.org; Additional tel.: (800) 544-7447; URL: http://www.ncpanet.org

Foundation type: Public charity
Limitations: Scholarships and research grants to pharmacy students and pharmacists.
Financial data: Year ended 06/30/2004.
Assets, $3,688,228 (M); Expenditures, $427,264; Total giving, $101,800; Grants to individuals, 20 grants totaling $49,750 (high: $6,250, low: $2,000).
Fields of interest: Pharmacy/prescriptions.
Type of support: Conferences/seminars; Awards/prizes.
Application information: Deadline Aug. 24; Completion of formal application required.
Program descriptions:
Presidential Scholarships: Scholarships of $2,000 each are awarded to National Community Pharmacists Association (NCPA) students who are members of the association. Expenses are also paid for them to attend the annual NCPA convention.
Independent Pharmacist of the Year: $1,000 cash award, $1,000 scholarship and a commemorative plaque awarded to recipient pharmacist.
EIN: 366072250

6002
National Council of La Raza

1126 16th St., NW
Washington, DC 20036-3603 (202) 785-1670
Contact: Janet Murguia, Pres. and C.E.O.
FAX: (202) 776-1792; Fellowship application address: c/o Mid-Career Admissions, Harvard Univ., John F. Kennedy School of Govt., 79 John F. Kennedy St., Cambridge, MA 02138; tel.: (617) 495-1156; FAX: (202) 776-1792; URL: http://www.nclr.org/

Foundation type: Public charity
Limitations: Fellowship at the John F. Kennedy School of Government to Hispanic organizational leaders.
Publications: Annual report.
Financial data: Year ended 09/30/2004.
Assets, $56,317,557 (M); Expenditures, $23,492,634; Total giving, $5,598,728.

Fields of interest: Community development; Hispanics/Latinos.
Type of support: Fellowships.
Application information: Applications accepted. Application form required.
　Deadline(s): Apr. 13.
　Applicants should submit the following:
　　1) Resume
　　2) Transcripts
　　3) SAT
　　4) ACT
　　5) Letter(s) of recommendation
　Additional information: Applicants must apply to Harvard University's John F. Kennedy School of Govt. Master's in Public Admin. Prog., in addition to applying to NCLR.
Program description:
　Esteban E. Torres NCLR-Harvard Mid-Career Fellowship Program: Designed to strengthen the capacity of Hispanic community-based organizations by helping to develop the administrative and management skills and networks of Hispanic organizational leaders. The one-year program begins with a five-week Summer Session. The fellowship for the ten-month period will be from $22,000. Eligible persons are: individuals formerly associated with Hispanic community based organizations; NCLR staff; and individuals formerly associated with mainstream organizations, but whose work focuses on the Hispanic community. Recipients must commit to returning and working in their communities for at least two years following completion of the program. Applicants must have a minimum of seven years of work experience, including at least five years employment in the Hispanic community.
EIN: 860212873

6003
National Crime Prevention Council
1000 Connecticut Ave. N.W., 13th Fl.
Washington, DC　20006　(202) 466-6272
FAX: (202) 296-1356; E-mail: Bpereira@ncpc.org; URL: http://www.ncpc.org

Foundation type: Public charity
Limitations: Grants to support service-learning projects planned and implemented by youth who identify needs and create projects to address or prevent crime and drug abuse in their schools and communities.
Publications: Application guidelines; Annual report; Newsletter.
Financial data: Year ended 09/30/2004. Assets, $2,012,263 (M); Expenditures, $12,979,582.
Fields of interest: Crime/violence prevention; Crime/violence prevention, youth.
Type of support: Program development.
Application information: Applications accepted. Application form required. Application form available on the grantmaker's Web site.
　Initial approach: E-mail.
　Deadline(s): Nov. 1, Feb. 1, Apr. 1, June 1
　Applicants should submit the following:
　　1) Letter(s) of recommendation
　　2) Proposal
　　3) Budget Information
　Additional information: See Web site for additional program information.
Program description:
　TCC Crime Prevention Grant: The National Crime Prevention Council will award one hundred grants of up to $500. These grants are intended to encourage and promote crime prevention, community service, and civic responsibility. To be eligible for funding, youth must be participating in a

Community Works or Youth Safety Corps program or be in a youth group or class of six or more members. All participants must be between the ages of 11 to 19.
EIN: 133129302

6004
National Depressive and Manic Depressive Association
730 N. Franklin St., Ste. 501
Chicago, IL　60610-3526　(800) 826-3632
Contact: Lydia Lewis, Pres.
FAX: (312) 642-7243;
E-mail: questions@dbsalliance.org; URL: http://www.dbsalliance.org

Foundation type: Public charity
Limitations: Research grants to study depression and bipolar disorders.
Financial data: Year ended 12/31/2004. Assets, $1,192,528 (M); Expenditures, $2,876,994; Total giving, $58,854; Grants to individuals, totaling $3,000.
Fields of interest: Mental health, disorders; Depression.
Type of support: Research.
Application information:
　Initial approach: E-mail.
　Additional information: Contact foundation for application guidelines.
EIN: 363379124

6005
National Fish and Wildlife Foundation
1120 Connecticut Ave., N.W., Ste. 900
Washington, DC　20036　(202) 857-0166
Contact: Jeff Trandahl, Exec. Dir.
Additional tel.: (503) 417-8700, ext. 21
FAX: (202) 857-0162; URL: http://www.nfwf.org/

Foundation type: Public charity
Limitations: Awards by nomination only to outstanding leaders in the field of fish and wildlife preservation and grants to support research, management, conservation and education/outreach activities related to the conservation and recovery of whales.
Publications: Application guidelines; Annual report; Grants list; Informational brochure; Newsletter.
Financial data: Year ended 09/30/2004. Assets, $197,940,906 (M); Expenditures, $44,090,921; Total giving, $35,634,847.
Fields of interest: Natural resources; Animals/wildlife, preservation/protection.
Type of support: Research; Awards/prizes; Graduate support; Undergraduate support.
Application information: Application form required.
　Initial approach: Proposal.
　Deadline(s): Vary for nomination, May 12 for Grants
　Applicants should submit the following:
　　1) Essay
　Additional information: See Web site for complete programs and guidelines.
Program descriptions:
　Pacific Walrus Conservation Fund (PWCF): Awards of up to $60,000 to individuals for research and management programs for the conservation of the Pacific walrus and its habitat. To apply, applicant must submit a proposal of 250 words or less. Deadline Apr. 25. See Web site for further guidelines and information.
　Guy Bradley Award: Awards of $1,000 are presented to people whose dedication and service to the protection of the country's natural resources

provides outstanding leadership, extended excellence, and lifetime commitment to the field of wildlife law enforcement and whose actions advance the cause of wildlife conservation. Nomination deadline Feb. 9.
　Chuck Yeager Award: This award recognizes fish and wildlife professionals who make a difference in on-the-ground conservation. The award honors outstanding achievement in the field and includes $15,000 to be used for conservation programs at the recipient's directions.
　Budweiser Conservation Scholarship Program: Ten scholarships of up to $10,000 awarded to graduate and undergraduate students who are poised to make a significant contribution to the field of conservation. Awards are to cover expenses for tuition, fees, books, room and board and other direct expenses related to their studies. Awards will be made based on merit and will take into consideration the student's academic achievements and their ability and commitment to develop innovative solutions that are designed to address real and pressing issues affecting fish, wildlife and plant conservation efforts. Recipients must be U.S. citizens enrolled in an accredited institution of higher learning pursuing a graduate or undergraduate degree (sophomores and juniors in their current academic year only) in environmental science, natural resource management, biology, public policy, geography, political science, or related disciplines. Recipients are eligible for one year of scholarship support. For further information, contact lauren.guite@nfwf.org. Deadline Jan. 27.
EIN: 521384139

6006
The National Foundation for Infectious Diseases
(also known as NFID)
4733 Bethesda Ave., Ste. 750
Bethesda, MD　20814　(301) 656-0003
Contact: Leonard Novick, Exec. Dir.
FAX: (301) 907-0878; E-mail: info@nfid.org; URL: http://www.nfid.org/

Foundation type: Public charity
Limitations: Fellowships and grants for education and research in the field of infectious diseases.
Publications: Annual report; Informational brochure (including application guidelines); Newsletter.
Financial data: Year ended 06/30/2003. Assets, $3,451,356 (M); Expenditures, $3,089,714; Total giving, $96,240; Grants to individuals, totaling $96,240.
Fields of interest: Public health, epidemiology; Biomedicine; Medical research, institute; Medical research; Minorities.
Type of support: Fellowships; Research; Postdoctoral support.
Application information:
　Initial approach: Letter.
　Deadline(s): Jan. 15 and Feb. 15
　Additional information: See web site for additional application and program information.
Program descriptions:
　New Investigator Matching Grants: New scientists are provided with $2,000 each to be matched by their institution for pilot monies to help pay for supplies and equipment during the first year of independent research. Applicants must be legal residents or citizens of the U.S., with full-time junior faculty status at a recognized, accredited institution of higher education in the U.S. or Canada.
　NFID Fellowship in Infectious Disease: Encourages and assists young, qualified U.S. physicians who have completed at least three years

of postgraduate medical training to become specialists and researchers in infectious diseases. A $24,000 award is provided, plus $1,000 for travel and supplies.

NFID John P. Utz Postdoctoral Fellowship in Medical Mycology: Encourages and assists qualified U.S. physicians in becoming specialists and researchers in the field of medical mycology (fungi). A $29,000 award is given, plus $1,000 for travel and supplies. Applicants must be sponsored by a university-affiliated medical center.

Postdoctoral Fellowship in Emerging Infectious Diseases: A $50,000 stipend is provided to encourage and assist a qualified U.S. physician in becoming a recognized authority on emerging infectious diseases and epidemiology. The fellowship is awarded for a one-year period. Recipients will be assigned to the National Center for Infectious Diseases, CDC, in Atlanta, GA.

Postdoctoral Fellowship in Nosocomial Infection Research and Training: Provides a $24,000 stipend and $1,000 for travel and supplies to encourage and assist a qualified U.S. physician researcher in becoming a specialist and investigator in the field of nosocomial infections. The fellowship is awarded for a one-year period.

Colin L. Powell Minority Postdoctoral Fellowship in Tropical Disease Research: Awards a $30,000 stipend for one year (of which $3,000 may be used for travel and supplies) to a qualified minority researcher. Applicant must be an under-represented minority in the biomedical sciences; hold a doctorate degree from a recognized university; and be a permanent resident or citizen of the U.S. Each applicant will be required to have arranged for an American or foreign laboratory in which to conduct his/her research. The laboratory should be supervised by a recognized leader in tropical disease research qualified to oversee the work of the selected fellow.
EIN: 237198530

6007

National Foundation for Jewish Culture

330 7th Ave., 21st Fl.
New York, NY 10001-5010 (212) 629-0500
Contact: Richard Siegel, Exec. Dir.; For fellowships: Kristen L. Runk
FAX: (212) 629-0508;
E-mail: nfjc@jewishculture.org; URL: http://www.Jewishculture.org

Foundation type: Public charity
Limitations: Dissertation fellowships and publication support to scholars in the field of Jewish studies.
Publications: Newsletter.
Financial data: Year ended 12/31/2003. Assets, $3,757,603 (M); Expenditures, $2,984,045; Total giving, $385,870; Grants to individuals, 25 grants totaling $243,202 (high: $50,000, low: $1,500).
Fields of interest: Literature; Jewish agencies & temples.
Type of support: Publication; Fellowships; Research.
Application information: Applications accepted. Application form required.
Additional information: See Web site for program's current application guidelines and deadline.
Program descriptions:
Doctoral Dissertation Fellowships in Jewish Studies: Fellowships are intended to encourage scholarly research, publication and teaching in the various disciplines of Jewish studies. Since its inception in 1960, the foundation has awarded grants-in-aid and fellowships to over 500 scholars.

Ganz-Zahler Grant: Writers are invited to submit works of nonfiction that explore the Jewish experience, including history, philosophy, biography, and belles letters. The Ganz-Zahler Grant of $2,500 will support the publication of the nonfiction work, which can cover publication cost, research, editorial, printing, marketing, or distribution of the work. The author must be a U.S. citizen or permanent resident of the U.S.; the work must be nonfiction; and proposals must include a contract or letter from an established publisher indicating intent to publish the completed work.
EIN: 131927751

6008

National Geographic Society

(also known as National Geographic Society Education Foundation)
1145 17th St., N.W.
Washington, DC 20036-4688 (202) 857-7310
FAX: (202) 429-5701; E-mail: foundation@ngs.org;
URL: http://www.nationalgeographic.com/foundation/

Foundation type: Public charity
Limitations: Grants to teachers for projects that will improve student achievement through geography literacy, and cultural understanding.
Financial data: Year ended 12/31/2004. Assets, $1,072,298,034 (M); Expenditures, $479,983,175; Total giving, $10,886,701; Grants to individuals, 163 grants totaling $5,954,016 (high: $150,000, low: $500).
Fields of interest: Education; Environmental education.
Type of support: Seed money.
Application information: Completion of formal application required, including seven copies of application with cover sheet.
Program description:
Teacher Awards: Awards of $5,000 to teachers for innovative geography education projects. The foundation primarily funds projects which promote geographic knowledge through education, and which promote stewardship of natural and cultural resources.
EIN: 530193519

6009

National Headache Foundation

820 N. Orleans St., Ste. 217
Chicago, IL 60610 (888) 643-5552
Contact: Carolyn Smith, Exec. Asst.
E-mail: info@headaches.org; URL: http://www.headaches.org

Foundation type: Public charity
Limitations: Grants to applicants with an extensive background in headache research.
Publications: Grants list; Informational brochure; Newsletter.
Financial data: Year ended 07/31/2004. Assets, $7,569,611 (M); Expenditures, $2,319,570; Total giving, $38,938; Grants to individuals, 4 grants totaling $38,938.
Fields of interest: Medical research.
Type of support: Research.
Application information:
Initial approach: E-mail or letter.
Additional information: Contact foundation for further application guidelines.
EIN: 237073022

6010

National Italian American Foundation, Inc.

Peter Secchia Bldg.
1860 19th St., N.W.
Washington, DC 20009-5501 (202) 387-0600
Contact: John Salamone, Exec. Dir.
FAX: (202) 387-0800; E-mail: info@niaf.org;
URL: http://www.niaf.org/scholarships

Foundation type: Public charity
Limitations: Grants for teaching of Italian language in schools; and for projects related to Italian-American culture or heritage.
Financial data: Year ended 12/31/2003. Assets, $6,529,555 (M); Expenditures, $6,836,817; Total giving, $3,884,058; Grants to individuals, totaling $2,091,314.
Fields of interest: Cultural/ethnic awareness; History/archaeology; Language (foreign).
Type of support: Program development.
Application information:
Initial approach: Grant query of one page to learn if project is one NIAF would consider funding; if response is positive applicant will be asked to submit full application by deadline.
Deadline(s): May 31 and Nov. 30
Program descriptions:
Italian Language Study Grants: This matching grant program is open to individuals who wish to launch or expand the teaching of Italian in the local public or private elementary, intermediate, or high schools. Grants of $500 to $2,000 per year may be used to purchase teaching materials, pay teacher and/or teacher's aide's salaries, etc. The language program may be held before, after, or during school hours, full- or part-time.
Culture and Heritage Grant Awards: Available to individuals pursuing projects to promote, research, educate or preserve Italian-American culture, history, or heritage. Examples include: documentaries, doctoral research, exhibits, conferences, books, media stereotyping/anti-defamation surveys, campaigns, plays, and course syllabi. Grants range from $2,000 to $15,000.
EIN: 521071723

6011

National Kidney Foundation of Eastern Missouri and Metro East, Inc.

1423 Hanley Industrial Ct.
St. Louis, MO 63144 (314) 961-2828
Contact: Barbara McQuitty, C.E.O.
FAX: (314) 961-0888; E-mail: mail@nkfstl.com;
URL: http://www.nkfstl.com

Foundation type: Public charity
Limitations: Research grants for the study of kidney disease, MO.
Publications: Annual report; Informational brochure; Newsletter; Occasional report.
Financial data: Year ended 06/30/2004. Assets, $1,017,099 (M); Expenditures, $841,974; Total giving, $167,254; Grants to individuals, totaling $107,237.
Fields of interest: Kidney research.
Type of support: Research.
Application information: Contact foundation for current application deadline/guidelines.
EIN: 436066368

6012

National Kidney Foundation of Georgia
2951 Flowers Rd. S., Ste. 211
Atlanta, GA   30341   (770) 452-1539
Contact: Charles C. Starr, C.E.O.
E-mail: info@kidney.org; Toll-free tel.: (800)
633-2339; URL: http://www.nkfg.org

Foundation type: Public charity
Limitations: Research grants to study kidney
disease.
Financial data: Year ended 06/30/2004.
Assets, $989,833 (M); Expenditures,
$1,387,332; Total giving, $97,658; Grants to
individuals, totaling $15,158.
Fields of interest: Kidney research.
Type of support: Research.
Application information: Contact foundation for
current application deadline/guidelines.
EIN: 237077237

6013

National Kidney Foundation of Illinois, Inc.
215 W. Illinois St., Ste. 1C
Chicago, IL   60610   (312) 321-1500
Contact: Willa Iglitzen Lang, Exec. Dir.
FAX: (312) 321-1505; E-mail: kidney@nkfi.org;
URL: http://www.nkfi.org

Foundation type: Public charity
Limitations: Research grants for the study of kidney
disease, primarily in IL.
Publications: Annual report; Informational brochure
(including application guidelines); Newsletter.
Financial data: Year ended 06/30/2003.
Assets, $3,275,443 (M); Expenditures,
$1,542,690; Total giving, $76,900.
Fields of interest: Kidney research.
Type of support: Fellowships; Research.
Application information: Application form required.
   Additional information: Contact foundation for
      current application deadline/guidelines.
EIN: 366009226

6014

National Kidney Foundation of Indiana, Inc.
911 E. 86th St., Ste. 100
Indianapolis, IN   46240-1840   (317) 722-5640
Contact: Margie Fort, Exec. Dir.
FAX: (317) 722-5650; E-mail: nkfi@myvine.com;
Additional tel.: (800) 382-9971; URL: http://
www.kidneyindiana.org

Foundation type: Public charity
Limitations: Research grants to physicians,
nurses, social workers and dieticians to assist in
working towards a cure for kidney and urological
diseases, primarily in IN.
Financial data: Year ended 06/30/2005.
Assets, $623,717 (M); Expenditures,
$1,215,100; Total giving, $425,506; Grants to
individuals, totaling $425,506.
Fields of interest: Kidney research.
Type of support: Research.
Application information: Application form required.
   Initial approach: E-mail.
   Deadline(s): Fall
   Additional information: Contact foundation for
      exact application deadline.
EIN: 351180274

6015

National Kidney Foundation of Louisiana
8200 Hampson St., Ste. 425
New Orleans, LA   70118   (504) 861-4500
Contact: K. Trevor From M.D., Pres.
FAX: (504) 861-1976; E-mail: info@kidneyla.org;
Toll-free tel.: (800) 462-3694; URL: http://
www.kidneyla.org

Foundation type: Public charity
Limitations: Research grants to support
postdoctoral work on kidney disease.
Financial data: Year ended 06/30/2004.
Assets, $605,839 (M); Expenditures, $655,308;
Total giving, $37,863; Grants to individuals,
totaling $37,863.
Fields of interest: Kidney research.
Type of support: Research; Postdoctoral support.
Application information: Contact foundation for
current application deadline/guidelines.
EIN: 720649707

6016

National Kidney Foundation of Maryland, Inc.
1107 Kenilworth Dr., Ste. 202
Baltimore, MD   21204-2186   (410) 494-8545
Contact: Raquel McGuire, Exec. Dir.
FAX: (410) 494-8549;
E-mail: rmcguire@kidneymd.org; URL: http://
www.kidneymd.org

Foundation type: Public charity
Limitations: Research grants for the study of kidney
disease, primarily in MD.
Financial data: Year ended 06/30/2005.
Assets, $5,017,051 (M); Expenditures,
$1,467,972; Total giving, $264,691; Grants to
individuals, 14 grants totaling $259,691 (high:
$40,000, low: $5,000).
Fields of interest: Kidney research.
Type of support: Research.
Application information: Contact foundation for
current application deadline/guidelines.
EIN: 526069952

6017

National Kidney Foundation of Massachusetts, Rhode Island, New Hampshire and Vermont, Inc.
11 Vanderbilt Ave., Ste. 105
Norwood, MA   02062   (781) 278-0222
Contact: BJ Weiss, C.E.O.
FAX: (781) 278-0333;
E-mail: bjweiss@kidneyhealth.org; Additional tel.:
(800) 542-4001; URL: http://
www.kidneyhealth.org

Foundation type: Public charity
Limitations: Grants to individuals for research into
all areas pertaining to kidney and urological
diseases, including hypertension and
transplantation, primarily giving in MA, NH, RI and
VT.
Publications: Annual report; Informational
brochure; Newsletter.
Financial data: Year ended 06/30/2003.
Assets, $374,640 (M); Expenditures,
$1,214,253; Total giving, $40,000; Grant to an
individual, 1 grant totaling $35,000.
Fields of interest: Kidney research.
Type of support: Research.
Application information: Application form required.
   Deadline(s): Feb. 1.
   Applicants should submit the following:

   1) Proposal
Program description:
   Research Awards: The following grants award
$35,000 each to an individual for research
pertaining to kidney and/or urological diseases:
   · Joseph E. Murray Grant
   · Joseph Shankman Grant
   · Volunteer/Donor Research Awards
   · Theodore I. Steinman Clinical Research
     Award
   · Pediatric Renal Research Awards: Awards
     $35,000 to an individual for research
     pertaining to pediatric kidney and/or
     urological diseases. While all childhood
     renal diseases will be considered within
     the scope of this award, a special
     emphasis has been placed on research
     addressing the pathophysiology and
     treatment of Nephrotic syndrome in
     children.
EIN: 042305643

6018

National Kidney Foundation of Michigan, Inc.
1169 Oak Valley Dr.
Ann Arbor, MI   48108   (734) 222-9800
Contact: Daniel M. Carney, Pres. and C.E.O.
FAX: (734) 222-9801; E-mail: mgerlach@nkfm.org;
Toll-free tel.(in MI): (800) 482-1455; URL: http://
www.nkfm.org

Foundation type: Public charity
Limitations: Research grants for the study of kidney
disease, primarily in MI.
Financial data: Year ended 06/30/2005.
Assets, $5,713,195 (M); Expenditures,
$3,440,343; Total giving, $228,847; Grants to
individuals, totaling $228,847.
Fields of interest: Kidney research.
Type of support: Research.
Application information: Contact foundation for
current application deadline/guidelines.
EIN: 381559941

6019

National Kidney Foundation of Northern California
611 Mission St., 3rd Fl.
San Francisco, CA   94105   (415) 543-3303
Contact: Christopher Kelley, C.E.O.
E-mail: melanie@kidneynca.org; FAX: (415)
543-3331; E-mail: info@kidneyca.org; URL: http://
www.kidneynca.org

Foundation type: Public charity
Limitations: Research grants to study nephrology,
urology and transplantation.
Publications: Application guidelines; Annual report;
Financial statement; Informational brochure
(including application guidelines); Newsletter.
Financial data: Year ended 06/30/2003.
Assets, $663,559 (M); Expenditures,
$1,253,452; Total giving, $265,154; Grants to
individuals, totaling $75,256.
Fields of interest: Kidney research.
Type of support: Research.
Application information: Contact foundation for
current application deadline/guidelines.
Program description:
   Research Fellowship Program: Annual
fellowships are granted to researchers with
sponsors at Stanford University, the University of
California at San Francisco and Davis, and the VA
Hospitals in San Francisco and Palo Alto. Research

awards are also available through the Small Grants Program. Research fellowship applications are available from the NKF national office at www.kidney.org.
EIN: 946130713

6020
National Kidney Foundation of Ohio, Inc.
1373 Grandview Ave., Ste. 200
Columbus, OH   43212-2804   (614) 481-4030
Contact: Orelle Jackson, Exec. Dir.
E-mail: info@nkfofohio.org; Additional tel.: (800) 242-2133; URL: http://www.nkfofohio.org

Foundation type: Public charity
Limitations: Research grants to individuals in OH for the study of nephrology.
Financial data: Year ended 06/30/2003.
Assets, $787,096 (M); Expenditures, $729,828; Total giving, $62,703; Grants to individuals, totaling $56,103.
Fields of interest: Kidney research.
Type of support: Research.
Application information: Contact foundation for current application deadline/guidelines.
EIN: 311197264

6021
National Kidney Foundation of Southern California
17100 Ventura Blvd., Ste. 222
Encino, CA   91316-4017   (818) 783-8153
Contact: Linda P. Small, Assoc. Dir.
FAX: (818) 783-8160; Additional tel.: (800) 747-5527; URL: http://www.kidneysocal.org

Foundation type: Public charity
Limitations: Research grants for the study of kidney disease, primarily in CA.
Financial data: Year ended 06/30/2004.
Assets, $535,279 (M); Expenditures, $993,642; Total giving, $336,400; Grants to individuals, totaling $147,489.
Fields of interest: Kidney research.
Type of support: Research.
Application information: Contact foundation for current application deadline/guidelines; Completion of formal application required.
EIN: 951998472

6022
National Kidney Foundation of Upstate New York, Inc.
15 Prince St.
Rochester, NY   14607   (585) 697-0874
Contact: Jan Miller M.S., Ed., Exec. Dir.
FAX: (585) 607-0895;
E-mail: kidneyinfo@kidneynyup.org; Additional tel.: (800) 724-9421; URL: http://www.kidneynyup.org

Foundation type: Public charity
Limitations: Research grants for the study of kidney disease, primarily in NY.
Publications: Annual report; Informational brochure; Newsletter; Program policy statement.
Financial data: Year ended 06/30/2003.
Assets, $911,752 (M); Expenditures, $1,296,409; Total giving, $64,540; Grants to individuals, totaling $34,540.
Fields of interest: Kidney research.
Type of support: Research.
Application information: Application form required.

Additional information: Contact foundation for current application deadline; See Web site for further information.
EIN: 161169134

6023
National Kidney Foundation, Inc.
30 E. 33 St., Ste. 1100
New York, NY   10016   (212) 889-2210
FAX: (212) 689-9261; E-mail: info@kidney.org; Additional tel.: (800) 622-9010; URL: http://www.kidney.org

Foundation type: Public charity
Limitations: Research grants and fellowships to young physician scientists for training assistance in kidney disease.
Financial data: Year ended 06/30/2003.
Assets, $17,819,332 (M); Expenditures, $19,415,700; Total giving, $2,002,832; Grants to individuals, totaling $2,002,832 (high: $50,000).
Fields of interest: Kidney research.
Type of support: Fellowships; Research.
Application information: Application form available on the grantmaker's Web site.
   Deadline(s): Dec. 15 for letter of intent, and Feb. 1 for grant proposal
Program descriptions:
Clinical Scientist Award: Awards $50,000 stipend to an advanced investigator who has demonstrated outstanding clinical or basic research to promote their independent researchers. Applicants must devote at least 75 percent of their time to research, be a U.S. citizen or permanent resident, hold an M.D. or equivalent domestic or foreign degree, and be a full-time staff member at a U.S. institution.
Franklin McDonald/Fresenius Medical Care Clinical Research Awards: Awards of $50,000 annually to nephrologists who have demonstrated the ability to conduct research to advance the treatment of kidney disease and who have a long-term commitment to clinical investigation as one of their career goals. Applicants must hold full-time faculty appointments at a university or equivalent positions as scientists on the staff of a research organization.
Nephrology Fellows Travel Grant Program: Fellowships of up to $600 awarded for educational travel, depending on travel distance, to assist recipients in attending the Clinical Nephrology meetings to be held in IN.
Research Fellowship Award: Awards $35,000 annual stipend for new recipients who have completed no more than 4.5 years of post-doctoral research training (after receipt of M.D., Ph.D., D.O. or equivalent degree) at time of the activation of the award. Reapplicants (competitive renewal) must have completed no more than 5.5 years of post-doctoral training.
Young Investigator Award of Singapore: Awards $50,000 to an investigator from Asia who holds an M.D. or Ph.D. and who is studying glomerulonephritus, particularly IgA nephropathy, or diabetic nephropathy resulting from type II diabetes.
Young Investigator Grant Program: Awards a $50,000 grant per year to individuals who have completed research fellowship training in nephrology, urology, or closely-related fields prior to the start of the grant award, who intend to pursue directly-related research, and who hold a full-time appointment to a faculty position at a university or an equivalent position as a scientist on the staff of a research-oriented institution no more than four years old at the start of the award.
EIN: 131673104

6024
National Medical Fellowships, Inc.
5 Hanover Sq., 15th Fl.
New York, NY   10004   (212) 483-8880
Contact: Jeanne A. Reynolds, Dir., Devel. and Comm.
FAX: (212) 483-8897; E-mail: info@nmfonline.org; URL: http://www.nmf-online.org

Foundation type: Public charity
Limitations: Fellowships and awards by nomination only to minority medical students by nomination or recommendation by medical school deans.
Financial data: Year ended 06/30/2003.
Assets, $4,496,240 (M); Expenditures, $3,494,661; Total giving, $1,293,233; Grants to individuals, totaling $1,243,233.
Fields of interest: Medical school/education; Minorities; African Americans/Blacks.
Type of support: Awards/grants by nomination only; Awards/prizes; Graduate support; Stipends.
Application information: Application form required.
   Additional information: Contact foundation for current application deadline.
Program descriptions:
Hugh J. Andersen Memorial Scholarships: Two need-based merit scholarships including a certificate of merit and $2,500 stipend are annually presented to Minnesota residents enrolled in any accredited U.S. medical school or students attending Minnesota medical schools. Eligible candidates must be underrepresented, minority students enrolled beyond their first year in an accredited U.S. medical school. Candidates must demonstrate outstanding leadership, community service, and financial need. Medical school deans must nominate students. Nominations are requested in Aug. Schools are required to submit letters of recommendation as well as official academic and financial aid transcripts. Candidates must submit personal essays and a resume. A special committee that is responsible for selecting the winners reviews candidate dossiers.
Franklin C. McLean Award: One award that includes a certificate of merit and a $3,000 stipend is presented annually to a senior student in recognition of outstanding academic achievement, leadership and community service. Competition is open to senior underrepresented minority students enrolled in accredited U.S. medical schools. Candidates must demonstrate outstanding academic achievement and leadership and be nominated by medical school deans.
William and Charlotte Cadbury Award: This award is presented annually to a senior medical student in recognition of outstanding academic achievement, leadership, and community service. Competition is open to senior, underrepresented minority students enrolled in accredited U.S. medical schools. Candidates must demonstrate outstanding academic achievement and leadership. One award is presented annually; the designated Cadbury Scholar is honored during the annual meeting of the Association of American Medical Colleges. The award includes a certificate of merit and $2,000 stipend (not renewable). Medical school deans must nominate students. Nominations are requested in June. Schools are required to submit letters of recommendation and official academic transcripts and resumes for each candidate. Candidate dossiers are reviewed by a special committee, the members of which individually review and rank each candidate.
Ralph W. Ellison Memorial Prize: This prize is presented to a graduating underrepresented medical student. Candidates must demonstrate outstanding academic achievement, leadership, and potential to make significant contributions to

medicine. One prize is presented each year; the honor includes a certificate of merit and a $500 stipend (not renewable). Medical school deans must nominate students. Application requirements include a letter of nomination that fully explains the candidate's academic and leadership accomplishments during medical school, an official academic transcript, and a personal statement of at least 500 words, written by the student, that discusses his or her motivation for a career in medicine and short- and long-range career plans. Nominations are reviewed by a special committee, the members of which individually review and rank each candidate.

Fellowship Program in Academic Medicine for Minority Students: The program encourages academically outstanding minority medical students to pursue careers in biomedical research and academic medicine and fosters mentor relationships between these students and prominent biomedical scientists. Each fellow spends eight to 12 weeks working in a major research laboratory. Competition is open to second- and third-year underrepresented minority students attending accredited U.S. medical schools who have demonstrated academic achievement and show promise for careers in research and academic medicine. Thirty-five $6,000 fellowships are awarded (not renewable). The medical school deans must recommend candidates. Mentors must submit letters of commitment in support of students' fellowship applications with detailed descriptions of proposed research projects. Students must obtain a third letter of recommendation from a faculty member who knows them well. Schools must submit an official academic transcript for each nominee. Candidates are required to complete fellowship applications including a personal statement and a resume.

Irving Graef Memorial Scholarship: This two-year scholarship is presented annually to a third-year student and recognizes outstanding academic achievement, leadership, and community service. The scholarship is renewable in the fourth year if the award winner continues in good academic standing. This scholarship is open only to rising third-year minority medical students who received NMF financial assistance during their second year. Candidates must demonstrate outstanding academic achievement and leadership. One new scholarship is awarded annually; this honor includes a certificate of merit and annual stipend of $2,000 (renewable). Medical school deans must nominate students. Nominations are requested in July. Schools are required to submit letters of recommendation as well as official academic transcripts. Candidates must submit a personal essay and resume.

Metropolitan Life Foundation Awards Program for Academic Excellence: Fourteen need-based scholarships for $4,000 each are awarded annually to second- and third-year underrepresented minority students in recognition of outstanding academic achievement and leadership. This scholarship program is open to second- and third-year underrepresented minority students who attend medical schools or have legal residence in cities that are annually designated by the Metropolitan Life Foundation. Candidates must demonstrate outstanding academic achievement, leadership, and potential for distinguished contributions to medicine. Students must also provide documented proof of financial need. Scholarships are not renewable. Medical school deans must nominate students. Schools are required to submit letters of recommendation as well as official academic transcripts. Candidates are required to submit scholarship applications, including personal statements and verification of financial need.

National Medical Association Special Awards Programs: The association annually recognizes and rewards African American medical students for extraordinary accomplishments, academic excellence, leadership, and potential for outstanding contributions to medicine. The NMA Merit Scholarships also have a need component. Eligibility is limited to African American medical students who are attending accredited M.D. or D.O. degree-granting schools in the U.S. Applicants must be U.S. citizens. The number of awards for each program varies from year to year. All candidates must request letters of recommendation from the dean and official academic transcripts. All candidates are required to complete program applications, including personal essays, and provide copies of income tax forms for themselves, their parents, and/or their spouses. Candidates for the NMA Merit Scholarships must also submit documentation of financial need. Applicants for the Slack awards must also submit copies of work that demonstrate skill in journalism.
EIN: 362125449

6025
National MPS Society, Inc.
P.O. Box 726
Bangor, ME 04402 (207) 947-1445
Contact: Barbara A. Wedehase, Exec. Dir.
FAX: (207) 990-3074;
E-mail: info@mpssociety.org; URL: http://www.mpssociety.org

Foundation type: Public charity
Limitations: Awards three, two-year grants of $60,000 each for the study and cure of mucopolysaccharidosis (MPS) and mucolipidosis (ML).
Financial data: Year ended 12/31/2003. Assets, $1,037,922 (M); Expenditures, $703,599; Total giving, $360,000; Grants to individuals, 12 grants totaling $360,000 (high: $41,250, low: $8,750).
Fields of interest: Medical research, institute; Nerve, muscle & bone research.
Type of support: Fellowships; Research.
Application information: Application form required.
Deadline(s): May 1
Additional information: See Web site for further information.
EIN: 112734849

6026
National Multiple Sclerosis Society
733 3rd Ave.
New York, NY 10017-3288 (212) 986-3240
Contact: Michael J. Dugan, Pres.
FAX: (212) 986-7981;
E-mail: patricia.olooney@nmss.org; Additional tel.: (800) 344-4867; URL: http://www.nationalmssociety.org

Foundation type: Public charity
Limitations: Research grants to investigators for the study and eventual cure of multiple sclerosis.
Publications: Annual report; Financial statement; Informational brochure; Newsletter; Program policy statement.
Financial data: Year ended 09/30/2003. Assets, $56,700,970 (M); Expenditures, $79,141,538; Total giving, $29,446,615; Grants to individuals, 67 grants totaling $94,500 (high: $3,000, low: $1,410).
Fields of interest: Multiple sclerosis research.
Type of support: Research.

Application information:
Initial approach: Letter or telephone.
Deadline(s): Feb. 1 and Aug. 1
Additional information: See Web site for program guidelines.
EIN: 135661935

6027
National Organization for Rare Disorders, Inc.
55 Kenosia Ave.
P.O. Box 1968
Danbury, CT 06813 (203) 744-0100
Contact: Linda Cataldo, Field Svcs. Coord.
FAX: (203) 798-2291;
E-mail: orphan@rarediseases.org; Additional tel.: (800) 999-6673 (voicemail only); URL: http://www.rarediseases.org

Foundation type: Public charity
Limitations: Research grants and fellowships to academic scientists and physicians specializing in rare diseases.
Publications: Application guidelines; Annual report; Grants list; Informational brochure; Newsletter; Program policy statement.
Financial data: Year ended 12/31/2003. Assets, $6,595,546 (L); Expenditures, $3,538,509; Total giving, $1,320,332; Grants to individuals, 35 grants totaling $733,709 (high: $29,000, low: $750).
Fields of interest: Diseases (rare) research.
Type of support: Fellowships; Research.
Application information:
Initial approach: Letter.
Deadline(s): Spring
Additional information: See Web site for further application information.
Program descriptions:
The Nord/Roscoe Brady Lysosomal Storage Diseases Fellowships: Awards $50,000-$70,000, with the possibility for a second year of funding, to physicians who wish to establish careers in lysosomal storage diseases clinical medicine.
Research Grants: Provides seed money to academic scientists studying new treatments or diagnostics for rare diseases.
EIN: 133223946

6028
National Parkinson Foundation, Inc.
1501 NW 9th Ave.
Bob Hope Rd.
Miami, FL 33136-1494 (305) 243-6666
Contact: Daniel Arty C.P.A.; For Research: Pam Olmo C.P.A.
Additional tel.: (305) 243-3886, fax: (305) 243-1103, e-mail: iiresearchgrants@parkinson.org
FAX: (305) 243-5595;
E-mail: contact@parkinson.org; URL: http://www.parkinson.org

Foundation type: Public charity
Limitations: Grants to scientists for Parkinson disease research.
Financial data: Year ended 06/30/2005. Assets, $31,539,710 (M); Expenditures, $9,867,552; Total giving, $4,187,594.
Fields of interest: Parkinson's disease; Parkinson's disease research.
Type of support: Research.
Application information: Applications accepted. Application form required. Application form available on the grantmaker's Web site.

Initial approach: Letter or e-mail.
Deadline(s): Mar. 13
Applicants should submit the following:
  1) Letter(s) of recommendation
  2) Curriculum vitae
  3) Budget Information
  4) Proposal
Additional information: See Web site for complete program description.

Program descriptions:
Investigator-Initiated Research Grants: Grants of up to $40,000 for the study of causes of and a cure for Parkinson disease. Both basic research and clinical research proposals are eligible for support. Preference will be given to scientists who are at an early stage of their professional careers.

The Fight Goes On: Grants up to $1,000,000 over a period of up to three years for targeted, time-limited pre-clinical or clinical studies directly relevant to studying the cause and cure for Parkinson disease. A premium will be placed on collaborative ventures involving researchers from more than one institution.
EIN: 590968031

6029
National Patient Safety Foundation

1120 MASS MoCa Way
North Adams, MA 01247 (413) 663-8900
Contact: Diane C. Pinakiewicz M.B.A., Pres.
FAX: (413) 663-8905; E-mail: info@npsf.org;
URL: http://www.npsf.org

Foundation type: Public charity
Limitations: Awards and research grants to study human and organizational error and prevention of accidents in health care.
Financial data: Year ended 12/31/2003.
Assets, $2,839,744 (M); Expenditures, $3,300,431; Total giving, $224,062; Grants to individuals, 2 grants totaling $199,062 (high: $100,000, low: $99,062).
Fields of interest: Safety, education.
Type of support: Awards/prizes.
Application information:
  Initial approach: E-mail or letter.
  Additional information: Contact foundation for further program information.

Program description:
James S. Todd Memorial Award for Patient Safety Research: This award goes to researchers who seek to understand the phenomenon of practice errors in occupational and physical therapy, explore preventive strategies, and develop a learning model and disseminate educational materials in an effort to improve patient safety.
EIN: 367166993

6030
National Press Foundation, Inc.

1211 Connecticut Ave., N.W., Ste. 310
Washington, DC 20036 (202) 663-7280
Contact: Nolan Walters, Dir., Progs.
Additional tel.: (202) 530-2355; Fax: (202) 530-2855; E-mail: nolan@nationalpress.org;
URL: http://www.nationalpress.org/index.htm

Foundation type: Public charity
Limitations: Awards by nomination only to accomplished, working journalists in various areas, and support to working professional journalists for professional development.
Publications: Annual report; Financial statement; Informational brochure; Occasional report.

Financial data: Year ended 12/31/2003.
Assets, $3,446,946 (M); Expenditures, $1,083,932; Total giving, $36,985.
Fields of interest: Journalism/publishing; Drawing; Literature; International affairs, information services; Science; Government/public administration.
Type of support: Fellowships; Awards/grants by nomination only; Awards/prizes; Grants for special needs.
Application information:
  Initial approach: E-mail.
  Deadline(s): For awards by nomination only applications by letter accepted throughout the year
  Additional information: For professional development support programs applications by letter, including brief biography, letter of support from supervisor (including a statement that applicant will be released from other duties for the seminar), and three clippings or other work samples accepted throughout the year; See Web site for current application and program information.

Program descriptions:
Sol Taishoff Award for Excellence in Broadcast Journalism: A prestigious lifetime achievement award for distinguished service to broadcast journalism. Recipients are pre-selected and applications are not accepted for this award.

Beveridge Editor of the Year Award: Recognizes significant achievements that enhance the quality of journalism in the U.S. The award is given to editors at any level, in recognition of imagination, professional skill, ethics, and an ability to motivate staff. Recipients are pre-selected and applications are not accepted for this award.

Clifford K. Berryman & James T. Berryman Award for Editorial Cartoonists: Open to editorial cartoonists of newspapers and magazines in recognition of work that exhibits power to influence public opinion, good drawing, and striking effect. Journalists are invited to apply for this award.

Evert Clark/Seth Payne for Young Science Journalists Award: A $1,000 award intended to encourage young science writers by recognizing outstanding reporting and writing in any field of science. Journalists age 30 or younger are invited to apply for this award. Deadline Dec. 10.

Thomas L. Stokes Awards for Best Newspaper Writing on Energy: A $1,000 prize given annually for the best writing "in the independent spirit of Tom Stokes" on subjects of interest to him, including energy and natural resources. Journalists are invited to apply for this award.

Everett McKinley Dirksen Awards for Distinguished Reporting of Congress: Intended to recognize individuals whose work shows thoughtful appraisal and insight into the workings of the U.S. Congress. Recipients are pre-selected and applications are not accepted for this award.

Kiplinger Distinguished Contribution to Journalism Award: Given to honor persons who have, through their vision and leadership, strengthened American journalism and furthered the efforts to establish quality in American journalism. Recipients are pre-selected and applications are not accepted for this award.

Chairman's Citation: Confers recognition on individuals whose accomplishments fall outside the traditional categories of excellence. It is only given when merited.

Kaiser Mini-Fellowships: Unsuccessful applicants for the Kaiser Media Fellowship (administered by the Henry J. Kaiser Family Foundation) are automatically considered for these mini-fellowships, which are administered by the National Press Foundation. Working, professional

journalists may apply for these funds to undertake a specific research project and report on a health policy or public health issue. The grant is intended to cover project-related travel and expenses. Recipients, selected by the National Press Foundation, receive limited grants, typically $5,000 each. Priority is given to projects that otherwise are unlikely to be undertaken or completed, and which have a high likelihood of being published/aired and of reaching a mass audience. Applicants must apply to Penny Duckham, Exec. Dir., Kaiser Media Fellowships Program, Henry J. Kaiser Family Foundation, 2400 Sand Hill Rd., Menlo Park, CA 94025; Tel.: (650) 854-9400; Fax: (650) 854-4800; E-mail: pduckham@kff.org.

Paul Miller Washington Reporting Fellowships: The foundation provides round-trip travel, living expenses, and material to recipients of this fellowship. Through seminars, demonstrations, and field trips, Paul Miller Fellows unlock the intricacies of the nation's Capitol and the federal government, thereby enriching their reporting for readers, listeners, and viewers back home. Fellows dedicate one day a month for nine months, Sept. through May, in intensive study sessions on such subjects as the federal budget and appropriations processes, campaign finance, congressional lobbying, and the federal court system. The emphasis is always on translating what happens in Washington into news of value to regional news organizations. To be eligible, journalists must be regional reporters in Washington (or becoming one), have the backing of a supervisor, and be willing and able to attend all fellowship sessions. There is no cost to the fellow. Deadline June 1.

Wharton Seminars for Business Writers: Awards three fellowships to working professional journalists worldwide to study finance at the Wharton School of Business, PA.

World Hot Spots: Awards 15 fellowships to journalists for attendance at a four-day seminar on various current global conflicts. Includes airfare, hotel, and most meals. Deadline Nov. 14.
EIN: 521069481

6031
National Science Teachers Association

1840 Wilson Blvd., 2nd Fl.
Arlington, VA 22201-3000
Contact: Gerald F. Wheeler, Exec. Dir.
FAX: (703) 243-7177; URL: http://www.nsta.org/

Foundation type: Public charity
Limitations: Awards to teachers for exemplary teaching in science education.
Financial data: Year ended 05/31/2004.
Assets, $19,490,195 (M); Expenditures, $19,296,460; Total giving, $1,157,200; Grants to individuals, 90 grants totaling $508,500 (high: $10,000, low: $500).
Fields of interest: Education; Science.
Type of support: Program development; Awards/prizes.
Application information: Deadline Dec. 16; Application by proposal focusing on a classroom project used to help students learn science while engaging in issues related to health.
EIN: 526055229

6032
National Society of Professional Engineers Educational Foundation

(formerly National Society of Professional Engineers)
1420 King St.
Alexandria, VA   22314-2794   (703) 684-2800
Contact: Mary Maul
FAX: (703) 836-4875; E-mail: mmaul@nspe.org;
URL: http://www.nspe.org

Foundation type: Public charity
Limitations: Awards by nomination only to engineers who have made significant contributions to the field.
Financial data: Year ended 06/30/2004. Assets, $1,069,174 (M); Expenditures, $84,211; Total giving, $59,541; Grants to individuals, 12 grants totaling $59,541.
Fields of interest: Engineering school/education; Community development; Engineering/technology.
Type of support: Awards/grants by nomination only; Awards/prizes.
Application information: Applications accepted. Application form required.
  Deadline(s): Vary
  Additional information: See Web site for complete guidelines and nomination forms.
Program descriptions:
  Distinguished Service Award: This award was established to recognize NSPE's members for their exceptional technical contributions to the engineering profession, their contributions to their communities, and to NSPE. Persons holding the membership grade of Member, Life, or Privileged Member in good standing are eligible for selection. Candidates must be recommended by a state society, with endorsement from two other state societies. In addition to completing the nomination, the following biographical information on each candidate should be provided: 500-word personal statement suitable for use as a press release; education; professional achievements; professional and technical society activity; and humanitarian and civic contributions. Each nomination must be made by a NSPE-affiliated state society and endorsed by two other state societies. Nominations should be sent to Attn.: NSPE Honor Awards Committee. The original and 10 copies of the nomination must be submitted. Deadline Feb. 2.
  Engineering Education Excellence Award: This national award recognizes one to two faculty members who have demonstrated an ability to link engineering education with professional practice. The recipients must be licensed and have a tenure-track faculty appointment in an ABET-EAC accredited engineering program. This award recognizes mid-career individuals who are 45 years or younger in age at the deadline for submission of the award. The recipients of the award will be recognized at the NSPE Annual Meeting, will receive a cash prize of $5,000, and will receive travel expenses to attend the awards ceremony. Deadline Apr. 6.
  Federal Engineer of the Year Award: All federal agencies employing at least 50 engineers worldwide are eligible to compete. Individual agency nominees must be presently engaged in the practice of engineering as an employee of the federal government in either managerial or technical positions. Only licensed professional engineers (P.E. or E.I.T.) are eligible for nomination to the Top Ten Finalists, and therefore Federal Engineer of the Year. However, non-licensed engineers are eligible to participate in the awards ceremony if they are chosen as Engineer of the Year within their agencies. Engineers who will have

retired within 12 months of the ceremony are eligible for nomination. All nominations must be typed, an original and eight copies submitted on the official form. Deadline Nov. 1.
  NSPE Award: This award is presented to an engineer who has made outstanding contributions to the engineering profession, the public welfare, and/or humankind. All engineers of recognized standing are eligible for nomination, provided that they are citizens of the U.S. and are preferably licensed professional engineers. Officers and directors of NSPE are ineligible. Nominations may be made by any member in good standing, but must be approved by the candidate's state society. A state society is not limited to the approval of a single candidate. Nominations should be sent to Attn.: NSPE Honor Awards Committee. Deadline Feb. 2.
  Young Engineer of the Year Award: This award recognizes young NSPE members who have made outstanding contributions to the engineering profession and their communities during the early years of their careers. Any licensed professional engineer or engineer-in-training (P.E. or E.I.T.) NSPE member in good standing who is 35 years of age or younger as of Jan. 1 is eligible for nomination. Nominations are to be submitted by an NSPE-affiliated state society or must contain an endorsement from the state society. Only one submission per state will be accepted. The committee makes the selection of the recipient based on the following criteria: 1) educational and collegiate achievements; 2) professional and technical society activities; 3) civic and humanitarian activities; 4) continuing competence; and 5) engineering achievements. Nominations should be sent to Attn.: NSPE Honor Awards Committee. The original and 10 copies of the nomination must be submitted. Deadline Feb. 2.
EIN: 526056276

6033
National Society to Preven Blindness

(also known as National Society to Prevent Blindness)
211 W. Wacker Dr., Ste. 1700
Chicago, IL   60606   (847) 843-2020
Contact: Hugh R. Parry, Pres. and C.E.O.
E-mail: info@preventblindness.org; Toll-free tel.: (800) 331-2020; URL: http://www.preventblindness.org/

Foundation type: Public charity
Limitations: Research grants and fellowships to graduate students, postdoctoral fellows and other beginning investigators for research on eye conditions and diseases.
Publications: Annual report; Newsletter.
Financial data: Year ended 03/31/2005. Assets, $9,425,927 (L); Expenditures, $4,976,671; Total giving, $543,577; Grants to individuals, 18 grants totaling $543,577 (high: $81,643, low: $3,000).
Fields of interest: Eye research.
Type of support: Fellowships; Research; Postdoctoral support; Graduate support.
Application information:
  Initial approach: Proposal.
  Additional information: Contact foundation for current application deadline/guidelines.
EIN: 363667121

6034
National Trust for Historic Preservation

1785 Massachusetts Ave., N.W.
Washington, DC   20036   (202) 588-6000
Contact: Richard Moe, Pres.
FAX: (202) 588-6223; E-mail: pr@nthp.org;
Additional tel.: (800) 944-6847; URL: http://www.nthp.org

Foundation type: Public charity
Limitations: Awards by nomination only to individuals for achievement in preservation of historical landmarks.
Publications: Application guidelines; Annual report; Corporate giving report; Grants list; Program policy statement.
Financial data: Year ended 09/30/2004. Assets, $194,747,474 (M); Expenditures, $57,204,344; Total giving, $7,573,111.
Fields of interest: Historic preservation/historical societies.
Type of support: Awards/grants by nomination only; Awards/prizes.
Application information: Application form required.
  Deadline(s): Nov. 1 for Great American Main Street Awards
  Additional information: See Web site for further application information.
Program description:
  National Preservation Honor Awards: Awards to individuals whose skill and determination have given new meaning to their communities through preservation. These efforts include citizen attempts to save and maintain important landmarks; craftsmen whose work restores the richness of the past; the vision of public officials who support preservation projects and legislation in their communities; and educators and journalists who help Americans understand the value of preservation. Deadline May 1.
EIN: 530210807

6035
National Urea Cycle Disorders Foundation

4841 Hill St.
La Canada, CA   91011   (818) 248-9970
Contact: Cindy LeMons, Exec. Dir.
E-mail: info@nucdf.org; URL: http://www.nucdf.org

Foundation type: Public charity
Limitations: Grants to medical doctors and other scientific professionals for research into urea cycle disorders.
Financial data: Year ended 12/31/2003. Assets, $158,580 (M); Expenditures, $54,791; Total giving, $12,500; Grants to individuals, 2 grants totaling $12,500 (high: $10,000, low: $2,500).
Fields of interest: Genetics/birth defects; Diseases (rare); Genetics/birth defects research; Diseases (rare) research.
Type of support: Research; Postdoctoral support.
Application information: Contact foundation for current application deadlines/guidelines.
EIN: 411661444

6036
The NEA Foundation for the Improvement of Education

1201 16th St. N.W.
Washington, DC   20036-3207   (202) 822-7840
Contact: Harriet Sanford, Pres. and C.E.O.
FAX: (202) 822-7779;
E-mail: info@neafoundation.org; URL: http://www.neafoundation.org

Foundation type: Public charity
Limitations: Professional development support to teachers and education professionals.
Publications: Application guidelines; Annual report; Financial statement; Grants list; Informational brochure; Occasional report.
Financial data: Year ended 08/31/2005. Assets, $46,837,721 (M); Expenditures, $4,008,972.
Fields of interest: Education.
Type of support: Grants to individuals.
Application information: Applications accepted throughout the year; Initial approach by letter or e-mail; Completion of formal application required.
Program descriptions:
Jordan Fundamentals Grant Program: These $2,500 grants are awarded to public secondary school teachers in grades 6 to 12. Eligibility is restricted to teachers or paraprofessionals in schools where forty percent or more of the student population qualifies for the free or reduced school lunch program.
Leadership Grants: These $1,000 grants are given to underwrite professional development opportunities for public school teachers, public education support personnel, and public higher education faculty and staff, enabling them to provide collegial leadership in efforts to improve teaching and learning. Grants may be used to fund activities for 12 months from the award date.
Arts@Work Grant Program: Up to 12 grants of $5,000 each awarded to U.S. public secondary school teachers whose primary assignment is to teach one or more art forms (music, dance, theater, visual arts or folk arts). Applicants must identify and collaborate with a partner. Applicants and their partners will incorporate technology (including computer, multimedia, video, hand-held, and internetworking technology) into standard-based arts curriculum. Grants may be used for hardware, software, consultants, release time or other costs directly related to the development of standards-based curriculum that integrates the arts and technology. Deadline Mar. 3.
EIN: 237035089

6037
Nevada Humanities Committee

P.O. Box 8029
Reno, NV   89507   (775) 784-6587
Additional tel.: (800) 382-5023; FAX: (775) 784-6527; URL: http://www.nevadahumanities.org

Foundation type: Public charity
Limitations: Grants to support research by scholars and other individuals working in humanities-related research, primarily in NV.
Financial data: Year ended 10/31/2003. Assets, $464,236 (M); Expenditures, $989,381; Total giving, $103,133.
Fields of interest: Humanities.
Type of support: Research.
Application information: Application form required.
  Deadline(s): Mar. 10 and Oct. 10.
  Applicants should submit the following:
    1) Letter(s) of recommendation
  Additional information: Application should include three- to five-page outline of research project, explanation of how results will be made available to NV audiences, resume, and a one-page bibliography; Applicants must send 25 copies of the entire application packet; Applicants are encouraged to discuss proposals with staff.

Program description:
Research Grants: Up to six $1,000 research stipends per year are awarded to scholars and others to support research in the humanities. Research on NV topics is encouraged but not required. Applicants may not seek support for work leading to a degree. An advanced degree or academic affiliation is not required. Recipients may not apply in consecutive years.
EIN: 237358959

6038
New England Biolabs Foundation

8 Enon St., No. 2B
Beverly, MA   01915-1116   (978) 927-2404
Contact: Martine Kellett, Exec. Dir.; Susan Foster, Asst. Dir.
FAX: (978) 998-6837; E-mail: fosters@nebf.org; Additional E-mail: kellett@nebf.org; URL: http://www.nebf.org

Foundation type: Company-sponsored foundation
Limitations: Limited support to individuals, in the Boston area and outside of the U.S., for projects which focus on grassroots and art efforts to bring about change. See program description for further limitations.
Publications: Application guidelines; Grants list; Informational brochure (including application guidelines).
Financial data: Year ended 12/31/2004. Assets, $8,179,330 (M); Expenditures, $544,971; Total giving, $351,017.
Fields of interest: Arts; Natural resources; Agriculture; Science; Marine science; Women.
Type of support: Program development; Seed money; Research.
Application information:
  Deadline(s): Mar. 1 and Sept. 1.
  Applicants should submit the following:
    1) Curriculum vitae
    2) Letter(s) of recommendation
  Additional information: Application should also include specific project details, bank references, list of the other grants applied for over past two years, and personal materials relevant to the project.

Program description:
Research Program: Grants are given for grassroots projects involving the arts, the environment, education, science, and social change. The foundation is especially interested in marine conservation, sustainable economic development, sustainable organic agriculture, education in women's health issues for developing counties, and environmental education for teachers. Support is only given to individuals and organizations in the New England region of the U.S., Cambodia, Cameroon, the Caribbean (excluding Haiti, U.S. Virgin Islands, and the Dominican Republic), Central America (excluding Mexico, Costa Rica, and Belize), Ghana, Tanzania, Madagascar, Philippines, Papua New Guinea, South America (excluding Argentina, Brazil, French Guiana, Suriname, Uruguay, and Venezuela) and Vietnam. Grants typically range from $500 to $30,000, with an average amount of $8,000.
EIN: 042776213

6039
The New World Foundation

666 West End Ave.
New York, NY   10025   (212) 249-1023
Contact: Colin Greer, Pres.
FAX: (212) 472-0508; E-mail: info@newwf.org; URL: http://www.newwf.org

Foundation type: Public charity
Limitations: Fellowships to those nominated or employed by qualified, tax-exempt organizations.
Publications: Biennial report (including application guidelines).
Financial data: Year ended 09/30/2003. Assets, $24,025,649 (M); Expenditures, $4,343,296; Total giving, $1,154,250.
Fields of interest: Education; Health care; AIDS; AIDS research; Human services; Children/youth, services; Minorities/immigrants, centers/services; International peace/security; Arms control; Race/intergroup relations; Civil rights; Community development; Public policy, research; Minorities.
Type of support: Program development; Conferences/seminars; Seed money; Fellowships; Awards/grants by nomination only.
Application information: Applications not accepted.
EIN: 131919791

6040
Nickel Producers Environmental Research Association, Inc.

2605 Meridian Pkwy., Ste. 200
Durham, NC   27713-2203   (919) 544-8500
Contact: Hudson K. Bates, Exec. Dir.
FAX: (919) 544-7724; E-mail: nipera@nipera.org; Additional tel.: (919) 544-7722; URL: http://www.nipera.org

Foundation type: Independent foundation
Limitations: Research grants for projects that investigate the toxicity of nickel and nickel compounds. Most grants are given over several years.
Financial data: Year ended 12/31/2003. Assets, $2,484,354 (M); Expenditures, $2,959,232; Total giving, $133,802; Grant to an individual, 1 grant totaling $12,000.
Type of support: Research.
Application information:
  Deadline(s): Contact association for current application deadline
  Additional information: NIPERA invites known researchers in the field to submit proposals including a budget, details of the project, and an estimated timetable.
EIN: 133070077

6041
North Dakota Humanities Council

418 E. Broadway, Ste. 8
P.O. Box 2191
Bismarck, ND   58502-2191   (701) 255-3360
Contact: Janet F. Daley, Exec. Dir.
FAX: (701) 223-8724; E-mail: council@nd-humanities.org; Toll-free tel.: (800) 338-6543; URL: http://www.nd-humanities.org

Foundation type: Public charity
Limitations: Fellowships to research a humanities topic, primarily in MN and ND.
Publications: Application guidelines.
Financial data: Year ended 10/31/2004. Assets, $350,293 (M); Expenditures, $512,819; Total giving, $160,150; Grants to individuals, 10

grants totaling $24,000 (high: $3,000, low: $2,000).

Fields of interest: Humanities.

Type of support: Fellowships.

Application information: Contact foundation for current application deadline; Completion of formal application required, including resume and letters of recommendation.

Program description:

Fellowship Awards: Applicants must have a minimum of a Master's Degree in a humanities discipline. Fellowship recipients are given a $5,000 honorarium.

EIN: 450318487

6042

The Northern California DX Foundation

4220 Chardonnay Ct.
Napa, CA 94558
Contact: Len Geraldi, Pres.
Application address: 9705 Old Redwood Hwy., Penngrove, CA 94951
FAX: (707) 794-8033; E-mail: info@ncdxf.org; URL: http://www.ncdxf.org

Foundation type: Operating foundation

Limitations: Research and travel grants to scientists for international scientific expeditions which use radio communications to advance and promote education, science and international goodwill.

Financial data: Year ended 12/31/2002. Assets, $329,368 (M); Expenditures, $11,238; Total giving, $2,550; Grants to individuals, 3 grants totaling $2,550 (high: $2,000, low: $250).

Fields of interest: Media/communications; Radio; Science, research.

Type of support: Research; Travel grants.

Application information: Applications accepted. Application form required. Application form available on the grantmaker's Web site.

Initial approach: Proposal.

Program description:

Research Grants: Grants are usually for well-designed amateur radio DXpeditions to rare and unusual locations which are high on the most-wanted list of various organizations in the world. Past sites of expeditions have included Burma, Eritrea, Korea, and Albania. The expedition participants should have a significant financial stake in their expedition, and the expedition should be likely to proceed even without financial support from the foundation. The foundation also offers a $1,000 scholarship for a collegiate amateur operator.

EIN: 942853576

6043

Northwest Health Foundation

1500 S.W. 1st Ave., Ste. 850
Portland, OR 97201-5884 (503) 220-1955
Contact: Thomas Aschenbrener, Pres.
FAX: (503) 220-1335; E-mail: nwhf@nwhf.org; URL: http://www.nwhf.org

Foundation type: Public charity

Limitations: Fellowships to advance the research careers of health practitioners who serve communities in OR and southwest WA. Two-year fellowships of $150,000 will be awarded.

Financial data: Year ended 12/31/2004. Assets, $61,286,389 (M); Expenditures, $4,436,347; Total giving, $2,815,502.

Fields of interest: Health care, research.

Type of support: Fellowships.

Application information: Applications accepted. Application form required. Application form available on the grantmaker's Web site.

Initial approach: E-mail.

Deadline(s): Apr. 24

Applicants should submit the following:

1) Curriculum vitae
2) Resume
3) Transcripts
4) Essay
5) Budget Information
6) Letter(s) of recommendation

Additional information: Contact foundation for further application guidelines.

EIN: 911854545

6044

Northwest Minnesota Foundation (NWMF)

4225 Technology Dr. N.W.
Bemidji, MN 56601 (218) 759-2057
Contact: Tim Wang, Dir., Finance; For grants: Jim Steenerson, Grants Specialist; For grants: Peggy Crandall, Grants Svcs. Assoc.
FAX: (218) 759-2328; E-mail: nwmf@nwmf.org; Additional tel. for MN residents: (800) 659-7859; Grant request E-mails: peggyc@nwmf.org and jims@nwmf.org; URL: http://www.nwmf.org

Foundation type: Community foundation

Limitations: Support to entrepreneurs to encourage business development in the northwestern MN, region.

Publications: Application guidelines; Annual report; Grants list; Informational brochure; Newsletter.

Financial data: Year ended 06/30/2004. Assets, $35,256,914 (M); Expenditures, $2,910,120; Total giving, $1,401,256; Grants to individuals, 73 grants totaling $44,075 (high: $5,000, low: $100).

Fields of interest: Agriculture; Business/industry.

Type of support: Program development; Seed money; Scholarships—to individuals.

Application information: Applications not accepted.

Additional information: Contact foundation for current application deadline/guidelines.

Program description:

Northwest Minnesota Foundation Program: The foundation provides support to entrepreneurs through the following programs, open only to businesses located within the 12-county service region of northwestern MN. Business Loans: Gap financing is available for business start-ups and expansions that create new jobs leading to long term community impact, diversification of the economy and that leverage other sources of funds to increase total capital investment in the region. Up to $200,000 is available with private funders for businesses engaged in:

- value-added manufacturing
- technologically innovative industries
- agri-processing
- agricultural marketing
- information industries
- tourism
- essential services (non-competing 'anchor' businesses)

Business relocation, agricultural production, and general retail businesses are not eligible. Entrepreneur Micro-Loans & Technical Assistance: Loans up to $35,000 are available to help entrepreneurs develop small businesses and self-employment opportunities. Staff will work directly with entrepreneurs to develop their business and will provide on-going assistance and training. Loan eligibility and terms:

- Retail, service, manufacturing and other business types are generally eligible
- Loan funds can be used for inventory, working capital, equipment and other fixed assets
- Loan terms can be up to five years and payments may be graduated for start-up businesses
- Refinancing is not eligible

Equity Investment: Investments are available to encourage start-up businesses and the expansion of firms focusing on new and emerging technologies, techniques and products. Equity investments are available where business growth would otherwise be hampered with debt financing and the owner is willing to involve others in ownership of the company. Generally, up to $50,000 is available and may be used for the acquisition of equipment, working capital for product development, manufacturing, marketing or other assets. New Product Development: Through a partnership with Minnesota Technology, Inc., small investments (generally $25,000 or less) are available to individuals and companies for activities necessary to determine the viability of a new product in the market place. Eligible activities include:

- prototype development
- patent searches
- product cost analysis
- test market research
- patent filing

Application review criteria include the following items: Market potential of the project, viability of the product, and abilities of the applicant. Generally, the repayment is deferred during the development period.

EIN: 411556013

6045

Northwest Osteopathic Medical Foundation

1410 S.W. Morrison St., Ste. 700
Portland, OR 97205 (503) 222-7161
Contact: Dennis Lavery, Exec. Dir.
FAX: (503) 222-2841; E-mail: info@nwosteo.org; Additional tel.: (888) 696-7836; URL: http://www.nwosteo.org

Foundation type: Public charity

Limitations: Scholarships and grants to students and professionals residing in AK, ID, MT, OR or WA in the area of osteopathic medicine.

Publications: Application guidelines; Annual report; Grants list; Informational brochure (including application guidelines); Newsletter.

Financial data: Year ended 12/31/2004. Assets, $7,516,504 (M); Expenditures, $692,898; Total giving, $95,229; Grants to individuals, totaling $95,229.

Fields of interest: Medical school/education; Health organizations.

Type of support: Program development; Research; Graduate support; Doctoral support.

Application information: Deadlines Mar. 1 and Nov. 1 for Osteopathic Professional, contact foundation for others; Application by letter or request for Osteopathic Professional, contact foundation for other guidelines.

Program descriptions:

Osteopathic Education: Scholarships and student loans are provided to osteopathic medical students in the Northwestern U.S.

Osteopathic Professional Grants: Grants are given to encourage accessible opportunities for continuing and graduate medical education and for research and development.

Rural Rotation Program: $500 scholarships are offered to osteopathic medical students who wish to serve four-week elective rural rotations intended for AK, ID, MT, OR, and WA. To be eligible, students must have completed at least one year of school and remain in good academic standing. Recipients are matched locally with physicians who have offered to serve as preceptors.
EIN: 930882138

6046
John & Mary O'Brien Foundation for Academic Excellence
P.O. Box 9598
Amarillo, TX 79105
Contact: Fay Moore, Treas.
Application address: 800 Monroe, Amarillo, TX 79105, tel.: (806) 372-3877

Foundation type: Independent foundation
Limitations: Grants to teachers who have taught in the public schools of Amarillo, TX, for at least three years and who will continue to teach for three additional years in Amarillo.
Financial data: Year ended 12/31/2004.
Assets, $349,723 (M); Expenditures, $26,507; Total giving, $25,000; Grants to individuals, totaling $25,000.
Fields of interest: Education.
Type of support: Grants to individuals.
Application information:
Initial approach: Letter.
Deadline(s): Feb. 1
Additional information: Interviews required; Application must be mailed to the main address or hand delivered to the application address.
Program description:
Research Grants: Grants are awarded on the basis of the quality of past performances and references. Use of funds is not restricted to formal study. Application letter should include background and qualifications, purpose of grant, and amount requested. Applicant must also enclose a letter of endorsement from one of the following: the PTA/PTO/Excellence Council, principal, a group of three or more peers in the same field of study from the public school system, or a group of three professors from higher education institutions.
EIN: 752156810

6047
Ohiyesa Corporation
P.O. Box 11
Norwich, VT 05055
Contact: Dean J. Seibert, Dir.

Foundation type: Operating foundation
Limitations: Fellowships for the enhancement of verbal skills while learning about medical services in Central America.
Financial data: Year ended 12/31/2002.
Assets, $117,021 (M); Expenditures, $59,513; Total giving, $20,474; Grants to individuals, 27 grants totaling $20,474 (high: $1,893, low: $314).
Fields of interest: Language (foreign); Health care.
Type of support: Fellowships; Travel grants.
Application information: Contact foundation for current application deadline/guidelines; Initial approach by letter or proposal.
Program description:
Fellowship Program: Approximately ten language fellowships will be made annually. The program is designed to enhance verbal skills, cultural appreciation, and an understanding of the

organization of medical services in Central America. Each award will cover travel expenses to Guatemala and living expenses during the six-week period.
EIN: 311586691

6048
The George and Carol Olmsted Foundation
150 S. Washington St., Ste. 403
Falls Church, VA 22046-2921
Contact: RADM. Larry R. Marsh, Pres.
FAX: (703) 536-5020;
E-mail: scholars@olmstedfoundation.org; Toll-free tel.: (877) 656-7833; URL: http://www.olmstedfoundation.org

Foundation type: Independent foundation
Limitations: Foreign study scholarships by nomination only to career military officers in the Armed Forces.
Publications: Annual report; Informational brochure.
Financial data: Year ended 12/31/2004.
Assets, $50,165,289 (M); Expenditures, $2,616,283; Total giving, $1,644,214.
Fields of interest: Language (foreign); Military/veterans' organizations.
Type of support: Awards/grants by nomination only; Graduate support.
Application information: Individual applications not accepted; Applications available through Military Services representatives; Funds largely committed.
Program description:
Olmsted Scholar Program: Offers educational grants for two years of graduate study and other educational experiences in a foreign country. Each year, three or more career officers from each of the four military departments (Army, Navy, Air Force, U.S. Marine Corps) are competitively selected. The spouses of married Scholars also receive grants for language training and to defray other expenses incident to their participation in their spouses' educational endeavors. The Olmsted Scholars are nominated by their military services to study in foreign universities chosen by them and approved by their services. Final selection of Scholars, designation of the foreign universities they will attend, and their areas of study are made by the Board of Directors of the foundation. The Olmsted Scholars enroll as full-time students and study in a language other than English while interacting with the residents of the countries in which they are living. By the end of two successive years of study abroad, the Scholar is eligible for assistance in completing degree requirements at any university in the U.S., under an advanced degree program.
EIN: 546049005

6049
The Oncologic Foundation of Buffalo, Inc.
c/o Jaeckle, Fleischmann and Mugel, LLP
12 Fountain Plz., Fleet Bank Bldg.
Buffalo, NY 14202-2292   (716) 856-0600
Contact: Ray Reichert, Secy.

Foundation type: Independent foundation
Limitations: Grants to individuals for cancer research at research institutes and universities.
Financial data: Year ended 04/30/2005.
Assets, $712,036 (M); Expenditures, $175,782; Total giving, $165,890.
Fields of interest: Cancer research.
Type of support: Research.
Application information: Application form not required.
Deadline(s): None
Applicants should submit the following:

1) Curriculum vitae
Additional information: Applications should be sent by proposal and should also include details of proposed research, description of facilities available to applicant, and an itemized budget.
EIN: 161183425

6050
The One Foundation
75 W. Center St.
Provo, UT 84601

Foundation type: Independent foundation
Limitations: Research grants to individuals for genealogy study.
Financial data: Year ended 12/31/2004.
Assets, $198,934 (M); Expenditures, $65,181; Total giving, $64,650; Grant to an individual, 1 grant totaling $64,650.
Fields of interest: Genealogy.
Type of support: Research.
Application information: Applications not accepted.
EIN: 870576575

6051
Open Society Institute
400 W. 59th St.
New York, NY 10019   (212) 548-0600
Contact: Inquiry Mgr.
FAX: (212) 548-4600; URL: http://www.soros.org

Foundation type: Operating foundation
Limitations: Fellowships to individuals for research, program support, and professional development.
Publications: Annual report; Newsletter; Program policy statement.
Financial data: Year ended 12/31/2004.
Assets, $329,344,522 (M); Expenditures, $124,835,453; Total giving, $83,470,616; Grants to individuals, 1,194 grants totaling $13,052,819 (high: $107,920, low: $44).
Fields of interest: International economic development.
Type of support: Fellowships.
Application information:
Initial approach: Proposal for New York City Community Fellowships and Lindesmith Fellowships.
Deadline(s): Vary
Additional information: Completion of formal application required for Soros Justice Fellows and Palliative Care Fellowships; Interviews required.
Program descriptions:
Soros Justice Fellowships: Awards one- and two-year stipends for the following:
- Media Fellowship: Awards up to $3,000 for one year to journalists working in print, photography, radio and documentary film to improve the quality of media coverage of incarceration and criminal justice issues. Journalists with at least three years experience are eligible to apply. Deadline Sept.
- Senior Fellowship: Awards $45,000 - $60,000 for one year to support activists, lawyers, academics and community leaders to raise the level of national discussion and scholarship and prompt policy debate on issues of incarceration and criminal justice. Deadline Sept.
- Soros Justice Advocacy Fellowships: Awards a one-time payment of $1,200 for relocation costs, a stipend of $37,500, a

$2,000 professional development budget, a $2,500 health insurance budget, and $6,000 to help with graduate school loan debt per year for two years to outstanding individuals in law, organizing, public health, public policy, and other disciplines. Fellows work in partnership with large and small nonprofits whose missions are related to criminal justice. Applicants must have three years experience with the issues and communities they wish to work. Deadline Sept.

Baltimore Community Fellowship Program: Awards fellowships to individuals wishing to apply their education and professional experiences to serve disadvantaged communities. The goals of these fellowships are to encourage public and community service careers, expand the number of mentors and role models available to youth in inner-city neighborhoods, and promote entrepreneurial initiatives that empower communities to increase opportunities and improve the quality of life for their residents. OSI will award up to 10 individuals to implement innovative projects that seek to improve the circumstances and capacity of a marginalized or disadvantaged community in Baltimore City. Applicants may either apply for a fellowship: 1) to work under the auspices of a nonprofit organization in Baltimore City; or 2) to work independently. In cases where the fellowship takes place at an organization in Baltimore, applicants must secure sponsorship from that organization. Recipient's project must be harmonious with the mission of host organization. Fellowship awards are in the amount of $48,750 for a term of 18 months. Applicants may come from any field, including, but not limited to, business management, law, medicine, education, architecture and engineering. OSI strongly encourages individuals from disadvantaged communities and people of color to apply. Applicants need not be from Baltimore City, but should be knowledgeable about social and economic justice issues affecting Baltimore communities. Individuals currently receiving wages or a salary to undertake the proposed project are ineligible. Fellows may not use stipends to supplant funding for activities or projects that the host organization is already implementing. The program does not award fellowships to conduct research or implement lobbying initiatives. Fellows must be willing to participate fully in meetings scheduled by OSI for Community Fellows. Deadline Apr. 7. See Web site for further information and guidelines.

International Pain Policy Fellowship: This fellowship provides candidates with the knowledge and skills necessary to develop and implement a project to improve the availability of pain medications for pain relief and palliative care in their country. It is intended for health professionals (e.g. oncologists, AIDS clinicians, pain and palliative care physicians), health care administrators, managers, policy experts, or lawyers from low or middle income countries with an interest in drug policy advocacy to improve availability of opioid analgesics for pain relief and palliative care. Two-year awards will be made to either the institution or to the fellow directly.
EIN: 137029285

6052
Optical Society of America
2010 Massachusetts Ave. N.W.
Washington, DC   20036-1023   (202) 223-8130
Contact: Elizabeth A. Rogan, Exec. Dir.
FAX: (202) 223-1096; E-mail: info@osa.org;
URL: http://www.osa.org

Foundation type: Public charity
Limitations: Awards by nomination only to individuals who have made outstanding contributions in the field of optics.
Financial data: Year ended 12/31/2004. Assets, $50,311,616 (M); Expenditures, $22,453,724; Total giving, $590,917; Grants to individuals, 93 grants totaling $96,527 (high: $10,000, low: $100).
Fields of interest: Eye research.
Type of support: Awards/prizes.
Application information: Application form required.
   Deadline(s): June 15 for Engineering Excellence, Aug. 10 for John Tyndall, Oct. 1 for all others
   Additional information: Nominations accepted throughout the year; Completion of formal nomination required.
Program descriptions:
Allen Prize: Presented to a person who, while a graduate student, has made outstanding contributions to atmospheric remote sensing using electro-optical instrumentation especially for conceiving new and unique devices, for the development of new measuring techniques, or for perceptive analysis of remote sensing measurements. Candidates must have received their Ph.D. no more than three years prior to the award deadline. This award consists of a certificate and $1,500.

Max Born Award: Presented to a person who has made outstanding contributions to physical optics, theoretical or experimental. It consists of a silver medal, a certificate, and $1,500.

Esther Hoffman Beller Medal: Presented for outstanding contributions to optical science and engineering education. Consideration is given to outstanding teaching and/or original work in optics education that enhances the understanding of optics. The scope of the award is international. The award consists of a silver medal, a certificate, and $2,500.

Distinguished Service Award: Presented to individuals who, over an extended period of time, have served the OSA in an outstanding way, especially through volunteer participation in its management, operation, or planning in such ways as editorship of a periodical, organization of meetings, or other service to the society.

Engineering Excellence Awards: These awards recognize technical achievements in optical engineering. Nominations are solicited in: products, engineering publication, process, software, patents, engineering education, contributions to society, engineering management, and furthering public appreciation of optical engineering. The award consists of a certificate and a glass sculpture.

Joseph Fraunhofer/Robert M. Burley Prize: The Burley prize is presented to the winner of the Joseph Fraunhofer award to recognize significant accomplishments in the field of optical engineering. The award consists of a silver medal, certificate, and $1,500.

Nicholas Holonyak, Jr. Award: Presented to an individual who has made significant contributions to optics based on semiconductor materials, including basic science and technological applications.

Frederic Ives Medal/Quinn Endowment: Recognizing overall distinction in optics, the medal is the highest award of the society. The medalist is asked to present a plenary address at the OSA's annual meeting. The award consists of a silver medal, certificate, and $10,000.

Edwin H. Land Medal: Recognizes individuals in the science of optics, the mechanisms of vision, the properties and use of light, or the creation and manipulation of images who have demonstrated, from a base of scientific knowledge, pioneering

entrepreneurial creativity that has had major public impact. The entrepreneurial activity can be carried on in an industrial or business setting, in academe, or in government. It consists of a silver medal, a certificate, and $10,000.

Ellis R. Lippincott Award: Presented to an individual who has made significant contributions to vibrational spectroscopy as judged by his or her influence on other scientists. Innovation must also be demonstrated by candidates for the award. The award is presented at the national meeting of one of the sponsoring societies and consists of a crystal box and $1,500.

Adolph Lomb Medal: Presented to the person who has made a noteworthy contribution to optics. The contribution must either be published or accepted for publication before he or she has reached the age of 30; the candidates cannot have reached the age of 32 on Jan. 1 of the year in which the award is presented. The award consists of a silver medal, a certificate, and $1,500.

C.E.K. Mees Medal: Presented biennially to a recipient who exemplifies the thought that "optics transcends all boundaries," interdisciplinary and international alike. The award consists of a silver medal, a certificate, and $1,500.

William F. Meggers Award: For outstanding work in spectroscopy. The award consists of a silver medal, a certificate, and $1,500.

OSA Leadership Award/New Focus Prize: The award recognizes: 1) An individual or group of optics professionals whose actions or policy outside the technology arena has made a significant contribution to society (this contribution may be social, economic, political, or humanitarian) or 2) An individual or group whose action, policy, or support has made a significant impact on the field of optics. Either a single contribution or a cumulative record of achievements may be recognized. It consists of a commissioned piece of optical art, a scroll, and a lifetime OSA membership.

OSA New Focus Student Award: The award was established to encourage research excellence, presentation prowess, and leadership in the optics community among OSA student members. At the OSA annual meeting each year, three student finalists will be awarded a top prize of $10,000 each; five finalists each will receive a check of $2,500. All of the following criteria must be met: 1) only an OSA member can nominate a student for this award; 2) The nominated student must submit an abstract or a paper or poster to be presented at the OSA annual meeting, following the guidelines in the annual meeting Call for Papers; 3) The person nominated must be an OSA student member when the nomination is made and when the paper/poster is presented at the Annual Meeting; 4) The preliminary nomination package must be received by OSA no later than May 16; and 5) A complete nomination package, if requested by the OSA New Focus Awards Committee, must be received by OSA no later than July 28. For more information, contact Program Development at (202) 416-1960 or awards@osa.org.

David Richardson Medal: Recognizes those who have made significant contributions primarily to technical optics, but not necessarily in a manner manifested by an extensive publication record or traditional academic reputation. The prize consists of a silver medal, a certificate, and $1,500.

Edgar D. Tillyer Award: Presented not more than once every two years to a person who has performed distinguished work in the field of vision, including (but not limited to) the optics, physiology, anatomy, or psychology of the visual system. The award consists of a silver medal, a certificate, and $1,500.

Charles Hard Townes Award: Given to an individual or a group of individuals for outstanding experimental or theoretical work, discovery, or invention in the field of quantum electronics. The award consists of a silver medal, a certificate, and $5,000.

John Tyndall Award: Recognizes an individual who has made pioneering, highly significant, or continuing technical or leadership contributions to fiber optics technology. The award includes a glass sculpture, a certificate, and $3,100.

R.W. Wood Prize: Recognizes an outstanding discovery, scientific or technical achievement, or invention in the field of optics. The accomplishment for which the prize is given is measured chiefly by its impact on the field of optics generally, and therefore the contribution is one that opens a new era of research or significantly expands an established one. The prize consists of a silver medal, a certificate, and $1,500.

EIN: 530259696

6053
Oregon Council for the Humanities

812 S.W. Washington St., Ste. 225
Portland, OR 97205-3210 (503) 241-0543
Contact: Christopher Zinn, Exec. Dir.
FAX: (503) 241-0024; E-mail: och@oregonhum.org;
Additional tel.: (800) 735-0543; URL: http://
www.oregonhum.org

Foundation type: Public charity
Limitations: Research grants to professional scholars who reside and/or are employed in OR, with training in one or more fields of the humanities.
Publications: Application guidelines; Annual report; Newsletter.
Financial data: Year ended 10/31/2004.
Assets, $463,173 (M); Expenditures, $757,542; Total giving, $94,453; Grants to individuals, 9 grants totaling $21,000 (high: $5,000, low: $2,000).
Fields of interest: Humanities.
Type of support: Research.
Application information: Application form required.
  Initial approach: Letter.
  Deadline(s): Contact foundation for current application deadline
Program description:
  Professional Scholars Awards: Awards two grants of $5,000 each to professional scholars with training in one or more fields of the humanities or those aspects of the social sciences that use historical and philosophical approaches. Grants are not made to finance work by graduate students or for degree-related study. Applicants must not have been awarded a Research Grant in the previous year, nor have done research on the same topic under an earlier award.
EIN: 930716419

6054
Organic Farming Research Foundation

P.O. Box 440
Santa Cruz, CA 95061 (831) 426-6606
Contact: Steve Ela, Pres.
URL: http://www.ofrf.org

Foundation type: Public charity
Limitations: Grants to individuals for research on organic farming and food systems. Preference is given to American researchers, but there is a limited amount of funding for exceptional international projects.

Financial data: Year ended 12/31/2004.
Assets, $462,674 (M); Expenditures, $907,777; Total giving, $138,445.
Fields of interest: Agriculture/food, research.
Type of support: Research.
Application information: Applications accepted. Application form not required.
  Copies of proposal: 7
  Deadline(s): July 15 and Dec. 15
  Additional information: Application by proposal; See Web site for further information.
EIN: 770252545

6055
Organization of American Historians

112 N. Bryan Ave.
P.O. Box 5457
Bloomington, IN 47408-5457 (812) 855-7311
Contact: Lee W. Formwalt, Exec. Dir.
FAX: (812) 855-0696; E-mail: oah@oah.org;
URL: http://www.oah.org

Foundation type: Public charity
Limitations: Awards, fellowships, prizes, and grants to scholars and professionals specializing in American history.
Financial data: Year ended 06/30/2005.
Assets, $2,227,457 (M); Expenditures, $2,842,495.
Fields of interest: Historical activities.
Type of support: Fellowships; Awards/prizes.
Application information: Application form required.
  Deadline(s): Vary
  Additional information: See Web site for further application and program information.
Program description:
  Historian Grants:
  · Willi Paul Adams Award
  · Erick Barnouw Award
  · Ray Allen Billington Prize
  · Binkley-Stephenson Award
  · Avery O. Craven Award
  · Huggins-Quarles Dissertation Award
  · Japanese Residencies
  · Richard W. Leopold Prize
  · Lerner-Scott Dissertation Prize
  · Horace Samuel & Marion Galbraith Merrill Travel Grants
  · Louis Pelzer Memorial Award
  · Mary K. Bonstel Tachau Precollegiate Teaching Award
  · David Thelen Award
  · Frederick Jackson Turner Award
  · White House Historical Association Fellowships.
EIN: 470426520

6056
Osteogenesis Imperfecta Foundation, Inc.

804 W. Diamond Ave., Ste. 210
Gaithersburg, MD 20878-1414
(301) 947-0083
Contact: Heller An Shapiro, Exec. Dir.
FAX: (301) 947-0456; E-mail: bonelink@oif.org;
Additional tel.: (800) 981-2663; URL: http://
www.oif.org

Foundation type: Public charity
Limitations: Fellowships to individuals for research on osteogenesis imperfecta (OI).
Publications: Application guidelines; Annual report; Grants list; Newsletter; Occasional report.
Financial data: Year ended 06/30/2003.
Assets, $1,942,514 (M); Expenditures, $1,116,704; Total giving, $146,320; Grants to

individuals, 3 grants totaling $146,320 (high: $60,000, low: $47,000).
Fields of interest: Nerve, muscle & bone research.
Type of support: Seed money; Fellowships; Research.
Application information: Applications accepted. Application form required. Application form available on the grantmaker's Web site.
  Deadline(s): Nov. 1.
  Additional information: Application should include letter and curriculum vitae from applicant's mentor.
Program descriptions:
  Michael Geisman Research Fellowships: Awards up to $50,000 per year ($35,000 toward investigator's salary and up to $15,000 per year for supplies). Second year funding may be available.
  Seed Grants: Awards up to $60,000 for one year (grants do not support independent investigator salaries)
  Clinical Seed Grants: Awards up to $120,000 for two years (grants do not support independent investigator salaries). In addition to projects at institutions, these grants offer an opportunity to study people with OI (osteogenesis imperfecta) and their families at the foundation's National Conference.
EIN: 237076021

6057
Osteopathic Founders Foundation

744 W. 9th St., H-295
Tulsa, OK 74127 (918) 599-5288
Contact: Sherri L. Wise, Pres.
Additional E-mail (for Sherri L. Wise):
swise@osteopathicfounders.org; URL: http://
www.osteopathicfounders.org

Foundation type: Public charity
Limitations: Scholarships by nomination only to fourth-year osteopathic medical students.
Publications: Annual report; Newsletter.
Financial data: Year ended 12/31/2004.
Assets, $12,918,895 (M); Expenditures, $584,917; Total giving, $211,088.
Type of support: Awards/grants by nomination only; Doctoral support.
Application information: Nominations accepted throughout the year. Nomination should be submitted by the dean.
Program description:
  Osteopathic Founders Foundation Program: Students must attend the alma mater, or another medical college chosen by the Foundation's Physician of the Year.
EIN: 730583936

6058
PADI Foundation

(also known as Professional Association of Diving Instructors Foundation)
9150 Wilshire Blvd., Ste. 300
Beverly Hills, CA 90212-3414
Contact: Charles P. Rettig, Pres.
E-mail: rettig@taxlitigator.com; URL: http://
www.padifoundation.org

Foundation type: Operating foundation
Limitations: Research and project grants primarily in the fields of ecology and marine science.
Publications: Application guidelines; Financial statement.
Financial data: Year ended 05/31/2005.
Assets, $2,448,470 (M); Expenditures, $190,045; Total giving, $158,539; Grants to

individuals, 38 grants totaling $140,839 (high: $9,860, low: $964).
Fields of interest: Natural resources; Marine science.
Type of support: Program development; Research.
Application information: Contact foundation for current application deadline; Application by letter.
EIN: 954326850

6059

The Paideia Foundation
c/o Klesman, Halper & Co.
7110 W. 127th St., Ste. 230
Palos Heights, IL 60463
Contact: John Dongas, Secy.
Application address: 15621 W. Mallord Ln., Lockport, IL 60441

Foundation type: Independent foundation
Limitations: Grants to teachers employed at the Koraes School in Palos Hills, IL, for work benefiting elementary child education.
Financial data: Year ended 12/31/2004.
Assets, $495,706 (M); Expenditures, $35,737; Total giving, $28,581.
Fields of interest: Elementary school/education; Education.
Type of support: Employee-related scholarships.
Application information: Applications accepted.
Initial approach: Letter or telephone.
Deadline(s): None
Additional information: Contact foundation for current application guidelines.
EIN: 363884185

6060

Pancreatic Cancer Action Network, Inc.
2141 Rosecrans Ave., Ste. 7000
El Segundo, CA 90245 (310) 725-0025
Contact: Julie Fleshman, Pres. and C.E.O.
FAX: (310) 725-0029; E-mail: info@pancan.org;
Toll-free tel.: (877) 272-6226; URL: http://www.pancan.org

Foundation type: Public charity
Limitations: Research grants to physicians and academics who specialize in pancreatic cancer.
Publications: Annual report; Grants list; Newsletter.
Financial data: Year ended 06/30/2005.
Assets, $1,845,791 (M); Expenditures, $2,706,569; Total giving, $314,400; Grants to individuals, totaling $314,400.
Fields of interest: Cancer research; Organ research.
Type of support: Fellowships; Research.
Application information: Applications accepted. Application form required.
Deadline(s): Nov.
Additional information: See Web site for further application and program information.
EIN: 330841281

6061

John A. & Irene Papines Scholarship Trust-Ermoupolis
c/o Bank of America, N.A.
P.O. Box 441
Ridgefield Park, NJ 07660-9984

Foundation type: Independent foundation
Limitations: Scholarships to residents of Ermoupolis, Island of Syra, Greece, who are pursuing a career in medicine.

Financial data: Year ended 12/31/2004.
Assets, $252,348 (M); Expenditures, $14,783; Total giving, $11,000; Grants to individuals, totaling $11,000.
Fields of interest: Medical school/education.
Type of support: Foreign applicants; Graduate support.
Application information: Application form required.
Deadline(s): June 1
EIN: 226321386

6062

Parapsychology Foundation, Inc.
P.O. Box 1562
New York, NY 10021-0043 (212) 628-1550
Contact: Eileen Coly, Chair.
FAX: (212) 628-1559;
E-mail: info@parapsychology.org; URL: http://www.parapsychology.org

Foundation type: Operating foundation
Limitations: Research and scholarship grants for study in parapsychology including clairvoyance, clairaudience, telepathy, precognition, retrocognition, psychokinesis, poltergeist, out-of-body experiences, spontaneous phenomena, mediumship, survival, psychology, psychiatry, unorthodox healing, altered states of consciousness, hypnosis, drugs, and dreams.
Publications: Application guidelines; Annual report (including application guidelines); Informational brochure; Informational brochure (including application guidelines); Newsletter.
Financial data: Year ended 12/31/2003.
Assets, $3,177,175 (M); Expenditures, $664,182; Total giving, $11,000; Grants to individuals, 6 grants totaling $11,000 (high: $3,000, low: $500).
Fields of interest: Psychology/behavioral science.
Type of support: Research; Scholarships—to individuals.
Application information: Applications accepted. Application form required.
Initial approach: Letter.
Copies of proposal: 2
Additional information: Applications accepted throughout the year, however, two copies of the proposal should be submitted between Jan. and Mar.
Program description:
Research Grants: Grants are awarded to scientists and others engaged in study, research, and experiments on original projects pertaining to parapsychology and parapsychological phenomena. Applicants should submit a prospectus outlining the nature and objectives of the project, biographical and professional data, and estimated expenditures. Grants are approved for one year only. The $3,000 Eileen J. Garrett Scholarship is offered annually to any student attending an accredited college or university who plans to pursue undergraduate or graduate parapsychology studies. The award not only provides financial assistance to the student but affords the foundation an opportunity to encourage pursuit of a study program in disciplines adaptable to research in parapsychology.
EIN: 131677742

6063

Robert J. and Claire Pasarow Foundation
211 Spalding Dr., Ste. 420N
Beverly Hills, CA 90212
Contact: Claire Pasarow, C.F.O.

Foundation type: Independent foundation

Limitations: Grants to individuals for medical and scientific research.
Financial data: Year ended 10/31/2005.
Assets, $1,309,358 (M); Expenditures, $170,858; Total giving, $150,000; Grants to individuals, 3 grants totaling $150,000 (high: $50,000, low: $50,000).
Fields of interest: Medical research, institute; Science, research.
Type of support: Research.
Application information: Deadline Aug. 31; Application by letter, including resume and statement of achievements in applicant's field.
EIN: 954079676

6064

Alicia Patterson Foundation
1025 F Street NW, Ste. 700
Washington, DC 20004 (202) 393-5995
FAX: (301) 951-8512;
E-mail: director@aliciapatterson.org; URL: http://www.aliciapatterson.org

Foundation type: Operating foundation
Limitations: Fellowships to U.S. citizens who have worked professionally as print journalists for at least five years.
Publications: Application guidelines; Annual report; Grants list; Informational brochure; Newsletter.
Financial data: Year ended 12/31/2003.
Assets, $5,100,189 (M); Expenditures, $396,152; Total giving, $242,222; Grants to individuals, 8 grants totaling $214,907 (high: $34,999, low: $2,916).
Fields of interest: Journalism/publishing.
Type of support: Fellowships.
Application information: Application form not required.
Additional information: Deadline Oct. 1; Initial approach by letter, telephone, or e-mail; Recipients are chosen by an annual competition; Completion of formal application required; Interviews for finalists required; Recipients notified in early Dec.
Program description:
Alicia Patterson Journalism Fellowships: The program awards five to seven new fellowships each year to newspaper, magazine, wire service, and freelance journalists, photographers, or editors for a year of travel and inquiry into significant foreign or domestic issues. Fellows write articles on their chosen subject for the APF Reporter, a quarterly magazine published by the foundation. The Reporter is circulated to newspaper and magazine editors and other interested people in business, government, and the professions throughout the U.S. All articles appearing in the magazine may be reprinted freely with proper credit. Fellowships include a $30,000 stipend. Fellows must take a leave of absence from their employer. Past research topics have included organized crime, abortion, immigrants, and issues in Haiti, Mexico, Hungary, and other nations.
EIN: 136092124

6065

Pediatric Brain Tumor Foundation of the United States, Inc.
(formerly Ride For Kids Foundation, Inc.)
302 Ridgefield Ct.
Asheville, NC 28806-2243 (828) 665-6891
Contact: Mike Traynor, Pres.
FAX: (828) 665-6894;
E-mail: research@pbtfus.org; URL: http://www.pbtfus.org/

Foundation type: Public charity
Limitations: Research grants to investigators for projects that demonstrate the potential to advance basic scientific research in brain tumors.
Publications: Informational brochure; Newsletter.
Financial data: Year ended 12/31/2004. Assets, $6,724,088 (M); Expenditures, $3,967,407; Total giving, $1,806,388; Grants to individuals, 37 grants totaling $81,564 (high: $3,750, low: $895).
Fields of interest: Brain research.
Type of support: Research.
Application information: Application form required. Application form available on the grantmaker's Web site.
Deadline(s): May 14
Program description:
Research Program: Awards are for $50,000 a year for two years not to exceed $100,000. Funds may be used to start up projects or as supplementary funding for the support of no more than five basic laboratory research projects exhibiting outstanding scientific merit. Preference will be given to studies that have direct relevance to pediatric brain tumors.
EIN: 581966822

6066
PENCIL Foundation

(also known as Public Education: Nashville Citizens Involved In Leadership)
421 Great Circle Rd., Ste. 100
Nashville, TN   37228-1407   (615) 242-3167
Contact: Connie Williams, Exec. Dir.
FAX: (615) 254-6748;
E-mail: pencilfd@bellsouth.net; URL: http://www.pencilfd.org

Foundation type: Public charity
Limitations: Awards and grants to Davidson County, TN, teachers and principals.
Publications: Application guidelines; Grants list; Informational brochure.
Financial data: Year ended 06/30/2004. Assets, $881,082; Expenditures, $1,886,872; Total giving, $62,112; Grants to individuals, totaling $44,947.
Fields of interest: Elementary school/education; Secondary school/education; Education.
Type of support: Program development; Awards/grants by nomination only; Awards/prizes.
Application information: Applications accepted. Application form required.
Deadline(s): Jan. 25.
Additional information: Interviews required.
Program descriptions:
Educator Awards: Awards of up to $5,000 are given to individual educators or teams of educators as they pursue programs of study that are designed to enhance administrative or teaching proficiencies. Teams consisting of four or more educators will be eligible to apply for grants of up to $20,000. Study programs may include, but are not limited to, site or program visits, consultations with experts, and attendance at workshops and seminars. Eligible educators are classroom teachers, guidance counselors, librarians, principals, assistant principals, and key administrators from Metropolitan Nashville Public Schools and member schools of the Independent Schools of the Nashville Area. See the foundation's Web site for current selection priorities.
Foundation Teacher Awards: Grants of up to $5,000 each are given to teachers in Metro Nashville Public Schools as well as in member schools of the Independent Schools of the Nashville Area for programs of independent study

during the summer. The study may be in an established training program or may be a completely self-designed project. Teachers may apply as individuals or in teams.
EIN: 581475675

6067
The People Technology Foundation, Inc.

219 South St.
New Providence, NJ   07974   (908) 665-4061
Contact: Frank J. Ponzio, Pres.

Foundation type: Operating foundation
Limitations: Paid internship opportunities to Eastern Europeans, with emphasis on individuals from Romania, who want to gain experience in the computer field by working as an intern in the U.S. for a summer.
Financial data: Year ended 12/31/2002. Assets, $115,235 (M); Expenditures, $47,116; Total giving, $13,600; Grants to individuals, totaling $13,600.
Fields of interest: Computer science.
Type of support: Internship funds.
Application information:
Deadline(s): None.
Additional information: Contact foundation for current application guidelines.
EIN: 223273424

6068
Henry S. Pernot Scholarship Fund

c/o U.S. Bank, N.A.
P.O. Box 3168
Portland, OR   97208

Foundation type: Independent foundation
Limitations: Scholarships by nomination only to medical students who have completed their first two years at the Oregon Health Sciences University.
Financial data: Year ended 06/30/2005. Assets, $368,347 (M); Expenditures, $23,851; Total giving, $18,500; Grants to individuals, totaling $18,500.
Fields of interest: Medical school/education.
Type of support: Support to graduates or students of specific schools; Awards/grants by nomination only; Graduate support.
Application information: Applications not accepted.
Additional information: Students are preselected by the Dean of the Oregon Health Sciences University; The fund then makes the final selection and determines the amount of each scholarship.
EIN: 237385854

6069
Peters Valley Craftsman, Inc.

19 Kuhn Rd.
Layton, NJ   07851   (973) 948-5200
Contact: Jimmy Clark, Exec. Dir.
FAX: (973) 948-0011; E-mail: pv@warwick.net;
URL: http://www.pvcrafts.org

Foundation type: Public charity
Limitations: Tuition scholarships to art teachers for attendance at the Center's workshops.
Financial data: Year ended 09/30/2003. Assets, $182,115 (M); Expenditures, $865,736.
Fields of interest: Folk arts; Visual arts; Ceramic arts.
Type of support: Conferences/seminars; Workstudy grants.

Application information: Application form required.
Initial approach: E-mail.
Deadline(s): Apr. 1
Additional information: Application must include letter of intent, slides of recent work and SASE.
Program description:
Tuition Scholarship for Art Teachers: Peters Valley will offer tuition scholarships to four art teachers. One scholarship will be awarded in each of the following four categories: Elementary, Middle (Jr. High), High, and "Other", which may include special art programs. These four teachers will receive free workshop tuition and free housing for a three to five day workshop of their choice during the summer. Recipients will be responsible for all other associated costs such as material fees and meals. The applicant must show active involvement in their field outside the classroom, as well as strong desire to enhance their school program.
EIN: 221920050

6070
Petra Foundation Charitable Trust

c/o Law Firm of Hill & Barlow
1 International Pl., 21st Fl.
Boston, MA   02110-2600
Application address: c/o Muriel Morisey Spence, Chair., Award Comm., P.O. Box 11579, Washington, DC 20008, tel.: (202) 364-8964

Foundation type: Independent foundation
Limitations: Awards by nomination only to individuals, in recognition of community activism and organization work, in the areas of social justice and civil and human rights.
Financial data: Year ended 03/31/2004. Assets, $295,637 (M); Expenditures, $193,363; Total giving, $30,000; Grants to individuals, totaling $30,000.
Fields of interest: International human rights; Civil rights, advocacy.
Type of support: Awards/grants by nomination only; Awards/prizes.
Application information: Deadline Jan 15; Completion of formal application required.
EIN: 046603552

6071
The Philadelphia Award

c/o PNC Advisors
1600 Market St.
Philadelphia, PA   19103-7240
Contact: William J. Marrazzo, Tr.
Application address: c/o WHYY Inc., Independence Mall W., 150 N. 6th St., Philadelphia, PA 19106

Foundation type: Independent foundation
Limitations: An award by nomination only, to recognize a resident of the Philadelphia, PA, area for his or her public service.
Financial data: Year ended 12/31/2004. Assets, $1,859,897 (M); Expenditures, $104,791; Total giving, $25,500; Grants to individuals, totaling $25,500.
Fields of interest: Leadership development.
Type of support: Awards/grants by nomination only; Awards/prizes.
Application information: Deadline Dec. 15; Nomination by letter.
Program description:
The Philadelphia Award Program: An annual award is given to a resident of Philadelphia who has "performed or brought to culmination an act or contributed a service calculated to advance the

best and largest interest of the community of which Philadelphia is the center.".
EIN: 236414396

6072
Philippe Foundation, Inc.
405 Lexington Ave., 35th Fl.
New York, NY 10174 (212) 687-3290
Contact: Beatrice Philippe, V.P.

Foundation type: Independent foundation
Limitations: Grants primarily for cancer research to French and American physicians and scientists. Living and travel expenses, and supplemental support are also given to recipients of research grants.
Publications: Application guidelines.
Financial data: Year ended 12/31/2004. Assets, $5,684,818 (M); Expenditures, $251,594; Total giving, $242,269.
Fields of interest: Health care, association; Medical research, institute; Science, research.
Type of support: Research; Exchange programs; Travel grants.
Application information: Applications by letter, including education and research background, publications, marital status, letter of acceptance at proposed research laboratory, at least two letters of recommendation from persons who worked with applicant, other sources of funds available to applicant, and the amount requested from the foundation, accepted throughout the year.
Program description:
Research Grants: The foundation is primarily concerned with the exchange of physicians and scientists between the U.S. and France, and with advanced study and scientific research, emphasizing cancer research. Except for the most unusual circumstances, grants are not intended to provide the principal source of support. Grants help pay for travel and living expenses in connection with advanced studies and research.
EIN: 136087157

6073
Phillips Foundation, Inc.
1 Massachusetts Ave. N.W., Ste. 620
Washington, DC 20001
Contact: John W. Farley, Secy.
Contact for scholarships: D. Jeffrey Hollingsworth, Asst. Secy., tel.: (202) 250-3887, ext. 628, E-mail: jhollingsworth@phillips.com
FAX: (202) 216-9188; E-mail: jfarley@phillips.com; Additional tel.: (202) 250-3887; URL: http://www.thephillipsfoundation.org

Foundation type: Company-sponsored foundation
Limitations: Fellowships to professional journalists with less than five years of experience who are U.S. citizens.
Financial data: Year ended 09/30/2004. Assets, $11,205,349 (M); Expenditures, $661,734; Total giving, $372,500; Grants to individuals, 60 grants totaling $372,500 (high: $35,000, low: $1,000).
Fields of interest: Journalism/publishing; History/ archaeology; Environment, public policy; Crime/law enforcement, research.
Type of support: Fellowships.
Application information: Applications accepted. Application form required. Application form available on the grantmaker's Web site.
Initial approach: Letter or telephone.
Deadline(s): Mar. 1
Applicants should submit the following:
1) Letter(s) of recommendation

2) Proposal
3) Curriculum vitae
4) Budget Information
Additional information: Application must also include three work samples.
Program description:
The Phillips Foundation Journalism Fellowship Program: The foundation awards full-time $50,000 fellowships and part-time $25,000 fellowships to working journalists with less than five years of professional experience in print journalism. Journalism projects are delivered in four quarterly installments with the potential to be published sequentially in periodical or all together as a book. Projects will focus on journalism supportive of American culture and a free society. The foundation awards a separate Environmental Fellowship for a writing project on the environment from a free-market perspective. In addition, The foundation has also created the Gilder Lehrman Journalism Fellowship for a writing project focusing on American history and the principles of the American founding; and a Law Enforcement Fellowship for a writing project focusing on some aspect of law enforcement in the United States.
EIN: 521707001

6074
Pine Family Foundation
c/o Ray Pine
401 W. 37th St.
Austin, TX 78705-1313 (512) 467-6166
Contact: Sharron Pine Catledge, Secy.
Application address: 1000 JoJo Rd., Pensacola, FL 32514; URL: http://www.pinefamilyfoundation.org

Foundation type: Independent foundation
Limitations: Scholarships and grants for Alzheimer's or AIDS research.
Financial data: Year ended 12/31/2004. Assets, $908,370 (M); Expenditures, $60,779; Total giving, $50,000; Grants to individuals, totaling $50,000.
Fields of interest: AIDS research; Alzheimer's disease research.
Type of support: Research.
Application information: Deadline Mar. 15; Completion of formal application required, including organization/institution prospectus if other than a college or university, an explanation of audit procedures at the organization/institution, a statement that animals used in experiments were cared for per UCSF and NIH guidelines, and financial records if requested.
Program description:
Research Program: The foundation's grants and scholarships are awarded to researchers and graduate students who are working toward a cure for Alzheimer's disease or AIDS. To apply for a scholarship, ($500 to $2,500), applicants must: be engaged in active research towards the cure of Alzheimer's or AIDS; be working on a graduate degree; submit a letter from the supervising professor; submit a personal resume; submit a letter detailing how funds are to be used; designate a person to oversee the spending of funds, and submit a progress report and final report. To apply for a grant, ($500 to $10,000), applicants must: conduct research on Alzheimer's or AIDS; use no more than five percent of funds for administrative purposes; submit a letter detailing how funds are to be used; designate a person to oversee the spending of funds, and submit a progress report and final report. Scholarship/grants will be awarded in June and the funds usually distributed in Aug.
EIN: 742697612

6075
The Virginia G. Piper Charitable Trust
6720 N. Scottsdale Rd., Ste. 350
Scottsdale, AZ 85253 (480) 948-5853
Contact: Judy Jolley Mohraz Ph.D., C.E.O. and Pres.
FAX: (480) 348-1316; E-mail: info@pipertrust.org; URL: http://www.pipertrust.org

Foundation type: Independent foundation
Limitations: Fellowships to Maricopa County, AZ, nonprofit executives.
Publications: Annual report; Biennial report; Grants list; Newsletter.
Financial data: Year ended 03/31/2005. Assets, $552,859,276 (M); Expenditures, $27,064,867; Total giving, $23,769,757.
Fields of interest: Nonprofit management.
Type of support: Fellowships.
Application information: Applications accepted.
Initial approach: E-mail or telephone.
Deadline(s): Sept. 15
Applicants should submit the following:
1) Letter(s) of recommendation
2) Budget Information
3) Resume
4) Essay
Additional information: Application by letter.
Program description:
Piper Fellows Program: The program offers five fellowships of up to $30,000 each to support the professional development of outstanding senior executives of established nonprofit organizations who serve the people of Maricopa County, AZ, in the areas of human services, health, education, religion, and arts and culture. The awards are intended to provide the executive with a minimum of one month to a maximum of two months of work release time plus expenses for study and travel in order to enhance their skills and rejuvenate. Piper Fellows are encouraged to draw on national, regional and local educational resources for professional development during their sabbatical.
EIN: 866247076

6076
Minnie Stevens Piper Foundation
1250 N.E. Loop 410, Ste. 810
San Antonio, TX 78209-1539 (210) 525-8494
Contact: Joyce M. Ellis, Secy. and Exec. Dir.
FAX: (210) 341-6627; E-mail: mspf@mspf.org; URL: http://www.mspf.org

Foundation type: Independent foundation
Limitations: Scholarships to financially needy students and cash awards to college teachers, both by nomination only. Recipients must be U.S. citizens or permanent residents, residents of TX, and attend or teach at TX colleges and universities.
Publications: Application guidelines; Occasional report; Program policy statement.
Financial data: Year ended 12/31/2004. Assets, $22,952,803 (M); Expenditures, $1,872,923; Total giving, $588,500.
Fields of interest: Education, research; Education.
Type of support: Awards/prizes; Undergraduate support.
Application information:
Applicants should submit the following:
1) Letter(s) of recommendation
2) Resume
3) ACT
4) Transcripts
Additional information: Application must include class rank; See program description for information on specific programs.

Program descriptions:

Piper Professors Program: Provides 10 annual awards of $2,500 each to professors for excellence in teaching at the college level. Selection is made on the basis of nominations submitted by president of each college and university in TX. Deadline Nov.

Piper Scholars Program: Awards four-year scholarships to academically superior high school seniors who reside in and plan to attend colleges or universities in TX. Recipients must maintain at least a "B" average to remain eligible. Upon invitation, nominations are made by principals or counselors from selected TX high schools. Selection is made by the foundation's Scholarship Committee which reviews high school records, achievement tests, and letters of evaluation. Deadline Sept.
EIN: 741292695

6077
PKD Foundation
(formerly Polycystic Kidney Research Foundation)
9221 Ward Pkwy., Ste. 400
Kansas City, MO   64114-3367   (800) 753-8273
Contact: Daniel Larson, Pres. and C.E.O.
FAX: (816) 931-2655;
E-mail: pkdcure@pkdcure.org; URL: http://www.pkdcure.org

Foundation type: Public charity
Limitations: Grants and fellowships to investigators for research on the cause, improved clinical treatment, and cure of polycystic kidney disease.
Publications: Application guidelines; Financial statement; Grants list; Informational brochure; Newsletter.
Financial data: Year ended 12/31/2003. Assets, $4,363,431 (M); Expenditures, $5,077,681; Total giving, $2,315,904; Grants to individuals, totaling $2,315,904 (high: $65,000, low: $50,000).
Fields of interest: Kidney research.
Type of support: Conferences/seminars; Fellowships; Research.
Application information: Application form required.
Initial approach: Letter or telephone.
Deadline(s): Aug. 1
EIN: 431266906

6078
Plastic Surgery Educational Foundation
444 E. Algonquin Rd.
Arlington Heights, IL   60005   (847) 228-9900
Contact: Bruce M. Achauer M.D., Pres.
Additional tel.: (888) 4-PLASTIC; URL: http://www.plasticsurgery.org/

Foundation type: Public charity
Limitations: Grants to plastic surgeons for research within their field.
Financial data: Year ended 12/31/2003. Assets, $11,919,834 (M); Expenditures, $3,769,311; Total giving, $326,600; Grants to individuals, totaling $326,600.
Fields of interest: Surgery research.
Type of support: Fellowships; Research.
Application information:
Initial approach: Telephone.
Deadline(s): Varies
Additional information: Contact foundation for current application guidelines; See Web site for deadlines and further information.
Program descriptions:
Basic Research Grants: Awards of up to $5,000 to plastic surgeons for basic scientific research related to plastic and reconstructive surgery.

Research Fellowship Grants: Awards fellowships to individuals for the purpose of encouraging research and academic career development in plastic and reconstructive surgery.
Smile Train Cleft Research Initiative: Awards up to $20,000 to provide funds for healthcare professionals to perform meritorious research projects in the areas of etiology, treatment or care of individuals with cleft lip and palate.
EIN: 596144450

6079
Ploughshares Fund
Fort Mason Ctr., Bldg. B, Ste. 330
San Francisco, CA   94123   (415) 775-2244
Contact: Naila Bolus, Exec. Dir.
FAX: (415) 775-4529;
E-mail: ploughshares@ploughshares.org;
URL: http://www.ploughshares.org

Foundation type: Public charity
Limitations: Research grants to individuals who seek to prevent the spread and use of nuclear, chemical, biological and other weapons of war, and to prevent conflicts that could lead to the use of weapons of mass destruction.
Publications: Annual report (including application guidelines); Grants list; Informational brochure (including application guidelines); Newsletter.
Financial data: Year ended 06/30/2004. Assets, $26,583,383 (M); Expenditures, $5,178,975; Total giving, $3,866,229; Grants to individuals, 11 grants totaling $459,931 (high: $182,360, low: $700).
Fields of interest: Arms control.
Type of support: Program development; Seed money; Research.
Application information: Application form required.
Initial approach: Letter.
Copies of proposal: 1
Deadline(s): Varies
Applicants should submit the following:
1) Financial information
Additional information: Contact foundation for current application deadline.
Program description:
The Ploughshares Fund Program: The fund will not support film, video, or book production, or research and writing for academic dissertations.
EIN: 942764520

6080
Poncin Scholarship Fund
c/o Bank of America, N.A.
P.O. Box 34345
Seattle, WA   98124-1345
Contact: Andrea Grosso
Application address: c/o Bank of America, N.A., P.O. Box 24565, Seattle, WA 98124, tel.: (206) 358-0648

Foundation type: Independent foundation
Limitations: Research grants to individuals engaged in medical research in a recognized institution of learning in WA.
Publications: Application guidelines.
Financial data: Year ended 12/31/2004. Assets, $7,376,641; Expenditures, $365,651; Total giving, $313,369.
Fields of interest: Medical research, institute.
Type of support: Research.
Application information: Applications accepted throughout the year; Application by proposal, including approval from the head of the educational

institution's research institute; Recipients notified eight weeks after deadline.
EIN: 916069573

6081
The Lois Pope Life Foundation
6274 Linton Blvd., Ste. 103
Delray Beach, FL   33484   (561) 865-0955
FAX: (561) 865-0938; E-mail: life@life-edu.org;
URL: http://www.life-edu.org

Foundation type: Independent foundation
Limitations: Awards to scientists whose research has led to clinical applications. Awards are presented on an annual basis, usually in the amount of $100,000.
Financial data: Year ended 12/31/2004. Assets, $795,796 (M); Expenditures, $1,256,345; Total giving, $882,235.
Fields of interest: Medical research, institute.
Type of support: Research; Awards/prizes.
Application information: Unsolicited requests for funds not accepted.
EIN: 137086087

6082
The Price Family Charitable Fund
(formerly The Sol & Helen Price Foundation)
7979 Ivanhoe Ave., Ste. 520
La Jolla, CA   92037
Contact: James Cahill, V.P.

Foundation type: Independent foundation
Limitations: Fellowships primarily to residents of San Diego, CA.
Financial data: Year ended 12/31/2002. Assets, $106,994,019 (M); Expenditures, $1,221,800; Total giving, $259,462; Grants to individuals, 140 grants totaling $52,135 (high: $4,000, low: $50).
Type of support: Fellowships.
Application information: Applications not accepted.
EIN: 953842468

6083
Primate Conservation, Inc.
1411 Shannock Rd.
Charlestown, RI   02813-3726   (401) 364-7140
Contact: Noel B. Rowe, Dir.
FAX: (401) 364-6785; E-mail: nroaw@primate.org;
URL: http://www.primate.org

Foundation type: Independent foundation
Limitations: Research grants and seed money to qualified conservationists, primatologists, and graduate students for projects pertaining to the study of rare and endangered primates, and their conservation.
Publications: Application guidelines; Grants list; Newsletter.
Financial data: Year ended 12/31/2004. Assets, $505,308 (M); Expenditures, $77,347; Total giving, $74,298; Grants to individuals, totaling $71,298.
Fields of interest: Animals/wildlife, preservation/protection; Science, research.
Type of support: Program development; Seed money; Research; Grants to individuals; Foreign applicants; Graduate support; Project support.
Application information: Application form required. Application form available on the grantmaker's Web site.
Initial approach: E-mail.

Copies of proposal: 4
Deadline(s): Feb. 1 and Sept. 20
Applicants should submit the following:
1) Proposal
2) Curriculum vitae
3) Budget Information
Additional information: Application should also include proposal cover sheet, background information, project descriptions, methods, timetable, bibliography, necessary permits and permissions for research, three potential references for proposal, and if needed, completed and signed institution agreement form; Applications should be sent by e-mail in Microsoft .doc file; Recipients notified May 15 and Dec. 15.

Program description:
Research Grant: Primate Conservation, Inc. funds field research that supports conservation programs for wild populations of primates. Priority will be given to projects that study the least known and most endangered species in their natural habitats. In particular, field studies in West Africa and Asia may receive priority. The involvement of citizens from the country in which the primates are found will be a plus. The intent of the foundation is to provide support for original research that can be used to formulate and to implement conservation plans for the species studied. The majority of funded proposals fall into the general category of behavior and ecology of primates. Most grants are given to individuals through the educational and nonprofit organizations with which they are associated, but direct applications by individuals without institutional support are accepted. Proposals are evaluated on a competitive basis, first by outside reviewers and then by the foundation's Scientific Advisory Board. Recipients are selected on the basis of their project's conservation and scientific merit. The maximum grant amount is $5,000. Projects with larger budgets will not be considered. Funds may not be used for conferences, travel to scientific meetings, legal actions, tuition, salaries, or overhead costs at institutions.
EIN: 113152696

6084
Priority Healthcare Foundation, Inc.
250 Technology Park, Ste. 124
Lake Mary, FL 32746-6232

Foundation type: Independent foundation
Limitations: Grants to doctors for infertility research and education.
Financial data: Year ended 12/31/2004.
Assets, $18,662 (L); Expenditures, $726,805; Total giving, $396,764.
Fields of interest: Pediatrics research.
Type of support: Research.
Application information: Contact foundation for current application deadline/guidelines.
EIN: 593573517

6085
Pro Deo Guild, Inc.
P.O. Box 304
Hartsdale, NY 10530-0304

Foundation type: Independent foundation
Limitations: Financial assistance only to Roman Catholic missionaries in the U.S. and abroad.
Financial data: Year ended 02/28/2005.
Assets, $255,563 (M); Expenditures, $240,375; Total giving, $237,200; Grants to individuals, 89

grants totaling $188,300 (high: $2,200, low: $100).
Fields of interest: Roman Catholic agencies & churches.
Type of support: Grants to individuals.
Application information: Applications not accepted.
EIN: 133311305

6086
Project Tomorrow
15707 Rockfield, Ste. 330
Irvine, CA 92618 (949) 609-4660
Contact: Julie Evans, Secy. and Exec. Dir.
FAX: (949) 609-4665; E-mail: pt@tommorow.org;
Additional e-mail: jevans@tomorrow.org;
URL: http://www.tomorrow.org

Foundation type: Public charity
Limitations: Awards by nomination only to principals and science teachers for exemplary work in the Orange County, CA, area.
Publications: Annual report; Informational brochure; Newsletter.
Financial data: Year ended 08/31/2004.
Assets, $1,136,068 (M); Expenditures, $547,081; Total giving, $164,474; Grants to individuals, 6 grants totaling $30,000 (high: $5,000, low: $5,000).
Fields of interest: Education; Science.
Type of support: Awards/grants by nomination only; Awards/prizes.
Application information: Contact foundation for current application deadline/guidelines.
Program description:
Vision for Excellence: Awards of $5,000 to teachers and principals for their visionary leadership and to exemplary K-12 science educators for their ability to engage students and inspire them to achieve excellence through innovative, inquiry-based science. Recipients also receive an invitation to work with Project Tomorrow in shaping the future of Orange County science education. Teachers and principals must be nominated by their district.
EIN: 954581958

6087
Prostate Cancer Foundation
(formerly Association for the Cure of Cancer of the Prostate)
1250 4th St.
Santa Monica, CA 90401 (310) 570-4700
Contact: Michael Milken, Chair.
FAX: (310) 570-4701;
E-mail: info@prostatecancerfoundation.org;
Toll-free tel.: (800) 757-2873; URL: http://www.prostatecancerfoundation.org

Foundation type: Public charity
Limitations: Research grants to scientists studying treatments for prostate cancer.
Publications: Application guidelines; Annual report; Newsletter.
Financial data: Year ended 12/31/2004.
Assets, $14,812,116 (M); Expenditures, $21,315,467; Total giving, $11,309,814.
Fields of interest: Prostate cancer; Prostate cancer research.
Type of support: Research.
Application information: Applications accepted. Application form required. Application form available on the grantmaker's Web site.
Initial approach: E-mail.
Deadline(s): Dec. 2
Applicants should submit the following:

1) Budget Information
2) Proposal
3) Essay
Additional information: Submit all forms electronically via email, in an attachment as an Adobe PDF document.
Program description:
Competitive Awards: The Prostate Cancer Foundation favors research applications focused on translational and clinical programs with potential for near term benefit for patients with recurrent prostate cancer. However, the PCF will continue to fund outstanding and novel basic science that we believe is the cornerstone in the discovery of a cure for prostate cancer. Prior work in the area of cancer is not a prerequisite. Applications from individuals with or without institutional affiliations will be considered. The awards are typically for a period of one year and range from $25,000 to $100,000. The amount requested should be justified by the budget submitted in the application.
EIN: 954418411

6088
Public Entity Risk Institute
11350 Random Hill Rd., Ste. 210
Fairfax, VA 22030-6044 (703) 352-1846
Contact: Gerard Hoetmer, Exec. Dir.
E-mail: creiss@riskinstitute.org; URL: http://riskinstitute.org

Foundation type: Public charity
Limitations: Scholarships to staff and officials of small local governments, schools, and nonprofit organizations for attendance at the Public Risk Management Association annual conference.
Publications: Application guidelines; Grants list; Informational brochure; Newsletter; Program policy statement.
Financial data: Year ended 12/31/2003.
Assets, $21,454,693 (L); Expenditures, $2,857,336; Total giving, $596,482; Grants to individuals, 59 grants totaling $59,000 (high: $1,000, low: $1,000).
Fields of interest: Insurance, providers.
Type of support: Travel grants.
Application information: Application form required.
Deadline(s): Feb. 27
Additional information: See Web site for further application information and for application form.
Program description:
Risk Management Awards:
· Recipients must be an employee or official of a municipality with a population of 50,000 or fewer, a county with a population of 100,000 or fewer, or a school district with an average daily attendance of 4,000 or fewer
· Recipients must be an employee or board member of a community-serving nonprofit organization with an annual operating budget of $2 million or less
· Recipients must have not attended a PRIMA Annual Conference within the past three years; and have direct or indirect responsibility for the risk management and/or insurance function for the organization.
Each recipient receives:
· $1,000 direct financial assistance to be applied to any of the costs if attending the conference, including travel, lodging, and registration expenses
· discounted registration fee of $495

• if not already a member of PRIMA, a complimentary six-month membership to PRIMA.
EIN: 411873459

6089
Puffin Foundation, Ltd.
20 E. Oakdene Ave.
Teaneck, NJ 07666
Contact: Gladys Miller-Rosenstein, Exec. Dir.
FAX: (201) 836-1734;
E-mail: puffingrant@mindspring.com; URL: http://www.puffinfoundation.org

Foundation type: Independent foundation
Limitations: The Puffin/Nation prize carries a $100,000 cash award and is given annually to an American citizen who has challenged the status quo "through distinctive, courageous, imaginative, socially responsible work of significance.".
Publications: Application guidelines; Informational brochure.
Financial data: Year ended 12/31/2003. Assets, $14,421,182 (M); Expenditures, $946,545; Total giving, $354,221.
Type of support: Awards/prizes.
Application information:
Initial approach: E-mail.
Additional information: Contact foundation for further program information.
EIN: 133155489

6090
Radio and Television News Directors Foundation
1600 K St., N.W., Ste. 700
Washington, DC 20006-2838   (202) 659-6510
Contact: Barbara Cochran, Pres.; For Scholarships: Irving Washington
E-mail for scholarships: irvingw@rtndf.org
FAX: (202) 223-4007; E-mail: rtndf@rtndf.org;
URL: http://www.rtndf.org

Foundation type: Public charity
Limitations: Fellowships to radio and television journalists.
Publications: Application guidelines; Annual report.
Financial data: Year ended 12/31/2004. Assets, $3,757,134 (M); Expenditures, $2,499,317; Total giving, $263,010.
Fields of interest: Media/communications; Journalism/publishing.
Type of support: Fellowships.
Application information: Application form required.
Initial approach: Letter, e-mail or telephone.
Deadline(s): Apr.
Program description:
Fellowship Programs: The foundation administers the following fellowship programs:
· Sherlee Barish Fellowship
· Michael Burke News Management Fellowship
· Michele Clark Fellowship
· Environmental and Science Reporting Fellowship
· Sandra Freeman Geller and Alfred Geller Fellowship
· Jaque I. Minnotte Health Reporting Fellowship
· Vada and Barney Oldfield Fellowship for National Security Reporting.
EIN: 381860090

6091
The Radius Foundation, Inc.
101 Central Park W. 2D/E
New York, NY 10023

Foundation type: Operating foundation
Limitations: Grants to individuals for research of and publications of Islam.
Financial data: Year ended 12/31/2003. Assets, $97,050 (M); Expenditures, $103,497; Total giving, $19,186; Grants to individuals, 3 grants totaling $16,686 (high: $15,786, low: $900).
Fields of interest: Islam.
Type of support: Publication; Research.
Application information: Contact foundation for current application deadlines/guidelines.
EIN: 760723998

6092
Rainforest Alliance, Inc.
665 Broadway, Ste. 500
New York, NY 10012-2420   (212) 677-1900
Contact: Tensie Whelan, Exec. Dir.
FAX: (212) 677-2187; E-mail: canopy@ra.org;
Additional tel.: (888) MY-EARTH; URL: http://www.rainforest-alliance.org

Foundation type: Public charity
Limitations: Fellowships for forestry research in Latin America.
Financial data: Year ended 06/30/2003. Assets, $2,459,890 (L); Expenditures, $7,687,406; Total giving, $196,447; Grants to individuals, totaling $20,515.
Fields of interest: Natural resources; Environment, forests.
Type of support: Fellowships; Research.
Application information: Applications accepted. Application form not required.
Deadline(s): Contact foundation for current application deadline.
Applicants should submit the following:
1) Curriculum vitae
2) Budget Information
Additional information: A five-page maximum proposal, including project description, abstract review of literature, references, and two letters of recommendation, all written in English.
Program description:
The Kleinhans Fellowship for Research in Tropical Non-Timber Forest Products: Fellowships of $15,000 per year for two years are available to individuals with master's degrees in forestry, ecology, environmental science or appropriate related fields. Doctoral and postdoctoral researchers are preferred. Applicants may substitute relevant experience for degrees. Support is given for research involving any tropical forest type, wet or dry, in Latin America.
EIN: 133377893

6093
Ramakrishna Foundation
1918 Granville Ave.
Los Angeles, CA 90025-1806   (310) 473-4479
Contact: Gary W. Kemper, Secy.
URL: http://www.geocities.com/rkfoundation

Foundation type: Public charity
Limitations: Grants to swamis, monks and brahmacharis to cover expenses for their religious work in India.

Financial data: Year ended 09/30/2003. Assets, $30,556 (M); Expenditures, $133,297; Total giving, $132,137.
Fields of interest: Hinduism; Religion.
Type of support: Foreign applicants; Grants for special needs.
Application information: Contact foundation for current application deadline/guidelines.
EIN: 954587617

6094
Rasmuson Foundation
301 W. Northern Lights Blvd., Ste. 400
Anchorage, AK 99503   (907) 297-2700
Contact: Diane S. Kaplan, C.E.O. and Pres.
FAX: (907) 297-2770;
E-mail: rasmusonfdn@rasmuson.org; URL: http://www.rasmuson.org

Foundation type: Independent foundation
Limitations: Sabbatical grants to executive directors and chief executive officers of health and human service agencies in AK.
Publications: Application guidelines; Grants list; Informational brochure (including application guidelines); Newsletter.
Financial data: Year ended 12/31/2004. Assets, $513,459,645 (M); Expenditures, $26,359,024; Total giving, $22,555,934.
Fields of interest: Philanthropy/voluntarism, management/technical aid; Philanthropy/voluntarism, administration/regulation.
Type of support: Stipends.
Application information: Applications accepted. Application form required. Application form available on the grantmaker's Web site.
Deadline(s): Oct. 1
Additional information: Application by proposal.
Program description:
Nonprofit Leader Sabbatical Program: The foundation will award sabbatical grants of up to $30,000. To be eligible, an individual must be employed through a 501(c)(3) organization in the health and human services field in AK. Grants will be used to cover the executive's salary and expenses during the sabbatical, which may run from two to six continuous months. Recipients will be selected based on two primary criteria: the benefit of the sabbatical to both the organization and the executive; and the demonstrated ability of the organization to sustain itself during the executive's absence.
EIN: 916340739

6095
The Reebok Human Rights Foundation
(formerly The Reebok Foundation)
1895 J.W. Foster Blvd.
Canton, MA 02021   (781) 401-7707
Contact: Geri Noonan, Assoc. Exec. Dir.
E-mail: rhrfoundation@reebok.com; Tel. for Human Rights Award: (781) 401-4377; URL: http://www.reebok.com/x/us/humanRights/foundation

Foundation type: Company-sponsored foundation
Limitations: Awards by nomination only to young activists for their contributions to human rights causes.
Publications: Application guidelines.
Financial data: Year ended 12/31/2004. Assets, $102,362 (M); Expenditures, $1,778,160; Total giving, $1,415,210.
Fields of interest: International human rights; Civil rights.
Type of support: Seed money; Awards/grants by nomination only; Awards/prizes.

Application information: Applications accepted. Application form required.

> *Deadline(s):* May 31
>
> *Applicants should submit the following:*
> 1) Letter(s) of recommendation
>
> *Additional information:* See Web site for nomination guidelines; Nomination may be submitted in English, French, or Spanish; Additional tels.: (781) 401-4910, (781) 401-5061, fax: (781) 401-4806, e-mail: rhraward@reebok.com.

Program description:

> *Reebok Human Rights Award:* Awards of $50,000 by nomination only to individuals 30 years of age or younger who have made significant contributions to human rights causes through non-violent means. The award aims to generate positive international attention for the recipients and their efforts.

EIN: 043073548

6096
Christopher Reeve Foundation

(formerly Christopher Reeve Paralysis Foundation)
636 Morris Tpke., Ste. 3A
Short Hills, NJ 07078 (973) 379-2690
Contact: Megan Sandow, Dir., Opers.
FAX: (973) 912-9433;
E-mail: info@ChristopherReeve.org; Additional tel.: (800) 225-0292; URL: http://www.christopherreeve.org
Additional URL: http://www.apacure.org/

Foundation type: Public charity
Limitations: Research grants to investigators for the study and development of effective therapies for paralysis associated with spinal cord injury and other central nervous system disorders.
Publications: Annual report; Newsletter.
Financial data: Year ended 12/31/2004. Assets, $15,888,965 (M); Expenditures, $17,384,523; Total giving, $8,784,584; Grants to individuals, 40 grants totaling $6,439,768 (high: $500,000, low: $3,245).
Fields of interest: Spine disorders research; Neuroscience research.
Type of support: Program development; Fellowships; Research; Postdoctoral support.
Application information: Application form required.

> *Deadline(s):* June 15 and Dec. 15
>
> *Additional information:* See Web site for further information.

Program description:

> *Research Program:* As part of its research program, the foundation supports an international individual grants program designed to: 1) encourage promising new investigators to undertake research on regeneration and recovery, particularly with respect to the spinal cord; 2) encourage researchers who are well-established in other areas to transfer their ideas and develop pilot data for seeking larger awards from NIH and other funding sources. The development of treatments for chronic injury is a high priority for the organization, however, funding will also be provided for studies more relevant to the acute phase of injury. Basic research will be supported if it has clear potential to accelerate progress at the applied end of the continuum and/or if it reflects a research "change of direction". Senior scientists, young investigators and postdoctoral fellows may serve as principal investigator. Two-year awards are available for senior scientists and young investigators at a maximum funding level of $75,000 per year. Postdoctoral fellowships are available at a minimum funding level of $60,000 per year.

EIN: 222939536

6097
Research Corporation

4703 E. Camp Lowell, Ste. 201
Tucson, AZ 85712 (520) 571-1111
Contact: Daniel Gasch, C.F.O.
FAX: (520) 571-1119; E-mail: awards@rescorp.org; URL: http://www.rescorp.org

Foundation type: Operating foundation
Limitations: Grants and awards for faculty research in the natural sciences (physics, chemistry, and astronomy) at colleges and universities in the U.S. and Canada. Awards are intended to help strengthen the linkage between research and teaching from high school through the graduate level, and Research Opportunity Awards by nomination only.
Publications: Annual report; Newsletter; Occasional report.
Financial data: Year ended 12/31/2004. Assets, $154,535,723 (M); Expenditures, $9,813,093; Total giving, $5,542,493.
Fields of interest: Education; Science, research; Science; Physical/earth sciences; Astronomy; Chemistry; Physics.
Type of support: Program development; Research; Awards/grants by nomination only; Awards/prizes.
Application information:

> *Deadline(s):* Sept. 1 for Cottrell Scholars Awards, May 1 for Research Innovation Awards, May 1 and Oct. 1 for Research Opportunity Awards.
>
> *Additional information:* Contact foundation for current application guidelines; See program description for General Awards application procedures.

Program descriptions:

> *Research Innovation Awards:* This program awards up to $35,000 to faculty at public and private research universities who propose innovative research that promises significant discoveries.
>
> *Cottrell Scholars Award:* This program awards $50,000 to beginning faculty members who wish to excel at both teaching and research. Recipients must be tenure track assistant professors at a Ph.D.-granting department of astronomy, chemistry, or physics who have begun or will begin their third year during the calendar year of application. Applications are accepted once yearly, in the fall.
>
> *Cottrell College Science Awards:* These awards support research in chemistry, physics, and astronomy by faculty at non-Ph.D.-granting departments. The involvement of students in the research is encouraged. Awards include equipment costs, summer stipends, and supplies.
>
> *Research Opportunity Awards:* Awards by nomination only to mid-career astronomy, chemistry, and physics faculty at Ph.D. granting institutions to explore new areas of experimental research. Candidates must be nominated by their department chair; Nomination must be accompanied by candidate's statement and curriculum vitae; Applications will be invited from a select group of nominees for review by Research Corporation's spring or fall advisory committee; Consult Web site for application guidelines.
>
> *General Awards:* This program supports projects that fall outside other program guidelines, but that promise to advance science or improve its infrastructure. Occasionally, proposals may also be encouraged for research projects that are exceedingly novel, that run counter to scientific paradigms, and are unlikely to achieve support from more traditional sources. Only the most challenging and innovative proposals are likely to have success. Requests for funding that might be obtained from other more appropriate sources, to supplement already substantial funding, or to simply extend

funding for mature projects, are not encouraged. Applicants should submit a concise preliminary letter proposal setting forth the nature of the project, the significance of the problem, the schedule and plan of procedure. A breakdown of the financial needs, along with a synopsis of sources of funding, including Research Corporation, should be provided. A brief vita or description of the credentials and background of the Principal Investigator for the project will also be helpful. After internal evaluation, formal applications will be invited from those that are of further interest.

EIN: 131963407

6098
Research Foundation of The City University of New York

230 W. 41st St., 7th Fl.
New York, NY 10036 (212) 417-8300
Contact: Richard F. Rothbard, Pres.
E-mail: questions@rfcuny.org; URL: http://www.rfcuny.org

Foundation type: Public charity
Limitations: Funds for research and creative projects to all permanent full-time faculty members of City University of New York, NY.
Publications: Annual report.
Financial data: Year ended 06/30/2004. Assets, $157,042,833 (M); Expenditures, $320,013,268; Total giving, $40,947,755; Grants to individuals, totaling $40,947,755.
Type of support: Research.
Application information:

> *Initial approach:* Letter or e-mail.
>
> *Applicants should submit the following:*
> 1) Proposal
>
> *Additional information:* Contact foundation for program descriptions and application procedures.

Program description:

> *CUNY Research:* Applications will be judged on the scholarly/creative merit of the project and on the ability of the applicant to perform such work successfully, and on the potential for the research to be awarded funding from external agencies or attain national or international prominence. Criteria:
> - a well-conceived research or creative design suggesting a reasonable promise of successful execution
> - potential contribution of the proposed work in the field
> - evidence of scholarly or creative promise and/or productivity
> - for research projects, demonstrated familiarity with the literature in the field
> - overall availability of program funds

EIN: 131988190

6099
Research Institute for the Study of Man

c/o Lambros Comitas
162 E. 78th St.
New York, NY 10021-0406 (212) 678-4040
FAX: (212) 535-0084

Foundation type: Operating foundation
Limitations: Grants to graduate students and advanced social scientists for research on the Caribbean region and other sociocultural settings.
Financial data: Year ended 12/31/2003. Assets, $7,791,106 (M); Expenditures, $528,911; Total giving, $87,000; Grants to individuals, totaling $84,000.

Fields of interest: History/archaeology; Social sciences; Anthropology/sociology; Political science.

Type of support: Research.

Application information: Contact institute for current application deadline; Application by letter, including statement of objective and methods, budget, evidence of good standing as a student or faculty member, evidence of academic performance, and names of references.

Program description:

RISM Grant Program: General RISM grants are normally restricted to graduate students and professional social scientists (e.g. anthropologists, sociologists, political scientists, economists, social psychologists and historians).

EIN: 131874676

6100

Restless Legs Syndrome Foundation, Inc.

819 2nd St., SW

Rochester, MN 55902-2985 (507) 287-6465

Contact: Monica Herman, Dir., Devel.

FAX: (507) 287-6312; E-mail: herman@rls.org;

URL: http://www.rls.org

Foundation type: Public charity

Limitations: Research grants to postdoctoral candidates for RLS research.

Publications: Annual report; Financial statement; Grants list; Informational brochure; Newsletter.

Financial data: Year ended 09/30/2005.

Assets, $777,307 (M); Expenditures, $1,453,555; Total giving, $230,378; Grants to individuals, 4 grants totaling $230,378 (high: $80,132, low: $30,000).

Fields of interest: Medical specialty research.

Type of support: Research.

Application information: Application form required.

Initial approach: Letter of intent.

Copies of proposal: 1

Deadline(s): Dec. 1 for Letter of Intent; Feb. 28 for full proposal

Additional information: See Web site for additional application information.

Program description:

Research Grants: Funds three to five grants for basic and clinical research studies of restless legs syndrome to postdoctoral candidates. Potential areas of research include: Epidemiology, Neurophysiology, Dopamine, Genetics, Iron, Treatment Models, and Circadian Rhythm.

EIN: 561784846

6101

Rett Syndrome Research Foundation

4600 Devitt Dr.

Cincinnati, OH 45246 (513) 874-3020

Contact: Craig Robertson, Exec. Dir.

FAX: (513) 874-2520; E-mail: craig@rsrf.org;

URL: http://www.rsrf.org

Foundation type: Public charity

Limitations: Fellowships and research grants for the treatment and cure of Rett Syndrome.

Financial data: Year ended 12/31/2003.

Assets, $1,486,052 (M); Expenditures, $1,933,678; Total giving, $1,680,071; Grants to individuals, totaling $1,116,293.

Fields of interest: Lung research; Diseases (rare) research; Neuroscience research.

Type of support: Fellowships; Research; Postdoctoral support; Travel grants.

Application information: Application form required.

Initial approach: Letter.

Deadline(s): Jan. 31 for letter of intent and May 31 for application

Additional information: See Web site for letter of intent information.

Program descriptions:

Postdoctoral Fellowships: Provides $50,000 ($40,000 salary plus $10,000 for expenses) for two years to postdoctoral students for research relevant to Rett Syndrome.

Research Grants: Provides $50,000 for up to two years to individuals for research on Rett Syndrome, as well as technical support, supplies, equipment and relevant travel necessary. Research should encompass innovative therapeutic approaches and state of the art diagnostic techniques that will result in a better understanding of the underlying pathology of Rett Syndrome and lead to an amelioration of the symptoms and a cure, and internal biomedical research aimed at understanding the nature of the breathing difficulties often seen in Rett Syndrome.

EIN: 311682518

6102

Rex Foundation

P.O. Box 29608

San Francisco, CA 94129-0608

(415) 561-3134

Contact: Sandy Sohcot, Exec. Dir.

FAX: (415) 561-3136;

E-mail: info@rexfoundation.org; URL: http://www.rexfoundation.org

Foundation type: Public charity

Limitations: Awards by nomination only to humanitarians and cultural leaders.

Financial data: Year ended 12/31/2003.

Assets, $280,990 (M); Expenditures, $158,900; Total giving, $151,500; Grant to an individual, 1 grant totaling $10,000.

Fields of interest: Music; Arts; International affairs.

Type of support: Awards/grants by nomination only; Awards/prizes.

Application information: Unsolicited applications not accepted.

Program descriptions:

Ralph J. Gleason Award: Awards are given to individuals for their outstanding contributions to culture, particularly in the area of music.

Bill Graham Award: Awards to organizations and individuals working to assist children who are victims of political oppression and human rights violations.

EIN: 680033257

6103

Z. Smith Reynolds Foundation, Inc.

147 S. Cherry St., Ste. 200

Winston-Salem, NC 27101-5287

(336) 725-7541

Contact: Thomas W. Ross, Secy.

FAX: (336) 725-6069; E-mail: info@zsr.org;

Additional tel.: (800) 443-8319; URL: http://www.zsr.org

Foundation type: Independent foundation

Limitations: Awards by nomination only to NC individuals who demonstrate leadership in their communities. Sabbaticals to leaders of NC nonprofit organizations.

Publications: Annual report (including application guidelines); Informational brochure; Informational brochure (including application guidelines); Occasional report.

Financial data: Year ended 12/31/2004.

Assets, $15,844,319 (M); Expenditures, $18,934,199; Total giving, $16,555,726.

Fields of interest: Community development, volunteer services; Nonprofit management.

Type of support: Awards/grants by nomination only; Awards/prizes; Grants for special needs.

Application information: Application form available on the grantmaker's Web site.

Initial approach: Letter or telephone.

Deadline(s): June 1 for NSR awards, Dec. 1 for Sabbatical program

Additional information: Nomination forms required for NSR awards; Completion of formal application required for Sabbatical program.

Program descriptions:

Nancy Susan Reynolds Awards: This program awards individuals who sacrifice their personal time and energy to make a difference in their communities and beyond. In seeking nominations, the foundation looks beyond traditional business or civic leaders or those people who already have received significant recognition and public visibility. The awards are $25,000 total, with $5,000 going to the individual and the rest donated to charitable organizations in NC as designated by the award recipient. Recipients must be nominated.

Z. Smith Reynolds Foundation Sabbatical Program: This program is for leaders of nonprofit organizations. Recipients are selected on the basis of need for a break from the daily stress and challenges of their work, the degree of difficulty of their work environment, and their potential to continue to make a significant contribution in their chosen field. Each of these leaders receives a $15,000 award, enabling them to take a leave of absence of three months to a year from their organizations and to return recommitted to the challenges and rewards of public service.

EIN: 586038145

6104

The Rhode Island Foundation

(also known as The Rhode Island Community Foundation)

1 Union Station

Providence, RI 02903 (401) 274-4564

Contact: Karen Voci, Sr. V.P., Prog.; For artists: Claude Elliott

FAX: (401) 331-8085; Artist grants E-mail: celliott@rifoundation.org; URL: http://www.rifoundation.org

Foundation type: Community foundation

Limitations: Awards by nomination only to outstanding Providence, RI, police officers and firefighters.

Publications: Application guidelines; Annual report (including application guidelines); Grants list; Informational brochure; Newsletter; Occasional report; Program policy statement.

Financial data: Year ended 12/31/2004.

Assets, $428,970,585 (M); Expenditures, $26,734,100; Total giving, $22,400,000.

Fields of interest: Crime/law enforcement, police agencies.

Application information: Application form required. Application form available on the grantmaker's Web site.

Initial approach: Letter.

Deadline(s): Contact foundation for current nomination deadline.

Program descriptions:

Rhea Archambault Memorial Fund: For outstanding Providence, RI, police officers.

Deputy Assistant Chief Anthony V. Sauro Award: For an outstanding Providence, RI, firefighter.
EIN: 222604963

6105
Oscar C. Rixson Foundation, Inc.
12 Pintail Ct.
Hendersonville, NC   28792-2839
Contact: Thomas J. Elliott Sr., Pres.
FAX: (828) 692-7876; E-mail: oldtom@mchsi.com

Foundation type: Independent foundation
Limitations: Project support in the form of grants to missionaries, teachers, and laymen engaged in the spread of the gospel throughout the world.
Financial data: Year ended 12/31/2004. Assets, $2,982,134 (M); Expenditures, $262,353; Total giving, $209,200; Grants to individuals, 132 grants totaling $60,900 (high: $600, low: $300).
Fields of interest: Christian agencies & churches.
Type of support: Program development.
Application information: Application form not required.
> *Deadline(s):* None.
> *Additional information:* Applications by letter, including details of use and financial information.
EIN: 136129767

6106
Raymond Rosenberger Award Foundation
c/o National City Bank
P.O. Box 94651
Cleveland, OH   44101-4651

Foundation type: Independent foundation
Limitations: Awards to individuals in the Fort Wayne, IN, area.
Financial data: Year ended 06/30/2005. Assets, $1,476,489 (M); Expenditures, $79,767; Total giving, $67,712; Grants to individuals, 4 grants totaling $26,856 (high: $8,464, low: $1,464).
Type of support: Awards/prizes.
Application information: Applications not accepted.
EIN: 356627244

6107
Milton B. Rosenbluth Foundation, Inc.
955 Lexington Ave.
New York, NY   10021
Contact: Michael J. Samek, Treas.

Foundation type: Independent foundation
Limitations: Grants to senior medical students in NY to secure clinical and research experience in developing countries.
Financial data: Year ended 12/31/2004. Assets, $642,654 (M); Expenditures, $61,671; Total giving, $54,600; Grants to individuals, totaling $37,800.
Fields of interest: Medical school/education.
Type of support: Research; Doctoral support.
Application information: Contact foundation for current application deadline/guidelines.
EIN: 133460707

6108
The Rotary Foundation of Rotary International
1 Rotary Ctr.
1560 Sherman Ave.
Evanston, IL   60201-3698   (847) 866-3000
Contact: Edwin H. Futa, Genl. Secy.
FAX: (847) 328-8554; URL: http://www.rotary.org/foundation

Foundation type: Public charity
Limitations: Support for projects initiated by Rotarians, foundation alumni, Rotaractors, and university teachers.
Publications: Annual report.
Financial data: Year ended 06/30/2005. Assets, $674,700,000 (M); Expenditures, $128,100,000; Total giving, $94,500,000.
Fields of interest: Education; Community development, volunteer services; Mutual aid societies, volunteer services.
Type of support: Exchange programs; Travel grants.
Application information: Applications accepted. Application form required.
> *Initial approach:* Letter, FAX, or e-mail.
> *Additional information:* Contact foundation for current application deadline/guidelines.
Program descriptions:
Group Study Exchange Program: Travel grants are provided to teams of young professionals who participate in a four- to five-week international exchange program which exposes them to how their careers are practiced overseas. The program also increases their cultural awareness through stays with host families.
Grants for Rotary Volunteers: Grants are available to subsidize the expenses of Rotarians, foundation alumni, and Rotaractors who volunteer their services in another country.
Rotary Grants for University Teachers: These grants are given to faculty members to teach in a developing nation for three to 10 months.
3-H Planning Grants: Grants are available to Rotarians to go toward planning costs for proposed projects which meet all 3-H criteria but can be developed on a larger scale or make a larger impact with preliminary funding.
EIN: 363245072

6109
Rotch Travelling Scholarship, Inc.
c/o Fiduciary Trust Co.
P.O. Box 1647
Boston, MA   02105-1647
Contact: Hugh Shepley, V.P.
Application address: Alexandra Lee, Admin., c/o Boston Society of Architects, 52 Broad St., Boston, MA 02109
URL: http://www.rotchscholarship.org

Foundation type: Operating foundation
Limitations: Grants to practicing architects under 35 years of age, with educational or professional experience in MA for foreign travel and study in architecture.
Publications: Informational brochure (including application guidelines).
Financial data: Year ended 12/31/2003. Assets, $1,539,259 (M); Expenditures, $143,415; Total giving, $75,000; Grants to individuals, 3 grants totaling $55,000 (high: $31,000, low: $7,000).
Fields of interest: Architecture.
Type of support: Travel grants.
Application information: Application form required.

Initial approach: Letter requesting application form and eligibility requirements.
Deadline(s): Jan. 1
Additional information: Recipients notified by Apr. 20.
Program descriptions:
Rotch Travelling Studio: Provides grants to faculty members in schools of architecture for study by their students in a foreign country. Grants are provided to enable faculty member to lead a "studio" for a group of students from the faculty member's school of architecture. Grant maximum $20,000.
Rotch Travelling Scholarship: Awarded annually to provide for eight months of foreign travel and study in the field of architecture. First place award is in the amount of $35,000 for 8-12 months of foreign travel. Second prize is $15,000, when awarded. Applicants must be U.S. citizens who have either received a degree from an accredited school of architecture and have one full year of professional experience in a MA architectural office, or received a degree from an accredited MA school of architecture and have at least one full year of professional experience in an architectural office anywhere in the U.S. Applicants receiving a certificate from the Boston Architectural Center before the degree-granting program are required to have four years experience in an architectural office.
EIN: 046062249

6110
Royal Oak Foundation for Public Education
P.O. Box 1363
Royal Oak, MI   48068-1363

Foundation type: Independent foundation
Limitations: Grants to teachers at Royal Oak, MI, public schools for programs in their classroom or school.
Financial data: Year ended 12/31/2002. Assets, $107,085 (M); Expenditures, $23,215; Total giving, $13,218; Grants to individuals, 16 grants totaling $13,218.
Fields of interest: Education.
Type of support: Program development; Grants to individuals.
Application information: Applications not accepted.
EIN: 383147156

6111
Salt Lake Education Foundation
440 E. 100 South
Salt Lake City, UT   84111-1891
(801) 578-8599
Contact: Daphne R. Williams, Dir.
FAX: (801) 578-8248; URL: http://www.slc.k12.ut.us/depts/comminv/foundation.html

Foundation type: Public charity
Limitations: Research grants to teachers in the Salt Lake City, UT, area, for the development of educational curricula.
Financial data: Year ended 06/30/2004. Assets, $3,307,611 (M); Expenditures, $2,061,599; Total giving, $20,289; Grants to individuals, 21 grants totaling $20,289.
Fields of interest: Education.
Type of support: Program development; Research.

Application information: Deadlines vary; Application by proposal; See Web site for further guidelines.
EIN: 742563849

6112
The San Carlos Foundation
1065 Creston Rd.
Berkeley, CA 94708 (510) 525-3787
Contact: Davida Coady, Pres.
FAX: (510) 525-3278; E-mail: dcoady@igc.org;
URL: http://sancarlos.nonprofitoffice.com/

Foundation type: Public charity
Limitations: Grants for living expenses to professionals (nurses, lawyers, engineers, teachers, etc.) who volunteer to train residents of the developing world.
Financial data: Year ended 12/31/2003. Assets, $85,171 (M); Expenditures, $340,786; Total giving, $340,186; Grants to individuals, 25 grants totaling $131,000 (high: $12,000, low: $1,500).
Fields of interest: International affairs, volunteer services; International affairs, formal/general education; International affairs, goodwill promotion.
Type of support: Travel grants; Stipends.
Application information: Applications accepted. Application form required. Application form available on the grantmaker's Web site.
  Initial approach: E-mail.
  Applicants should submit the following:
    1) Resume
    2) Proposal
Program description:
  Program: Volunteers must be professionally qualified, fluent in the appropriate language, have two year's experience in the developing world, be U.S. citizens with primary residence in the U.S., have secured a volunteer position of at least one year's duration; and have no other means of financial support.
EIN: 680040121

6113
The San Diego Foundation
(formerly San Diego Community Foundation)
1420 Kettner Blvd., Ste. 500
San Diego, CA 92101-9693 (619) 235-2300
Contact: Robert A. Kelly, C.E.O.; For scholarships and project grants: Valerie Attisha
FAX: (619) 239-1710;
E-mail: info@sdfoundation.org; Additional tel.: (858) 385-1595 (for North County); URL: http://www.sdfoundation.org

Foundation type: Community foundation
Limitations: Project grants to San Diego County, CA, K-6 elementary public school teachers and 9-12 public high school art teachers.
Publications: Annual report; Financial statement; Grants list; Informational brochure; Newsletter.
Financial data: Year ended 06/30/2005. Assets, $451,470,000 (M); Expenditures, $49,765,000; Total giving, $41,106,000; Grants to individuals, 444 grants totaling $1,890,700 (high: $156,000, low: $250).
Type of support: Program development.
Application information: Application form required. Application form available on the grantmaker's Web site.
  Initial approach: E-mail.
  Deadline(s): June
  Applicants should submit the following:
    1) Work samples
    2) Transcripts

3) Proposal
4) Letter(s) of recommendation
5) Essay
6) Budget Information
  Additional information: Contact foundation for further application guidelines.
EIN: 952942582

6114
San Luis Obispo County Community Foundation
1401 Higuera St.
P.O. Box 1580
San Luis Obispo, CA 93406-1580
(805) 543-2323
Contact: David Edwards, Exec. Dir.; For grants: Janice Fong Wolf, Dir., Grants & Progs.
FAX: (805) 543-2346; E-mail: info@sloccf.org;
Additional E-mails: dave@sloccf.org and jwolf@sloccf.org; URL: http://www.sloccf.org

Foundation type: Community foundation
Limitations: Awards to individuals of San Luis Obispo County, CA, who have made a significant contribution to bettering the environment.
Publications: Application guidelines; Annual report; Grants list; Informational brochure; Newsletter.
Financial data: Year ended 12/31/2004. Assets, $17,981,139 (M); Expenditures, $2,344,426; Total giving, $1,797,948.
Fields of interest: Environment.
Type of support: Awards/prizes.
Application information: Applications not accepted.
  Additional information: Unsolicited requests for funds not considered or acknowledged.
EIN: 770496500

6115
The Stanley J. Sarnoff Endowment for Cardiovascular Science, Inc.
731 G-2 Walker Rd.
Great Falls, VA 22066 (703) 759-7600
Contact: Dana Boyd, Exec. Dir.
FAX: (703) 759-7838;
E-mail: dana.boyd@verizon.net; Additional tel.: (888) 4SARNOF; URL: http://www.SarnoffEndowment.org

Foundation type: Public charity
Limitations: Grants to cardiovascular researchers.
Publications: Application guidelines; Grants list; Informational brochure; Informational brochure (including application guidelines); Newsletter; Occasional report.
Financial data: Year ended 06/30/2004. Assets, $28,184,120 (M); Expenditures, $917,908; Total giving, $283,000; Grants to individuals, 9 grants totaling $283,000 (high: $90,000, low: $21,000).
Fields of interest: Heart & circulatory research.
Type of support: Fellowships; Research.
Application information: Applications accepted. Application form required. Application form available on the grantmaker's Web site.
  Deadline(s): Jan. 19 for Fellowships; Dec. 1 for Transitional Scholars Program
Program descriptions:
  Sarnoff Fellowships: Recipients conduct one year of cardiovascular research at a U.S. institution other than the medical school (s)he attends. Medical students enrolled in any accredited medical school in the U.S. may apply for this fellowship, which consists of a yearly $25,000 stipend, a $2,000 allowance for moving costs, a

$2,000 allowance for travel costs associated with selecting a laboratory, funds to attend the Annual Scientific Meeting and the Annual American Heart Association Scientific Sessions, funds to enable the Fellow to present a paper at two national conferences, and funds to help cover the cost of health insurance.
  Sarnoff Scholar Transition Award: The program provides salary support for up to four consecutive years for full-time research. The award is designed to continue the longitudinal commitment of the Sarnoff Endowment to support the training and career development of new physician-scientists. For the first two years, as a Fellow, the stipend will be $45,000 per year. The stipend will then increase to $67,000 a year for up to two years when the fellow becomes a junior faculty member. In addition to the annual stipend, Scholars will also receive an annual budget of up to $10,000 for laboratory supplies and professional journal subscriptions, monetary support to attend the Annual Scientific Meeting of the Stanley J. Sarnoff Society of Fellows, an annual allowance of up to $750 to attend the annual American Heart Association Scientific Sessions, up to $1,500 annually to defray the cost of health insurance and travel funds of up to $1,000 to enable the Scholar to present a paper, based on Scholar's research, at a national conference within two years of completing the program.
EIN: 521254078

6116
Robert Schalkenbach Foundation, Inc.
149 Madison Ave., Ste. 601
New York, NY 10016-6713 (212) 683-6424
Contact: Mark A. Sullivan, Secy.
FAX: (212) 683-6454;
E-mail: msullivan@schalkenbach.org; Toll free tel.: (800) 269-9555; Additional E-mail: staff@schalkenbach.org; URL: http://www.schalkenbach.org/

Foundation type: Operating foundation
Limitations: Grants to individuals for academic projects related to the economic and social justice ideals of Henry George. Projects may focus upon urban or rural landscapes.
Publications: Application guidelines; Annual report; Grants list.
Financial data: Year ended 06/30/2004. Assets, $11,436,563 (M); Expenditures, $726,643; Total giving, $203,222; Grants to individuals, 3 grants totaling $20,760 (high: $15,000, low: $1,760).
Fields of interest: Education, research; Economics; Political science; Urban studies; Public policy, research.
Type of support: Publication; Research.
Application information: Applications accepted. Application form required. Application form available on the grantmaker's Web site.
  Initial approach: E-mail.
  Deadline(s): Quarterly
  Applicants should submit the following:
    1) Work samples
    2) Resume
    3) Proposal
    4) Curriculum vitae
    5) Budget Information
    6) Letter(s) of recommendation
  Additional information: See Website for further application information.
Program description:
  Project Awards: Projects may include books and articles on the economics, philosophy and historical importance of Henry George and like-minded thinkers. Projects may also include

fiscal and administrative reform proposals involving: downtaxing sales, payrolls and buildings and raising revenues from land and resource values instead; instituting pollution and congestion taxes; and managing resources in the public domain, like timberland, park land, mineral deposits, water supplies, the electromagnetic spectrum, aircraft routes and landing slots, and streets and other urban public space. Generally, grants are for $2,000 to $10,000 for projects to be completed within a year. Researchers will be awarded with 501 (c)(3) organizations to serve as fiscal sponsors.
EIN: 131656331

6117
Hans E. Schapira, M.D. Foundation, Inc.
3333 Henry Hudson Pkwy., Apt. 17S
Riverdale, NY   10463   (718) 796-3633
Contact: Ruth Schapira, Pres.

Foundation type: Independent foundation
Limitations: Grants for medical research projects, with preference given to urological research, primarily in NY.
Financial data: Year ended 02/28/2005.
Assets, $497,513 (M); Expenditures, $70,379; Total giving, $52,750.
Fields of interest: Medical research, institute.
Type of support: Research.
Application information:
   Deadline(s): Sept. 30.
   Additional information: Application by proposal.
EIN: 133338059

6118
The Schweppe Foundation
1127 S. Mason Rd.
St. Louis, MO   63131   (314) 878-5805
Contact: Gary H. Kline, Treas.
FAX: (314) 878-5807;
E-mail: schweppefnd@aol.com; URL: http://www.schweppefoundation.org

Foundation type: Independent foundation
Limitations: Medical research project support to individuals of junior rank who hold faculty or fellowship appointments at Chicago, IL, area medical schools or university-affiliated hospitals.
Publications: Application guidelines; Grants list; Informational brochure.
Financial data: Year ended 12/31/2004.
Assets, $12,699,313 (M); Expenditures, $770,141; Total giving, $580,000.
Fields of interest: Medical research, institute.
Type of support: Program development; Fellowships; Research.
Application information: Applications accepted. Application form required.
   Deadline(s): Sept. 1
   Additional information: Interviews required.
Program description:
   Medical Research Program: All grants are disbursed to institutions on behalf of individuals. Grants support medical research projects carried on by individuals of junior rank (not above that of Assistant Professor) who hold faculty or fellowship appointments in the university or hospital, and who have been assured the use of the physical facilities of the sponsoring institution. Grants last for three years, subject to annual approval.
EIN: 366014667

6119
Scleroderma Foundation, Inc.
300 Rosewood Dr., Ste. 105
Danvers, MA   01923   (978) 463-5843
Contact: Donna Kohli, Pres. and C.E.O.
FAX: (978) 463-5809;
E-mail: sfinfo@scleroderma.org; Toll-free tel.: (800) 722-4673; URL: http://www.scleroderma.org

Foundation type: Public charity
Limitations: Research grants to improve treatment and find a cure for scleroderma.
Publications: Application guidelines; Annual report.
Financial data: Year ended 12/31/2004.
Assets, $7,531,670 (M); Expenditures, $4,603,326; Total giving, $1,324,860; Grants to individuals, 19 grants totaling $1,324,860 (high: $50,000).
Fields of interest: Diseases (rare) research.
Type of support: Research.
Application information:
   Initial approach: E-mail or letter.
   Additional information: Contact foundation for further application information.
EIN: 521375827

6120
Scottish Rite Educational and Fellowship Program of Texas
2801 W. Waco Dr.
Waco, TX   76707-0080
Contact: For fellowships: Claude Ervin
Application address: P.O. Box 3080, Waco, TX 76707, tel.: (254) 754-3942

Foundation type: Operating foundation
Limitations: Fellowships to educators who are permanent residents of TX for doctoral studies in public school administration at accredited universities in TX. Special consideration will be given to individuals with family Masonic connections.
Financial data: Year ended 12/31/2003.
Assets, $0 (M); Expenditures, $11,702; Total giving, $4,900; Grants to individuals, 9 grants totaling $4,900 (high: $1,200, low: $100).
Fields of interest: Education, administration/regulation; Business/industry; Fraternal societies.
Type of support: Fellowships; Doctoral support.
Application information:
   Deadline(s): Mar. 1
   Additional information: Completion of formal application required, including financial information, three references, personal essay, transcripts, photograph, and an approved degree plan for the doctorate; Interviews may be required.
Program description:
   Fellowship Program: The program encourages recipients to enroll in a two-year course of study under the full-time grant to complete their doctoral degree at the earliest possible date. It is strongly recommended that the degree be completed within a 42-month period for those who elect to become part-time students. All recipients must profess a belief in a supreme being. Part-time students receive up to $6,000 ($100 per semester hour) and full-time students receive up to $9,000 ($150 per semester hour). In addition, both full- and part-time students receive $500 for dissertation typing and printing costs, provided one copy of the dissertation is deposited in the Texas Scottish Rite Library in Waco, TX. The following accredited TX universities offer approved doctoral degree programs in public school administration: Texas A&M University, Commerce, Texas A&M University, College Station, Texas Tech University, University of Houston,

University of North Texas, Dention, University of Texas at Austin, University of Texas at San Antonio, and Sam Houston State University. Fellowships are awarded on the basis of public school teaching experience, academic excellence, and financial need. All fellowship recipients must provide enrollment verification in an approved public school administration doctoral program at an accredited university in the state of TX.
EIN: 742177244

6121
Scotts Miracle-Gro Foundation
c/o Rob McMahon
800 Port Washington Blvd.
Port Washington, NY   11050

Foundation type: Independent foundation
Limitations: Awards by nomination only to community gardeners and teachers integrating gardening into their curriculum.
Financial data: Year ended 12/31/2004.
Assets, $421,214 (M); Expenditures, $162,620; Total giving, $160,000.
Fields of interest: Environment, volunteer services; Horticulture/garden clubs; Environment, beautification programs.
Type of support: Awards/grants by nomination only; Awards/prizes.
Application information: Applications accepted. Application form required. Application form available on the grantmaker's Web site.
   Initial approach: Telephone.
   Deadline(s): Dec. 2
   Additional information: Each winner will receive a $5,000 cash prize and public recognition for their work. Each of two finalists in each category will receive a $2,500 cash prize and public recognition for their work. See Web site for nomination forms.
Program descriptions:
   Scotts Classroom Gardener of the Year: This program salutes elementary through high school teachers who have integrated a school gardening program into their curriculum.
   Scotts Good Neighbor Gardener of the Year: This program salutes gardeners who donate produce to feed the hungry in their own communities.
   Scotts Urban Greenup Gardener of the Year: This program salutes volunteers working in an urban area who have successfully used community gardening to address the various challenges of an inner-city neighborhood.
   Scotts Community Beautification Gardener of the Year: This program salutes volunteers who have helped beautify a main street, park or neighborhood within their city limits, and in the process significantly contributed to community pride.
EIN: 311799491

6122
Scripps Howard Foundation
P.O. Box 5380
312 Walnut St., 28th Fl.
Cincinnati, OH   45201   (513) 977-3035
Contact: Judith G. Clabes, C.E.O. and Pres.; Patty Cottingham, Secy. and Exec. Dir.
FAX: (513) 977-3800;
E-mail: clabes@scripps.com; Application addresses: Contact for Roy W. Howard National Reporting Competition, Internships, and Top 10 Scholarship: Sue Porter, V.P. Progs., tel.: (800) 888-3000, E-mail: porters@scripps.com, Contact for Jack R. Howard Fellowships in International Journalism: Josh Friedman, Dir., International

Program, Columbia Graduate School of Journalism, E-mail: jf125@columbia.edu; Additional tel.: (513) 997-3048, (800) 888-3847; URL: http://foundation.scripps.com/foundation/

Foundation type: Company-sponsored foundation
Limitations: Awards only to professional print/broadcast journalists and college cartoonists.
Publications: Application guidelines; Annual report (including application guidelines).
Financial data: Year ended 12/31/2004. Assets, $73,350,056 (M); Expenditures, $6,685,626; Total giving, $5,356,837; Grants to individuals, totaling $710,737.
Fields of interest: Journalism/publishing; Drawing.
Type of support: Awards/grants by nomination only; Awards/prizes.
Application information: Contact foundation in the fall for current application deadline/guidelines.
Program description:
 Award Programs: The foundation administers numerous awards. See Web site for further information.
EIN: 316025114

6123

The Sendzimir Foundation, Inc.

c/o Clark, Schaefer, Hackett & Co.
105 E. 4th St., Ste. 1600
Cincinnati, OH 45202
Contact: Jan Peter Sendzimir, Pres.
E-mail: office@sendzimir.org.pl; Additional E-mail: gisela.bosch@chello.at; URL: http://www.sendzimir.org.pl/

Foundation type: Independent foundation
Limitations: Grants to individuals to conduct research to address problems of ecology and the environment, with particular emphasis on the environment of Eastern Europe.
Publications: Application guidelines; Grants list.
Financial data: Year ended 06/30/2004. Assets, $344,767 (M); Expenditures, $100,122; Total giving, $63,080; Grants to individuals, 9 grants totaling $10,600 (high: $5,000, low: $400).
Fields of interest: Environment; Eastern Europe.
Type of support: Research.
Application information: Applications by proposal accepted throughout the year.
EIN: 223309860

6124

The Servant Leadership Foundation

950 E. Westglow Ln.
Greenwood Village, CO 80121-1375
(303) 806-0607
Contact: Dan Jessup, Dir.

Foundation type: Independent foundation
Limitations: Scholarships to individuals in full-time ministry, as well as grants to reduce personal debt of individuals with at least ten years experience in the ministry.
Financial data: Year ended 12/31/2002. Assets, $104,247 (M); Expenditures, $544,353; Total giving, $499,286; Grants to individuals, 31 grants totaling $437,220 (high: $35,000, low: $1,420).
Fields of interest: Christian agencies & churches.
Type of support: Scholarships—to individuals; Grants for special needs.
Application information: Applications by letter accepted throughout the year.
EIN: 841400820

6125

SHOPA Kids In Need Foundation

(formerly SHOPA Foundation for Educational Excellence)
3131 Elbee Rd.
Dayton, OH 45439-1900 (937) 297-2250
Contact: Scott Walters, Exec. Dir.
E-mail: info@shopa.org; Additional tel.: (800) 854-7467; URL: http://www.shopa.org/shopa_foundation

Foundation type: Public charity
Limitations: Grants to teachers for innovative classroom support.
Financial data: Year ended 12/31/2003. Assets, $566,879 (M); Expenditures, $24,340,498; Total giving, $66,821; Grants to individuals, totaling $66,821.
Fields of interest: Elementary/secondary education.
Type of support: Grants to individuals.
Application information: Applications accepted. Application form required. Application form available on the grantmaker's Web site.
EIN: 311437587

6126

Mary S. Sigourney Award Trust

c/o James D. Devine
P.O. Box 10206
Bainbridge Island, WA 98110-0206
URL: http://www.sigourney.org/

Foundation type: Independent foundation
Limitations: Awards to individuals nominated by a reputable psychoanalytic society who have published or contributed in a significant way within the last ten years to clinical psychoanalysis or psychoanalytical research, including their application to the field of medicine or related sciences such as psychiatry and psychotherapy.
Publications: Annual report.
Financial data: Year ended 12/31/2004. Assets, $4,689,616 (M); Expenditures, $227,088; Total giving, $150,000; Grants to individuals, 6 grants totaling $150,000 (high: $30,000, low: $15,000).
Fields of interest: Mental health, treatment; Psychology/behavioral science.
Type of support: Research; Awards/grants by nomination only; Awards/prizes.
Application information: Individual applications not accepted; Awards by nomination only.
EIN: 776054596

6127

The Skadden Fellowship Foundation, Inc.

(formerly Skadden, Arps, Slate, Meagher & Flom Fellowship Foundation)
4 Times Sq., Rm. 40-228
New York, NY 10036 (212) 735-2956
Contact: Susan Butler Plum, Dir.
FAX: (917) 777-2956; URL: http://www.skaddenfellowships.org/

Foundation type: Company-sponsored foundation
Limitations: Fellowships to graduating law students and outgoing judicial clerks who want to work in the public interest for organizations that provide civil legal services to the poor, including the homeless, the elderly, the disabled, and those deprived of their civil or human rights.
Publications: Application guidelines; Informational brochure; Multi-year report.
Financial data: Year ended 12/31/2004. Assets, $3,958,670 (M); Expenditures,

$2,903,344; Total giving, $2,573,040; Grants to individuals, 83 grants totaling $2,573,040 (high: $58,607, low: $5,000).
Fields of interest: Law school/education; International human rights; Civil rights, advocacy; Leadership development.
Type of support: Fellowships.
Application information: Application form required.
 Deadline(s): Oct. 8
 Additional information: Completion of formal application required, including law school transcript, two letters of recommendation (one from a law school advisor and one from a former employer), commitment letter from the potential sponsoring institution, copy of the institution's 501(c)(3) tax-exempt letter, resume, and responses to three essay questions; Interviews required; Recipients notified by Dec. 12.
Program description:
 Fellowship Awards: The foundation awards 25 fellowships annually. Selection is based upon each applicant's academic performance and demonstrated commitment to the public interest as well as project quality. Grants are made to the public interest organizations chosen by the fellows. Thus, applicants must secure a potential position with a sponsoring public interest organization before applying for a fellowship. Selection is based not only on the qualifications of the applicant, but also on the demonstrated effectiveness of the sponsoring organization. Fellowships are awarded for one year, with the exception of renewal for a second year, provided the fellow remains in good standing with the sponsoring organization. Each fellow's salary is $37,500. The program also pays all fringe benefits to which an employee of the sponsoring organization would be entitled as well as all debt service on law school loans for the duration of the fellowship. Fellows may not receive any other fellowships or prize money for the duration of the fellowship.
EIN: 133455231

6128

Skidmore, Owings & Merrill Foundation

224 S. Michigan Ave., Ste. 1000
Chicago, IL 60604 (312) 427-4202
Contact: Lisa Westerfield, Admin. Dir.
FAX: (312) 360-4545;
E-mail: somfoundation@som.com; URL: http://www.somfoundation.som.com

Foundation type: Company-sponsored foundation
Limitations: Fellowships and travel grants by nomination only for research relating to architecture or architectural engineering; also giving in the United Kingdom.
Publications: Newsletter.
Financial data: Year ended 08/31/2004. Assets, $3,111,150 (M); Expenditures, $147,068; Total giving, $73,634; Grants to individuals, 15 grants totaling $73,634 (high: $13,500, low: $750).
Fields of interest: Architecture; Design; Literature; Urban studies.
Type of support: Fellowships; Research; Awards/grants by nomination only; Travel grants.
Application information: Application form required.
 Deadline(s): Contact foundation for current nomination deadline
 Additional information: Nomination forms with deadlines are sent to select schools every spring for awards given in Mar. and May; Schools nominate students in early spring; Interviews required; Nominations available on Web site.

Program descriptions:

Interior Architecture Traveling Fellowship Program: The $7,500 fellowship is awarded annually to a student in architecture or design with a specific interest in interior design. It will allow the Fellow to visit buildings and settings that are central to his or her area of interest and study. To be eligible, each candidate must meet the following qualifications:

· be graduated with and prior to the beginning of the fellowship, a bachelor's or master's degree from an accredited U.S. architectural school or Foundation for Interior Design Education Research (FIDER) accredited U.S. school of interior design within a school of design or architecture in the U.S.

· be nominated by the faculty and endorsed by the chair of the department from which he/she has received the aforementioned degree

To apply, students should follow the requirements of the Traveling Fellowship Awards and should also include two copies of a letter of recommendation from the faculty of the student's school.

Urban Design Traveling Fellowship Program: This program awards $7,500 annually to a student or recent graduate of an urban design program. Students must have received an architectural degree and a master's concentrating in urban design from an accredited program. To apply, students should follow the requirements of the Interior Architecture Traveling Fellowship Program and should also include two copies of a transcript.

Architecture Traveling Fellowship Awards: There are two annual fellowships of $15,000 each awarded to undergraduate and graduate students in accredited architecture programs in the U.S.: Bachelor Degree Traveling Fellowship: Available to students of accredited undergraduate programs who are obtaining a bachelors degree in architecture Master of Architecture Degree Fellowship: Available to individuals who are graduating with a masters degree from an architecture professional degree program. Each candidate is required to submit the following:

· a portfolio limited to 12 one-sided pages, not to exceed 11" x 17" without information identifying the applicant (black binder format)

· a one-page detachable cover sheet containing name, category, and school affiliation

· two copies of a proposed travel itinerary with sites of study. One copy is to have all names, school affiliations, sex, color, creed, or any other identifying information blanked out. The second copy is to be the original with all information intact

· a signed copyright release statement provided by the foundation.

EIN: 362969068

6129

The Skin Cancer Foundation, Inc.

245 5th Ave., Ste. 1403
New York, NY   10016   (212) 725-5176
Contact: Mary Stine, Exec. Dir.
FAX: (212) 725-5751; E-mail: info@skincancer.org;
URL: http://www.skincancer.org

Foundation type: Public charity
Limitations: Research grants to individuals for basic research, clinical studies, and educational programs related to skin cancer.
Publications: Annual report; Newsletter.

Financial data: Year ended 12/31/2004. Assets, $4,276,770 (M); Expenditures, $2,882,327; Total giving, $156,136; Grants to individuals, totaling $35,000. Subtotal for research: 4 grants totaling $35,000 (high: $10,000, low: $5,000).
Fields of interest: Cancer research; Skin disorders research.
Type of support: Research.
Application information: Applications accepted. Application form required. Application form available on the grantmaker's Web site.
  Initial approach: Letter of intent.
  Copies of proposal: 6
  Deadline(s): Oct. 15
  Applicants should submit the following:
    1) Essay
    2) Curriculum vitae
  Additional information: Applications by e-mail not accepted; See Web site for further information.

Program description:

Research Grants: Awards various one-year research grants ranging from $5,000 to $10,000. Contact foundation for more information.
EIN: 132948778

6130

Alfred P. Sloan Foundation

630 5th Ave., Ste. 2550
New York, NY   10111-0242   (212) 649-1649
Contact: Ralph E. Gomory, Pres.
FAX: (212) 757-5117; URL: http://www.sloan.org

Foundation type: Independent foundation
Limitations: Fellowships by nomination only to regular faculty members in chemistry, physics, computer science, mathematics, economics, and neuroscience at colleges and universities in the U.S. and Canada.
Publications: Annual report; Grants list; Informational brochure (including application guidelines).
Financial data: Year ended 12/31/2004. Assets, $1,505,602,994 (M); Expenditures, $75,324,032; Total giving, $59,742,875; Grants to individuals, 235 grants totaling $4,799,197 (high: $40,000, low: $17,609).
Fields of interest: Neuroscience; Chemistry; Mathematics; Physics; Computer science; Biological sciences; Economics.
Type of support: Fellowships; Research.
Application information:
  Deadline(s): Sept. 15 for Sloan Research Fellowships, Oct. 15 for Sloan Industry Center Fellowships.
  Additional information: Completion of formal nomination required; Individual applications not accepted.

Program descriptions:

Sloan Research Fellowships: This program aims to stimulate fundamental research by young scholars of outstanding promise at an early stage of their careers. Candidates may be no more than 32 years of age as of nomination, unless special circumstances such as military service, a change of field, or child rearing are involved, or unless they have held a faculty appointment for less than two years. They are required to hold a Ph.D. (or equivalent) in chemistry, physics, computer science, economics, neuroscience, molecular biology or mathematics. They must be members of the regular faculty of a college or university in the U.S. or Canada. Candidates are nominated by department heads or other senior scholars. Direct applications are not accepted. No formal research proposal is required. Fellowships are for $40,000

and are usually paid over two years. Funds are awarded directly to the Fellow's institution and may be used by the Fellow for such purposes as equipment, technical assistance, computer time, professional travel, trainee support, or any other activity directly related to the Fellow's research.

Sloan Industry Center Fellowships: Awards up to five fellowships annually to extend participation at Sloan Industry Centers. Candidates may be new Ph.D.'s, pre-tenure or post-tenure faculty. Fellowships include a $50,000 stipend to be awarded to the fellow's institution on his or her behalf and a $7,500 grant to be used in providing benefits to the fellow, related research funding, or administrative or other appropriate expenses at the discretion of the Center. Candidates must be nominated by the Director of a Sloan Industry Center or by another faculty member. No direct applications are accepted.
EIN: 131623877

6131

The Sloan Foundation

1 Westminster Pl.
Lake Forest, IL   60045   (847) 295-4317

Foundation type: Independent foundation
Limitations: Project support for Irish cultural pursuits, primarily in IL.
Financial data: Year ended 06/30/2004. Assets, $162,880 (M); Expenditures, $26,639; Total giving, $22,150; Grants to individuals, 6 grants totaling $10,300 (high: $4,000, low: $100).
Fields of interest: Arts; Ireland.
Type of support: Program development.
Application information: Applications accepted.
EIN: 363490527

6132

SMBC Global Foundation, Inc.

(formerly Sumitomo Bank Global Foundation)
277 Park Ave.
New York, NY   10172
Contact: Elizabeth Usui, Admin.
E-mail: globalfoundation@smbcgroup.com

Foundation type: Company-sponsored foundation
Limitations: Scholarships to citizens and residents of Asian countries, including but not limited to China, Thailand, Vietnam, Singapore, Indonesia and Malaysia.
Financial data: Year ended 12/31/2004. Assets, $13,494,936 (M); Expenditures, $718,993; Total giving, $504,690; Grants to individuals, 280 grants totaling $50,000 (high: $275, low: $150).
Type of support: Scholarships—to individuals; Foreign applicants.
Application information: Application form required.
  Deadline(s): Contact foundation for current application deadline
  Additional information: Application should include biographical record and supporting material, report on academic and professional careers, detailed statement of academic plans and plans after completion of academic program, letters of reference (including from instructors), list of extracurricular activities, and other pertinent information.
EIN: 133766226

6133
Florence Gay Smith Foundation
2191 E. Iverson Woods Pl.
Salt Lake City, UT 84117

Foundation type: Operating foundation
Limitations: Grants for prevention of child abuse and community education projects, primarily in UT.
Financial data: Year ended 12/31/2002.
Assets, $385,202 (M); Expenditures, $37,280;
Total giving, $34,583.
Fields of interest: Child abuse; Children/youth, services; Community development, volunteer services.
Type of support: Program development.
Application information:
    Initial approach: Letter or telephone.
    Additional information: Contact foundation for current application deadline/guidelines.
EIN: 870368865

6134
H. L. Snyder Medical Research Institute
1407 Wheat Rd.
Winfield, KS 67156 (620) 221-4080
Contact: Toya Smith, Admin.
FAX: (620) 221-2684;
E-mail: tsmith@snydermri.org; URL: http://www.snydermri.org/sp.html

Foundation type: Operating foundation
Limitations: Grants to residents of Winfield, KS, who are healthcare professionals including hospital or nursing home employees, lab and x-ray techs, aides, nurses, and LPNs who wish to advance their knowledge and skills in caring for their patients.
Financial data: Year ended 06/30/2004.
Assets, $7,586,962 (M); Expenditures, $335,309; Total giving, $10,615; Grants to individuals, totaling $10,615.
Fields of interest: Health care, formal/general education.
Type of support: Research.
Application information: Applications accepted. Application form required. Application form available on the grantmaker's Web site.
    Initial approach: Letter.
    Applicants should submit the following:
        1) Essay
        2) Budget Information
    Additional information: See Web site for complete program information.
EIN: 480622380

6135
Social Philosophy and Policy Foundation
P.O. Box 938
Bowling Green, OH 43402 (419) 372-2536
Contact: Fred D. Miller, Jr., Pres.

Foundation type: Public charity
Limitations: Research grants to scholars for study in the areas of social philosophy and policy.
Financial data: Year ended 12/31/2003.
Assets, $19,222,146 (M); Expenditures, $1,323,610; Total giving, $363,217; Grants to individuals, 4 grants totaling $30,717 (high: $9,696, low: $5,000).
Fields of interest: Philosophy/ethics; Social sciences, public policy.
Type of support: Research.
Application information: Contact foundation for current application deadline/guidelines.
EIN: 341502497

6136
Social Science Research Council
(also known as SSRC)
810 7th Ave.
New York, NY 10019 (212) 377-2700
Contact: Gail Kovach, Dir., Admin. Svcs.
FAX: (212) 377-2727; E-mail: info@ssrc.org;
URL: http://www.ssrc.org

Foundation type: Public charity
Limitations: Fellowships and grants to social science scholars and advanced students for interdisciplinary research, and Prizes awarded for promising dissertation work to recipients of fellowships from an ACLS/SSRC sponsored program.
Publications: Application guidelines; Informational brochure; Newsletter.
Financial data: Year ended 06/30/2004.
Assets, $36,267,050 (M); Expenditures, $16,063,786; Total giving, $2,820,881; Grants to individuals, totaling $2,820,881.
Fields of interest: Humanities; Arts; Crime/violence prevention; International peace/security; International affairs; Computer science; Economics; Psychology/behavioral science; Political science; Social sciences; Minorities; Immigrants/refugees.
Type of support: Fellowships; Research; Awards/prizes; Postdoctoral support; Graduate support; Doctoral support.
Application information: Applications accepted. Application form required.
    Deadline(s): Varies
    Additional information: See Web site for additional programs, further information and guidelines.
Program descriptions:
    Abe Fellowship Program: This program supports professional research in the social sciences or humanities on contemporary policy-relevant issues. Abe Fellows will be eligible for up to 12 months of full-time support. Fellowships are intended for projects by individual researchers regardless of whether those individuals are working alone or in collaboration with others. Candidates should propose to spend at least one-third or more of fellowship tenure in Japan or the U.S. Abe Fellows will be expected to affiliate with an American or Japanese institution appropriate to their research. Fellowship funds may also be spent on additional residence and fieldwork in third countries, as appropriate to individual projects.
    Eurasia Postdoctoral Language Training Fellowships: These awards support postdoctoral scholars in their desire to broaden existing, or advance new research projects that require additional language acquisition. Funds are available for new language acquisition and/or for increased language competency in one or more languages of the Eurasian region. Regions and countries currently supported include Armenia, Azerbaijan, Belrus, Georgia, Kazakhstan, Kyrgyzstan, Moldova, Russian Federation, Tajikistan, Turkmenistan, Ukraine, and Uzbekistan.
    Eurasia Teaching Fellowship: The program supports faculty members at all career levels who wish to create and implement significantly revised or wholly new university courses on, or related to, any of the New States, Eurasia, the Soviet Union, and/or the Russian Empire. Applicants must be U.S. citizens of permanent residents. Regions and countries currently supported by the program include Armenia, Azerbaijan, Belarus, Georgia, Kazakhstan, Kyrgyzstan, Moldova, Russian Federation, Tajikistan, Turkmenistan, Ukraine and Uzbekistan.

International Dissertation Field Research Fellowship Program (IDRF): This program provides 50 fellowships of up to $20,000 to support full-time graduate students in the humanities and social sciences who are enrolled in doctoral programs in the U.S., and who are conducting dissertation field research in all areas and regions of the world.
    JSPS Fellowship Program: The program provides recent Ph.D. recipients (and, with proper eligibility, A.B.D.s) with opportunities to conduct research in Japan under the leadership of a host researcher. Applicants are welcomed from all social science and humanities disciplines and need not be explicitly related to the study of Japan. Scholars who have received the Ph.D. no more than six years prior to Apr. 1, and who are U.S. citizens or permanent residents may apply for 12- to 24-month fellowships. Scholars who have received the Ph.D. no more than 10 years prior to Apr. 1 and who are U.S. citizens or permanent residents may apply for 3- to 11-month fellowships.
EIN: 131325070

6137
Society for Analytical Chemists of Pittsburgh
300 Penn Ctr. Blvd., Ste. 332
Pittsburgh, PA 15235-5503 (412) 825-3220
Contact: Charles L. Holifield, Chair.
FAX: (412) 825-3224; E-mail: sacpinfo@pitton.org;
URL: http://www.sacp.org/

Foundation type: Independent foundation
Limitations: Grants to PA science teachers and undergraduate science researchers.
Publications: Informational brochure.
Financial data: Year ended 06/30/2005.
Assets, $174,764 (M); Expenditures, $478,723; Total giving, $330,086; Grants to individuals, 75 grants totaling $56,834 (high: $5,000, low: $69).
Fields of interest: Education; Science; Chemistry.
Type of support: Program development; Research; Undergraduate support.
Application information: Contact society or consult Web site for current application deadline/guidelines.
Program descriptions:
    Analytical Chemistry Professor Starter Grant: The society awards one grant of $20,000 per year to an assistant professor in the field of analytical chemistry. The purpose of this grant is to encourage high-quality, innovative research by a new analytical chemistry professor and to promote the training and development of graduate students in this field.
    Elementary/Middle School Science Equipment Grants: The society invites every teacher who teaches science in selected counties of OH, PA, and WV to apply for an SACP Elementary/Middle School Equipment Grant. Applicant need not be designated as an official science teacher. The grant is for a maximum of $500, and at least 60 proposals will be funded.
    Undergraduate Analytical Research Program (UARP) Grant: The society has established a $10,000 annual grant to promote high-quality, innovative undergraduate research in the field of analytical chemistry and to promote training and development of undergraduate students in the field of analytical chemistry. Chemistry faculty at U.S. colleges and universities not having a graduate program in the chemical sciences are eligible to apply.
EIN: 256072976

6138
Society of Cosmetic Chemists
120 Wall St., Ste. 2400
New York, NY 10005-4088 (212) 668-1500
Contact: Theresa Cesario, Exec. Dir.
FAX: (212) 668-1504; E-mail: SCC@sccconline.org;
URL: http://www.sccconline.org

Foundation type: Public charity
Limitations: Fellowships to students of science.
Financial data: Year ended 08/31/2003.
Assets, $1,630,942 (M); Expenditures,
$1,512,452; Total giving, $40,000; Grants to
individuals, totaling $40,000.
Fields of interest: Medical school/education;
Pharmacy/prescriptions; Physical/earth sciences;
Chemistry; Engineering; Biological sciences;
Psychology/behavioral science.
Type of support: Fellowships; Graduate support.
Application information: Deadline Feb. 1; See Web
site for additional application information.
Program description:
Graduate Research Fellowship Program: A
fellowship of $20,000 per year for up to two years
to provide students with stipends and support for
dissertation research. Graduate fellowships are
awarded for research leading to doctoral degrees in
the physical, chemical, biological, medical,
pharmaceutical, or behavioral sciences or
engineering.
EIN: 131976655

6139
Society of Economic Geologists Foundation, Inc.
7811 Shaffer Pkwy.
Littleton, CO 80127

Foundation type: Independent foundation
Limitations: Awards, lectureships, and travel grants
to graduate students and researchers of the
science of economic geology.
Publications: Application guidelines; Informational
brochure; Newsletter; Occasional report.
Financial data: Year ended 12/31/2004.
Assets, $4,573,246 (M); Expenditures,
$289,243; Total giving, $200,014.
Fields of interest: Science, research; Economics.
Type of support: Awards/prizes; Travel grants.
Application information: Applications by letter
accepted throughout the year.
EIN: 516020487

6140
Society of Manufacturing Engineers Education Foundation
(also known as SME Education Foundation)
1 SME Dr.
P.O. Box 930
Dearborn, MI 48121-0930 (313) 425-3300
Contact: Sherril K. West, Pres.
FAX: (313) 425-3411;
E-mail: foundation@sme.org; URL: http://
www.sme.org/foundation

Foundation type: Public charity
Limitations: Awards by nomination only to faculty
members and authors in the area of manufacturing
coursework development and textbooks, and grants
to full-time engineering faculty members for work in
the area of manufacturing design methodologies.
Publications: Application guidelines; Annual report;
Grants list; Program policy statement.
Financial data: Year ended 12/31/2004.
Assets, $23,309,005 (M); Expenditures,

$1,651,514; Total giving, $729,302; Grants to
individuals, totaling $218,330.
Fields of interest: Literature; Education;
Engineering; Government/public administration.
Type of support: Program development;
Fellowships; Research; Scholarships—to
individuals; Awards/prizes; Graduate support;
Technical education support; Undergraduate
support.
Application information: Contact foundation for
current application deadline/guidelines.
Program descriptions:
*M. Eugene Merchant Manufacturing Textbook
Award:* A $2,500 award is given each year to
recognize an author of a first edition manufacturing
textbook published in North America. Recipients are
selected by a special review committee.
Sargent Americanism Award: One $2,500 award
is provided each year to a faculty member in
recognition of unusually significant and innovative
coursework which develops a better understanding
and appreciation of the American private enterprise
system among college and university students.
*Edward S. Roth Manufacturing Standards Grant
Award:* One $2,500 grant is provided to a full-time
engineering faculty member to accelerate the
application of design for manufacturing
methodologies using concurrent engineering and
geometric dimensioning and tolerancing.
EIN: 382746841

6141
Special Libraries Association
(also known as SLA)
331 S. Patrick St.
Alexandria, VA 22314-3501 (703) 647-4900
Contact: Janice R. Lachance, C.E.O.
FAX: (703) 647-4901; E-mail: sla@sla.org;
URL: http://www.sla.org

Foundation type: Public charity
Limitations: Professional development grants and
awards to librarians.
Publications: Application guidelines; Annual report;
Financial statement; Informational brochure;
Newsletter.
Financial data: Year ended 12/31/2004.
Assets, $14,233,375 (M); Expenditures,
$6,733,548; Total giving, $30,500; Grants to
individuals, 6 grants totaling $30,500 (high:
$6,000, low: $500).
Fields of interest: Libraries/library science;
Libraries (special); Computer science; Minorities.
Type of support: Program development;
Publication; Awards/prizes.
Application information: Application form required.
Initial approach: letter.
Deadline(s): Jan. 8 for Diversity Awards and Dec.
8 for other awards
Program descriptions:
*Mary Adeline Conner Professional Development
Scholarship:* One or more scholarships, not to
exceed $6,000 in total, are available each year for
post-M.L.S. certificate or degree programs in any
subject area, technological skills, or managerial
expertise relevant to applicant's career needs and
goals in special librarianship. Scholarships may
include a travel stipend. Applicants must be
members of the Special Libraries Association who
have the M.L.S. degree and have worked in special
libraries for at least five years.
*Diversity Leadership Development Program
Award:* Awarded to an active member or members
of the Association from multicultural backgrounds
who display excellent leadership abilities in the
profession and demonstrate a willingness to
develop and strive for leadership opportunities

within the Association. Cash award of $1,000 and
stipend for Annual Conference and/or Continuing
Education is presented.
*Factiva Leadership Award - 21st Century
Competencies in Action:* A cash award of $2,000 is
presented annually to an individual member or
members who exemplify leadership as a special
librarian through examples of personal and
professional competencies. This award requires a
separate application, which can be acquired by
calling Barbara Burton at (609) 627-2341; E-mail:
barbara.burton@factiva.com.
Innovations in Technology Award: A cash award of
$1,000 is granted to an individual member or
members for innovative use and applications of
technology in a special library setting.
H.W. Wilson Company Award: A cash award of
$500 is presented to the author(s) of an
outstanding article published in Information
Outlook during the publication year.
EIN: 135404745

6142
Spencer Community School Foundation
23 E. 7th St.
Spencer, IA 51301 (712) 262-8950
Contact: Glen Lohman, Secy.

Foundation type: Operating foundation
Limitations: Grants to Spencer, IA, teachers for
innovative projects that improve students' and
teachers' learning experiences.
Financial data: Year ended 12/31/2002.
Assets, $942,918 (M); Expenditures, $80,384;
Total giving, $66,584; Grants to individuals, 64
grants totaling $59,397 (high: $3,750, low: $200).
Fields of interest: Elementary/secondary
education.
Type of support: Program development.
Application information: Applications accepted.
Application form required.
Deadline(s): Mar. 3
Applicants should submit the following:
1) Budget Information
Additional information: See Web site for further
application information and application form.
EIN: 421306327

6143
The Spencer Foundation
625 N. Michigan Ave., Ste. 1600
Chicago, IL 60611 (312) 337-7000
Contact: Michael S. McPherson, Pres.
FAX: (312) 337-0282;
E-mail: information@spencer.org; URL: http://
www.spencer.org

Foundation type: Independent foundation
Limitations: Research grants and dissertation,
postdoctoral fellowships to individuals working
under the auspices of an institution. The foundation
supports research that yields new knowledge about
education broadly defined to include all the
situations and institutions in which learning occurs
throughout the lifespan and around the world.
Publications: Annual report (including application
guidelines); Informational brochure.
Financial data: Year ended 03/31/2005.
Assets, $411,018,768 (M); Expenditures,
$20,592,979; Total giving, $15,066,829; Grants
to individuals, 11 grants totaling $1,981,760 (high:
$681,600, low: $37,500).
Fields of interest: Education, research; Education,
reform.
Type of support: Fellowships; Research;
Postdoctoral support.

Application information: Applications accepted.
Initial approach: Telephone.
Deadline(s): None
Additional information: Application procedures differ by program. See the foundation's Web site for details.

Program descriptions:

NAE/Spencer Dissertation and Postdoctoral Fellowships: Awards fellowships to talented scholars with the purpose of increasing the number of scholars prepared to pursue research that gives promise of yielding new knowledge leading to the improvement of education.

Spencer Dissertation Fellowship Program: This program encourages a new generation of scholars from a variety of fields to undertake research relevant to the improvement of education. A brochure detailing eligibility and application procedures is available from the foundation and from college campuses. Dissertation-year fellowships are administered by the foundation directly.

NAE/Spencer Postdoctoral Fellowships: This program is open to scholars anywhere in the world who have received their doctoral degree within the past five years, and who wish to conduct research relevant to education. These fellowships are administered by the National Academy of Education, School of Education, New York University, 726 Broadway, 5th Fl., New York, NY 10003-6652, tel.: (212) 998-9035.

Small Grants Program: This program was designed to increase the number of able scholars working on problems in education. It is intended to facilitate investigators in pursuing exploratory research, problem-finding research, pilot research, modest projects, and the initial phases of larger investigations. Grants made under this program range from $1,000 to $35,000. Inquiries about this program should be directed to the Small Grants Admin., at the foundation address.

RAND/Spencer Postdoctoral Fellowship in Education Policy: Awards fellowships to enable outstanding new scholars in education policy to sharpen their analytic skills, learn to communicate research results effectively, and advance their research agendas. Housed within RAND Education and co-sponsored by the Spencer Foundation, the program blends formal and informal training and extensive collaboration with distinguished researchers in a variety of disciplines. Fellows spend 60 percent of their time on an appropriate RAND Education project and 40 percent of their time on their own research. Staff mentors will meet regularly with fellows to ensure that the fellows' programs reflect their own research interests and provide opportunities for them to make substantive contributions on their project teams. Fellowships are for one year, renewable for a second, and will be in RAND's Santa Monica, CA, or Washington, DC, office. Each fellow receives a yearly stipend of $50,000 plus a research and travel allowance. Fellows must have completed a Ph.D. in a relevant discipline such as education, psychology, sociology, economics, statistics, anthropology or political science within the last five years. To apply, send a letter of interest that includes a description of how your research agenda would complement RAND's research focus, a curriculum vitae, writing sample, and, under separate cover, two letters of reference to: Gretchen Thompson, Mgr., Recruitment. E-mail: research-jobs@rand.org; FAX: (310) 451-7070. Indicate within the subject line of your e-mail that you are applying for the RAND/Spencer Postdoctoral Fellowship in Education Policy. Reference letters may be included in e-mail, or may be mailed or faxed separately to: Sharon

Koga, RAND, 1700 Main St., P.O. Box 2138, Santa Monica, CA 90407-2138, FAX: (310) 393-4818.
EIN: 366078558

6144
State Farm Companies Foundation
1 State Farm Plz.
Bloomington, IL 61710 (309) 766-2161
Contact: Kristy Funk, Asst. Secy.
Address for Hispanic College Fund: 55 2nd St., Ste. 1500, San Francisco, CA 94105, tel.: (877) 473-4636
FAX: (309) 766-2314;
E-mail: kristy.funk.cm3n@statefarm.com;
Additional E-mail: home.sf-foundation.494b00@statefarm.com;
URL: http://www.statefarm.com/foundati/foundati.htm

Foundation type: Company-sponsored foundation
Limitations: Doctoral awards by nomination only to students at the dissertation stage in insurance or business. Candidates must be U.S. citizens.
Publications: Corporate giving report (including application guidelines); Informational brochure.
Financial data: Year ended 12/31/2005. Assets, $11,607,830 (M); Expenditures, $20,692,272; Total giving, $20,423,517.
Fields of interest: Business school/education; Insurance, providers.
Type of support: Fellowships; Awards/grants by nomination only; Graduate support; Doctoral support.
Application information: Application form required.
Deadline(s): Mar. 31
Applicants should submit the following:
   1) Transcripts
Additional information: Applications without nominations will not be considered; Completion of formal nomination required, including three letters of recommendation and doctoral dissertation proposal for doctoral awards; See program description for further information.

Program descriptions:

Doctoral Dissertation Award in Business: This program provides $10,000 to students at the dissertation stage of their doctoral program in a graduate school of business, to be used for educational purposes. A $3,000 grant is made to the recipient's graduate institution. Students can be majoring in finance, marketing or management, including business administration and organization behavior. Applicants must be U.S. citizens. Applications will be sent to directors or deans of doctoral programs in business and insurance at participating schools in Dec. Winners will be announced in May. An independent committee of educators selects recipients based on scholastic achievement, quality of the dissertation proposal, and recommendation from the dissertation advisor and faculty members.

The Doctoral Dissertation Award in Insurance: This program is designed to stimulate research and the development of knowledge in the insurance industry and to increase the number of qualified teachers of insurance in U.S. colleges and universities. The award provides $10,000 to the recipient and a grant of $3,000 to student's college or university. The award is available to doctoral candidates who have completed a major portion of their doctoral program and are at the dissertation stage. They also must major in insurance or a related field of study. Applicants must be U.S. citizens. Applications will be sent to directors or deans of doctoral programs in business and insurance at participating schools in Dec. Winners

will be announced in May. An independent committee of educators selects recipients based on scholastic achievement, quality of the dissertation proposal, and recommendation from the dissertation advisor and faculty members.
EIN: 366110423

6145
Ruth & Milton Steinbach Fund, Inc.
c/o Tanton & Co.
37 W. 57th St., 5th Fl.
New York, NY 10019

Foundation type: Independent foundation
Limitations: Research grants by nomination only to support basic biomedical research in loss of vision, specifically macular degeneration.
Financial data: Year ended 10/31/2004. Assets, $24,160,331 (M); Expenditures, $1,331,158; Total giving, $1,100,000.
Fields of interest: Eye diseases; Biomedicine research; Disabilities, people with.
Type of support: Research; Awards/grants by nomination only.
Application information: Contact fund for current nomination deadline/guidelines.
EIN: 136028785

6146
Stony Wold-Herbert Fund, Inc.
136 E. 57th St., Rm. 1705
New York, NY 10022 (212) 753-6565
Contact: Cheryl S. Friedman, Exec. Dir.
FAX: (212) 753-6053;
E-mail: director@stonywold-herbertfund.com;
URL: http://www.stonywold-herbertfund.com

Foundation type: Independent foundation
Limitations: Research grants and fellowships to doctors, teachers, and scientific investigators in the greater New York, NY, area working in respiratory and pulmonary fields.
Publications: Application guidelines; Annual report; Informational brochure; Newsletter.
Financial data: Year ended 12/31/2004. Assets, $6,679,346 (M); Expenditures, $391,610; Total giving, $241,311; Grants to individuals, totaling $46,125.
Fields of interest: Lung diseases; Lung research.
Type of support: Fellowships; Research; Technical education support; Undergraduate support.
Application information: Applications accepted. Application form required.
Deadline(s): Oct. 15
Additional information: Application must include references and description of nature and purpose of research; Interviews required; See program descriptions for further application information.

Program description:

Research Grants and Fellowships: In order to assist the scientific community in its battle against respiratory disease, the Stony Wold-Herbert Fund usually awards two fellowships and five grants-in-aid in the New York City area. Research grants are available for all basic disciplines which relate to respiratory diseases as well as for clinical investigation. Past awards have ranged up to $25,000 per annum. Fellowships promote the training of teachers, scientific investigators, and clinicians in the field of lung disease. Past awards have ranged up to $30,000 per annum. Contact the fund directly for an application form. Deadline is Oct. 15. In Nov., the Medical Advisory Committee makes its recommendations to the Board for the

one-year period beginning the following July. The term is one year, with the possibility of renewal.
EIN: 132784124

6147
Storkan/Hanes Research Foundation
(formerly The Richard C. Storkan Foundation)
8770 Hwy. 25
Hollister, CA 95024
Contact: Donald E. Munnecke, C.E.O.
Application address: c/o Dept. of Plant Pathology, University of California, Riverside, CA 92521, tel.: (714) 787-3125

Foundation type: Independent foundation
Limitations: Scholarships and research grants to graduate students who are residents of the U.S. and who demonstrate interest in soil-borne diseases. Research must be done in the U.S.
Financial data: Year ended 12/31/2004. Assets, $175,912 (M); Expenditures, $26,961; Total giving, $20,000; Grants to individuals, totaling $20,000.
Fields of interest: Biological sciences.
Type of support: Research; Graduate support.
Application information:
Deadline(s): May 1
Additional information: Application should include research proposal showing studies in soil-borne diseases and biographical letter.
EIN: 770193922

6148
Studenica Foundation
535 4th St.
San Rafael, CA 94901 (415) 451-6900
Contact: Michael D. Djordjevich, Pres.
Application address: 1299 4th St., San Rafael, CA 94901

Foundation type: Independent foundation
Limitations: Scholarships and publishing support to individuals in the Federal Republic of Yugoslavia.
Financial data: Year ended 12/31/2003. Assets, $1,047,725 (M); Expenditures, $300,883; Total giving, $276,040; Grants to individuals, 46 grants totaling $276,040 (high: $31,000, low: $300).
Type of support: Publication; Scholarships—to individuals; Foreign applicants.
Application information: Contact foundation for current application deadline/guidelines.
EIN: 943186334

6149
Surdna Foundation, Inc.
330 Madison Ave., 30th Fl.
New York, NY 10017-5001 (212) 557-0010
Contact: Edward Skloot, Exec. Dir.
FAX: (212) 557-0003; E-mail: request@surdna.org; URL: http://www.surdna.org

Foundation type: Independent foundation
Limitations: Fellowships to art teachers for artistic development.
Publications: Annual report (including application guidelines); Grants list.
Financial data: Year ended 06/30/2004. Assets, $681,880,246 (M); Expenditures, $36,740,021; Total giving, $30,238,622.
Fields of interest: Arts education.
Type of support: Program development; Fellowships.

Application information:
Initial approach: Proposal.
Deadline(s): Nov. 24
Additional information: Application by letter of intent, including general information form, resume or curriculum vitae, and school information; See Web site for further application information.
Program description:
Arts Teachers Fellowship Program: Awards fellowships of up to $5,000 each (with a complementary grant of $1,500 to the Fellow's school to support post-fellowship activities) to 20 recipients. Awards may be used to defray the costs of tuition and other fees, room and board, travel, purchase of materials and/or equipment for personal art-making, childcare and other relevant expenses. The Fellowship program includes: the professional development experience, post-fellowship activity in the Fellow's home school during the subsequent academic year and the convocation.
EIN: 136108163

6150
The Greater Tacoma Community Foundation
950 Pacific Ave., Ste. 1200
P.O. Box 1995
Tacoma, WA 98401-1995 (253) 383-5622
Contact: For grants: Kristen Corning, Community Progs. Coord.
FAX: (253) 272-8099; E-mail: kcorning@gtcf.org; Grant application E-mail: sherrana@gtcf.org; URL: http://www.tacomafoundation.org

Foundation type: Community foundation
Limitations: Grants to individuals, primarily women in the greater Tacoma-Pierce county area, for programs and projects that provide opportunities for women and girls to achieve their full potential.
Publications: Application guidelines; Annual report; Informational brochure (including application guidelines); Newsletter.
Financial data: Year ended 06/30/2005. Assets, $53,106,556 (M); Expenditures, $3,943,719; Total giving, $2,854,618; Grants to individuals, totaling $178,236.
Fields of interest: Women.
Type of support: Program development.
Application information:
Deadline(s): Oct. 3
Additional information: Completion of formal application required, including financial information and narrative; See Web site for further application information.
EIN: 911007459

6151
Tamer Foundation
56 S. Groesbeck Hwy.
Clinton Township, MI 48036

Foundation type: Independent foundation
Limitations: Grants for religious development, MI.
Financial data: Year ended 04/30/2005. Assets, $10,966,925 (M); Expenditures, $617,831; Total giving, $585,950; Grants to individuals, 24 grants totaling $64,400 (high: $6,008, low: $691).
Fields of interest: Christian agencies & churches; Religion.
Type of support: Grants to individuals.

Application information: Contact foundation for current application deadline/guidelines.
EIN: 382679633

6152
TAPPI Foundation, Inc.
15 Technology Pkwy. S.
Norcross, GA 30092-2928 (770) 209-7289
Contact: Mary Lynn Miller, Exec. Dir.
FAX: (770) 446-6947;
E-mail: foundation@tappi.org; URL: http://www.tappi.org/index.asp?pid=16129&ch=15

Foundation type: Public charity
Limitations: Awards by nomination only to TAPPI members who have significantly and demonstrably contributed to the advancement of the association.
Publications: Annual report.
Financial data: Year ended 08/31/2005. Assets, $3,523,535 (M); Expenditures, $210,108; Total giving, $181,729; Grants to individuals, 38 grants totaling $180,729 (high: $74,695, low: $48).
Fields of interest: Voluntarism promotion; Leadership development.
Type of support: Awards/grants by nomination only; Awards/prizes.
Application information: Nominations are only accepted from TAPPI chapter members.
Program description:
Herman L. Joachim Distinguished Service Award: The recipient receives $25,000, a silver medallion, a white gold ring, a lapel pin, a plaque, an honorary life membership in the association, and is designated a TAPPI Fellow.
EIN: 581886221

6153
TDC Research Foundation
P.O. Box 1008
Blacksburg, VA 24063
Contact: Thomas Hudlicky, Pres.
Tel. for Thomas Hudlicky, Ontario, Canada: (905) 682-4180

Foundation type: Operating foundation
Limitations: Research grants by nomination only for study in chemistry.
Financial data: Year ended 12/31/2003. Assets, $31,649 (M); Expenditures, $4,711; Total giving, $3,706; Grants to individuals, totaling $3,706.
Fields of interest: Chemistry.
Type of support: Fellowships; Research; Awards/grants by nomination only.
Application information: Applications not accepted.
EIN: 541574776

6154
The Teachers Network
285 W. Broadway
New York, NY 10013 (212) 966-5582
FAX: (212) 941-1787; URL: http://www.teachersnetwork.org

Foundation type: Public charity
Limitations: Awards to public school teachers in New York, NY, for curriculum projects.
Publications: Newsletter.
Financial data: Year ended 08/31/2004. Assets, $2,209,417 (M); Expenditures, $1,592,310; Total giving, $221,809.

Fields of interest: Education, public education; Education.

Type of support: Program development; Awards/ prizes.

Application information: Applications accepted. Application form required. Application form available on the grantmaker's Web site.

Deadline(s): Contact foundation for current application deadline.

Additional information: See Web site for program descriptions.

Program descriptions:

Disseminator Grants: Awards of $650 to New York City public school teachers for curriculum projects that have been tested and proven successful in the classroom. Projects must be the original creation of the applying teacher. These grants are available for math, science or new media (technology) curriculum projects.

Adaptor Grants: Awards of $250 to New York City public school teachers to assist them in adapting and implementing an award-winning curriculum project from the Catalog of Creative Teacher-Developed Programs.

EIN: 133312788

6155

Teachers of English to Speakers of Other Languages, Inc.

700 S. Washington St., Ste. 200
Alexandria, VA 22314 (703) 836-0774
FAX: (703) 836-7864; E-mail: info@tesol.org;
Toll-free tel.: (888) 547-3369; URL: http:// www.tesol.org

Foundation type: Public charity

Limitations: Awards and grants to English language teaching professionals.

Publications: Annual report; Informational brochure.

Financial data: Year ended 10/31/2004. Assets, $4,125,566 (M); Expenditures, $4,721,751; Total giving, $50,590; Grants to individuals, 60 grants totaling $36,870 (high: $2,567, low: $200).

Fields of interest: Education.

Type of support: Awards/grants by nomination only; Awards/prizes.

Application information: Application form required.

Initial approach: Letter or telephone.

Deadline(s): Sept. 15 for Alatis Award and Nov. 1 for all others

Applicants should submit the following:
1) Letter(s) of recommendation

Additional information: See Web site for additional guidelines for application and nomination.

Program descriptions:

James E. Alatis Award: This award acknowledges outstanding and extended service by TESOL members at international, regional, and local levels.

The TESOL Virginia French Allen Award: This award honors an ESOL teacher who has shared scholarship and provided service at the affiliate level.

D. Scott Enright TESOL Interest Section Service Award: This award acknowledges outstanding extended service to and leadership in TESOL interest sections.

The TESOL Leadership Mentoring Program: This program helps underrepresented groups within TESOL become more involved in the work of the association. At the TESOL convention, the Leadership Mentoring Program (LMP) pairs selected individuals with mentors who guide recipients throughout the year as they contribute

their time and expertise to TESOL and its varied activities and projects.

The TESOL Thomson Heinle Award for Excellence in Teaching: This award honors educators considered by their colleagues to be excellent teachers.

EIN: 237003530

6156

John Templeton Foundation

300 Conshohocken State Rd., Ste. 500
West Conshohocken, PA 19428
(610) 941-2828
Contact: Grant Admin.
FAX: (610) 825-1730; E-mail: info@templeton.org;
URL: http://www.templeton.org

Foundation type: Independent foundation

Limitations: Research grants to scholars of psychology who hold a Ph.D. degree, and awards by nomination only to individuals who show extraordinary originality in advancing humankind's understanding of God.

Publications: Application guidelines; Annual report; Financial statement; Informational brochure; Newsletter.

Financial data: Year ended 12/31/2003. Assets, $337,359,840 (M); Expenditures, $27,593,849; Total giving, $21,426,052; Grants to individuals, 6 grants totaling $37,076 (high: $13,576, low: $100).

Fields of interest: Psychology/behavioral science; Religion.

Type of support: Research; Grants to individuals; Awards/grants by nomination only; Awards/prizes.

Application information:

Deadline(s): Apr. 16 for Research grants

Additional information: Application by proposal, including six copies of curriculum vitae, for Templeton Prize, applications accepted throughout the year; Initial approach by letter outlining financial need; See http:// www.templetonprize.org/ for nomination forms and further information.

Program descriptions:

Martin P. Seligman Award: Awards a grant of $1,000 to a scholar who has completed a Ph.D. dissertation in any area of research related to positive psychology in the last three years and who plans to continue research in this area. Dissertations must have been completed after Mar. 31.

Templeton Prize: This award is given annually to individuals for outstanding originality in advancing the world's understanding of God or spirituality. The award is intended to encourage the concepts that resources and manpower are needed to accelerate progress in spiritual discoveries, which can help people to learn over 100-fold more about divinity. The foundation hopes that by learning about the lives of the awardees, millions of people will be uplifted and inspired toward research and more discoveries about aspects of divinity. Recipients must possess the following qualities: freshness, creativity, innovation and effectiveness.

EIN: 621322826

6157

The Texas Area Fund Foundation, Inc.

P.O. Box 283
Palestine, TX 75802
E-mail: txfoundation@goquest.com; URL: http:// www.tourism-tools.com/TAFF.htm

Foundation type: Community foundation

Limitations: To improve Anderson County, Texas through donor advised funds and projects.

Financial data: Year ended 12/31/2004. Assets, $1,951,046 (M); Expenditures, $82,137; Total giving, $60,564; Grants to individuals, 12 grants totaling $19,000 (high: $4,000, low: $500).

Type of support: Awards/prizes.

Application information: Contact fund for current application deadline/guidelines.

EIN: 752834546

6158

Texas Council for the Humanities

(formerly Texas Committee for the Humanities)
Banister Pl. A
3809 S. 2nd St.
Austin, TX 78704-7058 (512) 440-1991
Contact: Monte K. Youngs, Exec. Dir.
FAX: (512) 440-0115;
E-mail: postmaster@public-humanities.org;
URL: http://www.public-humanities.org

Foundation type: Public charity

Limitations: Awards by nomination only to humanities teachers.

Publications: Application guidelines; Biennial report; Financial statement; Informational brochure (including application guidelines); Newsletter; Occasional report.

Financial data: Year ended 10/31/2003. Assets, $783,419 (M); Expenditures, $1,174,934; Total giving, $237,171.

Fields of interest: Humanities; Education.

Type of support: Awards/grants by nomination only; Awards/prizes.

Application information:

Initial approach: Letter or telephone.

Deadline(s): Mar. 1.

Additional information: Contact council for current nomination guidelines.

Program description:

Outstanding Teaching of the Humanities Awards: In recognition of excellence in elementary and secondary humanities teaching, six $2,000 awards are given each year. The award is shared equally between the teacher and the teacher's school, to purchase instructional materials for the improvement of humanities courses and programs. Recipients are selected by nomination only and receive their awards in May.

EIN: 751493438

6159

Toshiba America Foundation

c/o Prog. Office
1251 Ave. of the Americas, 41st Fl.
New York, NY 10020 (212) 596-0620
Contact: Laura Cronin, Mgr.
FAX: (212) 221-1108;
E-mail: foundation@tai.toshiba.com; URL: http:// www.taf.toshiba.com

Foundation type: Company-sponsored foundation

Limitations: Grants for the creation of projects designed by classroom teachers to improve science and mathematics education for students in grades K through 12.

Publications: Grants list; Informational brochure (including application guidelines); Newsletter; Occasional report.

Financial data: Year ended 03/31/2004. Assets, $11,387,486 (M); Expenditures, $606,584; Total giving, $506,490.

Fields of interest: Elementary/secondary education.

Type of support: Program development; Project support.
Application information: Applications accepted. Application form required. Application form available on the grantmaker's Web site.
  Initial approach: E-mail, telephone, or letter.
  Deadline(s): Feb. 1, Aug. 1, Oct. 1
  Applicants should submit the following:
    1) Proposal
  Additional information: See Web site for complete program description and application procedures.
EIN: 133596612

6160
Trinity Health Foundation

(formerly T.R.H. Development Foundation)
802 Kenyon Rd.
Fort Dodge, IA 50501
URL: http://www.trmc.org/body.cfm?id=51

Foundation type: Public charity
Limitations: Scholarships to individuals residing in IA for studies that further the mission of Trinity Regional Hospital.
Financial data: Year ended 12/31/2003. Assets, $12,483,329 (M); Expenditures, $774,797; Total giving, $376,238; Grants to individuals, totaling $10,404.
Fields of interest: Health sciences school/education.
Type of support: Awards/grants by nomination only.
Application information: Unsolicited requests for funds not considered or acknowledged.
EIN: 421222381

6161
Alice Livingston Trout Family Memorial Fund

c/o Fulton Financial Advisors, N.A.
P.O. Box 3215
Lancaster, PA 17604-3215
Contact: Vincent Lattanzio, Trust Off., Fulton Financial Advisors, N.A.

Foundation type: Independent foundation
Limitations: Grants to doctors in eastern PA for medical research.
Financial data: Year ended 02/28/2005. Assets, $419,281 (M); Expenditures, $25,108; Total giving, $20,206.
Fields of interest: Medical research, institute.
Type of support: Research.
Application information: Application by letter, stating purpose of the medical research program, accepted throughout the year.
EIN: 237660671

6162
Tsadra Foundation

P.O. Box 20192
New York, NY 10014

Foundation type: Independent foundation
Limitations: Fellowships to advanced Western students of Tibetan Buddhism.
Financial data: Year ended 12/31/2003. Assets, $23,382 (M); Expenditures, $908,621; Total giving, $182,250; Grants to individuals, 7 grants totaling $182,250 (high: $40,000; low: $10,000).
Fields of interest: Foundations (private grantmaking); Buddhism.

Type of support: Program development; Publication; Fellowships.
Application information: Applications not accepted.
Program description:
  Fellowship Program: Provides grants to advanced western students of Tibetan Buddhism with significant contemplative training. Grants support a number of activity areas, such as the translation of authentic and authoritative text from Tibetan into English and French, and the further development of contemplative training through long retreats.
EIN: 137224970

6163
Elizabeth Tuckerman Foundation

c/o Wells Fargo Bank, N.A.
P.O. Box 63954
San Francisco, CA 94163
Application address: c/o Rosa Vongchanglor, Wells Fargo Bank, N.A., 333 S. Grand Ave., Los Angeles, CA 90071, tel.: (213) 253-3154

Foundation type: Independent foundation
Limitations: Scholarships to students from Wales and Great Britain who wish to pursue postgraduate studies in the U.S.
Financial data: Year ended 11/30/2005. Assets, $1,816,693 (M); Expenditures, $72,359; Total giving, $59,330; Grants to individuals, totaling $59,330.
Type of support: Foreign applicants; Postgraduate support.
Application information: Deadline May 12; Completion of formal application required; Applications distributed by universities.
EIN: 956601661

6164
U.S. Advisory Committee for International Carbohydrate Symposia, Inc.

2829 Bentbrook Ln.
West Lafayette, IN 47906-5275
Contact: James N. BeMiller, Pres.

Foundation type: Independent foundation
Limitations: Awards by nomination only to carbohydrate scientists for excellence in research.
Financial data: Year ended 12/31/2004. Assets, $210,136 (M); Expenditures, $13,000; Total giving, $10,000; Grants to individuals, 2 grants totaling $10,000 (high: $5,000; low: $5,000).
Fields of interest: Science, research.
Type of support: Conferences/seminars; Research; Awards/grants by nomination only.
Application information:
  Deadline(s): Apr. 30
  Additional information: Nomination by letter, including supporting documentation concerning excellence in carbohydrate research.
EIN: 371131168

6165
Unity Scholars

c/o Joanne Jaccaci
626 Penney Rd.
New Gloucester, ME 04260

Foundation type: Operating foundation
Limitations: Grants by nomination only to individual activists who employ general systemic principles for social change.

Publications: Informational brochure.
Financial data: Year ended 12/31/2005. Assets, $4,421 (M); Expenditures, $108,253; Total giving, $81,489.
Fields of interest: Arts; International exchange, arts; Social sciences.
Type of support: Program development; Publication; Fellowships; Internship funds; Research; Awards/grants by nomination only; Foreign applicants; Travel grants.
Application information: Applications by letter accepted throughout the year.
EIN: 222527441

6166
University of Delaware Research Foundation

162 Center Mall, Ste. 122
Newark, DE 19716-0099

Foundation type: Public charity
Limitations: Research grants to faculty members of the University of Delaware, DE.
Financial data: Year ended 12/31/2004. Assets, $8,466,248 (M); Expenditures, $383,349; Total giving, $380,349; Grants to individuals, totaling $380,349.
Type of support: Research.
Application information: Applications not accepted.
EIN: 516017306

6167
W. E. Upjohn Unemployment Trustee Corporation

300 S. Westnedge Ave.
Kalamazoo, MI 49007 (269) 343-5541
Contact: Randall W. Eberts, Exec. Dir.
FAX: (269) 343-3308;
E-mail: webmaster@upjohninstitute.org;
URL: http://www.upjohninstitute.org

Foundation type: Public charity
Limitations: Research grants to professional social scientists who have earned a Ph.D., or the equivalent, for studies on the causes, effects, prevention, and alleviation of unemployment.
Publications: Application guidelines; Program policy statement.
Financial data: Year ended 12/31/2003. Assets, $141,959,946 (M); Expenditures, $12,163,688; Total giving, $6,631,039; Grants to individuals, totaling $6,303,491.
Fields of interest: Employment, research; Social sciences.
Type of support: Research.
Application information: Application form required.
  Initial approach: three-page summary of project.
  Deadline(s): Feb. 1
  Additional information: FAX or e-mail submissions are not accepted.
Program descriptions:
  Grant Program: The foundation supports research into the causes, effects, prevention, and alleviation of unemployment through the W.E. Upjohn Institute for Employment Research. The grant program is aimed at supporting policy-relevant research expected to result in publication of a monograph by the Institute. In keeping with its charter, the Institute conducts research into the causes and effects of unemployment and measures for the alleviation of unemployment at the national, state, and local levels. The grant program is intended to extend and complement the internal research program at the Institute.

Applicants submit eight copies of a three-page summary of the proposed research and vitae describing their professional qualifications as a preliminary step. The selection committee evaluates these preliminary materials and then invites a subset of applicants to submit the full, 15-page proposal for evaluation. Full invited application submissions should include the following:

· statement of the problem or hypothesis to be investigated
· methodology in sufficient detail to make it possible to judge the workability of the proposal
· timetable
· budget
· curricula vitae of the principal investigators
· statement of research currently underway or proposed to other institutions in the subject areas of application

Applications are evaluated by an Institute grant committee on the basis of four equally weighted evaluation criteria: policy significance, technical merit, feasibility, and professional qualifications. The grant program does not fund dissertation research, international travel, multi-year projects, or conferences not initiated by the Institute.

Mini-Grants: Small amounts of funding (up to $5,000) are provided to meet special needs which, without support, would prevent untenured junior faculty researchers from pursuing the project. The funding can go towards summer compensation, to acquire special data sets, meet unusual computer processing or programming needs, or to cover travel to collect primary data. Special consideration will be given to those who use data from the Institute's "Employment Research Data Center". The authors are expected to submit their paper to a reputable journal, and to prepare a synopsis of their research for consideration as an article in the Institute's newsletter, "Employment Research".
EIN: 381360419

6168
The V Foundation
106 Towerview Ct.
Cary, NC   27513   (919) 380-9505
Contact: Nicholas P. Valvano, C.E.O.
FAX: (919) 380-0025; E-mail: info@jimmyv.org;
Additional tel.: (800) 454-6698; URL: http://
www.jimmyv.org

Foundation type: Public charity
Limitations: Research grants to support researchers at National Cancer Institute-designated facilities and selected institutions.
Publications: Annual report; Financial statement; Grants list; Informational brochure; Newsletter.
Financial data: Year ended 09/30/2004.
Assets, $13,145,195 (M); Expenditures, $4,896,972; Total giving, $3,209,570; Grants to individuals, 28 grants totaling $3,209,570.
Fields of interest: Cancer research.
Type of support: Research.
Application information: Application form not required.
Initial approach: Letter.
Applicants should submit the following:
  1) Proposal
  2) Letter(s) of recommendation
EIN: 133705951

6169
The Willard A. Van Engel Fellowship, Inc.
c/o VIMS, Dir.
P.O. Box 1346
Gloucester Point, VA   23062

Foundation type: Independent foundation
Limitations: Research fellowships to third and fourth year students at the Virginia Institute of Marine Sciences of the College of William and Mary, VA, who are concerned with crustacean biology.
Financial data: Year ended 06/30/2005.
Assets, $397,530 (M); Expenditures, $25,390; Total giving, $15,248; Grants to individuals, totaling $15,248.
Fields of interest: Marine science.
Type of support: Fellowships; Research; Support to graduates or students of specific schools.
Application information: Applications accepted. Application form required.
Initial approach: Letter or telephone.
Deadline(s): None
EIN: 541401233

6170
The Ann & Erlo Van Waveren Foundation, Inc.
210 E. 86th St., Ste. 204
New York, NY   10128   (212) 517-0060
Contact: Olivier Bernier, Pres.
FAX: (212) 876-0886; E-mail: obernier@aol.com

Foundation type: Independent foundation
Limitations: Grants for research, book projects, and the presentation of public programs related to Jungian psychology. No grants are given to undergraduates or for educational expenses.
Financial data: Year ended 12/31/2004.
Assets, $691,943 (M); Expenditures, $179,429; Total giving, $30,000; Grants to individuals, totaling $5,000.
Fields of interest: Psychology/behavioral science.
Type of support: Program development; Publication; Research.
Application information: Deadline Dec. 31; Contact foundation for current application guidelines; Initial approach by letter or telephone.
EIN: 133343738

6171
Vanguard Public Foundation
383 Rhode Island St., Ste. 301
San Francisco, CA   94103   (415) 487-2111
Contact: Hari Dillon, Pres.
FAX: (415) 487-2124;
E-mail: grants@vanguardsf.org; URL: http://
www.vanguardsf.org/

Foundation type: Public charity
Limitations: Sabbatical awards to outstanding community activists and leaders in northern CA and the Central Valley area to allow them to take a break from their overwhelming responsibilities.
Publications: Application guidelines; Annual report; Financial statement.
Financial data: Year ended 03/31/2004.
Assets, $2,466,794 (M); Expenditures, $3,508,621; Total giving, $169,619; Grant to an individual, 1 grant totaling $14,500.
Fields of interest: International human rights; Civil rights, advocacy.
Type of support: Awards/prizes.
Application information: Applications accepted. Application form required. Application form available on the grantmaker's Web site.
Deadline(s): Dec. 15

Additional information: Contact foundation for current application guidelines.
Program description:
  Social Justice Sabbatical Fund: Provides three- to four-month sabbatical awards of $12,000 to community leaders and activists who have made outstanding contributions and are in need of rest and rejuvenation.
EIN: 942369262

6172
Virginia Foundation for the Humanities
(also known as Virginia Foundation for the Humanities and Public Policy)
145 Ednam Dr.
Charlottesville, VA   22903-4629
(434) 924-3296
FAX: (434) 296-4714; E-mail: vfhinfo@virginia.edu;
URL: http://www.virginia.edu/VFH
http://www.virginiafoundation.org

Foundation type: Public charity
Limitations: Fellowships to individuals for research at the Center for the Humanities in Charlottesville, VA, and grants to non-profits engaged in the humanities.
Publications: Application guidelines; Annual report; Informational brochure (including application guidelines); Newsletter.
Financial data: Year ended 06/30/2004.
Assets, $3,105,104 (M); Expenditures, $2,535,553; Total giving, $471,938.
Fields of interest: Humanities.
Type of support: Seed money; Fellowships; Research.
Application information: Application form required.
Initial approach: Letter or telephone.
Deadline(s): Vary.
Program description:
  Center for the Humanities: Fellows are provided with offices, library privileges at the University of Virginia, modest administrative support, and a maximum stipend of $3,500 per month at the Center for the Humanities. Residencies range from one month to one semester. Affiliated and independent scholars, teachers, museum, government, library, media, and other professionals are encouraged to apply. All Fellows must be in residence at VFH.
EIN: 541435523

6173
Viz Dom Foundation
89 Country Club Dr.
Chula Vista, CA   91911-1401

Foundation type: Independent foundation
Limitations: Scholarships to residents of Croatia for technical, medical, and language studies.
Financial data: Year ended 12/31/2004.
Assets, $948,905 (M); Expenditures, $37,317; Total giving, $30,377; Grants to individuals, totaling $30,377.
Fields of interest: Language (foreign); Medical school/education; Engineering/technology.
Type of support: Foreign applicants; Graduate support; Technical education support; Undergraduate support.
Application information: Deadline July 15; Completion of formal application required; Applications are submitted to the Ministry of Education in Croatia.
EIN: 330516587

6174
VNA Foundation

(formerly Visiting Nurse Association of Chicago)
20 N. Wacker Dr., Ste. 3118
Chicago, IL   60606   (312) 214-1521
Contact: Robert N. DiLeonardi, Exec. Dir.
FAX: (312) 214-1529; E-mail: vnafund@aol.com;
URL: http://www.vnafoundation.net

Foundation type: Independent foundation
Limitations: Grants by nomination only to RN's who are practicing community/public health in Chicago or Cook, DuPage, Kane, Lake, McHenry or Will counties, IL.
Publications: Application guidelines; Annual report (including application guidelines); Grants list.
Financial data: Year ended 06/30/2005.
Assets, $465,569,268 (M); Expenditures, $2,528,304; Total giving, $1,812,833; Grants to individuals, 5 grants totaling $33,000 (high: $25,000, low: $1,000).
Fields of interest: Public health; Nursing care.
Type of support: Awards/grants by nomination only; Awards/prizes.
Application information: Application form required. Application form available on the grantmaker's Web site.
  Initial approach: Telephone, Web site or nomination form.
  Deadline(s): May 11
  Applicants should submit the following:
    1) Resume
    2) Curriculum vitae
    3) Letter(s) of recommendation
  Additional information: Completion of formal nomination required; Interviews required; Applications by fax or e-mail not accepted; Nominees notified by June 1; See Web site for further information.
Program description:
  Super Star in Community Nursing Award: Nominees must exhibit innovation and creativity, client advocacy, and client care. The award of up to $25,000 may be used for any purpose.
EIN: 362167943

6175
Dr. Ludwig Von Sallmann Memorial Fund Trust

c/o PNC Bank, N.A.
P.O. Box 96202
Washington, DC   20090-6202
Application address: Dr. Peter Gouras, Dept. of Ophthalmology, c/o Columbia University, College of Physicians and Surgeons, 630 W. 168th St., New York, NY 10032, tel.: (212) 305-5688

Foundation type: Independent foundation
Limitations: Prizes by nomination only awarded biennially to individuals for outstanding research in vision and ophthalmology.
Financial data: Year ended 12/31/2004.
Assets, $752,560 (M); Expenditures, $77,613; Total giving, $60,000; Grant to an individual, 1 grant totaling $60,000.
Fields of interest: Eye research.
Type of support: Research; Awards/grants by nomination only.
Application information: Application form required.
  Deadline(s): Mar. 1
  Additional information: Application must include description of nominee's achievements, curriculum vitae, and biography.
EIN: 521224404

6176
Wacker Foundation

8523 Thackery, No. 1115
Dallas, TX   75225   (214) 373-3308
Contact: John A. Wacker, Pres.

Foundation type: Independent foundation
Limitations: Research grants pertaining to the neurophysiological aspects of learning and behavior disorders.
Financial data: Year ended 12/31/2004.
Assets, $1,077,348 (M); Expenditures, $95,166; Total giving, $64,019; Grants to individuals, 3 grants totaling $64,019.
Fields of interest: Mental health, disorders; Neuroscience; Medical research, institute; Learning disorders research; Psychology/behavioral science.
Type of support: Fellowships; Research.
Application information:
  Deadline(s): None
  Applicants should submit the following:
    1) Proposal
    2) Budget Information
  Additional information: Applications should be sent by letter.
EIN: 237412635

6177
Waitt Family Foundation

P.O. Box 1948
La Jolla, CA   92037-1948   (858) 551-4400
Contact: Al Panico, C.A.O. and Dir., Grants
FAX: (858) 551-6871;
E-mail: grants@waittfoundation.org; Application address: c/o Siouxland Chapter, P.O. Box 1397, North Sioux City, SD 57049, tel.: (605) 232-9929; FAX: (605) 232-9486; URL: http://www.waittfoundation.org/

Foundation type: Independent foundation
Limitations: Awards to teachers and students for innovative ideas that enhance education in the classroom in the tri-state region of SD, NE and IA.
Financial data: Year ended 12/31/2003.
Assets, $157,342,483 (M); Expenditures, $8,652,514; Total giving, $6,549,647; Grants to individuals, 409 grants totaling $360,982 (high: $6,048, low: $42, average grant: $250-$2,500).
Fields of interest: Education.
Type of support: Awards/prizes; Precollege support.
Application information: Contact foundation for current application deadline; Completion of formal application required; Applications available on Web site.
Program descriptions:
  Teacher Recognition & Project Grant Awards: Project grants are awarded to teachers who propose an innovative classroom project that requires technology purchases. Each year, the program recognizes a number of teachers with financial awards:
    · Technology Innovator Awards: $2,500 each at a maximum of four awards
    · Technology Project Awards: Amounts and number of awards vary
To be eligible for either award, teachers must: 1. Teach high school full-time at Sioux City North, East, West, Central Campus, Heelan, South Sioux City, Sgt. Bluff-Luton or Dakota Valley, or at a middle or elementary school preparing students for one of the four named high schools. 2. Submit a PowerPoint portfolio or grant proposal (PowerPoint slides must be presented on a "zip" disk; slides must be developed in black and white with no graphics. 3. Not have previously received a major national or

state recognition award, or have a prior Waitt Family Foundation award of $2,500 or more (restriction applies only to applicants for Technology Innovator Award). 4. Sign a release form giving the foundation the right to publish their award-winning entries. For program details, including deadlines and selection process, see Web site.
  Student Education Essay Awards: A maximum of 10 awards of $500 each is presented to recognize innovative ideas, from high school students in their junior or senior year, that advance educational instruction and processes. The program challenges students to review their education to date and provide ideas that will improve instruction for tomorrow's students. The program also encourages students to "step into the teacher's shoes" by suggesting ideas that can improve classroom learning for years to come. Each year, the program recognizes a number of students with financial awards. To be eligible, students must:
    · Attend a "participating" high school at Sioux City North, East, West, Central Campus, Heelan, South Sioux City, Sgt. Bluff-Luton, or Dakota Valley
    · Presently be a junior or senior in a participating school
    · Submit a typed essay entitled "How I Would Improve Education." Essay must be from three to five pages long, double-spaced at 12 pt. font and submitted to high school teacher designated to administer essays for participating school. All essays should identify areas of their education that they view as positive and beneficial, those areas that need improvement, and make reasonable suggestions to correct those areas needed for improvement in public education. Participating schools will review all essays and submit the top five quality essays from each school to the Waitt Family Foundation for review by the selection committee
For program details, including deadlines and Selection process, see Web site.
EIN: 460428166

6178
Wal-Mart Foundation

(also known as SAM'S CLUB Foundation)
702 S.W. 8th St.
Bentonville, AR   72716-0150   (800) 530-9925
Contact: Brad Fisher, Dir.
FAX: (479) 273-6850; URL: http://www.walmartfoundation.org

Foundation type: Company-sponsored foundation
Limitations: Awards by nomination only to outstanding teachers throughout the U.S. and in areas where Wal-Mart stores or SAM'S CLUBS are in operation.
Publications: Informational brochure.
Financial data: Year ended 01/31/2005.
Assets, $18,881,075 (M); Expenditures, $155,212,734; Total giving, $154,537,406; Grants to individuals, 98 grants totaling $503,501 (high: $100,000, low: $1).
Fields of interest: Education.
Type of support: Awards/grants by nomination only; Awards/prizes.
Application information: Application form required.
  Deadline(s): Mar. 7
  Additional information: See www.pdkintl.org to download nomination form.
Program description:
  Teacher Award: Winning teachers receive a $1,000 educational grant to benefit their local school and an honorary Wal-Mart greeter's vest.

They also have the opportunity to apply for the state and national Teacher of the Year honors.
EIN: 716107283

6179
Walther Cancer Institute and Foundation, Inc.

3202 N. Meridian St.
Indianapolis, IN   46208-4646   (317) 921-2040
Contact: Fred Haslam, Exec. V.P.
For fellowships: Peggy Weber, Dir. of Prog. Devel.,
Tel.: (317) 274-7563, E-mail: bcog@walther.org
FAX: (317) 924-4688;
E-mail: fhaslam@walther.org; URL: http://www.walther.org

Foundation type: Public charity
Limitations: Fellowships to those who have behavioral research interests in the area of cancer research.
Publications: Annual report; Newsletter; Program policy statement.
Financial data: Year ended 06/30/2005.
Assets, $54,754,154 (M); Expenditures, $4,946,422; Total giving, $3,179,147; Grants to individuals, 16 grants totaling $164,050 (high: $30,000, low: $750).
Fields of interest: Cancer; Cancer research.
Type of support: Fellowships; Research.
Application information:
    Initial approach: E-mail.
    Additional information: Contact foundation for further application information.
Program descriptions:
    Mary Margaret Walther Program for Cancer Care Research: The mission of the Mary Margaret Walther Program for Cancer Care Research is to conduct behavioral research related to cancer care across the cancer continuum. It is important that this research integrate the specific talents of a variety of disciplines including, communication, dentistry, epidemiology, health services research, medicine, nursing, nutrition, pharmacy, psychology, public health, religion, sociology, and others. Of continuing importance is that the program be concerned with developing scientists who can, through research, training, become our future research scientists.
    Walther Fellowship: Walther Cancer Institute promotes learning in the cancer care continuum through fellowship and scholarship programs. This program establishes a yearlong fellowship for a postdoctoral student at one of the Walther-affiliated universities. This method of scholarship has proven very effective throughout the years and gives students direct contact with Walther scientists.
EIN: 351650570

6180
Washington Education Foundation

8610 N. 19th Ave.
Phoenix, AZ   85021-4294   (602) 347-4294
Contact: Thomas Pynn, Pres.; For Mini-grants: Lori Walk
FAX: (602) 347-2708;
E-mail: wesdfoundation@cox.net; URL: http://www.wesdfoundation.com

Foundation type: Public charity
Limitations: Grants to teachers in the Washington School District in Phoenix, AZ, area for the educational benefit of students in their classrooms.
Financial data: Year ended 06/30/2004.
Assets, $54,137 (M); Expenditures, $15,223;

Total giving, $11,966; Grants to individuals, 25 grants totaling $11,966 (high: $500, low: $368).
Fields of interest: Elementary/secondary education.
Type of support: Grants to individuals.
Application information: Applications accepted. Application form required. Application form available on the grantmaker's Web site.
    Deadline(s): Nov. 18 and Apr. 21
EIN: 860650710

6181
The Washington Post Company Educational Foundation

1150 15th St. N.W.
Washington, DC   20071
Contact: Tito Tolentino, Grants Coord.
Note: Applications not accepted

Foundation type: Company-sponsored foundation
Limitations: Awards by nomination only for educational leadership and excellence in teaching.
Financial data: Year ended 12/31/2004.
Assets, $44,799 (M); Expenditures, $599,271; Total giving, $236,932; Grants to individuals, 58 grants totaling $65,800 (high: $3,000, low: $400).
Fields of interest: Education; Leadership development.
Type of support: Awards/grants by nomination only; Awards/prizes.
Application information: Applications not accepted.
EIN: 521545926

6182
Waterford Foundation

1396 W. Herndon, Ste. 101
Fresno, CA   93711   (559) 436-0900
Contact: Dariush Assemi, C.E.O.

Foundation type: Independent foundation
Limitations: Donations to detectives and other professionals who support economically disadvantaged individuals and the Muslim community of the Fresno, CA, area.
Financial data: Year ended 12/31/2004.
Assets, $4,855,393 (M); Expenditures, $748,513; Total giving, $729,745.
Fields of interest: Islam; Economically disadvantaged.
Type of support: Grants to individuals.
Application information: Contact foundation for current application deadlines/guidelines.
EIN: 770437521

6183
Waterford Foundation for Public Education

P.O. Box 300681
Waterford, MI   48330-0681
Contact: Mary Lou Simmons, Pres.
URL: http://www.waterford.k12.mi.us/foundation/

Foundation type: Public charity
Limitations: Grants to teachers of the Waterford School District, MI, to fund educational enrichment programs.
Publications: Annual report; Financial statement.
Financial data: Year ended 06/30/2005.
Assets, $1,001,858 (M); Expenditures, $125,359; Total giving, $55,613; Grants to individuals, 3 grants totaling $7,500 (high: $2,500, low: $2,500).

Fields of interest: Elementary/secondary education.
Type of support: Project support.
Application information: Applications accepted.
    Initial approach: Letter.
    Deadline(s): Mar. 15
    Applicants should submit the following:
        1) Proposal
    Additional information: See Web site for further program information.
EIN: 382528009

6184
Richard Waterman Trust

c/o Tillinghast, Licht & Semonoff
10 Weybosset St.
Providence, RI   02903
Contact: Walter D. Waterman III, Mgr.
Application address: 493 Pleasant Valley Pkwy., Providence, RI 02908

Foundation type: Independent foundation
Limitations: Support to Baptist churches and individuals preaching the Calvinist Baptist doctrine within three miles of the late Richard Waterman's house in Greene, RI and also Coventry and Foster, RI.
Publications: Annual report.
Financial data: Year ended 12/31/2004.
Assets, $3,018,933 (M); Expenditures, $168,163; Total giving, $81,600; Grants to individuals, 2 grants totaling $23,100.
Fields of interest: Christian agencies & churches.
Type of support: Grants to individuals.
Application information: Application form not required.
    Initial approach: Letter.
    Copies of proposal: 1
    Deadline(s): None
    Applicants should submit the following:
        1) Proposal
    Additional information: Unsolicited applications from persons who have not established a reputation for preaching in the local area are rarely, if ever, granted.
EIN: 056040728

6185
The Thomas J. Watson Fellowship Program

(formerly The Thomas J. Watson Foundation)
293 S. Main St.
Providence, RI   02903-2910
Contact: Beverly Larson, Exec. Dir.
E-mail: TJW@WatsonFellowship.org; URL: http://www.watsonfellowship.org

Foundation type: Independent foundation
Limitations: Fellowships by nomination only to graduating seniors of specified colleges and universities for independent study and travel. Nominees must attend one of the specified colleges listed in program description.
Publications: Informational brochure.
Financial data: Year ended 05/31/2004.
Assets, $71,872,477 (M); Expenditures, $3,775,938; Total giving, $2,243,376.
Fields of interest: Leadership development.
Type of support: Fellowships; Support to graduates or students of specific schools; Awards/grants by nomination only; Undergraduate support; Travel grants.
Application information:
    Deadline(s): 1st Tues. in Nov.

Additional information: Individual applications not accepted; Completion of formal nomination required, including proposed plan of study, personal statement, two letters of recommendation, recent photograph, and college transcripts; On-campus interviews required during the late fall and winter.

Program descriptions:

Thomas J. Watson Fellowship Program: Enables up to 50 college graduates of unusual promise to engage in an initial postgraduate year of independent study and travel abroad. Candidates devise a focused and disciplined plan of travel. The experience is viewed as a break in which they might explore a particular interest, view their lives and American society in greater perspective, and develop a more informed sense of international concern. It is not intended for the Fellows to engage in extended formal study at a foreign university. It is intended to provide Fellows with an opportunity to immerse themselves in cultures other than their own for an entire year. A grant of $25,000 is provided for each Fellow ($35,000 for a Fellow accompanied by a dependent spouse or child). In the selection of Watson Fellows, individuals who demonstrate integrity, strong ethical character, intelligence, the capacity for vision and leadership, and potential for humane and effective participation in the world community are sought. A candidate's academic record, while not of primary importance, is considered together with those extracurricular activities that reflect both initiative and a commitment to his or her particular area of interest. The candidate's proposed project should involve investigation into an area of demonstrated concern and personal commitment. Furthermore, because the year's experience should not involve extended formal study at a foreign university or repeat earlier experiences, the project should be one which may be pursued with great independence and adaptability. In short, the project should be creative, feasible, and personally significant. The following institutions are invited to nominate candidates: Amherst College, Bates College, Berea College, Bowdoin College, Bryn Mawr College, California Institute of Technology, Carleton College, Colby College, Colgate University, The College of the Atlantic, College of the Holy Cross, The College of Wooster, Colorado College, Connecticut College, Davidson College, Earlham College, Grinnell College, Hamilton College, Harvey Mudd College, Haverford College, Hendrix College, Lawrence University, Macalester College, Middlebury College, Oberlin College, Occidental College, Pitzer College, Pomona College, Reed College, Rhode Island School of Design, Rhodes College, Rice University, Sarah Lawrence College, Scripps College, Spelman College, Swarthmore College, Union College, University of Puget Sound, The University of the South, Ursinus College, Vassar College, Washington and Lee University, Wellesley College, Wesleyan University, Wheaton College, Whitman College, Willamette University, and Williams College.

Jeanette K. Watson Summer Fellowships: This program builds on the experience of the Thomas J. Watson Fellowships and other selective awards that aim to develop talent, leadership, and motivation.
EIN: 136038151

6186
K. B. Weissman Foundation, Inc.
225 Westchester Ave.
Port Chester, NY 10573 (914) 937-6672

Foundation type: Operating foundation

Limitations: Grants to individuals for medical research, primarily in the New York, NY metropolitan area.
Financial data: Year ended 10/31/2003. Assets, $1,885; Expenditures, $6,104; Total giving, $3,275.
Fields of interest: Health care, research.
Type of support: Research.
Application information: Applications by letter accepted throughout the year.
EIN: 136161027

6187
The Robert A. Welch Foundation
5555 San Felipe, Ste. 1900
Houston, TX 77056-2732 (713) 961-9884
Contact: Norbert Dittrich, Pres.
FAX: (713) 961-5168; E-mail: dittrich@welch1.org;
URL: http://www.welch1.org

Foundation type: Independent foundation
Limitations: Awards by nomination only for basic chemistry research at educational institutions in TX.
Publications: Application guidelines; Annual report; Newsletter.
Financial data: Year ended 08/31/2005. Assets, $611,141,615 (M); Expenditures, $31,955,362; Total giving, $27,393,359; Grants to individuals, totaling $797,944.
Fields of interest: Chemistry.
Type of support: Awards/grants by nomination only; Awards/prizes.
Application information:
Initial approach: Letter.
Deadline(s): Contact foundation for current application deadline
Additional information: Individual applications not accepted; See program description for nomination guidelines.
Program descriptions:

Robert A. Welch Award in Chemistry: This award is granted to foster and encourage basic chemical research and to recognize, in a substantial manner, the value of chemical research with respect to the betterment of humankind. Generally, one award in the amount of $300,000 is given annually. The award may be omitted in any award period during which the Scientific Advisory Board and the Board of Directors are of the opinion that truly meritorious nominations have not been received. Nominations may be made by one of several chemistry and scientific organizations as well as by individuals, and should include a brief biographical sketch of the nominee, a list of 25 of the nominee's most important scientific publications, an outline of the nominee's contributions to research in chemistry, and three seconding letters of nomination. No direct application or self-nomination is accepted.

The Norman Hackerman Award in Chemical Research: This award is to encourage and recognize young chemical scientists in Texas for their past research endeavors.
EIN: 760343128

6188
Rob and Bessie Welder Wildlife Foundation
P.O. Box 1400
Sinton, TX 78387-1400 (361) 364-2643
Contact: D. Lynn Drawe, Dir.
FAX: (361) 364-2650; E-mail: welderwf@aol.com;
URL: http://hometown.aol.com/welderwf/welderweb.html

Foundation type: Operating foundation

Limitations: Fellowships to M.S. and Ph.D. candidates at accredited U.S. and Canadian colleges and universities to support research and further graduate-level education in wildlife problems and conservation, and to develop scientific methods for increasing wildlife populations.
Publications: Application guidelines; Biennial report; Informational brochure (including application guidelines); Multi-year report.
Financial data: Year ended 12/31/2004. Assets, $25,517,312 (M); Expenditures, $1,193,374; Total giving, $125,924; Grants to individuals, 13 grants totaling $125,924 (high: $18,520, low: $778).
Fields of interest: Animals/wildlife, preservation/protection.
Type of support: Fellowships; Internship funds.
Application information: Application form required. Application form available on the grantmaker's Web site.
Initial approach: Letter.
Copies of proposal: 2
Deadline(s): Oct. 1
Applicants should submit the following:
1) GPA
2) Budget Information
3) Proposal
4) Letter(s) of recommendation
5) Transcripts
Additional information: Application should also include GRE scores, timetable and biographical data.
Program description:

Fellowships: Applicants must be full-time students with a minimum GRE score of 1100 and at least a "B" average for the past two years of graduate or undergraduate study. Fellowship recipients may not receive any other financial assistance during the term of the fellowship, with the exception of GI Bill benefits. Recipients who are pursuing M.S. degrees receive a stipend of $1,300 per month. Recipients pursuing Ph.D. degrees receive a stipend of $1,400 a month. Stipends cover living expenses, tuition, fees, and books. In addition, all recipients receive up to $1,200 per year for travel expenses, or a prorated amount based on the number of months in which the recipient receives fellowship support. Recipients who are near the foundation will have access to a dormitory apartment, utilities, and available lab and field facilities. Project budgets cannot include overhead or indirect costs. If equipment is purchased with these funds, it will become the property of the foundation upon completion of the project. Project budgets can allow for expenses incurred up to $500 for one visit from the supervising professor to the research site. Also, the foundation will reimburse recipients for travel to one professional meeting at which he or she presents a paper. If permits are required to take specimens from the refuge, students and their professor must take responsibility for this. Progress reports and transcripts must be submitted biannually during the fellowship. After completion of the fellowship, student must provide the foundation with five 35mm slides showing the activities undertaken during the fellowship, and at least one cloth-bound copy of the final thesis for the library. A second copy of the thesis is also desired, although not required by the foundation. Students are responsible for printing and binding costs for the final thesis.
EIN: 741381321

6189
Wenner-Gren Foundation for Anthropological Research, Inc.
470 Park Ave. S., 8th Fl.
New York, NY 10016 (212) 683-5000
FAX: (212) 683-9151;
E-mail: inquiries@wennergren.org; URL: http://www.wennergren.org

Foundation type: Operating foundation
Limitations: Research grants, fellowships, and conference grants to scholars holding or enrolled for doctoral degrees in anthropology, for basic or dissertation research in all branches of anthropology, including cultural/social anthropology, ethnology, biological/physical anthropology, archaeology, anthropological linguistics, and related disciplines concerned with human origins, development, and variation.
Publications: Application guidelines; Annual report; Annual report (including application guidelines); Grants list; Informational brochure.
Financial data: Year ended 12/31/2004. Assets, $138,297,947 (M); Expenditures, $7,171,680; Total giving, $3,305,328; Grants to individuals, totaling $3,305,328.
Fields of interest: History/archaeology; Language/linguistics; Anthropology/sociology.
Type of support: Conferences/seminars; Publication; Seed money; Fellowships; Research; Awards/prizes; Postdoctoral support; Doctoral support.
Application information: Application form required. Application form available on the grantmaker's Web site.
Initial approach: Initial approach by letter or telephone.
Deadline(s): May 1 and Nov. 1 for Individual Research Grants
Additional information: Applications must be initiated at least nine months in advance of date of proposed research for fellowships; No set deadlines for other grants; Notification in six to eight months.
Program descriptions:
Individual Research Grants: Grants are available for basic research in all branches of anthropology. The foundation particularly invites projects employing comparative perspectives or integrating two or more subfields of anthropology. Under this program, the foundation offers Post-Ph.D. Grants, Dissertation Fieldwork Grants, and a limited number of Richard Carley Hunt Postdoctoral Fellowships.
Post-Ph.D. Grants: Grants of up to $25,000 are awarded to individual scholars holding the doctorate or equivalent qualification in anthropology or a related discipline. Qualified scholars are eligible without regard to nationality or institutional affiliation.
Dissertation Fieldwork Grants: Grants of up to $25,000 are awarded to individuals to aid dissertation or thesis research. Application must be made jointly with a thesis advisor or other scholar who will undertake responsibility for supervising the project. Awards are contingent upon the applicant's successful completion of all requirements for the degree other than the dissertation/thesis. Qualified students of all nationalities are eligible.
Richard Carley Hunt Memorial Postdoctoral Fellowships: Fellowships of up to $40,000 are awarded to scholars within ten years of receipt of the doctorate, to aid write-up of research results for publication. Qualified scholars are eligible without regard to nationality or institutional affiliation.
Professional Development International Award: These grants of up to $15,000 per year at the predoctoral level and $35,000 at the postdoctoral

level, are renewable for two years, are intended for scholars and advanced students from developing countries seeking additional training in anthropology, to enhance their skills or to expand or develop their areas of expertise. Candidates may pursue either a course of study leading to a degree or a specific nondegree plan for obtaining advanced training in any qualified institution in the world where appropriate training is available. Support is not normally provided for master's degree studies. Applications from students who have already had extensive training abroad will receive lower priority. Inquiries should be made by means of a one-page summary of purpose.
Conference Grants: Grants of up to $15,000 are available to the organizer(s) of conferences, which may be used to supplement other sources of support. Priority is given to working conferences that address research issues in anthropology and that provide for intensive interaction among participants. Symposia within larger professional meetings, lectures, and public events are generally not supported.
International Collaborative Research Grants: Grants of up to $30,000 a.e available to assist anthropological research projects undertaken jointly by two or more investigators from different countries. The purpose of the program is to encourage collaborations in which the principal investigators bring different and complementary perspectives, knowledge, and/or skills. Priority is given to those projects involving at least one principal investigator from outside North America and Western Europe, but other international collaborations will be considered. Both investigators must meet the qualification for Regular Grants (i.e., holding the doctorate or equivalent in anthropology or a related discipline)
EIN: 131813827

6190
West Foundation
P.O. Box 1675
Wichita Falls, TX 76307-1675
Contact: Reece A. West, Pres.

Foundation type: Independent foundation
Limitations: Awards by nomination only for excellence in teaching and leadership in public education in the Wichita Falls Independent School District, TX.
Financial data: Year ended 09/30/2004. Assets, $19,826,182 (M); Expenditures, $1,040,744; Total giving, $843,347; Grants to individuals, 20 grants totaling $70,000 (high: $3,500, low: $3,500).
Fields of interest: Education.
Type of support: Support to graduates or students of specific schools; Awards/grants by nomination only; Awards/prizes.
Application information: Applications not accepted.
Additional information: Awards by nomination only.
EIN: 237332105

6191
West Virginia Humanities Council, Inc.
1310 Kanawha Blvd. E.
Charleston, WV 25301-2703 (304) 346-8500
Contact: Kenneth Sullivan, Exec. Dir.
FAX: (304) 346-8504;
E-mail: sullivan@wvhumanities.org; URL: http://www.wvhumanities.org

Foundation type: Public charity

Limitations: Fellowships to humanities scholars for research support, and project grants to professors in WV.
Publications: Application guidelines; Annual report; Informational brochure; Newsletter.
Financial data: Year ended 10/31/2004. Assets, $1,392,961 (M); Expenditures, $1,273,229; Total giving, $456,246.
Fields of interest: Humanities; Education.
Type of support: Program development; Fellowships.
Application information: Applications accepted. Application form required.
Deadline(s): Vary.
Additional information: See Web site for complete application guidelines and forms.
Program descriptions:
Fellowships Program: Fellowships of up to $2,500 awarded on an annual basis to humanities scholars to provide support for individual research within a humanities discipline. The program offers opportunities for advanced study that will enhance scholars' capacities as teachers or interpreters of the humanities. Deadline Feb. 1.
Teacher Institutes Grants: Grants of up to $20,000 to college and university professors to develop and implement summer seminars on humanities topics suited to the teaching needs of elementary or secondary teachers. Deadline Sept. 1.
EIN: 550553594

6192
Western European Architecture Foundation
306 W. Sunset, Ste. 119
San Antonio, TX 78209
Contact: P.J. Fleming, Pres.

Foundation type: Independent foundation
Limitations: Prizes awarded to architects and students of architecture to study the preservation and construction of Western European and French Classical architecture in France.
Financial data: Year ended 12/31/2003. Assets, $1,845,084 (M); Expenditures, $119,969; Total giving, $10,000; Grants to individuals, 2 grants totaling $10,000 (high: $7,500, low: $2,500).
Fields of interest: Architecture.
Type of support: Awards/prizes.
Application information: Deadline Jan. 10; Application by letter detailing the amount of money requested and the specific use to which it will be applied.
Program description:
Gabriel Prize: Recipients shall either be owners of property which are examples of western European or French classical architecture (Board Opinion), or students of classical architecture who wish to study classical methods. Students are judged on their academic and practical experience. Owners are judged on their financial needs and their willingness to make property available for public inspection and study by architects, historians, and others in accordance with the foundation's goals. Recipients receive support for three months of study in France.
EIN: 742553016

6193
Wexner Foundation
8000 Walton Pkwy., Ste. 100
New Albany, OH   43054   (614) 939-6060
Contact: Larry Moses, Pres.
FAX: (614) 939-6066;
E-mail: info@wexnerfoundation.org; URL: http://
www.wexnerfoundation.org

Foundation type: Independent foundation
Limitations: Fellowships for Jewish religious
studies in North America. Fellowships to Israeli
government officials for study at Harvard
University's John F. Kennedy School of
Government.
Publications: Informational brochure; Program
policy statement.
Financial data: Year ended 12/31/2004.
Assets, $1,955,993 (M); Expenditures,
$9,621,276; Total giving, $5,178,016; Grants to
individuals, 133 grants totaling $822,417 (high:
$8,333, low: $1,083, average grant:
$6,667-$7,750).
Fields of interest: Government/public
administration; Leadership development; Jewish
agencies & temples.
Type of support: Fellowships; Support to graduates
or students of specific schools; Foreign applicants.
Application information: Application form required.
Initial approach: Letter.
Copies of proposal: 3
Deadline(s): Feb. 1 for Wexner Graduate
Fellowships, Dec. 15 for Wexner-Israel
Fellowships
Applicants should submit the following:
1) Essay
2) Transcripts
3) Letter(s) of recommendation
Additional information: Application should
include recent photograph, GRE scores, and
acceptance letter from graduate institution
applicant is attending; Israeli applicants must
also submit scores from a standardized
English proficiency test.
Program descriptions:
Wexner-Israel Fellowship Program: The program
enables up to ten Israeli government officials to
study for an M.A. at Harvard University's John F.
Kennedy School of Government. The goal of the
program is to provide Israel's next generation of
leaders with advanced public management training.
The program is open to outstanding Israeli
government and municipal officials and
professionals in other areas of the public sector
such as the Bank of Israel, the Israel Broadcast
Authority, the National Insurance Institute, and
Ports Authority. These officials should:
· have at least five years of substantial
professional experience in the public
sector or in public interest organizations
and be committed to careers in the public
interest
· have a professional career reflecting
significant demonstrated ability to perform
well in a rigorous, interdisciplinary
academic program
· pass a required English examination
showing language ability sufficient to meet
Harvard's standards
· be likely to achieve important leadership
positions in Israel upon their return
Recipients also obligate themselves to at least one
year's continued service in the Israeli public sector.
The fellowship covers tuition, fees, health
insurance, books, travel from Israel, and limited
moving costs. A living stipend of $1,600 per month
for single students or $2,000 per month for
participants with accompanying spouses is also

provided. Families with children will receive an
additional $200 per child per month. Living
stipends are subject to U.S. taxes. Fellowships are
for an 11-month period during which the Fellows will
complete the Mid-Career Master's in Public
Administration Program. This includes the Summer
Program and Foundation-sponsored seminars. The
Kennedy School ensures its students access to
courses in all the faculties of the University (Law,
Business, Arts & Sciences, Public Health, Media),
as well as to the Massachusetts Institute of
Technology and the Fletcher School of Law and
Diplomacy. Fellows will have access to all the
resources of Harvard University.
Wexner Graduate Fellowship Program: The
program is designed to attract the most promising
and talented Jewish men and women to prepare for
careers of professional Jewish leadership. The
leadership areas designated for Wexner Graduate
Fellows are: the rabbinate, the cantorate, Jewish
studies, Jewish communal service, and Jewish
education. The program provides generous
stipends for graduate study for two-year periods
which are renewable for a second two-year term.
Fellows will be expected to engage in full-time
graduate study with no independent employment
during the academic year. Fellows will also be
expected to participate in special programs held
during the course of the year and an annual
interdisciplinary institute, sponsored by the
foundation.
EIN: 237320631

6194
The Whitaker Foundation
1700 N. Moore St., Ste. 2200
Arlington, VA   22209   (703) 528-2430
Contact: Peter G. Katona Sc.D., C.E.O. and Pres.
E-mail: info@whitaker.org; URL: http://
www.whitaker.org

Foundation type: Independent foundation
Limitations: Research grants, fellowships and
internships to individuals in the U.S. or Canada in
the field of biomedical engineering.
Publications: Annual report.
Financial data: Year ended 12/31/2004.
Assets, $123,003,762 (M); Expenditures,
$67,071,768; Total giving, $63,876,625.
Fields of interest: Biomedicine research.
Type of support: Fellowships; Internship funds;
Research; Postdoctoral support; Graduate support;
Undergraduate support; Doctoral support.
Application information: Applications not
accepted.
Program description:
*Biomedical Engineering Summer Internship
Program:* In a partnership of the National Institute
of Health (NIH), a Biomedical Engineering Summer
Internship Program (BESIP) is being offered at the
NIH. This 10-week summer program (June 9 through
Aug. 15,) allows undergraduate biomedical
engineering students to participate, under the
mentorship of world class scientists in cutting edge
biomedical research projects in NIH laboratories in
Bethesda, MD. Please note: the BESIP is separate
from the NIH Summer Internship Program (SIP) in
Biomedical Research. Selected by a nationwide
competition, the 12 to 16 interns will have the
opportunity to indicate preferences from a list of
available NIH projects that involve areas of
engineering or physical science expertise. The
students will participate in group meetings, attend
planned lectures and laboratory visits, and be
encouraged to submit posters to the NIH Poster Day
where summer interns from all disciplines present

their projects. See Web site for deadlines and
further information.
EIN: 222096948

6195
Whitehall Foundation, Inc.
P.O. Box 3423
Palm Beach, FL   33480
Contact: George M. Moffett II, Pres.
E-mail: email@whitehall.org; Additional address:
380 S. County Rd., Ste. 201, Palm Beach, FL
33480; URL: http://www.whitehall.org

Foundation type: Independent foundation
Limitations: Support for scholarly research in the
life sciences, with emphasis on behavioral
neuroscience and invertebrate neurophysiology;
innovative and imaginative projects preferred.
Research grants are paid to sponsoring
institutions, rather than directly to individuals.
Publications: Grants list.
Financial data: Year ended 09/30/2005.
Assets, $96,630,000 (M); Expenditures,
$4,571,797; Total giving, $4,109,755.
Fields of interest: Science, research; Science.
Type of support: Research; Postdoctoral support.
Application information: Application form required.
Deadline(s): Jan. 15, Apr. 15, Oct. 1 for Letters
of Intent, and June 1, Sept. 1, and Feb. 15 for
applications
Additional information: Letters of Intent by e-mail
not accepted; See Web site for further
program and application information.
Program descriptions:
Research Grant: Available to established
scientists of all ages. Applications will be judged on
the scientific merit of the proposal and evidence of
the competence of the applicant. Grants are for a
period of three years. One two-year renewal may be
allowed, but is not automatic. Applications will not
be accepted from investigators who already have,
or expect to receive, substantial support from other
sources even though the support may be for an
unrelated project. Research grants will normally be
in the range of $30,000 to $75,000 per year.
Grant-in-Aid: Grants to researchers at the
assistant professor level who have not yet
established themselves and who, for this reason,
experience difficulty in competing for funds.
Grants-in-aid are also made to senior scientists or
retired researchers. In addition to scientific merit,
the major criteria upon which these applications are
judged are past performance and evidence of
continued productivity. Grants-in-aid are made for a
period of one year and do not exceed $30,000.
EIN: 135637595

6196
Marion and Jasper Whiting Foundation
c/o Rice, Heard & Bigelow, Inc.
50 Congress St., Ste. 1025
Boston, MA   02109-4002   (617) 227-1782
Contact: Robert G. Bannish, Tr.

Foundation type: Public charity
Limitations: Travel and training grants to college
and university professors.
Financial data: Year ended 10/31/2004.
Assets, $2,563,967 (M); Expenditures,
$106,024; Total giving, $83,748; Grants to
individuals, 19 grants totaling $83,748 (high:
$6,816, low: $2,547).
Fields of interest: College; University.
Type of support: Fellowships; Travel grants.
Application information: Application form required.

Initial approach: Letter or telephone.
Deadline(s): Feb. 1.
EIN: 046147345

6197
The Helen Hay Whitney Foundation
20 Squadron Blvd., Ste. 630
New City, NY 10956 (845) 639-6799
Contact: Robert Weinberger, Admin. Dir.
FAX: (845) 639-6798; E-mail: hhwf@earthlink.net;
URL: http://www.hhwf.org/

Foundation type: Independent foundation
Limitations: Fellowships to scientists in North America with less than one year of postdoctoral experience by application deadline. Applicants must be planning a career in biological or medical research, and have recently earned an M.D., Ph.D., or equivalent degree.
Publications: Application guidelines; Annual report; Financial statement; Informational brochure (including application guidelines).
Financial data: Year ended 06/30/2005. Assets, $46,149,070 (M); Expenditures, $3,239,449; Total giving, $2,486,105.
Fields of interest: Medical research, institute; Biomedicine research; Biological sciences.
Type of support: Fellowships; Research.
Application information: Application form required. Application form available on the grantmaker's Web site.
Deadline(s): July 15
Additional information: The Scientific Advisory Committee selects those candidates whose applications merit a personal interview. Each applicant is then assigned to a member of the Committee, who completes arrangements for the interview in Oct. Interview travel expenses from points in the U.S., Canada, and Mexico are paid by the foundation. Applicants not selected for interviews are advised on or about Oct. 1 that their application has been declined. Interview reports and applications are reviewed in Nov. and candidates are notified of the Committee's final decision by mid-Nov.
Program description:
Postdoctoral Support: The foundation supports early postdoctoral research training in all the basic biomedical sciences. To attain its ultimate goal of increasing the number of imaginative, well-trained, and dedicated medical scientists, the foundation grants financial support of sufficient duration to help further the careers of young men and women engaged in biological or medical research. Eligible candidates must live in North America and hold the M.D., Ph.D., or equivalent degree and seek to begin postdoctoral training in basic biomedical research. U.S. citizenship is not a requirement, but fellowships to resident noncitizens are awarded only for training in this country. Citizens may train abroad. Applications from established scientists or advanced fellows will not be considered. Because the fellowships are for early postdoctoral training only, applicants who have already had one year's postdoctoral laboratory training at the time of application deadline will not be considered. The foundation will not consider applicants who plan tenure of the fellowship in the same laboratory in which they received extensive pre- or postdoctoral training. Fellowship training is to be obtained in an academic setting. The selection of a commercial or industrial laboratory for the training experience is not acceptable. The Fellowship is normally for a period of three years. One- or two-year fellowships are not considered. July 1 is the usual starting date. With approval, a fellowship may be started at another date requested by the applicant, but in no event earlier than Apr. 1. An activation date earlier than July 1 is contingent upon availability of funds. The foundation provides funds for travel to the fellowship location for both the fellow and family. No payment is made for transportation of household goods. Recipients are awarded $41,000 for the first year, $42,500 for the second year, and $44,000 for the third year. An annual allowance of $2,500 is given to the fellow's laboratory to help defray research expenses. Its use is wholly at the discretion of the fellow's supervisor except that no part of it may be used for institutional overhead. Supplementation of the stipend is permitted. However, it is not acceptable to hold concurrently a full fellowship from another source. Nonresearch activities, such as teaching, must not occupy more than ten percent of the fellow's time. A two-day annual meeting of fellows is held in Nov. of each year, at which each third-year fellow presents the results of the research.
EIN: 131677403

6198
Wildlife Conservation Society
2300 Southern Blvd.
Bronx, NY 10460-1099 (718) 220-5100
Contact: Steven E. Sanderson, Pres. and C.E.O.
E-mail: fellowship@wcs.org; Additional tel.: (718) 220-6828; URL: http://www.wcs.org

Foundation type: Public charity
Limitations: Grants to support wildlife conservation field research in Africa, Asia, and Latin America (including Mexico).
Financial data: Year ended 06/30/2003. Assets, $576,753,581 (M); Expenditures, $139,510,005; Total giving, $4,985,780; Grants to individuals, 17 grants totaling $114,361 (high: $14,785, low: $730).
Fields of interest: Animals/wildlife, preservation/protection.
Type of support: Research; Foreign applicants.
Application information:
Deadline(s): Jan. 2 and July 1
Additional information: Completion of formal application required, including proposal, project outline, and abstract; See Web site for application information.
Program description:
Research Fellowship Program: The RFP supports field research in Africa, Asia, and Latin America. Traditionally the RFP has not supported research in North America, Australia or Europe, or their territories. However, the RFP has just begun to accept applications from Native Americans (U.S.) and First Nation Peoples (Canada) who intend to conduct work on native lands on issues of direct relevance to wildlife. Grants are for up to $25,000, and are for one year.
EIN: 131740011

6199
The Wiley Foundation, Inc.
c/o John Wiley & Sons, Inc.
111 River St.
Hoboken, NJ 07030
Contact: Deborah E. Wiley, Dir.
FAX: (201) 748-6940; E-mail: dwiley@wiley.com;
URL: http://www.wiley.com/legacy/wileyfoundation/

Foundation type: Company-sponsored foundation
Limitations: Prizes by nomination only to exceptional Ph.D. and M.D. scientists whose research has set the standard for excellence in the biomedical field.
Publications: Application guidelines.
Financial data: Year ended 04/30/2005. Assets, $396,415 (M); Expenditures, $57,027; Total giving, $26,500; Grants to individuals, 3 grants totaling $25,750 (high: $12,500, low: $750). Subtotal for research: 2 grants totaling $25,000.
Fields of interest: Biomedicine; Science.
Type of support: Research; Awards/grants by nomination only; Awards/prizes.
Application information: Application form not required.
Deadline(s): July 31
Additional information: Completion of formal nomination required, including short summary of 150 words or less, narrative of 5-10 pages, brief, one-page biography, including past positions, awards or recognition, list of six peer-reviewed journal references that substantiate the statements in nomination, at least two supporting letters from colleagues familiar with nominee's work and curriculum vitae; Applicant must submit one original and three copies of above requested materials.
Program description:
Wiley Prize in the Biomedical Sciences: Recipient's narrative (5-10 pages) must include detailed answers to the following questions:
· Why does nominee's work represent a major advance in the biomedical sciences?
· What are the unique aspects of the nominee's work that sets it apart from other notable advances in this award?
The award will consist of a $25,000 grant and the opportunity to deliver a lecture at Rockefeller University.
EIN: 134163744

6200
Charles K. Williams II Trust
c/o Mellon Bank, N.A.
P.O. Box 185
Pittsburgh, PA 15230-0185
Application address: c/o Mellon Financial Corp., 1735 Market St., Philadelphia, PA 19101, tel.: (215) 553-3344

Foundation type: Independent foundation
Limitations: Postgraduate fellowships for archaeology research and study.
Financial data: Year ended 11/30/2004. Assets, $96,764 (M); Expenditures, $202,185; Total giving, $202,130.
Fields of interest: History/archaeology.
Type of support: Fellowships; Research; Postgraduate support.
Application information: Applications by proposal accepted throughout the year.
EIN: 236758319

6201
Williams King Foundation, Inc.
407 W. Hwy. 131
Clarksville, IN 47129-1649
Contact: Willis C. Nale, Treas.
Application address: 930 Pennwood Dr., New Albany, IN 47150-2162, tel.: (812) 944-1878

Foundation type: Independent foundation
Limitations: Grants to individuals for Christian preaching and ministry.
Financial data: Year ended 12/31/2004. Assets, $208,073 (M); Expenditures, $55,654;

Total giving, $55,448; Grants to individuals, totaling $55,448.
Fields of interest: Christian agencies & churches.
Type of support: Grants to individuals.
Application information: Applications by letter accepted throughout the year.
EIN: 311044784

6202

The Woodrow Wilson National Fellowship Foundation

P.O. Box 5281
Princeton, NJ 08543-5281 (609) 452-7007
FAX: (609) 452-0066; E-mail: jlp@woodrow.org;
URL: http://www.woodrow.org

Foundation type: Public charity
Limitations: Awards and fellowships in a variety of areas to qualified individuals.
Publications: Annual report; Newsletter.
Financial data: Year ended 06/30/2005.
Assets, $20,737,668 (M); Expenditures, $15,097,337; Total giving, $10,155,178.
Fields of interest: Humanities; Minorities.
Type of support: Publication; Fellowships; Research; Awards/prizes; Postdoctoral support; Doctoral support; Grants for special needs.
Application information: Applications accepted. Application form required.
Deadline(s): Vary
Program descriptions:
Hans Rosenhaupt Memorial Book Award: This award of $2,000 is made biennially for a first book of wide humanistic interest, written by a scholar who has held one of the foundation's fellowships.
Humanities at Work Program—Practicum Grants: Provides up to 30 grants of $2,000 each to doctoral students who create meaningful internships in corporations or nonprofit organizations. Applications accepted throughout the year.
Charlotte W. Newcombe Doctoral Dissertation Fellowships: Original and significant study of ethical or religious values in the fields of the humanities and social sciences are encouraged. Successful proposals illuminate religious or ethical questions of broad significance and elucidate the ways in which these values inform choices and give meaning to people's lives. Each fellow receives a stipend of $18,000 for a year of uninterrupted research and writing leading to a timely completion of the doctoral dissertation. For more information, e-mail charlotte@woodrow.org.
Woodrow Wilson-Johnson & Johnson Dissertation Grants in Women's Health: $6,000 grants are available to individuals who are interested in the implications of research for the understanding of women's lives and its significance for public policy or treatment. Applicants must be students in doctoral programs such as nursing, public health, anthropology, history, sociology, psychology, and social work, who have completed all predissertation requirements. Deadline Oct. 11. For more information, e-mail wswhatt@woodrow.org. Applications must be filed electronically.
Woodrow Wilson Dissertation Grants in Women's Studies: These $3,000 grants are given to individuals to expand knowledge and scholarship about women in history, literature, art, science, and society. Applicants must be students in doctoral programs who have completed all predissertation requirements in any field of study at graduate schools in the U.S. Deadline Oct. 11. For more information, e-mail wswhatt@woodrow.org.
EIN: 210703075

6203

The Winn Feline Foundation

(formerly Robert H. Winn Foundation for Cat Research, Inc.)
1805 Atlantic Ave.
P.O. Box 1005
Manasquan, NJ 08736-0805 (732) 528-9797
Contact: Janet Wolf, Exec. Dir.
E-mail: winn@winnfelinehealth.org; URL: http://www.winnfelinehealth.org

Foundation type: Public charity
Limitations: Research grants for the study of feline diseases.
Financial data: Year ended 04/30/2004.
Assets, $1,113,370 (M); Expenditures, $248,534; Total giving, $184,123; Grants to individuals, 14 grants totaling $184,123.
Fields of interest: Animal welfare; Veterinary medicine.
Type of support: Research.
Application information: Application form required.
Deadline(s): Dec. 1
Additional information: See Web site for further application information.
Program description:
Veterinary Awards: Awards up to $15,000 to faculty veterinarians, post-doctoral fellows, practicing veterinarians or veterinary students. Applicants must submit 14 copies and a disk containing IBM Word format.
EIN: 237138699

6204

Wisconsin Medical Society Foundation, Inc.

(formerly State Medical Society Foundation)
330 E. Lakeside St.
P.O. Box 1109
Madison, WI 53701 (608) 442-3720
Contact: Renee Reback, Exec. Dir.
URL: http://www.wisconsinmedicalsociety.org/physician_resources/foundation

Foundation type: Public charity
Limitations: Grants to health care specialists in WI for state-wide projects which aim to improve public health through education, medical history and scientific projects. Awards are up to $20,000.
Publications: Application guidelines; Newsletter.
Financial data: Year ended 12/31/2004.
Assets, $7,749,797 (M); Expenditures, $378,318; Total giving, $48,350; Grants to individuals, 31 grants totaling $48,350; Loans to individuals, 64 loans totaling $320,000.
Fields of interest: Health care, research; Medicine/medical care, public education.
Type of support: Program development.
Application information:
Initial approach: Letter.
Additional information: Contact foundation for further application guidelines.
EIN: 396045649

6205

Women's Sports Foundation

Eisenhower Park
East Meadow, NY 11554 (516) 542-4700
Contact: Donna A. Lopiano Ph.D., Exec. Dir.
FAX: (516) 542-4716; E-mail: wosport@aol.com;
Additional tel.: (800) 227-3988; URL: http://www.womenssportsfoundation.org

Foundation type: Public charity

Limitations: Awards, grants, and research support to individuals working in the field of women in sports.
Publications: Application guidelines; Annual report; Financial statement; Grants list; Informational brochure; Newsletter.
Financial data: Year ended 12/31/2003.
Assets, $5,517,332 (L); Expenditures, $4,370,568; Total giving, $787,728.
Fields of interest: Athletics/sports, training; Athletics/sports, equestrianism; Women.
Type of support: Research.
Application information: Contact foundation or see Web site for current application deadline/guidelines.
Program descriptions:
AQHA Female Equestrian Award: A $2,000 grant is awarded to honor and reward an outstanding female equestrian for her accomplishments as a horsewoman and as an athlete. Female equestrians with national ranking who exhibit leadership, sportsmanship, and commitment to the sport and its athletes are eligible. Deadline June 30.
Lilo Leeds Women's Sports and Fitness Participation Endowment Research Grant: Grants of $500 to $1,000 are provided for research that creates a greater understanding of the factors that influence the participation of girls and women in sports and fitness activities. Any bona fide researcher is eligible, whether university-affiliated, organizationally affiliated, or independent.
Women's Sports Foundation Girls and Women in Sports Research Grants: Grants of $1,000 to $2,500 for research pertaining to girl's and women's sports and fitness are available to any bona fide researcher, including those who are university-affiliated, organizationally affiliated or independent. Deadline June 30.
Women's Sports Foundation Travel and Training Fund: Financial assistance is provided to aspiring female athletes and teams for coaching, specialized training, equipment, and travel. Any female athlete or team with a regional or national ranking or with successful competitive records who has the potential to achieve higher performance levels and rankings is eligible, with the exception of schools and colleges or university varsity teams. Individuals receive $2,000 and teams receive $4,000.
EIN: 237380557

6206

Woodlawn Foundation

524 North Ave., Ste. 203
New Rochelle, NY 10801-3410
(914) 632-3778
FAX: (914) 632-5502

Foundation type: Public charity
Limitations: Grants to individuals in support of Opus Dei activities.
Publications: Financial statement; Occasional report.
Financial data: Year ended 06/30/2004.
Assets, $13,726,605 (M); Expenditures, $12,048,357; Total giving, $11,051,826; Grant to an individual, 1 grant totaling $13,902.
Fields of interest: Christian agencies & churches.
Type of support: Program development.
Application information: Contact foundation for current application deadline/guidelines.
EIN: 133055729

6207
World Food Prize Foundation
666 Grand Ave., Ste. 1700
Des Moines, IA 50309 (515) 245-3783
Contact: Judith Pim, Dir., Secretariat Operations
FAX: (515) 245-3785;
E-mail: wfp@worldfoodprize.org; URL: http://www.worldfoodprize.org

Foundation type: Independent foundation
Limitations: Prize for research in the field of agriculture.
Publications: Informational brochure; Informational brochure (including application guidelines).
Financial data: Year ended 12/31/2004. Assets, $11,696,129 (M); Expenditures, $1,448,704; Total giving, $250,000; Grants to individuals, 2 grants totaling $250,000 (high: $125,000, low: $125,000).
Fields of interest: Agriculture.
Type of support: Research; Awards/prizes.
Application information: Contact foundation for current application deadline/guidelines.
Program description:
   The World Food Prize: The Prize recognizes contributions in any field involved in the world food supply- food and agriculture science and technology, manufacturing, marketing, nutrition, economics, poverty alleviation, political leadership and the social sciences.
EIN: 421356715

6208
World Hunger Year, Inc.
(also known as WHY)
505 8th Ave., Ste. 2100
New York, NY 10018-6582 (212) 629-8850
Contact: William Ayers, Exec. Dir.
FAX: (212) 465-9274;
E-mail: WHY@worldhungeryear.org; Additional tel: (800) 548-6479; URL: http://www.worldhungeryear.org

Foundation type: Public charity
Limitations: Awards to members of the media.
Publications: Application guidelines; Annual report; Financial statement; Grants list; Informational brochure (including application guidelines); Newsletter.
Financial data: Year ended 03/31/2005. Assets, $333,441 (M); Expenditures, $1,599,694; Total giving, $15,000.

Fields of interest: Media/communications; International affairs; Poverty studies.
Type of support: Awards/prizes.
Application information: Deadline Feb. 2; Initial approach by telephone or e-mail; Completion of formal application required; Nominations also accepted.
Program description:
   Harry Chapin Media Awards: Given to encourage, honor, and reward those members of the print and electronic media who have made significant contributions in bringing the issues of world hunger and poverty to the attention of the public.
EIN: 132805575

6209
World of Children, Inc.
5131 Post Rd., Ste. 340
Dublin, OH 43017 (614) 339-1096
Contact: Suzan Nocella, Dir., Opers.
E-mail: suzan@worldofchildren.org; URL: http://www.worldofchildren.org

Foundation type: Public charity
Limitations: Awards, by nomination only, of $15,000 to students under 21 who have at least three years of consecutive service to children.
Financial data: Year ended 03/31/2005. Assets, $258,263 (M); Expenditures, $580,865; Total giving, $265,000.
Fields of interest: Youth development; Children/youth, services.
Type of support: Awards/grants by nomination only; Awards/prizes.
Application information:
   Deadline(s): Apr. 26.
   Additional information: Completion of formal nomination required.
EIN: 311772381

6210
Wurtman Ner David Foundation, Inc.
(formerly Wurtman Foundation)
c/o Robert Finkel
233 Needham St., 4th Fl.
Newton, MA 02464
URL: http://www.rikma.org.il/foundation.php

Foundation type: Operating foundation

Limitations: Fellowships to leaders of Jewish communities in Israel and the U.S. Fellowships also to those who unite Israelis and Americans.
Financial data: Year ended 06/30/2003. Assets, $34,432 (M); Expenditures, $268,472; Total giving, $41,782; Grants to individuals, 7 grants totaling $41,782 (high: $12,059, low: $1,200).
Fields of interest: Jewish agencies & temples; Israel.
Type of support: Fellowships; Foreign applicants; Travel grants.
Application information: Applications not accepted.
   Additional information: Unsolicited requests for funds not considered or acknowledged.
EIN: 650881769

6211
Youth Venture, Inc.
1700 N. Moore St., Ste. 2000
Arlington, VA 22209 (703) 527-4126
Contact: Roy Gamse, Acting Pres.
FAX: (703) 527-8383;
E-mail: info@youthventure.org; URL: http://www.youthventure.org

Foundation type: Public charity
Limitations: Seed money to individuals between the ages of 12 and 20 for the creation of new, youth-led civic-minded organizations, clubs or ventures.
Publications: Application guidelines; Informational brochure; Newsletter.
Financial data: Year ended 12/31/2003. Assets, $228,081 (M); Expenditures, $567,675; Total giving, $58,259.
Fields of interest: Youth development, community service clubs; Community development.
Type of support: Seed money; Precollege support.
Application information: Application form available on the grantmaker's Web site.
   Deadline(s): Mar. 22
   Additional information: Completion of formal application required, including essay, budget, and two references; See Web site for further application information.
Program description:
   Award Program: Awards 20 start-up grants of up to $1,000 each. Projects must be new, sustainable, assets to the community.
EIN: 541744720

APPENDIX

This appendix lists those grantmakers that appeared in the 14th edition of *Foundation Grants to Individuals*, but were excluded from this 15th edition for the reasons stated. Reasons for exclusion include grantmakers that terminated, those whose status has changed, those no longer making grants to individuals, or those for which no recent information could be obtained. **Grantmakers listed here should not be considered possible sources of funding for individuals.**

A-P-A Transport Educational Foundation, NJ
The foundation no longer provides funding to individuals.

AASCIN
See American Association of Spinal Cord Injury Nurses

ABC Foundation, NC
The foundation gave less than $2,000 to individuals in 2004.

Abramson Family Foundation, The, FL
The foundation gave less than $2,000 to individuals in 2004.

Adams Trust, John & Hester, IN
The foundation no longer provides funding to individuals.

Adhesive & Sealant Council Education Foundation, MD
The foundation does not provide funding to individuals.

Adrian Kiwanis Foundation, Inc., MI
The foundation did not provide funding in 2004.

Agape Foundation, TX
The foundation gave less than $2,000 to individuals in 2004.

Air Liquide America Foundation, Inc., TX
(Formerly Big Three Industries Foundation, Inc.)
The foundation does not provide funding to individuals.

Albany-Schenectady League of Arts, Inc., NY
The organization terminated in 2004.

Amarillo Area Foundation, Inc., TX
The foundation does not provide funding to individuals.

AMDG Charitable Foundation, VA
The foundation gave less than $2,000 to individuals in 2004.

American Association of School Administrators, VA
(Formerly Leadership for Learning Foundation)
The association terminated in 2003.

American Association of Spinal Cord Injury Nurses, NY
(Also known as AASCIN)
The foundation has discontinued its research program.

American Bar Foundation, IL
The foundation did not provide funding to individuals in 2003.

American Pediatric Surgical Association Foundation, Inc., MI
The foundation gave less than $2,000 to individuals in 2003.

Ames Foundation, MA
The foundation did not provide funding in 2004.

Ardell Foundation, Kenneth, WA
The foundation did not provide funding in 2005.

Arnold Memorial Scholarship Fund, Teresa Youtz, PA
The foundation did not provide funding in 2004.

Arnold Scholarship Trust Fund, Robert T., CT
The foundation gave less than $2,000 to individuals in 2004.

ArtServe Michigan, MI
The foundation no longer provides funding to individuals.

Baker Memorial Fund Trust, Margaret, PA
The foundation no longer provides funding to individuals.

Bankus Memorial Scholarship Fund, Elmer, OR
The foundation did not provide funding to individuals in 2004.

Batterton Fund Trust, Fred (B. A.), KY
The fund no longer gives grants for general welfare support.

Bean Foundation, Inc., A. H., AL
The foundation no longer provides funding to individuals.

Beatty Trust, Cordelia Lunceford, OK
The trust does not give grants for general welfare support.

Beaumont Employees Trust Fund, Louis D., MO
The foundation no longer provides funding to individuals.

Bell Charitable Trust, Virginia, IL
The foundation gave less than $2,000 to individuals in 2004.

Bellinger Trust, Clarence H., RI
The foundation did not provide funding in 2004.

Best Student Loan Fund, OR
(Formerly Best Student Loan Fund, Woodie L. & Mabel)
The foundation did not provide funding in 2005.

Best Student Loan Fund, Woodie L. & Mabel
See Best Student Loan Fund

Big Three Industries Foundation, Inc.
See Air Liquide America Foundation, Inc.

Blue Mountain Foundation, CA
The foundation did not provide funding in 2004.

Blue Shield of California Foundation, CA
(Formerly California Physicians' Service Foundation)
The foundation does not provide funding to individuals.

BOSE Foundation, Inc., MA
The foundation does not provide funding to individuals.

Box of Rain Foundation, The, NY
The foundation no longer provides funding to individuals.

Brakeman Scholarship Fund, WI
The foundation no longer provides funding to individuals.

Bridgewater Improvement Association, Inc., MA
The foundation did not provide funding to individuals in 2003.

Burkett Trust, George W., IN
The foundation gave less than $2,000 to individuals in 2004.

Business Women's Home, The, MS
(Formerly Hough Home - Business Women's Home, Joseph W.)
The organization terminated in 2005.

Cade Foundation, Inc., Robert and Mary, FL
The foundation no longer gives grants for general welfare support.

California Physicians' Service Foundation
See Blue Shield of California Foundation

Camp Fund, Caleb J., CT
The fund terminated in 2004.

Cancer Aid and Research Fund, AZ
The foundation did not provide grants to individuals in 2004.

Carmine Trust, John Harry & Edith Carter Lewis, VA
The foundation did not provide funding to individuals in 2003.

Carnation Company Scholarship Foundation
See Nestle Scholarship Foundation

Carnegie Corporation of New York, NY
The foundation no longer provides funding for educational support.

Carr Trust Fund for Scholarships, Elizabeth S., RI
(Formerly Carr Trust Fund for Scholarships, Roy W. Carr & Elizabeth S.)
The foundation does not provide funding to individuals.

Carr Trust Fund for Scholarships, Roy W. Carr & Elizabeth S.
See Carr Trust Fund for Scholarships, Elizabeth S.

Center for Advanced Studies in Leukemia, CA
The foundation did not provide funding in 2004.

Center for Land Use Interpretation, The, CA
The foundation gave less than $2,000 to individuals in 2004.

Chamberlin Scholarship Trust, Ruth W.
See Chamberlin Scholarship Trust, Ruth W. & Alice I.

Chamberlin Scholarship Trust, Ruth W. & Alice I., NY
(Formerly Chamberlin Scholarship Trust, Ruth W.)
The foundation gave less than $2,000 to individuals in 2005.

Checketts Foundation, Stan and Sandy, The, UT
The foundation gave less than $2,000 to individuals in 2004.

Chela Financial Resources, CA
The foundation terminated in 2005.

Chen International Law Foundation, Inc., Kwen, NY
The foundation no longer provides funding to individuals.

Chiefs Children's Fund, MO
The foundation does not provide funding to individuals.

Christenson Family Organization, Alvin, UT
The foundation gave less than $2,000 to individuals in 2004.

Christian Business Ministries, CA
The foundation did not provide funding to individuals in 2003.

Citizens Committee for New York City, Inc.
See Citizens for NYC

Citizens for NYC, NY
(Formerly Citizens Committee for New York City, Inc.)
The foundation has discontinued its award program.

Clarke Trust, John, RI
The foundation does not provide funding to individuals.

CMI Foundation, The, SC
The foundation no longer provides funding to individuals.

Cochems Trust, Jane Nugent, OR
The foundation did not provide funding to individuals in 2002 and 2003.

Coffee Memorial Fund, Inc., William Marshall & Mildred, KY
The foundation gave less than $2,000 to individuals in 2004.

Columbiana County Public Health League Trust Fund, WI
The foundation did not provide funding in 2005.

Community Foundation for Southeastern Michigan, MI
The foundation no longer funds the WDIV Outstanding Teacher Awards and the Weber Fund.

Community Foundation for the Capital Region, Inc., The, NY
The foundation no longer gives grants for general welfare support.

Compassion and Choices, CO
(Also known as End of Life Choices)
The foundation no longer provides funding to individuals.

Compassion and Choices, CO
(Formerly Hemlock Foundation, The)
The foundation no longer provides funding to individuals.

Conover Scholarship Trust, Pauline W., IN
The trust terminated in August 2003..

ContiGroup Companies Foundation, NY
(Formerly Continental Grain Foundation)
The foundation does not provide funding to individuals.

Continental Grain Foundation
See ContiGroup Companies Foundation

Cooper Wood Products Foundation, Inc., VA
The foundation did not provide funding in 2004.

Cultural Society, Inc., The, FL
The society's scholarship fund has been discontinued.

Cumber Family Foundation, Aftab and Gul, FL
The foundation does not provide funding to individuals.

Czado Catholic Education Fund, Mary, MI
The foundation did not provide funding to individuals in 2003.

Dake Education Foundation, The, NY
The foundation gave less than $2,000 to individuals in 2004.

Dallas Cotton Exchange Trust, NY
The trust terminated in 2004.

Daniels Foundation, Inc., Lucy, NC
The foundation did not provide funding in 2004.

Davidson Foundation, Inc., Lorimer & Betty Gael, DC
The foundation does not provide funding to individuals.

Davidson Trust, Frank H., MO
The foundation did not provide funding in 2004.

Deafness Foundation
See Shea Clinic Foundation

Deffenbaugh Foundation Trust, Roy A., IL
The foundation did not provide funding in 2004.

Department of Neurological Surgery Research Foundation, OH
The foundation gave less than $2,000 to individuals in 2004.

Des Moines I Have a Dream Foundation, IA
The foundation no longer provides funding to individuals.

Devine Foundation, Mae
See Finks Foundation

DiGregorio Scholarship Fund, Brian A., MA
The foundation gave less than $2,000 to individuals in 2004.

DiMauro Foundation, Inc., Orazio, CT
The foundation did not provide funding in 2005.

Dobson Trust, Nellie, OK
The foundation no longer provides funding to individuals.

Dodge Foundation, Inc., Geraldine R., NJ
The foundation has discontinued its Humane Action Awards program.

Doerflinger Foundation, Inc., Thomas, The, NJ
The foundation did not provide funding to individuals in 2004.

Douroucouli Foundation, The, CA
The foundation did not provide funding to individuals in 2004.

Dubbs Scholarship Fund, Sallie, NC
The foundation does not provide funding to individuals.

E.D. Foundation, NY
The foundation did not provide funding to individuals in 2004.

Eberhardt I for Scholarship Fund, PA
(Also known as Eberhardt Trust I for Scholarship Fund, Melville A.)
The fund terminated in 2003.

Eberhardt Trust I for Scholarship Fund, Melville A.
See Eberhardt I for Scholarship Fund

Edge Scholarship Foundation, Oscar N., The, AL
The foundation did not provide funding in 2005.

Elmer Scholarship Fund, WI
The foundation gave less than $2,000 to individuals in 2005.

End of Life Choices
See Compassion and Choices

Envirosafe Services of Ohio, Inc. Foundation, OH
The foundation gave less than $2,000 to individuals in 2004.

EOC of Schuylkill
See Schuylkill Community Action

Finks Foundation, AZ
(Formerly Devine Foundation, Mae)
The foundation no longer provides funding to
individuals.

Flamingo Foundation, UT
The foundation gave less than $2,000 to individuals in
2004.

Flinn Trust, Peter G., WI
The trust terminated in 2004.

Florida Humanities Council, The, FL
The foundation no longer provides funding to
individuals.

Foot & Ankle Association, Inc.
See Institute for Foot and Ankle Studies, Inc.

For a New Social Science, FL
The foundation gave less than $2,000 to individuals in
2003.

Forrest Foundation, Inc., Thomas W., FL
The foundation did not provide funding in 2004.

**Foundation for International Medical
Education, CA**
The foundation no longer provides funding to
individuals.

Frasier Foundation, Julia Fredin, OK
The foundation did not provide funding in 2004.

Gale Foundation, William G., PA
The foundation did not provide funding in 2004.

Garbe Foundation, NJ
(Also known as Rotary-Garbe Foundation, Inc.)
The foundation does not provide funding to individuals.

**Gentry Endowment Scholarship Fund, Ben &
Lucille, IN**
The foundation gave less than $2,000 to individuals in
2003.

**German Marshall Fund of the United States,
The, DC**
Current information not available.

Graco Foundation, The, MN
The foundation does not provide funding to individuals.

Grattan Weaver Foundation, Margaret, VA
The foundation did not provide funding to individuals in
2004.

**Gray Family Scholarship Fund Trust, Sidney H.
& Mary L. Langille**
See Gray Family Scholarship Fund, Sidney H. & Mary L.

**Gray Family Scholarship Fund, Sidney H. &
Mary L., PA**
(Formerly Gray Family Scholarship Fund Trust, Sidney H.
& Mary L. Langille)
The foundation did not provide funding to individuals in
2004.

Gund Memorial Fund, William L. & Ethel, IA
The foundation did not provide funding in 2005.

H.E.I. Charitable Foundation
See Hawaiian Electric Industries Charitable Foundation

Hamilton Foundation, John Clifford, CA
The foundation gave less than $2,000 to individuals in
2004.

Harbor Branch Foundation
See Harbor Branch Oceanographic Institution, Inc.

**Harbor Branch Oceanographic Institution, Inc.,
FL**
(Formerly Harbor Branch Foundation)
The foundation terminated in 2003.

Harkham Foundation, CA
The foundation did not provide funding to individuals in
2003 and 2004.

Harless Foundation, Inc., James H., WV
The foundation no longer provides student loans to
individuals.

Harris Foundation, Ltd., The, HI
The foundation terminated in 2004.

**Hawaiian Electric Industries Charitable
Foundation, HI**
(Also known as H.E.I. Charitable Foundation)
The foundation does not provide funding to individuals.

Hazelton Charitable Trust, Della Lucille, NV
Current information not available.

Headliners Foundation of Texas, TX
Awards are now administered by the Associated Press.

Heinz Family Foundation, PA
The foundation no longer provides funding to
individuals for its General Welfare program.

Hemlock Foundation, The
See Compassion and Choices

Hess Scholarship Fund, Frances, MI
The foundation did not provide funding in 2004.

Higby Trust, WA
The foundation gave less than $2,000 to individuals in
2004.

Higgins Trust for Buren Fund, William, WI
The foundation gave less than $2,000 to individuals in
2004.

Hobgood Educational Trust, T. H. & Allie, MS
The foundation gave less than $2,000 to individuals in
2004.

**Hough Home - Business Women's Home,
Joseph W.**
See Business Women's Home, The

Hudson-Webber Foundation, MI
Current information not available.

Huff Fund, Ruth B. & George T., NC
The foundation did not provide funding in 2004.

Huguenot Society of America, The, NY
The foundation does not provide funding to individuals.

Hurley Foundation, Ed E. & Gladys, WI
The foundation did not provide funding in 2004.

Huyck Preserve, Inc., Edmund Niles, NY
The foundation did not provide funding to individuals in
2002.

I Have a Dream Foundation - Seattle, WA
The foundation gave less than $2,000 to individuals in
2002.

Ihrig Memorial Scholarship Fund, Lester H., WI
The foundation terminated in 2004.

Institute for Foot and Ankle Studies, Inc., MD
(Formerly Foot & Ankle Association, Inc.)
The foundation gave less than $2,000 to individuals in
2004.

International Documentary
See International Documentary Association

International Documentary Association, CA
(Formerly International Documentary)
The foundation did not provide funding to individuals in
2003.

James Award, Morris C. & Juliet L., CA
The foundation did not provide funding in 2005.

Johnson Foundation, Barbara Piasecka, NJ
The Foundation has suspended their grantmaking due
to lack of funding.

Joshua Foundation, Inc., The, NY
The foundation gave less than $2,000 to individuals in
2005.

Julius Trust, Tony, CA
The foundation did not provide funding in 2004.

Kebo Foundation Scholarship Trust, ME
The foundation gave less than $2,000 to individuals in
2004.

Keith Charitable Trust, Lenna M., IL
The foundation gave less than $2,000 to individuals in
2004.

Kent Medical Foundation, MI
The foundation did not provide funding to individuals in
2004.

Kids Fund, NM
The foundation gave less than $2,000 to individuals in
2005.

Kingsbury Temperance Fund, MA
The foundation did not provide funding in 2004.

Kissler Charitable Trust, L. H. & F., ID
The foundation did not provide funding in 2004.

Kluge Foundation, John W., The, MD
The foundation did not provide funding to individuals in
2004.

Kristianson Testamentary, Hanna R., MN
(Formerly Kristianson Trust, Hanna R.)
The foundation gave less than $2,000 to individuals in
2004.

Kristianson Trust, Hanna R.
See Kristianson Testamentary, Hanna R.

Laprade Educational Trust, J. M. and E. H., FL
The foundation did not provide funding to individuals in
2002.

Last Resort, Inc., TX
The foundation gave less than $2,000 to individuals in
2004.

Leadership for Learning Foundation
See American Association of School Administrators

Lezzer Memorial Foundation, Kenneth L., PA
The foundation terminated in 2004.

Liberty Mutual Scholarship Foundation, MA
The foundation did not provide funding to individuals in
2003.

Little Scholarship Foundation, William S., NC
The foundation did not provide funding to individuals in 2004.

Maier Foundation, Edward J. and Alice M., MI
The foundation terminated in 2004.

Maka'ainana Foundation, The, HI
The foundation did not provide funding in 2005.

Maloofs & You! Foundation, The
See Sacramento Kings Foundation

Mary Kay Foundation, TX
The foundation no longer provides funding to individuals.

MBE Foundation for Children's Initiatives
See We Deliver Dreams Foundation

McRae Foundation, AZ
The foundation gave less than $2,000 to individuals in 2004.

Meftah Scholarship Foundation, FL
The foundation terminated in 2004.

Mellinger Medical Research Memorial Fund, R. &. R., PA
The foundation does not provide funding to individuals.

Merck Company Foundation, The, NJ
The foundation has discontinued its fellowship program.

MetLife Foundation, NY
(Formerly Metropolitan Life Foundation)
The foundation did not provide funding in 2004.

Metropolitan Life Foundation
See MetLife Foundation

Miedema Trust, Madeline, CA
The foundation did not provide funding in 2004.

Milam Foundation, The, TX
The foundation did not provide funding in 2004.

Miller Foundation, F. Eugene, The, WA
The foundation did not provide funding in 2004.

Miller Scholarship Trust, John Scarborough, NE
The foundation did not provide funding in 2005.

Milton Society for the Blind, John, NY
The foundation did not provide funding to individuals in 2003.

Miskoff Foundation, John, FL
The foundation did not provide funding to individuals in 2002 and 2003.

Missouri Scholarship Foundation of Phi Gamma Delta, The, MO
The foundation did not provide funding in 2004.

Mitrani Foundation, Jacques H.
See Mitrani Foundation, Jacques H. & Selma

Mitrani Foundation, Jacques H. & Selma, PA
(Formerly Mitrani Foundation, Jacques H.)
The foundation no longer provides funding to individuals.

Moore Educational Fund, Marjorie
See Moore Trust, Marjorie

Moore Trust, Marjorie, RI
(Formerly Moore Educational Fund, Marjorie)
The foundation gave less than $2,000 to individuals in 2005.

Morrill Fund, Louisa S., KY
The foundation did not provide funding in 2004.

Moyer Charitable Trust, Marilyn, OR
The foundation has discontinued its scholarship program.

Music Foundation of San Antonio, Inc., TX
The foundation did not provide funding in 2004.

Nacca Trust, Louise C., NC
The foundation did not provide funding to individuals in 2004.

NATSO Foundation, The, VA
The foundation no longer provides funding to individuals.

Nestle Scholarship Foundation, WA
(Formerly Carnation Company Scholarship Foundation)
The foundation does not provide funding to individuals.

Newcastle Scholarship Trust, TX
The trust terminated in 2005.

Newstead Foundation, Inc., RI
The foundation did not provide funding to individuals in 2003.

Noyes Scholarship Fund, John Calvin, PA
The fund does not provide funding to individuals.

O'Brien Foundation, Inc., Lincoln, NM
The foundation no longer provides funding to individuals.

O'Brion Trust, Frank, CT
The foundation does not provide funding for research and professional support.

O'Daniel Foundation, F. A., AR
The foundation no longer provides funding to individuals.

Open Society Institute, NY
The institute closed its Documentary Fund and transferred it to the Sundance Institute.

Oshkosh Area Community Foundation, WI
(Formerly Oshkosh Foundation)
The foundation no longer administers a general welfare program.

Oshkosh Foundation
See Oshkosh Area Community Foundation

Ottaway Foundation, Inc., Nicholas B., NY
The foundation gave less than $2,000 to individuals in 2004.

Ozanich Crippled and Burned Children's Scholarship Fund Charitable Foundation, John G., OH
The foundation gave less than $2,000 to individuals in 2004.

Pace Trust for Community Creative Visual Arts, KY
The foundation gave less than $2,000 to individuals in 2004.

Pacers Basketball Corporation Foundation, Inc.
See Pacers Foundation, Inc.

Pacers Foundation, Inc., IN
(Formerly Pacers Basketball Corporation Foundation, Inc.)
The program has been suspended.

Pacific West Cancer Fund, Inc., LA
The foundation did not provide funding to individuals in 2004.

Pack Foundation, CA
The foundation no longer provides funding to individuals.

Park Charitable Foundation, Clyde, NY
(Formerly Park Trust, Clyde)
The foundation did not provide funding in 2004.

Park Ridge Organization Scholarship Fund, Inc., The, NY
The foundation gave less than $2,000 to individuals in 2004.

Park Trust, Clyde
See Park Charitable Foundation, Clyde

Peterson Scholarship Trust, Bradley A. & Birdell A., WI
The foundation did not provide funding to individuals in 2004.

Phoenix Swim & Sports Foundation
See Phoenix Swim Club

Phoenix Swim Club, AZ
(Also known as Phoenix Swim & Sports Foundation)
The foundation gave less than $2,000 to individuals in 2003.

Pope Foundation, UT
The foundation no longer provides funding to individuals.

Progress Village Foundation
See Progress Village Foundation, Inc.

Progress Village Foundation, Inc., FL
(Formerly Progress Village Foundation)
The foundation did not provide funding in 2004.

Proshek Foundation, Charles E., MN
The foundation did not give fellowships in 2003.

Rawlins Memorial Trust, Mary W., DE
The foundation gave less than $2,000 to individuals in 2004.

River Charitable Trust, NY
The foundation did not provide funding to individuals in 2004.

Robertson Foundation, Lois and Edward, FL
The foundation terminated in 2005.

Rockefeller Foundation, The, NY
The foundation no longer provides funding to individuals.

ROFEH, Inc., MA
The foundation does not provide funding to individuals.

Rohame Foundation, The, AZ
The foundation gave less than $2,000 to individuals in 2003.

Ronald McDonald House Charities of Greater Washington, DC, Inc., DC
The foundation has discontinued its general welfare program.

Ross Scholarship Fund, Edith L. and H. Danforth, RI
The foundation did not provide funding to individuals in 2003.

Ross Scholarship Trust, Ed & Eda, OR
The foundation gave less than $2,000 to individuals in 2004.

Rotary-Garbe Foundation, Inc.
See Garbe Foundation

Roth Foundation, FL
The foundation no longer provides funding to individuals.

Rouch Boys Foundation, A. P. and Louise
See Rouch Foundation

Rouch Foundation, AZ
(Formerly Rouch Boys Foundation, A. P. and Louise)
The foundation gave less than $2,000 to individuals for its relief assistance program 2002.

Rowan Charitable & Educational Fund, Inc., C. L., TX
The foundation did not provide funding to individuals in 2004.

Rural Kentucky Medical Scholarship Fund, KY
The foundation did not provide funding to individuals in 2004.

Ryan Foundation, Irene, CA
The foundation did not provide funding in 2004.

S.L. Scholarship Foundation, Inc., CA
The foundation gave less than $2,000 to individuals in 2004.

Sacramento Kings Foundation, CA
Maloofs & You! Foundation, The
The foundation did not provide funding in 2004.

Saint Louis Community Foundation, Greater, MO
(Formerly St. Louis Community Foundation)
The foundation did not provide funding to individuals in 2002 and 2003.

Saint Paul Foundation, Inc., The, MN
The foundation no longer gives grants to individuals.

Sappington Foundation II, Maurice Marion, OK
The foundation did not provide funding to individuals in 2003.

Scadron Memorial Educational Foundation, Irene Haas, FL
The foundation did not provide funding to individuals in 2002.

Schnepp Memorial Trust Fund, Danny, IA
The foundation gave less than $2,000 to individuals in 2004.

Schuette Family Foundation, Inc., WI
The foundation terminated in 2004.

Schuylkill Community Action, PA
(Formerly EOC of Schuylkill)
The foundation no longer provides funding to individuals.

Scripps Howard Foundation, OH
The foundation no longer administers this program.

Shattuck Foundation, W. L., OR
The foundation gave less than $2,000 to individuals in 2004.

Shea Clinic Foundation, TN
(Formerly Deafness Foundation)
The foundation gave less than $2,000 to individuals in 2003.

Shield Athletic Scholarship Fund, Inc., Daniel, CT
The foundation gave less than $2,000 to individuals in 2003.

Shriner-Smith Scholarship Trust, OK
The foundation did not provide funding in 2005.

Simmons Welfare Fund, Ralph & Mary, OH
The fund no longer provides support for general welfare.

Siskind Foundation, Aaron, NJ
The foundation did not provide funding to individuals in 2003.

Skokie Cable TV Foundation, IL
The foundation did not provide funding in 2005.

Slaughter Scholarship Trust, IN
The foundation did not provide funding in 2004.

Snyder Foundation, The, WA
The foundation gave less than $2,000 to individuals in 2005.

Snyder Scholarship Fund, Melda, RI
The foundation did not provide funding in 2004.

South Central Community Foundation, KS
The foundation no longer provides funding to individuals.

Speak Foundation, Alfred J., NC
The foundation terminated in 2003.

St. Louis Community Foundation
See Saint Louis Community Foundation, Greater

St. Martin Foundation, Michael X. & Virginia, LA
The foundation gave less than $2,000 to individuals in 2004.

Standish Scholarship Trust, Lawrence, OH
The foundation did not provide funding in 2005.

Starr Foundation, The, NY
The foundation no longer provides funding to individuals.

Steiner Educational Foundation, CT
The foundation no longer provides funding to individuals.

Stockton Rush Bartol Foundation, PA
The foundation did not provide funding to individuals in 2003 and 2004.

Swanson Fund f/b/o Fresno Lodge No. 247, F. & A. M, Christina Annette, CA
(Also known as Swanson Fund, Annette Monson)
The foundation gave less than $2,000 to individuals in 2004.

Swanson Fund, Annette Monson
See Swanson Fund f/b/o Fresno Lodge No. 247, F. & A. M, Christina Annette

Sweeney Trust Fund, Veda, WI
The foundation gave less than $2,000 to individuals in 2004.

Tacoma Community Foundation, Greater, The, WA
The foundation no longer gives grants to individuals.

Tauber, M.D. Charitable Foundation, Inc., Laszlo N., MD
The foundation terminated in 2004.

Third Wave Foundation, NY
(Also known as Third Wave, Inc.)
The foundation has discontinued its scholarship program.

Third Wave, Inc.
See Third Wave Foundation

Thomas Memorial Scholarship Trust, Albert L. Thomas and Hazel A., OH
The foundation no longer provides funding to individuals.

Thomson Foundation, John Edgar, The, NC
The foundation did not provide funding to individuals in 2002.

Tiffany Foundation, Louis Comfort, The, NY
The foundation did not provide funding in 2004.

Timm Charitable Trust, John E., IL
The foundation no longer provides funding to individuals.

Tweed Scholarship Endowment Trust, Ethel H. and George W., FL
The foundation did not provide funding in 2004.

UCLA Public Interest Law Foundation, CA
The foundation terminated in 2005.

Urann Foundation, RI
The foundation did not make grants for this program in 2002.

Vatras Educational Foundation, RI
The foundation no longer provides funding to individuals.

von Liebig Foundation, Inc., William J., The, FL
The foundation gave less than $2,000 to individuals in 2003.

Waldroup Educational Fund, R. M. & Hattie L., NC
The foundation no longer provides funding to individuals.

We Deliver Dreams Foundation, CA
(Formerly MBE Foundation for Children's Initiatives)
The foundation no longer makes employee-related scholarships to individuals.

Wheaton Foundation, Donald & Edna, WA
The foundation merged into Grays Harbor Community Foundation.

Whitecotton Scholarship Fund, Earl B. & Marie C., WI
The fund terminated in 2003.

Whitelight Foundation, The, CA
The foundation terminated in 2004.

Whitten Trust, Kathryn M., CA
The foundation did not provide funding in 2004.

Wilhelm Charitable Foundation, Werner, MI
The foundation terminated in 2005.

Wilken-Harding Educational Foundation, WI
The foundation gave less than $2,000 to individuals in 2004.

Willmott Memorial Trust I, James Worthington, OH
The foundation did not provide funding in 2004.

Wingate Foundation, The, SC
The foundation did not provide funding in 2004.

Winslow Foundation, Inc., John, NY
The foundation did not provide funding to individuals in 2002.

Winter Family Foundation, Harry A., OH
The foundation did not provide funding to individuals in 2003.

Wolf Aviation Fund, Alfred & Constance, PA
The foundation did not provide funding to individuals in 2004.

Wolf Foundation, Inc., Judith & Richard, NY
The foundation did not provide funding in 2004.

Wrightsman Educational Fund, Inc., C. J., TX
The foundation does not provide funding to individuals.

Wyatt Trust, Maria Veg, NC
The foundation terminated in 2005.

GEOGRAPHIC FOCUS INDEX

The sequence numbers in this index refer to grantmakers which restrict their giving to particular states. State listings are further subdivided by broad categories of giving. Boldface type indicates giving on a national, regional, or international basis. Grantmakers that restrict their giving to particular states, counties, or cities are listed in lighter type following the states in which they give.

Alabama

Education: 53, 155, 166, 317, 432, 513, 690, 1154, 1184, 1194, 1303, 1370, 1437, 1492, 1546, 1754, 1886, 1960, 2029, 2051, 2225, 2572, 2594, 3012, 3353, 3409, 3491, 3717, 4003, 4009, 4107, 4155, 4186, 4226, 4261, 4341, 4423, 4530
Welfare: 4573, 4660, 4805, 4917, 4938
Research: 5733

Alaska

Education: 3, 56, 64, 174, 522, 724, 769, 954, 1157, 1714, 1907, 2276, 2772, 2943, 3023, 3272, 3609, 3644, 3779, 3999, 4018
Arts and Culture: 5352, 5450
Research: 5753, **5896**, 6094

Arizona

Education: 76, 178, 179, 182, 250, 291, 330, 447, 709, 758, 867, 943, 1099, 1151, 1226, 1420, 1788, 1808, 2024, 2377, 2549, 3115, 3169, 3193, 3261, 3648, 3739, 4201, 4202, 4338
Welfare: 5006
Arts and Culture: 5231
Research: 5636, 6075, 6180

Arkansas

Education: 58, 89, 184, 185, 248, 333, 612, 643, 957, 1369, 1562, 1701, 1842, 1926, 1986, 2645, 2841, 3024, 3030, 3532, 3658, 3721, 3895, 3960, 4029, 4036, 4053, 4125, 4222, 4287, 4395, 4412
Welfare: 4587, 4588, 4891, 5134

California

Education: 21, 44, 78, 99, 188, 199, 228, 229, 247, 268, 285, 303, 324, 374, 393, 440, 442, 447, 455, 489, 496, 533, 566, 567, 568, 574, 584, 605, 617, 618, 622, 623, 624, 660, 697, 742, 765, 774, 784, 828, 849, 851, 918, 921, 925, 934, 963, 977, 1002, 1014, 1119, 1126, 1155, 1169, 1191, 1254, 1258, 1262, 1307, 1324, 1422, 1470, 1471, 1500, 1540, 1549, 1553, 1575, 1657, 1670, 1673, 1681, 1752, 1803, 1831, 1856, 1867, 1881, 1922, 1927, 1968, 2026, 2041, 2098, 2105, 2177, 2209, 2220, 2231, 2261, 2278, 2328, **2348**, 2375, 2381, 2405, 2406, 2429, 2458, 2491, 2506, 2579, 2733, 2735, 2743, 2765, 2776, **2798**, 2806, **2876**, 2877, **3042**, 3049, 3104, 3156, 3157, 3183, 3224, 3238, 3269, 3290, 3294, 3302, 3314, 3318, 3336, 3340, 3403, 3433, 3467, 3500, 3510, 3524, 3528, 3537, 3538, 3539, 3540, 3541, 3542, 3543, 3544, 3550, 3557, 3608, 3623, **3671**, 3677, 3704, 3705, 3709, 3731, 3767, 3804, 3839, 3863, 3866, 3871, 3899, 4165, 4188, 4190, 4193, 4197, 4229, 4251, 4300, 4347, 4411, 4420, 4488, 4511, 4520, 4556, 4559
Welfare: 4575, 4589, 4600, 4605, 4634, 4776, 4840, 4850, **4862**, 4871, 4872, 4903, 4919, 4923, 4951, 4970, 4982, 4987, 4992, 5026, 5038, 5042, 5046, 5160
Arts and Culture: 5214, 5231, 5239, 5252, 5311, 5339, 5363, 5399, 5462, 5465, 5469, 5489, 5501, 5509, 5529
Research: 5608, 5609, 5664, 5669, 5672, 5680, 5713, 5760, 5797, 5822, 5823, 5850, 5854, 5887, **5896**, 5923, **5940**, 5975, 6021, 6050, 6082, 6113, 6114, 6182

Colorado

Education: 240, 297, 397, 447, 452, 540, 639, 679, 715, 786, 851, 852, 916, 1017, 1035, 1037, 1160, 1252, 1301, 1322, 1388, 1423, 1642, 1676, 1716, 1757, 1806, 1808, 1811, 1844, 1887, 1901, 1903, 1956, 2199, 2325, 2344, 2462, 2465, 2632, 2749, 2768, 3169, 3208, 3373, 3452, 3495, 3583, 3853, 3958, 3994, 4111, 4136, 4325, 4396, 4499
Welfare: 4574, 4590, 4602, 4615, 4672, 4673, 4692, 4835
Arts and Culture: 5209, 5504
Research: 5655, 5862

Connecticut

Education: 36, 95, 132, 191, 194, 226, 230, 277, 278, 321, 417, 564, 576, 577, 613, 642, 687, 708, 732, 782, 896, 1013, 1024, 1025, 1137, 1168, 1201, 1212, 1219, 1265, 1293, 1439, **1477**, 1557, 1613, 1653, 1792, 1865, 1970, 1985, 2090, 2117, 2154, **2187**, 2204, **2260**, 2406, 2421, 2451, 2464, 2476, 2481, 2483, 2494, 2503, 2627, 2673, 2674, 2676, 2710, 2724, 2754, 2834, 2838, 2885, 2922, 3001, 3005, 3085, 3087, 3136, 3197, 3273, 3303, 3342, 3408, 3445, 3499, 3553, 3699, 3710, 3770, 3771, 3867, 3868, 3875, 3882, 3966, 4043, 4054, 4087, 4090, 4112, 4321, 4355, 4384, 4422, 4428, 4453, 4491, 4528
Welfare: 4612, 4618, 4619, 4620, 4621, 4644, 4652, 4737, 4743, 4838, 4934, 5055, 5150, 5156, 5165
Arts and Culture: 5341, 5378, 5439, 5443
Research: 5771, 5924

Delaware

Education: 97, **1008**, **1083**, 1085, 1791, 1864, 1904, 2002, 2451, 2784, 3249, 3300, 3947
Welfare: 4701
Research: 6166

District of Columbia

Education: 410, 1122, 1358, 1954, 2091, 3025, 3450, 3468, 3555, 4312, 4317, 4528
Welfare: 5090
Arts and Culture: 5242, 5505
Research: 5531, 5778, 5848

Florida

Education: 80, 201, 240, 246, 258, 286, 314, 329, 330, 443, 454, 532, 602, 614, 807, 850, 865, 899, 901, 931, 984, 1026, 1040, 1047, 1060, 1121, 1179, 1223, 1278, 1279, 1316, 1371, 1397, 1398, 1400, 1420, 1577, 1600, 1655, 1656, 1683, 1709, 1769, 1882, 1900, 1972, 1973, 1988, 2016, 2192, 2214, 2249, 2338, 2451, 2504, 2507, 2527, 2583, 2585, 2588, 2596, 2620, 2639, 2808, 2821, 2977, 2986, 3011, 3026, 3030, 3034, **3055**, 3063, 3079, 3334, 3335, 3353, 3400, 3445, 3477, 3482, 3500, 3507, 3513, 3528, 3646, 3652, 3730, 3753, 3818, 3881, 4008, 4073, 4096, 4220, **4329**, 4460, 4528
Welfare: 4680, 4691, 4702, 4706, 4790, 4791, 4906, 4942, 5002, 5010, 5025, 5038, 5065, 5163
Arts and Culture: 5275, 5429, 5517
Research: 5647, 5724, 5938, 5954

Georgia

Education: 267, 330, 426, 513, 517, 763, 770, 803, 812, 862, 904, 922, 1048, 1087, 1174, 1206, **1296**, 1506, 1532, 1533, 1690, 1863, 2092, 2096, 2105, 2120, 2218, 2363, 2507, **2563**, 2647, 2659, 2773, 2903, 3030, 3335, 3500, 3551, 3660, 3823, 3876, 4044, 4110, 4186, 4225, 4367, 4454, 4464, 4528, 4531
Welfare: 4585, 4660, 4667, 4719, 4729, 4765, 4784, 5038, 5045
Research: 5666, 5733, 5820, 5839

Hawaii

Education: 164, 225, 284, 447, 470, 588, 748, 761, 1524, 1553, 1707, 1759, 1772, 1773, 1961, 3239, 3458, 4088, **4098**, 4276, 4330
Welfare: 4803
Arts and Culture: 5231, 5344
Research: **5541**, 5841

Idaho

Education: 31, 701, 702, 970, 1162, 1284, 1475, 1766, 1808, 2006, 2243, 2389, 2648, 2757, 2865, 3272, 3319, 3443, 3644, 3698, 3886, 4152
Welfare: 4796, 4967
Arts and Culture: 5352

Illinois

Education: 11, 74, 88, 92, 153, 282, 288, 345, 356, 359, 407, 467, 468, 482, 484, 534, 544, 549, 560, 582, 597, 698, 734, 736, 739, 764, 822, 946, 1011, 1034, 1045, 1067, 1068, 1081, 1082, 1115, 1123, 1127, 1138, 1144, 1214, 1221, 1243, 1248, 1280, 1289, 1305, 1308, 1343, 1384, 1449, 1512, 1528, 1569, 1621, 1648, 1669, 1692, 1700, 1746, 1749, 1828, 1849, 1888, 1891, 1908, 1915, 1936, 1942, **1943**, 1992, 1996, 2008, 2009, 2010, 2011, 2012, 2013, 2103, 2166, 2226, 2268, 2277, 2301, 2322, 2347, 2367, 2512, 2513, 2536, 2544, 2545, 2569, 2581, 2600, 2611, 2617, 2625, 2636, 2729, 2781, 2807, 2857, 3000, 3018, 3030, 3056, 3064, 3072, 3091, 3118, 3158, 3169, 3206, 3232, 3289, 3293, 3301, 3306, 3330, 3367, 3368, 3371, 3384, 3385, 3410, 3426, 3438, 3439, **3460**, 3462, 3465, 3478, **3571**, 3581, 3600, 3646, 3667, 3702, 3777, 3795, 3802, 3842, 3850, 3930, 3940, 3942, 3957, 3961, 3984, 4006, 4015, 4017, 4028, 4085, 4089, 4099, 4176, 4190, 4267, 4274, 4283, 4298, 4336, 4363, 4376, 4476, 4493
Welfare: 4655, 4727, 4735, 4789, 4792, 4820, 4828, 4867, 4868, 4973, 5053, 5070, 5101
Arts and Culture: 5300, 5493
Research: 5690, **5937**, 6013, 6059, 6131

Indiana

Education: 19, 26, 30, 66, 75, 96, 109, 210, 253, 274, 299, 361, 366, 413, 414, 438, 453, 462, 473, 476, 531, 538, 539, 545, 562, 570, 592, 636, 682, 725, 744, 754, 756, 834, 836, 871, 872, 878, 881, 888, 889, 891, 906, 907, 944, 1005, 1063, 1064, 1077, **1078**, 1147, 1186, 1221, 1264, 1286, 1306, 1344, 1393, 1446, 1462, 1510, 1515, 1547, 1565, 1566, 1603, 1638, 1661, 1682, 1719, 1738, 1745, 1817, 1825, 1832, 1935, 1957, 1967, **1982**, 1983, 1999, 2018, 2033, 2053, 2100, 2155, 2159, 2181, 2183, 2229, 2235, 2254, 2266, 2282, 2295, 2305, 2329, 2401, 2402, 2404, 2424, 2438, 2492, 2499, 2513, 2520, 2684, 2723, 2742, 2767, 2777, 2804, 2855, 2859, 2907, 2941, 2960, 2963, 2984, 3000, 3002, 3008, 3013, 3019, 3030, **3047**, 3057, 3059, 3065, 3092, 3102, 3121, 3133, 3171, 3220, 3225, 3242, 3245, 3295, 3305, 3355, 3357, 3374, 3401, 3406, 3407, 3415, 3416, 3428, 3476, 3487, 3578, 3602, 3632, 3633, 3663, 3685, 3697, 3802, 3811, 3829, 3870, 3903, 3913, 3932, 3935, 4013, 4058, 4074, 4083, 4134, 4175, 4185, 4224, 4230, 4275, 4357, 4381, 4403, 4407, 4427, 4431, 4448, 4462, 4537
Welfare: 4658, 4678, 4817, 4881, 4893, 4945, 5023, 5033, 5153, 5154
Research: 5725, 5798, 5945, 6014, 6106

Iowa

Education: 143, 144, 151, 157, 252, 327, 332, 403, 406, 408, 488, 555, 581, 591, 670, 717, 818, 994, 1003, 1084, 1095, 1096, 1099, 1111, 1173, 1237, 1247, 1250, 1271, 1341, 1513, 1551, 1667, 1676, 1680, 1694, 1717, 1731, 1783, 1826, 1853, 1876, 1923, 1928, 1965, 1996, 2035, 2036, 2038, 2073, 2097, 2118, 2129, 2179, 2234, 2310, 2334, 2339, 2399, 2479, 2480, 2500, 2508, 2523, 2548, 2633, 2669, 2685, 2693, 2770, 2789, 2840, 2846, 2850, 2990, 3000, 3107, 3205, 3257, 3265, 3278, 3301, 3313, 3330, 3362, 3395, 3480, 3559, 3560, **3575**, 3582, 3594, 3610, 3719, 3723, 3724, 3773, 3802, 3890, 3941, 3951, 3985, 3986, 4062, 4140, 4160, 4198, 4223, 4235, 4284, 4331, 4359, 4377, 4497
Welfare: 4798, 4830, 4841, 5161
Arts and Culture: 5232
Research: 5968, 6142, 6160

Kansas

Education: 254, 270, 283, 328, 429, 461, 483, 508, 558, 699, 1056, 1113, 1114, 1131, 1139, 1170, 1240, 1260, 1262, 1467, 1468, 1624, 1644, 1713, 1858, 1874, 1917, 1993, 1996, 2076, 2132, **2178**, 2213, 2224, 2252, 2460, 2496, 2601, 2622, 2651, 2721, 2762, 2771, 2799, 2828, 2911, 2914, 2997, 3028, 3097, 3109, 3117, 3132, 3155, 3199, 3244, 3488, 3506, 3552, 3646, 3747, 3785, 3848, 3892, 3910, 3983, 4094, 4123, 4135, 4161, 4234, 4466, 4549
Welfare: 4711, 4947, 5064, 5155
Arts and Culture: **5365**, 5414
Research: 6134

Kentucky

Education: 273, 319, 435, 436, 513, 654, 658, 856, 890, 1110, 1280, **1296**, 1430, 1443, 1776, 2056, 2172, 2433, 2530, 2598, 2642, 2688, 2796, 2802, 2970, 3016, 3070, 3106, 3125, 3181, 3323, 3388, **3460**, 3635, 3821, 4061, 4149, 4435, 4544
Welfare: 4567, 4740, 4769, 4898, 4901, 4911, 5032, 5143

Louisiana

Education: 58, 276, 316, 384, 552, 946, 1057, 1587, 1909, 1979, 1986, 2477, 2537, 3143, 3296, **3460**, 4039, 4297, 4475, 4558
Welfare: 4788, 4930, 4948, 5151
Arts and Culture: 5211
Research: 5622, 5831, 5928, 5954

Maine

Education: 146, 217, 236, 331, 492, 564, 587, 707, 777, 817, 821, 1188, 1414, 1637, 1708, **1775**, 1846, 1930, 2057, 2202, 2264, 2410, 2484, 2485, 2547, 2558, 2658, 2692, 2728, 2753, 2922, 2976, 3166, 3237, 3360, 3404, 3493, 3713, 3759, 3893, 3918, 4003, 4050, 4151, 4278, 4301, 4414, 4425, 4458, 4490, 4525
Welfare: 4582, 4603, 4618, 4621, 4686, 4762, 4928, 5003, 5004, 5132
Arts and Culture: 5378
Research: 5744

Maryland

Education: 279, 410, 452, 514, 685, 688, 714, 876, 1175, 1420, 1491, 1537, 1950, 2205, 2246, 2595, 2605, 2703, 2727, 2788, 2792, 3286, 3450, 3507, 3718, 3889, 3908, 3978, 4132, **4252**
Welfare: 4585, 4811, 4864, 4904, 4927, 5135
Arts and Culture: 5444
Research: 5933, 6016

Massachusetts

Education: 12, 43, 127, 152, 187, 235, 247, 251, 272, 313, 318, 322, 411, 418, 419, 465, 516, 529, 564, 600, 637, 647, 673, 706, 731, 762, 814, 838, 941, 967, 968, 986, 987, 1000, 1001, 1024, 1025, 1044, 1072, 1142, 1166, 1172, 1181, 1193, 1196, 1198, 1299, 1325, 1326, 1339, 1342, 1343, 1348, 1377, **1391**, 1392, 1403, 1410, 1416, 1438, 1469, 1516, 1526, 1538, 1554, 1559, 1590, 1594, 1601, 1744, 1756, 1781, 1897, 1906, 1919, 1925, 1938, **1943**, 1976, 1998, 2014, 2061, 2082, 2128, 2131, 2186, 2193, 2219, 2245, 2436, **2455**, 2456, 2488, 2489, 2497, 2510, 2542, 2553, 2555, 2599, 2624, 2709, 2732, 2736, 2755, 2761, 2769, 2805, 2810, 2823, 2831, 2849, 2872, 2888, 2921, 2922, 2951, 2954, 2971, 2973, 2998, 3004, 3014, 3041, 3051, 3078, 3083, 3096, 3110, 3127, 3161, 3162, 3164, 3178, 3210, 3223, 3240, 3267, 3270, 3276,

3297, 3299, 3341, 3391, 3393, 3396, 3414, 3424, 3445, 3457, 3464, 3481, 3517, 3590, 3642, 3656, 3744, 3750, 3778, 3806, 3836, 3844, 3927, 3950, 3993, 4002, 4012, 4032, 4072, **4098**, 4139, 4187, 4192, 4215, 4254, 4281, 4299, 4305, 4306, 4374, 4387, 4390, 4432, 4500, 4504, 4513, 4550
Welfare: 4582, 4592, 4617, 4618, 4621, 4626, 4637, 4690, 4696, 4717, 4750, 4754, 4771, 4773, 4809, 4825, 4826, 4831, 4882, 4902, 4905, 4909, 4926, 4962, 4995, 4996, 4997, 5000, 5009, 5024, 5030, 5040, 5041, 5043, 5051, 5057, 5081, 5088, 5093, 5098, 5099, 5103, 5106, 5168
Arts and Culture: 5339, 5342, 5348, 5378
Research: 5761, 5771, 5915, 5964, 6017

Michigan

Education: 13, 205, 298, 310, 320, 325, 326, 346, 354, 402, 423, **460**, 494, 501, 596, **689**, 807, 833, 845, 861, 864, 880, 886, 892, 905, 910, 913, 1064, 1100, 1109, 1177, 1307, 1317, 1357, 1419, 1435, 1452, 1498, 1544, 1549, 1556, 1561, 1580, 1596, 1617, 1621, 1628, 1703, 1725, 1752, 1802, 1855, 1905, 1920, 1966, 1987, 1991, 2001, **2039**, 2050, 2052, 2072, 2108, 2118, 2254, 2275, 2289, 2303, 2306, 2312, 2342, 2368, 2463, 2514, 2515, 2519, 2538, 2551, 2695, 2697, 2698, 2718, 2720, 2795, 2822, 2858, 2939, 2993, 3000, 3009, 3030, **3033**, 3124, 3128, **3147**, 3169, 3176, 3302, 3359, 3479, 3486, 3500, 3512, 3525, 3527, 3549, 3589, 3730, 3754, 3802, 3816, 3827, 3872, 3995, 3998, 4003, 4004, 4017, 4027, 4049, 4056, 4124, 4129, 4145, 4186, 4206, 4216, 4236, 4256, 4320, 4324, 4349, 4350, 4366, 4404, 4416, 4471, 4522
Welfare: 4594, 4842, 4954, 4961, 4979, 5038, 5060, 5083, 5116, **5170**
Research: 5729, 5801, 5973, 6018, 6110, 6151, 6183

Minnesota

Education: 4, 24, 27, **91**, 111, 138, 141, 168, 203, 421, 692, 727, 751, 755, 965, 1040, 1094, 1136, 1176, 1268, 1295, 1405, 1417, 1620, 1736, 1756, 1827, 1958, 1996, 2021, 2081, 2118, 2280, 2281, 2311, 2744, 2895, 3027, 3058, 3080, 3120, 3177, 3200, 3287, 3312, 3372, 3425, 3723, 3797, 3802, 3813, 3814, 3859, 4003, 4070, 4078, 4104, 4156, 4342, 4380, 4467, 4496
Welfare: 4583, 4780, 4793, 4846, 4982, 5001, 5123, 5164
Arts and Culture: 5200, 5202, 5247, 5312, 5349, 5373, 5402, 5403
Research: 5724

Mississippi

Education: 269, 399, 425, 477, 663, 710, 946, 993, 1450, 1787, 2593, 2756, 3797, 4003, 4039, 4307
Welfare: 4639, 4885, 4976, 4990, 5016

Missouri

Education: 40, 121, 288, 335, 352, 401, 469, 480, 513, 530, 569, 585, 627, 659, 792, 795, 843, 911, 956, 971, 1113, 1114, 1115, 1128, 1134, 1145, 1163, 1179, 1215, 1220, 1230, 1270, 1354, 1372, 1461, 1466, 1481, 1543, 1601, 1624, 1625, 1632, 1641, 1679, 1689, 1723, 1782, 1806, 1861, 1896, 1917, **1943**, 1969, **1990**, 1996, 2125, 2135, 2171, **2178**, 2189, 2203, 2236, 2250, 2263, 2384, 2439, 2534, 2535, 2589, 2683, 2708, 2871, 2965, 3030, 3053, 3122, 3154, 3243, 3315, 3333, 3434, 3500, 3556, 3595, 3596, 3611, 3612, 3613, 3614, 3615, 3616, 3617, 3618, 3619, 3620, **3628**, 3694, 3735, 3760, 3854, 3855, 3865,

Welfare: 4585

Rhode Island

Education: 240, 247, 564, 583, 987, 988, 1880, 1898, 1941, 2540, 2845, 2888, 2922, 3389, 3390, 3763, 4067
Welfare: 4618, 4621, 4908, 5015, 5063, 5087, 5113, 5142
Arts and Culture: 5378, 5457
Research: 6017, 6184

South Carolina

Education: 50, 58, 90, 140, 240, 261, 610, 633, 648, 691, 712, 811, 812, 978, 1106, 1108, 1156, 1317, 1321, 1362, 1366, 1409, 1484, 1639, 1747, **1943**, 1981, 2022, 2200, 2211, 2783, 2786, 3006, 3030, 3934, 4121, 4169, 4524
Welfare: 4630, 4664, 4665, 4681, 4758, 4977, 5077
Research: 5539, 5742

South Dakota

Education: 1146, 1614, 1615, 1631, 1765, 1940, 1996, 2118, 2288, 2637, 2823, 3723, 3724, 3796, 3802, 3809, 3939, 4295
Welfare: 4709, 4935, 5067
Arts and Culture: 5247

Tennessee

Education: 376, 426, 456, 478, 721, 815, 879, 946, 1125, 1327, 1459, 1733, 1762, 1776, 1787, 1890, 1902, 1997, 2113, 2141, 2903, 3030, 3094, 3165, 3423, **3654**, 3682, 3732, 3864, 3880, 4091, 4148, 4169, 4285, 4322, 4343, 4437, 4468, 4485, 4501
Welfare: 4660, 4707, 4747, 4832, 4852, 4879, 4940, 5017, 5061, 5068
Research: 5684, 5861, 5918

Texas

Education: 57, 58, 147, 215, 221, 296, 372, 388, 395, 448, 580, 629, 635, 667, 669, 703, 704, 705, 737, 801, 807, 810, 850, 873, 930, 945, 946, 950, 995, 1006, 1023, 1027, 1035, 1080, 1102, 1190, 1203, 1227, 1244, 1245, 1246, 1338, 1364, 1413, 1483, 1497, 1578, 1579, 1611, 1643, 1675, 1705, 1718, 1731, 1770, 1798, 1843, 1850, 1862, 1878, 1937, 1953, 1986, 2104, 2105, 2190, 2195, 2232, 2238, 2259, 2265, 2291, 2309, 2315, 2397, 2409, 2412, 2422, 2474, 2526, 2568, 2584, 2606, 2670, 2714, 2731, 2750, 2766, 2778, 2797,

2809, 2837, 2904, 2952, 2956, 3030, 3040, 3067, 3099, 3119, 3139, 3151, 3163, 3179, 3192, 3213, 3235, 3241, 3255, 3325, 3363, 3453, **3460**, 3472, 3500, **3502**, 3528, 3534, 3536, 3646, 3666, 3711, 3725, 3726, 3815, 3874, 3879, 3924, 3953, 3970, 4014, 4031, 4035, 4038, 4039, 4040, 4119, 4141, 4150, 4171, 4190, 4247, 4258, 4292, 4304, 4347, 4444, 4455, 4469, 4486, 4487, 4512, 4517, 4535, 4540, 4559, 4563, 4565
Welfare: 4646, 4675, 4684, 4724, 4739, 4741, **4746**, 4747, 4800, 4847, **4853**, 4891, 4914, 4930, 4955, 4978, 4999, 5038, 5075, 5096, 5105, 5109, 5166
Arts and Culture: 5287
Research: 5817, 5840, 5917, 5929, 5984, 6157, 6190

Utah

Education: 280, 291, 300, 1037, 1420, 1705, 1728, 1808, 2028, 2134, **2178**, 2273, 2539, 2856, 3756, 3810, 4510
Welfare: 4653, 4804, 4836
Research: 5728, 5730, 6111, 6133

Vermont

Education: 355, 446, 564, 729, 732, 802, 951, 1192, 1224, 1276, 1297, 1527, 1763, 2062, 2197, 2374, 2816, 2888, 2922, 2966, 3267, 3630, 3684, 3762, 4034, 4199, 4217, 4231, 4232, 4303, 4399, 4447, 4450, 4542
Welfare: 4618, 4621, 4683, 5008, 5125, 5136
Arts and Culture: 5378, 5497
Research: 5584, 6017

Virginia

Education: 58, 69, 109, 240, 258, 410, 433, 472, 492, 590, 620, 638, 726, 787, 829, 851, 854, 912, 917, 949, 1004, 1074, 1143, 1148, 1225, 1281, 1282, 1337, 1634, 1652, 1660, 1785, 1822, 1912, 2121, 2144, 2196, 2198, 2373, 2379, 2403, 2441, 2449, 2457, 2506, 2522, **2564**, 2641, 2644, 2654, 2746, 2801, 2811, 2866, **2942**, 2987, **3042**, 3081, 3160, 3173, 3231, **3307**, 3331, 3449, 3450, 3484, 3489, 3518, 3547, 3576, 3762, 3801, 3860, 3888, 3921, 3937, 4007, 4017, 4063, 4116, 4166, 4233, 4272, 4337, 4421, 4433, 4528
Welfare: 4581, 4585, 4630, 4641, 4807, **4865**, 4879, 4966, 5091, 5115
Research: 5849, 6169

Washington

Education: 142, 177, 196, 262, 307, 437, 447, 490, 528, 615, 650, 733, 776, 824, 839, 853, 1039, 1040, 1066, 1187, 1233, 1267, 1472, 1511, 1627, 1659, 1688, 1691, 1714, 1893, 1945, 2064, 2110, 2112, 2191, 2194, 2215, 2217, 2341, 2448, 2571, 2694, 2726, 2812, 2814, 2991, 3044, 3073, 3108, 3141, 3144, 3247, 3258, 3272, 3335, 3497, 3563, 3599, 3604, 3644, 3787, 3873, 3886, 4003, 4024, 4060, 4126, 4143, 4144, 4152, 4244, 4262, 4270, **4314**, 4318, 4353, 4389, 4440, 4506
Welfare: 4698, 4767, 4786, 4796, 4818, 4840, 4877, 4886, 4932, 4967, 5028, 5138, 5144, 5145
Arts and Culture: 5205, 5242, 5311, 5352
Research: 5634, **5896**, 6043, 6080, 6150

West Virginia

Education: 192, 357, 472, 668, 671, 680, 752, 870, 961, 1004, 1518, 1735, 2003, 2074, 2445, 2590, 2598, 2746, 2803, 2826, 2996, 3010, 3084, 3106, 3275, 3383, 3450, 3492, 3718, 3877, 3914, 3915, 3921, 3936, 3938, 4507
Welfare: 4651, 4715, 4806, 4876, 5019, 5072, 5095
Research: 6191

Wisconsin

Education: 46, 60, 163, 176, 211, 216, 292, 338, 513, 557, 595, 923, 1009, 1010, 1051, 1088, 1109, 1176, 1189, 1231, 1314, 1352, 1361, 1386, 1415, 1444, 1494, 1549, 1582, 1609, 1629, 1630, 1687, 1761, 1804, 1823, 1877, 1899, 1948, 2060, 2114, 2118, 2123, 2140, 2157, 2185, 2270, 2272, 2292, 2313, 2340, 2461, 2463, 2513, 2517, 2523, 2525, 2543, 2667, 2839, 2912, 2913, 2955, 2958, 3000, 3003, 3030, 3060, 3089, 3167, 3169, 3180, 3191, 3264, 3283, 3291, 3309, 3327, 3350, 3381, 3447, **3460**, 3471, 3496, **3522**, 3593, 3609, 3622, 3662, 3663, 3664, 3665, 3728, 3758, 3802, 3869, 3884, 3964, 4003, 4005, 4045, 4057, 4153, 4228, 4242, 4289, 4344, 4361, 4362, 4418, 4451, 4472, 4473, 4474
Welfare: 4814, 5037, 5049, 5079, 5086, 5162
Arts and Culture: 5247, 5449
Research: 5718, 5724, 6204

Wyoming

Education: 145, 563, 783, 819, 1037, 1236, 1567, 1642, 1676, 1978, 2101, 2150, 2391, 2392, 2637, 2737, 2908, 3134, 3159, 3208, 3817
Welfare: 4643

INTERNATIONAL GIVING INDEX

List of terms: The names of countries, continents, or regions used in this index are drawn from the complete list below. Terms may appear on the list but not be present in the index.

Index: In the index itself, grantmakers are listed under the countries, continents, or regions in which they have demonstrated giving interests. Within these country or regional groupings, grantmakers are arranged by sequence number. This index indicates support going directly overseas; to learn more about the international interests of grantmakers, see the Subject Index for more information.

Afghanistan	Comoros	Indian Subcontinent & Afghanistan	Namibia
Africa	Congo	Indonesia	Nauru
Albania	Costa Rica	Iran	Nepal
Algeria	Croatia	Iraq	Netherlands
Andorra	Cuba	Ireland	Netherlands Antilles
Angola	Curacao	Isle of Man	New Caledonia
Anguilla	Cyprus	Israel	New Zealand
Antarctica	Czech Republic	Italy	Nicaragua
Antigua & Barbuda	Denmark	Ivory Coast	Niger
Arctic Region	Developing countries	Jamaica	Nigeria
Argentina	Djibouti	Japan	North Korea
Armenia	Dominica	Jordan	Northeast Africa
Aruba	Dominican Republic	Kazakhstan	Northern Ireland
Asia	Eastern Europe	Kenya	Norway
Australia	Ecuador	Kiribati	Oceania
Austria	Egypt	Korea	Oman
Azerbaijan	El Salvador	Kuwait	Pakistan
Bahamas	England	Kyrgyzstan	Panama
Bahrain	Equatorial Guinea	Laos	Papua New Guinea
Bangladesh	Eritrea	Latin America	Paraguay
Barbados	Estonia	Latvia	Peoples Dem. Rep. of Yemen
Belarus	Ethiopia	Lebanon	Peru
Belgium	Europe	Leeward Islands	Philippines
Belize	Fiji	Lesotho	Poland
Benin	Finland	Liberia	Portugal
Bermuda	France	Libya	Qatar
Bhutan	French Guiana	Liechtenstein	Romania
Bolivia	Gabon	Lithuania	Russia
Bonaire	Gambia	Luxembourg	Rwanda
Bosnia-Herzegovina	Georgia (Republic of)	Macedonia	Saint Kitts-Nevis
Botswana	Germany	Madagascar	Saint Lucia
Brazil	Ghana	Malawi	Saint Vincent & the Grenadines
Brunei	Gibraltar	Malaysia	Samoa
Bulgaria	Gilbert Islands	Maldives	Saudi Arabia
Burkina Faso	Global programs	Mali	Scandinavia
Burundi	Greece	Malta	Scotland
Cambodia	Greenland	Marianas	Senegal
Cameroon	Grenada	Marshall Islands	Serbia
Canada	Guadeloupe	Martinique	Seychelles
Cape Verde	Guam	Mauritania	Sierra Leone
Caribbean	Guatemala	Mauritius	Singapore
Caroline Islands	Guernsey	Mexico	Slovakia
Cayman Islands	Guinea	Micronesia	Slovenia
Central Africa	Guinea-Bissau	Middle East	Solomon Islands
Central African Republic	Guyana	Moldova	Somalia
Central America	Haiti	Monaco	South Africa
Chad	Honduras	Mongolia	South America
Chile	Hong Kong	Montserrat	South Korea
China	Hungary	Morocco	Southeast Asia
China & Mongolia	Iceland	Mozambique	Southern Africa
Colombia	India	Myanmar (Burma)	Soviet Union (Former)

Spain
Sri Lanka
Sub-Saharan Africa
Sudan
Suriname
Swaziland
Sweden
Switzerland
Syria
Tahiti
Taiwan

Tajikistan
Tanzania
Thailand
Togo
Tonga
Trinidad & Tobago
Tunisia
Turkey
Turkmenistan
Turks & Caicos Islands
Tuvalu

Uganda
Ukraine
United Arab Emirates
United Kingdom
Uruguay
Uzbekistan
Vanuatu
Vatican City
Venda
Venezuela
Vietnam

Wales
West Bank/Gaza
Western Africa
Western Samoa
Yemen Arab Republic
Yugoslavia (Federal Republic of)
Yugoslavia (Former)
Zaire
Zambia
Zimbabwe

Africa
Arts and Culture: 5215, 5482
Research: 5673, 5885, 5886, 5934, 6083, 6198

Albania
Research: 5563

Algeria
Education: 169, 170

Argentina
Research: 5795, 5860

Armenia
Education: 16, 197, 445, 1307, 1898, 2278, 4010
Research: 5564

Asia
Education: 103
Arts and Culture: 5215, 5219
Research: 5624, 5651, 5886, 5952, 5969, 5978, 6132, 6198

Australia
Education: 1078, 3533
Arts and Culture: 5427
Research: 5614, 5703, 5893, 6065

Austria
Arts and Culture: 5427
Research: 5614

Azerbaijan
Education: 3035
Research: 5564

Bahamas
Research: 5786

Belarus
Education: 3035

Belgium
Education: 350, 2329
Arts and Culture: 5427
Research: 5614

Belize
Research: 5802

Brazil
Welfare: 4887
Research: 5682, 5860

Bulgaria
Education: 3035
Research: 5563

Cambodia
Research: 6038

Cameroon
Education: 2947
Research: 6038

Canada
Education: 85, 124, 186, 349, 1149, 1408, 1775, 1883, 2260, 2283, 2794, 2897, 2932, 3042, 3211, 3379, 3672, 3789, 4329
Welfare: 4896, 5056, 5170
Arts and Culture: 5263, 5338, 5405, 5526
Research: 5530, 5549, 5590, 5614, 5661, 5674, 5677, 5681, 5710, 5764, 5795, 5860, 5881, 6065, 6097, 6130, 6194

Caribbean
Arts and Culture: 5338
Research: 5885, 5963, 6038, 6099

Central America
Education: 2557
Research: 5802, 5963, 6038

Chile
Research: 5614, 5795, 5860

China
Education: 746, 747, 869, 2382, 3731, 4521
Research: 5563, 5697, 6132

Costa Rica
Research: 5530

Croatia
Education: 998, 3035
Arts and Culture: 5215, 5427
Research: 6173

Cuba
Arts and Culture: 5271

Cyprus
Research: 5927

Czech Republic
Education: 1487
Arts and Culture: 5345
Research: 5563

Denmark
Education: 1161, 2990

Developing countries
Education: 869
Welfare: 4839, 5029
Research: 5623, 5678, 5825, 5826, 5959, 6108, 6112, 6189

Eastern Europe
Education: 3463, 4010
Welfare: 4704
Arts and Culture: 5328, 5490
Research: 5563, 5821, 6067, 6123

Egypt
Welfare: 4722

El Salvador
Research: 5802

England
Education: 1407, 2794
Research: 5874, 5927, 6163

Estonia
Education: 1300, 3463
Welfare: 4731
Research: 5563

Europe
Education: 1394
Arts and Culture: 5233, 5328, 5486, 5490
Research: 5614, 5784, 5795, 5821, 5860, 5927, 6192

France
Education: 76, 339, 1148, 1161, 1408, 1465, 1477, 2329, 2450, 3379, 3789
Welfare: 4763

Arts and Culture: 5223, 5253, 5322, 5385, 5427, 5488
Research: 5614, 5821, 5875, 5927, 5978, 6072, 6192

French Guiana
Research: 6038

Georgia (Republic of)
Education: 3035
Research: 5564

Germany
Education: 1407, 1537
Welfare: 4575
Arts and Culture: 5186, 5188, 5427
Research: 5614, 5679, 5821, 5885, 5927, 5978

Ghana
Research: 6038

Global programs
Education: 243, 415, 1041, 1056, 4023, 4098, 4515
Welfare: 4723
Arts and Culture: 5204, 5227, 5277, 5295
Research: 5561, 5617, 5626, 5628, 5640, 5649, 5689, 5723, 5731, 5743, 5749, 5766, 5784, 5819, 5881, 5989, 6042, 6064

Greece
Education: 759, 1052, 1312, 1426, 1487, 1538, 2167, 2332, 2935, 3098, 3792
Welfare: 4572
Research: 5611, 5876, 5978, 5990, 6061

Guatemala
Research: 5802

Haiti
Education: 4096

Honduras
Research: 5802

Hong Kong
Education: 1487
Research: 5893

Hungary
Education: 119, 750, 2187
Research: 5563, 5821

India
Education: 486, 1496, 2478, 3638
Arts and Culture: 5190
Research: 5577, 5631, 5719, 5874,
    5977, 6093

Indonesia
Education: 2019
Research: 6132

Ireland
Education: 2794
Arts and Culture: 5427
Research: 6131

Israel
Education: 99, 116, 498, 1149, 1442,
    2088, 2168, 2210, 3715, 4159
Welfare: 4734, 4861
Arts and Culture: 5394
Research: 5530, 5594, 5632, 5688,
    5811, 5895, 5911, 5927, 5939,
    6193, 6210

Italy
Education: 967, 1038, 1356, 1495,
    2045, 2884, 2935, 3805, 3994
Welfare: 4842, 5107
Arts and Culture: 5223, 5241, 5427
Research: 5530, 5726, 5821, 5927,
    5978, 6010

Jamaica
Education: 1921

Japan
Education: 623, 2957, 3516
Arts and Culture: 5219, 5223, 5427,
    5486
Research: 5563, 5624, 6136

Jordan
Education: 99
Welfare: 4669

Kazakhstan
Education: 3035

Kenya
Education: 137

Korea
Education: 1118, 2223, 2228, 2869,
    3503
Arts and Culture: 5427
Research: 5913

Kyrgyzstan
Education: 3035
Research: 5564

Latin America
Arts and Culture: 5215, 5338, 5486

Research: 5804, 5885, 5886, 6092,
    6198

Latvia
Education: 3035
Research: 5563

Lebanon
Education: 1685, 1726

Libya
Education: 99

Lithuania
Education: 2408, 3035
Research: 5563

Macedonia
Education: 3035, 3792

Madagascar
Research: 6038

Malaysia
Research: 6132

Mexico
Education: 186, 660, 1681, 2557,
    2681, 3318, 4338
Arts and Culture: 5223, 5263
Research: 5764, 5802, 5860, 5886,
    5893, 6198

Middle East
Education: 169, 170
Research: 5895

Moldova
Education: 3035

Mongolia
Education: 3035

Morocco
Education: 169, 170

Myanmar (Burma)
Education: 3035

Nepal
Education: 2916
Welfare: 4937

Netherlands
Education: 1161, 2919
Arts and Culture: 5419, 5427
Research: 5530

New Zealand
Education: 2216
Research: 5703

Nicaragua
Education: 263

Northeast Africa
Education: 169, 170

Norway
Education: 2992, 3723
Welfare: 4706

Papua New Guinea
Research: 6038

Philippines
Research: 5541, 6038, 6083

Poland
Education: 2283, 3233
Research: 5563, 5821, 5897, 5925

Portugal
Education: 1489
Research: 5821

Romania
Education: 3035
Research: 5563, 6067

Russia
Education: 2285, 3035
Welfare: 4704, 4862, 5036
Arts and Culture: 5490

Scandinavia
Education: 4288
Research: 5607

Scotland
Education: 773, 3626
Welfare: 4714, 5051

Serbia
Welfare: 5056

Singapore
Research: 5614, 6023, 6132

Slovakia
Education: 3035
Arts and Culture: 5345
Research: 5563

South America
Education: 3810
Research: 5963, 6038

Southeast Asia
Education: 1610
Arts and Culture: 5219
Research: 5952

Soviet Union (Former)
Research: 5784

Spain
Education: 3341
Arts and Culture: 5427
Research: 5614, 5821

Sweden
Education: 339, 1161, 4288
Research: 5853

Switzerland
Education: 3988
Welfare: 5101
Arts and Culture: 5427
Research: 5614, 5927

Syria
Education: 99

Taiwan
Education: 2382, 3731
Arts and Culture: 5345, 5427

Tajikistan
Education: 3035

Tanzania
Research: 6038

Thailand
Education: 486
Research: 6132

Turkey
Research: 5530, 5880

Ukraine
Education: 2284, 3035
Arts and Culture: 5201
Research: 5564

United Kingdom
Education: 2174, 3474
Welfare: 4621
Research: 5614, 5661, 5703, 5726

Uzbekistan
Education: 3035
Research: 5564

Venezuela
Research: 5860

Vietnam
Education: 4238
Research: 6038, 6083, 6132

Wales
Education: 2794
Research: 6163

West Bank/Gaza
Education: 99, 1442, 2084
Research: 5895

Yugoslavia
Research: 5563, 6148

COMPANY NAME INDEX

The numbers following the company names in this index refer to the sequence numbers of entries in the Descriptive Directory section. The specific companies or corporations listed here provide funding directly to employees, former employees, and families of employees.

SPECIFIC SCHOOL INDEX

The numbers following the school names in this index refer to the sequence numbers of entries in the Descriptive Directory section. The index refers to institutions that give educational support only to the graduates of specific high schools or school districts, or students of specific institutions of higher education.

Harper Creek public high schools, MI, 4465
Harrisburg Academy, PA, 17
Harrisburg area high schools, PA, 2437, 3691
Harrisburg High School, IL, 2511
Harrisburg High School, OR, 804
Harrisburg high schools, PA, 17
Harrison County high schools, WV, 4507
Hartford County public and private schools, CT, 1485
Hartford public high schools, CT, 1439
Hartselle High School, AL, 1754
Hartwick College, NY, 2080, 3634
Harvard University, John F. Kennedy School of
    Government, MA, 6002, 6193
Harvard University, MA, 419, 1744, 1756, 1835,
    2624, 3083, 3341
Harwich High School, MA, 647
Haskell High School, TX, 2618
Hauser High School, IN, 3997
Havana High School, IL, 2367
Haverford College, PA, 6185
Haverhill High School, MA, 1000
Hawkins County high schools, TN, 1733
Hayes (Rutherford B.) High School, OH, 4280
Hayes County high schools, NE, 1712
Haywood Community College, NC, 2575
Haywood County High School, TN, 815
Helena High School, MT, 3153
Helias High School, MO, 3617, 3618, 3619
Hemingford High School, NE, 1259
Henderson County High School, KY, 3323
Henderson County High School, NC, 1112
Henderson County public high schools, NC, 2136
Hendricks County high schools, IN, 1819
Hendrix College, AR, 6185
Henlopen High School, DE, 1083
Henrico County public schools, VA, 1822
Henrico County secondary schools, VA, 2403
Henry (Patrick) High School, MN, 1827
Henry County High School, IN, 725
Heritage Christian School, IN, 756
Herkimer County Community College, NY, 826
Herkimer County High School, NY, 826
Hermantown High School, MN, 2758
Herrin High School, IL, 1746, 2511
Herscher High School, IL, 4476
Hesperia High School, MI, 1463
Hiawatha High School, KS, 2787
Hibbing high schools, MN, 111
Hidalgo Independent School District, TX, 1843
Higbee High School, MO, 3053
High Point University, NC, 959
High School in Union County, NJ, 4174
High Sky Girls Ranch, TX, 1203
Highland County School System, OH, 675
Highland High School, IN, 2471
Highland Springs High School, VA, 3801
Hill (Arthur) High School, MI, 1544
Hill City High School, MN, 421
Hill City high schools, MN, 421
Hill County high schools, TX, 1850
Hill High School, The, PA, 3253
Hill School, PA, 4417
Hill-Murray School, MN, 3514
Hillcrest Middle School, CT, 4355
Hillsdale College, MI, 2967
Hinckley-Big Rock High School, IL, 238
Hingham High School, MA, 814
Hinsdale Central School, NY, 3887
Hitchcock high schools, NE, 1712
Hobart College, NY, 791
Hocking Technical College, OH, 2217
Hofstra University, NY, 3976
Holland Central High School, NY, 3365
Holland Christian High School, MI, 1617
Holland-Zeeland School District, MI, 910
Holliston County high schools, MA, 3464
Holmes Community College, MS, 946
Holy Family High School, CO, 1903
Holy Rosary Catholic School, MO, 2189
Holy Spirit High School, NJ, 3766
Holyoke High School, MA, 2805
Home on the Range for Boys, ND, 1203
Homedale High School, ID, 2865
Homestead High School, IN, 2963

Homestead High School, WI, 1444, 2182
Hood College, MD, 449
Hood River County high schools, OR, 953
Hoosac High School, MA, 3778
Hoover High, CA, 1575
Hope (Bob) High School, TX, 1203
Hope College, MI, 1463, 2967
Hopedale High School, MA, 1919
Hopkinton County high schools, MA, 3464
Hornell High School District, NY, 1665
Hornell High School, NY, 575
Houghton College, NY, 1943
Houlton High School, ME, 2484
Houston area public high schools, TX, 4246
Howard County high schools, IN, 30, 888, 3225
Howard County high schools, MO, 1969
Howard High School of Technology, DE, 1083
Howard University College of Medicine, DC, 5848
Howard University, DC, 2149
Hudson High School, FL, 1882
Hudson public high schools, MA, 1998
Humboldt County high schools, IA, 2399
Humphreys County high schools, TN, 3864
Hunterdon Central Regional High School, NJ, 1336
Huntington Beach Unified High School District, CA,
    1155
Huntington North High School, IN, 4448
Huron County high schools, MI, 3754
Husson College, ME, 2484
Hutchinson Community College, KS, 3132
Hutchinson High School, KS, 1056
Hyde Park High School, MA, 3270

I.U. Bedford N. Lawrence high school, OH, 1995
Ida Grove High School, IA, 1923
Illinois University, IL, 1308
Illinois Wesleyan University, IL, 3667
Illion High School, NY, 518
Ilwaco High School, WA, 1699
Imlay City School District, MI, 1435
Immokalee High School, FL, 2016
Independence-Monmouth School District 13J, OR,
    4051
Indian River County public high schools, FL, 1316
Indian River County schools, FL, 1371
Indian River Schools, DE, 1083
Indiana County high schools, PA, 311
Indiana Institute of Technology, IN, 1515
Indiana State University, Kelley School of Business, IN,
    1077
Indiana University School of Medicine, IN, 888
Indiana University, IN, 906, 1682, 1999, 3047, 3220,
    3407
Indiana University, South Bend, IN, 906
Indiana University-Purdue University, IN, 1515
Institute of Metallurgy Academica Sinica, Shanghai,
    China, 2382
Intermediate Middle School, CT, 4355
Interstate 35 High School, IA, 717
Iola High School, KS, 4549
Iowa High School, IA, 4062
Iowa Mennonite School, IA, 2508
Iowa Valley Community School District, IA, 406
Iron Mountain High School, MI, 1703
Ironton High School, MO, 1220
Ironton Public Schools, MO, 1220
Ironwood Area School District, MI, 2039
Iroquois County high schools, IL, 3385
Iselboro High School, ME, 2484
Island County high schools, WA, 3073
Isothermal Community College, NC, 2575
Itasca high schools, MN, 1620
Ivy Tech State College, IN, 894
Ivy Tech, IN, 3407

Jackson (Stonewall) High School, VA, 510
Jackson Community College, MI, 3793
Jackson County high schools, IN, 889
Jackson County high schools, OR, 3603
Jackson County high schools, WV, 3106
Jackson High School, OH, 2468
Jackson High School, WY, 1567

Jackson Memorial High School, NJ, 439
Jackson State University, MS, 883
Jamestown College, ND, 1765
Jamestown High School, NY, 645
Janesville High School, WI, 903
Janesville public high schools, WI, 2063
Jay County High School, IN, 3245
Jefferson (Thomas) High School, PA, 990
Jefferson (Thomas) University, Jefferson Medical
    College, PA, 780, 1585
Jefferson (Thomas) University, OR, 1331
Jefferson College, MO, 3793
Jefferson County high schools, WI, 1051
Jefferson County high schools, WV, 2580
Jefferson County public high schools, KY, 500
Jefferson High School, OR, 4310
Jeffersonville High School, IN, 1393
Jersey Community High School, IL, 684
Jersey Shore Area School District, PA, 3755
Jewell County high schools, KS, 3983
John Adams High School, IN, 906
Johns Hopkins University, MD, 1835
Johnson and Wales University, CO, 240
Johnson and Wales University, FL, 240
Johnson and Wales University, NC, 240
Johnson and Wales University, RI, 240
Johnson and Wales University, SC, 240
Johnson and Wales University, VA, 240
Johnson County high schools, IN, 2100, 3138
Johnson County schools, WY, 2101
Johnson Creek High School, WI, 60
Johnson High School, NJ, 301
Johnston City High School, IL, 2511
Joliet Junior College, IL, 1891
Jordan School District, UT, 2134
Josephinum High School, IL, 3209
Juilliard School of Music, The, NY, 3771
Juilliard School, The, NY, 4554
Julesburg High School, CO, 639
Julliard School, NY, 2395
Juneau Business High School, WI, 2182
Jupiter High School, FL, 865
Justin-Siaena High School, CA, 921

K.B. Beit Haemek, Israel, 2168
Kalama High School, WA, 2448
Kalamazoo County high schools, MI, 2152
Kalamazoo County schools, MI, 2357
Kalamazoo Valley Community College, MI, 2357, 3793
Kanabec County high schools, MN, 4104
Kaneland High School, IL, 238, 1248
Kaneland high schools, IL, 1289
Kansas State University, KS, 1262, 2162, 3910
Kansas University, KS, 2178
Kaskaskia College, IL, 3842
Katahdin High School, ME, 2484
Kearsley area schools, MI, 880
Keene public schools, NH, 2300
Keiser College, FL, 808
Kellogg Community College, MI, 3793
Kemmerer High School, WY, 4526
Kendall College of Art and Design, MI, 1621
Kennebec County high schools, ME, 2484
Kennedy (John F.) High School, OH, 2446
Kennedy (John F.) High School, OR, 2820
Kennett High School, NH, 1821
Kennett Public Schools, MO, 3315
Kennewick School District, WA, 3399
Kent County colleges, MI, 1419
Kent School District, WA, 3787
Kent School, CT, 4417
Kern County high schools, CA, 963, 2950
Kerr County High School, TX, 1643
Key West High School, FL, 2214
Key West high school, FL, 4680
Keystone Central School District, PA, 3215
Keystone High School, PA, 4227
Keystone Junior College, PA, 711
Keytesville Township School District, MO, 1372
Kilgore High School, TX, 2628
Killingly High School, CT, 3273
Kimberly High School, ID, 3580
King (Rufus) High School, WI, 2182

Pottstown High Schook, PA, 3253
Pottsville Area High School, PA, 753
Pottsville Area School District, PA, 1727
Powell County high schools, MT, 3361
Prairie Central Community Unit District 8 schools, IL, 2166
Prairie Grove High School, AR, 3203
Prairie Heights Community School Corporation School District, IN, 2305
Pratt County Community College, KS, 3244
Pratt County high schools, KS, 2622
Prattsburg Central School District, NY, 2578
Prescott Christian High School, AZ, 3261
Presentation College, SD, 1940
Presque Isle High School, ME, 2484, 3166
Princeton area secondary schools, NJ, 2623
Princeton Senior High School, WV, 3275
Princeton University, NJ, 1835
Proctor High School, MN, 2758
Proctor High School, NY, 1015
Profile High School, NH, 3800
Protestant Episcopal Theological Seminary of Virginia, VA, 2746
Providence Catholic High School, IL, 3091
Provincetown High School, MA, 647
Pueblo County high school, CO, 1716
Pueblo County high schools, CO, 1811
Puget Sound Christian College, WA, 142
Pullman Free School of Vocational Training, IL, 3293
Punxsutawney Area High School, PA, 1117, 2040
Punxsutawney School District, PA, 1152
Punxytawney Area High School, PA, 3052
Purdue University, IN, 1077, 1078, 1197, 1715, 2329, 2499
Purdue University, School of Mechanical Engineering, IN, 906
Purnell School, NJ, 4417
Putnam County Community Unit School District no. 535, IL, 3930
Putnam County High School, IL, 482

Queens College, NY, 6185
Quincy University, IL, 1308

Raceland-Worthington Independent School System, OH, 2774
Racine County high schools, WI, 3768
Racine Unified School District, WI, 3309
Radcliffe College, MA, 419
Raleigh high schools, NC, 2813
Randolph County high schools, IN, 897, 2791
Randolph High School, NE, 3413
Randolph Township Board of Education schools, NJ, 2827
Randolphe Southern High School, IN, 3913
Rayen High School, OH, 3101
Raymond High School, WA, 1893
Read Middle School, John, CT, 4355
Reading High School, PA, 1555
Reading Senior High School, PA, 1760, 1884
Red Bank Regional High School, NJ, 1650, 4406
Red Willow County high schools, NE, 1712
Redfield School District, SD, 3939
Reed College, OR, 3653, 6185
Reedsburg Webb High School, WI, 2958, 3167
Refugio County high schools, TX, 3453
Regis High School, IL, 1144
Reinbeck public schools, IA, 2548
Remer High School, MN, 421
Rensselaer County School District No. 1, NY, 3382
Rensselaer Polytechnic Institute, NY, 1835
Republic County high schools, KS, 3983
Republic high schools, WA, 196
Revere High School, MA, 1438
Revere High School, OH, 1505
Revere Junior-Senior High School, CO, 639
Reynolds High School, OR, 2713
Rhinelander High School, WI, 1494, 3350, 4289
Rhode Island School of Design, RI, 6185
Rhodes College, TN, 449, 946
Rice High School, TX, 4469
Rice University, TX, 1835, 6185

Richburg Central School, NY, 2819
Richland College, TX, 4041
Richland County high schools, MT, 1266
Richland County School District, ND, 3647
Richland High School, MS, 883
Richland School District, WA, 3399
Ricker Classical Institute, ME, 3404
Ricker College, ME, 3404
Ricker Junior College, ME, 3404
Ridgedale High School, OH, 4106
Ridgefield High School, CT, 277, 3408
Ridgewood High School, OH, 420, 2413
Rimrock High School, ID, 2865
Ringgold High School, PA, 383
Ripley High School, TN, 721
Ripley High School, WV, 3877
Rising Sun High School, IN, 274, 3019
Ritchie County high schools, WV, 3106
Ritenour Senior High School, MO, 971
River Valley High School, OH, 4106
River Valley High School, WI, 292
Riverside University High School, WI, 2182
Riverside-Brookfield High School, IL, 11
Riverview High School, OH, 420
Roane County high schools, WV, 3106
Roberts (Owen J.) High School, PA, 3253
Robstown High School, TX, 4119
Rochester Community High School, IN, 3092
Rochester High School, MI, 886
Rochester high schools, MN, 3058
Rochester high schoools, MN, 755
Rock Springs High School, WY, 4526
Rock Valley College, IL, 3439
Rock Valley Community School, IA, 3560
Rockefeller University, NY, 5856
Rockland District High School, ME, 271, 2484, 4414
Rockland High School, MA, 1976
Rockport High School, MA, 12
Rockville High School, CT, 2724
Rockwell Independent School District, TX, 1774
Rocky Mountain College, MT, 607
Rogers High School, RI, 4067
Rome Free Academy, NY, 1199, 4218
Rome High School, GA, 2614
Romeo School District, MI, 1435
Roosevelt High School, CA, 3290, 3318
Roosevelt High School, OR, 2764
Rosary High School, IL, 238
Roscoe Central School District, NY, 1216
Rose City School District, MI, 1580
Roseville High School, CA, 1169
Roxbury High School, NJ, 2630
Rush County high schools, IN, 836, 2438
Rush County high schools, KS, 270
Russell High School, KY, 654
Russell School System, OH, 2774
Ryan Middle School, TX, 3325
Rye High School, NY, 3501

Sacred Heart High School, MO, 792
Saddleback Community College, CA, 3623
Saginaw County school districts, MI, 2467
Saginaw Valley State University, MI, 325, 354, 2562
Saint Cloud High School, FL, 4073
Saint Joseph County high schools, IN, 476
Salem Central High School, NY, 586
Salem College, NC, 2207, 2349
Salem High School, MO, 4543
Salem High School, NJ, 657, 1743
Salem high schools, MA, 4432
Salinas Valley high schools, CA, 584
Saline County high schools, AR, 89
Saline County high schools, KS, 2771
Salisbury High School, MO, 1990
San Bernardino high schools, CA, 1720
San Diego County high schools, CA, 1345, 2253, 3537
San Diego County schools, CA, 1014
San Diego State University, CA, 392
San Francisco Bay Area high schools, CA, 1835
San Fransisco State University, CA, 209
San Lorenzo Valley High School, CA, 3183
San Mateo County high schools, CA, 566
San Rafael High School, CA, 765

Sandburg (Carl H.) High School, IL, 153
Sandburg High School, Carl, IL, 3091
Sandora high schools, IL, 698
Sandwich High School, MA, 647
Sanford High School, ME, 2484
Sangamon County High School, IL, 1700
Sangamon County high schools, IL, 2581, 2600
Sanilac County high schools, MI, 845, 3549
Santa Barbara County high schools, CA, 3550, 3586
Santa Cruz High School, CA, 1208, 3104
Santa Monica College, CA, 3394
Santaluces High School, FL, 865
Santiam High School, OR, 804
Saranac Lake School District, NY, 5044
Sarasota County high schools, FL, 899, 2364, 3652
Saratoga High School, CA, 2220
Saratoga Springs high schools, NY, 1780
Sargent College of Rehabilitation, MA, 647
Sauk County Normal School, The, WI, 2958
Sauquoit School District, NY, 4266
Savannah high schools, MO, 335
Sayre High School, OK, 3845
Scarborough High School, ME, 2484
Schalick High School, NJ, 2730
Schenectady County high schools, NY, 3569
School District No. 60, MO, 795
School of Medicine, Indiana University, IN, 3415
School of Podiatric Medicine, PA, 780
Schulenburg High School, TX, 3874
Scio High School, OR, 804
Scotch Plains-Fanwood High School, NJ, 3625
Scotts Bluff High School, NE, 3046
Scripps College, CA, 3394, 6185
Searsport High School, ME, 2484
Seattle Pacific College, WA, 142
Seattle School District No. 1, WA, 650
Sedgwick County high schools, CO, 639
Sedgwick County high schools, KS, 2911
Seneca Valley High School, PA, 4219
Sequoia Union High School District, CA, 3294
Seton Hall University School of Law, NJ, 1298
Sevier County High School, TN, 1140
Sevier County high schools, TN, 376
Seward High School, NE, 4277
Seymour Community School District, WI, 3662
Seymour High School, IN, 3428, 3663, 3687
Seymour High School, TN, 1140
Shamokin Area Senior High School, PA, 681
Shasta College, CA, 2579
Shasta County high schools, CA, 1657
Shasta High School, CA, 3671
Shelby County High School, KY, 3181
Shelby County high schools, IA, 2944
Shelby County high schools, OH, 900
Shelbyville High School, IL, 2258
Shelton High School, CT, 4355
Shenandoah Community School District, IA, 2310
Shenandoah County public schools, VA, 3576
Shenandoah High School, IA, 144, 1551, 2069
Shepard High School, Alan B., IL, 3091
Shepaug Valley High School, CT, 613
Sheridan College, WY, 3208
Sheridan County high schools, MT, 3683
Sheridan County high schools, WY, 3159, 4409
Sherman County high schools, OR, 1055
Shiloh C.U.S.D. No. 1, IL, 1127
Shriner High School, TX, 4486
Sikellamny High School, PA, 2366
Sikeston High School, MO, 2683
Silver Lake Regional High School, MA, 647
Silverton High School, OR, 2415
Simsbury High School, CT, 1265, 1970
Sinai Academy, NY, 2210
Sinclair Community College, OH, 5066
Sinslaw High School, OR, 4379
Sinton High School, TX, 3725
Sioux Falls high schools, SD, 1146
Skagit County high schools, WA, 3073
Skaneateles High School, NY, 458
Skyview High School, ID, 2865, 3698
Slippery Rock University, PA, 3740
Slocomb High School, AL, 1960
Smackover High School, AR, 4173
Smith (William) College, NY, 791

Trenton Public School System, NJ, 398
Tri-Central High School, IN, 3829
Tri-County Technical College, NC, 2575
Tri-State University, IN, 1661
Trinity Bible College, ND, 1765
Trinity College, CT, 2187
Trinity College, DC, 3468
Trinity University, TX, 4171
Trinity Valley College, TX, 4041
Trinity-Pawling School, NY, 4417
Triton High School, IN, 2282
Triton High School, MA, 600
Triton School Corp., IN, 2266
Troup County, GA, 628
Troup High School, TX, 2628
Troy High School, ID, 3319
Trumbell High School, CT, 4355
Trumbull High School, CT, 1493, 4355
Tufts University School of Medicine, MA, 1343
Tufts University, University College of Citizenship,
    Public Service, MA, 1193
Tulane University, LA, 946
Tulane University, Newcomb College, LA, 6185
Tulare District high schools, CA, 1803
Tulare high schools, CA, 618
Tullahoma High School, TN, 1890, 4485
Tupelo High School, MS, 993
Tuscarawas County high schools, OH, 1932
Tuscola County high schools, MI, 845
Twin Cedars Junior Senior High School, IA, 2789
Twin Falls County high schools, ID, 3745
Twin Lakes High School, IN, 1602, 3121
Two Harbors High School, MN, 2758, 4156
Tyler Junior College, TX, 4041

Ukiah High School, CA, 728
Umatilla County high schools, OR, 4257
Unified School District No. 290, KS, 3432
Unified School District No. 416, KS, 3155
Union 32 School District, VT, 3684
Union College, KY, 449, 1776
Union College, NE, 4354
Union College, NY, 6185
Union County High School, KY, 1443
Union High School, IN, 3913
Union High School, MI, 1621
Union Joint School District, PA, 2371
Union-Endicott High School, NY, 519
Uniontown High School, PA, 509
Unionville-Sebewaing Area High School, MI, 325
Universal Technical Institute, NE, 4354
University of Alabama, AL, 3068
University of Alaska, AK, 55
University of Arizona, AZ, 178, 3739
University of Arkansas at Little Rock, AR, 4412
University of Arkansas, AR, 4036, 4441
University of Arkansas, Fayetteville, AR, 643
University of California at Berkeley, CA, 1191
University of California at Davis, CA, 2978
University of California at San Francisco, CA, 5923
University of California System, CA, 623
University of California, Berkeley, CA, 228, 621, 3394,
    4188
University of California, CA, 623, 1835, 2320, 3832
University of California, Davis, CA, 303, 3394
University of California, Irvine, CA, 3394
University of California, Los Angeles, CA, 3394
University of California, Riverside, CA, 3394
University of California, San Diego, CA, 3394
University of California, Santa Barbara, CA, 3394,
    3706
University of California, Santa Cruz, CA, 5991
University of Central Florida, FL, 984, 2475
University of Charleston, VA, 2156
University of Charleston, WV, 2746
University of Chicago, IL, 1621, 1835, 3460, 3571,
    4493
University of Cincinnati Medical School, OH, 4242
University of Colorado at Boulder, CO, 3793
University of Colorado Medical School, CO, 2632
University of Colorado, CO, 778, 3973
University of Connecticut School of Law, CT, 3882
University of Dayton, OH, 5066

University of Delaware, DE, 1083, 1791, 2002, 3947
University of Denver, CO, 766, 778, 2462
University of Detroit Mercy, McAuley School of Nursing,
    MI, 2882
University of Detroit Mercy, MI, 325
University of Evansville, IN, 906, 3355
University of Florida, FL, 1400
University of Georgia, GA, 4110, 4454
University of Hawaii, HI, 103, 1815
University of Hong Kong, China, 1487
University of Idaho, ID, 3886
University of Illinois at Urbana-Champaign, IL, 92,
    1115, 1835, 4552, 5829
University of Illinois, College of Medicine, IL, 3439
University of Illinois, IL, 88, 544, 1138, 4363
University of Indianapolis, IN, 1957
University of Kansas, KS, 1114, 3199, 3506, 3910,
    4441
University of Las Vegas, NV, 520
University of Louisville, KY, 3635
University of Maine at Farmington, ME, 2484
University of Maine, ME, 2484, 4003
University of Massachusetts, Boston, MA, 3304
University of Massachusetts, MA, 4299
University of Memphis, Loewenberg School of Nursing,
    TN, 2882
University of Memphis, TN, 946
University of Miami School of Medicine, FL, 5647
University of Michigan, MI, 149, 325, 1177, 1463,
    1621, 4145
University of Minnesota Institute of Technology, MN,
    4015
University of Minnesota, MN, 1218, 2758, 3027, 4003
University of Minnesota, Twin Cities Campus, MN,
    1835
University of Mississippi, MS, 663
University of Missouri, Kansas City, MO, 2589
University of Missouri, MO, 3154, 4092
University of Missouri—Rolla, MO, 3793
University of Missouri-Columbia, MO, 480, 1215, 3596
University of Missouri-Rolla, MO, 480, 1601, 1782,
    3793
University of Montana at Missoula, MT, 607
University of Nebraska College of Law, NE, 2321
University of Nebraska College of Medicine, NE, 5921
University of Nebraska, NE, 788, 4354
University of Nevada, NV, 2920
University of Nevada, Reno, NV, 1098
University of Nevada- Las Vegas, NV, 2751
University of Nevada- Reno, NV, 2751
University of North Carolina at Asheville, NC, 2575
University of North Carolina at Chapel Hill, NC, 3182
University of North Carolina at Chapel Hill, The, NC,
    2794
University of North Carolina at Greensboro, NC, 2575
University of North Carolina at Wilmington, NC, 3837
University of North Carolina, Greensboro, NC, 3909
University of North Carolina, NC, 2349
University of North Dakota, Grand Forks, ND, 3483
University of North Dakota, John D. Odegard School of
    Aerospace, ND, 1200
University of North Texas, TX, 3793
University of Notre Dame, IN, 906
University of Oklahoma, OK, 2533, 4441
University of Oregon School of Architecture, OR, 304
University of Paris, Sorbonne, France, 1477
University of Pennsylvania School of Medicine, PA, 780
University of Pennsylvania, PA, 775, 1555, 1585,
    3718
University of Phoenix, AZ, 4189
University of Pittsburgh School of Medicine, PA, 781,
    3256
University of Pittsburgh, OH, 1750
University of Pittsburgh, PA, 2626, 3718
University of Pittsburgh, School of Library and
    Information, PA, 3772
University of Puget Sound, WA, 6185
University of Richmond, VA, 449
University of Rio Grande, OH, 2217
University of Rochester, NY, 1835, 2899
University of South Carolina School of Medicine, SC,
    955
University of South Florida, FL, 2596
University of Southern California Law Center, CA, 3394

University of Southern California School of Medicine,
    CA, 3394
University of Southern California, CA, 1262, 2735,
    3394
University of Southern Maine, ME, 2484
University of St. Francis, IN, 1515
University of St. Thomas, MN, 168
University of Tennessee Knoxville, TN, 439
University of Tennessee, TN, 1776
University of Texas at Arlington, TX, 1608
University of Texas at Austin, TX, 1718, 1790, 2567
University of Texas at San Antonio, TX, 1798
University of Texas, TX, 1835
University of the Pacific, CA, 3394
University of the South, The, TN, 6185
University of Toledo, OH, 348, 1504, 3591
University of Tulsa, OK, 2533, 4441
University of Tulsa, The, OK, 471
University of Utah, UT, 67
University of Vermont, VT, 2062
University of Virginia College of Law, VA, 3921
University of Virginia, VA, 2746
University of Washington Medical School, WA, 1267,
    4440
University of Washington, WA, 1835, 2814, 2957,
    3886, 4003
University of Wisconsin - Marshfield, WI, 2523
University of Wisconsin, Stevens Point, WI, 923
University of Wisconsin, WI, 1051, 1823
University of Wisconsin-Madison Medical School, WI,
    4242
University of Wisconsin-Madison, WI, 1835
University of Wisconsin-Stevens Point, WI, 4003
University of Wyoming, WY, 2150, 3208, 4526
Upper Darby School District, PA, 2665
Upper Valley Joint Vocational School, OH, 4408
Ursuline College, OH, 2045
Utica public and parochial high schools, NY, 3675
Utica public and parochial schools, NY, 474
Utica public schools, NY, 1015

Valley High School, WA, 615
Vallivue High School, ID, 2865
Valparaiso University, IN, 3793
Van Buren High School, AR, 1701
Van Wert County high schools, OH, 4210
Vanderbilt University, TN, 1835
Vanderburgh County high schools, IN, 545
Vassar College, NY, 4002, 6185
Venango County high schools, PA, 1744, 4429
Vernonia High School, OR, 1889
Verona-Vernon-Sherrill High School, NY, 4218
Vienna High School, IL, 2511
Villanova University, PA, 1585
Vincennes University, IN, 1738
Vincent High School, WI, 2182
Vintage High School, CA, 921
Virginia Beach high schools, VA, 69
Virginia School for the Deaf and the Blind, VA, 312
Virginia Secondary School Independent School District
    No. 70, MN, 2281
Vista Community College, CA, 374
Voorhees High School, NJ, 1336

Wabash High School, IN, 636, 2492, 2742
Wabash high schools, IN, 531
Waco high schools, TX, 4565
Waco Roman Catholic schools, TX, 1080
Wahconah Regional High School, MA, 986
Wake Forest University, Bowman Gray School of
    Medicine, NC, 4468
Wake Forest University, NC, 2207, 3946, 4468
Waldo County high schools, ME, 1637
Walhalla High School, SC, 4524
Walla Walla County high schools, WA, 4126
Wallington High School, NJ, 2393
Walpole High School, MA, 3393
Walsh (Archbishop) High School, NY, 3887
Waltham High School, MA, 967
Walton Central High School, NY, 1501, 1721, 4293
Walton Central School District #1, NY, 785
Walton Central School District No. 1, NY, 3135

TYPE OF SUPPORT INDEX

The numbers under the types of support in this index refer to the sequence numbers of entries in the Descriptive Directory section of this book. Grantmakers that give nationally or regionally are indicated in boldface type following the states in which they are located. Grantmakers that restrict their giving to particular states, counties, or cities are listed in lighter type following the states in which they give. This index is generated to denote the types of support a grantmaker might provide to individuals and does not include the types of support the grantmaker provides to organizations.

Awards/grants by nomination only

Alabama: 2560
Arizona: 867, 3968, **6097**
Arkansas: 6178
California: 566, 1474, 2381, **2712**, 3542, 3943, 4300, **5139**, 5183, 5250, 5297, 5310, 5399, 5608, 5609, **5656**, 5672, **5826**, **5827**, **5828**, **5830**, 5850, 5854, **5855**, 5923, **5949**, 5962, 6086, 6102
Colorado: 1903, **3645**, 5655, **5698**, **5756**, **5884**, **5983**
Connecticut: **350**, 902, **5631**
Delaware: 5702
District of Columbia: 100, **1872**, **4113**, **5325**, 5555, **5557**, **5565**, 5597, **5775**, **5821**, **5873**, **5890**, 6030, **6034**, **6175**, 6181
Florida: **171**, **805**, 3334, 3818, 5724, **5804**
Georgia: 770, 2659, **3661**, **5799**, **6152**
Hawaii: **5541**
Idaho: 2700
Illinois: 2011, **2287**, **2881**, 3293, **5437**, **5488**, **5549**, **5579**, **5586**, **5757**, 5829, **5919**, **5956**, **6128**, **6144**, 6174
Indiana: 366, 889, 6164
Iowa: 5968, 6160
Kansas: 1468, 1814
Kentucky: 2056, 2642
Louisiana: **4016**, 5928, 5954
Maine: 236, **6165**
Maryland: 666, 3889, **5860**, 5933
Massachusetts: **4095**, 4432, 5420, **5526**, **5749**, **5908**, **5930**, **6070**, **6095**
Michigan: 1463, **2882**, 3232, 4236, 4366, **5330**, **5346**, **5748**, **5819**
Minnesota: 168, 5397, 5971
Mississippi: 883, 2593
Missouri: 1220, 2493
Montana: 1387, 1807, 2825
Nebraska: 980, 1235, **5660**, 5921
Nevada: 1788
New Jersey: 1153, 3992, 4417, **5254**, 5734, 5867, **5898**, **6199**
New Mexico: **5374**, 5671
New York: 416, 439, 575, 779, 868, 908, 964, 979, 1328, 2080, 2345, **2382**, **2450**, 2734, **2874**, 3710, 3729, 3833, **3973**, 4808, 4900, 5078, **5178**, 5185, **5187**, **5217**, **5222**, 5240, **5284**, 5290, **5295**, **5314**, **5317**, **5331**, **5336**, 5388, **5395**, **5415**, **5427**, **5430**, **5438**, **5458**, 5472, **5492**, 5496, **5513**, 5528, **5563**, **5573**, 5641, 5659, **5668**, **5710**, **5717**, **5740**, **5741**, **5784**, 5816, **5825**, **5832**, **5866**, **5879**, **5910**, **5927**, **5932**, 5941, **5952**, **5955**, **5960**, **6024**, **6039**, **6121**, **6145**

North Carolina: 1195, 2531, 2621, 2794, 3419, 4439, **5661**, 5683, 5848, 6103
Ohio: 1202, 1995, 2215, **3184**, 3277, 4210, 4591, 5119, **5510**, 5894, 5988, **6122**, **6209**
Oklahoma: 6057
Oregon: 2833, 4912, 6068
Pennsylvania: 6, 509, 1061, 1092, 3790, 4831, 5272, **5304**, 5354, 5657, **5674**, **5732**, **5846**, 6071, **6156**
Puerto Rico: 4170
Rhode Island: 968, 2245, 3499, 3882, **5544**, 5814, **6185**
Tennessee: 456, 3094, 5861, 6066
Texas: 521, 1227, 1774, 2343, 2797, 3953, 5329, 5787, 6158, 6187, 6190
Vermont: 1527, 4447
Virgin Islands: **5836**
Virginia: **948**, **5627**, **5701**, 5704, **5707**, **5999**, 6032, **6048**, 6153, **6155**
Washington: 653, 4389, 5234, **6126**
West Virginia: 1518
Wisconsin: 2472, 3008, 3309, 3665, 3728, 3739, 4369, 4436

Awards/prizes

Alaska: 5450, 5540
Arizona: 3968, **6097**
Arkansas: 2841, 6178
California: 209, 440, **2712**, **3320**, 5183, 5239, 5297, **5305**, 5306, 5310, 5311, **5318**, 5391, 5399, **5426**, 5463, 5465, 5529, **5548**, 5608, 5609, **5642**, 5665, 5672, 5714, **5795**, **5827**, **5830**, **5844**, 5850, **5855**, **5870**, **5888**, **5949**, 5962, 6086, 6102, 6114, 6171, 6177
Colorado: 5243, 5655, **5756**, **5884**, **6139**
Connecticut: 511, **5484**, **5542**, **5985**
Delaware: **1083**, **5358**, 5702, 5856, **5889**
District of Columbia: 130, **135**, **169**, 1122, **1872**, **3624**, **4260**, **5201**, **5282**, **5406**, 5431, 5505, **5556**, **5557**, **5558**, **5564**, **5565**, 5597, 5648, **5785**, **5815**, **5821**, **5824**, **5873**, **5890**, **6005**, 6030, **6034**, 6052, 6181
Florida: 899, 3114, **5416**, 5724, **5802**, 5938, **6081**
Georgia: **5799**, **6152**
Hawaii: 748, 1773
Illinois: 92, **128**, **3466**, **5335**, **5437**, 5493, 5494, **5549**, **5579**, **5586**, **5681**, **5689**, 5746, **5757**, **5806**, 5829, **5865**, 5868, **5919**, 6174
Indiana: 2100, 2183, 4230, 5725, **6055**
Iowa: 1731, 5968, **6207**
Kansas: 1056, 1713, 4030, **5357**, **5365**, 5414
Kentucky: **2030**
Louisiana: 5211, 5532, 5831, 5928, 5954

Maryland: 5210, **5353**, 5444, **5559**, **5578**, **5613**, 5715, **5759**, **5763**, **5764**, **5788**, **5796**, **5891**
Massachusetts: 125, 3162, 3298, **4095**, **5307**, 5342, **5522**, **5749**, 5834, **5899**, **5908**, **6029**, **6070**, **6095**
Michigan: 880, 1463, 2327, **3834**, **5194**, **5199**, 5236, **5330**, **5346**, 5653, **5783**, **5819**, 5973, **6140**
Minnesota: 5264, 5312, 5397, 5402, 5403, 5753, **5970**, 5971
Mississippi: 883
Missouri: 573, 911, **5184**
Montana: 1807, 2825
Nebraska: 1099
New Jersey: 1153, 2443, **3703**, **5254**, **5424**, 5491, 5645, 5734, 5867, **5898**, **6089**, **6199**, 6202
New Mexico: **5374**, **5466**, 5671
New York: 439, 719, 908, **1426**, 1885, **2382**, 2660, **2874**, 2891, 2923, 3562, **3570**, 4250, **4413**, **5178**, **5187**, **5193**, **5217**, **5218**, **5222**, 5240, 5242, **5258**, **5266**, 5268, 5286, 5290, 5293, **5296**, 5301, **5314**, **5316**, **5321**, **5322**, **5331**, **5333**, 5347, 5360, **5395**, **5415**, **5417**, **5418**, **5422**, **5427**, **5430**, **5438**, 5448, **5458**, **5475**, **5490**, **5492**, **5507**, **5513**, 5571, **5573**, 5583, **5598**, **5606**, **5607**, **5641**, **5646**, 5658, 5659, **5710**, **5711**, **5784**, 5807, 5816, 5851, **5879**, **5901**, **5932**, 5941, **5943**, **5955**, **5960**, **5993**, **6024**, **6121**, **6136**, **6154**, **6189**, **6208**
North Carolina: **3707**, 5683, 6103
Ohio: 377, 435, 1070, **2394**, 2431, 2892, 4210, **5510**, 5721, 5894, **5947**, 5988, 6106, **6122**, **6209**
Oklahoma: 2853
Oregon: 3045, 5381, **5881**
Pennsylvania: 695, **983**, 2979, 3790, 4831, 5377, 5436, **5441**, **5674**, **5732**, **5846**, 5914, **5946**, 6071, **6156**
Rhode Island: 2219, 3390, **5544**, 5814
South Dakota: 3723
Tennessee: 5861, 6066
Texas: 2797, 3797, 5225, 5280, 5329, **5640**, 5787, 6076, 6157, 6158, 6187, 6190, **6192**
Utah: **5486**
Virgin Islands: **5836**
Virginia: 120, **2546**, **2878**, **2900**, 3888, 4079, **5192**, **5221**, 5567, **5596**, **5602**, **5627**, 5704, **5707**, **5999**, **6001**, **6031**, 6032, **6141**, **6155**
Washington: 2361, 5205, **5263**, 5352, **5803**, **6126**
West Virginia: 3106
Wisconsin: 3447, 3914, 4473, 5718
Wyoming: 3919

Kansas: **5357**
Kentucky: 3635
Louisiana: 5532
Maine: 6025, **6165**
Maryland: 3048, 5444, **5570**, 5601, **5676**, 5715, **5763**, **5764**, **5767**, **5796**, **5869**, **5994**, **6006**, **6056**
Massachusetts: 125, 3341, 3757, **5307**, **5487**, **5522**, **5553**, **5560**, 5587, **5594**, **5731**, **5749**, 5765, **5808**, **5833**, **5908**, 5915, **5930**, 6196, **6210**
Michigan: 5653, **5748**, **5907**, **6140**
Minnesota: **5189**, 5202, 5247, **5253**, 5373, 5425, **5635**, 5662, 5753, **5989**
Missouri: **6077**, 6118
Montana: 5244
New Hampshire: 2924, **5878**
New Jersey: 1160, 4443, **5511**, **5643**, 5734, 5738, **5898**, **5953**, **5996**, 6202
New Mexico: **5466**, 5479
New York: 779, **840**, **1619**, **2382**, **2385**, **2450**, **2874**, **2919**, 3288, **3788**, **3807**, **4288**, **5178**, **5179**, **5186**, **5193**, **5204**, 5208, **5215**, **5219**, 5240, 5241, 5262, **5271**, **5284**, 5292, **5317**, **5338**, **5384**, **5422**, **5445**, **5495**, **5507**, 5512, **5519**, **5563**, 5571, **5591**, **5606**, **5607**, **5624**, **5646**, **5667**, **5668**, **5673**, **5679**, **5700**, **5703**, **5711**, **5717**, **5726**, **5740**, **5741**, **5751**, **5770**, **5780**, **5784**, **5793**, **5825**, **5837**, 5851, 5863, **5864**, **5866**, **5879**, **5886**, **5916**, 5924, **5925**, **5927**, **5936**, **5952**, **5955**, **5978**, **5993**, 6000, **6007**, **6023**, **6039**, **6051**, **6092**, **6127**, **6130**, **6136**, **6138**, 6146, **6149**, **6162**, **6189**, **6197**
North Carolina: 5582, **5661**, **5875**, 5906
North Dakota: 6041
Ohio: 5838, **5845**, **6101**, **6193**
Oklahoma: 259
Oregon: 5267, 5381, 5454, **5881**, 6043
Pennsylvania: 781, 3898, 5354, 5433, **5554**, **5593**, **5614**, **5628**, 5872, **6200**
Rhode Island: **1149**, 3882, 5457, **6185**
South Carolina: 5216
South Dakota: **5309**
Tennessee: 5684, 5861
Texas: **935**, **4023**, 5280, **5409**, 5840, 6120, 6176, **6188**
Utah: **5486**
Vermont: **5499**, **6047**
Virginia: **2025**, **2854**, **2900**, **2945**, 5149, 5552, **5596**, **5604**, **5629**, **5692**, **5766**, **5800**, **6115**, 6153, 6169, 6172, **6194**
Washington: 5205, 5234, 5327, **5651**, **5812**
West Virginia: 6191
Wisconsin: 3471, 4473, 5920

Foreign applicants
California: **1610**, 1968, **2216**, **2285**, **2681**, **5345**, **5870**, **5934**, **6093**, **6148**, **6163**, **6173**
Colorado: **4937**
Connecticut: **750**
District of Columbia: **2084**, 5406, **5561**, **5564**, **5810**, **5821**, **5885**, **5890**
Florida: **243**, **1921**, **3533**, **4722**, **5786**, **5802**
Georgia: **3211**, **4669**
Hawaii: **103**, **5541**
Idaho: **2106**
Illinois: **2332**, **5611**
Maine: **6165**
Maryland: **1300**, **3715**, **5860**
Massachusetts: 3341, **5594**, **5731**, **6210**
Michigan: **5330**
Minnesota: **5948**
Missouri: **83**
New Hampshire: **5386**
New Jersey: **2168**, **4033**, **4975**, **5897**, **5963**, **6061**
New York: **116**, **486**, **2019**, **2032**, 2080, **2187**, **2450**, 3634, **3672**, **4288**, **4572**, **4734**, **4861**, 5089, **5219**, **5271**, **5277**, **5338**, **5400**, **5427**, **5438**, **5495**, **5563**, **5624**, **5703**, **5719**, **5811**, **5886**, **5910**, **5911**, **5925**, **5942**, **6132**, **6198**
Ohio: **6193**
Pennsylvania: **5789**

Rhode Island: **1149**, **5544**, **6083**
Tennessee: **5107**
Texas: 976, **5246**, **5270**
Utah: 3810
Vermont: **5257**, **5340**
Virginia: **5629**
Washington: **263**, **3463**
Wisconsin: **1078**

Graduate support
Alabama: 52, **308**, 772, 3068, 3353
Alaska: 769, 1971, 2276, 3779
Arizona: 250, 1151, 2632, 3469, 3648, 4142
Arkansas: 1926, 3658
California: **190**, 199, **219**, 479, 567, 623, 1258, 1584, 1657, 1670, **1835**, 1856, 1927, 2278, 2314, **2348**, 2381, 2522, 2604, 2619, 2733, 2765, **2916**, 2978, 2982, 3146, 3156, **3320**, 3336, 3394, 3542, 3706, 3764, 4177, 4229, 4300, 4302, 4515, 5580, **5716**, 6147, **6173**
Colorado: 165, **773**, 916, 2823, 3508, 4529, **5230**
Connecticut: **350**, 511, 896, **1407**, **3638**
Delaware: **1083**, 1904
District of Columbia: **105**, **131**, **135**, **169**, **526**, **929**, **1118**, **2084**, 2320, **2573**, **2879**, **2884**, **3310**, **3805**, 3949, **5406**, **5561**, **5565**, 5597, **5723**, **6005**
Florida: 123, **243**, 477, 504, **1135**, 1351, 1690, **1797**, 2239, 2338, **2564**, 2585, 2596, **3246**, 3324, 3400, 3513, 3861, **5786**, **5802**
Georgia: 628, 813, **1318**, 2647, **3186**, **3211**, 3954
Hawaii: 225, 1772, 2151, 3239, 3458, 3631
Illinois: **23**, 88, **102**, **104**, **107**, **108**, **124**, **128**, 238, 381, 549, 678, 698, 736, 1081, 1082, **1434**, 1512, 1715, **2287**, 2569, 2603, 2656, **2896**, 2917, 3064, **3174**, **3460**, **3466**, **3571**, 3708, 4352, 4493, 5494, **5566**, **5611**, **6033**, **6144**
Indiana: **87**, 438, 453, 878, 906, **2165**, **2316**, **3047**, 3171, 3602, **4290**, 4381, 4431
Iowa: 2353, 2479, 2500, 3278, 5968
Kansas: 1139, 2496, 2911
Kentucky: 319, 436, 890, 2208, 2970
Louisiana: 384, 2087, 2323, 4146
Maine: **2452**
Maryland: **113**, **126**, **136**, **1340**, 1740, **3042**, **3326**, 4071, **5613**, **5764**, **5767**, 5933
Massachusetts: **39**, 125, 802, 1166, 1238, 1416, 1906, 2117, 2542, 2888, 3162, 3981, **4095**, 4117
Michigan: 13, 205, 325, 402, 880, 892, 1307, **1495**, 1725, 2152, 2695, 3176, 3232, **5748**, **6140**
Minnesota: 93, **495**, 1218, 2321, 3080, 3226, 3917, 4342, 5264, **5989**
Mississippi: 1349, 2756
Missouri: 121, 1093, 1163, 1601, 2589, 3565, **3657**, 3980, **5184**
Montana: 3651
Nebraska: 1263, 2759, 2857, 5921
Nevada: 1155, 2920
New Hampshire: 1428, 2532, 2924, 4532
New Jersey: 227, 830, 1298, 1662, **2478**, 2498, 2704, 2722, 3103, 3503, **4000**, 4372, 4443, **5315**, **5897**, **6061**
New Mexico: 378, 1812
New York: **7**, 41, 65, **114**, **233**, 571, 719, 779, **840**, 863, 908, 960, 1232, 1576, 1586, **1619**, **2019**, 2068, 2089, 2164, **2283**, 2376, **2382**, **2385**, **2390**, **2450**, 2502, 2862, **2893**, **2919**, 2937, 2962, 3116, 3267, 3288, **3456**, 3566, **3570**, 3592, **3672**, **3789**, **3807**, **3830**, 3907, **3973**, 4081, 4271, **4308**, **4456**, 4482, **5284**, **5418**, 5521, **5563**, **5568**, **5607**, **5668**, **5711**, **5719**, **5780**, 5859, **5879**, **5886**, 6024, **6136**, **6138**
North Carolina: 340, 835, 927, 955, 1429, 2646, 2786, **3707**, **4181**, 4468, **4547**, 5848
North Dakota: 3601, 3647
Ohio: **38**, 451, 798, 800, 884, 1177, 1379, 1895, 2383, **2394**, 2570, 2668, 2717, 2892, 3101, 3237, 3494, 3591, 4268
Oklahoma: 1829, 2853

Oregon: 405, 640, **1693**, 2079, 2109, 2597, 3720, 4257, **5881**, 6045, 6068
Pennsylvania: 780, 781, 914, 920, 1545, 1585, 1589, 1741, 1809, 1834, 2040, 2437, 2613, 2643, **2690**, 2715, 2784, 2918, **3093**, 3198, 3256, 3691, 3740, 3780, 3898, 4243, 4386, 4548, 4560, 4778
Rhode Island: 235, 271, 2482, 3390, 3763, 3882, 3991, 4192, **6083**
South Carolina: 811, 1747, 2200, 3847
South Dakota: 3723
Tennessee: 1503, 1842
Texas: 461, 521, 704, **935**, 946, 976, 1190, **1228**, 1705, **1724**, 1851, 1937, 1986, 2721, 3040, 3216, 3397, **3621**, 4171, 4190
Utah: 2567
Vermont: 1192, 2062, **2557**
Virginia: **48**, 69, **101**, **133**, 343, **738**, **948**, **1041**, 1148, 1432, **2025**, 2396, **2854**, **2898**, **2900**, 2968, 3160, 3321, **3824**, **4180**, 4489, **5766**, **6048**, **6194**
Washington: 304, 404, 437, 1062, 1627, 2571, 2738, 2814, 3417, **3463**, 3475, 3485, 3886, 4143, 4440, 5327
West Virginia: 1353, 2156, 3084, 3268, 3936, 4715
Wisconsin: 211, 752, **1078**, **1502**, 1630, 2272, 2400, 3415, 3471, 3884, 4207, 4473
Wyoming: 819

Grants for special needs
Alabama: 4573, 4917, 4938
Arizona: **4571**, 4586, 4636, 5006, 5117
Arkansas: 4587, 4588, 5134
California: 1844, **1870**, 2041, 4575, 4589, 4594, 4598, 4600, 4605, 4628, 4634, 4693, 4720, 4721, **4752**, 4760, 4824, 4840, **4843**, 4850, 4857, **4862**, 4872, 4903, 4919, 4923, 4951, 4959, 4970, **4989**, 4992, 5026, 5039, 5042, **5050**, **5052**, 5062, 5411, **5477**, 5489, 5501, 5887, **6093**
Colorado: 4574, 4590, 4602, 4615, 4672, 4673, 4692, 4860, **4937**, **5080**, **5094**, 6124
Connecticut: 3039, 4612, 4619, **4622**, 4652, 4670, 4737, 4833, 4838, 4939, 4998, 5014, 5055, 5150, 5156, 5165
Delaware: 4701, **4823**, 5010, **5758**
District of Columbia: 4577, **4676**, **5012**, 5090, 6030
Florida: 4595, **4596**, 4680, 4691, 4702, 4710, 4712, **4713**, **4722**, 4753, 4790, 4791, 4849, 4906, **4933**, 4942, 5002, 5025, 5038, 5065, 5115, 5126, 5163, 5938
Georgia: 4627, **4669**, 4719, 4729, 4765, 4784, 4943, 5045, 5839
Hawaii: 1707, 4803, 4810, 4829, 4944, 5344
Idaho: **5137**
Illinois: 3007, **3825**, **4569**, 4655, 4671, 4727, 4730, 4735, 4736, 4745, **4783**, 4789, 4828, 4867, 4868, **4897**, 4930, 5020, **5056**, 5070, 5101
Indiana: 2855, 4658, 4678, 4881, 4883, 4893, 4945, 5023, 5033, 5053, 5112, 5153, 5154
Iowa: 4584, 4798, 4830, 4841, 4946, 5060, 5161
Kansas: 4666, 4711, 4947, 4980, 5064, 5155
Kentucky: 4608, 4740, 4769, 4898, 4911, 5032, 5469
Louisiana: 4788, 4948, 5151
Maine: 4603, 4686, 4768, 4928, 4949, 5003, 5004, 5008
Maryland: **4579**, 4625, 4716, 4807, 4811, 4864, **4866**, 4894, 4927, **5092**, 5135
Massachusetts: 3836, 4592, 4617, 4618, 4621, 4632, 4637, 4690, 4694, 4742, 4743, 4750, 4754, 4771, 4772, 4773, 4809, 4825, 4826, 4882, 4902, 4905, 4962, 4985, 4991, 4996, 4997, 5000, 5009, 5030, 5040, 5041, 5043, 5051, 5081, 5088, 5098, 5099, 5103, 5120, 5348
Michigan: 4349, 4916, 4954, 4961, 4979, 5083, 5116, **5170**
Minnesota: 2895, 4583, 4657, 4780, 4781, 4793, **4921**, **4922**, 4982, 5123, 5164, **5337**
Mississippi: 4639, 4885, 4976, 4990, 5016, **5743**

Missouri: 911, 4130, 4607, 4613, 4649, **4797**, 4816, 4874, **4936**, 4941
Montana: **4624**, 5054
Nebraska: 4957
New Hampshire: 4725, 4795, 4870, 4878, 4907
New Jersey: **4597**, 4633, 4714, 4738, 4748, **4848**, **4975**, 5011, 5073, 5076, 5171, 6202
New Mexico: **5464**
New York: **116**, **486**, 3974, 4570, **4572**, 4593, 4601, **4614**, 4623, 4638, 4654, 4661, 4663, 4682, 4695, 4703, 4708, 4718, **4731**, **4734**, 4774, 4785, 4808, 4821, 4834, **4854**, 4863, 4880, 4884, 4895, 4900, 4925, 4958, 4965, **4968**, 4969, 4972, 5022, 5031, **5036**, 5044, 5048, 5078, 5089, 5108, 5110, 5118, 5122, 5131, 5141, **5146**, 5159, 5174, **5180**, **5206**, 5256, 5273, **5289**, 5334, 5412, **5413**, **5430**, **5438**, **5458**, 5512, **5523**
North Carolina: 267, 3526, 4679, 4685, 4697, 4758, 4787, **4888**, 4950, 5102, 5666, 6103
North Dakota: 4728, 5127
Ohio: 4567, 4578, 4582, 4591, 4650, 4656, 4700, 4732, 4755, 4762, 4770, 4794, 4892, 4901, 4918, 4931, 4952, 4953, 4973, **5007**, 5047, 5059, 5066, 5111, 5119, 5147, 5169
Oklahoma: 2148, 4759, 4855, 4858, 5013, 5152, 5158
Oregon: 4640, 4662, 4749, 4912, 4932, 4974, 5082, 5157, 5259
Pennsylvania: 4599, 4609, 4610, 4645, 4677, 4744, 4763, 4764, 4777, 4778, 4802, 4851, 4913, 4920, **4956**, 4963, 4993, 4994, 5018, 5069, 5084, 5093, 5104, 5148, **5442**
Rhode Island: 3390, 4620, 4626, 4644, 4689, 4696, 4908, 4926, 4934, 5015, 5024, 5063, 5087, 5113, 5132, 5142
South Carolina: 4664, 4665, 4681, **4766**, 4977, 5077
South Dakota: 4935, 5067
Tennessee: **4576**, 4660, 4819, 4832, 4852, 4879, 4940, 5017, 5061, 5085, **5107**
Texas: 2309, 4647, 4675, 4684, 4739, 4741, **4746**, 4747, 4800, 4822, **4839**, 4847, **4853**, **4887**, **4890**, 4914, 4955, 4978, **4981**, **4984**, 4986, 5075, 5096, 5105, **5129**, 5166
Utah: 4653, 4804, 4836, 4899
Vermont: 4683, 4929, 5125, 5136, **5278**
Virginia: 4641, **4704**, 4706, **4865**, 5091
Washington: 4767, 4786, 4796, 4877, 4886, 4967, 5028, **5114**, 5138, 5144, 5145, 5327
West Virginia: 2074, 4651, 4715, 4876, 5019, 5072
Wisconsin: **4779**, 4792, 4814, 4817, 4835, **4896**, 4964, 5037, 5049, 5079, 5086, 5140, 5143, 5162
Wyoming: 4643

Grants to individuals

Alaska: 1907
Arizona: 6180
California: **1610**, 5251, **5318**, **5356**, 5428, **5483**, **5518**, 5745, **5855**, **5871**, **5958**, 6182
Connecticut: 3039, **5631**
District of Columbia: **5173**, **6036**
Florida: 454, **5416**, 5517, **5802**
Illinois: 4659, 4820, **5335**, 5736, 5777
Indiana: 871, **6201**
Iowa: 5232
Maryland: **4915**, 5210
Massachusetts: 3967, **4723**, 5168
Michigan: 4842, 6110, 6151
Minnesota: **5189**
Mississippi: 5068
Nebraska: 5167
New Jersey: 743, 4889
New York: 3071, **3570**, **3851**, **4019**, 5035, 5089, **5191**, 5207, **5219**, 5242, 5274, 5339, **5372**, 5380, 5382, **5404**, **5419**, 5515, **6085**
North Carolina: 4756
Ohio: 1323, 1995, 2308, 2607, 3185, 4086, 5119, 5485, **6125**
Oklahoma: **5977**
Pennsylvania: 4611, **6156**

Rhode Island: **6083**, 6184
South Carolina: 5543
South Dakota: 4709
Tennessee: **1425**
Texas: 4455, 4724, 4812, 6046
Utah: 4642
Vermont: 5497
Virginia: 120, **2031**, 2457, 5538, 5552, 5616, 5652
Washington: 4698, 4818, 5205, 5634
Wisconsin: 4473

Internship funds

Alaska: 769, 2587
Arkansas: **4158**
California: 3524, **5328**, **5888**, 5902
Delaware: **5758**
District of Columbia: **169**, **929**, **1487**, **3310**, **5558**, **5821**, **5824**, **5885**
Florida: **5416**
Georgia: **3186**
Illinois: **112**
Indiana: **85**, **87**
Iowa: 3301
Maine: **6165**
Maryland: 5444
Massachusetts: 2542, **4095**, **5908**
Minnesota: 5650
Missouri: 911
New Jersey: 1160, 4443, 5738, **6067**
New York: **161**, 3288, **3973**, **4494**, **5418**, **5445**, **5519**, **5679**, **5879**, **5952**
Oregon: **2317**
Pennsylvania: **3219**
Texas: 5225, **6188**
Virginia: **2025**, **6194**
Washington: 2361

Loans—to individuals

Arizona: 180, 3373
California: **4705**
Indiana: 1007
Minnesota: **5189**
New York: 5226
Virginia: 4966
Wyoming: 563

Postdoctoral support

Arizona: **5986**
California: 3156, **5328**, 5580, **5621**, 5797, 5854, **5934**, **5974**, **6035**
Connecticut: **5542**, **5696**
District of Columbia: **5562**, **5576**, **5821**, **5880**, **5995**
Florida: **243**, 5546, 5647, **5802**, **6195**
Georgia: 5839
Illinois: 4493, **5335**, **5626**, 5720, **5853**, **5937**, **6033**, **6143**
Iowa: 5794
Louisiana: 6015
Maryland: **5613**, 5715, **5764**, **5767**, **6006**
Massachusetts: **5553**, **5731**, **5808**, **5833**, 5915, **5930**
Minnesota: **5791**, **5989**
New Jersey: **6096**, 6202
New York: **5563**, **5568**, 5571, **5607**, **5667**, **5668**, **5711**, **5717**, **5726**, **5741**, **5790**, **5837**, 5851, 5863, **5864**, **5879**, **5901**, **5993**, **6136**, **6189**
North Carolina: **5875**
Ohio: 5931, **6101**
Oregon: **5881**
Pennsylvania: **5593**
South Carolina: 1747
Virginia: **3824**, 5567, **5766**, **6194**
Washington: **5812**

Postgraduate support

Alabama: 3068, 5733
California: 567, 3156, **5328**, **5656**, **6163**
Colorado: 5615

Connecticut: 3039
District of Columbia: **5561**, **5562**
Florida: **5802**
Georgia: 5820
Hawaii: 225
Illinois: 381, **3466**
Iowa: 2353
Maryland: **126**, **136**, **3042**, **5767**, **5869**
Michigan: 1621
Nebraska: 1263
Nevada: 1155
New Jersey: **5897**
New York: **2283**, **2919**, **5607**, **5688**, 5805, **5811**, **5879**
Ohio: 1504, 1995, 5739
Pennsylvania: **2223**, **2690**, **6200**
Texas: 3874, **5409**, **5969**
Virginia: 69, **2025**, **5537**, **5766**, **5800**
Washington: **3463**
Wisconsin: 4473

Precollege support

Alabama: 52, 166
Alaska: 55, 1907, 2772, 5540
Arizona: 76, 182, 183, 758, 2024, 2625
California: 324, 970, 2294, 2381, **3320**, 3668, 3804, **4508**, 4515, 4556, 6177
Colorado: 5470
Connecticut: 511, 924, 1137, **1407**
District of Columbia: 130, **391**, 410, 4315, 4316
Georgia: 1534, 1863
Hawaii: 748, 972, 1961
Illinois: **1256**, 2009, 2189
Indiana: 535, 682, 872, 2305, 2520, 3663, 4185
Iowa: 909
Kentucky: 890, 3821
Maine: 236, **2221**
Maryland: 514, 666, **5559**
Massachusetts: **39**, 649, 1142, 1906, **5908**
Michigan: 310, **503**, 1307, 2515, 2993, 4027, 4124, 4815
Minnesota: 1040
Missouri: 3384
Nebraska: 2097, 3955
New Jersey: 2630, **3172**, 4417, 5738
New Mexico: 1333
New York: 61, 387, **745**, 1249, 1721, 3348, **3789**, 5326
North Carolina: 2
North Dakota: 3601
Ohio: 800, 1384, **2394**
Oklahoma: 337
Oregon: 3045
Pennsylvania: 97, 1261, 1269, 2369, 4401
Rhode Island: 3390, 4108
Texas: 215, 737, 2309, 2315, 3797, 4042
Utah: 3810
Vermont: 1784, **2557**, 4232
Virginia: **948**, **2546**, 3160, **5999**, **6211**
Washington: **3207**, 4097
Wisconsin: 1630, 2472, 2523, 3914

Professorships

Illinois: **5569**
New York: **5219**, **5740**, **5784**, **5879**
North Carolina: **5661**
Virginia: 2801, 5567

Program development

Alaska: 5450, 5540
Arizona: 5456, **6097**
California: 918, **5029**, 5250, 5251, 5252, 5306, **5356**, 5391, 5432, 5489, **5644**, **5697**, **5705**, 5760, 5823, 5975, 5987, **6058**, **6079**, 6113
Colorado: **5230**, 5243
Connecticut: **4527**, 5439, 5443
Delaware: **1083**
District of Columbia: **5561**, 5564, 5592, **5821**, 6003, **6010**

Florida: 5275, 5754
Illinois: 4493, **5335**, 5494, **5566**, **5689**, 5691, **5806**, 5829, **5965**, 6131
Indiana: 5945
Iowa: 909, 6142
Kentucky: 890, 5367
Louisiana: 5532, 5622, 5831, 5928
Maine: **6165**
Maryland: **5570**, **5767**, **5860**
Massachusetts: **5248**, 5420, **6038**
Michigan: 5212, 5801, 5903, 6110, **6140**
Minnesota: 5247, 5752, **5948**, 6044
Missouri: 6118
New Jersey: 5446, 5514, 5734, **5963**, 5976, **6096**
New Mexico: **5374**, **5939**
New York: 719, **5191**, **5215**, **5219**, **5227**, 5242, **5260**, **5279**, **5314**, 5320, 5339, **5355**, 5364, 5375, **5376**, **5385**, 5387, **5405**, **5417**, 5448, **5460**, **5471**, **5490**, **5503**, **5507**, **5519**, 5571, **5573**, **5607**, 5618, 5658, **5668**, 5693, 5712, **5717**, **5751**, **5784**, **5901**, **5942**, **6039**, **6149**, **6154**, **6159**, **6162**, **6170**, **6206**
North Carolina: 5906, **6105**
Ohio: 2607, 4086, 5894
Oklahoma: 5639, 5912
Oregon: 5454, 6045
Pennsylvania: **2690**, 5377, **5628**, 5950, 6137
Rhode Island: **6083**
South Carolina: 5539
Tennessee: 5918, 6066
Texas: 5929
Utah: 5967, 6111, 6133
Vermont: **2557**, 5498
Virginia: **2878**, 5704, 5769, **5800**, 5849, **6031**, **6141**
Washington: 6150
West Virginia: 6191
Wisconsin: 4473, 5920, 6204

Project support

California: 5842
Connecticut: 3039, **4527**
Florida: **5416**, **5802**
Illinois: **5335**
Maine: **2452**
Michigan: 6183
Minnesota: 5202, 5312, 5362
New York: 5208, **5942**, **6159**
Ohio: 5119
Rhode Island: **6083**
Virginia: **5766**
Washington: 5205, 5327

Publication

California: **5705**, 5842, **6148**
Colorado: **5230**
District of Columbia: **5772**
Illinois: **5335**
Maine: **6165**
Massachusetts: **5526**, 5761
New Jersey: 6202
New Mexico: **5374**
New York: **4288**, **5178**, **5507**, **5519**, **5573**, **5673**, **5700**, 5712, **5879**, **6007**, **6091**, **6116**, **6162**, **6170**, **6189**
North Carolina: **5661**
Pennsylvania: **2690**, **5876**
Virginia: **6141**
Washington: 5327

Research

Alabama: 5733
Alaska: 769, 5181
Arizona: **5551**, 5636, **5986**, **6097**
California: 4419, **5328**, **5530**, **5536**, **5574**, 5580, 5608, **5610**, **5621**, **5642**, **5644**, 5669, **5697**, **5705**, **5706**, 5714, **5776**, **5795**, 5797, **5818**, **5826**, **5828**, 5854, **5870**, **5888**, **5934**, **5974**, 5987, 5991, **5997**, 6019, 6021, **6035**, **6042**, **6054**, **6058**, **6060**, **6063**, **6079**, **6087**, 6147

Colorado: **5230**, **5533**, 5615, **5980**
Connecticut: 750, **4527**, **5542**, 5735, **5985**, **6027**
Delaware: 5856, **5889**, 6166
District of Columbia: 5555, **5562**, **5565**, **5576**, **5592**, 5597, **5625**, **5632**, 5708, **5709**, **5723**, **5772**, **5775**, **5821**, **5824**, **5873**, **5880**, **5883**, **5885**, 5895, **5909**, **5961**, **5995**, **6005**, **6175**
Florida: **243**, 4680, 5546, 5647, **5802**, **6028**, **6081**, **6084**, **6195**
Georgia: **5620**, **5637**, **5675**, 5839, 6012
Hawaii: 5841
Illinois: 4493, **5335**, 5494, **5534**, **5549**, **5566**, **5569**, **5579**, **5586**, **5589**, **5590**, **5603**, **5681**, **5689**, 5690, **5694**, 5699, 5736, 5746, **5773**, **5806**, **5813**, 5868, **5937**, **5965**, **5972**, 6004, **6009**, 6013, **6033**, **6078**, **6128**, **6143**
Indiana: 5722, 5798, 6014, 6164, **6179**
Iowa: 2036, 5794, **6207**
Kansas: **5550**, 6134
Kentucky: **5882**
Louisiana: 6015
Maine: 6025, **6165**
Maryland: **136**, **5572**, 5575, **5588**, **5605**, **5613**, **5617**, **5630**, 5715, **5759**, **5764**, **5767**, **5788**, **5796**, **5860**, **5869**, **6006**, 6016, **6056**
Massachusetts: 2888, 3341, **4095**, **5560**, **5594**, **5670**, 5685, **5749**, 5761, **5808**, **5833**, **5899**, **5908**, 5915, **5930**, 6017, **6038**, **6119**
Michigan: 205, 2152, 5535, 5653, **5748**, **5779**, **5783**, **5819**, 6018, **6140**, **6167**
Minnesota: 5247, **5635**, **5791**, **5948**, **5970**, 5981, **6100**
Missouri: 4941, 5581, **5905**, **5957**, 6011, **6077**, 6118
Nevada: 5682, 5713, 5835, 6037
New Hampshire: **5878**
New Jersey: 1160, **5643**, **5663**, 5734, **5874**, **5898**, **5996**, **6096**, **6199**, 6202, **6203**
New York: **2874**, **3789**, **5219**, **5395**, **5507**, **5563**, **5568**, 5571, **5573**, 5583, **5591**, **5598**, **5606**, **5607**, **5624**, **5633**, **5646**, 5659, **5667**, **5668**, **5673**, **5686**, **5695**, **5703**, **5711**, 5712, **5717**, **5726**, **5740**, **5741**, 5747, 5768, **5770**, 5771, **5774**, **5781**, **5784**, **5793**, 5807, **5811**, **5825**, **5832**, **5837**, **5857**, 5859, 5863, **5864**, 5877, **5879**, **5901**, **5904**, **5911**, **5916**, **5925**, **5932**, 5935, **5936**, **5942**, **5943**, **5955**, **5966**, **5990**, **5993**, 6000, **6007**, 6022, **6023**, **6026**, 6049, **6062**, **6072**, **6091**, **6092**, 6098, **6099**, 6107, **6116**, 6117, **6129**, **6130**, **6136**, **6145**, 6146, **6170**, 6186, **6189**, **6197**, **6198**, 6205
North Carolina: 5582, **5661**, **5677**, 5750, **5875**, **6040**, 6065, **6168**
Ohio: **5845**, 5931, 6020, **6101**, **6123**, 6135
Oklahoma: 5912
Oregon: 4974, **5881**, 6045, 6053
Pennsylvania: **2223**, **2690**, **3219**, **5547**, **5554**, **5593**, **5628**, **5654**, 5680, **5792**, **5876**, 5892, 5914, 5951, 6137, **6156**, 6161, **6200**
Rhode Island: **5544**, **6083**
Tennessee: **5545**
Texas: 4455, **5619**, **5640**, 5840, 5917, **5922**, **5969**, 5984, 6074, 6176
Utah: 5728, 5730, **5900**, 6050, 6111
Vermont: 5584
Virginia: **2878**, 5552, 5567, **5595**, **5596**, **5600**, **5604**, **5623**, **5692**, **5766**, 5769, **5800**, **5992**, **6115**, 6153, 6169, 6172, **6194**
Washington: **3463**, **5803**, **5896**, 6080, **6126**
Wisconsin: 4473, **5585**
Wyoming: **5649**

Residencies

Arkansas: **5524**
California: 5175, 5183, **5198**, **5302**, 5323, **5324**, **5345**, 5363, **5407**, **5477**
Colorado: 5470
Connecticut: **5508**
Delaware: **5285**
District of Columbia: **5325**, **5366**
Florida: **5223**, **5368**, 5429

Illinois: **5195**, 5300, 5449, **5488**
Maine: **5506**
Maryland: 5229, **5299**, 5392, 5444, **5447**
Massachusetts: **5288**, **5307**, 5420, **5527**, **5553**
Michigan: **5332**, **5435**, **5737**
Minnesota: **5189**, 5196, 5200, 5202, 5238, **5253**, **5276**, **5319**, 5349, 5401, 5423, 5425
Nebraska: **5235**
New Hampshire: **5386**
New Jersey: **5434**
New Mexico: **5459**, **5525**
New York: **2283**, **5178**, **5182**, **5203**, **5204**, **5215**, **5219**, 5241, 5245, 5261, 5268, **5277**, 5286, **5294**, **5295**, **5296**, 5301, **5303**, **5321**, **5343**, 5347, **5350**, **5379**, **5384**, **5385**, **5398**, **5400**, **5408**, **5427**, 5461, **5468**, **5471**, **5474**, **5482**, **5490**, **5502**, **5519**
North Carolina: **5396**
Ohio: **5281**, **5510**
Oregon: 5249, **5440**, **5473**, **5476**
Pennsylvania: **5269**, **5304**, **5393**, **5467**, **5520**
South Carolina: 5216
Texas: **5246**, **5270**, 5287, **5351**, **5409**, 5478
Utah: **5452**, 5486
Vermont: **5257**, **5340**
Virginia: **5500**, **5516**
Washington: 5176, **5265**, **5298**, **5410**, **5481**
West Virginia: 5224
Wyoming: **5361**

Sabbaticals

California: 5665, 5745

Scholarships—to individuals

Alabama: 51, 432, 1154, 1194, 1303, 1437, 1492, 1546, 2051, 2652, 3012, 3409, 3491, 4155, 5638, 5733
Alaska: 64, 522, 626, 954, 1076, 3727, 4018, 4164
Arizona: **98**, 182, **1381**, 1570, 2155, 2625, 3115, 3195, 4201, 5456
Arkansas: 89, 248, 2124, 2842, 3532, 4053, 4279
California: 21, 99, 199, 229, 371, 393, 440, 489, 567, 584, 605, 619, 624, 697, 742, 828, 918, 925, 1119, 1254, 1422, **1431**, **1496**, 1500, 1540, **1542**, 1583, **1610**, **1616**, 1673, 1681, 1752, 1840, 1844, 1922, 2026, **2034**, 2041, 2209, 2220, **2285**, 2490, 2619, 2678, **2681**, **2712**, 2743, **2916**, 3049, 3156, **3227**, 3316, 3340, **3349**, 3370, 3403, 3433, 3510, 3524, 3537, 3541, 3543, 3557, 3586, 3608, **3671**, 3767, 3840, 3922, 4148, 4197, 4251, 4488, 4520, 4594, 5390, 5462, 5529, **5687**, 5979, **6148**
Colorado: 452, 540, 715, 1017, 1037, **1375**, 1956, 2419, 2832, **2880**, 3495, 3737, 3853, 3958, 3994, 5504, 6124
Connecticut: 321, 322, 576, 932, 1079, 1137, 1403, 1485, 1490, 2090, 2204, 2464, 2673, 2754, 3005, 3039, 3342, 3445, **3791**, 3867, 3868, 4112, 4254, 4321, 4365, 4737
Delaware: 1085, 1795, 2002
District of Columbia: 49, **213**, 443, **601**, 869, 1209, **1442**, **1871**, **2741**, 3025, **3188**, **3965**, **4113**, **5012**, 5895
Florida: **9**, 72, 329, 433, 492, 532, 931, 1026, 1103, **1105**, 1279, 1397, 1600, 1655, 1810, 1900, 1972, **2143**, 2378, 2451, 2504, 2507, **2563**, 2620, 2654, 2808, 2867, 2977, 3082, 3477, 3489, 3531, **3533**, 3753, 4076, 4096, 4220, 4249, 4460, 4528, 4680, **5416**
Georgia: **84**, 497, 628, **816**, 862, 904, 1048, 1087, 1506, 1533, 2096, 2120, 2773, 3551, 3660, 3823, 4225, 4367, 4719
Hawaii: 47, 470, 588, 761, 1524, 1654, 3659, 4276
Idaho: 31, 701, 1284, **2106**, 2648
Illinois: **102**, 282, 381, 484, 534, 560, 735, 822, 1011, 1068, 1127, 1221, 1243, **1256**, 1275, 1449, 1528, 1569, **1742**, 1828, 1849, 1888, 1942, 2008, 2013, 2103, 2123, 2138, 2226, 2268, 2301, 2322, **2386**, 2461, 2512, 2544,

2545, 2602, 2611, 2807, 2852, 3018, 3072, 3158, 3209, 3462, **3466**, 3930, 3961, 4085, 4176, 4336, 4352, 4376, **5972**
Indiana: 30, **82**, **85**, 96, 438, 473, 538, 539, 716, 871, 878, 881, 891, 906, 907, 1147, 1255, **1421**, 1510, 1825, 1935, 2181, 2295, 2305, 2402, 2723, 2780, 2855, 3002, 3102, 3295, 3305, 3374, 3406, 3407, 3416, 3476, 3487, 3578, 3685, 3903, 4083, **4183**, 4185, 4335, 4357, 4403, 4449
Iowa: 144, 151, 157, 403, 408, 818, 937, 994, 1731, 1876, 1928, 2035, 2036, 2037, 2129, 2334, 2508, 2770, 2850, 3107, 3265, 3301, 3594, 3724, 3890, 3941, 4160, 4198, 4235, 4284, 4377, 4497
Kansas: **370**, 429, 483, 1170, 1624, 1917, 2622, 2787, 2997, 3506, 4118, 4466
Kentucky: 5, 273, 3125, 3388, 4149
Louisiana: 552, 1909, 2432, 3296
Maine: 217, **290**, 777, **2452**, 2484, 2485, 3360
Maryland: 688, 714, 787, 829, 876, 1143, 1954, 2205, 2595, 2788, 3194, 3286, 3555, 3908, **5559**, **5570**, **5764**
Massachusetts: **39**, 43, 234, 318, 465, 529, 1024, 1025, 1044, 1072, 1142, 1172, 1181, 1299, 1339, 1342, 1348, 1392, 1526, 1594, 1925, 1938, **1943**, 2128, 2186, 2624, 2761, 2849, 2863, 2951, 2973, 3004, 3014, 3161, 3210, 3223, **3280**, **3304**, 3341, 3379, 3391, 3396, 3424, 3517, 3927, 3950, 3967, **3972**, 4072, **4095**, 4153, 4387, 4390, 5120, 5359
Michigan: 320, 346, 354, 644, 864, 905, 1012, 1034, **1396**, 1435, **1535**, **1573**, 1596, 1855, 1905, 1920, 1934, 1966, 1987, 2145, 2254, 2289, 2303, 2306, **2362**, 2463, 2514, 2519, 2586, 2686, 2697, 2795, 2822, **2882**, 3009, 3124, **3308**, 3512, 3589, 3872, 3998, 4049, 4056, 4349, 4416, 5729, **6140**
Minnesota: 4, 24, 751, 1136, 1218, 1295, **1622**, 1736, 1958, 2118, 2744, 2895, 3226, 3287, **3584**, 3610, 3813, 4228, 6044
Mississippi: 399, 425, 883, 3732
Missouri: 40, 335, 585, 627, 911, 974, **1090**, 1128, 1145, 1163, 1215, 1220, 1367, 1543, 1679, 1839, 1896, 2125, 2135, 2236, 2247, 2384, 2516, 2534, **3152**, 3616, 3854, 3855, 4077, 4080, 4255, 4265, **5451**
Montana: 693, 3977
Nebraska: 609, 981, 1059, 1161, 1237, 1566, 1695, 1778, 2380, 2649, 2675, 2702, 2940, 3418, 3582, 4470
Nevada: 1098, 1129, 1155, 1788, 1994, 2328, 3593, 3603, 4127, **4238**
New Hampshire: 553, **603**, 1132, 1428, 1946, 2319, 2929, 3322, 3912, 4878
New Jersey: 77, **79**, 115, 266, 380, **449**, 1210, 1401, 1402, 1664, 1684, 1975, 2044, 2147, 2926, **2932**, 3098, 3148, 3236, 3274, 3503, 3696, **4010**, 4065, 4174, 4555, 5421, 5734, **5926**
New Mexico: 696, 2093, 2470, 2930, **5464**
New York: 175, 224, 244, 255, 257, 672, 683, **689**, 719, **720**, 723, 740, 779, 908, 969, 1038, 1216, 1293, 1328, 1347, 1493, 1560, 1581, 1786, **2004**, **2032**, 2048, 2158, 2279, 2345, 2416, **2565**, 2640, 2815, 2851, 2861, 2923, 2936, 2985, 3135, 3248, 3260, 3281, 3284, 3429, **3456**, **3474**, 3546, 3558, 3562, **3570**, 3636, 3771, 3798, 3885, 3971, 3974, 4128, **4159**, **4237**, 4241, 4248, 4250, **4288**, 4393, **4494**, **4521**, **4546**, **4731**, 4958, 4972, **5188**, 5228, 5313, **5418**, **5445**, 5455, 5472, 5480, **5563**, 5805, **5811**, **5925**, **6062**, **6132**
North Carolina: 314, 763, 823, 832, 882, 887, 915, 1060, 1112, 1116, 1167, 1180, 1195, 1251, **1312**, 1355, 1360, 1558, 1916, 1931, 2042, **2167**, **2174**, 2614, 2676, 2727, 2860, 2972, 3149, 3234, 3449, 3484, 3490, 3526, 3883, **3956**, 4001, 4392, 4452, **5197**
North Dakota: 1272, 1294, 1417, 4184, 4368
Ohio: 19, 66, 331, 336, 365, 382, 430, 435, 462, 587, 654, 794, 799, 842, 893, 966, 1019, 1046, 1075, 1110, **1234**, 1274, 1291, 1323, 1384, 1412, 1499, **1685**, 1748, 1847, 1930, 2130,

2212, 2460, 2509, 2612, 2636, 2663, 2671, 2692, 2705, **2847**, 2868, 2946, 2964, 3131, 3382, 3428, 3441, 3468, 3519, **3522**, 3545, 3678, 3713, 3756, 3843, 3878, 3893, 4086, 4210, 4278, 4296, 4345, 4348, 4378, 4425, 4435, 4438, 4458, 4461, 4514, 4533
Oklahoma: 1448, 1829, 2077, **2107**, **2875**, 3022, 4333, 4551, 4759, **5998**
Oregon: 1031, 1039, 1411, 1552, **2317**, 2389, 2486, 2752, 3075, 3398, 3461, 3579, 3599, 4346
Pennsylvania: 193, 309, 368, 481, 550, 551, 556, 598, 730, 827, 1054, 1150, 1152, 1269, 1287, 1377, 1390, 1424, 1457, 1465, 1521, 1636, 1753, 1796, 1911, 2075, 2318, 2366, 2661, 2918, **3219**, **3230**, 3253, 3339, 3369, 3446, 3457, 3529, 3585, 3607, 3674, 3680, 3736, 3923, 4055, 4105, 4157, 4219, 4332, 4430, 4481, 4538, **5628**
Puerto Rico: 1359
Rhode Island: 139, 226, 245, 247, 251, 417, 445, 583, 759, 1001, 1013, 1325, 1507, 1516, 1607, 1880, 2240, 2476, 2540, 2674, 2709, 2728, 2736, 3087, 3136, 3276, 3299, 3414, 3605, 3750, 3772, 3778, 4087, 4192
South Carolina: 140, 648, 691, 712, 1106, **1914**, 2691, 4121, 4977
South Dakota: 1614, 4295
Tennessee: **86**, 426, 1140, 1327, 1762, 2113, 2115, 2141, 2175, **3654**, 4343, 4437, 4457
Texas: 57, **237**, 487, 629, 705, 801, 950, 995, 1023, 1035, 1080, 1102, 1114, 1241, 1244, 1578, 1579, 1677, 1702, 1794, 1813, 2291, 2559, 2568, 2584, 2638, 2670, 2714, 2873, 3017, 3067, 3099, 3119, 3151, 3163, 3325, 3332, 3375, 3397, **3502**, 3535, **3639**, 3895, 3970, **4023**, 4031, 4035, 4038, 4040, 4041, 4150, 4190, 4258, 4292, 4455, 4487, 4512, 4559, **5129**, 5817
Utah: 252, 2028, 2273, 2716, 4510
Vermont: 564, 1211, 1527, 2197, 2374, 3010, 4303, 5136
Virginia: 120, **134**, 212, 620, **757**, **806**, 1282, 1337, 1785, **2031**, 2403, 2441, 2457, 2641, 2644, 2801, **2854**, 2866, **2942**, 2968, 2987, **3036**, 3173, 3518, 3762, 4007, 4063, 4116, **5221**, **5800**
Washington: 42, 177, 447, 653, 702, 839, 853, 895, 1162, 1511, 1691, 1714, 2194, 2370, 2740, 2990, 3258, 3272, 3644, 4060, 4213, 4244, 4270, 4318, 5327
West Virginia: 472, 680, 870, 1004, 2003, 2074, 3084, 3271, 3877
Wisconsin: 46, 176, 327, 357, 543, 557, 848, 1009, 1231, 1304, 1415, 1522, 1694, 1936, 1955, 2185, 2523, 2529, 2912, 3191, 3283, 3317, 3442, 3492, 3496, 3632, 3665, 3700, 3733, 3869, 4099, 4140, **4167**, 4242, 4472, 4473, 5389
Wyoming: 1065, 1236, 2391, 2392, 2908

Seed money

California: **5237**, 5291, 5489, **5888**, **6079**
District of Columbia: **5561**, **6008**
Florida: **5802**
Indiana: 889
Iowa: 909, 4841
Maine: **2452**
Maryland: **6056**
Massachusetts: **6038**, **6095**
Minnesota: 5453, 6044
Missouri: 911, **5957**
New York: **5255**, 5571, **5740**, **5751**, 5768, **5942**, **6039**, **6189**
North Carolina: 5582
Pennsylvania: 695
Rhode Island: **6083**
Virginia: **2900**, 6172, **6211**
Washington: **5896**

Stipends

Alaska: 6094

California: **5324**, 5378, **6112**
Colorado: 5209
Connecticut: **5508**
District of Columbia: **929**, **5557**, **5890**
Florida: 5275, **5416**
Georgia: **5678**
Maryland: 5229, 5392, **5796**
Massachusetts: **5527**, **5553**
Minnesota: **5253**, 5423, 5425
New Mexico: **5459**
New York: 5208, 5261, 5268, 5286, **5321**, 5326, **5333**, **5404**, **5422**, **5474**, **5563**, **5568**, **5646**, **6024**
Ohio: 5283
Oregon: 2991
Rhode Island: 5457
Texas: **5246**
Utah: **5486**
Vermont: 4629
Virginia: **1458**, **2878**, **5516**, **5596**
Washington: 5176
Wyoming: **5361**

Student loans—to individuals

Alabama: 1184
California: 199, 268, 1575, 2088, 3269, 3586, 3731, 3871
Colorado: 916
Connecticut: 2469, 3039, 3875, 3966
District of Columbia: **601**, 1122
Florida: **243**, 710, 1091, 1399, 2808, 3753
Georgia: 1506, 2092, **3186**, 3954, 4282
Illinois: 381, 444, 684, 1604, 1648, 2277, 2617, 3371, 3940, 4068
Indiana: **82**, **85**, 253, 2183, 4431
Iowa: 581, 1826, 1853, 2234, 2399, 2480, 2770, 3265, 3278, 3301, 3559
Kansas: 270, 2622, 3097, 3244
Kentucky: 3070
Louisiana: 2477
Maine: 4050
Maryland: **1726**, 2595, 3673, 3908
Massachusetts: 239, 1919, 2922, 3391
Michigan: 1217, 2050, 2072, 2188, 2822, 3359, 4216
Minnesota: 27, 965, 3351, 4342
Mississippi: 1069
Missouri: 1700, 1992, 2020, 2439, 3735, 3990, 4077
Nebraska: 2633
Nevada: 2328
New Jersey: 36, 1210, 1686, 1894, 2583
New Mexico: 652
New York: 387, 837, 1879, 2578, 2640, 3032, 3105, 3577
North Carolina: 590, 823, 955, 1043, 1360, 1646, 1951, **2167**, 3168, 4052, 4356, 4468
North Dakota: 548
Ohio: 167, **170**, 207, 293, 430, 893, 1373, 2592, 2671, 2739, 2804, 3444, 3689, 3752, 3878, 4434
Oklahoma: 1548, 1764, 2102
Oregon: 953
Pennsylvania: 29, 358, 1389, 1545, 2501, 2629, 2793, 3329, 3459, 3680, 4538, 4778
Rhode Island: 821, 1410
South Carolina: 3006, 3847
South Dakota: 982, 2288
Tennessee: 2333, 4343
Texas: 450, 580, 643, 1114, 1115, 2195, 2526, 2559, 2672, 2731, 3130, 3154, 3666, 3924, 3987, **4023**, 4040
Vermont: 951
Virginia: 949, 1074, 2198, 2457, 2644, 4433, 4966
Washington: 528, 1233, 3653
West Virginia: 3761
Wisconsin: 1006, 1045, 4473
Wyoming: 563, 783, 1018, 3159

Support to graduates or students of specific schools

Alabama: 155, 317, 1370, 1754, 1886, 1960, 2225, 2594, 3068, 3717, 4009, 4261, 4530

Alaska: 55, 3609

Arizona: 178, 562, 1444, 1626, 2377, 2549, 2632, 3121, 3193, 3261, 3714, 4189

Arkansas: 89, 333, 612, 1369, 1562, 1701, 1926, 3203, 4036, 4125, 4173, 4222, 4412

California: 8, 78, 81, 188, 209, 228, 303, 305, 374, 392, 440, 442, 480, 541, 584, 618, 621, 623, 697, 728, 765, 792, 807, 849, 898, 921, 934, 963, 1014, 1126, 1169, 1208, 1345, 1575, 1612, 1657, 1670, 1720, 1803, **1835**, 1844, 1924, 1968, 2023, 2055, 2149, 2159, 2177, 2220, 2231, 2253, 2261, 2375, 2405, 2429, 2444, 2491, 2579, 2619, 2735, 2806, 2950, 3156, 3202, 3290, 3294, 3318, 3394, 3433, 3524, 3537, 3550, 3557, 3586, 3623, **3671**, 3706, 3709, 3832, 3863, 4109, 4188, 4300, 4411, 4420, 4488, **4508**, 4556, **5477**, 5923

Colorado: 397, 639, 766, 778, 786, 851, 916, 942, 975, 1252, 1301, 1322, 1388, 1716, 1887, 1901, 1903, 2150, 2325, 2344, 2388, 2465, 2832, 3495, 3583

Connecticut: 191, 322, 523, 687, **791**, 808, 986, 1137, 1403, 1439, 1485, 1613, 2407, 2421, 2627, 3039, 3164, 3273, 3408, 3966, 4043, 4355, 4453

Delaware: **1083**, 1599, 1795, 1864, 2561

District of Columbia: 1193, **1487**, 2320, 4312

Florida: 80, 94, 172, 201, 330, 488, 899, 901, 984, 1026, 1103, 1121, 1203, 1278, 1316, 1371, 1400, 1577, 1656, 1769, 1882, 1988, 2016, 2121, 2214, 2364, 2596, 2608, 2639, 2821, 2848, 3026, 3063, 3079, 3334, 3393, **3628**, 3652, 3938, 3969, 4073, 4536

Georgia: 862, 922, 1108, 1532, 2903, 4003, 4110, 4385, 4454, 4464

Hawaii: **103**, 748, 1707, 1815, **4098**

Idaho: 1475, 1766, 2757, 2865, 3319, 3580, 3745

Illinois: 88, 92, 149, 153, 345, 356, 359, 424, 467, 482, 505, 544, 582, 684, 698, 734, 739, 971, 1123, 1127, 1138, 1144, 1214, 1243, 1248, 1289, 1305, 1308, **1434**, 1454, 1512, 1528, 1669, 1692, 1723, 1746, 1783, 1820, 1891, 1915, 1942, 2013, 2146, 2166, 2189, 2258, 2277, 2347, 2367, 2461, 2511, 2521, 2536, 2545, 2581, 2600, 2729, 3007, 3091, 3158, 3206, 3209, 3212, 3289, 3306, 3315, 3367, 3368, 3371, 3385, 3426, 3434, 3438, 3439, **3460**, 3465, 3478, **3571**, 3581, 3600, 3667, 3777, 3795, 3850, 3902, 3984, 4015, 4062, 4267, 4283, 4363, 4493, **4502**, 4552

Indiana: 30, **87**, 232, 253, 361, 453, 531, 535, 545, 570, 592, 682, 744, 756, 878, 881, 888, 889, 891, 894, 897, 906, 907, 1073, 1077, 1186, 1197, 1264, 1286, 1462, 1547, 1565, 1638, 1682, 1719, 1738, 1816, 1817, 1832, 1935, 1999, 2033, 2100, 2235, 2282, 2295, 2305, 2401, 2402, 2424, 2471, 2492, 2499, 2777, 2791, 2907, 2941, 2963, 3013, 3019, **3047**, 3059, 3133, 3220, 3225, 3242, 3245, 3323, 3355, 3357, 3406, 3407, 3633, 3663, 3687, 3746, 3870, 3903, 3913, 3935, 3997, 4275, 4407, 4427, 4431, 4449, 4462, 4537

Iowa: 144, 157, 315, 403, 406, 555, 581, 591, 670, 717, 1003, 1084, 1095, 1111, 1247, 1551, 1965, 2069, 2162, 2179, 2304, 2310, 2414, 2479, 2508, 2548, 2685, 2693, 2789, 2846, 2850, 2910, 2944, 2980, 3205, 3278, 3313, 3560, **3575**, 3686, 3719, 3828, 3951, 3985, 3986, 4223, 4331, 4359

Kansas: 14, 195, 254, 270, 558, 1056, 1240, 1262, 1468, 1644, 1814, 1818, 1858, 1874, 1944, 1980, 2132, 2224, 2252, 2423, 2496, 2622, 2651, 2762, 2771, 2787, 2799, 2828, 2911, 2914, 2920, 3117, 3132, 3155, 3199, 3244, 3432, 3488, 3506, 3747, 3848, 3892, 3910, 3920, 4030, 4135, 4234

Kentucky: 856, 1430, 1443, 1508, 2230, 2433, 2642, 3181, 3401, 3821, 4358, 4544

Louisiana: 276, 384, 594, 1979, 2323, 4146, 4558

Maine: 1708, **2452**, 3404, 3435, 3643, 4490

Maryland: 279, 854, 1051, 1491, 1634, 1740, 1950, 1954, 2605, 2662, 2792, 3081, 3286, 3889, 4132, 4233, **4252**, **5764**

Massachusetts: 12, 152, 158, 260, 313, 411, 418, 419, 600, 649, 673, 762, 802, 967, 1072, 1181, 1196, 1198, 1207, 1335, 1392, 1469, 1554, 1897, 1919, **1943**, 1976, 1998, 2131, 2497, 2510, 2599, 2624, 2707, 2769, 2954, 2971, 3004, 3041, 3078, 3083, 3110, 3162, 3178, 3215, 3223, 3270, **3304**, 3464, 3481, 3744, 3844, 4012, 4032, **4095**, 4187, 4215, 4299, 4305, 4306, 4374, 4410, 4432, 4504, 4513, 4550

Michigan: 11, 150, 298, 326, 354, 355, 402, 423, **460**, 596, 833, 845, 880, 886, 910, 1064, 1419, 1452, 1463, 1498, 1544, 1561, 1580, 1621, 1703, 1801, 1841, 1967, 2001, **2039**, 2050, 2052, 2108, 2152, 2266, 2342, 2357, 2551, 2562, 2686, 2699, 2718, 2795, 2805, 2858, **2882**, 2967, 2993, **3033**, 3052, 3104, 3128, 3176, 3183, 3232, 3479, 3486, 3525, 3549, 3681, 3754, **3793**, 3827, 3852, 3995, 4084, 4124, 4145, 4206, 4320, 4325, 4366, 4465, 4471, 4522

Minnesota: 27, 111, 141, 421, 755, 1094, 1136, 1146, 1268, 1405, 1620, 1756, 1827, 1948, 1958, 2081, 2281, 2321, 2758, 3027, 3054, 3058, 3120, 3177, 3514, 3802, 3814, 3896, 4070, 4078, 4104, 4156, 4380, 4405, 4467, 4496

Mississippi: 883, 993, 1787, 2593

Missouri: 121, 288, 352, 401, 795, 911, 974, 1134, 1163, 1215, 1220, 1367, 1372, 1461, 1481, 1601, 1632, 1700, 1782, 1969, **1990**, 1992, 2020, 2171, 2203, 2247, 2250, 2263, 2384, 2439, 2459, 2528, 2609, 2683, 2708, 2952, 3053, 3122, 3243, 3565, 3595, 3596, 3611, 3612, 3613, 3614, 3615, 3617, 3618, 3619, 3620, 3760, 3842, 3904, 3990, 4092, 4543

Montana: 264, 790, 1029, 1266, 1387, 1777, 1807, 1857, 1929, 1989, 2864, 3361, 3431, 3448, 3963, 3982, 4102

Nebraska: 476, 788, 1259, 1271, 1306, 1602, 1712, 1717, 1838, 1923, 2097, 2119, 2229, 2719, 2742, **3046**, 3092, 3413, 3548, 3983, 4138, 4277, 4340, 4354

Nevada: 520, 615, 1098, 2726, 2751, 3113, 3392, 3603, 3787, 4127, 4310, 4564

New Hampshire: 351, 825, 1132, 2610, 3561, 3800

New Jersey: 36, 242, 301, 369, 398, **449**, 718, 830, 838, 1021, 1310, 1574, 1633, 1650, 1661, 1894, 2054, **2168**, 2286, 2398, 2473, 2623, 2630, 2730, 2790, 3126, 3254, 3266, 3523, 3625, 3688, 3992, 4119, 4204, 4205, 4273, 4406, 4417, 4549

New Mexico: 62, 396, 652, 1696, 1789, 2428, **3147**, 3509

New York: 61, 240, 241, 265, 422, 431, 439, 458, 491, **498**, 507, 518, 519, 575, 577, 586, 613, 645, 771, 785, 826, 837, 868, 908, 960, 1015, 1168, 1171, 1199, 1204, 1205, 1216, 1232, 1440, 1455, 1493, 1501, 1519, 1560, 1571, 1581, 1665, 1678, 1721, 1767, 1780, 1859, 1885, 2048, 2068, 2080, 2164, 2173, 2210, 2251, 2279, 2293, 2395, 2454, 2502, 2640, 2809, **2893**, **2899**, 2935, 2988, 3105, 3111, 3135, 3251, 3252, 3337, 3365, 3366, 3377, 3472, 3501, 3568, 3634, 3729, 3771, **3788**, 3856, 3976, 4022, 4075, 4081, 4133, 4218, 4224, 4266, 4271, 4293, 4482, 4483, **4521**, **5222**

North Carolina: 54, 90, 277, 385, 427, 459, 602, 711, 797, 955, 1112, 1156, 1159, 1223, 1251, 1336, 1343, 1376, 1409, 1436, 1453, 1555, 1557, 1597, 1647, 1651, 1668, 1704, 1710, 1734, 1837, 1952, 2133, 2136, 2207, 2349, 2352, 2354, 2411, 2449, 2531, 2550, 2614, 2621, 2631, 2748, 2794, 2813, 3069, 3137, 3149, 3165, 3182, 3419, 3421, 3482, 3749, 3755, 3765, 3794, 3837, 3838, 3909, 3934, 3946, 4191, **4329**, 4373, 4524, 4562, 5848

North Dakota: 3483, 3647, 3683

Ohio: 22, 34, 45, 66, 74, 148, 159, 167, 207, 208, 231, 274, **275**, 299, 348, 377, 382, 383, 420, 515, 524, 641, 651, 654, 675, 707, 789, 900, 985, 1049, 1058, 1070, 1117, 1177, 1188, 1202, 1291, 1309, 1311, 1373, 1384, 1460, 1476, 1504, 1505, 1509, 1515, 1556, 1658, 1697, 1737, 1750, **1775**, 1836, 1846, 1847, 1918, 1932, 1933, 1949, 1959, 1964, 2045, 2083, 2160, 2184, 2212, 2215, 2217, 2233, 2248, 2255, 2324, 2329, 2371, 2413, 2425, 2431, 2467, 2468, 2554, 2566, 2576, 2577, 2582, 2655, 2689, 2753, 2767, 2774, 2781, 2785, 2836, 2844, 2859, 2946, 2964, 3057, 3100, 3101, 3129, 3150, 3166, 3170, 3190, 3237, 3277, 3405, 3428, 3468, 3473, 3591, 3677, 3701, 3702, 3712, 3759, 3769, 3776, 3829, 3846, 3858, 3887, 4046, 4047, 4093, 4106, 4209, 4210, 4212, 4214, 4280, 4309, 4398, 4400, 4408, 4426, 4448, 4463, 4476, 4498, 4503, 4519, **6193**

Oklahoma: 259, 471, 1363, 2533, 3845

Oregon: 37, 67, 173, 363, 364, 607, 640, 796, 804, 847, 855, 953, 997, 1593, 1688, 1698, 1806, 1811, 1889, 2015, 2462, 2764, 2820, 3090, 3311, 3411, 3461, 3574, 3820, 3906, 3944, **4051**, 4152, 4196, 4257, 4328, 4346, 4375, 4379, 4446, 4506, 6068

Pennsylvania: 17, 29, 311, 358, 368, 375, 475, 525, 536, 556, 606, 681, 753, 775, 780, 781, 817, 936, 990, 999, 1016, 1086, 1152, 1242, 1277, 1385, **1477**, 1514, 1572, 1585, 1727, 1741, 1743, 1744, 1760, 1791, 1833, 1845, 1854, 1884, 1962, 2040, **2223**, 2244, 2337, 2365, 2366, 2369, 2404, 2437, 2456, 2518, 2574, 2590, 2591, **2626**, 2657, 2665, 2680, 2793, 2800, 2830, 2843, 2909, 2915, 2953, 2979, 3218, 3221, 3253, 3256, 3343, 3369, 3454, 3459, 3573, 3674, 3676, 3691, 3718, 3740, 3774, 3808, 3862, 3929, 3933, 3947, 3952, 3989, 4048, 4055, 4131, 4137, 4157, 4208, 4211, 4219, 4221, 4227, 4253, 4351, 4402, 4429, 4479, 4484, 4509, 4518, 4560

Puerto Rico: 4170

Rhode Island: 187, 271, 272, 306, 474, 814, 820, 968, 988, 1000, 1212, 1265, 1410, 1414, 1438, 1507, 1559, 1637, 1653, 1730, 1792, 1799, 1821, 1941, 1947, 1970, 2111, 2154, 2202, 2219, 2245, 2410, 2482, 2488, 2494, 2547, 2553, 2558, 2709, 2724, 2732, 2736, 2810, 2817, 2819, 2872, 3051, 3085, 3087, 3096, 3204, 3303, 3389, 3390, 3499, 3553, 3572, 3675, 3742, 3766, 3770, 3772, 3778, 3784, 4002, 4067, 4108, 4139, 4281, 4414, 4428, 4500, **6185**

South Carolina: 50, 261, 959, 2783

South Dakota: 982, 1631, 1765, 3723, 3796, 3939

Tennessee: 376, 663, 721, 725, 815, 885, 1140, 1459, 1503, 1733, 1776, 1890, 1902, 2113, 3094, 3423, 3864, 3880, 4091, 4285, 4485, 4501

Texas: 147, 221, 294, 296, 323, 328, 353, 409, 450, 461, 580, 635, 643, 667, 704, 705, 857, 945, 946, 976, 1027, 1113, 1114, 1115, 1141, 1158, 1190, 1239, 1246, 1338, 1364, 1413, 1483, 1497, 1608, 1643, 1675, 1718, 1771, 1774, 1790, 1798, 1843, 1850, 1862, 1878, 1937, 2259, 2309, 2397, 2422, 2618, 2628, 2672, 2766, 2778, 2779, 2797, 2956, 2965, 3130, 3139, 3154, 3192, 3241, 3325, 3453, 3534, 3649, 3722, 3725, 3726, 3815, 3874, 3879, 4014, 4038, 4041, 4042, 4123, 4171, 4245, 4246, 4304, 4469, 4486, 4517, 4540, 4565, 6190

Utah: 280, 300, 2134, **2178**, 2567

Vermont: 446, 1211, 1224, 1276, 1297, 1763, 2062, 2816, 3630, 3684, 4034, 4199, 4447

Virginia: 69, 258, 312, 343, 510, 917, 1281, 1652, 1660, 1822, 2144, 2403, 2801, 2866, 2968, 3231, 3576, 3801, 3937, 3945, 4337, 6169

Washington: 142, 196, 262, 304, 307, 437, 490, 528, 650, 776, 824, 947, 1055, 1187, 1267, 1290, 1531, 1659, 1699, 1739, 1875, 1892, 1893, 1978, 2112, 2116, 2127, 2191, 2341, 2370,

2415, 2448, 2635, 2713, 2812, **2883**, 2957, 3073, 3153, 3258, 3399, 3563, 3653, 3656, 3698, 3782, 3886, 4024, 4126, 4144, 4244, 4286, 4370, 4389, 4440, 5327
West Virginia: 589, 668, 1518, 1735, 1860, 2580, 2746, 2803, 2996, 3084, 3106, 3275, 3383, 3911, 3936
Wisconsin: 32, 33, 60, 163, 210, 292, 295, 357, 500, 501, 546, 595, 636, 671, 836, 903, 961, 1063, 1165, 1189, **1200**, 1250, 1280, 1352, 1357, 1361, 1386, 1393, 1479, 1494, 1609, 1630, 1687, 1732, 1761, 1804, 1823, 1877, 1899, 1957, 2063, 2157, 2182, 2270, 2292, 2299, 2313, 2339, 2340, 2438, 2669, 2725, 2768, 2837, 2839, 2913, 2949, 2955, 2958, 3003, 3008, 3060, 3065, 3138, 3167, 3283, 3291, 3309, 3327, 3350, 3395, 3415, 3662, 3664, 3669, 3693, 3728, 3739, 3768, 3857, 3914, 3921, 3932, 3964, 4013, 4045, 4057, 4136, 4242, 4289, 4344, 4369, 4418, 4436, 4473, 4507, 4516
Wyoming: 145, 783, 1563, 1567, 2101, 2391, 3134, 3159, 3208, 3919, 4409, 4526

Technical education support

Alabama: 52, **308**
Alaska: 55, 373, 769, 1157, 1971, 2276, 2297, 2587, 2943, **3641**
Arizona: 2549, 3469, 4122
Arkansas: 1926, 3721
California: 567, 568, 574, 1395, 1575, 1793, 1922, 2088, **2916**, 2950, 3076, 3156, 3668, 4229, 4302, **6173**
Colorado: 916, 942, **1375**, 1423, 4529
Connecticut: 132, 511, 708, 4090, **4527**
Delaware: **1083**
District of Columbia: **2084**, **2573**
Florida: **243**, 477, 865, 1203, 1988, 2373, 3324, 4415, 4528
Georgia: 517, **1318**
Idaho: 3580
Illinois: 874, 1123, 1723, 2426, 2581, 3091, 3293, 3434, 4006, 4015, 4240
Indiana: 189, 860, 872, 889, 891, 894, 1005, 1073, 1077, 1446, 2100, 2282, 2305, 2360, 2471, 2886, 3245, 3716, 3903, 4230, 4264
Iowa: 406, 909, 1030, 1341, 1667, 2069, 2353, 2548, 2944, 3362
Kansas: 1131, 1713, 2126, 2252, 3097, 3109, 3155, 3892, 4094
Kentucky: 890, 2056
Louisiana: 2477
Maryland: 1175, 1491, 1740, 4071
Massachusetts: **39**, 464, 731, 1906, 3626, 3962, **4021, 4095**
Michigan: 205, 325, 880, 892, 913, 1663, 2152, 3176, 3827, **6140**
Minnesota: 421, 727, 755, 1176, 3080, 3425, 3831
Missouri: 508, 795, 911, 1163, 1220, 2871, 3384, 3612, 3619
Montana: 790, 3963
Nebraska: 1271, 1464, **3046**, 4354
Nevada: 1155, 2257, 2418, 2920
New Hampshire: 2300, 2924, 4532, 4542
New Jersey: 222, 632, 3254, 3688, 3783
New Mexico: 1283, 1333, 1368, 4239
New York: 431, 831, 908, 1780, 1939, **3456**, 6146
North Carolina: 340, 1429
North Dakota: 2524, 3601
Ohio: 22, 641, 884, 1768, 1895, 1932, 2217, 2233, 2383, 2413, 2566, 2576, 2931, 3781, 4106, 4408, 4448, 4498
Oklahoma: 1829
Oregon: 855, 953, 1031, 1050, 1411, **1693**, 4257, 4375
Pennsylvania: 15, 97, 502, 914, **933**, 2040, 2590, 2591, 3112, 3387, 3587, 3597, 3780, 3929, 4211, 4227, 4477
Rhode Island: **1489**, 3096, 3925, 4523
South Carolina: 1747, 2211, 3948
South Dakota: 1631, 1940, 3723
Tennessee: 4501

Texas: 353, 1774, 2265, 2412, 3179, 3397, 3528, 4245, 4326
Utah: 3810
Vermont: **2557**, 2966, 4034, 4399, 4450
Virginia: 312, 343, **738**, 1432, **3050**, 3160, 3321, 3547, 3576, 3888, 4489
Washington: 3, 302, 1380, 1699, 2326, 2442
West Virginia: 1353, 1735, 2156, 2331
Wisconsin: 338, 546, 674, **1200**, 1630, 1877, 2063, 2206, 2513, 2523, 3060, 3061, 4474, 4516
Wyoming: **940**, 1018, 3817, 4526

Travel grants

Arizona: 3968
California: **339**, 3224, 4515, 5231, **5345, 5621, 5697, 5870, 5888, 5974**, 5979, **6042, 6112**
Colorado: 4529, **5230, 5698, 6139**
Connecticut: **750**
District of Columbia: **213**, **929**, **3037**, **5220**, 5555, **5564, 5821, 5880, 5885**, 5895
Florida: **5416**, 5546, **5802, 5944**
Georgia: **5678**
Hawaii: **103**
Illinois: 3330, **3466, 5335, 5579, 5689, 5972, 6108, 6128**
Iowa: 909, 4841
Louisiana: 5532
Maine: 2452, **6165**
Maryland: 4915, **5613, 5764**
Massachusetts: **5233**, 5420, **5553, 5749**, 5761, 6109, 6196, **6210**
Michigan: **5783**
Minnesota: 5202, 5362, 5403, **5635**
Missouri: 5982
New Hampshire: **5386**
New Jersey: 5734
New York: **2032, 2283, 3474, 3789**, 4900, **5215, 5219, 5398, 5490, 5507, 5563, 5607, 5673, 5703, 5726, 5790**, 5859, **5879, 5893, 6072**
Ohio: **1234, 5755, 6101**
Oregon: **5881**
Pennsylvania: **5554, 5628**, 5657
Rhode Island: 3390, **6185**
South Carolina: 1747, 5216
Tennessee: 5684
Texas: **237, 4839**
Vermont: **6047**
Virginia: **2025, 5596, 6088**
Washington: 5327, **5896**

Undergraduate support

Alabama: 52, 155, **308**, 317, 344, 690, 772, 1370, 1754, 1886, 1960, 2029, 2046, 2225, 2560, 2594, 3068, 3717, 4009, 4226, 4261, 4341, 4530
Alaska: 55, 174, 373, 769, 1157, 1971, 2276, 2297, 2587, 2943, 3023, 3609, **3641**, 3779, 3999
Arizona: 76, 178, 179, 181, 291, 562, 709, 867, 1151, 1226, 1394, 1444, 1626, 2377, 2549, 3121, 3193, 3261, 3469, **3567**, 3648, 3714, 3849, 3959, 4122, 4202, 4338
Arkansas: 184, 185, 333, 1369, 1562, 1701, 1926, 2645, 3024, 3203, 3658, 3721, 3960, 4029, 4036, 4125, **4158**, 4173, 4222, 4287, 4395, 4412, 4423
California: 8, 78, 81, 188, 209, 228, 303, 305, 324, **339**, 374, 392, 434, 441, 455, 479, 480, 496, 541, 566, 567, 568, 574, 617, 621, 622, 623, 625, 660, 728, **746**, 747, 765, 784, 792, 807, 849, 898, 921, 925, 934, 963, 977, 1014, 1126, 1169, 1191, 1208, 1213, 1258, 1324, 1345, 1395, 1470, 1471, 1474, 1553, 1575, 1584, 1612, 1623, 1657, 1670, 1793, 1803, 1831, 1840, 1844, 1867, **1870**, 1881, 1922, 1924, 1968, 2023, 2055, 2071, 2088, 2098, 2105, 2139, 2149, 2159, 2177, 2209, 2228, 2231, 2253, 2261, 2278, 2294, 2314, **2348**, 2356, 2375, 2381, 2405, 2444, 2458, 2491, 2579, 2604, 2619, **2712**, 2733, 2735, 2776, **2798**, 2806, 2869, **2876**, 2877, 2890, **2916**,

2947, 2950, 2978, 2982, 3038, 3076, 3123, 3146, 3156, 3157, 3224, 3238, 3279, 3290, 3294, 3314, 3318, **3320**, 3347, 3394, 3467, **3470**, 3505, 3538, 3539, 3540, 3542, 3544, 3550, 3586, **3598**, 3623, **3637**, 3655, 3668, **3671, 3690**, 3705, 3706, 3709, 3731, 3764, 3775, 3804, 3832, 3839, 3863, 3899, 3901, 3943, **3975**, 4100, 4109, 4165, 4188, 4229, 4300, 4302, 4411, 4420, **4508**, 4511, 4556, **5477, 6173**
Colorado: 165, 297, 397, 639, 766, **773**, 778, 851, 852, 916, 942, 975, 1252, 1322, **1375**, 1388, 1423, 1642, 1676, 1716, 1757, 1887, 1901, 1903, 2150, 2199, 2325, 2344, 2388, 2465, 2749, 2823, 2832, 3452, 3508, 3583, **3645**, **3803**, 3866, 4529, 4673
Connecticut: 95, 132, 191, 230, 278, 511, 523, 686, 708, **750**, 782, **791**, 808, 896, 902, 932, 986, 1201, **1407**, 1439, 1485, 1613, 1985, **2260**, 2350, 2407, 2421, 2483, 2503, 2627, 2710, 2834, 2885, 2998, 3164, 3273, 3408, **3436**, **3638**, 3966, 4043, 4054, 4090, 4321, 4355, 4384, 4422, 4453, 4491, **4527**, 4737
Delaware: **1083**, 1302, 1599, 1864, 2070, 2453, 2561
District of Columbia: 100, **105, 106**, 118, **131, 135, 169, 391, 526**, 858, **929, 1118, 1427, 1487, 1869, 1872, 1883**, 1913, **2049, 2084, 2170**, 2320, **2573, 2879, 2884, 3188, 3310**, 3450, **3624, 3805**, 3949, 4312, 4315, 4317, **5406**, 5505, **5565, 6005**
Florida: 59, 80, 94, 123, **171**, 172, 201, 286, 330, 477, 504, 614, **805**, 865, 899, 984, 1026, **1135**, 1203, 1278, 1316, 1351, 1371, 1398, 1568, 1577, 1600, 1656, 1683, 1690, 1706, 1709, 1769, **1797, 1805**, 1882, **1921**, 1988, 2016, 2121, 2214, 2239, 2249, 2364, 2373, 2475, 2527, **2564**, 2585, 2588, 2608, 2821, 2848, 2986, 3026, 3034, 3063, 3079, 3324, 3331, 3334, 3335, 3393, 3500, 3513, **3628**, 3652, 3730, 3818, 3861, 3881, 3938, 3969, 4008, 4073, 4272, 4415, 4528, 4536, 4680
Georgia: 1, **25, 466, 485**, 517, 628, 803, 813, 862, 922, 1174, 1206, **1296, 1318**, 1863, 2218, 2363, 2659, **3186**, 3201, **3211**, 3954, 4003, 4044, 4327, 4367, 4454, 4464
Hawaii: **103**, 164, 284, 972, 1482, 1759, 1772, 1773, 1815, 1961, 2151, 3239, 3458, 3516, 3631, 3996, 4088, **4098**, 4561
Idaho: 1475, 1766, 2006, 2243, 2700, 2757, 2865, 3319, 3580, 3745
Illinois: **23**, 88, 92, **107, 108, 112**, 149, 153, 154, 238, 341, 345, 356, 359, 407, 424, 467, 468, 482, 505, 544, 582, 597, **655**, 678, 684, 698, 734, 736, 739, 874, 971, 1032, 1067, 1081, 1123, 1138, 1144, 1214, 1248, **1256**, 1308, **1434**, 1454, 1669, 1692, 1715, 1723, 1746, 1749, 1783, 1820, 1891, 1908, 1973, 2009, 2094, 2146, 2166, 2258, 2277, **2332**, 2367, **2408**, 2426, 2511, 2521, 2536, 2569, 2581, 2600, 2602, 2656, 2729, 2852, **2896**, 3007, 3056, 3064, 3091, 3118, 3169, **3174**, 3206, 3212, 3289, 3293, 3306, 3315, 3330, 3367, 3368, 3385, 3410, 3426, 3434, 3438, 3465, **3466**, 3478, 3581, 3600, 3667, 3708, 3777, 3795, **3825**, 3850, 3902, 3942, 3957, 3979, 3984, 3988, 4006, 4015, 4017, 4062, 4089, 4176, 4240, 4267, 4283, 4298, 4363, 4493, **4495**, 4552, 4566, 5494, 5829
Indiana: 26, **87**, 96, 189, 232, 253, 361, 366, 413, 414, 438, 453, 531, 545, 570, 592, 744, 756, 764, 834, 860, 872, 878, 881, 888, 889, 891, 894, 906, 907, 944, 1005, 1073, 1077, 1186, 1264, 1286, 1344, 1446, 1462, 1525, 1547, 1565, 1638, 1682, 1719, 1738, 1745, 1816, 1817, 1819, 1832, **1982**, 1983, 1999, 2018, 2033, 2053, 2067, 2100, **2165**, 2183, 2227, 2282, 2295, 2302, 2305, **2316**, 2360, 2372, 2401, 2424, 2471, 2492, 2499, 2520, 2777, 2791, 2886, 2907, 2941, 2960, 2963, 3013, 3059, 3074, 3133, 3220, 3225, 3242, 3245, **3292**, 3295, 3323, 3355, 3357, 3602, 3633, 3687, 3716, 3746, 3799, 3811, 3870, 3903,

4246, 4304, 4326, 4455, 4469, 4486, 4517, 4535, 4540, 4563, 4565, 6076

Utah: 280, 300, 1107, 1728, 1808, **2178**, 2539, 2567, 2856, 3810

Vermont: 446, 729, 1192, 1224, 1276, 1297, 1763, 2062, **2557**, 2816, 2966, 3629, 3630, 3684, 4034, 4199, 4217, 4231, 4399, 4447, 4450

Virginia: **48**, **68**, 69, **101**, **133**, 258, 312, 343, 510, 634, **646**, **738**, **806**, 912, 917, **948**, **1041**, 1097, 1148, 1281, 1432, **1456**, 1598, 1652, 1660, **2025**, 2196, 2358, 2379, 2396, 2430, **2711**, 2811, **2897**, **2898**, **2900**, 2968, **3050**, 3160, **3307**, 3321, 3376, 3547, 3576, 3801, 3860, 3888, 3937, 4079, **4180**, **4195**, 4337, 4421, 4489, 5091, **5599**, **5999**, **6194**

Washington: 3, 56, 142, 196, **263**, 302, 304, 307, 342, 404, 437, 490, 650, 653, 733, 774, 824, 947, 1055, 1187, 1290, 1380, 1472, 1531, 1627, 1659, 1699, 1739, 1875, 1892, 1893, 1945, 1978, 2064, 2112, 2116, 2127, 2191, 2326, 2341, 2415, 2442, 2448, 2556, 2571,

2635, 2694, 2713, 2738, 2812, 2814, **2883**, 2957, 3073, 3144, 3153, **3207**, 3247, 3250, 3399, **3463**, 3485, 3563, 3604, 3656, 3698, 3782, 3873, 4024, 4066, 4126, 4143, 4144, 4262, 4286, 4311, 4313, **4314**, 4353, 4440, **5114**

West Virginia: 394, 589, 1353, 1518, 1735, 1860, 2156, 2331, 2445, 2580, 2746, 2803, 2996, 3084, 3106, 3268, 3275, 3383, 3911, 3936, 4715

Wisconsin: 32, 33, 60, 210, 211, 256, 292, 295, 338, 500, 501, 546, 579, 595, 636, 671, 674, 749, 752, 836, 903, 923, 961, 1010, 1057, 1063, 1130, 1165, 1189, **1200**, 1225, 1250, 1280, 1314, 1357, 1361, 1386, 1393, 1441, **1473**, 1479, 1494, **1539**, 1549, 1582, 1609, 1629, 1630, 1687, 1732, 1761, 1804, 1823, 1877, 1899, 1957, 2063, 2114, 2157, 2172, 2182, 2269, 2270, 2271, 2272, 2292, 2299, 2313, 2339, 2340, 2400, 2438, 2446, 2472, 2513, 2523, 2525, 2667, 2669, 2725, 2768, 2837,

2839, 2913, 2949, 2955, 2958, 3003, 3008, 3060, 3061, 3065, 3089, 3138, 3167, 3291, 3317, 3327, 3350, 3395, 3447, 3471, 3496, 3622, 3662, 3664, 3665, 3669, 3693, 3728, 3739, 3758, 3768, 3857, 3884, 3915, 3932, 3964, 4013, 4045, 4057, 4136, 4289, 4344, 4361, 4362, 4369, 4418, 4436, 4473, 4474, 4499, 4507, 4516

Wyoming: 145, 819, **940**, 1018, 1563, 1567, 2101, 2737, 3134, 3208, 3817, 3919, 4409, 4526

Workstudy grants

Alaska: 1971
Colorado: **5230**
Illinois: **2896**
Minnesota: 5403
New Jersey: **6069**
New York: 3634, **5418**, **5879**
Virginia: **5221**

SUBJECT INDEX

The numbers under the subject headings in this index refer to the sequence numbers of entries in the Descriptive Directory section of this book. Grantmakers that give nationally or regionally are indicated in boldface type following the states in which they are located. Grantmakers that restrict their giving to particular states, counties, or cities are listed in lighter type following the states in which they give. This index is generated to denote the fields of interest a grantmaker might support that are relevant to an individual's needs and does not include the giving interests the grantmaker provides to organizations.

Adoption

Colorado: **5094**
Illinois: 4745
Wisconsin: **4779**

Adult education—literacy, basic skills & GED

Delaware: **5889**
Massachusetts: 464
New Jersey: 4103

Adult/continuing education

California: **4705**
Colorado: 5615
Georgia: 862
Kentucky: 890, **2030**
New Jersey: 632
New Mexico: 396
Ohio: 800
Oregon: 1411
Virginia: **101**
Washington: 3873
Wisconsin: 4516

Adults, men

Ohio: 3185

Adults, women

New Jersey: **5953**
Ohio: 4309
Pennsylvania: 3923, 5377

African Americans/Blacks

California: 1840, **1870**, **5328**
Colorado: 3508
Connecticut: 932
District of Columbia: 410, **2049**
Florida: 865, 2475, 2608, 3335
Hawaii: **4098**
Illinois: 1715, **5972**
Maryland: 28, 3048, **5353**
Michigan: 1621
Minnesota: 5423
New Jersey: **5424**, **5926**
New York: **7**, 2862, **2874**, **2893**, **2899**, 3267, **4308**, **5482**, **6024**
North Carolina: 2
Ohio: 1070
Oregon: **5881**
Pennsylvania: 15

South Carolina: 811
Texas: 2474, 4246
Virginia: **646**, **4180**

Aging

California: **4843**, 4871, 4903, 4959, 4970, 5042
Connecticut: 5055
Florida: 4712, 5126
Georgia: 5045
Hawaii: 4810, 4829
Illinois: **4568**, 4730, 4930, **5056**, 5101
Indiana: 4881, 4893
Kansas: 5064
Kentucky: 4911
Maine: 5003
Maryland: 4716, 4894, 5135
Massachusetts: 4592, **4723**, 4742, 4826, 4905, 4996, 5000, 5030, 5040, 5098, 5099
Missouri: 4607
New Jersey: **4597**, **4975**, **5898**
New York: 4570, 4601, 4638, 4821, 4895, 5044, 5089, 5110, 5118, **5146**, **5295**, **5523**
Ohio: 4755, 4770, 4892, **5007**, 5047, 5059, 5169
Oregon: 4912
Pennsylvania: 4744, 4763, 4920, 5148
Rhode Island: 4689, 4696, 5024, 5113
Vermont: 4683
Virginia: **4865**, 5149
Washington: 4698, 5145, 5205
Wisconsin: 4817

Aging, centers/services

Texas: 4986
Virginia: **4865**

Agriculture

Arkansas: 185, **4158**
California: 441, 479, 619, 898, 963, 3764, **5795**
District of Columbia: **5821**
Hawaii: 1772
Illinois: 1891, 2569, 4085
Indiana: 860, 3245
Iowa: 2035, 2508, **6207**
Kentucky: 890
Louisiana: 2323, 2432
Maine: 2484
Maryland: **5764**
Massachusetts: **6038**
Michigan: 1463, 2696
Minnesota: 93, **495**, 3425, **5948**, 6044
Missouri: 4092
Ohio: 985, 1949, 2383, 2739, 4210, 4212

Oklahoma: 5912
Pennsylvania: 1741, 3774
Rhode Island: 4192
South Carolina: 633
Texas: 296, 1190, 2447
Washington: 1290, 4244
Wisconsin: 327, 1630, 3191, 4516

Agriculture, farm bureaus/granges

Kentucky: 4740
Missouri: 508

Agriculture, livestock issues

Georgia: **3211**
New Hampshire: 1946

Agriculture/food

California: 3123
Wisconsin: 4516

Agriculture/food, formal/general education

California: 4511
Florida: 4249
Georgia: **3211**
Illinois: 2094
Indiana: 1077, 2305
Massachusetts: 3836
Michigan: 3176
Minnesota: 4
New Jersey: 4549

Agriculture/food, reform

New York: 5816

Agriculture/food, research

California: **6054**

AIDS

Florida: 5065
Maryland: **5869**
Massachusetts: 4632
New York: **5430**, 5816, **6039**
Vermont: **5278**
Virginia: 5704
Washington: 4886

AIDS research

District of Columbia: **5824**
New York: 5747, **5790**, **6039**
Texas: 6074
Virginia: **5600**

AIDS, people with

Alabama: 4573
California: 5062, **5902**
Maryland: 4811

Alcoholism

New York: 656

Allergies

California: **5870**

Allergies research

Arizona: **5551**
Illinois: **5806**

Alzheimer's disease

California: 4970
Maryland: **4579**

Alzheimer's disease research

Arizona: **5551**
Maryland: 5575
Texas: 6074
Virginia: **5600**

American studies

Indiana: **3047**
Michigan: **5783**

Anesthesiology research

Minnesota: **5791**
New York: **5573**

Animal welfare

California: **5705**
New Jersey: **6203**
New York: **161**
Wyoming: **5649**

Animals/wildlife, endangered species

Wyoming: **5649**

Animals/wildlife, exhibition

Florida: **1135**

Animals/wildlife, preservation/protection

California: **5795**, **5830**
District of Columbia: **6005**
Minnesota: **5948**
Montana: **3440**
New York: **3973**, **6198**
Ohio: 2383, 4046
Pennsylvania: 1963
Rhode Island: **6083**
Texas: **5640**, **6188**
Wyoming: **5649**

Animals/wildlife, research

Maryland: **5764**
Massachusetts: 5685
Michigan: **5535**

Animals/wildlife, training

Florida: **1135**

Anthropology/sociology

California: **5934**
District of Columbia: **5821**
Florida: **5802**
Hawaii: 3631
Illinois: 3426, **3460**
Massachusetts: 1166
New Jersey: 4443
New Mexico: **5466**
New York: **5563**, 5877, **6099**, **6189**
Virginia: 5552
Washington: **5803**

Architecture

California: 1968, 3542, 5323, **5407**
Connecticut: **5913**
District of Columbia: 100, 2320
Illinois: **655**, **5335**, **5865**, **6128**
Maryland: **5763**
Massachusetts: 6109
Minnesota: 93
Missouri: 121
New Hampshire: **5386**
New Jersey: 838, 2330
New York: **2385**, 2936, **3474**, **5219**, 5241, **5271**,
    5422, 5521, **5563**, **5726**, **5879**
Ohio: 4210
Pennsylvania: 1962, 2518
Texas: **6192**
Virginia: 1432
Washington: 304
West Virginia: 5224

Armenia

California: 2278
Michigan: 1307
Rhode Island: 1898

Arms control

California: **6079**
New York: **6039**

Art & music therapy

Illinois: 2852

Art conservation

California: **5328**
Colorado: **5230**
New York: **5219**, **5460**, **5927**, **5978**
West Virginia: 5224

Art history

California: **5328**
Colorado: **5230**
Illinois: **5488**
Massachusetts: 2058
New Jersey: **5315**
New York: 840, **5186**, **5219**, 5284, **5316**, **5460**,
    5563, **5726**, **5927**, **5978**
North Carolina: **5875**
Texas: **5969**

Arthritis

California: 5760

Arthritis research

California: **5621**
Florida: 5647
Georgia: **5620**

Tennessee: **5545**

Arts

Alaska: 5181
Arizona: 3648
California: 541, 5252, 5291, 5297, **5318**, **5328**,
    5356, 6102
Colorado: 916, 5243, 5504, 5655
Connecticut: 5341, 5439, **5508**
District of Columbia: **2170**, 5431
Florida: 865, 1398, **3246**, 3818, 5275, 5429
Hawaii: 1772, 5344
Illinois: **655**, 1289, 6131
Indiana: 860, 1264, 5213
Kentucky: 5367, 5469
Louisiana: 5211
Maine: **6165**
Maryland: 279
Massachusetts: **5307**, 5348, 5420, **5487**, **6038**
Michigan: 5212
Minnesota: 5196, 5202, 5247, 5312, 5373, 5397,
    5401, 5423, 5453, 5971
Nebraska: 1263
New Jersey: 743, **3172**, **5434**, 5446, **5511**, 5514
New Mexico: 1789, **5466**, 5671
New York: **3570**, 5110, **5186**, **5187**, 5207, 5208,
    5215, **5219**, 5261, **5271**, 5286, **5295**, **5296**,
    5301, **5303**, 5326, **5331**, **5334**, **5338**, 5339,
    5384, **5404**, **5422**, **5427**, **5460**, 5461, 5496,
    5515, 5521, **5607**, **5942**, **6136**
Ohio: 1070, 2671, **2847**, **5281**, **5510**
Oregon: 1036, 5249, 5259, 5454
Pennsylvania: 1092, 5377, **5393**, 5436, **5520**, **5846**
South Carolina: 712, 5216
Texas: 3819, **5246**, 5280, **5351**, 5478
Utah: **5486**
Vermont: 5497, 5498
Washington: 2738, 2990, 3247, 5205, **5263**, **5265**,
    5481
West Virginia: 3106
Wisconsin: 903, 3471, 5389

Arts education

Arizona: 867
California: **219**, 3542, 5462
Colorado: 916, **5230**, 5470, 5504
Connecticut: 932
Florida: 201, 1026, 1398, **3246**
Hawaii: 1772
Illinois: 1289, **3825**, 4176, 5494
Indiana: 1077, 2282
Kansas: 4030
Massachusetts: 411, 1044, 2058
Michigan: 325, 1621
Minnesota: 5264
Nevada: 3603
New Jersey: 838, 5421
New Mexico: 1789
New York: 719, 1356, **5418**, 5521, **6149**
Ohio: 4210
Pennsylvania: 4332
Rhode Island: 3390
South Carolina: 712
Tennessee: 5861
Vermont: 5136
Virginia: **3036**, 4079
Washington: 262, 5634

Arts, administration/regulation

Minnesota: 5650
New York: **5215**
Oregon: 5454

Arts, alliance

California: 5463

Arts, artist's services
California: 918, 5175, 5250, 5252, **5318**, 5391, 5411, 5432, 5501, **5518**
Colorado: 5243, 5470
Florida: 5275, **5416**, 5429
Illinois: **5190**
Maine: 2484
Maryland: 5444
Massachusetts: **5307**, 5348
Michigan: 5212
Minnesota: 5247, 5312, 5362
New Jersey: 5734
New Mexico: **5525**
New York: **5180**, **5206**, 5207, **5215**, **5219**, 5273, 5274, **5314**, 5320, 5326, **5334**, **5372**, **5385**, **5405**, **5422**, **5438**, 5448, 5461, **5471**, 5512, 5515, **5519**, 5521, **5624**
Ohio: 5485
Pennsylvania: 5272, 5354, 5433
Texas: 5280
Vermont: **5278**

Arts, formal/general education
Delaware: **1083**
Nebraska: **3046**
New York: **5303**

Arts, management/technical aid
District of Columbia: **5220**, **5366**
Oregon: 5454

Arts, public education
Florida: 5429
New York: **5460**

Arts, research
California: 5987
New York: **5215**, **5395**, **5563**
Texas: **5969**

Asia
Texas: **5969**

Asians/Pacific Islanders
California: 209, 623, 747, 977, 2869, 3731
District of Columbia: **1118**
Hawaii: **103**, 3239
Illinois: **5972**
Nevada: **4238**
New York: **7**, 3267
Virginia: **4180**
Washington: 2957

Asthma
North Carolina: 5582

Asthma research
Arizona: **5551**
Illinois: **5689**, **5806**
New York: 5583

Astronomy
Arizona: **6097**
California: **1835**
Maryland: **5578**
Pennsylvania: 4548
Virgin Islands: **5836**

Athletics/sports, academies
Indiana: 2360
Vermont: 4217

Athletics/sports, amateur competition
New York: 3071

Athletics/sports, amateur leagues
District of Columbia: **5012**

Athletics/sports, baseball
Alaska: 55
California: 5823
Michigan: 325
New York: **4604**
Pennsylvania: 2487

Athletics/sports, basketball
Indiana: 2305
Michigan: 1463

Athletics/sports, equestrianism
Maryland: **5092**
Nebraska: 1161
New York: **4854**, **6205**
Tennessee: 2115
Texas: **129**
Virginia: 4641
Washington: **2883**

Athletics/sports, football
Louisiana: 594
Texas: 4647

Athletics/sports, golf
California: **4508**
Delaware: 1085
Indiana: 894
Kentucky: 273
Michigan: 325
New Jersey: 4394
New York: 1164
North Carolina: 2042
South Carolina: 811
Tennessee: 478

Athletics/sports, Olympics
New York: 3071

Athletics/sports, professional leagues
District of Columbia: **5012**
Florida: 4710

Athletics/sports, racquet sports
California: **3671**

Athletics/sports, school programs
Indiana: 906, 1077
Louisiana: 594
Maine: 2484
Michigan: 1463
New York: 2962
Rhode Island: 988
Washington: 490

Athletics/sports, soccer
Michigan: 4236

Athletics/sports, training
California: 898, 3901
Colorado: 452
Connecticut: 1137
Delaware: 1085

Florida: 865, 4460
Hawaii: 1772
Indiana: 872, 1264, 2282, 2360, 3074
Kansas: 1624
Maine: 5008
Michigan: 162, 325
Missouri: 911, 2161
Montana: 2825
New Jersey: 4204
New York: 868, 908, **6205**
North Carolina: 4468
Ohio: 1515
Oregon: 2486
Pennsylvania: 1016
Rhode Island: 988
South Dakota: 3723
Tennessee: 2115
Texas: **129**, 4647
Virginia: 4641
West Virginia: 3106, 4651

Athletics/sports, water sports
Florida: **1921**
Michigan: 880
New York: 3071
Oregon: 796

Athletics/sports, winter sports
California: 2490
Maine: 5008
Michigan: 880
Oregon: 2486

Australia
New York: **5893**

Autism research
California: 5714
Maryland: **5630**
New Jersey: **5996**

Bahamas
Florida: **5786**

Ballet
Delaware: **1083**
New York: 5480
Ohio: 5283

Belgium
Ohio: 2329

Belize
Florida: **5802**

Big Brothers/Big Sisters
Wisconsin: 2185

Biological sciences
California: **1835**, **5642**, **5828**, 5923, 6147
Delaware: 5856
District of Columbia: **2879**
Florida: 3969
Georgia: **5637**
Illinois: **655**, **5757**
Indiana: 232
Maryland: **5860**
Massachusetts: **5833**, **5930**
Minnesota: 93
New Jersey: 3103, **5643**
New York: **5641**, **5740**, 5768, **6130**, **6138**, **6197**

North Carolina: 4468, **5661**, 5742
Ohio: 3237, 4426
Pennsylvania: 3774
Virginia: **5692**
Wisconsin: 327

Biomedicine

Maryland: **6006**
Massachusetts: **5833**
Nevada: 5835
New Jersey: **6199**

Biomedicine research

Delaware: 5856
Illinois: **5972**
Maryland: **5860**
Massachusetts: 5915
Minnesota: **5948**
Missouri: **5957**
Nevada: 5835
New Jersey: **5996**
New York: 5771, **5932**, **6145**, **6197**
North Carolina: **5661**
Virginia: **6194**

Botanical/horticulture/landscape services

California: **3690**
Minnesota: 5971

Botany

Missouri: 3980

Boy scouts

Arizona: 562
Michigan: 880
New York: 3798

Boys & girls clubs

Georgia: **485**
Ohio: **1775**
Rhode Island: 445

Boys clubs

Missouri: 2534

Brain disorders

Georgia: **3211**
Minnesota: 5981

Brain research

New York: **5717**, 5807
North Carolina: **6065**

Brazil

Nevada: 5682

Buddhism

New York: **6162**

Burn centers

District of Columbia: **5883**

Business school/education

Alabama: 1960
Alaska: 55
Arkansas: **4158**
California: 574, 2026, 2209, 2444, **3671**, **5656**
Colorado: 3737

Connecticut: **3436**, **5727**
District of Columbia: **5775**
Florida: 865, 1203, 4415
Georgia: 517, **3211**
Hawaii: 1482, 1772
Illinois: **2287**, 2426, 3708, **6144**
Indiana: 860, 894, 3245, 4264
Kentucky: 890
Maryland: 28
Massachusetts: 158
Michigan: 325, 880, 1621, 1725, 2695, 3176, 4404
Minnesota: 138, 3226
Mississippi: 883, 2756
Missouri: 1230
Nebraska: 4354
New Jersey: 718, 3783, 4174, **5898**, **5926**
New York: 719, 868, **2032**, **3830**, **4288**
North Carolina: 835, 2352, 5742
Ohio: 985, 1070, 3150
Oklahoma: **2875**
Oregon: 67, 3043
Pennsylvania: 17, 481, 3597, 3718
Tennessee: 885
Texas: **935**
Virginia: **134**, **806**, **2897**, **2898**, **5701**, 5769, **5992**
Washington: 1699, 2713, 4244
Wisconsin: 903, 4472

Business/industry

California: 574, 1584, 2088, 3038, 3709, **5949**
Colorado: 4383
District of Columbia: 118
Illinois: **2287**, **2896**
Kentucky: **2030**, **5882**
Maine: 217
Maryland: 28
Massachusetts: 1906, 4618
Minnesota: 2543, 6044
Mississippi: 2756
Missouri: 3053
New Hampshire: 2925
New Jersey: 2330, 4443, **5926**
New Mexico: 1333
New York: 908, 3267, 3344, **4288**, **4456**, 5021, **5146**, **5679**, **5770**
North Carolina: 54
Ohio: 884, **2394**, 4210, **5947**
Oregon: 3043
Pennsylvania: 3774, 4913
Rhode Island: 2674, 3390, 5142
South Carolina: 811
South Dakota: 3723
Texas: 6120
Virginia: 1432, **5629**, **5692**
Wisconsin: 256, **1078**

Business/industry, trade boards

Ohio: 884

Cameroon

California: **2947**

Camps

Illinois: 3330, 4655
Maine: **2221**
Texas: 5096
Vermont: 5136

Canada

New Hampshire: 1408
New Jersey: **2932**
Rhode Island: **1149**
Virginia: **2897**

Cancer

Arizona: 4636

Florida: 4849
Georgia: 4627
Illinois: 4655
Indiana: **4290**, 4883, **6179**
Louisiana: 4788
Michigan: 4979
Minnesota: **4922**
Missouri: **4936**
New Jersey: 5171
New York: 4900, **5686**
Tennessee: 4832
Texas: **2274**, **5619**
Vermont: 4629
Virginia: **5623**
Washington: 4877

Cancer research

California: **5574**, **5706**, **5776**, **5888**, **5974**, **6060**
Colorado: **5980**
Connecticut: **5542**, **5696**, **5985**
District of Columbia: **5576**
Indiana: **4290**, **6179**
Maryland: **5796**
Massachusetts: **5670**
Michigan: **5819**
New York: **5606**, 5659, **5667**, **5668**, 5747, **5904**, **5936**, **5955**, 6000, 6049, **6129**
North Carolina: **6168**
Pennsylvania: **5554**, 5914
Texas: **5619**, 5917, **5922**
Virginia: **5623**

Cemeteries/burial services

Texas: **4984**

Ceramic arts

Maine: **5506**
Massachusetts: 2058
Michigan: **5332**, **5435**
Minnesota: **5337**, 5425
Montana: 5244
New Jersey: **3172**, **6069**
New York: **5495**
North Carolina: **5396**
Pennsylvania: **5269**
Texas: **5351**

Chemistry

Arizona: **6097**
California: **1835**, 3623, **5642**, 5923
Colorado: 766, 1676
Florida: 3335, 3969
Illinois: 424, **655**, **1742**
Michigan: 2686
Minnesota: 93
Missouri: 911
New York: **5740**, **6130**, **6138**
North Carolina: 5742
Pennsylvania: 550, 3774, 3790, 6137
Rhode Island: 2219
Texas: 6187
Virginia: 6153
Wisconsin: 2299

Child abuse

Utah: 6133

Children

Delaware: 4701
Minnesota: **4922**
New Jersey: 4738
Pennsylvania: 1796

Children, services

California: 2733, 4589, **5139**

Colorado: 4590
Florida: 4906
Hawaii: 1961
Missouri: **4797**
Nevada: 1994
New York: 3284, **5793**
Rhode Island: 4644
Tennessee: 4660
Virginia: **4704**

Children/youth

Florida: 5938
Georgia: 5839

Children/youth, services

Alabama: 2652
California: 2088, 3541, 4575, 4598, 4605, 5026,
    5039, **5855**
Colorado: 4692
Connecticut: **1407**
District of Columbia: **1872**
Florida: 329
Illinois: 3007, 4655, 4735, 4736
Indiana: 4883, 5112
Iowa: 408
Kentucky: 5032
Louisiana: 4788
Maine: 5003
Maryland: 4807, 4927
Massachusetts: 4991
Michigan: 4815, 4961
Minnesota: **4921**
Nebraska: 4957
New Jersey: 4443
New York: **4019**, 4708, 4821, 4972, **5036**, **5832**,
    6039
North Carolina: 4758
Ohio: 4378, 4582, 4931, **6209**
Oklahoma: 4858, 5158
Oregon: 4974
Pennsylvania: 4802, 5018, 5069, 5950
Rhode Island: 4908
Texas: 3953, 4800, 5096
Utah: 6133
Vermont: 1784, 4929, 5136
Virginia: 5091
Washington: **5114**
West Virginia: 3106, 4651, 4715
Wisconsin: 4792, 4964, 5086

China

California: 3731, **5697**

Chiropractic research

Iowa: 5794

Choreography

Alaska: 5450
Colorado: 5209
Connecticut: 5439
Massachusetts: **5288**, **5527**
Minnesota: 5247
New York: **5227**, **5277**, **5422**

Christian agencies & churches

Alabama: 2652
California: 229, 1422, **1610**, 2765, **4862**, 4924,
    4959, **5029**, **5687**, 5887
Colorado: **3803**, 6124
Connecticut: 1485
Delaware: 1904
District of Columbia: **1442**
Florida: **1797**, 2808, **4596**, **5944**
Georgia: **5637**
Hawaii: 225
Illinois: 4659

Indiana: 4058, **6201**
Iowa: 1928
Maryland: 1143
Michigan: 2050, **2362**, 6151
Minnesota: 4657
Mississippi: **5743**
Missouri: 1839, 2247, 2609
New Jersey: 2583, 4633
New York: 3692, 4708, **6206**
North Carolina: 1180, 2575, 4468, **6105**
Ohio: 3444, 4061, 4086, 4210, 5111
Oregon: 2597
Pennsylvania: 1741, 3529, 4430
Rhode Island: 445, 1001, 6184
South Carolina: 2200, 4665
South Dakota: 3723, 4295
Tennessee: 1327, 5918
Texas: 487, 857, 976, 1608, 3017, 3970, **4746**,
    4747, **4839**, 5075, 5096
Washington: 447
Wisconsin: 295, 3768, 3857, **4167**, 4207, 5049

Civil liberties, right to die

New York: 5924

Civil rights

California: **5827**
Massachusetts: **6095**
New York: **6039**

Civil rights, advocacy

California: 6171
Massachusetts: **6070**
New York: 863, **5910**, **6127**

Civil rights, formal/general education

New York: **4308**

Civil rights, gays/lesbians

California: **5855**

Civil rights, minorities

California: **4508**
New York: **5405**

Civil rights, women

District of Columbia: **5561**
Kentucky: 5367
Massachusetts: **3304**
New York: **5405**
Virgin Islands: **5836**

College

California: 3202
Indiana: 1255
Kansas: 270
Maine: 3435
Massachusetts: 6196
Michigan: **503**
New Jersey: 3148, 3274
Virginia: **2942**
Wisconsin: 3008

College (community/junior)

California: 2490
Nebraska: **3046**
North Carolina: 915
Virginia: **948**

Community development

Alaska: 5181

Connecticut: 3342
District of Columbia: 169, **5775**, **5873**, **6002**
Illinois: **5965**
Maryland: **5891**
Minnesota: 5164
New York: 5387, 5816, **6039**
North Dakota: 3683
Ohio: 2671, 5838
Tennessee: 5918
Virginia: **5999**, 6032, **6211**

Community development, real estate

New York: 3344, 5021

Community development, volunteer services

California: 3550, 5463, 5962
Colorado: 5655
Connecticut: 2627
District of Columbia: **1872**
Illinois: 5690, **6108**
Massachusetts: **3280**
Minnesota: 3080
Missouri: 573
New Jersey: **449**, 718
New Mexico: 62, 5671
New York: 779
North Carolina: 1429, 6103
Ohio: 1070
Rhode Island: 3390
Texas: 703
Utah: 6133

Computer science

Arkansas: **4158**
California: **1835**, 1840
Colorado: 3737, **5756**
Florida: 3335
Georgia: **3211**
Massachusetts: **5288**
Michigan: 1435, 2686, 3176
Minnesota: 93
Missouri: 3053
Nebraska: 2380, 4354
New Jersey: **6067**
New York: 3267, **5279**, 5387, **5422**, **5866**, **6130**,
    6136
North Carolina: 5742
Virginia: **134**, **6141**

Continuing education

New Mexico: 62

Courts/judicial administration

District of Columbia: 4577

Crime/law enforcement

Florida: 3114
Georgia: **5799**
New York: 2934, 4969

Crime/law enforcement, association

Virginia: **133**, **5599**

Crime/law enforcement, formal/general education

California: **3671**
Indiana: 906

Crime/law enforcement, police agencies

Florida: **9**
Massachusetts: 2831
New Jersey: 218, 632

New York: 362, 2934, 4960, 4969
Ohio: 435, 1070
Rhode Island: 2845, 6104
Texas: 5787

Crime/law enforcement, reform
District of Columbia: **5961**

Crime/law enforcement, research
District of Columbia: **6073**

Crime/violence prevention
California: 4605
District of Columbia: 6003
New York: **5837, 6136**

Crime/violence prevention, youth
District of Columbia: 6003

Croatia
Pennsylvania: 998

Cultural/ethnic awareness
California: **5305**
District of Columbia: **6010**
Florida: **5802**
New York: **5215, 5219, 5482**

Cystic fibrosis research
Maryland: 5715

Dance
California: 5183, 5432, 5489
Connecticut: 5439
District of Columbia: **5282**
Florida: 1398
Iowa: **3352**
Kansas: **5365**
Massachusetts: 5359, 5420, **5527**
Michigan: 325
Minnesota: 5264, 5362
Nebraska: **3046**
New Jersey: **5254**
New York: **5219, 5227**, 5228, 5241, 5242, 5245,
    5255, 5314, 5350, 5408, 5445, 5480, **5563**
Ohio: 1070

Day care
California: 4589
Massachusetts: 4985
Mississippi: 5068
New York: 4718, 4972
Pennsylvania: 5018, 5950
Vermont: 4929

Deaf/hearing impaired
Oregon: 4974

Dental care
California: 4589, 4850, 5039, 5042
Colorado: 4692
Connecticut: 5055
District of Columbia: **106, 5565**
Florida: 4595, **4713**, 4906
Illinois: **107, 5534, 5566**
Indiana: 5033
Maine: 4928, 5003
Massachusetts: 3162
New York: 5044
Ohio: 884

Utah: 4642

Dental school/education
California: **1431**
Connecticut: 4365
Delaware: 1904
District of Columbia: **106, 5565**
Florida: 1091, 2239, 3969
Georgia: 813, 1532
Hawaii: 1772
Illinois: **23**, 2569, **5566**
Indiana: 4431
Kansas: 4234
Maryland: **5860**
Michigan: 880
Missouri: 1093, 1839, 2589
Nebraska: 2857
North Carolina: 3358
Ohio: 985
Oklahoma: **2107**
Oregon: 3108
Pennsylvania: 550, 775, 1741, 2793, 2918
South Carolina: 3847

Depression
Illinois: 6004
New Jersey: **5898**

Design
California: 3542
District of Columbia: **135**
Illinois: **5335**, 5777, **6128**
Kansas: **5365**
Massachusetts: 2058, **5288**
Michigan: 1463
Minnesota: 5247
New York: **3474, 5334, 5350, 5422, 5438**, 5521
Pennsylvania: **5304**
Rhode Island: 3390
Virginia: 4079
Wisconsin: 3138

Developing countries
California: **5029**

Developmentally disabled, centers & services
District of Columbia: **5909**

Diabetes
Maine: 4768

Diabetes research
Arizona: **5551**
Illinois: **5813**
New York: **5901**
Oregon: 4974
Virginia: 5567

Diagnostic imaging research
Virginia: **5604**

Digestive disorders research
Maryland: **5796**
New York: 5659, **5711**

Disabilities, people with
Arizona: **4571**
California: **190**, 849, 4488, 4598, **4705**, 4992, 5026,
    5046
Colorado: 5504
Connecticut: 932

Delaware: 4701, **4823**
District of Columbia: 105, **4260, 5557, 5558, 5909**
Florida: 865, 1600, **4596**, 4710, 4753, 4791
Georgia: 2218, **3211**, 5045
Illinois: **3825**, 4730, 4867, 4930, **5056, 5590**
Indiana: 2100
Iowa: 408
Kansas: 4666
Kentucky: 5032, 5469
Maine: 5003
Maryland: **136**, 4716, 4807
Massachusetts: 2296, 4991
Michigan: 2697, 4349, 4842
Minnesota: 1218, **4921**, 5200
Mississippi: 4639
Missouri: **3657**, 4130
Nebraska: 3029, **5235**
New Hampshire: 4870
New Jersey: 1298, 1358, 2928, 3511, 5778
New York: **114, 2390**, 2969, 4218, **4572**, 4972,
    5031, 5412, **5523, 5943, 6145**
North Carolina: 4468, 4648, 4758
Ohio: **1775**, 4578, 4582, 4770, 4794, 4931, 4973,
    5066
Oklahoma: 4855, 5158
Oregon: 4749, 4974, 5082
Pennsylvania: 1796, 4610, 4802, 4920
South Carolina: 5077
Tennessee: 4660
Texas: 1244, 2232, 4986
Virginia: 312, 3376, **4704**
Washington: 4967
West Virginia: 3911
Wisconsin: 546, 4792, 4835, 5086, 5143

Disasters, 9/11/01
Minnesota: **3584**
New York: 2906, 4880
Virginia: **948**

Disasters, fire prevention/control
District of Columbia: **2573**
Florida: 1203, **4713**
Nebraska: 4291
New Jersey: 632
New York: 2933, 4880, 5122
Ohio: 435
Rhode Island: 3390
West Virginia: 5095

Disasters, floods
California: 5058
District of Columbia: **5173**
West Virginia: 5095

Disasters, Hurricane Katrina
District of Columbia: **5173**

Disasters, preparedness/services
North Carolina: 4630

Disasters, search/rescue
Pennsylvania: 4831

Diseases (rare)
California: **6035**

Diseases (rare) research
California: **6035**
Connecticut: **6027**
Massachusetts: **6119**
New York: 5659
Ohio: **6101**

Domestic violence

California: 4605
Massachusetts: **3304**

Drawing

District of Columbia: 6030
Massachusetts: **5526**
New Mexico: **5459**
New York: **5186**, **5430**
Ohio: **6122**

Ear & throat diseases

Missouri: **3657**
Oklahoma: 2148
Oregon: 4974

Ear & throat research

District of Columbia: **5723**
Florida: 5546
Illinois: **5590**
Maryland: **136**, **5605**, **5796**
Oregon: 4974

Early childhood education

District of Columbia: 410
Illinois: 5691
Oklahoma: 337
Pennsylvania: 5950
Texas: 737

Eastern Europe

Ohio: **6123**

Economic development

Missouri: 5982

Economically disadvantaged

Alabama: 4341
Arizona: 183
Arkansas: 4587, 4588
California: 1681, 2105, 4600, 4628, 4721, 4760, **4843**, 4850, **4862**, 4872, 4970, 5046, **5052**, **5128**, 5160, **5477**, 6182
Colorado: 4615, 4672, 4860, **5080**
Connecticut: 924, 4054, 4619, 4833, 5014, 5150
District of Columbia: 3025, 4316
Florida: 4702, 4712, **4722**, 5126, 5163
Georgia: 4719, 4765, 4784
Hawaii: 4810, 4829
Illinois: **3825**, **4568**, 4671, 4727, 4735, 4736, 4789, 4868, **5056**
Indiana: 894, 2855, 4658, 4893, 5023, 5033
Kansas: 4711, 5064, 5155
Kentucky: 5469
Louisiana: 5151
Maine: 4603, 4686, 4928
Maryland: 4927, 5135
Massachusetts: 4637, 4690, 4742, 4773, 4809, 4902, 4905, 4962, 4997, 5000, 5009, 5040, 5041, 5043, 5051, 5081, 5098, 5099, 5120
Michigan: 4815, 4842, **4859**, 4916, 5083, 5116, **5170**
Minnesota: 4657, 4869
Mississippi: 4885, 4976
Missouri: **4797**
Nebraska: 1235, 1306, 5167
New Hampshire: 2532, 4725, 4878, 4907
New Jersey: **449**, **4478**, **4597**, 4738, 4748, **4848**, 5011, 5076
New Mexico: 3451
New York: **116**, **745**, 841, 3116, 3284, 3971, 4241, 4570, **4572**, 4593, 4623, 4638, 4654, 4682, 4708, 4808, 4834, **4861**, 4863, 4895, 4925,

5021, **5036**, 5071, 5110, 5118, **5130**, 5131, 5141, 5412, 5521, 5816, **5966**
North Carolina: 3526, 4685, 4697, 4758
North Dakota: 4728
Ohio: 4578, 4650, 4700, 4794, 4892, 4918, 4973, 5047, 5111, 5169
Oklahoma: 2148
Oregon: 4640, 4662, 4912, 4974
Pennsylvania: 97, 4611, 4802, 5018, 5084, **5124**, 5148
Rhode Island: 4626, 4689, 4926, 5015, 5024, 5063, 5087, 5113, 5142
South Carolina: **4766**, 4977, 5077
South Dakota: 4709, 4935
Tennessee: 4819, 4832, 5061, **5107**
Texas: 2606, 4675, 4684, 4741, 4822, **4853**, 4914
Utah: 2273, 4804, 4836
Virginia: 4706, **4865**, 4966, 5091, 5149
Washington: 4786, 5028, 5144
West Virginia: 4651, 5072
Wisconsin: 4817, **4896**, 5079, 5086, 5143
Wyoming: 4643

Economics

California: **5949**
Colorado: **6139**
District of Columbia: **1487**, **5815**, **5821**
Hawaii: 3631
Illinois: **2287**, 3708
Maryland: 28, **5994**
Michigan: 325, 880, 1725
New Jersey: 4443
New York: 719, **5563**, **5679**, **5726**, **5770**, 5877, **6116**, **6130**, **6136**
North Carolina: 5742, **5875**
Pennsylvania: 3718, 3774, **5846**
Virginia: **134**, 5769

Education

Alaska: 769, 2772, 5540
Arizona: 3373, 3648, 5782, **6097**
Arkansas: 2841, 4173, 4294, 6178
California: 440, 970, 1844, **2712**, 2982, 3146, 3586, 5297, 5609, 5672, 5850, 6086, 6177
Colorado: **5080**, **5094**
Connecticut: 932, **4527**, 4737, 4833
District of Columbia: 213, **1872**, **5821**, **6008**, **6036**, 6181
Florida: 3861, 5754, 5938
Georgia: 2096, **3661**, 4385, 4719
Hawaii: 1961
Illinois: **128**, **655**, 736, 1144, 1888, **2896**, 5691, 5829, **5919**, 6059, **6108**
Indiana: 4335, 4357, 5725, 5945
Iowa: 1731, 1876, 2399, 3142, 3828, 5968
Kansas: 1056
Louisiana: 5532, 5622, 5831, 5928
Maryland: 1175, **5559**
Massachusetts: 234, 1919, 2973, 3757, **4723**, 5088, 5348
Michigan: 1855, 2463, 2514, 5801, 5903, 5973, 6110, **6140**
Minnesota: 1136, 2758, 4583, 5164, 5752
Mississippi: 883, 4885
Missouri: 5982
Nebraska: 1099, 1838, 2222, 2675
Nevada: **4238**
New Hampshire: 2929
New Jersey: 1153, 3148, 5734, 5738, 5976
New York: 719, 1879, 2506, 2935, 3562, 3634, **3807**, **3851**, 4133, 4972, 5159, 5618, 5658, **5710**, **5740**, **5793**, **5879**, **5942**, **6039**, **6154**
North Carolina: 882, 915, 1156, 1704, 2794, 2972, 3069, 3137, **4329**, 4468, 5683
North Dakota: 3647
Ohio: 377, 1202, 2308, 2607, 2835, 4770, 5894
Oklahoma: 5639
Pennsylvania: 551, 2369, **3230**, 3339, **4069**, 4401, 4611, **5442**, 5892, 6137
Rhode Island: 4620, 5814

South Dakota: 1765, 1940
Tennessee: 6066
Texas: 1115, 3163, 3535, **5129**, 6046, 6076, 6158, 6190
Utah: 4836, 6111
Vermont: 3010
Virginia: 2801, **2878**, 5704, 5849, **5999**, **6031**, **6155**
Washington: 3475, 4370
West Virginia: 668, 6191
Wisconsin: 1280, 1314, 2157, **2650**, 3884, 5718, 5920

Education, administration/regulation

Illinois: **2896**
Kentucky: 3635
Ohio: 5894
Texas: 6120
Virginia: **5999**

Education, association

New York: 683

Education, ESL programs

Massachusetts: 464

Education, gifted students

Hawaii: 972
Maryland: 666

Education, management/technical aid

Colorado: **5756**
South Carolina: 5543

Education, public education

Kentucky: 3635
New York: 5693, **6154**

Education, reform

District of Columbia: 5785
Illinois: **6143**

Education, research

California: 3550
Colorado: **5756**
Connecticut: 932
District of Columbia: **5564**, **5995**
Illinois: 1305, **3825**, 5829, **6143**
Maine: 2484
Michigan: 325
Missouri: 2161, 2247
New Jersey: 5734
New York: 719, 908, 3267, **3456**, **5717**, **5832**, **6116**
North Carolina: 1429
Ohio: 4210
Pennsylvania: 5892
Texas: 4487, 6076

Education, services

New York: 4958
Pennsylvania: 5018

Education, special

California: 1575, 2088
Connecticut: 932
Illinois: 3426
Kansas: 4666
Maryland: **3042**
Missouri: 2161
Nebraska: 3029
Pennsylvania: 3369
Texas: 2232, 5840
West Virginia: 3106

El Salvador
Florida: **5802**

Elementary school/education
Alabama: 166
Arizona: 3648
Delaware: **5889**
Hawaii: 1961
Illinois: 1305, 4424, 5691, 5829, 6059
Indiana: 96
Minnesota: 1040
Missouri: 1367, 2161
New Jersey: 5976
New York: **486**, 4133
Ohio: 2383, 2607, 5894
Tennessee: 6066
Vermont: 1784
Virginia: **2878**
West Virginia: 3106
Wisconsin: 5920

Elementary/secondary education
Arizona: 182, 183, 758, 6180
California: 2294, 5975
Delaware: **5889**
District of Columbia: 410, **5561**, **5564**
Florida: 5724
Iowa: 6142
Maine: **2221**, 2484
Michigan: **503**, 4124, 6183
New York: **745**, **6159**
Ohio: **6125**
Texas: 5929
Virginia: **2878**
Washington: 4818

Elementary/secondary school reform
District of Columbia: **5561**
New York: **5673**
Utah: 5967

Employment, research
Michigan: **6167**

Employment, services
California: **4705**
Florida: 4790

Employment, training
Florida: 4790

Energy
District of Columbia: **5821**
Minnesota: **5948**

Engineering
Arkansas: 4173
California: 1840, 3709
Colorado: 1676
Connecticut: 2469
District of Columbia: **3624**
Florida: 3335, 3969
Hawaii: 1772
Illinois: 3708
Indiana: 3602
Kansas: 1262
Massachusetts: 1998
Michigan: 892, **6140**
Missouri: 3053
New Jersey: 2330, 3783, 5867
New Mexico: 1789
New York: **233**, 863, 908, **2385**, 4115, **5866**, **6138**
North Carolina: 5742

Ohio: 884, **2394**, 4210
Oregon: 3108, **5881**
Pennsylvania: 550, 3774
Texas: 3354
Virginia: **5992**

Engineering school/education
Alabama: 4261
Alaska: 55
Arkansas: **4158**
California: **1835**, 3542
Colorado: 766
Connecticut: 2204
Delaware: **1083**
District of Columbia: **869**, **3624**
Florida: 1178, 1656, 3034
Georgia: 1533
Hawaii: 1772
Illinois: 424, 734, **1434**, **2287**, 4015
Indiana: 906, 1073, 1077, 2295, 2499, 3245
Iowa: 4223
Maryland: 1950
Michigan: 880, 1435, 2050, 2686, 3176, **3793**
Minnesota: 2311, 3200
Mississippi: 883
Missouri: 1601, 1782, 2516
Nebraska: 2380, 4354
Nevada: 2726
New Jersey: 1358, 5867
New York: 2640, **2874**, 2985, **5740**
Ohio: 985, 1070, 2329
Oklahoma: 4441
Pennsylvania: 1385, 1741, 2953, 3597
Rhode Island: 3572
Texas: **935**, **2870**, 3822, 4190
Virginia: 1432, **2898**, 6032
Washington: 1714
Wisconsin: 256, **1200**, 4289

Engineering/technology
Arizona: 3373
California: 1840, **6173**
District of Columbia: **5556**, **5561**
Florida: **243**
Idaho: 2700
Illinois: **655**, **5853**
Indiana: 232, 2100, 4264
Kentucky: 3016
Massachusetts: 125, 1172, **4021**, **5731**
Michigan: 880
Minnesota: **5635**, **5948**
New Jersey: **3703**, **5953**
New York: 719, 2985, **5296**, **5866**
North Carolina: 1429
Pennsylvania: **5846**
Texas: 4190
Virginia: **48**, 3743, **3826**, 6032

Environment
Alaska: 5540
California: 5548, **5795**, **5830**, 6114
District of Columbia: **5821**
Florida: 3818
Maryland: **5764**
Massachusetts: 5420
Minnesota: 5753
New Mexico: **5939**
New York: **2874**, **3973**, 5521, **5942**
Ohio: 2671, 4046, **6123**
Oregon: **5473**
Pennsylvania: 4645, **5467**, **5846**
Virginia: **2900**
Wisconsin: 256

Environment, beautification programs
New York: **6121**

Environment, forests
Alabama: 51
Michigan: 1498
Nevada: 2726
New Hampshire: 1635
New Jersey: 3103
New York: **6092**
Ohio: 2383, 4210
Washington: 2738
Wisconsin: 3191, 4516
Wyoming: 783

Environment, formal/general education
Massachusetts: **5749**
North Carolina: 5906

Environment, land resources
Minnesota: 5753

Environment, legal rights
New York: **3035**

Environment, public policy
District of Columbia: **6073**
New York: **3035**

Environment, reform
New York: **3035**

Environment, research
Massachusetts: **5749**
New York: 5859
Virginia: **5766**
Washington: **5896**

Environment, volunteer services
New York: **6121**

Environment, water resources
New York: 5859

Environmental education
California: 3542
District of Columbia: **2879**, **6008**
Illinois: 3169
Kentucky: 890
Maine: 2484
North Carolina: 5906
Oklahoma: 2533
Pennsylvania: **5467**
Texas: 1241
Wisconsin: 2299

Epilepsy
Illinois: 874
New York: **5916**

Epilepsy research
Illinois: 5699
Maryland: **5767**
New York: **5916**

Ethnic studies
Michigan: 880
Pennsylvania: **5593**

Europe
Utah: **5486**

Eye diseases
California: **5826**
District of Columbia: **105**
Massachusetts: 2296
New York: **114**, **2390**, **5825**, **5943**, **6145**
Ohio: **5845**
Oklahoma: 4858
Texas: **4981**

Eye research
California: 5797, **5826**
District of Columbia: 6052, **6175**
Georgia: 5839
Illinois: **6033**
Maryland: 5575, **5788**
New York: **5774**, **5780**, **5825**
Ohio: **5845**
Oregon: 4974
Virginia: 5567

Family services
Arizona: 5117
California: 4628
Maryland: 4927, **5676**
Massachusetts: 4997
New York: 4708
Tennessee: 4852
Virginia: 4966
West Virginia: 4806

Film/video
Alaska: 5540
California: **219**, **5177**, 5183, 5251, 5306, **5318**, **5324**, **5345**, **5356**, 5378, **5407**, **5426**, 5428, 5463, **5518**
Colorado: 5209
Illinois: 5494
Michigan: **5199**
Minnesota: 5247, **5253**, 5362
New Hampshire: **5386**
New Jersey: **5424**, 5446
New York: **1619**, **2237**, **5186**, **5219**, 5241, **5260**, **5277**, **5279**, 5301, **5303**, **5343**, **5350**, **5355**, 5382, 5387, **5400**, **5417**, **5422**, **5445**, **5474**, **5502**
Ohio: **5510**
Pennsylvania: 5433
Rhode Island: 3390, 5457
Texas: 5225
Utah: **5486**
Virginia: **2025**
Washington: 5176, **5263**, **5265**
West Virginia: 5224

Financial services
Connecticut: 3001
Rhode Island: 3390

Folk arts
Alaska: 5450
Hawaii: 1772
Minnesota: 5247
New Jersey: **3172**, **6069**
New York: **5422**
Rhode Island: 3390
Vermont: **5278**

Food distribution, groceries on wheels
California: 4720

Food services
Florida: 4702
Massachusetts: 5081
Michigan: 4961, **5170**

Minnesota: 5164
Ohio: 5147
Texas: 4986
Utah: 4836
Virginia: **738**
Wisconsin: 5079

Foreign policy
District of Columbia: **5821**

Foster care
Nebraska: 4957
Virginia: **3050**
Washington: **5114**

Foundations (non-grantmaking, non-operating)
Texas: **4984**

Foundations (private grantmaking)
New York: **6162**

France
Arizona: 76
New Hampshire: 1408
Ohio: 2329
Pennsylvania: 1465, 4763
Virginia: 1148

Fraternal societies
California: 625
Colorado: 852, 4673
Indiana: **2165**, **2316**
Maryland: **3530**, 4625
Massachusetts: **3972**
Montana: 1020
New Jersey: 1315, 2147
North Carolina: 4001
Pennsylvania: 1052
Rhode Island: 1880, 2540, 4908
Texas: 6120
Virginia: 4706

Fraternal societies (501(c)(8))
Michigan: **1573**

Genealogy
Connecticut: **1407**
Utah: 6050

Genetics/birth defects
California: **5642**, **5706**, **6035**
Illinois: 5746
Maryland: **5788**
New Hampshire: 1946
New York: **5960**
Washington: **5803**

Genetics/birth defects research
California: **6035**
Connecticut: **5542**
Georgia: **5678**
Massachusetts: **5808**
New York: 5851, **5864**, **5960**
Virgin Islands: **5836**

Geology
Arizona: 3373

Geriatrics
Tennessee: **1425**

Geriatrics research
Illinois: **5689**
Maryland: **5759**
New York: **5568**, **5573**

Germany
California: 4575
Maryland: 1537

Gerontology
California: **5828**
Oregon: 3579

Girls
District of Columbia: **391**, **5561**

Girls clubs
Illinois: **1256**

Global programs
Kansas: 1056
Mississippi: **5743**

Government/public administration
Delaware: 5702
District of Columbia: **5556**, **5821**, 6030
Hawaii: 3631
Illinois: 1308
Maine: 2484
Massachusetts: 5587, **5908**
Michigan: **6140**
Missouri: 911
New Jersey: 4443
New Mexico: 1333
New York: 2068, 5816
Ohio: 4463, **6193**
South Carolina: **1914**
Virginia: **5596**
Wisconsin: 903, 1441

Graduate/professional education
Connecticut: **350**
Georgia: 628
Michigan: **503**
Ohio: 3237

Greece
Massachusetts: 1538
New Jersey: 3098
New York: **1426**, 2935, 3792, **5990**
North Carolina: **1312**
Pennsylvania: 1052, **5876**
Rhode Island: 759

Guatemala
Florida: **5802**

Haiti
Florida: 4096

Health care
Alabama: 4917, 5638
Arizona: 3648
California: 1793, 1856, **3349**, 3524, 4594, 4600, 4628, **4705**, 4720, **4752**, 4776, 4850, 4857,

4871, **4989**, 5039, **5052**, 5160, 5411, **5548**, 5664, **5818**
Colorado: 4602, 4692, **5080**, 5655
Connecticut: 4612, 4619, 4737, 5055, 5150
Florida: 899, 3818, 4595, 4702, 4710, **4713**, 4906, 5025, 5938
Georgia: 4719, 4784, **5678**
Hawaii: **5541**
Illinois: **4783**, 4789, **4897**, 4930, 5720, **5843**
Indiana: 4658, 5033
Iowa: 1826, 4584, 4841
Kansas: 2911, 4711, **5550**
Kentucky: 4898
Maine: 4928, 5003
Maryland: **4579**, 4716, 4807, **5617**
Massachusetts: 4690, 4694, 4742, 5000, 5348
Michigan: 880, 2306, **2882**, 4979, 5083, 5653
Minnesota: 138, 4583, 4780, 4781, 4982
Mississippi: 4885, 4976, 5016
Missouri: **4936**
Montana: **4624**
Nebraska: 1592
New Hampshire: 4795
New Jersey: 4443, **4848**, 5011, **5898**
New Mexico: **5464**
New York: 2089, 3267, 3566, 4593, 4661, 4663, 4695, 4703, **4734**, 4965, **5703**, **5932**, **6039**
North Carolina: 267, 4468, 4685, 4697, 4758, 4787, 5102
North Dakota: 5127
Ohio: 884, 4762, 4794, 4918, 5119
Oklahoma: 3916, 4855
Oregon: 2109, 2991, 3579, 4932, 4974, 5082
Pennsylvania: 2661, 4645, 4777, 4778, 4802, 4851, 4963, 4993, 5093
Rhode Island: 4644, 4934, 5063, 5087, 5142
Tennessee: 4819, 5017, 5085, **5107**
Texas: 461, 4741, 4891, 4986, **5129**
Utah: 4804
Vermont: **6047**
Virginia: **4865**, 5091
Washington: 4767, 4967, 5028, 5138, 5144
West Virginia: 3106
Wisconsin: 1314, 4964, 5079, 5086
Wyoming: 4643

Health care, alliance
Indiana: 894

Health care, association
California: 4992, 5760
Georgia: **5959**
Massachusetts: **5594**, 5915
New York: **6072**
Pennsylvania: 4994
Rhode Island: **5544**
South Carolina: 5077

Health care, ethics
New York: 5924

Health care, financing
California: 5760
Connecticut: 4670
Kentucky: 4898

Health care, formal/general education
California: **5844**
Kansas: 3785, 6134
New Hampshire: 1428
Virginia: **5537**

Health care, home services
New York: 5044

Health care, management/technical aid
New Jersey: **5898**

Health care, organ/tissue banks
Missouri: 4941

Health care, patient services
Maryland: **4579**
Massachusetts: 4772, 4991
Missouri: **4936**

Health care, public policy
New Jersey: **5898**
New York: **5703**

Health care, research
Connecticut: 5735
Maryland: **5588**
New Jersey: **5898**
New York: 6186
Oregon: 6043
Wisconsin: 6204

Health organizations
Arizona: 4142
Illinois: **5589**
Iowa: 3301
Michigan: 1703
Minnesota: 5662
New York: 723
North Carolina: **5661**
Oregon: 6045
Texas: 1937, **4981**

Health organizations, volunteer services
California: 3238

Health sciences school/education
Alabama: 1546
California: 3076, 3238, **3349**
Colorado: 2419
District of Columbia: **5562**
Florida: 286, 2239
Georgia: 862, 4367
Hawaii: 47, 1772, 4561
Illinois: **108**, **655**
Indiana: 189, 1077, 2067, 2305, 3245
Iowa: 6160
Kansas: 4234
Kentucky: 2598, 3016
Maryland: **113**, **5570**, 5933
Massachusetts: 2186, 3981
Michigan: 1463, 1621, 1703, 2312, 3176, 5653
Minnesota: 4, 1268, **5948**
New Hampshire: 1428
New Jersey: 1358, 2201, 3274, 4443
New York: 1171, 2089, 2985, 4248
North Carolina: 2575, 5742
Ohio: 2130, 3494
Oregon: 3521
Pennsylvania: 695, 920, 1331, 2661, 3196, 4011
Tennessee: 4437
Texas: 1241, 3375, **3639**, 4014
Virginia: 343, 3321
Washington: 4286
West Virginia: 2074

Heart & circulatory diseases
Maryland: **4866**, 5617
West Virginia: 2074

Heart & circulatory research
Florida: 5647
Illinois: **5694**
Maryland: 5575
New York: 5659, **5741**
Utah: 5728
Virginia: **6115**
West Virginia: 2074

Hemophilia
Wisconsin: 4814

Higher education
Arizona: 3195
Arkansas: 1701
California: 624, 1395, **1542**, 2071, 3316, 3340, 3403, 3538
Colorado: 679
District of Columbia: 1193, 1209, **1871**
Florida: 246, 1655, 2378, 2867
Georgia: 862, 3551, 3660
Hawaii: 3458
Illinois: 282, 3942, 5829
Indiana: 1255, 1525, **4183**
Iowa: 1319
Maryland: 2043, 2246
Massachusetts: 2761, 2863, 3950, 3967
Michigan: 1313, 2289, 2519, 5729
Mississippi: 1349, 3732
Missouri: **3152**
Nebraska: 2380
New Jersey: 3274
New York: 928, 1038, 2985, **4494**
North Carolina: 915, 3011, 3234, 4052, 4452
Ohio: 1964, 2663, 2689
Oklahoma: **938**
Oregon: **1693**
Pennsylvania: 1288, 1383, 1521, 1545
Rhode Island: 583
South Carolina: 50
Texas: 995, 1023, 1851, 2195, 2873, 3099, 3504, 3650
Virginia: 212, 2441
Washington: 56, 895, 2110

Hinduism
California: **6093**

Hispanics/Latinos
California: 1840, **1870**, **2681**, 3038, 3076, 3542, **5328**, 5390
Colorado: 916
District of Columbia: **929**, **1869**, **1871**, **5885**, **6002**
Florida: 1026, **3055**
Illinois: **5972**
New Jersey: **5926**
New Mexico: 3451
New York: 7, **2874**, **2893**, 3267
Oregon: **5881**
Texas: **1868**, 3151, 4246
Virginia: **4180**

Historic preservation/historical societies
District of Columbia: **135**, **6034**
Florida: 3818
Illinois: 2010
Indiana: 906
Iowa: 5232
New York: **5781**
Virginia: 1097

Historical activities
California: 5251
Delaware: **5758**
Florida: **5802**

Illinois: 5868
Indiana: **3047**, **6055**
Massachusetts: **5553**

History/archaeology

California: 4419
Delaware: **5758**
District of Columbia: **5562**, **6010**, **6073**
Florida: **5802**
Hawaii: 3631
Illinois: 5868
Indiana: 860, 5722
Massachusetts: **5749**, 5761
Michigan: 325
New York: 1885, **5219**, 5241, **5563**, 5712, **5726**, **5857**, 5927, 5935, **5990**, **6099**, **6189**
North Carolina: **5875**
Pennsylvania: 1092, **5876**, **5946**, **6200**
Texas: **5969**
Utah: **5900**
Washington: 142

Home economics

Arizona: 4338
Georgia: **3211**
Illinois: 3158, 4085
Michigan: 325
Ohio: 4210, 4212

Homeless

Illinois: 4727

Homeless, human services

Alabama: 4573

Honduras

Florida: **5802**

Hong Kong

New York: **5893**

Horticulture/garden clubs

Illinois: **112**, **5569**
Michigan: **1396**
New Jersey: 3103
New York: **6121**
Ohio: 4210
Texas: 4041
Washington: 1290, 4244

Housing/shelter

California: 4720, **4752**, 4760, 4824, 4923, 5411
Connecticut: 4619, 4737, 4833
District of Columbia: **5775**
Florida: 4790, 4791
Georgia: 4784
Indiana: 4658, 5023
Iowa: 5161
Maine: 5003
Maryland: 4716
Massachusetts: 4617, 4985, 5081
Michigan: 4961
North Carolina: 5102
Ohio: 5119
Texas: 4741
Vermont: 4683
Virginia: 4966
West Virginia: 4876
Wisconsin: 5049, 5079

Housing/shelter, development

Maryland: **5763**
Michigan: 1905

New Jersey: 3783

Housing/shelter, expense aid

California: 4720, 4760, 4919
Connecticut: 5055
Illinois: 4730
Maryland: **4915**
Massachusetts: 4909
New York: 5131
North Carolina: 4685
Ohio: 4650
Pennsylvania: 4764
Texas: 4986

Housing/shelter, formal/general education

California: 622

Housing/shelter, management/technical aid

Massachusetts: **39**

Housing/shelter, reform

New York: 5816

Housing/shelter, repairs

California: 4760
Indiana: 5023
Massachusetts: **39**
Pennsylvania: 4963

Housing/shelter, services

Maine: 4603
Pennsylvania: 4764

Housing/shelter, temporary shelter

California: 4720

Human services

Alabama: 52
Arizona: 5006
California: 4589, **4705**, **4752**, 5665, **5827**, 5887
Colorado: 5862
Connecticut: 4737
Florida: 3818
Illinois: 3426, **3460**, 4828, **5566**
Iowa: 2508
Maryland: **5676**
Massachusetts: 4825, 5081, **5248**, 5348
Michigan: **5170**
Minnesota: 5164, 5971
Missouri: 2247, 4874
Montana: **4624**
New Hampshire: 4532
New Jersey: 4714, 4748, **4848**
New Mexico: **5939**
New York: 908, 4718, **4731**, **6039**
North Carolina: 5102
Ohio: 2671, 5147, 5838
Oregon: 4640
Pennsylvania: **1478**
Utah: 4653, 4899
West Virginia: 3106

Human services, emergency aid

California: 4720
Colorado: 4673
Connecticut: 4652
Georgia: 4667
Massachusetts: 4985
Ohio: 4567, 4591
Pennsylvania: 4764
Texas: **4984**
Washington: 1627

Human services, gift distribution

California: 4720
Connecticut: 5150

Human services, transportation

California: 4720
Texas: 4986

Human services, victim aid

Ohio: 4567

Humanities

Alaska: 5181
California: 2088, 3706, 4419, **5328**, **5940**
Colorado: 5655
Connecticut: 932
District of Columbia: **5564**, **5709**, **5995**
Hawaii: 5841
Illinois: **3571**
Maryland: 5210
Massachusetts: **5553**
Michigan: **5748**
Nevada: 6037
New Jersey: 4443, 5514, 6202
New Mexico: 5671
New York: **2385**, **3035**, **5219**, **5338**, **5503**, **5563**, **5700**, **6136**
North Dakota: 6041
Ohio: 4463
Oklahoma: 259, 4441
Oregon: 607, 3045, 6053
Pennsylvania: **1478**, 5433, **5593**, **5846**
Tennessee: 5861
Texas: 6158
Virginia: **2025**, 6172
Washington: 1892
West Virginia: 6191
Wisconsin: 2271

Hungary

New Jersey: **119**
New York: **2187**

Immigrants/refugees

California: **2285**
District of Columbia: **169**
Maryland: **4915**
New York: **486**, 2089, **3807**, **5793**, **6136**

Immunology

New York: **5668**

Immunology research

California: **5706**, **5870**
Illinois: **5806**
New York: **5717**
Ohio: 5931

India

California: **1496**
Connecticut: **3638**
New Jersey: **2478**

Insurance, providers

Illinois: **6144**
Pennsylvania: **983**
Virginia: **6088**

International affairs

California: **5305**, 6102
District of Columbia: **1273**, **1487**, **5709**, 5762, **5821**

Hawaii: 1772, 3631
New Hampshire: **5878**
New Jersey: 4443
New Mexico: 5671
New York: **2382**, **4288**, **6136**, **6208**
North Carolina: **5875**
Pennsylvania: **1478**
Virgin Islands: **5836**

International affairs, formal/general education
California: 4515, **6112**
Illinois: 678

International affairs, goodwill promotion
California: **6112**

International affairs, information services
District of Columbia: 6030

International affairs, public policy
District of Columbia: **1487**

International affairs, volunteer services
California: **6112**

International conflict resolution
District of Columbia: **1273**, 5762

International development
Florida: **5804**
New York: **5673**

International economic development
Florida: **5804**
New York: **6051**

International exchange
Florida: **5223**
Pennsylvania: **5789**

International exchange, arts
Maine: **6165**

International exchange, students
Connecticut: **350**
District of Columbia: **1487**, 5895
Hawaii: **103**
Illinois: **3466**
Michigan: 4027
New York: **2019**, **2382**, **2450**, 3634, **3789**, **4288**, **5719**, **5925**
Rhode Island: **1149**, **1489**
Texas: 976
Washington: **3463**

International human rights
California: **5827**, 6171
Massachusetts: **6070**, **6095**
New York: 863, **5430**, **5910**, **6127**

International peace/security
District of Columbia: **1273**, 5762
Hawaii: 1772, 3631
New York: **5673**, **6039**, **6136**

International relief
New York: **486**

Texas: **4984**
Virginia: **4865**

International studies
California: **746**, **5697**
Illinois: 3708
New York: **5219**, **5563**, **5952**

Ireland
Illinois: 6131

Islam
California: 6182
Colorado: **5230**
Florida: 4691
Georgia: **1318**
New York: **5673**, **6091**
Texas: 4724

Israel
California: 99
Massachusetts: **6210**
New Mexico: **5939**
New York: 2210, **4734**, **5394**, **5811**, **5911**

Italy
Colorado: 3994
Massachusetts: 967
Michigan: **1495**, 4842
New York: 1038, 2935
Tennessee: **5107**

Jamaica
Florida: **1921**

Japan
California: 623
Utah: **5486**

Jewish agencies & temples
California: 2088, **3598**
Georgia: **4669**
Illinois: 3330, 4868
Kentucky: 890
Louisiana: 2087
Maryland: 2091
Massachusetts: 1348, **6210**
Michigan: 2562
Missouri: 1367
New Jersey: 830, **2168**, 4555
New Mexico: **5939**
New York: **498**, 1249, 1347, 2086, 2089, 2210, **4019**, **4159**, 4179, **4861**, 4863, 4958, **5417**, **5688**, **5710**, **5811**, **5911**, 5935, **5966**, **6007**
North Carolina: 385
Ohio: 4514, **6193**
Pennsylvania: 1390, 1589, 2437, 3457, 4851
Texas: **4853**, 4914
Washington: 1511

Jordan
California: 99

Journalism school/education
California: 1575, 2490
Georgia: 862, **3211**
Indiana: 2305
Mississippi: 883
Nebraska: **3046**
Virginia: **2025**
Washington: 3873

Journalism/publishing
California: 5463, **5902**, **5949**
Connecticut: 932, **4622**
District of Columbia: **1487**, **3310**, 5648, 5708, **5810**, **5815**, **5821**, **5885**, **5890**, 6030, **6064**, **6073**, 6090
Florida: 865, 1026, **1135**
Georgia: **5675**, **5678**
Hawaii: 1772
Illinois: 2138, 2146
Indiana: **87**, 872
Maryland: **5578**, **5763**
Massachusetts: 360, 4606
Michigan: 325, 892, **5783**
Mississippi: 883
New Jersey: 1153, 4406, 5738
New York: 719, **5146**, **5218**, 5360, 5387, **5430**, **5475**, **5523**, **5679**, **5910**
North Carolina: **5197**
Ohio: 884, 1070, **6122**
Pennsylvania: 3774
Rhode Island: 2674
Texas: 1790
Virginia: **1458**, **2945**, **5602**
Wisconsin: 2299

Kidney diseases
Alabama: 4938
Arizona: 181, 4586
California: 2890, 4951
Connecticut: 2885, 4939
Florida: 4942, 5025
Georgia: 4943
Hawaii: 4944
Indiana: 2886, 4945
Iowa: 4946
Kansas: 4947
Louisiana: 4948
Maine: 2887, 4949
Massachusetts: 2888
Missouri: 4941
North Carolina: 2889, 4950
Ohio: 4952
Tennessee: 4940
Utah: 1107

Kidney research
California: 6019, 6021
Georgia: 6012
Illinois: 6013
Indiana: 6014
Louisiana: 6015
Maryland: 6016
Massachusetts: 2888, 6017
Michigan: 6018
Missouri: 6011, **6077**
New York: 2891, 6022, **6023**
Ohio: 6020
Texas: 5917
Utah: 5730

Korea
Connecticut: **5913**
Pennsylvania: **2223**

Labor unions/organizations
California: 3775
District of Columbia: 858, **1883**, **3965**, **4676**
Hawaii: 470
New Jersey: 2122, 2330
New York: 4115, 4393
Pennsylvania: 204, 4020

Landscaping
District of Columbia: 2320
New York: **3474**, 5241

Language (classical)
New York: 5241

Language (foreign)
Arizona: 76
California: **6173**
District of Columbia: **2884, 5821, 6010**
Florida: 865
Indiana: 3245
New Jersey: 4443
New York: **1426, 3789, 5322, 5430, 5563**
North Carolina: **5875**
Ohio: 4463
Vermont: **6047**
Virginia: 1148, **6048**
Washington: 2990, **3463, 5651**
Wisconsin: 903

Language/linguistics
Delaware: **5889**
District of Columbia: **1118, 5772**
Florida: **5802**
Maryland: **136**
New York: **5563, 6189**
North Carolina: **5875**
Pennsylvania: **5593**

Latin America
Utah: **5486**

Law school/education
Alabama: 52
Arizona: 180
California: 2522, 3038, **3671**
Delaware: **1083**, 1904
District of Columbia: 1122
Florida: 865, 1399
Georgia: 813
Illinois: **102, 104**, 1512, 2569, 3064
Indiana: **87**, 1525, 3171
Massachusetts: 1172, 2542
Michigan: 892, 3176, **3308**
Minnesota: 2321
Nebraska: 2759, 2857
New Jersey: 1298, 4406
New York: 65, **2385**, 2862, **4308, 6127**
North Carolina: 4468
Ohio: 985, 2636, 3545
Oregon: 67
Pennsylvania: 550, 1741, 2953
Rhode Island: 3882
Texas: 3354, 4246
Virginia: **757**
Washington: 2361, 3417
Wisconsin: 3921, 4418

Law/international law
California: **5871**
Georgia: **5799**
Hawaii: 3631
New York: **5563, 5679**, 5712, **5726**
Rhode Island: 3882
Virgin Islands: **5836**

Leadership development
Alaska: 5540
California: 228, 1856
Colorado: 786
Delaware: 5702
District of Columbia: **929, 5873**, 6181
Florida: 865
Georgia: **6152**
Illinois: 5690
Indiana: **2165**
Massachusetts: **5908**

Michigan: **5907**
Minnesota: 5662
Missouri: **83**, 2493
New Jersey: 718, 4443
New York: 779, **5751**, 5816, **6127**
Ohio: **6193**
Pennsylvania: 6071
Rhode Island: **6185**
Virginia: **134**
Wisconsin: 5920

Learning disorders
Colorado: 1956
New York: 4128
Pennsylvania: 4645
Texas: 215, 3953

Learning disorders research
California: **281**
Minnesota: 1218
Texas: 6176

Lebanon
Ohio: **1685**

Legal services
Colorado: 4672

Legal services, public interest law
District of Columbia: 5531
New York: 3288
Pennsylvania: 5872
Washington: 2361

Leukemia
Florida: 4849
Illinois: 4655

Leukemia research
Connecticut: **5542**
Illinois: **5937**
New York: 5863, **5936**
Washington: **5812**

LGBTQ
California: 1922, 3542, **5318, 5818**
Illinois: 3018
New York: 4965, **5222, 5405**
Pennsylvania: 499
Washington: 3644

Libraries (medical)
Illinois: **5972**

Libraries (public)
District of Columbia: 1122

Libraries (school)
Illinois: **5972**

Libraries (special)
Virginia: **6141**

Libraries/library science
District of Columbia: 1122
Illinois: **124**, 468, 2010, **5579, 5972**
Massachusetts: 5964
New York: 2937

Rhode Island: 3772
Virginia: **3824, 6141**

Libya
California: 99

Literature
Alaska: 5450, 5540
Arizona: 867
Arkansas: **5524**
California: 3146, **3320**, 3550, 4419, **5198**, 5250, 5251, **5345**, 5363, 5391, **5407**, 5509
Colorado: 5209
Connecticut: 932, 5439
Delaware: **5358**
District of Columbia: **5201, 5325**, 5431, 6030
Florida: **5223**, 5275, **5368**
Illinois: **5437**, 5449, 5493, **6128**
Indiana: 1264
Maine: 2484
Maryland: **5353**
Massachusetts: **5288, 5307, 5522, 5553, 5908**
Michigan: **5194, 5346, 6140**
Minnesota: 5196, 5238, 5247, **5253**, 5264, **5276**, 5362, 5402
New Hampshire: **5386**
New Jersey: 5446
New Mexico: **5374**
New York: 387, 1678, **3570, 5178, 5182, 5204, 5222**, 5226, 5241, 5256, **5258, 5271, 5277, 5289**, 5290, **5294, 5314, 5316, 5322**, 5326, **5338, 5350**, 5360, **5376, 5400, 5405, 5415, 5417, 5422**, 5430, 5461, **5502, 5503, 5513, 5523, 5563, 5646, 5719, 5726, 5879, 6007**
North Carolina: **5197, 5875**
Ohio: 2383, 4210, 4426
Oregon: 5381, 5454, **5476**
Pennsylvania: 1092, 1962, 2518
Rhode Island: 5457
South Dakota: **5309**
Texas: 2238, 3797
Utah: **5452, 5486**
Vermont: **5340, 5499**
Virginia: 2025, **5221, 5500, 5602**
Washington: **5265, 5298**, 5327, 5352, **5481**
West Virginia: 5224
Wyoming: 3919, **5361**

Lithuania
Illinois: **2408**

Liver research
Florida: 5546
Maryland: **5796**

Lung diseases
Louisiana: 5151
New York: 3931, 6146
Wisconsin: **5585**

Lung research
California: 5580
Florida: 5546
Illinois: **5689**
Missouri: 5581
New York: 5583, 6146
North Carolina: 5582
Ohio: **6101**
Pennsylvania: 5951
Texas: 5917
Utah: 5728
Vermont: 5584

Lupus research
Florida: 5647

Illinois: 6004
Maryland: **5613**
Texas: 6176
Virginia: **5595**

Mental health, treatment
California: 1856
Indiana: 5053
Maryland: 5933
New York: **846**
Washington: **6126**

Mental health/crisis services
California: 5026
New York: **5832**

Mental health/crisis services, formal/general education
Maine: 2484

Mental health/crisis services, research
Georgia: **5675**
Pennsylvania: 3898

Mentally disabled
New Jersey: 3175

Mexico
Arizona: 4338
California: 660, 1681, 3318
Florida: **5802**
New York: **5893**

Military/veterans
Illinois: 874

Military/veterans' organizations
California: **4705**
Connecticut: 808, 4491, **4668**, 5165
District of Columbia: 49
Florida: 1203, **4713**
Iowa: 151, 4584
Louisiana: 5954
Maine: 2484, 5004
Maryland: **1382**
Massachusetts: 1299, 2921
Missouri: 911
New York: **1042**, 5941
North Carolina: 4468
North Dakota: 5127
Oregon: 2059
Pennsylvania: 1536
Texas: **1374**, 1798, **4984**
Virginia: **48**, **1456**, **2711**, **4195**, **6048**

Minorities
California: 2149, **4508**, **5328**, **5902**
Connecticut: **4527**
District of Columbia: 2320, **2741**, **5556**
Florida: 865, 1972, 4249
Georgia: 2363
Illinois: **23**, **102**, **104**, 2008, **5972**
Indiana: **3047**
Kentucky: 2056
Maryland: **136**, **6006**
Massachusetts: 125, 318, 2888, **3280**
Michigan: **1053**, 2153, **2882**, **3834**
Minnesota: 4467
New Jersey: 1153, **5926**, **5953**, 6202
New York: **7**, 571, 2080, **2874**, 3267, 3430, 3634, **4494**, **5405**, 5512, 5521, **6024**, **6039**, **6136**
North Carolina: 2575, 5742

Ohio: **170**
Oklahoma: 2077
Oregon: 1039
Pennsylvania: 1854
South Carolina: 811
Texas: 3192
Virginia: **3824**, **5596**, **6141**
Washington: 1380
Wisconsin: 4516

Minorities/immigrants, centers/services
New York: **6039**

Multiple sclerosis
Florida: **4933**
Minnesota: 2895
New York: **2894**
Texas: 4955

Multiple sclerosis research
Michigan: 4954
New York: **6026**

Muscular dystrophy
Arizona: **5986**
Maryland: 4807

Muscular dystrophy research
Arizona: **5986**

Museums
California: **5328**
District of Columbia: **5557**

Museums (art)
California: **5302**, **5328**
New York: **5978**

Museums (children's)
Indiana: 744

Museums (science/technology)
California: **5302**

Music
Alaska: 55
Arizona: 867
California: 199, 1470, 1752, 2375, 2491, 3543, **3671**, 5183, 5239, 5252, 5291, 5390, 5399, **5407**, 5411, 5432, 5529, 5987, 6102
Colorado: 975, 5209
Connecticut: 5439, 5443, **5484**
District of Columbia: **4260**, **5366**, **5406**, 5505
Florida: 984, 1398
Illinois: **655**, 735, 2852, 4176
Indiana: 1077, 2492
Iowa: 1876, **3352**
Kansas: 4397, **5365**, 5414
Maine: 2484
Massachusetts: 647, 3812, 4387, **5233**, **5288**, 5342, 5348
Michigan: 162, **5330**, **5332**
Minnesota: 5264, 5362, 5403
Missouri: **5451**
Nebraska: **3046**
Nevada: 3603
New Jersey: 743, 838, 5421, 5446
New Mexico: **5464**
New York: 257, 387, **415**, 416, 439, 1015, **2283**, 2506, 2851, 3771, 4554, 4601, 5185, **5191**, **5193**, **5204**, **5219**, 5240, 5241, **5266**, **5279**,

5293, 5313, **5314**, **5343**, 5364, 5375, 5380, 5412, **5413**, **5415**, 5455, **5458**, **5507**, 5528, **5563**, **5726**
North Carolina: 915, **3707**
Ohio: 1177, 1556, 2255, 3712, 4210
Oklahoma: 2853, 4441
Oregon: 5267, **5473**
Pennsylvania: 1092, 1911, 1962, 2518, 3262, 3339, 3806, **5442**
Rhode Island: 245, 3390
Tennessee: 885, 1140, 5861
Virginia: **3036**
Washington: 702, 3399, 3873, **5265**, **5481**
West Virginia: 5224
Wisconsin: 2299, 2446, 3442, 5389

Music (choral)
California: 3543, 5231, **5477**
Michigan: 2515
New York: **5186**
Ohio: 1556
Virginia: **5516**

Music composition
Alaska: 5450
Arkansas: **5524**
California: **5407**
District of Columbia: **5366**
Illinois: 5493
Kansas: **5357**
Minnesota: **5189**, 5247, **5253**
Missouri: **5184**
New Hampshire: **5386**
New York: 439, 2851, **5182**, **5191**, **5217**, 5240, **5266**, **5271**, **5277**, 5292, **5294**, **5350**, **5376**, **5398**, **5400**, **5422**
Rhode Island: 5457
Utah: **5452**
Vermont: **5340**
Virginia: **5192**
Washington: **5265**

Music ensembles/groups
California: 5231
Connecticut: 5443
New Jersey: 5421
New York: **5179**, **5266**
Oregon: 5267

Mutual aid societies
Illinois: **1256**
New York: 5048

Mutual aid societies, volunteer services
Illinois: **6108**

Myasthenia gravis
Minnesota: **5989**

Myasthenia gravis research
Minnesota: **5989**

Native Americans/American Indians
Alaska: 174, 373, 626, 769, 954, 1971, 2276, 2297, 2943, **3641**, 3779, 3999, 4018, 5540
California: 1840, **5328**
Colorado: **5308**
Hawaii: 3239
Illinois: **5972**
Maryland: **1340**
Michigan: 325
Minnesota: 3514, 5753
Nevada: 1788
New Jersey: **5926**

New Mexico: **5466, 5479**
New York: **7, 2874, 2893,** 3267
North Carolina: 1355, 3490
North Dakota: 1294
Oregon: **5881**
South Dakota: 3723, **5309**
Vermont: **2557**
Virginia: 120, **1458, 4180**
Washington: 3, 2442
Wisconsin: 4473

Natural resources

Alaska: 5540
California: 3542, **5795, 5830, 6058**
District of Columbia: **2879, 5821, 6005**
Massachusetts: 3162, **5749, 6038**
Minnesota: **5948**
New Hampshire: **603,** 2924
New Jersey: 718
New Mexico: **5939**
New York: **3973, 5641, 6092**
Ohio: 2383, 4046
Pennsylvania: **1478,** 1963
South Dakota: 3723
Tennessee: 1140
Texas: 1190
Virginia: **2900, 5707**
Washington: 2738
Wisconsin: 256, 3191

Neighborhood centers

Florida: 329

Nepal

California: **2916**

Nerve, muscle & bone diseases

Arizona: **5986**
New York: **4614, 5633, 5695**

Nerve, muscle & bone research

Arizona: **5986**
California: **5610**
Maine: 6025
Maryland: **6056**
New Jersey: **2927**
New York: **5591, 5633, 5695**
Pennsylvania: **5614**

Netherlands

New York: **2919, 5419**

Neuroscience

District of Columbia: **1118**
Illinois: 4493, 5746
Massachusetts: **5833**
Minnesota: 93
New York: **846, 5916, 5993, 6130**
Texas: 6176
Virgin Islands: **5836**

Neuroscience research

Minnesota: **5970**
New Jersey: **6096**
New York: 5659, **5916, 5993**
Ohio: **6101**

Nonprofit management

Arizona: 6075
Delaware: **1083**
District of Columbia: **5625**
North Carolina: 6103

Norway

New York: **2992**
South Dakota: 3723
Virginia: 4706

Nursing care

Alabama: 5638
Colorado: 165, 5615
Illinois: 6174
Maryland: **5588**
Massachusetts: **5594**
New Jersey: **5898**
New York: 3856, **4968,** 5805
Ohio: 884
Pennsylvania: 311
Rhode Island: 3390

Nursing home/convalescent facility

New York: 4661
Pennsylvania: 5069

Nursing school/education

Arizona: **98,** 250, **5551**
Arkansas: **4158,** 4173
California: 1324, 1856, 1968, 2314, 2490, 2978,
   3076, 5580
Colorado: 916, 2419, 4383
Connecticut: 932
Delaware: **1083**
Florida: 504, 1203, 1351, 2848, 3513
Hawaii: 1772, 4561
Illinois: 874, 1067, 1082, 2347, 2569, 2602, 3426,
   4068, 4352
Indiana: 30, 1077, 1344, 1510, 2053, 2100, 2282,
   2305, 3225, 3245, 4264, 4381, 4431
Iowa: 1030, 1530, 3107
Kansas: 4234
Kentucky: 890, 2970
Louisiana: 4146
Maine: 2484, 3360
Massachusetts: 2555, 3162, 3626, 5103
Michigan: 325, 354, 880, 1663, 2357, **2882,** 3176
Minnesota: 93, 755, 4228, **5989**
Missouri: 1839
Nebraska: 2857, 4354
New Hampshire: 1635, 4532
New Jersey: 1650, 1662, 2704, 2722, 3783
New York: 719, 908, 2089, 2985, 3248, 4248, 5805
North Carolina: 927, 1429, 2575, 4468
Ohio: 966, 1117, 1274, 2264, 2383, 3150, 3494,
   3752, 4154, 4210, 4448, 4519, 5739
Oregon: 3579, 3720
Pennsylvania: 17, 914, 1253, 1727, 1809, 2366,
   2657, 2918, 3862, 3929, 4055, 4137, 4539
Rhode Island: 247, 386, 3572, 3925, 4414
South Dakota: 1615
Tennessee: 4437
Texas: 461, 521, 1794, 2474, 4469
Utah: 280
Virginia: 343, 4489
Washington: 142, 2713
Wisconsin: 557, 903, 1479, 1630, 1877, 3138, 4099,
   4361
Wyoming: 783, 819, 4526

Nutrition

Arizona: 4338
California: 5026
District of Columbia: **5576**
Hawaii: 1773
Illinois: **108**
Indiana: 2100, 4658
Michigan: 1621
New York: 5659
North Carolina: **5661**
Ohio: 4210
Texas: 5984
Virginia: **738, 5692**

Wisconsin: **1078,** 3138

Opera

Arizona: 867
California: 199, 5465
Connecticut: **5484**
New Jersey: 5491
New York: **5186, 5188,** 5380, 5455, 5472, **5492**
Virginia: **3036, 5516**
Washington: **5265**

Optometry/vision screening

California: 5026
Georgia: 5839
Maine: 4928, 5003
Massachusetts: 5088
New Jersey: 5076
Oregon: 4974, 5082
Pennsylvania: 5018
Texas: **4981,** 4986
West Virginia: 4651
Wisconsin: 4835

Orchestra (symphony)

California: 5529
Connecticut: 5443
Michigan: **3834,** 5236
New York: 2851, **5217, 5398,** 5528
Pennsylvania: **5441**

Organ diseases

Georgia: **3211**
Pennsylvania: **4956**

Organ research

California: **6060**

Orthodox Catholic agencies & churches

New Jersey: **5963**

Orthopedics

Tennessee: 5684

Orthopedics research

Indiana: 5798
New York: **5573**
North Carolina: 5750

Painting

California: **5483**
Florida: **3246**
Illinois: **5488**
Kansas: **5365**
Massachusetts: 2058, **5288**
Michigan: **5332**
Minnesota: 5238, **5276**
New Jersey: 838, **5315**
New Mexico: **5459**
New York: **5333,** 5347, **5385, 5404, 5422, 5438,**
   5461
North Carolina: **5396**
Vermont: **5499**
Washington: 5234, **5263**

Parasitic diseases

North Carolina: **5661**

Parkinson's disease

Florida: **6028**
New York: **5633**

Parkinson's disease research
Florida: **6028**
New York: **5633**, 5807

Pathology
Missouri: **3657**

Pediatrics
California: **5706**
District of Columbia: **5824**
Georgia: **3211**
New York: **5832**
Virginia: **5692**

Pediatrics research
Alabama: 5733
Florida: **6084**
Illinois: 5736
Maryland: 5715

Pensions, teacher funds
Texas: 5109

Performing arts
Alaska: 5450
Arizona: 867, 5456
California: **3637**, **5052**, 5214, 5250, 5252, **5302**, **5345**, 5432
Colorado: 5209, 5243
District of Columbia: **5325**, **5366**
Florida: **5223**, 5275, 5517
Illinois: 2852, **5190**
Indiana: 1264
Iowa: **3352**
Kansas: **5365**, 5414
Maryland: 5210, 5392
Massachusetts: 5342, 5348, **5553**
Minnesota: 5200, 5238, 5264
Missouri: **5451**
New Jersey: 5421, 5446
New York: **5180**, **5215**, **5219**, 5268, **5279**, **5296**, **5314**, **5321**, 5326, **5350**, 5375, 5382, **5419**, **5422**, **5879**
Ohio: **5510**
Pennsylvania: 1092, 5354
Rhode Island: 5457
South Dakota: **5309**
Texas: 5287
Washington: **5265**

Performing arts (multimedia)
New York: **5277**, **5279**, **5385**
Washington: 5176

Performing arts centers
District of Columbia: **5366**
New York: **5350**

Performing arts, education
Arizona: 5456
California: 1470, 1752, 2375, 2491, 3550, 5239, 5399
Colorado: 975
Delaware: 2561
District of Columbia: 5505
Florida: 865, 984, 1026
Illinois: 735, 4176
Indiana: 2282, 3242, 3746
Iowa: **3352**
Massachusetts: 3812, 4387, 5359
Michigan: 325, 880, 1621
Minnesota: 5264
Nevada: 3603

New York: 257, **415**, 416, 719, 3771, 4554, **5188**, 5228, 5293, **5317**, 5455, 5472, 5480
North Carolina: 73
Ohio: 1177, 1556, 2255, 2383, 3712, 4210, **5755**
Oklahoma: 2853, 4441
Oregon: 67
Pennsylvania: 1277, 1911, 1962, 3339, 3806
Rhode Island: 245, 3390
Vermont: 3630, 5136
Washington: 702, 3399
Wisconsin: 1630, 2299, 2446, 3442

Pharmacy/prescriptions
California: 584, 2314, 5026
District of Columbia: **5592**
Indiana: 2282, 4883
Iowa: 2036
Kentucky: 658
Maryland: **113**, **5570**, 5601, **5788**
Massachusetts: 4985
Michigan: 4129
New Jersey: 2704, **4597**, 5011, 5076
New York: 3577, **6138**
North Carolina: 3182, **5661**
Vermont: 4929
Virginia: **4865**, **6001**

Philanthropy/voluntarism
District of Columbia: **5873**
Ohio: 5988

Philanthropy/voluntarism, administration/ regulation
Alaska: 6094

Philanthropy/voluntarism, formal/general education
Virginia: **5537**

Philanthropy/voluntarism, management/ technical aid
Alaska: 6094

Philosophy/ethics
California: **3320**, 4419
Hawaii: 3631
Michigan: **5332**
New York: **4413**, 5241, **5563**, **5857**
Ohio: 6135
Pennsylvania: **5593**

Photography
California: 5251, **5305**, 5463
Massachusetts: 2058
Michigan: **5332**
Minnesota: 5238, 5247, **5253**
New Hampshire: **5386**
New Jersey: 5446
New Mexico: **5459**
New York: **5219**, 5262, **5379**, **5385**, **5422**, 5461, **5475**, **5502**
North Carolina: **5396**
Ohio: 1070
Vermont: **5499**
Washington: 2738, **5263**, **5265**

Physical therapy
California: 4598
Illinois: **5965**
Kansas: 4666
Maryland: **126**
Michigan: 325, 4349, 5083
New York: 3566

Ohio: 4931
Pennsylvania: 1331
Virginia: **5800**

Physical/earth sciences
Arizona: **6097**
California: **1835**
Florida: 3969
Hawaii: 1772
Massachusetts: 125, 5587, 5834
Michigan: 2686
Minnesota: 93
New York: 5768, **6138**
Pennsylvania: 3774
Texas: **935**, 3822

Physically disabled
Florida: 1600, 3818, 4791
Indiana: 894, 1983
Minnesota: 5123
New Jersey: 3175

Physics
Arizona: 3373, **6097**
California: **1835**, 3623
Florida: 3335, 3969
Illinois: 424
Maryland: **5559**, **5578**
Missouri: 911
New Jersey: **3703**
New York: **6130**
North Carolina: 5742
Pennsylvania: 3774, 4548
Texas: 3822
Wisconsin: 3739

Podiatry
Pennsylvania: 780, **3230**

Poland
New Jersey: **5897**
Pennsylvania: 3233

Political science
District of Columbia: 1487, 2879, **5815**, **5821**
Hawaii: 3631
Illinois: **655**, 3708, **5773**
Maine: 2484
Michigan: **5783**
New Jersey: 4443
New York: **5563**, **5679**, **5726**, **6099**, **6116**, **6136**
Ohio: 4463
Pennsylvania: 3774
Texas: 3354
Wisconsin: 1441

Population studies
Minnesota: **5948**

Portugal
Rhode Island: **1489**

Poverty studies
California: **5871**
New York: **6208**
North Carolina: 5102

Prostate cancer
California: **6087**

Prostate cancer research
California: **6087**

Protestant agencies & churches
Alabama: 5733
California: 4100, **5958**
Connecticut: **3791**
Florida: 3531
Hawaii: 225, 1772
Illinois: 1454, 4363
Indiana: 894, 2941, 3245
Iowa: 1928, 3265
Kansas: 1751
Maryland: 1143
Massachusetts: 4390, **5899**
Michigan: 1463, 2254, 2357, 2551, 2562, 3028, 4216
Minnesota: **1622**
Missouri: 3865
Montana: 1989
Nebraska: 1566, 5921
New Jersey: 2498, 3783
New York: 1332, 4884
North Carolina: 267, 1060, 1116, 1180, 1453
Ohio: 1591, **3522**, 4309
Oregon: 3906
Pennsylvania: 3356, 4430, 5084
Rhode Island: 3136, 4626
South Carolina: **4766**
South Dakota: 3723, 4295
Texas: 57, 521, **1724**, 1986, 2409, 2606, 4487, **4746**
Virginia: 69, 5652
Washington: 302
West Virginia: 1518, 3936
Wisconsin: 1006, 2185, 4362, **4896**

Psychology/behavioral science
California: **5644**
District of Columbia: 130, 5597, **5995**
Georgia: **3211**
Hawaii: 3631
Maryland: **136**
Nebraska: 1237
New York: 846, **5563**, 5571, **5832**, **5837**, **6062**, **6136**, **6138**, **6170**
North Carolina: **5661**, **5677**
Pennsylvania: **6156**
Rhode Island: 4926
Texas: 6176
Virginia: **5596**
Washington: 2738, **6126**

Public affairs
District of Columbia: **929**, **5885**
Indiana: **87**
Virginia: **2898**

Public affairs, administration/regulation
New York: **5679**

Public affairs, citizen participation
New York: **5784**
North Carolina: 3419
Ohio: 3769
Pennsylvania: 3587
South Carolina: **1914**
Texas: 2797
Wisconsin: 903

Public affairs, formal/general education
Mississippi: 883

Public affairs, government agencies
Alaska: 5540
Ohio: 5721

Public affairs, reform
District of Columbia: **5961**
New York: **5673**

Public health
California: **5844**
Georgia: **5678**
Illinois: 2511, 6174
Kentucky: 2208
Massachusetts: **5749**
New York: **3570**, **5932**

Public health school/education
California: 2149
Georgia: **3211**
Minnesota: 1268
New Jersey: 1358

Public health, epidemiology
Connecticut: 5735
Maryland: **6006**
New Jersey: **5898**

Public health, occupational health
Kentucky: 2208

Public policy, research
District of Columbia: **5909**
Maryland: **5676**
Massachusetts: **5908**
New Jersey: 4443
New York: **5703**, **6039**, **6116**
Ohio: 4463
Pennsylvania: **5846**
Virginia: **2025**

Race/intergroup relations
California: 4575
Michigan: 325, 1621
New York: **6039**
North Carolina: 3909

Radio
California: **6042**
District of Columbia: **526**
New York: 41
Pennsylvania: 5433
Washington: 1380

Reading
California: 2088
Connecticut: 932
Illinois: 3426
Kansas: 4666
Missouri: 2161
West Virginia: 3106

Recreation
California: 898
District of Columbia: **2170**
Florida: 4710
Indiana: 3476
Kentucky: 273
Michigan: 3346
Ohio: 2308
Oregon: 2833
Pennsylvania: 311

Virginia: **5999**

Recreation, community facilities
Illinois: 3007

Recreation, social clubs
Indiana: 2360

Religion
Arizona: 758
Arkansas: 3658
California: 4419, **6093**
Colorado: **5698**
Connecticut: **5631**
Florida: 865, **4596**, **5944**
Illinois: **3460**
Indiana: 539, 2401
Iowa: 4284
Maine: **2452**
Michigan: **2362**, **5194**, 6151
Minnesota: 755, 4657
Mississippi: **5743**
Missouri: 2247
New Jersey: 4443, **5963**
New York: **4413**, 4958, **5219**, **5688**
North Carolina: 1916, 4756
Ohio: 884, 3345, 3444
Oklahoma: **5977**
Pennsylvania: **6156**
South Dakota: 4295
Tennessee: 5061
Texas: **4023**, 4747, **5129**

Religion, formal/general education
Georgia: **3211**
Illinois: 3169, **3460**
Indiana: 682
Missouri: 3616
New York: 683
North Carolina: 657
Ohio: 4061
Texas: 857, 4724

Religion, interfaith issues
Minnesota: **5189**

Religion, research
Massachusetts: 5761
New York: **5563**, **5811**, **5966**

Reproductive health
District of Columbia: **5562**
Pennsylvania: 5680

Reproductive health, prenatal care
District of Columbia: **5562**

Reproductive health, sexuality education
California: 1793

Residential/custodial care
Arizona: 3469, **4571**
California: 2733
Georgia: 497
Hawaii: 1961, 4829
Maryland: 4625
Massachusetts: 239, 4617
Nevada: 1994
New Mexico: 4239
New York: 1249
Ohio: 365

Pennsylvania: 4610
South Carolina: 610
Texas: 3895
Wisconsin: 3632

Roman Catholic agencies & churches

Alaska: 2772
Arizona: 2625
Colorado: 3853
Florida: 3334
Illinois: 5070
Indiana: 682, 716, 1719, 2941
Iowa: 315, 3559
Massachusetts: 649, 1172, 2193, **2455**
Michigan: 13, 310, 1841, 4324
Missouri: 3616, 3842
Nebraska: 2229
New Hampshire: 1408
New Jersey: **5963**
New York: 428, 683, **2565**, 3348, **6085**
Ohio: 1384, 2329, 3000, 3468
Pennsylvania: 2241, 2456, 4055, **5789**
Rhode Island: 187, 2219
South Carolina: 811
Texas: 1080
Wisconsin: 5049

Rural development

District of Columbia: **1427**

Russia

California: **2285**, **4862**
New York: **5036**

Safety, automotive safety

Michigan: **1053**

Safety, education

Massachusetts: **6029**
New York: 4162

Safety/disasters

California: **4845**
District of Columbia: **4676**, 4837
Florida: **4971**, 5038
Kansas: 4711, 4980
Massachusetts: 4909
Mississippi: 4885
New York: 4960
North Carolina: 4648, **4888**
Ohio: 5119
Virginia: 3376
West Virginia: 5095

Safety/disasters, ethics

Pennsylvania: 4831

Safety/disasters, public education

District of Columbia: **5173**

Safety/disasters, research

Illinois: **5603**

Schizophrenia

New York: 5993

Scholarships/financial aid

California: 4594
New Jersey: 266, 1684
Virginia: **2031**

Science

Alaska: 174
Arizona: 3648, 3968, **6097**
Arkansas: 184
California: **1835**, 2375, 3290, 3623, **3671**, 3706, **5328**, **5642**, **5656**, 6086
Colorado: 1676, 5655
Connecticut: 4355
Delaware: 5702
District of Columbia: **5201**, **5556**, **5561**, 6030
Florida: 1656, 3335, **6195**
Hawaii: 1772
Idaho: 2700
Illinois: 424, **1742**, 2581, **5853**
Indiana: 531, 2295, 4264
Kansas: 4397
Kentucky: 3016
Maryland: **5796**
Massachusetts: 125, 1172, 2193, **4021**, 4390, **5731**, **6038**
Michigan: 325, 2050, 2686, 3176
Minnesota: 3200, 3351
Missouri: 530, 2516
Nebraska: 1263
New Hampshire: 1946
New Jersey: 1358, 1633, 5778, **6199**
New Mexico: 62
New York: 908, 1356, **2385**, **5296**, **5726**, **5837**, **5866**, **5932**, **5942**
North Carolina: 1931, 4468, **5661**, 5742, **5875**
Ohio: 4448
Oklahoma: 1480
Oregon: 1036, 3108
Pennsylvania: 3774, 3790, 6137
South Carolina: 712
Texas: **935**, 2238, **2870**, 4190, 4512
Utah: **5486**
Virginia: **48**, **6031**
Washington: 1892, **5265**
Wisconsin: 2157, 2271, 3739

Science, formal/general education

District of Columbia: **3624**
Indiana: 1077
Maryland: **5860**
New York: 868
Ohio: 1504, 2689, 3237

Science, public policy

District of Columbia: 2879

Science, research

Arizona: **6097**
California: **1835**, **5642**, 5934, **6042**, **6063**
Colorado: **6139**
Florida: **6195**
Indiana: 6164
Massachusetts: **5930**
Minnesota: **5635**, **5948**
New York: **5338**, 5768, **6072**
North Carolina: **5661**
Rhode Island: **6083**

Scotland

Colorado: **773**
Massachusetts: 5051
New Jersey: 4714

Sculpture

California: **5483**
Florida: **3246**
Kansas: **5365**
Maryland: 5229
Massachusetts: 2058, **5288**
Michigan: **5332**, **5435**
Minnesota: 5238, 5247, **5276**, **5319**, 5423

Montana: 5244
New Jersey: 838
New Mexico: **5459**
New York: **5182**, **5186**, **5295**, **5334**, 5347, **5385**, **5404**, **5418**, **5422**, **5438**, **5468**, **5503**
North Carolina: **5396**
Pennsylvania: 5377
Vermont: **5257**, **5499**
Washington: **5263**, **5265**

Secondary school/education

Alabama: 166, 2046
Connecticut: 932
Georgia: 1863
Hawaii: 1961
Illinois: 1305, 4424
Michigan: 2699
Minnesota: 1040
Missouri: 1367, 2161
New Jersey: 4417
New York: **486**, 928, **4133**, **5710**
Ohio: 1384, 2383, 2607, 5894
Pennsylvania: 1261, 1521
South Carolina: 5539
Tennessee: 6066
Vermont: 1784
Virginia: **2546**
Washington: 4097
West Virginia: 3106
Wisconsin: 5920

Senior continuing care

Massachusetts: 5168

Serbia

Illinois: **5056**

Single parents

Arkansas: 3721
Oklahoma: 5013
Texas: 4822, 4847

Skin disorders research

California: **5974**
Illinois: **5549**
New York: **5598**, **6129**
Pennsylvania: **5792**

Social sciences

California: **5328**
Connecticut: 1079
District of Columbia: **5709**, **5995**
Maine: **6165**
Maryland: **5767**
Michigan: **5779**, **6167**
New Jersey: 4443, 5645
New York: **2385**, **3035**, **5338**, **5563**, **5837**, 5877, **6099**, **6136**
North Carolina: **5875**
Ohio: 1309
Oregon: 607
Washington: 1892, **5265**
Wisconsin: 1441

Social sciences, interdisciplinary studies

New York: **5832**

Social sciences, public education

District of Columbia: **5564**

Social sciences, public policy

Ohio: 6135

Social sciences, research
Michigan: **5748**
New York: **5563, 5832**
Pennsylvania: **5593**

Social work school/education
Connecticut: **3638**
Florida: **1797**
Georgia: 862, **3211**

South America
Utah: 3810

Space/aviation
California: 1681
Florida: 1577
Maryland: 3048
Michigan: 2686
Minnesota: 93, **5948**
Ohio: 799
Pennsylvania: 4548
Virginia: **48, 101, 2031**, 5538
Wisconsin: **1200**

Spain
Massachusetts: 3341

Speech/hearing centers
Maryland: **136**
Michigan: 4349
Missouri: **3657**

Spine disorders
California: **5050**

Spine disorders research
California: 5608
Illinois: **5681**
New Jersey: **6096**

Students, sororities/fraternities
California: 228, 392, 393, 621
Florida: 1091
Georgia: **84, 3186**
Illinois: 88
Indiana: **82, 85, 87, 1421**
Iowa: 2162
Massachusetts: 3590
Michigan: 325
Missouri: 911, **1090, 1229**
New Hampshire: 3561
New York: **4237, 4553**
North Carolina: **3707**, 4468
Ohio: 798, 3185
Pennsylvania: 775
Rhode Island: 3390
Tennessee: **86, 4576, 5545**
Texas: 1089

Substance abuse, services
New Jersey: **5898**
Ohio: 884

Substance abuse, treatment
California: 5411
New York: 656
Texas: 3953

Suicide
New York: 5571

Surgery
Massachusetts: 5915
New York: **5573, 5893**
Pennsylvania: **4956, 5614**

Surgery research
California: **5536**
Illinois: **5626, 6078**
Indiana: 5798
Massachusetts: **5560**

Switzerland
Illinois: 5101

Syria
California: 99

Taiwan
California: 3731

Teacher school/education
Arkansas: 4173
California: 1575, 3038
Colorado: 297, 1301, 2344
Connecticut: **3638**
Florida: 865
Georgia: 862, **3211**
Hawaii: 1772
Illinois: 2569, **3460**
Indiana: 96, 906, 1077, 1462, 2305, 3245, 4431
Iowa: **3575**
Kansas: 3432
Maine: 3493
Maryland: 2605, 3286, 3555
Michigan: 880, 1463, 2153, 2357, 2515
Missouri: **83**, 911, 1839
Nebraska: 3029
New Jersey: 718, 3274
New York: 868, 3569, 4133
North Carolina: 3069, 3358
Ohio: 524, 800, 985, 1070, 1750, 2184, 2383, 3702, 4214, 4400
Pennsylvania: 551, 2953, 3369, 4430
Rhode Island: 245, 4414
Tennessee: 4343
Utah: 2567
Vermont: 3630
Virginia: **2878**, 3801, 4421
Washington: 142, 3475
Wisconsin: 500, 749, 903, 1494, 2157, 3138

Telecommunications
District of Columbia: **1427**

Television
District of Columbia: **526**
New York: 41
Washington: 1380

Theater
California: 5183, 5252, **5407**, 5489, 5509
Delaware: **1083**, 5702
District of Columbia: **4260, 5220**
Florida: 1398, 5517
Iowa: **3352**
Kansas: 4030
Massachusetts: 5348
Michigan: 1621
Minnesota: 5362
Missouri: 3865
Nebraska: **3046**
New Jersey: 838

New York: 1678, **5186, 5219**, 5241, 5245, **5279, 5314, 5317, 5350, 5417, 5445, 5490, 5563, 5726**
Ohio: **1234, 5755**
Oregon: 67, 1698
Pennsylvania: 1962, 2518
Texas: 5329

Theater (musical)
New York: **5187, 5217**, 5240, **5376**

Theater (playwriting)
California: **5407**
Minnesota: 5238, 5247
New York: **5182, 5289, 5415, 5422, 5430, 5445, 5490, 5503**
Virginia: **2025**
Washington: **5265, 5298**, 5352

Theological school/education
Alabama: 5733
California: 1856, 2765, 3290, **5687, 5958**
Connecticut: 2204, **3638, 3791**
Delaware: 1904
Florida: 1351, **1797**, 4220
Georgia: 1048, **5637**
Hawaii: 225
Illinois: **3460**
Indiana: 716, 2181
Iowa: 2129, 4284
Kentucky: 4608
Maryland: 1143, **3042**
Massachusetts: 1172, 2922, 3379
Michigan: 13, 1034, 1463, 2050, 2357
Minnesota: **1622**
Missouri: 1839, 2125, 2609, 3616
Nebraska: 1529, 5921
Nevada: 3593
New Jersey: 115, 2498, 2583, 4555
New York: 498, **2565, 5688, 5710, 5966**
North Carolina: 1060, 1453, 1916, 3934, **4181, 4547**
Ohio: 985, 1384, 1591, 2668, 2836, **3522**, 4086, 4210
Oregon: 2597
Pennsylvania: 2953, 3529, 4055, 4430, **5628**
South Carolina: 2200
South Dakota: 4295
Tennessee: **3654**
Texas: 976, 1608, **1724**, 1986, 3017, 4171, 4487
Washington: 302, 447, 3653, 4213
West Virginia: 2746, 3761
Wisconsin: 211, 1006, **1502**, 2299, **4167**, 4207

Theology
Indiana: 2295
Maine: 2484
New York: **5563**

Transportation
District of Columbia: **131**
Florida: 4791
Illinois: **2287**
Virginia: **2901, 3826**

Ukraine
District of Columbia: **5201**
Pennsylvania: **2284**

United Kingdom
New York: **5726**
North Carolina: **2174**

University
Arizona: 1394

California: 3202
Kansas: 270
Maine: 3435
Massachusetts: 6196
Michigan: **503**
New Jersey: 3274
Virginia: **2942**

Urban studies
Illinois: **5335, 6128**
Maryland: **5763**
New York: **6116**

Urban/community development
Maryland: **5763**
New York: 5816

Veterinary medicine
California: 199, 2678
Colorado: **5533, 5983**
Florida: 3969
Georgia: **5678**
Illinois: 381, 560, 1082, 3064
Indiana: 3602, 4431
Maine: 2484, 2485
Michigan: 1064, 1966
Missouri: 1215, 1839
New Jersey: 5734, **6203**
Ohio: 985, 4046, 4210
Pennsylvania: 4137

Vietnam
Nevada: **4238**

**Visitors/convention bureau/tourism
promotion**
New York: **2004**

Visual arts
Alaska: 5450
Arizona: 867
California: 4300, 5175, 5183, **5198**, 5214, **5237**,
    5250, 5252, **5302**, 5310, 5311, **5328, 5345**,
    5363, 5378, **5407**, 5432
Colorado: 5243, **5308**, 5470
Connecticut: **5508**
Delaware: **5285**
District of Columbia: **5325**
Florida: 1398, **3533, 5223**, 5275, **5416**
Illinois: 4176, **5195**, 5300, 5449, **5488**
Kansas: **5365**
Maryland: 5210, **5299**, 5392, **5447**
Massachusetts: 2058, **5288, 5307, 5553**
Michigan: 2327, **5332**
Minnesota: 5200, 5238, 5247, **5253**, 5264, 5349,
    5362
Missouri: **5184**
Nebraska: **5235**
New Hampshire: **5386**
New Jersey: 838, **3172, 6069**
New Mexico: **5374, 5459, 5479**
New York: 840, 4250, **5182, 5203, 5204, 5206**,
    5215, 5219, 5222, 5241, 5262, 5268, **5271**,
    5277, 5279, 5284, 5286, **5294, 5295, 5303**,
    5314, 5321, 5326, **5334, 5336, 5343**, 5347,
    5385, 5388, **5400, 5404, 5405, 5417, 5419**,
    5422, 5427, 5438, 5474, 5512, **5879**
Ohio: 1070, **5510**
Oregon: **5440, 5473**
Pennsylvania: 1092, **5269, 5304**, 5354, 5377, **5393**,
    5467
Rhode Island: 5457
South Dakota: **5309**
Texas: **5246, 5270**, 5287, **5409**
Utah: **5452**
Vermont: **5340**

Virginia: 4079
Washington: 3873, 5176, 5205, 5234, **5410**
West Virginia: 5224
Wyoming: **5361**

Vocational education
Alabama: 1754
Alaska: 1157, 1971, 2297
Arizona: 3469
California: 574, 1922, 2055, 2088, 2261, 2444,
    2604, 2950, 3202, 3269, 3550, 4229
Colorado: 916, 4383
Connecticut: 4090
Delaware: **1083**, 1599
District of Columbia: **601, 2573**
Florida: 865, 899, 1203, 2373, 3324, 3331, 4415
Georgia: 517, 862, 3551, 3954
Hawaii: 1772
Illinois: 1275, 1454, 1723, **1742**, 2347, 2426, 2581,
    2896, 3293, 3315, 3434, 4240
Indiana: 189, 2791, 3245, 3487, 3663, 3799
Iowa: 151, 406, 1030, 1667, 2069, 2353, 2548,
    2944
Kansas: 270, 1131, 1713, 2076, 2126, 2252, 3097,
    3109, 3155, 3432
Kentucky: 890, 3388
Maine: 2484, 3435
Maryland: 1491, 1740, **2017**, 3673
Massachusetts: 411, 3626, 3962, 4012, **4021**
Michigan: 325, 596, 1663, 2145, 3124, 3827, 4186
Minnesota: 203, 421, 727, 1176, 3080, 3372, 3425,
    3831
Missouri: 508, 795, 911, 2871, 3384, 3565, 4130
Montana: 264, 790, 1989, 3963
Nebraska: 1271, 1602, 4354
Nevada: 2257, 2335, 2418
New Hampshire: 2242, 2300, 2924, 4532, 4542
New Jersey: 222, 632, 1574, 2330, 3688
New Mexico: 1333, 4239
New York: 831, 868, 1780, 1939, 2640, 3885, 3931,
    4456
North Carolina: **2167**, 2352, 2575, 2995, 4001
North Dakota: 2524
Ohio: 159, 336, 1070, 1188, 1412, 1768, **1775**,
    1846, 2217, 2371, 2383, 2554, 2576, 2931,
    3150, 4046, 4408, 4498
Oklahoma: 1363
Oregon: 796, 953, 1031, 1050, 1698, 3043, 3894,
    4196, 4257, 4375
Pennsylvania: 6, 15, 17, 502, **933**, 1433, 2040, 3249,
    3387, 3597, 3780, 4211
Rhode Island: 2558, 3096, 3925
South Carolina: 2211
South Dakota: 1631, 3723
Tennessee: 1595
Texas: 353, 705, 2265, 2412, 3179, 4245, 4326,
    4455, 4986, 5917
Vermont: 2966, 4399, 4450
Virginia: 312, 1432, **2711**, 3547, 4166, 4489, **5692**
Washington: 42, 302, 1699, 2326, 2713, 2990, 4286
West Virginia: 589, 1353, 1735, 2156, 3877
Wisconsin: 546, 674, 1479, 1630, 2063, 2269, 2438,
    4474, 4516
Wyoming: 563, **940**, 1018

Vocational education, post-secondary
California: 1575, 1673, 1968, 2209
Florida: 1988
Georgia: **25**
Indiana: 1005, 2018
Iowa: 1341
Kansas: 4037, 4094
Michigan: 3176
Missouri: 3619
Montana: 1989
Nebraska: 4291
New York: 431
Oklahoma: 662
Oregon: 855
Tennessee: 4501

Texas: 3163, 3528
Washington: 3873

Vocational school, secondary
Delaware: **1083**
Florida: 2608
Massachusetts: 1906

Voluntarism promotion
Alabama: 772
Georgia: **6152**
Indiana: 2100
New Jersey: **449**, 718

Waste management
Virginia: **5766**

West Bank/Gaza
California: 99
District of Columbia: **2084**

Women
Alabama: 2652, 3068, 4341
Arizona: 4338
Arkansas: 4412
California: **190**, 792, 3146, 3394, 3550, **3671**, 4411,
    4575, 4605, 4903, 4919, **5518**
Colorado: 1301
Connecticut: 932, 2350, 5156, 5165
District of Columbia: 601, 4577, **5556, 5561, 5562**,
    5565, 5890
Georgia: 84, 862, **3186**, 3954, 5045
Hawaii: **103**, 1772, 2151, 3239
Illinois: 1067, 1715, 2301, 2917, **3571**, 4493, 5449
Indiana: 894, 2282, 2855, 4881, 4893
Kansas: 1131, 1980, 3199, 4030
Kentucky: 890, 3388, 4911, 5469
Louisiana: 2477
Maine: 2484, 5744
Maryland: 4625, 4716, **5092**, 5135
Massachusetts: 2755, **3304**, 4592, 4617, 4742,
    4743, 4826, 4996, 5009, 5030, 5040, 5098,
    6038
Michigan: 162, 355, 880, 2805
Minnesota: 5238
Mississippi: 1787
Missouri: **83**, 2171, 2952
Nebraska: 2649
Nevada: 2920
New Hampshire: 1132
New Jersey: **79**, 4443, **5963**
New Mexico: 4239, **5466**
New York: **7**, 439, 868, **1042**, 1232, 1328, 2089,
    3248, **4494**, 4965, 5078, 5110, **5222, 5405**,
    6205
North Carolina: 952, 3909, 4120
Ohio: **38**, 842, **1685**, 3468, 4210, 4770, **5007**, 5059,
    5169, 5721, 5739
Oregon: 67, **5476, 5881**
Pennsylvania: 1150, 1261, 1269, 1277, 1390, 3339,
    3457, 3806, 3923, 4386, 4609, 4744, 4913,
    5069, 5377, 5680
Rhode Island: 194, 2245, 3136, 4414, 4626, 4696,
    4908, 5015
South Carolina: 959
Tennessee: 2141, **4576**
Texas: 3192, 4847
Vermont: 4447
Virginia: **2898, 4865**
Washington: 177, 895, 1267, 1739, 2112, 3475,
    4318, 5138, 5205, 6150
Wisconsin: 1630, 2339, 4516

Women's studies
District of Columbia: **5561**
New Jersey: 4443

New York: **5405**

Women, centers/services
Virginia: **4865**

YM/YWCAs & YM/YWHAs
Rhode Island: 445

Young adults, female
Mississippi: 883
Virginia: **3050**

Young adults, male
Arizona: 562
Nebraska: 476
Texas: 705

Youth development
Alaska: 5540
California: 4598, **5855**
District of Columbia: **5909**
Hawaii: 1772
Maryland: **5676**, **5891**
New Jersey: 718
New York: **5832**
Ohio: **6209**
Pennsylvania: 97
Virginia: **5999**
Wisconsin: 2472

Youth development, adult & child programs
New York: 3636

Youth development, centers/clubs
Washington: 3656

Youth development, community service clubs
North Carolina: 2
Virginia: **6211**

Youth development, ethics
District of Columbia: **391**

Youth development, services
Virginia: **5999**

Youth, services
New Jersey: 3236
Ohio: 4794

GRANTMAKER NAME INDEX

This alphabetical index lists all grantmakers with full entries in this volume, as well as those that appeared in the 14th edition, but no longer qualify and are listed in the Appendix. Numbers following the grantmaker names refer to sequence numbers of entries in the Descriptive Directory section. The letter "A" following a grantmaker name refers to the Appendix.

Alternatives Research and Development Foundation, PA, 5547

Altman Foundation, Jenifer, CA, 5548

Alumnae Association of the College of St. Teresa Scholarship Fund, MN, 91

Alumni Foundation Fund of the Illinois Chapter of Alpha Delta Phi, IL, 92

Alworth Memorial Fund, Marshall H. and Nellie, MN, 93

Amadeus Fund, Inc., The, NY, 5185

Amarillo Area Foundation, Inc., TX, A

Amateis Foundation, Edmond, FL, see 94

Amateis Irrevocable Trust Foundation, Edmond, FL, 94

Ambler Trust, Elizabeth Raymond, CT, 95

Amburn Memorial Scholarship Fund, Clifford L. & Daisie B., IN, 96

AMDG Charitable Foundation, VA, A

Ameche Memorial Foundation, Alan, PA, 97

America West Airlines Education Foundation, Inc., AZ, see 4194

American Academy & Institute of Arts and Letters, NY, see 5187

American Academy in Berlin, NY, 5186

American Academy of Arts and Letters, NY, 5187

American Academy of Dermatology, Inc., IL, 5549

American Academy of Family Physicians Foundation, KS, 5550

American Academy of Nurse Practitioners Foundation, AZ, 98, 5551

American Anthropological Association, VA, 5552

American Antiquarian Society, MA, 5553

American Arabic Educational Foundation, CA, 99

American Architectural Foundation, Inc., The, DC, 100

American Association for Cancer Research, Inc., PA, 5554

American Association for Clinical Chemistry, DC, 5555

American Association for the Advancement of Science, DC, 5556

American Association of Airport Executives Foundation, VA, 101

American Association of Law Libraries, IL, 102

American Association of Museums, DC, 5557

American Association of People with Disabilities, DC, 5558

American Association of Physics Teachers, MD, 5559

American Association of Plastic Surgeons, MA, 5560

American Association of School Administrators, VA, A

American Association of Spinal Cord Injury Nurses, NY, A

American Association of State Troopers Scholarship Foundation, Inc., FL, see 9

American Association of University Women Educational Foundation, DC, 5561

American Association of University Women Honolulu Branch Educational Fund, HI, 103

American Association of University Women Legal Advocacy Fund, DC, 4577

American Bar Association Fund for Justice & Education, IL, 104

American Bar Foundation, IL, A

American Berlin Opera Foundation, Inc., The, NY, 5188

American College of Obstetricians and Gynecologists, DC, 5562

American Colloid Company Foundation, IL, see 341

American Composers Forum, MN, 5189

American Council of Learned Societies, NY, 5563

American Council of the Blind, Inc., DC, 105

American Councils for International Education, DC, 5564

American Dental Association Health Foundation, IL, see 23

American Dental Association Health Foundation, IL, see 4569

American Dental Association Health Foundation, IL, see 5534

American Dental Education Association, DC, 106, 5565

American Dental Hygienist Association Institute for Oral Health, IL, 107, 5566

American Diabetes Association, VA, 5567

American Dietetic Association Foundation, IL, 108

American Digestive Health Foundation, MD, see 5796

American Electric Power System Educational Trust Fund, The, OH, 109

American Express Foundation, NY, 110

American Federation for Aging Research, Inc., NY, 5568

American Federation of Riders, OH, 4578

American Finnish Workers Society Memorial Educational Trust, MN, 111

American Floral Endowment, IL, 112, 5569

American Foundation for Pharmaceutical Education, MD, 113, 5570

American Foundation for Suicide Prevention, NY, 5571

American Foundation for the Blind, NY, 114

American Foundation for Urologic Disease, Inc, MD, 5572

American Friends of Even Yisroel Charitable Foundation, NJ, 115

American Friends of Needy Israeli Sephardic Children, The, NY, 116

American General Finance Foundation, Inc., IN, 117

American General Finance, Inc.—Richard E. Meier Foundation, Inc., IN, see 117

American Geriatric Society, Inc., NY, 5573

American Head and Neck Society, Inc., The, CA, 5574

American Health Assistance Foundation, MD, 4579, 5575

American Hotel and Lodging Educational Foundation, DC, 118

American Hotel and Lodging Foundation, DC, see 118

American Hungarian Foundation, NJ, 119

American Indian Heritage Foundation, VA, 120

American Institute for Cancer Research, DC, 5576

American Institute of Architects Scholarship Fund, MO, 121

American Institute of Indian Studies, IL, 5190, 5577

American Institute of Physics, Inc., MD, 5578

American Legion Charles F. Moran Post No. 475, Scholarship Trust and Baseball Trust, PA, see 122

American Legion Charles F. Moran Trust, PA, 122

American Legion Memorial Scholarship Funds, Inc., FL, 123

American Library Association, IL, 124, 5579

American Lung Association of California, CA, 5580

American Lung Association of Eastern Missouri, MO, 5581

American Lung Association of North Carolina, NC, 5582

American Lung Association of the City of New York, Inc., NY, 5583

American Lung Association of Vermont, VT, 5584

American Lung Association of Wisconsin, Inc., WI, 5585

American Massage Therapy Association Foundation, IL, see 5965

American Medical Association Foundation, IL, 5586

American Meteorological Society, MA, 125, 5587

American Music Center, Inc., NY, 5191

American Nurses Association Foundation, MD, see 5588

American Nurses Foundation, Inc., MD, 5588

American Occupational Therapy Foundation, MD, 126

American Optical Foundation, MA, 127

American Osteopathic Association, IL, 5589

American Osteopathic Foundation, IL, 128

American Otological Society, IL, 5590

American Paint Horse Association Youth Development Foundation, TX, 129

American Parkinson's Disease Association, NY, 5591

American Pediatric Surgical Association Foundation, Inc., MI, A

American Pharmacists Association Foundation, DC, 5592

American Philosophical Society, PA, 5593

American Physicians Fellowship for Medicine in Israel, MA, 5594

American Psychiatric Association, VA, see 5596

American Psychiatric Foundation, Inc., VA, 4580, 5595

American Psychiatric Publishing, Inc., VA, 5596

American Psychological Foundation, DC, 130, 5597

American Road & Transportation Builders Association Foundation, DC, 131

American Savings Charitable Foundation, Inc., CT, see 132

American Savings Foundation, CT, 132

American Skin Association, Inc., NY, 5598

American Society for Industrial Security Foundation, VA, 133, 5599

American Society for Military Comptrollers, VA, 134

American Society for the Defense of Tradition, Family, and Property, The, PA, see 5789

American Society of Consultant Pharmacists Research & Education Foundation, VA, 5600

American Society of Health-System Pharmacists Research and Education Foundation, MD, 5601

American Society of Interior Designers Foundation, DC, 135

American Society of Newspaper Editors Foundation, VA, 5602

American Society of Safety Engineers Foundation, IL, 5603

American Society of Therapeutic Radiologists Education and Development Foundation, VA, 5604

American Speech-Language-Hearing Association Foundation, MD, 136, 5605

American String Teachers, Inc., VA, 5192

American Symphony Orchestra League, NY, 5193

American Thread Educational Foundation, Inc., NC, see 812

American Welding & Manufacturing Company Foundation, PA, see 1457

American-Italian Cancer Foundation, NY, 5606

American-Scandinavian Foundation, The, NY, 5607

Ameritec Foundation, CA, 5608

Ames Charitable Foundation, D. Baker, FL, 4581

Ames Foundation, MA, A

Ames Trust, Dorothy, OH, 4582

amfAR & AIDS Research Foundation & American Foundation for AIDS Research, NY, see 5790

Amgen Foundation, Inc., CA, 5609

Amis Foundation, Everett L., MN, 137

AMJ Trust, MN, 4583

Amundson Scholarships, L. A., Inc., MN, 138

Amy Foundation, MI, 5194

Amyotrophic Lateral Sclerosis Association, The, CA, 5610

Anagnos Educational Foundation, Christina and John, The, IL, 5611

Anchor Graphics, Inc., IL, 5195

Anctil Foundation, J. Wilfred, RI, 139

Anderson Center for Interdisciplinary Studies, Inc., MN, 5196

Anderson Chapter 75 (1896) United Daughters of the Confederacy Trust, Dick, SC, 140

Anderson Educational Trust, Harold C., MN, 141

Anderson Educational Trust, Sophie L., WA, 142

Anderson Family Scholarship Trust u/w of Barbara Olson, IA, 143

Anderson Foundation, Kay M., IA, 144

Anderson Foundation, Sherwood, NC, 5197

Anderson Memorial Educational Trust, WY, 145

Anderson Memorial Scholarship Fund, Carrie and Frances, OH, see 148

Anderson Prize Foundation, The, CA, 5612

Anderson Scholarship Foundation, E. & E., OH, 146

Anderson Scholarship Foundation, Eugene and Daniela, TX, 147

Anderson Scholarship Fund, The, OH, 148

Anderson Scholarship Trust, Elizabeth M., IL, 149

Anderson Scholarship Trust, Olson L. Anderson and Catherine Bastow, MI, 150

Anderson Veterans Trust, Ralph W., IA, 151, 4584

Andona Society, MA, 152

Andrew Family Foundation, The, IL, 153

Andrew Foundation, Aileen S., IL, 154

Andrews Foundation, Lillian P., The, AL, 155

Andrews Memorial Foundation, Emily B., The, NC, 156

Andrews Scholarship Trust, Leah, IA, 157

Andrews Trust, Marie B., MA, 158

Andrus Foundation, Alice A., OH, 159

Angelo Brothers Company Founders Scholarship Foundation, The, PA, 160

Angels Gate Cultural Center, Inc., CA, 5198

Animal Welfare Trust, NY, 161

Ann Arbor Area Community Foundation, MI, 162

Ann Arbor Area Foundation, MI, see 162

Ann Arbor Film Festival, MI, 5199

AnnMarie Foundation, WI, 163

Anodyne Artist Company, MN, 5200

Anonymous Fund, WI, *see* 4896
Anthony Foundation, Barbara Cox, The, HI, 164
Antonovych Foundation, Inc., The, DC, 5201
Anverse, Inc., GA, 4585
Anxiety Disorders Association of America, MD, 5613
AO North America, Inc., PA, 5614
Aorn Foundation, CO, 165, 5615
APF, MA, *see* 5594
APhA Foundation, The, DC, *see* 5592
APICS Educational & Research Foundation, VA, 5616
Aplastic Anemia & MDS International Foundation, Inc., MD, 5617
Aplastic Anemia Foundation of America, Inc., MD, *see* 5617
Applefield Charitable Trust, Bryan and Helen, The, AL, 166
Appleton Student Loan Fund, Grace G., OH, 167
Aquinas Foundation, MN, 168
Arab American Institute Foundation, DC, 169
Arab Student Aid International Corp., OH, 170
Arby's Foundation, Inc., FL, 171
Arcadian Foundation, The, FL, 172
Archer Scholarship Trust Fund, Virginia A., OR, 173
Arctic Education Foundation, AK, 174
Ardell Foundation, Kenneth, WA, A
Area Fund of Dutchess County, The, NY, 175, 5618
Area Fund, The, NY, *see* 175
Area Fund, The, NY, *see* 5618
Ariens Foundation, Ltd., WI, 176
Arise Charitable Trust, The, WA, 177
Arizona Community Foundation, AZ, 178
Arizona Cowpuncher's Scholarship Organization, Inc., The, AZ, 179
Arizona Foundation for Legal Services and Education, AZ, 180
Arizona Kidney Foundation, AZ, 181, 4586
Arizona Scholarship Fund, AZ, 182
Arizona School Choice Trust, Inc., AZ, 183
Arkansas Eastman Scholarship Trust, AR, 184
Arkansas Farm Bureau Scholarship Foundation, AR, 185
Arkansas Human Development Corporation, AR, 4587
Arkansas Single Parent Scholarship Fund, Inc., AR, *see* 3721
Arkema Inc. Foundation, PA, 186
Arlington Catholic High School Scholarship Fund, RI, 187
Armstrong Family Foundation, CA, 188
Armstrong Foundation, Cecil, IN, 189
Armstrong Foundation, Ethel Louise, Inc., CA, 190
Armstrong Foundation, Lance, Inc., TX, 5619
Armstrong Trust, Benjamin A., CT, 191
Arnold Educational Trust, George S., NC, 192
Arnold Foundation, PA, 193
Arnold Memorial Fund, Maude E., RI, 194
Arnold Memorial Scholarship Fund, Teresa Youtz, PA, A
Arnold Memorial Scholarship, Heather Lynn, KS, 195
Arnold Scholarship Trust Fund, Robert T., CT, A
Arnold Trust for Memorial Fund, Maude E., RI, *see* 194
Arnsberg Scholarship Trust, WA, 196
Arpajian Armenian Educational Foundation, Jack, Inc., PA, 197
Arps Memorial Fund, Ernest G., NC, 198
Arques Charitable Education Trust, CA, 199
Arrow International, Inc. Scholarship Fund, PA, 200
Arrowhead Regional Arts Council, The, MN, 5202
Art in General, Inc., NY, 5203
Art League of Marco Island, Inc., FL, 201
Art Omi International Art Center, NY, 5204
Art/Omi, Inc., NY, *see* 5204
Arthritis Foundation, Inc., GA, 5620
Arthritis National Research Foundation, CA, 5621
Arthur's Enterprises, Inc. Scholarship Foundation, WV, 202
Artist Trust, WA, 5205
Artists Fellowship, Inc., NY, 5206
Artists Space, Inc., NY, 5207
Arts & Cultural Council for Greater Rochester, Inc., NY, 5208
Arts Alive Fort Collins, CO, 5209
Arts and Humanities Council of Montgomery County, MD, 5210

Arts and Humanities Council of Southwest Louisiana, Inc., LA, 5211
Arts Council of Greater Kalamazoo, MI, 5212
Arts Council of Indianapolis, Inc., IN, 5213
Arts Council Silicon Valley, CA, 5214
Arts International, Inc., NY, 5215
Arts Partnership of Greater Spartanburg, The, SC, 5216
ArtServe Michigan, MI, A
Arvac, Inc., AR, 4588
Arvig Memorial Scholarship Fund, Royale B. and Eleanor M., MN, 203
Arvig Memorial Scholarship Fund, Royale B., MN, *see* 203
Asbestos Workers Local 14 Scholarship Fund, PA, 204
ASCAP Foundation, The, NY, 5217
Ascension Fund, Inc., The, LA, 5622
ASCO Foundation, VA, 5623
ASCP Foundation, The, VA, *see* 5600
Ash Foundation, Stanley and Blanche, MI, 205
Ashcraft Foundation, Inc., MT, 206
Ashland County Community Foundation, OH, 207
Ashland Trusts, PA, *see* 3606
ASHP Research and Education Foundation, MD, *see* 5601
Ashtabula Foundation, Inc., The, OH, 208
Asia Society, The, NY, 5218
Asian Cultural Council, NY, 5219, 5624
Asian Pacific Fund, CA, 209
ASIS Foundation, VA, *see* 133
ASIS Foundation, VA, *see* 5599
Askren Memorial Scholarship Trust, George W., WI, 210
Askren Trust, Caroline L., WI, *see* 210
Aslakson Scholarship Trust, Hazel, WI, 211
Asparagus Club, VA, 212
Aspen Institute, The, DC, 213, 5625
Aspire Foundation, The, PA, 214
Assistance League of Houston, TX, 215
Assistance League of Newport-Mesa California, CA, 4589
Assistance League of Pueblo, Inc., CO, 4590
Associated Banc-Corp Founders Scholarship, Inc., WI, 216
Associated Charities of Findlay, Ohio, OH, 4591
Associated General Contractors of Maine, Inc. Education Foundation, ME, 217
Association for Surgical Education Foundation, IL, 5626
Association for the Cure of Cancer of the Prostate, CA, *see* 6087
Association for the Relief of Aged Women of New Bedford, MA, 4592
Association of Former New Jersey States Troopers Educational Fund, NJ, *see* 218
Association of Former State Troopers Educational Fund, NJ, 218
Association of Higher Education Facilities Officers, VA, 5627
Association of Moving Image Archivists, CA, 219
Association of Performing Arts Presenters, DC, 5220
Association of the Wall & Ceiling Industry-Foundation Office, VA, *see* 1432
Association of Theological Schools in the U.S. & Canada, PA, 5628
Association of Writers and Writing Programs, VA, 5221
Assurant Foundation, NY, 220
Astin Charitable Trust, Nina Heard, TX, 221
Astle Memorial Scholarship Foundation, Edward Thatcher, NJ, 222
Astraea Lesbian Foundation for Justice, Inc., The, NY, 5222
ASTRAEA, National Lesbian Action Foundation, NY, *see* 5222
ASTRO, VA, *see* 5604
AT&T Foundation, TX, 223
Athanasiades Cultural Foundation, Inc., NY, 224, 4593
Athena Charitable Trust, CA, 4594
Atherton Family Foundation, HI, 225
Atkins Charities, Grace, RI, 226
Atlanta Community Foundation, Metropolitan, Inc., GA, *see* 862
Atlantic Center for the Arts, Inc., FL, 5223

Atlantic County Medical Society Scholarship Fund, NJ, 227
Atlas Economic Research Foundation, VA, 5629
ATO Foundation of Berkeley, Inc., CA, 228
Atofina Chemicals, Inc. Foundation, PA, *see* 186
ATP Tour Charities, Inc., FL, 4595
Atsinger Family Foundation, CA, 229
Atwood Fund, Eugene, CT, 230
Atwood Trust for Brooks Scholarship Fund, Florence D., OH, 231
Auburn Foundry Foundation, IN, 232
Audio Engineering Society Educational Foundation, Inc., NY, 233
Auerbach Youth Foundation, Red, Inc., MA, 234
August Charitable Trust, Fannie, RI, 235
Augusta Kiwanis Scholarship Foundation, ME, 236
Aurora Foundation, The, IL, 238
Aurora Foundation, TX, 237
Aurora Ministries, Inc., FL, 4596
Aurora Project, Inc., WV, 5224
Austin Film Society, TX, 5225
Austin Trust, William Harold Francis, MA, 239
Authier Trust, Jean B., NY, 240
Authors League Fund, The, NY, 5226
Autism Society of America Foundation, MD, 5630
Avatar Meher Baba Foundation, Inc., CT, 5631
Aventis Pharmaceuticals Health Care Foundation, NJ, 4597
Avery Scholarship Foundation, NY, 241
Avery-Fuller Children's Center, CA, *see* 4598
Avery-Fuller-Welch Children's Foundation, CA, 4598
Avoda Club of Atlantic County, The, NJ, 242
AWS Foundation, FL, 243
Axelrod Family Foundation, Inc., The, NY, 244
Ayer Trust, Waldo & Alice, RI, 245
Aylesworth Foundation for Advancement of Marine Sciences, Inc., FL, 246
Ayres Foundation, Lucy C., Inc., The, RI, 247
Ayres Home for Nurses, Lucy C., Inc., The, RI, *see* 247
Ayres Memorial Foundation, Mabel Brickey, Inc., AR, 248
Ayres Student Fund, Dr. Samuel & Mildred L., TX, 249
Ayres Trust, Mildred L., TX, *see* 249
Aysr Foundation, PA, 4599
AZHHA Education Foundation, AZ, 250

B'nai B'rith, DC, 5632
B-G Foundation, The, NC, *see* 2449
B. A. Hochmark Scholarship Trust, WA, *see* 1875
Babcock Fund, John C., RI, 251
Babcock Memorial Endowment, William, CA, 4600
Babcock Memorial Fund, Quintus C., UT, 252
Babcock Trust, Betsey E., RI, *see* 251
Baber Foundation, Weisell, Inc., IN, 253
Babson's Midwest Memorial Foundation, Inc., KS, 254
Bachmann-Strauss Dystonia and Parkinson Foundation, Inc., Inc., The, NY, 5633
Bacon Scholarship Fund, Daisy S., NY, 255
Badger Mining Scholarship Trust, WI, 256
Bagby Foundation for the Musical Arts, Inc., The, NY, 257, 4601
Bailey Family Foundation, Inc., The, VA, 258
Bailey Family Memorial Trust, OK, 259
Bailey Foundation, MA, 260
Bailey Foundation, The, SC, 261
Bainbridge Arts & Crafts, Inc., WA, 262, 5634
Bainbridge-Ometepe Sister Islands Association, WA, 263
Bair Memorial Trust, Charles M., MT, 264
Baker Educational Fund, Jessie H., NY, 265
Baker Family Foundation, Thomas E. and Linda O., NJ, 266
Baker Foundation, Clark and Ruby, NC, 267
Baker Memorial Fund Trust, Margaret, PA, A
Baker Memorial Scholarship Loan Fund Trust, Carl & Grace, CA, 268
Baker Memorial Trust, Charles Milton, MS, 269
Baker Trust, J. H., KS, 270
Baker Trust, Lillian M., RI, 271
Baker-Adams Scholarship Fund, RI, 272
Baker/Geary Memorial Fund, Inc., KY, 273
Bakes Scholarship Trust Fund, John E., OH, 274
Bakken Library of Electricity in Life, MN, *see* 5635

Bundy Scholarship Trust, Jesse David & Katie B., NC, 578

Bunn Memorial Fund, Henry, WI, 579

Burch-Setton Student Loan Fund, TX, 580

Burchfield Trust, Daisy L., IA, 581

Burgess Fund, Laura A., RI, 4626

Burgess Memorial Scholarship Fund, William, Agnes & Elizabeth, The, IL, 582

Burke Foundation, Thomas C., GA, 4627

Burke Memorial Fund, John P., RI, 583

Burke-Weber Memorial Fund, CA, 584

Burkett Trust, George W., IN, A

Burkhalter Educational Fund, The, MO, 585

Burks Charitable Trust f/b/o Fresno Lodge No. 247, F. & A. M., CA, 4628

Burlington Cancer Relief Association, Inc., VT, 4629

Burlington Industries Foundation, NC, 4630

Burnett Foundation, Belle C., NY, 586

Burnham Educational Trust, John & Ellen, OH, 587

Burns Foundation, John A., HI, 588

Burnside Foundation, Warren and Betty, Inc., The, WV, 589

Burroughs Educational Fund, N. R., NC, 590

Burroughs Wellcome Fund, NC, 5661

Burrows Memorial Trust, IA, 591

Burst Educational Foundation, Fran & Jean, Inc., IN, 592

Burtman Charity Trust, Abraham, NH, 593

Burton Foundation, William T. and Ethel Lewis, The, LA, 594

Burton Trust, Lila Draper, WI, 595

Busch Family Foundation, MI, 596

Busey-Mills Community Foundation, IL, 597

Bush Foundation, MN, 5247, 5662

Bush Memorial Scholarship Fund, William E. and Margaret N., PA, 598

Bush Memorial Scholarship Trust, Elizabeth B., OH, 599

Bushee Foundation, Florence Evans, Inc., MA, 600

Business and Professional Women's Foundation, The, DC, 601

Business Women's Home, The, MS, A

Butler Foundation, Alice, NC, 602

Butler Foundation, The, NH, 603

Butler Manufacturing Company Foundation, MO, 604, 4631

Butler Memorial Scholarship Foundation, J. D. and Alice, NC, see 602

Butte Creek Foundation, CA, 605

Butterer Educational Trust, M. Verna, PA, 606

Butterworth Foundation, Inc., MA, 4632

Buttrey Memorial Trust, Jane, OR, 607

Butts Memorial Home Association, Gertrude, NJ, 608, 4633

Butts Scholarship Foundation, Art & Clara, NE, 609

Byrnes Foundation, James F., SC, 610

C & E Foundation, PA, 611

C J Foundation for SIDS, Inc., NJ, 5663

Cabot Scholarship Foundation, AR, 612

Cabot Scholarship Fund, NY, 613

Cabot Trust, Ella Lyman, Inc., MA, 5248

Cade Foundation, Robert and Mary, Inc., FL, 614, A

Cady Educational Trust, George A., NV, 615

Cafaro Family Foundation, William M. & A., The, OH, 616

Cahp Foundation, CA, 617

Cain Family Foundation, The, CA, 618

Calcot-Seitz Foundation, CA, 619

Caldera, OR, 5249

Caleb Foundation, Inc., The, VA, 620

California Alpha Delta Phi Memorial Foundation, CA, 621

California Association of Realtors Scholarship Foundation, CA, 622

California Community Foundation, CA, 5250

California Council for the Humanities, CA, 5251

California HealthCare Foundation, CA, 5664

California Institute of Contemporary Arts, CA, 5252

California Japanese-American Alumni Association, CA, 623

California Job's Daughters Foundation, CA, 624

California Masonic Foundation, CA, 625

California Soldiers' Widows Home Association, CA, see 4919

California Wellness Foundation, The, CA, 5665

Californian Humanitarian Foundation for Holocaust Survivors, CA, 4634

Calista Scholarship Fund, AK, 626

Calkins Foundation, Ina, MO, 627

Callaway Foundation, Fuller E., GA, 628

Callaway Professorial Chairs, Trust for Fuller E., The, NC, 5666

Callejo-Botello Foundation Charitable Trust, TX, see 629

Callejo-Botello Foundation, TX, 629

Calvert Memorial Merit Scholarship Foundation, Stephen G., PA, 630

Calvi Memorial Foundation, Francis L., NJ, 631

Camargo Foundation, The, MN, 5253

Camden County Hero Scholarship 200 Club, Inc., NJ, 632

Camden Home for Senior Citizens, ME, 4635

Camellia Foundation, CA, see 2681

Cameron Educational Foundation, Dave, The, SC, 633

Camp Foundation, VA, 634

Camp Fund, Caleb J., CT, A

Camp Mohawk Scholarship Trust, TX, 635

Camp Trust, Lucille, WI, 636

Campanelli Charitable Foundation, Alfred, MA, 637

Campbell Charitable Trust, Ruth Camp, NY, 638

Campbell Foundation, Ernest and Lillian E., CO, 639

Campbell Scholarship Fund for Linfield College Students, W. C. & Pearl, OR, 640

Campbell Scholarship Fund, J. Colin, The, OH, 641

CAN, CA, see 5714

Canaan Exchange Club Charitable Trust, MA, 642

Cancer Aid and Research Fund, AZ, 4636, A

Cancer Research Fund of the Damon Runyon-Walter Winchell Foundation, NY, 5667

Cancer Research Institute, Inc., NY, 5668

Cannon Scholarship Foundation, Jesse W., TX, 643

Canton Community Foundation, MI, 644

Cantor Art Foundation, B. G., The, CA, see 5669

Cantor Foundation, Iris & B. Gerald, CA, 5669

Cantor Foundation, Jasmine L., Inc., NY, 645

CAP Charitable Foundation USA, VA, 646

Cape Cod Foundation, The, MA, 647

Cape Cod Times Needy Fund, Inc., MA, 4637

Capezio/Ballet Makers Dance Foundation, Inc., NJ, 5254

Capital Newspapers Public Benefit Fund, Inc., NY, 4638

Capricorn Foundation, The, SC, 648

Carco 31 Charitable Foundation, Robert C., MA, 649

Care Consistency Foundation, Inc., MS, 4639

Care To Share, OR, 4640

Career Transition for Dancers, NY, 5255

Carhart Memorial Fund Trust, Amory S., VA, 4641

Caring for Carcinoid Foundation, Inc., MA, 5670

Caring Foundation for Children, UT, 4642

Caring Foundation of Wyoming, WY, 4643

Caring Foundation, Inc., The, UT, see 4642

Carkeek Trust, Florence Lewis, WA, 650

Carleton College, Board of Trustees of, OH, 651

Carlisle Trust for Children of Goshen Trust, Alice L., RI, 4644

Carlsbad Foundation, Inc., NM, 652, 5671

Carlston Family Foundation, CA, 5672

Carman Scholarship Trust, Nellie Martin, WA, 653

Carmine Trust, John Harry & Edith Carter Lewis, VA, A

Carnegie Corporation of New York, NY, 5673, A

Carnegie Fund for Authors, NY, 5256

Carnegie Hero Fund Commission, PA, 5674

Carney Scholarship Fund, Helen K., OH, 654

Carpe Diem Foundation of Illinois, IL, 655

Carpenter Foundation, Milton, Inc., NY, 656

Carpenter Trust, John S., NC, 657

Carpenter-Dent Trust Fund, KY, 658

Carr Foundation, Clinton J., Inc., MO, 659

Carr Trust Fund for Scholarships, Elizabeth S., RI, A

Carreon, M.D. Foundation, Reynaldo J., CA, 660

Carrier & Bryant Distributors' Educational Foundation, NY, 661

Carrier Charitable Trust, Glen, OK, 662

Carrier Foundation, Robert M. and Lenore W., TN, 663

Carroll Foundation, Anne, Inc., The, MA, 664

Carson Electric Education Foundation, Kit, Inc., NM, 665

Carson Scholars Fund, Inc., MD, 666

Carter & Graham Smith Memorial Scholarship Fund, Eula, TX, 667

Carter Center, Inc., The, GA, 5675

Carter Family Foundation, WV, 668

Carter Memorial Foundation, Charles Wentz, PA, 4645

Carter Star-Telegram Employees Fund, Amon G., TX, 669, 4646

Carter Trust Fund, Marie L. & John L., IA, 670

Carter Trust, Evelyn C., WI, 671

Carver Scholarship Fund, Inc., NY, 672

Carving Studio & Sculpture Center, The, VT, 5257

Cary Educational Fund, Isaac Harris, MA, 673

Casey Foundation, Annie E., The, MD, 5676

Casper Foundation, William J. & Gertrude R., WI, 674

Cassner Foundation, The, OH, 675

Castele Foundation, Dr. and Mrs. Theodore J., OH, 676

Castelli Charitable Trust, PA, 677

Casten Family Foundation, Inc., IL, 678

Castle Pines Scholarship Foundation, CO, 679

Castrodale Scholarship Foundation, Dante, The, WV, 680

Catawissa Lumber & Specialty Co., Inc. College Educational Fund, PA, 681

Catholic Education Foundation Diocese of Evansville, IN, 682

Catholic Teachers Association of the Diocese of Brooklyn, Inc., NY, 683

Catt Educational Fund, Frank & Edith, IL, 684

Cattell Fund, James McKeen, NC, 5677

Cave Canem Foundation, Inc., NY, 5258

Caves Valley Scholars Foundation, Inc., MD, 685

Cawasa Grange Memorial Scholarship Fund, Inc., The, CT, 686

CB Trust, The, TX, 4647

CCBCC Relief Foundation, Inc., NC, 4648

CCSU Foundation, Inc., CT, 687

CDC Foundation, The, GA, 5678

CDS International, Inc., NY, 5679

Cecil County Bar Foundation, Inc., MD, 688

Celebration Foundation, The, OR, 5259

Center for Advanced Studies in Leukemia, CA, A

Center for Alternative Media and Culture, NY, 689, 5260

Center for Book Arts, Inc., NY, 5261

Center for Land Use Interpretation, The, CA, A

Center for Photography of Woodstock, Inc., The, NY, 5262

Center for Research on Women and Newborn Health Foundation, PA, 5680

Center on Contemporary Art, WA, 5263

Central Alabama Community Foundation, Inc., AL, 690

Central Carolina Community Foundation, SC, 691

Central Minnesota Arts Board, MN, 5264

Central Minnesota Community Foundation, MN, 692

Central Minnesota Initiative Fund, MN, see 2021

Central Missouri Counties Human Development Corporation, MO, 4649

Central Montana Foundation, MT, 693

Central National-Gottesman Foundation, The, NY, 694

Central Susquehanna Community Foundation, PA, 695

Central Valley Electric Education Foundation, NM, 696

Central Valley High School Scholarship Fund, CA, 697

Centralia Foundation, IL, 698

Centrum Foundation, WA, 5265

Century Brass Sunshine Fund, RI, see 5034

Cervical Spine Research Society, IL, 5681

Cessna Foundation, Inc., KS, 699

Cestone Foundation, Ralph M., Inc., The, PA, 700

CFEF, TX, see 1023

Chadwell-Townsend Private Foundation, OH, 4650

Chadwick Foundation, ID, 701

Chaffer Scholarship Foundation, Joyce A., WA, 702

Chairman's Award Foundation, TX, 703

Chalone Wine Foundation, CA, see 4511

Chamber Music America, NY, 5266

Chamber Music Northwest, Inc., OR, 5267

Chamberlin Scholarship Fund, Frank A. & Gladys F., TX, 704

Chamberlin Scholarship Trust, Ruth W. & Alice I., NY, A

Chambers Charitable Trust, Mary Cecile, The, TX, 705
Chambers Foundation, Roy, The, WV, 4651
Chambers Scholarship Fund, Mary Cecile, The, TX, see 705
Champion International Corporation, TX, see 3504
Chandler Trust, Esther, RI, 706
Chaney Scholarship Trust, Hazel M., OH, 707
Chapman Foundation, The, AZ, see 709
Chapman Foundation, William H., CT, 708
Chapman Fund, AZ, 709
Chapman Trust Fund, FL, 710
Chappell Memorial Fund, Corabelle, NC, 711
Charitable Foundation Corporation, A, NV, 5682
Charitable Society in Hartford, CT, 4652
Charleston Scientific & Cultural Educational Fund, SC, 712
Charlevoix County Community Foundation, MI, 713
Charlotte Advocates for Education, NC, 5683
Charlotte Hall School Board of Trustees, Inc., MD, 714
Charlotte-Mecklenburg Education Foundation, NC, see 5683
Charter Fund, The, CO, 715
Chartrand Memorial Scholarship Trust Fund, Bishop Joseph, The, IN, 716
Chase Family Scholarship Fund, Hal S., IA, 717
chashama, Inc., NY, 5268
Chatham Kiwanis Scholarship Fund, NJ, 718
Chattanooga Orthopedic Educational and Research Foundation, TN, 5684
Chautauqua Region Community Foundation, Inc., NY, 719
Chazen Foundation, The, NY, 720
Checketts Foundation, Stan and Sandy, The, UT, A
Cheek, Jr. Scholarship Fund, T. Franklin, TN, 721
Chela Financial Resources, CA, A
Chelonian Research Foundation, MA, 5685
CHEMCENTRAL Charitable Trust, IL, 722
Chemotherapy Foundation, Inc., NY, 5686
Chen International Law Foundation, Kwen, Inc., NY, A
Chenango County Medical Society & Otsego County Medical Society, Trustees for the Van Wagner Scholarship, NY, 723
Chenega Future, Inc., AK, 724
Chenoweth Foundation, Elizabeth, Inc., TN, 725
Cherith Christian Private Foundation, CA, 5687
Cherokee & Walker Foundation, The, UT, 4653
Chesapeake Corporation Foundation, VA, 726
Chesed Avrhom Hacohn Foundation, NY, 5688
Chesley Foundation, B. H., MN, 727
Chessall Memorial Scholarship Fund, William A., CA, 728
Chest and Foundation of the Fur Industry of the City of New York, Inc., NY, 4654
Chest Foundation, IL, 5689
Chester Academy, Trustees of, VT, 729
Chester County Community Foundation, PA, 730
Chester High School Alumni Association, MA, 731
Chester Springs Studio, PA, 5269
Chesterfield Charitable Foundation, NH, 732
Chevelle Foundation, Judge C. C., WA, 733
Chicago Community Trust, The, IL, 5690
Chicago Engineers' Club Foundation, IL, see 734
Chicago Engineers' Foundation of the Union League Club, IL, 734
Chicago Foundation for Education, IL, 5691
Chicago Symphony Orchestra, IL, 735
Chicago White Metal Charitable Foundation, IL, 736
Chico Community Hospital Foundation, CA, see 2978
Chiefs Children's Fund, MO, A
Child Development Center of the Houston-Galveston Psychoanalytic, TX, 737
Child Nutrition Foundation, VA, 738, 5692
Children at the Crossroads Foundation, IL, 739
Children for Children, NY, 5693
Children's Aid Association of Amsterdam, NY, NY, 740
Children's Aid Society, NY, 741
Children's Educational Opportunity Foundation, CA, 742
Children's Foundation for the Arts, Inc., NJ, 743
Children's Health Fund, CA, see 5026
Children's Heart Foundation, The, IL, 5694
Children's Museum of Indianapolis, Inc., The, IN, 744
Children's Oncology Services, Inc., IL, 4655

Children's Scholarship Fund, NY, 745
Children's Seedling Fund, The, CO, see 5094
Children's Tumor Foundation, NY, 5695
Childs Memorial Fund for Medical Research, Jane Coffin, The, CT, 5696
China Times Cultural Foundation, CA, 746, 5697
Chinati Foundation, The, TX, 5270
Chinese American Citizens Alliance Foundation, CA, 747
Ching Foundation, Hung Wo & Elizabeth Lau, HI, 748
Chmielewski Educational Foundation, Melanie V., WI, 749
Cholnoky Foundation, Thomas, Inc., The, CT, 750
Chong Foundation, Stanley & Marvel, MN, 751
Christ Scholarship Fund, Albert A., WI, 752
Christ Scholarship Fund, Elmer S. and Frances R., PA, 753
Christamore Aid Society, Inc., IN, see 754
Christamore House Guild, Inc., IN, 754
Christenson Family Organization, Alvin, UT, A
Christian Business Ministries, CA, A
Christian BusinessCares Foundation, OH, 4656
Christian Community Foundation, CO, 5698
Christian Fellowship Foundation of the Peace United Church of Christ, Inc., MN, 755
Christian Foundation of Indiana, IN, 756
Christian Legal Society, VA, 757
Christian Scholarship Fund of Arizona, AZ, 758
Christian Services, Inc., MN, 4657
Christy Scholarship Fund, Van and Joanna, RI, 759
Chubb Foundation, The, NJ, 760
Chung Kun Ai Foundation, HI, 761
Church Memorial Fund, Bradford & Dorothy, MA, 762
Churches Homes Foundation, Inc., NC, 763
CIACO, Inc., IN, 764, 4658
Ciatti Memorial Foundation, Joseph D., CA, 765
Cibrowski Family Foundation, CO, 766
Cilley Trust, Elwin L., RI, 767
Cintas Foundation, Inc., NY, 5271
Circuit City Foundation, VA, 768
CIRI Foundation, The, AK, 769
Cismoski Foundation, Bish & Frannie, IL, 4659
Citizens for NYC, NY, A
Citizens Scholarship Foundation, KS, see 3747
Citizens Union Bank Foundation, Ltd., GA, 770
Citizens United for Research in Epilepsy, IL, 5699
Citizens' Scholarship Foundation of America, MN, see 3584
City College 21st Century Foundation, Inc., The, NY, 771
Civitan Child Welfare Auxiliary, Inc., TN, 4660
Civitan International Foundation, AL, 772
Clan MacBean Foundation, The, CO, 773
Clancy Scholarship Foundation, Helen Miller, WA, 774
Clareth Fund: The Philadelphia Association of Zeta Psi Fraternity, The, PA, 775
Clark Community College District 14 Foundation, WA, 776
Clark Family Memorial Fund, Alvin T., WY, see 783
Clark Foundation, B. M., ME, 777
Clark Foundation, James T., CO, 778
Clark Foundation, The, NY, 779, 4661
Clark League Trust, Mary, PA, 780
Clark Medical Education Foundation, Henry H., PA, 781
Clark Medical Memorial Fund, Welsford Starr and Mildred M., CT, 782
Clark Memorial Fund, Alvin T., WY, 783
Clark Memorial Scholarship Fund, Claude, CA, 784
Clark Memorial Trust Fund, W. S. Clark & M. M., CT, see 782
Clark Memorial Trust, Royce W., The, NY, 785
Clark Scholarship Fund, CO, 786
Clark Scholarship Trust, Donald, NE, 788
Clark Scholarship Trust, Grace W. Clark, Thomas R. & Elsie T., MD, see 787
Clark Scholarship Trust, MD, 787
Clark-AFF League Memorial Fund, PA, see 780
Clarke Endowment Fund, Louis G. & Elizabeth L., OR, 4662
Clarke Testamentary Trust/Fund Foundation, Elizabeth Church, The, NY, 4663
Clarke Trust, John, RI, A
Clarke Trust, Rachel Fiero, OH, 789

Clarkson Scholarship Foundation, George M. and Florence M., MT, 790
Class of 1968 Scholarship, Inc., CT, 791
Claudia Foundation, The, CA, 792
Clay Scholarship & Research Fund, William L., MO, 793
Clayman Family Foundation, Inc., OH, 794
Clayton Scholarship Trust, Bernard and Anna, MO, 795
Clemens Foundation, The, OR, 796
Clements Scholarship Fund, H. Loren, NC, 797
Clemson Community Care, Inc., SC, 4664
Clergy Society, SC, 4665
Cleveland Alumnae Panhellenic Endowment Fund, Inc., OH, 798
Cleveland National Air Show Charitable Foundation, Inc., OH, 799
Cleveland Scholarship Programs, Inc., OH, 800
Clifford Foundation, Inc., TX, 801
Clifford Scholarship, Ted & Elinor, MA, 802
Clifton Trust, GA, 803
Cline Memorial Scholarship Fund, Charles O. & Hazel E., OR, 804
Clint Foundation, The, FL, 805
Cloud County Children's Trust, KS, 4666
Clover Foundation, NY, 5700
Club Foundation, The, VA, 806, 5701
Club of Hearts, Inc., GA, 4667
CMCD Scholarship Foundation, CA, 807
CMI Foundation, The, SC, A
Coast Guard Foundation, Inc., CT, 808, 4668
Coastal Banc Foundation, The, TX, 809
Coastal Bend Community Foundation, TX, 810
Coastal Community Foundation of South Carolina, SC, 811
Coastal Jewish Foundation, Inc., GA, 4669
Coats North American Educational Foundation, NC, 812
Cobb Educational Fund, Ty, GA, 813
Cobb Memorial Scholars, Frank and Ellen, RI, 814
Coburn Scholarship Trust, E. B., TN, 815
Coca-Cola Scholars Foundation, Inc., GA, 816
Cochems Trust, Jane Nugent, OR, A
Cochran Trust, Gifford A., PA, 817
Code Scholarship Fund, IA, 818
Cody Medical Foundation, WY, 819
Coe Fund, Marion Isabelle, CT, 4670
Coe Medical & Surgical Fund for Education, William H., RI, 820
Coe Trust, Helen R., RI, 821
Coeli Foundation, Regina, Inc., IL, 822, 4671
Coffee Memorial Fund, William Marshall & Mildred, Inc., KY, A
Coffey Foundation, Inc., The, NC, 823
Coffman Scholarship Trust, John F., WA, 824
Cogan Trust, George T., NH, 825
Cogar Foundation, Inc., NY, 826
Cohen Family Foundation, Martin D., PA, 827
Cohen Foundation, David J. and Rosetta Adler, The, CA, 828
Cohen Scholarship Fund, Sarah, MD, 829
Cohen Scholarship Trust Fund, Rueben J. and Dorothy S., NJ, 830
Colburn Education Foundation, Deo B., NY, 831
Colburn Memorial Fund, William Cullen, NC, 832
Cold Heading Foundation, The, MI, 833
Cole Foundation, Olive B., Inc., IN, 834
Cole Scholarship Trust, Harold M., NC, 835
Coleman Scholarship Trust, Lillian R., WI, 836
Coleman Scholarship Trust, William S. and Lillian R., WI, see 836
Coleman Student Fund, Inc., NY, 837
Coles Foundation, Mary D., NJ, 838
Colf Family Foundation, WA, 839
College Art Association of America, Inc., NY, see 840
College Art Association, NY, 840
College Careers Fund of Westchester, Inc., NY, 841
College Club of Cleveland Foundation, The, OH, 842
College Club of St. Louis, MO, 843
College First Foundation, TX, 844
Coller Foundation, MI, 845
Collins Foundation, Joseph, NY, 846
Collins McDonald Trust Fund, OR, 847
Collins Trust No. 2, Paul and Mary, WI, 848
Collister Scholarship Trust, Roberta, CA, 849

Council for Advancement and Support of Education, DC, 5708

Council of American Overseas Research Centers, DC, 5709

Council of American Research Centers, DC, see 5709

County North Foundation, OH, 973

Covenant Foundation, The, NY, 5710

Covington Memorial Scholarship Trust, MO, 974

Cox Charitable Trust, Edith May, CO, 975

Cox Charitable Trust, Opal G., TX, 976

Cox Family Foundation, Marshall G., The, CA, 977

Cox Foundation, James M., NE, 980

Cox Foundation, SC, 978

Cox Foundation, William J. and Dorothy H., Inc., The, NY, 979

Cozad Public Schools Foundation, NE, 981

Cozard Educational Scholarship Trust, William & Ruth, SD, 982

CPCU- Harry J. Loman Foundation, PA, see 983

CPCU- Loman Education Foundation, PA, 983

Craft Emergency Relief Fund, Inc., VT, 5278

Craig Memorial Fund for the Arts, Jennifer, Inc., FL, 984

Crain Family Scholarship Fund, J. P., OH, 985

Crane Fund for Student Aid, Zenas, CT, 986

Crane-Rogers Foundation, The, NH, see 5878

Cranston Foundation, The, RI, 987

Cranston High School Athletic Scholarship Fund, RI, 988

Cranston/Theophilus T. Pitman Fund, Robert B., RI, 4689

Crary Foundation, Bruce L., Inc., NY, 989

Crawford Memorial Scholarship Fund, G. Kenneth Crawford and Margaret B., PA, 990

Crawley Memorial Educational Fund, Ethel W., NC, 991

Creamer & Son Scholarship Foundation, J. Fletcher, NJ, 992

Create Christian Research Education Action Technical Enterprise, Inc., MS, see 993

CREATE Foundation, MS, 993

Creative Capital Foundation, NY, 5279

Credit Bureau of Fort Dodge Trust, IA, 994

Crescent Moon Foundation, Inc., The, TX, 995

Crescent Scholarship Foundation, TX, 996

Crist Trust, Luther E. Crist and Phyllis C., MA, 4690

Criswell Scholarship Fund, OR, 997

Croatian Fraternal Union Scholarship Foundation, Inc., PA, 998

Crohn's & Colitis Foundation of America, Inc., NY, 5711

Cromwell Foundation for the Research of the Law and Legal History of the Colonial Period of the U.S.A., William Nelson, NY, 5712

Cross Scholarship Fund, Alton & Mildred, PA, 999

Croston Scholarship Fund, R. Elaine, RI, 1000

Croston Trust, Mary G., RI, 1001

Croul Family Foundation, CA, 1002

Crozier Educational Trust, Robert Lloyd Crozier and Myrtle Madge, IA, 1003

Cruise Charitable Foundation, George M., WV, 1004

Crume Trust, Roy L., IN, 1005

Crump Fund, Joe and Jessie, WI, 1006

CSP, OH, see 800

CTS Foundation, IN, 1007

CTW Foundation, Inc., DE, 1008

Cuan Foundation, Inc., WI, 1009

Cultural Arts Council of Houston/Harris County, TX, 5280

Cultural Society, Inc., The, FL, 4691, A

Culver's V.I.P. Foundation, Inc., WI, 1010

Cumber Family Foundation, Aftab and Gul, FL, A

Cummings Foundation, Nicholas & Dorothy, The, NV, 5713

Cunningham Foundation, Cameron, IL, 1011

Cunningham Scholarship Foundation, Louis, The, MI, 1012

Cuno Foundation, RI, 1013

Cure Autism Now, CA, 5714

Curley Foundation, The, CA, 1014

Curran Music Scholarship Fund, NY, 1015

Curran Trust f/b/o Curran Music School, Gertrude D., NY, see 1015

Curtis Athletic Scholarship Fund, T. Manning, PA, 1016

Curtis Foundation, Charles Curtis & Patricia Morse, CO, 1017

Curtis Foundation, Frances Blayney, The, WY, 1018

Curtis Trust Fund, Effie H. and Edward H., CO, 4692

Curves Community Fund, Inc., The, TX, see 1800

Curves Community Fund, Inc., The, TX, see 4812

Cushwa Foundation, Charles B. & Margaret E., OH, 1019

Cut Bank Elks Lodge Charitable Corp., MT, 1020

Cutter Memorial Trust Fund, Albert B., CA, 4693

Cutter Trust Fund, William H. & Sadie R., Inc., NJ, 1021

Cuyahoga Valley National Park Association, OH, 5281

CVS Charitable Trust, Inc., RI, see 1022

CVS/pharmacy Charitable Trust, Inc., RI, 1022

Cypress-Fairbanks Educational Foundation, TX, 1023

Cystic Fibrosis Foundation, MD, 5715

Czado Catholic Education Fund, Mary, MI, A

D'Amour Fellowship Foundation, Paul H., The, MA, 1024

D'Amour Founders Scholarship for Academic Excellence, Gerald and Paul, The, MA, 1025

Dade Community Foundation, Inc., FL, 1026

Dade Foundation, FL, see 1026

Dailey College Scholarship Fund, Frank C., TX, 1027

Daiwa Securities America Foundation, NY, 1028

Dake Education Foundation, The, NY, A

Dale Trust, Samuel S., MA, 4694

Dales Foundation, George F., CA, 5716

Daley Scholarship Foundation, Jim & Doris, MT, 1029

Dallas Cotton Exchange Trust, NY, A

Dallas Scholarships, Margaret E., IA, 1030

Daly Educational Fund, Bernard, OR, 1031

Damato Scholarship Trust, Elizabeth J., IL, 1032

Dana Corporation Foundation, OH, 1033

Dana Foundation, Charles A., Inc., The, NY, see 5717

Dana Foundation, The, NY, 5717

Dance/USA, DC, 5282

Dancey Memorial Foundation, Opal, MI, 1034

Danciger Charitable Foundation, David Kendall, TX, 1035

Danforth Memorial Fund, Josiah H., NY, 4695

Danicas Foundation, Inc., OR, 1036

Daniels Foundation, CO, see 1037

Daniels Foundation, Lucy, Inc., NC, A

Daniels Fund, CO, 1037

Dante Foundation of Nassau County, Inc., NY, 1038

Darcey Foundation, Joseph and Sharon, Inc., WI, 5718

Darcey Foundation, Joseph, Inc., WI, see 5718

Dargan Minority Scholarship Fund, Thomas R., OR, 1039

Das Foundation, Taraknath, NY, 5719

Dasburg Foundation, Meredyth Anne, MN, 1040

Datatel Scholars Foundation, VA, 1041

Daughters of the Cincinnati, NY, 1042

Davenport Area Foundation, IA, see 909

Davenport Charitable Trust, George W., RI, 4696

Davenport Educational Family Foundation, Henry & Sidney T., NC, 1043

Davenport Educational Fund, Henry & Sidney T., NC, see 1043

Davenport Foundation, John K. and Thirza F., MA, 1044

Davey Scholarship Foundation, WI, 1045

David Family Foundation, The, OH, see 1046

David Foundation, Paul & Carol, The, OH, 1046

Davidson Foundation, Lorimer & Betty Gael, Inc., DC, A

Davidson Krueger Foundation, The, NY, 1047

Davidson Trust, Frank H., MO, A

Davies Educational Foundation of Friendship Class of Peachtree Road Methodist Church, Daisy, GA, see 1048

Davies Educational Fund, Daisy, GA, 1048

Davies Foundation, John and Shirley, OH, 1049

Davies Memorial Scholarship, Walter L. J., OR, 1050

Davies Scholarship Foundation, Joe, MD, 1051

Davis Charitable Trust, R. L., Inc., NC, 4697

Davis Charitable Trust, William G., PA, 1052

Davis Education Foundation, Edward, MI, 1053

Davis Education Trust, Grace, PA, 1054

Davis Educational Foundation, Charles E., WA, 1055

Davis Foundation, James A. and Juliet L., Inc., KS, 1056

Davis Foundation, Jones S., WI, 1057

Davis Foundation, Lewis J. & Nelle A., OH, 1058

Davis Foundation, William E. & Rose Marie, NE, 1059

Davis Medical School Scholarships, WA, see 1062

Davis Memorial Foundation, Fred W., NC, 1060

Davis Memorial Foundation, Thomas & Helen, PA, see 4402

Davis Scholarship Fund, Dorothy, PA, 1061

Davis Scholarship Trust No. 3, Helen S., WA, 1062

Davis Trust Fund, Margaret L., WI, 1063

Davis Trust, Jean M., MI, 1064

Davis, M.D. Education & Research Foundation, James E., IL, 5720

Davis-Roberts Scholarship Fund, Inc., WY, 1065

DaVita Children's Foundation, WA, 1066

Dawson Nursing Scholarship Fund, Blanche L., IL, 1067

Dawson Scholarship Trust, Muriel R., IL, 1068

Day Trust, Carl and Virginia, The, MS, 1069

Daystar Northwest, WA, 4698

Dayton Foundation, The, OH, 1070, 5283, 5721

Dayton Masonic Foundation, OH, 1071

de Kay Foundation, The, NY, 4699

Dead Sea Scrolls Foundation, IN, 5722

Deafness Research Foundation, DC, 5723

Deane Scholarship Fund, Faye H., MA, 1072

Dearborn Community Foundation, IN, 1073

Dearborn County Community Foundation, IN, see 1073

Dearing Educational Trust Fund, W. G., VA, 1074

Deaver Foundation, Marion Park Deaver and Harry Gilbert, FL, 5724

DeBartolo Memorial Scholarship Foundation, Edward J., The, OH, 1075

Debenham-Alaska Scholarships, Inc., AK, 1076

Decatur County Community Foundation, Inc., IN, 1077

DeCrane Family Foundation, Colleen, OH, 4700

Dedalus Foundation, Inc., NY, 5284

Deem Scholarship Fund, C. H., WI, 1078

Deering Foundation, Inc., CT, 1079

Deering Foundation, Mark, TX, 1080

Deffenbaugh Foundation Trust, Roy A., IL, A

DeHaan Family Foundation, Christel, IN, 5725

DeKalb County Community Foundation, IL, 1081

DeKalb County Producers' Supply and Farm Bureau Scholarship Trust Fund, IL, 1082

Delaware Center for the Contemporary Arts, Inc., DE, 5285

Delaware Community Foundation, DE, 1083

Delaware County Community Foundation, Greater, IA, 1084

Delaware Foundation for Retarded Children, Inc., DE, 4701

Delaware State Golf Association Scholarship Fund, Inc., DE, 1085

Delaware Valley Senior Citizens Scholarship Trust, PA, 1086

Dellinger Scholarship Fund, Ray, Inc., GA, 1087

Delmas Foundation, Gladys Krieble, The, NY, 5726

Deloitte & Touche Foundation, CT, see 5727

Deloitte Foundation, CT, 5727

DeLong Foundation, James E., Inc., WI, 1088

Delta Delta Delta Foundation, TX, 1089

Delta Phi Educational Fund, Inc., NY, see 3851

Delta Phi Epsilon Educational Foundation, MO, 1090

Delta Sigma Delta Educational Foundation, FL, 1091

Demarest Trust, Elizabeth B., PA, 1092

Demolay Foundation, Inc., MO, 1093

Denfeld Foundation, Greater, Inc., MN, 1094

Densch Charities, Wayne M., Inc., FL, 4702

Denton Scholarship Trust, Robert E. & Olive L., IA, 1095

Department of Neurological Surgery Research Foundation, OH, A

Des Moines Golf and Country Club Educational Foundation, IA, 1096

Des Moines I Have a Dream Foundation, IA, A

Descendants of the Signers of the Declaration of Independence, VA, 1097

DeSeranno Educational Foundation, Inc., MI, see 833

Deseret Foundation, The, UT, 5728

Desert Valley Charitable Foundation, CA, see 3349

DeSio Foundation, Anthony W. DeSio & Delores J., NV, 1098

deStwolinski Family Foundation, NE, 1099

Detroit Diesel Scholarship Foundation, Inc., MI, 1100

Detroit Golf Club Caddie Scholarship Foundation, MI, 5729
Dettman Foundation, Leroy E., Inc., FL, 1101
Deupree Foundation, Daniel B., TX, 1102
DeVoe Buick Cadillac Scholarship Trust, Dick, FL, 1103
Dewuhs-Keckritz Educational Trust, OR, 1104
DeYoung Educational Foundation, Murray, Inc., FL, 1105
Dial Educational Trust, Albert, SC, 1106
Dialysis Research Foundation, UT, 1107, 5730
Dibner Institute, Inc., MA, 5731
Dickens Family Foundation, The, GA, 1108
Dickinson Area Community Foundation, MI, 1109
Dickinson County Area Community Foundation, MI, see 1109
Dickinson Trust, Dorothy, NY, 4703
Dickson Trust for Dickson Prizes, Joseph Z. & Agnes F., PA, 5732
Diederich Educational Trust Fund, John T. and Ada, OH, 1110
Diehl Trust, Harlan O., IA, 1111
Diema's Dream Foundation, VA, 4704
Dietrich Trust, Emma Fanny, NC, 1112
Dieu Donne Papermill, NY, 5286
Diffenbaugh Trust for Baker University, H. J., TX, 1113
Diffenbaugh Trust for Kansas University, H. J., TX, 1114
Diffenbaugh Trust for University of Illinois, H. J., TX, 1115
DiGregorio Scholarship Fund, Brian A., MA, A
Dilcher Student Loan Fund, Harry J. and Mollie S., NC, 1116
DiMauro Foundation, Orazio, Inc., CT, A
Dinger Scholarship Fund, Max E. & Maude M., OH, 1117
Dingwall Foundation, William Orr, Inc., DC, 1118
Dinwiddie Scholarship Trust, CA, see 1119
Dinwiddie Scholarship Trust, Nancy, CA, 1119
Disabled American Veterans Charities of Los Angeles, CA, 4705
Disney Company Foundation, Walt, The, CA, 1120
Disney Foundation, CA, see 1120
Distilled Spirits Wholesalers of Florida Education Foundation, Inc., FL, 1121
District Lodge No. 3, Sons of Norway Charitable Trust, VA, see 4706
District Lodge No. 3, Sons of Norway Foundation, VA, 4706
District of Columbia Library Association, DC, 1122
District One Foundation for Quality Education, IL, 1123
Diverseworks, Inc., TX, 5287
Dixie Foundation, Inc., NC, 1124
Dixie Group Foundation, Inc., The, TN, 1125, 4707
Dixie Yarns Foundation, Inc., TN, see 1125
Dixie Yarns Foundation, Inc., TN, see 4707
Dixon Educational Foundation, George & Addie, CA, 1126
Dixon Foundation, The, AL, 5733
Do While Studio, MA, 5288
Dobson Trust, Nellie, OK, A
Doctors Hospital of Lakewood Foundation, CA, see 2314
Dodd Educational Trust, W. J. and Amy C., IL, 1127
Dodd Foundation, MO, 1128
Dodd Foundation, Norris E., NV, 1129
Dodd Scholarship Trust, Verna Lilly, WI, 1130
Dodge City Business & Professional Women's Club-Elma Schmidt Fund, KS, 1131
Dodge Foundation, Geraldine R., Inc., NJ, 5734, A
Dodge Scholarship Trust for Girls, NH, 1132
Dodge Scholarship Trust, Adelaide, NH, see 1132
Doe Charitable Trust, Hans & Margaret, CA, 1133
Doerflinger Foundation, Thomas, Inc., The, NJ, A
Doerhoff Scholarship Trust, Ray and Rosetta, MO, 1134
Dog Writers Educational Trust, FL, 1135
Doherty Scholarship Fund, James E., MN, 1136
Dolan & Gladys Saulsbury Foundation, Sabina, Inc., CT, 1137
Dole Scholarship Trust, Stephen Dexter and Emily Jane Tipton, IL, 1138
Dolechek Medical Scholarship Trust Fund, Christine A., The, KS, 1139
Dollywood Foundation, The, TN, 1140

Donaghey Foundation, Henry & Elizabeth, TX, 1141
Donaghue Medical Research Foundation, Patrick and Catherine Weldon, The, CT, 5735
Donnell Trust, Kenneth S., MA, 1142
Donovan Scholarship Fund, Herbert A. "Mike", MD, 1143
Doody Foundation, Donald J., The, IL, 1144
Doolin Foundation, Clifford, Inc., MO, 1145
Doolittle Private Foundation, Blanche, MN, 1146
Dora Foundation, James and Shirley, The, IN, 1147
Dorfman Foundation for Children, Emily, IL, 5736
Dornhecker Foundation, Marie A., The, VA, 1148
Dorot Foundation, RI, 1149
Dotson, M.D. Fund, John, PA, 1150
Dougherty Foundation, Inc., AZ, 1151
Douroucouli Foundation, The, CA, A
Dove Givings Foundation, NY, 4708
Doverspike Charitable Foundation, J. & R., PA, 1152
Dow Creativity Foundation, Alden B. and Vada B., MI, 5737
Dow Home, Baron & Emilie, Inc., SD, 4709
Dow Jones Newspaper Fund, Inc., NJ, 1153, 5738
Downing Educational Trust, Adrian & Marie, AL, 1154
Doyle Foundation, Frank M., Inc., The, NV, 1155
Doyle Memorial Fund, Dr. Edgar Clay Doyle and Mary Cherry, NC, see 1156
Doyle Memorial Fund, Mary, NC, 1156
Doyon Foundation, The, AK, 1157
Drag Racing Association of Women, FL, 4710
Drake Scholarship Trust, Lily E., OH, 5739
Dramatists Guild Fund, Inc., NY, 5289
DRAW, FL, see 4710
Dreams Scholarship Foundation, TX, 1158
Dreher Memorial Scholarship Fund, Grace D., NC, 1159
Dreman Foundation, David, NJ, see 1160
Dreman Foundation, Inc., The, NJ, 1160
Dressage Foundation, Inc., The, NE, 1161
Dreyfus Foundation, Camille and Henry, Inc., The, NY, 5740
Driscoll, Jr. Scholarship Trust, John Lynn, WA, 1162
Drowns Educational Foundation, Bruce V., MO, 1163
Druckenmiller Foundation, NY, 1164
Drummond Foundation, Alfred A. & Tia Juana, WI, 1165
DSGA Junior Golf Scholarship Fund, Inc., DE, see 1085
Du Bois Charitable Trust, Cora, MA, 1166
Dubbs Scholarship Fund, Sallie, MA, A
Duclos Foundation, Leva & Frank, KS, 4711
Dudley Foundation, The, NC, 1167
Dudley Fund, Grace Norton, NY, 1168
Dudley-Vehmeyer-Brown Memorial Foundation, Inc., CA, 1169
Duer Foundation, D. C., KS, 1170
Duffy Foundation, George, NY, 1171
Dugan Foundation, Martin W., MA, 1172
Dugan Trust, Martin W., MA, see 1172
Duggan Scholarship Trust, Cornelius, IA, 1173
Duke Charitable Foundation, Doris, NY, 5741
Duke Energy Foundation, NC, 5742
Duke Power Company Foundation, NC, see 5742
Duke Scholarship Fund, Margaret S., Inc., GA, 1174
Dulany Memorial, John H., Inc., MD, 1175
Duluth-Superior Area Community Foundation, MN, 1176
Dumesnil Trust, Evangeline L., OH, 1177
Dunbar Scholarship Trust A, Howard W., FL, 1178
Duncan Foundation, Harry F., Inc., MD, 1179
Duncan Trust, Dewey C., NC, 1180
Dungannon Foundation, Inc., NY, 5290
Dunham Educational Trust, Arlenn and Arthur H., MA, 1181
Dunkin' Donuts Charitable Trust, MA, 1182
Dunlap Foundation, Frank R. "Bo", Inc., OH, 1183
Dunlap, Jr. Memorial Trust, David R., AL, 1184
Dunlop Scholarship Trust, Mary Frances, MO, 1185
Dunn Memorial Fund Trust, Dr. Ferrell W., IN, 1186
Dunn Scholarship Fund, Margaret, WA, 1187
Dunnaway Foundation, Danny M., MS, 5743
Dunton Scholarship Fund, Caroline F., OH, 1188
Dupee Foundation, Mabel E., Inc., WI, 1189
Duplessis Scholarship Fund, ME, 5744
duPont Foundation, Alfred I., Inc., FL, 4712
Dupre Permanent Educational Scholarship Fund Trust, Naasson K. & Florrie S., The, TX, 1190

Duran Foundation, CA, 1191
Durfee Foundation, The, CA, 5291, 5745
Durfee Scholarship Fund, Hildegard, VT, 1192
Dutchess County Arts Council, Inc., NY, 5292
Dutka Arts Foundation, Joyce, Inc., NY, 5293
Dutko Memorial Foundation, Dan, The, DC, 1193
Duvall Family Foundation, AL, 1194
DuVall Scholarship Fund, Fred H., NC, 1195
Duxbury Yacht Club Charitable Foundation, MA, 1196
Dye Foundation, James W. & Betty, Inc., IN, 1197
Dyer Trust, J. Franklin, MA, 1198
Dyett Foundation, Herbert T., Inc., NY, 1199
Dystonia Medical Research Foundation, IL, 5746

E & WG Foundation, NY, 5747
E.D. Foundation, NY, A
EAA Aviation Foundation, Inc., WI, 1200
Eagle Foundation, Inc., The, CT, 1201
Eagle Scholarship Trust, Edna & Harvey, OH, 1202
Eagles Memorial Foundation, Inc., FL, 1203, 4713
Eagleton War Memorial Scholarship Fund, Inc., NY, 1204
Earhart Foundation, MI, 5748
Earl & Frances Smith Scholarship Fund, Harrison, NY, 1205
Earthwatch Expeditions, Inc., MA, see 5749
Earthwatch Institute, MA, 5749
East Lake Community Foundation, Inc., GA, see 1206
East Lake Foundation, Inc., GA, 1206
East Longmeadow Rotary Memorial Scholarship Foundation, MA, 1207
Eastcliff Foundation, CA, 1208
Eastern Choral Society, DC, 1209
Eastern Frontier Educational Foundation, Inc., NY, 5294
Eastern Scientific & Education Foundation, NC, 5750
Eastern Star Charity Foundation of New Jersey, NJ, 1210, 4714
Eastern West Virginia Community Foundation, WV, 4715
Easthampton Home for Aged Women, Inc., MA, see 5168
Eastman Memorial Scholarship Fund, Arthur G., VT, 1211
Eaton & Reed Scholarship Fund Trust, RI, 1212
Eaton Fund, Inc., The, MD, 4716
Eaton Memorial Fund, Georgiana Goddard, MA, 4717
Eaton Society, Annie, Inc., The, NY, 4718
Ebell of Los Angeles Scholarship Endowment Fund, CA, 1213
Eberhardt I for Scholarship Fund, PA, A
Eberhardt Trust, Elsie C., IL, 1214
Ebert Memorial Fund, Hazel C., MO, 1215
Echoing Green Foundation, NY, see 5751
Echoing Green, NY, 5751
ECI Scholarship Foundation, TX, see 1228
Eckert Memorial Fund, Dr. Robert R., NY, 1216
Eckmann Foundation, CA, see 1422
Ecolab Foundation, MN, 5752
Ecotrust Foundation, MN, 5753
Eddy Family Memorial Fund, C. K., MI, 1217
Eddy Foundation Charitable Foundation, MN, see 1218
Eddy Foundation, MN, 1218
Eder Foundation, Sidney and Arthur, Inc., The, CT, 1219
Edgar Charitable Foundation, William, MO, 1220
Edgar County Bank & Trust Foundation, IL, 1221
Edge Scholarship Foundation, Oscar N., The, AL, A
Edgerton Area Foundation, OH, 1222
Edmonds Scholarship Trust, George Walter & Violet C., NC, 1223
Edmondson-Telford Foundation, GA, 4719
Edmunds Scholarship Trust, V. Faith, VT, 1224
Edmunds Testamentary Trust, T. Murrell, WI, 1225
Educare Scholarship Fund, AZ, 1226
Education Foundation of Palm Beach County, The, FL, 5754
Educational Advancement Foundation, TX, 1227
Educational Communications Scholarship Foundation, TX, 1228
Educational Foundation of Alpha Gamma Rho, MO, 1229
Educational Foundation of the Missouri Society of Certified Public Accountants, Inc., MO, 1230

Educational Foundation, Inc. at Ozaukee Bank, The, WI, 1231

Educational Fund for Children of Phillips Petroleum Company Employees, OK, see 938

Educational Fund of the Rochester New York Branch of the American Association of University Women, NY, 1232

Educational Loan Foundation of Spokane, Inc., WA, 1233

Educational Theatre Association, OH, 1234, 5755

EducationQuest Foundation, NE, 1235

EDUCAUSE, CO, 5756

Edwards Foundation, Glade M., Inc., WY, 1236

Edwards Foundation, Winifred, Ruth, Frances & Dorothy, Inc., The, NE, 1237

Edwards Scholarship Fund, MA, 1238

Edwards Scholarship Trust, Marguerite R., TX, 1239

EFAF, MO, see 4613

Eggleston Educational Trust, KS, 1240

Ehlers Foundation, V. M., TX, 1241

Ehlers Memorial Fund, V. M., Inc., TX, see 1241

Ehrler Foundation, Dr. Glenn G., IL, 5757

EIA Research and Education Foundation, VA, see 5766

Eisenhauer Scholarship Fund, PA, 1242

Eisenhauer, et al. Scholarship Fund, John Henry & Clarissa A., PA, see 1242

Ekstrand Educational Trust, Marie and Margaret, IL, 1243

El Monte-South El Monte Emergency Resources Association, CA, 4720

El Paso Community Foundation, TX, 1244

El Paso County Salute to Education, TX, 1245

El Puente Charitable Foundation, CA, 4721

El-Mahdawy Foundation, Ahmed M. & Fawzia A., Inc., FL, 4722

Elam Scholarship Trust Fund, E. O., TX, 1246

Elbert Trust, Louis J., IA, 1247

Elburn Scholarship Fund, IL, 1248

Elderhostel, Inc., MA, 4723

Elec Material Hirtzel Memorial Foundation, PA, see 1866

Elenberg Foundation, Charles and Anna, Inc., NY, 1249

Eleutherian Mills-Hagley Foundation, Inc., DE, 5758

Elfarouq Foundation, TX, 4724

Elfers Scholarship Trust No. 2, Jessie, WI, 1250

Elizabeth City Foundation, NC, 1251

Elizabeth Foundation for the Arts, The, NY, 5295

Elizondo Scholarship Trust, Maria, CO, 1252

Elk County Community Foundation, PA, 1253

Elk Grove Community Foundation, CA, 1254

Elkhart County Community Foundation, Inc., IN, 1255

Elks National Foundation, IL, 1256

Ella Mount Burr Trust, NC, 1257

Elliott Educational Foundation, Mabel M., CA, 1258

Elliott Trust Fund, Mary E., NH, 4725

Elliott-Hemingford Scholarship Foundation, NE, 1259

Ellis Foundation, Danny and Willa, KS, 1260

Ellis Grant and Scholarship Fund, Charles E., PA, 1261

Ellis Gratuity Fund, Rudolph, NC, 4726

Ellis Scholarship Fund, John G., KS, 1262

Ellis Trust, Jeffrey Wallace, NE, 1263

Ellison Medical Foundation, The, MD, 5759

Ellison Scholarship Fund, Harold, IN, 1264

Ellsworth Scholarship Fund, Henry E., RI, 1265

Elm Trust, Henry, MT, 1266

Elmer Scholarship Fund, WI, A

Elvins Scholarship Trust, Catherine Marie Elvins and Naomi Libby, WA, 1267

Ely-Winton Hospital Association Scholarship Fund Trust, MN, 1268

Emergency Aid of Pennsylvania Foundation, Inc., The, PA, 1269

Emergency Fund for the Needy People, IL, see 4727

Emergency Fund, IL, 4727

Emerson Charitable Trust, MO, 1270

Emerson Foundation, Harland and Genevieve, NE, 1271

Emerson Trust, Thomas H., CA, 5760

Emmons County Sports Alumni, Inc., ND, 1272, 4728

Empty Stocking Fund, GA, 4729

Endowment for Biblical Research, Boston, MA, 5761

Endowment of the U.S. Institute of Peace, DC, 1273, 5762

Energy Assistance Foundation, IL, 4730

Engel Nurse Scholarship Fund, Mildred, OH, 1274

Engine Rebuilders Educational Foundation, The, IL, 1275

England Scholarship Fund, Frank F., VT, 1276

England Trust, Elizabeth R., PA, 1277

Englewood BPO Elks Scholarship Trust, FL, 1278

Englewood Youth Foundation, Inc., FL, 1279

English Charitable Trust, Fenton E., WI, 1280

English Foundation, The, VA, 1281

English Foundation-Trust, The, VA, see 1281

English Scholarship Foundation, W. C., The, VA, 1282

ENMR Education Foundation, NM, 1283

ENMR Telephone Education Foundation, NM, see 1283

Ensemble Studio Theatre, Inc., The, NY, 5296

Enterprise Foundation, The, MD, 5763

Entertainment Industry Foundation, The, CA, 5297

Entomological Foundation, MD, 5764

Environmental Leadership Program, Inc., MA, 5765

Environmental Research and Education Foundation, VA, 5766

Envirosafe Charitable Trust, ID, see 1284

Envirosafe Services of Idaho, Inc. Charitable Trust, ID, 1284

Envirosafe Services of Ohio, Inc. Foundation, OH, A

EOG Scholarship Fund, TX, 1285

Epilepsy Foundation of America, MD, 5767

Epler Scholarship Fund, Mabel S., IN, 1286

Eppley Foundation for Research, Inc., The, NY, 5768

Epstein Foundation Trust, Samuel, PA, 1287

Equipment Leasing and Finance Foundation, Inc., VA, 5769

ERI Educational Foundation, PA, 1288

Erickson Charitable Foundation, Arnold & Mildred, Inc., IL, 1289

Erickson Scholarship Educational Fund, Carl J., WA, 1290

Erickson Scholarship Fund, Leroy, OH, 1291

Erie Community Foundation, The, PA, 1292

Erk Charitable Education Trust, Alfred, NY, 1293

Ernst & Young Foundation, NY, 5770

Ernst Charitable Trust, Helen R., ND, 1294

Ernst Memorial Educational Trust Fund, Catherine, MN, 1295

Eshe Fund, The, NY, 5771

Esperantic Studies Foundation, Inc., DC, 5772

Espy Foundation, Dacy, Inc., GA, 1296

Espy Literary Foundation, Willard R., WA, 5298

Essex Classical Institute, VT, 1297

Essex County Bar Foundation, NJ, 1298

Essex Veterans of World War II, MA, 1299

Estonian Relief Committee, Inc., NY, 4731

Estonian-Revelia Academic Fund, Inc., MD, 1300

Ethnic Voice of America, OH, 4732

Ethridge Scholarship Foundation, The, CO, 1301

Etnier Charitable Trust, Oliver, DE, 1302

Euro Brokers Relief Fund, Inc., NY, 4733

Evans Educational Trust, Zelia Stephans, AL, 1303

Evans Scholarship Award Trust, Clyde R., WI, 1304

Evans Teacher's Scholarship Trust, LaVerna, IL, 1305

Evans-Moss Fund, NE, 1306

Evereg-Fenesse Mesrobian-Roupinian Educational Society, Inc., MI, 1307

Everett Improvement Company Scholarship Trust, WA, see 4024

Everett McKinley Dirksen Endowment Fund, IL, 1308, 5773

Evergreen House Foundation, Inc., The, MD, 5299

Everhart Scholarship Fund Trust, Andree T. & Gladys E., OH, 1309

Everly Scholarship Fund, Inc., NJ, 1310

Evers Trust, Paul B., OH, 1311

Evinrude Foundation, Ole, The, WI, see 3030

Evrytanian Association of America, NC, 1312

Ewald Foundation, H. T., MI, 1313

Exacto Foundation, Inc., WI, 1314

Excelsior Scottish Rite Bodies Charity Fund, Inc., NJ, 1315

Exchange Club of Vero Beach Scholarship Foundation Trust, The, FL, 1316

Experimental Sound Studio, IL, 5300

Experimental Television Center, Ltd., NY, 5301

Exploratorium, The, CA, 5302

Eye Research Foundation, The, NY, 5774

Eyebeam Atelier, The, NY, 5303

Ezer M'Zion, Inc., NY, 4734

Fabela Family Foundation, The, IL, 4735

Fabela Foundation, Elssy, The, IL, 4736

Fabri-Kal Foundation, MI, 1317

Fabric Workshop and Museum, The, PA, 5304

Fadel Educational Foundation, Inc., The, GA, 1318

Fahrney Education Foundation, Charles E., IA, 1319

Fahrney Education Foundation, IA, see 1319

Fairbanks-Horix Charitable Trust, OH, 1320

Fairey Educational Fund, Kittie M., NC, 1321

Fairfield - Meeker Charitable Trust, Freeman E., CO, 1322

Fairfield County Community Foundation, Inc., CT, 4737

Fairfield County Foundation, OH, 1323

Fairmount Tire Charitable Foundation, Inc., CA, 1324

Fales Educational Trust, Herbert, RI, 1325

Fallon Foundation, MA, 1326

Family Outreach Foundation, The, NJ, 4738

FAMSI, FL, see 5802

Fannie Mae Foundation, DC, 5775

Fanning Foundation, Charlotte, Inc., TN, 1327

Fanning Orphan School, TN, see 1327

Fansler Foundation, Kate, Inc., The, NY, 1328

Fansteel Scholarship Foundation, IL, 1329

Fant Foundation, The, TX, 4739

Faranna Scholarship Trust, Charles C., OK, 1330

Farber Foundation, Anne & Jason, Inc., CA, 5776

Farber Foundation, Inc., PA, 1331

Farm Bureau-Arkansas Scholarship Foundation, Inc., AR, see 185

Farm Income Improvement Foundation, Inc., KY, 4740

Farmen Trust/ St. Marks Church, Elizabeth, NY, 1332

Farmer Relief Fund, E. D., TX, 4741

Farmer Trust, Edwin S., MA, 4742

Farmers' Electric Education Foundation, NM, 1333

Farnam Trust, Henry, MA, 4743

Farrell Charitable Trust, Juli Ann, IA, 1334

Farrington Trust, Eleanor E., MA, 1335

Farrow Trust, Ruth T., NC, 1336

Fary Memorial Scholarship Fund, VA, 1337

Fashion Group Foundation of Chicago, Inc., The, IL, 5777

Fasken Foundation, The, TX, 1338

Fassino Foundation, Inc., The, MA, 1339

Fast Scholarship Foundation, Ethel & Emery, Inc., MD, 1340

Father Daily Scholarship Foundation, IA, 1341

Faunce Trust, Harriet M., MA, 1342

Fava Scholarship Foundation, NC, 1343

Fava Scholarship Foundation, Philip V. Fava and Nancy Owen D., NC, see 1343

Fayette County Foundation, IN, 1344

FCCF, CT, see 4737

Fed-Mart Foundation, CA, see 1345

Federal Employees Scholarship Foundation, Inc., CA, 1345

Federated Church of Columbus Foundation, Inc., The, NE, 1346

Federman Scholarship Fund, NY, 1347

FEF, IL, see 1434

Feiga-Olch Trust, MA, 1348

Feild Co-Operative Association, Inc., MS, 1349

Fellman Charitable Foundation Trust, Bruce M., NE, 1350

Fellows Memorial Fund, J. Hugh and Earle W., FL, 1351

Female Association of Philadelphia, The, PA, 4744

Feng Li Li Foundation, IL, 4745

Fenner Educational Trust, Gertrude A., WI, 1352

Feoppel Educational Loan Trust, Charles H., WV, 1353

Feraldo Memorial Fund, William Pablo, MO, 1354

Ferebee Endowment, Percy B., NC, 1355

Ferguson Foundation, Arch L., The, TX, 4746

Fermi Educational Fund of Yonkers, Enrico, Inc., NY, 1356

Fernstrum Scholarship Foundation Trust, Robert W. & Caroline A., WI, 1357

Ferraro Foundation for Science and the Disabled, Inc., The, NJ, 1358, 5778

Ferre Foundation, Luis A., Inc., The, PR, 1359

Ferree Educational & Welfare Fund, NC, 1360

Ferris Foundation, Clifford G. and Grace A., The, WI, 1361
FesteCapital Foundation, The, TX, 4747
Fetzer Foundation, John E., Inc., MI, see 5779
Fetzer Institute, John E., Inc., MI, 5779
Fieldcrest Cannon Foundation, NC, 1362
Fieldcrest Foundation, NC, see 1362
Fields Trust, Laura, OK, 1363
FiftyCrows Foundation, CA, 5305
Fight for Sight, Inc., NY, 5780
Files Foundation, TX, 1364
Film Arts Foundation, CA, 5306
Findlay Hancock County Community Foundation, OH, 1365
Findlay-Conso Education Foundation, The, FL, 1366
Fine Arts Work Center in Provincetown, Inc., MA, 5307
Fingersh Charitable Trust Fund, Morris, MO, see 1367
Fingersh Scholarship Fund, Morris, MO, 1367
Finis Heidel Trust, NM, 1368
Finkbeiner Memorial Fund for Benton High School Graduates, Henry J. & Helen, AR, 1369
Finks Foundation, AZ, A
Finlay Foundation, Curtis, Inc., AL, 1370
Finley Foundation, Rose McFarland, The, FL, 1371
Finnell Trust, Dred and Lula, The, MO, 1372
Firestone Charitable Trust, J. B., OH, 1373
First Brokers Good Samaritan Fund, NJ, 4748
First Command Educational Foundation, TX, 1374
First Data Western Union Foundation, CO, 1375
First Gaston Foundation, Inc., NC, 1376
First Nations Development Institute, CO, 5308
First People's Fund, SD, 5309
Fischer Foundation, Blanche, OR, 4749
Fischer Trust, Karl, PA, 1377
Fishburn Foundation, Velma Klamm & Ruth, OK, 1378
Fishel Scholarship Trust, Myron, The, OH, 1379
Fisher and Fuel Society of Beverly, MA, 4750
Fisher Broadcasting Minority Scholarship Fund, WA, 1380
Fisher Foundation, Steven and Lynn, The, AZ, 1381
Fisher House Foundation, Inc., MD, 1382
Fitch Charitable Foundation, James Marston, NY, 5781
Fitch Memorial Scholarship Fund, T. S., PA, 1383
Fitzgerald Scholarship Trust, Father James M., OH, 1384
Fitzpatrick Memorial Scholarship Fund, Rev. William J., PA, 1385
Fix Scholarship Fund, Alois A. and Nina M., WI, 1386
Flamingo Foundation, UT, A
Flathead Educational Foundation, MT, 1387
Flatirons Foundation, The, CO, 1388
Fleetwood Memorial Foundation, Inc., TX, 4751
Flegal Educational Trust, Clark, PA, 1389
Fleisher Trust No. 2, Foreman, PA, see 1390
Fleisher Trust, Foreman, PA, 1390
Fleishhacker Foundation, CA, 5310
Fleming Insurance Trust, Albert W., MA, 1391
Fleming Scholarship Trust for Holy Cross College, Mary E. Fleming & John J., MA, 1392
Fleshman Memorial Scholarship Fund, WI, 1393
Flinn Foundation, The, AZ, 1394, 5782
Flinn Trust, Peter G., WI, A
Flint Scholarship Endowment Fund, Ebell of Los Angeles/Charles N., The, CA, see 1395
Flint Scholarship Endowment Fund, Mr. & Mrs. Charles N., CA, 1395
Flintridge Foundation, CA, 5311
Floor Covering Industry Foundation, CA, 4752
Floriculture Industry Research and Scholarship Trust, MI, 1396
Florida Air Academy Scholarship Fund, Inc., FL, 1397
Florida Alliance for Arts Education, Inc., FL, 1398
Florida Bar Foundation, The, FL, 1399
Florida Endowment Foundation for Vocational Rehabilitation, FL, 4753
Florida Humanities Council, The, FL, A
Florida Land Surveyors Scholarship Foundation, Inc., FL, 1400
Flying Horse Foundation, Inc., NJ, 1401
Flynn Scholarship Fund, Joseph G. & Clara T., CT, see 1403
Flynn Scholarship Fund, Margaret and Thomas, NJ, 1402

Flynn Scholarship Trust, Joseph G. & Clara T., CT, 1403
FMI Scholarship Foundation, Inc., NJ, 1404
Foley Scholarship Foundation, Harry, MN, 1405
Follett Educational Foundation, IL, 1406
Folsom Foundation, Maud Glover, Inc., CT, 1407
Fond Rev. Edmond Gelinas, Inc., NH, 1408
Food Industry Scholarship Fund of New Hampshire, NH, see 2925
For a New Social Science, FL, A
Forbes Foundation, Stuart and Margaret L., Inc., NC, 1409
Forbes Kirkside Foundation, Inc., The, MA, 4754
Forbes Trust f/b/o Westborough High School, Fannie, RI, 1410
Forbes Trust, Fannie E., RI, see 1410
Ford Family Foundation, The, OR, 1411
Ford Foundation, Gerald R., MI, 5783
Ford Foundation, The, NY, 5784
Ford Fund, S. N. Ford and Ada, The, OH, 1412, 4755
Fordham Foundation, Thomas B., DC, 5785
Fore-Christ, Inc., NC, 4756
Forecast Public Artworks, MN, 5312
Foreman U.S. Scholarship Trust, Myron Jacob, FL, 5786
Formosa Plastics Corporation, Texas—Calhoun High School Scholarship Foundation, Inc., TX, 1413
Forrai Foundation, Olga, Inc., NY, 5313
Forrest Foundation, Thomas W., Inc., FL, A
Forsyth Educational Fund, RI, 1414
Forsyth Educational Trust Fund, Fred, RI, see 1414
Fort Atkinson Community Foundation, WI, 1415
Fort Pierce Memorial Hospital Scholarship Foundation, Inc., FL, see 2239
Fort Wayne Community Foundation, IN, see 881
Fort Worth Police Officers' Award Foundation, TX, 5787
Fortin Memorial Foundation, Ernest, Inc., MA, 1416
Fortis Foundation, NY, see 220
Forum Communications Foundation, ND, 1417
Foss Memorial Employees Trust, Donald J., OH, 4757
Foss Memorial Trust, Ralph H., OR, 1418
Foster Foundation, MI, 1419
Foster Welfare Foundation, MI, see 1419
Foulger Foundation, Sid & Mary, Inc., MD, 1420
Foundation Chapter of Theta Chi Fraternity, Inc., The, IN, 1421
Foundation Fighting Blindness, Inc., MD, 5788
Foundation for a Christian Civilization, Inc., PA, 5789
Foundation for AIDS Research, Inc., The, NY, 5790
Foundation for Anesthesia Education and Research, MN, 5791
Foundation for Basic Cutaneous Research, The, PA, 5792
Foundation for Child Development, NY, 5793
Foundation for Chiropractic Education & Research, Inc., IA, 5794
Foundation for College Christian Leaders, The, CA, 1422
Foundation for Contemporary Arts, NY, 5314
Foundation for Deep Ecology, CA, 5795
Foundation for Digestive Health and Nutrition, MD, 5796
Foundation for Educational Advancement, The, CO, see 1757
Foundation for Educational Excellence, CO, 1423
Foundation for Educational Funding, Inc., NE, see 1235
Foundation for Enhancing Communities, The, PA, 1424
Foundation for Eye Research, CA, 5797
Foundation for Geriatric Education, The, TN, 1425
Foundation for Hand Research and Education, IN, 5798
Foundation for Hellenic Culture, Inc., The, NY, 1426
Foundation for Improvement of Justice, Inc., GA, 5799
Foundation for International Medical Education, CA, A
Foundation for Physical Therapy Research, The, VA, see 5800
Foundation for Physical Therapy, Inc., The, VA, 5800
Foundation for Rural Education & Development, Inc., DC, 1427
Foundation for Saline Area Schools, MI, 5801
Foundation for Seacoast Health, NH, 1428
Foundation for Surgical Hand Research, IN, see 5798
Foundation for the Advancement of Mesoamerican Studies, Inc., FL, 5802
Foundation for the Art Renewal Center, Inc., NJ, 5315

Foundation for the Carolinas, NC, 1429, 4758
Foundation for the Future, WA, 5803
Foundation for the Jan Mitchell Prize, Inc., The, NY, 5316
Foundation for the National Capital Region, The, DC, see 869
Foundation for United Methodists, Inc., KY, 1430
Foundation for Visions, The, OK, 4759
Foundation Francisco Marroquin, FL, 5804
Foundation of Greater Greensboro, Inc., The, NC, see 882
Foundation of the Alumnae Association of Mount Sinai Hospital School of Nursing, Inc., NY, 5805
Foundation of the American College of Allergy, Asthma, and Immunology, IL, 5806
Foundation of the Pierre Fauchard Academy, CA, 1431
Foundation of the Wall & Ceiling Industry, VA, 1432
Foundation, Jones, Inc., KS, see 2126
Foundation, The, CA, 4760
Founders Memorial Fund of the American Sterilizer Company, PA, 1433
Foundry Educational Foundation, The, IL, 1434
Four County Community Foundation, MI, 1435
Four County Foundation, MI, see 1435
Fouts Scholarship Fund, Sadie and Hobert, NC, 1436
Fowler Charitable Trust, Blanche N., AL, 1437
Fox & Julian Karger Scholarship Fund, Louis B., RI, 1438
Fox & Julian Karger Trust, Louis B., RI, see 1438
Fox Foundation for Parkinson's Research, Michael J., NY, 5807
Fox Foundation, Jacob L. & Lewis, CT, 1439
Fox Foundation, William and Eva, The, NY, 5317
Fraites Foundation, Evelyn, Inc., NY, 1440
Frameline, CA, 5318
Francies Scholarship Fund, WI, 1441
Franciscan Foundation for the Holy Land, DC, 1442
Francisco Educational Trust, Elenore, KY, 1443
Franconia Sculpture Park, MN, 5319
Frank Family Memorial Scholarship, AZ, 1444
Frank Foundation, Andrea, Inc., The, NY, 5320
Frank Scholarship Fund, Jacob, Lillian & Nathan M., IN, 1445
Frank Scholarship Fund, Simon, AZ, see 1444
Franklin County Community Foundation, Inc., IN, 1446
Franklin Electric—Edward J. Schaefer and T. W. Kehoe Charitable and Educational Foundation, Inc., The, IN, 1447
Franklin Foundation, Anna Collins, OK, 1448
Franklin Furnace Archive, Inc., NY, 5321
Franklin Mutual Insurance Scholarship Foundation, Inc., NJ, see 1404
Franklin Park Rotary Club Foundation, IL, 1449
Franks Foundation Fund, OR, 1451
Franks Foundation, MS, 1450
Fraser Area Educational Foundation, MI, 1452
Fraser Fund, Hugh A., OH, 4761
Frasier Charitable Foundation, William G. & Margaret B., NC, 1453
Frasier Foundation, Julia Fredin, OK, A
Frautschy Scholarship Trust Fund, John Cowles, IL, 1454
Fraxa Research Foundation, Inc., MA, 5808
Fredenburgh Scholarship Fund, Harry S., NY, 1455
Frederick Trust Fund, Lena P., OH, 4762
Freedom Alliance, VA, 1456
Freedom Forge Corporation Foundation, PA, 1457
Freedom Forum, Inc., The, VA, 1458, 5809
Freels Scholarship Awards Trust, J. C., TN, 1459
Freer Memorial Scholarship Trust, Isabel, OH, 1460
Frees Educational Fund, Charles, MO, 1461
Frees Teaching Scholarship Trust, Irene, IN, 1462
Fremont Area Community Foundation, MI, 1463
Fremont Area Community Foundation, NE, 1464
Fremont Area Foundation, The, MI, see 1463
French Benevolent Society of Philadelphia, The, PA, 1465, 4763
French Charitable Foundation, Ed, Inc., MO, 1466
French Family Educational Foundation, R. E., KS, 1467
French Scholarship Foundation, Blanche E., KS, 1468
French Trust f/b/o Susan E. French Scholarship, Henry W., MA, 1469
French-American Foundation, NY, 5322

Gordy Family Educational Trust Fund, George E., DE, 1599

Gore Family Memorial Foundation, FL, 1600, 4791

Gorham Memorial Fund, Charles N., WI, 4792

Gorman Foundation, MO, 1601

Goslee Student Loan Fund, Alva O., Adie E. & Mary J., NE, 1602

Goss Educational Testamentary Trust, Beatrice I., MI, 1603

Gossett Foundation, Earl J., IL, 1604

Gottlieb Foundation, Adolph and Esther, Inc., NY, 5334

Gould Inc. Foundation, OH, 1605

Gould Scholarship Fund, Norman J. and Anna B., NY, see 1606

Gould Scholarship Fund, Norman J. and Anna B., RI, 1607

Gould Scholarship Fund, NY, 1606

Gourley Scholarship Foundation, Mary I., The, TX, 1608

Governor's Funding, Inc., LA, 5831

Graber Irrevocable Scholarship Trust, John N., WI, 1609

Grace Foundation, CA, 1610

Graco Foundation, The, MN, A

Graff Educational Foundation, Inc., TX, 1611

Graham & Clemma B. Fancher Scholarship Fund, Florence B., CA, 1612

Graham Foundation for Advanced Studies in the Fine Arts, IL, 5335

Graham Foundation, Inc., The, CT, 1613

Graham Scholarship Fund, Dorothy D., SD, 1614

Gramberg-Millner Scholarship Fund, SD, 1615

GRAMMY Foundation, The, CA, 1616

Grand Haven Area Community Foundation, Inc., MI, 1617

Grand Island Community Foundation, Inc., NE, 1618

Grand Marnier Foundation, The, NY, 1619

Grand Rapids Area Community Foundation, MN, 1620, 4793

Grand Rapids Community Foundation, MI, 1621

Grand Rapids Foundation, The, MI, see 1621

Grand Rapids Home Builders Association Foundation, Greater, MI, see 1905

Grannis-Martin Memorial Foundation, Inc., MN, 1622

Granoff Foundation, Leon L., CA, 1623

Grant Foundation, Tom, KS, 1624

Grant Foundation, William T. & Frances D., MO, 1625

Grant Foundation, William T., NY, 5832

Grass Foundation, The, MA, 5833

Grasso Memorial Scholarship Foundation, Arthur E., The, AZ, 1626

Grattan Weaver Foundation, Margaret, VA, A

Graves Foundation, Nancy, Inc., NY, 5336

Gravity Research Foundation, MA, 5834

Gray Family Scholarship Fund, Sidney H. & Mary L., PA, A

Grays Harbor Community Foundation, WA, 1627

Great Basin Foundation for Biomedical Research, NV, 5835

Great Commission Foundation, Inc., OH, see 4086

Great Commission Foundation, Inc., OH, see 5111

Great Lakes Castings Corporation Foundation, MI, 1628

Greatbatch Foundation, Eleanor and Wilson, NY, see 5747

Grede Foundation, Inc., WI, 1629

Green Bay Community Foundation, Greater, Inc., WI, 1630

Green Charitable Trust, Walter & Frances, SD, 1631

Green Foundation, Allen P. & Josephine B., MO, 1632

Green Scholarship Fund, Anna C. & R. J., MD, 1634

Green Scholarship Fund, NJ, 1633

Green Scholarship Trust, George B., NH, 1635

Green Scholarship Trust, Marcella, PA, 1636

Greenlaw Trust, Vera Grace, RI, 1637

GreenPoint Foundation, Inc., The, NY, see 2975

Greenwalt Foundation, Nora, OH, see 4794

Greenwalt Trust, Nora, OH, 4794

Greenwell Scholarship Trust, E. E. & Maud, IN, 1638

Gregg-Graniteville Foundation, Inc., SC, 1639

Griffin Educational Fund, Abbie M., NH, 1640

Griffin Family Foundation, Inc., IN, 1641

Griffin Foundation, Inc., The, CO, 1642

Griffin Foundation, Neil and Elaine, The, TX, 1643

Griffin Hospital Fund, Abbie M., NH, 4795

Griffis Memorial Scholarship in Art and Theatre, The, KS, see 4030

Griffith Foundation, Lewis, Philip and Andrew, The, KS, 1644

Griffith Scholarship Fund, Paul and Mary, IA, 1645

Grim Educational Fund, Clifford D. and Virginia S., NC, 1646

Grim Educational Fund, Clifford D. Grim and Virginia S., NC, see 1646

Grimley Scholarship Trust, NC, 1647

Griswold Trust, Jessie E., IL, 1648

Groeniger College Scholarship Fund, Mike & Bev, CA, 1649

Groff Foundation, Frank and Louise, NJ, 1650

Groff Scholarship Trust, Mary S., NC, 1651

Grogan Educational Fund, Beverly W. Grogan & Mabel Tudor, Inc., The, VA, 1652

Gromack Scholarship Fund, RI, 1653

Gromet Fund for Disadvantaged Children, Janice & Ben, The, HI, 1654

Groot Foundation, Candice B., MN, see 5337

Groot Foundation, Virginia A., MN, 5337

Gross Scholarship Fund, Mary Sullivan, FL, 1655

Grossman Scholarship Foundation, Alexander J., FL, 1656

Grotefend Scholarship Fund, George, CA, 1657

Group Health Community Foundation, WA, 4796

Group Health Foundation, The, WA, see 4796

Grove Scholarship Fund, Thomas O., OH, 1658

Grow Memorial Scholarship Fund, Freeman and Emma, WA, 1659

Growing Family Foundation, Inc., MO, 4797

Grubb Charitable Foundation, Stephen R., Inc., IA, 4798

Grubbs Charitable Trust, Augusta Schultz, VA, 1660

Gruber Foundation, Peter, VI, 5836

Gruenberg Foundation, Inc., The, NJ, 1661

Grupe Foundation, William F., Inc., NJ, 1662

GSBA, WA, see 3644

Guardian Industries Educational Foundation, MI, 1663

Gubitosi Charitable Fund, Paul, Inc., NJ, 1664

Guenther Scholarship Fund, The, NY, 1665

Guertin Trust, Ernest, RI, 1666

Guest Educational Trust, W. H. Guest & E. M., IA, 1667

Guest Educational Trust, William H. Guest & Edith M., IA, see 1667

Guggenheim Foundation, Harry Frank, The, NY, 5837

Guggenheim Memorial Foundation, John Simon, NY, 5338

Guggenheim Scholarship Fund, Simon, NC, 1668

Guiliani Scholarship Foundation, Albert, IL, 1669

Gund Foundation, George, The, OH, 5838

Gund Memorial Fund, William L. & Ethel, IA, A

Gunk Foundation, The, NY, 5339

Guslander Masonic Lodge Scholarship Fund, A. B., CA, 1670

Guthrie Scholarship Fund, Dwight R. & Julia, OH, 1671

Gygi and von Wyss Foundation, MI, 1672

Gygi Foundation, Hans, MI, see 1672

H.E.R.O. Scholarship Fund, CA, 1673

H.O.P.E. Foundation of Darke County, OH, 1674

Haas Foundation, Paul and Mary, TX, 1675

Habig Foundation, The, IN, see 2227

Hach Scientific Foundation, CO, 1676

Hachar Charitable Trust Fund, D. D., TX, 1677

Hacker Memorial Scholarship Fund, Starr, NY, 1678

Haddad Welfare Trust Fund, Edna, MO, 1679

Haeseler Memorial Fund, Louise H., NC, 4799

Hagedorn Trust, Mary Catherine, IA, 1680

Hager Hanger Club Foundation, CA, 1681

Haggerty Memorial Scholarship Fund, Roy, IN, 1682

Hahn Foundation, Robert L., Inc., FL, 1683

Haines Memorial Scholarship Trust, William, NJ, 1684

Hajjar Foundation, Jeanette, The, OH, 1685

Hale Memorial Foundation, Jen, Inc., The, NJ, 1686

Hale Memorial Scholarship Fund, Benton & Louise, WI, 1687

Hall Children's Crisis Foundation, F. V. Hall, Jr. & Marylou, TX, 4800

Hall Educational Trust, Martha K., OR, 1688

Hall Eye Foundation, James H., GA, 5839

Hall Family Foundation, MO, 1689, 4801

Hall Farm Center for Arts and Education, The, VT, 5340

Hall Trust, John T., FL, 1690

Haller Foundation, Albert, WA, 1691

Halsey Educational Trust, James & Lena, IL, 1692

Halton Foundation, OR, 1693

Halverson Scholarship, John Alvin, WI, 1694

Hambay Foundation, James T., PA, 4802

Hamilton Community Foundation, Inc., NE, 1695

Hamilton Foundation, John Clifford, CA, A

Hamilton Foundation, Robert W., NM, 1696

Hamilton Fund, Esther, OH, 1697

Hamilton Memorial Fund, Joann, OR, 1698

Hamilton Scholarship Fund, Marie H., WA, 1699

Hamilton Teachers Scholarship Fund, Helen and June, MO, 1700

Hamm Foundation, Harry O., AR, 1701

Hamman Foundation, George and Mary Josephine, TX, 1702

Hammel-Delangis Scholarship Trust, MI, 1703

Hammers Charitable Trust, C. Arthur and Elizabeth, NC, 1704

Hammill Foundation, Donald D., TX, 5840

Hammond Foundation, W. R., TX, 1705

Hampton Pitching In Foundation, Mike, FL, 1706

Hana Maui Trust, HI, 1707, 4803

Hancock Scholarship Fund, Sumner O., ME, 1708

Hand Foundation, Inc., The, FL, 1709

Hand II Memorial Scholarship Fund, Cecelia Hand Nelson and Morgan, NC, 1710

Handyside Memorial Scholarship Foundation, George T., The, PA, 1711

Hanks Foundation, Marion D. and Maxine C., Inc., The, UT, 4804

Hansen Charitable Foundation, Albert G. and Bernice F., NE, 1712

Hansen Foundation, Carl M., Inc., WA, 1714

Hansen Foundation, Dane G., KS, 1713

Hansen-Furnas Foundation, Inc., IL, 1715

Hanson Foundation, E. L. & Maudean, CO, 1716

Hapke Educational Fund, NE, 1717

Haraldson Foundation, The, TX, 1718

Harber Educational Trust Foundation, Anna M., IN, 1719

Harbert Employees Reaching Out Foundation, AL, 4805

Harbison Scholarship Trust, CA, 1720

Harbor Branch Oceanographic Institution, Inc., FL, A

Harby Scholarship Fund, Ralph Dean & Evelyn Peake, NY, 1721

Harden Foundation, Inc., NY, 1722

Hardin Memorial Scholarship Foundation, IL, 1723

Harding Foundation, The, TX, 1724

Harding Scholarship Fund, George, The, MI, 1725

Hariri Foundation, MD, 1726

Harkham Foundation, CA, A

Harless Foundation, James H., Inc., WV, 4806, A

Harley Nursing Scholarship Fund, Sylvia M., PA, 1727

Harmon Scholarship Foundation, Carlyle and Delta, UT, 1728

Harmon Women's Scholarship Fund, UT, see 1728

Harness Horsemen International Foundation, Inc., NJ, 1729

Harney/P. J. Harney Scholarship Trust, Laura Brooks, RI, 1730

Harper Brush Works Foundation, Inc., IA, 1731

Harper Trust, Carrie M., WI, 1732

Harrell Educational Fund, Clyde W., TN, 1733

Harrelson Memorial Scholarship Trust, Dwight H., NC, 1734

Harries & Eleanor Tippens Scholarship Trust, Adolph & Edith, WV, 1735

Harrington Foundation, The, MN, 1736

Harrington Scholarship Fund, Charles M. & Julia C., OH, 1737

Harris & Alice Faye Scholarship Foundation, Phil, Inc., IN, 1738

Harris Charitable Foundation, George M. Harris & Faye Tabor, WA, 1739

Harris Educational Fund, Ray M., MD, 1740

Harris Educational Trust, Raymond J., PA, 1741

Harris Foundation, H. H., IL, 1742

Harris Foundation, Ltd., The, HI, A

Harris Scholarship Fund, PA, 1743

International Association of Fire Fighters Burn Foundation, DC, 5883

International Burn Foundation of the United States, CO, 5884

International Center for Journalists, Inc., The, DC, 5885

International Council of Airshows Foundation, Inc., VA, 2031

International Council of Shopping Centers Educational Foundation, Inc., NY, 2032

International Documentary Association, CA, A

International Fellowships Fund, NY, 5886

International Gospel Mission, CA, 5887

International Medical Outreach, Inc., TX, 4839

International Myeloma Foundation, CA, 5888

International Palace of Sports, Inc., IN, 2033

International Reading Association, Inc., DE, 5358, 5889

International Women's Media Foundation, DC, 5890

International Youth Foundation, MD, 5891

Intuit Scholarship Foundation, The, CA, 2034

Ioan Foundation, The, CA, 4840

Iowa Foundation for Agricultural Advancement, IA, 2035

Iowa P.E.O. Project Fund, Inc., IA, 4841

Iowa Pharmacy Foundation, IA, 2036

Iowa West Foundation, IA, 2037

Ireland Scholarship Trust, A. G. & Rosalee W., NE, 2038

Ironwood Area Scholarship Foundation, MI, 2039

Irvin Scholarship Foundation, Mary Ann, PA, 2040

Irwin Memorial Fund, Agnes and Sophie Dallas, PA, 5892

Irwindale Educational & Scholarship Foundation, CA, see 2041

Irwindale Educational Foundation, CA, 2041

Isaac Scholarship Foundation, Betty & Kan, Inc., NC, 2042

Isaacs Scholarship Fund, Harry Z., Inc., MD, 2043

Islami, M.D. Foundation, Abdol H., Inc., NJ, 2044

Italian American Cultural Foundation, OH, 2045

Italian American Delegates, Inc., MI, 4842

Italian Welfare Agency, Inc., CA, see 4843

Italian-American Community Services Agency, CA, 4843

ITT Rayonier Foundation, The, FL, see 3335

Ittleson-Beaumont Fund, NY, 4844

ITVS, CA, see 5356

Ivey Memorial Foundation, Caroline Lawson, Inc., AL, 2046

Ivy Foundation of Suffolk/Nassau Counties, NY, 2047

IYF, MD, see 5891

J & B Fund for Disadvantaged Children, HI, see 1654

J & J Charitable Foundation, PA, see 827

Jachym Scholarship Fund, Amelia G., NY, 2048

Jack and Jill of America Foundation, DC, 2049

Jack in the Box Foundation, CA, 4845

Jackson Community Foundation, The, MI, see 2050

Jackson County Community Foundation, The, MI, 2050

Jackson Foundation, C. Daniel, AL, 2051

Jackson Foundation, Corwill and Margie, MI, 2052

Jackson Foundation, Greater, MS, see 883

Jackson Memorial Trust Fund, Dr. J. M., IN, 2053

Jackson Scholarship Foundation, George, NJ, 2054

Jackson Scholarship Fund, Colonel William J. & Helen, CA, 2055

Jackson Scholarship Trust, James A. Jackson and Beatrice D., OH, see 2057

Jackson Scholarship, Beatrice, KY, 2056

Jackson Trust, George, NJ, see 2054

Jackson Trust, James A., OH, 2057

Jackson Trust, Wilhelmina W., MA, 2058

Jackson-Gen. George A. White Student Aid for Children of War Veterans Foundation, Maria C., OR, 2059

Jacob's Pillow Dance Festival, Inc., MA, 5359

Jacobus Family Foundation, Charles D., WI, 2060

Jaffe Foundation, Rona, The, NY, 5360

Jaffray Employees Trust, Clive T., MN, 4846

James 1:27 Foundation, The, TX, 4847

James Award, Morris C. & Juliet L., CA, A

James Foundation, William E. and Janet Burrows, MA, 2061

James IV Association of Surgeons, Inc., NY, 5893

James Scholarship Fund, William & Glenna, VT, 2062

Janesville Foundation, Inc., WI, 2063

Janson Foundation, WA, 2064

Janssen Ortho Patient Assistance Foundation, Inc., NJ, 4848

Janssen, Sr. Memorial Foundation, Donald, NJ, 2065

Jarvis Memorial Scholarship Foundation, Gregory B., CA, 2066

Jasper Foundation, Inc., IN, 2067

Javits Foundation, Jacob K., Inc., The, NY, 2068

Jay Fund Foundation, Tom Coughlin, Inc., FL, 4849

Jay Memorial Trust, George S. & Grace A., IA, 2069

JBL Scholarship Trust, DE, 2070

Jefferies Educational Grant Program, Boyd & Stephen, CA, 2071

Jeffers Memorial Education Fund, Michael, MI, 2072

Jefferson County Community Foundation, Greater, IA, 2073

Jefferson County Tuberculosis Association, Inc., WV, 2074

Jefferson Endowment Fund, John Percival and Mary C., CA, 4850

Jefferson Scholarship Fund, Ethel, PA, 2075

Jellison Benevolent Society, Inc., KS, 2076

Jeltz Scholarship Foundation, Wyatt F. & Mattie M., OK, 2077

Jemez Mountains Electric Foundation, NM, see 2093

Jenkins Scholarship Fund, Melvin H. & Thelma N., PA, 2078

Jenkins Student Aid Fund, OR, 2079

Jenkins Trust, Carolyn, NY, 2080

Jenniges Education Trust, Vernon & Leoma, MN, 2081

Jennings Foundation, John J. & Nora, Inc., The, MA, 2082

Jennings Foundation, Martha Holden, The, OH, 5894

Jentel Foundation, WY, 5361

Jentes Scholarship Fund, Robert H., The, OH, 2083

Jerome Foundation, MN, 5362

Jerusalem Fund for Education and Community Development, The, DC, 2084, 5895

Jerusalem Fund, The, DC, see 2084

Jerusalem Fund, The, DC, see 5895

Jewell Memorial Foundation, Daniel Ashley and Irene Houston, The, TN, 2085

Jewish Children's Home of Rochester, New York, Inc., Fund, NY, 2086

Jewish Endowment Foundation, LA, 2087

Jewish Family and Children's Services of San Francisco, the Peninsula, Marin and Sonoma Counties, CA, 2088

Jewish Family Assistance Fund, PA, 4851

Jewish Family Services, Inc., TN, 4852

Jewish Federation of Galveston County, Inc., TX, 4853

Jewish Foundation for Education of Women, NY, 2089

Jewish Home for Children, Inc., CT, 2090

Jewish Social Service Agency, MD, 2091

JFCS, CA, see 2088

Ji Ji Foundation, The, WA, 5896

Jinks Foundation, Ruth T., GA, 2092

JMEC Foundation, NM, 2093

Jo Daviess County Extension & 4-H Foundation, IL, 2094

Jockey Club Foundation, The, NY, 4854

Johns Manville Fund, Inc., CO, 2095

Johns Scholarships, Marvin A. and Lillie Mae, GA, 2096

Johnson Charitable Trust, Donald K., NE, 2097

Johnson Charitable Trust, Ralph and Marguerita, The, CA, 2098

Johnson Controls Foundation, WI, 2099

Johnson County Community Foundation, Greater, IN, see 2100

Johnson County Community Foundation, Inc., IN, 2100

Johnson County High School Scholarship Fund Charitable Trust, WY, 2101

Johnson Educational and Benevolent Trust, Dexter G., OK, 2102, 4855

Johnson Educational Trust, Ethan Allen Johnson and Caroline H., IL, 2103

Johnson Family Foundation, TX, 2104

Johnson Foundation, Barbara Piasecka, NJ, 5897, A

Johnson Foundation, Inc., The, ID, 2106

Johnson Foundation, Magic, Inc., CA, 2105

Johnson Foundation, Paul and Louise, The, OK, 2107

Johnson Foundation, Paul T. and Frances B., The, MI, 2108

Johnson Foundation, Robert Wood, The, NJ, 5898

Johnson Foundation, Samuel S., The, OR, 2109

Johnson Matthey Electronics Employee's of Spokane Scholarship Foundation, WA, 2110

Johnson Memorial Fund for Scholarly Research on Christian Science, Marlene F., MA, 5899

Johnson Memorial Fund Trust, Alfred N., RI, 2111

Johnson Memorial Scholarship Fund, Ray & Vesta, WA, 2112

Johnson Scholarship Foundation, Inc., TN, 2113

Johnson Scholarship Fund, Ervin W., WI, 2114

Johnson Scholarship Fund, Ray & Nell, WA, 2116

Johnson Scholarship Fund, Sandra and Bill, Inc., The, TN, 2115

Johnson Scholarship Trust Fund, Magda M., MA, 2117

Johnson Scholarship Trust, Gladys L., MN, 2118

Johnson Scholarship, Morton, GA, see 2120

Johnson Student Scholarship & Loan Foundation, NE, 2119

Johnson Trust, Addie Kate M., GA, 2120

Johnston Foundation, F. W., FL, see 2121

Johnston Scholarship Fund, F. W., FL, 2121

Joint Council No. 73 Scholarship Fund, NJ, 2122

Jones Charitable Foundation, Thomas B. Jones & Grace Stevenson, IL, 2123

Jones Charitable Trust No. 2, Harvey and Bernice, The, AR, 2124

Jones Educational Fund, Emmett & Beulah, MO, 2125

Jones Foundation, Walter S. and Evan C., KS, 2126

Jones Loan Fund, Claude R. and Sadie B., WA, 2127

Jones Memorial Trust, Clinton O. & Lura Curtis, MA, 2128

Jones Ministerial Trust, Adora S., IA, 2129

Jones Scholarship Fund, Joseph, OH, 2130

Jones Trust, Addie M., MN, see 4583

Jones Trust, Grace B., MA, 2131

Jordaan Foundation, Inc., KS, 2132

Jordan Charitable Trust, Roderick J. & Gertrude B., NC, 2133

Jordan Education Foundation, UT, 2134

Jordan Scholarship & Monument Fund, Leon M., Inc., MO, 2135

Jordan Scholarship Fund, B. N. & W. L., The, NC, 2136

Joshua Foundation, Inc., The, NY, A

Joshua Tree National Park Association, CA, 5363

Jostens Foundation, Inc., The, MN, 2137

Journal Publishing Company Employees Welfare Fund, Inc., OR, 4856

Journalism Foundation of Metropolitan St. Louis, IL, 2138

Joyard Foundation, The, CA, 2139, 4857

Jozwiak Scholarship Trust, Melvin S., WI, 2140

JSA Foundation, TN, 2141

JSJ Family Foundation, MO, 2142

JSW Adoption Foundation, Inc., The, WI, see 4779

Judge Foundation, Bryan W. & Minnie, FL, 2143

Judges Athletic Association, VA, 2144

Juhl Scholarship Fund, George W. & Sadie Marie, MI, 2145

Julius Trust, Tony, CA, A

Jurassic Foundation, Inc., The, UT, 5900

Just Foundation, IL, 2146

Just Scholarship Foundation, F. Ward, IL, see 2146

Justice Lodge No. 285 F. & A.M., Educational Trust, NJ, 2147

Juvenile Diabetes Research Foundation International, NY, 5901

JWF Quanza Foundation, Inc., OK, 2148

Kaiser Family Foundation, Henry J., The, CA, 2149, 5902

Kaiser Foundation, Inc., CO, 2150

Kaiulani Home for Girls Trust, HI, 2151

Kalamazoo Community Foundation, MI, 2152

Kalamazoo Foundation, MI, see 2152

Kalamazoo Public Education Foundation, MI, 2153, 5903

Kamenski Trust, Stephanie, RI, 2154

Kaminski Foundation, Sylvester and Tessie, AZ, 2155

Kampel Foundation, Clarisse B., Inc., NY, 5364

Kanawha Valley Foundation, Greater, The, WV, 2156

Kander Scholarship Fund, Stephen D., WI, 2157
Kane Paper Scholarship Fund, Inc., NY, 2158
Kang Scholarship Trust, S. Y., CA, 2159
Kanhofer Trust, L., OH, 2160
Kansas City Community Foundation and Affiliated Trusts, Greater, The, MO, see 2161
Kansas City Community Foundation, Greater, MO, 2161
Kansas Cultural Trust, KS, 5365
Kansas State Alpha Tau Omega Students' Aid Endowment Fund, IA, 2162
Kaplan Foundation, Lazare and Charlotte, Inc., NY, 2163
Kaplan Scholarship Foundation, Seymour L., The, NY, 2164
Kappa Alpha Theta Foundation, IN, 2165
Karnes Memorial Fund, The, IL, 2166
Karyae Benevolent Foundation, NC, 2167
Kasser Family Foundation, NJ, 2168
Kathwari Foundation, Irfan, Inc., NY, 2169
Kattar Memorial Fund, Kerri Ann, Inc., DC, 2170
KATU Thomas R. Dargan Minority Scholarship Fund, OR, see 1039
Katz Foundation, Abraham J. & Phyllis, NY, 5904
Kauffman Foundation, Ewing Marion, MO, 5905
Kauffman Scholarship Foundation, Gene, Inc., MO, 2171
Kaufman & Coffman Scholarship Fund, WI, 2172
Kautz Foundation, Charles and Pauline, NY, 2173
Kautz Trust, Jessie B., PA, see 3774
KCPQ-TV/Kelly Foundation of Washington, WA, see 2191
Keasbey Memorial Fund, H. G. and A. G., NC, 2174
Kebo Foundation Scholarship Trust, ME, A
Keel Foundation, The, TN, 2175
Keen Charitable Trust, Loris and Pauline, OK, 4858
Keen Family Scholarship Foundation, Harold and Berta, The, PA, 2176
Keena Trust, Lorene Lobner, CA, 2177
Keener Foundation, Robert W. Keener and Barbara J., UT, 2178
Keep North Carolina Clean and Beautiful, Inc., NC, 5906
Keig Scholarship Trust, E. R. Keig and Alice, IA, 2179
Keith Charitable Trust, Lenna M., IL, A
Keith Scholarship Fund, Ruth, PA, 2180
Keitzer Memorial Trust C, Charles B. & Lenore M., IN, 2181
Kelben Foundation, Inc., WI, 2182
Keller Foundation, Lucille L., IN, 2183
Keller Scholarship Fund, Melvin G. & Mary F., OH, 2184
Keller Scholarship Trust, Clarence, WI, 2185
Kelley Foundation, Edward Bangs Kelley and Elza, Inc., MA, 2186
Kellner Foundation, The, NY, 2187
Kellogg Company 25-Year Employees Fund, Inc., MI, 4859
Kellogg Foundation, W. K., MI, 5907
Kelly Charitable Trust, C. L., MI, 2188
Kelly Family Charitable Foundation, IL, 2189
Kelly Family Foundation, TX, 2190
Kelly Foundation of Washington, WA, 2191
Kelly Foundation, Inc., FL, 2192
Kelly Foundation, Stephen P. and Sandra Lu, TX, see 2190
Kelly Scholarship Fund, Mary A., MA, 2193
Kelsey Foundation, Forest C. & Ruth V., The, WA, 2194
Kempner Fund, Harris and Eliza, Inc., TX, 2195
Kengla Foundation, Edward R., Inc., VA, 2196
Keniston and Dane Educational Fund, VT, 2197
Kennard Educational Fund, Inc., VA, 2198
Kennedy Center for the Performing Arts, John F., DC, 5366
Kennedy Foundation, CO, 2199
Kennedy Foundation, Francis Nathaniel and Katheryn Padgett, SC, 2200
Kennedy Health Care Foundation, Inc., NJ, see 2201
Kennedy Health System, Inc., NJ, 2201
Kennedy Library Foundation, John F., Inc., MA, 5908
Kennedy Scholarship Trust, Margaret, RI, 2202
Kennedy, Jr. Foundation, Joseph P., The, DC, 5909
Kennestone Regional Foundation, Inc., GA, see 4367
Kennett Educational Fund, Arthur, MO, 2203

Kenney Scholarship Fund, Walter J., CT, 2204
Kenny Education Fund, Monsignor Simon E., MD, 2205
Kenosha Scholarship Foundation, Inc., WI, 2206
Kent Foundation, Senah C. and C. A., NC, 2207
Kent Medical Foundation, MI, A
Kentucky Foundation for Women, Inc., KY, 5367
Kentucky Safety & Health Network Foundation, Inc., The, KY, 2208
Kerber Memorial Foundation, Ralph A., CA, 2209
Kerby and Robert S. Potter Fund, William F., The, NY, 5910
Keren America, CO, 4860
Keren Keshet - The Rainbow Foundation, NY, 4861, 5911
Keren Tifereth Yisroel Foundation, NY, 2210
Kerman Bible Studies, CA, 4862
Kerouac Writers in Residence Project, Jack, Inc., The, FL, 5368
Kerr Center for Sustainable Agriculture, Inc., The, OK, 5912
Kershaw County Vocational Education Foundation, Inc., SC, 2211
Keshet Foundation, NY, 4863
Kessel Scholarship Fund, Edgar E., OH, 2212
Kessel Trust, Edgar E., OH, see 2212
Key Charitable Trust, KS, 2213
Key West Rotary Foundation, Inc., FL, 2214
Keyes Trust, Bernice A. B., OH, 2215
Kia Ora Foundation, CA, 2216
Kibble Foundation, OH, 2217
Kids Campaign, Inc., MD, 4864
Kids Fund, NM, A
Kids' Chance, Inc., GA, 2218
Kiely Trust, Helen U., RI, 2219
Kiersted Memorial Scholarship Fund, Robert W., CA, 2220
Kieve Affective Education, ME, see 2221
Kieve-Wavus Education, Inc., ME, 2221
Kiewit Foundation, Peter, NE, 2222
Kil Chung-Hee Fellowship Fund, Inc., PA, 2223
Kilgore-Ramsey Scholarship Trust, KS, 2224
Killgore Scholarship Trust Fund, J. A. & Ophelia, AL, 2225
Kilts Foundation, The, IL, 2226
Kim Architectural Fellowship Foundation, Tai Soo, Inc., CT, 5913
Kimball International—Habig Foundation, Inc., The, IN, 2227
Kimbo Foundation, The, CA, 2228
Kimmel Foundation, Sidney, The, PA, 5914
Kimmel Scholarship Trust, Eugene E., NE, 2229
Kincaid Charitable Foundation, Kent Rogers, CA, see 2231
Kincaid Foundation, Inc., KY, 2230
Kincaid Foundation, Kent Rogers, CA, 2231
Kincaid Foundation, The, TX, 2232
Kindler Charitable Fund, Alice, OH, 2233
King Benevolent Fund, Inc., VA, 4865
King Cardiac Foundation, Larry, The, MD, 4866
King Charity Fund, Jane R., IA, 2234
King Education Trust, Maurice & Evelyn, IN, 2235
King Educational Trust, William Toben, MO, 2236
King Family Foundation, Charles & Lucille, Inc., NY, 2237
King Foundation, Carl B. and Florence E., TX, 2238
King Pharmaceuticals Benevolent Fund, VA, see 4865
King Scholarship Foundation, Basil L., Inc., FL, 2239
King Scholarship Fund, Cora E., RI, see 2240
King Scholarship Fund, RI, 2240
King Trust, Charles A., MA, 5915
King-St. Ferdinand College Scholarship Foundation, George Leech, PA, 2241
Kingsbury Fund, NH, 2242
Kingsbury Scholarship Fund, Mr. & Mrs. Henry B., ID, 2243
Kingsbury Temperance Fund, MA, A
Kinney Scholarship and Library Science Reference Fund, Clair H., PA, see 2244
Kinney Scholarship Fund, Clair H., PA, 2244
Kinsley Educational Foundation, James Edward, RI, see 2245
Kinsley Trust, James Edward, RI, 2245
Kirchner Family Foundation, Inc., The, MD, 2246

Kirkside, Inc., The, MA, see 4754
Kirschner Educational Trust, John E., MO, 2247
Kiser Memorial Fund, Clara Louise, OH, 2248
Kissler Charitable Trust, L. H. & F., ID, A
Kittredge Educational Fund, John Anson, ME, 5369
Kiwanis of Little Havana Foundation, FL, 2249
Kiwanis Scholarship Fund, OH, see 4463
Klapmeyer Grandview High School Foundation, Ray & Mary, MO, 2250
Kleban Foundation, Inc., The, NY, 5370
Kleeman, Jr. Scholarship Fund, A. M., NY, 2251
Klein Trust Fund, Arlen Francis, IL, 4867
Kleppe Scholarship Fund, Cecil H., KS, 2252
Klicka Foundation, Jessie, CA, 2253
Kling Scholarship Fund, Verne O. & Dorothy M., MI, 2254
Kling Trust, Louise, OH, 2255
Klingensmith Charitable Foundation, Agnes, OR, see 2317
Klingenstein Fund, Esther A. & Joseph, Inc., The, NY, 5916
Kluge Foundation, John W., The, MD, A
Knabusch Scholarship Foundation, Edward M. and Henrietta M., MI, 2256
Knapp Foundation Trust, Russell and Edna, NV, 2257
Knapp Foundation, NV, see 2257
Knecht Trust, Beulah, IL, 2258
Knight Scholarship Trust, Louise, TX, 2259
Knights of Columbus Charities, Inc., CT, 2260
Knoche-Guett Scholarship Fund, CA, 2261
Knoll Charitable Foundation, The, PA, 2262
Knoop Scholarship Fund, MO, 2263
Knowledge is Power Foundation, CA, see 3156
Knowles Trust B, Leonora H., OH, 2264
Knox-MKB Foundation, Ellen Beck, TX, 2265, 5917
Knoxville Christian Community Foundation, TN, 5918
Koch Bomarko Founders Scholarship Fund, Robert & Margaret, MI, 2266
Koch Foundation, Fred C. and Mary R., Inc., The, KS, 2267
Koch Foundation, Fred C., The, KS, see 2267
Koehler Fund, John G., IL, 2268
Kohen Non-Exempt Charitable Trust, Elsie, IL, 4868
Kohl Education Foundation, Dolores, IL, 5919
Kohl Educational Foundation, Herb, WI, 2269, 5920
Kohl Scholarship Trust, Leila, WI, 2270
Kohler Foundation, Inc., WI, 2271
Kolasinski Scholarship Trust, Cynthia McKinley, WI, 2272
Kolob Foundation, The, UT, 2273
Komarek Charitable Trust, NE, 5921
Komen Breast Cancer Foundation, Susan G., TX, 2274, 5922
KOMO Radio and Television Minority Scholarship Fund, WA, see 1380
Kondur Memorial Foundation, Louis and Ella I., Inc., MI, 2275
Koniag Education Foundation, AK, 2276
Kooi Education Fund, Elmer J. Kooi, Beatrice A. Kooi and Robert J., The, IL, 2277
Koomruian Armenian Education Fund, CA, 2278
Koomruian Education Fund, CA, see 2278
Koon Scholastic Fund, Alice W. C., NY, 2279
Koran Trust, Ida C., MN, 2280, 4869
Kornberg Family Foundation, CA, 5923
Kornfeld Foundation, Emily Davie and Joseph S., NY, 5924
Korpy Foundation, Ellen, Inc., MN, 2281
Kosciusko County Community Foundation, Inc., IN, 2282
Kosciuszko Foundation, Inc., NY, 2283, 5925
Kotur Foundation, Eugene R., PA, 2284
Koulaieff Educational Fund, Trustees of Ivan V., The, CA, 2285
Koussevitzky Music Foundation, Inc., NJ, 5371
Kovach Memorial Trust, Judith Kirsch, NJ, 2286
KPMG Foundation, The, NJ, 5926
KPMG Peat Marwick Foundation, The, NJ, see 5926
Krambles Transit Scholarship Fund, George, IL, 2287
Kramer Educational Fund, Louie & Frank, SD, 2288
Krause Foundation, Cmdr. and Mrs. Robert, MI, 2289
Krausman Scholarship Trust, Essie W., FL, 2290

Logan County Nurses Scholarship Association, CO, 2419

Lokoff Child Care Foundation, Terri Lynne, PA, 5950

London Educational Foundation, George & Frances, NC, 2420

Long Community Health Foundation, Wesley, Inc., NC, see 927

Long Trust, Dr. Ralph F. Long and Pearl A., CT, 2421

Long Trust, L. A., TX, 2422

Loofbourrow Educational Trust, KS, 2423

Loogootee Community School Scholarship Trust, IN, 2424

Lorain Foundation, The, OH, 2425

Lord Educational Fund, IL, 2426

Lord Scholarship Fund Trust, Henry C., RI, 2427

Los Alamos Community Foundation, NM, 2428

Los Altos Community Foundation, CA, 2429

Los Padres Foundation, VA, 2430

Loser Memorial Scholarship Fund, Alfred J., OH, 2431

Louisiana Poultry Industries Educational Foundation, Inc., LA, 2432

Louisville Community Foundation, Inc., KY, see 890

Louisville Male High School Foundation, Inc., KY, 2433

Love Family Foundation Incorporated, PA, 5951

Love Foundation, Lucyle S., The, SC, 2434

Lowe Memorial Educational Fund, Mary Friese, MA, 2435

Lowell 10th Clause Trust, Amy, MA, 2436

Lowengard Scholarship Fund, Leon, PA, 2437

Lower East Side Printshop, Inc., NY, 5384

Lower Manhattan Cultural Council, Inc., NY, 5385

Lower Memorial Scholarship Fund, Ora T. & Dessie H., WI, 2438

Lowrie Student Loan Fund, Pearl, MO, 2439

Lucas, Jr. Foundation, Sam J., The, TX, 2440

Luce Foundation, Henry, Inc., The, NY, 5952

Luce Policy Institute, Clare Boothe, VA, 2441

Luce Trust, Charles and Nancy Oden, WA, 2442

Lucent Technologies Foundation, NJ, 2443, 5953

Lucky Scholarship Trust, Oatha & Una, CA, 2444

Ludwig Educational Trust, Merwin C., WV, 2445

Luick Trust, Mary Jane, IN, 4893

Luley Scholarship & Educational Fund, Founces M., WI, 2446

Luling Foundation, The, TX, 2447

Lundquist Scholarship Testamentary Trust, Walter E., WA, 2448

Lundy Foundation, Turner and Louise, The, NC, 2449

Lupo Foundation, Commodore Thomas J., LA, 5954

Lurcy Charitable and Educational Trust, Georges, NY, 2450

Lyden Foundation, Inc., FL, 2451

Lyman Fund, Inc., ME, 2452

Lymphoma Research Foundation of America, Inc., NY, see 5955

Lymphoma Research Foundation, NY, 5955

Lynch Scholarship Foundation, John B., DE, 2453

Lynch Scholarship Fund, Cornelius T. & Elizabeth, NY, 2454

Lynch Scholarship Trust, Cornelius T. & Elizabeth, NY, see 2454

Lynch Trust, William A., MA, 2455

Lynch Trust, William A., PA, 2456

Lynchburg Community Trust, Greater, VA, 2457

Lynn Foundation, Berneice U., CA, 2458

Lyons Memorial Foundation, Charles, Inc., MO, 2459

Lyons Scholarship Fund, Marguerite Gambill, The, OH, 2460

Lyons Scholarship Fund, Ray C., Maude E. & Genevieve, The, IL, 2461

Lytle Scholarship Trust, Carl H., OR, see 2462

Lytle Scholarship Trust, OR, 2462

M & M Area Community Foundation, MI, 2463

M.I.G. Scholarship Foundation, TX, see 1608

Mac, Incorporated, MD, 4894

MacArthur Foundation, John D. and Catherine T., IL, 5956

MacCurdy-Salisbury Foundation, Inc., The, CT, 2464

MacDowell Colony, Inc., NH, 5386

MacGregor Charitable Trust, Muriel L., CO, 2465

MacGregor Ranch, CO, see 2465

Mack Industrial School, MA, 2466

Mackey Educational Awards Foundation, Helen H., OH, 2467

MacKinnon Fund, Mary W., NY, 4895

Mackley Memorial Scholarship Fund Trust, Arthur Rhodes, OH, 2468

MacPherson Trust, A. F., WI, 4896

Macristy Foundation, William & Ellen E., CT, 2469

Maddox Foundation, J. F, NM, 2470

Made in Dover Foundation, The, NJ, see 4478

Madison County Community Foundation, IN, 2471

Madison Rotary Foundation, WI, 2472

Madison Scholarship Committee, NJ, 2473

Maffett Scholarship Trust, Minnie L., TX, 2474

MAG Foundation, GA, see 2647

Magic Action Community Fund, Inc., FL, see 2475

Magic Action Team Community Fund, Inc., FL, 2475

Magraw Trust, Marguerite, RI, 2476

Maguire Trust, Agnes T., LA, 2477

Mahajan Memorial Trust, Varoon, Inc., NJ, 2478

Mahana Congregational Church Scholarship Foundation, IA, 2479

Mahanay Educational Trust, Dora L., IA, 2480

Mahoney Trust, B. William, NY, 2481

Maier Foundation, Edward J. and Alice M., MI, A

Main 1917 Scholarship Fund, Charles, RI, 2482

Main Street Community Foundation, CT, 2483

Maine Community Foundation, Inc., The, ME, 2484

Maine Veterinary Education Foundation, ME, 2485

Majid Family Foundation, IL, 4897

Major Junior Hockey Education Fund of Oregon, Inc., OR, 2486

Major League Baseball Equipment Managers Association, PA, 2487

Maka'ainana Foundation, The, HI, A

Makinson Trust, Emma F., RI, 2488

Malachi Foundation, The, TX, see 4747

Mallinckrodt, Jr. Foundation, Edward, MO, 5957

Mallory-Taylor Foundation, Inc., KY, 4898

Malone Foundation for Kids, Karl, UT, 4899

Maloney Foundation, William E., MA, 2489

Mammoth Lakes Foundation, CA, 2490

Mancini Trust, Ione, CA, 2491

Mang Foundation, So, CA, 5958

Manhattan Community Access Corporation, NY, see 5387

Manhattan Neighborhood Network, NY, 5387

Manley Music Scholarship Trust, IN, 2492

Mann Foundation, Rema Hort, Inc., NY, 4900, 5388

Mann, Jr. Memorial Fund, Joe L., MO, 2493

Mannweiler Trust for Emil Mannweiler Scholarship Fund, Mary B., RI, 2494

Manpower Foundation, Inc., WI, 2495

Mansfield Family Foundation, KS, 2496

Mansfield Fund for the Aged, Mary, OH, 4901

Manuel Trust, Viola G., MA, 2497

Manwiller Trust, Lloyd R. and Stella Gibboney, NJ, 2498

MAP International, GA, 5959

Maple Point Foundation, Inc., IN, 2499

Maquoketa Area Community Foundation, IA, 2500

Maquoketa Area Foundation, IA, see 2500

Marblehead Female Humane Society, Inc., MA, 4902

March Education Fund, William A., PA, 2501

March of Dimes Birth Defects Foundation, NY, 5960

March Scholarship Fund, Clara A., NY, 2502

Marciano Scholarship & Charitable Trust, Arthur & Ann, CT, see 2503

Marciano Scholarship Fund, Arthur and Ann, CT, 2503

Marco Island Women's Club Foundation, FL, 2504

Marcum Scholarship Fund, Joseph L., Inc., OH, 2505

Marcus Foundation, Adele, Inc., The, NY, 2506

Marcy Trust, Susan H. & Wilbur H., FL, 2507

Marek Trust Fund, IA, 2508

Marguerite Home Association, The, CA, see 4903

Marguerite Home, a Charitable Trust, The, CA, 4903

Mari's Foundation, WI, 5389

Mariachi Heritage Foundation, CA, 5390

Marietta Community Foundation, OH, 2509

Marijuana Policy Project Foundation, DC, 5961

Marin Community Foundation, CA, 5962

Marino Scholarship Fund, Maria, MA, 2510

Marion Memorial Health Foundation, IL, 2511

Maris Scholarship Foundation, Irena, IL, 2512

Markos Foundation, Inc., The, WI, 2513

Marquette Area Public Schools Education Foundation, MI, 2514

Marquette Community Foundation, MI, 2515

Marsch Charitable Trust, Louis & Temple, MO, 2516

Marshall & Ilsley Bank Foundation, Inc., WI, see 2517

Marshall & Ilsley Foundation, Inc., WI, 2517

Marshall & Margaret Hughes Scholarship Foundation, W., PA, 2518

Marshall Civic Foundation, MI, see 2519

Marshall Community Foundation, MI, 2519

Marshall County Community Foundation, Inc., IN, 2520

Marshall Educational Trust Fund, The, IL, 2521

Marshall Foundation, Judge Elliott D., The, CA, 2522

Marshfield Area Community Foundation, WI, 2523

Martell Memorial Foundation, C. F., ND, 2524

Marth Foundation, Ltd., WI, 2525

Marti Foundation, TX, 2526

Martin Charitable Trust, G. Roxy & Elizabeth C., FL, 2527

Martin Charitable Trust, Loy Crump, MO, 2528

Martin Education Trust, WI, 2529

Martin Endowment Fund, S. J., KY, 2530

Martin Foundation for the Creative Arts, Peter and Madeleine, CA, 5391

Martin Foundation, Glenn L., MD, 4904

Martin Fund, Henry B., Inc., MA, 4905

Martin Marietta Corporation Foundation, MD, see 2417

Martin Memorial Foundation, Inc., FL, 4906

Martin Scholarship Trust Fund, Albert and Jessie D., NC, 2531

Martin Trust 1, Mary R., NH, 4907

Martin Trust No. 2, Mary R., NH, 2532

Martin, Jr. Foundation, Karl & Georgia Martin, Sr., Anna Belle Flynn, Karl & June, OK, 2533

Martino Trust, Joseph W., MO, 2534

Mary Kay Foundation, TX, A

Mary's Pence, NJ, 5963

Maryland Hall for the Creative Arts, Inc., MD, 5392

Marymount Foundation, Mother Joseph Rogan, MO, 2535

Mason Scholarship Fund, Daisy, IL, 2536

Mason Scholarship Fund, IL, see 2536

Masonic Educational Foundation, Inc., LA, 2537

Masonic Foundation of Michigan, Inc., MI, 2538

Masonic Foundation of Utah, UT, 2539

Masonic Grand Lodge Charities of Rhode Island, Inc., RI, 2540, 4908

Massachusetts Automatic Merchandising Council Scholarship Fund, MA, 2541

Massachusetts Bar Foundation, Inc., MA, 2542

Massachusetts Charitable Fire Society, MA, 4909

Massachusetts Library Aid Association, MA, 5964

Massage Therapy Foundation, Inc., IL, 5965

Master Brewers Association of the Americas Scholarship Foundation, Inc., MN, 2543

Master Educational Assistance Foundation, IL, 2544

Masters Trust Fund, Edith L., IL, 2545

MATHCOUNTS Foundation, VA, 2546

Matheson Scholarship Fund, Margaret & Donald, RI, 2547

Matheson Scholarship Trust Fund, James Matheson & Marian, IA, 2548

Mathiesen Charitable Trust, Carol Hay, AZ, 2549

Mathis Memorial Trust, Charles B., NC, 2550

Matson Trust, Lorraine D., MI, 2551

Matthews Trust, Ernestine, MD, 2552

Mattress Factory, Ltd., The, PA, 5393

Matz Foundation, Israel, NY, 5394

Maude Children's Fund, Frances, RI, 2553

Mauger Insurance Fund, OH, 2554

Mavrogenis Trust Fund, Dennis & Marion, MA, 2555

Maxwell Foundation, Edmund F., WA, 2556

May Employees Trust Fund, David, MO, 4910

Maya Educational Foundation, VT, 2557

Maybury Trust, Imogene M., IL, 2558

Mayer Foundation, Chaim, Inc., NY, 5966

Mayfield Foundation, M. L. Mayfield and Jessie Star, The, TX, 2559

Mayson Scholarship Grant Fund, Charles G. & Alice R., The, AL, 2560

Maysteel Foundation, Ltd., WI, see 3758

MBE Foundation for Children's Initiatives, CA, see 5139

MBNA Foundation, The, DE, 2561

MCCA, MD, see 4927

McCabe Charitable Foundation, Donald C. and Helene Marienthal, MI, 2562

McCabe Testamentary Trust - Georgia, E. R. Warner, FL, 2563

McCabe Testamentary Trust - Virginia, E. R. Warner, FL, 2564

McCaddin-McQuirk Foundation, Inc., The, NY, 2565

McCall Foundation, Penny, Inc., The, NY, 5395

McCallay Educational Trust Fund, Edwin L. and Louis B., OH, 2566

McCarthey Dressman Education Foundation, The, UT, 2567, 5967

McCaulay Memorial Masonic Fund, TX, 2568

McClain Scholarship Trust, Pauline Linebarger & Riley, IL, 2569

McClain Trust, J. Allen, OH, 2570

McCleary Medical Scholarship Fund of the Mary Ball Chapter for the Daughters of the American Revolution, Frank, WA, 2571

McClendon, Sr. Memorial Scholarship Foundation, Glenn R., AL, 2572

McClennan Scholarship Fund, W. H. "Howie", DC, 2573

McClintock Home, Kate, KY, 4911

McCloskey Memorial Scholarship Fund, Charles A., PA, 2574

McClure Educational and Development Fund, James G. K., Inc., NC, 2575

McColl Center for Visual Arts, NC, 5396

McComas Foundation, Sophia Byers, OR, 4912

McComb Memorial Scholarship Fund, Lucille, OH, 2576

McConahay Educational Foundation, Ann, OH, 2577

McConnell Foundation and Scholarship Fund, Lynn E. and Mattie G., The, NY, 2578

McConnell Foundation, The, CA, 2579

McCormick Scholarship Fund, Robert W., WV, 2580

McCourtney Trust, Flora S., IL, 2581

McCoy Scholarship Trust, Clark & Laura, OH, 2582

McCready Scholarship Fund, Stephen F., NJ, 2583

McCrory Trust for Gonzales County, TX, Dorsey, TX, 2584

McCune Scholarship Foundation Trust, C. N., FL, 2585

McCurdy Memorial Scholarship Foundation, MI, 2586

McCurdy Scholarship Foundation, Edna P., AK, 2587

McCurry Foundation, Inc., The, FL, 2588

McDavid Dental Education Trust, G. N. and Edna, MO, see 2589

McDavid Dental Educational Trust, MO, 2589

McDonald Charitable Trust Memorial Scholarship Fund for Weir High School, Joan B. and Frank E., PA, 2590

McDonald Charitable Trust Memorial Scholarship Fund for Wheeling Park High School, Joan Bieberson, PA, 2591

McDonald Memorial Fund Trust, OH, 2592

McDonald Memorial Scholarship Fund, Katrina Overall, MS, 2593

McDonald Memorial Trust, Angus C., OH, see 2592

McDonald Scholarship Fund, Sam & Carrie, AL, 2594

McDonough Charity School, Trustees of, The, MD, 2595

McDougall Charitable Trust, Ruth Camp, NY, see 638

McDougall Medical Scholarship Foundation, Frances and Ina, FL, 2596

McDowell Corporation, Verne Catt, OR, 2597

McDowell Foundation, Ephraim, KY, 2598

McElaney Trust f/b/o Town of Avon, John, MA, 2599

McElroy Charitable, William E., IL, 2600

McElroy Trust, R. J., IA, 5968

McFadden Scholarship Fund, William Preston and Belvah, KS, 2601

McFarland Charitable Foundation, IL, 2602

McFarland Medical Trust, IL, 2603

McFarlane Scholarship Fund, John & Agnes, CA, 2604

McGeehin Educational Foundation, Inc., The, MD, 2605

McGill, Jr. Agape Foundation, Donald Ray, The, TX, 2606

McGinty Family Foundation, OH, 2607

McGinty Foundation, Alice and Patrick, Inc., OH, see 2607

McGinty Scholarship Fund Trust, Ellanora, FL, 2608

McGlothlan Trust, Arthur B. & Anna F., MO, 2609

MCH Foundation, Inc., The, TX, 5969

McIninch Scholarship Fund, The, NH, 2610

McInnes College Scholarship Fund, Eva E., IL, 2611

McIntire Educational Fund, John, OH, 2612

McKaig Foundation, Lalitta Nash, PA, 2613

McKay Memorial Scholarship Fund, Edward Nixon, NC, 2614

McKee Educational Foundation, TN, 2615

McKee Educational Trust, John W., OR, 2616

McKee Foundation, Ella G., IL, 2617

McKenney Scholarship Trust, Elmer, TX, 2618

McKesson Foundation, Inc., CA, 2619

McKesson HBOC Foundation, Inc., CA, see 2619

McKinney Charitable Foundation, Edgar & Nona, FL, 2620

McKinney Foundation, Charles Cecil, NC, 2621

McKinney Scholarship Trust, Lee, OH, see 2160

McKinnis Educational Trust, Ira and Dena, The, KS, 2622

McKnight Endowment Fund for Neuroscience, The, MN, 5970

McKnight Foundation, The, MN, 5397, 5971

McLane Association, Dorothea van Dyke, NJ, 2623

McLaughlin Foundation, MA, 2624

McLoraine Family Educational Trust, AZ, 2625

McMannis Educational Trust Fund, William J. McMannis and A. Haskell, PA, 2626

McMaster-Moulthrop Scholarship Fund, CT, 2627

McMillan, Jr. Foundation, Bruce, Inc., TX, 2628

McMillen Foundation, Wendell W., PA, 2629

McMurtrie Foundation, Lucy J., NJ, 2630

McMurtrie Scholarship Fund, NJ, see 2630

McNair Memorial Fund Trust, John F., NC, 2631

McNaught Scholarship Fund, Dr. Francis, AZ, 2632

McNaught Scholarship Fund, Grace I. McNaught-Dr. Francis, AZ, see 2632

McNay Educational Trust, Harry & Winnie, NE, 2633

McNeil Scholarship Fund, Roy and Yvonne, ND, 2634

McRae Foundation, AZ, A

McRae Scholarship Fund, Gertrude L., WA, 2635

McRoberts Memorial Law Scholarship Fund, OH, 2636

MDU Resources Foundation, ND, 2637

Mead Educational Trust, Beth Rowell, TX, 2638

Mead Scholarship Trust, Edwin Budge, FL, 2639

Meade Memorial Science Fund, Joseph F., NY, 2640

Meador Scholarship Trust, L. & M., VA, 2641

Mears Trust, Edith, KY, 2642

Measey Foundation, Benjamin and Mary Siddons, The, PA, 2643

Meat Cutters Educational Trust, TX, see 4163

Mecklenburg Scholarship Association, Inc., VA, 2644

Medallion Foods Competitive Edge Scholarship Trust, AR, 2645

Medic Educational Foundation, The, NC, 2646

Medical Association of Georgia Foundation, Inc., GA, 2647

Medical Education Scholarship Trust, The, ID, 2648

Medical Library Association, IL, 5972

Medical Research Foundation, Inc., NE, 2649

Meehan Family Foundation, Inc., WI, 2650

Meehan Foundation, Daniel E., Inc., WI, see 2650

MEEMIC Foundation for the Future of Education, MI, 5973

Meet The Composer, Inc., NY, 5398

Meftah Scholarship Foundation, FL, A

Mehaffy Foundation, Amy E., Inc., The, KS, 2651

Meharg Scholarship Trust, Lena Y., AL, 2652

Mehta Family Foundation, Bhupat and Jyott, TX, 2653

Meiller Educational Trust, Lucy E., FL, 2654

Melanoma Research Foundation, CA, 5974

Melish Trust, J. Robert and Rose Marie, The, OH, 2655

Mellinger Educational Foundation, Edward Arthur, Inc., IL, 2656

Mellinger Medical Research Memorial Fund, R. &. R., PA, A

Mellinger Scholarship Fund, Gertrude & Clarence, PA, see 2657

Mellinger Scholarship Fund, PA, 2657

Melmac Education Foundation, ME, 2658

Melton Scholarship Foundation, Jenny, GA, 2659

Melville House, Inc., NY, 2660

Memorial Hospital of Bedford County Foundation, PA, 2661

Memorial Scholarship Foundation of the Music Teachers Association of California, Alameda County Branch, CA, 5399

Memorial Scholarship Foundation of the Rotary Club of Westminster, Maryland in Memory of Colonel Sherman E. Flanagan, Jr., MD, 2662

Menard Memorial Scholarship Fund, Becky, The, OH, 2663

Menasha Corporation Foundation, WI, 2664

Mendenhall-Tyson Scholarship Foundation, PA, 2665

Menlo Park-Atherton Education Foundation, CA, 5975

Menn Foundation, Gregory, WI, 2666

Menomonie Area Community Foundation, Greater, Inc., WI, 2667

Mentzer Memorial Foundation, OH, 2668

Mentzer Memorial Trust, Charles T., OH, see 2668

Mentzer Scholarship Trust, John P., WI, 2669

Mercado Scholarship Foundation, Suzy, The, TX, 2670

Mercer County Civic Foundation, Inc., The, OH, 2671

Mercer Texas A & M Educational Foundation, Vandal and Winifred, TX, 2672

Merchants Fund, PA, 4913

Merchants-Oliver Fund, PA, see 4913

Merck Company Foundation, The, NJ, A

Merck Institute for Science Education, Inc., NJ, 5976

Meriden Foundation, The, CT, 2673

Meriden Record Journal Foundation, RI, 2674

Merrick Foundation, Inc., NE, 2675

Meserve Memorial Fund, Albert & Helen C., NC, 2676

Messenger of Salvation, OK, 5977

MetLife Foundation, NY, A

Metropolitan Museum of Art, The, NY, 5978

Metta Enlightenment Foundation, Inc., NY, 2677

Metz Foundation, Henry James and Christie M., CA, 2678

Metz Scholarship Trust, CA, see 2679

Metz Scholarship Trust, Rene, CA, 2679

Metzger Scholarship Fund, Stella E., The, PA, 2680

Mexico Foundation, The, CA, 2681

Meyer Foundation, Roy E. and Merle, The, MN, 2682

Meyer Scholarship Trust, Paul & Regina, MO, 2683

Meyer Trust, Charles, TX, 4914

Meyer Trust, Edward E., OH, 2684

Meyer, Jr. Foundation, Robert Benson, Inc., The, MD, 4915

Meyerhoff Charitable Trust, IA, 2685

Meyers Foundation, Allen H. and Nydia, MI, 2686

Meyers Foundation, Allen H., MI, see 2686

MFA Foundation, MO, 2687

MFU Training Plan Trust, CA, 5979

MGM Charitable/Scholarship Foundation, KY, 2688

Miami County Foundation, OH, 2689

Michael Foundation, Inc., The, PA, 2690

Michaels Scholarship Fund, Frank J., SC, 2691

Michaud Charitable Trust, The, OH, 2692

Michels Family Educational Trust, IA, 2693

Michels Scholarship Foundation, Jimmie, WA, 2694

Michigan Accountancy Foundation, MI, 2695

Michigan Agri-Business Association Educational Trust Fund, MI, 2696

Michigan Agri-Dealers Educational Trust, MI, see 2696

Michigan Dental Association Relief Fund, MI, 4916

Michigan Elks Association Charitable Grant Fund, MI, 2697

Michigan Gateway Community Foundation, MI, 2698

Michigan Health Care Education and Research Foundation/MHCERF, MI, see 5653

Michner Educational Foundation, Joseph & Lottie, MI, 2699

Micron Technology Foundation, Inc., ID, 2700

Mid-Columbia Health Foundation, OR, 2701

Mid-Nebraska Community Foundation, Inc., NE, 2702

Mid-Shore Community Foundation, Inc., MD, 2703

Middlesex County Medical Society Foundation, Inc., NJ, 2704

Middleton Fund, Kate Kinloch, AL, 4917

Middleton Trust, Ambrose, OH, 4918

Middletown Community Foundation, OH, 2705

Midwest Foundaton for Higher Education, NE, 2706

Miedema Trust, Madeline, CA, A

Mihos Youth Foundation, Christina M., MA, 2707

Milam Foundation, The, TX, A

Miles Educational Foundation, MO, 2708

Murphy Scholarship Trust, Dennis L. & Hildreth M., IA, 2846

Murray Fine Arts Educational Fund, Albert K., The, OH, 2847

Murray Memorial Scholarship Trust Fund, William H., FL, 2848

Murray Scholarship Fund, F. Leo Murray & Irene D., MA, 2849

Murray Trust, IA, 2850

Muscular Dystrophy Association, Inc., AZ, 5986

Museum of Fine Arts, Houston, The, TX, 5409

Museum of Glass, WA, 5410

Music Center of the North Shore, IL, see 2852

Music for Youth Foundation, Inc., The, NY, 2851

Music Foundation of San Antonio, Inc., TX, A

Music Institute of Chicago, IL, 2852

Musical Research Society Endowment Foundation, Inc., OK, see 2853

Musical Research Society Endowment Fund, Inc., OK, 2853

Musicares Foundation, Inc., CA, 5411, 5987

Musicians Emergency Relief Fund-Local 802, NY, 5412

Musicians Foundation, Inc., NY, 5413

Muskegon County Community Foundation, Inc., MI, see 864

Muskingum County Community Foundation, OH, 5988

Mustard Seed Foundation, Inc., VA, 2854

Mutual Service Foundation Trust, IN, 2855

My Brother's Keeper Foundation, UT, 2856

Myasthenia Gravis Foundation of America, Inc., MN, 5989

Mycenaean Foundation, Inc., NY, 5990

Myers Charitable Trust, NE, 2857

Myers Church Scholarship, MI, 2858

Myers Memorial Scholarship Trust, G., OH, 2859

Myers Oceanographic & Marine Biology Trust, CA, 5991

Myers Scholarship Fund, Malcolm W. & Anna G., NC, 2860

Myers-Ti-Caro Foundation, Inc., NC, see 1376

N Foundation, Inc., The, NY, 2861

NAA Foundation, VA, see 2945

NAACP Legal Defense and Education Fund, Inc., NY, 2862

NAC Scholarship Fund, Inc., MA, 2863

Nacca Trust, Louise C., NC, A

NACME, NY, see 2874

Nadeau & Louise E. Nelson Scholarship Foundation, Stella M. Nelson, MT, 2864

Nadeau & Louise E. Nelson Senft Scholarship Foundation, Stella M. Nelson, MT, see 2864

Naftzger Fund for Fine Arts, Inc., KS, 5414

Nagel Family Foundation, SD, 4935

Nahas Educational Scholarship Foundation, Robert T., ID, 2865

NAIW (International), OK, see 2875

NAIW (International), OK, see 5998

Nancy and John Foundation, TX, see 5075

Nansemond Charitable Foundation, Inc., VA, 2866

NAPHCC Educational Foundation, VA, 5992

Naples Yacht Club Blue Gavel Scholarship Fund, FL, 2867

Naples, Sr. Educational Foundation, Richard T., Inc., OH, 2868

Nara Bank Scholarship Foundation, The, CA, 2869

NARAS Foundation, The, CA, see 1616

NARSAD, The Mental Health Research Association, NY, 5993

NASA College Scholarship Fund, Inc., TX, 2870

NASB Foundation, Inc., MO, 2871

Nasdaq Stock Market Educational Foundation, Inc., The, MD, 5994

Nash Scholarship Fund, Clayton, RI, 2872

Nation Foundation (Corporation), TX, 2873

National Academy of Education, The, DC, 5995

National Action Council for Minorities in Engineering, Inc., NY, 2874

National Alliance for Autism Research, Inc., NJ, 5996

National Alliance for Research on Schizophrenia and Depression, NY, see 5993

National Alopecia Areata Foundation, CA, 5997

National Arts Club, The, NY, 5415

National Association of Insurance Women (International) Education Foundation, OK, 2875, 5998

National Association of Retail Druggists, VA, see 6001

National Association of Secondary School Principals, VA, 5999

National Cancer Center, Inc., NY, 6000

National Charity League, Inc., CA, 2876

National Charity League-Newport Chapter, CA, 2877

National Children's Cancer Society, Inc., MO, 4936

National Community Pharmacists Association Foundation, VA, 6001

National Council of La Raza, DC, 6002

National Council of Teachers of Mathematics, VA, 2878

National Crime Prevention Council, DC, 6003

National Depressive and Manic Depressive Association, IL, 6004

National Fish and Wildlife Foundation, DC, 2879, 6005

National Foundation for Advancement in the Arts, FL, 5416

National Foundation for Infectious Diseases, The, MD, 6006

National Foundation for Jewish Culture, NY, 5417, 6007

National Foundation, Inc., CO, 2880, 4937

National Fund for the CDC, Inc., GA, see 5678

National Geographic Society Education Foundation, DC, see 6008

National Geographic Society, DC, 6008

National Headache Foundation, IL, 2881, 6009

National Healthcare Scholars Foundation, MI, 2882

National Hispanic Scholarship Fund, Inc., CA, see 1870

National Institute for the Food Service Industry, IL, see 2896

National Intercollegiate Rodeo Foundation, Inc., WA, 2883

National Italian American Foundation, Inc., DC, 2884, 6010

National Kidney Foundation of Alabama, AL, 4938

National Kidney Foundation of Connecticut, CT, 2885, 4939

National Kidney Foundation of East Tennessee, TN, 4940

National Kidney Foundation of Eastern Missouri and Metro East, Inc., MO, 4941, 6011

National Kidney Foundation of Florida, FL, 4942

National Kidney Foundation of Georgia, GA, 4943, 6012

National Kidney Foundation of Hawaii, HI, 4944

National Kidney Foundation of Illinois, Inc., IL, 6013

National Kidney Foundation of Indiana, Inc., IN, 2886, 4945, 6014

National Kidney Foundation of Iowa, IA, 4946

National Kidney Foundation of Kansas and Western Missouri, KS, 4947

National Kidney Foundation of Louisiana, LA, 4948, 6015

National Kidney Foundation of Maine, ME, 2887, 4949

National Kidney Foundation of Maryland, Inc., MD, 6016

National Kidney Foundation of Massachusetts, Rhode Island, New Hampshire and Vermont, Inc., MA, 2888, 6017

National Kidney Foundation of Michigan, Inc., MI, 6018

National Kidney Foundation of North Carolina, NC, 2889, 4950

National Kidney Foundation of Northern California, CA, 2890, 4951, 6019

National Kidney Foundation of Ohio, Inc., OH, 4952, 6020

National Kidney Foundation of Southern California, CA, 6021

National Kidney Foundation of Upstate New York, Inc., NY, 2891, 6022

National Kidney Foundation, Inc., NY, 6023

National Machinery Foundation, Inc., OH, 2892, 4953

National Medical Fellowships, Inc., NY, 2893, 6024

National MPS Society, Inc., ME, 6025

National Multiple Sclerosis Society Michigan Chapter, Inc., MI, 4954

National Multiple Sclerosis Society, Minnesota Chapter, MN, 2895

National Multiple Sclerosis Society, North Central Texas Chapter, TX, 4955

National Multiple Sclerosis Society, NY, 2894, 6026

National Neurofibromatosis Foundation, Inc., NY, see 5695

National Organization for Rare Disorders, Inc., CT, 6027

National Osteopathic Foundation, IL, see 128

National Parkinson Foundation, Inc., FL, 6028

National Patient Safety Foundation, MA, 6029

National Press Foundation, Inc., DC, 6030

National Psychiatric Endowment Fund, Inc., MD, see 5933

National Restaurant Association Educational Foundation, IL, 2896

National Science Teachers Association, VA, 6031

National Sculpture Society, Inc., NY, 5418

National Society of Accountants Scholarship Foundation, VA, 2897

National Society of Professional Engineers Educational Foundation, VA, 2898, 6032

National Society of Professional Engineers, VA, see 2898

National Society of Professional Engineers, VA, see 6032

National Society of Public Accountants Scholarship Foundation, VA, see 2897

National Society to Preven Blindness, IL, 6033

National Society to Prevent Blindness, IL, see 6033

National Tourism Foundation, MA, see 4095

National Transplant Assistance Fund (NTAF), PA, 4956

National Trust for Historic Preservation, DC, 6034

National Urban League, Inc., NY, 2899

National Urea Cycle Disorders Foundation, CA, 6035

National Wildlife Federation, VA, 2900

NATSO Foundation, The, VA, 2901, A

Navarro Family Foundation, Inc., CT, see 924

NC Beautiful, NC, see 5906

NCR Scholarship Foundation, OH, 2902

NCTM's Mathematics Education Trust (MET), VA, see 2878

NEA Foundation for the Improvement of Education, The, DC, 6036

Neal Memorial Scholarship Fund, Ed, GA, 2903

Nearburg Foundation, Charles and Dana, The, TX, 2904

Nebraska Friends of Foster Children Foundation, NE, 4957

Nebraska Medical Foundation, Inc., NE, 2905

Needham September 11th Scholarship Fund, NY, 2906

Neel Scholarship Fund, Harold M. Neel and Katharine Klepinger, IN, 2907

NEFA, MA, see 5420

Neilson Foundation, Adeline L., WY, 2908

Neinken Scholarship Grant & Loan Foundation, Maurice A., PA, 2909

Neinken Scholarship Grant, Maurice A., PA, see 2909

Neiswanger Educational Foundation, Walter E., IA, 2910

Neiswanger Educational Trust, IA, see 2910

Nell Educational Trust, Zola N. & Lawrence R., KS, 2911

Nelson Foundation, Inc., WI, 2912

Nelson Scholarship Fund, Victor and Mary D., WI, 2913

Nelson Scholarship Trust, Hazel T., KS, 2914

Nelson Scholarships, Catherine Hayes, Inc., PA, 2915

Nepal Educational Fund, Inc., CA, 2916

Nesbitt Medical Student Foundation, IL, 2917

Neskowin Coast Foundation, OR, see 5473

Neslab Charitable Foundation, NH, see 603

Nestle Scholarship Foundation, WA, A

Nestor Foundation, Mary Margaret, PA, 2918

Netherland-America Foundation, Inc., The, NY, 2919, 5419

Netzach Foundation, NY, 4958

Nevada Humanities Committee, NV, 6037

Nevada Women's Fund, NV, 2920

New Bedford Port Society, Ladies Branch of the, MA, 2921

New England Biolabs Foundation, MA, 6038

New England Education Society, MA, 2922

New England Foundation for the Arts, MA, 5420

New England Society in the City of Brooklyn, NY, 2923

New Hampshire Charitable Foundation, The, NH, 2924

New Hampshire Food Industries Education Foundation, NH, 2925

New Horizons Foundation, CA, 4959

New Jersey Nets and Devils Foundation, NJ, 2926

New Jersey Nets Foundation, Inc., NJ, see 2926

New Jersey Osteopathic Education Foundation, NJ, 2927

New Jersey Performing Arts Center, Corp., NJ, 5421

New Jersey State Elks Crippled Children's Committee, NJ, 2928

New London Service Organization, Inc., NH, 2929

New Mexico Community Foundation, The, NM, 2930

New Orphan Asylum Scholarship Foundation, OH, 2931

New World Foundation, The, NY, 6039

New World Gospel Mission, Inc., NJ, 2932

New York City "Bravest" Scholarship Fund, NY, 2933

New York City Police Foundation, Inc., NY, 2934

New York Classical Club, Inc., The, NY, 2935

New York Foundation for Architecture, Inc., NY, 2936

New York Foundation for the Arts, NY, 5422

New York Library Association, NY, 2937

New York Mills Arts Retreat, MN, 5423

New York Music For Youth Foundation, Inc., The, NY, see 2851

New York Stock Exchange Fallen Heroes Fund, NY, 4960

New York Times Company Foundation, Inc., The, NY, 2938

Newark Museum Association, The, NJ, 5424

Newaygo County Community Services, MI, 4961

Newaygo Public Schools Educational Advancement Foundation, MI, 2939

Newblom Foundation, Darold A., NE, 2940

Newburyport Howard Benevolent Society, MA, 4962

Newcastle Scholarship Trust, TX, A

Newell Scholarship Trust Fund, Daniel James and Lavonne, IN, see 2941

Newell Scholarship Trust, IN, 2941

Newhouse Scholarship Trust Fund, VA, 2942

Newlin, Sr. Memorial Trust, Robert "Aqqaluk", AK, 2943

Newmeyer Trust, Marie, IA, 2944

Newspaper Association of America Foundation, VA, 2945

Newstead Foundation, Inc., RI, A

Newton Scholarship Fund, Horace & Letitia, OH, 2946

NFID, MD, see 6006

Ngwebifor Foundation, Bobe, CA, 2947

Niagara Falls Rotary Foundation, Inc., NY, 2948

Niccum Educational Trust Foundation, WI, 2949

Nicholas Family Foundation, PA, 4963

Nicholl Memorial Foundation, James R., WI, 4964

Nichols Scholarship Trust, Howard & Mamie, CA, 2950

Nichols Trust, Mary, MA, 2951

Nichols, Jr. Scholarship Foundation, Robert L., MO, 2952

Nickel Producers Environmental Research Association, Inc., NC, 6040

Nicklies Scholarship Fund, L. E., PA, 2953

Nicolai Memorial Scholarship Fund, David K., AK, see 626

Niconchuk Scholarship Trust, Anna, MA, 2954

Niederkorn Scholarship Trust, William J. & Myra L., WI, 2955

Nielson Scholarship Fund, Karl A. Nielson and Karen J., TX, see 2956

Nielson Scholarship Fund, TX, 2956

Nikkei Alumni Association, U. W., WA, 2957

Nishan Scholarship Trust, Freda, WI, 2958

Nixon Memorial Education Fund, PA, 2959

NMC Projects, Inc., WI, see 2912

Noble County Community Foundation, IN, 2960

Noble Foundation, Samuel Roberts, Inc., The, OK, 2961

Nolan Foundation, Robert J., Inc., NY, 2962

Noll Foundation, John H., IN, 2963

Nolley Educational Scholarship Fund, Gilbert and Evelyn, OH, 2964

Norby Scholarship Fund, Swan C., TX, 2965

Nordic Educational Trust, VT, 2966

Nordman Charitable Trust, Amos, MI, see 2967

Nordman Foundation Charitable Trust, Amos, MI, 2967

Norfolk Foundation, The, VA, 2968

Norman Trust for Visually Impaired Students, Kathleen, The, NY, 2969

Norris Fund, Shelley R. and Alice S., Inc., KY, 2970

North American Philips Foundation, NY, see 3187

North American Savings Bank Foundation, Inc., MO, see 2871

North Attleboro Scholarship Foundation, Inc., MA, 2971

North Carolina Community Foundation, NC, 2972

North Central Massachusetts Community Foundation, Inc., MA, 2973

North Dakota Community Foundation, ND, 2974

North Dakota Humanities Council, ND, 6041

North Fork Community Foundation, NY, 2975

North Fork Women for Women Fund, Inc., NY, 4965

North Haven Foundation, ME, 2976

North Orange Memorial Hospital Tax District Trust, FL, 2977

North Valley Health Education Foundation, CA, 2978

Northeast High School Alumni Foundation, PA, 2979

Northeast Iowa Charitable Foundation, IA, 2980

Northeastern New York Community Trust, NY, 2981

Northern California DX Foundation, The, CA, 6042

Northern California Scholarship Foundation and the Scaife Scholarship Foundation, The, CA, see 2982

Northern California Scholarship Foundation, The, CA, 2982

Northern Chautauqua Community Foundation, Inc., NY, 2983

Northern Clay Center, MN, 5425

Northern Indiana Fuel and Light Company, Inc. Fund and Trust, Inc., OH, 2984

Northern New York Community Foundation, Inc., NY, 2985

Northern Palm Beach County Youth Foundation, Inc., The, FL, 2986

Northern Virginia Community Foundation, VA, 2987

Northern Virginia Family Service, VA, 4966

Northrup Educational Foundation, Inc., NY, 2988

Northwest AIDS Foundation-Chicken Soup Brigade, WA, see 4886

Northwest Bancorp, Inc. Charitable Foundation, PA, 2989

Northwest Danish Foundation, WA, 2990

Northwest Health Foundation, OR, 2991, 6043

Northwest Lions Foundation for Sight & Hearing, WA, 4967

Northwest Minnesota Foundation (NWMF), MN, 6044

Northwest Osteopathic Medical Foundation, OR, 6045

Norwegian Children's Home Association of New York, Inc., The, NY, 2992

Novi Educational Foundation, MI, 2993

Noyes Scholarship Fund, John Calvin, PA, A

NRC Foundation, Inc., CT, 2994

Nucor Foundation, NC, 2995

Nugent Educational Fund, Adaline C., WV, 2996

Nurses House, Inc., NY, 4968

Nuttycomb Charitable Trust No. 2, S. T. & Mabel I., KS, 2997

NYContemporary Glass Center, Inc., NY, see 5495

Nye Scholarship Trust, Grace Swift Nye & Alfred Gibbs, CT, 2998

NYS Fraternal Order of Police Empire State Foundation, NY, see 2999

NYS Fraternal Order of Police Empire State Foundation, NY, see 4969

NYS Fraternal Order of Police Foundation, NY, 2999, 4969

O'Brien Foundation for Academic Excellence, John & Mary, TX, 6046

O'Brien Foundation, Lincoln, Inc., NM, A

O'Brien-VRBA Scholarship Trust, The, OH, 3000

O'Brion Trust, Frank, CT, 3001, A

O'Connor Educational Trust, Charles D. & Gertrude H., IN, 3002

O'Daniel Foundation, F. A., AR, A

O'Hara Trust, John and Blanche, WI, 3003

O'Leary Scholarship Fund Trust, Catherine G., MA, 3004

O'Meara Foundation, Inc., The, CT, 3005

O'Neill, Jr. Education Fund, L. Arthur, SC, 3006

Oak Park/River Forest Community Foundation, IL, 3007

Oakes Foundation, Frank L., WI, 3008

Oakland County Community Trust, MI, 3009

Oakland Foundation, Inc., VT, 3010

Oakley Foundation, Mary, Inc., The, CA, 4970

Oates Scholarship Fund, L. R., NC, 3011

Oates Scholarship Trust, Forrest C. Oates & Minnie Less, AL, 3012

Oberdorfer Scholarship Trust Fund, Julia S., IN, 3013

Oblinger Trust f/b/o Stephen Dexter and Emily Jane Tipton Dole Scholarship, Emily, IL, see 1138

Ocean State Power Scholarship Foundation, Ltd., MA, 3014

Ochoco Charitable Fund, OR, 3015

Ochoco Scholarship Fund, OR, see 3015

Office Depot Disaster Relief Foundation, FL, 4971

Ogden College Foundation, KY, 3016

Oglesby Foundation, Robert and Willora, Inc., TX, 3017

Ohadi Memorial Foundation, Jean Paul, IL, 3018

Ohio County Community Foundation, Inc., IN, 3019

Ohiyesa Corporation, VT, 6047

Oilgear Ferris Foundation, WI, 3020

Ojai Film Festival, CA, 5426

Oklahoma Communities Foundation, Inc., OK, see 859

Oklahoma Elks Major Project, Inc., OK, 3021

Oklahoma Scholarship Fund, OK, 3022

Old Harbor Scholarship Foundation, AK, 3023

Olds Foundation, Inc., AR, 3024

Olender Foundation, Jack H. & Lovell R., DC, 3025

Olliff Foundation, Matred Carlton, FL, 3026

Olmsted Foundation, George and Carol, The, VA, 6048

Olson Trust, C. P. & Irene, MN, 3027

Olson Trust, Iona, MI, 3028

Omaha Volunteers for Handicapped Children, NE, 3029

OMC Foundation, The, WI, 3030

Omega Charitable Foundation, NY, 3031

Oncologic Foundation of Buffalo, Inc., The, NY, 6049

One Foundation, The, UT, 6050

Ontario Children's Home, NY, 3032, 4972

Ontonagon Area Scholarship Foundation, The, MI, 3033

Oocea Foundation, Inc., FL, 3034

Open Society Institute, NY, 3035, 6051, A

Operafestival Roma, Inc., VA, 3036

Oppenheim Trust, Louis S., OH, 4973

Optical Society of America, DC, 3037, 6052

Orange County Community Foundation, CA, 3038

Orange Foundation, CT, 3039

Orange Memorial Hospital Corporation, TX, 3040

Orange Scholarship Foundation, MA, 3041

Order of the Alhambra Charity Fund, Inc., MD, 3042

Oregon Association of Public Accountants Scholarship Foundation, OR, 3043

Oregon Community Foundation, The, OR, 3044

Oregon Council for the Humanities, OR, 3045, 6053

Oregon Lions Sight and Hearing Foundation, Inc., OR, 4974

Oregon Trail Community Foundation, Inc., NE, 3046

Organic Farming Research Foundation, CA, 6054

Organization of American Historians, IN, 3047, 6055

Organization of Black Airline Pilots, MD, 3048

Oro Grande Foundation, CA, 3049

Orphan Foundation of America, VA, 3050

Orr Foundation, The, RI, 3051

Orris Memorial Scholarship Trust Fund, Dr. Donald J., MI, 3052

Orscheln Industries Foundation, Inc., MO, 3053

Orson A. Hull & Minnie E. Hull Educational Foundation, MN, 3054

Ortega Charitable Foundation, FL, 3055

Orum Memorial Foundation, Stig P., Inc., IL, 3056

Osborn Memorial Trust, Louise & Lane, OH, 3057

Osborn Scholarship Trust, Joyce L., MN, 3058

Osborn Scholarship Trust, Lawrence L., IN, 3059

Oshkosh Area Community Foundation, WI, 3060, A

Oshkosh B'Gosh Foundation, Inc., WI, 3061

Oshkosh Foundation, WI, see 3060

Ostberg Foundation, Inc., The, NJ, 4975

Osteogenesis Imperfecta Foundation, Inc., MD, 6056

Osteopathic Founders Foundation, OK, 6057

Osteopathic Institute of the South, GA, see 5820

Otero County Electric Education Foundation, NM, 3062

Ott Scholarship Foundation, Richard F., FL, 3063

Ott Scholarship Fund, Raymond J., IL, 3064

Ott Scholarship Trust, Harlan, Ruby & Phil E., WI, 3065

Ott Scholarships, Phil E., WI, see 3065
Ottaway Foundation, Nicholas B., Inc., NY, A
Outer Banks Community Foundation, Inc., NC, 3066
Owen Educational Scholarship Trust, Jack & Charlotte, TX, 3067
Owen Foundation, Herman & Hazel, MS, 4976
Owens Foundation, Elizabeth Anne, AL, 3068
Owens Scholarship Trust Co., NC, 3069
Owenton Rotary Student Loan Fund, KY, 3070
Oxford Foundation, Inc., IN, see 4058
Oyster Bay Sailing Foundation, The, NY, 3071
Ozanich Crippled and Burned Children's Scholarship Fund Charitable Foundation, John G., OH, A
Ozaukee Bank Educational Foundation, Inc., WI, see 1231
Ozinga Memorial Scholarship Foundation, Janet, IL, 3072

P.S. 1 Contemporary Art Center, Inc., NY, 5427
Pace 8-591 Fallen Workers Memorial Scholarship, WA, 3073
Pace Trust for Community Creative Visual Arts, KY, A
Pacers Basketball Corporation Foundation, Inc., IN, see 3074
Pacers Foundation, Inc., IN, 3074, A
Pacific N.W. Kiwanis Foundation, OR, 3075
Pacific Pioneer Fund, CA, 5428
Pacific West Cancer Fund, Inc., LA, A
PacifiCare Health Systems Foundation, CA, 3076
Pack Foundation, CA, A
Packaging Machinery Manufacturers Institute, VA, see 3228
Paddington Foundation, PA, 3077
Padelford Scholarship Trust Fund, Arline P., MA, 3078
PADI Foundation, CA, 6058
Padolf Foundation, Lou & Lillian, FL, 3079
Page Education Foundation, MN, 3080
Page Trust, Frank E., MD, 3081
Pagliara Charitable Foundation, The, FL, 3082
Paideia Foundation, The, IL, 6059
Paine Scholarship Fund Trust, Charles J., MA, 3083
Pais Family Educational Foundation, John and Lucia, Inc., The, WV, 3084
Palen-Klar Scholarship Fund, Countess Frances Thorley, RI, 3085
Palestine Temple Charities Trust, RI, see 5063
Palm Beach County Community Foundation, FL, see 865
Palm Beach County Cultural Council, FL, 5429
Palmer Foundation, Ann, NV, 3086
Palmer Fund Trust, Isaac E., RI, 3087
Palmer Memorial Scholarship Fund, C. Paul, OH, 3088
Palmer Scholarship Trust, Walter Curtis, WI, 3089
Palmer Trust, Marvin O., OR, 3090
Palmetto Electric Trust, SC, 4977
Palos Bank Foundation, Inc., IL, 3091
Paltz Memorial Scholarship Trust, Irene A., NE, 3092
Pan-Icarian Foundation, PA, 3093
Panasonic Tennessee-Japan Cultural Exchange Foundation, TN, 3094
Pancreatic Cancer Action Network, Inc., CA, 6060
Panizza Family Foundation, PA, 3095
Pape Charitable Foundation, Robert, RI, 3096
Pape Educational Fund Trust, Arthur F., KS, 3097
Papines Scholarship Trust, John A. & Irene, NJ, 3098
Papines Scholarship Trust-Ermoupolis, John A. & Irene, NJ, 6061
Parapsychology Foundation, Inc., NY, 6062
Pardee Cancer Treatment Association of Greater Brazosport, TX, 4978
Pardee Cancer Treatment Fund of Bay County, MI, 4979
Paris Education Foundation, TX, 3099
Park Charitable Foundation, Clyde, NY, A
Park Foundation, OH, 3100
Park Ridge Organization Scholarship Fund, Inc., The, NY, A
Park Technical Student Fund, Willis H., OH, 3101
Parke County Community Foundation, Inc., IN, 3102
Parker & Parsley Scholarship Foundation, TX, see 3213
Parker Scholarship Foundation, Winston E., NJ, 3103
Parker Scholarship Fund, Winston E., NJ, see 3103
Parker Scholarship Trust, Henry & Louise, MI, 3104
Parker Trust, Pauline R., NY, 3105

Parkersburg Area Community Foundation, WV, 3106
Parks Trust for the Education of Nurses, Ruth, IA, 3107
Parrett Scholarship Fund, OR, see 3108
Parrett Scholarship Trust Fund, Arthur and Doreen, OR, 3108
Parsons Community Foundation, KS, 4980
Parsons Scholarship Foundation, W. N., KS, 3109
Partridge Academy in Duxbury, Trustees of, MA, 3110
Partridge Memorial Scholarship Fund, William G. & Rhoda B., NY, 3111
PARTS Scholarship Foundation, PA, 3112
Pasarow Foundation, Robert J. and Claire, CA, 6063
Patch Scholarship Trust, Grace, NV, 3113
Patterson Charitable Trust, Charles A. & Odette W., FL, 3114
Patterson Foundation, Alicia, DC, 6064
Patterson Foundation, Father Joseph, Inc., AZ, 3115
Patterson Perpetual Fund, Nicholas, NY, 3116
Patterson Trust, Frances, KS, 3117
Patterson Trust, G. F., IL, 3118
Patton Scholarship Foundation Trust, Minnie, TX, 3119
Patton Scholarship Fund, George W. & Mary B., MN, 3120
Patton Scholarship Fund, MN, see 3120
Patton Scholarship Trust, AZ, 3121
Paul Foundation, Josephine Bay Paul and C. Michael, Inc., NY, see 5641
Paul Memorial Trust, Thomas M., MO, 3122
PAULA Difference Scholarship Fund, CA, 3123
Paulsen Trust, MI, 3124
Pawating Health Foundation, MI, see 2312
Paxton Memorial Scholarship Fund, Jack, Inc., KY, 3125
Payne Scholarship Fund, Charles K., Inc., NJ, 3126
Peabody Foundation, Grace & Bill, Inc., The, MA, 3127
Peacock Educational Trust, Louise, MI, 3128
Peak Scholarship Fund, Walter G. and Ella M., OH, 3129
Pearce Educational Foundation, Jack & Katherine, TX, 3130
Pearce Foundation, OH, 3131
Pearce Trust, George & Belle, KS, 3132
Pearle Vision Foundation, Inc., TX, 4981
Pearson Scholarship Trust, Edwin & Gladys, IN, 3133
Pearson Scholarship Trust, Viola, WY, 3134
Peck Memorial Fund, Abel E., NY, 3135
Peck Trust, Katherine L., RI, 3136
Peckitt Scholarship Trust, Hattie M., NC, 3137
Peckitt Scholarship Trust, Leonard Carlton, NC, see 3137
Pediatric AIDS Foundation, DC, see 5824
Pediatric Brain Tumor Foundation of the United States, Inc., NC, 6065
Peeples Trust, Marion A. & Eva S., WI, 3138
Peery Memorial Scholarship Fund, Bulah, TX, 3139
Pehna Scholarship Trust, Charles, OH, 3140
Pekema Memorial Scholarships, Andrew, WA, 3141
Pella Rolscreen Foundation, IA, 3142
Pellerin Foundation, Willis & Mildred, LA, 3143
PEMCO Foundation, WA, 3144
PEN American Center, Inc., NY, 5430
PEN/Faulkner, DC, 5431
Penasco Valley Telephone Education Foundation, NM, 3145
PENCIL Foundation, TN, 6066
Peninsula Community Foundation, CA, 3146, 5432
Peninsula Foundation, The, NM, 3147
Penn Jersey Youth Umpires School, Inc., NJ, 3148
Pennsylvania Auto & Truck Salvage Association Scholarship Foundation, PA, see 3112
Pennsylvania Humanities Council, PA, 5433
Pennsylvania Industrial Chemical Corporation-Chester High School Scholarship Fund, NC, 3149
Pennsylvania Industrial Chemical Corporation-Clairton High School Scholarship Fund, OH, 3150
Penrose Foundation, TX, 3151
People in Business Care, Inc., MN, 4982
People Technology Foundation, Inc., The, NJ, 6067
People to People International, MO, 3152
People's Fund, The, PA, see 499
Peoria Area Community Foundation, IL, see 874
Pequot Community Foundation, Inc., The, CT, see 902

Percival Scholarship Fund, H. Stanley & Marie, WA, 3153
Percy Franklin Lucas Memorial Student Loan Fund, The, TX, 3154
Percy Memorial Trust, Lottie King Lucas, TX, see 3154
Perdue Education Fund, Evelyn, KS, 3155
Performing Arts Foundation, Inc., CA, 3156
Pergo Foundation, The, CA, 3157
Perisho - Nina Rall McConkey Scholarship Trust, Mary, IL, 3158
Perkins Foundation, B. F. & Rose H., WY, 3159, 4983
Perkins Memorial Trust, James W., The, VA, 3160
Perley Free School, Trustees of the, MA, 3161
Permanent Endowment Fund for Martha's Vineyard, MA, 3162
Permian Basin Area Foundation, TX, 3163
Pernot Scholarship Fund, Henry S., OR, 6068
Perot Foundation, The, TX, 4984
Perpetual Benevolent Fund, The, MA, 4985
Perron Memorial Trust f/b/o Graduates of High School Serving the City of North Adams, Charles A., CT, see 3164
Perron Memorial Trust, Charles & Olivina, CT, 3164
Perry Memorial Scholarship Fund, NC, 3165
Perry Memorial Scholarships, Frank H. & Annie Belle Whilhelm, NC, see 3165
Perry Scholarship Foundation, OH, 3166
Perry Scholarship Trust, Mildred R., WI, 3167
Perry Scholarship, Nathan F. & Edna L., OH, see 3166
Perry-Griffin Foundation, The, NC, 3168
Peters Foundation Corp., Herman & Katherine, The, IL, 3169
Peters Scholarship B Fund, Ruth R., OH, 3170
Peters Trust, Glenn D., IN, 3171
Peters Valley Craftsman, Inc., NJ, 3172, 5434, 6069
Petersburg Methodist Home for Girls, VA, 3173
Peterson Charitable Foundation, Alan & Mildred, IL, 3174
Peterson Foundation, John P., NJ, 3175
Peterson Scholarship Trust, Bradley A. & Birdell A., WI, A
Petoskey-Harbor Springs Area Community Foundation, MI, 3176
Petra Foundation Charitable Trust, MA, 6070
Petraborg Educational Trust Fund, Hans & Thora, MN, 3177
Pettee-Chace Memorial Scholarship Fund, MA, 3178
Pewabic Society, Inc., MI, 5435
Peyton Foundation, Mary L., The, TX, 3179, 4986
Pfaffinger Foundation, CA, 4987
Pfister & Vogel Tanning Company, Inc. Foundation, WI, 3180
Pflughaupt Charitable Foundation, Eugene B. and Margery Ames, Inc., KY, see 3181
Pflughaupt Charitable Foundation, Inc., KY, 3181
Pharmacy Network Foundation, Inc., The, NC, 3182
Phelps Trust, Winifred Y., MI, 3183
Phi Delta Theta Educational Foundation, OH, 3184
Phi Kappa Tau Foundation, OH, 3185
Phi Mu Foundation, GA, 3186
Philadelphia Award, The, PA, 6071
Philadelphia Foundation, The, PA, 4988
Philanthropic Ventures Foundation, CA, 4989
Philippe Foundation, Inc., NY, 6072
Philips Electronics North American Foundation, NY, 3187
Phillips Foundation, Edwin, MA, 4991
Phillips Foundation, Inc., DC, 3188, 6073
Phillips Foundation, MS, 4990
Phillips Memorial Charitable Trust, Stephen, MA, 3189
Phillips Scholarship Fund, V. E. & Betty, The, OH, 3190
Phillips Trust, Russell, WI, 3191
Phillips-Hernandez Scholarship Foundation, TX, 3192
Phoenix Foundation Trust Fund, AZ, 3193
Phoenix Scholarship Foundation, Inc., MD, 3194
Phoenix Suns Charities, Inc., AZ, 3195
Phoenix Swim Club, AZ, A
Phoenixville Community Health Foundation, PA, 3196
Photronics Scholarship Foundation, Inc., FL, 3197
Physicians Aid Association of the Delaware Valley, The, PA, 4993
Physicians Aid Association, CA, 4992
Physicians' Relief Fund, PA, 3198, 4994

Pi Beta Phi Educational Foundation, Inc., KS, 3199
Pick Foundation, Vernon J., The, MN, 3200
Pickett & Hatcher Educational Fund, Inc., GA, 3201
Pickle Memorial Scholarship Fund, Elva and Herbert, CA, 3202
Pierce Charitable Foundation, Mills O. Pierce & Mount Vernon, AR, 3203
Pierce Company Employees Aid Fund, S. S., PA, 4995
Pierce Trust, Beatrice D., RI, 3204
Pierce Trust, Frank, IA, 3205
Pierce Trust, Katharine C., MA, 4996
Pierson Trust, Julia, IL, 3206
Pigott Scholarship Foundation, Paul, WA, 3207
Pilch Foundation, Walt and Olga, WY, 3208
Pilchard Foundation, A. Franklin, IL, 3209
PILF, NY, see 3288
Pilgrim Foundation, The, MA, 3210, 4997
Pilot International Foundation, Inc., GA, 3211
Pine Family Foundation, TX, 6074
Pingel Educational Fund, Edward H. Pingel & Cora W., The, IL, 3212
Pioneer Fund, Inc., CA, see 5428
Pioneer Natural Resources Scholarship Foundation, TX, 3213
Pipe Line Contractors Association Scholarship Foundation, TX, 3214
Piper Charitable Trust, Virginia G., The, AZ, 6075
Piper Foundation, Inc., MA, 3215
Piper Foundation, Minnie Stevens, TX, 3216, 6076
Piqua Community Foundation, The, OH, 3217
Piqua-Miami County Foundation, OH, see 2689
Pitcairn High School Alumni - R. J. Conrad Scholarship Fund, PA, 3218
Pitney Bowes Relief Fund Charitable Trust, The, CT, 4998
Pittsburgh Foundation, The, PA, 3219
Pittsburgh Glass Center, Inc., PA, 5436
Pitzer Trust, John, IN, 3220
PKD Foundation, MO, 6077
Plank Trust f/b/o C. Plank Scholarship Trust, Elsie L., PA, 3221
Plastic Surgery Educational Foundation, IL, 6078
Plexon Corp. Charitable Foundation, Inc., WI, see 3222
Plexus Corp. Charitable Foundation, Inc., WI, 3222
Plimpton Educational Fund, Alice H., MA, 3223
Plitt Southern Theatres, Inc. Employees Fund, TX, 4999
Plotkin Memorial Foundation, Peter & Masha, CA, 3224
Ploughshares Fund, CA, 6079
Plummer Scholarship Fund, IN, 3225
PLUS Foundation, MN, 3226
Plymouth Fragment Society Trust, MA, 5000
PMC Foundation, The, CA, 3227
PMMI Education and Training Foundation, VA, 3228
PNC Memorial Foundation, PA, 3229
Podiatry Foundation of Pittsburgh, The, PA, 3230
Poff Scholarship Foundation, Bess R., VA, 3231
Polakovic Charitable Trust, John, MI, 3232
Polaris Foundation, The, MN, 5001
Police Officer Assistance Trust, FL, 5002
Polish American Board of Education of Berks County, PA, PA, 3233
Polk County Community Foundation, Inc., The, NC, 3234
Polk Foundation, Annie M. & Clarke A., TX, 3235
Pollock-Krasner Foundation, Inc., The, NY, 5438
Polonsky Brothers Foundation, The, NJ, 3236
Polycystic Kidney Research Foundation, MO, see 6077
Pomeroy Scholarship Fund Trust, Harriet & Fred, OH, 3237
Pomona Valley Community Hospital LTD-Womens Auxiliary, CA, 3238
Poncin Scholarship Fund, WA, 6080
Pope Foundation, UT, A
Pope Life Foundation, Lois, The, FL, 6081
Pope Memorial Scholarship Fund, Ida M., HI, 3239
Pope Scholarship Fund, Thomas H., MA, 3240
Port Arthur Higher Education Foundation, Inc., TX, 3241
Porter Art Foundation, IN, 3242
Porter Educational Fund, Edwin M., MO, 3243
Porter Fund, Martha Boschen, Inc., The, CT, 5439
Porter Trust, Laura E., KS, 3244
Portland Female Charitable Society, ME, 5003

Portland Foundation, The, IN, 3245
Portland Institute for Contemporary Art, OR, 5440
Portland Seamen's Friend Society, ME, 5004
Portland Valley Acacia Fund, Inc., OR, 5005
Posey Foundation, Leslie T. & Frances U., FL, 3246
Positive Impact, Inc., AZ, 5006
POSSCA, Inc., WA, 3247
Post Trust, Ralph B., NY, 3248
Postles Scholarship Fund, Howard and Edna, PA, 3249
Potlatch Foundation for Higher Education, WA, 3250
Potter Foundation, Philip E., The, NY, 3251
Potter Memorial Foundation, Stephen J., Inc., NY, 3252
Pottstown Foundation, Greater, The, PA, 3253
Pottstown Symphony Orchestra, PA, 5441
Poucher Memorial Fund, Frank C. Poucher and Lillian S., NJ, 3254
Poujol Foundation, The, TX, 3255
Powell Trust, Mary E., OH, 5007
Power Scholarship Fund, Howard A., PA, 3256
Powers Foundation, Ross, ME, 5008
Poweshiek Community Foundation, Greater, IA, 3257
Poynter Fund, The, FL, see 3861
Prater Scholarship Fund, Guy and Nyda, WA, 3258
Pratt Trust, Fannie B., MA, 5009
Precision Rubber Products Foundation, Inc., TN, 3259
Preferred Mutual Insurance Company Foundation, NY, 3260
Prescott Christian School Scholarship Foundation, AZ, 3261
Presser Foundation, The, PA, 5442
Pressman Foundation, William, PA, 3262
Prest Educational Trust Fund, Joe, OH, 3263
Presto Foundation, The, DE, 3264
Preston Educational Trust, Elmer O. & Ida, IA, 3265
Preston Trust, Evelyn W., CT, 5443
Prevent Blindness America, IL, see 6033
Previti Family Charitable Foundation, A. A., Inc., NJ, 3266
Price Chopper's Golub Foundation, NY, 3267
Price Educational Foundation, Herschel C., WV, 3268
Price Family Charitable Foundation, Inc., The, DE, 5010
Price Family Charitable Fund, The, CA, 6082
Price Foundation, Inc., CA, 3269
Price Foundation, Sol & Helen, The, CA, see 6082
Price Scholarship Fund, Joseph R. and Florence A., MA, 3270
Price Trust, Albert M., WV, 3271
Pride Foundation, The, WA, 3272
Primate Conservation, Inc., RI, 6083
Prince George's Arts Council, Inc., MD, 5444
Prince Trust No. 2, Nathan D., CT, 3273
Princess Grace Foundation - U.S.A., NY, 5445
Princeton Area Community Foundation, Inc., NJ, 3274
Princeton Area Foundation, Inc., The, NJ, see 3274
Princeton High School Class of 1926 Scholarship Fund, WV, 3275
Pringle Charitable Foundation, C., RI, 3276
Pringle Foundation, Charles G., RI, see 3276
Prior Memorial Scholarship Trust, Beatrice O., OH, 3277
Pritchard Educational Fund, IA, 3278
Pritchett Trust, Scott R., CA, 3279
Private Colleges and Universities Foundation, MA, 3280
Pro Deo Guild, Inc., NY, 6085
Procrit Foundation, Inc., NJ, 5011
Professional Association of Diving Instructors Foundation, CA, see 6058
Professional Athletes Foundation, DC, 5012
Professional Horsemen's Scholarship Fund, Inc., NY, 3281
Progress Village Foundation, Inc., FL, A
Progressive Business Publications Foundation, PA, 3282
Prohaska Scholarship Foundation, WI, 3283
Project Reach Youth, Inc., NY, 3284
Project Single Parent, Inc., OK, 5013
Project Tomorrow, CA, 6086
Promotional Products Education Foundation, TX, 3285
Proshek Foundation, Charles E., MN, A
Prostate Cancer Foundation, CA, 6087
Protein Foundation, CT, 5014
Provenzano Scholarship Fund, Josephine, NJ, see 2122

Providence Female Charitable Society, RI, 5015
Pryde Scholarship Fund, John and Elizabeth, MD, 3286
Pryor Foundation, Mark R., Inc., MN, 3287
Public Education: Nashville Citizens Involved In Leadership, TN, see 6066
Public Entity Risk Institute, VA, 6088
Public Interest Law Foundation at Columbia, NY, 3288
Puckett Foundation, IL, 3289
Puckett Memorial Fund, Leta Potter, CA, 3290
Puckett, Jr. Family Foundation, Allen B., Inc., MS, 5016
Puffin Foundation, Ltd., NJ, 5446, 6089
Pugh Foundation Scholarship Fund, Hazel & Ben, WI, see 3291
Pugh Foundation Scholarship Fund, WI, 3291
Pugliese Medical Foundation, Sarah L., TN, 5017
Pulaski County Community Foundation, IN, 3292
Pullman Educational Foundation, George M., IL, 3293
Pursuit of Excellence, CA, 3294
Putnam County Community Foundation, The, IN, 3295
Putnam Cultural Endowment, Oscar Lee, LA, 3296
Putnam Free School, Trustees of the, MA, 3297
Putnam Prize Fund for the Promotion of Scholarship, William Lowell, MA, 3298
Putnam Trust, Franklin H., RI, 3299
Pyle Trust, Joseph P., PA, 3300
Pyramid Atlantic, Inc., MD, 5447

Quad City Osteopathic Foundation, IA, 3301
Quaker Chemical Foundation, The, PA, 3302
Queens Council on the Arts, Inc., NY, 5448
Quin Foundation, Robert D. & Margaret W., PA, 5018
Quinn Scholarship Fund, Thomas P., RI, 3303

R.O.S.E. Fund, Inc., The, MA, 3304
Raab Educational Trust, Herbert and Gwendolyn, IN, 3305
Rabideau Education Scholarship Fund, Omer E., IL, 3306
Racey Foundation, J. L. & Helen B., Inc., VA, 3307
Rachor Family Foundation, Ltd., MI, 3308
Rachor Professional School Scholarship Fund, Michael Garry, Ltd., MI, see 3308
Racine Community Foundation, Inc., WI, 3309
Racine County Area Foundation, Inc., WI, see 3309
Radio and Television News Directors Foundation, DC, 3310, 6090
Radius Foundation, Inc., The, NY, 6091
Ragdale Foundation, The, IL, 5449
Ragel Scholarship Fund, Robert L., OR, 3311
Rahr Foundation, MN, 3312
Raider Memorial Trust, Helen, IA, 3313
Raies-Murr Educational Trust, The, CA, 3314
Rainey Memorial Trust, Bish, IL, 3315
Rainey Scholarship Fund, Micki, Inc., CA, 3316
Rainforest Alliance, Inc., NY, 6092
Raleigh County Community Action Association, Inc., WV, 5019
Ramakrishna Foundation, CA, 6093
Ramirez, Jr. Family Foundation, Agustin A., WI, 3317
Ramona's Mexican Food Products Scholarship Foundation, CA, 3318
Ramsdale Scholarship Fund, Edward, Inc., ID, 3319
Rand Institute/The Center for the Advancement of Objectivism, Ayn, CA, 3320
Randolph Foundation, John, VA, 3321
Randolph Foundation, The, NH, 3322
Randolph Memorial Scholarship Trust, IN, 3323
Rangeley Educational Fund, FL, 3324
Ranger-Ryan Scholarship Foundation, TX, 3325
Raskob Foundation, Bill, Inc., The, MD, 3326
Rasmuson Foundation, AK, 5450, 6094
Rathke Irrevocable Scholarship Trust, Edward F., WI, 3327
Ratner, Miller, Shafran Foundation, The, OH, 3328
Rau Trust, Alexander and Cassia, PA, 3329
Rauch Family Foundation II, Inc., IL, 3330
Rawlins Memorial Trust, Mary W., DE, A
Rawls Educational Trust, Walter C. & Ella, FL, 3331
Rawls Scholarship Foundation, Jerry S., The, TX, 3332
Ray-Carroll County Grain Growers Scholarship Fund, Inc., MO, 3333
Rayni Foundation, Inc., The, FL, 3334

Rayonier Foundation, The, FL, 3335
RCI Foundation, IN, see 5725
RCL Foundation, CA, 3336
Reaching Up, Inc., NY, 3337
Reade Industrial Fund, IL, 5020
Reader's Digest Foundation, NY, 3338
Reading Musical Foundation, PA, 3339
READY Foundation, Inc., NJ, see 3412
Reagan Presidential Foundation, Ronald, The, CA, 3340
Real Colegio Complutense, Inc., MA, 3341
Real Estate Educational Foundation, Inc., The, CT, 3342
Realize Your Dream Foundation, PA, 3343
Realty Foundation of New York, NY, 3344, 5021
REC Music Foundation, MO, 5451
Record School Foundation, George J., OH, 3345
Recreational Boating Industries Educational Foundation, MI, 3346
Red Rock Mesa, UT, 5452
Redding Family Foundation, CA, 3347
Reddington Scholarship Fund & Trust, John A., NY, 3348
Reddy Charitable Foundation, Dr. Prem, CA, 3349
Redfield Trust, Richard F., WI, 3350
Redwood Area Communities Foundation, Inc., MN, 3351
Reebok Foundation, The, MA, see 6095
Reebok Human Rights Foundation, The, MA, 6095
Reed Foundation for the Performing Arts, Donna, The, IA, 3352
Reed Foundation, Peter S., Inc., NY, 5022
Reed Medical Scholarship Trust, Joanna F., AL, 3353
Reese Foundation, Spence, TX, 3354
Reeve Foundation, Christopher, NJ, 6096
Reeve Paralysis Foundation, Christopher, NJ, see 6096
Reeves Foundation Trust, Sophia K., PA, 3356
Reeves Foundation, IN, 3355
Reeves Foundation, Inc., IN, 3357
Region 2 Arts Council, MN, 5453
Regional Arts and Culture Council, OR, 5454
Rehfuss Memorial Fund, Heinz and Suze, NY, 5455
Reich Education Foundation, Edgar and Lois, NC, 3358
Reid Educational Trust, M. C. & A. A., MI, 3359
Reid Scholarship Fund, W. Scott, The, ME, 3360
Reierson Foundation, Olive Rice, MT, 3361
Reifel-Ellwood Education Trust, IA, 3362
Reilly Family Foundation, The, TX, 3363
Reilly Foundation, IN, 3364
Reiner Foundation, Inc., The, IN, 5023
Reinhardt Family Scholarship Trust, The, NY, 3365
Reinhart Memorial Scholarship Foundation, Floyd J., NY, 3366
Reinheimer Trust, Mildred, IL, 3367
Reiss Foundation, William M., IL, 3368
Reitnauer Scholarship Fund, Henry K. & Evelyn, PA, 3369
Relevance Foundation, The, CA, 3370
Relief Association Trust, RI, 5024
Relief Association, Inc, RI, see 5024
Reller Memorial Scholarship Fund, Elizabeth, IL, 3371
Remmele Foundation, MN, 3372
Renaissance Performing Arts Company, AZ, 5456
Renal Assistance, Inc., FL, 5025
Rennie Scholarship Fund, Waldo E., AZ, 3373
Rentschler Scholarship Fund, Brent & Helen, The, IN, 3374
REO Education Fund, IL, see 3306
Research & Education Foundation of the American Association for the Surgery of Trauma, TX, 3375
Research Corporation, AZ, 6097
Research Foundation of CFA Institute, The, VA, 3376
Research Foundation of The City University of New York, NY, 3377, 6098
Research Fund of the American Otological Society, Inc., IL, see 5590
Research Institute for the Study of Man, NY, 6099
Rest Haven Preventorium for Children, Inc., CA, 5026
Restless Legs Syndrome Foundation, Inc., MN, 6100
Retired Officers Association Scholarship Fund, The, VA, see 2711
Retiring Fund for the Women in the Diaconate of the Episcopal Church, SC, see 4766

Rett Syndrome Research Foundation, OH, 6101
Reuther Memorial Fund, Walter and May, MI, 3378
Reverend Boutin Brothers Trust, MA, 3379
Rex Foundation, CA, 6102
Rexam Corporation Foundation, NC, see 3380
Rexam Foundation, The, NC, 3380
Rexnord Foundation Inc., WI, 3381
Reynolds Estate Residuary Trust, Edith Grace, OH, see 3382
Reynolds Estate, Edith Grace, OH, 3382
Reynolds Foundation, Z. Smith, Inc., NC, 6103
Reynolds Medical Scholarship Fund, Dr. & Mrs. Charles O., WV, 3383
Reynolds Trust, Harry Bertram, MO, 3384
Reynolds-Barwick Scholarship Fund, IL, 3385
Rhoad Testamentary Trust, Robert L., OH, 3386
Rhoads Foundation, T. L., PA, 3387
Rhoads Scholarship Trust, KY, 3388
Rhode Island Building Industry Scholarship Fund, RI, 3389
Rhode Island Community Foundation, The, RI, see 3390
Rhode Island Community Foundation, The, RI, see 3390
Rhode Island Community Foundation, The, RI, see 6104
Rhode Island Foundation, The, RI, 3390, 5457, 6104
Rhythm and Blues Foundation, Inc., The, NY, 5458
Rice Aid Fund, William B., Inc., MA, 3391
Rice Trust, James C. & Irene M., NV, 3392
Rich Charitable Foundation, Raymond A., NY, see 3031
Richardi Scholarship Trust, Richard, FL, 3393
Richards Scholarship Fund, Mabel Wilson, The, CA, 3394
Richards Scholarship Trust, Clarence & Olive, WI, 3395
Richardson Fund Corporation, Mary T. & William A., MA, 3396
Richardson Memorial Fund, Sid, TX, 3397
Richardson Memorial Trust, Bob, OR, 3398
Richardson Musical Education Scholarship Fund, WA, 3399
Richardson Scholarship Foundation, Inc., FL, 3400
Richardt Charitable Trust, Charlotte M., KY, 3401
Richland County Foundation of Mansfield, Ohio, The, OH, see 3402
Richland County Foundation, OH, 3402
Richman Brothers Foundation, OH, 5027
Richmond Community Foundation, Greater, VA, see 917
Richmond Community Foundation, Greater, VA, see 5704
Richmond Educational Foundation, CA, 3403
Ricker College Endowment Fund, ME, 3404
Rickert Memorial Scholarship Fund, Gladys & Evelyn, OH, 3405
Ricketts Scholarship Fund, Raymond and Helen, IN, 3406
Riddleberger Scholarship Trust, Faye, IN, 3407
Ride For Kids Foundation, Inc., NC, see 6065
Rider Trust, Frank, WA, 5028
Ridgefield Scholarship Group, Inc., The, CT, 3408
Rieben Memorial Scholarship Fund, Albert, Inc., AL, 3409
Rieger Foundation, Herman I., IL, 3410
Rietman Charitable Foundation, Carl and Camilla, OR, 3411
Rigorous Educational Assistance for Deserving Youth Foundation, Inc., NJ, 3412
Riley Foundation, Grace O. & Harry D., The, NE, 3413
Rimmele Scholarship Fund, Robert, RI, 3414
Rinker Medical Scholarship Fund, Dr. E. B., WI, see 3415
Rinker Trust, Lila, WI, 3415
Ripley County Community Foundation, Inc., IN, 3416
Risley Educational Trust, Jean, WA, 3417
Riss Trust, Lois E., NE, 3418
Ritchie Memorial Fund, Lieutenant Robert Bolenius, NC, 3419
Rivendell Stewards' Trust, CA, 5029
River Charitable Trust, NY, A
Riverwood International Corporation Philanthropic Fund, GA, 3420
Rixson Foundation, Oscar C., Inc., NC, 6105
Rixstine Charitable Trust, Mary Amanda Hawke, NC, see 3421
Rixstine Charitable Trust, NC, 3421
Roach Memorial Scholarship Fund, Ruth E., OH, 3422

Roark Scholarship Fund Trust, Mary E., TN, 3423
Robbins Trust, Charlotte M., MA, 5030
Robbins Trust, Fred L., MA, 3424
Roberg Endowment Trust, Louis A., MN, 3425
Roberts Scholarship Foundation, Mary K., IL, 3426
Roberts Student Aid Fund, NJ, 3427
Robertson Family Memorial Fund, A. F., OH, 3428
Robertson Foundation, Lois and Edward, FL, A
Robins Educational Scholarship Foundation, Beatrice & Samuel, The, NY, 3429
Robinson Foundation, Jackie, Inc., NY, 3430
Robinson Fund, Fred L., MT, 3431
Robinson Scholarship Trust, Florence M., KS, 3432
Robinson Trust, Harry W. and Virginia, CA, 3433
Robinson Trust, Mary H., IL, 3434
Robinson Welfare Trust, John W., ME, 3435
Robinson, Jr. Memorial Foundation, Angus, Inc., CT, 3436
Robustelli Family Foundation, NJ, 3437
Rochester Area Community Foundation, Greater, MI, see 886
Rochester Female Charitable Society, NY, 5031
Rochetta-Wessies Scholarship Foundation, The, IL, 3438
Rockefeller Foundation, The, NY, A
Rockford Health Careers Foundation, IL, 3439
Rocky Mountain Elk Foundation, Inc., MT, 3440
Roddick Fund, OH, 3441
Roesch Vocal Scholarship Trust, Polly W., WI, 3442
ROFEH, Inc., MA, A
Rogers Brothers Foundation, ID, 3443
Rogers Memorial Student Loan Fund, Bruce & Mary, OH, see 3444
Rogers Trust, Ada M., OH, 3444
Rogow Birken Foundation, Inc., The, CT, see 3445
Rogow Greenberg Foundation, Inc., The, CT, 3445
Rohame Foundation, The, AZ, A
Rohrer, Jr. Educational Foundation, William G., PA, 3446
Rolfs Educational Foundation, Ltd., WI, 3447
Rolfson Scholarship Trust, Mars & Verna, MT, 3448
Rollison Educational Scholarship Trust, John W., NC, 3449
Ronald McDonald House Charities of Greater Washington, DC, Inc., DC, 3450, A
Ronald McDonald House Charities of New Mexico, NM, 3451
Roof Memorial Scholarship Fund, Freda T., CO, 3452
Rooke Foundation, Inc., TX, 3453
Rooney Scholarship Fund, Art, PA, 3454
Roosevelt County Electric Education Foundation, NM, 3455
Roothbert Fund, Inc., The, NY, 3456
Rose Foundation, Scott, Inc., KY, 5032
Rose Ladies Aid Society, IN, 5033
Rosenberger Award Foundation, Raymond, OH, 6106
Rosenbluth Foundation, Milton B., Inc., NY, 6107
Rosenfeld Trust, Max C., PA, 3457
Ross Foundation, John M., HI, 3458
Ross Loan Fund, The, PA, 3459
Ross Scholarship Fund, Edith L. and H. Danforth, RI, A
Ross Scholarship Trust, Ed & Eda, OR, A
Ross Trust, Charles M., IL, 3460
Rossman Fund for Pacific University, George, OR, 3461
Rostra Engineered Component Sunshine Fund, RI, 5034
Roswell Museum and Art Center Foundation, NM, 5459
Rot Foundation, Albert J. and Susan E., IL, 3462
Rotalia Foundation, WA, 3463
Rotary Club Education Fund of Framingham, MA, 3464
Rotary Club of Marshall Finney Educational Trust Fund, IL, 3465
Rotary Foundation of Rotary International, The, IL, 3466, 6108
Rotary Service Foundation of San Mateo, CA, 3467
Rotch Travelling Scholarship, Inc., MA, 6109
Roth Foundation, FL, A
Rothschild Foundation, Judith, The, NY, 5460
Rottenberg Foundation, Herman & Lenore, Inc., NY, 5035
Rotterman Trust, Helen L. & Marie F., OH, 3468
Rouch Boys Foundation, A. P. and Louise, AZ, see 3469
Rouch Foundation, AZ, 3469, A

Rowan Charitable & Educational Fund, C. L., Inc., TX, A
Rowan Family Foundation, CA, 3470
Rowland Foundation, Pleasant T., Inc., WI, 3471
Roy Scholarship Fund, Mildred C., OH, 3473
Roy Scholarship Fund, NY, 3472
Royal Oak Foundation for Public Education, MI, 6110
Royal Oak Foundation, NY, 3474
Royston Permanent Scholarship Foundation of Alpha Sigma State of the Delta Kappa Gamma Society International, Rachel, The, WA, 3475
RPW Foundation, Inc., IN, 3476
Rubenstein Memorial Scholarship Foundation, David, CA, see 1584
Rubin Foundation, J. M., Inc., FL, 3477
Rudy Scholarship Fund, Lillian & Harold, IL, 3478
Ruf Scholarship Trust, Clara A., MI, 3479
Rufer Scholarship Trust, Merlin & Ethyl, IA, 3480
Ruffini Charitable Foundation, Esther and Alcide, MA, 3481
Ruffini Charitable Foundation, MA, see 3481
Ruge Education Foundation, Edgar G. W., NC, see 3482
Ruge Trust, Isabel R., NC, 3482
Ruger Trust, Dr. Henry Hobert, ND, 3483
Rumbough Fund, James Hickey, NC, see 3484
Rumbough Trust, Constance H., NC, 3484
Runyon Cancer Research Foundation, Damon, NY, see 5667
Rural American Scholarship Fund, WA, 3485
Rural Kentucky Medical Scholarship Fund, KY, A
Rusch Family Scholarship, John, The, MI, 3486
Rush County Community Foundation, Inc., IN, 3487
Rush Educational Trust, David and Mary P., KS, 3488
Rush Testamentary Trust, Lonza L., FL, 3489
Rush Trust, R. Roy, FL, see 3489
Ruskin Trust, Gertrude Marion, NC, 3490
Russell Educational and Charitable Foundation, Benjamin and Roberta, Inc., AL, see 3491
Russell Foundation, Benjamin and Roberta, AL, 3491
Russell Scholarship Fund, Clyde, ME, 3493
Russell Scholarship Fund, Helen B. & Robert H., WI, see 3492
Russell Scholarship Fund, WI, 3492
Russian Children's Welfare Society, Inc., NY, 5036
Rutan Foundation, Mary, OH, 3494
Rutherford Foundation, CO, 3495
Rutledge Charity, Edward, WI, 3496, 5037
Ryan Charitable Foundation, Dorothy and Robert, The, OR, 3497
Ryan County Scholarship Fund, H. L. and K. G., NC, 3498
Ryan County Scholarship Fund, Katherine G., NC, see 3498
Ryan Foundation, Irene, CA, A
Ryan Fund f/b/o Portland High School, V. Gerard, RI, see 3499
Ryan Fund, V. Gerard, RI, 3499
Ryder System Charitable Foundation, Inc., The, FL, 3500, 5038
Rye Rotary Foundation, Inc., NY, 3501
Ryka Rose Foundation, MA, see 3304
Ryrie Foundation, The, TX, 3502
Ryu Family Foundation, Inc., NJ, 3503

S.D. Scholarship Fund, TX, 3504
S.L. Scholarship Foundation, Inc., CA, A
Saak Trust, Charles E., CA, 3505, 5039
Sabatini Family Foundation, KS, 3506
Sacco Scholarship Fund, Joseph, MD, 3507
Sachs Foundation, CO, 3508
Sacramento Kings Foundation, CA, A
Sacramento Mountain Scholarship Fund, Inc., NM, 3509
Sacramento Region Community Foundation, CA, 3510
Sacramento Regional Foundation, CA, see 3510
Saddle River Valley Lions Charities, Inc., NJ, 3511
Saginaw Community Foundation, MI, 3512
Sailfish Point Foundation, Inc., FL, 3513
Saint Louis Community Foundation, Greater, MO, A
Saint Paul Foundation, Inc., The, MN, 3514, A
Saks Incorporated Foundation, AL, 3515
Sakumoto Charitable Trust, Toyo, HI, 3516
Salah Family Foundation for the Town of Canton, James and Beatrice, Inc., MA, 3517

Sale Foundation, Lucy Pannill, The, VA, 3518
Salem Community Foundation, Inc., OH, 3519
Salem Female Charitable Society, MA, 5040
Salem Foundation, The, OR, 3520
Salem Hospital Foundation, OR, 3521
Salem Lutheran Foundation, OH, 3522
Saletra Scholarship Fund, Mary M., NJ, 3523
Salick Health Care Foundation, CA, 3524
Salisbury Memorial Scholarship Fund, Burl E., MI, 3525
Salisbury-Rowan Community Service Council, Inc., NC, 3526
Sallness Memorial Scholarship Fund, Fritchof T. Sallness and Marian M., MI, 3527
Salt Lake Education Foundation, UT, 6111
Saltonstall Foundation for the Arts, Constance, Inc., NY, 5461
Salute to Education, Inc., TX, 3528
SAM'S CLUB Foundation, AR, see 4279
SAM'S CLUB Foundation, AR, see 6178
Samaritan Foundation, The, AZ, see 5636
Samaritan Society, The, MA, 5041
Samer Trust, Spero, PA, 3529
Samet Foundation, Jerold J. & Margaret M., MD, 3530
Sample Scholarship Trust, Adrian M., FL, 3531
Sampley Educational Foundation, R. E. & Catherine Woodson, Inc., AR, 3532
Samstag Fine Arts Trust, Gordon, FL, 3533
San Antonio A & M Club Foundation, TX, 3534
San Antonio Area Foundation, TX, 3535
San Antonio Spurs Foundation, The, TX, 3536
San Carlos Foundation, The, CA, 6112
San Diego Community Foundation, CA, see 3539
San Diego Community Foundation, CA, see 6113
San Diego County Citizens Scholarship Foundation, CA, 3537
San Diego County Salute to Education, CA, 3538
San Diego Foundation, The, CA, 3539, 6113
San Diego Martin Luther King Jr. Foundation, CA, 3540
San Felipe del Rio, Inc., CA, see 3541
San Felipe Humanitarian Alliance, CA, 3541
San Francisco Children's Art Center, CA, 5462
San Francisco Family Foundation, The, CA, 5042
San Francisco Foundation, The, CA, 3542, 5463
San Francisco Girls Chorus, CA, 3543
San Luis Obispo County Community Foundation, CA, 3544, 6114
Sanders Fund, Inc., MA, 5043
Sandusky County Bar Association, OH, 3545
Sandy Hill Foundation, NY, 3546
Sanford Scholarship Foundation, Andrew and Martha, VA, 3547
Sanford Scholarship Foundation, Joe & Babe, NE, 3548
Sanilac County Community Foundation, MI, 3549
Santa Barbara Foundation, CA, 3550
Santa Claus Club Scholarship Fund, OH, see 1697
Santa Cruz County Community Foundation, Greater, CA, see 898
Santa Fe Jazz Foundation, Inc., NM, 5464
Sapelo Foundation, Inc., The, GA, 3551
Sapelo Island Research Foundation, Inc., GA, see 3551
Sappington Foundation II, Maurice Marion, OK, A
Saranac Lake Voluntary Health Association, Inc., NY, 5044
Sarasota County Community Foundation, Inc., The, FL, see 899
Sarnoff Endowment for Cardiovascular Science, Stanley J., Inc., The, VA, 6115
Sarver Charitable Trust, KS, 3552
Sasso Consolidation Fund Trust, RI, see 3553
Sasso Scholarship Fund Trust, RI, 3553
Sauvain Scholarship Fund, NC, see 3554
Sauvain Trust, Walter H., NC, 3554
Savannah Widows Society, GA, 5045
SAW Community Foundation, VA, see 3888
Sawyer Teacher Scholarship Fund, Lillie Murray, MD, 3555
Sayles Foundation, Ryan W., MO, 3556
SBC Foundation, TX, see 223
Scadron Memorial Educational Foundation, Irene Haas, FL, A
Scaife Scholarship Foundation, The, CA, 3557
Scalp and Blade Scholarship Trust, NY, 3558
Scanlan Foundation, IA, 3559

Scanlan Memorial Scholarship Fund, Trusteeship of Emmett R. Scanlan & Catherine D., IA, 3560
Scarlett Scholarship Fund, Andrew J., NH, 3561
Scarsdale Foundation, NY, 3562
Scatena Memorial Fund for San Francisco School Teachers, Virginia, CA, 5046
Schack Memorial Scholarship Fund, Margaret Lobdell, WA, 3563
Schaeneman, Jr. Memorial Scholarship Foundation, Lewis G., Inc., MA, 3564
Schafer Scholarship Fund, Frank and Elizabeth, MO, 3565
Schalkenbach Foundation, Robert, Inc., NY, 6116
Schapira, M.D. Foundation, Hans E., Inc., NY, 6117
Schechter Foundation, The, NY, 3566
Scheffler Family Foundation, AZ, 3567
Schenck Estate Trust, Jane, NY, 3568
Schenck Estate, Jane, NY, see 3568
Schenectady Foundation, The, NY, 3569
Schepp Foundation, Leopold, NY, 3570
Scherer Foundation, Karla, The, IL, 3571
Schiff Scholarship Fund, William J. Schiff and Elizabeth, RI, 3572
Schiffner Scholarship Fund, Helen M., PA, 3573
Schilling Family Foundation, OR, see 3574
Schilling Family Scholarship Fund, OR, 3574
Schlagenbusch Scholarship Trust, Marjorie, IA, 3575
Schlarb Scholarship Trust, Earle J., VA, 3576
Schlotterer Memorial Education Fund, Raymond C. & Dorothy I., NY, 3577
Schlotterer Trust, Raymond C. & Dorothy I., NY, see 3577
Schmidek Charitable Foundation, Damir I. Schmidek and Virginia A., CA, 5465
Schmidt Foundation, Walter C. and Marie C., OR, 3579
Schmidt Foundation, William E., Inc., IN, 3578
Schmidt Scholarship Trust Fund, Lee, ID, 3580
Schmidt Trust, Walter F., IL, 3581
Schmoker Trust, Cecil Mae, NE, 3582
Schneider Memorial Scholarship Fund, Roland R., CO, 3583
Schnepp Memorial Trust Fund, Danny, IA, A
Schnurmann Foundation, Cornelia, OH, 5047
Schoellkopf Silver Wedding Fund, J. F., NY, 5048
Scholarship America, MN, 3584
Scholarship Foundation of Erie Scottish Rite, PA, 3585
Scholarship Foundation of Santa Barbara, CA, 3586
Scholarship Foundation of the Union League of Philadelphia, The, PA, 3587
Scholarship Foundation, The, NJ, 3588
Scholarship Fund of Flint Plumbing and Pipefitting Industry, MI, 3589
Scholarship Fund of Kappa Sigma Fraternity, MA, 3590
Scholarship Fund, Inc., OH, 3591
Scholarships Foundation, Inc., The, NY, 3592
Scholz Family Foundation, NV, 3593
School Food Service Foundation, VA, see 738
School Food Service Foundation, VA, see 5692
School of American Research, NM, 5466
Schooler Scholarship Trust Fund, Karl, IA, 3594
Schooley Trust Fund, Paul, The, MO, 3595
Schowengerdt Family Scholarship Fund, MO, 3596
Schramm Foundation, PA, 3597
Schreibman Foundation, Jake J., CA, 3598
Schroeder Memorial Trust, J. P. and Maude V., OR, 3599
Schroeder Scholarship Trust, William Archie, IL, 3600
Schuette Family Foundation, Inc., WI, A
Schuetze Foundation, Maude M., ND, 3601
Schuller Fund, Inc., CO, see 2095
Schulte Foundation, Theodore & Catherine, WI, 5049
Schultz Trust, Kate W., IN, 3602
Schulz Trust, Irmgard, NV, 3603
Schumacher Scholarship Fund for Men, Herman Oscar, WA, see 3604
Schumacher School Fund, Herman Oscar, WA, 3604
Schuyler Child Educational Fund Trust, Byron S., RI, 3605
Schuylkill Area Community Foundation, PA, 3606
Schuylkill Center for Environmental Education, The, PA, 5467
Schuylkill Community Action, PA, A
Schwab Foundation, John, PA, 3607

Schwab-Rosenhouse Memorial Foundation, CA, 3608
Schwantes Scholarship Fund, Elmer & Ruth, AK, 3609
Schwartz Foundation, Ernie P., MN, 3610
Schwartze Linn High School Scholarship Fund Trust I,
    A. J., MO, 3611
Schwartze Scholarship Fund Trust II, A. J., MO, 3612
Schwartze Scholarship Fund Trust III, A. J., MO, 3613
Schwartze Scholarship Fund Trust IV, A. J., MO, 3614
Schwartze Scholarship Fund Trust, A. J., MO, 3615
Schwartze Seminary Scholarship Fund, A. J., MO, 3616
Schwartze Trust Helias High School Scholarship Fund
    II, A. J., MO, 3617
Schwartze Trust Helias High School Scholarship Fund
    III, A. J., MO, 3618
Schwartze Trust Helias High School Scholarship Fund,
    A. J., MO, 3619
Schwartze Trust Linn High School Scholarship Fund II,
    A. J., MO, 3620
Schwarz Charitable Trust for Education, Evalee C., The,
    TX, 3621
Schwarz Trust f/b/o Stockbridge High School, Faythe,
    WI, 3622
Schweppe Foundation, The, MO, 6118
SCI Special Fund, CA, 5050
Science Scholarship Foundation, CA, 3623
Science Service, Inc., DC, 3624
Scleroderma Foundation, Inc., MA, 6119
Scotch Plains Fanwood Scholarship Foundation, NJ,
    3625
Scots' Charitable Society, MA, 3626, 5051
Scott & Stringfellow Educational Foundation, VA, 3627
Scott Foundation, Richard L. & F. Annette, FL, 3628
Scott Fund, Olin, Inc., VT, 3629
Scott Memorial Trust, Arthur H., The, VT, 3630
Scott Scholarship Fund - Gertrude S. Straub Trust
    Estate, M. M., HI, 3631
Scott Trust, Ethel Voris, WI, 3632
Scott Trust, Gordon and Ann, IN, 3633
Scott-Jenkins Fund, NY, 3634
Scottish Rite Educational and Fellowship Program of
    Texas, TX, 6120
Scottish Rite Foundation in Kentucky, KY, 3635
Scottish Rite Oregon Consistory Almoner Fund, Inc.,
    OR, see 5005
Scotts Miracle-Gro Foundation, NY, 3636, 6121
Screen Actors Guild Foundation, The, CA, 3637, 5052
Scripps Howard Foundation, OH, 6122, A
Scudder Association, Inc., The, CT, 3638
Sculpture Space, Inc., NY, 5468
SDMS Educational Foundation, TX, 3639
Seabee Memorial Scholarship Association, MD, 3640
Sealaska Heritage Foundation, AK, see 3641
Sealaska Heritage Institute, AK, 3641
Seamen's Long Point Charitable Foundation, Inc., MA,
    3642
Searls Scholarship Foundation, William, ME, 3643
Seattle Business Association Scholarship Fund,
    Greater, WA, 3644
Seay Foundation, CO, 3645
Security Benefit Group Charitable Trust, KS, 3646
Sedler Scholarship Fund, Theodore H., ND, 3647
Seed Money for Growth Foundation, Inc., AZ, 3648
Seely Charitable Trust, R. Q. & L. A., TX, 3649
Seely Trust, Roger Q. & Lovye A., TX, see 3649
Seibel Foundation, Abe and Annie, The, TX, 3650
Seidner Charitable Foundation, Bette Lou, IN, 5053
Selah Charitable Trust, MT, 3651, 5054
Selby Foundation, William G. Selby and Marie, FL, 3652
Selling Scholarship Loan Fund, Ben, WA, 3653
Sells Foundation, Inc., TN, 3654
SEMA Memorial Scholarship Fund, CA, 3655
Sendzimir Foundation, Inc., The, OH, 6123
Senior Services of Stamford, Inc., CT, 5055
Sequim Masonic Lodge Foundation, WA, 3656
Serbian Brothers Help, Inc., IL, 5056
Serpent Source Foundation for Women, KY, 5469
Sertoma Foundation, MO, 3657
Servant Leadership Foundation, The, CO, 6124
Servant-Leader Scholarship Trust, AR, 3658
Servco Foundation, HI, 3659
Service League of Cherokee County, GA, 3660
Seven Oaks Foundation, Inc., GA, 3661
Sexton Can Company Employees Aid Fund, MA, 5057

Seymour Community School Scholarship Trust, WI,
    3662
Seymour Trust Fund, Greater, IN, 3663
Shafer Trust, Allen J., WI, 3664
Shaklee Cares, CA, 5058
Shallow Scholarship Foundation, Moses and Caroline,
    Inc., WI, 3665
Shanor Foundation, M. L., The, TX, 3666
Shapiro Testamentary Scholarship Trust, Ida, IL, 3667
Share the Dream Foundation, CA, 3668
Sharp Trust, Robert G., WI, 3669
Sharpe Art Foundation, Marie Walsh, The, CO, 5470
Shartzer Scholarship Fund, Helen B., PA, 3670
Shasta Regional Community Foundation, CA, 3671
Shatford Memorial Trust, J. D., NY, 3672
Shattuck Foundation, W. L., OR, A
Shaulis Foundation, Fred S., Inc., The, MD, 3673
Shaull Education Foundation, Clyde L. and Mary C., PA,
    3674
Shea Clinic Foundation, TN, A
Sheadle Trust, Jasper H., OH, 5059
Shearwater Foundation, Inc., The, NY, 5471
Sheehan Scholarship Fund, John P., RI, 3675
Sheen Scholarship Fund, Howard J. & Ruth H., PA,
    3676
Sheil Memorial Fund, Edward J. & Lavelette Rockwell,
    OH, 3677
Shelby Foundation, OH, 3678
Shelter Insurance Foundation, MO, 3679
Shenango Valley Community Foundation, PA, 3680
Shenango Valley Foundation, PA, see 3680
Shepard Scholarship Fund Foundation, Leon and
    Josephine Wade, Inc., MI, 3681
Shepherd Scholarship Committee, Elizabeth Buford,
    TN, 3682
Sheridan County Memorial Educational Trust, ND,
    3683
Sheridan Memorial Scholarship, Harry R., VT, 3684
Sherman Educational Fund, IN, 3685
Sherman Educational Fund, Mabel E., IA, 3686
Sherwood Trust, Nellie R., IA, 5060
Shiel Trust, John F. & Mary E., The, IN, 3687
Shield Athletic Scholarship Fund, Daniel, Inc., CT, A
Shifler Memorial Foundation, Howard & Christine, NJ,
    3688
Shiloh Ministries International, Inc., TN, 5061
Shingu Foundation, Ronald, The, CA, 5062
Shinnick Educational Fund, William M., OH, 3689
Shinoda Memorial Scholarship Foundation, Joseph,
    CA, 3690
Shoemaker Trust for Shoemaker Scholarship Fund, Ray
    S., PA, 3691
SHOPA Foundation for Educational Excellence, OH, see
    6125
SHOPA Kids In Need Foundation, OH, 6125
Shoppers Village/Maureen Nolan Memorial Fund, NY,
    3692
Short Scholarship Fund, J. Leo, WI, 3693
Shoshana Foundation, Inc., NY, 5472
Shouse Memorial Scholarship Fund, Helen Shacklet,
    TX, 3694
Show Foundation, Victoria Livestock, Inc., TX, 3695
Shreve Foundation, William A & Mary A., Inc., NJ, 3696
Shriner-Smith Scholarship Trust, OK, A
Shriners of Rhode Island Charities Trust, RI, 5063
Shroyer Scholarship Fund, Benjamin F. & Emma B., IN,
    3697
Shultz Eagle Scout Foundation, Bernard E., WA, 3698
Shultz Scholarship Fund, Ruth A., MA, 3699
Shumaker Foundation, Paul and Adelyn C., The, WI,
    3700
Shunk Association, John Q., OH, 3701
Sidwell Charitable Trust, KS, 5064
Siebenthal Scholarship Charitable Trust, Agnes Cecelia
    J., OH, 3702
Sieber Foundation, Fred B., The, FL, 5065
Siemens Foundation, NJ, 3703
Sierra Pacific Foundation, CA, 3704
Sierra Pacific Soroptimist Foundation, CA, 3705
Siff Educational Foundation, Philip and Aida, CA, 3706
Siff Educational Foundation, Philip Francis, CA, see
    3706
Sightless Children Club, Inc., OH, 5066

Sigma Alpha Iota Philanthropies, Inc., NC, 3707
Sigma Chi Foundation, IL, 3708
Signer Memorial Trust Fund, John J., CA, 3709
Sigourney Award Trust, Mary S., WA, 6126
Silver Shield Foundation, Inc., NY, 3710
Silverthorne Foundation, Rose, TX, 3711
Simmons Charitable Trust, Esther N., OH, 3712
Simmons Welfare Fund, Ralph & Mary, OH, 3713, A
Simon Educational Trust Foundation, AZ, 3714
Simon Family Foundation, The, MD, 3715
Simon Youth Foundation, Inc., IN, 3716
Simpson Foundation, The, AL, 3717
Simpson Foundation, William G. & M. Virginia, The, PA,
    3718
Sinek Scholarship Trust, Joseph J., IA, 3719
Singer Student Nurses Fund, Bertha P., OR, 3720
Single Parent Assistance Fund, Inc., OK, see 5013
Single Parent Scholarship Fund of Washington County,
    Inc., AR, 3721
Singleton Scholarship Trust, M. E., TX, 3722
Sioux Falls Area Community Foundation, SD, 3723,
    5067
Siouxland Community Foundation, IA, 3724
Siouxland Foundation, IA, see 3724
Sipes Memorial Student Loan Fund, Bedford W., TX,
    3725
Siros Foundation, Clara Lou Vena, TX, 3726
Siskind Foundation, Aaron, NJ, A
Sitka Center for Art and Education, OR, 5473
Sitnasuak Foundation, AK, 3727
SIU Scholarship Foundation and Trust, MD, see 3507
Sivyer Trust for Boys Trade Technical High School, Ida
    M., WI, 3728
Skadden Fellowship Foundation, Inc., The, NY, 6127
Skadden, Arps, Slate, Meagher & Flom Fellowship
    Foundation, NY, see 6127
Skahan Memorial Fund, Joan, NY, 3729
Skandalaris Family Foundation, FL, 3730
SKB Foundation, CA, 3731
Skelton Charitable Foundation, Homer, MS, 3732,
    5068
Skelton Scholarship Fund, WI, 3733
Skelton Trust Fund, Ila M., WI, see 3733
Skeuse Scholarship Fund, Thomas J. Skeuse and Rita
    T., Inc., The, NJ, 3734
Skidmore, Owings & Merrill Foundation, IL, 6128
Skillman Scholarship Fund, Chris A., MO, 3735
Skillman Scholarship, Frank Foster, PA, 3736
Skin Cancer Foundation, Inc., The, NY, 6129
Skinner Foundation, WA, see 5234
Skokie Cable TV Foundation, IL, A
SLA Foundation, CO, 3737
SLA, VA, see 3824
SLA, VA, see 6141
Slaughter Scholarship Trust, IN, A
Sleeper & Lottie S. Hill Fund, Josiah, PA, 5069
Slemp Foundation, The, OH, 3738
Slipher Testamentary Trust, V. M., WI, 3739
Slippery Rock Foundation, Inc., PA, see 3740
Slippery Rock University Foundation, Inc., PA, 3740
Sloan Foundation, Alfred P., NY, 6130
Sloan Foundation, The, IL, 6131
Sloan, Jr. Foundation, O. Temple, NC, 3741
Slovak Catholic Charitable Organization, IL, 5070
Slowinski Charitable Foundation, RI, 3742
Slowinski Estate Fund Trust, RI, see 3742
Smack Mellon Studios, Inc., NY, 5474
SMACNA College of Fellows Foundation, VA, 3743
Smalley Foundation, Inc., MA, 3744
Smallwood Scholarship Foundation, ID, 3745
SMBC Global Foundation, Inc., NY, 6132
SME Education Foundation, MI, see 3793
SME Education Foundation, MI, see 6140
Smelser Scholarship Fund, Hazel Dell Neff, IN, 3746
SMF Foundation, Inc., NY, 5071
SMFG Foundation, Inc., AZ, 3648
Smick Memorial Loan Fund, KS, 3747
Smith Charitable Trust, Jean and Verne, SC, 3748
Smith Charitable Trust, Tom C., WV, 5072
Smith Charitable Trust, William Harold, NC, 3749
Smith Education Fund, Jennie, RI, 3750
Smith Educational Foundation, Charles C., NJ, 3751
Smith Educational Fund, RI, see 3750